WHO WAS WHO

VOL. VI

1961-1970

WHO'S WHO

AN ANNUAL BIOGRAPHICAL DICTIONARY

FIRST PUBLISHED IN 1849

WHO *WAS* WHO

VOL. I. 1897–1915

VOL. II. 1916–1928

VOL. III. 1929–1940

VOL. IV. 1941–1950

VOL. V. 1951–1960

VOL. VI. 1961–1970

PUBLISHED BY

ADAM & CHARLES BLACK

WHO WAS WHO. VOL. VI

WHO WAS WHO
1961-1970

A COMPANION TO

WHO'S WHO

CONTAINING THE BIOGRAPHIES
OF THOSE WHO DIED DURING
THE DECADE 1961-1970

ADAM & CHARLES BLACK
LONDON

FIRST PUBLISHED 1972
BY A. AND C. BLACK LIMITED
4, 5 AND 6 SOHO SQUARE LONDON W.1

ISBN 0 7136 1202 9

PRINTED IN GREAT BRITAIN

PREFACE

This is the sixth volume of biographies removed from *Who's Who* on account of death. It contains the entries of those who died in the years 1961–1970. It also includes, in Addenda I on page xxix, the biographies of a number of those who died before 31 December 1960 but whose deaths were not known to us until after the publication of the second edition of *Who was Who* Vol. V 1951–1960. Addenda II, page xxxiv, contains the entries of those who died in 1961–1970 but whose deaths were not reported to us until after this volume had been made up for press; cross-references for these, however, are printed on the pages where their biographies should occur.

The entries are for the most part as they last appeared in *Who's Who*, with the date of death added and in some cases further additional information to bring them up to date. In rare instances the date of death could not be ascertained and information regarding such dates is welcomed for inclusion in a subsequent edition.

With the first five volumes of *Who was Who*, covering the years 1897–1915, 1916–1928, 1929–1940, 1941–1950, and 1951–1960, the present book should enable the enquirer to dispense with the earlier annual volumes of *Who's Who*, research into which for a particular entry may be a considerable task, especially if the date of death be unknown. A further volume of *Who was Who* will be published at the close of each decade.

ADAM AND CHARLES BLACK

CONTENTS

ABBREVIATIONS USED IN THIS BOOK

Some of the designatory letters in this list are used merely for economy of space and do not necessarily imply any professional or other qualification

A

AA . . Anti-Aircraft; Automobile Association; Architectural Association; Augustinians of the Assumption
AAA . Amateur Athletic Association
AA&QMG . Assistant Adjutant and Quarter-master-General
AAAS . . American Association for Advancement of Science
AACCA . . Associate of the Association of Certified and Corporate Accountants
AAF . . Auxiliary Air Force (now RAux AF)
AAG . . Assistant Adjutant-General
AAI . . Associate of Chartered Auctioneers' and Estate Agents' Institute
AAMC . . Australian Army Medical Corps
A&AEE . Aeroplane and Armament Experimental Establishment
AASA . . Associate of Australian Society of Accountants
AAUQ . . Associate in Accountancy, University of Queensland
AB . . Bachelor of Arts (US); able-bodied seaman
ABA . . Amateur Boxing Association
ABC . . Australian Broadcasting Commission
ABCA . . Army Bureau of Current Affairs
ABCFM . . American Board of Commissioners for Foreign Missions
Abp . . Archbishop
AC . . *Ante Christum* (before Christ)
ACA . . Associate of the Institute of Chartered Accountants
Acad. . . Academy
ACAS . . Assistant Chief of the Air Staff
ACCM . . Advisory Council for the Church's Ministry (formerly CACTM)
ACCS . . Associate of Corporation of Secretaries (formerly of Certified Secretaries)
ACDS . . Assistant Chief of Defence Staff
ACF . . Army Cadet Force
ACG . . Assistant Chaplain-General
ACGI . . Associate of City and Guilds of London Institute
ACII . . Associate of the Chartered Insurance Institute
ACIS . . Associate of the Chartered Institute of Secretaries
ACOS . . Assistant Chief of Staff
ACS . . Additional Curates Society
ACSEA . . Allied Command SE Asia
ACSM . . Associate of the Camborne School of Mines
ACT . . Australian Capital Territory; Australian College of Theology; Associate of the College of Technology
ACWA . . Associate of the Institute of Cost and Works Accountants
AD . . *Anno Domini*
ADC . . Aide-de-camp
ADCM . . Archbishop of Canterbury's Diploma in Church Music
AD Corps . Army Dental Corps
Ad eund. . . *Ad eundem gradum* (admitted to the same degree); and *see under* a e g
ADFW . . Assistant Director of Fortifications and Works
ADGB . . Air Defence of Great Britain
ADGMS . . Assistant Director-General of Medical Services
ADH . . Assistant Director of Hygiene
Adjt . . Adjutant
ADJAG . . Assistant Deputy Judge Advocate General
Adm. . . Admiral
ADMS . . Assistant Director of Medical Services
ADOS . . Assistant Director of Ordnance Services
ADPR . . Assistant Director of Public Relations
ADS&T . . Assistant Director of Supplies and Transport
Adv. . . Advisory; Advocate
ADVS . . Assistant Director of Veterinary Services
ADWE&M . Assistant Director of Works, Electrical and Mechanical
AEA . . Atomic Energy Authority; Air Efficiency Award
AEAF . . Allied Expeditionary Air Force
AEC . . Agricultural Executive Council; Army Educational Corps (now RAEC)
AEF . . Amalgamated Union of Engineering and Foundry Workers; American Expeditionary Forces
a e g . . *ad eundem gradum* (to the same degree—of the admission of a graduate of one university to the same degree at another without examination)
AEGIS . . Aid for the Elderly in Government Institutions
AEI . . Associated Electrical Industries
AEM . . Air Efficiency Medal
AER . . Army Emergency Reserve
AERE . . Atomic Energy Research Establishment (Harwell)
Æt., Ætat. . *Ætatis* (aged)
AEU . . Amalgamated Engineering Union
AFA . . Amateur Football Alliance
AFAIAA . Associate Fellow of American Institute of Aeronautics and Astronautics (and *see under* AFIAS)
AFC . . Air Force Cross; Association Football Club
AFCAI . . Associate Fellow of the Canadian Aeronautical Institute
AFD . . Doctor of Fine Arts (US)
AFHQ . . Allied Force Headquarters
AFIA . . Associate of Federal Institute of Accountants (Australia)
AFIAS . . (now *see under* AFAIAA) (formerly) Associate Fellow Institute of Aeronautical Sciences (US)
AFICD . . Associate Fellow Institute of Civil Defence
AFM . . Air Force Medal
AFRAeS . . Associate Fellow Royal Aeronautical Society
AFV . . Armoured Fighting Vehicles
AG . . Attorney-General
AGH . . Australian General Hospital
AGI . . Artistes Graphiques Internationales; Associate of the Institute of Certificated Grocers
AGSM . . Associate of Guildhall School of Music
AHQ . . Army Headquarters
AH-WC . . Associate of Heriot-Watt College, Edinburgh

AIA . . Associate of the Institute of Actuaries; American Institute of Architects
AIAL . . Associate Member of the International Institute of Arts and Letters
AIB . . Associate of the Institute of Bankers
AIBD . . Associate of the Institute of British Decorators
AIBP . . Associate of the Institute of British Photographers
AIC . . Agricultural Improvement Council; also formerly Associate of the Institute of Chemistry (*see* ARIC)
AICA . . Associate Member Commonwealth Institute of Accountants; Association Internationale des Critiques d'Art
AICE . . Associate of the Institution of Civil Engineers
AICTA . . Associate of the Imperial College of Tropical Agriculture
AIEE . . Associate of the Institution of Electrical Engineers
AIF . . Australian Imperial Forces
AIG . . Adjutant-Inspector-General
AIIA . . Associate Insurance Institute of America
AIL . . Associate of the Institute of Linguists
AILA . . Associate of the Institute of Landscape Architects
AILocoE . . Associate of Institution of Locomotive Engineers
AIME . . American Institute of Mechanical Engineers
AIMarE . . Associate of the Institute of Marine Engineers
AIOB . . Associate of the Institute of Builders
AInstP . . Associate of Institute of Physics
AInstPI . . Associate of the Institute of Patentees (Incorporated)
AISA . . Associate of the Incorporated Secretaries' Association
AIWSP . . Associate Member of Institute of Work Study Practitioners
AJAG . . Assistant Judge Advocate General
AKC . . Associate of King's College (London)
ALA . . Associate of the Library Association
Ala . . Alabama (US)
ALAS . . Associate of Chartered Land Agents' Society
ALCD . . Associate of London College of Divinity
ALCM . . Associate of London College of Music
ALFSEA . . Allied Land Forces South-East Asia
ALI . . Argyll Light Infantry
ALS . . Associate of the Linnaean Society
Alta . . Alberta
AM . . Albert Medal; Master of Arts (US); Alpes Maritimes
AMA . . Associate of the Museums Association; Australian Medical Association
Amb. . . Ambulance
AMBritIRE . (now *see under* AMIERE) (formerly) Associate Member of British Institution of Radio Engineers
AMC . . Association of Municipal Corporations
AMet . . Associate of Metallurgy (Sheffield University)
AMF . . Australian Military Forces
AMGOT . . Allied Military Government of Occupied Territory
AMIAgrE . Associate Member of Institution of Agricultural Engineers
AMICE . . Associate Member of Institution of Civil Engineers (formerly lower rank of corporate membership of Instn, now *see under* MICE; change dated July 1968)
AMIChemE . Associate Member of Institution of Chemical Engineers
AMIEA . . Associate Member of Institute of Engineers, Australia
AMIED . . Associate Member of Institution of Engineering Designers
AMIEE . . Associate Member of Institution of Electrical Engineers (formerly lower rank of corporate membership of Instn, now *see under* MIEE; change dated Dec. 1966)
AMIE(Ind) . Associate Member, Institution of Engineers, India
AMIERE . Associate Member of Institution of Electronic and Radio Engineers (and *see under* AMBritIRE)
AMIMechE . Associate Member of Institution of Mechanical Engineers (formerly lower rank of corporate membership of Instn, now *see under* MIMechE, change dated April 1968)
AMIMinE . Associate Member of Institution of Mining Engineers
AMIMM . . Associate Member of Institution of Mining and Metallurgy
AMInstBE . Associate Member of Institution of British Engineers
AMInstCE . Associate Member of Institution of Civil Engineers (changed 1946 to AMICE)
AmInstEE . American Institute of Electrical Engineers
AMInstR . . Associate Member of Institute of Refrigeration
AMInstT . . Associate Member of the Institute of Transport
AMIStructE . Associate Member of the Institution of Structural Engineers
AMRINA . Associate Member of Royal Institution of Naval Architects
AMS . . Assistant Military Secretary; Army Medical Service
AMTPI . . Associate of Town Planning Institute
ANA . . Associate National Academician (America)
Anat. . . Anatomy; Anatomical
ANECInst . Associate of NE Coast Institution of Engineers and Shipbuilders
Anon. . . Anonymously
ANU . . Australian National University
ANZAAS . Australian and New Zealand Association for the Advancement of Science
AO . . Air Officer
AOA . . Air Officer in charge of Administration
AOC . . Air Officer Commanding
AOC-in-C . Air Officer Commanding-in-Chief
AOD . . Army Ordnance Department
AOER . . Army Officers Emergency Reserve
APD . . Army Pay Department
APS . . Aborigines Protection Society
APTC . . Army Physical Training Corps
AQMG . . Assistant Quartermaster-General
AR . . Associated Rediffusion (Television)
ARA . . Associate of the Royal Academy
ARAD . . Associate of the Royal Academy of Dancing
ARAeS . . Associate of the Royal Aeronautical Society
ARAM . . Associate of the Royal Academy of Music
ARAS . . Associate of the Royal Astronomical Society
ARBA . . Associate of the Royal Society of British Artists
ARBC . . Associate Royal British Colonial Society of Artists
ARBS . . Associate Royal Society of British Sculptors
ARC . . Architects' Registration Council; Agricultural Research Council; Aeronautical Research Council
ARCA . . Associate Royal College of Art; Associate Royal Canadian Academy

ARCamA . Associate Royal Cambrian Academy (formerly ARCA)
ARCE . . Academical Rank of Civil Engineers
Archt . . Architect
ARCM . . Associate Royal College of Music
ARCO . . Associate Royal College of Organists
ARCO(CHM) . Associate Royal College of Organists with Diploma in Choir Training
ARCS . . Associate Royal College of Science
ARCST . . Associate Royal College of Science and Technology (Glasgow)
ARCVS . . Associate of Royal College of Veterinary Surgeons
ARE . . Associate of Royal Society of Painter-Etchers and Engravers
ARIBA . . Associate of the Royal Institute of British Architects
ARIC . . Associate of the Royal Institute of Chemistry
ARICS . . Professional Associate of the Royal Institution of Chartered Surveyors
Ark . . Arkansas (US)
ARMS . . Associate of the Royal Society of Miniature Painters
ARP . . Air Raid Precautions
ARPS . . Associate of the Royal Photographic Society
ARRC . . Associate of the Royal Red Cross
ARSA . . Associate Royal Scottish Academy
ARSM . . Associate Royal School of Mines
ARTC . . Associate Royal Technical College (Glasgow) (name changed) *see under* ARCST
ARVIA . . Associate Royal Victorian Institute of Architects
ARWA . . Associate Royal West of England Academy
ARWS . . Associate Royal Society of Painters in Water-Colours
AS . . Anglo-Saxon
ASAA . . Associate of the Society of Incorporated Accountants and Auditors
ASAM . . Associate of the Society of Art Masters
AScW . . Association of Scientific Workers
ASE . . Amalgamated Society of Engineers
ASIA(Ed) . Associate, Society of Industrial Artists (Education)
ASLEF . . Associated Society of Locomotive Engineers and Firemen
ASLIB . . Association of Special Libraries and Information Bureaux
ASO . . Air Staff Officer
ASSET . . Association of Supervisory Staffs, Executives and Technicians
AssocISI . . Associate of Iron and Steel Institute
AssocMCT . Associateship of Manchester College of Technology
AssocMIAeE . Associate Member Institution of Aeronautical Engineers
AssocRINA . Associate of the Royal Institution of Naval Architects
AssocSc . Associate in Science
Asst . . Assistant
ASTMS . . Association of Scientific, Technical and Managerial Staffs
Astr. . . Astronomy
ASW . . Association of Scientific Workers
ATA . . Air Transport Auxiliary
ATC . . Air Training Corps
ATCL . . Associate of Trinity College of Music, London
ATD . . Art Teachers' Diploma
ATI . . Associate of Textile Institute
ATII . . Associate Member of the Institute of Taxation
ATS . . Auxiliary Territorial Service
ATV . . Associated TeleVision
AUS . . Army of the United States
AVD . . Army Veterinary Department
AVR . . Army Volunteer Reserve

B

b . . . born; brother
BA . . Bachelor of Arts
B&FBS . . British and Foreign Bible Society
BAFO . . British Air Forces of Occupation
BAI . . Bachelor of Engineering (*Baccalarius in Arte Ingeniaria*)
BALPA . . British Air Line Pilots' Association
BAO . . Bachelor of Art of Obstetrics
BAOR . . British Army of the Rhine (formerly *on* the Rhine)
BARC . . British Automobile Racing Club
Bart or **Bt** . Baronet
BAS . . Bachelor in Agricultural Science
BASc . . Bachelor of Applied Science
Batt. . . Battery
BB&CIRly . Bombay, Baroda and Central India Railway
BBC . . British Broadcasting Corporation
BC . . Before Christ; British Columbia
BCE (Melb) . Bachelor of Civil Engineering (Melbourne Univ.)
BCh or **BChir** . Bachelor of Surgery
BCL . . Bachelor of Civil Law
BCMS . . Bible Churchmen's Missionary Society
BCOF . . British Commonwealth Occupation Force
BCom . . Bachelor of Commerce
BComSc . . Bachelor of Commercial Science
BCS . . Bengal Civil Service
BCURA . . British Coal Utilization Research Association
BD . . Bachelor of Divinity
Bd . . Board
BDA . . British Dental Association
Bde . . Brigade
BDS . . Bachelor of Dental Surgery
BDSc . . Bachelor of Dental Science
BE . . Bachelor of Engineering; British Element
BEA . . British East Africa; British European Airways
BEAMA . . British Electrical and Allied Manufacturers' Association
BEc . . Bachelor of Economics (Australian)
BEd . . Bachelor of Education
Beds . . Bedfordshire
BEE . . Bachelor of Electrical Engineering
BEF . . British Expeditionary Force
BEM . . British Empire Medal
BEngEE . . Bachelor of Electrical Engineering (Canada)
Berks . . Berkshire
BFPO . . British Forces Post Office
BGS . . Brigadier General Staff
BHS . . British Horse Society
BIF . . British Industries Fair
BIM . . British Institute of Management
BIS . . Bank for International Settlements
BISF . . British Iron and Steel Federation
BISFA . . British Industrial and Scientific Film Association
BISRA . . British Iron and Steel Research Association
BJ . . Bachelor of Journalism
BJSM . . British Joint Services Mission
BL . . Bachelor of Law
BLA . . British Liberation Army
BLE . . Brotherhood of Locomotive Engineers
BLitt . . Bachelor of Letters
BM . . British Museum; Bachelor of Medicine
BMA . . British Medical Association
BMH . . British Military Hospital
BMJ . . British Medical Journal
Bn . . Battalion
BNAF . . British North Africa Force
BNC . . Brasenose College
BNEC . . British National Export Council
BNOC . . British National Opera Company
BOAC . . British Overseas Airways Corporation
BomCS . . Bombay Civil Service
BomSC . . Bombay Staff Corps

BoT . . Board of Trade
Bot. . . Botany; Botanical
Bp . . . Bishop
BPharm . . Bachelor of Pharmacy
BR . . . British Rail
Br. . . . Branch
BRA . . Brigadier Royal Artillery
BRCS . . British Red Cross Society
Brig. . . Brigadier
BritIRE . . (now *see under* IERE) (formerly) British Institution of Radio Engineers
BRS . . British Road Services
BS . . Bachelor of Surgery; Bachelor of Science
BSA . . Bachelor of Scientific Agriculture; Birmingham Small Arms
BSAA . . British South American Airways
BSAP . . British South Africa Police
BSC . . British Steel Corporation; Bengal Staff Corps
BSc . . Bachelor of Science
BSc (Dent) . Bachelor of Science in Dentistry
BSE . . Bachelor of Science in Engineering (US)
BSF . . British Salonica Force
BSI . . British Standards Institution
BSJA . . British Show Jumping Association
Bt . . . Baronet; Brevet
BTA . . British Tourist Authority (*formerly* British Travel Association)
BTC . . British Transport Commission
BTh . . Bachelor of Theology
BVM . . Blessed Virgin Mary
Bucks . . Buckinghamshire
BWI . . British West Indies (now WI; West Indies)
BWM . . British War Medal

C

(C) . . . Conservative; 100
c . . . Child; cousin
CA . . . Central America; County Alderman; Chartered Accountant (Scotland, and Canada)
CACTM . . Central Advisory Council of Training for the Ministry (*now see* ACCM)
CALE . . Canadian Army Liaison Executive
Cambs . . Cambridgeshire
CAMC . . Canadian Army Medical Corps
CAMW . . Central Association for Mental Welfare
Cantab . . Of Cambridge University
CAS . . Chief of the Air Staff
CASI . . Canadian Aeronautics and Space Institute
Cav. . . Cavalry
CB . . . Companion of the Bath
CBE . . Commander Order of the British Empire
CBI . . Confederation of British Industry (and *see under* FBI)
CBSA . . Clay Bird Shooting Association
CC . . Companion of the Order of Canada; City Council; County Council; Cricket Club; Cycling Club; County Court
CCC . . Corpus Christi College; Central Criminal Court; County Cricket Club
CCF . . Combined Cadet Force
CCG . . Control Commission Germany
CCPR . . Central Council of Physical Recreation
CCRA . . Commander Corps Royal Artillery
CCS . . Casualty Clearing Station; Ceylon Civil Service
CD . . Canadian Forces Decoration
CDEE . . Chemical Defence Experimental Establishment
Cdre . . Commodore
CDS . . Chief of the Defence Staff
CE . . . Civil Engineer
CEF . . Canadian Expeditionary Force
CEGB . . Central Electricity Generating Board
CEI . . Council of Engineering Institutions
CEIR . . Corporation for Economic and Industrial Research
CEMA . . Council for the Encouragement of Music and the Arts
CEMS . . Church of England Men's Society
CEng . . Chartered Engineer
Cento . . Central Treaty Organisation
CERN . . Conseil (now Organisation) Européenne pour la Recherche Nucléaire
CETS . . Church of England Temperance Society
CF . . Chaplain to the Forces
CFA . . Canadian Field Artillery
CFE . . Central Fighter Establishment
CFR . . Commander of Federal Republic of Nigeria
CFS . . Central Flying School
CGIA . . City and Guilds of London Insignia Award
CGS . . Chief of the General Staff
CH . . Companion of Honour
Chanc. . . Chancellor; Chancery
Chap. . . Chaplain
ChapStJ . . Chaplain of Order of St John of Jerusalem (now ChStJ)
ChB . . Bachelor of Surgery
Ch. Ch. . . Christ Church
Ch. Coll. . . Christ's College
(CHM) . . *See under* ARCO(CHM), FRCO(CHM)
ChM . . Master of Surgery
Chm. . . Chairman
ChStJ . . Chaplain of Order of St John of Jerusalem
CI . . . Imperial Order of the Crown of India; Channel Islands
CIAD . . Central Institute of Art and Design
CIAgrE . . Companion, Institution of Agricultural Engineers
CIAL . . Corresponding Member of the International Institute of Arts and Letters
CID . . Criminal Investigation Department
CIE . . Companion of the Order of the Indian Empire
CIGRE . . Conférence Internationale des Grands Réseaux Electriques
CIGS . . (formerly) Chief of the Imperial General Staff (now CGS)
CIMarE . . Companion of the Institute of Marine Engineers
CIMechE . . Companion of the Institution of Mechanical Engineers
C-in-C . . Commander-in-Chief
CIR . . Commission on Industrial Relations
CIV . . City Imperial Volunteers
CJ . . Chief Justice
CJM . . Congregation of Jesus and Mary (Eudist Fathers)
CL . . Commander of Order of Leopold
c.l. . . . *cum laude*
Cl. . . . Class
CLA . . Country Landowners' Association
CLit . . Companion of Literature (Royal Society of Literature Award)
CM . . Medal of Courage (Canada); Congregation of the Mission (Vincentians); Master in Surgery; Certificated Master; Canadian Militia
CMA . . Canadian Medical Association
CMB . . Central Midwives' Board
CMF . . Commonwealth Military Forces; Central Mediterranean Force
CMG . . Companion of St Michael and St George
CMO . . Chief Medical Officer
CMS . . Church Missionary Society
CNAA . . Council for National Academic Awards
CNR . . Canadian National Railways
CO . . . Commanding Officer; Commonwealth Office (from Aug. 1966) (*see also* FCO); Colonial Office (before Aug. 1966); Conscientious Objector

Co. . . County; Company
C of E . . Church of England
C of S . . Chief of Staff
CoID . . Council of Industrial Design
Co.L or Coal.L Coalition Liberal
Col . . Colonel
Coll. . . College; Collegiate
Colo . . Colorado (US)
Col.-Sergt . Colour-Sergeant
Com . . Communist
Comd . . Command
Comdg . . Commanding
Comdr . . Commander
Comdt . . Commandant
Commn . . Commission
Commnd . . Commissioned
CompIEE . Companion of the Institution of Electrical Engineers
CompIERE . Companion of the Institution of Electronic and Radio Engineers
CompTI . . Companion of the Textile Institute
Comr . . Commissioner
Comy-Gen. . Commissary-General
CON . . Cross of Order of the Niger
Conn . . Connecticut (US)
Const. . . Constitutional
COPEC . . Conference of Politics, Economics and Christianity
Corp. . . Corporation; Corporal
Corr. Mem. or Fell. . Corresponding Member or Fellow
COS . . Charity Organization Society
COSA . . Colliery Officials and Staffs Association
COSSAC . Chief of Staff to Supreme Allied Commander
COTC . . Canadian Officers' Training Corps
Co.U or Coal.U Coalition Unionist
CP . . Central Provinces; Cape Province
CPA . . Commonwealth Parliamentary Association; Chartered Patent Agent; also (formerly) Certified Public Accountant (Canada) (now merged with CA)
CPR . . Canadian Pacific Railway
CPRE . . Council for the Preservation of Rural England
CPSU . . Communist Party of the Soviet Union
CR . . Community of the Resurrection
cr . . created or creation
CRA . . Commander, Royal Artillery
CRASC . . Commander, Royal Army Service Corps
CRE . . Commander, Royal Engineers
Cres. . . Crescent
CRO . . Commonwealth Relations Office (before Aug. 1966; *now see* CO)
CS . . . Civil Service
CSB . . Bachelor of Christian Science
CSC . . Conspicuous Service Cross
CSI . . Companion of the Order of the Star of India
CSIR . . Commonwealth Council for Scientific and Industrial Research (re-named: Commonwealth Scientific and Industrial Research Organisation; *see* below)
CSIRO . . Commonwealth Scientific and Industrial Research Organization (and *see* above)
CSO . . Chief Scientific Officer; Chief Signal Officer
CSP . . Chartered Society of Physiotherapists; Civil Service of Pakistan
CSSp . . Holy Ghost Father
CSSR . . Congregation of the Most Holy Redeemer (Redemptorist Order)
CStJ . . Commander of the Order of St John of Jerusalem
CTA . . Chaplain Territorial Army
CTC . . Cyclists' Touring Club
CTR (Harwell) Controlled Thermonuclear Research
CU . . Cambridge University
CUAC . . Cambridge University Athletic Club
CUAFC . . Cambridge University Association Football Club
CUBC . . Cambridge University Boat Club
CUCC . . Cambridge University Cricket Club
CUF . . Common University Fund
CUHC . . Cambridge University Hockey Club
CUP . . Cambridge University Press
CURUFC . Cambridge University Rugby Union Football Club
CVO . . Commander of the Royal Victorian Order
CWS . . Co-operative Wholesale Society

D

D . . . Duke
d . . . Died; daughter
DA . . Diploma in Anaesthesia, Diploma in Art
DAA&QMG . Deputy Assistant Adjutant and Quartermaster-General
DAAG . . Deputy Assistant Adjutant-General
DA&QMG . Deputy Adjutant and Quartermaster-General
DACG . . Deputy Assistant Chaplain-General
DAD . . Deputy Assistant Director
DADMS . . Deputy Assistant Director of Medical Services
DADOS . . Deputy Assistant Director of Ordnance Services
DADQ . . Deputy Assistant Director of Quartering
DADST . . Deputy Assistant Director of Supplies and Transport
DAG . . Deputy Adjutant-General
DAMS . . Deputy Assistant Military Secretary
DAQMG . Deputy Assistant Quartermaster-General
DASc . . Doctor in Agricultural Sciences
DATA . . Draughtsmen's and Allied Technicians' Association
DBE . . Dame Commander Order of the British Empire
DC . . District of Columbia (US)
DCAe . . Diploma of College of Aeronautics
DCAS . . Deputy Chief of the Air Staff
DCG . . Deputy Chaplain-General
DCGS . . Deputy Chief of the General Staff
DCh . . Doctor of Surgery
DCH . . Diploma in Child Health
DCIGS . . (formerly) Deputy Chief of the Imperial General Staff (now DCGS)
DCL . . Doctor of Civil Law
DCLI . . Duke of Cornwall's Light Infantry
DCM . . Distinguished Conduct Medal
DCMG . . Dame Commander of St Michael and St George
DCnL . . Doctor of Canon Law
DCS . . Deputy Chief of Staff; Doctor of Commercial Sciences
DCSO . . Deputy Chief Scientific Officer
DCT . . Doctor of Christian Theology
DCVO . . Dame Commander of Royal Victorian Order
DD . . Doctor of Divinity
DDL . . Deputy Director of Labour
DDME . . Deputy Director of Mechanical Engineering
DDMI . . Deputy Director of Military Intelligence
DDMS . . Deputy Director of Medical Services
DDMT . . Deputy Director of Military Training
DDNI . . Deputy Director of Naval Intelligence
DDO . . Diploma in Dental Orthopædics
DDPR . . Deputy Director of Public Relations
DDPS . . Deputy Director of Personal Services
DDRA . . Deputy Director Royal Artillery

DDS . . Doctor of Dental Surgery; Director of Dental Services
DDSc . . Doctor of Dental Science
DDSD . . Deputy Director Staff Duties
DDST . . Deputy Director of Supplies and Transport
DDWE&M . Deputy Director of Works, Electrical and Mechanical
DE . . Doctor of Engineering
DEA . . Department of Economic Affairs
Decd . . Deceased
DEconSc. . Doctor of Economic Science
DEd . . Doctor of Education
Del . . Delaware (US)
Deleg. . . Delegate
DEng . . Doctor of Engineering
DenM . . Docteur en Médicine
DEOVR . . Duke of Edinburgh's Own Volunteer Rifles
DEP . . Department of Employment and Productivity
Dep. . . Deputy
DèsL . . Docteur ès lettres
DèsS . . Docteur ès sciences
DesRCA . . Designer of the Royal College of Art
DFA . . Doctor of Fine Arts
DFC . . Distinguished Flying Cross
DFM . . Distinguished Flying Medal (Canada)
DG . . Dragoon Guards
DGAMS . . Director-General Army Medical Services
DGMS . . Director-General of Medical Services
DGMT . . Director-General of Military Training
DGMW . . Director-General of Military Works
DGNPS . . Director-General of Naval Personal Services
DGP . . Director-General of Personnel
DGS . . Diploma in Graduate Studies
DGStJ . . (formerly) Dame of Grace, Order of St John of Jerusalem (now DStJ)
DHL . . Doctor of Humane Letters; Doctor of Hebrew Literature
DHQ . . District Headquarters
DIC . . Diploma of the Imperial College
DIG . . Deputy Inspector-General
DIH . . Diploma in Industrial Health
Dio. . . Diocese
DipCD . . Diploma in Civic Design
DipEd . . Diploma in Education
DipPA . . Diploma of Practitioners in Advertising
DipTPT . . Diploma in Theory and Practice of Teaching
DisTP . . Distinction Town Planning
Div. . . Division; divorced
DJAG . . Deputy Judge Advocate General
DJStJ . . formerly Dame of Justice of St John of Jerusalem (now DStJ)
DJur . . Doctor Juris
DL . . Deputy-Lieutenant
DLC . . Diploma Loughborough College
DLES . . Doctor of Letters in Economic Studies
DLI . . Durham Light Infantry
DLitt or DLit . Doctor of Literature; Doctor of Letters
DLO . . Diploma in Laryngology and Otology
DM . . Doctor of Medicine
DMD . . Doctor of Medical Dentistry (Australia)
DME . . Director of Mechanical Engineering
DMI . . Director of Military Intelligence
DMJ . . Diploma in Medical Jurisprudence
DMR . . Diploma in Medical Radiology
DMRE . . Diploma in Medical Radiology and Electrology
DMRT . . Diploma in Medical Radio-Therapy
DMS . . Director of Medical Services
DMus . . Doctor of Music
DMT . . Director of Military Training
DNB . . Dictionary of National Biography
DNE . . Director of Naval Equipment.
DNI . . Director of Naval Intelligence
DO . . Diploma in Ophthalmology
DObstRCOG . Diploma Royal College of Obstetricians and Gynaecologists
DOC . . District Officer Commanding
DocEng . . Doctor of Engineering
DOL . . Doctor of Oriental Learning
Dom. . . *Dominus*
DOMS . . Diploma in Ophthalmic Medicine and Surgery
DOR . . Director of Operational Requirements
DOS . . Director of Ordnance Services
Dow. . . Dowager
DPed . . Doctor of Pedagogy
DPA . . Diploma in Public Administration; Discharged Prisoners' Aid
DPEc . . Doctor of Political Economy
DPH . . Diploma in Public Health
DPh or DPhil . Doctor of Philosophy
DPM . . Diploma in Psychological Medicine
DPR . . Director of Public Relations
DPS . . Director of Postal Services; also (formerly) Director of Personal Services
DQMG . . Deputy Quartermaster-General
Dr . . Doctor
DRAC . . Director Royal Armoured Corps
DrIng . . Doctor of Engineering (Germany)
DrOEcPol . Doctor OEconomiæ Politicæ
DSAO . . Diplomatic Service Administration Office
DSC . . Distinguished Service Cross
DSc . . Doctor of Science
DScA . . Docteur en sciences agricoles
DSD . . Director Staff Duties
DSIR . . Dept. of Scientific and Industrial Research (now *see under* SRC)
DSM . . Distinguished Service Medal
DSO . . Companion of the Distinguished Service Order
DSP . . Director of Selection of Personnel; Docteur en sciences politiques (Montreal)
d.s.p. . . *decessit sine prole* (died without issue)
DSS . . Doctor of Sacred Scripture
DSSc . . Doctor of Social Science (USA)
DST . . Director of Supplies and Transport
DStJ . . Dame of Grace, Order of St John of Jerusalem; Dame of Justice, Order of St John of Jerusalem; and *see* GCStJ
DTD . . Dekoratie voor Trouwe Dienst (Decoration for Devoted Service)
DTech . . Doctor of Technology
DTH . . Diploma in Tropical Hygiene
DTheol . . Doctor of Theology
DThPT . . Diploma in Theory and Practice of Teaching (Durham University)
DTM&H . . Diploma in Tropical Medicine and Hygiene
DUniv . . Doctor of the University
DUP . . Docteur de l'Université de Paris
DVH . . Diploma in Veterinary Hygiene
DVM . . Doctor of Veterinary Medicine
DVSM . . Diploma in Veterinary State Medicine

E

E . . East; Earl
e . . eldest
EAP . . East Africa Protectorate
Ebor . . (*Eboracensis*) of York
EC . . East Central (postal district); Emergency Commission
ECA . . Economic Co-operation Administration
ECAFE . . Economic Commission for Asia and the Far East
ECE . . Economic Commission for Europe

ECGD	Export Credits Guarantee Department
ECSC	European Coal and Steel Community
ECU	English Church Union
ED	Efficiency Decoration; Doctor of Engineering (US)
EdB	Bachelor of Education
EDC	Economic Development Committee
EdD	Doctor of Education
Edin.	Edinburgh
Edn	Edition
Educ	Educated
Educn	Education
EEC	European Economic Community
EEF	Egyptian Expeditionary Force
EETS	Early English Text Society
EFTA	European Free Trade Association
e.h.	*ehrenhalber*; see under *h.c.*
EI	East Indian; East Indies
EICS	East India Company's Service
E-in-C	Engineer-in-Chief
EMS	Emergency Medical Service
Ency.Brit.	Encyclopaedia Britannica
Eng.	England
Engr	Engineer
ENSA	Entertainments National Service Association
ENT	Ear, Nose and Throat
er.	elder
ER	Eastern Region (BR)
ERC	Electronics Research Council
ERD	Emergency Reserve Decoration (Army)
ESRO	European Space Research Organization
ESU	English-Speaking Union
Euratom	European Atomic Energy Commission
Ext.	Extinct

F

FA	Football Association
FAA	Fellow of the Australian Academy of Science; also (formerly) Fleet Air Arm
FAAAS	Fellow of the American Association for the Advancement of Science
FACC	Fellow of the American College of Cardiology
FACCA	Fellow of the Association of Certified and Corporate Accountants
FACCP	Fellow of American College of Chest Physicians
FACD	Fellow of the American College of Dentistry
FACE	Fellow of the Australian College of Education
FACI	(Changed to) FRACI
FACP	Fellow of American College of Physicians
FACR	Fellow of American College of Radiology
FACS	Fellow of American College of Surgeons
FAGS	Fellow American Geographical Society
FAHA	Fellow, Australian Academy of the Humanities
FAI	Fellow of Chartered Auctioneers' and Estate Agents' Institute
FAIA	Fellow of American Institute of Architects
FAIAA	Fellow of American Institute of Aeronautics and Astronautics (and *see under* FIAS)
FAIAS	Fellow of Australian Institute of Agricultural Science
FAIM	Fellow of the Australian Institute of Management
FAIP	Fellow of Australian Institute of Physics
FAMS	Fellow of the Ancient Monuments Society
FAmSCE	Fellow of the American Society of Civil Engineers
FANY	First Aid Nursing Yeomanry
FAO	Food and Agriculture Organization
FAPHA	Fellow American Public Health Association
FAPI	Fellow of the Australian Planning Institute
FARELF	Far East Land Forces
FAS	Fellow of the Antiquarian Society
FASA	Fellow of Australian Society of Accountants
FASCE	Fellow of the American Society of Civil Engineers
FBA	Fellow of the British Academy
FBCS	Fellow of the British Computer Society
FBHI	Fellow of the British Horological Institute
FBI	Federation of British Industries (*see under* CBI, in which now merged)
FBIM	Fellow of the British Institute of Management (formerly FIIA; Fellow of the Institute of Industrial Administration)
FBOA	Fellow of British Optical Association
FBOU	Fellow British Ornithologists Union
FBritIRE	(formerly) Fellow of British Institution of Radio Engineers
FBPsS	Fellow of British Psychological Society
FBS	Fellow Building Societies Institute
FBSI	Fellow of Boot and Shoe Institution
FBSM	Fellow of the Birmingham School of Music
FCA	Fellow of the Institute of Chartered Accountants
FCASI	(formerly FCAI) Fellow of the Canadian Aeronautics and Space Institute
FCCS	Fellow of Corporation of Secretaries (formerly of Certified Secretaries)
FCGI	Fellow of City and Guilds of London Institute
FCGP	Fellow of the College of General Practitioners
FCH	Fellow of Coopers Hill College
FChS	Fellow of the Society of Chiropodists
FCIC	Fellow Chemical Institute of Canada (formerly Canadian Institute of Chemistry)
FCII	Fellow of the Chartered Insurance Institute
FCIPA	(formerly used for) Fellow of the Chartered Institute of Patent Agents (now *see* CPA)
FCIS	Fellow of the Chartered Institute of Secretaries
FCO	Foreign and Commonwealth Office (departments merged Oct. 1968)
FCP	Fellow College of Preceptors
FCPath	Fellow of the College of Pathologists (now *see* FRCPath)
FCP(SoAf)	Fellow of the College of Physicians, South Africa
FCPSO(SoAf)	(and *see* FCP(SoAf) and FCS(SoAf) Fellow of the College of Physicians and Surgeons and Obstetricians, South Africa
FCRA	Fellow of the College of Radiologists of Australia
FCS or **FChemSoc**	Fellow of the Chemical Society
FCSP	Fellow of the Chartered Society of Physiotherapy
FCS(SoAf)	Fellow of the College of Surgeons, South Africa
FCST	Fellow of the College of Speech Therapists
FCT	Federal Capital Territory (now ACT)
FCTB	Fellow of the College of Teachers of the Blind

FCU . . Fighter Control Unit
FCWA . . Fellow of the Institute of Cost and Works Accountants
FDS . . Fellow in Dental Surgery
FDSRCS . Fellow in Dental Surgery, Royal College of Surgeons of England
FDSRCSE . Fellow in Dental Surgery, Royal College of Surgeons of Edinburgh
FEAF . . Far East Air Force
FEIS . . Fellow of the Educational Institute of Scotland
FES . . Fellow of the Entomological Society; Fellow of the Ethnological Society
FF . . Field Force
FFA . . Fellow of Faculty of Actuaries (in Scotland)
FFARACS . Fellow of Faculty of Anaesthetists, Royal Australian College of Surgeons
FFARCS . Fellow of Faculty of Anaesthetists, Royal College of Surgeons of England
FFARCSI . Fellow of Faculty of Anaesthetists, Royal College of Surgeons in Ireland
FFAS . . Fellow of Faculty of Architects and Surveyors, London
FFDRCSI . Fellow of Faculty of Dentistry, Royal College of Surgeons in Ireland
FFF . . Free French Forces
FFHom . . Fellow of Faculty of Homœopathy
FFI . . French Forces of the Interior
FFR . . Fellow of Faculty of Radiologists
FGA . . Fellow Gemmological Association
FGI . . Fellow of the Institute of Certificated Grocers
FGS . . Fellow of Geological Society
FGSM . . Fellow of Guildhall School of Music
FHA . . Fellow of the Institute of Hospital Administrators
FHAS . . Fellow of Highland and Agricultural Society of Scotland
FH-WC . . Fellow of Heriot-Watt College (now University), Edinburgh
FIA . . Fellow of Institute of Actuaries
FIAAS . . Fellow of the Institute of Australian Agricultural Science
FIAA&S . . Fellow of the Incorporated Association of Architects and Surveyors
FIAgrE . . Fellow of the Institution of Agricultural Engineers
FIAI . . Fellow of the Institute of Industrial and Commercial Accountants
FIAL . . Fellow of the International Institute of Arts and Letters
FIArb . . Fellow of Institute of Arbitrators
FIAS . . (now *see under* FAIAA) (formerly) Fellow Institute of Aeronautical Sciences (US)
FIB . . Fellow of Institute of Bankers
FIBD . . Fellow of the Institute of British Decorators
FIBP . . Fellow of the Institute of British Photographers
FIBiol . . Fellow of Institute of Biology
FIC . . *See* FRIC
FICA . . Fellow of the Commonwealth Institute of Accountancy; Fellow of the Institute of Chartered Accountants in England and Wales (but *see* FCA)
FICD . . Fellow of the Institute of Civil Defence; Fellow of the Indian College of Dentists
FICE . . Fellow of the Institution of Civil Engineers (*see also* MICE)
FICeram . . Fellow of the Institute of Ceramics
FICI . . Fellow of the Institute of Chemistry of Ireland; Fellow of the International Colonial Institute
FICS . . Fellow of Institute of Chartered Shipbrokers; Fellow of the International College of Surgeons
FIE . . Fellow of Institute of Engineers
FIEE . . Fellow of the Institution of Electrical Engineers (*see also* MIEE)
FIEEE . . Fellow of Institute of Electrical and Electronics Engineers (NY)
FIEI . . Fellow of the Institution of Engineering Inspection
FIES . . Fellow of Illuminating Engineering Society
FIFST . . Fellow of Institute of Food Science and Technology
FIGCM . . Fellow Incorporated Guild of Church Musicians
FIHsg . . (formerly) Fellow of Institute of Housing (now *see under* FIHM)
FIHE . . Fellow of Institute of Health Education
FIHM . . Fellow of Institute of Housing Managers
FIIA . . Fellow of Institute of Industrial Administration (now FBIM: Fellow of the British Institute of Management)
FIInst . . Fellow of the Imperial Institute
FIL . . Fellow of the Institute of Linguists
FILA . . Fellow of the Institute of Landscape Architects
FIM . . Fellow of the Institution of Metallurgists
FIMA . . Fellow of the Institute of Mathematics and its Applications
FIMechE . Fellow of the Institution of Mechanical Engineers (*see also* MIMechE)
FIMI . . Fellow of the Institute of the Motor Industry (formerly FIMT: Fell. Inst. of Motor Trade)
FIMinE . . Fellow of the Institution of Mining Engineers
FIMIT . . Fellow of the Institute of Music Instrument Technology
FIMTA . . Fellow of the Institute of Municipal Treasurers and Accountants
FIN . . Fellow of the Institute of Navigation
FInstBiol . . Fellow of Institute of Biology (now *see* FIBiol)
FInstD . . Fellow of Institute of Directors
FInstF . . Fellow of Institute of Fuel
FInstM . . Fellow of the Institute of Meat
FInstMSM . Fellow of the Institute of Marketing and Sales Management (formerly FSMA)
FInstMet . Fellow of Institute of Metals
FInstP . . Fellow of Institute of Physics
FInstPet . . Fellow of the Institute of Petroleum
FInstPI . . Fellow of the Institute of Patentees (Incorporated)
FInstPS . . Fellow of Institute of Purchasing and Supply
FInstW . . Fellow of the Institute of Welding
FIOB . . Fellow of Institute of Builders
FIPA . . Fellow of the Institute of Practitioners in Advertising
FIPHE . . Fellow of the Institution of Public Health Engineers
FIPM . . Fellow of the Institute of Personnel Management
FIPR . . Fellow of Institute of Public Relations
FIRA(Ind) . Fellow of Institute of Railway Auditors and Accountants (India)
FIRE(Aust) . (now *see under* FIREE (Aust)); (formerly) Fellow of the Institution of Radio Engineers (Australia)

FIREE(Aust) . Fellow of the Institution of Radio and Electronics Engineers (Australia) (and *see under* FIRE(Aust))
FIRI . . Fellow of the Institution of the Rubber Industry
FIS . . Fellow of the Institute of Statisticians (formerly Assoc. of Incorporated Statisticians)
FISA . . Fellow of the Incorporated Secretaries' Association
FISE . . Fellow Institution of Sanitary Engineers
FIST . . Fellow of the Institute of Science Technology
FIWM . . Fellow of the Institution of Works Managers
FIWSc . . Fellow of the Institute of Wood Science
FJI . . Fellow of Institute of Journalists
FKC . . Fellow of King's College (London)
FLA . . Fellow of Library Association
Fla . . Florida (US)
FLAS . . Fellow of the Chartered Land Agents' Society
FLCM . . Fellow of the London College of Music
FLHS . . Fellow of the London Historical Society
FLS . . Fellow of the Linnaean Society
Flt . . Flight
FM . . Field-Marshal
FMA . . Fellow of the Museums Association
FMS . . Federated Malay States
FMSA . . Fellow of the Mineralogical Society of America
FNI . . Fellow of National Institute of Sciences in India
FNZIA . . Fellow of the New Zealand Institute of Architects
FNZIAS . . Fellow of the New Zealand Institute of Agricultural Science
FNZIC . . Fellow of the New Zealand Institute of Chemistry
FNZIE . . Fellow of the New Zealand Institution of Engineers
FO . . Foreign Office (*see also* FCO); Field Officer; Flying Officer
FOIC . . Flag Officer in charge
FPhS . . Fellow of the Philosophical Society of England
FPS . . Fellow of the Pharmaceutical Society
FPhysS . . Fellow of the Physical Society
FRACI . . Fellow of the Royal Australian Chemical Institute (formerly FACI)
FRACP . . Fellow of the Royal Australasian College of Physicians
FRACS . . Fellow of the Royal Australasian College of Surgeons
FRAD . . Fellow of the Royal Academy of Dancing
FRAeS . . Fellow of the Royal Aeronautical Society
FRAgSs . . Fellow of the Royal Agricultural Societies (*i e* of England, Scotland and Wales)
FRAHS . . Fellow Royal Australian Historical Society
FRAI . . Fellow of the Royal Anthropological Institute
FRAIA . . Fellow of the Royal Australian Institute of Architects
FRAIC . . Fellow of the Royal Architectural Institute of Canada
FRAM . . Fellow of the Royal Academy of Music
FRAS . . Fellow of the Royal Astronomical Society; Fellow of the Royal Asiatic Society
FRASB . . Fellow of Royal Asiatic Society of Bengal
FRASE . . Fellow of the Royal Agricultural Society of England
FRBS . . Fellow of Royal Society of British Sculptors; Fellow of The Royal Botanic Society
FRCGP . . Fellow of the Royal College of General Practitioners
FRCM . . Fellow of the Royal College of Music
FRCO . . Fellow of the Royal College of Organists
FRCO(CHM) . Fellow of the Royal College of Organists with Diploma in Choir Training
FRCOG . . Fellow of the Royal College of Obstetricians and Gynaecologists
FRCP . . Fellow of the Royal College of Physicians, London
FRCPath. . Fellow of the Royal College of Pathologists
FRCP(C) . Fellow of the Royal College of Physicians of Canada
FRCPE and FRCPEd . Fellow of the Royal College of Physicians of Edinburgh
FRCPGlas . Fellow of the Royal College (formerly Faculty) of Physicians and Surgeons, Glasgow (and *see under* FRFPSG)
FRCPI . . Fellow of the Royal College of Physicians in Ireland
FRCPS(Hon) . Hon. Fellow of Royal College Physicians and Surgeons (Glasgow)
FRCS . . Fellow of the Royal College of Surgeons of England
FRCSE and FRCSEd . Fellow of the Royal College of Surgeons of Edinburgh
FRCSGlas . Fellow of the Royal College of Surgeons of Glasgow
FRCSI . . Fellow of the Royal College of Surgeons in Ireland
FRCSoc . . Fellow of the Royal Commonwealth Society
FRCUS . . Fellow of the Royal College of University Surgeons (Denmark)
FRCVS . . Fellow of the Royal College of Veterinary Surgeons
FREconS . Fellow of Royal Economic Society
FREI . . Fellow of the Real Estate Institute (Australia)
FRES . . Fellow of Royal Entomological Society of London
FRFPSG . (formerly) Fellow of Royal Faculty of Physicians and Surgeons, Glasgow (now Royal College of Physicians and Surgeons, Glasgow) (and *see under* FRCPGlas)
FRGS . . Fellow of the Royal Geographical Society
FRHistS . . Fellow of Royal Historical Society
FRHS . . Fellow of the Royal Horticultural Society
FRIAS . . Fellow of the Royal Incorporation of Architects of Scotland
FRIBA . . Fellow of the Royal Institute of British Architects
FRIC . . (formerly FIC) Fellow of Royal Institute of Chemistry
FRICS . . Fellow of the Royal Institution of Chartered Surveyors
FRIH . . Fellow of Royal Institute of Horticulture (NZ)
FRIPHH. . Fellow of the Royal Institute of Public Health and Hygiene
FRMCM . Fellow of Royal Manchester College of Music
FRMedSoc . Fellow of Royal Medical Society
FRMetS . . Fellow of the Royal Meteorological Society
FRMS . . Fellow of the Royal Microscopical Society
FRNS . . Fellow of Royal Numismatic Society
FRNSA . . Fellow Royal School Naval Architecture
FRPS . . Fellow of the Royal Photographic Society
FRPSL . . Fellow of the Royal Philatelic Society, London
FRS . . Fellow of the Royal Society
FRSA . . Fellow of Royal Society of Arts
FRSAI . . Fellow of the Royal Society of Antiquaries of Ireland

FRSanI	Fellow of Royal Sanitary Institute (*see* FRSH)
FRSC	Fellow of the Royal Society of Canada
FRSCM	Fellow of the Royal School of Church Music
FRSE	Fellow of the Royal Society of Edinburgh
FRSGS	Fellow of the Royal Scottish Geographical Society
FRSH	Fellow of the Royal Society for the Promotion of Health (formerly FRSanI)
FRSL	Fellow of the Royal Society of Literature
FRSM or **FRSocMed**	Fellow of Royal Society of Medicine
FRSNZ	Fellow of Royal Society of New Zealand
FRSSAf	Fellow of Royal Society of South Africa
FRST	Fellow of the Royal Society of Teachers
FRSTM&H	Fellow of Royal Society of Tropical Medicine and Hygiene
FRVIA	Fellow Royal Victorian Institute of Architects
FRZSScot	Fellow of the Royal Zoological Society of Scotland
fs	Graduate of Royal Air Force Staff College
FSA	Fellow of the Society of Antiquaries
FSAA	Fellow of the Society of Incorporated Accountants and Auditors
FSAM	Fellow of the Society of Art Masters
FSArc	Fellow of Society of Architects (merged with the RIBA, 1925)
FSAScot	Fellow of the Society of Antiquaries of Scotland
FSASM	Fellow of the South Australian School of Mines
fsc	Foreign Staff College
FSDC	Fellow of Society of Dyers and Colourists
FSE	Fellow Society of Engineers
FSG	Fellow of the Society of Genealogists
FSGT	Fellow Society of Glass Technology
FSI	Fellow of Royal Institution of Chartered Surveyors (changed Aug. 1947 to FRICS)
FSIA	Fellow of Society of Industrial Artists and Designers
FSMA	Fellow Incorporated Sales Managers' Association; *see* FInstMSM
FSMC	Freeman of the Spectacle-Makers' Company
FSS	Fellow of the Royal Statistical Society
FTCD	Fellow of Trinity College, Dublin
FTCL	Fellow of Trinity College of Music, London
FTI	Fellow of the Textile Institute
FTII	Fellow of the Institute of Taxation
FTS	Flying Training School
FUMIST	Fellow of University of Manchester Institute of Science and Technology
FWA	Fellow of the World Academy of Arts and Sciences
FZS	Fellow of the Zoological Society
FZSScot	(Changed to) FRZSScot

G

Ga	Georgia (US)
GAPAN	Guild of Air Pilots and Air Navigators
GATT	General Agreement on Tariffs and Trade
GB	Great Britain
GBA	Governing Bodies Association
GBE	Knight or Dame Grand Cross Order of the British Empire
GC	George Cross
GCB	Knight Grand Cross of the Bath
GCH	Knight Grand Cross of Hanover
GCIE	Knight Grand Commander of the Indian Empire
GCMG	Knight or Dame Grand Cross of St Michael and St George
GCON	Grand Cross, Order of the Niger
GCSI	Knight Grand Commander of the Star of India
GCStJ	Bailiff or Dame Grand Cross of the Order of St John of Jerusalem
GCVO	Knight or Dame Grand Cross of Royal Victorian Order
GDC	General Dental Council
Gdns	Gardens
Gen.	General
Ges.	Gesellschaft
GFS	Girls' Friendly Society
g g s	Great grandson
GHQ	General Headquarters
Gib.	Gibraltar
GIMechE	Graduate Institution of Mechanical Engineers
GL	Grand Lodge
GLC	Greater London Council
Glos	Gloucestershire
GM	George Medal; Grand Medal (Ghana)
GMC	General Medical Council; Guild of Memorial Craftsmen
GMIE	Grand Master of Indian Empire
GMSI	Grand Master of Star of India
GOC	General Officer Commanding
GOC-in-C	General Officer Commanding-in-Chief
GOE	General Ordination Examination
Gov.	Governor
Govt	Government
GP	General Practitioner; Grand Prix
GPDST	Girls' Public Day School Trust
GPO	General Post Office
GQG	Grand Quartier Général (French GHQ)
Gr.	Greek
Gram. Sch.	Grammar School
GRSM	Graduate of the Royal Schools of Music
GS	General Staff
g s	Grandson
GSM	Guildhall School of Music
GSO	General Staff Officer
GTS	General Theological Seminary (New York)
GUI	Golfing Union of Ireland
GWR	Great Western Railway

H

HAA	Heavy Anti-Aircraft
HAC	Honourable Artillery Company
Hants	Hampshire
HARCVS	Honorary Associate of the Royal College of Veterinary Surgeons
Harv.	Harvard
HBM	His (or Her) Britannic Majesty (Majesty's)
hc	*honoris causa*
HCF	Hon. Chaplain to the Forces
HDA	Hawkesbury Diploma in Agriculture (Australian)
HDD	Higher Dental Diploma
HE	His Excellency; His Eminence
HEH	His Exalted Highness
HEIC	Honourable East India Company
HEICS	Honourable East India Company's Service
Heir-pres.	Heir-presumptive
Herts	Hertfordshire
HFARA	Honorary Foreign Associate of the Royal Academy
HFRA	Honorary Foreign Member of the Royal Academy
HG	Home Guard
HH	His (or Her) Highness; His Holiness

HHD . . Doctor of Humanities (US)
HIH . . His (or Her) Imperial Highness
HIM . . His (or Her) Imperial Majesty
HJ . . Hilal-e-Jurat (Pakistan)
HLI . . Highland Light Infantry
HM . . His (or Her) Majesty, or Majesty's
HMAS . . His (or Her) Majesty's Australian Ship
HMC . . Headmasters' Conference; Hospital Management Committee
HMHS . . His (or Her) Majesty's Hospital Ship
HMI . . His (or Her) Majesty's Inspector
HMOCS . . His (or Her) Majesty's Overseas Civil Service
HMS . . His (or Her) Majesty's Ship
HMSO . . His (or Her) Majesty's Stationery Office
Hon. . . Honourable; Honorary
HP . . House Physician
HPk . . Hilal-e-Pakistan
HQ . . Headquarters
(HR) . . Home Ruler
HRCA . . Honorary Royal Cambrian Academician
HRH . . His (or Her) Royal Highness
HRHA . . Honorary Member of Royal Hibernian Academy
HRI . . Honorary Member of Royal Institute of Painters in Water Colours
HROI . . Honorary Member of Royal Institute of Oil Painters
HRSA . . Honorary Member of Royal Scottish Academy
HRSW . . Honorary Member of Royal Scottish Water Colour Society
HS . . House Surgeon
HSH . . His (or Her) Serene Highness
Hum. . . Humanity, Humanities (Latin)
Hunts . . Huntingdonshire
Hy . . Heavy

I

I . . . Island
Ia . . . Iowa (US)
IA . . . Indian Army
IAF . . Indian Air Force; Indian Auxiliary Force
IAHM . . Incorporated Association of Headmasters
IAMC . . Indian Army Medical Corps
IAMTACT . Institute of Advanced Machine Tool and Control Technology
IAOC . . Indian Army Ordnance Control
IAPS . . Incorporated Association of Preparatory Schools
IARO . . Indian Army Reserve of Officers
IAS . . Indian Administrative Service
IATA . . International Air Transport Association
Ib. or **Ibid.** . *Ibidem* (in the same place)
IBRD . . International Bank for Reconstruction and Development (World Bank)
i/c . . . In charge
ICA . . Institute of Contemporary Arts
ICAA . . Invalid Children's Aid Association
ICAO . . International Civil Aviation Organization
ICE . . Institution of Civil Engineers
Icel. . . Icelandic
ICFTU . . International Confederation of Free Trade Unions
IChemE . . Institution of Chemical Engineers
ICI . . Imperial Chemical Industries
ICOM . . International Council of Museums
ICRC . . International Committee of the Red Cross
ICS . . Indian Civil Service
ICSV . . International Council of Scientific Unions
ICT . . International Computers and Tabulators Ltd
Id . . Idaho (US)
IDA . . International Development Association
idc . . Completed a Course at, or served for a year on the Staff of, the Imperial Defence College
IEE . . Institution of Electrical Engineers
IEEE . . Institute of Electrical and Electronics Engineers (NY)
IERE . . Institution of Electronic and Radio Engineers (and *see under* BritIRE)
IES . . Indian Educational Service; Illuminating Engineering Society
IFS . . Irish Free State; Indian Forest Service
IG . . Instructor in Gunnery
IGU . . International Geographical Union
ILEC . . Inner London Education Committee
Ill . . Illinois (US)
ILO . . International Labour Office
ILP . . Independent Labour Party
IMA . . International Music Association
IMEA . . Incorporated Municipal Electrical Association
IMechE . . Institution of Mechanical Engineers
IMinE . . Institution of Mining Engineers
IMF . . International Monetary Fund
IMMTS . . Indian Mercantile Marine Training Ship
Imp. . . Imperial
IMS . . Indian Medical Service
IMTA . . Institute of Municipal Treasurers and Accountants
IMunE . . Institution of Municipal Engineers
IN . . Indian Navy
Inc. . . Incorporated
Incog. . . *Incognito* (in secret)
Ind. . . Independent; Indiana (US)
Insp. . . Inspector
Inst. . . Institute
InstT . . Institute of Transport
Instn . . Institution
InstnMM . Institution of Mining and Metallurgy
IODE . . Imperial Order of the Daughters of the Empire
I of M . . Isle of Man
IOGT . . International Order of Good Templars
IOM . . Isle of Man; Indian Order of Merit
IOOF . . Independent Order of Oddfellows
IOP . . Inst. of Painters in Oil Colours
IoW . . Isle of Wight
IPCS . . Institution of Professional Civil Servants
IPI . . International Press Institute
IPM . . Institute of Personnel Management
IPPS . . Institute of Physics and The Physical Society
IPS . . Indian Police Service; Indian Political Service
IPU . . Inter-Parliamentary Union
IRA . . Irish Republican Army
IRC . . Industrial Reorganization Corporation
IREE(Aust) . Institution of Radio and Electronics Engineers (Australia)
IRO . . International Refugee Organization
Is . . . Island(s)
IS . . . International Society of Sculptors, Painters and Gravers
ISC . . Imperial Service College, Haileybury; Indian Staff Corps
ISE . . Indian Service of Engineers
ISMRC . . Inter-Services Metallurgical Research Council
ISO . . Imperial Service Order
IStructE . . Institution of Structural Engineers
IT . . . Indian Territory (US)
ITA . . Independent Television Authority
Ital. or **It.** . Italian

ITO . . International Trade Organization
IUCW . . International Union for Child Welfare
IUP . . Association of Independent Unionist Peers
IW . . . Isle of Wight
IWGC . . Imperial War Graves Commission
IY . . . Imperial Yeomanry
IZ . . . I Zingari

J

JA . . . Judge Advocate
JAG . . Judge Advocate General
Jas . . James
JCB . . *Juris Canonici Bachelor* (Bachelor of Canon Law)
JCS . . Journal of the Chemical Society
JCD . . *Juris Canonici Doctor* (Doctor of Canon Law)
JD . . . Doctor of Jurisprudence
JDipMA . Joint Diploma in Management Accounting Services
JInstE . . Junior Institution of Engineers
jls . . . Journals
JMN . . *Johan Mangku Negara* (Malaysian Honour)
Joh. or **Jno.** . John
JP . . . Justice of the Peace
Jr . . . Junior
jsc . . . Qualified at a Junior Staff Course, or the equivalent, 1942–46
JSLS . . Joint Services Liaison Staff
jssc . . Joint Services Staff Course
JWS or **jws** . Joint Warfare Staff
JUD . . *Juris Utriusque Doctor,* Doctor of Both Laws (Canon and Civil)
Jun. . . Junior
Jun. Opt. . . Junior Optime

K

Kans . . Kansas (US)
KAR . . King's African Rifles
KBE . . Knight Commander Order of the British Empire
KC . . King's Counsel
KCB . . Knight Commander of the Bath
KCC . . Commander of Order of Crown, Belgian and Congo Free State
KCH . . King's College Hospital; Knight Commander of Hanover
KCIE . . Knight Commander of the Indian Empire
KCL . . King's College, London
KCMG . . Knight Commander of St Michael and St George
KCSG . . Knight Commander of St Gregory
KCSI . . Knight Commander of the Star of India
KCSS . . Knight Commander of St Silvester
KCVO . . Knight Commander of the Royal Victorian Order
KDG . . King's Dragoon Guards
KEH . . King Edward's Horse
KG . . Knight of the Order of the Garter
KGStJ . . formerly Knight of Grace, Order of St John of Jerusalem (now KStJ)
KH . . Knight of Hanover
KHC . . Hon. Chaplain to the King
KHDS . . Hon. Dental Surgeon to the King
KHNS . . Hon. Nursing Sister to the King
KHP . . Hon. Physician to the King
KHS . . Hon. Surgeon to the King; Knight of the Holy Sepulchre
K-i-H . . Kaisar-i-Hind
KJStJ . . formerly Knight of Justice, Order of St John of Jerusalem (now KStJ)
KORR . . King's Own Royal Regiment
KOSB . . King's Own Scottish Borderers
KOYLI . . King's Own Yorkshire Light Infantry
KP . . Knight of the Order of St Patrick (now held only by Dukes of Windsor and Gloucester)
KRRC . . King's Royal Rifle Corps
KStJ . . Knight of Order of St John of Jerusalem; and *see* GCStJ
KS . . . King's Scholar
KSG . . Knight of St Gregory
KSLI . . King's Shropshire Light Infantry
KSS . . Knight of St Silvester
KT . . Knight of the Order of the Thistle
Kt or **Knt** . Knight
Ky . . . Kentucky (US)

L

(L) . . . Liberal
LA . . Los Angeles; Literate in Arts; Liverpool Academy
La . . . Louisiana (US)
(Lab) . . Labour
LAC . . London Athletic Club
L-Corp. or **Lance-Corp.** Lance-Corporal
Lancs . . Lancashire
LCC . . London County Council (now *see under* GLC)
LCh . . Licentiate in Surgery
LCJ . . Lord Chief Justice
LCL . . Licentiate of Canon Law
LCP . . Licentiate of the College of Preceptors
LDiv . . Licentiate in Divinity
LDS . . Licentiate in Dental Surgery
LDV . . Local Defence Volunteers
LEA . . Local Education Authority
LesL . . Licencié ès lettres
LH . . Light Horse
LHD . . (*Literarum Humaniorum Doctor*) Doctor of Literature
LI . . Light Infantry; Long Island
LicMed . . Licentiate in Medicine
Lieut . . Lieutenant
Lincs . . Lincolnshire
Lit. . . Literature; Literary
LitD . . Doctor of Literature; Doctor of Letters
Lit. Hum. . *Literae Humaniores* (Classics)
LittD . . Doctor of Literature; Doctor of Letters
LJ . . . Lord Justice
LLA . . Lady Literate in Arts
LLB . . Bachelor of Laws
LLCM . . Licentiate London College of Music
LLD . . Doctor of Laws
LLL . . Licentiate in Laws
LLM . . Master of Laws
LM . . Licentiate in Midwifery
LMBC . . Lady Margaret Boat Club
LMCC . . Licentiate of Medical Council of Canada
LMR . . London Midland Region (BR)
LMS . . London, Midland and Scottish Railway (*see* BR); London Missionary Society
LMSSA . . Licentiate in Medicine and Surgery, Society of Apothecaries
LMTPI . . Legal Member of the Town Planning Institute
(LNat) . . Liberal National
LNER . . London and North Eastern Railway (*see* BR)
LRAM . . Licentiate of the Royal Academy of Music
LRCP . . Licentiate of the Royal College
LRAD . . Licentiate of the Royal Academy of Dancing
L of C . . Lines of Communication
LPTB . . London Passenger Transport Board
Physicians, London
LRCPE . . Licentiate Royal College of Physicians, Edinburgh
LRCS . . Licentiate of the Royal College of Surgeons of England

LRCSE Licentiate of the Royal College of Surgeons, Edinburgh

LRFPS(G) (formerly) Licentiate of the Royal Faculty of Physicians and Surgeons, Glasgow (now Royal College of Physicians and Surgeons, Glasgow)

LRIBA Licentiate Royal Institute of British Architects

LSA Licentiate of the Society of Apothecaries

LSE London School of Economics

Lt Light (*e.g.* Light Infantry)

Lt or **Lieut** Lieutenant

LT Licentiate in Teaching

LTB London Transport Board

LTCL Licentiate of Trinity College of Music, London

Lt-Col Lieutenant-Colonel

Lt-Gen. Lieutenant-General

LTh Licentiate in Theology

(LU) Liberal Unionist

LUOTC London University Officers' Training Corps

LXX Septuagint

M

M Marquess; Member; Monsieur

m married

MA Master of Arts

MAAF Mediterranean Allied Air Forces

MACE Member of the Australian College of Education

MACI Member of the American Concrete Institute

MACS Member of the American Chemical Society

MAEE Marine Aircraft Experimental Establishment

Mag. Magnetism or Magazine

MAI Master of Engineering (*Magister in Arte Ingeniaria*)

MAIAA Member of American Institute of Aeronautics and Astronautics (and *see under* MIAS)

MAICE Member of American Institute of Consulting Engineers

MAIChE Member of the American Institute of Chemical Engineers

Maj.-Gen. Major-General

Man Manitoba (Canada)

MAO Master of Obstetric Art

MAOU Member American Ornithologists' Union

MAP Ministry of Aircraft Production

MArch Master of Architecture

Marq. Marquess

MASAE Member American Society of Agricultural Engineering

MASCE Member American Society of Civil Engineers

MASME Member American Society of Mechanical Engineers

Mass Massachusetts (US)

Math. Mathematics; Mathematical

MB Bachelor of Medicine

MBE Member of the Order of the British Empire

MBIM Member of the British Institute of Management (formerly MIIA: Member of the Institute of Industrial Administration)

[illegible]BOU Member British Ornithologists' Union

[illegible]BritIRE (now *see under* MIERE) (formerly) Member of British Institution of Radio Engineers

[illegible] Military Cross

[illegible]C Marylebone Cricket Club

[illegible](Melb) Master of Civil Engineering (Melbourne University)

[illegible]r MChir Master in Surgery

[illegible]th Master of Orthopaedic Surgery

[illegible]A Master in Chemical Analysis

[illegible] Master of Civil Law

[illegible] Member of Civil and Mechanical Engineers' Society

MCom Master of Commerce

MConsE Master of Association of Consulting Engineers

MCP Master of City Planning (US)

MCPA Member of the College of Pathologists of Australia

MCPath Member of College of Pathologists

MCPS Member College of Physicians and Surgeons

MCS Madras Civil Service; Malayan Civil Service

MD Doctor of Medicine; Military District

Md Maryland (US)

MDS Master of Dental Surgery

Me Maine (US)

ME Mining Engineer; Middle East

MEAF Middle East Air Force

MEC Member of Executive Council

MEc Master of Economics

Mech. Mechanics; Mechanical

Med. Medical

MEd Master of Education

MEF Middle East Force

MEIC Member Engineering Institute of Canada

MELF Middle East Land Forces

MEng Master of Engineering

MetR Metropolitan Railway

MEXE Military Engineering Experimental Establishment

MFGB Miners' Federation of Great Britain

MFH Master of Foxhounds

MGA Maj.-Gen. i/c Administration

MGC Machine Gun Corps

MGGS Major-General, General Staff

MGI Member of the Institute of Certificated Grocers

Mgr Monsignor

MHA Member of House of Assembly

MHR Member House of Representatives

MI Military Intelligence

MIAeE Member Institute of Aeronautical Engineers

MIAgrE Member of Institution of Agricultural Engineers

MIAS (now *see under* MAIAA) (formerly) Member Institute of Aeronautical Science (US)

MIBF Member Institute of British Foundrymen

MIBritishE Member Institute of British Engineers

MICE Member of Institution of Civil Engineers (formerly the higher rank of corporate membership of the Institution, now the lower rank; *see also* FICE; change dated July 1968)

MICEI Member of Institution of Civil Engineers of Ireland

Mich Michigan (US)

MIChemE Member of the Institution of Chemical Engineers

MIEAust Member Institution of Engineers, Australia

MIEE Member of Institution of Electrical Engineers (formerly the higher rank of corporate membership of the Institution, now the lower rank; *see also* FIEE; change dated Dec. 1966)

MIEEE Member of Institute of Electrical and Electronics Engineers (NY)

MIEI Member of Institution of Engineering Inspection

MIE(Ind) Member of Institution of Engineers, India

MIERE Member of Institution of Electronic and Radio Engineers (and *see under* MBritIRE)

MIES Member Institution of Engineers and Shipbuilders, Scotland

MIEx Member Institute of Export

MIH Member Institute of Hygiene

MIHVE Member Institution of Heating and Ventilating Engineers

MIIA Member of the Institute of Industrial Administration (now *see under* MBIM)

Mil. Military

MILocoE Member of Institution of Locomotive Engineers

MIMarE Member of the Institute of Marine Engineers

MIMechE Member of Institution of Mechanical Engineers (formerly the higher rank of corporate membership of the Institution, now the lower rank; *see also* FIMechE; change dated April 1968)

MIMI Member of Institute of Motor Industry

MIMinE Member of the Institution of Mining Engineers

MIMM Member Institution of Mining and Metallurgy

MIMunE Member Institution of Municipal Engineers

Min. Ministry

MIN Member of the Institute of Navigation

Minn Minnesota (US)

MInstCE Member of Institution of Civil Engineers (changed Feb. 1940 to MICE)

MInstF Member of Institute of Fuel

MInstGasE Member Institution of Gas Engineers

MInstHE Member of the Institution of Highway Engineers

MInstM Member of Institute of Marketing

MInstME Member of Institution of Mining Engineers

MInstMet Member of the Institute of Metals

MInstPet Member of the Institute of Petroleum

MInstPI Member of the Institute of Patentees (Inc.)

MInstR Member of the Institute of Refrigeration

MInstRA Member of the Institute of Registered Architects

MInstT Member of the Institute of Transport

MInstW Member Institute of Welding

MInstWE Member of the Institution of Water Engineers (now MIWE)

MINucE Member of Institution of Nuclear Engineers

MIOB Member of the Institute of Builders

MIPA Member of the Institute of Practitioners in Advertising

MIPlantE Member of the Institution of Plant Engineers

MIPM Member of the Institute of Personnel Management

MIPR Member of the Institute of Public Relations

MIProdE (formerly MIPE) Member of the Institution of Production Engineers

MIRE (now *see under* MIERE) (formerly) Member of the Institution of Radio Engineers

MIREE(Aust) Member of the Institution of Radio and Electronics Engineers (Australia)

MIRTE Member of Institute of Road Transport Engineers

MIS(India) Member of the Institution of Surveyors of India

MISI Member of Iron and Steel Institute

Miss Mississippi (US)

MIStructE Member of the Institution of Structural Engineers

MIT Massachusetts Institute of Technology

MIWE Member of the Institution of Water Engineers

MJI Member of Institute of Journalists

MJIE Member of the Junior Institute of Engineers

MJS Member of the Japan Society

ML Licentiate in Medicine; Master of Laws

MLA Member of Legislative Assembly

MLC Member of Legislative Council

MLitt Master of Letters

Mlle *Mademoiselle* (Miss)

MLO Military Liaison Officer

MM Military Medal

MME Master of Mining Engineering

MMechE Master of Mechanical Engineering

Mme Madame

MMet Master of Metallurgy

MMGI Member of the Mining, Geological and Metallurgical Institute of India

MMSA Master of Midwifery Society of Apothecaries

MN Merchant Navy

MNAS Member of the National Academy of Sciences (US)

MO Medical Officer

Mo Missouri (US)

MoD Ministry of Defence

Mods Moderations (Oxford)

MOH Medical Officer(s) of Health

MOI Ministry of Information

Mon Monmouthshire

Mont Montana (US); Montgomeryshire

MOP Ministry of Power

Most Rev. Most Reverend

MoT Ministry of Transport

MP Member of Parliament

MPBW Ministry of Public Building and Works

MPP Member Provincial Parliament

MPS Member of Pharmaceutical Society

MR Master of the Rolls; Municipal Reform

MRAIC Member Royal Architectural Institute of Canada

MRAS Member of Royal Asiatic Society

MRC Medical Research Council

MRCOG Member of Royal College of Obstetricians and Gynaecologists.

MRCP Member of the Royal College of Physicians, London

MRCPE Member of the Royal College of Physicians, Edinburgh

MRCPGlas Member of the Royal College (formerly Faculty) of Physicians and Surgeons, Glasgow

MRCS Member Royal College of Surgeons of England

MRCSE Member of the Royal College of Surgeons, Edinburgh

MRCVS Member of the Royal College of Veterinary Surgeons

MREmpS Member of the Royal Empire Society

MRI Member Royal Institution

MRIA Member Royal Irish Academy

MRIAI Member of the Royal Institute of the Architects of Ireland

MRICS Member of the Royal Institution of Chartered Surveyors

MRINA Member of Royal Institution of Naval Architects

MRSanI Member of Royal Sanitary Institute (*see* MRSH)

MRSH Member of the Royal Society for the Promotion of Health (formerly MRSanI)

MRST Member of Royal Society o[f] Teachers

MRUSI Member of the Royal Unite[d] Service Institution

MS Master of Surgery; Master [of] Science (US)

MS, MSS Manuscript, Manucripts

MSA Master of Science, Agricul[ture] (US); Mineralogical So[ciety] of America

MSAE Member of the Societ[y of] Automotive Engineers (U[S])

MSAICE Member of South Afri[can Insti]tution of Civil Engineer[s]

MSAInstMM Member of South Afric[an Insti]tute of Mining and Me[tallurgy]

MS&R Merchant Shipbuilding [and Re]pairs

MSAutE . . Member of the Society of Automobile Engineers
MSC . . Madras Staff Corps
MSc . . Master of Science
MScD . . Master of Dental Science
MSE . . Master of Science in Chemical Engineering (US)
MSH . . Master of Stag Hounds
MSIA . . Member Society of Industrial Artists
MSINZ . . Member Surveyors' Institute New Zealand
MSIT . . Member Society of Instrument Technology
MSM . . Meritorious Service Medal; Madras Sappers and Miners
MSR . . Member Society of Radiographers
Mt . . Mountain
MT . . . Mechanical Transport
MTAI . . Member of Institute of Travel Agents
MTCA . . Ministry of Transport and Civil Aviation
MTPI . . Member of Town Planning Institute
MusB . . Bachelor of Music
MusD . . Doctor of Music
MusM . . Master of Music
MV . . Merchant Vessel, Motor Vessel (naval)
MVO . . Member of the Royal Victorian Order
Mx . . Middlesex

N

(N) . . Nationalist; Navigating Duties
N . . . North
n . . . Nephew
NA . . National Academician (America)
NAACP . . National Association for the Advancement of Colored People
NAAFI . . Navy, Army and Air Force Institutes
NABC . . National Association of Boys' Clubs
NALGO (Nalgo) . National and Local Government Officers' Association
NAPT . . National Association for the Prevention of Tuberculosis
NASA . . National Aeronautics and Space Administration (US)
NATCS . . National Air Traffic Control Services
NATO . . North Atlantic Treaty Organisation
Nat.Sci. . . Natural Sciences
NB . . New Brunswick
NBA . . North British Academy
NBC . . National Book Council (now National Book League); National Broadcasting Company (of America)
NBL . . National Book League (formerly National Book Council)
NBPI . . National Board for Prices and Incomes
NC . . North Carolina (US)
NCB . . National Coal Board
NCLC . . National Council of Labour Colleges
NCU . . National Cyclists' Union
NDA . . National Diploma in Agriculture
NDak . . North Dakota (US)
ndc . . National Defence College (Canada)
NDD . . National Diploma in Dairying; National Diploma in Design
NDH . . National Diploma in Horticulture
NE . . . North-east
NEAC . . New English Art Club
NEAF . . Near East Air Force
Neb . . Nebraska (US)
NECInst . North-East Coast Institution of Engineers and Shipbuilders
NEDC . . National Economic Development Council; North East Development Council
NEL . . National Engineering Laboratory
NERC . . National Environment Research Council
Nev . . Nevada (US)
New M . . New Mexico (US)
NFER . . National Foundation for Educational Research
NFS . . National Fire Service
NFU . . National Farmers' Union
NFWI . . National Federation of Women's Institutes
NH . . New Hampshire (US)
NI . . . Northern Ireland; Native Infantry
NIAB . . National Institute of Agricultural Botany
NID . . Naval Intelligence Division; National Institute for the Deaf; Northern Ireland District
NJ . . . New Jersey (US)
NL . . . National Liberal
NLF . . National Liberal Federation
Northants . Northamptonshire
Notts . . Nottinghamshire
NP . . Notary Public
NPFA . . National Playing Fields Association
NPk . . Nishan-e-Pakistan
NPL . . National Physical Laboratory
NRA . . National Rifle Association; National Recovery Administration
NRD . . National Registered Designer
NRDC . . National Research Development Corporation
NRR . . Northern Rhodesia Regiment
NS . . . Nova Scotia; New Style in the Calendar (in Great Britain since 1752); National Society
ns . . . Graduate of Royal Naval Staff College, Greenwich
NSA . . National Skating Association
NSPCC . . National Society for Prevention of Cruelty to Children
N/SSF . . Novice, Society of St Francis
NSW . . New South Wales
NT . . New Testament; Northern Territory of South Australia
NTDA . . National Trade Development Association
NUGMW . National Union of General and Municipal Workers
NUI . . National University of Ireland
NUM . . National Union of Mineworkers
NUPE . . National Union of Public Employees
NUR . . National Union of Railwaymen
NUT . . National Union of Teachers
NUTG . . National Union of Townswomen's Guilds
NUTN . . National Union of Trained Nurses
NW . . North-west
NWFP . . North-West Frontier Province
NWP . . North-Western Provinces
NWT . . North-Western Territories
NY . . New York—City or State
NYC . . New York City
NZ . . New Zealand
NZEF . . New Zealand Expeditionary Force
NZIA . . New Zealand Institute of Architects

O

O . . . Ohio (US)
o . . . only
OA . . Officier d'Académie
OAS . . On Active Service
O & E . . Operations and Engineering (US)
O & O . . Oriental and Occidental (Steamship Co)
ob. . . . died
OBE . . Officer Order of the British Empire

OBI . . Order of British India
o c . . only child
OC and o/c . Officer Commanding
OCF . . Officiating Chaplain to the Forces
OCTU . . Officer Cadet Training Unit
ODA . . Overseas Development Administration
ODI . . Overseas Development Institute
ODM . . Ministry of Overseas Development
OECD . . Organization for Economic Co-operation and Development (formerly OEEC)
OEEC . . Organization for European Economic Co-operation; *see* OECD
OFM . . Order of Friars Minor
OFS . . Orange Free State
OHMS . . On His (or Her) Majesty's Service
OL . . Officer of the Order of Leopold
OM . . Order of Merit
OMI . . Oblate of Mary Immaculate
Ont . . Ontario
OON . . Officer of the Order of Niger
OP . . *Ordinis Praedicatorum*—of the Order of Preachers (Dominican Ecclesiastical Title); Observation Post
ORC . . Orange River Colony
Ore . . Oregon (US)
o s . . only son
OSA . . Ontario Society of Artists
OSB . . Order of St Benedict
OSFC . . Franciscan (Capuchin) Order
OSNC . . Orient Steam Navigation Co.
OSRD . . Office of Scientific Research and Development
OStJ . . Officer of Order of St John of Jerusalem
OT . . Old Testament
OTC . . Officers' Training Corps
OU . . Oxford University
OUAC . . Oxford University Athletic Club
OUAFC . . Oxford University Association Football Club
OUBC . . Oxford University Boat Club
OUCC . . Oxford University Cricket Club
OUDS . . Oxford University Dramatic Society
OUP . . Oxford University Press
OURC . . Oxford Union Rifle Club
OURFC . . Oxford University Rugby Football Club
Oxon . . Oxfordshire; of Oxford

P

PA . . Pakistan Army
Pa . . Pennsylvania (US)
pac . . passed the final examination of the Advanced Class, The Military College of Science
PASI . . Professional Associate Chartered Surveyors' Institution (changed August 1947 to ARICS)
PC . . Privy Councillor; Police Constable; Perpetual Curate; Peace Commissioner (Ireland)
pc . . *per centum* (by the hundred)
PCMO . . Principal Colonial Medical Officer
PdD . . Doctor of Pedagogy (US)
PEI . . Prince Edward Island
PEN . . (Name of Club: Poets, Playwrights, Editors, Essayists, Novelists)
PEng . . Registered Professional Engineer (Canada)
PEP . . Political and Economic Planning
PEST . . Pressure for Economic and Social Toryism
PF . . Procurator-Fiscal
pfc . . Graduate of RAF Flying College
PH . . Presidential Medal of Honour (Botswana)
PhB . . Bachelor of Philosophy
PhC . . Pharmaceutical Chemist
PhD . . Doctor of Philosophy
Phil. . . Philology, Philological; Philosophy, Philosophical
PhM . . Master of Philosophy (USA)
Phys. . . Physical
PIB . . Prices and Incomes Board (*see* NBPI)
PICAO . . Provisional International Civil Aviation Organization
pinx. . . (He) painted it
Pl . . Place; Plural
PLA . . Port of London Authority
Plen. . . Plenipotentiary
PMG . . Postmaster-General
PMN . . *Panglima Mangku Negara* (Malaysian Honour)
PMO . . Principal Medical Officer
PMRAFNS . Princess Mary's Royal Air Force Nursing Service
PMS . . President Miniature Society
PNBS . . *Panglima Negara Bintang Sarawak*
PNEU . . Parents' National Educational Union
P&O . . Peninsular and Oriental Steamship Co.
P&OSNCo. . Peninsular and Oriental Steam Navigation Co.
PO . . Post Office
Pop. . . Population
POW . . Prisoner of War; Prince of Wales's
PP . . Parish Priest; Past President
Pp . . Pages
PPCLI . . Princess Patricia's Canadian Light Infantry
PPE . . Philosophy, Politics and Economics (Oxford Univ.)
PPIStructE . Past President of the Institution of Structural Engineers
PPRA . . Past President of the Royal Academy
PPRBA . . Past President of the Royal Society of British Artists
PPRE . . Past President of the Royal Society of Painter-Etchers and Engravers
PPS . . Parliamentary Private Secretary
PPSIA . . Past President of the Society of Industrial Artists
PPTPI . . Past President Town Planning Institute
PQ . . Province of Quebec
PRA . . President of the Royal Academy
PRCS . . President of the Royal College of Surgeons
PRE . . President of the Royal Society of Painter-Etchers and Engravers
Preb. . . Prebendary
Pres. . . President
PRHA . . President of the Royal Hibernian Academy
PRI . . President of the Royal Institute of Painters in Water Colours
PRIA . . President of the Royal Irish Academy
Prin. . . Principal
PRO . . Public Relations Officer; Public Records Office
Proc. . . Proctor; Proceedings
Prof. . . Professor
PROI . . President of the Royal Institute of Oil Painters
Pro tem. . . *Pro tempore* (for the time being)
Prov. . . Provost; Provincial
Prox. . . *Proximo* (next)
Prox. acc. . *Proxime accessit* (next in order of merit to the winner, or a very close second)
PRS . . President of the Royal Society; Performing Right Society Ltd
PRSA . . President of the Royal Scottish Academy
PRSE . . President of the Royal Society of Edinburgh
PRSH . . President of the Royal Society for the Promotion of Health
PRSW . . President of the Royal Scottish Water Colour Society

PRUAA . . President of the Royal Ulster Academy of Arts
PRWS . . President of the Royal Society of Painters in Water Colours
PS . . Pastel Society
ps . . . passed School of Instruction (of Officers)
psa . . . Graduate of RAF Staff College
psc . . . Graduate of Staff College (†indicated Graduate of Senior Wing Staff College)
PSIA . . President of the Society of Industrial Artists
psm . . Certificate of Royal Military School of Music
PSMA . . President of Society of Marine Artists
PSNC . . Pacific Steam Navigation Co.
Pte . . . Private (soldier)
Pty . . . Proprietary
PWD . . Public Works Department
PWO . . Prince of Wales's Own

Q

Q . . . Queen
QAIMNS . Queen Alexandra's Imperial Military Nursing Service
QALAS . . Qualified Associate Chartered Land Agents' Society
QARANC . Queen Alexandra's Royal Army Nursing Corps
QARNNS . Queen Alexandra's Royal Naval Nursing Service
QC . . Queen's Counsel
QHC . . Queen's Honorary Chaplain
QHDS . . Queen's Honorary Dental Surgeon
QHNS . . Queen's Honorary Nursing Sister
QHP . . Queen's Honorary Physician
QHS . . Queen's Honorary Surgeon
Qld . . Queensland
QMAAC . Queen Mary's Army Auxiliary Corps
QMC . . Queen Mary College (London)
QMG . . Quartermaster-General
Q(ops) . . Quartering (operations)
QPM . . Queen's Police Medal
Qr . . . Quarter
QRV . . Qualified Valuer, Real Estate Institute of New South Wales
QS . . . Quarter Sessions
qs . . . RAF graduates of the Military or Naval Staff College (symbol omitted if subsequently qualified psa)
QUB . . Queen's University, Belfast
qv . . . *quod vide* (which see)

R

(R) . . . Reserve
RA . . . Royal Academician; Royal Artillery
RAAF . . Royal Australian Air Force
RAAMC . Royal Australian Army Medical Corps
RAC . . Royal Automobile Club; Royal Agricultural College; Royal Armoured Corps
RACGP . . Royal Australian College of General Practitioners
RAChD . . Royal Army Chaplains' Dept
RACP . . Royal Australasian College of Physicians
RACS . . Royal Australasian College of Surgeons
RADA . . Royal Academy of Dramatic Art
RAE . . Royal Australian Engineers; Royal Aircraft Establishment
RAEC . . Royal Army Educational Corps
RAeS . . Royal Aeronautical Society
RAF . . Royal Air Force
RAFO . . Reserve of Air Force Officers (now Royal Air Force Reserve of Officers)
RAFRO . . Royal Air Force Reserve of Officers
RAFVR . . Royal Air Force Volunteer Reserve
RAIA . . Royal Australian Institute of Architects
RAIC . . Royal Architectural Institute of Canada
RAM . . (Member of) Royal Academy of Music
RAMC . . Royal Army Medical Corps
RAN . . Royal Australian Navy
R&D . . Research and Development
RANVR . . Royal Australian Naval Volunteer Reserve
RAOC . . Royal Army Ordnance Corps
RAPC . . Royal Army Pay Corps
RARO . . Regular Army Reserve of Officers
RAS . . Royal Astronomical or Asiatic Society
RASC . . (formerly) Royal Army Service Corps (now *see under* RCT)
RASE . . Royal Agricultural Society of England
RAuxAF . Royal Auxiliary Air Force
RAVC . . Royal Army Veterinary Corps
RB . . Rifle Brigade
RBA . . Member Royal Society of British Artists
RBC . . Royal British Colonial Society of Artists
RBS . . Royal Society of British Sculptors
RBSA . . Royal Birmingham Soc. of Artists
RC . . Roman Catholic
RCA . . Member Royal Canadian Academy; Royal College of Art
RCAF . . Royal Canadian Air Force
RCAC . . Royal Canadian Armoured Corps
RCamA . . Member Royal Cambrian Academy (formerly RCA)
RCAS . . Royal Central Asian Society
RCGP . . Royal College of General Practitioners
RCHA . . Royal Canadian Horse Artillery
RCHM . . Royal Commission on Historical Monuments
RCM . . Royal College of Music
RCN . . Royal Canadian Navy
RCNC . . Royal Corps of Naval Constructors
RCNR . . Royal Canadian Navy Retd
RCNVR . . Royal Canadian Naval Volunteer Reserve
RCO . . Royal College of Organists
RCOG . . Royal College of Obstetricians and Gynaecologists
RCP . . Royal College of Physicians, London
RCPath . . Royal College of Pathologists
RCPE and RCPEd . Royal College of Physicians of Edinburgh
RCPGlas. . Royal College of Physicians and Surgeons, Glasgow
RCS . . Royal College of Surgeons of England; Royal Corps of Signals; Royal College of Science
RCSE and RCSEd . Royal College of Surgeons of Edinburgh
RCSI . . Royal College of Surgeons in Ireland
RCT . . Royal Corps of Transport
RCVS . . Royal College of Veterinary Surgeons
RD . . Rural Dean; Royal Navy Reserve Decoration
Rd . . . Road
RDA . . Royal Defence Academy
RDC . . Rural District Council
RDF . . Royal Dublin Fusiliers
RDI . . Royal Designer for Industry (Royal Society of Arts)
RDS . . Royal Dublin Society
RE . . . Royal Engineers; Fellow of Royal Society of Painter-Etchers and Engravers
Rear-Adm. . Rear-Admiral
REconS . . Royal Economic Society
Rect. . . Rector
Reg. Prof. . Regius Professor
Regt . . Regiment

REME . . Royal Electrical and Mechanical Engineers
RERO . . Royal Engineers Reserve of Officers
RES . . Royal Empire Society (now Royal Commonwealth Society)
Res. . . Resigned; Reserve; Resident; Research
Rev. . . Reverend; Review
RFA . . Royal Field Artillery
RFC . . Royal Flying Corps (now RAF); Rugby Football Club
RFPS(G) . *see under* FRFPSG (formerly)
RFU . . Rugby Football Union
RGA . . Royal Garrison Artillery
RGS . . Royal Geographical Society
RHA . . Royal Hibernian Academy; Royal Horse Artillery
RHB . . Regional Hospitals Board
RHG . . Royal Horse Guards
RHR . . Royal Highland Regiment
RHS . . Royal Horticultural Society; Royal Humane Society
RI . . . Member Royal Institute of Painters in Water Colours; Rhode Island
RIA . . Royal Irish Academy
RIAM . . Royal Irish Academy of Music
RIAS . . Royal Incorporation of Architects in Scotland
RIASC . . Royal Indian Army Service Corps
RIBA . . Royal Institute of British Architects
RIBI . . Rotary International in Great Britain and Ireland
RIC . . Royal Irish Constabulary; Royal Institute of Chemistry
RICS . . Royal Institution of Chartered Surveyors
RIE . . Royal Indian Engineering (College)
RIF . . Royal Irish Fusiliers
RIIA . . Royal Institute of International Affairs
RIM . . Royal Indian Marine
RIN . . Royal Indian Navy
RINA . . Royal Institution of Naval Architects
RIPH&H . Royal Institute of Public Health and Hygiene
RM . . RoyalMarines;ResidentMagistrate
RMA . . Royal Marine Artillery; Royal Military Academy Sandhurst (now incorporating Royal Military Academy, Woolwich)
RMC . . Royal Military College Sandhurst (now Royal Military Academy)
RMCS . . Royal Military College of Science
RMedSoc . Royal Medical Society, Edinburgh
RMetS . . Royal Meteorological Society
RMFVR . . Royal Marine Forces Volunteer Reserve
RMLI . . Royal Marine Light Infantry
RMO . . Resident Medial Officer(s)
RMPA . . Royal Medico-Psychological Association
RMS . . Royal Microscopical Society; Royal Mail Steamer; Royal Society of Miniature Painters
RN . . Royal Navy; Royal Naval
RNAS . . Royal Naval Air Services
RNAY . . Royal Naval Air Yard
RNC . . Royal Naval College
RNEC . . Royal Naval Engineering College
RNIB . . Royal National Institute for the Blind
RNLI . . Royal National Life-boat Institution
RNR . . Royal Naval Reserve
RNT . . Registered Nurse Tutor
RNVR . . Royal Naval Volunteer Reserve
RNVSR . . Royal Naval Volunteer Supplementary Reserve
RNZN . . Royal New Zealand Navy
RNZNVR . Royal New Zealand Naval Volunteer Reserve
ROC . . Royal Observer Corps
ROF . . Royal Ordnance Factories
R of O . . Reserve of Officers
ROI . . Royal Institute of Oil Painters
RoSPA . . Royal Society for the Prevention of Accidents
(Rot.) . . Rotunda Hospital, Dublin (after degree)
Roy. . . Royal
RP . . Member Royal Society of Portrait Painters
RPC . . Royal Pioneer Corps
RPGMS . . Royal Postgraduate Medical School (formerly PGMS)
RPS . . Royal Photographic Society
RRC . . Royal Red Cross
RRE . . Royal Radar Establishment (formerly TRE)
RRS . . Royal Research Ship
RSA . . Royal Scottish Academician; Royal Society of Arts
RSAI . . Royal Society of Antiquaries of Ireland
RSanI . . *See* RSH
RSC . . Royal Society of Canada
RSCM . . Royal School of Church Music
RSCN . . Registered Sick Children's Nurse
RSE . . Royal Society of Edinburgh
RSF . . Royal Scots Fusiliers
RSFSR . . Russian Socialist Federated Soviet Republic
RSGS . . Royal Scottish Geographical Society
RSH . . Royal Society for the Promotion of Health (formerly Royal Sanitary Institute)
RSL . . Royal Society of Literature
RSM . . Royal Society of Medicine; Royal School of Mines
RSMA . . (formerly SMA) Royal Society of Marine Artists
RSO . . Rural Sub-Office; Railway Sub-Office; Resident Surgical Officer.
RSPB . . Royal Society for Protection of Birds
RSPCA . . Royal Society for Prevention of Cruelty to Animals
RSSAILA . Returned Sailors, Soldiers and Airmen's Imperial League of Australia
RSW . . Member Royal Scottish Water Colour Society
Rt Hon. . . Right Honourable
RTO . . Railway Transport Officer
RTR . . Royal Tank Regiment
Rt Rev. . . Right Reverend
RTS . . Religious Tract Society; Royal Toxophilite Society
RU . . Rugby Union
RUI . . Royal University of Ireland
RUSI . . Royal United Services Institute for Defence Studies (formerly Royal United Service Institution)
RWA (RWEA) Member of Royal West of England Academy
RWAFF . Royal West African Frontier Force
RWF . . Royal Welch Fusiliers
RWS . . Member Royal Society of Painters in Water Colours
RYA . . Royal Yachting Association
RYS . . Royal Yacht Squadron

S

(S) . . . (in Navy) Paymaster
S . . . Succeeded; South; Saint
s . . . Son
SA . . . South Australia; South Africa; Société Anonyme
SAAF . . South African Air Force
SACSEA . Supreme Allied Command, SE Asia
SADG . . Société des Architectes Diplômés par le Gouvernement
Salop . . Shropshire
SAMC . . South African Medical Corps
Sarum . . Salisbury
SAS . . Special Air Service
SASO . . Senior Air Staff Officer

SB . . . Bachelor of Science (US)
SBAC . . Society of British Aircraft Constructors
SBStJ . . Serving Brother, Order of St John of Jerusalem
SC . . . Senior Counsel (Eire); South Carolina (US)
sc. . . . Student at the Staff College
SCAO . . Senior Civil Affairs Officer
SCAPA . . Society for Checking the Abuses of Public Advertising
ScD . . Doctor of Science
SCF . . Senior Chaplain to the Forces
Sch. . . School
SCL . . Student in Civil Law
SCM . . State Certified Midwife; Student Christian Movement
Sculpt. . . Sculptor
SDak . . South Dakota (US)
SDB . . Salesian of Don Bosco
SDF . . Sudan Defence Force; Social Democratic Federation
SE . . South-east
SEAC . . South-East Asia Command
SEALF . . South-East Asia Land Forces
SEATO . . South-East Asia Treaty Organization
Sec. . . Secretary
SEN . . State Enrolled Nurse
SESO . . Senior Equipment Staff Officer
SG . . . Solicitor-General
SGA . . Member Society of Graphic Art
Sgt . . . Sergeant
SHAEF . . Supreme Headquarters, Allied Expeditionary Force
SHAPE . . Supreme Headquarters, Allied Powers, Europe
SIB . . Shipbuilding Industry Board
SITA . . Société Internationale de Télécommunications Aéronautiques
SJ . . . Society of Jesus (Jesuits)
SJAB . . St John Ambulance Brigade
SJD . . Doctor of Juristic Science
SL . . . Serjeant-at-Law
SM . . Medal of Service (Canada); Master of Science; Officer qualified for Submarine Duties
SMA . . Society of Marine Artists (now *see under* RSMA)
SME . . School of Military Engineering
SMIEEE . Senior Member of Institution of Electrical and Electronic Engineering (US)
SMIRE . . Senior Member Institution of Radio Engineers (New York)
SMMT . . Society of Motor Manufacturers and Traders Ltd
SMO . . Senior Medical Officer; Sovereign Military Order
SNCF . . Société Nationale des Chemins de Fer Français
SNP . . Scottish Nationalist Party
SO . . . Staff Officer
SOAS . . School of Oriental and African Studies
Soc. . . Society
SOE . . Special Operations Executive
s.p. . . *sine prole* (without issue)
SP . . Self-Propelled (Anti-Tank Regt)
SPCK . . Society for Promoting Christian Knowledge
SPD . . Salisbury Plain District
SPG . . Society for the Propagation of the Gospel (now USPG)
SPk . . Sitara-e-Pakistan
SPRC . . Society for Prevention and Relief of Cancer
sprl . . *société pour responsabilité limité*
Sq. . . Square
SR . . . Special Reserve; Southern Railway (*see* BR); Southern Region (BR)
SRC . . Science Research Council (formerly DSIR)
SRN . . State Registered Nurse
SRO . . Supplementary Reserve of Officers
SRP . . State Registered Physiotherapist
SS . . . Saints; Straits Settlements; Steamship
SSA . . Society of Scottish Artists
SS&AFA . Soldiers', Sailors', and Airmen's Families Association
SSC . . Solicitor before Supreme Court (Scotland); Sculptors Society of Canada
SSJE . . Society of St John the Evangelist
SSM . . Society of the Sacred Mission
SSO . . Senior Supply Officer
SSRC . . Social Science Research Council
SSStJ . . Serving Sister, Order of St John of Jerusalem
St . . Street; Saint
STB . . *Sacrae Theologiae Bachelor* (Bachelor of Sacred Theology)
STC . . Senior Training Corps
STD . . *Sacrae Theologiae Doctor* (Doctor of Sacred Theology)
STh . . Scholar in Theology
Stip. . . Stipend; Stipendiary
STL . . *Sacrae Theologiae Lector* (Reader or a Professor of Sacred Theology)
STM . . *Sacrae Theologiae Magister*
STP . . *Sacrae Theologiae Professor* (Professor of Divinity, old form of DD)
STRIVE . Society for Preservation of Rural Industries and Village Enterprises
STSO . . Senior Technical Staff Officer
Supp. Res. . Supplementary Reserve (of Officers)
Supt . . Superintendent
Surg. . . Surgeon
Surv. . . Surviving
SW . . South-west
Syd. . . Sydney

T

T . . . Telephone; Territorial
TA . . Telegraphic Address; Territorial Army
TAA . . Territorial Army Association
TAF . . Tactical Air Force
T&AFA . . Territorial and Auxiliary Forces Association
TANS . . Territorial Army Nursing Service
TANU . . Tanganyika African National Union
TARO . . Territorial Army Reserve of Officers
T&AVR . . Territorial and Army Volunteer Reserve
TA&VRA . Territorial Auxiliary and Volunteer Reserve Association
TC . . . Order of the Trinity Cross (Trinidad and Tobago)
TCD . . Trinity College, Dublin (University of Dublin, Trinity College)
TCF . . Temporary Chaplain to the Forces
TD . . Territorial Efficiency Decoration; Efficiency Decoration (T&AVR) (since April 1967); (Teachta Dala) Member of the Dail, Eire
Temp. . . Temperature; Temporary
Tenn . . Tennessee (US)
Tex . . Texas (US)
TF . . . Territorial Forces
TFR . . Territorial Force Reserve
TGO . . Timber Growers Organisation
TGWU . . Transport and General Workers' Union
ThL . . Theological Licentiate
TP . . Transvaal Province
TPI . . Town Planning Institute
Trans. . . Translation, Translated
Transf. . . Transferred
TRC . . Thames Rowing Club
TRE . . (now *see under* RRE) (formerly Telecommunications Research Establishment
TRH . . Their Royal Highnesses
Trin. . . Trinity
tsc . . . passed a Territorial Army Course in Staff Duties
TSD . . Tertiary of St Dominick
TUC . . Trades Union Congress
TV . . . Television
TYC . . Thames Yacht Club

U

(U) . . Unionist
u . . Uncle
UAR . . United Arab Republic
UC . . University College
UCH . . University College Hospital (London)
UCL . . University College, London
UCW . . University College of Wales
UDC . . Urban District Council
UDF . . Union Defence Force
UF . . United Free Church
UGC . . University Grants Committee
UJD . . *Utriusque Juris Doctor,* Doctor of both Laws (Doctor of Canon and Civil Law)
UK . . United Kingdom
UKAC . . United Kingdom Automation Council
UKAEA . . United Kingdom Atomic Energy Authority
UN . . United Nations
UNA . . United Nations Association
UNCIO . . United Nations Conference on International Organisation
UNCSAT . United Nations Conference on the Application of Science and Technology
UNCTAD (Unctad) . United Nations Commission for Trade and Development
UNDP . . United Nations Development Programme
UNESCO (Unesco) . United Nations Educational, Scientific and Cultural Organisation
UNICEF (Unicef) . United Nations Children's Fund (formerly United Nations International Children's Emergency Fund)
Univ. . . University
UNRRA . . United Nations Relief and Rehabilitation Administration
UNRWA . United Nations Relief Works Agency
UNSCOB . United Nations Special Commission on the Balkans
UP . . . United Provinces; Uttar Pradesh; United Presbyterian
US . . United States
USA . . United States of America
USAAF . . United States Army Air Forces
USAF . . United States Air Force
USAR . . United States Army Reserve
USDAW . . Union of Shop Distributive and Allied Workers
USMA . . United States Military Academy
USN . . United States Navy
USNR . . United States Naval Reserve
USPG . . United Society for the Propagation of the Gospel (formerly SPG)
USS . . United States Ship
USSR . . Union of Soviet Socialist Republics
UTC . . University Training Corps
(UU) . . Ulster Unionist

V

V . . . Five (Roman numerals); Version; Vicar; Viscount; *Vice*
v . . . *Versus* (against)
v or vid. . *Vide* (see)
V&A . . Victoria and Albert
Va . . . Virginia (US)
VAD . . Voluntary Aid Detachment
VC . . . Victoria Cross
VCAS . . Vice-Chief of the Air Staff
VD . . . Royal Naval Volunteer Reserve Officers' Decoration (now VRD); Volunteer Officers' Decoration; Victorian Decoration
VDC . . Volunteer Defence Corps
Ven. . . Venerable (of an Archdeacon).
Very Rev. . Very Reverend (of a Dean)
Vet. . . Veterinary
VG . . Vicar-General
VHS . . Hon Surgeon to Viceroy of India
Vice-Adm. . Vice-Admiral
Visc. . . Viscount
VM . . Victory Medal
VMH . . Victoria Medal of Honour (Royal Horticultural Society)
Vol. . . Volume; Volunteers
VP . . . Vice-President
VQMG . . Vice-Quartermaster-General
VR . . *Victoria Regina* (Queen Victoria)
VRD . . Royal Naval Volunteer Reserve Officers' Decoration
VSO . . Voluntary Service Overseas
Vt . . . Vermont (US)

W

W . . . West
WA . . Western Australia
WAAF . . Women's Auxiliary Air Force (now WRAF)
Wash . . Washington State (US)
W/Cdr . . Wing Commander
WEA . . Workers' Educational Association; Royal West of England Academy
WEU . . Western European Union
WFTU . . World Federation of Trade Unions
WHO . . World Health Organization
WhSch . . Whitworth Scholar
WI . . West Indies (formerly BWI: British West Indies)
Wilts . . Wiltshire
Wis . . Wisconsin (US)
WLA . . Women's Land Army
WLF . . Women's Liberal Federation
Wm . . William
WO . . War Office
Worcs . . Worcestershire
WOSB . . War Office Selection Board
WR . . West Riding; Western Region (BR)
WRAC . . Women's Royal Army Corps
WRAF . . Women's Royal Air Force (formerly WAAF)
WRNS . . Women's Royal Naval Service
WRVS . . Women's Royal Voluntary Service (previously WVS)
WS . . . Writer to the Signet
WSPU . . Women's Social and Political Union
WVa . . West Virginia (US)
WVS . . Women's Voluntary Services (*now see* WRVS)
Wyo . . Wyoming (US)

X

X . . . Ten (Roman numerals)

Y

y . . . youngest
Yeo. . . Yeomanry
YHA . . Youth Hostels Association
YMCA . . Young Men's Christian Association
Yorks . . Yorkshire
yr . . . younger
yrs . . . years
YWCA . . Young Women's Christian Association

ADDENDA: I

The following biographies are of those whose deaths occurred before 31st December 1960, but were not reported until after the volume of *Who was Who* covering the years 1951-1960 had been published.

CAMPBELL, Percy Gerald Cadogan; *see* p. xxxiii.

de SILVA, Sir Albert Ernest, Kt., *cr.* 1946; *b.* 26 Nov. 1887; *s.* of Albert Emmanuel de Silva; *m.* 1913, Evadne Lukshmini, *d.* of S. D. S. Gunasekera; two *s.* four *d.* *Educ.:* Royal College, Colombo; Clare College, Cambridge. B.A. (Cantab.) 1910; Barrister-at-Law, Inner Temple, 1912. Chairman, Bank of Ceylon, since 1939; Chairman, State Mortgage, Bank of Ceylon, since 1935. *Recreations:* billiards; stamp collecting. *Address:* Sirimethipaya, Flower Road, Colombo, Ceylon. *Clubs:* Orient, Ceylon Turf (Colombo). [*Died* 9 *May* 1957.

GANDHI, Prof. Nagardas P., M.A., B.Sc., A.R.S.M., D.I.C., F.I.M., M.I.E. (Ind.) M.Inst. M.M., M.Inst.Met., M.I.S.I.; Consulting Mining Engineer and Metallurgist, Bombay; Director, Industrial Research Laboratory, Devlali, since 1947; *b.* 22 Dec. 1886; *m.* Shiv Kunvar; four *s.* *Educ.:* Bahauddin College, Junagad; Wilson Coll., Bombay; Royal School of Mines (Imperial College of Science and Technology), London. General Manager, Tata Sons' Wolfram and Tin Mines, Tavoy, Burma, 1916-19; Head of the Department of Mining and Metallurgy, Benares Hindu University, 1919-42; President, Geology Section, Indian Science Congress, 1933; President, Geological, Mining and Metallurgical Society of India, 1935-36. President, Bombay Metallurgical Society, 1945-48; Corr. Mem. for India of Inst. of Metals, London, 1942-55; Chairman of Indian Non-ferrous Metals Standardization Cttee., 1948-51; Hon. Mem. Indian Inst. of Metals, 1954. Hon Mem., Bombay Metallurgical Soc., 1957. *Recreations:* tennis, cricket and photography. *Address:* Kennaway House, Proctor Rd., Girgaon, Bombay, 4. *T.:* 70845; 183 Lam Road, Devlali, India. [*Died* 26 *June* 1960.

GIBSON, Alexander James, M.E. (Hon. Queensland), M.Inst.C.E., M.I.E. Aust.; Consulting Engineer; *b.* 18 Dec. 1876; *s.* of E. Morris Gibson, Solicitor, Sutton, Surrey; *m.* 1902, Marion Helen (*d.* 1947), *d.* of T. J. Hitchman, Sydney, N.S.W.; two *s.* two *d.*; *m.* 1954, Ann Muriel, (*d.* 1957), *d.* of A. C. Dent, Rockhampton, Qld. *Educ.:* Dulwich College. Apprentice, Thames Ironworks and Shipbuilding Co., Ltd., Blackwall, London; Eng. Draftsman, S. C. Farnham & Co., Shanghai, China; Public Works Dept. N.S.W., 1900-03; Lecturer, Engineering Design, Univ. of Sydney, 1903-10; Prof. of Engineering, University of Queensland, 1910-18; Commonwealth Defence Department, Munitions Service, England, 1917; Acting General Manager, Chief Engineer, Commonwealth Arsenal, 1918; Superintendent of Construction, Broken Hill Pty. Co., Ltd., Steel Works, Newcastle, N.S.W., 1919-22; Past Chm. Standards Assoc. of Australia, 1940-48; Past President Institution of Engineers, Australia; P.N. Russell Medal; Fellow of Senate of University of Sydney, 1934-39; Past Chm. of Advisory Council, Sydney Central Technical Coll., 1936-42; Past Mem. of Council and Chm. of Advisory Cttee., N.S.W., Council for Scientific and Industrial Research. *Address:* Julius, Poole & Gibson, Consulting Engineers, 906 Culwulla Chambers, Castlereagh Street, Sydney, N.S.W. *T.A.:* Jupag, Sydney. [*Died* 2 *Dec.* 1960.

GILL, Robert Carey Chapple; High Sheriff, Montgomeryshire, 1924; senior partner, R. & C. Gill, Liverpool; Member of Liverpool and New York Cotton Exchanges; *b.* 19 July 1875; *s.* of late Chapple Gill, of Lower Lee, Woolton; *m.* 1908, Mildred, 3rd *d.* of William Pretty, The Goldrood, Ipswich; two *s.* one *d.* *Educ.:* private. Formerly: Chairman of the Liverpool Committee of Lloyds Bank; Deputy Chairman, Thos. Taylors, Ltd., Wigan; Trustee Blue Coat Hospital, Liverpool; Director: Liverpool Storage Company; Liverpool Warehousing Co. Ltd.; The Sandon Motor Co. Ltd. *Recreations:* shooting, hunting and general. *Address:* Brynderwen, Bwlch-y-Cibau, Montgomeryshire: Ford House, Bath Street, Southport. *T.A.:* Chesterlie, Liverpool. *T.:* Llanfyllin 226; Cent. Liverpool 3129. Southport 4770. *Club:* Old Hall (Liverpool). [*Died* 5 *Nov.* 1960.

GOWEN, Rev. Herbert H., D.D., F.R.G.S.; Professor Oriental Languages and Literature, Univ. of Washington, 1914; Prof. Emeritus, 1944; *s.* of late H. C. Gowen, Great Yarmouth, England; *m.* 1892, Annie Kate Green of Great Yarmouth; three *s.* two *d.* *Educ.:* Priory School, Great Yarmouth; S. Augustine's College, Canterbury. Missionary in Honolulu and in charge of Chinese Church in this city, 1886-90; Curate at S. Nicholas', Gt. Yarmouth, 1891-92; Rector of S. Barnabas', New Westminster, B.C., 1892-96; Trinity, Seattle, Wn., 1896-1914; Priest in charge of S. Mark's Parish, 1919-20; Priest-in-charge Memorial Chapel, Seattle; Associate Editor Anglican Theological Review; retired from Parochial work, 1936; Hon. Canon St. Mark's Cathedral, Seattle, 1950. President Washington State Philological Association; American Or. Soc., Society for Oriental Research, Japan Society of New York, R.G.S., Royal Asiatic Society, etc. *Publications:* Temperantia, 1891; The Paradise of the Pacific, 1892; The Kingdom of Man, 1893; Biography of Bishop Sillitoe, 1899; Idylls of Love and Death in Hawaii, 1908; The Revelation of S. John the Divine, 1910; Stella Duce, 1911; The Day of His Coming, 1907; The Revelation of the Things that Are, 1908; Sonnets for the Sundays, 1916; The Book of the Seven Blessings, 1919; An Outline History of China, 1914; The Napoleon of the Pacific, 1919; Sonnet Stories from the Chinese, 1920; Christ and Colosse, 1922; The Universal Faith, 1926; Asia: a Short History, 1926; An Outline History of Japan, 1927, French Edition, Spanish Edition, 1939; The Little Grey Lamb, and other Christmas Poems, 1928; The Psalms, or Book of Praises, 1929; A History of Indian Literature, 1931; A History of Religion, 1934; Five Foreigners in Japan, 1936; Asia, a Short History, revised and enlarged edition, 1936, French edition, 1937. *Recreations:* botanising, walking, gardening. *Address:* 2205, 74th Ave., S.E. Mercer Is., Washington, U.S.A. *Clubs:* Authors'; University Faculty, Monday, University (Seattle). [*Died* 6 *Nov.* 1960.

GUNN, Col. John Alexander, C.B. 1919; O.B.E. 1918; Consulting Surgeon, Winnipeg General Hospital and St. Boniface Hospital; Emeritus Prof. of Surgery, Manitoba University; *b.* 1878; *m.* 1920, Armorel M. Thomas; two *s.* Served European War, 1914-19 (despatches twice, O.B.E., C.B., 1914-15 Star, two medals). Retired, 1953. *Address:* 1 Rossmore Apts., Winnipeg 1, Canada. *Club:* Manitoba (Winnipeg).
[*Died Aug.* 1960.

HAGUE, Professor Bernard, Ph.D.; D.Sc.; Professor of Electrical Engineering, The University of Glasgow, since 1946; *b.* Barnsley, Yorks., 7 July 1893; *s.* of Joe and Amy Florence Hague; *m.* 1922, Muriel Thorne Grose; one *d.* *Educ.:* Grammar School, Eccles; Central Higher Grade School, Rochdale; City and Guilds College, South Kensington. Ph.D. (Glasgow) 1926, D.Sc. (London) 1927; F.C.G.I. 1936; M.I.E.E. 1929; M.Amer.I.E.E. 1930. Workshop training, Carter Bros., Rochdale, 1908-10; drawing office, Ferranti Ltd., Hollinwood, 1911-13; City and Guilds Coll., London, 1913-16; technical asst., Royal Aircraft Establishment, 1916-20; City and Guilds Coll., Lecturer, 1920-23; Univ. of Glasgow, Lecturer, 1923-29; Visiting Prof., Polytechnic Institute, Brooklyn, N.Y., 1929-30; Univ. of Glasgow, Senior Lecturer, 1930-46. *Publications:* Alternating Current Bridge Methods, 1st edn., 1923, revised 6th edn. 1957; Electromagnetic Problems in Electrical Engineering, 1929; Instrument Transformers, 1936; Introduction to Vector Analysis, 1st edn. 1939; 5th edn. 1951. Some 24 papers in Jl.I.E.E., Electrician, World Power, Engineering; numerous reviews and abstracts. *Recreations:* orchestral music (oboe); handicrafts in wood and metal. *Address:* 1 Princes Terrace, Glasgow, W.2. *T.:* Western 3354. *Club:* Authors'. [*Died* 29 *Sept.* 1960.

HARRIS, John Redford Oberlin; Headmaster, Hutchins School, Hobart, 1929-1942, retired 1942; *b.* 4 Dec. 1877; *s.* of Rev. John Oberlin Harris and Mary Hunt; *m.* 1917, Helen Mackenzie; two *d.* (one *s.* killed in action with R.A.A.F., 1942). *Educ.:* Christ's Coll. and Hutchins School, Hobart; Univ. of Tasmania (Classical Scholar). B.A. 1898, 1st Class Hons. in Classics; M.A. 1900. Junior Master, Hutchins School, 1895 and 1897; Classical Master at Launceston Church Gram. Sch., 1899-1902; Master at Melbourne Gram. Sch., 1903; Church of England Gram. Sch., Sydney, 1904-29; served with the A.I.F. in Egypt, France, and Belgium, 3rd Bn. Inf., rank of Major, 1915-18 (despatches); promoted Lt.-Col. on retirement, 1937. Member, Council, Univ. of Tasmania; an examiner to Univ. of Melbourne. Chief State Comr. of Boy Scouts, Tas. *Address:* 9 Lysterville Av., Malvern S.E.4, Melbourne, Vic., Australia. [*Died* 8 *Aug.* 1960.

INCE, Sir Godfrey Herbert, G.C.B., *cr.* 1951 (K.C.B., *cr.* 1946; C.B. 1941); K.B.E., *cr.* 1943; B.Sc.; Hon. LL.D. (London); Permanent Secretary, Ministry of Labour and National Service, 1944-Jan. 1956; Member of Economic Planning Board, 1947-Jan. 1956, retd.; Chairman of Cable and Wireless, Ltd., and its associated companies, since 1956; Member of Senate of London University; *b.* 25 Sept. 1891; *er. s.* of G. A. R. Ince, J.P., Reigate, Surrey; *m.* 1918, Doris, 2nd *d.* of late C. Maude, Northallerton, Yorkshire; three *d.* *Educ.:* Reigate Grammar School; University College, London (Surrey County Scholar), Sherbrooke University Scholar (Mathematics), 1912; Mayer de Rothschild Scholar (Pure Mathematics), 1913; Ellen Watson Memorial Scholar (Applied Mathematics), 1913; Joseph Hume Scholar (Political Economy), 1914; Senior Mathematics Prizeman, 1913, Senior Physics Prizeman, 1914, at University College; B.Sc. First Class Hons. Mathematics, 1913; served European War, 1915-19, Commission in Yorkshire Regt., 1915; transferred to East Lancashire Artillery; service in France attached to Royal Engineers, Field Survey (wounded); entered Ministry of Labour as Assistant Principal, 1919; Private Secretary to Sir David Shackleton (Chief Labour Adviser), 1920-23; Principal Private Secretary to Ministers of Labour, 1930-33; Assistant Secretary, Ministry of Labour, 1933; Chief Insurance Officer under Unemployment Insurance Acts, 1933-37; Adviser to the Commonwealth of Australia on Unemployment Insurance, 1936-37; also visited New Zealand to advise N.Z. Government, 1937; Principal Assistant Secretary, Ministry of Labour, 1938; Under Secretary, Ministry of Labour and National Service, 1940; seconded to offices of War Cabinet, to take charge of Production Executive Secretariat, Jan. 1941; Director-General of Man Power, Ministry of Labour and National Service, June 1941-44; Deputy Secretary, 1942. *Publications:* Report on Unemployment Insurance in Australia, 1937; Ministry of Labour and National Service, 1960; papers on Manpower in Gt. Britain, in Proc. Manchester Statistical Soc., 1945 and 1953. *Recreations:* cricket, lawn tennis, association football. *Address:* The Witterings, 138 Copse Hill, Wimbledon, S.W.20. *T.:* Wimbledon 1713. *Clubs:* Athenæum, Royal Commonwealth Society.
[*Died* 20 *Dec.* 1960.

INSH, George Pratt, C.B.E. 1944; B.Litt.; Historian; *b.* 17 Oct. 1883; *s.* of George Pratt Insh of Longside, Aberdeen, and Isabella Forbes Smith of Inverurie; *m.* 1911, Alice Louisa Dummer (*d.* 1952); one *s.* one *d.* *Educ.:* Crossmyloof School; Queen's Park School; Glasgow Univ. M.A. Glasgow, 1906; Carnegie Essay Prize of £100, 1921; D.Litt. 1922; Research Fellow, History, 1922; Teacher Glasgow Elementary Schools, 1904-1910; History Master, Hutchesons' Grammar School, 1910-23; Prin. Lect. History, Jordanhill Training College, 1923-45. President Educational Inst. of Scotland, 1938-39. Member Advisory Council Scottish Records, 1944; Historical Section of Cabinet, 1945-1946. President, The Forty-Five Association, 1955. Rifleman 1st Lanark R.V., 1902-5; Rifleman Cameronians, Captain Highland Light Infantry, 1914-19; Captain and Adjt. 11th Cameronians Sept. 1939-Dec. 1940, Staff Capt. (Educ.), Scottish Command, 1941, Instructor (Major) Army School of Education; Wakefield, 1941-42; Staff Officer (Educ.); Major, Galloway Area and Lothian and Border District, 1943. *Publications:* Scottish Colonial Schemes, 1922; Darien Shipping Papers (Scottish Hist. Soc.), 1924; School Life in Old Scotland, 1925; Carmina Glottiana: Poems of Avondale and Clydeside, 1928; Educational Values, 1932; The Company of Scotland trading to Africa and the Indies, 1932; The Study of Local History and other Essays, 1932; Scotland and the Modern World, 1932; The Clyde, the Elusive River, 1933, 3rd edition, 1946; Scotland, an Essay in Interpretation, 1936; Lanarkshire, 1937; Historian's Odyssey, 1938; The Challenge to Education, 1939; A Richard Jefferies Anthology, 1945; Thomas Henderson: an Appreciation, 1946; The Darien Scheme, 1947; Men, Moods and Movements, 1947; The Scottish Jacobite Movement: A Study in Economic and Social Forces, 1952; The Wartime History of the Scottish Red Cross, 1952. *Recreations:* walking, travel, historical research. *Club:* Literary (Glasgow). [*Died* 19 *March* 1956.

JAMESON, Ven. Francis Bernard; Archdeacon of Waterford and Lismore since 1955; Examining Chaplain to Bishop of Cashel; *b.* 14 July 1889; 4th *s.* of Rev. Thomas Edward Jamieson; *m.* 1921, Dorothy Elizabeth Sayers; two *s.* one *d.* *Educ.:* Leeds

Grammar School; University Coll., Durham; St. Augustine's College, Canterbury. S. Michael's Church, Wakefield, 1914-17; S.P.G. Missionary and Chaplain, Tinnevelly Diocese, Madras, 1917-33; Rector Aughrim, Diocese Clonfert, 1934-39; Dunmore East, Diocese of Waterford, 1939; Precentor and Prebendary of Corbally, 1942. *Address:* Dunmore East Rectory, Co. Waterford. *T.:* Dunmore East 7329. [*Died* 25 *Oct.* 1960.

JONES, Rev. Gilbert Basil; Incumbent of Trinity Church, St. Agathe des Monts, P.Q., Canada, since 1950; *b.* 7 Oct. 1894; *s.* of Rev. Thomas Jones, Vicar of Penbryn, Cardiganshire; *m.* 1921, Katherine, *d.* of William Douglas, Baldovan, Perthshire; one *d. Educ.:* St. Andrew's, Tenby; Lancing College; University London; Balliol College, Oxford; B.A. (Lond.), 1st Class Hons. in Philosophy, 1917; B.A. Oxon, 1st Class Hons. in Theology, 1920; M.A. 1925; D.C.L. (Bishop's University), 1941. Deacon, 1918; Priest, 1919; Chaplain and Tutor, St. Edmund Hall, Oxford, 1919-20; Sub-Warden of St. Michael's College, Llandaff, 1921-22; Warden of Church Hostel, Bangor, 1923-30; Examining Chaplain to Bishop of Bangor, 1922-30; Special Lecturer in Philosophical Theism, Univ. College of N. Wales, 1923-30; Warden of the Central Society of Sacred Study (Bangor Diocese), 1923-30; Welsh Church Scholarship Examiner, 1925-31; Examiner for first B.D. (Wales) 1925-31; Rector of South Luffenham, Rutland, 1931-36; Dean of Divinity, and Harold Professor, Bishop's Univ., Lennoxville, Que., 1936-49; Vice-Principal, 1941. General Ordination Examaminer of English Church Assembly, 1933-34. *Publication:* Church Ceremonial: Four Addresses, 1942. *Recreations:* travelling, golf. *Address:* St. Agathe des Monts, P.Q., Canada. [*Died Oct.* 1958.

KING, Lt.-Col. Giffard Hamilton Macarthur, C.M.G. 1915; D.S.O. 1918; V.D.; late 1st Field Artillery Brigade, Australian Imperial Force; Accountant Taxation Dept., New South Wales; *b.* 15 Jan. 1885; *m.* Frankun, *d.* of E. P. Pearce, Parramatta, N.S.W. Served European War (Dardanelles), 1914-18 (despatches, C.M.G., D.S.O.). *Address:* 13 Olova Avenue, Vaucluse, Sydney, N.S.W. [*Died* 12 *Oct.* 1956.

KUKDAY, Col. Sir Krishnaji Vishnoo, Kt., *cr.* 1939; C.I.E. 1926; Indian Medical Service, retired; Retired Inspector General of Civil Hospitals, Central Provinces India; *b.* 1870; *m.* 1886, Mainabai Gandhi; one *s.* two *d. Educ.:* Grant Medical College, Bombay; Edinburgh; London. Served British East Africa; European War, 1914-19 (despatches). *Address:* Maharajbag Club, Nagpur, C.P., India. [*Died* 4 *May* 1958.

LEVER, Richard Hayley, N.A., R.B.A., R.W.A. 1908; *b.* Adelaide, South Australia, 28 Sept. 1876; *s.* of Albion and Catherine Lever; *m.* 1906, Aida Smith Gale (*d.* 1949), St. Austell, Cornwall, England; one *s. Educ.:* Prince Alfred College, Adelaide. Came to St. Ives, Cornwall, 1899; Exhibitor, Venice International, Pittsburg International, Nice International, and Great White City Exhibitions, London; Royal Academy, New York Academy, Philadelphia Academy, International Exhibition, Toronto, New Salon, and Old Salon, Paris, etc. Represented in many galleries and museums in Australia, England and America, including Schumann Collection, Boston, Mass., Hon. Mention International Exhibition, Carnegie Institute, Pittsburgh, 1913; $500 Carnegie Prize, National Academy, New York, 1915; Silver Medal, National Arts Club, New York, 1914, and Gold Medal, 1916; Gold Medal, San Francisco Exp. 1915; Sesnam Gold Medal, Philadelphia Academy, U.S.A.; Temple Gold Medal, Pennsylvania Academy of Fine Arts, 1925; Bronze Medal, Philadelphia Sequistennial, 1926; Philadelphia Water-colour Prize, 1918, Bronze Medal Amsterdam Olympic Exhibition; Montclair Art Medal, New Jersey, 1930; Potter Palmer Marine Prize, National Academy, New York, 1936 and 1938; Newark (New Jersey) Art Club Marine Prize, Special Exhibition, Newark Centenary, 1936; 1st Hon. Mention Internat. Exhib. of Water Color, Chicago Inst., 1940; Instructor, Art Students' League (Hon. Life Member), New York; Instructor, Newark Art Club, N.J.; Hon. Member of Mt. Vernon Art Association, 1957-. 1st Award $1000 Annual Exhib. of Contemporary Amer. Artists, Studio Club Galleries, 1949; 1st Prize Westchester Art Centre, N.Y., 1953. *Recreations:* cricket, fishing, yachting. *Address:* National Arts Club (Life Mem.), Gramercy Park, N.Y., U.S.A. [*Died* 6 *Dec.* 1958.

MACAN-MARKAR, Hadji Sir Mohamed, Kt., *cr.* 1938; Director of the Bank of Ceylon; Merchant; Governing Director in the firm of O. L. M. Macan Markar Ltd., Colombo; Director of Macan Markar Buildings Ltd.; Member of The Ceylon Senate; Director of Moslem Educaional Society Ltd.; Director of the Galle-Face Land and Building Co., Ltd.; *b.* 7 Sept., 1879; *e. s.* of late Osuman Lebbe Marikar Macan Markar, and of Aamina Umma, *d.* of Mudaliyar Cassile Bronc. Cassie Lebbe Marikar; *m.* 1910, Noorul Neima (*decd.*), *e. d.* of late S. L. Naina Marikar Hadjiar; three *s.* four *d. Educ.:* Wesley College, Colombo. Consul for Turkey, 1903-15; member of Galle Municipal Council, 1906-31; returned as the first Muslim member to Ceylon Legislative Council, 1924-30; member for Batticoloa South seat, State Council, 1931-36; Minister of Communication and Works, 1931-1936; Chairman of now defunct Ceylon Electricity Board, 1966-67. *Recreations:* played for the Wesley College Cricket Eleven, 1898 and 1899; cricket and walking. *Address:* Muirburn, Turret Road, Cinnamon Gardens, Colombo; G.O.H. Buildings, Fort, Colombo. *T.A.:* Macan, Colombo. *T.:* 4897 and 4975. [*Died* 11 *May* 1952.

McKENDRICK, Archibald, J.P., F.R.C.S.Ed., D.P.H., L.D.S.Ed., F.R.S.Ed.; Consulting Radiologist, Edin. Royal Infirmary, Medical Referee for the Lothians and Peebles under Workmen's Compensation Acts; *b.* 1 June 1876; *s.* of Jas. D. McKendrick, Dental Surgeon, Kirkcaldy; *m.* 1906, Gertrude Maud Smith; two *s.* Medals in Surgery, Medicine, Midwifery, Chemistry, Materia Medica, Physiology, Medical Jurisprudence and Public Health; Late Demonstrator in Anatomy, Out-Patient Resident Surgeon, Resident Gynæcological Surgeon, Clinical Asst. Ear and Throat wards, Lock wards, and Surgeon in Charge X-Ray Department, Edinburgh Infirmary; Lecturer in Medical Physics; Examiner for Royal College of Surgeons, Edinburgh. *Publications:* Public Health Law and Vital Statistics Book; Volumes on Malingering, Back Injuries, and Medico-legal Injuries, X-Ray Atlas; Numerous publications in Medical Journals. *Recreations:* golf, shooting, and fishing. *Address:* 24 Murrayfield Gardens, Edinburgh 12. *T.:* Donaldson 4955. [*Died* 2 *Nov.* 1960.

MARCUS, Michael; Barrister-at-Law of the Middle Temple; Chairman Finsbury, Shoreditch Rent Tribunal, Oct. 1946-Oct. 1952; *b.* 9 Nov. 1894. *Educ.:* St. Leonard's Public Board School; George Heriot's School, Edinburgh; Edinburgh University, LL.B. Elected to Edinburgh Town Council for St. Leonard's Ward, 1926; formerly solicitor in practice in Edinburgh; election agent for late Rt. Hon. Wm. Graham, 1923-28; Hon. Solicitor to Edinburgh Trades and Labour Council, 1926-30; M.P. (Lab.) Dundee, 1929-31; Parliamentary Private Secretary to Mr. J. Westwood, M.P., Under-Secretary of State for Scotland, 1931;

contested Dundee in Labour interest in Parliamentary elections of 1931 and 1935; joined Edinburgh Central Branch of I.L.P., 1918 (Chairman, 1919); served on numerous parliamentary and political committees; Member of British Institute of Philosophy. *Publications:* Legal Aspects of Trade Unionism; numerous articles on economic, social, political, and philosophical subjects. *Recreations:* books, walking, tennis, gardening. *Address:* 42 Glenloch Road, Hampstead, N.W.3. [*Died Nov.* 1960.

NAIRAC, Sir (George) Edouard, Kt., *cr.* 1938; Q.C.; *b.* 15 March 1876; *s.* of Edouard Nairac and Laurence Couve; *m.* 1904, Marie Pauline Eva Rousset; six *s.* two *d.* *Educ.:* Royal College, Port Louis, Mauritius (Scholar). Called Bar, Middle Temple, 1898; Practised Mauritius Bar, 1898-1927; Member Legislative Council, 1911-27; Mayor of Port Louis, 1913, 1921, 1922; K.C. 1926; Procureur and Advocate General, 1927; M.E.C., 1927-36; Acting Colonial Secretary, 1929; Acting Chief Judge, 1930; Chief Justice, Mauritius, 1936-39; Pres., Fighting French Committee in Mauritius. *Publications:* Mauritius Law Reports, 1906-39; Digest of the Mauritius Law Reports, 1902 to 1925; Editor, Vol. IX, of Revised Laws of Mauritius (1930 to 1935); Causeries du Mercredi (Radio Talks in 1941 and 1942). *Address:* Schifanoia, Vacoas, Mauritius. *T.A.:* Vacoas Mauritius. [*Died* 1960.

POLLARD, Captain Alfred Oliver, V.C. 1917; M.C., D.C.M.; late R.A.F.; *s.* of J. A. Pollard, Tidbury, Wallington, Surrey; *b.* 4 May 1893; *m.* 1st, 1918, Mary, *d.* of Mr. Ainsley, Trefilan, Purley; 2nd, 1925, Violet Irene, *yr. d.* of R. A. Swarbrick, Elbury, Craven Avenue, Ealing, W. *Educ.:* Merchant Taylors' School. Served European War, 1914-18 (M.C. and bar, D.C.M., V.C.). *Publications:* Pirdale Island; Rum Alley; Murder Hide-and-Seek, 1931; Fire Eater; The Memoirs of a V.C., 1932; The Death Flight, 1932; The Riddle of Loch Lemman, 1933; The Phantom Plane, 1934; The Royal Air Force, 1934; Murder in the Air, 1935; The Secret of Castle Voxzel, 1935; Unofficial Spy; Boy's Romance of Aviation, 1935; The Death Game; Hidden Cipher, 1936; Romantic Stories of Air Heroes, 1936; The Murder Germ; Flanders Spy, 1937; Black-out; Air Reprisal, 1938; The Secret Formula; Murder of a Diplomat, 1939; The Secret Pact; A.R.P. Spy; Epic Deeds of the R.A.F., 1940; Bombers Over the Reich, 1941; Secret Weapon, 1941; Wanted by the Gestapo, 1942; Invitation to Death, 1942; The Death Squadron, 1943; Gestapo Fugitive, 1944; The Fifth Freedom, 1944; Blood Hunt, 1945; Double Cross, 1946; A Deal in Death, 1947; The Iron Curtain, 1947; The Death Curse; David Wilshaw investigates; The Secret Vendetta; Dead Man's Secret; Red Hazard, 1950; The Poisoned Pilot, 1950; The Death Parade, 1951; The Golden Buddha, 1951; Death Intervened, 1951; Counterfeit Spy, 1952; Criminal Airman, 1953; The Dead Forger, 1952; The Buckled Wing, 1953; Homicidal Spy, 1954; The Missing Diamond, 1955; Sinister Secret, 1955; Smugglers' Buoy, 1958; Wrong Verdict, 1960. *Address:* Linkwood, 18 Queen's Park Gardens, Bournemouth. [*Died* 4 *Dec.* 1960.

ROBIQUET, Jean; French art historian and essayist; Honorary Keeper of Musée Carnavalet and of Musée of Ile-de-France; *b.* Meudon (Seine-et-Oise), 6 July 1874; *s.* of late Paul Robiquet, Officer, Legion of Honour, and late Marie Lombard; *m.* 1908, Raymonde Berthelot; no *c.* *Educ.:* Lycée Henri IV; Faculté des Lettres, Paris (Licencié ès Lettres). Entered Musée Carnavalet, 1897, Keeper, 1919-34; helped to organise exhibitions in Paris, 1900, Turin, 1911, Gand, 1912, Wiesbaden, 1921, Liege, 1930, Paris, 1937; organised many exhibitions at the Orangerie des Tuileries and Musée Carnavalet. Hon. Pres., Association de la Presse artistique française; Hon. Pres., French Assoc. of Museum Conservators. Officer, Legion of Honour. *Publications:* L'Œuvre inédit de Gavarni, 1912; Les Vieux Hôtels du Marais, 1927; Louis XIV et la Faculté; La Révolution de 1789; La Femme dans la peinture française, 1938; La Vie quotidienne pendant la Révolution, 1938; La Vie quotidienne au temps de Napoléon 1er, 1943; L'Impressionnisme vécu, 1948, etc. *Address:* c/o Musée Carnavalet, 23 rue de Sévigné, Paris III, France. *Club:* Cercle des Escholiers (Hon. Pres.). [*Died* 10 *Oct.* 1960.

SANDERS, Henry Arthur; Professor of Latin, University of Michigan, 1911-Feb. 1939, Emeritus from 1939; Chairman of the Dept. of Speech and General Linguistics since 1932; Visiting Professor of Latin, University of Illinois, 1942; *b.* Livermore, Maine, U.S.A., 22 Oct. 1868; *s.* of John Sanders and Luretta Gibbs; *m.* 1913, Charlotte Ione Poynor; one *d.* *Educ.:* University of Michigan (A.B. 1890, A.M. 1894); University of Berlin, 1895-96; University of Munich (Ph.D. 1897); Hon. L.H.D. Colby, 1940. Teacher of Latin, Central High School, Minneapolis, 1890-2; and Greek, Kansas City, 1892-93; Instructor, University of Michigan, 1893-95; Minnesota, 1897-99; Michigan, 1899-1902; Assistant Professor, 1902-8; Junior Professor, 1908-11; Acting Director of the School for Classical Studies in the American Academy in Rome, 1915-16; Professor in charge of the School of Classical Studies of American Academy in Rome, 1928-31; Member, Amer. Editorial Board of Internat. Project to Establish a Critical Apparatus of the Greek New Testament, 1948-; Member: Amer. Philosophical Soc., Archeological Soc. of Amer., Philological Society, Society Biblical Research and Exegesis, Oriental Society, American Academy of Arts and Sciences, Council of several learned societies. *Publications:* Præfatio zu den Quellencontamination im xxi. xxii. Büche des Livius (The Lost Epitome of Livy), Berlin, 1897; Die Quellencontamination im xxi. xxii. Büche des Livius, Berlin, 1898; University of Michigan Studies, Vol. I. Roman Historical Sources, 1904; IV. Roman History and Mythology, 1908; VIII. I. Washington MS. of Deuteronomy and Joshua, 1910; II. Washington MS. of the Psalms, 1917; IX. I. Washington MS. of the Four Gospels, 1912; II. Washington MS. of the Epistles of Paul, 1917; XXI. Minor Prophets in the Freer Collection and Berlin Fragment of Genesis, 1927; XXXVIII. A Third Century Papyrus Codex of the Epistles of Paul, 1935; XLVIII. (P.Mich. Vol. VII.) Latin Papyri in the University of Michigan Collection, 1947. Facsimile of the Washington MS. of Deuteronomy and Joshua, 1910; Facsimile of the Washington MS. of the Four Gospels, 1912; Facsimile of the Minor Prophets in the Freer Collection and of the Berlin Fragment of Genesis, 1927; Hugo Grotius, The Law of War and Peace, translated by Francis W. Kelsey, Henry A. Sanders, and Arthur E. Boak, Carnegie Peace Foundation, Washington, 1927; Beati in Apocalipsin Libri Duodecim, Papers and Monographs of the American Academy in Rome, vol. vii, 1929. *Address:* 2037 Geddes Avenue, Ann Arbor, Michigan, U.S.A. *Clubs:* University, Golf (Ann Arbor). [*Died* 16 *Nov.* 1956.

SMITH, Theodore Clarke; Professor of American History, Williams College, Mass., 1904-38, Emeritus since 1938; Member Mass. Hist. Soc.; *b.* 18 May 1870; *s.* of Azariah Smith and Sophia Elizabeth Van Duzer. Unmarried. *Educ.:* Roxbury Latin School, Boston, Mass.; Harvard (B.A. 1892; M.A. 1893; Ph.D. in Political Science, 1896). Assistant in History at Harvard, 1893-94; Fellow in History at University of Wisconsin, 1895; studied, as holder of a travelling fellowship from Harvard, at University of

Paris, 1896-97, and University of Berlin, 1897; Instructor at University of Michigan, 1898; Instructor at Vassar College, 1899-1900; Assistant-Professor at Ohio State University, 1902-3. *Publications:* The Free Soil Party in Wisconsin, 1895; The Liberty and Free Soil Parties in the North-West, 1898; Expansion after the Civil War, 1902; Political Reconstruction, in Cambridge Modern History, vol. vii.; Politics and Slavery, 1951-59, 1906; Wars Between England and America, 1914; Life and Letters of James Abram Garfield, 1925; United States as a Factor in World History, 1941. *Address:* Williams College, Williamstown, Mass.
[*Died* 19 *Nov.* 1960.

SOUNDY, Hon. Sir John, Kt., *cr.* 1954; C.B.E. 1943; *b.* Dorchester, England, 14 November 1878; *s.* of J. T. Soundy; *m.* 1907, Edith, *d.* of Rev. George Wainwright; two *s.* five *d.* *Educ.:* Friends' School, Hobart. Lived in South Africa, 1903-7; returned to Tasmania and went into business (drapery and furnishings). Coroner to Hobart, 1911; M.H.A. for Hobart, 1925-1946; Alderman of Hobart City Council, 1917; Mayor of the City of Hobart, 1924 and 1929, elected by fellow Aldermen; first Mayor elected by Citizens, 1930-32; Lord Mayor of Hobart, 1938-46; M.L.C. 1946; J.P. Tasmania; retired from public affairs, 1952. O.St.J. *Recreations:* fishing, shooting, and bowls. *Address:* 92 Newdegate Street, Hobart, Tasmania. *T.:* Res. 31345 and Business 33268.
[*Died* 25 *Oct.* 1960.

STRONG, Rev. Canon Edward Herbert, M.A., B.Litt.; Canon-Emeritus, St. Peter's Cathedral, Hamilton, N.Z., 1941; Officiating Priest, Diocese of Dunedin; *b.* Winscombe, Somerset; *s.* of late Samuel Herbert and Mary Strong; unmarried. *Educ.:* Nelson College; University College, Auckland; St. John's College, Oxford; Cuddesdon Theological College. Deacon, 1906; Priest, 1907; Assistant Curate St. Barnabas, Balsall Heath, Birmingham, 1907-8; Sub-Warden St. John's College, Auckland, 1909-14; Chaplain King's College, Auckland, 1914-19; Vice-Principal Wells Theological College, 1919-20; Archdeacon of Tonga, 1920-22; Chaplain Boys' High School, New Plymouth, N.Z., 1922-32; Vicar of St. Mary's, New Plymouth, 1927-32; Warden of St. John's College, Auckland, 1932-38; Canon of Auckland Cathedral; P. in C. Dunedin Cathedral, 1939; Rector and Canon, Rockhampton Cathedral, 1940; Member of General Synod of N.Z., 1910, 1925, 1928, 1931, 1937, 1940, 1943, 1946, 1949, 1952; Commissary to Bishop of Melanesia since 1935. *Recreations:* golf and tennis. *Address:* c/o Diocesan Office, Stuart Street, Dunedin N.Z.
[*Died* 6 *Nov.* 1960.

WALMSLEY, Ben, C.B.E. 1920; *b.* 1871; *m.* 1906, Laura W. Champernowne, *d.* of late Rev. John Willington, Fen End House, Knowle. Was a Section Director (Pig Iron), a Director Iron and Steel Contracts, and Controller Ferrous Metals, Ministry of Munitions. 1916-19. *Address:* Stone Cottage, Halse, nr. Taunton. *T.:* Bishops Lydeard 203.
[*Died* 19 *Dec.* 1960.

YATES, Lt.-Col. Donald, C.M.G. 1943; M.C.; Consulting Engineer; *b* 27 Feb. 1893; *s.* of Thomas Yates, Adelaide; *m* 1916, Norah, *d.* of J. H. Crowe, Adelaide; one *s.* one *d.* *Educ.:* St. Peter's School Collegiate, Adelaide; Adelaide University (B.E.); School of Mines, Adelaide (F.S.A.S.M.). Served European War, 1st Tunnelling Co., A.I.F., Capt. (M.C.); B.H.P. Pty. Ltd., Newcastle, 1919-27; B.H.A.S. Pty. Ltd., Port Pirie, 1927-44; War of 1939-45; rejoined 2/A.I.F. Sept. 1942, Lt.-Col. S.O.R.E.; V.D.C. Bn. Comdr. (Home Guard), 1940-42. Sen. Mem., Australasian Institute of Mining and Metallurgy (Pres. 1937). *Recreations:* rowing, football in former years; golf and tennis. *Address:* 224 Young St., Unley, South Australia. *T.:* UA 7827. *Clubs:* Adelaide, Naval and Military (Adel.).
[*Died* 22 *Nov.* 1960.

CAMPBELL, Percy Gerald Cadogan, M.A. (Oxford); Docteur de l'Université de Paris; Hon. LL.D. (Queen's); Prof. Emeritus of French, Queen's Univ., Canada; *b.* 8 Jan. 1878; *e. s.* of Rev. C. Cadogan Campbell; *m.* 1910, Evelyn Amy, *d.* of Frank Jessup Rogers; two *s.* *Educ.:* France; Rossall; Balliol College, Oxford, Chancellor's Essay, 1902; University of Paris. Went to Queen's University on taking B.A. at Oxford, 1902; Commandant Fort Henry Internment Station, 1915-16; O.C. 253rd Battalion, C.E.F., 1916-17; Seconded to Imperial Forces in France, 1917-18; O.C. Queen's C.O.T.C., 1928-32. Treasurer of Diocese of Ontario, 1933-59. *Publication:* L'Epitre d'Othéa de Christine de Pisan. *Address:* 420 Earl Street, Kingston, Ontario, Canada.
[*Died* 1960.

ADDENDA: II

The following biographies are of those whose deaths occurred between 1st January 1961 and 31st December 1970, but were not reported until after the body of this book went to press.

BECKETT, John Warburton; *b.* 11 Oct. 1894; *s.* of Wm. Beckett, Thurlwood, Cheshire, and Dorothy Salmon, London; *m.*; two *s.* two *d.* *Educ.:* Latymer School. Journalist and Company Director. Served 1914-17, K.S.L.I.; M.P. (Lab.) Gateshead 1924-29, Peckham 1929-31; past Member Hackney Borough Council. *Recreations:* reading, walking. *Address:* 187 Queen's Gate, Kensington, S.W.7.
[*Died Dec.* 1964.

BOWMAN, Robert Ritchie, C.B.E. 1945; Chairman, Northern Ireland Paper Box Wages Council; Chm., Joint Advisory Councils for Local Authority Services, 1954-1964; *b.* Belfast, 1883; 2nd *s.* of late Alexander and Rose Bowman; *m.* 1913, Margaret, *yr. d.* of Henry Page; no *c.* *Educ.:* Belfast and Oxford. Entered service of Labour Dept., Board of Trade, 1911; Secretary Irish Trade Boards, 1919-21; Assistant Secretary, Ministry of Labour (Northern Ireland), 1922-39; Permanent Secretary, Ministry of Labour and National Insurance, Northern Ireland, 1939-49; Member of N. Ireland National Assistance Board, 1949-52. Sec. and later memb. of Commission on the Natural and Industrial Resources of Northern Ireland, 1923-26. Represented Govt. of Northern Ireland at Int. Labour Organisation Conferences, 1934-1948. *Address:* 8 Garranard Park, Belfast 4. *T.:* Belfast 653712. [*Died* 5 *Oct.* 1970.

BOYD, William, C.M.G. 1943; C.B.E. 1919; *b.* 1876; *s.* of Robert F. Boyd; *m.* Helen (*d.* 1954), *d.* of William Bow, J.P.; three *d.* Was Deputy Director-General, British Ministry of Shipping, New York, 1916-18; Dep. Rep. Min. of War Transport in U.S.A., 1939-1945, Representative, 1945. *Address:* 1143 Fifth Avenue, New York City. [*Died* 1961.

BRACEGIRDLE, Rear-Admiral Sir Leighton Seymour, K.C.V.O., *cr.* 1947; C.M.G. 1935; D.S.O. 1916; *b.* Balmain, Sydney, 31 May 1881; 4th *s.* of late Captain Frederick Bracegirdle of Kaikoura, East Balmain; *m.* 1910, Lilian Anne (*d.* 1966), 2nd *d.* of late Paterson Saunders, The Hill, Newcastle, New South Wales; two *s.* *Educ.:* Sydney High School. Joined New South Wales Naval Forces as Naval Cadet, 1898; Midshipman, 1900; Midshipman with Naval Brigade in China (Boxer War Tientsin and Peking), 1900-1 (China Medal); Attached British Forces S. African War 1901-2 (Queen's medal with 3 clasps); Sub-Lt., 1902; Lt., 1911; Naval Staff Officer with Naval Brigade landed to attack German New Guinea, Sept. 1914, and later succeeded to command (prom. Acting Lt.-Comdr.); commanded 1st Royal Australian Naval Bridging Train, abroad 1915-17; present at first landing Suvla Bay, Gallipoli, and evacuation (despatches thrice, D.S.O.), also at defence of Suez Canal and advance on Palestine; Commander, 1917; Captain, 1924; Rear-Admiral, retired list, Royal Australian Navy, 1945; Military and Official Secretary to the Governor-General of Australia 1931-1945; Official Secretary to the Duke of Gloucester, Governor-General of Australia, 1945-47; Personal Assistant to Governor of Victoria (late Lord Dugan), 1948. Pres. Commonwealth Coal Bd. in Qld. 1918, and in S. Aust. during coal shortage, 1919-20; Dir. of Naval Reserves and Mobilisation, Navy Office, Melb., 1922-31; Director: Peter Lloyd Ltd.; Consultant to Internat. Combustion Aust. Ltd., Syd., and Taubmans Industries Ltd., Syd.; Vice-Pres. Roy. N.S.W. Instn. for Deaf and Blind Children. *Recreations:* fishing and gardening. *Address:* Green Hills, Forest Way, French's Forest, N.S.W., Aust. *Club:* Union (Syd.).
[*Died* 22 *March* 1970.

CARBERY, 10th Baron, *cr.* 1715; **John Evans Carberry,** Bt. 1768; *b.* 20 May 1892; *s.* of 9th Baron and Mary (who *m.* 2nd, Arthur W. Sandford; she *d.* 1949), 2nd *d.* of Henry J. Toulmin, of The Pré, St. Albans; *S.* father, 1898; *m.* 1st, 1913, José (marr. diss. 1920), *d.* of Evelyn James Metcalfe; one *d.*; 2nd, 1922, Maïa Ivy (*d.* 1928), *d.* of Alfred Anderson; one *d.*; 3rd, 1930, June Weir Mosley. *Educ.:* Osborne Naval College; Leipzig. Name changed by deed poll, 1921, Kenya Colony, to John E. Carberry. A Citizen of Republic of S. Africa since 1957. *Heir:* *n.* Peter Ralfe Harrington Evans-Freke [*b.* 20 March 1920; *m.* 1941, Joyzelle Mary, *o. c.* of late Herbert Binnie; three *s.* two *d.*]. *Address:* 65 Oxford Rd., Saxonwold, Johannesburg, S. Africa.
[*Died* 25 *Dec.* 1970.

CARTER, Alexander Scott, R.C.A. 1927 (A.R.C.A. 1922); M.R.A.I.C.; F.R.S.A.; architect and artist; *b.* Harrow, Middlesex, 1879; *e. s.* of late Alexander Carter. *Educ.:* Royal Academy School of Architecture (two silver medals and other prizes). Practised architecture in London; went to Canada, 1912; exhibited at the Royal Academy, London, Royal Canadian Academy, The Art Gallery of Toronto, Canadian National Exhibition, Los Angeles Museum, etc.; represented in the collections of The Queen, Duke of Devonshire, and others; represented in the National Gallery, Ottawa, The Art Gallery of Toronto, and in universities, churches, and large corporations in Canada and U.S.A.; Member of The Essex Archæological Society and the Society of Genealogists, London. Awarded The Roy. Architectural Inst. of Canada Allied Arts silver medal for 1959. F.R.S.A. *Address:* 2 Washington Avenue, Toronto, Ont., Canada. *Clubs:* Arts and Letters, (Hon.) Faculty Union, University of Toronto (Toronto).
[*Died* 1969.

CAWTHORN, Major.-Gen. Sir Walter (Joseph), Kt. 1958; C.B. 1946; C.I.E. 1943; C.B.E. 1941; retired; *b.* 18 June 1896; *s.* of William Cawthorn, Rokeby, Victoria, Australia; *m.* 1927, Mary Wyman Varley (*née* Gillison); (one *s.* decd.). *Educ.:* Melbourne. Served European War, 1914-18, with 22 Battalion Australian Imperial Force, in Gallipoli, Egypt, France, and Belgium (wounded, despatches, 1914-15 Star, G.S. and Victory Medals); N.W. Frontier of India, 1930; Mohmand, 1935 (medal and clasp); War of 1939-45, Egypt, 1939-41 (C.B.E., despatches); Head of Middle East Intelligence Centre, 1939-41; Director of Intelligence, India Command, 1941-45 and Deputy Director of Intelligence South-East Asia Command, 1943-45 (C.I.E., C.B., despatches); Member India Delegation to U.N. conference, San Francisco, 1945; Representative of Commander-in-Chief in India on Joint Chiefs of Staff in Australia, 1946-47; Dep. Chief of Staff, Pakistan Army, 1948-51; retd. 1951. Director Jt. Intelligence Bureau, Dept. of Defence, Australia, 1952-54; High Comr. for Austr. in Pakistan, 1954-58; High Commissioner for Australia in Ottawa, 1959-1960. *Address:* Little Tocknells, Kallista, Australia. *Clubs:* United Service; Melbourne, Naval and Military (Melbourne). [*Died* 4 *Dec.* 1970.

COLLISON, Levi, J.P.; lately retired as Chairman of companies; *b.* Preston, 1875; *s.* of S. Collison, Preston; *m.* (widower); two *s.* two *d.* *Educ.:* private school. Art publisher; founder of Collisons, Ltd.; contested Penrith Division bye-election; M.P. (L.) Penrith and Cockermouth Division, 1922-23; Trustee Preston Savings Bank. *Recreation:* golf. *Address:* Brooklands, Watling Street Road, Fulwood, Preston, Lancs. *Club:* Reform (Preston). [*Died* 22 *Oct.* 1965.

CORLETTE, Brig. James Montagu Christian, C.M.G. 1919; D.S.O.; V.D.; Chevalier Légion d'Honneur; B.E., D.Eng., M.I.C.E., Hon. M.I.E.Aust.; Cons. Engineer; Brig. (Ret.) Aust. Mil. Forces; *b.* 25 Aug. 1880; *s.* of Rev. Canon J. C. Corlette, D.D. Oxon., and Mrs. F. E. Corlette, *d.* of late Sir Wm. Montagu Manning, K.C.M.G., etc.; *m.* 1914, Ruby, *d.* of Paterson J. Saunders, Newcastle, N.S.W.; one *s.* *Educ.:* Sydney Grammar School; Univ. of Sydney; graduate B.E. in Civil and Mining Engineering. Over 40 years service with Australian Military Forces; i/c first 750 sq. miles of Australian Military Topographical Survey, 1910-11. Served European War, 1914-18, with Aust. Engineers; left with first contingent from Australia; Gallipoli, France, and Belgium; C.R.E. 2nd Australian Division, 1917-18 (C.M.G., D.S.O., Chevalier Légion d'Honneur, despatches five times, 1914-15 Star); Group Commander (Col.) on staff of Volunteer Defence Corps, War of 1939-45. Chief Engineer of Water Supply and Sewerage Board, Newcastle, N.S.W., 1925-45. Pres. Instn. of Engineers, Australia, 1930 (Warren Memorial prizeman, 1945; P.N. Russell Memorial medallist, 1947; Hon. Mem., 1960). Hon. D.Eng. Newcastle Univ., N.S.W., 1966. *Publication:* articles on Engineering subjects. *Recreation:* football blue at University. *Address:* The Terrace, Newcastle, N.S.W., Australia. *T.:* B.2035. *Clubs:* University (Sydney); Newcastle, United Service (Newcastle, N.S.W.). [*Died* 11 *Dec.* 1969.

CRUTE, Robert; Town Clerk, Leeds, 1952-1964; *b.* 28 May 1907; 6th *s.* of late Richard Rutter Crute, Solicitor, Sunderland, Co. Durham, and late Mary A. G. Crute; *m.* 1936, Eleanor Haswell, *er. d.* of late William Moore and late Mary Moore, Newcastle upon Tyne; two *s.* *Educ.:* Bede Collegiate School, Sunderland; Durham University. Asst. Solicitor, County Borough of Sunderland, 1930-34; Chief Asst. Solicitor, Sunderland, 1934-38; Dep. Town Clerk and Dep. Clerk of the Peace, Bolton, Lancs., 1938-47; Dep. Town Clerk, Leeds, 1947-52. Chm., Associate Sect., Soc. of Town Clerks, 1950-51. *Clubs:* Royal Over-Seas League; Leeds (Leeds). [*Died June* 1967.

EBRAHIM, Sir Fazulbhoy Currimbhoy, Kt., *cr.* 1913; C.B.E. 1918; Millowner and Merchant, Bombay; *b.* 1873; 2nd *surv. s.* of Sir (Huscinali) Currimbhoy Ebrahim, 1st Bt.; *m.* 1889, Sakinabal (*d.* 1930), *d.* of Datoobhoy Ebrahim, of Cutch Mandvi; five *s.* Formerly Fellow of Bombay Universitty Past Pres., Corporation of Bombay. [*Died* 1970.

ELLIOTT, Rt. Rev. Anthony Blacker, D.D.; *b.* 1887; *s.* of Canon A. L. Elliott. *Educ.:* Trent College, Derbyshire; Trinity College, Dublin (M.A., D.D.). Curate, Aston, Birmingham, 1910-12; Missionary, Church Missionary Society, India, from 1913; Archdeacon of the Deccan, 1930; Asst. Bishop in Dornakal Diocese, 1935; Bishop of Dornakal, 1945-47; Bishop in Dornakal, 1947-55, in Krishna-Godavari, 1955-59, Church of South India. *Publication:* Hebrews. *Recreations:* birds, stars. *Address:* C.S.I., Alir S.C. Rly., Nalgonda District, A.P., India. [*Died* 19 *Dec.* 1970.

ELLIS, Malcolm Henry, C.M.G. 1956; Hon. D.Lit., Newcastle, Aust.; historian; *b.* Narine, Queensland, 21 Aug. 1890; *e. s.* of Thomas James Ellis and Constance Ruegg; *m.* 1st, Melicent Jane, *d.* of Major J. W. Ayscough, Brisbane; one *d.*; 2nd, Gwendoline Mary, *y. d.* of Harry and Sarah Wheeler. *Educ.:* Brisbane Grammar School. Chief Special Correspondent of Sydney Daily Telegraph, 1922-28; Mem. of Australian Meat Council's Delegate Cttee. to British Ports, 1926; in command Daily Telegraph motor expedition across Australia, 1924 (first complete double crossing of the continent by motor car) and of semi-official British motor expedition, London-Delhi, 1927; Director of the Electrical Development Association of N.S. Wales, 1929-31; Member of Government Committee of Inquiry into Municipal Trading in Electrical Appliances, 1930; Staff of Sydney Bulletin, 1933-65; Mem., Australian editorial delegation to Korea, 1951-52. Life Member: N.S. Wales United Service Institution; Australian Pioneers' Club; Hon. Member, Aust. Humanities Research Council. Hon. Sec., N.S. Wales and Canberra Group, Order of St. Michael and St. George; Macrossan Lecturer, University of Queensland, 1942; Harbison - Higinbotham Research Award (Melbourne University), 1948. *Publications:* The Long Lead, 1927; Express to Hindustan, 1929; The Red Road, 1932; The Beef Shorthorn in Australia, 1932; The Defence of Australia, 1933; Lachlan Macquarie (Macrossan Lectures), 1942; The Life and Times of Lachlan Macquarie, 1947; The Life of Francis Greenway, 1948; The Garden Path, 1949; John Macarthur, 1955; The Torch, 1957; The Drama of Coal, 1959; various historical papers. A Prior Prize for best manuscript of the year (Australia), 1940, for Life of Lachlan Macquarie. *Address:* 18 Reed Street, Cremorne, Australia. *T.:* 90-6261. *Clubs:* Australian (Sydney); Savage (Melbourne). [*Died* 18 *Jan.* 1969.

ETZEL, Franz; Grand Cross of Order of The Federal Republic (Germany), 1958; Partner of Bankhaus Friedrich Simon, Düsseldorf, since Nov. 1961; lawyer; *b.* 12 Aug. 1902; *s.* of Franz Etzel and Hélène (*née* Roepling); *m.* 1932, Hilde (*née* Lehnen); two *s.* one *d.* *Educ.:* studied law at Frankfort, Münich and Munster. First Law Exam., Hamm, 1925; final, Berlin, 1930. Barrister, Duisburg Dist. and Municipal Court, 1930-52; Notary public at Duisburg, 1939-62. War of 1939-45, German Army (last rank First Lieut.). Chm. Duisburg Dist. Gp. of Christian Democratic Union (C.D.U.), 1945-48; Mem. Exec. Cttee. Rhineland Section, C.D.U., 1946-53; Chm. C.D.U.'s Economic Policy Cttee. for Brit. Zone of Germany, 1947-49; Chm. C.D.U.'s Economic Policy Cttee. for whole of Germany, 1949-; Mem. First German Bundestag and Chm. Bundestag's

Economic Policy Cttee., 1949-53; First Vice-Pres. of High Authority of European Coal and Steel Community, 1952-57; Federal Minister of Finance, German Federal Republic, 1957-61. Holds Grand Cross of various foreign orders, etc. *Address:* Wittlaer, bei Düsseldorf, Am Töllershof 10, Federal Republic of Germany. *T.:* Düsseldorf 401076. *Club:* Rotary (Luxemburg). [*Died May* 1970.

EVANS, Herbert Edgar, C.M.G. 1957; Q.C. (N.Z.) 1946; *b.* Sudbury, Suffolk, 21 Nov. 1884; *s.* of Capt. E. J. Evans (Shaw Savill Line) and Ada E. G. Evans (*née* Green); *m.* 1912, Ella Mary Harman, West Acton, London; two *s.* *Educ.:* Whitgift Grammar School, Croydon; Victoria University College, Wellington, N.Z. B.A., 1906, LL.M. 1910. Univ. of New Zealand. Arrived in New Zealand (Wellington), 1902. Entered office of Bell, Gully, Bell and Myers (Barristers and Solicitors), 1903; admitted Barrister and Solicitor, 1910; Partner in successors to that firm, 1922-45; Solicitor-General for New Zealand, 1945-57; Chancellor of Anglican Diocese of Wellington, 1946-64. *Recreation:* gardening. *Address:* Flat 110, Lichfield, Selwyn Village, Point Chevalier, Auckland, New Zealand. *T.:* 80.119. [*Died* 28 *Oct.* 1970.

FAIR, Hon. Sir Arthur, Kt., *cr.* 1951; M.C.; Q.C. (New Zealand); Judge of the Supreme Court of New Zealand, 1934-55, retired; *s.* of J. W. Fair and Teresa Fair of Westport, New Zealand. *Educ.:* Nelson College; Victoria Univ. College, N.Z. LL.B., barrister and solicitor, 1907; Crown Solicitor, 1921; Principal Law Officer of Crown, 1923; K.C. 1925; Solicitor-General of N.Z., 1925-34; served 1914-19, Inns of Court Officers' Training Corps, 8th Batt.Suffolk Regiment, 1/5th Batt. Suffolk Regiment (T.F.), Egypt and Palestine (temporary Captain and Adjutant; M.C. 1918). *Publication:* History 1/5th Batt. Suffolk Regt. (with E. C. Wolton). *Recreations:* golf, motoring. *Address:* 19 Upland Road, Kelburne, Wellington, N.Z. *Club:* Wellington (Wellington, N.Z.). [*Died* 27 *March* 1970.

FARROW, G. Martin, C.B.E. 1934; J.P.; F.I.C.S.; *b.* 10 April 1896; *s.* of George Frederick and Ruth Jane Eleanor Farrow; *m.* 1923, Dorothy Elaine Drysdale; two *d.* *Educ.:* Sydney, New South Wales. Served with the 18th Bn. A.I.F. in Egypt, Gallipoli, and France (wounded at Anzac and Pozieres); Chairman, War Pensions Inquiry, 1931; Federal President, Limbless Soldiers Assoc., 1924-38; Trustee of the Anzac Memorial, 1926-37; Member of War Pensions Entitlement Appeal Tribunal, 1937-38. *Address:* 8 Esther Road, Balmoral Beach, N.S.W., Australia. *T.:* Sydney 96-8351. *Club:* Legacy (Sydney). [*Died* 5 *May* 1969.

FINLAY, Sir George Panton, Kt., *cr.* 1955; **Hon. Mr. Justice Finlay;** Senior Puisne Judge, Supreme Court, New Zealand, since 1943; *b.* 7 Aug. 1886; *m.* 1912, Mabel Florence (*née* Duder); one *d.* *Educ.:* Thames High School, N.Z. *Address:* 103 Mountain Road, Epsom, Auckland, N.Z. *T.:* 61.292. *Clubs:* Northern, Auckland (Auckland, N.Z.). [*Died* 9 *Nov.* 1970.

FITZGERALD, Sir (Adolf) Alexander, Kt., 1955; O.B.E. 1953; Chairman, Commonwealth Grants Commission, 1946-60; Commissioner, State Electricity Commission of Victoria, 1955-68; Member of firm of Fitzgerald Gunn and Partners, Chartered Accountants, 1916-66; President, Graduate Union, Univ. of Melbourne, 1961-1965; Professor of Accounting, University of Melbourne, 1955-58; *b.* 26 October 1890; *s.* of Michael and Mary Ann Fitzgerald; *m.* 1916, Ivy Alice Brunstein; three *d.* *Educ.:* Victorian State School; Box Hill Grammar School; University of Melbourne. In practice as a public accountant, 1916-66; Lectr. in Accountancy, Univ. of Melbourne, 1925-1951; B.Com. (Melb.) 1926. Gen. Pres., Commonwealth Inst. of Accountants, 1940-1941 (Victorian State Pres., 1928-30 and 1934-37); Victorian State Pres., Australasian Inst. of Secretaries, 1940. Mem. Roy. Commn. on Country Water Supply, Vic., 1936-37; Dep. Dir., Dept. of War Organization of Industry, 1942-46. Editor, Australian Accountant, 1936-54. Dir. or Chm. of public and private cos. Melbourne Rotary Vocational Service Award, 1967; Aust. Inst. Management John Storey Medal Award, 1967. *Publications:* Statistical Methods as Applied to Accounting Reports, 1940; Analysis and Interpretation of Financial and Operating Statements, 1946; (jointly) Form and Contents of Published Financial Statements, 1948; Current Accounting Trends, 1952; (jointly) Classification in Accounting, 1952; (Ed.) Fitzgerald's Accounting. Numerous articles in Australian Accountant, etc. *Recreations:* reading, writing, bowls. *Address:* 572 Whitehorse Road, Surrey Hills, Vic. 3127, Australia. *T.:* 89. 1736. *Clubs:* Melbourne, Melbourne Savage, University House, Australian-American (Melbourne). [*Died* 22 *Aug.* 1969.

GREGORY, William King, Ph.D., D.Sc.; Da Costa Professor emeritus of Vertebrate Palæontology, Columbia University, since 1945; Curator emeritus of Comparative Anatomy, American Museum of Natural History, and Curator emeritus of Ichthyology, 1944; *b.* New York, 19 May 1876; *s.* of George Gregory and Jane King; *m.* 1st, 1899, Laura Grace (decd.), *d.* of Daniel Foote, Mystic, Conn., no *c.*; 2nd, 1938, Angela, *d.* of Charles E. Du Bois, Kingston, N.Y. *Educ.:* Trinity School, New York City; School of Mines, School of Arts, Graduate School, Columbia Univ. Member of the National Academy of Sciences, American Philosophical Society, New York Academy of Sciences (President, 1932-33), New York Zoological Society, A.A.A.S.; Geological Society of America, American Association of Physical Anthropologists (President, 1941-1943), American Soc. of Herpetologists and Ichthyologists (President, 1936-38), Internat. Assoc. of Dental Research, etc.; foreign F.Z.S.; foreign F.G.S.; foreign member, Linnean Soc., London, etc.; member Royal Soc. of Sciences of Upsala, State Russian Palæontological Soc., etc.; Explorers Club; Phi Beta Kappa; Sigma Xi,; Delta Upsilon. Research Associate, Lerner Marine Zoolog. Laboratory, Bimini, Bahamas, 1949. *Publications:* The Orders of Mammals, 1910; Studies on the Evolution of the Primates, 1916; On the Structure and Relations of Notharctus, an American Eocene Primate, 1920; The Origin and Evolution of the Human Dentition, 1922; The Dentition of Dryopithecus and the Origin of Man (with Milo Hellman), 1926; Our Face from Fish to Man, 1929; Fish Skulls; A Study of the Evolution of Natural Mechanisms, 1933; Man's Place among the Anthropoids, 1934; A Half Century of Trituberculy, 1934; In Quest of Gorillas, 1937; Studies on the Origin and Early Evolution of Paired Fins and Limbs (with H. C. Raven), 1941; Pareiasaurs versus Placodonts as Near-ancestors to the Turtles, 1946; The Roles of Motile Larvae and Fixed Adults in the Origin of the Vertebrates, 1946; The Monotremes and the Palimpsest Theory, 1947; Evolution Emerging: A Survey of Changing Patterns from Primeval Life to Man, 2 vols., 1951; Essays presented to D. M. S. Watson, 1958 (London); Cone Shells and their Color Patterns—an Approach to Evolution and Natural Philosophy, 1959-61. *Address:* Box 35, Woodstock (N.Y.), New York 12489, U.S.A. [*Died* 29 *Dec.* 1970.

HELY, Air Vice-Marshal William Lloyd, C.B. 1964; C.B.E. 1953; A.F.C. 1938;

p.s.c., i.d.c.; retired as Air Member for Personnel, R.A.A.F. Headquarters, Canberra, A.C.T. (1960-66); *b.* Wellington, N.S.W., 24 Aug. 1909; *s.* of late Prosper F. Hely, Sydney; *m.* 1938, Jean A., *d.* of F. McDonald; two *d.* *Educ.:* Fort Street High School, Sydney; R.M.C., Duntroon. Pilot Officer, R.A.A.F., 1930; grad. flying training, Pt. Cook, 1931; comdg. R.A.A.F. Detachment, N. Aust. Aerial and Geological Survey, 1936; conducted air search and rescue operations in Northern Territory, 1937; R.A.F. Staff College, Andover, 1939; H.Q. Coastal Command, 1939 (Sqdn. Leader); Director: Air Staff Policy, H.Q., R.A.A.F., 1943-46; Personal Services, R.A.A.F., 1946-1950; Personnel Services, Dept. of Air, Melbourne, 1947-48; A.O.C. Western Area, 1951-53; Deputy Chief of the Air Staff, 1953; A.O.C. Trng. Comd., R.A.A.F., 1956-1957; Head of Australian Joint Services Staff, Washington, 1957-60. *Address:* 4 Hamelin Crescent, Narrabundah, A.C.T. [*Died* 20 *May* 1970.

JOSE, Sir Ivan Bede, Kt. 1963; M.C.; M.B., M.S. (Adelaide), F.R.C.S. (Eng., Edin., and Australasia); Hon. Cons. Surg., Roy. Adelaide Hosp., 1950; Mem. Medical Board of South Australia, 1963-67; President Australian Post-Graduate Federation Med., 1957-60 and 1965-66 (Gov., 1962); Mem. of Council, Univ. of Adelaide, 1953-65; Chm., South Australian Division Australian Red Cross, 1964 (Mem. Exec., 1942); *b.* Ningpo, China, 13 Feb. 1893; *s.* of late Very Rev. G. H. Jose; *m.* Imogen Mervyn, *d.* of W. G. Hawkes, Koonoona Station, S.A.; two *s.* one *d.* *Educ.:* Privately (Oxford); Queen's School, St. Peter's College, University of Adelaide; London Hospital; studied surgery London, Vienna, Paris, and U.S.A. Served European War, 1914-18, Egypt, France (despatches M.C.); Major, 1918; Lt.-Col., A.A.M.C., 1931; Squadron-Leader (temp.) R.A.A.F., 1940; Group Capt. 1953, R.A.A.F. Reserve. Surgical and Medical Registrar, Adelaide Hosp., 1923-24; Asst. Hon. Surgeon, 1925-30; Hon. Surgeon, 1930-50; Director and Lecturer in Surgery, Univ. of Adelaide, 1936-50, Dean of the Faculty of Med., 1948-49; Pres., Roy. Australasian Coll. of Surgeons, 1955-57 (Mem. Council, 1943-57); Visiting Urologist, Repatriation Hosp., 1946-1963. President, S.A. branch of B.M.A., 1954-55. *Publications:* papers in Australian Medical Journal. *Recreations:* cricket, golf, tennis. *Address:* 58 Brougham Place, North Adelaide, South Australia. *Club:* Adelaide (Adelaide). [*Died* 23 *Nov.* 1969.

KEATING, Brigadier Harold John Buckler, C.B.E. 1945; E.D. 1945; *b.* 15 March 1893; *s.* of Col. John B. Keating, O.B.E.; *m.* 1915, Gwladys M. Weston; two *s.* one *d.* *Educ.:* Portland, Maine, U.S.A. Joined Permanent Force of Canadian Army, 1912; retired 1922; Investment Business, 1922-39. Canadian Army Active, 1939; Dep. Q.-M.-G., National Defence H.Q., Ottawa; retired, 1946. *Recreations:* fishing, tennis, hunting. *Address:* Kenall, Wolfville, Nova Scotia. [*Died* 24 *Jan.* 1970.

LANE POOLE, Charles Edward; *b.* 1885; *s.* of late Stanley Lane-Poole and Charlotte Bell Wilson; *m.* 1911, Ruth Pollexfen; three *d.* *Educ.:* St. Columba's Coll., Dublin; Forest School, Nancy. South African Forest Dept., 1906; Conservator of Forests, Sierra Leone, 1910; Western Australia, 1917; commissioned by Commonwealth Govt. to report on Forests of Papua and New Guinea, 1922; Forestry Adviser Commonwealth Govt., 1925; Inspector-General of Forests of the Commonwealth of Australia, 1927-45; Consulting Forester Sydney, 1946; represented Commonwealth at the 1920 Empire Forestry Conference in London; Vice-chm. of the Third Empire Forestry Conference in 1928 in Australia; represented the Commonwealth at Fourth Empire Conference, in S. Africa, Chm. Silvicultural Cttee., 1935; reported on eucalypt plantations of S. Africa, 1935. *Publications:* Trees, Shrubs and Climbers of Sierra Leone; Kiln Drying of Jarrah; Forest Resources of Papua and New Guinea; Forests of Norfolk Island; Forest Policy for Capital Territory and Jervis Bay; Forests and Water; Statistical Methods, Forest Problems. *Address:* 15 Fairlight Cres., Fairlight, N.S.W., Aust. *Club:* Alpine (Canberra). [*Died* 22 *Nov.* 1970.

MACKINTOSH, William Archibald, C.C. (Canada), 1967; C.M.G. 1946; *b.* 21 May 1895; *s.* of William and Agnes Cowie Mackintosh; *m.* 1928, Jean Easton; one *d.* *Educ.:* Queen's Univ., Kingston (M.A. 1916); Harvard University (Ph.D. 1922). Department of Political and Economic Science, Queen's University, Kingston, Ont., Canada, 1920-51; Vice-Chancellor and Principal, 1951-61; Vice-Chancellor, 1961-65; Mem. of Nat. Employment Commission, 1936-38; Research Adviser, Royal Commission on Dominion-Provincial Relations, 1938-39; on leave of absence, 1939-46 to serve in various capacities in Departments of Finance and Reconstruction and Supply, Ottawa. Chairman of Council, Association of Universities of British Commonwealth, 1954. Pres. Royal Society of Canada, 1956-57. Mem. Canada Council, 1957-60. Mem. Cttee. on Organization of Govt. of Ontario, 1958-59; Mem. Roy. Commn. on Banking and Finance, 1962-64; Director, Bank of Canada, 1964-. Canada Council Medal, 1966; Innis-Gerin Medal, Roy. Soc. of Canada, 1967. *Publications:* Agricultural Cooperation in Western Canada, 1924; Prairie Settlement (Canadian Frontiers of Settlement), 1934; Economic Problems of the Prairie Provinces (Canadian Frontiers of Settlement), 1935; Economic Background of Dominion-Provincial Relations (Appendix 2 of Report of Royal Commission on Dominion-Provincial Relations), 1940. *Address:* Alwington Place, Kingston, Canada. [*Died* 29 *Dec.* 1970.

MAJOR, James Perrins, C.B.E. 1937; M.D.; F.R.A.C.P.; Cons. Physician; Hon. Phys. to In-Patients and Lecturer in Clinical Medicine, Alfred Hospital, Melbourne; Lecturer in Therapeutics, University of Melbourne; *b.* 22 Dec. 1878; *s.* of Frank Major, Melbourne; *m.* 1933, Beatrice, *d.* of John Lloyd Williams; one *s.* one *d.* *Educ.:* Cumloden; University of Melbourne. Member of Standing Committee of Convocation, University of Melbourne; Past-Pres. of Victorian Branch of B.M.A.; Lt.-Col., A.A.M.C., 2 A.I.F., is also Director of Australasian Medical Publishing Company; Member, Board of Management of Q.M. Infectious Diseases Hospital. *Address:* 12 Collins Street, Melbourne, C.1, Australia; 3 Moonga Road, Toorak, S.E.2, Australia. [*Died* 1964.

MEREDITH, Margaret; Composer; *d.* of late Ralph Elliot and Mrs. T. H. Lewin; *m.* 1892, W. M. Meredith (*d.* 1937), *s.* of late George Meredith; one *s.* *Educ.:* Cheltenham College; musical studies pupil of Dannreuther and Ernst Pauer. Founder of the Independent Music Club for the protection and advancement of art and artists, also of the Independent Musical World, the monthly journal issued in connection with the I.M.C. *Compositions,* as follows: The Pilgrim's Way, a musical allegory; Symphonic Tone Poem, Sursum Corda; Recessional, Rudyard Kipling's words; Sacramentum Supremum, words by Sir Henry Newbolt; Requiem on the death of Queen Victoria; Passing of King Edward VII; quintet flute, clarinet, violin, violoncello, piano; oratorio, The At-one-ment; The Immortelle or The Children's Heritage, A Musical Idyll; violin rhapsody, a symphony, an oratorio, a pageant and many songs, etc. *Recreations:* reading, chamber music, and lawn tennis. *Address:* 13 Pembroke Gardens, W.8. [*Died* 16 *March* 1964.

MOONEY, George Stuart; *b.* 5 Oct. 1900; *s.* of Richard Stuart Mooney and Grace Sowden; *m.* 1925, Tessie Tait; three *d.* *Educ.:* McGill University, Montreal; Sir George Williams College, Montreal. Exec. Dir. Canadian Federation of Mayors and Municipalities, 1936-; Exec. Sec., Montreal Y.M.C.A., 1922-35; Director Planning and Research, Montreal Metropolitan Commission, 1935-38; Director, Montreal Industrial and Economic Bureau, 1938-58; Consultant War Time Prices Trade Bd., Canada, 1940-42; Mem. of Faculty Sir George Williams Coll., Montreal (Public Finance and Administration), 1937-48; Member Federal Govt. Committee on Reconstruction (Canada), 1943-44. Director Greater Montreal Economic Council, 1942-58. Exec. Sec. Administrative Council U.N.R.R.A. and Head of Secretariat, 1944-46; Director of Research, Bd. of Research on Traffic and Mass Transportation (Montreal), 1949-52; Director, St. Lawrence Municipal Bureau (Montreal), 1955-1958. Chm. Nat. Exec., U.N. Assoc. in Canada, 1948-50; Vice-Pres., Community Planning Assoc. of Canada, 1948-49; Member Associate Cttee. Nat. Building Code Nat. Research Council), 1948; Dir. of Research; Commn. on Problems, Metropolitan Govt., Greater Montreal, 1953-58; Mem. Bd. of Governors, Canadian Welfare Council, 1959-. *Publications:* Co-operatives; To-day and To-morrow, 1937; Our Cities: Their Role in the National Economy, 1940; Municipal Finance in Canada, 1942; Municipalities and Reconstruction, 1943; A Housing Programme for Canada, 1944; Public Finance in Canada (1930-1948), 1950. *Recreations:* golf, fishing. *Address:* 3790 Côte des Neiges Rd., Montreal, Canada. *T.:* WE 5-8089. *Clubs:* Allies, Royal Automobile; Mount Stephen, Reform, Royal St. Lawrence Yacht (Montreal). [*Died Aug.* 1965.

MUKERJEE, Most Rev. Arabinda Nath, D.D.; *b.* 23 May 1892; Indian; *m.* 1919, Pronoy Protima Pyne; five *s.* three *d.* *Educ.:* University of Calcutta. Headmaster, St. Stephen's High School, 1919-25; deacon, 1923; priest, 1924; Principal, Delhi United Christian High School, 1926-36; Financial Secretary, Cambridge Mission to Delhi, 1936-1939; Head of Cambridge and S.P.G. Mission, 1939-44; Canon of Lahore Cathedral, 1940-44; Asst. Bishop of Lahore and Archdeacon of Delhi, 1944-47; Bishop of Delhi, 1947-50; Bishop of Calcutta and Metropolitan of India, Pakistan, Burma and Ceylon, 1950-62, retired. Episcopal Canon of St. George's Cathedral, Jerusalem, 1948. Hon. D.D. Univ. of Toronto, 1954. D.D. Lambeth, 1958. *Address:* Hill Crest, Nagpur 1, Maharastra, India. [*Died* 21 *Aug.* 1970.

NAIR, Rt. Hon. Sir C. Madhavan, P.C. 1941; Kt., *cr.* 1939; B.A.; Barrister-at-law; *b.* 24 Jan. 1879; *s.* of U. Raman Menon (landlord, Malabar); *m.* 1907, *e. d.* of Sir Sankaran Nair, C.I.E.; two *s.* one *d.* *Educ.:* Madras Christian College; University College, London; Middle Temple. Enrolled as Advocate, Madras High Court, 1904; officiated as Vice-Principal, Madras Law College, 1909; Law Reporter, High Court, 1915-16; Professor, Law College, 1916-20; for some time, Examiner in Law and Chairman of the Law Examination Board, Univ. of Madras, and Pres. the Law Coll. Council; officiating Principal, Law College, 1920; Secretary Students Advisory Committee; Government Pleader, High Court, Madras, 1920-23; Advocate-General, 1923-24; Judge, High Court, Madras, 1924-39; Pres. Railways Rates Advisory Board, 1940; Member Judicial Cttee. of Privy Council, 1941-50. *Address:* Lynwood, 52 Kodembakkam High Rd., Madras 34, India. *Clubs:* Athenæum, National Liberal; Cosmopolitan (Madras). [*Died* 5 *March* 1970.

OSSIANNILSSON, Karl Gustav, Plaquette of the Swedish Flag; Stipendiate of the Swedish State since 1908; Stipendiate of the Swedish Academy and of the Bonnier and the Kraemer Societies; Grand Prix of the Kraemer Society, 1933; Swedish State Artist Reward, since 1966; *b.* Lund, Sweden, 1875; *s.* of Rasmus Nilsson, manager of a church organ manufactory, and Elise Timelin; *m.* Naemi Arnman (*d.* 1961); three *s.* (two *s.* decd.); *m.* Vivi Eklund. *Educ.:* University of Lund. Teacher, 1897-1900; first book, 1900, since then independent writer (playwright, lyrist, novelist, romances, critic, politician, translator); journeys in Europe and U.S., 1901-; wrote 1917-18 against the German Propaganda in Sweden, and pleaded vigorously the cause of Swedish independence and friendship with England; member of the Association of Swedish Authors; Hon. F.R.S.L. (Great Britain), in 1919; Médaille du Roi Albert (Belgium). *Publications:* Barbarskogen, 1908, 1909, 1919, 1927, 1937, and four score of other novels and historical romances; several of these or other works translated into English, French, German, Russian, Finnish, Dutch, Danish, and Norwegian; Jörgen Kock, Tigerhuden (performed), Thomas Thorild (performed) and other plays; fifteen volumes of lyric, two of criticism, some of short stories, three political pamphlets; Collected Poems, four vols., 1920; Selected Poems, 1934 and 1954; two volumes of Memoirs, 1945 and 1946; Modern Swedish Poetry, part II. (translated by C. D. Locock), 1936; translations from Browning, Swinburne, Bennett, Pepys, Addison, Steele, Corneille, Verhaeren; Reviewer, Swedish papers and Mercure de France. *Recreation:* gardening. *Address:* Linghem, Sweden. *T.:* Linköping 70027. [*Died* 14 *March* 1970.

OWEN, Harrison; Dramatic author and journalist; *b.* Geelong, Australia, 24 June 1890; *s.* of late Albert Thomas Owen and Elizabeth Ann Harrison Swindells; *m.* Esther (*d.* 1964), *d.* of George Arthur Dyson, Melb., Australia. *Educ.:* Private schools. Dramatic critic and special writer for various Australian newspapers; came to London, 1920; leader-writer, Daily Sketch, 1921-32; returned to Australia, 1940. Leader-writer Melbourne Sun, 1940-55. *Publications:* The Mount Marunga Mystery, 1919; Tommyrot Rhymes, 1920; The Playwright's Craft, 1940; Plays: The Gentleman-in-Waiting, 1925; The Happy Husband, 1927; Doctor Pygmalion, 1932; Edge of the Night, 1959. *Recreations:* reading, play-going, golf. *Address:* 1/54 Hotham St., East St. Kilda, Melbourne, Australia. [*Died* 30 *May* 1966.

PHELAN, Major-Gen. Frederick Ross, C.B. 1945; D.S.O. 1919; M.C. 1916; V.D. 1931; *b.* 8 Aug. 1855; *s.* of Frederick Edward Phelan and Lillian Catherine Prevost; *m.* 1910, Mary Marshall Johnston (*d.* 1948); no *c.*; *m.* 1950, Vera Pearl Scott, A.R.R.C. *Educ.:* Public Schools, Montreal. Served European War, 1914-18 (despatches twice, M.C., D.S.O., French Croix de Guerre); Post-war: commanded Canadian Grenadier Guards and Brigade of Canadian Guards; served War of 1939-45, Deputy Adjutant-General, Ottawa, 1940; Deputy Adjutant-General, London, 1940-41; Commander Canadian Reinforcement Units, Aldershot, 1941-43; General Officer Commanding Canadian and Newfoundland Forces, 1943; Dir. Gen. Reserve Army, Canada, 1943-45; retired, 1945. C.St.J. *Address:* The Priory, St. Andrews East, P.Q., Canada. *Club:* The Mount Royal (Montreal). [*Died* 11 *Dec.* 1970.

REED, Hon. Sir Geoffrey (Sandford), Kt. 1953; retired; *b.* 14 March 1892; *s.* of late Rev. William Reed; *m.* 1918, Kathleen Jennie Matthews; one *s.* one *d.* *Educ.:*

Prince Alfred College, Adelaide; Adelaide University (LL.B.). Called South Australia Bar, 1914; Law Society of South Australia: Hon. Sec., 1924-27; Mem. Statutory Cttee., 1929-35; Vice-Pres. 1934. Lectr. in Private Internat. Law and Law of Evidence and Procedure, Adelaide Univ., 1928-34. Actg. Judge, Supreme Court of S.A., April 1935-July 1937; K.C. 1937. Chm. S.A. Nat. Security Advisory Cttee., 1941-45; Chm. or Comr., a number of Roy. Commissions and Bds. of Inquiry, State and Commonwealth Govts., 1943-48; Judge, Supreme Court of S. Australia, 1943-62. Dir.-Gen. of Security, Commonwealth of Australia, March 1949-June 1950. *Recreation:* golf. *Address:* 17 Briar Avenue, Medindie, S. Australia. *Club:* Adelaide (Adelaide). [*Died* 31 *Dec.* 1970.

RICHARDS, Hon. Mrs. Noel Olivier, M.D.; Hon. Consulting Physician, Westminster Children's Hospital, 1958, retd.; *b.* 1892; *d.* of 1st and last Baron Olivier; *m.* 1920, William Arthur Richards, F.R.C.S.; one *s.* four *d.* *Educ.:* Bedales School; University College, London; London School of Medicine for Women, M.B., B.S. 1917; L.R.C.P., Lond., M.R.C.S. Eng. 1917; M.D. Lond. 1921; M.R.C.P. Lond. 1922. Formerly: Consultant Physician, Westminster Children's Hosp.; Pædiatrician Westminster Med. School; Physician, Children's Department, Elizabeth Garrett Anderson Hospital; Out-patients' Physician and Senior Resident Medical Officer, Victoria Hospital for Children. *Publication:* (jt.) Healthy Babies, 1940. *Recreation:* Natural History. *Address:* Greenoge, 40 Swakeleys Road, Ickenham, Uxbridge. *T.:* Ruislip 39211. [*Died* 11 *April* 1969.

ROGERS, Lindsay; *b.* Baltimore, Maryland, 23 May 1891; *s.* of George Wilson Rogers and Emma K. Gore; *m.* 1917, Oona Carolyn Staples; no *c.* *Educ.:* Johns Hopkins Univ., A.B. 1912, Ph.D. 1915, LL.D. 1948; Univ. of Maryland, LL.B., 1915. Associate Professor of Political Science, Univ. of Virginia, 1915-20; Lecturer on Government, Harvard University, 1920-21; Associate Professor of Governments, Columbia Univ., 1921, and Burgess Professor of Public Law, 1929-59; Page Barbour Lecturer Univ. of Virginia, 1932; Visiting Professor on the Walgreen Foundation, Univ. of Chicago, 1939; Deputy Administrator, National Industrial Recovery Administration, 1933-34; Chairman, Board of Labour Review, Federal Emergency Administration of Public Works, 1934-37; Assistant Director of I.L.O., 1942-47. Consultant, U.S. Senate Committee on Foreign Relations, 1952-53 and 1956-62. Visiting Prof., Political Science, Johns Hopkins University, 1960; Occidental College, 1962-63. James Lecturer, University of Illinois, 1955. Mem. Bar, U.S. Supreme Court. *Publications:* The Postal Power of Congress, 1916; America's Case against Germany, 1917; The New Constitutions of Europe (with H. L. McBain), 1922 (Japanese translation); The American Senate, 1926; Crisis Government, 1934 (Czech transl.); The Pollsters, 1949. *Recreation:* contract bridge. *Address:* 88 Morningside Drive, New York, N.Y. 10027. *Clubs:* Athenæum; Century (New York); Cosmos (Washington). [*Died* 26 *Nov.* 1970.

SEFTON-COHEN, Arthur, C.B. 1935; barrister-at-law; *b.* 20 May 1879; *s.* of George Sefton-Cohen and Eliza Steavenson; *m.* 1922, Leonora Carlow; no *c.* Called to Bar, 1901; Assistant Director of Public Prosecutions, 1931; retired, 1944. Served European War, 1914-17. *Recreations:* fishing, rowing, swimming. [*Died* 1968.

SMART, D. I., R.E. Studied etching and engraving under Sir F. Short, R.A., P.R.E.; exhibitor at R.A. and International Exhibitions; has works in print rooms of National collections at London, Oxford and Cambridge. *Address:* 13 Clifton Road, Lee-on-the-Solent, Hants. [*Died.* 29 *Aug.* 1970.

SOUTHERN, Ralph Lang, C.B.E., 1952; Accountant and Comptroller-General of Inland Revenue, 1949-54; *b.* 14 May 1893; *s.* of James Lang Southern; *m.* 1919, Dora, *d.* of Albert Smith, J.P.; one *s.* two *d.* Entered Revenue Department, 1909. *Address:* 52 Sea Lane, Goring-by-sea, Sussex. [*Died* 22 *Oct.* 1968.

SOVEREIGN, Rt. Rev. Arthur Henry, M.A., D.D., F.R.G.S.; retired; *e. s.* of Freeman and Helen Sovereign; *b.* 1881; *m.* 1913, Ellen Fearnaught, *e. d.* of Hon. Price Ellison; one *s.* three *d.* *Educ.:* Toronto University; Wycliffe College, Toronto; Post-graduate course at Oxford University. Ordained Curate at Christ Church Cathedral, Vancouver, B.C., 1906; First Rector, St. Mark's Church, Vancouver, B.C., 1909; Professor and Lecturer, Anglican Theological College, Vancouver, B.C., 1920-31; service with Y.M.C.A. (Canadian); Canon of Christ Church Cathedral, Vancouver, B.C., 1929; Bishop of Yukon, 1932-33; Bishop of Athabasca, 1933-50. *Recreations:* mountain-climbing, photography. *Address:* 2501 23rd Street, Vernon, B.C., Canada. [*Deceased.*

TAYLOR, Rt. Hon. Sir Alan Russell, P.C. 1963; K.B.E., 1955; **Hon. Mr. Justice Taylor;** Justice of the High Court of Australia since 1952; *b.* 25 November 1901; *m.* 1933, Ceinwen Gertrude Williams; one *s.* one *d.* *Educ.:* University of Sydney, N.S.W. Admitted to N.S.W. Bar, 1926; Challis Lecturer, Sydney University Law School; Equity and Company Law, 1933-34; Legal Interpretation, 1935-38. K.C. 1943 (Q.C. 1952). President N.S.W. Bar Association, 1948-49; Justice of the Supreme Court of N.S.W., 1952-. *Recreations:* golf, bowls. *Address:* 7 Wentworth Road, Vaucluse, Sydney, N.S.W., Australia. *T.:* FU 2369. *Clubs:* Australian, Royal Sydney Golf, Elanora Country (Sydney); Athenæum (Melb.). [*Died* 3 *Aug.* 1969.

TAYLOR, Herbert, C.M.G. 1959; Chartered Accountant; now retired; *b.* 11 May 1885; *s.* of R. H. W. Taylor; *m.* 1919, Doris Madeline Brock; three *s.* *Educ.:* Caulfield Grammar School, Victoria. Clerk, W. J. Bush & Co., Melbourne, 1904-07; clerk, Flack & Flack, Melb. & Perth, 1907-12; Young & Outhwaite, 1913, admitted Partner, 1918. Life Governor, Roy. Victorian Inst. for the Blind and of Freemasons Hosp.; President: Assoc. Chambers of Commerce of Australia, 1945-47; Melbourne Chamber of Commerce, 1943-44. Past Member: Melbourne University Council (Chairman of Finance Cttee.); Council, Institute of Public Affairs; Past Coun. and Finance Committee, Victorian Red Cross Soc. *Publications:* The Organisation of a Chartered Accountants Office, 1933; The Audit of Sharebrokers Accounts, 1937; The Businessman and His Investments, 1945. *Recreations:* gardening, bowls. *Address:* (private) 10 Glenbrook Avenue, East Malvern, S.E.5, Victoria, Australia. *T.:* 25-3429; (business), 51 Queen Street, Melbourne, C.1, Victoria. *T.:* 61-2771. *Clubs:* Melbourne, West Brighton, Royal Automobile of Victoria (Past Pres., Life Member), Portsea Golf (Portsea, Vic.) (Life Mem.); Metropolitan Golf (Oakleigh, Vic.) (Capt., Pres., Life Mem.); Senior Golfers' Society of Victoria (Cttee.); Melbourne Cricket. [*Died* 27 *July* 1970.

VANDRY, Rt. Rev. Mgr. Ferdinand, C.M.G. 1946; *b.* Quebec, 8 Dec. 1887; *s.* of late Joseph Ulric Vandry and Caroline (*née* Fraser), Quebec City. *Educ.:* Seminary of Quebec; Laval University. B.A. 1910; L.Ph. 1911; D.Th. 1921; Priest of Roman

Catholic Church, 1914; Prof. of Philosophy and Theology from 1916; Superior of Grand Seminary of Quebec, 1938-45; created by the Pope, Apostolic Protonotary in 1945. Formerly Vicar-Gen., Dio. Quebec. Rector of Laval Univ., 1945-54, then Pres., Vice-Pres. Hon. LL.D. Universities of Fordham (N.Y.), Ottawa (Can.), Toronto (Can.), 1947; University of Oxford (England), 1948; Universities of Western Ontario (Can.), Edmonton (Alberta, Can.), 1949; Queen's (Kingston, Can.), Montreal, 1951; McGill, Manitoba, 1952; St. Francis-Xavier (Antigonish, N.S.); Bishop's Univ. (Lennoxville, P.Q.). Hon. Ph.-Lit.D., Louvain, 1949. Fellow Unattached, R.S.C., 1952. Knight of the Legion of Honour (France). *Address:* c/o Laval University, Quebec, Canada.
[*Died* 13 *Jan.* 1967.

WATTS, Arthur Frederick, C.M.G. 1949; *b.* 26 May 1897; *s.* of Arthur Joseph Watts, L.D.S. (Ire.), and Martha Kathleen Watts; *m.* 1st, 1924, Dorothy Furness Thomson (*decd.*); one *s.* one *d.*; 2nd, 1948, Ida Gladys O'Halloran. *Educ.:* Government School, Katanning, W.A.; Guildford Grammar School, W.A. M.L.A. for Katanning 1935 - 50, for Stirling, 1950-. Leader Country Party and Leader Opposition, 1942-47; one of two W.A. reps. to Constitutional Convention, Canberra, A.C.T., 1942, Deputy Premier, Minister for Education, Local Government and Industries, West Australian State Government, 1947-1953; Deputy Premier, Minister for Education and Attorney-General, April 1959-resignation, Feb. 1962. Chairman of State Licensing Court, W.A., 1962-. *Recreations:* literature, motoring. *Address:* 8 Edna Rd., Dalkeith, West Australia.
[*Died June* 1970.

WHITESIDE, Sir Cuthbert William, Kt., *cr.* 1921; *b.* 26 Oct. 1880; *o. s.* of late Rev. Jos. Whiteside; *m.* 1909, Janet, *d.* of late Edward Humpage; one *s.* two *d.* *Educ.:* Grey College, Port Elizabeth, S.A. Solicitor of the Supreme Court, 1901; practising at Grahamstown; retired, 1944; J.P. District of Albany, S.A.; Town Councillor, 1912; Mayor of City of Grahamstown, 1918-22. *Recreation:* tennis. *Address:* Leisure Isle, Knyana, S. Africa. [*Died* 25 *Oct.* 1969.

YOUNG, William, C.M.G. 1953; J.P., Fruit Grower and Company Director, Australia; *b.* 9 Nov. 1885; *s.* of Joseph Young; *m.* 1913, Christina Beveridge; one *s.* *Educ.:* Albert Public School, Glasgow, Scotland; Scotch College, Melbourne, Victoria. *Address:* Marina Rd., Mentone, Vic., Australia.
[*Died* 1 *Jan.* 1965.

YUSUF, Sir Mohamad, Kt., 1915; Indian landowner; *s.* of Haji Ismail. Founded Ismail College, first Muslim College in Western India at Bombay; Marine College, Seamen's Orphanage, Hospital, Sanatorium, Schools, etc., on Island of Novha, and other Charitable Institutions in Bombay. Formerly Head of Bombay Steam Navigation Co. Now living in retirement on the Island of Novha which he owns. *Address:* Novha House, Bombay.
[*Died* 15 *Sept.* 1965.

WHO WAS WHO, 1961-70

A

AALTONEN, Prof. Wäinö (Valdemar); Finnish sculptor and painter; Hon. Prof. Finland, 1940; Commander of White Rose of Finland (1st cl.); *b.* 8 Mar. 1894; *s.* of Matti Aaltonen and Ida Katarina Värri; *m.* 1st, 1920, Aino Pietiläinen (marr. diss.); one *s.* three *d.*; 2nd, 1931, Elsa Rantalainen (marr. diss.); 3rd, 1942, Elvi Brunila (marr. diss.); 4th, 1961, Elisabeth Maasik. *Educ.:* Turku Art Society's Art Sch. Works exhibited in many cities of Europe including Wäinö Aaltonen-Museum in Turku; special exhibitions; Helsinki, Stockholm, 1927; Paris, 1928; Eskilstuna, Malmö, Gothenburg, 1941; New York and San Francisco, 1939 (World Fairs); Copenhagen, 1950; Oslo, 1951; Philadelphia, 1948; Gt. Britain, Roy. Scottish Acad. of Arts, 1950; Germany, 1952; Washington, 1952, Moscow, Leningrad, 1953; England, 1954; Venice (Biennale), 1954; Rome, 1955; Tampere, 1957; Prague, 1957; China, 1958, etc. Works include: portrait busts: Jean Sibelius, League of national officials, authors and artists, Finnish Presidents, and Swedish Royalty; sculptures: Paavo Nurmi, Lilja, Aleksis Kivi statues, in Tampere, Turku and Helsinki; 4 bridgehead figures in Tampere; 5 statues in Finnish Parliament House and big marble relief in Univ. of Helsinki; 5 figures in The United Northern Bank, Helsinki; Genius leads the Youth in Turku University; monuments, since 1938, including Delaware Monument; Co-operative monument and Tying of Friendship monument in Gothenburg and Turku; Gutenberg portrait in Gutenberg Museum, Mainz. Several war memorials including war monuments in Lahti and Kuusankoski, the gravestones of Marshal Mannerheim of Finland, and President Risto Ryti, 1954, Gold Medal, Vienna Exhibition, 1936; Grand Prix, Paris World Fair, 1937; Internat. Prize of Peace (Budapest), 1953. Member of Finnish Academy, Finnish Academy of Arts; Swedish and Danish Royal Acad. of Arts; Salon Tuiliers; Brazilian Acad. of Arts; Hon. Mem., U.S.S.R. Acad. of Arts; Hon. Mem. and gold medal: Il Cenacolo Ceccardo Roccatagliata Ceccardi (Carrara); Int. Gutenberg Assoc.; Artists' Society and Sculptors' Association. Member Légion d'Honneur (France), Prins Eugen medal (Sweden); Comdr. of St. Olav (Norway) 1st Class; Stella della solidarieta Italiana. *Address:* Marsalkantie 1, Kulosaari, Helsinki, Finland. *T.:* 688257. [*Died* 29 *May* 1966.

ABADY, Jacques, Q.C. 1935; *b.* Manchester, 2 Oct. 1872; *m.* (wife decd.); one *s.* *Educ.:* Manchester Grammar School; Birkbeck Inst. Apprenticed as engineer; formerly M. Inst. Mech. E.; invented several scientific instruments; gold and silver medallist, Institution of Gas Engineers; called to Bar, 1905; Bencher, Middle Temple, 1941; Member Westminster City Council, 1906-12 and 1916-59; Mayor, 1927-28; J.P. for County of London. *Publications:* Clauses and Precedents in Private Bill Legislation; Gas Analyst's Manual and many papers and articles on scientific subjects. *Address:* Farrars Bldg., Temple, E.C.4. *T.:* Central 1684; 2 The Little Paddocks House, Beehive Lane, Ferring, Sussex. *Clubs:* Hurlingham, Constitutional. [*Died* 15 *April* 1964.

ABBISS, Sir George, Kt., *cr.* 1941; O.B.E. 1933; Knight of Order of St. John, 1941; *b.* 1884. Joined Metropolitan Police, 1905; appointed Chief Constable, 1930; Deputy Assistant Commissioner, 1933; Assistant Commissioner, 1936-46; retired, 1946. Police Adviser to the Secretary of State for the Colonies, 1948-60. *Address:* Bearwood, The Causeway, Potters Bar, Herts. *T.:* Potters Bar 52696. *Clubs:* Royal Automobile, Old Fold Golf. [*Died* 6 *Oct.* 1966.

ABBOTT, Colonel Rev. Preb. Herbert Alldridge, M.B.E.; Preb. of Marney (or Mornays) in Prebendal Church of St. Endellion, Cornwall, June 1946-Dec. 1958, and Vicar of Lanhydrock, Bodmin, Cornwall, Sept. 1946-Dec. 1958, resigned; *b.* 16 Mar. 1881; *s.* of B. C. Abbott; *m.* 1909, Gabrielle van der Weegen (*d.* 1958); one *s.* one *d.* *Educ.:* King's Coll., London; Queens' Coll., Cambridge (Exhibitioner). B.A. 1904, M.A. 1907, Hist. Tripos Parts I and II; Tutor and Lecturer, Training College, Chester, 1906-8; Asst. Master, Queen Elizabeth Grammar School, Blackburn, 1908-11; Headmaster, Eggars Grammar School, Alton, Hants., 1911-18; Headmaster Palmer's School, Grays, Essex, 1918-46. Deacon, 1909; Priest, 1910. Royal Fusiliers, 1899-1903; Captain 1st V.B. Hampshire Regt.; Executive Officer National Reserves, 1914; Essex Cadet Committee, 1918-46; Colonel T.A.R.O. and O.C. Palmer's School Cadet A.A. Regt. R.A. (formerly 10th Cadet Bn. Essex Regt.), 1919-50; Hon. Colonel of Essex Army Cadet Force, 1950; O.C. No. 2 Company, National Defence Companies, 6th Bn. Essex Regt., 1936-39; Attached to 2nd Bn. Coldstream Guards, 1921. District Commissioner Boy Scouts Assoc., 1919-34; Chairman Thurrock Youth Committee, 1940-46; President Thurrock Sea Cadet Corps since 1940 and Chairman, 1940-46; Chaplain 106 (Orsett Hundred) Squadron A.T.C.; Organised and conducted first Schoolboy Party to Canada, 1926. (Life) F.R.Hist.S. 1907; Founder Vice-Pres. (1930-31) and Pres. (1931-32) Thurrock Rotary Club; Vice-Pres. (Grays Branch) British Legion; Member Headmasters' Conference since 1926; Member Inc. Assoc. of Headmasters since 1911; Jubilee Medal, Cadet Long Service Award, Defence Medal, Cadet Forces Medal and Clasp. *Address:* c/o Mrs Fysh, 37 Lime Tree Grove, Shirley, Croydon, Surrey. [*Died* 31 *Dec.* 1962.

ABBOTT, Brig. Reginald Stuart, C.I.E. 1937; M.C.; B.A.; J.P.; I.A., retired; *b* 12 Nov. 1882; *o. surv. s.* of Sam Abbott Buenos Aires; *m.* 1933, Marjorie MacLeod (*d.* 1956), *y. d.* of John Macdonald, Portree, Isle of Skye; two *d.* *Educ.:* Tonbridge; Balliol College, Oxford. 2nd Lt R.A. 1904; Lt. Central India Horse, 1909; Capt 1913; Bt. Major, 1917; Major, 1919; Bt. Lt.-Col. 1923; Lt.-Col. 1930; Col. 1931; p.s.c.; Commander Kohat Brigade, 1935-1938; A.D.C. to the King, 1936-38; retired, 1938; recalled to Army Service, Oct. 1939-Feb. 1942; commanded East Midland Area. D.L. Leicestershire, 1951-55. *Address:* The Court

House Litton Cheney, Dorset. *T.:* Long Bredy, 367. [*Died* 2 *March* 1964.

ABBOTT, William, C.M.G. 1951; O.B.E. 1941; Ph.D., B.Sc., M.I.Mech.E.; M.R.I.; Director of Studies in connection with oversea scholarships scheme of F.B.I. since 1953; *b.* 9 Feb. 1891; *s.* of William Augustus and Alice Abbott, formerly of Portsmouth; *m.* Joan Helene (*d.* 1961); one *s.*; two *d.* (and one *d.* decd.). *Educ.:* H.M. Dockyard Sch. and Municipal Coll., Portsmouth. Admiralty, 1905-24; Coll. Lectr., 1924-34; H.M. Inspector of Schools, 1934-39; H.M. Staff Inspector for Engineering, Min. of Educn., 1939-53. Missions to U.S.A., Canada, Afghanistan, Pakistan, the Sudan, Central Africa. *Publications:* various works on geometry, perspective and engineering design. *Recreations:* walking, sailing; painting; foreign travel. *Address:* St. Andrews House, Billingshurst, Sussex. [*Died* 20 *Oct.* 1963.

ABDUL MALIKI, Alhaji, C.B.E. 1960; Ambassador for Nigeria in Paris since 1966; *b.* Okene, Nigeria, 1914; *m.*; *c.* *Educ.:* Okene Elementary School; Katsina Training College. Local Government Course, U.K., 1950. Clerk, 1935-36; Supervisor, N.A. Works, 1936-39; Clerical duties Provincial Office, Lokoja, 1939-40; Wakilin Atta Igbirra, Okene, 1940-45, first member for Igbirra. Northern Nigeria House of Assembly and Nigeria House of Representatives, 1951-55; Commissioner for Nigeria, 1958-60, High Commissioner, 1960-1966, in the U.K. *Recreation:* photography. *Address:* The Embassy of Nigeria, 91 Faubourg St. Honoré, B.P. 267-08, Paris 8e, France. [*Died* 28 *Aug.* 1969.

ABEL SMITH, Reginald Henry Macaulay, M.C. 1917; J.P. Herts; Director of Arbuthnot, Latham & Company Ltd. (Merchant Bankers), 10 Old Jewry, E.C.2, since 1920; *b.* 28 April 1890; *e. surv. s.* of late Reginald Abel Smith, Goldings, Hertford, and of Margaret Alice, *d.* of 1st Viscount Knutsford; *m.* 1st, 1913, Myrtle Vere (*d.* 1920), *d.* of Sir Robert Abercromby, 7th Bart.; 2nd, 1922, Beatrice, *d.* of late Francis Pelham Whitbread and of Hon. Mrs. Whitbread; three *d.* *Educ.:* Eton; Trinity College, Cambridge. Served European War, 1914-18, Herts Yeomanry, Captain; Egypt, Gallipoli, Palestine (despatches). High Sheriff of Hertfordshire, 1940; Hon. Treasurer British Red Cross and St. John Joint War Organisation (Hertfordshire), 1940-46. Member of Council of Haileybury and Imperial Service College. Director: Anglo-American Securities Corporation Ltd., etc. *Recreations:* fishing, shooting, etc. *Address:* Datchworth Close, Datchworth, Knebworth, Herts. *T.:* Knebworth 2103. *Club:* City of London. [*Died* 12 *March* 1964.

ABELL, Sir Westcott (Stile), K.B.E., *cr.* 1920; R.C.N.C., ret.; M.Eng.; Hon. Vice-Pres. Inst. N.A.; Fellow N.E. Coast Inst. of Shipbuilders and Engineers; Hon. M.I.Struct.E.; *b.* 16 Jan. 1877; *s.* of Thomas Abell; *m.* 1902, Beatrice (*d.* 1953), *d.* of Joseph Wyld Davenport; one *s.* two *d.* (and one *d.* decd.). *Educ.:* West Buckland School; Royal Naval Engineering College, Devonport; Royal Naval College, Greenwich. Appointed to Royal Corps of Naval Constructors, 1900; Professional Secretary to Director of Naval Construction, 1904-7; Instructor in Naval Architecture, Royal Naval College, 1907-10; Professor of Naval Architecture, University of Liverpool, 1910-14; Chief Ship Surveyor, Lloyd's Register of Shipping, 1914-28; Prof. of Naval Architecture, Armstrong College, Newcastle upon Tyne, 1928-41; Member of Board of Trade Committee on the Internationalisation of the Load Line of Ships, 1913; Member of Board of Trade Committee on Shipping and Shipbuilding, 1916; Member of Merchant Shipbuilding Advisory Committee appointed by Ministry of Shipping, 1916; Technical Adviser to the Controller of Shipping, 1917 (by arrangement with Lloyd's Register); Member of Admiralty Shipbuilding Council, 1917; President of Institute of Marine Engineers, 1924-25; Member of Board of Trade Load Line Committee, 1927; British Delegate International Conference on the Safety of Life at Sea, London, 1929; Master of the Worshipful Company of Shipwrights, 1931; President of Devonshire Association, 1933; Pres. Smeatonian Society of Civil Engineers, 1941. *Publications:* The Safe Sea, 1932; The Shipwright's Trade, 1948; The Ship and her Work; contributions to Transactions of Institution of Naval Architects and other societies. *Address:* 95 Kenton Road, Gosforth, Newcastle upon Tyne 3. *T.:* 53510. [*Died* 29 *July* 1961.

ABEOKUTA, The Alake of, (Ademola II); Sir Ladapo Ademola, K.B.E. 1954 (C.B.E. 1935); C.M.G. 1945; Member of Western House of Chiefs since 1954; *b.* 1873; married; *c.* Member of the former Western House of Assembly, and of the Legislative Council, 1946-51. The accolade was bestowed by the Queen during the Royal Tour, February, 1956. *Address:* Ibadan, Western Nigeria. [*Died* 27 *Dec.* 1962.

ABERCROMBY, Bt.-Col. Sir George (William), 8th Bt., *cr.* 1636; D.S.O. 1917; Gordon Highlanders; Lord Lieutenant of Banffshire since 1946; *b.* 18 Mar. 1886; *s.* of 7th Bt. and Florence Anita Eyre, C.B.E. (*d.* 1946), *o. d.* of Eyre Coote (she *m.* 2nd, 1899, 2nd Earl of Northbrook (*d.* 1929)); *S.* father, 1895; *m.* 1935, Eleanor, *o.d.* of late Sir Arthur Anderson, C.I.E., Roffey Place, Horsham. Served in Scots Guards, 1905-14; A.D.C. to G.O.C. Forces in Ireland, 1910-12; served European War in 8th Black Watch 1916-18 (D.S.O.); Commanded 6th (T.) Gordon Highlanders, 1920-27, Hon. Col., 1931-44. Owns about 12,000 acres. *Heir:* *b.* Robert Alexander, M.C. [*b.* 15 Aug. 1895; *m.* 1st, 1923, Hon. Diamond Hardinge (*d.* 1927) *o. d.* of 1st Baron Hardinge of Penhurst, K.G.; 2nd, 1929, Pamela (*d.* 1944), *o. d.* of late John Lomax; 3rd, 1951, Mrs. Elizabeth Lawrence. *Educ.:* Sandhurst]. *Address:* Forglen House, Turriff, Aberdeenshire; Birkenbog, Banffshire. [*Died* 9 *Sept.* 1964.

ABERDEEN and TEMAIR, 2nd Marquis of (*cr.* 1916); **George Gordon,** O.B.E.; J.P.; Viscount Formartine, Lord Haddo, Methlic, Tarves and Kellie, Earl of Aberdeen, 1682, Peerage of Scotland; Viscount Gordon of Aberdeen, 1814; and Earl of Haddo, 1915, Peerage of the United Kingdom, Baronet of Nova Scotia, 1642; K.St.J. 1949 (Prior of Scottish Priory of Order, 1951-57); Lord-Lieut. and Pres. T. and A.F.A. of Aberdeenshire, 1934-59, resigned; Mem. for Tarves, Aberdeenshire C.C., 1945-59; Chm. Aberdeenshire Education Committee, 1950-55; D.L. for County of City of Aberdeen since 1935; Hon. LL.D., Aberdeen, 1954; L.C.C. (P.) Peckham, 1910-25; (M.R.) West Fulham, 1931-34; Alderman (M.R.), 1925-1931; Deputy Chm. of the Council, 1923-1924; Chm. of the Parks and Open Spaces Com., 1927-29; Chm. of Town Planning Cttee., 1929-34; co-opted Member of Housing Committee, 1934-37; one of the L.C.C. Representatives on, and Vice-Chairman of, the Greater London Regional Planning Committee, 1929-33, and Chairman of the reconstituted Committee, 1933-34, co-opted, 1934-36; one of the L.C.C. Representatives on the Metropolitan Water Board, 1913-46 (Vice-Chairman of the Board's Finance Committee, 1919-22, and Chairman of Finance Committee, 1922-25; Vice-Chairman of General Purposes Committee, 1925-1928); a Governor (L.C.C.) of the Polytechnic, Regent Street, 1920-46 (City Parochial Foundation), since 1947; Trustee (L.C.C.) for the Crystal Palace, 1914-24, and 1926-51; a Vice-President of the National

Council of Y.M.C.A.s, and late Chairman of its Metropolitan Committee; Vice-Pres. Metropolitan Union Y.M.C.A.; Chairman of Council of Charity Organisation Society, 1934-37 and 1938-39; a "B" member of Royal Observer Corps, 1939-46 (Head Observer, 1939-43); President National Service Committee, Aberdeenshire, 1939; *b.* 20 Jan. 1879; *e. s.* of 1st Marquis; *S.* father, 1934; *m.* 1st, 1906, Mary Florence (*d.* 1937), *widow* of E. S. Cockayne, Sheffield; 2nd, 1940, Sheila (*d.* 1949), *widow* of Capt. J. W. Guy Innes, R.N., of Maryculter House, Kincardineshire, and *d.* of late Lt.-Col. Forbes of Rothiemay. *Educ.:* Harrow; St. Andrews University; Balliol College, Oxford. Contested (L.) East Berkshire, 1906. *Heir: b.* Lt.-Col. Lord Dudley Gordon, D.S.O. *Address:* Braehead, Bridge of Don, Aberdeen. *T.:* Aberdeen 43230. *Club:* Royal Northern (Aberdeen). [*Died* 6 *Jan.* 1965.

ABRAHAM, George Dixon; retired 1960, as Chairman and Managing Director of G. P. Abraham, Ltd., specialists in Alpine and mountain photography; *b.* Keswick, 7 Oct. 1872; *m.* 1st, 1901, Winifred E. Davies (*d.* 1939), B.Sc.Lond.; two *d.*; 2nd, 1940, Clara Young. *Educ.:* Manchester Grammar School; Manchester School of Art. With younger brother, A. P. Abraham, was first to obtain and publish detail photographs of routes up various climbs in England, Scotland, Wales, and the Alps of Austria, Italy, France, and Switzerland; leader of first ascents up numerous new climbs, especially in England, Scotland, and Wales. Hon. Mem., Alpine Club, Climbers' Club, Fell and Rock Climbing Club. *Publications:* The Complete Mountaineer; Mountain Adventures at Home and Abroad; On Alpine Heights and British Crags; British Mountain Climbs (7th ed. 1947); Swiss Mountain Climbs; First Steps to Climbing; Motoring in the English Lake District (5th ed. 1947); Motorways at Home and Abroad; Modern Mountaineering, 1933 (3rd ed. 1947); and regular contributor to Strand, Sphere, and leading magazines. *Recreations:* mountaineering, cricket, golf, and motoring at home and abroad; made 101st ascent of Pillar Rock a unique record, April 1926. *Address:* Idwal, Chestnut Hill, Keswick, Cumberland. *Clubs:* Royal Automobile; Swiss Alpine. [*Died* 4 *March* 1965.

ABRAHAM, James Johnston, C.B.E, 1919; D.S.O. 1918; M.A., Litt.D., M.D. (Dub.). F.R.C.S. (Eng.); Consulting Surgeon, Princess Beatrice Hospital; Chairman and Managing Director, Wm. Heinemann Medical Books Ltd.; Lt.-Col. late R.A.M.C.; Knight of Grace Order of St. John of Jerusalem; Officer Order of St. Sava; Fellow Roy. Society of Medicine; *b.* Coleraine, Co. Derry, 16 Aug. 1876; *e. s.* of Wm. Abraham, J.P., and Elizabeth Ann Morrison; *m.* 1920, Lilian Angela, *e. d.* of Dr. Alexander Francis, London; one *d.* *Educ.:* Coleraine Academy; Trinity College, Dublin (Senior Moderator, B.A., Gold Medallist in Natural Science); London Hospital. European War, 1914-18: Surgeon 4th Reserve Hospital, Uskub, Serbia, 1914-15; Surgical Specialist Queen Alexandra's Military Hosp., London, 1915-16, and 24th Stationary Hospital Egypt, 1916-17; A.D.M.S. Lines of Communication Egyptian Expeditionary Force, 1917-19; served Macedonia, Egypt, Palestine, Syria (despatches thrice). Pres. Irish Medical Graduates Association, 1939-50; Thomas Vicary Lecturer, Royal Coll. of Surgeons, England, 1944; Vice-Pres. Medical Soc. of London, 1940-42; Orator, 1946, Secretary for Foreign Correspondence, 1951, Hon-Librarian, 1956; Lloyd-Robert, Lecturer, 1948. Arnott Medal, 1949. Trustees Hunterian Collection, R.C.S., 1954. *Publications:* The Surgeon's Log, 1911; The Night Nurse (a novel), 1913 (Film versions: Norah O'Neale, in America; Irish Hearts, in Europe, 1935); The Golden Age of Henry the Navigator (translated, with W. E. Reynolds, from the Portuguese of Oliveira Martins), 1914; My Balkan Log, 1921; Lettsom, his Life and Times, 1933; Ninety-Nine Wimpole St., 1937; Surgeon's Journey, an autobiography 1957; several technical works; scientific papers in British and Amer. Medical Journals. Has also written under pseudonym of James Harpole (translated into many European languages); Leaves from a Surgeon's Case Book, 1937; The White Coated Army, 1938; (American title, Body Menders), Behind the Surgeon's Mask, 1940; A Surgeon's Heritage, 1953. *Recreations:* medical history and collecting old books. *Address:* 75 Wimpole Street, W.1; 30 Campden Hill Court, W.8; Glenhurst, Frinton-on-Sea. *Clubs:* Athenæum, Garrick; University (Dublin). [*Died* 9 *Aug.* 1963.

ABRAHAMS, Sir Adolphe, Kt., *cr.* 1939; O.B.E. 1919; M.A., M.D., B.Chir. (Camb.), F.R.C.P. (Lond.); Consulting Physician; Cons. Physician to Westminster Hosp., to Hampstead General Hosp., and to L.C.C. Hosps.; F.R.S.M. (ex-President Section of Medicine); F.R.P.S.; Hon. Medical Adviser, International Athletic Board, and Hon. Medical Officer, British Olympic Athletic Team; President, Brit. Assoc. Sport and Medicine, and United Hosps. Athletic Club; *b.* Cape Town, 6 Feb. 1883; *s.* of late Isaac Abrahams; *m.* 1922, Adrienne Walsh; one *s.* one *d.* *Educ.:* Bedford School (Exhibitioner); Emmanuel Coll., Cambridge (Foundation Scholar and Prizeman, First Class Honours Natural Sciences Tripos, 1906); St. Bartholomew's Hospital; Vienna. House Surgeon and House Surgeon Ear, Nose and Throat Dept., St. Bartholomew's Hosp.; late Physician Royal Chest Hosp.; Former Censor, R.C.P.; Arris and Gale Lecturer, R.C.S., 1928; Lumleian Lecturer, R.C.P., 1951. War service, 1915-20; Major R.A.M.C.; in charge Medical Div., Connaught Hosp., Aldershot, and District Cons. Physician Aldershot Command (despatches); M.O. in charge British Olympic Athletic Team, Stockholm, 1912, Paris, 1924, Amsterdam, 1928, Berlin, 1936, London, 1948; European Championships, Paris, 1938, Berne, 1954, Stockholm, 1958. Ex-Editor St. Bartholomew's Hosp. Journal and Post-Graduate Med. Jl.; Ex-Joint Lecturer, Tutor and Demonstrator of Medicine and Dean in the Medical School, Westminster Hosp.; formerly Cons. Phys. to Chislehurst, Orpington and Cray Valley Hosp. Sometime Examiner in Medicine, Universities of Liverpool and Cambridge, and in Medicine and in Applied Pharmacology and Therapeutics, University of London; ex-Pres. British Assoc. of Gastro-Enterologists. *Publications:* The Photography of Moving Objects and Advanced Hand-camera Work, 1910; Chronic Colitis (with late Dr. G. Herschell), 1913; Indigestion, 1920; A Manual of Urinary Diseases (with A. C. Morson), 1921; Training for Athletes (with H. M. Abrahams), 1928; Exercise, 1930; Diseases and Disorders of Digestion, 1931; Training for Health and Athletics (with H. M. Abrahams), 1936; Fitness for the average man and the super-athlete, 1952; Woman—Man's equal?, 1954; The Human Machine, 1955; Disabilities and Injuries of Athletics and Sport, 1960; Duodenal Ulcer and other Alimentary Canal Disorders, 1961; articles on medical, scientific, athletic, and photographic subjects. *Recreations:* athletics, journalism. *Address:* 55 Kingston House, Princes Gate, S.W.7. *T.:* Kensington 7917. *Club:* Achilles. [*Died* 11 *Dec.* 1967.

ABRAHAMSON, Sir Martin Arnold, K.B.E., *cr.* 1920; Director, Copenhagen; *b.* 12 Sept. 1870; *s.* of late Arnold Abrahamson, of London and Copenhagen; *m.* 1903,

Emma, *d.* of late Bernhard Hirschsprung of Copenhagen; one *s.* one *d.* *Educ.:* London; Copenhagen. *Address:* 1 Mynstersvej, Copenhagen V. *Clubs:* Royal Over-Seas League, Constitutional; British Centre (Copenhagen). [*Died* 4 *Dec.* 1962.

ABUBAKR, Seiyid Sir, K.B.E. 1953 (C.B.E. 1958); **bin Sheik al Kaf;** Has rendered public services in Aden Protectorate; State Councillor of the Kathiri State, Eastern Aden Protectorate. [*Died Dec.* 1965.

ACHESON, Anne Crawford, C.B.E., 1919; F.R.B.S., A.R.C.A.; sculptor; *b.* Ireland; unmarried. *Educ.:* Royal College of Art, South Kensington. Diploma (Sculpture); Exhibitor at Royal Academy, Salon, etc.; Degree in Modern Literature in Royal University of Ireland; war work at the Surgical Requisites Association, Mulberry Walk, Chelsea (C.B.E.). *Address:* Glebe House, Glenavy, Co. Antrim, N. Ireland. [*Died* 13 *March* 1962.

ACKERMANN, Gerald, R.I., watercolour painter; *b.* Blackheath, 1876; *s.* of Arthur Ackermann. *Educ.:* New College, Eastbourne. Studied at Heatherley's and Royal Academy Schools; while there won the Creswick prize and Landseer scholarship; exhibited at the Royal Academy and held exhibitions at the Leicester Galleries and the Fine Art Society. Official purchases: Wellington (N.Z.), New South Wales, and provincial galleries in England. Enlisted in the Artists Rifles O.T.C. and held commission in the Royal Air Force. *Recreation:* walking. *Address:* Santa Claus, Blakeney, Norfolk. *Club:* Chelsea Arts. [*Died* 27 *Dec.* 1960.

ACKNER, Brian Gerard Conrad, M.A., M.D., F.R.C.P., D.P.M.; Consultant Physician to Maudsley and Bethlem Royal Hospitals since 1948; Physician in charge, Department of Psychological Medicine, Hammersmith Hospital and, Lecturer at the Postgraduate Medical School of London, since 1950; *b.* 1 Nov. 1918; *s.* of Dr. Conrad and Rhoda Ackner; *m.* 1943, Jean, *d.* of late Walter Marley; one *s.* one *d.* *Educ.:* Rugby School; Clare Coll., Cambridge; Guy's Hosp., London. Schol. Guy's Hosp., 1939; House Officer, 1942. Served R.A.F., 1943-46; Wing Comdr., Command Psychiatrist R.A.F. Middle East and Med. Forces, 1946. Governor, Maudsley and Bethlem Roy. Hosps., 1960. Member: Mental Nurses Cttee. of Gen. Nursing Council, 1960; Council of Roy. Medico-Psychological Assoc., 1962. Examiner in Psychological Med., R.C.P., 1964. F.R.Soc. Med. *Publications:* articles in medical journals; (Ed.) Handbook for Psychiatric Nurses, 1964. *Recreations:* squash, tennis, skiing, gardening, photography. *Address:* 130 Harley Street, W.1. *T.:* Welbeck 3349; Holmbury, Peter Avenue, Oxted, Surrey. *T.:* Oxted 3503. [*Died* 29 *Aug.* 1966.

ACLAND, Arthur Geoffrey Dyke; Chairman Executive Committee Liberal Party, 1954; a Vice-President, Liberal Party, 1963; *b.* 17 May 1908; *m.* 1932; four *s.* (and one *d.* decd.). *Educ.:* Rugby; Trinity College, Cambridge. *Recreation:* ski-ing. *Address:* Hundhow, Burneside, Kendal, Westmorland; Liberal Party H.Q., 58 Victoria Street, S.W.1. *Club:* National Liberal. [*Died* 14 *Sept.* 1964.

ACLAND, Eng.-Rear-Adm. Edward Leopold Dyke, C.B. 1937; M.V.O. 1913; *b.* 7 Dec. 1878; *e. s.* of late Rev. Henry Dyke Acland and Adelaide, *d.* of late Richard Vaughan Davis; *m.* 1910, Phyllis Mary, *d.* of late Connell Whipple; one *d.* Served European War; commanded R.N. Engineering College at Keyham, 1930-33; on staff Commander-in-Chief, The Nore, 1934-37; retired list, 1937. *Address:* Lanherne, Haines Hill, Taunton, Somerset. *T.:* Taunton 4464. [*Died* 11 *March* 1968.

ACLAND, Sir William Henry Dyke, 3rd Bt., *cr.* 1890; *b.* 16 May 1888; *o. s.* of 2nd Bt. and late Emily Anna (author of several novels), *d.* of late Viscountess Hambleden and late Rt. Hon. W. H. Smith; *S.* father, 1924; *m.* 1916, Margaret (*d.* 1967), *d.* of late Theodore Barclay, of Fanshaws, Hertford; three *d.* (and one *d.* decd.). *Educ.:* Eton; Christ Church, Oxford, M.A. 1909. Royal Scots Greys; late Col. Royal Devon Yeomanry Artillery, R.F.C. and R.A.F.; Imperial Defence Coll., 1939; served European War (Military Cross, Air Force Cross, 4th Class Order of St. George, despatches); served War of 1939-45. J.P. and D.L. Herts, retd. from Aldermanic Bench, Herts C.C., 1966. High Sheriff of Hertfordshire, 1951; Governor Police College. *Heir:* *b.* Capt. Hubert Guy Dyke Acland. *Address:* Ellacombe, Seaview, Isle of Wight. *Clubs:* Athenæum; Royal Yacht Squadron, Seaview Yacht. [*Died* 4 *Dec.* 1970.

ACLAND-TROYTE, Lieut.-Col. Sir Gilbert John, Kt., *cr.* 1945; C.M.G. 1917; D.S.O. 1916; late King's Royal Rifle Corps; J.P. Devon; *b.* 1876; 3rd *s.* of late Col. C. A. W. Troyte; *m.* 1909, Gwladys Eleanor Quicke. *Educ.:* Eton; Trinity Hall, Cambridge. Served in S. African War (wounded); Somaliland Campaign, 1903-4; European War (despatches, C.M.G., D.S.O., Bt. Lieut.-Col., Croix de Guerre); Home Guard, 1940-44. County Alderman for Devon; M.P. (C.) Tiverton, 1924-45; contested (C.) Tiverton Division at by election, June 1923, and at General Election, Dec. 1923: President Central Landowners' Association, 1937-39. Joint Master of Tiverton Foxhounds, 1946-50. *Recreations:* hunting, shooting. *Address:* Huntsham Court, Tiverton, Devonshire. *Club:* Army and Navy. [*Died* 27 *April* 1964.

ACOMB, Henry Waldo, M.A.; Tutor, Davies, Laing & Dick, London, since 1960; *b.* 28 July 1891; *s.* of the Reverend W. J. Acomb and Emma Rebecca, *e. d.* of Allan Charles Brown, Redditch. *Educ.:* privately; Fitzwilliam Hall, Cambridge. Assistant, Trinity College Library, Cambridge, 1924-1926; County Librarian, Cornwall and Shropshire, 1926-28; Bookseller, 1928-29; Librarian, Gladstone Library, National Liberal Club, 1929-34; Lecturer on Cataloguing, School of Librarianship, Univ. Coll., London, 1929-34; Warden, Univ. Coll. Hall, W.5, 1932-33; Univ. Librarian, Durham, 1934-1945; T.A. (Gen. List) Commission, 1931-37; Lieut. R.A. 1940; Capt. A.E.C. 1941-42; full-time Lecturer for Central Advisory Council for Education in H.M. Forces, 1942. Seconded to British Council, Jan. 1943; Librarian and Administrative Officer, British Institute, Madrid, Feb.-June 1943; Books Officer in Portugal for British Council, June 1943-June 1944; Head of Administrative and Inspectorate Section of Education Branch Allied C. C. for Germany and Austria (British Elements), 1945-46. Editorial Manager, Burns Oates & Washbourne, 1946-47. Librarian, R.A.F. College, Cranwell, 1949-50; Professor of English, École de l'Air, Salon-de-Provence, France, 1950-55; Teacher of English, Davies's School of English, Cambridge, 1955-56; Director English School, Taranto, 1956; Teacher, Davies's School of English, London, 1956-57; Master Trinity House School, Hull, 1957-58. Médaille de l'Aéronautique, 1954. *Publications:* (with J. H. Quinn) A Manual of Cataloguing, 1933; miscellaneous reviews and articles, chiefly bibliographical. *Club:* National Liberal. [*Died* 27 *March* 1962.

ACWORTH, Capt. Bernard, D.S.O. 1917; Royal Navy, retired; Founder and President Emeritus Evolution Protest Movement; *b.* 1885; 2nd *s.* of late Reverend Herbert Sumner Acworth and Rose Charlotte, *d.* of late Colonel Roney-Dougal of Ratho; *m.* Phyllis Doreen Bousfield (*d.* 1962), 2nd *d.* of George Samuel Long, The Chipping, Wotton-under-Edge; two *s.* two *d.* (and three *s.* decd.). *Educ.:* H.M.S. Britannia; Royal Naval College, Greenwich. Served for 18 years in submarines and commanded the Anti-Submarine Flotilla: four years in the Torpedo Div. of the Naval Staff and closely associated with original Asdic development; late Naval Correspondent of the Morning Post, Observer and Yorkshire Post; contested (L.) Pontypridd, 1931, and (Ind.) Putney, 1942. *Publications:* This Bondage, 1929; Navies of To-day and To-morrow, 1931; Back to the Coal Standard, 1932. The Navy and the Next War—A Vindication of Sea Power, 1934: This Progress — The Tragedy of Evolution, 1934; The Restoration of England's Sea Power, 1936; Britain in Danger, 1937; How the War will be won; What we are fighting for; etc., 1940; The Cuckoo and Other Bird Mysteries, 1944; Butterfly Miracles and Mysteries, 1947; Life of Dean Swift, 1948; Bird and Butterfly Mysteries, 1955 (Amer. Edn. 1956). *Address:* Layton House, Avenue Road, Farnborough Park, Hants. *T.:* Farnborough 509. [*Died* 16 *Feb.* 1963.

ADAIR, Edward Robert, M.A.; F.R.Hist.S.; *b.* 26 April 1888; *o. s.* of Col. Edward Adair; *m.* Margaret Wilson; no *c.* *Educ.:* University of London; Peterhouse, Cambridge (Scholar). Gladstone Prizeman, Hugo de Balsham Student. Army VI. Master, Felsted School, Essex; Senior Assistant in History, University College, London, 1919-25; Member of the Boards of Studies and of Examiners in History, University of London, 1920-25; Special Lecturer for the English Association in Holland, 1922 and 1925; Member of the Council of the Historical Association, 1920-25. Formerly Professor of History, McGill University, Montreal; retired, 1954. President of the History Association of Montreal, 1930-32, 1943-45, Hon. President, 1936-53; Member of the Council of the Canadian Historical Association, 1931-42, Pres. 1935-36; Member of the Editorial Board of the Canadian Historical Review, 1932-33, 1935-36, 1939-40; Member, University Senate and Fellow of McGill, 1944. Lecturer at Universities of Michigan, Texas, Indiana and Northwestern. *Publications:* Sources for the History of the King's Council in the 16th and 17th Centuries; William Thomas: A Biography (in Tudor Studies); The Exterritoriality of Ambassadors in the 16th and 17th Centuries; articles in English Historical Review on History of 16th and 17th Centuries and in Canadian Historical Review on French-Canadian History and Art. *Recreations:* travelling, tramping, church architecture. *Address:* 6222 North Lamar, Austin, Texas, U.S.A. [*Died Nov.* 1967.

ADAM, Frederick Edward Fox, C.M.G. 1939; *b.* 9 Feb. 1887; *s.* of Charles Fox Frederick Adam, Counsellor in H.M. Diplomatic Service, and Juliet, *d.* of James Croxall Palmer, Surgeon General of the U.S. Navy; unmarried. *Educ.:* Rugby; Balliol College, Oxford. Entered the Foreign Office, 1910; acting 3rd Secretary, H.M. Legation at Athens, 1917-18; returned to Foreign Office, 1918; 1st Secretary, 1920; Counsellor of Embassy, Lisbon, 1929-34; H.M. Minister to Panama and Costa Rica and Consul-General for the Panama Canal Zone, 1934-1939. *Address:* 7 Oakley Gardens, Chelsea, S.W.3. *T.:* Flaxman 7829. *Clubs:* Travellers', Brooks's. [*Died* 5 *July* 1969.

ADAM, Karl; Professor of Dogmatics, University of Tübingen, 1919, Emeritus, 1949; *b.* Pursruck, Bavaria, 22 Oct. 1876; *s.* of Clemens Adam and Babette Sturm. *Educ.:* Amberg Gymnasium; Phil. Theol. Hochschule, Regensburg; University of Munich. Privatdozent, Faculty of Catholic Theology, Munich, 1908; Extraordinary Professor, 1915; Professor of Moral Theology, University of Strassburg, 1918. *Publications:* Der Kirchenbegriff Tertullians, 1907; Die Eucharistielehre des heiligen Augustin, 1908; Die kirchliche Sündenvergebung nach dem heiligen Augustin, 1917; Die geheime Kirchenbusse nach dem heiligen Augustin, 1921; Glaube und Glaubenswissenschaft im Katholizismus, 2nd edn., 1923; Die geistige Entwicklung des heiligen Augustin, 1931 (Eng. trans., 1932); Christus und der Geist des Abendlandes, 2nd edn., 1932; Pfingstgedanken, 2nd edn., 1933; Jesus Christus und der Geist unserer Zeit, 2nd edn., 1935; Die sakramentale Weihe der Ehe, 3rd edn., 1937; Kirchenmüdigkeit?, 2nd edn., 1940; Das Wesen des Katholizismus, 13th edn., 1957 (Eng. trans. 1932, etc.); Jesus Christus, 8th edn., 1950: Glaube und Liebe, 4th edn., 1947; Una Sancta zur Wiedervereinigung im Glauben, 1947; Christus, unser Bruder, 8th edn., 1950 (Eng. trans., 1931, etc.); Der Christus des Glaubens, 1956, 2nd edn. 1957 (Eng. trans., The Christ of Faith, 1958); numerous articles in learned journals. *Address:* c/o Patmos Verlag, Charlottenstrasse 82-86, Düsseldorf, Germany; Schönblick 6, Tübingen, Germany. [*Died* 1 *April* 1966.

ADAMS, Bernard; Hors Concours (Paris Salon); R.P.; R.O.I.; F.R.S.A.; N.S.; portrait and landscape painter; founder and Hon. Secretary, National Society Painters, Sculptors, Engravers and Potters; Hon. Secretary, Artists of Chelsea; *b.* London; *y. s.* of Robert Henry Adams, artist, and Louisa Fanny, *e. d.* of John William Chandler, Bungay, Suffolk; *g.s.* of Thomas Adams, artist and designer; *m.* 1912, Meri Olga Johanna, *o. d.* of Lieut.-Col. Berndt Standertskjöld, Helsingfors, Finland; two *s.* one *d.* (and one *d.* died as result of active service, 1945). *Educ.:* Chapel Royal, Savoy. Studied Westminster School of Art, Antwerp Academy, Silver Medallist Kennington and Allan Fraser Scholarship; Student of George Harcourt, R.A., and Philip de Laszlo; Exhibits London and Provinces. Médaille d'Argent, Paris Salon, 1957, Médaille d'Or, Soc. French Artists, 1958. *Recreations:* billiards, conjuring, ventriloquism. *Address:* 38 Longmore Point, Putney, S.W.15. *T.:* Putney 1712; (studio) 43 Roland Gardens, S.W.7. *Clubs:* Chelsea Arts, London Sketch; Royal Thames Yacht. [*Died* 10 *April* 1965.

ADAMS, Commander Henry William Allen, R.N. (retd.); *b.* 1884; *o. s.* of Col. A. N. Adams, King's Own Scottish Borderers; *m.* 1920, Hon. Charlotte M. L., *er. d.* of 1st Baron Glentanar and *widow* of Hon. Lionel Walrond, M.P., *o. s.* of 1st Baron Waleran. *Educ.:* Aysgarth; H.M.S. Britannia. Younger Brother Trinity House. *Recreation:* yachting. *Address:* La Carrière, St. Jean-Cap-Ferrat, A.M. France. *T.:* 82.52.05. *Clubs:* United Service; Royal Yacht Squadron (Cowes). [*Died* 25 *Sept.* 1962.

ADAMS, Comdr. Sir Jameson Boyd, K.C.V.O. *cr.* 1948 (C.V.O. 1938); C.B.E. 1928; D.S.O. 1918; R.N.R. (retired); *b.* 1880; *s.* of George Norris Adams, M.D.; *m.* 1914, Phebe Carnac Thompson (*d.* 1952), *d.* of late Rt. Rev. George Carnac Fisher, D.D., Burgh House, Fleggburgh, Norfolk; one *s.* one *d.* Joined R.N.R. 1895; 2nd in command Antarctic Expedition, 1907-9; entered Civil Service, 1909; served European War, 1914-18 (despatches, D.S.O., Croix de Guerre); re-employed, 1939. Secretary of King George's Jubilee Trust, 1935-48. *Clubs:* White's, Brooks's, Pratt's. [*Died* 25 *Sept.* 1962.

ADAMS, James Elwin Cokayne; *b.* 3 Dec. 1876; *s.* of Borlase Hill Adams, Barrister-at-law, and Mary Anne Staveley; *m.* 1919, Susan Mercer, *d.* of late James Archer Porter, Belfast; three *s.* one *d.* *Educ.:* Winchester; New College, Oxford. Barrister-at-law, 1900; Assistant Commissioner, Charity Commission, 1919-32; Secretary, Charity Commission, 1932-1939; Charity Commissioner, 1939-45. *Address:* 26 Montague Road, Richmond, Surrey. *T.:* Richmond 0917. [*Died* 14 *April* 1961.

ADAMS, John Roland, C.B.E. 1950; J.P. (N.S.W. and Queensland); United Kingdom Trade Commissioner (1) at Sydney, 1945-55; *b.* 29 Dec. 1894; *s.* of Alexander Annan Adams; *m.* 1927, Gwynneth Marguerite, *d.* of Archibald Johnson, Melbourne, Australia; one *d.* *Educ.:* Cranleigh School, Surrey; London University; Germany. Served European War, 1914-18; entered Board of Trade, 1918, appointed to Trade Commissioner Service overseas, 1919; serving at Singapore, 1919-20, Montreal, 1920-26, Sydney, 1927-37, Brisbane, 1937-45. *Publications:* Defence at Auction Bridge, 1930; and various publications on bridge and commercial subjects. *Recreations:* contract bridge, golf, photography. *Address:* 19 Prince Albert Street, Mosman, Sydney, N.S.W. *Club:* Australian (Sydney). [*Died* 18 *Dec.* 1961.

ADAMS, Stanley John; Director, Midland Bank; Deputy Chairman, Guardian Insurance; also Director of some other companies; *b.* 1 March 1893; 2nd *s.* of late Jonathan Adams; *m.* Lady Goulding, *widow* of Sir Lingard Goulding, Bt. *Educ.:* Privately and in Paris. Enlisted 1914, Royal Fusiliers; served throughout European War; Managing Director Prisoners of War Department of British Red Cross, 1941-42. *Address:* Eaton House, Upper Grosvenor Street, W.1; Staplegordon, Seale, Surrey. *Club:* Carlton. [*Died* 1 *June* 1965.

ADAMS, Sir Theodore Samuel, Kt., *cr.* 1942; C.M.G. 1937; *b.* 1885; *s.* of Rev. George Adams; *m.* 1923, Isabel Grace Portman; no *c.* *Educ.:* King's School, Canterbury; All Souls College, Oxford. Malayan Civil Service, 1908; Acting Under-Secretary, 1930-31; British Resident, Selangor, 1932; Chief Commissioner Northern Provinces, Nigeria, 1937-43; War Cabinet Office, 1944-1945. *Recreations:* cricket, squash, tennis. *Address:* Orchard Portman, Taunton, Somerset. *Clubs:* United University, East India and Sports. [*Died* 17 *May* 1961.

ADAMS, William B.; *see* Bridges-Adams.

ADAMS, Prof. William George Stewart, C.H. 1936; Hon. D.C.L. (Oxford); Hon. LL.D. (Glasgow and Manchester); Warden 1933-45, Fellow 1910-33, and Hon. Fellow since 1945, of All Souls College; *b.* 8 Nov. 1874; *s.* of John Adams, Gilbertfield, Hamilton, Lanarkshire; *m.* Muriel, *d.* of late Wm. Lane, Stonehurst, Killiney, County Dublin; one *s.* *Educ.:* St. John's Grammar School, Hamilton; The University of Glasgow; Balliol College, Oxford (Snell Exhibitioner). Lecturer and Tutor, Borough Road Training College, 1901-02; Lecturer in Economics in the Graduate School, The University of Chicago, 1902; Lecturer in Economics and Secretary of University Extension, The University of Manchester, 1903-04; Superintendent of Statistics and Intelligence, Department of Agriculture and Technical Instruction for Ireland, 1905-10; Reader in Political Theory and Institutions, Oxford University, 1910-12; Gladstone Professor of Political Theory and Institutions, Oxford, 1912-33; and Member of the Hebdomadal Council, Oxford University, 1912-24; Member of the Committee to advise the Cabinet on Irish Finance, 1911; Founder and Editor of The Political Quarterly, 1914-16; Ministry of Munitions, 1915; Secretary to the Prime Minister, 1916-19; Editor of the War Cabinet Reports, 1917 and 1918; Member of the Committee on the Examination for the Civil Service, 1918; Member of the Royal Commission on Oxford and Cambridge Universities, 1919-22; Member of the Agricultural Tribunal of Investigation, 1923-24; Chairman of the National Council of Social Service, 1920-49; Chairman National Federation of Young Farmers' Clubs, 1928-46; Member of the Development Commission, 1923-49; Stevenson Lecturer in Citizenship, The University of Glasgow, 1923-24; Lowell Lecturer, Boston, U.S.A., 1924; Graduates Society Lecturer, McGill University, Canada, 1931; Member of Delegation to China from the Universities China Committee, 1931-32; Chairman Universities China Committee in London, 1942; Visiting Professor, University of Toronto, 1949; visiting Universities in the Union of South Africa, 1953 and 1957. *Address:* Fahan House, Fahan, Co. Donegal; All Souls College, Oxford. [*Died* 30 *Jan.* 1966.

ADAMS, Canon William J. T. P.; *see* Phythian-Adams.

ADAMS, Rear-Admiral (Retd.) William Leslie Graham, C.B. 1955; O.B.E. 1942; Director of Civil Defence, Southern Region (Reading), 1955-63; *b.* 20 April 1901; *s.* of Leonard Graham Adams; *m.* 1928, Erica Margaret Hawkins. *Educ.:* Christ's Hospital. Special Entry into Navy, 1919; Commander, 1935; Captain, 1943; Rear-Admiral, 1952; despatches, 1942, 1949; Flag Officer Training Squadron, Home Fleet, 1953-54; retired, 1955. Commander of Oranje-Nassau (Dutch), 1947. Younger Brother of Trinity House, 1951. *Recreation:* fishing. *Address:* Greensleeves, Crondall, Hants. *T.:* Crondall 385. *Clubs:* United Service; Berkshire (Reading). [*Died* 28 *March* 1963.

ADAMSON, Mrs. Jennie Laurel; *m.* 1902, William Murdoch Adamson, formerly M.P. for Cannock Staffs and a Lord Commissioner of the Treasury (*d.* 1945). M.P. (Lab.) Dartford Division of Kent, 1938-1945; Bexley, 1945-46; additional Parliamentary Private Secretary to Sir Walter Womersley, Minister of Pensions, 1940-45; Parliamentary Sec., Ministry of Pensions, 1945-46; Deputy Chairman Assistance Board, 1946-53. *Address;* 13 Mill Vale, Bromley, Kent. [*Died* 25 *April* 1962.

ADAMSON, John; C.A.; formerly a Senior Partner in McClelland Ker & Co., Chartered Accountants, 120 St. Vincent Street, Glasgow, C.2, and 23 Lawrence Lane, Cheapside, E.C.2; formerly Director of several Companies; retd.; *b.* 23 Jan. 1886; *s.* of late William Adamson and late Elizabeth Watson, Kinross; *m.* 1915, Elsie (*d.* 1969), 2nd *d.* of late James Glendinning, Trinidad, British West Indies; one *s.* one *d.* *Educ.:* George Watson's Coll.; Edinburgh Univ. Pres. of Scottish Chartered Accountants in London, 1938-46; Controller of Fish Supplies, 1941-1943; a Governor of B.B.C., 1947-52. Governor and Member Finance and General Purposes Committee of Charing Cross Hosp., 1947-60; retd. 1960. *Address:* Wellcroft End, Chapel Row, Bucklebury, Reading, Berks. *Club:* Bath. [*Died* 29 *Oct.* 1969.

ADAMSON, Hon. Chief Justice (John Evans Adamson); Chief Justice of Manitoba, 1955-61, retd.; *b.* 9 September 1884; *s.* of Alan Joseph Adamson and Julia Turriff; *m.* 1912, Mary Turriff; four *d.* *Educ.:* St. John's College and Manitoba University. Called Manitoba Bar, 1910; Saskatchewan Bar, 1915; apptd. to Bench, 1922; Chm. Mobilization Bd., 1940; apptd. to Manitoba Court of Appeal, 1948. Chm.

Electoral Boundaries Commn. LL.D. (*h.c.*), University of Manitoba, 1955; Hon. Fellow of St. John's College, Manitoba. *Recreations:* golf, shooting. *Address:* Court House, Winnipeg, Canada. *T.:* 840, 307; 254 Kingsway Avenue, Winnipeg 9, Canada. *Clubs:* St. Charles Country, Manitoba (Winnipeg). [*Died* 22 *Dec.* 1961.

ADAMSON, John Evans; *see* Adamson, Hon. Chief Justice.

ADAMSON, Robert Stephen, M.A., D.Sc. Edin.; M.A. Cantab.; F.R.S.S. Af.; F.L.S.; Professor emeritus, University of Cape Town; *b.* Manchester, March 1885; *e. s.* of late Professor Robert Adamson; *m.* 1923, Margaret Heron, *yr. d.* of late Patrick Spence Mudie, Dundee. *Educ.:* Kelvinside Academy, Glasgow; University of Edinburgh; Emmanuel College, Cambridge. Lecturer, Botany, University of Manchester, 1912-23; Harry Bolus Professor of Botany, University of Cape Town, 1923-50. President Royal Society S. Africa, 1946-48. *Publications:* Vegetation of South Africa, 1938; Flora of the Cape Peninsula, 1950; articles in Botanical and Bacteriological journals. *Address:* The Brae, Jedburgh, Roxburghshire, Scotland. *T.:* Jedburgh 3105. [*Died* 6 *Nov.* 1965.

ADCOCK, Sir Frank (Ezra), Kt., *cr.* 1954; O.B.E. 1917; F.B.A. 1936; M.A., Litt.D., Hon. D.Litt. (Durham, Leicester); Hon. Litt.D. (Dublin and Manchester); Vice-Provost, Dec. 1951-July 1955, and Fellow, King's Coll., and Professor of Ancient History, 1925-51, University of Cambridge; *b.* 15 Apr. 1886; *s.* of late T. D. Adcock, Leicester. *Educ.:* Wyggeston School, Leicester; King's College, Cambridge; Berlin and Munich. Craven Scholar, 1908; Chancellor's Medallist, 1909; Craven Student, 1910; Fellow (since 1911), Dean (1913-19), Classical Lecturer (1911-25), King's College, Cambridge. Employed in Admiralty Intelligence Division, 1915-19; Lieutenant-Commander, R.N.V.R., 1917-19; employed by Foreign Office, 1939-1943; President of Society for Promotion of Roman Studies, 1929-31; Pres. Classical Assoc., 1947-48; Member of German Archæological Institute; Joint-editor of the Cambridge Ancient History. *Publications:* Papers on Ancient History; Chapters in Cambridge Ancient History; The Roman Art of War; Caesar as Man of Letters; The Greek and Macedonian Art of War; Roman Political Ideas and Practice; Thucydides and His History; Marcus Crassus, Millionare. *Recreations:* golf, chess. *Address:* King's College, Cambridge. *T.:* Cambridge 50411. *Club:* Savile. [*Died* 22 *Feb.* 1968.

ADDINGTON, 3rd Baron (*cr.* 1887), **John Gellibrand Hubbard;** Member of Bucks County Council since 1929, also Member of Buckingham Borough Council; formerly Captain, Bucks Batt. Oxon Light Infantry; late Major T.F. Reserve, T.D.; formerly partner in Egerton Hubbard & Co., Petrograd; *b.* 7 June 1883; *s.* of 2nd Baron and Mary Adelaide (*d.* 1933), *d.* of Sir Wyndham S. Portal, 1st Bt.; *S.* father, 1915; unmarried. *Educ.:* Eton; Christ Church, Oxford, M.A. Served European War, 1914-1918 (O.B.E., despatches); British Custodian of Enemy Property in China, 1923-28; Mayor of Buckingham, 1932-33, 1933-34, 1943-46 and 1951-52. *Heir:* *b.* Hon. Raymond Egerton Hubbard. *Address:* House of Lords, S.W.1. [*Died* 19 *July* 1966.

ADDISON, Maj.-Gen. George Henry, C.B. 1933; C.M.G. 1918; D.S.O. 1915; late R.E.; *b.* 13 May 1876; *s.* of Lt.-Col. G. W. Addison, R.E.; *m.* 1905, Margaret (*d.* 1946), *d.* of R. Henderson; one *s.* decd. one *d.* decd.; *m.* 1947, Winifred (*d.* 1962), *widow* of Col. A. D. Legard and *d.* of Col. Sir William Morris, K.C.M.G., C.B. *Educ.:* Wellington; R.M. Academy, Woolwich; Fellow-Commoner, King's College, Cambridge, 1920-23, B.A. (Honours Mech. Sc.), 1922; M.A. 1927. Entered army, 1895; Lieutenant, 1898; Capt., 1904; Adjutant, 1914; Major, 1914; Lt.-Colonel, 1922; Colonel, 1926; Major-General, 1931; A.A.G. at War Office, 1927-1930; Chief Engineer, Aldershot, 1930-31; Engineer-in-Chief, India, 1932-36; retired pay, 1936; Financial Adviser Army Headquarters, India, 1936-37; recalled to Active List, Sept. 1939; reverted to retired pay, 1941; Col. Comdt. R.E., 1940-46. Served South Africa, 1899-1902 (Queen's medal 3 clasps, King's medal 2 clasps); European War, 1914-18 (D.S.O., Bt. Lt.-Col., C.M.G.); awarded 3rd class Order of St. Anne of Russia (with swords), Sept. 1916; Légion d'Honneur (Chevalier), 1919; Ordre de Leopold (Officier), and Belgian Croix de Guerre, 1919; M.I.Mech.E. 1924; Hon. M.I.Struct.E. 1940. *Address:* Lyon House, Aldersey Road, Guildford. *T.:* Guildford 3041. *Clubs:* Army and Navy, M.C.C.; County (Guildford). [*Died* 5 *Feb.* 1964.

ADDISON, Hon. William, C.M.G. 1958; O.B.E. 1946; M.C. 1918; D.C.M. 1916; retired; Speaker, Legislative Assembly, Southern Rhodesia, 1954-60; *b.* 1 Nov. 1890. Editor, Bulawayo Chronicle, 1923-26; Editor, Rhodesia Herald, 1927-30; Manager, Rhodesian Printing and Publishing Co., 1930-1939. War Service: Chief Recruiting Officer, Controller Industrial Manpower, Director Demobilisation. Editor, The Star, Johannesburg, 1945-50. *Recreation:* walking. *Address:* Dunluce Farm Salisbury, Rhodesia; P.O. Box 1964, Salisbury. *T.:* 20693-22. *Clubs:* Bulawayo, Salisbury (Rhodesia). [*Died* 19 *July* 1966.

ADDISON, Rev. William Robert Fountaine, V.C. 1916; Rector of Coltishall with Great Hautbois, 1938-58, and Rural Dean of Ingworth, 1948-58, retired; *s.* of late W. G. Addison and Mrs. Addison, Cranbrook, Kent; *m.* 1917, Marjorie (*d.* 1959), *d.* of late E. W. Wallis, A.R.I.B.A., Caterham; two *s.* *Educ.:* Sarum College. Ordained, 1913; curate of St. Edmund, Salisbury, 1913; served European War, 1915-18 (V.C., Order of St. George); Permanent Chaplaincy, 1919; S.C.F., Bulford Camp, 1920-23; Aldershot, 1923-25; Malta, 1925 and 1926-27; Khartoum, 1926; Shanghai, 1927; S.C.F., C. of E., Shorncliffe Camp, 1929-30; C.F., Shoeburyness Garrison, 1930-31; Tidworth, 1931-32; promoted to 2nd class, 1932; C.F. Bulford, 1932-34; Senior Chaplain to Forces, Bordon, 1934-38; retired, 1938; S.C.F., Bordon, 1939-42; D.A.C.G., 1942; retired to Coltishall, 1942. *Address:* Flat 2, 13 Albert Rd., Bexhill-on-Sea, Sussex. [*Died* 7 *Jan.* 1962.

ADEMOLA, Sir Ladapo; *see* Abeokuta, The Alake of.

ADENAUER, Konrad; *b.* 5 January 1876; twice widowed; seven *c.* *Educ.:* Freiburg, Munich and Bonn Universities (Law). Practised law, Cologne; Dep. Mayor, 1906; Senior Dep. Mayor, 1909; Lord Mayor, 1917-33; Member Provincial Diet of Rhine Province, 1917-33, and of Exec. Cttee. of Centre Party until 1933; Member Prussian Herrenhaus, 1917-18, of Prussian State Council, 1918-33 (Pres. 1920-1933). Dismissed from all offices by Goering, 1933; temporarily imprisoned for political reasons, 1933 and 1944. Lord Mayor of Cologne, 1945; Foundation Member, Christian Democratic Party of Rhineland, 1945; Christian Democratic Union: Pres., in Rhine-Westphalia, 1946-48; Pres., in Fed. Republic of Germany, 1950-66; Mem. and Pres of Parliamentary Council of Bonn, 1948-49; Member of German Council of European Movement, 1949. Federal Chancellor, 1949-63 and Foreign Minister, 1951-55, of the Republic of Germany. Dr.rer. pol. (h.c.), Dr. med. (h.c.), Dr. jur. (h.c.), Dr. phil. (h.c.), Dr. nat. (h.c.), from Cologne Univ.; Dr. ing. (h.c.) from Berlin-Charlottenburg. Has also received numerous hon. degrees from foreign countries. Freedom of Cities of Cologne and Bonn on 75th birthday; Hon. Fell., Weizmann Inst. of Science, Israel, 1966. Hon. G.C.M.G. 1957. *Publication:* Erinnerungen 1945-55, 1965 (Eng. trans., Memoirs, 1966). *Relevant Publication:* Konrad Adenauer: die autorisierte Biographie, by Paul Weymar, 1956. *Recreation:* gardening. *Address:* Dr. Konrad Adenauer-Weg 8a, Rhöndorf am Rhein, Germany. [*Died* 19 *April* 1967.

ADENEY, Bernard; Artist, Painter; *b.* London; *s.* of W. F. Adeney, M.A., D.D.; *m.* 1920, Noel Gilford, artist, novelist; one *s.* one *d.* *Educ.:* Privately; Royal Academy; Slade; Julians, Paris. Pictures in Contemporary Arts Society; Tate Gallery; Bradford Municipal Gallery; Whitworth Gallery, Manchester; and many private collections. Founder Member of the London Group, 1913 (late Pres.); Founder Member of the National Society of Painters; Founder Member of the London Artists Association, inaugurated 1925, by Maynard Keynes and Samuel Courtauld. Appointed, 1952, Governor of Hammersmith School of Building and Arts and Crafts, to represent the London Group. War Museum, 1917-18; head of School of Textiles L.C.C. Central School of Arts and Crafts, 1930-47. *Recreations:* walking, conversation, reading. *Address:* 34 Crooms Hill, Greenwich, S.E.10. *T.:* Greenwich 0160 [*Died* 4 *April* 1966.

ADLER, Saul, O.B.E. 1947; F.R.S. 1957; Professor of Parasitology, Hebrew University, Jerusalem, Israel, since 1928; *b.* 17 May 1895; *m.* 1924, Sophie Isobel Husdar; two *s.* one *d.* *Educ.:* Univ. of Leeds; Liverpool Sch. of Tropical Medicine. M.B.,Ch.B., Leeds, 1917; D.T.M., Liverpool, 1920; M.R.C.P. 1937, F.R.C.P. 1958. R.A.M.C. (Capt.), 1917-20. Asst., Hebrew Univ., 1924; Kala-azar Commn., Royal Society, 1930-34; Chalmers Medal Royal Society of Tropical Medicine and Hygiene, London, 1933. Order of Cross of Phœnix, Greece. *Publications:* contributions to journals mainly dealing with tropical medicine. *Recreations:* chess, walking. *Address:* Talbieh, Jerusalem, Israel. *T.:* Jerusalem 32042. [*Died* 25 *Jan.* 1966.

ADLERCRON, Brig.-Gen. Rodolph Ladeveze, C.M.G. 1918; D.S.O. 1916; late Queen's Own Cameron Highlanders; *b.* 1873; *s.* of George Rothe Ladeveze Adlercron, of Moyglare; *m.* 1910, Hester Bancroft (*d.* 1939), Boston, Mass., U.S.A.; three *d.* *Educ.:* Eton. Entered Army, 1894; Captain, 1899; Major, 1913; Lieut.-Col. Comd. attached 6th West Riding Regiment, 1915; commanded 148th and 124th Infantry Brigades; Brigade Major, Lincoln and Leicester Brigade, 1911-15; served Nile Expedition, 1898 (despatches, 2 medals 2 clasps); S. African War, 1899-1901, with Mounted Infantry (despatches, Queen's medal with 4 clasps); European War, 1914-18 (despatches 7 times, D.S.O. and bar, C.M.G., Bt. Lt.-Col., French Croix de Guerre, Belgian Croix de Guerre); retired pay, 1920; Col. Reserve of Officers, 1920; Hon. Col. 6th Bn. Duke of Wellington's Regt. (T.F.). J.P., D.L. Lincs. *Recreations:* hunting, fishing, ski-ing, golf. *Address:* Wyberton Park, Boston, Lincs. *Club:* United Service. [*Died* 12 *June* 1966.

ADRIAN, Lady; Hester Agnes Adrian, D.B.E. 1965; B.E.M.; M.A., J.P.; *b.* 16 Sept. 1899; *o. d.* of late Hume C. Pinsent, Birmingham, and late Dame Ellen Pinsent, D.B.E.; *m.* 1923, Edgar Douglas Adrian (*see* 1st Baron Adrian); one *s.* two *d.* *Educ.:* Crofton Grange; Somerville College, Oxford (M.A.). J.P. City of Cambridge, 1936-; Chm. of Bench, 1955-58; Chm., Juv. Ct. Panel, 1948-58. W.V.S. Billeting Officer, Camb. City, 1938-45. Member: Coun. of Magistrates' Assoc., 1947-; Bd. of Mans., Kneesworth Approved School, 1950- (Chm., 1956-64); Cttee. of Mangt., Camb. Inst. of Criminology, 1960-; Ingleby Cttee. on Children and Young Persons, 1956-60; Tucker Cttee. Proceedings before Examining Magistrates, 1957-58; Roy. Commn. on Penal System in Eng. and Wales, 1964-66; President, Howard League for Penal Reform, 1959-. Member: E. Anglian Regl. Hosp. Bd., and Chm. Mental Health Cttee., 1947-; Fulbourn Ment. Hosp. Mangt. Cttee., 1947- (Chm., 1951-57); Bd. of Govs., United Camb. Hosps., 1950- (Chm., 1963-); Coun. of Nat. Assoc. for Mental Health, 1946- (Vice-Chm. and Chm. Exec. Cttee., 1962-); Cambs. Mental Welfare Assoc. (Hon. Sec. 1924-34, Chm. and Pres. 1948-); Roy. Commn. on Mental Health, 1954-57; Chairman, Trng. Coun. for Teachers of Mentally Handicapped, 1963-. Manager, Camb. Special Schools, 1935-64 (Chm., 1960-64). *Address:* Burrells End, 58A Grange Road, Cambridge. *Club:* University Women's. [*Died* 20 *May* 1966.

AGAR, Captain Augustus Willington Shelton, V.C. 1919; D.S.O. 1919; R.N.; *b.* 4 Jan. 1890; *s.* of John Shelton Agar, of Ceylon and Woodmount, Co. Kerry; *m.* Baroness Furnivall, *q.v.*; *m.* Ina Margaret, *d.* of late Robert Lindner, and *g. d.* of late Francis Logie-Pirie of Tottingworth Park, Heathfield, Sussex. Entered Royal Navy, 1905 (H.M.S. Britannia). Served European War, 1914-19 (despatches, V.C., D.S.O.); served War, 1939-45 (despatches); Captain, H.M.S. Dorsetshire, 1941-42; Commodore-President, Royal Naval College, Greenwich, 1943-46. Vice-President Sailors' Home and Red Ensign Club, 1957. Younger Brother of Trinity House, 1936. Contested (C.) Greenwich, 1945. *Publications:* autobiography: Footprints in the Sea, 1960; Showing the Flag, 1962; Baltic Episode, 1963. *Address:* Anstey Park House, Alton, Hants. *T.:* Alton 2376. *Clubs:* Athenæum; Royal Yacht Squadron (Naval Member); R.M.Y.C. (Hon. Life Member). [*Died* 30 *Dec.* 1968.

AGAR, Charles Phipp, C.M.G. 1956; J.P.; Company Director; *b.* 24 May 1886; *s.* of John James Agar, London; *m.* Julia, *d.* of George and Julia Iles, Christchurch, N.Z. Member N.Z. Dairy Products Marketing Commission, 1952-57. One time Dep. Mayor of Christchurch and C.C., 1919-26; J.P. 1914-. Freeman of City of London, 1951. *Address:* Merivale, Christchurch, N.Z. *Clubs:* Canterbury (Christchurch); Wellesley (Wellington); County (Ashburton). [*Died* 21 *Jan.* 1963.

AGARWALA, Sir Clifford Manmohan, Kt. 1943; *b.* 5 February 1890; *e. s.* of Dr. M. L. Agarwala, barrister-at-law, Allahabad, U.P.; *m.* 1918, Dorrie Muriel Lall; two *d.* *Educ.:* Aldenham School, Elstree. Called to Bar, Gray's Inn, 1911; barrister at Patna, 1912; official law reporter in the High Court, 1916; Standing Counsel to the Income Tax Dept., 1925; Asst. Govt. Advocate, 1927; Puisne Judge, High Court, Patna, 1932-46; Chief Justice, 1946-50. Chairman, Central Board of Film Censors, Govt. of India, 1951-54. *Publications:* Trial by Jury (India); Law of Evidence (India); Law of Limitation (India). *Address:* 17 Hill Drive Hove 4, Sussex. *Club:* Royal Over-Seas League. [*Died* 19 *March* 1964.

AGLIONBY, Rt. Rev. John Orfeur, D.D., M.C.; *b.* 16 Mar. 1884; *s.* of late Canon F. K. Aglionby. *Educ.:* Westminster School; Queen's College, Oxford, M.A.; Bishop's Hostel, Auckland. Curate of Holy Trinity, South Shields, 1911-15; Private,

R.A.M.C., 1915; C.F., 1915-18; Vicar Ven. Bede, Monkwearmouth, 1917-24; Chaplain 7th D.L.I., 1921-24; Bishop of Accra, 1924-1951; retired, 1951. *Recreations:* walking, cycling. *Address:* Crofton Lodge, Crofton Lane, Orpington, Kent. [*Died* 15 *May* 1963.

AGNEW, Alan Graeme; Chairman, Bradbury Agnew & Co. Ltd., Proprietors of Punch since 1938; *b.* 6 Dec. 1887; *m.* 1913, Dorothy Cecil (*née* Strode) (*d.* 1959); one *s.* one *d.* *Educ.:* Rugby; Trinity Hall, Cambridge. Joined Constable & Co. Ltd., 1909, retired, 1932; joined Bradbury Agnew, 1923. Chairman: Thos. Agnew & Sons Ltd., Art Dealers, 1932-55, retired; The Countryman Ltd., 1943-56; The Gardeners' Chronicle Ltd., 1945-55; The Leagrave Press Ltd., Luton, 1951-55; President Periodical Proprietors' Association, 1951-52. Joined Herts R.A., T.A., 1909; served European War, 1914-18, R.A. (T.A.) (despatches twice); retired as Major. *Recreations:* shooting, gardening. *Address:* 38 Brompton Square, S.W.3. *Clubs:* Bath, M.C.C. [*Died* 6 *May* 1962.

AGNON, (Shmuel) Yosef Halevi; Hebrew writer; *b.* Galicia, 17 July 1888; *s.* of Shalom Mordecai Czaczkes and Esther, *née* Farb-Hacohen; adopted pen-name of Agnon, 1909; *m.* 1919, Esther Marx; one *s.* one *d.* Mem., Hebrew Language Acad.; Pres., Mekitzei Nirdamim Soc., 1950- ; Hon. Citizen of Jerusalem, 1962. Bialik Prize of Tel Aviv, 1935, 1951; Ussishkin Prize, 1950; Israel Prize, 1950, 1958; Nobel Prize for Literature (jointly), 1966. Holds hon. degrees from Hebrew Univ., Jerusalem, and six other institutes. *Publications:* (untranslated): Agunot (Forsaken Wives), 1909; Ve-Haya ha-Akov le-Mishor (And the Crooked shall be Made Straight), 1912; Agadat ha-Safer (Legend of the Scribe), 1919; Giv'at ha-Hol (The Sandy Hill), 1919; Maase Rabi Gradiel ha-Tinok (Story of Rabbi Gadiel, the Infant), 1920; Mehamat ha-Metzik (The Oppressor), 1921; Al Kapot ha- Man'ul (Upon the Handles of the Bar), 1922; Be-Sod Yesharim (Council of the Honest), 1923; Maase ha-Ez (Story of the Goat), 1924; Pollania (Poland), 1925; Ha-Niddah (The Outcast), 1926; Sefer ha-Massim (Book of Stories), published in 1930s; Eilu Ve-Eilu (Both These and the Other Things); Al Kappot HaMan'ul (Upon the Handle of the Lock); Temol Shilshom (In Times Past), 1945; Samukh VeNir'eh (Nigh and Visible); Ad Henah (Thus Far); HaEsh VeHa'etzim (The Fire and the Wood); (Ed.) Sefer, Sofer, ve-Sippur (Book, Writer, and Story), 1937; (Ed.) Atem Re'item, 1959; (in translation): The Bridal Canopy, N.Y., 1937, London, 1968; In the Heart of the Seas, N.Y., 1947, London, 1967; Days of Awe, N.Y., 1948; (with others) Tehilla, and other Israeli Tales, London, 1956; Two Tales, N.Y., London, 1965; A Guest for the Night, N.Y., London, 1968; Twenty-One Stories, 1970 (posthumous). *Address:* Talpiot, Jerusalem, Israel. [*Died* 17 *Feb.* 1970.

AHEARNE, Christopher Dominic, C.M.G. 1939; *b.* 1886. *Educ.:* Christian Schools, Cork; Trinity College, Dublin (Scholar, B.A. 1909). Cadet, Straits Settlements, 1910; Federal Secretary, Federated Malay States, 1936-39; retired, 1939. *Address:* Mount Ophir, Bishopstown Avenue, Cork, Ireland. [*Died Dec.* 1964.

AHERN, Maj.-Gen. (temp.) Donal Maurice, C.B.E. 1962; D.S.O. 1944; Deputy Director of Medical Services, Eastern Command, since 1966; *b.* 30 March 1911; 2nd *s.* of Lt.-Col. M. D. Ahern, O.B.E., Glanmire, Co. Cork; *m.* 1940, Joyce Douglas, *d.* of F. Chaplin, Plymouth; two *s.* one *d.* *Educ.:* Ampleforth College; Dublin University. M.B. 1933. Commissioned into R.A.M.C., 1934; served N.W.F.P., India, 1936-37; Burma and North West Europe, 1939-45; Inspector of Army Med. Services, 1963-65; D.D.M.S., 1 (British) Corps, Germany, 1965-66. *Address:* c/o Glyn, Mills & Co., Kirkland House, Whitehall, S.W.1. [*Died* 31 *Oct.* 1966.

AHMED, Sir Syed Sultan, K.C.S.I. 1945; Kt. 1927; Doctor of Law, 1930; *b.* 24 December 1880; *s.* of Khan Bahadur S. Khairat Ahmed of Gaya (India); *m.* 1900. Called to the Bar in 1905; Deputy Legal Remembrancer to the Government of Bihar and Orissa, 1913; Government Advocate, 1916-37; late Advocate-General, Bihar; Member in Charge of Information and Broadcasting, Governor - General's Executive Council, India, 1943-46; acted as Judge, Patna High Court, 1919-20; Vice-Chancellor Patna University, 1923-30; Member Hartog Education Committee, 1928-29; Delegate Indian Round Table Conferences, 1930-31; Acting Member of Executive Council of Governor of Bihar and Orissa, 1932; Acting Member of Executive Council of Governor-General in charge of Railways and Commerce, 1937; Law Member, 1941-43; Degree of Doctor of Laws conferred by the Patna University, 1931. *Publication:* A Treaty between India and the United Kingdom. *Clubs:* Athenæum: Calcutta; New Patna. [*Died* 27 *Feb.* 1963.

AIKEN, John Macdonald, R.S.A. 1935; R.I. 1944; A.R.E. 1924; painter, etcher, and stained-glass worker; *s.* of John Lamont and Elizabeth Glen Macdonald Aiken; *m.* Isobel W. Calder (*d.* 1960). *Educ.:* Robert Gordon's College, Aberdeen; Gray's School of Art, Aberdeen; Royal College of Art, London, under Professor Gerald Moira. Head of Gray's School of Art, Aberdeen, 1911-14; served European War, 1915-19; Médaille d'Argent, Paris Salon, 1928. *Address:* 36 Upperkirkgate, Aberdeen; The Anchorage, Viewforth Place, Pittenweem, Fife. [*Died* 11 *Dec.* 1961.

AIKMAN, Sir Alexander, Kt., *cr.* 1941; C.I.E. 1936; *b.* 7 May 1886; *s.* of late Matthew and Agnes Aikman, Colinton, Midlothian; *m.* 1921, Beatrice Baggs; no *c.* *Educ.:* Daniel Stewart's Coll.; Edinburgh Univ. Chartered Accountant, Edinburgh, 1908; served European War, France, 1914-1918; Member, Legislative Assembly Indian Central Legislature, 1936-40, Leader European Gp., 1938-40. *Recreation:* fly-fishing. *Address:* 72 Eaton Square, S.W.1. *T.:* Belgravia 1687. *Club:* Carlton. [*Died* 26 *Dec.* 1968.

AIKMAN, Robert Gordon, C.M.G. 1951; *b.* 28 Aug. 1905; *s.* of late Matthew Aikman, Physician and Surgeon, Plymouth, Devon, and late Mary Aikman; *m.* 1940, Eaditha Sheila, *d.* of A. McB. McClelland, Cottesloe, W. Australia; one *s.* one *d.* *Educ.:* Cheltenham Coll.; Univ. of Bristol. Cadet, Sarawak Civil Service, 1926; District Officer, 1936; Resident, 1940; Deputy Chief Secretary, 1947; Chief Secretary, Sarawak, 1950-55, retired (ill health). Member, Supreme Council, 1941. *Address:* Lionel Road, Darlington, Western Australia. *T.:* Darlington 292. [*Died* 20 *April* 1962.

AILESBURY, 6th Marquess of (*cr.* 1821), **George William James Chandos Brudenell-Bruce;** D.S.O.; T.D.; Bt. 1611; Baron Brudenell, 1628; Earl of Cardigan, 1661; Baron Bruce, 1746; Earl of Ailesbury, 1776; Viscount Savernake, 1821; *b.* 21 May 1873; *o. s.* of 5th Marquess of Ailesbury and Georgiana Sophia Maria, *d.* of G. H. Pinckney; *S.* father, 1911; *m.* 1st, 1903, Sydney (*d.* 1941), *o. d.* of John Madden, Hilton Park, Co. Monagh; one *s.* two *d.*; 2nd, 1945, Irene (*d.* 1954), *d.* of J. S. Lindsay, Wrexham; 3rd, 1955, Alice Maude Emily (*d.* 1960), *d.* of late Capt. John Forbes Pinkey, 51st L.I., and *widow* of Col. Rowland Money, O.B.E., The King's Own Royal Regt. *Educ.:* Westminster. Late 3rd Bn. Argyll and Sutherland Highlanders, Royal Wilts Yeomanry, Middlesex Yeomanry, Wilts Regt. (S.B.), R.A.S.C. and R.F.A. (T.); served South Africa, 1899-1900 (despatches); served France, Belgium and Germany, 1915-19 (despatches); Knight of Grace Order of St. John of Jerusalem. *Heir: s.* Earl of Cardigan D.L. *Address:* Les Sillettes, Mont Cochon, Jersey, C.I. [*Died* 4 *Aug.* 1961.

AINSWORTH, Harry, Journalist; *b.* Darwen, Lancashire 1 Aug. 1888; *m.* Isabella Davidina Graham (*d.* 1965); two *d. Educ.:* Darwen Gram. Sch. Began as a reporter on local press and migrated to London via Dundee and Manchester, 1913; Features and News with D. C. Thomson & Co., Dundee, 1911-19; News Editor and Features Writer, Weekly Dispatch, 1919-22; Editor of John Bull, 1922-25; Editor of The People, 1925-1958; resigned as Director of Odhams Press Ltd. and as Editorial Director, Odhams newspaper group, 1961. *Address:* The Pantiles, Givon's Grove, Leatherhead, Surrey. [*Died* 4 *Aug.* 1965.

AIRD, Ian, Ch.M., F.R.C.S.; F.R.C.S.E.; F.A.C.S.; Professor of Surgery, University of London, since 1946; Director of Surgical Unit, Postgrad. Med. Sch. of London, Hammersmith Hosp.; *b.* 4 July 1905; *s.* of William Aird and Jean Elizabeth Binnie; *m.* 1936, Margaret, *d.* of late William Goodman Cowes, Buenos Aires; one *s.* one *d. Educ.:* George Watson's College; Universities of Edinburgh, Paris, Vienna and Washington (St. Louis, Mo.) M.B., Ch.B. (Edin.) 1928; Thomson Scholarship, Wightman Prize and Annandale Gold Medal; Rockefeller Travelling Fellow; Olof af Akrel Medal (Swedish Surgical Society). F.R.C.S. (Ed.) 1930; Ch.M. 1935; F.R.C.S. (Eng.) ad eundem 1947; Hon. Fellow (and Mem. Steering Cttee. for foundn. of) College General Pract., 1956; American College of Surgeons, 1957; Assoc. of Surgeons of East Africa; Pres. James IV Surgical Assoc. Inc., 1958-61; Member: Council (1953) and Court of Examiners (1950-56), Examiner, Primary Fellowship (Physiol.) (1960), Roy. Coll. of Surgeons of England; Council, Royal Society of Medicine, 1954-57; Grand Council and Scientific Advisory Committee, British Empire Cancer Campaign; Corr. Member: Société Chirurgie de Lyon; Soc. Chir. de Belgique; Hon. Member: Minneapolis Surgical Society; Swedish Surgical Society; Danish Surgical Society; President International Surg. Group; Mem. Internat. Soc. Surgery; Fell. Assoc. Surg. Gt. Brit. and Ireland. Examiner: Royal College of Surgeons, Edinburgh, and Universities of London (1950), Birmingham (1949-52), Malaya (1952), Edinburgh (1957-1961), Makerere (Uganda) (1960). Nuffield Visitor to S. African Med. Schools, 1953; Visiting Prof.: University of Illinois, Chicago, U.S.A., 1957; Indiana, 1959; Coll. Med. Evang., Los Angeles, 1959; Balfour Lectr., Univ. Toronto, 1961. R.A.M.C. 1939-43. Lieut.-Colonel (despatches twice). *Publications:* books, papers and articles on surgical, biological, historical and philosophical subjects. *Address:* British Postgraduate Medical School, Hammersmith Hospital, Ducane Rd., W.12. *T.A.:* Posgradmed Chisk London. *T.:* Shepherds Bush 1260. *Club:* Athenæum. [*Died* 17 *Sept.* 1962.

AIRLIE, 12th Earl of (*cr.* 1639), (*de facto* 9th Earl, 12th but for the Attainder), **David Lyulph Gore Wolseley Ogilvy,** K.T. 1942; G.C.V.O. 1938 (K.C.V.O. 1929); M.C. 1916; J.P.; Baron Ogilvy of Airlie, 1491; Lord Chamberlain to the Queen Mother, 1952-65 (apptd. Lord Chamberlain to the Queen 1937); Representative Peer for Scotland, 1922-63; H.M. Lieutenant for County of Angus, 1936-67; Chancellor of Order of Thistle, 1956-66; Lt.-Col. R. of O. Scots Guards; Bt. Col. Reserve T.A.; late Captain 10th Royal Hussars; *b.* 18 July 1893; *s.* of 11th Earl and Lady Mabell Frances Elizabeth Gore (*d.* 1956); *S.* father, 1900; *m.* 1917, Lady Alexandra Marie Bridget Coke, *d.* of 3rd Earl of Leicester, G.C.V.O.; three *s.* three *d. Educ.:* Eton. A Lord-in-Waiting, 1926-29; Deputy Governor, British Linen Bank, 1930-47, Governor, 1947-63; Director Barclay's Bank, 1947-63; Chairman, British Legion (Scotland), 1934-45; Chairman, Agricultural Wages Board for Scotland, 1937-1940; Commandant Army Cadet Force in Scotland, 1942-43; Chm. North of Scotland Hydro-Electric Board, 1943-45; served European War, 1914-19, (wounded, despatches, M.C.); Capt. 10th Hussars, 1919-1920; War of 1939-45, re-employed, 1940; Major, Scots Guards; Lt.-Col., 1942; Lieut. Queen's Body Guard for Scotland, Royal Company of Archers. Hon. LL.D., Univ. of St. Andrews, 1958. Grand Cross Knight of Legion of Honour and various other foreign decorations. Owns about 40,000 acres. *Heir: s.* Lord Ogilvy. *Address:* Airlie Castle, Kirriemuir, Angus. [*Died* 28 *Dec.* 1968.

AIRY, Anna, R.I., 1918; R.O.I., 1909; R.E., 1914 (A.R.E., 1908); Member P.S. 1907; R.P., 1913; Member The Royal Glasgow Institute of the Fine Arts, 1952; painter, portraits and figure, etcher, pastellist; *b.* 6 June 1882; *o. d.* of Wilfrid Airy, M.Inst.C.E.; *g.d.* of Sir George Biddell Airy, K.C.B., Astronomer-Royal. *Educ.:* Slade School of Art, London. Slade Scholarship, 1902; Melville Nettleship Prize at the Slade School of Art, 1900, 1901, 1902; all Slade first prizes for portrait, figure, and other subjects; exhibited Royal Academy and elsewhere in 1905, and each subsequent year; also International Exhibitions Continental, Colonial, and American. Represented in British Museum; S. Kensington (Victoria and Albert); Imperial War Museum, five large works; National Gallery of New South Wales (twice); Auckland, N.Z.; Vancouver; Ottawa; and in the Corporation Art Galleries of Liverpool (twice), Leeds, Huddersfield, Birkenhead, Blackpool, Rochdale, Ipswich (three times), Doncaster, Lincoln (twice), Harrogate, Paisley, Newport, Mon. Commissioned by Canadian War Memorials Fund, 1917; commissioned by Ministry of Munitions, 1940. President Ipswich Art Club, 1945; President Ipswich Museums. *Publications:* The Art of Pastel; Making a Start in Art. *Address:* The Cottage, Playford, near Ipswich, Suffolk. *T.:* Kesgrave 4059. [*Died* 23 *Oct.* 1964.

AITCHISON, Professor James, D.D.Sc.; Professor of Dental Surgery, 1951-64, Emeritus Professor since 1964, and Director of Dental Studies, 1947-64, in the University of Glasgow; Director of Glasgow Dental Hospital, 1947-64 and Consultant, Western Regional Hospitals Board; *b.* 24 March 1899; *s.* of Charles and Helen Aitchison; *m.* 1929, Esther, *d.* of James and Theresa Wilson; no *c. Educ.:* Hutchesons' Grammar School, Glasgow; Glasgow Dental School. L.D.S. 1924; H.D.D. 1937; D.D.O. 1949; B.Sc. 1949; F.D.S. 1951; D.D.Sc. (Melb.), 1961; F.F.D., 1964. Member of National Panel of Consultants for Scotland. Hon. Vice-President Dental and Medical Hypnosis Society. Examiner in Dental Anatomy and in Dental Surgery, Roy. Faculty of Physicians and Surgeons of Glasgow; Examiner in Dental Anatomy and in Dental Surgery, R.C.S. (Edin.). Member of Dental Council of Royal Faculty of Physicians and Surgeons, Glasgow. Formerly: Examiner in Dental Surgery, Liverpool and Leeds Univs.; Radio Dentist to B.B.C.; Postgraduate Lecturer in Eastman

Dental Clinic, London; Nuffield Vis. Prof., Melbourne Univ., Australia, and Otago Univ., N.Z. Associate Editor of Dental Record; Editor, Dental Magazine and Oral Topics, 1964-. Fellow, British Dental Association. Knight (1st Class), Order of St. Olav, Norway. *Publications: teätbooäs:* Dental Anatomy for Students, 1940, new edn. 1951; Dental Histology, 1944; articles in medical, dental and scientific jls. *Recreations:* golf, drama. *Address:* 10 Park Terrace, Glasgow, C.3. *T.:* Douglas 8771. *Clubs:* Royal Scottish Automobile, University (Glasgow). [*Died* 14 *June* 1968.

AITKEN, Alexander Craig, F.R.S. 1936; F.R.S.E.; Hon. F.R.S.N.Z.; M.A. (New Zealand); D.Sc. (Edin.); Hon. D.Sc. (N.Z.); Hon. LL.D. (Glas.); Hon. F.F.A.; Hon. F.S.E.; Professor of Mathematics, University of Edinburgh, 1946-65; Professor Emeritus since 1965; *b.* 1 April 1895; *s.* of William Aitken, Dunedin, New Zealand; *m.* 1920, Mary Winifred, *d.* of Alfred Betts, Nelson, N.Z.; one *s.* one *d.* *Educ.:* Otago Boys' High School; Otago University; Edinburgh Univ. M.A. (N.Z.), 1920; D.Sc. (Edin.), 1925; Lecturer and Reader in Statistics and Mathematical Economics, Univ. of Edinburgh, 1925-46. *Publications:* Gallipoli to the Somme, 1963. Books and memoirs on statistical and numerical mathematics, algebra, and other topics. *Recreation:* music. *Address:* 36 Primrose Bank Road, Edinburgh 5. *T.:* Granton 3419. [*Died* 3 *Nov.* 1967.

AITKEN, Major Nigel Woodford, D.S.O. 1917; M.C.; *b.* 10 Dec. 1882; *s.* of late Edward Aitken of Mayen, Banffshire, and Florence, *d.* of James Wheler Woodford Birch; *m.* 1911, Enid, *y. d.* of Sir Henry Pipon-Scholes; two *d.* *Educ.:* Harrow; R.M. Academy, Woolwich. Commissioned, 1902; served European War, 1914-18 (despatches four times, M.C., D.S.O.); sick list, 1919 and 1920; retired, 1921. *Recreations:* fishing, shooting. *Address:* Fairholt, South Newton, Nr. Salisbury, Wilts. *Club:* Army and Navy. [*Died* 31 *July* 1963.

AITKEN, Sir William Traven, Kt. 1963; M.P. (C.) Bury St. Edmunds Division of Suffolk since 1950; Manager London Express, News and Feature Services; *b.* Canada, 1905; *s.* of M. Aitken, Toronto, Canada; *m.* 1938, Hon. Penelope Loader Maffey, M.B.E., J.P., *o. d.* of 1st Baron Rugby, *q.v.*; one *s.* one *d.* *Educ.:* Upper Canada Coll.; Univ. of Toronto. Served War of 1939-45, R.A.F., Fighter Reconnaissance Pilot (wounded). Contested West Derbyshire, 1945. Director: Shop Investments Ltd., Western Ground Rents Ltd., etc. *Address:* Playford Hall, Nr. Ipswich, Suffolk; House of Commons, S.W.1. *Clubs:* Travellers', Pratt's, Carlton, Brooks's. [*Died* 19 *Jan.* 1964.

AKERMAN, Air Vice-Marshal Walter Joseph Martin, C.B. 1956; C.B.E. 1944; *b.* 17 October 1901; *s.* of R. F. M. Akerman, F.R.C.O., Windsor; *m.* 1929, Dorothy Dulcie, *d.* of Major R. E. Webb, York and Lancaster Regt. *Educ.:* St. George's, Windsor Castle; Imperial Service College, Windsor; R.A.F. College, Cranwell. Commissioned, December 1921; served India, 1925-31; Adjt. Electrical and Wireless School, Cranwell, 1931-35; Staff Coll., Andover, 1936; comd. No. 38 and 115 Sqdns., Marham, 1937-38; Training Staff, H.Q. Bomber Comd., 1938-39; Admin. Staff, H.Q. 40 Gp., Andover, 1939; comd. 114 Sqdn. 1940; Air Staff, No. 5 Gp., Bomber Comd., 1940-41; comd. R.A.F. Station, Scampton, 1941; Sen. Personnel Staff Officer, Egypt, 1941-45; A.O.C. 87 Gp., France, 1946-47; Air Officer i/c R.A.F. Records, 1947-49; A.O.C. No. 65 London Gp., 1949-50; Dir. of Organisation (Establishment), Air Min., 1950-51; A.O.A. Far East Air Force, Singapore, 1952-55; retd. with rank of Air Vice-Marshal, 1956. Commandeur, Légion d'Honneur, France, 1946. *Recreation:* yachting. *Address:* Westlands, Warblington Avenue, Warblington, Hants. *T.:* Havant 1310. *Club:* R.A.F. Yacht (Hamble). [*Died* 9 *Dec.* 1964.

ALANBROOKE, 1st Viscount, *cr.* 1946, of Brookeborough; 1st Baron, *cr.* 1945; **Field-Marshal Alan Francis Brooke,** K.G. 1946; G.C.B., *cr.* 1942 (K.C.B., *cr.* 1940; C.B. 1937); O.M. 1946; G.C.V.O., *cr.* 1953; D.S.O. 1917; Chancellor of Queen's University, Belfast, since 1949; Director of Midland Bank Ltd., 1947-63; Chm. Belfast Banking Co. Ltd., 1947-63; Director: National Discount Co., 1948-63; Hudson's Bay Co., 1948-59; Triplex Glass Co. Ltd., 1954-56; Lowland Tanker Co. Ltd., 1954; *b.* Bagnères de Bigorre, France, 23 July 1883; *s.* of late Sir Victor Brooke, Bart., and Lady Brooke-Colebrooke, Brookeborough, Co. Fermanagh; *m.* 1st, 1914, Jane Mary (*d.* 1925), *d.* of Col. Richardson, Rossfad, Ballinamaliard, Co. Fermanagh; one *s.* one *d.*; 2nd, 1929, Benita, *widow* of Sir Thomas Lees, 2nd Bt., and *e. d.* of Sir Harold Pelly, 4th Bt.; one *s.* (one *d.* decd.). *Educ.:* abroad; R.M.A., Woolwich. Joined R.F.A., 1902; served first four years in S. of Ireland; transferred to India, 1906; posted to Royal Horse Artillery (N Battery), 1909; proceeded to war in France with Secunderabad Cavalry Brigade; landed Marseilles, Sept. 1914, in command of ammunition column; posted Adjutant, 2nd Indian R.H.A. Brigade, Feb. 1915; Brigade-Major, 18th Divisional Artillery, Nov. 1915; G.S.O.2, Royal Artillery, Canadian Corps, Feb. 1917; G.S.O.1, R.A., First Army, 1 July 1918-31 March 1919 (despatches six times, bar to D.S.O., Brevet Lt.-Colonel); Delhi Durbar Medal, 1914 Star, 1935 Jubilee Medal, and Belgian Croix de Guerre; Staff College, Camberley, 1919; G.S.O.2, Northumbrian Division T.A., 1920-23; Staff College, Camberley, 1923-27; Imperial Defence College, 1927; Regimental duty, 1928; Commandant, School of Artillery, 1929-32; Army Instructor Imperial Defence College, 1932-34; Commander 8th Infantry Brigade, 1934-35; Inspector of Royal Artillery, 1935-36; Director of Military Training, War Office, 1936-37; Comdr. of Mobile Division, 1937-38; Commander, Anti-Aircraft Corps, 1938-39; G.O.C.-in-C. Anti-Aircraft Command, 1939; G.O.C.-in-C. Southern Command, 1939 and 1940; Comdr. of Second Army Corps, B.E.F., 1939-40; C.-in-C. Home Forces, 1940-41; Chief of Imperial General Staff, 1941-46; A.D.C. General to the King, 1942-46; Field Marshal, 1944; Colonel Comdt., R.A., 1939-57; R.H.A., 1940-57, Glider Pilot Regiment, 1942-51, and H.A.C., 1946-54. President of the Zoological Society of London, 1951-54; a Government Director of Anglo-Iranian Oil Co., 1946-54; Constable of the Tower of London, 1950-55; H.M. Lieutenant, County of London, 1950-57. Master Gunner, St. James's Park, 1946-56. Pres., Corps of Commissionaires, 1960. Recipient of Hon. Degrees from Oxford, Cambridge, Bristol, London, Leicester, Queen's Universities and Edinburgh University. Commander of Parade for Coronation, and Lord High Constable of England in Coronation Abbey Ceremonies, 1953. Presented with replica of Boyne Medal by Parliament of Northern Ireland, 1960. 1st Class Order of Polonia Restituta; 1st Class Order of Zovorof; Grand Cordon of Order of Leopold; Grand Commander of Legion of Honour; Order of White Lion of Czechoslovakia, 1st Class; Victory Star of White Lion; 1st Class Order of the Redeemer of Greece; Knight Grand Cross of the Order of the Netherlands; Knight Grand Cross of the Order of the Dannebrog; Knight Grand

Cross, Royal Order of North Star (Sweden); 1st Class Order of Trinity, Ethiopia; Grand Cross of The Military Order of Christ (Portugal); Belgian Croix de Guerre; French Croix de Guerre; Czechoslovakic Croix de Guerre. *Relevant Publications:* The Turn of the Tide, 1957 (by Sir Arthur Bryant; based on the war diaries of Field-Marshal Viscount Alanbrooke); Triumph in the West, 1959 (by Sir Arthur Bryant). *Recreations:* riding, shooting, and fishing. *Heir:* *s.* Hon. Thomas Brooke, *b.* 9 Jan. 1920. *Address:* Ferney Close, Hartley Wintney, Hants. *Clubs:* Army and Navy, Cavalry, Naval and Military, Bath, White's, United Service. [*Died* 17 *June* 1963.

ALBAN, Sir Frederick (John), Kt., *cr.* 1945; C.B.E. 1932; J.P. Glamorgan Chairman Wales Regional Hospital Board (National Health Service Act, 1946), 1947-59 (retired); *b.* 11 Jan. 1882; *s.* of David and Hannah Alban; *m.* 1906, Alice Emily Watkins; four *s.* two *d.* *Educ.:* Abergavenny (Mon.) National School; privately. Numerous appointments in Local Government, and in Government service; Deputy Accountant, Welsh National Insurance Commissioners, 1912-16; Consulting Accountant and Registrar, Taf Fechan Water Supply Board; Financial Adviser to Local Authorities; Senior Partner of Alban & Lamb, Chartered Accountants of Newport and Cardiff. First Prizeman, Final Examination, 1907, Institute of Municipal Treasurers & Accountants (Inc.) (Hon. Fell., 1954); F.C.A.; Gold Medallist, 1909, Pres. 1947-49, Soc. of Incorporated Accountants; Hon. Life Member, Certified Public Accountants' Association of Ontario; Member: Ministry of Health Departmental Cttee. on Greater London Water Supplies, 1947; Electricity Arbitration Tribunal (Electricity Act, 1947); Gas Arbitration Tribunal; Steel Arbitration Tribunal (Iron and Steel Act, 1949); Chartered Inst. of Secretaries (Pres. 1957); Chm. Finance Cttee., Welsh Nat. Sch. of Medicine; Vice-Pres., Institute of Public Administration. Hon. LL.D. Univ. of Wales, 1956. *Publications:* Income Tax as Affecting Local Authorities, 1936; The Organisation of the Waterworks Undertaking, 1926; Financial Editor, Knight's Local Government Chronicle, etc. *Recreation:* golf. *Address:* White Lodge, 894 Newport Road, Rumney, Cardiff. *T.:* 77852. *Clubs:* National Liberal; Cardiff and County. [*Died* 2 *May* 1965.

ALBAN DAVIES, Jenkin; Welsh Member of the Independent Television Authority, 1956-64; *b.* 24 June 1901; *s.* of D. Alban Davies, LL.D., Llanrhystyd, Cardiganshire; *m.* 1939, Margaret, *d.* of Capt. John Davies, Aberaeron; two *s.* *Educ.:* Merchant Taylors' School; and in U.S.A. Entered family business of Hitchman's Dairies Ltd., 1925; Underwriting Member of Lloyd's. Founder, Abermad Sch., 1948; Treas. of the Welsh League of Youth, 1950; Treas., Univ. Coll. of Wales, 1955; Mem. of the Council, National Museum of Wales, 1954; Member of Council of National Library of Wales, 1955; Trustee of National Eisteddfod of Wales, 1955. Treasurer, Coleg Harlech, 1957. Chm. Council for the Preservation of Rural Wales; Leader of Welsh Delegn. to Patagonia. High Sheriff, Cardiganshire, 1951. Hon. LL.D. Univ. of Wales, 1964. *Recreation:* gardening. *Address:* Brynawelon, Llanrhystyd, Cardiganshire. *T.:* Llanon 224; 71 Harley St., W.1. *Clubs:* East India and Sports'; St. David's (Aberystwyth). [*Died* 26 *May* 1968.

ALBERT-BUISSON, Dr. François; Grand Officer of the Legion of Honour; Member of the French Academy, 1955; *b.* 3 May 1881; *m.* 1908, Andrée Labrin; three *d.* (one *s.* decd.). *Educ.:* Coll. Issoire; Univ. of Paris, Docteur de l'Univ., Docteur en Droit; Lauréat de l'Institut (Acad. des Sciences); Lauréat de l'Acad. de Médecine. Served European War, 1914-18. Dir. du Cabinet, Min. Finance, 1924; Pres. Commercial Court of the Seine, 1930-34; Mem. Institut, 1936; Pres. Acad. des Sciences Morales et Politiques, 1944 (Sec. Perpétuel, 1951-56); Chanc. Institut de France, 1953. Chief of French Deleg., Conf. of London, 1924; Mem. French Mission to Washington and Berlin, 1931; Deleg. of Acad. des Sciences Morales et Politiques to Nat. Commn. U.N.E.S.C.O. *Publications:* Le Problème des poudres, 1913; Les Crises économiques, 1926; Mercuriales, 1931-34; Le Chancelier Antoine Duprat, 1935; Michel de l'Hospital, 1950; Le Cardinal de Retz, 1954; Les Quarante au Temps des Lumières, 1960. (Collab.) Revue des Deux-Mondes; numerous academic treatises. *Address:* 105 avenue Henri-Martin, Paris (16e). [*Died* 23 *May* 1961.

ALBERY, Sir Irving James, Kt., *cr.* 1936; M.C.; Major retd. Yeomanry; Member of the Stock Exchange, 1902-64; *b.* London, 12 May 1879; *s.* of James Albery, dramatic author, and late Mary Moore, afterwards Lady Wyndham; *m.* Jill Mary (*d.* 1967), *d.* of late Henry Arthur Jones; two *s.* one *d.* *Educ.:* Uppingham School; Freiburg Univ. M.P. (U.) Gravesend, 1924-45; contested Bow and Bromley, 1923 Election; served South Africa, 1900; European War, 1914 to Armistice (M.C., despatches). *Recreation:* sailing. *Clubs:* Carlton; Royal Corinthian Yacht. [*Died* 14 *Nov.* 1967.

ALBU, Major Sir George Werner, 2nd Bt., *cr.* 1912; Chairman and Managing Director, General Mining and Finance Corporation, Ltd., Van Ryn Gold Mines Estate, Ltd., and West Rand Consolidated Mines, Ltd.; *b.* 3 Sep. 1905; *o. surv. s.* of Sir George Albu, 1st Bt.; *S.* father, 1935; *m.* 1928, Betty (*d.* 1956), *d.* of E. C. Dicey; one *s.* four *d.* *Educ.:* Rugby; Trinity Hall, Cambridge. *Heir:* *s.* George, *b.* 5 June 1944. *Address:* P.O. Box 1242, Johannesburg. *Clubs:* Rand (Johannesburg); Kimberley. [*Died* 18 *Feb.* 1963.

ALDENHAM, 4th Baron (*cr.* 1896); 2nd Baron Hunsdon (*cr.* 1923) of Hunsdon; **Walter Durant Gibbs;** Director: Antony Gibbs & Sons (Chairman, 1939-65); Westminster Bank (Chm., 1950-61); English Scottish Australian Bank, etc.; Pres., British Assoc. of Bankers, 1954, 1955; *b.* 11 Aug. 1888; *e. s.* of 1st Baron Hunsdon and Anna Maria (*d.* 1938), 4th *d.* of Richard Durant Sharpham, Devon, and High Canons, Herts; *S.* father 1935 and cousin, Baron Aldenham, 1939; *m.* 1919, Beatrix Elinor, *d.* of Herbert Paul, and *widow* of Algernon Villiers; one *s.* (and *er. s.* killed in action, 1944). *Educ.:* Eton; Trinity College, Cambridge. Served European War, Herts Yeomanry, Gallipoli, Palestine, Persia, 1914-18 (despatches). *Heir:* *s.* Hon. Antony Durant Gibbs, R.N.V.R. [*b.* 1922; *m.* 1947, Mary Elizabeth, *o. d.* of late Walter Parkyns Tyser; three *s.* one *d.*]. *Address:* Briggens, Ware, Herts. *T.:* Roydon 2107. *Clubs:* Brooks's, City of London. [*Died* 30 *May* 1969.

ALDER, Wilfred, C.I.E. 1923; O.B.E. 1919. *Educ.:* Trinity College, Cambridge, M.A. Entered Indian Civil Service, 1900; Accountant-General, Bihar and Orissa, 1912; Punjab, 1913; Bombay, 1917; United Provinces, 1917; officiating Controller of Currency, Calcutta, 1919; retired, 1926. *Club:* East India and Sports. [*Died* 25 *Feb.* 1962.

ALDERMAN, Harry Graham, (gazetted Kt. 1962, but did not receive accolade); Q.C. (S. Aust.) 1943, (Vict. and N.S.W.) 1950; Barrister; Partner in legal firm of Alderman, Clark, Ligertwood & Rice; *b.* 24 Sept. 1895; *s.* of Thomas and Anne Alderman; *m.* 1919,

Mary Philomena, *o. d.* of Michael and Catherine Farrelly; three *s.* two *d.* (and one *s.* decd.). *Educ.:* Christian Brothers' Coll., Adelaide; Univ. of Adelaide. Admitted S. Australian Bar, 1917, to Victorian Bar and N.S.W. Bar, 1950. Pres. Law Society of S. Australia, 1945-47 (Mem. Council, 1930-34); Pres. Law Council of Australia, 1950-51. *Recreation:* Law. *Address:* 212 Napier Terrace, Unley Park, S. Australia. *T.:* 7-5668. *Clubs:* Naval, Military and Air Force (Adelaide); Stock Exchange (Adelaide).
[*Died* 15 *June* 1962.

ALDERSON, Rt. Rev. Cecil William; Bishop of Mashonaland since 1957; Dean, Prov. of Central Africa, 1961; *b.* 11 March 1900; *s.* of William James and Elizabeth Constance Alderson; unmarried. *Educ.:* Merchant Taylors' School; St. John's College, Oxford (Scholar and Exhibitioner); Ely Theological College. 1st class Class. Mods., 1921; B.A. (2nd cl. Lit. Hum.), Liddon Studentship, 1923; 1st Cl. Hons. Theology, 1924; M.A. 1926. Deacon, 1925; Priest, 1926; Curate, St. Matthew, Westminster, 1925; Vice-Principal, Ely Theol. Coll., 1925-30; Curate, Church of Ascension, Lavender Hill, 1930-33; Univs. Mission to Cent. Africa, Likoma, 1933-35; Manda, 1935-36; Permission to Officiate, Diocese of London, 1936-38; Warden, St. Paul's College, Grahamstown, 1938-43; Examining Chaplain to Bishop of George, 1942; Vice-Provost and Rector of Coll. Church of St. Mary the Virgin, Port Elizabeth, 1943-49; Archdeacon of Port Elizabeth and Canon of Grahamstown, 1944-49; Bishop of Damaraland, 1949-51, of Bloemfontein, 1951-57. Sub-prelate, Order of St. John of Jerusalem. Order of St. Mark of Alexandria, 1966. *Address:* Bishop's Mount, P.O. Box 7, Salisbury, Rhodesia. *Clubs:* Royal Over-Seas League; Salisbury (Rhodesia).
[*Died* 12 *Feb.* 1968.

ALDINGTON, Hubert Edward; C.B. 1947; M.Inst.C.E.; M.I.Mun.E.; M.Inst.T.; Consulting Civil Engineer; Member Board of Amalgamated Roadstone Corporation, and associated cos., 1949-65, retd.; *b.* 9 Sept. 1883; 2nd *s.* of late Rev. J. Arthur Aldington; *m.* 1913, Emily (*d.* 1967), 2nd *d.* of late Jas. Wm. Graham, Hong Kong and Northumberland; no *c.* *Educ.:* Kingswood School, Bath. Served several years on staff of G. W. Rly., also on Australian State Rly., in Adelaide. Served European War, 1914-19 (despatches), Major, R.E. County Surveyor of Cornwall. Chief Highway Engineer, Ministry of Transport, 1945-49. President, Inst. Highway Engineers, 1957-59. Jubilee Medal, 1935; Coronation Medal, 1937. *Address:* 22 High East Street, Dorchester, Dorset. *Club:* Royal Automobile.
[*Died* 20 *Sept.* 1967.

ALDINGTON, Richard; *b.* 1892; *m.* 1st, 1913, "H. D." (divorced 1937); 2nd, Netta, *d.* of late James McCulloch, Ashley Bank, Pinner; one *d.* *Educ.:* Dover College; London University. Served European War, 1916-18. *Publications:* Images, Old and New, 1915; War and Love, 1918: Images of Desire, 1919; Exile, and other Poems, 1923; Literary studies, 1924; A Fool i' the Forest, 1925; French studies, 1925; Voltaire, 1926; Collected Poems, 1928; Death of a Hero, 1929; A Dream in the Luxembourg, 1930; Roads to Glory, 1930; The Colonel's Daughter, 1931; Last Straws, 1931; The Eaten Heart, 1931; Soft Answers, 1932; All Men are Enemies, 1933; Women Must Work, 1934; The Spirit of Place, compiled from prose of D. H. Lawrence, 1935; Life Quest, 1936; Artifex, 1936; Very Heaven, 1937; Seven Against Reeves, 1938; Rejected Guest, 1939. U.S.A.: Life for Life's Sake, 1940; Poetry of English-Speaking World, 1941; A Wreath for San Gemignano, 1945; The Romance of Casanova, 1946; Great French Romances, 1946; Wellington, 1946 (awarded James Tait Black memorial prize, 1947); Poetry of the English-Speaking World, 1947; The Strange Life of Charles Waterton, 1949; Portrait of a Genius, But . . ., 1950; Pinorman, 1954; Lawrence of Arabia, A Biographical Enquiry, 1955; Introduction to Mistral, 1956 (Prix de Gratitude Mistralienne, 1959); Frauds, 1957; Portrait of a Rebel, 1957. Also translations. *Address:* c/o P. A. G. Aldington, 25 Castle St., Dover.
Died 27 *July* 1962.

ALDRIDGE, Sir Frederick, Kt. 1946; Adviser Manufactured Foods, Ministry of Food, 1941-62; Retired Director Co-operative Wholesale Society Ltd.; *b.* 24 May 1891; *s.* of William Aldridge, Portsmouth; *m.* 1913, Laura Violet, *d.* of Edward James, Cardiff; two *s.* one *d.* *Educ.:* St. Mary's, Portsmouth. Portsea Island Co-operative Society Ltd., 1905-9; Gillingham Co-operative Society Ltd., 1909-1911; General Manager and Secretary Grays Co-operative Society Ltd., 1911-34. A member of advisory committees grocery, bacon, butter and cheese, Food Defence Plans Dept., 1938-39; Ministry of Food, 1939-41; National Coal Advisory Committee, 1938-41. Chairman: Bacon Information Council; Min. of Agric., Fisheries and Food Sports and Social Council. Kt. of Merit, Order of Dannebrog (Denmark). *Recreations:* golf, bowls. *Address:* Brynhill College Avenue, Grays, Essex. *T.:* Grays Thurrock 2433. *Club:* Civil Service (Chm.).
[*Died* 23 *April* 1966.

ALERS HANKEY, Richard Lyons, C.B. 1957; Deputy Treasury Solicitor since 1964; *b.* 7 Oct. 1906; *s.* of Sydney George Alers Hankey and Theodosia (*née* Abdy); *m.* 1937, Margaret Lavender Reyne (*née* Barr); one *s.* *Educ.:* Westminster; Trinity Hall, Cambridge (M.A., LL.B.). Called to Bar, Middle Temple, 1929. Established in Civil Service (Treasury Solicitor's Office), 1939; subsequently a Principal Asst. Solicitor, Office of H.M. Procurator-General and Treasury Solicitor, until 1963. *Address:* 16 Baronsmead Road, Barnes, S.W.13. *T.:* 01-748 3503. *Club:* Oxford and Cambridge.
[*Died* 14 *Nov.* 1969.

ALEXANDER OF HILLSBOROUGH, 1st Earl, *cr.* 1963; 1st Viscount, *cr.* 1950, of Hillsborough, Sheffield; 1st Baron, *cr.* 1963, of Weston-super-Mare; **Albert Victor Alexander,** K.G. 1964; P.C. 1929; C.H. 1941; LL.D.; an Elder Brother of Trinity House since 1941; *b.* Weston-super-Mare 1 May 1885; *s.* of Albert Alexander, artisan engineer; *m.* 1908, Esther Ellen, C.B.E., *y. d.* of late George Chapple, of Tiverton; one *d.* *Educ.:* Barton Hill Elementary School, Bristol; St. George Technical Classes. M.P. (Co-op.) Hillsborough Div. of Sheffield, 1922-1931 and 1935-50; Parliamentary Sec. to the Board of Trade, 1924; First Lord of the Admiralty, 1929-31, 1940-45, and 1945-46; Minister of Defence, 1947-50; Chancellor of the Duchy of Lancaster, 1950-51; Leader of Labour Peers (formerly Deputy Leader), House of Lords, 1955-. President, U.K. Council of Protestant Churches, 1956. Mem. of Cabinet Delegation to India and Paris Peace Conference, 1946; formerly Sec. of the Parl. Cttee. of the Co-operative Congress; formerly on the staff of the Education Committee of the Somerset County Council; for many years Baptist lay preacher; served in the army; gazetted out with hon. rank of Captain. Formerly Vice-Chm., Roy. Inst. of Internat. Affairs; Hon. M.I.Mar.E.; Hon. F.G.I.; Hon. Freeman, City of Sheffield, and Borough of Weston-super-Mare. Master, Worshipful Company of Bakers, 1957-58. *Publications:* articles on co-operative and political subjects. *Heir:* none. *Address:* Wellhouse Farm, West Mersea, Essex.
[*Died* 11 *Jan.* 1965 (*ext.*).

ALEXANDER OF HILLSBOROUGH, Countess; C.B.E. 1947; **Esther Ellen Alexander;** *d.* of late George Chapple, Tiverton, Devon; *m.* 1908, 1st and last Earl Alexander of Hillsborough, K.G., P.C., C.H. (*d.* 1965); one *d.* Formerly President of the London and Home Counties King George's Fund for Sailors. *Address:* 101 Old Park Avenue, Enfield, Mddx. [*Died* 18 *Oct.* 1969.

ALEXANDER OF TUNIS, 1st Earl, *cr.* 1952; 1st Viscount, *cr.* 1946, of Errigal; 1st Baron Rideau, *cr.* 1952, of Ottawa, and of Castle Derg in Co. Tyrone; **Field-Marshal Harold Rupert Leofric George Alexander,** K.G. 1946; P.C. 1952; P.C. (Can.) 1952; G.C.B. 1942 (K.C.B. 1942; C.B. 1938); O.M. 1959; G.C.M.G., 1946; C.S.I. 1936; D.S.O. 1916; M.C.; H.M. Lieutenant, Greater London, 1965-66 (of County of London, 1957-65); Grand Master of the Order of St. Michael and St. George, 1960-67 (Chancellor, 1956-60); Constable, H.M. Tower of London, 1960-1965; *b.* 10 Dec. 1891; 3rd *s.* of 4th Earl of Caledon and Lady Elizabeth Graham Toler, *d.* of 3rd Earl of Norbury; *m.* 1931, Lady Margaret Diana Bingham, G.B.E. *cr.* 1954, D.St.J., *yr. d.* of 5th Earl of Lucan, P.C., G.C.V.O., K.B.E., C.B.; two *s.* one *d.* (and one adopted *d.*). *Educ.:* Harrow; Sandhurst. Served European War (France), 1914-18 (wounded thrice, despatches five times, D.S.O., M.C., Legion of Honour, Order of St. Anne, 2nd Class, with swords, Russia); Loe-Agra Operations, N.W. Frontier, 1935 (despatches, C.S.I.); Mohmand Operations, 1935 (despatches); Staff College, 1926-27; Commanding Regiment and Regimental District of Irish Guards, 1928-30; Imperial Defence College, 1930; General Staff Officer 1st Grade, Northern Command, 1932-34; Commander Nowshera Brigade, Northern Command, India, 1934-38; A.D.C. to the King, 1936-37; Col. 3rd Bn. 2 Punjab Regt., 1937; Major-General, 1937; Commander of the 1st Division, 1938-40; Lt.-Gen. 1940; Cmdr. 1st Corps, 1940 (despatches); G.O.C. in-C. Southern Command, 1940-42; General, 1942; G.O.C. Burma, 1942; C.-in-C., Middle East, 1942-43; C.-in-C. 18th Army Group, North Africa, 1943; C.-in-C. Allied Armies in Italy (15th Army Group), 1943-44; Field-Marshal, 1944; Supreme Allied Commander, Mediterranean Theatre, 1944-45; A.D.C. General to the King, 1944-46; Col. Irish Guards, 1947. Governor-General of Canada, 1946-52; Minister of Defence, 1952-54. Governor, Securicor Ltd., 1968-. K.J.St.J.; numerous medals, foreign orders and hon. degrees; Freeman of cities of: London, Belfast, Londonderry, Manchester, Edinburgh, Crosby, and Bologna; Hon. Freedom and Livery of Haberdashers' Company; Hon. Bencher of Lincoln's Inn; Hon. Freedom of Grocers' Company, Painters, Stainers' Company and Mercers' Company; Hon. M.I.C.E.; Hon. Fellow Roy. Coll. of Physicians and Surgeons of Canada; Hon. Member Cdn. Bar Assoc.; Governor of Harrow School, 1952-62. *Publication:* The Alexander Memoirs, 1940-1945, 1962. *Heir: s.* Lord Rideau. *Address:* Winkfield Lodge, Windsor Forest, Berkshire. *T.:* Winkfield Row 2240. *Clubs:* Guards', White's, Bath. [*Died* 16 *June* 1969.

ALEXANDER, Rear-Admiral Charles Otway; retired; *b.* 1888; *s.* of Capt. J. F. Alexander, 17th Lancers, Edwinstowe, Notts; *m.* 1915, Antonia Marie, *d.* of A. Geermans, The Hague, Holland; one *s.* two *d.* *Educ.:* H.M.S. Britannia. Joined R.N. 1902; served War of 1914-18; Comdr. 1919; Capt. 1927; Rear-Adm. 1939; retired 1939; re-employed 1939-45. *Publications:* various articles in sporting press. *Recreations:* shooting, fishing, golf, gardening. *Address:* Wilford Rise, Woodbridge, Suffolk. *T.:* 865. *Club:* United Service. [*Died* 13 *April* 1970.

ALEXANDER, Maj.-Gen. Edward Currie, C.B. 1928; C.I.E. 1919; D.S.O. 1902; Indian Army, retired; *b.* 15 Sep. 1875; *s.* of N. S. Alexander, late I.C.S.; *m.* 1914, Isabella (Sybil) Katherine, *d.* of late Major G. O. Stoney; one *d.* Entered army, 1895; served N.W. Frontier, India, 1897 (medal with two clasps); Mahsud Waziri operations, 1902 (D.S.O., despatches, clasp); Mohmand Expedition, 1908 (medal and clasp); European War, 1914-18 (despatches 4 times, Bt. of Lt.-Col., C.I.E.); Kurdistan, 1919 (despatches); Irak, 1920 (despatches); retired, 1934. *Address:* Old Pollard Moor, Cadnam, Hampshire. [*Died* 21 *March* 1964.

ALEXANDER, Henry Clay; Lawyer, Banker (retired); Director: Morgan Guaranty Trust Co. of New York; General Motors Corporation; Johns-Manville Corporation; Standard Brands Inc.; *b.* Murfreesboro, Tennessee, 1 August 1902; *s.* of Ellis De Witt Alexander and Nannie Eliza Snell; *m.* 1934, Janet Hutchinson; three *s.* one *d.* *Educ.:* Vanderbilt Univ., Nashville, Tenn. (A.B. 1923); student, Law Sch., 1922-1924; Yale Univ. (LL.B. 1925). Admitted to N.Y. Bar, 1926; assoc. with Davis, Polk, Wardwell, Gardiner & Reed, New York, 1925-1939, partner, 1935-39; partner, J. P. Morgan & Co., Feb. 1939 to incorporation, March 1940, Pres., Dir., Chief Executive Officer, J. P. Morgan & Co. Inc., 1950-55; Chm. and Chief Executive Officer: J.P. Morgan & Co. Inc., 1955-59; Morgan Guaranty Trust Company of New York, 1959-65 (Chm. Exec. Cttee., 1965-67). Vice-Chm.. U.S. Strategic Bombing Survey, 1944-45 (Presidential Citation, Medal for Merit, 1946). Mem. Board of Trustees, Presbyterian Hospital; Trustee Emeritus, Metropolitan Museum of Art; Mem. Board of Trustees, Alfred P. Sloan Foundation; Vice-Pres. Bd. of Trust, Vanderbilt Univ.; Member: Amer. and N.Y. State Bar Assocs., Bar Assoc. of City of N.Y., N.Y. County Lawyers Assoc., Kappa Alpha (Southern), Phi Delta Phi. *Address:* 23 Wall St., N.Y., 10015, U.S.A. *Club:* The Links. [*Died* 14 *Dec.* 1969.

ALEXANDER, Lieut.-Col. Hon. Herbrand (Charles), D.S.O. 1914; late 5th Lancers; *b.* and *heir-pres.* of 5th Earl of Caledon; *b.* 28 Nov. 1888; *m.* 1st, 1919, Millicent Valla (whom he divorced, 1927), *o. d.* of Sir Henry Meredyth, 5th Bart.; one *s.*; 2nd, 1937, Hon. Mrs. Domvile, Loughlinstown, Co. Dublin. *Educ.:* Harrow; R.M.C., Sandhurst. 2nd Lieut. 5th Lancers, 1909; Captain, 1914; served European War, 1914-19 (despatches, D.S.O.); Maj., 1921; Temp. Lt.-Col. 1941; Lt.-Col. 1945. *Address:* Carrickmines House, Carrickmines, Co. Dublin. *T:* Dublin 894257. *Clubs:* Cavalry; Kildare Street (Dublin). [*Died* 6 *May* 1965.

ALEXANDER, James Browning, M.D., F.R.C.P. (Lond.); Consulting Physician, London Chest Hospital and Prince of Wales's General Hospital; Hon. Consultant Physician St. Mark's Hospital; late Dean and Lecturer in Clinical Medicine, North-East London Post-Graduate Coll.; late Lecturer in Diseases of the Chest, Institute of Chest Diseases, London Chest Hospital; Consultant Physician Concert Artists Association; Member B.M.A.; F.R.S.M.; Fellow, London Medical Soc. and Hunterian Soc.; Fellow and Dean, Royal Institute of Public Health and Hygiene; Medical Editor of Jl. of Roy. Inst. of Public Health and Hygiene; *b.* Langbank, 1888; *s.* of late Rev. Dr. A. B. D. Alexander; *m.* Mary Beatrice, *d.* of late Lewis Bull, Suffolk; one *d.* *Educ.:* Univs. of Glasgow, Edinburgh, Caen. Diploma with Honours in French Language and Literature, 1905; M.B., Ch.B., 1911; M.D. (Glasgow), 1915; M.R.C.P., 1921; F.R.C.P. (Lond.), 1941. Served European War, 1914-18, R.A.M.C.

with the rank of Major; Officer in Charge of Medical Div. of No. 10 General Hosp., and sometime Deputy Consulting Physician to Rouen Base. Hon. F.R.I.P.H.H. *Publications:* papers in medical journals; edited Pneumonia, by the late R. M. Leslie, M.D. *Recreation:* golf. *Address:* 2 Meads Court, Eastbourne. *T.:* Eastbourne 458.
[*Died* 30 *Sept.* 1962.

ALEXANDER, Professor Peter, C.B.E. 1964; M.A.; F.B.A. 1951; Regius Professor of English Language and Literature, Glasgow University, 1935-63; Emeritus Professor since 1963. *Publications:* Shakespeare's Life and Art, 1939; Hamlet: Father and Son, 1955; Shakespeare, 1964. *Address:* 5A Gillespie Terrace, St. Andrews, Fife.
[*Died* 18 *June* 1969.

ALEXANDER, (Richard) Charles, C.B.E. 1944; LL.D.; Emeritus Professor of Surgery, University of St. Andrews; Consultant Surgeon (emeritus), Dundee Royal Infirmary and Perthshire Hospitals; *b.* 18 Sept. 1884; *s.* of Richard Alexander, Edinburgh, and Martha Wallace; *m.* 1917, Marjorie Linda, *d.* of late W. A. Morgan, Cardiff; two *s.* one *d.* *Educ.:* George Watson's College, Edinburgh; Univ. of Edinburgh (Crichton and Thomson Bursar, Vans Dunlop Scholar); Paris. M.A. (Edin.) 1904; M.B., Ch.B. (Hons.) Edin. 1908; House Surgeon Royal Infirmary, Edinburgh, 1909-10; R.S.O. Chalmers Hospital, Edinburgh, 1910-11; F.R.C.S. Edinburgh, 1911; Asst., Dept. of Surgery, Univ. of Edinburgh, 1911-21; Tutor in Clinical Surgery, Royal Infirmary, Edinburgh, 1912-19; Crichton Research Scholar (jointly), 1913; Major R.A.M.C., Surgical Specialist, B.E.F. France, 1916-18 (despatches twice); Assistant Surgeon, Chalmers Hospital, Edinburgh, 1919-1921; Professor of Surgery, University of St. Andrews, 1936-51; Surgeon, Royal Infirmary, Dundee, 1921-51; Surgical Director, E.M.S. Eastern Region of Scotland, 1939-45. Vice-President Royal College of Surgeons of Edinburgh, 1954-57; President Forfarshire Medical Association, 1957-58. Hon. LL.D. St. Andrews, 1952. *Publications:* Articles on Surgical Subjects, in Lancet, British Journal of Surgery, British Journal of Urology, Edinburgh Medical Journal, *Recreation:* golf. *Address:* 261A Perth Road, Dundee. *T.:* 67453. *Club:* Royal and Ancient Golf (St. Andrews).
[*Died* 14 *Feb.* 1968.

ALEXANDER, Lieut.-Col. Robert Donald Thain, D.S.O. 1917; O.B.E. 1919; T.D. 1919; F.K.C., M.Inst.C.E., M.I.E. (Ind.); The London Scottish (retired); Deputy Chief Engineer Indian State Railways and Chief Engineer and Acting Agent, Bengal Nagpur Railway (retired 1933); *b.* 29 Sept. 1878; *e. s.* of late Thomas Alexander, Acting Inspector-General of Constabulary, Jamaica, and of Aberdeen; *m.* 1914, Lilian Margaret Beatrice, *e. d.* of late A. J. W. Storie, advocate, Aberdeen; two *s.* decd. (*er. s.* killed in action, France, 1940; *yr. s.* killed in air crash, 1967). *Educ.:* Dulwich College; King's College, Univ. of London. Trained in Engineering Works in America and England; entered Indian Public Works Dept. (Railway Branch), 1904; engaged on construction of the Nagda-Muttra State Railway, Frontier Surveys and the Lower Ganges Bridge, Bengal; served throughout European war in India, Mesopotamia, Egypt, and the War Office, disembodied on conclusion of operations in Kurdistan, 1919 (despatches four times, D.S.O., O.B.E., T.D.); Lieut.-Col. Apr. 1917, and appointed Assistant Director of Inland Water Transport, Mesopotamian Expeditionary Force; served in Mahsud Campaign (Waziristan), 1920; Assistant Secretary Railway Board (India), 1920-21; Services lent by Government as Chief Engineer, Bengal Nagpur Railway, 1921; acted as Agent (Gen. Manager), 1931. President: the Institution of Engineers (India), 1928-29; British Commonwealth Rifle Club, 1947. Member of Council: (for India) Institution of Civil Engineers, 1927-30; N.R.A. of Gt. Brit., 1936-. F.K.C. 1938. Weapon Training Officer L.D.V. and Home Guard, 1940-44. *Publication:* (with late Lieut.-Col. A. Martin-Leake, V.C., V.D.) Some Signposts to Shikar, 1932. *Recreations:* golf, shooting. *Address:* c/o National and Grindlay's Bank Ltd., 13 St. James's Square, S.W.1. *Club:* Royal Calcutta Turf (Calcutta).
[*Died* 20 *Feb.* 1969.

ALEXANDER, Walter, C.M.G. 1963; Speaker, Legislative Assembly of S. Rhodesia, since 1959; *b.* 20 Dec. 1895; *er. s.* of Walter Alexander, St. Andrews, Fife, and Mary Josephine (*née* Allsop); *m.* 1942, Margaret Isabelle Mary Wilson; no *c.* *Educ.:* Madras Academy, St. Andrews, Fife. M.B., Ch.B. 1919, D.P.H. 1921, St. Andrews; M.D. (*Summa cum Laude*) 1924. Medical Officer, Rezende Mine, Penhalonga, S. Rhodesia, 1925-55. K.S.G. 1955. *Recreations:* golf, bowls. *Address:* Abbotsford, Box 32, Odzi, S. Rhodesia. *T.:* Odzi 0-1823. *Club:* Umtali (S. Rhodesia).
[*Died* 22 *May* 1964.

ALFIERI, Major-General Frederick John, C.I.E. 1945; *b.* 25 May 1892; *s.* of Frederick Alfieri, B.A., and Minnie E. Benjafield; *m.* 1919, Florence Marguerite, *d.* of Major F. J. W. Porter, D.S.O., R.A.M.C.; no *c.* *Educ.:* Privately. 34th Royal Sikh Pioneers, I.A.; Regtl. Duty and Staff Appts. and R.I.A.S.C.; A.Q.M.G.; A.A.G.; Director of Organisation (India); Major-General i/c Administration; Deputy Quartermaster-General, India, 1943-45; Director of Supplies and Transport, India, 1945-46; retired, 1947. *Publications:* Service only. *Recreations:* shooting, fishing, riding. *Address:* c/o Lloyds Bank Ltd., 6 Pall Mall, S.W.1; Queens Oak, Northiam, Sussex. *Club:* United Service.
[*Died* 17 *March* 1961.

ALFORD, Prebendary Charles Symes Leslie; Prebendary in Wells Cathedral since 1947; *b.* 7 Feb. 1885; *s.* of late J. G. Alford, Canon Residentiary of Bristol; *m.* 1911, Annie Lisette, *d.* of late Dr. Charles Welford, Barnard Castle, Co. Durham; one *s.* *Educ.:* Marlborough; Corpus Christi College, Cambridge. Curate Barnard Castle, 1908-10; Royal Army Chaplains' Dept., 1910-27; Hon. Chaplain to Bishop of Ripon, 1925-27; Vicar of Marshfield, Glos., 1927-33; Sec. Bristol Diocesan Board of Finance, 1929-38; Archdeacon of Bristol and Rector of Christ Church with St. Ewen, 1938-41; Hon. Chaplain to Bishop of Bristol, 1934-38; Rector of Staple Fitzpaine, 1941-45; Rector of Shipham with Rowberrow, 1945-52; Chaplain to High Sheriff (Somerset) 1958-59. *Recreation:* trout fishing. *Address:* Gaye's Cottage, Rowberrow, Winscombe, Somerset.
[*Died* 16 *May* 1963.

ALGEO, Sir Arthur, Kt. 1966; C.B.E. 1949; J.P.; Managing Director, Robert Holmes, Ltd., since 1933; Member, Ulster Transport Authority, since 1953 (Chairman, since 1963); Member, Electricity Board for Northern Ireland, since 1948; Member, Pigs Marketing Board, since 1958; Director, Northern Ireland Farmers' Bacon Co., Ltd., since 1958 (Chairman since 1963); *b.* April 1903; *s.* of Thomas Henry Algeo, Fortlea, Enniskillen, Northern Ireland; *m.* 1947, Rosemary Ivy Shaw, *d.* of Albert Palmer, Edgware, Middlesex; two *s.* two *d.* *Educ.:* Sligo Model School; Sligo Technical College, President, Ulster Farmers' Union, 1946-47, 1951-52, 1954-55, 1963-64. J.P. Antrim, 1934. *Recreations:* fishing, shooting, reading. *Address:* The Gables, Ballymoney, Co. Antrim, Northern Ireland. *T.:* Ballymoney 3147.
[*Died* 5 *Nov.* 1967.

ALI, Mohammed; Foreign Minister, Pakistan since 1962; *b.* Barisal, E. Bengal, 19 October 1909; *s.* of Altaf Ali; *m.*; three *s.* one *d.* *Educ.:* Islamia College, India; Presidency College, Calcutta University (B.A. 1930). Began career as Chm. District Board of Bogra, 1932; Parliamentary Secretary to Premier of E. Bengal, 1944-45; President Bogra School Board, 1945; Finance Minister of Bengal, 1946-47 (Premier for short periods); Member Constituent Assembly of Pakistan. 1947-49; first Pakistani Ambassador to Burma, 1948; Pakistani High Commissioner in Canada, 1949-52; Ambassador to U.S., 1952-53 (re-apptd. 1955); Prime Minister and Minister of Defence, 1953-54; Prime Minister and Minister of Foreign Affairs, 1954-55; Pakistani Ambassador to the United States, 1955-1959; to Japan, 1959-62. Led Pakistan Delegation to the U.N., 1955; Pakistan's Delegate to U.N. Commn. for Unification and Rehabilitation of Korea. *Address:* Foreign Office, Karachi, Pakistan.
[*Died* 23 *Jan.* 1963.

ALISON, Comdr. Sir Archibald, 4th Bt., *cr.* 1852; O.B.E. 1930; R.N. retd.; *b.* 5 Nov. 1888; *s.* of 3rd Bt. and Georgina (*d.* 1939), *y. d.* of late J. Bond Cabbell of Cromer Hall, Norfolk; *S.* father, 1921; *m.* 1919, Isa Margery, *d.* of late Sir Charles Tyrrell Giles, K.C., D.L., J.P. *Educ.:* H.M.S. Britannia. Served Persian Gulf, 1913; European War, 1914-18; Baltic, 1919; charge of tow of Admiralty Crane Lighter, Devonport to Singapore, 1928 (received thanks of Lords of the Admiralty); a Naval Assistant to Hydrographer, Admiralty, 1929-1931; retired list, 1932. Recalled for War service, 1939-44; Senior Naval Liaison Officer, Fighter Command Headquarters, R.A.F., 1939-41; Assistant King's Harbour Master, 1941, and King's Harbour Master, Milford Haven and Pembroke Dock, 1942-44. *Heir:* *b.* Comdr. Frederick Black Alison, R.N. retd. [*b.* 5 Aug. 1893; *m.* 1919, Lilian Phœbe, *d.* of L. C. Phillips, South Africa; one *d.*]. *Address:* Possil House, Marine Parade, Budleigh Salterton, Devon. *T.:* Budleigh Salterton 3138. *Club:* United Service. [*Died* 9 *Dec.* 1967.

ALISON, Sir Frederick (Black), 5th Bt. *cr.* 1852; R.N., retired; *b.* 5 Aug. 1893; *s.* of Sir Archibald Alison, 3rd Bt., and Georgina (*d.* 1939), *y. d.* of late J. Bond Cabbell, Cromer Hall, Norfolk; *S.* brother, 1967; *m.* 1919, Lilian Phoebe, *d.* of late L. C. Phillips, S. Africa; one *d.* *Educ.:* R.N. Colleges, Osborne and Dartmouth. *Heir:* none. *Address:* Dormers, Camber, Rye, Sussex. [*Died* 13 *Jan.* 1970 (*ext.*)

ALLAN, Douglas Alexander, C.B.E. 1954; D.Sc.; Ph.D.; Director of the Royal Scottish Museum, Edinburgh, 1945-61; *b.* 28 January 1896; 2nd *s.* of James Allan, Falkland, Fife, and Agnes Annie Logan; *m.* 1932, Gwendoline Hesketh, B.A., *er. d.* of Rev. R. H. Hesketh, B.A., vicar of Beckermet, Cumberland. *Educ.:* George Watson's Coll. and Boroughmuir Student Centre, Edinburgh; Edinburgh University. Served Department of Explosives Supply, Ministry of Munitions, and R.F. Artillery; served as geologist on three Scottish Expeditions to Spitzbergen, 1919-21; Asst. to the Regius Prof. of Geology, Univ. of Edinburgh, 1921-1924; Lectr. in Geology, Armstrong College, Univ. of Durham, Newcastle upon Tyne, 1925-29; Dir. City of Liverpool Public Museums, 1929-44. Falconer Memorial Fellow of the Univ. of Edinburgh, 1923-25; Hon. Gen. Sec. Univ. of Durham Phil. Soc., 1927-29; Swiney Lecturer in Geology, British Museum, 1929-30 and 1948-49; President of the Lancashire and Cheshire Federation of Museums and Art Galleries, 1931; President, Liverpool Geological Society, 1939; Hon. Treasurer, Museums Association, 1936-42; President, 1942-46; Pres., Roy. Scottish Geographical Soc., 1954; Council for Design in Industry; Governor, Scottish Nat. Memorial to David Livingstone; Pres., Conf. of Delegates, Brit. Assoc., 1951, 1953, 1964, 1965; Dir. U.N.E.S.C.O. Seminar, New York, 1952; British member Executive Committee Internat. Council of Museums, 1952-62; Chairman: British National Committee International Council of Museums, 1953-59 (Vice-Chairman, 1959-67); Council National Trust for Scotland, 1955, 1962; Council Roy. Soc. Edinburgh, 1955; Representative British Association to Ceylon and India, 1957-58; Council British Association, 1959; Representative Museums Assoc. to Canada and U.S.A., 1960, to Central Africa, 1961; Chm. Scottish Field Studies Assoc., 1962-65; President, Edinburgh Geological Soc., 1965-67. Kt. of Danish Order of the Dannebrog, 1951; Comdr. Order of Vasa, Sweden, 1962. Neill Medal, Royal Society, Edinburgh, 1944; Medal, Liverpool Geological Society, 1944; Medal, Royal Soc. of Arts, 1949; F.R.S.G.S.; F.R.S.E.; Hon. F.M.A.; Hon. Fellow Heriot-Watt College (now University), 1962; Hon. LL.D. (Edin.), 1958. *Publications:* Geographical articles on Denmark, Norway, and Spitzbergen; General and detailed articles on Museums and Adult Education; Geological papers in scientific jls. *Address:* 48 St. Alban's Rd., Edinburgh 9. *T.:* Newington 3770. *Club:* New (Edin.).
[*Died* 30 *July* 1967.

ALLAN, F. L., M.B.E.; M.C.; M.A.; Secretary of Headmasters' Conference and Incorporated Association of Head Masters since 1960; *b.* 2 Sept. 1893; *s.* of Rev. T. P. Allan and Agnes Willis; *m.* 1923, Kathleen Elsie, *d.* of J. H. Bodger; two *s.* *Educ.:* Newcastle Royal Grammar School; Emmanuel College, Cambridge. Active service with Northumberland Fusiliers, France, Belgium, Italy, North Russia (wounded, despatches, M.C.), 1914-19; Tutor at Ordination Test School, Knutsford, 1920-22; Assistant Master, Worcester Royal Grammar School, 1922-28; Headmaster, Heanor Grammar School, Derbyshire, 1929-34; Headmaster, Wallasey Grammar School, 1934-60. Staff Officer, War Office, 1941-45; played Rugby football for Northumberland and North Midlands and captain Worcestershire and Herefordshire. *Address:* 14 Garden Close, Cassiobury, Watford. *T.:* Watford 23552. *Club:* Junior Army and Navy.
[*Died* 9 *March* 1964.

ALLAN, Lt.-Col. William David, O.B.E. 1918; *b.* 4 Nov. 1879; *s.* of late James Allan, Highfield, Elgin; *m.* Eve, *d.* of late Maj. B. R. Crozier, Royal Scots Fusiliers; three *s.* *Educ.:* Elgin Academy; Blundells, Tiverton. Served South African War, 1900-2 with Seaforth Highlanders; 2nd Lieut. Black Watch, 1902; served European War, 1914-19 with the Black Watch; Major, 1917; Lt.-Col., 1928; Chief Constable of Bootle, Liverpool, 1919-20; Argyll. 1920-27; H.M. Inspector of Constabulary for Scotland, 1927-30; H.M. Inspector of Constabulary for England and Wales, 1930; Assistant Commissioner of Police of the Metropolis, 1931; H.M. Inspector of Constabulary for England and Wales, 1931-38. *Address:* Braelossie, Elgin, Morayshire.
[*Died* 9 *Jan.* 1961.

ALLARDYCE, Lady, C.B.E. 1945, **(Elsie Elizabeth);** *d.* of James Farquharson Stewart, Windsor Place, Dundee; *m.* 1st, Adam Goodfellow (*d.* 1913); one *s.*; 2nd, Sir William Lamond Allardyce, G.C.M.G. (*d.* 1930). Lady of Grace of St. John of Jerusalem. *Address:* Wick Vale, Finchampstead, Berks. *T.:* Eversley 3259. *Club:* Forum.
[*Died* 16 *July* 1962.

ALLCHIN, Sir Geoffrey Cuthbert, K.B.E., *cr.* 1954; C.M.G. 1945; M.C. 1917; *b.* 10 May 1895; *s.* of late T. C. Allchin, Longfield, Kent; *m.* 1940, Hon. Muriel Letitia Swinfen Eady (*d.* 1957), *d.* of 1st Baron Swinfen of Chertsey; no *c.* *Educ.:* Haileybury; Trinity, Cambridge. European War, 1914-1919, Royal West Kent Regiment and R.E. in France and Belgium, Capt. (M.C.); B.A. (Hons.) Cambridge, 1920; entered H.M. Consular Service, 1919; served in Morocco, 1920-30; Foreign Office, 1931; Head of Consular Dept., 1943-46; Inspector, 1947-49; H.M. Minister, Grand Duchy of Luxembourg, 1949-55, Ambassador, Sept. 1955, retired. Grand Cross Order Adolph of Nassau, 1953. *Address:* Longfield, Kent. *T.:* 2116. *Club:* Oxford and Cambridge. [*Died* 10 *Jan.* 1968.

ALLEN, Sir Carleton (Kemp), Kt., *cr.* 1952; M.C.; Q.C. 1945; F.B.A. 1944; F.R.S.L. 1951; M.A., D.C.L.; Hon. LL.D. (Glasgow); J.P. City of Oxford; of Lincoln's Inn (Hon. Bencher), Barrister-at-Law; Hon. Fellow of University College, Oxford; *b.* 7 Sept. 1887; *y. s.* of late Rev. William Allen, Sydney, Australia, and Martha Jane Holdsworth; *m.* 1st, 1922, Dorothy Frances Halford, B.E.M., Hon. M.A. (Oxon.) (*d.* 1959); one *s.* one *d.*; 2nd, 1962, Hilda Mary Grose. *Educ.:* Newington Coll., Sydney; Univ. of Sydney; New Coll., Oxford. First Class, Honour School of Jurisprudence, 1912; Eldon Law Scholar, 1913; European War, Western Front, 13th Middlesex (Capt. and Adjt.), 1914-19; Fellow, University Coll., Oxford, from 1920; Junior Proctor, 1925; Tagore Professor, University of Calcutta, 1926; Professor of Jurisprudence, Univ. of Oxford, 1929-31; Oxford Secretary to Rhodes Trustees and Warden of Rhodes House, Oxford, 1931-52. *Publications: legal:* Law in the Making, 1927 (7th edn., 1964) (Swiney Prize, R.S.A., 1944); Bureaucracy Triumphant, 1931; Legal Duties, 1931; Law and Orders, 1945 (3rd edn., 1965); The Queen's Peace (Hamlyn Lectures), 1953; Law and Disorders, 1954; Administrative Jurisdiction 1956; Aspects of Justice, 1958; articles, legal and other periodicals; *non-legal:* The Judgement of Paris (novel), 1924; Democracy and the Individual, 1943; pamphlets, short stories and articles in various periodicals. *Recreations:* travel, motoring. *Address:* 114 Banbury Road, Oxford. *T.:* Oxford 55319. *Club:* Reform. [*Died* 11 *Dec.* 1966.

ALLEN, Edgar Malpas, C.M.G. 1946; retired; *b.* 9 April 1883; *s.* of John Gray Allen, Formby, Lancs; *m.* 1940, Eva Helen Spears; one *s.* *Educ.:* Merchant Taylors', Crosby. Entered Alfred Holt & Co., Liverpool, 1900; Junior Partner, Wm. Stapledon & Sons, Port Said, also Suez (Steamship Agents), 1919; Senior Partner, 1925; retired, 1945. Deputy Representative British Ministry of War Transport, Port Said, 1940-1945. *Recreations:* horticulture, fishing and shooting. *Address:* Orchard Lodge, Orchard Hill, Bideford, North Devon. *Club:* East India and Sports'. [*Died* 2 *Aug.* 1967.

ALLEN, Colonel Edward Watts, C.B.E. 1919; Col. R.A.S.C., 1914-19; Hon. Adviser to Q.M.G. Organisations, 1939-45; retired as Chairman Civil Service Supply Association, 1958; *b.* 1883; *m.* 1909, Edith Jane, *d.* of Charles Denyer, Upham, Sidcup; five *d.* *Educ.:* Eltham. Director, Food Production, 1916; Mem. War Office Cttee. on Cost Accounting, 1918; Chm. Retail Distributors, 1928; Mem. Advisory Cttee., Board of Trade, 1928-. *Address:* Wood Norton, Fleet, Hants. *Clubs:* Constitutional, Portland. [*Died* 6 *Aug.* 1965.

ALLEN, Edwin Hopkins; *b.* Newbury, Berkshire, 21 May 1878; *m.* Lucy (*d.* 1942), *d.* of late D. Dillingham. *Educ.:* The British School, Newbury; Westminster Training Coll. Taught in elementary schools, 1899-1913. Joined staff of Teachers World as regular contributor, 1911; assistant editor, 1913; editor, 1915; first editor of Child Education, 1924. Formerly a Man. Dir. of Evans Brothers, Ltd., and Editor-in-Chief, Evans Brothers' Publications; Editor of Teachers World, 1915-45; Editor of Preparatory Schools Review, 1948-63. *Recreations:* walking, theatre, cinema. *Address:* National Liberal Club, Whitehall Place, S.W.1. *T.:* Whitehall 9871. *Clubs:* National Liberal, Royal Commonwealth Society. [*Died* 3 *April* 1967.

ALLEN, Frank, F.R.S.C.; first Professor of Physics, Univ. of Manitoba, Winnipeg, 1904-1944, Prof. Emeritus, 1944; *b.* Meductic, N.B., 6 Feb. 1874; *s.* of late Rev. John S. Allen and Charlotte N. Tuttle; *m.* 1903, Sarah Estelle (*d.* 1915), *d.* of late D. S. Harper, of New Brunswick; two *s.* one *d.* *Educ.:* public schools of N.B.; University of New Brunswick, Fredericton (B.A. 1895, with highest honours in Physics and Chemistry; Alumni gold medallist in Latin; M.A. 1897); Cornell University, Ithaca, N.Y. (University Scholar in Physics, 1899; M.A. 1900; President White Fellow in Physics, 1900; Ph.D. 1902); Hon. LL.D. Manitoba, 1924; Univ. of New Brunswick, 1945. Principal, High School, N.B., 1895-99; Instructor in Physics, Cornell, 1902-04; Member of Council, and Chairman of University Faculty, 1910-14, University of Manitoba; Member, National Research Council of Canada, 1932-37; Henry Marshall Tory Medallist, Royal Soc. of Canada, 1944. *Publications:* The Universe: from Crystal Spheres to Relativity; papers on Physiological Optics and Acoustics, and on the senses of Touch, Taste, Temperature, Pain, Muscle, Glands, etc., in scientific journals and Transactions. *Address:* University of Manitoba, Winnipeg, Canada. [*Died* 19 *Nov.* 1965.

ALLEN, Sir George (Vance), Kt., *cr.* 1952; C.B.E. 1946; Secretary, British Association for the Advancement of Science, 1954-1963; *b.* 16 April 1894; *s.* of late Rev. S. Allen and of E. A. Allen (*née* Vance); *m.* 1st, 1922, Sybil May Seaton (*d.* 1953); one *s.* one *d.*; 2nd, 1954, Orlane Frances, *d.* of late Rev. Cecil Henry Tomkins, Sissinghurst, Kent. *Educ.:* Methodist College, and Q.U.B. M.B., B.Ch., B.A.O. (Belfast) 1917, M.D. M.B., B.Ch., B.A.O. Belfast, 1917, D.T.M. & H. London, 1920; M.D. Belfast, 1927. Served War of 1914-18, Captain R.A.M.C. (German East Africa); interned by Japanese in Singapore, 1942-45. Bacteriologist, Medical Research Laboratory, Nairobi, 1921; Senior Bacteriologist, Nairobi, 1925; Bacteriologist, Institute for Medical Research, Kuala Lumpur, F.M.S., 1927; Principal, College of Medicine, Singapore, 1929-47; President, Raffles College, Singapore, 1932-34 and again 1947-49; Vice-Chancellor, University of Malaya, 1947-52; Mem. Inter-University Council for Higher Education Overseas, 1952-57; Hon. Treas. Assoc. of Univs. of the British Commonwealth, 1954-61; Chm., Council of Queen Elizabeth College, Univ. of London, 1958-64; Deputy Pro-Chancellor, Univ. of Kent; Governor: Christ Church College, Canterbury; College of Art, Canterbury; Pres. Kent Post-Graduate Medical Centre, Canterbury, 1963-1967. Fellow, Queen Elizabeth Coll., London, 1964. Hon. LL.D.: Malaya, 1952; Belfast, 1958; Aberdeen, 1963; Hon. D.Sc. Kent, 1969. *Address:* 13 Herne Bay Road, Tankerton, Kent. *T.:* Whitstable 3572. [*Died* 2 *Oct.* 1970.

ALLEN, Rear-Admiral Hamilton Colclough; reverted to retired list, 1948; *b.* 10 Aug. 1883; *e. s.* of late Dr. W.

Hamilton Allen, Stanmore, Mx.; *m.* Kathleen Mary, *d.* of late A. Crust, J.P., Lincolnshire; one *s.* *Educ.:* H.M.S. Britannia. Hon. M.A. (Cantab.) 1944. Mid., 1898; Lieut., 1904; Lieut. Comdr., 1912; Comdr., 1916; Capt. 1924; Rear-Adm., 1935. Served Boxer Rebellion, China, 1900 (despatches); European War, 1914-18; Capt. of R.N. School of Physical and Recreational Training, 1929-31; Captain of R.N. College, Greenwich, 1931-33; H.M.S. Iron Duke, 1933-35; Comd. Reserve Fleet, Nore, 1935; Naval A.D.C. to the King, 1935; Commodore of Convoy, 1939-41; Admiralty, 1941-48. *Recreations:* golf, tennis, squash rackets. *Address:* Cairns, Hythe, Hants. *T.:* Hythe 3108. [*Died* 7 *Dec.* 1964.

ALLEN, Herbert Warner, C.B.E. 1920; Journalist and Author; *b.* 8 March 1881; *e. s.* of Captain George Woronzow Allen, R.N.; *m.* Ethel, *d.* of Warwick Pemberton; one *s.* *Educ.:* Charterhouse, University College, Oxford (Scholar). 1st Class Hon. Mods., 1902; Taylorian Scholar in Spanish. Paris Correspondent of the Morning Post, 1908-14; Official Representative of the British Press on the French Front, 1915-16; accredited to French G.H.Q. for Morning Post and other London papers, 1916-17; with British Expeditionary Force in Italy and Italian Armies, 1917-18; with American Expeditionary Force in France and Germany, Aug. 1918-March 1919; Foreign Editor of the Morning Post, 1925-28; London Editor of the Yorkshire Post, 1928-30. Sept. 1939, Acting Wing Commander, R.A.F.V.R.; Assistant Deputy Director, Foreign Division, M.O.I., 1940-41; Chevalier of the Legion of Honour. *Publications:* Celestina, Edition of Mabbe's translation, 1908; The Unbroken Line, 1916; Our Italian Front (with Captain Martin Hardie), 1920; The Wines of France, 1924; The Devil that Slumbers, 1925; Italy from End to End, 1927; The Nymph and the Satyr, 1927; Gentlemen, I give you Wine, 1930; The Romance of Wine; Rum, the Englishman's Spirit, 1931; Sherry: Mr. Clerihew, Wine Merchant, 1933; Trent's Own Case (with E. C. Bentley), 1936; The Uncounted Hour, 1936; Death Fungus, 1937; The Timeless Moment, 1946; Lucy Houston, D.B.E., 1947; The Happy Issue, 1948; The Uncurtained Throne, 1950; Number Three St. James's Street, 1950; A Contemplation of Wine, 1951; Natural Red Wines, 1951; White Wines and Cognac, 1952; Sherry and Port, 1952; Through the Wine Glass, 1954; Good Wine from Portugal, 1957; History of Great Vintage Wines from Homer to the Present Day, 1961; The Wines of Portugal, 1962. *Recreations:* wine and crosswords. *Address:* Iden House, Sotwell, Wallingford, Berks. *T.:* Wallingford 3127. *Club:* Saintsbury. [*Died* 12 *Jan.* 1968.

ALLEN, John Ernest; *b.* 1872; *o. c.* of late John Allen of Highfield, Shepton Mallet; *m.* 1913, Helen Garnett, 2nd *d.* of late Alfred Hirst. *Educ.:* Clifton Coll.; Wadham, Oxford, Lit. Hum. (2nd Class). Also M.A. of Peterhouse, Cambridge; Barrister-at-law, Inner Temple; contested (L.) South West Sussex in 1905 and 1906; Hon. Secretary of British Association Committee on the Effect of the War on Credit, Currency, and Finance, 1915-22. *Publications:* County Elections, 1906; The War Debt, 1919; British War Budgets (with F. W. Hirst), 1926. *Recreation:* lawn tennis. *Address:* 2 St. Peter's Ter., Cambridge. *T.:* Cambridge 2019. *Clubs:* National Liberal, All England Lawn Tennis. [*Died* 12 *June* 1962.

ALLEN, Leslie Holdsworth, M.A. (Syd.), Ph.D. (Lpzg.); Lecturer in English and Classics, Canberra Univ. Coll. 1931-51, now Emeritus; *b.* 1879; *s.* of Rev. William Allen and Martha Jane Holdsworth; *m.* 1915, Dora, *d.* of Rev. Rainsford Bavin and Emma Buddle; one *d.* *Educ.:* Newington College, Stanmore, Sydney. First Class Honours, Classics and English, University of Sydney, 1904; James King of Irrawang Travelling Scholarship, 1904; graduated Ph.D., Leipzig, 1907; Lecturer in English and Classics, Teachers' College, Sydney, 1911; Professor of English, Royal Military College, Duntroon, Federal Territory, Australia, 1918-30. *Publications:* Gods and Wood Things, 1913; Verse Translation of Hebbel's Herod and Mariamne, and Gyges and his Ring, 1914; Phaedra, and other Poems, 1921; Araby, and other Poems, 1924; Billy Bubbles, Child Songs, 1924; William Blake, 1927; Patria: Poems, 1941; introd. to Marcus Clarke's For the Term of his Natural Life, 1952. *Address:* 6 Griffith Flats, Griffith, Canberra, Federal Territory, Australia. *T.:* Canberra X. 1584. *Club:* University (Sydney). [*Died* 6 *Jan.* 1964.

ALLEN, Commandant Mary Sophia, O.B.E. 1917; *b.* 12 March 1878; *d.* of Thomas Isaac Allen, Manager, Great Western Railway, and Margaret Carlyle, Cheltenham. *Educ.:* Princess Helena College, Ealing. Cofounder with Margaret Damer Dawson, 1914, of Women Police in London; Sub-Commandant, 1914-19; Commandant, 1919-38. *Publications:* Pioneer Policewomen; Lady in Blue; Women at the Cross-roads. *Recreations:* driving and flying. *Address:* 4 Birdhurst Road, Croydon, Surrey. *T.:* Croydon 2277. *Clubs:* (formerly) Ladies Carlton, Forum. [*Died* 16 *Dec.* 1964.

ALLEN, Colonel Sir Stephen Shepherd, K.B.E., *cr.* 1933; C.M.G. 1919; D.S.O. 1918; J.P.; *b.* 1882; *o. surv. s.* of late Wm. S. Allen, M.P.; *m.* 1918, Mary Isabel Hay (*d.* 1946), *d.* of A. L. Foster, Auckland, N.Z.; (one *s.* died on active service) one *d.* *Educ.:* privately; Pembroke College, Cambridge (M.A., LL.B.). Served European War, 1915-18 (D.S.O. and bar, C.M.G.); Commander 1st (N.Z.) Infantry Brigade, 1920-24 and 1933-37 Hon. A.D.C. to Governor-General, 1925-28; Mayor of Morrinsville, 1927-28; Administrator of Western Samoa, 1928-31; member of Central Transport Licensing Authority, New Zealand, 1932-34; Chairman Transport Co-ordination Board, 1935-37; War of 1939-45, served as Staff Capt. Salisbury Plain Area, 1939-40 and as Military Secretary 2nd N.Z.E.F., 1940-41; employed at Ministry of Home Security, Birmingham, 1942. *Publication:* Early Morrinsville, 1959. *Address:* La Signy Farm, Morrinsville, New Zealand. *Clubs:* United University; Northern (Auckland). [*Died* 4 *Nov.* 1964.

ALLEN, William Gilbert; Sheriff of the City of London, 1955-56; *b.* 6 Oct. 1892; *s.* of William Gilbert Allen; *m.* 1922, Winifred Margaret Anita, *d.* of Dr. Meredith-Henshall, Quebec, Canada; two *s.* *Educ.:* Quernmore School, Bromley, Kent; Haileybury College. Articled Clerk, Maurice Jenks, Percival & Co., Chartered Accountants, 1911. Served European War, 1914-18, in Royal Artillery (wounded); Adjutant of Trade Test Centre, Woolwich, 1917; invalided out as Captain, 1918. Re-joined Maurice Jenks, Percival & Co.; Junior Partner, 1923-32; founded own firm (Gilbert Allen & Co.), 1932. Liveryman: Worshipful Company of Haberdashers; Worshipful Company of Glass Sellers (Master 1950-51). Comdr Military Order of Christ (Holy See): (3rd class) Order of Al Rafidain (Iraq). *Address:* 3 Heath Rise, Kersfield Road, Putney, S.W.15. *T.:* 01-789 1639. ***Clubs:* City Livery (Life Member), Royal Automobile; Lucifer Golfing Society; Old Haileyburian Golfing Society.** [*Died* 27 *Feb.* 1970.

ALLFREY, Lieutenant-General Sir Charles Walter, K.B.E., *cr.* 1946; C.B. 1943; D.S.O. 1933; M.C. 1917 and Bar 1918; D.L.; J.P.; Col. Comdt. R.A., 1947-57; Col. Comdt. R.H.A., 1948-57; *b.* 24 Oct.

1895; *s.* of late Captain Henry Allfrey, 60th Rifles, Hemingford, Warwickshire, and Kathleen Hankey; *m.* 1935, Geraldine Clare, *er. d.* of late Col. Lucas-Scudamore and of Mrs. Lucas-Scudamore, Kentchurch Court, Hereford; one *s.* one *d.* *Educ.:* R.N. College, Dartmouth. Joined Royal Artillery Aug. 1914; Capt. 1917; Bt. Major 1931; Major 1933; Bt. Lt.-Col. 1935; Col. 1939; acting Lt.-Gen. 1942; Maj-Gen. 1943; temp. Lt.-Gen. 1943; Lt.-Gen. 1946; served in France 1914-18 (wounded twice, M.C. and Bar); Operations in N. Kurdistan, 1932 (D.S.O.); Commanded 5 Corps, N. Africa and Italy, 1942-44; G.O.C. British Troops in Egypt, 1944-48; retired 1948. *Address:* Lower Hazel, Rudgeway, Bristol. *Club:* Cavalry.
[*Died* 2 *Nov.* 1964.

ALLINGHAM, Margery Louise; *b.* 1904; *er. d.* of Herbert John Allingham and Emily Jane Hughes; *m.* 1927, Philip Youngman Carter. *Educ.:* Perse High School for Girls, Cambridge. *Publications:* Blackkerchief Dick; The Crime at Black Dudley; Mystery Mile; Look to the Lady; Police at the Funeral; Sweet Danger; Death of a Ghost; Flowers for the Judge; The Case of the Late Pig; Dancers in Mourning; The Fashion in Shrouds; Mr Campion and Others; Black Plumes; Traitor's Purse; The Oaken Heart; Dance of the Years; Coroner's Pidgin; More Work for the Undertaker; The Tiger in the Smoke (1956); filmed, The Beckoning Lady; Hide My Eyes; The China Governess; The Mysterious Mr. Campion (omnibus); The Mind Readers; Mr. Campion's Lady (omnibus); Cargo of Eagles; The Allingham Case Book (published posthumously). *Address:* d'Arcy House, Tolleshunt d'Arcy, Essex.
[*Died* 30 *June* 1966.

ALLISON, Sir John; *see* Allison, Sir W. J.

ALLISON, Captain John Hamilton, D.S.O. 1940, and Bar, 1942; R.N. retired; Managing Director, Zephyr Road Haulage Ltd.; a Younger Brother of Trinity House; *b.* 13 January 1902; *s.* of W. H. D. Allison and Isabella Wetherill; *m.* 1931, Barbara, *d.* of Rev. F. E. Skyrme; one *s.* one *d.* *Educ.:* Osborne; Dartmouth. Royal Navy from September 1915; served war of 1939-45, 16th, 5th, 7th, 14th, and 2nd Destroyer Flotillas (despatches twice, D.S.O. and Bar), Commander of Order of St. Olaf, 1944. Senior British Naval Officer, Ceylon, 1950 and 1951. A.D.C. to the Queen, 1952; Manager Guided Weapons Division of English Electric Co. Ltd., Salisbury, South Australia, 1953-59. *Address:* The Old Rectory, Withiel, Bodmin, Cornwall. *T.:* Lanivet 229. *Club:* United Service.
[*Died* 24 *Feb.* 1968.

ALLISON, Sir (William) John, K.B.E. 1959; Kt. 1954; Chairman since 1952, Managing Director since 1947 of Permewan Wright Ltd.; *b.* 7 March 1903; *s.* of Alfred James Allison and Florence Nightingale Gray; *m.* 1930, Olive Dorothy Becroft; two *s.* (one *d.* decd.). *Educ.:* Middle Park State School; Melbourne Univ. Joined staff of Permewan Wright Ltd., 1916; Chm.: N.S.W. Wholesale Sugar Distributors' Assoc., 1936-40; Victorian Wholesale Sugar Distributors' Assoc., 1944-47; Defence Business Board, Defence Department, 1953-; President: Associated Chambers of Commerce of Australia, 1951-53; Melbourne Chamber of Commerce, 1952-55; Vice-Pres. Roy. Commonwealth Soc., 1955-; Councillor, Melbourne City Council, 1954-58; Mem. Council, Melbourne Univ.; Pres. Australian Div., Institute of Directors, 1964-65; Chairman of Export Development Council, 1958-65; Dir., Petersville Australia Ltd., 1960-; Chm., Wrightcel Ltd., 1962-. Coronation Medal, 1953. *Recreations:* swimming, reading. *Address:* 50 Rowland St., Kew, Melbourne, Victoria, Australia. *T.:* 80-4442. *Clubs:* Australian, West Brighton, Hawthorn (Melbourne); Commonwealth (Canberra).
[*Died* 20 *Sept.* 1966.

ALLSOP, Hon. Sir James Joseph Whittlesea, Kt., *cr.* 1945; *b.* 1887; *s.* of late James George Whittlesea Allsop; *m.* 1913, Jessie Annie Delmerick. *Educ.:* London University. Entered Indian Civil Service, 1910; Puisne Judge, High Court, Allahabad, 1934-47. *Address:* Longmead, Meadow Road, New Milton, Hants.
[*Died* 28 *Aug.* 1963.

ALLT, Dr. Wilfrid Greenhouse, C.B.E. 1962; Principal and Controller of Examinations, Trinity College of Music, London, 1944-65; *b.* 29 Sept. 1889; *m.* 1915, Elsie Bayes Crowe; two *d.* *Educ.:* Collegiate School and Tutors, Wolverhampton; Edinburgh Univ. (Mus. Doc. 1930). Conductor, Recitalist, Lecturer, Adjudicator Musical Festivals. Sub-Organist Norwich Cathedral, 1910-14; Organist, St. John's, Princes St., Edinburgh, 1915-22; Master of the Music, St. Giles' Cathedral, 1923-44; Organist to Edinburgh Univ., 1923-44. Conductor University Musical Society and Royal Choral Union for 30 years. Director of Music at State and Civic Ceremonies in the Scottish Capital; Overseas and Home Examiner, Trinity College of Music, London; many times toured the Americas and Africa. European War, 1914-18, served in R.N.R.; War of 1939-1945, Civil Defence Warden, Music Director for City of Edinburgh Corporation Entertainments for H.M. Forces. President: Incorporated Soc. of Musicians, 1955; Incorporated Assoc. of Organists, 1956-58; Union of Graduates in Music, 1957-; National Music Council of Great Britain, 1959-68; London Assoc. of Organists, 1960-62; Roy. Coll. of Organists, 1962-64; Vice-Pres., Roy. Musical Assoc.; Chairman: Nat. Music Council of Great Britain, 1956-; Central Music Advisory Cttee. of B.B.C., 1956-62; Church Music Soc., 1955-; Musicians' Benevolent Fund, 1959-, Royal Concert Cttee., 1960-; Board of Studies in Music, Univ. of London, 1964-67. Fellow and Member: R.S.A.; R.C.O.; Royal School of Church Music; Fellow: Trinity College of Music; R.C.M.; London Coll. of Music; Birmingham School of Music; Curwen Memorial Coll. Hon. Member: Royal Acad. of Music, 1959; Guildhall School of Music, 1961; Hon. Internat. Mem. Amer. Guild of Organists. *Publications:* Thesis: The Organ and its Music from Mediaeval Times to John Sebastian Bach; The Treatment of Ground (Royal Musical Assoc. Publication 1945-46); Music and Worship; The Place of Music in a University (address to Convocation of University of London). Contrib. to learned journals. *Recreations:* books, travel. *Address:* 36 Holland Park, W.11. *T.:* Park 5083.
[*Died* 21 *Dec.* 1969.

ALLUM, Frederick Warner, C.B.E. 1919; retired; *b.* 25 June 1869; *s.* of Major E. W. Allum, Royal Bengal Artillery; *m.* 1894, *e. d.* of Captain J. H. Fairley; three *d.* (three *s.* decd.). *Educ.:* Mussoorie School. Entered Indian Public Works Department through Thomason College, Roorkee, 1891; served as an engineer of Indian Railways in India and Burma; in charge of the railway extension from Nushki to Duzdap, 1916-20 (despatches); in charge of survey for railway connection between Assam and Upper Burma, 1920-22; Chief Engineer, Railway Board, 1922-24. *Address:* c/o Lloyds Bank, 6 Pall Mall, S.W.1.
[*Died* 19 *Aug.* 1963.

ALLUM, Horace Benjamin, C.B.E. 1939 (O.B.E. 1929); M.V.O. 1936; *b.* 23 Oct. 1884; *m.* 1923, Mary Josephine Frances Dineen (*d.* 1953); two *s.* (and *e. s.* killed in action, 1945); *m.* 1954, Margaret Alice Ells. Lately Principal Asst. Sec., Ministry of Works and Buildings; Controller of Supplies, H.M. Office of Works, 1925-42. *Recreations:* golf, fishing. *Address:* 49 Beeches Avenue, Worthing, Sussex. [*Died* 22 *Jan.* 1966.

ALLWORTHY, Rev. Thomas Bateson, M.A., B.D. (Camb. and T.C.D.); *b.* 13 Sept. 1879; *s.* of Edward and Anna Allworthy of Belfast; *m.* 1912, Agnes, *d.* of James Medland and Priscilla Taylor of Manchester; three *d. Educ.:* Belfast Royal Academy; Christ's College, Cambridge. Ordained, 1902; Curate of St. Helen, Auckland, 1902-6; Holy Trinity, Hurdsfield, 1906-7; Licensed preacher, Diocese Manchester, 1907-8; Founder and First Warden of St. Anselm's Hostel, Manchester, 1908-14; Vicar of Martin, Lincoln, 1914-15; Director Religious Education in Diocese of Ely, 1915-24; Chaplain, Girton College, Cambridge, 1917-24; Rector of St. Mary-at-Stoke, Ipswich, 1924-34; Vicar of St. Andrew the Great, Cambridge, 1934-45; Select Preacher, Cambridge Univ., 1943. *Publication:* Women in the Apostolic Church, 1917. *Address:* 94 Thornton Road, Cambridge. *T.:* Cambridge 76255. [*Died* 12 *March* 1964.

ALMOND, Sir James, Kt., *cr.* 1941; *b.* 28 September 1891; *s.* of George Almond, Belmont, Bolton; *m.* 1925, May Victoria Howard, *e. d.* of Rev. S. H. Baker; three *s.* one *d. Educ.:* Bolton Grammar School; Emmanuel College, Cambridge. Entered I.C.S. 1915; Judical Commissioner, N.W.F.P., 1937-46; retd., 1946. *Recreation:* music (Mus.B., F.R.C.O.). *Address:* 10 Richmond Road, Bexhill-on-Sea. *T.:* Bexhill 1906. [*Died* 30 *Oct.* 1964.

ALPASS, Joseph Herbert, C.B.E. 1951; Auctioneer, Estate and Business Transfer Agent; *b.* Bristol, 1873; *s.* of Thomas Alpass, Berkeley; *m.* L. A. T., *d.* of John Neale, Berkeley; one *s. Educ.:* Merchant Venturers' College, Bristol. Contested Cirencester and Tewkesbury Division, 1918, 1924; Thornbury Div., 1923; M.P. (Lab.) Bristol Central, 1929-31; member: Gloucestershire County Council 42 years (16 years Alderman); Thornbury R.D.C. and Board of Guardians seven years; Gloucestershire War Agricultural Executive Cttee.; Chairman Gloucestershire Farmers' Union, 1917-18; M.P. (Lab.) Thornbury Division of Gloucestershire, 1945-50; ex.-member Labour Party's Agricultural Committee. *Address:* Elberton, 87 Ormerod Road, Stoke Bishop, Bristol 9. *T.:* 682357. [*Died* 31 *May* 1969.

ALSTON, Brigadier-General Francis (George), C.M.G. 1919; D.S.O. 1916; *b.* 19 July 1878; *s.* of late Sir Francis Alston, K.C.M.G., of the Foreign Office; *m.* Antoinette Tarn; one *s.* two *d. Educ.:* Eton; abroad. 2nd Lieut. Scots Guards, 1900; Capt. 1906; Major. 1915; Lt.-Col. 1921; Col. 1922; served S. Africa, 1900-2 (Queen's medal 3 clasps, King's medal 2 clasps); European War, 1914-18 (despatches, C.M.G., D.S.O., Bt. Lt.-Col., Croix de Guerre. Order of Leopold); on London District Staff, 1911-14 and Dec. 1918-June 1920; Instructor Senior Officers School, 1925-27; Assistant Adjutant-General, War Office, 1927 and 1939-1941; Colonel commanding Scots Guards, 1927-1931; A.Q.M.G. Western Command, 1932-35; retired pay, 1935. *Address:* Sandacre, Sandling, near Hythe, Kent. *Club:* Guards. [*Died* 10 *March* 1961.

ALSTON, Brigadier Llewilyn Arthur Augustus, C.B.E. 1945; D.S.O. 1919; M.C. 1918; *b.* 1890; *o. s.* of Arthur Alston, late of Witley Lodge, Up-Hatherley, Glos.; *m.* 1926, Ivetta (*d.* 1965), *o. d.* of Dr. E. A. Saunders, Pembroke Dock. *Educ.:* Cheltenham College. 2nd Lieutenant Royal Welch Fusiliers, 1909. Served European War, 1914-18, Western Front (despatches twice, D.S.O., M.C.); North West Frontier, India, 1920-23; War of 1939-45, North Africa and Italy (C.B.E.); Lt.-Col. 1937; Col. 1939; Brig. 1939; Comdr. Inf. Bde., 1939-41; Comdr. E. Central Area, Sheffield Sub-District, 211 Sub-Area; retired, 1946. Col. the Royal Welch Fusiliers, 1947-48 (relinquished owing to ill health). Officer Legion of Merit (U.S.), 1946. *Address:* Llanwysg House, Llangattock, Crickhowell, Breconshire. [*Died* 18 *March* 1968.

ALTHAM, Harry Surtees, C.B.E. 1957; D.S.O. 1918; M.C.; *b.* 30 Nov. 1888; *s.* of Lt.-Gen. Sir Edward Altham, K.C.B., K.C.I.E.; *m.* Alision Livingstone-Learmonth, Cadlington, Horndean, Hants; one *s.* two *d. Educ.:* Repton School; Trinity Coll., Oxon. Taught, Winchester College, May 1913–Aug. 1949; 60th Rifles, Aug. 1914; served European War in France, 1915-19 (M.C., D.S.O., despatches thrice). President M.C.C., 1960, Treas., 1950; Chairman: M.C.C. Youth Cricket Assoc. 1951; Board of Control Selection Committee, 1954. *Publications:* A History of Cricket, 1926; (jointly) Hampshire County Cricket, 1957. *Recreations:* cricket, golf. *Address:* Kingsmead, Winchester. *T.:* Winchester 2611. [*Died* 11 *March* 1965.

ALUN ROBERTS, Professor Robert, C.B.E. 1962; Ph.D.; Emeritus Professor since 1960; Professor of Agricultural Botany, Univ. Coll. of N. Wales, Bangor, 1945-60; Member of team on Research Survey of Common Lands, The Nuffield Foundation, 1961-66; *b.* 10 Mar. 1894; *y. s.* of Robert Owen and Jane Roberts, Glangors, Llanllyfni, Caernarvonshire; *m.* 1924, Jeannie, *d.* of J. M. Williams, Cae Mawr, Penygroes, Caernarvonshire; one *d. Educ.:* Penygroes Gram. Sch.; Univ. Coll. of N. Wales, Bangor. B.Sc., Ph.D. (Wales), 1928. Ministry of Agriculture, 1917-19. Lecturer, Univ. Coll. of N. Wales, Bangor, Dept. of Agricultural Botany, 1919-26; Independent Lecturer and Head of Dept., 1926-40. Executive Officer, Caernarvon War Agricultural Exec. Cttee., 1940-43; Min. of Education, 1943-45; Professor at Bangor, 1945-60. Committee for Wales Forestry Commission, 1946-53; first Chairman of Welsh Cttee. of Nature Conservancy until 1955; Member: Welsh Land Sub Commn., 1954-63; Roy. Commn. on Common Land, 1955-58; Welsh Advisory Water Cttee., 1958-61; Council of the National Library of Wales, 1959-; The Council for Wales and Monmouthshire, 1959-62. High Sheriff, Caernarvonshire, 1955-1956. *Publications:* Y Tir a'i Gynnyrch, 1930; Welsh Homespun, 1931; Hafodydd Brithion, 1947; contrib. to learned journals on plant ecology and the history of land use and of the Welsh countryside; prose essays in Welsh; Commons and Village Greens (jt. author), 1967. *Recreations:* golf, angling. *Address:* Hafod-y-Coed, Victoria Drive, Bangor, Caernarvonshire. *T.:* Bangor 3524. [*Died* 15 *May* 1969.

AMOR, Arthur Joseph, C.B.E. 1950; M.D., M.Sc.; Medical Adviser, London Electricity Board, since 1960; *b.* 1 Dec. 1897; *s.* of late A. E. Amor and of late Emma Amor, M.B.E.; *m.* 1926, Ivetta Esca Mary, *d.* of late James W. Kilmister; one *d. Educ.:* County School, Barry; University of Wales; University of London. M.D. (Lond.); M.Sc. (Wales); Hon. D.I.H. Society of Apothecaries. Commissioned Royal Artillery, 1917; Pilot, Royal Flying Corps, 1917-19. Medical Officer, Mond Nickel Co. Ltd., 1926-1946; Chief Medical Officer, Ministry of Supply, London, 1941-45; Principal Medical Officer, I.C.I. Ltd., London, 1946-60; late Examiner in Industrial Medicine, Society of Apothecaries. *Publications:* An X-ray Atlas of Silicosis, 1940; The Chemical Aspects of Silicosis, 1942. Section on Industrial Medicine, Garland and Philips

Textbook of Medicine, 1951. *Recreation:* gardening. *Address:* Beaumont, 6 Furze Hill, Purley, Sy. *T.:* Uplands 4049. [*Died* 8 *April* 1966.

AMWELL, 1st Baron *cr.* 1947, of Islington; **Frederick Montague,** C.B.E. 1946; *b.* Clerkenwell, London, 1876; *s.* of John Montague; *m.* Constance Craig (*d.* 1964), Runcorn; one *s.* two *d.* Self-educated. Newsboy; shop-assistant; free-lance journalist; with leading London Agencies as advertisement copy-writer; Parliamentary Agent, Labour Party; Political Organiser; joined 18th Bn. (S.) K.R.R.C., 1915; served France and Belgium; commissioned 1917; served Egypt and Palestine; Egyptian Military Schools (full Lieut.; teacher Commercial Subjects). M.P. (Lab.) West Islington, Dec. 1923-31, and 1935-47; Under-Secretary of State for Air, 1929-31; Parliamentary Secretary, Ministry of Transport, 1940-41; Parliamentary Secretary, Ministry of Aircraft Production, 1941-42; Alderman Islington Borough Council, 1919-25. Councillor, People's Dispensary for Sick Animals; Founder-Trustee Homeopathic Educational Trust; Member, Society for Psychical Research; Associate, Inner Magic Circle; *Heir:* *s.* Hon. Frederick Norman Montague, *b.* 6 Nov. 1912. *Address:* 27 Howitt Rd., Belsize Park, N.W.3. *T.:* Primrose 8291; 33 Cork Street, W.1. *T.:* Regent 6916 [*Died* 15 *Oct.* 1966.

ANDERSON, Sir Alexander (Greig), K.C.V.O., *cr.* 1956 (C.V.O. 1951); M.D., Ch.B.; D.L. Aberdeen 1952; Hon. Consultant Aberdeen Royal Infirmary; *s.* of late James Anderson, Mains of Annochie, Auchnagatt, Aberdeenshire; unmarried. *Educ.:* Robert Gordon's College, Aberdeen; University of Aberdeen; Berlin. M.A. Aberd. 1905; M.B., Ch.B. 1909; M.D. 1914; F.R.C.P. Lond. 1930; LL.D. Aberd. 1949; various resident hospital appointments; joined R.A.M.C., 1915; served at Cambridge Hospital, Aldershot, and later with 43rd and 52nd General Hospitals, British Salonika Force; officer in charge of Medical Division of these hospitals (despatches); Assistant Physician Aberdeen Royal Infirmary, 1919. Formerly: Physician to Royal Infirmary, Aberdeen; Physn. to Morningfield Hospital; Hon. Cons. Physn. Scottish Command; Hon. Physician to H.M.'s Medical Household in Scotland, 1936-1955. Pres. and Founder, Aberdeen Old People's Welfare Council. *Publications:* various, in medical journals. *Recreations:* travel, books. *Address:* 11 Albyn Terrace, Aberdeen. *T.:* Aberdeen 22455. *Club:* University (Aberdeen). [*Died* 21 *May* 1961.

ANDERSON, Sir Alexander James, Kt., *cr.* 1924; C.S.I. 1918; V.D. 1921; *b.* 24 March 1879; *s.* of late Alexander Gavin Anderson; *m.* 1925, Vera Latimer, *d.* of Rev. C. P. Eden. *Educ.:* Marlborough. Manager, Bombay Burmah Trading Corporation, Ltd., 1909-25; Member, Legislative Council, Burma, 1923-25; Member, Burma Retrenchment Committee, 1923; Chairman, Burma Chamber of Commerce, 1923-25; Vice-Chairman, Commissioners for the Port of Rangoon, 1924-25; served European War (Mesopotamia, Major Volunteer Artillery Battery; Kut; prisoner Turkey), 1914-18 (despatches, C.S.I.). *Address:* Moors Cottage, Elstead, Godalming, Surrey. *T.:* Elstead 3151. *Club:* Oriental [*Died* 27 *Feb.* 1965.

ANDERSON, Major-Gen. Alexander Vass, C.B. 1945; C.M.G. 1949; M.B.E. 1923; *b.* 17 Nov. 1895; *s.* of late Lt.-Col. A. V. Anderson, Stonehaven, Scotland; *m.* Aileen Elizabeth, *d.* of late Stanley Stevenson, Edinburgh; one *d.* 2nd Lt. R.E. 1914; Capt. 1917; Major 1929; Lt.-Col. 1937; Col. 1940; Temp. Maj.-Gen. 1943; Brig. 1947; retired pay, hon. rank of Maj.-Gen., 1949. Served European War, 1915-18 (despatches); Malabar, 1921-22. Served in Home Forces, British Army Staff, Washington, D.C., and War Office, 1939-46. *Address:* Les Vallées Cottage, St. Martin, Jersey, C.I. [*Died* 17 *Oct.* 1963.

ANDERSON, Arthur Emilius David, D.S.O. 1918; M.C.; late K.O.S.B.; Member H.M. Body Guard for Scotland (Royal Company of Archers); *b.* 1886; *s.* of late Rev. Prebendary David Anderson, Rector of St. George's, Hanover Sq.; *m.* 1916, Jean Douglas (*d.* 1967), *d.* of James Patrick McIntyre; four *d.* *Educ.:* Eton; Trinity Coll., Camb. Served European War, 1914-18 (despatches, M.C., D.S.O.); War of 1939-45, until 1942. *Address:* Fairseat Manor, Fairseat, Wrotham, Kent. *T.:* Fairseat 256. *Club:* Brooks's. [*Died* 21 *Oct.* 1967.

ANDERSON, Charles Martin, C.V.O. 1961; Counsellor, U.K. High Commission, New Delhi, since Dec. 1958; *b.* 1 July 1918; *o. s.* of T. J. Anderson; *m.* 1948, Beryl June Kimber; two *d.* *Educ.:* Gresham's School, Holt; Trinity Hall, Cambridge. Entered Consular Service, 1939, appointed probationer Vice-Consul, Bangkok, Oct. 1939; Vice-Consul, Tananarive, Madagascar, 1943-45; Foreign Office, 1945; Foreign Office Resident Clerk, 1946-48; Private Sec. to Chancellor of the Duchy of Lancaster, 1947-48; First Sec., Bangkok, 1949; U.K. Delegation to U.N., N.Y., 1951; U.K. mem., U.N. Children's Fund Executive Bd., 1951-53; 1st Sec. and Consul, British Embassy, Luxembourg, 1953-1955; Foreign Office, 1956; Asst. Head of Western Dept., 1956-58; seconded to Commonwealth Relations Office, Nov. 1958. *Recreation:* children. *Address:* 14 Holland Park Road, W.14. *Clubs:* Travellers', Royal Automobile. [*Died* 31 *July* 1961.

ANDERSON, Lieut.-Gen. Sir Desmond (Francis), K.B.E., 1943; C.B. 1938; C.M.G. 1919; D.S.O. 1915; *b.* 5 July 1885; *o. s.* of late Frank H. Anderson; *m.* 1915, Mary Hope Prisca, 2nd *d.* of Rev. S. W. Wentworth Wilkin, C.F., York; one *s.* one *d.* *Educ.:* Rugby School; R.M.C. Sandhurst. Entered army, Devon Regt., 1905; Captain E. Yorks. Regt., 1910; Adjutant, 1912-15; General Staff, 1915-20; Bt. Lt.-Col., 1921; Lt.-Col., 1927; Bt.-Col. and Col., 1931; Maj.-General, 1937; Lieut.-General, 1941; Staff College, 1921; served European War, 1914-1918 (C.M.G., D.S.O., Bt.-Major, Chevalier Legion of Honour, Russian Order of St. Stanislas (2nd Class)); Commanded 1st Batt. The E. Yorks. Regt., 1927-31; A.Q.M.G. Aldershot Command, 1932-33; General Staff Officer, 1st Grade, 5th Division, 1933-34; Deputy Director of Military Operations and Intelligence, War Office, 1934-36; Deputy Director of Military Intelligence, 1936-38; Major-General in charge of Administration Eastern Command, 1938-39; Major-General General Staff, Home Forces, 1939-40; Commander, 45th Division, 1940; Assistant Chief of Imperial General Staff, 1940; Commander 46th Division, 1940; Commander 3rd Corps, 1940-43; Commander 2nd Corps, 1943-44; retired pay, 1944. Colonel of East Yorkshire Regt., 1940-48. Trustee of Imperial War Museum, 1945-56. *Address:* Faulkners, Chailey Green, Nr. Lewes, Sussex. *T.:* Newick 373. *Club:* United Service. [*Died* 29 *Jan.* 1967.

ANDERSON, Emily, O.B.E. 1944; *b.* 17 March 1891; 2nd *c.* of late Alexander Anderson, LL.D., President of University College, Galway, and late Emily (*née* Binns). *Educ.:* privately, then at Universities of Berlin and Marburg. Modern Language Mistress, Queen's College, Barbados, B.W.I., 1915-17; Lecturer in German, University College, Galway, 1917-20; Civil Service,

Foreign Office, 1923, until retirement in 1951. Seconded to War Office, 1940-43, for Intelligence Work in the Middle East. *Publications:* English edn. of Benedetto Croce: Goethe, 1923; English edn. of the Letters of Mozart and his Family, in 3 vols., 1938; English edn. of the Letters of Beethoven, in 3 vols., 1961; articles in various music reviews. *Recreations:* music, languages, travelling. *Address:* 4 Ellerdale Court, 24 Ellerdale Road, Hampstead, N.W.3. *T.:* Hampstead 2463. [*Died* 26 *Oct.* 1962.

ANDERSON, Francis Sheed, C.B. 1949; Chairman, Bacon Market Council since 1964; Director, British Sugar Corporation Ltd., since 1960; *b.* 1897; *s.* of James Anderson, Aberdeen; *m.* 1921, Helen Forbes, *e. d.* of William Wattie, Strathdon, Aberdeenshire; no *c.* *Educ.:* Aberdeen Grammar School. Served European War, 1914-17; in Indian Army, 1917-19; retd., 1919 (Capt.). Director of several Scottish companies, 1920-54; Pres. Aberdeen Granite Manufacturers Assoc., 1933-36. Contested West Renfrewshire, 1929; J.P. County of City of Aberdeen, 1935-53; Member Aberdeen Town Council and Aberdeen Harbour Board, 1935-40; Divisional Food Officer, North East Scotland, 1940-43; Director of Fish Supplies, Ministry of Food, 1943-45; Under Secretary, Ministry of Food, 1946-54; Executive Director, International Sugar Council, 1954-57; Chm. Internat. Wheat Council, 1949-59. *Address:* Tornashiel, Cults, Aberdeen. *T.:* Aberdeen 47815. *Clubs:* Caledonian, United Service. [*Died* 12 *Sept.* 1966.

ANDERSON, Sir Frederick, Kt., *cr.* 1943; C.S.I. 1937; C.I.E. 1925; B.Sc.; *b.* 19 June 1884; *m.* 1908; one *s.* one *d.* (and one *s.* decd.). *Educ.:* George Watson's College; Edinburgh University, B.Sc. Joined Indian Service of Engineers, 1905; Chief Engineer, United Provinces, 1931-37; retired, 1937; Chief Engineer, Bahawalpur State, India; retired 1944. *Address:* 25 Murrayfield Gardens, Edinburgh. *T.:* Donaldson 6713. [*Died* 26 *Feb.* 1961.

ANDERSON, Rev. Frederick Ingall, C.M.G. 1916; M.A.; Chaplain to King George VI, 1937-52, and to the Queen until Aug. 1952; late Chaplain to the Forces, 1st class, and Assistant Chaplain-General; *m.* 1903, Annie Ethel Dora, *e. d.* of Gen. G. N. Channer, V.C., C.B.; three *s.* (and one *s.* decd.). *Educ.:* Bradfield College; Jesus College, Cambridge (Rustat and Kay Scholar); Senior Optime, 1896; 3rd Class Theological Tripos, 1898. Ordained, 1898; Curate of St. Sepulchre, Cambridge, 1898-1901; Northam and Westward Ho ! 1901-3; Cairo: 1904-9; Shorncliffe, 1909-14; Caterham, 1914; served European War, 1914-19 (C.M.G., despatches five times); Chaplain to King George V, 1919; retd. pay, 1926; Vicar of Boldre, Hants, 1926-32; Vicar of St. Michael's, Sutton Court, Chiswick, 1932-37. Chaplain i/c St. John's, Eastbourne, and serving in H.G., 1941-45. Asst. Chaplain in Parish of Wynburg, Cape, South Africa, 1946-50. *Recreations:* Cambridge University and Corinthians Association F.C., 1895-1896. *Address:* c/o Lloyds Bank, Chiswick, W.4; The Planche Nursing Home, Thurston, Bury St. Edmunds, Suffolk. [*Died* 29 *Dec.* 1961.

ANDERSON, Lieut.-Colonel Henry Stewart, C.M.G. 1918; late R.A.M.C.; F.R.G.S.; *b.* 15 April 1872; *s.* of Rev. Samuel Anderson, Dunmurry, Ireland; *m.* 1910, Cicely Mary, *d.* of Rev. Otho W. Steele, Lichfield, Staffs.; one *s.* *Educ.:* St. Columba's College, Dublin; Queen's College, Belfast; L.R.C.P., L.R.C.S. (Ed.); L.R.F.P.S. (Glas.) 1898. Served South African War, 1899-1902; European War, 1914-19 (C.M.G.); retired, 1924. *Address:* c/o Glyn, Mills & Co., Whitehall, S.W.1. [*Died* 24 *May* 1961.

ANDERSON, Ian, O.B.E. 1946; M.C.; D.L.; *b.* 23 Dec. 1891; *er. s.* of late T. J. Anderson, Elgin, Morayshire; *m.* 1917, Mona, *d.* of late Lieut.-Col. G. C. Daintry, East Yorkshire Regt.; one *s.* one *d.* (and *yr. s.* killed on active service, 1945). *Educ.:* Highgate School. Served European War, 1914-18; H.A.C., 1914; 1st Bn. Seaforth Highlanders, 1915-18 (wounded, M.C., despatches); War of 1939-45: O.C. 9th Surrey (Oxted) Bn. Home Guard, and, on standing down of Home Guard, apptd. Chm. Council of Voluntary War Work for N.W. Europe. Member London Stock Exchange for 33 years; retired, 1946. High Sheriff of Surrey, 1942 and 1948. Member of Queen's Body Guard for Scotland. Director of Public Companies. D.L., County of Surrey, 1955. *Address:* Wilderwick Farm House, nr. East Grinstead, Sussex. *Club:* New (Edinburgh). [*Died* 11 *May* 1970.

ANDERSON, Sir James Drummond, K.C.I.E. *cr.* 1944 (C.I.E. 1939); late I.C.S.; *b.* 10 Aug. 1886; *s.* of late James Drummond Anderson, I.C.S., and Frances Louisa Cordue; *m.* Jean, *d.* of late W. C. Macpherson, of Blairgowrie, C.S.I., I.C.S.; three *s.* one *d.* *Educ.:* St. Paul's School; Wadham College, Oxford. Passed Civil Service examination, 1909; served in the Panjab as Assistant Commissioner, Settlement Officer, Deputy Commissioner, Sessions Judge, Legal Remembrancer, and Commissioner. Additional Secretary to Government of India, Defence Department, and Secretary of Legislative Dept.; Financial Commissioner, Punjab, 1941-46; retd. 1946. *Address:* 29 Furzefield Crescent, Reigate, Surrey. *T.:* Reigate 46096. [*Died* 20 *Oct.* 1968.

ANDERSON, Sir John, 1st Bt., *cr.* 1920; J.P.; *b.* Glasgow, 8 May 1878; *s.* of late Peter Anderson, J.P.; *m.* 1st, Janet Barr (*d.* 1940), *o. d.* of late Alexander Bilsland, J.P.; 2nd, 1941, Muriel Stanley-Wiggins (*d.* 1953), Shoreham-by-Sea, Sussex. *Educ.:* Allan Glen's School and University, Glasgow. Writer and lecturer on the philosophy of "Thought" as a vital power which governs the lives of humanity. *Recreations:* music, art, and writing poems. *Address:* St. James' Court, S.W.1. *T.:* Victoria 2360. *Clubs:* Caledonian, Royal Automobile. [*Died* 11 *April* 1963 (*ext.*).

ANDERSON, Sir John, K.B.E. 1959; C.B. 1953; Chairman, Board of Customs and Excise, since 1963; *b.* 12 March 1908; *s.* of J. J. Anderson, Montrose; *m.* 1933, Margery Theodora, *d.* of late H. C. Lewin; one *s.* one *d.* *Educ.:* Rugby Sch.; Christ's Coll., Camb. Civil Service (Scottish Office), 1931; Private Sec. to Parliamentary Under-Sec. of State, 1934-36; Principal, 1936; Asst. Sec., 1942; Under-Sec., 1948; Deputy-Secretary Scottish Home Department, 1953-56; Secretary, Department of Health for Scotland, 1956-1959; Secretary, Scottish Home Department, 1959-63. Chairman of Customs' Co-operative Council, 1964. *Address:* Deep Cutting, Farnborough Hill, Kent. *T.:* Farnborough, Kent 54884. [*Died* 27 *Jan.* 1965.

ANDERSON, Rt. Rev. John Ogle, M.C. 1945; D.D.; *b.* 11 Nov. 1912; *s.* of Ven. J. Anderson, D.D., and Edith Alice More; *m.* 1941, Elizabeth Swalwell; one *s.* one *d.* *Educ.:* St. John's Coll., Winnipeg (D.D. 1949); University of Manitoba. Deacon 1936, Priest 1937. Rupert's Land, 1936; St. Anne's, Wandsworth, 1939; All Saints', Winnipeg, 1940; Chaplain to H.M. Forces, 1942; Rector St. Aidan's, Winnipeg, 1946; Dean of Rupert's Land, 1949; Dean of Ottawa, 1954; Bishop Suffragan of Rupert's Land, 1962-67; Bishop Coadjutor, 1967-69; Bishop of British Columbia, 1969. Dep. Prolocutor, General Synod, 1959. Colonel Commandant, Royal Canadian Army Chaplain Corps (Protestant), 1964. Hon. D.D. Emmanuel Coll., Toronto, 1969. *Recreation:* Canadian Legion. British Commonwealth Ex-Services League (Dominion Officer, 1950-60; Dominion Pres., 1954-56). *Address:* 227 Waverley Street, Winnipeg 9, Manitoba, Canada. *T.:* GR 4-3104. *Clubs:* Royal Canadian Military Inst. (Toronto); Manitoba (Winnipeg). [*Died Nov.* 1969.

ANDERSON, Major Joseph Ringland, M.C. 1918; attached R.A.A.F. Hqrs., 1941; Consulting Ophthalmic Surgeon, Alfred Hospital, Melbourne, Australia; Con. Ophthalmologist, R.A.A.F.; Cons. Ophthalmologist, R.A.N.; *b.* Lilydale, Victoria, 29 Oct. 1894; *s.* of Rev. J. R. Anderson, M.A., Mont Albert, Victoria; *m.* 1919, Mary, *e. d.* of R. B. McComas, 29 Mary Street, Hawthorn, and Commonwealth Bank Board; two *d.* *Educ.:* Scotch College, Melbourne; University of Melbourne, M.B., B.S. 1916. Enlisted A.I.F. Jan. 1917; served France R.M.O., 45th Bn.; acting Sqd.-Ldr. R.A.A.F., 1940-46, attached Hqrs.; postgraduate study, Edinburgh and London, 1919-21, 1950, 1954; F.R.C.S. Edinburgh, 1919; D.O.M.S. London, 1921; F.R.C.S. Australasia, 1929; M.D. Melbourne, 1934. *Publications:* Detachment of Retina, 1931; Anterior Dialysis of the Retina; Congenital Glaucoma or Hydrophthalmia; Ocular Vertical Deviations; Treatment of Nystagmus; various papers in scientific journals. *Recreation:* golf. *Address:* 108 Collins Street, Melbourne, C.1, Victoria, Australia. *T.:* M.F. 5869. *Clubs:* Melbourne, Naval and Military (Melbourne); Peninsula Country Golf (Frankston). [*Died* 14 *May* 1961.

ANDERSON, Professor Mark Louden, M.C. 1918; Professor of Forestry, Edinburgh University, since 1951; *b.* 16 April 1895; *s.* of Rev. J. C. Anderson, Kinneff, Scotland, and Jeanie (*née* Boyd); *m.* 1918, Mabel Watkins; two *s.* one *d.* *Educ.:* Edinburgh University. B.Sc. 1919, D.Sc. 1924. Served European War, Army, 1914-19. Research Officer, Forestry Commission, 1919-31; Chief Inspector and Director of Forestry, Ireland, 1931-46; Lecturer, Imperial Forestry Institute, Oxford, 1946-51. Hon. M.A. (Oxon) 1946, Member of Lincoln College. F.R.S.E. 1952. *Publications:* The Natural Woodlands of Britain and Ireland, 1932; State Control of Private Forestry in European Democracies, 1949: The Selection of Tree Species, 1950; (Ed.) Forest Trees by the 6th Earl of Haddington, 1952; (Ed.) The James Carmichael Collection of Proverbs in Scots, 1957. Various translations of text-books and papers in Forestry technical jls. *Recreations:* adagiology and etymology. *Address:* 133 Mayfield Road, Edinburgh 9. *T.:* Newington 4491. [*Died* 9 *Sept.* 1961.

ANDERSON, Lieutenant-Colonel Sir Neville, Kt., *cr.* 1947; C.B.E. 1923; *b.* 11 Jan. 1881; *s.* of late W. M. Anderson of Burghfield, Oxted, Surrey; *m.* 1906, Dorothy (*d.* 1930), *d.* of late R. Rowell, Oxford; one *s.* *Educ.:* Rugby: Oriel College, Oxford. Called to Bar, 1903; Midland Circuit; 2nd Lt. London Rifle Brigade, 1914; France, 1916-19; D.A.A.G. 1st Army Headquarters; M.B.E. 1917; O.B.E. 1918; despatches thrice; seconded for special service in Ireland with rank of Lt.-Col. 1920; Ireland, 1920-22; gazetted out of Army with rank of Lt.-Col. A Special Commissioner of Income Tax, 1919-1950; Presiding Special Commr. of Income Tax, 1946-50; retired, 1950. *Address:* 4 Ralston Street, Chelsea, S.W.3. *T.:* Flaxman 2365. *Clubs:* Brooks's; Royal St. George's Golf (Sandwich). [*Died* 7 *April* 1963.

ANDERSON, Colonel Patrick Campbell, D.S.O. 1918; M.C.; late Seaforth Highlanders; Director M. Samuel and Co. Ltd., Shell House, Bishopsgate, 1930-64; *b.* Nov. 1894; *m.* 1919, Gladys Erica, *o. d.* of Sir H. B. Abdy, 4th Bt. *Educ.:* Harrow School; R.M.C., Sandhurst. Served European War, 1914-18 (despatches, D.S.O., M.C. and bar); Belgian Croix de Guerre. War of 1939-45. *Address:* Lanchester Court, Seymour St., W.1. *Club:* White's. [*Died* 12 *Feb.* 1965.

ANDERSON, Rudolph Martin; Zoologist; Hon. Curator in Mammalogy, National Museum of Canada, from 1946; *b.* Winneshiek County, Iowa, 30 June 1876; *e. s.* of John E. and Martha Ann Johnson Anderson; *m.* 1913, M. B. Allstrand, B.A., M.A.; three *d.* (one *s.* decd.). *Educ.:* Public and High Schools; State University of Iowa; Ph.B. 1903, Ph.D. 1906; U.S. Volunteer Army (Infantry) for duration of Spanish-American War, 1898; Assistant in Zoology, Museum of Natural History, University of Iowa, 1902-6; National Guard, Iowa, Militia, 1900-6, instructor and assistant commandant Blees Military Academy, and captain National Guard of Missouri, 1906-8; explorer, field agent and assistant in mammalogy, Amer. Museum of Natural History, N.Y. City, 1908-13, explorations for Museum in N.W. Territories, Canada, and Alaska, 1908-12, for Geol. Surv. of Can., 1913-16 (zoologist, 1913-1920); Chief Div. of Biology, Nat. Museum of Canada and Consulting Zoologist, Lands, Parks and Forests Branch, Department of Mines and Resources, Ottawa, 1920-46; Chief of Southern Party of the Canadian Arctic Expedition, 1913-16, and general editor of the Government scientific reports of the expedition, 1919-48; Chairman Library Committee, Bureau of Geology and Topography and National Museum of Canada, 1920-46; Naturalist of Canadian Arctic Expedition of 1928 (Greenland and Eastern Arctic); field work in every Province and Territory of Canada; Member of Advisory Board on Wild Life Protection, Canada, 1917-46; Associate editor in Zoology, 1918-26, Canadian Field-Naturalist, Mammalogy, 1927; M.A.O.U., 1917-; Biological Soc. of Washington, 1919-; Cooper Ornithological Club of California, 1916-; Pacific Northwest Bird and Mammal Soc.; Member (charter) American Soc. of Mammalogists, 1919, Member Board of Directors, 1919-40, 1944-46; Vice-Pres. 1946; Hon. (life) Member, 1947-; Member of American Society of Ichthyologists and Herpetologists, 1937, Member Board of Governors, 1938; Member Wildlife Society, 1937-; Hon. Member, Arctic Inst. N. America, 1957; F.R.S.C., 1939; Corresponding Member Zoological Society of London, 1939, and of Société Provancher d'Histoire Naturelle du Canada, Quebec, 1940; Mason, Ancient Free and Accepted Masons, 1904-, Royal Arch Masons, 1908-. *Publications:* Birds of Iowa, 1907; Report on the Natural History Collections of the 1908-12 Arctic Expedition, 1913; Recent Explorations on the Canadian Arctic Coast, 1917; Methods of collecting and preserving vertebrate animals, Nat. Mus. Canada, Bull. 69, Biol. Ser. 18, 1932, 2nd revised ed., 1948; Mammals of Quebec, 1940; Catalogue Canadian Recent Mammals, National Museum of Canada, Bull. No. 102, Biol. Ser. 31, 1946 (issued 1947); zool. ed. names of fur and fur-bearing animals Webster's Internat. Dict.; contributions to Encyclopædia Britannica and many scientific journals and bulletins. Knight Officer of International Order of St. Hubert, Vienna, 1951. *Recreations:* Arctic research, natural history. *Address:* National Museum of Canada, and 58 Government Driveway, Ottawa, Canada. [*Died* 21 *June* 1961.

ANDERSON, Stanley, C.B.E. 1951; R.A. 1941 (A.R.A. 1934); R.E.; *b.* 11 May 1884; *m.* 1910, Lilian Phelps, London; two *s.* *Educ.:* Merchant Venturers Technical College, and Municipal School of Art, Bristol; Roy. Coll. of Art, and Goldsmiths' Coll. of

Art, London. Much against his will, apprenticed to father's business as a heraldic engraver at the age of 15; not able to take up art seriously until 1909; won The British Institution Etching Scholarship and came to London, 1909. Has exhibited paintings and line engravings at the principal galleries in England and Scotland, including the International Society, National Portrait Society, Vienna, Hamburg, and Dresden, and has held shows in U.S.A.; works acquired by Print Room, British Museum, Victoria and Albert Museum, National Portrait Gallery, Bradford Art Gallery, Bristol Art Gallery, National Gallery Australia, California State Library, Southport Art Gallery, Manchester Art Gallery, Fitzwilliam Museum, Cambridge, the Art Galleries of Hereford, Rochdale, Bradford, Exeter, Cheltenham, Sheffield, etc.; Ashmolean Museum, Oxford (collection of his prints and drawings presented by Arthur Mitchell, Esq., 1963); Chicago Art Institute, and Prague Museum, Adelaide, Birmingham, and Sydney Art Galleries, Museum of Modern Art, Venice, chief Art Galleries in the U.S.A. and National Museum, Stockholm; chosen by the British Council as sole representative of British Line Engraving and dry point at Venice Biennial International Art Exhibition, 1938; retrospective exhibition of his prints and drawings at Cheltenham Art Gallery, 1949; twice winner of The International Medal and first prize, Chicago Soc. of Etchers International Exhibition, 1931 and 1934; winner of Silver Medal, Los Angeles International Exhibition, 1932; awards at the National Academy, U.S.A., 1946. Member of the Engraving faculty, British School at Rome, 1930-52. *Recreations:* lawn tennis and billiards. *Address:* Darobey, Church Lane, Chearsley, Nr. Aylesbury, Bucks. *Club:* Arts. [*Died* 4 *March* 1966.

ANDERSON, Brig. Thomas Stephen James, C.B.E. 1946 (O.B.E. 1944); M.A.; Controller of Manpower Development, Vickers Ltd., since 1962; *b.* Dublin, 3 November 1909; 2nd *s.* of late Rev. Wm. Anderson, M.A.; *m.* 1938, Elizabeth Johnston, *yr. d.* of late Wm. Baird, Lurgan, N. Ireland; two *s.* *Educ.:* Mountjoy School, Dublin; Trinity Coll., Dublin. Asst. Master, Stamford School, 1933-39; Teacher of Mathematics, Stamford Technical School, 1933-39; embodied Royal Lincolnshire Regt. T.A., Aug. 1939; B.E.F. France, Mar-June 1940; M.E.F., Oct. 1942-March 1946 (C.B.E.). External Registrar, University of London, 1946-48; Director of Studies, R.M.A., Sandhurst, 1948-62. Member Board of Governors, Welbeck College, 1952-62. University of London's Representative on Governing Body of St. Albans School, and Trustees of Kentish's Educational Foundation; Mem. Advisory Council of Overseas Services Resettlement Bureau. *Recreations:* golf, swimming. *Address:* Windlemere, Westwood Road, Windlesham, Surrey. *T.:* Ascot 656. [*Died* 30 *June* 1969.

ANDERSON, Sir William (Hewson), Kt. 1965; C.B.E. 1950; J.P.; retired; *b.* 13 March 1897; *s.* of Rev. W. A. S. Anderson, B.A.; *m.* 1922, Elizabeth Catherine Shea; two *s.* one *d.* *Educ.:* Fort Street High School, Sydney; Sydney University (B.Ec.). Shell Company of Australia Ltd., 1920-57; Member of the Board, Reserve Bank of Australia, 1959-. Federal President of the Liberal Party of Australia, 1951-56. *Recreation:* golf. *Address:* 87 Kerferd Street, East Malvern, Melbourne, Australia. *Clubs:* Athenæum, Savage (Melbourne). [*Died* 25 *March* 1968.

ANDREAE, Herman Anton; Banker from 1897; Formerly Partner and Director Kleinwort Sons & Co. Ltd., Bankers, 1948-1961, retd.; *b.* 2 Sept. 1876; 2nd *s.* of John Charles Andreae and Sophie Charlotte Kleinwort; *m.* 1st, 1904, Christiana Candida (*née* Ahrens); 2nd, 1934, Joy Amelia (*née* Hounsell); one *s.* three *d.* (and one *s.* decd.). *Educ.:* Dulwich College; privately and abroad. Master of Hampshire Hunt, 1944-52. Grand Cross Merito Civil (Spain). *Recreations:* yachting, hunting. *Address:* Moundsmere Manor, Basingstoke, Hants. *T.:* Preston Candover 207. *Clubs:* Boodle's; Royal Yacht Squadron. [*Died* 9 *Sept.* 1965.

ANDREW, Ian Graham, M.A.; *b.* 6 Sept. 1893; *s.* of Rev. John Graham Andrew, M.A., and Isabella Ironside; *m.* Elizabeth May, *y. d.* of Alfred Smith, O.B.E., Woodworth, Keighley; two *s.* *Educ.:* Glasgow High School and Glasgow University. Enlisted in Cameron Highlanders, Sept. 1914; 2nd Lieut. 5th Scottish Rifles, 1916; Senior Supervising Officer, Physical and Recreational Training, North of Ireland, with rank of Captain, 1918; wounded at Loos, 1915 and Arras, 1916; graduated with Honours in English and Philosophy, 1919 (Glasgow University); Rector of Elgin Academy, 1922-33; Headmaster, Robert Gordon's Coll., Aberdeen, 1933-43; Headmaster, George Watson's Coll., Edinburgh, 1943-53; Chairman of Society in Scotland for Propagating Christian Knowledge (S.S.P.C.K.); Vice-President The School Library Assoc.; Convener of Education Cttee. of Highlands and Islands Education Trust; Vice-Chairman Scottish Old People's Welfare Cttee. Officier d'Académie Française, 1951. *Address:* 35 Barnshot Road, Colinton, nr. Edinburgh. *T.:* Colinton 2224. [*Died* 22 *May* 1962.

ANDREW, Sir John, K.B.E. 1963 (C.B.E. 1957); sheep-farmer; *b.* 19 Aug. 1896; *s.* of David Andrew; *m.* 1944, Joan Margaret, *d.* of William Mathewson; two *s.* two *d.* *Educ.:* Mosgiel District High School. Director, Primary Producers' Co-operative Society; Member, New Zealand Meat Producers' Board; President, Sheep-farmers' Federation; formerly President, Federated Farmers of New Zealand and International Federation of Agricultural Producers. Served European War, 1914-18 in Palestine, with New Zealand Mounted Rifles. *Address:* Box 12, Hyde, Central Otago, New Zealand. [*Died* 5 *Aug.* 1968.

ANDREW, John Harold, D.Sc.; Professor of Metallurgy, and Dean of the Faculty of Metallurgy, Sheffield University, 1932-50; Emeritus Professor since 1950; *b.* 14 Jan. 1887; *s.* of John Andrew; *m.* 1915, Sarah Elsie, *d.* of H. K. Shaw. *Educ.:* Manchester University (1st class honours in Chemistry, M.Sc., Dalton Scholar). Research Fellow and Demonstrator, 1910; Carnegie Scholar, Iron and Steel Institute (Bessemer Gold Medal for 1949); Chief of the Metallurgical Research Department of Sir W. G. Armstrong, Whitworth & Co., Ltd., Manchester, 1914-20; Professor of Metallurgy, Royal Technical College, Glasgow, 1920-32. *Address:* Sea Tor, West Shore, Llandudno, N. Wales. [*Died* 5 *May* 1961.

ANDREW, Brig. Leslie Wilton, V.C. 1917; D.S.O. 1942; i.d.c.; retd., as Comdr. Central Mil. District, N.Z.; *b.* 23 March 1897; *s.* of William Jeffrey Andrew and Francis Hannah MacNeil; *m.* 1918, Bessie, 2nd *d.* of T. Ball, Brinsley, Notts; two *s.* two *d.* *Educ.:* Ashhurst State School; Wanganui District High School and Wanganui Collegiate School. Served in the N.Z. Expeditionary Force during European War, 1914-18; New Zealand Staff Corps, Oct. 1919; served in Egypt, France, Belgium, and India; commanded 22nd Bn., 2nd New Zealand Expeditionary Force, 1940; Middle East, 1941-42 (despatches, D.S.O.). *Recreations:* Rugby football, rowing, swimming. *Address:* 47 King's Drive, Levin, Manawatu, New Zealand. *Club:* Levin (N.Z.). [*Died* 8 *Jan.* 1969.

ANDREW, Colonel Richard Hynman, C.B.E. 1941; M.C.; Solicitor 1910; *b.* 2 May 1885; *er. s.* of Rev. Canon Henry Andrew, Griston, Norfolk; *m.* 1915, Aline, *e. d.* of Sir Henry F. Jervis-White-Jervis, 5th Bt.; two *d.* *Educ.:* Haileybury; Jesus College, Cambridge. Served European War, 1914-19; B.E.F., 1914-17; E.E.F., 1917-19; (despatches thrice, O.B.E., M.C., Order of the Nile 3rd Class); War of 1939-45: M.E.F., 1940-42; Persia-Iraq Force, 1942-43 (despatches thrice, C.B.E.). *Address:* Buttfield, Nazeing, Essex. *T.:* Nazeing 2130. *Clubs:* Oxford and Cambridge; Royal Harwich Yacht. [*Died* 26 *Jan.* 1964.

ANDREW, Rev. Canon William Shaw, M.C. 1918; M.A.; D.D. (Hon.) St. Andrews, 1952; *b.* 6 Feb. 1884; *s.* of Robert Andrew and Lucy Shaw, Sheffield; *m.* 1st, 1917, Gladys Barnard Barnard-Smith; 2nd, 1945, Margaret Simpson Baker-Jones. *Educ.:* Sheffield Grammar School; Wadham College, Oxford (Classical Exhib.); Bishop's Hostel, Liverpool. 2nd Cl. Class. Mods. 1905; B.A. (3rd Cl. Lit. Hum.) 1907; M.A. 1910; Deacon, 1908; Priest, 1909; Curate, St. Luke Evang., Walton-on-the-Hill, Liverpool, 1908-11; Beccles, 1911-17; T.C.F., 1917-19; Hon. C.F., 1920; Rector, Boxford, with Hadleigh Hamlet, 1919-32; Rural Dean of Hadleigh, 1924-32; Rector Ingham, with Culford, Timworth, and Culford Heath, 1932-35; Exam. Chap. to Bp. of St. Andrews, 1941-56 and to Bp. of Moray, 1949-56. Rector of St. Andrews, St. Andrews, 1935; Canon, 1943; Dean of Dio. of St. Andrews, Dunkeld, and Dunblane, 1943-59, Hon. Canon, 1959. King Haakon VII Liberty Medal, 1947. *Address:* The Old Farm, Amport, nr. Andover, Hants. [*Died* 19 *July* 1963.

ANDREWS, Sir Ernest Herbert, Kt., *cr.* 1950; C.B.E. 1946; retd. Mayor of the City of Christchurch, New Zealand, 1941-50; Chairman: Prudential Building and Investment Society, since 1932; Canterbury Terminating Building Society; *b.* Nelson, N.Z., 25 June 1873; *s.* of late Thomas Andrews; *m.* 1st, 1900, Caroline (*d.* 1937), *d.* of late E. H. Couzins, Christchurch; two *s.* one *d.*; 2nd, 1951, Florence May Emmett. *Educ.:* Ashburton Public Schools; Normal Training College, Christchurch, New Zealand; Canterbury University College, Christchurch. Teacher in Primary and Secondary Schools in Ashburton, Christchurch, Hastings, Nelson, 1890-1907; founded printing and publishing business of Andrews, Baty & Co. Ltd., Christchurch. City Councillor of Christchurch 1919- (Chairman of committees and Deputy Mayor); Chm. of Christchurch Tramways Board, 1930-36; Member: Christchurch Unemployment Committee; Christchurch Fire Board; Governor of Christchurch Technical College; Member Canterbury Board of Education for 18 years (several terms Chm.); Founder, S. Island Local Bodies' Assoc. (10 yrs. Pres., now Life mem.); Pres. S. Island Publicity Assoc.; Life mem. Canterbury Progress League. J.P. New Zealand. During War of 1939-45, was District Controller, Emergency Precautions Service. Jubilee medal, 1935. *Publications:* N.Z. Road Guide, 1912; Quaint Characters, 1952; Local Centennial Histories, 1953; Eventful Years, 1958. *Recreation:* representative cricketer in younger days. *Address:* 464 Armagh Street, Christchurch, N.Z. [*Died* 9 *Nov.* 1961.

ANDREWS, James Peter, C.B.E. 1964; D.Sc.; *b.* 18 Mar. 1902; *s.* of John Andrews and Emily Sarah (*née* Drake); *m.* 1925, Ruth Cohen; one *s.* *Educ.:* Leyton County High Sch.; Queen Mary Coll., Univ. of London (B.Sc. 1st Cl. Hons. Physics, 1921; D.Sc. 1931). Research Asst., British Cotton Industry Research Assoc., Didsbury, 1922; Lecturer in Physics, Queen Mary College, 1922-1934; Professor of Physics, Ceylon Univ. Coll., 1934-37; research under Prof. Sir E. V. Appleton, at Cavendish Lab., Cambs., 1937-39; Scientific Officer, Admiralty, 1939; Head of Physics Dept., Bradford Technical Coll., 1939-44; Asst. Prof. of Physics, Queen Mary Coll., 1944-49; Prof. of Physics, Univ. Coll., Ibadan, Nigeria, 1949-52; Principal Kumasi Coll. of Technology, 1952-54; Prof. of Physics, Makerere Coll., 1954-62; Dep. Principal, 1962-64; Emeritus Prof. of Physics, 1964. Acting Principal, Malta College of Arts, Sciences and Technology, Malta, 1967; retired. Chairman, West African Examinations Council, 1953. *Publications:* some 25 in Proc. Physical Soc., Philosophical Magazine, and other Physical Jls. *Recreation:* sketching. *Address:* 15 Round Hill Road, Torquay, Devon. [*Died* 25 *Nov.* 1968.

ANDREWS, John Alban, M.C., M.B., Ch.B. Edin., F.R.C.S. Eng.; Hon. Consulting Surgeon: St. Peter's Hospital for Stone, London; Genito-Urinary Department Queen Mary's Hospital for the East End; Senior Fellow Assoc. of Surgeons of Great Britain and Ireland; late Hon. Surgeon Association Retired Naval Officers; Member International Urological Association and British Association of Urological Surgeons; *m.* 1st, Sarah Helen Davies, M.B., B.S., London (*d.* 1949); two *d.*; 2nd, Ruth Catherine Townshend, M.B., B.S. Lond., D.P.H. *Educ.:* Dean Close School, Cheltenham; Edinburgh University; King's College, London. House Physician, Edinburgh Royal Infirmary; Demonstrator Anatomy, Edinburgh University; Sen. Res. Med. Officer, Royal Free Hospital, London; Res. Surgic. Officer, St. Peter's Hospital; Capt. R.A.M.C. att. 2nd Bn. Gren. Gds. (M.C., despatches). *Address:* 100 Outram Road, Croydon, Surrey. [*Died* 14 *Aug.* 1964.

ANDREWS, John Launcelot; *b.* 18 Dec. 1893; *s.* of Launcelot Andrews and Maud Wisden; *m.* 1929, Bertha Margaret Happold; one *s.* one *d.* *Educ.:* Rugby School; Peterhouse, Cambridge (Exhibitioner). 1st Div. Class II Historical Tripos Part I; served European War, 1914-19; Capt. 5th Hampshire Regt. (T.F.) and 72nd Punjabis, Indian Army; Staff Capt. 1st Peshawar Infantry Brigade (Khyber Movable Column), 1916-17; Palestine E.E.F., 1917-18 (wounded), passed Home Civil Service Examination, 1919; Assistant Principal, Board of Education, 1920-21; Temp. Assistant Master, Rugby School, 1922; Assistant Master, Marlborough College, 1923-27; Headmaster, Exeter School, 1927-49. *Recreations:* cricket, tennis, walking, archæology, modern languages. *Address:* 1 Manston Terrace, Exeter. *T.:* 7/3334. [*Died* 18 *Aug.* 1968.

ANDREWS, Rear-Admiral Robert Walter Benjamin, C.B. 1930; retd., 1931; *b.* 24 March 1876; *s.* of late Robert Henry Andrews, Engineer Manager, H.M. Dockyard, Devonport, of Elburton Cross, South Devon; *m.* 1902, Edith Margaret Hunter, *d.* of James Davisson, late of Rochester; four *s.* *Educ.:* Sir Joseph Williamson's Mathematical School, Rochester; Naval Engineering College, Devonport. Assistant Engineer Empress of India, 1895-1900; Engineer, Wildfire, 1901-03; Senior Engineer Queen, 1903-06; at Armstrong, Whitworth & Co., Elswick Works and Naval Ordnance Dept., Admiralty, 1907-10; Engineer Lieutenant and Eng. Lt. Commander, Lyra, 1911-1913; Gun Mounting Overseer, Coventry Ord. Works, 1913-17; Engineer Officer Agamemnon and Lord Nelson Flagship, Eastern Mediterranean and Black Sea, 1917-1919; Engineer Inspector, Naval Ordnance Dept. Admiralty, 1919-21; Engineer Officer, Revenge, 2nd Flagship Atlantic Fleet, 1921-1922; Eng. Captain, 1922; Gun Mounting Overseer Messrs. Armstrong, Whitworth &

Co., Elswick, Newcastle up on Tyne during construction of the gun machinery of Nelson and Rodney and 8-inch cruisers, 1922-27; Senior Engineer Inspector, Naval Ordnance Dept., Admiralty, 1927-31; Eng. Rear Admiral 1928; Admiralty Regional Officer (Northern), 1940-46. President, British Sailors' Soc., 1930-65. *Address:* c/o Mrs. Earnhsaw, 19 Morton Road, Exmouth, Devon. [*Died* 7 *June* 1965.

ANDREWS, Roland Stuart, C.M.G. 1957; DSc., M.I.Chem.E., F.R.A.C.I.; F.Inst.F.; F.A.A.; Chairman and Managing Director, Gas and Fuel Corporation of Victoria, since 1952; *b.* Granville, N.S.W., 27 Sept. 1897; *s.* of T. J. Andrews, Lindfield, N.S.W.; *m.* 1926, Kathleen May, *d.* of W. A. F. Waitt, Lindfield, N.S.W.; two *s.* *Educ.:* Sydney Technical High School; Sydney Univ. Chemist and Plant Engineer, Broken Hill Proprietary Co. Ltd., Newcastle, N.S.W., 1919-25; Head Teacher of Chemistry, Sydney Technical Coll., 1925-27; Chief Chemist, Metropolitan Gas Co., Melbourne, 1927-50; Chief Technical Officer, Gas and Fuel Corp., 1950-51. Chm. Coal Utilization Cttee., 1945; Pres. Vic. Branch, Aust. Chem. Inst., 1946-47; Chm. Victoria Cttee., C.S.I.R., 1950; Pres. Australian Gas Inst., 1950. *Publications:* Coal Utilization Research, Vols. I and II, 1945; technical articles. *Address:* 1499 High Street, Glen Iris, Victoria, Australia. *Clubs:* Australian, Athenæum (Melbourne, Vic.). [*Died* 14 *Oct.* 1961.

ANEY, Madhao Shrihari, B.A., B.L.: Padmavibhushan, 1968; *b.* 29 Aug. 1880; *m.* 1898, S. Yamunabai (*d.* 1925); two *s.* *Educ.:* Morris College, Nagpur. Teacher, Kashibai Private High School, Amraoti, 1904-7; joined Bar, 1908, at Yeotmal; Vice-Pres. Indian Home Rule League; President, Berar Provincial Congress Committee, 1921-1930; joined Civil Disobedience Movement; Acting President, Indian National Congress, 1933; M.L.A. for Berar, 1924-26, 1927-30, and 1935; Member Congress Working Committee, 1924-25 and 1931-34; Member, for Indians Overseas, of Executive Council of Governor-General, 1941-43; Representative of Govt. of India in Ceylon, 1943-47; Governor of Bihar, 1948-52. Founded Yeotmal District Assoc., 1916; Member Nehru Committee; Vice-Pres., Responsivist Party; General Secretary, Congress Nationalist Assembly Party, 1935; Leader, Congress Nationalist Assembly Group, 1935; General Secretary, Anti-Communal Award Conference of Working Committee, 1935. Member Lok Sabha, to 1967. Member of Nagpur University Court since 1935 and of Hindu University Court, Benares, since 1938. Hon. D.Lit., Benares Hindu University; LL.D., Nagpur University. *Publications:* Speeches and Writings, 1931; Speeches as Governor of Bihar, 1948-52; Mahrinja Memorial Lectures II of the Benares Hindu Univ., 1966. *Address:* c/o D. M. Aney, Member Industrial Tribunal, Bel Haven, New Marine Lines, Bombay 1, India. [*Died* 26 *Jan.* 1968.

ANGELL, Sir Norman, Kt. 1931; LL.D.; author and lecturer; *b.* 26 Dec. 1874; *s.* of late Thomas Angell Lane, J.P., Mansion House, Holbeach. *Educ.:* privately; Lycée de St. Omer, France; Geneva. Youth passed in Western America, first ranching and prospecting, and later in newspaper work; returned to Europe, 1898, as correspondent various American newspapers; Editor, Galignani's Messenger, 1899-1903; staff of Eclair, Paris, 1903-5; General Manager Paris Daily Mail, 1905-14; Editor, Foreign Affairs, 1928-1931; M.P. (Lab.) North Bradford, 1929-31; Member of the Council of Royal Institute of International Affairs, 1928-42; Co-Pres., Comité mondial contre la guerre et le fascism. Nobel Peace Prize for 1933. Inventor of The Money Game, a series of card games which teach the principles of elementary economics, particularly of banking and currency. *Publications:* Patriotism under Three Flags, 1903; Europe's Optical Illusion, 1909; The Great Illusion, 1910; Peace Theories and the Balkan War, 1912; The Foundations of International Polity, 1914; Prussianism and its Destruction, 1914; America and the New World State: A Plea for American Leadership in International Organization, 1915; The World's Highway, 1915 (in America); The Dangers of Half-Preparedness, 1916 (in America); Why Freedom Matters, 1916; War Aims, 1917; The Political Conditions of Allied Success, 1918; The Economic Chaos and the Peace Treaty, 1919; The Fruits of Victory, 1921; If Britain is to Live, 1923; Must Britain Travel the Moscow Road?, 1926; The Public Mind, Its Disorders: Its Exploitation, 1926; The Story of Money, 1930; Can Governments Cure Unemployment?, 1931 (with Harold Wright); The Unseen Assassins, 1932; The Press and the Organisation of Society, 1933; The Great Illusion, 1933, 1933; From Chaos to Control, 1933; The Menace to Our National Defence, 1934; Preface to Peace, 1935; The Money Mystery, 1936; The Money Game, 1936; This Have and Have-not Business, 1936; The Defence of the Empire, 1937; Peace with the Dictators?, 1938; You and the Refugee (with Dorothy Buxton), 1939; For What do we Fight?, 1939; America's Dilemma, 1940; Let the People Know, 1943; The Steep Places, 1947; After All, 1951; Defence and the English-Speaking Rôle, 1958. The Great Illusion has appeared in England, America, France, Germany, Holland, Denmark, Sweden, Spain, Italy, Russia, Japan, and China, as well as in Hindi, Bengali, Urdu, Marathi, and Tamil. *Recreation:* small yacht cruising. *Address:* The Stone Cottage, Fernden Hill, Haslemere, Surrey. *T.:* Haslemere 2710. [*Died* 7 *Oct.* 1967.

ANNALY, 4th Baron (*cr.* 1863), **Luke Henry White;** late 11th Hussars; *b.* 7 Aug. 1885; *s.* of 3rd Baron Annaly and Hon. Lilah Georgiana Augusta Constance Agar-Ellis (*d.* 1944), *d.* of 3rd Viscount Clifden; *S.* father, 1922; *m.* 1919, Lady Lavinia Spencer (*d.* 1955), 2nd *d.* of 6th Earl Spencer, K.G.; one *s.* one *d.* Entered Army, 1906; Captain, 1915; Major, 1921; retd., 1921; was A.D.C. to Lord Methuen in South Africa; served European War, 1914-18 (Officer Legion of Honour, M.C.). *Heir:* *s.* Hon. Luke Robert White [*b.* 15 March 1927; *m.* 1st, 1953, Lady Marye Pepys (who obtained a divorce, 1957; she died, 1958), *e. d.* of 7th Earl of Cottenham; one *s.*; 2nd, 1960, Jennifer, *d.* of Rupert Carey; two *d.*]. *Address:* 37 Pattison Road, N.W.2. *Clubs:* Turf; Kildare Street (Dublin). [*Died* 4 *May* 1970.

ANNESLEY, Capt. John Campbell, D.S.O. 1918; R.N., retd.; *b.* 2 Aug. 1895; *s.* of late William Gore Annesley; *m.* 1920, Cicely Anne Walton Craig, *d.* of late James Craig, The Glen House, Crawfordsburn, Co. Down (marriage dissolved, 1947); one *s.* *Educ.:* Eastman's, Southsea; R.N. Colleges. Served European War, 1914-19 (wounded at Zeebrugge, despatches, D.S.O., Croix de Guerre); War of 1939-45 (despatches; Royal Norwegian Order of St. Olav); retired, 1948. *Address:* c/o Coutts & Co., 440 Strand, W.C.2. [*Died* 26 *April* 1964.

ANNOIS, Leonard Lloyd, R.W.S. 1958 (A.R.W.S. 1952): artist in watercolour, lithography and fresco mural painting; *b.* Malvern, Vic., 1 July 1906; *s.* of William Alfred Annois; *m.* 1928, Mavis Martha, *d.* of Frank Henry Nunn, Melbourne; one *s.* one *d.* *Educ.:* Melbourne High School; Melbourne National Gallery Art School. Crouch Prize, 1949-50; Bendigo Prize, 1947-50; Albury Prize, 1949; W.A. Gallery Prize, 1949;

Melb. Herald Drawing Prize, 1949; Dunlop Prizes, 1950, 1953, 1954; Victorian Artists' Prize, 1959; Wholahan Prize, 1960, 1962; Maitland Prize, 1961; Wynne Prize for Water Colours, N.S.W., 1962 and 1964. Watercolours in all Aust. Nat. and Provincial Galleries, University collections, Victoria, N.S.W., W.A., Queensland and Canberra; also represented in collection of Queen Elizabeth the Queen Mother and Mertz collection, U.S.A. Murals in fresco in schools, colleges, banks and public buildings in Victoria, Canberra and Northern Territory; *official purchases:* Australian Govt., 1953, 1954, 1959; Ministry of Works, 1952. Pres. National Gallery Society of Victoria, 1960 and 1961. *Recreations:* cricket and watching cricket. *Address:* 5 Longview Rd., North Balwyn, Victoria, Australia. *T.:* WL 2040. *Clubs:* Melbourne Savage, T-Square (Pres. 1960). [*Died* 10 *July* 1966.

ANSERMET, Ernest; Commander of the Legion of Honour; Conductor; *b.* Vevey, Switzerland, 1883. Conductor Montreux Kursaal, 1912; Subscription Concerts, Geneva, 1915-18; toured with Diaghileff Ballet, from 1915, in France, Spain, England, Italy and America; founded Orchestre de la Suisse-Romande, Geneva, 1918. Mayer Lecturer, British Institute of Recorded Sound, 1963. Guest-conductor in all important concert institutions in Europe and America. *Publication:* Les Fondements de la Musique dans la Conscience Humaine (Neuchâtel, Munich). *Address:* 11 Rue Bellot, Geneva. [*Died* 20 *Feb.* 1969.

ANSTEAD, Rudolph David, C.I.E. 1927; M.A.; *b.* Wisbech, Cambridgeshire, 2 June 1876; *s.* of Walter Henry Anstead, H.M. Inspector of Schools; *m.* 1904, Louisa Lofting (*d.* 1953); no *c.* *Educ.:* Giggleswick Grammar School; Christ's College, Cambridge (Scholar and Prizeman), 2nd Class in Natural Science Tripos; Research Chemist, Barbados, British West Indies, 1901; joined the Imperial Department of Agriculture, British West Indies, as Sugar Chemist, 1902; Superintendent of Agriculture, Grenada, in same Dept., 1906; transferred to Indian Agricultural Service as Deputy Director of Agriculture, Planting Districts, 1909; Director of Agriculture, Madras Agricultural Dept., 1922-31; retired, 1931; Member Indian Coffee Market Expansion Board, 1937, retired 1946. Formerly Fellow, Madras Univ. *Publications:* various in scientific journals. *Recreations:* fives, cricket, tennis; hobby: botany and gardening. *Address:* St. Alkelda, 5 Maple Av., Bishop's Stortford. *T.:* Bishop's Stortford 520. *Club:* Royal Commonwealth Society. [*Died* 6 *Jan.* 1962.

ANSTRUTHER, Brigadier (Retd.) Alexander Meister, C.B. 1953; O.B.E. 1946; *b.* 26 July 1902; *s.* of Arthur Wellesley Anstruther, C.B.; *m.* 1939, Barbara Ivy, *d.* of H. Ashman. *Educ.:* Malvern; R.M.A., Woolwich. Commissioned as 2nd Lt. in Royal Engineers, 1923, Lt. 1925, Capt. 1934, Maj. 1939, Lt.-Col. 1941, Col. 1945, Brig. 1951. Chief Engineer Singapore District, 1947-48, Chief Engineer British Troops in Egypt, 1950-53; Chief Engineer, Western Command, U.K., 1953-56; retired 1956. Dir., Nubold Development Ltd. *Recreations:* shooting, sailing, fencing. *Address:* The Old Post Cottage, Fawley, Henley-on-Thames, Oxon. *T.:* Henley 4654. *Clubs:* Royal Ocean Racing, Special Forces. [*Died* 24 *Oct.* 1969.

ANTHONY, Herbert Douglas, M.A. (Cantab.), B.Sc., Ph.D. (Lond.), F.R.A.S.; Col. (Research) Army Education, 1949-Dec. 1951, retd.; now Extra-mural Lecturer, Reading University and London University; *b.* 24 June 1892; *s.* of Thomas Michell Anthony; *m.* 1968, Mrs. Nora Jackson. *Educ.:* Latymer Upper School, Hammersmith; Queens' College, Cambridge (Mathematical Schol. and Prizeman, Ryle Reading Prize); King's Coll., London. Loyal North Lancashire Regt. (Asst. and Acting Adjutant); Royal Engineers (Sound-ranging, Western Front); Assistant Tutor, Richmond College; Mathematical Lecturer, Westminster College; Headmaster, Elmfield School, York; Headmaster Kilburn Grammar School; Territorial Army Anti-Aircraft; Senior Military Testing Officer, W.O.S.B.; Chief Inspector, Army Education; Panel of Asst. Examiners in Mathematics, London University; Examiner, L.C.C.; Hon. Local Sec., Geography Section, British Association, York Meeting, 1932; District Comr., Boy Scouts, Selby and Richmond, Surrey; M.R.S.T., etc. *Publications:* Relativity and Religion, an inquiry into the implications of the theory of relativity with respect to religious thought, 1927; Is Christ Final?, 1929; Science and its Background, 1948 (4th edn. 1961); Sir Isaac Newton, 1960. *Recreations:* walking, swimming, motoring. *Address:* 102 Norcot Road, Tilehurst, Reading. *T.:* Reading 27194. [*Died* 10 *June* 1968.

ANTROBUS, Captain Sir Philip Humphrey, 6th Bt., *cr.* 1815; M.C.; late Irish Guards; *b.* 22 July 1876; *s.* of late R. C. Antrobus; *S.* cousin, 1939; *m.* 1919, Olive, *d.* of late Louis Dillon FitzGibbon. *Educ.:* Eton. Served European War, 1914-1919. *Heir: cousin,* Philip Coutts Antrobus [*b.* 10 April 1908; *m.* 1937, Dorothy Margaret Mary, *d.* of late Rev. W. G. Davis; two *s.* one *d.*]. *Address:* West Amesbury House, Amesbury, Wilts. *T.:* Amesbury 2260. [*Died* 11 *July* 1968.

AP ELLIS, Group Capt. Augustine C.B.E. 1925; late R.A.F.; *b.* Westerdale, 1886; *s.* of Rev. John Rathbone Ellis, Westerdale, Yorks; *m.* 1910, Mary Catherine, *d.* of Captain James White; one *s.* *Educ.:* Market Bosworth Grammar School; Worksop College. Commissioned in the London Irish, 1909; attached to the R.F.C. from the Royal Engineers, 1915; served in France, 1915-16; Air Ministry; Directorates of Training and Demobilisation, 1917-19; permanent commission R.A.F. as Squadron Leader, 1919; Headquarters Inland Area, 1919-22; in command No. 208 Squadron, 1922-23; Headquarters Iraq Command, 1924-26; Headquarters Air Defence of Great Britain, 1926-29; Directorate of Staff Duties, Air Ministry, 1929-31; Group Capt. 1931; in command No. 5 Flying Training School, 1931-32; No. 4 Flying Training School, Egypt, 1932-35; No. 6 Flying Training School, 1935-40; No. 34 S.F.T.S., 1941-1944; retired from R.A.F. 1945. Mentioned for War Service, 1918; Belgian M.C. (1st Class), 1943; Commander of Order of Orange Nassau (Holland), 1947; Military Medal of Merit, 1st Class (Czechoslovakia), 1947. *Address:* 18 Heene Way, West Worthing, Sussex. *T.:* Worthing 35485. *Club:* Royal Air Force. [*Died* 20 *Dec.* 1969.

APPLEBY, Lieut.-Col. John Pringle, C.M.G. 1945; late Postmaster-General, Ceylon, retired 1947; *b.* 27 Sept. 1891; *m.* 1917; one *s.* one *d.* Entered Post Office at Morpeth, Northumberland, 1907. Mobilised with Northumberland Hussars, Aug. 1914; served with Royal Signals until Jan. 1920; Supplementary Reserve (L. of C. Signals), 1928-44. Headquarters G.P.O., London, 1921-33; Head Postmaster, Okehampton, Devon, 1933-36; Asst. P.M.G. Ceylon, 1936-1940. *Recreations:* golf, riding. *Address:* 3 Waterpark Court, Gorseway, Sidmouth, Devon. *T.:* Sidmouth 1451. [*Died* 29 *March* 1966.

APPLEBY, Sir Robert Rowland, K.B.E., *cr.* 1942 (C.B.E. 1937); President of Robert Appleby & Co. Inc. (Exporters & Importers), New York; *b.* London, England, 26 Dec. 1887; *s.* of George William

Appleby and Esther Weatherhead; *m.* 1912, Hilda Victoria Parsons; no *c.* *Educ.:* in England. Director, Past. Pres. and Chairman of the Board of The British Empire Chamber of Commerce in the U.S.A., New York; Founder and Vice-Pres. British War Relief Soc. of U.S.A.; Member St. George's Society (Past Pres.). *Recreation:* golf. *Address:* Pelham Manor, New York. *T.A.:* Ronappleby Newyork *T.:* Plaza 7-2270. *Clubs:* Pilgrims of America, English-Speaking Union, Bankers, British, Canadian (New York); Wykagyl Country (New Rochelle, N.Y.). [*Died* 1 *July* 1966.

APPLETON, Sir Edward (Victor), G.B.E., *cr.* 1946; K.C.B., *cr.* 1941; F.R.S. 1927; M.A., D.Sc., Hon. LL.D. (Aberdeen, Birmingham, St. Andrews, London, Glasgow, Liverpool, Dalhousie (Can.); Hon. Doctor, Montreal; Hon. D.Sc. (Oxford, Brussels, Leeds, Sydney, Sheffield and Laval); Hon. Sc.D. (Camb.): Hon. Litt.D. (Cincinnati); Hon. D.Eng. (Hanover); Hon. F.R.C.S.Ed.; Hon. F.R.S.E.; Hon. M.Inst.C.E.; Hon. M.I.E.E.; Hon. M.I.Mech.E.; Hon. A.R.I.B.A.; Hon. F.R.I.C.; Hon. Member R.I.A.; Hon. Fellow of St. John's College, Cambridge; Fellow of King's College, London; Principal and Vice-Chancellor, University of Edinburgh, since 1949; *b.* 6 September 1892; *s.* of Peter Appleton, Bradford, Yorks; *m.* 1915, Jessie (*d.* 1964), *d.* of late Rev. J. Longson; two *d.*; *m.* 1965, Mrs. Helen Allison. *Educ.:* Hanson School, Bradford; St. John's Coll., Cambridge (Scholar and Exhibitioner); Natural Science Tripos, Parts I. and II. (Physics), 1913 and 1914. Served European War, 1914-18, West Riding Regt. and Capt. R.E.; Assistant Demonstrator in Experimental Physics, Cavendish Laboratory, 1920; Wheatstone Professor of Physics, University of London, 1924-36; Jacksonian Professor of Natural Philosophy, Cambridge University, 1936-1939; Secretary, Department of Scientific and Industrial Research, 1939-49. President of British Association, 1953; Pres. Radio Industry Council, 1955-57. Morris Liebmann Memorial Prizeman (1929) and Vice-President (1932) American Inst. Radio, Eng.; Hughes Medallist of Royal Society, 1933, and Royal Medallist, 1950; Faraday Medallist, Institution of Electrical Engineers, 1946; Ewing Medallist, Institute of Civil Engineers, 1949; Nobel Prize for Physics, 1947; Gunning Victoria Jubilee Prize, R.S.E. 1960; Medal of Honour, Inst. of Radio Engineers of America, 1962; Kelvin Medal (Jt. Engineering Instns. award), 1963; Keith Medal of Roy. Scottish Soc. of Arts, 1963. Hon. Freeman of Bradford, Yorks, 1947. D.L. County of City of Edinburgh. Medal of Merit (U.S.A.); Legion of Honour (France); Cross of Freedom (Norway). Commander with star, Order of Saint Olav, Class II (Norway); Knight Commander with star, Icelandic Order of Falcon. *Publications:* various original papers on electricity and the scientific problems of wireless telegraphy. *Address:* Old College, The University, Edinburgh. *Clubs:* Athenæum; Caledonian; New (Edinburgh).
[*Died* 21 *April* 1965.

APPLETON, Brigadier Gilbert Leonard, C.B. 1947; O.B.E. 1941; J.P.; p.s.c.; *b.* 24 Nov. 1894; *s.* of late Charles Sewell Appleton, Paignton, Devon; *m.* 1918, Dorothy Essington, *d.* of late William Vosper, Merafield, Plympton, Devon; no *c.* *Educ.:* Blundell's School; R.M.A., Woolwich; Staff College, Camberley. Devon R.E. (T.A.); 2nd Lieut., 1913; Captain, 1915. R.A.: 2nd Lieut. 1917 (1915); Captain 1926; Bt. Major and Major, 1935; actg. Lt.-Col. 1939; actg. Brig. 1940; Lt.-Col. 1942; Col. 1944; Brigadier, 1948. Served European War, France and Belgium, 1914-18 (3 medals); Military Secretary to Governor of Malta, 1923-26; Gen. Staff, War Office, 1930-32; Bde. Major 12th Inf. Bde., 1932-34; Gen. Staff, British West Indies, 1935-38; Gen. Staff War Office, 1938-39; G.S.O.1. and Brig. Gen. Staff, A.A. Command, 1939-42 (O.B.E.); Dep. Director R.A., War Office, 1942-44; Bde. Comdr., A.A. Command, 1944; Brig. Air Disarmament Staff, S.H.A.E.F., 1944-45 (3 medals); Brig. Flak Disarmament 2nd T.A.F. and B.A.F.O., Germany, 1945-46 (C.B.); Director of Technical Training, War Office, 1946-48; retired, 1949. County Councillor, Devon, 1954-67; County Comr., Boy Scouts, 1955-1961. J.P. 1954. Member, Council of Magistrates' Assoc. O.St.J. 1926. *Address:* Gaddon Uffculme, Cullompton, Devon. *T.:* Craddock 267. *Clubs:* United Service, Sesame. [*Died* 23 *Oct.* 1970.

APPLEYARD, Col. Kenelm Charles, C.B.E. 1940 (O.B.E. 1937); T.D. 1942; D.L. County of Durham; J.P.; Consulting Industrial Adviser; Member Advisory Committee, Industrial Estates Limited, Nova Scotia, Canada; Company Director; President of Société Birtley, Brussels; ex-Pres. Instn. of Production Engineers; *b.* 25 March 1894; *s.* of Charles Wormald and Ada Leonora Clare Appleyard; *m.* 1920, Monica Mary, *d.* of late Professor Henry Louis; one *s.* *Educ.:* St Paul's School; privately. Entered works of C. A. Parsons and Co. Ltd., 1912; later with Sir W. G. Armstrong Whitworth and Co. Ltd., as a Production Manager; Gen. Manager and Managing Dir. Birtley Co. Ltd., 1919-47; Chm. and Dir. North Eastern Trading Estates, Ltd., and Northern Director of Special Areas Reconstruction Association, 1936-48; Chairman N.E. Coast Engineering Employers Association, 1929-39; Member of the Management Board, Engineering and Allied Employers National Federation, 1929-1939. Chairman of the Central Conference; M.I.Mech.E.; A.M.I.Min.E.; Pres. Junior Institution of Engineers, 1944-45; Member of the Iron and Steel Institute, the American Institute of Mining and Metallurgical Engineers and other societies; Member of the Durham County Council, 1922-25; Chairman of Highways and Works Committee, 1922-25; Vice-Chairman Durham County Unionist Association, 1923-30; Vice-President Durham Municipal and County Federation; Member of Council N.E. Coast Development Bd.; Military Member of Durham Territorial and Air Force Assoc., 1922-51; Lt.-Col. Royal Engineers (T.A.) and C.R.E. 50th (Northumbrian) Division, 1931-36, Hon. Col. 1937-64; Bt.-Col. 1935; Col. 1937; Brig. 1939; local Maj.-Gen. 1940; Chief Engineer Field Force Component R.A.F., B.E.F., France, 1939-40 (despatches). Director of Labour Supply and International Labour Branch, Ministry of Labour, 1940-41; lent to Ministry of Works as Director of Emergency Works, 1941; Dir. of Opencast Coal Production, 1942-45; Adviser on Regional Organisation, 1945-46. Hon. Freedom, City of Halifax, Nova Scotia, Canada, 1966. *Publications:* Miners, Owners and Mysteries, 1936; numerous technical papers before instns. in this country and the United States on coal preparation and other subjects relating to mechanical problems in mining. *Recreations:* shooting, tennis, travel. *Address:* 85 Fountain House, Park Lane, W.1. *T.:* Mayfair 5371-2; Point View, Chester-le-Street, Co. Durham. *T.:* Chester-le-Street 2196; Coach Lamps, The Quillot, Burwood Park, Walton-on-Thames, Surrey. *T.:* Walton 23417. *Clubs:* Army and Navy; County (Durham). [*Died* 20 *Dec.* 1967.

APSLEY, Lady; Violet Emily Mildred Bathurst; C.B.E. 1952; President, Glos. Women's Section, British Legion, and Life Mem. Central Cttee.; Member Glos. T.A. Assoc.; Governor Royal Agricultural Coll., Cirencester, since 1944; Joint Master V.W.H. (Earl Bathurst's) Hunt 1946-56; Mem. Roy.

Inst. of Foreign Affairs, 1944-; Governor Burden Neurological Inst., 1950-60; Pres. Cirencester and Tewkesbury Conservative Assoc., 1948-; *er. d.* of late Capt. B. C. S. Meeking, Richings Park, Colnbrook, Bucks, and late Mrs. Herbert Johnson, M.B.E., Marsh Court, Stockbridge, Hants; *m.* 1923, Lord Apsley, D.S.O., M.C., M.P. (killed on active service, 1942), *e. s.* of 7th Earl Bathurst, C.M.G.; two *s.* Succeeded to Richings Park, Colnbrook, Bucks, on the death of her grandfather, 1910. V.A.D. at Marsh Court Military Hospital, European War, 1914-18. Drove in Light Car Trials; President of Southampton Women's Conservative Association, 1924-29; President Links of Empire, 1926-38; "A" certificated air pilot, 1930; County Commandant A.T.S. for Glos. 1938-39; Group Cdr. A.T.S., 1939-40 (rank of Chief Commander) senior A.T.S. Welfare Officer, County of Glos., 1940-43; Hon. Sec. A.T.S. Benevolent Fund, 1941-44; District Councillor Sodbury R.D.C., 1941-43. M.P. (C.) Central Div. of Bristol, 1943-45. Member: Films Council (Board of Trade), 1943-46; Central Council, Victoria League, 1952-54. National Chm. Women's Section, British Legion, 1942-48. Conservative and National Liberal Candidate, Bristol N.E., 1947-51; Pres. Bristol Women's Conservative Assoc., 1932-52; Pres. Women's Electrical Assoc. (Bristol Branch), retired 1950. Director of Western Airways, 1936-1955. Pres. Cirencester Drama Club; Lady of the Manor of Iver, Bucks. *Publications:* The Amateur Settlers (with Lord Apsley), 1925; To Whom the Goddess, 1932; Bridleways through History, 1936; Fox Hunters Bedside Book, 1949; articles in Country Life, Field, Light Car, etc. *Recreations:* country life, travel. *Address:* Hullasey House, Tarlton, Cirencester. *T.:* Kemble 274.
[*Died* 19 *Jan.* 1966.

ARBERRY, Arthur John, M.A., Litt.D., F.B.A.; Sir Thomas Adams's Professor of Arabic, University of Cambridge, since 1947; *b.* 12 May 1905; *y. s.* of late William Arberry, R.N., Portsmouth; *m.* 1932, Sarina Simons, Braila, Roumania; one *d.* *Educ.:* Portsmouth Grammar School; Pembroke College, Cambridge (Senior Scholar). 1st Class, Classical Trip. Pt. I, 1925, 1st Class, Classical Trip., Pt. II (with distinction in Literature), 1927, 1st Class, Oriental Languages Tripos, Pts. I and II, 1929; Sir William Browne Medallist, E. G. Browne Scholar, 1927; Wright Student, 1929; Senior Goldsmiths' Student, 1930: Fellow of Pembroke College, 1931; Head of Dept. of Classics, Cairo Univ., 1932; Asst. Librarian, India Office, 1934; seconded to: W.O. (Postal Censorship) 1939; M.O.I., 1940; Prof.: of Persian, Univ. of London, 1944; of Arabic, Univ. of London, and Head of Near and Middle East Dept., School of Oriental and African Studies, 1946; Corr. mem. of the Egyptian and Persian Academy, Arab Academy of Damascus; Vice-Pres.: Unesco Translations Cttee.; British Inst. of Persian Studies; Chairman, Middle East Centre, Cambridge. Hon. D.Litt. (Malta), 1963; Nishan-i Danish, 1st Class (Iran), 1964. *Publications:* Majnun Layla, 1933; ed. al-Kalabadhi, Kitab al-Ta'arruf, 1934; Niffari, Mawaqif and Mukhatabat, 1935; The Doctrine of the Sufis, 1935; Catalogue of Arabic MSS. in the India Office Library, Vol. II, Pt. 2, 1936; Poems of a Persian Sufi, 1937; ed. al-Muhasibi, Kitab al-Tawahhum, 1937; Kharraz, the Book of Truthfulness, 1937; Catalogue of Persian Books in the India Office Library, 1937; The Library of the India Office, 1938; 'Iraqi, The Book of Lovers, 1939; Specimens of Arabic and Persian Palaeography, 1939; The Muslim Attitude to the War, 1940; British Contributions to Persian Studies, 1942; British Orientalists, 1943; co-editor, Islam To-day, 1943; Introduction to the History of Sufism, 1943; Modern Persian Reader, 1944; Kings and Beggars, 1945; Asiatic Jones, 1946; Fifty Poems of Hafiz, 1947; The Tulip of Sinai, 1947; Pages from the Kitab al-Luma', 1947; The Cambridge School of Arabic, 1948; Immortal Rose, 1948; Ruba'iyat of Omar Khayyam, 1949; Ruba'iyat of Jalal al-Din Rumi, 1949; Persian Psalms, 1949; Spiritual Physick of Rhazes, 1950; Modern Arabic Poetry, 1950; Sufism, 1951; Avicenna on Theology, 1951; Omar Khayyám, a New Version, 1952; Second Suppl. Handlist of Muhammadan MSS. in Cambridge, 1952; Ring of the Dove, 1953; Holy Koran, 1953; Moorish Poetry, 1953; Mysteries of Selflessness, 1953; (ed.) Legacy of Persia, 1953; Scheherezade, 1953; Persian Poems, 1954; Handlist of Arabic MSS., Chester Beatty Library, 7 vols., 1955-64; The Koran Interpreted, 1955; Salaman and Absal, 1956; Reason and Revelation in Islam, 1957; The Seven Odes, 1957; Classical Persian Literature, 1958; Romance of Rubáiyát, 1959; Maltese Anthology, 1960; Oriental Essays, 1960; Discourses of Rumi, 1961; Tales from the Masnavi, 1961; Dun Karm, Poet of Malta 1961; (ed.) Catalogue of Persian MSS., Chester Beatty Library, 1962; More Tales from the Masnavi, 1963; Humay-nama, 1963; Aspects of Islamic Civilization, 1964; Arabic Poetry, 1965; Javid-nama, 1966; Muslim Saints and Mystics, 1966; Poems of al-Mutanabbi, 1967; The Koran Illuminated, 1967; Mystical Poems of Rumi, 1968; (ed.) Religion in the Middle East, 1969; A Sufi Martyr, 1969; articles in learned journals and encyclopædias. *Address:* 12 Gurney Way, Cambridge. *T.:* Cambridge 57484.
[*Died* 2 *Oct.* 1969.

ARBUCKLE, Sir William (Forbes), K.B.E. 1961; C.B. 1956; F.R.S.E. 1963; Secretary, Scottish Education Department, 1957-1963, retd.; *b.* Edinburgh, 30 August 1902 *s.* of William Arbuckle and Grace Forbes; *m.* 1950, Flora May Inch; no *c.* *Educ.:* Daniel Stewart's College, Edinburgh; Edinburgh University; Merton College, Oxford. H.M. Inspector of Schools, Scottish Educn. Dept., 1931; seconded to Dept. of Health for Scotland, 1939-43; Asst. Sec., 1941; Asst. Sec., Scottish Educn. Dept., 1943; Under-Secretary, 1952-57. Trustee, National Museum of Antiquities of Scotland, 1964; Chm. Scottish National Camps Association, 1965. *Recreation:* hill-walking. *Address:* 1 Murrayfield Gdns., Edinburgh, 12. *T.:* DONaldson 4849. *Club:* New (Edinburgh).
[*Died* 3 *May* 1966.

ARBUTHNOT, Brigadier Alexander George, C.M.G. 1917; D.S.O. 1914; late R.F.A.; Major, 2nd Batt. Somerset Home Guard, 1940-44; *b.* 30 Nov. 1873; *s.* of late Gen. Sir Charles Arbuthnot, G.C.B., Col. Commandant, R.A.; *m.* 1905, Olive Mary Hay, *d.* of Col. W. H. Burton, R.E. *Educ.:* Marlborough; Woolwich. Entered Army, 1893; Captain, 1900; Adjutant, 1904-07; Major, 1910; Col., 1920; Col. Comdt., 1924; Comdg. R.A., Highland Div., 1923, 1st Div., 1924-28; Dist. Comdt., Kenya Defence Force, 1928-33; served European War, 1914-19 (despatches five times, severely wounded Ypres, 1917; Order of Karageorge, 1916; D.S.O., C.M.G.); retired pay, 1929. *Publications:* Contributor to Sportsman's Book for India, 1904, and Big Game Hunting in Himalayas, 1921. *Recreations:* big game hunting, racing, hunting. *Address:* Carrig-Uis-Nach, Ballycastle, Co. Antrim, N. Ireland.
[*Died* 3 *May* 1961.

ARBUTHNOT, Robert Wemyss Muir, M.C. 1917; Merchant Banker; *b.* 1889; *s.* of Robert George Arbuthnot; *m.* 1915, Mary Coghill; one *s.* two *d.* *Educ.:* Eton; Trinity College, Cambridge. Director: Arbuthnot Latham & Co. Ltd.; Demodera Tea Co. Ltd.; John K. Gilliat & Co. Ltd.; Served European War, 1914-18, Captain; French Croix de Guerre, 1917. *Address:* The

Old House, Catcott, Near Bridgwater, Somerset. *Club:* Brooks's. [*Died* 10 *Jan.* 1962.

ARBUTHNOTT, 15th Viscount of, *cr.* 1641; **Maj.-General Robert Keith Arbuthnott,** C.B. 1945; C.B.E. 1944; D.S.O. 1938; M.C.; Lord Lieutenant of Kincardineshire since 1961; *b.* 21 Aug. 1897; *s.* of John Campbell Arbuthnott, C.I.E.; *S.* cousin, 1960; *m.* 1924, Ursula *d.* of late Sir William Collingwood, K.B.E.; three *s.* one *d.* *Educ.:* Fettes; Sandhurst. Joined Black Watch, 1915; Lieut. 1917; Capt. 1924; Maj. 1938; Lt.-Colonel, 1944; Colonel, 1945; subst. rank of Maj.-Gen. Dec. 1946 antedated to Apr. 1945; retired, 1952. Served European War, 1916-18 (despatches, M.C., wounded); Palestine, 1938 (D.S.O.); Italy, 1943-45 (C.B.E., C.B.); Commander 78 Inf. Div., 1944-46; Chief of British Military Mission to Egyptian Army, 1946-47; Chief of Staff, Scottish Command, 1948-49; Commander 51st Highland Div and Highland Dist., 1949-52. Colonel of The Black Watch, 1960-1964. D.L. Kincardineshire, 1959. Comdr. Legion of Merit (U.S.A.). *Heir:* *s.* Master of Arbuthnott, D.S.C. *Address:* Arbuthnott House, Laurencekirk, Kincardineshire. [*Died* 15 *Dec.* 1966.

ARCHER, His Honour Francis Kentdray, Q.C. 1923; retired; *b.* 1882; *m.* 1906, *d.* of F. S. Champion, Burgess Hill; one *s.* *Educ.:* St. Peter's, Adelaide; London University, LL.B. Called to Bar, Lincoln's Inn, 1912; Bencher, 1925. Judge of County Courts (Circuit No. 50), 1937-54, retired Nov. 1954. *Address:* Church Street, Uckfield, Sussex. [*Died* 23 *June* 1962.

ARCHER, Sir Geoffrey (Francis), K.C.M.G., *cr.* 1920 (C.M.G. 1913); *b.* 1882; 2nd *s.* of Bradley Archer, Somers Place, Hyde Park, W.; *m.* 1916, Olive Mary, *e. d.* of late Colonel Charles Bulkeley Godman, Woldringfold, Horsham. Entered Colonial Civil Service as Assistant Collector, East Africa Protectorate, 1902; attached Secretariat; District Commissioner, 1907; Officer in Charge, Northern Frontier, 1911; sent to Somaliland to administer Government, 1912; Deputy Commissioner, Somaliland, 1913; Commissioner and Commander-in-Chief, 1914; present at action at Shimber Berris, 1915 (African General Service medal and clasp); Member of British Mission at Coronation of the Empress Zauditu of Abyssinia; awarded Cuthbert Peak Grant by the Royal Geographical Society in 1918 for surveys in East Africa connecting Major Gwynn's Abyssinian triangulation with the triangulation of East Africa; Governor, 1919; directed operations against Mullah, 1920, resulting in the destruction of the Dervish power in Somaliland (K.C.M.G., clasp to A.G.S. medal); Governor and Commander-in-Chief, Uganda, 1922-24; Governor-General of the Sudan, Dec. 1924-26; has Grand Cordon of Star of Ethiopia (1917) and of Egyptian Order of Ismail (1926). *Publications:* The Birds of British Somaliland and the Gulf of Aden (with Eva M. Godman), 2 Vols., 1938, 2 Vols., 1960; Personal and Historical Memoirs of an East African Administrator, 1964. *Address:* Palais des Dunes, Bloc G, 7ieme Étage-Droite, La Croisette, Cannes, A.-M., France. [*Died* 1 *May* 1964.

ARCHER, John Mark, C.B.E. 1962; Treasurer, Company of Merchants of City of Edinburgh, since 1963; Vice-President, Royal Zoological Society for Scotland, since 1964; Director of United Biscuits Ltd. since 1965, and of several private companies; Director of Scottish National Orchestra since 1955; Governor of Melville College since 1957; *b.* 7 Aug. 1908; *s.* of late Sir Gilbert Archer and Isabella Bald (*née* Purves); *m.* 1938, Marjorie Carmichael, *d.* of late Sir William MacDonald Baird; one *s.* three *d.* *Educ.:* Melville College; Edinburgh University. B.Com. 1930. Hon. Treasurer, Roy. Zoological Soc. for Scotland, 1953-64. Director, Edinburgh Chamber of Commerce, 1949-54. Commissioner of Leith Harbour and Docks, 1957-63; Chm. Nat. Savings Cttee. for Scotland, 1959-1965. *Recreations:* fishing, shooting. *Address:* Belvedere, Stanley Road, Leith, Edinburgh 6. *T.:* Granton 4633; Drumelzier Haugh, Broughton, By Biggar. *T.:* Broughton 247. *Clubs:* Royal Automobile; New (Edinburgh). [*Died* 28 *Aug.* 1965.

ARCHER, Wing Commander John Oliver, C.B.E. 1920 (O.B.E. 1919); R.A.F. retd.; *b.* Walton-on-the-Naze, 22 Sept. 1887; *s.* of late John Archer; *m.* 1st, 1916, Esther (*d.* 1930), *d.* of late C. S. Chilton; one *d.*; 2nd, 1939, Kathleen, *d.* of J. E. A. Sissmore. *Educ.:* Felsted School; University of London. B.Sc. Engineering (Honours), 1909. Enlisted Seaforth Highlanders, 1914; commissioned R.F.A., S.R. 1915 and transferred R.F.C.; served in France, Egypt, Palestine, and South Russia (despatches four times); Commanding No. 3 Indian Wing, 1926-30; retired list, 1935; Group Captain R.A.F.O., 1940-46. *Recreations:* fishing, beekeeping, gardening. *Address:* Cornhill Cottage, Melbury Abbas, Shaftesbury, Dorset. *T.:* Shaftesbury 2009. [*Died* 15 *Sept.* 1968.

ARCHER, Norman Ernest, C.M.G. 1944; O.B.E. 1937; *b.* 1892; *s.* of late Walter E. Archer, C.B.; *m.* 1925, Hon. Ruth Evelyn Pease, 2nd *d.* of 1st Baron Daryngton, P.C.; one *s.* one *d.* *Educ.:* R.N. Colleges, Osborne and Dartmouth. Lieut. R.N. 1913 (six 1st class certificates); 1909-20 served in Mediterranean and Home Fleets and attached Russian Navy; Lieut.-Comdr. (retd.), 1921; Colonial Office, 1921; Dominions Office, 1925; Secretary to British Economic Mission to Australia, 1928-29; Admve. Asst. Sec. Imperial Conferences, 1930, 1932 and 1937; Sec. Office of United Kingdom High Commissioner to Canada, 1932-36; acting High Commissioner during parts of 1934, 1935 and 1936; Private Sec. to Sec. of State for Dominion Affairs (Mr. Eden), 1939-40; Principal Sec., Office of United Kingdom Representative to Eire, 1941 and 1944-48; Assistant Under-Secretary of State, Commonwealth Relations Office, 1948-49; retired, 1949. *Recreations:* fishing, sailing. *Address:* White Gates, Longbridge Deverill, Warminster, Wilts *T.:* Sutton Veny 304. [*Died* 15 *Feb.* 1970.

ARCHER-JACKSON, Lieut.-Col. Basil, D.S.O. and M.C. 1919; *b.* 1884; *y. s.* of late John Archer-Jackson. *Educ.:* Wellington Coll. Entered Militia, 1904; served Shropshire Light Infantry; European War, 1914-1918, France and Belgium and Macedonia; Captain and Adjutant, 8th Shropshire Light Infantry; Major, 2nd in command, 1916; Lt.-Col., and commanding 9th King's Own Royal Lancaster Regt. (despatches four times, D.S.O., M.C., French Croix de Guerre avec Palmes). *Club:* Naval and Military. [*Died* 29 *Jan.* 1965.

ARCHIBALD, John Gordon; Solicitor; Fellow of All Souls College, Oxford, since 1908; *b.* 1 January 1885; *s.* of Hon. John Sprott Archibald, late Chief Justice of the Superior Court, Montreal; *m.* 1922, Gilda Conti Varesi (*d.* 1965); no *c.* *Educ.:* McGill University, Montreal; New College, Oxford. Rhodes Schol., 1904; First Cl. Lit. Hum. 1906; Second Cl. Jurisprudence, 1907; All Souls Fellowship, 1908; Licencié en Droit, Paris, 1910. Called to Bar, Inner Temple, 1910; served European War Ministry of Blockade and Ministry of Shipping, 1914-18, Ministry of Justice, Cairo, 1918-19; admitted Solicitor, 1921; Lecturer in Private International Law, Oxford, 1919-22; Member: Statute Law Cttee., 1927-60; Lord Chancellor's Cttee. on Arbitration, 1926; and on Arrestment of Property, 1927; Lord Chancellor's and Board of Trade Cttee. on Restraint of Trade, 1930; Treasury Cttee. on Industrial Assurance, 1931-32; Lord Chancellor's Cttee. on Reciprocal Enforcement of Judgments, 1931; Royal Commission on Business in the King's Bench Division, 1934 36. Honours Examiner to Law Soc., 1929-39. *Address:* 25 Oakwood Court, W.14. *T.:* Western 6752. *Club:* Athenæum. [*Died* 8 *June* 1970.

ARCHIBALD, His Honour Myles; County Court Judge, retired; *b.* 8 April 1898; *e. s.* of Charles Falcon and Harriett Mary Archibald, Rusland Hall, nr. Ulverston, N. Lancs.; unmarried. *Educ.:* Oundle; University of Leeds. Admitted Solicitor, 1923; called to Bar, Inner Temple, 1934; Chairman Agricultural Land Tribunal, 1948-52; Chairman East Riding Quarter Sessions, 1956; County Court Judge, Circuit No. 12 Bradford, etc., 1952-58. *Recreations:* gardening, foreign travel. *Address:* Rusland, Ulverston, N. Lancs. *T.:* Satterthwaite 216. [*Died* 14 *March* 1961.

ARDEN-CLARKE, Sir Charles Noble, G.C.M.G. 1952 (K.C.M.G. 1948; C.M.G. 1941); Kt. 1946; *b.* 25 July 1898; *e. s.* of Rev. C. W. Arden Clarke, Bournemouth; *m.* 1924, Georgina Dora Reid; one *s.* two *d.* Name changed by Deed Poll to Arden-Clarke. *Educ.:* Rossall. Joined Machine Gun Corps, served France, Germany and military mission to Southern Russia, temporary Captain (despatches), 1917-20; joined Colonial Administrative Service, 1920; Administrative Officer, Northern Nigeria, 1920-33; Actg. Principal Asst. Sec., Nigerian Secretariat, 1934-36; Asst. Resident Commissioner and Government Secretary, Bechuanaland Protectorate, 1936; Resident Commissioner, Bechuanaland Protectorate, 1937-42; Resident Commissioner, Basutoland, 1942-46; Governor and C.-in-C. of Sarawak, 1946-49; Governor and Commander-in-Chief, Gold Coast, 1949-57; First Governor-General and Commander-in-Chief of Ghana, March-May 1957. Chm. Royal African Society, 1959-; Chm. Royal Commonwealth Society for the Blind, 1959-; Chm. National Council for the Supply of Teachers Overseas, 1960-. Mem., Monckton Commission, 1960. K.St.J., 1952. Hon. D.C.L. Durham, 1958. *Recreations:* gardening, philately. *Address:* Syleham House, nr. Diss, Norfolk. *Club:* Athenæum. [*Died* 16 *Dec.* 1962.

ARIS, Ernest Alfred, F.Z.S.; S.G.A. artist; *b.* 22 April 1882; *s.* of Alfred Aris and Emily Wright; *m.* 1913, Winifred Archer Ould; one *s.* *Educ.:* Technical College and School of Art, Bradford (Diploma); Royal College of Art, London. Started as a portrait painter; later drifted into commercial art, book illustrations, magazines, etc.; later specialised in animals and writing and illustrating story books and nature articles; Art Director, Windermere; Art Master, Internat. Correspondence School. Exhibitor at many galleries. *Publications:* about 150 books for children; Bunny o' the Cosy Corner Series, 1920; Tales for Tiny Tots; The Dainty Series, 1921; Rock-a-bye Stories, 1919; The Bunny o' the Bracken Series, 1920; The Woodland Series, 1919; That Little Animal Series, 1915; Famous Animal Tales re-pictured by Ernest Aris, including stories by E. A., 1935; Fishing, 1946; The Brambledown Tales, 1946; Ernest Aris's Nature Series, 1947; The Art of the Pen, 1948, etc. *Recreations:* angling, entomology, swimming, collecting old furniture, gardening, travel. *Address:* 9 Oak Avenue, Priory Road, Hornsey, N.8. [*Died* 14 *April* 1963.

ARMITAGE, Sir Cecil; *see* Armitage, Sir S. C.

ARMITAGE, Rev. Cyril Moxon, M.V.O. 1948; M.A.; Dip.Th.; Rector, St. Bride's Church, Fleet Street, 1954-62, retired; Dean of Guild of St. Bride since 1962; Deputy priest to King George V, 1934-1935; Priest in Ordinary, 1935-62; *b.* 4 June 1900; *s.* of late Harry and late Charlotte Elizabeth Armitage, St. John's, Wakefield; *m.* 1931, Eva, *e. d.* of Herbert John and Winifred Brinsmead, Hendon; one *s.* one *d.* *Educ.:* Queen Elizabeth's School, Wakefield; St. Chad's College, Durham. Diploma in Theology, 1923. Deacon, 1923; Priest, 1924; Assistant Curate S. Augustine's, Kilburn, 1923-31; Deputy Minor Canon of Westminster, 1931; Minor Canon, 1932-51; Precentor of Westminster Abbey, 1934-51; Priest-in-charge, St. Bride's Church, Fleet Street, 1951-54. Asst. Sec. Church Lads' Brigade, 1931; Gen. Sec. and Headquarters Staff Chaplain, Church Lads' Brigade, 1932-1935; Chaplain R.N.V.R. Royal Marines, Plymouth Division, 1940-42; Chaplain H.M.S. Definace, Devonport, 1942; Chaplain H.M.S. Lynx, Dover Patrol, 1945; Proctor in Convocation for the diocese of London, 1950; Chairman, Association of Minor Canons, 1949-52; Pres., London Central Area of St. John Ambulance Brigade. 1953-54; O.St.J. 1954. Freeman of the City of London. Formerly Chaplain: Fleet Street Column Club; Institute of Journalists; Press Club (Hon. Chaplain, 1966); Soc. of Yorkshiremen, London; Chartered Institute of Secretaries. Late R.N.V.R. Licensed to officiate, Dio. Canterbury, 1963. *Publications:* Courage, 1942; The Church of Westminster, 1951; Beauty for Ashes, 1952. *Recreations:* music, architecture. *Address:* Willow Bend, Dymchurch, Kent. *T.:* Dymchurch 3185. *Clubs:* London Press, R.N.V.R., Royal Automobile, Fleet Street Column. [*Died* 7 *June* 1966.

ARMITAGE, Hugh Traill, C.M.G. 1941; Director of: Telephone and Electrical Industries Pty. Ltd. and of several other companies; *b.* 17 Feb. 1881; 2nd *s.* of late C. C. Armitage, Colombo, Ceylon; *m.* 1906, Edith J Callow; one *s.* one *d.* *Educ.:* St. Philip's Church of England Grammar School, Sydney. Joined Bank of New South Wales in 1897. Left in order to assist with organisation of Commonwealth Bank of Australia at its inception in 1912; successively Chief Accountant, Secretary, Head Office Manager, Chief Inspector, Deputy Governor, Governor Commonwealth Bank of Australia, 1941-48; retired, 1948. *Recreations:* golf, swimming, boating. *Address:* 21 Boyle Street, Cremorne, Sydney, New South Wales. *T.:* XY 2050. *Clubs:* Royal Automobile, Royal Commonwealth Society. [*Died* 17 *Oct.* 1963.

ARMITAGE, Sir (Stephen) Cecil, Kt., *cr.* 1953; C.B.E. 1943; D.L., J.P. Notts. Alderman and Hon. Freeman, Nottingham; *b.* 16 July 1889; *s.* of Stephen and Margaret Armitage; *m.* 1920, Irene Bowen Smith; one *s.* two *d.* *Educ.:* Rugby School. Solicitor, 1911; served European War, Capt. T.F., 1914-19 (despatches). Commerce, 1919-High Sheriff, Nottinghamshire, 1953-54 *Recreations:* Rugby, cricket, hockey, shooting. *Address:* Hawksworth Manor Nottingham. *Club:* Farmers'. [*Died* 6 *May* 1962.

ARMITAGE, Valentine Leathley, M.A. (Oxon); Diplomé ès lettres (Rennes); *b* Feb. 1888; *s.* of late Rev. A. L. Armitage; *m.* 1st, 1921, Evelyn Muriel (*d.* 1954), *d.* of late R. C. Nichols, Yockleton Hall, Salop; no *c.*; 2nd, 1955, Venetia Mary Stanley Errington Hunter-Gowan, *widow* of Capt. C. H. B. Gowan, Royal Navy. *Educ.:* King's School, Canterbury; Balliol College, Oxford. Teaching and Lecturing at Rennes University, 1909-11; Grange, Folkestone and Gore Court, Sittingbourne, 1911-13; Rossall School, 1914-15; War Service, England and France and Germany, Northamptonshire Regt. and Provost Corps, 1915-19; Rossall,

Housemaster, 1919-22; St. Bees School, Housemaster, Senior Modern Language Master, 1922-25; Headmaster, Bloxham School, 1925-40; Member of the Headmasters Conference, 1929-40; Member of Education Committee of County of Oxford, 1937-39; military appointment Intelligence Corps, 1939; Lieut.-Colonel and T.D., 1944; demobilised 1947 with rank of Lt.-Col.; in Germany with Office of Educational Adviser (Foreign Office, German Section), 1947-50. *Recreation:* cooking. *Address:* c/o Barclays Bank, Exeter. [*Died* 2 *Feb.* 1964.

ARMOUR, Rt. Rev. Thomas Makinson, B.A., Th. Soc.; Bishop of Wangaratta since 1943; *b.* 8 August 1890; *s.* of William John and Catherine Armour; *m.* 1944, Flora H. M. Calder, M.D., *d.* of late George and Catherine Calder, Edinburgh. *Educ.:* St. Chad's College, Durham. Deacon, 1916; Priest, 1917; Asst. Curate, Warrington, 1916-22; temp. C.F., 1918-19; hon. C.F., 1920-23 and from 1927; Chaplain T.A., 1923-27; Vicar of Orford, Lancs, 1922-28; Member of Brotherhood of the Good Shepherd, Dubbo, N.S.W., 1928-29; Principal, 1929-36; Dean of Newcastle, N.S.W., 1936-43. *Recreation:* walking. *Address:* Bishop's Lodge, Wangaratta, Victoria, Australia. *T.A.:* Wangaratta, Australia. *T.:* 43. *Club:* Melbourne (Melbourne). [*Died* 20 *Jan.* 1963.

ARMSTRONG, Sir Alfred Norman, Kt. 1966; C.B.E. 1962; Chairman, Export Development Council, since 1965 (Member, since 1958; Deputy Chairman, 1962-65); *b.* 6 March 1899; *s.* of W. Armstrong, Sydney. Commonwealth Bank of Australia: General Manager, Industrial Finance Department, 1945-51; Assistant Governor (Commercial Banking), 1951-53; Member, Capital Issues Advisory Committee, 1945-; Member, Advisory Council, 1949-; General Manager, Commonwealth Trading Bank of Australia, 1953-59; Deputy Managing Director, Commonwealth Banking Corporation, 1959-65. Deputy Chairman, Decimal Currency Board, 1963-; Member: Australian Wool Board, 1963- (Dep. Chairman 1964-); International Wool Secretariat Board, 1964-; Chairman, Australian Meat Board Selection Committee, 1964-. A Director, N.S.W. Division, National Heart Foundation of Australia, 1958-; Vice-President, Medical Foundation of University of New South Wales, 1963-. Director: Australian United Corporation Ltd.; Bradford Cotton Mills Ltd.; John A. Gilbert Holdings Ltd.; Member, Australian Board, Legal & General Assurance Society Ltd. *Address:* Kindersley House, 33 Bligh Street, Sydney, New South Wales, Australia. *Club:* Union (Sydney). [*Died* 1 *July* 1966.

ARMSTRONG, Edmond Arrenton, C.B. 1952; C.B.E. 1947; *b.* 5 April 1899; 2nd *s.* of late Rev. Thomas Armstrong, St. Fillans, Perthshire; *m.* 1924, Lillie Carson; one *d.* *Educ.:* Morrison's Academy, Crieff; Edinburgh Univ. M.A., 1st Cl. Hons. (Classics), 1921. Served European War, 1914-18, in Royal Field Artillery. Appointed to the War Office, 1924; served in Scottish Office, 1935-1941, and War Cabinet Office, 1941-47; Dep. Adviser to Viceroy on War Admin. in India, 1943-44; Under Secretary, Ministry of Transport and Civil Aviation, 1947, Controller, Civil Aviation Ground Services, 1957-60, retired. Attended the Malta and Yalta Confs. 1945. *Recreations:* golf, hill climbing. *Address:* 16 Oxgangs Road, Edinburgh 10. *T.:* Fairmilehead 2388 *Club:* Scottish Conservative. [*Died* 17 *June* 1966.

ARMSTRONG, Frederick Ernest; Member Stock Exchange, London; formerly Senior Partner in the firm of Killik and Co., stockbrokers; *b.* 26 Aug. 1884; *o. s.* of late Frederick and Louisa Armstrong; *m.* 1st, 1910, Elizabeth Marion (*d.* 1954), *e. d.* of late Thomas Daniel Follett; three *s.* two *d.*; 2nd, 1960, Audrey Viola Scott, *widow*; one *step d.* *Educ.:* Portsmouth, Plymouth and London. Authority on Stock Exchange procedure and lecturer on Exchange Law and Practice. Governor of City of London Coll.; late Examiner to Institute of Bankers. Contributor to the Press on financial matters. *Publication:* The Book of the Stock Exchange. *Recreations:* motoring, sport, and travel. *Address:* 4 Challoners Close, Rottingdean, Sussex. *T.:* Rottingdean 3916; *T.A.:* Myopia London. *T.:* National 0861. [*Died* 3 *April* 1962.

ARMSTRONG, Sir Godfrey, Kt., *cr.* 1944; O.B.E. 1919; Chairman Madras Port Trust, 1928-48; retired, 1948; *b.* 3 Oct. 1882; *s.* of James Armstrong, senior partner of Sandilands & Co., solicitors, London; *m.* 1919, Margaret Gardiner, C.B.E. 1946; two *s.* *Educ.:* Bradfield Coll.; Oriel Coll., Oxford. Joined Madras Railway Traffic Dept., 1905; Army in France, 1915-19, last position Lt.-Col. General Service, Asst. Director of Railway Traffic, Calais area. Traffic Dept. of Madras and Southern Mahratta Railway to 1928. Attached Govt. of India as Special Officer for Ports, 1944-46; retired, 1946. *Address:* Hale Edge North, South Nutfield, Surrey. [*Died* 18 *June* 1964.

ARMSTRONG, Col. John Cecil, C.B. 1918; C.M.G. 1916; *b.* 28 Aug. 1870; *y. s.* of late Maj.-General John Armstrong, C.B.; *m.* 1st, 1890, Minnie (*d.* 1936), *d.* of late Charles Morrell, J.P., The Manor, Dorchester; one *s.*; 2nd, Dorothy, *d.* of late W. O. Aves. *Educ.:* Wellington College; R.M.C., Sandhurst (Queen's Cadet). Joined Royal Inniskilling Fusiliers, 1890; Seconded A.P.D., 1898. Served S. Africa, 1899-1902 (Queen's medal 3 clasps, King's medal 2 clasps); European War, 1914-18 (C.M.G., C.B.); Chief Paymaster, War Office, and Officer in charge of Records, R.A.P.C., 1924-28; retired pay, 1930; Col.-Comdt. R.A.P.C., 1928-43. *Address:* Clandon, Tutshill, Chepstow, Mon. [*Died* 28 *April* 1961.

ARMSTRONG, Sir John D. H.; *see* Heaton-Armstrong.

ARMSTRONG, John Elliot, C.I.E. 1927; O.B.E. 1923; *b.* 21 Sept. 1875; *s.* of the late Lt.-Col. Mansel Armstrong, 20th Hussars and Bengal Staff Corps. Joined Indian Police Service, 1897; Deputy Inspector-General C.I.D., Bengal, 1920; Commissioner of Police, Calcutta, 1926; retired, 1929; Director-General of Police, Hyderabad, 1927-1935. King's Police Medal, 1926. *Address:* c/o Lloyds Bank Ltd., 6 Pall Mall, S.W.1. [*Died* 5 *March* 1962.

ARMSTRONG, Katharine Fairlie, S.R.N., S.C.M., Diploma of Nursing, London University; *b.* 6 July 1892. *Educ.:* Kendrick Girls School, Reading; University of Reading. After 4 years' teaching experience started to train as a nurse at King's Coll. Hosp., London, S.E.5, in 1916; took midwifery training, 1919-20; Ward Sister, King's College Hospital, 1920-22; Sister Tutor, Royal Northern Hospital, 1922-23; Sister Tutor, King's College Hospital, 1923-37; Member of the College of Nursing; Chairman of the Sister Tutor Section, College of Nursing 1934-37; Editor, The Nursing Times, 1937-1947; President of the Nat. Council of Nurses, 1948-51; Examiner to General Nursing Council. *Publications:* Teaching in Schools of Nursing (with M. Jackson); Aids to Surgical Nursing, 1938; Aids to Anatomy and Physiology, 1939; Aids to Bacteriology (with E. Joan Bocock), 1959; A Handbook of First Aid and Bandaging (with A. Belilios and D. Mulvany), 1941; British Red Cross Elementary Anatomy and Physiology Manual (with A. Belilios and D. Mulvany), 1945; Ed. Nurses Aid Series; Baillière's Atlas of

Female Anatomy (6th edn.), 1960; Baillière's Atlas of Male Anatomy (5th edn.), 1967. *Recreations:* gardening, painting. *Address:* Old Jordans, Nr. Beaconsfield, Bucks.
[*Died* 24 *Oct.* 1969.

ARMSTRONG, Terence I. F.; *see* Gawsworth, John.

ARMSTRONG-JONES, Ronald Owen Lloyd, M.B.E. 1944; Q.C. 1954; D.L.; Lord Chancellor's Visitor (Legal), 1955-63, retd.; Appointed Member of Industrial Disputes Tribunal, 1956; *b.* 18 May 1899; *s.* of late Sir Robert Armstrong-Jones, C.B.E., F.R.C.S., F.R.C.P.; *m.* 1st, 1925, Anne (marr. diss., 1934), *o.d.* of Lt.-Col. Leonard Charles Rudolph Messel, O.B.E., T.D., M.A., Cuckfield, Sussex; one *s.* one *d.*; 2nd, 1936, Carol Akhurst (marr. diss., 1959), *d.* of Sir Thomas Melrose Coombe, Glenelg, S. Australia; 3rd, 1960, Jenifer, *d.* of Basil Unite; one *s.* *Educ.:* Eton; Magdalen College, Oxford (M.A.). Called to Bar, Inner Temple, 1922. Served War, 1917-19; gunner 1917, 2nd Lieutenant, R.A., 1918; served War of 1939-45: 2nd Lieut. 1940, K.R.R.C. 1940, Major 1941, Deputy Judge Advocate, S.E. Army, 1942-44 (M.B.E.); Deputy Judge Advocate, 21 Army Group, serving in Normandy and Airborne H.Q., 1944; then invalided. High Sheriff, Caerns., 1936; Senior Warden, Clothworkers Company, 1957-58. Governor St. Bartholomew's Hospital. D.L. Caernarvonshire, 1961. *Recreations:* rowing (winning Grand Crew, Henley, 1921), shooting and wildfowling. *Address:* Plas Dinas, Caernarvon, North Wales. *Clubs:* Garrick, Royal Automobile; Leander; Royal Welsh Yacht.
[*Died* 27 *Jan.* 1966.

ARMYTAGE, Lt.-Col. Vivian B. G.; *see* Green-Armytage.

ARNO, Peter; Cartoonist for The New Yorker since 1925, and for numerous publications in America and abroad; *b.* 8 Jan. 1906; *s.* of Hon. Curtis Arnoux Peters and Edith Theresa Haynes; *m.* 1927, Lois Long (divorced 1931); one *d.*; *m.* 1935, Mary Livingston Lansing (divorced 1939). *Educ.:* Hotchkiss School, Lakeville, Conn.; Yale College. Has held 56 exhibitions throughout America and in London and Paris. *Publications:* Peter Arno's Parade, 1930; Peter Arno's Hullabaloo, 1932; Peter Arno's Circus, 1933; Peter Arno's Favorites, 1934; Peter Arno's For Members Only, 1935; Peter Arno's Cartoon Revue, 1941; Peter Arno's Man in the Shower, 1944; Peter Arno's Pocket Book, 1946. *Recreations:* color photography, piano, composing, riding, swimming. *Address:* New Yorker Magazine, 25 W. 43 St., N.Y.C., U.S.A. *Club:* Yale (New York). [*Died* 22 *Feb.* 1968.

ARNOLD, Major-Gen. Allan Cholmondeley, C.I.E. 1947; C.B.E. 1941; M.C.; *b.* 23 May 1893; *s.* of Lt.-Col. A. S. Arnold, late Indian Army; *m.* Dorothy Hamilton, *o. d.* of Arthur Webster-Wedderburn, Deputy Inspector-General Police, Jamaica; no *c.* *Educ.:* Wellington College, Berks; Royal Military College, Sandhurst. 2nd Lt. Middlesex Regt., 1912; Captain, 1915; Bt. Major, 1919; Subs. Major, Royal Fusiliers, 1930; Bt. Lt.-Col., 1935; Colonel, 1938; Acting Maj.-General, 1942; Temp. Maj.-Gen., 1943; retd. pay, 1946. Served European War, 1914-18 (M.C., despatches thrice); North Russia, 1919 (O.B.E., despatches); Indian Frontier, 1921-22 (medal and 2 clasps); War of 1939-45 (despatches. C.B.E.). Joined Govt. of India Food Dept., 1946; Ministry of Food, 1949-1954. *Recreations:* shooting, fishing. *Address:* The Well House, Bayford, nr. Wincanton, Somerset. *Club:* Army and Navy.
[*Died* 29 *Jan.* 1962.

ARNOLD, Arthur, A.M.I.Mech.E.; A.M.I.E.E.; F.Inst.F.; Editor of Power and Works Engineering; *b.* 31 Aug. 1891; *s.* of Arthur and Maria Arnold, Lymington; *m.* 1919, Elsie Milnes; one *s.* one *d.* *Educ.:* King Edward VI. Grammar School, Southampton. Pupil to late J. H. Bolam, M.Sc., M.I.E.E., at Weymouth Corporation Electricity Works; subsequently on Technical Staff of various electricity undertakings; two years during the 1914-18 War with Grand Fleet; Eng.-Lt. R.N.; joined The Power Engineer, 1919. *Publications:* technical books; sundry papers to technical societies; many articles in technical press. *Address:* 249 Horseshoe Lane, Garston, Watford, Herts.
[*Died* 6 *April* 1961.

ARNOLD, Sir Frederick (Blackmore), K.C.M.G. 1966 (C.M.G. 1954); O.B.E. 1943; M.A.; Indian Civil Service (retired); *b.* 26 June 1906; *e. s.* of late L. F. and A. E. Arnold, Dorking; *m.* 1st, 1929, Mary, *d.* of late H. H. Austin, Harpenden; one *s.* one *d.*; 2nd, 1948, Jacqueline, *d.* of late A. G. Barr, O.B.E., Edinburgh; one *d.* *Educ.:* Bishops Stortford; Trinity Hall, Cambridge (Scholar). Entered I.C.S. and appointed to Burma, 1929; Dep. Comr., Magwe, 1936-37; Dep. Sec. Finance Dept., 1937-39; Controller of Prices, Imports, Civil Supplies, 1939-42; Sec. to Govt. Reconstruction Dept., 1942-45, Commerce and Supply Dept., 1946-47; Retd. from I.C.S. and appointed to Trade Comr. Service of U.K. Bd. of Trade, 1947; Trade Comr., Colombo, 1948, Calcutta, 1948-1949, Bombay, 1949-50; Senior Trade Comr. in Pakistan, 1950-58; Minister (Commercial) and Sen. Trade Comr. in Australia, 1958-66. Transf. to H.M. Diplomatic Service, 1966; retd. 1966. *Recreations:* thrillers, gardening, golf. *Address:* Orana, Cuckmere Rd., Seaford, Sussex. *T.:* Seaford 5468. *Club:* East India and Sports. [*Died* 31 *March* 1968.

ARNOLD, Ralph Crispian Marshall; Author and former Publisher; *b.* 26 Oct. 1906; *s.* of late R. A. Arnold and Olive Grey Arnold; *m.* 1936, Constantia Pamela, *y. d.* of late Mark Fenwick; no *c.* *Educ.:* Loretto; Trinity Coll., Oxf. On staff of Roy. Institute of International Affairs, 1929-34. Joined Constable & Co., Ltd., 1936; Chm., 1958-62; Retired, 1962. 2nd Lt. the Cameronians (Scottish Rifles), 1939; Personal Asst. to C.I.G.S., 1939-40, to C.-in-C., Scottish Command, 1941-1942; A.D.P.R., XIV Army, 1943; D.D.P.R., H.Q. S.E.A.C., 1944; demobilised with rank of Colonel. *Publications:* *novels.* House with the Magnolias, 1931; Hands Across the Water, 1946; Spring List, 1956; *topography:* The Hundred of Hoo, 1947; A Yeoman of Kent, 1949; *history:* Kings, Bishops, Knights and Pawns, 1963; A Social History of England, 55 B.C. to 1215 A.D., 1967; *biography:* The Unhappy Countess, 1957; Northern Lights, 1959; The Whiston Matter, 1961; *autobiography:* A Very Quiet War, 1962; Orange Street and Brickhole Lane, 1963. *Recreations:* reading, writing, local history. *Address:* Swerford Old Rectory, Oxfordshire. *T.:* Hook Norton 398.
[*Died* 23 *Sept.* 1970.

ARNOLD, Ronald Nathan, D.Sc. (Glasgow); D.Eng., Ph.D. (Sheffield); M.S. (Illinois); F.R.S.E.; M.I.Mech.E.; M.I.C.E.; Regius Prof. of Engineering, Univ. of Edinburgh since 1946; Member of University Court, 1956-59; *b.* Glasgow, 23 Dec. 1908; *s.* of Arnold Attwood and Ada Louisa Arnold, Glasgow; *m.* 1940, Jessie Beattie Blake, Edinburgh; one *s.* *Educ.:* Shawlands Academy, Glasgow; Royal Technical Coll., Glasgow; Univ. of Sheffield; Univ. of Illinois. Engineering apprenticeship with Mirrlees Watson Co. Ltd., Glasgow. B.Sc. 1st Class Hons. in Mechanical Engineering, Glasgow Univ., 1932; elected an Associate of Royal Technical College and awarded Mont-

gomerie Neilson Gold Medal in Mechanical Engineering, 1932; Sir James Caird Senior Travelling Scholar, Sheffield Univ., 1932-34 (Ph.D. in Engineering, 1934); Commonwealth Fund Fellow, Univ. of Illinois, 1934-1936 (M.S. in Theoretical and Applied Mechanics, 1936); elected to Sigma Xi and Phi Kappa Epsilon Scholastic Fraternities of U.S.A.; Assistant Lecturer in Engineering, Royal Technical College, Glasgow, 1936-40; Gold Medal of Institution of Engineers and Shipbuilders in Scotland, 1940; Thomas Lowe Gray Prize, 1940, and Thomas Hawksley Gold Medal, 1946, of Institution of Mechanical Engineers. Research staff of Metropolitan Vickers Elec. Co., Manchester, 1940-44; D.Sc., Glasgow Univ., 1943; Professor of Engineering, University College of Swansea, 1944-46; D.Eng., Sheffield Univ., 1947; Member of Mechanical Engineering Research Board. 1948-52; Dean of Faculty of Science, Edinburgh University, 1949-53 and 1955-56. *Publications:* Gyrodynamics and its Engineering Applications, 1961. Papers in Engineering periodicals and Proc. of Learned Societies dealing with: Embrittlement in Steels; Impact Stresses; Mechanical Vibration; Cutting of Metals; Dynamical Balancing; Gyroscopic motion. *Recreations:* sketching, ciné photography, chess. *Address:* The University, Edinburgh.
[*Died* 30 *Dec.* 1963.

ARNOLD, Thurman Wesley, LL.D. (Wyoming); Lawyer, firm Arnold & Porter, Washington, D.C., since 1945; *b.* 2 June 1891; *s.* of Constantine Peter Arnold and Annie Brockway; *m.* 1917, Frances Longan; two *s.* *Educ.:* Princeton; Harvard; Yale. A.B. (Princeton), 1911; LL.B. (Harvard), 1914; M.A. (Yale), 1931; LL.D. (Wyoming) 1943. Practice of law, Chicago, Illinois, 1914-17; practice of law, Laramie, Wyo., 1919-27; Dean, Coll. of Law, West Virginia Univ., 1927-30; Prof. of Law, Yale Univ., 1930-38; Asst. Attorney-General i/c Anti-trust Div., Dept. of Justice, 1938-43; Assoc. Justice, U.S. Court of Appeals (D.C.), 1943-45; member Wyoming Legislature, 1921; Mayor of Laramie, Wyoming, 1923. *Publications:* The Symbols of Government, 1935; Cases on Trials, Judgements and Appeals, 1936; The Folklore of Capitalism, 1937; The Bottlenecks of Business, 1940; Democracy and Free Enterprise, 1942; Fair Fights and Foul, 1965. *Recreation:* golf. *Address:* (office) 1229 19th Street, N.W. Washington, D.C. *T.:* 223-3200; 301 S. St. Asaph St., Alexandria, Va., U.S.A. *T.:* Temple 6-7773. *Clubs:* National Press (Washington, D.C.); Princeton (New York).
[*Died* 7 *Nov.* 1969.

ARNOLD, Tom (Thomas Charles Arnold) O.B.E. 1969; theatrical manager; *s.* of George Henry and Louise Arnold; *m.* Helen Breen Moore. Commenced show business in office of Sir Walter de Frece; started in own management touring revues, 1922; produced over 300 revues and musical shows. Later successes include Ivor Novello series: The Dancing Years, Perchance to Dream, King's Rhapsody, Gay's the Word. Presented big Ice Shows prior to War of 1939-45, and resumed with bigger Ice Shows, 1946, doing four seasons at Stoll Theatre, London, and ultimately big-scale Ice Entertainment at Wembley Stadium. Inaugurated mammoth Christmas circus for annual presentation at Harringay Arena, 1947, and presented first Operette on Ice, Rose Marie, 1950; produced Noel Coward's Ace of Clubs (musical play), Cambridge Theatre, London, 1950; presented American-style Rodeo show at Harringay Arena, 1952; musical show, starring Anna Neagle, 1952; first stage presentation of Life with the Lyons, 1952. Took over Julian Wylie Productions Ltd., 1935, presenting major pantomimes annually in principal provincial cities; jointly presents annual Latin Quarter Revue at London Casino. Joint proprietor with Emile Littler of Palace, Casino and Cambridge Theatres, London; Proprietor, Sports Stadium, Brighton. Director: Piccadilly Theatre, London; New Britannia Pier, Great Yarmouth; Brighton Palace Pier; Brighton West Pier; Ramsgate Olympia, Ltd.; Radio Manx, etc. *Clubs:* City Livery, Hurlingham, Press, Green Room, Savage, etc.
[*Died* 2 *Feb.* 1969.

ARNOLD-FORSTER Major Francis Anson, D.S.O. 1918; T.D.; Engineer; *b.* 1890; *s.* of late E. P. Arnold-Forster; *m.* 1921, Helen Frances Broadbent Maufe (*d.* 1946); *m.* 1947, Phyllis, *widow* of Lt.-Col. R. I. H. Kinloch, O.B.E., and *d.* of late F. W. Hackforth-Jones, J.P. Served in R.A., T.A., 1914-19 and again, 1939-49. *Address:* Brookside, West Wittering, nr. Chichester, Sussex. *T.:* West Wittering 2112.
[*Died* 4 *Sept.* 1966.

ARNOLD-FORSTER, Commander Hugh Christopher, C.M.G. 1946; Royal Navy (retd.); Member of London Stock Exchange, 1925-59; *b.* 9 Dec. 1890; *s.* of Rt. Hon. H. O. Arnold-Forster, P.C.; *m.* 1923, Marcia Sophia Buddicom (marriage dissolved, 1948); one *s.* three *d.*; *m.* Frances Ann, *o. d.* of Eng Vice-Adm. Sir Harold Brown, G.B.E., K.C.B. *Educ.:* Bradfield College; R.N. Colleges, Osborne and Dartmouth. Naval Cadet, 1903; Commissioned, 1911. Served Atlantic Fleet, Home Fleet and China Squadron; retired, Jan. 1914; rejoined, July 1914; served throughout war; Assistant Naval Attaché, Washington, 1918-1919; retired, 1919; rejoined R.N., Sept. 1939; Assistant Director of Naval Intelligence, 1942-45; retired, 1945. *Address:* Salthrop House, Wroughton, Wilts. *Club:* Garrick.
[*Died* 21 *July* 1965.

ARNOTT, Sir Robert John, 4th Bt., *cr.* 1896; *b.* 19 Aug. 1896; *s.* of Sir John Alexander Arnott, 2nd Bt., and Caroline, D.B.E. (*d.* 1933), *e. d.* of Sir F. M. Williams, 2nd Bt. of Tregullow; *S.* brother (Sir Lauriston John Arnott, 3rd Bt.) 1958; *m.* 1926, Emita Amelia (*d.* 1948), *d.* of Francis James, formerly of Royston, Hertfordshire; two *s.* Formerly Lieutenant and Adjutant, King's Royal Rifle Corps. Served European War of 1914-18, in France and Salonika, 1915-16. *Heir:* *s.* John Robert Alexander Arnott, *b.* 9 April 1927. *Address:* Ounavarra, Lucan, Co. Dublin, Ireland. [*Died* 25 *July* 1966.

ARP, Jean (Hans); Chevalier de la Légion d'Honneur, 1960; sculptor; painter; engraver; writer of poetry and prose; *b.* Strasbourg, 16 Sept. 1887; *s.* of Pierre Arp; *m.* 1st, 1921, Sophie Taeuber (*d.* 1943); 2nd, 1959, Marguerite Hagenbach; no *c.* *Educ.:* Lycée, Strasbourg; Acad. of Art, Weimar; Acad. Julian, Paris. A Founder, Dada Movement, Switzerland, 1916-20; Mem. Surrealist Movement, Paris, 1932; Mem. Cttee., Salon des Réalités Nouvelles, 1946. 1948; Mem. Salon de la jeune Sculpture, Paris, 1950-52. *Work in permanent collections:* Tate Gallery, London; Museum of Modern Art, New York; Musée d'Art Moderne, Paris; and many others in N. and S. America, Europe, Japan. Mural Reliefs for Unesco Bldg., Paris, etc. Retrospective Exhibn., Musée Nationale d'Art Moderne, Paris, 1962, following numerous exhibns. in Europe and America. Great International Prize for Sculpture, 27th Venice Biennale, 1954; Stephan Lochner Medaille (Cologne), 1961; Grand Prix National des Arts (Paris), 1963; Grosser Bildhauerpreis des Landes Nordrhein-Westphalen, 1964; Citoyen d'Honneur de Locarno, 1965. *Publications:* Le Siège de l'Air, 1946 (On My Way, 1948); various, 1953 onwards; Gesammelte Gedichte, Band

1, 1963 (Zürich). *Recreations:* lecturing, travel. *Address:* 21 rue des Châtaigniers, Meudon, Seine et Oise, France; 5 Lange Gasse, Basle, Switzerland; Ronco dei Fiori, Solduno-Locarno, Switzerland.
[*Died* 7 *June* 1966.

ARROWSMITH, Rev. Preb. Walter Gordon; Commissary of Bishop of Fulham in jurisdiction of N. and Central Europe since 1952; Chaplain to the Queen since 1952 (to King George VI, 1946-52); Prebendary in St. Paul's Cathedral since 1946; Hon. Freeman of Chelsea, 1952; *b.* 17 Sept. 1888; *s.* of late Walter Arrowsmith; *m.* 1915, Lilian Mary, *d.* of Rev. T. H. H. Elliott; two *d.* *Educ.:* Gonville and Caius College, and Ridley Hall, Camb. (M.A.). Curate of Clifton, 1912-14. European War, 1914-18, C.F. (B.E.F., France, Aug. 1914). Rector St. Michael's, Bristol, 1918-23; Vicar St. John's, Sparkhill, Birmingham, 1923-28; Hon. Chaplain of Bishop of Birmingham, 1926; Hon. Canon in Birmingham Cathedral and Rector of Handsworth, 1928-30; Clerical Sec. Birmingham Dio. Conf., 1927-30; Rector of Chelsea, 1930-51. Councillor Borough of Chelsea, 1941, Alderman, 1945-1950. *Address:* Topsham Bridge, Nr. Kingsbridge, Devon. [*Died* 1 *June* 1964.

ARSENAULT, Hon. Aubin Edmond, M.A.; Barrister-at-law; *b.* 28 July 1870; *s.* of late Hon. Joseph O. Arsenault and Gertrude Gaudet; *m.* 1907, Bertha Rose Galland; two *s.* nine *d.* *Educ.:* St. Dunstan's College, Charlottetown P.E.I.; St. Joseph's College, Memramcook, N.B. Studied law with M'Leod Morson and M'Quarrie, Charlottetown and Sir Charles Russell, Bart., London, England; admitted Bar of Prince Edward Island 1898; entered upon practice of law in Summerside, P.E. Island, 1900; Assistant-Judge Supreme Court and Vice-Chancellor Court of Chancery and Member Appeal Court of Prince Edward Island, 1921-1946; retired from Bench, 1946. Elected Legislative Assembly, Prince Edward Island, 1908, 1911, 1915, bye-election 1917, and 1919; Member of Government, P.E.I., 1911; Premier and Attorney-General of Prince Edward Island, 1917-19; Leader of the Opposition, 1919-21; Member of Conservation Commission of Canada, 1913; Director Canadian National Geographic Society. Hon. LL.D.: Laval, St. Joseph and St. Dunstan's. Member Editorial Committee Canadian Geographical Journal. *Recreations:* reading and fishing. *Address:* 139 Upper Prince Street, Charlottetown, Prince Edward Island.
[*Died* 27 *April* 1969.

ASBURY, William, C.M.G. 1951; Member of the National Assistance Board since 1950 (Deputy-Chairman since 1954); *b.* 1889; *s.* of William Asbury, Edingale; *m.* 1917, Mary Bryce, *d.* of James Wright, Sheffield; one *s.* one *d.* *Educ.:* Wakefield. Member Royal Commission on Unemployment Insurance, 1930-32; Deputy Regional Commissioner for Civil Defence, Southern Region, 1942-45; Member of the Assistance Board, 1945 46; Land Commissioner, North Rhine-Westphalia, C.C.G., 1946-48, Schleswig-Holstein, 1948-50. Member Sheffield City Council, 1924-42; J.P. Sheffield, 1931. *Address:* 195 Frimley Road, Camberley, Surrey. *T.:* 21395.
[*Died* 19 *May* 1961.

ASCROFT, Professor Peter Byers, M.B.E. 1942; Professor of Surgery in the University of London and Director of the Surgical Unit, Middlesex Hospital Medical School, since 1947; *b.* 4 Sept. 1906; *o. s.* of James Arthur Ascroft, Bootle, Lancs, and Hannah Byers, Oulton, Cumberland. *Educ.:* Worksop; Middlesex Hospital; University of Strasbourg. M.R.C.S., L.R.C.P.; M.B., B.S., Hons. in Surgery, 1930; F.R.C.S., Eng., M.S. London, Univ. Gold Medal, 1931; Senior Broderip Scholar. Prosector to the Royal College of Surgeons and University of London; House Surgeon, House Physician, and Assistant in the Bland-Sutton Institute of Pathology, Middlesex Hospital; French Government Scholar; House Surgeon to the Department of Neurosurgery, London Hospital, 1933; Surgical Registrar, Middlesex Hospital, 1934-36; formerly Hon. Asst. Surgeon to Middlesex Hospital, 1937. Rockefeller Travelling Fellow in Neurosurgery, Yale University; Streatfield Research Scholar, 1937, Hunterian Professor, 1938, and Leverhulme Research Scholar, 1946, at Royal College of Surgeons; Member: British Medical Association; Society of British Neurological Surgeons; Fellow: Royal Society of Medicine, Association of Surgeons of England, Medical Society of London. War Service: 1940-46, Lieut.-Colonel, Royal Army Medical Corps; served in Middle East, North Africa and Italy; Adviser in Neurosurgery, Mediterranean theatre of operations, 1944-45. *Publications:* contributions to professional journals. *Recreations:* gardening, photography. *Address:* Surgical Unit, Middlesex Hospital, W.1; 20 Hallam Street, W.1. *T.:* Museum 8333, ext. 349.
[*Died* 27 *Oct.* 1965.

ASH, Edwin Lancelot Hopewell-, M.D., B.S.Lond.; M.R.C.S. Eng.; practised in Harley Street for 35 years as physician and nerve-specialist; *b.* 16 Jan. 1881; *m.* 1st, 1907, Mabel (*née* Streeter); three *s.*; 2nd, 1952, Christine (Chryssoula) (*née* Diamandis). *Educ.:* University Coll. School, London; St. Mary's Hospital, London (Cheadle Gold Medal). Chairman Westminster and Holborn division B.M.A., 1938-1939. *Publications:* many books and articles on general health, nervous breakdown and self-help. *Address:* West Parley, Dorset.
[*Died* 7 *Aug.* 1964.

ASHBY, Robert Claude, C.B.E. 1937; J.P.; F.R.G.S.; Company Director; *b.* 26 May 1876; *s.* of Robert Ashby, Staines, Middlesex; *m.* 1911, Frances Laeta Hunnybun. *Educ.:* Oliver's Mount School (Friends' School), Scarborough. Has been engaged since 1903 in Social and Philanthropic work through Statutory and Voluntary Committees, particularly those concerned with Housing, the Welfare of Young People, etc.; served in France during European War, 1914-18. *Address:* Park House, Palmerston Street, Romsey, Hants. *T.A.* and *T.:* Romsey 2354. *Clubs:* Alpine, Royal Commonwealth Society. [*Died* 23 *Dec.* 1963.

ASHCOMBE, 3rd Baron, *cr.* 1892; **Roland Calvert Cubitt,** D.L. for the County of Surrey; Lieutenant late Coldstream Guards; *b.* 26 Jan. 1899; *e. s.* of 2nd Baron Ashcombe, C.B., and Maud (*d.* 1945), *d.* of late Col. Calvert, Ockley Court; *S.* father, 1947; *m.* 1st, 1920, Sonia Rosemary (who obtained a divorce, 1947), *yr. d.* of late Lt.-Col. Hon. George Keppel, M.V.O.; two *s.* one *d.*; 2nd, 1948, Mrs. Idina Mills (*d.* 1954), *d.* of late Colonel R. E. Myddelton, J.P., D.L.; 3rd, 1959, Mrs. Jean Garland. *Recreations:* hunting, golf. *Heir:* *s.* Hon. Henry Edward Cubitt [*b.* 31 March 1924; *m.* 1955, Mrs. Ghislaine Alexander, *o. d.* of Cornelius Dresselhuys and of Viscountess Kemsley. *Educ.:* Eton. Late R.A.F. *Address:* Denbies, Dorking. *T.:* Dorking 2655. *Clubs:* Buck's, White's. [*Died* 28 *Oct.* 1962.

ASHCROFT, Alec Hutchinson, D.S.O. 1919; Hon. LL.D. (St. Andrews) 1939; Headmaster of Fettes College, 1919-45; *b.* 1887; *s.* of C. W. Ashcroft of Burwood, Oxton, Cheshire; *m.* 1915, Bertha Elizabeth (*d.* 1959), *d.* of Charles Tillard, Bathford, Bath; two *s.* one *d.* *Educ.:* Birkenhead chool; Gonville and Caius Coll., Camb. (open classical scholarship).

First-Class First Part Classical Tripos; First-Class Second Part Historical Tripos. Was an Assistant Master at Fettes College; served European War, Gallipoli, Egypt and France (despatches thrice, D.S.O., Order of the Crown of Italy). *Recreation:* played Rugby football for Eng. and Cambridge Univ. *Address:* Monkton Court, Monkton Combe, nr. Bath. *T.:* Limpley Stoke 2288. [*Died* 18 *April* 1963.

ASHCROFT, D(udley) Walker, E.R.D.; F.R.C.S.; Senior Consultant Ear, Nose, and Throat Surgeon, Westminster Hospital and Medical School, S.W.1, Westminster Children's Hospital and Chelsea Hospital for Women; *b.* 21 Nov. 1904; *s.* of late Peter Ashcroft and late Florence Ashcroft (*née* Gaucher); *m.* 1937, Enid Jessie (*d.* 1956), 2nd *d.* of late James Patrick and of late Jessie Dick Patrick (*née* Blair); one *s.*; *m.* 1957, Nancy Clarke, 2nd *d.* of late Alban Alfred Clarke and Frances Elizabeth Clarke (*née* Harris). *Educ.:* Knox College and University of Otago, Dunedin, New Zealand; Middlesex Hospital, W.I. M.B., Ch.B., New Zealand, 1929; D.L.O., Royal College of Physicians and Surgeons (Eng.), 1933; F.R.C.S. (Eng.) 1936. Lecturer in Otorhinolaryngology, Univ. of London. Bernhard Baron Research Scholar, Ferens Inst. of Otolaryngology, Middlesex Hosp., W.1, 1933; Streatfeild Scholar, Roy. Colls. of Physicians and Surgeons (Eng.), 1936. Late Mem. Council British Assoc. of Otolaryngologists; Member B.M.A.; Fellow Roy. Soc. Med. (late Sec. and Mem. of Council of Section of Laryngology); late Member of Council of Section of Otology. Served throughout War of 1939-45: Specialist in Otology, R.A.M.C. (S.R.) (despatches). *Publications:* papers on surgical and experimental physiological subjects in various scientific and med. jls. *Recreations:* golf, cricket, fishing. *Address:* (home) Bowling Green Cottage, Hurst Road, Horsham, Sussex. *T.:* Horsham 2261; (consulting rooms) 44 Wimpole Street, W.1. *T.:* Welbeck 6969. [*Died* 7 *May* 1963.

ASHCROFT, Thomas; *b.* Southport, 1890; *m.* *Educ.:* Elementary School; Southport Grammar School; London Labour College. Entered service Lancashire and Yorkshire Railway Company and became member of National Union of Railwaymen, 1914; Lecturer, London Labour College, 1924, and Principal, 1926-29; Editor of Railway Review, 1933-50. *Publications:* Text-Book of Modern Imperialism, 1922; English Art and English Society, 1936. *Recreations:* walking, theatre. *Address:* 27 Clinning Road, Birkdale, Southport, Lancs. [*Died* 3 *Jan.* 1961.

ASHLEY-BROWN, Ven. William, Th.L.; retd.; *b.* 22 Feb. 1887; *s.* of James Brown, J.P.; *m.* 1st, 1910, E. M. Gregson (*d.* 1923); 2nd, 1926, Alice May Preston; two *s.* two *d.* *Educ.:* St. John's Coll., Armidale, N.S.W.; Australian College of Theology. Deacon, 1910; Priest, 1911; Curate Christ Church Cathedral, Grafton; Vicar of Walgett; Coff's Harbour, N.S.W.; Chaplain of Poona, 1931-38; Archdeacon of Bombay, 1934-39; Rector of Smeeth, 1938-39; Dean of Gibraltar, 1943-45; Vicar of Cranbrook, 1939-47; Rural Dean of West Charing, 1945-47; served European War, A.I.F., 1915-17; Indian Ecclesiastical Establishment, 1917-1938; Past District Grand Warden (Bombay); Past Assistant Grand Chaplain (England). *Publications: novels:* The Hole in the Board; Zaudi, Princess of Abyssinia; *history:* On the Bombay Coast and Deccan; *memoirs:* Memory be Green; *miscellaneous:* articles, verse and essays. *Recreations:* surfing, bush-hikes, painting. *Address:* St. Michael's, 310 The Round Drive, Avoca Beach, via Gosford, N.S.W., Australia. *Club:* Imperial Service (Sydney). [*Died* 2 *Sept.* 1970.

ASHTON, Rt. Rev. John William, M.A., D.D. Oxon; *b.* Wakefield, Yorks, 1866; *m. e. d.* of J. G. Anderson, M.A., I.S.O., Under-Secretary of Education, Queensland; four *s.* two *d.* *Educ.:* Wakefield Grammar School; Univ. Coll., Oxford, (Scholar). First Class Mathematical Finals, 1889; D.D. (hon.) Oxford, 1924. Curate of All Saints', Northampton, 1892-95; Market Harborough, 1895-96; Rector, St. Andrew's, S. Brisbane, 1896-1900 and 1906-11; Christ Church, Bundaberg, Brisbane, 1900-3; Curate of Huddersfield, 1903-4; Hon. Canon of Brisbane, 1910-11; Vicar of All Saints', East St. Kilda, Victoria, 1911-21; Diocesan Missioner, Examining Chaplain, 1914-21; Rural Dean of St. Kilda, 1920-21; Bishop of Grafton, 1921-38; Director of Rel. Education, Dioc. of Melbourne, 1941-42. *Address:* 47 Bellett Street, Camberwell, E.6, Victoria, Australia. [*Died* 20 *March* 1964.

ASHTON, Thomas Southcliffe, M.A. (Manchester); F.B.A. 1951; Emeritus Professor of Economic History, University of London, since 1954 (Prof. 1944-54); *b.* 11 January 1889; 2nd *s.* of Thomas and Susan Ashton, Ashton-under-Lyne; *m.* 1915, Marion Hague, *d.* of Joseph Slater, Ashton-under-Lyne; one *s.* *Educ.:* Ashton-under-Lyne Secondary School; Univ. of Manchester. Asst. Lectr. in Economics, Univ. of Sheffield, 1912-19; Lectr. and Tutor in Economics and Political Science, Univ. of Birmingham, 1919-21; Sen. Lectr. in Economics, Univ. of Manchester, 1921-27; Reader in Currency and Public Finance, Univ. of Manchester, 1927-44. Pres. Manchester Statistical Society, 1938-40; Dean of Faculty of Commerce and Administration in Univ. of Manchester, 1938-44; Visiting Professor of Economics, The Johns Hopkins University, 1952; Ford's Lecturer in English History, Oxford, 1953-54; Raleigh Lectr., British Academy, 1955; Hon. Vice-President Royal Historical Society, 1961; President Economic History Society, 1960-1963; Vice-President Royal Economic Society, 1964; Hon. D.Litt. (Nottingham), 1963; Hon. Litt.D. (Manchester), 1964; Hon. Dr. Philosophy (Stockholm), 1964. *Publications:* Iron and Steel in the Industrial Revolution, 1924; The Coal Industry of the Eighteenth Century (with Joseph Sykes), 1929; Economic and Social Investigations in Manchester, 1833-1933, 1934; An Eighteenth-Century Industrialist: Peter Stubs of Warrington, 1756-1806, 1939; The Industrial Revolution, 1948; An Economic History of the Eighteenth Century, 1955; Economic Fluctuations in England, 1700-1800, 1959; ed. E. B. Schumpeter's English Overseas Trade Statistics, 1697-1808, 1960. *Address:* Tredwells, Blockley, Gloucestershire. *T.:* Blockley 334. [*Died* 22 *Sept.* 1968.

ASHTON, Sir William, Kt. 1960; O.B.E. 1941; H.R.O.I. 1948 (R.O.I. 1913); artist (Will Ashton); *b.* York, 1881; *s.* of James Ashton, artist and art teacher, Adelaide, S.A; *m.* May, *d.* of late James Millman, S. Australia; three *s.* *Educ.:* Prince Alfred College, Adelaide. Studied in England under Julius Olsson and Algernon Talmage, and in Paris with Professors Baschet and Schommer; exhibitor Roy. Academy, Paris Salons, Royal Society of British Artists, Royal West of England Academy, International Society of Painters, Sculptors and Gravers, Royal Institute of Oil Painters; Carnegie Institute, Pittsburgh (hon. mention 1914), Goupil Gallery, London, etc.; Wynne Prize for best Landscape of the year 1908, 1930 and 1939, Sydney; awarded Godfrey Rivers Memorial Prize, Brisbane, 1933; Society of Artists' Medal, Sydney, 1944. Represented in National Galleries, Sydney, Melbourne, Adelaide, Brisbane, Perth, Bendigo, Ballarat, Geelong and Castlemaine: Christchurch, Auckland, New Zealand; also in other galleries and art collections. Chairman Art Advisory Board to Commonwealth Government of Australia; acted as one of the Art Advisers to Board of Governors of National Gallery, Adelaide, in 1913-16, and purchased works for National Collection; Director, National Art Gallery of New South Wales, 1937-44. *Address:* Bossiney, Tivoli Street, Mosman, Sydney, N.S.W. *T.:* X.M. 4774. *Club:* Chelsea Arts. [*Died* 1 *Sept.* 1963.

ASHTON, Winifred; *see* Dane, Clemence.

ASHTOWN, 4th Baron (*cr.* 1800). **Robert Power Trench;** *b.* 27 April 1897; ***e. surv. s.*** of 3rd Baron and Violet (*d.* 1945), ***d.*** of Col. R. G. Cosby; S. father 1946; *m.* 1st, 1926, Geraldine (whom he divorced in 1938; she died 1940), 4th *d.* of late Sir Henry Foley Grey, 7th Bt.; 2nd, 1950, Oonah Anne Green-Wilkinson. *Educ.:* Eton. Served European War as Lieut. 3rd Batt. The Queen's (Royal West Surrey Regt.). *Heir:* *b.* Lt.-Col. Hon. Dudley Oliver Trench, O.B.E. *Address:* Landsdown, Nenagh, Co. Tipperary. *Club:* Kildare Street (Dublin).
[*Died* 3 *Nov.* 1966.

ASKEW, William George, C.B.E. 1951 (O.B.E. 1936); Secretary of St. Dunstan's, 1919-55; *b.* 27 July 1890; *e. s.* of late William Askew; *m.* 1917, Eleanor, *d.* of late William Gale; one *s.* Governor of St. Dunstan's; Member of Working Party appointed by Minister of Labour and National Service on the Employment of Blind Persons, 1948-50. *Address:* 11 Spinfield Park, Marlow, Bucks. *T.:* Marlow 3099. [*Died* 29 *Aug.* 1968.

ASKWITH, Lady (Ellen), C.B.E. 1918; *d.* of Archibald Peel, *g.d.* of Rt. Hon. General and Lady Alice Peel and of Sir Roger and Lady Palmer; *m.* 1st, Major Henry Graham, 20th Hussars; two *s.*; 2nd, Lord Askwith, K.C.B., K.C., D.C.L., LL.D. (*d.* 1942); one *d.* *Educ.:* Home. Worked as one of Y.M.C.A. Lady Presidents, European War, 1914-18; ran five canteens in the docks and one hostel; started the National Kitchens, taken over by the Government; joined the Dockers' Trades' Union as a member; served on several Government Committees, Women's Unemployment, War Savings, War Memorials Committees, and two Safeguarding Committees: Gloves and Translucent Pottery. Was Sub-Editor of the Onlooker. *Publications:* The Tower of Siloam; Disinherited of the Earth. *Address:* 14 Walton St., S.W.3. *T.:* Kensington 9968.
[*Died* 12 *Jan.* 1962.

ASKWITH, Rt. Rev. Wilfred Marcus, K.C.M.G. 1958; M.A. (Camb.); D.D. (Lambeth); Prelate of the Order of St. Michael and St. George since 1951; Bishop of Gloucester since 1954; *b.* 24 April 1890; *s.* of Preb. Henry and Louisa Alloway Askwith; *m.* 1928, Margaret Sibyl Luis, *d.* of George Walker Luis Fernandes, Haddon Lodge, Dorset; no *c.* *Educ.:* Bedford School; Corpus Christi College, Cambridge. Curate of St. Helens Parish Church, Lancs., 1913-1915; Master and Assistant Chaplain Bedford School, 1915-20; Rector of Stalbridge, Dorset, 1920-25; Chaplain to Europeans at Nakuru, Kenya Colony, 1925-1932; Hon. Canon of Mombasa, 1931-32; Vicar of Sherborne, Dorset, 1932-39; Vicar and Rural Dean of Leeds, 1939-42; Hon. Canon of Salisbury, 1938-41; of Ripon, 1941-42; Bishop of Blackburn, 1942-54. Hon. Fellow, Corpus Christi College, Cambridge, 1951. Chairman of the National Society, 1960. *Address:* Palace House, Pitt Street, Gloucester. *T.:* Gloucester 24598. *Club:* Athenæum.
[*Died* 16 *July* 1962.

ASQUITH OF YARNBURY, Baroness, *cr.* 1964 (Life Peeress); **Helen Violet Bonham Carter,** D.B.E. 1953; Governor of the Old Vic since 1945; President, Royal Institute of International Affairs since 1964; Patron United Nations Association; Trustee of Glyndebourne Arts Trust, since 1955; *b.* 15 April 1887; *er. d.* of Rt. Hon. H. H. Asquith, 1st Earl of Oxford and Asquith, and Helen Kelsall Melland; *m.* 1915, Sir Maurice Bonham Carter, K.C.B., K.C.V.O. (*d.* 1960); two *s.* two *d.* *Educ.:* home; Dresden and Paris. Governor of B.B.C., 1941-46. President of Women's Liberal Federation, 1923-1925, 1939-45; Pres. of Liberal Party Organisation, 1945-47; Mem. of Mr. Churchill's Focus in Defence of Freedom and Peace, 1936-39; Member of Executive of League of Nations Union up to 1941; Member Royal Commission on the Press, 1947-49; Delegate to Commonwealth Relations Conference in Canada, 1949. Contested (L.) Wells Division of Somerset, 1945, and Colne Valley, 1951. Falconer Lectures, Toronto, 1953; Romanes Lecture, Oxford, 1963. Hon. LL.D. (Sussex), 1963. *Publications:* Winston Churchill as I Knew Him, 1965; various articles in newspapers, magazines and other periodicals. *Address:* 21 Hyde Park Square, W.2. *T.:* 01-723 1881. [*Died* 19 *Feb.* 1969.

ASQUITH, Hon. Anthony; Film Director; a Governor of British Film Institute; President, Association of Cinematograph, Television, and Allied Technicians; *b.* 9 Nov. 1902; *y. s.* of 1st Earl of Oxford and Asquith. *Educ.:* Winchester; Balliol College, Oxford. Has directed the following films: Shooting Stars, Underground, A Cottage on Dartmoor, Dance Pretty Lady, Tell England, Moscow Nights, Pygmalion, French Without Tears, We Dive at Dawn, Quiet Wedding, The Demi-Paradise, The Way to the Stars, While the Sun Shines, The Winslow Boy, The Woman in Question, The Browning Version, The Importance of Being Earnest, The Net, The Final Test, The Young Lovers, Carrington, V.C., Orders to Kill, The Doctor's Dilemma, Libel, The Millionairess, Guns of Darkness, The V.I.P.s; The Yellow Rolls-Royce. Produced Carmen, Covent Garden, 1953. F.R.S.A.; Fellow, British Film Academy. Commander of the Order of Al Merito della Repubblica (Italy). *Recreations:* music and golf. *Club:* Brooks's. [*Died* 20 *Feb.* 1968.

ASQUITH, Cyril Edward, C.B.E. 1939; Author; *b.* 17 July 1902; *y. s.* of late James Edward and Gertrude Asquith, Stratford-on-Avon; *m.* 1923, Jeanne Marie Louise (marriage dissolved 1950), *o. d.* of François De Launoit, Brussels; two *d.*; *m.* 1954, Dorothy Henrietta Ward Stibbs. *Educ.:* Warwick School. Founder Member and Hon. Secretary, American and British Commonwealth Association; Hon. Sec. E.N.S.A. Council, 1941-45; Director, National Labour Organisation, 1936-46. Member of Council and Executive Committee English-Speaking Union, 1946-50. Joint Hon. Sec. the American Memorial Chapel Fund, 1946-50. *Publications:* The Forgotten Leader; Medicine's Great Revolution. *Films:* Thoroughbred; The City Beautiful; Come With Me series. *Recreation:* fishing. *Address:* 10 Grand Avenue, Hove, Sussex. [*Died* 7 *July* 1967.

ASTBURY, Rev. Canon (Harold) Stanley, M.C. 1916; M.A.; retired; *b.* 23 October 1889; *s.* of Canon George Astbury and Matilda Ingram Moody; *m.* 1917, Ida Gladys, *d.* of late F. J. Gibson, J.P., Wolverhampton; three *s.* two *d.* *Educ.:* King Edward's School, Birmingham; Christ's College, Cambridge; Lichfield Theological College. Deacon, 1912; Priest, 1914; Chaplain to H.M. Forces, 1914-19 (M.C.); Assistant Master at King Edward School, Birmingham, 1920-23; Vicar of

St. Mary's, Bearwood, Birmingham, 1923-1925; Smethwick, Birmingham, 1925-26; St. Paul's, Durban, Natal, 1926-31; Assistant Master and Chaplain at Charterhouse, 1931-35; Principal of Diocesan Training College Chester, 1935-53; Rector of Compton Greenfield, Bristol, 1953-60, retired. First Cmmoandant of Royal Army Chaplains Dept. Reception Centre and Depot, 1940; D.A.C.G., N. Wales Area, 1942; A.C.G. Eastern Command, India, 1943-44; relinquished Commission, 1945, Hon. C. F., First Class; Hon. Canon Chester Cathedral, 1946; Canon Emeritus, 1953. *Publications:* The Pocket Padre; A Short History of Chester College; A History of the College Chapel. *Recreation:* gardening. *Address:* Sedgeley, Olveston, Bristol. *T.:* Almondsbury 3377. [*Died* 31 *Aug.* 1962.

ASTBURY, Herbert Arthur; *b.* 14 Dec. 1870; *s.* of Thomas Astbury and Laura Welch; *m.* 1901, Emily Laura Stephens; two *s.* two *d.* *Educ.:* King Edward's High School, Birmingham. Has held managerial positions in Midland Bank at Cardiff, Derby, Leicester, and Birmingham; Assistant General Manager, 1920; Joint General Manager, 1924; Chief General Manager, 1938-43. Late Director Midland Bank Ltd., Midland Bank Executor and Trustee Company Ltd. *Recreations:* motoring, reading, bridge. *Address:* Hydro Hotel, Eastbourne, Sussex. [*Died* 17 *Jan.* 1968.

ASTBURY, Rev. Canon Stanley; *see* Astbury, Rev. Canon H. S.

ASTBURY, William Thomas, F.R.S. 1940; F.Inst.P.; M.A., Sc.D.(Cantab.); Professor of Biomolecular Structure and Hon. Reader in Textile Physics, Univ. of Leeds, since 1945; *b.* Longton, Stoke-on-Trent, 25 Feb. 1898; *e. s.* of W. E. Astbury; *m.* 1922, Frances, *d.* of D. Gould, Ballintemple, Cork; one *s.* one *d.* *Educ.:* Longton High School, Stoke-on-Trent; Jesus College, Cambridge (Scholar). Demonstrator in Physics, University College, London, and Assistant to Sir William Bragg, 1921-23; Assistant to Sir William Bragg at Davy-Faraday Laboratory of Royal Institution, 1923-28; Lecturer in Textile Physics, University of Leeds, 1928; Reader in Textile Physics, 1937, and Director of Textile Physics Research Laboratory, 1928, University of Leeds; Royal Society Croonian Lecturer, 1945; Member: Council of Royal Society, 1946-47; Food Investigation and Forest Products Research Boards, 1946-55; Royal Society of Sciences, Uppsala, 1946; Joint Services Materials Advisory Board, 1954-58; Hon. Life Member New York Academy of Sciences, 1950; Corresp. Member Istituto Lombardo di Scienze e Lettere, 1951; Foreign Member, Swedish Royal Academy of Sciences, 1956; Hon. Mem. British Biophysical Soc., 1960. Sc.D. (Cantab.), 1937; D. (h.c.), Univ. of Strasbourg, 1946; Medal of Univ. of Lille, 1933; Gold Medal of Company of Dyers, 1934; Warner Memorial Medal of Textile Institute, 1935; Actonian Prize of Royal Institution of Great Britain, 1935; Silvanus Thompson Medal of British Institute of Radiology, 1948; Medal of University of Brussels, 1949; Internat. Scientific Relations Medal, American Soc. of European Chemists, 1953; T. Duckett Jones Memorial Award, U.S., 1961. *Publications:* Fundamentals of Fibre Structure, 1933; Textile Fibres under the X-rays, 1943; many scientific papers on crystal structure, fibres, proteins and molecular biology. *Recreation:* music. *Address:* The University, Leeds 2. *T.:* 31751. *Clubs:* Athenæum, Royal Automobile. [*Died* 4 *June* 1961.

ASTELL, Richard John Vereker; *b.* 7 Sept. 1890; *s.* of late William Harvey Astell, Lieutenant Grenadier Guards, and Hon. Elizabeth M. Vereker, *d.* of 4th Viscount Gort (who married, 2nd, 1902, Philip, 3rd Baron De L'Isle and Dudley); *m.* 1922, Joan Evelyn, *o. c.* of James Crichton-Stuart. *Educ.:* Eton; Christ Church, Oxford. Attaché in H.M. Diplomatic Service, 1913; 3rd Secretary, 1915; 2nd Secretary, 1919; resigned, 1919; Served 1939-45 as Capt. in R.A. (A.A.) and War Office. *Address:* Woodbury Hall, Sandy, Beds. *Club:* Naval and Military. [*Died* 18 *June* 1969.

ASTOR, 3rd Viscount, *cr.* 1917, of Hever Castle; **William Waldorf Astor;** Baron, *cr.* 1916; Lt.-Comdr. R.N.V.R. (Sp.) 1939; *b.* 13 Aug. 1907; *e. s.* of 2nd Viscount Astor and of late Nancy, Viscountess Astor, *S.* father, 1952; *m.* 1st, 1945, Hon. Sarah Katharine Elinor Norton (marriage dissolved, 1953), *d.* of 6th Baron Grantley; one *s.*; 2nd, 1955, Philippa Victoria (marriage dissolved, 1960), *o. d.* of Lt.-Col. Henry Hunloke, T.D., and Lady Anne Holland-Martin; one *d.*; 3rd, 1960, Janet Bronwen Alun, *y. d.* of Judge Sir Alun Pugh; two *d.* *Educ.:* Eton; New College, Oxford. On Staff of Pilgrim Trust, 1930-31; Secretary to Earl of Lytton on League of Nations Commn. of Enquiry in Manchuria, 1932; in Unemployment Dept. of National Council of Social Service, 1933-34; M.P. (U.) East Fulham, 1935-45; Parliamentary Private Secretary to Sir Samuel Hoare when First Lord of the Admiralty, 1936-37, and when Home Secretary, 1937-39; M.P. (C.) Wycombe Div. of Bucks, 1951-52. Director: North British and Mercantile Insurance Co.; Trust Corp. of Bahamas; Chairman, Council of R.N.V.R. Officers' Assoc., 1944; Member, Board, Hosp. for Sick Children. Governor of The Peabody Trust. High Steward of Maidenhead. Grand Cross of Merit of the Sovereign Military Order of Malta, 1957; C.St.J. 1958. *Heir:* *s.* Hon. William Waldorf Astor, *b.* 27 Dec. 1951. *Address:* 45 Upper Grosvenor Street, W.1; Cliveden, Maidenhead, Berks. *Clubs:* White's, Carlton, Buck's, Pratt's. [*Died* 8 *March* 1966.

ASTOR, Nancy, Viscountess; (Nancy Witcher), C.H., 1937; M.P. (U.) Plymouth, Sutton Div., 1919-45; first woman M.P. to sit in Imperial Parliament; *d.* of late Chiswell Dabney Langhorne, Mirador, Greenwood, Va.; *m.* 1st, 1897, Robert Gould Shaw (*d.* 1930; from whom she obtained a decree of divorce, 1903); one *s.*; 2nd, 1906, 2nd Viscount Astor (*d.* 1952); four *s.* one *d.* Hon. LL.D., College of William and Mary, Williamsburg, Va., 1928; Univ. of Birmingham, 1930; Univ. of Exeter, 1959; Hon. D.Litt. Reading, 1937. *Publication:* My Two Countries, 1923. *Address:* 100 Eaton Square, S.W.1. *T.:* Belgravia 2228. [*Died* 2 *May* 1964.

ATCHERLEY, Air Marshal Sir Richard Llewellyn Roger, K.B.E., *cr.* 1956 (C.B.E. 1945; O.B.E. 1941); C.B. 1950; A.F.C. 1940 and bar 1942; Norwegian War Cross; Royal Air Force retired; *b.* 11 January 1904; *s.* of late Colonel (Hon. Major-General) Sir Llewellyn W. Atcherley, C.M.G., C.V.O.; unmarried. *Educ.:* Oundle; R.A.F. College, Cranwell. 29 (F) Squadron and 23 (F) Squadron, 1924-25; Central Flying School Instructor, 1925-28; High Speed Flight for Schneider Trophy race, 1928-29; won King's Cup Air Race with Flight Lt. Stainforth, 1929; 23 (F) Sqn., Kenley, 1929-1930; 14 Squadron, Amman, Jordan, 1930-34; R.A.E. Farnborough. 1934-37; R.A.F. Staff College, 1937-38; H.Q. Training Command: Air Staff Officer to Insp.-Gen., 1938-39; O.C. 219 Night Fighter Squadron, 1939-40; Norway, Garrison Commander Badu-Foss (Narvik), 1940; O.C. R.A.F. Station, Drem, 1940; O.C. No. 54 Night Fighter O.T.U. Church Fenton, 1941; Sector Commander, Fairwood Common, 1942; Sector-Commander, Kenley, 1942; A.O.C. 211

Group Desert Air Force, 1943; Air Support Training H.Q., A.E.A.F., 1944; Comdt., Central Fighter Establishment, 1945; Comdt. R.A.F. College, Cranwell, 1946-48; C.-in-C., Royal Pakistan Air Force, 1949-51; A.O.C. No. 12 Group, Fighter Command, 1951-53; Commander Royal Air Force Staff, British Joint Services Mission, Washington, 1953-Dec. 1955; A.O.C.-in-C., Flying Training Command, 1955-58, retd. Co-ordinator, Anglo American Community Relations, 1959-1961; Sales Director, Folland Aircraft Co., 1959-65. *Address:* Portesbery Woods, Camberley, Surrey. *T.:* Camberley 5846. *Club:* Royal Air Force. [*Died* 18 *April* 1970.

ATHENAGORAS, Archbishop (Archbishop of Thyateira); Metropolitan of Thyateira and Exarch of Western and Central Europe, Greek Orthodox Church, since 1951. Formerly Orthodox Bishop of Boston (U.S.A.), and became Metropolitan of Philadelphia (Venice). *Address:* (temp.) Flat 36, 56 Porchester Terrace, London, W.2. [*Died* 16 *Oct.* 1962.

ATKINS, Col. Sir John, K.C.M.G., *cr.* 1919 (C.M.G. 1916); K.C.V.O., *cr.* 1937; M.B. (Lond.), F.R.C.S. (Eng.), L.R.C.P. (Lond.); Physician in Ordinary to the late Duke of Connaught; Fellow Royal Society of Medicine; Vice-President West London Medico-Chirurgical Society; *b.* 1875; *m.* 1904, Elizabeth May (*d.* 1962), *d.* of late James Davies Smith; one *s.* *Educ.:* Guy's Hosp.; House Physician. Asst. House-Surgeon, and Clinical Assistant there; 1st Class Hons. Materia Medica and Pharmaceutical Chemistry, 1st M.B.; First Fellow of Queen Elizabeth College, Univ. of London; Member of Council, Queen Elizabeth College since 1912, and Chairman of Council, 1922-1958. Served South African War on staff of Imperial Yeomanry Hospital; European War, 1914-19, on Personal Staff of Commander-in-Chief (Earl of Ypres) while in France; subsequently appointed Assistant Director-General, Army Medical Service; Deputy Director of Medical Services, Great Britain (despatches four times, C.M.G., K.C.M.G.); member of Experiments Committee (British Army in the Field), Anti-Gas Committee and a Military Representative on the Central Medical War Committee and Central Professional Committee. *Publications:* Value of Examination of the Blood during Typhoid Fever, 1905; Paracentesis in Pleural and Pericardial Effusions, 1906; Angio-Neurotic Oedema, 1906; Defence against Gas Attacks, 1916; Gas-proof Dug-outs, 1916; The Origin and Development of Queen Elizabeth College, Univ. of London, 1956. *Recreation:* fly-fishing. *Address:* 95 Oakwood Court, W.14. *T.:* Western 4080. [*Died* 20 *April* 1963.

ATKINSON, Hon. Sir Cyril, Kt., *cr.* 1933; *b.* 9 May 1874; 2nd *s.* of Leonard William Atkinson of Bowdon, Cheshire; *m.* 1900, Kathleen O'Neill (*d.* 1947), *e. d.* of Michael Longridge; one *s.* (one *d.* decd.); *m.* 1948, Florence Morton Henderson, *widow* of Col. Michael Henderson. Stephen Heelis Gold Medallist, 1895; Studentship Bar Final, 1897. Called to the Bar, 1897; Bencher of Lincoln's Inn; Northern Circuit; K.C. 1913; Doctor of Laws (London); M.P. (C.) Altrincham Division of Cheshire 1924-33; late Referee under Part I. of Safeguarding of Industries Act; Judge of High Court of Justice, King's Bench Division, 1933-48; Member of Church Assembly, 1950-55; Lay Reader, Dioceses of St. Edmundsbury and Ipswich and Southwark; Past President Churches' Fellowship for Psychic Study. *Address:* Woodlands, Harley Place, Perth. *T.:* Perth 921940. *Club:* Royal Over-Seas League. [*Died* 29 *Jan.* 1967.

ATKINSON, Donald, B.A. (Oxon.); M.A. (Manchester); Professor of Ancient History, Victoria University of Manchester, 1929-51; Emeritus Professor, 1951; Curator, Corinium Museum, Cirencester; *b.* Birmingham, 13 Sept. 1886; *s.* of William Henry and Amelia Toy Atkinson; *m.* 1932, Kathleen Mary Tyrer Chrimes. *Educ.:* King Edward's School, Birmingham; Brasenose College, Oxford. Classical Master, Stamford Grammar School, 1909-12; Research Fellow in Archæology and Lecturer in Classics, University College, Reading, 1913-19; Reader in Ancient History, University of Manchester, 1919-29. *Address:* High St., Bampton, Oxon. [*Died* 4 *Feb.* 1963.

ATTLEE, 1st Earl *cr.* 1955; Viscount Prestwood, *cr.* 1955; **Clement Richard Attlee,** K.G. 1956; P.C. 1935; O.M. 1951; C.H. 1945; F.R.S. 1947; *b.* Putney, 3 Jan. 1883; 4th *s.* of late Henry Attlee, Solicitor, Westcott, Putney; *m.* 1922, Violet Helen (*d.* 1964), *d.* of late H. E. Millar, Heathdown, Hampstead; one *s.* three *d.* *Educ.:* Haileybury College; Univ. Coll., Oxford) 2nd Class Honours Modern History, M.A., Hon. Fellow, 1942). Called to Bar, Inner Temple, 1906; Hon. Bencher, 1946; practised until 1909. Secretary, Toynbee Hall, 1910; Lecturer, Ruskin College, 1911; Tutor and Lecturer in Social Science at London School of Economics, 1913-23; served European War in South Lancashire Regiment and Tank Corps, Gallipoli, Mesopotamia (wounded), and France, 1914-19; Major, 1917; first Labour Mayor of Stepney, 1919, 1920; Alderman, 1920-27; First Chairman of London Labour Mayors' and ex-Mayors' Assoc., 1919; joined Fabian Society, I.L.P. and Nat. Union of Clerks, 1908. M.P. (Lab.) Limehouse Division of Stepney, Nov. 1922-Feb. 1950, West Walthamstow, 1950-55. Parliamentary Private Secretary to the Leader of the Opposition (Rt. Hon. J. Ramsay MacDonald), 1922-24; Under-Secretary of State for War, 1924; Chancellor of the Duchy of Lancaster, 1930-31; Postmaster-General, 1931; Member of the Indian Statutory Commission, 1927; Deputy Leader of the Labour Party in the House of Commons, 1931-35; Leader of the Opposition, 1935-40; Lord Privy Seal, 1940-42; Sec. of State for Dominion Affairs, 1942-43; Lord President of the Council, 1943-45; Deputy Prime Minister, 1942-45; Prime Minister and First Lord of the Treasury, 1945-51; Minister of Defence, 1945-46; Leader of the Opposition, 1951-55. Attended San Francisco Conference, April 1945; Potsdam Conference as Representative of Opposition, June 1945, and as Prime Minister, July 1945; visited Ottawa and Washington for discussions with Mr. Mackenzie King and President Truman on Atomic Energy, Nov. 1945; Leader of U.K. Deleg. to Gen. Assembly of U.N., London, 1946; Leader of U.K. Deleg. to Paris Peace Conf., 1946. An Elder Brother of Trinity House, 1948; Hon. D.C.L., Oxf., 1946; Hon. LL.D.: Camb., 1946; Lond., 1947; Wales, 1949; Glasg., 1951; Nottingham, 1953; Aberdeen, 1956; Madras, 1956; Hull, 1958; Bristol, 1959; Ceylon, 1961; Hon. D.Litt., Reading, 1948; Hon. F.R.I.B.A.; Hon. Fellow: Univ. Coll., Oxford, 1942; Queen Mary Coll., Univ. of London, 1948; London School of Economics and Political Science, 1958. Azad Memorial Lectr., Delhi, 1961. Pres. Assoc. of Municipal Corpns., 1961-64. Freeman: Cities of Birmingham, Leeds, Manchester, Oxford, Aberdeen, Bristol, and of various boroughs; Hon. Freeman of City of London; Freeman and Liveryman of Worshipful Company of Innholders, 1946. K.G.St.J. 1946. *Publications:* The Social Worker; The Town Councillor (with W. A. Robson); The Will and the Way to Socialism; The Labour Party in Perspective, 1937; The Labour Party in Perspective—and Twelve Years Later, 1949; Purpose and Policy

(collected speeches); As It Happened (autobiography), 1954. *Heir:* s. Viscount Prestwood. *Address:* 1 King's Bench Walk, Temple, E.C.4. *T.:* City 5575. *Clubs:* Athenæum, Oxford and Cambridge.
[*Died* 8 *Oct.* 1967.

ATTLEE, Wilfrid Henry Waller, M.A., M.D., B.Ch. (Camb.), M.R.C.P. (Lond.), M.R.C.S. (Eng.); formerly Cons. Physician King Edward VII Hospital, Windsor; Cons. Physician Staines Cottage Hospital; *b.* 1876; *s.* of John Attlee, Dorking; *m.* 1920, Emily Bridget (*d.* 1952), *yr. d.* of Charles Cornelius Maconochie, C.B.E., K.C., Avontoun, Linlithgow; one *s.* two *d.* *Educ.:* Amersham Hall; St. John's College, Cambridge; St. Bartholomew's Hosp. Medical School. Senior Resident Medical Officer Metropolitan Hosp., 1901; House Surgeon and Extern Midwifery Assistant St. Barts. Hospital, 1902; Chairman Eton College Medical Board, 1920-45; in practice at Eton, 1905-45, except while holding temporary commission in R.A.M.C. in France, 1914-18 (despatches) retiring as Major. *Publications:* Various articles in Medical Books and Periodicals. *Recreation:* fishing. *Address:* c/o Westminster Bank, New Milton, Hants.
[*Died* 27 *Feb.* 1962.

ATTWATER, Harry Lawrence; Hon. Urological Surgeon Westminster Hosp., All Saints' Urological Centre; retired; late Cons. Urological Surgeon, Margaret Street Hospital for Diseases of the Chest; *b.* 1885; *s.* of late Thomas Henry Attwater, M.A., Barr.-at-Law, and late Edith J. Attwater; *m.* 1st, 1915, Nora Collingdon (*d.* 1929), *d.* of late Dr. W. Hawkins, Dorset; 2nd 1933, Doris Emily Winter, *d.* of late George Callaway. *Educ.:* Merchant Taylors' (Scholar); Pembroke Coll., Cambridge (Nat. Science Exhibitioner). B.A., 1906, Nat. Science Tripos, Part 1; M.A., 1909; M.R.C.S., L.R.C.P., 1909; F.R.C.S., 1912; M.Chir. Cantab., 1913; Temp. Capt. R.A.M.C., 1915-19, France and England; F.Z.S., F.R.S.M. (President of urological section, 1942-1943); Member of Medical Society of London, Harveian Soc., Chelsea Clinical Society, International Urological Society; Treasurer of West London Medico Chirurgical Society; President of Hunterian Society; Member of Executive Council of British Health Resorts Association; Member of B.M.A. *Publications:* numerous papers in medical journals. *Recreations:* photography and model engineering. *Address:* 59 Lichfield Court, Richmond, Surrey. *T.:* Richmond 0551; 51 Harley Street, W.1. *T.:* Langham 3711. [*Died* 22 *May* 1961.

ATTWELL, Mabel Lucie, (Mrs. Harold Earnshaw); Artist—child studies, illustrator; writer—children's stories and verse; *b.* London, 4 June 1879; sixth *c.* of Augustus and Ann Attwell; *m.* 1908, Harold Earnshaw (*d.* 1937); one *s.* one *d* (and one *s.* decd.). *Educ.:* Coopers' Company School; privately. Studied painting and life drawing at Regent Street Art School, Heatherley's, etc.; has illustrated Charles Kingsley's Water Babies, Hans Andersen's Fairy Tales, Grimm's Fairy Tales, Lewis Carroll's Alice in Wonderland, Queen of Roumania's Fairy Tale Books, Sir J. M. Barrie's Peter and Wendy, etc.; The Lucie Attwell's Annual, 1922-62; child studies published by Tatler, Graphic; textiles, china and toys. *Address:* Fowey, Cornwall. *T.:* Fowey 3218.
[*Died* 5 *Nov.* 1964.

ATTWOOD, Harold A. F.; *see* Freeman-Attwood.

ATUKORALA, Nandasara Wijetilaka, C.M.G. 1955; C.B.E. 1954 (O.B.E. 1951; M.B.E. 1948); J.P.; B.Sc. (Lond.); Economic Affairs Officer, Ceylon Embassy, Washington, D.C., U.S.A.; *b.* 18 August 1915; *s.* of A. W. Atukorala; *m.* 1948, Ione Surangani, *d.* of Justice E. W. Jayewardena; two *s.* *Educ.:* University College, Ceylon. Assistant Settlement Officer, Ceylon, 1938-1941; Secretary, Ministry of Agriculture and Lands, Ceylon, 1941-47; Secretary to the Prime Minister, Ceylon, 1947-54; Secretary to the Governor-General, Ceylon, 1954-62, retired. Manager, Mackinnon Mackenzie & Co. of Ceylon Ltd., Colombo, 1962-68, retd. S.B.St.J. 1954. *Address:* Embassy of Ceylon, 2148 Wyoming Avenue N.W., Washington, D.C. 20008, U.S.A. [*Died* 4 *Aug.* 1969.

ATWOOD, Clare; Hon. Life Member New English Art Club; *b.* Richmond, Surrey, 14 May 1866; *o. d.* of late Frederick Atwood, architect. Studied under L. C. Nightingale, and at Westminster and the Slade School under Professor Frederick Brown; exhibitor at the Tate Gallery, and principal London Exhibitions, and in the Provinces; also in Scotland, Ireland, France, Italy, Germany, Austria, America, Australia. Work purchased by National Gallery, New Zealand, 1940; painter of interiors with figures, portraits, and still-life; commissioned to paint for the Canadian Government, 1919, and for the Imperial War Museum, London, 1920. *Recreations:* music and the theatre. *Address:* Leyborne Lodge, Kew, Surrey. [*Died* 2 *Aug.* 1962.

AUBOYNEAU, Admiral Philippe Marie Joseph Raymond, K.C.B. (Hon.) 1946; Commandant les Forces Maritimes Françaises de la Méditerranée, 1955; Member of Conseil Supérieur de la Marine, and of Conseil Supérieur des Forces Armées; *b.* 9 Nov. 1899; *s.* of Gaston Auboyneau and Germaine de la Motte-Ango de Flers. *Educ.:* Lycée Carnot, Paris. Entered École Navale, 1917; Enseigne de Vaisseau, 1918; served in torpedo-boats and destroyers in the Channel till Nov. 1918; Lt. de Vaisseau, 1925; Brevet École de Guerre Navale, 1934; Capitaine de Corvette, 1935; Capitaine de Frégate, 1939; Capitaine de Vaisseau, 1940; Rear-Admiral, 1942; Vice-Adm., 1945; Vice-Amiral d'Escadre, 1952; Admiral, 1957; Commands: Motor Launch Flotilla of the Danube and Black Sea, 1919-20; Survey Ship Alidade, 1926-27; Gunboat Doudart de Lagree (Yangtse Flotilla), 1930-32; Destroyer Orage, 1937-39; Light Cruiser Le Triomphant and 1st Light Cruiser Division, 1940-42; C.-in-C. Fighting French Naval Forces, 1942-44; 3rd Div. of Cruisers, 1944-45; C.-in-C. French Naval Forces in the Far East, 1945-47; Inspector of French Naval Aviation, 1947-49; C.-in-C. French Forces (Army, Navy, Air Force), Indian Ocean, 1949-51; Gen. Inspector of French Navy, 1951-52. C.-in-C., French Naval Forces in Far East, 1952-54. *Publications:* Rôle de la marine française sur le Yang-Tse-Kiang, 1933; Guerre de succession de Pologne—Campagne de la Baltique, 1935. *Recreations:* yachting, golf, etc. *Address:* 74 Rue Raynouard, Paris, 16e. *Clubs:* Hon. member of various London. [*Died* 22 *Feb.* 1961.

AUBREY, Sir Stanley James, Kt., *cr.* 1939; Member of the Committee of Lloyd's; Trustee, Lloyd's Patriotic Fund; Treas. and Member of Council, King George's Fund for Sailors; Fellow of Chartered Insurance Institute; *b.* 3 Oct. 1883; 2nd *s.* of late James Warren Aubrey; unmarried. *Educ.:* privately. Entered Lloyd's, 1901; Underwriting Member of Lloyd's, 1910; first served on Committee of Lloyd's, 1927; Deputy Chm. of Lloyd's, 1934, 1943, 1944, 1948, 1949, 1950; Chairman, 1935, 1938 and 1939; awarded Lloyd's Gold Medal, 1939. Member of Board of Trade Committee on Compulsory Insurance, 1936-37. *Address:* 232 Cranmer Court, S.W.3. *T.:* Kensington 4736; Lloyd's, E.C.3. *T.:* Mansion House 7615. *Clubs:* City of London, Garrick.
[*Died* 14 *Sept.* 1962.

AUBREY-FLETCHER, Maj. Sir Henry Lancelot, 6th Bt. *cr.* 1782; C.V.O.

1957; D.S.O. 1918; late Grenadier Guards; Lord Lieutenant of Buckinghamshire, 1954-1961; *b.* 10 Sept. 1887; *e. surv. s.* of Sir Lancelot Aubrey-Fletcher, 5th Bt., and Emily Harriet (*d.* 1911), *d.* of late Rev. Nugent Wade; *S.* father, 1937; *m.* 1st, 1911, Mary Augusta (*d.* 1963), *e. d.* of Rev. R. W. Chilton, Rector of Great Horkesley, Colchester; four *s.* one *d.*; 2nd, 1965, Mrs. Nancy Cecil Reynolds, *y. d.* of Joseph Cecil Bull. *Educ.:* Eton; New College, Oxford. Joined 1st Batt. Grenadier Guards, 1908; retired, 1920; served European War, 1914-1918 (twice wounded, despatches, D.S.O., Brevet Major, French Croix de Guerre); served also, 1940-45; J.P. Bucks; Co. Alderman, Bucks; High Sheriff of Bucks, 1925, Lt., H.M. Body Guard of the Hon. Corps of Gentlemen-at-Arms, 1956-57 (Standard Bearer, 1955). *Publications:* A History of the Foot Guards to 1856; author of several novels under pen-name of Henry Wade. *Heir:* *s.* John Henry Lancelot Aubrey-Fletcher. *Address:* Barnfield, Delly End, Hailey, nr. Witney, Oxon. *T.:* Ramsden 389.
[*Died* 30 *May* 1969.

AUDLEY, 23rd Baron, Eng., *cr.* 1312-13; **Thomas Percy Henry Touchet Tuchet-Jesson,** M.B.E. 1945; Major (temp.) Worcester Regt.; *b.* 15 Sept. 1913; *s.* of late Thomas Touchet Tuchet-Jesson; *S.* kinswoman, 1942; *m.* 1st, 1952, Mrs. J. de Trafford (marr. diss., 1958), *d.* of late R. S. Chaplin; 2nd, 1962, Sarah, *d.* of Sir Winston Churchill, *q.v.* *Educ.:* Lancing College; Hertford College, Oxford. *Heir: sister,* Hon. Mrs. John Macnamee (Rosina Lois Veronica) [*b.* 10 July 1911; *m.* 1943, John Archibald Joseph Macnamee]. *Address:* 47 Clabon Mews, S.W.1; Upper Mill, Ashbury, Wilts.
[*Died* 3 *July* 1963.

AULD, Lieut.-Col. Samuel James Manson, O.B.E.; M.C.; D.Sc., Ph.D.; Chemical Engineer; *b.* Kilmarnock, 25 July 1884; *s.* of David Auld and Sara Manson; *m.* 1st, 1911, Ethel, 2nd *d.* of E. Montague Edwards, J.P.; two *s.*; 2nd, 1932, Mrs. Annie Lawrence Lewis (*d.* 1955); *m.* 1958, Mary Voshell-Flock, New York City. *Educ.:* Queen Mary College (University of London) (Drapers' Scholar); Universities of Würzburg and Leipzig. Scientific Staff, Imperial Institute, 1905-10; Head of Chemical Dept., South-Eastern Agricultural Coll., Wye, Kent. 1910-12; Professor of Agricultural Chemistry, Reading University, 1912-14; with Anglo-Persian Oil Company, 1919-28; Vacuum Oil Co. Ltd. 1930-52; Past-President, Oil Industries Club and London Ayrshire Society; Commission, Unattached List, 1909; 4th Royal Berks Regiment, 1913-21; Regular Army Reserve of Officers, R.E., 1921-39; Regimental, 1914-15; C.A. G.H.Q. and D.A.D.G.S., 1915-17; C.A. 3rd Army, 1917; Commanding British Gas Warfare Mission to U.S.A., and attached American Army, 1917-19; War Office, 1919-20 (despatches, M.C., O.B.E., American Distinguished Service Medal). Technical Adviser Petroleum Board, Petroleum (Warfare) Dept., Member War Cabinet Technical Sub-committee on Axis Oil, Chairman Enemy Oils and Fuels Committee, etc., Chairman Lubricating Oil Pool Technical Committee, 1939-46; Consultant and Dir. of Companies, 1949-; President, Institute of Petroleum, 1937 and 1954; Mem. Scientific Advisory Council, Min. of Fuel and Power, 1955, Min. of Power, 1958-; Mem. Admiralty Fuel and Lubricants Advisory Cttee., 1953-. *Publications:* publications in Proceedings Royal Society, Journal of Chemical Society, Journal of Agricultural Science, Journal of Institute of Petroleum, etc.; Gas and Flame in Modern Warfare, 1917; papers on Gas Warfare in R.E. Journal, Washington Academy of Science, etc. *Recreation:* fishing. *Address:* Bedford Court Mansions, Bedford Square, W.C.1. *Clubs:* Athenæum, Royal Automobile.
[*Died* 19 *Aug.* 1963.

AURIOL, Vincent, Grand Cross of Legion of Honour; Member of the Constitutional Council of the French Republic; *b.* 1884; *m.* 1912, Michelle Aucouturier; one *s.* *Educ.:* Toulouse Univ. (D. en Droit, L. ès L. Philosophie). Dep. for Haute Garonne, 1914; Gen. Sec. S.F.I.O. (Socialist Group) in Chamber of Deputies, 1919-36; Pres. of Finance Cttee. until resigned, 1925; Member of Financial Delegation to U.S., 1925; Minister of Finance in Blum Cabinet, 1936-1937; Minister of Justice in Chautemps Cabinet, 1937; Minister of Co-ordination of Services to Presidency of Council, March-April 1938. Voted against French Surrender, 1940; interned; escaped to London, 1943; Member French Provisional Consultative Assembly in Algiers and in Paris; President Foreign Affairs Committee, 1945; President Socialist Group; Minister of State (provisional de Gaulle Govt.), 1945; President: The two Constituent Assemblies, 1946; National Assembly, 1946; President of the French Republic, Jan. 1947-54. Patron (Pres. of Honour). World Veterans' Federation, 1954. Hon. D.C.L. Oxford, 1954, etc.; (Hon.) G.C.B. 1950; numerous other foreign decorations. *Address:* Cap Bênat par Bormes les Mimosas (Var), France.
[*Died* 1 *Jan.* 1966.

AUSTEN, General Sir Alfred R. G.; *see* Godwin-Austen.

AUSTEN, Winifred M. L., R.I. 1933; R.E. 1922; animal painter; *d.* of Josiah Austen, Staff Surgeon, R.N., and Fanny Mann; *m.* 1917, Oliver O'Donnell Frick (*d.* 1923). Member Royal Society of Painter Etchers and Engravers, Fellow of the Zoological Society, Member of the Royal Society for the Protection of Birds. *Works:* Paintings of animal life at the Royal Academy, Paris Salon, and other exhibitions. *Address:* Wayside, Orford, Suffolk. *T.:* Orford 258.
[*Died* 1 *Nov.* 1964.

AUSTEN-LEIGH, Richard Arthur, F.S.A.; F.R.S.L.; *b.* 17 May 1872; 2nd *s.* of Cholmeley Austen-Leigh and Melesina Mary, *d.* of Most Rev. R. C. Trench, sometime Archbishop of Dublin; *m.* 1st, 1906, Vera Mercedes (*d.* 1927), *e. d.* of Arthur Trench; 2nd, 1941, Margaret, *d.* of Col. E. H. Thruston. *Educ.:* Eton; King's College, Cambridge. 1st Class Classical Tripos, 1894; President of Amateur Dramatic Company (Cambridge), 1894; Clerk in the House of Commons, 1897-1900; President of the British Federation of Master Printers, 1922-1923; has represented the Federation at congresses in France, Belgium, Holland, Sweden, Germany, and the United States; Chairman of the Joint Industrial Council of the Printing Trade, 1927-28; President, Festival of Printers' Pension Corporation, 1941; President of the Bibliographical Society, 1934-36; President of the Huguenot Society, 1934-37; Treasurer and Chairman of Committee of Management of National Benevolent Institution, 1936-45; Chairman of the Council of the International Bureau of the Federations of Master Printers, 1934-49; Master, Stationers' Company, 1954-55. Chevalier, Order of Leopold (Belgium); Commandeur de Mérite Commercial (France). *Publications:* Eton College Register: I. 1698-1752 and II 1753-1790; The Eton Guide, 1904; Bygone Eton, 1905; Life and Letters of Jane Austen (with W. Austen-Leigh), 1913; The Story of a Printing House, 1911; Austen Papers, 1704-1856, 1942; Jane Austen and Lyme Regis, 1943; Jane Austen and Southampton, 1949; editor of the Master Printers Annual since 1920 and of *Etoniana* since 1904. *Address:* Isel Hall, Cockermouth, Cumberland. *T.:* Cockermouth 2159. *Club:* Athenæum.
[*Died* 18 *Oct.* 1961.

AUSTIN, Major-General Arthur Bramston, C.B. 1946; F.D.S.R.C.S.; *b.* 22 Aug. 1893; *s.* of late Arthur Frederick Austin, Chigwell, Essex; *m.* 1918, Gladys Mary, *d.* of late Henry Thomas Appleby, Bournemouth; two *d.* *Educ.:* The School, Bishop's Stortford; London University. House Surgeon, Royal Dental Hospital, 1915; Lieut. Army Dental Corps, 1915; Capt. 1919; Major, 1927; Lt.-Col. 1935; Col. 1940; Maj.-Gen. 1942. Served European War, Macedonia, 1916-18; Asst. Director of Dental Services, Southern Command, 1939-1940; Deputy Director of Dental Service, B.E.F., France, 1940; Asst. Director of Dental Service, Aldershot Command, 1940-1941; South-Eastern Command, 1941-42; Director Army Dental Service, War Office, 1942-48; retired pay, 1948; Col Comdt. Royal Army Dental Corps, 1951-58. K.H.D.S., 1946-48. Councillor, Salisbury City Council, 1960. *Recreation:* golf. *Address:* Littlecott, Bouverie Close, Harnham, Salisbury, Wilts. [*Died* 5 *Aug.* 1967.

AUSTIN, Warren Robinson; lawyer, United States; Member Atomic Energy Commission; *b.* Highgate, Vermont, 12 Nov. 1877; *s.* of Chauncey Goodrich Austin and Ann Mathilda Robinson; *m.* 1901, Mildred Mary, *d.* of Edward Fenton Lucas; two *s.* *Educ.:* Brigham Academy, Bakersfield, Vt.; Univ. of Vermont (Ph.B. 1899). Studied law and practised in his father's firm, C. G. Austin & Sons, St. Albans, Vt., until 1916; admitted to Vermont Bar, 1902; legal representative in China for American International Corporation, 1916; during European War, 1914-18, lectured on military law, and 1925-28, on med. jurisprudence at Univ. of Vermont; practised at Burlington, Vt., 1917-31. State's Attorney for Franklin County, 1904-06; U.S. Commissioner, 1907-15; Chm. Republican State Convention, 1908; U.S. Senator, 1931-46; Special Ambassador of the President and Adviser to the Acting Representative of U.S. to United Nations, 1946-47; Representative of United States at the seat of United Nations with rank of Ambassador, 1947-53; Hon. Chm., Vermont Council on World Affairs, 1953-. Chm. Advisory Cttee., Permanent H.Q., U.N.; U.S. Representative in the Security Council; Delegate to conferences; member of many legal associations. Recipient of many honours and awards; Hon. LL.D. or D.C.L. of numerous universities. *Recreation:* his apple orchard. *Address:* 43 Williams Street, Burlington, Vermont, U.S.A. *T.:* Burlington 2-1419. *Clubs:* Alibi, Allfalfa (Washington, D.C.); Ethan Allen (Burlington, Vermont), etc. [*Died* 25 *Dec.* 1962.

AUSTRAL, Florence; Dramatic Soprano, Grand Opera and Concert Artist, retd.; *b.* Richmond, Melbourne, Victoria, Australia, 26 Apr. 1894; *m.* 1925, John Amadio (*d.* 1964), solo flautist; no *c.* *Educ.:* Melbourne. Studied Singing, Harmony, and Pianoforte at University Conservatorium, Melbourne, and later studied opera at London School of Opera; studied Italian opera in New York under Signor Sibella; made début in Grand Opera at Covent Garden with British National Opera Co. as Brünnhilde in Wagner's Valkyrie, 1922; subsequently sang Brünnhilde in Wagner's complete cycle of the Ring at Covent Garden and throughout Great Britain; also sang Aida in Verdi's Aida with B.N.O.C.; toured England as soloist with Sir Landon Ronald and Royal Albert Hall Orchestra; appeared frequently at Albert Hall and Queen's Hall Concerts with Sir Henry Wood's Queen's Hall Orchestra and London Symphony Orchestra, also at Manchester Hallé and most of the principal concerts throughout Great Britain; American début, May 1925; sang at Evanston and Cincinnati Festivals, toured America, 1926; also appeared as Brünnhilde in Valkyrie and Siegfried, State Opera House, Berlin, 1930; has made six successive tours of U.S.A. and Canada; has toured Australia twice and Holland several times. *Recreations:* reading, needlework, and cooking. *Address:* 52 Caldwell Street, Merewether, New South Wales, Australia. [*Died* 16 *May* 1968.

AUTEN, Captain Harold, V.C. 1918; D.S.C. 1918 (for services in command of H.M.S. Stock Force, a "mystery ship"); Royal Naval Reserve; Executive Vice-Pres. J. Arthur Rank Organisation Inc., New York; Younger Brother of Trinity House; *m.*; one *s.* one *d.* *Educ.:* Wilson's Grammar School; *Publication:* Q Boat Adventures, 1919. *Address:* 245 West 52nd Street, New York City; Bushkill, Pike Co., Pennsylvania. *Clubs:* Savage; Lotos, Whitehall (New York). [*Died* 3 *Oct.* 1964.

AVERY, Brigadier Henry Esau, C.M.G. 1919; C.B.E. 1943; D.S.O. 1916; *b.* Wellington, N.Z., 1885; *s.* of Joseph Avery, Wellington, N.Z; *m.* 1913, Alice Maude, *d.* of Mrs. Annie Draper, Blenheim, N.Z.; three *s.* four *d.* *Educ.:* Wellington College, Wellington, N.Z. Served as Staff-Officer in N.Z. Staff Corps; served European War, with N.Z. Division H.Q., 1914-18 (despatches, D.S.O., C.M.G.); graduated Staff College, Camberley, 1920; represented Wellington Province, North Island of N.Z., and New Zealand (1910) at Rugby football; General Manager, Avery Motors, Ltd., 1924-36; President of Wellington Returned Soldiers Association, 1930-32; Secretary and Assistant Manager, N.Z. Centennial Exhibition, 1937-40; Quartermaster General, N.Z. Military Forces, 1940-45; General Manager War Assets Realisation Board, 1945-48; retired 31 Dec. 1948. *Address:* 151 Main Road, Eastbourne, Wellington, New Zealand. [*Died* 22 *March* 1961.

AVEZATHE, Gerald Henry, C.M.G. 1943; *b.* 1889; retired 1953, as director: Elder Dempster Lines Ltd. (Dep. Chm.); Elder Dempster Lines (Canada), Ltd.; West African Lighterage and Transport Co. Ltd. M.L.C. and M.E.C., Nigeria, 1942-46; formerly Ministry of War Transport Rep. in Lagos. *Address:* Walcheren, 52 Park Avenue, Broadstairs, Kent. [*Died* 17 *Feb.* 1966.

AWBERY, Stanley Stephen, J.P. Glamorgan; *b.* 19 July 1888; two *s.* three *d.* Trade Union official since 1920; Chairman Swansea Labour Assoc., 1921; Chairman of Swansea General and Eye Hospital, 1922; contested Clitheroe Div., 1931 and 1935; Alderman Barry Borough Council, 1939-45; Mayor Barry, 1941; Port Labour Inspector, South Wales Ports, 1941-42. M.P. (Lab.) Bristol Central, 1945-64. *Publications:* Labour's Early Struggles in Swansea, 1949; Let Us Talk of Barry, 1954; Llancarfan, the Village of a Thousand Saints, 1957; The Story of St. Athan and Aberthaw, 1959; I Searched for Llantwit Major, 1965; St. Donat's Castle and the Stradlings, 1966; The Baptists in Barry for 150 Years, 1967; Fourteen Talks about Barry, 1968. *Address:* 37 Woodland Road, Barry, Glam. *T.:* Barry 2812. [*Died* 7 *May* 1969.

AYALA, Ramon Pérez de; Spanish diplomatist and author, critic and poet; *b.* Oviedo, Spain, 9 Aug. 1880; *m.* Mabel Rick; two *s.* *Educ.:* The University, Oviedo. Spanish Ambassador at the Court of St. James, 1931-1936; Director of Prado Museum, 1931-36; resident in South America, 1938-54. Member of the Spanish Academy of Language, 1928. Awarded Juan March Foundation Prize, 1960. *Publications:* verse: La Paz del sendero, 1904; El sendero innumerable, 1915; El sendero andante, 1921; novels, essays and short stories: Tinieblas en las cumbres, 1907; A.M.D.G., 1910 (translated into German, Italian, and French); La pata de la raposa, 1911 (translated into English); Troteras y danzaderas, 1912; Prometeo, 1915 (short stories translated into English, French, Italian, etc.); Herman encadenado, 1917 (travels on the Italian front during the War); Las mascaras, 1920 (essays and criticisms on dramatic literature); Politica y Toros, 1920 (essays); Belarmino y Apolonio, 1921 (translated into French, Russian, Italian, English, Japanese and German); Luna de miel, 1922; Urbano y Simona (translated into Italian), 1922; El ombligo del mundo, 1925 (short stories translated into English, German, etc.); Tigre Juan, 1926 (translated into English); El curandero de su honra, 1926 (translated into English). Literary contributions made to A.B.C. *Recreations:* duty and life in itself. *Address:* c/o A.B.C., Calle de Serrano 61, Madrid, Spain; Gabriel Lobo 11, Madrid, Spain. [*Died* 5 *Aug.* 1962.

AYERS, Charles William, C.I.E. 1937; C.B.E. 1945; *b.* 18 Aug. 1880; *s.* of late William Henry Ayers and Jane A. R. Wakefield, Snodland, Kent; *m.* 1st, 1910, Harriet Higgs; 2nd, 1921, Evelyn Flint; four *d.* (and one *d.* decd.) *Educ.:* Tudor House School, Snodland. Assistant Officer of Excise, 1901; Assistant Surveyor of Taxes, 1905; Seconded to Government of India as Expert Adviser on Income Tax Subjects, Oct. 1935-Feb. 1937 (C.I.E.); Senior Principal Inspector of Taxes, 1937; retired 1940; Excess Profits Tax Adviser to Government of India, 1940-48. *Recreation:* gardening. *Address:* High Ridge, Yelling, Huntingdon. [*Died* 21 *Dec.* 1965.

AYKROYD, Sir Alfred Hammond, 2nd Bt., *cr.* 1920; late Major, Royal Field Artillery; Director of Martins Bank, Ltd. (Manchester Board); *b.* 3 June 1894; *s.* of Sir William Henry Aykroyd, 1st Baronet of Grantley Hall, Ripon, and Emma Louisa, *d.* of Erza Waugh Hammond; *S.* father, 1947; *m.* 1919, Sylvia, *d.* of late Francis Walker, Huddersfield, and *widow* of Lt.-Col. Foster Newton Thorne; one *s.* one *d.* *Educ.:* Charterhouse. High Sheriff of Yorkshire, 1952; Pres. Yorkshire Agric. Soc., 1954. *Recreations:* hunting (M.F.H., 1948-53), shooting. *Heir:* *s.* Lt. William Miles Aykroyd, M.C. [*b.* 24 Aug. 1923. *Educ.:* Charterhouse]. *Address:* Linton Spring, Wetherby, Yorks. *T.A.:* Aykroyd, Wetherby. *T.:* Wetherby 2006. *Club:* Boodle's. [*Died* 29 *April* 1965.

AYLEN, Mrs. H. C.; *see* Romanné-James.

AYLWEN, Sir George, 1st Bt., *cr.* 1949; Kt. 1942; Treasurer, St. Bartholomew's Hospital Old Voluntary Board, since 1937; Treasurer and Chairman, St. Bartholomew's Hospital, 1937-60; President, Medical Coll. of St. Bartholomew's Hospital, 1937-60; elected hon. Perpetual Student, 1960; Member of Council, King Edward's Hospital Fund for London, since 1944 (Member Management Cttee., 1944-60); Gov. Christ's Hospital; *s.* of late Arthur and Elizabeth Aylwen; *m.* Edith (marriage dissolved; she *d.* 1963), *d.* of late George Thomas Hill, Ipswich; one *d.* (and one *d.* decd.); *m.* 1951, Mme. Elena Bulgarides, *d.* of late Prof. Alexander Bulgarides; one step *s.* *Educ.:* privately. Past Master, Merchant Taylors' Co.; Alderman Langbourn Ward, 1941-51; Liveryman, Soc. of Apothecaries of London; Sheriff of City of London, 1946-47, Lord Mayor, 1948-49; one of H.M. Lieutenants of City of London, since 1932; Chairman, Voluntary Hospitals Committee for London, 1941-48; (First) Chairman Legal Aid Advisory Committee to Lord Chancellor, 1950-1956. Formerly partner in J. & A. Scrimgeour, E.C.4. Freeman, City of Philadelphia. Knight of Order of St. John of Jerusalem. Served South African War, 1900-02, with 2nd Royal Fusiliers, Lieutenant (Queen's medal four clasps); European War, 1914-18, with 11th Bn. Royal Fusiliers; Major retired, 1918. *Address:* 39 Green Street, W.1. *Clubs:* Pratt's, Eccentric (Hon.), Pilgrims. [*Died* 27 *Sept.* 1967.

AYNSLEY, Sir Charles M. M.; *see* Murray-Aynsley.

AYRES, Sir Reginald John, K.B.E. 1958 (C.B.E. 1949; O.B.E. 1946); C.B. 1955; Part-time Member National Coal Board since May 1961; *b.* 1900. Deputy Secretary, Ministry of Power, 1955-61, retd. *Address:* 7 Berrylands Road, Surbiton, Surrey. *Club:* Royal Automobile. [*Died* 25 *June* 1966.

B

BABER, Lt.-Colonel John Barton, C.B.E. 1949; M.C. 1915; T.D.; T.A. retd.; Under-Secretary, Ministry of Agriculture and Fisheries, 1951-54; *b.* 23 March 1892; *s.* of Harry Baber, Barrister-at-law, and Clara, *d.* of Major-Gen. Charles Barton, R.A.; *m.* 1st, 1926, Joyce, *d.* of Harvey Collingridge; two *s.*; 2nd, 1940, Jocelyn, *d.* of Major Ashley Dodd. *Educ.:* Marlborough; Trinity Coll., Cambridge (M.A.). Served European War, 1st Queen's Westminster Rifles, 1914-19, France and Belgium; War of 1939-45, 1st Queen's Westminsters and R.A.F. regiment, Normandy and Germany. Ministry of Agriculture and Fisheries, 1919-39 and 1945-54. *Publication:* (with wife) Castello, Portofino, 1965. *Address:* 4 Albert Terrace, N.W.1; Prattshayes House, Littleham, Nr. Exmouth, Devon. *Clubs:* United University, M.C.C. [*Died* 4 *July* 1967.

BABINGTON, Air Marshal Sir Philip, K.C.B., *cr.* 1943 (C.B. 1941); M.C. 1916; A.F.C. 1919; *b.* Feb. 1894; 4th *s.* of Charles H. Babington and Grace Damaris, *d.* of John Tremayne, Heligan and Sydenham; *m.* 1918, Joan, O.B.E. 1946, 3rd *d.* of Henry Avereil Daniell, Ledgers, Warlingham; (one *s.* Royal Air Force, killed on active service, May 1942) three *d.* *Educ.:* Eton. Joined Hampshire Regt. in 1914; transferred Dec. 1914 to Royal Flying Corps; served throughout European War, 1914-18 (despatches thrice, M.C., A.F.C.); Asst. Commandant R.A.F. College, Cranwell, 1931-35; Director of Postings, Air Ministry, 1936-40; Air Member for Personnel, 1940-42; A.O.C.-in-C. Flying Training Command, 1942-45; retired from R.A.F. Dec. 1945. *Address:* Glebe House, Chiddingstone, Kent. *T.:* Penshurst 457. *Club:* Royal Air Force. [*Died* 25 *Feb.* 1965.

BACHARACH, Alfred Louis, M.A., F.R.I.C.; *b.* 11 Aug. 1891; *s.* of Otto Leonhard and Alice Eva Bacharach; *m.* 1931, Elizabeth Owen; two *s.* *Educ.:* private school, Hampstead; St. Paul's School; Clare College, Cambridge. Wellcome Chemical Research Laboratory, 1915-18; Wellcome Chemical Works, 1918-19; Joseph Nathan & Co., Ltd., subsequently Glaxo Laboratories, Ltd., 1920-1956. Past Pres. Nutrition Soc.; past Chm., Food Group, Society of Chemical Industry; former Vice-Pres.: Royal Institute of Chemistry; Soc. of Chemical Industry; Society for Analytical Chemistry; Vice-President: Hampstead Scientific Society; Research Defence Society; Hon. Member, Working Men's College, N.W.1; Governor: Borough Polytechnic; Kynaston School. *Publications:* Science and Nutrition, 1938; (joint translator), Chromatography, 1941; Editor of: The Nation's Food, 1946 (joint ed.); Hormones in Blood, 1961 (joint ed.); Evaluation of Drug Activities, 1964 (joint ed.); Exploration Medicine, 1965 (joint ed.);

The Physiology of Human Survival, 1965 (joint ed.); The Musical Companion, 1934; Lives of the Great Composers, 1935; British Music of Our Time, 1946; The Music Masters, 1948-54; scientific papers in Biochemical Jl., Analyst, Brit. Jl. of Nutrition, etc.; scientific broadcasts. *Address:* 26 Willow Road, N.W.3. *T.:* Hampstead 3889. *Club:* Savage. [*Died* 16 *July* 1966.

BACKHAUS, Wilhelm; Pianist; *b.* **Leipsic, 26 March 1884;** *s.* **of Guido and Clara Schönberg;** *m.* **Alma Herzberg.** *Educ.:* **Leipsic Conservatoire under Alois Reckendorf; Frankfort-on-Maine under Eugen d'Albert. Won the Rubinstein Prize in Paris, 1905; Professor of the Piano, Royal College of Music, Manchester, 1905.** *Recreations:* **walking, motoring, bridge.** *Address:* **Villa Wellingtonia, Lugano, Switzerland.** [*Died* 5 *July* 1969.

BACKHOUSE, Lt.-Col. Miles Roland Charles, D.S.O. 1902 and bar, 1917; T.D.; Lt.-Col. T.A. (retd.); formerly Vice-President International Sleeping Car Co.; Director: Brixton Estate Ltd.; La Protectrice Insurance Co., Paris; *b.* 24 Nov. 1878; 4th *s.* of late Sir Jonathan Edmund Backhouse, 1st Bt. and Florence, *d.* of Sir W. Salusbury-Trelawny, 9th Bt. of Trelawne, Cornwall; *m.* 1904, Olive (*d.* 1954), 2nd *d.* of late Geoffrey F. Buxton, C.B.; three *s.* one *d.* *Educ.:* Eton; Trinity Hall, Cambridge. Served in the 14th Squadron Imperial Yeomanry in South Africa, 1900-2 (wounded, despatches, D.S.O., Queen's medal three clasps, King's medal two clasps); Hon. Capt. in Army, 1902; European War, 1914-18, Northumberland Hussars, North Somerset Yeomanry, and 8th Battn. Yorkshire Regt. (despatches four times, bar to D.S.O.). *Address:* 12 Cheyne Court, Flood Street, S.W.3. *T.:* Flaxman 8778. *Clubs:* Travellers'; Travellers' (Paris). [*Died* 15 *May* 1962.

BACON, Janet Ruth, M.A.; *b.* 26 Oct. 1891; *d.* of Richard Bacon, Oxford. *Educ.:* Oxford High School; Girton College. Classical Tripos, 1915, 1916; Assistant Mistress, King Edward VI.'s High School, Birmingham, 1916-18; Director of Studies and Lecturer in Classics, Girton College, 1919-35; University Lecturer in Classics, 1926-35; Principal, Royal Holloway College, (Univ. of London), 1935-44. *Publications:* The Voyage of the Argonauts, 1925; articles in classical periodicals. *Address:* 14 Rawlinson Road, Oxford. [*Died* 25 *Jan.* 1965.

BACON, Sir Roger (Sewell), Kt. 1958; M.B.E. 1943; Retd.; *b.* 23 Jan. 1895; *er. s.* of Sewell Bacon; *m.* 1946, Catherine Grace, *e. d.* of Hon. Sir James Connolly. *Educ.:* Rugby; Balliol College, Oxford. Called to Bar (Middle Temple), 1923. Temporary Commissions: Aug. 1914-Feb. 1919 (Cheshire Regt.); Jan. 1940-Feb. 1946 (Staff). A Deputy Judge Advocate, 1940-43; Legal Adviser to D.C.A., War Office, 1944-46. Chief Legal Adviser, C.A.B., G.H.Q., M.E.F., 1945; Chief Justice, Gibraltar, 1946-55; Justice of Appeal, East African Court of Appeal, 1955-57. *Publication:* Commercial Arbitrations, 1925. *Address:* Ca na Catalina, Pollensa, Mallorca, Baleares, Spain; c/o Martins Bank Ltd., 16 Whitehall, S.W.1. *Clubs:* Naval and Military, Royal Automobile. [*Died* 17 *Feb.* 1962.

BADCOCK, Brigadier Gerald Eliot, C.B.E. 1919; D.S.O. 1917; *b.* Murree, India, 26 Aug. 1883; *y. s.* of General Sir Alexander Badcock, K.C.B., C.S.I.; *m.* 1919, Beatrice (*d.* 1957), *y. d.* of J. Badger Clark; two *s.* one *d.* *Educ.:* Wellington College; Pembroke College, Cambridge. Joined R.A.S.C. 1904; Capt. 1912; Adjutant, 1914; Major, 1918; Bt. Lt.-Colonel 1918; Lt.-Col. and Col. 1931; D.A.D.T., M.E.F., Feb.-Sept. 1915; A.D.T., M.E.F. and E.E.F., 1915-19; D.A.D.T. War Office, 1919-22; served European War, 1914-1918, Gallipoli, Egypt, Palestine, Syria (despatches, C.B.E., D.S.O., Bt. Lt.-Col.); Officer Administrating the Government of Bermuda, June-Aug. 1922; Member of the Executive Council, Bermuda, 1922-23; O.C. R.A.S.C. Independent Brigade, China, 1927; Chief Instructor R.A.S.C. Training College, Aldershot, 1929-31; Instructor Senior Officers' School, Sheerness, 1931-33; A.Q.M.G. (Movements) War Office, 1934-36; retired pay, 1936; Bursar, Clifton College, 1936-39; re-employed Sept. 1939; Director of Salvage, War Office, 1940-44. *Publication:* A History of the Transport Services of the Egyptian Expeditionary Force, 1916-18. *Recreations:* cricket, hunting (Master Senior Officers' School Beagles, 1931-33), walking, ornithology, gardening. *Address:* Hilltop, Cattistock, Dorchester, Dorset. [*Died* 13 *Jan.* 1966.

BADDELEY, Sir Frank Morrish, K.B.E. *cr.* 1930; Kt., *cr.* 1928; C.M.G. 1925; *b.* 30 Nov. 1874; 4th *s.* of late Frank Baddeley, Liverpool; *m.* 1st, 1906, Frances Gertrude (*d.* 1920), *d.* of W. C. Quiggin, Liverpool; 2nd, 1926, Audrey Frances, *d.* of late Edward Arnold, Omagh, Co. Tyrone; one *s.* *Educ.:* Liverpool Institute; Magdalene Coll., Cambridge (Scholar); M.A.; 21st Wrangler, Mathematical Tripos, 1896). Malayan Civil Service, 1897-1924; Chief Sec. to Govt., Nigeria, 1924-30; retd., 1930; Barrister-at-Law, Inner Temple, 1913; acting Governor of Nigeria, 1925, 1927, 1928-29; represented Nigeria at Colonial Office Conference, 1930. *Address:* Windrush, Elgin Road, Weybridge, Surrey. *Club:* Athenæum. [*Died* 18 *April* 1966.

BADDELEY, Sir Vincent (Wilberforce), K.C.B., *cr.* 1921 (C.B. 1911); *b.* 24 Sept. 1874; *e. s.* of late Rev. J. J. Baddeley, Rector of Chelsfield, Kent; *m.* 1933, Katharine Angela, M.B.E., *er. d.* of late Maj.-Gen. Sir Reginald Thynne, K.C.B. *Educ.:* Marlborough (Scholar); Pembroke College, Oxford (Scholar). Clerk War Office, 1897; transferred to Secretariat Admiralty, 1899; Private Secretary to successive First Lords of the Admiralty (Lords Selborne, Cawdor, Tweedmouth, and Mr. M'Kenna), 1901-11; Principal Clerk of the Admiralty, 1910-11; Assistant Secretary for Finance Duties, 1911-20; Assistant Secretary of the Admiralty, 1920-21; First Principal Assistant Secretary, 1921-31; Deputy Secretary, Admiralty 1931-35; Director of Alliance Assurance Company, 1935-53; Prime Warden of the Fishmongers' Company, 1936-37; Hon. Fellow of Pembroke College, Oxford, 1937. *Address:* 60 Harley House, N.W.1. *T.:* Welbeck 3611. *Clubs:* Travellers'; (Hon.) Royal Yacht Squadron. [*Died* 25 *July* 1961.

BADEN-POWELL, 2nd Baron, *cr.* 1929, of Gilwell; **Arthur Robert Peter Baden-Powell,** Bt., *cr.* 1922; F.R.S.A.; *b.* 30 Oct. 1913; *o. s.* of 1st Baron Baden-Powell of Gilwell, O.M., G.C.M.G., G.C.V.O., K.C.B. and of Olave St. Clair, G.B.E., *d.* of Harold Soames; *S.* father, 1941; *m.* 1936, Carine Crause, *d.* of late C. H. C. Boardman, Johannesburg, South Africa; two *s.* one *d.* *Educ.:* Dane Court, Woking; Charterhouse; R.M.C., Sandhurst. Served in British S. Africa Police (Southern Rhodesia), 1934-37, Native Affairs Department (Southern Rhodesia), 1937-45; British South Africa Company, 1945-46. Chief Scout's Commissioner and Asst. Dist. Comr. (Farnham), Boy Scouts Assoc.; Guildmaster B.-P. Scout Guild; President, City of Westminster Boy Scouts Local Assoc.; Pres. and Founder, Commonwealth Students' Assoc., 1960; President, Youth Camping Association; Member Camping Club of G.B. and I.; Deputy-Chairman Rhodesia Fairbridge Memorial College (London Council); Member (Sgt.) City of London Special Constabulary; Fell. Roy. Commonwealth Soc.; Director City Share Trust Ltd., and Irene Mfg. Co.

Ltd.; Director of Contracts, Twentieth Century (Joinery and Packing) Co. Ltd.; Chairman, British Safety Council, 1962; Member Council: Japan Society, British Caribbean Assoc.; Member: Victoria League; British Commonwealth Rifle Club; Farnham Rifle Club; Council, National Rifle Association; English XX Rifle Club; Vice-President, Surrey Rifle Association; Liveryman Worshipful Company of Mercers, London. *Recreations:* camping, rifle-shooting, etc. *Heir:* *s.* Hon. Robert Crause Baden-Powell, *b.* 15 Oct. 1936. *Address:* Abbotts Corner, Dockenfield, nr. Farnham, Surrey. *T.:* Frensham 242.
[*Died* 10 *Dec.* 1962.

BADLEY, John Haden, M.A.; *b.* 1865; *s.* of James P. Badley, Surgeon, Dudley; *m.* 1892, Amy Garrett (*d.* 1956); one *s.* *Educ.:* Rugby School (Exhibitioner); Trinity Coll., Cambridge (Scholar). 1st Class Classical Tripos, 1887; Assistant Master at the New School, Abbotsholme, 1889-92; Headmaster of Bedales School, 1893-1935. *Publications:* Education after the War; School Talks in Peace and War; Bedales, a Pioneer School; The Will to Live; The Will to Fuller Life; These Make Men's Lives; A Schoolmaster's Testament; Form and Spirit; Memories and Reflections; The Bible: selected and re-arranged with a commentary (three volumes). *Address:* Fairhaven, Steep, Petersfield, Hants. *T.:* Petersfield 156.
[*Died* 6 *March* 1967.

BAERLEIN, Henry; *b.* Manchester, 1 April 1875. *Educ.:* Charterhouse; Trinity College, Cambridge. *Publications:* In Pursuit of Dulcinea, 1904; The Shade of the Balkans, 1904; The Diwan of Abu'l Ala, 1908; Yrivand, 1908; On the Forgotten Road, 1909; The Singing Caravan, 1910; Mexico, the Land of Unrest, 1913; Abu'l Ala the Syrian, 1914; London Circus, 1914; Windrush and Evenlode, 1915; Rimes of the Diables Bleus, 1917; A Difficult Frontier, 1922; The House of the Fighting Cocks, 1922; Under the Acroceraunian Mountains, 1922; The Birth of Yugoslavia, 1922; Box o' Lights, 1923; The Raft of Love, 1923; Over the Hills of Ruthenia, 1923; Mariposa, 1924; Here are Dragons, 1925; The March of the Seventy Thousand, 1926; Memoirs of the Marquise de Keroubec, 1927; Mariposa on the Way, 1927; Heine: The Strange Guest, 1928; In Search of Slovakia (called in America, Dreamy Rivers), 1929; Spain: Yesterday and To-morrow, 1930; And Then To Transylvania, 1931 (called in America, Enchanted Woods); The Endless Journey, 1933; Belmonte the Matador, 1934; Bessarabia and Beyond, 1935; No Longer Poles Apart, 1936; In Czechoslovakia's Hinterland, 1938; In Old Romania, 1940; Travels without a Passport, 1941; Travels without a Passport (second series), 1942; Baltic Paradise, 1943; The Caravan Rolls On, 1945; The Romanian Scene, 1945; Leaves in the Wind, 1946; So Many Roads, 1947; Romanian Oasis, 1948; The Problem of South Slesvig, 1948; Landfalls and Farewell, 1949; All Roads lead to People, 1951; The Squire of Piccadilly, 1951; Laugh, and the ghosts laugh with you . . ., 1951; Today in Greece, 1954; Travel News: Madeira, Luxembourg, 1955; Denmark, Land of Islands, 1956; Finland, Land of a Thousand Lakes, 1957; Malta, the British Riviera, 1957; Portugal, the Land of Wine and Sunshine, 1958. *Recreations:* primitive pleasures. *Club:* Bath.
[*Died* 9 *Dec.* 1960.

BAGGE, Sir (John) Picton, 5th Bt., *cr.* 1867; C.M.G. 1929; *b.* 19 Oct. 1877; *s.* of late Sir Alfred T. Bagge, 3rd Bt. of Stradsett Hall, Norfolk; *S.* brother 1939; *m.* 1910, Olive Muriel Mary (*d.* 1965), *d.* of late Samuel Mendel; two *s.* *Educ.:* Eton; King's College, Cambridge. Entered Consular Service, 1905; served in Russia, 1905-18; Commercial Secretary in Russia, 1918; transferred to Berne, 1921; to Brussels, 1922; Director of Foreign Division, Department of Overseas Trade, 1928-37; retired 1937. J.P. Norfolk, 1941-61. *Recreation:* bridge. *Heir:* *s.* John Alfred Picton Bagge [*b.* 27 Oct. 1914; *m.* 1939, Elizabeth Helena (Lena), 2nd *d.* of late D. James Davies, C.B.E.; three *s.* three *d.*]. *Address:* Finstall, Wokingham, Berkshire. *T.:* Wokingham 110. *Club:* Boodle's.
[*Died* 23 *Dec.* 1967.

BAGGE, Sir Picton, Bt.; *see* Bagge, Sir J. P.

BAGGOTT, Ven. Louis John; Archdeacon Emeritus since 1962; *b.* 3 February 1891; *s.* of John Baggott, Civil Engineer; *m.* 1918, Janet Borland, *d.* of Harrup McLaren; one *s.* one *d.* *Educ.:* Queens' College, Cambridge; Ridley Hall, Cambridge. B.A. 1914; M.A. 1918. Deacon 1915, Priest 1916, York; Curate of St. Andrew, Drypool, 1915-19; Temp. Chaplain to the Forces, 1918-20; Chaplain, Tower of London, 1919-20; Curate of Bath Abbey, 1920-23; Vicar of Christ Church, Sefton Park, 1923-28; Rector of Newcastle-under-Lyme, 1928-33; Vicar of Clifton, Glos., 1933-36; Rural Dean of Clifton, 1935-36; Vicar of Beverley Minster with Tickton, 1936-42; Vicar of Gt. Yarmouth, 1942-55; Hon. Canon of Norwich, 1943-55; Archdeacon of Norfolk and Residentiary Canon of Norwich, 1955-62. Hon. C.F. *Publications:* The Faith for the Faithful, 1928; This Generation and Its Spiritual Needs, 1937; Jesu, Joy of Man's Desiring, 1947; A New Approach to Colossians, 1961; The Seven Penitential Psalms, 1963; Spiritual Priorities, 1963; Pilgrim in the Modern World, 1963. *Address:* Norvic, Station Road, Droxford, Hants. [*Died* 9 *April* 1965.

BAGLEY, Edward Albert Ashton; *b.* 1876; *s.* of Thomas Ashton Bagley of Coningsby, Lincolnshire. Was Organising Secretary, 1915-19, of the Lancashire, North-Western Counties Division of the Tariff Reform League; M.P. (U.), Farnworth Division, Lancaster, 1918-22; served European War, 1915-19. *Address:* 2 St. Michaels, Cambridge Road, Bournemouth. [*Died* 5 *Nov.* 1961.

BAGOT, 6th Baron (*cr.* 1780); **Caryl Ernest Bagot,** 11th Bt. 1627; *b.* 9 March 1877; *s.* of late Rev. Lewis Richard Charles and Cecilia Cator Bagot; *S.* cousin, 1946; *m.* 1st, 1911, Margaret, *d.* of J. McMenemy; 2nd, 1940, Nancy Constance Spicer. *Educ.:* Radley College. Lt. Irish Guards, 1916-19. *Heir:* *cousin,* Capt. Harry Eric Bagot [*b.* 1894; *m.* 1951, Kathleen Elizabeth Saddler, *widow* of N. M. Puckle, Melbourne, Austr.]. *Address:* 16 The Gateways, Chelsea, S.W.3.; Blithfield, Rugeley, Staffs.
[*Died* 5 *Aug.* 1961.

BAGSHAWE, Lt.-Col. Herbert Vale, C.B.E. 1919; D.S.O. 1916; late R.A.M.C.; *b.* 31 Aug. 1874; *m.*; one *s.* two *d.* Served European War, 1914-18 (D.S.O., despatches, Bt. Lt.-Col.); Lt.-Col. 1924; retired pay, 1929. *Address:* c/o Messrs. Glyn, Mills, Currie, Holt & Co., Kirkland House, Whitehall, S.W.1.
[*Died* 17 *March* 1962.

BAGULEY, Sir John Minty, Kt. 1939; barrister-at-law; *b.* London, 21 June 1880; *s.* of John Edward Baguley, London and County Bank, and Pauline, *d.* of W. H. Minty, H.M. Civil Service; *m.* Laura May (*d.* 1959), *d.* of Rev. F. De Mille Crawley, Pt. Amelia, Sydney Nova Scotia; no *c.* *Educ.:* St. Paul's School; Pembroke Coll., Cambridge. Passed into I.C.S., 1903; arrived in Burma, 1904; first officiated in the High Court in 1924; Judge of the High Court of Judicature at Rangoon, 1930-40; retired 1940. *Recreations:* winter sports and cards. *Address:* 76 Highlands Heath, Putney, S.W.15. *Club:* East India and Sports.
[*Died* 13 *April* 1964.

BAHAWALPUR, General His Highness Al-Haj Nawab Sir Sadiq Mohammad Khan V Abbasi Bahadur, Ameer of, N.Q.A. (Nishan-i-Qaid-i-Azam, Pakistan), 1959; G.C.S.I. 1941 (K.C.S.I. 1929); G.C.I.E. 1931; K.C.V.O. 1922; *b.* 1904; *m.* 1921, *d.* of Sahibzada Faiz Muhammad Khan Abbasi. *Educ.:* Aitchison Chiefs Coll., Lahore. Succeeded as Ruler of Bahawalpur State, 1906; A.D.C. to Prince of Wales during his Indian Tour, 1921; invested with full Ruling Powers, 1924; Mem. Standing Cttee. Indian Princes' Chamber, 1933-47; Mem. Indian Defence Council, 1940-46. Attended Coronation Durbar, Delhi, 1911; Silver Jubilee, London, 1935; Coronation, London, 1937, 1953. Colonel-in-Chief of all Bahawalpur Units now part of Pakistan Army; served during War of 1939-46; Major-Gen., British Army, 1946; General Pakistan Army, 1955. Is entitled to numerous decorations including War Medals and Stars for 1939-45 War; Grand Cordon of Rafeyadain, Iraq, 1941; Order of Cedars, Lebanon, 1947. Hon. LL.D.: Punjab Univ., Pakistan; Aligarh Univ., India. *Recreations:* motoring, polo, shooting, philately. *Heir:* Brigadier Sahibzada Mohammad Abbas Abbasi, *b.* 1924. *Address:* Sadiq Garh Palace (Bahawalpur), West Pakistan. [*Died* 24 *May* 1966.

BAHR, Sir Philip M.; *see* Manson-Bahr.

BAHRAIN, Ruler of; H.H. Shaikh Sulman bin Hamad Al Khalifah, Hon. K.C.M.G., *cr.* 1952; Hon. K.C.I.E., *cr.* 1943; *e. s.* of late Shaikh Sir Hamad-bin Isa Al Khalifah, K.C.I.E., C.S.I.; *S.* father, 1942; *m.*; three *s.* Salute of 13 guns. K.St.J. Order of Rafidain, 1st Class. Grand Cross of Order of the Dannebrog (Denmark). *Address:* Manama Palace, Bahrain, Arabian Gulf. *T.A.:* Bahrstate [*Died* 2 *Nov.* 1961.

BAILEY, Charles Thomas Peach; *b.* 5 Mar. 1882; *s.* of Joseph Bailey, late of Board of Education; *m.* 1st 1915, Cecilia, *d.* of Dr. G. H. Charlesworth, J.P.: one *s.*; 2nd, 1932, Kathleen Mary, *e. d.* of Jonathan Cape. *Educ.:* St. Paul's School. Assistant Keeper in Victoria and Albert Museum, 1900; Deputy Keeper, 1935; Keeper, Department of Metalwork, 1937-44; served European War, 1914-1918, with Royal West Kent Regiment and Machine Gun Corps; Gallipoli, Egypt and Palestine; Major, 1918. Prime Warden, Worshipful Company of Goldsmiths, 1947-48. *Publications:* Knives and Forks, 1927; Contributor on art subjects to numerous papers and magazines. *Address:* Hedgelands, Hillfield Road, Selsey, Sussex. *T.:* Selsey 2103. [*Died* 15 *Nov.* 1968.

BAILEY, Sir Edward (Battersby), Kt., 1945; M.C. 1916; F.R.S. 1930; M.A., D.Sc., LL.D.; Chevalier Légion d'Honneur; Croix de Guerre; *b.* 1881; *s.* of Dr. J. B. Bailey; *m.* 1914, Alice Meason (*d.* 1956); one *s.* one *d.* *Educ.:* Kendal Grammar Sch.; Clare Coll., Cambridge (Scholar; Double First, 2nd Part Tripos, Geology and Physics; Harkness Scholar). H.M. Geological Survey, 1902-29 and 1937-45; Director of Geological Survey of Great Britain and Museum of Practical Geology, 1937-45; War service with R.G.A., 1915-19 (wounded twice, despatches twice); retired Lt., 1919; Pres. of Section C, British Association, 1928; Hon. Mem. Edinburgh Nat. Hist. Soc., 1928; Professor of Geology, University, Glasgow, 1930-1937; Correspondent Geological Socy., America, 1932; Chairman, Scot. Youth Hostels Ass., Glasgow District, 1932-37 and Vice-President, 1937; President Precambrian Association, 1934, 1937; Hon. Member Geologische Vereinigung-Frankfurt, 1935; Hon. D.S., Harvard, 1936; Hon. Fellow of R. Geol. Soc. Cornwall, 1937; Hon. Mem. N. England Inst. Min. and Mech. Engineers, 1937, Geol. Soc. Liverpool, 1937; Corr. Soc. belge de Géologie, de Paléontologie et d'Hydrologie, 1938 (Hon. Member 1946); For. Member Norwegian Academy Science and Letters at Oslo, 1938; Joly Memorial Lecturer, Trinity, Dublin, 1939; Hon. D.Sc., Birmingham, 1939; Lt. Commanding G.S.M. & L.R. Unit, 58th County of London Bn., Home Guard, 1940-42; Hon. Fell. Nat. Inst. Sciences, India, 1941; Royal Medal of Royal Society, 1943; Hon. Fellow, Clare College, 1944; For. Asste., National Acad. Sc. at Washington, 1944; Hon. Mem. Instn. R.E., Chatham, 1944; Vice-President, Royal Society, 1945; Associé Étranger, Soc. Géol., France, 1945; Asste., Acad. Roy., Belgique, 1945; Hon. LL.D., Glasgow, 1946; Hon. D.Sc., Queen's, Belfast, 1946; Hon. Fellow, Geol. Soc., Edinburgh, 1947; Wollaston Medal, Geol. Soc., London, 1948; Hon. Mem. Soc. Helvétique des Sciences Naturelles (Académie Suisse des Sciences), 1948; Hon. Pres. Scot. Youth Hostels Assoc., 1948; Hon. D.Sc., Cambridge, 1952; Guest Lecturer, Ceylon Association for Advancement of Science, 1954; Hon. F.G.S., Glasgow, 1958; Hon. D.Sc., Edinburgh, 1964. *Publications:* Tectonic Essays, Mainly Alpine, 1935; Regionale Geologie der Erde: Northwestern Europe Caledonides (with O. Holtedahl), 1938; Introduction to Geology (with J. Weir and W. J. McCallien), 1939; Geological Survey of Gt. Britain, 1952; Charles Lyell, 1962; Memoirs of the Geological Survey and communications to scientific journals. *Recreation:* reading science. *Address:* 76 Hampstead Way, N.W.11. *T.:* Speedwell 4458. [*Died* 19 *March* 1965.

BAILEY, Lt.-Col. Frederick Marshman, C.I.E. 1915; *b.* 3 Feb. 1882; *e. s.* of late Lieut.-Colonel F. Bailey, R.E.; *m.* 1921, Hon. Irma Cozens-Hardy, *o. c.* of 2nd Baron Cozens-Hardy. *Educ.:* Edinburgh Academy; Wellington College; Sandhurst. 17th Bengal Lancers, 1901-3; 32nd Sikh Pioneers, 1903-5; Tibet Expedition, 1903-4 (medal and clasp); exploration party to Western Tibet, 1904-5; Indian Political Department, 1905; British Trade Agent at Gyantse, Tibet, 1905-9; explored in Western China, South Eastern Tibet and Mishmi Hills, 1911; awarded Gill Memorial by Royal Geog. Soc., 1912; Abor Expedition, 1911 (medal and clasp); with late Capt. Morshead, R.E., explored course of Brahmaputra in Southern Tibet, 1913; awarded Macgregor Medal by Royal United Service Institution of India, 1914, and Gold Medal by Royal Geographical Society, 1916; served with Indian Expeditionary Force in Flanders and Gallipoli, 1915; N.W. Frontier Province, 1916-17; Political Officer in Mesopotamia and Persia, 1917-18; Mission in Central Asia, 1918-20; Livingstone Gold Medal, Royal Scottish Geographical Soc., 1920; Commander of the Crown of Roumania; Political Officer, Sikkim, 1921-28; Political Agent, Central India, and Resident, Baroda, 1930-1932; Resident in Kashmir, 1932-33; Envoy Extraordinary and Minister Plenipotentiary at the Court of Nepal, 1935-38; retired, 1938; King's Messenger in Central and S. America, 1942-43. *Publications:* China-Tibet-Assam; Mission to Tashkent; No Passport to Tibet. *Address:* Warborough House, Stiffkey, Norfolk. *Club:* United Service. [*Died* 17 *April* 1967.

BAILEY, George Buchanan, O.B.E. 1944; D.F.C.; D.L.; Chairman, C. H. Bailey Ltd.; Dir., Bailey (Malta) Ltd.; *b.* 14 July 1898; 3rd *s.* of late Charles Henry Bailey, Newport, Mon.; *m.* 1924, Dorothy Margaret, *d.* of late Sir John Cecil Davies, C.B.E., The Mount, Gowerton and later Stelvio, Newport, Mon.; two *s.* one *d.* *Educ.:* Malvern. Marine Engineer. Chairman: Bailey Shipbuilding Development Co. Ltd.; Bailey Aircraft Ltd.; Director: Mountstuart Dry Docks Ltd. and Associated Cos.; Plas-Winton Ltd.; Monkswood Nurseries Ltd. *Recreations:* yachting, fishing. *Address:* Church View, Monkswood, Near Usk, Mon. *Clubs:* East

India and Sports; Island Sailing (Cowes); Lloyds Yacht, Royal Southern Yacht. [*Died* 1 *Feb.* 1969.

BAILEY, Sir George Edwin, Kt. 1944; C.B.E. 1941; M.Sc.; M.I.Mech.E.; M.I.E.E.; M.I.P.E.; late Chairman Associated Electrical Industries Ltd., Metropolitan-Vickers Electrical Co. Ltd., and other companies; late Dep. Chm. The British Thomson Houston Co. Ltd.; *b.* 1879; *m.* 1910, Margaret Fanny Bolesworth; one *d.* *Educ.:* Loughborough Grammar School. Past President, British Electrical and Allied Manufacturers' Association; Engineering and Allied Employers' National Federation; Institution of Production Engineers; Manchester District Engineering Employers' Assoc.; Mem. of following Cttees. during War of 1939-45: Engineering Industrial Panel, Ministry of Labour and National Service; Committee on Skilled Men in the Services (Beveridge Committee); Industrial Panel, Ministry of Production; North West Regional Board, Ministry of Production; Chm. Manchester Local Reconstruction Panel of the Emergency Services Organization. Hon. M.Sc., Manchester. *Address:* Downside, Compton, Nr. Newbury, Berks. [*Died* 14 *Oct.* 1965.

BAILEY, Hamilton, F.R.C.S. (Eng.), F.A.C.S., F.I.C.S., F.R.S.E.; Emeritus Surgeon, Royal Northern Hospital; General Surgeon, Metropolitan Ear, Nose and Throat Hosp.; Senior Surgeon St. Vincent's Clinic; Consulting Surgeon, Italian Hosp. London; formerly External Examiner in Surgery, University of Bristol and the General Nursing Council; Hunterian Professor Royal College of Surgeons; *b.* 1 Oct. 1894; *s.* of late Dr. H. J. Bailey, Brighton; *m.* 1925, Veta Gillender *Educ.:* St. Lawrence College, Ramsgate; London Hospital. Late Hon. Assistant Surgeon, Surgical Registrar and Tutor, Liverpool Royal Infirmary; Surgical Registrar and First Surgical Assistant, London Hospital; Fellow of the Association of Surgeons of Great Britain and Ireland; Vice.-Pres. International College of Surgeons; Vice-Pres. British Medical Students Assoc.; Fellow, Medical Society of London; Member Société d'Urologie; served European War, with 1st Belgian Unit British Red Cross, 1914 (prisoner); Surgeon Royal Navy, H.M.S. Inflexible and Monitor 19; Gillson Scholar Society of Apothecaries, 1926-28. *Publications:* Physical Signs in Clinical Surgery, 13th edition, 1960; Branchial Cysts, and other Essays; Emergency Surgery, 7th edition, 1958; A Short Practice of Surgery, 12th edition, 1960 (with R. J. McNeill Love); Operation Surgery, 3rd edition, 1961; Surgery for Nurses, 8th edition, 1954; Recent Advances in Genito-Urinary Surgery (jointly), 1936; Diseases of the Testicle, 1936; Clinical Surgery for Dental Practitioners, 1937; Editor of Pye's Surgical Handicraft, 18th edition, 1960; Surgery of Modern Warfare, 3rd edition, 1943; papers on Surgical Subjects in the British Jour. Surgery and other medical periodicals. *Recreations:* swimming, golf, fishing. *Address:* Long Meadow, Hawkinge, Nr. Folkestone, Kent; Las Golondrinas, Fuengirola, Malaga, Spain. [*Died* 26 *March* 1961.

BAILEY, Henry Christopher; author; *b.* London, 1 Feb. 1878; *o. s.* of Henry and Jane Dillon Bailey; *m.* 1908, Lydia Haden Janet, *y. d.* of late Dr A. Haden Guest, Manchester; two *d.* *Educ.:* City of London School; Corpus Christi College, Oxford (Scholar); 1st Class Final Classical School 1901. On staff of The Daily Telegraph, 1901-46. *Publications:* My Lady of Orange; Karl of Erbach; The Master of Gray; Rimingtons; Beaujeu; Springtime; Raoul; The God of Clay; Colonel Stow; Storm and Treasure; The Lonely Queen; The Suburban; The Sea Captain; The Gentleman Adventurer; The Highwayman; The Gamesters; The Young Lovers; The Pillar of Fire; Barry Leroy; Call Mr. Fortune; His Serene Highness; The Fool; The Plot; Mr. Fortune's Practice; The Rebel; Knight at Arms; Mr. Fortune's Trials; The Golden Fleece; The Merchant Prince; Mr. Fortune, Please; Bonaventure; Judy Bovenden; Mr. Fortune Speaking; Mr. Fortune Explains; Garstons; Mr. Cardonnel; Case for Mr. Fortune; The Red Castle; The Man in the Cape; Mr. Fortune Wonders; Shadow on the Wall; Mr. Fortune Objects; Sullen Sky Mystery; Clue for Mr. Fortune; Black Land, White Land; Clunk's Claimant; This is Mr Fortune; The Great Game; The Veron Mystery; Mr. Fortune Here; The Bishop's Crime; The Little Captain; No Murder; Dead Man's Shoes; Slippery Ann; Dead Man's Effects; The Wrong Man; The Life Sentence; Honour Among Thieves; Saving a Rope; Shrouded Death; Mr. Fortune Finds a Pig. *Recreations:* walking, gardening. *Address:* Bernina, Llanfairfechen, North Wales. [*Died* 24 *March* 1961.

BAILEY, Sir John, Kt. 1965; retired; former National Secretary, Co-operative Party; *b.* 1 Jan. 1898; *s.* of John and Sarah Ann Bailey; *m.* 1926, Anne Glaser; one *s.* two *d.* *Educ.:* Miskin Mixed Elementary School; London Labour College. Councillor, Mountain Ash, 1924-25; Secretary, Bradford Co-operative Party, 1925; National Organiser, Co-operative Party, 1936-42; National Secretary, Co-operative Party, 1942-62. Member Bradford City Council, 1928-31 and 1933-38. President Co-operative Union Congress, 1964. Director Enfield Highway Co-operative Soc., 1952-. Editor Co-operative Party Journal, Monthly Letter, 1943-62. Served S. Wales Borderers, 1916-19, France 1917-18. *Publications:* The British Co-operative Movement, 1955; many political pamphlets and contribs. to Co-operative publications. *Recreations:* gardening and filling in forms! *Address:* Osborne Lodge, 41 Hatton Road, Cheshunt, Herts. *T.:* Waltham Cross 22361. [*Died* 18 *Jan.* 1969.

BAILEY, Kenneth, F.R.S. 1953; Ph.D., Sc.D.; Reader in Biochemistry, University of Cambridge, since 1948, and Lecturer, Trinity College, since 1948; *b.* 18 Aug. 1909; *er. s.* of Bertram Bailey and Florence Elizabeth Buckley. *Educ.:* Orme Boys' Sch., Newcastle-under-Lyme; Univs. of Birmingham, London (Roy. Coll. of Science), Harvard and Cambridge, B.Sc., Ph.D. (Birm.); M.Sc. (Lond.), D.I.C.; Ph.D., Sc.D. (Cantab.); Beit Scientific Research Fellow, 1933; Imperial Chemical Industries Research Fellow, 1945; Alan Johnston, Lawrence and Moseley Research Fellow of the Royal Society, 1947; Fellow of Trinity College, 1948; Walker-Ames Professor of the University of Washington, 1953. Pres. Commn. on Proteins, Internat. Union of Pure and Applied Chemistry, 1959-61. Researches connected with chemistry of proteins, mechanism of muscle contraction and of blood coagulation. *Publications:* Co-Editor of: The Biochemical Journal, 1945-48; Advances in Protein Chemistry; The Proteins (2 vols.), 1953. *Recreations:* music, ski-ing. *Address:* Trinity College, Cambridge. *T.:* 58201. [*Died* 22 *May* 1963.

BAILEY, Lionel Danyers, C.B. 1935; M.C., T.D.; M.R.C.S. (Eng.), L.R.C.P. (Lond.), 1904, D.P.H. (Lond.), 1919; Fellow Roy. Soc. Med.; *b.* 17 Oct. 1879; *s.* of Alfred and Fanny Margaret Bailey. *Educ.:* St. Paul's School; St. George's Hospital. Territorial Army, R.A.M.C., gazetted Lieut. 1909; Capt. 1913; European War, M.O. 1/5 The Queen's Royal Regt., 1 914-19 (M.C., Croix de Guerre avec Palme); O.C. 140th Co. of London Field Ambulance, 1924-28; A.D.M.S., 47th Division, 1928-34; Hon. Physician to the King, 1931-36. Formerly: Med. Supt. Physio-Therapy

Department, St. George's Hospital; Medical Officer in charge Electrical Dept., National Hospital, Queen Square; Physician in charge Physio-Therapy and Rehabilitation Depts., E.M.S. (St. Bart.'s Hospital), Hill End, St. Albans; Physician in Charge Physiotherapy and Rehabilitation Dept., Willesden General Hospital; Medical Office and Lecturer to Physiotherapy Unit, National Institute for the Blind, 1926; Medical Officer i/c Sir Oswald Stoll Mansions, 1920. Hon. Life Mem. British Assoc. of Physical Medicine; Formerly: Mem. Council and Chm. Education Cttee.; Chm. Chartered Soc. of Physiotherapy, 1939-44. Col., T.A., retired, 1936. *Publications:* The Importance of Electrical Reactions. Practitioner, 1924; Massage in General Practice, Practitioner, 1934; After Care in Acute Medical Diseases, Practitioner, 1942. *Recreations:* golf, fishing, shooting. *Address:* 18 Sandy Lodge Way, Northwood, Middlesex. *Club:* Union. [*Died* 27 *May* 1967.

BAILEY, Victor Albert, M.A., D.Phil. (Oxon), F.Inst.P.; F.A.A.; Emeritus Prof., formerly Research Professor of Physics, University of Sydney; Visiting Professor of Engineering Research, The Pennsylvania State University, U.S.A., 1953-54; Fulbright Research Scholar, 1953; *b.* 18 Dec. 1895; *s.* of William Henry and Susanna Bailey; *m.* 1934; Joyce, *d.* of W. C. Hewitt, Auckland, N.Z., two *s.* two *d.* *Educ.:* King Edward VI. School, Southampton; Queen's College, Oxford (scholar). School Sports Champion; Pioneer in Royal Engineers; studied Engineering Science and Physics; Demonstrator in the Electrical Laboratory, Oxford; occasional Lecturer of Queen's College; Walter Burfitt Prize of Royal Society of N.S.W.; T. K. Sidey Medal and Prize of Roy. Soc. of N.Z.; Archibald Ollé Prize of Roy. Soc. of N.S.W., 1962. Director of Radio Physics Training of Australian Army, Navy, and Air Force personnel at Sydney Univ., 1941-44. *Publications:* numerous in scientific journals on physical, astronomical and biological subjects. *Recreations:* golf, tennis, swimming, yachting. *Address:* University of Sydney, Australia. *T.:* XY 2176 (Sydney). *Club:* University (Sydney). [*Died* 7 *Dec.* 1964.

BAILEY, Wilfrid Norman, M.A, Sc.D. (Cantab.); D.Sc. (Manch.); M.Sc. (Lond.); Professor of Mathematics at Bedford College in Univ. of London, 1944-58, retired; Professor Emeritus since 1958; *b.* Consett, Durham, 5 Sept. 1893; *s.* of B. and H. R. Bailey; *m.* 1918, Elsie Marion, *d.* of late T. R. Ogden, Blackpool; one *s.* one *d.* *Educ.:* Trinity Coll., Cambridge (Senior Scholar); Mathematical Tripos, Part II, b*, 1915. Instructor Lieut. R.N. 1915-19 (present at Battle of Jutland); Lecturer in Mathematics at Birmingham University and Lecturer and Senior Lecturer in Mathematics at Manchester University, Leverhulme Research Fellow, 1935; formerly Hon. Editor, Hon. Librarian, Hon. Sec., and Vice-Pres., London Mathematical Society. *Publications:* A Cambridge mathematical tract, entitled Generalized Hypergeometric Series, 1935; Papers on analytical subjects in Pure Mathematics, in various mathematical journals. *Address:* 1 Baldwin Avenue, Eastbourne, Sussex. *T.:* Eastbourne 1471. [*Died* 23 *Oct.* 1961.

BAILLIE, Col. Duncan Gus, C.M.G. 1919; D.S.O. 1918; T.D.; *b.* 1872; *s.* of late Lt.-Gen. Duncan Baillie, Loch Loy, Nairn; *m.* 1919, Mary Evelyn, *d.* of Capt. Blair Onslow Cochrane, O.B.E.; one *s.* *Educ.:* Wellington Coll. Qualified as W.S.; J.P. Nairnshire. Served with C.I.V.'s, S. African War, 1900; European War, 1914-1918 (despatches, C.M.G., D.S.O.). Col. Comdt. Lovat Scouts, 1938-45. *Address:* Ardmore, Nairn. [*Died* 3 *July* 1968.

BAILLIEU, 1st Baron, *cr.* 1953, of Sefton in the Commonwealth of Australia and Parkwood in the County of Surrey; **Clive Latham Baillieu,** K.B.E. 1938 (O.B.E. 1918); C.M.G. 1929; President, Dunlop Rubber Company Ltd., 1957-66 (Chm. 1949-57, Dep.-Chm. 1945-49, Dir. 1929-45); Dep.-Chm., Central Mining & Investment Corporation Ltd., 1959-65 (Chm. 1945-59); Jt. Dep.-Chm., Rio Tinto-Zinc Corp. Ltd., 1962-1965; Jt. Pres., Dalgety & New Zealand Loan Ltd., 1962 (Director, 1961-62); Director: Zinc Corporation Ltd., 1924-49; Consolidated Zinc Corp. Ltd., 1949-62 (Dep.-Chm., 1961-62); The New Zealand Loan & Mercantile Agency Co. Ltd., 1924-61; The London & Lancashire Insurance Co. Ltd., 1955-62; English, Scottish & Australian Bank Ltd., 1929-; Midland Bank Ltd., 1944-; and other companies; President, Federation of British Industries, 1945-46-47 (Dep.-Pres., 1944-45); *b.* 24 September 1889; *e. s.* of late Hon. William Lawrence Baillieu, Melbourne, Australia; *m.* 1915, Ruby (*d.* 1962), *d.* of late William Clark, formerly of Windlesham Moor, Windlesham, Surrey; three *s.* one *d.* *Educ.:* Church of England Gram. Sch., Melbourne; Trinity Coll., Melbourne University; Magdalen Coll., Oxford (M.A.). Oxford VIII, 1913. Barrister, Inner Temple, 1914. Major (retired) Australian Forces; served European War Australian Imperial Forces and R.A.F. 1915-18 (despatches, O.B.E.). Representative of H.M. Govt. in Commonwealth of Australia on Imperial Communications Advisory Cttee., 1929-39; one of Australian representatives on Imperial Economic Cttee., 1930-47. Exec. mem. Export Council, 1940; Dir.-Gen., British Purchasing Commn., Washington, 1941-42; Head, British Raw Materials Mission, Washington, 1942-43; British rep. on Combined Raw Materials Board, Washington, 1942-43; Mem. British Supply Council in N. America, 1941-43; acted as Chairman, Fairey Aviation Co., Nov. 1943-May 1945; Head, British Trade Mission to the Argentine, 1948; Mem. National Investment Council, 1946-48; Chm. Departmental Cttee. on the establishment of a Central Institute of Management, 1946; Mem. first Council of British Inst. of Management, 1947; First Pres. British Inst. of Management, 1959; Hon. Fell. Brit. Inst. of Management, 1960; Mem. Nat. Production Advisory Council on Industry, 1945-53; Mem. Gen. Advisory Council of B.B.C., 1947-52; Chm., American British Commonwealth Assoc. until amalg. with E.S.U., 1944-47. Dep. Pres., The English-Speaking Union, 1965- (Dep. Chm., 1947-51, Chm., 1951-65); Chairman Executive Committee, American Memorial Chapel Fund, 1944-61; President Instn. of the Rubber Industry, 1952-56; President Research Association of British Rubber Manufacturers, 1954-1956; Chm. Commonwealth Council of Mining and Metallurgical Instns., 1946-61; Pres. Soc. of British Gas Industries, 1953; Hon. Member: Australasian Inst. of Mining and Metallurgy (Inc.); Instn. of Mining and Metallurgy (Gold Medal of the Instn., for 1960); Inst. of Metals; Governor, Nat. Inst. of Economic and Social Research, 1958-. *Recreations:* golf, shooting, fishing. *Heir:* *s.* Hon. William Latham Baillieu [*b.* 10 Dec. 1915; *m.* 1945, Anne Bayliss (marriage dissolved, 1961), *d.* of Leslie William Page, Southport, Qld.; two *s.*; *m.* 1962, Mrs. Delia Muriel Champion. *Educ.:* Winchester; Magdalen College, Oxford (M.A.)]. *Address:* Parkwood, Englefield Green, Surrey; Sefton, Mount Macedon, Victoria, Australia. *Clubs:* Athenæum, Bath; Leander (Henley); Melbourne (Australia); Athenæum (Australia). [*Died* 18 *June* 1967.

BAILY, Francis Evans; writer; *m.* Helen Marion (May) Edginton (*d.* 1957); one *s.* *Educ.:* St. George's College, Weybridge; Queen Elizabeth's School, Kingston-on-Thames (Schol.). Joined staff of Rapid Review; sub-editor of the Royal Magazine;

subsequently Editor. Enlisted R.A.S.C. (M.T.), 1916; and subsequently commissioned; left England for German East Africa (Tanganyika Territory), April 1917; took part in advance from Kilwa to the Portuguese border in operations of Aug.-Dec. 1917; invalided home, Aug. 1918; demobilised, Mar. 1919; and returned to editorship of Royal Magazine; resigned editorship, June 1927. Recalled from A.O.E.R. Sept. 1939 and given rank of Temp. Emergency 2nd Lt.; attached to P.R. (War Office) and detailed to Military Affairs Service, Ministry of Information; released after some months' service. *Publications:* over seventy novels and biographies; various articles, serials, short stories, and verse in England and the United States of America. *Recreations:* none. *Address:* c/o Curtis Brown, Ltd., 13 King Street, W.C.2. *Club:* Royal Automobile.
[*Died* 6 *July* 1962.

BAIN, Donald Charles, M.C. 1941; Q.C. 1961; Recorder of Cambridge since 1963; *b.* 8 Sept. 1913; *o. s.* of late Major and Mrs. L. G. Bain, Long Walk House, Windsor; *m.* 1945, Margaret Josephine Farrow, B.Sc. (Econ.); two *d.* *Educ.:* Clifton College, Bristol; Pembroke College, Cambridge (M.A.). Served War of 1939-45, R.A., T.A. (Hon. Major). Called to Bar, 1946; Chancellor of Dio. St. Edmundsbury and Ipswich, 1955-; Dep.-Chm. Essex Quarter Sessions, 1959; Chm. Agricultural Land Tribunal, Eastern Area, 1959-61; Chancellor of Dio. of Winchester, 1962-; Recorder of Rochester, 1961-63. *Recreations:* motoring, gardening, mountain climbing. *Address:* Pentlow Hall, Cavendish, Suffolk. *T.:* Glemsford 255; 1 Paper Buildings, Temple, E.C.4. *T.:* Central 3728. *Club:* Garrick.
[*Died* 24 *Oct.* 1964.

BAIRD, General Sir Douglas; *see* Baird, General Sir Harry B.D.

BAIRD, General Sir (Harry Beauchamp) Douglas, K.C.B., *cr.* 1935 (C.B., 1929); C.M.G. 1918; C.I.E. 1920; D.S.O 1915, p.s.c.; I.A., retired; *b.* 4 Apr. 1877; *o. surv. s.* of late Col. A. W. Baird, C.S.I., F.R.S., R.E., of Palmers' Cross, Elgin, N.B.; *m.* 1915, Ethel Mary Frances (*d.* 1935), *d.* of Captain Andrew E. Caldecott, Oxford; one *s.* one *d.* *Educ.:* Clifton College; R.M.C., Sandhurst; Staff College, Quetta. Entered Army, 1897; Lt. I.A., 12th Bengal Cavalry, 1899; Capt. 1906; Major, 1915; Lt.-Col. 1920; Col. 1920; Maj.-Gen. 1928, Lt.-Gen. 1935; Gen. 1937; Brig.-Maj. to the Inspector-General of Cavalry in India, 1910-11; A.D.C. to G.O.C. in C. Aldershot, 1912-14; General Staff Officer, 2nd Grade 1914; O.C. 1/8th A. and S. Hrs, 1915-16; Bde. Comdr. B.E.F. Nov. 1916-Feb. 1918; G.S.O. 4th Quetta Div. Nov 1918; B.G.G.S. Baluchistan Force, May 1919; served Tirah, 1897-8 (medal, 2 clasps); European War, 1914-18 (despatches 6 times, Croix de Guerre avec Palme, D.S.O., C.M.G., Bt. Lt.-Col.); Afghan War, 1919 (C.I.E., medal and clasp); operations in Zhob, Nov.-Dec. 1920 (clasp); Lt. Col. Commandant 28th Punjabis, May 1920; Colonel Commandant Zhob area, 1920-23; Commandant Senior Officers School, India, 1924-28; D.A.Q.M.G. India, 1929-1930; Commander Kohat District, India, 1930-32; Commander Deccan District 1932-34; General Officer Commanding-in-Chief, Eastern Command, India, 1936-40; A.D.C. General to the King, 1938-40; retired 1940; Morayshire Home Guard, 1940-42; Colonel of South Lancashire Regiment, 1940-47; late Colonel 4/5th Mahratta Light Infantry. *Recreations:* golf, fishing, shooting, etc. *Address:* Palmers Cross, Elgin, Morayshire. *T.:* Elgin 7240. *Club:* United Service. [*Died* 2 *July* 1963.

BAIRD, Sir James Hozier Gardiner, of Saughton Hall, Midlothian, 9th Bt., *cr.* 1695; *b.* 25 Nov. 1883; *s.* of 8th Bt. and Hon. Arabella Rose Evelyn Hozier (*d.* 1916), *d.* of 1st Baron Newlands; *S.* father, 1921; *m.* 1st, 1921, Peggy B. C. (*d.* 1922), *d.* of late John L. Denton; 2nd, 1923, Violet, *d.* of Thomas Barker. Capt. 4th Battalion Argyll and Sutherland Highlanders, retired; rejoined the army as Captain 4th Bedfordshire Regiment, 1914 (wounded at Neuve Chapelle, despatches, Military Cross). *Heir:* *n.* James Richard Gardiner, Lieut. R.A. [*b.* 12 July 1913; *m.* 1941, Mabel Ann, *d.* of A. Algernon Gill, Toronto]. *Address:* Waterfall House, Waterfall, Bantry, Co. Cork, Eire.
[*Died* 3 *Aug.* 1966.

BAIRD, John; L.D.S.; R.F.P.S. Glasgow, 1929; Dental Surgeon; Editor of Free Algeria; *b.* 26 September 1906; *s.* of Alexander and Mary A. T. Baird; *m.* 1933, Agnes F., *d.* of Baillie Kerr, Castle Douglas; one *s.* one *d.* *Educ.:* Council School; St. Mungo's Medical College. Active in politics since 1928. M.P. (Lab.) Wolverhampton East, 1945-50, Wolverhampton North-East, 1950-64. Served War of 1939-45 with Army Dental Corps. *Recreations:* gardening, books. *Address:* 293 Green Lanes, Palmers Green, N.13. *T.:* Palmers Green 0770; 6A Belsize Park Gdns., N.W.3. *T:* Primrose 8650.
[*Died* 21 *March* 1965.

BAIRD, William James; *b.* 1893; *s.* of William Baird of Elie, Fife, and Cambusdoon, Ayrshire; *m.* 1st, 1918, Audley Porter Porter (marriage dissolved, 1936; she *d.* 1952); one *d.*; 2nd, 1937, Hon. Barbara, O.B.E. 1944, *y. d.* of 1st Viscount Harcourt (she *m.* 1st, 1925, Capt. Robt. Chas. Horace Jenkinson, from whom she obtained a divorce, 1936). *Educ.:* Harrow; Sandhurst. 12th Royal Lancers, 1914-18. Master of the Cottesmore Hounds, 1921-31. High Sheriff of Rutland, 1925; County Councillor, 1931-46. *Address:* Langston House, Chadlington, Oxford. *T.:* Chadlington 36; Elie, Fife. *Clubs:* Turf; New (Edinburgh). [*Died* 2 *Feb.* 1961.

BAIRSTOW, Sir Leonard, Kt., *cr.* 1952; C.B.E. 1917; F.R.S. 1917; Emeritus Professor of Aviation, University of London; *b.* Halifax, Yorkshire, 25 June 1880; *m.* 1st, Eleanor Mary Hamer (*d.* 1926); one *s.* one *d.*; 2nd, 1930, Florence Katharine, *e. d.* of D. J. Stephens, Llandaff. *Educ.:* Royal College of Science, Diploma in Mechanics. Late Professor of Aerodynamics at the Imperial College of Science and Technology; Vice-President Royal Aeronautical Society, 1930-34. *Publications:* a text-book of Applied Aerodynamics; papers to Advisory Committee for Aeronautics and Royal Society on the Fatigue of Materials, etc. *Address:* Halidean, 227 Winchester Road, Chandler's Ford, Hants.
[*Died* 8 *Sept.* 1963.

BAKER, Rev. Albert Edward; Canon of York; Rector of Moor Monkton since 1939; Exam. Chap. to Archbishop of York; Proctor in Convocation, 1929-55; *b.* London, 10 March 1884; *s.* of Charles James Baker, Ipswich, and Laura, *e. d.* of Fred Miller, Ipswich; *m.* 1910, Julia Susan, 4th *d.* of William Macintyre, Co. Tyrone, N. Ireland; two *d.* *Educ.:* Trinity College, Cambridge. Vicar of Wetwang; then of St. Michael le Belfrey, York; Chaplain and Lecturer, St. John's College, York; Visiting Lecturer at Berkeley Divinity School, New Haven, Conn., U.S.A. *Publications:* How to Understand Philosophy, 1925; Psychoanalysis explained and criticised, 1926; Jesus, 1933; The Teaching of Jesus for Daily Life, 1933; Prophets for an Age of Doubt, 1934; The Divine Christ, 1937; St. Paul and His Gospel, 1940; Science, Christianity, and Truth, 1942; Prophets for a Day of Judgment, 1944; etc. *Address:* Moor Monkton Rectory, York. *T.:* Rufforth 243. [*Died* 25 *March* 1962.

BAKER, Arthur Harold; Chief of Parliamentary Staff of The Times, Jan. 1934-Dec.

1955; *b.* 1 Dec. 1890; *s.* of late James Baker, Manor House, Othery, Somerset; *m.* 1st, 1916, Margaret Muriel (*d.* 1958), *o. d.* of late Dr. A. R. Down, Bampton, Tiverton and Exeter, Devon; one *s.*; 2nd, 1960, Elsie Emma Wills, Moretonhampstead, Devon. *Educ.:* Taunton School. Engaged in journalism since 1910; reporter on the Tiverton Gazette, 1910-14; Western Morning News, Plymouth, 1914; joined Inns of Court O.T.C., 1915; served European War, 1915-18, Lieut. Prince Albert's Somerset L.I., 1915-18; joined editorial staff of The Times, 1919. Fellow of Institute of Journalists; Chairman of London District, 1936; Chairman of executive committee, 1937-40; Chairman of Parliamentary Press Gallery, 1941. *Publication:* The House is Sitting, 1958. *Address:* Hillcrest, Speen, Aylesbury, Bucks. *T.:* Hampden Row 251. [*Died* 4 *Jan.* 1962.

BAKER, Bevan B. B.; *see* Bevan-Baker.

BAKER, Bryant; sculptor; *b.* London, 8 July 1881; *s.* of John Baker, sculptor, and Susan Bryant; unmarried. *Educ.:* City and Guilds Technical Institute, London; Royal Academy of Arts, London. Medals and prizes for design and portraiture, 1908-10; executed heroic marble bust of King Edward VII. for Queen Alexandra, and many copies for Royal family; heroic statue of King Edward VII., Huddersfield, 1912; Middlesex Memorial Edward VII.; Hemming Robeson recumbent memorial, Tewkesbury Abbey; marble bust Prince (now King) Olaf of Norway, Oslo; also busts many notable persons in England; made busts from life of President Coolidge, Col. John Coolidge, General John H. Pershing, Chief-Justice William Howard Taft, Herbert Hoover, Percival Lowell, Ambassador George Harvey, Chief-Justice E. D. White; heroic statues, Grover Cleveland, Millard Fillmore and Young Lincoln, Buffalo, N.Y.; Patriots of Delaware, Statuary Hall, Washington, D.C.; Bishop Freeman's Memorial effigy, Washington National Cathedral; Pioneer Woman, 16ft. bronze statue, Ponca City, Oklahoma; Colossal Statue of George Washington in Washington; Masonic Nat. Memorial at Alexandria, Virginia; heroic bronze statue, President John F. Kennedy, City Park, McKeesport, Pa.; bronze busts of Winston Churchill, Washington and Fulton, Mo.; many ideal figures, heroic statues and busts in numerous U.S. States and in various countries. Works in permanent collections: 6 bronze busts in the National Portrait Gallery, Washington, D.C.; Eros, Manchester City Art Gallery; Memory, Hull City Art Gallery, England. From 1908 Exhibitor at Royal Academy; also Paris Salon, Corcoran Art Gallery, Washington, etc. National Academician (N.A.); Fellow National Sculpture Society; formerly Mem. R.B.S., London (retired); Hon. F.R.B.S. 1964. Many medals and citations for outstanding achievements. Came to U.S. 1916; Sergeant, M.C., U.S.A., 1918-19. *Recreations:* gardening, tarpon and other deep sea fishing. *Address:* Gainsborough Studios, 222 W. 59th Street, New York City 19, U.S.A. [*Died* 29 *March* 1970.

BAKER, Charles Gaffney, O.B.E. 1945; M.D., F.R.C.P.; Guy's Hospital: Physician, since 1949; Physician to the Cardiac Dept.; Warden of the Hostels; Consultant Cardiologist, King Edward VII Convalescent Home for Officers, Osborne; *b.* 17 June 1907; *o. s.* of Alfred Charles Baker and Marion Gaffney; *m.* 1966, Jean Elizabeth Bailey, 2nd *d.* of late Rev. T. H. Bailey and Ellen Margery Bailey. *Educ.:* Christ's Hospital. Schol., Guy's Dental Sch., 1925; L.D.S., R.C.S., 1930; M.R.C.S., L.R.C.P. 1932; M.B., B.S. (Lond.) 1935; M.R.C.P. 1936; M.D. (Lond.) 1937; F.R.C.P. 1948. Medical Registrar, Guy's, 1936; Phys., Selly Oak Hospital, Birmingham, 1938-46. War service, 1939-45 (O.B.E.). Lt.-Col. R.A.M.C. Med. Sub-Dean, Guy's, 1946-56. Member: Brit. Cardiac Society; Assoc. of Physicians; Vice-Pres., Medical Defence Union. *Publications:* Section on Cardiovascular Disease in Conybeare's Text Book of Medicine; contributions to various Medical Journals. *Recreations:* tennis, ski-ing, music. *Address:* The Warden's House, Guy's Hospital, 11 St. Thomas's Street, S.E.1. *T.:* 01-407 0353. *Clubs:* Athenæum, M.C.C. [*Died* 21 *Oct.* 1969.

BAKER, Rt. Rev. Donald, D.D., M.A.; Archdeacon of Geelong, Dio. Melb., Vic., 1938-59; *b.* Southsea, Eng., 1882; *s.* of late Archdeacon W. G. Baker; *m.* 1913, Rosa Catherine, *o. d.* of Canon Mervyn Archdall, Sydney; two *s.* two *d.* *Educ.:* privately in Colonies; Cambridge. Ordained 1905; Curacies, Sydney, Cambridge, Summer Hill, N.S.W.; Rector of S. George's, Hobart, 1913-20; Bishop of Bendigo, 1920-38; Principal of Ridley College, Melbourne, 1938-1953; Theol. Lectr. at Trin. Coll., 1960-62, and Ridley Coll., 1960-. *Address:* 3 Berwick St., Camberwell, Vic., 3124, Australia. [*Died* 19 *June* 1968.

BAKER, Major Edwin Godfrey Phipps, D.S.O. 1918; M.C.; Q.C. 1943; Barrister-at-law, Manitoba; Bencher and past Pres. Manitoba Law Soc.; Member, Bar of British Columbia; *b.* Winnipeg, 21 April 1885; *s.* of Geo. W. Baker, K.C., and Jennie Eastman; *m.* Mary Allison Hough; three *s.* one *d.* *Educ.:* St. John's College School, Winnipeg; London and Cambridge Universities. Barrister, Victoria, B.C. prior to war; served Canadian Expeditionary Force, France, Major in 47th Infantry (despatches, D.S.O. M.C., two medals). *Address:* 1210 Beach Drive, Victoria, B.C., Canada. *Clubs:* Manitoba (Winnipeg); Union (Victoria, B.C.). [*Died* 30 *Oct.* 1963.

BAKER, Sir Frederick Spencer Arnold, Kt., *cr.* 1954; Master of the Supreme Court of Judicature (Queen's Bench), 1926-Oct. 1958, retired; Senior Master and Queen's Remembrancer, 1951-Oct. 1958; *b.* 1 April 1885; 3rd *s.* of late Fredrick Arnold Baker, 3 Crosby Square, E.C., and Flutters Hill, Long Cross, and late Helen Catherine, *d.* of late Captain Alex. Nairne, R.N., H.E.I.C.S.; unmarried. *Educ.:* Hildersham House, Thanet; Winchester; Oriel College, Oxon; M.A. 1910 Called to Bar, Inner Temple, 1909; joined Western Circuit; 2nd Lieut. 3rd (S.R.) Batt. Seaforth Highlanders, 1914; Lieut., 1915; Captain, 1916 (despatches); Major (S.O.2) 3rd Brigade R.A.F., 1918; Private Secretary to Maj.-Gen. Sir F. H. Sykes, K.C.B., Chief of Staff, Air Ministry, 1919; Board of Management Seamen's Hospital Society (Dep. Chm. 1947); Chm. Seamen's Hospitals Management Cttee., 1948. Lt.-Col., Home Guard, 1941. *Recreations:* shooting, fishing, golf. *Address:* 2 Down Street, Mayfair, W.1. *Clubs:* Junior Carlton, Lansdowne, Royal Air Force, Royal Thames Yacht; Sunningdale Golf (Sunningdale); Royal St. George's Golf (Sandwich). [*Died* 9 *Dec.* 1963.

BAKER, Air Vice-Marshal George Brindley Aufrere, C.B. 1942; C.B.E. 1943; M.C. 1917; *b.* 25 July 1894; *s.* of late Col. W. W. Baker, R.E.; *m.* 1924, Charlotte Marian, *d.* of A. M. Anderson, Long Crendon, Bucks; one *d.* *Educ.:* Cheltenham College. Served European War, 1914-18 (M.C.); Chief of Staff Mediterranean Allied Air Force, 1944-45; Director of Training (Plans), in Dept. of Air Member for Training, 1945; retired list, 1946. *Address:* Queen Anne Cottage, Friday Street, Henley-on-Thames, Oxon. [*Died* 23 *Oct.* 1968.

BAKER, Hon. Sir Henry Seymour, K.C.M.G. 1961 (C.M.G. 1946); D.S.O. 1919; President of the Legislative Council of

Tasmania, since 1960; M.L.C. for Queenborough, Tasmania, from 1948; *b.* 1 September 1890; 4th *s.* of Rev. Sidney James Baker, Melbourne; *m.* 1920, Effie Millicent, *d.* of late George William Sharp, Hobart, Tasmania; three *s.* one *d.* *Educ.:* Tasmanian University, LL.M. Served European War, 1915-18 (despatches, D.S.O.); Attorney-General and Minister of Education, Tasmania, 1928-34; Leader of Opposition, 1936-45. M.H.A. for Franklin, 1928-46. Chancellor of the University of Tasmania, 1956-63. *Address:* 393 Sandy Bay Road, Hobart, Tasmania. *Club:* Tasmanian (Hobart). [*Died* 20 *July* 1968.

BAKER, H(enry) Wright, D.Sc., C.Eng., F.I.Mech.E.; ex-Mem. Internat. Coll. of Production Engineering Research (C.I.R.P.); Prof. of Mechanical Engineering Coll. of Science and Technology and Univ., Manchester, 1939-60, now Emeritus; *b.* 4 November 1893; *e. s.* of Harry Baker, F.C.S., F.I.C., and Mary Eccles; *m.* 1928, Kathleen M. Drew, D.Sc.; one *s.* one *d.* *Educ.:* Liverpool College; Manchester University. 4 years Head of Transport Dept., Friends War Victims Relief Committee. Assistant Lecturer, Lecturer, Senior Lecturer in Mechanical Engineering, University of Manchester. United Nations Chief adviser at the Central Mechanical Engineering Research Institute, Dungarpur, West Bengal, Nov. 1960-Feb. 1964. *Publications:* books on Thermodynamics, Workshop Technology, etc. Papers dealing with researches into problems chiefly relating to I.C. engines, education and metrology. *Recreations:* wood-carving, photography, lecturing and many others; opened Bronze scrolls from Dead Sea. *Address:* 26 Old Broadway, Withington, Manchester 20. *T.:* 061-445 2714. [*Died* 1 *May* 1969.

BAKER, Sir Jack (Croft), Kt. 1958; C.B.E. 1949; Retired; *b.* 25 Feb. 1894; 2nd *s.* of late Henry Croft Baker and Alderman Mrs. Ada Baker, J.P.; *m.* 1914, Doris Ann, *d.* of late Harry Beales; two *s.* two *d.* *Educ.:* Clee Grammar School; Elmfield College, York. Vice-Pres. British Trawlers Federation, 1940-44, President, 1944-57. Elected Mem. Cleethorpes Urban District Council, 1928 (Chairman of U.D.C., 1933-34); elected Mem. Cleethorpes Borough Council (Charter of Incorporation, 1936), 1936; Alderman, 1940; Mayor, 1940-41; resigned, 1945; elected Mem. Lindsey County Council, 1934; resigned, 1946; Chairman Grimsby, Cleethorpes and District Water Board, 1942-44. *Recreations:* music, photography and bowls. *Address:* The Crossways, 16 Lindum Rd., Cleethorpes, Lincs. *T.:* Cleethorpes 6118. *Club:* Royal Over-Seas League. [*Died* 18 *Feb.* 1962.

BAKER, Maj.-Gen. Jasper, C.B. 1932; C.B.E. 1919; *b.* 1877. 2nd Lt. Royal Marines, 1895; Lt. R.M., 1896; Capt. R.M., 1901; Capt. A.O.D., 1911; Major, 1912; served European War, 1914-19 (despatches four times, Bt. Lt.-Col., C.B.E.); Temp. Lt.-Col. 1915; Col. 1917; actg. Lt.-Col. 1919; Lt.-Col. 1922; Bt. Col. 1925; Col. 1927. Inspector of Army Ordnance Services, War Office, 1929-31; Maj.-Gen. 1932; War Office, 1932-35; retired pay, 1936; Deputy Director, Ordnance Services, 1940; Col. Comdt. R.A.O.C., 1935-45; Lt.-Col. commanding 9th Bn. Devon Home Guard, 1940-42; Hon. H.G. Lt.-Col., 1946. *Address:* Rooklands, St. Michael's Road, Torquay, Devon. [*Died* 21 *Jan.* 1964.

BAKER, Reginald Tustin, D.Mus. (Dunelm); F.R.C.O.; Organist and Master of the Choristers, Sheffield Cathedral since 1937; *b.* Gloucester, 1900. *Educ.:* King's School, Gloucester. Chorister of Gloucester Cathedral, 1911-15; articled to Sir Herbert Brewer (Organist of Gloucester Cathedral), 1915-18; sixteen months Army Service; returned to Gloucester Cathedral as Assistant Organist, 1920-26; Organist and Choirmaster, St. Luke's Church, S. Francisco, U.S.A., 1926-28; Hexham Abbey, 1928-29; Halifax Parish Church, 1929-37. *Publications:* Church Anthems and Services; part-songs and carols. *Address:* Greenhills, Dene Lane, Hathersage, Via Sheffield. [*Died* 18 *Dec.* 1966.

BAKER, Lt.-Gen. Sir William Henry Goldney, K.C.I.E., *cr.* 1944; C.B. 1941; D.S.O. 1917; O.B.E. 1937; *b.* 1888; *m.* 1924, Dorothy, 3rd *d.* of late J. H. Lace, C.I.E., Imperial Forest Service; one *s.* one *d.* Entered Indian Army, 1910; Major, 1925; Bt. Lieut.-Colonel, 1930; Lieut.-Colonel, 1935; Colonel, 1938; Major-Gen., 1940; Lt.-Gen. 1942; served European War, 1914-18 (despatches, D.S.O., Brevet Maj.); Marri Campaign, 1918; Afghan War 1919 (despatches); Waziristan Operations, 1936-37 (despatches, O.B.E.); Comdr. Delhi (I) Brigade Area, 1938; A.D.C. to the King, 1940; Adjutant-General in India, 1941; retired, 1944; p.s.c. 1921; i.d.c. 1933. *Address:* The Lodge, Thorverton, nr. Exeter. [*Died* 28 *Dec.* 1964.

BALCH, Emily G(reene); Hon. International President of Women's International League for Peace and Freedom since 1936; *b.* Boston, Massachusetts, 8 January 1867; *d.* of Francis V. Balch and Ellen Maria Noyes; unmarried. *Educ.:* Bryn Mawr Coll. (B.A.). Nobel Peace Prize (joint), 1946. *Publications:* Public Assistance of the Poor in France, 1893; Our Slavic Fellow-Citizens, 1910; (jointly) Women at The Hague, 1915; Approaches to the Great Settlement, 1918; (jointly) Occupied Haiti, 1927; Refugees as Assets, 1939; The Miracle of Living (poems), 1941 *Address:* 8 Dana St., Cambridge, Mass., U.S.A. [*Died* 9 *Jan.* 1961.

BALCHIN, Brigadier Nigel Marlin; *b.* 3 Dec. 1908; *s.* of William E. and Ada Elizabeth Balchin; *m.* 1st, 1933, Elisabeth Evelyn Walshe (from whom he obtained a divorce, 1951); three *d.*; 2nd, 1953, Yovanka Zorana Tomich; one *s.* one *d.* *Educ.:* Dauntsey's; Peterhouse, Cambridge (Exhibitioner and Prizeman in Natural Science). During War of 1939-45 was engaged in scientific work for the Army, ending as Dep. Scientific Adviser to Army Council. *Publications:* No Sky, 1933; Simple Life, 1934; Lightbody on Liberty, 1936; Income and Outcome, 1937; Darkness Falls from the Air, 1942; The Small Back Room, 1943; Mine Own Executioner, 1945; Lord, I was Afraid, 1947; The Borgia Testament, 1948; A Sort of Traitors, 1949; The Anatomy of Villainy, 1950; A Way Through the Wood, 1951; Sundry Creditors, 1953; Last recollections of my Uncle Charles, 1954; The Fall of the Sparrow, 1955; Seen Dimly before Dawn, 1962; In the Absence of Mrs. Petersen, 1966; Kings of Infinite Space, 1967. Under the pseudonym Mark Spade: How to Run a Bassoon Factory, 1934; Business for Pleasure, 1935. *Recreations:* golf, wood carving. *Address:* 48 Regent's Park Road, N.W.1. *T.:* 01-722, 5754. *Club:* Savile. [*Died* 17 *May* 1970.

BALD, Robert Cecil, M.A., LL.B., D.Litt (Adelaide); Ph.D. (Camb.); Prof. of English Monash Univ., Australia, since 1965; *b.* 25 January 1901; *s.* of George R. Bald, Melbourne, Australia, and Rebecca Grieve; *m.* 1928, Beatrice, *d.* of H. W. H. Hale, Melbourne; one *d.* *Educ.:* Scotch College, Melbourne; Ormond College, University of Melbourne; Clare College, Cambridge. Lecturer in English, University of West Australia, 1922; University of Adelaide, 1923-24 and 1927-33; University College of South West of England, 1933-35; Prof. of

English, University of Stellenbosch, 1935-1937, Cornell University, 1937-52; University of Chicago, 1952-65; Research Fellow, Folger Shakespeare Library, 1937; Guggenheim Foundation Fellow, 1946-47, 1960-61; Research Fell., Huntingdon Library, 1951-1952; Foyle Fell., Shakespeare Inst., Stratford-upon-Avon, 1955-56; Member, Institute for Advanced Study, Princeton, 1960-61; Alexander Lectr., Univ. of Toronto, 1961; Vis. Prof., Princeton Univ., 1963. *Publications:* Editions of Middleton's Game at Chesse, 1929, Hengist, King of Kent, 1938, and Honorable Entertainments, 1953, Shakespeare's Hamlet, 1 Henry IV, and King Lear 1946-49, Measure for Measure, 1955; Southwell's Humble Supplication, 1953; Literary Friendships in the Age of Wordsworth, 1932; Seventeenth-Century English Poetry, 1959; The Knave in Graine, 1961. Bibliographical Studies in the Beaumont and Fletcher Folio, 1938; Donne and the Drurys, 1959; articles in learned periodicals. *Recreations:* collecting, music. *Address:* Monash University, Clayton, Vic., Australia. [*Died* 23 *Aug.* 1965.

BALDWIN, Sir Archer Ernest, Kt. 1958; M.C.; D.L.; Chairman of Russell, Baldwin & Bright, Auctioneers and Land Agents, Hereford, Tenbury, Leominster, and Hay; Chairman of Underley Farms Ltd., farming 800 acres; *b.* 30 Dec. 1883; *s.* of William and Elizabeth Baldwin; *m.* 1911, Minnie Powell Baldwin; two *d.* (one *s.* decd.). *Educ.:* Lucton School, Herefordshire. Fellow of the Auctioneers' Institute. On Council of Three Counties Show. Served two years in European War, 1914-18, with T. Battery Royal Horse Artillery (wounded, M.C.). M.P. (C.) Leominster Division of Herefordshire, 1945-September 1959, retired. D.L. County of Hereford, 1960. Governor, Lucton School. *Address:* Underley, Tenbury Wells. *T.:* Kyre 237. *Clubs:* Royal Commonwealth Society, Farmers'. [*Died* 27 *March* 1966.

BALDWIN, Professor Ernest H. F.; Professor of Biochemistry, University College, University of London, since 1950; *b.* 29 March 1909; *e. s.* of Hubert C. Baldwin, Gloucester; *m.* 1938, Pauline Mary, *y. d.* of Walter Bushby Edwards; one *s.* one *d.* *Educ.:* The Crypt Gram. Sch., Gloucester; St. John's Coll., Cambridge. Prize and Open Exhibitioner, St. John's College, 1928-30, Foundation Scholar, 1930 - 32, Henry Humphreys Prize for Research, 1933, Hutchinson Research Student, 1932-35. Senior Student of the Royal Commission for the Exhibition of 1851, 1933-35. Fellow of St. John's College, 1936-41; Univ. Demonstrator in Biochemistry, Cambridge, 1936-43, Univ. Lecturer in Biochemistry, 1943-50. Senior Fellow of the Lalor Foundation (U.S.A.), 1948; Visiting Prof. Univ. of California, U.S.A., 1956-57; Rose Morgan Prof. Univ. of Kansas, 1965. Fellow of New York Academy of Sciences, 1963. *Publications:* An Introduction to Comparative Biochemistry, 1st Edn. 1937, 4th Edn. 1963; Dynamic Aspects of Biochemistry, 1st Edn., 1947, 2nd Edn., 1952 (Cortina Ulisse Prize), 5th Edn., 1967; The Nature of Biochemistry, 1963, 2nd Edn., 1967; (Ed. with Dr. Joseph Needham) Hopkins and Biochemistry, 1949; (with Dr. D. J. Bell) Cole's Practical Physiological Chemistry (10th Edn.), 1955; original papers in Biochem. J., Proc. Roy. Soc., J. exp. Biol. and elsewhere. *Address:* 8 Crofters Rd., Moor Park, Northwood, Middlesex. *T.:* Northwood 21057.
[*Died* 6 *Dec.* 1969.

BALFOUR, 3rd Earl of, *cr.* 1922, and Viscount Traprain of Whittingehame; **Robert Arthur Lytton Balfour,** F.R.S.A.; Chairman and Managing Director, Bruntons (Musselburgh) Ltd., since 1957; Chairman, Scottish Division, N.C.B., 1946-51 (Part-time Dir., 1952-62); *b.* 1902; *o. s.* of 2nd Earl and Lady Betty (*d.* 1942), *d.* of 1st Earl of Lytton; *S.* father, 1945; *m.* 1925, Jean (separated 1961), 4th *d.* of late Canon J. J. Cooke-Yarborough; one *s.* two *d.* *Educ.:* Eton; Trinity College, Cambridge. Cox, Cambridge Eight, 1923. Grand Master Mason, Scotland, 1939-42; served as Lieut., R.N.V.R., 1939-1942; Chm., Scottish Special Housing-Assoc., 1938-44; Chm, Roy. Commission on Scottish Affairs 1952-54; National Governor B.B.C. for Scotland, 1956-60; Director Scottish Gas Board, 1958-65. *Recreation:* yachting. *Heir:* *s.* Viscount Traprain. *Address:* The Tower, Whittingehame, Haddington, Scotland. *Clubs:* Naval and Military; Royal Cruising; Royal Forth Yacht; Royal Ocean Racing; Cambridge Cruising; East Lothian Yacht; Leander.
[*Died* 27 *Nov.* 1968.

BALFOUR of Burleigh, 11th Baron, *cr.* 1607, (*de facto* 7th Baron. 11th but for the Attainder); **George John Gordon Bruce**; Hon. D.C.L. (Durham), 1949; D.L., J P. for Clackmannanshire; Representative Peer for Scotland, 1923 - 63; Alderman, Kensington Borough Council, until 1963; Director, Lloyds Bank, 1945-63 (Chairman, 1946-54); Chm., Bd. of Land Tax Commissioners for City of London; Comr. for Gen. Purposes of Income Tax Acts for City of London; Vice-Pres. Assoc. of Municipal Corporations; Vice-Pres. Building Societies Assoc.; Hon. Member: Roy. Instn. of Chartered Surveyors; Instn. of Municipal Engineers; Soc. of Housing Managers; Member Royal Company of Archers (Queen's Body Guard for Scotland); Treasurer Royal Scottish Corporation; *b.* 18 Oct. 1883; *o. surv. s.* of 10th Baron and late Lady Katherine Gordon, *sister* of 1st Marquis of Aberdeen; *S.* father, 1921; *m.* 1919, Dorothy, *d.* of R. H. Done; two *s.* four *d.* Pres. Institute of Bankers, 1948, 1949; Chairman of Medical Research Council, 1936-48; Mem. of Central Housing Advisory Committee to 1945; Councillor Kensington Borough Council, 1924-49; Chairman Kensington Housing Trust, 1926-49; Pres. of Royal Sanitary Institute, 1931-41; Chairman Scottish Hill Sheep Farming Committee, 1943; Director L. & N.E. Rly. until nationalisation; Chairman: Cttee. of London Clearing Bankers, 1950; Hill Lands (North of Scotland) Commission; Pres. British Bankers Assoc., 1950. Mem. Select Cttee. of the House of Lords on the Powers of the House in relation to the Attendance of its Members; Mem. Cttee. on Administrative Tribunals and Enquiries; Chm. Departmental Cttee. on Export of Live Cattle, 1957. Capt. Royal and Ancient Golf Club of St. Andrews, 1949. Freeman, Roy. Borough of Kensington, 1965. Served European War, 1914-19 (despatches, four times, Bt.-Major, 1914 Star, Legion of Honour, wounded). *Heir:* *s.* Master of Burleigh. *Address:* Brucefield, Clackmannan. *T.:* Kincardine-on-Forth 228; 14 Parkside, S.W.1. *Clubs:* Carlton; New (Edinburgh). [*Died* 4 *June* 1967.

BALFOUR, Alfred; retd. as M.P. (Lab.) W. Div. of Stirling and Clackmannan (1945-Sept. 1959); *b.* 7 Sept. 1885; *s.* of William Balfour, shoemaker; *m.* 1913, Margaret Grant; three *d.* *Educ.:* Elem. schools; Evening Classes, Workers' Educational Classes, and National Council Labour Colleges Classes. Baker's message boy; sawmill worker; tannery worker; carter; railwayman. Formerly: Representative on Trades Council, Local Labour Party, and National Conferences of such; Secretary Aberdeen Branch N.U.R. 20 years; Mem. National Executive Cttee. N.U.R. Ex-member Aberdeen Town Council. *Recreations:* boxing, running, swimming, walking, reading. *Address:* 12 Union Grove, Aberdeen.
[*Died* 26 *Jan.* 1963.

BALFOUR, Lieut.-Col. Francis Cecil Campbell, C.I.E. 1919; C.V.O. 1953; C.B.E. 1931; M.C.; *b.* 1884; *s.* of late Col. Eustace J. A. Balfour and late Lady Frances Balfour, *d.* of 8th Duke of Argyll; *m.* 1920, Hon. Phyllis Evelyn Goschen, *d.* of 2nd Viscount Goschen, P.C., G.C.S.I., G.C.I.E.; one *s.* one *d.* *Educ.:* Eton. Joined P.W.D., Sudan Govt., 1906; trans. to Political Service, 1912; was in 6th (T.F.) Batt. Northumberland Fusiliers, and retired 1921 with rank of Lt.-Col. in the Army; served in Mesopotamia, 1917-20; Military Governor of Baghdad, 1919-20; Military Secretary to Viscount Goschen, Governor of Madras, 1924-26; Deputy-Governor Red Sea Province Sudan, 1926-27; Governor, 1927-28; Governor, Mongalla Province, 1929-30; retired from Sudan Political Service, 1931; Representative of the Peruvian Corporation in Peru and Bolivia, 1931-36; First British Delegate on International Sugar Council, Chairman, 1937-38; Chairman of Sugar Commission under Sugar Industry Reorganisation Act, 1936-40; Ministry of Food, Sept. 1939-51. Served with U.N.R.R.A. in Greece and Egypt, 1944-45; Order of the Lion and the Sun, Persia, 2nd class; Order of the Nile, Egypt, 3rd class. *Address:* Old Peans, Robertsbridge, Sussex. *T.:* Robertsbridge 248. [*Died* 16 *April* 1965.

BALFOUR-BROWNE, Vincent R.; J.P.; Artist; Hon. Sheriff Substitute, Dumfries and Galloway; 2nd *s.* of late J. H. Balfour-Browne, K.C., Goldielea, Dumfries. *Educ.:* Radley; Magdalen College, Oxford. *Publications:* A Day's Stalking; The Story of a Stag. *Recreations:* stalking and shooting. *Address:* Dalskairth, Dumfries. *Clubs:* Athenæum; New (Edinburgh). [*Died* 9 *April* 1963.

BALFOUR-BROWNE, William Alex Francis, M.A. (Oxon et Cantab); F.R.S.E., F.Z.S., F.E.S., F.L.S., F.R.M.S.; Barrister-at-law; *b.* London, 27 Dec. 1874; *s.* of late J. H. Balfour-Browne, K.C., D.L., LL.D., and late Caroline Emma, *d.* of late Lord Justice Lush; *m.* 1902, Elizabeth Lochhead Carslaw (*d.* 1947); one *s.* two *d.* *Educ.:* St. Paul's School; Magdalen College, Oxford, 2nd class Honours in Botany, 1896. Called to Bar 1898; returned to Oxford to study Zoology, 1899; went to the Marine Biological Association's Laboratory at Plymouth as Assistant Naturalist, 1900; Director of the Sutton Broad Laboratory, Norfolk, 1902; Naturalist to Ulster Fishery and Biology Dept., N. Ire.; Assistant in Biology at Queen's College, Belfast, 1906, and then Lecturer in Botany at Queen's University, Belfast; Lecturer in Entomology in Department of Zoology, University of Cambridge, 1913; University Lecturer in Zoology (Entomology), 1917; joined 1st London Sanitary Company, R.A.M.C., 1915; went out as Sanitary Officer with 40th Division, 1916; Professor of Entomology, Imperial College of Science and Technology, S.W.7, 1925-30; President Royal Microscopical Society, 1934-1935; Vice-President, Freshwater Biological Society, 1933; Vice-Pres., Royal Entomological Society, 1934-35; Pres., Zoological Section of British Association and of Association of British Zoologists, 1935; Pres., Society for British Entomology, 1939; Pres., South-Eastern Naturalists' Union, 1947. *Publications:* Keys to the Orders of Insects; Concerning the Habits of Insects; Vol. on Insects in Home University Library Series; Vol. on Insects in Benn's Sixpenny Series; Textbook of Practical Entomology, 1932; British Water-Beetles (Ray Soc., 1940); many scientific papers, mostly on Entomology. *Recreations:* fishing and insect collecting; represented Oxford Univ. against Cambridge at Hockey in 1894 and 1895; Half Blue for cycling, 1894. *Address:* Brocklehirst, Collin, Dumfries, Scotland. *T.A.* and *T.:* Mouswald 247. [*Died* 28 *Sept.* 1967.

BALIOL SCOTT, Edward; Editor of the Mining Journal, 1901-54; Chairman Mining Journal Ltd. since then; *b.* 1873; *o. s.* of Capt. L. H. Scott, 11th Regt.; *m.* 1902, Gladys Agnes, *d.* of William C. P. Grant, Paymaster-in-Chief R.N.; two *s.* *Educ.:* Geelong Grammar School; Bath College; University College, Oxford (Hon. Mods., Greats). Called to Bar, Middle Temple, 1897, Oxford Circuit. *Recreations:* golf, motoring. *Address:* Flat 5, 9 Cleveland Square, W.2. *T.:* Paddington 0373. *T.A.:* Tutwork. London. *T.:* Monarch 2567. [*Died* 23 *Dec.* 1963.

BALL, Sir (George) Joseph, K.B.E., *cr.* 1936 (O.B.E. 1919); Chairman of Henderson's Transvaal Estates Ltd. and of 5 subsidiary companies; Chairman: Lake View & Star Ltd.; Director: Consolidated Goldfields of South Africa Ltd.; Beaumont Property Trust Ltd. and subsidiaries; *b.* 1885; *s.* of late George Ball, Salisbury. *Educ.:* King's Coll. School, Strand; King's Coll. London. Called to Bar, Gray's Inn (1st Cl. Hons.), 1913; European War, 1914-19 (O.B.E.). Director of Conservative Research Department, 1930-39; Deputy Chairman National Publicity Bureau, 1934-39; Deputy Chairman Security Executive, 1940-42; Chairman Hampshire Rivers Catchment Board and Hampshire River Board, 1947-53. *Address:* The Old Mill, Ramsbury, Wilts. *Clubs:* Flyfishers', Pratt's, City of London, Bath, Army and Navy; Royal Lymington Yacht. [*Died* 10 *July* 1961.

BALL, Sir Joseph; *see* Ball, Sir G. J.

BALL, Willet, J.P.; *b.* Lincoln, 1873; *m.*; two *s.* one *d.* *Educ.:* Lincoln Middle School. Entered the service of the Great Northern Railway Company as a clerk, 1888; became a member of the National Union of Railwaymen and Social Democratic Federation, 1893; Sub-Editor of the Railway Review, 1900; Editor, 1917-33; Labour candidate Luton Division of Beds. Dec. 1918 and Dec. 1923. Governor: of Secondary Schools (Boys); of Secondary Schools (Girls). *Recreation:* bowling. *Address:* 52 Waller Avenue, Luton, Beds. [*Died* 1 *June* 1962.

BALLARD, Albert, C.B.E. 1955; Chairman United Sheffield Hospitals' Board of Governors, 1948-63; Lord Mayor of Sheffield, 1957-58; *b.* 2 Aug. 1888; father a brick-maker, mother a silk weaver; *m.* 1912, May Painting Conder; two *s.* one *d.* *Educ.:* Hillfoot elementary school, Sheffield; tutorial classes of the W.E.A. Member research group on educational standard of Sheffield working-class, 1917; Chm. National Co-operative Party, 1955-57; City of Sheffield Education Cttee.; Member: Sheffield City Council; Council of Sheffield Univ.; Association of Municipal Corporations. Hon. LL.D. (Sheffield University), 1959. *Recreations:* gardening and rambling. *Address:* 93 Ringstead Crescent, Sheffield 10. *T.:* Sheffield 31732. [*Died* 7 *Jan.* 1969.

BALLENTINE, Major-General John Steventon, C.B. 1947; C.I.E. 1946; *b.* 10 May 1897; *s.* of John G. Ballentine and Maud Katherine Steventon, Ballymena, Co. Antrim; *m.* 1920, Lilian Alicia (Kaisar-i-Hind Medal, 1947), *o. d.* of late Lieutenant-Colonel R. L. Benwell. *Educ.:* Portora Royal School, Enniskillen; R.M.C. Sandhurst. Commissioned Indian Army 1916, 17th Cavalry. Served European War, 1914-1918; Waziristan, 1921. Transferred to The Royal Deccan Horse, 1927; Staff Coll., Quetta, 1931-32; D.A.A. & Q.M.G. Western Comd., India, 1934-37; G.S.O. 2 Lahore Dist., 1938-40; War of 1939-45; Comdt. R. Deccan Horse, 1940-41; A.A. & Q.M.G. 31 Ind. Armd.

Div., 1941-42; Dep. Dir. of Military Trng., India, 1942-43; B.G.S., N.W. Army, 1943-44. Maj.-Gen. i/c Administration, Eastern Comd.; 1945-47; Q.M.G. (India), 1947. Colonel, 1946, Major-General, 1947; retired, 1948. Defence Secretary, E. Africa High Commission, 1949-1951; Special Commissioner of Lands, Kenya, 1951-55. Cross of Merit, 1st Class with Crown of Order of Malta, 1957. *Address:* Villa Dorada, Torre, Cascais, Portugal. *Club:* Naval and Military.

[*Died* 2 *Feb.* 1965.

BALSTON, Thomas, O.B.E. 1919; M.C. 1917; Writer; *b.* 30 July 1883; *s.* of William Edward Balston and Emily Julia Whitehead. *Educ.:* Eton (K.S.); New College, Oxford (Exhibitioner). Tutor in Italy to the Counts Gianbattista and Cesare Spalletti, 1906-07. Called to the Bar, Inner Temple, 1909. Secretary to T. Fisher Unwin, Publisher, 1912-14. Served European War, 1914-19, France and Belgium, Lieut. 12th Glos. Regt.; Staff Capt. 96th Inf. Bde., 1915-17; D.A.A.G. 3rd Div., 1917-18, and 3rd Corps, 1918-19; recalled to Southern Command as Staff Captain, Dec. 1939, but disabled after 3 months by pneumonia. With Duckworth & Co., Publishers, 1921-34 (Partner, 1923; Director, 1924); Orig. Mem., Double Crown Club, 1924, Pres. 1933. Started to paint, 1934; one-man exhibition, Redfern Gallery, 1938. Organised and catalogued: exhibn. of Wood-Engraving in Modern English Books, Nat. Book League, 1949; Mark Gertler Memorial Exhibn., Whitechapel Art Gall., 1949; John Martin Exhibn., Whitechapel Art Gall., 1953; spent forty years forming Collection of Victorian Staffordshire Portrait Figures, accepted by National Trust, 1963, and established at Stapleford Park near Melton Mowbray. *Publications:* Sitwelliana, 1928; The Life of Jonathan Martin, Incendiary of York Minster, 1945; John Martin, his Life and Works, 1947; The Wood-Engravings of Robert Gibbings, 1949; English Wood-Engraving 1900-1950, 1951; The Cambridge University Collection of Private Press Types, 1951; Dr. Balston at Eton, 1952; (Ed.) Susanna Whatman, Her Housekeeping Book, 1952; William Balston, Paper-Maker, 1954; James Whatman, Father and Son, 1957; Staffordshire Portrait Figures of the Victorian Age, 1958 (Supplement, 1963); contribs. to New Paths in Book Collecting (Ed. John Carter); History Today; The Book-Collector's Quarterly; The Library; The Fleuron; Signature; Image; Alphabet and Image; D.N.B. *Address:* Flat 64, 3 Whitehall Court, S.W.1. *T.:* Whitehall 3160. *Clubs:* Garrick, Savile. [*Died* 4 *Oct.* 1967.

BAMBRIDGE, Sir George, Kt., *cr.* 1941; M.C. 1917; V.D.; *b.* 21 Oct. 1883; *s.* of George Edmund Bambridge, F.R.A.M., F.T.C.L. (Director of Studies, Trinity Coll. of Music), and Marie Bambridge; *m.* 1918, Doris Mary Wrigley (*d.* 1956); one *s.* one *d.* *Educ.:* St. Paul's. Went out to Madras in 1907 to join the firm of Binny & Co. Ltd.; retired from India in 1941. Sometime Sheriff of Madras; Chairman: Madras Chamber of Commerce; Employers Federation of Southern India; Finance Committee, Madras Governor's War Fund; Trustee Port of Madras; member, Madras and Central Boards of Imperial Bank of India; Commanding Officer, Madras Artillery and Madras Signals, Auxiliary Force (India) and Hon. A.D.C. to H.E. the Viceroy of India. *Address:* Walnut Tree Cottage, Marnhull, Dorset. *Clubs:* Junior Army and Navy; Madras (Madras).

[*Died* 16 *Nov.* 1961.

BAMFORD, Lt.-Col. Harry William Morrey, C.B.E. 1933 (O.B.E. 1918); M.C.; *b.* 1882. Cape Mounted Riflemen, South African War; Transvaal Mounted Rifles, Zululand 1906; Adjutant Natal Light Horse, German South-West African Campaign; commanded 2nd South African Infantry and South African Composite Regiment, Egypt and France (three times wounded, despatches thrice, O.B.E., M.C., Croix de Guerre avec palme); Commissioner of Police, Malta 1919-1922; Commandant Northern Territories Constabulary, Gold Coast, 1922-24; Inspector General of Police, Gold Coast, 1924-38; appointed a member of the Legislative Council of the Gold Coast (now Ghana), 1936. Silver Jubilee Medal, 1935; Coronation Medal, 1937; King's Police Medal, 1937; War Service with Union Defence Force, 1941-1943. *Address:* Kokstad, East Griqualand, South Africa. *Club:* United Service.

[*Died* 25 *Aug.* 1968.

BANCROFT, Sir Oswald Lawrance, Kt., 1951; *b.* 1888; *y. s.* of Joseph Richard Bancroft, Barbados; *m.* Sybil, *o. d.* of Nigel Bruce Burnside, I.S.O.; one *s.* *Educ.:* Harrison Coll., Barbados; Trinity Coll., Camb. (M.A.). Called to Bar, Inner Temple, 1910; K.C. Bahamas, 1945. Barrister-at-law and Solicitor Supreme Court, British Columbia, 1911; Magistrate, Barbados, 1925 and 1931; Deputy Registrar Supreme Court of Tanganyika Territory, 1926; Crown Counsel, Northern Rhodesia, 1928; Magistrate, Bahamas, 1937; Attorney-General, British Honduras, 1941; Labour Officer, Bahamas, 1944; Attorney-General, Bahamas, 1944; Chief Justice of the Bahamas, 1946-51; retired, 1951, private practice in Bahamas. *Recreation:* fishing. *Address:* P.O. Box 437, Nassau, New Providence, Bahamas. *Clubs:* West Indian (London); Bahamas Country, Balmoral (Bahamas).

[*Died* 19 *Oct.* 1964.

BANFORD, Leslie Jackson, C.B.E. 1952; Director of Contracts, Air Ministry. *Address:* 26 Elm Grove Road, Ealing, W.5; Air Ministry, Adastral House, Theobalds Road, W.C.1. [*Died* 23 *April* 1961.

BANKART, Vice-Admiral (Retd.) Sir (George) Harold, K.C.B., *cr.* 1949; C.B.E. 1943; *b.* 1 March 1893; *er. s.* of late Charles J. Bankart, Leicester; *m.* 1924, Dorothy Gordon (*d.* 1964), *d.* of late Lieut.-Colonel W. H. D. Jones, 2nd Bombay Lancers, I.A.; two *s.* one *d.* *Educ.:* St. Helen's Coll., Southsea. Entered R.N. 1910; served on staff of Admiral of the Fleet Earl Jellicoe, 1914-16, and subsequently in secretarial and supply appointments; Secretary to Admiral of the Fleet Sir Charles M. Forbes, 1930-43; Fleet Supply Officer, Home Fleet, 1945-46; Command Supply Officer, Portsmouth, 1947-48; Naval A.D.C. to the King, 1946-48; Director-General Supply and Secretariat Branch, Admiralty, 1948-51; retired, 1951. *Address:* Heath Ridge, Graffham, nr. Petworth, Sussex.

[*Died* 17 *Dec.* 1964.

BANKART, Sir Harold; *see* Bankart, Sir G. H.

BANKS, Col. Hon. Charles Arthur, C.M.G. 1946; Mining Engineer; *b.* New Zealand, 1885; *s.* of late John Edward and Elizabeth Banks of London, England, and New Zealand; *m.* Jean, *d.* of late Count de Montalk, Paris. Served European War, 1914-19, Royal Engineers in France. Lieutenant-Governor of British Columbia, 1946-50, retired. Chairman (formerly Managing Director), Placer Development Ltd. K.St.J. *Address:* 700 Burrard Bldg., 1030 West Georgia Street, Vancouver 5, B.C., Canada. *Clubs:* Pacific Union (San Francisco); Vancouver (Vancouver, B.C.); Union (Victoria, B.C.). [*Died* 29 *Sept.* 1961.

BANKS, Colonel Cyril, M.B.E. 1942; Company Director, retired; *b.* 12 Aug. 1901

(British); *m.* 1930, Gladys Drackley; no *c.* *Educ.:* University of Sheffield. Banks Equipment Ltd. (Man. Dir.), 1935-39. Ministry of Food, Asst. Dir. Wartime Meals Div., 1940-1943; War Office, Civil Affairs Branch, 1943, (Lieut.-Col.) Cossac, 1943, (Colonel) S.H.A.E.F. Supply, 1944. Member for Otley, West Riding County Council, 1946-49. M.P. (C.) Pudsey, 1950-September 1959 (Ind. 1956-58). Joint Parliamentary Private Sec. to Minister of Transport and Civil Aviation, 1952-53. *Recreation:* golf. *Address:* 25 Holly Park, Huby, Leeds, Yorkshire. *T.:* Huby 563. *Club:* Constitutional. [*Died* 23 *Oct.* 1969.

BANKS, Edward Bernard, F.I.E.E.; Deputy Chairman, The English Electric Co. Ltd., since 1967; Joint Managing Director, since 1962; *b.* 5 Jan. 1901; *yr. s.* of late Dr. William Banks, Falmouth, Cornwall; unmarried. *Educ.:* Haileybury College; Bradford Technical College. Joined English Electric Co. Ltd. as apprentice, 1919; subsequently held numerous administrative posts at home and abroad. In India, 1923-35; Manager at Calcutta, 1929-35, returned to England, 1935. Production Manager, 1935-1937; General Manager at Preston, 1937-40; Dep. Chief Commercial Manager, 1940-46; Chief Commercial Manager, 1946-62; Deputy Man. Dir., April 1962. Director: Nuclear Design & Construction Ltd. (Dep. Chm.); D. Napier & Son Ltd.; The English Electric, Babcock & Wilcox and Taylor Woodrow Atomic Power Construction Co. Ltd. Member of Council, British Electrical and Allied Manufacturers' Assoc., 1961- (Pres. 1964-65); Member Economic Development Cttee. for electrical manufacturing industry. *Recreations:* reading, music. *Address:* Aston Grove, Newport, Shropshire. *T.:* Newport (Shropshire) 2265. [*Died* 15 *Dec.* 1968.

BANNATYNE, Maj.-Gen. Neil Charles, C.B. 1934; C.I.E. 1932; *b.* 24 Jan. 1880; *s.* of Col. John Millar Bannatyne (late 8th Foot), Milheugh, Blantyre, Scotland; *m.* 1917, Theodora, *d.* of late Rev. R. G. Wood; three *d.* *Educ.:* Cheltenham College; R.M.C., Sandhurst. Commissioned 1899; Military Secretary, Army Headquarters, India, 1936-40; retired 1940; Chief Censor, India, 1940-42; Deputy Chief Commissioner, Indian Red Cross, 1942-46. *Address:* Belsaye Hotel, Ratton Road, Eastbourne, Sussex. [*Died* 22 *Aug.* 1970.

BANNER, Hubert Stewart, B.A.; Author, Journalist and Lecturer; *b.* 1891; *s.* of Rev. Francis Stewart Banner, M.A., and Sophia Banner; *m.* 1922, Peggy Regina Lipton (decd.); (one *s.* decd.); *m.* 1957, Winnifred Van Ess, Oakland, Cal. *Educ.:* Haileybury Coll.; Brasenose Coll., Oxford. Joined British import firm in Java, 1913; Far Eastern Political Intelligence Service, 1914-1925; founded and edited The Java Palpitator, sole English periodical in Java; Publicity Officer, Malayan Govt. Agency, London, 1926-34; on staff of Editorial Services, Ltd 1935-37; Gen. Sec., Rotary Internat. in Gt. Brit. and Ireland, 1937-39; Chief Regional Information Officer, Min. of Information, S.-E. Region, 1939-43; served in 22nd (Kent) Bn. Home Guard, 1940-42; Director, The Netherlands House, London, 1943-46; lecturing in U.S.A. and Canada, 1946-48; Public Relations Officer, Hudson's Bay Co., Vancouver, B.C., 1948-49; Gen. Manager, Vancouver Civic Theatre Soc., 1949-1954; engaged in real estate business in Vancouver, 1954-57. *Publications:* Ten Poems, 1916; Guide to Brambanan Temples, 1920; Horrid Rhymes for Torrid Climes, 1924; Romantic Java as it Was and Is, 1927; The Mountain of Terror, 1928; A Tropical Tapestry, 1929; Red Cobra, 1929; Great Disasters of the World, 1931; The Ocean Wind, 1931; Flamboyante, 1932; Calamities of the World, 1932; Wanted on Voyage, 1933; Masonry in the Malay Peninsula and Archipelago, 1933; Amy Johnson, 1933; These Men Were Masons, 1934; Hell's Harvest, 1934; Tidal Wave, 1935; Raffles of Singapore (radio play), 1936; Kentish Fire, 1944; Thus My Orient, 1945. *Recreations:* study of Oriental mythology, folklore and comparaive religion; music and art. *Address:* 1205 Sunnyhills Rd., Oakland 10, California, U.S.A. *T.:* TEmplebar 2-6247. [*Died* 9 *May* 1964.

BANNERMAN OF KILDONAN, Baron *cr.* 1967 (Life Peer), of Kildonan in the County of Sutherland; **John MacDonald Bannerman,** O.B.E. 1952; J.P.; M.A., B.Sc.; Farmer; Joint President, Scottish Liberal Party since 1965 (Chairman 1956-1965); Forestry Commissioner, 1942-57; *b.* 1 September 1901; *s.* of late Roderick and Mary Bannerman; *m.* 1931, Ray, *d.* of late Walter Mundell, Swordale, Evanton, Ross-shire; two *s.* two *d.* *Educ.:* Shawlands Academy; Glasgow High School; Glasgow University; Balliol College, Oxford. Lord Rector Aberdeen University, 1957-60; Hon. LL.D. Aberdeen University, 1959. *Recreation:* Rugby football. *Address:* Ola Manse, Balmaha, Stirlingshire. *T.:* Balmahd 210. *Clubs:* Reform; Liberal (Edinburgh); Royal Scottish Automobile (Glasgow). [*Died* 10 *May* 1969.

BANNISTER, Frederick Allan, M.A., Sc.D., F.Inst.P.; *b.* 14 May 1901; *m.* 1927, Lesley M. Gordon; two *d.* *Educ.:* Whitgift School, Croydon; Clare Coll., Cambridge, Denman-Baynes student of Clare Coll., Cambridge, 1923-24; Production of water-cooled thermionic valves, Western Electric Company, 1924-27; British Museum (Natural History), 1927. *Publications:* various papers giving X-ray data for minerals. *Address:* Chantry House, Vicarage Lane, Horley, Surrey. *T.:* Horley 3000. [*Died* 4 *Oct.* 1970.

BARBER, Lt.-Col. Charles Harrison, D.S.O. 1919; M.A., D.M., B.Ch. (Oxon), M.R.C.S., L.R.C.P.; Indian Medical Service, retired; Lecturer on Tropical Diseases, King's College Hospital and West London Hospital Medical Schools; *b.* 1877; *s.* of late Richard Augustus Barber, Leicester, and Mary Ann, *d.* of Thos. Harrison, Leicester; *m.* 1st, Mercedes del Biot (marr. diss.); two *d.*; 2nd, Myra L. Griffin; one *s.* *Educ.:* Wyggeston School; Oxford University; King's College Hospital, London. Served N.W. Frontier, India-Zakka Khel Expedition, 1908; Mohmand Expedition, 1908; European War, 1914-18, Mesopotamia, siege of Kut-el-Amara, prisoner with Turks, exchanged, 1916 (despatches three times, D.S.O.); Army Specialist Operative Surgery; Professor, Medicine, Lucknow University, 1919-20. *Publications:* Professional—Tropical and Subtropical Diseases, Penetrating Gunshot Wounds of Abdomen, and other papers; General—Besieged in Kut and after; contributions to Blackwood, etc. *Recreation;* travel. *Address:* Starbank House, Thame, Oxon. *T.:* 270. *Clubs:* East India and Sports, Union (Oxford). [*Died* 1 *Jan.* 1965.

BARBER, Lieut.-General Sir Colin Muir, K.B.E., *cr.* 1952; C.B. 1945; D.S.O. 1940; D.L.; late Cameron Highlanders; retired; *b.* 27 June 1897; *s.* of late John Barber, Bromborough; *m.* 1st, 1929, Mary Edith Nixon (*d.* 1949); one *s.* one *d.*; 2nd, Mrs. Anthony Milburn. *Educ.:* Uppingham School. Served in France and Belgium with Liverpool Scottish and 1st Cameron Highlanders, 1917-19; India, 1919-1931, Staff College, Quetta, 1929-30; held Staff appointment in Scottish and Southern Command; Palestine, 1936; war of 1939-45 B.E.F. with 51st (Highland) Div. (D.S.O.); N.W. Europe, in command 15th Scottish Div. (Bar to D.S.O., C.B.); Commander

Highland District (Scottish Command), 1946-49; Director of Infantry and Military Training, W.O., 1949-52; G.O.C.-in-C., Scottish Command and Governor of Edinburgh Castle, 1952-55; retired 1955. Lt.-Gen. 1952. D.L., York, 1959. *Recreations:* shooting, golf. *Address:* Quarry Moor Lodge, Ripon; Glyn, Mills and Co., Kirkland House, Whitehall, S.W.1. *Club:* Naval and Military. [*Died* 5 *May* 1964.

BARBER, Eric Arthur, F.B.A. 1936; Hon. Litt.D. (Dublin); *b.* 18 Oct. 1888; *s.* of Arthur Mitchell Barber and Edith Mary Ferguson; *m.* 1924, Alice Madeleine, *d.* of Emile Gaudard, Conseiller National, Vevey; one *s. Educ.:* Shrewsbury School (Old Salopian Scholar); New College, Oxford (Open Scholar, Hon Fellow, 1946); 1st Class Hon. Classical Moderations, 1908; 1st Class Literae Humaniores, 1910; Craven Scholar, 1908; Ireland Scholar, 1909; Derby Scholar, 1910; Charles Oldham Prize, 1911; Fellow of Merton College, 1910-13, Hon. Fellow, 1944; Fellow, Tutor and Lecturer in Classics, Exeter College, 1913-43; Sub-Rector, 1914-15 and 1919-24; Rector, 1943-56; Hon. Fellow 1956. Served 4th K.S.L.I. and Intelligence Corps (Macedonia) (despatches). *Publications:* Properti Carmina; Co-Editor, New Chapters in the History of Greek Literature, also Second Series; Oxford Book of Greek Verse; The Elegies of Propertius: contributor to The Hellenistic Age; Cambridge Ancient History, Vol. VII; Greek Poetry and Life; Fifty years of Classical Scholarship. *Address:* Two Trees, Hernes Road, Oxford. *T.:* Oxford 55601. [*Died* 24 *May* 1965.

BARBER, Capt. James William, C.B.E. 1920; Company director; *s.* of late James Barber, Cardiff; *m.* 1st, 1907, Daisy Florence (*d.* 1942), *d.* of Frederick Harman, St. Leonards-on-Sea; 2nd, 1946, Sybil Gladys Tharby, Stoke d'Abernon, Surrey. *Educ.:* Cardiff; University of South Wales. Engineer by profession; Captain (General Service); Director National War Aims Committee, 1917-19; Designer, organiser and responsible for touring Cinemas used for propaganda purposes throughout the world during the War; Keith Lecturer Royal Scottish Society of Arts; Chairman Cinematograph Exhibitors' Association, 1922 and 1923; Chairman Radio Manufacturers' Association, 1930; Chairman British Plastic Moulding Trade Association 1932 and 1933; Commercial delegate, Imperial Conference, Ottawa, 1932. *Recreations:* yachting and fishing. *Address:* Tuffs Hard, Bosham, Sussex. *Club:* Royal London Yacht (Cowes). [*Died* 23 *Oct.* 1962.

BARBER, Leslie Claud Seton, M.B.E. 1944; *b.* London, 23 Nov. 1894; *m.* 1920, Helen Feleki, Budapest, Hungary; one *s. Educ.:* in England and abroad. Joined Foreign Service, 1919; Assistant Commercial Secretary at H.M. Legation, Budapest, 1919-1924, at Stockholm, 1924-45; Commercial Secretary, H.M. Embassy, Oslo, 1945-50; Consul-General, Boston, 1950-54, retired 1954. *Recreations:* travel, sociological studies. *Address:* Rua Sampaio Bruno 14.7.E., Lisbon, Portugal. [*Died* 14 *Oct.* 1968.

BARBER, Prof. Mary; Professor of Clinical Bacteriology, Postgraduate Medical School of London, since 1964; *b.* 3 April 1911; *d.* of Dr. Hugh Barber, Derby, and Ethel Mary (*née* Howlett). *Educ.:* Alice Ottley School, Worcester; Royal Free Hospital Medical School. M.R.C.S., L.R.C.P. 1934; M.B., B.S. Lond. 1936; M.D. Lond. 1940; F.Inst. Biol. 1964; F.C. Path. 1964. House Physician, Resident Pathologist and A. M. Bird Scholar in Pathology, Royal Free Hospital, 1934-37; Asst. Pathologist, Archway Group Laboratory, 1938-40; Asst. in Dept. of Pathology and later Lecturer in Bacteriology, British Postgraduate Medical Sch., 1940-48; Reader in Bacteriology, St. Thomas's Hosp. Med. Sch., 1948-57; Reader in Clinical Bacteriology, Postgraduate Med. Sch. of London, 1957-64. *Publications:* Antibiotic and Chemotherapy (with L. P. Garrod), 1963; Editor Section of Bacteriology, Recent Advances in Clinical Pathology, Series III, 1960, Series IV, 1964; numerous contribs. to med. jls. on Antibiotics and Drug-Resistant Bacteria. *Recreations:* Christian socialism and William Blake. *Address:* 10D Bracknell Gardens, N.W.3. *T.:* Hampstead 1624. [*Died* 11 *Sept.* 1965.

BARBER, Sir Philip, 1st Bt.; *see* Barber, Sir T. P.

BARBER, Sir (Thomas) Philip, 1st Bt. *cr.* 1960; D.S.O. 1918; T.D., D.L. Notts; *b.* Jan. 1876; *e. s.* of Thomas Barber; *m.* Beatrice Mary, *d.* of Lt.-Col. W. I. Merritt; one *s.* three *d.* (and one *s.* decd.). *Educ.:* Eton; Trinity College, Cambridge. Served S. African War, 1900-01 with Imperial Yeomanry (despatches, Queen's medal 4 clasps); European War, 1914-18 (despatches twice, wounded, D.S.O.); High Sheriff of Notts, 1907. Pro-Chancellor, (Hon.) LL.D., Nottingham Univ., 1955. *Heir: s.* Lt.-Col. William Francis Barber, T.D., J.P. [*b.* 20 Nov. 1905; *m.* 1936, Diana, *d.* of late Lt.-Col. T. O. Lloyd, C.M.G., Minard, Argyll; one *s.* one *d.*]. *Address:* Lamb Close, Eastwood, Notts. *Club:* Bath. [*Died* 11 *July* 1961.

BARBIROLLI, Sir John (Giovanni Battista), C.H.1969; Kt. *cr.* 1949; F.R.A.M. 1928 (A.R.A.M. 1923); F.T.C.L.; Permanent Conductor of Hallé Orchestra, Manchester, 1943-58, Principal Conductor, 1958-68; appointed Conductor Laureate for Life, 1968; *b.* London, Dec. 1899, of Italian and French parentage; *m.* 1939, Evelyn Rothwell. *Educ.:* Royal Academy of Music. First public appearance as violoncello soloist at Queen's Hall, 1911; later toured British Isles and Europe as member of the International String Quartet; founded and conducted Barbirolli Chamber Orchestra, 1925; joined British National Opera Company as conductor, 1926; Conductor and Musical Director, Scottish Orchestra, 1933-36; Permanent Conductor and Music Director New York Philharmonic Symphony Orch., 1937-42. Conductor in Chief, Houston Symphony Orchestra, 1961-67, now Conductor Emeritus. Hon. D.Mus.: Manchester, 1950, Dublin, 1952, Sheffield, 1957, London, 1961, Leicester, 1964. Freedom of City of Manchester, 1958; Hon. Freedom of Musicians' Company, 1966. Hon. Academician, Accad. Nazionale di St. Cecilia, 1960. Gold Medal, Royal Philharmonic Society, 1950; Bruckner Medal, Bruckner Society of America, 1959; Mahler Medal, Mahler-Bruckner Society of America, 1965. Grand Star and Collar of Commander 1st Class of White Rose of Finland, 1963; Comdr., Order of Merit, Italian Republic, 1964; Officer, Arts and Letters (France), 1966; Officier de l'Ordre National de Mérite, 1968. *Publications:* several arrangements of old classical music. *Recreations:* reading, cricket. *Address:* c/o 30 Cross St., Manchester 2. *Club:* Lord's Taverners'. [*Died* 29 *July* 1970.

BARCLAY, John Stephen, T.D. 1950; Clerk to the Fishmongers' Company since 1949; *b.* 24 Dec. 1908; *er. surv. s.* of late Lt.-Col. R. W. Barclay; *m.* 1940, Patricia, *yr. d.* of late George Slade, solicitor, London; one *s.* two *d. Educ.:* Harrow: Trinity College, Cambridge. Called to the Bar, 1932; served War of 1939-45, Westminster Dragoons. Clerk to the Governors of Gresham's School, Holt; Hon. Sec. Salmon and Trout Association, and of

Oyster Merchants and Planters' Association; joint Hon. Sec., Central Council for Rivers Protection. *Recreations:* fishing, golf. *Address:* Fishmongers' Hall, London Bridge, E.C.4. *T.:* 01-626 8591; The Cottage, Shere, Surrey. *T.:* Shere 2250. *Club:* Fly-fishers'. [*Died* 5 *Aug.* 1968.

BARCLAY, Major Maurice Edward, C.B.E. 1950; T.D.; D.L.; B.A.; late 2nd in command Norfolk Yeomanry (Order of the Nile; despatches twice); *b.* 1886; *s.* of late Edward E. Barclay, M.A., D.L.; *m.* 1916, Margaret Eleanor, 5th *d.* of Marlborough R. Pryor, M.A., D.L., J.P., of Weston Park, Herts; one *s.* (and one killed on active service) one *d.* *Educ.:* Ludgrove; Eton; Cambridge University, B.A. Became joint M.F.H. of the Puckeridge Foxhounds with his father, 1910, now Joint Master with his son, Capt. C. G. E. Barclay; acted as land-agent to his father, 1910. J.P., D.L. Hertfordshire. Chm. Hertfordshire War Agricultural Exec. Cttee. 1941 (later Herts. Agricultural Exec. Cttee. until Feb. 1958 when retired). *Recreations:* all games and sports, particularly hunting. *Address:* Brent Pelham Hall, Buntingford, Herts. *T.:* Brent Pelham 220. *T.A.:* Brent-Pelham. *Club:* Boodle's. [*Died* 9 *Nov.* 1962.

BARCLAY-HARVEY, Sir (Charles) Malcolm, K.C.M.G., *cr.* 1939; Kt., *cr.* 1936; D.L. and J.P. Co. Aberdeen; Member of Queen's Body Guard for Scotland (Royal Company of Archers); *b.* 2 March 1890; *s.* of late James Charles Barclay-Harvey of Dinnet, Aberdeenshire, and Ellen Marian, *d.* of Frank Clarke Hills of Redleaf, Penshurst, Kent; *m.* 1st, 1912, Margaret Joan (*d.* 1935), *yr. d.* of Henry de la Poer Beresford Heywood, of Wrentnall Pontesford, Salop; one *d.*; 2nd, 1938, Lady Muriel Liddell-Grainger, widow of Capt. H. H. Liddell-Grainger, *o. d.* of 12th Earl of Lindsey. *Educ.:* Eton; Christ Church, Oxford. 7th Batt. Gordon Highlanders, T.F., 1909-15; Home Staff, 1915-16; Ministry of Munitions, London, 1916-18; Paris, 1918-19; M.P. (U.) Kincardineshire, and West Aberdeenshire, 1923-29, and 1931-1939; Parliamentary Private Secretary to Sir John Gilmour, 1924-29, and to Sir Godfrey Collins, 1932-36; Governor of South Australia, 1939-44; Hon. Col. 4th Bn. Gordon Highlanders, 1939-45; adopted prospective Unionist candidate, East Aberdeenshire, 1914. Member Aberdeen County Council, 1945-55; Grand Master Mason, Freemasons Scottish Constitution, 1949-53. K.St.J., 1964, Prior of the Order of St. John, in Scotland. *Recreations:* fishing, shooting. *Address:* Dinnet, Aberdeenshire. *T.:* Dinnet 332. *Clubs:* Carlton; New (Edinburgh); Royal Northern (Aberdeen).
[*Died* 17 *Nov.* 1969.

BARDSWELL, Hugh Rosser, M.A.; I.C.S., retired; *b.* 10 June, 1874; 4th and *y. s.* of late Charles William Bardswell, M.A., Recorder of Kingston, and Frances Anne Bardswell; *m.* 1915, Bessie Frances (*d.* 1947), *d.* of late Col. Alexander Sinclair Grove, D.S.O.; one *d.* (decd.). *Educ.:* King's College School; Lincoln College, Oxford (Exhibitioner). 2nd Class Modern History, 1896; passed into I.C.S., 1897; served in Madras Presidency from 1898, also in Coorg; District and Sessions Judge, 1914-32; Judge of the Madras High Court (acting), 1930, 1932-33; (permanent) 1933; retired, 1934; officiating Administrator, Pudukkottai State, S. India, April-Oct. 1938; Special Officer under Madras Government, Sept. and Oct. 1941; Tutor to the Raja of Pudukkottai, 1942-44; employed under Court of Wards, Madras, 1944-45; Member of the Legislative Assembly, 1923; Long Service Medal. *Recreation:* looking on. *Address:* 5 Parkhill Road, East Croydon, Surrey. *T.:* Croydon 3918. *Clubs:* M.C.C., Oriental.
[*Died* 29 *Dec.* 1962.

BARDWELL, Capt. William Scot, D.S.O. 1942 (and Bar 1944); M.V.O. 1929; R.N., retd.; *b.* 21 April 1892; *y. s.* of late T. N. F. Bardwell, J.P., D.L., of Bolton Hall, E. Yorks; *m.* 1st, 1921, Ellen Louise (*d.* 1964), *d.* of Dr. C. Manville Pratt, Towanda, Pennsylvania, U.S.A.; one *s.* one *d.*; 2nd, 1966, Phyllis Mary, *e. d.* of late E. G. Hamilton, Lynch House, Kensworth, Beds. *Educ.:* Cheam School; R.N.C., Osborne and Dartmouth (awarded King's Medal). Served on Australian, West Indies, China, Mediterranean and African Stations. *Club:* Army and Navy. [*Died* 24 *Oct.* 1968.

BARE, Lt.-Col. Alfred Raymund, D.S.O. 1918; M.C.; late Loyal Regiment; *b.* 26 March 1886; *s.* of Thomas E. Barre Alperton, Middlesex; *m.* 1st, 1914, May Josephine (*d.* 1946), 5th *d.* of F. W. Dolman, Parkstone, Dorset; no *c.*; 2nd, 1955, Evelyn Nancy, *o. d.* of late J. G. Swanton, Salisbury. *Educ.:* King's College School. Joined Artists Rifles, 1903; British South Africa Police, 1910; Lieutenant, 22nd London Regiment, 1914; Captain, Loyal Regiment, 1916; served European War, 1914-19; Major 1931; retired pay, 1936; commanded 4th Bn. Loyal Regt., 1936-38. *Recreation:* golf. *Address:* East View, South Newton, Salisbury, Wilts. [*Died* 10 *April* 1967.

BARKER, Aldred Farrer, F.T.I.; first President of the Textile Society of Australia; *b.* Oulton, near Leeds, 1868; *s.* of Benjamin Barker of Leeds; *m.* 1899, Eveline, *d.* of William Bradshaw of Bramley and Ilkley; two *s.* *Educ.:* private and public schools; Univ. of Leeds (M.Sc.). First Headmaster of the Textile Department, Saltaire Technical School; Professor of Textile Industries at the Bradford Technical College, 1892-1914; Prof. of Textile Industries, Leeds University, 1914-1933, Emeritus Professor since 1933; Medallist of the Textile Institute; Member of the Weavers' Company and Citizen of London; Vice-President of various Textile Societies; foundation member of the Thoresby Society, Leeds, and member of other local societies, being specially interested in architectural studies. *Publications:* A Summer Tour (1919) through the Textile Districts of Canada and the United States; The Educational Value of Textile Studies; Cloth Analysis; An Introduction to the Study of Textile Design; The Wool Year Book; Textiles; Wool Carding and Combing; Wool and the Textile Industries (in four languages); Woollen and Worsted Spinning; University Ideals; Genetics and Wool Production; Peru as a Sheep-breeding and Wool-growing Country; The Sheep and Wool of S. Africa, Rhodesia, and Kenya Colony; Ornamentation and Textile Design; The Cottage Textile Industries of Kashmir; The Textile Industries of China; Camping with Motor Car and Camera; Leaves from a Northern University; Justice to Japan; Re-orientation etc. *Address:* Lewis Court, Wellington Rd., Portland, Vic., Australia. [*Died* 22 *July* 1964.

BARKER, Anthony Raine; painter, etcher, lithographer, and wood engraver; *b.* 4 Sept. 1880; *m.* 1916, Patricia Russell; one *s.* one *d.* *Educ.:* Framlingham. Soane medal, Institute of Architects, 1909. *Publications:* First Italian Portfolio (etchings), 1912; First Belgian Portfolio (lithographs), 1914; The Fairyland Express, 1925; Hidden Gold. *Recreations:* Restoration of old houses and bee-keeping. *Address:* Watermill House, Benenden, Kent.
[*Died* 9 *Aug.* 1963.

BARKER, Bertie Thomas Percival, C.B.E. 1952; M.A., Hon. F.R.H.S.; Professor of Agricultural Biology, University of Bristol, 1912-43, Emeritus Professor, 1943; Director of the National Fruit and Cider Institute, 1904-1943; *b.* 9 Aug. 1877; *s.* of Thomas Burch Edwin Barker, Cambridge; *m.* 1st, 1904, Ethel (*d.* 1937), *e. d.* of William Tibbit Norman, Cambridge; one *s.* three *d.* (and one *s.* decd.); 2nd, 1938, Alicia Erskine, *d.* of Capt. Ernest Maunsell, St. Albans; one *d.* *Educ.:* Perse and Gonville and Caius College, Cambridge (Scholar). Engaged in botanical research under late Prof. H. Marshall Ward, M.A., F.R.S., at the University Botanical Laboratory, Cambridge, 1899-1904; Walsingham Gold Medallist for Research, Cambridge University, 1901. *Publications:* Cider Apple Production; Annual Reports of the National Fruit and Cider Institute; numerous papers in scientific journals on results of researches. *Recreations:* golf, chess, music. *Address:* The Mead, Long Ashton, Bristol. *T.A.:* Barker, Long Ashton. *T.:* Long Ashton 3133. [*Died* 19 *Dec.* 1961.

BARKER, Colonel Ernest Francis William, C.B.E. 1924; D.S.O. 1916; A.M.I.E.E.; late Royal Corps of Signals and Yorkshire Light Infantry; *b.* 2 July 1877; *e. s.* of late Colonel Sir Francis Barker; *m.* 1914, Enid (*d.* 1948), 2nd *d.* of Col. Boyce, R.E. *Educ.:* Restoration House and Dover College. Entered Army, 1898; Lieut. 1899; Captain, 1901; Major, 1915; Lt.-Col 1920 (with R.C. of S.); Colonel, 1924; served S. African War, 1899-1902, with the K.O.Y.L.I., (Queen's medal 3 clasps, King's medal 2 clasps); Occupation of Crete; European War, 1914-18, (despatches thrice, D.S.O., Brevet Lt.-Col. 1918). Bronze Medal of Royal Humane Society for saving life off the coast of Crete, 1904; Commanded 14th Div. Signal Coy. till Oct. 1916, then A.D. Signals 1st Corps till Dec. 1917, thence O.C. Signal Depôt, Abbeville; Assistant Signal Officer in Chief, G.H.Q., B.E.F., 1918; Chief Signal Officer Aldershot, 1919-20; Chief Signal Officer Allied Forces of Occupation, Turkey, 1921-23 till evacuation; Commandant S.T.C. Jubbulpore, 1926-31; Chief Signal Officer, Northern Command, India, 1931-34; retired, 1937. War of 1939-45: Ministry of Supply; A.R.P. and ex-Officer's Employment Bureau. *Address:* 59 Cadogan Square, S.W.1. *T.:* Sloane 4782. [*Died* 13 *Dec.* 1961.

BARKER, John, F.R.S. 1953; M.A., Ph.D. (Trinity College, Cambridge); Sc.D.; Emeritus Reader in Plant Physiology in the University of Cambridge. *Address:* 67 Grantchester Str eet, Cambridge; The Botany School, Downing Street, Cambridge. [*Died* 30 *Dec.* 1970.

BARKER, Major-Gen. Richard Ernest, C.B.E. 1941; *b.* Christchurch, New Zealand, 3 Oct. 1888; *s.* of A. L. Barker, Wainui, Winchester, N.Z.; *m.* 1920, Dorothy Enid, *d.* of F. J. Millton, Fallgate, Orari, N.Z.; three *s.* one *d.* *Educ.:* Wanganui Collegiate School, N.Z.; Sherborne School, Dorset. Joined N.Z. Mounted Rifles, 1907; Commissioned South Lancashire Regt., 1911; served with Indian Signal Corps, 1915-18; in Mesopotamia; Political Officer, Mesopotamia, Kurdistan and Persia, 1918-20; Ireland, 1920-22; transferred to R. Signals, 1921; Palestine, 1936-37; Colonel, 1936; Signal Officer in Chief, Middle East (Acting Maj.-Gen.), 1940-41; C.S.O. Scottish Command, 1942; C.S.O. Home Forces, 1944; retired pay, 1944. *Recreation:* farming. *Address:* Wainui, Geraldine R.D., New Zealand. *Club:* Army and Navy. [*Died* 6 *April* 1962.

BARKER, Sir Robert (Beacroft), Kt., *cr.* 1950; O.B.E. 1944; Minister without portfolio, Jamaica, Nov. 1957-Dec. 1958 (resigned); *b.* 18 May 1890; *s.* of John and Hannah Barker, Yorks., England; *m.* 1919, Nina Gladys (*née* Alexander); one *s.* *Educ.:* Blackburn Gram. School; Victoria Univ. of Manchester. B.A. 1911, M.A. 1912. Commissioned in Royal Garrison Artillery, European War, 1914-19. Settled in Jamaica, 1919; Nominated Member Legislative Council, Jamaica, 1942-45; Nominated Member Legislative Council, Jamaica (New Constitution), 1945-58 (resigned); Member Executive Council, 1945-57. *Address* 5 Devon Road, Half-Way-Tree, Jamaica. *Clubs:* Jamaica, Liguanea (Jamaica). [*Died* 11 *Dec.* 1960.

BARKER, Lt.-Col. Robert Hewitt, J.P.; *b.* 1887; *m.* 1916, Violet, *d.* of late C. Gartside, Ashton-under-Lyne; one *s.* three *d.* *Educ.:* Bedford School. M.P. (Ind.) Sowerby Division of Yorks, 1918-22; served European War, Egypt, Gallipoli, and France. *Recreations:* formerly member of county Rugby football team, golf. *Address:* 35 St. Albans Terrace, Rochdale, Lancs. [*Died* 14 *Feb.* 1961.

BARKER, Tom Battersby, C.B.E. 1920; Deputy Director of Raw Materials, War Office, during European War; afterwards Controller of Disposals, Ministry of Munitions; Order of the Crown, Belgian. *Clubs:* National Liberal, Queen's, Royal Automobile, All England Lawn Tennis. [*Died* 5 *Oct.* 1968.

BARKER-BENFIELD, Brig. Karl Vere, C.B.E. 1945; D.S.O. 1916; M.C.; p.s.c.; *b.* 20 Oct. 1892; *s.* of late F. J. Barker-Benfield, M.A.; *m.* Gladys, *d.* of late Brig.-Gen. H. E. B. Lane, C.M.G.; two *s.* one *d.* *Educ.:* Privately abroad; R.M.A. Joined Royal Artillery, 1913; served European War, 1914-19 (D.S.O. and Bar, M.C.). Staff College, Camberley; Military Attaché, Vienna, Budapest and Berne, 1935-38; Inspector of Intelligence Training, 1941-42; Brigadier in charge Intelligence, 1943; Special Operations Greece, 1944; Commander Crete Force, 1944-45; retired, 1945. *Recreation:* interested in Central European and Middle Eastern affairs. *Address:* Ridge House, Morchard Bishop, Devon. *T.:* 224. [*Died* 11 *Feb.* 1969.

BARKWAY, Rt. Rev. James Lumsden, B.A. (Vict. and Liverpool); M.A. (Cantab.); Hon. D.D. (St. Andrews); *b.* 9 July 1878; *s.* of Alexander Bannerman Barkway and Jane Thom; *m.* 1906, Mary (*d.* 1959), *d.* of Principal Oswald Dykes; two *s.* *Educ.:* Univ. Coll., Liverpool; Westminster Coll., Cambridge. Assistant Minister, Marylebone Presbyterian Church, London; Sefton Park Presbyterian Church, Liverpool; Minister of Redcar Presbyterian Church, 1906-16; Curate of St. Albans Cathedral, 1916-18 and 1923-27; Vicar of Christ Church, Luton, 1918-23; Rector of Little Gaddesden, 1928-34; Hon. Canon of St. Albans Cathedral, 1929; Diocesan Missioner, St. Albans, 1934; Bishop of Bedford, 1935-38; Bishop of St. Andrews, Dunkeld, and Dunblane, 1938-49. Select Preacher, Cambridge, 1936. Hon. D.D. (St. Andrews), 1949. *Publications:* The Creed and its Credentials; The Christian Belief about Christ; An Introduction to the Inner Life. *Address:* Woodcote Grove House, Coulsdon, Surrey. [*Died* 12 *Dec.* 1968.

BARLOW, Sir Alan, Bt.; *see* Barlow, Sir J. A. N.

BARLOW, Disney Charles; High Sheriff of Leicestershire, 1939; Director, District Bank, Ltd.; Chairman Liberty Shoes, Ltd.; *b.* 23 June 1880; 2nd *s.* of Rev. Thomas Disney Barlow, B.A., T.C.D.; *m.* 1905, Ethel Mabel, *d.* of Alfred Sexton, J.P., Dublin; one *s.* (and one *s.* decd.). *Educ.:* privately; Wyggeston School, Leicester. *Recreations:* shooting, fishing, golf. *Address:* The Chace, Woodhouse Eaves, Loughborough. *T.A.* and *T.:* Woodhouse Eaves 232. *Clubs:* Royal Over-Seas League; Leicestershire (Leicester). [*Died* 16 *Feb.* 1965.

BARLOW, Sir (James) Alan (Noel), 2nd Bt., *cr.* 1900; G.C.B., 1947 (K.C.B., 1942; C.B. 1928); K.B.E., 1938 (C.B.E. 1918; M.A.; J.P.; F.S.A.; *b.* 25 Dec. 1881; *s.* of Sir Thomas Barlow, 1st Bt.; *S.* father

1945; *m.* 1911, Emma Nora (editor of The Beagle Diary, 1933, Charles Darwin and the Voyage of the Beagle, 1946, and The Autobiography of Charles Darwin, 1958), *d.* of late Sir Horace Darwin, K.B.E.; four *s.* one *d.* (one *d.* decd.). *Educ.:* Marlborough; Corpus Christi College, Oxford (Hon. Fellow). Clerk in House of Commons, 1906; Junior Examiner, Board of Education, 1907; Private Secretary to Parliamentary Secretary of Board of Education, 1914; to Parliamentary Secretary, Ministry of Munitions, 1915; and to Minister of Munitions, 1916; Principal Assistant Secretary, Ministry of Labour; Principal Private Secretary to the Prime Minister, 1933-34; Under-Secretary, Treasury, 1934; joint Second Secretary, 1938-48; Member Iron and Steel Board, 1946-48. Trustee, National Gallery, 1948-55 (Chm., 1949-51); Member of Court of Univ. of London, 1949-56. LL.D. (hon.) Glasgow. *Heir: s.* Thomas Erasmus Barlow, D.S.C., R.N. [*b.* 23 Jan. 1914; *m.* 1955, Isabel, *d.* of late T. M. Body, Middlesbrough; two *s.* two *d.* Served European War, 1939-45]. *Address:* Boswells, Wendover, Bucks. *T.:* Wendover 2119. *Clubs:* Athenæum, Savile. [*Died* 28 *Feb.* 1968.

BARLOW, Sir Thomas D., G.B.E. 1946 (K.B.E. 1934); retired as Chairman of District Bank Ltd., 1960 (still Mem. London Cttee.); Director (late Chm.) Barlow & Jones Ltd., Manchester; *b.* 23 Feb. 1883; *s.* of Sir Thomas Barlow, 1st Bt., and Ada Helen Dalmahoy; *m.* 1911, Esther Sophia (*d.* 1956), *d.* of Henry Gaselee, barrister-at-law; one *s.* two *d.* *Educ.:* Marlborough; Trinity College, Cambridge. Director-General of Civilian Clothing, 1941-45. *Address:* 49 Strand on the Green, W.4. *T.:* Chiswick 1655. *Club:* Athenæum. [*Died* 22 *Nov.* 1964.

BARNARD, 10th Baron (*cr.* 1698); **Christopher William Vane,** C.M.G. 1930; O.B.E. 1955; M.C.; T.D.; Lord Lieut., County of Durham, 1958-64; County Comr., Durham County Boy Scouts Assoc.; M.F.H. Zetland Hunt, 1920-63; *b.* 28 Oct. 1888; *s.* of 9th Baron and Lady Catharine Sarah Cecil (*d.* 1918), *d.* of 3rd Marquess of Exeter; *S.* father, 1918; *m.* 1920, Sylvia Mary, *o. d.* of late Herbert Straker; two *s.* one *d.* *Educ.:* Eton; Trinity College, Cambridge, B.A. Served European War, Westmorland and Cumberland Yeomanry (wounded, M.C.); Bt.-Col., comd. 6th Durham L.I., 1926-1931. *Heir: s.* Hon. Harry John Neville Vane [*b.* 21 Sep. 1923; *m.* 1952, Hon. Davina Mary Cecil, *e. d.* of 6th Marquess of Exeter, K.C.M.G.; one *s.* three *d.*]. *Address:* Raby Castle, Staindrop, Darlington, Co. Durham. *Club:* Brooks's. [*Died* 19 *Oct.* 1964.

BARNARDO, Fleming; *see* Barnardo, F.A.F.

BARNARDO, (Frederick Adolphus) Fleming, C.I.E. 1918; C.B.E. 1919; M.A., B.Sc., M.D., M.R.C.P., F.R.C.S.; Lieut.-Col. late Indian Medical Service; Consulting Physician; *b.* 4 June 1874; *s.* of late George Charles Ferdinand Barnardo; *m.* 1910, Violet Kathleen Ann (*d.* 1942), *d.* of late Henry Teviot Kerr of Monteviot, Darjeeling, India; four *d.* (one *s.* killed at Alamein, 1942). *Educ.:* Edinburgh University (M.A., B.Sc.); M.B. 1899; M.D., 1904; F.R.C.S., 1912; M.R.C.P., 1913. Resident Surgeon, Simpson Memorial Hospital, Edinburgh, 1899; Resident Surgeon, Victoria Hospital for Children, Stepney, 1899; Fife and Forfar Light Horse: served South Africa, 1900-2, and Civil Surgeon (Queen's medal with three clasps; King's medal with two clasps); late Surgeon-Captain, 2nd County of London Yeomanry; King's coronation, 1902; served Somaliland, 1903-4 (medal with two clasps); Lieut., Indian Medical Service, 1902; Captain 1905; Civil Surgeon, Darjeeling, 1912; Major, 1913; Bt. Lt.-Col. 1917; Colonel 1922; Honorary Magistrate and J.P., Bombay, 1916; Hon. Associate, St. John's Ambulance Association, 1917; Assistant Director of Medical Services (Embarkation), Bombay, 1917; served Mesopotamia, 1916; East Africa, 1917; Afghanistan, 1918 (despatches); Assistant Director of Medical Services, A.H.Q., Simla, 1918-19; Civil Surgeon, Simla, 1920-21; Principal, Medical College, Calcutta, and Professor of Medicine; Superintendent, Medical College Hospitals; First Physician to Medical College Hospitals, 1921-27; retired, 1929; Fellow, Calcutta University; President, Calcutta Rotary Club, 1926; late Dean Faculty of Medicine, Calcutta University; Fellow, Royal Society of Medicine; Fellow Royal Society of Tropical Medicine. *Publications:* Shock; Enteric Fever in the Tropics; Enteric Fever and its diag. in the Tropics; The Importance of Mixed and Multiple Infections in Tropical Diseases. *Address:* 19 Cavendish Square, W.1. *T.:* Langham 3969. *Club:* Oriental. [*Died* 27 *April* 1962.

BARNES, Barry K., (Nelson Barry Mackintosh Barnes); actor, stage and screen; *b.* Chelsea, 27 Dec. 1906; *s.* of Horatio Nelson Barnes and Anne Mackintosh; *m.* 1st, Joan Cobb (marriage dissolved); 2nd, Diana (Josephine) Churchill. *Educ.:* City of London Sch.; Dollar Acad.; Royal Academy of Dramatic Art. First stage appearance in Paul I, 1927; played in repertory for 2 years and then in West End. Went to Australia, 1932, playing Robert Browning in The Barretts of Wimpole Street. Subsequently continued acting in London, and toured in 1944. Has appeared in numerous films since 1937, his first film being The Return of the Scarlet Pimpernel. *Address:* c/o Al. Parker, 50 Mount Street, W.1. [*Died* 12 *Jan.* 1965.

BARNES, Dr. Bertie Frank, D.Sc., Ph.D. (Lond.), F.L.S.; *b.* 19 July 1888; *m.* 1923; one *d.* *Educ.:* Private; Birkbeck Coll., University of London. Teacher since 1908; served R.E., France, 1915-19; Demonstrator and Lecturer in Botany, Birkbeck Coll., 1922-1933; Head, Department of Biology, Chelsea Polytechnic, S.W.3, 1934-52. B.Sc. (1st Class Honours), 1922; Ph.D., 1928; D.Sc. 1933; President, British Mycological Society, 1934; Vice-Pres., Linnean Society, 1937-38, 1942-44, 1951-52; Deputy-Treasurer, 1941-45; Botanical Secretary, 1944-51; Secretary, Section K., Brit. Association, 1929-34; Recorder, Section K., British Association, 1935-45; Member of Council, Linnean Society, 1935-39, 1941-52; of Scientific Committee, Royal Horticultural Society, 1936-55. *Publications:* The Structure and Development of the Fungi (with Prof. Dame Helen Gwynne-Vaughan), 1927, 2nd Edition, 1937, reprinted, 1949, 1950, 1958; articles in Annals of Botany, Journal of Botany, New Phytologist, Transactions British Mycological Society, Discovery, etc. *Recreation:* gardening. *Address:* North Bank, June Lane, Midhurst, Sussex. [*Died* 19 *March* 1965.

BARNES, Harry Elmer, Ph.D.; Educator; Publicist; Author; Lecturer; *b.* Auburn, New York, 15 June 1889; *s.* of William Henry Barnes and Lulu Carlotta Short; *m.* 1st, 1916, L. Grace Stone; one *s.*; 2nd, 1935, Jean Hutchison Newman. *Educ.:* Syracuse Univ., A.B., 1913; Harvard Univ.; Columbia Univ., Ph.D. 1918. Instructor in Historical Sociology, Syracuse University, 1913-15; Fellow, Columbia University, 1915-1917; Lecturer in History, Columbia University and Barnard College, 1917-18; Associate Professor of History, Clark University, 1918-1919; Professor, New School for Social Research, 1919-20, Clark University, 1920-23; Amherst College, 1923-25; Smith College, 1923-30; Lecturer in Education, Teachers College, Columbia Univ., 1937-38; Professor of Sociology, Temple Univ., 1946; Visiting Lecturer, Univ. of Colorado, 1948-49; Visiting Professor, Indiana University, 1951, Washington State College, 1954-55. Editorial Dept., Scripps-Howard Newspapers, 1929-40; Head consultant Prison War Program Branch, War Production Board, 1943-1944; Consultant and Historian, Smaller War Plants Corporation, 1945; Vice-President A.A.A.S., 1928; member of many American and foreign learned societies; associate editor and bibliographic editor of several professional journals. *Publications:* History of New Jersey Penal Institutions, 1918; Sociology and Political Theory, 1923 (German trans. 1927); The New History and the Social Studies, 1925; History and Social Intelligence, 1926; The Genesis of the World War, 1926 (new editions, 1927, 1929; French, German and Norwegian translations, 1928); The Repression of Crime, 1926; The Evolution of Penology in Pennsylvania, 1927; An Economic and Social History of Europe (with M. M. Knight and Felix Flügel), 1928; Living in the Twentieth Century, 1928; In Quest of Truth and Justice, 1928; The Twilight of Christianity, 1929; World Politics in Modern Civilisation, 1930; The Story of Punishment, 1930 (rev. edn. 1968); Can Man Be Civilised?, 1932; A History of Western Civilization, 2 vols., 1935; An Economic History of the Western World, 1937; The History of Historical Writing, 1937 (rev. edn., 1962); Intellectual and Cultural History of the Western World, 1937 (enlarged edn., 3 vols., 1965); Social Thought from Lore to Science, 2 vols. (with H. Becker), 1938 (enlarged edn., 3 vols., 1961); Society in Transition, 1939 (new rev. edn., 1952); Social Institutions, 1942; The American Way of Life (with O. Ruedi), 1942 (new enlarged edn., 1950); New Horizons in Criminology (with N. K. Teeters), 1943 (new edn., 1968); Prisons in Wartime, 1944; A Survey of Western Civilization, 1947; Historical Sociology: Its Rise and Development, 1948; co-author and ed., Contemporary Social Theory (with H. Becker), 1940; Introduction to the History of Sociology, 1947; Handbook of Correctional Design and Construction, 1950; Perpetual War for Perpetual Peace, 1953; Editor: History of Political Theories: Recent Times (with C. E. Merriam), 1924; revised edition of Ploetz's Manual of Universal History, 1925; The History and Prospects of the Social Sciences, 1926; A History of Civilization, 100 vols., 1926 *et seq.* (with C. K. Ogden); An Introduction to Sociology (with Jerome Davis), 2 vols., 1928; Studies in American Imperialism, 7 vols., 1928-36; Illustrated World History (with J. A. Hammerton), 1937; The Human Comedy, by James Harvey Robinson, 1937; Universal World History (with J. A. Hammerton), 6 vols., 1940; History of the Smaller War Plants Corporation, 1946; numerous historical vols. dealing with the Second World War, 1950-63; contributed chapters to numerous works; contributor to Encyclopedia Americana; Encyclopædia Britannica, etc. *Recreations:* hunting, fishing, motoring. *Address:* 31509 W. Pacific Coast Highway, Malibu, Calif., U.S.A. *Clubs:* Authors'; P.E.N. (N.Y.). [*Died* 25 *Aug.* 1968.

BARNES, Sir James (Horace), K.C.B. 1948; K.B.E. 1946; *b.* 14 Dec. 1891; *s.* of late Richard Barnes, Pendleton, Manchester; *m.* 1st, 1941, Jane Ellen Stevenson (*d.* 1964); 2nd, 1965, Elsie Doris McKenzie. *Educ.:* Manchester Grammar School; Merton College, Oxford (Open Classical Postmaster, 1st Class Honour Moderations, M.A.). Air Ministry, 1919. Permanent Under-Secretary of State for Air, 1947-55; retired, 1955. Governor Westminster Hospital, Chm. Nursing Cttee. *Recreations:* golf, bridge, reading; watching cricket, Association and Rugby football. *Address:* 7 Fitzwilliam House, Little Green, Richmond, Surrey. *T.:* Richmond 1538. *Clubs:* Royal Automobile; Royal Mid-Surrey; Swinley Forest. [*Died* 4 *Feb.* 1969.

BARNES, Nelson Barry Mackintosh; *see* Barnes, Barry K.

BARNES, Sir Thomas James, G.C.B., *cr.* 1948 (K.C.B., *cr.* 1938); Kt., *cr.* 1927; C.B.E. 1920; H.M. Procurator-General and Treasury Solicitor, 1934-53; *b.* 21 Mar. 1888; *s.* of Thomas Barnes; *m.* 1924, Elsie Margaret, *d.* of John Alexander. Assistant Solicitor Board of Inland Revenue, 1919; Legal Adviser Ministry of Shipping, 1918-20; Solicitor Board of Trade, 1920-33. Commander of the Order of Orange Nassau (Netherlands). Member Evershed Committee on Supreme Court Practice and Procedure, 1947-53; Member Monopolies and Restrictive Practices Commission. *Address:* 2 Whitehall Court, S.W.1. *T.:* Whitehall 8160. *Club:* Athenæum. [*Died* 4 *Feb.* 1964.

BARNETT, Prof. Cyril Harry; Professor of Anatomy, St. Thomas's Hospital Medical School, University of London, since 1970; *b.* 30 Oct. 1919; *m.* 1950, Sheila Catherine Arnold; one *s.* one *d. Educ.:* Selhurst Gram. Sch.; St. Catharine's Coll., Cambridge; Westminster Medical School. R.A.M.C., 1944-47. Demonstrator, then Lectr. in Anatomy, St. Thomas's Hosp. Med. Sch., 1947-55; Lectr., Univ. of Melbourne, 1956-57; Reader, St. Thomas's Hosp. Med. Sch., 1955-64; Foundation Prof. of Anatomy, Univ. of Tasmania, 1964-67; Prof. of Functional Morphology, St. Thomas's Hosp. Med. Sch., 1967-70. *Publications:* Synovial Joints (jtly.), 1961; The Human Body (jtly.), 1966; Practical Embryology, 1969. *Recreations:* painting, golf. *Address:* 21 Bessels Way, Bessels Green, Sevenoaks, Kent. *T.:* 56926. [*Died* 23 *Oct.* 1970.

BARNETT, Sir Geoffrey (Morris), Kt., 1953; Solicitor; Chm., Dobson Hardwick Ltd., and other cos.; *b.* 5 May 1902; *s.* of Harold Darracott Morris Barnett and Ethel Mary Barnett (*née* Woolley); *m.* 1941, Isobel Morag Marshall; one *s. Educ.:* Haileybury Coll. Served War of 1939-45, Major. Judge Advocate General's Dept. Leicester C.C., 1934-, Alderman, 1945-55; Lord Mayor of Leicester, 1952-53. *Recreations:* golf, shooting. *Address:* The White House, Cossington, Leicestershire. *T.:* Sileby 222. *Clubs:* International Sportsmen's; Leicestershire (Leicester). [*Died* 18 *May* 1970.

BARNETT, Sir George (Percy), Kt. 1952; H.M. Chief Inspector of Factories 1947-1957; *b.* 19 Oct. 1894; *s.* of E. B. and M. J. Barnett, Winchester; *m.* 1920, Florence, *d.* of R. J. and J. Simcock, Liverpool. *Educ.:* Peter Symonds Sch., Winchester; Univ. College, Southampton. Served European War, 1914-18, Lieut. in 15th London Regt. Entered Factory Dept., Home Office 1920; District Inspector, 1928; Superintending Inspector, 1941; Deputy Chief Inspector, 1944; Chairman Manchester and District Industrial Accident Prevention Cttee., 1941-1944; Chairman Cttee. on Conditions in Cotton Mills, 1944-47. Vice-Pres. Royal Society for the Prevention of Accidents, 1955. *Address:* 5 Grimston Avenue, Folkestone, Kent. [*Died* 19 *Oct.* 1965.

BARNEWALL, Sir Reginald J., 12th Bt., *cr.* 1622; Landowner and Grazier; *b.* 8 June 1888; *s.* of Sir John R. Barnewall, 11th Bt., and Grace Blennerhasset; *S.* father, 1936; *m.* 1922, Jessie Ellen Fry; one *s. Educ.:* Thornton (private). *Heir: s.* Reginald Robert, *b.* 1 Oct. 1924. *Address:* 5 Hansen St., Kew, Victoria, Australia. [*Died* 1 *Nov.* 1961.

BARNSLEY, Major-General Robert Eric, C.B. 1944; M.C.; M.A.; M.B., B.Ch.; *b.* 25 April 1886; *s.* of late Brig.-Gen. Sir

John Barnsley, Edgbaston, Birmingham. *Educ.*: Rydal School; Trinity College, Cambridge; St. Bartholomew's Hospital. Served European War, B.E.F., France and Belgium, 1915; B. Salonica Force, 1915-18; Army of Black Sea, 1918-21 (M.C., Brevet Major, despatches); Leishman Memorial Medal and Montefiore Prize, R.A.M. College, 1929; D.A.D.M.S. British Troops in Egypt, 1934-37; A.D.M.S. Northern Command, 1937; War of 1939-45, A.D.M.S., D.D.M.S., and D.M.S. East Africa Force, 1940-41 (despatches); D.D.M.S. Southern Command; K.H.S. 1941-47; retired, 1946. Hon. Col. Territorial Army, 1949-53; Col. Comdt. R.A.M.C., 1948-51. American Legion of Merit (degree of Officer), 1946. *Address:* c/o Holt & Co., Kirkland House, Whitehall, S.W.1. *Club:* Junior Army and Navy.
[*Died* 11 *Sept.* 1968.

BARODA, State of; Maj.-Gen. H.H. Maharaja Sir Pratapsinha Gaekwar Sena Khas Khel Shamsher Bahadur, G.C.I.E. 1941; LL.D. 1940; *b.* 29 June 1908; *S.* 1939; *m.* 1929, H.H. Maharani Shantadev Saheb, Kolhapur; *m.* 1943, H.H. Maharani Sita Devi (marriage dissolved, 1956). *Educ.*: Rajkumar College, Rajkot; Baroda College; Deccan College, Poona; in England. Major-General, Indian Army. Full responsible government granted to State, 1948; State merged with Bombay, 1949. *Address:* Laxmi Vilas Palace, Baroda, India. [*Died* 19 *July* 1968.

BARON, Sir Edward S., Kt. 1942; retired; President, formerly Chairman and Managing Director, of Carreras Ltd.; Director Guardian Assurance Company; *b.* 22 June 1892; *m.* 1916, Bertha Schaul; two *d.* *Address:* 80 Eaton Square, S.W.1. *T.:* Sloane 4479. *Clubs:* St. James', Buck's.
[*Died* 27 *June* 1962.

BAROTSELAND, Litunga of, since 1948; **(Sir Mwanawina Lewanika III),** K.B.E. 1959; K.M. (Barotseland decoration); *b.* 7 February 1888; *s.* of Lewanika Lubosi; *m.* 1915, Akabana Mataa; six *s.* eight *d.* *Educ.*: Lovendale Coll., Cape Univ. of S.A. Sec. and Councillor to Paramount Chiefs Lewanika and Yeta; Representative of Barotse Native Government on Trust Fund, Mongu; Chief of District Kuta at Mankoya, 1937-48. Led Barotse War Carriers to East Africa Campaign during European War, 1914-18. During War of 1939-45 encouraged the war effort by the production of rubber and funds. *Recreations:* carpentry, fishing and hunting. *Address:* Lealui, Barotseland, Zambia, Central Africa.
[*Died* 13 *Nov.* 1968.

BARR, James Gordon, M.A., LL.B. (Cantab.); Solicitor and Parliamentary Officer, L.C.C., since 1951; *b.* 3 July 1908; *s.* of James Barr and Isobel Webb, Birkenhead and Linton, Cambs.; *m.* 1935, Mollie, *d.* of Arthur Evans, F.R.C.S., Liverpool; two *s.* one *d.* *Educ.*: Birkenhead School; Magdalene College, Cambridge. Articled to Town Clerk, Southport, 1930; Assistant Solicitor: Southport Corp., 1933; Brighton Corp., 1934; Dep. Town Clerk, Wolverhampton Corp., 1937; Town Clerk, and Clerk of the Peace, Ipswich, 1946. Hon. Solicitor, Roy. Soc. for the Prevention of Accidents. *Recreations:* fishing, gardening. *Address:* Ardlui, Cranley Road, Guildford. *T.:* 61846; County Hall, S.E.1. *T.:* Waterloo 5000, Ext. 410.
[*Died* 24 *Nov.* 1963.

BARR SMITH, Sir Tom Elder, Kt. 1959; Consul for Sweden, in South Australia, since 1948; Pastoralist; *b.* 28 Apr. 1904; *s.* of late Tom Elder Barr Smith, Adelaide; *m.* 1936, Nancy Leland (*d.* 1960), *d.* of late L. L. Greene, Melbourne; one *s.* three *d.* *Educ.*: Geelong Grammar Sch., Victoria; Trinity Hall, Cambridge. Chairman: Mutooroo Pastoral Co. Ltd.; Beltana Pastoral Co. Ltd.; Milo Pastoral Co. Ltd.; Lake Victoria Proprietors; Auchendarroch Pty. Ltd.; Cellulose Australia Ltd.; Chairman, Elder's Trustee & Executor Co. Ltd.; Dep. Chm., Adelaide Steamship Co. Ltd.; Director: Elder Smith Goldsbrough Mort Ltd.; Lensworth Finance Ltd.; Lensworth Mortgages Ltd.; Commercial Union Assce. Co. of Aust. Ltd. A.D.C. to Gov. of S. Aust., 1931-33. Kt., Roy. Order of Vasa, 1st Cl., Sweden. *Recreations:* golf, racing. *Address:* Birksgate, Glen Osmond, S. Australia. *T.:* Adelaide 51. 1319. *Clubs:* Oriental; Adelaide (Adelaide); Melbourne (Melbourne).
[*Died* 5 *March* 1968.

BARRATT, Air Chief Marshal Sir Arthur Sheridan, K.C.B. 1940 (C.B. 1937); C.M.G. 1919; M.C.; D.L.; Gentleman Usher to the Sword of State since 1946; *b.* 25 Feb. 1891; *e. s.* of Charles Henry Barratt, Clifton; *m.* 1916, Norah Lilian (marriage dissolved 1948), 3rd *d.* of Edgar Crew, Clifton; one *d.*; *m.* 1949, Judith Rhoda Cartmell, *widow* of Terence Horsley. *Educ.*: Clifton College; R.M.A., Woolwich; Staff Coll., Camberley. Seconded to R.F.C. 1914; served European War in France, 1914-18 (C.M.G., M.C., Officier de l'Ordre de la Couronne, Belgian Croix de Guerre, despatches four times); Chief Instructor, Royal Air Force, Staff College, Andover; commanded No. 1 (Indian) Group, Peshawar, 1931-32; Senior Air Staff Officer H.Q., R.A.F., India, 1932-1934; Director of Staff Duties, Air Ministry, 1935; Commandant R.A.F. Staff College, Andover, 1936-39; served War of 1939-45; A.O.C.-in-C. British Air Forces in France, 1940 (despatches); A.O.C.-in-C. Army Co-operation Command, 1940-43; A.O.C.-in-C. Technical Training Command, 1943-45; Inspector-General of the R.A.F., 1945-47; Air Chief Marshal, 1946; retired, 1947; p.s.a. D.L. Hants., 1956 Restituta Militari 2nd class (Polish); Grand Croix Légion d'Honneur; French Croix de Guerre. *Recreations:* field sports. *Address:* The Old Vicarage, Hambledon, Hants. *T.:* 432. *Club:* Army and Navy.
[*Died* 4 *Nov.* 1966.

BARRATT, Capt. Sir Francis H. G. L.; *see* Layland-Barratt.

BARRETT-LENNARD, Sir Fiennes, Kt., *cr.* 1926; Legal Assistant Ministry of Agriculture and Fisheries, 1943-55; *s.* of late Captain Thomas George Barrett Lennard, 5th Dragoon Guards, and *heir-pres.* to Sir Richard Barrett-Lennard, 5th Bt.; *m.* 1916, Winifrede, *d.* of late Alfred Berlyn; one *s.* *Educ.*: University of Bonn. Served in Anglo-Boer War (wounded severely and invalided); Bar, Lincoln's Inn, 1905; Judge of Supreme Courts of the Gold Coast (now Republic of Ghana) and in E. Africa, 1914-1915; served with local Field Force, 1915 and 1916; invalided, 1917; Bar, 1917-20; Justice of the Supreme Courts, Straits Settlements, Federated Malay States, and Johore (now State of Singapore and Federation of Malaya), 1920-26; Chief Justice of Jamaica, 1926-32; Lecturer Birkbeck College (Univ. of London). *Address:* 8 Vine Place, Brighton. *Club:* Athenæum. [*Died* 26 *Jan.* 1963.

BARRON, Evan Macleod, LL.D. (Aberdeen); J.P.; editor and proprietor of Inverness Courier from 1919 (succeeding his father); Mem. Council, Scottish History Society; *b.* Inverness, 1879; 2nd and *o. surv.* *s.* of late James Barron, Inverness Courier; *m.* 1923, Gladys Caroline Barron, *q.v.* *Educ.*: Inverness Royal Academy; Edinburgh Univ. Lord Rector's Historical Essay Prize, 1900; Editor of The Student, 1902-3; practised as solicitor, Inverness, 1903-11.

Publications: Inverness in the 15th Century, 1906; Inverness in the Middle Ages, 1907; Prince Charlie's Pilot, 1913; The Scottish War of Independence, 1914, 2nd Edition with new Introduction, 1934; A Highland Editor, 1927; Inverness and the Macdonalds, 1930; The Truth about the Highlands, 1931; The Betrayal of Scotland, An Exposure of Self-Government, 1932 (rev. edn., 1953); numerous articles in learned jls., etc., especially on matters relating to Highland and Scottish History and Highland Affairs. *Recreations:* walking, reading. *Address:* Westerlea, Nairn. *T.A.:* Courier, Inverness. *T.:* Inverness 31459: Nairn 2136. *Club:* Highland (Inverness). [*Died* 24 *April* 1965.

BARRON, Maj.-General Frederick Wilmot, C.B. 1936; O.B.E. 1919; p.s.c.; *b.* 22 June 1880; *s.* of Frederick Cadogan Barron and Anne Cother Rider; *m.* 1911, Eileen Ella (*d.* 1961), *e. d.* of late Brig.-Gen. R. B. Williams, C.B.; no *c.* *Educ.:* Abbey School, Beckenham; Radley College; Royal Military Academy, Woolwich. Commissioned in Royal Artillery, 1899; Captain, 1907; Major, 1914; Bt. Lt.-Col., 1918; Colonel, 1922; Maj.-Gen., 1934; served South African War, 1899-1902 (Queen's medal 3 clasps, King's medal 2 clasps); European War, 1914-19, France, Gallipoli, Mesopotamia, Persia (1914 Star, British War Medal, Victory Medal, O.B.E., Croix de Guerre avec palme, despatches five times); Gunnery Staff Course, 1906-7; Instructor in Gunnery (1st Class), 1909-13; Staff College, 1914; Staff, 1915-19; General Staff, War Office, 1920-1924; Staff, 1929-34; Inspector of Fixed Defences, War Office, 1934-38; retired pay, 1938; Inspector of Fixed Defences, G.H.Q. Home Forces and War Office, 1939-41; retired pay, 1941; Lt.-Col. Home Guard, 1941. Gold Medallist, R.A. Institution. *Recreations:* hunting, shooting, cricket, hockey, lawn-tennis, billiards. *Address:* Greystones, Whitchurch, Tavistock, Devon. *T.:* Tavistock 2083. *Club:* United Service. [*Died* 4 *Jan.* 1963.

BARRON, Gladys Caroline, A.R.B.S.; Sculptor; *o. d.* of late Maxwell Bellew Logan; *m.* 1923, Evan Macleod Barron, LL.D., J.P., *q.v.* *Educ.:* studied under Gilbert and Mrs. Bayes; St. John's Wood Art School. Frequent exhibitor at the R.A. and the Royal Scottish Academy. *Principal works: portraiture:* A. D. Mackintosh of Mackintosh; Rt. Hon. Thomas Johnston (in North of Scotland Hydro-Electricity HQ., Edin.); 19th Earl of Moray; Kurt Hahn (in Gordonstoun School); Sir Murdoch MacDonald, Sir Alexander MacEwen (both in Inverness Town Hall); Sir William Calder (in Edin. Univ. Library); Sir Thomas Taylor (in Aberdeen Univ. Library); Neil Gunn; John Birnie; A Man of the Polish Resistance, etc.; many portraits of children; *memorial plaques:* Maj. Hon. Robert Bruce; Sir Edward McColl (at Pitlochry Power Station); George Balfour (at Tummel Power Station). *Recreations:* motoring, country life, drama. *Address:* Westerlea, Nairn. *T.:* Nairn 2136. [*Died* 17 *Jan.* 1967.

BARROW, Rear-Adm. Benjamin Wingate, D.S.O. 1919; Royal Navy, retired; *b.* 21 Aug. 1878; *s.* of late F. H. Barrow, I.C.S.; *m.* 1908, Charlotte Constance, *d.* of late Ven. Richard Brooke; (*s.* killed in action in Burma in Jan. 1945) four *d.* *Educ.:* Clifton Coll.; H.M.S. Britannia. Naval Cadet, 1892; Lieut. 1901; Commander, 1914; Captain, 1920; Rear-Adm. 1932; commanded the Central Reserve of Mine-sweepers at Sheerness, 1925-27; Captain-Superintendent of Contract-built Ships, 1927-29; Superintendent Sheerness Dockyard, 1929-30; commanded H.M.S. Harebell, 1930-32; retired list, 1932; Commodore of Atlantic Fleet Convoys, Sept. 1939-April 1942; Commodore-in-Charge, Simonstown, 1942; reverted to retd. list, Oct. 1944. *Address:* Bonaventure, Bertha Avenue, Claremont, C.P., S. Africa. [*Died* 23 *Jan.* 1966.

BARRY, Charles, (pseudonym of Charles Bryson), writer of detective fiction; B.B.C. European Service, 1950; *b.* 1887; *s.* of George Bryson, Royal Irish Constabulary, and Mary Donnelly, Belfast; *m.* Dora, *d.* of J. Savi, Calcutta. *Educ.:* St. Macarten's, Monaghan; Dublin; Paris. Professor of Modern languages in Imperial Russian Education Dept. till 1914; Imp. Russian Horse Artillery, 1914-17; North Russian Exped. Force, 1918-19, Intelligence Corps, 1939-48 (M.B.E., despatches, Order of St. George, Order of St. Anne 4th Cl. with inscription For Bravery, Order of St. Vladimir 4th Class, with crossed swords and knot, Order of St. Stanislas 2nd Class, with crossed swords, Officer of the Crown of Rumania, Knight of the Star of Rumania, Polonia Restituta). *Publications:* The Corpse on the Bridge; The Clue of the Clot; The Witness at the Window; The Avenging Ikon; The Ghost of a Clue; Murder on Monday; Death in Darkness; The Wrong Murder Mystery; The Shot from the Door; Death of a First Mate; Death Overseas; A Case Dead and Buried; Nicholas Lattermole's Case; The Dead Have no Mouths; Secrecy at Sandhurst; Unsought Adventure, etc. *Address:* 118 Delaware Mansions, W.9. *T.:* Cunningham 7155. [*Died* 17 *Jan.* 1963.

BARRY, Sir (Claude) Francis, 3rd Bt., *cr.* 1899; *b.* 16 Dec. 1883; *er. s.* of Sir Edward Barry, 2nd Bt., and Kathleen Ellen (*d.* 1885), *d.* of Percy Bicknell; *S.* father, 1949; *m.* 1st, 1908, Angela Doris Manners (marriage dissolved, 1927), *e. d.* of Herbert C. Hume-Spry of Nunney, Frome, Somerset; one *s.* two *d.*; 2nd, 1927, Violet Gwendoline Pretyman (*d.* 1957), *yr. d.* of late Alfred Darby, of Brentwood, Essex. *Educ.:* Harrow. Artist, oil painter, etcher. Member R.B.A.; regular exhibitor Paris Salon. *Recreation:* croquet (champion cup 1919 and 1921). *Heir:* *s.* Rupert Rodney Francis Tress Barry, M.B.E. [*b.* 6 Dec. 1910; *m.* 1st, 1936, Diana Madeline (*d.* 1948), *o. d.* of R. O'Brien Thompson; one *s.* one *d.*; 2nd, 1951, Sheila Georgina Veronica, *o. d.* of Maj. G. J. F. White; three *s.* two *d.* Served War, 1939-40 (prisoner)]. *Address:* c/o Lloyds Bank, St. Ives, Cornwall; c/o Brisley Rise, Willesborough Lees, Ashford, Kent. [*Died* 25 *Oct.* 1970.

BARRY, Sir Gerald (Reid), Kt. 1951; Journalist; *b.* 20 Nov. 1898; *s.* of Rev. G. D. Barry, B.D.; *m.* 1st, 1922, Gladys, *y. d.* of late G. Chisholm Williams, M.D., F.R.C.S.; one *s.*; 2nd, Helen Jepson, *o. d.* of Mr. Justice Rigg; 3rd, 1944, Mrs. Vera Burton; one *s.*; 4th, 1959, Mrs. Diana Wotton Schlumberger. *Educ.:* Marlborough; Corpus Christi College, Cambridge (Scholar). Served European War, R.F.C. and R.A.F., 1917-19; Capt. 1918. Executive, Granada Television Ltd.; Chairman, International Literary Management; Director, New Statesman and Nation; Chairman, New Barbican Committee; Chairman, Cities Redevelopment Research Ltd.; Dep. Chm. Committee on reform of Obscene Libel Laws; radio and television programmes, I.T.A. and B.B.C. Asst. Editor, Saturday Review, 1921-1924; Editor, 1924-30; founded Week-end Review, 1930, and edited it 1930-34; Editor News Chronicle, 1936-47; Dir.-Gen., Festival of Britain, 1948-51; Consultant to L.C.C. on re-development of Crystal Palace site, 1952-56; adviser on public policy to N.F.U., 1952-57; Co-founder of P.E.P. (Political and Economic Planning); appointed Mem. Govt. Cttee. on scope of Town and Country Planning, 1948; F.R.I.B.A. (Hon.); F.R.S.A. *Publications:* A Week-end Calendar (edit.), 1933; This England (edit.), 1934; (co-editor with Sir Francis Meynell) Week-end Book. 1955 edn. *Recreations:* people, places and buildings. *Address:* 4 Mount Street, W.1. *Clubs:* Garrick, Savile. [*Died* 21 *Nov.* 1968.

BARRY, Iris; author; *b.* Birmingham, March 1895; *m.* 1st, 1923, F. Alan Porter, author; no *c.*; 2nd, 1934, John E. Abbott; no *c.* *Educ.:* Ursuline Convent, Verviers, Belgium. Film critic of Daily Mail, 1925-30; Librarian of Museum of Modern Art, New York, 1932-35; director of Film Library, Museum of Modern Art, 1935-51. Chevalier de la Légion d'Honneur, 1949. *Publications:* Splashing into Society, 1923; Let's Go to the Pictures, 1928; Portrait of Lady Mary Montagu, 1928; Here is thy Victory, 1930; D. W. Griffith: American Film Master, 1940. *Recreation:* talking. *Address:* Fayence (Var), France. [*Died* 22 *Dec.* 1969.

BARRY, Hon. Sir John (Vincent William), Kt. 1961; Judge of Supreme Court of Victoria, Australia, since 1947, Senior Puisne Judge, since 1966; Chairman, Department of Criminology, Melbourne University, since founding in 1951; Chairman, Parole Board of Victoria since creation of Board in 1957; *b.* Albury, N.S.W., 13 June 1903; *s.* of late William Edward Barry and late Jeannette Barry; *m.* 1st, 1930, Ethel May Pryor (*d.* 1943); one *s.* one *d.*; 2nd, 1951, Nancy Lorraine Hudson; one *d.* *Educ.:* St Patrick's Coll., Goulburn, N.S.W.; University of Melbourne; LL.B.; LL.D. 1969. Admitted as barrister, Victoria, 1926 and N.S.W., 1946; K.C. (Victoria) 1942; K.C. (N.S.W.) 1946. Leader Austr. delegn. to 1st (Geneva, 1955) and 2nd (London, 1960) U.N. Congresses for Prevention of Crime and Treatment of Offenders. Member: Internat. Criminological Soc.; adv. bd., Brit. Jl. of Criminology. 1st Pres., Australian and N.Z. Soc. of Criminology, 1967-. Fellow, Royal Historical Soc. of Victoria. *Publications:* Alexander Maconochie of Norfolk Island, 1958 (O.U.P.); The Life and Death of John Price, 1964 (Melb. U.P.); (co-author) An Introduction to the Criminal Law in Australia, 1948 (Gt. Brit.). Contributor, Pioneers in Criminology, 1960 (Gt. Brit.); Australian Dictionary of Biography. Articles in Australian, English, Canadian and American legal and criminological jls. *Recreation:* historical and sociological research. *Address:* Judges' Chambers, Supreme Court, Melbourne, Victoria, Australia. *T.:* 60-0311; 39 Hampden Road, Armadale, Victoria 3143, Australia. *T.:* 50-5601. *Clubs:* (all in Melbourne): Athenæum, Victoria Golf, University House, E.S.U. House. [*Died* 10 *Nov.* 1969.

BARSTOW, Sir George Lewis, K.C.B., *cr.* 1920 (C.B. 1913), LL.D.; *b.* 20 May 1874; *m.* 1904, Hon. Enid Lilian Lawrence, *o. d.* of 1st Baron Trevethin; one *s.* one *d.* (and one *s.* killed in action, 1941). Controller of Supply Services Treasury, 1919-27; Government Director of Anglo-Iranian Oil Co., 1927-46; Chairman of the Board of Directors of the Prudential Assurance Co., 1941-53. *Address:* Chapel House, Builth, Breconshire. [*Died* 29 *Jan.* 1966.

BARSTOW, Percy Gott; *b.* 25 Oct. 1883; *s.* of an engine-driver; *m.* 1922; one *s.* two *d.* *Educ.:* Leeds Higher Grade School. Engine cleaner; clerk and later Office Manager at H.Q. of National Union of Railwaymen; thirty-seven years trade unionist and co-operator; contested Barrow-in-Furness in 1935; M.P. (Lab.) for Pontefract Division of Yorkshire, 1941-50. *Address:* Vectis, Jason Hill, Chesham, Bucks. *T.:* Chesham 2986. [*Died* 2 *Jan.* 1969.

BARTH, Karl, D.Theol., D.D., LL.D., Dr. ès Lettres; Professor of Theology, University of Basle, 1935-62, retired; *b.* 10 May 1886; *s.* of Friedrich Barth and Anna Sartorius; *m.* 1913, Nelly Hoffmann; five *c.* *Educ.:* Freies Gymnasium, Bern; Universities of Bern, Berlin, Tübingen, and Marburg. Assistant at Die Christliche Welt, Marburg, 1908-09; Minister at Genf, 1909-11, at Safenwil, 1911-21; Hon. Professor, Göttingen, 1921; Professor, Münster, 1925, Bonn, 1930-35. *Publications:* Der Römerbrief, 1919; Das Wort Gottes und die Theologie, 1923; Die Auferstehung der Toten, 1924; Erklärung des Philipperbriefs, 1927; Die Theologie und die Kirche, 1927; Christliche Dogmatik I, 1927; Fides quaerens intellectum, 1932; Kirchliche Dogmatik I. 1, 1932; Theologische Existenz heute, 1933; Credo, 1935; Kirchliche Dogmatik I, 2, 1938; Gotteserkenntnis und Gottesdienst nach dem Schottischen Bekenntnis, 1938 (Eng. trans., The Knowledge of God and the Service of God According to the Teaching of the Reformation, 1938); Kirchliche Dogmatik II, 1, 1940; A Letter to Gt. Brit. from Switzerland, 1941; Kirchliche Dogmatik, II, 2, 1942; Eine Schweizer-stimme, 1945; Kirchliche Dogmatik III, 1, 1945; Die protestantische Theologie im 19. Jahrhundert, 1947; Dogmatik im Grundriss, 1947; Die christl. Lehre nach dem Heidelberger Katechismus, 1948; Kirchliche Dogmatik III, 2, 1948; Fürchte dich nicht! (Predigten), 1949; Kirchliche Dogmatik, III, 3, 1950, III, 4, 1951, IV, 1, 1953, IV 2, 1955; IV, 3, 1959 (all vols. are now in Eng. trans. as: Church Dogmatics I/1-IV/3, 1936-1962). Against the Stream, 1954; Wolfgang Amadeus Mozart, 1956; Kurze Erklärung des Römerbriefs, 1956; Theologische Fragen und Antworten, 1957; Den Gefangenen Befreiung!, 1959; Philosophie und Theologie, 1960; Einführung in den Heidelberger Katechismus, 1961; Einführung in die Evangelische Theologie, 1962; Rufe mich an! Predigten, 1965; Kirchliche Dogmatik, IV, 4 (Fragment). *Address:* Bruderholzallee 26, Basel, Switzerland. *T.:* 35.27.79. [*Died* 9 *Dec.* 1968.

BARTHOLOMEW, John, C.B.E. 1960; M.C. 1915; M.A. 1919; J.P., Midlothian, 1943; Chairman and Cartographical Head of Geographical Institute, Edinburgh (Messrs. J. Bartholomew & Son Ltd.); *b.* 12 Feb. 1890; *s.* of late J. G. Bartholomew, LL.D., and late Janet Macdonald; *m.* 1920, Marie, 3rd *d.* of late Léon Sarolea, M.D., Hasselt, Belgium; four *s.* one *d.* (and one *d.* decd.). *Educ.:* Merchiston Castle School, Edinburgh; Universities of Leipzig, Paris and Edinburgh. Served European War from Aug. 1914; Capt. 1915, 1st Bn. The Gordon Highlanders and Staff (despatches thrice). Succeeded, on his father's death in 1920, to management of family cartographical business. Appointed Cartographer to King George V, 1921. Member Permanent Cttee. on Geographical Names, London (under R.G.S.), since 1926; Member National Cttee. on Geography (under Roy. Soc.) since 1941. Pres. Roy. Scottish Geog. Soc., 1950, after serving since 1920 as Hon. Sec. and since 1946 as Trustee. *Publications:* The Times Survey Atlas, 1922 (started by his father); The Handy Reference Atlas, 1922-49; Citizens Atlas of World, 1924-47; Survey Gazetteer of British Isles, 1927-43; The Times Handy Atlas 1935; Advanced Atlas of Modern Geography, 1950, The Compact Atlas of the World, 1954, etc. Various papers on projections and travel. *Recreations:* travel and photography. *Address:* The Manor House, Inveresk, Musselburgh, Midlothian. *T.:* Musselburgh 101. *Clubs:* Athenæum; New (Edinburgh). [*Died* 9 *Feb.* 1962.

BARTHOLOMEW, Gen. Sir William Henry, G.C.B. *cr.* 1939 (K.C.B. *cr.* 1934; C.B. 1919); C.M.G. 1917; D.S.O. 1917; *b.* 16 March 1877; *e. s.* of late J. S. Bartholomew, Moorlands, Devizes; *m.* Violet Alice (*d.* 1960), *d.* of Maj.-Gen. H. E. Penton, I.A.; one *s.* one *d.* *Educ.:* Newton College, S. Devon; R.M. Academy, Woolwich. Entered R.A. 1897; graduated Staff College, Quetta, 1909-10; served European War, 1914-18, G.S.O. 1 4th Division (France), B.G.G.S. XX Corps, 1917-18, B.G.G.S., E.E.F., 1918 (despatches, Bt. Lt.-Col. and Col., C.B., C.M.G., D.S.O., Officer Legion of Honour, Croix de Guerre, Belgian Croix de Guerre, Order of the Nile, Order of the Crown (Belgium), Order of El Nahda, Sacred Treasure of Japan); comd. 6th Inf. Bde., 1923-26; A.D.C. to the King, 1926; Maj.-Gen., 1926; Dir. of Recruiting and Organisation, W.O., 1927-28; Commandant Imperial Defence College, 1929-31; Director of Military Operations and Intelligence, War Office, 1931-34; Colonel Commandant Royal Artillery, 1934-47; Lt.-Gen. 1933; Chief of General Staff, India, 1934-37; General, 1937; G.O.C.-in-C. Northern Command, York 1937-40; A.D.C. General to the King, 1938-40; retired pay, 1940; North Eastern Regional Commissioner for Civil Defence 1940-45. *Address:* Sandell's House, West Amesbury, Salisbury, Wilts. *T.:* Amesbury 3166. *Club:* Army and Navy. [*Died* 31 *Dec.* 1962.

BARTIMEUS; *see* Ritchie, Capt. Sir Lewis Anselmo.

BARTLE, Anita; *b.* near Birmingham; *e. c.* of George Henry Bartle, Valencia, and Rebecca Wood; *m.* 1906, A. G. Brackenbury (she obtained a divorce, 1924; he died 1952); one *s.* one *d.* *Educ.:* privately, in Clifton; Valencia, Spain. *Publications:* This is my Birthday, in the Daily Chronicle, 1900-03; Our Christmas Cracker Party, 1902; contributions to Punch; This is my Birthday, in book form, Oct. 1902; The Madonna of the Poets, 1906; The Lover's Book of Verse: culled from the Poets of Seven Centuries; (with the translator, John Christopher, Ph.D., D.Litt.) The Akathistos Hymn from the Ancient Greek, 1922. *Recreations:* gardening, chess, reading aloud, listening to music. *Address:* c/o P. S. Brackenbury, Esq., 13A, Earls Court Square, S.W.5. *T.:* Fremantle 6781. [*Died* 16 *Nov.* 1962.

BARTLETT, Rev. Canon Donald Mackenzie Maynard; Canon Emeritus since 1966, formerly Hon. Canon, and Librarian of Ripon Cathedral; *b.* 25 August 1873; *s.* of late Reverend J. E. P. Bartlett, J.P., Rector of Barnham Broom and Kimberley, and Isabella Brewster Meadows; *m.* 1905, Sybil Langley Hunt, J.P., *d.* of late J. W. Hunt, M.D.; two *d.* *Educ.:* Haileybury; Clare College, Cambridge (M.A.); Wells Theological College. Deacon, 1896; Priest, 1897; Assistant Priest at St. Matthew's, Bethnal Green, 1896-99; Ashill, 1899-1900; Leeds Parish Church, 1900-4; Vicar of St. Mark's, Leeds, 1904-19; T.C.F., 1914-16, Dardanelles Expeditionary Force; Vicar of St. Wilfrid's Church, Harrogate, 1919-40; Hon. Canon of Ripon, 1929; Fellow of Woodard Corporation, 1932; Rural Dean of Knaresborough, 1935; Archdeacon of Leeds, 1937-40; Archdeacon of Richmond, 1940-51; Canon Residentiary of Ripon Cathedral, 1940-61. *Publications:* Isaac Heron, 1900; Two Recent Gypsy Funerals, 1934; Munster's Cosmographia Universalis, 1952; occasional contributions to Journal of the Gypsy Lore Society. *Recreations:* reading, sketching. *Address:* Hampden House, Harrogate. *T.:* Harrogate 66965. [*Died* 16 *Oct.* 1969.

BARTLETT, Sir Frederic Charles, Kt., *cr.* 1948; C.B.E. 1941; F.R.S. 1932; M.A. Hon. D.Phil. Athens, 1937; Hon. D.Sc. Princeton, 1947; Hon. D.Psy. Louvain. 1949; Hon. D.Sc. London, 1949; Hon. LL.D., Edinburgh, 1961; Hon. D.Sc. Oxford. 1962; Hon. D.Ed. Padua, 1965; Fellow of St. John's Coll., Cambridge; Professor of Experimental Psychology, 1931-1952, and Director of the Psychological Laboratory, Univ. of Cambridge, 1922-52; *b.* 20 Oct. 1886; 2nd *s.* of William Bartlett, Stow-on-the-Wold, Glos.; *m.* Emily Mary, *d.* of William Henry Smith, J.P., Helmshore, Lancs; two *s.* *Educ.:* private; St. John's College, Cambridge. B.A. London, 1st Class Hons. Philosophy, 1909; M.A. London, with special distinction in Sociology and Ethics, 1911; 1st Class Moral Sciences Tripos, Cambridge, 1914; Assistant to the Director of the Psychological Laboratory, Cambridge, 1914; Reader in Experimental Psychology in the University of Cambridge, 1922; Editor of the British Journal of Psychology, 1924-48; President, Section J, British Association, 1929; membre associé étranger de la Société Française de Psychologie, 1930; Member American Philos. Soc. Philad., 1946; For. Associate American National Academy of Sciences, 1947; For. Hon. Mem. Amer. Acad. of Arts and Sciences, 1958. Hon. Fell. Brit. Psych. Soc., 1954 (Pres. 1950); Hon. Mem. Swedish Psych. Soc., 1952, Spanish Psych. Soc., 1955, Swiss Psych. Soc., 1956, Turkish Psych. Soc., 1957, Internat. Assoc. for Applied Psychology, 1958; Experimental Psychological Society, 1960; Italian Psych. Society, 1963. Baly Medal, 1943; Huxley Medal, 1943; Royal Medal, 1952; Longacre Award, Aero Medical Association, 1952; Gold Medal, International Academy of Aviation and Space Medicine, 1964. Huxley Lecturer, Birmingham, 1957-58. *Publications:* Exercises in Logic, 1913, Psychology and Primitive Culture, 1923; (with Dr. C. S. Myers) Text-Book of Experimental Psychology, Part II, 1925; Psychology and the Soldier, 1927; Remembering: An Experimental and Social Study, 1932, The Problem of Noise, 1934; (edited, with others) The Study of Society, 1939; Political Propaganda, 1941; The Mind at Work and Play, 1951; Thinking: An Experimental and Social Study, 1958; contributions to various psychological journals. *Recreation:* walking. *Address:* 161 Huntingdon Rd., Cambridge. *T.:* Cambridge 53909. [*Died* 30 *Sept.* 1969.

BARTLETT, Joseph Leslie, C.B.E. 1952; *b.* 13 Feb. 1889; *s.* of John Bartlett, Plymouth; *m.* 1918, Dorothy Maria Perry. Became Member Royal Corps of Naval Constructors, 1912 after completion of 3 years' course at R.N. College, Greenwich. Service with Admiralty in various capacities, mainly on Warship Design. Deputy Director of Naval Construction, 1951-53; retired 1953. *Address:* 3 The Circus, Bath. [*Died* 17 *July* 1968.

BARTLEY, Lieutenant-Colonel Bryan Cole, C.B.E. 1919; M.I.Mech.E.; Managing Director of East Clare Estates, Ltd., Rhodesia; *s.* of late Sir George C. T. Bartley, K.C.B.; *m.* 1st, 1901, Gertrude Strickland (*d.* 1943), S. Africa; two *s.* two *d.* (and one *d.* decd.); 2nd, 1945, Elizabeth Cecil, *o. d.* of Noel C. Dowson, Taplow, Bucks; one *d.* *Educ.:* Haileybury. Engineering career, England and S. Africa; served S. African War (Capt. Railway Pioneers); European War, Admiralty, France, Air Bd., Asst. Controller of Supplies, Aircraft Production, 1917-19 (C.B.E.). Joined S. African Air Force, 1940-1941; Head Administrator of York Aircraft Repair Depot, 1944-45; Freeman City of London, 1945. *Publication:* Marine Engineers Record Book. *Recreations:* golf, etc. *Address:* Le Mottée, St. John's, Jersey, C.I. *Clubs:* Carlton, Royal Automobile; Rand (Johannesburg); Bulawayo (Bulawayo); Salisbury (Salisbury). [*Died* 13 *Aug.* 1968.

BARTLEY, Sir Charles, Kt., *cr.* 1942; J.P.; I.C.S., retd.; barrister-at-law; *b.* 18

Dec. 1882; *e. s.* of C. Bartley, Enniskillen; *m.* 1916, Marjorie, *d.* of W. Flowers Hamilton; two *s.* two *d.* *Educ.:* St. Columb's College, Londonderry; Methodist College, Belfast; Trinity College, Dublin (Sch. Sen. Mod. Classics and Mod. Lit.). Entered Indian Civil Service, 1907; District and Sessions Judge, Bengal, 1921; Assam, 1929; Legal Remembrancer, Bengal, 1931; Judge, High Court, Calcutta, 1932-42. *Address:* Garden Flat, Brook House, Ardingly, Sussex. *T.:* Ardingly 238. [*Died* 2 *Sept.* 1968.

BARTLEY, William, C.M.G. 1937; M.B.E. 1919; B.A. Dublin; *b.* Belfast, Northern Ireland, 3 Jan. 1885; *s.* of Charles Bartley, Fairview, Enniskillen; *m.* 1918, Leslie Marion, *d.* of Robert Brown, Wogganora and Kahanoo, Queensland; one *d.* *Educ.:* St. Columb's College; Trinity College, Dublin. Straits Settlements Civil Service, 1908; Director of War Trade, Straits Settlements, 1915; Agent Food Controller, Singapore, 1919; Acting Collector General of Income Tax, 1920; Assistant Adviser, Kelantan, 1922; Commissioner of Lands, Straits Settlements, 1926; Under Secretary to Govt., Straits Settlements, 1930; Acting Colonial Secretary, S.S., 1930; President Municipal Commissioners Singapore, 1931-39; attached to War Office, 1944; Senior Civil Affairs Officer, British Military Administration, Singapore, 1945; President Municipal Commissions, Singapore, 1946; retired 1946. *Publication:* Singapore in the War. *Recreations:* tennis, golf, fishing. *Address:* 28 Brisbane Avenue, Lindfield, Sydney, N.S.W. *Club:* East India and Sports. [*Died* 21 *March* 1961.

BARTON, Most Rev. Arthur William, D.D.; Archbishop of Dublin, and Primate of Ireland, 1939-56, retired; *b.* 1 June 1881; *s.* of Rev. Arthur Robinson Barton and Annie Hayes; *m.* 1914, Zoe Dorothy Victoria Cosgrave; one *s.* two *d.* *Educ.:* St. Columba's College, Dublin; Trinity College, Dublin. Curate, St. George's, Dublin, 1904; Curate in charge, Howth, Co. Dublin, 1905; First Head, Trinity College Mission, Belfast, 1912; Rector of St. Mark's, Dundela, 1914; Canon of Down, 1922; Rector of Bangor, 1925-30; Archdeacon of Down, 1927-30; Bishop of Kilmore, 1930-39. *Address:* 71 Wellington Road, Dublin [*Died* 22 *Sept.* 1962.

BARTON, Cecil Molyneux, B.A., LL.B.; *b.* 12 Oct. 1883; *e. s.* of late Molyneux Barton and Charlotte, *d.* of Captain Edmond Yates Peel and *g. d.* of General Jonathan and Lady Peel, *d.* of Marquis of Ailsa; *m.* 1920, Una Alys, *d.* of late George Morgan Harvey, Eburru, Kenya; (one *s.* killed on active service, 1941). *Educ.:* Shrewsbury; Dublin University. Barrister-at-law, King's Inns, Dublin, 1906; entered Colonial Service as Assistant District Commissioner, Kenya, 1913; Resident Magistrate, Kenya, 1914-22; Legal Adviser, Gambia and Member of Executive and Legislative Councils, 1922-29; Circuit Judge, Ashanti and Northern Territories, Gold Coast, 1929-34; Judge of the Supreme Court of Gold Coast Colony; retired; Member of West African Court of Appeal; Captain, Special Reserve of Officers (retired). Jubilee Medal, 1935; Coronation Medal, 1937. *Recreations:* shooting, golf, tennis. *Address:* 8A York Road, Farnham, Surrey. *T.:* Farnham 4926. *Club:* Constitutional. [*Died* 29 *March* 1962.

BARTON, Frederick Sherbrooke, C.B.E. 1953; retired; Consultant and Director of Companies; *b.* 13 May 1895; *s.* of Prof. E. H. Barton, Nottingham, and Mary Ann Barton (*née* Stafford); *m.* 1927, V. I. G. Hedges, *e. d.* of A. J. Hedges, M.B.E., Asst. Chief Constable of Berkshire; one *s.* *Educ.:* Nottingham High School; St. John's Coll., Cambridge (Foundation Schol.). M.A. (Cantab.); B.Sc. (London). Sub.-Lieut., R.N.V.R., 1917; Capt. R.A.F., 1918; Technical Officer, Instrument Design Establishment, Biggin Hill 1920; Royal Aircraft Establishment (Radio Dept.), 1922; Director of Radio Engineering, British Air Commission, Washington, 1941-46; Director Communications Development, Ministry of Supply, 1946-50; Principal Director Electronics Research and Development, Ministry of Supply, 1950-55; Adviser, Defence Supplies, to U.K. High Commissioner in Canada, 1955-59; Counsellor, Defence Research and Supply to U.K. High Comr. in Canada, Jan.-June 1960. M.I.E.E.; F.Inst.P. Fellow (Vice-Pres. 1943) Inst. of Radio Engineers (U.S.); U.S. Medal of Freedom with Silver Palm, 1947. *Recreations:* walking, handicrafts, photography. *Address:* The White House, Broomfield Park, Sunningdale, Berks. *T.:* Ascot 20964. [*Died* 6 *June* 1969.

BARTON, George Samuel Horace, C.M.G. 1935; *b.* Vankleek Hill, Ontario, 29 June 1883; *s.* of John M. Barton and Margaret Allen of Vankleek Hill, Ont.; *m.* 1912, Mabel Pauline Loveridge (*d.* 1960). *Educ.:* Ontario Agricultural College; Toronto University, B.S.A.; Laval University, D.Sc. (Hon.). Joined staff of Macdonald College as Assistant Lecturer, 1907; Professor of Animal Husbandry, 1911-32; Dean of the Faculty of Agriculture, McGill University, 1925-32; Deputy Minister of Agriculture, Dominion Government, Ottawa, 1932-49; Special Assistant to Minister of Agriculture, Dominion Government, Ottawa, 1949-52; retired, 1952. Member Co-ordinating Cttee., F.A.O., Rome, 1954. Commander, Agricole Mérite, Quebec; Pres. (C.S.T.A.) Canadian Society of Technical Agriculturists, 1923-25; Vice-Pres. 1920-23. *Publications:* Various papers on Animal Husbandry, Agriculture, and Rural Sociology. *Recreations:* golf, curling and out-door life. *Address:* 243 McLeod St., Ottawa, Canada. *Clubs:* Rideau Curling, Canadian (Ottawa). [*Died* 4 *Jan.* 1962.

BARTON, Sir Harold (Montague), Kt. 1947; F.C.A.; formerly Senior Partner in Barton, Mayhew & Co., Chartered Accountants, of which he was joint founder with Sir Basil Mayhew, 1908, retired Sept. 1954; *b.* Hull, 24 Sept. 1882; 3rd *s.* of late Major Bernard Barton, J.P.; *m.* 1927, Joyce, 2nd *d.* of late W. H. Wale, Lapworth; one *s.* one *d.* *Educ.:* Oundle. Member of Council of Institute of Chartered Accountants, 1928-57, Vice-Pres. 1942-43 and 1943-44, Pres. 1944-45; London Region, Price of Goods Committee, 1939-42; Financial Director, National Dock Labour Corporation Ltd., 1941-47; Higher Appointments Cttee., Ministry of Labour and National Service, 1943-44; Authorised Controller, General Aircraft Ltd. (appointed by Minister of Aircraft Production), 1943-45; Chm. Unlicensed Residential Establishments Wages Board, 1946-50; Vice-Chairman National Dock Labour Board, 1947-49; Member of Tribunal to determine compensation payable under Cable & Wireless Act, 1946; Member of the two Railway Conciliation Boards appointed by the Min. of Labour and Nat. Service, 1949; Chm. British Film Production Fund, 1950-58. Chm. Society of Yorkshiremen in London, 1929 and 1930. Mem. Court of Governors, L.S.E., 1943-. K.St.J. 1947. *Address:* 17 Montagu Square, W.1; Alderman's House, Bishopsgate, E.C.2. *Clubs:* City, Constitutional. [*Died* 20 *Oct.* 1962.

BARTON, Ven. Harry Douglas; Archdeacon of Sudbury since 1962; Rector of Sudbury, 1957-67; *b.* 1 Dec. 1898; *s.* of late Canon Harry Barton and Mrs. Barton (*née* Oakley); *m.* 1925, Edith Florence Ward Maxwell; three *s.* one *d.* *Educ.:* King's

School, Ely; Corpus Christi College, Cambridge (M.A.); Ridley Hall. Deacon 1923, priest 1924; Curate, Swansea St. Mary; Curate, Bradford Cathedral, 1928; Rector of St. Thomas, Birmingham, 1930; Vicar of Coleshill, Warwicks., 1938; Army Chaplain, 1939-45, S.C.F., D.A.C.G.; Hon. C.F., 2nd class, 1945. Rural Dean of Sutton Coldfield, 1947; Hon. Sec., Diocesan Conf., Birmingham, 1948; Hon. Canon of Birmingham Cathedral, 1948; Proctor in Convocation for Birmingham, 1949-57; Rural Dean of Sudbury, 1957-62; Hon. Canon of St. Edmundsbury Cathedral, 1957-62. *Recreation:* stamp collecting. *Address:* 2 Gainsborough Road, Bury St. Edmunds, Suffolk. *T.:* Bury St. Edmunds 3903. [*Died* 16 *March* 1968.

BARTON, John Saxon, C.M.G. 1933; retired; *b.* Melb., 1875; *s.* of Rev. John Barton, Congregational Minister; *m.*; one *s.* four *d.* *Educ.:* Melbourne. Arrived in New Zealand, 1903; Stipendiary Magistrate, 1918-37; Stipendiary Magistrate, Wellington, N.Z. 1933-37. Chairman of several Royal Commissions including especially Napier Rehabilitation Commission (following earthquake destruction) and Bondholders Incorporation Commission. *Publications:* 20th Century Commerce and Book-keeping; N.Z. Company Secretary; N.Z. Land Agent. *Address:* 70 Penrose Street, Lower Hutt, New Zealand. [*Died* 2 *Sept.* 1961.

BARUCH, Bernard Mannes; *b.* 19 Aug. 1870; *s.* of Simon Baruch and Belle Wolfe; *m.* 1897, Annie Griffen, N.Y. City; one *s.* two *d.* *Educ.:* A.B., College City of N.Y., 1889. Appointed by President Wilson, Member Advisory Commission of Council National Defence, 1916; Chairman Commission on Raw Materials, Minerals, and Metals; also Commissioner in Charge of Raw Materials for War Industries Board; Chairman of the Allied Purchasing Commission; Chairman War Industries Board, 5 March 1918; resigned 1 Jan. 1919; connected with American Commission to Negotiate Peace as Member Drafting Committee of Economic Section; Member Supreme Economic Council and Chairman of its Raw Materials Division; American Delegate on Economics and Reparation Clauses; Economic Adviser for the American Peace Commission; Member President's Conference for Capital and Labour, Oct. 1919; President's Agricultural Conference, Jan. 1922. War of 1939-45: War and Post War, Rubber and Manpower Reports. Amer. Representative on Atomic Energy Commission. *Publications:* Making of Economic and Reparation Sections of Peace Treaty, 1920; My Own Story, Vol. I, 1957; Vol. II, The Public Years, 1960; also pamphlets, public addresses, etc., on agricultural and economic subjects. *Address:* 597 Madison Avenue, New York, 22 N.Y., U.S.A. [*Died* 20 *June* 1965.

BASHFORD, Sir Henry Howarth, Kt., *cr.* 1938; M.D., F.R.C.P., Lond.; *b.* 1880; *s.* of late Frederick Bashford, Northaw, Herts, and *g.s.* of late Rev. Henry Howarth, B.D., Rector of St. George's, Hanover Square, and Chaplain in Ordinary to Queen Victoria; *m.* Margaret Eveline (*d.* 1955), *d.* of Ernest Sutton of Basildon, Berks; one *s.* three *d.* *Educ.:* Bedford Modern School; London Univ.; London Hosp. Chief Medical Officer to the Post Office, 1933-43; Treasury Medical Adviser, 1943-45; Hon. Physician to King George VI, 1941-44; K.G.St.J.; late Hon. President Post Office Ambulance Centre, St. John Ambulance Association. *Publications:* The Corner of Harley Street; Pity the Poor Blind; Vagabonds in Périgord; Half-past Bedtime; The Happy Ghost; Behind the Fog; The Harley Street Calendar; Lodgings for Twelve; Fisherman's Progress; Wiltshire Harvest: contributions to Lancet; The Ideal Element in Medicine (Hunterian Oration); Adolescent Albuminuria; The Physique of Young Londoners; Health Standards in Industry; The Contribution of Industry to Medicine (Proceedings of Royal Society of Medicine); and to other magazines and journals. *Address:* The White House, Easton Royal, Pewsey, Wilts. [*Died* 15 *Aug.* 1961.

BASING, 3rd Baron (*cr.* 1887), **John Limbrey Robert Sclater-Booth,** T.D. 1946; D.L. 1959; County Alderman, Dorset County Council, since 1961 (Member of Dorset C.C., since 1947); Bt. Maj. Reserve of Officers; late Bt. Col. commanding 43rd Wessex Divisional Signals (T.A.), retd., 1934; late Hon. Col.; D.L., Hants, 1939-50; *b.* 3 Dec. 1890; *S.* father, 1919; *o. s.* of 2nd Baron and Mary (*d.* 1904), *d.* of John Hargreaves, Maiden Erlegh, Berks, and Whalley Abbey, Lancashire; *m.* 1924, Mary (Molly) Alice Erle, *yr. d.* of late Lt.-Col. Richard Erle Benson, East Yorks Regt.; three *d.* *Educ.:* Eton; Royal Military College, Sandhurst. Capt. 1st Royal Dragoons. Served European War (France), 1914-18; served in Movement Control in 1939-45 War as D.A.Q.M.G. (Movement), D.L. Dorset, 1959. *Heir: cousin* George Lutley Sclater-Booth [*b.* 7 Dec. 1903; *m.* 1938, Jeannette (*d.* 1957), *d.* of late N. B. MacKelvie, New York; one *s.* (*b.* 16 Jan. 1939)]. *Address:* The Malt House, Gillingham, Dorset. *Clubs:* Army and Navy; Dorset County (Dorchester). [*Died* 2 *Oct.* 1969.

BASSER, Sir Adolph, Kt. 1962; C.B.E. 1955; Company Director; *b.* 26 June 1887; *s.* of Leo Wolf Basser; *m.* 1912, Miriam Nelson; one *s.* *Educ.:* Cracow, Poland. Optometrist and Jeweller. Hon. D.Sc. Univ. of Sydney, 1955. *Recreations:* golf, bowls. *Address:* Castlefield, 343 Edgecliff Rd., Edgecliff, N.S.W., Australia. *Clubs:* Tattersall's (Sydney); Royal Automobile of Australia; Double Bay Bowling [*Died* 20 *Oct.* 1964.

BASSETT, Arthur Tilney, O.B.E.; Chevalier Ordre de Léopold (Belgium); *b.* 13 Oct. 1869; *s.* of late Henry Tilney Bassett, Norwich; *m.* Mary (*d.* 1954), *d.* of late William Barton. *Educ.:* privately; Trinity College, Dublin. Sec. to Gladstone Trustees, 1907-14; War Refugees Cttee., 1915-19; London Defences C.P.O., R.N.V.R. (Anti-Aircraft Corps); Italian Red Cross; Metropolitan Observation Service; Secretary, British Committee of Russian Red Cross, 1919-20; Secy. to Mr. Asquith, General Election, 1922; Secretary Welsh Church Fund, 1920-26. *Publications:* Life of John Edward Ellis, 1914; Gladstone's Speeches, 1916; St. Barnabas, Oxford, 1919; A Victorian Vintage, 1930; The Gladstone Papers, 1930; Gladstone to his Wife, 1936; Catalogue of the Gladstone Papers (British Museum), 1953; edited various works; many contributions to reviews and magazines. *Recreations:* billiards, chess. *Address:* 2 Castelnau, Barnes, S.W.13. *T.:* Riverside 3371. *Club:* Athenæum. [*Died* 17 *Nov.* 1964.

BASSETT, Henry, D.Sc., Ph.D., D. ès Sc.; F.R.I.C.; Emeritus Professor, University of Reading; *b.* 1 May 1881; *s.* of Mary Kate and Henry Bassett, consulting chemist; *m.* 1915, Violet Muriel, *d.* of H. B. Fleming, M.B., Omagh, Co. Tyrone; two *s.* one *d.* (and one *s.* killed on active service, 1944). *Educ.:* University College School and University College, London; Universities of Munich and Nancy. 1st Class Honours, B.Sc. London, 1901; 1851 Exhibition scholar, 1903-5; Demonstrator and Assistant Lecturer in Chemistry, University of Liverpool, 1905-12; Professor of Chemistry, Univ. of Reading, 1912-46; temp. Professor of Chemistry, Univ. Coll., Hull, Oct.-Dec. 1946; Director of Research and Development, Peter Spence

& Sons Ltd., Widnes, Lancs., 1947-50; Mineralogist Chemist, Geological Survey, Dodoma, Tanganyika, 1950-54. Defence Medal (1939-45). *Publications:* Papers on Chemical, Geological, and Hydrographic subjects in various scientific journals. *Recreations:* pedestrian and cycle touring and camping; climbing; geologising. *Address:* 282 Wokingham Road, Reading. *T* Reading 62017. [*Died* 23 *Feb.* 1965.

BASSETT, Ralph Henry, C.M.G. 1951; C.B.E. 1949 (O.B.E. 1943); Retired Permanent Secretary, Ministry of Industries and Fisheries, Ceylon Government; *b.* 16 Feb. 1896; *s.* of Rev. H. J. Bassett, Vicar of East Kirkby, Lincs., and G. M. Brown, Glentworth, Lincs.; *m.* 1917, Norah Marion Madden; three *d.* *Educ.:* Haileybury College; Nottingham University. Served European War, 1914-19; joined Duke of Cornwall's L.I., Aug. 1914; demobilized as Captain, 1919. Joined Colonial Administrative Service, Dec. 1920; service in Ceylon, 1921-51, as: Magistrate, Land Settlement Officer, Assistant Government Agent, Marketing Commissioner, Permanent Secretary; started and developed the Marketing Department. Colonial Auxiliary Forces Long Service Medal. Civil Defence Officer, Dursley, R.D.C., 1951-61. Civil Defence Chief Warden for S. Gloucestershire from 1951. *Publications:* Romantic Ceylon, 1930; The Rare Romances of Nariya the Jackal, 1933; The Mechanised Historian, 1950. *Recreations:* archæology, ornithology, gardening, journalism (antiquarian subjects), volunteer soldiering. *Address:* Glentworth, Coombe, Wotton-under-Edge, Glos. *T.:* Wotton-under-Edge 3227. [*Died* 18 *July* 1962.

BATCHELOR, Rev. Alfred Williams, M.A., D.C.L.; Hon. Canon of Christ Church, Oxford; *b.* 31 Oct. 1864; 4th *s.* of late Rev. Henry Batchelor, Glasgow; *m.* 1st, Agnes Lowe (*d.* 1928); two *s.*; 2nd, 1934, Mabel Florence Leith (*d.* 1950). *Educ.:* Blackheath; University of Durham. B.A. 1884; M.A., B.C.L., 1891; D.C.L. 1900; Headmaster of Kingston School, Yeovil, 1896-99; Deacon, 1897; Priest, 1898; Headmaster of Taplow Grammar School, 1900-10; Vicar of Cookham, Berks., 1910-31; Rector of Launton, Bicester, Oxon, 1931-39; Rural Dean of Bicester, 1934; retired, 1939. Editor of the Oxford Diocesan Magazine, 1933-49. *Publication:* A Paper on Tithe, 1932. *Recreation:* motoring. *Address:* The Cottage, Westfield Road, Maidenhead. *T.:* Maidenhead 2294. [*Died* 15 *Aug.* 1961.

BATCHELOR, Denzil Stanley; Author and Journalist; *b.* 23 Feb. 1906; *o. s.* of Sir Stanley Batchelor, Judge of High Court, Bombay, and Maud Alice (*née* Batty), *d.* of Mr. Justice Batty, Judge of High Court, Bombay; *m.* 1939, Eleanor Bowes, *d.* of R. F. Pack, Chm. Northern States Power Co., Minneapolis, Minn., U.S.A.; two *s.* *Educ.:* Trent Coll., Derbyshire; Worcester Coll., Oxford. Columnist, book and film critic, Sydney Sunday Sun, Woman, Sydney Morning Herald, 1930-37; served War of 1939-45, War Office (M.1 and P.R. Directorates), retiring with rank of Major; Sports Editor and Asst. Editor, Leader Magazine, 1946-49; Sports Editor, Picture Post, 1949-1957. Has appeared on many broadcast and television programmes. Writer on wine for The Field; Homes and Gardens; author of a number of broadcast plays. *Publications:* Poems, 1926; The Test Match Murder, 1936; The Game Goes On, 1945; British Boxing; Days Without Sunset; The Match I Remember; Game of a Lifetime; The Book of Cricket; C. B. Fry; The Picture Post Books of The Test, 1953-56; Soccer; The Turf of Old; Big Fight; Jack Johnson; They Laugh that Win; This My Son; The Taste of Blood; Everything Happens to Hector; The Man Who Loved Chocolates; Babbled of Green Fields; The English Inn; On the Brink; London in Colour (Text); For What We are about to Receive; The Test Matches of 1964; The Delicate Flower; The Sedulous Ape; Sportsman's London; The Changing Face of Cricket (with Sir Learie Constantine). Edited: The Picture Post Book of Wimbledon; Best Boxing Stories; Maxims and Reflections (Churchilliana); The Boxing Companion; Guide to Good Living in London; Best Cricket Stories. Contrib. to many magazines and newspapers. *Recreation:* being driven. *Address:* 52 Onslow Square, S.W.7. *T.:* Kensington 0860. *Clubs:* Savile, M.C.C. [*Died* 6 *Sept.* 1969.

BATE, Brig.-Gen. Thomas Reginald Fraser, C.M.G. 1919; D.L., J.P.; *b.* 1881; *o. s.* of late Major Henry Reginald Bate, Somersetshire Light Infantry; *m.* 1914, Mary Ulric. Alicia, *y. d.* of Charles Fitzwilliam of Cilgwyn, Newcastle-Emlyn, S. Wales; one *s.* *Educ.:* Wellington College; Royal Military Academy, Woolwich. Major and Brevet Lieut.-Col. R.A.; retired, 1920, as Brig.-General; served European War, 1914-19 (despatches, C.M.G., Officer of Order of Leopold of Belgium, medal of La Solidaridad of Panama); D.L. (Monmouthshire) 1932, J.P. 1934; C.C. (Herefordshire) 1947, D.L. 1948; High Sheriff of Herefordshire, 1953. *Address:* Glanmonnow House, Garway, Herefordshire. *T.A.:* Glanmonnow, Skenfrith. *T.:* Skenfrith 205. *Club:* Naval and Military. [*Died* 3 *March* 1964.

BATEMAN, Maj.-Gen. Donald Roland Edwin Rowan, C.I.E. 1946; D.S.O. 1940, Bar, 1943; O.B.E. 1942; *b.* 21 Jan. 1901; *s.* of late C. R. Bateman and Mrs. G. M. Manfield; *m.* 1930, Violet May Chapman; two *d.* *Educ.:* Dulwich College; R.M.C., Sandhurst. Commissioned India Army, 1920; posted Baluch Regt.; Operations in Waziristan, 1921-24 (medal and clasp); Staff College, Quetta, 1933-34; Bt. Major, 1937; War of 1939-45: Middle East Forces (4th Indian Division), 1939-43; Central Mediterranean Forces (Italy), 1943-44 (despatches thrice, D.S.O. and Bar, O.B.E.). Acting Lt.-Col. 1941; Acting Brig. 1942; Acting Maj.-Gen. 1944; Lt.-Col. 1946; Director of Military Training G.H.Q., India Command; retired, 1948, as Hon. Maj.-Gen. *Recreations:* various. *Address:* c/o National and Grindlay's Bank Ltd., 13 St. James's Square, S.W.1. [*Died* 18 *Feb.* 1969.

BATEMAN, George Cecil, C.M.G. 1946; O.B.E. 1943; LL.D. Queen's University, 1944; B.Sc.; Consulting Engineer; Director: Canada Steamship Lines (Mem. Exec. Cttee.); Algoma Steel Corp.; White Pass and Yukon Corp.; The Eastern Trust, Company; Associate Metals Controller, Dir.-Gen. Washington Office Department of Munitions and Supply (now Dept. of Reconstruction and Supply), and also as Canadian Dep. Member Combined Production and Resources Board, 1944-46; *b.* Sutton, Ontario, 25 Dec. 1882; *s.* of George Arthur Bateman, Kingston, Ontario; *m.* 1908, Agnes, *d.* of I. L. Rogers, Gananoque, Ontario; one *s.* two *d.*; *m.* 1944, Sarah Evelyn Bourne (*née* Rust). *Educ.:* Queen's University, Kingston, Ontario. Secretary-Treasurer Ontario Mining Association, 1924-1943; on loan as Metals Controller for Canada under Department of Munitions and Supply, Ottawa, 1940-44. *Address:* The Château, Montreal, Canada. *Club:* St. James's (Montreal). [*Died* 4 *Feb.* 1963.

BATEMAN, Henry Mayo; Black and White Artist and Caricaturist; *b.* Sutton Forest, New South Wales, Australia, 15 Feb. 1887; *s.* of Henry Charles Bateman and Rose Mayo; *m.* 1926, Brenda Mary Collison

Weir: two *d.* *Educ.:* Forest Hill House, S.E. Studied drawing and painting at the Westminster and New Cross Art Schools, and in the studio of Charles van Havenmaet for several years; commenced drawing for reproduction 1906, since when has contributed numbers of humorous drawings to most of the leading weeklies and monthly magazines; has designed several theatrical posters; many humorous story and book illustrations. *Publications:* Burlesques; A Book of Drawings; Suburbia; More Drawings; Considered Trifles; Himself, 1937; The Evening Rise, 1960, etc. *Recreations:* golf, fishing. *Address:* Sampford Courtenay, Okehampton, Devon. [*Died* 11 *Feb.* 1970.

BATES, Lieutenant-Colonel Austin Graves, D.S.O. 1918; M.C.; R.A.; Director Thos. & Jno. Brocklebank Ltd.; *b.* 1891; 6th *s.* of late Sir E. P. Bates, Bt.; *m.* 1920, Jean M. C., *e. surv. d.* of Col. James Hunter, Antons Hill, Coldstream, Berwickshire; two *s.* Served European War, 1914-18 (wounded, M.C., D.S.O.); retired pay, 1930, but served again; Chairman General Council of British Shipping, 1951. Formerly Dir., Cunard Steamship Co. Ltd. *Address:* P.O. Box 23, Liverpool. *Club:* United Service. [*Died* 11 *Sept.* 1961.

BATES, Air Vice-Marshal Sir Leslie John Vernon, K.B.E., *cr.* 1956 (C.B.E. 1948); C.B. 1950; p.s.a.; R.A.F. retd.; *b.* 1896; *s.* of George William Bates, Mus.Doc., Stourbridge, Worcs.; *m.* 1917, Celia Ellen, *d.* of J. Pollard, Drakes, Little Waltham, nr. Chelmsford. *Educ.:* New College School, Oxford. Served European War, 1914-18, with R.N.A.S. and R.A.F. Deputy Commander of Mediterranean Air Transport Service, 1943-44; Director of Equipment at the Air Ministry, 1944-49; Air Officer Commanding No. 40 Group, Maintenance Command, 1949-52; Director-General of Equipment, Air Ministry, 1952-55. Air Commodore 1946; Acting Air Vice-Marshal, 1949; Air Vice-Marshal, 1951. Legion of Merit (U.S.A.), 1946. *Address:* Newlands, Crawley Ridge, Camberley, Surrey. *Club:* Royal Air Force. [*Died* 18 *Nov.* 1966.

BATESON, Sir Dingwall Latham, Kt., *cr.* 1953; C.B.E. 1946; M.C. 1918; Partner, Walters & Hart, Solicitors, 18 Mansfield St., W.1; *b.* 7 July 1898; 3rd *s.* of late Mr. Justice Bateson; *m.* 1922, Naomi Judith, *e. d.* of late Sir Walter G. Alcock, M.V.O.; two *s.* one *d.* *Educ.:* Rugby. Served European War, 1914-18, officer in 60th Rifles (M.C.). President Law Soc. 1952-53; Chm., Racecourse Betting Control Bd., 1951-61 (Member, 1949-); Mem. Horserace Totalisator Board, 1961-. *Recreations:* shooting and golf. *Clubs:* Carlton, Portland, All England Lawn Tennis. [*Died* 29 *Jan.* 1967.

BATHER, Rear-Adm. Rowland Henry, C.B.E. 1919; Royal Navy; *b.* Nov. 1873; *s.* of Arthur H. Bather, Assistant Accountant-General of the Navy; *m.* 1st, 1906, Evelyne Alice Eleanor (*d.* 1931), *y. d.* of late Sir Owen T. Burne; two *s.* one *d*; 2nd, 1932, Hilda, *d.* of late Ward Brook, Highfield House, Morley, Yorks. *Educ.:* Summerfield School, Oxford. Retired list, 1922. *Address:* Garavan, Greenhill Road, Farnham, Surrey. [*Died* 25 *Dec.* 1961.

BATHURST, Hon. William Ralph Seymour, T.D.; J.P.; M.A., F.S.A., F.G.S.; local Director, Barclays Bank Limited, Bristol; *b.* 1903; 2nd *s.* of 7th Earl Bathurst, C.M.G.; *m.* 1932, Helen Winifred, *er. d.* of Lieutenant-Colonel Harry William Ludovic Heathcoat Amory, Dulverton, Somerset. *Educ.:* Eton; Trinity College, Oxford. Capt. Roy. Gloucestershire Hussars, 1939. County Councillor, Glos., 1949-55; High Sheriff, 1952. Fell. of Soc. of Antiquaries, 1953; Master, Soc. of Merchant Venturers of Bristol, 1958-59. *Address:* Cold Ashton Manor, Chippenham, Wiltshire. *T.:* Marshfield 262. *Clubs:* Athenæum, Leander. [*Died* 10 *Sept.* 1970.

BATT, His Honour Judge Francis Raleigh, LL.M. (Wales); County Court Judge, Circuit No. 8 (Manchester and Leigh), since 1958; J.P. Cheshire and Lancs.; a Deputy Chairman of Lancashire Quarter Sessions; *b.* 9 June 1890; *y. s.* of late H. E. Batt, Heavitree, Exeter; *m.* 1st, 1921, Amy Isabel (*d.* 1941), 2nd *d.* of late James Aird, Montreal; 2nd, 1959, Mary Teresa Corrigan, Castlewellan, Northern Ireland. *Educ.:* Mount Radford School, Exeter; Law Society's School of Law, London. Articled to the late Richard Tapley, Solicitor, of Exeter, 1906; Daniel Reardon, Clements Inn and Clabon Prizeman, Law Society, June 1911; Assistant Lecturer in Law, University College of Wales, Aberystwyth, 1911-1913; Lecturer in Law University of Sheffield, 1913-19; Professor of Commercial Law in the University of Liverpool, 1919-42; Dean of the Faculty of Law, 1925-42; Hon. Professor of Common Law, 1942-45; called to the Bar, Gray's Inn, 1917; elected to Northern Circuit, 1920; one of the founders and first Hon. Secretary of the Association of University Teachers; President of the Society of Public Teachers of Law, 1939-46; Assistant Recorder of Liverpool, 1940-42; appointed to sit as Tribunal to examine Aliens in Lancashire and Westmorland, 1939; County Court Judge, Circuit No. 10 (Lancashire and Cheshire), 1942-1958. *Publications:* Law of Master and Servant, 1928, 4th ed., 1950; Law of Negotiable Instruments, 1931; Editor of Chalmer's Bills of Exchange, 1946. *Address:* 34 Hawthorn Lane, Wilmslow, Cheshire. *T.:* Wilmslow 3006. *Club:* University (Liverpool). [*Died* 25 *March* 1961.

BATT, William Loren, C.M.G. (Hon.) 1946; Gantt Medalist, 1946; Hoover Medal, U.S., 1951; Bok Award, 1942; Engineer and Politician, retd.; *b.* Salem, Ind., 31 July 1885; *s.* of George McLelland and Hettie Markland Batt; *m.* 1st, 1909, Ruby, Burroughs (*decd.*); two *s.* three *d.*; 2nd 1950, Madeleine Clark Batt. *Educ.:* Purdue University (M.E.). Dr. Eng. 1933; Dr. Eng. Stevens Inst. of Technology; Sc.D. Drexel Inst., Univ. of Penn.; Dr. Sci. Rose Poly Inst. Hess-Bright Mfg. Co. and its successor, S.K.F. Industries Inc. from 1907 to retirement 1950, President 1923-50. On leave of absence with U.S. Govt., 1940-46; Defense Advisory Commission, Office of Production Management, War Production Board, Combined Production and Resources Board, Combined Raw Materials Board, Member President's Special Mission to Moscow, 1941; Chief, Mutual Security Agency Mission to U.K. 1950-52, and Minister of Economic Affairs, American Embassy, London, 1951-1952; subseq. U.S. Rep. to NATO, and Minister for Finance and Econ. Affairs. Hon. Member: Am. Soc. Mech. Engrs., Brit. Inst. Mech. Engrs., Engring. Inst. of Canada; Hon. Life Mem. American Management Assocn.; Benjamin Franklin Fellow, R.S.A. *Address:* 1407 Kenilworth Apts., Philadelphia, U.S.A. *Clubs:* Metropolitan (Washington); Union League (Philadelphia). [*Died* 10 *Feb.* 1965.

BATTCOCK, Col. Grenville Arthur, C.B.E. 1928; T.D.; D.L.; *b.* 1882; *s.* of George Arthur Battcock, Maidenhead; *m.* 1912, Margaret Hester Yowo, *d.* of R. C. Peake, J.P., Cumberland House, Redbourn, Herts. *Educ.:* Winchester; Trinity College, Oxford, B.A. Admitted a solicitor, 1910; served European War, 1914-19 (despatches thrice), D.L. Bedfordshire. *Address:* Witts End Close, Eversholt, Bletchley, Bucks. *T.:* Ridgmont 272. [*Died* 15 *Nov.* 1964.

BATTEN, Colonel Herbert Copeland Cary, D.S.O. 1918; D.L., J.P., B.A.; late Dorset Regiment (Special Reserve); *b.* 5 Dec. 1884; 2nd and *y. s.* of late Col. H. C. G. Batten, O.B.E., of Abbots Leigh, Bristol, and of Keyford, Yeovil, and first wife, Eleanor Frances, *d.* and *heiress* of John Beardmore of Uplands, Hants; *m.* 1912, Dorothy Lilian Hyde (*d.* 1951), 3rd and *y. d.* of late Rev. E. A. Milne; one *s.* one *d.*; *m.* 1952, Mrs. Betty Richards, *yr. d.* of John Fletcher-Mossop, Cumberland, and *widow* of Nigel Richards, R.A.F.V.R., Hamlet House, Chetnole, Dorset. *Educ.:* Winchester Coll.; Trinity Hall, Cambridge. Served European War, 1914-18 (D.S.O., despatches five times). *Recreation:* hunting. *Address:* Aldon, Yeovil, Somerset. *T.A.:* Aldon, Yeovil. *T.:* Yeovil 89. *Club:* Boodle's. [*Died* 30 *Nov.* 1963.

BATTERSBY, Rev. Prebendary Gerald William, O.B.E. 1946; Rector of Weston super Mare, Somerset, since 1951; Chaplain to the Queen since 1956; Prebendary of Wells Cathedral since 1957; *b.* 23 May 1911; *o. s.* of William and Anne Battersby, Preston, Lancs; *m.* 1933, Constance, *e. d.* of Herbert and Maude Shuttleworth; one *s.* one *d.* *Educ.:* Bury Grammar School, Lancs; London University. B.A. London, 1933; B.D. (Hons.), 1938. Deacon 1935, priest 1936, Manchester Diocese; curate, Christ Church, Manchester, 1935-38; Temp. Chaplain to the Forces, Aldershot, 1938; Arborfield, 1939; B.E.F., France, 1939-40 (despatches); O.C.T.U., Shrivenham, 1940-41; S.C.F. 11th Armoured Div., 1941-42; Staff Chaplain, War Office, 1942; Chief Staff Chaplain to Chaplain General, 1942-46; Chaplain of the Royal Military Academy, Sandhurst, 1947-49; D.A.C.G., Canal Zone, Egypt, 1949-51. Examining Chaplain to the Bishop of Bath and Wells, 1954. *Address:* The Rectory, Weston super Mare, Somerset. [*Died* 14 *July* 1961.

BATTLE, George Frederick Newsum, C.B.E. 1952; Director, British Sugar Corporation Ltd., 1940 (Exec. Dir., 1940-62); *b.* 25 Feb. 1897; 3rd *s.* of late F. G. Battle, J.P.; *m.* 1933, Mary Dere Howard; three *s.* *Educ.:* Repton. Served European War: Lincolnshire Yeomanry, 1915-17; 1st Life Guards, 1917-19; in France, 1918. Farming in partnership, in Lincolnshire, since 1918. *Recreation:* shooting. *Address:* Greystones, Nettleham, Lincoln. *T.:* Nettleham 342. [*Died* 13 *March* 1966.

BATTY, Archibald Douglas George Staunton, M.V.O. 1922; O.B.E. 1926; actor; *b.* 6 Nov. 1887; *s.* of late Rev. G. Staunton Batty, North Mymms, Hatfield, Herts; *m.* 1927, Mary, *o. d.* of late George Miller. *Educ.:* Trent College, Derbyshire; Magdalene College, Cambridge (B.A. History Tripos). Served Waziristan Field Force, 1917; N.W. Frontier, 1918; A.D.C. to Sir Harcourt Butler, Governor of the United Provinces, 1919-22; Officer on Special Duty in charge of arrangements Prince of Wales' visit to the United Provinces, 1921-22; H.E. the Viceroy's visit to Burma, 1923; Military Sec. to Prince Arthur of Connaught during his tour in India, 1924-25; Staff of H.E. the Governor of Burma, 1925-26; Staff Capt. War Office, 1940; A.M.S. (Lt.-Col.), 1943-45. *Address:* 2 Bloomsbury Place, Bloomsbury Square, W.C.1. *T.:* Museum 9066. *Clubs:* Garrick, Leander; Royal Calcutta Turf (Calcutta). [*Died* 24 *Nov.* 1961.

BATTY, Rt. Rev. Francis de Witt, O.B.E. 1959; M.A.; Bishop of Newcastle, N.S.W., 1931-58, retd.; *b.* 10 Jan. 1879; *y. s.* of Rev. William Edmund Batty, M.A. and Frances Beatrice Jebb; *m.* 1925, Elizabeth Meredith, *d.* of Percy Stanislaus Davis, Brisbane; no *c.* *Educ.:* St. Paul's School; Balliol College, Oxford; Wells Theological College. Deacon, 1903; Priest, 1904; Assistant Curate, Hornsey, 1903-04; Domestic Chaplain to Archbishop of Brisbane, 1904-15; Canon Residentiary and sub-dean of Brisbane Cathedral, 1915-25; Dean, 1925-30; Coadjutor-Bishop of Brisbane, 1930-31. *Publications:* The Diocese of Brisbane, 1909; The Ministry of Healing, 1922; Christianity and the Home, 1930; St. Clair Donaldson (with C. T. Dimont), 1939; Human Nature (Moorhouse Lectures, 1939), 1941; Australian Proposals for Intercommunion, 1948; and various pamphlets. *Recreations:* music, walking, cabinet-making. *Address:* 41 Manning Road, Double Bay, N.S.W., Australia. *Clubs:* Union (Oxford); Australian (Sydney). [*Died* 3 *April* 1961.

BAUDOUIN, Charles; Professor, Institut J.-J. Rousseau, Geneva, Switzerland, since 1915; Director, Institut International de Psychagogie et de Psychothérapie, 1924; Editor of Action et Pensée, and of the Cahiers du Carmel; *b.* Nancy, 1893; *s.* of Antoine Baudouin and Pauline Desfossez; *m.* 1918, Marie-Laurence Geoffray; two *s.* *Educ.:* Nancy; Paris. Taught at Collège de Neufchâteau, France, 1914; Private Docent, 1920, Prof. 1961, Faculty of Letters, Univ. Geneva. Chevalier, Légion d'Honneur, 1950. *Publications:* Suggestion et auto-suggestion; Qu'est-ce que la suggestion? Études de psychanalyse; Psychanalyse de l'art; Tolstoi éducateur; La Force en nous; Le Symbole chez Verhaeren; Contemporary Studies; Mobilisation de l'énergie: l'Ame enfantine et la pyschanalyse; Carl Spitteler: essai; la Psychanalyse; Découverte de la personne; Douceur de France; Psychanalyse de Victor Hugo; L'Ame et l'action (prix Amiel, 1943); Éclaircie sur l'Europe; Introduction à l'analyse des rêves; Le Mythe du moderne; Reconnaissances lorraines; Le Voile de la danse; De l'instinct à l'esprit; le Triomphe du héros; Y a-t-il une science de l'âme?; Psychanalyse du symbole religieux; Livre d'heures; Blaise Pascal ou l'ordre du cœur; Paroles sur de vieux airs; Jean Racine, l'enfant du Désert. *Address:* Saconnex d'Arve, Geneva, Switzerland. [*Died* 25 *Aug.* 1963.

BAUME, Frederick Ehrenfried, (Eric Baume), O.B.E. 1966; Author, journalist, broadcaster; Television Commentator, Australia; Columnist and Lecturer; *b.* Auckland, N.Z., 29 May 1900; *e. s.* of late F. E. Baume, K.C., M.P., LL.B., and Rosetta L., Ph.B., *d.* of Capt. Hon. Charles M. Leavy; *m.* 1921, Mary Caroline Jack; one *s.* two *d.* *Educ.:* Waitaki Boys High School, Oamaru, N.Z.; Auckland Univ. Coll. Reporter N.Z. Herald, 1917, Waipa Post 1918-19, Dominion 1920, Christchurch Sun 1921; Editor, Timaru Herald, 1922-23; News Editor, Sydney Daily Guardian, 1924-1929; Editor, Sunday Sun, Sydney, to 1939; European Editor, Truth, 1939-49; Editorial Dir., 1949-58. Exec. Editor, 2 GB-Macquarie Radio Network, 1962; Australia, U.S.A., Britain, B.B.C. postscripts; accredited British war correspondent, with B.E.F., France, prior to German invasion 1940, with British 2nd Army, France, Belgium, Holland, 1944, Norway 1945, with 1st Airborne Div. F.R.G.S. *Publications:* Tragedy Track, 1932; Half-Caste, 1934; Burnt Sugar, 1934; I lived These Years, 1942; I Lived Another Year, 1943; Sydney Duck, 1944; 5 Graves at Nijmegen, 1945; Mercia Wade, 1947; Ponty Galler, 1947; Devil Lord's Daughter, 1948; Unrehearsed Incident, 1949; The Mortal Sin of Father Grossard, 1950. *Address:* c/o 2 GB, Sydney, N.S.W. *Clubs:* Press, British Military Historical Society; Imperial Service, Tattersalls, Sports (N.S.W.). [*Died* 25 *April* 1967.

BAUMER, Lewis C. E.; *b.* 8 Aug. 1870; *m.* 1896, Edith Margaret (*d.* 1955), *d.* of late Rev. Canon Venn; one *s.* one *d.* *Educ.:* Univ. Coll. School; St. John's Wood Art Schools; Royal Academy Schools. Work in black and white for Punch and most of the magazines, also paints portraits and flower pieces in oils, water-colour and pastel; Member Pastel Society; Member of the Royal Institute of Painters in Water-colours. *Address:* Rupert's Guard, Henley-on-Thames. *T.:* Henley 164. *Club:* Arts.
[*Died* 25 *Oct.* 1963.

BAX, Clifford, F.R.S.L.; F.S.A.; *b.* 13 July 1886; 3rd *s.* of Alfred Ridley Bax, F.S.A., and Charlotte Ellen Lea; *m.* 1st, 1910, Gwendolen Bishop (*née* Bernhard Smith) (*d.* 1926); one *d.* 2nd, 1927, Vera May Young, *d.* of late Col. Claude Rawnsley, C.M.G., C.B.E., D.S.O. *Educ.:* privately. Studied art at the Slade School and Heatherley's. Subsequently lived in Germany, Belgium, and Italy; elected Chairman of the Incorporated Stage Society, 1929; abandoned painting and concentrated upon literary and dramatic work; first play to be produced in the commercial theatre, The Poetasters of Ispahan, 1912; subsequent productions: Polly, with music by Frederick Austin, 1923; The Insect Play, adapted in collaboration with Nigel Playfair, 1923; Midsummer Madness, with music by Armstrong Gibbs, 1924; Mr. Pepys, with music by Martin Shaw, 1926; Waterloo Leave, with music by Martin Shaw, 1928; Socrates, 1930; The Venetian, 1931; The Immortal Lady, 1931; The Rose without a Thorn, 1932; The House of Borgia, 1935. *Publications:* Twenty-five Chinese Poems, 1910; Shakespeare (play in collaboration with H. F. Rubinstein), 1921; four comedies by Goldoni (edited and part-translated), 1922; Midsummer Madness, 1924; Inland Far (memoirs), 1925; Mr. Pepys, 1926; Many a Green Isle (short stories), 1927; Socrates (play), 1930; Valiant Ladies (three plays), 1931; Twelve Short Plays, 1932; Leonardo da Vinci (monograph) 1932; Pretty Witty Nell (Nell Gwyn), 1932; Farewell, My Muse (collected poems), 1932; Ideas and People, 1936; Highways and Byways in Essex, 1939; The Life of the White Devil, 1940; Evenings in Albany, 1942; Time with a Gift of Tears (novel), 1943; Whither the Theatre?, 1945; The Beauty of Women, 1946; Golden Eagle (play and book), 1946; The Silver Casket (Mary Stuart's Letters and Sonnets), 1946; Hemlock for Eight, radio play, 1946; The Buddha (radio-play), 1947; Rosemary for Remembrance, 1948; Circe (play), 1948; Some I Knew Well, 1951; W. G. Grace, 1952. *Recreations:* music, and reading history. *Address:* F2 Albany, W.1.
[*Died* 18 *Nov.* 1962.

BAX, Adm. Robert Nesham, C.B. 1918; Royal Navy, retired; *s.* of Captain Bonham Bax, Royal Navy, and Emily Harris, *d.* of Col. Nesham, Rifle Brigade; *m.* Helinor Marjorie, *d.* of late Colonel W. F. Parker, Rifle Brigade, of Delamore, Ivybridge, S. Devon; two *s.* one *d.* *Educ.:* Kelly College, Tavistock. Joined H.M.S. Britannia, 1889; Lieut. 1896; Commander, 1906; Captain, 1913; Rear-Adm., 1923; Director of the Mobilisation Department at the Admiralty, 1924-26; Vice-Adm. 1928; retired list, 1928; Admiral, retired 1932; Naval A.D.C. to the King, 1922-3; served European War in Channel Squadron, Dardanelles operations, Anzac landing, Adriatic Squadron, and in Aegean Squadron (C.B.); appt. under Central Electricity Board, 1928-1933; Hon. Organiser Swale Statutory Joint Committee (A.R.P.), 1937-39; recalled to Royal Navy, 1940, and served as Resident Naval Officer Whitstable and Margate; reverted to retired list, 1945. J.P. Faversham division of Kent, Supplementary list. *Address:* 4 South Close, The Precincts, Canterbury, Kent. *T.:* 64202. *Clubs:* United Service; Kent County Cricket.
[*Died* 21 *Sept.* 1969.

BAXTER, Sir (Arthur) Beverley, Kt., *cr.* 1954; M.P. (C.) Borough of Southgate since 1950; F.R.S.L.; *b.* Toronto, 8 Jan. 1891; *s.* of James B. and Meribah Baxter; *m.* 1924, Edith Letson, Vancouver; one *s.* one *d.* *Educ.:* Canada. Served as Lieut., Infantry, Canadian Engineers, with Canadian Expeditionary Force, and with R.E. 1918; joined London Daily Express, 1920; Managing Editor, Sunday Express, 1922; Managing Editor, Daily Express, 1924; Editor-in-Chief, Inveresk publications, 1929; Editor-in-Chief and Director, The Daily Express, 1929-33; Public Relations Counsel Gaumont British Picture Corporation Ltd., 1933-35; Editorial Adviser Allied Newspapers, 1938. M.P. (C.) Wood Green, 1935-45 and 1945-50. *Publications:* The Parts Men Play (novel); The Blower of Bubbles (collection of short stories); Strange Street (autobiography); Men, Martyrs and Mountebanks; First Nights—and Noises Off (collection of critical articles); First Nights and Footlights (collection of critical articles); It Happened in September (play). *Recreations:* music, golf, bridge. *Address:* 19 Oakwood Court, W.14. *T.:* Western 2655. *Clubs:* Carlton; Royal Canadian Yacht (Toronto).
[*Died* 26 *April* 1964.

BAXTER, Sir Beverley; *see* Baxter, Sir A. B.

BAXTER, Charles William, C.M.G. 1939; M.C.; *b.* 16 Feb. 1895; *s.* of John Henry Baxter, Gilston, Largoward, Fifeshire; *m.* 1924, Patience Violet, *d.* of Sir Henry Lambert, K.C.M.G., Larklands, Banstead, Surrey; two *s.* one *d.* *Educ.:* Charterhouse; Trinity College, Cambridge. Served in Army, Aug. 1914 - March 1919; Third Secretary, Tehran, 1919; Second Secretary, 1920; Foreign Office, 1922; First Secretary, 1928; in Berlin, 1932-33; Foreign Office, 1933; British Minister to Iceland, 1947-50; retired, 1950. *Address:* Edgehill, 20 Bereweeke Ave., Winchester, Hants. *T.:* Winchester 61378. [*Died* 21 *April* 1969.

BAXTER, George Herbert, C.M.G. 1949; C.I.E. 1942; M.A. (Oxon); *b.* 30 Nov. 1894; *s.* of late Rev. A. W. Baxter, M.A., Vicar of St. James's, Rochdale, and Alice, *d.* of William Gadd, C.E., F.R.M.S.; *m.* 1928, Gwendolen, *d.* of H. V. Layton; two *s.* *Educ.:* Manchester Grammar School (scholar); New College, Oxford (classical scholar), 1st class Final Honour School of Jurisprudence, 1920; Student of Lincoln's Inn. President of Stubbs Society (Oxford Univ. Historical Society), 1920. War service: enlisted Sept. 1914, R. Fusiliers; commissioned Jan. 1915, Royal Artillery; served in France; commanded Anti-aircraft Defences of City of London, 1918; entered India Office, 1920; Principal, 1924-33; Financial Sec. 1933-43; Assistant Under-Secretary of State for India, 1943-47, and for Commonwealth Relations, 1947-55; retired, Sept. 1955. Undertook special mission to Baghdad, 1921; Secretary of Royal Commission on Indian Currency and Finance 1925-26; Adviser to British Govt. Delegation, Indian Round Table Conference, 1931-32; Secretary of the Lord Privy Seal's Conference (U.K.) on Air Raid Shelter Policy 1939; Member of Standing Committee for Administration of Occupied Territories, 1941-1943; visited India with Rt. Hon. A. Henderson, for discussions with Govt. of India about the Services, Jan. 1947; Chm. of Conf. on Closer Association in Cent. Africa, Mar. 1951; visited: Cent. Africa for Victoria Falls Conf., Sept. 1951; Rhodesia, by invitation of Federal Govt., Feb. 1954; Swaziland (all districts) and Union of South Africa,

March 1954; Nyasaland, Feb. 1959. Vice-Pres. Cornhill Club. Dir., Rhodesia & Nyasaland Committee (London), 1957-62. *Publications:* India and Pakistan—External Economic Relations, 1949; Oxford & Cambridge Miscellany, 1920 (joint editor and contributor); contributions to the International Gold Problem, 1931, and to the Press on Commonwealth and other subjects. *Recreation:* travel. *Address:* 20 Woodcote Avenue, Wallington, Surrey. *T.:* Wallington 1639. *Club:* Union. [*Died* 8 *Aug.* 1962.

BAXTER, James, C.M.G. 1942; M.A.; **b.** 1 Oct. 1886; **s. s. of late James Baxter Mauchline, Ayrshire; unmarried. *Educ.:* St. Andrews University; 1st class honours in Mental Philosophy and 1st class honours in** Political Economy: Berry Scholar in Philosophy, 1910; Carnegie Research Scholar in Economics, 1911. Assistant Lecturer in Economics at Sheffield University, 1911-12; Professor of Economics, Law School, Cairo, 1912; Lieutenant, 3rd Batt. Gordon Highlanders, 1915-19; Assistant Financial Secretary to Egyptian Government, 1919-24; Financial Secretary to Egyptian Government, 1924-28; Financial Adviser to the Government of Siam, 1932-35; Financial Assistant to Governor of Burma, 1936-37; Financial Adviser to Governor of Burma, 1937-43; Financial and Economic Expert to Egyptian Government, 1943-46. *Address:* Sieur Nikola, Kyrenia, Cyprus [*Died* 18 *Sept.* 1964.

BAYER, Sir Horace, Kt., 1922; *b.* 1878; *s.* of Charles Bayer; *m.* 1901, Florence, *d.* of William Adair, Londonderry; one *d.* (and one *d.* decd.). *Educ.:* Dulwich College; Bar-le-Duc, Meuse, France. High Sheriff of Londonderry City, 1914-24. *Address:* Southwood, Silverdale, Sydenham, S.E.26. *Club:* Northern Counties (Londonderry). [*Died* 11 *March* 1965.

BAYKOV, Professor Alexander M.; Professor of Russian Economic Studies, Birmingham University, since 1955; *b.* 30 Aug. 1899; *s.* of Michael Baykov and Iulia Gorbaneva; *m.* 1st, 1927, Hala Mazurenko Bogolujbova (marriage dissolved); one *s.* one *d.*; 2nd, 1948, Inna Arian; one *s.* *Educ.:* Polytechnical Institute, Kiev; Agricultural Institute, Kharkov; Russian Faculty of Law, Prague. Jur.Dip. 1927; Ph.D. Birmingham, 1942. In the Army, and, afterwards, the Navy, of Russian Southern Government, 1919; evacuated to Tunis, 1920; Prague, 1922-39: Research Fellow, Russian Economic Research Service, Prague, 1927-39; Fellow of Economic Department, Slavonic Institute (Slovansky Ustav), Prague, 1933-47; Lecturer in Russian Economics and Institutions, Czech Technical University (Faculty of Commerce), Prague, 1934-39; Hon. Research Fellow, Birmingham University, 1939-45; Research Associate, National Institute of Economic and Social Research, London, 1941-45; Senior Lecturer, 1945, and Reader in Russian Economic Studies and Head of Department of Economics and Institutions of the U.S.S.R., Faculty of Commerce and Social Science, University of Birmingham, 1948. *Publications:* The Development of the Soviet Economic System, 1946, 1950 (Spanish trans., 1948, Italian, 1952, Japanese, 1954); Soviet Foreign Trade, 1946; over 100 articles. *Recreations:* mountaineering, swimming. *Address:* The University, Birmingham; 2 Elmdon Rd., Selly Park, Birmingham 29. *T.:* Birmingham, Selly Oak 0583. *Club:* Birmingham University Staff. [*Died* 2 *March* 1963.

BAYLEY, Maj.-Gen. Kennett, C.B. 1953; **C.B.E. 1945; D.L.; J.P.; retd.; *b.* 8 Nov. 1903; *s.* of Kennett Champain Bayley, Durham. *Educ.:* Rugby; R.M.C., Sandhurst. Commnd. Oxford and Bucks. L.I., 1924; Brig. 1949; Maj.-Gen. 1953; A.D.C. to H.M., 1949-52. Served War of 1939-45 (wounded twice); France and Burma; Brig., Gen. Staff, and Bde. Comdr. (despatches). Chief of Staff, British Troops, Egypt, 1949-1951; Director Personnel Administration, War Office, 1951-55, retired; Director, Boys Training, War Office, 1955-57. J.P. Durham, 1961. D.L. County of Durham, 1964. *Recreations:* golf, shooting, travel. *Address:*** The Mill House, Bedburn, Bishop Auckland, Co. Durham. *T.:* Witton-le-Wear 223. *Club:* Army and Navy. [*Died* 29 *March* 1967.

BAYLEY, Vernon Thomas, C.M.G. 1963; O.B.E. 1945 (M.B.E. 1941); Foreign Service, 1946-66; *b.* 7 Oct. 1908; *s.* of Col. Lytton Bayley; *m.* 1934, Viola, *d.* of Lewis Powles, A.R.A.; two *s.* two *d.* *Educ.:* Blundells. Entered Indian Police, 1928. Frontier Constabulary (N.W.F.P.), 1934; Asst. Political Officer, Hangu, 1935; Govt. of India, 1937; U.K. High Commn., Delhi, 1947; Brit. Embassy, Ankara, 1949; Brit. Legation, Beirut, Lebanon, 1950; Brit. Embassy, Paris, 1951; Political Office, M.E.F., Cyprus, 1958; Brit. Embassy, Stockholm, 1960. King's Police Medal for Gallantry, 1932. *Recreations:* golf, gardening, gramophones. *Address:* Rother Cliff, Rye, Sussex. *T.:* Rye 2204. [*Died* 25 *Oct.* 1966.

BAYLISS, William, C.B.E. 1949; D.L.; J.P.; President, Nottingham Area, National Union of Mineworkers since 1946; Member of the National Coal Board since 1952; *b.* 19 Dec. 1886; *m.* 1905, Florence Amelia Dexter; one *s.* one *d.* *Educ.:* Nailstone Elementary School. Chairman Nottinghamshire County Council, 1945-. Executive Member, National Union of Mineworkers, 1940-. D.L. County of Nottingham, 1955. *Address:* 3 Ridsdale Rd., Sherwood, Nottingham. [*Died* 12 *Feb.* 1963.

BAYNES, Edward William, C.B.E. 1928 (O.B.E. 1920); *b.* 1880; *s.* of late Edward Baynes, Commissioner of Montserrat, West Indies; *m.* Dorothy Margaret (*d.* 1957), *d.* of late F. W. Beauchamp; one *s.* Clerk in Colonial Service, Leeward Islands, 1899-1912; transferred to Home Civil Service; National Health Insurance Commission, 1912; Private Secretary to Secretary, Ministry of Shipping, 1917; Superintending Clerk, Ministry of Health, 1920; Secretary, Discovery Committee, Colonial Office, 1923; Colonial Secretary of the Leeward Islands, 1925-35; Acting Governor, Leeward Islands, Apr.-Sept. 1930, May-Oct. 1932, May-Sept. 1934; Administrator of St. Lucia, 1935-38; Acting Governor, Windward Islands, June-Oct. 1936; retired, 1938; Sec. Assocn. of Consulting Engineers, 1940-45. *Club:* New (Cheltenham). [*Died* 30 *March* 1962.

BAYNES, Frederic William Wilberforce, C.I.E. 1946; I.C.S. (retd.); *b.* 4 Aug. 1889; *s.* of William Wilberforce Baynes, D.L., J.P., Pickhurst Wood, Bromley, Kent; *m.* 1st, 1914, Jessie Hariet Maud (*d.* 1958), *d.* of Lt.-Col. F. G. Cunningham, O.B.E., Hove; two *d.*; 2nd, 1958, Beatrice Mary Joly, M.D., M.R.C.P., F.R.C.S.(E.), *d.* of E. T. C. Joly, Beirut. *Educ.:* Harrow School; Gonville and Caius Coll., Cambridge. Entered I.C.S., 1913; Comr., Meerut Div., U.P., India, 1943-47; retired, 1947. *Address:* The Chase, Dockenfield, nr. Farnham, Surrey. *T.:* Frensham 2257. [*Died* 22 *Nov.* 1967.

BAYNES, Norman Hepburn, F.B.A.; Hon. D.D. (St. Andrews); Hon. D.Litt. (Oxford) and (Durham); Hon. Litt.D. (Cambridge); Hon. Lit.D. (London); *b.* 29 May 1877; *s.* of Alfred Henry Baynes (*d.* 1914) and Emma Katherine Baynes; unmarried. *Educ.:* Eastbourne Coll.; New Coll., Oxford. M.A. (Oxon); Lothian Essay

Prize, 1901; Arnold Essay Prize, 1903; Barrister-at-law. *Publications:* Cambridge Mediæval History, Vol. I., chapters iii. and viii., Vol. II., chapter ix.; Editor of The Claim of Antiquity; The Byzantine Empire (Home University Library), 1926; The Historia Augusta, its Date and Purpose, 1926; Israel amongst the Nations, 1927; A Bibliography of the Works of J. B. Bury, 1929; Constantine the Great and the Christian Church, 1931; Cambridge Ancient History, Vol. XII. chapters xix. xx., 1939; Intellectual Liberty and Totalitarian Claims, 1942; Hitler's Speeches (translations), 1942; the Hellenistic Civilization and East Rome, 1946; The Thought-World of East Rome, 1947; (with Dr. Elizabeth Dawes) Three Byzantine Saints, 1948; ed. (with H. St. L. B. Moss), Byzantium, 1948; Byzantine Studies and Other Essays, 1955. *Address:* 4B Abercorn Place, N.W.8. *Club:* Athenæum. [*Died* 12 *Feb.* 1961.

BAYNHAM, Brigadier Cuthbert Theodore, D.S.O. 1918; J.P.; late Royal Artillery; *b.* 7 Jan. 1889; *s.* of late Rev. J. F. Baynham, Charlton, Dover; *m.* Elsie Dorothea, *o. d.* of late Lieut.-Colonel C. Conyers, Royal Irish Fusiliers, of Castletown Conyers, Co. Limerick; two *s.* *Educ.:* Dover College; Jesus College, Cambridge (B.A.). Commissioned R.A. 1911; proceeded to France, 4th Div., 1914; Bde. Maj., R.A. 31st Div. (D.S.O., despatches thrice); Instructor in Gunnery, Western Command, 1924-27; Instructor in Gunnery, China Command, 1930-1933; Commander 45th A. A. Brigade; retired pay, 1942; late Deputy Regional Controller (S.W. Region), Ministry of Supply; retd. 1948. J.P., Somerset. *Address:* Charmwood, West Hill, Wraxall, Somerset. *T.:* Nailsea 2046. [*Died* 26 *Sept.* 1966.

BAZARRABUSA, Byabasakuzi Timothy, M.B.E. 1960; High Commissioner for Uganda since 1962; *b.* 28 March 1912; *s.* of Paulo and Sofu Byabasakuzi; *m.* 1st, 1943, Caroline Lwanga (*d* 1945); two *d.*; 2nd, 1948, Janey Kulnbya; two *s.* two *d.* *Educ.:* Nyakasura, Makerere, Uganda; Exeter University College; Lawers School of Agriculture, U.K. Schoolmaster, Nyakasura, 1934-42; Headmaster, Kabarole Primary Sch., 1943-46; Asst. Schools' Supervisor and Visiting Teacher, 1947-50; Schools' Supervisor for Church of Uganda Schools, 1951-61. M.L.C., Uganda, 1954-61. Commonwealth Parliamentary Course, Westminster, 1958; Minister of Education, Toro Kingdom, Uganda, Jan.-Oct. 1962. *Publications:* Akaana Akatabunga (travel), 1940; Ihanga Rukanga (citizenship), 1945; Onyuunye Omale (Saltworks) 1957; Mungenzoomu (Lone Traveller), 1962; Hamunwa Gw'Ekituuro, 1963; Kalyaki na Marunga (novel), 1964. *Recreations:* mountaineering, writing. *Address:* Uganda House, Trafalgar Square, W.C.2. *T.:* Trafalgar 1963, (house) Hampstead 9195. *Club:* Alpine. [*Died* 25 *April* 1966.

BEA, Cardinal, His Eminence Agostino, S.J.; Cardinal Deacon since 1959; *b.* Riedböhringen, Baden, Germany, 28 May 1881. *Educ.:* Univ. of Fribourg; Jesuit College, Valkenburg; Univs. of Innsbruck and Berlin. Ordained priest, 1912. Jesuit Provincial for Upper Germany, 1921-24; Dir. Higher Studies, Jesuit College, Rome, 1924-28; Prof. at Pontifical Biblical Inst., 1924-59 (Rector, 1930-49). Editor, Biblica. Mem. of several Sacred Congregations, Rome; Mem. or Hon. Mem. various socs. Grand Cross, Sovereign Order of Malta. *Publications:* De Pentateucho, 1928; De Inspiratione S. Scripturae, 1935; Pontificii Instituti Biblici de Urbe Quinque Prima Lustra, 1935; Liber Psalmorum cum Canticis Breviarii Romani, 1944-45; Il Nuovo Salterio Latino, 1946 (trans. French, German, Spanish, Portuguese, Polish); Liber Ecclesiastae . . . nova interpretatio latina cum notis criticis et exegeticis, 1950; Il Trasformismo, 1950; Canticum Canticorum, 1953; Officium Parvum B.V.M., 1953; Unione dei cristiani, 1962 (trans. several langs.); Unity in Freedom, 1964 (trans. several langs.); Il cammino all'Unione dopo il Concilio, 1966 (trans. several langs.); La Chiesa e il popolo ebraico, 1966 (trans. several langs.); La Chiesa e l'Umanità, 1967 (trans. several langs.); La Parola di Dio e l'Umanità, 1967 (trans. several langs.); Ecumenismo nel Concilio, 1968 (trans.); numerous articles in various reviews and learned jls. *Address:* Via Aurelia 527, Rome, Italy. [*Died* 16 *Nov.* 1968.

BEACH, Lady Victoria A. H.; *see* Hicks-Beach.

BEACHCROFT, (Philip) Maurice, O.B.E. 1919; LL.D. (Hon.) Leeds University, 1955; *b.* 1879; *s.* of Philip Edward Beachcroft, Sheen Wood, and Mary, *d.* of Robert Bonnor-Maurice, Bodynfoel Hall, Llanfechain; *m.* 1st, Patience Wilson; two *d.* (three *s.* decd. of whom two were killed in action or on active service, 1942 and 1943); 2nd, Judith Hammond Swingler, C.St.J. *Educ.:* Uppingham; Magdalen College, Oxford (M.A.). Barrister-at-Law, 1903; President Hardwicke Society, 1910; served 1914-18 War: France and Belgium, Maj. R.A. (despatches, O.B.E.); seconded Royal Air Force, first Air Ministry Staff, i/c Legal Discipline, 1918. Secretary, Royal Masonic Inst. for Girls, 1920-47; Board R. Mas. Hosp., 1920-1953; Chapter-General Order of St. John, 1936-; Chairman St. John Council, Buckinghamshire, 1947-50, and St. John Council Sussex, 1956-60. Master of Worshipful Company of Clothworkers, 1945-46; Chairman Finance Committee, 1946-56; Chairman Trusts and General Superintendence committee, 1956-64; Court of Leeds University, 1952-67; Council and Delegacy City and Guilds Inst., Imperial College of Science and Technology, 1943-64; Gov., Mary Datchelor School, 1945-67, and Chairman of Govs., 1956-64. K.St.J. *Address:* Sun House, Chelwood Gate, Sussex. *T.:* Chelwood Gate 344. [*Died* 22 *Dec.* 1969.

BEAK, Maj.-Gen. Daniel Marcus William, V.C., D.S.O. 1918, M.C.; late The King's Regiment and Royal Scots Fusiliers; *b.* 1891; *m.* 1923, Matilda Catherine Frances Ritchie (*d.* 1930), *o. d.* of late Lt.-Col. Hugh Robert Wallace of Busbie, D.S.O., J.P., D.L.; two *s.* Served European War as Commander R.N.V.R., 1914-18 (despatches, M.C. with bar, D.S.O., V.C.); commanded 1st Battalion South Lancashire Regt. (Prince of Wales's Volunteers), 1939-40; G.O.C. Malta, 1942; retired pay, 1945. *Address:* c/o Lloyds Bank, Cox's Branch, 6 Pall Mall, S.W.1. [*Died* 3 *May* 1967.

BEAL, Vice-Adm. Alister Francis, C.B. 1926; C.M.G. 1919; *b.* 1875; *s.* of late Rev. Canon Samuel Gilbert Beal, Rector of Romaldkirk, Darlington; *m.* 1904, Mabel (*d.* 1952), *d.* of late Charles Youl of Oakdene Park, Launceston, Tasmania. Served European War, 1914-19; Executive Officer, H.M.S. Princess Royal, 1912-15; Admiralty War Staff, 1915-18; Commanded H.M.S. Weymouth, British Adriatic Squadron, 1918-19 (C.M.G., Officer of Legion of Honour, Italian Silver Medal for Military Valour); and on the South American Station, 1920-21; Deputy Director Operations Division, Admiralty, 1921-23; First Naval Member of Royal New Zealand Naval Board and Commodore in command of New Zealand Station, 1923-26; Retired List, 1926; A.D.C. to the King, 1925-26; Vice-Adm., retired, 1931; one of the Delegates for New Zealand on the Conference for the limitation of Naval Armament at Geneva, June 1927. *Club:* United Service. [*Died* 18 *Oct.* 1962.

BEALE, Sir Samuel Richard, K.B.E., *cr.* 1942; *b.* 7 Feb. 1881; *s.* of James Samuel Beale and Margaret Field; *m.* 1908, Sylvia Constance Bell (*d.* 1953); three *s.* *Educ.:* Marlborough; Trinity College, Cambridge. Rowed Cambridge University Boat, 1903; President, Glasgow Chamber of Commerce, 1929-30; President Association of British Chambers of Commerce, 1934-35 and -36; Director various companies. *Recreations:* shooting, gardening. *Address:* Drumlamford, Barrhill, Ayrshire. *T.:* Barrhill 220. *Clubs:* Junior Carlton, Leander; Western (Glasgow). [*Died* 10 *Oct.* 1964.

BEAMENT, Brig. Arthur Warwick, C.B.E. 1944; V.D. 1929; C.D. 1954; Barrister, etc.; *b.* 1 April 1898; *s.* of Thomas Arthur Beament and of Edith Louise Belford; *m.* 1938, Dorothy Violet Wisbey; one *s.* one *d.* by former marriage. *Educ.:* Ottawa Collegiate Institute; Univ. of Toronto; Osgoode Hall. Served Canadian Exped. Force, 1915-19 (Inf. and M.G.). Called to bar (Ontario) and admitted as solicitor, 1921; K.C. (Ontario), 1937. Canadian Militia, 1920-37 (Royal Canadian Signals); proceeded to C.M.H.Q., London, 1940; Deputy Adjutant-Gen. 1941-1943; O. i/c Cdn. Sec. 1 Ech. 15 Army Gp., 1943-44; Officer i/c Canadian Section 1 Ech. 21 A. Gp., 1944; Control Commission for Germany (B.E.), 1944-45. Pres. Canadian Signals Assoc., 1949-51; Chm. Conference of Defence Assocs., 1953-54. Hon. Col. Comdt., Roy. Canadian Corps of Signals, 1954-61; Hon. Colonel, 3rd Signal Regt., Royal Canadian Corps of Signals, 1963-. *Address:* 95 Lakeway Drive, Rockcliffe, Ottawa, Canada. *T.:* SH 749-8881. *Clubs:* Royal Ottawa Golf, Country (Ottawa); United Services (Montreal). [*Died* 24 *May* 1966.

BEAMISH, Air Marshal Sir George Robert, K.C.B. 1955 (C.B. 1944); C.B.E. 1942; R.A.F. (Retd.); A.O.C.-in-C. Technical Training Command, 1955-58; *b.* 29 April 1905; *s.* of late F. G. Beamish, Coleraine, County Londonderry. *Educ.:* Coleraine Academical Institution. Cadet Royal Air Force College, Cranwell, 1923-1924; Commission, 1924; Squadron Leader, 1936; R.A.F. Staff College, 1937; served War of 1939-45; Wing-Commander, 1940; Group Capt. 1941; acting Air Commodore, 1942; Addtl. Air A.D.C. to the King, 1944; Temp. Air Cdre., 1944; Air Cdre., 1947; A.O.C., R.A.F. Cranwell and Comdt. of the R.A.F. College, 1949-50; A.O.C., A.H.Q. Iraq, 1950-52; Director-General of Personnel (II), Air Ministry, 1952-54; A.O.C.-in-C., Transport Command, 1954-55; Air Vice-Marshal, 1950; actg. Air Marshal, 1955; Air Marshal, 1956. High Sheriff, Co. Londonderry, 1962. Officer: Order George I of Greece, 1942; Legion of Merit, U.S.A., 1944. *Recreations:* Rugby football (Irish International, 1925-33), golf. *Address:* Rocklea, Castlerock, Co. Londonderry. *Club:* R.A.F. [*Died* 13 *Nov.* 1967.

BEAN, Charles Edwin Woodrow, M.A.; B.C.L.; Litt.D. Melbourne; Hon. LL.D. Australian National University; *b.* Bathurst, N.S.W., 18 Nov. 1879; *e. s.* of late Rev. Edwin Bean, formerly Headmaster Brentwood School, Essex, 1891-1913; *m.* 1921, Ethel, 2nd *d.* of James Young, Tumbarumba, N.S.W. *Educ.:* All Saints' College, Bathurst; Brentwood Grammar School; Clifton Coll.; Hertford College, Oxford (Classical Scholar). M.A., B.C.L.; Litt.D. (of Grace), Melb., Asst. Master Brentwood Sch., 1903; Sydney Gram. Sch., 1904; called to Bar, Inner Temple, 1903; admitted to Bar of Supreme Court of N.S.W., 1904; Associate to Sir Wm. Owen, 1905-07; junior reporter Sydney Morning Herald, 1908; correspondent in London, 1910-13; leader-writer, 1914; official correspondent with the Australian Force, 1914-18; led Australian Historical Mission to Gallipoli, 1919; Acting-Director, Australian War Museum, 1919; Official Historian of the First World War for the Australian Government, 1919-42; Member of Council of National Fitness, N.S.W., 1937-44; attached to Dept. of Information, 1940, to establish Press liaison with Service Chiefs. Chm. Australian War Memorial Board, 1952-59; founder of Parks and Playgrounds Movement of N.S.W.; Hon. Fellow Royal Australian Historical Society; Member of Australian Services Education Council, 1945-46; Chm., Australian War Archives Cttee., 1942-46; Chm., Commonwealth Archives Cttee.; Chm., Promotion Appeal Bd., Aust. Broadcasting Commn. 1947-58; Pres. Inst. of Journalists, N.S.W., 1944-49; Chm., N.S.W. Standing Conf. on Community Centres, 1944-1947; awarded Chesney medal by Royal United Service Instn., 1931. *Publications:* On the Wool Track, 1910; The Dreadnought of the Darling, 1911; Flagships Three, 1913; Letters from France, 1917; In Your Hands, Australians! 1919; Official History of Australia in the War of 1914-18, Vols. I. and II. (Anzac), 1922 and 1925; Vols. III., IV., V. and VI. (France 1916-18), 1929, 1933, 1937, and 1942; War Aims of a Plain Australian, 1943; Anzac to Amiens (shorter history of Australia's part in War of 1914-18), 1946; Gallipoli Mission, 1948; Here, my Son (Independent Schools of Australia), 1950; Two Men I Knew, 1957. *Recreations:* formerly cricket, lawn tennis, walking. *Address:* 24 Suffolk Ave., Collaroy, Sydney, N.S.W., Australia. *Club:* Imperial Service (Sydney). [*Died* 30 *Aug.* 1968.

BEAN, John Harper, C.B.E. 1918; *b.* 1885; *o. s.* of late Sir George Bean, J.P., and Mary, *d.* of John Harper, Dudley. *Address:* Lawnswood House, nr. Stourbridge, Worcs. [*Died* 19 *March* 1963.

BEANLAND, Maj.-Gen. Douglas, C.I.E. 1946; O.B.E. 1932; Indian Army (retd.); *b.* 4 March 1893; *s.* of Fred Beanland, Harrogate and Sandsend, Whitby, Yorks; *m.* 1st, 1917, Annie Sybil (*d.* 1919), *d.* of Arthur Harrowing, Whitby, Yorks; one *d.*; 2nd, 1922, Elizabeth Grace (marriage dissolved 1953), *d.* of George Longstaff, Newbiggin, Northumberland; one *s.* one *d.*; 3rd, 1953, Beryl Enid, widow of T. B. Russell, I.C.S. *Educ.:* Marlborough College, Wilts; R.M.C. Sandhurst (Sword of Honour). 2nd Lt. Indian Army, 1913; Adjt. and Qr.-Mr. Cadet College, Quetta, 1918-19; Adjt. and Qr.-Mr. Staff College, Quetta, 1919-24; Student Staff College, Quetta, 1927-28; D.A.A. and Q.M.G. Burma Dist., 1931-35; Commandant 10 Bn. 14 Punjab Regt., 1938-40; A.A.G. G.H.Q. (India), 1940-42; Commander (Brig.) 106 L. of C. Area, 1942-44; Maj.-Gen. i/c Administration, North-Western Army, 1944-1945; Deputy Quartermaster-General in India, 1945-47. *Recreation:* bird-watching. *Address:* The Close, Weedon, Aylesbury, Bucks. *T.:* Whitchurch 272. [*Died* 9 *April* 1963.

BEARD, James Robert, C.B.E. 1950; M.Sc., M.I.C.E.; Hon. M.I.E.E.; Consultant with Merz and McLellan, Consulting Engineers, 32 Victoria St., S.W.1; *b.* 19 Sept. 1885; *e. s.* of late James Hogg Beard, Manchester; *m.* 1912, Gertrude, *d.* of late W. H. Robinson, Middlesbrough; one *s.* one *d.* *Educ.:* Manchester Gram. Sch.; University of Manchester. With North Eastern Electric Supply Co. and Cleveland and Durham Electric Power Co. before joining Merz and McLellan; partner, 1930, senior partner, 1940-61. Closely associated with design and construction of Grid system and Scottish hydro-electric schemes and of numerous electric power supply and traction schemes in Great Britain, South Africa, India, and elsewhere; Pres. Institution of Electrical Engineers, 1940;

Past-Chm. N.E. Centre; Pres. British Electrical Power Convention, 1953-54; Chm. Assoc. of Consulting Engineers, 1945-46; Pres. Assoc. of Supervising Electrical Engineers, 1937-39; Chm. (appointed by Minister of Works) of Council for Codes of Practice for Buildings, Construction and Engineering Services, 1947-49; Chairman of various committees of British Standards Institution and President British Electrical and Allied Industries Research Assoc., 1961-1962. Member of Engineering Advisory Committee of the War Cabinet, 1941-45. Master, Worshipful Company of Makers of Playing Cards, 1961-62. Fellow, Amer. Inst. Electrical Engineers. *Publications:* various papers on electricity generation, transmission and distribution before Institution of Electrical Engineers, World Power Conference, Paris E.H.T. Conference and elsewhere. *Address:* Amberhurst, Broom Close, Esher, Surrey. *T.:* Esher 2739. *Clubs:* Athenæum, Reform, Royal Automobile; Union (Newcastle upon Tyne).

[*Died* 22 *Sept.* 1962.

BEARD, John Stanley Coombe, J.P.; F.R.I.B.A. 1927; retired; Founder of J. Stanley Beard, Bennett & Wilkins, Chartered Architects London; *b.* 17 July 1890; *e. s.* of Percy Edward Beard, Rayleigh, Essex; *m.* 1st, 1914, Amelia Cheer; one *s.* (and one *s.* killed on active service, 1942; two *d.* decd.); 2nd, 1935, Mildred Evelyn, *d* of Aubrey Bertram Drayton, Montevideo; one *s.* one *d.* *Educ.:* King Alfred's School, Wantage. F.I.Arb. 1935. Served European War in Royal Artillery (wounded in France, 1918). Commenced practising in London in 1910. Has specialised in the designing of theatres, music-halls, and cinemas, and has been responsible for the design of a large number of commercial buildings, including factories, offices, and flats. On St. Marylebone Borough Council, 1932-37; commanded Grayshott contingent of Home Guard, 1940-1944; Hon. District Representative of Royal Air Force Benevolent Fund in the Counties of Hampshire, Surrey, and Sussex, 1942; General Commissioner of Income Tax for Hampshire; Council of the London Society, 1943, Council of Architects Benevolent Society, 1944; Chm. several Property Cos. Formerly of Grayshott Hall, Nr. Hindhead. Purchased Compton Acres, Dorset, 1950, reconstructed the 7 famous gardens and opened these to the public, 1952. *Address:* Colliston House, Canford Cliffs, Dorset. *T.:* Canford Cliffs 77411. *Clubs:* M.C.C.; Royal Motor Yacht. [*Died* 22 *Nov.* 1970.

BEARD, Wilfred Blackwell, O.B.E. 1948; General Secretary, United Patternmakers' Association, 1941-66; Member T.U.C. General Council, 1947-67 (Chairman, 1955-1956; Vice-Chm., 1956-57); *b.* Manchester, 1892; *m.*; one *d.* *Educ.:* Ardwick Higher Grade School, Manchester. Patternmaker (apprenticed). Full-time area official, United Patternmakers' Assoc., Lancashire and Cheshire, 1929-41; Chairman T.U.C. Educational Cttee. and Educl. Trust, 1950-. Member: Board of Governors, Welbeck College, Loughborough College, Ruskin College; various T.U.C. and government committees. Pres. Confedn. of Shipbuilding and Engineering Unions, 1958-59. *Recreations:* music, reading. *Address:* Mount Royal, 15 Cleve Road, West Hampstead, N.W.6. *T.:* Maida Vale 7085.

[*Died* 16 *Dec.* 1967.

BEARDMORE, Rt. Rev. Harold, O.B.E. 1941; *b.* 13 Nov. 1898; *s.* of A. E. Beardmore, Wolverhampton, Staffs.; *m.* 1930, Nona Vivienne, *d.* of R. W. Douglas, Plumstead, Cape Province, South Africa; one *s.* *Educ.:* Berkhamsted and Wolverhampton Schools; King's Coll., London; Wycliffe Hall, Oxford: H.M.S. Conway Training Ship. Cadet and Midshipman, 1915-19 (took part in naval raid on Zeebrugge and Ostende, 1918). Chaplain, Royal Navy, 1927-47. Dean of Port of Spain, Trinidad, B.W.I., 1947. Archdeacon of Basutoland, 1952. Bishop of St. Helena, 1960-67. War of 1939-1945: Chaplain: H.M.S. Hood, Nelson, King George V and Excellent. Retired at own request from Royal Navy, 1947. A.K.C. London. *Publication:* The Waters of Uncertainty, 1945. *Recreations:* golf and riding; formerly played Rugby football for London Univ. and United Services. *Address:* Stuart Cottage, Bray, Berks. *Clubs:* Junior Army and Navy, Royal Over-Seas League; Civil Service (Cape Town).

[*Died* 17 *Nov.* 1968.

BEARE, Josias Crocker, R.C.A., A.R.I.B.A.; Painter in Water Colour and retired Architect; *b.* Newton Abbot, 10 Jan. 1881; *s.* of late Henry Beare, Engineer; *m.* Audrey H. Petherbridge; one *s.* three *d.* *Educ.:* Torquay. Exhibited at R.A., R.C.A., R.W.A., W.A.G., Liverpool, Oldham, and other galleries; one man show Walker's Galleries, London; war service in R.E. (T.F.), 1915-19. *Recreations:* gardening and travel. *Address:* Culver Lodge, Newton Abbot, Devon. *T.:* 897.

[*Died* 13 *April* 1962.

BEARE, Professor William; Professor of Latin in the University of Bristol since 1931; *b.* 20 April 1900; *s.* of William and Maria Beare, Bandon, Co. Cork; *m.* 1934, Sylvia Joan Gibson; one *s.* two *d.* *Educ.:* Bandon Grammar School; Cork Grammar School; Trinity Coll., Dublin. Appointed Asst. lecturer in Classics, University of Manchester, 1924, Senior Lecturer in Latin, 1929; occasional lecturer for Ministry of Information, 1940. Dean of the Faculty of Arts, Univ. of Bristol, 1946-49; Public Orator of the University, 1949-; Pro-Vice-Chancellor of the University, 1955-58. Co-opted mem. Bristol Education Cttee., 1949. Charles Eliot Norton Lectr., Archaeological Inst. of Amer., 1955-56. F.I.A.L., 1960. President of Classical Assoc., 1961-62. Hon. D.Litt. University of Leeds, 1962. *Publications:* articles in Oxford Classical Dictionary, 1949; The Roman Stage, 1950 (3rd edn., 1963); articles in Oxford Companion to the Theatre, 1951; articles in Cassell's Encyclopædia, 1953; articles in Encyclopædia Britannica, 1957-58 and 1963; Latin Verse and European Song, 1957; The Roman Achievement, 1959; Scholars and Scientists (Presidential address to Classical Assoc.), 1962, etc.; various articles in Classical Review, Classical Quarterly, Hermathena, Revue de Philologie, Classical Philology. *Address:* 27 Belgrave Road, Bristol 8.

[*Died* 28 *July* 1963.

BEATTY, Sir (Alfred) Chester, Kt., *cr.* 1954; F.S.A.; Hon. LL.D.: Dublin, Birmingham; Hon. D.Sc. Columbia, 1928; Vice-Patron (formerly Pres.) of Royal Cancer Hospital; *b.* New York City, 1875; *s.* of John Cuming Beatty, New York, and Hetty, *d.* of William Gedney Bull; naturalized Englishman, 1933; *m.* 1st, 1900, Grace Madeline (*decd.*), *d.* of Alfred Rickard, Denver; one *s.* one *d.*; 2nd, 1913, Edith (*d.* 1952), *d.* of John Dunn, N.Y. City. *Educ.:* Westminster School, Dobbs Ferry, New York; Columbia School of Mines, E.M., 1898; Princeton Univ. Has done much work in America and Northern Rhodesia in connection with mines; Grand Cordon of the Order of St. Sava, 1930; Commander of the Order of Leopold II, 1932; Columbia Univ. Medal, 1933; Gold Medal, Institution of Mining and Metallurgy, 1935; Columbia Engineering School Alumni Association Egleston Medal, 1948. Former Chairman: Selection Trust Ltd.; Consolidated African Selection Trust Ltd.; Sierra Leone Selection Trust Ltd. M.Inst.M.M.; M.Inst.Met. *Recreations:* interested for many

years in collecting Oriental manuscripts, specialising particularly in manuscripts of artistic merit from the point of view of miniatures and calligraphy. *Address:* 10 Ailesbury Road, Dublin, Eire. *Clubs:* Pilgrims', Roxburghe; Kildare St. (Dublin).
[*Died* 19 *Jan.* 1968.

BEATTY, Sir Chester; *see* Beatty, Sir A. C.

BEATTY, Sir Kenneth James, Kt., *cr.* 1926; *s.* of William Beatty, J.P., Yackandandah, Victoria, Australia; *m.* 1919, Gladys, *d.* of B. F. Simpson of Little Friston, East Dean, Eastbourne; one *d.* decd. *Educ.:* Melbourne University. Barrister-at-law, Middle Temple; Public Prosecutor, Transvaal, 1902; Assistant Resident Magistrate, Transvaal, 1903-7; Police Magistrate and Registrar-General, Sierra Leone, 1908; Puisne Judge, Gold Coast Colony, 1921-24; Chief Justice: Bermuda, 1924-27; the Bahamas, 1927-31; Gibraltar, 1931-41; served South African War; Natal and Zululand Rebellion, 1906; European War, 1915-1918. *Publication:* Human Leopards. *Address:* Street Farm House, South Warnborough, nr. Basingstoke, Hants.
[*Died* 17 *Oct.* 1966.

BEAUBIEN, Justine Lacoste (Madame L. de G.), C.B.E. 1943; Bene Merenti, 1927; Doc. (h.c.) Univ. of Montreal, 1936; Pres., Board of Administration, Hôpital Sainte-Justine, Montreal, 1907; *b.* 1 Oct. 1877; *d.* of Sir Alexandre Lacoste and Marie-Louise Globensky; *m.* 1899, L. de G. Beaubien. *Educ.:* Sisters of the Holy Names of Jesus and Mary's Convent, Hochelaga, Montreal. Graduated, 1894. Hon. Fellow American College of Hospital Administrators, 1939; Hon. Member: Amer. Hospital Association, 1948; Canadian Nurses Assoc., 1960, Canadian Conference on Children, 1961; Quebec Hospital Assoc., 1962; Pro Ecclesia & Pontifice, 1949. Dame of Magistral Grace of the Sovereign and Military Order of Malta, 1958. *Address:* 448 St. Catherine Rd., Outremont, P.Q., Can. *T.:* 272-6325.
[*Died* 17 *Jan.* 1967.

BEAUFOY, Samuel Leslie George, C.B.E. 1947; F.R.I.B.A.; M.T.P.I.; Chief Housing and Planning Inspector to Ministry of Housing and Local Government since 1958; Chief Technical Planner, 1947-58; *b.* 28 July 1899; *s.* of Charles Edwin Beaufoy, O.B.E., and Edith Mary (*née* Chidwick); *m.* 1st, Ethel Gwendolin, *d.* of Frederick Barton Dell; one *s.* one *d.*; 2nd, Phyllis Shaw, *d.* of John William Harwood. *Educ.:* Dover Grammar School. R.I.B.A. Distinction in Town Planning; Diploma in Town Planning and Civic Design, London University. R.F.C. and R.A.F. 1917-19. Architectural Assistant to Professor S. D. Adshead, M.A., with whom associated in preparation of numerous Town Planning Schemes. Town Planning Officer, Liverpool Corporation, 1927-33; Min. of Health, Housing and Town Planning Inspector and Chief Inspector, 1933-42; Asst. Sec., Min. of Town and Country Planning, 1942-47. Dir. of Technical Services (Planning) and Chief Technical Planner, 1947-58. Past Pres. T.P.I. *Publications:* Six Aspects of Town Planning, 1932. Contrib. to Technical Press on Town Planning and Civic Design. *Address:* 805 Nelson House, Dolphin Sq., S.W.1. *T.:* Victoria 3800 (Nelson 805).
[*Died* 31 *May* 1961.

BEAUMONT, Air Commodore Frank, C.B. 1947; R.A.F. (retd.); Director British Information Service, Bipartite Control Office, Frankfurt, 1949; *b.* 1896; *s.* of Frederick Gommersall Beaumont; *m.* Baroness Emilia Konitz-Vanek; one *d.* *Educ.:* Cranleigh; Lille; Leipzig. Served European War, 1914-1918, R.F.C. 1915; R.A.F. 1919. Air Attaché, Prague, Vienna, Belgrade, 1934-38. Bomber Command, 1939-42; Director Allied Air Co-operation and foreign liaison, 1942-45; Air Attaché, Belgrade, 1945-48. *Address:* 7 Thieme Strasse, Munich 23, Bavaria, Germany.
[*Died* 27 *Dec.* 1968.

BEAUMONT, Kenneth Macdonald, C.B.E. 1949; D.S.O. 1918; M.A. (Oxon), F.R.P.S.L., F.R.S.A., A.F.R.Ae.S., F.I.D.; Senior partner (since 1936) in law firms of Beaumont & Son and Clarke Rawlins & Co., E.C.2; *b.* 10 Feb. 1884; *s.* of Macdonald Beaumont and Emily (*née* Antonini); *m.* Madeleine St. John (*nee* Brodrick); one *s.* one *d.* *Educ.:* Harrow; Trinity Coll., Oxford. Admitted Solicitor, 1910. Legal adviser of Imperial Airways Ltd., 1925-40; and Director of Imperial Airways (Africa) Ltd. and other subsidiaries; original mem. Legal Cttee. of Internat. Air Traffic Assoc., 1925-45; Rapporteur Général of Air Transport Cttee. of Internat. Chamber of Commerce for about ten years; U.K. rep. on Comité International Technique des Experts Juridiques Seriens from 1945 until Cttee. was dissolved, and thereafter (from 1947-57) U.K. rep. on Legal Cttee. of Internat. Civil Aviation Organization (Chm. 1954-57); first Chm. of Legal Commn. of P.I.C.A.O., 1946; first Chm. London Aeroplane Club (1926-45) and first man to obtain *ab initio* pilot's Licence under Light Aeroplane Club Scheme, 1925. Chm. Air Law Cttee. of Internat. Law Assoc. from its inception; Jt. Chm. Air Law Cttee. of Internat. Bar Assoc.; Chm. British Nat. Cttee. on Air Transport of Internat. Chamber of Commerce; Mem. Legal Cttee. of Internat. Chamber of Commerce; Chm. Board of Westminster Fire Office; President Royal Philatelic Society, London, 1953-56; first Pres. Great Britain Philatelic Society; elected to Roll of Distinguished Philatelists, 1955; Pres. Nat. Skating Assoc. of Gt. Brit., and former member Council Internat. Skating Union. Freeman of the City of London and Past Master of the Cutlers' Company. *Publications:* (with C. N. Shawcross, Q.C.) Air Law; (jointly) The Postage Stamps of Great Britain, Parts III and IV. *Recreations:* formerly rowing (Trial Eights, Oxford, 1904; Capt. College Boat, 1906; skating (rep. Gt. Brit. in figure-skating, singles and pairs, with Mrs. Beaumont, at Olympic Winter Games, 1920; winner Pair-Skating Championship of Gt. Brit., 1921 and 1922). *Address:* 187 Queen's Gate, S.W.7; 15 Devonshire Square, E.C.2. *Clubs:* City of London, Royal Aero, Vincent's; Leander; Walton Heath (only surv. orig. mem.).
[*Died* 24 *April* 1965.

BEAVER, Sir Hugh Eyre Campbell, K.B.E 1956; Kt. 1943; M.Inst.C.E.; M.I.Chem.E.; F.S.A.; F.R.Econ.S.; F.S.S.; F.R.S.A.I.; Director, Richard Thomas & Baldwins Ltd.; Vice-Pres. British Institute of Management; Mem. of Court of Govs. of London Sch. of Economics; Mem. of Council and Treasurer, Univ. of Sussex; Chairman of Council, Tavistock Institute of Human Relations; Hon. Treasurer and Member, The Lister Institute of Preventive Medicine; *b.* 4 May 1890; *s.* of Hugh Edward Campbell Beaver, Bryn Glas, Montgomeryshire, and Cerise, *d.* of John Eyre, Eyrecourt, Co. Galway; *m.* 1925, Jean Atwood (*decd.*), *d.* of Maj. Atwood Beaver, O.B.E., M.D., Pathhead House, Cockburnspath, Berwickshire; two *d.* *Educ.:* Wellington College. Partner in Sir Alexander Gibb and Partners, Consulting Engineers, 1932-42; Director General and Controller General, Ministry of Works, 1940-1945; Managing Director, Arthur Guinness, Son & Co. Ltd., 1946-60, retired. Served as co-opted member Lord Reith's Committee on New Towns, 1946-47; Member Building Industry Working Party, 1948-50; Director, Colonial Development Corporation, 1951-60; Chm. Cttee. on Power

Station Construction, 1952-53; Chm. Cttee. on Air Pollution, 1953-54; Pres., F.B.I., 1957-59; Chm. of Governing Body, Ashridge College, 1958-63; formerly Chm.: Advisory Council for Scientific and Industrial Research; Industrial Fund for Advancement of Scientific Education in Schools; Public Schools Appts. Bureau; formerly Mem., Cttee. of St. Catherine's College, Oxford. Pres., Institution of Chemical Engineers, 1957-59; Pres., Engineers' Guild, 1960-62; formerly, Chm. Council British Inst. of Archaeol., Ankara. Hon. LL.D. (Cantab., T.C.D.); Hon. D.Econ.Sc. (N.U.I.). Hon. Fellow, L.S.E., 1960; Hon. Fellow, St. Catherine's Coll., Oxford. *Address:* Luxford, Crowborough, Sussex. *T.:* Crowborough 373. *Club:* Athenæum. [*Died* 16 *Jan.* 1967.

BEAVERBROOK, 1st Baron, *cr.* 1917, of Beaverbrook, New Brunswick, and Cherkley, Surrey; **William Maxwell Aitken,** P.C. 1918; Bt., *cr.* 1916; Kt., *cr.* 1911; E.D. (Can.), C.D.; *b.* Maple, Ont., Canada, 25 May 1879; 3rd *s.* of late Rev. William Aitken, Minister at Newcastle, New Brunswick, Canada, and Jean Noble of Vaughan, Canada; *m.* 1st, 1906, Gladys (*d.* 1927), 3rd *d.* of late General Charles William Drury, C.B., Halifax, N.S.; one *s.* one *d.* (and one *s.* decd.), 2nd, 1963, Marcia Anastasia, *widow* of Sir James Dunn, 1st Bt., and *d.* of John Christoforides, Leyswood, Withyham, Sussex. *Educ.:* Public (Board) School, Newcastle, New Brunswick. With Canadian Expeditionary Force as Eye-Witness, 1915; Canadian Government Representative at the Front, 1916; Officer in charge Canadian War Records, 1917; M.P. (U.) Ashton-under-Lyne, 1910-16; Chancellor of the Duchy of Lancaster and Minister of Information, 1918; Minister for Aircraft Production, 1940-41; Minister of State, 1941; Minister of Supply, 1941-42; Lord Privy Seal, Sept. 1943-July 1945; Chancellor of University of New Brunswick, 1947-53 (Hon. Chancellor, 1954). Hon. Col. The 1st Bn. of Royal New Brunswick Regt. Hon. LL.D., New Brunswick, 1921, Toronto, 1947, St. Thomas, 1953; Lit.D., Mount Allison, 1948; D.C.L. Bishops Univ., P.Q., 1950. Order of Suvorov (1st Class). *Publications:* Canada in Flanders, 1916; Vol. II, 1917; Success, 1921; Politicians and the Press, 1925; Politicians and the War, 1928; Vol. II, 1932; Resources of the British Empire, 1934; Don't Trust to Luck, 1954; Three Keys to Success, 1956; Men and Power, 1956; Friends, 1959; Courage: The Story of Sir James Dunn, 1961; The Divine Propagandist, 1962; The Decline and Fall of Lloyd George, 1963. *Heir: s.* Hon. Max Aitken, D.S.O. *Clubs:* St. James's (Montreal); Halifax, Toronto, Union (St. John); Royal St. Lawrence Yacht, Royal Kennebecassis Yacht (Canada). [*Died* 9 *June* 1964.

BEAZELEY, Lieut.-Col. George Adam, D.S.O. 1918; *b.* 7 July 1870; *s.* of late Michael Beazeley, M.I.C.E., Civil Engineer, and late Janet Martin Beazeley; *m.* 1900, Annette Cortlandt Anderson (*d.* 1950); four *d.* *Educ.:* Chigwell Grammar School; Cherbourg School, Malvern; Harrow; R.M.A. Woolwich. Commissioned in Royal Engineers, 1890; School of Military Engineering, 1890-92; Cork Harbour, 1892-94; Submarine Mining India, 1894-97; Survey of India, 1897-1925; Somaliland Field Force, 1903-4 (despatches); European War (Mesopotamia) 1916-18, shot down while flying, 2 May 1918, captured by Turks and taken prisoner; repatriated 16 Nov. 1918 (despatches, D.S.O.); on special duty with Air Force, 1919, 1921-22; retired on pension, 1925; Sudan Air Survey, 1929-30; Left Jersey June 1940; A.R.P. work, 1938-42; War work in office of Frank Curtis, Ltd., Totnes, 1942; returned to Jersey, July 1945. *Publication:* Air Reconnaissance and Sketching, Survey of India publications. *Recreations:* formerly interested in most forms of land and water sports; geology, model ship construction; trained in A.R.P. *Address:* Grouville Hall Hotel, Grouville, Jersey, C.I. *T.:* East 35. [*Died* 8 *May* 1961.

BEAZLEY, Col. Sir Geoffrey; *see* Beazley, Col. Sir J. G. B.

BEAZLEY, His Honour Sir Hugh Loveday, Kt. *cr.* 1953; *b.* 16 Oct. 1880; *er. s.* of late Robert Clover Beazley and late Harriett Gertrude Beazley; *m.* 1911, Beatrice Constance Veasey; one *s.* one *d.* (and one *s.* presumed killed, Burma, War of 1939-45, one *d.* (decd.). *Educ.:* Cheltenham College; Oriel College, Oxford; M.A. Called to Bar, Inner Temple, 1905; Master of Bench, Inner Temple, 1941; served in France, 1917-19, King's Liverpool Regiment, Staff First Army Headquarters (despatches); Member of Bar Council, 1924-27; County Court Judge. Circuit No. 16 (Hull and East Riding of Yorks) 1927-34; Circuit No. 38 (Middlesex, Essex and Herts) 1934-37; Judge of Mayor's and City of London Court, 1937-42; Common Serjeant of City of London, 1942-53. President Cheltonian Society, 1947-48. J.P. Herts. *Recreation:* fishing. *Address:* 7 Mill Lane, Broxbourne, Herts. *Club:* Oxford and Cambridge. [*Died* 17 *July* 1964.

BEAZLEY, Col. Sir (James) Geoffrey (Brydon), Kt., *cr.* 1954; M.C.; T.D.; D.L., J.P. Cheshire; Senior Partner, Gracie Beazley Co., Liverpool; *b.* Birkenhead, 23 Sept. 1884; *s.* of late Edwin Arthur Beazley; *m.* 1910, Lilian Edgar, *d.* of late James Edgar Gordon, The Manor, Great Sutton, Wirral, Cheshire; one *s.* one *d.* *Educ.:* Marlborough; Oriel Coll., Oxf. (M.A.). Chairman: Reliance Marine Assurance Co. Ltd.; Director: Liverpool Grain Storage & Transit Co. Ltd.; retired, December 1959, from Mersey Docks and Harbour Board (Chairman 1951-54); Chairman Liverpool Steamship-Owners' Association, 1933 and 1934; President, Liverpool Shipbrokers' Benevolent Soc., 1935 and 1936; Past Pres. Dock-Harbour Authorities Assoc.; High Sheriff, Cheshire, 1944; Pres., Royal Liverpool Seamen's Orphan Institution. Served in Volunteers and T.A., 1906-27; European War, 1914-19, Staff (M.C.); commanded 7th Bn. The King's Regt. (Liverpool), 1923-27; Bt. Col., 1927. Late Hon. Col. 40th (The King's) R.T.R. *Recreations:* shooting and golf. *Address:* Holmfield, Great Sutton, Wirral, Cheshire. *T.A.:* Little Sutton. *T.:* Hooton 3132. *Clubs:* Palatine (Liverpool); Royal Liverpool Golf (Hoylake). [*Died* 29 *March* 1962.

BEAZLEY, Sir John Davidson, C.H. 1959; Kt., 1949; M.A., Hon. D.Litt., Oxford; F.B.A. 1927; Professor of Classical Archæology, Oxford University, 1925-56; Hon. Fell. of Balliol Coll., Oxford; Hon. Fell. of Lincoln Coll., Oxford; Hon. Student of Christ Church, Oxford; *b.* Glasgow, 13 Sept. 1885; *e. s.* of Mark Beazley and Mary Catherine Davidson; *m.* 1919, Marie (*d.* 1967), *d.* of Bernard Bloomfield. *Educ.:* Christ's Hospital; Balliol College, Oxford (Classical Scholar, 1903); Ireland Scholar, 1904; Craven Scholar, 1904; First Class Classical Moderations, 1905; Hertford Scholar, 1905; Gaisford Prize (Prose), 1907; First Class Literæ Humaniores, 1907; Derby Scholar, 1907; Student and Tutor of Christ Church, Oxford, 1908-1925; Sather Professor, Univ. of California, 1949. Hon. Vice-Pres. Greek Archæological Society; Foreign Associate of Académie des Inscriptions et des Belles-Lettres; Foreign Mem. of American Philosophical Soc., Philadelphia, of Amer. Acad., of Archæological Institute of America, of Pontificia Accademia Romana, of Accademia dei Lincei, of Royal Danish Acad., of Austrian Acad. and of Athens Acad.; Hon. Student of the British School at Athens; Hon. Fell. Metropolitan Museum, New York; Petrie Medal, 1937; Kenyon Medal (for Classical Studies) British Academy, 1957. Hon. degrees: Litt.D. Cambridge; LL.D. Glasgow; D.Litt., Durham and Reading; Dr., Paris; Dr., Lyons; Dr.Phil. Marburg; Dr.Phil., Thessalonike; Antonio Feltrinelli Foundation Prize, 1965. *Publications:* Attic Red-figured Vases in Amer. Museums, 1918; The Lewes House Collection of Ancient Gems, 1920; Attische Vasenmaler des rotfigurigen Stils, 1925; Corpus Vasorum Antiquorum, Oxford, I.-II., 1927-31; Greek Vases in Poland, 1928; Attic Black-figure: a Sketch, 1929; Der Berliner Maler, 1930; Der Pan-Maler, 1931; Attic Vase Paintings in Boston (with Caskey), 1931-63; Greek Sculpture and Painting (with Ashmole), 1932; Der Kleophrades-Maler, 1933; Campana Fragments in Florence, 1933; Attic White Lekythoi, 1938; La raccolta Guglielmi (with Magi), 1939; Attic Red-figure Vase-painters, 1942 and 1963; Potter and Painter in Ancient Athens, 1945; Etruscan Vase-painting, 1947; The Development of Attic Black-figure, 1951; Attic Black-figure Vase-painters, 1956; The Berlin Painter, 1965; Paralipomena: additions to Attic Black-figured Vase Painters and to Red-figured Vase Painters, 1969. *Address:* 100 Holywell, Oxford. [*Died* 6 *May* 1970.

BEAZLEY, Lt.-Col. Walter Edwin, C.I.E. 1932; M.C.; I.A., retired; *b.* 26 June 1886; *s.* of late J. H. Beazley, Noctorum, Cheshire; *m.* 1st, 1922, Ida (*d.* 1923), *d.* of Arthur Bazett, Grayshott, Hants; 2nd, 1925, Harriet Huger, *d.* of late Robert Hinshaw-Wilkie, Bricklehampton Hall, Worcs, and Ingleton, Woolton; two *d.* *Educ.:* Rugby; R.M.C., Sandhurst. 2nd Lieut. Indian Army, 1905; joined 54th Sikhs (Frontier Force), 1906; served Zakka Khel Expedition, 1908 (medal with clasp); Captain, 1914; Commandant Indian Signal Service Depot, 1914-15; East African Expeditionary Force, Commandant Divisional Signal Company and Brigade Major, 1915-18 (despatches twice, M.C., Bt. Major); Brigade Major, India, 1919-21; Afghan War, 1919; operations on N.W. Frontier, India, 1920 (two clasps); Staff Officer to Military Adviser-in-Chief, Indian States Forces, 1928-31; Lt.-Col. 1931; Member of the Indian Delegation to Disarmament Conference, 1932-33; retired 1934. *Address:* Reeds, Liss, Hants. *Clubs:* Flyfishers', United Service. [*Died* 8 *June* 1969.

BÉCHERVAISE, Alderman Albert Eric; M.P. (Lab.), 1945-50; *b.* 15 July 1884; *s.* of Richard Rundle Béchervaise; *m.* 1911, Lilian Winifred Lee; one *s.* one *d.* *Educ.:* Mayville School, Leytonstone. Reeve of Leyton Section Epping Forest; Hon. Freeman of Borough of Leyton, 1949 and Hon. Freeman of Borough Waltham Forest; Mem. Metropolitan Water Bd., 1954-1960. *Publications:* articles in local Bulletin. *Recreations:* swimming, cycling, books. *Address:* 347 Cannhall Road, Leytonstone, E.11. *T.:* Maryland 3526. [*Died* 20 *Dec.* 1969.

BECKE, Major Sir Jack, Kt., *cr.* 1944; C.B.E. 1941 (O.B.E. 1931); *b.* 1878; *s.* of Capt. J. Becke, 24th (Marine Bn.) Bombay Native Infantry; *m.* 1908, Enid Mary Margaret, *d.* of Edwyn Jones, Barrister, Bencher Gray's Inn; one *d.* (two *s.* both killed in action, 1944). *Educ.:* Cheltenham. Served in South African War, 1899-1902, trooper Ceylon Mounted Infantry, Lieutenant 32nd Bn. Imperial Yeomanry; joined 4th Lancs Fus., 1903; A.D.C. and Staff Officer, Leeward Islands, 1906-7; served European War, 1914-18 (wounded), 2nd in command 2nd South Lancs; War Office, M.I.5, 1916-18; retired 1918; barrister Gray's Inn, 1918; Chief Constable of Shropshire, 1918-35; Chief Constable of Cheshire, 1935-1946; King's Police Medal, 1937; Silver Jubilee Medal, 1935; King George VI Coronation Medal, 1937. *Recreations:* golf, gardening, tennis, shooting. *Address:* Yew Tree House, Over Tabley, Knutsford, Cheshire. [*Died* 29 *March* 1962.

BECKETT, Sir Eric; *see* Beckett, Sir W. E.

BECKETT, Geoffrey Bernard, C.M.G. 1951; *b.* 28 November 1903; *s.* of Edward Henry Beckett, J.P. and Maude Marion Beckett; *m.* 1933, Phyllis Doreen Mitchell; one *s.* two *d.* *Educ.:* Felsted School; Reading University. Took up ranching and tobacco planting, Northern Rhodesia, 1925; Member or Chairman many farming organisations, 1930-48; President, Northern Rhodesia Farmers' Union, 1947-48. Nominated to Legislature of N. Rhodesia, 1945; elected Member for S.W. Electoral Area, 1948; Member of Executive Council, 1949; Member of delegation to London: on constitutional changes, 1948; on B.S.A. Co. mineral royalties, 1949; Member for Agriculture and Natural Resources, Legislature of Northern Rhodesia, 1949-52. *Recreations:* riding, shooting. *Address:* Momba Farm, Choma, Zambia; Kabulanga, Lusaka, Zambia. *T.:* Choma 14A; Lusaka 2391. *Clubs:* Farmer's; Lusaka (Lusaka, Zambia). [*Died* 9 *July* 1965.

BECKETT, James, C.I.E. 1944; *b.* 25 March 1891; *s.* of William Beckett; *m.* Gwendoline Pauline, *d.* of Wm. Whately, Barrister, Master, Supreme Court, London; one *s.* one *d.* *Educ.:* Villiers School, Limerick. 2nd Div., Home Civil Service, R.I.C. Office, 1910-11; entered Indian Police, 1911; Asst. Insp.-Gen., 1927-30; Deputy Insp.-Gen., 1939-44; retired, 1944. *Recreations:* shooting, golf, bridge. *Address:* c/o National and Grindlay's Bank Ltd., 13 St. James's Square, S.W.1. *T.:* Bishops Cleeve 2510. *Clubs:* East India and Sports; New (Cheltenham). [*Died* 16 *Jan.* 1970.

BECKETT, John Warburton; *see* Addenda: II.

BECKETT, Ronald Brymer; Art Historian; *b.* 17 Jan. 1891; *s.* of James Robertson Beckett and Annie Bertha Murray; *m.* 1918, Norah Ford Anderson; two *d.* *Educ.:* Woodbridge School; Lincoln College, Oxford; University College, London; Middle Temple. Entered Indian Civil Service, 1913; Guardian to the Nawab of Mamdot; Under-Sec. to Government, Punjab, 1921-22; Secretary to Municipal Cttee., Lahore; Dep. Comr., Montgomery, and Colonization Officer, Lower Bari Doab Canal; Registrar, High Court, Lahore, 1927-30; Legal Remembrancer to Government, Punjab, 1937-40; Acting or Additional Judge, High Court, Lahore, 1934-41; Puisne Judge, 1941-46. British Academy award, 1963. *Publications:* Hogarth, 1949; Lely, 1951; annotated vols., Constable's correspondence, 1953-68; (under name of John Anthony) The Story of Hassan, 1928; The Story of Maryam, 1930. *Address:* 7 Farncombe Road, Worthing, Sussex. *T.:* Worthing 1314. *Clubs:* Athenæum, Royal Automobile. [*Died* 1 *Dec.* 1970.

BECKETT, Sir (William) Eric, K.C.M.G., *cr.* 1948 (C.M.G. 1931); Q.C. 1946; M.A.; Legal Adviser to Foreign Office, 1945-53, retired, *b.* 1896; *s.* of late T. A. Beckett, Riverside, Chester; *m.* 1925, Katharine Mary, *y. d.* of late Sir Henry Erle Richards, K.C.S.I., K.C.; two *s.* one *d.* *Educ.:* Sherborne School; Wadham College, Oxford (Scholar). Lieutenant 3rd Battalion The Cheshire Regiment, 1914-18; Capt. 1918; served in France and Salonika; G.S.O. 3, 27 Division, 1918 (Caucasus); 1st class school of Jurisprudence; Eldon Law

Scholar; Fellow of All Souls College, 1921-1928; called to Bar, Inner Temple, 1922; Assistant Legal Adviser Foreign Office, 1925; 2nd Legal Adviser, 1929-45. *Publications:* Articles on Legal Subjects. *Address:* King-o-Mill, Keinton Mandeville, Som. [*Died* 27 *Aug.* 1966.

BEDALE, Rear-Admiral Sir John Leigh, K.B.E., *cr.* 1948; C.B. 1946; *b.* 14 July 1891; *s.* of late Canon F. and Mary Bedale; *m.* 1920, Mary Stewart, Sydenham Hill, S.E.; one *s.* one *d.* *Educ.:* Royal Naval Colleges, Osborne, Dartmouth, and Greenwich. Lieut. 1914; present at battles of Heligoland Bight 1914, Gallipoli 1915, Jutland 1916; Director of Aircraft Maintenance and Repair, Admiralty, 1940-45; A.D.C. to The King, 1944; Rear-Admiral, Reserve Aircraft and Technical Training, 1945; retired list, 1948; F.R.S.A. 1948. *Address:* Four Ways, Somerset West, Cape, S. Africa. [*Died* 7 *July* 1964.

BEDALE, Rev. Stephen Frederick Burstal, S.S.M.: Tutor Kelham Theological College since 1952; *b.* 25 July 1888; *e.s.* of Rev. Frederick Bedale (afterwards Canon of Coventry) and Mary Sarah Eliza Burstal, Ramsgate. *Educ.:* Weymouth Coll.; Exeter Coll., Oxford. Mitchell Exhibitioner, 3rd Cl. Hon. Mods., 2nd Class Hon. Theology, B.A. 1912. Deacon, 1913: Priest, 1914; Assist. Curate St. Thomas, Coventry, 1913-15; Tutor Kelham Theological College, 1916; Temporary Chaplain R.N., 1917-19; Warden of Theological College of Sacred Mission, Kelham, 1922-42; Rector of Averham with Kelham, 1942-43; Director-General of Society of the Sacred Mission, 1943-52; Member Central Advisory Council of Training for the Ministry, 1944-57. *Address:* House of the Sacred Mission, Kelham, Newark, Notts. *T.:* Newark 350. [*Died* 1 *March* 1961.

BEDDINGTON, Mrs. Claude; (Frances Ethel Beddington); *d.* of Francis Berry Mulock, J.P. Bellair, Ballycumber, King's Co. Ireland, and Ethel Annie, *d.* of Rt. Hon. Sir Edward Braddon, P.C., K.C.M.G. *m.*; one *d.* (two *s.* decd.). *Educ.:* mostly on the Continent. Fellow, Royal Philharmonic Society (London). *Publication:* Book of reminiscences, All that I have Met, 1929. *Recreations:* riding, music (amateur pianist), the theatre, yachting, reading, collecting sixteenth-century furniture; launching young artists; helping Under-Dogs; working for Lost Causes; writing; gardening; conversation in four languages; listening to radio; organising. *Address:* 11 Welbeck House, Welbeck Street, W.1. *T.:* Welbeck 8385. *Club:* Bath. [*Died* 19 *Dec.* 1963.

BEDDINGTON, Brigadier Sir Edward Henry Lionel, Kt., *cr.* 1956; C.M.G. 1919; D.S.O. 1917; M.C.; late 16th Lancers; *b.* 1884; *s.* of late Henry Edward Beddington; *m.* 1907, Elsie (*d.* 1955), *d.* of late Raoul H. Foà; two *s.* (and one *s.* decd.). *Educ.:* Eton; Royal Military College, Sandhurst. Served European War, 1914-19 (despatches six times, C.M.G., D.S.O., M.C., Legion of Honour, Commander of Order of Aviz, Order of Sacred Treasure, Bt. Major and Lt.-Col.); served again, 1940-45. D.L. and J.P. Hertfordshire; Chairman Herts C.C., 1952-58; High Sheriff of Hertfordshire, 1948-49. *Address:* Anstey Hall, Buntingford, Herts. *Club:* Cavalry. [*Died* 25 *April* 1966.

BEDDINGTON, Reginald, C.B.E. 1939 (O.B.E. 1920); *b.* 1877; *s.* of late David Lionel Beddington, 4 Sussex Square, W.2; *m.* 1901, Sybil Elizabeth (*d.* 1939), *d.* of late David Quixano Henriques; two *s* one *d.*; *m.* 1951, Betty Inkpen. *Educ.:* Rugby; Corpus Christi College, Oxford. Barrister-at-Law, Lincoln's Inn; Pres. Nat. Assoc. of Fishery Boards, 1930-46; Pres. Freshwater Biological Assoc. of British Empire since 1930; late Member Central Advisory Water Committee and other departmental committees relating to rivers and fisheries; Vice-Pres. Middlesex Hospital, W.1; Chm. Dresden Homes for Poor Ladies, Hove, 1915-; late Headquarters Staff, Metro. Special Constabulary (30 years' service); Organised Fishing for the Forces, 1939-45; late Member Basingstoke R.D.C.; late Pres. Old Basing Horticultural Society; Pres. Old Basing Youth Centre; Vice-Pres. Basingstoke Div., St. John Ambulance Bde. Previously joint editor of Prideaux's Precedents in Conveyancing. *Recreations:* fishing, gardening. *Address:* The Paddock, Old Basing, Hants. *T.:* Basingstoke 786. *Clubs:* Flyfishers', Royal Automobile. [*Died* 11 *March* 1962.

BEDDINGTON-BEHRENS, Sir Edward, Kt. 1957; C.M.G. 1953; M.C.; Ph.D., M.A.; Major; R.A.; student Middle Temple; *b.* 7 Feb. 1897; *s.* of late Walter Behrens, Pres. British Chamber of Commerce in Paris, and Evelyn, *d.* of late S. H. Beddington; *m.* 1st, 1931, Barbara, *d.* of Sir Montague Burton; one *d.*; 2nd, 1944, Princess Irena Obolensky (marriage dissolved, 1957); one *s.* one *d.*; 3rd, 1958, Mrs. Renèe Kane. *Educ.:* Charterhouse; R.M.A., Woolwich U(nder-Officer); Christ Church, Oxford (blue, athletics); London Univ. (Ph.D. Econ.). Served European War, 1915-18 (despatches, M.C. and bar); War of 1939-45, served as regimental officer Belgian Campaign and Dunkirk and G.S.O. with G.H.Q., B.E.F. Permanent Secretariat of League of Nations (I.L.O.), 1921-24; rep League of Nations at numerous internat. confs.; occasional lectr. London Sch. of Economics; instrumental in forming Nat. Housing Cttee., 1934, and Army League, 1937; Vice-Pres. European League for Economic Co-operation; Chm. Central and Eastern European Commission, 1952; Vice-Chm. and one of founder members of European Movement; Chief Organiser Commonwealth Conf. of European League for Economic Co-operation, 1951, and Central and Eastern European Conf., 1952, Chairman: European Industrial Conf., 1958; Polit. and Economic Conf. of the Seven, 1960; Conf. on Central and Eastern Europe, Brussels, 1963; Conf. on European Co-operation in Advanced Technology, 1965; European Telecommunications Conf., 1967. Former President, Army League; President of the European Atlantic Group. Chairman: Jeremiah Ambler Ltd.; Ocean Trust Co. Ltd.; Bedco Ltd. *Publications:* Look Back, Look Forward, 1963; Why Britain must join Europe, 1966; numerous articles on political and economic questions. *Recreations:* ski-ing, music, archæology; translating French books. *Address:* Chesham House, Chesham Place, S.W.1. *T.:* Belgravia 5667; Park House, Abinger Common, Surrey. *T.:* Abinger 412 and 401. *Clubs:* Reform, Queen's, Hurlingham; Union Interalliée (Paris). [*Died* 28 *Nov.* 1968.

BEDDOW, Lt.-Col. (Hon. Col.) Arnold Bellamy, C.I.E. 1935; V.D.; *b.* 1883; *s.* of Frederick Beddow, St. Lawrence, Isle of Wight; *m.* Marie Virginia (*d.* 1941), *d.* of J. J. Meagher of Montreal; one *d.*; 2nd, 1946, Anne St. John Hickman. *Address:* The Dairy House, Dedham, Essex. *T.:* Dedham 2271. [*Died* 28 *Oct.* 1965.

BEDFORD, Richard Perry, R.W.A., F.S.A.; *b.* 15 Nov. 1883; 2nd *s.* of George Bedford, Headmaster of Torquay School of Art; *m.* 1914, Ethel Pearl Donisthorpe (*d.* 1964); two *s.* one *d.* *Educ.:* Dean Close Sch., Cheltenham. Appointed to Victoria and Albert Museum, 1903; Keeper, Dept. of Sculpture, 1924-38, Dept. of Circulation,

1938-46; Curator of Pictures, Ministry of Works, 1947-48. Exhibited sculpture at Royal Academy, Lefèvre Galleries (one-man show, 1936), Leicester, Beaux-Arts, New Burlington, and Princes Galls., Open Air Sculpture Exhibition, Battersea Park, 1948; The Minories, Colchester (one-man show), 1960. Drawings in the Victoria and Albert Museum. B.B.C. (Television), at Empire Exhibition, Glasgow, Hamburg, and elsewhere. *Publications:* St. James the Less, 1911; articles and reviews in Dictionary of National Biography, Encyclopaedia Britannica, Burlington Magazine, Connoisseur, Artwork, Kunstkronik, Thieme's Künstlerlexikon, etc. *Recreation:* gardening. *Address:* Daisybank, Firs Chase, West Mersea, Essex.
[*Died* 3 *Oct.* 1967.

BEDSON, Sir Samuel Phillips, Kt., *cr.* 1956; F.R.S. 1935; M.D., M.Sc., B.S., Hon. D.Sc. (Belfast and Durham); F.R.C.P.; Professor Emeritus of Bacteriology, London University, since 1952; *b.* 1 Dec. 1886; *s.* of late Peter Phillips Bedson; *m.* 1926, Dorothea Annie Hoffert; three *s.* *Educ.:* Abbotsholme School; Armstrong College and Durham University College of Medicine, Newcastle on Tyne. B.Sc. (Distinction in Zoology), 1907; M.B., B.S. (Hons.) 1912; M.D. (Gold Medal) and M.Sc., 1914; studied bacteriology at Pasteur Institute, Paris, 1912-13; British Medical Research Scholar at Lister Institute, 1913-14; War Service, 1914-19; commission in Northumberland Fusiliers (8th Bn.), 1914-16; wounded Gallipoli, 1915; transferred to R.A.M.C., 1916; Assistant Adviser in Pathology, 5th Army, 1918; Assistant in the Department of Bacteriology, College of Medicine, Newcastle on Tyne, 1919; Assistant Bacteriologist, Lister Institute, London, 1921; seconded for service with the Foot and Mouth Research Committee, 1942; Senior Freedom Research Fellow, London Hospital, 1926; Goldsmiths' Co. Prof. of Bacteriology, University of London (London Hospital and Medical Coll.), 1934-52; Adviser in Pathology to Ministry of Health, 1949-60; Research appointment (Virology) Middlesex Hospital Medical College, 1953-62. Hon. Fell. R.S.M. *Publications:* (jointly with Downie, MacCallum and Stuart Harris) Virus and Rickettsial Diseases, 1950; numerous scientific papers, mainly on viruses and virus diseases. *Recreations:* gardening, fishing. *Address:* 37 Woodruff Avenue, Hove 4, Sussex.
[*Died* 11 *May* 1969.

BEEBE, William; Director of the Society's Department of Tropical Research and Hon. Curator of Birds of the New York Zoological Society since 1899; *b.* Brooklyn, 29 July 1877; *m.* 1927, Elswyth Thane, novelist. *Educ.:* Columbia University; D.Sc., etc. *Publications:* Two Bird Lovers in Mexico, 1905; The Bird, 1906; The Log of the Sun, 1906; Our Search for a Wilderness, 1910; Tropical Wild Life, 1917; Monograph of the Pheasants, 1918; Jungle Peace, 1919; The Edge of the Jungle, 1922; Galápagos World's End, 1924; Jungle Days, 1925; The Arcturus Adventure, 1926; Pheasants: Their Lives and Homes; Pheasant Jungles, 1927; Beneath Tropic Seas, 1928; Nonsuch: Land of Water, 1932; Exploring with Beebe, 1932; Field Book of Bermuda Shore Fishes, 1933; Half Mile Down, 1934; Zaca Venture, 1938; A Book of Bays, 1942; The Book of Naturalists, 1944; High Jungle, 1949; Unseen Life of New York, 1953; Adventuring with Beebe, 1955; besides several hundred technical scientific monographs and treatises. *Address:* N.Y. Zoological Park, New York City 60. *Club:* Explorers' (New York).
[*Died* 4 *June* 1962.

BEECH, Francis William, C.B.E. 1952; *b.* 5 June 1885; *e. s.* of Zachariah and Emma Beech; *m.* 1st, 1914, Florence Hannah Mary Jenkins (*d.* 1963); one *d.*; 2nd, 1963, Phyllis Alexandra Cooper. *Educ.:* Long Ashton, Bristol; Lewis School, Pengam. Solicitor, 1911. Served European War, 1915 and on to 1926; M.P. (C.) West Woolwich, 1943-45; Major and Staff Paymaster, R.A.P.C.; Dep. Chm. L.C.C., 1952-53. Freeman, City of London; J.P., Co. London. Freeman, Metropolitan Borough of Woolwich, 1952; Mayor of Woolwich, 1955-56. Serving Brother, Order of St. John of Jerusalem. *Recreations:* reading and motoring. *Address:* 6 Shelley Court, Parkleys, Ham Common, Surrey. *Club:* Royal Automobile.
[*Died* 21 *Feb.* 1969.

BEECHAM, Sir Thomas, 2nd Bt., *cr.* 1914; Kt. 1916; C.H. 1957; conductor, composer, and operatic impresario; *b.* 29 April 1879; *s.* of 1st Bt. and Josephine Burnett (*d.* 1934); *S.* father 1916; *m.* 1st, 1903, Utica (from whom he obtained a divorce at Boise, Idaho, 1943), *d.* of Dr. Charles S. Welles, New York, and Ella Celeste Miles; two *s.*; 2nd, 1943, Betty (*d.* 1958), *d.* of Dr. and Mrs. Morg n Humby, London; 3rd, 1959, Shirley Hudson. *Educ.:* Rossall; Wadham College, Oxford. *Publications:* A Mingled Chime, 1944; Frederick Delius, 1958. *Relevant Publications:* Thomas Beecham: An Independent Biography (by Charles Reid), 1961; Sir Thomas Beecham (by Neville Cardus), 1961. *Recreations:* writing, composing. *Heir:* *s.* Adrian Beecham. *Address:* c/o Philip Emanuel, 74 Great Russell Street, W.C.1.
[*Died* 8 *March* 1961.

BEECHMAN, Captain Nevil Alexander (Alec), M.C.; Q.C. 1947; *o. surv. s.* of late N. C. and Emily Beechman; *m.* Mrs. Mary Gwendolen Caradoc Williams, *widow* of Capt. Garth Caradoc Williams, R.E. *Educ.:* Westminster School (King's Scholar); Balliol Coll., Oxford (Domus Exhibitioner in Classics; M.A.). Pres. Oxford Union, 1921; first post-war chm. Oxford Univ. Liberal Club; chairman Union of University Liberal Societies, 1922; served in France and Belgium during European War with King's Royal Rifle Corps; Captain, 1917 (M.C., wounded); subsequently instructor of officer cadets; Member of Select Committee on National Expenditure (Naval Services sub-Committee); M.P. (L. Nat.) St. Ives, 1937-1950; formerly Parliamentary Private Secretary to Minister of Overseas Trade; Parliamentary Private Secretary to Under-Secretary of State, Dominions Office, 1940; to Minister of Health, 1941-42; Chief Whip of Liberal National Party, 1942-45; a Lord Commissioner of the Treasury, 1943-45; mem. St. Ives Local Authority. *Address* Wharf House, St. Ives, Cornwall.
[*Died* 6 *Nov.* 1965.

BEEMAN, Eng. Rear-Adm. Sir Robert, K.B.E. *cr.* 1935; C.B. 1935; C.M.G. 1919; R.N., retd.; *m.* 1944, Vera, *widow* of Baron Jules de Catelin. Late Naval A.D.C. to the King; served European War, 1914-19 (C.M.G.); Eng. Rear-Adm. 1931; Deputy Engineer-in-Chief, Admiralty, 1932-35; retired list, 1935; Special Director of Vickers-Armstrongs, Ltd., and engineering manager of Barrow works, 1935-44, retired, 1944. *Club:* Athenæum.
[*Died* 10 *Sept.* 1963.

BEER, Harry, C.B. 1949; Under-Secretary, Board of Trade, 1946-56; *b.* 23 April 1896; *m.* 1929, Dorothy, *d.* of J. O. H. Foster; two *s.* *Educ.:* Ipswich Middle School. Admiralty, 1914; R.N.V.R. 1918-19; Reparations Commission, 1920-23; Board of Trade, 1923; Private Secretary to President, 1938-1940; Private Secretary to Minister of Supply, 1940-41. Principal Assistant Secretary, Ministry of Supply, 1941; Board of Trade, 1946. *Recreation:* walking. *Address:* Hillside, Churston Rise, Seaton, Devon. *T.:* Seaton 583.
[*Died* 3 *Jan.* 1970.

BEEVOR, Rt. Rev. Humphry; Rector of Litchborough with Maidford since 1964;

b. 24 Aug. 1903; *s.* of Rowland and Margaret Frances Beevor; *m.* 1955, Mary Elizabeth Seaton. *Educ.:* Winchester; Oriel College, Oxford. B.A. 1926; M.A. 1929. St. Stephen's House, Oxford, 1926-28; Deacon, 1928; Priest, 1929; Assistant Curate, St. Mark's, Swindon, 1928-30; Librarian, Pusey House, Oxford, 1930-37; Chaplain, Shrewsbury School, 1937-41. Served War of 1939-1945, Chaplain, R.N.V.R. (in H.M.S. Malaya, Valiant, Adamant), 1941-46. Assistant Editor, Church Times, 1947, Editor, 1948-50; Priest-in-charge, St. Mary and St. George, West Wycombe, 1950-52; Bishop of Lebombo, 1952-57; Senior Chaplain, The King's School, Canterbury, 1957-60; Chaplain: St. John's Church, Montreux, 1961; St. George's Châtelard Schools, 1961-1964; *Publications:* (Ed.) Catholic Sermons, 1932; The Anglican Armoury, 1933; Peace and Pacifism, 1937; Lord of our Life, 1948. *Recreations:* foreign travel; Victorian novels. *Address:* Litchborough Rectory, Towcester, Northants. *Clubs:* Bath; R.N.V.R.; Stephen's Green (Dublin).

[*Died* 12 *June* 1965.

BEHAN, Brendan; author in Irish and English; *b.* 9 Feb. 1923; *s.* of Stephen and Kathleen Behan; *m.* 1955, Beatrice Salkeld; one *d.* *Educ.:* French Sisters of Charity, North William St., Dublin. Member of I.R.A. from 1937; sentenced three years Borstal, Liverpool, 1939; fourteen years by military court, Dublin, 1942. *Publications:* The Quare Fellow (play), 1956 (filmed 1962); Borstal Boy (novel), 1958; The Hostage (play), 1959; Brendan Behan's Island: An Irish Sketch-book, 1962; Hold Your Hour and Have Another, 1963; The Big House (play), 1963; Brendan Behan's New York (illus. Paul Hogarth, posthumous), 1964. *Relevant Publication:* Brendan Behan by Ulick O'Connor, 1970. *Recreations:* drinking, talking, and swimming. *Address:* 5 Anglesea Rd., Dublin.

[*Died* 20 *March* 1964.

BEHRENS, Sir Edward B.; *see* Beddington-Behrens.

BELCH, Alexander, C.B.E. 1943; Controller, The Shipbuilding Conference, 1952-57, retired (Dep. Chm. 1937-52, Actg. Chm. 1939-44); *e. s.* of late David B. Belch; *m.* 1st, 1915, Agnes Wright Ross (*d.* 1935); two *s.* one *d.*; 2nd, 1937, Freda Walker Jones (*d.* 1954). Sec. Shipbuilding Employers' Fedn., 1931-37. Founder Member, British Institute of Management; Life Mem. Inst. of Journalists; Life M.I.Mar.E.; Life Mem. R.S.A.; Mem. Worshipful Company of Shipwrights; Freeman of London (as Mem. Shipwrights Livery); Hon. Pres., London Ayrshire Soc., 1957-60 (Sec. for 20 years until 1939); Mem. Governing Body of Navy League (10 years until 1963 inclusive); Associate Mem. of Council, R.I.N.A., until 1961; Mem. of Finance Cttee. of R.I.I.A. until 1961. *Address:* West Lindores House, Upper Flat, 158 Finnart St., Greenock, Renfrewshire.

[*Died* 15 *Oct.* 1967.

BELCHER, Sir Charles Frederic, Kt., *cr.* 1931; O.B.E. 1923; M.A., LL.B.; *b.* Geelong, Australia, 11 July 1876; *s.* of George Frederick Belcher, M.L.C., Victoria; *m.* 1908, Sara (*d.* 1965), *d.* of Harman Visger, London; one *s.* one *d.* *Educ.:* Geelong; Trinity Coll., Melbourne (Final Scholarship, Classics and Comparative Philology, 1897; Shakespeare Scholarship, 1898). Admitted to practise Victoria, 1902; called to Bar, Gray's Inn, 1909 (Certificate of Honour); Conveyancer, Uganda, 1914; Magistrate, Uganda, 1916; Assistant Judge, Zanzibar, 1920; acting Puisne Judge Kenya, 1920; Member of H.M.'s Court of Appeal for Eastern Africa, 1920 and 1925; Attorney-General, Nyasaland, 1920; Judge of the High Court, Nyasaland, 1924-27; Chief Justice of Supreme Court of Cyprus, 1927-30; Presided H.M.'s Court of Appeal for Egypt, June 1928; Chief Justice of Trinidad and Tobago, and President West India Appeal Court, 1930-36; retired, 1937. Chairman, Kenya Customs Frauds Enquiry Commission, 1940; Coffee Control Commission, 1941; Defence Advisory Committee, 1939-45; Kenya Museums Trustees, 1941-45; Central and Coast Rent Control Boards, 1949-50; Immigration Appeals Tribunal, 1947-50; Air Transport Licensing Advisory Tribunal, 1947-51. Chief Legal Adviser, Civil Affairs Branch, East Africa Command, 1942-45. Jubilee Medal, 1935. *Publications:* Birds of the District of Geelong, Australia, 1914; Nyasaland Birds, 1930. *Recreation:* field ornithology. *Address:* 143 Hope Street, Kokstad, Cape Province, South Africa.

[*Died* 7 *Feb.* 1970.

BELCHER, John William; *b.* 1905; *e. s.* of John Thomas and Lillie Belcher, Chakrata, Heathside, Hounslow; *m.* 1927, Louise Moody; one *s.* two *d.* *Educ.:* Latymer Upper School, Hammersmith; London University. Railway Official. Lecturer, M.O.I., 1940-45; Parliamentary Secretary, Board of Trade, 1946-48; M.P. (Lab.) Sowerby Division of West Riding of Yorks, 1945-49. Fellow Royal Economic Soc. *Publications:* various contributions to Trade Union Journals and Press. *Recreations:* gardening, music. *Address:* 34 Bycullah Road, Enfield, Mx. *T.:* Enfield 8823.

[*Died* 26 *Oct.* 1964.

BELCHER, Rt. Rev. Wilfrid Bernard, M.C. 1918; Rector of Ovington with Itchen Stoke with Abbotstone, Alresford, since 1961; *m.* 1940, Mary Calway, M.A. 1920; Bishop's College, Cheshunt, 1920; Deacon, 1921; Priest, 1922; Vicar of Rickmansworth, 1934-41; of Cheshunt, 1941-45; Chaplain Royal Masonic Institute for Girls, 1934-41; Rural Dean of Watford, 1936-40; Proctor in Convocation, St. Albans, 1941-45; Vicar of St. Thomas, Durban, 1946-47; Bishop of North Queensland, 1947-1952; Assistant Bishop of Norwich and Rector of Diss, 1953-55; Vicar of York cum Ravensworth, Natal, 1955-58, retired. *Address:* Ovington Rectory, Alresford, Hants.

[*Died* 28 *Jan.* 1963.

BELDEN, Rev. Albert David, B.D. London University; D.D. Ursinus, U.S.A.; Founder Director Pax Christi League; *b.* 109 Gt. Dover Street, 17 Feb. 1883; *s.* of William Belden, boot tree and last manufacturer of Great Dover Street, London, S.E., and Esther Belden; *m.* 1st, 1909, Doris Hunter (*d.* 1961), *d.* of James W. Richman, Ramsgate; one *s.*; 2nd, 1962, Cecily Maud Glenister. *Educ.:* Wilson's Grammar School, Camberwell; New College, Hampstead. In business, 1897-1902; six years at New Coll., Hampstead, Univ. of London, B.D.; Minister of South Bar Church, Banbury, 1908-12; first Minister of Crowstone Congregational Church, Westcliff-on-Sea, 1912-27; Superintendent Minister, Whitefield's Central Mission Church, Tottenham Court Road, London, 1927-39; Pilgrim Fathers Memorial Chruch, Southwark, S.E.1, 1956-58, Minister Emeritus Vice-Pres. Univ. of London Soc., Examiner and Chm. Philosophical Soc. of England, Pres. British Union Abolition of Vivisection, Exec. Mem. Labour Peace Fellowship; Dir. St. Pancras Bldg. Soc. *Publications:* George Whitefield, the Awakener; Does God Really Care?; The Greater Christ; God's Better Thing; The Religious difficulties of Youth; Voices of the Great Creator; When Power Comes; The Harmony of Life; The Commands of the King; The Teachings of the King; The Way to Live; The Boys and Girls of the Bible; The Game of Life; What is your Name?; Banners of Gold; The Silver

Lining; Chalices of Cheer, Pax Christi; The Practice of Prayer; Pilgrims of the Impossible; The Paradoxes of Jesus; One Hundred Tales Worth Telling; More Tales Worth Telling, etc.; contributor to religious press in England, Dominions, and America; columnist Manchester Evening News. *Address:* 1 Ulva Road, Putney, S.W.15. *T.:* Putney 0889. [*Died* 14 *Dec.* 1964.

BELGRAVE, Sir Charles (Dalrymple), K.B.E., *cr.* 1952 (C.B.E. 1936); Financial Adviser to the Govt. of Bahrain, 1926-57; *b.* 9 Dec. 1894; *s.* of Dalrymple James Belgrave, Barrister-at-law, and Isabel Richardson; *m.* 1926, Marjorie Lepel, Kaisar-i-Hind medal, silver, 1945, *o. d.* of Sir (Richard) Fynes Barrett-Lennard, 4th Bt.; one *s.* *Educ.:* Bedford; Lincoln College, Oxford. Served European War in various Camel Corps, in the Sudan, Egypt and Palestine, Darfur Expedition, 1915 (Sudan medal and clasp); seconded for services with the Egyptian Government in the Frontier Districts Administration, Siwa Oasis, 1920-21; Administrative Officer in Tanganyika Territory, 1924-25. Order of Al Rafidain (Iraq), 1952; Commander of Order of Dannebrog (Denmark), 1957. Lawrence of Arabia Medal, Royal Central Asian Society, 1967. *Publications:* Siwa, The Oasis of Jupiter Ammon, 1923; Personal Column, 1960; The Pirate Coast, 1966; numerous contributions to journals and magazines on eastern subjects. *Address:* 53 Victoria Rd., W.8. *Clubs:* Travellers'; Guerrière (Boston, U.S.A.). [*Died* 28 *Feb.* 1969.

BELHAVEN and STENTON, 12th Baron, *cr.* 1647; **Robert Alexander Benjamin Hamilton;** Lt.-Col., retd.; *b.* 16 Sept. 1903; *o. s.* of 11th Baron Belhaven and Stenton, C.I.E., and Kathleen Gonville (*d.* 1935), *d.* of Col. Sir Benjamin Bromhead, 4th Bt., C.B., Thurlby Hall, Lincoln; *S.* father 1950; *m.* 1st, 1926, Heather Mildred Carmichael, *d.* of Lt.-Col. R. C. Bell, D.S.O., O.B.E.; one *s.*; 2nd, 1942, Cyrilla Mary, *d.* of late Raymund Binns, The Green Howards; one *d.* decd. *Educ.:* Eton; R.M.C. Sandhurst (Sword of Honour, 1924). R.S.F., 1924-34; seconded to Aden Protectorate Levies, 1931; A.D.C. etc., British Mission to Yemen, 1934; retired from Army, 1934; Colonial Administrative Service (Aden Protectorate), 1934; retired, 1946. War of 1939-45, Africa, Italy stars; Lt.-Col. Comdg. Mil. Mission 106, which failed, 1940-41; sick list, 1941-42; Capt. W.O. Selection Bds., 1943; Major A.M.G.O.T., N. Africa, 1943; Mil. Governor, Caserta District, 1943-44; Lt.-Col. Provincial Comr., Province of Grosseto, 1944; Provincial Comr., Pistoia and Lucca Provinces, 1945; Liaison Officer for Allied Commn. with Gen. Officer Comdg. N. Italy, 1946; retd. from Army, 1946. *Concittadino* of cities of Caserta, Grosseto, Lucca and Viareggio. Chm. Motherwell and Wishaw Unionist Assoc., 1946-51; Exec. Scottish Covenant Assoc. F.R.G.S.; F.R.C.A.S. *Publications:* The Old House (novel), 1936; The Arabian Carpet and Other Verses; The Kingdom of Melchior, 1950; The Eagle and the Sun (historical novel), 1951; The Uneven Road, 1955; various lectures and articles. *Heir:* *s.* Master of Belhaven. *Address:* Barlay, Balmaclellan, Kirkcudbrightshire. [*Died* 10 *July* 1961.

BELL, Arthur Doyne Courtenay, M.A., D.M. (Oxford); F.R.C.P.; Consulting Physician (lately Physician in Charge of Children's Department), Charing Cross Hospital; Physician Belgrave Children's Hospital; Hon. Physician, Children's Department, Queen Mary's Hospital for the East End of London; Member of Board of Governors and Chairman of Planning Committee, Charing Cross Hospital; Examiner in Medicine and Child Health, Royal College of Physicians: Examiner in Pædiatrics, Univ. of Birmingham; *b.* 15 June 1900; *s.* of Robert Arthur Bell and Evelyn Maud (*née* Richardson). *Educ.:* Gresham's School; St. John's College, Oxford (open Scholar and Adrian Graves Memorial Exhibitioner); St. Thomas's Hospital. Perkins' Travelling Fellowship, Vienna, 1931. Chief Asst., Children's dept., St. Thomas's Hosp., 1932; Examiner for Diploma in Child Health, R.C.S., 1947. Mem. of Worshipful Soc. of Apothecaries; Freeman of City of London; F.R.Soc.Med. Past Pres. Paediatric Section, Roy. Soc. Med.; Past Pres. W. London Med. Chirurgical Soc. *Publications:* communications to Med Jls. *Recreations:* angling and deipnosophism. *Address:* (residence) 14A Compton Road, Canonbury, N.1. *T.:* Canonbury 8731; 144 Harley Street, W.1. *T.:* Welbeck 9770. *Clubs:* Savile, United University; Wilton Fly-fishing. [*Died* 16 *Sept.* 1970.

BELL, Colonel Arthur Hugh, D.S.O. 1916; O.B.E. 1919; Chairman of G. Bell & Sons, Ltd., Publishers; late Royal Engineers; *s.* of late Edward Bell and Alice Hoets; *b.* Hampstead, 16 April 1878; *m.* 1905, Gabrielle, *d.* of late J. Kennedy, I.C.S. *Educ.:* Charterhouse; R.M.A. Woolwich. Commissioned 2nd Lieut. 1898; served S. African War, 1900-02 (Queen's medal with 3 clasps, King's medal with two clasps); European War, 1915-16 (wounded, D.S.O., despatches); engaged in military and public works on N.W. Frontier of India, 1916-20 (O.B.E., 1915 Star, G.S. medal, Victory medal, despatches); served in operations in Waziristan, 1917 (despatches); 3rd Afghan War, 1919 (medal, clasp, and despatches); Waziristan, 1919-20 (clasp, despatches); South Ireland during rebellion, 1920-21; Chanak, 1922-23; retired pay, 1928. *Publications:* a few articles in a military journal; translator of The Modern Dowser, Water Diviners and their Methods, The Elements of Dowsing, How to Dowse; editor, Practical Dowsing. *Recreations:* walking, archæology. *Address:* The Old Vicarage, Cuckfield, Sussex. *Club:* Bath. [*Died* 21 *Feb.* 1968.

BELL, Charles Francis, M.A., F.S.A., Hon. A.R.I.B.A.; *b.* 28 April 1871; 4th *s.* of Robert Courtenay Bell and Clara, *e. d.* of Ambrose Poynter, architect. Asst. Keeper, Ashmolean Museum, 1896; Keeper of Dept. of Fine Art, Ashmolean Museum, Oxford, 1909-31; Fellow of Magdalen College, 1905-1931; Sec. to Committee of Oxford Exhibitions of Historical Portraits, 1904-06; a Trustee of the National Portrait Gallery, 1910-40. *Address:* 4 Inverness Gardens, Vicarage Gate, W.8. [*Died* 3 *April* 1966.

BELL, Sir Charles R. F. M.; *see* Morrison-Bell.

BELL, Claude Waylen, M.C. 1916; President Bell's Asbestos and Engineering (Holdings), Ltd. (formerly Bell's Asbestos and Engineering Ltd.) since 1963 (a Director; Chairman, 1938-63); *b.* 22 February 1891; *s.* of late Francis Carbutt Bell and Maud Constance Bell (afterwards Baird); *m.* 1915, Marie Kathleen, *o. d.* of late C. H. West, C.I.E.; two *s.* (one *d.* decd.); *m.* 1956, Dolores Brenda Lamer (*née* Foreman). *Educ.:* Summerfields, Oxford; Eton. Asst. Manager in Forbes, Forbes, Campbell & Co. Ltd., at Karachi, 1910-15; Intelligence Corps, 1915-1918; Asst. Military Attaché, The Hague, 1916-17; Hon. rank of Capt. on demobilisation, 1919. Joined Bell's United Asbestos Co. Ltd., 1919-29; formed Bell's Asbestos and Engineering Ltd., 1929, and became first jt. Man. Dir., subsequently Chairman; Company floated publicly, 1948. *Recreation:* horse racing *Address:* 6 Farley Court, Melbury Road, W.14. *Clubs:* Eccentric, Royal Automobile; several race-course. [*Died* 12 *July* 1964.

BELL, Clive; writer on art and literature; *b.* 1881; *m.* 1907, Vanessa (*d.* 1961), *e. d.* of Sir Leslie Stephen, K.C.B.; two *s.* one *d.* *Educ.:* Marlborough; Trinity College, Cambridge (Exhibitioner, Earl of Derby student). Chevalier of Legion of Honour, 1936. *Publications:* Art, 1914; Peace at Once, 1915; Pot Boilers, 1918; Poems, 1921; Since Cézanne, 1922; On British Freedom, 1923; The Legend of Monte della Sibilla, 1920; Landmarks in Nineteenth Century Painting, 1927; Civilization, 1928; Proust, 1929; An Account of French Painting, 1931; Enjoying Pictures, 1934; Old Friends, 1956. *Address:* Charleston, Firle, Lewes, Sussex. *Clubs:* Beefsteak, Travellers'. [*Died* 18 *Sept.* 1964.

BELL, Enid Moberly, M.A. Cantab.; *b.* 24 March 1881; *d.* of late Charles Frederic Moberly Bell, sometime Managing Director of The Times, and Ethel Chataway. *Educ.:* Francis Holland School; Newnham College, Cambs. Taught Auckland House, Simla and Whitelands College School, Chelsea; Head Mistress, Lady Margaret School, Parsons Green, S.W.6., 1917-47. *Publications*. Life and Letters of C. F. Moberly Bell, 1927; History of Francis Holland School, 1939; Octavia Hill: A Biography, 1942; Flora Shaw, Lady Lugard 1947; Storming the Citadel, 1953; History of Church Schools Company, 1958; The Story of Hospital Almoners, 1961; Josephine Butler, a Biography, 1963. *Address:* 7 Mallord Street, Chelsea, S.W.3. *T.:* Flaxman 2163. *Club:* University Women's. [*Died* 13 *April* 1967.

BELL, Sir Francis Gordon, K.B.E., *cr.* 1953; M.C. 1917; F.R.C.S.; F.R.A.C.S.; Emeritus Professor of Surgery, University of Otago, New Zealand (Professor, 1925-52, retired); *b.* New Zealand, 1887; *s.* of W. Bell, Marlborough; *m.* 1916, Marion W. (*d.* 1968), *d.* of W. Austin, Edinburgh; one *s.* three *d.* *Educ.:* Marlborough Coll.; Edinburgh Univ. (M.D.); Vans Dunlop Scholar, Ettles Scholar, Goodsir Memorial Fellow Research Scholar and demonstrator in Anatomy. House Surgeon Royal Infirmary, Edinburgh; appts. Stanley and Salford Royal Hospitals, Liverpool; postgraduate study in Germany and at Mayo Clinic, U.S.; served European War, R.A.M.C. (despatches, M.C.). Surgeon Tutor, Royal Infirmary, Edinburgh, 1920-1923; Asst. Surg., 1924. *Publications:* contributions to medical jls., etc. *Address:* 45 Rewa Street, Dunedin, New Zealand. [*Died* 28 *Feb.* 1970.

BELL, Frank, M.A. (Cantab.); *b.* 1878; *s.* of late J. F. Bell, J.P., of North End, Durham; *m.* Esther Mary, *d.* of late Captain N. W. Apperley, M.V.O.; three *s.* one *d.* Served European War, 1914-18 (despatches); Hon. Capt. in Army; J.P.; D.L. Co. Durham; Joint-Master North Durham Hunt, 1918-23. *Address:* Little Newsham Hall, Winston, Darlington. [*Died* 16 *Feb.* 1961.

BELL, Sir (Harold) Idris, Kt., *cr.* 1946; C.B. 1936; O.B.E. 1920; F.B.A., M.A. (Oxon.), Hon. LL.D. (Liverpool), Hon. D.Litt. (Wales, Michigan, and Brussels); *b.* Epworth, Lincs., 2 Oct. 1879; *s.* of Charles Christopher Bell and Rachel Hughes; *m.* 1911, Mabel Winifred (*d.* 1967), *d.* of Ernest Ayling; three *s.* *Educ.:* Nottingham High School; Oriel Coll., Oxford; Univs. of Berlin and Halle. Assistant in the Department of MSS., British Museum, 1903; Deputy-Keeper of MSS., 1927; Keeper of the MSS. and Egerton Librarian, British Museum, 1929-1944; Hon. Reader in Papyrology, Oxford, 1935-50; Hon. Secretary of Egypt Exploration Society, 1923-27, Vice-President since 1945; corresponding member of the Bavarian (1928), Bologna (1934), Belgian (1945) and Norwegian (1946) Academies and of Fondation Égyptologique Reine Élisabeth, Brussels (1939); Member of the Archäologisches Institut des Deutschen Reiches (1934); Membre associé de l'Institut d'Égypte (1940); Foreign Member of the American Philosophical Soc. (1941); Corr. mem. Académie des Inscriptions et Belles-Lettres, Paris, 1947; Société Royale d'Archéologie d'Alexandrie, 1950; Österreichische Akademie der Wissenschaften, 1955; Instituto Sudamericano de Asuntos Legales, 1957; Pres. Hon. Soc. of Cymmrodorion, 1947-53, Vice-Pres., 1953-; Pres. of Soc. for Promotion of Roman Studies, 1937-45, Vice-Pres. since 1945; Vice-Pres. of Soc. for Promotion of Hellenic Studies since 1930; Vice-Pres. of Int. Council for Philosophy and Humanistic Studies, 1949-52; Pres. of Internat. Assoc. of Papyrologists, 1947-55, Hon.-Pres., 1955-; Hon. Fellow of Oriel Coll., Oxford, since 1936; Pres. of Brit. Acad., 1946-50; Mem. Governing Body of Church in Wales, 1950-; awarded Cymmrodorion Medal for services to Welsh literature, 1946; hon. member, as Druid, of Welsh Gorsedd since 1949. *Publications:* Vols. III (with Sir Frederic Kenyon), IV. and V. of the Catalogue of Greek Papyri in the British Museum; Jews and Christians in Egypt, 1924; Part XVI. of the Oxyrhynchus Papyri (with B. P. Grenfell and A. S. Hunt), 1924; Part XIX. (with E. Lobel, E. P. Wegener, and C. H. Roberts), 1948; Wadi Sarga (with W. E. Crum), 1922; Juden und Griechen im römischen Alexandreia, 1926; Fragments of an Unknown Gospel (with T. C. Skeat), 1935; A Descriptive Catalogue of the Greek Papyri in the Collection of Wilfred Merton, F.S.A., Vol. I (with C. H. Roberts), 1948, Vol. II (with B. R. Rees), 1958; Egypt from Alexander the Great to the Arab Conquest, 1948; Cults and Creeds in Graeco-Roman Egypt, 1953; edited Vita Sancti Tathei and Buchedd Seint y Katrin for Bangor Welsh MSS. Society, 1909; edited Traherne's Poems of Felicity, 1910; Poems from the Welsh (with C. C. Bell), 1913; Welsh Poems of the Twentieth Century in English Verse (with C. C. Bell), 1925; The Development of Welsh Poetry, 1936; Dafydd ap Gwilym: Fifty Poems (with David Bell), 1942; The Crisis of Our Time and Other Papers, 1954; Trans. with appendix, of T. Parry's A History of Welsh Literature, 1955; Two Welsh fairy-tales, viz. Dewi a'r Blodyn Llo Mawr, 1928 and Calon y Dywysoges, 1929; Trwy Diroedd y Dwyrain, 1946. *Recreation:* walking. *Address:* Bro Gynin, Iorwerth Avenue, Aberystwyth. [*Died* 22 *Jan.* 1967.

BELL, Herbert Clifford Francis, F.R.H.S.; B.A.; Toronto; M.A., Wesleyan; Ph.D. Pennsylvania; D.Lit. Bowdoin; L.H.D., Holy Cross; Professor of European History, Wesleyan University, Middletown, Connecticut, 1926-46; Professor Emeritus; *b.* 1881; *s.* of late William Bell, K.C., Hamilton, Ontario, Canada, and Emily Rogers; unmarried. *Educ.:* Hamilton Collegiate Institute; Univs. of Toronto, Pennsylvania and Paris. Took up residence in U.S. in 1903; Naturalised 1919; Instructor in History, Univ. of Wisconsin, 1909-12; Professor of History, Bowdoin College, 1912-26; Visiting Professor at Pennsylvania, 1925, and at Yale, 1927; interned in Germany and released on parole, 1914; served with Intelligence Section of American Army in France as Lieutenant and Captain, 1917-19 (citation from Commander-in-Chief); Major, O.R.C., 1919-35; President American Catholic Historical Association; member of Anglo-American Historical Committee; City Councilman of Middletown, Connecticut, 1946-48, Mayor, 1948-50. Trustee of the Church Peace Union (New York), 1947-. *Publications:* Lord Palmerston, 1936; Woodrow Wilson and the People, 1945; Principal compiler of Guide to West Indian Archival Materials, 1926; contributor to Encyc. of the Social Sciences, various historical reviews and other periodicals. *Address:* 22 Wyllys Avenue, Middletown, Conn., U.S.A. *T.A.:* Middletown,

Conn. *Clubs:* Century, Zeta Psi (New York). [*Died* 12 *April* 1966.

BELL, Sir Hugh (Francis), 4th Bt., *cr.* 1885; Lt. R.N.V.R.; *b.* 7 Dec. 1923; *er.* and *o. surv. s.* of late Rev. Hugh Lowthian Bell (2nd *s.* of 2nd Bt.) and of Frances Helena, *d.* of John William Morkill, J.P., D.L., Newfield Hall, Bell Busk, Yorks; *S.* uncle, 1944; *m.* 1947, Mary Helen, *d.* of A. Mathieson, 50 Clarendon Ct., N.W.; *m.* 1959, Mary Howson, M.B., Ch.B., The Hyde, Hambledon; four *s.* *Educ.:* Bryanston Sch., Blandford. Served R.N., 1942-46. *Recreation:* shooting. *Heir: s.* John Lowthian Bell, *b.* 14 June 1960. *Address:* Arncliffe Hall, Ingleby Cross, Northallerton, Yorks. *Club:* Royal Yorkshire Yacht (Bridlington). [*Died* 6 *Aug.* 1970.

BELL, Sir Idris; *see* Bell, Sir Harold I.

BELL, Isaac; *b.* 15 June 1879; *s.* of Isaac Bell of Newport, R.I., U.S.A.; *m.* 1909, Evadne Cane (*d.* 1959), of St. Wolstan's, Celbridge, Co. Kildare; one *d.* (and one *d.* decd.). *Educ.:* Harrow; Trinity Hall, Cambridge. Previously Master of Galway Blazers, Kilkenny Hound , South and West Wilts Foxhounds. *Address:* Readsland, Drumree, Co. Meath, Ireland. *Clubs:* Royal Thames Yacht; Kildare Street (Dublin). [*Died* 28 *Oct.* 1964.

BELL, James Alan, M.C.; J.P.; *b.* 28 Oct. 1894; *s.* of late C. W. Bell, Sunderland; *m.* 1923, Emily Norah (*d.* 1967), *widow* of Capt. A. T. E. Wyatt, Lincolnshire Regt.; one *d.* *Educ.:* Royal Grammar School, Newcastle upon Tyne; Downing College, Cambridge (B.A., LL.B.). 2nd Lt. Durham L.I. (T.F.), 1913; served France and Flanders, 1915-19, with 50th (Northumbrian) Division, Staff Captain and Brigade Major (wounded twice, M.C.); T.A.R.O., 1923; Barrister-at-law, Lincoln's Inn, 1920; North-Eastern Circuit; Commissioner of Escheat; Conservative Candidate, North-East Bethnal Green, 1926-31; Deputy County Court Judge, 1939-40; recalled to Army, 1940; Deputy Judge Advocate-General, Iceland Force, 1940-41; Judge, High Court of Judicature, Madras, 1941; retired, 1950; Judge, Federal Supreme Court, Libya, 1953-56. J.P. Norfolk. *Address:* Scarborough Cottage, Mundesley, Norfolk. *Clubs:* Savage; Madras (Madras). [*Died* 9 *Feb.* 1968.

BELL, James Young, C.B. 1926; late Principal Assistant-Secretary, General Post Office; *b.* 1877. *Educ.:* George Watson's College, Edinburgh; Edinburgh University; Balliol College, Oxford. *Address:* 6 Wonersh Court, Guildford. *T.:* Bramley 2440. [*Died* 14 *Dec.* 1966.

BELL, Laird, K.B.E. (Hon.) 1957; Member of Bell, Boyd, Lloyd, Haddad & Burns, lawyers, and predecessor firms; *b.* 6 Apr. 1883; *s.* of Frederic Somers and Frances Laird Bell; *m.* 1909, Nathalie Fairbank; four *d.* *Educ.:* St. Paul's School, Concord, New Hampshire; Harvard College (A.B.); University of Chicago (J.D.). Practice of law in present association, 1907- ; Director of various corporations and Chairman Weyerhaeuser Co., 1947-55. Amer. Red Cross, France, 1918; Mil. Govt., Germany, 1945. Alternate U.S. Deleg. to 10th Gen. Assembly of U.N.; Mem. Governing Boards: Harvard Coll.; Univ. of Chicago; Carleton Coll. (formerly chm. of last two); Director and ex-Pres. Chicago Council on Foreign Relations; Mem. Chicago Board, English-Speaking Union. Hon. degrees: LL.D.: Univ. of Chicago, 1954; Carleton Coll., 1955; Harvard Coll., 1955. Distinguished Civilian Service Award (U.S. Navy), 1946; Medal for Merit (U.S. Army), 1946. *Publications:* contrib. magazines, legal periodicals, etc. *Recreations:* various outdoor activities. *Address:* (home) 1350 Tower Rd., Winnetka, Ill., U.S.A. *T.:* Hillcrest 6-0183; (office) 135 S. La Salle St., Chicago 3, Ill. *T.:* Andover 3-1131. *Clubs:* Chicago, University (Chicago). [*Died* 21 *Oct.* 1965.

BELL, Maj.-Gen. Peter Harvey, C.B. 1944; D.S.O. 1918; *b.* Wanganui, N.Z., 27 June 1886; *s.* of William Bell, St. Johns Hill, Wanganui, N.Z.; *m.* 1910, Maude Vincent, *d.* of H. V. Gully; one *s.* two *d.* *Educ.:* Wanganui Collegiate School. Served in first N.Z.E.F., despatches thrice, D.S.O., French Croix de Guerre; N.Z. Staff Corps; Major, 1919; Major-General, 1942; Retired 1945. Commander, Legion of Merit, U.S., 1945. *Address:* 82 Victoria Avenue, Auckland, S.E.2, N.Z. [*Died* 15 *Jan.* 1963.

BELL, Lieut.-Colonel William Cory Heward, D.S.O. 1917; J.P.; D.L.; Lt.-Col. Royal Field Artillery (Reserve of Officers); *b.* 21 Oct. 1875; *s.* of late W. Heward Bell, J.P., D.L., of Cleeve House, Melksham, Wilts; *m.* 1903, Violet Mary (*d.* 1950), *d.* of late Capt. D. Bowly, R.E.; one *s.* one *d.* *Educ.:* Westminster; R.M.A., Woolwich. 2nd Lieut. R.A., 1895; appointed R.H.A., 1900; Captain, 1901; served S. African War (Queen's medal and 4 clasps); retired, 1911; rejoined on mobilisation, 3 Aug. 1914; proceeded to France, Nov. 1914, and served with the Artillery of the 1st Division until Jan. 1919 (despatches twice, D.S.O., 'cité' in orders of French 35th Corps, Oct. 1918, Croix de Guerre); M.P. (U.) Devizes Division, Dec. 1918-23; High Sheriff of Wilts, 1932; Wilts County Council, 1931-46. *Recreation:* shooting. *Address:* Cleeve House, Melksham, Wilts. *T.:* Seend 281. *Clubs:* Carlton, United Service. [*Died* 6 *Feb.* 1961.

BELLAMY, Dennis, C.B.E. 1958 (O.B.E. 1944); D.L.; Chairman, Bradford College of Advanced Technology, since 1962; Chairman Yorkshire Electricity Board, 1952-1962; *b.* 18 September 1894; *s.* of late Walter Bellamy, Kettering, and late Mary Jane Loasby; *m.* 1920, Edith Alice Bailey, Kettering, Northants; one *d.* Served European War, 1914-18, B.E.F., France. Commanded Company of the General Service Home Guard Battalions, 1940-41; H.G. Adviser, 65 A.A. Brigade. Lt.-Col. Comdg. 14 H.G. A.A. Regt., 1942-45. Hull Corporation Electricity Dept., 1919-48 (Gen. Manager, 1938-48); Dep. Chm. Yorkshire Electricity Board, 1948 (resigned same year and returned as Manager, E. Riding Area, Yorks.). Pres. Hull & E. Riding County Centre, St. John Amb. Assoc.; Hull Br. Roy. Soc. of St. George; Vice-Chm. Council of Order of St. John for E. Riding of Yorks.; O.St.J. 1957; holds local offices in British Legion, S.S.A.F.A., etc. Chairman Advisory Committee, British Limbless Ex-Servicemens' Assoc.; Chm. Gen. Council, and Trustee, Combined Services Welfare Trust. D.L. for E. Riding of Co. of Yorks and for City and Co. of Kingston-upon-Hull, 1945. F.Inst.Cost and Works Accountants, 1935; Comp. M.I.E.E. 1938; F.R.Econ.S. 1938; F.S.S. 1938; F.A.C.C.A. 1938. *Publications:* specialist and technical publications relating to electricity supply. *Recreations:* all sports, public service. *Address:* 274 Cottingham Road, Hull, Yorkshire. *T.:* Hull 43246. [*Died* 16 *March* 1964.

BELLASIS, Capt. Richard O.; *see* Oliver-Bellasis.

BELLENGER, Capt. Rt. Hon. Frederick John, P.C. 1946; M.P. (Lab.) Bassetlaw Division, Notts., since 1935; Surveyor; *b.* 23 July 1894; *s.* of Eugene Bernard Bellenger; *m.* 1922, Marion Theresa, *o. d.* of Generalkonsul Karl Stollwerck, Cologne; five *s.* one *d.* Served European War, 1914-19; Lieutenant Royal Artillery (twice wounded); Capt., France, 1940. Financial Sec., War Office, 1945-46; Secretary of State for War, 1946-47. *Address:* 198 Old Brompton Road, S.W.5. *Club:* Royal Automobile. [*Died* 11 *May* 1968.

BELLEW, Capt. Edward Donald, V.C. 1915; Irish Fusiliers of Canada, Vancouver, B.C., retired; prospector, and explorer; *b.* 28 Oct. 1882; *er. s.* of late Major Patrick Bellew, Bengal Army, H.E.I.C.S., and Assay-Master of the Bombay Mint, and of Exeter, England; *m.* Muriel Rees of London; no *c.* *Educ.:* Clifton College; R.M.C., Sandhurst. Served in India as a Lieutenant in the 18th Royal Irish Regiment; afterwards ranching and mining in British Columbia; joined 1st Canadian Contingent in Aug. 1914; Inspector of dredging in Fraser River for Public Works of Canada, 1919-22; Life Member Royal Canadian Military Institute, Toronto. Hon. Mem. The Royal Society of St. George, London. *Recreations:* fly-fishing, youth welfare, gardening. *Address:* Monte Creek, P.O., B.C., Canada. [*Died* 1 *Feb.* 1961.

BELLMAN, Sir Harold, Kt., *cr.* 1932; M.B.E.; D.L.; J.P.; LL.D.; Chairman, Abbey National Building Society; Vice-Lieut. County of Middlesex; *b.* Paddington, 16 Feb. 1886; *m.* 1911, Kate (*d.* 1959), *e. d.* of late Edwin Peacock, Brondesbury Park; two *s.* one *d.* First served on Coaching Staff, Railway Clearing House; lent to Ministry of Munitions during European War, 1914-19, and served as Principal Assistant Establishment Dept.; Fellow Royal Statistical Society; F.R.Econ.Soc.; F.R.S.H.; Hon. Fellow Valuers' Instn.; Director Legal and General Assurance Society Ltd. and Chairman Metropolitan Board; Director Messrs. Taylor Woodrow Ltd.; member Court of Governors of London School of Economics; Governor, Bedford College; Chm. of Governors of Queenswood School; Gov. Southlands Tr. Coll., Wimbledon. Chm. of Justices, Hampstead and St. Marylebone Div., 1958-60; Chm. London University Hostels and Halls of Residence Committee; Chm. of Cttee. and General Treas. National Children's Home; Chm. Council of Town and Country Planning Assoc.; Pres., Central Mx. Marriage Guidance Council; Member British National Committee, International Chamber of Commerce, 1928-30; President Savings and Loan Association of East Africa; Member of Ministry of Health Central Housing Advisory Committee, 1935-57; Member Inter-departmental Cttee. (Board of Trade and Ministry of Health) on Prices of Building Materials; Member Board of Trade Departmental Committee on the Registration of Accountants, 1930; President International Union of Building Societies, 1934-38; Chm., The Building Societies Association, 1933-1937; Major, 22nd Middlesex Bn., H.G.; Chevalier of Legion of Honour; Officer of the Austrian Order of Merit; First President British Building Societies Institute; First Hon. Member American Building and Loan Inst.; Hon. LL.D. The American University, Washington, D.C., 1939; President The Aldwych Club, 1935-36; President of Advertising Assoc. of Great Britain, 1939. *Publications:* Cornish Cockney; Christianity and Commerce; Culture *or* Anarchy; After School; The Silent Revolution; Architects of the New Age; The Building Society Movement; Capital, Confidence and the Community; The Thrifty Three Millions; Stars, Stripes, and Skyscrapers; African Angles; Baltic Backgrounds; Bricks and Mortals, etc. *Recreations:* gardening, travelling, reading. *Address:* The White House, London Road, Stanmore, Middlesex. *T.:* Grimsdyke 2161. *Clubs:* Reform, Co. of London, Magistrates. [*Died* 1 *June* 1963.

BELLO, Alhaji Sir Ahmadu, K.B.E. 1959 (C.B.E. 1953); Sardauna of Sokoto since 1938; Premier of Northern Nigeria since 1954; first Chancellor of Ahmadu Bello University, Zaria, since 1963; *b.* Rabah, 1909; *s.* of Ibrahim, District Head Rabah; *m.* 1932; two *d.* *Educ.:* Sokoto Provincial School; Katsina Training College. Teacher in Sokoto Middle School, 1931-34. District Head Raban, 1934-38; Member, House of Assembly, 1949-51, and since 1952; Member of the House of Representatives, Nigeria, 1952-54. First Northern Nigerian Minister of Works, Local Government and Development; one-time Member Nigerian Coal Board; Northern Region Production Development Board; Northern Region Development (Loans) Board; Marketing and Export Board; North Regional Scholarship Board. Vice-Pres., World Moslem League, 1961. Hon. Dr. of Law: Univ. of Nigeria, Nsukka; Univ. of Al Azhar, Cairo; Aligarh Muslim Univ., India; Ahmadu Bello Univ., Zaria; Hon. Ph.D. Univ. of Libya, Benghazi. *Publication:* My Life, 1962. *Recreations:* fives and cricket, at times. *Address:* Premier's Office, Kaduna, Northern Nigeria. [*Died* 15 *Jan.* 1966.

BELLOT, Hugh Hale, M.A. (Oxon.), Hon. LL.D. (Lond.); Professor Emeritus of American History in the University of London; Fellow of University College, London; Hon. Fellow of Lincoln College, Oxford; *b.* 26 January 1890; *o. surv. s.* of late Hugh H. L. Bellot, D.C.L., and Beatrice, *d.* of Charles Clarke. *Educ.:* Bedales School and Lincoln Coll., Oxford (Scholar). Temp. master, Battersea Polytechnic Secondary School and Bedales School, and temp. clerk, H.M. Customs and Excise, 1915-18; asst., dept. of History, University College, London, 1921; senior lecturer, 1926; Reader in Modern History, University of Manchester, 1927-30; Commonwealth Fund Prof. of American History in the Univ. of London, 1930-55; Sir George Watson Lecturer, Birmingham, 1938; Creighton Lecturer, University of London, 1954; Acting Principal, Board of Trade, 1940-44; Mem. of Senate of the Univ. of London, 1938-56, and of Court of the University, 1948-53; Chairman of the Academic Council, 1948-51; Vice-Chancellor, 1951-53; Hon. Sec., Royal Historical Soc., 1934-52; President, 1952-56; Member of Council: Westfield College, 1946-1965, Charing Cross Hospital Medical School, 1955-63; University College, Ibadan, 1948-1957. *Publications:* Selections from the Abrégé du projet de paix perpétuelle by C. I. C. de St. Pierre (trs.) 1927; University College, London, 1826-1926, 1929; The Study of American History, 1932; American History and American Historians, 1952. *Recreations:* gardening, walking, travel. *Address:* Wayside, Lyndale, N.W.2; The Mill, High Ham, Langport, Somerset. *Club:* Athenæum. [*Died* 18 *Feb.* 1969.

BELLVILLE, Captain George Ernest; *b.* Dec. 1879; *s.* of late W. J. and Mrs. Bellville, of 22 Berkeley Square, W.1; *m.* Madeleine Malvina, 3rd *d.* of Count Rodolph de Kerchove de Denterghem; two *d.* *Educ.:* Eton; Trinity College, Cambridge. Entered Army, 16th Lancers, 1900; served S. African War, 1900-1 (severely wounded); Adjutant, Westminster Dragoons Yeomanry, 1908-12; went to France with 16th Lancers, Aug. 1914, and severely wounded during retreat from Mons, being taken prisoner in hospital; repatriated in 1917 from Switzerland; joint master with Mr. Isaac Bell, Kilkenny Hounds, 1919-20; M.F.H. Woodland Pytchley Hounds, 1920-32; represented regiment at polo, 1904-14, and with Old Cantab. team won Hurlingham Champion cup four times; Sheriff of Northamptonshire, 1941. *Address:* Fermyn Woods, Brigstock, Northants. *Club:* Cavalry. [*Died* 28 *June* 1967.

BELOE, Vice-Adm. Sir (Isaac) William (Trant), K.B.E. 1965; C.B. 1963; D.S.C. 1945; *b.* 9 Dec. 1909; *s.* of late Reverend R. D. Beloe, sometime Headmaster of Bradfield Coll., and of late Mrs. C. Beloe, late of St. Nicholas, Winchester, *d.* of Reverend J. T. Bramston, Winchester; *m.* 1936, Ethel Diana, *d.* of Comdr. J. F. H. Cole (killed on active service, 1915) and of Mrs. Leggett (who *m.* late Vice-Adm. O. E. Leggett, C.B.); one *s.* one *d.* *Educ.:* R.N. College, Dartmouth. Joined R.N. 1923; Lieut. 1933; served War of 1939-45 (comd. H.M. Ships: Campbeltown, Vanity, Cotton; in Western Approaches, West Mediterranean and Russian convoys); comd. H.M. Ship Contest, 1945; Comdr. 1946; Capt., 1951; Dep. Director, R.N. Staff College, 1953-56; Comd. H.M. Ships Dainty and Ocean, 1956-57; Cdre. comdg. Pakistan Flotilla, 1957; Cdre., R.N. Barracks, Devonport, 1959; Rear-Adm. 1961; Flag Officer, Medway, and Adm. Superintendent, Chatham, 1961-63; Vice-Adm. 1963; N.A.T.O. Deputy Supreme Allied Commander, Atlantic, 1964-66. *Recreations:* travel and country life. *Address:* c/o Ministry of Defence, S.W.1.

[*Died* 3 *April* 1966.

BELTON, Rev. Francis George, B.A.; Vicar of St. Patrick's, Bordesley, Birmingham, 1912-45; Hon. Canon Birmingham Cathedral, 1923; *s.* of Francis William Belton; unmarried. *Educ.:* Lincoln School; Universities of Sheffield and Durham; President of the Union, Sheffield, 1906; Durham, 1909; Fellow of Chemical Society, 1905; Deacon, 1909; Priest, 1910; Hon. Demonstrator in Metallurgy, Birmingham University, 1916-18. *Publications:* A Manual for Confessors, 1916, revised and enlarged edition, 1931 and 1936; Present-Day Problems in Christian Morals, 1920; Belief and Conduct, 1926; So-called Rebels, a Record of Recent Events in the Diocese of Birmingham, 1930; Christian Ideals in Daily Life, 1933; Ommanney of Sheffield, 1936; (papers) The Existence of a Definite Lead Potassium Sulphate; The Estimation of Nickel in Aluminium Alloys. *Address:* 69 Livingstone Road, King's Heath, Birmingham 14. *T.:* Birmingham Highbury 2764.

[*Died* 29 *April* 1962.

BEMELMANS, Ludwig; painter and author; *b.* Merano, Tyrol, 27 Apr. 1898; *s.* of Lambert Bemelmans and Frances Fisher; *m.* 1935, Madeline Freund; one *d.* *Educ.:* Königliche Realschule, Regensburg and Rothenburg, Bavaria. Went to United States, 1914; naturalised, 1918. Exhibitions: New York; principal U.S. cities; Paris Gall. Durand Ruel; Düsseldorf, Malkasten Gallery. Work in most American museums. incl. Metropolitan, and private collections. Also paints theatre décors, interiors. *Publications:* (also illustrator) Hansi, 1934; Golden Basket, 1935; Castle Number Nine, 1936; Quito Express, 1937; My War with the U.S.A., 1937; Life Class, 1938; Madeline, 1939; Hotel Splendide, 1939; Small Beer, 1940; Fifi, 1940; The Donkey Inside, 1941; I love you, I love you, I love you, 1942; Now I lay me down to Sleep, 1943; The Blue Danube, 1944; How to Travel Incognito, 1952; Father, Dear Father, 1953; Madeline's Rescue, 1953; Sunshine; The High World, 1954; To the One I Love the Best, 1955; Parsley, 1955; The World of Bemelmans, 1955; The Woman of My Life, 1957; Madeline and the Bad Hat, 1958; My Life in Art, 1958; Madeline in London, 1961; Are You Hungry, Are You Cold, 1961; On Board Noah's Ark, 1962; Marina, 1962; The Street where the Heart lies, 1962. Contributor articles and pictures to Vogue, Town and Country, Stage, New Yorker, Holiday Magazine, etc. *Recreation:* travel. *Address:* New York; Paris; on board cutter Arche de Noé, France.

[*Died* 1 *Oct.* 1962.

BENAS, Bertram Benjamin Baron, C.B.E. 1954; B.A., LL.B.; Hon. LL.M. (Liverpool) 1952; J.P.; Barrister-at-Law (Northern Circuit, Lancashire Chancery Court, Equity Draughtsman and Conveyancer); *b.* Toxteth, Liverpool; *o. s.* of late Baron Louis Benas, J.P. Liverpool. *Educ.:* Liverpool College (Upper School); graduated Univs. of Manchester and Liverpool. Called to Bar, Middle Temple, 1906, Bencher, 1953; Mem. Council, 1941-47, of Cttees. since 1941, and of Court of Governors, Univ. of Liverpool; Life Governor, Liverpool College; Member of Cttee., Soc. of Public Teachers of Law, 1934-51; Lecturer in Law of Property and Conveyancing, Warrington and District Law Soc., 1925-26, and Equity and Jurisprudence, Univ. of Liverpool, 1926-1927; Pres., Literary and Philosophical Soc. of Liverpool, 1922, 1951, 1961; Pres., Athenæum, Liverpool, 1938; Pres., University Club, Liverpool, 1957; Chairman, Liverpool Music Guild, 1936-38, 1941; Chairman, Merseyside Music Council, 1962-; Chm. St. George's Hall Organ Club (Liverpool), 1958-; Chm. Executive Merseyside Civic Soc., 1947-59 (Vice-Pres. 1959-); Pres. Liverpool Jewish Literary Soc., 1914-21; Pres. Liverpool Branch, Anglo-Jewish Assoc., 1914-; President, Union of Jewish Literary Societies (London), 1923-25; first Pres. Merseyside Jewish Representative Council (1944-1946); Pres. Historic Soc. of Lancashire and Cheshire, 1963- (contrib. Later Records Jews in Liverpool and Centenary Address (1948) to Trans. Society); President Jewish Historical Soc. of England, 1951-53 (contrib. Survey of the Jewish Institutional History of Liverpool and district to Trans. Soc.); Chm., Liverpool and District Jewish War Services Cttee.; Mem. Council of Christians and Jews and Chairman Liverpool and District Executive; Chairman Liverpool Local Bar Association, 1947-; Chairman Liverpool Theatres and Public Entertainments (Licensing) Cttee., 1954-55; J.P. Liverpool, 1938-. *Publications:* (with late Judge Essenhigh) Precedents of Pleading; (with late Lord Justice Scott) The New Law of Property Explained; contrib. upon the Law of Property and Conveyancing Practice in Encyclopædia of Laws of England (3rd Edn.), and in Halsbury's Laws of England (3rd Edn.), The Law Journal and The Conveyancer; contribs. to legal Quarterlies and Annuals and to Proceedings and Transactions of Societies. *Recreations:* literature and music. *Address:* 10 Ullet Road, Dingle, Liverpool 8; 14 Cook Street, Liverpool 2; 8 Old Square, Lincoln's Inn, W.C.2. *Clubs:* Royal Commonwealth Society; Athenæum, University (Liverpool).

[*Died* 8 *Dec.* 1968.

BENDER, William E. G., C.I.E. 1936; M.B.E. 1919; V.D.; M.I.C.E.; A.C.G.I.; *b.* 11 Jan. 1885; *s.* of Charles Bender and Nancy Lancefield; *m.* 1927, Alison Cordeaux Dobbie; two *s.* one *d.* *Educ.:* Dulwich College; Central Technical College. Personal Assistant to F. E. Robertson, C.I.E., of Rendel and Robertson (now Rendel, Palmer, and Tritton), Consulting Engineers to Government of India, 1903; Assistant Engineer, B. and N.W. Railway, 1905; obtained commission in the I.A.R.O., 1916; served European War, N.W. Frontier India and Mesopotamia (Capt., despatches, M.B.E.); rejoined B. and N.W. Railway, 1919, Resident Engineer and Personal Assistant to the Agent and General Manager; Chief Engineer Bengal and N.W. Railway and Rohilkund and Kumaon Railway, 1933-40; retired, 1940; Designing Engineer Timbrol Ltd., Chemical Manufacturers, 1942-44; 1945, Consulting Engineer to same firm; restored Railway communications in Behar after earthquake of January 1934 (C.I.E.). Has now retired. *Recreations:* Reading and home workshop. *Address:* 16 Kintore St., Wahroonga, Sydney, N.S.W., Australia.

[*Died* 1 *April* 1961.

BENDERN, Count; Arnold Maurice; hereditary Count of Principality of Liechtenstein (Bendern on the Rhine); Baron de Forest, hereditary Baron of the former Austrian Empire, Barony confirmed for Great Britain by Royal Decree, 1900, use relinquished, 1920; *b.* 9 Jan. 1879; *m.* 1904, Hon. Ethel Catherine Gerard (*d.* 1966); *o. d.* of 2nd Baron Gerard; two *s.* *Educ.:* Eton; Christ Church, Oxford. Late Lieut. Prince of Wales's Own Norfolk Artillery Militia; Hon. Lieut. in the Army, 1900; transferred, 1903, to Staffords Imp. Yeo.; Lieut.-Commander R.N.V.R.; served in France (1914 star); attached Royal Naval Armoured Car Force, Sept. 1914; contested (L.) Southport, 1910; Member L.C.C. 1910-13 (Kennington Division, Lambeth); M.P. (L.) West Ham, North Division, 1911-18; naturalised in the Principality of Liechtenstein 1932; Principality Diplomatic Counsellor, 1936. *Heir: s.* Count Alaric Bendern. *Address:* Villa Espoir, Biarritz; Vaduz, Liechtenstein. [*Died* 6 *Oct.* 1968.

BENFIELD, Brig. Karl V. B.; *see* Barker-Benfield.

BENHAM, Frederic Charles Courtenay, C.M.G. 1950; C.B.E. 1945; Sir Henry Price Research Professor of International Economics, Royal Institute of International Affairs, since 1955; Temporary post as economic adviser to Comptroller for Development and Welfare in the West Indies, 1942-1945; Professor of Commerce (with special reference to International Trade) in the University of London, 1945-47; Economic Adviser to Commissioner-General for U.K. in South-East Asia, 1947-55. *Publications:* Economics; Great Britain under Protection; The National Income of Malaya; The Colombo Plan and other essays; A Short Introduction to the Economy of Latin America (part-author); Economic Aid to Underdeveloped Countries, etc. *Address:* 47 Gordon Square, W.C.1. *T.:* Euston 4100. [*Died* 7 *Jan.* 1962.

BENKA-COKER, Sir Salako Ambrosius, Kt. 1961; O.B.E. 1951; B.A. (Dunelm); Chief Justice, Sierra Leone, since 1960; *b.* 16 June 1900; *s.* of Ambrose Benka-Coker and late Iris Eglantine Benka-Coker (*née* Roberts); *m.* 1932, Hannah Ransolina Luke (*d.* 1952); two *s.* one *d.* (and one *s.* decd.). *Educ.:* Sierra Leone Grammar School (C.M.S.); Fourah Bay Coll., Sierra Leone. Called to Bar, Middle Temple, London, 1926. Practised Supreme Court, Gambia, 1926-35; Organiser and Comr., Boy Scouts, Gambia, 1927-35. Sierra Leone: private practice, Supreme Court, 1935-43; City Councillor, Freetown, 1941-43; Crown Counsel, 1943-53 (seconded Legal Adviser's Dept., Colonial Office, July 1947-Jan. 1948); Solicitor General, Sierra Leone, 1953-57; acted Attorney Gen., 1956, 1957; Actg. Judge, 1958; Puisne Judge, 1958-. Acting Governor-General, Sierra Leone in June 1961, July 1961, Sept.-Dec. 1962. Ex-Chm. Sierra Leone Football Assoc.; Chm. Cheshire Homes Trust, Sierra Leone, 1961-; Jt. Organiser Inter-Colonial Games, Gambia-Sierra Leone; Member Sierra Leone Sports Committee and Chairman Amateur Sports Council; Chm. Laymen's Cttee. of Church Chm. Bd. of Trustees Freetown Secondary School for Girls; Mem. C.M.S. Gram. Sch. Exec. Bd. Represented Govt. in Govt. Shaw Riot Commn. Enquiry and Kailahun Enquiry. *Recreations:* football, tennis, cricket, billiards. *Address:* R 4, Hill Station, Freetown, Sierra Leone; Chief Justice's Chambers, Law Courts, Freetown. *T.:* Freetown 2847. [*Died* 7 *Dec.* 1965.

BENN, Captain Sir Ion Hamilton, 1st Bt., *cr.* 1920; C.B. 1918; D.S.O. 1917; T.D., 1926; R.N.V.R.; *b.* 31 Mar. 1863; 3rd *s.* of late Rev. J. W. Benn, Rector of Carrigaline and Douglas, Co. Cork, and Maria Louisa, *d.* of Gen. Christopher Hamilton, C.B., and Hon. Sarah Hamilton, *d.* of 2nd Baron Castlemaine; *m.* 1st, 1885, Frances Charlotte (*d.* 1948), *o. d.* of N. Bridges, Wallington Manor, Surrey, and Blackheath, Kent; one *d.* (one *s.* decd.); 2nd, 1950, Katharine Winifred, *d.* of late Brockwill Grier, Montreal. Member of London Port Authority since 1909; member of Thames Conservancy, 1937-46; late Hon. Col. 20th Batt. County of London Regt.; Mayor of Greenwich, 1901-2; contested Greenwich (Unionist and Tariff Reformer), 1906; member of London County Council for Greenwich, 1907-10; M.P. (U.) Greenwich, 1910-22; member of the 1st Metropolitan Water Board, 1903-6; served European War, 1914-18; operations Belgian Coast (despatches three times, D.S.O., C.B., Croix de Guerre); Knight of the Order of St. John of Jerusalem, 1925; Director of Price and Pierce, Ltd., London; President, Seamen's Hospital, Greenwich (The Dreadnought), 1949- (Chairman 1937-46); President Tower Hill Improvement Fund; Rollesby Hall Estate Co. Ltd. *Recreations:* fishing, shooting, yachting. *Heir: g.s.* Capt. Patrick Ion Hamilton Benn, [*b.* 26 Feb. 1922; *m.* 1959, Edel Jørgine Løback, Vesteraalen, Norway]. *Address:* 18 Kingston House South, Ennismore Gardens, S.W.7. *T.:* Kensington 4039; 27 St. Clements Lane, E.C.4. *Clubs:* Royal Thames Yacht; Norfolk (Norwich). [*Died* 12 *Aug.* 1961.

BENNETT, Alfred Gordon, F.R.S.A.; Author; *b.* Warrington, Lancashire, 11 Dec. 1901; *s.* of late Arthur Bennett and Eliza Annie (Lily), *e. d.* of Edwin Richardson, Warrington; *m.* Gwendoline Evans-Williams, L.R.A.M., *y. d.* of late Captain W. Barrow Williams, Anglesey. *Educ.:* The Boteler Grammar School, Warrington; The Leys, Cambridge; but largely by personal observation of life and by travel in at least fourteen foreign countries. Pilot Officer (Intelligence) R.A.F.V.R., 1941; Flying Officer, 1943-45. Reporter on Liverpool Daily Post, 1920; articles on Travel, Science, and Film and Dramatic criticism, etc.; lectures and plays for Broadcasting; assisted in founding The Warrington Art Theatre, 1926; Founding Member and Member of the Council of the Institute of Amateur Cinematographers Ltd.; Founder and Chairman of Pharos Books, Ltd., Publishers, 1946. Fellow British Institute of Cinematography; Fellow Ancient Monuments Society. Awarded Gold Medal Société Académique d'Histoire Internationale of France, 1929. *Publications:* The Valley of Paradise, 1922; The Forest of Fear, 1924; The Sea of Sleep (in U.S.A. The Sea of Dreams), 1926; Thine is the Kingdom, 1928; Voices Off, 1929; Collected Poems, 1920-30, 1930; The Sword: A Poetical Play, 1931; Cinemania: Aspects of Filmic Creation, 1937; The Demigods, 1939 (French version and trans. by Tanette Prigent, Paris, 1951; Italian "Urania Edn.," trans. by Patrizio Dalloro, Milan, 1953; new revised English edition, 1955); Whom the Gods Destroy, 1946; Purple Testament (Poems), 1950; Focus on the Unknown, 1953 (Atlantic non-fiction Award semi-finalist, 1952-53; Italian trans. by Rossana De Michele, Milan, 1957); The Coil and other Strange Stories. *Plays:* Glory, 1926; Woman Nature (produced under the title, Derek Knoyle's Dilemma), 1927; A Touch of Sun, 1928. *Films:* The Valley of Paradise (U.S.A.), and many private productions; produced and directed pre-Service documentary, Round the Year with Youth, 1943-44. *Recreations:* motoring, keeping pet cats, and watching television. *Address:* Ty Gwyn, Upper Colwyn, N. Wales. *T.:* 2470. *Clubs:* Authors', Order of the Road, Veteran Motorists. [*Died* 11 *Aug.* 1962.

BENNETT, Cecil Harry Andrew; Hon. Mr. Justice Bennett; C.B.E. 1967; Q.C. 1952; British Member of the Arbitral Commission, Germany, since 1955; *b.* 14 March 1898; *s.* of H. G. D. Bennett, Allesley, Warwickshire; *m.* 1925, Katharine, *d.* of Lieut.-Colonel Selby Ormond; one *s.*; *m.* 1933, Cynthia, *d.* of Capt. F. Elton, R.N.; two *s.* one *d.* *Educ.:* Charterhouse; Pembroke Coll., Cambridge (B.A., LL.B.); Univ. of Paris (Licencié-ès-Droit). Commission in R.G.A. 1915; served in France and Flanders; demobilised with rank of Capt. 1919. Called to Bar, 1922. Advocate-General, Sudan Govt., 1936-40; Attorney-General, Sudan Govt., 1941-43; Chief Justice of the Sudan, 1944-46; Puisne Judge, High Court, Patna, 1946-47; Joint Legal Adviser to High Commissioners for the U.K. in India and in Pakistan, 1947; Legal Counsellor to Brit. Adm. and to Comrs. for U.N., Eritrea, 1952; Legal Adviser to Government of Eritrea, 1952; Brit. Mem. of Supreme Restitution Court for Berlin, 1953-62. *Address:* c/o Schiedskommission, Koblenz, Schloss, Germany. *Club:* Sesame Imperial and Pioneer. [*Died* 19 *Sept.* 1967.

BENNETT, Captain (Eugene) Paul, V.C. 1916, M.C.; late Worcester Regiment; Metropolitan Police Magistrate, 1935 - 61; barrister - at - law; *b.* Stroud, Gloucester, 4 June 1892; 4th *s.* of late Charles Bennett, Stroud; *m.* 1922, Violet, 2nd *d.* of late J. F. Forster, 30 Hamilton Terrace, N.W.; one *d.* (one *s.* decd.). *Educ.:* Marling School, Stroud. To France with 1st Artists, Oct. 1914; 2nd Lt. 2nd Worcesters, Dec. 1914 (M.C. in counter-attack, 26 Sept. 1915; Captain, March 1916; despatches, Victoria Cross, 5 Nov. 1916); called to Bar, 1923. *Address:* Villa Violetta, Via Roma, Marostica, Vicenza, Italy. [*Died* 4 *April* 1970.

BENNETT, Lt.-Gen. Gordon; *see* Bennett, Lt.-Gen. H. G.

BENNETT, Lt.-Gen. (Henry) Gordon, C.B. 1918; C.M.G. 1915; D.S.O. 1919; V.D. 1923; *b.* Balwyn, Victoria, Australia, 15 April 1887; *s.* of late G. J. Bennett; *m.* 1916, Bessie Agnes, *y. d.* of late Robert Buchanan, Canterbury, Australia; one *d.* *Educ.:* Hawthorn College, Victoria, Australia. Is a Company Director, Australia; President of Chamber of Manufacturers, N.S.W., 1931-33; President, Associated Chambers of Manufacturers of Australia, 1933-34; Civic Commissioner, city of Sydney, 1928-30; was 37 years in Militia (Commonwealth Military Forces with commissioned rank); served European War, 1915-18 (despatches eight times, C.M.G., C.B., D.S.O., V.D.); Order of Danilo, 3rd class; commanded 2nd Division Australian Military Forces, 1926-31; Commanded 8th Division A.I.F., 1940; G.O.C. Australian Imperial Force, in Malaya, 1941-42; Comdg. 3rd Australian Corps, 1942; past President and Fellow N.S.W. Division, The Australian Institute of Cost Accounts; President, 1931-32, and Fellow, N.S.W. Division, Institute of Chartered Secretaries, 1930-32. *Publication:* Why Singapore Fell, 1945. *Address:* The Chase Road, Turramurra, N.S.W., Australia. [*Died* 1 *Aug.* 1962.

BENNETT, Sir John (Cecil) Sterndale, K.C.M.G., *cr.* 1950 (C.M.G. 1926); M.C. 1917; Retired Ambassador, H.M. Foreign Service; *b.* Sheffield 25 April 1895; *s.* of Cornelius Bennett; *m.* 1926, Dorothy Mary, *e. d.* of late Cyril Payne. *Educ.:* King Edward VII. Sch., Sheffield; St. Catharine's Coll., Camb. Served in European War with Royal Naval Division, 1914-18 (M.C.). Entered Diplomatic Service, 1920; served in Stockholm, Santiago, Peking, Cairo and, as Minister, in Ankara. Head of Far Eastern Dept., Foreign Office, 1940-42 and 1944-46; British Political Representative, Bulgaria, 1947, Minister in Sofia, 1947-49; sen. civilian mem. on staff of Imperial Defence Coll., 1949-1950; Deputy Commissioner-General for the United Kingdom in South-East Asia, 1950-53; Head of British Middle East Office, 1953-55. *Address:* The Old Rectory, Netherfield, Battle, Sussex. *Club:* Travellers'. [*Died* 30 *May* 1969.

BENNETT, John Colburn, C.M.G. 1961; C.B.E. 1951; Director, Henry Gardner & Co. Ltd., 1942-67 (Man. Dir., 1950-62); *b.* 19 Apr. 1897; *m.* 1927, Joan Florence Mary (*d.* 1956), *d.* of late O. F. G. Stonor, C.M.G. *Educ.:* St. George's College, Weybridge. Director: Amalgamated Metal Corp. Ltd.; Sandilands Buttery & Co. Ltd. Adviser, Board of Trade, 1939-60; Chm. Rubber Trade Assoc. of London, 1945-46; Councillor, British National Cttee., Internat. Chamber of Commerce, 1957-60. *Address:* 2 Metal Exchange Buildings, E.C.3; 11 Lantern Close, Roehampton, S.W.15. [*Died* 25 *Aug.* 1969.

BENNETT, John Still, C.V.O. 1961; C.B.E. 1964 (O.B.E. 1959); High Commissioner in Barbados, since 1966; *b.* 22 March 1911; *m.* 1943, Danica (*née* Ribnikar) (*d.* 1967); no *c.* *Educ.:* Clifton Coll.; Peterhouse, Cambridge. Called to Bar, 1936. Served with H.M. Forces, 1939-43. Director, British Information Services, Istanbul, 1943-46; Information Officer: Bucharest, 1946-48; Stockholm, 1949-52; Consul: Houston, Texas, 1952-54; Khorramshahr, Iran, 1955-59; Regional Information Officer, Singapore and Bangkok, 1959-63; Ambassador to Burundi and to Rwanda, 1964-66. *Recreations:* golf, shooting, riding. *Address:* P.O. 95, Bridgetown, Barbados. *Club:* United Hunts. [*Died* 10 *Dec.* 1970.

BENNETT, Capt. Paul; *see* Bennett, Capt. E. P.

BENNETT, Percy R. L.; *see* Leigh-Bennett.

BENNETT, Reginald Robert, B.Sc., F.R.I.C.; pharmaceutical chemist; a Director of The British Drug Houses, Ltd., 1919-1948; *b.* Ashford, Kent, 28 March 1879; *s.* of George Bennett; *m.* 1904, Ethelwyn Phillips (*d.* 1959); one *s.* *Educ.:* Privately; University College and King's College, London. Called to Bar, Gray's Inn, 1913; Chairman, British Pharmaceutical Conference, 1928, 1929; Mem. British Pharmacopœia Commission, 1928-48. *Publications:* numerous contributions on pharmaceutical and technical subjects. *Address:* Longwood, Fairfield Road, Eastbourne. *T.:* 3390. [*Died* 27 *Jan.* 1966.

BENNETT, Thomas William Westropp; Chairman of Irish Agricultural Wholesale Society, 151 Thoms St., Dublin; *b.* 30 Jan. 1867; *e. s.* of Thomas Westropp Bennett, Ballymurphy, Limerick, late Captain H.M. 39th Regiment; *m.* 1st, Esther, *o. d.* of late Charles Moreton Macdonald of Largie Castle, Tayinloane, Kintyre; 2nd, Lillah Mary, *e. d.* of late William Alexander Happell, Indian Civil Service; one *s.* *Educ.:* St. John's College, Kilkenny; privately. Contested the Parliamentary constituency of East Limerick as an Independent candidate, 1910; served in Limerick County Council for nearly 20 years; was an active supporter of the Irish Co-operative Movement inaugurated by Sir Horace Plunkett, having served on the Cttee. of the Irish Agricultural Organisation for some 15 years; member of the Senate of the Irish Free State, 1922-36; Cathaoirleac (President), 1928-36. *Address:* Summerville, Kilmallock, Co. Limerick. *T.A.:* Summerville, Bruff. *Club:* (Pres.) Hibernian United Service (Dublin). [*Died* 13 *Feb.* 1962.

BENNEY, Ernest Alfred Sallis, R.B.A., 1936, A.R.C.A., F.S.A.E. Hon. F.I.B.D.;

Landscape Painter and Designer; formerly Director of Art Education to the Brighton Education Committee and Principal of the Brighton College of Art; *b.* 1894; *s.* of A. E. Benney, lecturer and schoolmaster; *m.* 1923, Aileen Mary Ward; two *s.* Studied art at Bradford School of Art and Royal College of Art, London. Headmaster of Northwich School of Art, 1918-23; Headmaster of the City of Salisbury School of Art, 1923-25; Director of Art Education (Gloucestershire) and Principal of Cheltenham School of Arts and Crafts, 1925-29; Principal of the City of Hull College of Art and Crafts and Art Adviser to the Hull Education Committee, 1929-34; Ministry of Education Examination Assessor, 1941-45. Exhibitor at the Roy. Acad., Roy. Soc. of British Artists, and leading provincial galleries; Official purchases by the Victoria and Albert Museum, Laing Art Gallery, Newcastle, Towner Art Gallery, Eastbourne, Hove Art Gallery, Worthing Art Gallery, Bradford Art Gallery and the Brighton Art Gallery. Trustee to the Federation of British Artists. *Address:* 19 Cornwall Gardens, Preston Park, Brighton, Sussex. *T.:* Brighton 52000. [*Died* 9 *March* 1966.

BENOIT, Pierre; novelist; member of French Academy since 1931; *b.* 1886. Former President of the Société des Gens de Lettres. *Publications:* Diadumène (poetry), 1914; Les Suppliantes (poetry), 1921; Novels: L'Atlantide (Grand Prix of Acad. Française), 1919; Pour Don-Carlos, 1920; La Chaussée des Géants, 1922; Mademoiselle de la Ferté, 1923; Les puits de Jacob, 1925; Alberte, 1926; Le Roi Lépreux, 1927; Axelle 1928; Erromango, 1929; Le Déjeuner de Sousceyrac, 1931; L'Ile Verte, 1932; Fort de France, 1933; Jamrose, 1948. *Address:* c/o Albin Michel, 22 rue Huyghens, Paris XIVe; 71 avenue du Président Roosevelt, Paris VIIIe; rue d'Assas, 120, Paris, VIe. [*Died* 3 *March* 1962.

BENSON, Hon. (Eleanor) Theodora Roby; Authoress; *b.* 21 Aug. 1906; *d.* of 1st Baron Charnwood. *Publications:* Earliest novels: Salad Days; Glass Houses; Shallow Water; Which Way?; Façade; Concert Pitch, 2 Novels with Hon. Betty Askwith: Lobster Quadrille; Seven Basketfuls. 3 Travel Books: Chip, Chip, my Little Horse; The Unambitious Journey; In the East my Pleasure lies. Edited 1 Book of Essays: The First Time I . . .; 3 Humorous Books with Hon. Betty Askwith: Foreigners, or the World in a Nut-shell; Muddling Through, or Britain in a Nut-shell and How to Succeed, or the Great in Nutshells. Best Stories of Theodora Benson, 1940. 1 book on women's part in war: Sweethearts and Wives, 1941; The Undertaker's Wife, 1948; The Man from the Tunnel and other stories, 1950; London Immortals, 1951; Rehearsal for Death, 1954. *Address:* 60 Richmond Court, Sloane Street, S.W.1. *T.:* Belgravia 2592. [*Died* 25 *Dec.* 1968.

BENSON, Percy George Reginald; *b.* 1872; 4th *s.* of J. R. Benson, of Brisbane, Qld.; *m.* 1901, Lillian (*d.* 1954), *d.* of A. F. Gault, of Montreal; one *s.* one *d.* *Educ.:* Rugby; Christ Church, Oxford. Served in West Somerset Yeomanry, 1910-20; Master Taunton Vale Fox Hounds, 1915-27. *Address:* Carrigane Lodge, Ballyduff, Co. Waterford, Eire. *T.:* Ballyduff 6. *Club:* Cavalry. [*Died* 22 *Sept.* 1961.

BENSON, Lieut.-Colonel Sir Rex (Lindsay), Kt. 1958; D.S.O. 1918; M.V.O. 1921; M.C.; late 9th Lancers; Director of Kleinwort, Benson, Lonsdale Ltd., Aldermanbury House, E.C.2.; Deputy President, English-Speaking Union of the Commonwealth; *b.* 1889; 2nd *s.* of late Robert Henry Benson and Evelyn, *d.* of Mr. Holford; *m.* 1932, Leslie Foster Nast, *d.* of Volney Foster, Lake Forest, Illinois, U.S.A.; two *s.* *Educ.:* Eton; Oxford. Served European War, 1914-18 (despatches, D.S.O., M.C., Legion of Honour, Croix de Guerre); served French Army, 1939-40. Mil. Attaché Washington, U.S.A., 1941-44. *Address:* Cucumber Farm, Singleton, nr. Chichester, Sussex; 30 Cadogan Place, S.W.1. *Clubs:* Bath, Buck's, White's. [*Died* 26 *Sept.* 1968.

BENSON, Stephen Riou; Barrister-at-law, Oxford Circuit; Recorder of Abingdon since 1929; Deputy Chairman, Court of Quarter Sessions for County of Oxford, since 1958; 2nd *s.* of late Ralph Beaumont Benson, of Lutwyche Hall, Much Wenlock, Salod; *m.* 1935, Phyllis May, *widow* of Edwin Cawston; two *s.* *Educ.:* Charterhouse. Served European War in Palestine, Egypt, Turkey, and under Generals Denikin and Wrangel in South Russia with the British Military Mission, attaining the rank of Captain; called to Bar, Inner Temple, 1923; contested (Nat. Con.), Upton Division of West Ham, 1935; Member L.C.C. (Municipal Reform) for Balham and Tooting, 1937. *Address:* 21 Cliveden Place, Eaton Sq., S.W.1; 2 Harcourt Buildings, Temple, E.C.4. [*Died* 29 *Nov.* 1961.

BENSON, Hon. Theodora; *see* Benson, Hon. E. T. R.

BENTHALL, Sir Edward Charles, K.C.S.I., *cr.* 1945; Kt., *cr.* 1933; Chairman Bird & Co., Ltd., Calcutta, and F. W. Heilgers & Co., Ltd., Calcutta; a Governor of the B.B.C. 1955-60; *s.* of Rev. Charles Francis Benthall and Annie Theodosia Benthall; *b.* 26 Nov. 1893; *m.* 1918, Hon. Ruth McCarthy Cable, *d.* of first Baron Cable of Ideford; one *s.* *Educ.:* Eton (King's Scholar); King's Coll., Cambridge. Joined White Star Line Office, Liverpool, 1913. Served European War, 1914-19; India, 1914-15; Mesopotamia 1916-18 (wounded); Staff War Office, 1918-19; Director, Imperial Bank of India, 1926-34; Governor 1928-30; Pres., Bengal Chamber of Commerce, 1932 and 1936, Vice Pres., 1931, 1934 and 1938; President, Associated Chambers of Commerce of India and Ceylon, 1932 and 1936; Delegate, Indian Round Table Conference, 1931-1932; Indian Army Retrenchment Committee, 1931; Council of State, 1932-33; Director, Reserve Bank of India, 1935-36; Vice-President, Employers' Federation, 1933-38; President European Association, 1938; Prospective Parl. Candidate (C.), N.W. Devon 1938-42; Ministry of Economic Warfare and Board of Trade, London, 1940-42; Member for War Transport, Governor-General's Executive Council, 1942-46; Leader of the House, Indian Assembly, 1946; Crown Representative on Governing Body of School of Oriental and African Studies, 1948-; Vice-Chairman, Devon River Board, 1950-55; High Sheriff of Devon, 1951. Leader, U.K. Mission to Middle East, 1953. *Recreations:* Rugby football, Cambridge University, Devon County and Reserve for England, 1914; gardening, fishing, travel. *Address:* Lindridge, Bishopsteignton, Devon. *Clubs:* Oriental; Bengal (Calcutta). [*Died* 5 *March* 1961.

BENTINCK, Baron, Adolph (Willem Carel); Commander of Order of Orange Nassau; Chevalier of Order of the Netherlands Lion; Netherlands Ambassador to France since September 1963; *b.* 3 September 1905; *s.* of Baron Rudolf Bentinck and Sigrid (*née* van Karnebeek); *m.* 1938, Baroness Gabrielle Thyssen-Bornemisza; one *s.* one *d.* *Educ.:* Nederlands Lyceum, The Hague; University of Utrecht (graduate in Law). After a few years with Netherlands Trading Society and subsequently Min. of Finance, joined Min. of Foreign Affairs, 1937. Netherlands Chargé d'Affaires *ad interim* at Budapest, 1939-40; Netherlands Chargé d'Affaires at Cairo, 1940-45; Minister-Counsellor, London, 1945-50; Minister of the Netherlands at Berne, 1951-56; Netherlands Member, European Commission for the Saar Referendum. Deputy-Secretary-General of N.A.T.O., 1956-58. Netherlands Ambassador to U.K. and Iceland, 1958-63. *Address:* 85 Rue de Grenelle, Paris VII. *Clubs:* Turf; De Haagse (The Hague); Jockey, Cercle de l'Union (Paris). [*Died* 7 *March* 1970.

BENTINCK, Arthur Harold Walter, C.I.E. 1926; 4th *s.* of late Walter Bentinck, formerly of Froyle House, Alton, Hants; *m.* 1st, 1903, Emma Elizabeth Kemble (*d.* 1932), *d.* of G. S. Hayes; one *s.* one *d.*; 2nd, 1933, Edith White (*d.* 1933); 3rd, 1937, Eunice Gosset (*d.* 1945). *Educ.:* Harrow; Balliol College, Oxford (M.A.). Entered Indian Civil Service, 1898; Political Officer, Abor Expedition, 1911-12; Member Assam Legislative Council, 1924; Commissioner of Revenue, Assam; retired 1933. *Address:* Elm Cottage, Bell Hill, Petersfield, Hants. *Club:* M.C.C. [*Died* 7 *June* 1964.

BENTLEY, Rt. Rev. David Williams Bentley, C.B.E. 1938. *Educ.:* University of Durham. Deacon, 1906; Priest, 1907; Curate, St. John's, Barrow-in-Furness, 1906-1910; St. James-the-less, 1910-14; Vicar of St. Mary's, Plaistow, 1914-16; Warden of St. Peter's Coll., Jamaica, 1917-27; Examining Chaplain to Bishop of Jamaica, 1918; Assistant Bishop of Jamaica, 1919; Bishop of Barbados, 1927-45. *Address:* Brigade House, Garrison, St. Michael, Barbados, W.I. [*Died* 14 *Nov.* 1970.

BENYON, Vice-Adm. Richard, C.B. 1946; C.B.E. 1941; *b.* 18 Jan. 1892; *s.* of Sir John Shelley, 9th Bt.; *m.* 1929, Eve Alice Gascoyne-Cecil, *d.* of late Lord William Cecil, Bishop of Exeter; four *s.*; changed his surname from Shelley to Benyon, by deed poll, 1964. *Educ.:* Royal Naval Colleges, Osborne and Dartmouth. Entered Royal Navy, 1904; Vice-Adm. (Retd.), 1948. D.L. 1953, High Sheriff of Bucks, 1958, Vice-Lieut., 1961-65. *Address:* The Lambdens, Beenham, Berkshire. *Club:* United Service. [*Died* 12 *June* 1968.

BERCOVICI, Konrad; writer; *b.* Braila, Roumania; *m.* Naomi Lebrescu; two *s.* two *d.* *Educ.:* Paris. Musician, teacher, journalist; New York World 1917-20; New York Evening Post, 1920-21. *Publications:* Ghitza, and six other volumes of short stories; *novels:* Story of the Gypsies, Alexander the Great, The Crusaders, The Exodus; It's the Gypsy in Me; On New Shores; Around the World in New York; Manhattan Side Show; That Royal Lover; Crimes of Charity; Savage Prodigal, etc. *Recreation:* farming. *Address:* Ridgefield, Connecticut, U.S.A. *Club:* Authors' (N.Y.). [*Died* 27 *Dec.* 1961.

BERESFORD, Maj.-Gen. Sir George de la Poer, Kt. *cr.* 1947; C.B. 1938; M.C.; p.s.c.; *s.* of Henry Tristram de la Poer Beresford; *m.* 1916, Margaret Ethel Granville (*d.* 1963), *d.* of late Rev. George Thynne; two *s.* *Educ.:* in Australia; R.M.C. Sandhurst. Served Hodson's Horse, 1907-31; Commander P.A.V.O. Cavalry F.F., 1933-34 and 4th Cavalry Brigade, 1934-38; D.A. and Q.M.G., Northern Command India, 1938; served European War, France, 1914-18; Palestine, 1918; Kurdistan, 1919; N.W. Frontier of India, 1919-20, 1930-31; District Commander, 1940; Iraq and Persia, 1940, 1941-42; retired 1942; re-employed, 1942. *Recreations:* polo, shooting, fishing, golf. *Address:* Murranumbla, Dalgety, N.S. Wales; c/o National and Grindlay's Bank, 54 Parliament St., S.W.1; Bank of N.S. Wales, Goulburn. *Clubs:* Naval and Military; Imperial Service (Sydney). [*Died* 29 *Sept.* 1964.

BERESFORD, Tristram de la Poer, Q.C. 1936; Barrister-at-law; Recorder of Folkestone since 1939; *b.* 29 Sept. 1887; *s.* of Cecil Hugh Wriothsley Beresford (late Judge of County Courts) and Caroline Felice Octavi White; *m.* 1912, Eileen Beatrice Rachel Ainslie Grant Duff, Delgaty Castle, Turriff, Aberdeen; two *s.* one *d.* *Educ.:* United Services College, Westward Ho; Trinity Hall, Cambridge. Called to Bar, Middle Temple, 1909; South Eastern Circuit; North London, Middlesex and Central Criminal Court Sessions; served overseas, 1915-19, Royal Flying Corps; Member of Deptl. Committee for revision of Army and Air Force Courts-martial, 1938; one of the Chairmen for the Examination of Germans and Austrians for Internment, 1939-40. Chairman of East Kent Quarter Sessions, 1940-; Chairman of West Kent Quarter Sessions, 1946-47, re-appointed, 1959; Chairman, Special Grants Committee, Ministry of Pensions and National Insurance, 1954-1958; Bencher Middle Temple, 1943. Member of the Chapter General, Order of St. John of Jerusalem; K.St.J. *Recreation:* golf. *Address:* 1 Paper Buildings, Temple, E.C.4. *T.:* Central 0165; 2 Essex Court, Temple. *T.:* 0661; 2 Prince of Wales Terrace, Deal, Kent. *T.:* Deal 517. *Clubs:* Carlton, Royal Air Force; M.C.C.; Royal Cinque Ports; Golf (Deal). [*Died* 23 *Sept.* 1962.

BERKELEY, Baroness (16th in line; 21st of orig. *cr.*), *cr.* 1421; **Eva Mary Fitzhardinge Foley;** *b.* 4 March 1875; *m.* 1903, Col. F. W. Foley, C.B.E., D.S.O. (*d.* 1949); two *d.* (co-heiresses to the Barony); *S.* to Barony, 1899, on death of her mother, who *m.* 1872, Major-General Gustavus Hamilton-Lockwood Milman, R.A. (*d.* 1915). *Address:* Pickade House, Kimble, Aylesbury, Bucks. [*Died* 4 *Dec.* 1964 (*abeyant*).

BERNARD, Anthony; Director and Conductor of The London Chamber Orchestra and The London Chamber Singers; Composer; *b.* London, 25 Jan. 1891; *m.* 1st, 1919, Marie Augustine Jourdan (marr. diss.), Langres, France; two *d.*; 2nd, 1950, Mary Catherine Beattie, Canonbie, Dumfriesshire. Studied under Granville Bantock, Leonard Borwick and John Ireland. A.R.C.O. 1912. Held various appts., 1909-16, as organist and choir director; appeared as pianist in London before creating London Chamber Orchestra, 1921; Professor, Royal College of Music, 1922-25. Has directed Orchestral and Choral Concerts for B.B.C., 1924-. Guest-Conductor, British Nat. Opera Co., 1926; has since appeared: The Hague, Paris, Athens, Madrid, Prague, Bratislava, Copenhagen, Geneva. Organized and directed Festival of Italian Music (of XI-XX Cent.) at Royal Academy, Burlington House, 1930; a similar series of historical Concerts was given by him at Queen's Hall, London, during French Exhibn., 1932, and at Victoria and Albert Museum during Exhibn. of French tapestries, 1947. Director of Music, Shakespeare Memorial Theatre, Stratford-on-Avon, 1932-1942; Canterbury Festival, 1947, 1954, 1956; Cambridge Festival, 1948; Festival of Britain, 1951, conducted at concerts in collaboration with Arts Council. Officier d'Académie, 1948. *Address:* 6 Emperor's Gate, S.W.7. *T.:* Fremantle 0927. [*Died* 6 *April* 1963.

BERNEY-FICKLIN, Maj.-General Horatio Pettus Mackintosh, C.B. 1942; M.C.; late Colonel, Royal Norfolk Regiment; *b.* 13 June 1892; *m.* 1917, Audrey Brenda Knyvet, *d.* of Brereton Knyvet Wilson (marriage dissolved, 1936); *m.* 1936, Ileana, *d.* of Gen. Bartolomei, Tsarskoe Selo, Russia. *Educ.:* Rugby; Jesus College, Cambridge. 2nd Lt. Norfolk Regt. 1914; served European War, 1914-18 (wounded thrice, despatches, Bt. Major, M.C., Legion of Honour); N.W. Frontier of India, 1935; Palestine, 1936-39 (despatches); War of 1939-45 (despatches). *Address:* 7 Eversley, Grove Ave., Claremont, Cape, S. Africa. *Club:* Army and Navy. [*Died* 17 *Feb.* 1961.

BERRIE, John Archibald Alexander, R.C.A. 1923 (A.R.C.A. 1912); F.R.S.A. 1950; portrait and landscape painter; *b.* Fallowfield, Manchester, 1887; *m.* 1915, Lilian, *d.* of Orr Williams; one *s.* one *d.* *Educ.:* Liverpool, London and Paris. Studied Liverpool School of Art, under Marmaduke Flower, Bushey, Herts, Marcel Bèranneau and Senor Casteluchio, Paris; Exhibitor Royal Academy, Paris, etc. Works include: portraits of King George V, Queen Mary, King Edward VIII, King George VI, Queen Elizabeth II; Sir Winston Churchill; The Viscount Bledisloe; The Duke of Abercorn; Admiral Earl Mountbatten of Burma; The Earl of Dartmouth; The Lord Cadman, The Lord Brocket, The Viscount Hailsham; General Sir Colin Barber; Sir Patrick Hannon, M.P.; Sir Frederick Hamilton; Sir Norman Vernon, Bt. (for Baltic Exchange); Sir Philip Mitchell; Sir John Hathorn Hall; Raphael Sabatini, etc.; sportsmen: Steve Donoghue, Gordon Richards, Bobby Jones, Henry Cotton, Bobby Locke, Dai Rees, etc.; many portraits of moderators Presbyterian Church; numerous portraits in Cambridge; a complete series of Presidents of Incorporated Accountants; Lord Mayors and Mayors in numerous Town Halls throughout the Kingdom; many portraits of people in Johannesburg. *Recreations:* motoring, golf. *Address:* Beverley Heights, Killarney, Johannesburg, Transvaal. *T.:* 412969. *Clubs:* Rotary; Artists' (Liverpool); Harrogate Golf; Nairobi, Royal Nairobi Golf (Nairobi, Kenya). [*Died* 3 *Feb.* 1962.

BERRY, Richard James Arthur, M.D. Edin., F.R.S. Edin., F.R.C.S. Edin.; Professor Emeritus; *b.* 30 May 1867; *m.* Beatrice Catherine (*d.* 1949), *e. d.* of Sir Samuel Brighouse; one *s.* two *d.* *Educ.:* privately; University of Edinburgh; Dublin; London and Berlin. Graduated in University of Edinburgh, 1891; House Surgeon Royal Infirmary; M.D. with honours and Gunning Victoria Prize in Surgery, 1894; Lecturer on Anatomy in the School of Medicine of the Royal Colleges, Edinburgh, 1896; Professor of Anatomy, University of Melbourne, 1905-29, and Dean of the Faculty of Medicine, 1923-29; Hon. Psychiatrist, Children's Hospital, Melbourne; Hon. Consulting Psychiatrist, Melbourne Hospital; Life Fellow of Eugenics Society, London; formerly Member of Council of B.M.A.; Board of Directors of B.M.J.; was Examiner in Anatomy, Universities of St. Andrews, Dundee, Aberdeen, New Zealand, Melbourne, and Adelaide, and R.C.S., Edinburgh. *Publications:* A Cerebral Atlas of Normal and Defective Brains, 1938; Your Brain and its Story, 1939; Recent Advances in the Study of the Brain as the Implement of Mind, Royal Society of Edinburgh, 1944; Brain and Mind, or the Nervous System of Man, 1928; The Beattie Smith Lectures on Insanity, University of Melbourne, Cornell University, N.Y.; Intelligence and Social Valuation, Training School, Vineland, N.J., 1920; Report on Mental Deficiency in the State of Victoria, 1929; many contributions to the scientific press in Anatomy, Anthropology, and Mental Science. *Address:* 3c All Saints Road, Clifton, Bristol 8. *T.:* 36237. *Club:* Royal Commonwealth Society. [*Died* 30 *Sept.* 1962.

BERRY, Rev. Sidney Malcolm, D.D. (Glas.); M.A.; *b.* Southport, 25 July 1881; *s.* of Dr. C. A. Berry, Wolverhampton; *m.* 1907, Helen Logan, Bedford Park, W.; two *d.* *Educ.:* Tettenhall College, Staffs.; Clare College, Cambridge; Mansfield College, Oxford. Minister of the following churches: Oxted and Limpsfield, Surrey, 1906-9; Chorlton-cum-Hardy, Manchester, 1909-1912; Carrs Lane Church, Birmingham, 1912-23; Mod. of Federal Council of Free Churches of Eng. 1934-35, Acting Moderator, 1941-42; Hon. Sec., Free Church Federal Council, 1935-44; Chm., Congregational Union of England and Wales, 1947-48; (Sec., 1923-48, and 1955-56); Moderator Internat. Congregational Council, 1944-50; Minister and Sec., 1948-55. *Publications:* Graces of the Christian Character; The Crucible of Experience; Revealing Light; Vital Preaching, 1936; The Great Issue, 1944. *Address:* 56 Claremont Road, Highgate, N. 6. *Club:* Athenæum. [*Died* 2 *Aug.* **1961.**

BERRY, Trevor T.; *see* Thornton-Berry.

BERTHON, Rear-Admiral Charles Pierre, C.B.E. 1945; retired; *b.* 15 Feb. 1893; *er. s.* of Claude Tinné Berthon; *m.* 1920, Ruth Euphemia Meldrum, 2nd *d.* of John Ferrier, Woodhayes, Wimbledon; one *s.* three *d.* *Educ.:* Royal Naval Colleges Osborne and Dartmouth. Joined R.N., 1906; served European War 1914-18, Home Fleet; War of 1939-45; Mediterranean Fleet, 1939-41; Staff of Admiral (Air), Lee-on-Solent, 1942-45 (despatches, C.B.E.); Director of Aircraft Maintenance and Repair, Admiralty, 1945-48. Captain (E), 1939; Rear-Admiral (E), 1946; retired, 1949. *Address:* The Leaden Porch House, Deddington, Oxford. *T.:* Deddington 261 [*Died* 11 *March* 1965.

BERTRAM, Lt.-Col. William Robert, C.M.G. 1919; D.S.O. 1917; late 8th Canadian Infantry Batt. and General Staff 2nd Canadian Div.; *b.* 1888; *s.* of late Maj. William Bertram of Nisbet and Kersawell; *m.* 1st 1917, Zoë Weldon L'Estrange (marr. diss., 1947), *y. d.* of late Maj.-Gen. William L'Estrange Eames, C.B., C.B.E., V.D.; four *d.*; 2nd, 1949, Ena, 2nd *d.* of W. T. Radford. *Educ.:* Wellington College; Royal Military Academy, Woolwich. Served in Gordon Highlanders, 1907-11, when relinquished commission and went to Canada; served European War, 1914-19 (despatches, C.M.G., D.S.O., Belgian Croix de Guerre, French Croix de Guerre with Palm). *Address:* Old Quay House, Hayle, Cornwall. *T.:* Hayle 2347. [*Died* 8 *Aug.* 1970.

BESICOVITCH, Abram Samoilovitch, F.R.S. 1934; Rouse Ball Professor of Mathematics at University of Cambridge, 1950-58, retired; Fellow of Trinity College; *b.* 24 Jan. 1891; *s.* of Samuel and Eva Besicovitch; *m.* 1928, Valentina Alexandrovna Denissova. *Educ.:* University of Petersbourgh. Academic career in Perm and Petersbourgh; emigrated from U.S.S.R. in 1925. Lectureship in Liverpool; Cayley Lecturer in Mathematics, Cambridge. Visiting Professor: Univ. of Pennsylvania, 1958-62; Dartmouth Coll., 1962-63; Oregon State Univ., 1964-65; Univ. of Wisconsin, 1965; Cornell University, 1965-66. Adams Prize, 1930; De Morgan Medallist of London Mathematical Soc., 1950; Sylvester Medallist of Royal Soc., 1952. *Publications:* Almost periodic functions, 1932; papers in mathematical periodicals. *Address:* Trinity College, Cambridge. *T.:* 58201. [*Died* 2 *Nov.* 1970.

BESLY, Ernest Francis Withers, C.M.G. 1941; Partner in firm of Trower, Still & Keeling, Solicitors, 5 New Square, Lincoln's Inn; *b.* 1891; 2nd *s.* of late Rev. Edward Frederick Seymour Besly, Stokesley Rectory, Yorkshire and Evelyn Georgina Moore; *m.* 1927, Helen Judith, *d.* of late D'Oyley Scott Ransom, Wyverton Hall, Notts.; one *s.* one *d.* *Educ.:* Winchester; Balliol College, Oxford. Called to Bar, Inner Temple, 1921. Legal Secretary to Judicial Adviser to Egyptian Government, 1926-37; Legal

Counsellor, British Embassy, Cairo, 1937-46; Judge of H.B.M. Consular Court in Egypt, 1938-46. U.K. Representative and Pres. Internat. Tribunal in the Saar, 1956-59. 2nd Class Order of the Nile, 3rd Class Order of Ismail. *Recreation:* golf. *Address:* Barton Hatch, Limpsfield, Surrey. *T.:* Limpsfield Chart 2262. *Club:* St. James'.
[*Died* 10 *Aug.* 1965.

BEST, Ven. Joseph; Archdeacon of Ballarat, 1926-50, now Archdeacon Emeritus; *b.* 1880; 3rd *s.* of Henry Best, J.P., one of Australia's pioneer settlers; *m.* 1910, Marjorie Jean Wallace; three *s.* two *d.* *Educ.:* Stawell T.S.; St. Aidan's College, Ballarat. Curate of Berringa, 1905-7; Vicar of Nhill, 1907-12; Linton, 1912-14; St. John's Ballarat, 1915-21; Rural Dean of Ballarat North, 1919; Archdeacon of Maryborough, 1921-26; served European War; Chaplain, 39th Battalion A.I.F. in France, 1916-17; Chaplain, 11th Regiment Australian Light Horse, Palestine, 1918; Senior Chaplain, Australian Mounted Division, 1918; Examining Chaplain to the Bishop of Ballarat, 1934-50; Vicar General of Diocese of Ballarat, 1947-50. *Publications:* The Apostolic Ministry; Big Business in Religion; What Every Anglican Should Know; Editor of the Ballarat Chronicle, 1926-37. *Recreations:* angling, geology, chess. *Address:* 413 Lydiard Street, Ballarat, Victoria, Australia. *T.A.:* Ballarat, Australia. *T.:* Ballarat 2.4911.
[*Died* 11 *July* 1965.

BESTE, Capt. Sir Henry A. B. D.; *see* Digby-Beste.

BETHAM, Lt.-Col. Sir Geoffrey Lawrence, K.B.E., *cr.* 1944; C.I.E. 1934; M.C; *b.* 8 Apr. 1889; *m.* 1915, Dorothy, *d.* of A. Cartwright; one *d.* *Educ.:* Dulwich College; R.M.C. Sandhurst. First commission, 1909: Political Agent Chagai, 1925, Sibi, 1927, Zhob, 1929; Commissioner, Ajmer-Merwara, 1933-34; Resident in Mewar, 1935-38; Min. in Nepal, 1938-44. *Publication:* The Golden Gallery (a Story of the 2nd Punjab Regiment, 1762-1947), 1956. *Address:* 64 Albert Hall Mansions, S.W.7. *T.:* Kensington 8285. *Clubs:* United Service, M.C.C.; I Zingari; Free Foresters; Band of Brothers; Rugby Football (Blackheath). [*Died* 6 *Nov.* 1963.

BETHELL, 2nd Baron of Romford, U.K., *cr.* 1922; **John Raymond Bethell;** Bt., *cr.* 1911; Director of Gillett Bros. Discount Co. Ltd.; *b.* 23 Oct. 1902; *er. s.* of 1st Baron Bethell and Florence (*d.* 1957), *d.* of James W. Wyles; *S.* father 1945; *m.* 1st, 1927, Veronica Eileen (marriage dissolved, 1948), *d.* of Sir James Connolly; one *s.* two *d.*; 2nd, 1948, Mrs. Joan Reid, *widow* of Lt.-Comdr. H. N. Reid, R.N., and *d.* of late Brig.-Gen. N. W. Webber, C.M.G., D.S.O. *Educ.:* Harrow; Jesus College, Cambridge. *Recreation:* shooting. *Heir:* *s.* Hon. Guy Anthony John Bethell, *b.* 17 Mar. 1928. *Address:* 40 Hill St., W.1. *T.:* Mayfair 4113. *Clubs:* Naval and Military, Public Schools.
[*Died* 30 *Sept.* 1965.

BETHELL, 3rd Baron, *cr.* 1922, of Romford; **Guy Anthony John Bethell;** Bt., *cr.* 1911; *b.* 17 March 1928; *S.* father, 1965. *Educ.:* Eton. Formerly Royal Irish Fusiliers, 2nd Lieutenant; served Palestine, 1947-48. *Heir:* *kinsman,* William Nicholas Bethell [*b.* 19 July 1938; *m.* 1964, Cecilia Mary Lothian Honeyman, *e. d.* of Prof. A. M. Honeyman]. [*Died* 2 *Dec.* 1967.

BETTERIDGE, Don; *see* Newman, Bernard.

BETTS, Reginald Robert; Masaryk Professor of Central European History in the University of London since 1946; *b.* 30 Oct. 1903; *e. s.* of Robert Frederick and Gertrude Emily Betts; *m.* 1930; one *s.* one *d.* *Educ.:* Norwich School; New College, Oxford. Assistant Master, Winchester College, 1927; Lecturer in History, University of Liverpool, 1929-31; Lecturer in Medieval History, Queen's Univ., Belfast, 1931-34; Professor of History, University College, Southampton, 1934-44; Service with European division of B.B.C. 1941-44; Professor of History, Univ. of Birmingham, 1945-46. *Publications:* Central and Southern Europe, 1945-1948; articles on Czechoslovak and Central European History in New Cambridge Modern History, Chambers's Encyclopedia and various historical jls. *Address:* The School of Slavonic and East European Studies, Senate House, University of London, W.C.1. *T.:* Museum 9782. [*Died* 15 *May* 1961.

BETTY, Vice-Adm. A. K.; *see* Kemmi Betty.

BEVAN, Ven. Hugh Henry Molesworth, M.A.; Prebendary of Hereford Cathedral, 1948-66; Vicar of Stanton-Lacy, 1954-66; Archdeacon of Ludlow, 1948-60, emeritus since 1960; Examining Chaplain to Bishop of London, 1939-61, and to Bishop of Hereford, 1948-66; Member of Nobody's Friends, 1946-64. Fellow of Sion Coll., 1945; *b.* 2 Aug. 1884; *s.* of late Ven. H. E. J. Bevan; *m.* 1917, Rachel Joyse, *d.* of late Rev. R. B. Knatchbull-Hugessen; three *s.* *Educ.:* Shrewsbury; Queen's Coll., Oxford; Cuddesdon. Deacon, 1908; Priest, 1909; Curate, Holy Trinity, Paddington, 1908-13; Chelsea Parish Church, 1913-16; Lecturer in Divinity (Whitelands College), 1915-17; Vicar of St. Dunstan's, E. Acton, 1916-28; Vicar of Hammersmith, 1928-48; Prebendary of Newington in St. Paul's Cathedral, 1942-48. Hon. Clerical Secretary of London Diocesan Conference, 1943-48; Rural Dean of Ealing, 1926-28; and of Hammersmith, 1928-42 and 1945-48; Hon. Chaplain to Bishop Winnington-Ingram, 1934-39. O.C.F., 1941-1945. *Address:* Corvedale, Croscombe, Wells, Somerset. [*Died* 15 *Jan.* 1970.

BEVAN-BAKER, Bevan Braithwaite, M.A., B.Sc. (Lond.), D.Sc. (Edin.); F.R.S.E.; *b.* 1890; *s.* of George Samuel Baker, Willesden; *m.* 1918, Margaret Stewart (*d.* 1961), *e. d.* of Dr. A. H. Freeland Barbour, Edinburgh; one *s.* three *d.* *Educ.:* Sidcot School, Somerset; University College, London; University of Münich. Assistant in Mathematics, University College, London, 1918-20; Lecturer in Mathematics, University of Edinburgh, 1920-24; Professor of Mathematics in the University of London, and Head of the Department of Mathematics, Royal Holloway College (University of London), 1924-44; Secretary of the Edinburgh Mathematical Society, 1921-24. *Publications:* (with E. T. Copson) The Mathematical Theory of Huygens' Principle, 1939; various memoirs in the Philosophical Magazine and the publications of the Edinburgh Mathematical Society, etc. *Recreation:* music. *Address:* 24 George Square, Edinburgh. *T.:* Newington 2588.
[*Died* 1 *July* 1963.

BEVERIDGE, 1st Baron, *cr.* 1946, of Tuggal; **William Henry Beveridge,** K.C.B., *cr.* 1919 (C.B. 1916); Das grosse Ehrenzeichen mit dem Stern (Austria); F.B.A. 1937; Barrister; Hon. LL.D. London, Aberdeen, Birmingham, Chicago, Columbia, Melbourne and Oslo; Hon. D.C.L. Oxford; Docteur (Hon.) Faculty of Law, Univ. of Paris; Hon. D.Litt. McGill and New Zealand; Hon. D.Litt. Hum. Pennsylvania; Hon. Dr. of Social Sciences, Brussels; Hon. Doctor of Economics, Rotterdam; Hon. Fellow Balliol, Nuffield and University Colleges, Oxford; Hon. Dr. Humanities, Brandeis; *b.* Rangpur, Bengal, 5 Mar. 1879; *e. s.* of Henry Beveridge, I.C.S. (*d.* 1929), and Annette (*d.* 1929), *d.* of William

Akroyd of Stourbridge (through whom held William Akroyd Founder's Kin Scholarship); *m.* 1942, Janet (*d.* 1959), *widow* of D. B. Mair and 3rd *d.* of William Philip, Newport, Fife. *Educ.:* Charterhouse, Balliol College, Oxford (1st Class Math. Mods.; 1st Class Classical Mods., 1st Class Lit. Hum. M.A., B.C.L. 1902). Stowell Civil Law Fellow of University College, Oxford, 1902-9; D.Sc. (Econ.) London, 1930; Sub-warden of Toynbee Hall, 1903-5; Leader-writer for Morning Post, 1906-8; Member of Central (Unemployed) Body for London, 1905-8, and first Chairman of Employment Exchanges Committee; in Board of Trade, 1908-16, as Director of Labour Exchanges, 1909-16, and Assist.-Sec. in charge of Employment Depart.; Assist. Gen. Sec. to the Ministry of Munitions, 1915-16; in Ministry of Food as Second Secretary, 1916-18; and Permanent Sec., 1919; Director of London School of Economics and Political Science, 1919-37; Vice-Chanc. of London Univ., 1926-28; Master of Univ. College, Oxford, 1937-45; M.P. (L.) Berwick-on-Tweed, 1944-45; Pres. Royal Economic Society, 1940-44; President Royal Statistical Society, 1941-43; Senator of London Univ., 1919-37 and 1944-48. Mem. of Royal Commission on Coal Industry, 1925; Chairman Unemployment Insurance Statutory Committee, 1934-44; Chairman of Sub-Committee of Committee of Imperial Defence on Food Rationing, 1936; Chairman of Committee on Skilled Men in Services, 1941-42; Fuel Rationing Enquiry for President of Board of Trade, 1942; Chairman of Inter-Departmental Committee on Social Insurance and Allied Services, 1941-42; undertook Voluntary Social Service Inquiry, 1947; Chm. Aycliffe Development Corp. under New Towns Act, 1947-53, and Peterlee Development Corp., 1949-51; Chm. Broadcasting Cttee., 1949-50. *Publications:* Unemployment: A Problem of Industry, 1909 (new edition, 1930); John and Irene: An Anthology of Thoughts on Woman, 1912; Swish (a submarine war game), 1916; The Public Service in War and in Peace, Peace in Austria, 1920; Insurance for All, 1924; British Food Control, 1929; Causes and Cures of Unemployment, 1931; Tariffs (in collaboration), 1931; Changes in Family Life, 1932; Planning under Socialism, 1936; The Unemployment Insurance Statutory Committee (pamphlet), 1937; Prices and Wages in England, Vol. I. (with others), 1939; Blockade and the Civilian Population (pamphlet); Peace by Federation? (pamphlet); Pillars of Security, 1943; Full Employment in a Free Society, 1944 (new Prologue, 1960); The Price of Peace, 1945; Why I am a Liberal, 1945; Germany: An Urgent Message (pamphlet), 1947; India Called Them, 1948; Voluntary Action, 1948; the Evidence for Voluntary Action, 1949; (with Janet Beveridge) On and Off the Platform, 1949; and Antipodes Notebook, 1949; Power and Influence, 1953; A Defence of Free Learning, 1959: London School of Economics and its Problems, 1960. Articles in Contempory Review, Economic Journal, Statistical Journal, Economica, Politica, Economic History Review, Universities Quarterly, etc. and introductions to numerous books by others. *Recreation:* country life. *Heir:* none. *Address:* Staverton House, 104 Woodstock Road, Oxford. *T.:* 56060. *Club:* Reform.

[*Died* 16 *March* 1963 (*ext.*).

BEVERIDGE, Maj.-Gen. Sir Wilfred William Ogilvy, K.B.E., *cr.* 1924 (C.B.E. 1919); C.B. 1915; D.S.O. 1902; Légion d'Honneur, Croix de Chevalier; Order of St. Stanislas: M.B., M.Ch. Edin.; D.P.H. Camb.; late Professor of Hygiene, Royal Army Medical College; late Director of Hygiene, W.O.; K.H.P. 1920; Corr. Member French Acad. of Medicine; *b.* Edinburgh, 16 Nov. 1864; *s.* of James Beveridge of Tillyochie and Helen Ogilvy; *m.* Mary (*d.* 1946), *d.* of George Spencer-Walker. *Educ.:* Kensington; Edin. University. Entered R.A.M.C. 1890; Major, 1902; Lt.-Col. 1912; Col. 1917; Major-General 1922; retired pay, 1924; served S. African War, 1899-1902 (despatches, D.S.O.); on General Headquarters Staff, European War, 1914-18 (despatches five times, C.B.); Vice-President Royal Society of Health; Vice-President Institute of Hygiene; Fellow Soc. of Medical Officers of Health; late Examiner in Public Health to Royal College of Physicians and Surgeons, London; Chadwick Gold Medallist, 1920. *Publications:* Hand book on analysis, 1911; and many papers on analysis of food and lethal gases. *Address:* 55 Earls Avenue, Folkestone, Kent. *T.:* Folkestone 51056.

[*Died* 23 *March* 1962.

BEVERS, Edmund Cecil, C.B.E. 1951; M.A., M.B., B.Ch. (Oxon); F.R.C.S. (Eng.); F.R.C.S. (Edin.); Consulting Surgeon, Radcliffe Infirmary, Oxford; Major, R.A.M.C.(T.); *b.* 1876; *s.* of late Edmund Augustine Bevers of Oxford; *m.* Tryphaena Letathea (*d.* 1954), *d.* of late Rev. Edward Seymour, Bratton Clovelly, Devon. *Educ.:* St. Edward's School, Oxford; Oxford Univ.; Guy's Hosp. After graduating held several Hospital appointments in London and Oxford, and for three years was engaged in teaching Anatomy in the University. *Publications:* Treatment of Acute Intestinal Obstruction; Conditions which mimic the Acute Abdomen; Traumatic Myositis Ossificans; Facio-Hypoglossal Anastomosis and other papers in medical journals. *Recreation:* fishing. *Address:* 39 Belsyre Court, Oxford. *Clubs:* Union Society (Oxford); Salcombe Yacht (Salcombe).

[*Died* 13 *Dec.* 1961.

BEVES, Donald Howard; University Lecturer, Cambridge; *b.* 6 March 1896; *s.* of Edward Leslie Beves, Brighton; unmarried. *Educ.:* Rugby; King's College, Cambridge (B.A. 1921). 8th Batt. Rifle Brigade, Dec. 1914-April 1919; France, 1915-16, Instructor No. 6 O.C.B. Oxford, Mar. 1917-Sept. 1918; Instructor, Central School of Instruction, Berkhamsted, Sept. 1918-April 1919; Clerk in the House of Commons, 1922-24; Fellow of King's College, Cambridge, 1924, Vice-Provost, 1946-51. *Recreations:* glass and silver collecting. *Address:* King's College, Cambridge. *T.:* Cambridge 4411. *Club:* Garrick.

[*Died* 6 *July* 1961.

BEVIN, Dame Florence (Anne), D.B.E., *cr.* 1952; *m.* (as Florence Townley), Ernest Bevin, later Rt. Hon. Ernest Bevin, P.C., M.P., Hon. LL.D., Secretary of State for Foreign Affairs, 1945-51, Lord Privy Seal, 1951, and former General Secretary of the T.G.W.U. (*d.* 14 April 1951); one *d.*

[*Died* 11 *Aug.* 1968.

BEVIR, Vice-Adm. Oliver, C.B. 1945; C.B.E. 1946; *b.* 16 February 1891; *s.* of late Ernest Bevir, Downhurst, Hendon, Middlesex, and Dyer Street, Cirencester; *m.* 1924, L. K. C. Raikes, Cefncoed, nr. Newport, Mon.; one *s.* *Educ.:* Heddon Court; R.N.C. Osborne and Dartmouth. Midshipman, 1908; Comdr. 1925; R.N. Staff Course, 1925-26; on Staff of Tactical School, 1926-28; 2nd in Command H.M.S. Renown, 1928-30; in Plans Division Admiralty, 1931-1932; Captain, 1932; Command of H.M.S. Leith; (N.Z. Station), 1934-37; Staff of R.N. War College, 1937-39; Command of H.M.S. Resolution, 1939-40; of H.M.S. Excellent, 1941; Director of Naval Ordnance, 1941-44; Rear-Admiral, 1942; Senior Officer, Royal Naval Establishments, India, 1944-46; retired Dec. 1945; Vice-Admiral, 1945. Secretary of the National Trust, 1946-1949. *Recreations:* fishing, gardening. *Address:* Hill House, Holcombe, nr. Bath. *Club:* United Service.

[*Died* 4 *Nov.* 1967.

BEWSHER, Paul; author and journalist; *b.* 12 Nov. 1894; *s.* of late James Bewsher, M.A., for 42 years Headmaster of Colet Court.

Educ.: Colet Court and St. Paul's School. Port of London Authority, 1912-14; Advertisers' Weekly, 1914; Royal Naval Air Service, 1915-18; Royal Air Force, 1918-19; Sub-Editor, Modern Transport, 1919; lectured in United States, 1919; lectured in Great Britain, 1919-20; joined staff of Daily Mail, 1920. *Publications:* The Dawn Patrol, and other Poems of an Aviator, 1917; The Bombing of Bruges, 1918; Green Balls: The Adventures of a Night Bomber, 1919. *Recreations:* walking in London and the country. *Address:* Northcliffe House, Tudor Street, E.C.4. [*Died* 18 *Jan.* 1966.

BEZZANT, Rev. Canon James Stanley, B.D., M.A. (Oxon.); B.D. (Cantab.); Lecturer in Divinity, Cambridge, 1953-64; Fellow of St. John's Coll. (Dean, 1952-64); Canon Emeritus of Liverpool Cathedral; *b.* 14 May 1897; *s.* of late Albert Edward and Jane Caroline Bezzant, formerly of Dover; *m.* 1928, Muriel Christine Turberville, *o. d.* of late Dr. W. T. Farncombe, Endon, Pershore, Worcestershire; one *s.* one *d.* *Educ.:* privately; Pembroke Coll., Oxon. Graduated in Mod. Hist. (S.C.), 1921, 1st Class Hon. School of Theology, 1923; Senior Denyer and Johnson Scholarship, 1927; Curate of Hartlebury, Worcs., 1923; Chaplain and Lecturer of Exeter College, 1927; Tutor in Theology to Pembroke College, 1927; Fellow of Exeter College, 1929; Vice-Principal of Ripon Hall, Oxon, 1925-33; Canon Residentiary and Chancellor of Liverpool Cathedral, 1933-52. Select Preacher, Cambridge, 1930-31, 1934-1935, 1953-54; Hulsean Preacher, Camb., 1954-55; Proctor in Convocation, for Camb. Univ., 1958-60. Select Preacher, Oxford, 1932-1934 and 1963-64; Examining Chaplain to Bishops of Worcester and Coventry, 1931-38; to Bishop of Bradford, 1931-33; to Bishop of Liverpool since 1932; to Bishops of Winchester, 1940-64; Examiner in Theology, University of London, 1932-34; Examiner in Honour School of Theology, Oxford, 1935-1938; Lectr. in Union Theol. Seminary, New York, 1935; W. B. Noble Lecturer, Harvard University, U.S.A., 1937-38 and 1950; Chaplain R.N.V.R., 1940-46. *Publications:* Explanations: A Companion to A Short Bible; Aspects of Belief; articles in Hibbert Journal and The Modern Churchman, Encyclopædia Britannica, Objections to Christian Belief, etc. *Address:* St. John's College, Cambridge. *T.:* Cambridge 58741. *Club:* Exchange (Liverpool). [*Died* 27 *March* 1967.

BHABHA, Homi Jehangir, Ph.D.; F.R.S. 1941; Padma Bhushan, 1954; Hon. D.Sc.: Patna, 1944; Lucknow, 1949; Banaras, 1950; Agra, 1952; Perth, 1954; Allahabad, 1958; London, 1960; Hon. Sc.D. Cambridge, 1959; Padova, 1961; Hon. F.R.S.E. 1957; Director and Professor of Theoretical Physics, Tata Institute of Fundamental Research, Bombay; Secretary to the Government of India, Department of Atomic Energy; Chairman, Atomic Energy Commission, India; Director, Atomic Energy Establishment at Trombay, Bombay; *b.* 30 Oct. 1909. *Educ.:* Cathedral and John Cannon High School, Elphinstone Coll., and Royal Inst. of Science, Bombay; Gonville and Caius College, Cambridge (B.A., Ph.D.). Rouse Ball Travelling Studentship in Mathematics, Cambridge, 1932; Isaac Newton Studentship from 1934; Sen. Studentship of Exhibition of 1851 from 1936. Became special Reader in Theoretical Physics, 1940, at Indian Institute of Science, Bangalore; Adams Prize, 1942; Professor, Cosmic Ray Research Unit, Indian Institute of Science, 1942-45; Hopkins Prize, 1948. Pres., Internat. Conf. on the Peaceful Uses of Atomic Energy, Geneva, 1955; Member: Scientific Advisory Cttee., Inter at. Atomic Energy Agency; U.N. Scientific Advisory Committee. Hon. Fellow: Gonville and Caius College, Cambridge, 1957; Roy. Soc. Edinburgh, 1957; American Academy of Arts and Sciences, 1959; Member: World Acad. of Arts and Sciences 1962, (Fellow); Scientific Advisory Cttee., Internat. Atomic Energy Agency; U.N. Scientific Advisory Cttee. *Publications:* on quantum theory, elementary physical particles, cosmic radiation. *Address:* 12 Little Gibbs Road, Bombay 6, India. [*Died* 24 *Jan.* 1966.

BICESTER, 2nd Baron, *cr.* 1938, of Tusmeor; **Randal Hugh Vivian Smith:** Managing Director, Morgan Grenfell & Co. Ltd., 1930-1967; Director until 1967: Vickers Ltd.; Shell Transport and Trading Co. Ltd.; Associated Electrical Industries; Chm., Royal National Pension Fund for Nurses, since 1963; *b.* 9 January 1898; *e. s.* of 1st Baron Bicester and the late Lady Sybil Mary McDonnell, *o. d.* of 6th Earl of Antrim; *S.* father 1956; *m.* 1922, Hon. Dorothea Gwenllian James, *e. d.* of 3rd Baron Northbourne; two *d.* *Educ.:* Eton; Sandhurst. High Sheriff County of Oxfordshire, 1945-46. Lieutenant 17th Lancers; invalided, 1920. O.St.J. 1944. *Recreation:* shooting. *Heir:* *nephew* Angus Edward Vivian Smith, *b.* 20 Feb. 1932. *Address:* Tusmore, Bicester, Oxon. *T.:* Fritwell 209. *Clubs:* Brooks's, Cavalry, Oriental. [*Died* 15 *Jan.* 1968.

BICKERSTETH, John Richard, C.B.E. 1952; D.L.; Land Agent; *b.* 1897; *s.* of late John Bickersteth, C.B.E., D.L., Cottingham House, Cottingham, E. Yorks., and Margaret, *d.* of 4th Earl of Ashburnham; *m.* 1925, Cecily, *d.* of late Michael O'Shea, Knocknasuff, Co. Cork, and *widow* of H. F. Percival. *Educ.:* Shrewsbury; Balliol Coll., Oxford. Served European War, 1914-18, in France with Yorkshire Hussars and R.F.C., retired with rank of Captain, 1919. C.A. East Sussex; Chairman East Sussex C.C., 1946-1949; J.P. Sussex 1945; D.L. 1956. Chairman East Sussex County Agricultural Executive Committee, 1946-58. F.L.A.S. *Address:* Agmerhurst House, Ashburnham, Battle, Sussex. *T.:* Ninfield 253. *Club:* United University. [*Died* 5 *Oct.* 1967.

BICKERSTETH, Rev. Kenneth Julian Faithfull, M.C., 1918; M.A.; Hon. C.F.; Chaplain to Her Majesty's Household from 1953; Archdeacon of Maidstone and Canon Residentiary of Canterbury Cathedral, 1943-58, retired; Hon. Canon, Canterbury Cathedral, since 1958; *b.* 5 July 1885; 3rd *s.* of late Rev. Dr. S. Bickersteth. *Educ.:* Rugby; Christ Church, Oxford, B.A. 1907, M.A. 1912; Wells Theological College. Formerly Assistant Curate, Rugby Parish Church; Chaplain and Assistant Master, Melbourne Grammar School; Brigade Chaplain and subsequently Senior Chaplain of the 56th (London) Territorial Division on the Western Front (M.C., despatches twice); Headmaster of St. Peter's College, Adelaide, 1919-33; Headmaster of Felsted School, Essex, 1933-43; Member of the Council of the University of Adelaide, 1921-33; Foundation Fellow of St. Mark's College, Adelaide, 1925; Senior Chaplain (C. of E.) Australian Military Forces, South Australia, 1930; Select Preacher, Cambridge, 1934-35; Council of Royal Empire Society, 1936; Select Preacher, Oxford, 1939-40. Fellow Corporation of SS. Mary and Nicolas, 1943; Chairman, Canterbury Diocesan Education Committee, 1944; Member, Council of Royal School of Church Music, 1944-52; Canterbury Cathedral, Treasurer, 1945-58. Hon. Fell. Australian Coll. of Education, 1960. *Address:* 2 Starr's House, The Precincts, Canterbury. *T.:* Canterbury 2089. *Club:* Athenæum. [*Died* 16 *Oct.* 1962.

BICKFORD, Right Rev. Monsignor Francis P., Protonotary Apostolic, 1960; M.C.; Chaplain, Tyburn Convent, W.2; Canon of Westminster since 1932; Domestic Prelate to H.H., 1935; *b.* 1889; *y. s.* of late Admiral A. K. Bickford, C.M.G. *Educ.:* St. Edmund's Old Hall. C.F. 47th

Lond. Div., 1915-19 (M.C., despatches); Vicar-Gen., Westminster 1937-43; Pres., St. Edmund's Coll. and Rector of Allen Hall, 1932-46. *Address:* 9 Hyde Park Pl., W.2. [*Died* 7 *Dec.* 1968.

BICKLEY, William Gee, D.Sc. (London), F.R.Ae.S.; A.C.G.I.; F.I.M.A.; Emeritus Professor since 1953; Professor of Mathematics in the University of London, at Imperial College of Science and Technology, 1947-53; *b.* 19 April 1893. *Educ.:* Council and County Schools, Wolverton, Bucks.; University College, Reading. B.S.c, 1912; First Cl. Hons. in Mathematics, 1913; M.Sc., 1920; D.Sc., 1930. Teacher of mathematics in secondary and public schools, 1914-19; Lecturer in Mathematics at Battersea Polytechnic, 1919-29; Asst. Prof. and Univ. Reader at Imperial Coll., 1930-47, became blind, 1949. Council of London Mathematical Society, 1942-46, Vice-Pres., 1946-1948; Member, Executive Council, R.N.I.B. *Publications:* Engineering Applications of Mathematics 1925; (part author) Rayleigh's Principle, 1933; Table of Powers, 1940; (editor and part author) Tables of Bessel Functions, Part II, 1952; (part author) Introduction to the Study of Vibrating Systems, 1961; Via Vector to Tensor, 1962; Matrices, their Meaning and Manipulation, 1964; original papers on mathematics and its applications; articles, and reviews of mathematical books. *Address:* 27 Cuckoo Hill, Pinner, Middx. [*Died* 4 *July* 1969.

BIDDLE, Major-General Anthony J. Drexel, LL.D.; Legion of Merit (U.S.); United States Ambassador to Spain, since 1961; *b.* Philadelphia, 17 Dec. 1896; *s.* of late A(nthony) J(oseph) Drexel Biddle and Cornelia Rundell Biddle (*née* Bradley); *m.* 1st, Mary Duke; 2nd, 1931, Margaret Thompson Schulze; 3rd, 1946, Margaret Atkinson Loughborough. *Educ.:* St. Paul's School, N.H. Grad. 1915. Engaged in shipping business, mining bus., S. Africa, 1931-1934; U.S. Minister to Norway, 1935-37; Ambassador to Poland, 1937; accompanied Polish Govt. in forced move from Warsaw to several capitals in Poland, 1939, and to Angers, France; Interim Ambassador to France, 1940, when French Govt. moved seat to Tours and thence to Bordeaux; U.S. Ambassador to govts. of Poland, Belgium, The Netherlands, Norway, Greece, Yugoslavia, Czechoslovakia (concurrently Minister to Luxembourg), 1941-44; ret. from diplomatic service, Jan. 1944. Asst. Sec., Dem. Nat. Convention, Philadelphia, 1936. Served with U.S. Army in War, 1917-18, advancing to rank of Capt.; on active duty as Lt.-Col., U.S. Army, 1944, advancing to Brig.-Gen., 1951; Deputy Chief, European Allied Contact Section, S.H.A.E.F.; chief, Allied Contact Section, U.S.F.E.T., 1945; Chief, Allied Contact Sect., E.U.C.O.M., 1946-48; Dep. Foreign Liaison Officer, Gen. Staff Corps, Dept. of Army, Washington, 1948; Foreign Liaison Officer, 1950-51; exec. Nat. Mil. Reps., S.H.A.P.E., 1951-53; Special Asst. to Chief of Staff, Dept. of Army, Washington, 1953-55; Adjutant General of Pennsylvania with rank of Maj.-General, U.S.A.R., A.U.S., 1955-61. Pres. Assoc. of U.S. Army, 1959-60. Chairman: Penna. Aeronautics Commn., 1958-61; State Armory Board, 1958-61; Governmental Reorganizaton Commn., 1958-61; Commr. to up-date Pennsylvania Laws on Drugs, Foods and Cosmetics, 1961; 100th Anniv. of Battle of Gettysburg and Lincoln's Gettysburg Address Commn., 1955-61; (Member, *ex officio*, State Veterans Commn. and of Board of Trustees, Soldiers' & Sailors' Home), 1955-1961; Member Board of Trustees, Temple Univ., Philadelphia; Hon. LL.D.: Temple Univ.; Drexel Inst. of Technology. Holds numerous foreign decorations including O.B.E. (Gt. Brit.). *Recreations:* (formerly) tennis (Court tennis champion of France, 1933). *Address:* Embassy of the U.S.A., Madrid, Spain. *Clubs:* Philadelphia, Racquet and Tennis (Phila.); Brook, Knickerbocker, Union, Racquet and Tennis, River (N.Y.C.); Travellers' (Paris). [*Died* 13 *Nov.* 1961.

BIDDLE, Francis; *b.* 9 May 1886; *s.* of Algernon Sydney and Frances Robinson Biddle; *m.* 1918, Katherine Garrison Chapin; one *s.* *Educ.:* Groton School, Mass.; Harvard College and Law School. Private Sec., Mr. Justice Holmes, U.S. Supreme Court, 1911-12; private practice of law, Philadelphia, 1912-39; Special Asst. U.S. Attorney Eastern Dist., Pa., 1922-26; Chm. Nat. Labor Relations Board, 1934-35; Member Board of Education, Phila., 1936-39; Class C director Federal Reserve Bank, Pa., and Deputy Chairman, 1938-39; Chief Counsel Joint Congressional Cttee. to investigate Tennessee Valley Authority, 1938-39; Judge U.S. Circuit Court of Appeals, Third Circuit, 1939-40; Solicitor-General, U.S., 1940-41; Attorney-General, U.S., 1941-45; U.S. Member Internat. Military Tribunal, 1945-46; Member, Permanent Court of Arbitration, 1951-57; Hon. Bencher Inner Temple, 1946; Mem. American Academy of Arts and Sciences. Nat. Chm., Americans for Democratic Action, 1950-54; Member, Franklin Delano Roosevelt Memorial Commn. (Chm., 1955-65). Hon. LL.D.: Boston University, 1942; Drexel Institute of Technology, Hobart and William Smith College, 1943; La Salle Coll.; Four Freedoms Award, 1942; Order of Merit, Italy, 1954. *Publications:* Llanfear Pattern (novel), 1927; Mr. Justice Holmes (biography), 1942; Democratic Thinking and the War (William H. White lectures), 1943; The World's Best Hope, 1949; The Fear of Freedom, 1951; A Casual Past, 1961; Justice Holmes, Natural Law and the Supreme Court, 1961; In Brief Authority, 1962; *Address:* 1669 31 Street, N.W. Washington 7, D.C., U.S.A. *T.:* Adams 43560. *Clubs:* Philadelphia; Coffee House (New York); Cosmos (Washington). [*Died* 4 *Oct.* 1968.

BIDDLE, Sir Reginald Poulton, Kt. 1957; C.B.E. 1944; T.D.; D.L., J.P. Southampton; Docks and Marine Manager, Southampton, retired; *b.* Jersey, Channel Islands, 4 Dec. 1888, *s.* of late Alfred Biddle; *m.* 1922, Kathleen, *d.* of Frederick Baker, Jersey. *Educ.:* Saunders Acad. in Jersey. Joined L. & S.W. Rly. Co. in Jersey, 1904. Transferred to Southampton, 1907; Lt.-Col. Engineer and Railway Staff Corps, 1936; Deputy Director of Ports, Ministry of War Transport, London, 1941; later Regional Port Director, North Western Ports. Officier Légion d'Honneur; American Medal of Freedom with Silver Palm, 1945; Chevalier de l'Ordre de Léopold, 1947; O.St.J., 1948. *Address:* Rozel, Brookvale Road, Southampton. *T.:* Southampton 54506. *Clubs:* M.C.C.; Royal Southampton Yacht (Southampton). [*Died* 11 *Sept.* 1970.

BIDWELL, Rear-Admiral Roger Edward Shelford, C.B.E. 1946; C.D. 1946; R.C.N.; Flag Officer Atlantic Coast (Canada), 1951-57, retd.; *b.* 14 Sept. 1899; *s.* of Rt. Rev. E. J. Bidwell, sometime Bishop of Ontario; *m.* 1923, Mary Grafton Bothamley; two *s.* one *d.* *Educ.:* Bishops College School and St. Albans School, Canada; Royal Naval College of Canada. Served European War, 1918; served in ships of R.N. and R.C.N. between wars; Staff Coll., 1938. Served ashore and afloat War of 1939-45. Commanded H.M.S. Puncher, 1943-46; i.d.c. 1947; N.D.C. of Canada, 1948-49; Director of Plans, Ottawa, 1948-50; Commodore Barracks, Esquimalt, 1951. Commanded Canadian Squadron at Spithead Coronation Review, 1953. Order of Merit, Degree of Officer (U.S.A.). Hon. D.C.L.

King's Univ., Halifax, N.S., 1951. *Recreations:* fishing, walking, sailing. *Address:* 6231 Watt St., Halifax, N.S., Canada. [*Died* 2 *Nov.* 1968.

BIGGAM, Maj.-Gen. Sir Alexander Gordon, K.B.E. *cr.* 1946 (O.B.E. 1920); C.B. 1944; Commander of Legion of Merit, 1945; Commander of the Order of the Nile; M.D. (Edin.), F.R.C.P.; Hon. F.R.C.P.E.; D.T.M. & H. (Eng.); F.R.S. Ed.; R.A.M.C., retd.; formerly Director of Study, Edin. Post-Grad. Board for Medicine; *b.* 1888; *s.* of late J. Biggam, Laigh Glenstockadale, Leswait Stranraer, Scotland; *m.* Margaret Frances, *d.* of late Lt.-Col. B. G. Patch, R.A.M.C.; one *s.* one *d.* *Educ.:* George Watson's College and the University, Edinburgh. House Physician and House Surg., Royal Infirmary, Edinburgh; entered R.A.M.C., 1912; served France (1914 Star), North-West Frontier India, Afghan Campaign, 1919, Waziristan Field Force, 1919-21 (Frontier Medal and three clasps, despatches, O.B.E.); formerly Director Medical Unit, Kasr-el-Aini Hospital, Cairo, and Prof. of Clinical Medicine, Egyptian Univ., 1926-33; sometime examiner in Medicine, Kitchener School of Medicine, Khartoum, and American Univ. of Beirut, Beirut; K.H.P. 1937-47: late Professor of Tropical Medicine and Consulting Physician to the Army; retired pay, 1947. Hon. LL.D. (Punjab), 1960. *Publications:* in various medical and scientific journals. *Address:* 24 Heriot Row, Edinburgh. [*Died* 22 *March* 1963.

BIGLAND, Eileen (Anne Carstairs); (Mrs. E. W. Bigland); author; Publisher's reader since 1930; *b.* 29 May 1898; *m.* 1923, Eric Walter Bigland (decd.). one *s.* one *d.* (and one *s* decd.). *Educ.:* George Watson's Ladies' Coll., Edinburgh. Trained for Ballet, 1915-21. Travel: Europe, 1921-30; Russia, Tropical Africa, China, Far East, 1930-39; Egypt, 1947; took George Borrow's journeys through Spain and Portugal, 1949; took Lord Byron's journeys through Europe to Greece, 1952. Lecturer, Ministry of Information staff, 1941-43; Lecturer to Services, 1944-45. *Publications: novels:* 10 published since 1931; *travel:* Laughing Odyssey, 1937; The Lake of the Royal Crocodiles, 1939; Into China, 1940; The Key to the Russian Door, 1941; Journey to Egypt, 1948; Russia Has Two Faces, 1960; *biography:* Ouida, 1950; George Borrow, 1951; Marie Corelli, 1953; The Indomitable Mrs. Trollope, 1953 (reprinted 1970); Lord Byron, 1957; Mary Shelley, 1959. *Address:* c/o A. P. Watt & Son, 26-28 Bedford Row, W.C.1. *Died* 11 *April* 1970.

BIGNOLD, Sir (Charles) Robert, Kt., 1938; D.L. (Norfolk); J.P. Norwich; *b.* 22 Aug. 1892; *s.* of Charles Arthur Bathurst-Bignold, D.L., J.P.; *m.* 1919, Ethel, *d.* of late W. H. Dale, Kensington. *Educ.:* Charterhouse. Captain 4th Bn. Norfolk Regt.; Lord Mayor of Norwich, 1925-26; sometime Leader and Chairman of Norwich Conservative Association; Hon. Life Governor, Norwich Union Insurance Socs.; Past Pres.: Norwich Union Life Insurance Society; Norwich Union Fire Insurance Society; Scottish Union and Nat. Insurance Company; Chairman, Royal Hotel Norwich Ltd.; Director: Anglia Television Ltd.; Securicor (Southern) Ltd. *Address:* Flat 1, Gwydyr Mansions, Holland Rd., Hove 2, Sussex. *Clubs:* Constitutional; Norfolk County (Norwich). [*Died* 26 *Dec.* 1970.

BIGSWORTH, Air Commodore Arthur Wellesley, C.M.G. 1919; D.S.O. 1915, and Bar 1917; A.F.C. 1919; Royal Air Force, retd.; *b.* 27 March 1885; *s.* of late Arthur Wellesley Bigsworth and Kate Box; *m.* 1920, Kathleen Eleanor, *widow* of Major E. Gardiner, R. E. *Educ.:* H.M.S. Worcester. Served for several years in the Mercantile Marine as an officer; joined the Royal Naval Reserve and later the Royal Navy as a Lieutenant; joined the Royal Flying Corps Naval Wing as Lieutenant, 1912; Royal Naval Air Service, 1914; served European War, first in France with No. 1 Naval Aeroplane Wing; siege of Antwerp, Lille, Ostend, etc.; was the first officer who succeeded in dropping bombs on a Zeppelin, 17 May 1915 (promoted to Squadron Commander); also the first officer to destroy a submarine with bombs, 26 Aug. 1915 (D.S.O.); bar to D.S.O., 1917; Air Commodore, 1930; Director of Equipment, Air Ministry, 1931-35; Dept. of Air Member for Supply and Organisation 1935; retired list 1935. *Recreation:* motoring. *Club:* United Service. [*Died* 24 *Feb.* 1961.

BILKEY, Paul Ernest; Editor Emeritus Montreal Gazette since 1943; *b.* St. George, Bermuda, 26 Jan. 1878; 2nd *s.* of Rev. Robert Anthony Bilkey and Lillian Rosa Wood; *m.* 1904, Sarah Esther Dalton, Ottawa; (one *s.* killed on active service (R.C.A.F.) 1940) three *d.* *Educ.:* Toronto and Bowmanville, Ontario. Entered journalism in Toronto, 1896; fourteen years parliamentary correspondent Canadian, American, and British newspapers; contributor Canadian correcan periodicals; President Parliamentary Press Gallery, 1909-10; Canadian correspondent London Morning Post for 25 years; joined editorial staff Montreal Gazette, 1917; Editor-in-Chief, 1926-43; Vice-President o the Gazette Printing Company, Ltd., 1934-1943. *Publications:* Persons, Papers and Things. *Recreations:* fishing, motoring. *Address:* Edgemere, Hudson Heights, P.Q., Canada. *Clubs:* Canadian, St. James's (Montreal). [*Died April* 1962.

BILL, Rt. Rev. Sydney Alfred, M.A.; *b.* 1884; *s.* of H. P. Bill, Streetly, Staffs.; *m.* 1st, 1911, Margaret (*d.* 1955), *d.* of Canon Ford; two *s.* one *d.*; 2nd, 1958, Hilda Smith, *Educ.:* Trinity College, Cambridge. M.A., 1909; Hist. Trip., Parts I. and II.; Deacon, 1907; Priest, 1908; Curate of St. George's, Birmingham, 1907; St. Leonard's, Bilston, 1909; Chaplain to H.M. Indian Government, 1911-38; Diocese of Lucknow at various stations; Senior Chaplain, All Saints' Cathedral, 1915-16, 1921-25; Canon of All Saints' Cathedral, 1922; Diocesan Inspector of Schools, 1925-28; Archdeacon of Lucknow, 1926-37; Vicar of St. Matthias, Plymouth, 1936-38; Bishop of Lucknow 1939-47; Rector of Instow, N. Devon, 1947-1955. *Address:* 3 Bath Terrace, Instow, N. Devon. [*Died* 3 *July* 1964.

BILLEN, Rev. Albert Victor, D.D. Oxon. Ph.D.; Rector of Shenington with Alkerton, Banbury, Oxfordshire, since 1959. *Educ.:* Univ. Coll., Oxford. Headmaster of Ellesmere College, Salop, 1927-35; Grinfield Lecturer in the University of Oxford, 1931-35; Headmaster of Wellingborough School, Northants, 1935-40; Deputy-Warden of St. Michael's, Tenbury, 1940-45. Speaker's Lecturer on Biblical Studies in the University of Oxford, 1948-51; Vicar of Fyfield and Tubney, and Rector of Kingston Bagpuize-Abingdon, Berkshire, 1949-59. *Publication:* The Old Latin Texts of the Heptateuch; 1000 years of Fyfield's History, 1956. *Address:* Shenington Rectory, Banbury, Oxfordshire. *T.:* Edge Hill 315. [*Died* 5 *June* 1961.

BILLINGHURST, Alfred John, R.B.A.; artist, portrait and landscape painter *b.* 1880; *s.* of Henry F. and Rosa A. Billinghurst; *m.* Gwen Woods Smyth; three *s.* *Educ.:* Slade School; Hanover and Paris. Pictures exhibited R.A., R.I., Paris Salon, etc.; The Pool of London, in Corporation Gallery, Plymouth; served European War, Lieutenant R.F.A. (despatches). Member of Art Workers

Guild, Ridley Art Club. *Recreations:* music, violin and viola. *Address:* 219 Sheen Lane, S.W.14. *T.:* Prospect 5677. [*Died* 30 *Dec.* 1963.

BILLMEIR, Jack Albert, C.B.E. 1953; Chairman and Managing Director: Stanhope Steamship Co., Ltd.; J. A. Billmeir & Co. Ltd.; E. Hughes & Sons, Ltd.; Lamorna Steamship Co. Ltd.; Director of several cos.; *b.* London, 1 Sept. 1900; *s.* of Joseph and Rosa Billmeir; *m.* 1921, Annie Margaret Gibbs. *Educ.:* St. Marylebone Sch. Business career: Shipbroker's office, City of London, 1914; shipbroker and shipowner, 1928; formed Stanhope Steamship Co. Ltd., 1934, and controls 75% of Issued Capital. Member Council Chamber of Shipping, 1948-; Chm. Intermed. Sect. of Chamber of Shipping, 1948-53; Mem. Shipowners' Advisory Panel of Lighthouse Commn., 1946-57; Mem. Baltic Exchange, 1927-, Director, Baltic Exchange, 1953-58; Underwriting Mem. Lloyd's F.I.C.S. 1932. Prime Warden, Shipwrights' Company, 1962-63. Hon. M.A. Oxford, 1958. *Recreations:* yachting, golf. *Address:* Westbrook, Elstead, Surrey. *T.:* Elstead 2262; Melfort, Argyll; Tillmouth Park, Northumberland; Basing Park, Hampshire; Parnham, Dorset. *Clubs:* Reform, International Sportsmen's; Royal Southampton Yacht (Commodore); Royal London Yacht. [*Died* 22 *Dec.* 1963.

BILSLAND, 1st Baron, *cr.* 1950, of Kinrara, Inverness-shire; **Alexander Steven Bilsland,** 2nd Bt., *cr.* 1907; K.T. 1955; M.C.; D.L., J.P.; Hon. LL.D. (Glas.) 1948, (Aberd.) 1956; Hon. A.R.I.B.A.; Chairman: Bilsland Bros., Ltd., Glasgow Stockholders Trust Ltd., Scottish National Trust Ltd., and other cos.; Past Director: Colvilles Ltd., Burmah Oil Co. Ltd.; John Brown & Co. Ltd.; Past Governor of the Bank of Scotland; President: Scottish Amicable Life Assurance Society. Hon. Fellow, St. John's College, Cambridge. Hon. Member, American Academy of Arts and Sciences; Member, Royal Company of Archers (Queen's Body Guard for Scotland); late Captain, 8th Scottish Rifles and Staff; *b.* Glasgow, 13 Sept. 1892; *s.* of Sir William Bilsland, LL.D., 1st Bt. and Agnes Anne (*d.* 1935), 3rd *d.* of Alexander Steven of Provanside, Glasgow; *S.* to father's baronetcy, 1921; *m.* 1922, Amy, *d.* of late David Colville, Jerviston House, Motherwell. *Educ.:* Glasgow; St. John's Coll., Cambridge. President Glasgow Chamber of Commerce, 1933-35; District Commissioner for Western District of Scotland under Civil Defence Regional Organisation, 1940-44. Freeman of Aberdeen, 1956. U.S. Medal of Freedom. *Heir:* none. *Recreations:* fishing and shooting. *Address:* Garden, Buchlyvie, Stirlingshire; Kinrara, Aviemore, Inverness-shire. *Clubs:* Brooks's, Caledonian; New (Edinburgh); Western (Glasgow); Northern (Inverness). [*Died* 10 *Dec.* 1970 (*ext.*).

BINDER, Sir Bernhard Heymann, Kt 1952; F.C.A.; Formerly Senior Partner in Binder, Hamlyn & Co. (Founder, 1918); retired, Dec. 1958; *b.* 24 November 1876; *s.* of late Henry and Sarah Binder (*née* Thomas), Nottingham; *m.* 1st, 1900, Florence May Miller (*d.* 1924); one *s.* one *d.*; 2nd, 1925, Amy Kathleen Moran; one *d.* *Educ.:* Privately. Passed first in order of merit in final Exam. of Inst. of Chartered Accountants in England and Wales, 1908; Member of Council of that Institute, 1932-57, Vice-President, 1947-48, President, 1948-1949. Was engaged on work in connection with financial reconstruction in Austria, and in particular in relation to Austrian League of Nations Loan and reorganization of Austrian Banks, after 1914-18 War. Visited Zanzibar and investigated and reported upon Clove industry for Colonial Office in 1936. First Chairman of South Wales Dist. Sales Control Board, 1936-42; Coal Supplies Officer, 1939-1942; Member of Capital Issues Cttee., 1944-1946; Member of Treasury Advisory Panel, 1951-59; attached to British Govt. Mission to Argentina, 1946. *Publication:* Random Rhymes, 1943. *Address:* 8 Stanhope Terrace, W.2. *Club:* Royal Automobile. [*Died* 11 *July* 1966.

BING, Prof. Gertrud, Ph.D. (Hamburg), 1921; Director of the Warburg Institute and Professor of the History of the Classical Tradition in the University of London, 1955-59, now Professor Emeritus; *b.* 7 June 1892; *d.* of Emma and Moritz Bing. *Educ.:* Hamburg; Universities of Munich and Hamburg. Librarian, Kulturwissenschaftliche Bibliothek Warburg, Hamburg, 1922-27; Asst. to Prof. Aby M. Warburg, 1927-29; Asst. Director of the Warburg Institute, 1927-55; Recognised Teacher of University of London, 1945-1955. Hon. D.Litt., Reading, 1959. *Publications:* Edn. of A. M. Warburg, Gesammelte Schriften, Vols. I and II, 1932; Reviews in A Bibliography of the Survival of the Classics, 1934-38; articles in Jl. of the Warburg and Courtauld Institutes; edn. of Lectures of Prof. Fritz Saxl (late Dir. Warburg Inst.), 1957; Fritz Saxl (A Memoir) in Fritz Saxl 1890-1948, A Volume of Memorial Essays, 1957; Aby M. Warburg, in Rivista Storica Italiana, Anno LXXII, 1960 (Naples). *Address:* Warburg Institute, University of London, Woburn Square, W.C.1. *T.:* Langham 9663. [*Died* 3 *July* 1964.

BINNS, Kenneth, C.B.E., 1964; F.L.A.; Librarian, Parliamentary and Commonwealth National Libraries, 1928, retired, 1947; *b.* Dunfermline, Scotland, 28 Nov. 1882; 3rd *s.* of late Rev. F. Binns; *m.* 1909, A. J. Higgins (decd.); one *s.* two *d.* *Educ.:* Sydney Grammar School; University of Sydney. Junior Assistant Librarian in Fisher Library, University of Sydney, 1900; Cataloguer in the Commonwealth Parliament Library, 1911; Assistant Librarian, 1918, and Librarian in charge of the Commonwealth National Library, 1923; Australian representative for the International Inst. for Intellectual Co-operation of League of Nations, 1930-39; Chairman, Commonwealth Literary Censorship Board, 1957-64 (Mem. 1937-); Commonwealth Literary Fund Cttee., 1939-53; Pres. Australian Institute of Librarians, 1941; Commonwealth Archives Cttee., 1943; J.P. 1943; Australian National Film Board, 1945-48; Member, National Cttee. for U.N.E.S.C.O., 1947. *Publications:* Commonwealth Parliamentary Handbook; Library Services in Tasmania, 1943; Annual Catalogue of Australian Publications, etc. *Recreations:* cabinet-making and bowls. *Address:* Arthur Circle, Canberra, A.C.T., Australia. *T.:* Canberra X 1586. [*Died* 27 *July* 1969.

BINNS, Rev. Leonard Elliott Elliott-, D.D.; *b.* Manchester, 18 Sept. 1885; *s.* of George and Margaret Binns; changed surname to Elliott-Binns by Deed Poll, 1936; *m.* 1915, Anna (*d.* 1957), *d.* of Charles Scott Kilner, M.B., J.P., Bury St. Edmunds; three *s.* one *d.* *Educ.:* Manchester Grammar School; Emmanuel College, Cambridge; Ridley Hall, Cambridge. Carus Prize, 1911; Carus Prize (Bach) and Crosse Scholar 1912; Jeremie Prize, 1913; Chaplain, Ridley Hall, 1913-15; Curate, St. Andrew, Plymouth, 1915-17; Vicar, Christ Church, Plymouth, 1917-1919; St Michael, Devonport, 1919-21; Hulsean Lecturer, Cambridge, 1921-22; Rector of North Cadbury, 1921-25 Vicar of West Ham, 1925-28; Rural Dean, West Ham, 1927-28; Vicar of Gedney, 1928-30; Rector of Great Hallingbury, 1933-34; Vicar of Newton St. Cyres, 1939-43; Vicar of St. Newlyn E. and Hon. Canon of Truro, 1943-1945; Canon Emeritus of Truro, 1945-48; Canon and Treasurer of Truro Cathedral, 1948-50; Examining Chap. to Bp. of Coventry, 1922-30,

Hereford, 1930-46; White Lecturer (St. Paul's), 1931; Hulsean Preacher, Cambridge, 1939-1940. *Publications:* Mr. Wells' Invisible King, 1919; Jeremiah (Westminster Commentaries), 1919; Erasmus the Reformer (Hulsean Lectures), 1923, 1928 (2nd ed.); Numbers (Westminster Commentaries), 1927; The Evangelical Party in the English Church (Faiths' Series), 1928; From Moses to Elisha, 1929; The Jewish People and their Faith, 1929; Innocent III., 1931; The Decline and Fall of the Medieval Papacy, 1934; Religion in the Victorian Era, 1936; The Reformation in England, 1937; England and the New Learning, 1937; The Church in the Ancient World, 1938; Jeremiah, a Prophet for Wartime, 1941; Reconstruction: the Church's Part, 1942; Divine Providence and Human Destiny, 1943; The Story of England's Church, 1945; The Beginnings of Western Christendom, 1948; The Development of English Theology in the Later Nineteenth Century, 1952; The Early Evangelicals, 1953; Medieval Cornwall, 1955; English Thought, 1860-1900: the Theological Aspect, 1956; Galilean Christianity, 1956; Contributor to the Encyclopædia Britannica. *Recreations:* walking and travel.
[*Died* 10 *April* 1963.

BIRCH, Sir Alan; *see* Birch, Sir J. A.

BIRCH, David; *see* Birch, W. H. D.

BIRCH, Col. Edward Massy, C.B. 1919; C.M.G. 1917; D.S.O. 1900; *b.* 12 Mar. 1875; *s.* of Lieut.-Col. E. A. Birch, M.D.; *m.* 1917, Violet *widow* of Alfred Evans Brown, Colonial Civil Service. Entered R.A. 1895; Lieut. 1898; Captain, 1901; Major, 1911; General Staff Officer, 2nd grade, Mauritius, 1911-1914; served South Africa, 1899-1902 (despatches, D.S.O.); European War, 1915-18 (C.B., C.M.G., Bt. Col.); Officer, Legion of Honour; Cross of St. Anne of Russia, 3rd Class; C.R.A. 42nd Div. (T.A.), 1920-24; retired pay, 1924. *Address:* Longdown, near Exeter. [*Died* 5 *April* 1964.

BIRCH, Sir (John) Alan, Kt. 1961; General Secretary, Union of Shop, Distributive and Allied Workers, since 1949; *b.* 20 Dec. 1909; *s.* of John and Florence Birch; *m.* 1940, Mildred Mary Crompton; two *s.* *Educ.:* Secondary School, Technical and Commercial Institute, Warrington. A.C.I.S., 1933; F.C.I.S. 1949; Area Organiser, National Union of Distributive and Allied Workers (N.U.D.A.W.), 1936; National Organiser, N.U.D.A.W. (later Union of Shop Distributive and Allied Workers), 1943. Sec., Trade Unions' Side, Nat. Conciliation Bds. for Cooperative Service; Member: Gen. Council of T.U.C., 1949-; Min. of Lab. and Nat. Service Nat. Jt. Advisory Council, 1949-; Central Price Regulation Cttee. of the Bd. of Trade, 1950-53; Bd. of Trade Standing Cttee. under Merchandise Marks Act (1926), 1952-61; Nat. Production Adv. Council on Industry, 1952-; British Productivity Council, 1952-; Bd. of Trade Cttee. on the Censuses of Production and Distribution, 1953-54: Monopolies Commission, 1953-59; Cttee. of Inquiry into working of Dock Labour Scheme, 1955-56; Economic Planning Board 1957-; National Coal Board, 1958-; B.B.C. General Advisory Council, 1960-. *Address:* U.S.D.A.W. Office, Oakley, 188 Wilmslow Road, Fallowfield, Manchester 14. *T.:* Rusholme 2804; Sorrento, 13 Stanley Avenue, Stockton Heath, Nr. Warrington, Lancs. *T.:* Grappenhall 94.
[*Died* 13 *Dec.* 1961.

BIRCH, (William Henry) David, R.O.I. 1945; Principal of Epsom and Ewell School of Art and Crafts, 1930-61; *b.* Epsom, 19 May 1894; *s.* of Joseph Henry and Jane Catherine Birch; *m.* Sybil Aida (*d.* 1956), *d.* of Henry Johnson Kaines, Guernsey; one *s.* *Educ.:* Epsom Collegiate School; Epsom Art School; Goldsmiths' College of Art, London. Served European War, September 1914-15 (invalided out). Continued art training but worked in H.M. Stationery Office for three years; book illustrator, and later, part-time art teacher in London. Particular study of landscape painting in Constable tradition since 1935; regular exhibitor at R.A. and other exhibitions since 1937, particularly of large panoramic paintings. Works acquired by public galleries: Eastbourne, Brighton, Epsom, Kingston, Newport, Shrewsbury. *Publications:* Painting Panorama, 1950; Lending Libraries of Pictures (publ. privately), 1950. Fine Art reproductions of landscape subjects. *Recreations:* painting and caravanning. *Address:* Netherfield, 47 Longdown Lane, Epsom, Surrey. *T.:* 21116.
[*Died* 10 *March* 1968.

BIRCHALL, Sir (Walter) Raymond, K.C.B., *cr.* 1946 (C.B. 1937); K.B.E., *cr.* 1939; *b.* 1888; *s.* of late Rev. John Birchall, Nottingham; *m.* 1911, Daisy (*d.* 1964), *d.* of late John Price, Wimbledon; one *s.* two *d.* *Educ.:* Westminster Sch.; Trinity Coll., Cambridge. Clerk 2nd Class Higher Division G.P.O., 1911; Asst. Secretary, G.P.O., 1934; Deputy Director-General, 1936-45; Director-General Post Office, 1946-49. *Recreation:* golf. *Address:* Trollheim, Kingston, Cambridge. [*Died* 1 *Aug.* 1968.

BIRCHAM, Sir Bertram Okeden, Kt., *cr.* 1932; Solicitor to the Ministry of Labour, 1926-42; *b.* 18 Oct. 1877; *s.* of F. T. Bircham, Gwentland, Chepstow; *m.* 1st 1921, Grace Louise (*d.* 1931), *d.* of J. Harris Sanders; 2nd 1935, Marjorie (*d.* 1956), *d.* of R. F. Webb. *Educ.:* Eton; New College, Oxford. Called to Bar, 1901; served European War, 1914-18 (M.C.). *Address:* Brockham, Betchworth, Surrey. [*Died* 16 *Oct.* 1961.

BIRD, Colonel Arthur James Glover, C.I.E. 1935; D.S.O. 1915; *b.* 4 Feb. 1883; *s.* of late C. P. Bird, I.C.S.; of Drybridge, Hereford; *m.* 1927, Eileen Julia, *yr. d.* of late Sir Edward Cameron, K.C.M.G., three *d.* *Educ.:* Cheltenham Coll. Entered Roy. Engineers, 1900; Capt., 1910; Bt. Lt.-Col. 1918; Lt.-Col. 1926; Col., 1930; served N.W. Frontier, India, 1908 (medal with clasp); European War, 1914-18 (despatches, D.S.O.); Brigadier, R.E., A.H.Q., India, 1931-32; Assistant Commandant, Indian Military Academy, 1932-35; retired 1935. *Address:* Sharling, Heath Road, Petersfield, Hants. [*Died* 5 *March* 1962.

BIRD, Sir C(yril) Handley, Kt. 1958; C.B.E. 1955; *b.* 3 June 1896; *s.* of H. Handley Bird; *m.* 1921, Signa Elaine Handley (*née* Garside); one *s.* one *d.* *Educ.:* St. Lawrence College, I. of Thanet; Bristol University. War Service with B.R.C.S., 1915-19. Commercial: Lagos, Nigeria, 1920-1924; E. Africa, 1928-55. President Uganda Chamber of Commerce, 1942-46; Founder Member, Uganda Electricity Board, 1948-55. Hon. Belgian Vice-Consul, 1937-43, Consul 1943-55. Member Uganda Legislative Council (Representative, 1947-55); Minister of Commerce and Works, Uganda Govt., Aug. 1955-Oct. 1958. Now retired from all business and political activities. Officer of Order of the Crown, Belgium, 1953; Chevalier of Order of Leopold, Belgium, 1955. *Address:* Makindye, Telham Lane, Battle, Sussex.
[*Died* 27 *March* 1969.

BIRD, (Cyril) Kenneth, C.B.E. 1946; B.Sc., F.S.I.A., F.K.C.; Lt. R.E. (retired); artist (*nom de plume* Fougasse); Editor of Punch 1949-1953, Art Editor, 1937-1949; *b.* 1887; *yr. s.* of late Arthur Bird, 9 Windsor Court, W.; *m.* Mary Holden, 2nd *d.* of late William Hay Caldwell, Morar Lodge, Morar, Scotland; no *c.* *Educ.:* Cheltenham College. *Publications:* A Gallery of Games, 1921; Drawn at a Venture, 1922; P.T.O., 1926; E. and O. E., 1928; Fun Fair, 1934; The Luck of the Draw, 1936; Drawing the Line Somewhere, 1937; Stop or go, 1938; Jotsam, 1939; The Changing

Face of Britain, 1940; And the Gate-post, 1940; Running Commentary, 1941; Sorry—No Rubber, 1942; Family Group, 1944; Home Circle, 1945; A School of Purposes, 1946; You and Me, 1948; Us, 1951; The Neighbours, 1954; The Good-Tempered Pencil, 1956; Between the Lines, 1958; (with A. W. Bird) Just a Few Lines, 1943; (with W. D. H. McCullough) Aces Made Easy, 1934; You Have Been Warned, 1935; (for the National Safety First Assn.) Many Happy Returns, 1936; Fancy Meeting You, 1947. *Address:* 115 Swan Court, Chelsea, S.W.3. *Club:* Garrick. [*Died* 11 *June* 1965.

BIRD, Sir Donald (Geoffrey), 3rd Bt. *cr.* 1922; retired; *b.* 3 July 1906; *s.* of late Geoffrey Bird (2nd *s.* of Sir Alfred Frederick Bird, 1st Bt. and of Elsie Hilda Bird (*née* Suckling); *S.* uncle, Sir Robert Bland Bird, 2nd Bt., 1960; *m.* 1930, Anne Rowena, *d.* of late Charles Chapman, Carlecotes Hall, Yorkshire, and of Cora Evelyn Chapman (*née* Beet); two *s.* one *d.* (and one *s.* decd.). *Educ.:* Uppingham; Christ Church, Oxford. Interests in food manufacture, engineering, scientific developments, and inventions. *Recreations:* yachting and golf. *Heir: er. surv. s.* Richard Geoffrey Chapman Bird [*b.* 3 Nov. 1935; *m.* 1957, Gillian Frances, *d.* of Bernard Haggett; three *d.*]. *Address:* Whitts End, Poolhead Lane, Tanworth in Arden, Warwickshire. *T.:* Tanworth 309. *Clubs:* Royal Cornwall Yacht (Falmouth); Copt Heath Golf (Solihull, Warwicks.). [*Died* 18 *Oct.* 1963.

BIRD, Eric Leslie, M.B.E. 1951; M.C. 1917; Consultant on Structural Fire Protection; Journalist; *b.* 10 June 1894; *s.* of W. F. Bird, M.S.A., architect, Midsomer Norton, Somerset; *m.* 1927, Elizabeth Mary, *d.* of late Rev. H. N. Startup, Vicar of Hillesden, Bucks; two *s.* one *d.* *Educ.:* Wycliffe Coll. Articled pupil, 1912-14; enlisted Glos. Regt. 1914; commissioned, 1915; seconded Machine Gun Corps, 1916 (M.C.); Capt. 1918. At Architectural Association School of Architecture, 1920-23; A.R.I.B.A. 1922; in practice, 1923-33; teacher of architecture on A.A. School staff, 1929-30; Assistant Editor, Architect and Building News, 1930-33; Technical Editor R.I.B.A. Journal and Public Relations Officer, 1933-39; Editor, R.I.B.A. Journal, 1946-56; Tech. Res. and Educn. Officer, the Building Centre, 1956-64. Mem. of Home Office Structural A.R.P. Cttee., 1937-39; Architectural Adviser, Research and Experiments Dept., Ministry of Home Security, 1939-45. As Hon. Wing Commander R.A.F.V.R. visited Sicily and France to study effects of Allied air attacks. Principal work on incendiary attack and fire. Member: Joint Committee of the Building Research Board and Fire Offices' Committee on Fire Grading of Buildings, 1942-49; Fire Research Board of D.S.I.R., 1947-50; of Forest Products Research Board of D.S.I.R., 1947-51; Vice-Pres., Architectural Assoc., 1943-45, 1947-48; Hon. Treasurer 1945-46; Hon. Sec. 1946 - 47. *Publications:* numerous articles, mostly anonymous, in technical and lay journals on architectural subjects and several Government publications; (with S. J. Docking) Fire in Buildings; (with Kenneth Holmes) Decorating for the Amateur; House Maintenance for the Intelligent Owner. *Recreations:* fruit growing and books. *Address:* Rose Tile, Bisham Road, Marlow, Bucks. *T.:* Marlow 2002. *Club:* Arts. [*Died* 22 *Nov.* 1965.

BIRD, Kenneth; *see* Bird, C. K.

BIRD, Captain Oliver, M.C. 1918; J.P. County of Warwick; *b.* 15 Feb. 1880; 3rd *s.* of Sir Alfred F. Bird, 1st Bt., M.P., and Lady Bird, Tudor Grange, Solihull; *m.* 1909, Gwendoline Heaton, *e. d.* of late W. A. Upton and late Mrs. A. A. Davis; no *c.* *Educ.:* King Edward's High School, Birmingham. Entered father's business, Alfred Bird & Sons Ltd., Birmingham, in 1898; resigned, 1947. Commission in Welsh Guards, 1916; served as Divisional Gas Officer, Guards Division, France, Belgium, and Germany, 1917-19 (M.C.); Sheriff of Warwickshire, 1943-44. *Recreations:* golf, cycling, shooting, owns 275 acres estate. *Address:* The Chase, Bentley Heath, Knowle, Warwickshire. *T.:* Knowle 2247. *Clubs:* Royal Automobile; Conservative (Birmingham). [*Died* 13 *April* 1963.

BIRDWOOD, 2nd Baron, *cr.* 1938, of Anzac and of Totnes; **Christopher Bromhead Birdwood,** Bt., *cr.* 1919; M.V.O. 1939; Lt.-Col., Probyn's Horse; *b.* 22 May 1899; *o. s.* of 1st Baron Birdwood, G.C.B. (Field-Marshal Lord Birdwood); *S.* father 1951; *m.* 1st, 1931, Vere Drummond (marr. diss., 1954; M.V.O. 1958), *o. d.* of Lt.-Col. Sir George D. Ogilvie; one *s.* one *d.*; 2nd, 1954, Joan Pollock Graham. *Educ.:* Clifton College; R.M.C. Sandhurst. European War, 1918 (despatches, Military Order of Aviz, 5th Class); N.W. Frontier, India, 1919-20 and 1936-37; retired from Indian Army, 1945, British Red Cross, Germany, 1947. Chairman, Anglo-German Association; Vice-Chm., Exec. Cttee. European-Atlantic Group. Mem. Roy. Inst. of Internat. Affairs; Member of Councils: East India Assoc.; Anglo-Arab Assoc.; Mem. British Delegation, U.N.O., 1959; Member Executive Committee, Commonwealth Migration Council; President London branch Inst. of Commercial and Industrial Managers; Fellow Royal Commonwealth Society. *Publications:* A Continent Experiments, 1946; The Worcestershire Regiment, 1922-1950; A Continent Decides, 1953; Two Nations and Kashmir, 1956; Nuri As-Said, 1959. *Recreations:* lecturer, international affairs; music and literature. *Heir: s.* Hon. Mark William Ogilvie Birdwood, *b.* 23 Nov. 1938. *Address:* 12 Warwick Avenue, W.2. *T.:* Ambassador 9841. *Club:* Cavalry. [*Died* 5 *Jan.* 1962.

BIRKETT, 1st Baron, *cr.* 1958, of Ulverston; **William Norman Birkett,** P.C. 1947; Kt. 1941; J.P. Bucks.; Chairman of the Court, University of London, since 1946; President of the Pilgrims since 1958; *b.* Ulverston, Lancashire, 6 Sept. 1883; *s.* of Thomas and Agnes Birkett; *m.* 1920, Ruth, *d.* of Emil and Anna Nilsson; one *s.* one *d.* *Educ.:* Barrow-in-Furness; Emmanuel College, Cambridge (M.A., LL.B., Historical and Law Tripos). President of the Cambridge Union 1910; called to the Bar, Inner Temple, 1913; Q.C. 1924; Judge of the King's Bench Division, High Court of Justice, 1941-50; Lord Justice of Appeal, 1950-57; contested (L.) Eastern Div. of Nottingham, Dec 1923-Oct. 1924 and 1929-31; Master, Company of Curriers, 1936, 1945, 1946 and 1957; Hon. Fell. of Emmanuel Coll., Cambridge, 1946; Treasurer, Inner Temple, 1956; Chm. Buckinghamshire Quarter Sessions, 1946-58. Hon. LL.D.: Univs. of London, Birmingham, Cambridge, Hull, Liverpool. *Recreations:* occasional golf, gentle walking, reading, writing. *Heir: s.* Hon. Michael Birkett [*b.* 22 Oct. 1929; *m.* 1960, Mrs. Junia Crawford, *d.* of Harold Elliott]. *Address:* Challens Green, Chalfont St. Giles, Buckinghamshire. *T.:* Little Chalfont 2023. *Clubs:* Athenæum; Savage (Hon. Life Mem.). [*Died* 10 *Feb.* 1962.

BIRT, Francis B. B.; *see* Bradley-Birt.

BIRTCHNELL, Sir Cyril (Augustine), K.C.M.G., *cr.* 1949; C.B. 1943; retd.; U.K. Member, Transport and Communications Commission, U.N.O., 1955 - 59; *b.* 1887; *s.* of late Frank Newman Birtchnell; *m.* 1923, Rita Hindmarsh, *d.* of late John Cobb Sutherland; no *c.* *Educ.:* Wimbledon College. Entered H.M Customs, 1906; Estate Duty Office, 1909; served

European War, 1914-18; Ministry of Transport, 1920; called to Bar, Lincoln's Inn, 1919; Member of Permanent Committee on Road Traffic, League of Nations, 1937; British member of Executive Board of European Inland Transport Organisation, 1945-46; Under-Secretary Ministry of Transport, 1946; Deputy Secretary, 1947-53. *Address:* 1 Roehampton Gate, S.W.15. *T.:* Prospect 2024. *Clubs:* Reform, Royal Automobile. [*Died* 3 *Oct.* 1967.

BISCOE, Walter Treweeke, C.I.E. 1946; retired; *b.* 8 Jan. 1892; *s.* of Charles Law Biscoe and Kate Roxborough; *m.* 1919, Elsie Elizabeth Bestall; two *d.* *Educ.:* Marlborough. Joined North Western Rly. of India, 1910. Served European War, 1914-1918 (despatches, 1914-15 Star). Served in America as Manager Indian State Rlys. Publicity Bureau, New York, 1930-35; Regional Controller, N.W. India, 1943 and 1944; Chief Operating Supt. of the North Western Rly., 1944-47; retired Jan. 1947. *Address:* 68 The Dell, Westbury-on-Trym, Bristol. [*Died* 7 *Jan.* 1969.

BISHOP, Arthur Henry Burdick, M.A.; Headmaster, Warwick School, 1936-62, retd.; *s.* of late Arthur Bishop, Callington, Cornwall; *m.* 1st, 1928, Olive Douthwaite, Felixstowe; two *s.* two *d.*; 2nd, 1965, Irene M. Titcomb, M.A., F.R.C.O.G. *Educ.:* Jesus Coll., Oxf. Commissioned to 4th Wiltshire Regt., 1917-20; served in France, Egypt, and Palestine; Commoner of Jesus Coll., Oxford, 1920-24; 1st Class Hons. in Natural Science, after research on Adsorption; Lecturer at Westminster College, London, 1924-25; Senior Chemistry master at Radley College, 1925-29; Headmaster of Magdalen College School, Brackley, 1930-36. *Publications:* An Elementary Chemistry; Introduction to Chemistry (both with G. H. Locket). *Recreations:* walking, reading, gardening. *Address:* Beehive Cottage, Bladon, Oxford. [*Died* 5 *June* 1969.

BISHOP, Lieut.-Commander Francis Charles, Royal Navy (retired); Consul-General, Lisbon, since 1960; *b.* 17 June 1905; *e. s.* of late Major Charles Gamble Bishop, D.S.O., St. Helens, Lancashire, and of Mrs. Pearl Hall Down, O.B.E.; *m.* 1934, Eleanor (Elizabeth) May Pargiter; no *c.* *Educ.:* Uppingham. Entered Royal Navy, 1923; Mediterranean Fleet, 1924; Atlantic Fleet, 1926; Africa Squadron, 1928; resigned commission, 1930, to study high-speed boats under H. Scott-Paine. Crossed France by high-speed boat in 6 days, 1930. Lecture tours in England, Scandinavia, and Western Europe, 1938-39. Rejoined Navy, 1941; Mediterranean, 1942; Admiralty, 1943 H.M. Consul, Malmo, Sweden, 1943; H.M. Consul, Bilbao, Spain, 1946; H.M. Consul with rank of Consul-General, Antananarivo, Madagascar, 1949-1951; First Secretary and H.M. Consul, H.M. Embassy, Copenhagen, 1951-54; H.M. Consul, Nantes, 1954-57; First Secretary, Mexico City, and Regional Information Officer, Mexico, Central America and the Caribbean Republics, 1957-60. *Publications:* articles in the Times, Motor Boat and several Scandinavian papers. *Recreations:* swimming, sailing, marine books. *Address:* c/o Foreign Office, S.W.1. *Clubs:* United Service, Goat; Royal British (Lisbon). [*Died* 30 *March* 1965.

BISHOP, George Walter; Theatre Correspondent, Daily Telegraph; *b.* London, 9 Nov. 1886; *e. s.* of George Bishop; *m.* 1st, 1915, Margaret (*d.* 1955), *d.* of Joseph Thornton Jones, Harrogate; two *d.*; 2nd, 1956, Margaret Mary, *d.* of Leonard Brinkman, New Zealand. Formerly editor of the Era; Special Correspondent, The Observer; Literary Editor of Daily Telegraph; Assistant Dramatic Critic to the Daily News for several years; has also written articles on dramatic subjects for the Sunday Times, New York Times, Berlingske Tidende (of Copenhagen), etc.; President, Critics' Circle, 1935-36. *Publications:* Barry Jackson and the London Theatre, 1933; My Betters, 1957. *Recreations:* collecting modern first editions. *Address:* 7 Elizabeth Close, W.9. *T.:* Cunningham 1208. [*Died* 26 *April* 1965.

BISHOP, Theodore Bendysh Watson, C.I.E. 1946; I.C.S. retd.; *b.* 13 Dec. 1886; *s.* of James Watson and Adelaide Mary Bishop, Oulton House, Stone, Staffs; *m.* 1916, Evelyn Isabel May Chesney. *Educ.:* Rugby School; Emmanuel College, Cambridge. 10th Wrangler, 1908. Indian Civil Service, United Provinces, 1911; Adviser to Governor, United Provinces, 1944-46. *Address:* The Cottage, Barnham, Sussex. *Club:* East India and Sports. [*Died* 12 *July* 1967.

BISSEKER, Rev. Harry, M.A.; *b.* Handsworth, Birmingham, 3 Oct. 1878; *s.* of T. J. Bisseker; *m.* 1909, Marian Doris, *d.* of late F. A. Holman, 3 Hyde Park Square, W., and Sydmonton Court, Newbury; one *s.* two *d.* *Educ.:* King Edward's School, Birmingham; Jesus College, Cambridge (Foundation Scholar). Carus Greek Testament Prizeman, 1st Class Theological Tripos; Chaplain at Leys School, Cambridge, 1901; Leysian Mission, London, 1904; Professor of New Testament Language and Literature, Richmond College, Surrey, 1910; Member of Faculty of Theology, London University, 1910; Headmaster of Leys School, Cambridge, 1919-34. *Publications:* Contributions to Hastings' Dictionary of Christ and the Gospels, and Encyclopaedia of Religion and Ethics, and to various volumes of essays on theology, education and social science; Problems of Discipleship; (with Basil Matthews) Christian Fellowship in Thought and Prayer; The Way of Discipleship. *Address:* The Old House, Harston, Cambridge. *T.:* Harston 288. [*Died* 27 *Nov.* 1965.

BISSET, Capt. Sir James Gordon Partridge, Kt., *cr.* 1945; C.B.E. 1942; LL.D.; R.D.; Royal Naval Reserve, retd.; *b.* 15 July 1883; *s.* of James Smith Bisset, Blairgowrie, Perthshire, and Ellen Butler, Liverpool; *m.* 1913, May Hodgson, London; no *c.* *Educ.:* Liverpool. Went to sea as apprentice in sailing ship, 1898; joined Cunard Line as Junior Officer, 1907; during European War served in R.N.R. and was in command of destroyer for over three years; appointed to first Cunard command, s.s. Aurania, in Canadian trade, 1929; retired from R.N.R. 1933 with rank of Capt.; commanded s.s. Queen Mary and Queen Elizabeth during War of 1939-45; Commodore of Cunard White Star Co. Ltd., Liverpool, 1944-47; commanded s.s. Queen Elizabeth on her maiden voyage, 1946. Hon. LL.D. Cambridge, 1947. U.S. Legion of Merit, 1949. *Publications:* Lifeboat Efficiency, 1920; Ship Ahoy, 1926; Sail Ho!, 1958; Tramps and Ladies, 1959; Commodore, 1960. *Recreation:* motoring. *Address:* Fairfield, Mid-Lavant, Chichester, Sussex. [*Died* 28 *March* 1967.

BISSETT, Maj.-Gen. Frederic William Lyon, C.B.E. 1940; D.S.O. 1918; M.C.; *b.* 4 June 1888. *Educ.:* Charterhouse; R.M.C. Sandhurst. Gazetted D.C.L.I. 1909; Major Northamptonshire Regt. 1926; served European war, 1914-19 (D.S.O., M.C., despatches) and War of 1939-45 (C.B.E., despatches). *Address:* 17 Albemarle St., W.1. [*Died* 27 *May* 1961.

BISSON, Laurence Adolphus; Professor of French and Romance Philology, Queen's University of Belfast, 1945-61; *b.* St. Heliers, Jersey, C.I., 21 Dec. 1897; *o. s.* of Adolphus Bisson and Lillian Marian Delorme; *m.* 1933, Isabella Jane, *d.* of Robert Smith, Oldmeldrum, Aberdeenshire; no *c.*

Educ.: Victoria College, Jersey; Pembroke College, Oxford (Scholar); Sorbonne, Paris; Université de Bordeaux. B.A. (Oxon.) 1921; M.A. 1922; Docteur de l'Université de Bordeaux, 1932; D.Litt. (Oxon.) 1945. Served European War, 1914-18, in R.E., 1917-18; temp. member of Secretariat, League of Nations, 1921-22; Lecturer in French, Queen's Univ., Kingston, Ont., 1922-23; Asst. Prof. of French, Trinity Coll., Toronto, 1923-26; Lecturer in French, Univ. of Birmingham, 1927-33; Univ. Lecturer in French, Oxford, 1933-38; University Reader in French Literature, Oxford, 1938-45; Lecturer in French, Pembroke College, Oxford, 1937-45. Leverhulme Fellow, 1948-50. Visiting Lecturer, Universities of Geneva, Neuchâtel and Lausanne, 1954. *Publications:* Le Romantisme littéraire au Canada français, 1932; Le Préromantisme étranger à Bordeaux (in Mélanges Laumonier), 1936; Amedée Pichot, 1942; A Short History of French Literature, 1943; a critical edition of Hugo: Les Feuilles d'Automne, 1944; Proust and Thomas Hardy (in Studies presented to Prof. R. L. G. Ritchie), 1949; numerous articles (especially on Marcel Proust) and reviews, in Mod. Lang. Review and French Studies. *Recreations:* travel, music. *Address:* Mallories, Stratton Audley, Bicester, Oxon. *Clubs:* Authors'; Union Society (Oxford). [*Died* 12 *Sept.* 1965.

BITHELL, Jethro, M.A.; sometime Reader in German, Univ. of London; *b.* 29 Jan. 1878 at Birchall Farm, Hindley, nr. Wigan; *s.* of John Bithell and Harriet Bithell (*née* Cubbin); *m.* 1st, 1910, Ethel Rose (*d.* 1946), *d.* of Frederick William Fisher, Maidenhead; 2nd, 1947, Alice Emily Eastlake, Ph.D., *d.* of Charles Bertrand Eastlake, London. *Educ.:* Wigan Mining School; Univ. of Manchester (M.A., 1st Class Honours, Modern Languages, 1900); University of Munich. Studied Scandinavian literatures at Copenhagen, 1901; Lecturer in Modern Languages, Salford Technical College, 1902-4; Lecturer in German, Univ. of Manchester, 1904-10; Head of Dept. of German, Birkbeck College, 1910-38; served as private, Royal Sussex Regt., Oct. 1916-Jan. 1919. *Publications:* The Minnesingers, 1909; Contemporary German Poetry, 1909; Contemporary Belgian Poetry, 1911; Contemporary French Poetry, 1912; Contemporary Flemish Poetry, 1917; Turandot, Princess of China, from the German of Karl Gustav Vollmoeller (produced by Sir George Alexander at St. James's Theatre, 1913); Life and Writings of Maurice Maeterlinck, 1913; Contemporary Belgian Literature, 1915; Helen of Sparta (in The Plays of Emile Verhaeren), 1915; German-English and English-German Dictionary, 1922, 5th edn., 1958; German Science Reader, 1925 (9th edn. 1956); A French Reader for Science Students, 1926; A Modern German Course, 1928; Advanced German Composition, 1929; Germany: a Companion to German Studies, 1932 (5th edn., enlarged, 1955); Modern German Literature, 1880-1938, 1939, 3rd edn., 1880-1950, 1959; An Anthology of German Poetry, 1880-1940, 1941; An Anthology of German Poetry, 1830-1880, 1947; German Pronunciation and Phonology, 1951; An Anthology of German Poetry, 1730-1830, 1957. *Recreation:* gardening. *Address:* 13 Fortescue Road, Preston, Paignton, Devon. [*Died* 26 *Feb.* 1962.

BLACHE, Jules Adolphe Lucien; Officier de la Legion d'honneur. Croix de Guerre, etc.; retd. as Rector, Univ. of Aix-Marseille; *b.* 28 January 1893; *m.* 1920, Lucile Bout; two *s.* *Educ.:* Faculté des Lettres, Grenoble. Teacher at the Lycée de Grenoble; subsequently Lecturer, Faculté des Lettres, Grenoble, and Professor, Faculté des Lettres, Nancy; Préfet of Meurthe-et-Moselle, 1944-1946. Agrégé de l'Université; Docteur ès Lettres. Hon. D.Litt. Oxford University, 1957. *Publications:* various geographical books on the Alps, North Africa and Scandinavia. *Address:* 125 rue de France, Nice. *T.:* 87-49-21. [*Died* 6 *April* 1970.

BLACK, Sir Archibald Campbell, Kt., cr. 1937; O.B.E. 1918; Q.C. 1926, LL.D. (Glas.); M.A., LL.B.; formerly Sheriff of Lanarks.; *s.* of Archibald C. Black, Glasgow; *m.* 1907, Charlotte Wyllie, *d.* of Sir Thomas Mason, Glasgow. Assistant Editor Encyclopaedia of the Laws of Scotland, 1926-34; Sheriff of Stirling, Dumbarton, and Clackmannan, 1933-37; Procurator for the Church of Scotland, 1936-37; Chm. Scottish Departmental Cttee. on the Training of Nurses, 1934; Chm. Conscientious Objectors Tribunal for S.W. Scotland, 1939-49. Pres. Roy. Philosophic Soc. of Glasgow, 1951-52 (now Hon. Vice-Pres.). *Address:* Thatched House, Wallis Wood, nr. Ockley, Dorking, Surrey. *T.:* Oakwood Hill 385. [*Died* 16 *Sept.* 1962.

BLACK, Rt. Hon. Arthur, P.C. (N.I.), 1947; M.A., LL.B. (Camb.); *b.* 6 Feb. 1888; *s.* of late Arthur and Mary Black. *Educ.:* Campbell College, Belfast; Sidney Sussex College, Cambridge (Scholar). Goldsmiths' Exhibitioner in Classics, 1908; First Class Classical Tripos, Part I, 1910; First Class (first place) Law Tripos, Part II, 1911; University (Whewell) Scholar in International Law, 1911. Called to Irish Bar; K.C. (Northern Ireland), 1929; M.P. for South Belfast, 1925-29, Willowfield Division of Belfast, 1929-41, Parliament of Northern Ireland; Attorney-General for Northern Ireland, 1939-41; Recorder of Belfast, 1941-43; Judge High Court of Justice, N. Ireland, 1943-49; Lord Justice of Appeal in Northern Ireland, 1949-64. *Address:* 20 Castlehill Road, Knock, Belfast 4. *T.:* Belfast 653914. [*Died* 15 *April* 1968.

BLACK, Hon. George, P.C. (Can.); Q.C. (Can.); practising law at Dawson, and Whitehorse, Yukon; M.P. (C.) Yukon Terr., Hse. of Commons of Canada, 1921-35, and 1940-49 (now retired from politics); Speaker, 1930-1935; *b.* Woodstock, N.B., 10 Apr. 1873; *s.* of William Andrew Black and Margaret Anne Bedell; *m.* 1904, Martha Louise Purdy (*d.* 1957), *d.* of George M. Munger, Chicago; *m.* 1958, Sadie Catherine King. *Educ.:* Public Schools, N.B. Yukon, 1898; practised law, and became identified with political affairs; elected to Territorial Council, 1905, 1907, and 1909, as leader of the Conservative party in the Council; Commissioner of Yukon Territory, 1912-16; organised Yukon Infantry Company, C.E.F., 1916; Company transferred to Machine Guns; commanded same in France as captain; on demobilisation resumed practice of law. *Recreations:* hunting and fishing, golf, photography. *Address:* 3410 Point Grey Road, Vancouver, British Columbia. *Club:* Vancouver (B.C.). [*Died* 23 *Aug.* 1965.

BLACK, Henry, C.B.E. 1935; apartment blocks owner and manager; *b.* 14 Feb. 1875; *s.* of William John and Elizabeth Johnston Black; *m.* 1910, Jennie Lenore Barker (*d.* 1950); four *s.* one *d.* *Educ.:* Public Sch., Grenville Co., Ont.; Business Coll., Brockville, Ont. Alderman of Regina, 1915-17, 1923-24; Mayor, 1918-19; Member General Hospital Board, 1918-23 and 1924; Member of the Library Board, 1917 and 1918; Chairman of the Saskatchewan Relief Commission, 1931-32 and 1933; Member of the Secondary School Board, 1930-38. *Address:* 2370 Lorne St., Regina, Sask., Canada. *T.:* Lakeside 2-3169. [*Died* 30 *July* 1960.

BLACK, Rt. Rev. James; Bishop of Paisley (R.C.), since 1948; *b.* 25 June 1894; *s.* of William Black and Catherine Black (*née* Queen). *Educ.:* St. Aloysius' College, Glasgow; Glasgow University; St. Peter's College,

Bearsden. Priest, 1920. *Address:* Bishop's House, Kilmacolm, Renfrewshire. *T.:* Kilmacolm 2494. [*Died* 29 *March* 1968.

BLACK, John Bennett, LL.D.; Fellow Royal Historical Society, 1920-54; Laureate and Hon. Corresp. Member of the Institut Historique et Héraldique de France; President of Historical Association of Scotland, 1937-40; Burnett-Fletcher Professor of History in the University of Aberdeen, 1930-1953, Emeritus Professor, 1953; Dean of Faculty of Arts (1939-42). Member of the Scottish Universities' Entrance Board, and member of the Court, Aberdeen University (1939-47); *b.* 1883; *s.* of late John Black, Glasgow; *m.* Margaret Ross 2nd *d.* of late J. B. Greig, Kirkcaldy, Scotland; one *s.* (*er. s.* killed on active service, 1943). *Educ.:* Glasgow University; Balliol College, Oxford; M.A. First Class Honours in English language and Lit. Glasgow University, 1907; Luke Fellow, 1907-10; B.A. First Class Hons. in Mod. Hist. Oxford, 1910; M.A. 1919; Beit Prize, 1910; Arnold Prize, 1913; Lecturer in British History, Glasgow University, 1910-19; Professor of Modern History, Queen's University, Kingston, Ont., Canada, 1919-20; Professor of Modern History, University of Sheffield, 1920-30; Dean of the Faculty of Arts and Public Orator, 1923-30; 2nd Lieutenant Glasgow University O.T.C. 1915-16; Lt. H.L.I. 1916-1918; P.O.W. 1918; Hon. LL.D. (Glasgow), 1949, and (Aberdeen), 1954. *Publications:* Elizabeth and Henry IV., 1914; The Art of History, 1926; contributor to Harmsworth's Universal History, 1927; Voltaire (Political and Social Ideas of Great French Thinkers of the XVIIIth Century, ed. Hearnshaw), 1929; contributor to English Historical Review, the Scottish Historical Review, the American Encyclopædia of the Social Sciences, The Spectator, History and other journals; The Reign of Queen Elizabeth, 1936 (2nd edn. 1958); Hector Boece's Scotorum Historiae (Aberd. Univ. Studies), 1937; Andrew Lang and the Casket Letters (Lang Memorial Lecture), 1949. *Recreations:* golf, motoring. *Address:* 3 Taleworth Road, Ashtead, Surrey. *T.:* Ashtead 5319. [*Died* 25 *Nov.* 1964.

BLACK, Sir John Paul, Kt., *cr.* 1943; *b.* 10 February 1895; *m.* 1943, Alicia Joan Pears, *d.* of Rt. Rev. J. H. Linton; three *s.* Served European War, 1914-18. Formerly Chairman and Managing Director Standard Motor Co. Ltd.; Deputy Chairman, Enfield Cables, 1954-55. Now farming. *Recreations:* shooting, fishing. *Address:* Dolbebin Farm, Llanbedr, Merioneth, Wales. [*Died* 24 *Dec.* 1965.

BLACK, Prof. Robert Alastair Lucien, D.S.C. 1943; B.Sc. (Eng.), A.R.S.M., M.I.M.M.; Professor of Mining, London University, since 1963; *b.* 31 Jan. 1921; *s.* of late Lt.-Col. C. H. G. Black, D.S.O., XIIth Royal Lancers; *m.* 1943, Margaret Katherine, *d.* of late H. N. Howorth; two *s.* *Educ.:* Stowe School; Imperial Coll. of Science and Technology, London Univ. Air Branch, Royal Navy as Lieut. (A) R.N.V.R., 1940-45. Mining Engineer, Central Mining and Investment Corp. Ltd., S. Africa, 1946-1956; Chamber of Mines Prof. of Mining Engineering, Univ. of Witwatersrand, 1956; Director S. African Govt. Miners Training Schools, 1956; Dean, Faculty of Engineering, Univ. of Witwatersrand, 1960. Mem. S. Africa Govt. Commn. of Enquiry into Methods of Training Engineers, 1960; Visiting Lectr., London Univ., 1962; Carnegie Travelling Fell., 1962; Visiting Lectr., Amer. Engineers Jt. Council, 1963. Council Mem., Instn. of Mining and Metallurgy, 1963. *Publications:* various scientific and technical papers in proceedings of professional institutes. *Recreations:* music, chess. *Address:* Royal School of Mines, S.W.7. *T.:* Kensington 5111. *Club:* Rand (Johannesburg). [*Died* 21 *June* 1967.

BLACK, Sydney, O.B.E. 1949; D.L.; J.P.; Partner of Knight & Co., Surveyors and Estate Agents; Director of Beaumont Property Trust Ltd., London Shop Property Trust Ltd., M.F. North Ltd., and numerous other Companies; *b.* 1908; *s.* of Robert Wilson Black, J.P., and Annie Louise (*née* North). *Educ.:* King's College School, Wimbledon; College of Estate Management. Joined R.A.F.V.R. (T.) 1941; Wing Comdr. 1948; O.C. Surrey Wing, A.T.C., 1947-55. Mem. Wimbledon Borough Council, 1947-; Deputy Mayor, 1951-52; Mayor, 1952-54; Alderman, 1953-65; Freedom of Borough of Wimbledon, 1964. C.C. 1949, J.P. 1949, D.L. 1960, C.A. 1961, High Sheriff 1962, Co. of Surrey; Vice-Chm. Surrey C.C., 1962-65; Chm. of Educn. Cttee., 1961-1965; Chm. Surrey C.C., 1965. Governor, King's College School, Wimbledon; Chm., Wimbledon Football Club. F.A.I. 1935; F.R.I.C.S. 1939. *Recreations:* public work and sport. *Address:* The Well House, 21 Arthur Road, Wimbledon, S.W.19. *T.:* Wimbledon 7819; Grattons, Dunsfold, Surrey. *T.:* Dunsfold 214. *Clubs:* Carlton, Royal Automobile, City Livery. [*Died* 4 *April* 1968.

BLACKBURN, Sir Arthur Dickinson, K.C.M.G., *cr.* 1938; C.B.E., 1935; *b.* 21 Oct. 1887; *s.* of Capt. Charles Henry Blackburn; *m.* 1st, 1913, Isabelle Piry (*d.* 1950); four *s.*; 2nd, 1953, Margaret Grizel Main. *Educ.:* Bedford School. Entered H.M. Consular Service in China, 1908; Called to Bar, Middle Temple, 1917; served as Vice-Consul and Consul Peking, Foochow and Shanghai, Chinese Counsellor, British Embassy, China; retired, 1944. *Address:* Old Manor House, Hythe, Kent. [*Died* 5 *March* 1970.

BLACKBURNE, Very Rev. Harry William, D.S.O. 1918; M.C. 1915; Dean of Bristol, 1934-51, emeritus since 1951; *b.* 25 Jan. 1878; *s.* of C. E. Blackburne, Oldham; *m.* 1904, Haidee Frances (*d.* 1958), *d.* of Maj.-Gen. W. Creagh, I.A.; two *s.* *Educ.:* Tonbridge; Clare Coll., Cambridge. Served as a trooper, W. Kent Imperial Yeomanry, South Africa, 1900 (Queen's medal); B.A. 1901; M.A. 1902; Deacon, 1901; Priest, 1902; Curate of Leamington, 1901-1903; Acting Chaplain to H.M. Forces, 1903; Chaplain to H.M. Forces, 1904; Aldershot, 1903-5; Bordon Camp, 1905-9; S. Africa, 1909-1912; Travelling Secretary, C.E.M.S., India, 1912; Chaplain to R.M.C. Camberley, 1913-14 and 1919-24; Vicar of Ashford, Kent, 1924-31; Rural Dean of East Charing, 1929; Canon of St. George's, Windsor, 1931-34; Chaplain to the King, 1920-1934; Select Preacher, Cambridge University, 1935 and 1947; European War, 1914-18 (despatches seven times, M.C., D.S.O., promoted 1st class Chap.). *Publications:* This also happened on the Western Front, The Padre's Story, 1932; The Romance of St. George's Chapel, Windsor Castle, 1933; Clergy in Wartime, 1939; A Thought for Sunday, 1942. *Recreations:* sailing, fishing. *Address:* 5 Grange Road, Clifton, Bristol 8. *T.:* Bristol 33444. *Club:* Naval and Military. [*Died* 31 *May* 1963.

BLACKER, L(atham) V(alentine) Stewart, O.B.E. 1920; T.D.; p.s.c.; A.F.R.Ae.S.; lately Comdr. LVIIIth (Sussex) Field Brigade, R.A.; *s.* of Major Latham Blacker; *g.g.s.* of Latham Blacker, of Lisnahanna, Co. Tyrone; *m.* 1927, Lady Doris, *o. d.* of 1st Earl Peel; twin *s.* two *d.* *Educ.:* Cheltenham; Bedford. Served North-West Frontier, 1908; Aeroplane pilot, 1911; raised and commanded 1st Divisional Signals, 1910; with Q.O. Corps of Guides, Buner, 1913-14, Russia, 1914; France and Flanders, as Flying Officer, R.F.C., 1915-16 (wounded); Captain 57th Wilde's

Rifles Frontier Force, April-Aug. 1915 (severely wounded); Staff Captain, Aeronautics, War Office, 1916; with R.F.C., 1916-1917 (very severely injured); commanded detachment Q.O. Corps of Guides in Turkistan, 1918-20; at Tashkent with Red Army during 1918; in command during pursuit and capture of hostile party in Kuen-Lun, 1918; first explored Shakshu; served in Transcaspia, Merv, 1918-19; Afghan War, Herat Frontier, 1919 (medal and clasp); commanded Independent Force in operations Khorasan-Turkistan frontiers, 1920 (medal and clasp, O.B.E.); acting Lt.-Col., 1919-20; Govt. of India's Macgregor medal, 1920; addressed Royal Geographical Society, 1921; British Association. 1921; Royal Society, 1933; propounded Parachute Infantry, 1922; Staff College, 1922; Jowaki Valley operations, 1923 (clasp); Imperial General Staff, 1924-28; Kajuri Afridi operations, 1930-31 (clasp); has traversed much of Central Asia and Russia; took part in Mt. Everest flight, 1933; Geographical Society's Gold Medal, Paris; Times' Medal; Membre d'honneur Royal Geog. Soc. of Antwerp; invented the Blacker Bombard, the Hedgehog (anti-submarine), the P.I.A.T. and the Petard of the A.V.R.E. *Publications:* On Secret Patrol in High Asia, 1921; Tales from Turkistan, 1924; (jointly) First over Everest, 1933. *Recreations:* thinking and organisation. *Address:* Cold Hayes, Liss, Hants. *T.:* Liss 2299. *Clubs:* Royal Air Force, Royal Automobile, Airborne Forces: Shikar. [*Died* 19 *April* 1964.

BLACKETT, Sir Charles Douglas, 9th Bt. *cr.* 1673; D.L.; Major, retired; *b.* 15 Aug. 1904; *e. s.* of Sir Hugh Douglas Blackett, 8th Bt., and Helen Katherine Lowther (*d.* 1943); *S.* father, 1960; *m.* 1935, Ursula Mary, *d.* of Major M. F. Cely-Trevilian; two *d.* (one *s.* decd.). *Educ.:* Eton; Sandhurst. 2nd Lt. The Queen's Bays, 1924; Capt. 1936; Adjt. The Northumberland Hussars, 1937-40; Major 1940. Served in France and N. Africa with The Queen's Bays, 1940-42. Prisoner of War, 1942-45; retired 1947. High Sheriff of Northumberland, 1953; D.L., 1954. *Recreations:* hunting, shooting. *Heir:* *b.* George William Blackett [*b.* 26 April, 1906; *m.* 1933, Euphemia Cicely Robinson (*d.* 1960); no *c.*]. *Address:* Halton Castle, Corbridge, Northumberland; Matfen Hall, Newcastle upon Tyne. *Clubs:* Cavalry; Northern Counties (Newcastle upon Tyne). [*Died* 26 *Dec.* 1968.

BLACKLEDGE, Geoffrey Glynn, M.C. 1915; Q.C. 1950; Presiding Judge of the Liverpool Court of Passage since 1950; *b.* 11 July 1894; *s.* of W. T. Blackledge, M.B.E., M.B., Liverpool, and Sarah Elizabeth, *d.* of Isaac Taylor, J.P., Flint; *m.* 1939, Madeleine, *e. d.* of J. V. Ellis, Workington, Cumberland; one *d.* *Educ.:* Shrewsbury School; St. John's Coll. Oxf. Served 1914-19 6th Bn. The King's Regt. (Liverpool) (despatches, M.C. and Bar); B.A. Oxford 1919; M.A. 1920; called to Bar, Middle Temple, 1920; Northern Circuit; Stipendiary Magistrate for Liverpool, 1946-47; returned to practise at Bar, 1947; J.P. for Cheshire, 1948-50. *Address:* 10 King's Bench Walk, Temple, E.C.4. *T.:* Central 2775; Surrey Cottage, Chiddingfold, Surrey. *Clubs:* Leander, Oxford and Cambridge. [*Died* 25 *June* 1964.

BLACKMAN, Vernon Herbert, F.R.S. 1913; Sc.D. (Cantab.); Hon. D.Sc. (Benares and Allahabad); *b.* 8 Jan. 1872; *s.* of Frederick Blackman, M.R.C.S., L.R.C.P., and Catherine Frost; *m.* 1st, 1901, Edith Delta Emett (*d.* 1940); one *s.* one *d.*; 2nd, 1941, Thérèse Elizabeth, *e. d.* of late S. G. S. Panisset. *Educ.:* City of London School; King's College School; St. John's College, Cambridge (Fellow, 1898-1904); Walsingham Medallist, 1898; Assistant in Department of Botany, British Museum (Natural History), 1896-1906; Lecturer in Botany, Birkbeck and East London Colleges, and Lecturer in Vegetable Cytology, University College, London, 1906-07; Professor of Botany, Leeds University, 1907-11; Professor of Plant Physiology, Imperial College of Science and Technology, 1911-37; Emeritus Professor of Plant Physiology, University of London, 1937; Director of the Research Institute of Plant Physiology, Imperial College of Science and Technology, London, 1913-42; Member: Advisory Council, Dept. Scientific and Industrial Research, 1926-30, Chairman, 1930; Water Pollution Research Board, 1927-44; Forest Products Research Board, 1931-47 (Chairman, 1939-47). Editor, Annals of Botany, 1922-47; Pres., Section of Botany, British Assoc., 1924; Hon. Treasurer, The English Association, 1953-59. *Publications:* contrib. to scientific jls. *Address:* 17 Berkeley Place, S.W.19. *T.:* 01-946 2685. *Club:* Athenæum. [*Died* 1 *Oct.* 1967.

BLACKMORE, Sir Charles Henry, Kt., *cr.* 1932; C.B.E. 1921; *b.* 1880. Formerly Private Secretary to Parliamentary Secretary, Ministry of Pensions, and Financial Secretary, Admiralty; late Secretary, Prime Minister, Northern Ireland; also Secretary, Cabinet of Northern Ireland and Clerk of Privy Council thereof, 1925-39. *Address:* Clanbrassil, Cultra, Co. Down. *T.:* Holywood 2388. *Clubs:* Constitutional; Ulster Reform (Belfast). [*Died* 13 *May* 1967.

BLACKMUR, Richard Palmer; author, critic, poet; Professor of English, Princeton University, since 1951; Fellow of Library of Congress; Member National Institute of Arts and Letters, 1956; *b.* 21 Jan. 1904; *s.* of George Edward Blackmur and Helen (*neé* Palmer); *m.* 1930, Helen Dickson (marr. diss., 1951). Guggenheim Fellowships, 1936-1938. Princeton University: Res. Fell., 1940-43, 1946-48; Assoc. Prof. of English, 1948-51. Pitt Professor of American History and Institutions, Cambridge Univ., 1961-62 (M.A. (Cantab), 1961); Fell. of Christ's Coll. Camb., 1961. Hon. Litt.D. Rutgers Univ., 1958. *Publications:* The Double Agent, 1935; From Jordan's Delight, 1937; The Expense of Greatness, 1940; The Second World, 1942; The Good European, 1947; Languages as a Gesture, 1952; The Lion and the Honeycomb, 1955; Anni Mirabiles, 1956; Form and Value in Modern Poetry, 1957. Many articles of criticism. *Address:* 53 McCosh Circle, Princeton, N.J., U.S.A. [*Died* 2 *Feb.* 1965.

BLADON, Air Cdre. Graham Clarke, C.B. 1959; C.B.E. 1951; R.A.F. retd.; *b.* 13 Sept. 1899; *s.* of J. J. Bladon; *m.* 1937, Muriel, *d.* of T. A. Clibbens; one *s.* Served War (despatches, 1920). Air Force Adviser to Ceylon Government, 1950-58; Commander, Royal Ceylon Air Force, 1951-58. *Recreation:* golf. *Address:* c/o The Air Ministry, Adastral House, Theobalds Road, W.C.1; Rosemary, Limpley Stoke, Bath, Somerset. *Club:* Royal Air Force. [*Died* 11 *Oct.* 1967.

BLAGDEN, His Honour John Basil; retired as Judge of County Courts; *b.* Holmleigh, Yelverton, S. Devon, 8 Oct. 1901; *o. s.* of late John James Blagden, M.R.C.S., 5 King's Buildings, Chester, and late Jessica, *o. d.* of Rt. Hon. Mr. Justice Murphy; *m.* 1st, 1929, Nellie Sydney (*d.* 1959), *o. d.* of late Charles Hignett, Huntingdon, Hunts; no *c.*; 2nd, 1960, Eleanor Mary (Mollie), *e. d.* of late Willis James Bull; no *c.* *Educ.:* Shrewsbury (Scholar); Brasenose College, Oxford (Scholar, 2nd Class Moderations 1922, 1st Class Jurisprudence 1924, Senior Hulme Scholar 1924). Eldon University Scholar 1924; Fellow of All Souls College, 1924-31; B.A. 1924, M.A. 1927; called to the Bar, Inner Temple, 1925; Oxford Circuit; Assistant Reader in Criminal Law Evidence and Procedure to Council of Legal Education, 1928-39; pending call-up by R.N.V.S.R. served as stretcher-bearer to

Battersea Borough Council and assistant legal adviser to Minister of Food, 1939; Officiating Judge, High Court, Calcutta, June-Sept. 1942, and Bombay, 1942-44; Puisne Judge, High Court, Rangoon, 1940-44, and 1946-48 High Court, Bombay, 1944-46; Judge of County Courts, circuits 37 and 40, 1948, circuit 41, 1949-50; circuit 44, 1950; retired 1964. Chairman (1955-57) Board of Trade Committee on Bankruptcy Law Amendment. *Publications:* with Sir W. N. Stable, 1932, 14th, and with J. M. Buckley, 1938, 15th editions of Williams on Bankruptcy. *Recreations:* gardening, and shove halfpenny; formerly sailing, field sports, rowing and running: ran (cross-country) for Oxford, 1922. *Address:* Beldhamland, Loxfold, W. Sussex. *Clubs:* Garrick; Vincent's (Oxford). [*Died* 29 *July* 1964.

BLAIN, Hon. Sir Eric (Herbert), Kt. 1965; Q.C. 1961; **Hon. Mr. Justice Blain;** a Judge of the High Court of Justice, Queen's Bench Division, since 1965; *b.* 7 May 1904; *o. s.* of late Sir Herbert E. Blain, C.B.E., and late Lady Blain; *m.* 1930, Dulcie Hylda ("Bunty"), *o. d.* of late R. W. Paton, Bishop's Stortford. *Educ.:* Uppingham; King's College, Cambridge. Called to the Bar, Middle Temple, 1927; Bencher, Middle Temple, 1957. Served War of 1939-45, Suffolk Regiment and General Staff. Judge of the Court of Appeal of the Bailiwick of Guernsey and of the Court of Appeal of the Island of Jersey, 1964-65. *Address:* Royal Courts of Justice, Strand, W.C.2; 80 Eaton Square, S.W.1. *T.:* 01-235 2601. *Clubs:* St. James', Portland. [*Died* 19 *Nov.* 1969.

BLAIR, Dame Emily Mathieson, D.B.E. *cr.* 1943; R.R.C. 1938. *Educ.:* Glasgow Joined R.A.F. 1918. Served in hospitals at home and abroad; Matron-in-Chief, Princess Mary's R.A.F. Nursing Service, 1938-43 (despatches); O.St.J. 1944; Matron-in-Chief Joint War Organisation, 1943-47, subsequently Matron-in-Chief British Red Cross Society to 1953. Awarded Florence Nightingale Medal, 1947. *Address:* 189 Grove End Gardens, N.W.8. *Club:* United Nursing Services. [*Died* 25 *Dec.* 1963.

BLAIR, Sir Reginald, 1st Bt., *cr.* 1945; Kt., *cr.* 1921; D.L. Mddx., J.P. Mddx. and Bucks; late Chairman, Racecourse Betting Control Board; *b.* 8 Nov. 1881; *y. s.* of late George MacLellan Blair, J.P., Glasgow; *m* 1905, Mabel (*d.* 1936), *y. d.* of late Geo. Bradley Wieland; one *d.* (three *s.* decd. of whom two died during War of 1939-45). *Educ.:* Kelvinside Acad.; Glasgow Univ. A member of the Institute of Accountants and Actuaries in Scotland; M.P. (C.) Bow and Bromley, 1912-22; M.P. (C.) Hendon Division of Middlesex, 1935-45; Chairman London Municipal Society, 1919-29. Hon. Freedom of Hendon, 1946. Served with British Expeditionary Force, 1914-16 (despatches), as a field cashier and on Staff of Paymaster-in-Chief at War Office, with temporary rank of Major, 1917-18. *Recreations:* shooting, golf. *Clubs:* Carlton, Royal Automobile. [*Died* 18 *Sept.* 1962.

BLAIR-FISH, Wallace Wilfrid; *pseudonym* **Blair;** Playwright; *b.* 1889; *m.* 1st, Hilary Margaret, *y. d.* of late C. R. Burgis of Leamington Spa; one *s.* one *d.*; 2nd, Hilary May, *e. d.* of late Ralph Heaton of The Mint, Birmingham. *Educ.:* Privately; Pembroke Coll., Oxford. Editor of The Varsity, 1910; contributor to Punch, 1908-17; literary staff of Sunday Times and Sunday Chronicle; Food Economy Department, Ministry of Food, 1917; Chief of Labour Section, 1918; Director, Transport, Labour and Materials Branch, 1919; Mission to Near East, Supreme Economic Council, 1919; Joint Managing Director and Publisher, Shakespeare Head Press, Ltd., 1921-22; Director, Rural Industries Bureau, 1926-27; Sec. of Rotary International: Association for Great Britain and Ireland, 1928-37, Editor of the same, 1928-42. *Plays:* Consarnin' Sairey 'Uggins, 1914; Whimsies, 1915; The Private Life of P.C. Pettifer, 1916; Old King Cole, 1942; The Beggar Maid, Gather Ye Rosebuds, 1943; Blimpton Won't Budge, Genius Ltd., 1945; Born Again, Ivory Tower, Civvy Street, 1949; Pyrrhus Had Three Wives, 1959; Tragedy at Evesham (1265), 1965. Over 30 Radio Plays from 1943. *Publications:* various volumes of light verse and poetry, including Poets on the Isis, Black and White Magic, Herbs of Grace, The Life and Death of Mrs. Tidmuss; also plays, including the Death of Shakespeare and Gather ye Rosebuds. *Recreations:* reading, plays, sports, TV. *Address:* Fladbury Mill, near Pershore, Worcs. *T.:* Cropthorne 311. [*Died* 9 *April* 1968.

BLAKE, Vice-Admiral Sir Geoffrey, K.C.B. 1937 (C.B. 1929); D.S.O. 1916; *b.* 1882; *s.* of Thomas Naish Blake, Bramley House, Alverstoke; *m.* 1911, Jean St. John (*d.* 1963), *d.* of Sir W. St. J. Carr; two *d.* *Educ.:* Winchester Coll. Entered Navy, 1897; Lieut., 1904 Commander, 1914; Captain, 1918; Rear-Adm. 1931; Vice-Adm. 1935; served European War; Gunnery Commander H.M.S. Iron Duke, 1914-17 (despatches, D.S.O., Order of St. Anne, Russia); Battle of Jutland, 1916; H.M.S. Queen Elizabeth, 1917-19; Naval Attaché to U.S.A., 1919-21; commanded H.M.S. Queen Elizabeth, Fleet Flagship of Atlantic Fleet, 1921-23; served on Staff of War College, 1923-25; Deputy Director, Royal Naval Staff College, 1925-26; Director, 1926-27; Chief of Staff, Atlantic Fleet, 1927-29; Commodore in command of New Zealand Station and First Naval Member, New Zealand Naval Board, 1929-32; Fourth Sea Lord and Chief of Supplies and Transport, 1932-35; Vice-Adm. Comdg. Battle Cruiser Squadron, and Second-in-Command Mediterranean Fleet, 1936-38; retired 1938; a Lord Commissioner of the Admiralty and additional Assist. Chief of Naval Staff, 1940; Flag Officer Liaison United States Navy in Europe, 1942-45 (Legion of Merit, Degree of Chief Commander). Gentleman Usher of the Black Rod, 1945-49. *Address:* 42 Burton Court, S.W.3. *Club:* United Service. [*Died* 18 *July* 1968.

BLAKE, George; novelist; *b.* Greenock, 28 Oct. 1893; *m.* 1923, Ellie Malcolm Lawson: two *s.* one *d.* Acting Editor John o' London's Weekly, 1924-28; Strand Magazine, 1928-30; Director, Faber and Faber, publishers, 1930-32. *Publications:* Vagabond Papers, 1922; Mince Collop Close, 1923; The Wild Men, 1925; Young Malcolm, 1926; Paper Money, 1928; The Path of Glory, 1929; The Seas Between, 1930; Returned Empty, 1931; Sea Tangle 1932; Rest and Be Thankful, 1934; The Heart of Scotland, 1934; The Shipbuilders, 1935; David and Joanna, 1936; Down to the Sea, 1937; Late Harvest, 1938; The Valiant Heart, 1940; The Constant Star, 1945; The Westering Sun, 1946; The Five Arches, 1947; The Paying Guest, 1949; Mountain and Flood: History of the 52nd (Lowland) Division, 1950; The Piper's Tune, 1950; Barrie and the Kailyard School, 1951; The Firth of Clyde, 1952; The Voyage Home, 1952; The Innocence Within, 1955; B.I. Centenary History, 1956; The Ben Line, 1956; The Last Fling, 1956; The Peacock Palace, 1958; History of Lloyd's Register of Shipping, 1960; The Loves of Mary Glen, 1960. *Address:* 75 Queen Margaret Drive, Glasgow, N.W. [*Died* 29 *Aug.* 1961.

BLAKE, Sir Ulick Temple, of Menlough, Galway, 16th Bt., *cr.* 1622; Lt. R.A., T.A.; late 4/7 Dragoon Guards; *b.* 6 Aug. 1904; *s.* of 15th Bt. and Evelyn Winifred, *y. d.* of L. G. Stewart, late Lieut. R.E.; *S.*

father, 1925; *m.* 1940, Betty, 2nd *d.* of Arthur Gordon, Blundellsands, Lancs.; one *s.* *Heir:* *s.* Thomas Richard Valentine, *b.* 7 Jan. 1942. *Address:* Saltergill, Yarm-on-Tees.
[*Died* 5 *Oct.* 1963.

BLAKE-REED, Sir John (Seymour), Kt., *cr.* 1950; O.B.E. 1919; retired; *b.* 26 Nov. 1882; *e. s.* of John Howard Reed and Ada Lavinia Blake; *m.* 1913, Emma Beatrice (*d.* 1947), *o. d.* of Alfred Stanley Purcell, Manchester; no *c.* *Educ.:* Manchester Gram. Sch. Jesus Coll., Oxford (Scholar). M.A.; Hon. Fell., 1960. Called to Bar, Gray's Inn, 1907; Northern Circuit, Palatine Court of Chancery. Served European War, 1914-18, Lieut. R.N.V.R. Judge in Egyptian Native Courts, 1919-24; President Land Court, Palestine, 1925; Judge in Mixed Court, Cairo, 1926-32; Judge, Mixed Court of Appeal, Alexandria, 1932-49. Grand Officer Order of the Nile. *Publications:* Twenty-five Odes of Horace, 1942; More Odes of Horace, 1945. *Recreation:* water-colour painting. *Address:* 7 Canterbury Road, Oxford. *Clubs:* Turf (Cairo); Union (Alexandria). [*Died* 8 *March* 1966.

BLAKELOCK, Denys (Martin); Actor, writer, poet; *b.* 22 June 1901; *s.* of Reverend Martin Ogle Blakelock and Constance Rose (*née* Pike). *Educ.:* Aldenham. Trained R.A.D.A. First appearance Philip in You Never Can Tell, 1920; Hugo in The World of Light, 1931; Aristophanes in Acropolis, 1933; Aguecheek in Twelfth Night, 1942; Bob Acres in The Rivals, 1943; Androcles in Androcles and the Lion, 1943; Title role in The Magistrate, 1943; Title role in The Bread-Winner, 1944; Cecil Graham in Lady Windermere's Fan, 1945; The Dean in Dandy Dick, 1948; Mr. Goldfinch in A Pair of Spectacles, 1948; Lamprett Bellboys in A Penny for a Song, 1951. Teacher of Audition Technique and Diction, Royal Academy of Dramatic Art, 1947-62. Has appeared in numerous films and on television; also broadcasts. *Publications:* The Waters (collected poems), 1955; The Chastening (collected poems), 1957; Advice to a Player (letters to a young actor), 1957; Finding My Way (A Spiritual Journey), 1958; Choosing Your Piece (auditions anthology), 1960; Acting My Way (further letters to a young actor), 1964; Making the Stage Your Career, 1965; Eleanor: Portrait of a Farjeon, 1966; Round the Next Corner (autobiography), 1967. *Recreations:* walking, antique-collecting. *Address:* 42 Lancaster Close, St. Petersburgh Place, W.2. *T.:* 01-229 4695. *Clubs:* Garrick, B.B.C. [*Died* 7 *Dec.* 1970.

BLAKER, Cedric, C.B.E. 1958; M.C. 1918; E.D. 1946; retired from Gilman & Co. Ltd. Hong Kong, East India Merchants, 1958 (Chm., 1947-58); *b.* 19 Feb. 1889; *er. s.* of Rev. Cecil Renshaw Blaker, Turners Hill, Sussex; *m.* 1921, Louise Douglas, *e. d.* of Dr. W. A. Chapple, Wellington, N.Z.; two *s.* *Educ.:* Haileybury Coll. Served European War with Army Service Corps and 2nd Bn. Roy. Sussex Regt., France, 1915-18; War of 1939-45, with Hong Kong Vol. Defence Corps; Hon. Col. Hong Kong Regt., 1954-58. Retired as Chairman: Hongkong & Shanghai Banking Corp. (1953-1958); Union Insurance Soc. of Canton Ltd. (1954-58); South China Morning Post, Ltd. (1950-58); Rediffusion (Hongkong) Ltd. (1953-58); and as Director numerous other public cos. in Hong Kong. Chm. Hongkong General Chamber of Commerce, 1953-54, 1956-58; Mem. Hongkong Executive Council, 1953-54, and Legislative Council, 1953-58. Hon. Consul-General for Sweden, 1938-54; Hon. Consul for Greece, 1946-58. Commander Royal Order of Wasa (Sweden), 1954; Golden Cross, Royal Order of King George (Greece), 1961. *Address:* Town House Farm, Scaynes Hill, Sussex. *T.:* Dane Hill 415. [*Died* 18 *June* 1965.

BLAKISTON, John Francis, C.I.E. 1937; *b.* 21 March 1882; *s.* of John Rochfort Blakiston; *m.* 1937, Margaret Dora, *er. d.* of Rev. G. A. Ward-Jackson, Heyford, Oxon.; one *s.* two *d.* *Educ.:* Wellington College; Switzerland. Architect, Indian Archæological Survey, India; Director General of Archæology in India, 1935-37; retired, 1937. *Publications:* edited several Archæological reports. *Recreations:* gardening, etc. *Address:* Anelog, Aberadron, Nr. Pwllheli, N. Wales. *T.A.:* Angelo, Aberdaron. *T.:* Aberdaron 347.
[*Died* 8 *Jan.* 1965.

BLAMPIED, Edmund, R.B.A. 1938; R.E. 1921, now Hon. Retired Fellow; artist; *b.* Jersey, Jersey parents, 30 March, 1886; *m.* 1914, Marianne Van Abbe, Holland; no *c.* *Educ.:* Jersey. Studied at the Lambeth Art school; exhibited in the Royal Academy and French Salon. Lived in Jersey during German occupation; designed Jersey Occupation stamps (six—known as the Pictorial Set), also one of Channel Islands Liberation stamps, issued 10 May 1948. *Recreations:* chess, billiards. *Address:* 1 La Haule Court, St. Aubin, Jersey, C.I. [*Died* 26 *Aug.* 1966.

BLAND, Charles Heber, C.M.G. 1946; Chairman, Civil Service Commission of Canada, from 1935, retired; *b.* 6 Sept. 1886, English-Welsh; *m.* 1912, Ethel Farrow; three *s.* *Educ.:* Queen's Univ., Kingston, Ontario. Entered Civil Service, 1909. Served overseas during European War, 1914-18, with 20th Battery, C.F.A. Chief Examiner, Civil Service Commission, 1921; Civil Service Commissioner, 1933. *Publications:* Public Personnel Administration in Canada, 1935; Two Years of Wartime Personnel Administration in Canada, 1942; Training for Administrative Posts in the Public Service of Canada, 1945. *Recreations:* fishing, curling. *Address:* 828 Echo Drive, Ottawa. *T.:* CE 4-5904.
[*Died* 3 *Feb.* 1966.

BLAND, Francis Armand, C.M.G. 1958; M.A., LL.B.; Emeritus Prof. of Government, Sydney University; *b.* 24 August 1882; *s.* of C. E. Bland; *m.* 1st, 1908, Elizabeth Bates Jacobs; one *s.*; 2nd, 1912, Lillian Victoria Orr; one *s.* two *d.* (and two *s.* decd.); 3rd, 1954, Ida Mary Warby (*née* Bland); 4th, 1960, Gertrude Rollins. *Educ.:* Greigs Flat and Kogarah State Schools; Sydney Univ.; London Sch. of Economics. Private enterprise, 1897; N.S.W. Public Service, 1900; University Lectr. in Public Administration, Sydney, 1912; Tutorial Class Lectr., Oxford Univ., 1916-17; Asst. Dir. Tutorial Classes, Sydney, 1918; First Prof. of Public Admin. at Sydney Univ., 1935. M.P., Federal Parliament (Canberra) for Warringah, 1951-61; elected Chairman Parliamentary Public Accounts Cttee., 1952. Visiting Prof. of Government, Washington Square Coll., New York, 1929-30. Hon. Lectr., Lond. Sch. of Economics, 1947. Vice-Pres. Roy. Inst. Public Administration, London, 1933. Life Vice-Pres. N.S.W. Br. Roy. Inst. Public Admin., 1947. *Publications:* Shadows and Realities of Government, 1923; City Government by Commission, 1928; Budget Control, 1931; Planning the Modern State, 1934; Government in Australia, 1939; Editor, Australian Highway, 1918-35; Editor Jl. of Public Admin., 1935-47. Contributor to many books and jls. *Recreation:* gardening. *Address:* Llandaff, 59 Barker Rd., Strathfield, N.S.W., Aust. *T.:* U.M. 7198. *Clubs:* University (Sydney); Commercial Travellers' (Melbourne).
[*Died* 9 *April* 1967.

BLAND, Sir Thomas (Maltby), Kt. 1961; T.D.; D.L.; Deputy Chairman, Barclays Bank Ltd. (and Local Director, Ipswich); Director: Barclays Bank of California; Société Financière Européenne; Intercontinental Banking Services Ltd.; Chairman: Tollemache and Cobbold Breweries

Ltd.; Clive Discount Co. Ltd.; *b.* 1906; 2nd *s.* of late Francis Lawrence Bland, J.P., Copdock, Ipswich; unmarried. *Educ.:* Eton; Magdalene Coll., Cambridge. President, Institute of Bankers, 1956-58. Vice-Chairman, East Suffolk County Council, 1957-63 (C.C., 1945-50; C.A., 1951-; Chm., Finance and General Purposes Committee, 1948-61); a Vice-Pres. County Councils Association (Chm., 1960-63; Vice-Chm., 1956-60; Chairman of its Police Committee, 1953-60 and 1963-67); Chm., Suffolk Police Authority, from 1967; Mem. Police Council for Gt. Britain; a Gov., Police Coll.; Pres. East Anglian Assoc. of Building Societies; Hon. Life Pres., Ipswich Chamber of Commerce & Shipping (Pres., 1951-65); Pres. League of Friends of Ipswich Hospitals; Chm. Ipswich Gp. Hosp. Management Cttee., 1948-55; Pres., Suffolk Agricultural Association, 1955-56; Member British National Export Council, 1964-68; Chm., Financial Advisory Panel on Exports, 1964-68; Chm., Cttee. on Invisible Exports, 1966-67. Served War of 1939-45, Major, Royal Artillery. High Sheriff of Suffolk, 1952; D.L., Suffolk, 1958. *Address:* Rookwood, Copdock, Ipswich. *T.:* 266; 1 St. James's Street, S.W.1. *Clubs:* Brooks's, Pratt's, Royal Automobile. [*Died* 29 *June* 1968.

BLANDY, Air Commodore Lyster Fettiplace, C.B. 1924; D.S.O. 1915; late R.E. and R.A.F.; *b.* 21 Sep. 1874; *s.* of late Adam F. Blandy of The Warren, Abingdon; *m.* 1905, Violet Mary, *d.* of Charles Vernon, British Columbia. *Educ.:* Haileybury; Woolwich. Entered Army, 1895; Captain, 1904; Major, 1914; Brevet Lt-Col., 1916; Colonel, 1921; retired pay, 1928; employed with Canadian Forces, 1906; Inspector R.E. Stores, 1911-13; European War, 1914-18 (D.S.O., Officer Legion of Honour, Order of Crown and Croix de guerre, Belgium); re-empl., 1939. [*Died* 7 *June* 1964.

BLANDY, Richard Denis, C.M.G. 1951; O.B.E. 1942; *b.* 3 Dec. 1891; *s.* of Richard Ridpath Blandy and Ada Eliza Penfold; *m.* 1st, 1916, Millicent Joyce Kidd (*decd.*); one *d.* (one *s.* decd.); 2nd, Agnes M. Douglas; twin *s.* *Educ.:* Victoria College, Jersey. Indian Police, 1911-24; Seconded Indian Army Reserve of Officers, 1915-18; retired on proportionate pension, 1924, under Reforms Scheme; in business, Madeira, 1924-28; Chief Tangier International Police, 1928; Assistant to British Resident Commr. New Hebrides, 1929-40; British Resident Commissioner, New Hebrides Condominium, 1940-51; retired, 1951. Asst. Bursar, St. Peter's Coll., Adelaide, 1954; School Bursar, 1957-60. *Recreation:* golf. *Address:* 28 Church Terrace, Walkerville, S. Australia. [*Died* 7 *Sept.* 1964.

BLANK, Abraham Lewis; *b.* 19 May 1891; *o.* *s.* of Joseph Blank and Matilda Jacobs; *m.* 1920, Deborah Freda Schulmann; three *d.* *Educ.:* City of London School; Wadham College, Oxon. (Exhibitioner). B.A. 1914; M.A. 1920; joined I.C.S. 1915; I.A.R.O. 1916-19; confirmed as District and Sessions Judge 1926. Called to Bar, Middle Temple, 1930; Commissioner for Workmen's Compensation, Bengal, 1931; Secretary to Government and Legal Remembrancer, Assam, 1935, Bengal, 1939; Acting Judge, Calcutta High Court, 1942; Puisne Judge, Calcutta High Court, 1944-50; resigned from I.C.S., 1950. *Recreation:* reading. *Address:* 46 Westminster Court, St. Albans, Herts. *T.:* 59751. [*Died* 27 *Jan.* 1967.

BLATCH, Sir William Bernard, Kt., 1942; M.B.E. 1920; Solicitor of Inland Revenue, 1939-52; *b.* 12 Dec. 1887; *s.* of late Frank Blatch, Basingstoke, Hants; *m.* 1915, Madeleine Dorothy Ross; two *s.* (and one *s.* killed in War of 1939-45). *Educ.:* Brighton Coll.; Queen's Coll., Oxf. *Address:* Raglan, Gerrards Cross, Bucks. [*Died* 8 *Sept.* 1965.

BLAXLAND, Major-General Alan Bruce, C.B. 1945; O.B.E. 1926; I.A. retd.; *b.* 17 Oct. 1892; *s.* of Rev. Bruce Blaxland; *m.* 1919, Lilian Alice Lucy, *d.* of M. M. Ferguson; two *d.* *Educ.:* Shrewsbury; Oxford (B.A.). 2nd Lieut. unattached list I.A. 1913 (University Commn.); Lieut. Indian Army, 1915; Capt. 1917; Major, 1931; Lt.-Col. 1938; Col. 1941; local Lt.-Gen. 1942; Temp. Maj.-Gen. 1943; retired with Hon. rank of Maj.-Gen. 1947. Served European War, 1914-19 (wounded, despatches): France and Flanders, South Persia and Persian Gulf; Waziristan, N.W. Frontier, India, 1921-22; Small Arms School, India, 1922-25; Mil. Adviser, Central India States Forces, 1929-33; Mohmand Operations, 1933; comd. 1/7 Rajput Regt. (despatches). Served War of 1939-45; comd. 4/7 Rajput Regt., Egypt and Desert, 1938-1940; 2nd Comd. Mersa Mtruh Fortress, 1940; comd. 27th Indian Inf. Bde., Iraq and Persia, 1941-42; comd. 10th Indian Inf. Div., Desert and Cyprus, 1942-43; comd. 25th Corps, Cyprus; invalided to India, 1943; G.O.C. Lahore District, 1943-46. Collar Badge of Order of Cloud and Banner (China), 1945. *Address:* c/o National and Grindlay's Bank, 54 Parliament St., S.W.1; Pleasaunce, Kingsdown, Kent. *Club:* Junior Army and Navy. [*Died* 2 *Sept.* 1963.

BLAXTER, Kenneth William, C.M.G. 1950; Assistant Secretary, Colonial Office, 1942-56; retired April 1956; *b.* 1 Sept. 1895; *s.* of late W. F. Blaxter, J.P., Warminster, Wilts.; *m.* 1924, Janet, *er. d.* of late Dr. Hollis, Wellingborough; two *s.* one *d.* *Educ.:* Malvern Coll.; Magdalene Coll., Cambridge. Classical scholar, Malvern College; scholar Magdalene College, Cambridge. Served European War, 1914-18, Army, 1915-19; Lieut. R.F.A., in France and Italy (wounded). Entered Home Civil Service, 1920; Ministry of Transport, 1920-22; Secretary Royal Commission on Suffering and Damage by Enemy Action, 1922-24; Colonial Office, 1924-56. Member Cell Barnes and Harperbury Group Hospital Management Cttee., 1956-64; Board of Governors, Univ. Coll. Hosp., 1959-63. *Recreation:* tennis. *Address:* Pathside, Frithesden Copse, Berkhamsted Herts. *T.:* Berkhamsted 79. *Clubs:* St. Stephen's; Hawks (Cambridge). [*Died* 3 *April* 1964.

BLEASE, W. Lyon, LL.M.; Barrister-at-law; *b.* Liverpool, 1884; *s.* of Walter and Mary Cecilia Blease; *m.* 1918, Harriott Davies; three *d.* *Educ.:* Parkfield School, Liverpool; Shrewsbury; Liverpool University. Awarded the Studentship at Bar Final Examination, 1906; contested Chorley Division of Lancashire, 1910; served with hospital units in Serbia, 1915; and in Russia and Roumania, 1916-18; Assistant Editor of The New East, Tokyo, 1918; Lecturer in the Law and Custom of the Constitution in Liverpool University, 1910; Queen Victoria Prof. of Law, Liverpool Univ., 1919-49; Public Orator, 1931-49; a Governor of the British Film Institute, 1936. Contested (L.) East Toxteth Division of Liverpool, 1945; Garston Division of Liverpool, 1950; Chm. Liverpool Philharmonic Society, 1950-51; Chm. Exec. Council for Liverpool under National Health Service Act, 1952-60; Member Management Committee of Executive Councils Association (England), 1960-. *Publications:* Liverpool Vestry Books, Vol. I, 1908 (in collaboration); The Emancipation of English Women, 1910; A Short History of English Liberalism, 1913; A Red Cross Unit in Serbia, 1916 (in collaboration); Suvorof, 1921. *Address:* 12 Eaton Road, Cressington Park, Liverpool. *T.:* Cen. 7213; Cressington 3545. [*Died* 12 *April* 1963.

BLIGH, John Murray, M.D., F.R.C.P.; formerly Physician to Ormskirk County Hosp. and Belmont Hosp., Liverpool; Consulting

Physician to Royal Liverpool United Hospital (Northern Hospital); Consulting Physician to Royal Liverpool Children's Hosp.; formerly Physician to Lourdes Hospital, Royal Liverpool Babies' Hospital; Consulting Physician to Southport Infirmary; Lecturer and Examiner in Clinical Medicine and Clinical Pediatrics, Univ. of Liverpool; Physician to Stanley Hospital; *s.* of Alexander Murray Bligh, M.R.C.S., and Mary Agnes Brady; *m.* 1926, Elizabeth Emily Underwood; three *s.* *Educ.:* Castleknock College; University of Liverpool. President Students' Representative Council of University of Liverpool, 1902; attached No. 12 Indian General Hospital, Mesopotamia, 1918; President Liverpool Medical Institution, 1934; Editor Liverpool Medico-Chirurgical Journal, 1934-1948; Hon. Mem. Manchester Medical Soc.; Fellow of Royal Society of Medicine; Sen. Member of Assoc. of Physicians; Hon. Member of British Paediatric Assoc.; Master of Guild of St. Luke, St. Cosmas, and St. Damian, 1938-48. J.P. City of Liverpool, 1938-49. *Publications:* Richet's Anaphylaxis (Translation); papers on Children's Diseases. *Recreation:* fishing. *Address:* Thornbury, Freshfield Rd., Formby, Lancs. *T.:* Formby 2303. [*Died* 9 *Jan.* 1968.

BLIGH, Sir Timothy (James), K.B.E. 1963 (O.B.E. 1945); D.S.O. 1945; D.S.C. 1944 (and Bar 1944); Assistant Managing Director, Thomson Organisation since 1966 (Dir., 1964-66); *b.* 2 September 1918; *er. surv. s.* of Sir Edward Bligh; *m.* 1945, Ruth Pamela Robertson; two *s.* one *d.* *Educ.:* Winchester; Balliol College, Oxford (Scholar; B.A.). R.N.V.R., 1939-45 (twice wounded, despatches four times, D.S.C. and Bar, D.S.O., O.B.E.); served in destroyers, Norway and Western Approaches; Sub-Lieutenant, 1940; in motor launches, Channel Convoys, 1941; and motor torpedo boats and motor gun boats, Mediterranean, Lieut., 1942, Lieut.-Comdr., 1944. Assistant Principal, H.M. Treasury, 1946; Principal, 1947; Secretary to Three Advisers, 1948; Private Secretary to Permanent Secretary to the Treasury and Official Head of H.M. Civil Service, 1949; Assistant Secretary, 1954; Under-Secretary, 1959; Principal Private Secretary to the Prime Minister, 1959-64; Dep. Under-Sec. of State (Air) during Aug. 1964. Alderman, G.L.C. 1967. *Recreations:* cricket, golf, music, amateur theatricals, doing-it-himself. *Address:* The Priory, Swanley Village, Kent. *T.:* Swanley 2187. *Clubs:* R.N.V.R., M.C.C. [*Died* 12 *March* 1969.

BLISS, Cuthbert Vivian, C.I.E. 1918; *b.* 1878; *s.* of Lewis Hill Bliss; *m.* 1906, Daisy Violet (decd.), *d.* of Charles Sheen; one *s.* Served European War, 1914-19, in Mesopotamia (despatches). Formerly Agent of Delhi Electric Supply and Traction Co. *Address:* 40 Stafford Court, Kensington, W.8. [*Died* 18 *Aug.* 1963.

BLISS, Brigadier Philip Wheeler, C.B.E. 1942; *b.* 27 Nov. 1887; *s.* of late Sir H. W. Bliss, K.C.I.E., I.C.S. (retd.); *m.* 1919, Monica Mary Hunt; one *s.* *Educ.:* Eton; R.M.A., Woolwich. Commissioned 1905 in R.E.; five years in India, five in France, and two months in Russia in European War, 1914-18; five years, Malta, 1923-1928; Iceland, 1940-42; retd. pay, 1943. *Address:* Fairlynch, Budleigh Salterton, Devon. *Club:* Army and Navy. [*Died* 18 *July* 1966.

BLOCH, Sir Maurice, Kt., *cr.* 1937. *Educ.:* Harris Academy, Dundee. J.P. for County of City of Glasgow, 1921-49; Hon. Pres. and Treasurer, Glasgow Jewish Board of Guardians; Convener, Consumptive Fund; Hon. President, Glasgow Jewish Institute; Pres. Maryhill Unionist Assoc.; Vice-Pres. Glasgow Unionist Assoc.; Member of Council, City of Glasgow Society of Social Service; Member of Committee, A.T.C.; Income Tax Commissioner for City of Glasgow; Chairman, Jewish War-Services Committee for Scotland. Contested (U.) Gorbals Division of Glasgow, 1929, 1931, and 1935. *Address:* 39 Newark Drive, Pollokshields, Glasgow. *T.:* Pollok 0648. [*Died* 19 *Feb.* 1964.

BLOCKEY, Air Vice-Marshal Paul Sandland, C.B. 1955; C.B.E. 1945; Senior Air Staff Officer, R.A.F. Technical Training Command, 1959-60, ret.; *b.* 23 Feb. 1905; *s.* of Albert and Mabel Blockey; *m.* 1926, Ella Temple; three *s.* (one *d.* decd.). *Educ.:* Dulwich Coll.; Trinity Hall, Cambridge (Mech. Sciences Tripos, 3rd class). Commissioned R.A.F., 1924; Officers' Engineering Course, 1929-31; R.A.F. Staff College, 1939. A.O.C., No. 230 Maintenance Group, 1943-45; Senior Technical Staff Officer, Transport Command, 1948-50; Dir. Aircraft Engineering, 1950-54; Senior Technical Staff Officer, M.E.A.F., 1954-56; Deputy Director-General of Aircraft Research and Development (R.A.F.), Ministry of Supply, 1956-59. *Recreations:* shooting, tennis. *Address:* Van Common, Fernhurst, Haslemere, Surrey. *T.:* Fernhurst 267. [*Died* 10 *Oct.* 1963.

BLOIS, Captain Sir Gervase (Ralph Edmund), 10th Bt., *cr.* 1686; M.C. 1944; with I.C.I. Ltd., 1929-39 and 1946-53; *b.* 6 June 1901; *s.* of Sir Ralph Barrett Macnaghten Blois, 9th Bt., and Freda (*d.* 1963), *y. d.* of late Col. E. Hegan Kennard; *S.* father 1950; *m.* 1st, 1938, Audrey Winifred Johnson (marr. diss.); two *s.* one *d.*; 2nd, 1948, Margaret Lucia, *o. c.* of late Maj. Hon. C. J. White. *Educ.:* Wellington; Sandhurst. Commissioned Scots Guards, 1921; served on Military Inter-Allied Commn. of Control, Berlin, 1924-25; A.D.C. to Governor of Bengal, 1925-28; R.A.R.O., 1929; re-employed, 1939-46; served in N. Africa, Italy, France and Germany; Personal Liaison Officer to C.-in-C. French Zone, Germany, 1945-46. Chevalier Légion d'Honneur, Croix de Guerre avec Palme (France), 1945. *Recreations:* shooting, bridge. *Heir:* *s.* Charles Nicholas Gervase Blois [*b.* 25 Dec. 1939; *m.* 1967, Celia Helen Mary, *o. d.* of C. G. F. Pritchett]. *Address:* Cockfield Hall, Yoxford, Suffolk. *T.:* Yoxford 354. *Clubs:* Guards, International Sportsmen's, M.C.C. [*Died* 22 *May* 1968.

BLOND, Neville, C.M.G. 1950; O.B.E. 1945; *b.* Hull, Yorks, 11 Feb. 1896; *s.* of Bernard and Rachel Blond; *m.* 1st, 1927, Eileen Reba, *d.* of V. di H. Nahum (Italy); two *s.*; 2nd, 1944, Elaine, *d.* of Michael Marks. *Educ.:* Manchester Grammar School; Switzerland. Served European War, 1914-18, with Royal Horse Guards, Major (despatches twice, Croix de Guerre avec Palme, Officier de la Légion d'Honneur). Liaison Officer Ministère de la Guerre, Paris, 1918-21; Family business of Blond Brothers, Textile Manufacturers, Manchester; travelled throughout Europe, America and Canada. Vice-Pres. N.W. Area, British Legion, 1933-1948. Served War of 1939-45, 1940-42 R.A.F. (Fighter Command), Wing Comdr. Ministry of Production, London, 1942-45; Board of Trade, 1945; lent to Central Economic Planning Staff, 1947; U.K. Trade Adviser in the U.S., 1948-49; late Hon. Trade Adviser to Board of Trade on North American Exports, resigned 1951; late Special Trade Adviser to the High Commissioner in Canada. Chairman of English Stage Co. Ltd. Freeman of City of London; Past Master, Worshipful Company of Pattenmakers. *Publication:* History of the Rubber Proofed Clothing Industry, 1928. *Recreations:* horseracing, golf and tennis. *Address:* Gotwick Manor, East Grinstead, Sussex. *T.:* East Grinstead 23408. *Clubs:* R.A.F., Naval and Military. [*Died* 4 *Aug.* 1970.

BLOOD, Sir Hilary Rudolph Robert, G.B.E., *cr.* 1953; K.C.M.G., *cr.* 1944 (C.M.G 1934); Hon. LL.D. Glasgow University, 1944; *b.* 1893; *e. s.* of late Canon A. F. Blood, Rector, Holy Trinity Church, Kilmarnock; *m.* 1919, Alison Farie, *y. d.* of late W. Boyd Anderson, Ayr; one *s.* two d, *Educ.:* Irvine Royal Academy; Glasgow University, M.A. Served European War, 1914-19, Capt. R. Scots Fusiliers; Ceylon Civil Service, 1920-30; Colonial Secretary, Grenada, 1930-34; Colonial Secretary, Sierra Leone, 1934-42; Governor and C.-in-C. in the Gambia, 1942-47; Barbados 1947-49; Mauritius, 1949-54. Constitutional Commissioner: British Honduras, 1959; Zanzibar, 1960; Chm. Constitutional Commn. on Malta, 1960: Chm. Royal Commonwealth Society for the Blind, 1962-65; Chm. Royal Soc. of Arts, 1963-65; Vice-Pres., Royal Commonwealth Society, 1963. K.St.J., 1946. *Recreations:* bridge, sailing. *Address:* Glovers, Kennington, Kent. *T.:* Kennington 289. *Clubs:* Athenæum, Pilgrims, Royal Commonwealth Society. [*Died* 20 *June* 1967.

BLOSSE, Sir Henry Lt., Bt.; *see* Lynch-Blosse.

BLOSSE, Sir Robert (Geoffrey) Lynch-, 14th Bt., *cr.* 1622; *b.* 1 April 1915; *s.* of Sir Robert Cyril Lynch-Blosse, 13th Bt., and Dorothy Mary (*d.* 1926), *d.* of late Edward Cunliffe-Owen, C.M.G.; *S.* father, 1951; unmarried. *Educ.:* St. Aubyn's, Rottingdean, Sussex; The Nautical College, Pangbourne, Berks. Anglo-Iranian Oil Co., 1932-35; Anglo-Saxon Petroleum Co., 1936-39. Royal Navy, 1939-51, demobilised with rank of Lieut.-Comdr., 1951. The British Motor Corporation (Australia and Oxford), 1953-59; Associated British Combustion Ltd., Portchester, Hants., 1960. *Heir: cousin* Henry Lynch-Blosse [*b.* 29 Oct. 1884; *m.* 1914, Cicely Edith Bircham; two *d.*]. *Address:* Brambles, Newlands Rd., New Milton, Hants. [*Died* 21 *April* 1963.

BLOUNT, Vice-Admiral George Ronald, D.S.O. 1917; R.N. retired; *b.* Belvedere, Kent, 8 Oct. 1877; *s.* of George Bouverie Blount and Annie C. Attenburrow; *m.* 1912, Cecilia Frances, *d.* of Frederick Hore, of Ewell Manor, West Farleigh, Kent; two *s.* one *d.* *Educ.:* Cordwalles, Maidenhead; H.M.S. Britannia. Commander 1912; Assistant to D.N.O., Admiralty, 1912-14; served in H.M.S. Revenge and on staff of Vice-Admiral, Dover, 1914-15; in command of H.M.S. Lord Clive and Marshal Soult, Belgian coast operations (Captain, 1917, D.S.O., French Croix de Guerre, Officier Belgian Order of Leopold, despatches twice); in command of H.M.S. Commonwealth, 1918-20; Devonport Gunnery School, 1920-23; Naval Ordnance Department, Admiralty, 1923-25; in command of H.M.S. Ramillies and Barham, 1926-28; A.D.C. to the King, 1928; promoted to Rear-Admiral and retired at own request, 1928; Vice-Admiral, retd., 1933; served at Ministry of Pensions (Officers' Friend Branch), 1939-45. *Address:* East Hill Lodge, Tenterden, Kent. *Club:* United Service. [*Died* 8 *Jan.* 1964.

BLOUNT, Lieut.-General Harold, D.S.O. 1917; late Royal Marines; *b.* 11 Oct. 1881; *y. s.* of George Bouverie and Annie Christina Blount. *Educ.:* Malvern College. 2nd Lieut. Royal Marine Artillery, 1898; Captain, 1909; Major, 1917; Lt.-Col. Royal Marines, 1928; Col., 1931; Brigadier, 1934; Maj.-Gen., 1937; Lt.-Gen., 1938; Mediterranean Station, 1901-3; Cape of Good Hope, 1904-7; Assistant to Professor of Fortification, R.N.C., Greenwich, 1907-9; Royal Naval College, Dartmouth, in charge of a term of cadets, 1909-11; round the world in H.M.S. New Zealand, 1913; served in her throughout the Great War, being present at Heligoland, Dogger Bank and Jutland (D.S.O., Russian Order of St. Stanislas); Instructor of Musketry, R.M.A., 1919-22; Fleet R.M. Officer, Mediterranean, 1922-24; Brigade Major, R.M., Plymouth, 1924-28; Fleet R.M. Officer, Mediterranean, 1928-30; Colonel 2nd Commandant, Chatham, 1931-34; Commandant Depot, Royal Marines, 1934-1937; A.D.C. to the King, 1935-37; retired, 1939; Hon. Secretary Whaddon Chase Hunt, 1940-46; Company Commander Home Guard, 1940-44. *Address:* Woughton House, Bletchley, Bucks. *Club:* United Service. [*Died* 13 *Aug.* 1967.

BLOW, Sydney; Author; *m.* Hilda Trevelyan (*d.* 1959). *Educ.:* Westminster. *Plays:* The Officers' Mess; Lord Richard in the Pantry; Oh, I say!; Little Miss Llewelyn; Live Wire; Kiki; Old Jig; (with Douglas Hoare) The Unseemly Adventure; All that Glitters; (with Edward Royce) Fritzi, 1935; (with Gordon Whitehead) As Husbands Go, 1938. *Publications:* The Ghost Walks on Fridays (autobiography), 1935; Through Stage Doors (autobiography), 1959. *Recreations:* fishing, gardening. *Address:* c/o National Provincial Bank, 24 Bedford Row, Bloomsbury, W.C.1. [*Died* 31 *May* 1961.

BLUNDELL, Rev. Canon E. K.; Canon of diocese of Johannesburg, 1949-58, retired; Rector of St. Peter's, Mossel Bay, 1953-58; *b.* England, 11 Nov. 1886; *m.* 1916; one *s.* three *d.* *Educ.:* King's College, Wimbledon; Selwyn College, Cambridge; Theological College, Wells, 1910-11; B.A. 1908; M.A. 1927. Curate St. James, Fulham, 1911-14; Sub-Warden at St. Paul's Theological College, Grahamstown, 1915-16; Curate at Cathedral, Grahamstown, 1916-17; Chaplain to Forces, 1917-18; Curate at St. Saviour's, Claremont, Cape, 1917-20; Rector of King Williamstown, S. Africa, 1920-28; Dean and Archdeacon of Grahamstown, 1928-33; Vicar of St. Paul's, Leicester, 1933-38; Rector of St. Aidan's, Yeoville, Johannesburg, 1938-44; of St. George's, Parktown, Johannesburg, 1945-52; of Van der Byl Park, Transvaal, 1952-53. *Recreation:* tennis, half blue (Cambridge), 1905-8. *Address:* 58 Darling Street, George, Cape Province, South Africa. [*Died* 5 *Dec.* 1961.

BLUNDELL, Col. Frederick Blundell Moss, C.M.G. 1918; D.S.O. 1917; M.A., LL.D.; solicitor; D.L. East Riding of Yorks; *b.* 21 September 1873; 2nd *s.* of John Seymour Moss Blundell of Hessle, J.P.; *m.* 1925, Mrs. Katharine Maude Prudence Jameson (*d.* 1939). *Educ.:* Rugby; Trinity College, Cambridge. Proceeded to France in command of 251st Brigade R.F.A., April 1915 (despatches five times, D.S.O., C.M.G.); Colonel (T.A.). 1918. *Address:* 157 Boothferry Road, Hull. Yorks. *T.:* Hull 51153. [*Died* 6 *Oct.* 1964.

BLUNDELL, Sir Robert (Henderson), Kt. 1961; Barrister-at-Law; Chief Metropolitan Stipendiary Magistrate since 1960 (a Metropolitan Stipendiary Magistrate, 1949-60); *b.* 19 Jan. 1901; *s.* of Robert Charles Blundell, Horley, Sy., and Catherine Davidson Henderson, Edinburgh. *Educ.:* Westminster Sch.; Trinity Coll., Camb. (M.A.). Called to Bar (Inner Temple), 1924; Central Criminal Court Bar Mess; South-eastern Circuit; Surrey quarter sessions: Recorder of Colchester, 1947-49. Member, Board of Governors, Nat. Hospitals for Nervous Diseases. *Recreation:* deipnosophism. *Clubs:* Brooks's, M.C.C., United University. [*Died* 19 *June* 1967.

BLUNT, Davenport Fabian Cartwright, C.B. 1947; *s.* of Henry Blunt; *m.* 1911, Edith Isobel, *d.* of Lawrence Harris; one *s.* five *d.* (and one *d.* decd.). *Educ.:* Bedford Modern School. Under-Secretary H.M. Treasury, 1946-48; retired, 1948. *Address:* 21 Bishopsthorne Rd., S.E.26. *T.:* Sydenham 7300. [*Died* 28 *Dec.* 1965.

BLUNT, Denzil Layton, C.M.G. 1945; Minister of Forest Development, Game and Fisheries, Kenya, 1955-60, retired; Nominated M.L.C., Kenya; *b.* 1 July 1891; *s.* of H. Layton Blunt, Orton Longueville, Hunts; *m.* 1917, Gwendolen Mary Edwards, Devoran, Cornwall; one *s.* two *d.* *Educ.:* Shrewsbury; King's Coll., Cambridge. Indian Education Dept., 1912-1914; European War, 1915-19, R.A.S.C.; farming in England, 1919-22; Agricultural Research, School of Agriculture, Cambridge, 1922-26; Senior Agricultural Officer, Kenya, 1926-33; Director of Agriculture, Cyprus, 1933-37; Nyasaland, 1937-39; Kenya, 1939-1949; retired, 1949. *Publications:* papers in Agricultural Journals. *Recreations:* rowing, golf. *Address:* Kiwanda, Limuru, Kenya. [*Died* 16 *June* 1968.

BLUNT, Brigadier Gerald Charles Gordon, D.S.O. 1916; O.B.E. 1919; A.M.I.Mech.E.; *b.* St. Andrews, 10 June 1883; *s.* of Gerald H. Blunt and Augusta Louisa, *d.* of late Sir Henry Gordon, K.C.B.; *m.* 1921, Kate Annie Wilson, *e. d.* of Major Charles James Fox; one *d.* *Educ.:* Sedbergh; Sandhurst. Entered A.S.C., 1902; served European War, France, 1914-20; Commanded 1st Indian Cavalry Supply Column, Oct. 1914-July 1916 (despatches twice, D.S.O.); commanded XI. Army Corps Ammunition Park Headquarters, Aug.-Sept. 1916; commanded Base M.T. Depot, Calais, 1916-20 (despatches twice, O.B.E.); D.A.D.T. War Office, 1922-26; A.A.G. and A.D.S. & T. War Office, 1932-36; Commandant, R.A.S.C. Training Centre, Aldershot, 1936-38; Assistant Director of Supplies and Transport, Aldershot Command, 1938-39; A.D.C. to H.M. the King, 1938-39; retired, Aug. 1939; Deputy Director of Supplies and Transport, Aldershot, Sept.-Nov. 1939; Director of Supplies, G.H.Q., B.E.F., France, Dec. 1939-May 1940 (despatches); Deputy Director of Supplies and Transport, Western Command, July 1940-43; G.S.O. 1 Civil Affairs, War Office, July 1943; Director of Supply, Civil Affairs, S.H.A.E.F., Nov. 1943-June 1944; reverted to retired pay, 1945; Head of Relief Supplies branch, Ministry of Supply, 1945-49. Médaille de Sauvetage, en vermeil, France; Commander of the Military Order of Avis, Portugal. *Address:* Overponds Cottage, Puttenham, Guildford, Surrey. *Club:* United Service. [*Died* 10 *June* 1967.

BLUNT, Sir John Lionel Reginald, 10th Bart., *cr.* 1720; *b.* 28 May 1908; *s.* of Sir John Blunt, 9th Bt. and Maud Julia (*d.* 1935), *e. d.* of late Sir David Lionel Goldsmid-Stern-Salomons, 2nd Bart., of Broomhill, Tunbridge Wells; *S.* father, 1938; *m.* 1932, Heather Alice, (from whom he obtained a divorce, 1941), *y. d.* of Capt. J. B. Harrison-Broadley; *m.* 1947, The Hon. Mrs. Esmond Harmsworth. *Heir:* *b.* Richard David Harvey Blunt [*b.* 22 Oct. 1912; *m.* 1st, 1936, Elisabeth Malvine Ernestine, *er. d.* of Com. F. M. Fransen Van de Putte, Royal Netherlands Navy (retired); one *s.*; 2nd, 1943, Margaret, *e. d.* of Jack Dean, Nutbeam, Cirencester; two *d.*]. *Address:* Cross Farm, Waldron, Nr. Heathfield, Sussex. [*Died* 29 *Sept.* 1969.

BLYTH, Robert Henderson, R.S.A. 1958 (A.R.S.A. 1949); R.S.W. 1950; Head of Drawing and Painting, Gray's School of Art, Aberdeen, since 1954; *b.* 21 May 1919; *s.* of William Blyth and Susan McGown; *m.* 1948, Isabel Mary Izatt; one *d.* *Educ.:* Glasgow Sch. of Art; Hospitalfield Art College. On staff of Edinburgh Coll. of Art, 1946-54. *Address:* 106 Desswood Place, Aberdeen AB2 4DQ. *T.:* 21735. *Clubs:* Royal Northern (Aberdeen); Scottish Arts (Edinburgh). [*Died* 18 *May* 1970.

BLYTON, Enid Mary; author and educationist; *d.* of Thomas Carey Blyton; *m.* 1924, Major Hugh Alexander Pollock; two *d.*; *m.* 1943, Kenneth F. Darrell Waters, F.R.C.S.E. (*d.* 1967). Entered journalism, specialising in educational and juvenile literature, and in natural history; writer of educational, nature and juvenile books and of stage plays. *Publications:* numerous books for children; edited Modern Teaching; associate editor of Pictorial Knowledge; editor and part author of Two Years in the Infant School; author of children's pantomime Noddy in Toyland, produced London and elsewhere at Christmas-time; also of Famous Five Adventure, play for older children, and of various films. *Recreations:* gardening, reading, bridge and golf. [*Died* 28 *Nov.* 1968.

BOAG, Sir George Townsend, K.C.I.E., *cr.* 1941 (C.I.E. 1928); C.S.I. 1936; *b.* 12 Nov. 1884; *e. s.* of late Rev. George Boag, Vicar of Winster, Westmorland, and late Frances Sophia, *d.* of John Townsend, Wimbledon; unmarried. *Educ.:* Westminster; Trinity College, Cambridge. 1st class, Div. II., in Classical Tripos Part I., 1906; passed into Indian Civil Service, 1907; arrived in Madras, 1908; Special Settlement Officer, 1912-18; served under Indian Munitions Board as Controller of Tanstuffs, 1918-1919; Provincial Superintendent of Census Operations, Madras, 1920-22; Commissioner of the Madras City Corporation, 1923-25; Secretary to the Madras Government, 1925-1928, 1930, 1933-34 and 1935-37; Collector and District Magistrate, Madras, 1929-30 and 1934; Member Indian Tariff Board, 1931-33; Member Board of Revenue, Madras, 1935; Secretary to the Governor of Madras, 1937-38; Chief Secretary to Govt. of Madras, 1936, 1938-39; Adviser to Governor of Madras, 1939-42; Dewan of Cochin State, 1943-47. *Address:* 30 St. James' Court, S.W.1. *Clubs:* East India and Sports; Madras (Madras); Ootacamund (Ootacamund). [*Died* 28 *April* 1969.

BOAS, Guy, M.A. (Oxon); F.R.S.L.; Headmaster of Sloane School, Chelsea, 1929-61 (produced there 15 of Shakespeare's plays); formerly Sen. English Master St. Paul's Sch., and Lectr. in English Literature to the Oxford Univ. Extension Delegacy; "G. B." of Punch; Vice-President, English Association; Originator and Associate Editor of English, 1936-65; *b.* 9 December 1896; *s.* of late Frederick S. Boas, O.B.E.; *m.* Cicely, *e. d.* of late Sir J. Beethom Whitehead, K.C.M.G.; one *s.* *Educ.:* Summer Fields; Radley College (Exhibitioner); Christ Church, Oxford (Scholar). Honours Final School of English; Lieutenant Oxfordshire Hussars, 1916-18; member of Oxford University Centaurs Football Club. *Publications:* The Garrick Club, 1831-1964, 1964; Selected Light Verse, 1964; A Teacher's Story, 1963; Shakespeare and the Young Actor, 1955; Lays of Learning, 1926; A Punch Anthology, 1932; An English Book of Light Verse, 1944. Article on Light Verse in Chambers's Encyclopædia; General Editor of The Scholar's Library. *Recreations:* music, philately. *Address:* 73 Murray Road, Wimbledon, S.W.19. *T.:* Wimbledon 1407. *Clubs:* Garrick, Oxford and Cambridge University, Royal Automobile. [*Died* 26 *March* 1966.

BOASE, Lieut.-Gen. Allan Joseph, C.B.E. 1942; p.s.c.; *b.* Gympie, Queensland, 19 Feb. 1894; *s.* of Charles Boase and Harriet J. Hughes; *m.* 1922, Ena, *d.* of H. D. Norman; one *s.* one *d.* *Educ.:* Brisbane Grammar School; Royal Military College, Duntroon. Commissioned in P.M.F. and posted to A.I.F. Aug. 1914; Active Service 1914-18 in Egypt, Gallipoli (wounded in landing at Anzac), Sinai, France and Flanders (Bt. Major); staff appts. in Australia, 1918-23; at Staff College, Camberley, 1924-25; staff appts. up to G.S.O. 1 in Australia, 1926-36; Exchange Officer in India, 1937-38; G.S.O. 1 4 Aust. Div., Feb.-Oct. 1939; Commandant, Com-

mand and Staff School, Aust., Nov. 1939-Mar. 1940. Seconded to 2nd A.I.F. as A.A. and Q.M.G., 7 Aust. Div. April 1940; Active Service in Palestine and Syria, 1940-42; commanded Australian Forces in Ceylon, Mar.-July 1942, and G.O.C. 6 Aust. Div. Aug. 1942 (C.B.E.); M.G.G.S. First Aust. Army, 1942-43; G.O.C. 11 Aust. Div., New Guinea, 1943-45; G.O.C. Western Comd.' Australia, 1945-46; Australian Army Rep' in U.K., 1946-48. Australian Defence Rep., London, 1948; G.O.C., Southern Command, Australia, 1949-50. *Recreation:* golf. *Address:* 26 Ardoch, 226 Dandenong Rd., Melbourne, S.16, Australia.
[*Died* 1 *Jan.* 1964.

BOASE, Colonel George Orlebar, C.B.E. 1919; late R.F.A.; *b.* 23 July 1881; *s.* of George William Boase, J.P., Dundee; *m.* Alice Eleanor Bernard, M.A., M.B.E. (*d.* 1963), *d.* of late Most Rev. and Rt. Hon. the Provost of Trinity Coll., Dublin; one *s.* (*er. s.* killed in action, Oct. 1944) one *d.* *Educ.:* Cargilfield and Fettes College, Edinburgh. Bt. Lt.-Col. 1918; Lt.-Col. 1928; Col. 1930; retired, 1938; Asst. Suptd. of Design, Woolwich, 1914-23 and 1925-28; C.R.A. Aden, 1929; Dep. Ch. Suptd. of Research Dept., 1930-33; Member of Ordnance Board, 1934-1943. *Address:* Curles, Barnhorn Road, Little Common, Bexhill.
[*Died* 4 *Nov.* 1966.

BOCQUET, Guy Sutton, C.I.E. 1918; V.D.; M.Inst.T.; F.R.S.A.; Traffic Manager, Eastern Bengal Railway (Government), Calcutta, 1925-36; *b.* 14 May 1882; 3rd *s.* of late William Bocquet, Liverpool and Baroness Van Zuylen van Neveldt de Gaesbeck, Brussels; *m.* Gwynneth Macredie; no *c.* *Educ.:* Bedford. Two years under training on the London-North Western Railway (England); subsequently as Officer of the Traffic Department, Indian State Railways; during the War, 1914-18, Temp. Lt.-Col. and Deputy Director Railways, Mesopotamia (despatches); Colonel comdg. E.B.R. Auxiliary Force, India, 1925-32; Hon. A.D.C. to the Viceroy of India, 1928-32; Silver Jubilee Medal, 1935. *Recreations:* golf, tennis, the fine arts. *Address:* Looking West House, Crowborough, Sussex. *T.:* Crowborough 553; c/o Lloyds Bank, 6 Pall Mall, S.W.1. *Club:* Bengal (Calcutta). [*Died* 18 *Jan.* 1961.

BODDIE, Rear-Adm. Ronald Charles, C.V.O. 1931; D.S.O. 1918; M.I.Mech.E.; R.N. Retd.; *b.* 1886; *e. s.* of C. L. Boddie, Coleraine; *m.* 1922, Jenny (*d.* 1964), *o. d.* of A. B. Gowan, Newcastle upon Tyne; one *s.* two *d.* Joined Royal Naval Engineering College, Keyham, 1902; served European War, 1914-18 in H.M.S. Hercules and H.M.S. Thetis; Naval Control Commission, Berlin, 1919-22; H.M. Yacht Victoria and Albert, 1923-32; A.D.C. to the King, 1936; commanding R.N. Engineering College, Keyham, 1933-36; retired from R.N., 1936. Superintending Engineer and Constructor of Shipping R.A.S.C., Fleet, 1936-51. *Address:* Watergall, Campbeltown, Argyll.
[*Died* 9 *May* 1967.

BODKIN, Thomas Patrick, K.S.G.; M.R.I.A.; D.Litt. (Honoris Causa) and LL.D. (Honoris Causa) the National University of Ireland; Litt. D. (Honoris Causa) the University of Dublin; Barrister-at-law, formerly Barber Professor of Fine Arts, Director of Barber Inst., and Public Orator Univ. of Birmingham; Emeritus Professor, 1953; Hon. Professor of History of Fine Arts, Trinity College, Dublin; Professor of the History of Art to the Royal Hibernian Academy (hon. R.H.A.); Hon. A.R.I.B.A.; Hon. M.R.I.A.I. Trustee of the National Library of Ireland; a Governor and Guardian of the National Gallery of Ireland; Life Governor of the University of Birmingham; Officier de la Légion d'Honneur; Membre du Comité des Musées Royaux de la Belgique; *b.* Dublin, 21 July 1887; *e. s.* of late Mathias Bodkin, County Court Judge of Clare, M.P. for North Roscommon, and the late Arabella (*née* Norman); *m.* 1917, Aileen, 3rd *d.* of Joseph Cox, M.P.; five *d.* *Educ.:* Belvedere College; Clongowes Wood College; Royal Univ., Ireland. Auditor, Literary and Historical Society, University College, Dublin, 1908; Gold medal for Oratory; Auditor Law, Students' Debating Society of Ireland, 1911, Gold medals for Oratory and Legal Debate; Prize medal for Legal Essay, Lord Chancellor's Prize; graduated R.U.I., 1908; called to Bar, King's Inns, 1911; practised for five years; Director of the National Gallery of Ireland, 1927-35; Secretary to the Commissioners of Charitable Donations and Bequests in Ireland, 1916-35; a member of the Commission since 1925; Member of Commission to advise the Minister of Finance on Coinage, 1926; Member of Committees to advise the Minister of Education on National Museum organisation, 1927; on Art Education, 1927; appointed by the Irish Govt. in 1949 to report on the various Institutes and activities concerned with the Arts in Ireland; Vice-President of Council of Friends of National Collections of Ireland; Chairman of Council of Birmingham Civic Society. Rowland Hughes Lecturer, Bangor, 1936; George Cadbury Memorial Lecturer, Selly Oak, 1937; Ferens Lecturer, Hull, 1946; Donnellan Lecturer, T.C.D., 1947; Hermione Lecturer, Dublin, 1918, 1928, 1938, and 1948; Sydney Jones Lecturer, Liverpool, 1948; Bertram Cox Memorial Lecturer, R.P.S., London, 1961. *Publications:* May it Please Your Lordships, a volume of reproductions of modern French poetry, 1917; Four Irish Landscape Painters, 1920; A Guide to Caper, 1924; The Approach to Painting, 1927, rewritten, 1945 and 1954; Hugh Lane and his Pictures, 1932, rewritten, 1934 and 1956; The Paintings of Jan Vermeer, 1940; My Uncle Frank, 1941; Dismembered Masterpieces, 1945; Virgin and Child, Flemish Painters, 1946; The Wilton Diptych, 1947; The Noble Science, 1948; Report on the Arts in Ireland, 1949. *Address:* 259 Hagley Road, Birmingham 16. *T.:* Edgbaston 0727. *Clubs:* Athenæum, Saintsbury; Union (Birmingham); United Arts, Stephen's Green (Dublin); Ulster Arts (Belfast).
[*Died* 24 *April* 1961.

BODKIN, Hon. Sir William (Alexander), K.C.V.O. 1954; New Zealand barrister and solicitor; Member of the National Party; *b.* 28 April 1883; *m.* 1920, Elizabeth L. McCorkindale; one *d.* *Educ.:* Wilson's College, Christchurch; Otago University (matriculated 1905). Admitted Barrister and Solicitor, 1909; purchased practice of J. R. Bartholomew S.M., 1910; contested Central Otago seat, 1914; M.P. Central Otago, 1928-54; Chairman of Cttees., 1929-1931; Member Empire Parliamentary Deleg., 1935; Minister of Civil Defence, War Cabinet; Minister of Internal Affairs, 1949; Minister of Social Security, 1950; Minister of Tourist and Health Resorts, 1951; retired. *Address:* Alexandra, Central Otago, N.Z.
[*Died* 15 *June* 1964.

BOEGNER, Marc, D.Theol.; Grand Officier, Legion of Honour; French ecclesiastic; *b.* Epinal, 21 February 1881; *m.* 1st, Jeanne Bargeton (*d.* 1933); three *s.* one *d.*; 2nd, Mary Thurneyssen (*d.* 1951). *Educ.:* Orléans; Paris. Ordained Pastor, Reformed Church of France, 1905; Pastor, Aouste, 1905-11; Prof. of Theology, Coll. of Soc. of Evangelical Missions, Paris, 1911-18; Pastor of Church of Passy, 1918-53. President: French Fedn. of Student Christian Assocs., 1922-39; Fedn. of French Protestant Churches, 1929-61; Nat. Coun. of Reformed Church of France, 1938-50; World Coun. of Churches, 1948-54. Mem. French Inst., 1946; Mem. French Acad., 1962. Hon.

D.D.: Edinburgh, Toronto, North Western, Aberdeen; Hon. D.Theol.: Prague. Bonn, Geneva. *Publications:* La Vie et la Pensée de T. Fallot, vol. 1, 1914, vol. 2, 1926; Dieu, l'éternel tourment des hommes, 1929; Jésus-Christ, 1930; Qu'est-ce que l'Église, 1931; L'Église et les questions du temps présent, 1932; La Vie chrétienne, 1933; Le Christ devant la souffrance et la joie, 1935; Le Problème de l'Unité chrétienne, 1947; La Prière de l'Église universelle, 1951; La Vie Triomphante, 1954; Le Chrétien et la Souffrance, 1955; Les Sept Paroles de la Croix, 1957; Notre Vocation à la Sainteté, 1958. *Recreation:* travelling. *Address:* 34 Avenue d'Eylau, Paris 16e, France. [*Died* 18 *Dec.* 1970.

BOEVEY, Sir Lance L. V. H.; *see* Crawley-Boevey.

BOFFA, Sir Paul, Kt. 1956; O.B.E. 1941; M.D. Roy. Univ. of Malta; *b.* 1890; *s.* of Carmel Boffa; *m.* 1921, Genevieve Cecy; two *s.* two *d.* Served European War (1914-18 Star, Victory Medal, War Medal). Leader of Labour Party, Malta, until 1950; M.P. (Lab.), 1921-35; during War of 1939-45: M.E.C.; regional protection officer, dockyard area (Defence Medal, O.B.E.). Prime Minister of Malta, 1947-50; Minister of Health, 1950-55; retired from politics, 1955. C.St.J. 1950; Coronation Medals, 1937, 1953. *Address:* 118 Tarxien Rd., Casal Paula, Malta. [*Died* 6 *July* 1962.

BOGGIS-ROLFE, Douglass Horace; Barrister-at-law; *b.* 1874; *y. s.* of late F. D. Boggis-Rolfe, of The Grange, Wormingford; *m.* 1909, Maria Maud, *o. d.* of late Capt. Christopher William Bailey, of Moorock, King's Co.; two *s.* one *d.* *Educ.:* Westminster. Called to Bar, Middle Temple, 1897; Assistant District Auditor, Local Government Board, 1903; District Auditor, 1904; Secretary National Insurance Audit Department, 1912; Acting Chief Auditor, 1915; Chief Auditor, 1918-26; Seconded to Reparation Commission (Maritime Service), 1920; Secretary-General Delegation of the Committee of Guarantees (Berlin), 1922-24; Manager, Export Credits Department (Department of Overseas Trade), 1924-26; Government representative Hire Claims Committee, 1917-25; Master Worshipful Company of Woolmen, 1925, expert adviser Company of Woolmen, 1925; Expert Adviser on Government Accounts to the Government of Antioquia, 1928; Alderman, L.C.C., 1928-34. *Publication:* Handbook to the Old Age Pensions Act. *Address:* The Grange, Wormingford, Colchester. *T.:* Bures 303. [*Died* 14 *June* 1966.

BOHR, Niels Henrik David; Professor in Theoretical Physics, University of Copenhagen, since 1916; Director of Institute for Theoretical Physics in Copenhagen since 1920; *b.* 7 Oct. 1885; *s.* of Professor Christian Bohr, Prof. in Physiology, Univ. of Copenhagen, and Ellen Adler; *m.* 1912, Margrethe, *d.* of A. Nørlund, Slagelse; four *s.* *Educ.:* Copenhagen. Dr. phil. Copenhagen, 1911; Lecturer in Copenhagen, 1913; Lecturer in Manchester, 1914-16; Nobel Prize in Physics, 1922; Atoms for peace Award, 1957. President of Royal Danish Academy of Science; Pres. Danish Cancer Cttee.; Chm. Danish Atomic Energy Commn. Foreign Member of Royal Society, Royal Institution and of Academies in Amsterdam, Berlin, Bologna, Boston, Edinburgh, Göttingen, Helsingfors, Budapest, München, Oslo, Paris, Rome, Stockholm, Upsala, Vienna, Washington, Harlem, Moscow, Trondhjem, Halle, Dublin, Liége, Cracow. Hon. Mem. many other societies. Dr. (*h.c.*), Technical Univ. of Denmark and Univs. of Cambridge, Oxford, Manchester, Liverpool, Edinburgh, Aberdeen, Oslo, Kiel, Berkeley, Birmingham, London, Paris, Providence, Princeton, Montreal, Glasgow, Athens, Lund, New York, Basel, Aarhus, Bombay, Calcutta. *Publications:* Theory of Spectra and Atomic Constitution, 1922; Atomic Theory and Description of Nature, 1935; Atomic Physics and Human Knowledge, 1958; scientific papers on atomic theory. *Address:* Copenhagen, Gl. Carlsberg, Denmark. *Club:* Athenæum. [*Died* 18 *Nov.* 1962.

BOILEAU, Brigadier-General Guy Hamilton, C.B. 1919; C.M.G. 1918; D.S.O. 1915; late R.E.; *b.* 27 Sept. 1870; *s.* of late Major C. H. Boileau, 61st Regiment; *m.* 1909, Violet Mary Irene, *d.* of Col. W. J. Smyth Fergusson, late King's Dragoon Guards. Entered army, 1890; Captain, 1901; Major, 1910; Col. 1920; served West Africa, 1892 (despatches); Gambia, 1892 (despatches); Chitral, 1895; China, 1900 (despatches, medal with clasp); European War, 1914-18, Afghan War, 1919 (D.S.O., Bt. Lt.-Col., C.M.G., C.B.); retd., 1927; holds Order of Danilo, 3rd class. *Address:* Rosehill House, Par, Cornwall. *Club:* Naval and Military. [*Died* 5 *Dec.* 1962.

BOILLOT, Félix, (Félix de Grand' Combe), M.C.; L.-ès-L., M.A., Officier de la Légion d'Honneur, Croix de Guerre with two bars; Polish Cross for Valour; Médaille d'or de l'Académie Française; Inspecteur Général honoraire de l'enseignement, United Nations; Emeritus Prof. of French Language and Literature, late Director Sch. and Higher S.C. Exams., The Univ., Bristol; *b.* 1880; *m.*; one *s.* two *d.* (and two *s.* decd.). Past Examiner to the Universities of Sheffield, Wales, Ireland, etc.; Liaison Officer to B.E.F. Western Front; late Assistant to the French Military Attaché, French Embassy, London; Deputy Assistant Quarter Master General, Polish Army; Major on Staff of Allied Military Committee, 1939-40; Major F.F.F., 1941-46; membre de l'Assemblée Consultative; Vice-Président du Groupe Interparlementaire franco-britannique; membre de la Société des gens de lettres: délégué de la Société des orateurs et conférenciers; ex-Vice-Pres. British Legion, Gloucestershire. Membre du Conseil Supérieur des Français de l'Etranger. *Publications:* Le Patois de la Grand' Combe, Doubs (couronné par l'Institut de France); Quelques heures de français dans une université anglaise; The Methodical Study of Literature; Les Impressions sensorielles chez La Fontaine; Un Officier d'infanterie à la guerre; Les Métaphores topographiques; Le Français régional de la Grand' Combe; Le Vrai Ami du traducteur; Psychologie de la construction; Le Second Vrai Ami du traducteur. Under the pen-name of Félix de Grand' Combe: Tu viens en Angleterre; En croyant aux roses; Modestes Conseils à un conférencier; Tu viens en France (Recomp. par l'Ac. des Sc. Mor. et Pol.); J'ai souvenance, vols. I and II; Bir Hakeim; The Three Years of Fighting France; Tu viens en Amérique; Tu viens en Espagne; Superstition. *Address:* 6 Place Sully, Maisons-Laffitte, S.-et-O., France; Grand' Combe-Châteleu (Doubs). [*Died* 17 *Aug.* 1961.

BOISSIER, Léopold; President of the International Committee of the Red Cross, 1955-64; *b.* 16 July 1893; *m.* 1924, Renée E. Grand d'Hauteville; one *s.* one *d.* *Educ.:* Universities of Geneva and Zürich. Diplomatic career with Federal Political Dept. (Foreign Affairs), 1918-; Secretary of Gustave Ador, Federal Councillor at Peace-Conference, 1919; Attaché, Swiss Legation, London; 1933-53: Secretary-General of Inter-Parly. Union; former Pres. and Vice-Pres. International Red Cross; Lectr., later Prof., Univ. Geneva. Corresp. Mem. Institut de France; Mem. Inst. international de droit public, etc. Holds many foreign distinctions. *Publications:* L'Avènement de la démocratie en Suisse, 1918; Le Contrôle de la politique étrangère, 1924; La Situation

politique du monde (annually since 1933); Regards vers la paix, 1943; Nouveaux Regards vers la paix, 1944, etc. *Recreation:* riding. *Address:* 6 rue des Granges, Geneva. *T.:* 25.63.14. *Club:* Terrasse (Geneva).
[*Died* 22 *Oct.* 1968.

BOLDERO, Sir Harold (Esmond Arnison), Kt., *cr.* 1950; M.A. (Oxon); D.M., B.Ch.; F.R.C.P. (London); Hon. Consultant Physician to Middlesex Hospital, and formerly Dean of the Middlesex Hospital Medical School; Consulting Physician to Evelina Hospital for Children and to St. Saviour's Hospital; Registrar, Royal College of Physicians; Member: North West Metropolitan Regional Hospital Board; General Medical Council; *b.* Aug. 1889; *er. s.* of late John Boldero, J.P., Frankham, Mark Cross; *m.* 1917, Margery (*d.* 1950), *er. d.* of late Arthur T. B. Dunn, Ludgrove, and Helen Malcolmson; one *surv. s.* *Educ.:* Sandroyd; Charterhouse; Trinity College, Oxford; Middlesex Hospital. Represented Oxford University, Athletics. 1911 and Hockey, 1912; served European War, B.E.F., 1915-19; Units and Field Ambulance, later Deputy Assistant Director of Medical Services, Major R.A.M.C. (despatches twice); House Physician, Clinical Assistant and Medical Registrar, Middlesex Hospital; Member of Association of Physicians of Great Britain and Ireland; F.R.S.M. late Treasurer, Royal College of Physicians; Fellow (late Hon. Sec.) Medical Society of London; Physician to St. Saviour's Hospital, 1921-34; Physician to Evelina Hospital for Children, 1921-34; Clinical Assistant, Hospital for Sick Children, 1921; formerly Examiner in Medicine, Universities of Oxford, Cambridge and Birmingham; Member of Senate of Univ. of London. *Publications:* Infective Endocarditis in Congenital Heart Disease (jointly) Lancet, 1924; Treatment of Chorea, ibid.; Associated Organisms causing Empyema (jointly) ibid. 1926. *Recreation:* fly fishing. *Address:* 39 Hill Street, Berkeley Square, W.1. *Clubs:* Athenæum; Vincent's (Oxford).
[*Died* 30 *Nov.* 1960.

BOLITHO, Lt.-Col. Sir Edward Hoblyn Warren, K.B.E., *cr.* 1953; C.B. 1943; D.S.O. 1919; late R.A.; J.P.; *e. s.* of Captain E. A. Bolitho, Royal Navy, 2nd *s.* of T. S. Bolitho of Trengwainton; *m.* 1914, Agnes Hamilton (*d.* 1950), *d.* of G. Randall Johnson; one *s.* one *d.*; *m.* 1950, Sheila Désirée, *d.* of late Capt. Rt. Hon. R. C. Bourne and of Lady Hester Bourne, Old Mill House, Bradford Abbas, Sherborne; one *s.* three *d.* *Educ.:* Harrow; R.M.A., Woolwich. Entered R.A., 1900; retd. 1919; served European War (despatches thrice, twice wounded, D.S.O.); High Sheriff of Cornwall, 1931; Chairman, Cornwall County Council, 1941-52; Chm. China Clay Council, 1951-63. Lord Lieutenant of Cornwall, 1936-62. K.St.J., 1952. *Recreations:* fishing, shooting. *Address:* Trengwainton, Penzance, Cornwall. *T.:* 3106. *Clubs:* Army and Navy, United Service. [*Died* 18 *Dec.* 1969.

BOLITHO, Captain Richard John Bruce (formerly J. B. Bolitho); Reserve of Officers, Royal Corps of Signals; *b.* 28 Nov. 1889; *s.* of Capt. E. A. Bolitho, R.N., of Rockbeare House, nr. Exeter; *m.* Roselle, *d.* of R. R. Lempriere of Rozel Manor, Jersey; one *s.* one *d.* (*er. s.* killed in action, 1942). *Educ.:* Wellington College. Studied Engineering; 2nd Lieut. Devon Regt., 1912; Served European War, 1914-18, in Infantry, Flying Corps and Signals (wireless); served war of 1939-45, lent to Royal Navy, 1942-46. *Recreation:* yachting. *Address:* Rosel Manor, Jersey, C.I. *T.:* Jersey, Five Oaks 992. *Clubs:* United Service; Royal Yacht Squadron (Cowes). [*Died* 7 *Sept.* 1965.

BOLTON, 6th Baron (*cr.* 1797), **Nigel Amyas Orde-Powlett;** *b.* 1900; *o. surv. s.* of 5th Baron and Hon. Elizabeth Mary Gibson (*d.* 1943), *d.* of 1st Baron Ashbourne; *S.* father 1944; *m.* 1928, Victoria Mary (*d.* 1933), *d.* of Henry Montagu Villiers, M.V.O.; two *s.* *Educ.:* Eton; Cambridge. *Heir:* *s.* Hon. Richard William Algar Orde-Powlett [*b.* 11 July 1929; *m.* 1951, Hon. Christine Weld-Forester, *e. d.* of Baron Forester; two *s.* one *d.*]. *Address:* Bolton Hall, Leyburn, Yorks. [*Died* 15 *June* 1963.

BOLTON, Brigadier Charles Arthur, C.B.E. 1920; *b.* 3 Jan. 1882; *s.* of late Charles Walter Bolton, C.S.I., Indian Civil Service, and late Alice Emma Wilford Brett; *m.* 1st, 1912, Ada Violet Emily (*d.* 1946), *d.* of late Sir Henry Jourdain, K.C.M.G.; one *d.* (and one *s.* one *d.* decd.) 2nd, 1961, Mrs. Jay Campbell, (widow). *Educ.:* Marlborough; New College, Oxford; Commissioned Manchester Regiment, 1902; transferred R. Tank Corps, 1923; Lieut.-Col. 1927; Col. 1931; passed Staff College, 1913-14; served on Staff in European War, 1914-18; France, 1914; Gallipoli, France, 1916; Macedonia, Palestine (despatches 4 times; Bt. Lt.-Col.; C.B.E.; Commandeur de l'Ordre de Saint Sauveur, Greece; 3rd Class Order of the Nile, Egypt); O.C. 5th Bn. Royal Tank Corps, 1927-1931; Commandant Royal Tank Corps Centre, 1931-35; retired pay, 1935; recalled 1940-41. D.P.L. G.H.Q. Middle East (despatches twice). *Recreations:* Rugby football, England International, 1908-9. *Address:* c/o Lloyds Bank. Ltd., Cox's and King's Branch, 6 Pall Mall, S.W.1; 16 St. Brelades, Trinity Place, Eastbourne, Sussex. *Clubs:* United Service, M.C.C., Free Foresters, Barbarians.
[*Died* 23 *Nov.* 1964.

BOLTON, Elizabeth, C.B.E. 1935; M.D., B.S.; Consulting Surgeon, Elizabeth Garrett Anderson Hospital; *b.* Leeds, 1878; *d.* of William Bolton, M.A., Congregational Minister, and Ellen Warrick. *Educ.:* Stoneygate College, Leicester; Bedford College for Women; London (Royal Free Hospital) School of Medicine for Women. Dean of the London (Royal Free Hospital) School of Medicine for Women until Oct. 1945, President until 1957. *Address:* c/o National Provincial Bank Ltd., Eastbourne, Sussex. [*Died* 25 *May* 1961.

BOLTON, Sir (Horatio) Norman, K.C.I.E., *cr.* 1926 (C.I.E. 1916); C.S.I. 1918; *b.* 1 Feb. 1875; *s.* of late Preb. C. N. Bolton; *m.* 1911, Ethel Frances, *d.* of late Captain J. C. H. Mansfield, Castle Wray, Co. Donegal; one *d.* *Educ.:* Rossall; Corpus Christi College, Oxford (B.A.). Entered I.C.S. 1897; Deputy Commissioner Dera Ismail Khan, 1904; Kohat, 1909; Sessions Judge, Peshawar, 1910-11; Political Agent Dir, Swat, and Chitral, 1911-12; Deputy Commissioner, Peshawar, 1912-19; Revenue Commissioner N.W. Frontier Province, 1920-23; Chief Commissioner N.W.F.P., 1923-30; retired 1931. *Recreations:* fishing, yachting. *Address:* Kyson Point, Woodbridge, Suffolk. *T.:* Woodbridge 328. [*Died* 24 *May* 1965.

BOND, Lieutenant-General Sir Lionel Vivian, K.B.E., *cr.* 1942; C.B. 1938; p.s.c.; *b.* 1884; *s.* of Maj.-General Sir Francis Geo. Bond, K.B.E., C.B., C.M.G., late R.E.; *m.* 1925, Dorothy Isabel May (*d.* 1953). *d.* of Maj. James Townshend Reilly, O.B.E., D.L., J.P.; no c. *Educ.:* Cheltenham College; R.M.A. Woolwich. Joined R.E., 1903; operations in Zakka Khel and Mohmand Areas. 1908 (despatches); served European War, Mesopotamia (despatches, brevet of Major and Lt., Colonel); General Officer Commanding Chatham Area, Comdt. School of Military Engineering and Inspector of the Royal Engineers, 1935-39; G.O.C. Malaya, 1939-41; retired, 1941, Colonel Commandant, Royal Engineers, 1940-1950. *Club:* United Service.
[*Died* 4 *Oct.* 1961.

BOND, Sir Ralph Stuart, Kt., *cr.* 1946; C.B.E. 1932; retired solicitor; *b.* 2 July 1871; 4th *s.* of Erasmus Bond, Architect, London; *m.* 1st, 1900 (silver wedding, 1925), Maud (*d.* 1926), *yr. d.* of George Denbigh Hicks, M.R.C.S.; 2nd, 1928 (silver wedding, 1953), Rose Elizabeth, *yr. d.* of Samuel Hill; two *d. Educ.:* Charterhouse. Admitted solicitor, 1894 (honours), retired 1953. Staff Captain in Remount Department, War Office, 1917-19; Member of Council of Royal Commonwealth Soc. since 1910; Hon. Treasurer, 1927-38; a Vice-Pres. since 1938; Deputy Chairman of Council, 1938-43, Acting Chairman, 1942; Chairman of Finance Committee, Empire Societies War Hospitality Committee, 1940-46; Hon. Mem. and Mem. Advisory Council of English-Speaking Union. Hon. Mem. Royal Over-Seas League. *Address:* Cranley Mansion, 160 Gloucester Rd., S.W.7. *T.:* Fremantle 2767. [*Died* 1 *April* 1968.

BONE, Lady; Gertrude Helena; *b.* Holyhead; *d.* of Rev. Benjamin Dodd; *m.* 1903, Sir Muirhead Bone (*d.* 1953); one *s.* decd. *Educ.:* Trinity Hall, Southport. *Publications:* Provincial Tales; Children's Children; Women of the Country; The Furrowed Earth (poems); Mr. Paul; Oasis; This Old Man; Of the Western Isles; The Hidden Orchis; The Cope; Old Spain; Days in Old Spain; Came to Oxford. *Recreation:* reading. *Address:* 140 Haverstock Hill, N.W.3. [*Died* 25 *Feb.* 1962.

BONE, James, C.H. 1947; London Editor of the Manchester Guardian, 1912-45; Hon. A.R.I.B.A.; *b.* Glasgow, 1872; *s.* of David Drummond Bone, journalist, Glasgow; *m.* 1903, Annie M. (*d.* 1950), *d.* of John McGavigan, Lenzie. *Educ.:* Glasgow. *Publications:* (part author) Glasgow in 1901; author, Edinburgh Revisited (afterwards revised and republished as The Perambulator in Edinburgh); The London Perambulator; London Echoing. *Address:* Abbot's Holt, Tilford, Surrey. *T.:* Frensham 412. *Club:* Press. [*Died* 23 *Nov.* 1962.

BONIWELL, Martin Charles, C.B.E. 1936; *b.* Surbiton, England, 1883; *s.* of late C. E. Boniwell, Hobart, Tasmania; *m.* 1912, Ruby Mary, *y. d.* of late Joseph Okines, Hobart; four *d. Educ.:* Hutchins Grammar School (Church of England); University of Tasmania. LL.B., 1911; Barrister and Solicitor, Australia, 1924; entered Public Service of Tasmania, 1899; Attorney-General's Department, Commonwealth Public Service, 1912; Assistant Secretary, and Assistant Parliamentary Draftsman, Commonwealth of Australia, 1932-38; acted as Solicitor-General of Commonwealth for six months, 1937; Legal Adviser to Australian Delegation to Seventh Assembly of League of Nations, 1926; Public Service Arbitrator, 1939-45; Parliamentary Draftsman, Commonwealth of Australia, 1946-48. *Recreations:* golf, gardening. *Address:* 9 Seacombe Grove, Brighton, Victoria, Australia. [*Died* 6 *Jan.* 1967.

BONNETARD, Sir (Nicolas Patrick) France, Kt. 1964; **Hon. Mr. Justice Bonnetard;** Chief Justice, Seychelles, 1958-66; *b.* Seychelles, 20 Feb. 1907; *s.* of late Gustave Bonnetard and Amelie Moulinié; *m.* 1949, Madeleine Mauvis. *Educ.:* Saint Louis College, Seychelles; privately in England. Called to Bar, Gray's Inn, 1928; entered private practice at the Bar, Seychelles, 1929; various magisterial appointments until 1945; subsequently Crown Prosecutor for short period; Q.C. 1954; Acting Chief Justice, 1954. Formerly nominated unofficial member of Legislative Council and Executive Council. *Address:* c/o Supreme Court, Seychelles. [*Died* 9 *Oct.* 1969.

BONSER, Rev. Henry; Minister of Findon Valley Free Church, Worthing, 1949-60, retd.; *b.* 26 May 1884; *s.* of Henry Bonser, Derby; *m.* 1st, 1916, Constance Ellen Millar; two *s.*; 2nd, 1932, Elizabeth Annie Bertha Borley. *Educ.:* Rawdon College. Minister, Stepney Baptist Church, King's Lynn, 1910-14; Minister, New North Road Baptist Church, Huddersfield, 1915-23; Gen. Supt., N.E. Area, 1923-49; Secretary, Rawdon College, 1919-23; Pres., Yorkshire Assoc. of Baptist Churches, 1922-23; Moderator, Northern Baptist Assoc., 1947-48; Pres., Baptist Union of Great Britain and Ireland, 1953-54. *Publications:* various addresses and sermons. *Recreations:* tennis and golf. *Address:* 1 Loompits Way, Saffron Walden, Essex. *T.:* Saffron Walden 2362. [*Died* 16 *Feb.* 1966.

BOON, Sir Geoffrey Pearl, Kt. 1966; C.B.E. 1959; Q.C. (W.I.) 1965; *b.* 19 July 1888; 2nd *s.* of Walter Rodwell Boon and Alicia Margaret (*née* Roger); *m.* 1919, Marie Ismée Thurston; one *s.* two *d. Educ.:* St. Christopher Gram. Sch.; St. Albans, Toronto, Canada. Colonial Civil Service, Leeward Is. Colony, B.W.I., 1907-15. Called to the Bar, Middle Temple, 1920. Attorney-General, Leeward Is., 1929-30; Mem. Federal Legislative and Exec. Councils of Leeward Is., and of Legislative and Exec. Councils of the Presidencies, 1929-30; Mem. Federal Legislative and Exec. Councils and of Legislative and Exec. Councils of Presidency of St. Christopher Nevis Anguilla, 1930-1947, 1956-66. Chm. St. Christopher Forestry Bd. and St. Christopher Sugar Industry Rehabilitation Cttee. Served European War, 1914-18 as Lt. R.F.A. (wounded, invalided). *Address:* Romneys, St. Christopher, W.I. *Clubs:* Naval and Military; New (Antigua); St. Kitts. [*Died* 26 *April* 1970.

BOOTH, Alderman Alfred, J.P.; Congregational Lay Preacher; *b.* 24 Feb. 1893; *m.* 1927, Anne Webster; one *d. Educ.:* St. James, Bolton. Elected Bolton Town Council, 1933; J.P. 1940; Mayor of Bolton, 1941-42, Alderman, 1945. Pres. Bolton Council of Christian Congregations, 1942; Chm. Bolton National Savings Constituency, 1943-; Chm. Bolton Y.M.C.A. Executive, 1949; Pres. Bolton Labour Party, 1935; M.P. (Lab.) Bolton East, 1950-51. Vice-Pres., The Cremation Society. Served European War of 1914-18, Lancashire Fusiliers (wounded, prisoner). *Recreations:* soccer, cricket. *Address:* 29 Halliwell Road, Bolton, Lancs. *T.:* Bolton 26822. *Club:* Y.M.C.A. (Bolton). [*Died* 19 *Dec.* 1965.

BOOTH, Sir Charles (Sylvester), Kt. 1969; C.B.E. 1964; Director, Australian Paper Manufacturers Ltd., since 1944; *b.* 23 Feb. 1897; *s.* of John T. Booth, Halifax and Birmingham, England, and Ada, *d.* of Charles Wilson; *m.* 1939, (Ellen) Myra Grant; no *c. Educ.:* King Edward's Sch., Birmingham. Served War of 1914-18 (despatches); Royal Engineers, France (Major, Staff Officer, R.E.). Trained as Mechanical Engineer with Armstrong Whitworth (England); Armstrong Whitworth Contracting Co. (Australia), 1923-28; Australian Rep. of Walmsleys (Bury) Ltd. (Papermaking Machinery), 1923-46; Dir., Australian Paper Manufacturers Ltd., 1944- (Asst. Man. Dir., 1946; Man. Dir., 1948-58; Chm., 1959-66). Dir., Melbourne Bd., Bankers & Traders' Insurance Co. Ltd., 1949- (Chm. Melbourne Bd., 1962-). Mem. Council, Australian Administrative Staff College, 1958- (Chm., 1959-69). Knight, Order of White Rose of Finland, 1960. *Recreations:* gardening, motoring, collection of oils and water colours. *Address:* 12 Huntingfield Road, Toorak, Victoria 3142, Australia. *T.:* 20 6114. *Clubs:* Melbourne, Australian (Melbourne); Union, Australian (Sydney); Commonwealth (Canberra). [*Died* 27 *June* 1970.

BOOTH, Dr. Edgar Harold, M.C. 1917; D.Sc. (Syd.); F.Inst.P.; International Counsellor; *b.* 12 Feb. 1893; *s.* of John and Maud T. Booth, Montrose, Scotland; *m.* 1924, Jessie Annie Wilcox; one *s.* one *d.* *Educ.:* Old Fort Street School and Sydney University, Sydney, N.S.W. Served European War, 1915-19, A.I.F. France and Belgium, Artillery; Staff Captain 5th Australian Division Artillery, 1918 (despatches). Senior Lecturer in Physics, University of Sydney, 1919-37; Pres. Sydney Univ. Union, 1922-1925; member Sydney Univ. Eclipse Expedition to Goondiwindi, 1923; President Science Teachers' Association of N.S.W. 1928-32, Life Vice-President, 1933-; Consultant Seismic section, Imperial Geophysical Experimental Survey, 1929-31; Consulting Physicist to N.S.W. Government, 1930-; President Royal Soc. of N.S.W., 1936-1937, Hon. Life Member, 1955-; Chairman of Committees, Standards Association of Australia, 1919- and Member of Council, 1957-; President Northern N.S.W. Cttee. of Services Education Advisory Council 1940-45; Warden and Pres. New England Univ. Coll., Armidale (Univ. of Sydney, N.S.W.), 1937-45; Chairman, International Wool Secretariat, and Overseas Representative Australian Wool Board, 1945-48 Fellow A.N.Z.A.A.S. and Member of Council; Vice-Pres. Inc. Society London Fashion Designers, 1946-49; Foundation Vice-Pres. Clothing Institute, U.K., 1948-, and Chm. Provisional Council, 1947-48. D.Sc. (*h.c.*) Univ. of New England, 1955. *Publications:* Physics—Fundamental Laws and Principles, 1931 (16th Edn. 1962); Elementary Physics, 1932 (5th Edn. 1950); Elementary Science—Physics, 1935; Geophysical Prospecting Seismic Methods, 1931 (Camb. Univ. Press). Founder, editor and contributor, Environment, Journal of Science, 1933-38; contributor to scientific, technical and educational journals and learned societies and general Press, as well as many minor technical and popular smaller publications on scientific and educational subjects. *Recreations:* golf, gardening, children. *Address:* Hills and Dales, Mittagong, New South Wales; 59 Hopetoun Avenue, Vaucluse, N.S.W. *T.:* 37-1341. *T.A.:* Intercouns Sydney (Australia). *Clubs:* Junior Carlton, Royal Automobile; Australian (Sydney).
[*Died* 18 *Dec.* 1963.

BOOTH, John Bennion, LL.B.; author and journalist; *b.* 24 Feb. 1880; *e. s.* of late John Bennion Booth, M.D. M R.C.S. L.R.C.P. L.M., and Esther, *d* of Henry Deacon of Appleton House, Widnes; unmarried. *Educ.:* Liverpool College; Liverpool University. Solicitor; joined editorial staff of Sporting Times, 1905, assistant editor and dramatic critic; with late Colonel Newnham-Davis, late Arthur Binstead, and late Horace Lennard, founded Town Topics, 1912. *Publications:* Old Pink 'Un Days; Master and Men; Tramps of a Scamp (with Edward Michael); The Show Shop; Myself and Others (with Jessie Millward); The Gentle, Cultured German; Miss Billie Tuchaud, Her Letters; London Town, 1929; Through the Box Office Window (with W. H Leverton); Arms and the Woman (with E. V H. S. Culling); Pink Parade, 1933; Bits of Character, 1936; A Pink 'Un Remembers, 1937, Sporting Times, 1938; Life, Laughter, and Brass Hats, 1939; The Days We Knew, 1943; Editor of Seventy Years of Song, 1943; Palmy Days, 1957; short stories and articles. *Recreations:* theatre, sailing. *Address:* 5 Morley Road, Hesketh Park, Southport. *Club:* Royal Temple Yacht (Ramsgate). [*Died* 24 *July* 1961.

BOOTH, John Reginald Trevor, C.I.E. 1934; *b.* 14 Aug. 1883. *Educ.:* Bromsgrove School; Worcester College, Oxford. Entered I.C.S. 1906; Postmaster-General, Bengal and Assam, 1919; Punjab, 1925: Senior Deputy Director-General, Posts and Telegraphs, India, 1931-36; Postmaster-General Bombay Circle from 1936. [*Died* 8 *Feb.* 1963.

BOOTH, Most Rev. Joseph John, C.M.G. 1954; *b.* 1886; *s.* of Joseph and Mary Booth; *m.* 1919, Beryl Gertrude Bradshaw; three *d.* *Educ.:* Hugh Bell School, Middlesbro; Melbourne University, B.A. Fellow, Aust. College of Theology, 1935; D.D. (Lambeth), 1944. Business and industry until 1912; ordained, 1914; Chaplain to the Forces, 1916-19 (M.C.); Vicar of Fairfield, Victoria, 1919; Geelong, 1923; Archdeacon of Dandenong, 1932; Bishop of Geelong, 1934-42; Archdeacon of Melbourne, 1936-42; Deputy Asst. Chaplain-General with A.I.F. in Middle East, 1941-42; Archbishop of Melbourne, 1942-56; acted as Administrator, Melbourne, during 1957. *Address:* 2 Manning Road, East Malvern, S.E.5, Victoria, Australia.
[*Died* 30 *Oct.* 1965.

BOOTH, Mary Booth, C.B.E. 1919; has had charge of the Salvation Army Work, Germany, West Indies, and Denmark; 2nd *d.* of General and Mrs. Bramwell Booth; *b.* Hadley Wood, Barnet, 22 April 1885. *Educ.:* privately. After course in International Training College, became an Officer of The Salvation Army and commanded several Corps in the United Kingdom, attaining rank of Colonel. Was the first woman to address prisoners at Parkhurst Gaol; jointly responsible for Army's work amongst troops in France (C.B.E.); has addressed large gatherings in Europe and on the American Continents; was in charge Salvation Army work in Belgium at outbreak of war; taken prisoner by the Germans in June 1940; reached England, April 1943. *Publications:* With the B.E.F. in France; My Bible in a German Prison. *Recreations:* music and modelling. *Address:* North Court, Finchampstead, Berks. [*Died* 31 *Aug.* 1969.

BOOTH, Major Sir Paul, Kt., *cr.* 1937; M.I.Mech.E.; M.I.B.F.; D.L. Essex; Vice-Pres. National Liberal Club; Trustee Gladstone Library; Governor: Northern Polytechnic; National Coll. of Rubber Technology; Alderman Essex County Council; Guild of Freemen; *b.* 28 July 1884; 2nd *s.* of James Wilson Booth, Cork; *m.* 1917, Agnes Ellen, *d.* of George Affleck Gray, York; two *d.* *Educ.:* Oakfield. Engineer and Ironfounder; Managing Director Booth-Brookes Ltd., Mildmay Iron Works, Burnham-on-Crouch, Essex, etc.; Past Pres. Federation British Music Industries; War Service R.N.R. 1914. Civil Defence, Westminster, 1938-42; Army Welfare Officer, 1943-48. Member Worshipful Company of Founders. Council City Livery Club. Chairman Council St. John, Essex; K.St.J. *Recreations:* yachting, travel. *Address:* The Limes, Burnham-on-Crouch, Essex. *T.:* Burnham-on-Crouch 2197. *Clubs:* United Wards, National Liberal, Royal Commonwealth Society, English-Speaking Union, City Livery; Royal Naval Yacht; Royal Naval Sailing Assn.; Royal Burnham Yacht, Royal Corinthian Yacht (Burnham-on-Crouch); City Livery Yacht (Founder Cdre.).
[*Died* 2 *July* 1963.

BOOTH, Walter Reynolds, M.A.; *b.* 14 Sept. 1891, *e. s.* of James Booth, of Thornton, Bradford; *m.* 1934, Aline Margaret, *d.* of H. W. Morley, Bradford; two *s.* two *d.* *Educ.:* Bradford Grammar School; Corpus Christi College, Cambridge (Scholar), 1910; Natural Science Tripos, 1st class in Part I., 1912, and Historical Tripos, 2nd class (Div. I.), Part II., 1913; Tutor and Assistant Master, Wellington College, Berks, 1914-23; Headmaster of Wolverhampton Grammar School, 1923-28; Master of Dulwich College, 1928-41; Headmaster of Cockermouth Grammar School, 1943-

1956; War Service, 1914-18, B.E.F., R.F.A. (T.F.). *Address:* Fern Bank, Cockermouth. [*Died* 13 *June* 1963.

BORASTON, Lieut.-Colonel John Herbert, C.B. 1919; O.B.E. 1918; Barrister-at-law; *b.* Liskeard, Cornwall, 1885; *o. s.* of late Sir John Boraston, of Ringwood, Beckenham, Kent; *m.* 1916, Honor Emily Muriel, *d.* of late Charles FitzRoy Doll, J.P., of Hadham Towers, Much Hadham, Herts; two *s.* (one *d.* decd.). *Educ.:* Malvern; Merton College, Oxford (History Postmaster), M.A., B.C.L. Called to Bar, Inner Temple, 1909; served European War, 1914-19; Foreign Service, France, 1916-19 (despatches four times); attached for special duties G.H.Q., France, Sept. 1916; G.S.O. 2, G.H.Q., France, Oct. 1918; Private Secretary to F.M., C. in C., France, Feb. 1919; to F.M., C. in C. Forces in Great Britain, May 1919-Feb. 1920; served War of 1939-45, England, France and Germany (despatches); Chevalier Légion d'Honneur, 1920; Croix de Guerre, 1945. Hon. Freeman of Borough of Holborn, 1957. *Publications:* (with G. A. B. Dewar) Sir Douglas Haig's Command, 1915-18, 1922; (with C. E. O. Bax) The Eighth Division in War, 1914-1918, 1927; editor of Haig's Despatches; Hood and Challis's Property Acts, 8th Edition, 1938. *Address:* Marrick, Church Road, Tiptree, Essex. *T.:* Tiptree 578; 15 Old Square, Lincoln's Inn, W.C.2. *T.:* Holborn 4814. *Club:* Oxford and Cambridge. [*Died* 18 *March* 1969.

BORDEAUX, Henry; Commander of the Legion of Honour; novelist; member of the French Academy since 1919; *b.* Thonon (Haute-Savoie) 25 Jan. 1870; *m.* 1901; three *d.* *Educ.:* Thonon College; Sorbonne and Paris Law Faculty. Lawyer, 1890-1900; then writer; during War of 1914-18, Commandant, then Staff Major, twice mentioned in despatches; Grand Officer and Commander of many foreign orders; hon. Dr. of University of Montreal, etc. *Publications:* Le Pays natal; La Voie sans retour; La Peur de vivre; L'Amour en fuite; Le Lac noir; La Petite Mademoiselle; Les Roquevillard; L'Écran brisé; Les Yeux qui s'ouvrent; La Croisée des chemins; Le Carnet d'un stagiaire; La Robe de laine; La Neige sur les pas; La Maison; La Nouvelle Croisade des enfants; Ménages d'après-guerre; La Résurrection de la chair; La Chair et l'esprit; Les Derniers Jours du fort de Vaux; La Bataille devant Souville; Les Captifs délivrés; Vie de Guynemer; Sur le Rhin; La Maison morte; Le Fantôme de la rue Michel-Ange; Yamile sous les cèdres; La Vie est un sport; La Chartreuse du reposoir; Le Cœur et le sang; L'Amour et le bonheur; Les Jeux dangereux; le Barrage; Rap et Vaga; le Calvaire de Cimiez; Andromède et le monstre; Châteaux en Suède; Sous les pins aroles; La Claire Italie; Valombré; L'Abbé Fouque; Visages français; Tuilette; Murder-Party (celle qui n'était pas invitée); La Revenante; La Goutte d'eau; Les Ondes amoureuses, Les Déclassés, Le Chêne et les roseaux, Le Miracle du Maroc; Le Pays sans ombre; Les Trois Confesseurs; L'Intruse; Henry de Bournazel; Au pays des Élisabeth; Le Parrain; Le Maître de l'amour; L'Affaire de la rue Lepic; L'Air de Rome et de la mer; Le Gouffre; La Cendre chaude; Crimes involontaires; La Sonate au clair de lune; Mariage de guerre; L'Ombre sur la maison; Les Yeux voilés; Vie et mort de Bayart; Notre Dame de la vie; Le Remorqueur; Un Crime sous la Directoire; Le Visage du Maroc; Reines et femmes; Marie Mancini; Cas de conscience; Le Jeu de massacre; Profits de héros; Le Double Aveu; La Lumière au bout du chemin; Vie de saint Louis roi de France; Images romaines; Paris aller et retour (mémoires); Les Trois Sœurs des îles; Le Fil de la Vierge (trans.: A Pathway to Heaven); La Marche à l'abime; La Brebis égarée; La Fille du prisonnier; Cette voix du cœur; Reconstructeurs et mainteneurs; Le Mystère de St. Louis, drame; Proverbes et scènes d'amour; Mémoires, Vols. II et III, Le Garde de la maison et la douceur de vivre menacée (1896-1914); Vol. IV, La Guerre incertaine (1914-1916); Vol. V, Verdun; Vol. VI, L'année ténébreuse; Vol. VII, La Victoire et le Traité de Versailles; Vol. VIII, L'enchantement de la Victoire. *Recreations:* Alpinism; automobile. *Address:* 8 Chaussée de la Muette, Paris; Chalet du Maupas à Cognin (Savoie). [*Died* 29 *March* 1963.

BORDEN, Mary, (Lady Spears); *d.* of William Borden, Chicago; *m.* George Douglas Turner; three *d.*; *m.* 1918, Maj.-Gen. Sir Edward Spears, 1st Bt., K.B.E., C.B., M.C.; one *s.* (decd.). *Publications:* Jane—Our Stranger; Three Pilgrims and a Tinker, 1924; Jericho Sands, 1925; Four o'Clock, 1926; Flamingo, 1927; Jehovah's Day, 1928; The Forbidden Zone, 1929; A Woman with White Eyes, 1930; Sarah Gay, 1931; Mary of Nazareth, 1933; The King of the Jews, 1935; Action for Slander, 1936; The Black Virgin, 1937; Passport for a Girl, 1939; Journey Down a Blind Alley, 1946; No. 2, Shovel Street, 1949; For the Record, 1950; Martin Merriedew, 1952; Margin of Error, 1954; The Hungry Leopard. 1956. *Address:* St. Michael's Grange, Warfield, Berks.; 12 Strathearn Place, W.2. [*Died* 2 *Dec.* 1968.

BORDET, Jules; Director of the Pasteur Institute, Brussels, since 1901, honorary since 1940; Professor of Bacteriology at the University of Brussels, honorary since 1935; *b.* Soignies, Belgium, 13 June 1870; *m.* 1899; one *s.* two *d.* *Educ.:* Brussels. Doctor of Medicine, 1892; member of the Pasteur Institute of Paris, 1894-1901; foreign Fellow Royal Society; foreign member Institut de France; member of several foreign Academies and scientific societies; Nobel Prize, Medicine, 1919. *Publications:* Traité de l'Immunité dans les maladies infectieuses, 2nd ed. 1939; a great number of medical (especially bacteriological) publications. *Address:* Avenue de l'Université 57, Bruxelles, Belgium. [*Died* 6 *April* 1961.

BOREEL, Sir Alfred, 12th Bt., *cr.* 1645; *b.* 22 July 1883; *s.* of late Robert Eugene Boreel; *S.* brother 1941; *m.* 1st, 1911, Countess Aletta Cornelia Anna (*d.* 1913), *d.* of Count Francis David Schimmelpenninck; 2nd, 1919, Countess Reiniera Adriana (*d.* 1957), *d.* of Count Francis David Schimmelpenninck; one *s.* one *d.* *Heir:* *s.* Francis David, *b.* 14 June 1926. *Address:* L. Couperusplein 36, The Hague, Holland. [*Died* 20 *Aug.* 1964.

BOREHAM, Ven. Frederick; Emeritus Archdeacon of Cornwall; Emeritus Canon Missioner of Truro; Hon. Chaplain to the Queen since 1952 (to King George VI, 1941-52); *b.* 7 June 1888; *s.* of Francis and Fanny Boreham; *m.* 1918, Caroline Mildred-Slater (*d.* 1943); two *s.* one *d.* *Educ.:* King Charles School, Tunbridge Wells; Durham University, St. John's College. Curate Holy Trinity Church, Hull, 1913; C.M.S. Missionary in Szechuan, China, 1917; Archdeacon of West Szechuan, 1930; Principal of C.M.S. College, West China Union University, Chengtu, 1932; Home Superintendent British and Foreign Bible Society, 1935-37; Vicar of Holy Trinity, Hull, 1937-1947; Rural Dean of Kingston-upon-Hull, 1939-47; Canon of York, 1941-47; Canon of Truro, 1947-65; Archdeacon of Cornwall, 1949-65. *Recreations:* walking, gardening. *Address:* 11 Marlborough Crescent, Falmouth. *T.:* 849. [*Died* 1 *Feb.* 1966.

BORING, Edwin G(arrigues), M.E., Ph.D., Sc.D.; Edgar Pierce Professor of Psychology Emeritus, Harvard University, since 1957; *b.* Philadelphia, 23 Oct. 1886; *s.* of Edwin M. Boring and Elizabeth G. Truman; *m.* 1914, Lucy M. Day, West Newton, Mass.; two *s.* one *d.* (and one *d.* decd.). *Educ.:* Cornell Univ. (M.E. 1908; Ph.D. 1914). Instructor in Psychology, Cornell University, 1912-18; Captain, psychological service, U.S. Army, 1918-19; Professor of Experimental Psychology, Clark University, 1919-22; Associate Prof. of Psychology, 1922-28; Director of the Harvard Psychological Laboratory, 1924-49, Professor of Psychology, 1928-56, Edgar Pierce Professor of Psychology and Lowell Television Lectr., 1956-57, Harvard University; Phi Beta Kappa Visiting Scholar, 1958-59. Hon. Pres. XVII International Congress of Psychology, 1963. Member: National Academy of Sciences, Amer. Philosophical Society, Amer. Academy of Arts and Sciences, etc. American Psychological Foundation Gold Medal, 1959. *Publications:* A History of Experimental Psychology, 1929 (2nd ed., 1950); The Physical Dimensions of Consciousness, 1933, 1963; Sensation and Perception in the History of Experimental Psychology, 1942; Psychologist at Large, 1961; History, Psychology and Science, 1963; (with R. J. Herrnstein) Source Book in the History of Psychology, 1965; Editor of Boring, Langfield and Weld, Foundations of Psychology; Psychology for the Fighting Man; Editor, Contemporary Psychology, 1956-61; Consulting Editor, Basic Books, 1961-; articles in psychological jls. *Address:* William James Hall, Harvard Univ., Cambridge, Massachusetts 02138, U.S.A. *T.A.:* Harvard, Cambridge, U.S.A. *T.:* Cambridge, Mass. University 868-7600. *Clubs:* Harvard (New York); Harvard (Boston). [*Died* 1 *July* 1968.

BORN, Max, F.R.S. 1939; F.R.S.E.; M.A. (Cantab.); Dr.phil. (Göttingen); Hon. Sc.D (Bristol); Hon. Dr. ès sc. (Bordeaux); Hon D.Sc. (Oxford); Hon. LL.D. (Edinburgh); Hon. Dr. rer. nat. (Freiburg i.B.); Hon. Dr.ing. (Stuttgart); Hon. D Sc. (Oslo); Hon. D.Sc. (Bruxelles); Hon. Dr. rer. nat. (Humboldt Univ., Berlin); Tait professor of natural philosophy University of Edinburgh, 1936-53; Professor Emeritus, 1953; Nobel Prize for Physics (jointly), 1954; *b.* 11 Dec. 1882; *s.* of Gustav Born, Dr. med., Prof. at the Univ. of Breslau, Germany, and Margarethe Kauffmann; *m* 1913 Hedwig Ehrenberg; one *s.* two *d.* *Educ.:* Gymnasium, Breslau; Univs. of Breslau, Heidelberg, Zürich, Göttingen, Cambridge. Privat-Dozent Göttingen, 1909; Professor Extraord. Berlin, 1915; Professor Ord. Frankfurt a.M. 1919; Göttingen, 1921; Stokes Lecturer of Applied Mathematics, Cambridge, 1933; Fellow: Gesellschaft der Wissenschaften, Göttingen since 1920; Russian Academy of Sciences since 1925; German Academy of Sciences, Berlin, since 1929; Roy. Swedish Acad. since 1953; Honorary Fellow of Indian Academy of Sciences since 1937; Rumanian Acad. of Sciences since 1937; Acad. de Ciencias Lima, Peru, since 1939; Royal Irish Academy since 1941; Royal Danish Academy of Science since 1947; Associate of National Academy of Science, Washington, since 1955; Amer. Acad. of Science and Art, since 1959. *Publications:* 20 books, some in German, many translated in different languages; English: Einstein's Theory of Relativity, 1924; Problems of Atomic Dynamics, 1926; Mechanics of the Atom, 1927; Atomic Physics, 1935; The Restless Universe, 1936; Natural Philosophy of Cause and Chance, 1949; A General Kinetic Theory of Liquids (with H. S. Green), 1949; Theory of Crystal Lattices (with Kun Huang), 1954; Physics in my Generation, 1956; Principles of Optics (with E. Wolf), 1959; Physics and Politics, 1962; Ausgewählte Abhandlungen (Selected Papers), 1963; My Life and my Views, 1968; about 300 papers in various periodicals. *Recreation:* music. *Address:* Marcard Str. 4, Bad Pyrmont, Germany. [*Died* 5 *Jan.* 1970.

BORTON, Air Vice-Marshal Amyas Eden, C.B. 1922; C.M.G. 1919; D.S.O. 1915; A.F.C. 1918; Royal Air Force (retired); late Black Watch (Royal Highlanders); *b.* 20 Sept. 1886; *yr. s.* of late Lt.-Col. A. C. Borton, J.P., of Cheveney; *m.* 1923, Muriel Agnes, *d.* of late Canon H. B. Streatfeild. *Educ.:* Eton. Served European War, 1914-18 (despatches, severely wounded, D.S.O.; Bt. Lt.-Col.; 3rd Class Order St. Stanislas (with Swords); 3rd Class Order of Nile; C.M.G.; 3rd class Order of El Nahda); D.L. Kent; Chairman Kent Ter. and A.F. Assoc., 1938-49. *Address:* Salters Cross, Yalding, Kent. *T.:* Hunton 368. *Club:* United Service. [*Died* 15 *Aug.* 1969.

BORWICK, 3rd Baron, *cr.* 1922; **(Robert) Geoffrey Borwick;** Bt., *cr.* 1916; *b.* 1 July 1886; *y. s.* of 1st Baron Borwick of Hawkshead; *S.* brother 1941; *m.* 1st, 1913, Irene Phyllis (from whom he obtained a divorce), *d.* of late T. M. Patterson; one *s.* two *d.*; 2nd, Margaret Elizabeth, *d.* of late G. R. Sandbach, Liverpool; two *s.* *Educ.:* Eton; R.M.C., Sandhurst. Lieut. 20th Hussars, retired; served in 1st Hertfordshire Regt. in European War, 1914-16; and then in R.F.A. up to Armistice. *Recreation:* gardening. *Heir:* *s.* Major Hon. James Hugh Myles Borwick, M.C. [*b.* 12 Dec. 1917; *m.* 1954, Hyllarie Adàlia Mary, *yr. d.* of late Lieut.-Col. W. H. H. Johnston. *Educ.:* Eton; R.M.C. Sandhurst. M.C. 1945; Highland L.I., retd. 1947]. *Address:* Sawyers Wood, Pangbourne, nr. Reading. *T.:* Pangbourne 233. [*Died* 30 *Jan.* 1961.

BORWICK, Lt.-Col. George Oldroyd, D.S.O. 1917; *b.* 7 Mar. 1879; *e. s.* of J. C. Borwick; *m.* 1915, Hon. Mary Cavendish, *e. d.* of 4th Baron Waterpark. *Educ.:* Harrow; Trinity College, Oxford. Contested Poplar, 1906; Limehouse, Jan. 1910; Surrey Yeomanry, 1901-24; served with them in France, Jan.-Nov. 1915, and in Salonica till armistice (D.S.O., Legion of Honour, despatches thrice); M.P. (C.U.) North Croydon, Dec. 1918-22. *Address:* Dudley Hotel, Hove. *Club:* Bath. [*Died* 27 *June* 1964.

BOSANQUET, Theodora, M.B.E. 1919; B.Sc. (Lond.); *b.* 3 Oct. 1880; *d.* of late Frederick C. T. Bosanquet and Gertrude Mary, *d.* of William Darwin Fox. *Educ.:* Ladies' College, Cheltenham; University College, University of London. Secretary to late Henry James, O.M., 1907-16; Assistant, "Who's Who" Section, War Trade Intelligence Depart., 1917-18; Assistant to Secretary, Ministry of Food, 1918-20; Executive Secretary International Federation of University Women, 1920-35; Literary Editor, Time and Tide, 1935-1943; a Director, Time and Tide, 1943-58. *Publications:* Spectators (with Clara Smith), 1916; Henry James at Work, 1924; Harriet Martineau, 1927; Paul Valéry, 1933. *Address:* c/o Lloyds Bank Ltd., 164 King's Rd., S.W.3. *Clubs:* Arts Theatre, P.E.N., English-Speaking Union. [*Died* 1 *June* 1961.

BOSSOM, Baron *cr.* 1960 (Life Peer); 1st Bt. 1953; **Alfred Charles Bossom;** F.R.I.B.A.; J.P.; Hon. LL.D. (Pittsburgh, U.S.A.), 1952; Hon. Fellow, University College, London, 1953; *b.* London, 16 Oct. 1881; *s.* of Alfred Henry Bossom and Amelia Jane Hammond; *m.* 1910, Emily (*d.* 1932), *d.* of Samuel G. Bayne, Pres. Seaboard National Bank, New York; one *s.* (and two *s.* decd.). *Educ.:* St. Thomas Sch., Charterhouse, E.C.1; Roy. Acad. of Arts. Formerly an architect with internat. practice. Went to U.S. 1903; architect: of rehousing of workers of U.S. Steel Co., Pittsburgh, 1904; for several of early skyscrapers;

undertook restoration of Ft. Ticonderoga, 1908; supervising architect U.S. Shipping Bd. 1917-18; architect Magnolia Petroleum Co. Building (Dallas, Tex.), Seaboard National Bank (New York); Treas. Architectural League, New York, 1923-26; Founder of Co-operation in Govt. Movement in U.S.; Chm. Exec. Cttee., Amer. Mid-European Assoc.; Hon. Sec. Amer. Baltic League, 1920-23; Pres. and Founder Anglo-Baltic Soc., 1933; Alderman L.C.C., 1930-34; Chm. Slum Clearance Sub-Cttee., L.C.C., 1930-34; Vice-Chm. L.C.C. Improvement Sub-Cttee., and of Housing Cttee. M.P. (C.) Maidstone Div. of Kent, 1931-Sept. 1959. Mem. Brit. Building Mission to U.S.A., 1943; Chm.: S.E. Provincial Area Conservative and Unionist Assocs., 1949-52; Kent Cons. and Unionist Assocs., 1947-49; Pres. Rochester and Chatham Cons. Association, 1959-60; Pres. Assoc. of Men of Kent and Kentish Men; Founded Alfred C. Bossom Travelling Scholarship awarded annually by R.I.B.A.; Trustee of Antarctic Film Trust; Pres. of the R.D.I., 1958-59; Chm. Roy. Soc. of Arts. 1957-59; Pres. Anglo-Turkish Soc.; Pres, Anglo-Texan Soc.; Life Vice-Pres. Anglo-Brazilian Soc.; Pres. Iran Soc.; Chm. Anglo-Luxembourg Group, Inter-Parl. Union 1953-1959; Council, Luxembourg Soc.; Chm. Anglo-Belgian Section, Inter-Parl. Union, 1951-59; Chm. Anglo-Belgian Union, 1956-1960; Chm. European-Atlantic Group, Chm., 1959-61 (now a Vice-Chm.); Sec. H.G. Parl. Cttee. Lords and Commons, 1942-44; Mem. of Parl. Select Cttee. on Nat. Expenditure, 1939. 1945; Mem. Paviors' and Armourers' and Brasiers' London City Companies; Life Mem-Court of Guild of Freemen of City of London; Master, Needlemakers' Co., 1959-60; Underwriter at Lloyd's; Grand Prior of The Primrose League; Pres. Assoc. of Public Health Inspectors, 1957-60; Life Mem., Roy. Soc. of Health; Hon. Fellow: Inst. of Quantity Surveyors; Faculty of Building; Pres. Modular Soc.; Life Governor, Imperial Cancer Research Fund; Governor, Queen Elizabeth's Training College for the Disabled; President of various Rifle Leagues and Assocs.; Vice-Chm., Nat. Small-Bore Rifle Assoc.; Council Mem., Nat Rifle Assoc.; President Pitman Fellowship, 1959; Hon. Freeman. Borough of Maidstone; Hon. Vice-Pres. Kent Br. First or Grenadier Guards Comrades Association; Major Kent Home Guard and Liaison Officer for County of Kent Home Guard; Vice-Pres. Maidstone Rural Dist. Coun.; Mem. Exec. Cttee. Kent War Org., B.R.C.S. and Order St. John; Mem. Chapter General and Bailiff Grand Cross of Order of St. John; Grand Bailiff of England, Order of St. Lazarus of Jerusalem. Real Academia de Nobles Artes de San Fernando, Spain; Officier Légion d'Honneur; Comdr' Order of Crown (Belgium); Order of Merit (Chile); Cavalier of Crown (Italy); Cavalier Order of White Lion (Czecho-Slovakia); Order of Eagle Cross (Estonia), 2nd class; Order of Lithuanian Grand Duke Gediminas, 2nd class; Comdr. of Order of Grand Cross of the Three Stars (Latvia); Order of Merit (Latvia); Commander Order of White Rose (Finland); Diploma and Gold Medal of Les Invalides Prévoyantes (Belgium); Firdausi Medal, Persia; Order of Taj (2nd Grade) Iran; Order of Christ (Portugal); Defence Medal; Bronze medal of Union Départementale des Sapeurs-Pompiers du Pas-de-Calais; Hon. Citizen of Texas, U.S.A., etc. *Publications:* An Architectural Pilgrimage in Old Mexico, 1923; Building to the Skies; A Bird's Eye View of Europe; Our House, an introduction to Parliamentary Procedure, 1948; Some Reminiscences; articles on architectural and political subjects. *Recreations:* travel and investigation of educational and economic subjects. *Heir* (to Baronetcy only): *s.* Major Hon. Clive Bossom, M.P. *Address:* 1 St. John's House, Smith Square, S.W.1. *T.:* Whitehall 9364; Stoneacre, Otham, nr. Maidstone, Kent. *T.:* Otham 256. *Clubs:* Carlton, Garrick; Kent County (Maidstone); Pilgrims, British Schools and Universities (New York).

[*Died* 4 *Sept.* 1965.

BOSTOCK, Geoffrey, F.C.A.; Senior Partner, Annan, Dexter & Co. since 1934; *b.* 6 Aug. 1880; *s.* of Henry Bostock and Alice Susannah Marson; *m.* 1907, Vera Lough, *d.* of late William Ingram James, Stafford; four *s.* two *d.* *Educ.:* Solihull School. Joined Annan, Dexter & Co. as a partner, 1904; also, in 1904, admitted partner of Deloitte, Plender, Griffiths, Annan & Co. (S. Africa). Chairman: Burberrys Ltd., 1937-54; Mirror Laundries, 1942-53; Power Plant Co. Ltd., 1950-; Royal Free Hospital, 1950-56 (Vice-Chm. 1948). Hon. Treas. Melanesian Mission, 1939-; Past Grand Treas., Grand Lodge of England (1941); Member Bd. of Management Royal Masonic Instn. for Boys. 1942-; Member General Counc of King Edward's Hospital Fund for London, 1953-57. *Recreations:* photography and gardening. *Address:* 3 Rosslyn Hill, Hampstead, N.W.3. *T.:* Hampstead 1820. *Club:* Gresham.

[*Died* 24 *May* 1961.

BOSTOCK, Air Vice-Marshal William Dowling, C.B. 1942; D.S.O. 1948; O.B.E. 1935; R.A.A.F. (retd.); Member Federal Parliament (Canberra) for electorate of Indi (Victoria), 1949-58; Grazier; *b.* Sydney, 5 Feb. 1892; *m.* 1919, Gwendolen, *d.* of F. H. Meade-Norton; two *d.*; *m.* 1951, Nanette Mary, *d.* of Edward O'Keefe; three *s.* Served European War, A.I.F., 1914-15, R.F.C. and R.A.F., 1916-19 (Belgian Croix de Guerre); Deputy Chief of Air Staff R.A.A.F., 1939-42; Chief of Staff Allied Air Forces, S.W.P.A., 1942; Air Officer commanding R.A.A.F. Command, Allied Air Forces, S.W.P.A., 1943. American Medal of Freedom (Silver Palm). *Address:* Gwill, Molyullah, Victoria, Australia. *Club:* Naval and Military (Melbourne). [*Died* 28 *April* 1968.

BOSTON, Sir Henry (Josiah) Lightfoot, G.C.M.G. 1962 (C.M.G. 1959); Governor-General of Sierra Leone, 1962-67; *b.* 19 August 1898; *yr. s.* of late Reverend N. H. Boston, M.A., L.Th., and Mrs. Lauretta Boston; *m.* 1946, Christiana Muriel Songo Davies, M.B.E. (*d.* 1965). *Educ.:* C.M.S. Gram. Sch., and Fourah Bay Coll., Freetown, Sierra Leone. Called to the Bar, Lincoln's Inn, London, 1926. M.A., B.C.L., Dunelm; LL.B. 1st class hons. London; Barstow. Scholar, Council of Legal Education, 1926. In private practice as Barrister and Solicitor, Sierra Leone, 1926-46; J.P 1936; Police Magistrate, Sierra Leone, 1946-57; Puisne Judge of Supreme Court, Sierra Leone, 1957; retired. Speaker, House of Representatives, Sierra Leone, 1957-62. K.St.J. 1965. *Recreation:* walking. *Clubs:* Royal Commonwealth Society; Reform (Freetown).

[*Died* 11 *Jan.* 1969.

BOSWALL, Major Sir Gordon H.; *see* Houstoun-Boswall.

BOSWELL, Alexander Bruce, M.A.; Professor Emeritus in the University of Liverpool; *b.* Ashbourne, Derbyshire, 1884; *s.* of Dr. Alexander Boswell; *m.* 1919, Clarice May Page; two *d.* *Educ.:* Rossall School; Lincoln College, Oxford. Assistant Librarian in the Zamoyski Library, Warsaw, 1908-13; Research Fellow in Polish, University of Liverpool, 1913-19; Assistant Editor, The Russian Review, 1913-14; Lecturer in Russian, University of Leeds, 1917-19; Professor of Russian in the University of Liverpool, 1919-49; Dean of the Faculty of Arts, 1921-24 and 1928-34; Member of Council, Liverpool University, 1926-28;

Chairman, Men's Hostel Committee, 1924-29; Examiner for Joint Matriculation Board, 1920-51; Sometime Examiner for the Civil Service and for Universities of Cambridge, Glasgow, London, Manchester and Sheffield; Chairman, Merseyside Anglo-Polish Society, 1941-55. *Publications:* The Poles, History of Nations, 1915; Poland and the Poles, 1919; Poland, 1050-1303, The Teutonic Order, and Poland, 1303-1500, in the Camb. Medieval History, Vols. VI, VII and VIII; Camb. History of Poland, Vol. I, Chaps. III, IV, VIII and XII; Articles on Poland in Encyc. Brit. (14th Edition, and in Chambers's Encyclopædia (new edn.); numerous articles and reviews in learned journals. *Recreations:* walking and lawn tennis. *Address:* Westlands, Sandybrook Road, Ashbourne, Derbyshire. *T.:* Ashbourne 634. *Club:* University (Liverpool). [*Died* 9 *Jan.* 1962.

BOSWORTH-SMITH, Nevil Digby, C.B. 1946; *b.* 17 Feb. 1886; *s.* of late R. Bosworth Smith (Author, Biographer), Bingham's Melcombe, Dorchester, Dorset; *m.* 1913, Gladys, *d.* of J. Francis Wood, Uffculme, Devon; one *s.* one *d.* (and *s. s.* decd.; 2nd *s.* killed in action, 1945). *Educ.:* Harrow School; Pembroke College, Cambridge. B.A. (First Class in Classical Tripos) 1907; Master at Gresham's School, Holt, 1908-9; entered Board of Education as Junior Inspector, 1911; Junior Examiner, 1912; Principal, 1919; Assistant Secretary, 1930; Principal Assistant Secretary, 1940. Under-Secretary, Ministry of Education, 1946-47; retired 1947. Was Private Secretary to late Marquess of Crewe (Secretary of State for India and Lord President of the Council), to Rt. Hon. H. A. L. Fisher (President of Board of Education) and Marquess Curzon of Kedleston (Lord President). *Recreations:* shooting, travel. *Address:* 18 Rochester Terrace, N.W.1. *T.:* Gulliver 1635. [*Died* 17 *June* 1964.

BOTHAM, Arthur William, C.S.I. 1926; C.I.E. 1918; J.P.; *b.* 10 Dec. 1874; *s.* of Rev. George William Botham; *m.* 1903, Mary Florence Hamilton (*d.* 1934). *Educ.:* Newcastle-under-Lyme; Magdalene College, Cambridge. Entered Indian Civil Service, 1898; Chief Secretary to the Government of Assam, 1919-25; Member of Executive Council of Assam, 1925-30. *Address:* Manor House, Alford, Lincs. *Club:* East India and Sports. [*Died* 25 *Aug.* 1963.

BOTTOME, Phyllis (Mrs. A. E. Forbes Dennis); novelist and lecturer; *b.* Rochester, 31 May 1884; *d.* of Rev. William Macdonald Bottome, New York and Margaret Leatham, of Leatham, Yorks; *g.d.* of Margaret Bottome, writer and philanthropist, foundress of the King's Daughters Society of U.S.A.; *m.* 1917, Captain A. E. Forbes Dennis, *g.s.* of General Sir John Forbes, G.C.B., of Inverernan. *Educ.:* Privately in England and America. Lived in England till age of nine; nine to thirteen in U.S.A.; subsequently in Switzerland, Italy, France, and Austria; Belgian Relief Work, 1914-15; lecturer for Ministry of Information, 1940-43. *Publications:* Raw Material, 1905; Captive; Secretly Armed; A Certain Star; A Servant of Reality; The Kingfisher; The Derelict and other Stories; The Perfect Wife; Old Wine; The Belated Reckoning; Wild Grapes; Strange Fruit; Tatter'd Loving; Windlestraws; Wind in His Fists, 1931 (re-published 1948, as The Devil's Due); The Advances of Harriet, 1933; Private Worlds, 1934; Innocence and Experience, 1935; Level Crossing, 1936; The Mortal Storm, 1937; Murder in the Bud, 1939; Alfred Adler; Apostle of Freedom, 1939; Masks and Faces, 1940; Heart of a Child, 1940; Formidable to Tyrants, 1941; London Pride, 1941; Within the Cup (American title, The Survival), 1943; From the Life, 1944; The Life-Line, 1946; Search for a Soul, 1947; Under the Skin, 1950; Fortune's Finger, 1950; The Challenge, Memoir, 1953; The Crystal Heart; Depths of Prosperity; Man and Beast (short stories), 1953; Against Whom? (American title, The Secret Stair), 1954; Not in Our Stars, 1955; Eldorado Jane, 1956; Walls of Glass (short stories), 1958; The Goal (Memoir), 1961; numerous short stories and articles in English and American magazines; works translated into French, German, Italian, Swedish, Hungarian, Norwegian, and Danish; special articles at request of Min. of Munitions, 1916. The Best Stories of Phyllis Bottome (selected by Dauphne du Maurier), 1963. *Recreations:* reading, conversation, travel. *Address:* Little Greenly, 95 South End Road, Hampstead, N.W.3. [*Died* 22 *Aug.* 1963.

BOTTOMLEY, Air Chief Marshal Sir Norman Howard, K.C.B., *cr.* 1944 (C.B. 1941); C.I.E. 1937; D.S.O. 1937; A.F.C. 1918; R.A.F. retired *b.* 18 Sept. 1891; *s.* of Thomas Bottomley, Ripponden, Yorks; *m.* 1927, Anne, *d.* of late Sir William B. Lang; one *s.* one *d.* *Educ.:* Halifax; Université de Rennes. Served European War, East Yorkshire Regiment, 1914-15; seconded R.F.C., 1915, France; Egypt, 1921-24; p.s.a. 1924; Dept. of Chief of Air Staff 1924-27; commanded No. 4 (A.C.) Squadron, 1928; i.d.c., 1930; Instructor R.A.F. Staff College, 1931-33; commanded No. 1 (Indian) Group, 1934-37 (despatches, D.S.O.); Senior Air Staff Officer, H.Q. Bomber Command, 1938-40; commanded a bomber group, 1940-41; Asst. Chief of Air Staff (operations), 1942-43; Deputy Chief of Air Staff, 1941 and 1943-45; A.O.C.-in-C. Bomber Command, 1945-47; Inspector-General, R.A.F., 1947-48; retired list, 1948. Director of Administration, B.B.C., 1948-56. Order of Merit (U.S.A.), 1945; Médaille de la Ville de Bordeaux, 1946. *Recreations:* golf, fishing, gardening. *Address:* Pipers Wing, Great Kingshill, Nr. High Wycombe, Bucks. *T.:* Holmer Green 3130. *Club:* Royal Air Force. [*Died* 13 *Aug.* 1970.

BOUCH, Thomas; *b.* April 1882; *o. s.* of late William Bouch, Ashorne, Warwick; unmarried; *Educ.:* Cheltenham; Magdalen College, Oxford; Served in 10th Hussars, 1904-07, 1914-1915. M.F.H. East Galway, 1908; M.F.H. Tipperary, 1909-10; Joint M.F.H. Atherstone, 1911; Belvoir, 1912-24; V. W. H. (Lord Bathurst's), 1933-34; Major attached to Headquarters, Cavalry Corps, B.E.F. *Publications:* Saved from the Waters; Cinderella, a play; Will o' the Wisp and the Wandering Voice; Storms in Teacups; Sentimentalities, 1926; Coat of Many Colours, 1953. *Address:* Ashorne, Warwick. *Clubs:* White's, Royal Automobile, Lansdowne. [*Died* 1 *May* 1963.

BOUCHARD, Hon. T. Damien; Supreme Governor of l'Institut Démocratique Canadien since 1943; Member Canadian Senate since 1944; *s.* of Damien Bouchard and Julie Rivard; *m.* late Corona Cusson; one *d.* *Educ.:* Seminary of St. Hyacinthe. Elected to Municipal Council of St. Hyacinthe, 1905; Mayor of St. Hyacinthe, 1917-1944; M.L.A. of Quebec for St. Hyacinthe, 1912-44; Pres. Legislative Assembly of Quebec, 1930-35; Minister of Municipal Affairs, Commerce and Industry, 1935-36; Minister of Lands and Forests, Municipal Affairs, Commerce and Industry, 1936; Leader of the Opposition, 1936-39; Minister of Public Works and Roads, 1939-42; Minister of Roads till 1944; belongs to Liberal Party; Editor of Le Clairon and Le Haut-Parleur, weeklies. *Publications:* Speeches in Pamphlet form. *Address:* 3155 Girouard Street, St. Hyacinthe, Que., Canada. *T.:* 4-6260. *Clubs:* Montreal Reform, Mount

Stephen (Montreal); Garrison (Quebec); St. Hyacinthe Golf, Canadien (St. Hyacinthe). [*Died* 13 *Nov.* 1962.

BOUCHER, Rear-Adm. Maitland Walter Sabine, D.S.O. 1919; R.N., retired; Nautical Assessor to Court of Appeal, House of Lords, 1947-53, and to Admiralty Court of Appeal, 1949-58; Managing Director of Trenean Estates Ltd.; *b.* 19 Dec. 1888; *s.* of late Walter E. and Mary L. S. Boucher, Belgrave Road, S.W.1; *m.* 1912, Vera H., *d.* of Commander E. C. H. Helby, R.N., Alverstoke, Hants; (one *s.* Captain J. Boucher, R.A., killed on active service, 19 Oct. 1945); one *d.* *Educ.:* Stubbington House School. Entered Navy as a cadet, 1904; Commander, 1923; Capt. 1930; Rear-Adm. 1941; served European War (wounded), North Sea, Eastern Mediterranean and N. Atlantic; Minesweeping, 1919 (D.S.O., despatches); Operations Division of Admiralty, 1923-24; qualified as Air Pilot in 1925; flying, 1925-43; Director; ate of Training, Air Ministry, 1929-31 - commanded H.M.S. Champion, 1931-32; Naval Air Division, Admiralty, 1933-34; Commanded H.M.S. Courageous, 1935-36-37: Director of Air Matériel Admiralty, 1938; A.D.C. to the King, 1940; Second Naval Member of Australian Naval Board, 1939-40; acting Chief of Australian Naval Staff during outbreak of war; retired list, 1941; served as Rear-Admiral until April 1941; afterwards joined Air Transport Auxiliary as a ferry pilot; served as Commodore R.N.R. in command of convoys, 1943-45; commanded many Arctic and other Convoys including that which led to the sinking of the German Battle Cruiser Scharnhorst. Younger Brother of Trinity House; A.F.R.Ae.S. *Address:* The Little House, White Waltham, Berks; Trenean, Nr. Looe, Cornwall. [*Died* 10 *May* 1963.

BOUCHER, Major-General Valentine, C.B. 1954; C.B.E. 1946; D.L.; Regional Director of Civil Defence, S.E. Region, since 1960; *b.* 14 February 1904; *s.* of late Franklin Coles Boucher, Rochester; *m.* 1933, Pamela Montfort, *d.* of late John Montfort Symns, Canterbury; two *s.* *Educ.:* Tonbridge; Royal Military College, Sandhurst. Joined Buffs, 1924; Burma (medal with clasp), 1930-32; Captain, 1935; served War, 1939-40 (O.B.E.), in France, as D.A.Q.M.G. (Movements); Director of Movements, General Headquarters, India, 1944-1946; Lt.-Col., 1946; Brigadier (temp.), 1946; Deputy-Director of Military Intelligence, War Office, 1948-50; comd. 24th Inf. Bde., 1950-53; Director of Military Intelligence, War Office, 1953-56; Commander of British Army Staff, British Jt. Services Mission, Washington, D.C., 1956-58. Maj.-Gen. 1954. Colonel The Buffs, 1953-61; D.L. Kent, 1961. *Address:* Lambden, Pluckley, Ashford, Kent. *T.:* Pluckley 373. *Club:* United Service. [*Died* 1 *April* 1961.

BOUGHTON, Sir Edward Hotham Rouse-, 13th Bt., *cr.* 1641; 5th Bt., *cr.* 1791; Maj. retired, 15th Hussars; *b.* 23 Aug. 1893 *o. s.* of Sir W. St. A. Rouse-Boughton, 12th Bt., and Eleanor Frances (*d.* 1930), *d.* of late Rev. F H. Hotham; *S.* father, 1937; *m.* 1916, Dorothy Alys, 2nd *d.* of late James H. Ismay; one *d.*; *m.* 1948, Mrs. Elizabeth Swaffer, *widow* of Geoffrey Swaffer. *Educ.:* Eton. 15th King's Hussars, 1913-19; served European War, France, 1914-18 (despatches); served R.N.R. 1939-40, Sub.-Lt.; 15/19th Hussars, 1941-1943, Major; Motor Boats, 1943-45, Major; now retired; Sheriff of Shropshire, 1940; M.F.H. Mendip, 1920-21; Wheatland, 1924-1929; North Ludlow, 1931-40. *Recreations:* hunting, shooting, sailing. *Heir:* none. *Address:* Anchor Gate, Seagrove Bay, Seaview, Isle of Wight; 39 Rutland Gate, S.W.7. [*Died* 17 *June* 1963.

BOULTER, Rev. Canon John Sidney, M.B.E. 1938; T.D.; M.A. (Oxon); Vicar of Sawrey, Lancashire, since 1962; Hon. Canon of Carlisle, since 1964; *b.* 16 August 1890; *s.* of Rev. Sidney Boulter, Rector of Poulshot, and Mary, *d.* of Charles Alcock, D.Litt.; *m.* 1939 Mary Joyce Thorn; one *s.* *Educ.:* St. John's, Leatherhead; Aldenham School; Keble College, Oxford. Assistant Master, St. Bees School, 1913; Second Master, 1934-38; Headmaster, St. Bees School, Cumberland, 1938-45. Deacon, 1954; Priest, 1954; Vicar of Rusland and Satterthwaite, 1955-62. *Recreations:* cricket, golf, walking. *Address:* Sawrey Vicarage, Ambleside, Westmorland. [*Died* 28 *Feb.* 1969.

BOULTON, Sir (Denis Duncan) Harold (Owen), 3rd Bart., *cr* 1905; *b.* 10 Dec. 1892; *s.* of Sir Harold Edwin Boulton, 2nd Bt., and Ida Davidson of Tulloch Castle, Dingwall, Scotland; *S.* father, 1935; *m.* 1918, Louise McGowan, U.S.A.; one *s.* (*yr. s.* killed in action in Italy 1944) one *d.* *Educ.:* Stonyhurst. For a time Hon. Equerry to Princess Louise, Duchess of Argyll. Flight Lieutenant R.A.F.V.R., 1940-42; then seconded to Foreign Office (American Hospitality); joined Home Security (C.D.) Commandant Civil Defence Unit, 1943-44; Chief Representative in N.Y. of British Travel Assoc., 1949-52; Agent in G.B. for Grosvenor Properties Canada, 1954-55. Commander Order of St. John of Jerusalem. *Recreations:* travelling, shooting. *Heir:* *er. s.* Sir Harold Hugh Christian Boulton, 4th Bt. *S.* 1968; late Captain Irish Guards [*b.* 29 Oct. 1918; now resides in Canada. *Educ.:* Ampleforth College, Yorks.]. *Address:* c/o The Westminster Bank Ltd., Leconfield House, Curzon Street, W.1. [*Died* 10 *Aug.* 1968.

BOUMPHREY, Geoffrey Maxwell; engineer, writer and broadcaster; *b.* 7 Aug. 1894; *s.* of Arthur Burrows Boumphrey and Alice Eleanor Whalley; *m.* 1st, 1917, Esther Mary Grandage; one *s.* 2nd, 1937, Sylvia Burnett (*née* Franklin) (*d.* 1942); 3rd, 1946, Diana Van Oss. *Educ.:* Radley (Exhibitioner). 2nd Lt.-Capt., South Lancashire Regiment, 1914; transferred to Royal Flying Corps (later Royal Air Force) as pilot, 1916; wounded, 1917; commenced writing, 1922; first broadcast, 1931; main interest, contemporary design—from a town to a teaspoon. Jt. Gen. Ed. Oxford Junior Encyclopædia, 1945-49; Ed., The Shell and B.P. Guide to Britain, 1962-64. *Publications:* The Log of the Ark (with K. M. Walker), 1923; Sea Farmers, 1929; The Story of the Wheel, 1932; The Story of the Ship, 1933; The Weekend Cookery Book, 1932; Along the Roman Roads, 1935; The House—Inside and Out, 1936; Down River, 1936; Your House and Mine, 1938; British Roads, 1938; Cunning Cookery, 1939; Town and Country Tomorrow, 1940; Open on Sundays, 1951; Engines and their Uses, 1959; many articles in the Spectator and other papers, technical and lay. *Recreations:* reading, eating, gardening. *Address:* Lower Farway, Chardstock, Nr. Axminster, Devon. [*Died* 29 *Nov.* 1969.

BOURDILLON, Francis Bernard, C.B.E. 1923; *b.* 3 March 1883; *s.* of late F. W. Bourdillon, Midhurst; *m.* Mary Dorothea, *d.* of late Joseph Armitage, M.D., Tasmania; one *s.* two *d.* *Educ.:* Charterhouse; Balliol College, Oxford. Lecturer in German, University College, Reading, 1908-1914; Modern Languages Lecturer, Balliol College, Oxford, 1913-15; Naval Intelligence Division, 1916-19; attended British Delegation, Paris Peace Conference, 1919; Upper Silesian Commission 1920-22; Irish Boundary Commission (Secretary), 1924-25; Secretary Royal Institute of International Affairs, 1926-29; Research Dept., Foreign Office,

1943-49. *Address:* Shotover, Dunchurch, Rugby, Warwicks. [*Died* 9 *June* 1970.

BOURKE, John Francis, J.P., Worcs.; Recorder of Shrewsbury, 1945-63; Chairman Worcs. Quarter Sessions, 1942-65; *b.* 1 Dec. 1889; *s.* of late Matthew J. Bourke, K.C., Recorder of Cork; *m.* 1923, Eileen Winifred, *d.* of Joseph George Beddoes, Edgbaston; three *s.* one *d.* *Educ.:* Clongowes Wood College; National University of Ireland. Called to Irish Bar, King's Inns, Dublin, 1916; English Bar, Gray's Inn, 1922; joined Oxford Circuit, 1922. *Address:* 1 Fountain Court, Birmingham 4; Westwood House, Droitwich. *T.:* 2102. [*Died* 27 *Nov.* 1967.

BOURNE, Gen. Sir Alan George Barwys, K.C.B. *cr.* 1941 (C.B. 1937); D.S.O. 1918; M.V.O. 1909; *b.* 25 July 1882; *s.* of late Rev. C. W. Bourne, Headmaster, King's College School, Wimbledon; *m.* 1911, Lilian Mary Poole (*d.* 1958), *d.* of late Colonel Poole Gabbett, R.A.M.C.; one *s.* *Educ.:* Cheltenham College. Entered Royal Marine Artillery, 1899; served on board H.M.S. Renown, 1905-6, on occasion of visit of Prince and Princess of Wales to India; appointed to R.N. College, Osborne, 1906; Capt. 1910; Major, 1917; Lt.-Col., 1929; Bt.-Col., 1932; Col. 1933; Maj.-Gen. 1938; Lt.-Gen., 1939; General, 1942; served on board H.M.S. Balmoral Castle during the visit of Duke and Duchess of Connaught to South Africa, 1910; graduated at Staff College, Camberley, 1915, and Imperial Defence College, 1931; A.A.G. Royal Marines, 1932-35; Col. Commandant, Portsmouth Division, Royal Marines, 1935-38; Adjutant-General, Royal Marines, 1939-43; Director Combined Operations, 1940; retired list, 1943; served European War (D.S.O.); Cavalier of the Order of St. Maurice and St. Lazarus; Italian Silver Medal for military valour. *Address:* Drove House, Cranborne, Wimborne, Dorset. *T.:* Cranborne 321. *Club:* United Service. [*Died* 24 *June* 1967.

BOURNE, Geoffrey, M.D., F.R.C.P.; Consulting Physician and Consulting Cardiologist to St. Bartholomew's Hospital; Consulting Cardiologist to British Air Corporations Joint Medical Service and to The Artists General Benevolent Institution, etc.; *b.* 1893; *s.* of late James Bourne and Ethel Ellen Bourne; *m.* 1st, Margherita Cotonio (*d.* 1952), New Orleans; 2nd, 1953, Patricia Mary, *d.* of late Rev. W. F. H. McCready, and of Mrs. McCready. *Educ.:* Highgate School; St. Bartholomews. M.D. (London), 1920; F.R.C.P. London 1929; Lawrence Research Scholar and Gold Medallist, 1919; Rockefeller Travelling Fellow, 1926-27, etc. *Publications:* Return to Reason, 1942; We met at Barts', 1963; Articles on Cardiac subjects in Quarterly Journal of Medicine, British Heart Journal, Lancet, British Medical Journal, etc. *Recreations:* fishing, painting. *Address:* 73 Harley St., W.1. *T.:* Welbeck 9942; (private) 61 Farley Court, Allsop Place, N.W.1. *T.:* Welbeck 2138. *Club:* English-Speaking Union. [*Died* 4 *Dec.* 1970.

BOURNE, Kenneth Morison, C.B.E. 1941; M.C.; *b.* Hong Kong, 1 Nov. 1893; *s.* of late Sir Frederick Bourne, C.M.G., H.B.M. Consular Service in China, and Asst. Judge of the Supreme Court of China and Korea; *m.* 1925, Marion Royston, *d.* of late Harold Porter, C.M.G., H.B.M. Consular Service in China; two *s.* *Educ.:* Clifton College; Royal Military College, Sandhurst. Gazetted to Prince of Wales Volunteers (South Lancashire Regt.) 1913; six months course at Royal Irish Constabulary, Dublin and Belfast; joined Shanghai Municipal Police, 1914; returned to England, and re-gazetted to 2nd Bn. Prince of Wales Volunteers, due to war; served France, 1915-18 (despatches, M.C. and Bar, Belgian Croix de Guerre); Regular Army Reserve of Officers, with rank of Major, 1919-35; returned to Shanghai Municipal Police, 1919; Deputy Commissioner, 1930; Commissioner of Police since 1938; proceeded on leave to Canada, Aug. 1941, and, owing to hostilities, joined Veteran Guards of Canada, 1942; transferred to Intelligence Corps (British Army); served Washington, D.C., India (1945), Burma (1946), and Malaya and India, 1947-48. Hon. Lt.-Col. *Address:* Stonecroft, Limehouse, nr. Georgetown, Ont., Canada. [*Died* 28 *Nov.* 1968.

BOUTFLOUR, Robert, C.B.E. 1952; M.Sc. (Dunelm); retired as Principal, Royal Agricultural College, Cirencester (1931-39 and 1945-58); *b.* 9 March 1890; *s.* of Robert Boutflour, High Throston, West Hartlepool; *m.* 1914, Mary Louisa Katherine, *d.* of William Somerville-Woodiwis, J.P.; two *s.* one *d.* *Educ.:* Barnard Castle School. Lectr. in Agriculture, Lancashire County Council, 1914-19; Lectr. in Agriculture, Univ. of Leeds, 1919-21; Agricultural Organiser, Lindsey, Lincoln County Council, 1921-22; Chief Agricultural Officer, Wilts County Council, 1922-26; Dir. of Dairy Husbandry, 1926-31; Professor of Agriculture, University of Bristol, 1935-40; Executive Officer for Glos. War Agricultural Committee, 1939-45. Sir Thomas Baxter Gold Medallist, 1955. Hon. Mem. R.A.S.E. 1958. *Publications:* various on Management and breeding of dairy cattle. *Recreation:* shooting. *Address:* Throston, Kirby-le-Soken, Nr. Frinton-on-Sea, Essex. [*Died* 25 *Oct.* 1961.

BOVELL, Vice-Admiral Henry Cecil, C.B. 1946; C.B.E. 1941; D.S.O. 1942; *b.* 4 Jan. 1893; *s.* of Sir Henry A. Bovell, K.C.; *m.* 1923, Beatrice Springman (*d.* 1952); one *d.* *Educ.:* R.N. Colleges, Osborne and Dartmouth. Midshipman H.M.S. Lord Nelson, 1910; Sub.-Lieut., 1913; Lieut., 1914; specialised in Gunnery, 1917; Commander, 1928; Captain, 1934; Imperial Defence College, 1935; Rear-Adm. 1944; Admiral Superintendent, H.M. Dockyard, Rosyth, 1944-47; retired list, 1947; Vice-Adm. retd. 1948. *Recreations:* fishing, shooting. *Address:* Boreham Grange, Warminster, Wilts. *T.:* Warminster 2260. *Club:* United Service. [*Died* 31 *March* 1963.

BOVELL-JONES, Thomas Boughton, C.M.G. 1956; *b.* 2 March 1906; *s.* of William Bovell-Jones and Ellen Jessica Cameron Dougall. *Educ.:* Bedford School; Brasenose College, Oxford. B.A. Hon. School of Jurisprudence, 1927. Nigerian Administrative Service, 1928-56; Senior Resident, Nigeria, 1952; retired, 1956. Coronation Medal, 1953. *Recreation:* fishing. *Address:* Poulstone Court, King's Caple, Hereford. *T.:* Carey 243. *Club:* East India and Sports. [*Died* 10 *Aug.* 1967.

BOVILL, Edward William; Chairman, R. C. Treatt & Co. Ltd., 1942-61; Director, Matheson & Co. Ltd., 1936-45; *b.* 25 Dec. 1892; *s.* of Edward Merewether Bovill and Mary Ellen Larkins; *m.* 1919, Sylvia Mary, *d.* of late Geoffrey Cheston; one *s.* one *d.* *Educ.:* Rugby; Trinity Coll., Camb. Served European War, 1914-19, with Xth Royal Hussars (S.R.), and W.A.F.F. Vice-Pres., Hakluyt Soc., 1964; Trustee and mem. Coun. Society for Nautical Research, 1954. Medallist Royal Soc. of Arts, 1935; F.S.A. *Publications:* Caravans of the Old Sahara, 1933; East African Agriculture (Jt. Ed.), 1950; The Battle of Alcazar, 1952; The Golden Trade of the Moors, 1958; The England of Nimrod and Surtees, 1959; English Country Life: 1780-1830, 1962; Missions to the Niger: F. Hornemann and A. Gordon Laing (Ed.) (Hakluyt Society), 1964; The Bornu Mission,

3 vols. (Ed.) (Hakluyt Society), 1965. *Address:* Brook House, Moreton, Ongar, Essex. *T.:* Moreton 221. *Club:* Travellers'. [*Died* 19 *Dec.* 1966.

BOWATER, Sir Eric Vansittart, Kt. 1944; Officier Légion d'Honneur; F.R.S.A.; Chairman, Bowater Paper Corporation Ltd., and Associated Cos., since 1927; Chairman, The Bowater Corporation of North America Ltd. and Subsidiary Companies; Director: Alliance Assurance Company, Lloyds Bank Ltd., British Newfoundland Corp. Ltd., Sun Alliance Insurance Ltd.; *b.* 16 Jan. 1895; *o. s.* of late Sir Frederick W. Bowater, K.B.E., and late Dame Alice Bowater; *m.* 1937, Margaret Vivian, *d.* of late Charles Perkins; one *s.* two *d.* *Educ.:* Charterhouse. Served in R.A., 1913-17; Min. of Aircraft Production, 1940 (Dir.-Gen.), Controller, 1945; a Vice-Pres. Empire Art Council; F.R.S.A. 1948. *Recreations:* farming, shooting. *Address:* Dene Place, West Horsley, Surrey. *T.:* East Horsley 4222; 1 Edinburgh Gate, S.W.1. *T.:* Knightsbridge 7070. *Clubs:* White's; Westward Ho Golf; Mount Royal (Montreal); Brook (New York). [*Died* 30 *Aug.* 1962.

BOWDEN, Frank Philip, C.B.E. 1956; F.R.S. 1948; D.Sc. (Tasmania), Ph.D., Sc.D. (Cantab); F.Inst.P.; Professor of Surface Physics and Director of Sub-Dept. of Surface Physics, Cavendish Laboratory, Cambridge University, since 1966; Professorial Fellow, Gonville and Caius College, Cambridge, 1957; *b.* 2 May 1903; *s.* of Frank Prosser Bowden and Grace Hill, Hobart, Tasmania; *m.* 1931, Margot Hutchison; three *s.* one *d.* *Educ.:* Hutchins School; Univ. of Tasmania; Gonville and Caius College, Cambridge. Demonstrator in Physics, Univ. of Tasmania, 1926; Overseas Exhibition of 1851 to Cambridge, 1927; Rockefeller Internat. Research Fellow and Senior 1851 Exhibition, 1930; Fellow, 1931; Director of Studies and College Lecturer in Chemistry, Gonville and Caius College, 1935; Humphrey Owen Jones Lecturer in Physical Chemistry, Cambridge, 1937; Beilby Memorial Award, 1938; Head of Tribophysics Laboratory of Council of Scientific and Industrial Research Australia, 1939-45; Reader in Physics and Director, Laboratory for Physics and Chemistry of Solids, Cambridge, 1946-65. Vice-Pres. Faraday Soc., 1953-56; Pres., Cambridge Alpine Club, 1965-. Res. Consultant, Tube Investments Res. Laboratories, 1953-; Chairman, Executive Committee National Physical Laboratory, 1955-62; Visitor, Electrical Research Assoc. 1963; Pres. Cambridge Philosophical Society, 1957; Member, Adv. Council on Scientific and Technical Develt., 1964-67; Director, The English Electric Co. Ltd., 1958-. Hawkesley Lectr., 1954; Kelvin Lectr., 1967. Redwood Medal of Institute of Petroleum, 1953; Elliott Cresson Medal of Franklin Institute, 1955; Rumford Medal of Royal Society, 1956; Medal of Société Française de Métallurgie, 1957; Glazebrook Medal of Physical Soc., 1968; Lewis Medal, Combustion Inst. of America, 1968. *Publications:* various scientific on surface and strength properties of solids, friction, and on solid state decomposition; (with D. Tabor) The Friction and Lubrication of Solids (Part I, 1950, Part II, 1964); Friction and Lubrication 1956; (with A. Yoffe) The Initiation and Growth of Explosion in Liquids and Solids, 1952; Fast Reactions in Solids (with Dr. Yoffe) 1958. *Recreations* mountaineering ski-ing. *Address:* Finella West, Queens' Road, Cambridge. *T.:* 53598. *Clubs:* Athenæum, Alpine. [*Died* 3 *Sept.* 1968.

BOWDEN, Norman Henry Martin, C.B.E. 1939 (O.B.E. 1934); retired; *b.* 17 May 1879; *er. s.* of Hule Nicolson Bowden, Balranald, New South Wales; *m.* 1914, Violet Westland; one *s.* one *d.* *Educ.:* Hawthorn College, Melbourne, Australia; Hale School, Perth, Australia. Western Australia Civil Service, 1897-1907; Papua Civil Service, 1907-11 (Resident Magistrate, 1910-11); Ceylon, Tea and Rubber planting, 1911-13; S. India, Deputy Ceylon Labour Commissioner, 1913 - 27; Commissioned Indian Army, 1918-19, on active service Persia-Turkestan Frontier; S. India, Ceylon Emigration Commissioner, 1927-39. *Publications:* Official reports only. *Recreations:* plain cooking, correspondence. *Address:* c/o Perpetual Trustees Assoc., 100 Queen St., Melbourne, Australia. [*Died* 21 *Oct.* 1968.

BOWDEN SMITH, Vice-Admiral William, C.B.E. 1918; J.P.; *b.* 28 Mar. 1874; *s.* of W. Bowden Smith of Brockenhurst and Louisa Sophia Prinsep; *m.* 1913, Ada Margaret, *d.* of late Charles Munro Sandham, Pulborough, and Mrs. Sandham, 13 Egerton Place; two *s.* one *d.* *Educ.:* Mr. Wilkinson's Preparation; H.M.S. Britannia. Went to sea, 1889; Sub-Lieutenant 1894; Lieutenant, 1896; Commander, 1906; Capt., 1913; Rear-Adm., 1923; Vice-Admiral, Retired List, 1928; served continuously during World War in H.M.S. Russell (sunk in Mediterranean), Grand Fleet, Dardanelles, H.M.S. Carnarvon, Atlantic Convoys; and as S.N.O. Tyne in command of anti-submarine flotillas; Commodore Hong Kong, 1920-22 (medals, Coronation 1911, Allied War, British War, 1914-15 Star, C.B.E., despatches); retired. *Recreations:* outdoor sports and games. *Address:* The Cottage, Horsham, Sussex. *T.:* Horsham 3896. *Clubs:* United Service, M.C.C. [*Died* 17 *March* 1962.

BOWDLER, (William) Audley; *b.* Kirkham, Lancs, 7 Sept. 1884; *s.* of W. H. Bowdler and E. A. Richards of Clifton, Lancs; *m.* 1918, Marguerite, *d.* of G. W. Parkes, Woldingham; one *s.* three *d.* *Educ.:* Rossall. M.P. (L.) Holderness, E. Yorks, 1922-23, M.R.C.S (Eng.), L.R.C.P. (Lond.); Major R.A. *Publications:* scientific and literary. *Address:* 25 Glenleigh Avenue, Bexhill-on-Sea. [*Died* 20 *Feb.* 1969.

BOWEN, Col. Arthur Winniett Nunn, C.B.E. 1919; D.S.O. 1917; late R.A.M.C.; L.R.C.S. and P. Ireland; *y. s.* of late George Edward Bowen, Portaferry; *m.* 1st, 1917, Edith (who obtained a divorce, 1926) *d.* of Lieut. S. A. Hickson, R.N.R., and *widow* of Capt. W. C. O. Phillips; 2nd, 1930, Gladys (*d.* 1939), *o. d.* of late W. M. Robertson, Cheltenham. Late Resident Surgeon, Meath Hospital, Dublin; served European War (D.S.O., C.B.E.); retired as Colonel, 1923. [*Died* 4 *Feb.* 1964.

BOWEN, Air Commodore James Bevan, C.B.E. 1937 (O.B.E. 1919); J.P.; retired; *b.* 20 March 1883; *e. s.* of late Sir George Bowen, K.B.E.; *m.* 1st, 1915, Noel (*d.* 1951), *er. d.* of L. Marshall, Nepicar House, Wrotham, Kent; two *s.* three *d.* 2nd, 1958, Muriel Ethelwyn Thomson, Monkton Old Hall, Pembroke. *Educ.:* Winchester College; Trinity College, Cambridge. Commissioned Pembrokeshire Yeomanry, 1910; Signals Officer, South Wales Mounted Brigade, 1914; attached R.F.C. 1916 (Served in France); Commandant Wireless School, R.F.C., 1917-21; mentioned for valuable War Services, 1918; permanent commission as Lt.-Col. R.A.F. 1919; Deputy Director Research (Instruments), 1921-25; R. M. Groves Aeronautical Research Prize, 1923; first Chief Instructor, Cambridge University Air Squadron, 1925-28; Group Captain, 1928; Senior Equipment Staff Officer, Iraq, 1928-30; commanded No. 3 Flying Training School, 1930-32; Air Commodore, 1932; Senior Air Staff Officer, Inland Area, 1932-33; Director of Signals, Air Ministry, 1933-37; commanded No. 1 Balloon Centre, Kidbrooke, 1937-41. Sometime Cdre. Ranelagh Sailing Club and Assoc.

of Pembrokeshire Yacht Clubs. D.L., 1932; V.L., 1952. H.M. Lieutenant, 1954-58, County of Pembroke. *Recreations:* fishing, sailing. *Address:* Monkton Old Hall, Pembroke. *T.:* 2339. [*Died* 12 *Aug.* 1969.

BOWEN, Sir (John) William, Kt., *cr.* 1953; C.B.E. 1939; J.P.; member London County Council 1940-61 (Chairman, 1949-1952, Alderman, 1951-61); *b.* Blackpill, near Swansea, 1876; *m.* 1903, Eva Sanger (*d.* 1953), Waunarlwydd, Swansea; three *s.* one *d.* *Educ.:* Gowerton Glam. Active in Labour, Trade Union and Co-operative movement; Friendly Society and National Health Insurance work; served on many Government Cttees., etc.; formerly Chairman North East (Met.) Regional Hospital Board; Fellow Chartered Institute of Insurance; Chairman Workers' Travel Association; Chairman Ruskin College, Oxford; formerly General Secretary Union of Post Office Workers; contested Newport, Mon., 1918, 1922 (twice), 1923, 1924, Crewe Div., 1929, 1931 and 1935; M.P (Lab.) Crewe Div., 1929-31. Commander Legion of Honour (France), 1950; Commander Order of Orange-Nassau (Holland), 1951; Commander Royal Order of Dannebrog (Denmark), 1951. *Address:* 18 Titchwell Rd., Wandsworth Common, S.W.18. *T.:* Vandyke 8440. [*Died* 1 *April* 1965.

BOWEN, Owen, R.C.A. 1916 (formerly President); R.O.I. 1916; *b.* Leeds, 28 April 1873; *s.* of George Bowen; *m.* Janet Wilson; one *s.* two *d.* *Educ.:* Leeds. *Address:* Evenholm, Collingham, Wetherby, Yorkshire. [*Died* 17 *Sept.* 1967.

BOWEN, Trevor Alfred, D.L., J.P. Co. Lond.; late Chairman and Managing Director, John Barker & Co, Ltd., Kensington, W.8; *m.* Daisy Maud (*d.* 1960), *d.* of G. Donnelly, Hastings; one *d.* *Educ.:* Monmouth. Freeman City of London; Hon. Freeman Borough of Monmouth. Past Master Worshipful Company of Bakers. Closely associated with 162nd Anti-Aircraft Territorial Battalion since its formation, the Air Force and Sea Cadets; late Governor or Vice-Pres. of many London Hospitals. *Address:* 13 Balliol House, Manor Fields, Putney, S.W.15. *Clubs:* City Livery, Royal Automobile. [*Died* 27 *April* 1964.

BOWEN, Sir William; *see* Bowen, Sir J. W.

BOWEN, Wm. Henry, M.B., M.S., F.R.C.S.; Consulting Surgeon (retired); Consulting Surg., Addenbrooke's Hospital and to Royston Co. Hospital; *b.* Moseley, Birmingham; 3rd *s.* of late Alderman J. Bowen, J.P.; *m.* 1914, K. E. Clark, of Harrogate; two *s.* one *d.* (and one *s.* decd.). *Educ.:* The Birmingham High School; Guy's Hosp. House Surgeon to Guy's Hospital; formerly: Surgeon to the East London Hospital for Children, and the Royal Ear Hospital; Supervisor and Examiner in Surgery, University of Cambridge; Member of Court of Examiners, R.C.S.; Hunterian Professor, R.C.S.; worked in the Imperial Cancer Research Fund for five years and contributed papers to their Scientific Reports (III.); Gold Medal in Clinical Surgery at Guy's Hospital; M.A. Camb. (hon.). *Publications:* Appendicitis: A Clinical Study, 1937; Charles Dickens; a Sympathetic Study, 1957; Traumatic Subdural Hæmorrhage (Guy's Hospital Reports); various other papers to Medical Journals on Surgical Subjects. *Address:* 24 Lensfield Road, Cambridge. *T.:* Cambridge 4856. [*Died* 31 *Dec.* 1963.

BOWEN, Maj.-Gen. William Oswald, C.B. 1946; C.B.E. 1945 (O.B.E. 1935); M.I.E.E.; Hampshire County Civil Defence Officer since 1954; *b.* 16 Nov. 1898; *y. s.* of late William Bowen, Llanelly; *m.* 1932, Ethel Gwenllian, *d.* of late Dr. J. L. Davies, Llanelly; three *s.* one *d.* *Educ.:* Llanelly; Royal Military College, Sandhurst. Commissioned 1917; with Gurkha Rifles until 1928; served European War, 1914-18 in France, Italy, N.W. Frontier India and Burma; transferred to Royal Signals, 1928; on active service Burma 1932 while seconded to Civil Govt. Burma and Palestine 1936-37; Lt.-Col. 1943; Col. 1946; Brig. 1949; Maj.-Gen. 1949; served throughout war of 1939-45 as Chief Signal Officer, Burma Front in Burma Army, Eastern Army and Fourteenth Army successively (despatches twice, C.B.E., C.B.). Chief Signal Officer, M.E.L.F., 1949-51; Director of Signals, War Office, 1951-54, retired 1954. *Recreation:* tennis. *Address:* Rowanhurst, St. Giles Hill, Winchester. [*Died* 14 *Jan.* 1961.

BOWEN, York; pianist, composer; Professor and Fellow of Royal Academy of Music; *b.* London, 22 Feb. 1884; *y. s.* of Edward Bowen; *m.* 1912, Sylvia, *o. d.* of Rev. J. P. Dalton, Rector of Creech St. Michael, Somerset; one *s.* Started serious musical training at age of fourteen, studying privately, at the Blackheath Conservatoire, and afterwards for a period of some seven years at the Royal Academy of Music, gaining two scholarships for the pianoforte and numerous prizes for composition and piano; orchestral works performed at London and provincial concerts, including Royal Philharmonic Society, London Symphony Orchestral Concerts, Promenade Concerts, Queen's Hall, and Hallé Concerts, Manchester; engagements as pianist in various towns and abroad, and regular Recitals in London, instituting joint Recitals with his wife (singer), 1912. B.B.C. broadcasts both as pianist and composer. *Publications:* five Suites for piano, and numerous other single pieces; two sonatas for viola and piano; sonatas for flute, oboe, violoncello, clarinet, recorder, horn and piano; songs, concertos for violin, viola, cello, piano, and orchestra; three symphonies, and chamber music; pieces for two pianos; concerto for horn and orchestra. *Address:* 25 Langland Gardens, N.W.3. [*Died* 23 *Nov.* 1961.

BOWEN-BUSCARLET, Air Vice-Marshal Sir Willett Amalric Bowen, K.B.E. 1960 (C.B.E. 1943); C.B. 1953; D.F.C. 1931; D.L.; late R.A.F.; *b.* 28 May 1898; *s.* of F. C. Buscarlet, Maybrook, Londonderry, N. Ireland; *m.* 1925, Violet Mary Montague; two *d.*; *m.* 1947, Christiane Marie Estler. *Educ.:* Sedbergh School; R.M.A., Woolwich. 2nd Lieut., R.A., 1916; seconded R.F.C. 1917; returned to R.A., 1919; re-seconded R.A.F., 1921; Air Commodore (temp.), 1943 (war subs. 1945); retired with rank of Air Vice-Marshal, 1946. D.L. County Palatinate of Lancaster, 1951. *Recreations:* mountaineering, motor racing. *Address:* The Manor House, Charwelton, Rugby, Warwickshire. *T.:* Byfield 600. *Clubs:* Royal Air Force, Royal Automobile, British Racing Drivers, Royal Aero. [*Died* 18 *Sept.* 1967.

BOWES-LYON, Hon. Sir David, K.C.V.O. 1959; Managing Director Lazard Bros. & Co. Ltd. (incorporating Edward de Stein & Co.); H.M. Lieutenant, County of Hertford, since 1952; Trustee of British Museum since 1953; *b.* 2 May 1902; 6th *s.* of 14th Earl of Strathmore, K.G., K.T., G.C.V.O.; *m.* 1929, Rachel Pauline, *y. d.* of Lt.-Col. Rt. Hon. H. H. Spender-Clay, P.C., C.M.G., M.P.; one *s.* one *d.* *Educ.:* Eton; Magdalen College, Oxford. Late Lt. Hertfordshire Regiment, 1939; Ministry of Economic Warfare, 1940-41; Head of Political Warfare Mission, Washington, 1942-1944. High Sheriff of Herts., 1950. Dir.: Times Publishing Co., Martin's Bank Ltd., Cunard Steamship Co., Dunlop Rubber Co.; Sub. Governor, Roy. Exchange Assnce. President Royal Horticultural Society.

Order of Leopold (Belgium), 1957. *Recreations:* shooting, gardening. *Address:* St. Paul's Walden Bury, Hitchin, Herts. *T.:* Whitwell 225; 11 Old Broad Street, E.C.2. *T.:* London Wall 2721. *Club:* Brooks's. [*Died* 13 *Sept.* 1961.

BOWKER, Sir Leslie Cecil Blackmore, K.C.V.O., *cr.* 1953; Kt., *cr.* 1948; O.B.E. 1928; M.C.; City Remembrancer, 1933-53; *s.* of Charles Edward Blackmore Bowker, solicitor, and Ellen Pearce; unmarried. *Educ.:* All Saints School; Moore Park School, Fulham. Entered Civil Service, 1906; served European War, 1914-19, with 2nd Bn. London Scottish, France, Salonika, Palestine, Captain (M.C.); called to Bar, Middle Temple, 1922; Liveryman of the Fanmakers and Plaisterers Companies; Chief Clerk to Law Officers of the Crown, 1925; Legal Secretary to Law Officers of Crown, 1932; President: London F.A.. London Football League. London Youth F.A.; London Schools' F.A.; Hon. Member Legion Club, Montreal; Order of Al Rafidain, 1933; Officer, Crown of Belgium, 1937; Commander: Star of Roumania, 1938; Legion of Honour, 1950; Order of Orange-Nassau, 1950; Order of The Dannebrog, 1951. *Recreation:* golf. *Address:* 23B Marine Drive, Rottingdean, Sussex. *T.:* Rottingdean 2772. [*Died* 23 *April* 1965.

BOWLBY, Capt. Cuthbert Francis Bond, C.M.G. 1956; C.B.E. 1945; D.S.C. and bar 1918; R.N. (Retd.); *b.* 23 Aug. 1895; *s.* of Rev. H. T. Bowlby; *m.* 1920, Isobel Murray Thorburn; one *s.* one *d.* *Educ.:* Summerfields, Oxford; R.N.C. Osborne and Dartmouth. Went to sea, 1912; served European War, 1914-18, Battle Cruiser Sqdn. and original coastal Motor Boat Flotilla, and War of 1939-45, Admiralty and Mediterranean H.Q., Egypt and Italy; retd. from Navy, 1945. Served in F.O., 1945-55; retd. 1955. *Recreations:* golf, shooting. *Address:* Round Hill Lodge, Bramshaw, nr. Lyndhurst, Hants. *T.:* Cadnam 3280. [*Died* 31 *May* 1969.

BOWLES, Baron (Life Peer) *cr.* 1964; **Francis George Bowles;** Captain of the Queen's Bodyguard of the Yeomen of the Guard since 1965; *b.* 2 May 1902; *s.* of late Horace Edgar Bowles, Freshwater, I.o.W.; *m.* 1950, Kay, *e. d.* of late E. H. Musgrove, and *widow* of Air Commodore E. D. M. Hopkins. *Educ.:* Highgate School; London Univ. LL.B. Lond., B.Sc. (Econ.); Admitted a solicitor, 1925. Contested (Lab.) Hackney North, 1929, 1931 and 1935, and Preston, 1936; M.P. (Lab.) Nuneaton Division of Warwickshire, 1942-64; Vice-Chairman Parliamentary Labour Party, 1946-48; Deputy Chairman of Ways and Means, 1948-50. *Address:* 88 St. James's Street, S.W.1; *T.:* 01-930 9134; House of Lords, S.W.1. [*Died* 29 *Dec.* 1970.

BOWMAN, Humphrey Ernest, C.M.G. 1936; C.B.E. 1919; M.A. (Oxon); Member: Royal Institute of International Affairs; Royal Central Asian Soc.; Vice-President Council, Anglo-Egyptian Assoc.; *b.* 26 July 1879; *er. s.* of late John Frederick Bowman of 25 Young St., Kensington, and Garramor, Arisaig, Inverness-shire, and late Cecilia (*née* Charrington); *m.* 1st, 1916, Frances Guinevere (*d.* 1923), *d.* of Col. A. H. Armytage; one *s.* one *d.*; 2nd, 1925, Elinor Marion (*d.* 1957), *e. d.* of Rev. Charles H. Conybeare, and *widow* of Arthur William Bowman. *Educ.:* Eton; New College, Oxford. Egyptian Civil Service (Ministry of Education), 1903-23; Inspector, Education Dept., Sudan, 1911-13; Director, Egyptian Students in England, 1913-14; Army Service (18th Batt. R. Fusiliers; Staff; France, India, Mesopotamia), 1914-18; Director of Education, Iraq, 1918-20; Director of Education, and member of Advisory Council, Palestine Govt., 1920-36; temp. employed in M.O.I., 1939; on special duty under the Foreign Office, 1941-45. Commander, of the Order of the Nile; K. St. J. *Publication:* Middle East Window, 1942. *Recreations:* fishing, gardening. *Address:* Glebe House, Chiddingfold, Godalming, Surrey. *T.:* Wormley 2040. *Club:* Athenæum. [*Died* 23 *March* 1965.

BOWMAN, Robert Ritchie; *see* Addenda: II.

BOWRING, Theodore Louis, C.M.G. 1955; O.B.E. 1948; *b.* 29 July 1901; 2nd *s.* of late John Bowring; *m.* 1931, Dagmar Hedwig, *y. d.* of H. W. L. Jarrand; one *d.* *Educ.:* Chatham House School Ramsgate; Thames Nautical Training Coll.; H.M.S. Worcester; Crystal Palace School of Practical Engineering. Served European War, 1918-19, Midshipman, R.N.R. Asst. Engineer, Messrs. Sir John Jackson Ltd., 1922-25; entered Colonial Government Service as Executive Engineer, Public Work Dept., Gold Coast, 1925; seconded for military service, 1939-41; Major R.E. (despatches 1940); Director of Public Works, British Honduras, 1941; Director of Public Works, Nyasaland, 1948; Director of Public Works, Hong Kong, 1950; retired 1957; Adviser on Engineering Appointments, Colonial Office, and later, Dept. of Technical Co-operation, 1958-61; Consultant, Scott & Wilson, Kirkpatrick & Partners, Consulting Civil and Structural Engineers, 1962-66. M.I.C.E. *Address:* 27 Flag Court, Kingsway, Hove 3, Sussex. [*Died* 24 *June* 1967.

BOWSTEAD, John, C.S.I. 1947; C.I.E. 1942; M.C. 1918; Secretary, Scottish Council of Social Service, 1967 and 1968; *b.* 16 Feb. 1897; *s.* of late Rev. A. K. Bowstead; *m.* 1925, Elsie, *d.* of late Sir Hugh McPherson; two *d.* *Educ.:* King's Sch., Worcester; Corpus Christi Coll., Camb., B.A. Commission in R.G.A., 1916-19 (M.C.); entered Indian Civil Service, 1921; posted to Bihar and Orissa; Under-Secretary to Govt. of Bihar and Orissa, 1925-27; Asst. Political Agent, Orissa States, 1928-32; Political Agent, 1932-35; Magistrate and Collector, 1936; Secretary to Governor of Orissa, 1938-40; Chief Secretary to Govt. of Orissa, 1940-44; Chief Secretary to Govt. of Bihar, 1945 and 1946. *Address:* c/o Lloyds Bank Ltd., 6 Pall Mall, S.W.1; 27 Wilton Road, Edinburgh 9. *T.:* 031-667 6100. [*Died* 14 *June* 1969.

BOWYER, Sir Eric Blacklock, K.C.B. 1954 (C.B. 1947); K.B.E. 1950; Permanent Secretary, Ministry of Pensions and National Insurance, 1955-64, retd.; *b.* 5 Nov. 1902; *s.* of late Frank L. Bowyer; *m.* 1939, Elizabeth Crane, *d.* of late J. Crane Nicholls; two *s.* two *d.* *Educ.:* Whitehill School, Glasgow; Glasgow Univ. B.Sc. 1923, M.A. (1st cl. hon. maths. and natural phil.), 1924; Colonial Office, 1926-33 and 1935-38; Dominions Office, 1933-34; Air Ministry, 1939; Ministry of Aircraft Production, 1940-45; Ministry of Supply, 1946-53; Permanent Secretary to Ministry of Materials, 1953-54. Hon. LL.D. Glasgow, 1959. *Recreations:* golf, gardening. *Address:* 10 Haydn Avenue, Purley, Surrey. *T.:* Uplands 8351. *Club:* Union. [*Died* 21 *April* 1964.

BOXER, Rear-Admiral Henry Percy; *b.* 14 Oct. 1885; *s.* of late Commander J. A. Boxer, R.N. (retd.), Folkestone; *m.* 1911, Enid Everard, *d.* of late Archdeacon A. E. Kitchin and Mrs. Kitchin, Hardingstone, Saxlingham, Norwich; one *s.* one *d.* Joined H.M.S. Britannia 1900; H.M.S. Terrible 1902 on China Station; saw Naval engagement off Chemulpho, Korea, when serving in H.M.S. Talbot; was in command of T.B.4 at Dover, also H.M. Ships Noble and Plover in the Grand Fleet, taking part in the Battle of Jutland and surrender of German Fleet; after serving in over 30 ships and in command of 19 of them was promoted to rank of Rear-Adm.

and retired 1939; rejoined in Sept. 1939 as Commodore R.N.R. and served in Convoys till 1940, when he was again retired through ill-health; A.R.P. Staff Officer Hampshire County, 1940-45. *Address:* Trees, Itchen Abbas, Winchester. *T.:* Itchen Abbas 304. [*Died* 30 *June* 1961.

BOXER, Captain Herbert Martyn, C.M.G. 1919; M.V.O. 1926; R.N., retired; recalled from retired list September 1939 and lent to Ministry of Economic Warfare, to Ministry of Shipping, 1940; H.M.S. Collingwood, 1941; *b.* 18 June 1882; 2nd *s.* of Paymaster-in-Chief W. E. Boxer, R.N.; *m.* 1910, Dorothy, *d.* of E. G. Woolhouse, Colonial Service; two *s.* one *d.* *Educ.:* George Watson's College, Edinburgh. Entered Royal Navy, 1900; Assistant Paymaster, 1903; Paymaster, 1915; Paymaster-Commander, 1921; Paymaster-Captain, 1931; retired 1937; Secretary to Rear-Admiral Commanding 7th and 2nd Cruiser Squadrons, 1916; to Vice-Admiral Commanding 3rd Battle Squadron, 1917; to 2nd Sea Lord of Admiralty, 1917-19; to Commander-in-Chief, Coast of Scotland, 1919-22; to Rear-Admiral Commanding H.M. Yachts, 1922-27; to Admiral commanding Reserves, 1929-31; to Commander-in-Chief, Home Fleet, 1931-33; to Commander-in-Chief, Portsmouth, 1934-36. *Address:* 32A Anglesey Road, Alverstoke, Hants. [*Died* 27 *Jan.* 1962.

BOYCE, Col. (Hon. Brig.) Charles Edward, D.S.O. 1917; D.S.M. (America); *b.* Nov. 1882; *m.* Joan; two *d.* *Educ.:* Haileybury Coll.; R.M. Academy, Woolwich. Served European War, 1914-19 (D.S.O., Bt. Lt.-Col.); Lt.-Col. 1929; Col. 1933; Commander R.A. 48th (South Midland) Div. T.A., 1934-38; retired pay, 1938. *Address:* 12 Downs Lodge Court, Epsom, Surrey. *Club:* Hurlingham. [*Died* 9 *Oct.* 1963.

BOYCE, Sir Richard (Leslie), 2nd Bt., *cr.* 1952; Engineer; *b.* 5 July 1929; *s.* of Sir (Harold) Leslie Boyce, 1st Bt., K.B.E., and Maybery, D.St.J., *d.* of late Edward Philip Bevan, Melbourne; *S.* father 1955; *m.* 1958, Jacqueline Anne, *o. d.* of Roland A. Hill, Brimscombe, Glos.; one *s.* one *d.* *Educ.:* Cheltenham College. National Service commission, Gloucestershire Regt., 1950. O.St.J. *Heir:* *s.* Robert Charles Leslie Boyce, *b.* 2 May 1962. *Address:* Highfields, 35 Rowan Way, Lisvane, Cardiff. *T.:* Cardiff 753024. [*Died* 12 *Oct.* 1968.

BOYD, Admiral Sir Denis (William), K.C.B. 1945 (C.B. 1943); C.B.E. 1941; D.S.C. 1917; Principal of Ashridge College, 1950-57, retired; *b.* 6 March 1891; *s.* of William John and Emily Eva Charlotte Boyd, Manchester; *m.* 1915, Audrey Edoline, *d.* of Lt.-Col. A. B. Shakespear, R.M. Artillery; one *s.* two *d.* (and one *s.* decd.). *Educ.:* Dartmouth Royal Naval Coll. Midshipman, 1906; Lt.-Comdr. 1919; Comdr. 1924; Capt. 1931; Rear-Adm. 1941; Vice-Adm. 1944; Adm. 1948. Served European War, 1914-18 (D.S.C.) 1st Lieut. H.M.S. Hood on her world cruise, 1923-25; lent to Australian Navy, 1926-28; Captain of a Destroyer Flotilla at Malta and in the Mediterranean during Spanish Civil War, 1936; at outbreak of war, 1939, was Captain of H.M.S. Vernon Torpedo School; Captain of Aircraft Carrier H.M.S. Illustrious, 1940, which he commanded at Taranto; Rear-Admiral commanding Mediterranean Aircraft Carriers, 1941 (despatches); Rear-Admiral, H.M.S. Indomitable; Fifth Sea Lord and Chief of Naval Air Equipment, 1943-45; Admiral (Air), 1945-46; C.-in-C. Far East Station, 1948-49 (C.-in-C. British Pacific Fleet, 1946-48); retired list, 1949. *Recreations:* hockey, tennis, golf, Rugby football. *Address:* 3 Castleton Court, Southsea Terrace, Southsea, Hants. *Club:* United Service. [*Died* 21 *Jan.* 1965.

BOYD, Douglas Thornley, C.M.G. 1951; Member of the Australian Wool Board, from its inception (formerly Chairman); Chairman International Wool Publicity and Research Executive from 1944; *b.* Melbourne, 19 Oct. 1896; *s.* of late William Boyd, Tarrone, Koroit, Victoria, Australia; *m.* 1st, 1920, Eina F., *d.* of Rev. George Pennicott; four *d.*; 2nd, 1951, Marjory, *d.* of R. Tait Sutherland. *Educ.:* Geelong Coll. Mem., Australian Woolgrowers' Council (Vice-President); Past President Council of Graziers' Federation, 1936-37. Chm., Wool Bureau, New York, 1949. *Address:* Deloraine, Beveridge, Vic., Australia. *Club:* Australian (Melbourne and Sydney). [*Died* 5 *June* 1964.

BOYD, James, C.B.E. 1951; retired as Chief Medical Officer to Ministries of Labour and Health and Local Government for Northern Ireland; *b.* 7 Feb. 1888; *s.* of late Wm. C. Boyd, J.P., Belfast; *m.* 1921, M. Gwendoline, *d.* of late I. Jenkins, Crickhowell, Brecon; no *c.* *Educ.:* Campbell College, Belfast; Queen's University of Belfast; University of Paris. B.A. 1908; M.A. 1910; B.Sc. 1911; M.B., B.Ch. 1916; D.P.H., 1919; M.D. 1923; M.R.C.P. (Ireland) 1934; F.R.C.P. (Ireland) 1936. Medical Officer, Bradfield Coll., Berks, 1919-21; Hon. Physician, Royal Gwent Hosp., Newport, 1922-30; Chief Medical Officer, Min. of Labour for N. Ire., 1930-54, Ministry of Health and Local Govt. for N. Ire., 1944-54. Chm. Jt. Nursing and Midwives Council for N. Ireland, 1943-55; General Medical Council, Crown Nominee for N. Ireland, 1946-56. K.H.P. 1947-50. *Address:* 18 Cadogan Park, Belfast. *T.:* 665133. [*Died* 26 *Oct.* 1963.

BOYD, James, M.A. B.Litt., (Oxon), Ph.D. (Heidelberg); Taylor Professor of German Language and Literature, Oxford University, 1938-59; Emeritus Professor in the University of Oxford; Emeritus Fellow of The Queen's College; *m.* 1915, Anna Maria Geertruida Josephina Smulders. *Educ.:* Oxford Univ., 1st class Honour School of Mod. Languages (with Distinction). Served European War, 1914-17 (wounded); Lektor University of Heidelberg, 1921-23; Professor of German, University of Cape Town, 1923-1926; Reader in German and Head of Dept. of German, Bristol University, 1926-31; Reader in German, Oxford University, 1931-1938. *Publications:* Goethe's Knowledge of English Literature, 1932; Ulrich Füetrer's Parzival; Material and Sources, Medium Aevum Monographs I, 1936; Goethe's Poems, 1942; Goethe's Iphigenie auf Tauris, an Interpretation and Critical Analysis, 1942; Notes to Goethe's Poems, Vol. I, 1944, Vol. II, 1949; Chamisso's Peter Schlemihl, 1956; articles and reviews in Modern Languages Review, etc. General Editor of Blackwell's German Texts and of Blackwell's German Plain Texts; Joint Editor of Modern Language Studies. *Recreation:* music. *Address:* 36 St. Margaret's Road, Oxford. *T.:* Oxford 58064. [*Died* 30 *Oct.* 1970.

BOYD, James Dixon; Professor of Anatomy, Cambridge University, since 1951; *b.* 29 Sept. 1907; *s.* of James Dixon Boyd and Grace Helen Smythe; *m.* 1933, Amélie Loewenthal, M.B., B.Sc., D.P.H.; four *s.* *Educ.:* Royal Belfast Academical Institution; Queen's University, Belfast. B.Sc., 1927 1st class hons.; M.B., B.Ch., B.A.O. 1930 hons.; Gold Medal in Surgery; Adami Medal in Pathology; M.Sc. 1932; M.D. (Gold Medal) 1934; D.Sc. *h.c.*, 1961; M.A. Cambridge, 1935; F.R.C.O.G. *h.c.*, 1963; Rockefeller Fellowship (Johns Hopkins University), 1934-35; University Demonstrator and Lecturer, Cambridge, 1935-38; Woodward Lecturer, Yale Univ., 1955; formerly Professor of Anatomy, Univ. of London, London Hosp.

Medical College; formerly Professor of Anatomy, Royal Academy, London; Professorial Fellow, Clare College, Cambridge; Fellow, Cambridge Philosophical Society; Fellow, Internat. Inst. of Embryology; Ex-Pres., Anatomical Soc. Great Britain and Ireland; F.Z.S.; one-time Examiner in Anatomy, Universities of Oxford, London, Glasgow, Cardiff and Birmingham and R.C.P. *Publications:* contributions to Anatomical Literature. *Address:* Anatomy School, Cambridge. *T.:* Cambridge 58761; Corrie, 21 Newton Rd., Cambridge. *T.:* Cambridge 50809. [*Died* 7 *Feb.* 1968.

BOYD, Sir John, Kt. 1961; solicitor; member of Russell & Duncan, Glasgow; Emeritus Professor of Mercantile Law, Univ. of Glasgow; *b.* Doura, Ayrshire; *s.* of William Boyd, B.A., and Janet McAlpine; *m.* Catherine, *d.* of John Mackinlay, Writer, Barrhead; three *s.* *Educ.:* Irvine Royal Academy; Glasgow University. M.A. (Hons.) 1912, LL.B. 1920. Served European War, 1914-18: with 1st Royal Dublin Fus., 1915, 7th H.L.I. 1916-1918. Vice-President, Law Society of Scotland, 1954-55; Dean, Royal Faculty of Procurators, Glasgow, 1955. Hon. LL.D. Glasgow Univ., 1958. *Recreation:* walking. *Address:* 3 Westbourne Gardens, Glasgow. *T.:* Glasgow Western 3803. *Clubs:* Glasgow Art, The Western, The Conservative (Glasgow). [*Died* 4 *Nov.* 1967.

BOYD, Sir John (Smith), Kt. 1947; M.A.; LL.B.; formerly Vice-President Shipbuilding Employers' Federation, 1931-56; *b.* Kilmarnock, 18 May 1886; *s.* of David Boyd and Janet Smith; *m.* 1915, Maggie Picken Neilson (*d.* 1961); one *s.* *Educ.:* Kilmarnock Acad.; Glasgow University (Robertson Scholar, 1912). President and Warden, Glasgow Univ. Students' Settlement; Solicitors Department, Caledonian Railway, 1909-14; General Manager's Office, North Eastern Railway, 1914-22; Staff Assistant to General Manager, 1922; Assistant to Superintendent, North-Eastern Area, London and North-Eastern Railway, 1923-27; Secretary, Shipbuilding Employers, Federation, 1927-31; Member of Home Office (Stewart) Departmental Committee on Workmen's Compensation, 1935-1938; Member of Ministry of Labour Departmental Committee on the Fair Wages Clause, 1937; Mem. of Roy. Commission on Workmen's Compensation, 1939-45; Member Ministry of Labour National Joint Advisory Council, 1939; Member Admiralty Central Consultative Committee Essential Work (Shipbuilding) Order, 1941-45; Member Home Office Departmental Committee on Alternative Remedies (Social Insurance), 1944; Member Shipbuilding Advisory Committee, 1946; Member National Insurance Advisory Committee, 1947-55. *Address:* 1 Grove Road, Northwood, Middlesex. *T.:* Northwood 25495. [*Died* 17 *May* 1963.

BOYD, Sidney Arthur, M.S. (London), F.R.C.S. Eng.; retd. as Cons. Surg., Hampstead General Hosp., Belgrave Hosp. for Children, Leatherhead Hosp., Mildmay Mission Hosp., Church Missionary Society (also Vice-Pres.), to St. John's School, Leatherhead, and Surgeon to St. Luke's Nursing Home for Clergy (also Trustee); *b.* 20 July 1880; *s.* of Albert Thomas and Marianne Boyd; *m.* 1910, Violet Evangeline Fox; one *s.* three *d.* *Educ.:* Bedford; London Univ., Charing Cross (Livingstone Scholar) and London Hospital; M.R.C.S., L.R.C.P., 1902; M.B., B.S. (Lond.), 1904 (Gold Medal); resident posts at Charing Cross Hospital and Surgical Registrar, 1906-09; served in R.A.M.C., 1914-19 (Temp. Major), Mediterranean and Egyptian Expeditionary Forces (despatches twice). Lecturer in Applied Anatomy, King's College, London, 1919-1925. F.R.Soc.Med. and Fellow of B.M.A.; Alderman of Hampstead Borough Council, Mayor, 1938-45 (seven years); Hon. Freeman, Metropolitan Borough of Hampstead; J.P. for County of London; Hon. Treas. Westfield Coll., Univ. of London. *Publications:* Various articles on Surgical Subjects in Medical Journals and in Proceedings of Royal Society of Medicine. *Address:* 10 Oakhill Avenue, Hampstead, N.W.3. *T.:* Hampstead 2020. [*Died* 2 *Nov.* 1966.

BOYD, William, C.M.G., C.B.E.; *see* Addenda: II.

BOYD, Col. Thomas Crawford, C.I.E. 1944; F.R.C.S. (Irel.), M.R.C.P. (Irel.), D.P.H., F.R.I.C.; I.M.S. (retd.); *b.* 26 Aug. 1886; *s.* of Evans Boyd, Ruane, New Ross, Co. Wexford; *m.* 1915, Dora, *d.* of Edward Godsall; one *d.* *Educ.:* St. Andrews, Tenby; Coleraine, Ulster. Indian Medical Service, 1908-43; France and Mesopotamia, 1914. Professor of Chemistry Medical Coll., Calcutta; Principal of Medical Coll., Calcutta; Inspector-General of Civil Hospitals, U.P., 1939-43. K.H.S., 1941-43. *Recreation:* yachting. *Address:* 4 Suffolk House, Brassey Road, Bexhill-on-Sea, Sussex. *T.:* Bexhill 4247. *Club:* Royal Calcutta Turf. [*Died* 9 *Nov.* 1967.

BOYD, William, M.A., B.Sc., D.Phil., LL.D.; Reader Emeritus in Education, University of Glasgow, Lecturer and Reader, 1907-46; *b.* Riccarton, Ayrshire, 1874; *m.* 1st, 1905, Isa S. Burt; one *d.*; 2nd, 1919, Dorothy Wilson, M.A.; two *s.* one *d.* *Educ.:* Kilmarnock Academy; Glasgow Univ. M.A. 1896; B.Sc. 1900; D.Phil. 1911; Hon. D.Litt. (Western Australia), 1937; LL.D. (Glasgow) 1945; Asst. Master in Blairgowrie High School, 1900-2; Science Master and Head of the Secondary Department in North Kelvinside Higher Grade School, Glasgow, 1902-7; Headmaster of Colston Public School, Glasgow, 1907; President of the Educational Institute of Scotland, 1920-21; Warden of Glasgow University Students' Settlement and afterwards President; Visiting Prof. of Education in Columbia Univ., New York, 1930-31. Consultant, Third Statistical Account of Scotland, 1947-50. *Publications:* An Introduction to the Republic of Plato, 1904; The Minor Educational Writings of Rousseau, 1911 (enlarged, 1962); The Educational Theory of Rousseau, 1911; From Locke to Montessori, 1914; The History of Western Education, 1921 (enlarged, 1950); Measuring Devices in Composition, Spelling, and Arithmetic, 1924; Edited Towards a New Education (the Report of the World Conference of the New Education Fellowship at Elsinore), 1930; America in School and College, 1933; edited The Challenge of Leisure, 1936; edited Evacuation in Scotland, 1944; (jt.) Ayrshire volume in the Third Statistical Account of Scotland, 1951; Emile for Today, 1956; Education in Ayrshire Through Seven Centuries, 1961; Plato's Republic for Today with Educational Commentary, 1962; also a number of articles on various aspects of child study. *Address:* Duncraig, East Ogwell, Newton Abbot, Devon. [*Died* 28 *Aug* 962

BOYER, Sir Richard (James Fildes), K.B.E., *cr.* 1956; M.A.; Chairman Australian Broadcasting Commission since 1945; *b.* Taree, New South Wales, Australia. 24 Aug. 1891; *s.* of Rev. F. C. Boyer, Manchester, England; *m.* 1920, Elenor Muriel, *d.* of John Underwood, Ashfield, Sydney; one *s.* one *d.* *Educ.:* Newington College, Sydney; University of Sydney (1st Final Honors European History, M.A. 1913). Served Australian Imperial Force 1st Infantry Bn. Gallipoli, France, 1915-18, Lieut. Established sheep-station Western Queensland 1920—personally managed to 1937. President United Graziers' Assoc. of Queensland, 1941-44; President Graziers' Federal Council of Australia, 1941; Vice-Pres. Australian League of Nations Union. Australian delegate Empire Relations Conference, 1938; Empire Producers Conference, Sydney, 1938; World Agricultural Conference, Dresden, 1939;

International Chamber of Commerce, Copenhagen, 1939; Wool Federation Conference, Brussels, 1939; Official Delegate League of Nations Assembly, 1939. Leader Australian Delegation, Pacific Relations Conferences, Montreal, 1942, and Hot Springs, Va., 1945; Delegate British Commonwealth Relations Conference, London, 1945. Hon. Director American Division, Australian Ministry of Information, 1941-45; Commissioner Australian Broadcasting Commission, 1940-45; Pres. Aust. Institute of International Affairs, 1946-48; Leader Aust. Delegation 9th U.N.E.S.C.O. Assembly, New Delhi, 1956. Chm. Cttee. of Inquiry into Commonwealth Public Service Recruitment, 1958-59. Vice-President Elizabethan Theatre Trust. *Address:* A.B.C. Broadcast House, Pitt St., Sydney, N.S.W. *Clubs:* Queensland (Brisbane); Melbourne (Victoria); Australian (Sydney). [*Died* 5 *June* 1961.

BOYLE, (Arthur) Brian, C.B.E. 1945; Q.C. 1958; Barrister-at-law, practising on the North Eastern Circuit; Recorder of Sunderland, 1960; Recorder of Newcastle upon Tyne, 1961; *b.* 16 August 1913; *o. s.* of Colonel Walter Boyle, O.B.E., T.D., and late Mrs. Boyle; unmarried. *Educ.:* Uppingham; Brasenose College, Oxford. 2nd Lieut. T.A., 49th Divisional Signals, 1932; M.A. (Oxon.); called to Bar, Middle Temple, 1936. T.A.R.O. 1938; War of 1939-45: Staff College, Camberley (War Course), 1939; 49th Divisional Signals, 1939-40; 2nd Divisional Signals, 1940; G.S.O. 3, G.H.Q., B.E.F., 1940; War Office, Directorate of Staff Duties, G.S.O. 3, 1940; G.S.O. 2, 1941; G.S.O. 1 (Lt.-Col.) Military Assistant to C.I.G.S. (Field-Marshal Viscount Alanbrooke), 1942-45. *Recreations:* travel, music. *Address:* 42 West Park Grove, Roundhay, Leeds 8. *T.:* 661830; 2 Harcourt Buildings, Temple, E.C.4. *T.:* Central 2548. *Club:* United University. [*Died* 1 *May* 1965.

BOYLE, Rear-Adm. Edward Courtney, V.C. 1915 (Operations in Sea of Marmora); *b.* 1883; *s.* of late Lt.-Col. Edward Boyle. Entered H.M.S. Britannia, 1898; Capt. 1920; Rear-Adm. 1932; retd. 1932. Flag Officer in Charge, London, 1939-1942. Officer Legion of Honour and St. Maurice and St. Lazarus, 1915. *Club:* Sunningdale Golf. [*Died* 16 *Dec.* 1967.

BOYNTON, Sir Griffith Wilfrid Norman, 13th Bart., *cr.* 1618; Comdr. R.N. (retired); *b.* 1889; *s.* of Sir Griffith Boynton, 12th Bt. and Euphemia Violet (*d.* 1930), *d.* of late J. Inglis Chalmers of Aldbar Castle, Brechin; *S.* father, 1937; *m.* 1914, Naomi, *d.* of late H. E. Nightingale. Entered R.N., 1904; served European War, 1914-19. War of 1939-45. *Club:* United Service. [*Died* 10 *March* 1966 (*ext.*).

BRABAZON OF TARA, 1st Baron, *cr.* 1942, of Sandwich; **John Theodore Cuthbert Moore-Brabazon,** P.C. 1940; G.B.E. *cr.* 1953; M.C.; *b.* 8 Feb. 1884; *s.* of Lt.-Col. J. A. H. Moore-Brabazon, of Tara Hall, Co. Meath; *m.* 1906, Hilda Mary, *o. d.* of late Charles H. Krabbé, Buenos Ayres; one *s.* (and one *s.* decd.). *Educ.:* Harrow; Trinity Coll., Camb. M.P. (U.) Chatham Div. of Rochester, 1918-29, Wallasey, 1931-42; Parly. Sec. to Min. of Transport, 1923-24, and Nov. 1924-27; Minister of Transport, 1940-1941; Minister of Aircraft Production, 1941-42; pioneer motorist and aviator; winner of Circuit des Ardennes motor race, 1907; first English aviator; holds No. 1 Certificate granted by the Royal Aero Club for pilots; won the Daily Mail £1000 for flying a circular mile on an all-English-made machine, 1909; also the first British Empire Michelin Cup. Served European War, 1914-1918 (despatches thrice, M.C., Legion of Honour); Lt.-Col.; responsible for the R.F.C. Photographic Section during the War and the development of aerial photography. Member of the original Civil Aviation Committee; Lord Weir's Advisory Committee; Chairman of the Air Mails Committee, 1923; Assessor R 101 Enquiry, 1930-31; President: Royal Aeronautical Society, 1935; Royal Aero Club, 1943-64; Royal Institution, 1948-63. Member L.C.C. St. George's Division, Westminster, 1931-32; President, English Golf Union, 1938; Capt. Royal and Ancient (St. Andrews), 1952-53; Pres. Professional Golfers' Assoc., 1954; Winner of Curzon Cup, St. Moritz, 1920, 1922, 1927; Chairman A.C.V.; Director: Kodak; E.M.I.; David Brown Corporation Ltd.; Leyland Motors; Chairman: Committee on post-war civil aircraft; Air Registration Bd.; Air Safety Bd.; President, Radio Industry Council. Gold Medal, Royal Aero Club, 1959; Wakefield Gold Medal (R.Ae.S.), 1963. Hon. LL.D. St. Andrews, 1959. *Publications:* The Brabazon Story, 1956; Glastonbury: a Legend (play), 1963. *Recreations:* golf, tobogganing, yachting. *Heir: s.* Hon. Derek Charles Moore-Brabazon, C.B.E. *Address:* 20 Berkeley Square, W.1. *T.:* Grosvenor 2326. *Clubs:* White's; Royal Yacht Squadron (Cowes). [*Died* 17 *May* 1964.

BRACKENBURY, Rev. Basil V. F.; *b.* 1889; *s.* of late Rev. F. Brackenbury; *m.* 1920, Evelyn, *d.* of late F. Winch, Cranbrook, Kent. *Educ.:* Dover College; Queens' College, Cambridge. Assistant Master at Rossall School, 1914-16; Housemaster, Marlborough College, 1916-28; Chaplain, 1927-1928; Headmaster of St. Lawrence College, Ramsgate, 1928-37; Headmaster of Grammar School, Ramsgate, 1938-47; Vicar of Freeland, April-Oct. 1955; resigned, 1955. Chm. of Council of Croquet Assoc., 1956-58. *Address:* Patchwork, Watlington, Oxford. *Club:* Hurlingham. [*Died* 26 *July* 1965.

BRACEGIRDLE, Rear-Adm. Sir Leighton Seymour; *see* Addenda: II.

BRACKENRIDGE, Sir Alexander, K.B.E. 1959 (C.B.E. 1951); M.C. and Bar, 1918; President, Morton Sundour Co. Inc., New York, 1943-63, retd.; *b.* Larkhall, Scotland, 14 June 1893; *s.* of Alexander Brackenridge and Catherine Hastie; *m.* 1923, Alice, *d.* of John Hogg, Cambuslang, Scotland; one *s.* two *d.* *Educ.:* Larkhall Acad.; Royal Technical Coll., Glasgow. Served European War, Scottish Horse Brigade, Royal Naval Division, 1915-1919. President, British Commonwealth Chamber of Commerce in the U.S.A., 1947-1951; Chairman U.S.A. Committee Scottish Council (Development and Industry), 1948-1963; Director: Bowater Paper Co. Inc., New York; Bowaters Southern Paper Corporation (U.S.A.), 1951-63; Josiah Wedgwood and Sons, Inc., 1951-63; Bowater Corporation of N. America Ltd. Member (in U.S.A.): of Dollar Exports Bd., 1950-51; of Dollar Exports Council, 1951-60. *Recreation:* golf. *Address:* 227 Turrell Avenue, South Orange, New Jersey, U.S.A. *Clubs:* Rockefeller Centre (New York); Rock Spring (West Orange, N.J.). [*Died* 22 *May* 1964.

BRADBEER, Sir Albert (Frederick), Kt. 1960; J.P.; *b.* 20 Nov. 1890; *s.* of Frank Bradbeer, compositor, and Cecilia (*née* Jones); *m.* 1919, Mary Cameron, Arpafeelie, Ross-shire. *Educ.:* St. Jude's Church School, Dalston, London; Noel Park Board School, N. London; Dame Alice Owen's School, Islington; King's College, London (evenings); London School of Economics (evenings). Alderman, Birmingham City Council, 1945; Lord Mayor of Birmingham, 1946-47. J.P. Birmingham, 1949. Freeman of the City of Birmingham, 1960. Birmingham Civic Soc. Gold Medal, 1951. *Publications:* articles in the press. *Recreations:* music, gardening. *Address:* 54 Woodbrooke Rd., Bournville, Birmingham 30. *T.:* Selly Oak 1748. [*Died* 15 *March* 1963.

BRADBURY, Surg. Rear-Adm. (Retd.) William, C.B.E. 1937; D.S.O. 1918; M.B.; R.N., retd. 1946; *b.* 1884; *y. s.* of Samuel Bradbury, Lisburn, Ireland; *m.* 1918, Norah Michael, *y. d.* of G. M. Williams; one *s.* (and one *s.* decd.). *Educ.:* Queen's College, Belfast. Served China, 1913 (medal); European War, with R.N.D. in Gallipoli and France, 1914-19 (despatches, D.S.O.). *Address:* c/o Admiralty, S.W.1. [*Died* 22 *Oct.* 1966.

BRADDELL, Darcy; *see* Braddell, T. A. D.

BRADDELL, Sir Roland (St. John), Kt., *cr.* 1948; Hon. D.Litt. (Malaya); M.A. (Oxon), F.R.G.S., F.R.A.S., F.R.S.A.; Advocate and Solicitor, Singapore and Federation of Malaya; *b.* 20 Dec. 1880; *e. s.* of late Sir Thomas De Multon Lee Braddell, Chief Judicial Commissioner, Federated Malay States, and Violet Ida Nassau; *m.* 1st, Dulcie Sylvia (decd.), *o. d.* of Dr. Lyttelton Stuart Forbes-Winslow, D.C.L., LL.D., M.D.; one *s.*; 2nd, Estell Vernon, *y. d.* of Isaac Payton, Montpelier, Vermont, U.S.A.; one *d.* *Educ.:* The King's School, Canterbury; Worcester College, Oxford. B.A., 2nd Class Hons. Jurisprudence, 1904; Barrister-at-Law, Middle Temple, 1905; Municipal Commissioner, Singapore, 1914-18; Member Housing Commission, Singapore (thanks of Secretary of State); Exec. Council and Council of State, Johore, 1932-40; Exec. Council, Singapore, 1949-50; First Class (Sri Paduka) of Order of Crown of Johore, 1947; legal adviser to United Malays National Organization during negotiations for Federation of Malaya (thanks of Sec. of State); has served on many Govt. Cttees and Commissions in Singapore. Chairman of Council, Univ. of Malaya, 1949-51 Pres. Malayan Branch, Royal Asiatic Soc., 1948-51; Private Legal Adviser to Conference of Rulers, Federation of Malaya 1948-51 1954-. *Publications:* Laws of the Straits Settlements, 2nd ed., 1931; Legal Status of the Malay States, 1931; Common Gaming Houses, 2nd ed., 1932; The Lights of Singapore, 6th ed., 1947; (co-editor and contrib.) One Hundred Years of Singapore, 1921; historical papers in Journal, Malayan Branch, Royal Asiatic Soc.; many Press articles *Address:* 85 Oakwood Court, Kensington W.14. [*Died* 15 *Nov.* 1966.

BRADDELL, (Rhomas Arthur) Darcy, F.S.A., F.R.I.B.A.; Architect; *b.* 4 Mar. 1884; 2nd *s.* of late Sir Thomas Braddell; *m.* 1914, Dorothy Adelaide Bussé; one *s.* one *d.* *Educ.:* St. Paul's School. Articled to late Sir Ernest George, R.A., 1902-05; entered private practice with H. Deane, 1910. Principally known as a designer of domestic architecture and interior decoration. Chief works comprise: Potter Street Hill, Northwood; Weston Corbett Place; Woodfalls, Romsey; Barleys, Offham; Creek House, Barton-on-Sea; Greatford Hall, Stamford; Lake House, Amesbury; Woodhall Park, Herts.; town houses in Chelsea Square, Lees Place, Cheyne Place; housing schemes at Sunbury-on-Thames; Great Hall, The King's School, Canterbury. Vice-President R.I.B.A., 1937; Vice-Chairman Architects Registration Council, U.K., 1937-44; Chm. R.I.B.A. Bd. of Architectural Education, 1935-38. Late External Examiner School of Architecture, Liverpool Univ. and Sheffield Univ.; late Mem. of Bd. of Studies and External Examiner, London Univ. Master, Art Workers' Guild, 1949. *Publication:* How to look at Buildings, 1932. *Address:* 8 Lansdowne Rd., Holland Park, W.11. *T.:* Park 5487. *Club:* Athenæum. [*Died* 20 *Feb.* 1970.

BRADDOCK, Mrs. Elizabeth Margaret, J.P.; M.P. (Lab.) Exchange Div. of Liverpool since 1945; Member Liverpool City Council, 1930-61, Alderman, 1955-61; *b.* 1899; *d.* of late Mary Bamber, J.P., National Organiser, N.U.D.A.W., and Hugh Bamber; *m.* 1922, John Braddock (*d.* 1963), Alderman, Leader Liverpool City Council; no *c.* *Educ.:* Liverpool Elementary. President Liverpool Trades and Labour Council, 1944. Director, Securicor North-West, 1967-. *Publication:* (with Jack Braddock) The Braddocks. *Recreations:* reading, housekeeping. *Address:* 2 Zigzag Road, Liverpool 12. *T.:* Stoneycroft 1247 [*Died* 13 *Nov.* 1970.

BRADDOCK, Geoffrey Frank, C.M.G. 1941; O.B.E. 1931; *b.* 9 Jan. 1881; *s.* of late George William Braddock, Martham, Norfolk; *m.* 1910, Mary (*d.* 1946), *d.* of late Hugh Mair, Borough Engineer of Hammersmith; (one *s.* decd.) *Educ.:* Latymer Upper School; privately. Entered Commercial Intelligence Branch of Board of Trade, 1914; lent to Army Contracts Dept. of War Office, 1915; Trade Officer, Dept. of Overseas Trade, 1917; Senior Trade officer, 1920; H.M. Trade Commissioner, Toronto, 1924-28; Assistant Director, Dept. of Overseas Trade, 1929-36; United Kingdom Trade Commissioner, Dublin, 1937-41; Senior United Kingdom Trade Commissioner in Eire, 1942-46; retd., 1946; conducted official mission in United States, Cuba, Brazil, Uruguay, Argentina, Chile, Peru, and Bolivia, 1918-19. *Recreations:* golf and gardening. *Address:* Kilteragh Mansions, Foxrock, Co. Dublin, Eire. *T.:* Dublin 893312. *Clubs:* Devonshire; Stephen's Green (Dublin); Royal Irish Yacht. [*Died* 13 *June* 1966.

BRADFIELD, Lt.-Gen. Sir Ernest W. C., K.C.I.E., *cr.* 1941 (C.I.E. 1928); O.B.E. 1918; I.M.S., retired; Hon. Indian Red Cross Commissioner in England, 1940; Knight Order of St. John of Jerusalem; *b.* 28 May 1880; *s.* of W. C. Bradfield, Moseley; *m.* Margaret Annie, *d.* of H. A. Barnard, Olton; two *d.* *Educ.:* London University, M.B., M.S. F.R.C.S. Ed.; F.R.C.S. 1962. Joined I.M.S. 1903; Prof. of Surgery in Medical Coll., 1924, and Superintendent of Government General Hospital, Madras; served N.W. Frontier of India, 1908 (medal with clasp); European War, 1914-1921; Mesopotamia, 1918-19 (despatches); operations against Upper Mohmands, 1933 (despatches); Assist. Director of Medical Services 1932-35; Surgeon-General, Bombay, 1935-37; Hon. Surgeon to the King 1935-39; Director-General I.M.S. 1937-39; retd., 1939; President Medical Council of India, 1937-39; Chairman, Tuberculosis Association of India in 1939, and Lady Minto's Indian Nursing Association, 1937-39; Surgeon-in-Chief, St. John Ambulance Brigade Overseas (India), 1937-39; Medical Adviser to Sec. of State and President Medical Board, India Office, 1939-46; Chairman Indian Red Cross Society, 1938-39. *Address:* 18 Exeter House, Putney Heath, S.W.15. *Club:* East India and Sports. [*Died* 26 *Oct.* 1963.

BRADFORD, Sir Thomas Andrews, Kt., *cr.* 1939; D.S.O. 1916; D.L.; J.P.; D.C.L. (Durham); late The York and Lancaster Regiment; *b.* 23 March 1886; *e. s.* of George Bradford, Milbanke, Darlington; *m.* 1915, Honor Rebe (*d.* 1943), *d.* of Colonel W. C. Blackett, Sacriston, Durham; one *s.*; *m.* 1945, Kathleen, *widow* of Col. Joscelyn E. S. Percy, D.S.O., M.C., and *d.* of late Vernon Ross. *Educ.:* Royal Naval School, Kent. Joined 8th Battalion The Durham Light Infantry, 1906; Captain, 1910; served European War, 1914-18 (wounded, despatches twice, D.S.O.); Brigade Major; contested (C.) Seaham Harbour and Durham Divisions; Sheriff of County Durham, 1942. *Recreations:* played cricket and Rugby football for Durham County for several years; field sports generally. *Address:* Aden Cottage, Durham. *Club:* Army and Navy. [*Died* 29 *Dec.* 1966.

BRADLEY, Col. Edward de Winton Herbert, C.B.E. 1948; D.S.O. 1919; M.C. 1917; D.L.; *b.* 1889; *m.* 1914, Margery, *d.* of late A. W. Moore, C.V.O.; one *s.* one *d.* *Educ.:* Marlborough. Late the K.O.Y.L.I. and Royal Signals; served European War, 1914-19 (despatches, D.S.O., M.C.); Col. 1933; Chief Signal Officer, Southern Command, 1934-38; retired pay, 1938. Secretary W. Lancs. T.A. and A.F. Assoc., 1938-49. D.L. County of Lancaster. *Address:* Ross Cottage, Sutton Benger, nr. Chippenham, Wilts. *T.:* Seagry 227. [*Died* 29 *Jan.* 1964.

BRADLEY, Leslie Ripley, C.B. 1961; C.B.E. 1947 (O.B.E. 1938; M.B.E. 1920); F.M.A., 1952; Director, Imperial War Museum, 1938-60, retd.; *b.* 22 October 1892; *m.*; one *s.* *Educ.:* Christ's Hospital; St. John's College, Oxford; R.M.C., Sandhurst. Served France, Middlesex Regiment, 1915-16; joined Staff of Imperial War Museum, 1917; Curator and Secretary, 1933-38. *Address:* 84 Ashurst Road, Cockfosters, Barnet, Herts. [*Died* 26 *Jan.* 1968.

BRADLEY, Lieut.-Colonel Robert Anstruther, C.M.G. 1919, late Prince of Wales' North Stafford Regt.; Lt.-Col. on retirement; *e. s.* of late Brig.-General C. E. Bradley, C.B.; *g.s.* of Major-General John Bradley, *g.-g.s.* of Dean Bradley of Merival and Atherston, Warwickshire; *m.* 1st, 1908, Marjory Fontaine, *y. d.* of T. Winch, Rochester; one *d.*; 2nd, 1930, Bridget, *d.* of late E. H. Clutterbuck, J.P., Hardenhuish Park, Chippenham. *Educ.:* Privately and in France. Served S. African War in 1st Argyll and Sutherland Highlanders (Queen's medal 5 bars, King's medal 2 bars); 2nd Lieutenant Prince of Wales's N. Stafford Regt., 1901; Operations S. Nigeria, 1902-3 (African General Service Medal and bar); European War in France, Egypt and Mesopotamia in Royal Flying Corps as Pilot; actions including advance on Kut, Relief of Kut; Major, 1916; commanded Royal Air Force, Mesopotamia and Persia, 1918-19 (despatches three times); Lieut.-Col. R.A.F., 1918. *Recreation:* yachting. *Address:* Butt Green Cottage, Painswick, Glos. [*Died* 7 *June* 1965.

BRADLEY-BIRT, Francis Bradley, M.A.; F.R.G.S.; *b.* 25 June 1874; *e. s.* of late John Bradley-Birt of Birtsmoreton Court, and The Berrow, Worcestershire; *m.* 1920, Lady Norah Spencer-Churchill (*d.* 1946), *d.* of 8th Duke of Marlborough and of Alberta, Marchioness of Blandford. *Educ.:* Brasenose College, Oxford. M.A. (Honours in History), 1896; M.A. 1941; entered Inner Temple, 1895; I.C.S. 1898; Asst. Magistrate and Collector, Bengal; several times on special duty as Magistrate and Collector, Khulna, Midnapore, Hooghly, and Calcutta; services lent to Commander-in-Chief in India; Lt.-Col. (despatches) 1918; Assistant Director of Local Resources, Mesopotamia; specially attached to British Legation, Teheran; Member of the Legislative Assembly of India, 1921-23; contested (C.) Merthyr Tydfil, 1929; President, Worcestershire Archaeological Society, 1939-42; Chm. Worcestershire Assoc., 1955-57. Is lord of the manors of Birtsmoreton and Berrow, and patron of Birtsmoreton, Worcestershire. *Publications:* Chota Nagpore, a little-known Province of the Empire, 1903; The Story of an Indian Upland, 1905; The Romance of an Eastern Capital, 1906; Through Persia from the Gulf to the Caspian, 1909; Twelve Men of Bengal, 1910; Sylhet Thackeray, 1911; Bengal Fairy Tales, 1920; Henry Louis Vivian Derozio, 1923: An Anthology of English Verse through Eight Centuries, 1925; Tewkesbury, 1931; A Worcestershire Anthology, 1934. *Address:* Birtsmoreton Court, Worcestershire. *Clubs:* Athenæum, Authors', 1900. [*Died* 11 *June* 1963.

BRADSHAW, Constance H., R.B.A.; R.O.I. *y. d.* of William Henry Bradshaw, M.A. (Cantab.), Bowdon, Cheshire. *Educ.:* Spenlove School. Exhibitor R.A., Paris Salon, Canada, New Zealand, and principal Provincial Galleries. Acting President Society of Women Artists, 1936-39. President of New Sussex Art Club. *Address:* Rostherne, Southlands Road, Bickley, Kent. *T.:* Ravensbourne 0374. *Club:* Forum. [*Died* 30 *Dec.* 1961.

BRADSHAW, Professor Eric, M.B.E. 1952; M.Sc.Tech., Ph.D.; M.I.E.E.; Professor of Electrical Engineering in the Faculty of Technology, University of Manchester, since 1952; *b.* 24 July 1909; 2nd *s.* of late Sir William Bradshaw; *m.* 1935, Joyce Ena Smith; no *c.* *Educ.:* King's School, Grantham; Manchester University. With British Thomson-Houston Co., Rugby, 1931-32; on staff of Royal Technical College, Glasgow, 1932-44; Lecturer and Senior Lecturer in High Voltage Engineering, Coll. of Technology, Manchester, 1944-52. Chm., N.W. Centre of Institution of Electrical Engineers, 1954-55; Organiser and Editor of Bulletin of Electrical Engineering Education (founded 1948). *Publications:* Electrical Units, 1952; papers in Proc. I.E.E. and other journals. *Address:* Lindis, Winnington Rd., Marple, Ches. [*Died* 15 *Aug.* 1961.

BRADSHAW, Maj.-Gen. William Pat Arthur, C.B. 1946; D.S.O. 1917; *b.* 8 March 1897; *s.* of late Arthur Bradshaw, 30 Park Lane, W.; *m.* 1938, Hon. Sybil Mary Cadman, *yr. d.* of 1st Baron Cadman, G.C.M.G., F.R.S.; two *s.* two *d.* *Educ.:* Eton; R.M.C. Sandhurst. Entered Scots Guards, 1914; served European War, Belgium, France, 1915-17 (despatches, D.S.O.); staff, Viceroy of India, A.D.C., 1928-29; commanded 2nd Bn. Scots Guards, 1935-38; Officer Commanding Scots Guards Regiment and Regimental District, 1938-39; Commanded Infantry Brigade, 1939-41; Commanded Infantry Division, 1942-45; retired, 1946. *Address:* Turweston Glebe, Brackley, Northants. *T.:* Brackley 2140. *Clubs:* Turf, Buck's. [*Died* 9 *April* 1966.

BRADSTOCK, Major George, D.S.O. 1919; M.C.; Chairman and Managing Director University Motors Ltd., 40 Conduit Street, W.1; *g. s.* of late Rev. J. R. Bradstock; *m.* Ursula Mary (*d.* 1957), *d.* of FitzHerbert Wright, The Hayes, Derbyshire; three *s.* *Educ.:* Blundell's School, Tiverton; Jesus College, Cambridge. Served in Royal Artillery, 1914-1919; served European War, 1914-19 (despatches, D.S.O., M.C. and bar). *Address:* Yokehurst, South Chailey, nr. Lewes, Sussex. *T.:* Plumpton 245. *Club:* Oxford and Cambridge. [*Died* 23 *March* 1966.

BRAIN, 1st Baron *cr.* 1962, of Eynsham; **Walter Russell Brain;** Bt. 1954; Kt. 1952; F.R.S. 1964 (Council, 1965); D.M. Oxon.; F.R.C.P. Lond.; Hon. F.R.C.P.Ed. and I.; Hon. F.R.C.S. Eng.; Hon. F.R.C.O.G.; Hon. F.R.A.C.P.; Hon. F.A.C.P.; Hon. F.C.P.S.A.; Hon. F.R.C.P.S.(G.); Hon. F.F.R.; Hon. F.B.Ps.S.; Hon. D.Sc.: Oxford, Manchester, Southampton; Hon. LL.D.: Wales, Belfast; Hon. D.C.L. Durham; Consulting Physician to London Hospital and to Maida Vale Hospital for Nervous Diseases; Member: Association of Physicians (President 1956); Association of British Neurologists (Pres. 1960); Internat. Soc. of Internal Medicine (Pres. 1958); American, French, German and Spanish Neurological Societies; Swiss Academy of Medicine; Hon. Fellow, New College, Oxford; Editor, Brain; Mem., Royal Commissions on Marriage and Divorce, Law relating to Mental Illness and Medical Services of Newfoundland and Labrador; *b.* 23 Oct. 1895; *s.* of Walter John Brain, Reading, and Edith Alice Smith; *m.* Stella, *er. d.* of Reginald

L. Langdon-Down, M.B.; two *s.* one *d.* *Educ.:* Mill Hill School; New College, Oxford; London Hospital. Theodore Williams Scholar in Physiology at the University of Oxford; Price Entrance Scholar in Anatomy and Physiology, the London Hospital; Bradshaw Lecturer, R.C.P., 1945; Harveian Orator, 1959; Manson Lecturer, British Inst. Philosophy, 1946 and 1960; Galton Lecturer, Eugenics Society, 1948; Rede Lecturer, Cambridge Univ., 1952; Riddell Lecturer, Durham Univ., 1958; Hughlings Jackson Lecturer, 1961. Osler Medal, Univ. of Oxford, 1961. Pres., R.C.P., 1950-1957; Pres., British Assoc., 1963; Pres., Family Planning Assoc.; Chm., Advisory Cttee. on Distinction Awards. *Publications:* Man, Society and Religion, 1944; Recent Advances in Neurology (7th Edn. 1962); Diseases of the Nervous System (6th Edn. 1962); Clinical Neurology (2nd Edn. 1964). Mind, Perception and Science, 1951; Tea with Walter de la Mare, 1957; The Nature of Experience, 1959; Some Reflections on Genius, 1960; Speech Disorders (2nd edn.), 1965; Doctors Past and Present, 1964; Science and Man, 1966. *Recreations:* bird watching, gardening. *Heir:* *s.* Hon. Christopher Langdon Brain [*b.* 30 Aug 1926; *m.* 1953, Susan Mary Morris]. *Address:* 86 Harley Street, W.1. *T.:* Welbeck 2215; Hillmorton, Coombe Hill Road, Kingston-upon-Thames. *T.:* Malden 5325. *Clubs:* Athenæum, Savile. [*Died* 29 *Dec.* 1966.

BRAINTREE, 1st Baron, *cr.* 1948; **Valentine George Crittall;** Kt. 1930; J.P.; Chairman Crittall Manufacturing Company, Ltd., Darlington and Simpson Rolling Mills, Ltd., and other Companies; *b.* Braintree, Essex, 28 June 1884; *s.* of late Francis Henry Crittall, J.P.; *m.* 1st, 1915, Olive Lillian (*d.* 1932), *d.* of late Charles Landay MacDermott, Comber, Ont., Can.; three *d.*; 2nd, 1933, Lydia Mabel (*d.* 1947), *d.* of Julian John Revy, and *widow* of Frank C. R. Reed, Hankow, China; 3rd, 1955, Mrs. Phyllis Dorothy Parker, Owls Hall, Blackmore End, Braintree. *Educ.:* Uppingham. Director, Bank of England, 1948-55; Past President Institution of Works Managers; M.P. (Lab.) Maldon Div., 1923-24; Parly. Private Sec. to Minister for Air, 1924. *Heir:* none. *Address:* Queen's Meadow, Bocking, Braintree, Essex. [*Died* 21 *May* 1961 (*ext.*).

BRAITHWAITE, Vice-Admiral Lawrence Walter, C.M.G. 1919; *b.* July 1878; *s.* of late Rev. J. M. Braithwaite, Vicar of Croydon; *m.* 1903; two *d.* *Educ.:* Hildersham House, Broadstairs; H.M.S. Britannia. Served as midshipman in H.M.S. Nile on the Mediterranean Station, 1894-97; Sub-Lieut. in H.M.S. Endymion on China Section, 1899-1900; landed with Adm. Seymour expedition during Boxer rising (severely wounded; specially promoted to Lieut. Nov. 1900); Commander, 1913; Commander of H.M.S. Cumberland, 1913-16; Naval Assistant to 4th Sea Lord at Admiralty, 1917-19; Captain, 1917; Flag Capt. and Chief of Staff to Commander-in-Chief, East Indies, 1919-21; Chief of Staff to the Commander-in-Chief, Plymouth Station; Senior Officer of the Reserve Fleet at the Nore, 1925-26; Commodore and Chief of Staff to Commander-in-Chief, China Station, 1927-29; retired list, 1929; Vice-Admiral, retired list, 1934. J.P. Plymouth, 1938. *Address:* 9 Penlee Gardens, Stoke, Devonport, Plymouth. *Clubs:* Army and Navy; Royal Western Yacht (Plymouth). [*Died* 18 *Jan.* 1961.

BRALEY, Rev. Evelyn Foley, O.B.E. 1958; M.A., LL.M.Cantab.; M.A. Wadham College, Oxon; LL.D. 1932; Canon Residentiary of Worcester since 1947; *b.* 15 Oct. 1884; *s.* of Francis Braley of Aylestone Park, Leicester; *m.* 1925, Margaret Isabel, *e. d.* of late E. C. Sawyer, Heywood Lodge, Berks, and Water Eaton Manor, Oxon; one *d.* *Educ.:* Downing College, Cambridge. Assistant Curate of Rushden, Northants, 1910-13; Secretary of Church of England Sunday School Institute, 1913-15; 2nd Master of Duke's School, Alnwick, 1915-16; Director of Religious Education in the Diocese of Southwell, 1916-20; Vice-Principal and Master of Method of Culham Training College, Oxford, 1920-25; Professor of Education, 1935-39, and Lecturer in Modern History in Durham Univ., 1926-39; Principal of the College of the Venerable Bede, Durham, 1925-47; Hon. Canon of Durham Cathedral, 1936-47. *Publications:* Church Teaching for the Christian Year; Sir Hobbard de Hoy; A Sunday School in Utopia; The State and Religious Education; The Teaching of Religion; A Policy in Religious Education; The School without the Parson; The Life and Teaching of Jesus; The Letters of Herbert Hensley Henson; More Letters of Herbert Hensley Henson. *Recreations:* fishing, gardening. *Address:* The Old Precentory, College Yard, Worcester. *T.:* 24874. [*Died* 17 *March* 1963.

BRAMBELL, Francis William Rogers, C.B.E. 1966; F.R.S. 1949; D.Sc. London; M.R.I.A.; Lloyd Roberts Professor of Zoology, University College of North Wales, Bangor, University of Wales, 1930-68, Emeritus Professor, 1968; *b.* Sandycove, Co. Dublin, 1901; *er. s.* of L. A. Brambell; *m.* 1927, Margaret Lilian, *e.d.* of W. Adgie, F.C.A., Leeds; one *s.* one *d.* *Educ.:* Aravon Sch.; Trinity Coll., Dublin (Foundation Scholar and Sen. Moderator in Natural Science); University Coll., London. Scholar, Royal Commn. for Exhibn. of 1851, 1924-26; Fellow, Internat. Educn. Bd., 1926-27; Lectr. in Zoology, King's Coll., London, 1927-30. Fellow, U.C.L. Pres., Section D, British Assoc. for the Advancement of Science, 1955; Chm., Technical Cttee. to inquire into conditions in intensive systems of livestock husbandry, 1964-65; Mem. Council, A.R.C., 1959-69. Hon. Dir., Unit of Embryology, Bangor, 1953-68. Mem., U.G.C., 1960-68. Ingleby Lectr., Univ. of Birmingham, 1966. Sc.D. *h.c.* Dublin, 1966. Royal Medal of Royal Soc., 1964. *Publications:* The Development of Sex in Vertebrates, 1930; Antibodies and Embryos, 1952; The Transmission of Passive Immunity from Mother to Young, 1970; various papers on cytology, sex-determination, mammalian reproduction and immunology, in scientific jls. *Recreation:* fishing. *Address:* Y Gwylain, Bangor, Caernarvonshire. *T.:* Bangor 3094. *Club:* Athenæum. [*Died* 6 *June* 1970.

BRAND, 1st Baron, *cr.* 1946, of Eydon; **Robert Henry Brand,** C.M.G. 1910; Hon. D.C.L. Oxford, 1937; *b.* 30 Oct. 1878; 4th (3rd *surv.*) *s.* of 2nd Viscount Hampden; *m.* 1917, Phyllis (*d.* 1937), *d.* of Chiswell Dabney Langhorne, of Virginia; two *d.* (one *s.* killed in action, 1945). *Educ.:* Marlborough; New Coll., Oxford. Fellow of All Souls Coll., Oxford; Hon. Fellow New College, Oxford. Served in South Africa 1902-9, first under Lord Milner, as Secretary of the Inter-Colonial Council of the Transvaal and Orange River Colony and Secretary of the Railway Committee of the Central South African Railways; then under Lord Selborne, and later under General Botha; Secretary to the Transvaal Delegates at the South African National Convention, 1908-9; member of the Imperial Munitions Board of Canada, 1915-18; Deputy-Chairman British Mission in Washington for nine months, 1917-18; Financial Adviser to Lord Robert Cecil, when Chairman of Supreme Economic Council, Peace Conference, Paris, 1919; Vice-Pres., International Financial Conference of League of Nations, Brussels, Sept. 1920; Financial Representative of South Africa at the Genoa Conference, 1922; member of Expert Committee advising German Government on stabilisation of the mark, 1922; Member of Macmillan Committee on Finance and Industry, 1930-31; Head of British Food Mission, Washington, Mar. 1941-May 1944, Representative of H.M. Treasury in Washington, May 1944-May 1946; Chairman, British Supply Council in North America, April-Nov. 1942, and June 1945-March 1946; U.K. delegate at Bretton Woods and Savannah Conferences. Mem. B.B.C. Gen. Advisory Council, 1951-56. President of Royal Economic Society, 1952-1953. Chairman, North British and Mercantile Insurance Co. Ltd. until 1957; Director of Lazard Bros. & Co. Ltd., until 1960; Director of Times Publishing Co. Ltd., until 1959; formerly Dir. of Lloyds Bank Ltd. *Publications:* The Union of South Africa, 1909; War and National Finance, 1921. *Address:* Eydon Hall, Eydon, nr. Rugby. *T.:* Byfield 282; 11 Old Broad Street, E.C.2. *Clubs:* Brooks's, Athenæum. [*Died* 23 *Aug.* 1963 (*ext.*).

BRAND, Maj-Gen. Charles Henry, C.B. 1918; C.M.G. 1916; C.V.O. 1927; D.S.O. 1915; *b.* 4 Sept. 1873; *s.* of late Charles Hayman Brand of Topsham, Exeter; *m.* Ella Arline, *d.* of late Charles Armstrong, Charters Towers, Queensland; two *d.* Served South African War, 1900-1 (Queen's medal 5 clasps); European War, Dardanelles, 1914-15; Western Front, 1916-1918 (Bt. Lt.-Col. and Bt.-Col., despatches eight times, C.M.G., C.B., D.S.O.); Second Chief of General Staff, Australian Military Forces, 1926-30; Quartermaster-General, Australian Military Forces, 1930-32; Additional A.D.C. to the King, 1931-33; retired, 1933; Senator for Victoria, 1934-47. *Address:* 1 Monomeith Avenue, Toorak, Melbourne, S.E.2, Australia. [*Died* 31 *July* 1961.

BRAND, Air Vice-Marshal Sir (Christopher Joseph) Quintin, K.B.E., *cr.* 1920; D.S.O. 1918; M.C., D.F.C.; R.A.F. (retd.); *grand-nephew* of late Sir John Brand; *b.* Beaconsfield, nr. Kimberley, 25 May 1893; *s.* of E. C. J. Brand, late Inspector C.I.D., Johannesburg; *m.* 1920, Marie (*d.* 1941), *d.* of late P. W. Vaughan, Somerset House, Goodmayes; one *s.* one *d.* (and one *s.* decd.); *m.* 1943, Mildred, *d.* of late P. W. Vaughan, Somerset House, Goodmayes, Essex; one *d.* *Educ.:* Marist Brothers, Johannesburg. Served European War, 1914-1919 (despatches, D.S.O., M.C., D.F.C.); destroyed a Gotha in the last air raid on England; flew from London to Cape Town, 1920; Director General of Aviation, Egypt, 1932-36; Director of Repair and Maintenance, Air Ministry, 1937-39; commanded No. 10 Fighter Group (Battle of Britain), 1939-41; retired, Nov. 1943. *Address:* Quo Vadis, P.O. Box 415, Umtali, Rhodesia. [*Died* 7 *March* 1968.

BRAND, Air Vice-Marshal Sir Quintin; *see* Brand, Air V-M. Sir C. J. Q.

BRANDON, Col. Oscar Gilbert, C.M.G. 1919; D.S.O. 1916; late R.E.; *b.* 1876; *m.* 1903, Margaret Irene (*d.* 1941), *e. d.* of C. Mordaunt Matthew; one *s.* two *d.*; *m.* 1949, Valerie Edith, *d.* of late C. G. H. de Mattos. Joined Army, 1896; Capt., 1905; Major, 1914; Lt.-Col., 1922; Col., 1926; Public Works Department, Railways in India, 1899-1903; Adjutant, South Midland R.E., 1911-1914; served European War (wounded, despatches seven times, C.M.G., D.S.O., Order of Crown of Belgium, Bt. Lt.-Col., 1918); Member of Royal Engineer Board, 1927-28; Deputy Chief Engineer, Eastern Command, 1928-32; retired pay, 1932. *Address:* c/o Lloyds Bank, 6 Pall Mall, S.W.1. [*Died* 16 *Oct.* 1968.

BRAQUE, Georges; French painter, sculptor and engraver; *b.* 1882. Served European War, 1914-18. First exhibited at Salon d'Automne and Salon des Indépendants, 1906; has frequently exhibited in French and foreign galleries since then. Is an exponent of classical cubism. Works represented in: Tate Gallery, Musée National d'Art Moderne, Paris, Museum of Modern Art, New York, Phillips Coll., Washington, D.C., Kunstmuseum, Bâle, Guggenheim Foundation, N.Y., and in other galleries and private collections. Grand Officier de la Légion d'Honneur. Dr. (*h.c.*) Oxford, 1956. Corresp. Member Argentine Acad. of Fine Arts, 1948. He completed three paintings on ceiling in the Louvre, 1953. Exhibition, Musée du Louvre, 1961. Has been awarded: Carnegie Prize, 1937; 1st Prize of Internat. Exhibition, San Francisco, 1939; Grand Prix, Internat. Venice Biennale, 1948, Prix de la Fondation Feltrinelli de l'Académie des Beaux-Arts de Rome 1958, etc. *Address:* c/o Curator, Galerie Maeght, 13 Rue de Téhéran, Paris VIII. [*Died* 31 *Aug.* 1963.

BRASSEY OF APETHORPE, 2nd Baron, *cr.* 1938; **Bernard Thomas Brassey,** Bt. 1922; M.C. 1945; T.D.; D.L.; Lt.-Col. late comdg. Leicestershire Yeomanry; *b.* 15 Feb. 1905; 5th and *er. surv. s.* of 1st Baron Brassey of Apethorpe and Lady Violet Mary Gordon Lennox (*d.* 1946), 2nd *d.* of 7th Duke of Richmond and Gordon; *S.* father 1958; *m.* 1st, 1931, (Crystal) Gloria (*d.* 1962), *d.* of late Lt.-Col. Francis William George Gore and Lady Constance Gore; two *s.*; 2nd, 1963, Barbara Westmorland, *y. d.* of late Leonard Jörgensen. *Educ.:* Eton. Served War of 1939-45 in North-Western Europe (wounded, M.C.); Lt.-Col., 1945. D.L. Northamptonshire, 1958; Hon. Col. The Leicestershire and Derbyshire Yeomanry, T.A., 1962-. *Heir:* *s.* Hon. David Henry Brassey [*b.* 16 Sept. 1932; *m.* 1958, Myrna Elizabeth, *o. d.* of Lt.-Col. John Baskervyle-Glegg]. *Address:* The Manor House, Apethorpe, Peterborough. *T.:* Kingscliffe 231. *Club:* White's. [*Died* 28 *June* 1967.

BRAUND, Sir Henry Benedict Linthwaite, Kt. 1945; M.A. (Oxon); Barrister-at-law; Judge of County Courts, Circuit No. 19, 1953-64, retd. (Circuit No. 46, 1950-53); *b.* 21 March 1893; *s.* of Marwood Leonard Boyd Braund; *m.* 1920, Isabel Margaret, *o. d.* of late Charles Henry Jones, C.B.E.; one *d.* *Educ.:* Rugby; St. John's Coll., Oxford. Served in the Army, European War, 1914-19. Practised at the Chancery Bar in London, 1920-34; Judge of High Court of Judicature, Rangoon, Burma, 1934-39; Judge of High Court of Judicature, Allahabad, United Provinces, India, 1939, retired; Chairman of Committee appointed to inquire into the Burma riots, 1938-39, 1939; Regional Food Commission, Eastern Region India, 1943-44; Chairman Bengal Foodgrains Policy Committee, 1944; Chairman War Pensions (Special Review) Tribunals. 1947-49. *Recreations:* golf, riding, fishing. *Address:* Etwall Lodge, Etwall, Nr. Derby. [*Died* 18 *April* 1969.

BRAUNHOLTZ, Gustav Ernst Karl, M.A.; Professor Emeritus, Oxford University; Emeritus Fellow of Worcester College, Oxford; *b.* 19 March 1887; *s.* of late E. G. W. Braunholtz; *m.* 1922, Mary, *d.* of late Professor C. H. Herford; three *s.* (one *d. decd.*). *Educ.:* Oundle Sch.; Emmanuel Coll., Camb.; Freiburg and Berlin Universities; George Charles Winter Warr Scholar, 1911-12; Assistant Lecturer, Lecterer, and Senior Lecturer in Classics, 1913-1924, and Lecturer in Indo-European Philology, 1919-24, Manchester University; War Service, 1916-19; Professor of Latin in University College of South Wales and Monmouthshire, 1924-25; Professor of Comparative Philology, Oxford University, 1925-52. *Recreations:* gardening, fell-walking. *Address:* Worcester College and 78 Old Road, Headington, Oxford. *T.:* Oxford 62885. [*Died* 21 *April* 1967.

BRAUNHOLTZ, Hermann Justus, C.B.E. 1951; M.A. (Camb.); Keeper, Dept. Oriental Antiquities and Ethnography, 1938-1945, and Dept. Ethnography, 1945-53, British Museum; *b.* 12 Oct. 1888; *s.* of E. G. W. Braunholtz; *m.* 1932, Joan, 4th *d.* of late Thomas Raymont; one *s.* one *d.* *Educ.:* Oundle School; St. John's College, Cambridge. Entered British Museum, 1913; European War, R.A.M.C., 1915-19; Hon. Editor, Royal Anthropological Institute, 1926-35; Pres. 1937-39 and 1941-43. *Publications:* Various articles and reviews on anthropology and archæology in scientific Journals; contributions to Encyclopædia Britannica, 13th and 14th editions, Oxford Junior Encyclopædia, 1948 and 1954, Chambers's Encyclopædia, 1950, Victoria Encyclopædia, and Enciclopedia Universale dell' Arte, 1959; joint translator of J. Strzygowski, Origin of Christian Church Art. *Recreations:* music, travel. *Address:* Torre House, 10 Avenue St. Nicholas, Harpenden, Herts. *T.:* Harpenden 3017. *Club:* Oxford and Cambridge Musical. [*Died* 4 *June* 1963.

BRAY, Captain Sir Jocelyn, Kt., *cr.* 1946; D.L.; Chartered Surveyor and Land Agent; Chairman Thames Conservancy Board, 1938-60; *b.* 7 April 1880; 3rd *s.* of Hon. Mr. Justice Bray, Manor House, Shere, Guildford; *m.* 1905, Sandra, *er. d.* of late Sir Alexander Onslow, Send Grove, Send, Surrey; one *s.* *Educ.:* Harrow; Trinity College, Cambridge. Chairman Guildford Rural District Council, 1933-48. Served in South African War, 1900, and in European War, 1914-18, with Surrey Yeomanry and 2nd Life Guards as Captain. *Address:* The Manor House, Shere, Guildford, Surrey. [*Died* 12 *Feb.* 1964.

BRAYNE, Albert Frederic Lucas, C.I.E. 1923; *b.* 1884; *e. s.* of Llewellyn Brayne of Roddington, Salop; *m.* 1909, Mary, *e. d.* of James Thomson, M.D., of Irvine, Ayrshire. *Educ.:* Irvine Royal Academy; Glasgow Univ. (M.A.); Trinity Coll., Oxford (B.A.); Lincoln's Inn. Entered I.C.S. 1907; Under-Secretary and Dep. Secretary to the Government of Bombay, 1916-20; Dep. Secretary to the Government of India, Finance Department, and attached to the Indian Retrenchment-Committee, 1920-23; Financial Adviser, Posts and Telegraphs, 1923-1924; Financial Adviser for the Army in India, 1924-29; Financial Secretary to the Government of India and Member, Council of State, 1926-27 and 1932; Army Secretary, 1928; Retrenchment Officer, Government of India, 1931; Chairman, Sind Conference, and on special duty in connection with the Indian Defence Expenditure Tribunal, 1932; Secretary, Indian Delegation, Monetary and Economic Conference, 1933; retired, 1935; temp. duty in Petroleum Department, Ministry of Fuel and Power, 1940-45. *Address:* Craigroy, Kilmacolm, Renfrewshire. [*Died* 18 *June* 1970.

BRAYNE, Charles Valentine, C.M.G. 1935; *b.* 17 Aug. 1877; *s.* of late Rev. R. T. W. Brayne, Rector of Combe Hay, nr. Bath; *m.* 1st, 1906, Amy Chanter Goodchild; 2nd, 1922, Blodwen Price; three *d.* *Educ.:* Monkton Combe School, Bath; Pembroke College, Cambridge, B.A. Cadet Ceylon Civil Service, 1901. Assistant Govt. Agent, Mullaitivu, 1906, Kalutara, 1916; Govt. Agent, E. Province, 1920; acting Controller of Revenue and Member of the Executive and Legislative Councils, Ceylon, 1927; Commissioner of Lands, Ceylon, 1931-35; retired, 1935. Member Leatherhead U.D.C., 1938-47. *Publication:* Social Justice First. *Address:* Wolverley, Gloucester Ave., Devonport, Tasmania, Australia. [*Died* 16 *Nov.* 1964.

BREAKEY, Air Vice-Marshal John Denis, C.B. 1944; D.F.C.; retd.; Assistant Chief of Air Staff (Technical Requirements), 1943; A.O.C. No. 222 Group S.E.A.C., 1945; A.O.C. Air Headquarters, Malaya, 1945-47; Air Officer in Charge of Administration, Bomber Command, 1947-51; Air Officer Commanding No. 21 Group, Flying Training Command, March-July 1951; Head of Air Force Staff, British Joint Services Mission, Washington, 1951-54. Group Capt. 1943; Air Commodore and Temp. Air Vice-Marshal, 1946; Air Vice-Marshal, 1947; retired, 1954. *Address:* 9 Eastbury Court, W.14. *T.:* Western 0049. [*Died* 8 *Jan.* 1965.

BREAKS, Rear-Admiral James, C.B.E. 1950; M.I.Mech.E.; R.N. retd.; *b.* 26 Feb. 1895; *s.* of late Capt. John Breaks, Newlands, Glasgow; *m.* 1922, Phyllis Margaret (*d.* 1962), *d.* of late Major H. Hobbs, M.B.E., V.D., Calcutta; one *s.* three *d.*; *m.* 1964, Mrs. Norma Maclean Bryceson. *Educ.:* Allan Glen's, Glasgow. Royal Navy, 1913. Served European War, 1914-18 and War of 1939-45; H.M.S. Shannon, Phaeton, Monarch, and Naval Air Arm. Commander (E), 1929; Capt. (E), 1940; Rear-Admiral (E), 1947; retired list, 1951. *Address:* 40 Earls Court Square, S.W.5. [*Died* 15 *Feb.* 1968.

BREEN, Air Marshal John Joseph, C.B. 1942; O.B.E. 1935; R.A.F. (retd.); *b.* 8 March 1896; *s.* of late Inspector-General T. J. Breen, R.N., Inspector-Gen. of Hospitals and Fleets. *Educ.:* Beaumont College; Royal Military College, Sandhurst. Royal Irish Regiment, 1915; seconded R.F.C., 1915; transferred to R.A.F., 1918; served European War, 1914-18, France and Italy, 1915-18 (despatches twice); R.A.F. Staff Coll., 1925; commanded 84 Squadron, Iraq, 1926-28, 33 Squadron, 1929-30; Imperial Defence College, 1931; Wessex Bombing Area, 1932-35; Sudan, 1935-38; War of 1939-45, A.O.C. No. 1 Bomber Group, 1940; Air Min. Dir. Gen. of Personnel, 1941-44; Head of post-war planning exec., 1944-45; retired list, 1946. *Address:* Windyridge, Greystones, Co. Wicklow, Ireland. *Club:* Royal Air Force. [*Died* 9 *May* 1964.

BREEN, Timothy Florence, C.B.E. 1933; M.C.; *b.* 8 Aug. 1885; *s.* of Michael Roche Breen; *m.* 1920, Maud Alice White; no *c.* *Educ.:* privately. Served European War, 1914-18; attached Military Mission, Berlin, April 1919, Major General Staff; Press Attaché (First Secretary), British Embassy, Berlin, 1921-37. *Recreation:* sailing. *Address:* Sark, Channel Isles. *T.:* Sark 44 [*Died* 8 *Nov.* 1966.

BREMNER, Lieutenant-Colonel Claude E. U., M.C.; *b.* 30 Aug. 1891; *s.* of late Bt. Col. H. J. Bremner and Edith, *d.* of late John Graham, Enniskillen; *m.* 1936, Anne Geraldine Stuart, *e. d.* of late Bertram Christian; one *s.* four *d.* *Educ.:* Bedford School. Entered army, 1911; 1st Bn. (44th Foot) Essex Regt.; exchanged to Indian Army, 1914 (29th Punjabis); served in East Africa, 1914-17 (despatches, M.C.); Marri Field Force, 1918; Palestine and Egypt, 1918-19; Punjab Rebellion, 1919; Afghan War, 1919; N.W. Frontier, 1930; joined the Foreign and Political Dept. (Govt. of India), 1919; served in Baluchistan, N.W.F. Province, Persia, Persian Gulf, Indian States; also on foreign service in Baroda State and as Consul in Portuguese India. Acting King's (Foreign Service) Messenger, 1944; retired 1945. Employed with Brit. Mil. Admin. (Libya), 1947-48; resigned 1948, to settle in S. Rhodesia; employed in S. Rhodesian and Rhodesian and Federal Govts. as temp. Civil Servant, 1948-61. Travelled in Europe, North, Central and East Africa, Middle East, U.S.A., Central and S. America. *Recreations:* philately, art, European and other languages. *Address:* Roffey Hurst, Roffey, Nr. Horsham, Sussex. *Club:* United Service. [*Died* 25 *April* 1965.

BRENTANO, Dr. Heinrich von; Grand Cross of Order of Merit of Federal Republic of Germany; Member of the Federal Parliament, since 1949; Chairman Christian Democrat/Christian Socialist Group (C.D.U./C.S.U.) of the Federal Parliament since 1961 (also 1949-55); barrister and notary; *b.* Offenbach, Hesse, 20 June 1904; *s.* of Otto von Brentano di Tremezzo, barrister and notary, Hessian Minister of the Interior and of Justice, member of German National Assembly and of German Reichstag. *Educ.:* Universities of Marburg, Munich and Giessen. Dr. of Law, Univ. of Giessen, 1930. Member: Hessian Provincial Council (group leader of the C.D.U., 1945-49); Governing Body of Christian Democratic Union, Hesse; Parliamentary Council, 1948-49; Federal Parliament, 1949-, President of the Parliamentary Section of the C.D.U., 1949-55; Foreign Minister, 1955-56. Pres. of Parl. Section of German Council of European Movement, 1954; Mem. and Vice-Pres. of Consultative Assembly of Council of Europe, 1950-55; Member General Assembly of European Coal and Steel Community, 1952-1955. Chairman of European Constitutional Cttee. (*ad hoc* Assembly of European Coal and Steel Community) 1952-53. LL.D. (*h.c.*) Georgetown University, 1957. Holds numerous foreign decorations. *Publication:* Deutschland, Europa und die Welt (Germany, Europe and the World), 1962 (Bonn). *Recreation:* collection of antique works of art. *Address:* Bundeshaus, Bonn, Germany. [*Died* 14 *Nov.* 1964.

BRERETON, Very Rev. Eric Hugh, O.B.E. 1919; M.A.; T.D.; Dean of Glasgow and Galloway, since 1959; Rector of St. Margaret's Church, Newlands, Glasgow, and its Missions, since 1933; Canon of St. Mary's Cathedral, Glasgow, 1936; *o. s.* of late Captain W. E. Brereton, R.A.; *b.* Dublin, 17 Nov. 1889; *m.* 1939, Adeline Susan May, *y. d.* of late Rev. John Matheson, Rector of St. Paul's Church, Strathnairn, Inverness-shire. *Educ.:* Private School; University College, Durham; Edinburgh Theological College. Ordained, 1912; Curate at St. James' Church, Leith, 1912-14; Assistant Priest and Senior Chaplain, St. Mary's Cathedral, Edinburgh, 1914-20; temporary Chaplain to the Forces, 1915-19; appointed Senior Chaplain 26th Division (despatches twice, O.B.E.); Chaplain to the Territorial Army, 1921-40; Hon. C.F. (3rd Class), 1940; Rector of Christ Church, Morningside, Edinburgh, 1921-27; Vice-Provost and Senior Canon of St. Mary's Cathedral, Edinburgh, 1927-33; Convener, Home Mission Committee, 1934-38. *Recreations:* motoring, fishing. *Address:* St. Margaret's Rectory, 22 Monreith Road, Newlands, Glasgow. *T.:* Langside 3292. *Club:* Caledonian United Service and Northern (Edinburgh). [*Died* 8 *Dec.* 1962.

BRETT, Lieut.-Gen. George H.; retired; *b.* 7 Feb. 1886; *s.* of William Howard Brett and Alice Allen; *m.* 1916, Mary Devol; three *c.* *Educ.:* Virginia Military Institute. 2nd Lt., Philippine Scouts, 1910; 2nd Lt., U.S. Cavalry, 1911: U.S. Air Force, 1915; 1st Lieut. 1916; Capt. 1917; Major, 1917; Lieut.-Col. 1934; Brig.-Gen. 1936; Col. 1938; Brig.-Gen. 1939; Maj.-Gen. 1940; Lieut.-Gen. 1942; retired 1946. Decorations: Distinguished Service Medal with Oak Leaf Cluster, Silver Star, Distinguished Flying Cross, K.C.B. (Great Britain), Order of Orange Nassau with swords (Netherlands), Presidential Citation with Oak Leaf Cluster. *Clubs:* Army and Navy (Washington, D.C.); University (Winter Park, Fla.); Club Union (Panama); Circular Militar (Buenos Aires). [*Died* 2 *Dec.* 1963.

BRETT, Henry James, C.M.G. 1928; *b.* Dublin, 13 July 1878; *s.* of late John Henry Brett. *Educ.:* Trinity College, Dublin. Appointed to H.M. Consular Service in China, 1901; Consul, 1918; Commercial Secretary to H. M. Legation, Peking, 1919-32; retired, 1932. *Address:* 125 Swan Court, S.W.3. [*Died* 10 *Nov.* 1963.

BRETT, Brigadier Rupert John, D.S.O. 1919; D.L.; J.P.; *b.* 14 November 1890; *s.* of late John Mansel Brett and Amy, *d.* of late John Gardiner of Queen's Gate, S.W.; *m.* 1923, Olive Barbara, *d.* of Joshua Hirst Wheatley of Berkswell Hall, Coventry; one *d.* *Educ.:* Eton; R.M.C., Sandhurst. Joined 52nd Light Infantry, 1910; served European War, 1914-18; Second-in-Command. 52nd Light Infantry and 17th Royal Fusiliers; commanded 1st Batt. Royal Berkshire Regiment (wounded, despatches. D.S.O., Croix de Guerre, Bt.-Maj.); graduated at Staff College, Dec. 1922; General Staff, War Office, 1923-24; Brigade Maj. 10th Infantry Brig. 1924-26; Adj. 43rd Light Infantry, 1926-28; D.A.A.G. War Office, 1928-32; Oxfordshire and Buckinghamshire Light Infantry, 1932-34; G.S.O. 2 British Troops in Egypt, 1934-37; Commanded 52nd Light Infantry, 1938: Brigadier Commanding 165th Infantry Brigade, 1940-1942; Directorate of Prisoners of War, War Office, 1942; Commandant A.T.S. Wing of the Staff College, 1943-45; A.D.C. to the King, 1942-45; retired, 1945. County Commandant Buckinghamshire Army Cadet Force, 1945-50. Committee Territorial and Auxiliary Forces Assoc. of Oxon, 1947; Vice-Chm., 1954; Alderman, Oxfordshire, 1961 (C.C., 1949-61); J.P. Oxon 1950; D.L. Oxon 1952. *Recreations:* shooting, fishing. *Address:* Langsmeade House, Milton Common, Oxford. *T.:* Great Milton 256. *Clubs:* United Hunts, M.C.C. [*Died* 10 *Nov.* 1963.

BRETTELL, Frederick Gilbert; chartered patent agent; *b.* 6 Dec. 1884; *s.* of late Frederick Brettell and Emma Gilbert; *m.* Elsie Margaret, *d.* of late William E. Jeff, Edgbaston, Birmingham, and Coleshill; one *s.* (and one killed in action) one *d.* *Educ.:* College School, Saltley; Technical Institute, Birmingham. Articled pupil of George Barker, engineer and chartered patent agent; qualified 1905; Fellow of the Chartered Institute of Patent Agents, 1910; Member of Council, 1921 President, 1932; Member of Board of Trade, Trade Marks Committee, 1933, to review Law of Trade Marks; President Midland Association of Mountaineers, 1933-35. *Address:* 32 Innage Road, Northfield, Birmingham 31. *T.A.:* Patent, Birmingham. *T.:* Priory 1702. *Club:* Alpine. [*Died* 11 *March* 1965.

BREUIL, Abbé Henri Édouard Prosper; Membre de l'Institut, France (Académie des Inscriptions), since 1938; Hon. Professor, Institut de Paléontologie Humaine (Ethnographie Préhistorique), since 1910; Hon. Professor, Collège de France, Paris (Préhistoire), 1929-47; *b.* Mortain (Manche), 28 Feb. 1877; *s.* of Albert Breuil, Magistrate, and Lucie Morio de l'Isle. *Educ.:* Collège St.-Vincent, Senlis (Oise); Séminaire St.-Sulpice, Paris; Faculté des Sciences, Sorbonne (Licencié ès Sciences Naturelles); Institut Catholique, Paris. Lecturer on Prehistory and Ethnography, University of Fribourg, 1905-10. Member, Société préhistorique de France; corresp. mem. and hon. mem. numerous foreign socs. Commandeur de la Légion d'Honneur. Elliot Gold Medal Amer. Acad. of Science, 1924; Huxley Memorial Medal, 1946; Prestwich Medal for Geology, 1947; Gold Medal, Archæological Soc., London. Hon. degrees, Oxford, Cambridge, Edinburgh, Cape Town, Lisbon and Fribourg Univs. *Publications:* Beyond the Bounds of History (Eng. trans.), 1949; 400 Siècles d'art pariétal, 1952 (Eng. trans. 1952); Les Hommes de la Pierre ancienne (Course at Univ. of Lisbon, 1942) (ed. with R. Lantier), 1952, 2nd edn. 1959; Les Roches peintes de Tassili-N-Agger (Sahara), 1955;

The White Lady of the Brandberg, S.W. Africa, 1955 (Eng. trans.); Taisab Ravine, S.W. Africa, 1959 (Eng. trans.); Quelques Dolmens de Morbihan, 1960; nombreux volumes sur les cavernes ornées de l'Age du Renne, les gravures et peintures sur roches paléolithiques, néo- et énéolithiques; nombreux articles sur les mêmes sujets, sur le Paléolithique ancien et supérieur, la géologie quaternaire, l'art mobilier de l'Age du Renne, l'art rupestre d'Afrique australe, etc. *Address:* 52 Avenue de la Motte-Picquet, Paris XV. [*Died* 14 *Aug.* 1961.

BREWER, Sir Henry Campbell, Kt., *cr.* 1954; M.B.E. 1944; F.I.C.S.; Director; J. A. Billmeir & Co. Ltd., shipowners; Burwood Steamship Co. Ltd.; Lamorna Shipping Co. Ltd.; Stanhope Steamship Co. Ltd.; St. Helen's Insurance Co. Ltd.; *b.* 1885; *s.* of Henry John Brewer; *m.* 1914, Gladys Mary, *d.* of William Edward Horn. Served European War, France and Belgium, 1914-19. Chm. The Baltic Exchange, 1948-1951; President Institute of Chartered Shipbrokers, 1953-56; Member of Exec. Council Shipping Federation; Hon. Shipping Adviser, Ministry of Food, 1945-55; Member of Sugar Board, 1956-. Prime Warden, Worshipful Co. of Shipwrights. *Address:* 9 St. Helen's Place, E.C.3. *T.:* London Wall 7721. *Club:* Royal Automobile. [*Died* 1 *Aug.* 1963.

BREWERTON, Elmore, F.R.C.S.; Consulting Ophthalmic Surgeon, Metropolitan Hospital and Royal Westminster Ophthalmic Hospital; late President Section of Ophthalmology Royal Society of Medicine; late Ophthalmic Surgeon, Fourth London General Hospital; *b.* Buenos Ayres, 1867; *s.* of Charles Brewerton of Whetstone, Middlesex; *m.* Olive, *d.* of late Dr. M'Ivor Tindall of Market Harborough; two *s.* three *d.* *Educ.:* Neuenheim College, Heidelberg; Univ. College School and St. Bartholomew's Hospital, London. Retired from practice Jan. 1945. *Publications:* A Text-book of Ophthalmic Operations (jointly); Ophthalmic Section in Carson's Modern Operative Surgery. *Recreations:* motoring and fishing. *Address:* Dromineen, 1 Ashley Rise, Walton on Thames. *T.:* Walton 3261. [*Died* 8 *Nov.* 1962.

BREWS, (Richard) Alan; Obstetric and Gynæcological Surgeon to the London Hospital since 1931; *b.* 22 June 1902; *s.* of Richard Vincent Brews and Edith Manifold; *m.* 1928, Gwyneth Grace, *d.* of Joseph Dixie Churchill, late Rector of Little Bentley, Essex; one *s.* *Educ.:* Merchant Taylors' School; London Hospital Medical College. M.D., M.S. (Lond.), F.R.C.P., F.R.C.S. (Eng.), F.R.C.O.G. Director of Obstetric Studies and Lecturer in Midwifery and Diseases of Women in London Hospital Medical School; Master, Soc. of Apothecaries of London, 1965-66. Examiner in Midwifery and Diseases of Women, Univ. of London and Royal College of Obstetricians and Gynæcologists. Lately examiner in Midwifery and Diseases of Women, Univs. of Cambridge, Liverpool, Durham, Hong Kong and the West Indies, and for Conjoint Bd. of England; Obstetric and Gynæcological Surgeon (part-time), North-East Metropolitan Regional Bd. *Publications:* (Ed.) Holland and Brews Manual of Obstetrics, 12th edn., 1963. *Recreations:* golf, bridge. *Address:* 149 Harley Street, W.1. *T.:* Welbeck 4444; Highlands, Sawyer's Hall Lane, Shenfield, Essex. *T.:* Brentwood 576. *Clubs:* Reform, Royal Automobile. [*Died* 25 *Dec.* 1965.

BRICKELL, Daniel Francis Horseman. O.B.E. 1945 (M.B.E. 1929); *b.* 4 Sept. 1893; *s.* of Robert Frederick Brickell and Mary Elizabeth Darby, Dublin; *m.* 1924, Maureen Rosemary Sherlock; (one *s.* decd.). *Educ.:* St. Mary's College, Dublin. Passed C.S. Examination and appointed to Estate Duty Office, 1913, and Foreign Office, 1914; 2nd Lt. R.F.C. 1917; Vice-Consul Levant Consular Service, 1923; served at Istanbul, Smyrna, Cairo, Suez, Athens, New York; Consul at Basra, 1936, and Rouen, 1940; Minister to Paraguay, 1940-43; 1st Secretary and Consul, Montevideo, Uruguay, 1944; Consul-General Detroit, U.S.A., 1945-49; H.M. Minister at San Salvador, 1949-50; Consul-Gen., Ahwaz, 1950, Philadelphia, 1951-53; retired 1953. Grand Officer Paraguayan Order of Merit. *Recreation:* golf. *Address:* 10 Thorncliffe Pk., Rathgar, Dublin. *Clubs:* Franklin Inn (Philadelphia); Milltown Golf. [*Died* 14 *July* 1967.

BRIDGE, Brigadier Charles Edward Dunscomb, C.M.G. 1938; D.S.O. 1918; M.C. 1916; p.s.c.; late R.A.; *b.* 22 Feb. 1886; *s.* of late Brig.-Gen. Sir Charles H. Bridge, K.C.M.G., C.B., and Elizabeth Dorcas, *d.* of Sir Edward Morris, K.C.B.; *m.* Georgena Canning, *y. d.* of late James Wesley Hall, Melbourne, Australia; one *s.* two *d.* *Educ.:* Bradfield; R.M.A., Woolwich. 1st Commission R.F.A. Dec. 1904; R.H.A. 1909; Gen. Staff, 1915; temp. Lt.-Col. 1918; served in France and Italy (despatches seven times); assistant Military Attaché, Washington, 1920-23; Military Attaché at Warsaw and Prague, 1927-28; retired pay, 1928; Secretary-General of the British Council from its foundation in Nov. 1934 until April 1940; Military Attaché at Rome, May 1940; Head of British Military Mission to Polish G.H.Q., July-Dec. 1940; Temp. Col., 1942; Control Commission for Germany, 1945; Order of Leopold, and French, Belgian, and Italian Croix de Guerre. *Address:* 18 Hale House, De Vere Gardens, W.8. *T.:* Western 7157. *Club:* Cavalry. [*Died* 31 *Jan.* 1961.

BRIDGEMAN, Caroline Beatrix, Viscountess, D.B.E., *cr.* 1924; J.P.; *d.* of Hon. Cecil Parker and Rosamond Longley; *m.* 1895, 1st Viscount Bridgeman (*d.* 1935); three *s.* *Educ.:* Private. Formerly Chairman Women's War Agricultural Committees London and Shropshire; Florence Nightingale Hospital for Gentlewomen; Council and Conference National Union of Conservative Associations; Member of Royal Commission on London Squares; late Governor British Broadcasting Corporation; Chm. Central Hospital Supply Service; Member of Council and Exec. Cttee. of Queen's Institute of District Nursing; late Member (formerly Vice-Chairman) House of Laity, Church Assembly. *Address:* 8 Knightsbridge Court, Sloane Street, S.W.1. *T.:* Sloane 2985. *Club:* Naval and Military. [*Died* 26 *Dec.* 1961.

BRIDGEMAN, Reginald Francis Orlando, C.M.G. 1917; M.V.O. 1914; *b.* 14 Oct. 1884; *e. s.* of late Colonel Hon. Francis Bridgeman; *m.* 1923, Olwen Elizabeth, *o. d.* of Maurice Jones, M.P.S.; one *s.* (and one *s.* killed in action in Italy, May 1944) two *d.* *Educ.:* Harrow. Appointed Attaché at Madrid, 1903; Clerk in the Foreign Office, 1904; transferred to Diplomatic Service, 1908; served in France, Greece, Austria, and Persia; Counsellor of Embassy, 1920; retired on pension, 1923; Chairman of Hendon Divisional Labour Party, 1927; contested (Lab.) Uxbridge Division of Middlesex, 1929, and as Workers' Candidate, 1931; Secretary of the League against Imperialism, 1933-37; Prospective Parliamentary Labour Candidate for Hendon, 1938-40. Member Nat. Union of Gen. and Municipal Workers, 1927-51; Member: British-Soviet Friendship Soc., Britain-China Friendship Assoc., Nat. Coun. for Civil Liberties; Harrow Campaign for Nuclear Disarmament. *Address:* 105 Waxwell Lane, Pinner. *T.:* Pinner 0117. *Club:* India. [*Died* 11 *Dec.* 1968.

BRIDGES, 1st Baron, *cr.* 1957; **Edward Bridges,** K.G. 1965; P.C. 1953; G.C.B.

1944 (K.C.B. 1939); G.C.V.O. 1946; M.C.; F.R.S. 1952; Hon. LL.D. (Bristol, London, Cambridge, Hong Kong, Leicester, Liverpool); Hon. D.Litt. (Reading); Hon. D.C.L. (Oxford); Chancellor, Reading University, 1959; *b.* 4 August 1892; *o. s.* of late Robert Bridges, O.M., Poet Laureate; *m.* 1922, Hon. Katherine D. Farrer, 2nd *d.* of 2nd Baron Farrer; two *s.* two *d.* *Educ.:* Eton; Magdalen College, Oxford (Hon. Fellow, 1946). Fellow of All Souls College, Oxford, 1920-27 and 1954-68, Hon. Fellow, 1968; Hon. Fellow, University Coll., Cambridge, 1965-; Hon. Fellow, L.S.E., 1969; Hon. F.R.I.B.A. European War, 1914-18, Captain, and sometime Adjutant 4th Bn. Oxford and Bucks L.I. (M.C.). Home Civil Service: Treasury, 1919-38; Secretary to the Cabinet, 1938-46; Permanent Secretary, H.M. Treasury, 1945-56; retired 1956. Chm.: Royal Fine Art Commn., 1957-58; British Council, 1959-67. A Trustee of Pilgrim Trust (Chairman, 1965-68. *Publications:* The Treasury (Whitehall Series), 1964; contrib. to Action This Day—Working with Churchill (ed. Wheeler-Bennett), 1968. *Heir:* *s.* Hon. Thomas Edward Bridges [*b.* 27 Nov. 1927; *m.* 1953, Rachel Mary, *y. d.* of Sir Henry Bunbury; two *s.* one *d.*]. *Address:* Goodman's Furze, Headley, Epsom. *Club:* Athenæum. [*Died* 27 *Aug.* 1969.

BRIDGES, Colonel George, C.M.G. 1917; D.S.O. 1900; R.H. and R.F.A.; *o. s.* of late Capt. Edward Bridges, of Caynham, Shropshire; *m.* 1st, 1919, Gwendoline Elizabeth (*d.* 1942), *widow* of Capt. Gordon Farrer, 18th Hussars; 2nd, Sheila Gladys, *d.* of I. W. Marcuson, Sutton Coldfield, Warwickshire. Served South Africa, 1899-1901 including Siege of Mafeking (wounded, despatches, D.S.O.): also in Ashanti and Malay States; on French Remount Commission to Argentine Republic, 1914-15; France and Belgium, 1915-18; commanded Kent Force Div. Artillery, 1918-19. C.R.A. Larkhill (despatches thrice, C.M.G.); retired, 1921. *Club:* Naval and Military. [*Died* 10 *Dec.* 1962.

BRIDGES-ADAMS, William, C.B.E. 1960; theatrical producer, designer and historian; *b.* 1 March 1889; *o. s.* of Walter and Mary Bridges-Adams; *m.* 1929, Marguerite Doris, *y. d.* of late W. H. Wellsted, J.P.; one *s.* *Educ.:* Bedales; Worcester Coll., Oxf. Joined stage from O.U.D.S. 1911; under managements of Laurence Irving, William Poel, Granville-Barker and Sir George Alexander; first London production, 1912; producer, Bristol repertory seasons, 1914-15; Joint Controller, Playhouse, Liverpool, 1916-17; designed settings for Gilbert and Sullivan revivals, London, 1919-24; Dir. of Shakespeare Festivals, Stratford upon Avon, 1919-1934; Gov. of Memorial (now Royal Shakespeare) Theatre since 1934. Mem. and hon. dramatic adviser of The British Council, 1937, in charge of foreign tours; served on Council staff during War of 1939-45. *Publications:* The Shakespeare Country, 1932; The British Theatre, 1944; Looking at a Play, 1947; The Lost Leader, 1954; The Irresistible Theatre and To Charlotte While Shaving (verse), 1957; The Edwardian Theatre (contrib. to Edwardian England), 1965; essays, reviews, broadcasts. *Recreations:* reading, fishing, carpentry. *Address:* Hermitage, Waterfall, Bantry, Co. Cork, Ireland. *Clubs:* Garrick, Savile. [*Died* 17 *Aug.* 1965.

BRIDGLAND, Sir Aynsley (Vernon), Kt. 1959; C.B.E. 1955; Chairman: Aynsley Trust Ltd.; Barholme Property Trust Ltd.; City and Colonial Trust Ltd.; Desimis Investments Ltd.; Haleybridge Invest. Trust Ltd.; Limes Property Invest. Ltd.; Metropolitan Ground Rents Ltd.; Planet Trust Ltd.; R.C.P. Holding Co. Ltd.; Real Property and Finance Corporation Ltd.; Regis Property Co. Ltd.; Section Four Co. Ltd.; Trustees of the London Clinic Ltd.; Forbes Campbell and Co. Ltd.; Forbes Campbell (Merchant Shippers) Ltd.; Director, Liverpool Exchange Co. Ltd.; *b.* 24 May 1893; *s.* of late Edward Thomas Bridgland; *m.* 1st, 1915, Dorothy Muriel Metters (decd.); 2nd, 1939, Kathleen Dickie Moffat (*née* Reid); three *s.* two *d.* *Educ.:* University High School, Melbourne; Adelaide University. *Recreation:* golf. *Address:* Kent Holme, The Bishop's Avenue, N.2. [*Died* 20 *July* 1966.

BRIDGMAN, Percy W., A.B.; A.M., Ph.D.; D.Sc.; *b.* 21 April 1882; *s.* of Raymond L. and Mary A. M. W. Bridgman; *m.* 1912, Olive Ware; one *s.* one *d.* *Educ.:* Newton Public Schools; Harvard Univ. Has been continually at Harvard Univ. since 1900, as student to 1908, then as assist. instructor and prof. of physics. Principal activity, experimental research in the field of high pressures. Also occupied with thermodynamics and critical analysis of the foundations of physics; Nobel Prize for Physics, 1946. Foreign member, Royal Society, 1949. Higgins University Prof. at Harvard University, retired 1954. *Publications:* Dimensional Analysis, 1923; Logic of Modern Physics, 1926; Physics of High Pressure, 1931; Thermodynamics of Electrical Phenomena in Metals, 1933; Nature of Physical Theory, 1936; Intelligent Individual and Society, 1938; Nature of Thermodynamics, 1941; Reflections of a Physicist, 1950, 2nd enlarged edn., 1955; Studies in Large Plastic Flow and Fracture, 1952; The Nature of some of our Physical Concepts, 1952; The Way Things Are, 1959; numerous articles in technical journals. *Address:* c/o Research Laboratory of Physics, Harvard University, Cambridge, Mass. [*Died* 21 *Aug.* 1961.

BRIDPORT, 3rd Viscount (*cr.* 1868); **Rowland Arthur Herbert Nelson Hood,** Baron Bridport, 1794; Lt.-Comdr. R.N. (Emergency List); *b.* 22 May 1911; *o. s.* of Lieut. Hon. Maurice Nelson Hood, R.N. Div. (killed in action 1915), and Eileen (*d.* 1931), *e. d.* of late Charles Kendall, Wokingham, Berks; *g.s.* of 2nd Viscount; *S.* grandfather, 1924; *m.* 1st, 1934, Pamela Aline Mary (marriage dissolved, 1945), *o. d.* of late Charles J. Baker, Wantage; (one *s.* decd.); 2nd, 1946, Sheila Jeanne Agatha, *widow* of Wing Commander James Hawyard Little, D.F.C., Aux. A.F., and *d.* of Johann van Meurs; one *s.* *Educ.:* R.N. College, Dartmouth. Midshipman H.M.S. Nelson, Home Fleet, 1928-31; Sub-Lieut. courses, 1931-32; H.M.S. Daring, Mediterranean Fleet, 1933, then transferred to Emergency List Royal Navy. Holds Board of Trade's Certificate of Master of a foreign-going ship. Inherited title and estates of the Dukedom of Bronte in Sicily 1937. Lord-in-Waiting to the King, 1939-40. War of 1939-45 (campaign stars for Atlantic, Africa, Burma): recalled to Royal Navy, Aug. 1939; Lieut. 1940 Lt.-Commander 1943; served in H.M.S. Newcastle, 1939-44; Press Division, Admiralty, 1944-45; reverted to Emergency List, 1946. Coronation Medal, 1953. *Heir:* *s.* Hon. Alexander Nelson Hood, *b.* 17 March 1948. *Address:* Castello di Maniace, Maniace di Bronte, 95030 (Catania), Sicily. *T.:* 095-691502. *T.A.:* Ducea Maletto. *Club:* Brooks's. [*Died* 25 *July* 1969.

BRIERLEY, Colonel Geoffrey Teale, C.M.G. 1919; D.S.O. 1901; late Royal Artillery; *s.* of late Rev. J. H. Brierley, Prebendary of Hereford; *m.* Eily, *o. d.* of late Insp.-Gen. Coppinger, R.N., and Mrs. Coppinger, of Wallington House, Fareham, Hants. *Educ.:* Rossall; Royal Military Academy, Woolwich. Entered Army, 1893; Capt. 1900; Col. 1923: served with Imperial Light Horse, South

Africa, 1900-2 (despatches thrice, wounded, D.S.O.); European War, 1914 (wounded at Ypres, 31 Oct. 1914); D.A.A.G. War Office, 1915-1917 (despatches); Air Ministry, 1918-22 (despatches, C.M.G.); A.A.G. War Office, 1924-28; Provost Marshal Commandant Corps of Military Police, 1928-30. Gold Staff Officer at the Coronation of King George VI. *Address:* Wallington House, Fareham, Hants. *Club:* Army and Navy. [*Died* 2 *Feb.* 1961.

BRIERLEY, Rev. Canon John; Rector and Rural Dean of Wolverhampton since 1935; Prebendary in Lichfield Cathedral since 1941; *b.* Antofagasta, Chili, 19 Oct. 1886; *s.* of late John Edward Brierley, Merchant, Rochdale; *m.* Constance Margaret, *d.* of Charles Henry Hamilton, Maeldune, Blundellsands; three *s.* one *d.* (and one *s.* decd.). *Educ.:* Liverpool College; Trinity College, Cambridge; Bishop's Hostel, Farnham, Surrey. B.A. 1909; M.A. 1913; Curate of Northwich, 1910-12; senior Curate of Newark-on-Trent, 1912-15; Hon. Secretary, Newark Deanery Chapter and Conference, 1912-15; Secretary, Southwell Diocesan Finance Association, 1914-15; Vicar of Greatham, 1915-18; Hon. Secretary, Hartlepool Deanery Chapter and Conference, 1915-18; Vicar of St. Faith's, Great Crosby, 1918-35; Hon. Clerical Secretary, Liverpool Diocesan Conference, 1928-35; Hon. Canon of Liverpool, 1931-35, Emeritus since 1935; Hon. Chaplain to Bishop of Liverpool, 1928-31; Member of the Governing Body of St. Chad's College, Durham, 1935; Chairman Brentwood School, Southport, 1945; Fellow of the Woodard Corporation, 1957; Proctor in Convocation, Diocese of Liverpool, 1935; Diocese of Lichfield, 1944; Church Commissioner, 1948; Chairman, House of Clergy, Church Assembly, 1955; Vice-Chairman, Lichfield Board of Finance, 1956. *Address:* The Rectory, Wolverhampton. *T.:* Wolverhampton 21918 (Home); Wolverhampton 23554 (Office). *Clubs:* Athenæum, Royal Commonwealth Society. [*Died* 9 *June* 1964.

BRIERLEY, William Broadhurst, D.Sc. (Manchester); Professor Emeritus of Agricultural Botany, The University, Reading; *b.* 19 Feb. 1889; *s.* of late Charles Henry Brierley and Elizabeth Broadhurst; *m.* 1922, Marjorie Flowers Ellis. *Educ.:* Manchester University. Lecturer in Economic Botany, Manchester University, 1911-1914; First Class Assistant, Royal Botanic Gardens, Kew, 1914-18; Head of Department of Plant Pathology, Rothamsted Experimental Station, Harpenden, 1918-32; President (1932-34) and Honorary Member of Association of Applied Biologists; Hon. Editor of Annals of Applied Biology, 1921-45 *Publications:* papers in scientific and literary journals. *Recreation:* gardening. *Address:* Rowling End, Newlands, Keswick, Cumberland. *T.:* Braithwaite 264. [*Died* 20 *Feb.* 1963.

BRIGHT, Rt. Rev. Humphrey Penderell; Bishop of Soli, since 1944, and Auxiliary Bishop to the Roman Catholic Archbishop of Birmingham; *b.* London, 27 Jan. 1903; *s.* of George Penderell Bright and Kathleen Emery. *Educ.:* Cotton Coll.; Oscott. Ordained, 1928; Staff, Cotton College, 1928-1935; Parish Priest, Trent Vale, Stoke-on-Trent, 1935-39; C.F., 1939-44. *Address:* The Presbytery, Queen's Avenue, Tunstall, Stoke-on-Trent. *T.:* Stoke-on-Trent 88357. [*Died* 26 *March* 1964.

BRIGHTEN, Lt.-Col. Edgar William, C.M.G. 1916; D.S.O. 1918; T.D.; retired; Bedfs. and Herts Regt.; *b.* 18 May 1880; *s.* of William Green Brighten, Solicitor, late Captain H.A.C.; *m.* 1905, Sarah Hirell (*d.* 1957), *d.* of Dr. Alfred James, Biggleswade, Beds; two *s.* one *d.* *Educ.:* Fauconberg School, Beccles; Christ's College, Blackheath. 2nd Lieut. 3rd Vol. Bn. Bedford Regt., 1898; served South African War as Lieut. commanding one of the Volunteer Service Companies attached to 2nd Bedford Regt.; saw service with Col. Rochford's Force operating in South-Western Transvaal, etc.; Captain, 1902; transferred to 5th Bedford Regt. on creation of Territorial Force; Major, 1912. Served European War (despatches, C.M.G., D.S.O.): Lieut.-Col. to command, 1915; Major (Regular Army), 1917; Bt. Lieut.-Col., 1919; Lieut.-Col., 1929; Instructor Senior Officers' School, India, 1924-28; retd. pay, 1933. Admitted Solicitor, 1904; practised until 1914 at Luton and London; Freeman of City of London; Member of Bakers' Company. *Recreations:* hunting, golf, etc. *Address:* Castle Base, Rusape, Rhodesia. [*Died* 22 *April* 1966.

BRIMBLE, Lionel John Farnham, B.Sc. (Lond.), B.Sc. (Reading); F.R.S.E.; F.R.S.A.; F.L.S.; F.I.Biol.; Associate of Univ. Coll., Reading; Certificate in Education (Oxford and Reading); Editor of Nature since 1938; *b.* Radstock, Somerset, 16 January 1904; *s.* of D. and late T. S. Brimble. *Educ.:* Sexey's School, Bruton; Universities of Reading and London. Lecturer in Botany, University of Glasgow, 1926-27; Lecturer in Botany, University of Manchester, 1927-30; Joint Editor of the North-Western Naturalist, 1930; Assistant Editor of Nature, 1931-38; Lectured in Universities of Calcutta (1945) and Cairo (1946); to troops in Britain, India and Burma (1942-48); in American Universities (1956) and Australian Universities (1958); Member New York Academy of Sciences; Member American Academy of Political and Social Science; Mem. Suffolk Naturalists Assoc.; Hon. Mem. of School Nature Study Union. *Publications:* Everyday Botany, 1934; General Science for Indian Schools (with Sir Richard Gregory, Bt., F.R.S.), 1939; Biological Readers, Books I-IV (with C. B. Rutley), 1942-45; Social Studies and World Citizenship (with F. J. May), 1944; Flowers in Britain, 1944; Trees in Britain, 1946; Science and Civilization (Lecture for the Anglo-Egyptian Union, Cairo), 1946; Science in a Changing World (series of lectures to Fouad I University, Cairo), 1946; Adult Education: The Record of the British Army (with Major T. H. Hawkins), 1947; The Floral Year, 1949; Reference Book to Enid Blyton Nature Readers, 1950; Nature Studies, 1951; Intermediate Botany (with Dr. S. Williams and Dr. G. Bond), 1953; Useful Animals of the World (with E. M. Edwards), 1956; School Course of Biology (with Dr. L. M. J. Kramer), 1957; Physiology, Anatomy and Health (with T. H. and Dr. K. Hawkins), 1957: articles in various journals; Editor of several scientific, medical, and educational books. *Address:* 401 Grenville House, Dolphin Square S.W.1. *T.:* Victoria 9105. *Clubs:* Athenæum, Savage. [*Died* 15 *Nov.* 1965.

BRIND, Admiral Sir (Eric James) Patrick, G.B.E., *cr.* 1951 (C.B.E. 1941); K.C.B., *cr.* 1946 (C.B. 1944); *b.* 12 May 1892; 3rd *s.* of Colonel E. A. Brind; *m.* 1918, Eileen Margaret Apperly (*d.* 1940); one *d.*; *m.* 1948, Edith Gordon, *widow* of Rear-Adm. H. E. C. Blagrove. *Educ.:* Osborne and Dartmouth Naval Colls. Capt., 1933; Rear-Adm., 1942; Vice-Adm., 1945; Admiral, 1949. Commanded H.M.S. Orion, Birmingham, Excellent; Chief of Staff to the C.-in-C. Home Fleet, 1940-42; an Assistant Chief of Naval Staff, 1942-44; commanded cruisers in British Pacific Fleet, 1945; President of Royal Naval College, Greenwich, 1946-48; Commander-in-Chief, Far East Station, 1949-51; Commander-in-Chief, Allied Forces, Northern Europe, 1951-1953; retired list, 1953. Served European War, 1914-18, in H.M. Gunboat Excellent, 1914-15, H.M.S. Malaya, 1916-18 and H.M.S. Sir John Moore, 1918. *Address:* Lye Green

Forge, Nr. Crowborough, Sussex. *Club:* United Service. [*Died* 4 *Oct.* 1963.

BRISBANE, Sir (Hugh) Lancelot, Kt. 1961; M.B.E. 1951; Chairman and Managing Director, H. L. Brisbane & Wunderlich Ltd.; Chairman: Local Board, Atlas Assurance Co. Ltd.; Chamberlain Industries Pty. Ltd.; Carba Dry Ice (W.A.) Pty. Ltd.; Director: Australian Fixed Trusts (W.A.) Pty. Ltd.; D.H.A. (W. Australia) Ltd.; North Kalgurli (1912) Ltd.; *b.* Fitzroy, Victoria, 16 March 1893; *s.* of H. Brisbane; *m.* 1921, Frances Leonard Hoyle; two *d.* *Educ.:* Perth Technical College, W.A. Served in European War, 1915-19. Founded H. L. Brisbane & Co. Ltd. (later H. L. Brisbane & Wunderlich Ltd.), 1929; Business Admin. Government Factories and Annexes, W. Australia, 1942-45; Chairman: Board Area Management, Ministry of Munitions, 1944-45; Trustees, Air Force Assoc.; Industrial Devel. Cttee., W.A. Govt., 1959-63; President: Nat. Heart Foundation of Australia (W.A. Div.); Asthma Foundation of Western Australia. Order of the Nile. *Recreations:* golf and fishing. *Address:* 53 Johnston Street, Peppermint Grove, Perth, Western Australia. *Clubs:* Weld, Perth, Karrinyup (all in W.A.). [*Died* 4 *Feb.* 1966.

BRISCO, Sir Hylton (Musgrave Campbell), 7th Bt. *cr.* 1782; *b.* 5 Dec. 1886; *s.* of late Arthur Hylton Brisco (5th *s.* of 3rd Bt.); *S.* cousin (Sir Aubrey Hylton Brisco, 6th Bt.) 1957; *m.* 1914, Kathleen, *d.* of W. Fenwick McAllum, New Zealand; one *s.* two *d.* (and one *s.* killed in action, 1943; three *d.* decd.). *Recreation:* outdoor bowls. *Heir:* *s.* Donald Gilfrid Brisco [*b.* 15 Sept. 1920; *m.* 1945, Irene, *o. d.* of Henry John Gage, Ermine Park, Brockworth, Gloucestershire; three *d.*]. *Address:* 208 Windsor Ave., Hastings, Hawke's Bay, New Zealand. [*Died* 8 *Jan.* 1968.

BRISCOE, Henry Vincent Aird, A.R.C.S; D.Sc.(Lond.); D.I.C.; M.Sc.(Dun.) F.R.I.C., F.Inst.F.; University Professor of Inorganic Chemistry, Imperial College, Royal College of Science, 1932-54, Professor Emeritus, 1954; Fellow of Imperial College of Science and Technology, 1958; Director of the Inorganic and Physical Chemistry Laboratories, 1938-54; *o. s.* of late W. H. Briscoe, Cross Keld, Robin Hood's Bay; *b.* Hackney, 24 Sept. 1888; *m.* 1915, Rebecca Kirkwood, *o. d.* of William Stevenson, Johnstone; one *s.* one *d.* *Educ.:* City of London School; Royal College of Science, South Kensington, 1906-09. Research Assistant to Sir T. E. Thorpe, 1909-11; Assistant Demonstrator, 1911-13; Demonstrator, 1913-1916; Lecturer in Engineering Chemistry at the Imperial College, 1916-18; Lecturer in charge of the Department of Organic Chemistry, Sir John Cass Technical Institute, 1917-19; Consulting Chemist and Chemical Engineer, 1916-21; Professor of Inorganic and Physical Chemistry, 1921-32, and Director of the Department of Chemistry, 1925-32, in Armstrong College, Newcastle upon Tyne, in the University of Durham; Professor of Chemistry, University of Durham College of Medicine, 1921-32; Secretary of the University of Durham School Examinations Board, 1923-32; Secretary and Director of Research of the Northern Coke Research Committee, 1926-32; Member of the Commission Internationale des Eléments Chimiques; Past President of the Paint Research Assoc., 1951-54. *Publications:* vol. i., part ii, The Inert Gases, of Text Books of Inorganic Chemistry; First Aid in the Laboratory and Workshop; Annual Reports on Inorganic Chemistry, 1922-28; contributions to Thorpe's Dictionary of Applied Chemistry and to scientific journals; (ed.) Supplement to Mellor's Comprehensive Treatise on Inorganic and Theoretical Chemistry. *Address:* Imperial College, S.W.7. *T.:* Kensington 5111 *Clubs:* Athenæum, Savage. [*Died* 24 *Sept.* 1961.

BRISTOW, Sir Charles (Holditch), Kt., *cr.* 1944; C.I.E. 1937; *b.* 28 Dec. 1887; *s.* of late H. B. Bristow, Chantry House, Steyning, Sussex; *m.* 1921, Alix Mildred, *d.* of H. J. Crafer, Houghton, Norfolk; one *s.* two *d.* *Educ.:* Bedford School; Christ's College, Cambridge. Entered Indian Civil Service, posted to Ahmedabad in Bombay Presidency, 1911; served European War in the I.A.R.O., attached to 2/4th P.W.O. Gurkha Rifles in Mesopotamia (wounded); served as Collector and District Magistrate Nasik, Poona, Satara and Sholapur; Settlement Commissioner, 1929; was Collector of Kanara and Secretary to Government, Home Dept.; Secretary to Governor of Bombay, 1935-38; Commissioner, Northern Division Bombay Presidency, 1938-40; Adviser to Governor of Bombay, 1941-46; acted as Governor of Bombay, Aug. 1945. *Recreations:* tennis, sailing. *Address:* Brinton Grange, near Melton Constable, Norfolk. [*Died* 18 *April* 1967.

BRISTOW, Ernest, C.M.G. 1933; *b.* 21 July 1873; *o. s.* of late Canon Bristow of Southwark Cathedral; *m.* 1926, Violet C., *d.* of late Richard Guy, Cork. *Educ.:* Merchant Taylors'; St. John's College, Cambridge. M.A. (Oriental Languages Tripos, 1897); Clerk to Legation, Tangier, 1897; Assistant Interpreter, 1902; Vice-Consul Zanzibar, 1907; Tangier, 1908; Resht, 1912; Consul, Tabriz, 1918; Consul-General, Isfahan, 1923-1934 when he retired on a pension. *Address:* Belsaye Private Hotel, Eastbourne, Sussex. *Club:* Royal Over-Seas League. [*Died* 9 *March* 1968.

BRISTOW, Sir Robert Charles, Kt., *cr.* 1941; C.I.E. 1935; *b.* 1880; *s.* of Robert Alfred Bristow and Laura Webb; *m.* 1925, Gertrude Kimpton; no *c.* In Admiralty service, Malta, Portsmouth, Dover, Rosyth and Whitehall; transferred to Government of India, 1920, for harbour work in South India; Administrative Officer and Harbour Engineer-in-Chief, Cochin Port, 1935-41. Hon. Vice-President, South Devon Literary and Debating Society. Retired in December 1961. *Publications:* The Real India; The Port of Cochin; The Mudbanks of Malabar; Sri Aurobindo, Mystic and Poet; The Only Way or National Teamwork; Westminster Hash or British Parliaments?; Cochin Saga (500 B.C.–1958 A.D.). *Recreations:* writing, music. *Address:* c/o National Provincial Bank Ltd., 15 Bishopsgate, E.C.2. [*Died* 3 *Sept.* 1966.

BRITTAIN, Frederick, Litt.D., M.A.; Fellow, and Keeper of the Records of Jesus College, Cambridge; *er. s.* of late William Brittain and Elizabeth (Daniels) Brittain; *m.* 1959, Muriel, *o. c.* of late Francis Octavius Cunnington and Hilda Jessie Cunnington (*née* Harper). *Educ.:* Queen Elizabeth's Grammar School, Barnet; Jesus College, Cambridge. Librarian of Jesus Coll., 1930-45; Steward, 1945-54; Prælector, 1954-64; Editor of the Cambridge Review, 1942-48; Pro-Proctor or Proctor of Cambridge Univ., 1943-48; Lectr. in Medieval Latin Literature, 1930-61. Vice-Pres. Hymn Soc. of Gt. Britain and Ireland. *Publications:* The Decadence of Europe (trans. from the Italian of F. S. Nitti), 1923; They Make a Desert (ditto), 1924; Saint Radegund, 1925; The Lyfe of Saynt Radegunde (ed.), 1926; Saint Giles, 1928; The Jesus College Boat Club (with H. B. Playford), 1928, vol. 2, 1962; Slowly Forward (points from Steve Fairbairn), 1929; Oar, Scull, and Rudder, a Bibliography of Rowing, 1930; History of South Mymms, 1931; (part author) No More Women (Footlights Revue), 1933; Latin in Church, the History of its Pronunciation, 1934 (enlarged 1955); The Medieval Latin and Romance Lyric, 1937 (2nd edn. 1951); A Short History of Jesus College, 1940; Babylon Bruis'd and Mount Moriah Mended (with B. L. Manning), 1940; Bernard Lord Manning, a Memoir, 1942; Arthur Quiller-Couch, a Biographical Study of "Q" 1947; "Q" Anthology, 194-; Tales of South Mymms and Elsewhere, 1952; Mostly Mymms, 1954; (with late Arthur Gray) A History of Jesus College, 1960; The Penguin Book of Latin Verse, 1962; The Penguin Handbook to Literature (Medieval Latin section), 1968. *Recreations:* acting and singing. *Address:* Jesus College, Cambridge; Ingham Lodge, South Mymms, Herts. *Club:* Footlights (Cambridge). [*Died* 15 *March* 1969.

BRITTAIN, Sir Herbert, K.C.B. *cr.* 1955 (C.B. 1941); K.B.E., *cr.* 1944; *b.* 3 July 1894; *s.* of late Rev. J. H. Brittain, of Rochdale, Everton (Beds.), and Welwyn Garden City; *m.* 1920, Annie Crabtree; one *s.* one *d.* *Educ.:* Rochdale Secondary School; Manchester University. Served in Royal Field Artillery, 1915-19; Major (despatches twice); entered Treasury, 1919; Second Secretary in the Treasury, 1953-57; retired, 1957. Chairman, Iron and Steel Holding and Realisation Agency; Member, Council on Tribunals; Chairman, Civil Service Insurance Society and associated Societies; Chairman, and later President, Civil Service Riding Club (1946-58). *Publication:* The British Budgetary System, 1959. *Address:* 8 Pont St., S.W.1. *T.:* Belgravia 8107. *Club:* Reform. [*Died* 6 *Sept.* 1961.

BRITTAIN, Vera, M.A.; Hon. D.Litt.; F.R.S.L.; Writer; *b.* Newcastle, Staffordshire; *o. d.* of late Thomas Arthur Brittain and Edith Mary Bervon; *m.* 1925, Prof. George E. G. Catlin; one *s.* one *d.* *Educ.:* St. Monica's, Kingswood; Somerville Coll., Oxf. (Exhibitioner). Lecture tours in U.S.A. and Canada, 1934, 1937, 1940, 1946, 1957, 1958, 1959; Holland, 1936, Scandinavia, 1945, Germany, 1947, India and Pakistan, 1949-50, India, 1963; addresses to University of Natal Jubilee Conference, Durban, South Africa, 1960; Director, Femina Books Ltd.; Hon. Life President, Society of Women Writers and Journalists; Pres., Married Women's Association; Vice-Pres., Women's Internat. League for Peace and Freedom; Vice-Pres., National Peace Council. *Publications:* Twenty-nine books, including: Testament of Youth, 1933; Honourable Estate, 1936; Thrice a Stranger, 1938; Testament of Friendship, 1940; England's Hour, 1941; Humiliation with Honour, 1942; Account Rendered, 1945. On Becoming a Writer, 1947; Born 1925: A Novel of Youth, 1949; In the Steps of John Bunyan (in U.S.A., Valiant Pilgrim), 1950; Search After Sunrise, 1951; Lady Into Woman: A History of Women from Victoria to Elizabeth II, 1953; Testament of Experience, 1957; The Women at Oxford, 1959; Selected Letters of Winifred Holtby and Vera Brittain (limited edn.), 1960; Pethick-Lawrence: A Portrait, 1963; The Rebel Passion: A Short History of some Pioneer Peacemakers, 1964; Envoy Extraordinary: a Study of Vijaya Lakshmi Pandit, 1965; Literary Testaments (Katja Reissner Lecture 1960) in Essays by Divers Hands, Vol. XXXIV, R.S.L., 1966; Radclyffe Hall: A Case of Obscenity?, 1968. *Recreations:* walking, travelling, politics. *Address:* 4 Whitehall Court, S.W.1. *Clubs:* Arts Theatre, P.E.N., Royal Commonwealth Society. [*Died* 29 *March* 1970.

BRITTON, Colonel; *see* Ritchie, Douglas Ernest.

BROAD, Philip, C.M.G. 1954; *b.* 18 Jan. 1903. *Educ.:* Clifton Coll.; St. John's Coll., Cambridge. Appointed a 3rd Sec. in Foreign Office. 1926; 2nd Secretary, 1931; 1st Secretary, 1938; Foreign Service Officer, Grade 6, 1946; Counsellor, 1949. Has served in Tokyo, Washington, Tehran, Cairo, Bari, Warsaw; also at various periods in Foreign Office; Political Adviser to A.F.H.Q., Italy, 1943; Political Adviser, Trieste, 1951-54; Counsellor in charge of Permanent Under-Secretary's Committee Secretariat, 1959; Consul-General at Istanbul, 1955-60, retd. *Club:* St. James'. [*Died* 25 *Feb.* 1966.

BROADFOOT, Hon. Sir Walter James, K.B.E. *cr.* 1955; Postmaster-General and Minister of Telegraphs, New Zealand, 1949-1954; *b.* Lower Hutt, New Zealand, 1881; widower; two *d.* *Educ.:* Auckland. Joined staff of Auckland Observer and served in Post and Telegraph Department; resigned to study law; practised with P. H. Watt at Hamilton, 1907; Te Kuiti, 1908; practised in partnership with G. P. Finlay (now Sir George Finlay) for 16 years. Mayor of Te Kuiti for 8 years (after being Deputy Mayor, 1923-25), also Chm. Te Kuiti Chamber of Commerce and President of New Zealand Tourist League. Interested in land settlement, immigration and tourist traffic. M.P. for Waitomo, N.Z., 1928-54; Minister of National Service, War Administration, 1942; Jun. Whip, 1936-41; Sen. Whip, 1941-49. *Recreations:* formerly hockey (Auckland rep.), cricket, lacrosse. *Address:* 4 Stormont Place, Kingston, Wellington, S.W.1., N.Z. [*Died* 10 *Sept.* 1965.

BROCK, Captain Donald Carey, C.B.E. 1943 (O.B.E. 1919); R.N. (retd.); Jurat, Royal Court, Guernsey, 1950-62; Conseiller of States of Guernsey, 1952-58; *b.* 5 July 1891; *y. s.* of late Rev. H. W. Brock, M.A., S. Pierre du Bois, Guernsey, C.I.; *m.* 1946, Annette, *yr. d.* of late Arthur Lecat, St. Brévin les Pins, Loire Inf., France; two *s.* twin *d.* *Educ.:* Elizabeth College, Guernsey; R.N. Colls., Osborne and Dartmouth. Midshipman, 1909; Lieut., 1914; Lt.-Comdr., 1922; retired with rank of Commander, 1931. Served European War, 1914-18 (O.B.E.); War of 1939-45, as Capt., R.N., operations in France, 1939-40 (despatches); Egypt, 1940-1943; as Commodore, R.N., Principal Sea Transport Officer, Middle East, 1943-44 (C.B.E.) and Mediterranean, 1944-45. Reverted to Retired List with rank of Capt. R.N., 1946. *Address:* 33B Bushey Hall Road, Bushey, Herts. *T.:* Watford 43753. [*Died* 29 *July* 1970.

BROCK, Dame Dorothy; *see* Brock, Dame M. D.

BROCK, Air Commodore Henry Le Marchant, C.B. 1931; D.S.O. 1916; late Royal Air Force; *b.* 5 May 1889; *s.* of late Rev. H. W. Brock of Guernsey; *m.* 1917, Daphne Fanshawe, *e. d.* of C. A. Carey, Guernsey; two *s.* one *d.* *Educ.:* Elizabeth College, Guernsey. 2nd Lieut. Royal Guernsey Militia, 1907; Royal Warwickshire Regt. 1909; R.F.C. 1913; Wing-Commander, 1916; Air Commodore, 1931; served European War, 1914-19 (D.S.O., despatches five times); N.W. Frontier Province, 1930 (C.B.); A.O.C. No. 22 (Army Co-op.) Group, 1931-36; A.O.A. Bomber Command, 1936-37; retired list, 1937; Deputy Commandant, Royal Observer Corps, 1938-42. *Address:* Wyk House, Rotherwick, Hants. *Club:* Athenæum. [*Died* 11 *March* 1964.

BROCK, Dame (Madeline) Dorothy, D.B.E., *cr.* 1947 (O.B.E. 1929); M.A. (Cantab), 1926; Litt.D. (T.C.D.), 1911; Hon. LL.M. (Lond.), 1947; Headmistress of Mary Datchelor School, Camberwell, S.E.5, 1918-1950; *b.* 18 Nov. 1886; *yr. d.* of late G. W. F. Brock, Afton, Bromley, Kent. *Educ.:* Bromley High School (G.P.D.S.T.); Girton College, Cambridge. Cambridge Classical Tripos; Part I, Class I, 1907, Part II, Class II, 1908;

held Research Studentships, 1908-10, at Girton; Classical Mistress at King Edward's High School, Birmingham, 1910-17; member of Prime Minister's Committee on Classics, 1919; Chairman of Committee of Association of Headmistresses, 1927-29; Vice-President of Classical Association since 1930; member of Lancet Commission on Nursing, 1931; Member of the Consultative Committee of the Board of Education, 1931-40; President of the Association of Head Mistresses, 1933-35; Chairman of Joint Committee of the Four Secondary Associations, 1935-37; Member B.M.A. Committee on Physical Education, 1936; Member of Secondary School Examinations Council of Board of Education, 1937-1951; Member of Inter-Departmental Committee on Nursing, 1937; of Departmental Committee on Public Schools, 1942-44; Director, Univ. of London Press, 1951-68. Honorary Freedom of Clothworkers' Company, and Freedom of City of London, 1936; Freedom of the Borough of Camberwell, 1950, now Southwark. *Publications:* Studies in Fronto and his age, 1911; The Girls' School: ch. vii. of The Schools of England, 1929; An Unusual Happening, 1946; Parts 3 and 6 of The Story of the Mary Datchelor School, 1877-1957, 1957. *Recreations:* music, reading. *Address:* Teasels, Tankerton Road, Tankerton, Whitstable, Kent. *T.:* Whitstable 3306. [*Died* 31 *Dec.* 1969.

BROCKET, 2nd Baron, *cr.* 1933, of Brocket Hall, County of Hertford; **Arthur Ronald Nall Nall-Cain,** 2nd Bt., *cr.* 1921; Barrister-at-law, Inner Temple, 1927; J.P. Hertfordshire; Chairman of Hertfordshire Soc.; Chairman: Brocket Estates Ltd.; O'Cahan Estates Ltd.; Carton Properties Ltd.; Eire Chemicals Ltd.; Liverpool Marine & Gen. Insce. Co. Ltd.; Vice-Chairman, Allied Breweries Ltd.; Director: Nat. Carbonising Co.; Midland Rexco Ltd.; Rexco Products Ltd.; Scottish Rexco Ltd.; Dublin Board of Century & Friends Provident Insurance Co. Ltd.; Member National Trust Historic Buildings Committee; Mem. Exec. Cttee. C.P.R.E.; *b.* 4 Aug. 1904; *o. s.* of 1st Baron and Florence (*d.* 1927), *y. d.* of late William Nall, Kegworth, Leics.; *S.* father 1934; *m.* 1927, Angela Beatrix (Order of Mercy and Bar), *yr. d.* of late Preb. W. G. Pennyman, Ormesby Hall, Yorks; one *s.* one *d.* (and one *s.* decd.). *Educ.:* Eton; Magdalen College, Oxford, B.A. 1925; M.A. 1930. M.P. (C.), Wavertree Division, 1931-1934; member of House of Lords Select Committee on Road Accidents, 1938-39. Member of Hertfordshire County Council, 1931-46; Member of Hertfordshire T.A. Assoc. 1935-46; Hon. Treas. of the League of Mercy, 1935-47; Chairman, Land Union, 1936-51; Chairman: Walker Cain Ltd., 1934-64; Tetley Walker Ltd., 1960-64; President Association of Land and Property Owners, 1960-; President of Hertfordshire Agricultural Society, 1935 and 1956, Chairman, 1936-46; President of Central and Associated Chambers of Agriculture, 1938-40; Chm. Appeals and Propaganda Cttee. of National Playing Fields Assoc., 1937-47; Pres. British Percheron Horse Society, 1938-39; on Herefordshire War Agricultural Executive Labour Cttee., 1941-44; Pres. Clun Forest Sheep Society, 1943-44; Pres. National Sheep Breeders Association, 1945-47; President Suffolk Sheep Society, 1961; President Ryeland Sheep Society, 1963. Patron of six livings; Knight of Justice of Order of St. John of Jerusalem, Order of Mercy. *Recreations:* shooting, stalking, golf, played golf for Oxford University *v.* Cambridge, 1923-24-25-26 (Captain, 1925), winner of Parliamentary golf cup, 1939. *Heir:* *g.s.* Charles Ronald George Nall-Cain, *b.* 12 Feb. 1952. *Address:* Brocket Hall, Welwyn, Hertfordshire. *T.:* Hatfield 3033; Carton, Maynooth, Co. Kildare. *T.:* Dublin 286-250. *Club:* Carlton. [*Died* 24 *March* 1967.

BROCKHOLES, J. W. F.; *see* Fitzherbert-Brockholes.

BROCKINGTON, Leonard Walter, C.M.G. 1946; Q.C. Alberta and Manitoba; B.A., LL.D.; D.C.L.; Counsel, Gowling, MacTavish, Osborne & Henderson, Barristers, Ottawa, since 1942; Rector of Queen's Univ., Canada; Pres., Odeon Theatres (Canada) Ltd., and J. Arthur Rank Organisation of Canada, Ltd. and subsidiary cos.; *b.* Cardiff, Wales, 6 April 1888; *s.* of Walter Brockington and Annie Walters; *m.* 1913, Agnes Neaves MacKenzie; two *s.* *Educ.:* Cardiff High School (Scholar and leaving exhibitioner); University College of South Wales and Monmouthshire (entrance scholar). B.A. University of Wales (Hons. Latin and Hons. Greek); Classics and English Master, Cowley Grammar School, St. Helens, Lancashire; emigrated to Canada, 1912; sometime journalist and civil servant; Gold Medallist Law Society of Alberta; called to Bar of Alberta, 1919; Hon. LL.D. Univs. of Alberta, Wales, Middlebury, U.S.A., Syracuse, U.S.A., Western Ontario, and Queen's, Canada; Hon. D.C.L. Bishop's; Hon. Life Member Canadian Legion; Hon. Bencher, Inner Temple, 1942; Hon. Member of American Bar Association; Member of Bars of Alberta, Manitoba, and Ontario; City Solicitor, Calgary, 1921-35; General Counsel, Northwestern Grain Dealers, Winnipeg, 1935-39; first Chairman, Board of Governors Canadian Broadcasting Corporation, 1936-39; Special War-time Assistant to Prime Minister of Canada, 1939-42; visited England Dec. 1941 as guest of the British Government. Returned to England as Adviser, Empire Division, M.O.I., London, July 1942. Hon. member Bar of City and State of New York; Hon. life member Canadian Bar Association, 1949. Canada Council Medal 1962. *Address:* (law office) 88 Metcalfe Street, Ottawa, Ontario, Canada; (office) 20 Carlton Street, Toronto, Ont., Canada. *Clubs:* Athenæum; Rideau (Ottawa); Ranchmen's (Calgary); Manitoba (Winnipeg); York (Toronto). [*Died* 15 *Sept.* 1966.

BRODIE, Neil, C.I.E. 1947; Chairman, Gladstone Wyllie & Co. Ltd., 26 Lime Street, E.C.3 (formerly Chairman of Board of Gladstone, Lyall & Co. Ltd., Calcutta); *b.* 3 Oct. 1900; *s.* of late Neil Brodie, Ayrshire; *m.* 1928, E. Katharine Emmert; two *s.* *Educ.:* Bearsden Acad. Served 4th Seaforths, 1918-1919; joined Gladstone Wyllie Co. (became a public company, 1948; now Gladstone Lyall & Co. Ltd.), Calcutta, 1924; partner, 1937. *Recreation:* golf. *Address:* April Cottage, Fredley Park, Mickleham, nr. Dorking. *T.:* Dorking 2706. *Clubs:* Oriental; Bengal, Tollygunge (Calcutta). [*Died* 17 *March* 1968.

BRODRICK, William John Henry, O.B.E. 1917; Metropolitan Police Magistrate, 1928-44; *b.* 25 Jan. 1874; 2nd *s.* of late Rev. Hon. Alan Brodrick; *heir-pres.* to Viscountcy of 2nd Earl of Midleton, M.C.; *m.* 1902, Blanche, *e. d.* of late F. A. Hawker; four *s.* *Educ.:* Charterhouse; Corpus Christi College, Oxford (M.A.). Bar, Lincoln's Inn, 1899; sometime Secretary Alien's Advisory Committee; Recorder of Bournemouth, 1924-28. Chevalier of Order of Crown of Belgium. *Address:* 12 Frognal Gardens, Hampstead, N.W.3. [*Died* 28 *Oct.* 1964.

BROKE-SMITH, Brigadier Philip William Lilian, C.I.E. 1937; D.S.O. 1916; O.B.E. 1918; Fellow Institute of Civil Defence; *b.* 1882; *s.* of Surgeon Major-General Philip Broke-Smith, Army Medical Staff; *m.* 1908, Dorothy Margaret, *d.* of Vice-Admiral G. O. Twiss; one *s.* two *d.* *Educ.:* Cheltenham College; Royal Military Academy, Woolwich. 2nd Lieut. R.E. 1900;

balloon pilot, 1902; man-lifting kite pilot, 1904; Airship pilot, 1910; Aeroplane pilot, 1912; air services, England and Gibraltar (R.E.), 1902-05; India (R.E.), 1907-08; England (R.E. and R.F.C.), 1910-12; Mesopotamia (R.F.C.), 1915-16; Military Works, N.W. Frontier of India, 1906-10, 1913-15 and 1916-19, including Mohmand Blockade and Afghan War, 1919 (A.D. Works, N.W.F. Force); A.D. Military Works, A.H.Q. India, 1919-24; C.R.E. Baluchistan District, Quetta, India, 1928-29; Deputy Engineer-in-chief, Army Headquarters, India, 1931-32; Chief Engineer, Eastern Command, India, 1932-36; retired 1936; Director Passive Air Defence, Ministry of Supply, 1939-45. *Publication:* History of Early British Military Aeronautics, 1952. *Address:* Summerhill Cottage, Lindfield, Haywards Heath, Sussex. *Club:* Royal Over-Seas League. [*Died* 10 *Nov.* 1963.

BROMHEAD, Lieut.-Colonel Alfred Claude, C.B.E. 1918; Commander Order of St. Maurice and St. Lazarus; Officer Orders of St. Anne and St. Stanislas; J.P. Richmond; Governor Star and Garter Home; Director Anglo-Scottish Investment Trust Ltd.; *b.* Southsea, 25 July 1876; 4th *s.* of late S. S. Bromhead; *m.* 1st, 1906, Olive (*d.* 1911), *d.* of late S. Guest; 2nd, 1914, Gertrude Carmela (*d.* 1947); two *s.* one *d.*; 3rd, Margaret Eileen Eaton. Joined 4th Queen's, 1899; retired as Captain, 1907; rejoined 24th London Regiment, The Queen's, 1914; seconded for special mission to Russian Armies, 1916; Riga to Caucasus-Roumania and Asia Minor, 1916-17; Lt.-Col., 1917; commanded British Special Mission to Italian Armies, 1918-19; Co-Founder with M. Leon Gaumont of the Gaumont Company, 1898; First Chm. Gaumont British Picture Corporation, also later Chairman Provincial Cinematograph Theatres Ltd., and associated Companies—retired from the above, 1929; Hon. Adviser to Films Div., M.O.I., 1939-45. *Address:* Douglas House, Petersham, Sy. *T.:* Richmond 0240; Hill End Farm, Sherborne St. John, Basingstoke. *T.:* Monk Sherborne 16. [*Died* 5 *March* 1963.

BROMLEY, Rear-Admiral Sir Arthur 8th Bt. *cr.* 1757; K.C.M.G. 1941 (C.M.G. 1919; K.C.V.O. 1953 (C.V.O. 1935); late R.N.; Ceremonial and Reception Secretary, Dominions (now Commonwealth Relations) and Colonial Office, 1931-52, retired; temporarily re-employed from 1 Dec. 1952 for special Coronation duties; a Gentleman Usher to the Queen since 1952 (to King George V, 1927; to King George VI, 1937-1952); *b.* 8 August 1876; 3rd *s.* of Sir Henry Bromley, 5th Bart.; *S.* brother (Sir Maurice Bromley-Wilson, 7th Bt.) 1957; *m.* 1904, Laura Mary (*d.* 1959), *d.* of Hon. James Dunsmuir, Hatley Park, Victoria, B.C.; one *s.* four *d.* *Educ.:* Farnborough School; H.M.S. Britannia; joined Navy, 1892; Lieutenant, 1898; Commander, 1908; Captain, 1915; served European War, 1914-18; H.M.S. Courageous, 1916-19; Flag Capt. to Vice-Admiral Napier commanding Light Cruiser Force (C.M.G.); retired list, 1922; Rear-Adm., retired, 1926; patron of two livings. *Recreations:* fishing, shooting. *Heir:* *s.* Rupert Howe Bromley [*b.* 31 Dec. 1910; *m.* 1935, Dorothy Vera, *d.* of Sir Walford Selby, K.C.M.G., C.B.; two *s.*]. *Address:* 59 Cadogan Square, S.W.1. *Club:* Turf. [*Died* 12 *Jan.* 1961.

BROMLEY, Sir Rupert (Howe), 9th Bt. *cr.* 1757; M.C. 1944; *b.* 31 Dec. 1910; *o. s.* of Rear-Admiral Sir Arthur Bromley, 8th Bt., K.C.M.G., K.C.V.O., and Laura Mary (*d.* 1959), *d.* of Hon. James Dunsmuir, sometime Lieut.-Governor of British Columbia; *S.* father, 1961; *m.* 1st, 1935, Dorothy Vera (marriage dissolved, 1960), *o. d.* of Sir Walford Selby, K.C.M.G.; two *s.*; 2nd, 1960, Ethel Maud, *d.* of Francis Stephens, Killarney, Co. Cork. *Educ.:* Eton. Served War of 1939-45 (M.C.): Grenadier Guards, 3rd Division, B.E.F., 1939-40; Major, 1940; Guards' Armoured Division, 1941-44 (wounded and evacuated from Normandy, 1944). Staff College, Haifa, 1945-46; Military Secretary's Branch, G.H.Q. Middle East Land Forces, 1946-47; retired, as Major, 1948. *Recreations:* hunting, shooting, ski-ing, sailing. *Heir:* *s.* Rupert Charles Bromley [*b.* 2 April 1936; *m.* 1962, Priscilla Hazel, *d.* of late Major Howard Bourne, H.A.C., and of Mrs. J. W. Pollock, Bridge House, Shoreham, Kent; two *s.*]. *Address:* Ashwell Estate, Glendale, Rhodesia. *T.:* Glendale 1840. *Club:* Guards. [*Died* 13 *June* 1966.

BROMWICH, Engineer Rear-Admiral George Herbert, D.S.O. 1900; O.B.E.; late R.N.; *s.* of Dr. E. Cockey, Frome, Somerset; *b.* Nov. 1871 [name changed to Bromwich by deed-poll, 1912]; *m.* Evelyn, *d.* of Richard Newton, Brisbane; one *s.* one *d.* *Educ.:* Bloxham, Banbury, Oxford. Assisted at salvage operations at Ferrol on board H.M.S. Howe in 1893; Australia in H.M.S. Karrakatta, 1894-97; served China, 1900 (D.S.O.); Superintendent Naval Yard, Sydney, 1913-19 (O.B.E.); Engineer Capt., 1921; Chief Engineer Naval Yard, Hong Kong, 1922-24; Admiralty Overseer, Manchester and Liverpool District, 1925-27; retired, 1926; Eng.-Rr. Adm., retired list, 1927. *Address:* 22 Bereweke Road, Felpham, Bognor Regis, Sussex. [*Died* 11 *Dec.* 1965.

BRONSON, Howard Logan, F.R.S.C.; Professor of Physics, Dalhousie College, Halifax, N.S., 1910-46, Emeritus since 1947; *b.* Washington, Connecticut, 12 July 1878; *s.* of Walter W. Bronson, merchant, and Helen M. Logan; *m.* 1st, 1910, Anna J. Baldwin (*d.* 1914), New Haven, Conn.; no *c.*; 2nd, 1925, Merle P. Colpitt. *Educ.:* Gunnery School, Washington; Yale University; B.A. 1900; Ph.D. 1904. Instructor in Physics, Lehigh University, 1900-1901; Assistant in Physics, Yale University, 1901-2; Sloane Fellow in Physics, 1902-4; Demonstrator, McGill University, 1904-7; Lecturer, 1907-9; Assistant Professor, 1909-10; Member American Association for Advancement of Science, American Physical Society, and N.S. Institute of Science. Hon. LL.D. Dalhousie Univ., 1947. *Publications:* Papers on Radio activity, Standards of High Resistance, and Standard Cells and Specific Heat in Proceedings of the Royal Society and scientific journals. *Address:* 1154 Studley Avenue, Halifax, N.S. [*Died* 7 *March* 1968.

BROOK, Captain Edward William, J.P., D.L. Dumfriesshire; Extra Equerry to Duke of Gloucester; *b.* 1895; *o. s.* of late Col. Charles Brook, T.D., J.P., Upperwood House, Greenfield, Yorks, and Kinmount, Annan, Dumfriesshire; *m.* 1933, Mary C. H., *yr. d.* of 1st Baron Gretton, P.C., C.B.E.; one *s.* one *d.* *Educ.:* Radley; Royal Military College, Sandhurst. Served Yorkshire Dragoons, 1914-15; 20th Hussars, 1915-22, France and Egypt. Member of Queen's Body Guard for Scotland (Royal Company of Archers); D.L. Dumfriesshire, 1951. *Recreations:* big game shooting, hunting, shooting, fishing. *Address:* 2 Mansfield Street, Portland Place, W.1. *T.:* Langham 3996; Carskiey, Southend, Argyll. *T.:* Southend (Argyll) 229; Kinmount, Annan, Dumfriesshire. *T.:* Cummertrees 246. *Clubs:* Cavalry, Puck's; Yorkshire (York). [*Died* 20 *Jan.* 1963.

BROOK, John Herbert, C.M.G. 1952; Assistant Secretary in Ministry of Education; *b.* 27 March 1912; *s.* of H. A. Brook, B.A., B.Sc., and Annie Brook; *m.* 1st, 1936, Isabel Black (*d.* 1959); three *s.*; 2nd, 1961, Elizabeth Woodville Wilson. *Educ.:*

Bablake Sch., Coventry; Christ's Coll., Cambridge (Scholar). B.A. (Cantab.) 1st Class Hons. Modern Langs. Tripos, 1932; 1st Class Hons. History Tripos, 1933. Entered Administrative Civil Service, 1934; Private Sec. to Secretary for Mines, 1940; Coal Representative, Allied C.C.G. (U.K. Element), Berlin, 1946; Coal Adviser, U.K. Delegation to Marshall Plan Conf., Paris, 1947; Chairman: Coal Cttee., Economic Commission for Europe (U.N.), 1949-51; Supply and Distribution Sub-Cttee., O.E.E.C., Paris, 1951; Petroleum Attaché, British Embassy, Washington, 1953-56; now in Welsh Dept., Ministry of Education. *Recreations:* historical research, painting foreign travel. *Address:* 39 Clarence Rd., Walton-on-Thames, Surrey. *T.:* Walton-on-Thames 21831. *Club:* English-Speaking Union. [*Died* 24 *Dec.* 1963.

BROOK, Bt. Colonel Reginald James, C.B.E. 1919; D.S.O. 1916; T.D. 1943; D.L.; late Royal Canadian Regt. and 56th (King's Own) Anti-Tank Regt., R.A. (T.A.); *b.* 1885; *s.* of Arthur Brook, Woodhouse, Weybridge; *m.* 1912, Eleanor Darlington; one *s.* two *d.* *Educ.:* Uppingham. Served European War, 1914-1918; Russia, 1918-19 (despatches, C.B.E., D.S.O. Czechoslovakia War Cross); War of 1939-45. *Address:* The Beeches, Aughton, Hornby, nr. Lancaster.
[*Died* 10 *Sept.* 1965.

BROOK, Rt. Rev. Richard, D.D., M.A.; *b.* 1880; *e. s.* of late Richard Brook, Bradford; *m.* 1928, Janet Moss, *e. d.* of W. Roscoe Hardwick, Huyton Lancashire. *Educ.:* Bradford School; Lincoln College, Oxford (Scholar). 1st Class Honours, Modern History, Oxford B.A. (M.A. 1906); Aubrey Moore student; Liddon Student, Oxford; 1st Class Honours, Theology, Oxford, 1904; ordained, 1905; Fellow and Tutor of Merton College, Oxford, 1906-19; Sub-Warden of Merton College, 1919; Lecturer of Oriel College, Oxford, 1911-14; Select Preacher to the University of Oxford, 1914-16, 1936-37; Univ. of Cambridge, 1940 and 1946; Examiner Honour School of Theology, Oxford, 1914-16; Chaplain to the Forces (mentioned twice), 1916-19; Head master of Liverpool College, 1919-28; Vicar of Doncaster and Canon of Sheffield, 1928-35; Rural Dean of Doncaster, 1934-35; Archdeacon of Coventry and Rector of St. Andrew with Holy Trinity, Rugby, 1935-40; Bishop of St. Edmundsbury and Ipswich, 1940-53; Examining Chaplain to Bishop of Wakefield, 1911-19; to Bishop of Manchester, 1921; to Bishop of Ripon, 1926; Chaplain to the King, 1935-41. Mem. of Board of Church Commissioners, 1948. *Publications:* (joint), Foundations, 1912; Contributor to Murray's Bible Dictionary, 1908, and Peake's Commentary on Bible, 1919. *Recreations:* canicure and washing-up. *Address:* Crag Close, Grasmere, Westmorland. *T.:* Grasmere 216. *Club:* Athenæum
9 [*Died* 31 *Jan.* 1969.

BROOKE (Bernard) Jocelyn; Author; *b* 30 Nov. 1908; *yr. s.* of late Henry Brooke and May Turner. *Educ.:* Bedales; Worcester College, Oxford. *Publications:* December Spring (poems), 1946; The Military Orchid, 1948; The Scapegoat, 1949; The Wonderful Summer, 1949; A Mine of Serpents, 1949; The Image of a Drawn Sword, 1950; The Wild Orchids of Britain, 1950; The Goose Cathedral, 1950; Ronald Firbank, 1951; The Flower in Season, 1952; The Denton Welch Journals (Ed.), 1952; The Elements of Death (poems), 1952; The Passing of a Hero, 1953; Private View, 1954; The Dog at Clambercrown, 1955; The Crisis in Bulgaria, 1956; Conventional Weapons, 1961; Denton Welch: A Selection from his Published Works (Ed. and Introduced), 1963; The Birth of a Legend, 1964. *Recreation:* botany. *Address:* Ivy Cottage, Bishopsbourne, Nr. Canterbury, Kent. *T.:* Bridge 377. *Club:* Oxford and Cambridge.
[*Died* 29 *Oct.* 1966.

BROOKE, Lieut.-General Sir Bertram Norman Sergison-, K.C.B., *cr.* 1942 (C.B. 1935); K.C.V.O., *cr.* 1937; C.M.G. 1919; D.S.O. 1915; *b.* 20 July 1880; *m.* 1st, 1915, Prudence (*d.* 1918), *e. d.* of late C. Sergison of Cuckfield Park, Sussex; one *d.*; 2nd, 1923, Hilda (*d.* 1954), *d.* of Mark Fenwick, Abbotswood, Stow-on-the-Wold; one *s.* Entered Army, 1899; Capt., 1907; Maj., 1914; Temp. Lt.-Col. Feb. 1916; Brig.-Gen. Aug. 1917-March 1919; Col. 1923; Maj.-Gen. 1934; served S. Africa, 1899-1902 (Queen's medal 3 clasps, King's medal 2 clasps); European War, 1914-18 (despatches, D.S.O., C.M.G., Bt. Lt.-Col.); commanded 1st (Guards) Brigade, Aldershot, 1928-31; Brigadier, General Staff, Eastern Command India, 1931-34; G.O.C. London District, 1934-38; Chm. of Royal Tournament, 1934-1938; retired pay, 1939; re-employed Sept. 1939; G.O.C. London District, 1939-42; British Red Cross Commissioner with Allied Army of Liberation, 1943-45. *Address:* The Manor House, Chipping Warden, Banbury. *T.:* Chipping Warden 227. *Clubs:* Turf, White's. [*Died* 26 *March* 1967.

BROOKE, Sir Charles Vyner, G.C.M.G., *cr.* 1927; Rajah of Sarawak, 1917-46; *b.* London, Sept. 1874; *s.* of H.H. Charles Brooke, G.C.M.G., 2nd Rajah, and Margaret, *d.* of Clayton de Windt, Blunsden Hall, Wilts; *S.* father, 1917; *m.* 1911, Hon. Sylvia Brett (author of Sylvia of Sarawak: An Autobiography, 1936; The Three White Rajahs, 1939), *d.* of 2nd Viscount Esher; three *d.* *Educ.:* Clevedon, Winchester; Magdalene College, Cambridge. Joined his father in Sarawak to study the duties of government, 1897; has led several expeditions into the far interior of the country to punish head hunters; understands the management of natives; ruled over a population of 500 000 souls and a country 40,000 sq. miles in extent. *Address:* 13 Albion Street, Bayswater Road, W.2. [*Died* 9 *May* 1963.

BROOKE, Major-General Geoffrey (Francis Heremon), C.B. 1938; D.S.O. 1918; M.C.; 16/5th Lancers; *b.* 1884; *s.* of late John Monk Brooke, of Castleknock, Ireland; *m.* 1st, 1908, Vera Mechin, *d.* of Baron de Soukhanov; one *s.*; 2nd, 1926, Dorothy Evelyn Searight (*d.* 1955), *d.* of Henry Vivian Gibson Craig. *Educ.:* Haileybury. Served European War, 1914-18 (despatches, D.S.O. and bar, M.C., Croix de Guerre, Brevet Major, Brevet Lieut.-Colonel); Comdr. Cavalry Brigade, Egypt, 1930-34; A.D.C. to the King, 1934-35; Inspector General of Cavalry, India, 1935-1939; retired pay, 1939. *Publications:* Horse Sense and Horsemanship of To-day, 1924; Horse Lovers, 1927; The Way of a Man with a Horse, 1929; A Hunting we will go, 1932; The Foxhunter's England, 1937; Horsemen All, 1939; The Brotherhood of Arms; The Glad Companion; Riding and Stablecraft; Good Company, 1955. *Address:* Malmesbury House, The Close, Salisbury. *Club:* Cavalry. [*Died* 26 *June* 1966.

BROOKE, Jocelyn; *see* Brooke, B. J.

BROOKE, Nevile John, C.B.E. 1957; retired as Puisne Judge, Supreme Court of Nigeria; *b.* 9 May 1891; *s.* of George Brooke, Barrister-at-law, of the Inland Revenue Dept., Somerset House; *m.* 1924, Gladys Edith Monckton. *Educ.:* Felsted School; Corpus Christi College, Cambridge. Colonial Service; Nigerian Administrative Service, 1915; Resident, 1932; Judge of High Court, 1934; Puisne Judge of Supreme Court, 1940; acted as Chief Justice, Nigeria;

Member of West African Court of Appeal, 1934-48; Comr. for Revision of Laws of Nigeria, 1948; Special Comr., Native Courts Commns. of Inquiry, Nigeria, 1949-52, Sierra Leone, 1953; Chm., Public Service Commn., Western Region, Nigeria, 1954; retired Dec. 1956. *Publications:* Census of Northern Provinces of Nigeria, 1931; Revised Edn. of Laws of Nigeria, 1948, Supplement 1949; Reports of Native Courts Commissions of Inquiry (Nigeria, 1952, Sierra Leone, 1953). *Address:* Keverstone Court, Manor Road, Bournemouth, Hants. *Clubs:* Royal Commonwealth Society, Junior Carlton. [*Died* 28 *June* 1968.

BROOKES, Captain Sir Ernest Geoffrey, Kt., *cr.* 1946; *b.* 1889; *s.* of A. E. Brookes, Gloucester; *m* 1920, Mabel Emily, *d.* of Louis Asiola, Sydney, N.S.W.; one *s.* one *d.* *Educ.:* Crypt Grammar School, Gloucester H.M.S. Conway. Joined British India S.N. Co., 1909; promoted to command, 1926; Commodore, 1944-46; retired, 1946. *Recreations:* bowling, gardening. *Address:* c/o British India S.N. Co., One, Aldgate, E.C.3. [*Died* 10 *July* 1969.

BROOKES, Sir Norman Everard, Kt., *cr.* 1939; Chevalier Légion d'Honneur; Chairman Australasian Paper and Pulp Co. Ltd., and North British Insurance Co.; Director of other companies; partner William Brookes & Co., graziers; retired; former world tennis champion; *b.* Melbourne 1877; *m.* 1911, Mabel Balcombe (*see* Lady Brookes), *d.* of late Harry Emmerton; three *d.* *Educ.:* Melbourne Church of England Grammar School. Commissioner for Australian Branch of British Red Cross in Egypt and France in 1915 and 1916; Asst. Commissioner of British Red Cross in Mesopotamia, 1917; Staff Major in B.E.F., 1918, in Mesopotamia, in Supply and Transport (Local Resources). Member management committee of Royal Melbourne Hospital; member executive council of Melbourne Symphony Orchestra; member Council for Australia of Royal Academy of Dancing. *Address:* 233 Domain Road, South Yarra, Melbourne, Australia. [*Died* 27 *Sept.* 1968.

BROOKING, Admiral Patrick W. B., C.B. 1948; D.S.O. 1942, Bar 1943; retd.; served with U.K. Atomic Energy Authority, 1950-64; *b.* 3 Oct. 1896; 2nd *s.* of Arthur H. Brooking, London; *m.* 1925, Mary Allan *d.* (1964): one *d.* *Educ.:* Lambrook, Bracknell; Royal Naval Colleges, Osborne and Dartmouth. Entered R.N., 1910; Lieut., 1919; Comdr., 1930; Capt., 1937; Rear Adm., 1946; Vice-Admiral, 1949. Commanded H.M.S. Sirius in War of 1939-45 (D.S.O. and Bar). Chief of Staff British Admiralty Delegation, Washington, U.S.A., 1946-48; Flag Officer and Admiral Supt., Gibraltar, 1948-50; retired list, 1950; Admiral, retired list, 1953. *Address:* Bramble Cottage, Sulham, Pangbourne, Berks. [*Died* 3 *Sept.* 1964.

BROOKS, General Sir Dallas; *see* Brooks, General Sir R. A. D.

BROOKS, John Birtwhistle Tyrrell C.I.E. 1945; *b.* 1889; *s.* of late Walter Tyrrell Brooks, M.A. Oxon., M.B.; *m.* 1924, Dorothy Howard (*d.* 1953), *d.* of late John W. Pickering, D.Sc.; one *d.* *Educ.:* Marlborough; Christ Church, Oxford. I.A.R.O. 2nd Lt. 1/6 Gurkha Rifles, Temp. Capt. 2/3 Gurkha Rifles, N.W.F.P., 1917-18. Entered Indian Forest Service, 1912; Chief Conservator of Forests, Bombay, 1944-45; retired 1945. *Recreations:* cricket, golf. *Address:* Grey Gables, Nyeri, Kenya. *Clubs:* East India and Sports; Sind (Karachi); Mombasa (Mombasa). [*Died* 7 *Jan.* 1962.

BROOKS, Lt.-Col. Marshall; *see* Brooks, Lt.-Col. T. M.

BROOKS, Ralph T. St. J.; *see* St. John-Brooks.

BROOKS, General Sir (Reginald Alexander) Dallas, G.C.M.G. 1963 (K.C.M.G. 1952; C.M.G. 1943); K.C.B. 1948 (C.B. 1946); K.C.V.O., 1954; D.S.O. 1918; Governor of Victoria, Australia, 1949-February 1961, and again August 1961-March 1963 (Administrator of the Commonwealth of Australia, February-August 1961); *o. s.* of late Rev. Dallas Brooks; *m.* 1924, Muriel Violet, C.St.J., *d.* of late Mrs. Turner Laing, Crathie Cottage, Cooden Beach, Sussex; one *d.* Commandant-General Royal Marines, 1946-49; retired list, 1949. Hon. LL.D. Melbourne, 1960. K.St.J. 1949. Croix de Guerre, 1918. *Clubs:* United Service, East India and Sports. [*Died* 22 *March* 1966.

BROOKS, Lt.-Col. (Bt. Col.) T(homas) Marshall, M.C. 1918; T.D.; D.L.; J.P.; Chairman, District Bank, 1960-67 (Deputy Chairman, 1951-60); *b.* 23 February 1893; *er. s.* of late Hon. Marshall Brooks; *m.* 1920, Evelyn Sylvia, *d.* of late Preb. Hon. Archibald Parker; one *s.* (one *d.* decd.). *Educ.:* Eton; New College, Oxford. Croix de Guerre avec Palme, 1918. *Address:* Portal, Tarporley, Cheshire. *T.:* Tarporley 425. [*Died* 15 *Sept.* 1967.

BROOKS, Van Wyck; Writer; *b.* Plainfield, New Jersey, 16 Feb. 1886; *s.* of Charles Edward and Sarah Ames Brooks; *m.* 1st, 1911, Eleanor Kenyon Stimson (*d.* 1946), two *s.*; 2nd, Gladys Rice Billings. *Educ.:* Harvard. Associate Editor, The Seven Arts, 1916-17; Literary editor, The Freeman, 1920-1924; Member: American Academy of Arts and Letters; American Philosophical Society; Fellow, Royal Society of Literature, American Academy of Arts and Sciences. *Publications:* The Wine of the Puritans, 1909; The Malady of the Ideal, 1913; John Addington Symonds, 1914; The World of H. G. Wells, 1915; America's Coming of Age, 1915; Letters and Leadership, 1918; The Ordeal of Mark Twain, 1920; The Pilgrimage of Henry James, 1925; Emerson, and others, 1927; The Life of Emerson, 1932; Sketches in Criticism, 1932; Three Essays on America, 1934; The Flowering of New England, 1936; New England: Indian Summer, 1940; Opinions of Oliver Allston, 1941; The World of Washington Irving, 1944; The Times of Melville and Whitman, 1947; A Chilmark Miscellany, 1948; The Confident Years, 1951; The Writer in America, 1953; Scenes and Portraits, 1954; John Sloan, a Painter's Life, 1955; Helen Keller: Sketch for a Portrait, 1956; Days of the Phoenix, 1957; From a Writer's Notebook, The Dream of Arcadia, 1958; Howells: His Life and World, 1959; From the Shadow of the Mountain, 1961; Fenollosa and His Circle, 1962; many translations. *Address:* c/o E. P. Dutton & Co., 300 Fourth Avenue, New York, U.S.A. [*Died* 2 *May* 1963.

BROOM, Cyril George Mitchell, M.A.; Secretary of Lord Kitchener National Memorial Fund and of its Kitchener Scholarships Cttee., 1956-67; *b.* 19 August 1889; *s.* of J. G. Broom and Margaret Mitchell, Bath; *m.* 1923, Agnes (*d.* 1964), *d.* of Agnes and James Hulland, Aldeburgh, Suffolk; one *s.* *Educ.:* King Edward VI School, Bath; Brasenose College Oxford (Scholar); 1st Class in Classical Moderations, 2nd Class in Lit. Hum. Senior Classical Master at Carlisle Grammar School, 1911, at Liverpool Institute, 1913; T. F. Commission, 1914 (unattached list for home service); Senior Classical Master, City of London School, 1917; Headmaster, Colfe's Grammar School, Lewisham, 1924-28; Examiner in Latin, London University, 1918-26; Headmaster of Emanuel School, 1928-53. F.R.S.A. 1949. Served on second Admiralty Interview Board, 1954-55. *Recreations:* reading, walking, travel.

Address: 1 Harold Avenue, Westgate-on-Sea, Kent. [*Died* 27 *July* 1968.

BROOMAN-WHITE, Richard Charles; M.P. (C.) Rutherglen Division of Lanarkshire since 1951; *b.* 16 February 1912; *s.* of late Major Charles James Brooman-White, C.B.E.; *m.* 1957, Rosalie Mary, *o. d.* of late Major-General T. W. Rees, C.B., C.I.E., D.S.O., M.C.; two *s. Educ.:* Eton; Trinity College, Cambridge. Journalist and political activities, 1935-38; Public Relations Officer, T.A., 1938. Served War of 1939-45, Intelligence Corps. Contested (C.) Bridgeton, 1945. Served in Foreign Office; Attaché, H.M. Embassy, Turkey, 1946-47. Parl. Private Sec. to Secretary of State for Scotland, 1955-57; Government Assistant Whip (Unpaid), 1957; a Lord Commissioner of the Treasury, 1957-1960; Vice-Chamberlain of H.M. Household, 1960; Joint Parliamentary Under-Secretary of State for Scotland, 1960-1963. *Recreations:* fishing, racing. *Address:* 17 Cheyne Place, S.W.3; Pennymore Farm, Furnace, Argyllshire, Scotland. *Clubs:* White's, Pratt's; New (Edinburgh); Conservative (Glasgow). [*Died* 25 *Jan.* 1964.

BROPHY, John; Author; *b.* Liverpool, 6 Dec. 1899; *o. s.* of John Brophy and Agnes Bodell; *m.* 1924, Charis Weare, *d.* of Rev. J. Grundy one *d. Educ.:* Holt School; University of Liverpool; University of Durham. Ran away from school in 1914, shortly before fifteenth birthday, and enlisted in King's Regiment; served as private solder in France and Belgium; after two lazy years teaching in Egypt, came home to work in a general store; entered advertising profession and wrote "copy" for the leading agency in U.K.; had intended to become a writer since schooldays, and commenced serious publication with a novel written in evenings after ten or more hours' work in a store. Formerly chief fiction critic of Daily Telegraph, B.B.C. and Time and Tide. During War of 1939-45, edited John o' London's and published Home Guard Training Manuals. Films from his novels: Immortal Sergeant, Waterfront, Turn the Key Softly, and The Day They Robbed the Bank of England. *Publications:* The Bitter End, 1928; Fanfare, 1930; Songs and Slang of the British Soldier, 1914-18 (with Eric Partridge), 1930 (rev. edn. as The Long Trail (with Eric Partridge), 1965); Flesh and Blood, 1931; English Prose, 1932; The Rocky Road, 1932; Waterfront, 1934; The World Went Mad, 1934; I Let Him Go, 1935; The Ramparts of Virtue,1936; Ilonka Speaks of Hungary, 1936; Felicity Greene, 1937; Behold the Judge, 1937; Man, Woman and Child, 1938; The Ridiculous Hat, 1939; The Queer Fellow, 1939; Gentleman of Stratford, 1939; Green Glory, 1940; Green Ladies, 1940; Immortal Sergeant, 1942; Spear Head, 1943; Britain's Home Guard (with Eric Kennington), 1944; Portrait of an Unknown Lady, 1945; The Human Face, 1945; The Woman from Nowhere, 1946; City of Departures, 1946; Body and Soul, 1948; Sarah, 1948; Julian's Way, 1949; The Mind's Eye, 1949; Windfall, 1951; Turn the Key Softly, 1951; The Prime of Life, 1954; The Nimble Rabbit, 1955; The Prince and Petronella, 1956; The Day They Robbed the Bank of England, 1959; The Front Door Key, 1960; The Human Face Reconsidered, 1962; The Face in Western Art, 1963; The Face of the Nude, 1965; A New Look at Murder, 1966 (posthumous). *Recreations:* walking, theatre-going, watching people. *Address:* 59 Coleherne Court, S.W.5. *Club:* Reform. [*Died* 12 *Nov.* 1965.

BROSTER, Lennox Ross, O.B.E. 1918; **M.A., D.M., M.Ch. (Oxon); F.R.C.S. (Eng.); Hon. Fellow American Surgical Association, 1942; Surgeon, Charing Cross Hospital; Consulting Surgeon, Chesham, Luton and Dunstable Hospitals, Church Army; formerly Surgeon, Queen's Hospital for Children; Governor of London House and of Sister Trust; Member: Management Committee Dominion Students Hall Truse and Sister Trust; Council British Post-graduate Medical Federation, Academic Council; Management Cttee., Post Graduate Medical School, Hammersmith; Medical Appeal Tribunal;** *b.* South Africa; *s.* of Charles John Broster and Emma Lois Freemantle; *m.* 1916, Edith M. V. Thomas; three *d. Educ.:* St. Andrew's College, Grahamstown, S. Africa; Trinity Coll., Oxford (Rhodes Scholar); Guy's Hosp. B.E.F. 1914-18, 44th Field Ambulance, D.A.D.M.S. in charge Tank Corps, Medical Admin. (O.B.E., despatches twice); Hunterian Professor, Royal College of Surgeons, 1934; ex-Examiner in Clinical Surgery, Universities of Oxford, Cambridge and Leeds; Court of Examiners, R.C.S. of Eng. and in Clinical Pathology; Tour of United States and Canada, 1936, lecturing on the Adrenal Gland, Mayo Foundation Lecture, Rochester, Min.; 1941, Lecture on War Surgery (by invitation Am. Surgical Assoc., White Sulphur Springs, W. Virginia, U.S.A.); Withering Lecturer to University of Birmingham, 1940, and to other universities; Tour of Union of South Africa by invitation of S.A. Med. Assoc.; address to Annual Congress in Pretoria, 1948; Visiting Prof. of Surgery to Univ. of Cairo, 1950; mem. surgical deleg. to Deutsche Gesellschaft für Chirurgie, Frankfurt 1950; Berlin, 1952-1954; Milan, 1953; Toronto, 1955. Ex-Chm. Management Cttee. of B.M.A. Empire Med. Advisory Bureau and Internat. Visitors' Bureau; ex-Mem. Council R.S.M. (ex-Hon. Sec. and Treas. and ex-Pres. endocrine section); ex-Mem. Council, B.M.A. and Assoc. of Surgeons of Great Brit. and Ire.; Mem. Internat. Soc. of Surgeons. Bronze medal S.A. Med. Assoc. Hon. F.R.Soc.Med. *Publications:* The Adrenal Cortex, with H. W. C. Vines, 1933; The Adrenal Cortex and Intersexuality (jointly), 1938; Endocrine Man, 1944; papers on general urgery in the medical journals. *Recreation:* Rugby football (Ox. *v.* Cam., 1912-13; ex-Pres. United Hosps. R.F.C.). *Address:* 24 Dunstall Road, S.W.20. *T.:* Wimbledon 0144. [*Died* 12 *April* 1965.

BROUGHAM AND VAUX, 4th Baron (*cr.* 1860); **Victor Henry Peter Brougham;** Major late Middlesex Regiment, T.A.; *b.* 23 Oct. 1909; *s.* of late Capt. Hon. Henry Brougham and Hon. Diana Sturt, *o. d.* of 2nd Baron Alington; *S.* grandfather, 1927; *m.* 1st, 1931, Violet Valerie (who obtained a divorce, 1934), *yr. d.* of Major Hon. E. Gerald French (one *s.* decd.); 2nd, 1935, Jean (who obtained a divorce, 1942; she *m.*, 1946, Felix Guépin), *d.* of late Brig.-Gen. G. B. S. Follett and Lady Mildred Fitzgerald; two *s.*; 3rd, 1942, Mrs. Richard Hart Davis. *Heir: s.* Hon. Michael John Brougham [*b.* 2 Aug. 1938; *m.* 1963, Olivia Susan, *d.* of Rear-Admiral Gordon Thomas Seccombe Gray, C.B., D.S.C.; one *d.*]. [*Died* 20 *June* 1967.

BROUGHTON-HEAD, Leslie Charles, M.B., Ch.B. (Glas.); L.D.S. (Eng.); Retired; late Surgeon Dentist in H.M. Medical Household in Scotland; Hon. Consulting Dental Surgeon, Royal Hospital for Sick Children, Glasgow; *s.* of late George and Mary Elizabeth Head, London; *m.* Dorothy, *e. d.* of late Geo. R. Bland, Brondesbury Park, London; one *s. Educ.:* St. Paul's School; Universities Edinburgh, Glasgow, and London; Middlesex and Royal Dental Hospitals. Past President, Odonto-Chirurgical Society of Scotland; Member (Past Vice-President) Odontological Section of Royal Society of Medicine; Member British Med. Assoc., etc.; late Temp. Capt., Royal Air Force Med. Service. *Publications:* contributions to various professional journals. *Recreations:*

walking, travel, reading. *Address:* 26 Wendan Road, Newbury, Berks. [*Died* 30 *Oct.* 1961.

BROUN, Sir (James) Lionel, 11th Bt., *cr.* 1686; *b.* 1875; *s.* of 10th Bt. and Alice, *d.* of late J. C. Peters, Hope House, Manly Beach, Sydney; *S.* father, 1918; *m.* 1925, Georgina, *d.* of Henry Law; one *s.* *Heir: s.* Lionel John Law, *b.* 25 April 1927. *Address:* Colstoun, Gunnedah, N.S. Wales; Coonimbia, Coonamble, N.S. Wales. *T.A.:* Gunnedah and Coonamble. *T.:* Gunnedah 72; Coonamble 813. [*Died* 8 *Aug.* 1962.

BROUN, Sir Lionel, Bt.; *see* Broun, Sir J. L.

BROUN LINDSAY, Major Sir (George) Humphrey (Maurice), Kt., *cr.* 1947; D.S.O. 1919; V.L. East Lothian; J.P.; late K.O.S.B.; retired, 1921; *b.* 23 Oct. 1888; *o. s.* of Alfred Lindsay; *g.s.* of Hon. Colin Lindsay; *m.* 1921, Edith Christian Broun Baird (O.B.E. 1964), Wellwood, Ayrshire; one *s.* *Educ.:* Cheltenham College; R.M.C., Sandhurst. Gazetted, 1909; Capt. 1915; Brevet Major, 1918; sailed with Expeditionary Force, 1914; served on Staff during European War in France and Italy, 1914-18, as Brigade Major and D.A.A. and Q.M.G. (despatches twice, D.S.O.); M.P. (U.) Partick Division of Glasgow, 1924-29. Assumed name of Broun on marriage (Broun Lindsay). *Address:* Colstoun, Haddington. *Club:* New (Edinburgh). [*Died* 23 *June* 1964.

BROUWER, Luitzen Egbertus Jan, Sc.D. (Camb.) *h.c.*; Dr.Sci. (Oslo) *h.c.*; Knight in the Order of the Dutch Lion, 1932; Professor Emeritus of the University of Amsterdam since 1951; *b.* 27 Feb. 1881; *s.* of Egbert Brouwer and Henderika Poutsma; *m.* 1904, Reinharda Bernardina Frederica Elisabeth de Holl (*d.* 1959); no *c.* *Educ.:* Secondary Sch. Hoorn and Haarlem; Gram. Sch. Haarlem; Univ. of Amsterdam (Dr. Sci. 1907). External Lecturer, 1909-12, Professor 1912-51, Univ. of Amsterdam. Mem. Royal Dutch Academy of Sciences, 1912. For. Mem., Hon. Mem., Non-resident Mem. or Corresp. Mem. of th following learned societies; Royal Society of London; Royal Society of Edinburgh; Edinburgh Mathematical Society; Calcutta Mathematical Society; American Philosophical Society and of many academies and societies of Europe. *Publications:* Leven, Kunst en Mystiek (Life, Art and Mysticism), 1905; Over de grondslagen der wiskunde (On the Foundations of Mathematics) (Dissertation), 1907; Wiskunde, Waarheid, Werkelijkheid (Mathematics, Truth, Reality), 1919; contributions to learned jls. mainly on mechanics, geometry, theory of aggregates, theory of functions, topology, and philosophy. *Recreations:* hiking; formerly swimming and football. *Address:* 72 Torenlaan, Blaricum, Netherlands. *T.:* 02953-2605. [*Died* 2 *Dec.* 1966.

BROWN, Col. Alexander Denis; *see* Burnett-Brown.

BROWN, Allan, F.R.C.O., F.G.S.M., L.R.A.M., A.R.C.M., L.Mus.T.C.L., M.R.S.T.; Organist Emeritus, St. Paul's, Onslow Square, S.W.7, since 1962 (Organist and Master of the Music, 1949-62); President of the Westminster Choral Society since 1955; Prof. and Examiner Guildhall School of Music and Drama, 1931-64; Examiner, Guildhall School of Music and Drama, since 1944; *b.* London, 1884; *m.* 1922, Beatrice Ashton, L.R.A.M., Professor of Singing; one *s.* one *d.* *Educ.:* Sir Walter St. John's School, Battersea. Deputy-Organist, St. Michael's, Wandsworth Common, S.W., 1896; Assistant Organist, St. Peter's, Battersea, S.W. 1899; Organist and Choirmaster, Hockliffe Parish Church, Beds, 1902; Weekday Organist, St. Mary, Aldermary, E.C., 1902 Organist, Methodist Church, Upper Tooting, S.W., 1903; Principal, The South Western Coll. of Music London, S.W. since 1911; Conductor, Balham Orchestral Soc., 1913; Organist and Choirmaster, Presbyterian Church of England, Regent Square, W.C., 1913; Organist and Musical Director, The City Temple, E.C.4, 1915-28; Organ Recitalist and Accompanist (Special Saturday Concerts), Methodist Central Hall, Tooting, S.W., 1915-28; Organist and Musical Director, Kingsway Hall, 1928-44; Professor Trinity College of Music, London, 1944-55; Conductor, Westminster Choral Society, 1944-1955; Choirmaster, St. Barnabas', Clapham Common, S.W., 1917; Founder and Conductor, The City Temple Choral Society, 1918 - 28; Organist, C.E.T.S. Choir, Queen's Hall, 1921-29; Organist, National Temperance Choral Union, Crystal Palace, 1921-31; Organist, The Bible Testimony Fellowship, Royal Albert Hall and Crystal Palace, 1923-45; Conductor and Founder, Kingsway Hall Choral Society, 1928-44; Organist and Musical Director, The "Dome" Mission, Brighton, 1945-47; Organ Recitalist of the Royal Albert Hall, Queen's Hall, etc.; coach for R.C.O. diplomas. *Publication:* Hints to R.C.O. Candidates. *Recreation:* golf. *Address:* 50 Queen Elizabeth's Drive, Southgate, N.14. *T.:* 01-886 4601. [*Died* 4 *Dec.* 1969.

BROWN, Armitage N. B.; *see* Bryan-Brown.

BROWN, Lt.-Col. Arthur M. W.; *see* Weber-Brown.

BROWN, Cedric C.; *see* Clifton Brown.

BROWN, Air Vice-Marshal Colin Peter, C.B. 1945; C.B.E. 1941; D.F.C. 1918; M.Brit.I.R.E.; Royal Air Force, retired; *b.* 20 December 1898; *e. s.* of John Duncan Brown and Margaret Bayne; *m.* 1924, Grace, *d.* of late Wm. Cuthbert, Perth; one *d.* *Educ.:* Dulwich College. Commissioned R.N.A.S. 1917; served in France, European War, 1917-18; p.s.a. 1928; Iraq, 1929-30; commanded No. 26 Squadron, 1935-36; R.A.F. Station, Catterick, 1937; on Air Staff, Air Ministry, 1938; Group Captain, 1940; Senior Air Officer, No. 60 Group R.A.F., 1940-42; Director of Radar, Air Ministry, 1943-45; Air Commodore, 1947; Chief Signals Officer, Middle East Air Force, 1949-50; Air Vice-Marshal, 1952; Assistant Controller of Supplies (Air), Min. of Supply, 1950; attached Air Ministry for special duty, 1953, retired 1954. *Recreations:* sailing, fishing. *Address:* 8 Hurst Way, Pyrford, Woking, Surrey. [*Died* 19 *Oct.* 1965.

BROWN, David Hownam, C.B.E. 1942; M.Inst.C.E.; ex-County Surveyor and Bridgemaster, Warwickshire C.C.; ex-Pres. Institution of Municipal and County Engineers; *b.* 9 May 1879; *s.* of David Hownam and Christina Brown; *m.* 1st, 1904, T. J. Y. Wallace; 2nd, 1933, Ethel Annie Evans; three *s.* *Educ.:* privately. Articled pupilage under Park & Son, Surveyors, Preston; Engineering Assistant, Preston Corporation; Assistant County Bridgemaster, Lancashire County Council; Deputy County Surveyor, Durham County Council. *Publications:* professional papers only. *Recreation:* golf. *Address:* The Glebe House, The Butts, Warwick. *T.:* Warwick 612. *Clubs:* Leamington and County Golf, Tennis Court (Leamington). [*Died* 21 *Nov.* 1961.

BROWN, Eden Tatton, C.M.G. 1929; *b.* Charlton, Kent, 31 Dec. 1877; *s.* of late Maj.-Gen. John Tatton Butler Brown, C.B., R.A.; *g.s.* of Gen. Tatton Brown; *m.* 1904, Pauline, *d.* of late Edward Stewart-Jones;

two *s.* one *d.* *Educ.:* Wellington College; King's College, Cambridge. 2nd Class Math. Tripos and B.A.; joined Ministry of Education, Egypt, 1901; Egyptian Customs Administration, 1910; Director-General Egyptian Customs Administration, 1924; Govt. Commissioner for Egyptian Customs, 1930; retired 1933; 3rd Class Order of the Nile, 1921; 2nd Class, 1933; Grand Officer of the Order of Leopold II, 1930. *Address:* Westergate Wood, Chichester. [*Died* 29 *Sept.* 1961.

BROWN, Major-General Eric Gilmour, C.B. 1955; C.B.E. 1948; retired 1957; Col.-Commandant R.A.O.C., 1957-62; *b.* 7 July 1900; *s.* of Edgar Allan Brown, Eastbourne; *m.* 1933, Erda Kirk Keep; two *d.* *Educ.:* Eastbourne College; R.M.A. Woolwich. Commissioned in R.G.A., 1920; transferred to R.A.O.C., 1929; served War of 1939-45: France, A.A. Command Middle East, Gibraltar, Australia. Inspector, R.A.O.C., 1948; Comdr., M.T.Org., R.A.O.C., 1954. Hon. Col. A. E. R. Units, R.A.O.C., 1956-61. *Recreations:* swimming (Vice-Pres. Army Swimming Union), music and horticulture. *Address:* Orchard Corner, Firgrove Hill, Farnham, Surrey. [*Died* 23 *Feb.* 1967.

BROWN, Rt. Hon. Ernest, P.C. 1935; C.H. 1945; M.C.; *b.* Torquay, 27 Aug. 1881; *e. s.* of William and Anna Brown; *m.* Isabel Eva, *e. d.* of R. B. Narracott, Torquay. *Educ.:* Torquay. Political lecturer; Liberal candidate, Salisbury, 1918 and 1922; Mitcham Election, Feb. 1923; Rugby, 1924; M.P. Rugby, Nov. 1923; M.P. (L.) Leith, 1927-31, (L. Nat.) 1931-45; Parliamentary Secretary, Ministry of Health, 1931-32; Secretary to Mines Department, 1932-35; Minister of Labour, 1935-40 and Minister of National Service, 1939-40; Secretary for Scotland, 1940-41; Minister of Health, 1941-1943; Chancellor of the Duchy of Lancaster, 1943-45; Minister of Aircraft Production, May-July 1945; Chairman, Select Committee on Procedure, House of Commons, 1931-32; Chairman, European Council U.N.R.R.A. 1944-45. Sportsman's Battalion, 1914; commissioned Somerset L.I. 1916 (M.C., Italian Silver Star, despatches). Baptist lay preacher and Brotherhood worker; Hon. Treasurer Baptist Missionary Society; Freeman of Borough of Torquay. *Recreations:* Rugby football, yachting. *Address:* 4 Exeter Mansions, 106 Shaftesbury Avenue, W.1. *T.:* Gerrard 6815. *Clubs:* National Liberal; Scottish Liberal (Edinburgh) [*Died* 16 *Feb.* 1962.

BROWN, Lt.-Col. and Hon. Brig.-Gen. Ernest C.; *see* Craig-Brown.

BROWN, Vice-Admiral Francis Clifton, C.B. 1919; C.M.G. 1917; *b.* 10 July 1874; 3rd *s.* of late Col. J. Clifton Brown, J.P., D.L., and Amelia, *d.* of Charles Rowe; *m.* 1913, Violet (*d.* 1952), *y. d.* of late W. P. Galton; no *c.*; *m.* 1952, Mrs. Margaret Maud Wood. *Educ.:* Cheam; H.M.S. Britannia. Capt. 1912. Rear-Adm. 1922; served European War, 1914-18 (C.B., C.M.G.); Head of Naval Mission to Greece: 1917-19; retired list, 1922; Vice-Admiral (retired list), 1927; High Sheriff of Berkshire, 1931; D.L., J.P. Berkshire. *Address:* The Paddocks, Pusey, Faringdon, Berks. *T.:* Buckland 217. [*Died* 6 *Sept.* 1963.

BROWN, Francis David Wynyard, C.M.G. 1959; Minister for U.K. Mission to U.N., 1965; *b.* 15 September 1915; *s.* of late Capt. W. K. Brown, I.A., and late Mrs. Brown (*née* Mabel Seymour); *m.* 1946, Ellen Ruth Trevenen Mills; three *s.* one *d.* *Educ.:* Wellington College; Trinity College, Cambridge. 3rd Secretary, Foreign Office, 1938-1940; served War of 1939-45: Coldstream Guards, 1940-45; Capt. 1940. Asst. Private Secretary to the Prime Minister, 1941-44; Asst. British Political Adviser at S.H.A.E.F. 1945; Political Div., Control Commission for Germany, Berlin, 1945-46; Foreign Office, 1946-49; 1st Sec., British Embassy, Paris, 1949-52; U.K. Deleg. to N.A.T.O., Paris, 1952-54; Counsellor, 1954; Inspector, 1955-1959; Minister, British Embassy, Ankara, 1959-62; Deputy Resident at Bahrain, 1962-1964. *Address:* Westbrook, Godalming, Surrey. *T.:* 1416. *Clubs:* Travellers', Guards. [*Died* 21 *April* 1967.

BROWN, His Honour Harold; Judge of County Courts, Circuit No. 6 (Liverpool), 1952-63, retd.; J.P. (Lancs.) 1952; *b.* 18 June 1895; *s.* of late Frank Bennett Brown, J.P., and Annie Brown, West Kirby; *m.* 1925, Hilda, *y. d.* of late Arthur James and Mary Ellen Beer, Wallasey; one *s.* two *d.* *Educ.:* King Edward VI Grammar School, Louth; Liverpool University; Merton College, Oxford (M.A. 1st Cl. Hons. Jurisprudence). Served European War, 1914-18, enlisted in King's (Liverpool) Regt., Sept. 1914; commissioned in The King's Own (Roy. Lancaster) Regt., 1917; in France and Belgium, 1915-19. LL.B. (Hons.) Liverpool Univ. (in absence), 1916; Bacon and Holt Schol., Gray's Inn, 1919, Arden Schol., 1920; called to Bar, Gray's Inn, 1921. Joined Northern Circuit, 1921; practised at bar (mainly in Chancery Court of County Palatine of Lancaster and in Chancery Div. of High Court) until 1952. Lecturer and Tutor in Law, Liverpool Univ., 1926-38. Served War of 1939-45, with R.A. and with Legal Div. of C.C.G. 1941-46, when demobilised with rank of Lt.-Col. Deputy of the Chancellor of the County Palatine of Lancaster, 1959. *Address:* 23 Carpenters Lane, West Kirby, Cheshire. *T.:* Caldy 8240. *Clubs:* Athenæum (Liverpool), Sandon. [*Died* 26 *Jan.* 1969.

BROWN, Harold Arrowsmith; *s.* of late J. P. Brown, C.B.E.; *m.* 1903, Margaret Alice (*d.* 1920), *d.* of late Arthur Brooke; one *s.* two *d.* (and two *s.* decd.). *Educ.:* Plymouth and Mannamead Coll., Plymouth; Caius College, Cambridge. Entered I.C.S., 1903; called to Bar, Inner Temple, 1920; Acted Judge, High Court, Rangoon, 1924; Puisne Judge, High Court of Judicature, Rangoon, 1927-33; retired 1933. *Address:* Avon View, Abbots Leigh, Bristol. *T.:* Pill 2207. *Club:* East India and Sports. [*Died* 30 *Dec.* 1968.

BROWN, Eng. Vice-Admiral Sir Harold Arthur, G.B.E., *cr.* 1939; K.C.B., *cr.* 1934 (C.B. 1932); *b.* 19 March 1878; *s.* of J. J. Brown; *m.* Marion Lillie (*d.* 1946), *d.* of Col. Forbes Macbean, 92nd Highlanders; one *d.* Engineer-in-Chief of the Fleet, Admiralty, 1932-36; retired list, 1936; Dir.-Gen. of Munitions Production, Army Council, War Office, 1936-39; Director-General of Munitions Production, Ministry of Supply, 1939-1941; Controller-General of Munitions Production, 1941-42; Senior Supply Officer and Chairman of Armament Development Board, Ministry of Supply, 1942-46; Chairman Fuel Research Board, 1947-50; Advisory Council, Ministry of Fuel and Power, 1949-51; Chairman Machine Tools Advisory Council, Ministry of Supply, 1948, and Board of Trade, 1957-58. *Address:* 4 Burton Court, S.W.3. *T.:* Sloane 9088. *Club:* Athenæum. [*Died* 15 *Feb.* 1968.

BROWN, Sir Harry Percy, Kt., *cr.* 1938; C.M.G. 1934; M.B.E. 1918; M.I.E.E.; *b.* 28 Dec. 1878; *s.* of George Brown; *m.* 1904, Emily Aldous (*d.* 1957); two *s.* one *d.* (and one *d.* decd.). *Educ.:* Bede College, Sunderland; Durham College, Newcastle upon Tyne. On staff of British Post Office for 25 years; visited India 1913-14 in connection with Telephone, Telegraph and Railway Traffic Control Communications; during European War, 1914-19, was responsible for

telephone plant of United Kingdom and emergency communications for Defence System; went to Australia in 1923 as technical adviser to Commonwealth Government in connection with Post Office matters; Director-General of Posts and Telegraphs, Commonwealth of Australia, 1923-39; as representative of Commonwealth Government attended International Radio-telegraph Conference at Washington U.S.A. 1927 and Imperial Cable and Wireless Conference in London, 1928; represented Commonwealth Government at Imperial Cable and Wireless Conference, London, 1937; Co-ordinator-General of Public Works, Commonwealth of Australia, 1940-45; full-time Chairman in Australia of British General Electric Company Proprietary Ltd., 1939-53, retired 1953. *Address:* 16 Luxor Parade, Roseville, N.S.W., Australia. *Clubs:* Tattersalls, Royal Automobile Club of Australia (Sydney).
[*Died* 5 *June* 1 67.

BROWN, Sir Henry Isaac Close, Kt. *cr.* 1938; P.C. (Jamaica), Q.C. 1911; *b.* 1874; 2nd *s.* of Phillpotts Brown, Solicitor, of Montego Bay, Jamaica. *Educ.:* York Castle, Jamaica; Pembroke College, Oxford. Called to Bar, Lincoln's Inn, 1899; late Registrar and Librarian Supreme Court, Jamaica; Puisne Judge, Supreme Court of Jamaica, 1922-34. *Address:* 6 Devon Rd., Halfway Tree, Jamaica, W.I. [*Died* 18 *March* 1962.

BROWN, Sir James Birch, K.C.I.E., *cr.* 1947 (C.I.E. 1931); C.S.I 1943; *b.* 18 Nov. 1888; *m.* 1931, Nancy Vera Oliver; no *c.* *Educ.:* Trinity College, Dublin. Entered I.C.S. 1912; Member, Board of Revenue, Madras; Secretary to Governor of Madras. *Address:* Penlee, 11 Drake's Avenue, Exmouth, Devon. [*Died* 28 *Nov.* 1968.

BROWN, Lt.-Col. James C. *see* Cross Brown.

BROWN, John Mason; Critic, Author, Lecturer; *b.* 3 July 1900; *s.* of John Mason Brown and Carrie Ferguson, Louisville Kentucky; *m.* 1933, Catherine Screven Meredith; two *s.* *Educ.:* Harvard University, U.S.A. (A.B.). Editor and Dramatic Critic, Theatre Arts Monthly, 1924-28; Dramatic Critic: New York Evening Post, 1929-41, New York World Telegram, 1941-42; Associate Editor and Dramatic Critic of The Saturday Review, U.S.A., 1944-55; Editor-at-large, 1956-. Has taught at Yale, at American Laboratory Theatre, at summer sessions at Harvard, Columbia, and University of Montana. Lieutenant U.S.N.R., 1942-44; on staff of Vice-Admiral Alan G. Kirk for invasions of Sicily and Normandy (Bronze Star). Lecturer; radio program, Of Men and Books, 1944-47; Transatlantic Quiz program, 1945-47, 1951. Television show, Critic-at-Large, 1948-49, The Last Word, 1957-59; President New York Drama Critics Circle, 1941-42 and 1945-49; President American Center of P.E.N., 1947-48. Member National Institute of Arts and Letters; Overseer of Harvard Coll., 1949-55; Mem. bd. of judges Book-of-the-Month Club, 1956-; Mem. Pulitzer Prize Drama Jury, 1956-1963; Trustee Metropolitan Museum of Art, 1951-56, New York Society Library, 1950-, Recording for the Blind, Inc., 1951-. Holds several Hon. Degrees. *Publications:* The Modern Theatre in Revolt, 1929; Upstage—The American Theatre in Performance, 1930; Letters from Greenroom Ghosts, 1934; The Art of Playgoing, 1936; Two on the Aisle, 1938; Broadway in Review, 1940; Accustomed As I Am, 1942; Insides Out, 1942; To All Hands, 1943; Many a Watchful Night, 1944; Seeing Things, 1946; Seeing More Things, 1948; The Portable Charles Lamb, 1949; Morning Faces, 1949; Still Seeing Things, 1950; Daniel Boone, The Opening of the Wilderness, 1952; As They Appear, 1952; Through These Men, 1956; The Ladies' Home Journal Treasury, 1956; Dramatis Personae, 1963; The Worlds of Robert E. Sherwood: Mirror to His Times, 1965. *Recreations:* reading, walking, fishing, talking. *Address:* 17 East 89th Street, New York, N.Y. 10028, U.S.A. *T.:* Lehigh 4-7469. *Clubs:* Harvard, Century Association, The Players (Hon.) (New York).
[*Died* 16 *March* 1969.

BROWN, Maud F. F.; *see* Forrester-Brown.

BROWN, Michael George Harold, B.A., F.C.A.; Chairman, Universal Grinding Wheel Group Holdings Ltd., since 1961; *b.* 24 Sept. 1907; 3rd *s.* of late Harold G. Brown; *m.* 1932, Dorothy Margaret, *d.* of Caesar Colston Douty; two *s.* *Educ.:* Rugby; Trinity Coll., Cambridge. Qualified as Chartered Accountant, 1932. Served War of 1939-45, France, Belgium, Holland and Germany: Comr. in Rangers (K.R.R.C.), Aug. 1939; transf. to Northants. Yeomanry, 1943. Chm., National Bank of New Zealand Ltd.; Dep. Chm., Dalgety and New Zealand Loan Ltd.; Chm. of London Bd., National Mutual Life Assoc. of Australasia Ltd.; Director: Lloyds Bank Ltd.; The Industrial & General Trust Ltd.; C. Tennant, Sons & Co. Ltd. *Recreations:* shooting, golf. *Address:* (home) Ladycross House, Dormansland, Surrey. *T.:* Dormans Park 314; (office) 42/43 Abbey House, Victoria St., S.W.1. *T.:* Abbey 3869. *Clubs:* Junior Carlton; Leander (Henley).
[*Died* 14 *Jan.* 1969.

BROWN, Sir Percival, Kt., *cr.* 1953; C.B.E. 1943; F.A.I.; Chairman, Northern Ireland National Assistance Board, since April 1956; *b.* 3 April 1901; *s.* of Thomas Brown, Belfast; *m.* 1951, Helen W., *d.* of D. McD. Lyon, Edinburgh; one *s.* two *d.* *Educ.:* Royal Belfast Academical Institution. Partner in firm of Ephraim Brown & Son, Estate Agents; member of Belfast Corporation, 1936-55; High Sheriff of County of City of Belfast, 1942; Chairman, Belfast Corpn. A.R.P. Cttee., 1939-40; Chm. Belfast Civil Defence Authority, 1940-46; Chairman Northern Ireland Tuberculosis Authority, 1946-51. Deputy Lord Mayor of Belfast, 1950-51; Lord Mayor, 1953-54 and 1954-55. *Address:* 14 Deramore Drive, Malone Road, Belfast. *Club:* Ulster Reform (Belfast).
[*Died* 4 *Oct.* 1962.

BROWN, Professor Raymond Gordon, F.R.I.B.A. 1954; M.A. (Edin.); architect; *b.* 18 March 1912; *s.* of Robert Gordon Brown and Christina Lawson Neill; *m.* 1937, Alison Margaret Brown; three *d.* *Educ.:* Clifton College, Bristol; Architectural Association School of Architecture (A.A. dipl.). Private Practice in London before 1939; Army, 1939-45; Principal Architectural Association School of Architecture, 1945-49; Town Planning Adviser to Govt. of British North Borneo; Architectural Practice in Hongkong and British North Borneo; Professor of Architecture, and Dean of Faculty of Architecture, Hongkong University, 1950-1957 resigned. Subsequently at University of Utah, Salt Lake City; also Consulting Architect to the President of Guatemala. Returned to Great Britain, setting up again in private practice, 1960. *Recreation:* sailing. *Address:* c/o R.I.B.A., Great Portland Street, W.1. [*Died* 17 *March* 1962.

BROWN, Ronald D. S.; *see* Stewart-Brown.

BROWN, Sir Samuel Harold, Kt., *cr.* 1946; Solicitor; Senior Adviser to Linklaters and Paines; *b.* 28 Dec. 1903; *s.* of late Harold George Brown; *m.* 1929, Barbara Compton Hays; one *s.* one *d.* *Educ.:* Rugby; Trinity College, Cambridge. Solicitor 1928; partner in Linklaters and Paines, 1928;

Principal, Ministry of Economic Warfare, 1939-40; Asst. Sec., Ministry of Aircraft Production, Jan. 1940; Principal Asst. Sec., Dec. 1940. Under-Secretary, 1943; returned to legal practice Aug. 1945. *Recreations:* golf, tennis. *Address:* Criplands, Gravelye Lane, Lindfield, Sussex. *T.:* Lindfield 3108. *Clubs:* Junior Carlton, Leander.

[*Died* 17 *Dec.* 1965.

BROWN, Rear-Adm. (retired) Sydney, C.B. 1951; Extra Naval Assistant to Second Sea Lord for Engineering Personnel, 1949-1953; *b.* 1899; *s.* of late Thomas Mitchell Brown, Bothwell, Lanarkshire; *m.* 1st, 1924, Iris Mary Hones (*d.* 1966); 2nd, 1968, Wilma Denise Brookes. *Educ.:* R.N. Colleges Osborne and Dartmouth. Entered R.N. as Cadet, 1912; Comdr. (E), 1931; Capt. (E), 1942; Rear-Adm. (E), 1949; retd. 1953. *Address:* Little Sussex Bell, Bell Vale, Haslemere, Surrey. *T.:* Haslemere 4300. [*Died* 14 *Aug.* 1970.

BROWN, Thomas G.; *see* Graham-Brown.

BROWN, Tom; (Thomas James); *b.* 12 August 1886; *m.* 1912; one *s.* one *d.* *Educ.:* Brunswick Schools, Hindley Green. Started work at the pits at the age of 12; at the age of 17 member of Branch Committee, later became its President, and then Secretary; Exec. Committee Miners' Federation of Great Britain, 1922 and 1938, rep. this at French Miners' Congress at Ales in 1938; Miners' Agent, 1937. Formerly: J.P. Lancs; Mem. Hindley U.D.C. etc.; M.P. (Lab.) Ince-in-Makerfield Div. of Lancs., 1942-64. *Address:* 393 Leigh Road, Hindley Green, nr. Wigan. *T.:* Wigan 55832.

[*Died* 10 *Nov.* 1970.

BROWN, Walter Russell, C.B.E. 1931; A.M. 1915; *b.* 12 May 1879; *s.* of Walter Edward Brown, formerly of Ringwood, Hampshire; *m.* 1908, Helen Maud Armstrong (*d.* 1965); one *s.* four *d.* *Educ.:* Private Schools. Student Interpreter in China, 1901; acting Vice-Consul, 1911-14; received Albert Medal of the 2nd class for gallantry in saving life on land in bringing about a suspension of hostilities during the street fighting at Chungking, 21 Sept. 1913; acting Consul at Kiukiang, 1916-18; in charge of Consulate at Wuhu, 1917-18; acting Vice-Consul at Hankow, 1918 and 1919; acting Consul-General, 1 July-22 Sept. 1918; one of H.M. Vice-Consuls in China, 1919; acting Consul-General at Hankow, 1919-20; acting Consul at Chefoo, 1920-21; Vice-Consul, Tientsin, from 1 Nov. 1921; one of H.M. Consuls in China, 1922; acting Consul-General at Tientsin, 1923; Senior District Officer and Magistrate at Weihaiwei, 4 Nov. 1923; Officer Administering the Government of Weihaiwai, 1923-27; in charge of Consulate at Chefoo, 29 Mar.-30 Sept. 1927, and 19 Nov. 1928-3 Feb. 1929; in charge of Consulate at Amoy from 5 March 1929; acting Consul-General at Hankow, 3 Feb.-7 Sept. 1930; one of H.M. Consuls-General in China, 1930; in Dept. of Overseas Trade, 1932; retired, 1932. J.P. Devonshire, 1943-48. *Recreations:* shooting and fishing. *Address:* 70 Links Road, Ashtead, Surrey. *T.:* Ashtead 3802 [*Died* 27 *Feb.* 1966.

BROWN, Ven. William A.; *see* Ashley Brown.

BROWN, Very Rev. William James, B.D.; Dean of Bocking, Rector of Hadleigh, 1946-61, and Rural Dean of Hadleigh, 1948-1961; then Dean Emeritus; F.K.C. Lond., 1928; *b.* 17 Apr. 1889; *y. s.* of Lewis James Brown, Forest Gate, E.; *m.* 1st, 1916 Elizabeth (*d.* 1954), *d.* of Louisa and Donald Calder, Caithness and London; one *s.* one *d.*; 2nd, 1957, Gladys, *widow* of Sydney Waller, Peyton Hall, Hadleigh. *Educ.:* High Schools, Leyton and Leytonstone: King's Coll. Univ. of London (Scholar Exhibitioner and Prizeman); A.K.C. (1st Class Honours), 1911; B.D. 1912, 1st Class Honours Philosophy of Religion, 1914; Deacon, 1912; Priest, 1913; Curate of Little Ilford, 1912-17; Holy Trinity, Paddington, and with B.E.F. France, 1917-19; Diocesan Inspector of Schools, Durham, 1920; Director of Religious Education, Wakefield, and Licensed Preacher, 1921; Chaplain to Lay-readers' Board, 1922; Canon of St. John of Beverley in Wakefield Cathedral, 1923 (emeritus 1946); Campden Lecturer and Christian Evidence Lecturer in Wakefield Cathedral, 1923; Proctor in York Convocation, 1928; Champney Lecturer, 1931; Vicar and Rural Dean of Dewsbury, 1932-46; Deputy Prolocutor York Convocation, 1943-46; Hon. O.C.F., 1940-45. *Publications:* Suggestions on Sunday School Work, 1928; The Gospel of the Infancy, 1923; Jeremy Taylor, 1925; Notes on Islam, 1926; Church Schools and Religious Education, 1929; The Labour Government, Education and Church Schools, 1929; Notes on the Ministry of the Church and Christian Reunion, 1930; A Handbook for Church School Managers, 1931 (revised and enlarged, 1933); An Introduction to the Christian Doctrine of God, 1932; Secondary Education and the Church of England, 1939; The Church and Religious Education: A Policy for Discussion, 1941; The Church and the Education Act, 1944; Rowland Taylor LL.D., 1959; The Clergy, Church and Nation, 1959; One Man's Life; a Personal Narrative (autobiography), 1962; articles and reviews on theology, philosophy, and education. *Recreation:* walking. *Address:* 51 Deanhill Avenue, Clacton-on-Sea, Essex. *T.:* Holland-on-Sea 2296.

[*Died* 13 *May* 1970.

BROWN, Sir William Scott, K.C.I.E., *cr.* 1947 (C.I.E. 1936); C.S.I. 1942; late I.C.S.; *b.* Kelso, Roxburghshire, 30 Sept. 1890; *s.* of William Brown; *m.* 1932, Evelyn Jessie Longmore; two *s.* *Educ.:* Aberdeen University; Christ Church, Oxford. I.C.S. 1914; Assistant and Sub-Collector, 1914-17; Military Duty, I.A.R.O., 1918-19; Sub-Collector and Under-Secretary to Government, 1919-24; Secretary, Board of Revenue, 1924-27; Collector and District Magistrate in various districts, 1928-34; Sec. to Govt. Public Works Dept., Madras, 1935-37; Sec. to Govt., Finance Dept., Madras, 1939-42; Mem. Bd. of Rev., Madras, 1942; Chief Sec. to Govt., Madras, 1946-47; retd., 1949; Rector's Assessor, Aberdeen Univ. Court, 1950-65. Hon. LL.D. (Aberdeen University), 1956. *Recreation:* golf. *Address:* 27 Rubislaw Den South, Aberdeen.

[*Died* 17 *May* 1968.

BROWNE, Rt. Rev. Arthur Henry Howe; *s.* of the Hon. Richard and Elise Howe Browne. *Educ.:* Winchester; Balliol College, Oxford; Cuddesdon. Assistant Curate of Witney, Oxon, 1905-8; St. John's, East Dulwich, 1908-9; Vicar, 1909-16; St. John the Baptist, Kensington, 1916-21; Vicar of St. John the Divine, Kennington, S.W.9, 1921-34; Rural Dean of Kennington, 1926-34; Hon. Canon of Southwark, 1926-33; Residentiary Canon of Southwark, 1933-34; Proctor in Convocation, 1932-34; Bishop of Bloemfontein, 1935-51; resigned, 1951. *Address:* 39 Woodlands, Highstead Road, Rondebosch, C.P., S. Africa.

[*Died* 8 *Sept.* 1961.

BROWNE, Denis; Barrister-at-Law; Queen Victoria Professor of Law, Liverpool University, since 1955; *b.* 25 Dec. 1903; *o. s.* of late G. D'E. Browne and of E. M. Browne; *m.* 1933 Edith Violet Sleap; two *d.* *Educ.:* Winchester; New College, Oxford. Called to Bar, Lincoln's Inn, 1928; Professor of Law, 1936-55, Pro-Vice-Chancellor, 1950-54, University of

Sheffield. *Publications:* 2nd Edition (with Author) McGillivray on Insurance Law, 1937; 3rd Edition (with Author) McGillivray on Insurance Law, 1947. *Recreations:* cricket, fishing, bridge. *Address:* Department of Law, The University, Liverpool. [*Died* 8 *May* 1965.

BROWNE, Sir Denis (John Wolko), K.C.V.O. 1961; M.B., F.R.C.S.; Surgeon, The Hospital for Sick Children, Great Ormond Street, W.C.1, 1928-57, Emeritus Surgeon 1957; *b.* 28 April 1892; *s.* of Sylvester Browne and Anne Catherine Stawell; *m.* 1st, 1927, Helen Simpson (*d.* 1940); one *d.*; 2nd, 1945, Lady Moyra Blanche Madeleine Ponsonby, O.B.E., *d.* of 9th Earl of Bessborough, P.C., G.C.M.G.; one *s.* one *d.* *Educ.:* The King's School, Paramatta; Univ. of Sydney (graduated in medicine). Served in Australian Army Medical Corps, 1914-19; Major, 1917; Fellow of Royal College of Surgeons, 1922; House-Surgeon, Surgical Registrar, and Superintendent to The Hospital for Sick Children; Arris and Gale Lecturer to the Royal College of Surgeons for 1934 and 1954, Hunterian Professor, 1947, 1949, 1950, 1951; Member: B.B.C. Gen. Advisory Council, 1952-56; Brit. Orthopædic Assoc.; British Pædiatric Assoc.; Brit. Assoc. Plastic Surgeons; Hon. Fellow: International College Surgeons (co-President, British section, 1962-; World President, 1967-); Royal Australasian Coll. of Surgeons; Pres. Brit. Assoc. Pædiatric Surgeons, 1954 1955, 1956 and 1957; Past Pres. Pædiatric Section, Royal Society of Medicine; Hon. Mem. French Soc. of Urology, 1961-; Past Chm., Medical Gp., Roy. Photographic Soc., 1963. Dawson Williams Prize for services to Pædiatrics, 1957; William E. Ladd Memorial Medal (U.S.A.) for Pædiatric Surgery, 1957. Chevalier, Légion d'Honneur, 1961. *Publications:* articles in medical journals. *Recreations:* various. *Address:* 16 Wilton Street, Grosvenor Place, S.W.1. *T.:* Belgravia 1419; 46 Harley Street, W.1. *T.:* Langham 1564. [*Died* 9 *Jan.* 1967.

BROWNE, Edith A.; author, exhibition organiser and cookery expert; *b.* Norwich. *Educ.:* Surrey House School, Norwich. Entered Civil Service. On retirement from Civil Service, visited the West Indies and British Guiana to devote attention to the cane-sugar industry, 1910; in 1911 went out to the Far East in the interests of the 2nd International Rubber Exhibition; in 1913 went to Brazil, the Argentine, etc., as representative of the 4th International Rubber Exhibition and 1st International Cotton Exhibition; courses of Popular Lectures on Our Tropical Industries at the Imperial Institute, London, 1916-18; in 1919 went to West Africa as special correspondent of the Times Trade Supplement, etc., to study the development of the cocoa, vegetable oils and other tropical industries, and as representative of the 5th International Rubber Exhibition; Commissaire Général 6th International Rubber Exhibition, Brussels, 1924, and 7th International Rubber Exhibition, Paris, 1927; Organising Manager Ideal Holidays Exhibition, 1930. *Publications:* Greek Architecture; Romanesque Architecture; Norman Architecture; Byzantine Architecture; Gothic Architecture (Great Buildings and How to Enjoy Them); Life of Sir W. S. Gilbert; Peep at Greece; Peep at Spain; Peep at Panama; Peep at South America; Sugar, Rubber, Tea, Cocoa, Vegetable Oils (Peeps at Industries); The World's Best Recipes. *Recreations:* travelling off the beaten track, international cookery, and life generally. *Address:* c/o Lloyds Bank Ltd., Town Hall Branch, Hove 3. [*Died* 15 *March* 1963.

BROWNE, Col. Sir Eric; *see* Gore-Browne.

BROWNE, Francis James; Emeritus Professor of Obstetrics and Gynecology in the University of London; Consulting Obstetrician and Gynecologist: Royal North Shore Hospital, Sydney; Royal Hospital for Women, Sydney; Royal Newcastle Hospital, N.S.W.; Hon. Fellow Edinburgh Obstetrical Soc.; Membre Honoraire de la Société Française de Gynécologie; Hon. Member, Section of Obstetrics and Gynæcology, Royal Society of Medicine; Hon. Fellow Ulster Medical Society; Hon. Member West Herts Medical Society; *s.* of William Browne, Tullybogley, Manor Cunningham, Co. Donegal; *m.* Mary (*d.* 1948), *e. d.* of John Gallaugher, Balleighan, Manor Cunningham, Co. Donegal; one *s.* (*yr. s.* killed (R.A.F. pilot) in 1941), two *d.*; *m.* 1951, Grace Cuthbert, Sydney, N.S.W. *Educ.:* Royal School, Raphoe; Foyle College, Londonderry; Aberdeen University, M.B., Ch.B., 1906. General practice in Welsh mining district, 1906; Lieut. R.A.M.C., 1915-1916; Research Pathologist, Edinburgh Royal Maternity Hospital, 1919-26; Assistant Physician, 1923; F.R.C.S. Edin. 1914, M.D., Highest Honours, 1919; D.Sc. Edin. 1925; F.R.C.O.G. Blair Bell Gold Medal, 1960. *Publications:* Ante-Natal and Post-Natal Care, 9th Edition, 1960; Obstetric Technique, 5th Edition, 1949; Advice to the Expectant Mother on the Care of her Health, 11th Edition, 1957; Postgraduate Obstetrics and Gynæcology, 3rd edn., 1963; numerous contributions to obstetrical literature, especially dealing with ante-natal pathology. *Recreations:* gardening, walking. *Address:* 2 Gillies St., Wollstonecraft, Sydney, N.S.W., Australia. [*Died* 17 *Aug.* 1963.

BROWNE, Prof. George Stephenson, M.C.; M.A. (Oxon); Dip. Ed. (Oxon, Lond., Melb.); Professor of Education, Univ. of Melbourne, 1934-December 1956, Emeritus Professor since retirement; Dean of the Faculty of Education and Chairman of the Schools Board at the University of Melbourne, retired Dec. 1956; commentator on Current Affairs since 1957, and "Improve Your English" since 1965, on TV, from Melbourne; *b.* Melbourne; *s.* of George Browne, Northumberland, and Lydia Mary Purcell Melbourne; *m.* 1923, Rosalind Haig, *d.* of A. W. Malcolm, Lancaster; one *d.* *Educ.:* Melbourne High School; Univ. of Melbourne; Balliol College, Oxford. High School Master in Victoria prior to 1914; served with Australian Imperial Force in France (M.C., severely wounded); awarded, at close of War, an Overseas Scholarship at Balliol College, Oxford; Vice-Principal Teachers College, Lancaster, 1920; Oxford Travelling Scholarship in Education; visited U.S.A. and Germany, 1922; Visiting lecturer in Education at University of California, 1931; educational adviser and lecturer to R.A.A.F. during War of 1939-45, visiting New Guinea, Northern Australia, the Pacific Islands and Borneo. In 1947 visited Japan and reported to Australian Department of External Affairs on moves to democratize Japanese education. Vis. Prof. at Portland, Oregon, U.S.A. 1953. *Publications:* A Survey of Education in Australia, 1927; Australia: A General Account, 1929; The Case for Curriculum Revision, 1932; The Making of an Army Instructor, 1943; Report on Democratic Tendencies in Japanese Education, 1947; (with N. H. Harper) Our Pacific Neighbours, 1953; Secondary Education To-Day and To-Morrow, 1953; (with President Cramer, Portland State College) Contemporary Education, 1956 and 1965 (2nd edn.). *Recreations:* tennis, golf. *Address:* 50 The Avenue, Parkville, N.2, Victoria, Australia. *Clubs:* Melbourne, Naval and Military, Legacy, Beefsteak (Melbourne). [*Died* 23 *May* 1970.

BROWNE, Brigadier-General John Gilbert, C.M.G. 1918; C.B.E. 1928; D.S.O. 1917; *b.* 1878; *s.* of Leonard G. Browne of Hoburne, Hants.; *m.* 1966, Adeline Iris, *d.* of late Ernest William Shipman, Taunton,

Somerset. *Educ.:* Wellington College; R.M.C., Sandhurst; Magdalen College, Oxford. Served South African War, 1899-1902 (Queen's medal seven clasps, King's medal two clasps); Northern Nigeria, 1906 (medal and clasp); European War, 1914-18 (despatches, D.S.O., Bt. Lt.-Col., C.M.G., 1914 Star, British War Medal, Victory Medal); Iraq, 1925-27 (C.B.E. Iraq, active service medal); Iraq, 1930-31 (clasp); Iraq, 1932 (British Medal and Clasp, Northern Kurdistan); Order of the Nile, 3rd Class; Knight of Grace of Order of St. John of Jerusalem; commanded 14th King's Hussars (now 14/20th King's Hussars), 1921-25; Comd. Iraq Levies, 1925-33; retired pay, 1933, with rank of Brig.-General; Employed under the League of Nations on Assyrian Settlement Scheme, 1933-35; Civil Defence and Home Guard List, II, 1939-45. J.P., Hampshire, 1936. *Publications:* History of the Iraq Levies, 1932; (Part Writer) History of the 14th King's Hussars, 1932. *Address:* Hoburne, Christchurch, Hants. *T.:* Highcliffe 2007. *Club:* United Service.
[*Died* 12 *Feb.* 1968.

BROWNE, Colonel Maurice, C.B.E. 1953; M.C. 1914; D.L.; *b.* 13 December 1884; 2nd *s.* of Brigadier-General E. S. Browne, V.C., C.B., 24th Foot, South Wales Borderers; unmarried. *Educ.:* Christ College, Brecon. Joined Middlesex Regt. (Duke of Cambridge's Own) from Guernsey L.I. Militia, 1905, and served in all ranks including Comd. 2nd Bn. Served European War, 1914-18 (despatches); on gen. staff, Home Forces and in War Office; on conclusion of Bn. Comd. apptd. Instructor Senior Officers' School, Sheerness, June 1935; retired, ill-health, Sept. 1935; War of 1939-45, commanded Regtl. Machine Gun Training Centre. O. St. J.; after retirement, J.P., D.L., Middlesex, 31 Dec. 1941; High Sheriff, County of Middlesex, 1948-49; Colonel, The Middlesex Regt. (Duke of Cambridge's Own), 1942-52. *Address:* Inglis Barracks, Mill Hill, N.W.7. *T.:* Finchley 2611; The Grange Hotel, 3 Hendon Avenue, Finchley, N.3. *Club:* United Service.
[*Died* 21 *Dec.* 1961.

BROWNE, Philip Austin, C.B 1953; *b.* 26 Jan. 1898; *y. s.* of late Edward Austin Browne. *Educ.:* Winchester; Magdalen Coll., Oxford; Roy. Coll. of Music. M.A., D.Mus., Oxon; Hon. A.R.C.M. Served European War, 1916-19, Lt. The Black Watch. Assistant Master, Stowe School, 1923; H.M. Inspector of Schools, 1929; Commonwealth Fellow, 1937-38; Divisional Inspector (Northern Division), 1944; Chief Inspector, 1946; retired 1959; Member, National Savings Cttee. 1946-59 Company Commander, 10th Cornwall Bn. Home Guard, 1940-44. Fell. Roy. Philatelic Soc. of London. *Publications:* Brahms, the Symphonies, 1933; articles in Music and Letters; various musical compositions. *Recreations:* bridge, philately. *Address:* 12 Redcliffe Square, S.W.10. *Clubs:* Athenæum, Hamilton.
[*Died* 4 *March* 1961.

BROWNE, Lt.-Col. Sir Stewart G.; *see* Gore-Browne.

BROWNE, Air Marshal Sir Thomas A. W.; *see* Warne-Browne.

BROWNE, Professor Thomas George, M.Sc. (T.C.D.), M.V.Sc. (N.U.I.), M.R.C.V.S., M.R.I.A.; Principal of the Veterinary College of Ireland, 1941-53; Prof. of Anatomy, 1915-53, retired 1953; *b.* 9 September 1888; *s.* of late John Browne and Jane Eakin, Moneymore, County Derry, Ireland; *m.* 1924, Margaret Power; one *s.* one *d.* *Educ.:* Intermediate School, Lisburn; Cookstown Academy; Veterinary Coll. of Ireland. M.R.C.V.S. 1913; ex-Pres. Irish Veterinary Council; ex-Member Council R.C.V.S.; ex-Pres. Veterinary Medical Assoc. of Ireland; formerly Member of Royal Irish Acad. Instrumental in initiating and effecting negotiations which culminated in affiliation of Veterinary College of Ireland with the two Dublin Universities, 1944-46; Pioneer in Ireland in use of Spinal Anæsthesia in Animals. *Publications:* Atlas of the Horse: its Anatomy and Physiology, 1918; Atlas of the Ox: its Anatomy and Physiology, 1927; many contributions to scientific journals. *Recreations:* golf and tennis. *Address:* 25 Rosmeen Gardens, Dun Laoghaire, Co. Dublin. *T.:* Dublin 87266.
[*Died* 9 *April* 1963.

BROWNE, Vincent R. B.; *see* Balfour-Browne.

BROWNE, Maj.-Gen. William; *see* Cave-Browne.

BROWNE, William A. F. B.; *see* Balfour-Browne.

BROWNE, Wynyard Barry; novelist and dramatist; *b* 6 Oct. 1911; *o. s.* of Rev. Barry Mathew Charles Sleater Browne and Ellinor Muriel Verena (*née* Malcolmson), *m.* 1948 Joan Margaret, *d.* of Dr. B. A. Yeaxlee, C.B.E.; one *d.* *Educ.:* Marlborough; Christ's College, Cambridge. Plays: Dark Summer, St. Martin's, 1947; The Holly and The Ivy, Duchess, 1950; A Question of Fact, Piccadilly, 1953; The Ring of Truth, Savoy, 1959. *Publications:* novels: Queenie Molson, 1934; Sheldon's Way, 1935; The Fire and the Fiddle, 1937. *Recreations:* conversation, reading, going to the theatre. *Address:* Wild Wood, Taverham, Norfolk. *T.:* Drayton 350. *Clubs:* Savile, Dramatists'.
[*Died* 19 *Feb.* 1964.

BROWNE-CAVE; *see* Cave-Browne-Cave.

BROWNE-WILKINSON, Rev. Arthur Rupert, M.C.; M.A.; Canon Residentiary of Chichester Cathedral since 1938; Precentor since 1945; *b.* 6 Aug. 1889; *s.* of late Rev. Henry Browne-Wilkinson; *m.* 1917, Mary Theresa Caroline, 2nd *d.* of late Rt. Rev. C. T. Abraham, late Bishop of Derby; one *s.* four *d.* *Educ.:* Lancing; Oxford and Cuddesdon. Curate of Bakewell, 1912; Lecturer at Bishop Heber College, Trichinopoly, 1915, temporary Chaplain to the Forces, 1917 (M.C., despatches); Vicar of St. Paul's, Daybrook, 1919, Diocesan Missioner of Southwell and Chaplain to the Bishop, 1923; Principal, S. Christopher's College, Blackheath, 1926-31; Rector of Bedale, North Yorks, 1931-38; Rural Dean of Bedale, 1937-38; Fellow of Woodard Corporation, Provost of Lancing, 1944. *Publications:* The Confirmation School; Pastoral Work among Children; With Due Preparation; contributor to the Teachers' Commentary, Christian Discipline, Liturgy and Worship, The Teaching of the Catechism, Prayer Book Preparation for Confirmation. *Recreation:* gardening. *Address:* The Residentiary, Chichester. *T.:* Chichester 2292. *Club:* Oxford and Cambridge University.
[*Died* 7 *April* 1961.

BROWNELL, Reginald Samuel, C.B. 1958; C.B.E. 1945; Permanent Secretary, Ministry of Education (Northern Ireland), 1939-58, retired; *b.* 5 Feb. 1893; *s.* of late Thomas and Susanna Brownell; *m.* 1924, Jessie, *d.* of Thomas Strachan; two *d.* *Educ.:* Mountjoy School, Dublin; Trinity College, Dublin. Hons. Degree in Classics, Dublin University, 1915. Egyptian Civil Service, 1915-23. Served European War, 1917-19. Passed Advanced Examination in Arabic of the Egyptian Government, 1922; resigned Egyptian Civil Service, and joined Ulster Civil Service, 1923; Private Secretary to Viscount Charlemont, Minister of Education

(N.I.), 1925; Assistant Secretary, Ministry of Edu ation (N.I.), 1938; Permanent Secretary and Civil Service Commissioner for Northern Ireland, 1939; Civil Commissioner for Northern Area of Northern Ireland, 1941. *Recreations:* gardening, reading, motoring. *Address:* Southcote, Caledon Road, Beaconsfield, Bucks. *T.:* Beaconsfield 484. [*Died* 20 *May* 1961.

BROWNFIELD, Vice-Admiral Leslie Newton, C.B. 1954; C.B.E. 1951; R.N. retd.; *b.* 29 Dec. 1901; *s.* of Harry Munyard Brownfield; *m.* 1929, Sylvia Kathleen Dore; one *s.* *Educ.:* Stubbington House, Fareham; H.M.S. Conway; R.N. College, Dartmouth. H.M.S. Ajax, as midshipman, 1918; qualified in Gunnery, 1927; served with Royal Australian Navy, 1935-37; Naval Attaché, Thailand, 1939-41; War of 1939-45, commanded H.M. Ships Ramillies and Apollo. Commodore-in-Charge, Hong Kong, 1949-51 A.D.C. to H.M., 1952; Rear-Adm. 1952; President Admiralty Interview Board, 1952-1954; Vice-Adm. 1955; Admiral Superintendent, Devonport, 1954-57, retired. *Address:* Brownfields, Westmark, Petersfield, Hants. [*Died* 28 *July* 1968.

BROWNING, Lieutenant-General Sir Frederick (Arthur Montague), G.C.V.O. 1959 (K.C.V.O. 1953); K.B.E. 1946; C.B. 1943; D.S.O. 1918; D.L.; Extra Equerry to the Queen and to the Duke of Edinburgh, since 1959; retired from Army, 1948; *b.* 20 December 1896; *s.* of late Colonel F. H. Browning, C.B.E.; *m.* 1932, Daphne, *d.* of late Sir Gerald du Maurier; one *s.* two *d.* Served European War, 1914-18 (despatches, D.S.O., Croix de Guerre); Adjutant, Royal Military College, Sandhurst, 1924-28; commanded: 2nd Bn. Grenadier Guards, 1935-39; Small Arms Schools, 1939-40; 24th Guards Brigade Group, 1940-41; 1st Airborne Division, 1941-43; British Airborne Corps, 1944; Deputy Commander First Allied Airborne Army, 1944; Chief of Staff, S.E.A.C., 1944-46; Military Secretary, War Office, 1946-48; Comptroller and Treasurer, Princess Elizabeth's Household, 1948-52; Treasurer to the Duke of Edinburgh, 1952-59. Civil Defence County Controller, Cornwall; Chm. Territorial Army Assoc., Cornwall; D.L., County of Cornwall, 1960. *Address:* Menabilly, Par, Cornwall. *Club:* Royal Fowey Yacht. [*Died* 14 *March* 1965.

BROWNLEE, John Donald Mackenzie; Singer; President of American Guild of Musical Artists Inc. since 1952; President, Manhattan School of Music, N.Y., since 1955; *b.* Geelong, Aust. (Scotch parentage); *s.* of James Watson Brownlee and Isabelle Finlayson Mackenzie; *m.* 1928, Donna Carla Oddone di Feletto; two *s.* one *d.* *Educ.:* Geelong Coll. Debut at Covent Garden in Bohème on the occasion of Dame Nellie Melba's Farewell, 1926; Debut Grand Opera House Paris in Thais, 1927; for ten years permanently attached to Paris Opera House, doing all principal baritone roles, later doing guest performances only; Principal Baritone of: Grand Opera House, Paris, 1927-36; Glyndebourne Festival Opera, 1934-39; Metropolitan Opera Co., N.Y., 1936-59; also Royal Opera House, Covent Garden; several concert tours of Australia, U.S.A., England, and S. America. Appointed by Pres. Eisenhower member of Advisory Committee on the arts, for National Cultural Center, Washington, D.C. Appointed by Pres. Kennedy member of U.S. Advisory Commission on International, Educational and Cultural Affairs. Hon. D.Mus Cincinnati, 1957. *Recreation:* golf. *Address:* 1 West 72nd Street, New York 23. *Clubs:* Sunningdale Golf; Maidstone (East Hampton, U.S.A.). [*Died* 10 *Jan.* 1969.

BROWNLEE, John Edward, Q.C., LL.D.; President and General Manager, United Grain Growers Ltd., since 1948; *b.* Port Ryerse, Ontario, 27 Aug. 1884; *s.* of William James Brownlee and Christina Shaw; *m.* 1912, Florence Agnes, *d.* of James V. Edy, Toronto; two *s.* *Educ.:* Sarnia, Ontario High School; Toronto University (B.A.). LL.D. (Hon.) Alberta University. Attorney-General, Alberta, 1921-25; Premier of Alberta, 1924-34; Vice-Pres. United Grain Growers Ltd., 1941. Member law firm Brownlee & Brownlee, Edmonton, Alberta. Director: Catelli Food Products Ltd., 1951; Canadian Board Royal Exchange Assurance, 1952; Mem. Advisory Cttee. Canadian Wheat Board. *Address:* Office of the President, United Grain Growers Ltd., Hamilton Building, Winnipeg, Manitoba, Canada. [*Died* 15 *July* 1961.

BROWNRIGG, Captain Thomas Marcus, C.B.E. 1943 (O.B.E. 1942); D.S.O. 1944; Royal Navy retired; i.d.c.; Director: Rediffusion (Holdings) Ltd.; Keith Prowse Music Publishing Co.; TV Publications Ltd.; *b.* 8 July 1902; *s.* of Col. H. J. W. Brownrigg and Evelyn Huleatt; *m.* 1926, Joyce, *d.* of Sidney Chiesman; one *s.* one *d.* *Educ.:* R.N. Colls., Osborne and Dartmouth. Midshipman, 1919; Lt., 1923. R.N. Staff Course, 1933; Comdr., 1936; Master of the Fleet to Admiral Sir Andrew Cunningham, 1939-42; Capt., 1942; Deputy Chief of Staff to Admiral Sir Andrew Cunningham, 1942-1943; commanded H.M.S. Scylla, 1944; R.N.A.S. Rattray, 1945; H.M.S. Theseus, 1946; Imperial Defence College, 1947; Director of Plans, Admiralty Naval Staff, 1948-49; Chief of Staff, Mediterranean, as Cdre. 1st Class, 1949-52; Naval A.D.C. to the Queen, 1952; retd. list, 1952. General Manager of Bracknell New Town Development Corporation, 1952. General Manager Associated Rediffusion, Ltd., 1954-63. *Address:* Vann House, Finchampstead, Berks; 56 Cranmer Court, S.W.3. *Club:* United Service. [*Died* 9 *Oct.* 1967.

BRUCE OF MELBOURNE, 1st Viscount, *cr.* 1947, of Westminster Gardens in the City of Westminster; **Stanley Melbourne Bruce,** P.C. 1923; C.H. 1927; M.C.; F.R.S. 1944; (first) Chancellor of the Australian National University, Canberra, 1951-61; *b.* 15 April 1883; *s.* of John Bruce, Melbourne; *m.* 1913, Ethel (*d.* 1967), *d.* of late Andrew Anderson. *Educ.:* Melbourne Grammar School; Trinity Hall, Cambridge, B.A., Hon. LL.D. 1923. Called to Bar, Middle Temple, 1906; Hon. Bencher Lincoln's Inn, 1932; served European War, 1914-17 (twice wounded, despatches, M.C., Croix de Guerre avec Palme); Member for Flinders, 1918-29 and 1931-33; represented the Commonwealth at the League of Nations Assembly, 1921, 1932, 1933, 1934, 1935, 1936, 1937, 1938; Australian Representative Council of League of Nations, 1933-36; President of Council, 1936; Commonwealth Treasurer, 1921-23; Prime Minister of Australia and Minister for External Affairs, 1923-29; Minister for Health, 1927-28; Minister for Trade and Customs, May-Nov. 1928; Minister for Territories, 1928-29; Minister without Portfolio, 1932-33; Australian Minister in London, 1932-33; High Commissioner for Australia in London, 1933-45, and Minister for Australia to Netherlands Government, 1942-45; represented Australia at the Imperial and Economic Conferences, London, 1923, 1926 and 1937, and Ottawa, 1932, and at World Economic Conference, 1933; Pres. Montreux Conference for revision of Straits Convention, 1936; Representative of Commonwealth Government in United Kingdom War Cabinet and on Pacific War Council, 1942-45; Chairman World Food Council, 1947-51. Chairman Finance Corporation for Industry, 1947-57. *Recreations:* riding, golf; rowed

in winning Cambridge Eight, 1904. *Address:* Flat 16, 7 Princes Gate, S.W.7. *Clubs:* Athenæum; Melbourne (Melbourne).
[*Died* 25 *Aug.* 1967 (*ext.*).

BRUCE, Colonel Hon. David; *b.* 11 June 1888; 4th *s* of 9th Earl of Elgin; *m.* 1919, Jennet Rawstorne, *d.* of late Right Rev. A. G. Rawstorne, Bishop of Whalley; one *s.* one *d.* *Educ.:* Eton; Sandhurst. Joined Seaforth Highlanders, 1908; served European War, being a member of the original Expeditionary Force in 1914; commanded the 7th Bn. Seaforth Highlanders, April 1918-May 1919 (thrice wounded, despatches, Brevet Major. Jan. 1919; Belgian Croix de Guerre); commanded 6th Bn. Seaforth Highlanders, T.A., 1928-32; commanded 8th Bn. (afterwards 30th Bn.) Seaforth Highlanders, 1939-42; D.L., County of Sutherland, Vice-Lieut., 1957-. *Recreations:* shooting, fishing. *Address:* Ballamor, Brora, Sutherland. *Club:* New (Edinburgh).
[*Died* 26 *Aug.* 1964.

BRUCE, Colonel Hon. Herbert Alexander, M.D., L.R.C.P. (Lond.); F.A.C.S.; F.R.C.S. England; LL.D. Toronto, Western and Queen's Universities; Colonel C.A.M.C.; Col. A.M.S.; Consulting Surgeon to British Armies in France during European War, 1914-1918; Emeritus Professor of Surgery, Univ. of Toronto; Governor, Univ. of Toronto, since 1930; *b.* Blackstock, Ontario; *s.* of Stewart Bruce and Isabella Morrow; *m.* Amy Angela Hall, Cornwall; one *s.* *Educ.:* University of Toronto (M.B. 1892, Univ. Gold Medal, Starr Medal); Univ. College, London. Consulting Surgeon Toronto General Hospital; President, Ontario Medical Association, 1911-12; Fellow, American Surgical Association; Pres., Academy of Medicine, Toronto, 1916-1917; A Founder and Regent of Amer. Coll. of Surgeons, 1913; late Inspector-General Canadian A.M.C., 1916; European War, 1916-19 (despatches twice); Lieutenant-Governor of Ontario, 1932-37; M.P. Canadian House of Commons, 1940-46. K.G.St.J. *Publications:* Politics and the C.A.M.C.; Our Heritage, 1934; Friendship, the Key to Peace, 1937; Varied Operations, 1958. *Address:* 18 Douglas Drive, Toronto 5, Ont. *T.:* Walnut 28952. *Clubs:* York, Toronto Hunt.
[*Died* 23 *June* 1963.

BRUCE, Howard; *b.* 31 Aug. 1879; *s.* of Albert C. Bruce and Mary Howard; *m.* 1912, Mary Graham Bowdoin; three *d.* *Educ.:* private schools; Virginia Military Institute, B.S. (Civil Eng.). Engineer with East River Gas Co., 1897; Asst. Engineer and Engineer of Construction, Consolidated Gas Co., N.Y., 1907; Gen. Man. Bartlett Hayward Co., Baltimore, Md., 1907, Vice-Pres. and Gen. Man., 1909-17, Pres. and Gen. Man., 1917-28, Chm. of Bd. from 1928 until firm was consolidated with Koppers Co. Served as Democratic Nat. Committeeman, State of Md., 1926-40. Army Service Forces, War Dept., 1942-45. Dep. Dir. of Materiel and Dir. of Materiel, 1943-45 (D.S.M.); Dep. Administrator Economic Co-operation Administration, 1948-49. Actively interested in civic work. Director and Chairman of Executive Committee: Worthington Corporation; The Baltimore and Ohio Railroad Company; Chairman of Board, Maryland Shipbuilding and Drydock Co.; Director: Baltimore National Bank; The Martin Company; Maryland Casualty Company. Hon. Mem. Board of Trustees of The Johns Hopkins Univ.; Member of Business Advisory Council, Dept. of Commerce, Washington, D.C.; Dir. Amer. Cttee. on United Europe. *Address:* 33 Warrenton Road, Baltimore 10, Md., U.S.A. *Clubs:* Maryland, Elkridge (Baltimore, Md.); Links, Jockey (New York).
[*Died* 17 *June* 1961.

BRUCE, Hon. John (Hamilton), C.B.E. 1951; K.St.J. 1936; Principal Secretary, Priory for Wales, Order of St. John of Jerusalem, since 1931; *b.* 14 June 1889; *s.* of 2nd Baron Aberdare and Constance Mary, *d.* of Hamilton Beckett; *m.* 1923, Cynthia Juliet Grant Duff Ainslie, D.St.J.; one *s.* one *d.* (and one *d.* decd.). *Educ.:* Winchester College; New College, Oxford. Lieut. Glamorgan Yeomanry, 1908-15. J.P. Glamorgan, 1928; D.L. Glamorgan, 1936. *Address:* Cefn Pennar House, Mountain Ash, Glamorgan. *Club:* Cardiff and County (Cardiff).
[*Died* 18 *April* 1964.

BRUCE, Brig.-General Thomas, C.M.G. 1919; D.S.O. 1918; late Royal Artillery; J.P. Dorset; *e. s.* of Capt. John Bruce, Royal Navy; *m.* Violet Augusta Bruce (*d.* 1964), *d.* of Alan Cameron Bruce Pryce, Nicholas, Glamorgan; two *s.* *Educ.:* Hilbrow, Rugby; Cheltenham College; R.M.A., Woolwich. First Commission, 1891; served Tirah Campaign, N.W. Frontier (medal two clasps); European War (despatches, Bt. Lieut.-Colonel, Bt. Colonel, St. Anne Russia, with swords, C.M.G., D.S.O.). *Recreations:* represented Woolwich in the Rugby Fifteen, Gymnasium and Sports Team against Sandhurst; won several Point to Point. *Club:* United Service.
[*Died* 7 *Aug.* 1966.

BRUCE LOCKHART, Sir Robert (Hamilton), K.C.M.G., *cr.* 1943; Author; *b.* 2 September 1887; *s.* of R. Bruce Lockhart, lately of Eagle House, Sandhurst, Berks. and Florence Stuart Macgregor; *m.* 1913, Jean Haslewood (marriage dissolved, 1938), *d.* of late Leonard Turner, Kinellan, Brisbane, Australia; one *s.*; *m.* 1948, Frances Mary, *er. d.* of Maj.-Gen. E. A. Beck. *Educ.:* Fettes College; Berlin; Paris. Passed a competitive examination and appointed a Vice-Consul in H.M. Consular Service, 1911; appointed to Moscow; Acting Consul-General there, 1915-17; proceeded to St. Petersburg and Moscow as Head of Special Mission to the Soviet Government, Jan. 1918; arrested by the Bolsheviks and imprisoned in the Kremlin, Sept. 1918; released and exchanged for Litvinoff, Oct. 1918; Commercial Secretary to H.M. Legation, Prague, Nov. 1919; resigned, Oct. 1922; banking in Central Europe, 1922-28; Editorial Staff Evening Standard, 1929-37; Political Intelligence Department, Foreign Office, 1939-40; British Representative with Provisional Czechoslovak Government, London, 1940-41; Deputy Under-Secretary of State, Foreign Office, and Director-General of Political Warfare Exec., 1941-45. *Publications:* Memoirs of a British Agent, 1932; Retreat from Glory, 1934; Return to Malaya, 1936; My Scottish Youth, 1937; Guns or Butter?, 1938; Comes the Reckoning, 1947; My Rod My Comfort, 1948; The Marines Were There, 1950; Jan Masaryk, 1951; Scotch, 1951; My Europe, 1952; Your England, 1955; The Two Revolutions, 1957; Friends, Foes and Foreigners, 1957; Giants Cast Long Shadows, 1960. *Address:* Brookside, Ditchling, Sussex. *Clubs:* St. James', Beefsteak.
[*Died* 27 *Feb.* 1970.

BRUCHE, Major-General Sir Julius Henry, K.C.B., *cr.* 1935 (C.B. 1919); C.M.G. 1917; Maj. Gen. A.M.F., retired; *b.* 6 March 1873; *y. s.* of late William Bruche, Melbourne; *m.* 1904, Dorothy Annette, *y. d.* of late Judge Alfred M'Farland of Sydney; one *d.* *Educ.:* Scotch College, Melbourne; Melbourne University. Admitted as Barrister and Solicitor Supreme Court of Victoria, 1898, held commission in Australian Citizen Forces for 8 years; commission in Permanent Forces since 1898; D.A.A.G. Victoria, 1904-10; exchange duty with British Army, Aldershot and War Office, 1910-1911; D.A.A.G., Tasmania, 1911-13; A.A.G., Queensland, 1913-14; Military Commandant, Western Australia, 1914-16; served in South-African War, 1899-1902 (Queen's medal 6 clasps); European War (despatches five times, C.B.,

C.M.G.); Military Commandant, New South Wales, 1920-21; Hon. A.D.C. to Governor-Gen., 1920-23; G.O.C. Field Troops, Queensland, 1921-1925, and District Base Commandant, 1922-25; Commanding 1st Division and District Base Commandant, N.S.W., 1926-27; Adjutant-General Military Board, Army Headquarters, 1927-29; Australian Representative on Imperial Gen. Staff, and temp. Major-Gen. in British Army, 1929-31; Commandant, Royal Military College, Sydney, 1931; Chief of the General Staff, 1931-35; retired list, 1936. *Address:* 4 Kensington Road, South Yarra, Victoria, Australia. [*Died* 28 *April* 1961.

BRUDENELL, George Lionel Thomas; *b.* 26 Aug. 1880; *e. surv. s.* of late Lord Robert Thomas Brudenell Bruce and Emma, *d.* of late Capel Hanbury Leigh, of Pont-y-pool Park, Monmouthshire; inherited the Cardigan Estates; dropped the surname and arms of Bruce; *m.* 1923, Mary, *d.* of Stephen Schilizzi, of Loddington Hall, Kettering; one *s.* one *d.* *Recreations:* forestry, agriculture, bibliophil. *Address:* Deene Park, Corby, Northants. *T.A.:* Deene Bulwick. *T.:* Bulwick 223. *Clubs:* Travellers'; New (Edinburgh). [*Died* 8 *Aug.* 1962.

BRUMWELL, George Murray, M.A.; journalist and author; *b.* 1872; *o. s.* of late G. M. Brumwell, M.D., J.P., and Mary, *d.* of G. Hyde; *m.* Cicely S. A., *d.* of J. Baker. *Educ.:* Manchester Grammar School; Trinity College, Oxford. Joined the Editorial Staff of The Times in 1902; Night Editor, 1908-22; Director, The Times Publishing Co. Ltd., 1914-1922; Assistant Editor of The Times, 1922-34. *Publications:* collaborated with late Canon Sheppard, Sub-Dean of the Chapels Royal, in the Life of the Duke of Cambridge. *Recreations:* golf, gardening. *Address:* Red Roofs, Budock Vean, near Falmouth. *Clubs:* Athenæum, United University. [*Died* 14 *Nov.* 1963.

BRUMWELL, Rev. Percy Middleton, C.B.E. 1941; M.C.; *b.* 22 Nov. 1881; *s.* of Rev. H. T. Brumwell; *m.* 1923, Marion Elizabeth Whittle; two *d.* *Educ.:* Kingswood School, Bath. Ceylon, 1904-14 (Officiating Chaplain to Troops); S.C.F. 12th Div. France, European War, 1915-19; S.C.F. 34th Div. Germany, Army of Occupation, 1919; C.F. in Ireland, 1921; Constantinople, 1922; Malta, 1923-27; Aldershot, 1927-29; C.F. 3rd Cl. Aldershot, 1929-31; C.F. 2nd Cl. 1931-36; Asst. Chaplain-General Western Command, Chester, 1936-39; Deputy Chaplain-General, War Office, 1940-42; retired pay, 1943; B.L.A. (Belgium and France), 1944; Chairman Council of Voluntary Welfare Work, with B.L.A. and B.A.O.R., 1945-50. O.C.F. Depot of R.A.M.C., Crookham, Aldershot, 1954-60. *Publications:* History of 12th Division (Compiler); The Army Chaplain. *Recreations:* cricket, tennis, boxing (Referee and Judge), chess. *Address:* Epworth, Fitzroy Road, Fleet, Hants. *T.:* Fleet 586. [*Died* 20 *March* 1963.

BRUNDLE, Frank Walter, C.B.E. 1944; *b.* 1 Sept. 1890; *e. s.* of late F. H. Brundle; *m.* 1914, Gladys May Bignold; one *s.* two *d.* *Educ.:* City of London School. *Address:* Newport, Downs Hill, Beckenham. [*Died* 2 *Dec.* 1963.

BRÜNING, Heinrich, Dr. phil., LL.D.; Prof. of Political Science, University of Cologne, 1951-55, Emeritus since 1955; Lucius N. Littauer Professor of Government, Harvard Graduate School of Public Administration, 1939-52, Emeritus since 1952; *b.* 26 Nov. 1885. *Educ.:* Univs. of München, Strassburg and Bonn; London School of Economics. Served European War, 1915-18 (Iron Cross 2nd and 1st Class); Prussian Ministry of Health, 1919-21; Adviser to the German Christian Trade Union Movement, 1922-29; member of Reichstag, 1924-33; Reich Chancellor, 1930-32; Lecturer on Government, Harvard University, 1937-39; Supernumerary Fellow and Lecturer in Political Theory, Queen's College, Oxford, 1937-39. *Address:* Seminar für Politische Wissenschaften der Universität zu Köln, Köln-Lindenthal, Albertus-Magnus-Platz, Germany. *T.:* 411221, ext. 344. [*Died* 27 *March* 1970.

BRUNNER, Professor Dr. Emil; Theologian; Honorary Professor of Zürich University; *b.* Switzerland, 23 December 1889; *s.* of Emil and Sophie Brunner; *m.* 1917, Margrit Lauterburg; two *s.* (and two *s.* decd.). *Educ.:* Gymnasium, Zürich. Studied theology at Zürich, Berlin, and New York. Theol. D., Zürich, 1913; Hon. D.D.: Münster, 1925; Edinburgh, 1931; Utrecht, 1936; Oxford, 1937; Oslo, 1946; Princeton, 1946; St. Andrews, 1950; Hon. Dr. of Law, Bern, 1948. Grand Cross, Order of Merit, Federal Republic of Germany, 1960. Minister, Swiss Reformed Church, 1912; teacher, High School, Leeds, England, 1913; Pastor, in Canton of Glarus, 1916-1924; Professor of Theology, Zürich University, 1924-53; Professor of Christian Philosophy, Tokyo, 1953-55. Pres. Swiss-American Soc. for Cultural Relations. *Publications:* The Mediator (German ed.), 1927; (English ed.), 1934; The Word and the World, 1931; The Divine Imperative, 1932 and 1934; Our Faith, 1936 and 1949; God and Man, 1936; The Philosophy of Religion from the Standpoint of Protestant Theology, 1937; Man in Revolt, 1937 and 1939; The Divine-Human Encounter, 1938 and 1944; Justice and the Social Order, 1943 and 1945; (with Karl Barth) Natural Theology, 1946; Revelation and Reason, 1941 and 1946; Christianity and Civilization, Pt. I, 1948, Pt. II, 1949; The Christian Doctrine of God, 1946 and 1949 The Christian Doctrine of Creation and Redemption, 1950 and 1952; The Christian Doctrine of the Church, Faith and the Consummation, 1960 and 1962; Communism, Capitalism and Christianity, 1949; the Misunderstanding of the Church, 1951 and 1952; Eternal Hope; the Letter to the Romans, 1960; Truth as Encounter, 1964. *Address:* University of Zürich, Switzerland; Hirslanderstrasse 47, Zürich. *T.:* (051) 531249. [*Died* 6 *April* 1966.

BRUNNER, Rt. Rev. George, Titular Bishop of Murustaga; *b.* Hull, 21 Aug. 1889; *s.* of late Englebert and Clara Brunner. *Educ.:* Ushaw College; Durham University. Ordained, 1917; served St. Charles's Hull, St. Mary's Hessle, St. Patrick's Hull; Parish Priest, St. Charles's Hull, 1937; Canon of Middlesbrough Chapter, 1935; Titular Bishop of Elide and Auxiliary Bishop to Bishop of Middlesbrough, 1946; Vicar-General, 1951-56; Bishop of Middlesbrough, 1956-67. *Address:* 16 Cambridge Road, Middlesbrough, Yorks. [*Died* 21 *March* 1969.

BRUNSKILL, Major-Gen. Gerald, C.B. 1945; M.C. 1918; D.L.; *b.* 2 June 1897; *s.* of late Gerald F. Brunskill, K.C., 1 Fitzwilliam Place, Dublin; *m.* 1925, Irene Dulcie Mary, *d.* of late M. McPhie, St. John's Wood. *Educ.:* Shrewsbury; Dublin Univ. 2nd Lt. R. Sussex Regt. 1914; European War, 1914-1919 (despatches, M.C.); Levant Co. Ltd., London, E.C.3, 1920; R. Ulster Rifles, 1921; Capt. 1923; Maj. 1934; p.s.c. 1932; Bde. Maj. N. Mid. Area, 1933-36; Palestine, 1937-1938 (despatches, medal and clasp); G.S.O. 2 Palestine, 1938-39; Lt.-Col. 1939 and Comd. 1st R. Ulster Rifles, N.W.F., India (medal and clasp); Bde Comd., 129 Inf. Bde., 1941-42; Dir. Special Weapons and Vehicles, War Office, 1942-45; G.O.C. British Troops, Siam, S.E.A.C., 1946; Deputy Master General of the Ordnance in India, 1947; Deputy Chief

of the General Staff in India, 1947-48. Col. 1943; Brig. 1947; Acting Maj.-Gen. 1943; Temp. Maj.-Gen. 1944; retired. 1948. Employed under Medical Research Council (National Institute for Medical Research, Mill Hill, N.W.7), 1949-56. D.L. Kent, 1962. Comr. for County of Kent, St. John Ambulance Bde. C.St.J. U.S. Legion of Merit, Degree of Comdr., 1945. *Address:* 6 Caroline Place Mews, W.2. *T.:* Bayswater 3600; The Chantry, Hawkhurst, Kent. *T.:* Hawkhurst 2283. *Club:* Army and Navy.
[*Died* 26 *Sept.* 1964.

BRUNT, Sir David, K.B.E. 1959; Kt. 1949; F.R.S. 1939; M.A., Sc.D.; Hon. D.Sc. (Wales and London); Secretary, Royal Society, 1948-57, Vice-President, 1949-57; Emeritus Professor of Meteorology, London University, 1952; Chairman of Electricity Supply Research Council, Electricity Council, 1952-59, Vice-Chairman, 1960-61; *b.* 17 June 1886; *m.* 1915, Claudia, *e. d.* of W. Roberts, Nantyglo, Monmouthshire; one *s.* (decd.). *Educ.:* University College of Wales, Aberystwyth (First Class Hons. Mathematics, 1907); Trinity College, Cambridge (Mathematical Tripos, Part II, 1910). Isaac Newton Student, 1911-13; Lecturer University of Birmingham, 1913-14; Lecturer Monmouthshire Training College, Caerleon, 1914-15; served European War; 1916-19 (despatches); Superintendent Army Meteorological Services, Air Ministry, 1919-1934; Professor of Meteorology, Imperial College of Science and Technology, South Kensington, 1934-52 (Fellow, 1954); Hon. Associate, Manchester Coll. of Technology, 1955. Chm. of Council of British Gliding Assoc., 1935-46; Pres. R.Met.S. 1942-44; Pres. Physical Society, 1945-47; Royal Medal (Royal Society), 1944; Buchan Prize, 1933, and Symons Gold Medal, 1947, of R.Met.S. Member of Kungl. Vetenskaps Soc., Upsala. *Publications:* Combination of Observations, 1917; Meteorology, 1928; Physical and Dynamical Meteorology, 1934; Weather Science for Everybody, 1936; Weather Study, 1942; scientific papers in various journals. *Club:* Athenæum.
[*Died* 5 *Feb.* 1965.

BRUTON, Charles Lamb, O.B.E. 1935; B.A.; *b.* Gloucester, 6 April 1890; *s.* of Henry William Bruton, Bewick House, Gloucester; *m.* 1926, Mona Mary, *d.* of L. W. Webster. *Educ.:* Radley Coll., Berks; Keble Coll., Oxford. Private Sec. to Bishop (Paget) of Stepney, 1913-14; Assistant District Commissioner, Uganda, 1914; District Commissioner, 1924; Provincial Commissioner, Eastern Province, 1936; Resident Commissioner, Swaziland, 1937-42; local rank of Lieutenant-Colonel, 1941; Commissioner East African Refugee Administration, 1942-47. Retired, 1947. *Recreation:* cricket (played cricket for Gloucestershire in 1922). *Address:* Rozel Cottage, Shiplake-on-Thames, Oxon. *Clubs:* M.C.C.; Vincent's (Oxford). [*Died* 26 *March* 1969.

BRUTTON, Charles Phipps, C.B.E. 1954 (O.B.E. 1946); retd. as Clerk of the Peace, Clerk of the C.C., Clerk to the Lieutenancy and County Solicitor for Dorset (1935-61); *b.* 20 Jan. 1899; *s.* of late Septimus Brutton, solicitor, Portsmouth; *m.* 1st, 1935, Jackie (marriage dissolved, 1943), *d.* of late Sir Alfred McAlpine; 2nd, 1943, Katharine (marriage dissolved, 1950), *d.* of late Ernest Arthur Oakman; one *d.*; 3rd, 1952, Barbara Mary (Miki), *d.* of late Jock Hood. *Educ.:* Copthorne School, Sussex; Winchester College. Served European War, Grenadier Guards (wounded when with 1st Bn., France, 1918). Solicitor, 1926; Asst. Solicitor, West Riding C.C., 1927-32; Dep. Clerk of the Peace and C.C. Cheshire, 1932-35. County A.R.P. Controller, 1939-45. *Publication:* A Police Constable's Guide to his Daily Work. *Recreations:* cricket (Hampshire, 1920-27; Gentlemen *v.* Players, Oval, 1926), football, rackets, golf. *Address:* 24 Campden St., Kensington, W.8. *T.:* Park 3634. *Clubs:* M.C.C., Butterflies C.C., Hants C.C.; Old Wykehamist G.S. [*Died* 11 *May* 1964.

BRYAN-BROWN, Armitage Noel, M.A.; Emeritus Fellow of Worcester College, Oxford; Fellow and Lecturer in Classics, 1922-67; *b.* 6 January 1900; *y. s.* of Reverend Willoughby Bryan-Brown; *m.* 1926, Teresa, *y. d.* of Professor Herbert Wildon Carr; two *s.* one *d.* *Educ.:* Marlborough College; Balliol College, Oxford. Scholar of Balliol, 1917. 2nd Lt. Royal Sussex Regt., 1918. Craven Scholar, 1921. Senior Proctor, 1939. Part-time Leading Fireman, 1939-45. Senior Tutor, Worc. Coll., 1947-61; Vice-Provost, 1958-67; Public Orator, 1958-67. *Publications:* contrib. to: The Mind of Rome, 1926; Some Oxford Compositions, 1947; More Oxford Compositions, 1964. *Recreations:* travel, mountaineering, hockey, golf, lawn-tennis, bee-keeping. *Address:* Arpinum, Eddystone Rd., Thurlestone, Kingsbridge, Devon.
[*Died* 25 *Aug.* 1968.

BRYANT, Marguerite (Mrs. Munn); *b.* Chippenham, Wilts, 1870; *d.* of G. R. Bryant; *m.* 1901, P. W. Munn (*d.* 1949); one *d.* one adopted *s.* *Publications:* A Great Responsibility, 1895; Morton Verlost; A Woman's Privilege; The Princess Cynthia, 1901; Louis Dural; Christopher Hibbault; Anne Kempburn; The Adjustment; The Dominant Passion; Felicity Crofton; Shadow on the Stone; A Courageous Marriage; Redemption of Richard; The Heights; Mrs Fuller; Chronicles of a Great Prince; Dear Idiot; Breakfast for Three; wrote and produced various plays for Women's Institute. *Address:* Amport Beeches, Broughton, Stockbridge, Hants. [*Died* 13 *Nov.* 1962.

BRYSON, Charles; *see* Barry, Charles.

BRYSON, George Murray, B.L.; S.S.C.; Sheriff Substitute of Stirling, Dunbarton and Clackmannan, at Dumbarton, 1966-69; *b.* 12 March 1904; *s.* of James Guthrie Bryson, Solicitor, Edinburgh, and Ellen Scott Murray; *m.* 1933, Marjorie Una Catharine Hayter; one *s.* two *d.* *Educ.:* Daniel Stewart's Coll. and University of Edinburgh. Practised as Solicitor in Edinburgh, 1929-56; Sen. partner of Bryson & Davie, W.S., Edinburgh; Vice-President, Society of Solicitors in Supreme Courts of Scotland, 1956; Mem. of Council of Law Soc. of Scotland, 1954-56; Sheriff-Substitute of Renfrew and Argyll at Dunoon, 1956-66. *Recreations:* sailing, fishing, golf. *Address:* Sea Bourne, Innellan, Argyll. *T.:* Innellan 205. *Club:* Royal Scottish Automobile.
[*Died* 25 *Feb.* 1970.

BUBER, Martin, Ph.D.; philosopher and author; Professor Emeritus of Social Philosophy at the Hebrew University, Jerusalem, since 1938; *b.* Vienna, 1878. *Educ.:* Univs. of Vienna, Berlin, Leipzig and Zürich. Editor of Welt (Vienna), 1901; Co-founder of Jüdischer Verlag; Founder (and Editor, 1916-24) of Der Jude; Professor of Comparative Religion, University of Frankfurt, 1923-33; Director of College of Jewish Studies, Frankfurt. Left Germany, 1938. Holds Hon. Doctorates in Law, Divinity, Letters and Medicine. *Publications:* I and Thou, 1937; For the Sake of Heaven, 1945; Moses, 1947; Between Man and Man, 1947; Tales of the Hasidim, I 1947, II 1948; Israel and the World, 1948; The Prophetic Faith, 1949; Paths in Utopia, 1949; The Way of Man, 1950; Two Types of Faith, 1951; Israel and Palestine, 1952; Images of Good and Evil, 1952; Right and Wrong, 1952; Eclipse of God, 1952; At the Turning, 1952; Pointing the Way, 1958; Hasidism and Modern Man, 1958; The

Origin and Meaning of Hasidism, 1960; Daniel, 1964; translated Bible into German (with Franz Rosenzweig); many works on the subjects of Hasidism and Zionism. *Address:* Talbiyeh, Jerusalem. *T.:* 33051
[*Died* 13 *June* 1965.

BUCHAN-HEPBURN, Sir John Karslake Thomas, 5th Bt., *cr.* 1815; *b.* 20 March 1894; *s.* of 4th Bt. and Edith Agnes (*d.* 1923), *o. d.* of late E. K. Karslake, K.C.; *S.* father, 1929; *m.* 1916, Jessie Lawrence, *d.* of late Francis William Smith, M.D. one *s.* one *d.* *Educ.:* Dulwich; privately. *Publications:* The Time of Life, 1945; The Young Naturalist, 1949. The Field Book of Country Queries (Editor). *Heir: s.* Ninian Buchan Archibald John [*b* 1922; *m.* 1958, Bridget, *e. d.* of late Sir Louis Greig and of Lady Greig, Binsness, Forres, Morayshire]. *Address:* (temp.) c/o Lloyds Bank Ltd., East Street, Chichester, Sussex
[*Died* 8 *Feb.* 1961.

BUCHANAN, Rear-Admiral Herbert James, C.B.E. 1953; D.S.O. 1940; Royal Australian Navy, retired; *b.* 10 March 1902; *s.* of H. J. Buchanan, Melbourne; *m.* 1932, Florence Knarhöi, *d.* of Florence Ellis, Melbourne, and late Godfrey William Ellis; two *s.* *Educ.:* Scotch Coll., Melbourne; Roy. Australian Naval Coll., Jervis Bay. Comdr. 1938; R.N. Staff Coll., 1939; Executive Officer H.M.S. Diomede, 1939; in command H.M.S. Valentine, 1940, lost by enemy action 15 May 1940 during operations off Flanders coast; evacuation of Dunkirk, 31 May-4 June 1940; in command H.M.S. Vanity, 1940; Naval Staff, Navy Office, Melbourne, 1941-43; in command H.M.A.S. Norman, 1943-44; Capt. 1944. H.M.A.S. Napier and (as Capt.) (D) 7th Destroyer Flotilla, 1944-45; Dep. Chief of Naval Staff, Melbourne, 1945-46; in command H.M.A.S. Shropshire, H.M.A.S. Australia, 1947-48; in command H.M.A.S. Sydney, 1952-53; I.d.c. London, 1949; Commodore Superintendent of Training, Flinders Naval Depot, Victoria, Australia, 1950-52; Second Naval Member (Cdre. 1st class), 1953; Flag Officer-in-Charge, East Australian Area, Sydney, 1955; Rear-Adm. 1955. Retired 1957. Managing Director of Bell's Asbestos and Engineering (Australia) Ltd.; Director: Trustees, Executors & Agency Co. Ltd.; Northern & Employers Assurance Co. Ltd. *Recreation:* yachting. *Address:* 1 Wentworth St., Point Piper, Sydney, N.S.W. *Clubs:* Australian (Sydney), Melbourne (Melb.); Royal Sydney Golf, Royal Sydney Yacht Squadron; Naval and Military (Vict.)
[*Died* 15 *March* 1965.

BUCHANAN, John Nevile, D.S.O. 1919; M.C. 1917; *b.* Grahamstown, South Africa, 30 May 1887; *s.* of late Sir John Buchanan, Judge of the Supreme Court, South Africa; *m.* 1915, Nancy Isabel, *d.* of late D. A. Bevan and Dame Maud Bevan, D.B.E.; two *s.* one *d.* (and one *s.* killed N. Africa, 1943). *Educ.:* Diocesan Coll. Sch., S. Africa; Charterhouse; Trinity College, Cambridge. B.A., LL.B. 1908. Called to Bar, 1910; practised, when not on active service, at Common Law Bar until 1922. Grenadier Guards Special Reserve 1914; served in France and Germany, 1914-19 (M.C., D.S.O.); Brigade Major, 3rd Guards Brigade and G.S.O. 2 Guards Division. Financial Director, Rio Tinto Company, 1925-47; Director, Rhokana Corp. Ltd. and Nchanga Copper Mines, from promotion of companies in 1931 to transfer to Africa, 1951; Chm. and Manager, Minerals Separation Ltd., 1947-1966. Temp. Wing Cdr., R.A.F., 1939-40. *Recreations:* cricket (Camb. Univ. XI, 1906-1909, Capt.); tennis (Cambridge v. Oxford, 1908); golf. *Address:* 17 Cavendish Avenue, St. John's Wood, N.W.8. *T.:* 01-286 2822. *Club:* White's.
[*Died* 31 *Oct.* 1969.

BUCHANAN, Sir John Scoular, Kt. 1944; C.B.E. 1934; F.R.Ae.S.; retd.; late Chm. London and South Eastern Regional Board for Industry, 1949-60; *b.* 23 Nov. 1883. *Educ.* Allan Glen's School and Royal Technical College, Glasgow. H.M. Inspector of Factories, 1908; Lieut.-Comdr. R.N.V.R.; Squadron Leader R.A.F.; Deputy Director of Research and Development of Aircraft, Director-General of Aircraft Production 1941; Assistant Chief Executive, Ministry of Aircraft Production, 1943-45; Technical Director Short Bros. Ltd., 1945-48. President, Royal Aeronautical Society, 1949-1950. *Address:* 11 St. Denis House, Manor Close, Melville Rd., Edgbaston, Birmingham. *T.:* Edgbaston 2676. [*Died* 5 *April* 1966.

BUCHANAN-JARDINE, Capt. Sir John W., Bt.; *see* Jardine.

BUCHER, Frederick Newell, Q.C. 1955; *o. s.* of Frank Greig Bucher and Sarah Newell, Edinburgh; *m.* 1939, Lydia Joy Acland Griffith. *Educ.:* Edinburgh Academy; Oriel College, Oxford. B.A. Oxon. 1932; M.A. Oxon. 1954. Called to the Bar, Middle Temple, 1936. 2nd Lt., R.A., 1939; Hon. Lt.-Colonel, R.A., 1945. Contested (C) Birkenhead East, 1945. Chairman Uganda Coffee Commission, 1957. Life Mem. British Legion, 1959; Director Equity & Law Life Assce. Soc. Ltd. *Recreations:* flyfishing and hacking. *Address:* Potash Farmhouse, Radwinter, Essex. *T.:* Radwinter 255. *Clubs:* Athenæum, Oxford and Cambridge University.
[*Died* 16 *Aug.* 1964.

BUCHMAN, Frank N. D.; leader of the Oxford Group; initiator of Moral Rearmament (MRA); *b.* Pennsburg, Pa., 4 June 1878; *s.* of Frank Buchman and Sarah A. Greenawalt. *Educ.:* Muhlenberg College, A.B., A.M., D.D., LL.D. (Oglethorpe); studied Cambridge University, 1921-22. Travelled in the Near East, including Turkey, Greece and Egypt, 1908; in charge of Christian work at Pennsylvania State College, 1909-15; made a tour of India, Korea and Japan, 1915-16; toured in the Far East, 1917-19; visited Oxford in 1921 where in following years the Oxford leadership grew; travelled, 1929, with a group of Oxford men in South Africa, where they were given the name Oxford Group by the press, their work since spreading to more than sixty countries; in South America, 1931; visited Canada and United States in charge of Oxford Group Team, 1932-33 and 1933-34; led teams to Scandinavia, 1934-35, and Holland, 1937; Near East and Geneva, 1938; inaugurated campaign for Moral Rearmament (MRA) East Ham Town Hall, London, June 1938; led Nordic Assembly for MRA, Visby, Sweden, Aug. 1938, World Assembly for MRA Interlaken, Switzerland, Sept. 1938; launched American campaign for MRA, New York, Washington, 1939; led Second World Assembly on the Monterey Peninsula, California, 1939; initiated You Can Defend America campaign for total defence, 1940; opened School for Home Defence, Maine, 1941; Mid-Western industrial morale-building campaign, 1942; conducted Summer Training Centre, Mackinac Island, 1942-47; presented industrial programme The Forgotten Factor, Washington, D.C., 1944, San Francisco, 1945; Europe, 1946; campaign Midlands, South Wales, 1948; World Congress, California, June 1948; presented ideological dramatisation of inspired democracy, The Good Road, in Germany and London, 1948; MRA World Assemblies, Caux, Switzerland, annually, 1946-, Mackinac Is., 1942; Nat. Assembly, Washington, D.C., 1951; Assembly of Americas, Miami, 1952; travelled Ceylon, India, Kashmir, Pakistan, Egypt, Iran, Turkey, with 200 from 25 countries at invitation national leaders, 1952-53; European Industrial Assembly for MRA, Italy, 1954; MRA Mission sent to Asia, Middle East and Africa, 1955; European Mission to France, Switzerland,

Germany, 1955; Scandinavia, Italy, Holland and Great Britain, 1956; travelled Australia, New Zealand; visited Japan and S.-E. Asia as guest of govts., 1956; prod. first full-length African colour film, Freedom, 1957; The Crowning Experience (technicolour, world release), 1960. S.-E. Asian Assembly, Philippines, 1957, 1958; Japan, 1959; Hemisphere Assembly, Miami, 1961. Comdr. Order of King George I of Greece; Chevalier, Legion of Honour; Grand Cross of Merit, Order of Merit of German Republic, 1953; Order of Rising Sun, Japan, 1956; Grand Cordon Order of Brilliant Star of China, 1956; Knight Grand Cross Crown of Thailand, 1956; Legion of Honour with Gold Medal of Philippine Republic, 1956; Comdr., Order of Crown of Iran, 1959. *Publications:* Rising Tide, 1937; Moral Rearmament, 1938; The Rise of a New Spirit, 1939; You Can Defend America, 1941; Remaking the World, 1942, 1947, 1958; The Fight to Serve, 1943; You can Fight for Canada, Battle Together for Britain, Fight On, Australia, 1943-44; The World Rebuilt, 1951; Where Do We Go From Here?; The Oxford Group and its Work of Moral Re-Armament; Remaking Men, 1954; America Needs An Ideology, 1957; Frank Buchman—80, 1959. New World News (quarterly). *Address:* 45 Berkeley Square, W.1; 2419 Massachusetts Ave., Washington 8, D.C. [*Died* 7 *Aug.* 1961.

BUCKHAM, Bernard; journalist, drama and radio critic, B.B.B. of the Daily Mirror (retd.); *b.* 9 Feb. 1882; *s.* of Edward Buckham, M.I.C.E.; *m.* Grace (*d.* 1963), *d.* of late William Bennett, Ipswich; one *d.* *Educ.:* Northgate, Ipswich. Positions on East Anglian Daily Times, Birmingham Mail, Birmingham Despatch, Daily Sketch, Evening Standard; London editor Daily Dispatch; Parliamentary correspondent Hulton Press; editor Sunday Herald, 1918-20. Member of the Critics Circle. *Publications:* Stories and sketches in periodical press. *Recreation:* building castles in the air. *Address:* 15 Knightscroft Avenue, Rustington, Sussex. *T.:* 364. [*Died* 28 *Dec.* 1963.

BUCKINGHAMSHIRE, 8th Earl of (*cr.* 1746), **John Hampden Mercer-Henderson,** Bt. 1611; Baron Hobart, 1728; Capt. Oxfordshire and Buckinghamshire L.I.; *b.* 16 April 1906; *o. s.* of 7th Earl and Georgiana (*d.* 1937), *o. c.* of Hon. H. Duncan Mercer Henderson (*s.* of 1st Earl of Camperdown); *S.* father, 1930. *Educ.:* Eton. Demobilised 1945 and worked as an officer in the Civil Control Commission in Germany until 1947. Dep. Chairman of Committees, House of Lords, 1952; Dep. Speaker, House of Lords, 1954. Owns about 3500 acres. *Heir: cousin,* Vere Frederick Cecil Hobart-Hampden, *b.* 17 May 1901. *Address:* Little Hampden Lodge, Great Missenden, Bucks. *Clubs:* Carlton; New (Edinburgh). [*Died* 2 *Jan.* 1963.

BUCKLAND, Captain Arthur Edgar, C.B.E. 1944; D.S.O. 1919; D.S.C. 1916; R.N., retd.; *b.* 4 Aug. 1890; *er. s.* of Rev. Arthur R. Buckland; *m.* 1921, Rona Elizabeth Tower. *Educ.:* Royal Naval College, Dartmouth. Naval Cadet, 1905; Midshipman, 1907; Sub-Lieut., 1910; Lieut., 1911; specialised in navigation, 1912; on outbreak of war was surveying in Australia in H.M.S. Fantome; proceeded to New Guinea with Australian Fleet; returned to U.K. Dec. 1914, and appointed to H.M.S. Pekin at Grimsby for mine-sweeping duties (despatches); H.M.S. Attentive III, at Dover for command of mine-sweeping vessels, Belgian coast, 1916 (D.S.C. and bar, Légion d'honneur); Port Mine-sweeping Officer, Dover, 1918 (Belgian Croix de Guerre, D.S.O.); on Armistice appointed Mine Clearance Officer, Dover area; Mine-sweeping Department, Admiralty, Aug. 1919; Lieutenant Commander, 1919; Command Mine-sweeping Section of the South African Division R.N.V.R. 1921; Commander, 1925; Training Commander at Portsmouth Naval Barracks, 1926-28; H.M.S. Magnolia in command, 1928-30; Operations Division of Naval Staff, 1931-33; Acting Captain, 1937; commanded Boom Defence Depot, Rosyth, 1934-1946; retired list, 1940. F.A.M.S., 1957. *Address:* City Yard House, Wing, Oakham, Rutland. *T.:* Manton 239. [*Died* 29 *Sept.* 1969.

BUCKLAND, Geoffrey Ronald Aubert, C.B. 1947; *b.* 8 Dec. 1889; *s.* of Francis Oke and Elizabeth Anna Buckland; *m.* 1918, Lelgarde Edith Eleanor Eden; one *s.* *Educ.:* Winchester College; New College, Oxford. Entered Civil Service (Local Government Board), 1914; transferred to Home Office, 1914; private sec. to Under-Secretaries and Secretaries of State, 1919-25; Asst. Under-Secretary of State, 1939; Under-Secretary, Ministry of Labour and National Service, 1946-53; Brit. Govt. Deleg. to Internat. Labour Conf., 1947, 1952 and 1953; retired 1953. *Recreations:* philately, music. *Address:* 22 Down St., W.1. *T.:* 01-499 5269. [*Died* 27 *Dec.* 1968.

BUCKLAND, Brigadier Gerald Charles Balfour, C.B. 1938; D.S.O. 1915; M.C.; *b.* 18 May 1884; *m.* 1921, Kathleen Lonsdale Sealy, *d.* of late Rev. Francis Edwin Waldie; one *s.* one *d.* *Educ.:* Rugby. Entered army, 1903; Bt. Lt.-Col. 1928; Lt.-Col. 1929; Colonel, 1932; served European War, 1914-1915 (wounded, despatches, D.S.O., M.C.); commanded 1st Batt. 8th Gurkha Rifles, 1929-32; General Staff Officer, 1st Grade, Lahore District, 1932-35; Comdr. Jullundur Brigade Area, India, 1935-38; retired 1938. *Address:* 4 Newlands Manor, Everton, Lymington, Hants. *Club:* United Service. [*Died* 13 *March* 1967.

BUCKLEY, Lieut.-Col. Albert, C.B.E. 1946; D.S.O. 1917; President of Morris and Jones, Ltd.; *b.* 10 April 1877; *s.* of late William Buckley, J.P., Blundellsands, Lancs; *m.* 1919, Elsie Juanita, 2nd *d.* of J. E. Fisher, Blundellsands, Lancs; three *s.* two *d.* *Educ.:* Merchant Taylors' School, Crosby; Aldenham School, Herts. Late Lt.-Col. 5th Batt. The King's Regiment (T.F.); served S. African War, 1901-2 (Queen's medal 3 clasps); European War, 1914-18 (wounded, D.S.O. and bar, despatches twice); M.P. (U.) Waterloo Division of Lancashire, 1918-23; Junior Unionist Whip, 1921-22; Junior Lord of the Treasury, 1922-23; Parliamentary Secretary Department of Overseas Trade, 1923; resigned Dec. 1923; Chairman, Liverpool Chamber of Commerce, 1924-28; Member Mersey Docks and Harbour Board, 1928-51; Liverpool National Savings Committee, 1931-1948. Formerly Chiraman: Bury Felt Company Ltd.; Liverpool Gas Co.; Liverpool Overhead Rly.; Birkenhead Brewery Co. *Address:* Rotherslade, Meols Drive, Hoylake, Cheshire. *T.:* Hoylake 1800. [*Died* 13 *Nov.* 1965.

BUCKLEY, Maj.-Gen. Sir Hugh Clive, Kt., *cr.* 1947; C.S.I. 1941; M.D.; F.R.C.S. Edin.; Medical Member, Special Review Pensions Tribunal; *b.* 31 Oct. 1880. *Educ.:* University of Edinburgh. Lieut. I.M.S. 1905; Capt. 1908; Major 1915; Lt.-Col. 1924; Col. 1933; Maj.-Gen. 1937; Hon. Physician to the King, 1937; Surgeon-General with Government of Bombay, 1937-40; retired, 1940; re-employed 1941-1946, Principal Medical College and Dean Faculty of Medicine, Agra, U.P. *Club:* East India and Sports. [*Died* 28 *Dec.* 1962.

BUCKLEY, Brigadier William Percy, D.S.O. 1914; D.L.; *b.* 13 Sept. 1887; *m.* 1920, Norah Kathleen, *o. d.* of late Maj.-Gen. W. M. Southey, C.M.G.; two *d.* Entered Army, 1907; Capt. 1915; Major, 1927; Bt. Lt.-Col. and Lt.-Col. 1932; Col. 1936;

served European War, 1914-18 (despatches, D.S.O. for gallantry at Beaupuits); Commanded 2nd Batt. The Duke of Cornwall's Light Infantry, 1932-36; A.A.G., Aldershot Command, 1937-39; Area Commander, 1939-1941; retired pay, 1942. D.L. Cornwall, 1957. *Address:* Keverall, Westhill, Ottery St. Mary, Devon. [*Died* 13 *May* 1968.

BUCKNILL, Right Hon. Sir Alfred Townsend, P.C. 1945; Kt. *cr.* 1935; O.B.E. 1919; *b.* 1880; *e. s.* of Rt. Hon. Sir T. T. Bucknill, P.C., and Dame Annie Bell Bucknill; *m.* 1905, Brenda (*d.* 1953), *d.* of H. P. Boulnois; one *s.* (one *d.* decd.). *Educ.:* Cheam Sch.; Charterhouse; Trinity Coll., Oxf. (Hon. Fellow 1944). M.A.; 1st Class Final School Modern History. Called to Bar, 1903; K.C. 1931; Judge of High Court of Justice (Probate, Divorce and Admiralty Division), 1935-45; Lord Justice of Appeal, 1945-1951, retired 1951; Lieutenant Surrey Yeo. 1914; served on Staff in France, Egypt, and Ireland, D.J.A.G. and D.A.A.G.; retired rank Major; Bencher Inner Temple, 1928, Treasurer, 1951. *Publications:* Law Relating to Tug and Tow; The Nature of Evidence. *Address:* 48 Melton Court, S.W.7. [*Died* 22 *Dec.* 1963.

BUDDEN, Lionel, B.A., Mus.Bac.; *b.* 8 June 1891; *s.* of Alfred Budden and Alice Maud Davis; *m.* 1926, Margaret I., *d.* of Frank A. Lane, J.P. *Educ.:* Wimborne Grammar School; Weymouth College. Qualified as solicitor, 1914; R.A.M.C. 1915-1919; attached Royal Serbian Army, 1916-18 (despatches); House Master, Senior Modern Languages Master and Games Master at Kirkham Grammar School, Lancs, 1919-32; Headmaster, Appleby Grammar School, 1932-43; Senior Modern Language Master at Poole Grammar School, Dorset, 1949-52; (Assistant Master, 1944-49), retired 1952. B.A. London, 2nd Class Hons. (Mediæval and Modern Languages) 1924; Mus.Bac. (Dunelm), 1946; Diploma in Education, Oxford, 1927; President Bournemouth Chamber Music Society; Vice-Pres. Bournemouth Music Competitions Festival; writer of Historical and Analytical notes for Symphony Concerts of Bournemouth Symphony Orchestra, 1947-63. *Recreations:* music, cricket, tennis, golf. *Address:* 19 Parkstone Avenue, Parkstone, Dorset. *T.:* 2349. [*Died* 5 *Jan.* 1966.

BUESST, Captain Aylmer, Hon. R.A.M., Hon. R.C.M.; F.G.S.M.; Conductor and Composer; late Intelligence Corps; *b.* Melbourne, 28 Jan. 1883; *s.* of William Augustine Buesst and Helen Violette Pett; *m.* 1st, 1907, Wanda Heiliger; 2nd, 1926, May Blyth; three *d.* *Educ.:* Melbourne, Brussels and Leipzig. Appeared publicly as a child pianist; studied violin with César Thomson in Brussels, and Wilhelmj in London; pupil of Arthur Nikisch in Leipzig and played in the Gewandhaus Orchestra under him; Opera conductor in Breslau, Görlitz, etc.; Moody-Manners and Beecham Opera companies and Covent Garden; War service; one of the founders of British National Opera Coy., Prof. at Royal Academy of Music, Royal College of Music, and Guildhall School of Music; Assistant Director of Music for B.B.C. 1933-1936. *Publications:* Songs and book, The Nibelung's Ring (Wagner). *Recreations:* Historical reading, Member Society of Genealogists, Heraldry Society. *Address:* 5 Homewood Road, St. Albans; Beechcroft, Birchington, Kent. *Club:* Savage. [*Died* 25 *Jan.* 1970.

BUGANDA, H.H. The Kabaka (Sir Edward Frederick William Walugembe Mutebi Luwangula Mutesa II) of, K.B.E.; First President and Commander-in-Chief of the State of Uganda from 1963 (deposed and came to England, June 1966); Comdr. of Order of Shield and Spears, Buganda; Hon. Lt.-Col., Grenadier Guards; *b.* 19 Nov. 1924; *s.* of H.H. the late Daudi Chwa II, Kabaka of Buganda, K.C.M.G., K.B.E.; *m.* 1948, Damali Kisosonkole. *Educ.:* King's Coll., Budo, Buganda; Makerere Univ. Coll., Uganda; Magdalene Coll., Cambridge. Kabaka of Buganda 1939- (crowned, 1942; exiled, 1953-55, and again in 1966, since when resident in England). Kt. Comdr., Order of British Empire, 1962; Kt. Grand Cross, Order of Phœnix (Greece); Grand Cordon, Order of Queen of Sheba (Ethiopia). *Publication:* The Desecration of My Kingdom (memoirs), 1967. *Club:* Guards (London). [*Died* 21 *Nov.* 1969.

BUISSON, Dr. François A.; *see* Albert-Buisson.

BUIST, H(ugo) Massac; Aviation and Motoring Pioneer and Publicist; *b.* Hampstead, 16 Apr. 1878; *o. s.* of late John Buist and late Marie Isabelle Massac; *m.* 1907, Muriel Rose, 3rd *d.* of late Col. Charles Thomas Wallis, D.L., J.P.; no *c.* Made the first motor mountaineering tour in the world, 1904; made Monte Carlo to London record with late Hon. C. S. Rolls, 1905; took part in first cross-Channel Motor Boat Trial, 1906; took the air in man-lifting kites, captive spherical balloons, kite balloons, free balloons, aeroplanes, seaplanes and airships before creation of Royal Flying Corps; pioneer advocate of mechanised artillery and military transport; high duty, multi-cylinder engines; supercharging; fourwheel braking; mechanical gear changing; fluid power transmission; motorised farming; motor shipping, etc.; on Lebaudy airship when wrecked May 1911; made special study of manufacturing problems at home, on the Continent, in U.S.A. and Canada; lectured on aircraft engine design, maintenance and use to officers and men of R.A.F. and R.N.A.S., 1914-18. Founder-member of Royal Aeronautical Soc. *Publications:* thousands of articles on aviation, motoring and manufacturing problems; The Illustrated Motoring Year Book, 1908; Aircraft in the German War, 1914; A Quarter of a Century of Success and Service, 1924; Motoring Memories: A Coming of Age Souvenir, 1925. *Recreations:* Studying heredity and mutation in horses and cattle (Animal Genetics), the play, travelling, reading, music, and collecting old English furniture and household equipment. *Address:* Flat 2, Savoy House, Mullion, Cornwall. *Clubs:* Savage, Farmers', Royal Aero, Royal Automobile, Royal Motor Yacht. [*Died* 5 *April* 1966.

BULL, Archibald William Major, C.B. 1953; retired; *b.* 26 Nov. 1888; *o. s.* of late John Major Bull and late Rosa Whitley; *m.* 1940, Kate Winch (*d.* 1964), *d.* of late Alfred Bostock and late Ellen Mary Fisher; no *c.* *Educ.:* Highgate School; Trinity Hall, Cambridge. Asst. Clerk, House of Commons, 1913; lent to War Office as Higher Division Clerk, 1915-19; Senior Clerk, 1926; Clerk of the Journals, 1948-53; retd., 1953. *Address:* Nazareth Hse., London Rd., Charlton Kings, Cheltenham, Glos. GL52 6YJ. *T.:* Cheltenham 56361. [*Died* 11 *Feb.* 1970.

BULL, Henry Cecil Herbert, M.C.; M.A., M.B., M.R.C.P.; Consulting Radiologist: Royal Waterloo Hospital; Southend General Hospital; *b.* 1892; *y. s.* of late Col. W. H. Bull, F.R.C.S., D.L., J.P., St. Oswald's House, Stony Stratford and late Emma, *d.* of T. H. Garde, Ballinacurra, Co. Cork; *m.* 1st, Eileen Clarke; two *d.*; 2nd, Dorothy Cunningham. *Educ.:* Stubbington House; Wellington College; Cambridge; St. George's Hospital. Late house-physician, house-surgeon, medical registrar, assistant curator and resident assistant physician, St. George's Hospital; served in the infantry in European War, Capt. 8th K.O.

Yorks L.I. (M.C.); after the war, appointed Fellow in internal medicine at the Mayo Clinic, Rochester, Minnesota, U.S.A. *Publications:* X-ray Interpretation, 1935; X-ray Diagnosis in Maingot's Post-Graduate Surgery, Vol. I.; various contributions to contemporary medical literature. *Address:* 87 Harley Street, W.1. *T.:* Welbeck 2606. [*Died* 4 *Oct.* 1964.

BULLARD, John Eric, C.B. 1953; *b.* 2 Nov. 1903; *e. s.* of Herbert John and Harriet Annie Bullard; unmarried. *Educ.:* Christ's Hospital; Trinity College, Camb. Entered H.M. Treasury as Assistant Principal, 1926; transferred to Unemployment Assistance Board, 1934; Under-Secretary, National Assistance Board, 1947; resigned 1954; Assistant Master, Christ's Hospital, 1954-. *Address:* Christ's Hospital, Horsham, Sussex. *Club:* Reform. [*Died* 5 *May* 1961.

BULLEID, Oliver Vaughan Snell, C.B.E. 1949; *b.* 1882; *e. s.* of late William Bulleid, Invercargill, N.Z., and Marian Bulleid, Llanfyllin, Mont., *d.* of late Oliver Vaughan Pugh; *m.* 1908, Marjorie Campbell Ivatt, *d.* of late H. A. Ivatt; two *s.* one *d.* (and one *s.* decd.). *Educ.:* Bridge of Allan; Accrington Tech. School; Leeds and Sheffield Univs. Served European War, France, 1914-18, Major, R.E. Lt.-Col. (retd.) Engineer and Railway Staff Corps, R.E. Chief Mechanical Engineer, Southern Railway and Southern Region, British Railways, 1937-49; Chief Mech. Eng., Coras Iompair Eireann, Dublin, 1949-58. Past President: Inst. Mech. Engrs.; Inst. Loco. Engrs.; Inst. of Welding; Hon. Member: Inst. Mech. Engrs.; Am. Soc. Mech. Engrs.; Inst. of Welding. Freedom of City of London; Liveryman of Goldsmiths' Company; former Member, Smeatonian Soc. of Civil Engineers. Hon. D.Sc. Bath, 1967. *Address:* Sandra, 55 St. Valentine Street, Balzan, Malta. [*Died* 25 *April* 1970.

BULLER, Lt.-Col. John Dashwood, C.M.G. 1918; D.S.O. 1917; re-employed under War Office and Ministry of Information from Sept. 1939; *b.* 17 Aug. 1878; *s.* of Col. James Hornby Buller, late Body-Guard, and Emily Augusta Dashwood; *m.* 1st, 1903, Sybil Collier (*d.* 1934); no *c.*; 2nd, 1938, Ruth, *e. d.* of late A. C. Verrières, C.I.E. *Educ.:* Eton. Served S. African War, 1900-2; European War, France, Aug. 1914-Feb. 1915; Gallipoli (R. Naval Div.), Mar. 1915 to evacuation in Jan. 1916; France, Apr. 1916-Mar. 1917 (D.S.O., C.M.G.); then War Office; retired pay, 1925. *Address:* Beech Cottage, Downs Wood, Tattenham Corner, Epsom, Surrey. [*Died* 11 *May* 1961.

BULLIN, Major Sir Reginald, Kt., *cr.* 1956; O.B.E. 1949; T.D. 1919; Chairman: Portsmouth Local Employment Cttee., 1937-1959; Portsmouth Disablement Advisory Cttee., 1947-63; a Vice-Pres. Magistrates Assoc. since 1954 (Dep.-Chm. 1946-54; Life Mem. 1928-); *b.* 20 Sept. 1879; *s.* of James Bullin, Portsmouth; *m.* 1st, 1911, Grace Bright Smith (*d.* 1942), Portsmouth; 2nd, 1945, Cissie Florence Oliver, Portsmouth; no *c.* *Educ.:* Skinners Sch., Tunbridge Wells. Admitted as Solicitor of Supreme Court, 1901. Commnd., 1905, as 2nd Lt. 6th (Duke of Connaught's Own) Territorial Bn., The Hampshire Regt. Served European War, 1914-18, as Captain and Major (mentioned for good services); subsequently retired with rank of Major. Hon. Sec. Port of Portsmouth Incorp. Chamber of Commerce, 1906-; Pres. Hampshire Inc. Law Society, 1929-30; Dep. Portsmouth Dist. High Court Registrar and Dep. Portsmouth Co. Court Registrar, 1921-1967; Chm. Portsmouth Appeal Tribunal (Nat. Assistance Bd.), 1934-51; Chm. Bd. of Governors Royal Portsmouth Hosp. 1939-46; Member Price Regulation Committee South Region (Board of Trade), 1940-52. Master of Worshipful Company of Glovers, 1964; Liveryman: Worshipful Company of Musicians; Worshipful Co. of Solicitors of City of London; Life Mem. Guild of Freemen of City of London; Life Mem. Assoc. of Brit. Chambers of Commerce. Mem. (apptd. by Law Society) of Management Cttee. of Solicitors' Clerks Pension Fund, 1949-62; Mem. Magistrates Courts Rules Cttee., 1951-. Mem. of the Court of the University of Southampton, 1953-62. Hon. F.T.C.L. 1957; Fell., Royal Commonwealth Society; F.R.S.A. J.P. Portsmouth, 1927- (Chairman of Justices, 1951-54); Officer Order of Three Stars of Latvia, 1938; Coronation Medal, 1953. *Recreation:* music. *Address:* 21 Havelock Road, Southsea, Hants. *T.:* Portsmouth 34119. *Clubs:* City Livery, Victory Ex-Services; Royal Naval, Nuffield United Services Officers' (Portsmouth). [*Died* 25 *Jan.* 1969.

BULLITT, William Christian; author; *b.* Philadelphia, Penna., 25 Jan. 1891; widower; one *d.* *Educ.:* Yale; Harvard; Graduated Yale, 1912; Harvard Law School, 1913; entered Dept. of State, 1917; American Peace Commission, Paris, 1919; sent on Special Mission to Russia by President Wilson, 1919; manager film company, 1921; author; Special Assistant to Secretary of State, 1933; American Ambassador to Russia, 1933-36; American Ambassador to France, 1936-41; President Roosevelt's special representative in Near East, 1941; Special Assistant Secretary of the Navy, 1942-43; Volunteered in French Armed Services, 1944; served as Major, Infantry (Croix de Guerre with palm); Commander Legion of Honor; LL.D. Temple University, Dartmouth, Georgetown, Univ. of Montreal and Univ. of Nancy, France. *Publications:* It's Not Done, 1926; Report to the American People, 1940; The Great Globe Itself, 1946. *Recreations:* tennis, riding, swimming, baseball, golf. *Address:* 1921 Kalorama Road, N.W., Washington, D.C. (Summer): Apple Hill Farm, Ashfield, Mass. *Club:* Rittenhouse (Philadelphia). [*Died* 15 *Feb.* 1967.

BULLOCK, Captain Sir (Harold) Malcolm, 1st Bt., *cr.* 1954; M.B.E. 1918; Hon. Col. of 336 Medium Regt., Royal Artillery; *o. s.* of late F. M. Bullock of Thursley; *b.* 10 July 1890; *m.* 1919, Lady Victoria (*d.* 1927), *widow* of Rt. Hon. Neil Primrose and *d.* of 17th Earl of Derby, K.G., P.C., G.C.B., G.C.V.O.; one *d.* *Educ.:* private; in Paris; Trinity College, Cambridge; M.A. Barrister-at-law, Inner Temple; Capt. Scots Guards, 1914-21 (M.B.E., Officier de la Légion d'Honneur, wounded); A.D.C. to F.M. Lord Methuen, 1915-16; attached Foreign Office, 1917-18; Military Secretary, British Embassy, Paris, 1918-20. M.P. (C.) Crosby Division of Lancashire, 1950-53 (Waterloo Div. of Lancashire, 1923-50). Hon. Secretary of United Associations of Great Britain and France, 1925-50; and on Committee of Anglo-German Association from its foundation until it was dissolved in 1933; Member of Royal Institute of International Affairs; Chairman of Sadler's Wells Society in support of Sadler's Wells and the Old Vic Theatres, 1930-46; Chm. of National Union of Conservative and Unionist Associations for North West Area, 1936-38; Chairman of Political Education Committee for North West Area, 1936; on Committee of Poplar Hosp., 1913-44; Chm. of Red Cross Hosp. Library War Organisation, 1939-44; attached to British Red Cross Commission with B.E.F. in France, 1940; Vice-Chairman of Franco-British Inter-Parliamentary Committee, 1945-49, Chairman, 1950-53; Vice-Chm. Maison de France, London, 1953-56. Commandeur Légion d'Honneur, 1954. *Publication:* Austria, 1918-1938, a Study in Failure, 1939. *Heir:* none. *Address:* Middlefield, Great Shelford, Cambridge. *T.:* Shelford 3236. *Clubs:* Buck's Turf. [*Died* 20 *June* 1966 (*ext.*).

BULMAN, Paul Ward Spencer, C.B.E. 1943; M.C. 1917, Bar 1918; A.F.C. 1918, Bars 1921 and 23; F.R.Ae.S.; Aircraft Test Pilot and C sultant; *b.* 8 April 1896; *s.* of Rev. Thomas Bulman, Canon Emeritus of St. Albans; *m.* 1920, Constance Dorothy, *d.* of E. Wiseman, Luton, Beds.; one *s.* *Educ.:* Bedford School. Served European War, 1914-19, H.A.C., Royal Flying Corps, and R.A.F.; Experimental Test Pilot, Royal Aircraft Establishment, S. Farnborough, 1919-25; latterly Chief Test Pilot, Hawker Aircraft Ltd.; Head of Aircraft Test Branch, British Air Commission, Washington, U.S.A., 1941-42. *Recreations:* flying and golf. *Address:* Lydele, Woodham Road, Woking. *T.:* Woking 69. *Clubs:* Royal Aero, R.A.F. [*Died* 6 *May* 1963.

BUNBURY, Sir Charles Henry Napier, 11th Bt., *cr.* 1681; late Coldstream Guards; *b.* 19 Jan. 1886; *s.* of Sir Henry Bunbury, 10th Bt., and Laura (*d.* 1938), *d.* of late General T. Wood, M.P., of Littleton, Middlesex, and Gwernyfed Park, Breconshire; *S.* father, 1930; *m.* 1914, Katherine, *d.* of late Herbert E. Reid; one *s.* two *d.* *Educ.:* Eton; Trinity College, Cambridge. Served European War; Sheriff of Suffolk, 1936. *Heir:* *s.* John William Napier, 2nd Lt. 60th Rifles [*b.* 3 July 1915; *m.* 1940, Margaret Pamela, *er. d.* of T. A. Sutton, Westlecott Manor, Swindon]. *Address:* Naunton Hall, Rendlesham, Suffolk. [*Died* 24 *June* 1963.

BUNBURY, Evelyn James, C.B.E. 1952; M.C., B.A. (Oxon); Knight of Malta; Director, Agricultural Mortgage Corp., Ltd.; Chm., National Mutual Life Assoc. of Australasia Ltd. (London Bd.); Director of companies; Member, Agricultural Marketing Facilities Committees for England and Great Britain; Lieut. City of London; Treasurer Gordon Boys School; *b.* 31 Oct. 1888; *s.* of Col. C. T. Bunbury, Rifle Brigade, and Lady Harriot Bunbury, sister of 1st Marquis of Zetland; *m.* 1928, Marjorie, *e. d.* of late Lt.-Col. E. B. North, C.M.G., D.S.O.; one *d.* *Educ.:* Oratory School, Edgbaston; Queen's College, Oxford; Caen Univ., France. Chairman Forbes Forbes Campbell Co. Ltd. Bombay, India; President Bombay Local Board, Imperial Bank of India; Chairman Bombay Telephone Co. Ltd.; Chairman Goodlass Wall (India) Ltd.; Chairman Asbestos (India) Ltd.; served European war, Lieut. (acting Captain) Grenadier Guards; Director Bank of England, 1937-38; Chairman London Tin Corporation Ltd., 1935-37; Chairman Anglo-Oriental Mining Corporation Ltd., 1935-37; Chairman Oriental Telephone and Electric Co. Ltd., 1949-57. Kaisar-i-Hind gold medal. Member of the Arbitration Tribunal set up under the Cables and Wireless Act, 1947; Member: Iraq Currency Board, 1938-49; Cttee. on National Stud, 1954. J.P. 1942. *Recreation:* piano playing. *Address:* Bracken Hill, Camberley. *Clubs:* M.C.C., Lansdowne. [*Died* 14 *July* 1965.

BUNBURY, Sir Henry Noel, K.C.B., *cr.* 1920 (C.B. 1913); *b.* 29 Nov. 1876; *s.* of late Thomas Henry Bunbury and Marion Martin; *m.* 1911, Dorothea (*d.* 1951), *d.* of late Walter Merivale, M.I.C.E.; seven *d.* *Educ.:* Merchant Taylors' School; St. John's College, Oxford (1st class Litt. Hum. 1899). Clerk, War Office, 1900; Exchequer and Audit Dept. 1903; Treasury Officer of Accounts, 1909; Accountant and Comptroller-General National Health Insurance Commission, 1912-13; National Health Insurance Commissioner (England), 1913; Accountant-General, Ministry of Shipping, 1917; Comptroller and Accountant-General of the Post Office, 1920-37; Director Czech Refugee Trust, 1939-40; President, British-Yugoslav Soc. Commander Legion of Honour; Commendatore Crown of Italy. *Publications:* Overhead Cost, 1931; Governmental Planning Machinery, 1938; Lloyd George's Ambulance Wagon, 1957; various articles and pamphlets on public affairs and economics. *Address:* Malt End Cottage, Church St., Ewell, Surrey. *T.:* Ewell 8271. *Club:* Reform. [*Died* 2 *Sept.* 1968.

BUNKER, Lieut.-Colonel Sidney Waterfield, D.S.O. 1919; M.C.; Technical Consultant; *b.* 20 August 1889; *e. s.* of late C. J. G. Bunker, Teddington; *m.* 1932, Mary Pamela, 4th *d.* of H. H. Owen, Wimbledon; three *s.* *Educ.:* St. Olave's; King's Coll., University of London. B.Sc. (Hons. Chem.) 1911; A.R.I.C. 1912; F.R.I.C. 1919; Member Council, R.I.C., 1928-30; F.C.S.; Commissioned Royal Fusiliers (S.R.) 1913; served 1st Batt. Royal Fusiliers, 1914-15 (France); seconded to Royal Engineers, 1915-19 (France) (D.S.O., M.C., despatches twice, Order of St. Maurice and St. Lazarus, Italy); resigned commission Nov. 1919; Assist. Agric. Chemist, Dept. of Agriculture, F.M.S., 1919-20; Chemist, Dept. of Technical Research, Malay Peninsula Agricultural Association, Malaya, 1920-25; Malay States Volunteer Regiment, 1921-26, Captain; Extra Aide-de-Camp to the Governor, Straits Settlements, and to the High Commissioner of the Federated Malay States, 1921-1924. Chief Warden, Sutton and Cheam, 1939-45. *Publications:* various scientific papers. *Recreation:* yachting. *Clubs:* East India and Sports, Royal Thames Yacht. [*Died* 29 *June* 1968.

BUNNING, Arthur John Farrant, C.M.G. 1946; M.Inst.T.; *b.* 2 Sept. 1895; *s.* of Charles Bunning, Pontypool; *m.* 1934, Evelyn Alma Smith. *Educ.:* Newport High School; Newport Tech. Coll. Great Western Railway, 1911-14; army service, 1914-18 (wounded); military railway service, Germany and Poland, 1919-20; joined Nigerian Rly. as Asst. Traffic Supt., 1921; Traffic Manager, Gold Coast Rly., 1939-42; Dep. Gen. Man., Nigerian Railway, 1942, General Manager, 1943-47; Adviser on Inland Transport, Colonial Office, 1948-52; General Manager, Transport and Harbours Department, British Guiana, 1952-54. Visited various parts of Africa and the Far East, 1948-50. *Publications:* reports on Transport in: Mauritius, 1949, Sierra Leone, 1950, The Gambia, 1952. *Recreation:* fishing. *Address:* c/o Bank of West Africa, 37 Gracechurch St., E.C.3. [*Died* 11 *Nov.* 1968.

BUNTING, D. G.; *see* George, Daniel.

BURBIDGE, Sir Richard (Grant Woodman), 3rd Bt., *cr.* 1916; C.B.E. 1946; Chairman of British Home Stores Ltd.; Director of Maple & Co. Ltd.; *b.* 23 June 1897; *s.* of Sir (Richard) Woodman Burbidge, 2nd Bt. (*d.* 1945) and late Catherine Jemima, *d.* of H. Grant, Sodbury House, Great Clacton, Essex; *S.* father, 1945; *m.* 1st, 1925, Gladys' *er. d.* of late C. F. Kearley; one *s.* one *d.*; 2nd, 1946, Mrs. Joan Elizabeth Hamilton. *Educ.:* Rugby. Studied retail business in America, 1919-20; joined Harrods, November 1920; General Manager, 1927; Chairman, 1945-59. *Recreations:* golf, yachting, real tennis. *Heir:* *s.* John Richard Woodman Burbidge [*b.* 5 Oct. 1930; *m.* 1956, Benita Roxane, *d.* of A. W. Mosselmans]. *Address:* Walnut Tree Cottage, Ashampstead, Nr. Reading, Berks. *Club:* Royal Thames Yacht. [*Died* 2 *Feb.* 1966.

BURDEN, 1st Baron, *cr.* 1950, of Hazlebarrow, Derby; **Thomas William Burden,** C.B.E. 1948; *b.* 1885; *m.* 1910, Augusta, *d.* of David Sime, Aberdeen; one *s.* Mayor of East Ham, 1935; M.P. (Lab.) Park Division of Sheffield, 1942-50. Second Church Estates Commissioner, 1945-50; Lord in Waiting to the King, 1950-51; Assistant Opposition Whip, House of Lords, 1951-64.

Heir: *s.* Hon. Philip William Burden [*b.* 21 June 1916; *m.* 1951, Audrey Elsworth, *d.* of Major W. E. Sykes; three *s.* three *d.*]. *Address:* Westwick House, Westwick Worle, Nr. Weston-Super-Mare, Somerset. *Club:* Reform. [*Died* 27 *May* 1970.

BURDETT, Scott Langshaw, C.B.E. 1950; M.C. 1918; *b.* 11 Feb. 1897; *e. s.* of late Josiah Burdett, Solicitor, 3-4 Gray's Inn Sq., London, and of late Lilian le Feuvre (*née* Tunstall); *m.* 1934, Frances Eileen Davis Workman; one *s.* *Educ.:* Marlborough College. Student Interpreter, China Consular Service, 1920. Served at Weihaiwei, Harbin, Chefoo, Shanghai, Hankow. Vice-Consul (Grade I), in China, 1932; Foreign Office, 1933-34; Consul (Grade II), in China, 1935; served at Changsha and Weihaiwei, 1935-37; Consul in China, 1937; Department of Overseas Trade, 1938-40; re-appointed Consul in China, 1941; served at Canton, Chefoo, Weihaiwei, 1941; Moscow, with local rank of 1st Secretary in the Diplomatic Service, 1943-45; Consul-General, 1945; served at: Tsingtao and Mukden, 1946-47; Tientsin, 1947-50; Shanghai, 1950-52; retired 1952. *Address:* Headlands, Polruan-by-Fowey, Cornwall. *Clubs:* Junior Carlton; Royal Fowey Yacht. [*Died* 2 *March* 1961.

BURGE, Milward Rodon Kennedy; *b.* 21 June 1894; *m.* 1st, 1921, Georgina Lee (*d.* 1924); 2nd, 1926, Eveline Schreiber Billiat; one *s.* *Educ.:* Winchester; New College, Oxford. Served European War, 1914-18, The Buffs, M.I. Directorate, War Office, G.S.O.3 (Croix de Guerre); Ministry of Finance, Cairo, 1919-20; International Labour Office, Geneva, 1920-24; Director, London Office of I.L.O., 1924-45; Dominions Office (Director of U.K. Information Office, Ottawa), 1943-44; London Editor, Empire Digest, 1945-49. *Publications:* numerous detective novels, etc., mainly under pseudonym Milward Kennedy. *Address:* Cousens, Rudgwick, W. Sussex. *T.:* Rudgwick 233. *Club:* Oxford and Cambridge. [*Died* 20 *Jan.* 1968.

BURGESS, Maj.-Gen. Sir William L. H.; *see* Sinclair-Burgess.

BURGIS, His Honour Sir Edwin Cooper, Kt. 1948; D.L.; M.A., B.C.L. (Oxon); LL.B. (Vict.); J.P. Lancashire and Cheshire; formerly Independent Chairman of Sandstone Industry Compensation Fund for North West of England; Independent Chairman of Byssinosis Compensation and Benefit Schemes; Member of Home Office Committee on Industrial Diseases (Workmen's Compensation); Deputy Chm. of Quarter Sessions of County of Cheshire; Chm. of Eddisbury Petty Sessions; Chm. of Cheshire County Licensing Cttee.; Chm. Conscientious Objectors, N. Western Div.; *b.* 1878; *e. s.* of late Edwin Burgis, Withington, Manchester; *m.* Edith May (*d.* 1955), 4th *d.* of late William Coxon, Bradley, Staffordshire; two *d.* *Educ.:* Lincoln Coll., Oxford. First Class Honours Modern History; Victoria University, First Class Honours Law, Dauntesey Legal Scholarship. Called to Bar, Gray's Inn, 1904; Certificate of Honour and Bacon Law Scholarship; practised on Northern Circuit; County Court Judge, 1924-50, Circuit No. 10 (parts of Lancashire, Cheshire and Yorkshire), 1924-40, No. 7 Circuit (Cheshire), 1940-50; retired, 1950; Lecturer in Common and Commercial Law, Manchester University, 1906-14; Fellow of Royal Horticultural Society; Member of National Rose Society. D.L., Cheshire. *Recreations:* gardening, motoring, carpentry. *Address:* The Small House, Cuddington, Cheshire. *T.:* Sandiway 3024. *Club:* Union (Manchester). [*Died* 4 *Feb.* 1966.

BURGMANN, Rt. Rev. Ernest Henry, C.M.G. 1961; *b.* 9 May 1885; *s.* of Henry and Mary Ann Burgmann; *m.* 1916, Edna Carey Crowhurst; two *s.* three *d.* *Educ.:* St. Paul's College, University of Sydney, M.A. Deacon, 1911; Priest, 1912; Curate at Gosford, N.S.W., 1911-12; Rector of Gundy, 1912-14; Curate at Holy Trinity, Wimbledon, Eng., 1914-15; Rector of Wyong, N.S.W., 1915-17; Travelling Sec., Australian Bd. of Missions, 1917-18; Warden of St. John's College, Armidale, N.S.W., 1918-25; Morpeth, N.S.W., 1925-34; Bishop of Canberra and Goulburn, 1934-60, resigned (name of diocese changed, from Goulburn, 1950). Warden of St. Mark's Library, Canberra, A.C.T., 1961-64, retired, 1964. *Publications:* Factors in the Making of the Christian Religion; Religion in the Life of the Nation; Jesus and God; Whither Australia; God in Human History; founder of the Morpeth Review; The People of God, 1935; The Beginning and the End of Things; What is the Gospel?; Providence and Judgement; The Regeneration of Civilization (Moorhouse Lectures for 1942); The Faith of an Anglican, 1943; The Education of an Australian, 1944; Founder of the Anglican Review, 1947; Anglican Belief and Practice, 1952; The Coronation of Her Majesty Queen Elizabeth II, 1952; St. Mark's Review, 1955. *Address:* 5 Gellibrand Street, Campbell, Canberra, A.C.T. *T.:* Canberra U1076. *Club:* University House (Canberra). [*Died* 14 *March* 1967.

BURGOYNE, Sir John, Kt., *cr.* 1956; O.B.E. 1946; retired; *b.* 25 Feb. 1875; *s.* of Thomas Burgoyne, Tipple Hill, Caddington, Beds.; *m.* 1902, Florence Emily (*d.* 1964), *d.* of William Farrow; one *s.* *Educ.:* Slip End County Sch., Beds. Straw Plait Merchant, retd. Councillor and Alderman, Luton Borough Council, 1931-55; Mayor, 1938-1944. Chairman: Luton Technical College Governors, 1937-58; of Education, 1938-54. Defence Medal, 1946; Hon. Freeman of Luton, 1946. Chief interest: Education. *Recreations:* social activities of many kinds. *Address:* Buckingham Hotel, Buxton, Derbyshire. [*Died* 5 *Dec.* 1969.

BURKE, Wilfrid Andrew; National Union of Allied and Distributive Workers. Contested Blackley Div. of Manchester, 1924 1929 and 1931; M.P. (Lab.) Burnley, 1935-Sept. 1959; Assistant Postmaster-General 1945-47. Member National Executive Committee, Labour Party (Chm. 1953-54). *Address:* 79 Crow Hill, Alkrington, Middleton, Manchester. [*Died* 18 *July* 1968.

BURKHARDT, Col. Valentine Rodolphe, D.S.O. 1917; O.B.E. 1928; *b.* 21 Dec. 1884; *s.* of L. R. Burkhardt and A. C. Caldwell; *m.* Edith Elspeth Joan Ewing; one *s.* one *d.* *Educ.:* Clifton College. 2nd Lieut. R.A., 1903; Lieut., 1906; Capt., 1914; Major, 1916; Lt.-Col., 1933; Col., 1937; Staff-Capt. R.A., 28 Division, 1914; D.A.A. & Q.M.G. 42nd Division, 1915-17; G.S.O. (2) British Mission with French Headquarters in France, 1918-19; served European War, 1914-18 (despatches thrice, D.S.O., Legion of Honour, Croix de Guerre); G.S.O. (2) British Mission with Marshal Foch, 1919; Interallie; Commission of Control, Germany, 1920-23; G.S.O. (2) and Brigade Major, North China, 1923-28; Military Attaché at Peking, 1932-1934; commanded 7th Heavy Brigade R.A. 1935; G.S.O. (1) China Command, 1936-39; retired pay, 1939; Military Attaché, China, 1939; reverted to retired pay, 1941; employed Admiralty T.C.O., 1943-46. *Publication:* Chinese Creeds and Customs (3 vols.), 1953, 1955 and 1958. *Address:* 86 Main Street, Stanley, Hong Kong. *Clubs:* Army and Navy; Peking; Hongkong. [*Died* 5 *Feb.* 1967.

BURKILL, Isaac Henry; *b.* Chapel Allerton, nr. Leeds, 1870; *s.* of I. H. Burkill of Thorpe, Ashbourne, Derby; *m.* Ethel Maud, 2nd *d.* of W. H. B. Morrison of St. John's, Wakefield one *s.* *Educ.:* Repton; Gonville and Caius College, Cambridge. B.A. Natural Sciences Tripos, 1891; Assistant Curator, University Herbarium, 1891; Walsingham medallist, 1894; M.A. 1895; a Technical Assistant, 1897, and a Principal Assistant, 1899, in the Royal Botanic Gardens, Kew; Assistant Reporter, 1901, and Officiating Reporter on Economic Products to the Government of India, 1902; Econ. Bot., in Bot. Survey of India, 1910; botanist on the Abor Expedition, 1911-12; Director of Gardens, Straits Settlements, 1912-25. Natural History Sec., Asiatic Soc. of Bengal, 1906-11; Paul Johannes Brühl Memorial Medal, 1934; Sec., Straits branch, Roy. Asiatic Soc., 1914-17, Hon. Mem. Malayan branch, 1952; Botanical Sec., Linnean Soc. of London, 1937-44; Hooker Lect., 1951; Linnean Medallist, 1952. *Publications:* A Dictionary of the Economic Products of the Malay Peninsula, 1935; Scientific and Technical papers in various journals *Address:* 43 The Mount, Leatherhead. [*Died* 7 *March* 1965.

BURN, Col. Harold Septimus, C.B. 1944; M.C. 1918; T.D. 1917; D.L. Carmarthenshire, 1937; *m.* 1924, Mary Frances Fleming; two *s.* *Educ.:* Sunderland High School. Served European War, 1914-19, with Royal Engineers. Chairman of Carmarthenshire T.A. Association, 1938-46. Army Welfare Officer, County of Carmarthen, War of 1939-45. *Address:* 6 Cilfig Avenue, Llanelli, Carmarthenshire, S. Wales. [*Died* 25 *Oct.* 1970.

BURN, Sir Harry Harrison, K.B.E. *cr.* 1947; Kt., *cr.* 1941; *b.* 22 Feb. 1888; *s.* of John Foster Burn, South Shields, Durham; *m.* 1917, Aimée Cecile, *d.* of Robert Riddell, M.D., Lond. and Belfast; (one *s.* killed in action, 1942). Fellow Inst. Chartered Accountants, Eng. and Wales; Chm. Calcutta Electric Supply Corp. Ltd.; Chm. McLeod & Co. Ltd., Calcutta, 1936-41; Chm. Indian Oxygen-Acetylene Co. Ltd., 1943-47; Pres. Imp. Bank of India, Bengal Local Bd., 1937, 1938, 1940, 1941; Dir.: I.C.I. (India) Ltd., 1942-47; Alkali & Chemical Corp. of India, 1944-47. Chm. Ind. Jute Mills Assoc., 1933-1937; Mem. Cttee., Bengal Chamber of Commerce, 1932 and 1939-45, Pres. 1939; Pres. Assoc. Chambers of Commerce of India, 1939. M.L.C. Bengal, 1930-35; Sheriff of Calcutta, 1940; Chm. Nat. Service Advisory Cttee., Bengal and Assam Area, 1939-47; Pres. E. India Fund for Brit. War Services, 1940-46; Mem. Advisory Cttee. to Dir.-Gen., Munitions Production, Govt. of India, Supply Dept., 1940-46; Mem. Advisory Cttee. and Amenities Adviser to Bengal War Purposes Fund, 1940-46. *Address:* Linchmere House, Haslemere, Surrey. *Clubs:* Oriental; Bengal (Calcutta). [*Died* 19 *Nov.* 1961.

BURN, Sir Sidney, Kt., *cr.* 1939; *b.* 19 June 1881; *s.* of John and Jane Burn, Wakefield; *m.* 1909, Clara Blanche (*d.* 1957), *d.* of late Dr. D. M. Williams, Liverpool; one *d.* *Educ.:* Queen Elizabeth's School, Wakefield; Queen's College, Oxford. Entered I.C.S., 1904; Assistant Resident Travancore and Cochin, 1907-9; Subcollector, 1910; Superintendent of Pudukkottai, 1915-22; District and Sessions Judge, 1924; Puisne Judge, High Court, Madras, officiating, 1932; Puisne Judge, High Court, Madras, 1934-42. Chairman, Madras Public Service Commission, 1946-47; retired, 1947. *Recreations:* lawn tennis, golf, bridge. *Address:* Delamere, Spitalfield Lane, New Romney, Kent. *Club:* Madras (Madras). [*Died* 12 *May* 1963.

BURN, Professor William Laurence; Professor of Modern History, University of Newcastle upon Tyne (formerly King's College, University of Durham), since 1944; *b.* Wolsingham, Co. Durham, 15 Oct. 1904; *o. s.* of Laurence Burn and Anne, *e. d.* of William Coates, Oakcroft, Wolsingham; *m.* 1933, Alice, *e. d.* of John Proud, Wolsingham; one *s.* *Educ.:* Durham School; Merton College, Oxford (Exhibitioner). B.A. 1925. M.A. 1932; Barrister-at-Law (Inner Temple), 1932; Rockefeller Fellow, 1932-33. Assistant, 1925-30, and Lecturer, 1930-37, in History, University of St. Andrews. In practice, North-Eastern Circuit (Newcastle upon Tyne) and Durham Chancery Court between 1937 and 1946. War of 1939-45: commissioned 2nd Lt. R.A.S.C. from Officers' Emergency Reserve, 1940; served overseas, 1940-41; subsequently employed under the Foreign Office; invalided, 1944. Weardale R.D.C. 1946-52; Chm. Wolsingham and Wear Valley Agricultural Soc., 1947-50. J.P., Co. Durham, 1946; Deputy Chairman, Durham Quarter Sessions, 1953-58, Chairman, 1958; Member Departmental Committee on Adult Education, 1953-54. Visiting Nuffield Professor, University Coll., Ibadan, 1956. Mem., Univ. Grants Cttee. on Latin American Studies, 1963-64; Visiting Hinkley Prof., Johns Hopkins Univ., 1965. Pres., Northern Rent Assessment Panel, 1965-. *Publications:* Emancipation and Apprenticeship in the British West Indies, 1937; The British West Indies, 1951; The Age of Equipoise, 1964; articles in historical and legal reviews and in the periodical press. *Recreations:* shooting, fishing. *Address:* Bombay House, Wolsingham, Co. Durham. *T.:* Wolsingham 273; The University, Newcastle upon Tyne, 1. *Clubs:* United University; Durham County. [*Died* 11 *July* 1966.

BURNAND, Sir (Richard) Frank, Kt. 1960; C.B.E. 1946 (O.B.E. 1918); M.A. Oxon; Barrister-at-law; retired as Senior Master of the Supreme Court and Queen's Remembrancer, 1957-60, having been Master, Queen's Bench Division, 1930-60; *b.* 16 Nov. 1887; *s.* of late Richard John Burnand; *m.* Léa Félicie, *d.* of late Félix Mudler, Brussels; no *c.* *Educ.:* Uppingham; Pembroke Coll. Oxford. Served European War with 5th Fusiliers and M.G.C. in France, 1914-19; promoted Major, 1916; Chief Instructor M.G.T.C., Grantham, 1918 (despatches, O.B.E.). Called to the Bar, Lincoln's Inn, 1919; practised on North Eastern Circuit and in London; Prosecuting Counsel to the Post Office on the North-Eastern Circuit, 1927-30; Recorder of Richmond, Yorks., 1928-30. Mem. of the General Council of the Bar, 1921-30. Hon. Lt.-Col. at War Office in connection with Army and R.A.F. Legal Aid Scheme, 1941-47. Editor of the Annual Practice, 1934-60, Chitty's Queen's Bench Forms, 1956, and Bullen and Leake's Pleadings, 1959. Member: Cttee. on Legal Aid and Advice (Rushcliffe Cttee.), 1945; Circuit Officers' Cttee. (Caldecote Cttee.), 1946; Cttee. on Law of Defamation (Porter Cttee.), 1948; Lord Chancellor's Advisory Cttee (under Legal Aid and Advice Act, 1949), 1950-62. Prescribed Officer for Election Petitions under the Representation of the People Act, 1949 (1957-59); Registrar of the Court constituted under the Benefices Act, 1898, (1957-60). *Recreations:* gardening, reading. *Address:* Shillong, Deneside, East Dean, Nr. Eastbourne, Sussex. [*Died* 24 *April* 1969.

BURNE, Ven. Richard Vernon Higgins, M.A.; F.S.A.; Archdeacon Emeritus and Canon Emeritus of Chester Cathedral since 1965; *b.* 19 Mar. 1882; 3rd. *s.* of late Colonel S. T. H. Burne, V.D., J.P., Loynton Hall, and Julia Susannah, *d.* of late Valentine Vickers, Offley Grove, Staffordshire; *m.* 1938, Mary Elizabeth Sibratha Goodwin. *Educ.:* Malvern College; Keble College, Oxford (Exhibitioner)

(1st class Mod. History) Cuddesdon Theological College. Curate of Upton-cum-Chalvey (Slough), 1907; Chaplain to the Bishop of Singapore, 1913; Diocesan Chaplain, Singapore, 1914; T.C.F. in France (2nd Cav. Div.), 1917; Tutor at the Ordination Test School, Knutsford, 1919; Principal of the Knutsford Test School, 1923-37; Rector of Tattenhall, 1937-40; Archdeacon of Chester, 1937-1965; Residentiary Canon of Chester Cathedral, 1940-65; Vice-Dean of Chester Cathedral, 1946-65. Examining Chaplain to the Bishop of Chester. *Publications:* Chester Cathedral; The Monks of Chester. *Address:* Simm's Cottage, Homington, Salisbury, Wilts. [*Died* 9 *Oct.* 1970.

BURNELL, Lieut.-Col. Charles Desborough, D.S.O. 1918; O.B.E. 1954; T.D.; D.L., J.P. Berkshire; *b.* 13 Jan. 1876; *s.* of George Edward Burnell; *m.* 1903, Jessie Backhouse Hulke (*d.* 1966); two *s.* two *d.* *Educ.:* Eton; Magdalen Coll., Oxford (M.A.). At Eton, won Junior Sculling, House Fours, rowed in VIII, winners of Ladies' Plate at Henley, 1894; Lieutenant E.C.R.V.; at Oxford, won Varsity Sculls, 1898; Head of River, 1895; Winning Varsity VIII, 1895-1898; Rowing successes: Grand Challenge, Henley, 1898 1901; Stewards, 1898-1900; Cork International Regatta, Leander VIII, 1902; Olympic Regatta VIII, 1908; joined London Rifle Brigade, 1894; retired as Major, 1913; rejoined as Captain, 1914; commanded 1st Batt. in France, 1917-18 (D.S.O., despatches twice, T.D.); Major, 12th Berks (U.T.P.) Bn. Home Guard; Chm. Wokingham R.D.C., 1941-64; Hon. Treas. Army Cadet Force Assoc., resigned, 1956; Pres., Oxford County Committee and S. Oxon Group British Legion, resigned, 1960; President: Leander Club, 1954-57; Henley Rowing Club. *Recreation:* rowing. *Clubs:* Leander (Henley-on-Thames), M.C.C., Junior Carlton. [*Died* 3 *Oct.* 1969.

BURNETT, Col. Allan Harrington, C.B. 1937; D.S.O. 1917; Indian Army, retired; *b.* 9 June 1884. Served S. Africa, 1902 (medal); European War, 1915-19 (despatches 5 times, D.S.O.); G.S.O. 1 at Army Headquarters, India, 1931-34; Assist. Comdt. Indian Military Academy, Dehra Dun, 1935-1938; retired, 1938; Chief of Staff H.E.H. The Nizam's Regular Forces, 1938-43. *Address:* Reedy, Dunsford, Nr. Exeter, Devon. [*Died* 17 *Aug.* 1966

BURNETT, Dame Ivy C.; *see* Compton-Burnett.

BURNETT, Brig. John Curteis, D.S.O. 1914; late The Duke of Wellington's Regt.; *b.* 5 Mar. 1882; *s.* of late Capt. Lindsay Robert Burnett, Sherwood Foresters, and Agnes Henrietta, *d.* of late Rev. S. Curteis, Sevenoaks, Kent; *m.* Mary Isabella (*d.* 1942), *d.* of late J. Haddon, J.P., Cheltenham; one *d.* *Educ.:* privately; R.M.C. Sandhurst. Entered army, 1901; Captain, 1909; Major, 1916; Lt.-Col. 1929; Col. 1933; served European War, 1914-19; trained and commanded the 5th Divisional Cyclist Company (despatches, D.S.O.); commanded E. Bn. Tank Corps; commanded 2nd Battalion the Duke of Wellington's Regiment (West Riding), 1929-33; commanded 147th 2nd (West Riding) Infantry Brigade T.A. 1933-1936; retired pay, 1936; served war of 1939-1945 as a Brigadier on General Staff, 1940-41, and subsequently on retirement under Home Office. *Recreations:* croquet, golf and gardening. *Address:* Southwood, Burley, Ringwood, Hants. [*Died* 3 *July* 1968.

BURNETT, John George, O.B.E. 1946; *b.* 30 March 1876; *s.* of George Burnett, LL.D., Lyon King of Arms; *m.* 1901, Helen (*d.* 1944), *o. d.* of Capt. D. M. Irvine, 17th Regiment; two *s.* two *d.* (one *d.* decd.). *Educ.:* Trinity College, Glenalmond; Magdalen College, Oxford. M.A., Barrister, Inner Temple; L.R.A.M., A.R.C.M., J.P. Aberdeen and Aberdeenshire; Aberdeen School Board, 1906-11; Secretary Aberdeen War Pensions Committee, 1915-20; Aberdeen Town Council, 1928-31; M.P. (U.) North Aberdeen 1931-1935; Member Scottish Departmental Committee on Housing, 1933; County Army Welfare Officer, Aberdeenshire and Kincardineshire, 1940-47. *Publication:* Powis Papers, 1952. *Address:* Powis Gate, Old Aberdeen. *T.:* Aberdeen 44064. [*Died* 20 *Jan.* 1962.

BURNETT-BROWN, Col. Alexander Denis, O.B.E. 1953; M.C., T.D.; Secretary Royal National Lifeboat Institution, 1947-60, retired; *b.* 1 July 1894; *er. s.* of late A. Burnett-Brown, F.S.I., Lennox House, Norfolk St., Strand, W.C.; *m.* 1926, Katharine Mary, *d.* of late Rev. Preb. W. G. Clark-Maxwell; one *s.* one *d.* *Educ.:* Haileybury **Coll.; Corpus Christi Coll., Oxford (M.A.). Civil Servant (Treasury), 1920;** Dep. Sec, **R.N.L.I., 1931; Buckinghamshire Bn. (T.A.) 1914-46. Served European War, 1914-18, and War of 1939-45. Lt.-Col. 1934; Bt. Col. 1938.** *Address:* Lacock Abbey, Chippenham, Wilts. *Club:* Oxford and Cambridge. [*Died* 23 *Nov.* 1966.

BURNEY, Commander Sir (Charles) Dennistoun, 2nd Bt., *cr.* 1921; C.M.G. 1917; R.N. (retired); *b.* 28 Dec. 1888; *o. s.* of Adm. Sir Cecil Burney, 1st Bt., and Lucinda Marion (*d.* 1944), 2nd *d.* of George R. Burnett; *S.* father, 1929; *m.* 1921, Gladys, *yr. d.* of George Henry High, Lake Shore Drive, Chicago; one *s.* Inventor of the paravane; M.P. (U.) Uxbridge Division of Middlesex, 1922-29; Responsible for design and construction of British Airship R. 100, 1924-28, and represented the builders on her acceptance flight from England to Canada and back in August 1930. *Publication:* The World, The Air, and The Future, 1929. *Heir:* *s.* Cecil Denniston Burney [*b.* 8 January 1923; *m.* 1957, Mrs. Hazel Marguerite de Hamel, *yr. d.* of late Thurman Coleman, Weymouth; two *s.*]. *Address:* Huntley Towers, Paget, Bermuda. *T.:* 2-5036; Little England, Darwendale, Rhodesia. *T.:* Darwendale 1202. [*Died* 11 *Nov.* 1968.

BURNHAM, 4th Baron, *cr.* 1903; **Major-General Edward Frederick Lawson**, Bt., *cr.* 1892; C.B. 1940; D.S.O.; M.C.; T.D.; D.L.; Director, The Daily Telegraph (Managing Director, 1945-61); *b.* 16 June 1890; *o. surv. s.* of 3rd Baron and Sybil Mary, *e. d.* of late Lieutenant-General Sir Frederick Marshall; *S.* father, 1943; *m.* 1920, Enid (*see* Lady Burnham), *o. d.* of Hugh Scott Robson, of Buenos Aires; two *s.* one *d.* *Educ.:* Eton; Balliol College, Oxford. M.A. Served European War, 1914-19 (despatches thrice, D.S.O., M.C.); Commander R.A. 48th (South Midland) Division T.A., 1938; served War of 1939-45, France and Belgium, 1940 (C.B.); commanded Yorkshire Division, 1941; Director of Public Relations in the War Office and Senior Military Adviser to Ministry of Information 1942-45. *Heir:* *s.* Hon. William Edward Harry Lawson, Lt.-Col. Scots Guards [*b.* 1920; *m.* 1942, Anne, *d.* of Major G. G. Petherick; three *d.*]. *Address:* Hall Barn, Beaconsfield, Bucks. [*Died* 4 *July* 1963.

BURNHAM, Cecil, O.B.E. 1953; F.R.C.S., M.B., Ch.B. (Ed.); Consulting Surgeon to Star and Garter Home since 1953; Hon. Consulting Surgeon to French Hospital, and to the Homœopathic Hospital, London; Fellow of Royal Society of Medicine; Officier d'Académie française; *b.* 22 September 1887; *s.* of Henry Beardmore Burnham and Annie Dell; *m.* 1918, Marion Paterson; two *d.*

Educ.: Glasgow Academy; Bruges; Edinburgh Univ. Graduated Edinburgh, 1911; Resident Surgical Officer Bolton Infirmary, King Edward VII Hospital, Windsor (15 months), etc.; London School of Tropical Medicine; Demonstrator of Anatomy, University of Edinburgh; served European War, 1914-19 (France, Belgium, Italy), Regimental M.O. 112th Brigade B.E.F.; Surgical Specialist; Surgical Divisional Officer, 62 General Hospital; Surgical Chest and Abdominal Specialist 2nd Army 1917; rank of Major on retirement; Ministry of Pensions, 1919-20; Confidential Asst. Director, Deputy Comm. (Orthopædics) West Midland Region; Edinburgh University, 1920-21, Asst. to Dr. Logan Turner (Ear and Throat) Royal Infirmary; Captain Indian Medical Service; Specialist in Ear, Nose and Throat, Eastern Command; late Senior Surgeon to the French and the Homœopathic Hospitals, London; Surgeon Queen Mary's Hospital, Roehampton. Surgical Adviser at H.Q. Ministry of Pensions, 1936-42; Commandant Star and Garter Home, Richmond, Surrey, 1942-52. *Publication:* The Ileo-Cæcal region (significance of appendicitis). *Recreations:* Edin. Univ. Blue (Association football), golf, tennis. *Address:* Manor Barn, Rustington, Sussex. *T.:* Rustington 5850.
[*Died* 20 *March* 1965.

BURNISTON, Surgeon Rear-Adm. Hugh Somerville, C.M.G. 1919; R.N. retired; *s.* of Captain Augustus John Burniston, R.N., formerly of Langford Cottage, Langford, near Bristol; *b.* 1870; *m.* 1922, Bertha Stanley (*d.* 1961), *yr. d.* of Edward Scafe Scorfield. *Educ.:* privately. M.B. and B.S. Durham, 1892; M.R.C.S. England and L.R.C.P. London, 1893. Served China, 1900; European War, 1914-18; retired list, 1925. *Address:* c/o National Provincial Bank, Portsea, Portsmouth.
[*Died* 1 *May* 1962.

BURNS, David, M.A. (Glas. et Dunelm); D.Sc. (Glas.); F.R.S.E.; J.P.; Emeritus Professor of Physiology, University of Durham, King's College, 1950; *b.* 4 September 1884; *e. s.* of Rev. David Burns; *m.* 1925, Clarice Margaret, *e. d.* of Joseph Dugdale, Upp Hall, Lancs; one *s.* *Educ.:* Collegiate School, Glasgow; Strathbungo School; Glasgow University. Muirhead Demonstrator in Physiology Lecturer in Biophysics, Grieve Lecturer in Physiological Chemistry, Glasgow University. *Publications:* Introduction to Biophysics; papers on Parathyroid Glands, etc. in Biochemical and Physiological Journals; The Assessment of Physical Fitness and papers relating thereto in Journal of Physiology. *Recreations:* Boy Scouts. *Address:* Upphall, 88 Westfield Drive, Gosforth, Newcastle upon Tyne 3. *T.:* Newcastle 52046. [*Died* 4 *April* 1969.

BURNS, George, C.M.G. 1965; Editor, Christchurch Star, Christchurch, New Zealand, since 1945; *b.* 16 Aug. 1903; *s.* of Donald and Marion Sutherland Burns; *m.* 1926, Barbara Raeburn Nisbet; (one *s.* decd.). *Educ.:* Oamaru North School; University of Canterbury. Reporter, Oamaru Mail, 1919-23; from 1923 successively: reporter, Parly. correspondent, chief sub-editor, asst. editor and editor, Christchurch Star. Member, N.Z. delegn., Imperial Press Conf., Canada, 1950; Smith-Mundt Scholar, Columbia Univ., New York, 1950; leader, N.Z. press delegn., Korea, 1952; leader, N.Z. Govt. mission, U.N. Commission on Human Rights, India, 1962. Mem., Bd. of Dirs., N.Z. Press Assoc., 1955-67 (chm. 1959-60, 1964-1965, 1966-67); Chm. N.Z. Section, Commonwealth Press Union, 1964-, and leader of delegation to conference, West Indies, 1965. Member, King George V Memorial Trust Board, 1956 (Chm. 1966); Foundation member, Shirley High School Bd. of Govs., 1957- (chm. 1959-61); Lecturer-in-charge, School of Journalism, Univ. of Canterbury, 1947-58. Major (retd. list), Canterbury Regt. *Recreations:* gardening, yachting. *Address:* 34 Glenelg Spur, Murray Aynsley Hill, Christchurch, New Zealand. *T.:* 35-553. *Clubs:* Canterbury, Canterbury Officers' (Christchurch); Banks Peninsula Cruising (Lyttelton, N.Z.). [*Died* 30 *Oct.* 1970.

BURNS, Brigadier Lionel Bryan Douglas, C.B.E. 1945 (O.B.E. 1940); D.S.O. 1938; M.C. 1918; R.A. retd.; *b.* 5 Dec. 1895; *s.* of Captain J. P. Burns, late R.A. and R.A.F.; *m.* 1st, 1926, Charlotte (*d.* 1961), *d.* of Alexander Goodwin; two *s.*; 2nd, 1963, Kathleen Reine Walsh. *Educ.:* St. Boniface's College, Plymouth. Joined R.A. 1915; Major, 1937; Lt.-Col. 1944; Col. 1946; served European War, 1914-18, France, Belgium, Balkans, and South Russia; acting Capt. 1917-19; acting Major, 1919 (despatches twice, M.C.); Adjutant Lancs. and Cheshire Heavy Bde. R.A. (T.A.), 1925-29; p.s.c. 1932; Staff Capt. India, 1936; Bde. Major India, 1936-39; N.W. Frontier of India, 1936-37 and 1937-39, Bde. Major Tochi Column (despatches twice, D.S.O.); served in France, 1940, N.W. Europe, 1944-45. G.S.O.1. 46 Div., 1940-41 (O.B.E.); C.R.A. 52nd (Lowland) Div., 1942-45 (despatches, C.B.E.); D.D.P.S.(A) War Office, 1946-49; retired pay, 1949. *Address:* East Lodge, Allerthorpe, York. *T.:* Pocklington 3383.
[*Died* 20 *Nov.* 1966.

BURNS, Professor Philip Leonard; Professor of Electrical Engineering, Queen's University, Belfast, since 1924; *b.* 17 May 1896; *s.* of M. and A. Burns; *m.* 1922, J. Mein; two *d.* *Educ.:* Manchester Grammar School; Manchester University; Oxford University. M.Sc. (Manchester), 1917. Metropolitan-Vickers, 1915-16. Served European War, 1914-18, R.N.V.R., 1917-19. With engineering firms, U.S.A. and Canada, 1919-21; Head of Electrical Engineering Dept., Rutherford Technical College, Newcastle upon Tyne, 1921-24. War of 1939-45; commissioned Royal Signals, 1940. Officer Comdg. R.E.M.E., Queen's Univ. Training Corps (T.A.). General Service and Victory Medals, 1919, Defence Medal, 1946; T.D. 1957. *Recreations:* Vice-Pres. of Rugby and Cricket clubs, Q.U.B. *Address:* 23 Conway Ave., Cleveleys, Blackpool, Lancs.
[*Died* 23 *Oct.* 1968.

BURNS, William, C.I.E. 1939; D.Sc. Edinburgh; F.R.S.E. 1945; *b.* 6 July 1884; *e. s.* of James Burns, Montrose, Scotland; *m.* 1912, Margaret Forrest Aitchison; two *s.* one *d.* *Educ.:* Montrose Academy; Edinburgh University. Assistant Lecturer in Botany, Reading University College, 1907-1908; entered Indian Agricultural Service as Economic Botanist to Bombay Government, 1908; Principal, Poona College of Agriculture, 1922-32; Joint Director of Agriculture, 1926-27; Director of Agriculture, Bombay, 1932-36; Agricultural Expert, Imperial Council of Agricultural Research, 1936-38, offg. Vice-Chairman, 1943; Agricultural Commissioner, Govt. of India, 1939-43; retired 1943; European War, 1917-19. Fellow Botanical Soc. of Edinburgh. *Publications:* numerous on agricultural and botanical matters in Agriculture and Livestock in India, Memoirs of the Indian Department of Agriculture, etc. *Address:* 29 Craiglea Drive, Edinburgh 10. *T.:* 031-447 2802.
[*Died* 8 *April* 1970.

BURRARD, Major Sir Gerald, 8th Bt., *cr.* 1769; D.S.O. 1915; F.R.G.S.; F.R.M.S.; late R.F.A.; *b.* Dehra Dun, India, 17 Jan. 1888; *o. s.* of Colonel Sir Sidney Burrard, 7th Bt., K.C.S.I., F.R.S., and Gertrude Ellen (*d.* 1928), *d.* of Maj.-Gen. C. Haig;

S. father, 1943; *m.* 1917, Hilda Elizabeth, *d.* of R. J. Mumm, Oxford Terrace, W.; one *d.* (one *s.* decd.). *Educ.:* Cheltenham College; R.M.A., Woolwich. Entered R.F.A., 1909; Captain, 1915; Major, 1918; served in India until outbreak of European War; went to France with Indian Expeditionary Force, Nov. 1914; actions of Givenchy, Neuve Chapelle, Ypres, Festubert, Loos (despatches, D.S.O.), and Somme (severely wounded); retired on account of wounds, 1919; Gun Expert to The Field, 1919-33; Editor of Game and Gun, 1924-45; Vice-Chm., N.R.A., 1946-48, Vice-Pres., 1949; Master of the Worshipful Company of Gunmakers, 1937-38 and 1948-49. *Publications:* Notes on Sporting Rifles, 1920, 2nd edition 1925, 4th edition 1953; The Tiger of Tibet, a novel, 1924; Big Game Hunting in the Himalayas and Tibet, 1925; The Mystery of the Mekong, a novel, 1928; In the Gunroom, 1930; The Modern Shotgun, 3 vols. 1931-32; The Identification of Firearms and Forensic Ballistics, 1934; Fly Tying: Principles and Practice, 1940. *Recreations:* shooting, fishing, photography. *Heir:* none. *Address:* Willow Lodge, Hungerford, Berks. *Club:* United Service. [*Died* 22 *Feb.* 1965 (*ext.*).

BURRARD, Col. Harry George, C.B. 1925; C.S.I. 1921; D.S.O. 1915; late A.D.C. to H.M.; *b.* 18 April 1871; 4th *s.* of late Lt.-Col. Sidney Burrard; *m.* 1900, Mabel (*d.* 1951), *d.* of Maj.-Gen. Charles Armstrong. Entered Army (Lancs. Fusiliers), 1893; A.S.C. 1895; Captain, 1900; Major, 1908; employed Gold Coast, 1898-99; served West Africa, 1897-98 (medal with clasp); S. African War, 1899-1902 (despatches, Queen's medal 3 clasps, King's medal 2 clasps); European War, 1914-1918 (despatches, D.S.O., Bt. Col.); Mesopotamia, 1920 (despatches, C.S.I.); Assistant Director of Supplies and Transport, Egypt, 1922-26; retired pay, 1926. *Address:* Artillery Mansions, 75 Victoria Street, S.W.1. [*Died* 28 *Jan.* 1963.

BURRELL, Robert Eric, Q.C. 1937; Barrister-at-law; *b.* 2 Jan. 1890; *s.* of John Burrell, London; *m.* 1922, Olga, *d.* of Dr. Robert Parry, J.P. Caernarvon; one *s.* one *d.* *Educ.:* Merchant Taylors' School, London; Trinity Hall, Cambridge (Scholar, 1st Class Law Tripos Part I., 1910, Law Studentship, 1911-1914, M.A., LL.M.); Berlin University (Science), 1911-13. Called to Bar, Inner Temple, 1913; Bencher, 1945. Served European war, 1914-17, Lt. Royal Welch Fusiliers; Capt. Army Cyclist Corps; Legal Adviser British Legation, Christiania, 1917-19. Secretary, Trade Marks, Patents and Designs Fedn., 1920-26. Successively Technical Adviser, Rapporteur and Vice-Pres., Industrial Property Commn. of Internat. Chamber of Commerce, Paris, 1921-55; Delegate of Internat. Chamber, at Diplomatic Confs. for Revision of Industrial Property Conventions, at the Hague, 1925, and London, 1934. Pres., British Group of Internat. Assoc. for the Protection of Industrial Property, 1928-1929 (Hon. Mem. 1958). Chairman, Trade Mark Cttee. of Internat. Law Assoc., 1946-51. Hon. Mem., Inst. of Trade Mark Agents. *Address:* Brantfell, Rockfield Drive, Llandudno, N. Wales; 2 Mitre Court Buildings, Temple, E.C.4. [*Died* 25 *July* 1968.

BURROUGHES, Dorothy Mary Burroughes-, R.B.A. 1925 (resigned 1936); Woman's Society of Artists; F.Z.S.; artist; *y. d.* of late James S. Burroughes and Rosabel Buttery. *Educ.:* London; Germany. Studied under late Professor Van Hier; Society of Women Artists, 1923; held exhibition Dorian Leigh Galleries, May 1923; Linocut exhibition at Dorian Leigh Gallery, April 1926; prints purchased by Victoria and Albert Museum; exhibited also Hull, Brighton, etc. *Publications:* Zoo Poster Designs for Underground Railways; illustrated Coral Island, Hans Brittermann and the Silver Skates, Heart of the Ancient Wood, Queer Beasts and Queer Birds, Eyes of the Wilderness, Hudson's Book of a Naturalist; designs and cartoons in Illustrated London News, Bystander, Sketch, Bookman, John o' London's Weekly; Poster for Reandean Production R.U.R., numerous cover designs; wrote and illustrated The Amazing Adventure of Little Brown Bear; The Journeyings of Selina and Her Friends; Jack Rabbit (Detective); The Odd Little Girl; More Adventures of the Odd Little Girl; Mary Jane Stubbs; Captain Seal; Harris the Hare; The Home the Moles Built, 1939; Niggs, the Little Black Rabbit, 1940; Teddy, the Refugee Mouse; Just Smith; The Little Gentleman in Black Velvet; The Pigs who Sailed Away; What Nature teaches you; The Magic Herb; The Conceited Frog; The Little White Elephant; illustrated in colour the Rose Fyleman book of Nursery Rhymes and Gardeners Frenzy by M. Pallister; Exhibition at the Fine Arts, Dec. 1934; illustrated, 1936, Earl Fortescue's Edition de Luxe of the Story of the Red-Deer; Lady Gorell's Bitty and the Bears, The Bear Garden and also her Stubbington Manor; Last Love: a dog story. *Recreations:* natural history and animal lore generally, listening to music. *Address:* Threeways, Turville Heath, Henley-on-Thames, Oxon. *T.:* Turville Heath 260. [*Died* 18 *July* 1963.

BURROW, Joseph le Fleming, M.D. (Edin.); F.R.C.P.(London); Professor Emeritus of Clinical Medicine, University of Leeds, since 1949 (Professor, 1936-49); Consulting Physician, General Infirmary, Leeds, since 1929; Adviser in Neurology, Ministry of Health, Yorkshire Region; Consulting Physician Leeds Public Dispensary and Hospital, etc.; *b.* Bowness, Windermere, 1888; *e. s.* of Robert Fleming Burrow, landowner and Sarah Mackeveth; *m.* 1st, 1913, Joan McClennan (*d.* 1926); one *s.* two *d.*; 2nd, 1932, Anne Lindsay; two *s.* *Educ.:* Rydal School, Colwyn Bay; Edinburgh University. House Physician and Clinical Assistant, Edinburgh Royal Infirmary; Medical Registrar, Leeds Infirmary; Tutor in Clinical Medicine University of Leeds; Hon. Physician Leeds Public Dispensary; Hon. Assistant Physician Leeds Infirmary; served European War, 1914-18, Captain R.A.M.C. (T.F.); 2nd Northern Gen. Hospital, 1915-17, Egypt, 33rd Mounted Brigade and i/c of Medical Div. Citadel Hospital, Cairo, 1916; Neurological Specialist i/c Dept. 2nd N. Gen. Hospital, 1917-18; Professor of Pharmacology and Therapeutics, Univ. of Leeds, 1929. *Publications:* War Injuries of Peripheral Nerves, 1918; 2000 Cases of Nerve Injury (with H. S. Carter); Chordama of the Clivus (with Prof. M. J. Stewart); Family Tabes Dorsalis, etc. *Recreations:* riding, hunting, fishing. *Address:* 30 Park Square, Leeds. *T.:* 26689; Edge Nook, Hartwith, Ripley, nr. Harrogate. *T.:* Darley 335. *Club:* Leeds (Leeds). [*Died* 20 *Jan.* 1967.

BURROWES, Rt. Rev. Arnold Brian, O.B.E. 1946; M.A. Oxon; Temp. Chaplain, R.N.V.R., 1941-45, Hon. Chaplain from 1947; *b.* 5 Oct. 1896; *o. s.* of late Brig.-Gen. Arnold Robinson Burrowes, C.M.G., D.S.O. *Educ.:* Wellington Coll.; Corpus Christi Coll., Oxford (Exhibitioner). Served the 4th and 1st Battns. Royal Irish Fusiliers, 1916-19 (France, 1916) Lieut. (Acting Captain) (General Service and Victory medals). B.A. 1920; M.A. 1921; Fellow, Lecturer, Dean and Chaplain of Pembroke College, Oxford, 1921-37; Senior Proctor Univ. of Oxford, 1931-32; Principal of Salisbury Theological College, 1937-49; Bishop of St. Andrews, Dunkeld and Dunblane, 1950-55; retired 1955; late Canon of Salisbury; officiating C.F. Portland, 1939-40. Hon. D.D. St.

Andrews Univ. *Address:* Moraybank, Institution Road, Elgin, Scotland. [*Died* 15 *Nov.* 1963.

BURROWS, Lionel Burton, C.B.E. 1931; B.A.; J.P.; *b.* Deposit, New York State, 12 Mar. 1883; *s.* of late Charles Benjamin Burrows, publisher, and late Lily Amelia Craymer; *m.* 1st, late Catherine Ella Frampton; one *d.*; 2nd, Ethel Fray. *Educ.:* St. Paul's School, Darjeeling; Elphinstone Coll., Bombay. Joined Bengal Civil Service, 1907; Deputy Collector, Kolhan, 1908-11; Assistant Settlement Officer, 1911-12; Sub-Divisional Officer, Vishnupur, 1912-15; Sub-Divisional Officer, Cox's Bazaar, 1915-16; Deputy Magistrate, Subordinate Judge and Superintendent, Jail, Darjeeling, 1916-20; Secretary Government of India Coal Committee, 1920; Deputy Director General of Commercial Intelligence, 1920; Deputy Administrator General, 1920-21; Additional District Magistrate, Chittagong, 1921-22; District Magistrate, Chittagong, 1923-24; Additional District Magistrate, Mymensingh and Dacca, 1924-25; District Magistrate, Faridpur, 1925-28; Midnapore, 1928-29; Manager, Kasimbazar Raj Wards' Estate, 1929-30; District Magistrate, Mymensingh, 1930; officiating Commissioner, Burdwan Division, 1931; Manager, Kasimbazar Raj Wards' Estate, 1931-32; Commissioner, Burdwan Division, Bengal, 1932-38; permanent Commissioner, 1936; Chairman, Government of India Coal Mining Committee, Nov. 1936 to April 1937; retired 1938; re-employed in Ministry of Home Security, 1939-41, Ministry of Information, 1941; Director of Administration, Far Eastern Bureau, New Delhi, 1943-45; Political Intelligence Department, Foreign Office, 1945; Ministry of Information, 1945-46; Principal (Establishment and Claims Depts.), Foreign Office, 1946-55; retired 1955. *Publications:* Round the Kacheri: Ho Grammar with Vocabulary; Indian Chikan Work. *Recreations:* dabbles in journalism and has done some more serious writing. *Address:* c/o National and Grindlay's Bank, 13 St. James's Square, S.W.1. [*Died* 13 *Oct.* 1970.

BURROWS, Lt.-Gen. Montagu Brocas, C.B. 1943; D.S.O. 1920; M.C.; M.A.; late 5th Royal Inniskilling Dragoon Guards; Dep. Chm., Le Bas Investment Trust Ltd.; Chairman: Brit. Steel Piling Co. Ltd.; Brit. Steel Piling Co. (Holdings) Ltd.; I. S. & G. Merchants Ltd.; J. Starkie Gardner Ltd.; Louverdrape Vertical Blinds Ltd.; Director: George Fischer (Gt. Brit.) Ltd., Britannia Iron & Steel Works Ltd.; Le Bas Tube Co. Ltd.; Keith Andrew & Co. Ltd.; Caledonian Insurance Co. (London Board); *b.* 1894; *s.* of late Sir Montagu Burrows, C.I.E.; *m.* 1932, Molly, *yr. d.* of late Edward Le Bas; two *s.* one *d.* *Educ.:* Eton Coll.; Balliol Coll., Oxford. Served European War, 1914-1918; North Russian Exped. Force, 1918-19; Murman Coast (despatches twice, M.C., D.S.O., Orders of St. George, St. Vladimir and St. Anne of Russia); Adjutant Oxford University O.T.C. 1920-22; Instructor, Royal Military Coll., Camberley, 1922-25; Student, Staff College, Camberley, 1925-26; A.H.Q. India, 1927; Brigade Major Nowshera Infantry Brigade, 1928-30; Brigade Major, 1st Cavalry Brigade, Aldershot, 1930-32; General Staff, War Office, 1935-38; Military Attaché, Rome, Budapest and Tirana, 1938-40; a Commander, 1940; Head of British Military Mission to U.S.S.R., 1944; G.O.C.-in-C. W. Africa Command, 1945-46. Commander of Order of Crown of Belgium, 1938; Ordine al Merito della Repubblica Italiana (Grande Ufficiale). *Address:* 10 Arlington House, Arlington Street, S.W.1. *T.:* Hyde Park 3159; Oakendene Manor, Cowfold, Sussex. *T.:* Cowfold 202. *Club:* White's. [*Died* 17 *Jan.* 1967.

BURROWS, Sir Robert (Abraham), K.B.E., *cr.* 1952; Kt., *cr.* 1937; J.P. County of Lancaster; Director: District Bank, Ltd. (ex-Dep. Chm.); National Boiler and General Insurance Co. Ltd. (Chairman); Alliance Assurance Co. Ltd.; Yorkshire Bank (ex-Chm.); *b.* 17 March 1884; *s.* of late Miles Formby Burrows and Gertrude, *d.* of late Robert Dawbarn; *m.* 1911, Eleanor Doris, *d.* of late A. E. Bainbridge; two *s.* two *d.* *Educ.:* Leys, Cambridge. After other business experience, started with Fletcher, Burrows and Co. Ltd., 1904, which in 1929 became part of Manchester Collieries Ltd.; one of the founders of the Lancashire and Cheshire Coal Research Association, 1918, and was its first President, 1918-28; Member of the Fuel Research Board, 1923-27; High Sheriff of Cheshire, 1940; Chairman L.M.S. Railway, 1946-47. C.St J. *Address:* 48 West Heath Road, N.W.3. *Club:* Brooks's. [*Died* 14 *Aug.* 1964.

BURT, Sir George Mowlem, K.B.E. 1955; Kt. 1942; President since Nov. 1961 (retired as Chairman) John Mowlem and Co., Ltd., 91 Ebury Bridge Road, S.W.1.; Dir. Builders' Accident Insurance, Ltd. and Director of other companies; *b.* 1884; *m.* 1911, Olave Charlotte Sortain, *d.* of Frederick E. Hulbert; one *s.* *Educ.:* Clifton. *Address:* 121 Cranmer Court, Sloane Avenue, S.W.3; Comforts Place, Blindley Heath, Lingfield, Surrey. [*Died* 1 *Sept.* 1964.

BURT, Rear-Admiral Gerald George Percy, C.B. 1943; *b.* 28 April 1888; *s.* of William Henry and Emily Burt, The Gables, Dartmouth, Devon; *m.* 1922, Minnie Victoria Olga (*d.* 1951), *d.* of Reuben William and Mary Baxter; *m.* 1954, Marion Ione, *o. d.* of George Henry Boyce and Marion Peters, The Towans, Aldwick, Bognor Regis. *Educ.:* Devonport High School; R.N.E. Coll., Keyham; R.N. College, Greenwich. Served European War, 1914-17; H.M.S. Highflyer; Assistant Engineer-in-Chief, Admiralty, 1939-1941; Engineer-in-Chief, Washington, D.C., and Deputy British Admiralty Maintenance Representative, British Admiralty Delegation, U.S.A., 1941; retd. list, 1946. Alderman, West Sussex County Council. Officer of U.S.A. Legion of Merit, 1946. *Recreation:* gardening. *Address:* Fircroft, A'Beckets Avenue, Bognor Regis, Sussex. *Club:* Army and Navy. [*Died* 25 *Dec.* 1965.

BURTON, Baroness (2nd in line, *cr.* 1886 and 1897 **Nellie Lisa Melles,** *née* **Bass**; *b.* 27 Dec. 1873; *d.* of 1st Baron and Harriet Georgina (*d.* 1931), 4th *d.* of Edward Thornewill, Dove Cliff, Staffordshire; *S.* father, 1909; *m.* 1st, 1894, J. E. B. Baillie, M.V.O. (*d.* 1931); one *s.* (and one *s.* and one *d.* decd.); 2nd, 1932, Major W. E. Melles (*d.* 1953). *Heir:* *g.s.* Michael Evan Victor Baillie, late Lieut. Scots Guards [*b.* 27 June 1924; *m.* 1948, Elizabeth Ursula Forster, *er. d.* of Capt. A. F. Wise; one *s.* four *d.*]. *Address:* Greenhill, Killearnan, Ross-shire. *T.:* Muir-of-Ord 206; Needwood House, Burton-on-Trent. *T.:* Hoar Cross 320. [*Died* 28 *May* 1962.

BURTON, Arthur Davis, M.B.E. 1959; Farmer; *b.* 16 Aug. 1887; *s.* of William and Amy Burton; *m.* 1911, Alice Clarke; one *s.* one *d.* *Educ.:* March Gram. Sch. Alderman of Isle of Ely C.C.; Member of Great Ouse River Board and also member of various other Drainage Boards and Public Bodies. High Sheriff of Cambs. and Hunts, 1949-50. *Recreation:* shooting. *Address:* Askham House, Doddington, Cambs. *T.:* Doddington (Cambs.) 269. *Clubs:* City and Counties (Peterborough), March and County (March, Cambs.). [*Died* 14 *July* 1962.

BURTON, Donald, M.B.E. 1920; D.Sc., F.R.I.C., F.R.S.A.; Professor of Leather Industries, The University of Leeds, 1951-September 1959, retired, now Emeritus Professor; *b.* 29 July 1892; *s.* of Arthur Angell Burton, B.A., LL.B., solicitor, Morley and Leeds; *m.* 1926, Ellen Alexandra Valentina Short; one *s.* *Educ.:* Leeds Boys' Modern Sch.; Bradford Gram. Sch.; University of Leeds. B.Sc. 1st Class Hons. Chemistry, 1914; D.Sc. (Leeds), 1925; F.R.I.C. 1926. Asst. to Prof. H. R. Procter, F.R.S. in Procter Internat. Research Laboratory, Leeds Univ., 1914; Asst. to Prof. J. W. Cobb, C.B.E.; Ministry of Munitions during European War; on staff of Leather Industries Dept., 1919-20; Head of Leather Section, C.W.S. Research Department, Manchester, 1920-25; Chief Chemist, Walker & Martin, Ltd., Rose Hill Tannery, Bolton, 1925-51; Hon. Director, Procter International Research Laboratory, 1955-1959. Part-time Lecturer on Leather Chemistry, College of Technology, Manchester, 1931-40. Member: Advisory Cttee. on Leather Subjects, City and Guilds of London Inst., 1927-; Hon. Member British Leather Manufacturers' Res. Assoc., 1964; Council British Boot, Shoe and Allied Trades' Research Assoc., 1951-65. Hon. Treasurer: Society of Leather Trades' Chemists, 1923- (Pres., 1942-45), Hon. Member, 1959; Internat. Union of Leather Chemists' Socs., 1948-64; Hon. Member, City and Guilds of London Institute, 1961. Governor, National Leathersellers' College, 1951-62; Hon. Member, American Leather Chemists Assoc., 1962. *Publications:* Sulphated Oils and Allied Products (in collaboration with G. F. Robertshaw), 1939; scientific and technical papers on Leather Subjects, Oils and Fats and Sulphated Oils, and dating of Dead Sea Scrolls (jointly), 1959. *Recreation:* philately. *Address:* Ousel Nest, 1 Blacklands Close, Saffron Walden, Essex. *T.:* Saffron Walden 2019. [*Died* 6 *Oct.* 1966.

BURTON, Professor Harold, D.Sc., Ph.D. (London), M.Sc. (Sheffield), F.R.I.C.; Professor of Chemistry, Queen Elizabeth College (formerly King's College of Household and Social Science), University of London, W.8, since 1947; *b.* 8 February 1901; *s.* of late William Walter and Annie Burton; *m.* 1927, Janet Elizabeth Beattie; no *c.* *Educ.:* Mexborough Grammar School; University of Sheffield. Chemist, Burroughs, Wellcome & Co., 1921-24; Research Chemist, Chemical Warfare Research Dept., 1924-26. Lecturer, 1927-42 and Senior Lecturer, 1942-1947 in Organic Chemistry, Univ. of Leeds. Honorary Secretary The Chemical Society, 1949-55. *Publications:* scientific papers in specialist journals since 1921. *Recreation:* gardening. *Address:* 69 Chevening Road, S.E. 19. *Club:* Savage. [*Died* 1 *Sept.* 1966.

BURTON, Mr. Justice Harold Hitz; Associate Justice of Supreme Court of the United States, 1945-58, retired; *b.* 22 June 1888; *s.* of Alfred E. Burton (late Dean of Mass. Inst. of Technology) and Gertrude Hitz; *m.* 1912, Selma Florence Smith; two *s.* two *d.* *Educ.:* Bowdoin Coll. (A.B., LL.D.); Harvard University (LL.B.). General Practice of the law in Cleveland, Ohio, 1912-14, 1919-45; Asst. Attorney for Utah Power & Light Co., Salt Lake City, Utah, 1914-16; Attorney for Idaho Power Co., Boise, Idaho, 1916-17; Lieut. and Capt. 361st Inf. 91st Div., 1917-19; served in France and Belgium (Order of the Purple Heart, Belgian Croix de Guerre). Member Board of Education, East Cleveland, O., 1928-29; Member Ohio House of Representatives, 1929; Director of Law, City of Cleveland, 1929-32; Mayor of Cleveland, 1935-40; U.S. Senator from Ohio, 1941-45. Instructor in Western Reserve University Law School, 1923-25. Member Board of Overseers, Bowdoin College; Member Board of Trustees: Hiram College; Fenn College. *Address:* Supreme Court of the United States, Washington, D.C. *T.:* Executive 3-1640 (Washington, D.C.). [*Died* 27 *Oct.* 1964.

BURTON, John Adam Gib, M.C.; LL.D.; St. Mungo Professor of Surgery, Univ. of Glasgow, 1935-53; *b.* 7 Jan. 1888; *s.* of John T. Burton and Christina B. Campbell; unmarried. *Educ.:* Glasgow High School; Glasgow University. House Surgeon and House Physician Royal Infirmary; Assistant Pathologist; then 5 years War service, France, Gallipoli, Egypt, Mesopotamia and North West Frontier of India; returned in 1920; took up surgery and pathology again; Assistant Surgeon in 1924; Surgeon, 1934. *Publications:* surgical and pathological. *Recreations:* tennis, golf. *Address:* 8 Woodside Place, Glasgow, C.3. [*Died* 28 *Nov.* 1962.

BURTON, Rt. Rev. Spence, S.S.J.E.; *b.* 4 October 1881; *s.* of Caspar Henry Burton and Byrd Waithman Spence; unmarried. *Educ.:* Franklin School, Cincinnati, Ohio; Harvard University (B.A., M.A.); General Theological Seminary, New York (B.D., S.T.D.). D.D. Nashotah House. Deacon, 1907; Priest, 1908; Asst. at Ch. S. John the Evangelist, Boston, Mass., 1907-08 and 1912-16; Novice of S.S.J.E., Cowley, Oxford, 1908-12; Master of Novices and of Lay Brothers American Congregation of S.S.J.E., 1916-22; Father Superior, Branch House, S.S.J.E., and Rector Church of the Advent, San Francisco, and Chaplain of California State Prison, San Quentin, 1922-24; Father Superior of American Congregation, S.S.J.E., Cambridge, Mass., 1924-39; Suffragan Bishop of Haiti and the Dominican Republic, 1939-42; Bishop of Nassau and The Bahamas, 1942-November 1961, resigned. *Publications:* Letters of Caspar Henry Burton, Jun., 1921; The Atonement, 1928. *Address:* c/o The Society for the Propagation of the Gospel in Foreign Parts, 15 Tufton St., S.W.1. *Clubs:* Harvard (New York); Queen City (Cincinnati); Porcupine (Nassau). [*Died* 15 *Feb.* 1966.

BURY, Viscount; Derek William Charles Keppel; D.L.; J.P.: Hon. Lieut.-Col., p.s.c.; *b.* 18 December 1911; *e.* *s.* of 9th Earl of Albemarle; *m.* 1st, 1940, Lady Mairi Vane Tempest Stewart, J.P. (marriage dissolved, 1958), *y.* *d.* of 7th Marquess of Londonderry, K.G., P.C., M.V.O.; two *d.*; 2nd, 1964, Marina (A.R.I.B.A., A.A.Dipl.), *yr.* *d.* of late Count Serge Orloff-Davidoff; one *s.* *Educ.:* Eton; Royal Military College, Sandhurst. Commissioned 13th/18th Royal Hussars, 1932; retired, 1947; seconded for service as pilot with R.A.F., 1938-41, Fl. Lt. 13 Sqdn. and 231 Sqdn. High Sheriff, County Down, 1949; sometime Master and Huntsman East Down Foxhounds. D.L., J.P., County Down. *Recreations:* sailing, golf. *Heir:* *s.* Hon. Rufus Arnold Alexis Keppel, *b.* 16 July 1965. *Address:* Rosa dei Venti, Cala Piccola, Porto S. Stefano, Grosseto, Italy. *T.:* Porto S. Stefano 72838. *Clubs:* White's; Royal Cornwall Yacht. [*Died* 8 *Nov.* 1968.

BURY, Lieut.-Col. Charles Kenneth Howard, D.S.O. 1918; J.P. and D.L. Co. Westmeath; *s.* of Capt. Kenneth Howard Bury, *g.s.* of 16th Earl of Suffolk and Berkshire, and Lady Emily Howard Bury, *d.* of 3rd Earl of Charleville; *b.* 15 Aug. 1883. *Educ.:* Eton; Sandhurst. Joined 60th Rifles, 1904; served European War, 1914-18 (D.S.O., despatches seven times), commanded 7th and 9th Batts. K.R.R.; prisoner of war, 1918; High Sheriff, King's County, 1921; travelled in

Tianshan, Chinese and Russian Turkestan, 1913; Leader of Mount Everest Expedition, 1921 (Founders Medal Royal Geographical Society, 1922, Gold Medals French Geographical Society and French Alpine Club); M.P. (U.) South Wolverhampton (Bilston Division), 1922-1924; Chelmsford Division of Essex, 1926-31; Parliamentary Private Secretary to Under-Secretary of State for War, 1922; Hon. Colonel 85th East Anglian Brigade T.A. 1927-32. *Publications:* Mount Everest, The Reconnaissance. *Recreations:* travelling, big-game shooting, gardening. *Address:* Belvedere House, Mullingar, Co. Westmeath. *T.:* Mullingar 386. *Club:* Travellers'. [*Died* 20 *Sept.* 1963.

BUSCARLET, Air Vice-Marshal Sir W. A. B. B.; *see* Bowen-Buscarlet.

BUSHBY, Walter Edwin, C.I.E. 1946; A.M.Inst.C.E.; A.C.G.I.; I.S.E. retired; *b.* 28 December 1889; British; *m.* 1924, Sybil Anne Cary; two *d.* *Educ.:* Tonbridge School, Kent. Graduated from City and Guilds Engineering Coll., South Kensington, 1912. Pupil, London and North-Western Rly., Crewe, 1912-13; Indian Public Works, 1913; P.W.D., Bombay, 1913; volunteered and posted to 2nd Sappers and Miners (R.E.); served European War, 1914-18, S. Baluchistan, N.W.F.P. and Mesopotamia; demobilized, 1919. Rejoined P.W.D., Irrigation on design of Sukkur Barrage, and Canal Construction; Dep. Sec., Bombay, 1923-24; Superintending Engineer, 1937, Chief Engineer, 1942; Chm. Port Trust, Karachi, 1942-45; retired, 1945; Manager for India, John Mowlem & Co. (U.K.), 1946-52; subsequently Managing Director Freemerchants Nicosia, Cyprus. *Address:* 11 St. Helier Court, St. Helier, Jersey, C.I.; National and Grindlay's Bank Ltd., 54 Parliament St., S.W.1. *Clubs:* Oriental; Surrey County Cricket; Royal Bombay Yacht (Bombay); Sind (Karachi); Madras (Madras); Gymkhana (Delhi). [*Died* 22 *Feb.* 1963.

BUSHE, Sir (Henry) Grattan, K.C.M.G., *cr.* 1936 (C.M.G. 1927); C.B. 1932; *b.* 1886; *s.* of John Scott Bushe, C.M.G.; *m.* 1914, Mary Kenrick Gibbons Chambers (one *s.* killed in action, 1944). *Educ.:* Aysgarth School; Denstone College. Called to Bar, 1909; Western and South-Eastern Circuits, 1910-1916; Herts and Essex Sessions, 1916; acting Legal Assistant, Colonial Office, 1917; Assist. Legal Adviser Dominions Office and Colonial Office, 1919-31, Legal Adviser, 1931-1941; Governor and C.-in-C., Barbados, 1941-1946. *Club:* Union. [*Died* 23 *Aug.* 1961.

BUSK, Air Commodore Clifford Westly, C.B. 1947; M.C. 1916; A.F.C. 1930; retd.; *b.* 19 Mar. 1898; *m.*; one *d.* *Educ.:* Marlborough; R.M.C., Sandhurst. Served European War, 1914-18; commissioned in Suffolk Regt. and seconded to R.F.C. 1916; served in No. 70 Sqdn., France, 1916; Central Flying School, Upavon, 1917-18; instructor, Sealand, 1919-1923; with No. 60 Sqdn., India, 1923-27; Armament Officer, No. 25 Group, 1928-33; Air H.Q. Iraq, 1933-35; H.Q. Flying Training Command, 1937-38; Deputy Director Training (Armament), Air Ministry, 1940-43; Station Commander, Bircham Newton, 1943; First Commandant Empire Air Armament School, 1944-46; A.O.A., Reserve Command, 1946-48; retired, 1950; Air Force Adviser to U.K. High Comr. and Senior Air Liaison Officer, U.K. Service Liaison Staff, Ottawa, Canada, 1948-50. *Address:* Farvane Cottage, Little Sandhurst, Camberley, Surrey. [*Died* 23 *Oct.* 1970.

BUTCHER, Sir Herbert (Walter), 1st Bt *cr.* 1960; Kt. 1953; Chairman of: Birmingham Wagon Co. Ltd.; Ideal Building & Land Development Co. Ltd.; Director: Abbey National Building Society; Beecham Group Ltd.; Haleybridge Investment Trust Ltd.; Victory Insurance Co. Ltd.; Newton, Chambers & Co. Ltd.; Member of Lloyd's; *b.* Bexhill, Sussex, 12 June 1901; *o. c.* of Herbert and Fanny Butcher; *m.* 1935, Mary, *yr. d.* of James Odom, Peterborough; three *d.* *Educ.:* Hastings Grammar School; College of Estate Management. Trained as surveyor and land agent; Gold Medallist Auctioneers Institute, 1922; Member of Soke of Peterborough County Council, 1931-37. M.P. (Nat. L.), 1937-50, (Nat. L.-C.), 1950-66, Holland-with-Boston division of Lincolnshire. Parliamentary Private Secretary to Robert Bernays, M.P., Parliamentary Secretary to Ministry of Health, 1938-39, and when Parliamentary Secretary to Ministry of Transport, 1939-40; a Lord Commissioner of the Treasury and Deputy Chief Government Whip, 1951-53. Member of Council on Aliens, 1940; joined R.N.V.R. (Sp. Br.) as Sub-Lieut., 1941. Member of Parliamentary Delegation to Australia and N.Z., 1944, Turkey, 1951; Member Select Committee on National Expenditure, 1944; member of Chairman's Panel, House of Commons, 1945-51 and 1959; Chm. Select Cttee. on Kitchen and Refreshment Rooms, House of Commons, 1959-64; Hon. Treas., U K. Branch, Inter-Parliamentary Union, 1959-61, Vice-Chm., 1961-62, Chm. 1962-65. Chm. of National Liberal Organisation, 1962- (Vice-Chm., 1952-62). *Address:* Chiltern Lodge, 4 Furze Hill, Purley, Surrey. *T.:* Uplands 8600. *Clubs:* Carlton, City Livery; Boston and County Boston. [*Died* 11 *May* 1966 (*ext.*).

BUTLER, Arthur Stanley George, F.R.I.B.A. 1924; Architect and Author; *b.* 23 Sept. 1888; *s.* of Prof. A. S. Butler of St. Andrews University; *g.s.* of Mrs. Josephine Butler, the feminist; unmarried. *Educ.:* Rugby; St. Andrews University; travel in Europe. Built or reconstructed a number of country houses, churches, libraries, etc. Consultant to Govt. of Gibraltar, 1934, and to university bodies. Exhibited in R.A., and in London and provincial galleries. Served European War, 1914-18 (wounded twice; disabled, 1917); Hon. Lieut. R.F.A. 1917. Served in London Fire Service, 1939-1945. *Publications:* Plain Impressions, 1919; The Substance of Architecture, 1926; Recording Ruin, 1942; The Architecture of Sir Edwin Lutyens (3 tomes), 1950; Portrait of Josephine Butler, 1954; John Francis Bentley: the architect of Westminster Cathedral, 1962. *Recreation:* sea-fishing. *Address:* 42 Bloomfield Terrace, S.W.1. *T.:* Sloane 8701. *Clubs:* Travellers', Chelsea Arts. [*Died* 30 *Sept.* 1965.

BUTLER, Sir (Charles) Owen, K.B.E., *cr.* 1951; C.M.G. 1947; E.D. 1928; *b.* 4 Feb. 1896; *yr. s.* of late Charles McArthur Butler; *m.* 1926, Margaret Blackburn. *Educ.:* privately. War Service, 1914-20, London Scottish and Black Watch; Colonial Administrative Service, Gold Coast, 1921-51; Chief Commissioner, Northern Territories, 1945; Chief Commissioner, Ashanti, 1946-51. *Address:* Crossways, Beacon Edge, Penrith, Cumberland. [*Died* 13 *Jan.* 1968.

BUTLER, Sir Frederick George Augustus, K.C.M.G., *cr.* 1920 (C.M.G. 1915); C.B. 1917; *b.* 5 April 1873; *s.* of Rev. A. M. Butler and Elizabeth Jane, *d.* of Rev. Thomas Mays; *m.* 1902, Florence (*d.* 1918), *o. d.* of George Leighton, Sedbergh, Yorks; one *s.* one *d.* *Educ.:* Bradford Grammar School; Trinity College, Oxford (1st class, Classica Moderations, 1st class, Final Classical School). Entered Colonial Office, 1897; Private Secretary to the Duke of Marlborough, Under-Secretary of State for the Colonies, 1904-5; Mr. Winston Churchill, M.P., 1905-6; Mr. Lewis Harcourt,

M.P., Sec. of State for the Colonies, 1912-15; Mr. Bonar Law, 1915-16; Deputy Comptroller-General, Dept. of Overseas Trade, 1917-22; Finance Officer, Foreign Office, 1922-38; Asst. Under-Secretary of State, 1933-38; retired, 1938; returned to Foreign Office for War work, Sept. 1939; finally retired Sept. 1940. *Address:* 50 Pelham Court, S W 3. *Club:* United University. [*Died* 30 *March* 1961.

BUTLER, Sir Gerald Snowden, Kt., *cr.* 1943; C.I.E. 1939; *b.* 8 April 1885; *s.* of James Butler of Kirkstall, Yorks. and Margaret Campbell Butler (*née* Pollock), Harrisburg, Penna., U.S.A.; *m.* 1910, Helen Veronica Shaw (*d.* 1963); one *d.* (one *s.* killed in action, one *s.* decd. 1963, and one *d.* decd.). *Educ.:* Sir Wm. Turner's Grammar School, Coatham; Keble College, Oxford (Scholar). B.A. (Hons.) 1908; Half Blue Cross Country, 1905, 1906, 1907. F.I.C. 1912; M.I.Chem.E. 1938. Apptd. Indian Ordnance Factories Service at the Cordite Factory, Aruvankadu 1910; Works Manager, 1920; Superintendent, 1930; Mem., for explosives, Cttee. for Rationalisation of 8 Indian Ordnance Factories, 1937-38; Director of Ordnance Factories, Army Headquarters, India, 1938; Dep. Dir.-Gen., Munition Production (Armaments), India, 1940; Addl. Dir.-Gen., Munition Production (Armaments), Dept. of Supply, India, 1943; retired 1943. A Governor, Lawrence Memorial Sch.; Viceroy's Visitor to Indian Inst. of Science; a magistrate. *Publications:* in Jl. of Chem. Soc. and Jl. of Soc. of Chem. Industry. *Address:* Great Maytham Hall, Rolvenden, Kent. *T.:* Rolvenden 224. [*Died* 19 *Dec.* 1969.

BUTLER, Hon. (Horace) Somerset Edmond, C.I.E. 1945; Commercial Adviser, Dept. of Food, Govt. of India; presently Chairman Anglo-American Combined Siam Rice Commission, Bangkok; *b.* 23 May 1903; 2nd (twin) *s.* of 7th Earl of Carrick; *m.* 1928, Barbara, *d.* of M. S. Jacomb-Hood, London; one *d.* *Educ.:* R.N. Colleges, Osborne and Dartmouth. *Club:* St. James'. [*Died* 26 *Aug.* 1962.

BUTLER, James Bayley, M.B.E. 1918; M.A., M.B., B.Ch., B.A.O., M.R.I.A., F.I.W.Sc.; Professor of Zoology, University College, Dublin, National University of Ireland (formerly Professor of Botany); retired 1956; Emeritus Professor, 1957; Consultant Technologist. Vice-President: Royal Zoological Soc. of Ireland; Royal Dublin Society; Technical Director, Biotox Ltd., Dublin. *Address:* (Consulting Room) 81 Ranelagh Road, Dublin, Ireland. *T.:* Dublin 972369; (home) Glenlion, Baily, Co. Dublin. *T.:* Dublin 323187 [*Died* 21 *Feb.* 1964.

BUTLER, Sir Owen; *see* Butler, Sir C. O.

BUTLER, Lieut.-Col. Patrick Richard, D.S.O. 1917; *b.* Plymouth, 7 Nov. 1880; *e. s.* of late Lt.-Gen. Rt. Hon. Sir Wm. Butler, G.C.B., and Lady (Elizabeth) Butler (painter of The Roll Call, and other pictures) (*d.* 1933); *m.* 1930, Rhona Lilian, 2nd *d.* of Hon. Assheton N. Curzon; one *s.* *Educ.:* Clongowes; Weybridge; Stonyhurst. Joined Roy. Irish Regt. from Militia, 1902; Capt., 1908; Major, 1916; Brevet Lt.-Col., 1919; Lt.-Col., 1927; served in Malta, South Africa, and India; went to Flanders with 7th Division, Oct. 1914; was in the retreat from Ghent to Ypres, and through the first battle of Ypres (severely wounded); served with his regiment during second battle of Ypres and in France, and subsequently at Salonika. Returned to France, July 1918, and served throughout the offensive (despatches 5 times, D.S.O., Bt. Lt.-Col.); commanded 2nd Batt. Royal Welch Fusiliers, 1927-31; retired, 1931; visited Southern Front, Nationalist Spain, 1938. *Publications:* A Galloper at Ypres, 1920; Contributor to many periodicals. *Address:* 31 Ennismore Gardens, S.W.7. [*Died* 14 *Dec.* 1967.

BUTLER, Hon. Sir Richard Layton, K.C.M.G., *cr.* 1939; Chairman, State Liquid Fuel Control Board, S. Australia; ex-Director of Emergency Road Transport, South Australia; Director: Adelaide Electric Supply Co. Ltd.; Cellulose (Aust.) Pty. Ltd.; *b.* Yattalunga Station, near Onetree Hill, S. Australia, 31 March 1885; 2nd *s.* of late Sir Richard Butler; *m.* Maud Draper; one *s.* two *d.* *Educ.:* Mallala Public School; Adelaide Agricultural School. Engaged in stock and station business, farming and grazing; represented South Australia at Silver Jubilee Celebrations, and Empire Parliamentary Association Conference, 1935; also at Coronation, 1937; Chairman South Australia Centenary Celebrations, 1936; elected as a Liberal for District of Wooroora, 1915, 1921, 1924, 1927, 1930, 1933, and 1936; Leader of the Opposition in the South Australian Parliament, 1925-27 and 1930-33; Premier, Treasurer, and Minister of Railways, S. Australia, 1927-30; Premier, Treasurer and Minister of Immigration, South Australia, 1933-38. *Address:* 35A Stephen Tce., Gilberton, S. Australia. [*Died* 21 *Jan.* 1966.

BUTLER, Hon. Somerset E.; *see* Butler, Hon. H. S. E.

BUTLER, Maj.-Gen. Stephen Seymour, C.B. 1936; C.M.G. 1919; D.S.O. 1917; *b.* 1880; *s.* of late Rev. G. H. Butler; *m.* 1913, Phyllis (*d.* 1963), *d.* of Capt. H. Critchley-Salmonson; two *s.* *Educ.:* Winchester. Joined 3rd Northumberland Fusiliers, 1897; Roy. Warwickshire Regt., 1899; S. African War (medal 5 clasps); King's African Rifles, 1905-7 (African G.S. Medal 2 clasps); explored Northern Arabia, 1907-08, disguised as a Bedu, and lectured to R.G.S. on return; transferred S. Staffordshire Regiment, 1908; Egyptian Army, 1909-15 (Sudan medal and clasp, Order of the Nile); European War, 1914-18, Egyptian Expeditionary Force, 1914-15, Dardanelles, 1915-16, France, 1916-1918; Dep. Chief Intelligence G.H.Q., 1918 (C.M.G., D.S.O., Order of Sacred Treasure, French Croix de Guerre, despatches 5 times, Bt. Lt.-Col., 1914-15 Star, Allies, War medals); Head of Naval Intelligence, Constantinople, 1919-20; A.M.S., N. Comd., India, 1921-23 (Indian G.S. Medal and clasp); Military Attaché, Bucharest, 1923-26; Inspector-General Royal West African Frontier Force, 1926-30; Kaid Sudan Defence Force, 1930-35; G.O.C. 48th Div., T.A., 1935-39; retired pay, 1939; re-employed Aug. 1939, War of 1939-45; Head of Mil. Mission to Turkey, 1939-40; Liaison, Africa, 1940-41; Head of British Military Mission, Ethiopia, 1941-43 (despatches twice, 1939-45 Star, Africa Star, Defence Medal, War Medal). *Recreation:* hunting. *Address:* Bury Lodge, Hambledon, Hants. [*Died* 16 *July* 1964.

BUTLER, Major-General Hon. Theobald Patrick Probyn, D.S.O. 1918; *b.* 3 July 1884; *y. s.* of 26th Baron Dunboyne; *m.* 1933, Hon. Vera Elizabeth Sanders, *er. d.* of 1st Baron Bayford. *Educ.:* Winchester; Royal Military Academy, Woolwich. Served European War, France, Palestine, Egypt, and Sudan (despatches twice, D.S.O., 3rd Class Order of the Nile), N W Frontier, India, 1930; Bt. Lt-Col. 1931; Lt.-Col., 1933; Col., 1937; Garrison Commander and Commandant R.A. Depot, Woolwich, 1937; District Commander, India, 1940 retired, 1942. *Address:* Kentisbeare House, Cullompton, Devon. [*Died* 18 *Oct.* 1970.

BUTLER, Victor Spencer, C.M.G. 1950; *b.* 1900; *s.* of late Sir (Spencer) Harcourt

Butler, G.C.S.I., G.C.I.E. *Educ.:* Harrow; Magdalen College, Oxford. Entered Civil Service, 1946; Under-Secretary, Ministry of Fuel and Power, 1946-54; Senior Executive, Shell Petroleum Company, 1955-61. *Address:* 9 Empire House, Thurloe Place, S.W.7. *T.:* 01-589 0217. *Club:* Garrick.
[*Died* 19 *June* 1969.

BUTT, Sir Alfred, 1st Bt., *cr.* 1929; Kt. 1918; Breeder of Bloodstock, Brook Stud; *b.* 20 March 1878; *o. s.* of F. Butt, Hampshire; *m.* 1st, 1902, Georgina Mary (*d.* 1960), *o. d.* of Frederick Say, Norwich; one *s.*; 2nd, 1960, Wilhelmine Wahl. Dir. Rationing, Min. of Food, 1917-18; M.P. (U.) Balham and Tooting Div. of Wandsworth, 1922-36. Chm. and Man. Dir., Theatre Royal, Drury Lane, and other Theatrical cos., 1925-31. *Heir: s.* Kenneth (Alfred) Dudley Butt [*b.* 7 July 1908; *m.* 2nd, 1948, Marie Josephine, *widow* of Ivor Watkins Birts and 2nd *d.* of John Bain]. *Address:* Clarehaven, Newmarket Suffolk.
[*Died* 8 *Dec.* 1962.

BUTT, Professor John Everett, B.Litt., M.A.; F.B.A. 1961; Regius Professor of Rhetoric and English Literature in the University of Edinburgh since 1959; *b.* Hoole, Cheshire, 12 April 1906; *s.* of Francis John Butt, M.B., C.M., and Charlotte Butt; *m.* 1941, Enid Margaret, *d.* of Alaric and Enid Hope, Goring on Thames; one *s.* two *d.* *Educ.:* Shrewsbury Sch.; Merton Coll., Oxford. Assistant Lecturer in English, Leeds Univ. 1929; Asst. Librarian, English School Library, Oxford, 1930; Lecturer in English, Bedford Coll., London Univ., 1930-46; temp. Admin. Asst., Min. of Home Security, 1941-43; temp. Principal, Home Office, 1943-45. Gen. Editor, Twickenham edn. of Pope's poetry, since 1932; Ed. of The Review of English Studies, 1947-54; visiting Professor: Univ. of California at Los Angeles, 1952; Yale Univ., 1962; Prof. of English Language and Literature at King's Coll. (University of Durham), Newcastle upon Tyne, 1946-59. *Publications:* A Bibliography of Izaak Walton's Lives, 1930; (ed. with G. Tillotson) Two Sermons on the Resurrection by Lancelot Andrewes, 1932; Pope's Taste in Shakespeare, 1936; (ed.) Imitations of Horace by Alexander Pope, 1939; (with H. V. D. Dyson) Augustans and Romantics, 1940; Translations of Voltaire's Candide, 1947, Zadig and L'Ingénu, 1964; The Augustan Age, 1950; (ed. with N. Ault) Pope's Minor Poems, 1954; Fielding 1954; Popes Poetical MSS (British Academy Warton Lecture), 1955; (with K. Tillotson) Dickens at Work, 1957; (ed.) Letters of Alexander Pope, 1960. *Address:* 15 Blacket Avenue, Edinburgh 9. *T.:* Newington 6135. *Club:* United University.
[*Died* 22 *Nov.* 1965.

BUTTERFIELD, Robert William Fitzmaurice, C.I.E. 1944; F.I.R.A. (Ind.); J.P.; Financial Adviser and Chief Accounts Officer, Bombay, Baroda and Central India Railway, Bombay (retired); *b.* 10 Jan. 1889; 2nd *s.* of late Alfred Lumsden Butterfield, Indian Police, and Caroline Butterfield; *m.* May Winifred Catley; two *s.* one *d.* Volunteer Long Service Medal, 1924. *Address:* 14A, St. Margaret's, London Rd., Guildford, Surrey. *T.:* Guildford 3861.
[*Died* 14 *Jan.* 1967.

BUTTERS, Sir John Henry, Kt., 1927; C.M.G. 1923; M.B.E. 1920; V.D.; M.I.C.E., F.I.E.E., M.I.E. Aust., F.A.S.C.E.; Consultant, Sydney, New South Wales; *b.* Alverstoke, Hants, 23 Dec. 1885; *s.* of late R. J. Butters; *m.* Lilian Gordon, *d.* of late T. W. Keele, M.I.C.E., Sydney; one *s.* three *d.* *Educ.:* Tauntons School; University College, Southampton. Chief Engineer and General Manager, Hydro-Electric Department, Tasmania, 1912-24; Chief Commissioner, Federal Capital, Canberra, 1924-29; Chairman of Associated Newspapers, Ltd., Sydney, 1940-56. Lieut.-Colonel Royal Australian Engineers (Retired). Hon. Cons. Mil. Eng., A.H.Q. Aust., 1927-43. President, Institution of Engineers, Australia, 1927. Director: General Motors Holdens Pty. Ltd.; Petrochemical Holdings Ltd.; Boral Ltd.; Chairman: Hadfields Steel Works Ltd.; North Shore Gas Co. Ltd.; Vunalama Plantations Ltd. *Address:* Alverstoke, Wahroonga, Sydney, N.S.W., Australia. *T.A.:* Sydney. *Clubs:* Australian, R.A.C.A. (Sydney).
[*Died* 29 *July* 1969.

BUTTON, Howard, C.B.E. 1920; Chartered Accountant, retd.; *b.* 20 Mar. 1875; *s.* of late John J. Button, Olton, Warwickshire; *m.* Beatrice Maud (*d.* 1959), *d.* of late Willoughby F. Ellis, Woodville; one *d.* *Educ.:* King Edward VI. Grammar School, Birmingham (Foundation Scholar). Director of Internal Audits and later Controller of Munitions Accounts in Ministry of Munitions of War. *Publication:* Notes on Principles of Profit Sharing. *Address:* Tudor Croft, 6 Wyvern Road, Sutton Coldfield, Warwicks.
[*Died* 21 *June* 1965.

BUXTON, Lady; *see* Noel-Buxton.

BUXTON, Major Anthony, D.S.O. 1916; D.L.; B.A.; J.P., Norfolk; *b.* 2 Sept. 1881; *y. s.* of late Edward North Buxton; *m.* 1926, Mary (*d.* 1953), *e. d.* of late Hon. Bernard Constable-Maxwell, Farlie House, Inverness; one *s.* three *d.* *Educ.:* Harrow; Trinity College, Cambridge; graduated Natural Science Tripos, 1904. Played in the Harrow Eleven, 1900, 1901; served for 11 years in the Essex Yeomanry; served European War with his regiment, 1914-18 (D.S.O.); attached 10th Royal Hussars, 1918-19; Secretariat, Headquarters, League of Nations, 1919-31; travelled in Asia Minor and the Caucasus. High Sheriff of Norfolk, 1945-46. *Publications:* Sport in Peace and War; Sporting Interludes at Geneva, 1932; Fisherman Naturalist, 1946; Travelling Naturalist, 1948; Happy Year, 1950; contributions to reviews and newspapers. *Recreations:* fishing, shooting, hunting, travel, natural history. *Address:* Horsey Hall, nr. Great Yarmouth, Norfolk. *Club:* Brooks's.
[*Died* 9 *Aug.* 1970.

BUXTON, Denis Alfred Jex; Director: Uganda Co. Ltd.; Cory's Associated Wharves; F.S.A.; *b.* 26 March 1895; *s.* of late Alfred Fowell Buxton; *m.* 1923, Emily Mary, *d.* of William Hollins, Berry Hill, Mansfield, Notts; one *s.* three *d.* *Educ.:* Rugby; Balliol Coll., Oxford. 1st Cl. Lit. Hum., 1921; served in the ranks in Gallipoli; Lt. W. Riding Regt., 1916-19. Raised and commanded one of the first London Balloon Squadrons (909 County of Essex). Hon. Treasurer, Magistrates' Assoc., 1942-63, and Council for British Archæology. D.L. Essex, 1943-57 (Sheriff 1944) and sometime J.P. for Essex. President, Norfolk and Norwich Archæological Soc. *Recreations:* natural history, archæology, and travel. *Address:* Caister Hall, Great Yarmouth, Norfolk. *Clubs:* Athenæum, Brooks's; Norfolk (Norwich).
[*Died* 2 *Sept.* 1946.

BUXTON, Lionel Gurney, M.V.O. 1905; M.C. 1916; retired from Board of Barclays Bank Ltd., Feb. 1954; Local Director in Barclays Bank Ltd., 1904-57; *b.* 6 Sept. 1876; *s.* of Samuel Gurney Buxton; unmarried. *Educ.:* Harrow; Trinity College Cambridge. Served South African War, 1901-2; European War, France, Oct. 1914-1918, 2nd Div. XIII Corps, 4th Army, Legion of Honour (France). *Recreations:* formerly hunting and shooting. *Address:* 42 Westbourne Terrace, W.2. *T.:* Paddington 6620. *Clubs:* Turf, Brooks's.
[*Died* 25 *April* 1962.

BUXTON, Captain Roden Henry Victor, C.B.E. 1942; R.N. (retd.); Order of Polonia Restituta 3rd class; *b.* 17 Dec. 1890; *s.* of Sir Victor Buxton, 4th Bt.; *heir-pres.* to Sir T. F. V. Buxton, 6th Bt.; *m.* 1st, 1917, Dorothy Alina (*d.* 1956), *d.* of Col. C. W. R. St. John, R.E.; two *s.* four *d.*; 2nd, 1957, Hilda, M.B.E., *d.* of late Charles Alfred Meadows, Rainham, Kent. *Educ.:* Cheam School; R.N.C., Osborne and Dartmouth. Midshipman, 1908; Lt., 1913; specialised in Signals; Grand Fleet, 1914-18; Flag Lt. and Signal Officer to Vice-Adm. Sir Roger Keyes, 1919-21; Fleet Signal Officer, Mediterranean and Atlantic Fleets, 1921-24; R.N. Staff Coll., 1925; R.A.F. Staff Coll., 1929; H.M.S. Enterprise East Indies, 1929-31; served at Admiralty Signal Dept.; Drafting Commander, Portsmouth; Admiralty as Director of Manning, 1940-43; Combined Operations H.Q. and Admiralty, as Director of Combined Operations Personnel, 1943-1946; Naval Mission to Greece, 1946-47. J.P. for Hants, 1948-57. *Recreations:* fishing, gardening. *Address:* Smallburgh Hall, Norwich, Norfolk. *T.:* Smallburgh 355. *Club:* United Service. [*Died* 10 *Nov.* 1970.

BUXTON, William Leonard, M.B.E. 1929; *b.* 15 August 1894; *e. c.* of late William D. Buxton, Brooklands, Highgate, Chairman of Ohlsson's Cape Breweries; *m.* 1924, Flora (Jock), *d.* of late John Morison, M.D., Haddon Court, Highgate; two *d.* *Educ.:* Highgate School; Pembroke College, Cambridge. Scholar, Pembroke Coll., 1913, B.A. 1919, M.A. 1947. Served European War, 1914-18, 2nd Lt. York and Lancaster Regt., Aug. 1914; severely wounded Suvla Bay landing, 1915; Lieut. 1915; Capt. British Mission to Italian Commando Supremo, 1917; Croce di Guerra, 1918; despatches 1919. Cricket Captain Pembroke, Cambridge, 1919. Asst. Principal Ministry of Labour, 1920; Private Sec. to Parliamentary Sec., 1921, and to Permanent Sec. 1922. On Secretariat of Lord Riverdale's Cttee. on Industry and Trade from its appointment in 1924 to final report in 1929. Principal 1928; Asst. Sec. 1937; Principal Asst. Sec., 1944; Under-Secretary, 1947. Appointed Member of the Industrial Disputes Tribunal, 1953-56. Chm. of Assoc. of First Division Civil Servants, 1935-37; U.K. representative on Governing Body of International Labour Organisation, 1937-38, whilst Sir Frederick Leggett was Chairman. Apptd. by I.L.O., Sept. 1953, under Technical Assistance Programme to advise Govt. of Burma on Labour Admin. and Inspection; reported March 1954. Served on I.L.O. Institute for Near and Middle East, stationed in Istanbul, October 1955-August 1956. *Publication:* Mearham (U.K. and U.S.A.), 1927. *Recreations:* now sedentary (owing to amputation of wounded leg, 1959). *Address:* Timsbury, Gordon Avenue, Stanmore, Middlesex. *T.:* Grimsdyke 1184. *Club:* Oxford and Cambridge. [*Died* 19 *May* 1964.

BUZZARD, Lieutenant-Colonel Charles Norman, C.M.G. 1919; D.S.O. 1918; *b* 29 April 1873; *s.* of T. Buzzard, M.D., F.R.C.P.; *m.* 1st, 1902, Isabel Mary d'Aguilar (*d.* 1922), *d.* of Maj.-Gen. G. D'A. A. Jackson; 2nd, 1922, Baroness Elizabeth Wrangell (*née* Baroness Elizabeth Hoyningen Huene), formerly Maid of Honour to the Empress of Russia; one *d.* (and one *d.* decd.). *Educ.:* S. Paul's School; R.M.A., Woolwich. Served European War, Dardanelles, Flanders, Italy (Bt. Lt.-Col., C.M.G., D.S.O., Chev. Légion d'Honneur, Cav. Mil. Ord., Savoy, Italy, Officer Ord. Corona Italy, desp. twice); retired, 1920. *Publications:* Shining Hours, 1946; articles in Blackwood, Cornhill, Vanity Fair, Pioneer, Country Life. *Recreations:* golf, sketching. *Address:* 150 Boulevard de la République, Vaucresson, S.-et-O., France. [*Died* 8 *April* 1961.

BYAM, William, O.B.E.; M.R.C.S., L.R.C.P.; Lt.-Col. R.A.M.C. (retd.); *o. s.* of Maj.-Gen. William Byam, C.B.; *b.* 19 Aug. 1882; *m.* 1st, 1915, Doris Mabert (*d.* 1950), 2nd *d.* of Edward Stiven, M.D., Harrow-on-the-Hill; two *d.* (one *s.* killed on active service, R.N.V.R. (A), 1941); 2nd, 1952, Dorothy Mary, *widow* of J. Oscar Thomas, M.C., T.D., M.D. *Educ.:* Wellington College; St. George's Hospital. Entered Royal Army Medical Corps, 1904; attached Egyptian Army, 1908-16; Operations S.E. Sudan, 1912 (despatches, Order 4th class Medjedieh); British Red Cross Unit to Bulgaria, 1912 (Order 4th class St. Alexander of Bulgaria); New Zealand Expeditionary Force, 1914-16 (despatches, Order 3rd class Nile); War Office Trench Fever Commission, 1918 (O.B.E.). Director Princess Tsehai Memorial Hospital, Addis Ababa, Ethiopia, 1951-53. *Publications:* Dr. Byam in Harley Street, 1962; The Road to Harley Street, 1963; Editor (with R. G. Archibald) Practice of Medicine in the Tropics; Trench Fever. *Recreations:* philately, gardening. *Address:* Cedar Hill, Mount Durand, Guernsey, C.I. *T.:* Central 3044. *Club:* Oriental. [*Died* 25 *Oct.* 1963.

BYNNER, Witter; author; *b.* Brooklyn, 10 Aug. 1881; *s.* of Thomas Edgarton Bynner and Annie Louise Brewer; unmarried. *Educ.:* Harvard (A.B.). Assistant editor McClure's Magazine, and literary editor McClure, Phillips & Co., 1902-06; advisory editor with Small, Maynard & Co., 1907-15; Instructor English, S.A.T.C. of California, 1918-19; contributor to many magazines; lecturer on poetry; Phi Beta Kappa poet, Harvard, 1911; University of California, 1919; Amherst, 1931; President of Poetry Society, America, 1921-22; Chancellor, Academy of American Poets, 1946- ; Regional Vice-Pres., Poetry Soc., America; Mem. Nat. Inst. of Arts and Letters, 1962. Hon. Lit.D. Univ. of New Mexico, 1962. *Publications:* (poems) Young Harvard, 1907; (plays) Tiger, 1913; The Little King, 1914; (poem) The New World, 1915; (play) Iphigenia in Tauris, 1915; Grenstone Poems, 1917; (poems) The Beloved Stranger, 1919; A Canticle of Pan, 1920; Pins for Wings (under *pseudonym* Emanuel Morgan), 1921; A Book of Plays, 1922; (from the French of Charles Vildrac, poems) A Book of Love, 1923; (poems) Caravan, 1925; (play) Cake, 1926; (poems) Indian Earth, 1929; (poem) Eden Tree, 1931; (poems) Guest Book, 1935; Selected Poems, 1936; (poems) Against the Cold, 1940; The Way of Life according to Laotzu (Tao Teh Ching), 1944; (poems) Take Away the Darkness, 1947; Journey with Genius: Recollections and Reflections concerning the D. H. Lawrences, 1951; England, 1953; Book of Lyrics, 1955; (new version of play Iphigenia in Tauris)Euripides II, 1956; New Poems, 1960. Co-author (with Arthur Davison Ficke, under *pseudonyms* Emanuel Morgan and Anne Knish, poems), Spectra, 1916; (with Julia Ellsworth Ford, play), Snickerty Nick, 1919; (with Dr. Kiang Kang-hu, translation from T'ang poets) The Jade Mountain, 1929; The Sonnets of Frederick Goddard Tuckerman (Editor), 1931. *Address:* 342 Buena Vista Road, Santa Fé, N.M., U.S.A. *T.:* 982-0577. *Clubs:* Harvard, The Players (New York); Book Club of California (San Francisco). [*Died* 1 *June* 1968.

BYRNE, Hon. Sir Laurence Austin, Kt., 1945; Judge of High Court, Queen's Bench Division, 1947-60, retd.; *b.* 17 Sept. 1896; *yr. s.* of late William Austin Byrne; *m.* 1928, Dorothy Frances, *d.* of late Joseph Harkness Tickell. Served in European War, Lieut. Queen's Royal West Surrey Regt.; called to Bar, Middle Temple, 1918; Bencher of Middle Temple, 1942; Reader, 1954. Counsel to Mint at the Central Criminal Court,

1928-30; Junior Prosecuting Counsel to Crown at Central Criminal Court, 1930-37; Second Senior Prosecuting Counsel, 1937-42; Senior Prosecuting Counsel, 1942-45; Recorder of Rochester, 1939-45; Judge of High Court, Probate, Divorce and Admiralty Division, 1945-47. *Address:* Gosfield Hall, Halstead, Essex. *T.:* Halstead 2542. [*Died* 1 *Nov.* 1965.

BYRNE, Air Commodore Reginald, C.B. 1946; M.C. 1917; *b.* 29 Oct. 1888; *er. s.* of late Bernard Byrne (Major R. W. Kent Regt.) and A. K. Byrne; *m.* 1913, Maud, *yr. d.* of late William Law, J.P., West Cross, Glam.; two *d. Educ.:* privately. Served European War, 1914-18, 6th Reserve Cavalry, and City of London Yeomanry (severely wounded); special staff duties, 1919-1920; transferred to R.A.F. 1921. Held many appointments at home and overseas mainly in H.Q. Staffs Inland Area, Middle East, British Forces, Aden, Wessex Bombing Area, Mediterranean, Training Command, France (despatches), Bomber Command, Flying Training Command, etc.; retd., 1946. Member Grants Cttee. R.A.F. Benevolent Fund. *Address:* Ingram House, Hampton Wick, Kingston-on-Thames. *T.:* Teddington Lock 4750. [*Died* 30 *April* 1965.

BYRT, Albert Henry, C.B.E. 1938; *b.* 18 March 1881; *e. s.* of Albert and Kate Byrt, Shepton Mallet, Somerset; *m.* 1912, Dorothy Muriel, *y. d.* of late R. Stafford Thorne, Kingston-on-Thames; one *s.* two *d. Educ.:* Privately. After initial work on home provincial newspapers, joined editorial staff of The Times of India (Bombay), 1904 and remained a member of it until retirement in 1938; assistant editor, editor, leader writer and special correspondent at Indian winter and summer capitals (Delhi and Simla), director; London correspondent, 1939-46; for several years correspondent of The Times and later of The Daily Telegraph, at Delhi and Simla, and Hon. Sec. of Himalayan Club. *Recreations:* walking, gardening, photography. *Address:* Kersbrook, 14 St. Winifred's Road, Bournemouth. [*Died* 28 *March* 1966.

BYWATERS, Dr. Hubert William, D.Sc. London; D.Sc. Bristol; PhD. Würzburg; F.R.I.C.; Director, C. R. Bywater, Ltd., Great Chesterford, Essex; *b.* 3 Feb. 1881; *m.* 1911, Olive Robertson (*d.* 1963); three *s.* one *d. Educ.:* Roy. Coll. of Science, London; University of Würzburg. Formerly Demonstrator of Physiology in the University of Bristol; chief chemist to J. S. Fry & Sons, Ltd., cocoa and chocolate manufacturers, Bristol; Works Manager, Geo. Bassett & Co., Ltd., Sheffield. *Publications* Modern Methods of Cocoa and Chocolate Manufacture, 1929; numerous articles in scientific journals. *Recreation:* gardening. *Address:* Fairstead, Great Chesterford, Essex. *T.:* Great Chesterford 320. *Club:* Royal Automobile. [*Died* 9 *Dec.* 1966.

C

CABLE, Eric Grant, C.M.G. 1938; *b.* 25 Feb. 1887; *s.* of Jas. Cable and Catherine Campbell; *m.* 1919, Nellie Margaret (*d.* 1963), *o. d.* of late Harry John Skelton, Hythe; two *s. Educ.:* Universities of Helsingfors, London and Heidelberg. Employed in the British Consulate at Helsingfors, 1904-7 and 1908-1912; Act -Consul there in 1909 and 1911; passed a competitive examination and appointed a Vice-Consul in the Consular Service, 1913; employed at Hamburg February to July, and at Rotterdam July to August 1914; Acting Consul in Iceland, 1914; Vice-Consul in Majunga (Madagascar), 1915 (did not proceed); in charge of French Vice-Consulate in Iceland, Aug. 1916-April 1917; Contraband Department, Foreign Office, 1917; H.M. Consul for Iceland, 1915-19; Acting Consul at Dunkirk, 1919-20; H.M. Consul at Riga, 1920; Consular Dep., Foreign Office, 1920-1922; H.M. Consul, Oslo, 1922-26; Acting Consul, Stockholm, 1925; H.M. Consul Danzig, 1926-29; Portland, Oregon, 1929-31; Seattle, Washington, 1932-33; H.M. Consul and Commercial Secretary to the British Legation, Copenhagen, 1933-39; Consul-General at Cologne, 1939, until outbreak of War: then at Rotterdam until three days after the German invasion of Holland in May 1940; employed by Ministry of Home Security at Birmingham and at headquarters, 1940-41; in the Northern Dept. Foreign Office, 1941-42; Consul-General at Zürich, 1942-47; retired from Foreign Service, 1947. *Address:* c/o Lloyds Bank Ltd., Bournemouth. [*Died* 7 *May* 1970.

CACCIA, Anthony, C.B. 1919; M.V.O. 1903; Chevalier Legion d'Honneur, 1918; Cavaliere S.S. Maurizio e Lazzaro, 1918; M.A. (Oxon); F.Z.S.; *b.* 1869. Joined the Indian Forest Service, 1889, as Assistant Commissioner of Forests; Deputy Commissioner, 1897; Conservator, 1913; Director of Forest Studies in England, 1911-26; joined H.M. Forces at commencement of War; Temp. Major, July 1915; Major on Staff, attached to British Military Mission at French Headquarters, 1916 (despatches); Assistant Director Timber Supplies, War Office, 1917; Secretary, Supreme War Council, Versailles, 1918; Peace Conference, Paris, 1919. *Address:* Elsmere, Crick Road, Oxford. [*Died* 30 *July* 1962.

CADBURY, Sir Egbert, Kt. 1957; D.S.C. 1916; D.F.C. 1918; D.L.; J.P.; M.A.; Managing Director Cadbury Bros. Ltd., 1943-1963, and J. S. Fry & Sons Ltd., 1920-63; Dir., British Cocoa & Chocolate Co. Ltd., 1921-1965 (Managing Director, 1921-62; Vice-Chm. 1959-62); *b.* 20 April 1893; British; *y. s.* of late George Cadbury, Birmingham; *m.* 1917, Mary *d.* of late Rev. Forbes Phillips, Vicar of Gorleston; one *s.* (and one *s.* decd.). *Educ.:* Leighton Park School, Reading; Trinity College, Cambridge. Joined Royal Navy as Able Seaman, 1914; served European War, 1914-18, Commission in R.N.A.S., 1915 (D.S.C.); transferred to R.A.F., 1918 (D.F.C.). Joined J. S. Fry & Sons, Ltd., 1919; Managing Dir., 1920; Dir., Lloyd's Bank, 1944-64; Ch. Bristol Cttee. Lloyds Bank, 1958-65. Director: E.M.B. Co. Ltd., Daily News Ltd., 1949, Keith Prowse and Co. Ltd., 1957, Willett Investments Ltd. (Chairman), 1960. Regional Controller for S. Western Region, Min. of Fuel and Power, 1941-50; Fire Prevention Officer for S. Western Region, 1940-1945; Chm., Central Transport Consultative Cttee., 1948-54; Chm. Bristol Fedn. of Boys' Clubs, 1933-53; Chairman of Governors, Claremont School (Hove) Ltd. 1961; Governor, Nuffield Nursing Homes Trust, 1961. Hon. Treasurer Bristol Royal Infirmary, 1922-48; Mem., Glos. Territorial Assoc., 1936-58; Master of Society of Merchant Venturers, 1947. Hon. Treas., United Bristol Hosps., 1948-. Chairman Bristol Wing, Air Training Corps., 1942-64; Hon. Air Commodore R.A.F.; Pres., Bristol Gliding Club. J.P. Somerset, 1928; Chm., Long Ashton Petty Sessions; D.L., Co. of Glos., 1950. *Recreations:* riding, shooting, golf, yachting. *Address:* The Manor House, Abbots Leigh, nr. Bristol. *T.:* Pill 2350; The Manor Farm, East Wellow, Hants. *T.:* West Wellow 254; The Foresters' Arms, Coleford Water, Lydeard St. Lawrence, Nr. Taunton, Som. *T.:* Lydeard St. Lawrence 239. *Clubs:* R.A.F., Royal Thames Yacht; Leigh Woods Yacht; Royal Yacht Squadron. [*Died* 12 *Jan.* 1967.

CADDY, Adrian, V.D.; M.D. (Lond.), F.R.C.S. (Eng.); Consulting Surgeon, Royal Westminster Ophthalmic Hospital; Consulting Ophthalmic Surgeon, Royal Nat. Orthopædic Hospital; late Ophthalmic Surgeon (temp.) St. George's Hospital; Consulting Ophthalmic Surgeon, Italian Hospital; Officer Order of St. John of Jerusalem; *b.* 10 Jan. 1879; *s.* of late Inspector-General John Turner Caddy, M.D., R.N., and late Florence Caddy; *m.* Evelyn Mary, *d.* of late Sir Charles A. Payton, M.V.O., British Consular Service; two *s.* one *d.* *Educ.:* St. Paul's School; St. George's Hospital (Entrance Scholarship). Late Surgeon Superintendent, Hindu Marwari Hospital, Calcutta; Lieutenant-Colonel (ret.) Indian Auxiliary Forces Medical Corps, attached Calcutta Light Horse; Honorary Life Governor and late temporary Surgeon, St. George's Hospital; late Member of Bengal Council of Med. Registration; late Mem. of the Faculty School of Tropical Medicine, Calcutta; late examiner D.O.M.S., Royal College of Surgeons, England. *Publications* several professional publications. *Address:* Harington, Kettlewell Hill, Woking. *T.:* 1021. *Club:* Oriental. [*Died* 24 *Feb.* 1966.

CADELL of Grange, Colonel Henry Moubray, O.B.E. 1940; J.P.; M.I.Mech.E.; *b.* 27 January 1892; *s.* of Henry Moubray-Cadell of Grange, V.D., J.P., D.L., LL.D., F.R.S.E. and Elinor, M.B.E., *d.* of David Simson, Bengal Civil Service; *m.* 1928, Christina Rose, *d.* of Alexander Nimmo, Westbank, Falkirk; three *s.* one *d.* *Educ.:* Merchiston Castle; R.M.A., Woolwich. Commissioned 2nd Lt. Royal Engineers, Dec. 1911; Served European War, 1914-18: France, 1914-15; Salonika and Palestine, 1916-17. Capt. 1917; Major 1928; Lt.-Col. 1935; Col. 1940. C.R.E., G.H.Q. Tps, France, 1939-40; A.D.F.W., War Office, 1940-41; retired 1942. Comd. 2nd West Lothian Bn. H.G. 1942 till Stand Down. J.P. 1939; D.L. West Lothian, 1943-67; H.M. Lieut. for County of West Lothian, 1952-64. Croix de Guerre (Fr.), 1916. *Address:* Grange, Linlithgow, West Lothian. *T.:* Linlithgow 44. *Club:* Caledonian United Service and Northern (Edinburgh). [*Died* 6 *Nov.* 1967.

CADELL, Sir Patrick Robert, Kt., *cr.* 1935; C.S.I. 1919; C.I.E. 1913; V.D.; Indian Civil Service, retired; *b.* 6 May 1871; *s.* of late Colonel Thomas Cadell, V.C., C.B., of Cockenzie. *m.* 1920, Agnes Aimée *d.* of late John Kemp (*d.* 1961), Barrister-at-law, 1, Onslow Square, S.W. *Educ.:* Edinburgh Academy; Haileybury; Balliol College, Oxford. Member of Oxford University Football XV., 1890-91; selected to play for South of England; service in India, 1891-1926; served in Bombay Presidency and in Calcutta; Hon Colonel, Indian Defence Forces; A.D.C. to Viceroy; Chairman, Bombay Port Trust; Acting Member Executive Council Bombay, 1924; Commissioner in Sind, 1925-26; retired, 1927; President of the Council, Junagadh State 1932-35: President of Council, Sangli State, 1937; Rajkot State, 1938. *Publications:* History of the Bombay Army, 1938; (joint) India: The New Phase; Letters of Meadows Taylor. *Recreations:* outdoor sports. *Address:* Cornriggs, Frilford Heath, Abingdon, Berks. *T.:* Frilford Heath 207. *Club:* East India and Sports. [*Died* 22 *Nov.* 1961.

CADMAN, 2nd Baron, *cr.* 1937, of Silverdale; **John Basil Cope Cadman;** *b.* 23 March 1909; *s.* of 1st Baron and late Lilian, *d.* of John Harragin, Trinidad; *S.* father 1941; *m.* 1936, Marjorie Elizabeth Bunnis; two *s.* *Educ.:* Harrow; Grenoble University. *Heir:* *s.* Hon. John Anthony Cadman, *b.* 3 July 1938. *Address:* 50 Stoke Road, Linslade, Leighton Buzzard. *Club:* Lansdowne. [*Died* 4 *April* 1966.

CADMAN, Rev. William Healey, B.Litt., M.A. (Oxon), D.Theol. (Strasbourg), Hon. D.D. (Aberdeen); B.D. (London); University Lecturer in New Testament Theology, Oxford, 1945-61; *b.* Aug. 1891; *e. s.* of Thomas and Sarah Ann Cadman, Wem, Salop; *m.* 1918, Lilian Julia, *d.* of Alderman John Yeo, J.P., Plymouth; no *c.* *Educ.:* privately; New Coll., London; St. Catherine's Coll. and Mansfield Coll., Oxford; University of Strasbourg. Tutor in New Testament Greek, 1923-29, and Lecturer in New Testament Language and Literature, 1929-31, and Research Fellow, 1932-44, Mansfield College; Professor of Biblical Studies, Mansfield College, Oxford, 1944-59. Examr., Univs. of Birmingham, 1932-34; Oxford, 1936-38, 1947, 1950-52; Nottingham, 1950-52; Aberdeen, 1950-52; Bristol, 1961. *Publications:* The Last Journey of Jesus to Jerusalem, 1923; contributor to Christian Worship, 1936, Studia Evangelica, 1959, Studia Patristica, 1961, and to theological journals. *Recreations:* fishing, walking. *Address:* 197 Woodstock Road, Oxford. [*Died* 12 *Sept.* 1965

CADOGAN, Rt. Hon. Sir Alexander George Montagu, P.C. 1946; O.M. 1951; G.C.M.G., *cr.* 1939 (K.C.M.G., *cr.* 1934; C.M.G. 1926); K.C.B., *cr.* 1941 (C.B. 1932); Director, National Provincial Bank, 1951-1964; *b.* 25 November 1884; *y. s.* of 5th Earl Cadogan; *m.* 1912, Lady Theodosia Acheson, *d.* of 4th Earl of Gosford; one *s.* three *d.* *Educ.:* Eton; Oxford. B.A. Hon. Fellow of Balliol College, Oxford, 1950; Hon. D.C.L. Toronto, 1947, McGill and Princeton, 1950. Envoy Extraordinary and Minister Plenipotentiary at Peking, 1933-35; Ambassador, 1935-36; Deputy Under-Secretary of State for Foreign Affairs, 1936-1937; Permanent Under-Secretary of State for Foreign Affairs, Jan. 1938-Feb. 1946; Permanent Representative of H.M. Govt. in the U.K. to the United Nations, New York, 1946-50; retired from H.M. Foreign Service, 1950; Government Director of Suez Canal Co., 1951-57; Chairman B.B.C., 1952-57. *Address:* 2 Westminster Gardens, S.W.1. *T.:* Victoria 2880. *Club:* St. James'. [*Died* 9 *July* 1968.

CADOGAN, Hon. Sir Edward (Cecil George), K.B.E., *cr.* 1939; C.B. 1921; J.P.; D.L. Co. London; B.A.; Barrister-at-law; Major Suffolk Yeomanry; late Secretary to the Speaker; Sec. Caledonian Canal Commission; Dep.-Chm. Law Union Insurance Company and Deputy Chairman of Great Western Railway; Member Indian Statutory Commission; Chairman of the Borstal Association; Temp. Chairman of Committees, House of Commons, 1931-35; Member of Joint Select Committee on the Indian Constitution; Member of Select Committee (House of Commons) on National Expenditure, 1941; Chairman of the Juvenile Organisations Committee (Board of Education): One of the original members of exec. council of Nat. Playing Fields Assoc.; served on King George V Memorial Playing Fields Cttee.; Chairman London and Greater London Playing Fields Assoc. for 25 years; Deputy Chairman of National Advisory Council on Physical Training; Chm. Home Office Cttee. on Corporal Punishment; Co-opted Member, L.C.C. Educn. Cttee.; Chm. No. 1 Advisory Committee, S.-E. London District Unemployment Assistance Board; Member of London Territorial Force Assoc.; Dep.-Chm. Council of Central After Care Assoc. (under the provisions of the Criminal Justice Act, 1948); Member, Royal Commission on Justices of the Peace, 1946; Member Committee of Enquiry into political activities of Civil Service, 1948; *b.* 15 Nov. 1880; 6th *s* of 5th Earl Cadogan. *Educ.:* Eton; Balliol College, Oxford. Bar, Inner Temple, 1905; contested (C.) King's

Lynn, 1910; M.P. Reading, 1922-23; Finchley, 1924-35; M.P. (U.) Bolton, 1940-45; contested Reading, 1923; served Dardanelles, Egypt, Palestine, 1915-19 (despatches); R.A.F.V.R., War of 1939-45. Vice-Lieutenant, County of London, 1945-58. Order of Al Rafidain, 1st class, Iraq, 1956. *Publications:* Makers of Modern History, 1905; Life of Cavour, 1907; The India We Saw, 1933; The Roots of Evil, 1937; Before the Deluge, 1961. *Address:* The Warren Farm, Lewknor, Oxon. *Clubs:* Carlton, Turf. [*Died* 13 *Sept.* 1962.

CAHAN, J(ohn) Flint; Associate Director of the Overseas Development Institute since 1960; *b.* 27 Dec. 1912; *s.* of John Flint Cahan and Beatrice Ellinor Daviss; *m.* 1st, Theresa Cobbold; one *d.*; 2nd, Eleri Wynn Williams; two *s.* one *d.* *Educ.:* Halifax County Acad. (Halifax, N.S.); Dalhousie Univ. (Halifax, N.S.); Univ. of London (Univ. Coll.). Sec., National Institute of Economic and Social Research, 1938-39; Ministry of Economic Warfare, 1939-44; H.M. Treasury, 1944-46; Deputy Director-General, Joint Export/Import Agency, Frankfurt-am-Main, 1947-49; Director of Trade and Payments, O.E.E.C., Paris, 1951-1956; Dep. Sec.-Gen., O.E.E.C., 1956-60. Order of Orange Nassau (Netherlands), 1946; Medal of Freedom (Bronze Palm) (U.S.), 1946. *Address:* 3 Reynolds Close, N.W.11. *T.:* Speedwell 8695. *Club:* Travellers'. [*Died* 3 *Feb.* 1961.

CAIN, Sir Ernest, 2nd Bt., *cr.* 1920; *b.* 25 Sept. 1891; *o. s.* of Sir William Ernest Cain, 1st Bt.; *S.* father, 1924; *m.* 1923, Enid Willoughby, *o. d.* of George Glasgow, Liverpool; three *d.* *Educ.:* Trinity Hall, Cambridge; B.A. 1915; Barrister-at-law, Gray's Inn, 1920. *Heir:* none. *Address:* White House, Ferry Lane, Wargrave, Reading, Berks. *T.:* Wargrave 2944. *Club:* Liverpool Conservative (Liverpool). [*Died* 8 *Sept.* 1969 (*ext.*).

CAINE, Gordon R. H.; *see* Hall Caine.

CAIRNEY, John, C.M.G. 1960; M.D.; D.Sc.; F.R.A.C.S.; Retired; *b.* 8 Oct. 1898; *s.* of John Cairney; *m.* 1920, Claris Dorothy Kempthorne; one *s.* two *d.* *Educ.:* Greymouth District High School; University of Otago, New Zealand. M.D. 1925; F.R.A.C.S. 1943; D.Sc. 1948. Demonstrator, Lecturer and Associate Prof. of Anatomy Univ. of Otago, 1921-27; Medical Supt., Hawera Hosp., 1927-36; Director of Clinical Services, Wellington Hosp., 1936; Med. Supt., Wellington Hosp., 1940; Supt.-in-Chief for Wellington Hosp. Bd., 1944-49, Director-Gen. of Health and Inspector-Gen of Hosps. for Dominion of New Zealand 1949-59, retd. *Publications:* Surgery for Students of Nursing, 1952; Gynaecology for Senior Students of Nursing, 1954; Anatomy and Physiology for Nurses (with W. P. Gowland), 1941; First Studies in Anatomy and Physiology (with John Cairney, Jnr.) 1956; The Human Body: A Survey of Structure and Function (with John Cairney, Jnr.), 1966; Papers in Jl. of Anat. and Jl. of Comparative Neurology. *Address:* 7 Lancaster Street, Karori, Wellington, W.3, New Zealand. *T.:* 78299. *Club:* Wellington (Wellington, N.Z.). [*Died* 5 *Aug.* 1966

CAITHNESS, 19th Earl of, *cr.* 1455; **James Roderick Sinclair;** C.V.O. 1963; C.B.E. 1951; D.S.O. 1944; D.L.; J.P.; Baron Berriedale, 1455; Bt. 1631; Factor for H.M. the Queen's Balmoral and Birkhall Estates, since 1955; Col. The Gordon Highlanders; Representative Peer for Scotland, 1950-63; Member Royal Company of Archers (Queen's Body Guard for Scotland); *b.* 29 Sept. 1906; *s.* of late Rev. Canon Hon. Charles Augustus Sinclair (*s.* of 16th Earl); *S.* uncle, 1947; *m.* 1st, 1933, Grizel Margaret (*d.* 1943), *d.* of Sir George Miller-Cunningham of Leithenhopes, K.B.E., C.B.; three *d.*; 2nd, 1946, Madeleine Gabrielle, *d.* of Herman Edward de Pury and *widow* of Capt. G. W. D. Ormerod, R.A.; one *s.* one *d.* *Educ.:* Marlborough; R.M.C Sandhurst. 2nd Lt. Gordon Highlanders, 1926; D.A.M.S. War Office, 1939-40; G.S.O. 3 and G.S.O. 2, 15 Scottish Div., 1940; Bde. Major, 46 Inf. Bde., 1940-42; Bde. Major 73 Ind. Inf. Bde., 1942-43; G.S.O. 1, H.Q. Southern Army, India, 1943: Comdg. 2 Bn. Gordon Highlanders, 1944; Comdg. 153 Bde., 51 (Highland) Div., 1944; Comdg. 6 Highland Bde., 2 Inf. Div., 1947; Brigadier Adviser, British Services Mission, Burma, 1948; Commander, Ceylon Army, 1949-52. Comdg. 51 Infantry Brigade, 1952-55; Deputy Commander Highland District, 1955; J.P. Aberdeenshire, 1956; D.L. Aberdeenshire, 1963. *Recreations:* shooting, fishing. *Heir:* *s.* Lord Berridale. *Address:* Baile-na-Coille, Balmoral, Aberdeenshire. *Club:* United Hunts. [*Died* 8 *May* 1965.

CALDER, George, C.B. 1947; *b.* 9 Nov. 1894; *e. s.* of late George Calder and Catherine Calder. *Educ.:* Edinburgh University (M.A., B.Sc.). Asst. Principal, Air Ministry, 1919; Private Secretary to successive Parliamentary Under Secretaries of State, 1927-33; Principal, 1933; Asst. Secretary, 1937; Ministry of Aircraft Production 1940; Principal Asst. Secretary, 1941; Board of Trade, Under Secretary, 1946; Directing Staff, Imperial Defence College, 1948; Second Secretary, Board of Trade, 1949-52; United Kingdom Commissioner, British Phosphate Commissioners, 1952-64. Member, Eastern Gas Board, 1953-64. *Recreations:* golf and curling. *Address:* 132 Swan Court, Chelsea, S.W.3. *T.:* Flaxman 1697. *Club:* Caledonian. [*Died* 9 *Oct.* 1968.

CALDER, Colonel (Hon.) James, C.M.G. 1948; retired; *b.* 1898; *s.* of James Calder, Glasgow, Scotland and Nelson, New Zealand; *m.* 1921, Emma Elvira Jacqueline de Weerdt, Mechelen, Belgium. *Educ.:* Glasgow University. M.A. 1921. Served European War, 1914-18, Belgium, France and Germany; Argyll and Sutherland Highlanders, 1917; Oxford and Bucks. Light Inf., 1918; D.L.I., 1918-19. Joined M.C.S., 1921; served in various posts including: Resident, Labuan, 1923-25; Magistrate, Seremban and Kuala Lumpur, 1935-36; Judge Supreme Court and Legal Adviser, Trengganu, 1938-39; Deputy Malayan Govt. Agent, Australia, 1942-44. Served War of 1939-45, as Col., Gen. List in India and Malaya (British Mil. Admin.), 1945-46; Chief Secretary to Government, North Borneo, 1946-53. Actg. Governor, North Borneo, periods 1946-52. Deputy Dominion Chief Comr., N.Z. Boy Scouts, 1958. *Address:* 27 Scotia St., Nelson, N.Z. [*Died* 24 *Jan.* 1968.

CALDER, Sir James Charles, Kt., *cr.* 1921; C.B.E. 1920; D.L., J.P., Kinross-shire; *b.* Alloa, Dec. 1869; *yr. s.* of James Calder of Ardargie, Forgandenny, Perthshire; *m.* 1904, Mildred Louise (*d.* 1938), *d.* of Col. Richard Manners, Royal Scots; no *c.* *Educ.:* St. Benedict's, Fort Augustus. Chairman, Calders Ltd., Edinburgh and London, timber merchants; ex-Dir. of Wilson's Brewery Ltd.; Deputy Timber Controller, Timber Supply Department, Board of Trade, 1917-19; Controller, 1919-1920; Director of Home Timber Production, 1940-41. Landowner at Ledlanet, Kinross, and Perthshire. *Recreations:* shooting, fishing. *Address:* Kinross, Ledlanet, Milnathort, Kinross-shire. [*Died* 22 *Aug.* 1962.

CALDWELL, Robert Nixon, C.M.G. 1947; M.C. 1916; retd.; *b.* 16 Aug. 1888; 3rd *s.* of Charles William Caldwell, Suva, Fiji; *m.* 1920, Leila Hope Duncan; one *s.* two *d.*

Educ.: Suva and Melbourne Grammar Schools; Marist Brothers, Suva. Immigration Dept., Fiji Govt., 1906; Secretariat, 1908; served European War, 1914-18, Samoa, Gallipoli, Mesopotamia, Belgium, France and Balkans; Major 4th South Wales Borderers (despatches twice, M.C.). Clerk to Legislative and Executive Councils, Fiji Govt., 1921; District Commissioner and Stipendiary Magistrate, 1923; Senior District Commissioner and Provincial Commissioner, 1940; Member Legislative and Executive Councils, 1946; formerly Deputy Secretary for Fijian Affairs, Fiji; retired 1953. Director W. R. Carpenter & Co. and Subsidiary Companies. Trustee, Coubrough and Mua Estates. *Address:* Suva, Fiji. *Club:* Fiji. [*Died* 4 *Jan.* 1967.

CALEDON, 5th Earl of, *cr.* 1800; **Erik James Desmond Alexander;** Baron Caledon, 1789; Viscount Caledon, 1797; Major late 1st Life Guards; *b.* 9 Aug. 1885; *e. s.* of 4th Earl and Lady Elizabeth Graham Toler (*d.* 1939), *d.* of 3rd Earl of Norbury; *S.* father, 1898. Lieut. 1st Life Guards; served European War, 1914-18 (wounded). Owns about 30,000 acres. *Heir: nephew* Major Denis James Alexander [*b.* 10 Nov. 1920; *m.* 1st, 1943, Ghislaine Dresselhuys (marr. diss., 1949); one *d.*; 2nd, 1952, Baroness Anne de Graevenitz (*d.* 1963); one *s.* one *d.*; 3rd, 1964, Marie Elisabeth Erskine (*née* Allen)]. *Address:* Castle Caledon, Tyrone, N. Ireland; Tyttenhanger Park, St. Albans. [*Died* 10 *July* 1968.

CALLAGHAN, Major-General Cecil Arthur, C.B. 1946; C.M.G. 1919; D.S.O. 1915; V.D.; *b.* 31 July 1890; unmarried. *Educ.:* Sydney Grammar School. Served European War, 1915-19 in Gallipoli, France, and Belgium (despatches five times, D.S.O., C.M.G., Bt. Major, Legion of Honour, 1914-15 Star, two medals); commanded 3rd Australian Field Artillery Brigade, 1920-21; 7th A.F.A. Brigade, 1921-26; Royal Artillery, 2nd Division, 1926-32; Commander 8th Infantry Brigade, Australia, 1934-39; served Malaya, 1942 (prisoner, C.B.). *Address:* Bushlands Avenue, Gordon, N.S.W., Australia. *Club:* Imperial Service (Sydney). [*Died* 1 *Jan.* 1967.

CALLANDER, Major William Henry Burn, M.B.E. 1945; D.L.; J.P.; *b.* 1890; *s.* of late Henry Burn Callander, D.L., J.P., Preston Hall, Ford, Midlothian; *m.* 1916, Christian (*d.* 1957), *d.* of late William Henry Garforth, J.P., Malton, Yorks, and late Hon. Hylda Maria Madeline, M.B.E., 3rd *d.* of 8th Baron Middleton; two *s.* (and one *s.* killed on active service, 1944). *Educ.:* Harrow; R.M.C. Sandhurst. Joined Roy. Scots Greys, 1910; served European War, 1914-18 (despatches twice, Bt.-Maj.); on staff. 1916-19; Adj. Cavalry Sch., and Cavalry Depot, 1919-26; retd. 1927. Served War of 1939-45, on staff (M.B.E.). Mem. Roy. Co. of Archers, Queen's Body Guard for Scotland. D.L. 1931, J.P. 1938, Vice-Lieutenant, 1957-65, Midlothian. Officier de la Légion d'Honneur. *Address:* Preston Hall, Ford, Midlothian. *Clubs:* Cavalry; New (Edinburgh). [*Died* 23 *Jan.* 1967.

CALVER, Sir Robert Henry Sherwood, Kt. 1953; Q.C. (Scot.) 1945; Sheriff of Lanarkshire since October 1952. *Address:* County Buildings, Glasgow. [*Died* 3 *July* 1963.

CALVERT, Hubert, C.S.I. 1933; C.I.E. 1925; B.Sc.; *b.* 1875; *s.* of late J. M. Calvert; *m.* 1902, Oclanis, *d.* of late Edward O'Brien, I.C.S.; four *s.* two *d.* *Educ.:* Univ. Coll., London; King's Coll., Camb. Entered I.C.S. 1897; Assist. Commissioner and Deputy Commissioner, Punjab; Special duty in Western Thibet, 1906; Registrar, Co-operative Societies, 1916-26; Member Legislative Assembly, 1923-26; Commissioner Rawalpindi, 1926; Financial Commissioner, Development, Punjab, 1929-33; retired 1933; Member Royal Commission on Agriculture, 1926-28; Chairman Committee on Co-operation in Burma, 1928-29; Finance Member, Punjab 1932; Registrar, Co-operative Societies, Ceylon, 1935-36. *Publications:* Law and Principles of Co-operation; Wealth and Welfare of the Punjab; articles relating to Co-operation and rural economics. *Address:* c/o National Provincial Bank, Exeter. [*Died* 9 *May* 1961.

CAM, Helen Maud, C.B.E. 1957; M.A. London; M.A., Litt.D. Cambridge; F.R.Hist.S.; F.B.A. 1945; Mediaeval Historian; Fellow Amer. Acad. of Arts and Sciences; Corr. Fellow of the Mediaeval Academy of America; *b.* 22 Aug. 1885; *d.* of Rev. William Herbert Cam, Head Master of Abingdon Grammar School, and Kate, *d.* of George Erving Scott. *Educ.:* home; Royal Holloway College, University of London (Scholar). D.Litt. (Hon.) Oxford; M.A. (Hon.) Harvard University; LL.D. (Hon.); Smith Coll.; Women's Coll., Univ. of North Carolina; Mount Holyoke Coll., Mass.: Fellow in History Bryn Mawr Coll., Pennsylvania, 1908-09; London M.A., 1909; Asst. Mistress in History, Ladies' Coll., Cheltenham, 1909-12; Asst. Lectr. in History, 1912-17, Staff Lectr. in History, 1919-21, Royal Holloway Coll.; Pfeiffer Research Fellow, Girton College, 1921-1926; Lectr. in History, Girton College, 1926-1948; Lectr. in History, Univ. of Cambridge, 1930-48; Zemurray Radcliffe Professor in History, Harvard University, 1948-54. Vice-Pres. Selden Society, 1962. Hon. Vice-Pres., Royal Historical Society, 1963-. Hon. Fell., Somerville Coll., Oxford, 1964-. *Publications:* Local Government in France and England, 1912; Studies in the Hundred Rolls, 1921; The Hundred and the Hundred Rolls, 1930; Liberties and Communities in Medieval England, 1944; England before Elizabeth, 1950; (Ed.) Crown, Community and Parliament in the Later Middle Ages by Gaillard T. Lapsley, 1951; (Ed.) Selected Historical Essays of F. W. Maitland, 1957; What of the Middle Ages is Alive in England today, 1961; Law-Finders and Law-Makers in Medieval England, 1962; Magna Carta (lecture to the Selden Soc.), 1965; articles in English Hist. Rev., History, Speculum, etc.; Borough of Northampton in Victoria County History, 1930; City of Cambridge in Victoria County History, 1959. *Recreations:* water-colour sketching, travelling. *Address:* Mochras, Grassy Lane, Sevenoaks, Kent. *T.:* Sevenoaks 54957; Girton College, Cambridge. [*Died* 9 *Feb.* 1968.

CAMBON, Roger, (Hon.) K.C.V.O. 1939 (C.V.O. 1927); Commander of the Legion of Honour; *b.* 24 August 1881; *s.* of late Jules Cambon, late French Ambassador in Berlin, and nephew of Paul Cambon, G.C.B., G.C.V.O., French Ambassador in London, 1898-1920; *m.* 1953, Mme. Sabline (*d.* 1966), *widow* of M. Eugène Sabline, late Counsellor of Russian Imperial Embassy, London. *Educ.:* École de Droit; École des Sciences Politiques and École des Langues Orientales, Paris. Entered French Diplomatic Service, 1905; Third Secretary, Lisbon, 1907; Constantinople, 1910; Second Secretary, London, 1913; a Minister Plenipotentiary and Counsellor to French Embassy, 1924-40. *Address:* 16 Thurloe Square, S.W.7. *T.:* 01-589 3523. *Club:* Travellers'. [*Died* 18 *July* 1970.

CAMERON, Archibald; Regius Professor of Greek in the University of Aberdeen since 1931; Member of North-Eastern Regional Hospital Board, 1952-64; Chairman, National Staff Advisory Cttee., Scottish Hospital Service, since 1960; Chairman, Board of Management, Aberdeen General Hospitals, since 1962; *b.* 4 January 1902;

s. of late Donald Cameron, Kirkintilloch, Dunbartonshire; *m.* 1935, Doreen Graham, *o. d.* of late John Mackintosh, I.S.O., Prison Commission for Scotland. *Educ.:* Glasgow Univ.; Sorbonne; Balliol College, Oxford. First Class Honours in Classics, Glasgow University, 1921; Diplôme d'Études Supérieures, Sorbonne, 1922; Ferguson Scholar; Snell Exhibitioner, Balliol College, Oxford; First Class Literae Humaniores, 1924; Assistant in Humanity, Aberdeen University, 1924-27; Lecturer in Humanity, Edinburgh University, 1927-31; Chm. Aberdeen Provincial Cttee. for the Training of Teachers, 1950-55. *Publication:* Monumenta Asiae Minoris Antiqua V (with Sir C. W. M. Cox). *Recreations:* fishing, gardening. *Address:* Greek Dept., King's College, Aberdeen; 16 The Chanonry, Aberdeen. *T.:* Aberdeen 43487. [*Died* 22 *May* 1964.

CAMERON, Charles, C.B.E. 1952; Professor, retired; *b.* 2 Jan. 1886; *m.* 1918, Agnes Wilson Wotherspoon; one *s.* *Educ.:* University of Glasgow. M.A. 1907; D.P.H. 1913; M.D. (Glas.), 1921; F.R.F.P.S.(G.), 1921; F.R.C.P.E., 1947; F.R.C.P. (Glas.), 1964. Lately Professor of Tuberculosis, University of Edinburgh. *Publications:* many articles on tuberculosis and allied conditions in professional journals. *Address:* 566 Upper Queen Street, London, Ontario, Canada. [*Died* 17 *July* 1968.

CAMERON, Sir Donald (Charles), Kt., *cr.* 1948; J.P.; Mayor of City of Dunedin, N.Z.; *b.* Dunedin, 12 May 1877; *s.* of D. C. Cameron, Dunedin; *m.* 1905, Frances Ellen Raines, Invercargill; three *s.* one *d.* *Educ.:* N.E. Valley and Normal Schools, Dunedin. Entered firm of Reid & Gray Ltd., Farm Implement Makers in 1891 as office boy, and retired in 1937, being then Chairman of Directors. Mayor of St. Kilda borough, 1910; City Councillor, 1931; Mayor of the City, 1944. Member Otago Education Board for 20 years; has always taken keen interest in Methodist Church; Vice-Pres. Church in N.Z., 1925. Chm. Armed Forces Appeal Board, Dunedin, War of 1939-45. Ex-Member Dominion Bowling Council and Pres. Dunedin Bowling Centre; Vice-Pres. S. Island Local Bodies Assoc.; Mayor of Dunedin, Centennial Year, 1948. Freedom of City of Edinburgh, 1949. *Recreations:* principally bowling. *Address:* 60 High St., St. Kilda, Dunedin, N.Z. *T.A.:* St. Kilda. *T.:* 22-315. [*Died Oct.* 1962.

CAMERON, Lieut.-Colonel Sir Donald Charles, K.C.M.G., *cr.* 1932 (C.M.G. 1919); D.S.O. 1917; V.D.; *b.* Brisbane, 19 Nov. 1879; *s.* of John Cameron, Longreach, Queensland; *m.* 1914, Evelyn Stella, *d.* of late Alexander Jardine, Brisbane. Served S. Africa, 1900-2 (despatches, Queen's medal with two clasps); European War, 1915-19 (despatches thrice, D.S.O., Order of the Nile); an Australian Delegate, League of Nations Assembly, Geneva, 1923 and 1932; Member House of Representatives, Commonwealth of Australia, 1919-31 and 1934-37. *Address:* 4 Rosemont Avenue, Woollahra, N.S.W. *Clubs:* Queensland (Brisbane); Union (Sydney). [*Died* 18 *Nov.* 1960.

CAMERON, Hon. Sir Ewen (Paul), Kt. 1961; M.L.C., East Yarra, Victoria, Australia, since 1948 (Chairman of Cttees., since 1961); State Minister of Health, 1955-61; *b.* 15 January 1892; *m.* 1920, Flora White; one *d.* Served European War, 1914-18, commissioned in 4 Light Horse, Australian Imperial Forces, 1915-19. Fellow, Commonwealth Institute of Valuers. *Address:* 10 Orrong Crescent, Camberwell, Victoria, Australia. [*Died* 18 *Jan.* 1964.

CAMERON, Sir James (Davidson Stuart), Kt. 1965; C.B.E. 1946; T.D. 1952; M.D., F.R.C.P. Edin. and Lond.; F.R.S.E.; *b.* 28 Dec. 1900; *e. s.* of Joseph Calder Cameron and Mary Fotheringham Davidson Cameron; *m.* 1929, Ester Johanne Frederickson Dover; no *c.* *Educ.:* Montrose Academy; Edinburgh University (M.D.; Gold Medal). Lectr., Dept. of Physiol., Edinburgh Univ., 1926-39. Cons. Phys., Roy. Inf., Edin., 1933-65, Hon. Cons. Phys., 1965-; also Borders Gp. of Hosps. Med. Specialist and Officer i/c Div., 1939-42; Brig. Cons. Phys., India Command, 1942-45; Hon. Cons., India and Burma Offices, 1946. Adviser, Post Grad. Medicine, Govt. of E. Pakistan, also Dir. and Prof., Inst. of Post Grad. Medicine, Dacca, E. Pakistan, 1965-1968. Examiner in Medicine: Univs. of Edinburgh, Aberdeen, Bombay, Dacca, Baghdad. R.C.P. Edin.; R.C.P. Lond.; R.C.S. Edin.; C.P.S. (Pak.). Pres., R.C.P. Edin., 1960-63; Verona Gow Fellow, 1963, and Cullen Prize, 1967, R.C.P. Edin. Hume Halliburton Lectr., Newcastle upon Tyne, 1963; Gwladys and Olwen Williams Lectr., Liverpool, 1963; Sir A. L. Mudaliar Foundn. Lectr., Madras, 1964. Hon. F.R.C.P.S. (Glas.) 1963; Hon. F.R.C.S. Edin. 1967. *Publications:* medical contrib. to Quarterly Jl. of Medicine, Lancet, Amer. Heart Jl., Edin. Med. Jl., etc. *Recreations:* golf, curling. *Address:* 91 Colinton Road, Edinburgh 10. *T.:* 031-337 3432. *Club:* Royal Commonwealth Society. [*Died* 13 *Feb.* 1969.

CAMERON, Sir John, 2nd Bt., *cr.* 1893; Barrister-at-law, Gray's Inn, 1926; Chairman, Holloway Sanatorium, Virginia Water; Chairman of Council, Roy. Holloway Coll., Univ. of London; *b.* 26 Nov. 1903; *s.* of 1st Bt. and late Blanche, *d.* of Arthur Perman; *S.* father, 1924. *Educ.:* Charterhouse; Christ's College, Cambridge. B.A., LL.B. 1924, M.A. 1946; Temp. Press Officer in Foreign Office News Dept. 1939-46; Metropolitan Stipendiary Magistrate since July 1954, South Western Magistrates' Court. *Heir:* none. *Address:* Halfacre House, Northcroft Road, Englefield Green, Surrey. *T.:* Egham 2525. *Club:* Reform. [*Died* 4 *Oct.* 1968 (*ext.*).

CAMERON, John Gordon Patrick, C.I.E. 1918; retired; *b.* 31 Jan. 1885; *s.* of late Donald Charles Cameron, Skye; *m.* 1918, Agnes Lucie (*d.* 1961), *d.* of late Edward Brown. *Educ.:* Dover Coll.; Royal Indian Engineering Coll., Coopers Hill. Telegraph Dept., Govt. of India, 1906-33; served European War, Mesopotamia, 1915-19 (C.I.E.); War 1939-45, with Signal Service of Admiralty. *Address:* 28 Albany Park Road, Kingston, Surrey. *T.:* 01-546 7681. *Clubs:* East India and Sports; Richmond (Richmond). [*Died* 16 *July* 1970.

CAMERON, Sir Roy, Kt. 1957; F.R.S. 1946; F.R.C.P.; Hon. Consulting Pathologist to University Coll. Hospital, London, since 1964; Emeritus Professor of Morbid Anatomy, University of London, since 1964; *b.* Vict., Australia, 30 June 1899; *s.* of late Rev. G. Cameron, Melbourne, Australia. *Educ.:* Kyneton High School, Vict., Australia; Univ. of Melbourne and Univ. of Freiburg i. Br., Germany. Scholar and Tutor, Queen's Coll., Univ. of Melbourne, 1916-28; Asst. Director, Walter and Eliza Hall Institute of Research, Melbourne, 1926-28; Reader in Morbid Anatomy, Univ. Coll. Hosp. Med. School, 1935-37, Prof., 1937-64. Assistant Editor, Journal of Pathology and Bacteriology, 1935-55. Member: Agricultural Research Council, 1948-56; Medical Research Council, 1952-56; Advisory Council, Beit Memorial Fellowship for Medical Research (Sec., 1959-64); Council, Imperial Cancer Research Fund 1948-. Foundation President, College of Pathologists, 1962-. Hon. LL.D.: Edin. 1956; Melb. 1962-. Hon. Fell., Univ. Coll., London, 1965. Royal Medal, Royal Society, 1960. *Pub-*

lications: Pathology of the Cell, 1952; Chemistry of the Injured Cell, 1961; Biliary Cirrhosis, 1962; numerous papers in Journal of Pathology and Bacteriology. *Recreations:* walking, interested in painting and music. *Address:* 56 Camlet Way, Hadley Wood, Barnet, Herts. *Club:* Athenæum. [*Died* 7 *Oct.* 1966.

CAMM, Sir Sydney, Kt. 1953; C.B.E. 1941; F.R.Ae.S.; Director, Hawker Siddeley Group Limited; Director of Design, Hawker Siddeley Aviation Ltd.; *b.* 1893. Joined Hawker Engineering Co. Ltd., 1923; made Chief Designer, 1925; Director, 1935; Chief Engineer, 1959; among aeroplanes produced are: Hart, Fury, Osprey and Nimrod, Henley, Hurricane, Typhoon, Tempest, Sea Fury, Sea Hawk, Hunter, P.1127 and P.1154 V.T.O. aircraft. Hon. Fellow and Member of Council of Royal Aeronautical Society (Vice-President 1950, 1951, Pres. 1954); Chm. of Technical Board, Society of British Aircraft Constructors, 1951-53. British Gold Medal for Aeronautics, 1949; Royal Aeronautical Society's Gold Medal, 1958. *Address:* Hawker Siddeley Aviation Ltd., Richmond Road, Kingston-on-Thames, Surrey. *T.:* Kingston 7741; Carradale, Embercourt Road, Thames Ditton, Surrey. *T.:* Emberbrook 1084. *Club:* Royal Aero. [*Died* 12 *March* 1966.

CAMOYS, 5th Baron, *cr.* 1264; **Ralph Francis Julian Stonor;** *b.* 28 Jan. 1884; *e. s.* of 4th Baron and Jessie Phillippa, 2nd *d.* of late Robert Russell Carew, Carpenders Park, Watford; *S.* father, 1897; *m.* 1911, Mildred (*d.* 1961), *d.* of late W. Watts Sherman, Rhode Island, U.S.A.; one *s.* two *d.* *Educ.:* The Oratory, Edgbaston; Balliol College, Oxford, Late Captain Oxfordshire Yeomanry, Lieut. Oxf. Yeo. attached R.A.F.; Captain Bucks Home Guard. *Heir:* *s.* Major Hon. (Ralph Robert Watts) Sherman Stonor. *Address:* Bellevue Avenue, Newport, R.I., U.S.A. *Club:* Knickerbocker (N.Y.). [*Died* 3 *Aug.* 1968.

CAMP, Harold Robert, C.B. 1951; retired from Civil Service; *b.* 21 Sept. 1893; *s.* of late John Patey Camp, Babbacombe, Devon; *m.* 1926, Mildred Doris, *d.* of late Walter Boon, Enfield, Middlesex; one *s.* *Educ.:* Wandsworth Technical Coll. Served European War, 1914-18, with R.A.M.C., France. G.P.O. 1911; Air Ministry, 1920; Ministry of Aircraft Production, 1940; Ministry of Supply, 1945; Under-Sec., Min. of Supply, 1947-53, retired. O.St.J. *Address:* Selden Lodge, Patching, Worthing, Sussex. *T.:* Patching 217. [*Died* 21 *Apr.* 1968.

CAMP, Instructor Captain J., C.B. 1931; R.N., retired; *b.* 15 March 1877; *s.* of late William Camp, Highgate; *m.* 1919, Léonie May, *d.* of late John May, Highgate; two *s.* two *d.* *Educ.:* Owen's School Islington; Peterhouse, Cambridge. Entered Royal Navy, 1898; served in various ships afloat till 1909; Head of Navigation Department, R.N. College, Dartmouth, 1909-14 and 1915-21; in H.M.S. Erin, Grand Fleet, 1914-15; in R.N. Training Establishment, Shotley, during 1922; Deputy Superintendent of Naval Examinations Admiralty, 1923-33; retired list, 1932; qualified as interpreter in French, 1902. *Address:* 115 Bridge Lane, Golders Green, N.W.11. *T.:* Speedwell 3976. [*Died* 17 *Feb.* 1962.

CAMPBELL, Mrs. Alan; *see* Parker, Dorothy.

CAMPBELL, Sir Alexander, Kt., *cr.* 1944; M.C.; E.D.; M.A.; Lt.-Col. I.E.S. (retired); *b.* 29 Jan. 1892; *s.* of late Hugh Ross Campbell and late Margaret Nightingale Campbell, Perth, Scotland; *m.* 1923, Mary Downie, *d.* of late Alexander and Margaret Boyd, Ayr, Scotland; one *s.* one *d.* *Educ.:* Perth Academy; Edinburgh Univ. M.A. (Hons.). Served in Burma in I.E.S., 1915-46; in incorp. and devel. of Rangoon Univ. Chm. Educ. Reform Cttee. (Campbell Report), Dir. of Public Instr. and Comr. of Exams, 1933, 1936, 1939-46; after re-occup. of Burma, re-established Rangoon Univ. and reformed Educ. System; Official M.L.C. Burma, 1939; Regtr. U. Coll. S.W. Eng., 1947-52; Principal of Staff College, The Chartered Bank, 1952-59. Military Service, 1915-19; German E. Africa (M.C.); O.C. 6th Burma Bn., T.F., 1924-33; War of 1939-45, Lt.-Col. Burma Auxiliary Force (E.D.); Burma Campaign, 1941-42 (despatches), attached R.A.F., subsq. directing Red Cross and Welfare Services; S.E.A.C., Civil Affairs Service (Burma), 1943-45; O.C. Advance Party, H.Q. Brit. Mil. Govt. Burma, Rangoon, 1945. *Address:* 5 Trundle Mead, Horsham. [*Died* 19 *July* 1963.

CAMPBELL, Alexander; Ex-Director Daily Mirror; Ex-Chm. Council Newspaper Press Fund; Fellow of Institute of Journalists; *b.* Halifax; *m.* Maud, *d.* of Arthur Smith; one *s.* *Educ.:* Ilkley Grammar School, etc. Assistant Editor, Leeds Mercury; Acting Editor, Daily Record, Glasgow; Director Sunday Pictorial for ten years; Assistant Editor, Sunday Pictorial; Editor Daily Mirror nearly eleven years; Special Correspondent home and abroad; writer on industrial, political, and social problems, etc.; Vice-President Victoria Hospital for Children; Life Governor Children's Hospital, Great Ormond Street; of the Royal Free Hospital and the East London Hospital for Children; etc.; Hon. Treasurer, Institute of Journalists, 1929-31. *Address:* 29 Burdon Lane, Cheam, Surrey. *Clubs:* Royal Automobile; Birdham Yacht. [*Died* 10 *Sept.* 1961.

CAMPBELL, Hon. Angus Dudley, C.B.E. 1939; J.P. 1942; Director: The Manchester Ship Canal; Martin's Bank; London Assurance; Sea Insurance; Haighton & Dewhurst Ltd.; Geo. & R. Dewhurst Ltd. (Chairman); *b.* 8 October 1895; *y. s.* of 1st Baron Colgrain; *m.* 1926, Joan Esther Sybella, J.P. Nantwich, 1949, *e. d.* of Col. Arthur Pakenham, C.M.G., Langford Lodge, Crumlin, Co. Antrim; three *d.* *Educ.:* Eton. Joined 2nd/1st Surrey Yeomanry 1914; 9th Lancers, 1916-20. Member: Lancs. Mission to India, 1933 (Chm., 1936, 1938 and 1955); Pres. Manchester Chamber of Commerce, 1940-41; U.K. Industrial Mission to Pakistan, 1950; Chm. U.K. Cotton Industries Mission to E. Africa, 1953. *Address:* Doddington Cottage, Nantwich, Cheshire. *T.:* Wybunbury 258; 60 Park Mansions, Knightsbridge, S.W.1. *Club:* Cavalry. [*Died* 5 *Dec.* 1967.

CAMPBELL, Archibald; retired Judge of the High Court of Lahore; *b.* 18 Jan. 1877; *y.* and *o. surv. s.* of late John Campbell of Kilberry; *m.* 1905, Violet (*d.* 1949), *y. d.* of Sir Cecil Beadon, K.C.S.I., Lieut.-Governor of Bengal; two *s.* one *d.* *Educ.:* Harrow; Pembroke College, Cambridge, M.A. Passed into Indian Civil Service, 1900; Assistant Commissioner, Punjab, 1901; Additional Judge High Court, 1921-25; Puisne Judge, 1925-28; retired, 1928; lecturer in Indian Law to Bd. of Indian Civil Service Studies, Cambridge Univ., 1929-41. *Address:* 1D The Mansions, Earl's Court Road, S.W.5. *Club:* Caledonian. [*Died* 24 *April* 1963.

CAMPBELL, Hon. Sir Charles (Rudolph), Kt. 1961; C.B.E. 1946; J.P.; P.C. (Jamaica), 1952-59 and 1962, as Senior Member of Privy Council of Jamaica; Director and Deputy Chairman, R. Hanna & Sons Ltd. and Associate Companies, since 1946; *b.* 11 Aug. 1885; *s.* of Robert Clark Campbell and Susan Emily, *d.* of Robert Hall; *m.* 1916, Lilian Gertrude, *d.* of Wm. Nash; three *d.* *Educ.:* private sch.; Mandeville

Middle Grade Sch. Clerk, Revenue Dept., 1906; Asst. Collec. of Taxes, 1920; Collector, 1934; Dep. Stamp Comr., 1938; Dep. Comr., Income Tax and Stamp Duties, 1940; Comr., 1943. Mem. Management Cttee. of Univ. Coll. of the W.I., 1948; Chm., Bd. of Management, Univ. Coll. of the W.I. Hosp., 1953-59; Chm. Wolmer's Trust (Schs.), 1953. Chm. Federal Public Service Commn., 1957-1959; Chm. Public Service Commn., Jamaica 1952-62. Hon. LL.D., Univ. of West Indies, 1967. *Recreations:* reading, photography, motoring, swimming (formerly also tennis, hiking). *Address:* (office) P.O. Box 235, Kingston, Jamaica. *T.:* 24031, 23624.
[*Died* 26 *June* 1969.

CAMPBELL, Rt. Hon. Sir David (Callender), P.C. 1963; K.B.E. 1950; Kt. 1945; C.M.G. 1944; M.P. (U.U.) South Belfast, since 1952; *b.* 29 Jan. 1891; *s.* of late William Howard Campbell and late Elizabeth Nevin Boyd; *m.* 1919, Ragnhild Gregersen. *Educ.:* Foyle College, Derry; Edinburgh University. Provincial Administration, Tanganyika, 1919; Assistant Chief Secretary, 1933; Deputy Chief Secretary, Uganda, 1936; Colonial Secretary, Gibraltar, 1942; Acting Lieut.-Governor, Malta, 1942; Lieut.-Governor of Malta, 1943-52. Officer Administering Government, Malta, March-July 1946, June-Sept. 1949 and June-Sept. 1951. Hon. LL.D. Queen's University, Belfast, 1961. *Recreations:* fishing, golf. *Address:* 19 Adelaide Park, Belfast.
[*Died* 12 *June* 1963.

CAMPBELL, Most Rev. Donald Alphonsus, Ph.D., D.D.; Archbishop of Glasgow (R.C.), since 1945; *b.* 1894; *s.* of Donald Campbell and Mary Mackintosh. *Educ.:* Blairs College, Aberdeen; Scots College, Rome. Ph.D., D.D. Gregorian Univ. R.C. Bishop of Argyll and the Isles, 1939-45. *Address:* Archbishop's House, 30 Langside Drive, Glasgow. [*Died* 22 *July* 1963.

CAMPBELL, Donald (Malcolm), C.B.E. 1957; Chairman, Norris Brothers, Ltd., consulting engineers, since 1954; Director: Stewart Smith & Co. (Home) Limited (Insurance Brokers at Lloyd's); *b.* March 1921; *o. s.* of late Major Sir Malcolm Campbell, M.B.E.; *m.* 1st, 1945, Daphne Margaret Harvey (marr. diss., 1952); one *d.*; 2nd, 1952, Dorothy, *d.* of Amos McKegg (marr. diss., 1957); 3rd, 1958, Antoinette Maria, *d.* of Antoine Joseph Beun. *Educ.:* Uppingham School. Enlisted Royal Air Force under training Pilot, 1939; invalided out, August 1940. With turbo-jet hydroplane Bluebird established world's unlimited water speed record of 202·32 m.p.h., Ullswater Lake, Cumberland, July 1955; raised the record on six successive occasions to 276·3 m.p.h. in Western Australia in 1964. With Proteus Bluebird established World Automobile Speed Record of 403·1 m.p.h. at Lake Eyre, South Australia in July 1964. *Publication:* Into The Water Barrier (with Alan Mitchell), 1955; *Relevant Publication:* Donald Campbell: An Informal Biography by Douglas Young-James, 1968. *Recreations:* golf, sailing, flying, photography. *Address:* Priors Ford, Leatherhead, Surrey. *T.:* Leatherhead 4747. *Clubs:* Royal Aero, Royal Automobile, British Sportsman's, Royal Motor Yacht.
[*Died* 4 *Jan.* 1967.

CAMPBELL, Captain Sir Eric Francis Dennistoun, 6th Bt. *cr.* 1831; Civil Service Dept. of Agriculture for Scotland, 1936-57; retired 1957; Hereditary Keeper of Barcaldine Castle; *b.* 17 Aug. 1892; *s.* of late Lt.-Col. F. J. B. Campbell, Indian Army and Ethel May, *d.* of late Surgeon General C. E. Raddock, Indian Medical Service; *S.* uncle, 1932; unmarried. *Educ.:* Wellington Coll.; Sandhurst. Served with the 1st Bn. S. Lancashire Regt., 1912-20. *Heir: cousin,* Ian Vincent Hamilton Campbell. *Address:* Faithfull House, Suffolk Square, Cheltenham, Glos.
[*Died* 11 *July* 1963.

CAMPBELL, George Archibald, Q.C. (Can.) 1912; Advocate; senior counsel legal firm of Laidley, Campbell, Walsh & Kisilenko, Montreal; *b.* Montreal, 26 Sept. 1875; *s.* of Rev. Robert Campbell, D.D., and Margaret Macdonnell; *m.* 1st, 1909, Amy G. (*d.* 1949), *d.* of Wm V. Dawson; one *s.*; 2nd, 1951, Phoebe M. B., *d.* of Charles A. Lewis. *Educ.:* Montreal High School, McGill Univ. Called to Bar of Lower Canada, 1901; K.C. 1912. Active practice in Montreal, 1902-. Hon. Treasurer Bar of Montreal, 1928-30; Batonnier of the Bar of Montreal, 1930-31; Batonnier-General of the Province of Quebec, 1930-31; Hon. Dir. The Royal Trust Company; Gov. Montreal General Hosp., Children's Memorial Hosp., Verdun Protestant Hosp. *Recreations:* golf, motoring. *Address:* 644 Argyle Avenue, Montreal 6. *T.A.:* Cammacco; Penzance, Hermitage Club, Lake Memphremagog, P.Q. *Clubs:* Mount Royal, University, Montreal (Montreal); Hermitage Country.
[*Died* 26 *June* 1964.

CAMPBELL, Sir George Ilay, 6th Bt. of Succoth, Dunbartonshire, *cr.* 1808; *b.* 20 Jan. 1894; *s.* of Sir Archibald S. L. Campbell, 5th Bt., and Harriet K. G. (*d.* 1940), *d.* of Col. Reynell-Pack, C.B.; *S.* father, 1941; *m.* 1926, Clematis (marriage dissolved by Court of Session, 1935), *e. d.* of late Walter Waring and late Lady Clementine Waring; one *s.* *Educ.:* Harrow; Christ Church, Oxford. Served European War of 1914-18 with Argyll and Sutherland Highlanders (Captain); Member, Queen's Bodyguard for Scotland, Royal Company of Archers; D.L. Argyll. J.P. Mem. Council, and Garden Cttee., Nat. Trust for Scotland; a Vice-President The Scottish Landowners' Federation. President Royal Scottish Forestry Society, 1937-41; war of 1939-45, Assistant Observer Group Officer, R.O.C., 1940-43. *Recreations:* forestry, gardening. *Heir: s.* Ilay Mark Campbell [*b.* 29 May 1927; *m.* 1961, Margaret Minette Rohais Anderson]. *Address:* Crarae Lodge, Inveraray, Argyll. *T.:* Minard 204. *Clubs:* Carlton; New (Edinburgh); Royal Highland Yacht (Oban).
[*Died* 1 *April* 1967.

CAMPBELL, Sir George Riddoch, K.C.I.E., *cr.* 1942; Kt., *cr.* 1936; C.I.Mar.E.; *b.* 4 April 1887; *s.* of George Campbell and Rose Young Henderson; *m.* 1915, Cynthia May Berry; two *s.* two *d.* (and one *s.*, Lieut. Scots Guards, *d.* of wounds, 1945). *Educ.:* Hamilton Acad. Joined Thos. Law & Co., Shipowners, Glasgow, 1903; came to India in 1909, to Mackinnon, Mackenzie & Co.; representative in India, Burma and Ceylon, of Ministry of War Transport, and Shipping Controller in India, 1939-41; Commercial Dir. of Sea Transport, Min. of War Transp., 1941-43; Regional Port Director, S.E. England, 1943-45. Mem., Council of State, New Delhi, 1935-36; Pres. Bengal Chamber of Commerce and Associated Chambers of Commerce of India, 1935-36 and 1938-1939; Leader, European Party, Bengal Legislative Assembly, 1937-39; Pres., Calcutta Burns Club, 1935-36; served in France with Q.O.R. Glasgow Yeomanry and Highland Light Infantry, 1916-18; N.W. Frontier India, 1918-19, with 31st D.C.O. Lancers, Captain. *Address:* Westcroft, Pyrford, Surrey. [*Died* 8 *July* 1965.

CAMPBELL, Sir Gerald, G.C.M.G. *cr.* 1942 (K.C.M.G., *cr.* 1934; C.M.G. 1923); F.R.G.S.; Hon. LL.D. Rutgers University, New Jersey, Queen's Univ., Kingston, Ont., McGill Univ., Montreal, Univ. of Toronto, New York Univ., Union Coll. Schenectady, Grove City College, Pennsylvania; Hon.

D.C.L. Univ. of Bishop's College, Lennoxville, P.Q.; Doctor of Humane Letters South Dakota School of Mines and Technology; *b.* 30 Oct. 1879; *s.* of Rev. Colin Campbell, Weston-super-Mare; *m.* 1911, Margaret C. (*d.* 1961), *d.* of Henry E. Juler, F.R.C.S., 23 Cavendish Square, W.1; three *d.* *Educ.:* Repton; Trinity College, Cambridge, B.A. Vice-Consul at Rio de Janeiro, 1907; Belgian Congo, 1908-13; Venice, 1913-15; Consul at Addis Ababa, 1915-19; Consul-General at Philadelphia, 1920-1921; San Francisco, 1922-31; New York, 1931-38; High Commissioner for the United Kingdom in Canada, 1938-41; Minister in Washington, 1941 and 1942-45; Director-General of British Information Services, New York, 1941-42; Officer of the Order of St. John of Jerusalem; Star of Ethiopia. Member Advisory Council of English-Speaking Union; Vice-President, Royal Commonwealth Society. *Publication:* Of True Experience (publ. in U.S.A.), 1947 (in London), 1949. *Recreations:* hockey, golf, tennis. *Club:* Travellers'.
[*Died* 4 *July* 1964.

CAMPBELL, H. Donald; lawyer and banker, U.S.A.; retired; Member Trust Advisory Board, Chase Manhattan Bank, New York, 1955-66; *b.* Danville, Illinois, 11 Jan. 1879; *s.* of Thomas Jefferson Campbell and Emma Luella English; *m.* 1919, Alice E. Calmus; no *c.* *Educ.:* Univ. of Minnesota, Minneapolis, Minn., A.B. 1902; University of Minnesota Law School, LL.B. 1904. Practised law with the firm of Brown and Kerr (Minneapolis), 1905-06; went to Seattle Washington as Business Manager, Independent Telephone Co., 1906-12; successively asst. sec., sec., vice-pres., and director Washington Mutual Savings Bank (Seattle), 1912-17; director, sec. and treas., later vice-pres. Mercantile Trust Co. (New York), 1917-22; vice-pres. and director Seaboard National Bank (New York), 1922-29; executive vice-pres. and trustee Equitable Trust Co. (New York), 1929-30; vice-pres. and director Chase National Bank (New York), 1930-34; pres., 1934-46; vice-chm., 1946-1947); Chairman Trust Committee, Board of Directors, The Chase National Bank, 1947-1955; Director of corporations; Trustee Stevens Institute of Technology (New Jersey), Leonard Wood Memorial for the eradication of Leprosy; Member Beta Theta Pi. *Address:* 435 East 52 St., New York; (Office) 1 Chase Manhattan Plaza, N.Y., U.S.A. *Clubs:* River, The Links, University, India House (New York); Wianno Golf (Mass.); Paradise Valley Country (Phœnix, Arizona).
[*Died* 3 *Feb.* 1969.

CAMPBELL, Captain Sir Harold George, G.C.V.O., *cr.* 1953 (K.C.V.O., *cr.* 1943; C.V.O. 1935); D.S.O. 1918; (retired) R.N.; *b.* 1888; *m.* 1912, Violet Albinia Lucy, *d.* of Canon John Otter Stephens. Served European War, 1914-18 (wounded, despatches, D.S.O.). Private Secretary to the Duke of York, 1933-36; Deputy Comptroller and Equerry, 1936; Extra Equerry to the Queen, 1954- (Groom of the Robes, Equerry to the Queen, 1952-54; to King George VI, 1937-52). *Address:* Strood House, Rolvenden, Kent.
[*Died* 9 *June* 1969.

CAMPBELL, Col. Hon. Ian (Malcolm), D.S.O. 1918; Lord Lieutenant of Nairnshire, 1949-58, retired; *b.* 17 Nov. 1883; 5th *s.* of 3rd Earl Cawdor; *m.* 1928, Marion Louisa, O.B.E. 1957, *d.* of late Major W. Stirling, Fairburn, Ross-shire, and *widow* of Capt. E. J. Brodie, Cameron Highlanders. *Educ.:* Eton; Trinity Coll., Cambridge (M.A.). Served European War, 1914-18 (D.S.O., despatches); Fellow and Bursar of Trinity Hall, Cambridge, 1919-28; Colonel (late Lovat Scouts); Commander 152nd (Seaforth and Cameron) Infantry Brigade, 1928-32. *Address:* Auchindoune, Cawdor, Nairn. *Club:* New (Edinburgh).
[*Died* 11 *March* 1962.

CAMPBELL, Maj.-Gen. James Alexander, D.S.O. 1916; *b.* 3 Dec. 1886; *s.* of James Campbell; *m.* 1920, Violet Constance Madeline Calthrop; one *s.* (and one killed, 1943, when a prisoner of war, escaping). *Educ.:* Brighton College; R.M.C., Sandhurst. 2nd Lt. Suffolk Regt. 1906; served in Malta, Egypt, Sudan; European War, 1914-18, with 1st Suffolk on Western Front and in Macedonia; Brigade-Major, Nov. 1916-Dec. 1917; commanded 9th East Lancashire Regt. 1918 (wounded twice, despatches thrice, D.S.O. and Bar, Bt. Major, Greek M.C.); Staff College, Quetta, 1920-21; Brigade-Major, India, 1922-24; D.A.A.G. Northern Command, 1924-26; G.S.O. 2 India, N. Ireland, R.M.C., Sandhurst, and War Office, 1927-34; Bt. Lt.-Col. 1932; commanded Northern Brigade, King's African Rifles and Local Forces, Kenya and Uganda, Dec. 1934-Oct. 1939; Bt.-Col. 1934; Subst. 1936; Brig. 1938; commanded Brigade of 15th (Scottish) Division, Dec. 1939-May 1941; 73rd Independent Brigade; South Highland Area, Dec. 1941; Lancashire and Border District, Dec. 1941-May 1944; retired, 1944. *Recreations:* hunting, polo, tennis. *Address:* The Old House, Benhall, Saxmundham, Suffolk. *Club:* Army and Navy.
[*Died* 3 *Feb.* 1964.

CAMPBELL, Sir James (Clark), Kt., *cr.* 1954; T.D. 1920; D.L.; Vice-President, Trustee Savings Bank Association; Governor Standard Life Assurance Co. since 1948; *b.* 26 December 1882; *s.* of late M. Pearce Campbell and Mary Helen Campbell, both of Glasgow; *m.* 1908, Jean (*d.* 1958), *d.* of James Lilburn, shipowner, Glasgow; three *d.* *Educ.:* Rugby. Was for 53 years with Campbells and Stewart & McDonald Ltd., Wholesale Textile Merchants, Glasgow; Chairman and Managing Director, retired 1957. Served 20 years with 5th Scottish Rifles; European War, France, 1914-15; War of 1939-45, comdg. 2nd Renfrewshire Bn. (Home Guard). D.L. for Renfrewshire, 1946. *Recreations:* yachting, shooting. *Address:* Glenlora, Lochwinnoch, Renfrewshire. *T.:* Lochwinnoch 313. *Clubs:* Junior Army and Navy; Western (Glas.); New (Edin.).
[*Died* 8 *March* 1964.

CAMPBELL, Rev. John McLeod, M.C.; D.D. (Lambeth); Master of Charterhouse since 1954; Chaplain to the Queen since 1952 (to King George VI, 1944-1952); Speaker's Chaplain since 1955; Hon. Canon of Canterbury since 1936. *Educ.:* Marlborough; Balliol College, Oxford. Late Fellow and Chaplain of Hertford College, Oxford, and formerly Senior Chaplain, Fourth Division, B.E.F.; Principal of Trinity College, Kandy, 1924-35; General Secretary, Overseas Council of Church Assembly, Church House, Westminster, S.W.1, 1935-53. Hon. D.D. Glasgow. *Publications:* Bridge-builders; Man-power in the 20th-Century Church; Christian History in the Making; Lambeth Calls; New Horizons; The Making of African History. *Address:* Charterhouse, E.C.1. *Club:* United University.
[*Died* 26 *Feb.* 1961.

CAMPBELL, John Ross, M.M. 1917; Editor Daily Worker, 1949-59; *b.* Paisley, 1894; *s.* of John Campbell and Mary Stevenson; *m.* 1920, Sarah Marie O'Donnell; two *d.* *Educ.:* Elementary School, Paisley. Joined British Socialist Party, 1912. Served European War, 1914-18. Ed. Glasgow Worker, 1921-24; Ed. Works Weekly, 1924-26; Member Executive Committee of Communist Party, 1923-64: Member of Executive Cttee. of Communist International, 1925-35; arrested and subsequently released, in Campbell case, 1924; served six months for seditious conspiracy, 1925-26. *Publication:* Soviet Policy and its Critics, 1939. *Recreations:* theatre, swimming and loafing. *Address:* c/o 16 King St., W.C.2.
[*Died* 18 *Sept.* 1969.

CAMPBELL of Strachur, Lt.-Col. Kenneth John, 23rd Chief of MacArthur Campbell's of Strachur (recognised by Lord Lyon King of Arms, 1950, and given authority to assume the feudal title as Representer of Baronial House of Campbell of Strachur in derivation from Sir Arthur Campbell 2nd of Strachur, 1296); *b.* 1878; *e. s.* of John Campbell of Strachur and Ardgartan (*d.* 1887), Argyllshire (Ardgartan sold, 1885, Strachur, 1899); *m.* 1915, Marie Sybil, *y. d.* of late Lawrence Dolan, St. Mary Cray; one *s.* *Educ.:* Pembroke College, Cambridge. Joined 42nd Royal Highlanders in India, 1901; served South Africa, 1901-2 (medal with four clasps); Captain, 1910; served European War as Adjutant 7th Argyll and Sutherland Highlanders, 1914-15 (General Service, Victory Medals, 1914-15 Star); commanded a Company of G.C.'s, R.M.C., Sandhurst, 1916-18; Major, 1916; commanded 11th Batt. Leicestershire Regt., British Army of the Rhine, 1919 (temp. Lieut.-Col.); Adjutant 5th Black Watch, 1920-22; Second-in-command, 2nd Black Watch, 1922-24; retired, 1924; Gold-Staff Officer, King George VI Coronation, 1937 (Medal). Recruiting Officer Hertfordshire, 1939-47. Defence Medal. *Recreations:* shooting, fishing, painting. *Address:* Old Ninnings, Bedmond, Herts. *T.:* Kings Langley 2747. *Club:* Army and Navy. [*Died* 23 *June* 1965.

CAMPBELL, His Honour Lawson; *see* Campbell, His Honour William L.

CAMPBELL, Sir Louis (Hamilton), 14th Bt. *cr.* 1628 (N.S.); *b.* 29 Sept. 1885; 4th *s.* of Sir Charles Ralph Campbell, 11th Bt. and Sara (*d.* 1927), *d.* of Hon. William Robinson, Cheviot Hills, N.Z.; *S.* brother, 1968; *m.* 1920, Margaret Elizabeth Patricia, *d.* of late Patrick Campbell; one *s.* (one *d.* decd.). *Educ.:* Eton; Oriel College, Oxford. Sheep Farmer, N. Canterbury, N.Z. R.N.V.R., Minesweepers, 1916-19; R.N.R., Minesweeping Office, 1939-44. *Recreations:* sailing, golf. *Heir:* *s.* Robin Auchinbreck Campbell [*b.* 7 June 1922; *m.* 1948, Rosemary (Sally), *d.* of Ashley Dean, Christchurch, N.Z.; one *s.* two *d.*]. *Address:* 15 Jacksons Road, Fendalton, Christchurch, N.Z. *Club:* Bembridge Sailing (Isle of Wight). [*Died* 13 *Oct.* 1970.

CAMPBELL, Sir Norman Dugald Ferrier, 13th Bt. *cr.* 1628; *b.* 1883; *s.* of Sir Charles Ralph Campbell, 11th Bt. and Sara, *d.* of Hon. William Robinson, of Cheviot Hills, N.Z.; *S.* brother, 1948. *Educ.:* Eton. *Heir:* *b.* Louis Hamilton Campbell [*b.* 1885; *m.* 1920, Margaret Elizabeth Patricia, *d.* of late Patrick Campbell; one *s.* one *d.*]. *Address:* Glen Dhu, Motunau, Canterbury, N.Z. [*Died* 20 *Jan.* 1968.

CAMPBELL, (Renton) Stuart; Editor of The People since 1958; Director, Odhams Press, since 1962 (Exec. Dir. 1959-62); *b.* 4 June 1908; *s.* of John and Florence Campbell, London; *m.* 1935, Joan Mary Algernon, Nottingham; one *d.* *Educ.:* London. After wide newspaper experience in the provinces joined the News Chronicle, Manchester, 1933; Daily Mirror, London, 1935; Assistant Editor Sunday Pictorial, 1937; Editor Sunday Pictorial, 1940-46; Managing Editor, The People, 1946-57. Member of Press Council, 1961-63. *Address:* 92 Long Acre, W.C.2. *T.:* Temple Bar 5400. *Club:* Greenfingers. [*Died* 1 *Feb.* 1966.

CAMPBELL, Maj.-Gen. Robin Hasluck, C.B. 1943; M.C.; *b.* 19 Sept. 1894; *s.* of Thomas Hinton Campbell; *m.* 1919, Thyrza Virginia, *d.* of Edward Banning Weston of Dayton, Ohio; one *d.* *Educ.:* Radley College. Joined Royal Marines, 1912; served European War, 1914-19. Major-Gen. 1944; retired, 1946. *Address:* Newton of Doune, Perthshire. *T.:* Doune 262. *Club:* M.C.C. [*Died* 16 *July* 1964.

CAMPBELL, Colonel Ronald Bruce, C.B.E. 1923; D.S.O. 1917; M.A. (Edin.); *b.* 1878; *m.* 1911, May, *d.* of late Col. W. Brockman; two *s.* *Educ.:* Bedford School. Served S. Africa, 1900-1 (Queen's medal with five clasps); European War, 1914-18 (despatches, D.S.O., Bt. Lt.-Col. Legion of Honour, Order of Avis of Portugal, Distinguished Service Medal of America, Order of the White Elephant of Siam, Order of the Crown (Officer) of Belgium); Col. 1922; late D.C.L.I. Gordon Hldrs. and Insp. of Physical Training; Joint Hon. Secretary National Association of Boys' Clubs, 1928-30; Director Physical Education, Edinburgh University, 1930-46. *Publications:* A Ten-Round Contest; The Foster-Brothers. *Address:* Tigh-Ur, Bonskeid, By Pitlochry, Perthshire. *T.:* Killiecrankie 242. *Clubs:* United Service, London Fencing. [*Died* 7 *March* 1963.

CAMPBELL, Stuart; *see* Campbell, R. S.

CAMPBELL, Maj.-Gen. William H. M. V.; *see* Verschoyle-Campbell.

CAMPBELL, His Honour (William) Lawson; retired as Judge of County Courts Circuit No. 35 (1937-62); Deputy-Chairman, National Advisory Council on the Training of Magistrates, since 1964; Chairman, Cambridgeshire and Isle of Ely Quarter Sessions, 1965; Deputy Chairman, Essex Quarter Sessions, 1964, 1965; *b.* 5 July 1890. *Educ.:* Harrow; Magdalen College, Oxford. B.A. 1913. Called to Bar, Lincoln's Inn, 1914; served European War, 1914-18, with 6th Black Watch, 51st Division. M.A. Trinity Hall, Cambs., 1939. Chairman, Isle of Ely Quarter Sessions, 1941-65; acting Chairman, Soke of Peterborough Quarter Sessions, 1942-65; Chairman, Cambridge Quarter Sessions, 1950-65. *Address:* 14 Woollards Lane, Gt. Shelford, Cambs. [*Died* 26 *Sept.* 1970.

CAMPION, Col. (hon. Brig.) Douglas John Montriou, D.S.O. 1919; *b.* 14 Dec. 1883; *s.* of John Montriou Campion; *m.* 1930, Evelyn Russell Halahan (*d.* 1961), *d.* of late Rev. Dr. F. W. B. Dunne. *Educ.:* Bedford; R.M.A., Woolwich. Date of first Commission, 1902 Lieut 1905; Capt., 1914; Major, 1916; Bt. Lt. Col., 1928; Lt.-Col 1932; Colonel, 1932; retired, 1939. *Address:* Little Lawn Cottage, West Parley, Dorset. [*Died* 22 *June* 1963.

CAMPNEY, Hon. Ralph Osborne, Q.C. (Can.); LL.D.; Barrister; *b.* 6 June 1894; *s.* of late Frank Campney and late Mary Emily Cronk; *m.* 1st, 1925, Vera Wilhelmina Farnsworth (*d.* 1961); one *s.*; 2nd, 1965, Mary Dudley. *Educ.:* Picton (Ont.) Collegiate Inst.; Queen's Univ., Kingston (B.A.); Osgoode Hall, Toronto. Called to Bar of Ont., 1924; Bar of B.C., 1929; K.C. (Can.) 1940; Sec. to late Rt. Hon. W. L. Mackenzie King, 1924-26; Private Sec. to late Hon. James Malcolm, Minister of Trade and Commerce, 1926-29. Member firm Campney, Owen & Murphy, 1936-. Chm. Nat. Harbours Bd., 1936-40. Elected to Parliament, 1949; re-elected, 1953; Parl. Asst. to Minister of Nat. Defence, 1951; Solicitor General of Canada, Oct. 1952; Associate Minister of National Defence, 1953-54; Minister of Nat. Defence, 1954-57. LL.D., Royal Military Coll., Kingston, Ont., 1964. *Recreations:* gardening, fishing; study of American Civil War. *Address:* Campney, Owen & Murphy, The Burrard Building, 1030 West Georgia St., Vancouver 5, B.C. *T.:* (office) Mutual 4-2511; 4629 West 2nd Ave., Vancouver 8, B.C. *T.:* (home) Castle 4.7000. *Clubs:* Vancouver (Vancouver); Rideau (Ottawa). [*Died* 6 *Oct.* 1967.

CANBY, Henry Seidel; Retired since 1954 from active pursuits; Chairman, Editorial Board, The Saturday Review, from 1938 and Board of Judges, Book-of-the-Month Club, from 1926; retired as Professor, Yale University; *b.* 1878; *s.* of Edward Tatnall and Ella Seidel Canby, Wilmington, Delaware, U.S.A.; *m.* 1907, Marion Ponsonby Gause; two *s.* *Educ.:* Yale University (Ph.B., Ph.D.). Dept. of English, Yale Univ., from 1900. Editor, Literary Review New York Evening Post, 1920-24; Founder and editor of The Saturday Review, 1924, advisory editor, 1936-; Asst. editor Yale Review, 1911, 1920. On Liaison work for the British Ministry of Information, 1918, and on the U.S. Office of War Information in Australia and New Zealand, 1945. President American P.E.N.; Associate Fellow Silliman College, Yale; Member Nat. Inst. of Art and Letters; F.R.S.L., Hon. Litt.D., Knox College; Hon. Litt.D. Univ. of Delaware. *Publications:* The Short Story in English, 1909; Education by Violence, 1919; American Estimates, 1929; Classic Americans, 1931; The Age of Confidence, 1934; Seven Years Harvest, 1936; Thoreau, a Biography 1939; The Brandywine, 1941; Walt Whitman, an American, 1943; American Memoir, 1947; (editor) The Literary History of The United States, 1948; Turn West, Turn East: Mark Twain and Henry James, 1951. *Recreations:* fishing, travel. *Address:* Deep River, R.F.D. 2, Connecticut, U.S.A.; (home) Killingworth, Connecticut. *T.:* Clinton, Montrose 9-8770. *Clubs:* Century (New York); Graduates, Elizabethan (New Haven). [*Died* 5 *April* 1961.

CANNAN, Joanna (Mrs. H. J. Pullein-Thompson); Novelist; 3rd *d.* of late Charles Cannan, Secretary to the Delegates of the Oxford University Press; *m.* 1918, Capt. H. J. Pullein-Thompson, M.C., late The Queen's Royal Regiment (*d.* 1957); one *s.* three *d.* *Educ.:* Wychwood School, Oxford. *Publications: Novels:* Frightened Angels; Ithuriel's Hour; High Table; No Walls of Jasper; They rang up the Police; Idle Apprentice; Death at the Dog; Blind Messenger; Little I Understood; Murder Included; Body in the Beck; Long Shadows; People to be Found; And be a Villain, etc.; *Children's Books:* A Pony for Jean; We Met Our Cousins, Gaze at the Moon, etc. *Address:* Hod Cottage, Stourpaine, Blandford Forum, Dorset.
[*Died* 22 *April* 1961.

CANNING, Sir Ernest R., Kt., *cr* 1939, D.L. Warwickshire; J.P.; President, W. Canning & Co. Ltd.; *b.* 7 Aug. 1876; *s.* of John and Ellen Canning, Binton, Warwickshire; *m.* 1st, 1909, Emily Gent (*d.* 1939) Somerset; 2nd, 1940, Mrs. John Hare Taunton. *Educ.:* King Edward's School, Aston, Birmingham. Commenced Political work under Joseph Chamberlain, 1899; entered City Council, 1930; Lord Mayor 1937-38; Gov., Birmingham Univ.; High Sheriff of Warwickshire for 1946-47. *Address:* Grey House, Handsworth Wood, Birmingham, 20. *T.:* Northern 0056. *Clubs:* Union, Conservative, St Paul's (Birmingham). [*Died* 25 *Dec.* 1966.

CANNING, Frederick, C.I.E. 1934; *b.* 31 Dec. 1882; *s.* of John Canning and Ellen Atherton; *m.* 1914, Georgina May, *d.* of Surgeon Major W. Deane, I.M.S.; two *s.* two *d.* *Educ.:* St. Lawrence; Cooper's Hill. Joined Indian Forest Service, 1903; Deputy Conservator of Forests, 1908; Conservator of Forests, 1920; Chief Conservator of Forests, United Provinces, India, 1929-37; nominated M.L.C.; Officiated Inspector General of Forests, Dehra Dun, 1936; retired, 1937. *Address:* Havards, Ferndown, Dorset.
[*Died* 27 *Jan.* 1968.

CANNON, George Harry Franklyn; *b.* London, 1885; *s.* of late Matthew and Fanny Cannon; *m.* Ivy (*d.* 1960), 2nd *d.* of late Rev. E. Botry Pigott, Rector of Ellisfield, Hants. *Educ.:* privately; St. John's Coll., Oxford (M.A.). Served European War of 1914-18, France and Italy, Captain Special List (despatches). Called to Bar, Inner Temple, 1921; Western Circuit; Stipendiary Magistrate and Coroner, Bahamas, 1928-31; Judge of the Supreme Court, Jamaica, 1934-1939; Judge of the Supreme Court, Ceylon, 1939-47. *Recreations:* hacking, gardening, music, reading. *Address:* Brocas, Ellisfield, Basingstoke, Hants. *T.:* Herriard 279. *Club:* Royal Automobile.
[*Died* 15 *Feb.* 1966.

CANNON, Herbert Graham, F.R.S. 1935; F.R.S. (Edin.); F.L.S.; Hon. F.R.M.S.; M.A., Sc.D. (Cantab.), D.Sc. (Lond.), M.Sc. (Manch.); Beyer Professor of Zoology and Director of Zoological Laboratory, Manchester University since 1931; Pro-Vice-Chancellor, 1946-50; *b.* 14 Apr. 1897; *y.* *s.* of late Alice and David William Cannon; *m.* 1927, Annie Helen, *o.* *c.* of Helen Fyfe and late Edwin J. Fyfe, Edinburgh; two *s.* two *d.* *Educ.:* Wilson's Grammar School, Camberwell; Christ's College, Cambridge (Scholar). Naturalist on Board of Fisheries (Ministry of Agriculture and Fisheries), 1918; Demonstrator in Zoology, Imperial College of Science and Technology, S. Kensington, 1920-1922 Lecturer, 1922-26; Professor of Zoology, Sheffield University, 1926-31; Crisp Medal of the Linnean Society, 1927; President North Western Naturalists Union, 1935-37; Pres. Zoology Section, British Assoc., 1948. Chairman Manchester Museum; Academic Sponsor, University College of N. Staffordshire, 1950-62. *Publications:* Lamarck and Modern Genetics, 1959; various papers on zoological subjects. *Recreations:* angling, Chinese and Japanese collecting. *Address:* Hollin Knowle, Chapel-en-le-Frith Derbyshire *T.:* Chapel-en-le Frith 222. *Club:* English-Speaking Union [*Died* 6 *Jan.* 1963.

CANNON, Sir Leslie, Kt. 1971. C.B.E. 1968; General President, Electrical Trades Union, since 1963; *b.* 21 Feb. 1920; *s.* of James and Ellen Cannon; *m.* 1949, Olga Julinava; two *s.* *Educ.:* Wigan and Dist. Tech. Coll. Electrical Trades Union: Shop Steward, 1940; District Committee, 1941, District Secretary, 1942; Area Committee, 1944; Executive Councillor 1945; Education Officer, 1954; working electrician, 1957. Student of Inner Temple, 1958, 1959. Chairman: Nat. Jt. Industrial Coun. for Electrical Contracting Industry, 1966-67; Nat. Jt. Ind. Coun., Elec. Supply Ind., 1967-68; Member: T.U.C. General Council, 1965-; Industrial Reorganisation Corp. (part-time), 1966-; Royal Commn. on Assizes and Quarter Sessions, 1966-; Committee of Inquiry into Shipping, 1967. F.R.S.A. 1967. *Recreations:* theatre, reading, music. *Address:* 78 Bolton Road, Chessington, Surrey. [*Died* 9 *Dec.* 1970.
[*Knighthood gazetted New Year* 1971.

CANTER, Bernard Hall; Editor, The Friend (the Quaker weekly), 1950-65, retd.; *b.* 1 Jan. 1906; *s.* of late James Canter, M.B.E., and Alice Mary Canter, Sanderstead, Surrey; *m.* 1936, Doris Alice, *d.* of William and Alice Ray, Norwich; two *s.* one *d.* *Educ.:* Strand School, London; King's College, London (B.A.). Editorial staff: Chatham News, 1928; Norwich Mercury, 1931; Eastern Daily Press and associated papers, 1932; Editor, Norwich Mercury Series, 1948. Worked with Society of Friends Relief Service, 1941-43. *Publication:* The Quaker Bedside Book, 1952. *Address:* (home) 5 Park North, Westerfield Rd., Ipswich, Suffolk. [*Died* 6 *Sept.* 1969.

CANTLIE, Admiral (retd.) Sir Colin, K.B.E., *cr.* 1946; C.B. 1941; D.S.C.; *b.* 8 May 1888; *s.* of late Sir James Cantlie, K.B.E., LL.D., F.R.C.S.; *m.* 1921, Agnes, *d.* of late Thomas Calder, J.P.; two *s.* one *d.* Joined Britannia, 1903; Captain, 1928; Rear-Admiral, 1939; Vice-Admiral (retired), 1942; served in submarines, 1909-33; Admiral (retired), 1945; chief staff officer to R.A. submarines, 1931-33; commanding Achilles, 1933-35; Director of Tactical Division, Admiralty, 1935-37; commanding Royal Oak, 1938-39; A.D.C. to the King, 1939; Admiral Superintendent H.M. Dockyard, Rosyth, 1939-44; Director-General, Shipbuilding and Repairs, India, 1944-46. Commander of Order of St. Olaf. *Address:* Kirklands of Coull, Tarland, Aberdeenshire; Thornby, Armstrong Road, Brockenhurst, Hants. [*Died* 9 *Oct.* 1967.

CANTOR, Eddie; actor, stage, screen, radio; *b.* N.Y.C., 31 Jan. 1892; *s.* of Michael and Minnie Cantor; *m.* 1914, Ida Tobias (*d.* 1962); five *d.* *Educ.:* public schools, New York City. Appeared in Gus Edwards Kid Kabaret and later played in vaudeville and burlesque, U.S.A.; made first appearance on legitimate stage in Canary Cottage, 1916; appeared in Broadway Brevities of 1920, Make it Snappy, 1922; played in following productions of Florenz Ziegfeld; Follies of 1917, 1918, 1919, and 1927, Kid Boots (1923-26), Whoopee (1929-30); reappeared, New York, in Banjo Eyes, 1941; presented Nellie Bly (with Nat Karson), 1946. Entered films, 1926. Films include: Kid Boots, Special Delivery, Whoopee, Palmy Days, Kid from Spain, Roman Scandals, Kid Millions, Strike Me Pink, Ali Baba Goes to Town, Show Business (producer), If You Knew Susie (producer). Has appeared on radio programmes, 1931-, one-man stage show, Forty Years in Show Business; television, 1950-. President of American Federation of Radio Artists; Member Actors Equity Association, Screen Actors Guild (Pres. 1934-35), Jewish Theatrical Guild (Pres.), Catholic Actors Guild (Life Member). *Publications:* My Life is in Your Hands, 1928; Caught Short, 1929; Yoo Hoo Prosperity, 1930; Take My Life (with Jane Kesner Ardmore), 1956; The Way I See It (with Phyllis Rosenteur), 1959; also articles in magazines. *Recreations:* Founder of Eddie Cantor Camp Committee, 1922, for poor and undernourished boys; director, Surprise Lake Camp. *Address:* 140 South Lasky Drive, Beverly Hills, California. [*Died* 10 *Oct.* 1964.

CANZIANI, Estella Louisa Michaela, R.B.A., F.R.G.S.; *d.* of Louisa Starr, portrait painter and late Commendatore Enrico F. Canziani, Milan; *b.* 12 Jan. 1887. *Educ.:* Sir Arthur Cope and Mr. Watson Nichol's school of art at South Kensington; Royal Academy Schools (medals). Artist, writer; Exhibited R.A., R.B.A. R.I. Liverpool, Milan, Venice, France, and other provincial galleries; painter of portraits, subject pictures, landscapes, illustrator and decorator; mediums for work, oil, tempera, water-colour and black and white; during the war of 1914-20 painted scientific water-colours of abnormal cases under different treatments, and made special moulded splints and casts of these cases for English and Australian museums and hospitals; principal works: Piper of Dreams Blue Badge of Courage, The Peace Baby, Portrait of Sir George Gibb and others: Decorations for the Retreat, York; Member of Council of Folk-Lore Society and of Anglo-Italian Society for Protection of Animals and Birds (formerly Hawksley Society). Social worker. *Publications:* Round About Three Palace Green (written and illustrated), 1939; Costumes, Traditions, and Songs of Savoy (written and illustrated) both in French and English; Piedmont (written and illustrated) both in Italian and English; Through the Apennines and the Lands of the Abruzzi (written and illustrated); illustrator of Walter de la Mare's Songs of Childhood; Oxford in Brush and Pen (illustrated and compiled, an anthology); etc. *Recreations:* Folk-lore, travelling, reading, nature study, fencing. *Address:* 3 Palace Green, W.8. *Club:* English-Speaking Union. [*Died* 23 *Aug.* 1964.

CAPE, Colonel Edmund Graves Meredith, D.S.O. 1917; E.D.; B.A.Sc.; M.E.I.C.; Chairman of E. G. M. Cape and Co., Engineers and Contractors; *b.* Hamilton, Ont., 1878; *s.* of John Cape; *m.* 1908, Elizabeth Lillian Guest Smith, Montreal; two *s.* one *d.* *Educ.:* McGill University (B.A.Sc. 1898). Assistant Engineer Lake Superior Power Co., Sault Ste. Marie, 1900; Chief Engineer during construction Canada Car Company; practised for some years as a Civil Engineer, Montreal; Life Member Engineering Inst. of Canada; recruited and commanded 3rd Canadian Siege Battery and took same overseas, 1915; trained in England and went to France, June 1916; battle of the Somme (despatches); Vimy Ridge (despatches, D.S.O.). Governor: Montreal Gen., Montreal Children's, Queen Elizabeth and Reddy Memorial Hosps. *Address:* The Ledges, Redpath Cres., Montreal, Canada. *Clubs:* St. James's, Royal Montreal Golf (Montreal). [*Died Sept.* 1962.

CAPEY, Reco, R.D.I. 1938; A.R.C.A.; F.R.S.A.; F.S.I.A.; Industrial Designer; Art Director, Yardley & Co. Ltd., London, 1928-58; *b.* 5 July 1895; *s.* of Catherine and George Capey; *m.* 1947, Muriel, *o. d.* of A. C. Compton, Bexhill, Sx. Served in France during European War, 1915-19. Student at Royal Coll. of Art, 1919-22; studied in France, Italy, and Sweden, 1923-25; Chief Instructor, Design, Royal College of Art, 1925-35; Industrial Liaison Officer, Royal College of Art, 1936-53; Chief Examiner, Industrial Design, Board of Education, 1937-40. Industrial Contracts, Europe and America; President Arts and Crafts Exhibition Society, 1938-42; exhibited Paintings, Sculpture, Royal Academy, Paris Salon, England, Europe, America, Asia. Represented in various galleries. *Publications:* Lacquer, 1925; Printing of Textiles, 1927. *Recreation:* tennis. *Address:* Down Laine, Alfriston, Sussex. [*Died* 11 *May* 1961.

CAPON, Maj.-Gen. Philip John Lauriston, C.B. 1959; Major-General late R.A.M.C.; Director of Army Health, Department of the Adjutant-General to the Forces, War Office, 1956-62; *b.* 3 Nov. 1902. St. Thomas's Hospital. M.R.C.S. Eng., L.R.C.P. Lond. 1926; D.P.H. Eng. 1935. War of 1939-45 (despatches). Formerly Professor of Army Health, Royal Army Medical Coll., London. Fellow of the Royal Society for the Promotion of Health (formerly Royal Sanitary Institute); Fellow of the Society of Medical Officers of Health. *Address:* 6 Collington Rise, Bexhill-on-Sea, Sussex; c/o Glyn Mills & Co., Whitehall, S.W.1. [*Died* 22 *Oct.* 1964.

CAPPER, Major Charles Francis; Ambassador to the Republic of Liberia, 1952-56, retd. (Minister, Dec. 1951-Sept. 1952); *b.* 26 May 1902; *s.* of late Henry Francis Everard Capper and late Margaret Baines; *m.* 1st, 1933, Rosamund Dorothy Howes (marriage dissolved, 1950); two *s.*; 2nd, 1951, Karen, *er. d.* of Svend Geleff, Nairobi. *Educ.:* Eton; Royal Military Academy, Woolwich. 2nd Lieut., Royal Artillery, 1923; served throughout War of 1939-1945 in India and Paiforce as Regimental Officer, with rank of Major; with B.A.O.R. in Military Govt., Germany, until 1947; retired from Army, with rank of Major, April 1947; continued to serve in C.C.G. until May 1948. Consul, Ahwaz, Persia, 1949. Consul-General, Khorramshahr, Persia, 1950-1951. *Recreations:* boxing (several times Army and Inter Services heavy-weight champion; heavy-weight champion, A.B.A., 1927); polo, tennis, golf, shooting. *Address:* P.O. Box 6327, Nairobi. *Club:* Army and Navy. [*Died* 30 *Dec.* 1964.

CAPPS, Frederick Cecil Wray, F.R.C.S.; Consulting Surgeon, Ear, Nose and Throat, St. Bartholomew's Hospital, E.C.1; Cons. Otolaryngologist to Royal Navy, Treasury Medical Service, and Civil Service Commissioners; late Surgeon to Ear, Nose and Throat Dept., Luton and Dunstable, West Suffolk General, Willesden General and Metropolitan Hospitals; *b.* 17 May 1898; *s.* of late Fleet Surgeon Fredk. A. Capps, R.N.; *m.* 1931, Gertrud Margareta Torell; two *s.* two *d.* *Educ.:* R.N. College, Osborne; Epsom College; St. Bartholomew's Hospital. Distinction in Physics, 1st M.B., London Univ.; Epsom Scholar; Senior and Junior Anatomy prizes; Brackenbury Scholarship in Surgery, St. Bart.'s Hosp. Surgeon Probationer, R.N.V.R., 1917-18; L.R.C.P. Lond. 1921; M.R.C.S. Eng. 1921; F.R.C.S. Eng. 1924. Sector Hospital Officer, Sector 3 E.M.S., 1945; Past Hon. Secretary and Vice - President British Association Otolaryngology; Hon. Sec. 4th International Congress of Otolaryngology, London, 1949; Examiner Part 1 Dipl. Laryngology and Otology; Mem. Court of Examiners, Royal College of Surgeons, 1952-58. Fell. Roy. Soc. Med. (Sec. and ex-Pres., Section of Laryngology; Pres. United Services Section, 1968-70). Semon Lecturer, Univ. of London, 1957. *Publications:* various papers in medical journals. *Recreations:* tennis, squash, ski-ing. *Address:* 108 Harley St., W.1. *T.:* Welbeck 7507. [*Died* 12 *June* 1970.

CARDELL, J(ohn) D(ouglas) Magor, F.R.C.S.; Hon. Consulting Surgeon, late Senior Surgeon, City Road Branch, Moorfields Eye Hospital; Ophthalmic Surgeon, Royal Masonic Hospital, 1935-61 (now retired), *b.* 13 February 1896; *s.* of Arthur John Cardell; *m.* 1928, Audrey Winifred Craig; three *d.* *Educ.:* Epsom Coll.; London University; St. Thomas's Hospital. Jenks, Tite and Peacock Scholarships, 1914; Surgeon Probationer, R.N.V.R., 1916-18; M.R.C.S., L.R.C.P., 1919; M.B., B.S. Lond., 1922; F.R.C.S. Eng., 1925; Medical Officer, London Scottish, 1924-28 (Capt. R.A.M.C.T.). Ophthalmic Surgeon: Park Prewett E.M.S. Hosp., 1939-45; Leatherhead E.M.S. Hosp., 1940-45; Senior Surgeon, Central London Eye Hosp., 1945-1947. *Publications:* Contributions and Papers in: Brit. Jl. Ophth.; Brit. Med. Jl.; Proc. Royal Soc. Med.; Proc. Ophth. Society of U.K. *Recreations:* fishing, golf. *Address:* Galleon, Mizen Way, Cobham, Surrey. *T.:* Cobham, Surrey 3064. *Club:* Royal Automobile. [*Died* 6 *March* 1966.

CARDELL-OLIVER, Hon. Dame (Annie) Florence (Gillies), D.B.E., *cr.* 1951; M.L.A.; Hon. Minister of Supply and Shipping, Western Australia, 1947-53; Minister of Health and of Supply and Shipping, 1949-1953; First woman appointed to Cabinet Rank in Australia; *m.* Dr. A. Cardell-Oliver (*decd.*); two *s.* *Educ.:* Victoria; England. Travelled for many years (Russia, Baltic, Balkan states, Europe, America). M.P. for Subiaco, W.A., 1936-56; Pres.: Free Milk Council of W.A.; Women's br. Liberal and Country League of Western Australia; Women Painters' Soc.; Women's Hockey Assoc. of W.A.; Past Pres. Perth br. Women's Service Guilds. Member: Victoria League; Roy. Instn. of Great Britain. *Publication:* Empire Unity or Red Asiatic Domination, 1934. *Recreation:* work. *Address:* St. Quentins Nursing Home, 92 Redcliffe Gardens, S.W.10. *Clubs:* Royal Over-Seas League; Karakatta (Perth, W.A.). [*Died* 12 *Jan.* 1965.

CARDEN, Major Sir Frederick Henry Walter, 3rd Bt., *cr.* 1887; late 1st Life Guards; *b.* 17 Oct. 1873; *s.* of 2nd Bt. and Rowena, *d.* of late R. Ronald and *widow* of Capt. A. L. Copland, 57th Regt.; *S.* father, 1909; *m.* 1901, Winifred Mary, 4th *d.* of late Philip Wroughton, Woolley Park, Berks; one *s.* one *d.* *Heir:* *s.* Lt.-Col. Henry Christopher Carden, O.B.E. 1945 [*b.* 16 Oct. 1908; *m.* 1st, 1943, Jane St. Clare (from whom he obtained a divorce, 1961), *yr. d.* of late T. E. St. C. Daniell, O.B.E., M.C.; one *s.* one *d.*; 2nd, 1962, Gwyneth Sybil, F.C.A., *widow* of Flt.-Lt. R. S. Emerson, R.A.F.V.R., Argentina (who was killed in action, 1944), and *er. d.* of H. A. D. Acland]. *Address:* Stargroves, Newbury. *T.A.:* Woolton Hill. *T.:* Highclere 203. *Club:* Guards. [*Died* 22 *Sept.* 1966.

CARDON, Philip Vincent; retired; *b.* 25 April 1889; *s.* of Thomas Barthelemy and Lucy Smith Cardon; *m.* 1913, Leah Ivins; one *s.* two *d.* *Educ.:* Utah State Agricultural College; University of California. Prof. of Agronomy, Montana State Agric. Coll., 1920-1921; Director, Utah State Experiment Station, Logan, 1928-33; Principal Agronomist, Forage Crops and Diseases, U.S. Dept. of Agric., 1935-39; Asst. Chief, Bureau of Plant Industry, U.S. Dept. of Agriculture, 1942-45. Research Administrator, Agric. Research Administration, U.S. Dept. of Agriculture, 1945-46 and 1948-51. Director, Graduate School, U.S. Dept. of Agriculture, 1952-53; Director-General of the Food and Agriculture Organisation of the United Nations, 1954-56. Hon. LL.D. Utah State Agric. Coll., 1948; Hon. D.Sc. Montana State Coll., 1953. Dist. Service Award, U.S. Dept. of Agric., 1948. *Publications:* articles for technical bulletins and journals; also to U.S. Dept. of Agric. Yearbook. *Recreations:* painting, gardening. *Address:* 1730 Crestwood Drive, Washington 11, D.C., U.S.A. *T.:* Randolph 6-8530. [*Died* 13 *Oct.* 1965.

CARDWELL, George; *b.* 30 Sept. 1882; British; *m.* 1913, Winifred Harridge Cayless; two *s.* *Educ.:* Baines' Grammar School, Poulton-le-Fylde, Lancs. Premium pupil, Brush Electrical Engineering Co. Ltd., Loughborough, Leics., 1901-4, then on Company's engineering staff until 1907; Gen. Man. Hartlepools Electric Tramways Co., 1907-12; Devonport and District Tramways Co., 1912-15; Aldershot and District Traction Co. Ltd., 1915-17. Commissioned Royal Engineers, 1917-19 (Capt.). Gen. Man., Macclesfield Branch of British Automobile Traction Ltd., later formed into North Western Road Car Co. Ltd., 1919-30; Executive, Thomas Tilling Ltd., 1930-32; Director Thomas Tilling Ltd. and many Cos. assoc. with passenger road transport, of some of which he was Chm., 1932-48; Member Road Transport Exec. (later Road Haulage Exec.), 1948-49; Chairman Road Passenger Executive, British Transport Commission, 1949-52. Formerly Chairman Midland General Omnibus Co., Ltd.; Mansfield District Traction Co.; Nottinghamshire & Derbyshire Traction Co.; Western National Omnibus Co., Ltd.; Southern National Omnibus Co., Ltd.; West Yorkshire Road Car Co., Ltd.; Keighley-West Yorkshire Road Services, Ltd.; retired from business, 1956. *Recreations:* football, golf, motoring. *Address:* Woodhouse, 3 Burdon Lane, Cheam, Surrey. *T.:* Vigilant 5653. [*Died* 7 *Oct.* 1962.

CAREY, Brig.-General Arthur Basil, C.M.G. 1915; D.S.O. 1917; late R.E.; Engineer and Inventor; *b.* 3 March 1872. Served Dardanelles, 1914-15 (despatches, C.M.G.); elsewhere, 1916-18 (D.S.O.); Mesopotamia, 1920 (Bt. Col.); Director of Military and Public Works, 1920-23; Chief Engineer, Scottish Command, 1923-27; retired with rank of Brig.-Gen., 1927. K.St.J. 1955. *Address:* 169 Ote, Calle 158, Colonia Montezuma, Mexico 9, D.F. [*Died* 29 *March* 1961.

CAREY, (Francis) Clive (Savill), C.B.E. 1955; B.A., B.Mus. (Cantab.), F.R.C.M.;

Hon. R.A.M.; retd.; *b.* 30 May 1883; *s.* of Francis Carey and Elizabeth Harrowell, Burgess Hill, Sussex; *m.* 1929, Doris, *d.* of Samuel Johnson, Adelaide S. Australia; no *c.* *Educ.:* King's College Choir Sch., Camb.; Sherborne School; Clare College, Cambridge (Organ Schol.). Grove Schol. (composition) at Royal College of Music under Stanford; continued studies abroad; in Italy with Pavesi (singing) and in Paris with Isnardon (singing) and Moszkowski (composition). Recital tours of English vocal music in Holland, Germany and Scandinavia. Collected English folk songs and dances. First Opera prod. The Magic Flute, Cambridge, 1911; with Bristol Repertory Co. 1914. Served European War, 1914-18, R.A.M.C. and R.A.O.C. (Maj., France and Italy. Prof. of singing, R.C.M., 1919; in original group of English Singers and toured Continent; prod. and sang in Operas at Old Vic; further study with Jean de Reszke at Nice, acting also as his accompanist and asst., 1920-24; Prof. of singing, Univ. Conservatorium, Adelaide till 1928; toured U.S. and Canada in The Beggar's Opera, 1928-29; also with English Folk Dance Soc. and individual recitals, winter of 1929-30; rejoined staff of R.C.M. and prod. opera at Sadler's Wells, 1932-39; rep. England as vocal adjudicator at Internat. Competitive Festival, Vienna, 1939; Adelaide Conservatorium, 1939; Albert St. Conservatorium, Melb., 1942 (Co-Dir., 1943-45); Director, Sadler's Wells Opera, 1945-46 season; Professor of Singing and Dir. of Opera School at Royal College of Music, 1946-53. Has adjudicated at Competitive Festivals since 1911 and examined for Associated Board of Royal Music Schools in Canada, Australia, N.Z. and S. Africa. Composed musical Fantasy, All Fools' Day (produced Theatre Royal, Bristol); incidental music to The Blue Lagoon, The Wonderful Visit, The Red Feathers (London productions), and other plays. *Publications:* various songs and part-songs, also folk-song arrangements; articles in Music and Letters and other journals. *Recreations:* gardening and photography. *Address:* 85 St. Mark's Rd., W.10. *T.:* Ladbroke 2766. *Club:* English-Speaking Union. [*Died* 30 *April* 1968.

CAREY, Gordon Vero, M.A.; *b.* 9 Oct. 1886; *yr. s.* of late Francis Carey, Burgess Hill; *m.* 1st, 1919, Eila (*d.* 1932), *d.* of late G. W. Reynolds; two *s.*; 2nd, 1934, Dorothy, 2nd *d.* of late Ernest Armstrong; one *s.* *Educ.:* King's Choir School, Cambridge (chorister); Eastbourne College (scholar); Caius Coll., Camb. (schol.); 2nd Class (1st Div.) Classical Tripos. Pt. I.; two years in Univ. Rugby XV.; Harlequins, 1906-10, Barbarians, 1909. Asst. Master at Eastbourne College and Trinity College, Glenalmond, 1909-13; Assistant Secretary, Cambridge University Press, 1913; Educational Secretary, 1922-29; Fellow of Clare College, Cambridge, 1919-25; Headmaster of Eastbourne College, 1929-38; on Governing Body of Felsted School, 1938-47; President of Society of Indexers, 1962-66. Commissioned in 8th Batt. The Rifle Brigade, 1914; wounded, 1915; Captain, 1915; Major, 1917; Acting Lieut.-Col.; attached R.F.C., 1917; Staff Officer in R.A.F., 1918-1919 (despatches, Belgian Croix de Guerre); commissioned in R.A.F.V.R., 1940; Squadron Leader, 1941; Librarian, R.A.F. Staff Coll., 1942-45. *Publications:* Mind the Stop, 1939, 1958; American into English, 1953; Cambridge Authors' and Printers' Guides: Making an Index, 1951, 1963, and Punctuation, 1957; compiled Cambridge University War List, 1921; part-author of An Outline History of the Great War, 1928. *Address:* 60 Houndean Rise, Lewes, Sussex. *T.:* Lewes 4727. *Clubs:* United Service, R.A.F. Reserves; Hawks (Cambridge). [*Died* 21 *Nov.* 1969.

CARGILL, Air Commandant Dame Helen Wilson, D.B.E. *cr.* 1951; R.R.C. 1945 (A.R.R.C. 1941); *b.* 1 October 1896; *d.* of late William Cargill, S.S.C., Edinburgh, and of late A. D. Cargill. *Educ.:* St. Bride's School, Edinburgh. General Training: St. George's Hospital, London, S.W., 1919-23; P.M.R.A.F.N.S., 1923-52; Matron-in-Chief, Princess Mary's Royal Air Force Nursing Service, 1948-52 C.St.J. 1949. *Address:* 6 Abbotsford Crescent, Edinburgh. [*Died* 4 *Dec.* 1969.

CARLETON, Ven. George Dundas, M.A., B.D.; Licensed Preacher in Diocese of London since 1947; *b.* 6 June 1877; *s.* of Rev. J. G. Carleton, D.D., Canon and Treasurer of St. Patrick's Cathedral, Dublin. *Educ.:* Trinity College, Dublin. Deacon, 1902; Priest, 1903; Tutor of House of Sacred Mission, Kelham, 1902-6 and 1908-1914; Curate of St. Matthew, Wallsall, 1906-8; Provincial Superior of the Society of the Sacred Mission in South Africa; Warden of the Modderpoort Training School; Theological Tutor in the Diocese of Blomfontein, 1915-23; Archdeacon of Modderpoort, 1921-23; A.C.C. Missioner, 1923-24; Temporary Foreign Secretary of S.P.G., 1925; Curate of All Saints', Notting Hill, 1925-27; Vicar-of-Bromley-by-Bow, E.3. 1927-47; Proctor in Convocation, 1936-60, *Publications:* Coram Deo; The King's Highway; The Spirit of Discipleship; The Fear of the Lord; Mother of Jesus; The English Psalter. *Address:* 43 Eden Grove, N.7. *T.:* North 1988. [*Died* 1 *Jan.* 1961.

CARLISLE, 11th Earl of (*cr.* 1661), **George Josslyn L'Estrange Howard;** J.P.; Viscount Howard of Morpeth, Baron Dacre of Gillesland, 1661; *b.* 6 Jan. 1895; *e. s.* of 10th Earl and Rhoda (*d.* 1957); *d.* of Col. Paget W. L'Estrange; *S.* father, 1912; *m.* 1st, 1918, Hon. Bridget Helen Hore-Ruthven, C.B.E., 1947 (from whom he obtained a divorce, 1947; she married, 2nd, 1947, Rt. Hon. Sir Walter Monckton and succeeded, 1956, as 10th Baroness Ruthven of Freeland), *e. d.* of 9th Baron Ruthven, C.B., C.M.G., D.S.O.; one *s.* one *d.*; 2nd, 1947, Esme Mary Shrubb Iredell, *d.* of Charles Edward Iredell, M.D., M.R.C.S., M.R.C.P.; one *d.* *Educ.:* Osborne; Dartmouth. Retired 1920 as Lieutenant on R. of O. (despatches, Croix de Guerre with palms); Lt.-Cdr. retired, 1924. *Heir: s.* Viscount Morpeth, M.C. *Address:* Naworth Castle, Carlisle. *T.:* Brampton 460. *Club:* White's. [*Died* 17 *Feb.* 1963.

CARMICHAEL, George Chapman, M.C. 1944; Q.C. (Scot.) 1962; Advocate since 1949; Sheriff-Substitute of Dumfries and Galloway at Kirkcudbright, Wigtown and Stranraer, since 1969; *b.* 9 March 1924; *s.* of late Alastair Macpherson Carmichael, Edinburgh; *m.* 1960, Ruth Isabell, *d.* of late John Albert Waters Smith, Edinburgh; one *s.* *Educ.:* Edinburgh Academy; Edinburgh University. Served in R.A. (Field) and, later, with 5th King's Own Scottish Borderers (52nd Div.), 1942-45. M.A. Edin., 1946; admitted to Faculty of Advocates, Nov. 1949. Hon. Sheriff-substitute at Glasgow, Aug. 1954-May 1957; Standing Junior Counsel to Min. of National Insurance, Dec. 1955-May, 1957; Extra Advocate-depute at Glasgow High Court Circuit, May 1957-Oct. 1958; Full Advocate-depute (Crown Office, Scotland), Oct. 1958-May, 1962. Lecturer at Scottish Senior Police College, 1952-. Chm. Disciplinary Cttee. of: Potato Marketing Bd., Sept., 1962-; British Egg Marketing Bd., Sept., 1962-; Scottish Milk Marketing Board, Oct., 1962-. *Recreations:* sketching, golf. *Address:* 12 Ainslie Place, Edinburgh 3. *T.:* 031-225 2067. *Clubs:* New, Caledonian United Services and Northern (Edinburgh). [*Died* 10 *Sept.* 1970.

CARMICHAEL, James, J.P.; *b.* 1894. M.P. (I.L.P.) 1946-47, (Lab.) 1947-61, retired, Bridgeton Div. of Glasgow. Mem. Glasgow City Council, 1929-47. J.P. Glasgow, 1935. *Address:* 31 Sandyhills Place, Glasgow, E.2. [*Died* 19 *Jan.* 1966.

CARMICHAEL, Sir William G. C.; *see* Gibson-Craig-Carmichael.

CARMONT, Hon. Lord; John Francis Carmont; Hon. LL.D. (Edin.); Senator of the College of Justice in Scotland since 1934; Chairman in Scotland of the Railway and Canal Commission, 1935-47; *b.* 1880; *y. s.* of late James Carmont, of Castledykes, Dumfries; *m.* 1929, Barbara Wilson Campbell, *yr. d.* of late D. Russell Malloy. *Educ.:* Abbey School, Fort Augustus, and abroad. Advocate, 1906; Hon. Sheriff-Substitute of Selkirkshire, 1909; K.C. 1924; served European War, 1914-19. Privy Chamberlain of the Sword and Cape, to H.H. The Pope, 1960. *Address:* Greenhill Gardens, Edinburgh. *Club:* Authors'. [*Died* 7 *Aug.* 1965.

CARNAC, Vice-Adm. James W. R.; *see* Rivett-Carnac.

CARNEGIE, Air Vice-Marshal David Vaughan, C.B. 1950; C.B.E. 1945; A.F.C.; p.s.a.; Director of Burghley House, Stamford; *b.* 7 February 1897; *s.* of Rev. J. D. Carnegie; *m.* 1942, Kathleen Pugson; two *d.* *Educ.:* Wyggeston. Sub-Lieut. in Royal Naval Air Service, 1917, and served as a pilot in North Sea Patrols until the Armistice; 202 and 267 Flying Boat Squadrons, Mediterranean, 1920-24; Flying Boat Test and Experimental Duties at M.A.E.E. 1924-27; Far East Flight, 1927-28, and R.A.F. Base, Singapore, until 1930; commanded Seaplane Training Unit, Calshot, 1930-31; Staff College, 1931; Air Defence of Great Britain H.Q., 1932-34; Air Ministry—War Training, 1935-37; commanded R.A.F. Station, Wittering, 1938-40; H.Q. Fighter Command, Air Staff, 1940-41; R.A.F. Delegation, Washington, 1941-42; Director of Flying Training, Air Ministry, 1942-45; Air Force Adviser to the U.K. High Commissioner, Ottawa, Canada, 1945-1948; A.O.C. No. 18 Group Coastal Command and Sen. Air Officer, Scotland, 1948-1950; Chief of Air Staff, Roy. N.Z. Air Force, 1950-53. Air Liaison Officer, British Oxygen Co., 1954-62. Member of Queen's Body Guard for Scotland, Royal Company of Archers. U.S. Legion of Merit, 1945. *Recreation:* golf. *Address:* Sibson House, Nr. Wansford, Peterborough; Dundarg Castle, New Aberdour, Aberdeenshire. *Club:* R.A.F. [*Died* 3 *Aug.* 1964.

CARNEGY, Rev. Canon Patrick Charles Alexander; Canon Emeritus of Coventry Cathedral since 1961, Canon Theologian, 1954-61; *b.* 1 June 1893; *s.* of late Col. C. G. Carnegy, M.V.O.; *m.* 1928, Joyce Eleanor Townsley; two *s.* one *d.* *Educ.:* Privately; Hertford College, Oxford. Deacon, 1918; Priest, 1919; Curate of Brighouse, 1918-21; Leeds Parish Church, 1921-23; S. Aidan's, Leeds, 1923-26; first vicar of S. Wilfrid's, Harehills, Leeds, 1926-32; vicar of S. Peter's, Blackburn, 1932-35; vicar of All Souls', Leeds, 1935-40; Canon Missioner and Champney Lecturer in Wakefield Cathedral, 1940-45; Vicar of Spalding, 1945-49; Canon of Lincoln and Prebendary of Aylesbury in Lincoln Cathedral, 1946-49; Rector of Rugby, 1949-61. Examining Chaplain to Bishop of Wakefield, 1942-45; Proctor in Convocation, 1943-45. *Publications:* The Assurance of God, 1940; Our Fellowship in the Gospel, 1944. *Recreation:* gardening. *Address:* Harrington House, Moulton, Spalding, Lincs. *T.:* Moulton 316. [*Died* 28 *May* 1969.

CARPENDALE, Vice-Admiral Sir Charles Douglas, Kt. *cr.* 1932; C.B. 1918; retired; *b.* 1874; *s.* of Rev. William Henry Carpendale; *m.* 1907, Christina Henrietta (*d.* 1952), *e. d.* of late James Stuart Strange, of Denham Court, Winchester; one *s.* Entered R.N. 1887; Lieutenant (five Firsts); served Mombasa (Naval Brigade), 1895 (medal); Flag Captain 5th (later 3rd) Cruiser Squadron, 1911-12; 2nd Cruiser Squadron, 1912-13; Naval Ordnance Dept., 1914; served European War (C.B.); retired list, 1923. Controller, Administration Division, British Broadcasting Corporation, 1923-35; Deputy Director-General, 1935-38; President Union Internationale de Radio-diffusion, 1925-35. *Address:* Holme Close, Pinkney's Green, Maidenhead, Berks. *Club:* United Service. [*Died* 21 *March* 1968.

CARPENTER, Ven. Horace John, M.A.; Archdeacon of Salop, 1945, emer. 1959; *b.* 30 July 1887; *s.* of Joseph Garratt and Marion Carpenter; *m.* Kathleen Clare, *d.* of Gerald Clare Moberley, LL.M., and Edith Maud Moberley; one *s.* one *d.* *Educ.:* privately; University College, London. B.A. (Lond.) Hons. Philosophy, 1913; M.A. 1914; Resident Tutor, London College of Divinity, 1915-20; lecturer in Philosophy and Biblical Theology, London Univ., 1915-1920; Curate, Christ Church, Penge, 1913-1915; C.F. 1916-19; Vicar of Holy Trinity, Anerley, 1920-29; Vicar of Wrangthorn, Leeds, 1929-35; Vicar and Rural Dean of Walsall, 1935-48; Vicar and Rural Dean of Penkridge, 1943-45; Prebendary of Lichfield Cathedral since 1938; Examining Chaplain to Bishop of Lichfield since 1937. *Address:* 102 Nyewood Lane, Bognor Regis, Sussex. [*Died* 26 *June* 1965.

CARPENTER, Major-General John Owen, C.B.E. 1942; M.C.; *b.* 20 June 1894; *s.* of late Owen and Alice Carpenter, Bexhill-on-Sea; *m.* 1922, Margaret Louisa Nora Douglass; two *s.*; *m.* 1948, Florence Blanche Paget (*d.* 1952), *y. d.* of late C. J. C. Douglas, formerly of 6 Royal Crescent, Bath. *Educ.:* Bradfield College; Royal Military College, Sandhurst. 2nd Lt. E. Surrey Regiment, 1914; served European War, 1914-18 (wounded, despatches, M.C.); Col. 1939; Temp. Brig. 1941; acting Maj.-Gen. 1942; retired pay, 1946. *Recreation:* gardening. *Address:* Hooper's Court, Beckley, Nr. Rye, Sussex. [*Died* 28 *Feb.* 1967.

CARPENTER, Percy Frederick; Senior Partner, W. B. Keen & Co., Chartered Accountants, since 1946; *b.* 3 Aug. 1901; 2nd *s.* of late Frederick John Carpenter, F.C.A.; *m.* 1925, Doris Kate, *e. d.* of late Frederick Richard Densham; one *s.* three *d.* (and one *s.* decd.). *Educ.:* St. Marylebone Grammar School (The Philological School). Inst. of Chartered Accountants in Eng. and Wales: Member 1923, Mem. of Council 1947, Vice-Pres. 1961, President 1962. Advisory Accountant, Railway Assessment Authority, 1940; Fellow, Roy. Statistical Soc., 1942; Chm., London and District Soc. of Chartered Accountants, 1943; Member, Palmer Cttee. on Prices of Building Materials, 1947. Hon. F.Z.S. 1960. Freeman of City of London, 1936; Member of Court: Loriners, 1961, Makers of Playing Cards, 1963; Warden, Guild of Freemen, 1962. Special Constabulary Long Service Medal 1943, Bar 1946. *Recreations:* gardening, walking, non-party local politics. *Address:* Finsbury Circus House, Blomfield Street, E.C.2. *T.:* London Wall 6356; Glendale, 2 Hillcrest Avenue, Pinner, Middlesex. *Clubs:* City of London, City Livery; Middlesex County Cricket. [*Died* 9 *Sept.* 1964.

CARPENTER, Percy Henry, C.I.E. 1946; O.B.E. 1942; F.R.I.C., F.C.S.; retired; *b.* 19 Feb. 1879; *s.* of Charles Percy

Carpenter and Zillah Eliza Cook; *m.* 1906, Constance Mary Jones. *Educ.:* City and Guilds College, London. Chemist Assistant to A. C. Chapman, F.R.I.C., F.R.S. (late President Institute of Chemistry); in 1909 to Scientific Dept. India Tea Association, Experimental Station, Assam, India; I.A.R.O., Indian Cavalry, Mesopotamia, 1915-19 (despatches). Chief Scientific Officer, 1920 and subsequently Director of the Tocklai Exp. Station (Indian Tea Association, Assam, India); retired, 1945. *Publications:* Quarterly Journal Indian Tea Association and scientific memoranda published by Indian Tea Association. *Address:* 3 Angrove House, Goldsmith Avenue, Crowborough, Sussex. *Club:* Royal Corinthian Yacht (Burnham on Crouch). [*Died* 6 *July* 1962.

CARPENTER-GARNIER, Right Rev. Mark Rodolph, D.D. (Lambeth), 1924; *b.* 1881; 3rd *s.* of late John Carpenter-Garnier, Rookesbury Park, Wickham, Hants.; *m.* 1940, Eveline (*d.* 1967), 2nd *d.* of late Piers Egerton-Warburton, Arley Hall, Cheshire. *Educ.:* Winchester; Oriel Coll., Oxford (B.A. 1903, M.A. 1906); Cuddesdon. Curate of St. Thomas, Portman Square, 1905-8; All Saints', Margaret Street, 1908-20; temp. Chaplain to the Forces, 1918-19; Librarian of Pusey House, Oxford, 1921-24; Bishop of Colombo, 1924-38; Principal of St Boniface Missionary College, Warminster, 1938-42; Canon of Salisbury, 1938-44; Chaplain of the Diocesan Training College, 1942-44. *Address:* Cutlers House, Wickham, Fareham, Hants. *Club:* Athenæum. [*Died* 11 *Oct.* 1969.

CARR, Sir Arthur S. C.; *see* Comyns Carr.

CARR, Sir Cecil Thomas, K.C.B., *cr.* 1947; Kt., *cr.* 1939; Q.C. 1945; Counsel to the Speaker, 1943-55; Bencher Inner Temple, 1944; *b.* 4 Aug. 1878; *s.* of late Thomas Carr, Twerton-on-Avon, Bath; *m.* 1911, Norah, *d.* of late Sir Alexander Binnie. *Educ.:* Bath College; Trinity College, Cambridge (scholar); 1st class Classical Tripos; Yorke Prize, 1902 and 1905. Called to Bar (Inner Temple), 1902; Western Circuit; LL.D. Camb.; Hon. LL.D., Columbia, 1940, London, 1952, Belfast, 1954; Hon. Fellow Trinity College, Camb., 1963. Served in India, 1914-19 (2/4th Wiltshire Regiment); Assistant to Editor of Revised Statutes, Statutory Rules and Orders, etc., 1919; Editor, 1923-43; Carpentier Lecturer, Columbia University, 1940; Chm. of Statute Law Committee, 1943-47; Chm. Cttee. on Electoral Law Reform, 1944-47. Visiting Lectr., Univs. of Cape Town and Witwatersrand, 1955. F.B.A. 1952. President Selden Soc., 1958-61. *Publications:* Law of Corporations, 1905; Collective Ownership, 1907; Select Charters of Trading Companies, 1913; Delegated Legislation, 1921; Administrative Law in England, 1941; Annual Summaries of U.K. Laws in Journal of Society of Comparative Legislation (1920-51); Clement's Inn Pension Book, 1960. *Address:* Rock, Wadebridge, Cornwall. *Club:* Athenæum. [*Died* 12 *May* 1966.

CARR, Edward Arthur, C.M.G. 1951; appointed Administrator of the Colony of Nigeria, 1947; retired, 1954; *b.* 7 April 1903; *s.* of Edward Crossley Carr; *m.* 1930, Margaret Alys Willson; one *s.* *Educ.:* Ermysted's Gram. School, Skipton; Christ's College, Cambridge. Exhibitioner of Christ's College, Cambridge, 1922; M.A. Cantab. Joined Colonial Administrative Service, 1925. *Address:* Porch House, Great Gransden, Near Sandy, Beds. [*Died* 5 *June* 1966.

CARR, Francis Howard, C.B.E. 1920; F.R.I.C.; D.Sc. (Manchester); F.C.G.I.; M.I.Chem.E; late Chairman British Drug Houses, Limited, London; Past Pres. Soc. of Chemical Industry and Association of British Chemical Manufacturers; *b.* Croydon, 13 March 1874; *s.* of Henry Carr; *m.* 1898, Hilda Mary Sykes; three *d.* *Educ.:* The Whitgift Gram. School; City and Guilds Coll., London. Salter's Research Fell., 1894-98; Chief Manufacturing Chemist to Burroughs, Wellcome & Co., 1898-1914; Director and Chief Chemist Boots' Pure Drug Co., 1914-19. Fellow of the Imperial College of Science. *Publications:* numerous contributions to Chemical Science and Technology; (joint) Organic Medicinal Chemicals. *Recreation:* gardening. *Address:* The White House, Petersfield, Hants. *T.:* Petersfield 4212. *Club:* Athenæum. [*Died* 26 *Jan.* 1969.

CARR, Henry Marvell, R.A. 1966 (A.R.A. 1957); R.P.; R.B.A.; A.R.C.A.; Landscape, Figure and Portrait Painter; *b.* Leeds, 16 August 1894; *s.* of Matthew and Clara Marvell Carr; *m.* 1920, Olive Rumble; one *s.* two *d.* *Educ.:* Leeds Modern School; Leeds College of Art; Royal College of Art, Kensington. Exhibits in R.A. and most London and provincial exhibitions. Gold medal Paris Salon, 1956. War service, 1914-18 in France in Royal Field Artillery. War artist with 1st Army in North Africa and Italy, 1942-45. *Publications:* Portrait Painting, 1952; Portrait Drawing, 1961. *Address:* Witchet Ford, Aylesbury, Bucks; 2A, Avenue Studios, Sydney Close, S.W.3. *T.:* 01-589 3048. *Clubs:* Athenæum, Chelsea Arts. [*Died* 16 *March* 1970.

CARR His Honour Norman Alexander; *b.* 7 Oct. 1899; *s.* of late Stephen Carr, Moseley, Birmingham; unmarried. *Educ.:* King Edward's Sch., Birmingham; Queens' Coll., Cambridge (M.A., LL.B.). Called to Bar, Gray's Inn, 1922, Oxford Circuit. Recorder of New Windsor, 1945-55; Judge of County Courts, 1955-69; Chairman, Northants Q.S., 1960-70 (Vice-Chm., 1955-60) Dep. Chm., Herefordshire Q.S., 1955-70. Chm., Courts of Referees, Min. of Labour, 1928-48, and of Military Service (Hardship) Tribunals, 1939-48; Referee, Min. of Health Evacuation Scheme, 1939-45; Chm. Local Tribunal, Min. of National Insurance, 1948-1951; Chm., Dispossession Appeal Tribunal, Min. of Agriculture and Fisheries, 1946-48 and of Agricultural Land Tribunal for West Midland Province, 1948-55; Chm. of Council, Mansfield Coll., Oxford, 1958-70; Governor, Tettenhall Coll. *Address:* Grazings, Churchill, near Kidderminster, Worcs. *T.:* Blakedown 244. [*Died* 29 *Sept.* 1970.

CARR, Surgeon Rear-Admiral William James, C.B.E. 1937; R.A.N.; Director of Naval Medical Services Royal Australian Navy since 1933; *b.* 30 Jan. 1883; *s.* of James Carr, Solicitor, Thornton House, Thornton-in-Craven, Yorkshire, and Mary Carr; *m.* 1919, Leonora Constance, *d.* of George Eddington, Melbourne, Vic.; one *s.* two *d.* *Educ.:* Marlborough; Trinity College, Cambridge; London Hospital. B.A. (Nat. Sci. Tripos), 1904; B.Chir. 1908; M.R.C.S., L.R.C.P., 1908; F.R.A.C.P. 1942; House Surgeon London Hospital; other hospital appointments; Surgeon R.A.N., 1912; served European War in H.M.A. ships Melbourne, Australia and Sydney; Surgeon Lieut. Comdr., 1918; Surgeon Comdr., 1924; Surgeon Captain, 1935; Surgeon Rear-Admiral, 1946; Retired, 1946. Hon. Physician to Governor-General of Australia, 1934; K.H.P. 1940. *Recreations:* bowls. cricket, golf, gardening. *Address:* 2 Grange Road, Frankston, Vic., Aust. *Clubs:* Melbourne, Naval and Military (Melbourne). [*Died* 16 *May* 1966.

CARR-HALL, Col. Ralph E.; *see* Hall.

CARR - SAUNDERS, Sir Alexander (Morris), K.B.E. 1957; Kt. 1946; F.B.A. 1946; M.A.; Hon. LL.D. Glasgow, Columbia, Natal; Hon. Litt.D. Dublin, Liverpool, Cambridge; Hon. D. en Droit Grenoble; Hon. D.Litt. Malaya; Hon. D.Sc. London; Hon. Fellow of Peterhouse, of University College of East Africa, and of The London School of Economics; Director of London School of Economics, 1937-56; *b.* 1886; *s.* of late J. Carr-Saunders of Milton Heath, Dorking; *m.* 1929, Teresa, *d.* of late Major E. H. Molyneux-Seel of Huyton Hey Manor, Lancashire; two *s.* one *d.* *Educ.:* Eton Coll.; Magdalen Coll., Oxford. Charles Booth Professor of Social Science, Liverpool Univ., 1923-37. Chairman: Statistics Cttee. of the Royal Commission on Population, 1944-49; Colonial Social Science Research Council, 1945-51; Commission on Univ. Educ. in Malaya, 1947; Cttee. on Commercial Educ. 1949; Commission on Higher Educ. for Africans in Central Africa, 1953; Inter-Univ. Council for Higher Educ. Overseas, 1951-56, Vice-Chm., 1946-51 and 1956-62; Mission on University Educ. in Northern Nigeria, 1961; Member: Commission on Higher Educ. in the Colonies, 1943-45; Royal Commission on Population, 1944-49; Committee on University of East Africa, 1962. *Publications:* The Population Problem, 1922; Eugenics, 1924; Social Structure, 1928; The Professions, 1933; World Population, 1936; Social Conditions, 1958; New Universities Overseas, 1961; memoirs and articles in scientific and other publications. *Recreation:* mountaineering. *Address:* 51 Brompton Square, S.W.3. *Clubs:* Athenæum, Alpine. [*Died* 6 *Oct.* 1966.

CARRICK, Alexander, R.S.A. 1929 (A.R.S.A. 1918); retired; sculptor. *Educ.:* Edinburgh Art School (scholar); South Kensington. *Address:* Tower Road, Darnick, Melrose. [*Died* 26 *Jan.* 1966.

CARRINGTON, Lt.-Gen., Sir Harold; *see* Carrington, Sir R. H.

CARRINGTON, Vice - Admiral John Walsh, D.S.O. 1916; O.B.E. 1942; *b.* 5 Jan. 1879; *e. s.* of late Sir John W. Carrington, C.M.G., Chief Justice of Hong-Kong; *m.* 1918, Mary, 2nd *d.* of Admiral C. J. Eyres, D.S.O., O.B.E.; one *s.* one *d.* *Educ.:* King's School, Canterbury; H.M.S. Britannia, Dartmouth. Served European War (D.S.O.); Capt. 1917; Rear-Adm. 1929; retired list, 1930; Vice-Adm. retired, 1934. Deputy Controller, Southampton Civil Defence, 1939-1945. *Address:* Forelands, Watlington, Oxon. *T.:* Watlington 85 [*Died* 15 *Nov.* 1964.

CARRINGTON, Lt.-Gen. Sir (Robert) Harold, K.C.B., *cr.* 1941 (C.B. 1938); D.S.O. 1916; D.L.; p.s.c.; *b.* 7 Nov. 1882; *m.* 1921, Elizabeth Ruby, *o. d.* of R. S. Mesham. *Educ.:* Winchester. 2nd Lieut. Royal Field Artillery, 1901; served with R.H.A., 1908-16; Lieut.-Colonel, 1929; Colonel, 1931; Major-General, 1936; Lt.-Gen., 1940; served South African War, 1901-02 (Queen's medal and 5 clasps); European War (despatches 4 times, D.S.O., promoted Bt. Lieut.-Col.); G.S.O. 1. 4th Division, 1931-32; Comdr. Royal Artillery 4th Division 1932-36; Maj.-Gen. R.A., A.H.Q., India, 1936-39; Deputy Adjutant-General War Office, 1939; Lt.-Gen., 1940; G.O.C.-in-C. Scottish Command and Governor of Edinburgh Castle, 1940; retired pay, 1941; employed under Ministry of Supply, 1942-45. Colonel Commandant R.A., 1940-50. D.L. Suffolk, 1952; High Sheriff, Suffolk, 1953. O.St.J. *Address:* Edwardstone House, Boxford, Suffolk. *Club:* Cavalry. [*Died* 4 *Sept.* 1964.

CARRITT, Edgar Frederick, F.B.A. 1945; M.A.; *b.* 27 Feb. 1876; *s.* of Frederick Blasson Carritt and Edith Price; *m.* 1900, Winifred Margaret Frampton Etty; three *s.* one *d.* (two *s.* one *d.* decd.). *Educ.:* Bradfield Coll.; Hertford Coll., Oxford. Fellow Emeritus of Univ. Coll., Oxford; late Univ. Lectr. in Philosophy; Visiting Prof., State University of Michigan, 1924-25; Phi Beta Kappa; Substitute Prof. of Moral Philosophy, Univ. of Aberdeen, Michaelmas Term, 1946. Hon. LL.D. (Aberdeen) 1950. *Publications:* The Theory of Beauty, 1914, enlarged edn., 1923, rev. edn. 1962; The Theory of Morals, 1928; Philosophies of Beauty from Socrates to Robert Bridges, 1931; What is Beauty?, 1932; Morals and Politics 1935; (edited) Letters of Courtship, 1838-43, 1933; Hertz Philosophical Lecture (British Academy): An Ambiguity of the Word Good, 1937; Ethical and Political Thinking, 1947; (Translation) Selected Essays of Benedetto Croce, 1949; Introduction to Aesthetics, 1949; A Calendar of British Taste, 1600-1800, 1949; articles in Mind, Law Quarterly Review, Philosophy, Chambers's Encyclopædia, Encyclopædia Britannica, Revue Internationale de Philosophie, British Journal of Aesthetics. *Address:* Wreyland, 37 Mayflower Way, Farnham Common, Bucks. *T.:* Farnham Common 544. [*Died* 19 *June* 1964.

CARROLL, Rt. Rev. Francis P., D.D.; Bishop of Calgary, (R.C.), 1936-66, retd.; *b.* Toronto, Ontario, 1890. *Educ.:* St. Michael's College, Toronto; St. Augustine's Seminary, Toronto; Biblical Institute of St. Stephen, Jerusalem. Ordained, 1917; Profes or of S. Scripture, St. Augustine's Seminary, 1918-1931; President of St. Augustine's Seminary, 1931-35; Vicar Capitular, Archdiocese of Toronto, 1934-35. *Address:* 910-7A St. N.W., Calgary, Alberta, Canada. [*Died* 25 *Feb.* 1967.

CARROLL, Paul Vincent; playwright; *b.* 10 July 1900; *s.* of late Michael Carroll, schoolmaster, and of late Kitty Sandys, dressmaker; both Irish; *m.* 1923; widower; one *s.* three *d.* *Educ.:* Dublin; supplemented by self-education in Glasgow later. Taught in State schools in Scotland, 1921-37; resigned and became full-time professional playwright. Casement Award of Irish Academy of Letters for Shadow and Substance, and New York Critics' Foreign Award for same play when it was running on Broadway, 1938. Foreign Award for The White Steed, on Broadway, 1939; returned to Britain, 1941. Now a Director of Glasgow Citizens' Theatre which he helped to found with James Bridie; chief interest lies in British Repertory movement rather than in Metropolitan Show Business. *Publications:* Things That Are Cæsar's; The Strings, My Lord, are False; The White Steed (in one vol. entitled Three Plays), 1945; Plays For My Children (New York); Shadow and Substance, 1942; The Old Foolishness, 1945; The Wise Have Not Spoken (in one vol. entitled Two Plays), 1947; Plays for Young and Old, 1947; The Devil Came From Dublin (play), 1952; The Wayward Saint (play), New York, 1955; Irish Short Stories and plays, New York, 1959; Farewell to Greatness (play), U.S. and Canada, 1968. *Recreations:* drinking beer in English country inns; going to Repertory productions of good plays. Dislikes all outdoor sports. *Address:* 22 Park Road, Bromley, Kent. *T.:* Ravensbourne 1682. [*Died* 20 *Oct.* 1968.

CARRON, Baron *cr.* 1967 (Life Peer), of City and Co. of Kingston-upon-Hull; **William John Carron,** Kt. 1963; M.A.; President, Amalgamated Engineering Union, 1956-67; a Director of the Bank of England, since 1963; *b.* 19 Nov. 1902; *s.* of John and Frances Ann Carron; *m.* 1931; two *d.* *Educ.:* St. Mary's R.C. Primary Sch.; Hull Technical Coll. Apprenticeship, Messrs. Rose, Downs & Thompson Ltd. Hull, 1918-23. Amalgamated

Engineering Union: Sec., Hull 4 Br., 1932-1945; District Pres., Hull District, 1941-45; Divisional Organiser, No. 12 Div., 1945-50; Mem., Exec. Council, 1950-56. Chairman: British Sect., Internat. Metal-workers Fedn., 1957-68; Foundn. on Automation and Employment, 1962-. Director: British Productivity Council, 1957-68 (Chm., 1959-); London Bd., Co-operative Printing Soc., 1956-68; Fairfields (Glasgow), 1966-68. Jt. Sec., Air Min. Nat. Industrial Whitley Council, 1950-66. Member: (and T.U. Vice-Chm.) N. Midlands Regional Bd. for Industry, 1945-50; Lincoln and District Employment Cttee., 1946-50 (Chm., 1949-1950); (and Vice-Chm.) Engineering Trades Jt. Council for Govt. Industrial Establishments, 1950-56; Nat. Jt. Council for Civil Air Transport, 1950-56; Exec. Council, Confedn. of Shipbuilding and Engineering Unions, 1951-68; Gen. Council of T.U.C., 1954-68. Part-time Member: E. Midlands Gas Bd., 1967-; U.K.A.E.A., 1967-; N.E.D.C., 1968-. Trustee, Churchill Coll., Cambridge, 1958; Vis. Fellow, Nuffield Coll., Oxford, 1959-68. Mem. Council, Air League of British Empire, 1958. F.R.S.A. 1962. Hon. D.Sc.: Loughborough, 1966; Salford, 1967. Kt. of St. Gregory The Great, 1959. *Recreation:* photography. *Address:* 174 Grierson Rd., Honor Oak Park, S.E.23. *T.:* 01-699 9305. [*Died* 3 *Dec.* 1969.

CARRUTHERS, Agnes Lucy Mary; F.J.I.; Vice-Pres. Newspaper Press Fund, 1935; *b.* 14 Aug. 1872; *m.* 1899; one *s.* Has been engaged in journalism since 1895; the only woman elected to the Council of the Institute of Journalists, 1910; first woman Treasurer of the London District during 1912; first woman Chairman of London District, 1913; first woman elected on Executive of the Council, 1919-42; first woman elected to Council of Newspaper Press Fund, 1924-38; first woman Chairman Newspaper Press Fund, 1935-36; first woman Chairman of Institute of Journalists Orphan Fund, 1931-1952 (first woman Trustee, 1947); Mem. Council, Inst. of Journalists, 1900-52 (Hon. Vice-Pres., 1950-57-58-59); member House of Laity of the Church Assembly, 1920-25. *Address:* 5 Westbourne Road, Peverell, Plymouth, Devon. [*Died* 3 *March* 1961.

CARRUTHERS, (Alexander) Douglas (Mitchell), Explorer and Naturalist; *e. s.* of late Rev. W. Mitchell Carruthers; *m.* 1st, 1915 Hon. Mrs Morrison (who obtained a divorce 1948), *y. d.* of 1st Lord Trevor; 2nd, 1948, Rose mary Arden, *o. d.* of late Lt.-Col. Ernest Charles Clay, C.B.E. *Educ.:* Haileybury; Trinity College, Cambridge. Worked as naturalist in Syria, 1904-5; attached to British Museum Expedition to Ruwenzori and the Congo, 1906-6; worked as naturalist in Russian Turkestan and Bokhara, 1907-8; explored and collected natural-history specimens in North-West Arabia, 1909; explored in Mongolia and Central Asia, 1910-11; travelled in Syria and Asia Minor, 1913; awarded the Gill Memorial by the Royal Geographical Society, 1910, and the Patron's Gold Medal, 1912. Sykes Medal, Roy. Central Asian Soc., 1936. F.R.G.S.; F.Z.S. *Publications:* Lectures before the R.G.S.; various articles on Travel and Natural History; Unknown Mongolia, 1913; The Desert Route to India, Hakluyt Society, 1930; Arabian Adventure, 1935; Northern Najd, 1938; Beyond the Caspian, 1949. *Address:* Elder Farm, Grimston, King's Lynn, Norfolk. *T.:* Hillington 340. [*Died* 23 *May* 1962.

CARRUTHERS, Douglas; *see* Carruthers, A. D. M.

CARSON, Sir Norman (John), Kt 1961; C.M.G. 1952; Past Chairman: Australian Wool Realization, Commission 1950-60; Carlton and United Breweries Ltd.; Carlton Brewery Ltd. *b.* 27 Aug. 1877; *s.* of David Carson; *m.* 1911, Edith, *d.* of James H. Riley; one *s.* two *d.* *Educ.:* Brighton Grammar School. Manager for Victoria of Australian Mercantile Land & Finance Co. Ltd., 1929-45, retired; Member Central Wool Committee, 1939-45; Chairman Sheepskin Sub-Cttee.; Dir., Union-Fidelity Trustee Co. of Australia, and other companies; Member Board of Management of Alfred Hospital; Counsellor, Toorak College. *Recreations:* gardening, golf. *Address:* Ryburn, 54 Charles Street, Kew, Victoria, Australia. *Clubs:* Australian, Rotary (Melbourne). [*Died* 28 *Jan.* 1964.

CARSON, Rachel L(ouise); author; naturalist; *b.* 27 May 1907; *d.* of Robert Warden and Maria McLean Carson. *Educ.:* Pennsylvania Coll. for Women (now called Chatham Coll.) (A.B. 1929); Johns Hopkins University (A.M. 1932). Assistant in zoology: University of Maryland, 1931-1936; Johns Hopkins University, 1930-36 (summers); Aquatic biologist, U.S. Fish and Wildlife Service, 1936-49; Editor-in-chief, 1949-52; Eugene Saxton Mem. Fellow, 1949-50; Guggenheim Fellow, 1951-52; Associate, Woods Hole Oceanographic Instn., 1952-; Associate Member, Bermuda Biological Station, 1952-. George Westinghouse Science Writing Prize, 1950; Henry G. Bryant Gold Medal, 1952; Nat. Book Award (non-fiction), 1952; John Burroughs Medal, 1952; Frances K. Hutchinson Medal, 1952; annual Book Award of Geog. Soc. of Chicago, 1952; Page One Award, 1952; Gold Medal, New York Zoological Soc., 1953; Silver Jubilee Medal, Limited Editions Club, 1954; Distinguished Service Alumnae Award, Chatham College, 1956; Achievement Award, Amer. Association of University Women, 1956; Literature Award, Council of Women of the United States, 1956; Schweitzer Medal of Animal Welfare Inst., 1962; Conservationist of the Year, Award of Nat. Wildlife Fedn., 1963; some Special Citations, 1963, etc. Hon. D.Lit., Chatham College, Pennsylvania, 1952; Hon. D.Sc., Oberlin College, 1952; Hon. Dr. of Letters, Drexel Institute of Technology, 1952; Hon. D.Lit., Smith College, 1953; F.R.S.L. 1952; Member: National Institute of Arts and Letters; Society of Women Geographers; Audubon Society; Wilderness Society, etc. *Publications:* Under The Sea Wind, 1941, republished 1952; The Sea Around Us, 1951 (film version, 1954); The Edge of the Sea, 1955; Silent Spring, 1962; contributor to various magazines since 1937. *Recreations:* field ornithology; interested in preservation of wilderness areas. *Address:* c/o Marie F. Rodell, 15 E. 48 St., New York 17, N.Y. [*Died* 14 *April* 1964.

CART DE LAFONTAINE, Lieut.-Col. (Ret.). Henry Philip L., O.B.E. 1920; T.D.; F.R.I.B.A.; P.P.T.P.I.; Officier de la Légion d'Honneur, Officier d'Académie; Architect and Town Planning Consultant; President Town Planning Institute, 1950; Member of Council International Union of Architects, 1949; President Franco-British Union of Architects, 1948-49; Chairman of Council Royal Drawing Society, 1947; Consulting Architect, Crafts Centre of Great Britain, 1947; Member of Council, T.P.I., 1947; Member, Research and Planning Group, T.P.I., 1940; Member, Inter-allied Committee for Physical Planning and Reconstruction, 1944 (Ministry of Town and County Planning): Master of Company of Gold and Silver Wyre Drawers, 1937; President: Old Comrades Assoc.; Imperial War Graves Commission, 1953; *b.* 30 March 1884; *s.* of late H. T. Cart de Lafontaine, M.A., F.R.S.L., etc., and F. E. Dawe; unmarried. *Educ.:* privately; in France, Italy, Switzerland. Articled to Sir Guy Dawber, R.A.; completed architectural studies at Ecole des Beaux Arts, Paris; commenced practice in London, 1911; served European War, 4th City

of London Regt. R.F. (T.A.), 1914-17, in Malta and France (despatches); Assistant Director, Directorate of Graves Registration and Enquiries, G.H.Q. France and Flanders, 1918-19; Chief Inspector of Works, Imperial War Graves Commission, France and Flanders, 1919-21; special duties, I.W.G.C., 1922-23; resumed private practice, 1923; Member of Council Royal Institute of British Architects, 1926-34; Secretary General Franco-British Union of Architects; Hon. Sec. (British Sec.) Permanent International Committee of Architects; Vice-Chairman, Foreign Relations Com., R.I.B.A.; Official Delegate H.M. Govt. International Congress of Architects, Rome, 1935; Paris, 1937; Architect to Messrs Coty (England) Limited; Member of Committee of Experts (League of Nations) for the regulation of Architectural competitions; Town Planning Adviser, Southampton Corporation for Special Area and Bargate Improvement Scheme, 1928-34; Hon. Corresponding Member: American Institute of Architects, Société des Architectes Diplômés par le Gouvernement (France); Association of Architects of Liège (Belgium); Sociėdad de Arquetetos (Uruguay); Hon. Surveyor Worshipful Company of Gold and Silver Wyre Drawers, 1959. *Publications:* National Planning and Re-development (Design for Britain Booklets), 1941; various articles. *Recreations:* sketching and travel, skating. *Address:* 17 Harewood Av., N.W.1. *Clubs:* Junior Army and Navy, City Livery.
[*Died* 2 *Feb.* 1963.

CARTER, Alexander Scott; *see* Addenda: II.

CARTER, Rev. Dr. Charles Sydney, M.A. (2nd Class Hons. Mod. Hist.); D.D. (Oxon), Hon. D.D. (Wycliffe Coll., Toronto); F.R.Hist.S.; Principal Clifton Theol. Coll., 1932-1946; *b.* 26 Dec. 1876; *s.* of late George Foster Carter, Stow Maries, Essex; *m.* Joanna Lilian (*d.* 1954), *o. d.* of late Sir Richard Thorne Thorne, K.C.B., F.R.S., Chief Medical Officer to the Local Government Board; one *s.* one *d.*; *m.* 1954, Henrietta Maureen, *e. d.* of late Dr. T. Westgate, D.D., of Winnipeg, Canada. *Educ.:* Private School; Brasenose College, Oxford; Wycliffe Hall, Oxford. Served in Banking business in London, New York, and Halifax, N.S., 1892-1901; Ordained, 1905; Incumbent St. Mary Magdalene, Bath, 1912-14; Rector of Aston Sandford, Bucks., 1914-16; Principal Bible Churchmen's Missionary and Theological Coll., Clifton, 1925-32 *Publications:* English Church in the XVIIth Century, 1909; English Church in the XVIIIth Century, 1910, 2nd Edit., 1948; The Caroline Church, 1913; English Church and the Reformation, 1912, 2nd Edition, 1925; Contributor to the Prayer Book Dictionary, 1912 and 1925; Ministerial Commission, 1922; The Anglican Viá Mediá, 1927; The Reformers and Holy Scripture, 1928; Co-Editor The Protestant Dictionary, 1932; The Reformation and Reunion, 1935, 2nd edn., 1938; Ed. revised edn., Bishop Ryle's Knots Untied, 1954; Our English Prayer Book, 2nd edn., 1950; Articles in various periodicals, e.g. Church Quarterly Review; Hon. Corresponding Mem. de L'Institut Historique et Heraldique de France: Great Silver Medal, 1933. *Recreations:* chess, carpentering. *Address:* 2 Alma Road, Clifton, Bristol. *T.:* Bristol 34221. *Clubs:* Royal Commonwealth Society; Union Society (Oxford). [*Died* 23 *April* 1963.

CARTER, Frederick; painter-etcher; *b.* near Bradford, Yorkshire. *Educ.:* Paris; Académie Royale des Beaux Arts; Antwerp. Educated as civil engineer and surveyor; at 19 went to Paris to continue study, but took more seriously to drawing from life; returned to England and took up work for poster printers, but resumed study and gained three successive gold medals in the National Competition, South Kensington. for book illustrations; studied etching under Sir Frank Short; Exhibitor oil paintings and a series of engraved portraits R.A., etc., and water-colours. *Publications:* A series of drawings and etchings on the Comedy of Masks; The Wandering Jew; The Dragon of the Alchemists, a book of drawings with prefatory essays on comparative symbolism; Eighteen Drawings; The Dragon of Revelation; D. H. Lawrence and the Body Mystical; Symbols of Revelation; Introduction and drawings for Byron's Manfred; Café Royal Cocktail Book; Heinrich Heine's Florentine Nights; Decorations for Cyril Tourneur's works and other books. *Address:* 66 Abbey Road, St. John's Wood, N.W.8.
[*Died* 9 *June* 1967.

CARTER, George Stuart, M.A., Ph.D., F.L.S., F.R.S.E., F.Z.S.; Fellow since 1930 of Corpus Christi College, Cambridge; *b.* 15 Sept. 1893; *s.* of Rev. G. C. Carter and Hilda E. Keane; unmarried. *Educ.:* Marlborough Coll.; Gonville and Caius Coll., Cambridge. Maths. Tripos, Part I, 1913; served European War, 1914-18, with 6th Leicestershire Regt., 1914-17, and R.E. (sound-ranging), 1917-19; Nat. Sci. Tripos, Part II (Zoology), 1921; Frank Smart Prize, 1921; Frank Smart studentship (Caius College), 1921-23; research at Stazione Zoologica, Naples, 1922-1923; Lecturer at Glasgow Univ., 1924-30; conducted an expedition to Brazil and Paraguayan Chaco for an investigation of tropical swamps, 1926-27; Director of Studies in Natural Sciences, 1933, Praelector, 1935-47, Acting Tutor, 1942-45, Dean of College, 1947-1948, Senior Tutor, 1948-51, of Corpus Christi College; Lectr. in Zoology, Cambridge Univ., 1938-60. Conducted a biological expedition to the forests of British Guiana, 1933. Council Linnean Soc., 1931-34, 1941-44, Vice-Pres., 1941, Linnean Gold Medal, 1966; Brit. Assoc. Council, 1962-67 (Pres., Section D, 1960). *Publications:* A General Zoology of the Invertebrates, 1940; Animal Evolution, 1951; The Papyrus Swamps of Uganda, 1955; A Hundred Years of Evolution, 1957; Structure and Habit in Vertebrate Evolution, 1967; and papers in various biological journals. *Address:* Corpus Christi College, Cambridge. *T.:* Cambridge 59418; 40 Grange Road, Cambridge. *T.:* Cambridge 50987. *Clubs:* Athenæum, Savile.
[*Died* 2 *Dec.* 1969.

CARTER, Humphrey G.; *see* Gilbert-Carter.

CARTER, Norman St. Clair; Portrait Painter and Designer in stained glass; Teacher of Drawing; Lecturer in Architectural School, Sydney Technical College, 1918-39; Lecturer in Architectural School, Univ. of Sydney, 1918-46; Hon. Mem. Soc. of Artists; Foundation Member, Aust. Acad. of Arts; *b.* Kew, Melbourne, Victoria, 30 June 1875; father English, mother Scotch; *m.* 1908; two *s.* three *d.* *Educ.:* Melbourne Church of England Gram. Sch. Served apprenticeship in stained glass designing; studied painting, Melbourne National Gallery School, under Bernard Hall and F. McCubbin; later at Melbourne School of Art under E. Phillips Fox. Moved to Sydney, 1903; exhibited portrait Société des Artistes Français, Paris 1913, awarded Bronze Medal; Royal Academy, London, 1914: painted two large panels of decoration, "The Philosophers," University of Sydney; King's Jubilee Medal. Represented in National Galleries of Sydney, Melbourne, Perth, Brisbane; windows in many metropolitan and country churches. *Recreations:* walking, carpentering, reading. *Address:* 29 Belmont Avenue, Wollstonecraft, Sydney, N.S.W. *T.:* JF 4655. *Club:* Society of Artists (Sydney). [*Died* 18 *Sept.* 1963.

CARTER, Dr. Octavius Cyril; retired from private general medical practice in Bournemouth after 40 years; Consultant Anaesthetist Emeritus at Royal Victoria and West Hants Hospital since 1925; Direct Representative on Gen. Med. Council;

b. 15 July 1893; *s.* of late O. Carter, Bournemouth; *m.* 1921, Gladys Ann Summer; two *d.* *Educ.:* Bishop's Stortford; London Hospital. Qualified, 1917; held house appointments at London Hospital. Served European War, 1914-18, Captain R.A.M.C.; surgical specialist in India. For two years after war worked on Ministry of Pensions Medical Boards and then started private general practice in Bournemouth. Hon. Sec. to Bournemouth Division of B.M.A. for 25 years; Member of Council of B.M.A. for 12 years; Fell. B.M.A. (Vice-Pres.); Pres. Wessex Branch B.M.A., 1960. Was a mem. of Spens Cttee. determining the remuneration of general practitioners under National Health Service. First Chairman of Family Doctor magazine. Late Co-opted Member Council of R.C.S. of Eng. *Recreations:* collecting pottery and books, and study of trees and plants. *Address:* 96 Bath Hill Court, Bath Road, Bournemouth. [*Died* 29 *July* 1964.

CARTER, Lieut.-Col. Robert Markham, C.B. 1918; F.R.C.S.; F.C.P.S.; L.R.C.P., D.T.M. Liv.; F.R.G.S.; F.Z.S.; F.R. Hort. S.; Fellow Royal Society of Medicine, also Royal Soc. Tropical Medicine and Hygiene; *b.* 18 Oct. 1875; *s.* of Arthur William Markham Carter and Rosalie Edmunds Bradley; *m.* Kate Elizabeth' *d.* of Alexander Michie Saunderson, Oak Hill Park, Liverpool; three *d.* (one *s.* decd.). *Educ.:* Epsom; St. George's and St. Bartholomew's Hospitals; London and Liverpool Universities. Entered I.M.S. 1902; Medical Officer 1st Bombay Lancers, 1902; M.O. Anglo-Turkish Boundary Commission, Aden, 1903; Runcorn Research Laboratory, 1904; Cancer Research Laboratory, 1905; M.O. 36th Cavalry, Jacob's Horse, 1906; Director and Assistant Director, Pasteur Institute of India, 1907-9; Resident Surgeon, St. George's Hospital, Bombay, 1911; Professor of Materia Medica and Pharmacy, Grant Medical College, 1912; 2nd Presidency Surgeon, Bombay; 2nd Physician, Sir Jamsetjee Jeejeebhoy Hospital, Bombay, 1913; 3rd Presidency Surgeon and Professor of Pathology and Morbid Anatomy, and Curator of Museum Grant Medical College, Bombay, 1914; Medical Officer, 1st Lancers, Skinner's Horse, 1915; Surgical Specialist and S.M.O., H.M.H.S. Syria, and S.M.O., H.M.H.S. Varela, 1915 and 1916; special duty under Marine Department, Government of India, Ocean-going Hospital Ships, 1916; special duty under India Office, Q.M.G. 2D, and M.R.3 War Office, 1917; River Hospital Fleet for Mesopotamia, Water Post System and Purification Plant, Ice-Making Fleet and Refrigeration Barges; special duty under D.C.A.S. and Controller-General of Merchant Shipbuilding, Admiralty, 1918; Admiralty National Shipyards and attendant camps; medical supervision of Labour and Housing under Third Civil Lord, Admiralty; Dean and Professor of Pathology and Morbid Anatomy, and Curator of Museum Grant Medical College, 1919; 1st Physician, Sir Jamsetjee Jeejeebhoy Hospital, and Professor of Medicine, G.M. College, 1920-24; 1st Presidency Surgeon, Bombay, and Consulting Physician European General Hospital, Bombay, 1925-26; retired, 1927; served Aden Hinterland, 1902-3; N.W. Frontier, India, Zakka Khel, 1906, wounded severely (medal and clasp); N W. Frontier, India, 1915; Egypt, Aden, France, 1915-16 (despatches three times, Bt. Lt.-Col., C.B.); Director, Medical Services, to M.R.3 War Office and C.G.M.S. Admiralty, 1916-18. *Publications:* papers on tropical medicine, and research work on tropical diseases. *Recreation:* shooting. *Address:* Paddock Cottage, High Street, Ascot, Berkshire. *T:* Ascot 1055; c/o Barclays Bank, 127 Edgware Road, W.2. *Clubs:* United Service, East India and Sports; Oriental; Bombay Yacht (Bombay). [*Died* 13 *March* 1961.

CARTER, Walter, C.B. 1949; C.B.E. 1937; Commander, Order of Orange-Nassau, 1948; *b.* Berwick-on-Tweed, 8 Dec. 1883; *s.* of Thomas Carter and Elizabeth Paulin. *Educ.:* George Watson's College, Edinburgh; Edinburgh University. Entered Board of Trade, 1906; Secretary to Committee on Subdivision of Merchant Ships, 1912-15, and to War Risks Insurance Advisory Committee, 1914; served on Secretariat of Peace Conference, Paris, 1918-19; participated in work of Government of India Secretariat Procedure Committee, Simla and Delhi, 1919, of British Delegation for negotiation of Commercial Agreement with Persia, Tehran, 1920, and of International Conference on the Limitation of Armament, Washington, 1921-22; Secretary to Balfour Committee on Industry and Trade, 1924-29; Delegate to third Internat. Conf. on Safety of Life at Sea, 1948, having been Sec.-Gen. of second Conf., 1929, and Asst. Sec. of first Conf., 1913-14; Asst. Sec., Mercantile Marine Dept., Board of Trade, 1930-39; Ministry of Shipping, 1939-41; Principal Asst. Secretary, Min. of Transport, 1941-48; retired 1948. Member of East Horsley Parish Council and Guildford Rural District Council, 1952-55. *Address:* 5 Comiston Springs Avenue, Edinburgh 10. [*Died* 16 *Nov.* 1964.

CARTER, Wilfred George, C.B.E. 1947; Technical Consultant, Gloster Aircraft Co., Ltd., retired. Apprenticeship with W. H. Allen Sons and Co., Ltd., of Bedford, 1906-12; Design of I.C. engines and transmission units, 1912-16; Chief Draughtsman of the Sopwith Aviation Co., Ltd., 1916-20; Chief Designer of the Hawker Engineering Co., Ltd., 1920-24; Designer (special project) with Short Bros., of Rochester, was responsible for the design of a high-speed seaplane for 1927 Schneider Trophy contest, 1924-28; Designer with the de Havilland Aircraft Co., Ltd., 1928-31; Designer with the Gloster Aircraft Co., Ltd., i/c of D.H.72 bomber design and construction which had been transferred from the de Havilland Co., 1931-1935; transferred from Gloster Aircraft to A. V. Roe and Co., Ltd., 1935-36; Chief Designer to Gloster Aircraft Co., Ltd., 1936-1948; Technical Director, Gloster Aircraft Co., Ltd., 1948-54. Awarded R.Ae.S. Silver Medal, 1947. *Publications:* Papers on high-speed flight research and lecture before R.Ae.S. *Address:* Haroldstone House, Crickley Hill, Gloucester. *T.:* Witcombe 3105. [*Died* 27 *Feb.* 1969.

CARTER, William Edward, J.P. Staffs.; *b.* 1885; *s.* of George William Carter, Eccleshall Castle; *m.* 1914, Rose Margaret Eleanor, *d.* of late C. E. Morris Eyton, J.P., Wood Eaton Manor, Staffs; one *s.* two *d.* *Educ.:* Harrow; Trinity College, Cambs. Called to Bar, Inner Temple, 1910; served European war, R.G.A., 1915-19; Court Martial Officer, Havre Area, 1919; High Sheriff of Staffordshire, 1940. *Recreations:* shooting and tennis. *Address:* Eccleshall Castle, Stafford. *T.A.:* Castle Eccleshall. *T.:* Eccleshall 204. *Club:* Bath. [*Died* 13 *June* 1965.

CARTLEDGE, Jack Pickering, C.M.G. 1947; LL.B.; Chairman South Australian Housing Trust; *b.* 3 July 1900; *s.* of Herbert Cartledge, Adelaide; *m.* 1923, Margerie, *d.* of A. C. Vortman; one *s.* *Educ.:* Adelaide High School; University of Adelaide. Admitted S. Australian Bar, 1921; Law Officer of Crown (S. Australia), 1922-65; Chairman, Local Govt. Advisory Committee, 1934-65. Chairman, Building Act Inquiry Cttee., 1937-40 and of Building Act Advisory Cttee., 1941-65; Member S. Australian Housing Trust, 1941 (Chm. since 1945). Editor South Australian Statutes since 1934. *Publications:* Consolidated Statutes of South Australia, 1837-1936 (with notes), 1937; Statutes of South Australia, 1937-65 (with notes). *Recreations:* reading.

music. *Address:* 5 St. Andrews Street, Walkerville, South Australia. [*Died* 23 *July* 1966.

CARTON DE WIART, Lieut.-General Sir Adrian, V.C. 1916; K.B.E., *cr.* 1945; C.B. 1919; C.M.G. 1918; D.S.O. 1915; *b.* Brussels, 1880; *s.* of Léon Carton de Wiart, Brussels and Cairo; *m.* Countess Frederica (*d.* 1949), *e. d.* of Prince Fugger Babenhausen and Nora, Princess Hohenlohe; two *d.*; *m.* 1951, Mrs. Joan Sutherland. *Educ.:* Edgbaston; Balliol College, Oxford. Served South Africa, 1901 (twice wounded); East Africa (Somaliland), 1914-1915 (severely wounded, D.S.O.); European War, 1915-18 (eight times wounded, V.C., C.M.G., C.B.); Croix d'Officier de l'Ordre de la Couronne, Croix de Guerre (Belgian decorations); commanded British Military Mission to Poland, 1918-24 (Virtuti Militari, Krzyz Walecznc); retired pay, 1924; served war of 1939-45: British Military Mission with Polish Army; commanded Central Norwegian Expeditionary Force; also in the Middle East (despatches twice, K.B.E., Polish Cross of Valour; prisoner 1941, but freed 1943); special military representative with Gen. Chiang Kai-shek, 1943-46; retired pay, 1947; Col. 4th/7th Dragoon Guards, 1940. Hon. LL.D. Aberdeen Univ.; Hon. M.A. Oxford Univ.; Commander of Legion of Honour and French Croix de Guerre. *Publication:* Happy Odyssey, 1950. *Address:* Aghinagh House, Killinardrish, Co. Cork, Eire. *Club:* White's. [*Died* 5 *June* 1963.

CARTWRIGHT-TAYLOR, General Sir Malcolm Cartwright, K.C.B. 1963 (C.B. 1961); Director, East Riding of Yorkshire Branch, British Red Cross Society, since 1968; *b.* 29 Oct. 1911; *s.* of J. A. Taylor, Bakewell, Derbyshire, and Annie Cartwright; *d.* of T. W. Cartwright, Nottingham; *m.* 1935, Barbara Mahon Copson Peake; one *s.* three *d.* *Educ.:* Rugby School. Joined Royal Marines, 1930; served H.M.S. Hood, 1933-1935; H.M.S. Queen Elizabeth, 1935-37; R. M. Portsmouth, 1937-39; H.M.S. Renown, 1939-41; R.M. Depot, Exton, 1942-43; H.Q. 117 Inf. Bde. (R.M.) 1944-45; Admiralty, 1945-47; R.M. Chatham, 1949-1950; H.M.S. Bermuda and Fleet R.M. Officer, S. Atlantic, 1950-53; H.Q. Portsmouth Group, R.M., 1953-55; Admty., 1955-1958; Infty. Trg. Centre, 1958-59; Maj.-Gen., R.M., Plymouth. 1959-62. Comdt.-Gen., Royal Marines, 1962-65. *Recreation:* golf. *Address:* Southfield House, Old Ellerby, Nr. Hull, E. Yorks. *Club:* Army and Navy. [*Died* 5 *Nov.* 1969.

CARVER, Sir Stanley (Roy), Kt. 1962; O.B.E. 1958; *b.* 7 Feb. 1897; *s.* of Arthur James Carver and Martha Ann Carver (*née* Studman); *m.* 1922, Frances H. (*née* Horberry); one *s.* one *d.* *Educ.:* Warren and Newcastle, N.S.W.; Sydney Univ. Govt. Statistician, N.S.W., 1938-62; Actg. Commonwealth Statistician on various dates, 1941-57; Commonwealth Statistician of Australia, 1957-62, ret. *Publications:* Commonwealth and N.S.W. Official Year Books; various official statistical publications. *Recreation:* golf. *Address:* 12 Campbell St., Eastwood, Sydney, Australia. *T.:* WL 1800. *Clubs:* Eastwood Bowling; Ryde Parramatta Golf. [*Died* 22 *July* 1967.

CARVER, Colonel William Henton; D.L.; J.P. East Riding of Yorks; *b.* 27 May 1868; 4th *s.* of late Benjamin Carver, J.P., of Polefield, Prestwich, Lancashire; *m.* 1st, 1895, Florence Rosalie (*d.* 1937), 2nd *d.* of late Edward Philip Maxsted, J.P., of The Cliff, Hessle, East Yorks; one *s.* two *d.*; 2nd, 1955, Veronica, 2nd *d.* of Rev. Charles Moor, Kensington. *Educ.:* Uppingham School. Joined 3rd King's Own Yorkshire Light Infantry, 1889-1908; in European War raised 10th Batt. the East Yorkshire Regiment, 1 Sept. 1914, and served in Egypt and France; retired March 1919 with rank of Major; M.P. (C.) Howdenshire Division, 1926-45; Hon. Colonel East Yorkshire Regt. since 1939; President, Hull Chamber of Commerce, 1925 and 1926; has been in business in Hull since 1890; member of East Riding County Council, 1915, retired, 1950, Alderman, 1940. Director, London and North Eastern Railway Co. until nationalization; formerly Dir. of Wilson's Brewery, Ltd., Manchester to 1953. *Address:* The Croft, North Cave, East Yorkshire. *T.:* North Cave 203. *Clubs:* Carlton; Yorkshire (York). [*Died* 28 *Jan.* 1961.

CARY, Hon. Philip Plantagenet; late Captain Grenadier Guards (S.R.); *b.* 24 Sept. 1895; 2nd *surv. s.* of 12th Viscount Falkland; *m.* 1920, Esther Mildred, *d.* of Sir George Leon, 2nd Bart.; one *d.* *Educ.:* Eton. Joined Grenadier Guards (S.R.) as 2nd Lt., 1914; served European War, 1914-18 (twice wounded); retired as Captain (S.R.) 1919; Bluemantle Pursuivant of Arms, 1919-23; York Herald, 1923-32; rejoined Grenadier Guards (O.E.R.) 1940, as Lt. *Address:* 16 Sprimont Place, S.W.3. [*Died* 21 *June* 1968.

CASALIS, Jeanne de; Stage, Film and Radio actress; *b.* 22 May 1898; *d.* of Dr. Lt.-Col. Casalis de Pury; *m.* 1929, Colin Clive (*d.* 1937); *m.* 1942, Squadron Leader C. D. Stephenson, A.F.C., B.A. *Educ.:* Paris. Has played a variety of stage parts; first appearance in Fata Morgana, 1926; entertainer in wireless programmes, notably as "Mrs. Feather"; film career began in film Settled Out of Court; has had many subsequent appearances. Adapted Frou-Frou, New Lindsey Theatre, 1951. *Publications:* Mrs. Feather's Diary, 1936; co-author of St. Helena, play written in collaboration with R. C. Sherriff, 1934; author and producer of Dearly Beloved Wife, 1938; Things I Don't Remember; Never Will She Be Unfaithful, 1955. *Recreations:* golf, flying, writing. *Address:* c/o Eric Glass Ltd., 28 Berkeley Square, W.1. [*Died* 19 *Aug.* 1966.

CASE, Colonel Horace Akroyd, C.M.G. 1919; C.B.E. 1927; D.S.O. 1917; *b.* 23 April 1879; 3rd *s.* of late James Case, formerly of Ufton, near Reading; *m.* 1911, Enid Edington (*d.* 1940), *o. d.* of F. J. H. Green, Johannesburg; one *s.* one *d.* *Educ.:* Camb. Univ. 2nd Lieut. Dorsetshire Regt., 1900; Lieut., 1901; Capt., 1909; Major, 1915; Lt.-Col. (Brevet), 1916; served S. African War, 1900-2 (Queen's medal four clasps, King's medal two clasps); operations in Somaliland, 1908-10 (African General Service Medal); European War, Mesopotamia, 1915-18, Palestine, 1918-19; commanded 9th Infantry Brigade, Feb.-May 1919 (1914-15 Star, British War Medal, Victory Medal, C.M.G., C.B.E., D.S.O., despatches); commanded Southern Brigade, East Africa, 1929-1933; re-employed, 1939-45 (despatches twice, Africa Star, 1939-45 Star). *Address:* c/o National and Grindlay's Bank Ltd., 13 St. James's Square, S.W.1. [*Died* 29 *April* 1968.

CASEMENT, Major-General Francis, D.S.O. 1917; late R.A.M.C.; *b.* 1881; *s.* of late Roger Casement, D.L., of Ballycastle, Co. Antrim; *m.* 1916, Mabel Harrison; one *s.* one *d.* *Educ.:* Academical Institution, Coleraine; Trinity College, Dublin (B.A. 1904, M.B. and B.Ch. 1906). Served European War, 1914-19, with Naval Division (despatches, D.S.O. with bar, Legion of Honour); Deputy Director-General, Army Medical Services, 1937-38; Deputy Director of Medical Services, Southern Command, 1938; Hon. Surgeon to the King, 1940-41; retired, 1941; High Sheriff, County Antrim,

1951. *Address:* c/o Glyn, Mills & Co., Kirkland House, Whitehall, S.W.1. [*Died* 14 *Aug*. 1967.

CASEY, Captain Denis Arthur, C.B.E. 1942; D.S.O. 1942; D.S.C. 1915; R.D. 1923; *b.* 25 Oct. 1889; *o. surv. s.* of Maurice Casey, J.P., Spring Garden, Tipperary; *m.* 1928, Marie Louise, *e. d.* of John Barnes, Lytham; two *s.* *Educ.:* Weybridge; H.M.S. Conway (Silver medallist). Midshipman R.N.R., 1907; Submarine Service, 1914-18 (D.S.C. and 3 war medals); Commodore, 1940; A.D.C. to the King, 1944; retired list, 1944. Master of Royal Mail Flagship Andes, 1948-49; retired, 1949. Younger Brother Trinity House. *Address:* Holly Tree House, High Park Rd., Ryde, Isle of Wight. [*Died* 20 *July* 1968.

CASH, Sir William, Kt. 1958; M.A.; F.C.A.; Consultant to Harmood-Banner, Cash, Stone & Mounsey, Chartered Accountants, London, E.C.2; *b.* 18 June 1891; *s.* of William Cash, Coombe Wood, Addington, Surrey; *m.* 1932, Hilda Mary Napier (M.A. Oxon.) (*d.* 1962), *d.* of Prof. A. S. Napier, Oxford. *Educ.:* Haileybury College; Balliol College, Oxford. Chairman: Abbey National Building Society, Amalgamated Asphalte Companies Ltd., Neuchatel Asphalte Co. Ltd. and Lambton Close Holdings, and director of associated companies; Director: Bournemouth & District Water Co.; South Essex Waterworks Co., etc. Chairman, Girls' Public Day School Trust; Hon. Sec., Association of Governing Bodies of Girls' Public Schools; Hon. Treas., National Trg. Coll. of Domestic Subjects; Vice-Chm. and Trustee, Industrial Christian Fellowship; Trustee, Oxford and Bermondsey Club. Licenced Lay Reader in dio. of London. Bursar, Oxford and Bermondsey Mission, 1914-19; Under Bd. of Trade in Spain, 1916; Supervisor of London Br., Disconto Gesellschaft, 1914-24; Croydon Board of Guardians and Godstone R.D.C., 1916-19; Ed., The Challenge, 1919-20; visited Germany for Society of Friends Student Relief, 1919-20. Parl. candidate, Saffron Walden div. of Essex, 1922-29; Essex C.C., 1925-28; Royal Commns. on Civil Service, 1929-31 and 1953-55; Masterman Committee on Political Activities of Civil Servants, 1948-49. *Recreations:* reading, travel. *Address:* 1 Bryanston Square, W.1. *T.:* Paddington 6336. [*Died* 4 *May* 1964.

CASH-REED, Bellamy Alexander, C.M.G. 1955; *b.* Plymouth, 1888; *s.* of William Cash-Reed, M.D., of London and Liverpool; *m.* 1916, Irene Cargill; one *s.* one *d.* (and elder son killed in War of 1939-1945). *Educ.:* Liverpool College. Commercial career in Argentina, India and other foreign countries with widely spaced periods of Government service, also overseas. Food and Agriculture Attaché, British Embassy, Washington, 1951-55. *Address:* Bexhill, Sussex. *T.:* Bexhill 3434 [*Died* 3 *Nov*. 1965.

CASS, Brigadier Edward Earnshaw Eden, C.B.E. 1944; D.S.O. 1918; M.C.; K.O.Y.L.I.; *b.* 3 Mar. 1898; *o.s.* of late Dr. E. Eden Cass, M.B., B.S., Goole; *m.* 1926, Catherine Dorothea Bond (*d.* 1959); one *s.* four *d.* *Educ.:* St. Bees; R.M.C., Sandhurst. Joined K.O.Y.L.I. 1916; France, 1917; wounded 1917, France, 1918 (D.S.O., M.C., despatches); Lieut. 1918; Acting Capt. 1918-1919; Capt. 1927; Major, 1938; Lt.-Col. 1945; Actg. Brig. 1942; Temp. Brig. 1942; Asst. Instructor Small Arms School, India, 1920; Chief Instructor, 1935-39; War of 1939-45 (wounded, despatches, Bar to D.S.O., C.B.E., U.S.A. Silver Star); Comdr., 11 Inf. (Assault) Bde., Algiers, N. Africa, Nov. 1942, and 8 Br. Inf. (Assault) Bde., Normandy, "D" Day, 1944. *Recreations:* game and rifle shooting:—won Alexandra N.R.A. meeting, 1926; A.R.A. Silver Jewel, 1925; in King's Hundred N.R.A. meeting, 1931; British Army Rifle Champion (India), 1935 and 1937; Winner A.R.A. Gold Jewel (I), N.R.A. Silver Medal, The King's Medal (I), 1937; Rugby football: played for Army, 1925, 1926, 1927. *Address:* The Pheasantry, Snainton, Scarborough, Yorks. *T.:* Snainton 286. [*Died* 31 *Aug*. 1968.

CASSEL, Sir Francis Edward, 2nd Bt., *cr.* 1920; concert pianist; *b.* 27 May 1912; *s.* of Rt. Hon. Sir Felix Cassel, 1st Bt., P.C., Q.C., and Lady Helen Grimston (*d.* 1947), *d.* of 3rd Earl of Verulam. *Educ.:* Harrow; Tobias Matthay Pianoforte School. Chairman: Management Committee Cassel Hospital for Functional Nervous Disorders, Ham Common, Richmond, Surrey; King Edward VII British-German Foundn. *Heir:* *b.* Harold Felix Cassel [*b.* 8 Nov. 1916; *m.* 1st, 1940, Ione Jean (marr. diss., 1963), *e. d.* of Capt. Evelyn Hugh Barclay, Colney Hall, Norwich, and Hon. Mrs. Barclay, *d.* of 1st Baron Somerleyton; three *s.* one *d.*; 2nd, 1963, Mrs. Eileen Smedley, *d.* of James H. R. Faulkner. Served European War, 1939-45, Captain R.A. Barrister, Lincoln's Inn, 1946]. *Address:* Putteridge Bury, Luton, Bedfordshire. *T.:* 20358. [*Died* 17 *April* 1969.

CASSELLS, Alexander, C.I.E. 1931; M.A.; Indian Civil Service; retired, 1933; *b.* 1883; *m.* Lilian M., *y. d.* of late Thomas Collishaw, Hickling, Notts. *Educ.:* Univ. of St. Andrews; Lincoln College, Oxford. Entered Indian Civil Service as Assistant Magistrate, Bengal, 1908; served as Under Secretary, Deputy Secretary, Magistrate and Collector, Finance Secretary, and Commissioner, Government of Bengal. *Recreation:* golf. *Address:* 4 S. Inverleith Avenue, Edinburgh. [*Died* 30 *Aug*. 1967.

CASSON, Sir Lewis, Kt., *cr.* 1945; M.C.; Hon. LL.D. (Glas.), 1954; Hon. LL.D. (Wales), 1959; Hon. D.Litt. (Oxford), 1966; Fellow of Imperial College, London, 1959; Actor and Theatrical Producer; *b.* 26 October 1875; *s.* of Major Thomas Casson, J.P., of Festiniog and Portmadoc; *m.* 1908, Sybil Thorndike; two *s.* two *d.* *Educ.:* Ruthin Grammar School; Central Technical College, South Kensington. Started stage career in 1900 after preliminaries as Teacher and Organ Builder; engagements include whole Vedrenne-Barker season Court Theatre, 1903-1907 (in original casts of Prunella, Man and Superman, Silver Box, etc.); Horniman Company, Gaiety, Manchester, 1907-9 and 1911-13 (original producer of Hindle Wakes, Jane Clegg, etc.); Glasgow Repertory, 1914 (original producer of Marigold); Chas. Frohman's Repertory, 1912; seasons in America with John Drew and with Helen Hayes; in management with Sybil Thorndike, Bronson Albery, Bruce Winston, etc., at Holborn Empire, Criterion, Ambassadors, New, Wyndham's, Strand, Empire, etc., including original production of Saint Joan and productions of Henry VIII (Sybil Thorndike), Macbeth (Ainley and Sybil Thorndike); produced Henry V at Drury Lane for Ivor Novello, 1938, and King Lear for John Gielgud at Old Vic, 1940; has played some hundreds of parts in most of the English-speaking countries and in France, Germany, Portugal, Italy, Egypt and Greece; recital tour of Australia, New Zealand, Africa, India, Malaya, Turkey and Israel with Dame Sybil Thorndike, 1954-56; season in New York, Spring, 1957; toured Australia and New Zealand in The Chalk Garden, 1957-58; London season: Eighty in the Shade, 1959; Waiting in the Wings, 1960; Teresa of Avila, Dublin and London 1961; Festival, Perth, W.A., with Dame Sybil Thorndike, 1962. Chichester Festival

Theatre, 1962 and 1963; Queen B, Windsor and tour, 1963; Arsenic and Old Lace, Vaudeville, 1966; Night Must Fall, 1968. President British Actors' Equity, 1941-45; Drama Director to C.E.M.A., 1942-44; Member Arts Council of Great Britain, 1945-1947; Member British Council Drama Committee. Fellow of the Imperial College. War ser vice,A.S.C., (M.T.), 1914-15 (to Sergt.), Royal Engineers (Special Brigade), 1916-19 (to Major). *Address:* 98 Swan Court, S.W.3. *T.:* Flaxman 1315. *Club:* Savage. [*Died* 16 *May* 1969.

CASSWELL, Joshua David, Q.C. 1938; J.P.; M.A.; *s.* of Joshua Joyce Casswell and Sarah Tate; *m.* 1919, Irene FitzRoy Hutton; three *s.* one *d.* *Educ.:* King's College School; Pembroke College, Oxford. Classical Scholar Pembroke College, Oxon., 1905; Hon. Mods, Classics, 1907; Honours degree Jurisprudence, 1909; called to Bar, 1910; Assist. Comdr. and Commander V Divn. Met. Special Constabulary 1914; Horse Transport, R.A.S.C. 1914-19; Capt. 1915; Major 1916 (despatches); returned to Bar, 1919; practised London and Western Circuit; Recorder of Salisbury, 1938-41, of Southampton, 1941-51; Official Referee of Supreme Court of Judicature, 1951-59. Bencher Middle Temple, 1947. Deputy Chairman Surrey Quarter Sessions, 1954-61. Represented Oxford 3 times, Long Jump. *Publication:* A Lance for Liberty, 1961. *Recreation:* odd jobs. *Address:* 110 Ridgway, S.W.19. *T.A.:* and *T.:* Wimbledon 0147. *Clubs:* Royal Wimbledon; Vincent's (Oxford). [*Died* 15 *Dec.* 1963.

CASTLE STEWART, 7th Earl (*cr.* 1800), **Arthur Stuart,** M.C.; Viscount Stuart, 1793; Barony, 1619; Baronetcy, 1628; *b.* 6 Aug. 1889; *e. surv. s.* of 6th Earl and Emma Georgiana (*d.* 1949), *d.* of Gen. Arthur Stevens; *S.* father, 1921; *m.* 1920, Eleanor May, *er. d.* of late S. R. Guggenheim, New York; two *s.* *Educ.:* Charterhouse; Trinity College, Cambridge; University of Paris. Served European War, 1914-18 (M.C.); M.P. (U.) Harborough Division of Leicestershire, 1929-33. *Heir:* *s.* Viscount Stuart. *Address:* Old Lodge, Uckfield, Sussex; Stuart Hall, Stewartstown, Co. Tyrone. [*Died* 5 *Nov.* 1961.

CATER, Sir John James, Kt., *cr.* 1946; *b.* 30 June 1885; *s.* of Thomas Cater, Chepstow, Mon.; *m.* 1909, Jessie Sheila MacDonald (*d.* 1948), *d.* of Dr. Robert Moodie, Stirling; one *s.* one *d.* *Educ.:* Newport (Mon.), High School; London University; Ph.D. Edinburgh University; entered Inland Revenue, 1906; Surveyor for Argyllshire, 1909-14; Inspector in Edinburgh, 1914-33; Inspector in City of London and at Somerset House, 1933-38; Deputy Chief Inspector, 1938-43; Chief Inspector of Taxes, Inland Revenue, 1943-47; retired, 1947. *Recreations:* chess, golf, fishing and mountaineering. *Address:* 94A Findhorn Place, Edinburgh. [*Died* 16 *Feb.* 1962.

CATOR, Lieutenant-Colonel Henry John, O.B.E. 1964; M.C. 1917; D.L.; J.P.; *b.* 25th January 1897; *s.* of late John Cator, D.L., J.P., Woodbastwick Hall, Norwich; *m.* 1st, 1925, Anne Laetitia Mary, B.E.M. (*d.* 1960), *d.* of Sir George Everard Arthur Cayley, 9th Bt., and Lady Mary Cayley (*d.* 1941); two *s.*; 2nd, 1961, Lady Joan Birkbeck, *widow* of Colonel Oliver Birkbeck, Massingham, Norfolk. *Educ:* Eton; R.M.C. Sandhurst. Served European War, 1915-18, 2nd Dragoons; Capt. Norfolk Yeo., 1923; re-employed, 1939 (despatches); Lt.-Col. Roy. Scots Greys, 1945. C.C. Norfolk, 1924-39 and 1946-49; D.L. 1948, J.P. 1930, High Sheriff, 1957, Norfolk. Hon. LL.D. Cambridge. *Recreations:* shooting and fishing. *Address:* Woodbastwick, Norfolk. *Club:* Buck's. [*Died* 27 *March* 1965.

CATROUX, Général Georges, Hon. G.C.B. 1946; Grand Croix de la Légion d'Honneur; Médaille Militaire; Compagnon de la Libération; Commander, Legion of Merit, U.S.; Grand Chancelier de la Légion d'Honneur, 1954-69; *b.* 1877. *Educ.:* St. Cyr. Served European War, 1914-16 (wounded, prisoner). Commanded 14th Infantry Div., French Army, 1936; later 19th Corps, Algiers; Gov.-Gen., Indo-China, 1939-40; Free French High Comr. and General de Gaulle's rep. in Near East, 1940; C.-in-C. Free French in Levant, 1941; Gov.-Gen. of Algeria, 1943-44; Comr. of State for Moslem Affairs, French Cttee. of Nat. Liberation, 1943; Minister for North Africa, French Provisional Govt., 1944; French Ambassador in Moscow, 1945-48; Conseiller du Gouvernement Français, 1948-49; French Resident Minister in Algeria, Jan.-Feb. 1956. *Publications:* Dans la Bataille de Méditerranée, 1949; J'ai vu tomber le rideau de fer, 1951; Lyautey le Marocain, 1952; Deux Missions en Moyen Orient, 1958; Deux actes du Drame Indochinois, 1959. *Address:* 7 rue Juliette Lamber, Paris XVII. [*Died* 21 *Dec.* 1969.

CATTERALL, Councillor Sir Robert, Kt., *cr.* 1952; M.B.E. 1937; J.P.; retired; *b.* 18 June 1880; *m.* 1905; two *d.* (one *s.* decd.). *Educ.:* privately. Volunteered and served: South African War, 1900-1902; European War, 1914-18: War of 1939-45 (despatches, Meritorious Service Medal); served as Chief Observer for Royal Observer Corps, 1937-45. Chairman: Nat. Union of Conservative and Unionist Assoc., 1944-45; Darwen Div. Conservative and Unionist Assoc., 1945-52; President Assoc. of Conservative Clubs, 1953 (Vice-Pres., 1951-53); President North Western Area of Conservative and Unionist Associations, 1949-1953. Member of Turton Urban District Council, 1924- (three times Chm.); Mem. of Divisional Planning Unemployment and War Pensions Cttees. and numerous other Cttees. Member Assoc. of Conservative Clubs. *Recreations:* lecturing and public service. *Address:* 16 Darwen Road, Bromley Cross, near Bolton, Lancs. *T.:* Turton 307. [*Died* 25 *May* 1962.

CATTERNS, Basil Gage; *b.* 20 June 1886; *m.* 1918, Evelyn Nancy, *d.* of late W. H. Dodd; one *s.* (Fl.-Lt. R.A.F., killed 1945) one *d.* *Educ.:* Trent College, Notts. Served War of 1916-19 in R.F.A. Mem. Transport Arbitration Tribunal, 1917-50; Director Bank of England, 1934-36 and 1946-48; Deputy Governor, 1936-45; Sheriff of County of London, 1940. *Address:* Clements Meadow, Marlborough, Wilts. *Club:* Public Schools. [*Died* 5 *Feb.* 1969.

CATTY, Col. Thomas Claude, C.M.G. 1919; D.S.O. 1917; *b.* 1879; *s.* of late James Edwards Catty; *m.* 1933, Eileen Dorothy, *d.* of late Dr. George Cole-Baker; two *s.* *Educ.:* Heidelberg; R.M.C. Sandhurst. Served European War, 1915-18: A.A. and Q.M.G. 7th (Indian) Div., in Mesopotamia and Palestine, 1917-19; A.A. and Q.M.G. 10th (Irish) Div., 1919-21; Comdg. 2nd Bn., 2nd Punjab Regt., 1921-26; A.Q.M.G. Eastern comd., India, 1926-27; Comdg. 7th (Dehra Dun) Inf. Bde., 1927; retired, 1929. *Recreations:* shooting, golf. *Address:* The Croft, Tenterden, Kent. *T.:* Tenterden 2167. *Club:* United Service. [*Died* 23 *April* 1967.

CAULFIELD, Sidney Burgoyne Kitchener, F.R.I.B.A.; architect; *s.* of late John and Helena Caulfield, London, and *g.-g.s.* of Joseph Caulfield, Master of the King's Musick to George III.; *m.* Mary Philippa (*d.* 1950), *o. d.* of late H. W. and Margaret Wynne Nevinson; one *d.* *Educ.:* Privately. Works: factory and warehouse buildings at Poplar, Bromley-by-Bow, Bow, Hackney, Holborn, Clerkenwell, St. Pancras, Hounslow, Edmonton, Worcester, etc.; many houses in and around London; flats in Kensington, St. John's Wood, Mayfair, Dulwich, Sydenham, and Chelsea, Wey Manor Estate, Weybridge; also hospitals, garages, offices; late Director of Architecture, Central School of Arts and Crafts. *Address:* 27 Emperor's Gate, S.W.7. *T.:* Fremantle 2727. [*Died* 14 *March* 1964.

CAVE - BROWNE, Major-General William, C.B.E. 1937; D.S.O. 1919; M.C.; late R.E.; *b.* 1884; *s.* of late E. R. Cave-Browne, C.S.I.; *m.* 1916, Muriel, *d.* of J. W. Wainwright, A.M.I.C.E.; one *s.* one *d.* (and two *s.* decd.). *Educ.:* Shrewsbury School; R.M.A, Woolwich. Served Abor Expedition, 1911-12 (despatches); European War, 1916-19 (despatches four times, M.C., D.S.O., Order of the Nile); Col. 1934; Chief Engineer, Malaya, 1935-38; Chief Engineer, Eastern Command, 1938; B.E.F., 1939-40 (despatches twice); Maj.-Gen. 1940; Director of Fortifications and Works, War Office; retired, 1941. *Address:* The Walled Garden, Wonersh, Guildford. [*Died* 1 *Nov.* 1967.

CAVE-BROWNE-CAVE, Air Vice-Marshal Henry Meyrick, C.B. 1936; D.S.O. 1918; D.F.C. 1918; *b.* 1 Feb. 1887; *y. s.* of late Sir T. Cave-Browne-Cave, C.B. *Educ.:* Dulwich College; Royal Navy. Served European War, 1914-18 (D.S.O., D.F.C.); Director of Technical Development, Air Ministry, 1931-34; Commandant R.A.F. College, Cranwell, 1934-36; A.O.C. No. 16 Group, 1937; No. 25 (Armament) Group, 1938; retired list, 1940; Regional Air Liaison Officer Regional Commission, Scotland, 1940-45. *Address:* Bassett Mount, Beechmount Road, Bassett, Southampton. [*Died* 5 *Aug.* 1965.

CAVE - BROWNE - CAVE, Wing Commander Thomas Reginald, C.B.E. 1919; *b.* 11 Jan. 1895; *e. s.* of late Sir Thomas Cave-Browne-Cave, C.B.; *m.* 1918, Marjorie Gwynne Wright (*d.* 1969); one *s.* one *d.* (and *er. s.* decd.); *m.* 1969, Elsie M. Ricks. *Educ.:* Dulwich Coll. Royal Navy Engineer Officer, 1901-13; transferred to Naval Wing, 1913, R.N.A.S., and to R.A.F. on formation; in charge of non-rigid airship design, construction, and trial till 1918; then on airship research at Admiralty and Air Ministry; served with Advisory Committee for Aeronautics, 1914-20; then on Aeronautical Research Committee; retired list, 1931; Professor of Engineering, University College, Southampton, 1931-50, retd. 1950. Various Home Office Committees on Structural Air Raid Precautions, 1938-39; Director of Camouflage, Ministry of Home Security, 1941-45; Fellow and Ex-Mem. of Council Royal Aeronautical Society; Ex-Member of Council, British Association; M.I.Mech.E. (Ex-Mem. of Council). Lecturer Airship Engineering, Imperial College of Science, 1921. *Publications:* various lectures to Royal Aeronautical Society, Royal Society of Arts, Inst. of Mechanical Engineers and British Association; Airship Section, Encyclopædia Britannica, 1922. *Address:* Bassett Mount, Southampton. *T.:* 68135. *Club:* Junior Army and Navy. [*Died* 26 *Nov.* 1969.

CAVENDISH, Colonel Ralph Henry Voltelin, C.B.E. 1944; M.V.O. 1910; D.L.; *s.* of late Brig.-Gen. A. E. J. Cavendish, C.M.G.; *b.* 27 Mar. 1887; *m.* 1926, Lady Gweneth Baring, *widow* of Hon. Windham Baring and *d.* of 8th Earl of Bessborough; (one *s.* died on active service, 1947). *Educ.:* Eton. Entered Grenadier Guards, 1906; retired, 1919; A.D.C. to Governor of Madras, 1912-14; served in European War, 1914-18 (despatches). Col. and Group Comdr. Home Guard (C.B.E.). D.L. Kent, 1952. *Address:* Ightham Court, Ightham, Kent. *Club:* Turf. [*Died* 21 *June* 1968.

CAWDOR, 5th Earl (*cr.* 1827); **John Duncan Vaughan Campbell;** Baron Cawdor (Gt. Brit.), 1796; Viscount Emlyn (U.K.), 1827; T.D. and clasps; F.S.A.; F.S.A.(Scot.); Convener, Nairn County Council, 1953-64; Chairman, Joint County Council of Moray and Nairn, 1958-64; Chairman, Historic Buildings Council for Scotland; Trustee, Nat. Museum of Antiquities of Scotland; Lieut.-Colonel Cameron Highlanders; *b.* 17 May 1900; *e. s.* of 4th Earl and Joan Emily Mary (*d.* 1945), *d.* of late John C. Thynne; *S.* father, 1914; *m.* 1st, 1929, Wilma Mairi (marriage dissolved, 1961), *e. d.* of late Vincent C. Vickers, 38 Princes Gate, S.W.7; two *s.* one *d.*; 2nd, 1961, Elizabeth Lady Gordon Cumming (who *m.* 1st, 1924, Major Sir Alexander Penrose Gordon Cumming, 5th Bt., M.C.). Served in R.N., 1913-1920. Major, Cameron Highlanders, 1934; War of 1939-45 (despatches); Lt.-Col. 1939. *Heir: s.* Viscount Emlyn. *Address:* Cawdor Castle, Nairn. *Clubs:* Brooks's, Pratt's; New (Edinburgh). [*Died* 9 *Jan.* 1970.

CAWOOD, Sir Walter, K.B.E. 1965 (C.B.E. 1953); C.B. 1956; Ph.D.; B.Sc.; F.R.Ae.S.; Chief Scientist, Ministry of Aviation, since 1965; *b.* 28 April 1907; *s.* of late Walter Cawood, York; *m.* 1934, Molly Johnson, York; one *s.* one *d.* *Educ.:* Archbishop Holgate's School, York; Univ. of Leeds. B.Sc. (Lond.); Ph.D. (Leeds); Cohen Prizeman (Leeds), 1931; Ramsay Memorial Fell., 1931-33; Moseley Scholar of Roy. Soc., 1933-38; Member of League of Nations International Atomic Weight Committee, 1937; joined staff of Air Ministry, 1938; Wing Commander, R.A.F.V.R., 1943; Deputy Director Armament Research, 1945; Deputy Director (Chief Scientific Officer), R.A.E., Farnborough, 1947-53; Prin. Dir. of Scientific Research (Defence), Min. of Supply, 1953-55; Director-General of Scientific Research (Air), 1955-57; Deputy Controller of Aircraft (Research and Development), Ministry of Supply, 1957-60; Chief Scientist, War Office, 1960-64; Chief Scientist (Army), Ministry of Defence, and Mem. Army Bd., 1964-65. *Publications:* many scientific papers on physical chemistry, 1932-38. *Recreations:* yachting, swimming, organising recreation. *Address:* White Eaves, Boyle Farm, Thames Ditton, Surrey. *T.:* Emberbrook 4727. *Clubs:* Athenæum, Royal Ocean Racing; Royal Southern Yacht. [*Died* 6 *March* 1967.

CAWTHORN, Maj.-Gen. Sir Walter Joseph; *see* Addenda: II.

CAWTHORNE, Sir Terence (Edward), Kt. 1964; F.R.C.S.; Consulting Adviser in Otolaryngology to Ministry of Health, 1948-1967; Aural Surgeon, National Hospital for Nervous Diseases, London, 1936-67; *b.* 29 Sept. 1902; *o. c.* of William Cawthorne and Annie (*née* England), Aberdeen; *m.* 1930, Lilian, *o. c.* of William and Ann Southworth, London; one *s.* one *d.* *Educ.:* Denstone College; King's College Hospital, London. F.R.C.S. Eng., 1930. Resident Anæsthetist, House Surgeon and Registrar, E.N.T. Dept., King's College Hosp., 1924-29; Consultant E.N.T. Surgeon: Metropolitan Hosp., London, 1930-34; Hostel of St. Luke, London, 1932-45; St. Giles' Hosp., London, 1932-45; Royal Hosp., Richmond, 1931-33; East Surrey Hospital, 1934-38; Hon. Cons. Surg., E.N.T. Dept., King's Coll. Hosp., London, 1932-64; Clin. Dir., Wernher Res. Unit on Deafness, M.R.C., 1958-64; Dean. King's Coll. Hosp. Med. Sch., 1946-48; Hunterian Professor, R.C.S., 1949, 1953; F.R.Soc.Med. (Hon. Sec., Laryng. Section, 1936-38, Otol. Section, 1940-42; Joint Hon. Sec., 1955-61; Mem. Council, 1940-42, 1949-

1951). Examiner Part I Dipl. Laryngol. and Otol., R.C.S., 1940-44, Part II, 1956-61. Hon. Member: Amer. Otol. Soc., 1946; Otoschlerosis Study Group, Amer. Acad. of Otolaryng.. 1951; Canadian Otolaryng. Soc., 1955; Chicago Laryng. and Otol. Soc., 1960; Austrian Otolaryng. Soc., 1960; Danish Otolaryng. Soc.; Corresp. Member: Portuguese Society of Oto-rhinolaryngology and Broncho-oesophagology, 1956; Société Française d'Oto-Rhino Laryngologie, 1959; Roy. Flemish Acad. of Med., Belgium, 1964; Roy. Acad. of Med., Toronto, 1966; Hon. Fellow: Amer. Rhinol. Laryngol. and Otol. Soc., 1946; Pacific Coast Oto-opthalmological Soc., 1962; Roy. Acad. of Med. of Ireland, 1964; Yugoslav. Soc. of Otolaryng., 1965. Hon. Member: Yugoslav Soc. of Otolaryng., 1968; South African Soc. of Oto-rhino-laryng., 1968; Finland Otolaryng. Soc., 1969; Corres. Fell., American Laryng. Assoc., 1968. Joint Hon. Secretary, R.S.M., 1956- (President, 1962-64; Hon. Fell., 1966; Pres., Section of Otol., 1958-59; Hon. Mem. 1969). Pres. Harveian Soc., 1960; Sec., Internat. Conf. on Audiology, 1949; Master, Second Brit. Academic Conf. on Otolaryng., 1967. Dalby Memorial Prize, R.S.M., 1953; James Yearsley Memorial Lectr.,1955; Patrick Watson-Williams Memorial Lectr., 1958; Robert Campbell Memorial Orator, Univ. of Belfast, 1961; First Wilkerson Memorial Lectr., Vanderbilt Univ., U.S.A., 1966; Harrison Medal for Otology, R.S.M., 1961; Gold Medal, Worshipful Soc. of Apothecaries, 1965: Sir William Wilde Memorial Lectr., 1961; Sir William Gowers Memorial Lectr., 1968; Award of Merit, Amer. Otolaryng. Soc., 1969. F.K.C., 1963. Hon M.D. (Uppsala), 1963; Hon. LL.D. (Syracuse, N.Y.), 1964. Hon. F.R.C.S. Ireland, 1966. *Publications:* articles in learned journals in England, America, France, Belgium, Sweden, Switzerland, Canada. *Recreations:* the arts, swimming. *Address:* 149 Harley St., W.1. *T.:* 01-935 4444. *Clubs:* Athenæum, Garrick, Royal Automobile. [*Died* 22 *Jan.* 1970.

CAYLEY, Sir Kenelm (Henry Ernest), 10th Bt., *cr.* 1661; *b.* 24 Sept. 1896; *S.* father 1917; 2nd *s.* of 9th Bt. and Lady Mary Susan, *d.* of Hon. F. D. Montagu-Stuart-Wortley and *s.* of 2nd Earl of Wharncliffe; *m.* 1929, Frances Elizabeth Edwyna, *e. d.* of Lt.-Col. F. B. Brewis, Norton Grove, Malton; seven *d.* Lieut. 3rd Batt. Suffolk Regt.; served European War, 1914-15 (prisoner); served War of 1939-45 in Pioneer Corps; retired owing to ill-health with rank of Major, 1941. *Heir: kinsman* Digby William David Cayley, *b.* 3 June 1944. *Address:* Malpas House, Brompton, Scarborough, Yorkshire. *T.:* Snainton 233. *Club:* Royal Automobile. [*Died* 27 *Dec.* 1967.

CAZAMIAN, Louis; Professor of English Language and Literature at the Sorbonne, Univ. of Paris, retired; *b.* Saint-Denis (île de la Réunion), 2 Apr. 1877. *Educ.:* Lycee Henri IV., Paris; University of Paris. Elève de l'école normale supérieure (Paris); Professeur d'anglais at the Lycées of Brest, Nevers, Lyon; Lecturer at the Universities of Lyon, Bordeaux, Paris; Licencié ès lettres; agrégé d'anglais; docteur ès lettres; officier de l'Instruction Publique; officier de la légion d'honneur; Hon. LL.D. (St. Andrews), D.Litt. (Durham); Litt.D. (Oxon); F.R.S.L. *Publications:* Le Roman social en Angleterre (1830-50), 1903; Kingsley et Thomas Cooper, 1903; A History of Civilisation in England, 1904; J. Michelet; L'Oiseau (Oxford Higher French Series), 1908; L'Angleterre moderne, 1911; Modern England, 1911; Carlyle (Les Grands Ecrivains Etrangers), 1913; Etudes de Psychologie Littéraire, 1913; La Grande-Bretagne et la guerre, 1917; L'Evolution Psychologique et la Littérature en Angleterre (1660-1914), 1920; Histoire de la littérature anglaise (with M. Emile Legouis), 1924; Carlyle: extracts from Heroes and Hero-Worship, with Introduction and notes, 1925; A History of English Literature, Part II (Modern), 1927; Ce qu'il faut connaître de l'âme anglaise, 1927; Criticism in the Making, 1929; The Development of English Humour, Part I., 1930; La Grande Bretagne, 1934; R. Browning, Hommes et Femmes (Men and Women), poèmes choisis, 1938; Essais en deux langues, 1938; la poésie romantique anglaise, 1939; L'humour anglais, 1942; Shelley, Prométhée délivré (Prometheus Unbound), traduit avec une Introduction, 1942; L'humour de Shakespeare, 1945; Anthologie de la Poésie Anglaise, 1946; Symbolisme et Poésie, 1947; W. Wordsworth, Le Prélude, traduit avec une introduction, 1949; The Development of English Humour, Parts I and II, 1952; A History of French Literature, 1955; Carlyle, Sartor Resartus, préface et traduction, 1958; Shelley, chosen Poems (trans. with M. L. Cazamian), 1960; G. Meredith, Poems, (Text and translation) with Introduction and notes (with M. L. Cazamian), 1965. *Address:* 11 rue Monticelli, Paris XIV. [*Died* 5 *Sept.* 1965.

CAZENOVE, Brigadier Arnold de Lerisson, C.B.E. 1943; D.S.O. 1940; M.V.O. 1936; J.P.; D.L.; *s.* of Arthur Philip Cazenove, London Stock Exchange, and Isabel, *d.* of Gen. Sir Charles Shute, K.C.B.; *m.* 1939, Elizabeth, *d.* of Sir Eustace Gurney, Walsingham, Norfolk; two *s.* two *d.* *Educ.:* Eton; R.M. Coll., Sandhurst. Joined Coldstream Guards, 1916; served European War in France, 1917 and 1918 (despatches); Adjt. 2nd Bn., 1922-25; General Staff, London Dist., 1926-29; Bde. Major, Bde. of Guards, 1933-36; Commandant Guards Depôt, 1937-1939; Commanding 1st Coldstream Guards, 1939-40; served War of 1939-45, in N.W. Europe (despatches); Deputy Commander, Aldershot District, 1947-50; A.D.C. to the King, 1949-50; retired pay, 1950. Bt. Lieut.-Col. and Lieut.-Col., 1939; Temp. Brigadier, 1940; Colonel, 1942; Brig. 1948. J.P., D.L. Somerset. Officer U.S. Legion of Merit; Comdr. Netherlands Order of Orange Nassau. *Address:* Ham Manor, nr. Shepton Mallet, Somerset. [*Died* 2 *April* 1969.

CECIL-WILLIAMS, Sir John (Lias Cecil), Kt. 1951; M.A., LL.B. (Cantab.); LL.D. Wales *h.c.* 1951; Solicitor; Member of Council since 1932 and Hon. Sec. since 1934, Honourable Soc. of Cymmrodorion; Hon. Sec. of Cttee. of Y Bywgraffiadur Cymreig (1953) and The Dictionary of Welsh Biography (1959) and their Supplements, since their inception in 1937; *b.* London, 14 Oct. 1892; *s.* of late Dr. John Cadwaladr Williams and Catherine Thomas, Cerrig-y-drudion, N. Wales and London; changed surname to Cecil-Williams by Deed Poll, 1935; *m.* 1935, Olive Mary, *o. d.* of Alderman Aneurin O. Evans, J.P., Whitehall, Denbigh, N. Wales; one *s.* *Educ.:* Cerrig-y-drudion; City of London Sch.; Gonville and Caius Coll., Cambridge. Enlisted Inns of Court O.T.C., 1914; Capt. Royal Welch Fusiliers; served European War, France and Belgium (wounded thrice), demobilised with rank of Capt. 1919. Admitted a Solicitor (hons.), 1920; retired, 1960. Member Courts of: University of Wales, National Library of Wales (Council), National Museum of Wales; Trustee, The Museum of The Royal Welch Fusiliers, Caernarvon Castle; Gorsedd of Bards of the Isle of Britain (Seisyllt). Established and conducted Cymmrodorion Welsh War Relief, 1940-46; Hon. Solicitor Kinsmen Trust, 1942-56; Mem. U.K. Jt. Consultative Cttee.. Virginia 350th Anniversay, 1956-57; Member British Goodwill Mission to U.S.A., 1957; Hopkins Medal, New York, 1957. Freeman of City of London (by presentation). 1917. Cymmrodorion Medal, 1962. President Amateur Football Alliance, 1959-; President Southern Olympian Amateur Football League, 1951-59. *Address:* 118 Newgate Street, E.C.1. *T.:* Monarch 0840;

6 Gainsborough Gardens, Hampstead Heath, N.W.3. *T.:* Hampstead 3173. *Clubs:* Reform; Union Society (Cambridge).
[*Died* 30 *Nov.* 1964.

CEMLYN-JONES, Sir E. Wynne, Kt., *cr.* 1941; Barrister-at-Law; Chairman Selection Committee of Anglesey County Council; Vice-President of County Councils Association; *b.* 16 May 1888; *s.* of John Cemlyn-Jones, Brynbella, Penmaenmawr; *m.* 1914, Muriel Gwendolin (*d.* 1930), *d.* of late Owen Owen, Liverpool and Penmaenmawr; two *s.* two *d.* *Educ.:* Shrewsbury School; London and abroad. Private Secretary to late Rt. Hon. Sir Ellis Griffith, M.P., at the Home Office, 1912-14; served in Royal Welch Fusiliers, 1914-18; contested (L.) South Croydon, 1923, and Brecon and Radnor, 1929. Member of Anglesey C.C., 1919, (Alderman, 1928-). Served on Milne Cttee. on Water Supplies; Athlone Committee on Nursing Services and Rushcliffe Committee on Nurses' Salaries; Chairman of Anglesey War Agricultural Exec. Cttee., 1941-46; Member of Central Advisory Water Cttee.; Member of Small Holdings Advisory Council; Vice-Pres. of National Museum of Wales and of Courts of University of Wales and National Library of Wales; Vice-Pres. of Univ. Coll. of North Wales; Mem. of Council, Welsh National School of Medicine; Member of Central Whitley Council for the Health Service. *Recreations:* travel and art. *Address:* Trewen, Penmaenmawr, Caerns. *Clubs:* Reform, National Liberal.
[*Died* 6 *June* 1966.

CENTLIVRES, Hon. Albert van de Sandt, B.A. (Cape and Oxon.); Chancellor of the University of Cape Town, since 1951; Chief Justice of South Africa, 1950-57; *b.* 13 Jan. 1887; *s.* of Frederick James Centlivres and Albertina Centlivres (*née* de Villiers); *m.* 1916, Isabel, *d.* of George Short; three *d.* (one *s.* decd.). *Educ.:* South African College School; South African College; New College, Oxford. Called to Bar, Middle Temple, London, 1910; admitted as an advocate of Supreme Court of S. Africa, at Cape Town, 1911. On active service in S.W. Africa, 1914-15. Parliamentary Draftsman to Houses of Parliament, S. Africa, 1920; Acting Judge in S.W. Africa, 1922, in Cape Provincial Div. of Supreme Court of S. Africa, 1932-34: Judge of Cape Province Div., 1935; Judge of Appeal, 1939-57. Chm. Law Revision Cttee., 1950-57. Hon. D.C.L. (Oxford); Hon. Fellow New College, Oxford; Hon. Master of the Bench, Middle Temple, 1953. Hon. LL.D.: Cape Town and Melbourne, 1951; Rhodes, 1957; Witwatersrand, 1964. *Recreation:* bowls. *Address:* Crescent Road, Claremont, Cape Town, South Africa. *T.:* 774612. *Clubs:* Civil Service, Western Province Sports (Cape Town).
[*Died* 19 *Sept.* 1966.

CERNY, Jaroslav, F.B.A. 1953; Ph.D.; Professor emeritus of Egyptology, University of Oxford and Emeritus Fellow of Queen's College, Oxford, since 1965; *b.* 22 August 1898; *m.* 1951, Marie Sargant. *Educ.:* Charles Univ., Prague. Lecturer in Egyptology, Charles University, Prague, 1929-46; attached to Czechoslovak Legation, Cairo, and Czechoslovak Ministry of Foreign Affairs, then in London, 1942-45. Edwards Professor of Egyptology, University College, London, 1946-51. *Publications:* Ostraca hiératiques, Catalogue Général du Musée du Caire, 2 vols. (Cairo), 1930-35; Ostraca hiératiques non littéraires de Deir el Médineh, 5 vols. (Cairo), 1935-51; Late Ramesside Letters (Bruxelles) 1939; Egyptian Religion (London) 1952; The Inscriptions of Sinai (2nd edn.), 2 vols., 1952-1955; Hieratic Ostraca (Oxford), 1957; Egyptian Stelae in the Bankes Collection (Oxford), 1958, etc. *Address:* 2 Linkside Avenue, Oxford. *T.:* Oxford 59329.
[*Died* 29 *May* 1970.

CHADWELL, Rt. Rev. Arthur Ernest; *b.* 1 Aug. 1892; *s.* of Edwin Herbert Chadwell; unmarried. *Educ.:* King's Coll., London; Bishop's Coll., Cheshunt. A.K.C. 1921. Deacon, 1922; priest, 1923, Diocese of Southwark; Curate of St. Andrew, Earlsfield, 1922-26; Priest-in-Charge: Chin-Chun, 1926-28; Paik-chun, 1928-31; Pyeng Yang, 1932-40; Vicar Rural of Northern Area, Korea, 1932-40; Curate of St. Michael, Polwatte, Colombo, 1941-43; Priest-in-Charge, 1943-45; Examining Chaplain to the Bishop of Colombo, 1943-45; Curate of St. John the Evangelist, Shirley, 1945-48; Archdeacon of Southern Provs. of Korea, 1949-51. Commissary in Korea to Archbp. of Canterbury, 1949-53; Assistant Bishop in Korea, 1951-63, retd. *Address:* Posudong 2 Ka, 65, Pusan, Korea.
[*Died* 21 *Nov.* 1967.

CHADWICK, Brigadier Cecil Arthur Harrop, C.B.E. 1943; Retd.; *b.* 13 August 1901; *s.* of late Major P. T. Chadwick, Hopton Brow, Mirfield, Yorks; *m.* 1924, Muriel Grace, *yr. d.* of Thomas R. David, London; one *d.* *Educ.:* Stanmore Park; Harrow School; Royal Military College, Sandhurst. 2nd Lt. K.O.Y.L.I., 1920; transferred Royal Corps of Signals, 1927; Captain, 1931; Major, 1938; Brigadier (temp.), 1942; Lt.-Col. 1945; Col. 1946; Brig. 1950. Served in India, 1921-24, in Egypt, 1928-33; Staff College, Camberley, 1936-37; G.S.O. 3 I.A.A. Division, 1938; G.S.O. 2 I.A.A. Division, 1939; G.S.O. 1 I.A.A. Div., 1940; B.G.S. A.A. Command, 1942; Bde. Comd., 1943; Regional Commander in Germany, 1945; A.A.G. War Office, 1946; C.S.O. British Troops in Egypt, 1948; C.S.O. Eastern Command, 1951. A.D.C. to the Queen, 1952-55. *Recreations:* shooting, golf. *Address:* 25 Bulstrode Court, Gerrards Cross, Bucks. *Club:* Naval and Military.
[*Died* 3 *Sept.* 1970.

CHADWICK, Sir Thomas, K.C.V.O., *cr.* 1953 (C.V.O. 1942); C.B.E. 1947 (O.B.E. 1933); Accountant, Treasury; retired 1953; *b.* 14 May 1888; *m.* 1912, Alice (*d.* 1933), *d.* of E. T. Woolley; one *s.*; *m.* 1935, Ethel, *d.* of F. Warnett, Kidbrooke; one *d.* *Address:* 5 Cosbycote Avenue, Herne Hill, S.E.24. *T.:* 01-274 6929.
[*Died* 20 *Dec.* 1969.

CHALLINOR, William Francis, D.S.O. 1916; M.A.; T.D.; D.L.; Lt.-Col. (retd.) T.A.; sub-Controller Area 6 Bucks. (Civil Defence); *b.* 20 June 1882; *s.* of William Edward Challinor, J.P., and Catherine Challinor; *m.* 1st, 1917, Florence Bertha (*d.* 1924), *e. d.* of late C. C. Ellis, Kniveden Hall, Leek; one *d.* (and one *d.* decd.); 2nd, 1925, Kathleen Constance Annesley (*d.* 1958), *er. d.* of late Col. Sir Stuart Sankey, K.B.E., C.V.O. *Educ.:* Rugby; Trinity Coll., Cambridge (M.A.). Joined 1st Vol. Batt. North Staffs. Regt., 1901; Major (T.F.) to command 3rd Staffs. Battery, R.F.A., formed 1908; embodied, Aug. 1914; served European War, 1914-17 (despatches, D.S.O.); J.P., Bucks., 1932-61; High Sheriff of Bucks., 1944; D.L. 1952. *Recreations:* reading, formerly shooting, farming and other out-of-door pursuits. *Address:* Blackwater Covert, Nr. Southwold, Suffolk. *Club:* United University.
[*Died* 4 *Oct.* 1967.

CHAMBERLAIN, Professor Digby, C.B.E. 1962; F.R.C.S.; Ch.M.; F.A.C.S. (Hon); Prof. Emeritus of Clinical Surgery, University of Leeds; Consultant Surgeon; *b.* 31 July 1896; *s.* of Digby Chamberlain; *m.* 1935, Sarah, *d.* of Edgar Gaunt, Hawksworth Hall, Guiseley; one *s.* two *d.* *Educ.:* Leeds School of Medicine. Hon. Surgeon to General Infirmary, Leeds, and consulting surgeon to various hosps. in Yorkshire; Hunterian Prof., R.C.S., 1940, Mem. Council, Mem. Court of Examiners, Vice-Pres. 1960-1962. Fell. Roy. Soc. Med. and Pres. of Surgical Section, 1949-50; Fell. Assoc. of Surgeons of Gt. Brit. and Ireland, and Pres., 1954; external examiner, University of Edinburgh, 1949-51. Member Leeds and West Riding Medico-Chirurgical Soc. (Pres., 1951-52). Late Major R.A. *Publications:* articles in medical journals. *Recreations:* shooting and golf. *Address:* Orchards, Huby, nr. Leeds. *T.:* Huby 321. *Clubs:* Bath; Leeds (Leeds).

[*Died* 15 *June* 1962.

CHAMBERLAIN, Francis Walter, C.B.E. 1942; D.L., J.P. Kent; Officer of Crown of Italy; Partner, Chamberlain & Co., Solicitors, Lincoln's Inn; *b.* 8 Nov. 1892; *m.* 1st, 1915, Mildred Hall (*d.* 1953); 2nd, 1958, Stella Jean Agnes Wickham, M.A., *d.* of late Prebendary A. P. Wickham, East Brent, Somerset. *Educ.:* Merchant Taylors' School. Solicitor, 1913; Commissioner for Oaths, 1919; Commissioner for Affidavits, Ontario, Canada. European War, 1914-18; Trooper, 1914; commissioned R.F.A. 1915, served in France and Belgium. Formerly (1925-31), Member of Bromley R.D.C. and later, Beckenham U.D.C.; Inspector, Special Constabulary, 1926. Chief-Warden, A.R.P., Beckenham South, 1937-40. War of 1939-1945; Col. and Sector Comdr. Home Guard, 1940-45. High Sheriff of Kent, 1949-50. County Chief Warden, Civil Defence, 1950-1951; Sector Comdr. Metropolitan Kent Home Guard, 1951-52. *Address:* The Glebe House, West Wickham, Kent. *T.:* 01-777 1122. *Clubs:* Boodle's, Farmers'.

[*Died* 2 *April* 1970.

CHAMBERS, Rt. Rev. George Alexander, O.B.E. 1953; D.D.; retd.; *s.* of William and Mary Chambers, Sydney, N.S.W.; *m.* Winifred Marian, *d.* of late Rev. Hon. W. Talbot Rice; two *s.* *Educ.:* St. Paul's College, University of Sydney. Curate St. Clements, Mosman, Sydney, 1902-4; Vice-Principal, Moore Theological College, Sydney, 1904-11; Rector Holy Trinity, Dulwich Hill, 1911-27; Bishop of Central Tanganyika, 1927-47; Chaplain of British Embassy Church in Paris, 1947-55; Rural Dean of France, 1948-55; Assisting at Holy Trinity, Windsor, 1957-59; Chaplain Iringa, Tanganyika, 1959. Warden Trinity Grammar School, Sydney, 1913-28; Examining Chaplain to the Archbishop of Sydney, 1911-27. *Address:* c/o Barclays Bank, Windsor, Berks. *Club:* Royal Commonwealth Society. [*Died* 5 *Dec.* 1963.

CHAMBERS, Prof. Jonathan David, Ph.D. (Lond.); Emeritus Professor of Economic and Social History, Nottingham University, since 1965 (Professor, 1958-1964); *b.* 13 October 1898; *m.* 1926, Dorothy Grace Cheston; one *d.* *Educ.:* Mundella Secondary School, Nottingham; University College, Nottingham. Sixth Form English Master Boys' Gram. Sch., Ashby-de-la-Zouch, Leics., 1920-22; Lecturer in Dept. of Adult Education, Univ. Coll., Nottingham, 1924-34; Asst. Dir. of Adult Education, Univ. Coll., Nottingham, 1934-40; Sixth Form History Master, Boys' Gram. Sch., Ashby-de-la-Zouch, 1940-47; Lecturer in Economic History, Univ. of Nottingham, 1947-52; Reader in Economic and Social History, 1952-58. *Publications:* Nottinghamshire in the Eighteenth Century, 1932 (2nd edn. 1966); Dictators in History, 1940; Modern Nottingham in the Making, 1945; The Vale of Trent, 1956; The Workshop of the World, 1961, 2nd. edn., 1968; (ed.) D. H. Lawrence: A Personal Record by E. T., 1965; (with E. G. Mingay) The Agricultural Revolution 1750-1880, 1966; (with P. Madgwick) Conflict and Community: Europe since 1750, 1968; articles in Economic History Review, Economica, etc. *Address:* 136 Park Side, Wollaton, Nottingham. *T.:* Nottingham 283307.

[*Died* 12 *April* 1970.

CHAMPION de CRESPIGNY, Air Vice-Marshal Hugh Vivian, C.B. 1943; M.C. 1916; D.F.C. 1918; *b.* 8 April 1897; *s.* of Philip Champion de Crespigny, of Victoria, Australia; *m.* 1926, Sylvia Ethel, (marriage dissolved, 1951), *d.* of Rev. Robert Usher, M.A.; three *s.* (and one *s.* decd. and one *s.* adopted). *Educ.:* Brighton, Victoria. 2nd Lieutenant R.F.C. 1915; served European War, 1914-19; transferred R.A.F. 1918 (M.C., D.F.C., French Croix de Guerre); Wing Comdr. 1930; Operations N.W. Frontier, 1930 (despatches); Comd. No. 2 (Indian) Wing Station, 1930-33; Air Staff H.Q. Inland Area, 1934-36; Group Capt. 1936-39; Air Commodore, 1939; Comdg. No. 25 Armament Group, 1939; Air Vice-Marshal, 1939; Air Officer Cdg. Iraq and Persia, 1942-43; A.O.C., No. 21 Group, 1943-44; Labour Candidate for Newark-on-Trent Parliamentary Division, 1945; Regional Commissioner for Schleswig-Holstein, Control Commission, Germany, 1946-47. *Clubs:* Victoria (Pietermaritzburg, Natal); R.A.F. (London).

[*Died* 20 *June* 1969.

CHAMPNESS, Captain Charles Henry, D.S.O. 1940; R.N. (retired); *b.* 30 Aug. 1889; *s.* of late Henry Robert Champness, M.V.O., and late Susan Augusta Quiller; *m.* 1920, Jessie Black, *d.* of late John Motherwell, coalmaster, Rawyards House, Rawyards, Lanarkshire. *Educ.:* Plymouth College; Dulwich College. Entered H.M.S. Britannia, 1904; served in Persian Gulf in suppression of gun-running, 1910-12 (Naval General Service Medal, Persian Gulf Bar); qualified as Navigation Specialist, 1913; in North Sea Destroyers, 1914-15 and Dec. 1916-Nov. 1918; White Sea, Nov. 1915-Dec. 1916 (Russian Order of St. Anne 3rd Cl. with crossed swords, 1914-15 Star, Victory and Allied Medals); Commander, 1925; qualified as a Staff Officer, 1928; retired with rank of Captain, 1935; Marine Superintendent to Scottish Fishery Board, 1935-39; Marine Superintendent to Scottish Home Dept., Sept. 1945-Dec. 1954. Called up for war appointment, 1939; landed for operations in Norway, April-May 1940 (D.S.O., despatches, 1939-45 Star). Jubilee Medal, 1935; Coronation Medal, 1953. *Recreation:* fishing. *Address:* Rawyards Cottage, Pitlochry, Perthshire.

[*Died* 13 *Aug.* 1963.

CHANCE, Kenneth Macomb, M.A. (Cantab.), F.C.S.; President British Industrial Plastics Ltd.; *b.* 16 July 1879; 2nd *s.* of Alexander Macomb Chance and Florence Mercer; *m.* 1905, Muriel Monkhouse, *e.d.* of late G. B. Monkhouse, Gosforth, Newcastle upon Tyne; two *s.* two *d.* (and one *s.* killed serving with R.A.F.). *Educ.:* Repton; Trinity College, Cambridge. Served on Govt. Cttees. on Nitrogen and Potash, 1915-18; Board of Trade Cttee. on Export, 1942; Pres. of Plastics Institute, 1938-43. First Chance Memorial Lecture, 1944; High Sheriff of Warwickshire, 1948. *Publications:* papers on potash and aminoplastics. *Recreations:* shooting, gardening. *Address:* Rose Hall, Bungay, Suffolk. *Clubs:* Athenæum, Bath. [*Died* 9 *Jan.* 1666.

CHANCE, Percival Vincent, C.I.E. 1943; B.A.; B.A.I., T.C.D.; *b.* 12 June 1888. Joined Indian Service of Engineers, 1911; Chief Engineer Central Provinces and Berar,

1937-43; retired, 1943. *Address:* Glenalla, Rock Road, Blackrock, Ireland. [*Died* 12 *April* 1970.

CHANCE, Sir Robert Christopher, Kt. *cr.* 1946; J.P.; B.A.; Chairman Ferguson Bros. Ltd., Carlisle; *b.* 28 Nov. 1883; *s.* of Sir F. W. Chance, K.B.E.; *m.* 1918, Marjorie Winnifred Bradshaw; two *s.* two *d.* *Educ.:* Malvern College; Trinity College, Cambridge. Army Service, 1918-19; County Commandant for Army Cadet Force, 1942-45; Textile Manufacturer. Mayor of Carlisle, 1929-30; High Sheriff of Cumberland, 1938; Lord Lieutenant, Cumberland, 1949-58. D.L. Cumberland, 1944. Hon. Freeman, City of Carlisle. Hon. LL.D. Dickinson Coll., Carlisle, Pa., U.S.A., 1952. *Address:* Morton, Carlisle. *T.:* Carlisle 25027. [*Died* 10 *Dec.* 1960.

CHANCE, Walter Lucas, J.P.; *b.* 2 Dec. 1880; *s.* of Arthur L. Chance, D.L., J.P., Great Alne Hall, Alcester; *m.* 1907, Rosa Edith, *d.* of Hamilton Fulton, Salisbury; two *s.* one *d.* *Educ:* Eton; Trinity College, Oxford (M.A.). Director: Chance Brothers Ltd., Glass and Lighthouse Works, 1909-53 (Chm. 1929-47); Fibreglass Ltd. until 1958; Pres., Brit. Glas Convention, 1930; Chm., Midland Regional Production Bd., 1940-42; Pres., Birmingham Chamber of Commerce, 1933-34; Mem. B.I.F. Management Cttee., 1933-56; and of Bd. of Trade Export Advisory Cttee., 1951-56; Master, Worshipful Co. of Spectacle-Makers, 1951-53; Pres., W. Bromwich Gen. Hosp., 1933-48, and several other hosp. appts.; a Comr. of Income Tax, 1938-56; Mem. Council, Birmingham Univ., 1932-56, and formerly on Council of F.B.I. and of Associated British Chambers of Commerce. J.P. Smethwick, 1916-. *Publications:* many articles for the Press of various countries. *Address:* Mill Green House, Wargrave, Berks. *T.:* Wargrave 232. *Clubs:* M.C.C.; Phyllis Court (Henley). [*Died* 8 *Dec.* 1963.

CHANDLER, Sir John (Beals), Kt., *cr.* 1952; *b.* 21 Feb. 1887; *s.* of John Chandler, Bunwell, Norfolk, England, and Mary Chandler; *m.* 1912, Lydia Isabel Parish: two *s.* (and two *s.* killed in action, War of 1939-45). *Educ.:* Bunwell. Chm.: Chandlers (Australia Ltd.) and Man. Dir. of its subsidiaries; J. B. Chandler Investment Co. Ltd.; Brisbane Freehold Properties Pty. Ltd.; Dir.: Queensland Trustees Ltd.; Macquarie Broadcasting Service Pty. Ltd.; and others cos. M.L.A. Hamilton, Qld., 1943-1947; Lord Mayor of Brisbane, 1940-52. Past Pres.: Qld. Patriotic and Australian Comforts Fund (Qld. Div.); Brisbane Chamber of Commerce; Australian Fedn. of Commercial Broadcasting Stations. *Recreations:* motoring and orchid culture. *Address:* Lamont Street, St. Lucia, Brisbane, Queensland, Australia. *T.:* U2244. *Clubs:* Queensland, Brisbane (Brisbane); Indooroopilly Golf. [*Died* 19 *Feb.* 1962.

CHANDLER, Sir John DeLisle, Kt. 1954; Sugar Planter, Barbados, W.I., since 1909; *b.* 12 January 1889; *s.* of Sir William Kellman Chandler, K.C.M.G., and Ella DeLisle Chandler, *d.* of Hon. Thomas Jones, M.L.C.; *m.* 1st, 1917, Winifred Marian, *d.* of Hon. A. S. Bryden, M.L.C.; one *s.* two *d.*; *m.* 2nd, 1943, Edith Marie Evelyn, *d.* of Arthur Gill. *Educ.:* Harrison College, Barbados; Malvern College, England. M.H.A., Barbados, 1917-35; Mem. Exec. Cttee., 1928-34; Dep. Speaker, House of Assembly, 1935; M.L.C. 1935-55; President Legislative Council, 1950-55; M.E.C., 1951-56. George V Jubilee Medal, 1935; Coronation Medals, 1937 and 1953. *Recreations:* horse racing (Sen. Steward, Barbados Turf Club), yachting. *Address:* Gun Site, Brittons Hill, Barbados, W.I. *T.:* 7373. *Clubs:* East India and Sports; Savannah, Bridgetown, Royal Barbados Yacht (Barbados). [*Died* 29 *May* 1967.

CHANEY, Major-General James E.; D.S.M. (U.S.); Legion of Merit (with Oak Leaf Cluster); United States Air Force, retired; *b.* Chaney, Maryland, 16 March 1885; *s.* of Dr. Thomas Morris Chaney; *m.* 1910, Miriam Clark; no *c.* *Educ.:* Baltimore City College; U.S. Military Academy. 2nd Lt. with 9th Infantry, 1908; served with American Expeditionary Force in France, 1918-19 (several U.S. medals); Air Attaché, American Embassy, Rome, 1919-24; Commandant Air Corps Flying Schools, Brooks Field and Kelly Field, Texas, 1926-30; Chief War Plans Division, Air Corps, Washington, 1932-34; Assistant Chief of Air Corps, 1934-38, and commanding Air Corps Training Center, San Antonio, Texas, 1935-38; commanded Mitchel Field, Long Island, N.Y., 1938-40; commanded first Air Defense, 1940-41; Special Army Observer in the British Isles, May 1941; Commanding United States Army Forces in the British Isles, December 1941; to Moscow (with rank of Minister) with Beaverbrook-Harriman Mission, 1941; Commanding General, First Air Force, 1942; Commanding General Army Air Force's Basic Training Center and Technical School and then of the Western Technical Training Command, 1943-44; Chief of U.S. Delegation of Anglo-American Mission to Portugal, Sept.-Nov. 1944; Commanding General Army Forces in the seizure, occupation and development of Iwo Jima, 1945; Commanding General Western Pacific Base Command, 1945; Member and president, Secretary of War's Personnel Board, Washington, D.C., 1945-47; retd. 1947. Holds foreign Orders. *Address:* 3410 Reservoir Rd., N.W., Washington, D.C., U.S.A. [*Died* 21 *Aug.* 1967.

CHANNER, Major-General George Osborne De Renzy, C.B.E. 1937 (O.B.E. 1935); M.C.; *b.* 25 Feb. 1890; *s.* of late Lt.-Col. O. H. Channer, I.M.S.; *m.* 1920, Florence Maud Lees, *d.* of Col. L. L. Hepper, D.S.O.; two *s.* *Educ.:* Wellington College, 2nd Lieut., 1909; joined 7th Gurkha Rifles; Maj.-Gen., 1940; Comdt. 1/3 Gurkha Rifles, 1933-35; A.D.C. to the King, 1940-42; retired, 1943; served European war, Egypt and Mesopotamia (despatches twice, M.C.); Burma Rebellion, 1932-33 (medal and clasp), Waziristan, 1936-37 (despatches twice). Served War of 1939-45, 1939-43. *Address:* Lane End, Putney Heath Lane, S.W.15. *Club:* United Service. [*Died* 9 *March* 1969.

CHAPLIN, Alan Geoffrey Tunstal, C.M.G. 1956; *b.* S. Africa, 27 Sept. 1908; *s.* of Albert Frederick Chaplin, London, and Hester Margaret Potts, Newcastle upon Tyne; *m.* 1939, Amy Elizabeth Collier (marr. diss.); two *s.*; *m.* 1962, Patty Dent Allen. *Educ.:* Michaelhouse, Natal. Basutoland Mounted Police, 1926; Admin. Service, Basutoland, 1928; First Asst. Sec., Basutoland, 1937; Rep. High Commission Territories, South Africa, 1940; Asst. Admin. Sec., High Commissioner, 1944; seconded to Colonial Office, 1948; Development Commissioner, British Honduras, 1950; Colonial Sec., Bermuda, 1954; Actg. Governor, Bermuda, Apr.-Oct. 1955; Resident Commissioner, Basutoland, 1956-62. *Recreations:* tennis, riding, bridge. *Address:* Bay House, Pembroke, Bermuda. *Club:* Royal Bermuda Yacht. [*Died* 20 *April* 1967.

CHAPMAN, Capt. Alex. Colin, C.B.E. 1943; R.N., retd.; *b.* 15 Sept. 1897; *s.* of Rev. Theodore Charles Chapman and Alice Barr Chapman; *m.* 1929, Janet Marion, *d.* of late Canon P. H. Chapman; one *s.* *Educ.:* Clifton College; R.N. Colleges. Osborne and Dartmouth. Midshipman, August 1914.

Specialised in Gunnery. Commanded H.M.S. Arethusa and Captain of the Fleet, Home Fleet, War of 1939-45 (despatches); Retired list, 1949. *Address:* Ravelston, The Marina, Deal. *Club:* United Service.
[*Died* 4 *Sept.* 1970.

CHAPMAN, Allan, M.A. (Cantab.); *b.* 1897; *s.* of late H. Williams Chapman; *m.* Beatrice, *d.* of late Edward Cox, D.L., Cardean. *Educ.:* Queens' College, Cambridge. M.P. (U.) Rutherglen division of Lanarkshire, 1935-45; Parliamentary Private Secretary to Secretary of State for Scotland, Feb. 1938; to Minister of Health, May 1938; to Sir John Anderson, 1938-41; Assistant Postmaster-General, 1941-42; Joint Parliamentary Under-Secretary of State for Scotland, 1942-45; served European War of 1914-18, R.F.C. and R.A.F. *Club:* Pratt's
[*Died* 7 *Jan.* 1966.

CHAPMAN, Dorothy; *b.* 1878. *Educ.:* University of St. Andrews; University College, London. Warden of Women Students, University College of North Wales, Bangor, 1909-11; Warden of University Hall and Special Lecturer in Latin, University of Liverpool, 1911-31; Principal of Westfield College, University of London, 1931-39. *Address:* Nevill's Cottage, Rotherfield, Crowborough, Sussex. *T.:* Rotherfield 432. *Club:* Forum. [*Died* 28 *Jan.* 1967.

CHAPMAN, Major-General John Austin, C.B. 1952; D.S.O. 1919 (Bar to D.S.O. 1941); retired; *b.* 15 Dec. 1896; *s.* of late Sir Austin Chapman, K.C.M.G. and late Lady C. J. Chapman; *m.* 1919, Helena M. Booten (*d.* 1960), Brussels and Paris; two *s.* one *d.* (and one *d.* decd.). *Educ.:* Christian Brothers Colls., Waverley, N.S.W. and East Melbourne, Vic.; Royal Military College, Duntroon, Australia. Graduated R.M.C., Duntroon, Lt., 1915; served European War, Egypt, France, Belgium, 1915-18; Staff College, Camberley, England, 1931-32; Comdt. Small Arms School, Australia, 1934-38; Instructor, Staff College, Minley Manor, England, 1939; War of 1939-45, Eng., Aust., and Middle East, 1939-45: G.S.O.1., 52nd Lowland Div., 1939; G.S.O.1., 7th Aust. Div., 1940-41; Comd. A.I.F.(M.E.) Base Area, 1941-42; D.A. & Q M.G., Adv. Landforce H.Q., 1942-44; D.C.G.S. Aust., 1944-45; Head Aust. Mil. Mission, Washington, U.S.A. and Chief, Joint-Service Staff, Aust.-U.S.A., 1946-50; Aust. U.N. Mission to Balkans, 1947; G.O.C. Central Comd. Aust., 1950; Quartermaster-General, 1951-53. Hon. Col. R.A.A.S.C., 1960. *Recreation:* photography. *Address:* 38 Awaba St., Mosman, N.S.W., Australia. *T.:* XM4593 (Sydney). *Club:* Imperial Service (Sydney).
[*Died* 19 *April* 1963.

CHAPMAN, Lewis, C.B.E. 1955; Director, Birmingham Small Arms Co. Ltd.; *b.* 1890; *m.* 1919; three *c.* *Educ.:* Sheffield. Steel works practical training on manufacture of High Quality Steels, 1905-10, followed by commercial posts. Man. Dir., Wm. Jessop & Sons Ltd., 1931-55. Chairman, 1955-. Chairman of High Speed Steel Alloys Ltd. and other companies. *Address:* 390 Sandygate Road, Sheffield. *T.:* 32276.
[*Died* 18 *Jan.* 1963.

CHAPMAN, Colonel Sir Robert, 1st Bt. *cr.* 1958; Kt. 1950; C.B. 1944; C.M.G. 1918; C.B.E. 1945; D.S.O. 1916; T.D.; D.L. Co. Durham; B.A. London; J.P. Durham County and South Shields; Chartered Accountant; *s.* of late Henry Chapman, J.P., Westoe, South Shields; *b.* 1880; *m.* 1909, Hélène Paris (J.P.), *d.* of late James George MacGowan; two *s.* *Educ.:* High School, South Shields. Served European War, Royal Artillery, 1914-18 (wounded, despatches four times, D.S.O., Legion of Honour, C.M.G.); Served Volunteer and Territorial Artillery, Colonel 1900-50; M.P. (Nat. U.) Houghton-le-Spring Division, Durham, 1931-35; High Sheriff of Durham, 1940-41; Vice-Lieutenant Durham, 1946-1958; Councillor, Alderman South Shields Town Council, 1921-52; Mayor of South Shields, 1931-32; Chairman, Durham Territorial Association, 1941-46; Durham County Army Welfare Officer, 1939-52; Chairman North Eastern Trading Estates Ltd., 1940-48, Chairman Durham County Orthopædic Association, Finchale Abbey Training Centre for the Disabled, Finchale Abbey, County Durham, 1937-58; Governor Sherburn Hospital, Durham; President: South Shields Cricket Club; Durham County Rowing Clubs Assoc. O.St.J. *Heir:* *s.* Robin (Robert Macgowan), C.B.E., T.D. *Address:* Undercliff, Cleadon, nr. Sunderland. *Clubs:* County (Durham); Northern Counties, Union (Newcastle upon Tyne).
[*Died* 31 *July* 1963.

CHAPMAN, Sydney, F.R.S., 1919; Advisory Scientific Director, Geophysical Institute, University of Alaska, since 1951, and staff member, High Altitude Observatory, Boulder, Colorado, since 1955; *b.* Eccles, Lancs., 29 Jan. 1888; *m.* 1922, Katharine Nora Steinthal (*d.* 1967); three *s.* one *d.* Fellow of Trinity Coll., Cambridge, 1913-19, Lecturer, 1914-19, Hon. Fellow since 1957; Chief Assistant, Greenwich Observatory, 1910-14; Professor of Natural Philosophy at: Manchester University, 1919-24, Imperial Coll., 1924-46, Oxford Univ., 1946-53; Fellow of Queen's Coll., Oxford, 1946-53, Hon. Fellow since 1954; Deputy Scientific Adviser to Army Council, 1943-45; Research Assoc., California Institute of Technology, 1950-51; Visiting Prof. or researcher Cairo, 1934, 1963, Michigan, 1953, 1957-63, New York, Istanbul, 1954, Iowa, 1955, Göttingen, 1956, Minn., 1959, 1961, Ibadan, 1964; Mexico, 1965. Smith's and Adams Prizes, Cambridge; Past President: London Mathematical, Royal Meteorological Roy. Astronomical and Physical Societies, and of Internat. Assocs. of Meteorology, 1936-48, and Terrestrial Magnetism and Electricity, 1948-51 and Internat. Union for Geodesy and Geophysics, 1951-54; Pres. Commn. for Internat. Geophysical Year (1957/8), 1953-59. Hon. Fell. Roy. Soc. Edin., 1954; Hon. Fell., Nat. Inst. of Sciences, India, 1954; Fellow Imperial College, 1956. Foreign member of Nat. Acad. Sci. of U.S.A., India, Norway, Sweden, Finland, and of Accademia dei Lincei, Rome, and of academies of Halle and Göttingen; Hon. Life Mem., N.Y. Acad. of Sciences. Medallist of Royal, Physical, London Mathematical and Royal Astronomical Societies; Bowie Medal, American Geophysical Union; Internat. Prize (of Foundation Antonio Feltrinelli, for Astronomy, Geodesy, Geophysics and Applications) awarded by Acad. dei Lincei, Rome, 1956; Copley Medal, Royal Society, 1964; Symons Memorial Gold Medal, Royal Meteorological Soc., 1965; Hodgkins Medal, Smithsonian Instn., 1965. Hon. degrees: Sc.D. Cambridge, 1958; D.Sc.: Alaska; Michigan, 1960; Colorado and Paris, 1962; Exeter, 1963; Newcastle, 1965; Sheffield, 1968; D.Tech. Brunel, 1968; LL.D. Manchester, 1969. *Publications:* The Earth's Magnetism, 1936, 1952; Mathematical Theory of Non-Uniform Gases (with T. G. Cowling), 1939, 1952; Geomagnetism (with J. Bartels), 1940; IGY: Year of Discovery, 1958; Solar Plasma, Geomagnetism and Aurora, 1964; also many scientific papers. *Address:* High Altitude Observatory, Boulder, Colorado, U.S.A. *Club:* Athenæum. [*Died* 16 *June* 1970.

CHAPPLE, Charles Roberts, M.A.; Emeritus Professor and formerly

Professor of Education and Head of the Department for the Training of Primary and Secondary Teachers, University College of Wales, Aberystwyth; *b.* St. Levan, Cornwall, 21 Feb. 1874; *e. s.* of Edwin and Cordelia Chapple; *m.* 1911, Dora (*d.* 1913), *d.* of H. F. Elenor, Winchester; no *c.* *Educ.:* University College of Wales, Aberystwyth; University College, London; University of Jena. Formerly Professor of Education at University College, Southampton; Principal of Federal Government Training College for Men, Catamarca, Argentine Republic; Life member of Court of Governors and for many years member of the Council, University College of Wales; of the Grammar School Governors, etc. *Publications:* Contributions to the Dictionary of National Biography, The Encyclopædia and Dictionary of Education, The Higher Education Journal, etc. *Address:* Woodville, Penglais Road, Aberystwyth. [*Died* 15 *June* 1965.

CHARLEMONT, 9th Viscount (*cr.* 1665); **Charles Edward St. George Caulfeild,** Baron Caulfeild of Charlemont, *cr.* 1620; F.S.S.; Honorary Vice-President, National Association of British Manufacturers, Director of Membership, 1919-50; *b.* Mauritius, 12 July 1887; *o. s.* of Hon. Hans St. George Caulfeild, M.I.C.E., and of Emily Bertha, *d.* of Edward James, M.D., of Edgbaston, Warwickshire; *g.s.* of Rt. Rev. Charles Caulfeild, D.D., Bishop of Nassau; *S.* cousin, 1949; *m.* 1911, Mabel, *e. d.* of James F. W. Hawthorn; two *d.* *Educ.:* Godolphin School; studied aviation, etc., at Christ Church, Oxford. Sometime Lt. R.F.C. (Military Wing); served on Administrative Staff, Eastern Command, 1916-18; loaned to the Ministry of National Service, 1918, to Command N.W. Wilts., Captain; served War of 1939-45 (Defence Medal); President (Sutton and Cheam Branch) Royal Air Forces Assoc., 1946-49. Owner of portraits by Kneller, Lely and Reynolds. *Recreations:* motoring, fishing. *Heir: cousin,* Robert Toby St. George Caulfeild, *b.* 30 Sept. 1881. *Address:* Ranby, 12 Milnthorpe Road, Eastbourne, Sussex. *T.:* Eastbourne 3493. [*Died* 18 *Jan.* 1964.

CHARLEMONT, 10th Viscount, *cr.* 1665 (Ireland); **Robert Toby St. George Caulfeild;** Baron Caulfeild of Charlemont, *cr.* 1620 (Ireland); *b.* 30 September 1881; 2nd *s.* of Henry St. George Caulfeild, Queensland C.S., and Jane, *d.* of William Goldsmith, Gravesend, England; *S.* cousin, 1964. *Educ.:* Von Schultz Grammar School, Bundaberg, Queensland, Australia. Retired as Inspector, Queensland National Bank (Limited), Brisbane. Sometime Lieutenant 47th Australian Infantry (Reserve). Served European War, 1914-19 (wounded). *Heir: b.* Charles St. George Caulfeild [*b.* 1884; *m.* 1915, Lydia Clara, *d.* of Charles James Kingston, Aramac, Queensland; two *d.* Retired Manager of the Bank of New South Wales, Cambooya, Queensland]. *Address:* c/o National Bank of Australasia, Bundaberg, Queensland, Australia. *Club:* Returned Soldiers' (Bundaberg). [*Died* 26 *Nov.* 1967.

CHARLES, Sir Arthur (Eber Sydney), Kt. 1965; C.B.E. 1956; Speaker of the Legislative Council of Aden since 1959, also Public Service Commissioner, Aden since 1959, and Public Service Commissioner, Federation of South Arabia since 1963; *b.* 6 Jan. 1910; *s.* of late Rev. Edward Eber Charles and Mrs. Winifred Sydney Charles; *m.* 1949, Mary Elise, *d.* of late Thomas Charles and Charlotte Fanny Sheppard. *Educ.:* Sherborne; Worcester College, Oxford. Appointed to Sudan Political Service, 1933; Assistant District Commissioner, Kordofan Province, 1933-37; Deputy Assistant Civil Secretary, 1937-38; seconded to Palestine Administrative Service as Assistant District Commissioner, 1938-41; Temporary Commission, British Army General List, 1941; Assistant District Commissioner, Equatoria Province, Sudan, 1941-43; Inspector of Establishments, 1943-46; District Commissioner, Northern Darfur District, 1946-51; Assistant Director of Establishments, 1952-53; Director of Establishments, 1953-55; Establishments Adviser, 1955-57; Chairman, Committee for Adenisation of Civil Service of Aden, 1957-59. *Address:* Al Jabaly Building, Crater, Aden. *Clubs:* Royal Commonwealth Society; United University. [*Died* 1 *Sept.* 1965.

CHARLES, Brigadier Eric Montagu Seton, C.M.G. 1919; D.S.O. 1917; late Royal Engineers; *s.* of late T. Edmondston Charles, M.D., Hon. Physician to H.M., Deputy Surgeon General, I.M.S., and *g.s.* of late General F. H. Rundall, C.S.I., R.E.; *b.* 22 Feb. 1878; *m.* 1911, Lola Beatrice (*d.* 1948), *d.* of W. F. Powell, Ottawa; one *d.* *Educ.:* Winchester; Royal Military Academy, Woolwich. 2nd Lieutenant Royal Engineers, 1898; Lieutenant, 1901 Captain, 1907 Major, 1914; Lieut.-Colonel, 1922; Colonel, 1927; served South Africa, 1900-02; France and Macedonia, 1915-17 and Palestine, 1917-18 (despatches 5 times, C.M.G., Bt. Lt.-Col., D.S.O.); Chief Engineer Southern Command, India, 1927-31; Commander 161st Essex Infantry Brigade T.A., 1932-35; A.D.C. to the King, 1932-35; retired, 1935. *Address:* Lightburn, Ulverston, N. Lancs. [*Died* 30 *July* 1964.

CHARLES, John Roger, M.A., M.D. Cantab.; F.R.C.P. Lond.; retired; formerly Consulting Physician, Royal Infirmary, Bristol; *e. s.* of John Smith Charles, Pelsall Hall, Staffs.; *b.* Oct. 1872; *m.* 1st, Alice M. G. (*d.* 1924), *d.* of Ven. R. Hodgson, late Archdeacon of Stafford and Canon of Lichfield; two *s.* (one *d.* decd.); 2nd, 1925, Hilda Mary Fisher. *Educ.:* Rugby; Caius Coll., Cambridge; St. Thomas's Hospital. Appointments at St. Thomas's Hospital; General Hospital, Birmingham; Royal Infirmary, Bristol. *Publications:* contributions to medical journals. *Address:* The Cottage, Churchill, nr. Bristol. *T.:* Churchill 273. [*Died* 8 *April* 1962.

CHARLES-ROUX, François; French diplomat and historian; President, Suez Canal Co., 1948-58, Hon. President, 1958; *b.* 1879. *Educ.:* University and École des Sciences Politiques, Paris. Attaché, St. Petersburg Embassy, 1902; Constantinople, 1905; Sec. Cairo, 1907; London, 1912; Counsellor, Rome, 1916; Inspector of Embassies, 1924; Del. Danubian Commn., 1925; Minister to Czechoslovakia, 1926-32; Ambassador to Holy See, 1932-40; Permanent Head Min. of Foreign Affairs, 1940; Suez Canal Admin., 1944-48. Member, Institut de France, 1934. *Address:* 7 bis, rue des Saints-Pères, Paris VI. [*Died* 26 *June* 1961.

CHARLESWORTH, Lilian E., C.B.E. 1954; Director, Thomas Wall Trust. *Educ.:* Clapham High School, G.P.D.S.T.; Royal Holloway College. Head Mistress of Kensington High School, 1931-39; Head Mistress, Sutton High School, G.P.D.S.T., 1939-59. President of Association of Head-mistresses, 1948-50. Chairman: Joint Committee of the Four Secondary Associations, 1952-54; Whitelands College Council; Charlotte Mason Schools Company. Member, Professional Classes Aid Council. Hon. Director, Royal Academy of Dancing, Teachers' Training Course. *Address:* 46 Beaufort Mansions, S.W.3 [*Died* 20 *Nov.* 1970.

CHARLTON, Brig.-General Claud Edward Charles Graham, C.B. 1924; C.M.G. 1919; D.S.O. 1917; D.L., Essex;

o. surv. s. of late Lieut.-Col. Richard Granville Charlton; *m.* Gwendoline, *d.* of Arthur Whitaker, 52 Cadogan Square, S.W.; one *s.* one *d.* *Educ.:* privately; Royal Military Academy, Woolwich. Joined R.A.; served in R.H. and R.F.A. in India and England; has held appointments of A.D.C. to the Sirdar and Governor-General, Sudan; military sec., Egyptian Army; commandant Artillery, Egyptian Army; served Tirah (medal and 2 clasps); expedition against Agar Dinkas, Sudan, 1902 (medal and clasp); European War in France, 1914-18 (D.S.O., C.M.G., despatches six times, Bt Col., Belgian Croix de Guerre); C.R.A. 16th (Irish) Div., 1917-19; C.R.A. W. Lancs Div. 1919-23; Military Attaché, British Embassy, Washington, 1923-27; retired pay, 1927; Essex Home Guard as Battalion Comdr., Group Comdr., Inspector, and Zone Comdr.; High Sheriff of Essex, 1947-48. Osmanieh, 3rd class; Medjidie, 4th class; King's Coronation medal; Defence medal. *Address:* Great Canfield Park, Takeley, Essex. *Club:* Naval and Military. [*Died* 26 *June* 1961.

CHARLTON, Henry Buckley, C.B.E. 1951; M.A., D. de Dijon, Litt.D.; sometime Fellow, University of Leeds; Professor of English Literature, University of Manchester, 1921-57; Pro Vice-Chancellor, 1936-1938; Dean of the Faculty of Arts, 1926-28, 1943-46; Visiting Professor, University of West Indies, 1957-58; Trustee and Gov. of the John Rylands Library; *b.* 5 May 1890; *e. s.* of late R. J. Charlton, of Bingley, Yorks.; *m.* Edith, 2nd *d.* of Samuel Town of Bingley, Yorkshire; three *s.* one *d.* *Educ.:* Universities of Leeds and Berlin. President Association of University Teachers, 1937-38; Chairman Northern Universities J.M.B., 1944-47; Clark Lecturer, Trinity College, Cambridge, 1947. *Publications:* Castelvetro's Theory of Poetry, 1912; (with Professor L. E. Kastner) Editor of The Poetical Works of the First Earl of Stirling, 1921-29; The Senecan Tradition in Renaissance Tragedy, 1921, re-issued 1946; The Art of Literary Study, 1924 (trans. into Arabic, 1946); List of the Writings of C. E. Vaughan; Shakespearian Comedy, 1938; Romeo and Juliet as an Experimental Tragedy (British Academy Shakespeare Lecture, 1939); The Tradition of Letters and Learning (in What We Defend, 1941); Shakespearian Tragedy, 1948; Portrait of a University, Manchester Centenary, 1951; edited Love's Labour's Lost and Winter's Tale; Taine's Introduction à l'histoire de la littérature anglaise; Ratseis Ghost (Rylands Facsimiles); and (with R. D. Waller) Marlowe's Edward II; Lectures on Browning (John Rylands Bulletin). *Address:* Priesthorpe, Marple Bridge, Cheshire. *Club:* National Liberal. [*Died* 17 *Aug.* 1961.

CHAROUX, Siegfried Joseph, R.A. 1956 (A.R.A. 1949); Sculptor: *b.* 15 Oct. 1896; *s.* of Joseph Charoux and Anna Kinich; *m.* 1925, Margarete Treibl; no c. *Educ.:* Vienna, Elementary and Secondary Schools, Academy of Fine Arts. Academy of Fine Arts, 1919-24; political cartoonist, 1923-26; first exhibition, 1925; Robert Blum Memorial, 1928; Matteotti Memorial, 1930; Prof. Herz Memorial, Univ. of Vienna, 1932; various commissions for sculpture on Municipal Buildings in Vienna, 1930-35; Winns Competition for Lessing monument, 1933; exhibited works in Austria, Germany, Belgium and Italy, 1932-35; unveiling of Lessing, 1935. Came to England and settled in London, September 1935; developed terra-cotta technique of his own; first life-size terra-cotta figure, 1937; first Exhibition, London Group, 1938; first Exhibition at Royal Academy, 1940; Highest award for sculpture, City of Vienna, 1948; Hon. Prof. Republic of Austria, 1958. Commissioned to make stone carving for New School of Anatomy, Univ. of Cambridge, 1938; other commissions: Amy Johnson Memorial; Hull; Lord Cecil bust for Chatham House; Portraits: Sir Stafford Cripps, Dr. Thomas Jones, C.H., Dr. Robert Gillespie Memorial for Guy's Hospital; Mary and Child Statue (Terra Cotta) for the Grail, Pinner, Mx. The Islanders (Colossal Group, 40 ft.) for Festival of Britain, 1950-51; Stone Carving on Salters' Hall, Wallbrook, City of London 9 figures 8½ ft. (Manual and Spiritual Labour), 1950-51; Stone Carving on Exchange Buildings, City of Liverpool (Two Groups, Portland Stone, 8 ft.), 1953; commission from Municipality of Vienna for Hugo Breitner Memorial, 1953, for Richard Strauss Memorial, 1956 (Richard Strauss Memorial unveiled, March 1958); The Cellist, placed South Bank (in front of Festival Hall), 1959. The Neighbours, L.C.C. Highbury Estate; The Motor Cyclist (Bronze), Shell Building, South Bank. Mediums worked: Stone Bronze and Terra Cotta. Works are included in Art Galleries and Museums in Vienna, Hamburg, Chicago; Tate Gallery; Newport Art Gallery; Belfast Art Gallery; Atkinson Art Gallery, Southport; Harris Art Gallery, Preston. Youth, purchased by Chantrey Bequest, 1948; The Judge, purchased by Chantrey Bequest, 1964. Open Air Exhibitions of Sculpture, Battersea Park, London, 1948, 1951, 1954, 1960, and Holland Park, 1957. *Recreation:* painting. *Address:* 26 Temple Fortune Hill, N.W.11. *Clubs:* Chelsea Arts, The Arts. [*Died* 26 *April* 1967.

CHARTERIS, Francis James, M.D., LL.D.; Emeritus Professor of Materia Medica, University of St. Andrews; *b.* 5 Dec. 1875; 2nd *s.* of late Mathew Charteris, M.D., Professor of Materia Medica and Therapeutics, Glasgow University, 1880-97; *m.* 1907, Annie Fraser, M.A., *e. d.* of Robert Kedie, J.P., D.L.; one *d.* *Educ.:* Glasgow and Leipsic Universities. *Publication:* Charteris' Practice of Medicine, 8th edit.; numerous contributions to medical journals. *Address:* Westlands, St. Andrews. *T.:* 192 St. Andrews. *Club:* Royal and Ancient (St. Andrews). [*Died* 4 *July* 1964.

CHARTERIS, Hon. Guy Lawrence; *o. surv. s.* of 11th Earl of Wemyss; *b.* 1886; *m.* 1st, 1912, Frances Lucy (*d.* 1925), *d.* of F. J. Tennant; one *s.* three *d.*; 2nd, 1945, Violet Porter. *Educ.:* Eton; Trinity College, Oxford, B.A. Late Scots Guards. *Address:* The Old House, Didbrook (near) Cheltenham, Gloucestershire. [*Died* 21 *Sept.* 1967.

CHARTERIS, Hugo Francis Guy, M.C.; writer; *b.* 11 Dec. 1922; *s.* of late Hon. Guy Lawrence Charteris, *q.v.*; *m.* 1948, Virginia, *d.* of Colin Gurdon Forbes Adam; one *s.* three *d.* (and one *s.* decd.). *Educ.:* Eton; University of Oxford. Scots Guards, 1941-1947; served in Italy (twice wounded); went as Public Relations Officer, Malaya, Java, etc. S.E.A.C. Journalist, Daily Mail, London and Paris, 1948-51. Went to live in Sutherland, 1951-59. Formerly contributor, Sunday and Daily Telegraph. Scottish Arts Council Prize, 1969. *Publications:* A Share of the World, 1952; Marching with April, 1955; Picnic at Porokorro, 1958; The Lifeline, 1961; Pictures on the Wall, 1963; The River-Watcher, 1965; Clunie (for children), 1963; Staying with Aunt Rozzie, 1964; The Coat, 1966; The Indian Summer of Gabriel Murray, 1968. Television plays, including The Connoisseur, Toggle, Cradle Song, There is also Tomorrow. Short stories in Cornhill, London Magazine; translations, adaptations, etc. *Recreations:* photography, gardening, shooting. *Address:* The Grange, Elvington, York. *T.:* Elvington 209. [*Died* 20 *Dec.* 1970.

CHARTERIS, Colonel Nigel Keppel, C.M.G. 1918; D.S.O. 1916; O.B.E. 1943; J.P. Hants; *b.* 10 Mar. 1878; *s.* of Capt. Hon. F. W. Charteris, R.N.; *y. s.* of 9th Earl of Wemyss, and Lady Louisa Keppel, *e. d.* of 6th Earl of Albemarle; *m.* 1904, Katherine Margaret (*d.* 1961), *e. d.* of Sir John Buchanan-Riddell, 11th Bt.; two *s.* two *d.* *Educ.:* Winchester; Christ Church, Oxford. Joined 3rd Bn. R. Scots Militia, 1897; Commission 1st R. Scots, 1899; served South African War, 1899-1902 (despatches twice, King's medal and 2 clasps, Queen's medal and 4 clasps); Adjutant 1st R. Scots, 1902-04; 8th R. Scots, 1907-11; Instructor School of Musketry, Hythe, 1913-14; served European War, 1914-18; Mediterranean Expeditionary Force, 1915; Egyptian Expeditionary Force, 1916; B.E.F. France, 1916 and 1918 (despatches thrice, D.S.O., Bt. Lt.-Col., C.M.G.); Chief Instructor, Machine Gun School, Grantham, 1917; Chief Instructor, Rifle Wing, Small Arms School, Hythe, Kent, 1921-1925; commanded 1st Bn. The Royal Scots, 1926-29; retired pay, 1929; commanded 24th Hants Home Guard. *Publication:* Some Lectures and Notes on Machine Guns, 1914. *Recreations:* shooting, golf, motoring. *Address:* c/o Coutts & Co., 440 Strand, W.C.2.
[*Died* 28 *Feb.* 1967.

CHASE, William Henry, C.B.E. 1934 (O.B.E. 1926); F.R.C.V.S.; *b.* Tiverton, 10 Nov. 1880; *s.* of Henry Paul and Myra Chase; *m.* 1st, 1907, Catherine Price (*d.* 1958); one *s.* one *d.*; 2nd, 1959, Rose Louisa Jessie Sabine. *Educ.:* Blundell's School. Assisted in his father's veterinary practice, 1896-97; entered Royal Veterinary College, London, 1897; M.R.C.V.S. 1901; diploma Royal Sanitary Institute 1902; F.R.C.V.S. 1905; Tutor in surgery Royal Veterinary College 1901; Government Veterinary Surgeon, Cape Colony, 1902; Chief Veterinary Officer, Bechuanaland Protectorate, 1905-35, and in addition Chief Agricultural Officer, 1926-1935. *Publication:* After investigating Molteno cattle disease in 1904 published The Poisoning of Stock by Senecio Burchelii. *Recreation:* shooting. *Address:* 3 Clarendon Court, Eastwood Street, Arcadia, Pretoria, S. Africa.
[*Died* 1 *Feb.* 1965.

CHATFIELD, 1st Baron *cr.* 1937, of Ditchling; **Admiral of the Fleet Alfred Ernle Montacute Chatfield,** P.C. 1939; G.C.B., *cr.* 1934 (K.C.B., *cr.* 1922; C.B. 1916); O.M. 1939; K.C.M.G., *cr.* 1919 (C.M.G. 1916); C.V.O. 1912; Hon. D.C.L. Oxford, 1934; Hon. LL.D. Cambridge, 1939; *b.* 27 Sept. 1873; *s.* of late Admiral A. J. Chatfield, C.B.; *m.* 1909, Lillian (C.St.J. 1957), *d.* of Major G. L. Matthews, T.F.; one *s.* one *d.* (and one *d.* decd.). Entered H.M.S. Britannia, 1886; Captain, 1909; Rear-Adm., 1920; Vice-Adm., 1926; Adm., 1930; Adm. of the Fleet, 1935. Captain H.M.S. Medina during tour of King George V and Queen Mary in India, 1911-12; served as Flag-Capt. to Sir David Beatty, H.M.S. Lion, during action off Heligoland, 1914, Dogger Bank action, 1915 (despatches, C.B.), and battle of Jutland, 1916 (despatches, C.M.G.); Flag Capt. and Fleet Gunnery Officer to Sir David Beatty (C.-in-C. Grand Fleet), H.M.S. Queen Elizabeth, 1917-19; 4th Sea Lord, 1919-20; Naval Representative, Washington Naval Conference, 1920; Assistant Chief of Naval Staff, 1920-22; Commanded Third Light Cruiser Squadron, 1923-25; Third Sea Lord and Controller of the Navy, 1925-28; C.-in-C. Atlantic Fleet, 1929-30; C.-in-C. Mediterranean, 1930-32; First Sea Lord and Chief of Naval Staff, 1933-38; Chairman of Expert Committee on Indian Defence, 1938-39; Minister for Co-ordination of Defence, 1939-1940, with seat in War Cabinet; Chairman of Civil Defence Honours Committee, 1940-1946; Chairman of Committee on Evacuation of Casualties in London Region Hospitals, 1940; Special Asst. Commissioner for Hampshire, 1941; President: Inst. of Naval Architects, 1941-48; War Memorials Advisory Committee, 1943-48; Chairman of Trustees of Imperial War Museum, 1943-50; Chm. Royal Empire Society, 1948-51; President of Garden Tomb Association, 1950-. D.L. Bucks, 1951. Freedom of Salters' Company, 1937. Gold Medal, R.S.A., 1947. Grand Cross of the Phœnix (Greece), 1933; Grand Cross of Aviz of Portugal, 1940. *Publications:* The Navy and Defence, 1942; Defence after the War, 1944; It Might Happen Again, 1947. *Heir:* *s.* Hon. Ernle David Lewis Chatfield [Lieut. R.N.V.R. and A.D.C. to Lord Athlone, Governor-General of Canada, 1940-44; *b.* 2 Jan. 1917]. *Address.* The Small House, Farnham Common, Bucks. *T.:* Farnham Common 269. *Club:* Army and Navy.
[*Died* 15 *Nov.* 1967.

CHAVASSE, Rt. Rev. Christopher Maude, O.B.E. 1936; M.C. 1916; T.D. 1940; D.L. 1959; D.D. (Lambeth); M.A.; Bishop of Rochester, 1940-60, retired; *b.* 1884; twin *s.* of late Rt. Rev. Francis James Chavasse (Bishop of Liverpool, 1900-23); *m.* 1919, Beatrice Cropper, *d.* of late William Edward Willink, J.P., Dingle Bank, Liverpool; three *s.* two *d.* *Educ.:* Magdalen College School, Oxford; Liverpool Coll.; Trinity Coll., Oxford; Bishop's Hostel, Liverpool. Played Lacrosse v. Cambridge 1905, 6, 7; represented Oxford in 100 yards, ¼-mile, 1906, 7, 8; represented England in 400 metres at Olympic games, 1908. Curate of St. Helens, Lancashire, 1910; played for the St. Helens Rugby Northern Union team, 1912; Domestic Chaplain to Bishop of Liverpool, 1913; T.C.F. 1914; Senior Chaplain, 62nd Division, 1916; Deputy Assistant Chaplain General, 9th Corps, 1918 (wounded, M.C., Croix-de-Guerre); Vicar of St. George's Barrow-in-Furness, 1919; Rector of St. Aldates, Oxford, 1922; Rector of St. Peter-le-Bailey, Oxford, 1928-39; Master of St. Peter's Hall, Oxford, 1929-39; Examining Chaplain to Bishop of Bristol, 1924-33; to Bishop of Oxford, 1925-39; Senior Chaplain (T.), 48th (S.M.) Division, 1933-37; Proc. Conv. Ox., 1936-39; Select Preacher, Cambridge, 1938 and 1955. Sub-Prelate of Order of St. John of Jerusalem since 1946. Hon. Fell. St. Peter's Hall, Oxford, 1949, and of Trinity College, Oxford, 1955. D.L. Kent, 1959. *Publications:* The Meaning of the Lessons and of the Psalms; A Letter from the Catacombs; Christ and Fairies; Five Questions before the Church; This is Our Faith; contributor to The Anglican Communion, to The Atonement in History and in Life and to Christianity in the Modern State; Editor of the Report of the Archbishops' Commission on Evangelism: Towards the Conversion of England (1945), and author of numerous pamphlets on the subject. *Address:* 14 Staverton Rd., Oxford. *T.:* Oxford 55359.
[*Died* 10 *March* 1962.

CHAWORTH-MUSTERS, Colonel John Nevile, D.S.O. 1918; O.B.E. 1951; T.D.; J.P.; Lt.-Col. R.A., T.A.; Vice-Lieut. of County of Nottingham, 1957-63; *b.* 1890; *s.* of late J. P. Chaworth-Musters, J.P., D.L., of Annesley Park, Notts; *m.* 1914, Daphne, O.B.E., *y. d.* of late Captain H. Wilberforce-Bell, Military Knight of Windsor; one *s.* (*er. s.* killed in action, 1943); two *d.* *Educ.:* Stubbington House. Served European War, 1914-18 (D.S.O.); Brevet-Colonel, 1932; commanded 107th (South Notts Hussars) Regt. R.A., T.A., 1928-33; Com. 150th (South Notts Hussars) Regt. R.A., 1939-41. High Sheriff of Nottinghamshire, 1936; J.P. 1922, D.L. 1931, Notts. *Address:* Annesley Park, Notts. *T.A.:* Annesley, Woodhouse. *T.:* Kirkby-in-Ashfield 2297. *Clubs:* Junior Carlton; Notts County (Nottingham).
[*Died* 12 *March* 1970.

CHAYTOR, Lt.-Col. John Clervaux, C.B.E. 1953; D.S.O., 1918; M.C. 1915; late South Staffordshire Regiment; Chief Constable, N. Riding, Yorks, 1929-58, retd.; *b.* 20 Nov. 1888; *s.* of late Lt.-Col. Robert James Chaytor and Frances Thomasina Chaytor; *m.* Agnes Mary (*d.* 1955), *widow* of J. H. Jaques, and *d.* of late Rt. Rev. James Macarthur, D.D., Bishop of Southampton; one *s.*; *m.* 1956, Mrs. Frederic Bell, O.B.E. *Educ.:* Cheltenham Coll. 2nd Lieut. South Staffordshire Regiment, 1908; Lieut. 1909; Captain, 1914; Brevet Major, 1916; Major, 1924; Lt.-Col. 1929; served European War, 1914-18 (despatches, D.S.O., M.C., Bt. Maj., Legion of Honour, Croix de Guerre); retired pay, 1929. *Address:* The Old Rectory, Sulham, Pangbourne, Berks. *T.:* Pangbourne 29. [*Died* 28 *Feb.* 1964.

CHEESEMAN, A. K. A.; *see* Wymark, Patrick C.

CHEESEMAN, Harold Ambrose Robinson, C.M.G. 1947; Malayan Education Service, retired; *b.* 7 Dec. 1889; *e. s.* of Reverend J. A. Cheeseman. *Educ.:* Perse School. Inspector of Schools, Penang, 1923; Supt. of Education, Johore, 1928; Senior Inspector of Schools, Singapore, 1934; Deputy Director of Educ., Straits Settlements and Federated Malay States, 1938; Educ. Officer, Singapore internment camp, 1942; Director of Educ., Federation of Malaya, 1946-49; retired, 1949. Headquarters Commr. Boy Scouts Assoc., Malaya, 1924; Scout Medal of Merit, 1926; Scout Silver Wolf, 1927; President Thanet South Scout Assoc.; Pres. Singapore Rotary Club, 1940-1942, Kuala Lumpur, 1949; Past Asst. District Grand Master, Masonic District of E. Archipelago; Past President, Ramsgate and Broadstairs Free Church Council; Member of Free Church Federal Council of England and Wales, 1954-. Hon. Sec. Malaya Cttee., Presbyterian Church of England; Session-Clerk, Ramsgate Presbyterian Church; Chm. Ramsgate U.N. Assoc. Member, Thanet Divisional Executive, Kent Education Cttee., 1954-. *Publications:* editor of a number of school textbooks for schools in Malaya; compiler of Bibliography of Malaya, 1960. *Recreations:* various. *Address:* 31 Granville House, Ramsgate, Kent. *T.:* Thanet 52851. *Clubs:* Royal Commonwealth Society; various in Malaya. [*Died* 23 *Nov.* 1961.

CHEESMAN, (Lucy) Evelyn, O.B.E. 1955; F.R.E.S. Entomologist, Author Lecturer *b.* 1881; 2nd *d.* of late Robert Cheesman, Westwell, Kent. Curator of Insects to the Zoological Society of London, 1920-26; Official Entomologist to the St. George Expedition to the Pacific, 1924-25; Expedition to the New Hebrides to collect insects for the British Museum (Natural History), 1929-31; Expedition to Papua, 1933-34; Expedition to the Cyclops Mts., Dutch New Guinea, 1936; Expedition to Waigeu and Japen, Dutch New Guinea; and Torricelli Mts., Mandated Territory, 1938-39; Expedition to New Caledonia, 1949-50; Expedition to Aneityum, New Hebrides, 1954-55; Hon. Associate of Entomological Dept., British Museum (Nat. Hist.), 1949. *Publications:* Everyday Doings of Insects, 1924; The Great Little Insect, 1924; Islands near the Sun, 1927; A First Book of Nature Study, 1931; Hunting Insects in the South Seas, 1932; Insect Behaviour, 1932; Backwaters of the Savage South Seas, 1933; The Two Roads of Papua, 1935; The Land of the Red Bird, 1938; Four Chapters in The Second World War on S.W. Pacific Operations, 1943-46; Camping Adventures in New Guinea, 1947; Marooned in Du-bu Cove, 1948; Six-legged Snakes in New Guinea, 1949; Sealskins for Silk; Insects Indomitable; Charles Darwin's Problems, 1953; Things Worth While, 1957; Time Well Spent, 1960; Look At Insects, 1960; Who Stand Alone, 1965; Entomological papers in various scientific pubns. *Address:* c/o The Royal Entomological Society of London, 41 Queen's Gate, S.W.7. [*Died* 15 *April* 1969.

CHEESMAN, Colonel Robert Ernest, C.B.E. 1935 (O.B.E. 1923); *b.* 1878; *s.* of late Robert Cheesman; *m.* 1927, Catherine (*d.* 1958), *d.* of late W. F. Winch of Cranbrook, Kent. *Educ.:* Merchant Taylors' School. Served European War, 1914-18, in India and Mesopotamia (despatches); Reserve of Officers, retired, 1928; Private Secretary to High Commissioner in Iraq, 1920-23; H.M. Consul for N.W. Ethiopia, 1925-34; Head of Ethiopian Section, Intelligence, Sudan Defence Force, 1940-42 (despatches); Oriental Counsellor British Legation, Addis Ababa, 1942; retired, 1944. Awarded Gill Memorial, 1924, and Patron's Medal, 1936, by Royal Geographical Society; Hon. Corr. Mem. Zoological Society of London; is a Commander of the Star of Ethiopia. *Publications:* In Unknown Arabia, 1926; Lake Tana and the Blue Nile, 1936. *Address:* Tilsden, Cranbrook, Kent. *T.:* Cranbrook 2170. [*Died* 13 *Feb.* 1962.

CHEETHAM, Canon Frederic Philip, M.A.; Hon. C.F.; Vicar of Hartford, Cheshire, 1939-58, resigned; Canon Emeritus of Manchester Cathedral, 1939; Examining Chaplain to the Bishop of Manchester, 1924-47 and to the Bishop of Chester 1945-58; *b.* 1890; 2nd *s.* of Walter and Ann Cheetham; *m.* 1930, Helen Elizabeth, *y. d.* of J. D. MacIntosh, Woodford Green; one *s.* *Educ.:* City of London School; St. John's College, Cambridge (Exhibitioner and Foundation Sch.); Ridley Hall, Cambridge. B.A. 1912; M.A. 1916; Browne Medallist, 1912; Carus Prizeman, 1913; Jeremie Prizeman, 1914; Deacon 1914; Priest, 1915; Curate, St. Barnabas, Mitcham, 1914-16; Tutor, St. Aidan's Coll., Birkenhead, 1916-20; Chaplain to Forces in France, 1918-19; Hon. C.F. 1920; Lecturer and Sub-Warden of Theological Hostel, King's College, London, 1920-1924; Principal of Egerton Hall, Manchester, 1924-39; Hon Canon of Manchester Cathedral, 1935-39; Rural Dean of Middlewich, 1951-57. Select preacher at Cambridge, 1941. *Address:* 515 The Ridge, St. Leonards-on-Sea, Sussex. [*Died* 29 *Dec.* 1970.

CHEETHAM, Major-General Geoffrey, C.B. 1946; D.S.O. 1918; M.C.; *b.* 1891; *m.* 1930, Constance Margaret, *d.* of A. C. Roberts; one *s.* two *d.* *Educ.:* Wellington College. Survey Duty, Gold Coast, 1920-24; Asst. Instructor at School of Military Engineering, 1924-25; served European War, 1914-18 (wounded, D.S.O., M.C., despatches twice); Lt.-Col. 1935; Col. 1938; Maj.-Gen. 1943; Director-General Ordnance Survey, 1943-49; retired pay, 1949. *Address:* Southwood, Hermitage, Nr. Newbury, Berks. [*Died* 4 *Aug.* 1962.

CHELMICK, William George Hamar, C.B.E. 1942; *b.* 26 Oct. 1882; *s.* of late W. T. H. Chelmick; *m.* 1906, Ivy, *d.* of late W. H. Burgess; one *s.* two *d.* *Educ.:* Owen's School, Islington. Inspector of Taxes, 1905-25; Accountant and Comptroller General, Inland Revenue, 1939-45. *Address:* Hope Villa, Barns Green, Nr. Horsham, Sussex. [*Died* 29 *April* 1969.

CHELMSFORD, 2nd Viscount, *cr.* 1921, of Chelmsford; **Andrew Charles Gerald Thesiger;** 4th Baron (U.K.), *cr.* 1858; *b.* 25 July 1903; *o. surv. s.* of 1st Viscount and Frances, Viscountess Chelmsford, G.B.E., C.I. (*d.* 1957); *S.* father, 1933; *m.* 1927, Gilian, *d.* of late Arthur Nevile Lubbock; one *s.* two *d.* *Educ.:* Winchester College; Christ's College, Cambridge. Lieut. R.N.V.R., 1940-45. *Heir:* *s.* Hon. Frederic Jan Thesiger [*b.* 7 March 1931; *m.* 1958, Clare Rendle, *d.*

of Dr. G. R. Rolston, Haslemere; one *s.* one *d.*]. *Address:* Hazelbridge Court, Chiddingfold, Surrey. [*Died* 27 *Sept.* 1970.

CHENEVIX-TRENCH, Colonel Arthur Henry, C.I.E. 1919; late R.E.; *b.* Dublin, 28 April 1884; *e. s.* of Rev. H. F. Chenevix-Trench, and *g.s.* of Archbishop Trench; *m.* 1913, Dorothy Pauline (*d.* 1950), *e. d.* of late A. G. Steel, K.C.; one *s.* two *d.* *Educ.:* Charterhouse; Woolwich. Served European War in Mesopotamia (C.I.E.). Inspecting Officer of Railways, Ministry of Transport, 1927-49. *Address:* Abbotsford, West Byfleet, Surrey. [*Died* 12 *Jan.* 1968.

CHENEVIX-TRENCH, Charles Godfrey, C.I.E. 1931; Indian Civil Service, retired; Revenue Commissioner, Udaipur State; *b.* 30 Dec. 1877; *s.* of Colonel Charles Chenevix-Trench, late R.A.; *m.* 1910, Margaret May, *e. d.* of John Holmes Blakesley, C.E. *Educ.:* Loretto; Lincoln College, Oxford, B.A. Entered Indian Civil Service, 1900; retired. 1926. *Publications:* Grammar and Glossary of the Gondi language, 1919. *Recreations:* Ornithology, languages, fishing and shooting. *Address:* Pudding Lane, Kelling, Holt, Norfolk. [*Died* 1 *Sept.* 1964.

CHENG, Tien-Hsi, (F. T. Cheng), LL.D.; Member of Panel for Inquiry and Conciliation of U.N. and Member of Permanent Court of Arbitration, Hague, since 1950; Adviser to Judicial Yuan (Council), Taiwan, since 1954; *b.* 10 July 1884; *m.*; three *s.* three *d.* *Educ.:* Canton, China; University of London. Called to Bar, Middle Temple, 1913; LL.D. (London) 1915; Quain Prizeman, 1916; admitted to Hong Kong Bar, 1917; Fellow of University College, London, 1936; Vice-Pres. London Inst. of World Affairs and International Law Assoc., London; Judge of the Supreme Court, Senior Member of the Law Codification Commission, Adviser to the Trade Mark Bureau and the Extra-territoriality Commission, Tutor of the Judicial Academy, Professor of English Law in the Peking University. Technical Expert of Chinese Delegation to the Washington Conference, 1921. Substitute Member of International Judicial Commission, 1926. Vice-Minister of Justice and sometime Acting Minister of Justice, 1931-34; Adviser to Ministry for Foreign Affairs and Ministry of Justice, 1934-36. Special Commissioner of Chinese Government for International Exhibition of Chinese Art in London, 1935; Delegate to 11th International Penal and Penitentiary Congress, Berlin, 1935 and to 6th International Congress on Unification of Penal Law, Copenhagen; Judge of Permanent Court of International Justice, 1936-45; Member of Board of Liquidation of League of Nations, 1945-47; Chinese Ambassador in London, 1946-50. Order of Brilliant Jade, 2nd Cl. with Grand Cordon; Hon. Bencher Middle Temple, 1946. *Publications:* Rules of Private International Law Determining Capacity to Contract, 1915; Civilization and Art of China, 1935; Laws of China (The Lawyers Directory, Cincinnati, Ohio); China Moulded by Confucius, 1946; East and West, 1951; Musings of a Chinese Gourmet, 1954; Reflections at Eighty, 1967. Translator of Chinese Supreme Court Decisions, Prize Court Judgments, First Draft Civil Code, etc. from Chinese into English. *Address:* 64 Northway, Hampstead Garden Suburb, N.W.11. *Clubs:* Athenæum, Reform. [*Died* 31 *Jan.* 1970.

CHERRY, Professor Sir Thomas (MacFarland), Kt. 1965; F.R.S. 1954; Pres., Australian Academy of Science, 1961-65; Professor of Applied Mathematics, University of Melbourne, 1929-63 (Emeritus since 1964); *b.* 21 May 1898; *s.* of Thomas Cherry, M.D., M.S., and Edith Sarah Cherry (*née* Gladman); *m.* 1931, Olive Ellen Wright; one *d.* *Educ.:* Scotch College, Melbourne. B.A. Melb. 1918; B.A. Camb. 1922; Ph.D. Camb. 1924; Sc.D. Camb. 1950. Fellow of Trinity College, Cambridge, 1924-28; Associate Professor of Applied Mathematics, Univ. of Manchester, 1924-25. Hon. D.Sc., Australian Nat. Univ., 1963; Univ. of W.A., 1963. *Publications:* papers in scientific journals, on Pure and Applied Mathematics. *Recreation:* mountaineering. *Address:* 7 Mountain Grove, Kew, Victoria, Australia. [*Died* 21 *Nov.* 1966.

CHESNEY, Lieut.-Col. Clement Hope Rawdon, D.S.O. 1916; late R.E.; *b.* India, 23 July 1883; *s.* of Col. H. F. Chesney, R.E.; *m.* 1914, Millicent Margaret, *d.* of late Captain A. G. Douglas, R.N., of Emsworth; *m.* 1959, E. M. King, *widow*, East London. *Educ.:* Blundell's School, Tiverton; Woolwich. Entered Army, 1901; Capt. 1912; Major, 1916; Lt.-Col., 1927; served European War, 1914-18 (despatches, D.S.O.); Afghan War, 1918; retired 1932. *Publication:* The Art of Camouflage, 1941. *Address:* c/o Standard Bank of South Africa, Terminus Street, East London, South Africa. [*Died* 17 *Oct.* 1962.

CHESTER, Cecil Harry, C.B.E. 1951 (O.B.E. 1943); Chairman, South Western Gas Board, since 1949; Chairman Plymouth Tar Distilleries Ltd. since 1952; Chairman, Bristol and West Tar Distilleries Ltd. since 1952; *b.* 12 Dec. 1900; *s.* of C. Chester; *m.* 1922, Evelyn Daniel; four *d.* *Educ.:* Wakefield Academy; Leeds University. Trained as Gas Engineer, 1917-1922; Asst. Engineer, Manager and Secretary, South Bank and Normanby Gas Co. Ltd., 1922-24; Deputy Engineer and Manager, Wakefield Gaslight Co., 1924-31; Engineer, General Manager and Secretary, and Director, Swindon United Gas Co., 1931-1949, and associated cos. Chartered Mechanical Engineer; Chartered Gas Engineer; Past Pres. Inst. of Gas Engineers, 1949-50. *Recreations:* golf and country life. *Address:* Hunterscombe, Turleigh, Nr. Bradford-on-Avon, Wilts. *Clubs:* United Sports; Bath and County (Bath). [*Died* 1 *March* 1964.

CHESTER-MASTER, Col. William Alfred, T.D. 1945; *b.* 27 Jan. 1903; *e. s.* of late Lt.-Col. Richard Chester Chester-Master, D.S.O., The Abbey, Cirencester, and Almondsbury, Glos.; *m.* 1927, Patience Mary, J.P., *e. d.* of late George S. Streeter, J.P., Thorley Place, Herts; one *s.* two *d.* *Educ.:* Harrow; R.M.C. Sandhurst. Formerly Lieut. King's Royal Rifle Corps; Lt.-Col. R. Gloucestershire Hussars, T.A.R.O., 1947; Brevet-Col. 1951. Chairman Glos. A.E.C. D.L. Glos., 1950; High Sheriff of Gloucestershire, 1957. *Address:* Norcote House, Cirencester, Glos. *T.:* 110. *Club:* Farmers'. [*Died* 18 *Jan.* 1963.

CHESTERTON, Mrs. Cecil (Ada Elizabeth), O.B.E. 1938; Journalist, Author, Playwright, Short-story Writer, Literary and Dramatic Critic and Lecturer; *b.* London; *d.* of late Frederick John Jones and Ada Charlotte; *m.* 1917, late Cecil Edward Chesterton. Has contributed special articles to leading London daily and weekly papers and magazines on topics of social, psychological, literary, and economic interest; Assistant Editor of New Witness; special correspondent for Daily Express in Poland, Soviet Russia, China and Japan and has lectured extensively on these countries; lived as down-and-out for Sunday Express, 1926, and published experiences later in book form; Founder and Life President of Cecil Houses (Inc.) Public Lodging Houses for women and girls who obtain a bed and bath at nominal prices, and no questions asked; two self-supporting houses now existing; also founded Cecil Residential Club for Working Girls and Residential Club for Old Age Women Pensioners in London. Member of China Council. *Publications:* In Darkest London, 1926; St. Theresa, 1927; Women of the Underworld, 1930; My Russian Venture, 1931; Young China and New Japan, 1933; Sickle or Swastika?, 1935; I lived in a Slum, 1936; This Thy Body, 1936; What Price Youth, 1939; The Chestertons, 1941; Salute the Soviet, 1942. Plays: The Man who was Thursday, from G. K. Chesterton's novel, produced 1926, and The Love Game, produced 1927, both with Ralph Neale; lectures: social, literary, dramatic and psychological subjects, also travel. *Recreation:* human intercourse. *Address:* 16 Phillimore Place, W.8. *T.:* Western 5373. *Clubs:* P.E.N., Critics' Circle. [*Died* 20 *Jan.* 1962.

CHETWYND, 9th Viscount (*cr.* 1717); **Adam Duncan Chetwynd**; Baron Rathdown, 1717; Peer of Ireland; F.S.A.; T.D. and first clasp, 1950; Royal Artillery; *b.* 14 Nov. 1904; *e. s.* of 8th Viscount and Hon. Mary Eden (*d.* 1925), 3rd *d.* of 4th Baron Auckland; *S.* father 1936; *m.* 1st, 1928, Joan Gilbert (from whom he obtained a divorce, 1951), *o. c.* of late H. A. Casson, C.S.I.; one *s.* two *d.*; 2nd, 1952, Dorothea Marianne Duncan-Johnstone; two *d.* *Educ.:* Eton; New College, Oxford. Served War of 1939-1945, R.A.; Captain 1939, Major 1941, Lt.-Col. 1946; Major R.A., T.A., 1946; Hon. Lt.-Col. R.A.; served with High Commission for Germany as R.B. Governmental Officer, Düsseldorf, 1946-47, and Chief Governmental Officer, Schleswig-Holstein, 1947-53. *Recreations:* motor sport, philately, photography. *Heir:* *s.* Hon. Adam Richard John Casson Chetwynd, *b.* 2 Feb. 1935. *Address:* Eastbury House, near Newbury, Berkshire. *T.:* Lambourn 204. *Clubs:* Naval and Military; British Racing Drivers.
[*Died* 12 *June* 1965.

CHETWYND-STAPYLTON, Granville Brian, C.B. 1949; O.B.E. 1947; T.D.; Colonel; Warden of Whiteley Village, Walton-on-Thames, 1936-59; *b.* 19 Sept. 1887; *s.* of late Granville Chetwynd-Stapylton; *m.* 1922, Catherine Lyne; three *d.* *Educ.:* Charterhouse. Member of London Stock Exchange, 1913-36. First Commission in 2nd Vol. Bn. the East Surrey Regt., 1906 (became 5th Bn. the East Surrey Regt. T.A. in 1908); served European War, 1914-18, Bde. Major, Nowshera Bde., N.W.F., India, 1916-17; G.S.O. (3) No. 2 Section Tigris Defences, M.E.F., 1917-18 (despatches); with unit in S. Kurdistan, 1919-1920; commanded 5th Bn. the East Surrey Regt., 1924-30; Chairman Surrey T. and A.F.A., 1939-43 and 1944-47; County Army Welfare Officer, Surrey, 1939-43; Command Welfare Officer, S.E. Command, 1943-45; Hon. Rank of Colonel, 1946. Hon. Colonel 381 (East Surrey) Light Regiment R.A., T.A., 1947-57. D.L. Surrey 1931; J.P. Surrey 1941; High Sheriff of Surrey, 1952-53. *Recreation:* gardening. *Address:* Brackensted, Sheet's Heath, Brookwood, Nr. Woking, Surrey. *T.:* Brookwood 2346.
[*Died* 20 *Jan.* 1964.

CHEW, Frederic Robert Gansel, C.V.O. 1968; M.A. Cantab.; Headmaster of Gordonsoun School, 1959-67; *b.* 4 May 1907; *s.* of late Robert George Chew, Dove Nest, Windermere, and Ethel Marion Symes; *m.* 1947, Eva Marie Mohr, *d.* of late Odd Gundersen Bergen, Norway, and of Marie Lütken; one *s.* *Educ.:* Sedbergh School; St. John's College, Cambridge. Asst. Master, Salem, Baden, Germany, 1929-33; Asst. Master and Housemaster, Gordonstoun School, 1934-59. Lieut. 5th Bn. Seaforth Highlanders. T.A., 1939; demobilised (Lieut.-Col.), 1945. Freedom Cross (Norway), 1945. *Recreations* mountaineering, tennis. *Address:* Thornthwaite Cottage, Troutbeck, Windermere, Westmorland. *T.:* Ambleside 3239. *Club:* Alpine. [*Died* 11 *Sept.* 1970.

CHEYNE, Brigadier (Retd.) Douglas Gordon, C.B.E. 1948 (O.B.E. 1930); M.C. 1918; M.D.; Ch.B.; D.P.H.; D.T.M. & H.; *b.* 30 October 1889; *s.* of late Walter Smith Cheyne, M.D., Aberdeen, Scotland; *m.* 1927, Helen Mary, *d.* of Rev. F. R. Lawrence, Atlow, Derbyshire; one *s.* *Educ.:* Grammar School, Aberdeen; Marischal College, University of Aberdeen, M.B., Ch.B., Aberdeen, 1910; House Surgeon, Royal Waterloo Hospital, City of London Maternity Hospital, etc.; M.D., D.P.H. 1914; entered R.A.M.C. 1914. Regular Commission, 1917; D.T.M. & H. (Cantab.), 1924; Major, 1926; Lt.-Col. 1938; Temp. Col. 1941; Brig. 1944; Subst. Col. 1944; on Active Service, France, Belgium, Italy, 1915-19; Shanghai Defence Force, 1927-30; India, 1919-23 and 1932-38; A.D.H., S. Command, 1938-42; A.D.M.S. 78 Div. 1942-43; Director Public Health A.M.G.O.T., Sicily, 1943; D.D.M.S. 13 Corps, 1944-45; D.D.M.S. Land Forces, Greece, 1945-46; formerly Public Health Branch, Control Commission, Germany; subsequently Ministry of Defence until 1963. O.St.J.; Officer Legion of Merit, U.S.A. *Publications:* numerous medical in journals. *Recreations:* music, travel, photography. *Address:* Flat 2, Comilla Court, 17 The Avenue, Branksome Park, Poole, Dorset. *T.:* Westbourne 65598.
[*Died* 26 *June* 1966.

CHICHESTER, Most Rev. Aston, S.J.; *b.* 22 May 1879; *y. s.* of Col. Hugh Arthur Chichester and Alice Stainforth, Templeton, Devonshire. *Educ.:* Mount St. Mary's College, Chesterfield. Entered the Society of Jesus, 1897; continued his classical and philosophical studies, 1899-1904; Assistant Master at Wimbledon College, 1904-10; theological studies, 1910-14; Headmaster of the Army Department, Wimbledon, 1915-17; Headmaster and Rector of Wimbledon College, 1917-21; Headmaster and Rector of Beaumont College, 1921-29. Titular Bishop of Ubaza and Vicar Apostolic of Salisbury, S. Rhodesia, 1931; Metropolitan of Prov. of S. Rhodesia, 1955-56, and Titular Archbishop of Velebusdo. *Address:* Box 8060, Salisbury, S. Rhodesia. *Club:* Public Schools.
[*Died* 24 *Oct.* 1962.

CHICHESTER-CONSTABLE, Brigadier Raleigh Charles Joseph, C.B.E. 1959; D.S.O. 1916; J.P. and D.L. East Riding, Yorkshire; late Rifle Brigade; late Commanding East Riding Yeomanry; *b.* 21 Dec. 1890; *e. s.* of late W. G. R. Chichester-Constable, J.P., D.L.; *m.* 1917, Gladys Consuelo (*d.* 1954), *e. d.* of Edward Hanly; one *s.*; *m.* 1955, Inez Quilter. Served European War, 1914-18 (D.S.O.); Regular Army Reserve of Officers, 1923; War of 1939-45 (bar to D.S.O.); 45th Lord Paramount of the Seigniory of Holderness. *Address:* Burton Constable, East Yorks; Wood Hall, Skirlaugh, East Yorks. *Club:* Boodle's.
[*Died* 26 *May* 1963.

CHICHESTER SMITH, Charles Henry, D.S.C. 1915; A.F.R.Ae.S.; Managing Director, The Fairey Co. Ltd. (Parent Co. of Fairey Group), since 1960; *b.* 22 Feb. 1897; *s.* of late Charles John Smith and Constance Langley; *m.* 1917, Nora Margaret Cubitt (dec.); one *d.* *Educ.:* Exeter School. Royal Aero Club Pilot's Cert., 1914. Joined R.N.A.S. (Sub. Lieutenant Pilot), 1914; Permanent Commn., R.A.F., 1918; Sec., Air Sect., Peace Conf., Versailles, 1919; Mem. Brit. Naval Mission to Greece, 1920-21; Mem. Brit. Air Mission to Japan, 1922-24; Rep.

John I. Thorneycroft Ltd., in Japan, 1925-1930; Export Man. and later Export Dir., Morris Motors Ltd., 1930-36; Dir. and Gen. Man., Vine Products Ltd.; Controller for M.A.P. Burtonwood Repair Depot, 1939-42; Fairey Aviation Co. Ltd.: Gen. Man., Stockport Div., 1942; Dir. and Gen. Man. of the Company, 1943; Jt. Asst. Man. Dir., Fairey Aviation, 1944-52; Dir.-in-Charge, Guided Weapon Div., Fairey Aviation Co. Ltd., 1953; Dir., Fairey Aviation Co. Ltd., 1956; Chairman, 1959; Chm., Fairey Engrg. Ltd., 1959. Gold Medal, R.Ae.S. of Japan, 1924. Order of the Rising Sun, 4th Cl. (Japan), 1924. *Recreations:* sailing (Mem. Brit. Internat. Dinghy Team, Canada, 1938), golf, travelling. *Address:* 65 Campbell Court, Queensgate Gardens, S.W.7. *T.:* Knightsbridge 5620. *Clubs:* Royal Aero; Royal Southern Yacht (Hamble); Island Sailing (Cowes); Itchenor Sailing (Hon. Life Mem.); Royal West Norfolk Golf (Brancaster).

[*Died* 18 *Jan.* 1966.

CHILDS-CLARKE, Rev. Septimus John; Rector of St. Columb Major, Cornwall, 1920-48, retd.; Hon. Canon of Truro, 1933, Canon emeritus, 1948; Rural Dean of Pydar, 1923-27; *b.* 18 Jan. 1876; *s.* of late Rev. S. Childs-Clarke; *m.* Harriett Ethel, 2nd *d.* of late Alfred Claude Taylor, M.D., of Nottingham; two *s.* one *d.* *Educ.:* King's College Choir School, Cambridge; Blundell's School, Tiverton; Sidney Sussex College, Cambridge; Ely Theological College. Curate of St. Matthew's, Nottingham, 1900-03; Organising Secretary, Church of England Mission to Corea, 1908-16; Minor Canon (1903), Succentor (1905), Junior Cardinal (1911), and Senior Cardinal (1914) of St. Paul's Cathedral; Organising Secretary Hospital Naval Fund; Chaplain, City of London National Reserve, 1913; Acting Chaplain, R.N., H.M.S. Vernon, Sept. 1914-Sept. 1916; H.M.S. Sandhurst for XVth Destroyer Flotilla, Grand Fleet, 1916-1917; R.N. College, Devonport, Oct. 1917; Hon. Secretary, Diocesan Maintenance Committee, 1921-29 and 1937-41; Hon. Organising Secretary, Truro Diocesan Board of Finance, 1927-28. Served in Home Guard from inception. *Publication:* The Public Schools and the Navy, 1918. *Address:* Ilton Court, Ilminster, Somerset.

[*Died* 4 *Dec.* 1964.

CHILTON, Vice-Admiral Francis George Gillilan, C.B. 1933; *b.* 8 July 1879; *s.* of late Capt. A. Chilton, R.A., and Caroline, *d.* of Samuel Gibson Getty; *m.* 1st, 1904, Ruth (*d.* 1922), *d.* of late Major Rochfort-Boyd, Manchester Regiment; three *s.*; 2nd, 1923, Elizabeth, *d.* of R. M. Downie, Knutsford, and *widow* of Lt. Mansel Bowly, R.N.; one *s.* *Educ.:* H.M.S. Britannia. Lt., 1901-1914; Comdr., 1914-19; Capt., 1919-31; Rear-Adm., 1931; Vice-Adm., 1936; served European War as Commander H.M.S. Berwick, 1914-15; Intelligence Division, Admiralty, 1915-17; in command H.M.S. Foresight, Mediterranean, 1918-19; Captain, 1919; Assistant Director, Mobilisation, 1919-22; in command H.M.S. Argus, 1922-24; President Naval Personnel Committee, 1924-26; Chief of Staff to Commander-in-Chief, Portsmouth, 1926-28; in command H.M.S. Repulse, 1928-29; A.D.C. to the King, 1931; Rear-Admiral and Senior Naval Officer, Yangtse, 1933-35; retired list, 1936. War of 1939-45, Admiralty Appointment. *Address:* 53 Drayton Gardens, S.W.10. *T.:* Fremantle 3998 *Clubs:* Naval and Military, M.C.C.; (Naval Member) Royal Yacht Squadron (Cowes).

[*Died* 23 *March* 1964.

CHILVERS, Rev. H. Tydeman; President of Spurgeon's Orphanage, 1927-51; *b.* Chelmsford, 12 Oct. 1872; *m.* (wife decd.); three *s.* (and two *s.* decd.); *m.* 1960, Elsie Millicent Springhall (*d.* 1962). Early years in London commercial life and grocery business; ordained as minister of Baptist Chapel, Keppel Street, Bloomsbury, 1894; Bethesda Baptist Chapel, Ipswich, 1903; Pastor of Metropolitan (Spurgeon's) Tabernacle, 1920-35; Pastor of Baptist Church, Holland Road, Hove, 1937-47; retd. from Pastoral Ministry, 1947. *Publications:* But Jesus Answered, 1923; The Great Confession, 1925; The Panoply of God, 1927; That Ye may Know; Is there a future for Calvinism? 12 Annual Vols. of Monthly Sermons. *Recreation:* chess. *Address:* 18 Chesham Close, Goring-by-Sea, Sussex. *T.:* Goring 44798.

[*Died* 22 *March* 1963.

CHINN, Wilfred Henry, C.M.G. 1951; *b.* 26 June 1901; *s.* of Henry Chinn, Birmingham; *m.* 1933, Rachel Mawd, *d.* of Rev. Canon T. S. Dunn; two *d.* *Educ.:* George Dixon Gram. School, Birmingham; Univ. of Birmingham. Probation Officer, Birmingham, 1924-35; Principal Probation Officer, Palestine, 1935; Adviser on Social Welfare, Palestine, 1941; Director of Social Welfare, Palestine, 1943,; Adviser on Social Welfare to Secretary of State for the Colonies, 1947-61; Adviser on Social Development, Ministry of Overseas Development, 1964-66 (Dept. of Technical Co-operation, 1961-64). *Address:* Yew Tree Cottage, Longnor, Shrewsbury. *T.:* Dorrington 495.

[*Died* 23 *Dec.* 1970.

CHINOY, Sir Sultan Meherally, Kt. 1939; Chairman: F. M. Chinoy & Co. Private Ltd.; The Bombay Garage Private Ltd.; Director, British India General Insurance Co. Ltd. and other Cos.; *b.* 16 Feb. 1885; *m.* Sherbanoo; one *s.* four *d.* *Educ.:* Bharda New High Sch.; Elphinstone Coll. Mainly responsible for introduction of Wireless Telegraphy in India on a commercial scale and founded Indian Radio and Cable Communications Co. Ltd.; Chm., Standing Cttee., Bombay Municipal Corporation, 1937-38; Mayor of Bombay, 1938-39; Member, Bombay Board of Film Censors, 1938-39; Member Bombay Hospital Maintenance Fund Committee; Committee Member of Children's Aid Society, Society for the Protection of Children in Western India; Member, City Committee, Bombay Branch Indian Red Cross Society, etc.; organised Pageants in 1937 and 1940 in aid of funds for Red Cross; Chairman, Rupee Fund Committee, King Emperor's Anti-Tuberculosis Fund, Bombay Presidency. Governor 89th District of Rotary International, 1944-45. *Publication:* Pioneering in Indian Business. *Recreation:* horse flesh. *Address:* Meher Buildings, Chowpatty, Bombay 7, India. *Clubs:* Willingdon Sports, Orient, Royal Western India Turf (Bombay).

[*Died* 2 *Sept.* 1968.

CHIPMAN, Warwick Fielding, Q.C. (Can.); B.A., B.C.L.; Hon. D.C.L. University of Bishop's College, Canada, 1942; Hon.LL.D. McGill Univ., Montreal, 1958; Barrister; *b.* 26 April 1880; *s.* of Warwick William Lawrence Chipman and Kathleen Anne Sweeny; *m.* 1922, Mary Somerset (*d.* 1949), *o. d.* of Mrs. J. Somerset Aikins, of Stanstead, P.Q., and late J. Somerset Aikins; four *s.* one *d.*; *m.* 1953, Ottilie Wright, *widow* of late Dr. Campbell Howard. *Educ.:* Eliock and Abingdon Schools; McGill University. Admitted to Bar, 1906; practising at Montreal; Batonnier General, Bar of P.Q., 1942-1943; Batonnier, Bar of Montreal, 1942-43; Canadian Ambassador to Chile, 1944-45; a Senior Adviser, Canadian Deleg., San Francisco Conf., 1945; Canadian Ambassador to Argentina, 1945-49; Canadian High Comr. to India, 1949-52; retired 1953. *Publications:* The Amber Valley (Poems), 1915; Beyond the Road's End, 1929; articles, and poems, in magazines; a Trans. of Dante's Inferno, 1961 (medal from Italian Govt., 1963). *Recreation:* golf. *Address:* (city) 1509 Sherbrooke Street West, Montreal 25;

(country) Oka, P.Q., Canada. *Clubs:* Authors'; University, Pen and Pencil, P.E.N., Royal Montreal Golf, Faculty (Montreal); Rideau (Ottawa).
[*Died* 13 *Jan.* 1967.

CHIPPINDALL, Sir Giles (Tatlock), Kt., *cr.* 1955; C.B.E. 1950; Chairman, Plessey Pacific Pty. Ltd.; *b.* 20 May 1893; *s.* of Giles Tatlock Chippindall, Gympie, Que., Australia; *m.* 1918, Grace Elizabeth, *d.* of W. H. Bayley; one *s.* one *d.* *Educ.:* Victorian State School; Prahran Business College. Postmaster-General's Department: Telegraph Messenger, 1908; various positions in many Branches in Victoria till 1920; Headqrs., Engineering and Telephone Branches, 1920-36; Chief Inspector (Personnel), 1936-41; Director-Gen., Dept. of War Organization of Industry, 1941-45; Chief Exec. Officer of Production Exec. of Cabinet, 1941-45. Member, 1941-45: Commonwealth War Commitments Committee; Commonwealth Prices Stabilization Cttee.; Allied Supply Council Standing Cttee.; Commonwealth Works Priorities Sub-Cttee. Sec. Dept. of Supply and Shipping, 1945-46; Chm. Australian Shipping Bd., 1945-46; Asst. Dir.-Gen., Posts and Telegraphs, 1946-1948; Dep. Dir.-Gen.. Posts and Telegraphs, 1948-49; Director-General, Posts and Telegraphs, Commonwealth of Australia, 1949-58; Chm. Commonwealth Disposals Commn., 1945-49; Vice-Chm. Aust. Overseas Telecomm. Commn., 1949-60, Chm. 1960-63; Mem. Aust. Nat. Airlines Commn., 1949-57, Vice-Chm., 1957-59, Chm. 1959-66. Vice-Chm. National Security Resources Board, 1950; President Australian Council on Ageing. *Recreations:* golf and fishing. *Address:* Kuranda, Pinschoff Lane, Mount Macedon, Victoria, Australia. *T.:* Mount Macedon 121. *Clubs:* Melbourne, Savage (Melbourne); Royal Sydney Yacht Squadron (Sydney); Kingston Heath Golf, Royal Automobile of Victoria (Melbourne).
[*Died* 20 *Dec.* 1969.

CHIRGWIN, Rev. Arthur Mitchell; Research Secretary, United Bible Societies, 19 Route de Malagnou, Geneva, Switzerland, 1951-55; *b.* 5 April 1885; *s.* of William Ladner Chirgwin and Mary Jennings; *m.* 1911, Flora Elizabeth Grigg; three *s.* *Educ.:* Dunheved College, Launceston; University College, University of London. Trained for the Ministry at Richmond Theological College, 1907-10; B.A. London Honours in Philosophy, 1916; M.A. 1920; Hon. D.D. (Aberdeen), 1943; Minister of Congregational Church, Ewell, Surrey, 1910-16; Zion Congregational Church, Bristol, 1916-20; Asst. Home Sec., London Missionary Soc., 1920, Foreign Sec., 1929, Gen. Sec., 1932-50, Chairman, 1951-52; visited U.S. in 1928, Canada in 1929, and paid a twelve months' visit to Africa and Madagascar in 1930-31; visited Newfoundland, Nova Scotia and U.S. in 1935; U.S., Japan and China in 1938; India and Egypt in 1939; Newfoundland, Canada and U.S. in 1947 and 1950; Norway, Sweden, and Finland in 1950; Turkey, Cyprus, Lebanon, Syria, India. Pakistan and Ceylon in 1952; Brazil, Panama, Costa Rica, El Salvador, Mexico, U.S.A. and Canada in 1953; Member British deleg. to meeting of Internat. Missionary Council, held in Madras, 1938, Geneva, 1946, and Whitby, Canada, 1947 and 1950; Member British deleg. to Amsterdam Conf. of World Council of Churches, 1948; Vice-Pres. British and Foreign Bible Society and of United Society for Christian Literature; Chairman Congregational Union of England and Wales for 1945-1946; Cornish Bard, 1946; Duff Lecturer on Missionary Strategy in Edinburgh and Glasgow, 1948; frequent broadcaster on missionary and international topics. *Publications:* Pioneers of Freedom, 1920; Beyond the Great Thirst Land, 1925; The Forward Tread, 1927; Wayfaring for Christ, 1931; An African Pilgrimage, 1932; On the Road in Madagascar, 1933; African Youth, 1935; Arthington's Million, 1935; Conflict: China, Japan and Christ, 1939; Under Fire: The Christian Church in a Hostile World, 1940; Into Action: The Church plans Advance, 1943; Coming Together: The Churches Cooperate, 1944; The Next Ten Years, 1945; The Decisive Decade, 1949; The Bible in World Evangelism, 1954; A Book in his Hand, 1955; For Everyman, 1958; contributions to papers and periodicals on missionary and international subjects. *Recreations:* football, played five times for Cornwall County, 1904-6; tramping, has walked much of the English coast; literary work, travel, study of international questions. *Address:* Ballard Glebe, Studland, Dorset. *T.:* Studland 289. *Club:* Royal Commonwealth Society.
[*Died* 29 *June* 1966.

CHISHOLM, Sir (Albert) Roderick, Kt., *cr.* 1947; retired Managing Director, Imperial Bank of India; *b.* 31 May 1897; *s.* of late Roderick Chisholm; *m.* 1924, Emily Ada Waller; one *d.* *Educ.:* Robert Gordon's College. *Address:* Tanglin, Dunblane, Perthshire; (business) c/o State Bank of India, 14/18 Gresham St., E.C.2. *Clubs:* Oriental; Royal and Ancient Golf (St. Andrews).
[*Died* 25 *July* 1967.

CHOLMELEY, Major Sir Hugh John Francis Sibthorp, 5th Bt., *cr.* 1806; C.B. 1963; D.S.O. 1944; J.P.; Vice-Lieut. of Lincolnshire, since 1963; Grenadier Guards R. of O.; Hon. Colonel, 4/6 Bn. The Royal Lincolnshire Regiment T.A., 1947-63; *b.* 7 Feb. 1906; *s.* of 4th Bt. and Mabel Janetta (she *m.* 2nd, Brig.-Gen. W. J. Lambert, D.S.O.), *e. d.* of late Montagu Richard Waldo Sibthorp of Canwick Hall, Lincoln; *S.* father, 1914; *m.* 1931, Cecilia, *er. d.* of W. H. Ellice, Ewhurst Manor, Shermanbury, Horsham; one *s.* *Educ.:* Eton; R.M.C., Sandhurst. J.P. and D.L., parts of Kesteven, Lincs., 1939; High Sheriff, Lincolnshire, 1961. Owns about 7,500 acres. *Heir:* *s.* Capt. Montague John Cholmeley, Grenadier Guards [*b.* 27 March 1935; *m.* 1960, Juliet Auriol Sally, *y. d.* of Brigadier E. J. B. Nelson and Lady Jane Nelson, Hackers House, Churchill, Oxon; two *d.*]. *Address:* The Dower House, Easton, Grantham. Lincs. *Club:* Guards.
[*Died* 1 *Feb.* 1964.

CHOLMONDELEY, 5th Marquess of (*cr.* 1815); **George Horatio Charles Cholmondeley,** G.C.V.O., *cr.* 1953; Bt. 1611; Viscount Cholmondeley, 1661; Baron Cholmondeley of Namptwich (Eng.), 1689; Earl of Cholmondeley, Viscount Malpas, 1706; Baron Newborough (Ire.), 1715; Baron Newburgh (Gt. Brit.), 1716; Earl of Rocksavage, 1815; Lord Great Chamberlain, 1936-37 and 1952-66; *b.* 19 May 1883; *e. s.* of 4th Marquess and Winifred Ida, O.B.E. (*d.* 1938), *y. d.* of Col. Sir Nigel Kingscote, K.C.B., and *g.d.* of 1st Earl Howe; *S.* father, 1923; *m.* 1913, Sybil (Supt. Women's Royal Naval Service, 1939-46, C.B.E. 1946), *sister* of late Rt. Hon. Sir Philip Sassoon, P.C., 3rd Bt., G.B.E., M.P.; two *s.* one *d.* Captain late 9th Lancers; served in South African War, 1901-02 (Queen's medal 3 clasps); and in European War, 1914-19; Major, 1920. *Heir:* *s.* Earl of Rocksavage. *Address:* 12 Kensington Palace Gardens, W.8. *T.:* Bayswater 4531; Houghton Hall, Kings Lynn, Norfolk.
[*Died* 16 *Sept.* 1968.

CHRISTIANSEN, Arthur; *b.* Wallasey, Cheshire, 27 July 1904; *s.* of Louis Neils and Sarah Ellen Christiansen; *m.* 1926, Brenda Winifred Shepherd; two *s.* two *d.* *Educ.:* Wallasey Gram. Sch. Wallasey Chronicle,

1920-24; Liverpool Courier, 1924-25; Liverpool Evening Express, London Editor, 1925-1926; Sunday Express, News Editor, 1926-1929; Assistant Editor, 1928-33; Editor of Daily Express, 1933-57; Editorial Director, Daily Express, 1957-59; Director Beaverbrook Newspapers Ltd., 1941-59; Editorial Adviser, Associated Television Ltd., 1960-62; Director, Independent Television News, 1960-1962. Technical Adviser and Actor in: The Day the Earth Caught Fire, 1961; 80,000 Suspects, 1963. *Publication:* Headlines All My Life, 1961. *Address:* 98 Mount Street, W.1.; Little Holland Hill, Holland on Sea, Essex. *Clubs:* Garrick, Press, Danish.
[*Died* 27 *Sept.* 1963.

CHRISTIE, Colonel Archibald, C.M.G. 1919; D.S.O. 1918; *b.* 1889; *e. s.* of Archibald Christie, I.C.S., and Ellen Ruth Coates; *m.* 1st, 1914, Agatha (who was granted a divorce, 1938), *d.* of Frederick Miller, New York and Torquay; one *d.*; 2nd, 1928, Nancy (*d.* 1958), *d.* of C. W. Neele, Croxley Green, Herts; one *s.* *Educ.:* Clifton Coll. Served in France, Aug. 1914-Sep. 1918 with R.F.C. and R.A.F. (C.M.G., D.S.O., Order of St. Stanislaus 3rd Class with Swords, despatches five times). *Address:* 59 Gresham St., E.C.2. *T.:* Monarch 6505.
[*Died* 20 *Dec.* 1962.

CHRISTIE, Major-General Campbell Manning, M.C. 1919; *b.* 3 Oct. 1893; *yr. s.* of Archibald Christie, I.C.S.; *m.* 1914, Dorothea, *y. d.* of Sir George Casson Walker, K.C.S.I.; one *d.* *Educ.:* Clifton; R.M.A., Woolwich. Commissioned in Royal Artillery, 1913. Served European War, 1914-18, in France and Macedonia; War of 1939-45, Commanding Artillery in Malta, 1942-44; Major-General, 1942; retired, 1946. *Publications:* (with wife) various plays and film scripts. Plays include: Someone at the Door, Grand National Night, His Excellency, Come Live With Me, Carrington, V.C., The Touch of Fear. *Recreations:* golf, shooting, fishing. *Address:* Crayshott, Woodlands Rd., West Byfleet, Sy. *T.:* Byfleet 43127. *Clubs:* Garrick, Army and Navy, M.C.C. [*Died* 20 *June* 1963.

CHRISTIE, Daniel Hall, C.B.E. 1950; D.L. Londonderry; Chairman Londonderry County Council (Member from 1920); Chm., County Education, County Finance and General Purposes, Roads and Public Works, Law, Planning and Highways Committees; Chairman: Association of County Councils, Northern Ireland; *b.* 31 January 1881; *s.* of Daniel and Emily Christie; *m.* 1st, 1905, Ena Church, *d.* of Henry Church Mann, Drumlamph House, Castledawson; one *s.*; 2nd, 1934, Jessie Elizabeth, *y. d.* of Thomas Parker, Coalbrookdale, Shropshire. *Educ.:* Coleraine; Manchester. Member and Chairman Coleraine Urban District Council, 1920-1928; Charter Mayor, 1929; and Mayor since Borough's re-Incorporation until 1938, also 1944, 1945 and 1946; Member for North Londonderry in N. Ireland Parliament, 1933-1938; High Sheriff for County of Londonderry, 1943; Ex-Master Route Hunt. Freedom of Borough of Coleraine, 1934. *Recreations:* rowing, golf, shooting, fishing, hunting. *Address:* Magherabuoy House, Portrush. *T.:* Portrush 2388.
[*Died* 22 *April* 1965.

CHRISTIE, John, C.H. 1954; M.C. 1915; Hon. D.Mus. Oxford, 1956; M.A.; *b.* 1882; *o. c.* of late Augustus Langham Christie and late Lady Rosamond Alicia Wallop, sister of 8th Earl of Portsmouth; *m.* 1931, Grace Audrey Louisa (*d.* 1953), *d.* of late Rev. Sir Aubrey Neville St. John Mildmay, 10th Bt.; one *s.* one *d.* *Educ.:* Eton; Trinity College, Cambridge. Served in the Boer War, 1900-02. Was a master at Eton; served European War, 1914-16 (M.C.); co-founder with Mrs. Christie of the Glyndebourne Festival. Mozart Medal, Vienna, 1954; Hon. Freedom of Lewes, 1954; Commander, Federal Order of Merit, Germany, 1959; Grand Commander, Cross of Merit, Austrian Republic, 1959. *Address:* Glyndebourne, Lewes, Sussex. *T.:* Ringmer 250; Tapley Park, Instow, N. Devon. *T.:* Instow 28. *Club:* Brooks's.
[*Died* 4 *July* 1962.

CHRISTIE, William Lorenzo; Owner of racehorses; *b.* 18 Dec. 1858; *o. s.* of Hector Christie, Jervaulx Abbey, Yorkshire; *m.* 1st, 1907, Eglantine Marie (*d.* 1908), *yr. d.* of Joseph Limoges, Montreal and Alberta; one *s.* one *d.*; 2nd, 1922, Rachel, *o. d.* of Capt. Frank Reynard, Camp Hill, Bedale, Yorks.; two *d.* *Educ.:* Eton; Christ Church, Oxford. J.P., W.R. Yorks., 1887, N.R. Yorks., 1916. Member, Bedale Hunt; sometime amateur jockey. Was the oldest Old Etonian when he died aged 103. *Address:* Jervaulx Abbey, Ripon. *Clud:* Cavalry.
[*Died* 20 *Feb.* 1962.

CHRISTIE-MILLER, Colonel Sir Geoffry, K.C.B. *cr.* 1951 (C.B. 1946); D.S.O. 1919; M.C.; D.L. Cheshire; *b.* 15 March 1881; *s.* of Wakefield and Mary Elizabeth Christie-Miller; *m.* 1908, Kathleen Olive (*d.* 1965), *e. d.* of late Ven. J. H. Thorpe, B.D., Archdeacon of Macclesfield; three *s.* one *d.* (and one *s.* killed in action). *Educ.:* Eton; Trinity Coll., Oxford (M.A.). Served European War, 1914-19 (D.S.O., M.C., despatches). *Address:* Acton Grange. Nantwich. [*Died* 2 *April* 1969.

CHRISTIE-MILLER, Samuel Vandeleur, C.B.E. 1965; D.L.; Chairman, Wiltshire County Council, since 1961; *b.* 12 Sept. 1911; *s.* of late Sidney Richardson Christie-Miller; *m.* 1947, Esmée Antoinette Fraser (*née* Hutcheson); one *s.* one *d.* *Educ.:* Eton. 2nd Lt., Royal Wilts. Yeo., 1939; Capt. 1942. High Sheriff of Wilts., 1949; D.L. Wilts., 1950. *Address:* Clarendon Park, Salisbury, Wiltshire. *T.:* Alderbury 217. *Club:* Turf. [*Died* 20 *Jan.* 1968.

CHRISTOPHERSON, Very Rev. Noel Charles, M.C.; Dean of Peterborough, 1943-1965; retd.; *s.* of W. B. Christopherson, Bondicarr, Blackheath Park, S.E.3. *Educ.:* Uppingham; St. John's College, Oxford. B.A. 1913; M.A. 1916; Curate of St. John's, Walworth; Domestic Chaplain to the Bishop of Newcastle upon Tyne; temp. Chaplain to the Forces, 4th class; Curate and Vicar St. John's, E. Dulwich; Archdeacon of Colombo and Incumbent of St. Peter's, City and Diocese of Colombo, 1929-35; Vicar of Eltham, 1935-43; Canon Residentiary and Vice-Provost in Southwark Cathedral, 1937-1943; Rural Dean of Woolwich, 1939-43. *Address:* 6 Selborne Place, Littlehampton, Sussex. *Club:* United University.
[*Died* 29 *May* 1968.

CHUBB, Gilbert Charles, D.Sc. Lond.; F.R.C.S. Eng.; late Cons. Surgeon, Ear, Nose and Throat Department, Westminster Hospital and to Throat Hospital, Golden Square; *s.* of late John Charles Chubb; *m.* 1917, Phyllis Grey Barker; two *s.* two *d.* *Educ.:* St. Paul's School; University College, London. Fellow of University College and Jodrill Gold Medallist in Comparative Anatomy; First Class Hons. at Final, and Double First Class Hons. at Intermediate B.Sc. Surgical Specialist, British Expeditionary Force, 1914-18; some time Aural Surgeon to London Fever Hospital and Plastic Surgeon to Queen's Hospital for Facial Injuries, Sidcup. *Publications:* Indications for the Cortical Mastoid Operation, The Problem of Otosclerosis, Ménière's Disease, and other papers in medical journals, Philosophical Transactions of Royal Society of London and Encyclopaedia Britannica. *Address:* 33 Mill Lane, Shoram-by-Sea, Sussex. [*Died* 22 *July* 1966.

CHULA-CHAKRABONGSE of Thailand, H.R.H. Prince, Hon. G.C.V.O. 1938; Knight of the Most Illustrious Order of the Royal House of Chakri, 1934; Knight Grand Cross of the Order of Chula Chom Clao, 1962; Major-General, Thai Army and Special A.D.C. to the King; Author and Journalist, Lecturer and Broadcaster: *b.* 28 March 1908; *s.* of Field Marshal H.R.H. Prince Chakrabongse of Thailand, Prince of Bisnulok, Hon. G.C.V.O., and Catherine Desnitsky, Kiev, Russia; *m.* 1938, Elisabeth Curling Hunter, London; one *d.* *Educ.:* Harrow School; Trinity College, Cambridge; Royal Military College, Bankok. B.A. Cantab. 1930; M.A. 1934. F.R.G.S. 1957. Served as Private in Cornwall H.G., 1942-44; Officer, Cornwall Army Cadet Force, 1943-54, commanding 4th Bn. 1949-54. Hon. Pres. Roy. Automobile Assoc. of Thailand; Hon. President of Association of former Thai students in England. Delegate of Thailand at 16th Session, United Nations Gen. Assembly, 1961. Chairman, Cornwall Branch, National Union of Journalists, 1963. Hon. Freeman, Bodmin, Cornwall, 1958. Military Grand Cross of Order of Leopold (Belgium), 1935; Grand Cross of the White Lion (Czechoslovakia), 1939. *Publications:* first Thai book, 1931; first English book, 1936: autobiography in English: Brought up in England, 1943; autobiography in English: The Twain Have Met, or An Eastern Prince Came West, 1956; First Class Ticket, 1958; Lords of Life: The Paternal Monarchy of Thailand, 1782-1932, 1960. Over 20 books (biographies, autobiography, essays, plays, and novels) in Thai; 5 books on Motor-Racing. *Recreation:* travelling. *Address:* Tredethy, near Bodmin, Cornwall. *T.:* St. Mabyn 232 and 262. *Clubs:* Brooks's, Royal Automobile, Chelsea Arts; British Racing Drivers'; Leander. [*Died* 30 *Dec.* 1963.

CHURCH, Rev. Leslie Frederic, B.A., Ph.D. (Lond.), F.R.Hist.S.; Editorial Board, Methodist Recorder; Chairman Methodist Press and Information Service; Hon. Editor, Methodist Church; Connexional Editor Methodist Church, 1935-53; Editor London and Holborn Quarterly Review, 1935-1953; *b.* Chester-le-Street, Co. Durham, 1886; *s.* of Rev. Frederick Church, Northampton; *m.* 1912, Ida, *d.* of E. Keightley, Wakefield; one *d.* *Educ.:* Liverpool College; Epworth College, Rhyl; Headingley Theological College, Leeds. Entered Methodist ministry, 1908; A.C.F. to H.M. Brigade of Guards, 1908-11; Chaplain Royal Navy, 1918-19; Minister of Methodist Churches, 1908-29; Resident Tutor and Tutor in Pastoral Theology and Church History, Richmond College, Univ. of London, 1929-35; Governor of Queenswood School, Hatfield; member of Institute of Historical Research, University of London; President Methodist Conference, 1943; Official Methodist Visitor to Troops in M.E. and Italy, 1944-45; Select Preacher, Cambridge Univ., 1950; Pres. Guild of Methodist Braillists, 1953-59. Broadcast on many occasions. *Publications:* The Protestant Churches, 1913; The Story of Serbia, 1915; A Mender of Hearts, 1914; The Story of Alsace Lorraine, 1915; Attention!, 1919; Très Bon, 1919; Oglethorpe, a Study in Philanthropy, 1932; If They had Known, Studies of Everyman at the Cross, 1936; Day by Day with F. W. Boreham, 1937; Knight of the Burning Heart, 1938 (new edn. 1960); In the Quietness, 1938; Percy C. Ainsworth, an Anthology, 1939; Before God's Throne, 1939; In the Storm, 1941; Yonder, 1942; Greetings from Home, 1943; Welcome Home, 1945; And Here a Rainbow, 1947; The Early Methodist People (Fernley-Hartley Lecture), 1948; More About the Early Methodist People, 1949; The Homely Year, 1949 (with Ida Church); Second Homely Year, 1950; Third Homely Year, 1951; Fourth Homely Year, 1952; Fifth Homely Year, 1953; Sixth Homely Year, 1954; The Promise Book, 1955; Listening at the Cross, 1955 (new edn. 1960); The Life of Jesus, 1957; Begin with a Hymn, 1958 (with Ida Church); various manuals for men on active service and for women in the Auxiliary Forces. *Recreations:* fishing, walking, reading. *Address:* Wiston, 45 Homefield Road, Worthing, Sussex. *T.:* Worthing 4507. [*Died* 17 *Jan.* 1961.

CHURCHILL, Captain Edward George Spencer-, M.C.; *s.* of Lord Edward Spencer-Churchill and Augusta Warburton, C.B.E., 1935 (*d.* 1941), *d.* of Lady Northwick; *b.* 21 May 1876. *Educ.:* Eton; Magdalen College, Oxford (B.A.). Joined Grenadier Guards, 1899; served through Boer War (2 medals and 7 clasps), and German War (M.C., Croix de Guerre with palm); contested (U.) Derby, 1906; Tynemouth, 1910; High Sheriff, 1924-25. A Trustee, National Gallery, 1943-50. *Publications:* Tarpon Fishing in Mexico and Florida; Home Industry; The Herbal of Apuleius Barbarus. *Address:* Northwick Park, Blockley, Gloucestershire. *T.:* Blockley 224. *Clubs:* Guards, Brooks's, Roxburghe, Pratt's. [*Died* 24 *June* 1964.

CHURCHILL, Brig. John Atherton, C.B.E. 1946; D.S.O. 1940; M.C.; retired; *b.* 10 Apr. 1887; *s.* of Col. A. G. Churchill, C.B., C.B.E. (late XII R. Lancers) and *d.* of Lt.-Gen. Sir William Payn, K.C.B.; *m.* 1920, Agnes Katharine Tulloch; one *s.* one *d.* *Educ.:* Summerfields; Eton; R.M.C. Sandhurst. Commissioned Durham L.I. 1906; served in India with 1st Bn., 1906-14; European War, 1914-18, with 19th Inf. Bde., Sig. and Staff Capt., 18 Division D.A.A.G. (M.C., Brevet Major, despatches thrice); Staff College 1919; Curragh as Bde. Major, 1920-21; Chester as D.A.A.G., 1921; Directing Staff, Staff College, 1922-25; 1 Bn. D.L.I., 1925-26; Shanghai Defence Force, D.A.A.G. and G.S.O. 2, 1927-28; Poona as G.S.O. 2 on H.Q. Southern Comd., 1929-32; 1st D.L.I. as second in command, then in command, 1934-35; Directing Staff, Senior Officers' School, 1936-37; Comd. 151 (D.L.I.) T.A. Bde., 1938-40; Comd. Somerset and Bristol Area, 1941; War Office Committee and D.D.T.I., 1942-46; retired 1946 (Dunkirk Medal, Defence Medal, D.S.O., C.B.E.); A.D.C. to the King, 1938-46; Jubilee and Coronation medals. Colonel, Durham Light Infantry, 1947-52. *Recreations:* polo (played in D.L.I., in winning team of Infantry Cup in India in 1912); hockey (Staff College, 1st D.L.I., English Trials 1920); tennis, golf. *Address:* Bindon Cottage, Headley Down, Bordon, Hants. *Club:* M.C.C. [*Died* 22 *May* 1965.

CHURCHILL, Hon. Randolph (Frederick Edward Spencer), M.B.E. 1944; Capt. (Temp. Major) 4th Q.O. Hussars; *b.* 28 May 1911; *s.* of late Rt. Hon. Sir Winston Churchill, K.G., P.C., O.M., C.H., F.R.S., and of Baroness Spencer-Churchill; *m.* 1st, 1939, Hon. Pamela B. Digby (marr. diss., 1946), *d.* of 11th Baron Digby; one *s.*; 2nd, 1948, June (marr. diss., 1961), *o. d.* of late Col. Rex Osborne, D.S.O., M.C., Malmesbury, Wilts; one *d.* *Educ.:* Eton; Christ Church, Oxford. Lectr., Journalist and Author; M.P. (C.) for Preston, 1940-45; contested (Ind. C.) Wavertree Div. of Liverp., Feb. 1935, (C.) West Toxteth Div. of Liverp., Nov. 1935, Ross and Cromarty Div. of Inverness-shire, Ross-shire and Cromarty, 1936, Preston, 1945 and Devonport Div. of Plymouth, 1950 and 1951. G.S.O. on Gen. Staff (Intelligence) at G.H.Q. Middle East, 1941; served in Western Desert, N. Africa, Italy and Yugoslavia. Trustee, Winston Churchill Memorial

Trust, 1967. Hon. Fell., Churchill Coll., Cambridge, 1965-. *Publications:* They Serve the Queen, 1953; The Story of the Coronation, 1953; Fifteen Famous English Homes, 1954; What I Said about the Press, 1957; The Rise and Fall of Sir Anthony Eden, 1959; Lord Derby, "King of Lancashire", 1960; The Fight for Tory Leadership, 1964; Twenty-One Years, 1965. Winston S. Churchill: Vol. I, Youth, 1874-1900, 1966; Vol. II, The Young Politician, 1901-1914, 1967; (ed.) Winston S. Churchill: Companion Volume I, Parts I and II, 1967; (with Winston S. Churchill jun.) The Six Day War, 1967. Also edited collections of his father's speeches: Arms and the Covenant, 1938; Into Battle, 1940; The Sinews of Peace, 1948; Europe Unite, 1950; In the Balance, 1951; Stemming the Tide, 1953; The Unwritten Alliance, 1961. *Address:* Stour, East Bergholt, Suffolk. *Clubs:* White's, Pratt's. [*Died* 6 *June* 1968.

CHURCHILL, Rev. Robert Reginald, C.B.E. 1944; *b.* 3 June 1890; *s.* of late Rev. Frank Churchill, Rector of Everdon, near Daventry; *m.* 1939, Charity, *d.* of Rev. W. H. Logan; no *c.* *Educ.:* Fonthill, East Grinstead; Radley; Keble College, Oxford; Cuddesdon. St. Mathew's, Northampton, 1913-14; Parish of Minehead, 1915; Temp. Naval Chaplain, 1915; H.M.S. Vindictive, 1915-16; H.M.S. Monarch, 1916-19; H.M.S. Marlborough, 1919-21; Chaplain R.N. 1921; H.M.S. Impregnable, 1921-22 and 1925-28; H.M.S. Carlisle and 5th Light Cruiser Squadron, 1923-25; H.M.S. Courageous, 1928-30; H.M.S. Nelson, 1930-35; Royal Naval Engineering College, Keyham, 1935-1939; Royal Naval Barracks, Portsmouth, 1939-42; Royal Naval Air Station, Worthy Down, 1942-46; Hon. Chaplain to the King, 1944; Chaplain to the King, 1946-52; Chaplain, The Royal Chapel, The Great Park, Windsor, 1946-49; Vicar of Lower Shuckburgh with Wolthamcote Flecknoe and Upper Shuckburgh, 1950-53; retired 1953. Chaplain to the Queen, 1952-60. *Address:* The Red Cottage, Wappenham, Towcester. [*Died* 27 *Jan.* 1970.

CHURCHILL, William Foster Norton, C.M.G. 1952; Colonial Administrative Service, retired; British Adviser, Kelantan, 1946-53; *b.* 9 April 1898; *s.* of late Col. A. B. N. Churchill; *m.* 1954, Ernestine Hallett, *d.* of Arthur Tilney Bassett, O.B.E. *Educ.:* Cheltenham College; Sidney Sussex College, Cambridge (B.A.). On Military Service, 1917-19, Lieut., R.F.A. Joined Malayan Civil Service, 1921. Order of Crown of Kelantan, 1st Class, 1952. *Address:* The Chartered Bank, 38 Bishopsgate, E.C.2. *Club:* East India and Sports. [*Died* 5 *July* 1963.

CHURCHILL, Rt. Hon. Sir Winston (Leonard Spencer), K.G. 1953; P.C. 1907; O.M. 1946; C.H. 1922; F.R.S. 1941; *b.* 30 Nov. 1874; *e. s.* of Rt. Hon. Lord Randolph Churchill, 3rd *s.* of 7th Duke of Marlborough; *m.* 1908, Clementine, G.B.E., *d.* of late Col. Sir H. M. Hozier, K.C.B., 3rd Dragoon Guards, and Lady Blanche Ogilvy, *d.* of 9th Earl of Airlie; one *s.* two *d.* (and two *d.* decd.). *Educ.:* Harrow; Sandhurst. Entered Army, 1895; served with Spanish forces in Cuba, 1895 (1st class (Spanish) Order of Military Merit); served, attached 31st Punjab Infantry, with Malakand Field Force, 1897 (despatches, medal with clasp); served as orderly officer to Sir W. Lockhart with Tirah Expeditionary Force, 1898 (clasp); served, attached 21st Lancers, with Nile Expeditionary Force, 1898, present at Battle of Khartoum (medal with clasp); served as Lieut. South African Lt. Horse; acted as correspondent Morning Post, South Africa, 1899-1900; taken prisoner, action 15 November, but escaped 12 Dec.; present at actions of Acton Homes, Venter's Spruit, Hussar Hill, Cingolo, Monte Cristo, and at Battles of Spion Kop, Vaal Krantz, and Pieters; engagements of Johannesburg and Diamond Hill, and capture of Pretoria (medal with six clasps); late Lieut. the 4th Queen's Own Hussars; Major, Queen's Own Oxfordshire Hussars; Lieut.-Col. commanding 6th Royal Scots Fusiliers, France, 1916 (medals); retired, 1916. Contested (C.) Oldham, 1899; M.P. (C.) Oldham, 1900-04, (L.) 1904-1906; (L.) N.W. Manchester, 1906-08; (L.) Dundee, 1908-18, (Co. L.) 1918-22; (Const.) Epping Div. of Essex, 1924-31, (C.) 1931-45; (C.) Woodford, 1945-64. Under-Sec. of State for the Colonies, 1906-08; Pres., Board of Trade, 1908-10; Home Secretary, 1910-11; First Lord of the Admty., 1911-15; Chancellor of Duchy of Lancaster, 1915; Minister of Munitions, 1917; Sec. of State for: War and Air, Jan. 1919-Feb. 1921; Air and the Colonies, Feb.-Apr. 1921; and for the Colonies until Oct. 1922; Chancellor of the Exchequer, 1924-29; First Lord of the Admiralty, 1939-40; Prime Minister, First Lord of the Treasury, and Minister of Defence, 1940-45; Leader of the Opposition, 1945-51; Prime Minister and First Lord of the Treasury, Oct. 1951-5 Apr. 1955, resigned; was also Minister of Defence, Oct. 1951-Jan. 1952. Elder Brother of Trinity House, 1913-; Lord Warden of the Cinque Ports, 1941-; Lord Rector of Aberdeen University, 1914-18, of Edinburgh Univ., 1929-32; Chancellor of Bristol University, 1929; Hon. Fellow Merton College, Oxford, 1942; Chairman of the Trustees, Churchill College, Cambridge, 1959; first Hon. Fellow of Churchill College, Cambridge, 1964. Hon. Bencher Gray's Inn, 1942. Grand Master Primrose League, 1943-; Hon. Academician Extraordinary of R.A., 1948; One-man show at Royal Academy, 1959; Hon. R.B.A.; F.R.I.B.A. 1941; Hon. F.R.C.S. 1943; F.Z.S. 1944; F.R.Ae.S. 1944; F.S.E., 1946; F.R.S.L., 1947; F.R.G.S. 1948; F.J.I. 1950; Hon. F.R.C.P. 1951; Hon. F.B.A. 1952; Hon. A.R.C.V.S. 1955; Hon. F.I.O.B. 1962. Hon. Member: of Lloyd's; of Instn. of Municipal and County Engrs.; of R. Instn. of Naval Architects; of Instn. of Mining and Metallurgy. Hon. Pres. U.N. Assoc.; Pres. Constitutional Club; Vice-Pres. R.A.F. Benevolent Fund, 1919-; Vice-Pres. London Library, 1948-; First President of the Victoria Cross Assoc., 1959; Liveryman of Mercers' Co., hon. Freeman of Shipwrights' Co., hon. Life Member of Assoc. of Men of Kent and Kentish Men; D.L. Kent, 1949; Pres., Franco-British Soc., 1951; Patron, Buck's Club, 1952; a Vice-Pres. Soc. of the Friends of St. George's and Descendants of the Knights of the Garter, 1953; Hon. Pres. Amateur Fencing Assoc., 1953; Pres., Westerham Br. British Legion, 1953. Col. 4th Queen's Own Hus., 1941-58; Col. The Queen's Royal Irish Hussars, 1958-; hon. Air Cdre. No. 615 (Co. of Surrey) Fighter Sqdn., R.Aux.A.F., 1939-; hon. Col. 63rd Oxf. Yeo. Anti-Tank Regt., R.A. (T.A.), 1942; 6th Bn. R. Scots Fus., 1940; 489 (Cinque Ports) H.A.A. Regt., R.A. (T.A.), 1947; 299 Fd. Regt. R.A. (Bucks and Oxf. Yeo.) T.A.; 4th/5th (Cinque Ports) Bn., R. Sussex Regt., 1941; 1st/4th Bn., Essex Regt., 1945; 6th (Cinque Ports) Cadet Bn. Buffs. Special award, Sept. 1945: 1939-45 Star, Africa Star, Italy Star, France and Germany Star, Defence Medal. Albert Gold Medal of R. Soc. of Arts, 1945; Grotius Medal (Netherlands), 1949; Sunday Times Literary Award and Medal, 1938 and 1949. Member of Jockey Club, 1950. Nobel Prize for Literature, 1953; Charlemagne Prize, 1955; Freedom House Award (U.S.A.), 1955; Williamsburg Award, 1955; Franklin Medal of City of Philadelphia, 1956; Humanitarian Award for 1954, 1956; Grand Seigneur of the Hudson's Bay Company, 1956; Theodor

Herzl Award, Zionist Organisation of America, 1964. Hon. Life Mem. Friendship Veterans Fire Engine Company of Alexandria, Virginia, U.S.A., 1960. C.Lit., 1961. *Hon. Degrees:* D.C.L.: Oxford, 1925, Rochester, U.S.A., 1941. Doctor of Laws: Queen's, Belfast, 1926, Bristol, 1929, Harvard, 1943, McGill, Canada, 1944, Brussels, Louvain, 1945, Miami, U.S.A., Westminster College, U.S.A., Columbia, U.S.A., Aberdeen, Leyden, 1946, St. Andrews, 1948, Liverpool, 1949, University of New York State, 1954. D.Phil. and Hist., Oslo, 1948. Litt.D., Cambridge, 1948. D.Lit., London, 1948. D.Phil., Copenhagen, 1950. *Freedoms:* Oldham, 1941; Edinburgh, 1942; City of London, 1943; Wanstead and Woodford, Brussels, Antwerp, 1945; Aberdeen, City of Westminster, Luxemburg, Blackpool, Birmingham, Beckenham, Stafford, 1946; Darlington, Ayr, Woodstock, Brighton, Manchester, 1947; Eastbourne, Perth, Aldershot, Cardiff, 1948; Kensington, Strasbourg, 1949; Bath, Worcester, Wimbledon, Portsmouth, 1950; Sheffield, Aberystwyth, Malden and Coombe, Deal, Dover, 1951; Leeds, 1953; Poole, 1954; Rochester, Londonderry, Belfast, Harrow, 1955; Douglas (I.O.M.), Margate, Hastings, 1957; Estcourt (Natal), 1964. *Hon. Citizen:* Cuba, 1941; Pinar Del Rio (Cuba), 1942; Paris, 1945; Athens, Marathon, Thebes, Aeglion, 1945; Naupactos (Gr.), 1946; Jacksonville, Florida, 1949; Nancy, 1950; Roquebrune-Cap Martin (A.-M.), 1956; U.S.A. and individual states of Maryland, Hawaii, West Virginia, New Hampshire, Nebraska, Tennessee, N. Carolina, 1963. *Hon. Mayor:* Cap d'Ail (A.-M.), 1952. Gold Medals of Cities of New York, Amsterdam and Rotterdam, 1946. Member, National Congress of American Indians, 1963. *Foreign Decorations:* Knight Grand Cross, Order of Leopold of Belgium; Knight Grand Cross, Order of the Netherlands Lion; Grand Cross, Ordre Grand-Ducal de la Couronne de Chêne, of Luxembourg; Grand Cross with Chain, Order of St. Olav, Norway; Kt., Order of Elephant, Denmark; Danish Liberation Medal; French Croix de Guerre avec Palme (1914); Belgian Croix de Guerre avec Palme (1915); Médaille Militaire of France; Mil. Medal of Luxemburg; Spanish Order of Mil. Merit (1st cl.); D.S.M.(U.S.A.); U.S.A.F. Pilot's Wings; Fr. Croix de la Libération; Order of Star of Nepal; Grand Sash of the High Order of Sayyid Mohammed bin Ali al Senussi. *Publications:* The Story of the Malakand Field Force, 1898; The River War, 1899; Savrola, 1900; London to Ladysmith via Pretoria, 1900; Ian Hamilton's March, 1900; Lord Randolph Churchill, 1906, 2nd ed. 1907; My African Journey, 1908 (reprinted and revised 1962); Liberalism and the Social Problem; The World Crisis, 4 vols., 1923-29 (abridged and revised edition in one vol., 1931); My Early Life, 1930; The Eastern Front, 1931; Thoughts and Adventures, 1932; Marlborough, vol. 1, 1933, vol. 2, 1934, vol. 3, 1936, vol. 4, 1938; Great Contemporaries, 1937, new edition 1938; Arms and the Covenant (Speeches), 1938; Step by Step, 1939; Into Battle (Speeches), 1941; The Unrelenting Struggle (Speeches), 1942; The End of the Beginning (Speeches), 1943; Onwards to Victory (Speeches), 1944; The Dawn of Liberation (Speeches), 1945; Victory, 1946; Secret Session Speeches, 1946; The Sinews of Peace (Speeches), 1948; Painting as a Pastime, 1948; Europe Unite (Speeches), 1950; In the Balance (Speeches), 1951; Stemming the Tide (Speeches, 1951-1952), 1953; The Unwritten Alliance (Speeches, 1954-), 1961. The Second World War: vol. 1, The Gathering Storm, 1948; vol. 2, Their Finest Hour, 1949; vol. 3, The Grand Alliance, 1950; vol. 4, The Hinge of Fate, 1951; vol. 5, Closing the Ring, 1952; vol. 6, Triumph and Tragedy, 1954. A History of the English-Speaking Peoples: vol. 1, The Birth of Britain, 1956; vol. 2, The New World, 1956; vol. 3, The Age of Revolution, 1957; vol. 4, The Great Democracies, 1958; Frontiers and Wars, 1962 (repr. in one vol., Malakand Field Force, The River War, London to Ladysmith and Ian Hamilton's March, slightly abridged). *Relevant Publications:* Winston S. Churchill: vol. I, Youth, 1874-1900, 1966; vol. II, The Young Politician, 1901-1914, 1967, by Randolph Churchill; vol. III, 1914-1916, 1971, by Martin Gilbert; vol. IV, 1916-1922, vol. V, 1923-1940, vol. VI, 1940-1965, by Martin Gilbert, *forthcoming*; Winston S. Churchill: Companion volume I, parts I and II, ed. Randolph Churchill, 1967; Companion volume II onwards, ed. Martin Gilbert, *forthcoming*. *Address:* 28 Hyde Park Gate, S.W.7; Chartwell, Westerham, Kent. *Clubs:* Athenæum, Carlton, Buck's, Boodle's.

[*Died* 24 *Jan.* 1965.

CHURCHMAN, Air Commodore Allan Robert, C.B. 1959; D.F.C. 1918; D.L.; R.A.F. Retd.; General Inspector, Ministry of Health and Local Government, Northern Ireland, 1946-61, retired; *b.* 2 Jan. 1896; *s.* of Andrew Churchman, London; *m.* 1918, Doris Greville (*d.* 1968); two *d.* *Educ.:* Froebel and Latymer. Enlisted in R.N.A.S., 1914; commissioned Royal North Devon Hussars, 1916; transferred to R.F.C., 1917; permanent commission in Royal Air Force, 1919. Squadron Leader 1931; Wing Commander, 1937; Group Captain, 1940; Air Commodore, 1942; retired from R.A.F., 1946. Served European War, 1914-18, France and Belgium; qualified as Flying Instructor, 1919. Commanded 16 sqdn., 1931, 45 Sqdn., 1935, No. 50 (Army co-operation) Wing, 1940. S.A.S.O. Air Headquarters, Bengal, 1942-43 and Ceylon, 1943-1944; A.O.C., R.A.F. N. Ireland, 1944. Pres., S.S.A.F.A., County of Cornwall. D.L. Belfast, 1955. *Recreations:* music, gardening, shooting. *Address:* Glyn House, Ruan Minor, Helston, Cornwall. *T.:* Ruan Minor 606. *Club:* United Hunts.

[*Died* 13 *Jan.* 1970.

CHUTE, Ven. John Chaloner, T.D.; Archdeacon of Sherborne, Diocese of Salisbury, 1941-61; and Prebendary of Salisbury Cathedral from 1941; *b.* 1881; 2nd *s.* of late Chaloner William Chute, D.L., J.P., The Vyne, Hants; *m.* 1922, Violet Mary, *d.* of late Richard Durnford, C.B., Hartley Wespall, Hants. *Educ.:* Eton; Balliol College, Oxford; Cuddesdon College. 1st Cl. Maths. Hon. 1903; B.A. (2nd Cl. Mod. Hist.) 1904; M.A. 1908, Oxford. Deacon, 1913; Priest, 1914. Asst. Chaplain, Eton College, 1913-36; Rector of Piddlehinton, 1938-57. *Address:* Hollies, Buckland Newton, Dorchester, Dorset. *T.:* Buckland Newton 214. *Club:* English-Speaking Union.

[*Died* 12 *Sept.* 1961.

CHUTER-EDE, Baron *cr.* 1964 (Life Peer); **James Chuter Chuter-Ede,** P.C. 1944; C.H. 1953; D.L. Surrey; *b.* Epsom, 1882; *s.* of late James and Agnes Mary Ede; *m.* 1917, Lilian Mary S. Williams (*d.* 1948); changed surname from Ede to Chuter-Ede by deed poll, 1964. *Educ.:* Epsom National Schools; Dorking High School; Battersea P.T. Centre; Christ's College, Cambridge. Assistant Master in Surrey Elementary Schools until 1914; Pres. of Surrey County Teachers' Assoc., 1914; Asst. Secretary, Surrey County Teachers' Association, 1919-45. Member of Epsom Urban Council, 1908-27, and 1933-37; Charter Mayor of Epsom and Ewell, 1937; Surrey County Council, 1914-49; Vice-Chm. 1930-33; Chm. 1933-37; Member of London and Home Counties Joint Electricity Authority, 1927-46; Chairman, 1934-40. M.P. (Lab.) Mitcham Div. of Surrey, March-Nov. 1923, South Shields, 1929-31 and 1935-1964; Parliamentary Secretary to Ministry of

Education, 1940-45; Home Sec., 1945-51; Leader of the House of Commons, March-Oct. 1951; Pres., British Electrical Development Assoc., 1937; Chm., Surrey and Sussex Area Cttee. for National Fitness; Chairman, Departmental Committee on Private Schools; Member, Departmental Committee on Garden Cities; President, Friends of Box Hill, 1950; Trustee, British Museum, 1951-63; Pres., County Councils Assoc., 1953-61; Pres. Commons, Footpaths and Open Spaces Preservation Soc., 1955-61; Pres. Internat. Assoc. for Liberal Christianity and Religious Freedom, 1955-58. Hon. Freeman, Borough of Wimbledon, 1937, of Epsom and Ewell, 1939, of Mitcham, 1944, and of South Shields, 1950. Hon. M.A., Camb., 1943; Hon. LL.D., Bristol, 1951, Sheffield, 1960; Hon. D.C.L., Durham, 1954; served during European War, 1914-18, as Sergeant in East Surreys and R.E.'s; contested Epsom Div., 1918; Dep. Leader of House of Commons, 1947. Dep. Chm. B.B.C. Gen. Advisory Council, 1952-59. *Publications:* Housing in Surrey, 1923; Agricultural Labourers' Guide to Wages Award (1918). *Recreations:* photography, motor-boating. *Address:* Tayles Hill, Ewell, Sy. [*Died* 11 *Nov.* 1965.

CLAPPERTON, T. J., F.R.B.S. 1938; *b.* 1879; *s.* of John Clapperton, Galashiels; *m.* Elizabeth, *d.* of Jas. Fairbairn, Galashiels; one *d.* *Educ.:* Gala High School, Galashiels; Galashiels School of Art; Glasgow School of Art; London; and with Sir Wm. Goscombe John, R.A.; Royal Academy Schools (Gold Medal and Travelling Studentship of £200, 1905); travelled and studied in France and Italy. *Principal Works:* Completion of Mungo Park Monument at Selkirk; War Memorials at Canonbie, Dumfriesshire, Minto, Roxburghshire, and in Church of St. John Lee, Hexham; War Memorial of 49th (W.R.) Reconaissance Regiment in Wakefield Cathedral; Bronze Statue to commemorate Flodden tradition at Selkirk; Marble Statue of Bishop Morgan for Cardiff City Hall; Stone Groups Mining and Shipping, also Stone Statue, Learning, for National Museum of Wales; sculpture for Liberty's new building, Regent Street, W.; Equestrian Group, Galashiels War Memorial; Statue of King Robert the Bruce at the gateway of Edinburgh Castle; Centenary Memorial to Sir Walter Scott at Galashiels; Portrait bust (bronze) the late Lord Tweedsmuir, Scottish National Portrait Gallery; Lord Tweedsmuir: (bronze), National Portrait Gallery, London, (marble) Brasenose College, Oxford, (bronze) Queen's University of Kingston, Ontario; Cat (black marble), Corporation Art Gallery, Glasgow. *Address:* Yair Cottage, The High Street, Upper Beeding, Sussex. *T.:* Steyning 3317 [*Died* 15 *Feb.* 1962.

CLARE, Mary (Mrs. L. Mawhood); actress, stage and films, retired; *b.* London, 17 July 1892; *m.* 1915, Lieut. L. Mawhood, Royal Inniskilling Fusiliers; one *s.* one *d.* *Educ.:* Secondary School, Wood Green. First London appearance, 1910, from which date frequently playing in the West End (Mary Fitton in Will Shakespeare, The Skin Game, The Likes of 'Er, etc.). Went to South Africa, autumn 1929 (Dolores Mendez in The Squall, The Matriarch, Countess Polda in The Lonely House, etc.). Other parts include: Julia Price in the Ghost Train, Linda in the Constant Nymph, Mrs. Bardell in Mr. Pickwick, Jane Marryot in Cavalcade, Tant Sannie in Story of an African Farm, Lady Macbeth, Ellen Creed in Ladies in Retirement, Agatha Payne in The Old Ladies. Entered films, 1931. *Films include:* The Skin Game, Constant Nymph, Passing of the Third Floor Back, A Girl Must Live, Old Bill and Son, Jew Süss, The Citadel, There Aint No Justice, Mrs. Pym of Scotland Yard, Young and Innocent, On The Night of the Fire, The Patient Vanishes, The Lady Vanishes, The Briggs Family, Mrs. Fitz-Herbert, The Hundred Pound Window, London Town, Cardboard Cavalier, Next of Kin, The Night Has Eyes, One Exciting Night, The Three Weird Sisters, My Brother Jonathan, Oliver Twist, Esther Waters, Penny Princess, Moulin Rouge, The Beggar's Opera, Mambo. Hon. Corres. Mem., Institut Littéraire et Artistique de France. *Recreations:* house furnishing and decoration, gardening. *Address:* 141 Coleherne Court, S.W.5. [*Died* 29 *Aug.* 1970.

CLARK, Sir Allen (George), Kt. 1961; Chairman and Managing Director, Plessey Co. Ltd. (Plessey Group of Companies), since 1946; Chairman, Automatic Telephone and Electric Co., since 1962; *b.* 24 Aug. 1898; *s.* of Byron George and Helen Peirce Clark; *m.* 1925, Jocelyn Anina Marie-Louise Culverhouse; two *s.* one *d.* *Educ.:* Felsted School. Established The Plessey Co. Ltd., 1920; Jt. Managing Dir., 1925. Member of Council: Telecommunication Engineering and Manufacturing Association, 1943; Society of British Aircraft Constructors, 1960. *Recreations:* fishing, shooting, golf. *Address:* Braxted Park, Near Witham, Essex. *Clubs:* Royal Aero, American. [*Died* 30 *June* 1962.

CLARK, Sir Arthur; *see* Clark, Sir W. A. W.

CLARK, Sir Beresford; *see* Clark, Sir J. B.

CLARK, Rear-Admiral (Retd.) Charles Carr, C.B. 1958; O.B.E. 1945; D.S.C. 1945; Director: Broken Hill Pty. Ltd.; Broken Hill By-Products Ltd.; Australian Iron and Steel Pty. Ltd.; Australian Wire Industries Pty. Ltd.; Tasmanian Electrical Metallurgical Co.; Commonwealth Aircraft Corp. Pty. Ltd.; *b.* 22 Aug. 1902; *s.* of George Carr Clark, Ellinthorp, Qld.; *m.* 1928, Margaret Granville Haymen; two *s.* two *d.* *Educ.:* Toowoomba Gram. Sch.; Royal Australian Naval College. Entered Navy, 1916; specialised in Engineering; Lieut. (E) 1925; Comdr. (E) 1936; Captain (E) 1946; Rear-Adm. (E.) 1953; 3rd Naval Member, Australian Naval Board, and Chief of Naval Construction, Australia, 1953-59, retired. *Recreations:* tennis, fishing. *Address:* Talgai, Northwood Rd., Seymour, Vic., Australia. *T.:* Seymour 87. *Clubs:* Imperial Service (Sydney); Melbourne (Melbourne). [*Died* 29 *Jan.* 1965.

CLARK, Cosmo; *see* Clark, John C.

CLARK, Colonel D'Arcy Melville, C.B.E. 1919; *e. s.* of late Alexander Melville Clark, F.C.I.P.A.; unmarried. *Educ.:* Cheltenham College; University College, London. Admitted a Fellow of the Chartered Institute of Patent Agents, 1907; The London Scottish, 1901-15; commissioned New Armies, 1915; France, 1914-19 (despatches, M.B.E., C.B.E.). *Address:* c/o Lloyds Bank Ltd., 58 High Holborn, W.C.1. [*Died* 19 *Feb.* 1964.

CLARK, George Albert, C.B. 1954; V.R.D.; M.D. (Dunelm); retired as Deputy Chief Medical Officer, Ministry of Health (1956-1958) (Principal M.O., 1946-56); Member of General Medical Council, 1938-62 (rep. Sheffield University, 1938-47; Crown nominee, 1947-62; Treas., 1955-62); *b.* 22 Apr. 1894; *s.* of George Atkinson Clark and Mary Lawson Bainbridge; *m.* 1918, Kate Stewart Henderson; three *s.* *Educ.:* Barnard Castle Sch.; Durham Univ. Coll. of Medicine, Newcastle upon Tyne. Surg. Sub.-Lieut. R.N.V.R., 1914-16; M.B. (Hons.), B.S., 1917; Surg. Lieut. R.N., 1917-19; R.N.V.R., 1920-39, resigning as Surgeon Commander; Demonstrator and Lecturer in Physiology, Durham University College of Medicine, 1920-24; M.D. (gold medal), 1922; Lecturer in Physiology, Sheffield University, 1924; Professor of Physiology and Dean of the Faculty of

Medicine, Sheffield University, 1933-46; Hon. Physiologist to Royal Sheffield Infirmary and Hospital and Jessop Hospital, 1933-46; Chairman, Sheffield School of Nursing, 1942-1946; Member of National Radium Commission, 1942-47; Chairman Sheffield Medical War Committee, 1943-46; Member Interdepartmental Committee on Social and Economic Research, 1947-51; Member Cope Cttees. on Medical Auxiliaries, 1949-50; Member, Commission on Health needs of Gold Coast, 1952; Chm., Cttee. on Health Services, British Guiana, 1954; Mem. Gov. Body of Brit. Post-Grad. Med. Fedn., 1948-58. *Publications:* papers of physiological interest on kidney function, blood sugar, adrenaline, pituitrin, etc. *Address:* Paddicks, Redwood Road, Sidmouth, Devon. *T.:* Sidmouth 1198. *Clubs:* Athenæum; Sidmouth (Sidmouth). [*Died* 9 *Feb.* 1963.

CLARK, James, (Jim Clark), O.B.E. 1964; Professional Racing Driver; *b.* 4 Mar. 1936; *s.* of James and Helen Clark, Kerchesters, Kelso. *Educ.:* Clifton Hall; Loretto. First motor race, 1956; Scottish National Speed Champion, 1958, 1959; joined Team Lotus, 1960; Formula Junior Champion, 1960; 3rd in Le Mans, 1960. First Grand Prix win at Pau, 1961; first in Rand, Natal and South African Grand Prix, 1961; numerous other 1961 wins while racing in 13 countries. Grand Prix wins in 1962: Belgium, Britain, United States, Mexico, Rand; other Formula I wins included Lombank Trophy, Aintree 200, Gold Cup. World record number of Championship Grand Prix wins in 1963, including: Belgian, Dutch, French, British, Italian, Mexican and South African; other Grand Prix wins in 1963: Pau, Imola, Swedish; many other Formula I wins. First in Milwaukee 200 and second in Indianapolis 500; World Champion Racing Driver, 1963. Awarded British Racing Drivers' Club Gold Star, British Automobile Racing Club Gold Medal, Ferodo Trophy; elected Daily Express Sportsman of the Year, Sports Writers' Assoc. Sportsman of the Year, Guild of Motoring Writers' Driver of the Year, Daily Mail Man of the Year. 1963. 1964 Grand Prix wins: British, Dutch, Belgian; British Saloon Car champion, 1964; Tasman Cup winner, 1965, 1967; Grand Prix wins: South African, Belgian, French, British, Dutch, German, Mexican/U.S. for second successive year; World Champion Racing Driver (again), 1965. *Publication:* Jim Clark at the Wheel, 1964. *Recreations:* shooting, water ski-ing, flying; parking in London. *Address:* 11 Murray Street, Duns, Berwickshire. *Clubs:* British Racing Drivers', British Automobile Racing, British Racing and Sports Car, Steering Wheel; Royal Scottish Automobile, Scottish Motor Racing, etc. [*Died* 7 *April* 1968.

CLARK, Jim; *see* Clark, James.

CLARK, Sir (John) Beresford, K.C.M.G. 1958; C.B.E. 1942; Director of External Broadcasting, B.B.C., 1952-64; *b.* 1902; *er. s.* of late Frederic and Lettia Clark; *m.* 1932, Edith Margery, *d.* of late Alfred and of Edith Cotton; no *c.* *Educ.:* Rydal School; King's College, London. President University of London Union, 1924; Governor of Rydal School, 1930; Member of Delegacy of King's College, 1964; joined B.B.C. at Cardiff, 1924; Adviser to Egyptian State Broadcasting, 1934; Director of B.B.C. Empire Service, 1935; Controller European Services, 1944-45; Deputy Director of Overseas Services, 1948-52. F.K.C. 1964. Chevalier Ordre de Léopold (Belgium). *Address:* 105 Oakwood Court, W.14. [*Died* 2 *Aug.* 1968.

CLARK, (John) Cosmo, C.B.E. 1955; M.C. 1918; R.A. 1958 (A.R.A. 1949); R.W.S. 1952 (A.R.W.S. 1950); Painter; Director of the Royal Industries Bureau, 1942-1963, retd.; *b.* 24 Jan. 1897; *s.* of James Clark, R.I., and Elizabeth Clark; *m.* 1924, Jean Manson Wymer; one *d.* *Educ.:* St. Mark's School, Chelsea; Goldsmiths' College School of Art; Académie Julian, Paris; Royal Academy Schools. Art Student, 1912-14. Joined London Regiment, 1914, served European War, 1914-18; commissioned Middlesex Regt., 1915; B.E.F., France, 1915-18 (M.C., Captain). Student in Paris and London, 1918-21; awarded Royal Academy Gold Medal in Painting and Travelling Scholarship, 1921. Numerous mural paintings and easel pictures, 1921-39, and Visiting Teacher Painting and Drawing at Camberwell School of Art; Head of Hackney School of Art, 1938; Deputy Chief Camouflage Officer, Ministry of Home Security, 1939-42. Elected member New English Art Club, 1946. Paintings purchased by Contemporary Art Society, Huddersfield Corporation Art Gallery, Sheffield Art Gallery, Stoke-on-Trent Art Gallery, Ministry of Works, Hinckley Art Gallery. Silver Medal, Royal Society of Arts, 1948. Trustee, Imperial War Museum, 1957. *Recreation:* studying various crafts. *Address:* 16 St. Peter's Square, Hammersmith, W.6. *Clubs:* Chelsea Arts (Chairman, 1946, 1947), Arts. [*Died* 7 *Aug.* 1967.

CLARK, John Maurice, Ph.D., L.H.D., LL.D., Litt.D., Dr. h.c., Paris, 1948; John Bates Clark Professor of Political Economy, 1951; Emeritus Professor, 1953-; *b.* 30 Nov. 1884; *s.* of John Bates Clark and Myra Smith; *m.* 1921, Winifred Fiske Miller; two *s.* *Educ.:* Amherst Coll. (A.B. 1905); Columbia Univ. (A.M. 1906, Ph.D. 1910). Instructor, Economics and Sociology, Colorado Coll., 1908-10; Associate Prof. of Econ., Amherst College, 1910-15; Assoc. Prof. of Pol. Econ., University of Chicago, 1915-1922, Professor 1922-26; Professor of Economics, Columbia University, 1926-53; Special Lecturer, 1953-57; Consultant Nat. Planning Board, 1934; N.R.A., 1934-35; Mem., Cttee. on Industrial Analysis, 1936; Consultant, Nat. Resources Planning Board, 1938-39; Consultant, Office of Price Administration, 1940-43; Member, Nat. Commission on Freedom of the Press, 1944-46; U.N. Cttee. of Experts on Full Employment, 1949; Attorney-Gen.'s Commn. on Antitrust Laws, 1954-55. President American Econ. Association, 1935; Francis A. Walker Medal of American Econ. Association, 1952; foreign member, Royal Swedish Academy of Science, 1938-; hon. Pres. Internat. Econ. Assoc., 1950-. *Publications:* Economics of Overhead Costs, 1923; Social Control of Business, 1926, 2nd ed. 1939; Costs of the World War to the American People, 1931; Economics of Planning Public Works, 1934; Strategic Factors in Business Cycles, 1936; Preface to Social Economics, 1937; Demobilization of Wartime Economic Controls, 1944; Alternative to Serfdom, 1948; Guide-Posts in Time of Change, 1949; Economic Institutions and Human Welfare, 1957; Competition as a Dynamic Process, 1961. *Recreations:* golf, sketching. *Address:* 41 Wright Street, Westport, Conn., U.S.A. *T.:* Westport CA7-4581. [*Died* 27 *June* 1963.

CLARK, Sir (William) Arthur (Weir), K.C.M.G. 1961 (C.M.G. 1952); C.B.E. 1948; Director of Information Services and Cultural Relations, Commonwealth Office, since 1964; *b.* 5 December 1908; *e. s.* of late Reverend W. W. Clark, B.D., Midcalder, Midlothian; *m.* 1935, Margaret Jean, *e. d.* of late Rev. W. Dobbie, Lanark; one *s.* one *d.* *Educ.:* Stewart's Coll., Edinburgh; Edinburgh Univ.; Trinity Coll., Oxf. M.A. (Hons. Classics). Dist. Officer, Kenya, 1931; Asst. Sec., Kenya, 1937; seconded to Dominions Office, 1939; Private Secretary to Rt. Hon. C. R. Attlee and to Viscount

Cranborne, 1942-45; Chief Secretary: Central African Council, 1945-48; to High Commissioner for Basutoland, Swaziland, and Bechuanaland, 1949-50; Commonwealth Relations Office, 1950; Assistant Under-Secretary of State, C.R.O., 1954-56, and 1958-1960; Dep. High Comr. for U.K. in Delhi, 1956-58. U.K. Representative in Cyprus, 1960-61. British High Commissioner in the Cyprus Republic, 1961-64. *Address:* The Old Vicarage, Wrotham, Kent. *T.:* Borough Green 2041. *Club:* Travellers'.
[*Died* 29 *May* 1967.

CLARK, Brigadier William Ellis, C.M.G. 1918; D.S.O. 1915; *b.* Catford, Kent, 30 April 1877; *s.* of late William John Hyne Clark. Barrister-at-law. *Educ.:* Dulwich; R.M. Academy, Woolwich. Entered Royal Artillery, 1896; served South African Campaign, 1899-1902 (Queen's medal, King's medal); European War, 1914-18 (despatches, C.M.G., D.S.O., 1914 Star); C.R.A. South Midland Division (T.A.), 1924-27; Brig. R.A. Southern Command, India, 1927-31. D.L. Co. Kent, 1941-65. County Commissioner, Boy Scouts, 1939-50. *Address:* 34 Elmstead Lane, Chislehurst, Kent. *T.:* 01-467 3476. *Club:* Army and Navy. [*Died* 14 *Jan.* 1969.

CLARK-HALL, Air Marshal Sir Robert (Hamilton), K.B.E., *cr.* 1934; C.M.G. 1919; D.S.O. 1918; *b.* London (Eng.) 1883; *m.* 1919, Lillias, *d.* of Colonel Eliot Lockhart, R.H.A., Lockerbie, Scotland; one *s.* (and one killed on operations with Royal Air Force 1944) one *d.* Learned to fly privately August 1911, Royal Aero Club certificate No. 127. Joined H.M.S. Britannia as naval cadet, 1897; midshipman on China Station, 1898-1901; landed with naval brigade for relief of Pekin, Boxer Rebellion, China, 1900, as midshipman; Lieut. 1903; Commander and Wing Commander, R.N.A.S. 1914; Wing Capt. 1918; transferred from R.N. to R.A.F. on its formation, 1918; Air Commodore, 1922; Air Vice-Marshal, 1931; Air Marshal, 1933; placed on retired list at own request and emigrated to New Zealand, 1934. Has held following commands: H.M.S. Ark Royal, aircraft carrier, in Dardanelles, 1914-15; No. 1 Wing, R.N.A.S. Dunkirk, 1917; Scottish Group, R.A.F. 1919-21; Egyptian Group, 1924; Mediterranean Area, 1925-29; Coastal Command, 1931-34. Joined R.N.Z.A.F. 1940, with rank of Wing Commander and commanded R.N.Z.A.F. Station, Harewood, 1940-43; Air Commodore, 1943; A.O.C. Southern (Training) Group, 1943-44; A.O.C. Islands Group in Pacific, 1944-45. Has also held following Staff appts.: Experimental Air Armament, R.N.A.S. 1913-14; Assistant Director, Air Dept., Admiralty, 1916; Fleet Aviation Officer, Grand Fleet, 1918-19; Asst. Commandant, R.A.F. Staff College, 1922-24; Director of Equipment, 1929-30. *Address:* Weyhill, Macmillan Av., Christchurch, N.Z.
[*Died* 8 *March* 1964.

CLARK-KENNEDY, Lt.-Col. W. H.; *see* Kennedy of Knockgray.

CLARKE, Brigadier Bowcher Campbell Senhouse, D.S.O. 1917; *b.* 19 April 1882; *s.* of Col. William Senhouse Clarke. *Educ.:* Wellington College. Served South Africa, 1901-2 (Queen's medal and four clasps); European War, 1914-18 (despatches thrice, D.S.O. with Bar, Bt. Maj.) commanded 2nd Bn. Worcestershire Regt., 1929-33; Commander 145th (South Midland) Infantry Brigade T.A. 1934-38; Col. 1933; Brigadier, 1937; retired pay, 1938; Hon. Flight-Lt. R.A.F.V.R., 1939; Brig. commanding North Aldershot Area, 1939-41; retired pay, 1941. B.B.C., 1941-44. Colonel, The Worcestershire Regiment, 1945-50. *Address:* Teme House, Hewlett Road, Cheltenham Spa.
[*Died* 16 *Jan.* 1969.

CLARKE, Charles Cyril; *b.* 25 Nov. 1882; *s.* of John Henry Clarke, Amherst House, Clifton, Bristol; *m.* 1915, Olga Helena (J.P. Som.), *d.* of Alfred R. Robinson, Backwell House, Som.; two *s.* two *d.* *Educ.:* Radley; Oriel College, Oxford (M.A.). Solicitor, 1908. Served European War, 1914-18, 2nd Lieutenant, R.G.A., 1917. Director, Bristol Water Works, 1922-64; Member Church Assembly, 1920-60; Chairman, Bristol Diocesan Board of Finance, 1927-51; Mem. Central Board of Finance (C. of E.), 1945-57. Master, Soc. of Merchant Venturers, Bristol, 1921; President various Bristol societies from 1929. Chm., Colston Girls' School, 1924-57; Chm., Bristol Royal Hosp., 1942-48; Chm., United Bristol Hospitals, 1948-54; Member of Council of Bristol Univ. 1943-65; Vice-Chm., Bristol Municipal Charities, 1954-64; Chm., Bristol Gram. Sch., 1955-59. *Publication:* The Society of Merchant Venturers of Bristol, 1922. *Recreations:* book collecting and gardening. *Address:* The Manor Farm, Stone Allerton, Nr. Axbridge, Som. *Club:* Oxford and Cambridge. [*Died* 28 *July* 1968.

CLARKE, Sir Charles N. A.; *see* Arden-Clarke.

CLARKE, Rear-Admiral Sir (Charles), Philip, K.B.E. 1954; C.B. 1950; D.S.O. 1944; M.I.E.E.; retd.; *b.* 1898; *s.* of C. P. Clarke, Solicitor, Taunton, Somerset; *m.* 1927, Audrey White, Torweston, Williton; one *s.* one *d.* *Educ.:* St. Peter's, Weston-super-Mare; Royal Naval Colleges, Osborne and Dartmouth. Midshipman, 1914; served European War, 1914-18, H.M.S. Queen, Dardanelles, 1915; H.M.S. Royal Sovereign, Grand Fleet, 1916-17; Sub-Lieutenant, H.M.S. Miranda, Dover Patrol, 1917-1918; Christ's College, Cambridge, 1919; Lieut., H.M.S. Coventry, 1920-22; specialised Torpedo, 1922-24; H.M.S. Durban, China, 1925-27; Lieut-Comdr. R.N. Staff College, 1927-29; Staff of Commodore, Atlantic Fleet Destroyers, 1929-30; H.M.S. Queen Elizabeth, 1930-32; Commander, 1932; staff jobs, 1932-36; H.M.S. Exeter, South America, 1936-39; Captain, 1938; War of 1939-45, H.M.S. Caledon (Northern Patrol, Med., Red Sea), 1939-41; senior officer, Red Sea, 1941 (despatches); Director Anti-Submarine Div., Admiralty, 1942-43; H.M.S. Glasgow, 1943-46, action Bay of Biscay, 1943 (D.S.O.), Normandy Landing, June 1944 (despatches); Director of Manning, Admiralty, 1946-48; Rear-Admiral, 1948; Flag Officer, Malta, 1948-50 (C.B.); Director of Naval Electrical Department, Admiralty, 1951-55, retired 1955. President, British Institution of Radio Engineers, 1954-56. Director of J. Langham Thompson Ltd., until 1961. *Address:* Pine Needles, Avon Run Rd., Christchurch, Hants. *T.:* Highcliffe 2026. *Club:* Royal Commonwealth Society.
[*Died* 13 *Nov.* 1966.

CLARKE, Commander Courtney; *see* Clarke, Commander H. C. C.

CLARKE, Dennis Robert; Master of the Supreme Court since 1954; *b.* 16 Jan. 1902. *Educ.:* Jesuit College of the Sacred Heart, Wimbledon. Admitted Solicitor, 1931; *m.* 1929, Caroline Alice Hill; three *s.* one *d.* Actg. P/O R.A.F.V.R., 1941; retired as Sqdn. Ldr., 1946. Senior Legal Assistant, H.M. Treasury Solicitor, 1946. *Recreations:* sailing, golf. *Address:* 43 Bedford Court Mansions, Bedford Avenue, W.C.1. *T.:* Langham 9731. *Clubs:* Devonshire; R.A.F. Yacht. [*Died* 7 *May* 1967.

CLARKE, Sir Douglas, Kt., *cr.* 1956; *b.* 17 Nov. 1901; *s.* of John Richard and Christina Clarke; *m.* 1938, Jean Meredyth Smith; one *s.* two *d.* *Educ.:* Shrewsbury School. *Recreations:* golf, gardening. *Address:*

Greenways, Hollies Lane, Dean Row Wilmslow, Cheshire. *T.:* Wimslow 23156. [*Died* 30 *May* 1969.

CLARKE, Captain Edward Denman, C.B.E. 1956; M.C. 1917; Managing Director, Saunders-Roe Ltd., Aircraft Constructors, etc., 1937-60; *b.* 21 May 1898; *s.* of late Alexander F. Clarke; *m.* 1946, Maureen Cowie Leitch; two *s* one *d.* *Educ.:* Eton. R.F.C., R.A.F., 1916-19. Canada, 1921-35. With Saunders-Roe, Ltd., since 1936. *Address:* Crossways, Binstead, Isle of Wight. *Club:* St. James'. [*Died* 5 *Sept.* 1966.

CLARKE, Commander H(enry) C(ecil) Courtney, D.S.O. 1918; R.N. retd.; *b.* 3 May 1890; 3rd *s.* of late Lieut.-Col. J. H. Courtney Clarke, 7th Royal Fusiliers (subsequently Clerk in Holy Orders), of Larch Hill, Co. Dublin, and late Arbella Walsh, Dundrum Castle, Co. Dublin; *m.* 1925, Euphane Scott (*d.* 1963), *d.* of late Capt. Scott Watson, Burnhead, Hawick; one *s.* (and one *s.* decd.). *Educ.:* Stubbington House; H.M.S. Britannia. Specialised in Gunnery, General Service Medal (Persian Gulf Clasp, 1909-14). Roy. Soc. Bronze life-saving medal, 1916. Served European War, 1914-18 (despatches); 1st Lt. (G.), H.M.S. Calypso (D.S.O.); 1st Lt.-Comdr. of both Chatham and Devonport Gunnery Schools and H.M.S. Iron Duke (Flagship Med.); retired list, 1933. Recalled for active service 1939-46 (2 war medals); served in Persian Gulf, India and U.K. Superintendent to River Tweed Commissioners, 1933-56. Hon. Sec. Berwickshire Unionist Assoc., 1937-39. Member: Council for Preservation of Rural Scotland, 1937 (Chm., 1950-67); government committee appointed to inquire into salmon and trout poaching, 1947-48; Exec. Cttee. of Assoc. of Scottish Salmon District Fishery Boards, 1934-56, and Scottish Salmon Anglers Federation, 1947-58; Panel of Fishery Advisers to North of Scotland Hydro-Elect. Board, 1953-; Scottish River Purification Advisory Cttee., 1956-67. *Recreation:* gardening. *Address:* Clairinsh, Melrose, Roxburghshire. *T.:* Melrose 227. *Clubs:* Army and Navy; New (Edinburgh). [*Died* 7 *March* 1968.

CLARKE, Ven. Herbert Lovell, M.A.; Archdeacon Emeritus; Honorary Chaplain to the Forces; *b.* 15 August 1881; *s.* of late Archbishop of Melbourne, Most Rev. Henry Lowther Clarke, D.D., D.C.L.; *m.* 1911, Phyllis Mary Fulford, M.A. (*d.* 1946); five *s.* one *d.*; *m.* 1950, Marguerite Charlotte Hélène Guigou, L.-ès-L. *Educ.:* Magdalen College School, Oxford (Choral Scholar); St. John's Coll., Cambridge (Scholar, 1st Class Classical Tripos). Assistant Missioner, Lady Margaret Church, Walworth, S.E., 1905-8; Curate of Wimbledon, S.W., 1908-13; Vicar of All Saints, Nottingham, 1913-23; in Army, 1918-19; 2nd Lieut.; wicar of Armley, 1923-33; Rector of Barwick-in-Elmet, 1933-42; Rural Dean of Whitkirk, 1938-43; Archdeacon of Leeds, 1940-50; Vicar of Horsforth, Leeds, 1944-51. President, Rotary Club of Leeds, 1934-35. *Address:* Thatchers, West Mill Lane, Cricklade, Wilts. *T.:* Cricklade 231. [*Died* 4 *April* 1962.

CLARKE, Sir Horace (William), Kt. 1956; Past Chairman, James Booth & Co. Ltd. (1953) (Man. Dir., 1922-58); Founder Member (1954-), Aluminium Industry Council; *b.* 6 Jan. 1883; *s.* of Charles Clarke; *m.* 1908, Teresa, *d.* of Timothy Flynn; one *s.* one *d.* *Educ.:* Woolwich Polytechnic; Goldsmiths' Coll., Univ. of London. Chairman: Wrought Light Alloys Association, 1937-; Grand Council F.B.I., 1937-; Materials Group Cttee. Soc. of Brit. Aircraft Constructors, 1942-; Court of Governors, Birmingham Univ. (elected Life Mem. 1946); Brit. Non-Ferrous Metals Fedn. (Founder Pres. 1945-1949); Aluminium Devel. Assoc. (Founder Pres. 1946); etc. Formerly Member: Council Inst. of Metals, 1937-42 (Vice-Pres. 1942-45); Director, Control of Fabricated Light Alloys (Aluminium and Magnesium), Min. of Aircraft Production, 1939-43. Hon. D.Sc. Birm. 1948; C.G.I.A. 1954; F.I.M. 1933; F.R.Ae.S. 1955. *Recreations:* golf, bridge. *Address:* Aranmore, 11 Church Road, Edgbaston, Birmingham 15. *T.:* Edgbaston 1292. *Club:* Junior Carlton. [*Died* 29 *July* 1963.

CLARKE, John Joseph, M.A., F.S.S.; of Gray's Inn and Northern Circuit; Barrister-at-Law; Legal Member, Town Planning Institute; Hon. Research Associate in Law of Housing and Planning, Univ. of London, since 1966; Lectr. in Local Government and Law of Land, Kingston-upon-Thames and Greater London Council; Examiner to Inc. Rating and Valuation Association, Building Societies' Institute, and Town Planning Institute; Assessor to Ministry of Education; Member Panel of Extension Lecturers and Tutorial Classes in University of London; Visiting Lecturer in Harvard and other Univs., U.S.A.; *b.* 2 April 1879; *o. s.* of late John Clarke, Fairfield, Liverpool; *m.* Edith, 3rd *d.* of late James Coole, shipbuilder, Castletown, I.O.M.; no *c.* *Educ.:* The University of Liverpool. Finance Staff, Corporation of Liverpool, 1897-1907; Assistant Finance Officer, 1907-11; Finance Officer, 1911-29, University of Liverpool; called to Bar, Gray's Inn, 1927; first lecturer in Liverpool in Citizenship, 1902; Local Government, 1909, and special lecturer in Law of Housing and Planning; in the University of Liverpool since 1920; University of London, 1935-66; Lectr. for University Extension Bd. *Publications:* Outlines of Local Government, 1918 (20th (Golden Jubilee) ed. 1969); Outlines of Central Government, 1919 (15th ed. 1968); Outlines of Industrial and Social Economics, 1920; Local Government of the United Kingdom, 1921 (15th ed.), 1955; The Housing Problem, 1920; Social Administration, 1922 (5th ed. 1950); The Rehousing of Slum Dwellers, 1923; Housing in Relation to Public Health and Social Welfare, 1926; Law of Housing and Planning, 1933 (5th ed. 1949); Public Assistance and Unemployment Assistance, 1934 (2nd ed. 1937); County Councils: Their Powers and Duties, 1939; Outlines of Housing and Planning, 5th ed. 1950; Introduction to Public Health Law, 1949; Planning Law: An Introduction, 1948 (2nd ed. 1954). Social Welfare, 1953; A History of Local Government, 1955; Building Law and Regulations, 1963 (2nd ed. 1967); Planning Law, 1962, 1963; The Gist of Planning Law, 1964 (3rd ed. 1969); The Gist of Housing Law, 1969; Articles in Chambers's Encyclopædia, 1950, Everyman's Encyclopædia, 1958. *Recreation:* walking. *Address:* 2 Mitre Court Buildings, E.C.4. *T.:* Central 4488; 10 Water Street, Liverpool. *T.:* Central 1983; Shenn Valla, Woolton Road, Wavertree. *T.:* Childwall 1678. *Clubs:* Athenæum, Authors' (Hon. Life Member, 1969). [*Died* 1 *Oct.* 1969.

CLARKE, Louis Colville Gray, F.S.A.; Fellow of Trinity Hall; *b.* 2 May 1881; 10th and *y. s.* of Stephenson Clarke and Agnes Maria Bridger; unmarried. *Educ.:* Trinity Hall, Cambridge. Curator of the Univ. Museum of Archæology and of Ethnology, Cambridge, 1922-37; Director of Fitzwilliam Museum, Cambridge, 1937-46; Travelled in Central and South America; to Abyssinia twice and other parts of Africa; excavated in New Mexico, U.S.A. in 1923 and on several occasions in Hungary; President of Cambridge Antiquarian Society, 1927-29 and 1938-45; Order of Merit of Hungary; Hon. Fellow of Soc. of Archæological and Historical Arts of

Hungary; Hon. LL.D. Cambridge, 1959. *Publications:* articles in journals. *Recreations:* interest in all forms of art. *Address:* Leckhampton House, Cambridge. *T.:* 5153. *Club:* Bath. [*Died* 13 *Dec.* 1960.

CLARKE, Rear-Admiral Sir Philip; *see* Clarke, Rear-Admiral Sir C. P.

CLARKE, Col. Sir Ralph Stephenson, K.B.E. 1955; T.D. (4 clasps); D.L.; *b.* 17 Aug. 1892; *e. s.* of late Stephenson R. Clarke, C.B.; *m.* 1921, Rebekah Mary, *d.* of Gerald Buxton, J.P., Birch Hall, Theydon Bois: two *s.* (one *d.* decd.). *Educ.:* Eton; King's College, Cambridge (Scholar). First class hons. Natural Science Tripos, 1913; M.A. 1919. Joined Sussex Yeomanry, 1914; served with them during European War in Gallipoli, Egypt and Palestine (wounded); A.D.C. Southern Command, 1918; Bt.-Col. 1937; Colonel 1938; re-employed as Lieutenant-Colonel R.A., 1939; Overseas July 1941; served in Iraq, Iran, and Sicily (despatches). Hon. Colonel of 258 (Sussex Yeomanry) L.A.A. Regiment R.A. (T.A.), 1947-58. D.L. Sussex 1932-; Member East Sussex C.C., 1934-63; Alderman, 1953, Chm. 1958-61. M.P. (U.) East Grinstead, 1936-55. Joint Master Old Surrey and Burstow Hunt, 1947-. Master, Clothworkers' Co., 1962-63. Hon. Treas., British Field Sports Soc., 1946-65. Member: Regional Adv. Cttee. for S.E. Conservancy of England, Forestry Commn., 1958-70 (Chm. 1964-70); Min. of Transport Adv. Cttee. on Landscape Treatment of Trunk Roads, 1956-69; Nature Conservancy Committee for England, 1960-1966; Council Royal Agricultural Society of England, 1954-64; Council Royal Forestry Society of England and Wales, 1957-63. Retd. Dir., Stephenson Clarke Ltd. *Address:* Borde Hill, Haywards Heath, Sx. *T.:* Haywards Heath 2828; 4 Grosvenor Cottages, Eaton Terrace, S.W.1. *T.:* Sloane 5468. *Club:* Junior Carlton. [*Died* 9 *May* 1970.

CLARKE, Rev. Septimus J. C.; *see* Childs-Clarke.

CLARKE, Ven. Thomas; Archdeacon of Macclesfield since 1958; Vicar of Macclesfield since 1953; *b.* 28 July 1907; *s.* of Thomas and Mary Clarke, Warrington, Lancs.; *m.* 1937, Nancy, *d.* of late William Calow, Repton, Derbys.; one *s.* one *d.* *Educ.:* Wycliffe Hall, Oxford. Curate of Farnworth Parish Church, Widnes, Lancs., 1941-43; Chaplain, Government Hostels for War Workers, 1943-45; Vicar of Thornton Hough, Wirral, and Chaplain Clatterbridge General Hospital, 1945-53; Rural Dean of Macclesfield, 1955-58; Proctor in Convocation and Member of Church Assembly, 1955-1958; Chaplain to High Sheriff of Cheshire, 1957-58. Represents Lord Lieutenant of Cheshire on Governing Body of The King's School, Macclesfield; Past President, Rotary Club of Macclesfield. Previously held administrative posts in local Government Service and was Boy Scouts' Assoc. Assistant County Commissioner for South-West Lancs. *Address:* The Vicarage, Macclesfield, Cheshire. *T.:* Macclesfield 3382. [*Died* 4 *April* 1965.

CLARKE, Lieut.-Gen. Sir Travers (Edwards), G.B.E., *cr.* 1926, K.C.B., *cr.* 1920 (C.B. 1917); K.C.M.G., *cr.* 1919; *b.* 1871; *m.* 1st, 1911, Edith Mary (*d.* 1918), *o. d.* of late Rt. Hon. Sir John Jordan, P.C., G.C.M.G., G.C.I.E., K.C.B.; one *s.*; 2nd, 1921, Irene, *widow* of Captain S. G. Roe, R. Inniskilling Fusiliers, and *y. d.* of late John Woodrow Cross, 15 Sussex Place, Regent's Park; one *s.* one *d.* (and one *s.* killed on active service, 1944). Served N.W. Frontier India, 1897-98 (medal and clasp), Tirah, 1897-98 (clasp); South African War, 1900-1902 (Queen's medal 4 clasps); European War, 1914-18 (despatches fourteen times, Bt. Lt.-Col., Bt. Col., Maj.-Gen., Lieut.-Gen., C.B., K.C.M.G.); Légion d'honneur, Croix de Commandeur; Order of White Eagle (2nd Class); Serbia, 1916; Grand Cross of White Eagle, Serbia, 1918; Grand Officer, Crown of Belgium; Grand Officer, Order of the Redeemer, Greece; Croix de Guerre (with palm), France; Croix de Guerre, Belgium; Grand Officer of Military Order of Aviz, Portugal; American Distinguished Service Order; Quartermaster-Gen. to the British Armies in France, 1917-19; Quartermaster-General to the Forces and member of the Army Council, 1919-23; retired pay, 1926; Col. Royal Inniskilling Fusiliers, 1923-41; Deputy Chairman and Chief Administrator to the British Empire Exhibition, 1923-25. *Address:* 6 Ashley Gardens, Westminster, S.W.1. *Club:* Army and Navy. [*Died* 2 *Feb.* 1962.

CLARKE, Rev. William Kemp Lowther, D.D.; Canon Residentiary of Chichester Cathedral, 1945-63; Prebendary of Chichester Cathedral since 1943; *b.* 1879; *s.* of Henry Lowther Clarke, late Archbishop of Melbourne; *m.* 1907, Dorothy Elizabeth, *d.* of Rev. Henry William Fulford, late Dean of Clare College, Cambridge; two *s.* two *d.* *Educ.:* Shrewsbury; Jesus College, Cambridge. 1st class Class. Tripos, 1902; 1st class Theol. Tripos, 1904; Carus Greek Testament prize, 1903; Jeremie Septuagint prize, 1903; Fellow of Jesus College, 1904-8; Curate of St. Matthew's, Moorfields, Bristol, 1904-6; Rector of Harlton, Cambridge, 1906-1908; Rector of Cavendish, Suffolk, 1908-15; Editorial Secretary of Society for Promoting Christian Knowledge, 1915-44; Hon. Canon of Canterbury, 1942-43; Chm. of Hymns Ancient and Modern, 1947-63. Serbian Order of St. Sava, 1919; D.D. Cambridge, 1925. *Publications:* St. Basil the Great, 1913; The Lausiac History of Palladius, 1918; The Ascetic Works of St. Basil, 1925; New Testament Problems, 1929; Liturgy and Worship, 1932; Divine Humanity, 1936; The First Epistle of Clement, 1937; Eighteenth Century Piety, 1944; Concise Bible Commentary, 1952; A History of the S.P.C.K., 1959. *Address:* Blackman House, Canon Lane, Chichester, Sussex. [*Died* 8 *April* 1968.

CLARKSON, Patrick Wensley, M.B.E.; M.B., B.S. (Lond.), F.R.C.S. (Eng.); Consultant Plastic Surgeon, Roehampton Plastic Centre (Westminster Hospital Group); Surgeon in charge of the Accident and Emergency Service, Emeritus Plastic Surgeon to the Accident Service, and in charge of Children's Burns Unit and of the Hand Clinic, Guy's Hospital; Hon. Civil Consultant Plastic Surgeon: Queen Alexandra Hospital, Millbank; Cambridge Military Hospital; President, Plastic Section of the R.S.M.; *b.* 20 Feb. 1911; *er. s.* of George Wensley Clarkson, Sheep Farmer, Meat Exporter, Christchurch, New Zealand and Ann Fraser O'Keeffe; *m.* 1st, 1937, Eileen Barbara, *d.* of Dr. N. Mutch; (marriage dissolved, 1953); two *s.*; 2nd, 1953, Elizabeth, *o. c.* of late A. C. Daubeny, Somerset, and of Mrs. A. C. Daubeny, London, W.1. *Educ.:* Christ College, N.Z.; Univs. of N.Z., Edin., London (Guy's Hosp.). Univ. Exhibnr., Guy's, 1932, Treasurer's Gold Medal, Guy's, in Med. and Surg., 1935; Physical, Laidlaw Prizes, 1935. Editor Guy's Hosp. Gazette, 1934-36. Full House Appts. Guy's, 1935-36; Med. Res. Coun. Grant, R.C.S., 1937; Surgical Tutor, Demons. Op. Surg. Anat., Guy's, 1937-39; Surgeon Cons., E.M.S. at Guy's, 1939. R.A.M.C. Jan. 1940-Mar. 1946; Surg. Specialist, C.C.S., France, 1940; attached H. Gillies Plastic Centre, Basingstoke, 1942; O.C. Army Maxillo-Facial (and Burns) Unit, N. Africa, Italy, 1942-45; Brit. Army Staff, Washington, Liaison to U.S. Army, Navy, Plastic Units, 1945 (after

V.J. Day; War Office, 1946. Hunterian Prof., R.C.S. (Face Wounds), 1946; Leverhulme Research Scholar, R.C.S. (Burns), 1946; Hunterian Prof., R.C.S. (The Burnt Child in London), 1965. Formerly Cons. Plastic Surg., L.C.C.; Recog. Teacher of Surgery, University of London. Army sponsored visits to Washington and U.S. Burns and Plastic Centres, 1951 and 1954; Visiting Professor of Plastic Surgery: Presbyterian Hosp., N.Y., 1963; Johns Hopkins Hosp., Baltimore, 1964. Hon. Member American Society for Surgery of the Hand; Hon. Assoc. Member: Surg. Socs. of Brussels, Madrid and Bordeaux; Assoc. Member, French Soc. Plastic and Reconstructive Surgery; Corr. Mem. Amer. Soc. of Plastic and Reconstructive Surgery; Member: British Association Plastic Surgeons; Internat. Soc. Plastic Surgeons; London Med. Society; Club for Hand Surgery in Gt. Brit.; F.R.Soc. Med. Examr. R.C.S. in Med. and Surg., L.D.S. and F.D.S.; Vice-President Edinburgh University Society, London. *Publications:* various papers on Burns, Hands, Plastic and Cosmetic Surgery. *Recreations:* reading, racing, sleep, sun; formerly boxing (Heavy Weight: Edin. Univ., 1930-31, won London United Hosp. Champ., 1933). *Address:* 107 Harley Street, W.1. *T.:* 01-935 2254. *Clubs:* Athenæum, Buck's; Travellers' (Paris).
[*Died* 28 *Dec.* 1969.

CLARKSON, Randolph Norman Macgregor, M.A.; *b.* 8 May 1889; *o. c.* of Dr. Thomas James Randolph Clarkson, J.P.; *m.* 1916, Gwendolyn Grace, *y. d.* of Joseph Franks; two *s.* one *d.* (and one *d.* decd.). *Educ.:* King Edward's School, New Street, Birmingham; Emmanuel College, Cambridge, M.A. 1911. Called to Bar, Gray's Inn, 1914; Oxford Circuit; served European War with M.T.R.A.S.C., France, 1916-19. Gov., Rugeley Gram. Sch., Staffs., 1958-1966; Stipendiary Magistrate, Staffordshire Potteries Petty Sessional Dist., 1939-60, and J.P. Co. Stafford, retd. 1961. *Recreations:* golf, motoring. *Address:* Bryn Celyn, Rhydyclafdy, Caerns. [*Died* 15 *May* 1967.

CLAUGHTON, Sir Harold, Kt., *cr.* 1948; C.B.E. 1923; M.A.; Officier de l'Académie Française; *b.* 28 Sept. 1882; *s.* of Rev. Thomas Legh Claughton, Canon Residentiary of Worcester, and Henrietta, *d.* of Capt. Edmond St. John Mildmay; *g.s.* of 1st Bishop of St. Albans and Hon. Julia Susannah, *sister* of 1st Earl of Dudley; *m.* 1913, Helen Henriette, *d.* of Sir George Henschel; one *d.* (one *s.* decd.). *Educ.:* Radley; Trinity Coll., Oxf. Ran in half-mile for Oxford v. Cambridge, 1905. Asst. Officer in charge, Imperial Record Dept., Government of India, 1906-11; writing, journalism, 1912-14; Military Intelligence Dept., War Office, 1915-18; Assistant Secretary, Surplus Government Property Disposal Board, 1919-20; Secretary, Disposal Board, 1920-23; Financial Officer and Secretary to the Senate, University of London, 1924-29; Clerk of the University Court, 1929-41; Acting Principal, 1941-43; Principal, 1943-47; Vice-Chm. Universities Bureau of British Empire, 1945-1947; Principal, Polish University College in London, 1951-53. Secretary, Standing Commission on Museums and Galleries, 1948-1960. Chm.: Advisory Council National Corporation for Care of Old People, 1949-63; Great Met. Ltd., 1948-63. Governor, Sadler's Wells, 1948-63. Governor, Imperial College of Science, 1948-66. *Address:* 49 Elm Park House, S.W.10. *T.:* Flaxman 1287.
[*Died* 10 *May* 1969.

CLAUSEN, Raymond John, M.C.; F.F.A.R.C.S. (Eng.), D.A. (Eng.); Hon. Consult. Anæsthetist to Charing Cross Hospital, Chelsea Hospital for Women and St. Paul's Hospital. *Educ.:* University College London; Westminster Hospital. M.B.; B.S. (Lond.) 1913; D.A. (Eng.) 1938; F.F.A.R.C.S. (Eng.) 1948; formerly House Physician Westminster Hospital; Resident Anæsthetist St. Bartholomew's Hospital; late Major, R.A.M.C. (Specialist Anæsthetist). *Address:* 8 Parkside, N.W.2.
[*Died* 29 *July* 1966.

CLAVERING, Maj.-Gen. Noel W. N.; *see* Napier-Clavering.

CLAY, Sir Geoffrey Fletcher, K.C.M.G. *cr.* 1951 (C.M.G. 1942); O.B.E. 1936; M.C.; *b.* 1895; *s.* of Frederick William and Hannah Clay, Radcliffe, Lancashire; *m.* Norah, *d.* of W. A. Lunn, Hull, Yorks; three *s.* *Educ.:* Bury Grammar School, Lancs.; Edinburgh and Cambridge Univs. B.Sc. (Agric.) Edin.; N.D.A., N.D.D. (Hons.). Served European War, 1914-19, 5th Battalion Duke of Wellington's Regt. (M.C.); Agricultural Officer, Uganda, 1924-31; Dep. Dir. of Agriculture, Uganda, 1931-36; Asst. Director of Agriculture, Nigeria, 1936-39; Director of Agriculture, Uganda, 1939-44; Vice-Chm. E. A. Production and Supply Council, 1942-44; Development Adviser for Northern Rhodesia and Nyasaland, 1944-46. Retired from Colonial Agricultural Service on appt. as Agricul. Adviser to Secretary of State for the Colonies, 1947. Member, U.K. delegn. to U.N. Conservation of Resources Conf., 1949; leader Abyan Mission, 1951; joint-leader of United Nations ission to Korea, to prepare 5-year plan for rehabilitation of Korean Agriculture, Forestry and Fisheries, 1952-53; Agricultural Adviser to Secretary of State for the Colonies, 1946-56; Mem., Admin. Council and Scientific Cttee., Empire Cotton Growing Corp., 1956-59; Mem. Council, Jt. E. and Central Africa Bd., 1957-59; Agricul. Consultant to Joint Mediterranean Development Project of F.A.O. and U.N.O., 1948-59; Controller of Rubber Research, Malaya, 1959-1962. *Recreation:* golf. *Address:* Gratwicke, 14 First Avenue, Worthing. *T.:* Worthing 30501. [*Died* 9 *Aug.* 1969.

CLAY, Col. John, C.B.E. 1919; T.D.; M.B.; F.R.C.S. *Educ.:* Cheltenham College; Durham University, M.B., B.S. Went to S. Africa, 1900, Lieut. R.A.M.C., serving until the peace. Served European War, 1914-19 (despatches, C.B.E.). *Address:* 6 Victoria Square, Newcastle upon Tyne.
[*Died* 6 *July* 1962.

CLAYTON, Arthur Ross, D.S.O. 1918; retd.; *b.* Yankalilla, S. Australia, 14 May 1876; 3rd *s.* of late J. Woods Clayton and Elizabeth Clayton; *m.* 1922, Nellie Mary Harbison, Wallaroo, S.A. *Educ.:* St. Peter's College and University, Adelaide. M.B. B.S., 1902; House Surgeon, Adelaide Hospital, 1903; at London Hospital, Whitechapel Road, 1905; M.R.C.S.; L.R.C.P.; Surgeon at Moonta, S.A.; Mayor of Corporation of Moonta, 1925-26 and 1939; in Egypt and France on active service, 1915-19 (Brevet-Major, D.S.O., despatches); Rank Lieut.-Colonel A.A.M.C., C.O., 8th Australian Field Ambulance. *Recreations:* fishing, bowls, golf. *Address:* Robert Street, Moonta, South Australia. *T.:* Moonta 14.
[*Died* 2 *Sept.* 1963.

CLAYTON, Major-General Edward Hadrill, C.B. 1949; C.B.E. 1943 (O.B.E. 1941); Managing Director Service Division, British Motor Corporation; Director: Morris Motors Ltd., B.M.C. Service Ltd.; Suez Contractors (Vehicles) Ltd.; *b.* 10 Oct. 1899; *o. s.* of late Frederick and Louise Clayton; *m.* 1928, Grace Gwyther; one *d.* *Educ.:* Brighton College; Royal Military Acad., Woolwich. Commissioned in R.A. 1918; Student on the 43rd Advanced Class, Military College of Science, 1924-27; Asst. Inspector, Armaments Inspection Dept., 1928-34; Staff College, Camberley, 1935-36;

G.S.O. III, War Office, 1937-38; Deputy Asst. Director of Munitions Production, War Office, and Min. of Supply, 1939; Asst. Director, Min. of Supply, 1939-40, Dep. Director, 1941; Dep. Controller-Gen., Army Provision Eastern Group, 1941-43; Director of Weapons and Equipment, General Staff G.H.Q. India, 1943-46; Director of Equipment and Requirements, War Office, 1946-47; Director-General of Fighting Vehicles, Min. of Supply, 1948-51; retired pay, 1951. *Address:* Old Victoria, North Moreton, Berks. *Club:* United Service. [*Died* 19 *Nov.* 1962.

CLAYTON, Harold, C.I.E. 1919; *b.* 7 May 1874; *s.* of late Bishop Clayton; *m.* 1917, Alice L. Chapman (*d.* 1956); one *d.* *Educ.:* Marlborough; Pembroke College, Cambridge. Entered Indian Civil Service, 1897; has served in Burma; last posts held: Director of Agriculture, 1912-16; Registrar of Co-operative Societies, 1916-19; Commissioner, 1919-22; Financial Commissioner, 1923-26; retired, 1926; Secretary, Church of England Men's Society, 1926-38. *Address:* c/o Lloyds Bank Ltd., Cox's and King's Branch, 6 Pall Mall, S.W.1. [*Died* 12 *March* 1963.

CLAYTON, Colonel Patrick Andrew, D.S.O. 1941; M.B.E. 1945; F.G.S.; F.R.G.S.; F.R.I.C.S.; retired 1953; *b.* 16 April 1896; *m.* 1927, Ethel Williamson Wyatt; one *s.* *Educ.:* University College School; London University. Served in Royal Field Artillery in Greece and Turkey, 1915-20; Inspector, Desert Surveys, Egypt, 1920-38; Survey Dept. Lands and Mines, Tanganyika Govt., 1938-40; recalled to Army to Long Range Desert Group under Gen. Wavell in Libya, 1940-41 (prisoner). Formerly Intelligence Corps. Gold medal for actes méritoires by King Fuad I for rescue of Arabs from Kufra 1931; Founders' medal, R.G.S., 1941, for maps used in 1940-43 campaigns in Libya. *Publications:* various monographs on work in Western Desert, and silica glass in conjunction with research with Dr. Spencer of British Museum. *Recreation:* travel. *Address:* Murzouk, Salisbury Rd., Hove 3, Sussex. [*Died* 17 *March* 1962.

CLAYTON, Reginald John Byard; late Malayan Civil Service; *b.* 10 Dec. 1875; *s.* of late R. B. B. Clayton, Maryborough, Queensland, Australia, and Little Hatchett, Beaulieu, Hants; *m.* Beatrice Dickens (*d.* 1936), *g.d.* of Charles Dickens; one *d.* *Educ.:* St. Paul's School; Brasenose College, Oxford (open scholar). Malayan Civil Service 1898; British Adviser to the Government of Kelantan; retired, 1930. *Publications:* Pamphlets on Rice supplies and on Toddy. *Recreation:* fishing. *Address:* Beach Warren, Milford-on-Sea, Hants. *T.:* 43. *Club:* Royal Commonwealth Society. [*Died* 25 *July* 1962.

CLAYTON, William Lockhart; late Under-Sec. of State for Economic Affairs, U.S.; *b.* on a cotton farm near Tupelo, Mississippi, 7 Feb. 1880; *m.* 1902, Susan Vaughan, Clinton, Kentucky; four *d.* Left school at 13 to work in office of Clerk and Master of Chancery Court, Jackson, Tennessee; Deputy Clerk and Master at 15; learned shorthand at night and became court reporter; American Cotton Company, New York, in various positions, 1896-1904; joined in forming, with family, firm of Anderson, Clayton & Co., Oklahoma City, 1904; headquarters moved to Houston, Texas, 1916: Member, Cttee. on Cotton Distribution of War Industries Board, during 1918 (temporarily withdrew as partner in firm); resigned as Chm. Anderson, Clayton & Co. to enter Govt. service, 1940; first with Nelson Rockefeller, coordinator of Inter-American affairs; second, as Deputy Federal Loan Administrator; third, as Asst. Sec. of Commerce; then as Administrator of Surplus War Property Administration; later as Asst. Sec. of State in Charge of Economic Affairs. *Address:* c/o Anderson, Clayton & Co., P.O. Box 2538, Houston 1, U.S.A. [*Died* 8 *Feb.* 1966.

CLEARY, Hon. Sir Timothy Patrick, Kt. 1959; Judge of the Court of Appeal, New Zealand, since 1958; *b.* Meanee, Hawkes Bay, New Zealand, 1900; *s.* of Patrick Cleary; *m.* 1933, Nea Constance Jervis. *Educ.:* St. Patrick's College, Wellington, New Zealand; Victoria University, Wellington, Practised Law in Wellington to 1957. Pres. N.Z. Law Society, 1953-57. *Address:* 47 Messines Road, Wellington, W.3, New Zealand. [*Died* 15 *Aug.* 1962.

CLEATHER, Edward Gordon; *b.* 1872; *s.* of late Gabriel Gordon and Emily Cleather; *m.* 1897, Ethel Lillis Scott (*d.* 1935); two *s.* four *d.* *Educ.:* Radley. Professor of Singing, Royal Irish Academy of Music, Dublin, 1893; came to London and appeared at principal concerts and in Opéra Comique at Daly's, Apollo, Prince of Wales, and other theatres, 1900; joined the R.N.V.R. June 1917. F.G.S.M.; Professor of Singing, Guildhall School of Music, 1913, now retired. *Recreations:* cricket, lawn tennis, played cricket for Co. Wicklow, and tennis for Middlesex and All England Club, Wimbledon. *Address:* 31 Queen's Gate Terrace, S.W.7. [*Died* 27 *Feb.* 1967.

CLEGG, Rear-Admiral John Harry Kay, O.B.E. 1919; Retired; *b.* 24 July 1884; *s.* of late Harry Clegg, Plas Llanfair, Anglesey; *m.* 1932, Josephine Claiborne Faust (*d.* 1946); *m.* 1947, Damaris Frederick Roberts, Christiansburg, Va., *widow* of J. Griggs Roberts. *Educ.:* H.M.S. Britannia. Joined Navy, 1899; retired, 1936, with rank of Rear-Admiral. *Address:* Flat 10, 62 Westbourne Terrace, W.2. *T.:* Ambassador 6148. [*Died* 2 *June* 1962.

CLEMENTS, His Honour Arthur Frederick; Judge of County Courts on Circuit No. 49 (Kent), 1930-50; retd; Special Commissioner Probate Division of High Court (Matrimonial Causes), 1946-50; Chm. Dover Licensing Planning Committee, 1946-60; *b.* Newark-on-Trent, 21 Jan. 1877; *s.* of Rev. John Clements; *m.* Kate Fynmore (*d.* 1957), *d.* of William Messenger Jenner, Sandgate, Kent; (one *d.* decd.). *Educ.:* privately and for a time in Univ. of Wales, but chiefly in his father's study. Admitted a Solicitor, 1899; called to Bar, Middle Temple, 1911; joined the Oxford Circuit; Recorder of Tewkesbury, 1927-30; Member of the General Council of the Bar, 1922-30; J.P. Kent; Chairman, East Kent Quarter Sessions, 1940-47. F.S.A. 1939. *Publication:* Tudor Translations: An Anthology, 1940. *Address:* Barham House, Barham, Kent. [*Died* 20 *Jan.* 1968.

CLEMINSON, Henry Millican; Solicitor and Parliamentary Agent, retired; Lloyd's Underwriter; *b.* 1885; *s.* of late Rev. J. R. Cleminson, Hull; *m.* 1917, Hester (*d.* 1945), *d.* of late Hon. Josiah Wood, New Brunswick, Canada, and *widow* of Lieut. Comdr. Bernard Harvey; one *s.* one step *s.* (and one *s.* decd.). *Educ.:* Kingswood. Subseq. under articles to Messrs. Woodhouse, Ashe and Ferens, Hull. General Manager, Chamber of Shipping of United Kingdom, 1916-41; Secretary, Shipowners' Parliamentary Committee, 1917-41, and Secretary, International Shipping Conference, 1921-1941; Member of firm of Botterell & Roche, London, and, as such, a Manager of the British Steamship Owners Association, 1913-1923; Legal Member of British Government Commercial Mission to Sweden, 1915; member of various war commissions and committees, 1916-22 and 1939-41; Member Board of Trade Merchant Shipping Advisory Committee, 1922-39; responsible in 1921 for institution of Internat. Shipping Conference (re-named the Internat. Chamber of Shipping); Member appointed by Ministry of Agriculture of East Suffolk Rivers Catchment Board, 1931-36; Vice-Chairman, River Blyth Drainage Board, 1934-36; Member Council, Catchment Boards Association, 1933-36; member of Council Town and Country Planning Association, 1943-49. Vice-Pres. of the Council for Visual Education (Chairman, 1942-54). *Recreations:* sailing and ornithology. *Address:* Whitebarn, Walberswick, Suffolk. *T.:* Southwold 2363. *Club:* Royal Norfolk and Suffolk Yacht (Lowestoft). [*Died* 30 *March* 1970.

CLEUGH, Eric Arthur, C.M.G. 1951; C.V.O. 1954 (M.V.O. 1939); O.B.E. 1945; *b.* 10 Nov. 1894; *s.* of late James Cleugh; *m.* 1938, Maxine, *d.* of Graham Harding; two *d. Educ.:* Dulwich College; abroad. Artists' Rifles, 1918; entered Consular Service, 1919; Montevideo, 1919; Paris, 1924; Mexico City, 1928; British Secretary to Anglo-Mexican Special Claims Commission, 1929; Panama, 1933; Chargé d'Affaires, British Legation, Panama, 1934; New York, 1935; Consul at Los Angeles, 1939 - 43; Consul - General there, 1943; Consul-General at Havana, Feb.-Oct. 1945; Danzig, 1945; Houston, 1946; British Embassy, Washington (on temp. duty, Feb.-Sept. 1947); Counsellor and Consul-General, British Embassy, Washington, 1948-50; Minister, British Embassy, Panama, 1950-53; British Ambassador to Panama, 1953-55; retired from Foreign Service, 1955. *Publications:* Without Let or Hindrance, 1960; Viva Mallorca, Yesterday and Today in the Balearic Islands, 1963. *Recreations:* golf, tennis, swimming, bridge. *Address:* c/o Barclay's Bank Ltd., 4 Vere Street, W.1. [*Died* 10 *Feb.* 1964.

CLEVERLY, Sir Osmund Somers, Kt., *cr.* 1951; C.B. 1939; C.V.O. 1937; *b.* 25 Oct. 1891; *e. s.* of late Charles F. M. Cleverly, Dunsborough, Ripley, Surrey; *m.* 1920, Priscilla, *e. d.* of late Professor F. M. Simpson, F.R.I.B.A.; two *s.* one *d. Educ.:* Rugby; Magdalen College, Oxford. Commissioned 5th Batt. The Queens Regt. (T.F.), 1912; served European War, Aug. 1914-Feb. 1919, India and Mesopotamia; Higher Division Clerk War Office, 1919; Principal, 1924; Private Sec. to Prime Minister, 1935; Principal Private Secretary to Prime Minister (Mr. Baldwin and Mr. Chamberlain), 1936-39; Deputy Secretary, Ministry of Supply, 1939-1941; Commissioner for Crown Lands, 1941-1952, and 1954-55. *Address:* Jesse's Hill, Gomshall, Surrey. *T.:* Abinger 288. [*Died* 21 *Oct.* 1966.

CLIFDEN, 7th Viscount (*cr.* 1781); **Francis Gerald Agar-Robartes,** K.C.V.O., *cr.* 1952 (M.V.O. 1909); Baron Clifden, 1776; Baron Mendip (Gt. Brit.), 1794; Baron Robartes, 1869; late Counsellor of Embassy Diplomatic Service; *b.* 14 Apr. 1883; *e. surv. s.* of 6th Viscount and Mary (*d.* 1921), *d.* of late Francis Henry Dickinson, Kingweston, Somerset; *S.* father, 1930. *Educ.:* Eton; Christ Church, Oxford. Attaché, 1906; appointed to Paris, 1907; 3rd Sec. 1908; 2nd Sec. 1914; 1st Sec. 1919; Assistant Private Secretary to the Secretary of State for Foreign Affairs, 1919-20 and 1922-23; Counsellor of H.M. Embassy, Madrid, 1926-27; a Lord-in-Waiting, 1940-1945; Member, C.C., Cornwall, 1934-52; Member of H.M. Council for the Duchy of Cornwall, 1939-52; Secretary to the British Delegates at the Third International Opium Conference at The Hague, 1914; County Director British Red Cross Society (Cornwall), 1939-46; Formerly: Pres. Roy. Hosp. and Home for Incurables, Putney; Roy. Cornwall Infirmary, Truro; Camborne-Redruth Miners' and Gen. Hosp.; E. Cornwall Hosp., Bodmin. O.St.J. *Heir:* *b.* Hon. (Arthur) Victor Agar-Robartes, M.C. *Address:* Lanhydrock, Bodmin; 7 Belgrave Square, S.W.1. [*Died* 15 *July* 1966.

CLIFF, Eric Francis, C.B. 1943; *b.* 6 May 1884; *s.* of late A. Cliff, H.M. Patent Office; *m.* 1912, Mima (*d.* 1959), *d.* of late J. Roulston, J.P.; two *s.* one *d. Educ.:* St. Albans Sch.; The Northampton College of Advanced Technology; Gray's Inn. Entered H.M. Patent Office, 1906; Inns of Court O.T.C. 1914; Commissioned R.A. 1915. Asst. Principal, Air Ministry, 1919; Private Sec. to late Marquess of Londonderry, K.G., M.V.O., Finance Member of the Air Council; Principal, 1921; Assistant Secretary, 1936; Assistant Under-Secretary of State, 1938; Principal Assistant Secretary, Treasury, 1943; Treasury Establishment rep. in Washington, 1943-45; retired, 1945. *Address:* 9 Marlborough Road, Southwold, Suffolk. *T.:* Southwold 3186. [*Died* 25 *Jan.* 1969.

CLIFFE, Michael; M.P. (Lab.) Shoreditch and Finsbury from 1958; Member of National Executive, National Union of Tailors and Garment Workers; *b.* 1904; British; *m.* 1932, Sophia Whitesman; two *s. Educ.:* Holliscroft School, Solly St., Sheffield. Worked in clothing industry up to the time of becoming Member of Parliament. Adult life devoted to Labour and Trade Union Movements, and during the past 12 years has been connected with Local Government at Finsbury; Mayor of Finsbury, 1956-57. *Recreations:* walking, reading. *Address:* 63 Hatfield House, Golden Lane Estate, E.C.1. [*Died* 9 *Aug.* 1964.

CLIFFORD OF CHUDLEIGH, 11th Baron (*cr.* 1672); **Charles Oswald Hugh Clifford,** *b.* 24 Apr. 1887; *e. s.* of 10th Baron and Catherine Mary, *d.* of R. Bassett; *S.* father 1943; *m.* 1st, 1917, Dorothy (*d.* 1918), *o. d.* of Alfred J. Hornyold, 97 Eaton Place, S.W.; one *d.*; 2nd, Clare Mary, *d.* of Capt. J. G. Mayne, Chagford, *g. d.* of Sir Frederick Weld, G.C.M.G., and *widow* of C. S. W. Ogilvie. *Educ.:* Downside. Served European War, 1914-18. *Heir:* *b.* Hon. Lewis Joseph Hugh Clifford, *q.v. Address:* Lawell House, Chudleigh, Devon; Ugbrooke Park, Chudleigh. [*Died* 1 *Feb.* 1962.

CLIFFORD OF CHUDLEIGH, 12th Baron *cr.* 1672; **Lewis Joseph Hugh Clifford;** *b.* 1889; 2nd *s.* of 10th Baron Clifford of Chudleigh; *S.* brother, 11th Baron, 1962; *m.* 1st, 1914, Amy (*d.* 1926), *er. d.* of John A. Webster, M.D.; one *s.* two *d.*; 2nd, 1934, Mary Elizabeth, *yr. d.* of late Rt. Hon. Sir Adrian Knox, P.C., K.C.M.G. *Educ.:* Zavier College, Melbourne. *Heir:* *s.* Colonel Hon. (Lewis) Hugh Clifford, O.B.E. [*b.* 13 April 1916; *m.* 1945, Hon. Katharine Fisher, *d.* of 2nd Baron Fisher; two *s.* two *d.*]. *Address:* Yarra Brae, Wonga Park, Victoria, Australia; El Reposo, San Roque, Province of Cadiz, Spain. *T.:* San Roque 188; (seat) Ugbrooke Park, Chudleigh, S. Devon. [*Died* 27 *Aug.* 1964.

CLIFFORD, Captain Hon. Sir Bede Edmund Hugh, G.C.M.G., *cr.* 1945 (K.C.M.G., *cr.* 1933; C.M.G. 1923); C.B. 1931; M.V.O. 1920; F.R.G.S.; Capt. R. of O., late Royal Fusiliers; *b.* 1890; *y. s.* of 10th Baron Clifford of Chudleigh; *m.* 1925, Alice Devin, *d.* of J. M. Gundry, Cleveland, Ohio; three *d.* Private and Military Secretary to Governor-General of Australia, 1919-20; Secretary to Prince Arthur of Connaught (Governor-General of South Africa), 1921-24; Secretary to Earl of Athlone, 1924; Imperial Secretary (South African High Commission) and Representative of H.M.'s Govts. of Great Britain and Northern Ireland in the Union of South Africa; Governor and Commander-in-Chief: Bahamas, 1932-37; Mauritius, 1937-42; Trinidad and Tobago, 1942-46; accompanied Lord Jellicoe's Naval Mission in Australia and South Sea Islands; led first British

Expedition across Kalahari Desert. *Publications:* Kalahari Desert, Ancient Forts of Bahamas, Irrigation and Hydro-Electric Resources of Mauritius; Proconsul (autobiography). *Recreations:* yachting, racing, tennis, golf, etc. *Clubs:* White's, Buck's; Royal Yacht Squadron (Cowes).
[*Died* 6 *Oct.* 1969.

CLIFFORD, Vice-Admiral Sir Eric (George Anderson), K.C.B., *cr.* 1956 (C.B. 1952); C.B.E. 1953; F.I.N.; a Lord Commissioner of the Admiralty and Dep. Chief of Naval Staff, 1954-57, retd.; *b.* 3 Sept. 1900; *s.* of Captain W. T. Clifford; *m.* 1936, Nita Marion Hill; one *d.* *Educ.:* Training Ship Worcester. H.M.S. Iron Duke, 1917; H.M.S. Colossus, 1918; specialised in Navigation, 1924; H.M.S. Nelson, 1928; H.M.S. Caradoc, 1929-30; completed Staff Coll. Course, 1932; H.M.S. Coventry, 1933-1935; Plans Div., Admiralty, 1935-37; Fleet Navigating Officer, China Fleet, 1938-40; Cmd. Mackay, Salisbury, Diadem, 1939-45; Naval Asst. Secretary, War Cabinet, 1941-1943; Chief of Staff, Hong Kong, 1945-46; Imperial Defence Coll., 1946; Comd. H.M. Navigation School, 1947-48; Comd. H.M.S. Illustrious, 1949-50; Assistant Chief of Naval Staff, 1951-52; Flag-Officer Commanding 5th Cruiser Squadron and Flag-Officer Second in Command, Far East station, 1952-1953. Captain, 1941; Rear-Admiral, 1951; Vice-Admiral, 1954. *Address:* Hammer Hill, Cuckfield, Sussex. *Clubs:* United Service; All England Lawn Tennis. [*Died* 7 *Sept.* 1964.

CLIFFORD, Col. Esmond Humphrey Miller, C.B.E. 1936 (O.B.E. 1928); M.C.; F.R.G.S.; late R.E.; *b.* 6 March 1895; *s.* of Miller Hancorne Clifford and Louisa Mann (*née* Peterson); *m.* 1921, Louise Marie Gilberte Phillips; one *s.* decd. *Educ.:* Clifton Coll.; R.M.A., Woolwich. Entered Army, 1914; Col., 1940; served European War, France and Belgium, 1915-17, Italy, 1917-19 (wounded, M.C., despatches twice); Assist. British Commissioner, Anglo-Italian Jubaland Boundary Commission 1925-1928 (O.B.E.); Senior British Commissioner, British Somaliland-Ethiopia Boundary Commission, 1931-36 (C.B.E.); War of 1939-45, went to Hong-Kong in 1940; P.O.W. 1941-1945. Retired, 1948; British Commissioner, Kenya-Ethiopia Boundary Commission, 1950-1957. *Recreations:* golf, shooting. *Clubs:* Army and Navy; Phyllis Court (Henley).
[*Died* 3 *Sept.* 1970.

CLIFFORD, Rev. Sir Lewis Arthur Joseph, 5th Bt., *cr.* 1887; S.J.; Headmaster of Beaumont College, Old Windsor, 1950-56 (formerly Bursar); *b.* 9 April 1896; 3rd *surv. s.* of Charles W. Clifford (3rd *s.* of 1st Bt.) and of Sicele Agnes De Trafford; *S.* uncle, 1944. *Educ.:* Beaumont College, Windsor, Berks. Served as Chaplain to the Forces during War of 1939-45, in France and Middle East. *Heir:* *b.* Roger Charles Joseph Gerrard Clifford, *b.* 1910. *Address:* Campion House, P.O. Box 54, Salisbury, Rhodesia.
[*Died* 8 *Dec.* 1970.

CLIFTON, Violet Mary (Mrs. Talbot Clifton); *b.* Nov. 1883; *d.* of William Nelthorpe Beauclerk, D.L., Little Grimsby Hall, Lincs, and Jane Rathborne; *m.* 1907, late John Talbot Clifton, of Lytham Hall, Lytham and Kildalton Castle, Isle of Islay; two *s.* three *d.* *Educ.:* Bruxelles. Travel in Andaman and Nicobar Islands and Malay, Burma, India, also Java, Sumatra, and Dutch Indian Islands: Mentawei Nias, Bali, Lombok, Sumbaya, Celebes, North-Pagi; French Africa, S. America, N. America, Honolulu, etc.; three medals for work in European War, 1914-18; became Roman Catholic. *Publications:* Pilgrims to the Isles of Penance; Islands of Queen Wilhelmina; The Book of Talbot (awarded Tait-Black Memorial Prize); Sanctity; Charister; Vision of Peru. *Address:* Lytham Hall, Lytham, Lancs. *T.:* Lytham 6748.
[*Died* 20 *Nov.* 1961.

CLIFTON BROWN, Cedric; J.P. Norfolk; *b.* 10 Dec. 1887; *y. s.* of late Col. Clifton Brown, Holmbush, Faygate, Sussex; *m.* 1938, Manie (O.B.E. 1960; County Alderman), *o. d.* of late Rev. J. A. Labouchere, M.A., Rector of Sculthorpe, 1902-20; two *s.* one *d.* *Educ.:* Eton; Trinity College, Cambridge. B.A. 1909. In office of Brown, Shipley and Co., Merchant Bankers, of Founders Court, Lothbury, E.C., 1909-19; served in European war with Sussex Yeomanry, Worcestershire Yeomanry and Grenadier Guards,1914-19; High Sheriff of Norfolk 1941; Member Norfolk County Council, 1934; Alderman, 1952; F.R.G.S.; F.R.Z.S. F.R.S.A. *Recreations:* shooting, cricket. *Address:* Congham Lodge, Hillington, King's Lynn. *T.A.:* Hillington. *T.:* Hillington 225. *Clubs:* Bath, Guards, Pratt's, M.C.C. [*Died* 22 *Oct.* 1968.

CLIVE, Lt.-Col. George W.; *see* Windsor-Clive.

CLIVE, Col. Harry, C.B. 1934; O.B.E.; T.D.; D.L., J.P.; Director of Companies; *b.* 7 May 1880; *s.* of Col. Robert Clement Clive and Mary Dale Clive; *m.* 1907, Dorothy (*d.* 1942), 13th child of Joseph Clive of Barston Hall, Warwickshire and Coombe Florey, Somerset; one *s.* two *d.* *Educ.:* Newcastle-under-Lyme High School. Joined 1st V B N Staff. Regt 1899; continuous service till mobilised Aug 1914; France, 1915; Northern Command, York 1918-19; commanded 5th Bn. N. Staffordshire Regt., 1923-28; commanded The (137th) Staffs Infantry Brigade, 1928-32. Hon. Col. 576 S L. Regt. (5 N. Staffs) R.A. (T.A.) 1947-50. *Recreations:* shooting, horticulture, philately. *Address:* Willoughbridge, Market Drayton, Salop. *T.A.:* Willoughbridge Woore. *T.:* Pipegate 237. [*Died* 2 *Jan.* 1963.

CLOAKE, Professor Philip Cyril; Emeritus Professor, University of Birmingham; Consulting Physician, United Birmingham Hospitals; *b.* 1890; *s.* of Alfred and Elizabeth Cloake; *m.* 1st, 1916, Blanche Macdonald; three *d.*; 2nd, 1958, Evelyn, *d.* of Sidney Roberson, Upper Colwall, Herefordshire. *Educ.:* London and Cambridge. Physician to the Queen's Hospital, later Birmingham United Hospital, 1925; Professor of Medicine, University of Birmingham, 1933-46; Professor of Neurology, University of Birmingham, 1946-55. Past President: Section of Neurology, Royal Society of Medicine; West Midlands Physicians Assoc.; British Br. of Internat. League against Epilepsy; British Electroencephalographic Society. *Address:* 9 Pakenham Road, Birmingham 15. *T.:* Calthorpe 3037. [*Died* 14 *March* 1969.

CLOTHIER, His Honour Wilfrid, Q.C. 1933; LL.M.; retired as Judge of County Courts Circuit No. 48 (Lambeth) (1947-1959); *b.* 19 February 1887; *s.* of late William Charles Clothier, Senior Surveyor H.M. Customs; *m.* 1st, 1913, Ada Millward (*d.* 1947), *d.* of late Edward Roberts, partner in Richard Williams & Co., timber merchants, Liverpool; no *c.*; 2nd, 1949, Kathleen Mary, 2nd *d.* of late Edward Ernest Godfrey, a Dir. of Cook, Son & Co. Ltd., wholesale textile merchants, St. Paul's Churchyard, E.C.4, and of late Mrs. Godfrey, formerly of Salcombe, Foxley Lane, Purley. *Educ.:* privately; Liverpool University (Exhibitioner). Honours LL.B., 1908; LL.M., 1909; Honours Solicitors' Final Exam., 1909; practised as a Solicitor in Liverpool until Army service with Honourable Artillery Company and later served as legal assistant to the Director-General of Recruiting; called to Bar, Inner Temple, 1920; K.C. 1933; Bencher, 1941; Treasurer, 1965. Recorder of Blackburn,

1944-47. Contested (C.) Edge Hill Division of Liverpool, 1945. *Recreations:* golf and motoring. *Address:* Aeolia, The Ridge, Woodcote Park, Epsom, Surrey. *Club:* Royal Automobile (Epsom). [*Died* 9 *Feb.* 1967.

CLOUGH, Arthur Harold, C.M.G. 1955; O.B.E. 1946; formerly Minister (Treasury Adviser) to U.K. Delegation to United Nations, New York; *b.* 2 April 1897; *s.* of Thomas George Clough and Mary Newth; *m.* 1929, Marjorie Violet Anderson; one *s.* one *d.* (and one *s.* decd.). *Educ.:* County Secondary School, Brockley; King's College, London. Inland Revenue Department, 1914-15; War Office, 1915-38; Royal Flying Corps and Royal Air Force, 1917-20; H.M. Treasury, 1938; Under-Secretary, 1951; Member of National Whitley Council for the Civil Service. Seconded to Foreign Office for service with U.K. Delegation to United Nations with rank of Minister, 1952-58. Mem. of U.N. Advisory Cttee. on Administrative and Budgetary Questions, and of U.N. Contribns. Cttee. Retired, 1958. *Recreations:* music, golf. *Address:* Kingsgarth, Kingswood Rd., Penn, Bucks. [*Died* 11 *Sept.* 1967.

CLOUGH, (Ernest Marshall) Owen, C.M.G. 1921; *b.* Huddersfield, Yorks, 26 June 1873; *s.* of late W. O. Clough, sometime M.P. for Portsmouth; *m.* 1908, Stella Irene, *d.* of late B. T. Bourke, Vierfontein, South Africa; three *d.* *Educ.:* Mercers School; Germany. Private Secretary to the late Hon. Sir R. Solomon, G.C.M.G., when Legal Adviser to the Transvaal Administration and to Lord Kitchener, C.-in-C., South Africa, and later when Attorney-General, Transvaal, 1901-3; accompanied S.A. Representative Delhi Durbar, 1903; Clerk of Executive and Legislative Councils (Transvaal) under Crown Colony Government, 1903-7; Clerk of Legislative Council (Transvaal) during responsible Government, 1907-10; Clerk of the Senate of the Union of South Africa, 1910-29; Hon. Sec. Union of South African Branch, Empire Parliamentary Association, 1911-29; on Parliamentary delegations to England, 1916, Southern Africa, 1924, Australia, 1926 and Canada, 1928; Editor, African Affairs Report, 1930-35; served S. Africa, 1900-1, H.A.C. Battery; German S.-W. Africa, 1914-15, C.G.A.; France and Italy, 1917-18, R.H. and F.A.; Staff Officer (Maj.) G.H.Q., Pretoria, 1941-44; Founder and Sec.-Treas. of Society of Clerks-at-the-Table in Empire Parliaments, Editor of its annual Journal, 1932-52, and Life Pres of the Society. Hon. LL.D. (Cape), 1954. *Address:* Tennant Rise, Kenilworth, Cape, S. Africa. *Club:* Civil Service (Cape Town). [*Died* 6 *Feb.* 1964.

CLOUGH, Howard James Butler, C.B.E. 1949; *b.* 26 July 1890; *o. s.* of George Frederick Butler-Clough and Katherine Mary (*née* Smyth); *m.* 1916, Frances Margaret, 3rd *d.* of Rev. T. E. Jones, Rector of Hope, Flintshire; two *s.* *Educ.:* Rugby School; Magdalen College, Oxford. Higher Division Clerk, War Office, 1914; Private Secretary to Sir Reginald Brade, Sec. of the War Office, 1916-20, and to Sir Herbert Creedy, Sec. of the War Office, Jan.-Oct. 1920; Principal, 1920; Principal Private Sec. to successive Secs. of State for War (Mr. Thomas Shaw, the Marquess of Crewe, and Viscount Hailsham), 1929-34; Assistant Secretary, 1934; Director of Finance, War Office, 1946; Under-Secretary, 1949; retired 1951. Silver Jubilee Medal, 1935; Coronation Medal, 1937. Chevalier Légion d'Honneur, 1920; Medal of Freedom with bronze palm (U.S.), 1946. *Address:* 4 Cissbury, Ascot, Berks. *T.:* Ascot 22317. *Club:* Royal Automobile. [*Died* 15 *Dec.* 1967.

CLOUGH, Owen; *see* Clough, E. M. O.

CLOUGH, Sir Robert, Kt., *cr.* 1921; *b.* 10 Feb. 1873; *m.* 1st, 1896, Edith Mary (*d.* 1908), *d.* of P. W. Musgrave, Otley; one *s.* one *d.*; 2nd, 1909, Alice, *d.* of James Mathers, Leeds; (one *s.* decd.). *Educ.:* Giggleswick; Stuttgart. Mayor of Keighley, 1907-08. M.P. (Democratic Unionist), Keighley Division, West Riding of Yorkshire, Dec. 1918-22. *Address:* Green Bank, Utley, Keighley. *Club:* Bradford (Bradford). [*Died* 27 *Sept.* 1965.

CLOVER, Major-General Frederick Sherwood, C.B. 1947; C.B.E. 1943 (O.B.E. 1942); A.M.I.Mech.E.; late R.A S.C.; *b.* 1894; *m.* 1917, Mildred Mary, *d.* of James Richard Carter; three *d.* *Educ.:* St. Andrew's Coll., Dublin; Royal Military College, Sandhurst. Commissioned R.A.S.C., 1913; served European War, 1914-19, France and Belgium; War of 1939-45, Middle East; D.D.S.T., 8th Army, 1941-42; D.S.T., 21 Army Group, 1943; D.S.T., War Office, 1946-48. A.D.C. to the King, 1945; retired pay, 1948. *Address:* Dormicot, The Sands, Farnham, Surrey. *T.:* Runfold 2077. [*Died* 13 *Jan.* 1962.

CLOWES, Lt.-Gen. Cyril Albert, C.B.E. 1943; D.S.O. 1918; M.C. 1917; *b.* 11 Mar. 1892; *s.* of Albert Clowes, Warwick, Queensland; *m.* 1925, Eva F. Magennis (*d.* 1963); one *d.* *Educ.:* Toowoomba Gram. Sch., Queensland; Royal Military College, Duntroon, Aust. Graduated R.M.C., Duntroon, and commissioned Aust. Staff Corps and 1st A.I.F., 1914; served War of 1914-19 in Egypt, Gallipoli and France in Field Artillery (despatches, M.C., D.S.O.); Aust. Staff Corps in various capacities, in Aust. and England, 1919-39; served War of 1939-45 2nd A.I.F. in Middle East (as Commander Corps Artillery, 1st Aust. Corps) including Libya, Greece, Syria, 1940-41; served New Guinea (includin goperations at Milne Bay, Aug.-Sept. 1942, as Commander), 1942-43 (despatches twice, C.B.E.); Adjutant-General, Aust. Military Forces, 1946; G.O.C., Southern Command, 1946-49. Retired List, Australian Military Forces, 1949. Servian White Eagle, 1916; Greek Military Cross, 1941. *Recreations:* golf, tennis, shooting, fishing. *Address:* 6 Hampden Road, Armadale, S.E.3, Victoria, Australia. *Clubs:* Royal Melbourne Golf; Naval and Military (Melbourne). [*Died* 19 *May* 1968.

CLOWES, Alderman Sir Harold, Kt. 1960; O.B.E. 1955; J.P.; Builder (retired); *b.* 19 March 1903; *s.* of Alderman Samuel Clowes, J.P., M.P. and Jane Clowes; *m.* (marriage dissolved, 1943); two *s.* one *d.* Lord Mayor of Stoke-on-Trent, 1959-60; Alderman, Stoke-on-Trent; J.P. 1953. Member of Council, Keele University; Mem. of Sub-Committee on Housing Standards, Central Housing Advisory Committee; Vice-Chairman, 1960, Rating Committee of Assoc. of Municipal Corporations. Chm., Building and Development Cttee. *Publications:* papers on Housing and Community Development. *Address:* The Old Rectory, Bucknall, Stoke-on-Trent. *T.:* Stoke-on-Trent 54461. [*Died* 16 *Sept.* 1968.

CLUBB, Hon. William Reid; Retd.; Chm. Manitoba Govt. Liquor Control Commission, 1941-57; *b.* Morris, Man., 7 Oct. 1884; *s.* of George G. Clubb and Alice Jex; *m.* 1913, Gertrude, *d.* of Peter Kastner, Morris, Man.; one *s.* four *d.* *Educ.:* Manitoba Public Schools; Winnipeg Business College; Manitoba Agricultural College. A Farmer; Member of the Council, Rural Municipality of Morris, Manitoba, 1916-20; Member of Manitoba Legislature, 1920; Minister of Public Works, Manitoba, 1922-40, and Labour, 1936-40. Religion, Member of United Church of Canada.

Recreations: curling, golf, hunting and fishing. *Address:* 1043 McMillan Ave., Winnipeg, Manitoba, Canada. [*Died* 11 *Aug.* 1962.

CLUNES, Alec Sheriff de Moro; *b.* 17 May 1912; *s.* of Alexander Sheriff Sydney Clunes and Georgina Sumner; *m.* 1949, Stella Richman (marriage dissolved, 1954); *m* 1956, Daphne Acott; one *s.* one *d.* *Educ.:* Cliftonville, Margate. After appearing with Ben Greet Players he went to Old Vic Company in 1934 playing a number of parts including Laertes in Hamlet, Clarence in Richard III, Autolycus in The Winter's Tale, Edmund in King Lear, Berowne in Love's Labour's Lost. Appeared in West End theatres in Hell - for - Leather (1936), George and Margaret (1937), The Road to Ruin (1937), Yes, My Darling Daughter (1937), I Killed the Count (1937). In 1938 played at the Malvern Festival in Music at Night, The Last Trump and Dunois in Saint Joan. Played in London production of In Good King Charles's Golden Days in 1939. In 1942 he founded the Arts Theatre Group of Actors at the Arts Theatre Club; plays under his production there include Macbeth, 1950 (Arts' 100th production; played title rôle); responsible for two productions—The Magistrate and Bird in Hand—at St. Martin's Theatre. Has appeared as Sir Harry Wildair in The Constant Couple, as Hamlet and as Don Juan in G. B. Shaw's Don Juan in Hell. Is part author of Exercise Bowler. Planned an extensive tour of Europe under auspices of the British Council, playing Hamlet and Iago: appeared (at author's suggestion) as Professor Higgins in Shaw's Pygmalion, Lyric, Hammersmith, 1947; leading parts in The Lady's not for Burning, Arts, 1948 (also in radio and television versions, 1950); Robert Browning in revival of The Barretts of Wimpole Street, Garrick, 1948; leading parts in Bridie's Gog and MacGog, 1948; The Diary of a Scoundrel, 1949; Macbeth, 1950—all at Arts Theatre; produced Queen Elizabeth by Hugh Ross Williamson, Arts, 1950; Old Vic Company, playing King Henry in Henry V, Orsino in Twelfth Night, Ford in Merry Wives of Windsor and Waspe in Bartholomew Fair, 1951. Moses in The Firstborn, Winter Garden, 1952; Sir Harry Wildair in The Constant Couple, Winter Garden, 1952. Arts Theatre, 1952-53: productions include: Don Juan in Hell (title rôle); Arms and The Man (chief rôle). Carrington, V.C. (title rôle), Westminster, 1953; relinquished post as Theatre Director of Arts Theatre, 1953; played chief rôle in The Facts of Life, Duke of York's, 1954; played Hastings, Richard III (film), 1955; Burgundy, Quentin Durward (film), 1955; The Brighton Story (film), 1955; played Claudius, Hamlet, Phoenix Theatre, 1955-56. Played Richard Hannay in radio serial, Island of Sheep, 1954; Woodes Rogers in TV serial The Buccaneers, 1955; The Professor in Who Cares, 1956. Stratford 1957 Season: The Bastard in King John, Brutus in Julius Cæsar. Caliban in The Tempest; also Caliban, Drury Lane, 1958; Professor Higgins in My Fair Lady, 1959-1960; Sir Lewis Eliot in The Affair, Strand, 1962; Soames in Getting Married, Strand, 1967; Bishop Bell in Soldiers, New, 1968. Numerous TV appearances. *Publication:* The British Theatre, 1964. *Recreation:* his theatre bookshop. *Address:* c/o London Management, 235-241 Regent Street, W.1. [*Died* 13 *March* 1970.

CLUTTON, Sir George (Lisle), K.C.M.G. 1959 (C.M.G. 1950); F.S.A.; *b.* 5 Mar. 1909; 2nd *surv. s.* of late Captain Ralph Clutton, R.N., and of Margaret Mary Clutton. *Educ.:* Bedford School; Merton Coll., Oxford. Employed in British Museum, 1934-39. On active service with H.M. armed forces, Sept. 1939-Jan. 1940; seconded to Foreign Office, 1940; transferred to Stockholm, 1944; First Secretary, Belgrade, 1946-48; Head of African Department, Foreign Office, 1948-1950; Minister at the U.K. Liaison Mission Japan, 1950-52; Minister employed in Foreign Office, 1952-55; Ambassador to the Republic of the Philippines, 1955-59; Ambassador to Poland, 1960-66. Kt. Cross with Star, Order of Polonia Restituta, 1970. *Publications:* various contributions to journals on early printing and woodcuts, and historical subjects. *Recreations:* walking and talking. *Address:* 15 St. James's Chambers, Ryder St., S.W.1. *T.:* 01-839 5354. *Clubs:* Brooks's, Beefsteak. [*Died* 9 *Sept.* 1970.

CLYDE, Col. Sir David, Kt., *cr.* 1947; C.I.E. 1941; M.D.; D.P.H.; *b.* 30 Mar. 1894. Lieut. I.M.S. 1920; Capt. 1920; Major 1928; Lt.-Col. 1936; Col. 1944. Civil Surgeon, United Provinces, 1929-47; Surgeon General, Bengal, 1947. Retired, 1948. *Address:* c/o National and Grindlay's Bank, 13 St. James's Sq., S.W.1. [*Died* 23 *Nov.* 1966.

CLYNE, Hon. Sir Thomas Stuart, Kt., *cr.* 1955; Judge of the Federal Court of Bankruptcy, Australia, since 1942; *b.* 1887. *Educ.:* Wesley College; Univ. of Melbourne (1st cl. hons. Law). Former Lecturer in European History, Univ. of Melbourne; formerly Judge of County Court of Victoria; Judge of Supreme Court of Australian Capital Territory, 1943-45; Chm. Commonwealth Marine War Risks Insurance Board; acted as Chm., Royal Commission on Industrial Insurance. Fellow, Queen's College, Univ. of Melbourne. *Address:* 621 Toorak Rd., Toorak, Victoria, Australia. *Clubs:* Australian, Yorick (Melbourne). [*Died* 12 *April* 1967.

COAD, Rev. Canon William Samuel; Canon Residentiary, Chester Cathedral, 1944-1963 (now Emeritus); *b.* 8 Dec. 1882; *s.* of Samuel and Mary Bray Coad, Salcombe, Devon; *m.* 1910, Mary, 4th *d.* of William Elliot Amies; three *d.* *Educ.:* Exeter; St. Edmund Hall, Oxford (M.A.). Master, Wyggeston School, Leicester, 1909. Deacon, 1911; Priest, 1912; Curate, St. Nicholas, Leicester, 1911-12, Bath Abbey, 1913-1920; T.C.F. 1916-19; Vicar, St. George's, Macclesfield, 1920-34, St. James', New Brighton, 1934-44; Proctor in Convocation, Chester, 1930-31; Hon. Canon, Chester Cathedral, 1943. Hon. Chaplain Chester Regiment, 1944. President, Cheshire Branch English-Speaking Union, 1960. *Recreation:* reading. *Address:* Cannington Vicarage, Bridgwater, Somerset. *Club:* Grosvenor (Chester). [*Died* 11 *Jan.* 1965.

COADE, Thorold Francis, M.A.; retired as Headmaster of Bryanston School, Blandford (1932-59); *b.* Dublin, 3 July 1896; *s.* of Rev. Charles Edward Coade, M.A., B.D., LL.D.; *m.* 1922, Kathleen Eleanor, *d.* of H. H. Hardy; two *d.* *Educ.:* Harrow School; Royal Military College, Sandhurst; Christ Church, Oxford; passed with distinction in the Honours School of English Literature (shortened War course at Oxford University, 1921). 1st Loyal North Lancashire Regt., 1915-19; Assistant Master, Harrow School, 1922-32. *Publications:* Latin Translation Simplified, 1924; Editor of Harrow Lectures on Education, 1930; Editor of, and Contributor to Manhood in the Making, 1939. *Recreation:* golf. *Address:* Old Bell Cottage, Milton, East Knoyle, Salisbury, Wilts. *T.:* East Knoyle 268. [*Died* 1 *Feb.* 1963.

COAST, James Percy Chatterton, C.B.E. 1938; *b.* 5 Jan. 1880; *y. s.* of late William Chatterton Coast; *m.* 1st, 1915, Gwendoline Violet Elphicke (*d.* 1925), *yr. d.* of Frederick C. W. Hunnibell, Tunbridge Wells; one *s.* one *d.*; 2nd, 1945, Kathleen Blanche Walters. *Educ.:* Marlborough College; Queens' College, Cambridge. B.A. 1904; M.A. 1935; Secretary, Newspaper Press Fund, 1906-19; Secretary, The Land Agents' Society, 1919-37; Queen's Royal West

Surrey Regt. and 1st Batt., Royal Warwickshire Regt. 1915-19; latterly Instructor 4th Army Musketry School at Pont Remy; Temporary Assistant Land Commissioner (and for 2 years Liaison Officer, Defence Departments), Ministry of Agriculture and Fisheries, 1941-45. Hon. Member Land Agents' Society, 1939. *Publication:* The Land Agents' Society, 1901-39. *Address:* Apple Tree Cottage, Plaxtol, Sevenoaks, Kent. *T.:* Plaxtol 473. [*Died* 1 *April* 1962.

COATALEN, Louis Hervé; President Lockheed Hydraulic Brakes and K.L.G. Sparking Plugs (for France); *b.* Concarneau, Finisterre, 1879; 2nd *s.* of J. Coatalen and Louise le Brise; *m.* 1st, Olive Mary Bath (who obtained a divorce, 1922); two *s.*; 2nd, 1923, Mrs Enid Florence van Raalte. *Educ.:* The Lycée, Brest; The Arts et Metiers, Paris. Served his time in the French army; engaged in the drawing office of the De Dion-Bouton firm, going from there to Clement and Panhard; started with the Humber Co. at Coventry, 1901; in 1907 entered into partnership with Mr. Hillman in the production of the Hillman-Coatalen car; joined Sunbeam Motor Car Co., Ltd., 1908; became Chief Engineer. The first products of his designing figured in competitions, 1909; bought a Henry Farman aeroplane and experimented with his engines, with the result that by 1914 Sunbeam-Coatalen aircraft engines were the only ones of native design produced by a firm with a big factory behind it, which had sufficient power to fly our sea-planes. *Publication:* Motor Car and Aircraft Engine Design, a lecture delivered to the Aeronautical Society of Great Britain. *Recreation:* motor yachting. *Address:* 7 Rue Lesueur, Paris 16e, France. [*Died* 23 *May* 1962.

COATES, David Wilson, C.B.E. 1918; M.A., LL.B.; *b.* 11 April 1886; *s.* of late Fletcher Coates; *m.* 1913, Mabel R. (*d.* 1961), *d.* of late Thomas Goodley; three *s.* two *d.* *Educ.:* Wycliffe College; Château de Lancy, near Geneva; St. John's College, Cambridge. Associate of Institute of Chartered Accountants, 1911: Fellow 1918. Partner in D. W. Coates, West, Grimwood and Co.; and formerly in Elles, Salaman, Coates and Co. Successively Chief Accountant, Financial Secretary and Financial Adviser to Mines Department of Board of Trade, 1917-21; Chief Accountant, Central Electricity Board, 1927-48, and British Electricity Authority, 1948-51; Hon. Accountant to Sea-Fish Commission for the United Kingdom, 1933-35; Member of Land Fertility Committee, 1937-41; Finance Director, Coal Division, Ministry of Fuel and Power, 1942-43. *Publication:* Excess Profits Duty Termination and Stock Adjustments, 1921. *Address:* Calvercote, Gunnerside, Richmond, Yorks. *T.:* Gunnerside 260. *Club:* Oxford and Cambridge. [*Died* 5 *Aug.* 1968.

COATES, Sir Eric Thomas, Kt. 1945; C.S.I. 1941; C.I.E. 1938; Chairman, Delhi Engineering College Trust, since 1959; *b.* 1 October 1897; *s.* of Reverend Scott and Hannah Coates; *m.* 1929, Edith Van Dyke; one *s.* one *d.* *Educ.:* Heath Grammar School, Halifax; Queen's College, Oxford. Served European War, France and Mesopotamia, 1916-20; joined I.C.S. 1921; Joint Magistrate, 1921-25; Under-Sec., Finance Dept., Govt. of Bengal; Dep. Controller of the Currency; Accountant-Gen. in various Indian Provinces; Addtl. Financial Sec. to Govt. of India; Financial Adviser, War and Supply Finance and ex-officio Financial Secretary to the Govt. of India; Secretary to the Governor-General's Executive Council, India; Finance Member, Governor-General's Executive Council, India, 1946; Chief of Finance Division, C.C.G. (B.E.), 1947-49; Chairman of Overseas Food Corporation, 1950-51; a Deputy Chairman, National Coal Board, 1951-55; Leader of British Steel Mission to India, 1955; Chm. Franco-Saar Arbitral Commn. on the Warndt, 1955-56; Member, Commonwealth Scholarship Commn., 1960-1963; Leader of British Heavy Engineering Mission to India, 1956-57; Chairman, Police Council of Great Britain, 1957-65. Chairman, East African Commission of Enquiry on Income Tax, 1956-57; Director, W. S. Atkins and Partners, 1957-59; Director, Thomas Cook & Son, 1959-64. *Recreation:* motoring. *Address:* 2 White Post Gardens, Ash, Canterbury, Kent. *T.:* 378. *Club:* East India and Sports. [*Died* 28 *Sept.* 1968.

COATES, Henry, Ph.D. (Lond.); musical professor, critic, writer, and composer; Member of Board of Studies, Faculty of Music, and Recognised Teacher, London University; Member of Trinity College Corporation and Board; Senator, Faculty Dean and Chairman, Board of Examiners in Music, University of London, 1949-55; *b.* London, 1880; *s.* of late Henry Coates of 8 Salisbury Court, E.C.; *m.* 1921, Kathleen Josephine Brophy (*d.* 1959). *Educ.:* City of London School; Christ's College, Cambridge (Scholar); honours in mathematical tripos; B.A. 1902; M.A. 1930. Musical critic of the Evening News, 1908; Daily Chronicle, 1909; Editor of the Musician, 1919; studied the organ under Edwin Lemare and composition under various teachers, and was for some time organist at various churches. Orchestral Compositions produced: Concert Overture, Symphonic March, Nocturne, Suite, etc. *Publications:* Palestrina, 1938; Chopin, 1940; contributor to Oxford History of Music and Grove's Dictionary of Music and other periodicals; various songs and compositions for organ, pianoforte, violin, and editions and arrangements of musical classics. *Address:* Villino, Vermont Way, East Preston, Sussex. *T.:* Rustington 4083. [*Died* 28 *Dec.* 1963.

COATES, Col. Sir William, K.C.B., *cr.* 1930 (C.B. (Civil), 1905; and (Military), 1918); C.B.E. 1920; V.D.; T.D.; D.L. Co. Palatine of Lancaster; Officier de la Couronne, Belgium; F.R.C.S. (Eng.) and L.R.C.P.; retd. 1953; late Chm. E. Lancs. Assoc. T.A.; Chm. E. Lancs. Joint Committee of the Order of St. John and B.R.C.S.; K.St.J. 1961 (C.St.J. 1952); Vice-Pres. Barrowmore Tuberculosis Colony; Mem.: V.A.D. Council; B.R.C.S. Council; Central Council of War Organization of B.R.C.S. and Order of St. John; Founder of East Lancashire Homes for totally disabled Ex-Service Men; late Pres. Manchester Medical Society, etc.; *b.* Worksop, Notts, 1860; *m.* 1896, Leonora Stilwell (*d.* 1949), *d.* of Frederick Stilwell Freeland, J.P., Chichester; two *s.* one *d.* *Educ.:* London Hospital Medical College, (anatomical schol. and Prizeman in surgery) and held many appointments at the London Hospital, and in practice in Manchester since 1884; was instrumental in forming the Manchester R.A.M.C.V. in 1886; Assist. Director of Medical Services, E. Lancashire Territorial Division, 1908-12; Assist. Director of Medical Services, Western Command, 1914-19. *Publications:* severe hæmorrhage combated by Intravenous Injection, Lancet, 1882; and many subsequent publications. *Address:* Ingleside, Whalley Range, Manchester. *T.:* Moss Side 2382; 17 St. John Street, Manchester. *T.:* Blackfriars 3076. *Clubs:* Naval and Military; Union (Manchester). [*Died* 13 *Jan.* 1962.

COATES, Sir William (Henry), Kt., *cr.* 1947; LL.B., B.Sc., Ph.D.; *b.* 31 May 1882; 2nd *s.* of T. Mallalieu Coates, M.R.C.V.S.; *m.* 1909, Claire (*d.* 1963), *e. d.* of Edward Ferris; two *d.* *Educ.:* Loughborough Grammar School. Entered Civil Service, 1900; War Office, 1900-4; H.M. Inspectorate of Taxes, Inland Revenue Department, 1904-19; Dir. of Statistics and Intelligence, Inland Revenue Department, 1919-25; Secretary, Nobel Industries Ltd., 1925-26; Treasurer, I.C.I.,

Ltd., 1927-29, subs. Director (Dep. Chm. 1945-50); Member of Senate, Univ. of London, 1929-33; Financial Adviser to High Commissioner in Canada, 1941. Chairman of Excess Profits Tax Refund Advisory Panel, 1946-56; Chairman, Agricultural Marketing Facilities Committee, 1952-56; Director, Carpet Manufacturing Co. Ltd., 1950-55; a Deputy Chairman Westminster Bank Ltd., 1950-57. *Recreation:* golf. *Address:* Burlington Hotel, Eastbourne.
[*Died* 7 *Feb.* 1963.

COATMAN, John, C.I.E. 1929; M.A.; *b.* 5 Nov. 1889; *s.* of John Randall Coatman, Stockport; *m.* 1918, Theodora (*d.* 1956), *d.* of Rev. S. Pitt, Salisbury; two *s.* *Educ.:* Manchester Grammar Sch.; Manchester University (Walters Scholar in Modern Languages); Pembroke College, Oxford. 1st Class Hon. School of Philosophy, Politics and Economics, Beit Prizeman; joined Indian Police Service, 1910; Frontier Constabulary, 1914-19; King's Police Medal, 1916; Mohmand, Tochi, Southern Waziristan Campaigns, 3rd Afghan War, 1919, Hazara Frontier, 1920; Bar to King's Police Medal, 1921; Director of Public Information, Govt. of India, 1926; Member of Indian Legislative Assembly, 1926-30; Member of Indian Cinematograph Enquiry Committee, 1927-28; Hon. Professor of Political Science, Delhi University; Secretary to Liberal Parliamentary Delegation to the Round Table Conference, 1930-32; Professor of Imperial Economic Relations, University of London, 1930-34; Chief News Editor of B.B.C., 1934-37; North Regional Controller of B.B.C., 1937-49; Chairman of Convocation, Manchester University, 1941-1945; Director of Research in the Social Sciences, St. Andrews University, 1949-54. *Publications:* Indian Moral and Material Progress Reports, 1925-30; The Indian Riddle, 1932; Years of Destiny, 1932; Magna Britannia, 1936; India, The Road to Self-Government, 1941; The British Family of Nations, 1950; Völkerfamilie Commonwealth Stuttgart, 1955; Police, 1959; A Commonwealth of Nations; Berlin, 1959. *Address:* Luttrell Cottage, Murcott, nr. Islip, Oxfordshire. *Club:* Royal and Ancient Golf (St. Andrews). [*Died* 1 *Nov.* 1963.

COATS, Sir James (Stuart), 3rd Bt., *cr.* 1905; M.C.; *b.* 13 April 1894; *o. surv. s.* of Sir Stuart Coats, 2nd Bt., and Jane Muir (*d.* 1958), *d.* of Thomas Greenlees, Paisley, Renfrewshire; *S.* father 1959; *m.* 1917, Lady Amy (Gwendoline) Gordon-Lennox, *e. d.* of 8th Duke of Richmond and Gordon, D.S.O., M.V.O.; three *s.* (and one *s.* decd.). *Educ.:* Downside; Magdalen College, Oxford. Served European War, 1914-18, with Coldstream Guards (wounded, despatches, M.C.), also served War of 1939-45, North-West Europe (despatches); Lieut.-Col. Coldstream Guards (Reserve). *Recreations:* fishing and golf. *Heir:* *s.* Alastair Francis Stuart Coats [*b.* 18 Nov. 1921; *m.* 1947, Lukyn, *d.* of Captain Charles Gordon; one *s.* one *d.* Served War, 1939-45; Captain, Reserve of Officers, Coldstream Guards]. *Address:* 32 Ennismore Gdns., S.W.7. *Club:* White's.
[*Died* 26 *Oct.* 1966.

COBBAN, Professor Alfred, M.A.; Ph.D.; Professor of French History, University College, University of London, since 1953; Head of History Department, 1961-66; Editor of History; *b.* 1901; *s.* of Robert and Edith Frances Cobban; *m.* 1929, Kathleen Muriel Hartshorn; two *d.* *Educ.:* Latymer Upper School; Gonville and Caius College, Cambridge. Scholar and Research Student, Gonville and Caius Coll., 1919-25; Lecturer in History, Univ. of Newcastle upon Tyne, 1926-37; Rockefeller Fellow, 1932-33; Reader in Modern French History, University of London, 1937-53; Visiting Professor: University of Chicago, 1947; Harvard, 1959. *Publications:* Edmund Burke and the Revolt against the Eighteenth Century, 1929; Rousseau and the Modern State, 1934; Dictatorship: its History and Theory, 1939; The Crisis of Civilization, 1941; National Self-Determination, 1945; The Debate on the French Revolution, 1950; Ambassadors and Secret Agents, 1954; History of Modern France, i. The Old Regime and the Revolution, 1957; ii. From the First Empire to the Second Empire, 1961; iii. France of the Republics, 1965; In Search of Humanity: The Role of Enlightenment in Modern History, 1960; The Social Interpretation of the French Revolution, 1964. Contributions to: English Historical Review, Political Science Quarterly, Internat. Affairs, History, etc. *Address:* 32 Windsor Court, Moscow Rd., W.2. *T.:* Bayswater 2392.
[*Died* 1 *April* 1968.

COBBOLD, Lady Evelyn; *sister* of 8th Earl of Dunmore, V.C.; *m.* 1891, John Dupuis Cobbold, D.L. (*d.* 1929); one *d.* (and one *s.* killed, Guards Chapel, 1945; one *d.* decd.). *Publications:* Pilgrimage to Mecca, 1934; Kenya: The Land of Illusion, 1935. *Address:* Glencarron Lodge, Ross-shire.
[*Died* 25 *Jan.* 1963.

COBDEN-RAMSAY, Louis Eveleigh Bawtree, C.I.E. 1914; I.C.S. (retired); *b.* 29 Oct. 1873; *m.* 1914, Dorothy Forster, *d.* of late C. J. Grieve, J.P., Branxholm Park, Hawick; one *s.* one *d.* *Educ.:* Dulwich College; Sidney Sussex College, Cambridge. Passed into the Indian Civil Service, 1896; Under-Secretary to Government of Bengal in the Revenue and General Department, 1900-2; Registrar Cooperative Credit Societies, 1905; Commissioner and Political Agent Orissa Feudatory States; Bihar and Orissa; retired, 1922. *Publication:* Gazetteer of the Orissa Feudatory States. *Address:* The Platts, Bodle Street, Hailsham, Sussex. *T.:* Herstmonceux 3104.
[*Died* 15 *May* 1962.

COBHAM, Ven. John Lawrence, M.A.; Archdeacon emeritus since 1937; Prebendary of Exeter, 1933-53; Prebendary emeritus since 1953; *b.* 12 May 1873; *s.* of John Cobham and Martha Ann Matches; *m.* 1898, Frances Eliza, *d.* of late Sir William Willis (Accountant General, Navy); two *c.* *Educ.:* Merchant Taylors' School, Great Crosby; Corpus Christi College, and Ridley Hall, Cambridge. Deacon, 1896; Priest, 1897; Curate of Gt. Yarmouth, 1896-1900; Christ Church, Gipsy Hill, 1900-04; Vicar of St. John Evangelist, Carl., 1904-12; T.C.F., 1917-18; St. Peter, Tunbridge Wells, 1912-19; Commissary, Uganda, 1912-22; Treasurer of Uganda Diocesan Fund, 1919-22; C.C.C.S. Chaplain at Entebbe, Uganda, 1920-21; Clarens, 1922; Rector of St. Mark's, Torwood, Torquay, 1922-38; Rural Dean of Ipplepen, 1928-33; Archdeacon of Totnes, 1933-47. *Address:* Inniscarra, 11 Southfield Avenue, Paignton, Devon. *T.:* Paignton 82316. [*Died* 27 *Dec.* 1960.

COBURN, Sir (Marmaduke) Robert, Kt., *cr.* 1947; C.S.I. 1945; C.I.E. 1939; O.B.E. 1919; *b.* 9 Mar. 1885; *s.* of John Coburn; *m.* 1931, Avis Mary Mildred, *d.* of Sir Thomas Ryan, C.I.E.; two *s.* *Educ.:* East London College; Hertford College, Oxford. Joined service of Govt. of India in 1910 in the Military Accounts Dept.; Financial Officer to Indian Munitions Board, 1916-20; Director of Establishments, Posts, and Telegraphs, 1926; Financial Adviser, Posts and Telegraphs, 1928; Military Accountant General, 1936; Additional Financial Adviser, Military Finance, Government of India, 1939-47; retired, 1947. *Address:* Salters, Rotherfield, Crowborough, Sussex. *T.:* Rotherfield 356.
[*Died* 26 *May* 1966.

COCHRAN, Alexander, C.B.E. 1919; *e. s.* of late James Taylor Cochran, of Birkenhead and Annan; *m.* 1st, 1908, E. L. Watson

(*d.* 1922); one *s.* two *d.*; 2nd, 1924, M. M. Hingston (*d.* 1943); one *d.*; 3rd, 1950, Kathleen Ruth, *o. d.* of late John Deazley Hanna. *Educ.:* Shrewsbury School. Joined the firm of Burn & Co., Ltd., Engineers, Howrah, India, 1902; partner firm of Burn & Co., 7 Hasting Street, Calcutta, 1913-24; Chairman Indian Engineering Association, 1913, 1918, 1923; Chairman Indian River-craft Board, 1916-18; Chairman Bengal Association of the Institution of Engineers, India, 1921; Vice-President of the Institution of Engineers, India, 1921; Member of Council of Institution of Engineers, India, 1923; Member of Bengal Legislative Council, 1921 and 1923; Member of Indian Legislative Assembly, 1924; Member of Institute o) Naval Architects and Institution of Engineers, India. *Address:* Cliff House, Paignton, S. Devon. *Clubs:* Oriental; Royal Dart Yacht (Kingswear)
[*Died* 28 *Jan.* 1961.

COCHRANE of Cults, 2nd Baron, *cr.* 1919; **Thomas George Frederick Cochrane,** D.S.O. 1919; Black Watch (S.R.); *b.* 19 Mar. 1883; *e. s.* of 1st Baron Cochrane and Lady Gertrude Boyle, O.B.E. (*d.* 1950), *d.* of 6th Earl of Glasgow; *S.* father 1951; *m.* 1st, 1920, Hon. Elin Douglas-Pennant (*d.* 1934), *y. d.* of 2nd Baron Penrhyn; three *s.*; 2nd, 1948, Mrs. M. A. M. Foster. *Educ.:* Eton; Christ Church, Oxford, M.A.; Bar. Inner Temple, 1908; served European War, 1914-1919 (wounded thrice, despatches thrice, D.S.O.). *Recreations:* shooting and travel. *Heir:* *s.* Hon. Thomas Charles Anthony Cochrane, *b.* 31 October 1922. *Address:* Crawford Priory, Cupar, Fife. *T.:* Cupar 3162. *Clubs:* Carlton, Brooks's; New (Edinburgh).
[*Died* 8 *Dec.* 1968.

COCKBILL, Ven. Charles Shipley, M.A.; Archdeacon of St. Albans, 1951-62; Archdeacon Emeritus, and Hon. Canon of St. Albans, 1962; *b.* 27 Jan. 1888; *s.* of Samuel Edward Cockbill and Hannah Maria Shipley; *m.* 1917, Phyllis, *y. d.* of Rev. Prebendary Bazell, Eastover Vicarage, Bridgwater, Somerset; no *c.* *Educ.:* Bristol Grammar School (Scholar); St. John Baptist College, Oxford (Mathematical Exhibitioner). Assistant Curate St. John's Bridgwater, 1911-17; Holy Trinity, Eltham 1917-18; Vicar of Oakhill, Somerset, 1918-23; Rector of Holy Trinity, Bath, 1923-30; Assistant Diocesan Inspector of Schools (Bath and Wells) 1918-30; Rector of Digswell, Herts, 1930-39; Hon Canon of St. Albans, 1935-42; Diocesan Director of Religious Education (St. Albans), 1935-48; Canon Residentiary of St. Albans, 1942-48; Hon. Canon of St. Albans 1948-51; Canon Residentiary and Diocesan Missioner, 1951-58. *Address:* 5 Seymour Road, St. Albans, Herts.
[*Died* 13 *March* 1965.

COCKBURN, Archibald William, Q.C. 1938; Chm., Co. of London Sessions, 1954-1959 (Dep. Chm., 1938-53); *b.* 6 June 1887; *e. s.* of Henry Cockburn and Ella, *d.* of Rev. Canon W. Chetwynd-Stapylton; *m.* 1st, 1933, Jacqueline Theodora (*d.* 1948) (O.St.J. 1939, J.P. Co. of London, member Chelsea Borough Council, 1937), *e. d.* of late Lt.-Col. Sir Henry Trotter, K.C.M.G., C.B.; 2nd, 1953, Phyllis, *y. d.* of late E. Bent Walker. *Educ.:* Eton; New College, Oxford (M.A.). President of Oxford Union Society, 1910; called to Bar, Inner Temple, 1913; went the Oxford Circuit; Bencher of the Inner Temple, 1935; K.C. 1938; Recorder of Ludlow, 1934-36; Recorder of Oxford, 1936-1938; Member of the Bar Council, 1919-28 and 1930-38; Secretary of Royal Commission on Importation of Store Cattle, 1921; Chm. of the Hops Reorganisation Commission for England, 1938; Dep. Chm. of the Home Office Advisory Cttee. (Defence Regulation 18B), 1940-45; Treasurer of the Inner Temple, 1959; served European War, R.G.A., France and Belgium. *Publications:* joint-editor of Pratt and Mackenzie's Law of Highways, 17th and 18th editions, and parts of Halsbury's Laws of England (2nd ed.), Halsbury's Statutes, and other legal works. *Address:* 1 Crown Office Row, Temple, E.C.4. *T.:* 01-583 1933.
[*Died* 19 *Sept.* 1969.

COCKBURN, Captain William, D.S.O. 1918; M.C.; *b.* 1893; *o. s.* of James Cockburn, Selkirk; *m.* 1924, Louisa Nellie Norris, Invercargill, New Zealand; one *s.* four *d.* *Educ.:* Private Schools. Served European War, 1914-18 (1914-15 Star, despatches, D.S.O., M.C., Croix de Guerre (French with Gold Star); twice wounded). A Founder and Hon. Treas. for 17 years, of the British Hospitals Contributory Assoc. *Publications:* Various articles on subjects dealing with Hospital Administration and Hospital History. *Recreations:* walking, Lieder singing, music. *Address:* c/o Lloyds Bank Ltd, Knightsbridge Branch, 79 Brompton Road, S.W.3. *Club:* The Club (Rugby).
[*Died* 4 *Feb.* 1970.

COCKCRAFT, Lt.-Col. Louis William la Trobe, D.S.O. 1916; M.V.O. 1945; R.A.; Military Knight of Windsor since 1940; *b.* 20 June 1880; *s.* of late Colonel W. la T. Cockcraft, Royal Marine Artillery; *m.*; one *s.* one *d.* Entered R.F.A. 1899; Captain 1908; Major, 1914; Lieut.-Colonel 1925; served S. Africa (last 6 months in Intelligence Department), 1900-2 (despatches); W. Africa, 1906-8; European War, Suez Canal, 1914; C. Helles, Gallipoli, 1915-16; (despatches, D.S.O.); France, 1916-18 (despatches, Belgian Croix de Guerre, Bt. Lt.-Col.); retired pay, 1929; re-employed Sept. 1939. *Address:* 8 Lower Ward, Windsor Castle, Berks.
[*Died* 15 *April* 1963.

COCKCROFT, Sir John (Douglas), O.M. 1957; K.C.B. 1953; Kt. 1948; C.B.E. 1944; F.R.S. 1936; M.A., Ph.D., M.Sc. (Tech.); Master of Churchill College, Cambridge, since 1959; President, Manchester College of Science and Technology, since 1961 Hon. Fellow of St. John's College, Cambridge *b.* 27 May 1897; *s.* of J. A. Cockcroft and A. M. Fielden; *m.* 1925, E. Elizabeth Crabtree; one *s.* four *d.* *Educ.:* Todmorden Secondary School; University of Manchester; St. John's College, Cambridge. Fellow of St. John's College, Cambridge, 1928-46; Jacksonian Professor of Natural Philosophy, Univ. of Cambridge, 1939-46. Chief Superintendent, Air Defence, Research and Development Establishment, Ministry of Supply, 1941-44; Director, Atomic Energy Division, National Research Council of Canada, 1944-46; Director of Atomic Energy Research Establishment, Ministry of Supply, at Harwell, 1946-58; Chm. Defence Research Policy Committee and Scientific Adviser Ministry of Defence, 1952-54; Mem., Advisory Council on Scientific Policy until 1963; Mem. for Scientific Research, United Kingdom Atomic Energy Authority, 1954-59 (Part-time mem., 1959-); Chancellor of Australian National University, Canberra, 1961-65. Member: B.B.C. Scientific Adv. Cttee., 1948-52; Governing Bd. of National Inst. for Research in Nuclear Science, 1957 1965; Court of London Univ., 1959-66; Hon. Mem., Parliamentary and Scientific Cttee., 1960. Pres., British Association, 1962; Pres., Inst. of Physics and Physical Society, 1960-62. Hon. Freedom of Todmorden, 1946; Freedom of City of London, 1958 D.Sc.(*h.c.*): Oxford, 1949; London, 1950; Trinity College, Dublin, 1951; Sidney, Canberra, 1952; Manchester, 1953; Birmingham, 1954; Leeds, 1956; Temple (Philadelphia), 1961; Western Australia, 1962; Saskatchewan, 1962; Rhodes (Grahamstown), 1964; Sc.D. (*h.c.*): Cambridge, 1953; Coimbra, 1955; Leicester, 1959; Hon. D.Eng., Sheffield, 1960; Hon. Dr. of Technical Science, Technical University, Delft, 1959; Hon. LL.D. (Toronto, Glasgow, Melbourne,

St. Andrews, Dalhousie). F.R.S.A. 1962. M.I.E.E.; Hon. M.I.Mech.E.; Hon. Associate, Manchester College of Technology (President 1962-); Hon. member: Institute of Marine Engineers; Institute of Civil and Mechanical Engineers; Inst. of Metals; R.I.B.A.; Salters' Company; Foreign member: Royal Swedish Academy; Royal Danish Academy; Australian Academy of Sciences. Foreign Hon. Member American Academy of Arts and Sciences. Hughes Medal, Royal Society; J. A. Ewing Medal of Institution of Civil Engineering, 1948; Royal Medal, Roy. Soc., 1954; Faraday Medal of Instn. of Electrical Engs., 1955; Kelvin Medal (Jt. Engineering Instns. award), 1956; Churchill Gold Medal of Soc. of Engineers, 1958; Wilhelm Exner Medal, Austria, 1961. U.S. Medal of Freedom (Golden Palms), 1947; Chevalier de la Légion d'Honneur, 1950; Knight Commander, Military Order of Christ, Portugal, 1955; Niels Bohr Medal, Denmark, 1958; Grand Cross, Order of Alfonso X (Spain), 1958. (With E. T. S. Walton) Nobel prize for physics, 1951; Atoms for Peace Award, 1961. *Publications:* Various papers on Nuclear Physics in Proceedings of the Royal Society; also on technical subjects, Journal Inst. Electrical Engineers. *Address:* Churchill College, Cambridge. *Clubs:* Savile, Athenæum. [*Died* 18 *Sept.* 1967.

COCKER, William Hollis, C.M.G. 1950; Barrister and Solicitor, Auckland, New Zealand; *b.* 26 February 1896; *s.* of James and Sarah Ann Cocker; *m.* 1934, Ada Vera Hay. *Educ.:* Auckland Grammar School (N.Z.); Canterbury University College (N.Z.); Emmanuel College, Cambridge (Scholar). Economics and Law Tripos. Served European War, 1914-18, with N.Z. Expeditionary Force. Member, N.Z. Broadcasting Board, 1935-36; President, Auckland District Law Society, 1941-42; President Auckland Univ. Coll. (Univ. of New Zealand), 1938-57; Chairman National Council of Adult Education of New Zealand, 1948-58; Member, Senate of University of New Zealand, 1938-1961; Chancellor Auckland University, 1957-61. Hon. LL.D. 1961. Director New Zealand St. Dunstan's, 1955-. *Address:* 124 Grafton Road, Auckland, N.Z. *T.:* 42382. *Club:* Northern (Auckland). [*Died* 19 *Dec.* 1962.

COCKERELL, Sir Sydney (Carlyle), Kt., *cr.* 1934; M.A.; Hon. Litt.D. Cambridge; Hon. Fellow of Downing College since 1937; *b.* 16 July 1867; 2nd *s.* of Sydney John Cockerell and Alice, *d.* of Sir John Bennett; *m.* 1907, Florence Kate Kingsford (*d.* 1949); one *s.* two *d.* *Educ.:* St. Paul's School. Coal merchant, 1889-92; Secretary to William Morris and to the Kelmscott Press, 1892-1898; in partnership with late Sir Emery Walker, 1900-4; Director, 1908-37, of the Fitzwilliam Museum, Cambridge; European Adviser to Felton Trustees of National Gallery of Victoria, 1936-39; Fellow of Jesus College, Cambridge, 1910-16, and of Downing College, 1932-37; a literary executor of William Morris, Wilfrid Scawen Blunt, and Thomas Hardy. *Publications:* various bibliographical monographs. *Relevant Publications:* Friends of a Lifetime: Letters to Sydney Carlyle Cockerell (ed. Viola Meynell), 1940; The Best of Friends (ed. Viola Meynell), 1956. *Recreations:* calligraphy and book-collecting. *Address:* 21 Kew Gardens Road, Kew, Surrey. *T.:* Richmond 5852. [*Died* 1 *May* 1962.

COCKIN, Rt. Rev. Frederic Arthur; *b.* 30 July 1888; *s.* of Charles Edward Cockin and Emma Dorothea Scott; *m.* 1920, Olive Mary Moberly; no *c.* *Educ.:* Marlborough; University College, Oxford; Cuddesdon. Hon. Fellow, University College, Oxford, 1950. Cambridge Mission to Delhi; Curate, St. Mary, Newington; Student Christian Movement; Canon Missioner, Diocese of Southwark; Vicar of Saint Mary-the-Virgin, Oxford, 1933-38; Canon of St. Paul's Cathedral, 1938-44; Secretary to Council of the Church Training Colleges, 1944-46, Chairman, 1947; Hon. Canon of Canterbury Cathedral, 1944-46; Chaplain to the King, 1937-46; Bishop of Bristol, 1946-58. *Address:* Finches, Marlborough, Wilts. [*Died* 15 *Jan.* 1969.

COCKS, John S. S.; *see* Somers Cocks.

COCTEAU, Jean; poète; Member of the French Academy since 1955; Member of the Royal Academy of Belgium, 1955; Dr. *h.c.* Oxford, 1956; Member various universities in the U.S.A. in Arts and Letters, also at Berlin, 1956; *b.* Maisons-Laffitte, 5 July 1889. *Educ.:* Lycée Condorcet. *Works: Poésie:* Le Cap de Bonne Espérance, 1919; La Rose de François, 1923; Vocabulaire, 1922; Plain Chant, 1923; Discours du grand sommeil, 1923; Prière mutilée, 1925; L'Ange Heurtebise, 1925; Opéra, 1927; Morceaux choisis, 1932; Allégories, 1941; Léone, 1945; La Crucifixion, 1946; Le Chiffre Sept, 1952; Clair obscur, 1954; Paraprosodies, 1958. *Poésie de Roman:* Le Potomak, 1919 (definitive edn., 1924); Le Grand Écart, 1923; Thomas l'Imposteur, 1923 (trans. as The Imposter, Gt. Brit. 1957); Les Enfants terribles, 1929; Fin de Potomak, 1939. *Poésie critique:* Visite à Barrès, 1921; Le Secret professionnel, 1922; Le Rappel à l'ordre, 1926; Le Mystère laïc, 1928; Opium, 1930 (trans. as Opium, Gt. Brit. 1957); Essai de critique indirecte, 1932; Portraits-Souvenirs, 1935 (trans. as Paris Album, 1900-1914, Gt. Brit. 1957); Mon Premier Voyage, 1936; La Difficulté d'être, 1947; Maalesh, 1949; La corrida du 1er mai, 1957. *Poésie de Théâtre:* Parade, 1917; Le Bœuf sur le toit, 1920; Les Mariés de la Tour Eiffel, 1921; Roméo et Juliette, 1924; Orphée, 1926; Antigone, 1922; Œdipe-Roi, 1928; La Voix humaine, 1930; La Machine infernale, 1934; Les Chevaliers de la table ronde, 1937; Les Parents terribles, 1938; Les Monstres sacrés, 1940; La Machine à écrire, 1941; Renaud et Armide, 1943; L'Aigle a deux têtes, 1946; Bacchus, 1952; Patmos (oratorio), 1962. *Poésie graphique:* Dessins, 1923; Le Mystère de Jean l'Oiseleur, 1924; Maison de santé, 1926; Portraits d'un dormeur, 1929; Dessins pour les enfants terribles, 1934. *Tapisseries aubusson:* Judith et Holopherne; Mère et fille dans un jardin; La chapelle Saint Pierre de Villefranche sur mer, 1957; La salle des mariages de la mairie de Menton, 1958. *Poésie cinématographique:* Le Sang du poète, 1932; L'Éternel Retour, 1943; La Belle et la bête, 1945; Les Parents terribles, 1948; Orphée, 1949; Les Enfants terribles, 1950; Ruy Blas, 1947; Le Testament d'Orphée, 1960; *Relevant Publication:* Jean Cocteau: An Impersonation of Angels, by Frederick Brown. *Address:* 36 rue de Montpensier, Palais Royal, Paris. [*Died* 11 *Oct.* 1963.

CODRINGTON, William Melville, C.M.G. 1946; M.C.; Lord Lieutenant of County of Rutland since 1951; Chairman Nyasaland Railways Ltd.; Director of other cos.; *b.* 16 Dec. 1892; 2nd *s.* of late Lieut.-Gen. Sir Alfred E. Codrington, G.C.V.O., K.C.B.; *m.* 1935, Kath. Theodosia, *er. d.* of late John Houston Sinclair; two *d.* (and one *d.* decd.). *Educ.:* Harrow; New Coll., Oxford (M.A.). Served European War in 16th Lancers and attached Signal Service (M.C., despatches); Cap. Reserve of Officers 16/5th Lancers; 3rd Sec. Diplomatic Service, 1918; served in Foreign Office; 2nd Sec. at British Agency, Tangier; resigned, 1925; member of Coal Commn., 1938-47. Served in Ministry of Economic Warfare, 1939; Chief Security

Officer (with rank of Acting Asst. Under Sec. of State, unpaid) in Foreign Office, 1940-45, and in War Cabinet Offices, 1942-45. High Sheriff of Rutland, 1947-48. *Recreations:* hunting, gardening. *Address:* City Wall House, 129 Finsbury Pavement, E.C.2. *T.A.:* Wilmecod Avenue, London. *T.:* Monarch 1292; Preston Hall, Uppingham. *T.:* Manton-Rutland 216. *Clubs:* Cavalry, Pratt's, City of London. [*Died* 29 *April* 1963.

CODRINGTON, Sir William Richard, 7th Bart., *cr.* 1721; farmer; Temp. Lt.-Cdr. R.N.V.R.; British Naval Liaison Officer, U.S. Navy Yard, Philadelphia; *b.* 22 April 1904; *s.* of Sir William Robert Codrington, 6th Bt., and Joan, *d.* of H. A. Rogers, Johannesburg; *S.* father, 1932; *m.* 1933, Joan Kathleen Birelli, *e. d.* of Percy E. Nicholas, 13 Dunstan Road, N.W.3; three *s.* one *d.* *Educ.:* Shrewsbury; Victoria College, Jersey. *Recreations:* tennis, shooting. *Heir:* *s.* William Alexander, *b.* 5 July 1934. *Address:* Mpongwe Estate, Fort Jameson, N. Rhodesia. [*Died* 23 *March* 1961.

COEN, Sir Terence B. C.; *see* Creagh Coen.

COFFEY, Thomas Malo, C.I.E. 1946; *b.* 4 May 1894; *s.* of P. M. Coffey, J.P., Ballinacree, Co. Tipperary; *m.* 1st, 1924, Isabel Anderson (*d.* 1947), *d.* of Rev. J. A. Graham, D.D., C.I.E.; three *s.*; 2nd, 1951, Margaret, *d.* of Neil Macinnes, Isle of Skye. *Educ.:* Mungret College, Limerick; Brasenose College, Oxford. Served European War, 1914-1918. Indian Forest Service, 1921-48. Farming since 1949. *Recreations:* farming, shooting, fishing. *Address:* 507 Carrington House, Hertford St., W.1. *T.:* Mayfair 2130. *Clubs:* East India and Sports; Tollygunge (Calcutta). [*Died* 25 *Sept.* 1968.

COGHLAN, Rt. Rev. Mgr. John, C.B.E. 1940; B.A.; *b.* 6 July 1887; 3rd *s.* of late Hugh Coghlan, Castlepollard, Westmeath, Ireland. *Educ.:* St. Finian's College, Navan; Maynooth College; Royal University of Ireland. Priest of diocese of Meath, 1913; C.F. 4th class, 1915; 3rd class, 1931; 2nd class, 1932; 1st class, 1938; served France and Flanders as S.C.F. (R.C.), 1915-17 (wounded, despatches); Egypt and Mesopotamia, 1918-19; Rhine army, 1922-25; S.C.F. (R.C.), Malta, 1926; Shanghai Defence Force, 1927-28; Eastern Command, 1929-30; Malta, 1930-32; Egypt, 1932-35; Northern Command, 1935-38; Aldershot, 1938-39; Assistant Deputy Chaplain-General and Principal Roman Catholic Chaplain, B.E.F., 1939-40 (despatches); Vicar-General, the British Army, 1940; Principal Roman Catholic Army Chaplain; retired pay, 1945. Croix de Guerre, 1st class, 1945 (Belgium). *Address:* Multyfarnham, Co. Westmeath, Eire. [*Died* 15 *April* 1963.

COHALAN, Most Rev. Daniel, Ph.D., D.C.L., J.U.D.; *b.* Jan. 1884. Bishop of Waterford and Lismore (R.C.), since 1943. *Educ.:* National School, Kilmichael; Presentation College, Cork; Irish College, Rome. Ordained 1906; remained in Rome until 1910 and secured Ph.D. and D.C.L. with special distinction; Dean of Residence in Cork University College, 1910; C.C. of St. Patrick's, 1922; Administrator of Cork Cathedral, 1929; P.P. of St. Finbarr's West, Cork, 1937. *Address:* Bishop's House, John's Hill, Waterford, Eire. *T.:* Waterford 4463. [*Died* 27 *Jan.* 1965.

COHEN OF BRIGHTON, Baron *cr.* 1965 (Life Peer); **Lewis Coleman Cohen;** Chairman and Managing Director, Alliance Building Society; *b.* 28 March 1897; *s.* of Hyam and Esther Cohen; *m.* 1st, 1939, Sonya Lawson (marriage dissolved); one *s.* two *d.*; 2nd, 1961, Renie, *d.* of Simon Frieze and *widow* of Leonard Bodlender; one step *s.* one step *d.* *Educ.:* Hastings Gram. Sch.; Brighton Gram. Sch. Brighton & Sussex Bldg. Soc.: Sec., 1929; Man. Dir., 1933 (Soc. changed name to Alliance Bldg. Soc., 1945); Chm. and Man. Dir., 1959. Mem., Brighton Town Council, 1930-; Alderman, 1964-; Mayor, 1956-57. Chm., Brighton Theatre Royal, 1946. Mem. Council Sussex Univ., and Chm. Buildings Cttee., 1965-; Chm. Agrément Board, 1965-. Contested (Lab.): Brighton and Hove, 1931 and 1935; Hastings, 1950; Brighton (Kemp Town), 1951, 1955, 1959. Mem. Dartmouth Street Trust. *Recreations:* walking, swimming, golf, travel. *Address:* 55 Dyke Road Avenue, Hove; Alliance Building Society, Princes House, North Street, Brighton. [*Died* 21 *Oct.* 1966.

COHEN, Sir Andrew (Benjamin), K.C.M.G. 1952 (C.M.G. 1948); K.C.V.O. 1954; O.B.E. 1942; Permanent Secretary, Ministry of Overseas Development, since Oct. 1964; *b.* 1909; *s.* of W. S. Cohen, Amersfort, Berkhamsted, Herts.; *m.* 1949, Helen Donington; one *s.* *Educ.:* Malvern; Trinity College, Cambridge (B.A.). Entered Inland Revenue Department, 1932; transferred Colonial Office, 1933; Asst. Sec., 1943; Supt. Asst. Sec., 1947; Asst. Under-Sec. of State, 1947-51; Gov. and C.-in-C., Uganda, 1952-57; Permanent British representative on Trusteeship Council, U.N., 1957-61; Dir.-Gen., Dept. of Technical Co-operation, 1961-1964. Hon. LL.D. Belfast. *Publication:* British Policy in Changing Africa, 1959. *Address:* c/o Ministry of Overseas Development, Eland House, Victoria, S.W.1. *Club:* Athenæum. [*Died* 17 *June* 1968.

COHEN, Mrs. Arthur M.; *see* Cohen, Mary Gwendolen.

COHEN, Lt.-Col. Charles Waley, C.M.G. 1919; 3rd *s.* of late Nathaniel Louis Cohen; *b.* 1879; *m.* 1909 (wife *d.* 1956). *Educ.:* Clifton Coll.; Balliol Coll., Oxford. Called to Bar, 1903; Mem. of Colonial Office Committee of Emigrants Information Board, 1904-10; Secretary of the Select Committee on Post Office Servants, 1906-1907 and 1912-13; Acting Judge in High Court at Karachi, 1910-11; in Army, 1915-21 (despatches, C.M.G., Légion d'honneur). *Recreations:* golf, tennis. *Clubs:* Athenæum, Savile. [*Died* 16 *Jan.* 1963.

COHEN, Harriet, C.B.E. 1938; Comdr. of Crown of Belgium, 1947; Order of White Lion (1st Cl.) of Czechoslovakia, 1947; Officier d'Académie Française, 1950; Freedom of City of London, 1954; Cavalier of Order of Southern Cross of Brazil, 1954; Stella della Solidarietà Italiana, 1955; Order of the Lion of Finland (Finlandia Medal), 1958; Lazo de Dama de la Orden Merito (Civil) (Spain), 1959; Medal of Sibelius Academy, 1955; Otto Andersson Medal of Abo Akademi (Finland), 1959; Dr. of Music (*h.c.*) National University of Ireland, 1960; F.R.A.M.; pianist; *e. d.* of Joseph Verney-Cohen, Aldershot, Hants., and Florence White, Norwich. *Educ.:* Roy. Acad. of Music, London. Mem. Advisory Council of Institute of Contemporary Arts; Chm., Harriet Cohen Internat. Music Awards; late Vice-Pres. Nat. Union of Townswomen's Guilds; Vice-Pres. Women's Freedom League; Vice-Pres. Children and Youth Aliyah. Chosen to appear for England at International Festivals at Salzburg, Washington, Strasbourg, Frankfurt-Homburg, Cheltenham and Chicago; has appeared in principal cities of Europe, U.S.A., U.S.S.R., Palestine. *Publications:* Music's Handmaid; Chapter on Piano Music in Life of Dvorák, produced by Czechoslovak Govt. in London; Solo Instrumentalist in A Career in Music (Elkin); Arrangement for Piano of the Organ Choral Preludes of Bach; gramophone records by Columbia; A Bundle of Time, 1969 (*posthumous*). *Address:* 8

Gloucester Place Mews, W.1. *T.:* Welbeck 2149. [*Died* 13 *Nov.* 1967.

COHEN, Sir Herbert (Benjamin), 2nd Bt., *cr.* 1905; O.B.E. 1919; T.D.; *b.* 26 April 1874; *s.* of 1st Bt. and Louisa Emily, *o. d.* of late Benjamin M. Merton; *S.* father, Sir Benjamin Louis Cohen, 1909; *m.* 1907, Hannah Mildred (*d.* 1963), 2nd *d.* of late Henry Behrens of 34 Gloucester Sq., W.; two *s.* (*er. s.* died, 1931; *yr. s.* died on active service in India, 1943). *Educ.:* Clifton College; King's Coll., Cambridge, M.A. Barrister, Inner Temple; Major, 4th R. West Kent Regt. (retired). *Address:* Highfield, Shoreham, Kent. *Clubs:* Junior Carlton; Kent County (Maidstone). [*Died* 23 *April* 1968 (*ext.*).

COHEN, Israel; author and lecturer; member Foreign Affairs Cttee. of Board of Deputies of British Jews since 1931 and Vice-Chairman since 1952; formerly General Secretary of World Zionist Organisation, London; *b.* Manchester, 24 April 1879; 2nd *s.* of Morris Cohen, Manchester; *m.* 1918, Theresa, *e. d.* of L. Jacobs; two *s.* *Educ.:* Manchester Grammar School; Jews' College and University College, London; graduated B.A. (Lond., Semit. Honours), 1904. On literary staff of The Tribune, 1906-8; English Secretary of Zionist Organisation Central Office, Cologne, 1910-11, Berlin, 1911-14; Berlin correspondent of Glasgow Herald and Globe, 1911-14; acted as special correspondent for The Times, Manchester Guardian, Westminster Gazette, etc.; interned in the Ruhleben Prison Camp, Germany, 1914-16; lectured on experiences in captivity and acted as Secretary of Ruhleben Prisoners' Release Committee, 1916-1918; travelled extensively on behalf of Zionist Organisation; raised nearly £120,000 for Palestine Restoration Fund, 1920-21; has lectured in five continents. *Publications:* Israel in Italien (Berlin, 1909); Zionist Work in Palestine (edited), 1911; Jewish Life in Modern Times, 1914 (revised edition, 1929); The Ruhleben Prison Camp, 1917; Report on the Pogroms in Poland, 1919; The Journal of a Jewish Traveller, 1925; A Ghetto Gallery, 1931; The Jews in Germany, 1933; The Jewish Tragedy, 1934; The Progress of Zionism (8th edn.), 1947; French edn., 1945); The Jews in the War, 1942 (rev. edn., 1943); Britain's Nameless Ally, 1942; History of the Jews in Vilna, 1943; The Zionist Movement, 1945; (French edn., 1946, Spanish edn., 1947, Italian edn., 1953, Hebrew edn., 1956); Contemporary Jewry, 1950; Revised edn. of Paul Goodman's History of the Jews, 1951; A Short History of Zionism, 1951 (Braille edn., 1952, Arabic edn. 1957); Travels in Jewry, 1952; The Re-birth of Israel (ed.), 1952; A Jewish Pilgrimage (autobiography), 1956; Theodor Herzl, 1958; numerous pamphlets on Jewish and Zionist questions; articles in Quarterly Review, Fortnightly Review, Nineteenth Century, Contemporary, New Statesman, etc. Contributor to Jewish Encyclopedia, Chambers's Encyclopedia, Britannica Year-Book, etc. *Address:* 29 Pattison Road, Child's Hill, N.W.2. [*Died* 26 *Nov.* 1961.

COHEN, Maj. Sir (Jack Benn) Brunel, K.B.E., *cr.* 1948; Kt., *cr.* 1943; *b.* 5 Oct. 1886; *s.* of Alderman L. S. Cohen, Liverpool; *g.s.* of Hon. L. W. Levy and of Samuel Cohen, M.P., of Sydney, Australia; *m.* 1914, Vera, *e. d.* of Sir Stuart Samuel, Bart.; two *s.* one *d.* *Educ.:* Cheltenham College. Joined 1st V.B., King's (Liverpool) Regt. in 1906, later 5th King's (Liverpool) Regt. T.A.; on Reserve on outbreak of war; active list, 22 Aug. 1914. Served European War, 1914-1917 (badly wounded, despatches); M.P. (U.) Fairfield Division, Liverpool, 1918-31; J.P. Liverpool, 1923-36; Hon. Treasurer of the British Legion, 1921-30, 1932-46, Vice-Chairman, 1930-32; Member of Board of Governors, St. Thomas's Hospital; Member of Executive Committee St. Dunstan's; Past Chairman National Advisory Council (Min. of Labour) on employment of Disabled; Past Chairman of Remploy Ltd.; Past Chairman Preston Hall Hosp. Management Cttee.; Life Member Cheltenham College Council; Past Master Worshipful Company of Gardeners. *Publication:* Count Your Blessings, 1956. *Recreation:* swimming. *Address:* 82 Portland Place, W.1. *Club:* Carlton. [*Died* 11 *May* 1965.

COHEN, Mary Gwendolen (Mrs. Arthur M. Cohen), O.B.E. 1945; Vice-President Scottish Association of Mixed Clubs and Girls' Clubs (Chairman, 1931-50); Vice-Chm. National Vigilance Assoc. of Scotland; Vice-President City of Glasgow Girl Guides Association; President Glasgow Branch National Council of Women, 1957; *b.* Salford, Lancs, 15 July 1893; *y. d.* of late Alderman Isidore Frankenburg; *m.* 1918, Arthur M. Cohen; three *d.* (one *s.* decd.). *Educ.:* Roedean School. President Glasgow and West of Scotland Union of Girls' Clubs, 1924-31; Mem. Scottish Central Council of Juvenile Organisations, 1926-42; Mem. Nat. Advisory Council for Physical Training and Recreation (Scotland), 1937-40; Emergency Officer for Youth, Glasgow, 1939-1943; Founder and 1st Chm. Glasgow Girls' Training Corps, 1942-45; Dep. Leader Glasgow W.V.S., 1944-46; Mem. Departmental Cttee. Homosexual Offences and Prostitution, 1954-57. *Recreations:* gardening and golf. *Address:* Mhor, Portencross, West Kilbride, Ayrshire. *T.:* West Kilbride 2277. *Clubs:* English-Speaking Union; Literary (Glasgow). [*Died* 16 *May* 1962.

COKE, Col. Jacynth d'Ewes Fitz-Ercald, C.M.G. 1918; C.V.O. 1924; C.B.E. 1927; late York and Lancaster Regt. and R.A.S.C.; *b.* 1879; *er. surv. s.* of Lt.-Col. Langton Coke, Brookhill Hall, Derbyshire; *m.* 1902, Elizabeth, *d.* of Albert Waller, of Shannon Grove, Banagher, Ireland; one *s.* two *d.* Served South African War, 1899-1902 (despatches, Queen's medal and 3 clasps, King's medal and 1 clasp); European War, 1914-18 (despatches, C.M.G., Legion of Honour); Commander of the Order of the Saviour; retired pay, 1919; Chief Constable of the West Riding of Yorkshire, 1919-29; Chief of the British Police Mission to the Greek Govt., 1929-31; Chief Constable of West Suffolk, 1932-37; one of H.M. Inspectors of Constabulary, 1937-45. H.M. Lieutenant for the City of London. *Address:* Elmhurst Cottage, Woodbridge, Suffolk. *T.:* 765. [*Died* 17 *May* 1963.

COKE, Captain Hon. Reginald, D.S.O. 1915; Barrister at law; one of the special Commissioners of Income Tax; *b.* 10 Nov. 1883; 8th *s.* of 2nd Earl of Leicester; *m.* 1924, Katharine, *y. d.* of Hon. E. A. D. Ryder and Lady Maud Ryder; two *d.* *Educ.:* Eton; Magdalen College, Oxford; B.A. Served European War in Scots Guards, 1914-19 (despatches twice, D.S.O.). *Address:* Tudor House, Cuddington Avenue, Cheam, Surrey. *T.:* Vigilant 0943. *Clubs:* Turf, Brooks's. [*Died* 30 *April* 1969.

COKE, Major Hon. Richard; formerly Capt. Reserve of Officers, Scots Guards; 5th *s.* of 2nd Earl of Leicester and Hon. Georgina Caroline Cavendish, *e. d.* of 2nd Baron Chesham; *b.* 20 Aug. 1876; *m.* 1st, 1907, Hon. Doreen O'Brien (who obtained a divorce, 1927; she died 1960), *y. d.* of 14th Baron Inchiquin; one *s.* two *d.* (and two *d.* decd.); 2nd, 1932, Elizabeth, *er. d.* of late Dr. Louis Leopold Martial B. and Hon. Mrs. de Beaumont; one *s.* two *d.* *Educ.:* Eton; Trinity College, Cambridge. Served South African War, 1899-1902; European War, 1914-1916 (wounded twice). *Address:* White House, Weasenham, King's Lynn, Norfolk. *T.:* Weasenham St. Peter 214. [*Died* 14 *June* 1964.

COKER, Sir Salako A. B.; *see* Benka-Coker.

COLE, Air Vice-Marshal (retd.) Adrian Trevor, C.B.E. 1937; D.S.O. 1942; D.F.C.; M.C.; *b.* 19 June 1895; *s.* of late Robert Hodgson Cole, M.D., LL.B., Malvern, Melb.; *m. cousin,* Katherine Shaw, *d.* of late Nicholas Cole, grazier, Cloven Hills, Camperdown; two *s.* two *d.* *Educ.:* Church of England Grammar Schools, Geelong and Melbourne, Victoria. Served European War, 1914-19, through all ranks to Captain in Australian Flying Corps; business as merchant, 1919; joined permanent Flying Corps as Flight Lieutenant, 1920; Director of Training, 3 years; acting 2nd member of Air Board, 1½ years; C.O. No. 1. Flying Training School, 3 years; C.O. No. 1. Aircraft Depot, 3 years; Air Member for Supply, Air Board, 3 years; passed R.A.F., Staff Coll., Andover, 1924; Organizer and Deputy Chm. McRobertson International Air Race, England to Australia, 1932/1934; O.C., R.A.A.F., Richmond, N.S.W., 2 years; Imperial Defence College, London, 1938; A.O.C. Central Area, Sydney, 1939-40; special duty, 1940, loaned R.A.F., in Middle East and Home Forces, Dieppe (D.S.O.); Commando raid in France, 1942 (wounded). *Recreation:* fishing. *Address:* 47 Caroline Street, South Yarra, Victoria, Australia. *Clubs:* Beefsteak, Melbourne, Naval and Military (Melbourne); Victoria Racing, Royal Melbourne Golf.
[*Died* 14 *Feb.* 1966.

COLE, Vice-Admiral Sir Antony (Bartholomew), K.B.E. 1964; C.B. 1962; D.S.C. 1941; *b.* 23 May 1909; *s.* of late Commander J. F. H. Cole, Royal Navy, Fell Court, Torquay and Ethel Sophie Bartholomew, Devizes; *m.* 1937, Barbara Mary Burstall; two *d.* *Educ.:* Winchester College. Joined Navy, 1927; Comdr. 1944; Capt. 1951; comd. H.M.S. Campania, 1952; Naval Attaché, Rome, 1953-55; comd. H.M.S. Albion, 1958-59; Assistant Chief of Naval Staff, 1959-62; Rear-Adm. 1960; Chief of Allied Staff, Mediterranean, 1962-65; Vice-Adm. 1963. Retd. 1965. *Recreations:* fishing, sailing, gardening. *Address:* Heathayne Farm, Colyton, Devon. *T.:* Colyton 543. *Clubs:* United Service; Royal Ocean Racing. [*Died* 24 *March* 1967.

COLE, Eric Kirkham, C.B.E. 1958; *b.* 4 July 1901; *o. s.* of Henry and Alice Laura Cole, Westcliff-on-Sea; *m.* 1925, Muriel (*d.* 1965), *d.* of Henry Bradshaw, Liverpool; one *s.* one *d.* *Educ.:* Southend High School. Founded the Ekco Radio Receiver Manufacturing Business, 1922; Dir., E. K. Cole Ltd., 1926-61, Past Chm. 1961; Past Dep. Chm. British Electronic Industries Ltd. (1960-61). Liveryman, Worshipful Cos. of Skinners and Horners. Hon. Mem., Instn. of Electronic and Radio Engineers. *Address:* Flat 82, Grosvenor House, Park Lane, W.1. *T.:* Grosvenor 6363; 16 Abbotts Kings Rd., Brighton, Sussex. *T.:* Brighton 25536. *Clubs:* City Livery; International Sportsmen's. [*Died* 18 *Nov.* 1966.

COLE, Percy Frederick, O.B.E. 1946; *b.* 4 June 1882; *s.* of late F. J. Cole, Five Ways House, Maidstone; *m.* 1st, 1914, Clara (*d.* 1957), *d.* of late Jonathan Redman, Hebden Bridge, Yorks.; 2nd, 1959, Georgina Dunbar, 25 Chelsea Gardens, S.W.1. *Educ.:* privately. Trained as journalist, South Eastern Gazette, Maidstone, and Central News; business training abroad. Chm., Parliamentary Press Gall., 1944-45; Editor, Official Report of Debates, House of Commons (Hansard), 1944-47. retired 1947. *Publication:* Four Decades in the Press Gallery, 1966. *Address:* 79 Burton Court, Chelsea, S.W.3. *T.:* 01-730 4786.
[*Died* 25 *Aug.* 1968.

COLE, Thomas Loftus, C.B.E. 1958; J.P.; Alderman Belfast Corporation. Formerly Chm. of Food Control Cttee.; Dep. Lord Mayor, 1937-39. M.P. (Ulster Unionist) East Belfast, 1945-50. Formerly M.P. (N. Ire.), Dock Div. of Belfast. *Address:* Elmfield House, Antrim Rd., Whitewell, Belfast. [*Died* 7 *March* 1961.

COLE, Walton Adamson; The Editor of Reuters since 1945; General Manager since 1959 (Deputy General Manager, 1958-1959); Managing Dir., Brit. Commonwealth Internat. Newsfilm Agency Ltd. (B.C.I.N.A.), since 1961; *b.* 28 June 1912; *s.* of late Robert Michael and Margaret Alyce Cole; *m.* 1936, Janet Clingan, *d.* of late John and late Agnes Clingan, Grangemouth, Stirlingshire; two *d.* *Educ.:* George Heriot's School; George Watson's College, Edinburgh. In journalism since 1927; Evening Dispatch and The Scotsman, Edinburgh, 1927-30; Reporter, Falkirk Herald, also contributor to Scottish newspapers and magazines, 1930-35; Reporter, The Press Association, 1935-37; Deputy News Editor, The Press Association, 1937; Day Supervising Editor, Press Association, 1938; Night Editor, Press Association, 1939-42; News Manager, Reuters, 1942. Member various press wartime cttees.; press member of delegation appointed by General Eisenhower to deal with press communications after D Day; Mem. U.K. Delegn. Commonwealth Press Union Confs., London 1946, Ottawa 1950, Canberra 1955. King Haakon VII Liberty Cross, 1947; Comdr. Order of Phœnix, Greece, 1961; Comdr. Order of Orange Nassau (Netherlands), 1961; Comdr. Order of the Crown, Belgium, 1962. *Recreations:* roving, reporting. *Address:* (home) 10 Pensioners Ct., The Charterhouse, Charterhouse Sq., E.C.1; (office) Reuters, 85 Fleet St., E.C.4. *T.A.:* Reuter London. *T.:* Fleet Street 6060. *Clubs:* Garrick, Press.
[*Died* 25 *Jan.* 1963.

COLE-DEACON, Gerald John, C.B.E. 1945; Solicitor; *b.* 2 December 1890; *s.* of William Cole-Deacon, Bedford; *m.* 1939, Phyllis Gertrude (*d.* 1954), *d.* of William Horton, Bryn Dinarth, Colwyn Bay, N. Wales. *Educ.:* Bedford School. Asst. Solicitor, Great Northern Railway, 1914-20; Assistant Solicitor, L.N.W. Rly., 1920-23; Chief Parliamentary Assistant to Chief Legal Adviser L.M.S. Rly. and Chief Assistant Solicitor for matters arising under the Railways Act, 1923-30; Secretary, Railway Companies Association, 1930-48; Secretary Railway Rates and Charges Committee, 1921-39; Sec. Railway Executive Committee, M.W.T., 1938-45. *Recreations:* fishing and yachting. *Address:* The Mansion House, Hingham, Norwich. *Clubs:* St. Stephen's, Flyfishers'; Royal Norfolk and Suffolk Yacht.
[*Died* 31 *Jan.* 1968.

COLEBROOK, Leonard, F.R.S. 1945; F.R.C.O.G., F.R.C.S.; Hon. D.Sc. Birm., 1950; *b.* 2 March 1883; *s.* of May Colebrook and Mary Gower; *m.* 1st, 1914, Dorothy Scarlett Campbell; no *c.*; 2nd, 1946, Vera Scovell; no *c.* *Educ.:* Grammar School, Guildford; High School, Bournemouth; Christ's College, Blackheath; St. Mary's Hospital. Assistant, Inoculation Dept., St. Mary's Hospital, 1907-14; Capt. R.A.M.C., serving in France, European War, 1914-18. Hon. Director of Laboratory, Queen Charlotte's Hospital, 1930-39; Col. R.A.M.C. 1939-42, Bacteriological Consultant to Army in France, 1939-40. Director Burns Investigation Unit, Royal Infirmary, Glasgow, 1942-43, and The Accident Hospital, Birmingham, 1944-48; Member Scientific Staff of Medical Research Council, 1920-48; retired, 1948. *Publications:* On the Technique of the Teat and the Capillary Glass Tube (with Sir A. E. Wright), 1921; On the Treatment of Streptococcal Infection by Organic Arsenicals, special report series, No.

119, Medical Research Council, 1928; Treatment of Puerperal Infections with Prontosil (with M. Kenny), Lancet, 1936; The Prevention of Puerperal Sepsis, 1936; Studies of Burns and Scalds, special report series No. 249 (with others), Medical Research Council, 1945; A New Approach to the Treatment of Burns and Scalds, 1950; Almroth Wright, 1954. *Recreations:* sketching, gardening. *Address:* Silverwood, Farnham Royal, Bucks. *T.:* Farnham Common 2220. [*Died* 29 *Sept.* 1967.

COLEMAN, Ephraim Herbert, C.M.G. 1944; Q.C. (Canada), 1929; LL.D.; Barrister; *b.* 21 July 1890; *s.* of James Doherty Coleman and Mary Doherty; *m.* 1934, Jean, *d.* of late Hon. Hugh Amos Robson; no *c.* *Educ.:* Public and High Schools, Arnprior, Ontario; Univ. of Manitoba, Winnipeg (LL.D. 1937). Barrister, Winnipeg, 1922-33; Secretary-Treasurer Canadian Bar Assoc., 1919-33; Hon. Executive Secretary Canadian Bar Assoc., 1934-49; Dean Manitoba Law School, 1929 - 33; Bencher Law Society of Manitoba, 1928-33; Under-Secretary of State and Deputy Registrar-General of Canada, 1933-49; Canadian Ambassador to Cuba, 1950-51 (Minister, 1949-50); Canadian Ambassador to Brazil, 1951-53. *Recreation:* reading. *Address:* 404 Laurier Avenu , E., Ottawa, Ontario, Canada. *Clubs:* Rideau (Ottawa); Manitoba (Winnipeg). [*Died* 4 *Dec.* 1961.

COLEMAN, Frank, M.R.C.S., L.R.C.P., F.D.S., R.C.S. (Eng.); Consulting Dental Surgeon St. Bartholomew's Hospital and Royal Dental Hospital; *b.* London, Feb. 1876; *s.* of Alfred Coleman, F.R.C.S. (Eng.). *Educ.:* Nelson College, N.Z.; Epsom College. Pres. Metropolitan Branch, British Dental Association. Late Pres., Royal Society of Medicine (Odontological section); late Lecturer on Materia Medica, Royal Dental Hospital, London; late Examiner in Dental Surgery at Univ. of London; late Member of the Bd. of Examiners in Dental Surgery, Royal College of Surgeons; Acting Lt.-Col. (M.C.) R.A.M.C. (T.F.), 6th Field Ambulance, 47th London Division. *Publications:* Extraction of Teeth (3rd edition), 1933; Nasal Administration of Nitrous Oxide, 1908; (with Dr. H. Hilliard) Anæsthetics in Dental Surgery, 1912; article, The Development of the Jaws and Teeth, in the Science and Practice of Dental Surgery, 1914 and 1931; Materia Medica for Dentists, 1936 (7th edition). *Address:* Empress Hotel, Exeter Road, Bournemouth. [*Died* 27 *Nov.* 1962.

COLEMAN, Rt. Rev. Michael Edward, D.D. (*hon. causa*) Trinity Coll., Hartford, Conn., 1942; D.D. (*hon. causa*) St. Chad's College, Regina; Vicar of N. and S. Pender Is. since 1960; *b.* April 1902; *s.* of Dr. James G. B. Coleman, M.D., and Rosa Hogg; *m.* 1938, Mary Garland King; two *s.* two *d.* *Educ.:* Bradfield College, Berks.; Bishop's Hostel, Lincoln. Deacon, 1927; priest, 1928; Curate, Hucknall Torkard, Southwell, 1927-1930; Chaplain to Toc H, Manchester, 1930-1935; Toc H Commissioner, W. Canada, 1935-37; Curate, All Hallows-by-the-Tower, London, E.C.3, 1937-39, actg. Vicar, 1939-43; Diocesan Missioner and John Albert Hall lecturer, Christ Church Cathedral, Victoria, B.C., 1943-49; Canon of Christ Church Cathedral, Victoria, 1943; Rector of Quamichan, B.C., 1949-50; Bishop of Qu'Appelle, 1950-1960. *Publications:* Faith under Fire, 1942; The Cross, the Eucharist and You, 1959. *Recreations:* golf, gardening. *Address:* Windsong, R.R. 1, Port Washington, B.C., Canada. [*Died* 3 *Feb.* 1969.

COLFOX, Lt.-Col. Sir (William) Philip, 1st Bt., *cr.* 1939; J.P., D.L. Dorset; *b.* 25 Feb. 1888; *e.* and *o. surv. s.* of late Col. T. A. Colfox, T.D., D.L., J.P., Coneygar, Bridport, and Constance, 2nd *d.* of late Edward Nettlefold, Birmingham; *m.* 1920, Mary Frances, J.P., *o. d.* of late Col. J. B. Symes-Bullen, Catherston, Charmouth; one *s.* two *d.* (and *er. s.* decd.). *Educ.:* Eton, R.M.A. Woolwich. Commissioned into R.F.A., 1908; Lieut., 1911; Capt., 1914; Major, 1918; Lt.-Col. Home Guard, 1940; served European War, 1914-17 (twice wounded), M.C.); M.P. (Co. U.) North Dorset, 1918-22, (U.) West Dorset, 1922-41; Assistant Government Whip, 1922; Parliamentary Secretary to Under-Secretary of State for the Colonies, 1921; to Minister of Pensions, 1920; Governor of Sherborne School; Alderman Dorset County Council; High Sheriff of Dorset, 1946-47. *Heir: s.* William John Colfox [*b.* 25 April 1924. *Educ.:* Eton. Served War, 1943-45, Lieut. R.N.V.R.]. *Address:* Symondsbury Manor, Bridport, Dorset. *T.:* 2685. *Club:* Army and Navy. [*Died* 8 *Nov.* 1966.

COLLARD, Vice-Adm. Bernard St. G., C.B. 1927; D.S.O. 1918; *b.* 27 Feb. 1876; 3rd *s.* of Rev. Canon John Marshall Collard; *m.* 1909, Rosamond (*d.* 1957), 3rd *d.* of John Fred. Starkey of Bodicote House, Banbury; one *s.* one *d.* *Educ.:* Clifton College. Entered Britannia, 1890; Capt., 1915; Rear-Adm., 1926; retired list, 1928; Vice-Adm., retired, 1931. *Address:* c/o Lloyds Bank, Ltd., Petersfield. [*Died* 12 *April* 1962.

COLLARD, Group Capt. (Retd.) Richard Charles Marler, D.S.O. 1942; D.F.C. 1941; M.P. (C. and Nat. L.) Central Norfolk since 1959; Director Handley Page Ltd., since 1958; *b.* 25 Aug. 1911; *s.* of late Charles John Collard; *m.* 1st, 1938, Suzette (*d.* 1958), *d.* of Alfred W. White, Spalding, Lincolnshire; one *s.*; *m.* 2nd, 1961, Mrs. Joan Mary Putt. *Educ.:* Haileybury. Commissioned R.A.F., 1931; Flying Instructor, 1936; O.C. No. 37 Squadron, 1941, No. 12 Squadron, 1942; shot down over Germany, 1942 (p.o.w.). Commanded: R.A.F. Goodwill Mission to U.S.A., 1946; R.A.F. Station, Stradishall, 1946-48; Group Capt. Ops., M.E.A.F., 1949-51; i.d.c., 1952; retd. at own request, 1953. King Haakon VII Liberty Cross, 1945. *Recreations:* sailing, walking, reading, history. *Address:* 7 Neville Terrace, S.W.7. *T.:* Kensington 4438. *Clubs:* Royal Automobile, Royal Aero; Norfolk (Norwich). [*Died* 9 *Aug.* 1962.

COLLEY, Richard, M.B., Ch.B. (Vict.), D.O.M.S., R.C.P.S.; Honorary Consultant Ophthalmic Surgeon to the South Western Regional Hospital Board; *b.* 30 October 1893; *s.* of Thomas and Esther Colley, Preston, Lancashire; *m.* 1929, Alice May Nuttall; three *s.* *Educ.:* Privately; Manchester University (John Henry Agnew Prize for Diseases of Children; Prosector of Anatomy, Medal in Practical Surgery; Medal in Pharmacology and Therapeutics). Captain R.A.M.C. (S.R.) European War, Mesopotamia (despatches); Visiting Ophthalmic Surgeon, Ministry of Pensions Hospital, Bath; House Physician, Hospital for Sick Children, Great Ormond St. London; Resident Surgical Officer and House Surgeon, Birmingham and Midland Eye Hospital; various appointments Manchester; Lately: Hon. Ophthalmic Surgeon, Roy. United Hosp., Bath; Hon. Ophthalmologist, Royal National Hospital for Rheumatic Diseases, Bath; Senior Hon. Surgeon Bath Eye Infirmary; Consulting Hon. Ophthalmic Surgeon, Chippenham and District Hospital; Oculist Wiltshire County Council; Oculist, Bath City Council; F.R.S.M. (Member of Council, Section of Ophthalmology, 1935-38); Member of Ophthalmological Society U.K. etc. *Publications:* Articles in Medical Press. *Recreation:* gardening. *Address:* Midmar, Richmond Road, Lansdown, Bath. *T.:* 4636. [*Died* 27 *June* 1964.

COLLIER, Lieut.-Col. Ernest Victor, D.S.O. 1917; M.E.I.C., F.R.G.S.; Canadian Engineers, retd.; Director: Alva Steamship Co. Ltd., Navigation & Coal Trade Co., Ltd., Navcot Ships Stores Ltd., Navcot Australia Pty. Ltd., Linolite Ltd.; *b.* Falmouth, 12 Sept. 1878; *s.* of late Capt. E. R. Collier, of H.M. Indian Marine, and Margaret Jeffrey; *m.* 1924, Fanny Gertrude (*decd.*), *widow* of Martin C. H. Nockolds Saffron Walden. *Educ.:* Falmouth Grammar School and private tuition. Went to Canada,1899; employed on public works, Winnipeg, 1900-2; Asst. Engineer, St. Lawrence Ship Channel, Hydrographic Surveys and Improvements, 1902-10; on private contracts, 1911-14; served European War with Canadian Expeditionary Forces, Infantry, Vimy and Hill 70 (wounded, despatches, D.S.O.); with Canadian Engineers, Amiens, Arras, and Cambrai battles; Capt. 1916; Major, 1916; Lt.-Col. 1919; retired in U.K. 1919; resigned Collier & Co. Ltd. 1921; Civil Engineer, Anglo-Persian Oil Co. Ltd., 1921; resigned, 1931. *Clubs:* Royal Thames Yacht; Royal Cornwall Yacht (Falmouth). [*Died* 11 *Aug.* 1964.

COLLIER, Frank Simon, C.M.G. 1956; C.B.E. 1949; Forestry Adviser to Secretary of State for the Colonies, 1951-57, retired for reasons of health; *b.* 24 Aug. 1900; *s.* of Charles Collier, Northampton, and Alice Murray Collier (*née* Smitheman); *m.* 1st, 1932, Gladys Eveline Moss (*d.* 1950); two *d.*; 2nd, 1953, Elfrida Frances Hilda (*née* Vicars-Miles), *widow* of Peter Hamblin Smith. *Educ.:* Masonic School, Bushey; Lincoln College, Oxford. Asst. Conservator, Nigeria, Colonial Forest Service, 1922; Capt. Nigeria Regt., 1941-43 (Nigeria only); Conservator of Forests, Nigeria, 1942; Chief Conservator of Forests, Nigeria, 1946. *Recreations:* those of a field naturalist, with pencil and water colour and formerly rifle. At one time rowing. *Address:* Black Bush, Burley, Ringwood, Hampshire. *T.:* Burley 3128. *Club:* Leander. [*Died* 7 *Feb.* 1964.

COLLIER, Joseph; President of United Drapery Stores Ltd., since 1966 (Chairman, 1959-66; Director, 1945-66); also Director of: Alexandre Ltd.; Allders Ltd.; Arding & Hobbs Ltd.; John Blundell Ltd.; Household Supplies Co. Ltd.; Prices Tailors Ltd.; Richard Shops Ltd.; William Whiteley Ltd., and many other cos. Has many charitable interests. Freeman Metropolitan Borough of Southwark. *Address:* 364/366 Kensington High St., W.14. [*Died* 27 *Aug.* 1967.

COLLIER, Most Rev. Patrick; Bishop of Ossory (R.C.), since 1928; *b.* 1880; *s.* of late John Collier, Camross, Leix. *Educ.:* St. Kieran's College, Kilkenny; Maynooth. (*Address:* Sion House, Kilkenny. [*Died* 10 *Jan.* 1964.

COLLINGWOOD, Sir Charles Arthur, Kt. 1950; M.A., LL.B.; a Judge of the High Court of Justice, Probate, Divorce, and Admiralty Division, 1950-62, retd.; *b.* 2 Nov. 1887; *m.* 1918, Angela, *d.* of late E. R. Longcroft, Hall Place, Havant, Hants. *Educ.:* Exeter School; Downing College, Cambridge (M.A., LL.B.). Hon. Fellow, Downing College, Cambridge, 1950. Called to Bar, Lincoln's Inn, 1912; South-Eastern Circuit. Served European War, 1914-18, Northumberland Fusiliers; War of 1939-45 on staff of Judge Advocate-General; Asst. Judge Advocate-General, 1943-45; County Court Judge, 1945-50. *Address:* Moormead, Blackhills, Esher, Surrey. *T.:* Esher 2068 *Clubs:* Athenæum, Oxford and Cambridge University. [*Died* 23 *May* 1964.

COLLINGWOOD, Sir Edward (Foyle), Kt. 1962; C.B.E. 1946; M.A., Ph.D., Sc.D., Camb.; F.R.S. 1965; F.R.S.E. 1954; D.L.; J.P.; Chairman: Council of Durham University, since 1963 (Council of Durham Colleges, 1955-63); Central Health Services Council since 1963 (Vice-Chm., 1959-63); Newcastle Regional Hospital Bd., 1953-68; Vice-Chm., Bd. of Governors of United Newcastle Hospitals; Vice-Pres. Internat. Hospital Federation, 1959-67; Mem. Med. Res. Council, 1960-68 (Treas., 1960-67); Mem., Royal Commission on Medical Education, 1965-68; *b.* 17 January 1900; *e. s.* of late Col. C. G. Collingwood, C.B., Lilburn Tower, Northumberland. *Educ.:* R.N.C. Osborne and Dartmouth; Trinity College, Cambridge. Midshipman R.N., 1916-17 (invalided); entered Trinity College, Cambridge, 1918; Rayleigh Prizeman, 1923; Rouse Ball Travelling Student, 1924-25; Lieut. Northumberland Hussars (Yeomanry), 1923-27; Steward of Trinity College, Cambridge, and Lecturer in Faculty of Mathematics, Cambridge University, 1930-38; Temp. Lieut. R.N.V.R. 1940; Lt.-Comdr. 1942; Comdr. 1942; Acting Capt. 1944; served as Dir. of Scientific Research with Admiralty Delegation in Washington, 1942; officer in charge of sweeping div., 1943, Chief Scientist, 1943-45, Admiralty Mine Design Dept. Vice-President London Mathematical Society, 1959-60, Treasurer, 1960-. Gibson Lecture, Univ. of Glasgow, 1961. High Sheriff of Northumberland, 1937; J.P. 1935, D.L. 1959, Northumberland. Hon. D.Sc. (Durham), 1950; Hon. LL.D. (Glasgow), 1965. Legion of Merit, Degree of Officer, U.S.A., 1946. Officier de l'Ordre de la Santé Publique, France, 1963. *Publications:* The Theory of Cluster Sets (with A. J. Lohwater), 1966; papers in Mathematical Journals. *Address:* Lilburn Tower, Alnwick, Northumberland. *T.:* Wooperton 226. *Clubs:* Travellers'; Northern Counties (Newcastle upon Tyne). [*Died* 25 *Oct.* 1970.

COLLINS, Maj.-Gen. Charles Edward; *see* Edward-Collins.

COLLINS, Prof. Douglas Henry, O.B.E. 1946; M.D., F.R.C.P., F.C.Path.; Professor of Pathology, University of Sheffield, since 1954; Consultant Pathologist, United Sheffeld Hospitals (Royal Infirmary) and Sheffield National Radiotherapy Centre, since 1954; *b.* 23 July 1907; *s.* of Dr. A. W. Collins, Ulverston, Lancs.; *m.* 1932, Jean Wright; one *s.* one *d.* *Educ.:* Rossall School; University of Liverpool. Mem. Central Health Services Council and its Standing Medical Advisory Cttee., 1958-; Mem. Sub. Cttee. on Staphylococcal Infections in Hospitals, 1958-59; Mem. Sub. Cttee. on Hospital Medical Records, 1961-64. W.H.O. Consultant, India, 1963. *Publications:* The Pathology of Articular and Spinal Diseases, 1949; Modern Trends in Pathology, 1959; The Pathology of Testicular Tumours (jtly.), 1964; medical articles. *Recreation:* music. *Address:* 54 Stumperlowe Crescent Road, Sheffield 10. [*Died* 1 *Aug.* 1964.

COLLINS, George Edward, R.C.A., 1941 (A.R.C.A., 1915); R.B.A., 1905; *b.* Dorking, 29 Oct. 1880; *s.* of late Charles Collins, R.B.A., A.R.C.A.; *m.* Clara Caroline, *d.* of late A. F. Perrin, R.C.A.; one *s.* one *d.* *Educ.:* Dorking High School; Epsom and Lambeth Schools of Art. Exhibited R.A., R.B.A., R.C.A., R.I., Melbourne, Adelaide, Brisbane, Liverpool, Birmingham, Southport, etc. Illustrated: The Natural History of Selborne, by Gilbert White, 1911; Green Fields and Fantasy, by Patrick R. Chalmers, 1934; Wild Life in a Southern County, by Richard Jefferies, 1937. *Recreations:* reading, woodworking. *Address:* Wayside, Wonham Way, Gomshall, near Guildford. [*Died* 1 *Feb.* 1968.

COLLINS, Brigadier Gerald; *see* Edward-Collins.

COLLINS, Herbert Frederick, C.M.G. 1950; Staff Inspector of Modern Languages,

Ministry of Education, since 1945; *b.* 2 Feb. 1890; *s.* of late Herbert Collins and Elizabeth Jane Collins; *m.* 1919, Winifred, *d.* of Harry Fenton Smith, Ecclesall, Sheffield. *Educ.:* Latymer Upper School, Hammersmith, W.; Universities of London and Paris. Senior Modern Language Master, Tottenham County School, 1919-25; Head of Modern Side, Manchester Grammar School, 1925-28; Headmaster, Chichester High School for Boys, 1928-34; H.M. Inspector of Schools (Board of Education), 1934. *Publications:* A French Course for Schools, 1929; Conteurs Français, 1932; Talma, 1964; articles on Modern Language Teaching Method and on French Literature. *Recreations:* walking, theatre going, reading. *Address:* Lannilis, Arlington Avenue, Goring-by-Sea, Sussex. *Club:* Authors'. [*Died* 21 *Aug.* 1967.

COLLINS, Herbert Jeffery, C.B. 1964; C.B.E. 1951; *b.* 27 March 1907; *s.* of late Harry Collins, Newbury, Berkshire; *m.* 1938, Meryem, *d.* of Antonin Besse; one *s.* one *d.* Formerly: Sub-Regional Security Officer, Hong Kong; Under-Secretary, Foreign Office, until 1963. *Address:* 52 Coleherne Court, Old Brompton Road, S.W.5. [*Died* 13 *Nov.* 1968.

COLLINS, Horatio John, M.C.; M.Sc., M.Inst.C.E., M.I.Mech.E., P.P.I.Struct.E., M.Cons.E., M.Am.Soc.C.E.; Chartered Civil Engineer; *b.* 17 July 1894; *s.* of late Horatio Collins, Trenuth, Truro, Cornwall; *m.* 1929, Edith Mary, 2nd *d.* of late Lt.-Col. H. J. Harvey, K.O.S.B.'s; one *s.* *Educ.:* Univ. of Birmingham; Univ. of London. Served European War, The Royal Warwickshire Regt., 1914-19, Captain; War of 1939-45, Royal Engineers, Major. Heslop Gold Medallist for Research; President Institution of Structural Engineers, 1946; lecturer in Bartlett School of Architecture, Univ. of London; Chadwick Prof. of Civil Engineering, Univ. Coll., Univ. of London, retd. 1959; Emeritus Professor, Univ. of London, 1960. Consultant in Collins & Mason, Consulting Engineers. *Publications:* The Principles of Road Engineering, 1936; various technical papers. *Recreations:* gardening, sea-fishing. *Address:* 27 Bentinck Close, St. John's Wood, N.W.8. *T.:* Primrose 3203. [*Died* 22 *Dec.* 1963.

COLLINS, Sir James (Patrick), Kt., *cr.* 1953; *b.* 8 Aug. 1891; *m.* 1935, Winifride Mary Mahoney; two *s.* *Educ.:* St. Peter's School, Cardiff. Entered Royal Navy, 1907; served European War, 1914-18 (War Service Medals). Post Office, 1913-53 (Imperial Service Medal). Lord Mayor of Cardiff, 1953-1954. Company Director. Coronation Medal, 1953. *Recreations:* walking, reading. *Address:* 57 Fairwater Grove East, Fairwater, Cardiff. *T.:* Cardiff 72127. [*Died* 1 *Dec.* 1964.

COLLINS, John Rupert; Physician Emeritus, Cheltenham College; formerly Consulting Physician, Cheltenham General and Eye Hospitals, Evesham Hospital, Cirencester Hospital and Cheltenham Children's Hospital; *s.* of Rev. T. R. S. Collins, B.D., Dublin; *m.* Agnes Mary Brandt; three *d.* *Educ.:* Trinity College, Dublin. M.A., M.D., Dublin University, F.R.C.P., London; President, Gloucestershire Branch, British Medical Association, 1926; President, Cheltenham Science Society, 1924, 1925; Acting Major, R.A.M.C.; Officer in charge, Medical Division 30, General Hospital, Calais, 1916-19; Former Consulting Physician and Chairman Medical Staff, Cheltenham College, Cheltenham Ladies' College, and Dean Close School. *Publications:* papers in medical periodicals. *Recreation:* golf. *Address:* Ashfield, Cheltenham. *T.:* Cheltenham 2282. *Clubs:* Steeplechase, Golf, Cotswold Hills (Cheltenham). [*Died Nov.* 1965.

COLLINS, Seymour John; Metropolitan Magistrate, W. London Court, since 1960; *b.* 15 March 1906; *s.* of late Arthur John Collins and of Alice Charlotte Dujardin Collins; *m.* 1936, Nancye Westray, *er. d.* of Albert Yarwood, Cheshire; one *s.* one *d.* *Educ.:* Lancing; Pembroke College, Camb. (M.A.). Called to Bar, Inner Temple, 1929; Western Circuit and Hants Sessions. Served War of 1939-45 in Army, U.K. and Central Mediterranean Force, 1940-45; Temporary Major. Metropolitan Magistrate, Bow Street, 1950; N. London Court, 1950-60. Member, Chairmen's Panel, Metropolitan Juvenile Courts, 1952-62. *Recreation:* horticulture. *Address:* Manor Heath, Knowl Hill, Woking, Surrey. *T.:* Woking 61930. [*Died* 28 *Jan.* 1970.

COLLINSON, William Edward, M.A. (Lond.), Ph.D. (Heidelberg); Prof. Emeritus, Univ. of Liverpool, since 1954; Fellow of University College, London; Membre de la Société de Linguistique; Korrespondierendes Mitglied der Deutschen Akademie; Member of Fryske Akademy; Member of Maatschappij der Nederlandse Letterkunde; Honora patrono de la Universala Esperanto-Asocio; Membro de la Esperanto-Akademio; Professor of German, Liverpool University, 1914-54, and Hon. Lecturer in Comparative Philology; John Buchanan Lectr. in Esperanto, 1931-54, 1962-64; Chm. of Faculty of Arts, 1921-22, 1943-44; *b.* Edgbaston, 4 Jan. 1889; *s.* of late Wm. Robert Collinson, F.C.I.S., and late Laura Frances Piper; *m.* 1919, Paula, *d.* of Hubert Erdle; one *s.* one *d.* *Educ.:* Dulwich College; University College, London; University of Bonn. English Lektor at the Handelshochschule, Cologne, 1910-13; Assistant Lecturer in German, Liverpool University, 1913-14; 2nd Lieut. 3rd Reserve Garrison Batt., R.W.F. seconded and lent Naval Intelligence Dept. 1917-19; Member Home Office Advisory Committee (Internment of Aliens and 18b), 1939-41; Member University Grants Cttee., 1943-48; Lewis Fry Memorial Lectr., Bristol Univ., 1962. *Publications:* papers in the Modern Languages Review, etc.; Die mnd. Katharinenlegende der Hs. II. 143 der kgl. Bibl. zu Brüssel. Texte und Untersuchungen (Heidelberg, 1915); Contemporary English—A Personal Speech-Record, 1927; La Homa Lingvo, Berlin, 1927; Spoken English and Ergänzungsheft, Leipzig, 1929; German Literature till 1748 (in Companion to German Studies, London, 1932); (with R. Priebsch) The German Language, London, 1934, 6th edn., 1966; Indication, a Study of Demonstratives, etc.; Baltimore, 1937; The German Language Today, 1953; Penguin English-German Dictionary, 1954. *Address:* 8 Aigburth Drive, Liverpool 17. [*Died* 4 *May* 1969.

COLLIP, James Bertram, C.B.E. 1943; F.R.S. 1933; Prof. and Head of Department of Medical Research, Univ. of Western Ontario (Dean of Medicine and Prof. and Head of Department of Medical Research, 1947; retired as Dean, 1961); Director, Division of Medical Research, National Research Council, 1946-57; *b.* Belleville, Ontario, 20 Nov. 1892; *s.* of J. D. Collip; *m.* 1915, Ray Vivian, *d.* of H. W. Ralph, Dundas; one *s.* two *d.* *Educ.:* Belleville High School; University of Toronto. Research Fellow Biochemistry, University of Toronto, 1912-15; Lecturer Biochemistry, University, Alberta, 1915-17; Assistant Professor, 1917-19; Associate Professor, 1919-21; Travelling Fellow Rockefeller Foundation, 1921-22; Professor of Biochemistry, University of Alberta, 1922-28; Professor of Biochemistry, McGill University, Montreal, 1928-41; Gilman Professor of Endocrinology and Dir. of Research Inst. of Endocrinology, McGill Univ., Montreal, 1941-47; Chm. Associate Cttee. on Medical Research of National Research Council of

Canada, 1941-46. *Publications:* numerous papers on blood and tissue chemistry and internal secretions: Insulin, the Parathyroid Hormone, Placental Hormones and Pituitary Hormones. *Address:* Univ. of Western Ontario, London, Ontario, Canada. [*Died* 19 *June* 1965.

COLLYMORE, Sir (Ernest) Allan, Kt., *cr.* 1943; Chief Justice Barbados and Judge West Indian Court of Appeal, 1936-1957, retd.; *b.* 1893; *e. s.* of late Ernest and Mary Collymore, Barbados; *m.* 1921, Margaret, *o. d.* of Sebert Evelyn, Barbados; no *c.* *Educ.:* Harrison College, Barbados; Merton College, Oxford. M.A. (Oxon.) 1919; served European War, 1914-19, Captain East Lancashire Regt.; called to Bar, Inner Temple, 1920; Magistrate, Barbados, 1925; Magistrate, Bahamas, 1927; Attorney-General, Barbados, 1928; K.C., Barbados, 1933. Pres. Barbados Cricket Assoc., 1944-59. *Address:* Clapham House, St. Michael, Barbados. *Club:* Royal Societies. [*Died* 23 *June* 1962.

COLMAN, Lieut.-Col. and Bt. Col. Frederick Gordon Dalziel, O.B.E. 1929; T.D.; *s.* of late F. E. Colman, North Park, Epsom Downs; *m.* Peggy, *d.* of late A. Brocklehurst; no *c.* *Educ.:* Eton. High Sheriff of Surrey, 1924-25; Master Surrey Union Hounds, 1904-10; served with Surrey Yeomanry throughout European War in Belgium, France, and Salonica (despatches twice); served 1939-42 with Royal Artillery; Joint Master, Duke of Rutland's Hounds, 1930-31; Master, 1931-34 and 1940; Joint Master, 1934-39. *Recreations:* hunting, shooting, fishing. *Address:* Scalford Hall, Melton Mowbray, Leicestershire. *T.:* Scalford 220; Tarvie, Bridge of Cally, Blairgowrie, Perthshire. *T.:* Strathardle 264. *Clubs:* Carlton, Cavalry, International Sportsmen's, Royal Automobile, M.C.C. [*Died* 23 *Feb.* 1969.

COLMAN, Sir (George) Stanley, Kt. 1965; C.B.E. 1937; General Manager and Australian Director Australian Estates Co. Ltd., Melb.; Chm. Amalgamated Sugar Mills Ltd., Queensland; *m.* 1916, Marion, *d.* of Hon. D. H. Dalrymple, Queensland; two *s.* one *d.* *Educ.:* St. John's Gram. Sch., Parramatta, N.S.W. Shipping and Merchandise business in New South Wales, Queensland and Philippine Islands; General Manager, Queensland Meat Export Co. Ltd., Brisbane, for eleven years; Vice-Consul for Argentine in Brisbane, 1923-1926. *Recreations:* golf and tennis. *Address:* 6 Gordon Grove, South Yarra, Melbourne, Australia. *Clubs:* Reform; Melbourne (Melbourne); Queensland (Brisbane); Union (Sydney). [*Died* 4 *Feb.* 1966.

COLMAN, Sir Jeremiah, 2nd Bt., *cr.* 1907; *b.* 1 January 1886; *o. c.* of Sir Jeremiah Colman, 1st Bt.; *S.* father, 1942; *m.* 1924, Edith Gwendolen, *e. d.* of Sir Alfred Tritton, 2nd Bt.; two *s.* one *d.* *Educ.:* Winchester; Trinity Coll., Cambridge. J.P., County of Southampton (Surrey, 1909-38). *Heir:* *s.* Michael Jeremiah [*b.* 7 July 1928. *m.* 1955. Judith Jean, *d.* of Vice-Adm. Sir Peveril William-Powlett; one *s.* one *d.*]. *Address:* Malshanger, Basingstoke. *T.:* Oakley (Hants) 241. *Club:* Reform. [*Died* 8 *Jan.* 1961.

COLMAN, Sir Nigel Claudian Dalziel, 1st Bt. *cr.* 1952; Director Reckitt & Colman Holdings Ltd.; *s.* of late Frederick Edward Colman, D.L., and late Helen, *e. d.* of Davison Octavius Dalziel; *m.* 1952, Nona Ann, *d.* of late Edward H. M. Willan. M.P. (C.) Brixton Division of Lambeth, 1927-45; London County Council Member for Brixton Division of Lambeth, 1925-28; Chairman of Central Council of National Union of Conservative and Unionist Associations, 1939; Chm. Council and Exec. Cttee. of Metropolitan Area, 1934-36, mem. Area Council, 1927-65, Hon. Treas., 1931-34; Chm. Exec. Cttee, of Nat. Union of Conservative and Unionist Assocs., 1945-51 (served on this Cttee. 1934-); Pres. London Conservative Union, 1952-59; Mem. Management Cttee., Conservative and Unionist Agents' Superannuation Fund 1937, (Chairman 1940-61, Chairman Trustees, 1961, and a Trustee 1942-). President of the London Surrey Society, 1935-36; President of the National Horse Association of Great Britain, 1935-45; President of Hackney Horse Society, 1923 and 1938; President of Royal Counties Agricultural Society, 1937; Chm. British Horse Soc., 1952-55. Medal of Honour, Brit. Horse Soc., 1953. *Recreations:* The breedings and exhibition of Harness Horses; yachting, shooting, golf. *Heir:* none. *Address:* 49 Grosvenor Sq., W.1. *T.:* Mayfair 2373; Broadleas, Reigate, Surrey. *Clubs:* Carlton, Royal Automobile; Royal Motor Yacht; Royal Yacht Squadron. [*Died* 7 *March* 1966 (*ext.*).

COLMAN, Sir Stanley; *see* Colman, Sir G. S.

COLOMBOS, C(onstantine) John, Q.C. 1950; LL.D. (Lond.); *b.* Valetta, Malta; *e. s.* of John C. Colombos and Calliope Ralli. *Educ.:* Flores's Coll., Lyceum and Royal University, Malta; Ecole des Sciences Politiques and Institut des Hautes Études Internationales, Paris. LL.D. London, 1926; Dr. of Laws, Univ. of Brussels and Paris. Called to Bar, Middle Temple, 1923, and has practised at English Bar since then. Hon. Master of the Bench, Middle Temple, 1963. Prof., The Hague Academy of International Law; Hon. Treas., Grotius Soc., 1934-45, Hon. Sec., 1944-56; Member: Inst. of Internat. Law; Académie Diplomatique Internationale; President Admiralty and Prize Law Committee of International Bar Assoc. Served European War, 1914-18, Legal Adviser to Admiral C.-in-C. Allied Fleets in Mediterranean, 1915-19; Legal Adviser to Govt. of Malta in London, 1922-27 and 1932-33; Hon. Adm. in Navy of Texas (U.S.A.). Chief Legal Adviser to Oecumenical Patriarch of Constantinople, 1953-. Hon. Member Chamber of Advocates, Malta, 1964. Member, Board of Trustees, Commonwealth Foundation, 1965. French Legion of Honour and Palmes d'Académie (1st Class); Belgian Order of the Crown; Netherlands Order of Orange-Nassau and other Allied decorations. *Publications:* A Treatise on the Law of Prize, 3rd edn., 1949; The International Law of the Sea, 6th revised edn., 1967; contrib. to 14th Edn. of Encyclopædia Britannica, to Halsbury's Laws of England (2nd edn.) and to British section of Diplomatic Biography of Académie Diplomatique Internationale; articles on International and Constitutional Law in Journal of Comparative Legislation, British Year Book of International Law, Trans. of Grotius Society and International Law Quarterly. *Recreations:* yachting, walking and art collecting. *Address:* 10 King's Bench Walk, Temple, E.C.4. *T.:* Central 2775. *Club:* Athenæum. [*Died* 18 *April* 1968.

COLQUHOUN, Robert; artist; *b.* Ayrshire, Scotland, 1914. *Educ.:* Glasgow School of Art; Italy; France; Holland; Belgium. His work has been bought by the Contemporary Art Society and is exhibited at the Tate Gallery; is represented in the Museum of Modern Art, New York. One-man show: (retrospective), Whitechapel Art Gallery, 1958; Museum Street Galleries, 1962. *Address:* c/o Museum Street Galleries, 47 Museum Street, W.C.1. *T.:* Holborn 3337. [*Died* 20 *Sept.* 1962.

COLSON, Surgeon Vice-Adm. Sir Henry St. Clair, K.C.B., *cr.* 1947 (C.B. 1946); C.B.E. 1942; F.R.C.P.;

M.B., B.S., D.P.H.; *b.* 29 July 1887; *s.* of Peter James Colson, Southampton; *m.* 1921, Vera Jessica, *d.* of W. F. Bergh, of South Africa; one *s.* *Educ.:* King Edward VI Grammar School, Southampton; Westminster Hospital. Joined Royal Navy, 1912; North America and West Indies, 1913-16; served with Royal Marines, Plymouth, 1916-18; 4th R.M. Battalion (Zeebrugge), 1918; South American Station, 1919-21; R.N. Hospital, Bermuda, 1921-24; Specialist in bacteriology, S. Africa, 1924-1927; R.N. Hospital, Chatham, 1928-30; Specialist in Hygiene, 1932-41; Surgeon Rear-Adm. in charge R.N. Hospital, Barrow Gurney, 1942-45; Medical Director General of the Navy, 1946-48; late K.H.P.; retired list, 1948. *Address:* c/o Ministry of Defence, Whitehall, S.W.1. [*Died* 27 *Feb.* 1968.

COLSTON, Sir Charles (Blampied), Kt., *cr.* **1950; C.B.E. 1946; M.C.; D.C.M.; F.C.G.I.; Chairman since 1937, and Managing Director since 1928, Hoover Limited, Perivale, Greenford, Middlesex and of all subsidiary Companies; retired 1954; Chairman, Charles Colston, Limited, since 1955; Chairman, Colston Appliances Limited,** since 1961; *b.* 31 October 1891; *m.* 1st, 1924, Elsie Foster Shaw, M.B.E., 1962 (*d.* 1964); one *s.* three *d.* 2nd, 1968, Margaret Sim. *Educ.:* Colston School, Bristol; City & Guilds Technical College, Finsbury. Enlisted Sept. 1914, in Royal Engineers; **Dardanelles Campaign; Suvla Bay, Gallipoli; (D.C.M., despatches); gazetted into R.E., 1916; served in France, Belgium and Italy, 1916-18 (despatches, M.C.); June 1919 joined newly-formed Company of Hoover Ltd., became Director, 1920; Managing Director, 1928; Chairman, 1937; Regional Controller Ministry of Production, and Chairman of L. & S.E. Regional Board, 1942-45.** *Recreations:* shooting, fishing. *Address:* A13, Albany, Piccadilly, W.1. *T.:* Regent 4369. [*Died* 14 *Feb.* 1969.

COLTART, Captain Cyril George Bucknill, C.V.O. 1939; R.N. (retd.); *b.* 9 May 1889; *s.* of W. W. Coltart, Epsom; *m.* 1928, Frances, *d.* of W. Forsythe, London and Ceylon; no *c.* *Educ.:* Epsom College; Royal Academy, Gosport. Joined Royal Navy, 1904; joined Submarine Branch, 1912; commanded various Submarines, 1915-25; in command of S/M tenders, depot ships and flotillas, 1925-38; commanded H.M.S. Glasgow (2nd Cruiser Squadron) 1938 and 1939, including escort duty during visit of King and Queen to Canada (C.V.O.); Commodore West Coast S. America. 1940; Command of H.M.S. Hecla, 1941; Commodore in Charge, Inveraray, Argyll, 1942-43; commanding H.M.S. Cochrane 1944; retired, 1946. *Address:* Corner Cottage, Stroud, Petersfield, Hants. *Clubs:* United Service; United Hunts. [*Died* 19 *June* 1964.

COLVILE, Ernest Frederick, C.M.G. 1927; J.P.; *b.* 20 May 1879; *s.* of Col. Charles F. Colvile, 16 Harrington Gardens, and Mary Eliza Rowe; *m.* 1922, Amy Evelyn, *d.* of Henry Blunt Howard of Bark Hart, Kent. *Educ.;* Westminster School; Christ Church, Oxford. Assistant Resident, Nyasaland Prot., 1905; Political Officer in German East Africa, 1916-17; Provincial Commissioner, Nyasaland, 1921; Member of Executive and Legislative Councils, 1925; Acting Governor, Nyasaland, 1926; Senior Commissioner, Nyasaland Protectorate; District Comr., Northern Palestine, 1928-31; Member West Suffolk County Council, 1937-1962. *Address:* Hedingham Castle, Nr. Halstead, Essex. *Club:* Oxford and Cambridge. [*Died* 19 *Feb.* 1967.

COLVILLE, Lady (Helen) Cynthia, D.C.V.O., *cr.* 1937; D.B.E., *cr.* 1953; President of Cecil Houses; *b.* 20 May 1884; *d.* of 1st and last Marquess of Crewe, K.G., P.C.; *m.* 1908, Hon. George Colville (*d.* 1943); three *s.* *Educ.:* home. Woman of the Bedchamber to Queen Mary, 1923-53. J.P. County of London; F.R.C.M.; LL.D. (Hon.) Leeds. *Publication:* Crowded Life, 1963. *Recreations:* sailing, attending concerts. *Address:* 4 Mulberry Walk, Chelsea, S.W.3. *T.:* Flaxman 6556. [*Died* 15 *June* 1968.

COLVIN, Sir George Lethbridge, Kt., *cr.* 1933; C.B. 1919; C.M.G. 1918; D.S.O. 1917; Consultant to firm of Long, Till & Colvin, 33 King St., E.C.2; Hon. Brig.-Gen. in Army; *b.* London, 27 Mar. 1878; *e. s.* of late Clement Sneyd Colvin, C.S.I., Secretary for Public Works, India Office, London; *m.* 1911, Katherine Isabella Mylne; one *s.* one *d.* *Educ.:* Westminster. Served in the Army in France and Italy during the European War, and from 1918 to termination of war was Director-General Transportation, B.E.F., Italy (despatches five times, D.S.O., C.M.G., C.B.); Commendatore, Order of S.S. Maurice and Lazzarus (Italy), 1921. Director of Development, Ministry of Transport, 1919-21; General Manager, East Indian Railway, 1921-33; A.D.C. to H.M. King George V, 1929-35. *Address:* Wellsbridge Cottage, Ascot. *T.:* Ascot 566. [*Died* 2 *March* 1962.

COLVIN, Major Hugh, V.C. 1917; late Cheshire Regt.; *b.* Burnley, Lancs., 1 Feb. 1887; father and mother both Aberdeenshire; *m.* 1921. *Educ.:* Hatherlow day school, Cheshire. Joined the service, 8th (King's Royal Irish) Hussars, 1908; served one year in England and in India with Regt. till 1914; served in France with Regt. till 1917, gaining the rank of Lance-Sergeant; commissioned April 1917 on the field to 2nd Batt. The Cheshire Regt.; retired pay, 1935. *Address:* 1 Sandhurst Avenue, Bispham, Blackpool, Lancashire. [*Died* 16 *Sept.* 1962.

COLWYN, 2nd Baron, *cr.* 1917; **Frederic John Vivian Smith,** Bt., *cr.* 1912; *b.* 26 Nov. 1914; *s.* of late Hon. Frederick H. Hamilton-Smith (*e. s.* of 1st Baron) and Hilda (*d.* 1964), *d.* of late John Ross (she *m.*, 2nd, 1932, Major J. F. Hardy-Smith, who *d.* 1945); *S.* grandfather, 1946; *m.* 1940, Miriam, *d.* of Victor Ferguson, Cheltenham; two *s.*; *m.* 1952, Hermione Sophia O'Bryen, *d.* of late C. B. E. Hoare and of Mrs. Hoare, d'Avigdor House, Hove, Sx.; *m.* 1955, Beryl, *d.* of late Harvey Walker and of late Mrs. Walker, Heathgate House, Heathgate, Shropshire. *Educ.:* Malvern Coll. Served War of 1939-45, London Scottish, Gordon Highlanders; Capt. 1941; France 1944 (wounded); left Army 1947. *Heir:* *s.* Hon. Ian Anthony Hamilton-Smith [*b.* 1 Jan. 1942; *m.* 1964, Sonia Jane, *er. d.* of P. H. G. Morgan, Braeside, Malvern, Worcs.]. *Address:* 144 Harley Street, W.1; 17 Cavendish Avenue, St. John's Wood, N.W.8. [*Died* 1 *June* 1966.

COMBE, Maj.-Gen. John Frederick Boyce, C.B. 1947; D.S.O. and Bar 1941; late Lt.-Col. 11th Hussars, R.A.C.; *b.* 1895; *m.* 1947, Helen Violet Gosling (*née* St. Maur), *widow* of Major Gosling. Served European War, 1914-18, 11th Hussars; War of 1939-1945, N. Africa (despatches), Italy; prisoner of war, 1941-44; C.M.F., 1944; Comdr. 2nd Armoured Bde., 78th Div. and 46th Div.; Dep. Comdr. B.T.A., 1946; retired pay, 1947. *Address:* Clanville Lodge, Andover, Hants. *Clubs:* Turf, Buck's, Cavalry. [*Died* 12 *July* 1967.

COMBE, Simon Harvey, M.C. 1943; Chairman, Watney Mann Ltd., since 1958; *b.* 1903; *s.* of Major Boyce Combe, Gt. Holt, Dockenfield, Farnham, Surrey; *m.* 1932, Silvia Beatrice Coke, *d.* of 4th Earl of Leicester; one *s.* one *d.* *Educ.:* Eton. *Address:* The Manor House, Burnham Thorpe, nr. King's Lynn, Norfolk. *T.:* Burnham Market 201; 1 Watney House,

Palace St., S.W.1. *T.:* Victoria 7858. *Clubs:* White's; Brancaster Golf (Brancaster). [*Died* 1 *April* 1965.

COMBERMERE, 4th Viscount (*cr.* 1826), **Francis Lynch Wellington Stapleton-Cotton**; Bt. 1677; Baron Combermere (U.K.) 1814; late Lieut. R.G.A.; *b.* 29 June 1887; *o. c.* of 3rd Viscount and Isabel Marian, 3rd *d.* of Sir George Chetwynd, 3rd Bt.; *S.* father, 1898; *m.* 1st, 1913, Hazel Louisa (marr. diss., 1926; she died 1943), *d.* of late Henry de Courcy Agnew; 2nd, 1927, Constance Marie Katherine (*d.* 1968), *y. d.* of late Lt.-Col. Sir Francis Dudley W. Drummond, K.B.E.; two *s.* Served European War, 1914-18 (wounded). Hon. Joint County Secretary, S.S.A.F.A., 1952-59; D.L. Hereford, 1953-60. *Heir:* *s.* Hon. Michael Wellington Stapleton-Cotton [*b.* 8 Aug. 1929; *m.* 1961, Pamela Elizabeth, *d.* of Rev. R. G. Coulson; two *d.* Served Palestine Police, 1947-48; Royal Canadian Mounted Police, 1948-49; joined R.A.F., 1950]. *Address:* 17 Chancellor House, Hyde Park Gate, S.W.7. [*Died* 8 *Feb.* 1969.

COMMON, Frank Breadon, Q.C.; M.A., B.C.L.; Counsel to firm of Ogilvy, Cope, Porteous, Hansard, Marler, Montgomery & Renault, Advocates; *b.* Montreal, 26 Nov. 1891; *s.* of William John Common, C.A., and Mary Elizabeth Breadon; *m.* 1917, Ruth Louise, *d.* of James Lang; two *s.* two *d.* *Educ.:* Montreal High School; McGill University (M.A., B.C.L. and Gold Medallist). Chm., Montreal Refrigerating & Storage Ltd.; Dir., Canadian Arena Co., etc. *Address:* The Royal Bank of Canada Bldg., Montreal 2, Canada. *T.A.:* Jonhall. *T.:* 875-5424; Apt. B-71, 3940 Cote des Neiges Rd., Montreal, Canada. *Clubs:* Mount Royal, St. James's, Mount Bruno Country, University, (Montreal); Racquet and Tennis (New York). [*Died* 25 *Feb.* 1969.

COMPER, Sir (John) Ninian, Kt., *cr.* 1950; Architect (not registered); *b.* 10 June 1864; *s.* of John Comper, founder and incumbent of St. Margaret's, Aberdeen, and Ellen, *d.* of John Taylor, merchant of Hull; *m.* 1890, Grace Bucknall; two *s.* one *d.* (and two *s.* and one *d.* decd.). *Educ.:* Glenalmond; Ruskin's School, Oxford; Royal School of Art, South Kensington, and with C. E. Kempe; then articled to G. F. Bodley and T. Garner. Principal works: St. Mary's, Wellingborough, following St. Cyprian's, Marylebone and its corollary St. Crispin's, Yerendawna, Poona, India, 1903; Wimborne St. Giles, 1910; St. Mary's, Rochdale, 1911; St. Martin's Chapel, Chailey, 1912; Stanton Memorial, St. Alban's, Holborn, 1918; work at Southwark Cathedral from 1922; Warriors' Chapel, Westminster Abbey, 1927, and Nave Windows from 1908; Welsh National War Memorial, Cardiff, 1928; Chapel of All Saints Sisters, nr. St. Albans, 1928; the abortive U.S.A. Cathedral for Aberdeen, 1930; St. Philip's, Portsmouth, 1937; and proposed Church of St. Frideswide, Bletchley, for the late Bishop of Oxford, designed 1950; Parliamentary War Memorial Window in Westminster Hall, 1952; Royal Window, Canterbury Cathedral, 1954; East Window, Holy Trinity Church, Coventry, 1955. *Publications:* Of the Atmosphere of a Church, 1947; Of the Christian Altar and the buildings which contain it, 1950; articles in transactions of ecclesiological societies. *Address:* The Priory, 67 Beulah Hill, Norwood, S.E.19. *T.:* Livingstone 1696. [*Died* 22 *Dec.* 1960.

COMPTON, Arthur H(olly); Professor-at-large, Washington University, Univ. of California (Berkeley), Coll. of Wooster, 1961-; Distinguished Service Prof. of Natural Philosophy, Washington Univ., 1954-61; Chancellor, 1945-53; *b.* Wooster, Ohio, 10 Sept. 1892; *s.* of Elias Compton, Ph.D., D.D., Professor of Philosophy and Dean of College of Wooster, and Otelia Catherine Augspurger, LL.D.; *m.* 1916, Betty Charity McCloskey (B.A.); two *s.* *Educ.:* College of Wooster (B.Sc. 1913); Princeton University (M.A. 1914, Ph.D. 1916). Instructor, Univ. of Minn., 1916-17; Research Engineer, Westinghouse Lamp Co., 1917-19; National Research Council Fellow, Cambridge Univ., 1919-20; Wayman Crow Professor of Physics and Head of Dept., of Physics, Washington Univ., St. Louis, 1920-23; Professor of Physics, Univ. of Chicago, 1923-45; Chairman, Dept. of Physics, Dean of Physical Sciences, Univ. of Chicago, 1940-45. Civilian Associate, U.S. Signal Corps, developing aeroplane instruments, 1917-18; Consultant, General Electric Co. 1926-45. Director, World Survey of Cosmic Rays, 1931-34; George Eastman Visiting Professor, Oxford Univ., 1934-35; Fellow, Balliol College, 1934-35; Director, Univ. of Chicago S. American Cosmic Ray Expeditions, 1941; Director, U.S. Government's Plutonium Research Project, 1942-1945. Has been special lecturer at various Universities. President: A.A.A.S., 1942; Amer. Physical Soc., 1934; Amer. Assn. Scientific Workers, 1939-40; Member Nat. Acad. of Sciences, 1927; Am. Philosophical Soc. 1927; hon. member many American and foreign academies. Protestant Co-Chairman, National Conference of Christians and Jews, 1938-47; General Chairman, World Brotherhood, 1950-55; North American Co-Chairman, 1955-; Regent, Smithsonian Institution, 1938-; Presidential Commission on Higher Education, 1946-48; Naval Research Advisory Cttee. 1946-53 (Chm., 1952-53); U.S. Deleg. to U.N.E.S.C.O., Paris, 1946; Mexico, 1947; Civilian Aide to Sec. of Army, 1952-53; attended many internat. science congresses. Chm., Amer. Deleg. India-America Relations Conf., New Delhi, India, 1949. Has numerous hon. degrees. Nobel Prize for physics, 1927; Rumford Gold Medal of Am. Acad. of Arts and Sciences, 1927; gold medal, Radiological Soc. N. America, 1928; Hughes Medal of R. Soc. London, 1940; Franklin gold medal of Franklin Inst., 1940; Franklin medal of Am. Philosophical Soc., 1945; U.S. Govt. Medal for Merit, 1946; Officer French Legion of Honour, 1947 and other U.S. and foreign awards. Has made some discoveries regarding X-rays; also directed development of first atomic chain reaction and of first quantity production of plutonium. *Publications:* Secondary Radiations Produced by X-rays, 1922; X-rays and Electrons, 1926, 2nd ed., 1928; X-rays in Theory and Experiment (with S. K. Allison), 1935; The Freedom of Man, 1935; On Going to College (co-author), 1940; Human Meaning of Science, 1940; Atomic Quest: A Personal Narrative, 1956. *Recreations:* tennis, astronomy, photography, music. *Address:* Washington University, St. Louis, U.S.A. *Clubs:* Country, University, Noonday, Round Table (St. Louis); University, Tavern (Chicago); Cosmos (Washington); University (New York). [*Died* 15 *March* 1962.

COMPTON, Joseph, C.B.E. 1952; M.A.; Educational Adviser, National Book League; formerly Director of Education, Ealing, 1937-1957, retd.; *b.* 18 Aug. 1891; *s.* of Samuel and Lena Elkin Compton. Served European War, 1914-18. Taught at Glasgow High School and Royal Academical Institution, Belfast, and, in 1921, became an Inspector of Schools in Manchester; appointed a Director of Education, 1925. Past Pres. Assoc. Education Officers. Formerly Chairman: Univ. of London Advisory Cttee. on Diploma in Diction and Dramatic Art; Board of Management, Poetry Book Society; Society for Italic Handwriting; National Book League. Formerly Mem. Exec. Cttee. Arts Council of Gt. Britain (chm. Poetry Panel) and Mem. Council, Royal College of Art. Mem. Royal Academy of Dancing.

Gov., Central School of Speech and Drama. *Publications:* Open Sesame, 1925; The Curtain Rises, 1927; Master Venturers, 1931; Chapters from Contemporary Novelists, 1932; Magic Sesame, 1932; Spoken English, 1941; contributions to literary and educational journals. *Recreations:* books, the theatre, music, travel, golf. *Address:* 3a Castlebar Road, Ealing, W.5. *T.:* Perivale 1918. *Clubs:* Savile; Denham Golf.
[*Died* 27 *Feb.* 1964.

COMPTON-BURNETT, Dame Ivy, D.B.E. 1967 (C.B.E. 1951); C.Lit. 1968; *d.* of late James Compton-Burnett and Katharine, *d.* of Rowland Rees. *Publications:* Novels: Pastors and Masters, 1925; Brothers and Sisters, 1929; Men and Wives, 1931; More Women than Men, 1933; A House and its Head, 1935; Daughters and Sons, 1937; A Family and a Fortune, 1939; Parents and Children, 1941; Elders and Betters, 1944; Manservant and Maidservant, 1947; Two Worlds and Their Ways, 1949; Darkness and Day, 1951; The Present and the Past, 1953; Mother and Son, 1955 (awarded James Tait Black Memorial Prize, 1956); A Father and His Fate, 1957; A Heritage and its History, 1959; The Mighty and their Fall, 1961; A God and His Gifts, 1963; The Last and the First, 1970; Dolores, 1970 (both posthumous). *Relevant Publication:* I. Compton-Burnett, by Charles Burkhart, 1965. *Address:* 5 Braemar Mansions, Cornwall Gardens, S.W.7. [*Died* 27 *Aug.* 1969.

COMYN, Col. Lewis James, C.M.G. 1918; D.S.O. 1916; K.O.S.B.; *b.* 1878; *s.* of late Andrew Nugent Comyn of Ballinderry, Co. Galway; *m.* 1914, Mary Esther, *d.* of Mr. de Courcey Duff of Riversdale, Co. Dublin; one *s.* one *d.* *Educ.:* Clongowes Wood College; Dublin Univ. Joined the Connaught Rangers, 1899; Lieut. 1900; Capt. 1906; Major, 1915; Bt.Lt.-Col. 1917; Lt.-Col. 1926; Col. 1930; D.A.A.G. 14th Div., Sept. 1914-Oct. 1915; A.A. and Q.M.G. 36th (Ulster) Division, Oct. 1915-Oct. 17; A.A.G. War Office, Oct. 1917 (despatches four times, D.S.O., Bt. Lt.-Col., C.M.G.); retired pay, 1934. *Recreations:* hunting, cricket. *Address:* Spring Cottage, Mallow, Co. Cork, Eire.
[*Died* 17 *March* 1961.

COMYN-PLATT, Sir Thomas; *see* Platt.

COMYNS, Louis, L.R.C.P., L.R.C.S. Ed.; L.R.F.P.S. Glas.; J.P.; Medical Practitioner. Member North-East Metropolitan Regional Hospital Board since 1948; Chairman, Hospital Management Committee (West Ham), Group 9, since 1948; Member West Ham Executive Council, since 1948; Alderman, County Borough West Ham, 1954; Member, Board of Governors, London Hospital, 1960. M.P. (Lab.) Silvertown Division of West Ham, 1945-50. *Address:* 23 Hermit Road, E.16. *T.:* Albert Dock 2028; 14 Hermitage Court, S. Woodford, Essex. *T.:* Wanstead 1301. [*Died* 10 *Feb.* 1962.

COMYNS CARR, Sir Arthur Strettell, Kt., *cr.* 1949; Q.C. 1924; Bencher of Gray's Inn, 1938; Vice-Treasurer of Honourable Society of Gray's Inn, 1951 (Treasurer 1950); *b.* 19 September 1882; *s.* of late J. W. Comyns Carr, dramatist, and late A. L. V. Comyns Carr, novelist; *m.* 1907, Cicely Oriana Raikes (*d.* 1935), *d.* of late R. R. Bromage, three *s.* *Educ.:* Winchester; Trinity Coll., Oxford. Called to Bar, Gray's Inn, 1908; M.P. (L.) East Islington, 1923-24. Chairman, Foreign Compensation Commn., 1950-58. *Publications:* National Insurance (part author), 1912; Escape from the Dole, 1930; Recent Mining Legislation (part author), 1931; Empire and World Currency (part author), 1932; Faraday on Rating (part author), 1934 and 1951. *Address:* 17 Springfield Place, Lansdown, Bath. *Club:* National Liberal.
[*Died* 20 *April* 1965.

CONAN DOYLE, Adrian M(alcolm); author; Trustee of Sir Arthur Conan Doyle Estates; engaged in arranging family archives and biographical records; Chm., Sir Arthur Conan Doyle Foundation; *b.* 19 Nov. 1910; 2nd *s.* of late Sir Arthur Conan Doyle and Lady Conan Doyle (*née* Jean Leckie); *g.s.* of Charles Altamont Doyle, Artist; *m.* 1938, Anna, *d.* of Adolf Gjols Andersen, Copenhagen. *Educ.:* preparatory school; private tutor. Held British dirt track record for cars, 1936. Expedition (zoological) to Cameroons, 1938-39. Expedition (big-game fish) with schooner, Mafia Channel and coast of S. Tanganyika, 1951-52; took Sherlock Holmes Exhibition to America, 1952; made two expedns. on Arab dhow, French Somaliland coast (brought back a 1500 lbs. tiger-shark), also expedn. along coast of the Hadramaut for specimens, 1961, both for the Geneva Museum. *Publications:* The True Conan Doyle, 1945; Heaven Has Claws, 1953; The Exploits of Sherlock Holmes, 1954; Tales of Love and Hate, 1960; Lone Dhow, 1963. Contributions to Cornhill, Life Magazine, etc. *Recreations:* ancient arms and armour, big-game fishing, shooting, motoring, boxing, zoology. *Address:* Château de Lucens, Lucens, Vaud, Switzerland. *Club:* Authors'. [*Died* 3 *June* 1970.

CONGLETON, 7th Baron (*cr.* 1841); **William Jared Parnell;** Bt. 1766; Lt. R.N. (Emergency List); *b.* 18 Aug. 1925; *e. s.* of 6th Baron and Hon. Edith Mary Palmer Howard, M.B.E., 1941 (she *m.* 2nd, 1946, Flight Lieut. Eric Rowland Aldridge, who died 1950), *y. d.* of late R. J. B. Howard and late Lady Strathcona and Mount Royal; *S.* father, 1932. *Educ.:* Eton College. *Heir:* *b.* Hon. Christopher Patrick Parnell [*b.* 11 March 1930; *m.* 1955, Anna Hedvig, *d.* of G. A. Sommerfelt, Röa, Oslo, Norway; two *s.* three *d.*] *Address:* 61 Furzecroft, George Street, W.1; Minstead Lodge, Lyndhurst, Hants. *T.:* Cadnam 2297. [*Died* 12 *Oct.* 1967.

CONNALLY, Tom (Thomas Terry); retired as United States Senator (Senate, 1929; Chairman Foreign Relations Committee; voluntarily retired, Jan. 1953); *b.* McLennan County, Texas, 19 Aug. 1877; *s.* of Jones Connally and Mary E. Terry; *m.* 1904, Louise Clarkson (*d.* 1935): one *s.*; *m.* 1942, Mrs. Lucile Sanderson Sheppard, widow of Senator Morris Sheppard, Texas. *Educ.:* Public Schools; Baylor University; University of Texas Law School. Admitted Texas Bar, 1898; prosecuting attorney for home county and a Representative in State Legislature, Enlisted and served in Spanish-American War and European War, 1914-18. Served on the House Cttee. on Foreign Affairs; member of Inter-parl. Union; Member of Cttee. on Foreign Relations during repealing of Arms Embargo, passing of Lend-Lease Act, declarations of war against Axis nations, and ratification of U.N. Charter by Senate. U.S. Delegate at many conferences and assemblies, including Vice-Chm. of U.S. Deleg. to U.N. Conf. on Internat. Organisation, San Francisco, 1945. Chairman and member of numerous committees. Hon. LL.D. Baylor Univ. and Howard Payne Coll., 1936; member of Phi Delta Theta Fraternity; former Grand Chancellor, Knights of Pythias of Texas; Thirty-third Degree Mason. *Address:* Marlin, Falls County, Texas U.S.A.
[*Died* 28 *Oct.* 1963.

CONNEL, John Arthur, B.Sc.; Vice-Chairman, Unilever Ltd. since 1960; Part-time Director, British Overseas Airways Corporation, since 1960; *b.* 7 Sept. 1903; *s.* of James Wallace Connel and Helen Walker Cuthbert; *m.* 1930, Jennie Jardine McCracken; two *d.* *Educ.:* Merchiston Castle School; Edinburgh University. Mem. of Board of Unilever Ltd., 1954-; Member of Board of N.V., 1954. *Address:* Tangley, West Road, St. George's Hill, Weybridge, Surrey. *T.:* Weybridge 4487. [*Died* 23 *July* 1961.

CONNELL, John; (John Henry Robertson); Author and Journalist; *b.* 10 Aug. 1909; *o. s.* of late T. R. Robertson, M.B., Ch.B. (Edinburgh) and Mary Connell Robertson; *m.* 1946, Ruth (*née* Epstein), LL.B., Barrister-at-law. *Educ.:* Loretto School; Balliol Coll., Oxford. Craigielands Scholar, Elton Exhibitioner, Balliol Coll.; B.A., 1931. Junior Treas., O.U.D.S. Joined staff of The Evening News, 1932; served War of 1939-45, London Scottish (T.A.), 1939; commissioned Royal Artillery, 1940; six years' service at home and overseas (M.E.F., India); Chief Military Press Censor, India, 1944; demobilised as Major, 1945. Leader-writer, The Evening News, London, 1945-59. Co-opted mem. L.C.C. Educn. Cttee., 1949-58; Alderman, St. Pancras Borough Council, 1949; Chm. St. Pancras Public Libraries and Education Cttee., 1949-50-51; Dep. Mayor St. Pancras, 1951-52. Trustee of Loretto School, 1963; Gov. of William Ellis Sch.; F.R.S.L. *Publications:* Lyndesay, 1930; Who Goes Sailing?, 1932; The Fortunate Simpleton, 1934; David Go Back, 1935; Tomorrow We Shall Be Free, 1938; The House by Herod's Gate, 1947; Midstream, 1948; W. E. Henley, 1949 (James Tait Black Memorial Prize, 1949); The Return of Long John Silver, 1949; Time and Chance, 1952; Winston Churchill, The Writer, 1956; The Most Important Country, 1957; The Office, 1958; Death on the Left, 1958; Auchinleck, 1959; Wavell: Scholar and Soldier, 1964; Wavell: Supreme Commander, 1941-43 (posthumous), 1969. *Address:* 7 William Street House, William Street, Lowndes Square, S.W.1. *T.:* Belgravia 3487. *Clubs:* Beefsteak, Oxford and Cambridge University, Special Forces. [*Died* 5 *Oct.* 1965.

CONNELL, Walter Thomas, M.D., F.R.C.P. (C.); Emeritus Professor of Medicine, Queen's University, since 1941; *b.* Spencerville, Ontario, 15 Dec. 1873; *s.* of Martin Connell, Spencerville; *m.* 1900, Florence, *y. d.* of R. M. Ford, Kingston, Ontario; one *s.* one *d.* *Educ.:* Queen's University, Kingston (M.D.); St. Bartholomew's Hospital (M.R.C.S.Eng., and L.R.C.P.). Lecturer on Pathology Queen's University, 1895; Professor of Pathology and Bacteriology, Queen's University, Kingston, Canada, 1896-1920; Bacteriologist, Eastern Dairy School, 1898-1920; Pathologist, General Hospital, Kingston, 1897-1920; Assistant Bacteriologist, Provincial Board of Health of Ontario, 1904-20; Prof. of Medicine, Queen's University, 1920-41; Lt.-Col. C.A.M.C. attached No. 5 Canadian Stationary Hospital at Shorncliffe, and in Egypt, 1915; O.C. Queen's Military Hospital, Kingston, Ontario, 1917-20. *Publications:* Practical Bacteriology, 1913; articles on Pathological, Bacteriological and Medical subjects in various medical journals. *Address:* 11 Arch St., Kingston, Ontario, Canada. *T.:* 548-4992. [*Died* 9 *April* 1964.

CONNELY, Willard, M.A. Oxon.; M.A. Harvard; F.R.S.L.; Director American University Union in London, 1930-46; retired, 1946; Consultant to State Dept., U.S.A., on European Universities, 1944; *b.* Atlantic City, U.S.A., 1888; *y. s.* of George Washington Connely and Anne, *y. d.* of Augustus Willard, M.D., a founder of American Medical Association and Pres New York State Medical Society; *m.* Agnes Lauchlan, actress, *o. c.* of late H. D. Lauchlan, L.R.C.P., London and Edinburgh. *Educ.:* Stevens Institute of Technology; Dartmouth College (B.Sc.); Harvard University; New College, Oxford; 2nd Class Final Honours, School of English Language and Literature. On staff Atlantic City Review, 1904-6; New York Sunday American, 1911-1913; Harper's Weekly, 1913-14; McClure's Magazine, 1913-15; International Film Service, 1915-16; U.S. Navy, 1917-18; Instructor in English, Harvard, 1920-25; Secretary Harvard Classical Club, 1923-24; a founder of the Bryce Club, Oxford, 1927; on staff Sunday Express, 1927-28; Official delegate to Harvard Tercentenary, 1936; Member Committee of: Horatian Society (Vice-Chairman); British-American Schoolboy Scholarship Exchange (English-Speaking Union); Medallist Carnegie Corporation of New York, 1936; founded 1931 (on Carnegie Endowment) Week-End Lectureships to British Universities for American professors on sabbatical leave; instituted, 1932 (on Carnegie Endowment), one-term professorships for American staff at British newer universities; Secretary to Carnegie Corporation International Conference on Examinations, 1931-38; Grantee of Carnegie Foundation for study of scholarships in British schools and universities, 1939; Grantee of American Council of Learned Societies for research on Colonial Americans (1654-1775) in Oxford and Cambridge, 1942; Byron Foundation lecturer, Nottingham Univ., 1936. Lecturer to H.M. Forces on America in the War, 1941-43; Hon. Phi Beta Kappa (Dartmouth Coll., N.H.). *Publications:* articles on aspects of Greek and Roman Literature, 1923-25; Brawny Wycherley, 1930; Sir Richard Steele, 1934; The True Chesterfield, 1939; The Reign of Beau Brummell, 1940; Young George Farquhar, 1949; Count D'Orsay, 1952; Beau Nash, 1955; Adventures in Biography, 1956; Laurence Sterne as Yorick, 1958; Louis Sullivan as He Lived: the Shaping of American Architecture, 1960. Contributor to Chambers's Encyclopædia (new ed.), 1946-1947; to Encyclopaedia Britannica (new ed.), 1962. *Address:* Whitegates, Godalming, Surrey. *T.:* Goldaming 213. *Club:* Athenæum. [*Died* 26 *March* 1967.

CONNOLLY, Air Cdre. Hugh Patrick, C.B. 1963; D.F.C. 1944 and Bar 1945; A.F.C. 1952; A.F.M. 1939; Commandant, Royal Air Force Halton, since 1967; A.D.C. to the Queen since 1967; *b.* 9 March 1915; *s.* of Capt. E. T. Connolly, I.A.; *m.* 1941, Margaret Stevens, Harrow, Middlesex; two *s.* *Educ.:* St. Joseph's Coll., Naini Tal, India; R.A.F. Entered R.A.F. as aircraft apprentice, 1931; Sergt. Pilot, 1937; Commnd. 1940; served with Pathfinder Force of Bomber Comd., 1943-45; Far East Air Force, 1945-47; R.A.F. Staff Coll., 1948; Planning duties, H.Q. Bomber Comd., 1948-1950; Jt. Services Staff Coll., 1950; commanded first Canberra Jet Bomber Wing, R.A.F. Binbrook, 1951-52; Staff duties, H.Q. No. 1 Group, Bomber Comd., 1953-54; Commanded R.A.F. Waddington, 1955-56; attended Imperial Defence Coll., 1957; Director of Air Staff Plans, Far East Air Force, 1958-60; A.O.C. and Comdt., Central Flying School, R.A.F., Little Rissington, 1961-63; Asst. Chief of Staff (Trg.), Combined Mil. Planning Staff, Cento, 1964-1965; Commandant, Officers and Aircrew Selection Centre, R.A.F. Biggin Hill, 1965-1967. *Recreations:* golf, sailing. *Address:* c/o Lloyds Bank, Hitchin, Herts. *Clubs:* Royal Air Force; Pathfinder. [*Died* 11 *Dec.* 1968.

CONNOLLY, Hon. Sir James Daniel, Kt., *cr.* 1920; *b.* Queensland, 2 Dec. 1869; 2nd *s.* of late Denis Connolly, J.P., Elphinstone and Woolowin, Qld; *m.* Catherine Charlotte (*d.* 1948), *d.* of John Edwards, St. Arnaud, Vic.; five *d.* *Educ.:* Warwick Catholic and National Technical Schools. After receiving training as a quantity surveyor and contractor was attracted to Western Australia by the newly discovered Coolgardie goldfields in 1893. First carried out Government contract, Perth; then entrusted with contract for first Government

building Post Office and Goldwardens Court in Coolgardie; engaged in contracting and gold-mining business in Coolgardie and Kalgoorlie Goldfields. M.L.C. for N.E. Province, 1901-14; M.L.A., Perth, 1914-17; Leader Upper House, Colonial Secretary, Minister for Commerce and Labour, Public Health, etc., 1906-12; initiated Public Health and Pure Foods Act; also author State Children Act, for the protection and care of homeless children, copied by other Dominions; the protection of and greatly improved conditions for the aborigines by purchase for their benefit of Cattle Station (Moola Bulla—Meat Plenty) and reservation of six million acres virgin Crown lands in the Kimberley district for their exclusive use; also Government Clinics were established on Bernier and Dorre Islands. Again became member of the Cabinet, 1916-17; resigned to take up position of Agent-General in London for Western Australia, 1917-24; Agent-General for Malta, 1929-32; created Knight of St. Silvester by Pius X., 1912; Commandeur de l'Ordre de la Couronne, Belgium, 1918. *Recreations:* golf, travelling, etc. *Address:* 26 Kensington Court Gardens, W.8. *Clubs:* Australia, The Challoner, Royal Over-Seas League, English-Speaking Union.
[*Died* 12 *Feb.* 1962.

CONNOR, Dame (Annie) Jean, D.B.E., *cr.* 1935; M.D.; Specialist on conservative orthopædics; Consultant in Physical Medicine, Royal Children's Hospital, Melbourne; Protagonist for use of Myxomatosis in Australia, 1933-51, for rabbit control; *b.* 1899; *d.* of John Macnamara; *m.* 1934, Joseph Ivan Connor, M.B., M.S., D.T.M. and H.; two *d.* *Address:* Springfield, 33 Murphy Street, South Yarra, Melbourne, S.E.1, Australia.
[*Died* 13 *Oct.* 1968.

CONNOR, Sir William (Neil), Kt. 1966; Journalist since 1935; *b.* 26 April 1909; *y. s.* of William Henry Connor and Isobella Littlejohn; *m.* 1938, Gwynfil Mair Morgan; two *s.* one *d.* *Educ.:* Glendale School. Advertising copywriter, Arks Publicity and J. Walter Thompson, 1929-35; Columnist (Cassandra), Daily Mirror, 1935-. R.A.C., R.A., British Army Newspapers, 1942-46. *Publications:* The English at War, 1940; Cassandra's Cats, 1960. *Recreations:* travel, old English bracket clocks. *Address:* The Old Rectory, Fingest, Nr. Henley-on-Thames, Oxon. [*Died* 6 *April* 1967.

CONOR, William, O.B.E. 1952; R.H.A.; P.R.U.A.A. since 1957; Member of the National Society of Painters and Sculptors, London; *b.* 7 May 1881. Studied at Belfast, London and Paris; has exhibited at R.A., Paris Salon, Venice, and New York Art Galleries; works acquired by the Belfast Municipal Art Gallery, Dublin Municipal Art Gallery, Manchester and Whitworth Galleries; also Brooklyn Museum, New York; Commissioned by War Artists' Committee at Ministry of Information to do a series of drawings illustrating War Effort in Northern Ireland. M.A., Q.U.B., 1957. *Address:* 107 Salisbury Ave., Belfast, Northern Ireland. *T.:* 76303. *Club:* Chelsea Arts.
[*Died* 5 *Feb.* 1968.

CONSTABLE, Brigadier R. C. J. C.; *see* Chichester-Constable.

CONSTANT, Hayne, C.B. 1958; C.B.E. 1951; F.R.S. 1948; M.A., F.R.Ae.S., M.I.Mech.E.; *b.* 26 September 1904; *s.* of Frederick Charles and Mary Theresa Constant; unmarried. *Educ.:* Queens' Coll., Cambridge. Lecturer, Imperial College of Science, 1934-36; started work on R.A.E. Gas Turbine Project, 1936; Head of Engine Dept., R.A.E., 1941; Head of Research Dept. Power Jets (Research and Devel.), 1944; Dep. Dir., 1946, Dir. 1948-60, Nat. Gas Turbine Estabt.; Scientific Adviser to the Air Min., 1960-64; Chief Scientist (R.A.F.), Ministry of Defence, 1964. Busk Memorial Prize (R.Ae.S.), 1932; Clayton Prize (I.Mech.E.), 1947; Gold Medal (R.Ae.S.), 1963. *Publications:* Gas Turbines and their Problems, 1948; contribs. to technical jls. and Govt. papers. *Recreations:* ski-ing and sailing. *Address:* Ripelhyrst, Kiln Way, Grayshott, Hindhead, Sy. *T.:* Headley Down 3359. *Club:* Athenæum. [*Died* 12 *Jan.* 1968.

CONSTANTINE, Sir George Baxandall, Kt. 1954; Barrister; *b.* 22 June 1902; *s.* of B. Constantine, sometime Ceylon Civil Service; *m.* 1955, M. A. Rahim (*née* Vatter). *Educ.:* Bradford Gram. Sch.; Balliol Coll., Oxford. Career in Civil Service of Pakistan. Formerly Chief Judge, Chief Court of Sind; Judge of High Court of W. Pakistan. *Recreations:* music and ball games. *Address:* c/o Midland Bank, Market Street, Bradford. *Clubs:* Sind (Karachi); Punjab (Lahore).
[*Died* 8 *Sept.* 1969.

CONWAY, Edward Joseph; F.R.S. 1947; D.Sc., M.D.; Director, Unit of Cell Metabolism, University College, Dublin; *b.* 3 July 1894; *s.* of William Francis and Mary McCready Conway; *m.* 1934, Mabel Edith Hughes; four *d.* *Educ.:* Blackrock College and University College, Dublin. Graduated in Physiology and Chemistry, 1916; M.Sc., 1917; graduated in Medicine, 1921; D.Sc. 1927. Asst. in Physiology, University College, Dublin, 1921; worked in Biochemical Inst. of Univ. of Frankfurt, 1928-29 (travelling studentship). Prof. of Biochemistry and Pharmacology, 1932, Prof. of Biochemistry, 1945, U.C., Dublin; re-appointed Prof. of Biochemistry and Pharmacology, 1947-64. Examr. in Biochemistry (Tripos II) to Cambridge University, 1959-62. Mem. Senate, and Chm. Graduates Assoc., National University of Ireland; Mem. Académie Septentrionale, 1958; Mem. Council, Roy. Irish Academy (M.R.I.A. 1939); Mem. Cancer Consultative Council (apptd. by Govt.); Mem. Pontifical Acad. of Sciences, 1961; Pres. Blackrock Coll. Union, 1961; Chm. Council, Dublin Inst. of Advanced Studies (apptd. by Govt.); Mem. Irish Nat. Commn. for Unesco (apptd. by Govt.). *Publications:* Micro-diffusion Analysis, 1939, 5th edn. 1961; Gastric Acid Secretion, 1953; various papers on subjects of biochemical, chemical and physiological interest in Biochemical Jour., Jour. of Physiology, Royal Irish Academy, etc. *Recreation:* fishing. *Address:* Woodbank, Killiney, Co. Dublin, Ireland. *T.:* Dun Laoghaire 803377. [*Died* 29 *Dec.* 1968.

CONWAY, Marmaduke Percy, Mus. Doc. (Dubl.), Mus. Bac. (Oxon.), F.R.C.O., A.R.C.M.; *b.* Walthamstow, Essex, 1885; *s.* of Rev. Samuel Conway, Walthamstow; *m.* 1954, Anne U. Fryer. *Educ.:* Bedford Grammar School; Roy. Coll. of Music, London (organ scholar). Organist, All Saints, Eastbourne, 1908; S. Andrew's, Wells Street, 1917; sub-organist, Wells Cathedral, 1921; Organist and Master of the Choristers, Chichester Cathedral, 1925-31; Organist of Ely Cathedral, 1931-49, retd. 1949. *Publications:* Playing a Church Organ; Church Organ Accompaniment; The Self-Taught Country Organist; Messiah, Organ Score; various articles relating to organ playing and literature in Musical Opinion and The Organ. *Recreations:* travel and chess. *Address:* The Rookery, Hilary Park, Douglas, Isle of Man.
[*Died* 22 *March* 1961.

CONWAY-GORDON, Col. Esme Cosmo William, C.I.E. 1921; Indian Army, retired; *b.* 29 Aug. 1875; *s.* of Col. Charles Vanrenen Conway-Gordon, Indian Army, and Anna Lumsden Roberdeau Conway-Gordon; *m.* May Kathleen Harrington (*d.* 1947); one *s.* one *d.*; *m.* Edith Lilian Sherlock.

Educ.: Charterhouse; Sandhurst. Commissioned, 1895; joined 3rd Bengal Cavalry, 1896; Staff College, 1909-10; Senior Instructor, Cavalry School, Saugor, 1912-14; G.S.O. 2nd Grade, 1st Indian Cavalry Division, B.E.F., Sept. 1914; G.S.O. 2nd Grade, 12th Division, B.E.F.,; 1916; G.S.O. 1st Grade, Poona Division, 1917; G.S.O. 1st Grade, 4th War Division, 1919; G.S.O. 1st Grade, Wazir and Tochi Columns, 1919-20; Commdt., 27th L.C. 1920; Commdt., 1st D.Y.O. Skinner's Horse, 1921; Comdt. Equitation School, Saugor, 1924-27; Subst. Col. 1924; served Tirah, 1897-98 (medal with three clasps); Somaliland, 1903-4 (medal with two clasps); European War, 1914-18 (despatches twice); Afghanistan, 1919 (despatches); Waziristan, 1919-20 (despatches, C.I.E.). *Recreation:* painting. *Address:* 11 Norton Road, Hove, Sussex.

[*Died* 31 *March* 1962.

CONYBEARE, Sir John Josias, K.B.E., *cr.* 1946; M.C.; D.M.; F.R.C.P. (Lond.); Consultant Physician Emeritus to Guy's Hospital; *b.* 13 Dec. 1888; *s.* of late F. C. Conybeare, 64 Banbury Road, Oxford. *Educ.:* Rugby; New College, Oxford; Guy's Hospital. Capt. 4th Batt. Oxfordshire and Buckinghamshire Light Infantry, 1908-16; Captain R.A.M.C. (S.R.) 1917-20; Air Vice-Marshal R.A.F.V.R. 1939-45. Hon. Civil Consultant to R.A.F. Warden of the College, Guy's Hospital, 1923-38; Rockefeller Travelling Fellowship, 1924. *Publications:* Editor of Textbook of Medicine; Manual of Diabetes. *Recreation:* travel. *Address:* 14 St. Thomas's St., S.E.1. *T.:* Hop 0808. *Clubs:* Athenæum, Royal Air Force; Huntercombe Golf (Henley-on-Thames).

[*Died* 6 *Jan.* 1967.

COOCH BEHAR, Lt.-Col. H.H. Maharaja Sir Jagaddipendra Narayan Bhup Bahadur, Maharaja of; K.C.I.E., *cr.* 1945; *b.* 15 Dec. 1915; succeeded, 1922. *Educ.:* Harrow; Trinity Hall, Cambridge. *Address:* Cooch Behar, Bengal, India.

[*Died* 11 *April* 1970.

COODE, Sir Bernard Henry, Kt., *cr.* 1953; C.B. 1949; retired; *b.* 18 Dec. 1887; *s.* of late Rev. Athelstan Coode; unmarried. *Educ.:* Radley College; New College, Oxford. 2nd Class, Honour School of Modern History, 1910. Clerk, House of Commons, 1912; Principal Clerk, House of Commons Public Bill Office, 1943-48; Principal Clerk, Committee Office, House of Commons, 1948-Dec. 1952; reappointed Senior Clerk, Jan. 1953. Served European War, 1914-18, in Army; France, 1915-18. *Publication:* This Sliding on Wood, 1937. *Recreation:* watching cricket. *Clubs:* Oxford and Cambridge; Surrey County Cricket (Kennington Oval). [*Died* 27 *April* 1962.

COOK, Rev. Canon Arthur Malcolm, M.A.; Hon. C.F.; Canon of Lincoln; *b.* 24 July 1883; *s.* of Charles Malcolm and Gertrude Emily Cook; *m.* 1914, Stella Sybil Shaw (*d.* 1949); two *s.* two *d.* *Educ.:* Bedford School; Hertford Coll., Oxford. Asst. Master, King's School, Grantham, 1905-9; Ordained 1908; Vicar of St. Peter in Eastgate, Lincoln, 1925-31; Vicar of Boston, Lincs., 1931-46; Subdean of Lincoln Cathedral, 1946-61. Chairman, Lincoln Civic Trust. Chaplain to H.M. Forces, 1915-16. *Publications:* Boston, Botolphstown; Lincolnshire Links with Australia; Lincolnshire Links with U.S.A. *Address:* 14 Minster Yard, Lincoln. *T.:* Lincoln 23735.

[*Died* 12 *April* 1964.

COOK, Lt.-Col. Sir Thomas Russell Albert Mason, Kt., *cr.* 1937; *b.* 1902; *s.* of Thomas Albert Cook; *m.* 1926, Gweneth Margaret (C.C. Reepham Divn. Norfolk 1931-46, joint master North Norfolk Hunt, 1926-40, D.St.J.). *o. d.* of late Spencer Evan Jones, of Banwell Abbey, Somerset, and of Mrs. Evan Jones, of Burnham Hall, Norfolk; one *s.* three *d.* *Educ.:* Eton; Worcester Coll., Oxford. 5th Bn. Royal Norfolk Regt., 1920-25; Staff Capt., 18th Divn., 1939; G.H.Q., France, 1940; Liaison Officer to Allied Forces, War Office, 1941-46. Master, North Norfolk Hunt, 1923-1940; Founder Chairman Anglo-Brazilian Society, 1943-49; Chairman Anglo-Egyptian Society and Luxembourg Society, also British Mexican Society, 1945-48; Chm. North Norfolk Conservative and Liberal Assoc., 1949-51; County Comr. St. John Ambulance Brigade, 1935-68; Chairman St John Council for Norfolk, 1946-69. Contested (C.) North Norfolk, 1924, 1929, (bye-election 1930), and 1945; M.P. (C.) Norfolk (Northern Div.), 1931-45; J.P. 1934 (Chm., Fakenham Bench, 1954); C.C. (Holt Div.), Norfolk, 1928-46. Proprietor The Norfolk Chronicle, 1935-55. Master, Worshipful Company of Glaziers, 1960. K.St.J.; Gr. Cross, St. Sava (Yugoslavia); Gr. Officer, Adolph Nassau and Gr. Officer, Order of Merit (Luxembourg); also has orders of: Southern Cross (Brazil); White Lion (Czechoslovakia); King Charles IV (Czechoslovakia); Oaken Crown (Luxembourg); Nile (Egypt); Christ (Portugal); King George I (Greece); Aztec Eagle (Mexico); Orange Nassau (Neth.); St. Olav (Norway); Civic Cross (Belgium); Medal of Military Merit (Czechoslovakia); Cross of Social Merit (France). *Address:* Sennowe Park, Guist, Norfolk. *T.:* Gt. Ryburgh 202. *Clubs:* Carlton; Norfolk (Norwich).

[*Died* 12 *Aug.* 1970.

COOKE, Amos John, C.M.G. 1953; General Manager, Buenos Aires Grain Future Market, since 1917; *b.* 24 Feb. 1885; *s.* of George Stanley and Caroline Louisa Cooke; *m.* 1912, Amy Dawson (*d.* 1937); *m.* 1942, Hilda Mabel Brown. Apprenticed to Grain Trade until 1908; Organiser and Asst. Man., Buenos Aires Grain Future Market, 1908-15; Tech. Adviser and Chief of Sales to Argentine Farm Bd., 1933-44 (Gold Plaque from Argentine Govt. for services rendered); Hon. Chm. Brit. Food Mission, Argentina, 1946-53. Chm. Telefonos Automaticos y Productos Electricos S.A., 1950. *Recreations:* rowing, tennis, golf, country pursuits. *Address:* Florida 1065, Buenos Aires, Argentina. *Clubs:* Canning; Tigre Boat, San Andres Golf, Jockey, English (Argentine).

[*Died* 13 *June* 1961.

COOKE, Brian K.; *see* Kennedy-Cooke.

COOKE, Rev. Leslie Edward, D.D.; LL.D.; Associate General Secretary of the World Council of Churches, and Director of the Division of Inter-Church Aid, Refugee and World Service, since 1955; *b.* 22 May 1908; *m.* 1936, Gladys Evelyn Burrows; no *c.* *Educ.:* Municipal Secondary School, Brighton; Lancashire Independent College, Manchester University. B.A. 1930. B.D. 1933 (Manchester); Hon. D.D. (Chicago Theol. Seminary) 1949; Hon. D.D. (Vict., Toronto) 1950; Hon. LL.D. (Mount Allison) 1954; Fondren Lecturer, Southern Methodist University, Dallas, Texas, 1959. Minister, Gatley Congregational Church, 1933-38; Minister, Warwick Road Congregational Church, Coventry, 1938-48; Associate Editor, Congregational Quarterly, 1946-1948; Secretary, Congregational Union of England and Wales, 1948-55. *Publications:* Faith Stakes a Claim; Token of our Inheritance; The Prophetic Ministry; Upon This Rock; The Church is There; Above Every Name. Contributions to Ecumenical Review, Holborn Review, Congregational Quarterly, etc. *Recreations:* golf, drama. *Address:* c/o World Council of Churches, 150 Route de Ferney, Geneva 20, Switzerland. *T.:* Geneva 33.34.00. *Club:* Athenæum.

[*Died* 22 *Feb.* 1967.

COOKE, Roger Gresham, C.B.E. 1953; M.P. (C.) Twickenham since Jan. 1955; Formerly Director, Society of Motor Manufacturers and Traders, and Joint Secretary National Advisory Council, Motor Manufacturing Industry; Dir., Kerry Group Ltd. since 1955; *b.* 26 Jan. 1907; *s.* of Arthur Cooke, F.R.C.S., of Cambridge; *m.* 1934, Anne, J.P., *d.* of late J. R. H. Pinckney, C.B.E.; two *s.* two *d.* *Educ.:* Winchester Coll.; New Coll., Oxf.; Trinity Coll., Camb. Barrister-at-Law, Inner Temple, 1930; practised until 1935. Secretary British Road Federation, 1935-38; Hon. Secretary German Road Delegation, 1937; Secretary United Steel Cos. Ltd., Sheffield, 1938-46; Major, Co. Comdr. H.G., 1940-44; Chairman Wentworth(Yorks.)Parliamentary Div. Cons. Assoc., 1945-46; Member: Council of Sheffield Univ., 1943-46; Grand Council F.B.I. 1946-55; Board of Trade Exhibition Advisory Cttee., 1947-55; Chm., Highways Cttee., British Road Federation, 1948-55. Parliamentary Private Secretary to Economic Secretary to the Treasury, 1957-58. Jt. Secretary Conservative Parliamentary Transport Committee, 1955-58; Member, Estimates Cttee.; Member, Council of Europe and Western European Union Assembly, 1962-64. Founder Council Mem., Inst. of Advanced Motorists; Deputy Chairman, Wider Share Ownership Council, 1950-68. President of the River Thames Society. President, Institute of Road Transport Engineers, 1962-64. Donor of Gresham Cooke Prize to Automobile Division, I.Mech.E. Vice-Pres., Royal Institution. Chm. Standing Conf., on Nat. Qualification and Title. *Publications:* (consulting editor) Law of Restrictive Trade Practices; articles on motor industry and roads; various. *Recreations:* golf, sailing (represented Oxford Univ. 1927 and 1928). *Address:* Turgis Court, Stratfield Turgis, Basingstoke, Hants. *T.:* Turgis Green 351; Flat 36, 35 Buckingham Gate, S.W.1. *T.:* Victoria 0073; The Friary, Blackeney, Norfolk. *T.:* Cley 320. *Clubs:* Calton, Royal Automobile; Oxford and Cambridge Sailing Society. [*Died* 22 *Feb.* 1970.

COOKE, William Charles Cyril, M.A. Cantab.; Headmaster, Northampton School, 1921-44; *b.* 26 March 1881; *s.* of late Rev. W. C. Cooke, Histon, Cambs. *Educ.:* King Edward's School, Birmingham; Queens' College, Cambridge. 2nd Class Classical Tripos, 1903 (Camb. Univ. Athletics, 1903); Classical master King's School, Peterborough, 1903; Caldy Grange Grammar School, 1908; Northampton School, 1910-21; 4th Bn. Northants Regt. 1915-19; Member H.M.C., I.A.H.M. *Publications:* occasional articles and verses. *Recreations:* walking and the Education Act, 1944. *Address:* 19 Abington Grove, Northampton. *T.:* 54071-1. [*Died* 7 *Feb.* 1966.

COOKE, Sir William Henry Charles Wemyss, 10th Bt., *cr.* 1661; D.L.; *b.* 21 June 1872; *S.* father, 1894; *m.* 1st, 1902, Lady Mildred Adelaide Cecilia Denison (who obtained a divorce, 1924) *y. d.* of 1st Earl of Londesborough; one *s.* (and *er. s.* decd.); 2nd, 1927, Margaret (*d.* 1964), *d.* of late Richard Ross; one *d.* Served Imp. Yeo., 1900-1901, and 8th Service Bn. Buffs, 1914-16. Owns about 5000 acres. *Recreations:* hunting and racing. *Heir: s.* Major Charles Arthur John Cooke [*b.* 12 Nov. 1905; *m.* 1932, Diana, *o. d.* of late Maj.-Gen. Sir Edward Maxwell Perceval, K.C.B., D.S.O.; one *s.* one *d.*]. *Address:* Wyld Court, Hampstead, Norris, Newbury, Berks. *Clubs:* Boodle's; Yorkshire (York). [*Died* 11 *June* 1964.

COOKMAN, Anthony Victor; Principal Dramatic Critic of The Times since 1939; *b.* 12 May 1894; *m.* Eva Murphy (*d.* 1959); three *s.* Joined editorial staff of the Manchester Guardian, 1919, acted as special correspondent in Ireland and elsewhere; joined editorial staff of The Times, 1925; assistant dramatic critic of The Times, 1928-29. *Recreations:* golf, walking. *Address:* 7A Ranelagh Gdns., S.W.6. *T.:* Renown 1707. *Club:* Garrick. [*Died* 29 *April* 1962.

COOKSON, Captain Claude Edward, C.M.G. 1932; retired Colonial official; *b.* 1879; 3rd *s.* of late Dr. Samuel Cookson, Stafford; *m.* 1st, 1922, Margaret Ellen, *d.* of Charles Lowe, Sugnall Hall, Staffs. (who obtained a divorce, 1929); one *d.*; 2nd, 1931, Lillian Sybil, *d.* of U. N. Holborow, Trowbridge; two *s.* one *d.* *Educ.:* Eton (King's Scholar). Joined Bedfordshire Regt., 1899; Captain, 1908; served in India, Aden and Gibraltar, 1899-1910; Assistant-Commissioner, Gold Coast Police, 1911-15; Assistant Colonial Sec. Gold Coast, 1915-20; served with Gold Coast Regt., as temporary Major in Togoland, 1917; Inspector-General of Prisons, Gold Coast, 1920-26; Called to Bar, 1921; Senior Asst. Colonial Secretary, Sierra Leone, 1926-30; Colonial Sec., Sierra Leone, 1930-34. Acting Governor, Sierra Leone, Dec. 1930-July 1931, and June-Dec. 1933. *Publications:* The Key to National Unity, 1938; A Heretic's Answer to Communism, 1953; articles in United Empire, 1912, Chambers's Journal, 1913, National Review, 1936, West African Review, 1935-37, Eastern World, 1956. *Address:* Trelawny's Cottages, Sompting, Lancing, Sussex. [*Died* 11 *March* 1963.

COOMBER, John Edward, M.A., LL.B. (Cantab.); Clerk to the Clothworkers' Company since 1950; *b.* 29 March 1901; *o. c.* of late William George Coomber and Arabella (*née* Berryman); *m.* 1st, 1930, Ethel (*d.* 1952), *d.* of late Charles Bray; one *d.*; 2nd, 1962, Dorothy Ann Fairhead, *d.* of late Arthur Oxford Hayward. *Educ.:* Highgate School; Magdalene College, Cambridge. Solicitor, 1926; Asst. Clerk to the Clothworkers Company, 1933-50. C.St.J. 1962 (O.St.J. 1956). *Recreation:* cricket. *Address:* 52 Lanchester Road, Highgate, N.6. *T.:* Tudor 5417. [*Died* 13 *April* 1963.

COOMBS, William Harry, C.B.E. 1947; Hon. Capt. R.N.R.: retd. as President Officers (Merchant Navy) Federation, 1958; C.C. West Suffolk since 1958; *b.* 15 July 1893; *yr. s.* of late John Coombs; *m.* 1936, Irene Helen, *e. d.* of Philip Vidal; no *c.* *Educ.:* Cadet Ship H.M.S. Conway. Master Mariner, Barrister at Law; called to the bar, Inner Temple, 1932. Served in Hooghli River Survey, 1909-13. Served European War, 1914-18, in Merchant Navy and R.N.R. as Lieut. After further service in Merchant Navy appointed Asst. Cartographer to Chinese Maritime Customs, 1920-21; originated Navigators Indemnity and founded Navigators and General Insurance Co., 1921; applied himself to reform and betterment of conditions of Shipmasters and Officers in Br. Merchant Navy, and in collaboration with late Adm. Philip Nelson-Ward, C.V.O., founded Officers (M.N.) Federation, 1928. Member of U.K. Delegations to: Internat. Maritime Confs., Geneva 1936, Copenhagen 1945, Seattle 1946; 2nd Internat. Conf. on Radio Aids to Navigation, N.Y., 1947; del. Internat. Conf. on Safety of Life at Sea, London, 1948. Pres., Internat. Mercantile Marine Officers Assoc., 1940-48; Younger Brother of Trinity House, 1948; Mem. National Maritime Board, Min. of Transp. Merchant Shipbuilding Adv. Council; Chm. Merchant Navy Officers Pension Fund. 1948-58; President: Navigators and General Insurance Co. Ltd.; Army, Navy and Gen. Assurance Assoc. Ltd.; Member of Court of the Hon. Co. of Master Mariners, and London Representative; Hon. Life Mem.: Soc. of Master Mariners (S. Africa); Soc. of Master Mariners (N.Z.); Trustee, Nat. Maritime Museum, 1959-67. Council of the Institute of Navigation (F.I.N., 1952), and of Inst. of Naval Architects; Chm. Transport Users Consultative Cttee. (East Anglia), 1951-63; Member: Worshipful Company of Shipwrights, 1951; Baltic & Mercantile Shipping Exchange, 1960; Member Governors' Boards of: H.M.S. Conway, Southampton University Nautical College, and "Cutty Sark" Society. *Publication:* The Nation's Key Men, 1925. *Recreations:* yachting, farming. *Address:* Reeves Hall, Hepworth, Diss, Norfolk. *T.:* Stanton (Suffolk) 217. *Clubs:* Royal Thames Yacht, City Livery Yacht (Vice-Commodore), Royal Automobile, Pilgrims; Lloyd's Yacht. [*Died* 23 *June* 1969.

COOMBS, Rev. Canon William Joseph Mundy, M.A.; Canon Emeritus of York Minster, 1957; Canon of Holme in York Minster, 1931; *b.* 16 Sept. 1871; *s.* of Joseph Coombs, The Firs, Radstock, Somerset; *m.* Elise Innes Hopkins (*d.* 1945). *Educ.:* privately; Downing College, Cambridge. Deacon, 1894; Priest, 1895; Assistant Curate of Norton, Stockton-on-Tees, 1894-1902; Whitby, 1902-7; Vicar of Norton juxta Malton, 1907-16; Sowerby, 1918-24; Surrogate since 1908; Rector of Holy Trinity, Goodramgate with St. Maurice, York, 1924-32; Rural Dean of York, 1931-1932; Vicar of Sutton-on-the-Forest, York, 1932-45; Rural Dean of Easingwold, 1936. *Address:* 8 Bradford Road, Winsley, Bradford-on-Avon, Wilts. [*Died* 4 *April* 1966.

COOPER, Rt. Rev. Alfred Cecil, C.B.E. 1956; Bishop in Korea, 1931-54; *s.* of Charles Philip Cooper, Civil Servant, Bombay, and Beatrice Maud Partridge. *Educ.:* Bradfield College; Christ's College, Cambridge, Hist. Trip. Pt. I, 3rd cl., Pt. II, 2nd cl., B.A. 1904, M.A. 1908; Cuddesdon Theological College. Curate St. Oswald's, West Hartlepool, 1905-1908; Korean Mission, 1908; had to leave diocese temp., 1941, owing to political situation; returned to Korea, 1946. Interned in North Korea by the Communists, 1950-April 1953; returned to Korea, Oct. 1953; resigned Dec. 1954; Chaplain to S.L.G., Burwash, 1955-61. *Address:* Homes of St. Barnabas, Dormans, Lingfield, Surrey. [*Died* 17 *Dec.* 1964.

COOPER, Sir Ernest Herbert, Kt., 1944; Director, Gillette Industries Limited; *b.* Clinton, Ont., Canada, 10 June 1877; *m.* 1st, 1903 (wife *d.* 1929); one *d.*; 2nd, 1936, Audrey Morten Bentley. *Educ.:* Toronto Univ. (graduated 1900). Came to England to reside, 1908; served in Canadian Exped. Force, European War, 1916-19, retired with rank of Capt. In Min. of Aircraft Production, 1940-41; Industrial Adviser to Govt. of Northern Ireland, 1941-43; Director of Information Services in London for the Govt. of Northern Ireland, 1943-46. *Address:* 66 Kingston House, Princes Gate, S.W.7. *Club:* Junior Carlton. [*Died* 7 *Sept.* 1962.

COOPER, Gary (Frank James); film actor; *b.* Helena, Montana, 7 May 1901; *s.* of Charles Henry and Alice Louise Cooper; *m.* 1933, Veronica Balfe, stage name Sandra Shaw; one *d.* *Educ.:* Boseman High School; Helena Wesleyan College; Grinnell College. Newspaper cartoonist, 1924; advertising salesman, Los Angeles; entered films and has taken leading parts in Farewell to Arms, Design for Living, Lives of a Bengal Lancer, Peter Ibbetson, Mr. Deeds goes to Town, The Adventures of Marco Polo, Bluebeard's Eighth Wife, Sergeant York, Meet John Doe, The Westerner, Ball of Fire, Casanova Brown, Along Came Jones, For Whom the Bell Tolls, Saratoga Trunk, Cloak and Dagger, Unconquered, Good Sam, The Fountainhead, The Bright Leaf, You're in the Navy Now, Dallas, Distant Drums, High Noon, Springfield Rifle, Return to Paradise, Blowing Wild, Garden of Evil, One Man Mutiny, Vera Cruz, The Court-Martial of Billy Mitchell, Friendly Persuasion, Love in the Afternoon, Man of the West, The Hanging Tree, They Came to Cordura, The Wreck of the Mary Deare; The Naked Edge. *Address:* Hollywood, Calif. [*Died* 13 *May* 1961.

COOPER, Capt. Sir George James Robertson, 2nd Bt., *cr.* 1905; *b.* 22 July 1890; *e. s.* of Sir George Alexander Cooper, 1st Bt., and Mary Emma, C.B.E. 1920 (*d.* 1948), *d.* of George S. Smith of Evanston, Illinois, U.S.A.; *S.* father 1940; *m.* 1923, Hon. Isolde Frances Borthwick (*d.* 1953), *d.* of 17th Baron Borthwick and Susanna, Duchess of Grafton. *Educ.:* Eton; Balliol Coll., Oxford. Gazetted to Royal Scots Greys, 1911; served European War, 1914-18 (despatches). J.P., D.L.; High Sheriff of Hampshire, 1937. *Recreations:* shooting, golf. *Address:* Merdon Manor, Hursley, Winchester. *T.A.:* Merdon Hursley. *T.:* Hursley 215. *Clubs:* Army and Navy; New (Edinburgh). [*Died* 5 *Jan.* 1961 (*ext.*).

COOPER, Giles Stannus, O.B.E. 1960; dramatist; *b.* Carrickmines, Co. Dublin, 9 Aug. 1918; *s.* of Comdr. G. E. Cooper, R.N., and Winifred Cooper (*née* Warren); *m.* 1947, Gwyneth Mary, *d.* of Rev. James A. Lewis, Canon of Llandaff; two *s.* *Educ.:* Lancing; Grenoble; Webber-Douglas School of Drama. Served War, 1939-46; Actor, 1946-52; Asst. Script Editor, B.B.C., Television, 1953; Assistant Script Editor, Associated Rediffusion, 1955. Working as a writer, 1955-; Guild of Television Producers Script Award, 1961. *Publications:* plays include: *theatre:* Never Get Out! 1950; Everything in the Garden, 1962; Out of the Crocodile, 1963; The Spies are Singing, 1966; Happy Family, 1966; *radio:* Mathry Beacon, 1956; Unman, Wittering and Zigo, 1958; *television:* The Lonesome Road, 1962; Carried by Storm, 1964; The Long House, 1965. Has also made numerous adaptations. *Recreation:* writing plays. *Address:* Oatscroft, Heyshott, Midhurst, Sussex. *Club:* Garrick. [*Died* 2 *Dec.* 1966.

COOPER, Sir Henry, Kt., *cr.* 1943; Member Chamber of Coal Traders since 1936 (Chm. 1936-50); Member Nat. Council of Coal Traders since 1934 (Chm. 1934-53); Member Merchants' Consultative Cttee. since 1941 (Chm., 1941-50); *b.* 1873; *s.* of Henry Cooper, Southwark; *m.* 1898, Jane (*d.* 1953), *d.* of William Dobson, Camberwell; one *d.* *Educ.:* Wilsons Grammar School. Formerly Mem. Industrial Coal Consumers Council, and Dir. Wm. Cory & Son, Ltd. (joined 1888). *Address:* 26 Flodden Road, S.E.5. *T.:* Brixton 5840. [*Died* 2 *March* 1962.

COOPER, Rev. Canon James Sidmouth; Canon Emeritus of Leicester Cathedral since 1958; resigned as Canon Residentiary of Leicester Cathedral (1945-58) and Master of Wyggeston Hospital, Leicester (1937-58); *b.* 2 Nov. 1869; *m.* 1898, Elizabeth Adeline Wood; one *s.* two *d.* *Educ.:* Kingswood School, Bath; Manchester University. *Recreations:* cricket and golf. *Address:* 39 Westminster Road, Leicester. *T.:* 76941. [*Died* 2 *July* 1961.

COOPER, Sir Patrick Ashley, Kt., *cr.* 1944; M.A. (Cantab.), LL.B. (Aberdeen); Director of Aron Electricity Meter Ltd. and other companies; a Lieut. and a Freeman of the City of London; *b.* Aberdeen, 18 Nov. 1887; *e. s.* of late Patrick Cooper and Mary, 2nd *d.* of John Cook; *m.* Kathleen, 2nd *d.* of James Spickett; one *s.* two *d.* *Educ.:* Fettes College; Trinity Hall, Cambridge; Aberdeen Univ. Hon. Fellow, Trinity Hall, Cambridge, 1950. Studied law; recruited and trained first section A.F.A. Cambridge O.T.C.,

1907; served European War, R.F.A. (wounded, despatches twice, Bt.Major); Asst. Dep. Director-Gen. Trench Warfare and Asst. Controller Gun Ammunition; engaged in financial and industrial reorganisation from 1919; Governor Guy's Hosp., 1926-53; Governor, Hudson's Bay Company, 1931-52; retired from the Bank of England, 1955, after serving for 23 years as a Director; Vice-Chm. and Chm. of Northern Assurance Co., 1936 1952; Member of Nat. Econ. Cttee., 1931; Mem. Bd. of Trade Advisory Cttee., 1929-32; Member Air Ministry Advisory Committee, 1936; Member of Rhodesia-Nyasaland Royal Commission, 1938; Trustee of Public Debt of the Federation of Rhodesia and Nyasaland and of Southern Rhodesia; Mem. of Supply Council and Director-General of Finance and Contracts, Ministry of Supply, 1939-42; Member London Passenger Transport Board, 1933-47; Ministry of Labour Appeals Tribunal, Further Education and Training Scheme, 1945. Member, Pilgrims of Great Britain; Director, Foundation for the Study of Cycles (U.S.A.). High Sheriff of County of London, 1944 and 1957; of Hertfordshire for 1946-47; Lord of the Manor of Hexton. *Recreations:* shooting, riding. *Address:* Hexton Manor, Hertfordshire. *T.:* Hexton 204. *Club:* Brooks's. [*Died* 22 *March* 1961.

COOPER, Robert William, O.B.E. 1919; M.C.; J.P.; past Dir. Ferranti, Ltd.; past Chm. British Aluminium Co. Ltd.; *b.* 6 Mar. 1877; *s.* of late Robert Cooper, J.P., Bexley; *m.* 1904, Violet (*d.* 1950), *e. d.* of late Maj.-Gen. H. B. Hayward; one *s.* *Educ.:* Cheltenham. D.A.Q.M.G. 1914-18. Croix de Guerre, with Silver Star, 1916; Order of Commander of St. Olav (Norway), 1933. *Recreation:* shooting. *Address:* Wood Hill House, Warninglid, nr. Haywards Heath, Sussex. *T.A.:* Warninglid 284.
[*Died* 21 *Dec.* 1970.

COOPER, William Edward Deck, C.I.E, 1936; *b.* Knodishall Hall, nr. Saxmundham, Suffolk, 3 Nov. 1877; *e. s.* of J. Eggar Cooper; *m.* 1911, Winifred Kathleen McWha; two *s.* one *d.* *Educ.:* Clifton College. Engineer; Tea Planter, 1901; Member Legislative Council Assam, 1927; Manager Eastern Cachar Tea Co.; Secretary Surma Valley Branch Indian Tea Association, 1917; occasionally leader of the planting group; retired, 1939. *Recreations:* all forms of sport, fishing and shooting for preference. *Address:* Field End, Leiston, Suffolk. *Club:* Royal Commonwealth Society.
[*Died* 15 *Jan.* 1962.

COOPER, Sir William Herbert, 3rd Bt., *cr.* 1905; J.P.; First Honorary President, Cooper McDougall and Robertson Ltd. since 1963 (Chm. 1945-62); Chairman, Ashmole Investment Trust, 1946-68; *b.* 7 March 1901; *e. s.* of Sir Richard Ashmole Cooper, 2nd Bart., and Alice E. (*d.* 1963), *d.* of Rev. E. Priestland, Spondon; *S.* father, 1946; *m.* 1948, Mrs. Eileen Dolores Patricia George, *d.* of late G. P. Hayes of Dunloe Castle, County Kerry. *Educ.:* Wellington; Trinity College, Cambridge. Joint-Master Hertfordshire Hunt, 1927-39; joined Royal Observer Corps, 1939; R.A.F.V.R., India, 1940-45 (Burma Star). President Royal Smithfield Club, 1964. High Sheriff of Hertfordshire, 1956. J.P. (Dacorum Division) County Hertford, 1957. *Recreations:* foxhunting, fishing, gardening. *Heir:* *b.* Francis Ashmole Cooper, Ph.D. [*b.* 9 Aug. 1905; *m.* 1933, Dorothy, *d.* of late Emile Deen; one *s.* three *d.*]. *Address:* Shenstone, Berkhamsted, Herts. *T.:* Berkhamsted 3067. *Club:* Carlton. [*Died* 8 *June* 1970.

COOTE, Rt. Rev. Mgr. Canon George; Rector of Church of Our Lady of Dolours, Hendon, since 1937; *b.* London, 1881. *Educ.:* St John's, Wonersh. Priest, 1905; served parishes of Deptford, Folkestone, Mortlake, 1905-12; transferred to Westminster and became second Private Secretary to Cardinal Bourne, 1912; Principal Private Secretary to Cardinal Bourne, 1926-35; made Privy Chamberlain by Pope Benedict XV., 1920; Canon of Westminster Cathedral, 1928; Domestic Prelate to the Pope, 1933; Knight Commander of Holy Sepulchre, 1924; Editor of Westminster Cathedral Chronicle, 1918-28; Westminster Diocesan Treasurer, 1935-36; Editor of the Catholic Directory, 1927-37. *Address:* 4 Egerton Gardens, Hendon, N.W.4.
[*Died* 18 *April* 1961.

COPE, Sir Anthony (Mohun Leckonby), 15th Bt., *cr.* 1611; *b.* 15 July 1927; *s.* of Capt. Sir Denzil Cope, 14th Bt., and Edna (she *m.* 2nd, 1951, Sir Geoffrey Peto, K.B.E., who *d.* 1956), *d.* of late Edward B. Hilton, Paris and New York; *S.* father, 1940; *m.* 1956, Angela Rose Elizabeth, *yr. d.* of James A. S. Wright, A F.C., F.D.S., R.C.S. Eng., London; one adopted *d.* *Educ.:* Ampleforth College, Yorks; Christ Church, Oxford. Served Rifle Brigade. *Heir:* *u.* Mordaunt Leckonby Cope, M.C. [*b.* 12 Feb. 1878; *m.* 1st, 1917, Frances Muriel (*d.* 1935), *d.* of late A. E. W. Darby, J.P., D.L., Adcote, Shrewsbury; 2nd, 1936, Eveline, *d.* of late Alfred Bishop, Gloucester]. *Address:* Doulting Manor, Shepton Mallet, Somerset. [*Died* 13 *May* 1966.

COPE, Brig.-General Sir Thomas George, 2nd Bart., *cr.* 1918; C.M.G. 1919; D.S.O. 1917; *b.* 1884; *e. s.* of 1st Bart. and Alice Kate (*d.* 1916), *d.* of George Walker, Walthamstow; *S.* father, 1924; *m.* 1923, Comtesse d'Abbans. *Educ.:* Eton; Trinity College, Cambridge. Commission in R. Fusiliers, 1906; served in India, 1906-12; Adjutant, 8th Batt. Royal Fusiliers on its formation at outbreak of war, Aug. 1914; Capt. November 1914; proceeded to France, May 1915; 2nd in command, 8th Batt. Royal Fusiliers, June 1915; wounded, March 1916; promoted Temp. Lieut. Colonel, April 1916, to command 6th Batt. The Buffs; wounded, Oct. 1916; bar to D.S.O. Jan. 1917; Temp. Brig.-Gen. June 1917; Bt. Lt.-Col. Jan. 1918; Lt.-Col. 1929; commanded 2nd Batt. Seaforth Highlanders, 1929-30; retired pay, 1930. *Recreations:* hunting, shooting. *Heir:* none. *Address:* Osbaston Hall, Nuneaton. *Club:* Army and Navy. [*Died* 23 *Aug.* 1966 (*ext.*).

COPELAND, Edwin Bingham, Ph.D.; LL.D.; retd. as Research Associate, University of California, Berkeley; *b.* Monroe, Wis., 30 Sept. 1873; *s.* of Prof. Herbert E. and Alice Bingham Copeland; *m.* 1900, Ethel Tilden Faulkner (*d.* 1953); three *s.* two *d.* *Educ.:* Universities of Wisconsin, Stanford, Chicago, Leipzig, and Halle, Taught botany in Univ. of Indiana, West Virginia Univ., and Stanford, 1897-1903; botanical work in Phillippines, 1903; Professor of Plant Physiology, and Dean, College of Agriculture, University of the Philippines, 1909-17; in charge of herbarium, University of California, 1928-32; Technical Adviser (Agriculture), botanist in charge of Economic Garden, Philippines Govt., 1932-1935. City Commons, Berkeley, Cal., Botanical Soc. (Pres. 1945). *Publications:* Elements of Philippine Agriculture, 1908; The Coconut, 1914; Rice, 1924; Natural Conduct, 1928; Fiji Ferns, 1929; Genera Filicum, 1947; Grammitis, 1951; Philippine Ferns, 1954; more than 150 papers, chiefly on plant physiology, ferns, and tropical agriculture. *Recreations:* mountaineering and collecting ferns. *Address:* 2727 Pacific Ave., San Francisco 15, California, U.S.A.; Butte Meadows, Cal., U.S.A.
[*Died* 15 *March* 1964.

COPELAND, Mrs. Ronald (Ida), F.R.S.A., Silver Medallist, 1934; *d.* of late C. Fenzi and late Mrs. Leonard Cunliffe; *g.d.* of late Sir Douglas

Galton, K.C.B.; *m.* 1915, R. Ronald J. Copeland, C.B.E. (*d.* 1958); one *s.* (and one *s.* decd.). Served on Internat. Council Girl Guides, 1920-28 and 1940-; Division Commissioner for N.W. Staffs. Division Girl Guides from 1918; Chairman of Stoke Division Women's Unionist Association, 1920; M.P. (U.) Stoke Division of Stoke-on-Trent, 1931-35; Chm. of Staffordshire Anglo-Polish Soc. 1943-; Pres. of Staffordshire Allotment Holders Assoc., 1948-; Pres. of Women's Advisory Council, Truro Div., 1955. Sister of Order of St. John of Jerusalem, 1949. Polish Gold Cross of Merit, 1952. *Recreations:* languages, travel, pottery, small boat sailing. *Address:* Trelissick, Feock, Truro. *Clubs:* Forum, Royal Aero. (Assoc. Mem.). [*Died* 29 *June* 1964.

COPEMAN, Constance Gertrude, A.R.E. 1895; *b.* Liverpool; *d.* of C. R. Copeman, solicitor; unmarried. *Educ.:* private schools, Liverpool and London. Studied Art under John Finnie, R.E., at the School of Art, Liverpool; Silver Medallist; 1st special Queen's Prize for Figure Composition, National Competition, 1892; Member of the Liverpool Academy and an exhibitor at the Royal Academy and provincial galleries; pictures in the permanent collections at Liverpool and Preston; Figure painter chiefly, in oil and pastel; Toy Designer. *Address:* 158 Upper Parliament Street, Liverpool 8. [*Deceased.*

COPEMAN, Vice-Adm. Sir Nicholas (Alfred), K.B.E. 1961; C.B. 1959; D.S.C. 1940; *b.* 28 Feb. 1906; *s.* of Dr. A. H. Copeman, M.D., D.L. City of London; *m.* 1933, Violet Lilian King; two *s.* *Educ.:* Royal Naval Colleges, Osborne and Dartmouth. Specialised in Torpedoes, 1932; served War of 1939-45 in H.M.S. Southampton, Warspite, Royalist and with Admiralty (Bath); Comdr. 1942; H.M.S. Victorious, 1946-47; Captain, 1947; Admiralty, London, 1948-49; Captain, Minesweeping, Mediterranean and in comd. 2nd Minesweeping Flotilla, 1950-51; Admiralty Interview Board, 1952; in comd. H.M.S. Vernon, 1953-54; in comd. 4th Destroyer Squadron, 1955-56; Rear-Adm. 1956; Vice-Controller of the Navy, Admiralty, Bath, 1956-58; Vice-Adm. 1960; a Lord Commissioner of the Admiralty, Fourth Sea Lord, and Vice-Controller, 1958-60; C.-in-C., S. Atlantic and S. America, 1960-63; retired list, 1963; Director of Civil Defence, North-Western Region (Manchester), 1963-66; Comdt., Civil Defence Staff Coll., 1966-68; Dir. of Administration, Civil Service Dept., Sunningdale Park, 1969; retd. 1969. A.M.I.E.E. 1948; F.I.C.D. Order of Merit (Chile), 1965. *Recreations:* golf and fishing. *Address:* New Mile Corner, Winkfield Road, Ascot, Berks. [*Died* 21 *Nov.* 1969.

COPEMAN, William Sydney Charles, C.B.E. 1965 (O.B.E. 1945); T.D.; J.P. (Co. London); M.A., M.D., F.R.C.P.; Emeritus Physician, Middlesex and West London Hospitals, and Hospital of St. John and St. Elizabeth; Pres., Arthritis and Rheumatism Council; Chairman: Kennedy Research Institute; Faculty of History of Medicine, Society of Apothecaries; *b.* 29 July 1900; *o. s.* of late Dr. S. Monckton Copeman, F.R.S., M.D., F.R.C.P., and Ethel, *d.* of Sir (Thomas) William Boord, Bart., M.P.; *m.* Helen, *d.* of late W. W. Bourne of Garston Manor, Herts; one *s.* two *d.* *Educ.:* Lancing College; Caius College, Cambridge; Paris; St. Thomas's Hospital. F.R.C.P. London, 1937; Asst. Etranger to Professor of Pædiatrics, Univ. of Paris; House Physician, Hospital for Sick Children, Great Ormond Street; Medical Registrar and Medical Registrar to Out-Patients, St. Mary's Hospital; Mem. Council (and FitzPatrick Lectr.) Royal Coll. Physicians; Mem. Assoc. of Physicians; late President Epidemiological and Historical, and Vice-Pres. Medicine Sections, Royal Society of Medicine; late Hunterian Prof. and Vicary Lectr., Roy. Coll. of Surgeons; Woodward Lectr., Yale Univ.; late Chm. Med. Res. Council Rheum. Cttee.; Past Pres. (late Orator) and Hon. Fellow Hunterian Soc. and Heberden Socs., Osler Club, and West London Medical Soc.; past Master of Apothecaries' Company; Chm., Faculty of History of Medicine; ex-Chm., Chartered Soc. of Physiotherapy; late Research Grantee, British Medical Assoc.; President and Vice-Pres., Ligue Européenne et Internationale contre le Rhumatisme; Ensign, Coldstream Guards, European War, 1914-18; Lieutenant-Colonel R.A.M.C., War of 1939-45 (despatches twice, O.B.E.); Adviser in Medicine, Malta Command, 1943; Heberden Research Medallist, 1940; awarded Gold Key of Amer. Congress of Physical Med., 1941. C.St.J. Comdr. Order of Merit, Knights of Malta. Patron living of Hadleigh, Essex. *Publications:* A Text-book of the Rheum. Dis. (4th Ed.), 1968; (Editor) The Treatment of Rheumatism in General Practice (4th Ed.), 1939; Cortisone and ACTH in Clinical Practice, 1954; Doctors and Disease in Tudor Times, 1960; A History of the Gout, 1964; Apothecaries: a History of the Worshipful Society of Apothecaries of London, 1617-1967, 1968; contribs. to Chief Medical Journals, article, Diseases of Locomotor System, Price's Text-book of Medicine, and British Encyclopædias of Medicine, and Surgery. Editor, Annals of Rheumatic Diseases. *Recreations:* shooting and travelling. *Address:* 129 Harley Street, W.1. *T.:* Welbeck 3470; Rapleys, Ockley, Surrey. *Club:* Athenæum. [*Died* 24 *Nov.* 1970.

COPLAND-GRIFFITHS, Brigadier Felix Alexander Vincent, D.S.O. 1940; M.C. 1917; D.L.; J.P.; *b.* 28 June 1894; 3rd *s.* of late Arthur Edward Copland-Griffiths, Meadowbank Grange, Melksham, Wilts.; *m.* 1st, 1922, Hon. Ursula Mary Ethel Devereux (*d.* 1957), *yr. d.* of 17th Visc. Hereford; 2nd, 1962, Maud Wishart (who *m.* 1st, 1922, 12th Baron Fairfax of Cameron; he *d.* 1939; two *s.*; 2nd, 1947, Maj. Cecil Wigan, M.C.; he *d.* 1958), *d.* of James McKelvie, Duckyls Park, East Grinstead. *Educ.:* Wellington; Trinity Coll., Camb. Joined Rifle Bde., 1914; transf. to Welsh Guards, 1915; served European War, 1914-18 (despatches); attached Military Intelligence, W.O., 1922; Major, 1931; Lt.-Col., 1938; Col., 1941; Brigadier, 1942; retired, 1947. Hon. Col. Hereford L.I. (T.A.), 1957. J.P. Herefordshire, 1950; High Sheriff, Herefordshire, 1954; D.L. Herefordshire, 1958. K.St.J. *Recreation:* shooting. *Address:* Bircher Hall, Leominster, Herefordshire. *T.:* Yarpole 218. *Club:* Guards. [*Died* 10 *April* 1967.

COPLANS, Major Myer, D.S.O. 1917; O.B.E. 1919; M.D. (State Medicine) Lond.; D.P.H. Camb.; late R.A.M.C., T.A.; Technical Consultant, Laboratoire des Vaccins Pasteur (pour l'Étranger) and Institut Pasteur, Paris; *m.* Estelle, *d.* of Alex. Leon; one *s.* one *d.* *Educ.:* University College and Guy's Hospital. Beit Fellow, 1914 and 1920; Demonstrator Bacteriology and Public Health, University of Leeds; Civil Surgeon, South African Field Force, 1902 (Queen's Medal and 4 clasps); served European War, 1914-19 (despatches five times, D.S.O., O.B.E.); O.C. First Mobile (Hygiene) Laboratory, B.E.F. France, 1914-16; also Sanitary Officer, Second Army, in charge Belgian Civilian Epidemic (Typhoid) Operations, 1914-15; D.A.D.M.S. (Sanitation) H.Qs. Second Army, B.E.F. France, 1916-17; Assistant Director of Medical Services (Sanitation), General Headqrs., Italian Expeditionary Force; Member of Chemical Warfare Committee of Medical Research Council; Chevalier of the Order of Leopold I. and Croix de Guerre, Belgium, Croce di Guerra and Italian Silver Medal (Al merito della Sanità Pubblica).

Publications: many reports and papers on bacteriological, public health, and other subjects in leading medical and chemical journals. *Address:* 3 The Approach, Hendon, N.W.4. *T.:* Hendon 8584. [*Died* 9 *March* 1961.

COPPINGER, Rear-Admiral Robert Henry, C.B.E. 1919; *b* 5 March 1877; 2nd *s.* of late Valentine John Coppinger, Barrister-at-law, Dublin; *m.* 1st, 1909, Georgiana K. G. Long; (one *s.* killed on active service in R.N., Sept. 1939); 2nd, 1939, Mrs. Vesta Atkinson, 2nd *d.* of late John Harrison, Aldwick House, Bognor. *Educ.:* H.M.S. Britannia. Entered Navy, 1893; Lieut. 1898; Commander, 1910; Captain, 1916; Rear-Admiral, retired, 1927; served European War (despatches). *Address:* c/o Barclay's Bank Ltd., Tunbridge Wells, Kent. [*Died* 18 *Dec.* 1967.

COPPLESON, Sir Victor (Marcus), Kt. 1964; M.B., Ch.M., F.R.C.S., F.R.A.C.S., F.A.C.S.; Consulting Surgeon; President, Australian Postgraduate Federation in Medicine since 1961; *b.* 27 Feb. 1893; *s.* of late A. A. Coppleson, Wee Waa, N.S.W.; *m.* 1924, Enid James; one *s.* one *d.* *Educ.:* University of Sydney. Lecturer in Anatomy, Clinical Surgery, University of Sydney, 1923-1953; Surgeon, St. Vincent's, Royal North Shore and other hospitals, 1923-53; Served European War, 1914-18, New Guinea, France; served War of 1939-45, Greece, Crete. Chairman and Hon. Director, Postgraduate Cttee. Medicine, University of Sydney, 1946-. *Publications:* Trends in Modern Medical Education, 1953; Shark Attack, 1958, 1962; various articles on surgical subjects in Medical Jl. of Australia, Lancet and Surgery Gynaecology and Obstetrics. *Address:* 231 Macquarie Street, Sydney, Australia. *T.:* BW. 5637. [*Died* 12 *May* 1965.

CORBIN, (André) Charles, G.C.V.O. (Hon.) 1938; G.B.E. (Hon.), 1966; Licencié-ès-Lettres et en Droit, Diplôme de l'École des Sciences Politiques; Président honoraire de l'Association France-Grande Bretagne. Né 4 décembre 1881. Attaché d'Ambassade, 1906; à Rome, 1906; Sécretaire d'Ambassade, 1908; Attaché au Cabinet du Min. des Affaires Étrangères, 1912; Off. d'Acad. 1914; Chef du Service de Presse, 1920; Conseiller d'Ambassade à Madrid, 1923; Sous-Directeur d'Europe, 1924; Ministre Plénipotentiaire, 1926; Directeur des Affaires Politiques et Commerciales, 1927; Ambassadeur à Madrid, 1929; Ambassadeur à Bruxelles, 1931; Ambassadeur à Londres, 1933-40; Grand Officier de la Légion d'Honneur, 1938. *Address:* 82 Rue de l'Université, Paris; Avenue Cézanne, Cannes. [*Died* 25 *Sept.* 1970.

CORBYN, Ernest Nugent; Sudan Political Service, retired; *b.* 2 April 1881; *s.* of late Lt.-Col. E. C. Corbyn, Bengal Staff Corps. *Educ.:* King William's Coll., Isle of Man; Trinity Coll., Cambridge (Scholar); 1st Class, 1st Division, Classical Honours Tripos, 1903; M.A. Joined Sudan Polical Service, 1904; operations on the Blue Nile, 1908 (4th Class Order of the Medjidieh, Sudan medal); Deputy Assistant Financial Secretary to the Sudan Government, 1915; Acting Governor of Kordofan Province while base of operations for the reconquest of Darfur, 1916 (despatches, 4th class Order of the Nile); Deputy Civil Secretary to the Sudan Government, 1917; Governor of the White Nile Province, 1919; Governor of the Khartoum Province, 1922; Commander of the Order of the Nile, 1924; Governor of the Fung Province, 1924-26; Head of Sudan Education Dept., and Principal of the Gordon College, Khartoum, 1926-27; retired 1927; Observer for the Sudan Government on the Colonial Secretary's Advisory Committee on Education in the Colonies, 1935-37; Public Relations consultant to the Sudan Govt. in London, 1944-51. Secretary of Royal African Society, 1939-41; elected Life Member for services to the Society. Member of Governing Body and Trustee of Gordon College, Khartoum; Member of Council, Executive and Scholarship Committees of the Lord Kitchener National Memorial Fund, 1934-41; Sec. of Fund and of its Kitchener Scholarships Cttee., 1942-56; Member of Finance Committee of the Empire Societies' War Hospitality Committee, 1939-46. *Publications:* Editor of Journal of the Royal African Soc., 1940-43; articles on African affairs. *Address:* c/o Barclays Bank, D.C.O., 1 Cockspur Street, S.W.1. [*Died* 26 *May* 1961.

CORDEAUX, Captain Edward Cawdron, D.S.O. 1940; O.B.E. 1941; D.L.; J.P.; R.N.; *b.* 24 July 1894; *er. s.* of late Colonel E. K. Cordeaux, C.B.E.; *m.* 1921, Marjorie Holmes Bennett; four *s.* *Educ.:* R.N. Colleges, Osborne and Dartmouth. Royal Navy, 1907-29; served European war, 1914-18, Dardanelles and Jutland; qualified Gunnery Specialist, 1919; Royal Naval Staff College, 1927; retired as Lieut.-Commander, 1929; entered Middlesex Hospital as student, 1930, M.B., B.S. London and M.R.C.S. England, L.R.C.P. London in 1935; House Surgeon and Casualty Medical Officer, Middlesex Hospital, 1935-36; General Practice, Southwold, Suffolk, 1937; Royal Navy as Commander, 1939; Acting Captain, 1940; served Dunkirk, 1940 (D.S.O.); Senior Officer Thames Local Defence Flotilla, 1940-43; Maintenance Captain on Staff of Commander-in-Chief The Nore, 1943-45; awarded Czechoslovak Air Force Pilot's Badge, 1942. C.C. for parts of Lindsey, Lincolnshire, 1949; D.L. County of Lincoln; J.P. Parts of Lindsey; Diocesan Lay Reader, Vice-Chm. Diocesan Trust and Bd. of Finance 1957-62; Mem Church Assembly, Diocese of Lincoln, 1950; Member Sheffield Regional Hospital Board, 1952-60; Chairman Horncastle Rural District Council, 1958-60; Chm. County Civil Defence Cttee., 1958; Chm. Grimsby Group Hospitals Management Cttee., 1960-62; Group Controller, Civil Defence, North Lincolnshire, 1960. High Sheriff of Lincolnshire, 1963. *Address:* Goulceby House, nr. Louth, Lincolnshire. *T.:* Stenigot 229. *Club:* United Service. [*Died* 8 *June* 1963.

CORDER, Philip, M.A., Litt.D.; Assistant Secretary of the Society of Antiquaries of London since 1943; Editor, Archaeologia and The Antiquaries Journal since 1943; *b.* Sunderland, 5 March 1891; *s.* of Herbert Corder and Mary Grace Dymond; *m.* 1915, Johanna A. van der Mersch; three *s.* *Educ.:* Bootham School, York; Bristol University; St. John's College, Cambridge. Certif. in Mech. Engineering, Bristol, 1911; Medieval and Modern Langs. Tripos, 1915; M.A. 1919; Litt.D. 1951; F.S.A. 1931-43. House Master, Bootham School, York, 1918-1938; Curator Verulamium Museum, 1938-1946. Editor, Archaeological Journal, 1939-1944; Member of Council: Soc. of Antiquaries, 1939-41; Roman Soc. 1934-61; Museums Assoc. 1945-48; Royal Archaeological Inst. 1944-49 (Pres., 1954-57); Vice-Pres. Council for British Archaeology, 1954-1957; Mem. Exec. Cttee. of Roman and Medieval London Excavation Council; Mem. Excavation Committees of Malton, Verulamium, Canterbury, York, etc. *Publications:* The Defences of the Roman Fort at Malton, 1930; The Roman Pottery at Crambeck, 1928; The Roman Villa at Langton (with J. L. Kirk), 1932; The Roman Town at Brough, 1934-37; The Roman Town and Villa at Great Casterton, 1951, 1954, 1961. Articles in Antiquity, Archaeological Jl., Antiquaries Jl. and other archaeological jls. *Address:* 108 Riddles-

down Road, Purley, Surrey. *T.:* Uplands 1150. *Club:* Athenæum.
[*Died* 28 *May* 1961.

CORDINER, Thomas Smith, F.R.I.B.A.; Architect, practising since 1931; *b.* 13 Dec. 1902; *m.* 1936 Margaret Violet Gillanders MacLean; two *s.* *Educ.:* Glasgow. Qualified as Architect, 1928. Pres., Glasgow Inst. of Architects, 1956-58; Pres., Royal Incorporation of Architects in Scotland, June 1961-May 1963. *Publications:* work illustrated in architectural journals. *Recreation:* golf. *Address:* 314 St. Vincent Street, Glasgow, C.3. *T.:* City 3441. *Club:* Art (Glasgow). [*Died* 24 *Nov.* 1965.

CORDINGLEY, Reginald Annandale, M.A.; Hon. Dip. Arch.; F.R.I.B.A.; M.T.P.I., F.R.S.A.; Professor of Architecture, Manchester University, since 1933; *b.* 12 Mar. 1896; *s.* of James Cordingley and Ellen Mary Annandale; *m.* 1925, Madeleine Eugenie Tardieu; one *s.* *Educ.:* Manchester University; B.A. Hons. Arch. first class, 1922. Articled pupil with R. J. MacBeath, M.S.A., F.R.I.B.A., Sale, Cheshire, 1911-14; war service, Royal Fusiliers and Royal Engineers, 1914-19; at Manchester University, 1919-22; Jarvis Scholar, 1920 and 1921; Institute of Builders (Manchester) Scholar, 1922; Associate Royal Institute of British Architects, 1922; Assistant Lecturer in Architecture, Manchester University, 1922-1923; Rome Scholar in Architecture, 1923; Society of Architects American Scholar, 1923; at the British School of Rome, 1923-26; Resident Architect, Durham Cathedral, and in private practice as architect, 1926; Master of Architecture at Durham University, 1929. *Publications:* papers, Architecture and Archæology; re-publication of A Parallel of the Orders of Architecture by C. Normand; The Story of Architecture, revision of a work by P. L. Waterhouse; revision of A History of Architecture on the Comparative Method, by Sir Banister Fletcher. *Address:* The University, Manchester. [*Died* 28 *Nov.* 1962.

COREA, Sir (George) Claude (Stanley), K.B.E. 1952; retired as Ambassador and Permanent Delegate of Ceylon to the United Nations, 1958-61; *b.* 5 Sept. 1894; *s.* of Alfred Winzer Corea and Sarah Elizabeth (*née* Herat); *m.* 1933, Karmanie Chitty; three *s.* *Educ.:* Wesley Coll., and Law School, Colombo. Began practice as lawyer, 1916; left Bar for politics, 1930, during which time was elected three times President of Ceylon National Congress; elected member Ceylon State Council, 1931, and acted during lifetime of that council as Minister of Home Affairs on two occasions; re-elected member State Council, 1936, and became Minister for Labour, Industry and Commerce, 1936-46; Established first State-aided Commercial Bank known as Bank of Ceylon and also Industrial and Agricultural Credit Corporation; Ceylon Government Representative in London, 1946-48; Ambassador of Ceylon in the U.S.A., 1948-54 (first Ceylonese Ambassador to U.S.); High Commissioner for Ceylon in the United Kingdom, 1954-57, also Minister of Ceylon to France and to the Netherlands. Chm. U.N. Interim Co-ordinating Cttee. for Internat. Commodity Arrangements, 1955-56; Chm. G.A.T.T., 1956-57; Ceylon Representative on the Security Council of the U.N. *Address:* 36 Alfred House Avenue, Colombo, Ceylon.
[*Died* 3 *Sept.* 1962.

CORFIATO, Hector Othon, F.R.I.B.A.; S.A.D.G.; F.S.A.; F.R.S.A.; Hon. F.I.B.D.; Professor of Architecture and Director School of Architecture, University of London (Univ. Coll.), 1946-60, Professor Emeritus, 1960; *m.* Lillian A. Barrett; one *d.* *Educ.:* École Nationale et Supérieure des Beaux Arts, Paris. Pupil of Atelier Daumet-Jaussely, School of Fine Arts, Paris: Medallist in Ornamental Drawing and Modelling; Medallist in Architectural Design; Medallist of the Sté. des Architectes Diplômés par le Gouvernement, Paris; Head of the first Atelier of Architecture, London, 1922; Professor of Architectural Design, University of London, University College, 1937. Member, French Academy of Architecture; Member, Board of Architectural Education, R.I.B.A.; Member, Board of Architectural Education, Architects' Registration Council. Freeman and Mem. Livery, Worshipful Co. of Masons of the City of London, 1956. Chevalier, Légion d'Honneur. *Works:* decorations: Greek Cathedral, London (designer); Notre Dame de France, Catholic Church in Beaufort Street, Chelsea; St. William of York, Stanmore, new Cathedral Debra Libanos, Ethiopia; mosques at Zaria and Gombe, and other religious buildings; additions to: University College, London; Biological Sciences Building and Faculty of Engineering (U.C.L.); College of Arts, Science and Technology, Nigeria, and various other buildings in West Africa; co-designer various buildings in Burma. *Publications:* (jointly) Art of Architecture; Design in Civil Architecture; Piranesi compositions; various papers on Ironwork, Mosaics, Gothic Architecture. *Address:* 15 Woburn Square, W.C.1. *T.:* Langham 5414-5-6. *Clubs:* Athenæum, Arts.
[*Died* 3 *May* 1963.

CORFIELD, Rt. Rev. Bernard Conyngham, M.A.; Chaplain of St. John's Hospital, Winchester, since 1962; *b.* Simla, India, 1890; 2nd *s.* of Reverend Egerton Corfield (C.M.S. India), and *g.s.* of Rev. F. C. Corfield and Rev. T. A. Anson, both of Derbyshire; *m.* 1920, Ethel Celia, *d.* of Rev. Henry D. Goldsmith (C.M.S. India); two *s.* one *d.* *Educ.:* St. Lawrence College, Ramsgate; Jesus College, Cambridge; Ridley Hall (Theological College), Cambridge; Short Service Scheme (Educational) in C.M.S., India, 1912-15; Temp. Lieut. R.F.A. during European War (despatches twice); Ordained, 1920; Principal of C.M.S. Schools in India, and Pakistan, 1921-35; Principal, during 1928-30 furlough, of St. Michael's, Limpsfield; Vicar of South Nutfield, Surrey, 1935-1938; Bishop of Travancore and Cochin, South India, 1938-44; Rector of Stratfieldsaye, 1944-50; Rector of St. Lawrence and St. Maurice, Winchester, 1950-62. *Address:* 1 Grafton Rd., Winchester, Hants.
[*Died* 22 *July* 1965.

CORFIELD, Gerald Frederick Conyngham, D.S.O. 1918; Lt.-Col. Royal Engineers; *b.* 14 June 1886; *y. s.* of late Rev. C. W. G. Corfield, M.A. of Heanor Rectory, Derbyshire; *m.* 1919, Isla, *e. d.* of G. Hartley; one *s.* one *d.* *Educ.:* privately. Eight years in Mercantile Marine; three years with the Chinese Maritime Customs; 2nd Lt. 1914; 9th Yorkshire Regt. 1915; transferred to Royal Engineers; served with the British Mission to Royal Serbian Army in Corfu and Salonika, 1916 (Distinguished Service Medal of Serbia); with Mesopotamian Expeditionary Force, 1916-19 (D.S.O., despatches twice); Assistant River Inspector, Chinese Maritime Customs, 1920-1936; Chairman, Pilotage Examination Board, Shanghai, 1934; Assistant River Inspector in charge Woosung-Hankow Pilotage District, 1934-35-36; River Inspector, Chinese Maritime Customs, 1938-42; retired, 1943. Re-commissioned, Royal Engineers, 1943; Chairman, Requisitioning Committee for Inland Water Craft, 1944; Chairman, Standing River Conservancy Board, Calcutta, 1945; released from Military Service, Sept. 1945. *Address:* 18 Hornton Court, Hornton St., W.8. *T.:* Western 5375.
[*Died* 21 *Jan.* 1961.

CORK and ORRERY, 12th Earl of (*cr.* 1620), **William Henry Dudley Boyle,** G.C.B. *cr.* 1936 (K.C.B. *cr.* 1931; C.B. 1918); G.C.V.O. *cr.* 1935; Baron Boyle of Youghall, 1616; Viscount Dungarvan, 1620; Viscount Kinalmeaky, Baron Boyle of Bandon Bridge and Baron Boyle of Broghill (Ireland), 1628; Earl of Orrery, 1660; Baron Boyle of Marston, 1711; President, Shaftesbury Homes and Arethusa Training Ship, 1943-53; *b.* 30 Nov. 1873; *s.* of late Col. Gerald E. Boyle and late Lady Theresa Pepys, *d.* of 1st Earl of Cottenham; *S.* cousin, 1934; *m.* 1902, Lady Florence Cecilia Keppel (*d.* 1963), *y. d.* of 7th Earl of Albemarle. *Educ.:* H.M.S. Britannia. Entered R.N. as Naval Cadet, 1887; Lieut. 1895; Commander, 1906; Capt. 1913; Rear-Admiral, 1923; Vice-Admiral, 1928; Admiral, 1932; served China, 1900; Naval Intelligence Department, 1909-11; Naval Attaché, Rome, 1913-15; a Naval A.D.C. to the King, 1922-23; was Senior Officer Red Sea Patrol (despatches), and commanded H.M.S. Repulse during European War; Rear-Admiral, 1st Battle Squadron, 1924-25; Rear-Admiral commanding 1st Cruiser Squadron, 1926-28; Vice-Admiral commanding Reserve Fleet, 1928-29; President of Royal Naval College, Greenwich, and Admiral commanding Roaly Naval War College, 1929-32; Commander-in-Chief Home Fleet, 1933-35; Commander-in-Chief, Portsmouth, 1937-39; First and Principal Naval A.D.C. to the King, 1936-38; Admiral of the Fleet, 1938; served at Admiralty and in Norway, 1939-40; comd. combined expedition for capture of Narvik, 1940; Home Guard, 1941-42. Order of St. Lazarus, Order of Nile, 3rd class (Egypt), 1916; Order of El Nadhr (Arabia), 2nd class, 1917; Grand Cross of Norwegian Order of St. Olav; Grand Cross of Legion of Honour; Croix de Guerre with palm. *Heir: n.* Patrick Reginald Boyle. *Address:* St. James's Court, S.W.1. *T.:* Belgravia 5537. *Club:* United Service. [*Died* 19 *April* 1967.

CORKERY, Daniel; dramatist; late Professor of English Literature, Univ. Coll., Cork, retd. 1947; *b.* Cork, 1878. *Plays:* The Labour Leader; The Yellow Bittern; The Onus of Ownership; Fohnam the Sculptor. *Novel:* The Threshold of Quiet. *Short Stories:* A Munster Twilight; The Hounds of Banba; Study of Irish Literature; The Hidden Ireland; Synge and Anglo-Irish Literature, 1931. *Address:* Baile an Chuainin, Co. Cork. [*Died* 31 *Dec.* 1964.

CORKEY, Very Rev. Rt. Hon. Prof. Robert, P.C. (N. Ire.) 1943; M.A., D.Phil., D.D.; Member of the Senate, N. Ireland, since 1943; Professor of Ethics and Practical Theology in the Presbyterian College, Belfast, 1917-51; *b.* 1881; *s.* of late Rev. Dr. Corkey, Glendermott, Londonderry; *m.* Nina Frances, *d.* of Rev. J. A. Allison, Monaghan; two *d.* *Educ.:* Foyle College, Magee College, Derry; Queen's Coll., Belfast; Edinburgh University. Minister of the Presbyterian Church in Ireland, Ballygawley, 1906-10; Monaghan, 1910-17; M.P. for Queen's University in the Parliament of Northern Ireland, 1929-43; Ulster Government Junior Whip, 1942-43; Minister of Education, Northern Ireland, and Leader of the Senate, 1943-44; Moderator of General Assembly of Pres. Church in Ireland, 1945-46. *Publications:* Paths to Power in Religious Education; Can World Peace be Won?; Social Credit Criticised; War, Pacifism and Peace; A Philosophy of Christian Morals for Today; articles in Hibbert Journal and Philosophy. *Address:* 44 Deramore Drive, Belfast 9. [*Died* 26 *Jan.* 1966.

CORKILL, Norman Lace, C.M.G. 1959; M.M. 1918; M.D.; *b.* 11 June 1898; *s.* of William Lace Corkill and Bessie Furness Corkill (*née* Jewell); *m.* 1930, Phyllis Rosalie White Lavis; two *s.* *Educ.:* Liverpool Institute; Liverpool University. Served King's (Liverpool) Regt., 1915-19 (M.M., M.S.M.). M.B., Ch.B. (Liverp.) 1925; M.D. (Liverp.) 1936. Iraq Health Service, 1927-30; Professor of Zoology, Royal College of Medicine of Iraq; Civil Staff Surgeon, Baghdad; Sudan Medical Service, 1930-46; Sudan Defence Force and R.A.M.C., Miralai and Lt.-Col., 1940-44; M.O.H., Khartoum, 1944; Asst. Director (Public Health) S.M.S., 1945-46; Sen. Lectr., Trop. Hygiene, Liverpool Sch. of Trop. Med., 1946-48; Quarantine Expert, Saudi Arabia, 1948-50; Short Term Consultant in Nutrition, W.H.O., 1951; Health Adviser, Aden Protectorate Health Service, 1951-52; W.H.O. Nutritionist, Teheran, 1962-63. Coronation Medal, 1953. Order of the Nile, 4th Class, 1944. *Publications:* Snakes and Snake Bite in Iraq, 1932; The Feeding of Sudanese Infants, 1946; contrib. on tropical medicine and ophiology. *Recreations:* snakes and folk medicine; formerly Shooting Blue, Liverpool University. *Address:* The White House, Poughill, Bude, Cornwall. *T.:* Bude 2474. *Clubs:* East India and Sports; North Cornwall Golf (Bude). [*Died* 26 *Sept.* 1966.

CORKILL, Thomas Frederick, C.M.G. 1964; M.C. 1917 (Bar, 1918); M.D., F.R.C.P.E., F.R.C.O.G.; in practice in Wellington, New Zealand, 1921-63, specialising in obstetrics and diseases of children; *b.* Manly, Sydney, 18 November 1893; *s.* of T. E. Corkill; *m.* 1919, Edith A., *d.* of J. L. Morrison; two *s.* two *d.* *Educ.:* Wellington College, Victoria Univ. of Wellington; Univ. of Edinburgh. M.B., Ch.B. 1915; M.D. Edin. 1920; M.R.C.P.E. 1920; M.R.C.O.G. 1934; F.R.C.O.G. 1937; F.R.C.P.E. 1952. Served with R.A.M.C., France and Italy, 1915-19 (M.C. and bar, Belgian Croix de Guerre, Chevalier of Order of Leopold). Hon. Phys., Wellington Children's Hosp., 1922-34; Hon. Phys. and Lectr. to Nurses, Alexandra Maternity Hosp., Wellington, 1922-42. Pres., N.Z. Obstetrical and Gynæcological Soc., 1936-37; Chm. of Council, N.Z., B.M.A., 1934-35; Chm., Cttee. of Inquiry into Maternity Services, 1946 (Vic -Chm., 1934-35). Sims-Black Travelling Prof. in Obstetrics, G.B., 1960. Sir C. Hastings Clinical Prize, B.M.A., 1935. *Publications:* Lectures on Midwifery and Infant Care, 1932 (6th edn. 1959); articles on obstetrical subjects in N.Z. Med. Jl., and in Jl. of Obstetrics and Gynæcology of the British Empire. *Recreations:* none outstanding. *Address:* 1A Trelissick Crescent, Wellington C.4, New Zealand. *T.:* 35-276. [*Died* 4 *Dec.* 1965.

CORLESS, Richard, C.B.E. 1946 (O.B.E. 1919); M.A.; retired; *b.* 10 Oct. 1884; *m.* 1912, Etheline Oaten; one *s.* one *d.* *Educ.:* Preston Grammar School; Sidney Sussex College, Cambridge (Scholar). 16th Wrangler, Mathematical Tripos, Part 1, 1906; B.A. 1906; 1st Class Natural Sciences Tripos, Part 1, 1907; M.A. 1910; Assistant Director Meteorological Office, Air Ministry, 1939-47. *Publications:* Papers in Quarterly Journal of Royal Meteorological Society, and in official publications of Meteorological Office. *Address:* 21 Wimborne Gardens, West Ealing, W.13. *T.:* Perivale 4522. [*Died* 11 *Dec.* 1967.

CORLETTE, Brig. James Montague Christian; *see* Addenda: II.

CORNEWALL, Sir William (Francis), 7th Bt., *cr.* 1764; *b.* 16 Nov. 1871; *y. s.* of Rev. Sir G. H. Cornewall, 5th Bt. and Louisa (*d.* 1900), *d.* of Francis Bayley, County Court Judge; *S.* brother, 1951. *Educ.:* Wellington College; New College, Oxford (B.A.). Called to the Bar, Inner Temple, 1896. Formerly Capt., The Herefordshire Regiment, T.F.; served European War, 1914-18. Patron of one living. *Recreations:* fishing, shooting. *Heir:* none. *Address:* Newcote, Moccas, Hereford. *T.:* Moccas 233. *Club:* Flyfishers'. [*Died* 18 *May* 1962 (*ext.*).

CORNWALL, Ernest; Director of National Provincial Bank Ltd.; retd. Chm., Finney's Seeds, Ltd.; *b.* 28 Jan. 1875; *s.* of Andrew Cornwall, Lapford, N. Devon; *m.* Florence Emily (*d.* 1955), *d.* of J. W. Read, Whitchurch, Salop. *Recreations:* golf and motoring. *Address:* 84 North Gate, Regent's Park, N.W.8. *T.:* Primrose 7207.
[*Died* 30 *April* 1966.

CORNWALL, Sir Reginald Edwin, 2nd Bt. *cr.* 1918; *b.* 31 May 1887; *s.* of Rt. Hon. Sir Edwin Cornwall, 1st Bt., P.C., and Ellen Mary (*d.* 1929), *d.* of John Day, Oxford; *S.* father, 1953; *m.* 1923, Nellie M. E. King, (*d.* 1956), *d.* of late David E. Morley, Mellis, Suffolk. *Address:* c/o Clyde and Mersey Investment Trust, 8 Gordon St., Glasgow, C.1. [*Died* 29 *Aug.* 1962 (*extinct*).
He never proved his succession to the Baronetcy.

CORNWALL, Major-General Richard Frank, C.B. 1953; C.B.E. 1951 (O.B.E. 1946; M.B.E. 1931); *b.* 3 April 1902; 3rd *s.* of Venerable Archdeacon Alan W. Cornwall; *m.* 1931, Mary Eileen Douglas; one *s.* *Educ.:* Marlborough College. Commissioned 2nd Lieut. R.M., 1920; Bt. Major, 1935; Bt. Lt.-Col., 1941; Maj.-Gen., 1951. Commander, Plymouth Group, R.M., 1951-1954; retired, Dec. 1954. Colonel Comdt., R.M., 1963-66. *Address:* Four Winds, Seale, Farnham, Surrey. *Club:* United Service.
[*Died* 17 *May* 1967.

CORRIE, Sir Owen Cecil Kirkpatrick, Kt. 1939; M.C.; B.A.; *b.* 3 March 1882; *s.* of late J. Owen Corrie, F.R.A.S., Barrister-at-Law, and Amy Constance, *d.* of Hull Terrell; *m.* 1921, Ivy Isabel (*d.* 1957), *y.d.* of late Henry Digges La Touche, M.I.C.E., Chief Engineer, Madras Presidency; two *s.* *Educ.:* Monkton Combe School; Trinity Coll., Cambridge (Mathematical Exhibitioner). Barrister-at-Law, Gray's Inn; served in France, Belgium, and Palestine with N. Somerset Yeomanry and R.F.A. (T.F.), 1915-1919 (M.C., despatches twice); demobilised with rank of Major; Judicial Officer, Nablus, Palestine, 1919; Vice-President, Court of Appeal, Jerusalem, 1919-24; Senior Puisne Judge, Supreme Court of Palestine, 1924-36; Member of H.B.M. Consular Court of Appeal for Egypt, 1933; Chief Justice of Fiji and Chief Judicial Commissioner for the Western Pacific, 1936-45; Adjutant, Fiji Home Guard, 1942-43; Judge, Supreme Court, British Zone of Control, Germany, 1946-51; Puisne Judge, Supreme Court, Kenya, 1953-1956; Chairman, Rent Control Boards, Kenya, 1956-59; acting as Judge of Court of Appeal for Eastern Africa, 1958-61. *Address:* 16 Springfield Place, Lansdown, Bath, Somerset. *Club:* English-Speaking Union.
[*Died* 28 *Aug.* 1965.

CORSER, Captain Charles Huskisson, C.I.E. 1937; Royal Indian Navy, retired; *b.* 1886; *s.* of Benjamin Corser; *m.* 1916, Mary Kathleen (*d.* 1960), *d.* of John Ward, Warrenpoint, Ireland; one *s.* one *d.* *Address:* c/o Midland Bank, Hythe, Kent.
[*Died* 17 *Jan.* 1962.

CORTOT, Alfred; pianist; professor (hon.) at the Paris Conservatoire; Président de l'École Normale de Musique; Médaille d'or of The Royal Philharmonic Society; Commandeur de la Légion d' Honneur; *b.* Switzerland, 1877. *Educ.:* Paris Conservatoire. Called to Bayreuth as director of the chorus; Madam Wagner confided to him the direction of the performance of Gotterdämmerung and Tristan, 1902; Tournées de Concerts dans le monde entier. *Publications:* French Piano Music, 3 vols.; éditions de travail des Œuvres de Chopin, Schumann et Liszt; Aspects de Chopin, Paris, 1949. *Address:* 5 Avenue de Jaman, Lausanne, Switzerland.
[*Died* 15 *June* 1962.

CORWIN, Edward Samuel; McCormick Professor of Jurisprudence, Princeton University, 1918-46; Emeritus Professor since 1946; *b.* Plymouth, Michigan, U.S.A., 19 Jan. 1878; *s.* of Frank Adelbert Corwin and Dora Lyndon; *m.* 1909, Mildred Sutcliffe Smith. *Educ.:* Public Schools of Michigan; Universities of Michigan (Ph.B. 1900) and Pennsylvania (Ph.D. 1905). Preceptor in History, Politics and Economics, Princeton University, 1905-11; Professor of Politics, 1911-18; Phi Beta Kappa, University of Michigan; Hon. LL.D., University of Michigan, 1925; Institut International de Droit Public, 1925; Carnegie Professor Yenching University, Peiping, and other Chinese Institutions, 1928-1929; President American Political Science Association, 1931; Irvine Lecturer, Cornell University, 1933; Storrs Lecturer, Yale University, 1934; Hon. Litt.D., Harvard Univ., 1936 (Ter-centenary); American Philosophical Society, 1936; Bacon Lecturer, Boston University, 1937; Schouler Lecturer, Johns Hopkins University, 1937; Cutler Lecturer, University of Rochester, 1937; Stokes Lecturer, New York University, 1937; Lecturer Juristic Theory, Claremont Colleges, 1941; Edward Douglass White Lecturer, Louisiana State University, 1943; Phillips Prize, American Philosophical Society, 1942; Walker Ames Prof. of Political Science, Univ. of Washington, 1945; W. W. Cook Lecturer, Univ. of Michigan, 1946; Visiting Prof. of History, Columbia Univ., 1947-48; Special Lecturer in Political Science, Univ. of Minnesota, 1949; Contributor to Univ. of Notre Dame Natural Law Institute, 1949, 1951; William H. White Lecturer, Law School, Univ. of Virginia, 1950; Visiting Prof. of Political Science, Emory Univ., 1951; Visiting Prof. Law School of New York Univ., 1952; Lecturer on Constitutional Theory, New School for Social Research, 1953. Lectr., Whittier College, Los Angeles, Calif., 1954. Editor in Legislative Reference Div. of Library of Congress, 1949-52; Mem. Permanent Cttee. on the Oliver Wendell Holmes devise, Library of Congress, 1958. Hon. LL.D. Princeton Univ. 1954. *Publications:* National Supremacy, 1913; The Doctrine of Judicial Review, 1914; French Policy and the American Alliance, 1916; The President's Control of Foreign Relations, 1917; John Marshall and the Constitution, 1919; The Constitution and What it Means To-day, 1920, 12th ed., 1958; (trans. in five foreign langs.); The President's Removal Power, 1927; The Twilight of the Supreme Court, 1934, 4th ed., 1937 (Sp. tr. Buenos Aires, 1947); The Commerce Power versus States Rights, 1936; Court over Constitution, 1938; The President, Office and Powers, 1940, 4th ed., 1957; Constitutional Revolution, Ltd., 1941, 2nd ed., 1945 (Ger. tr. Wiesbaden, 1949); The Constitution and World Organization, 1944; Total War and the Constitution, 1947; Liberty against Government, 1948; A Constitution of Powers in a Secular State, 1951; (Ed.) Constitution of United States of America, Annotated, 1953; (with Louis W. Koenig) The Presidency Today, 1956. Co-author of several volumes. Contributor to various other volumes, encyclopædias and reviews. *Recreation:* gardening. *Address:* Old Stone House, Stockton Rd., Princeton, N.J., U.S.A. *T.:* Princeton, N.J. WA4-0576. *Club:* Nassau (Princeton, N.J.). [*Died* 29 *April* 1963.

CORY, Lt.-Gen. Sir George (Norton), K.C.B., *cr.* 1943 (C.B. 1918); K.B.E., *cr.* 1925; D.S.O. 1900; late Royal Dublin Fus.; *b.* 26 Dec. 1874; *s.* of late Charles D. Cory of Halifax, N.S.; *m.* 1934, Laura Emily (*d.* 1949), *d.* of late Oscar John de Satgé and *widow* of Major Malcolm Dinwiddy. Entered Army, 1895; Captain, 1900; served South Africa, 1899-1902 (despatches twice, Queen's medal seven clasps, King's medal two clasps); Aden Hinterland, 1903; European War, 1914-18 (despatches seven times, Bt. Lt.-Col.

and Col., C.B.. Legion of Honour. Order of the Redeemer, Order of the White Eagle, French, Greek, and Belgian Military Crosses); D.A.G. and Director Personal Services, A.H.Q., India, 1921-22; Deputy Chief of General Staff, India, 1922-26; G.O.C. 50th Northumbrian Division T.A., 1927-28; Lt.-Gen., 1928; retired pay, 1931; Inspector and Chief Liaison Officer, Allied Contingents, 1940-43. Orders of Polonia Restituta, Orange Nassau, and St. Olaf. *Address:* Hempstead, Bearsted, Kent. *Club:* Naval and Military. [*Died* 17 *Nov.* 1968.

CORY, Surgeon Rear-Adm. Robert Francis Preston, C.B.E. 1941; Royal Navy, retd.; *b.* 3 Sept. 1885; *s.* of late Ven. C. P. Cory; *m.* 1916, Gertrude Pepper (*d.* 1946), Bangor, Co. Down, Ireland; one *s.*; *m.* 1948, Kathleen Horrex, *d.* of H. Bentham and Mrs. Bentham, O.B.E. *Educ.:* Sedbergh School; Caius College, Cambridge; St, Thomas's Hospital, London. Joined Royal Navy, 1912; Afloat and at R.N. Hospital, Gibraltar, during war of 1914-1918; Surgical Specialist, R.N. Hospital, Haslar, 1927-30; Surgeon Captain, 1934; Senior Medical Officer, Surgical Division R.N. Hospital, Chatham, 1937-41; Principal Medical Officer, R.N. Auxiliary Hospital, Minterne Magna, 1941; Surgeon Rear-Adm., 1942; M.O. in charge R.N. Auxiliary Hospital, Sherborne, 1941-45; Retired List, 1945. Asst. County Director, Suffolk Branch, B.R.C.S., 1947. *Recreation:* fishing. *Address:* 43 Through Duncans, Woodbridge, Suffolk. [*Died* 8 *May* 1961.

CORY-WRIGHT, Sir Geoffrey, 3rd Bt., *cr.* 1903; *b.* 26 Aug. 1892; *e. s.* of Sir Arthur Cory Cory-Wright, 2nd Bt. and Olive (*d.* 1928), *e. d.* of Henry Clothier, M.D.; *S.* father 1951; *m.* 1915, Felicity, 2nd *d.* of late Sir Herbert Tree; three *s.* (and two *s.* killed in action, 1944 and 1945). Captain, late 3rd Bn. The Buffs; late Flying Officer, R.F.C. Served European War, 1914-18 (wounded) *Heir: g.s.* Richard Michael Cory-Wright [*b.* 17 Jan. 1944; *s.* of Capt. Julian Cory-Wright, R.A. (killed in action, 1944), and of Susan Esterel, *d.* of Robert Elwes, Congham House, King's Lynn]. *Address:* Mulberry Tree Cottage, Knebworth, Herts. *T.:* 2315; The Cottage, Brancaster, Norfolk. *T.:* 245 [*Died* 23 *March* 1969.

COSGRAVE, William Thomas; Member of Dail Eireann for Counties Carlow and Kilkenny, 1922-27, for Cork, 1927-44; *b.* Dublin, 1880; *s.* of Thomas Cosgrave, T.C., P.L.G., 174 James's Street, Dublin; *m.* 1919, Louise (*d.* 1959), *d.* of Alderman Flanagan, Portmahon House, Dublin; two *s. Educ.:* Christian Brothers Schools. Member of Dublin Corporation, 1909-22; Alderman, 1920; resigned, 1922; Chairman of the Finance Committee, Dublin Corporation, 1916-22; M.P. (Sinn Fein) North Kilkenny, Dec. 1918-22, Kilkenny City, 1917-18; Minister for Local Government, Dail Eireann, 1917-21; Member of the Provisional Government, Jan. 1922, and Minister for Local Government; Chairman of the Provisional Govt., Aug. 1922; Pres. of Dail Eireann, Sep. 1922-5 Dec. 1922; held portfolios of Minister for Finance, 1922-23; and Minister for Defence, 1924; President of the Executive Council of the Irish Free State, 1922-32; created by His Holiness the Pope a Knight of the Grand Cross of the First Class of the Pian Order, 1925; Hon. LL.D. Catholic Univ., Washington, Columbia Univ., Cambridge Univ., the National Univ., and Trinity College, Dublin. *Address:* Beechpark, Templeogue, Co. Dublin. [*Died* 16 *Nov.* 1965.

COSGROVE, Dame Gertrude (Ann), D.B.E., 1947; *b.* 3 Oct. 1882; *d.* of James Geappen and Elizabeth Mary O'Brien; *m.* 1911, Hon. Sir Robert Cosgrove, *q.v.*; one *s.* two *d. Educ.:* Central School, Hobart, Tasmania. *Recreations:* reading, needlework and gardennig. *Address:* 11 Watkins Avenue, West Hobart, Tasmania. *T.:* 23500. [*Died* 21 *July* 1962.

COSGROVE, Hon. Sir Robert, K.C.M.G. 1959; retired as Premier of Tasmania (1939-1958) and Minister for Education (1948-58); *b.* 28 Dec. 1884; *s.* of Michael Thomas Cosgrove and Mary Ann Cosgrove (*née* Hewitt); *m.* 1911, Gertrude Ann Geappen (Dame Gertrude Cosgrove, D.B.E.) (*d.* 1962); one *s.* two *d.* (and one *s.* Flt.-Lt., R.A.F., killed in action). *Educ.:* St. Mary's Primary Sch., Tas. Elected Mem. for Denison in House of Assembly, 1919; Govt. Whip, 1926-28; Opposition Whip, 1930; Minister for Agriculture, 1934-39; held portfolio of Treasurer, 1939-48; Magistrate for the Territory and a Commissioner of the Peace for the State of New South Wales. *Recreations:* golf, swimming, racing. *Address:* 11 Watkins Avenue, West Hobart, Tasmania. *T.:* 23500. *Clubs:* Royal Auto Car of Tasmania, Workingmen's (Hobart); Tattersall's. [*Died* 25 *Aug.* 1969.

COSTAIN, Rev. Alfred James, M.A.; Headmaster, Rydal School, Colwyn Bay, 1915-1946; (in temporary quarters at Conway, 1939-1946); *b.* 31 August, 1881; *s.* of Richard Costain and Margaret Kneen; *m.* 1908, Netta Graham, *d.* of William Graham Clark and Catherine Maclaurin; two *s. Educ.:* Merchant Taylors' School, Crosby; Lincoln College, Oxford (Classical Exhibitioner, Hon. Mods.; Lit. Hum.). Entered Wesleyan ministry, 1904; Chaplain Leys School, Cambridge, 1904; Council and Court of Governors, University College of North Wales, 1917-54; Member of Central Welsh Board, 1919; Member Headmasters' Conference, 1923-46; Chairman North Wales Division of Toc H, 1929-36; Hon. Association Padre of Toc H; County Commissioner for Scouts, 1928-46; awarded Silver Acorn, 1940; President, North Wales Cricket Association, 1930-; Captain Denbighshire County Cricket Club, 1929; Founder-President, Rotary Club of Colwyn Bay, 1927, President, 1938 Chairman No. 5 District, Rotary International of the British Isles, 1929-30; Member Youth Committee of Denbighshire, 1940; Mem. Denbighshire Education Committee 1941-50. *Publications:* Notes on Rugby Football, 1906; Dr. Arthur Jackson of Manchuria, 1911; Men in the Making, 1913; The Daybreak Call, 1914; The Manx Poems, in T. E. Brown Centenary Volume, 1930; Rydal School Sermons, 1935 *Recreations:* cricket and Rugby football (talking about them), and golf. *Address:* Tremynys, Abersoch, Caernarvons. *T.:* Abersoch 144. [*Died* 7 *May* 1963.

COSTAIN, Sir Richard Rylandes, Kt. 1954; C.B.E. 1946; F.I.O.B.; Chairman, Richard Costain Ltd. since 1946; Chairman of Harlow Development Corporation, and a Director of Richard Costain & Sons (Liverpool) Ltd.; *b.* 20 Nov. 1902; *s.* of William Percy Costain and Maud May Smith; *m.* 1927, Gertrude, *d.* of William John Minto; one *s.* two *d. Educ.:* Rydal School; Merchant Taylors'. Joined firm of Richard Costain & Sons Ltd., 1920; a Director, 1924; Joint Managing Director in 1927. Pres. of London Master Builders' Assoc. 1950; Chm., Export Group for Constructional Industries, 1955-57. During the War served in Min. of Works, 1941-45, first as Dep. Dir. of Emergency Works and then as Deputy Director of Works. *Recreations:* golf and bridge. *Address:* 111 Westminster Bridge Road, S.E.1. *T.:* Waterloo 4977. *Clubs:* Royal St. George's, Sandwich Golf; Hankley Common Golf; Royal Salisbury Golf (S.R.). [*Died* 26 *March* 1966.

COSTAIN, Thomas Bertram; Author, U.S.A.; *b.* 8 May 1885; *s.* of John Herbert

Costain and Mary Costain (*née* Schultz); *m.* 1910, Ida Randolph Spragge; two *d.* *Educ.:* Brantford Collegiate Institute, Canada. Editor, Guelph Mercury, 1908-10; Editor, Maclean's Magazine, Toronto, 1910-20; Chief Associate Editor, Saturday Evening Post, 1920-34; Story Editor, 20th Century-Fox Film Corporation, 1934-36; became editor American Cavalcade, 1937; Advisory Editor, Doubleday & Co., 1939-46. Author since 1942 (full-time since 1945, both fiction and non-fiction). Hon. Doctor of Letters, Univ. of Western Ontario, 1952. *Publications:* For My Great Folly, 1942; Joshua, 1943 (with Rogers MacVeagh); Ride With Me, 1944; The Black Rose, 1945; The Moneyman, 1947; High Towers, 1949; The Conquerors, 1949; Son of a Hundred Kings, 1950; The Magnificent Century, 1951; The Silver Chalice, 1952; The White and the Gold, 1954; The Mississippi Bubble, 1955; The Tontine, 1955; Stories to Remember (with John Beecroft), 1956; Below the Salt, 1957; The Three Edwards, 1958; More Stories to Remember (with John Beecroft), 1958; The Darkness and the Dawn, 1959; The Chord of Steel, 1960; 12 Short Novels, 1961; The Last Plantagenets, 1962; 30 Stories to Remember (with John Beecroft), 1962; The Last Love, 1963. *Address:* c/o Doubleday & Co., Inc., 575 Madison Ave., New York 22, N.Y., U.S.A. *Clubs:* Coffee House, Regency, Canadian (New York). [*Died* 8 *Oct.* 1965.

COSTELLO, Prof. Desmond Patrick; Professor of Russian, University of Manchester, since 1955; *b.* Auckland, N.Z., 31 Jan. 1912; *s.* of Christopher and Mary Costello; *m.* 1935, Bella Lerner; three *s.* two *d.* *Educ.:* Auckland Grammar School; Auckland University College; Trinity College, Cambridge. Asst. Lecturer (Classics), University College, Exeter, 1936-40. War Service with 2 N.Z.E.F.: Greece, 1941; North Africa, 1941-43; Italy, 1943-44. Diplomatic service: Second, then First Secretary, New Zealand Legation, Moscow, 1944-50; First Secretary, New Zealand Legation, Paris, 1950-55. *Publications:* (2nd edn.) Oxford Book of Russian Verse; (ed.) Griboedor's Gore ot uma; articles on Russian literature in learned journals; translations. *Recreation:* reading. *Address:* 21 Rathen Road, Withington, Manchester 20. *T.:* Didsbury 1436. [*Died* 23 *Feb.* 1964.

COSTIN, William Conrad, O.B.E. 1957; M.C. 1916; M.A., D.Litt.; President of St. John's College, Oxford, 1957-63; Fellow of St. John's, 1922-57, Hon. Fell., 1963; Senior Tutor, 1945-56; Hon. LL.D., Univ. B.C.; *b.* 19 May 1893; *s.* of late W. A. and late F. H. B. Costin, Dumfries; unmarried. *Educ.:* Reading School; St. John's College, Oxford (Exhibitioner, Hon. Schol.). First Class Modern History, 1920. Served European War, Gloucestershire Regt., 1914-19 (M.C.). Proctor, Oxford University, 1935. *Publications:* Great Britain and China, 1833-60, 1937; (with J. S. Watson) The Law and Working of the Constitution: Documents, 1660-1914, 1952; History of St. John's College, 1598-1860, 1958. *Recreation:* walking. *Address:* 4 Wellington Place, St. Giles, Oxford. *T.:* 57027. *Clubs:* United University. [*Died* 6 *Oct.* 1970.

COSTLEY-WHITE, Very Rev. Harold, D.D.; Dean-Emeritus of Gloucester; *b.* 1878; *s.* of late R. W. Costley-White and Jessie, *d.* of Thomas Arnold Marten; *m.* 1913, Hope, *e. d.* of late Sir Washington Ranger, D.C.L.; one *s.* one *d.* *Educ.:* Malvern College; Balliol College, Oxford (Scholar); 1st Class Classical Mods.; 2nd Class Final Honours Lit. Hum. Distinguished mention for Hertford University Scholarship, 1899; Goldsmiths' Exhibition, 1901. Ordained 1902; Assistant Master Sherborne School; Assistant Master Rugby School, 1903-10; Head-master Bradfield College, 1910-14; Principal of Liverpool College, 1917-19; Headmaster of Westminster School, 1919-37; Canon of Westminster, 1936-38; Dean of Gloucester, 1938-53. Select Preacher, Oxford University, 1929-31, Cambridge University, 1927 and 1938; Chaplain to the King, 1932-38. *Publications:* (Joint) Periods of Old Testament History, 5 vols., 1908-10; Abraham of Ur, 1938; contributor to Education and Religion, 1924; to Public School Religion, 1933; to What is Patriotism?, 1935; various Essays on Educationa Subjects. *Address:* Little Fountains, Dulcote, Wells, Somerset. [*Died* 5 *April* 1966.

COTTAM, Rev. Maj.-Gen. Algernon Edward, C.B. 1949; C.B.E. 1946 (O.B.E. 1938); M.C. 1918; Rector of Bodiam, Sussex, 1955-63, retd.; *b.* 8 July 1893; 5th *s.* of Henry Philip Cottam, Barnet, Herts.; *m.* 1933, Margaret Eileen, *o. d.* of Noel Haselden, Minieh, Egypt; two *s.* one *d.* *Educ.:* Highgate School. Enlisted Artists Rifles (T.A.), 1912; 2nd Lieut., East Surrey Regt., 1915; Adjutant, E. Surrey Regt., 1918-20 and 1922-25; Captain, S. Staffordshire Regt., 1926; Sudan Defence Force, 1928-38; Brevet Major, 1937; various Staff appointments (1st and 2nd Grade), 1940-43; Member British Delegation to Ethiopia under Earl De La Warr, 1944; Head of British Military Mission to Ethiopia, 1943-49; temp. Maj-Gen., 1943; retired pay, 1949 (as Honorary Maj.-Gen.). Attended theological course at St. George's, Windsor Castle, July 1952-Sept. 1953; Deacon 1953; Curate, Wadhurst Parish Church, Sussex, from Sept. 1953; Priest 1954. *Recreations:* cricket, golf. *Address:* Apple Trees, Sponden Lane, Sandhurst, Hawkhurst, Kent. [*Died* 18 *May* 1964.

COTTENHAM, 7th Earl of, *cr.* 1850; **John Digby Thomas Pepys;** Bt. 1784 and 1801; Baron Cottenham (U.K.) 1836; Visc. Crowhurst, 1850; late Lt. 10th Royal Hussars; *b.* 14 June 1907; *y. s.* of 4th Earl and Lady Rose Nevill (*d.* 1913), *d.* of 1st Marquess of Abergavenny; *S.* brother, 1943; *m.* 1933, Lady Angela Isabel Nellie Nevill, *d.* of 4th Marquess of Abergavenny; one *s.* two *d.* (and one *d.* decd.). *Educ.:* Eton; R.M.C. Sandhurst. President, Arundel and Shoreham Division Conservative Assoc., 1961-65 (Chairman Thakeham Branch, 1947-1962); Late President: British Show Pony Soc.; Ponies of Britain Club; Tunbridge Wells and South-Eastern Counties Agricultural Soc. West Grinstead and District Agricultural Soc.; Queen's Park Rangers Football Club; Metropolitan and Southern Counties Amateur Athletic Assoc.; Member: National Hunt Cttee., 1954; National Hunt Finance Cttee., 1957-62; Tattersalls Cttee., 1957-62; Steward, National Hunt Committee, 1962, Senior Steward, 1964; Member, Turf Board, 1963-64. Director: Peter Merchant Ltd. (Chm. 1943-52, Man. Dir. 1933-52); Lockhart Group Ltd. (Chm. 1946-60, Man. Dir., 1946-52); Trust Houses Ltd., 1962; Lingfield Park Racecourse Ltd. *Recreations:* racing, shooting and forestry. *Heir:* *s.* Viscount Crowhurst. *Address:* Hill House, Somerton, Oxford. *T.:* Fritwell 210. *Club:* Turf. [*Died* 12 *May* 1968.

COTTER, Col. Edward, C.I.E. 1943; I.M.S., retd.,; M.B., B.Ch., B.A.O. National University of Ireland, 1915; D.P.H. Eng. 1923; *b.* 6 Nov. 1892; *s.* of late Eugene Cotter, Blarney, Co. Cork; *m.* 1927, Ada, *d.* of late Joseph Sullivan, Eglantine, Cork; one *s.* *Educ.:* University College, Cork Entered I.M.S. 1915; Capt. 1916; Major, 1927; Lt.-Col. 1935; Col. 1944; Deputy Public Health Commissioner with Govt. of India, 1937; Public Health Commissioner with Govt. of India, 1939-47. K.St.J. *Address:* Knockdrin, 134 Merrion Road, Dublin. *T.:* 680367. [*Died* 2 *June* 1961.

COTTERELL, Gilbert Thorp, M.Inst.C.E., M.R.San.I., F.Inst.San.E., M.Inst.W.E., M.Inst.Mun. and Cy. E., Hon. M.Inst.R.E.; Consulting Engineer A.P.I. Cotterell and Son; Sanitary Adviser to War Office since 1937; *b.* 8 Sept. 1891; *s.* of Albert Player Isaac and Annie M. Cotterell; *m.* 1920; no *c.* *Educ.:* Stramongate School, Kendal; Bristol University. Articled to A. P. I. Cotterell, M.Inst.C.E., F.S.I., etc.; Senior Partner in firm of Consultants A. P. I. Cotterell and Son dealing with works of sewerage and water supply from 1923. President Institution of Sanitary Engineers, 1936. *Address:* Watergate, Nairn Rd., Canford Cliffs, Bournemouth. *T.:* Canford Cliffs 77297; 54 Victoria Street, S.W.1. *T.:* Victoria 1983 and 7481. [*Died* 29 *March* 1963.

COTTERELL, Mabel, O.B.E.; *y. d.* of George Cotterell, York, and *sister* of late Cecil Bernard Cotterell, C.S.I., C.I.E. *Educ.:* York High School; private coaching. Took Honours in Theory and Practice of Education at Cambridge; taught for some years in large London school; on outbreak of war organised Girls' Patriotic Clubs at Ipswich, Chatham, and Hull; Lady Superintendent of the Welfare Department at H.M. Factory, Gretna, 1916-19; Organising Secretary to the Women Voters' League for Licensing Reform, 1919-23; Executive-Secretary to Anthroposophical Society of U.S.A., 1926-1928; Secretary to Council of Anthroposophical Society in Great Britain till 1938. *Publications:* short magazine stories and verses. *Address:* 35 Park Road, N.W.1. [*Died* 20 *May* 1968.

COTTON, Jack; Chairman, until July 1963, City Centre Properties, Ltd. (when he resigned for health reasons but remained a Director until Feb. 1964; subseq. Pres.); also Chairman or Director of a number of subsidiary associated and jt. cos.; *b.* Birmingham, 1 Jan. 1903; *s.* of late Marcus Cotton; *m.* 1928, Marjorie Rachel Mindleson; three *s.* one *d.* *Educ.:* King Edward School, Birmingham; Cheltenham College. Surveyor and Estate Agent, Birmingham, 1924; founded firm of Cotton Ballard & Blow, Architects. Responsible for extensive developments in Great Britain, Africa, America, The West Indies and Europe. Chm. of developments in U.S.A., including the erection of Grand Central City, The Pan Am Building. Benefactions: Chair of Architecture and Fine Arts, Hebrew University, Jerusalem; Chair of Bio-Chemistry, Roy. Coll. of Surgeons, London; Chair of Bio-Chemistry, Weizman Inst., Israel; Patron of the London Zoo, making possible the enlarging of amenities and restoration of environs (Gold Medal, 1963). Collector of Impressionist Paintings. *Recreations:* golf, gardening, conversing and listening. *Address:* Thames Lawn, Marlow, Bucks. *Clubs:* Constitutional, Eccentric; Midland Conservative (Birmingham). [*Died* 21 *March* 1964.

COTTON, Sir James Temple, Kt., *cr.* 1945; C.B. 1941; O.B.E. 1928; late Under-Secretary, Ministry of Aircraft Production; *b.* 12 Nov. 1879; *s.* of G. F. Cotton, New Southgate, Middx.; *m.* 1912, Laura Beatrice Dunnett; one *d.* decd. *Educ.:* Stationers' Company's School. Various appointments in Admiralty, Air Ministry, and Ministry of Aircraft Production; U.K. Representative, International Civil Aviation Organisation, 1946-47. *Recreations:* golf, motoring, bridge. *Address:* c/o Australia and New Zealand Bank, Ltd., Queen and Creek Streets, Brisbane, Queensland, Australia. [*Died* 15 *Sept.* 1965.

COTTON, Leo Arthur, M.A., D.Sc.; Professor of Geology, University of Sydney, 1925-48, Emeritus Professor, 1949; *b.* Nymagee, New South Wales, 11 Nov. 1883; *e. s.* of Frank Cotton, Hornsby, N.S.W.; *m.* 1910, Florence Edith Channon (*d.* 1930); three *s.* two *d.*; *m.* 1946, Lilian Reed. *Educ.:* Model Public School, Fort Street, Sydney; Univ., Sydney. B.A. 1906; B.Sc. 1908; M.A. 1916; D.Sc. 1920. Won a number of prizes and scholarships for Geology and Physics; accompanied Shackleton Expedition as member of ship's party in summer of 1907-8; carried out research as Linnean Macleay Fellow, 1909-1910; Lecturer at University, 1911; represented University of Sydney at First Pan-Pacific Science Congress at Honolulu, 1920, and Third Pan-Pacific Science Congress at Tokio, 1926; member and officer of a number of scientific societies; Chairman Australian National Research Council, 1943; President, Royal Soc. of N.S.W., 1929-30. Mem. Linnean Society of N.S.W.; Mem. Australian Geographical Soc. *Publications:* Doctorate Thesis, Earthquake Frequency and Tidal Stresses in the Lithosphere, published in Bulletin Seismological Society, America, 1922; numerous scientific papers. *Recreations:* swimming, golf, bowls, chess. *Address:* Newport Beach and University, Sydney, Australia. [*Died* 12 *July* 1963.

COTTON, Thomas Forrest, B.A., M.D., F.R.C.P.; D.Sc. (hon. causa) McGill; Major C.A.M.C.; Consulting Physician National Heart Hospital; Hon. Consultant Diseases of the Heart, Ministry of Pensions, Civil Service, Edgar Lee Home, Queen Alexandra Military Hosp.; Member War Office Appeal Board; *b.* Cowansville, P.Q.; *s.* of late Cedric L. Cotton, M.D., Member of the Legislative Assembly, Province of Quebec; *m.* 1928, Mary, *e. d.* of Dr. Robert Marshall, Douglas, Isle of Man. *Educ.:* Cowansville Academy; Montreal High School; McGill University; Berlin, Munich, and Paris; graduated in Medicine, McGill University, 1909; House Physician and House Surgeon, Montreal General Hospital; Demonstrator Clinical Microscopy and Director Clinical Electrocardiography, F.R.S.M. Served in France with C.A.M.C.; in charge of clinical services Military Heart Hospitals, Hampstead and Colchester; part time worker Medical Research Council; clinical assistant, University College Hospital. *Publications:* Observations on Hypertrophy; Clubbed Fingers, a Sign of Subacute Infective Endocarditis; Observations on Mitral Stenosis; many other contributions to Medical Science. *Recreation:* golf. *Address:* Lister House, 12 Wimpole St., W.1.; Marsham Ct., S.W.1. *Club:* Athenæum. [*Died* 25 *July* 1965.

COTTON, Lieutenant-Colonel (Bt. Col.) Vere Egerton, C.B.E. 1937; T.D.; Hon. LL.D.; J.P.; retired; Member, Liverpool Cathedral Committee; *b.* 5 May 1888; *s.* of late Charles Calveley Cotton; *m.* 1922, Elfreda Helen, *d.* of W. F. Moore three *s.* *Educ.:* Repton; Magdalene College, Cambridge (Exhibitioner), M.A. Hon. LL.D. (Liverpool) 1953. Served in Artillery T.A. 1911-36; European War, France, Belgium and Italy, 1915-19 (despatches thrice, O.B.E., Croix de Guerre, Croce di Guerra); Commanded 59th (4th W. Lancs) Medium Bde. R.A. T.A., 1932-36. Hon. Col. 470 L.A.A. Regt. (T.A.), 1952-56. Pro-Chancellor, Liverpool University, 1942-54; Chairman, Liverpool Libraries, Museums and Arts Committee, 1939-55, Co-opted Member, 1956-68; Member of Arts Council, 1954-59. Lord Mayor of Liverpool, 1951-52; High Sheriff of County Palatine of Lancashire, 1956-57; Hon. Alderman, Liverpool, 1964. *Publication:* Book of Liverpool Cathedral. *Recreation:* travel. *Address:* Langdale, Grassendale Park, Liverpool. *T.:* Cressington Park 1196. *Club:* Palatine (Liverpool). [*Died* 19 *Nov.* 1970.

COTTRELL, Brigadier (retired) Arthur Foulkes Baglietto, D.S.O. 1917; O.B.E. 1938; late Royal Artillery; *s.* of late Capt.

William Henry Cottrell, C.M.G., O.B.E., R.N.V.R.; *b.* 4 April 1891; *m.* 1916, Mary Barbara Nicoll; one *s.* (elder son killed in action, July 1943) three *d.* *Educ.:* King's School, Canterbury; Royal Military Acad., Woolwich. Second Lieut. 1911; Lt.-Col. 1938; Col. 1941; active service in France, Gallipoli, and Egypt (despatches 4 times; D.S.O., White Eagle of Serbia, Order of the Rafidain, Iraq, 1914-18 medal with Mons Star, General Service Medal, Victory Medal); retired pay, 1945. Councillor, East Ashford Rural District, 1949-. *Address:* Boughton Aluph Cottage, Ashford, Kent. *T.:* Kennington 234. [*Died* 19 *Feb.* 1962.

COTTRELL-HILL, Maj.-Gen. (retd.) Robert Charles, C.B. 1952; C.B.E. 1946 (O.B.E. 1944); D.S.O. and bar, 1945; M.C. 1938; *b.* 7 November 1903; *s.* of Lieutenant-Colonel J. R. Hill, Indian Army; *m.* 1933, Alice Mary Victoria Ellen Madge Durrant (*d.* 1955); *m.* 1957, Joan Mary Griffith (*née* Champneys). *Educ.:* Bedford School; Royal Military Coll., Sandhurst. Commissioned 2nd Lt. The Border Regiment, 1924; Adjutant, 1933; Brigade Major, 1940; Brigade Commander, 1944; Dep. Dir. Infantry, War Office, 1948-50; Chief of Staff, Malaya, 1950-53; Director of Military Training, War Office, 1953-55; General Officer Commanding Berlin (British Sector), Berlin, 1955-56; President, Special Board, War Office, 1957; President, Regular Commissions Board, Nov. 1957-59; retired, Dec. 1959. *Address:* Redholme, Heacham, Norfolk. *T.:* Heacham 362. *Club:* United Service. [*Died* 10 *Nov.* 1965.

COTTS, Sir (William) Campbell Mitchell-, 2nd Bt., *cr.* 1921; M.A.; late Lt. Black Watch (R.H.R.); *b.* 12 Apr. 1902; *s.* of 1st Bt. and Agnes Nivison, 2nd *d.* of late Robert Sloane; *S.* father, 1932; assumed by deed poll, 1932, the name of Mitchell-Cotts in lieu of Cotts; *m.* 1934, Princesse Hélène-Marie de la Trémoille (marriage dissolved, 1940), 3rd *d.* of Louis-Charles-Marie, Prince et IIe Duc de la Trémoille, IIe Duc de Thouars, Premier Duc de France. *Educ.:* Harrow; Trinity Hall, Cambridge; Wycliffe Hall, Oxford. Called to Bar, Inner Temple, 1928; unpaid private secretary to Mr. Duff Cooper at Geneva in September 1928; contested (C.) Forest of Dean Division of Gloucestershire, 1929; late Director of the London Mercury and Frederick Muller, Ltd.; Officer of St. John of Jerusalem; les Palmes d'Officier d'Académie. *Heir:* *b.* Robert Crichton Mitchell, M.A.; formerly Major Irish Guards [*b.* 21 Oct. 1903; *m.* 1942, Barbara, *o. d.* of late Capt. Herbert J. A. Throckmorton, R.N.; two *s.* three *d.* *Educ.:* Harrow; Balliol College, Oxford (M.A.)]. *Publications:* Surrender to Dreams, 1935; The Lute Player in Avalon, 1937; contributions to newspapers and magazines. *Address:* 13 Onslow Square, S.W.7. [*Died* 20 *Feb.* 1964.

COTY, René; formerly President of the French Republic (Dec. 1953-Jan. 1959); Member of the Constitutional Council since 1959; *b.* Le Hâvre, 20 March 1882; *m.* 1907, Germaine Corblet (*d.* 1955); two *d.* *Educ.:* The University, Caen. L. ès L. (philosophy); Licencié en Droit. Called to Bar, Le Hâvre, 1902; Municipal Council, Le Hâvre, 1908. Councillor-General, Seine-Inférieure, 1919; elected Dep. Seine-Inférieure, 1923; re-elected 1924, 1928, 1932; Senator, 1935. Took no part in politics, 1940-45. After the liberation became member of both Constituent Assemblies, then of 1st National Assembly. Minister of Reconstruction and Town Planning, 1947; elected Member, Council of Republic, 1948, re-elected, 1952; Vice-President, 1949. Served European War, 1914-18 (Croix de Guerre, Croix du Combattant volontaire). *Recreations:* music, walking. *Address:* 84 rue Gabriel Monod, Le Havre, France. [*Died* 22 *Nov.* 1962.

COUBROUGH, Anthony Cathcart, C.B.E. 1919; Retired; *b.* 1877; *s.* of late Anthony Sykes Coubrough, J.P., of Blanefield, Stirlingshire; *m.* 1932, Ariel Psyche, *d.* of late W. W. Kennedy, M.D., Calcutta. *Educ.:* Albany Academy, Glasgow; Glasgow University. M.A., B.Sc. and C.E.; M.I.E.E.; M.I.Mech.E.; M.I.E. (Ind.). *Address:* Chantry Wood Cottage, Witham, Essex. *T.:* Wickham Bishops 259. [*Died* 26 *Jan.* 1963.

COUDURIER DE CHASSAIGNE, Joseph, C.B.E. (Hon.) 1920; Chevalier de la Légion d'Honneur, 1913; Author and Journalist (*pseudonym* George Saint-Clair); lauréat de l'Académie Française; *b.* Lyon, France, 30 July 1878; *m.* 1933, Yvette Steffens (*d.* 1958). *Educ.:* Lycée Corneille de Rouen; B.-ès-L. (Paris), 1896. Faculté des Lettres de l'Université de Paris, 1897; Licencié ès Lettres (M.A.), 1900; Licencié des Langues Vivantes, 1901; Fellow of the Sorbonne, 1901-3; Private Secretary to M. Émile Boutmy, Directeur de l'École des Sciences Politiques, 1898-1900; Rédacteur à l'Événement, 1899-1900; London Correspondent of Le Figaro, 1903-19; Le Journal de Genève, 1904-19; l'Illustration, 1913-19, etc.; Editor of Le Cri de Londres, 1914-16; Foreign Editor of the Sunday Times, 1915-16; Hon. Delegate French Colonial Section Franco-British Exhibition, 1908; President, 1911-20, Hon. Pres. since 1920 of the Foreign Press Association in London; Chairman of Executive Committee of Foreigners' Section, National Service Department, 1917-18; Member Foreigners' Advisory Committee, Ministry of National Service, 1918; attached to the Prime Minister of Australia for the Peace Conference, 1919, Paris; Chargé de mission du Maréchal Lyautey Commissaire général de l'Exposition Coloniale Internationale (Paris, 1931) auprès du Gouvernement Britannique (1928-31); et auprès de la Section Britannique, 1931; Président de la Société Française de numismatique, 1933-35; Membre Sociétaire de la Société des gens de Lettres; Membre Correspondant de l'Académie des Sciences, Belles-Lettres et Arts de Lyon, 1938; Officier de l'Instruction Publique; Commandeur de l'Ordre de St. Sava; Commandeur de l'Ordre du Sauveur de Grèce, etc. *Publications:* French version of John de Kay's Judas, played by Sarah Bernhardt at Globe Theatre, N.Y., 1910; and of Raymond Roze's Jeanne d'Arc, Théâtre National de l'Opéra, Paris, 1917; Bonaparte et l'Épopée Impériale en Médailles, 1927; Les Picquet du Consulat Lyonnais au XVII Siècle, 1936 (prix Jean Chazière, 1937, Acad. de Lyon); Les Trois Chamberlain, 1939 (Couronné par l'Académie Française, Prix Vitet, 1939). *Address:* 14 rue Raynouard, Paris XVIe. [*Died* 1961.

COULTAS, Frederick George, C.M.G. 1944; *b.* 29 Feb. 1888; *s.* of late Rev. G. W. Coultas, Hangchow, China; *m.* 1919, Hilda Caroline Marsh; no *c.* *Educ.:* St. Lawrence College, Ramsgate; privately in France and Germany. Entered Consular Service, 1914. Served with London Rifle Brigade, 1914-19; Vice-Consul at Cologne and Valparaiso; Consul at Para, Seville, and Gothenburg; Minister at San José, Costa Rica, Dec. 1945-March 1948; retired, 1948. *Recreation:* gardening. *Address:* The Oast House, Wickhambreaux, Canterbury, Kent. [*Died* 15 *Sept.* 1961.

COUPER, John Duncan Campbell, C.B.E. 1919; M.A., M.Inst.C.E., M.I.Mech.E.; Consulting Engineer, retired; formerly Consultant to the firm of Livesey & Henderson; *b.* 1876; *s.* of late John Couper, M.D., F.R.C.S.; *m.* 1905, Muriel, 4th *d.* of late John Lloyd

Price of Holywell, North Wales; one *s.* one *d.* Resident Engineer, Great Northern, Piccadilly, and Brompton Railway (Kensington and Hammersmith Section), 1904; Resident Engineer, New Dock Works, Newport, Mon., 1905; Engineer to the Alexandra (Newport and South Wales) Docks and Railway Co., 1914; Colonel R.E., Deputy Director of Docks (Engineering), B.E.F., France, 1917; Director of Docks, B.E.F., France, 1919. *Address:* Hill Rising, Pangbourne, Berks. *T.:* Pangbourne 2. *Clubs:* Athenæum, United University. [*Died* 23 *April* 1962.

COURAGE, James (Francis); Writer (novelist); *b.* 9 Feb. 1903; *e. s.* of Frank Hubert Courage, Amberley, New Zealand, and Zoë Frances Courage (*née* Peache); unmarried. *Educ.:* Christ's College, Christchurch, N.Z.,; St. John's College, Oxford. Play, Private History, performed at Gate Theatre, London, 1938. *Publications: Novels:* One House, 1933; The Fifth Child, 1948; Desire Without Content, 1950; Fires in the Distance, 1952; The Young Have Secrets, 1954; The Call Home, 1956; A Way of Love, 1959; The Visit to Penmorten, 1961. *Recreations:* piano-playing; listening to conversation. *Address:* 67 Greenhill, Hampstead, N.W.3. *T.:* Hampstead 4928. [*Died* 5 *Oct.* 1963.

COURAGE, Lt.-Col. John Hubert; Director of Courage and Barclay Limited, 1924-1962; *b.* 28 Dec. 1891; *s.* of Edward Hubert Courage and Beatrice Mary Audrey; *m.* 1st, 1919, Rose Mary McNeil; two *s.*; 2nd, 1934, Helen Mary Belsham; one *d.* *Educ.:* Wellington College; R.M.A. Woolwich. Joined 1st Bn. Royal Welch Fusiliers, Oct. 1911; served European War, 1914 (wounded, despatches, P.O.W.); resigned commission, 1921. Joined family business, Courage & Co. Ltd., 1923 (subseq. Courage and Barclay) (Chm., 1947-59). War of 1939-45 (despatches): France, 1940; Mid. East, Greece, 1941. *Recreations:* farming, hunting, shooting, fishing. *Address:* Kirkby Fleetham Hall, Northallerton, Yorkshire. *T.:* Kirkby Fleetham 226. *Club:* Army and Navy. [*Died* 28 *April* 1967.

COURNOS, John; novelist, poet, critic; *b.* Kieff, Russia, 6 March 1881; *m.* 1924, Helen, *o. c.* of late Christian Kestner, LL.B., Lawyer. *Educ.:* left school at 13, self-taught. Lived in a Russian village until 10th year; then went with family to Philadelphia, where learnt the first English; became a journalist; in 31st year came to London, where began profession of author in dead earnest; began first novel at 35; member of Anglo-Russian Commission in Petrograd, 1917-18. *Publications—novels:* The Mask, 1919; The Wall, 1921; Babel, 1922; The New Candide, 1924; Miranda Masters, 1926; O'Flaherty the Great, 1927; Grandmother Martin is Murdered, 1930; Wandering Women, 1930; The Devil is an English Gentleman, 1932; *biography:* A Modern Plutarch, 1928; Autobiography, 1935; *poems:* In Exile, 1923; With hey, ho . . .; The Man with the Spats, 1963; The Lost Leader: an Elegy for John Fitzgerald Kennedy, 1964; *play:* Sport of Gods, 1925; Shylock's Choice (Imagist Anthology, 1930); *juveniles:* A Boy named John, 1941; (with Sybil Norton) Famous Modern American Novelists, 1952; Famous British Novelists, 1952; Famous British Poets, 1952; A Pilgrimage to Freedom: The Story of Roger Williams, 1953; A Candidate For Truth: The Story of Daniel Webster, 1953; John Adams: Independence Forever, 1954; *public affairs:* An Open Letter to Jews and Christians; translations and editing, etc.; translator of Russian novels of Feodor Sologub and Alexey Remizov; contributor of articles on art and literature to English and American periodicals; co-editor, The Best Short Stories (English), 1922-25; translator and editor Short Stories out of Soviet Russia, 1929; editor, American Short Stories of the 19th Century (Everyman's Library), 1930; editor, A Treasury of Russian Life and Humor, 1943; editor (with Sybil Norton), Best World Short Stories, 1947; editor (with Hiram Haydn) A World of Great Stories, 1947; translator of St. Petersburg, by Andrey Biely, 1958. *Address:* c/o Grove Press, 80 University Place, New York, N.Y., U.S.A. [*Died* 27 *Aug.* 1966.

COURTAULD, Sir Stephen (Lewis), Kt. 1958; M.C. 1918; *b.* 27 Feb. 1883; *s.* of Sydney Courtauld, Bocking Pl., nr. Braintree, Essex; *m.* 1923, Virginia, *d.* of Richard Peirano, Santa Margherita Ligure, Italy. *Educ.:* Rugby; King's College, Cambridge. Served European War, 1914-19, with Artists' Rifles, Worcestershire Regiment and Machine Gun Corps (despatches twice). Chairman of the Board of Trustees of the Rhodes National Gallery, Federation of Rhodesia and Nyasaland, 1953-61. *Recreation:* horticulture. *Address:* P.O. Box 295, Umtali, Rhodesia. *T.:* Penhalonga 250. *Clubs:* Oxford and Cambridge, Alpine; Royal Yacht Squadron. [*Died* 9 *Oct.* 1967.

COUSINS, Professor Donald, B.Com. (Birmingham); C.A.; Professor of Accounting and Administration, University of Birmingham, since 1931; *b.* 22 Sept. 1900; *er. s.* of Henry and Margaret Cousins; *m.* 1931, Winifred Maude, *er. d.* of Norman and Mabel Cumberbirch; no *c.* *Educ.:* Bablake School, Coventry; University of Birmingham. In accountancy profession, 1925-28; secretary and accountant of public companies, 1928-31. *Publications:* Bookkeeping and Accounts, 1936; Elements of Bookkeeping, 1938; Business Finance and Accounts, 1945; (edited) Office Organisation and Management, 1951; (ed.) The Accounting Field, 1954; Costing, 1954; various articles in The Accountant, etc. *Recreations:* walking and gardening. *Address:* 522 Warwick Road, Solihull, Warwickshire. *T.:* Solihull 1427. *Club:* University (Birmingham). [*Died* 20 *Feb.* 1964.

COUTTS, William Strachan, C.I.E. 1917; late I.C.S.; Barrister, 1911; J.P.; Hon. Sheriff Substitute; *b.* 1873; *m* 1st, Mabel (*d.* 1935); *e. d* of late David Alexander Howden; 2nd, 1936, Mrs. Alice Amy Peppé or Leslie, *widow* of John Leslie, Ranchi. *Educ.:* Dollar; Trinity College, Cambridge. Entered I.C.S. 1895; Joint Magistrate, 1905; District and Sessions Judge, Patna and Orissa, 1912; Registrar of Patna High Court, Patna, 1918; Puisne Judge, Patna High Court, 1918-24; retired, 1924. *Address:* 23 Chester St., Edinburgh. [*Died* 21 *May* 1963.

COVE, Captain George Edward, C.B.E. 1952; Master Mariner; retd.; Command of S.S. Queen Elizabeth, Cunard S.S. Co. Ltd., 1950-52; *b.* 1889; *s.* of George Cove and Annie Cole, Salcombe, Devon; *m.* 1916, Clara Maude Clegg, Liverpool; one *s.* two *d.* *Educ.:* Liverpool. Apprentice in sailing vessel Barque Criffel (McDiarmid & Co., Liverpool), 1905-9; Officer in cargo steamers, 1909-14; joined Cunard Line as Junior Officer, 1914; appointed to command of M.V. Britannic, 1948, S.S. Mauretania, 1946, S.S. Aquitania, 1947, R.M.S. Queen Mary, 1948; retd. 1952. *Recreation:* hobby—wood carving. *Address:* 2 Cliftonville, Devon Road, Salcombe, Devon. [*Died* 29 *March* 1967.

COVE, William George; *b.* Treherbert, Glamorganshire, 1888. *Educ.:* University Coll., Exeter. President N.U.T. 1922. M.P. (Lab.) Wellingborough, 1923-29, Aberavon Division of Glamorganshire, 1929-Sept. 1959, Chairman, Welsh Labour Parliamentary Group. Freeman, Borough of Port Talbot, 1957. *Address:* Valley Rd., Welwyn Garden City, Herts. [*Died* 15 *March* 1963.

COVERNTON, Alfred Laurence, C.I.E. 1926; M.A.; Indian Educational Service, retired; *b.* 11 June 1872; 4th *s.* of Alfred Hennel and Ellen Covernton, 21 Aberdeen Park, Highbury, London, N.: *m.* Olive Helena (*d.* 1939), 2nd *d.* of Dr. William Love, Hoddesden; one *s.* two *d.* *Educ.:* Merchant Taylors' School, London; St. John's College, Oxford (Exhibitioner). Second-class Hon. Moderations, 1893; First-class Literæ Humaniores, 1895; Assistant Master, Merchant Taylors' School, 1895-98; Professor of English and History, Elphinstone College, Bombay, 1898-1905; Inspector of European Schools, Bombay Presidency and Central Provinces, 1905-8; Principal and Professor of English, Elphinstone College, Bombay, 1908-13; Deputy Director of Public Instruction, Bombay, 1913-15; Principal, Elphinstone College, Bombay, 1915; retired 1927. *Address:* c/o Mr. and Mrs. Hatt-Cook, Young's Farm House, Whiteparish, Wiltshire.
[*Died* 2 *Jan.* 1961.

COWAN, James Macfarlane, Q.C. (Scot.) 1956; Sheriff-Substitute of Lanarkshire at Glasgow since 1958; *b.* 16 November 1912; *s.* of late D. G. Cowan, Cloberview, Milngavie; *m.* 1957, Margaret Geddes Hay; one *s.* one *d.* *Educ.:* Perth Academy; Glasgow University. Served War of 1939-45, Royal Artillery (Major). Member of Scottish Bar, 1946. *Recreation:* golf. *Address:* Benvue, Biggar, Lanarkshire. *T.:* Biggar 73. *Club:* Hon. Company of Edinburgh Golfers.
[*Died* 4 *Oct.* 1967.

COWELL, Hubert Russell, C.M.G. 1928; *s.* of Albert Cowell, Kidderminster; *m.* 1906, Irene Zeppie, *d.* of A. Cooke; one *s.* one *d.* *Educ.:* Malvern Coll. (scholar); Clare Coll., Cambridge (scholar). Appointed after competitive examination to Inland Revenue Department, 1901; transferred to Colonial Office, 1902; Secretary of Canada-West Indies Royal Commission, 1909-10; Assistant Secretary, Colonial Office, 1920-39. *Address:* Polruan, Walton-on-Thames.
[*Died* 6 *Nov.* 1967.

COWHAM, Hilda; artist, author, book illustrator; 2nd *d.* of late Joseph H. Cowham, LL.D., author of educational books; *g.d.* of Tinsley Cowham, of Friskney, Lincs.; *m.* Edgar Longley Lander (decd.), late Roy. Fusiliers, 2nd *s.* of late Henry Longley Lander, of Lincoln's Inn; one *s.* *Educ.:* Wimbledon College; Lambeth School of Art. Began drawing at a very early age; first publication, whilst at school, in the Queen; contributor to Punch, the Graphic, Sphere, Sketch, Tatler, etc.; the monthly magazines; designer of posters, also the Hilda Cowham dolls; exhibitor Royal Academy and other galleries. *Publications:* Fiddlesticks; Our Generals; Blacklegs; Curly Locks and Long Legs; Kitty in Fairyland, etc.; short stories in newspapers and magazines. *Recreations:* sketching, travel. *Address:* Ashley House, Shalford, Surrey. *T.:* Shalford 61406.
[*Died* 28 *Sept.* 1964.

COWIE, Col. Henry Edward Colvin, C.B.E. 1919; D.S.O. 1901; late R.E.; *b.* 17 Dec. 1872; *s.* of H. G. Cowie, of Indian Finance Department, and Tiverton, Devonshire; *m.* 1903, Mary Theodora, *e. d.* of Rev. Daniel G. Thomas. *Educ.:* Shrewsbury; R.M.A., Woolwich, 1891-1893. Entered Army, 1893; retired, 1927; served Chatham, 1893-95; China, 1900-3 (despatches, D.S.O.); India, 1895-1927, in Indian P.W.D. Railway branch; France, 1915-20 (despatches, C.B.E.). *Recreations:* Football XI. at Shrewsbury; Football XI. at R.M.A.; Woolwich; R.E. Training Battalion Association team, 1893-94. *Address:* 12 Broadway, Bramhall, Stockport, Cheshire.
[*Died* 16 *March* 1963.

COWLAND, Rear-Admiral (Wm.) Geoffrey, C.B. 1950; M.I.Mech.E.; *b.* 1 Oct. 1895; *s.* of late Wm. Cowland, Horam, Sussex; *m.*; two *s.* one *d.*; *m.* 1948, Isobel M. Masson. *Educ.:* Royal Naval Colleges, Osborne and Dartmouth. Entered Royal Navy, 1908; served European War, 1914-18 (war medals); Supt. Admiralty Engineering Laboratory, 1936-40, 1945-46, War of 1939-45 (war medals); Staff of C.-in-C. Mediterranean, 1940-41; Deputy Director, Coastal Forces, 1942-45; Rear-Admiral, 1946; Deputy Engineer in Chief of the Fleet, 1948-50; retired, 1950. *Recreation:* yachting. *Address:* Lamb Cottage, South Petherton, Somerset. *T.:* 227. *Clubs:* Royal Ocean Racing; Royal Corinthian Yacht.
[*Died* 20 *April* 1966.

COWLEY, 4th Earl (*cr.* 1857), **Christian Arthur Wellesley;** Baron Cowley (U.K.), 1828; Viscount Dangan, 1857; *b.* 25 Dec. 1890; *s.* of 3rd Earl and Lady Violet Neville (*d.* 1910), *d.* of 1st Marquis of Abergavenny; *S.* father, 1919; *m.* 1st, 1914, May Picard (*d.* 1946); one *s.* one *d.*; 2nd, 1933, Mary Elsie Himes; two *s.* *Educ.:* Radley College. Is a member of theatrical profession; late Lieut. 5th Lancers; enlisted in Artillery, 1915. *Heir:* *s.* Viscount Dangan. *Address:* c/o C. A. Wellesley, Crystal Bay, Nevada, U.S.A.
[*Died* 29 *Aug.* 1962.

COWLEY, 5th Earl, *cr.* 1857; **Denis Arthur Wellesley;** Baron Cowley (U.K.), 1828; Viscount Dangan, 1857; Past Director, City Prudential Building Society (Chm., 1960-1965; Man. Dir., 1962-65); *b.* 25 Dec. 1921; *e. surv. s.* of 4th Earl Cowley and (1st wife) May Picard (*d.* 1946); *S.* father, 1962; *m.* 1st, 1944, Elizabeth Anne (marr. diss., 1950), *widow* of Flt.-Lt. Stephen A. Hankey, R.A.F.; one *s.*; 2nd, 1950, Annette Nancy Doughty (*d.* 1959), *d.* of Maj. J. J. O'Hara; 3rd, 1961, Janet Elizabeth Mary Aiyar, *d.* of R. Duray Aiyar, F.R.C.S., Denbigh. *Educ.:* Oratory School. Late R.A.F. Served War of 1939-45, Coastal Command (B.E.M.). Called to the Bar, Lincoln's Inn, 1958. He was one of Press Representatives to first meeting of United Nations at Westminster; served on numerous cttees. with British Council in Barbados for furtherance of cultural and educational activities. Formerly Legal Adviser and a Vice-Pres., Fulham Conservative Assoc., 1960; retired as a practising member of the Bar, 1962. Associate Mem. Building Society's Inst. *Heir:* *s.* Viscount Dangan. *Address:* House of Lords, S.W.1.
[*Died* 23 *March* 1968.

COWLEY, Herbert; *b.* Wantage, Berks, 9 Jan. 1885. *Educ.:* King Alfred's School, Wantage. Student, Horticultural College, Swanley; trained J. Veitch & Sons; Royal Gardens, Windsor; Royal Botanic Gardens, Kew. Editor of The Garden, 1915-21; Editor Gardening Illustrated, 1923-36; Hon. Life Member Alpine Garden Society; Fellow Internat. Camellia Soc.; visited Bulgaria as guest of King Ferdinand and collected plants in the Rhodope Alps, 1911; collected in the Pyrenees, 1921 and Andorra, 1927; Dolomites, 1922, 1926, 1934, and 1935; Maritimes, 1923; Majorca, 1925; Leventina, 1929; Albania, 1930; Sierra Nevada, Spain, 1933, 1947; Apennines, 1956; San Marino, 1958; Sicily, 1959; Elba, 1960; Ischia, 1961; joined 12th London Regiment on outbreak of European War, 1914-1918 (twice wounded at Ypres). Enrolled in Exmoor Mounted Patrol, 1940. *Publications:* The Garden Year; Edited Kew Guild Journal, 1909-14. *Recreations:* the flower garden, travel. *Address:* Kara, Holwell Rd., Brixham, Devon. *T.:* Brixham 3783. *Club:* Horticultural.
[*Died* 1 *Nov.* 1967

COWLEY, Horace W.; *see* Wyndham, Horace Cowley.

COX, Alfred Innes, C.I.E. 1947; O.B.E. 1943; L.R.C.P., M.R.C.S., L.D.S. (R.C.S.); late Lt.-Col. I.M.S.; retired; *b.* 1 Nov. 1894; *s.* of Alfred Cox, Architect, late of Baker Street, London; *m.* 1923, Ella Irene Ratcliffe; one *s.* *Educ.:* University College School, London. European War, 1914-18, Surgeon Probationer; qualified Middlesex and Royal Dental Hospital; I.M.S. 1919; Civil, Madras, 1932; Dist. Med. Officer, Malabar, Coimbatore, Madura and Nilgris. *Publications:* contributions to Indian Medical Gazette, 1941-43. *Address:* Tern, 9 Oldfields, Salterton Rd., Exmouth, Devon. [*Died* 7 *Aug.* 1970.

COX, Arthur Hubert, F.G.S.; Emeritus Professor of Geology, Univ. Coll. of South Wales and Monmouthshire; *b.* Handsworth, Birmingham, 2 Dec. 1884; *e. s.* of Arthur James and Mary Cox; *m.* 1919, Florence Elizabeth, *y. d.* of Charles Edward Page. *Educ.:* King Edward VI. Grammar School, Camp Hill, Birmingham; University of Birmingham (B.Sc. 1904, M.Sc. 1905, University Scholar, Priestley Research Scholar); University of Strasburg (Ph.D.); D.Sc. (B'ham). Lecturer in Geology, University Coll., Aberystwyth, 1909; Assistant Lecturer in Geology, King's Coll., London, 1910; Lecturer in Petrology, 1915; Temp. Officer of H.M. Geological Survey, 1917; Professor of Geology, University College, Cardiff, 1918-1949; Lyell Geological Fund, 1917; J. B. Tyrrell Fund, 1931 and 1933; Lyell Medal, 1948; Member Iron-Ore Committee, 1918; Geophysical Committee, 1929; Geological Survey Board, 1938; Leverhulme Research Grant, 1949. *Publications:* Papers on the Lower Palæozoic Rocks of Wales: Coal Measures of South Wales, Underground Structure of the Midlands, natural resources of South Wales, Geological History of Glamorgan, South Staffordshire Fireclays, Incidence of Silicosis; Magnetic Disturbances and Geological Structure; Trials of geo-electrical methods for the detection of waterlogged areas in mines, etc., in the Philosophical Transactions of the Royal Society, and elsewhere. *Recreations:* travel, field geology, music. *Address:* Tan-y-rhiw, Rhiwbina Hill, near Cardiff. *T.:* Rhiwbina 650. [*Died* 14 *Feb.* 1961.

COX, Charles Leslie, C.B.E. 1935; M.Inst.C.E.; *b.* 12 Dec. 1880; *s.* of Charles Albert Cox and Emma Claridge; *m.* 1912, Dorothy Caldicott; one *s.* (and one *s.* killed on active service, Battle of Britain, 1940). *Educ.:* privately. Capt. R.E., 1915-19. Twenty-nine years Colonial Services; Director of Public Works and Member of Legislative Council, 1923-35, Nigeria; retired 1935; Ministry of Health, 1935-42. *Publications:* various technical. *Recreations:* work, fishing. *Address:* c/o Lloyds Bank, 6 Pall Mall, S.W.1. [*Died* 27 *May* 1963.

COX, Cuthbert Machell, M.A.: T.D.; Headmaster, Berkhamsted School until Dec. 1945; *b.* 29 Dec. 1881; *s.* of Rev. John Charles Cox, LL.D., F.S.A. *Educ.:* Berkhamsted School; Magdalen College, Oxford. *Address:* 4 Croft Rd., Thame, Oxon. *Club:* United University. [*Died* 13 *March* 1962.

COX, George Lissant, C.B.E. 1944; M.A., M.D. Camb.; late Chief Tuberculosis Officer, Lancs. C.C.; *b.* 14 Sept. 1879; *s.* of George H. Cox, Liverpool, and Isabella Richardson, Edinburgh; *m.* 1919, Sarah Marguerita Howarth; one *s.* two *d.* *Educ.:* Abbotsholme School; Christ's College, Cambridge; Liverpool. Qualified 1906; formerly Sen. Res. M.O. and Asst. Pathologist, Royal Infirmary, Liverpool; Hon. Asst. Phys. Consumption Hospital, Liverpool; Asst. Lectr. Pathol. and Bact., Liverpool; ex-Member and ex-Chm. Joint Tuberculosis Council Eng. and Wales; ex-Mem. Standing Advisory Cttee., Tuberculosis, of Minister of Health. Varrier-Jones Gold Medal, 1959. *Publications:* Lancashire County Council Reports on Prevention and Treatment of Tuberculosis since 1913; numerous papers in Medical Journals. *Recreations:* apple-growing in experimental orchards; rhododendron and rose species culture; fishing. *Address:* 2 Oaks Road, Battle Field, Church Stretton, Shropshire. [*Died* 27 *Sept.* 1967.

COX, Sir Ivor (Richard), Kt., *cr.* 1955; D.S.O. 1918; D.Sc. (*Honoris Causa*), University of Wales; M.I.Mech.E., A.M.I.C.E.; Deputy Chairman, Associated Electrical Industries Overseas Ltd., 1956-58; *b.* 28 March 1891; *s.* of Richard Cox, Cardiff; *m.* 1917, Elsie Dorothy Pearce; one *d.* *Educ.:* University College of South Wales and Monmouthshire, Cardiff. After graduating joined British Westinghouse Company as Engineer. Served European War, 1914-19, in R.G.A., France, Palestine, Salonica (despatches, D.S.O., French Croix de Guerre with palms), retd. with rank Major, 1919. Engineer, Metropolitan-Vickers Electrical Co. Ltd., 1919, and travelled U.S.A., Russia, Australia, N.Z., etc. Order of the Southern Cross, Brazil, 1955. *Address:* The Paddock House, West Common, Gerrard's Cross, Bucks. *T.:* Gerrard's Cross 4238. *Club:* Travellers'. [*Died* 11 *June* 1964.

COX, Leslie Reginald, O.B.E. 1958; F.R.S. 1950; Sc.D.; Deputy Keeper, Department of Palæontology, British Museum (Natural History), 1961-63; *b.* 22 Nov. 1897; *s.* of late Walter Cox and late Jessie Lucy Cox (*née* Witte); *m.* 1925, Hilda Cecilia, *d.* of late Rev. W. J. Lewis, Vicar of Mountsorrel, Leicester; one *s.* one *d.* (and one *d.* decd.). *Educ.:* Owen's School, London, E.C.1; Queens' Coll., Cambridge (scholar). Served European War, 1914-18, in Experimental Section R.N.A.S. and R.N., 1916-19; member assault party, Zeebrugge (wounded). Nat. Sci. Tripos (double first), 1920, 1921; Sc.D. (Cantab.), 1937. Asst. Keeper, Dept. of Geology, Brit. Museum (Natural Hist.), 1922; Senior Principal Scientific Officer, 1951. President Malacological Soc. of London, 1957-60 (Treas. 1926-51); awarded Murchison Fund of Geological Soc. of London, 1929; Lyell Medal, 1956. Hon. Librarian of Geologists' Assoc., 1940-53, Vice-Pres., 1953, Pres., 1954-56. Council of Geological Soc. of London, 1940-44 and 1950-55 (Vice-Pres. 1952-54); Vice-President: Palæontographical Soc., 1957-1962, 1963-; Palæontological Association, 1958-60 (President, 1964-). Corr. Mem. American Museum of Natural History, 1943-1948. Correspondent of Paleontological Soc. (U.S.A.), 1950-; Hon. Fell. Palæontological Soc. of India, 1956-. *Publications:* numerous papers and monographs published in various learned journals (British and foreign), dealing with palæontology of mollusca and with life and work of William Smith ("Father of English Geology"). *Recreations:* gardening, photography. *Address:* 30 Haslemere Avenue, Hendon, N.W.4. [*Died* 5 *Aug.* 1965.

COX, Brig. Sir Matthew (Henry), Kt. 1960; C.I.E. 1944; O.B.E. 1937; M.C. 1916; M.I.Mech.E.; F.Inst.D.; Indian Army, retired; *b.* 1892; *s.* of late Matthew Cox, Easton, Stamford, Lincs; *m.* 1924, Margaret Goddard, 2nd *d.* of late Ernest Sewell Gale, F.R.I.B.A.; two *s.* one *d.* *Educ.:* Easton School. 2nd Lieut. R.A.S.C., 1916; served European War, 1914-19 (despatches), France, Belgium, Italy. Transferred I.A. 1924; Bt. Major, 1932; Bt. Lt.-Col. 1937; Col. 1940; Brig. 1942. *Address:* c/o Lloyds Bank, 6 Pall Mall, S.W.1; 12 Fairmile Court, Henley-on-Thames, Oxon. [*Died* 10 *Sept.* 1966.

COX, Sir Reginald K. K.; *see* Kennedy-Cox.

COXWELL, Charles Blake, C.B. 1943; O.B.E. 1920; Retired Civil Servant, Admiralty; *b.* 11 Oct. 1889; *s.* of late C. F. Coxwell, M.D. (Cantab.), M.R.C.P. (Lond.); *m.* 1913, Marjorie Milne (*d.* 1948), *d.* of late J. H. Billinghurst, Upper Norwood; three *d.* *Educ.:* Blackheath Schools; Dulwich Coll.; Christ's Coll., Cambridge (Schol.); M.A.; First Class Classical Tripos, Part I, 1910; First Class Historical Tripos, Part II, 1911. Entered Admiralty, 1912; served as Private Secretary to successive Fourth Sea Lords, 1915-17; Commissioned in Royal Marines, 1918; a Principal, Admiralty, 1920; Principal Private Sec. to First Lord (Viscount Monsell), 1932-36; Asst. Sec., Admty., 1933; Principal Assistant Secretary, 1939; Director of Establishments, 1944; Under-Secretary, 1945; Principal Under-Secretary, 1946-51; retired, 1951. Director of Greenwich Hospital, 1951-54. Sometime Member Cttee. Royal Humane Society; sometime Member, Gen. Council, Royal Patriotic Fund Corp. and sometime Almoner of Christ's Hospital. *Address:* Red Roofs, Fearn Close, East Horsley, Leatherhead, Surrey. *T.:* East Horsley 2446. [*Died* 9 *Nov.* 1967.

CRABBE, Col. Sir John Gordon, Kt. 1957; O.B.E. 1944; M.C. 1916; T.D. 1951; *b.* 12 Aug. 1892; *er. s.* of late Lieut.-Col. John Crabbe, Duncow, Dumfries; *m.* 1919, Frances Mildred, *d.* of Colonel Charles Brook, Kinmount, Annan; two *d.* (one *s.* died of wounds, 1944). *Educ.:* Eton; R.M.C. Sandhurst. Joined Royal Scots Greys, 1912; served European War, 1914-18, Adjutant Bedfordshire Yeo., 1915-17; Staff, 1st Cavalry Div., 1917-19; Bt. Major, 1919; Major, 1925; retired, 1925. Joined Yorkshire Dragoons, 1926; commanded Yorkshire Dragoons, 1935-39; Colonel, 1939; War of 1939-45, H.Q. Home Forces, 1940; commanded 1st Lothians and Border Horse, 1940-44, Hon. Colonel, 1946-56; County Council, 1928-; Convener of Dumfries County Council, 1946-. Lieutenant, Queen's Bodyguard for Scotland. D.L. 1936, J.P. 1935; H.M. Lieutenant of County of Dumfries, 1949-. *Recreations:* shooting and fishing. *Address:* Duncow, Dumfries. *T.:* Amisfield 211. *Clubs:* Cavalry; New (Edinburgh). [*Died* 1 *Nov.* 1961.

CRABBE, Rt. Rev. Reginald Percy; *b.* 15 July 1883; *s.* of late Rev. Henry Brooksby Crabbe; *m.* 1912, Margaret Forbes, *d.* of Dr. John Wilson, Sheffield; one *s.* two *d.* *Educ.:* Trent College, Derbyshire; Corpus Christi College, Cambridge; Ridley Hall, Cambridge. Deacon, 1906; Priest, 1907; Curate of St. George's, Newcastle, Staffs., 1906-11; Domestic Chaplain to Bishop of Sierra Leone, 1911-14; Vicar of St. Mary's, Peckham, 1915-20; Vicar of St. Mary's, Sheffield, 1920-24; Vicar of St. Peter's, Brockley, 1924-30; Rural Dean of Greenwich, 1926-30; Chaplain of Alleyn's College of God's Gift, Dulwich, 1930-36; Rural Dean of Dulwich, 1935-36; Bishop of Mombasa, 1936-53; Vicar of Ventnor, Isle of Wight, 1953-58. Hon. Canon of Portsmouth Cathedral, 1954-58. *Recreations:* athletics and cross country Blue, represented Cambridge against Oxford in Athletics, 1903, 1904, 1905, 1906; represented Great Britain, Olympic Games, Athens, 1906. *Address:* 2 Linley Close, off Manor Road, Bexhill-on-Sea, Sussex. *T.:* Bexhill 4381. [*Died* 22 *Oct.* 1964.

CRACE, Admiral (retd.) Sir John Gregory, K.B.E., *cr.* 1947; C.B. 1941; *b.* 6 Feb. 1887; *s.* of late Edward Kendall Crace, Gininderra, N.S.W.; *m.* 1920, Carola Helen, *d.* of late Allan F. Baird, Glasgow; three *s.* *Educ.:* King's School, N.S.W.; H.M.S. Britannia. Joined Royal Navy, 1902; served European War, 1914-18; Commander, 1920; Captain, 1928; Rear-Adm., 1939; served in War of 1939-45 as Rear-Adm. commanding Australian Squadron (Coral Sea), 1939-42, and Admiral Superintendent, H.M. Dockyard, Chatham, 1942-46; Vice-Admiral, Retired List, 1942; Admiral, Retired List, 1945. *Address:* Longacre, Liss, Hants. [*Died* 11 *May* 1968.

CRADDOCK, Colonel Alexander Bainbridge, C.I.E. 1946; O.B.E. 1921; retd. pay; *b.* 1893; *s.* of late Thomas F. Craddock, formerly of Caverswall, Staffs; *m.* 1935, Noel, *d.* of late Rev. Lyonel D. Hildyard, Rowley, E. Yorks.; no *c.* *Educ.:* Clifton College; Exeter College, Oxford (B.A.). 2nd Lieut. Roy. Warwickshire Regt., 1913; p.s.c., 1928; served European War, 1914-18, Adjt. 10th Bn. R. Warwick Regt., 1914-15; attached Oxford and Bucks L.I., 1916-17; Iraq, 1917; D.A.Q.M.G. Afghanistan and N.W. Frontier, 1919, Waziristan, 1919-22 (despatches); Wana-Wazir Column, 1920-22 (despatches). 106th Hazara Pioneers, 1922; Waziristan, 1922-24; D.A.A.G. Baluchistan Dist., 1924, Meerut Dist., 1931-34; 1/14th Punjab Regt., 1934; comdg., 1936; Comdt., 1937-39. Invalided (active service), 1939. War of 1939-1945: Col. Gen. Staff, War Staff, India Office, 1941-47; Major, 2nd Hants. Home Guard Battalion, 1952-53. Joint Commissioner, Indian Military Widows' and Orphans' Fund, 1940-46. *Recreations:* golf, gardens. *Address:* Lime Tree Cottage, Hook, near Basingstoke, Hants. *T.:* Hook 100. [*Died* 22 *Dec.* 1962.

CRAIG, Edward Gordon, C.H. 1956; R.D.I. 1938; President, Mermaid Theatre, since 1964; *b.* 16 Jan. 1872; *s.* of Ellen Terry and E. W. Godwin, F.S.A.; Order of Dannebrog, 1930. *Publications:* The Page, 1898-1901; A Book of Penny Toys, 1899; The Art of the Theatre, 1905; many essays in The Mask, published in Florence, from 1908 to 1929; On the Art of the Theatre, 1911; A Living Theatre, 1913; Towards a New Theatre, 1913; The Marionnette, 1918; The Theatre Advancing, 1921; Scene, 1923; Woodcuts and some Words, 1924; Books and Theatres, 1925; A Production 1926, 1930; Henry Irving, 1930; Fourteen Notes, 1931; Ellen Terry and Her Secret Self, 1931; Index to the Story of My Days, 1957. *Address:* Le Mas André, Corniche du Malvan, Vence, A.M., France. [*Died* 29 *July* 1966.

CRAIG, Sir (Ernest) Gordon, Kt. 1929; Director British Movietone News; *b.* 13 June 1891. *Educ.:* King's, Peterborough. Served European War, 1914-18; a Vice-Pres. of the Old Contemptibles Association, and Ex-President of the Founder Branch of the Association; Freeman City of London; Liveryman of the Gold and Silver Wyre Drawers' Company. *Recreations:* shooting, golf, fishing. *Address:* Cockhaven Manor Hotel, Bishopsteignton, Devon. [*Died* 29 *April* 1966.

CRAIG, John Douglas, M.A. (Oxon), M.A., D.Litt. (St. And.); Firth Professor of Latin in the University of Sheffield, 1931-52, Dean of Faculty of Arts, 1936-39, retd.; now Emeritus Professor; *b.* The Manse of Ardentinny, Argyll, 31 May 1887; 3rd *s.* of late Rev. Robert Craig, M.A., and Susan Stuart Meldrum; *m.* Elizabeth Dalgliesh (*d.* 1968), *yr. d.* of late John Edgar, Prof. of Education in the University of St. Andrews; three *s.* one *d.* *Educ.:* Madras College, St. Andrews; St. Andrews and Oxford Universities; 1st Class Hons. in Classics, St. Andrews; Scholar of Jesus College, Oxford (1st Class Classical Moderations, 2nd Class Lit. Hum.). Assistant in Classics, St. Andrews, 1912-13; Assistant Professor of Classics, Queen's University, Kingston, Ont., 1913-15; Acting Professor of Latin, Queen's University, 1919-20. Lecturer in Classics, Sheffield University, 1920-1924; Lecturer in Latin, St. Andrews University, 1924-30; Commissioned in the

Royal Field Artillery, 1915; served in France, Jan.-Dec. 1916; took part in the Battle of the Somme; invalided home and served for a time as Intelligence Officer. Joined West Riding Home Guard, 1940. Town Councillor, St. Andrews, 1956-61. *Publications:* Jovialis and the Calliopian Text of Terence; Ancient Editions of Terence; various articles in the Classical Review and the Classical Quarterly. *Recreations:* trout angling, sea-fishing, boating. *Address:* East Scores House, St. Andrews.
[*Died* 13 *May* 1968.

CRAIG, John Manson, V.C. 1917; B.Sc.; Sqdn. Ldr. (War Subs.) R.A.F.V.R.; *b.* 5 March 1896; *s.* of John Craig, Innergeldie, Perthshire, and Margaret Eleanora McCosh; *m.* 1931, Elizabeth Melville Henderson; two *s.* one *d.* *Educ.:* Morrison's Academy, Crieff; Edinburgh University; Trinity College, Cambridge. Served in France with 6th Cameron Highlanders and in Palestine with 1/5th Royal Scots Fusiliers in European War, 1915-18 (V.C.; Royal Flying Corps, Instructor, 1918; demobilised, 1919). Served 1940-1945 with R.A.F. with acting rank of Wing Commander. *Recreations:* golf and gardening. *Address:* Coneyhill, Comrie, Perthshire.
[*Died* 17 *Feb.* 1970.

CRAIG, Colonel Noel Newman Lombard, D.S.O. 1917; O.B.E. 1919; LL.D.; *y. s.* of late William Alexander Craig, J.P., of Crotanstoun, County Kildare, and Frascati, Blackrock, County Dublin; *m.* 1926, Marian Eleanor, *d.* of late Edgar Clarke Quinby, of Titusville, Pennsylvania, U.S.A.; three *d.* *Educ.:* University School and Trinity College, Dublin, 1st Senior Moderator (Gold Medallist), Honours B.A., LL.B., LL.D. Joined Indian Army (Royal Munster Fusiliers), 1906 (Sword of Honour); Capt. 1914; T. Lt.-Col., A.Q.M.G., 1918; called to English Bar, Lincoln's Inn, 1915; served European War two years regimentally and subsequently as D.A.D.S. H.Qrs. Second Army France, D.A.D.S., Italy; D.A.A. and Q.M.G. Supreme War Council, Versailles (despatches thrice, D.S.O., O.B.E., Mons Star 1914 and Bar, 1914-18 War Medal, Victory Medal with Palm, Chevalier Legion of Honour, Officer Order of Leopold, Belgium, Officer Crown of Italy, Officer Crown of Belgium, Croix de Guerre with Palm, Croce di Guerra); Knight Comdr. Holy Sepulchre; subsequently employed as A.Q.M.G. Paris, A.Q.M.G. (actg. Col.), Brussels, Military Liaison Bureau, 1919-20, D.A.A.G., British Delegations, Inter-allied Commissions, Vienna and Buda-pest, 1920-22; retired pay, 1924; Attaché Diplomatic Service, British Legation, Riga, 1925; Oslo, 1926-27; to the Hague, 1927; Military Attaché at British Legation, Copenhagen, 1939; served War of 1939-45, with M.I. Branch, Copenhagen and London; made prisoner by German Army, Apr. 9, 1940; (war medals, 1939-45, and 1940); re-appointed to British Embassy, Copenhagen, 1945-51, and to British Embassy, Madrid, 1951-54. *Publications:* Gulfs (novel), 1932; Twilight in Vienna (novel), 1933; 50 short stories to British and American Magazines. *Address:* Titusville, Penn., U.S.A. *Club:* Kildare Street (Dublin).
[*Died* 31 *Oct.* 1968.

CRAIG, Thomas Joseph Alexander, C.I.E. 1932; *b.* 1881; 2nd *s.* of late James Craig, Banbridge, Co. Down; *m.* 1924, Mabel Frances, *e. d.* of late J. B. Quinnell, Edenburn, Co. Kerry; two *s.* *Educ.:* Dundalk; Banbridge. Joined the Indian Police, 1902; posted to Bengal; Supt. of Police, 1911; Dep. Insp. Gen. of Police, 1925; Insp. Gen. of Police, 1930-36; retd., 1936. *Recreation:* gardening. *Address:* Collette, Cooden, Bexhill, Sx. *T.:* Cooden 2243.
[*Died* 7 *March* 1970.

CRAIG-BROWN, Lt.-Col. and Hon. Brig.-Gen. Ernest, D.S.O. 1915; late the West India Regt. and Queen's Own Cameron Highlanders; *b.* 20 June 1871; *e. s.* of late T. Craig-Brown, Selkirk; *m.* 1903, Constance Ellen (*d.* 1964), *y. d.* of late Henry Guinness, Stillorgan, Co. Dublin; one *s.* two *d.* *Educ.:* Merchiston Castle School, Edinburgh; Edinburgh Univ.; Royal Military Coll., Sandhurst. Entered Army, 1895; Capt. 1899; Staff College, 1904-5; Major, 1914; Lt.-Col. 1921; General Staff Officer, 3rd grade, 1908-1912, 2nd grade, 1914; D.A.A.G. 1914; D.A.Q.M.G. 1915; served Sierra Leone, 1898 (severely wounded, medal with clasp); South African War, 1900-2 (Queen's medal 3 clasps, King's medal 2 clasps); European War, 1914-18 (D.S.O., despatches five times, Bt. Lt.-Col., Order of Danilo of Montenegro, 4th class); retired pay, 1925. *Address:* 33 Chester Street, Edinburgh 3. *T.:* Caledonian 7919. *Club:* Caledonian.
[*Died* 22 *April* 1966.

CRAMPTON, Harold Percy, M.A., M.D., B.Ch.Cantab.; M.R.C.S., L.R.C.P.; F.F.A.; R.C.S.; D.A.; Emer. Consulting Anæsthetist, late Hon. Anæsthetist and Lecturer on Anæsthetics, Middlesex Hosp.; *b.* London, 1878; *e. s.* of Percy and Florence Crampton; *m.* Muriel (*d.* 1961), *d.* of Rev. W. R. Tindal-Atkinson; one *s.* two *d.* *Educ.:* Brighton Coll.; Cambridge Univ.; Middlesex Hosp. Anæsthetist Central London Nose, Throat and Ear Hosp., 1908-20; temporary Capt., R.A.M.C., B.E.F., 1915-19; Anæsthetist E.M.S. 1939-45; retired, 1945. *Publication:* Chapter Anæsthesia, History of Great War, based on Official Documents, 1922. *Address:* Lindens, Kithurst Park, Storrington, Sussex.
[*Died* 17 *Sept.* 1969.

CRANKSHAW, Lieut.-Col. Sir Eric Norman Spencer, K.C.M.G., *cr.* 1939 (C.M.G. 1934); M.B.E. 1919; Secretary, Government Hospitality Fund, 1929-49, and Office Commandant, New Public Offices, 1940-49; *b.* 1 July 1885; *e. s.* of late R. L. Crankshaw, Dunlewy, Gweedore, Co. Donegal; *m.* 1912, Winifred Mary (*d.* 1927), *o. d.* of late G. H. Ireland, Mauritius; one *s.* one *d.* *Educ.:* Eton. Royal Fusiliers, 1905-21; served European War, 1915-18 (wounded, despatches twice); attached Army Signal Service, 1915-16; Camp Commandant (D.A.A.G.) 4th Army Corps, 1916-17; Camp Commandant (D.A.A.G.) Supreme War Council, Versailles, 1917-18; D.A.A.&Q.M.G., Peace Conference, Paris, 1918-20; Assistant Private Secretary to Secretary of State for War, 1920-21; Reserve of Officers, 1921 to 1936; re-employed, G.S.O.(1) M.I. War Office, 1939-40. Order of the Brilliant Star of Zanzibar, 4th class, 1929; Order of the Star of Ethiopia (Comdr.), 3rd class, 1932; Order of Al Rafidain, Iraq, 3rd class, 1933; Order of El Nahdah, Class III, Trans-Jordan, 1934. *Recreations:* hunting, shooting, fishing, cricket. *Address:* The Old Posting House, Speen, Newbury, Berks. *Clubs:* Turf, Bath, M.C.C.
[*Died* 24 *June* 1966.

CRANSTON, William Patrick, C.M.G. 1964; Counsellor, British Embassy, Jedda, since 1966; *b.* 5 Oct. 1913; *s.* of Col. W. J. Cranston, D.S.O., O.B.E. *Educ.:* Stonyhurst Coll.; R.M.C., Sandhurst. Commissioned in Indian Army, 1933; transf. to Indian Political Service, 1938; returned to I.A., Sept. 1939, but recalled to I.P.S., Aug. 1941. Served in Office of U.K. High Comr., Delhi, 1947; transf. to C.R.O., Dec. 1947; transf. to Admin. of African Territories Dept., Foreign Office, 1949; Asst. Political Sec., H.Q. Secretariat, Mogadishu, 1949-50; apptd. a Mem. Foreign Service, Oct. 1950; First Sec. and Consul, Damascus, 1952; N.A.T.O. Defence Coll., Paris, 1957; Foreign Office, 1957; Kuwait, 1960; in charge of British

Property in Egypt Section, Foreign Office, 1964. *Address:* c/o Foreign Office, S.W.1; 52 Eaton Place, S.W.1. *Clubs:* Athenæum, Cavalry. [*Died* 12 *Nov.* 1967.

CRANWORTH, 2nd Baron (*cr.* 1899), **Bertram Francis Gurdon,** K.G. 1948; M.C.; Vice-Lieut. of County of Suffolk since 1947; *b.* 13 June 1877; *e. s.* of 1st Baron and Emily (*d.* 1934), *d.* of R. Boothby Heathcote; *S.* father, 1902; *m.* 1903, Vera, C.B.E. 1945, *d.* of Arthur W. Ridley, of Eaton Place, S.W.; two *d. Educ.:* Eton; Trinity Coll., Cambridge. Served S. African War, 1900-1; B.E. Africa, 1906-11; European War, France and East Africa, 1915-18 (M.C., French Croix de guerre (with Palm), despatches twice). *Publications:* A Colony in the Making, 1912, second edition entitled Profit and Sport in British East Africa, 1919; Kenya Chronicles, 1940. *Heir: g.s.* Philip Bertram Gurdon [*b.* 1940; *s.* of late Hon. Robert Brampton Gurdon and Hon. Daisy Consuelo (Yoskyl) Pearson, *e. d.* of 2nd Viscount Cowdray; she *m.* 2nd, 1944, Lt.-Col. Alistair Gibb (*d.* 1955), *s.* of late Sir Alexander Gibb, G.B.E., C.B. and 3rd, 1962, 1st Baron McCorquodale of Newton, P.C.]. *Recreations:* shooting, fishing. *Address:* Grundisburgh, Woodbridge, Suffolk. *Club:* Brooks's. [*Died* 4 *Jan.* 1964.

CRASKE, A(rthur) H(ugh) Glenn; Metropolitan Magistrate since 1952; *b.* 11 June 1904; *o. s.* of Harold Craske, Letchworth, Herts, and Beatrice Isabella, *d.* of Henry Glenn; unmarried. *Educ.:* Clayesmore School; University College, London (LL.B. 1st class Hons. 1924). Called to Bar, Middle Temple, 1925; Bencher, 1951; South-Eastern Circuit. Served War of 1939-1945 in R.A.F.V.R., 1940-45, demobilised as Squadron Leader. Member, Council of Clayesmore School. *Recreation:* being lazy. *Address:* 48 Couchmore Avenue, Esher. *T.:* Emberbrook 1452. *Club:* Royal Automobile. [*Died* 9 *May* 1967.

CRAUFURD, Sir Alexander John Fortescue, 7th Bt., *cr.* 1781; *b.* 22 March 1876; *s.* of Sir Charles William Frederick Craufurd, 4th Bt., and Hon. Isolda Caroline Vereker (*d.* 1927), *e. d.* of 4th Viscount Gort; *S.* brother, Sir Quentin Charles Alexander Craufurd, 6th Bt., M.B.E., 1957; *m.* 1911, Alexa Campbell Little (*d.* 1955); two *d. Educ.:* Wellington; King's College, London; Camborne School of Mines. Mining and prospecting, 1899-1912. From 1913, partially incapacitated. *Heir: kinsman* James Gregan Craufurd [*b.* 23 Feb. 1886; *m.* 1931, Ruth Marjorie, *d.* of F. Corder, Ipswich; one *s.* two *d.*]. *Address:* c/o J. Clement, The Old Homestead, Ceres, C.P., South Africa. [*Died* 10 *July* 1966.

CRAUFURD, Sir James Gregan, 8th Bt., *cr.* 1781, of Kilbirney; Barrister, retired; *b.* 23 February 1886; *s.* of late Henry Robert Craufurd; *S.* kinsman, Sir Alexander John Fortescue Craufurd, 7th Bt., 1966; *m.* 1931, Ruth Marjorie, *d.* of Frederic Corder, Ipswich; one *s.* two *d. Educ.:* Harrow School; University College, Oxford (M.A.). Called to the Bar, Lincoln's Inn, 1914. J.P., County of Hertford, 1930-. *Recreations:* music, local history, local government. *Heir: s.* Robert James Craufurd [*b.* 18 March 1937; *m.* 1964, Catherine Penelope Westmacott; three *d.*]. *Address:* Brightwood, Aldbury, Tring, Hertfordshire. *T.:* Aldbury Common 262. *Club:* United University. [*Died* 7 *April* 1970.

CRAVEN, 6th Earl of, *cr.* 1801; **William Robert Bradley Craven;** Viscount Uffington, 1801; Baron Craven, 1665; Lieut. R.N.V.R.; *b.* 8 Sept. 1917; *s.* of 5th Earl and Mary Wilhelmina, *d.* of William George, Town Clerk, Invergordon; *S.* father, 1932; *m.* 1st, 1939, Irene *y.d.* of F.D.H. Meyrick, M.D.; one *d.*; 2nd, 1954, Elizabeth Johnstone-Douglas; two *s.* one *d. Educ.:* Downside. *Heir: s.* Viscount Uffington. *Address:* Hampstead Marshall, Newbury, Berks. [*Died* 27 *Jan.* 1965.

CRAVEN, Rt. Rev. George L., M.C.; Vicar General of the Westminster Archdiocese, Titular Bishop of Sebastopolis and Auxiliary to the Archbishop of Westminster since 1947; Provost of the Metropolitan Cathedral Chapter of Westminster since 1957; Assistant at the Pontifical Throne since 1964; *b.* 1884. *Educ.:* St. Wilfrid's Cotton Hall, Oscott; St. Sulpice, Paris. Priest, 1912; served mission at Westminster Cathedral; C.F. European War, 1914-18 (despatches, M.C.); Asst. Administrator, Crusade of Rescue, 1919, Administrator since 1920; Hon. Canon of Westminster, 1933; Adm. Westminster Diocesan Education Fund, 1938; Member Westminster Chapter, 1947; Ecclesiastical Adviser to Catholic Nurses' Guild of Great Britain, 1954. Chevalier, Légion d'Honneur, 1956 (Officier, 1963). Vicar Capitular, Westminster, 1963. *Address:* St. James's Rectory, 22 George Street, Manchester Square, W.1. [*Died* 15 *March* 1967.

CRAW, Sir Henry Hewat, K.B.E., *cr.* 1942; C.I.E. 1937; *b.* Whitsome, Berwickshire, 29 Oct. 1882; *m.* 1915, Kathleen Pleasant (*d.* 1945), *d.* of John Pollen, LL.D., C.I.E., I.C.S.; one *s.* one *d. Educ.:* George Watson's College, Edinburgh; Edinburgh University. Indian Civil Service, 1907; Military Service, 1917-19; Chief Secretary to Govt. of Burma, 1935-37; Counsellor to Governor of Burma, 1939-41; Adviser to Secretary of State for Burma, 1942-47. *Address:* 24 Langside Avenue, S.W.15. *Club:* Roehampton. [*Died* 28 *Jan.* 1964.

CRAWFORD, Arthur Muir, M.D., Ch.B., F.R.F.P.S.G.; retd.; Hon. Consulting Physician, Royal Infirmary, Glasgow; *b.* 1882; 2nd *s.* of Robert Crawford, J.P.; *m.* Jenny Lennox, *d.* of J. F. Beaumont; two *s. Educ.:* Ayr Academy; Glasgow University. Formerly Pathologist, Lanark District Asylum, Hartwood; House Surgeon and House Physician, and Physician to Out-Patient Department, Glasgow Royal Infirmary; Visiting Physician, Woodside Red Cross Hospital, Glasgow, 1915-16; Medical Specialist to 53rd C.C.S., B.E.F. (Maj. R.A.M.C.); Medical Specialist and Cardiologist to Ministry of Pensions; Professor of Materia Medica and Therapeutics, St. Mungo's College, Glasgow; Physician, Royal Infirmary, Glasgow; Hon. Lecturer in Clinical Medicine, University of Glasgow. *Publications:* Materia Medica for Nurses, 1927, 6th Ed., 1946; many papers in medical journals. *Recreations:* interest in music and general literature. *Address:* 9 Brean Down Avenue, Weston - super - Mare, Somerset. *Club:* Royal Scottish Automobile (Glasgow). [*Died* 12 *July* 1962.

CRAWFORD, Col. Edward William, C.B.E. 1926. D.S.O. 1918; member of firm of E. W. Crawford & Co., Chartered Accountants, 2 Coleman Street, E.C.2; *b.* 1879. Served European War, 1914-18 (despatches, D.S.O. and Bar, Croix de Guerre). *Address:* 15 Warwick Square, S.W.1. *T.:* Victoria 7105. [*Died* 10 *Oct.* 1961.

CRAWFORD, John Balfour, J.P. (County of City of Edinburgh); F.R.S.E.; *b.* 11 Nov. 1887; *s.* of late Alexander Crawford, Milngavie; *m.* 1918, Agnes, *d.* of late George Scrivener, Bearsden; two *s.* two *d. Educ.:* Allan Glen's School, Glasgow. Treasurer, Bank of Scotland, Edinburgh, 1942-52; President, Institute of Bankers in Scotland, 1945-47. *Address:* 30 Midmar Gardens, Edinburgh 10. *T.:* Edinburgh Morningside 7131. [*Died* 6 *June* 1962.

CRAWFORD, General Sir Kenneth Noel, K.C.B., *cr.* 1948 (C.B. 1944); M.C.; retd.; Chief Royal Engineer since 1958; Colonel Commandant Royal Engineers, 1951, Representative Colonel Commandant, 1955; *b.* 25 June 1895; *s.* of Henry Leighton Crawford, C.M.G., Ceylon Civil Service; *m.* 1921, Doris Margaret, *e. d.* of Joseph Parker, C.S.I.; two *s.* one *d.* *Educ.:* Clifton College; R.M.A., Woolwich. 2nd Lt. R.E., 1915; served European War, 1915-18 (M.C., despatches); Capt. 1918; Major, 1930; Bt. Lt.-Col. 1935; Col. 1938; Maj.-Gen. 1944 (Actg. 1942, Temp. 1943); Lt.-Gen. 1947; Gen. 1952. Director, Air (including Airborne Forces), W.O.. 1942-46; General Officer Commanding Land Forces, Greece, 1946-47; Deputy Chief of Imperial General Staff and member of Army Council, 1947-49; Controller of Supplies (Munitions), Ministry of Supply, 1949-53; Chairman. Royal Ordnance Factories Board of Management, 1952-1953; retired 1953. Chairman Edwin Danks (Oldbury) Ltd.; Chairman, Penman & Co. Ltd.; Director Cyanamid of Great Britain Ltd.; Director, Westland Aircraft Ltd. Vice-Pres. Parachute Regimental Association; Life Hon. Member, Australian Paratroopers Assoc. Hon. Colonel Parachute Bn. T.A., 1952-60. F.R.S.A. U.S. Legion of Merit. *Recreations:* Rugby football (Army XV, 1921; President Army Rugby Union, 1948-53), golf, shooting, fishing. *Address:* 1 Hamilton Mansions, Fourth Avenue, Hove, Sussex. *Clubs:* Army and Navy, Airborne Forces. [*Died* 5 *March* 1961.

CRAWFURD-PRICE, Walter Harrington; author and journalist; *b.* London, Jan. 1881; *o. s.* of Walter Henry Harrington Price and Mary, *d.* of late Captain James Crawfurd, R.A.; *m.* 1st, 1907, Margaret (*d.* 1938), *d.* of late James Allan, of Bishopbriggs, Lanarkshire, and Agnes Crawfurd; two *s.*; 2nd, 1945, Hélène Louise Léontine (*d.* 1965), *d.* of late Catherin Gaguin, Mâcon, France, *widow* of George Henry Mennell, Solicitor. *Educ.:* Norwich; University of Wales. Special Correspondent of Daily Mail, Turkish Counter Revolution, 1909; Correspondent of The Times in Macedonia and Greece, 1911-14; War Correspondent of The Times with the Turkish Army in first Balkan War, 1912; with the Greek Army in second Balkan War, 1913; with the Serbian Army in European War; represented the Sunday Times at Paris and subsequent Peace Conferences; Foreign Editor of the Sunday Times, 1920-25; travelled extensively in Europe and Near East and North Africa; Grand Officer of the Order of the Crown of Rumania; Commander of the Order of St. Sava (Serbia); Chevalier of the Orders of The Redeemer (Greece), and King George I of Greece. *Publications:* The Balkan Cockpit, 1914; Light on the Balkan Darkness, 1915; Venizelos and the War, 1916; Serbia's Part in the War, 1918; A Tangier Visit, 1935. *Address:* Oak Cottage, Hatfield Broad Oak, Nr. Bishop's Stortford, Herts. *Club:* Savage. [*Died* 12 *Oct.* 1967.

CRAWLEY-BOEVEY, Sir Lance (Launcelot) Valentine Hyde, 7th Bt., *cr.* 1784; Verderer of the Royal Forest of Dean; *b.* 26 Apr. 1900; *o. s.* of 6th Bt. and Eliza Barbara (*d.* 1962), *o. d.* of Valentine Blake McGrath; *S.* father, 1928; *m.* 1927, Elizabeth Goodeth, *d.* of Herbert d'Auvergne Innes, late Indian Police; two *s.* *Educ.:* Wellington College. *Heir:* *s.* Thomas Michael Blake Crawley-Boevey [*b.* 29 Sept. 1928; *m.* 1957, Laura Coelingh Van der Eijken; two *s.*]. *Address:* c/o Westminster Bank, Newnham, Glos.; Aloha, Finca el Capricho, Marbella, Malaga, Spain. *Club:* English-Speaking Union. [*Died* 4 *July* 1968.

CRAWSHAY-WILLIAMS, Lieut.-Col. Eliot; retired; F.R.G.S.; *e. s.* of Arthur John Williams and Rose H. T. Crawshay; *b.* 4 Sept. 1879; *m.* 1st, 1908, Alice (who obtained a divorce, 1914), *d.* of late James Gay-Roberts; one *s.* one *d.*; 2nd, 1915, Kathleen Isabella McNeale (who obtained a divorce, 1924), *o. c.* of late Wm. Rome; 3rd, Weeta, *d.* of late William Cattanach Donaldson; two *s.* *Educ.:* Eton; Trinity College, Oxford. Entered army, 1900; served England and India; returned overland through Persia and Russia, 1903-4; contested Chorley Division of Lancashire, 1906; Assistant Private Secretary to Rt. Hon. Winston Churchill at Colonial Office, 1906-8; Parliamentary Private Secretary to Rt. Hon. D. Lloyd George, Chancellor of the Exchequer, 1910; M.P. (L.) Leicester, Jan. 1910-13; J.P.; Lt.-Col. R.H.A. (T.); late Lieut. R.F.A., R.F.A. (M.), and R.F.R.A.; commanded 1st Leicestershire R.H.A., 1915-17, Egypt, Sinai; attached H.Q. Northern Command, 1918-20 (Lt.-Col.); Chief Civil Defence Officer, Treforest Trading Estate, 1941-43; Lecturer to H.M. Forces, 1943-45; Chm. Coed y Mwstwr (Approved) School, 1945-47. *Publications:* Across Persia, 1907; Problems of To-day, 1908; Songs on Service, 1917; Leaves from an Officer's Notebook, 1918; The Gutter and the Stars, 1918; Clouds and the Sun, 1919; Five Grand Guignol Plays, 1924; More Grand Guignol Plays, 1927; The Booby Trap, 1928; The Donkey's Nose, 1929; Night in the Hotel, 1931; The Rule of Three, 1931; Stay of Execution, 1933; First Passion, 1934; Parade of Virgins, 1935; Simple Story (Autobiography), 1935; Hotel Exit, 1935; Lobs' Pound, 1936; A Young Man's Fancy, 1936; They want to be Faithful, 1937; No One Wants Poetry, 1938; Votes and Virgins, 1939; Husbands Can't Help it, 1939; Speckled Virtue, 1940; Lapse into Lunacy, 1942; Strictly Confidential, 1944; Flak, 1944; Outrageous Fortune, 1944; Barrage, 1944; 'Tis Not in Mortals, 1945; Hywel and Gwyneth, 1945; Night in No Time, 1946; Borderline (short stories), 1946; The Wolf from the West, 1947; The Man who met Himself (short stories), 1947; This and That, 1947; No Apparent Motive, 1948; Love Affair, 1948; Heaven Takes a Hand, 1949; Rough Passage, 1950; Unusual Eugene 1952; The Stroud Case, 1953; various political and other articles. *Plays:* Rounding the Triangle, 1921; E. and O.E., 1921; Amends, 1922; The Compleat Lover (produced as Spring Cleaning), 1922; Cupboard Love, 1922; The Nutcracker Suite, 1922; This Marriage, 1924; The Man in the Next Room, 1924; After Bedtime, 1926; The Debit Account, 1926; Out East, 1929; The Donkey's Nose, 1929; Husbands can't Help it, 1946; Fascination (Film, 1931); Man of Mayfair (Film, 1931); Service for Ladies (part author, Film, 1931). *Recreations:* (past) lawn tennis, golf, shooting, riding. *Address:* Tybryn, Kingsdown, near Deal. *T.:* Kingsdown 202. *Clubs:* Brooks's, Eighty, National Liberal, Queen's, P.E.N., International L.T. [*Died* 11 *May* 1962.

CRAY, Rev. Canon Frank Maynard; Residentiary Canon of Leicester Cathedral since 1958; *b.* 6 April 1898; *s.* of Albert and Thirza Cray; *m.* 1929, Constance Mary Parker; no *c.* *Educ.:* S. Peter's School, Leicester; Alderman Newton School, Leicester; Univ. of Leeds; Leeds Clergy School; Westcott House, Cambridge. Asst. Curate: St. Margaret's, Leicester, 1924; St. Michael and All Angels, Belgrave, 1928; Vicar of St. Alban's, Leicester, 1932; Rector of Aylestone, 1950-65; Director of Religious Education Leicester Diocese, 1945-58. Hon. Canon of Leicester Cathedral, 1945. Canon Treasurer, 1953-54, Chancellor, 1954-58, of Leicester. *Address:* 134 Glen Rd., Oadby, Leicester. [*Died* 29 *Aug.* 1967.

CREAGH, Major-Gen. Sir Michael O'Moore, K.B.E., *cr.* 1941; M.C.; *b.* 16

May 1892. 2nd Lt. 7th Hussars, 1911; Capt., 1918; Major, 15th/19th Hussars, 1924; Bt. Lt.-Col., 1931; Lt.-Col., 1934; Colonel, 1938; Major-General, 1941; served European War, 1914-18 (despatches, M.C.); War of 1939-45, Operations in Middle East (despatches, K.B.E.); retired pay, 1944; U.N.R.R.A., 1944-46; Dep. Chief of Greece Mission; Chief of Emergency Supply Unit, European Regional Office; Chief of European Regional Office Voluntary Soc. Liaison Unit. *Address:* Pigeon Hill, Homington, Salisbury, Wilts. [*Died* 14 *Dec.* 1970.

CREAGH COEN, Sir Terence (Bernard), K.B.E. 1953; C.I.E. 1946; *b.* 31 March 1903; *s.* of late Rev. J. Creagh Coen, D.D., Rector of Hannington, Northampton. *Educ.:* Uppingham; Queen's Coll., Oxford. Entered Indian Civil Service (Punjab), 1927; Indian Political Service, 1935. Served in Indian States, 1935-41 and 1944-46; First Secretary, British Embassy, Washington, 1941-44. Deputy Secretary, Political Department, 1946-47. Transferred, 1947, to service of Government of Pakistan (Joint Secretary, Ministry of Foreign Affairs, 1947-50; Establishment Secretary, Cabinet Secretariat, 1950-53). Chief, U.N. public administration mission to Colombia, 1954-55. Chairman, Public Service Commission, Eastern Region, Nigeria, 1956-58. Fellow, St. Antony's College, Oxford, 1965-67. *Publication:* The Indian Political Service: a study in indirect rule, 1971 (posthumous). *Address:* 10 rue Sir Basil Scott, Tangier, Morocco. *Clubs:* Athenæum, Travellers'. [*Died* 27 *Sept.* 1970.

CREED, Richard Stephen, T.D. (with 4 clasps); D.M. (Oxon.); Emeritus Fellow, New College, Oxford (Fellow and Tutor, 1925-60); formerly Univ. Demonstrator and Lectr. in Physiology; Fellow of Winchester Coll., since 1945; *b.* 1898; 4th *s.* of Rev. C. J. Creed, M.A.; *m.* 1933, Sybil, *d.* of late Sir Edwin Cooper, R.A.; one *s.* three *d.* *Educ.:* Wyggeston School, Leicester; Trinity College, Oxford (Millard Scholar); St. Thomas' Hospital. Served in R.F.A., 1917-19 (France and Belgium); in R.A.M.C., 1939-45, B.E.F., M.E.F., C.M.F., and B.L.A.; 1st Class Hon. School of Natural Science (Physiology), 1921; Senior Demy, Magdalen College, 1921-24; Gotch Memorial Prize, 1921; M.R.C.S., L.R.C.P., 1923; B.M., B.Ch., M.A., 1923; D.M., 1930; Radcliffe Prize, 1933; formerly Casualty Officer and House Physician, St. Thomas' Hospital; Pres. Section I (Physiology), British Assoc., 1955. Chm. Management Cttee., Warneford Hosp., 1947-60; Chm. Editorial Bd., Journal of Physiology, 1951-56. *Publications:* papers in various scientific journals; translated and edited The Physiology of the Vestibular Apparatus by M. Camis, 1930; part-author of Reflex Activity of the Spinal Cord, 1932. *Address:* Church Farm House, Dry Sandford, Abingdon, Berks. [*Died* 7 *July* 1964.

CREED, Sir Thomas Percival, K.B.E., *cr.* 1946 (C.B.E. 1943); M.C.; Q.C. 1948; M.A.; Principal, Queen Mary College, Univ. of London, 1952-67, Fellow, 1967; Chm. Medical Appeal Tribunal, under National Insurance (Industrial Injuries) Act 1946, since 1948; *b.* 1897; 3rd *s.* of late Reverend C. J. Creed, M.A., Rector of Farthinghoe, Northants; *m.* 1928, Margaret, *er. d.* of A. Brewis; one *s.* two *d.* *Educ.:* Wyggeston School, Leicester; Pembroke College, Oxford (Classical Scholar). B.A. (Lit. Hum.), 1922; M.A. 1925; called to Bar, Lincoln's Inn; Hon. Bencher, Lincoln's Inn, 1967. Artists' Rifles, 1915; served with Leicestershire Regiment, 1915-1919 (M.C., twice wounded); Sudan Political Service, 1922; District Judge, 1926; Judge in Iraq Courts under Anglo-Iraq Judicial Agreement, 1931; Additional Judge, Baghdad; President of the Courts, Kirkuk, 1932; Mosul, 1934; Judge High Court, Khartoum, Sudan, 1935; Chief Justice of the Sudan, 1936-41; Legal Sec. Sudan Govt. and member Gov.-Gen.'s Council, 1941-47; periodically Actg. Governor-Gen.; Chief Rep. of Sudan Govt. at hearing of Egyptian case, Security Council, 1947; Secretary, King's College, London, 1948-51; Chm., Forest of Dean Cttee., Forestry Commn., 1955; Chm., Collegiate Council, 1955-57, Deputy Vice-Chancellor, University of London, 1958-61; Vice-Chancellor, 1964-67; Co-opted Member of Senate, 1968-. Chm. Council, Queen Elizabeth Coll., Univ. of London, 1968-. Mem., Commonwealth Scholarship Commn., 1967-. Hon. Fellow, Pembroke Coll., Oxford, 1950. Chm., Burnham Cttee., 1958-65. Hon. LL.D. (Leicester), 1965. Comdr., Order of the Nile, 1939. *Address:* 18 Wynnstay Gdns., W.8. *T.:* Western 0078. *Club:* Athenæum. [*Died* 11 *May* 1969.

CREIGHTON, Rev. Cuthbert; Headmaster of King's School, Worcester, 1919-36, and Hno. Headmaster, 1940-42; *b.* 25 July 1876; *s.* of Mandell Creighton, late Bishop of London and Louise von Glehn; *m.* 1913, Margaret Bruce, *d.* of Hon. F. J. Bruce; two *s.* *Educ.:* Marlborough; Emmanuel College, Cambridge. 2nd Class Classical Tripos; Assistant Master and Chaplain, Uppingham School, 1899-1918; Deacon, 1901; Priest, 1902; Examining Chaplain to Bishop of Worcester, 1919. *Recreations:* walking, foreign travel. *Address:* The Grange, Shalbourne, Marlborough. *T.:* Great Bedwyn 256. [*Died* 21 *April* 1963.

CREIGHTON, Rear-Adm. Sir Kenelm Everard Lane, K.B.E., *cr.* 1944; M.V.O.; J.P.; *b.* Malta, 10 Jan. 1883; 2nd *s.* of Major Fitzgerald Creighton; *m.* Gladys *e. d.* of G. P. Warren, Pitlochry, Perthshire; one *s.* one *d.* *Educ.:* Fermoy College, Ireland. H.M.S. Britannia, Midshipman, 1898; served in H.M. ships Venus, Jupiter; Sub-Lieut., 1902; Lieut. 1904; H.M.S. Rambler, and assisted in Survey of British North Borneo, 1904-6; Navigator of H.M. Ships Patrol, Talbot, 1908-10; Staff of Navigation School, 1910; Navigator of Cumberland Cadet Training Cruiser, 1911-14; Navigator of H.M. Battle Cruiser, New Zealand, 1914-18; took part in actions of Heligoland Bight, Dogger Bank, and Jutland (Croix de Guerre, promoted to Commander, 31 Dec. 1915); Navigating Officer H.M.A.S. Australia, Flagship of Sir Lionel Halsey, 1918; appointed H.M.S. Queen Elizabeth, Flagship of Sir David Beatty, as Navigator and Master of the Fleet, 1918; acted in this capacity at the surrender of the German Fleet, 21 Nov. 1918; Commander for Navigating duties of the Royal Yacht, H.M.Y. Victoria and Albert, 1919; Captain, 1921; Captain of R.N. College, Greenwich, 1928-29; Director of Navigation Admiralty, 1929-31; Captain of H.M.S. Royal Sovereign, 1932-33; Rear-Adm. and retired list, 1934; recalled, 1939; served as Commodore Ocean Convoys 1939-43 (despatches); Director-General of Ports and Lights Administration, Egypt, 1943-46. Younger Brother of Trinity House; A.D.C. to the King, 1933-34; Member of Hants County Council. *Publication:* Convoy Commodore 1957. *Recreations:* yachting, golf, tennis. *Address:* Glebe Meadow, Clovelly Road, Emsworth, Hants. *T.:* Emsworth 2159. *Club:* Royal Yacht Squadron (Cowes) (Naval Member). [*Died* 27 *Feb.* 1963.

CREMER, Herbert William, C.B.E. 1948; M.Sc., C.Eng.; F.R.I.C., M.I.Chem.E., F.Inst.F.; M.Cons.E.; Hon. F.Inst.W.P.C.; F.K.C., Lond.; Formerly Senior Partner, Cremer & Warner, Consulting Chemical Engineers; *b.* Faversham, Kent, 1893; *y. s.* of late Charles Cremer, Faversham; *m.* 1924, Dorothy (*d.* 1955), *y. d.* of late John Garment Nunns, London and Faversham; one *s.* *Educ.:* King's School,

Canterbury; University of London, King's College. Technical Staff, Department of Explosives Supply, 1915-18; Director Chemical Warfare Supplies, Dept. of Military Requirements, Ministry of Munitions, 1918; Headquarters Staff, Dept. of Scientific and Industrial Research, 1919-20; Lecturer in Chemistry, 1920, at King's Coll., London; inaugurated the study of Chemical Engineering at this College in 1928, occupying position of Director of Chemical Engineering Studies until 1939; Chemical Engineer to Sir Alexander Gibb & Partners on the design and construction of Royal Ordnance and other Factories, etc., 1939-46; Hon. Sec. Institution of Chemical Engineers, 1931-37, Pres., 1947-48. Osborne Reynolds Medal; list of the Institution; Joint Hon. Sec. Soc. of Chemical Industry, 1946; Vice-Pres. and Jubilee Memorial Lecturer of the Soc., 1947 Pres. Royal Inst. of Chemistry, 1951-53; Member: Organising and Technical Cttees. of First International Congress of Chemical Engineering, 1936; General Board, 1939-49, 1955-60, Executive Cttee., 1944-49, 1955-60, of Nat. Physical Laboratory; Technology Cttee., Univ. Grants Cttee., 1948-59; Chairman: Water Pollution Research Bd., 1946-1951, 1952-64; Thames Survey Cttee., 1948-1963. Chemical Engineering Research Cttee., D.S.I.R., 1949-53; Standing Tech. Cttee. on Synthetic Detergents, Min of Housing and Local Govt., 1956-; Member: Chemical Council, 1948-50, 1954-56; Nat. Cttee. for Chemistry, 1948-54; Council and Exec. Cttee. of the City and Guilds of London Inst., 1949-: Chem. Research Bd., 1952-58; Nat. Advisory Council for Educ. in Industry and Commerce, 1952-58; Gen. Council Brit. Standards Instn., 1955-59; Governing Body: Loughborough Coll. of Technology, 1954-66; Imperial Coll., London, 1957-. *Publications:* Joint Compiler of Technical Records of Explosive Supply (1915-19); Gen. Editor encyclop. on Chem. Eng. Practice, 1956-66; papers in Jl. Chem. Soc. and Trans. Instn. Chemical Engineers, etc. *Recreations:* gardening, yachting. *Address:* Bickley Court, Chislehurst Road, Bromley, Kent. *T.:* Imperial 5260. *Clubs:* Athenæum, Savage.

[*Died* 11 *Feb.* 1970.

CREMER, Robert W. K.; *see* Ketton-Cremer.

CRERAR, Gen. Henry Duncan Graham, C.H. 1945; C.B. 1943; D.S.O. 1917; C.D. 1950; LL.D., D.C.L.; p.s.c.; i.d.c.; *b.* 28 April 1888; *s.* of Peter Duncan Crerar and Marion Elizabeth Stinson; *m.* 1916, Verschoyle, *er. d.* of B. B. Cronyn, Toronto; one *s.* one *d.* *Educ.:* Highfield School, Hamilton; Upper Canada Coll., Toronto; Royal Military Coll., Kingston; Staff Coll., Camberley; Imperial Defence Coll., London. Served European War, 1914-18 (despatches, D.S.O.); Lieut., 4th Fd. Batt. C.A., 1910; Captain, 3rd Brigade C.F.A., C.E.F., 1914; Major and O.C., 11th Batt. C.F.A., C.E.F., 1916; Brigade Major, 5th Can. Div. Artillery, 1917; Lt.-Colonel and Counter Battery Staff Officer, Canadian Corps, 1918; Staff Officer, Artillery, Dept. of National Defence, 1920; General Staff Officer (2), War Office, 1925; Prof. of Tactics, R.M.C., Kingston, 1927; General Staff Officer (1), Dept. of National Defence, 1929-35; Technical Adviser Disarmament Conference, Geneva, 1932; Imperial Conference, London, 1937; Dir. of Mil. Operations and Intelligence, Dept. of National Defence, 1935-38; Comdt., Royal Military Coll., Kingston, 1938-39; Senior Officer, Canadian Military Headquarters, London, 1939-40; Chief of General Staff, Canada, 1940-41; G.O.C. 2nd Canadian Division Overseas, 1941; Commander I Canadian Corps, 1942-44; commanded I Canadian Corps, Mediterranean Area, 1943-44; commanded First Canadian Army, 1944-45; retired, 1946. A.D.C. General to King George VI, 1948-52, to Queen Elizabeth II, 1952. K.G. St. J. 1954. Hon. LL.D.: Queen's, Laval, McGill, Saskatchewan, Toronto, Western Ontario Universities, 1945-46; Hon. D.C.L. Oxford, 1946; Hon. D.Sc. Mil., R.M.C. Canada, 1962. Holds numerous foreign decorations. *Address:* 477 Manor Avenue, Rockcliffe, Ottawa. *Clubs:* Rideau (Ottawa); Hamilton (Hamilton); Mount Royal (Montreal).

[*Died* 1 *April* 1965.

CRESSY-MARCKS, Violet Olivia (Mrs. Francis Fisher), F.R.A.S., F.R.G.S., F.Z.S.; *o. d.* of William Ernest Rutley; *m.* 1st, Captain Cressy-Marcks (whom she divorced); one *s.*; 2nd, 1932, Francis Fisher (*d.* 1956); two *s.* Explorer; travelled in every country of the world, chiefly for purposes of scientific research; carried out archæological studies among the ruins of ancient civilisation, including those of Mesopotamia, Syria, Palestine, North Africa, Egypt, China, Persia, India, Java, Afghanistan, Ethiopia, the Aztec monuments, Khumer and those of the Inca and pre-Inca in Peru and Bolivia; studied in Arabia and other Arab countries. Expeditions, Cairo-Cape, 1925 (5 months); Albania and Balkans, 1927-28 (8 months); Lapland to Baluchistan, 1928-29 (9 months); drove reindeer N. Arctic to Russia, 1930; Brazil and Peru, 1929-30 (11 months); climbed 16,000 feet over the Andes to Huancayo and Lima; visited ruins of Manchu Picchu; made 4th journey around world, 1931-32 (7 months); revisited Angkor (Indo-China); 1933, revisited Spain; 1934, flew from England to India, flew from Kabul over the Hindu Khush and Samarkand to Tashkent, journeyed through Turkistan and flew from Moscow to England; 1935, took the first motor transport from Addis Ababa to Nairobi; 1936, visited the Ethiopian and Eritrean War Fronts; 1937, Mandalay to Pekin overland; 1938, Turkey to Tibet by motor, yak, and mule caravan; first English guest of Mao Tse Tung, Head of the Chinese Communist Party; visited Chinese war fronts, military hospitals, refugee camps, interviewing war lords and governors; travelled westwards to Kokonor Lake studying Lamaseries, Chinese, and Tibetan peoples. Served War of 1939-45, as driver; Special War Corresp. of Daily Express, 1943-45, throughout the East (H.Q. Chungking); accredited to W.O. as War Corresp. (Internat. Military Tribunal, Nuremburg; Paris Peace Conf.; Greek elections). Travelling in many countries, 1947-. Guest of King of Arabia at Riyadh; revisited Indo-China, Japan, Katmundu, 1953-54; 7th and 8th journeys around the world, 1955 and 1956. *Publications:* Up the Amazon and Over the Andes, 1932; Journey into China, 1940. *Recreations:* big game shooting, hunting, music, and collecting Eastern rugs and icons. *Address:* Hazelwood, Kings Langley, Herts. *T.:* Kings Langley 3111; 19 Prince's Gate, S.W.7. *T.:* 01-589 5960.

[*Died* 12 *Sept.* 1970.

CRESWELL, Rear-Adm. (retd.) George Hector, C.B. 1943; D.S.O. 1939; D.S.C.; Royal Navy; *b.* 17 June 1889; *s.* of late F. S. Creswell, Wimbledon; *m.* 1916, Katharine, *d.* of Major John Stuart, O.B.E., The Black Watch; three *s.* three *d.* *Educ.:* Sedbergh; Littlejohns, Blackheath; H.M.S. Britannia. Served European war, 1914-18 (D.S.C.); war of 1939-45. (D.S.O.). *Address:* Rivers Hall, Waldringfield, Woodbridge, Suffolk. *T.:* Waldringfield 259.

[*Died* 20 *April* 1967.

CREWDSON, Bernard Francis, C.B.E. 1920; M.A.; LL.B.; *b.* 9 July 1887; *s.* of F. W. Crewdson, Kendal, Westmorland; *m.* 1920, Audrey Newcombe (*d.* 1951), *y. d.* of C. J. Maltby, late of Travancore, India; one *d.* *Educ.:* Uppingham; King's College, Cambridge; History and Law Tripos. Lloyds Bank, 1909-14; Border Regiment,

1914-16; Irish Guards, 1917-18; beginning of 1919 to Poland with the British Relief Mission to that country and remained as Chief of that Mission until end of 1919; General Secretary, Information Service, Austrian Section Reparation Commission, 1920; now partner David A. Bevan, Simpson & Co. *Recreations:* archery, horticulture. *Address:* 23 Hertford Street, W.1. *Club:* Guards, Gresham. [*Died* 15 *Nov.* 1966.

CREWE, Marchioness of; (Margaret Etrenne Hannah), C.I. 1911; 2nd *d.* of 5th Earl of Rosebery, K.G., K.T., P.C.; *m.* 1899, as his 2nd wife, the 1st and last Marquess of Crewe, K.G., P.C. (*d.* 1945); one *d.* Chevalier of the Legion of Honour, France, 1947. *Address:* 50 Charles Street, W.1; West Horsley Place, Leatherhead, Surrey. [*Died* 13 *March* 1967.

CRIBBETT, Sir (Wilfrid Charles) George, K.B.E., *cr.* 1948; C.M.G. 1943; retired as: Director, B.O.A.C. Associated Companies Ltd. (1957-63); Director International Aeradio Ltd. (1960-63); Deputy Chairman, British Overseas Airways Corporation (1956-60); *b.* 1897; *s.* of Charles James Cribbett; *m.* 1923, Hilda Marion Kettley (*d.* 1963); one *d.* Served European War, 1915-18, London Regt. and R.A.F. Entered Exchequer and Audit Dept., 1919; Principal, Air Ministry, 1938; Dir. of Administration and Finance, R.A.F. Delegation, Washington, 1941-43; Asst. Under-Sec., of State, Air Ministry, 1943; Deputy Secretary, Ministry of Civil Aviation, 1946-56. Commander Order of Orange Nassau (Netherlands), 1948. *Address:* 12 Warborough Road, Churston Ferrers, Devon. *T.:* Churston 81707. [*Died* 23 *May* 1964.

CRICHTON, Hon. Arthur Owen; 3rd *s.* of 4th Earl of Erne; *b.* 15 Aug. 1876; *m* 1906, Katharine Helen Elizabeth (*d.* 1964), 3rd *d.* of late Col. Hon. Walter Rodolph Trefusis, C.B.; one *s.* one *d.* *Educ.:* Eton; Christ Church, Oxford. Late Lieutenant 3rd Battalion Gordon Highlanders; served South African War; European War (despatches, Order of the Crown of Belgium). Chairman of Association of Investment Trusts, 1941-52. *Club:* Carlton. [*Died* 11 *July* 1970.

CRICHTON, Lt.-Col. Gerald Charles Lawrence, C.S.I. 1947; C.I.E. 1946; *b.* 30 July 1900; *s.* of Alexander Baillie Crichton; *m.* 1930, Muriel Noreen, *d.* of H. H. James, Littlehampton, Sussex; three *d.* R.M.C. Sandhurst, 1919-21; Indian Army, 1921-26; Indian Political Service, 1926-48; Counsellor, H.M. Legation, Kabul, 1943-46; H.M. Chargé d'Affaires, Kabul, June-Dec. 1945; Joint Secretary, External Affairs Dept., Govt. of India, 1946. Officiating Secretary, External Affairs Dept., Apr.-Aug. 1947; Chairman, British Commonwealth-Siamese War Claims Cttee., Bangkok, 1949-50; Financial Adviser, Kuwait State, Persian Gulf, 1951-56. *Address:* Chases, Eastergate, Sussex. *T.:* Eastergate 2288. [*Died* 15 *Aug.* 1969.

CRICK, Very Rev. Thomas, C.B. 1943; C.B.E. 1937; M.V.O. 1922; M.A.; Dean Emeritus, 1958 (Dean of Rochester, 1943-58); Permission to officiate in the Diocese of London, 1958; Chaplain to the High Sheriff of Kent, 1959; *b.* 1885; *s.* of late Reverend Thomas Crick, and *g. s.* of late Rev. Thomas Crick, Public Orator of Cambridge Univ. and President of St. John's College; *m.* 1921, Elena Marjorie, *d.* of Charles Morgan, Barcelona; one *s.* *Educ.:* St. Edmund's School, Canterbury; Brasenose College, Oxford. Curate of Wigan, 1909; Chaplain, Royal Navy, 1911; served in H.M.S. King Edward VII., Flagship of International Force at occupation of Scutari, 1913; H.M.S. Malaya (Battle of Jutland, wounded); H.M.S. New Zealand (Naval Mission, under Earl Jellicoe, to India and the Dominions), 1919-20; H.M.S. Malaya (Duke of Connaught's visit to India), 1920-21; H.M.S. Renown (Prince of Wales' visit to India and Japan), 1921-22; Senior Chaplain of the Royal Naval College, Dartmouth, 1923-26, and 1929-32; Chaplain of His Majesty's Dockyard and Royal Marine Barracks, Chatham, 1926-28; of H.M.S. Excellent, H.M. Gunnery School, Portsmouth, 1932-1935; H.M. Dockyard, Portsmouth, 1935-38; Hon. Chaplain to the King, 1935-1940; Chaplain of the Fleet and Archdeacon for Royal Navy, 1938-43; Chaplain to the King, 1940-43. Hon. Chaplain, Royal Naval Association, 1952; Hon. Chaplain, Royal Marine Assoc., 1954. President St. Bartholomew's Hospital, Rochester, 1943-58. Gold Badge of the British Legion, 1958. *Address:* c/o Westminster Bank, Kingston-on-Thames. *Club:* United Service. [*Died* 13 *Nov.* 1970.

CRITCHLEY, Brigadier-General Alfred Cecil, C.M.G. 1919; C.B.E. 1943; D.S.O. 1916; *b.* Calgary, 1890; *s.* of late Major Oswald Asheton Critchley; *m.* 1st, 1916, Maryon, *e. d.* of John Galt (one *s.* killed in action in Libya, Dec. 1941); one *d.*; 2nd, 1927, Joan *yr. d.* of Mrs. Reginald Foster; one *s.* one *d.*; 3rd, 1938, Diana Fishwick; one *s.* one *d.* *Educ.:* St. Bees School, Cumberland. Commissioned Lord Strathcona's Horse (Royal Canadians) (Canadian Regular Forces), 1908; served European War, 1st Canadian Division; Adjutant of Strathcona's Horse, 1914-15; 1st and 3rd Canadian Divisions, General Staff, 1st, 2nd, and 3rd Grades, 1916-17; seconded to Royal Flying Corps from Canadian Forces, Feb. 1918; went to R. of O., Canadian Forces, 1919 (despatches, D.S.O., C.M.G., twice wounded); apptd. Air Commodore in R.A.F.V.R., 1939; organised and commanded the Initial Training of air crews for the R.A.F. until 1943. 1919-23, made a study of Mexico and Central America, carrying out works of development and colonisation in these countries; Director Associated and British Portland Cement Manufacturing Corporations, 1923; Vice-President of the British Portland Cement Association, 1925. Built and operated first greyhound race-track in Great Britain at Manchester, 1926; M.P. (Nat. Con.) Twickenham Division of Middlesex, 1934-35; Director-General of B.O.A.C., 1943-46; Chairman Skyways, Ltd., Air Charter Co., 1946-54; Deputy Chairman, Helicopter Services Ltd., 1954-57. Has travelled extensively. *Publication:* Critch!, 1961. *Recreation:* golf, won Surrey County Golf Championship, 1932, 1938, King William Medal, St. Andrews, 1932, French Amateur Golf Championship, 1933; French Open Mixed Foursomes, with Miss Fishwick, 1933, 1934, 1935, 1936, 1937; Belgian Amateur Championship, 1938; Dutch Amateur Championship, 1938 and again in 1939; German Open Mixed Foursomes, with Mrs. Critchley, 1938; Pro-Amateur Foursomes with Dai Rees, 1939; Social Clubs' Foursomes, with Wing Comdr. Lucas, 1948 (Rep. Bath Club); Pres. British Golf Foundation, 1953-; Capt. Wentworth Golf Club, 1954, 1955 and 1956. *Address:* Wentworth, Surrey. *T.:* Wentworth 2208. *Clubs:* Bath, Portland. [*Died* 9 *Feb.* 1963

CROCKER, Lieut.-Colonel Herbert Edmund, C.M.G. 1919; D.S.O. 1916; late Essex Regiment; *b.* 10 Sept. 1877; *s.* of H. J. Crocker and Blanche Greenhill; *m.* 1960, Eileen, *y. d.* of late R. A. Cilento, Adelaide, S.A. *Educ.:* St. Michael's School, Westgate-on-Sea; Shrewsbury School. Obtained Commission in Essex Regiment, 1900; served South African War (wounded, Queen's medal, 6 clasps); commanded 13th Signal Co. European War in Gallipoli (wounded, despatches, D.S.O.) and Mesopotamia (Bt. Lt.-Col.); commanded 8th Cheshire Regt. Mesopotamia Feb. 1917 to end of war (Bt. Lt.-Col., C.M.G., despatches

4 times); ret. pay, 1929. *Publications:* in Quarterly Rev., Time and Tide, Army Quarterly, etc. *Recreations:* writing and reading. *Address:* c/o Lloyds Bank, Ltd., 346 Strand, W.C.2. [*Died* 13 *May* 1962.

CROCKER, General Sir John Tredinnick, G.C.B., *cr.* 1948 (K.C.B., *cr.* 1947; C.B. 1943); K.B.E., *cr.* 1944 (C.B.E. 1940); D.S.O. 1918; M.C.; late Royal Tank Corps; Lord Lieutenant of Middlesex, since 1961; Vice-Chairman Commonwealth War Graves Commn., 1957-63; *b.* 3 January 1896; *y. s.* of late Isaac Crocker; *m.* 1920, Hilda May, *d.* of late E. J. Mitchell, Beckenham, Kent; (one *s.* killed on active service) one *d.* Served European War with the Artists' Rifles and Machine Gun Corps (M.C., D.S.O., despatches); posted to the Middlesex Regiment, 1920; transferred to Royal Tank Corps, 1923; commanded an Armoured Bde. in France, 1940, 9th Corps in Tunisia, 1942-43 (wounded), and 1st Corps throughout campaign in France and Germany, 1944-45; G.O.C.-in-C. Southern Command., 1945-47; C.-in-C. Middle East Land Forces, 1947-50; Adjutant-General to the Forces, 1950-53; A.D.C. General to the King, 1948-51. Legion of Honour (Commander), 1943; Virtuti Militari (Polish), 1945; Order of Orange-Nassau (Grand Officer), 1945; Croix de Guerre, 1946. *Address:* The King's House, Ingram Avenue, N.W.11. *T.:* Speedwell 5035. [*Died* 9 *March* 1963.

CROCOMBE, Leonard Cecil; Editor of various periodicals for George Newnes, 1918-46; *b.* 14 February 1890; *e. s.* of Edward Hammersley Crocombe; *m.* 1916, Marjorie Murtagh, *e. d.* of William Murtagh Stevens; one *s.* two *d.* First Editor, Radio Times, 1923-26. *Publications:* An Editor Goes West; Written for Fun; Slow Ship to Hong Kong; Australian Excursion. *Recreations:* travel, reading. *Club:* National Liberal. [*Died* 19 *Nov.* 1968.

CROFT, Sir Arthur, Kt., *cr.* 1953; Chairman, Crofts Engineers (Holdings) Ltd. and other cos.; *b.* 14 Mar. 1886; *s.* of late Frederick Lister Croft and late Lucy Croft, Bradford; *m.* 1920, Hilda, *d.* of late John Henry and Rose Anne Field, Oakenshaw, Bradford; one *s.* one *d.* *Educ.:* Hanson's School; Bradford Technical College. Served European War 1914-18; Major, R.A., France, in Heavy Artillery. Chm. North Bradford Conservative Association, 1941-47; Pres. Pudsey Conservative Association. Magistrate City of Bradford (retired). *Recreations:* interested in all sports. *Address:* Buckstone Hall, Rawdon, nr. Leeds, Yorks; *T.:* Rawdon 41. *Clubs:* Constitutional, Conservative (Bradford). [*Died* 12 *Feb.* 1961.

CROFT, Sir William Dawson, K.C.B., *cr.* 1948; K.B.E., *cr.* 1943; C.I.E. 1934; C.V.O. 1938; *b.* 16 August 1892; *s.* of William Bleaden Croft and Geraldine Elizabeth Dawson; *m.* 1st, 1919, Henriette Charlotte Elise Massé (*d.* 1920); 2nd, 1923, Dorothea Mavor (*d.* 1954); two *s.* one *d.* *Educ.:* Winchester College; Trinity College, Oxford. 2nd Cl. Hon. Mods.; 1st Cl. Literae Humaniores; Junior Clerk, India Office, 1919; Private Secretary to Permanent Under-Secretary of State; Principal, 1921; Private Secretary to Rt. Hon. Wedgwood Benn, 1931; to Rt. Hon. Sir Samuel Hoare, 1931; to Marquess of Zetland, 1935; Assistant Secretary, 1936; Assistant Under Secretary of State, 1940; Deputy Under Secretary of State, 1941-47; Chief Civil Asst. to Minister of State in Cairo, 1943-45; Chairman of Board of Customs and Excise, 1947-55, retired. Chm. Trade and Tariffs Commission, B.W.I., 1956-58. *Address:* 2 Kingsbury Sq., Wilton, Nr. Salisbury, Wilts. *Club:* Travellers'. [*Died* 18 *Aug.* 1964.

CROFT, Brig.-General William Denman, C.B. 1935; C.M.G. 1918; D.S.O. 1917; late Cameronians and Royal Tank Corps; *b.* 15 March 1879; *s.* of Sir Herbert Croft, 9th Bt., Croft Castle, Herefordshire; *m.* 1912, Esmé, *o. d.* of Sir Arthur Sutton, 7th Bt.; one *s.* two *d.* (and one *s.* died on active service, 1946). *Educ.:* Oxford Military College. First Commissioned, 1899; seconded with Nigerian Regiment, W.A.F.F., 1904-7; severely wounded by poisoned arrow, 1907; in France, 2 Nov. 1914; Adjt. 5th Scottish Rifles; commanded 11th Royal Scots, 4 Dec. 1915; commanding Lowland Brigade, 14 Sept. 1917 to end of War (despatches ten times, D.S.O. 3 bars, C.M.G., Légion d'Honneur, Croix d'Officier); G.S.O. 1. H.Q. India (Simla and Delhi), 1924-27; Instructor Senior Officers' School, 1927-29; Brigadier commanding Royal Tank Corps Centre, 1929-31; Nowshera Brigade, North-West Frontier Province, India, 1931-34; operations against Upper Mohmands, 1933 (despatches); retired pay, 1934; p.s.c. 1919; raised Home Guard, Cornwall, 1940; Group Comdr., Home Guard, Cornwall; Hon. County Commissioner Cornwall Boy Scouts. *Publication:* Three Years with the 9th Division. *Address:* Anchorage, Mawnan, Falmouth. *Club:* Army and Navy. [*Died* 14 *July* 1968.

CROFTON, Major Sir (Malby Richard) Henry, 4th Bt., *cr.* 1838 (orig. *cr.* 1661); D.S.O. 1916; late Royal Artillery; *b.* Sept. 1881; *e. s.* of Sir Malby Crofton, 3rd Bart. of Longford House, Co. Sligo, and Louisa, *d.* of R. J. Verschoyle, Tanrego, Co. Sligo; *S.* father, 1926; *m.* 1918, Katharine Beatrix, (*d.* 1961), *o. d.* of late George Sturges Pollard, J.P., Scarr Hall, nr. Bradford, Yorks.; one *s.* one *d.* *Educ.:* Aysgarth, Winchester; Roy. Military Acad., Woolwich. First Commn., 1900; served in Africa and India; served in France and Mesopotamia, 1914-18 (four times wounded, despatches twice, D.S.O. and Bar, direct award); in North Russia, 1919; retired pay, 1927; Pilot Officer R.A.F.V.R., 1940. *Heir:* *s.* Malby Sturges, *b.* 11 Jan. 1923. *Address:* Longford House, Co. Sligo. *T.A.:* Beltra; Berwick St. John Manor, Wilts. via Shaftesbury. *Club:* United Service. [*Died* 21 *Jan.* 1962.

CROMARTIE, Countess of (*cr.* 1861), **Sibel Lilian Mackenzie,** Viscountess of Tarbat, Baroness of Castlehaven and Macleod, *cr.* 1861; *b.* 14 Aug. 1878; *d.* of 2nd Earl of Cromartie and Lilian (*d.* 1926), *d.* of 4th Baron Macdonald [on the death of the 2nd Earl in 1893 the title fell into abeyance between his two daughters, which was terminated in favour of the present Countess, 1895]; *m.* 1899, Major E. W. Blunt-Mackenzie (*d.* 1949); one *s.* one *d.* (and one *s.* one *d.* decd.) *Publications:* The End of the Song, 1904; The Web of the Past; Sons of Milesians, 1906; The Days of Fire, 1908; Out of the Dark; Sword of the Crowns, 1910; The Golden Guard, 1912; The Decoy, 1914; The Temple of the Winds, 1926; Heremon, the Beautiful, 1929. *Heir:* *s.* Viscount Tarbat, M.C. *Address:* Tarbat House, Kildary, Ross-shire, Scotland. [*Died* 20 *May* 1962.

CROMB, David Lyall; *s.* of late James Cromb, journalist; *b.* Coupar Angus, Perthshire, 17 Aug. 1875; *m.* Catherine Millar; two *s.* two *d.* *Educ.:* Harris Academy, Dundee. Entered People's Journal, 1888; appointed sub-editor, 1900; editor, 1905-9; assistant editor National Press Agency, London, 1909-11; partner Cotterill and Cromb, literary agents. *Publications:* The Life Story of Hector Macdonald; The Highland Brigade (joint); several popular serial stories; short stories; for many years writer of cricket and football articles to Dundee Advertiser. *Address:* 20 Greenwood Road, Croydon. [*Died* 15 *Nov.* 1961.

CROMBIE, Sir James (Ian Cormack), K.C.B. 1957; K.B.E. 1950; C.M.G. 1947; formerly Chairman, H.M. Board of Customs and Excise (1955-62), retired; *b.* 10 December 1902; *s.* of late John Alexander Crombie, Aberdeen; *m.* 1928, Janet, 2nd *d.* of late Alexander McDonald, Fraserburgh, Aberdeenshire; one *s.* two *d.* *Educ.:* Aberdeen Grammar School; Aberdeen Univ. (M.A. 1925); Gonville and Caius Coll., Cambridge. Administrative Class, Home Civil Service, 1926; Served in War Office; H.M. Treasury; Ministry of Food; Foreign Office. Chm. Civil Service Sports Council, 1959-62. Hon. LL.D. Aberdeen Univ., 1957. *Recreations:* swimming, music. *Address:* 63 Grove Avenue, N.10. *T.:* Tudor 4422. *Club:* Oxford and Cambridge. [*Died* 22 *May* 1969.

CROMPTON, Richmal; *see* Lamburn, R. C.

CROMWELL, 5th Baron, *cr.* 1375 (called out of abeyance 1923); **Robert Godfrey Wolseley Bewicke-Copley;** D.S.O. 1944; M.C., D.L., J.P.; K.St.J.; late Major K.R.R.C.; Lord Lieutenant of Leicestershire, 1949-65. Director Martins Bank, Ltd.; Hon. Treasurer British Legion; County Alderman for Leicestershire; Col. Comdt. (Leicestershire) Army Cadets; Chairman: Leicester Advisory Committee National Assistance Board; Leicester Disablement Advisory Committee, Min. of Labour and National Service; President: Leicestershire T.A.; Leicestershire Red Cross; Leicestershire St. John Ambulance Bde.; Member Leicester War Pensions Committee; Chairman Leics. War Agricultural Executive Cttee.; Master, Worshipful Company of Farmers, 1961; *b.* 23 May 1893; *e. surv. s.* of late Brigadier-General Sir R. C. Alington Bewicke-Copley, K.B.E., C.B., and Selina Frances (*d.* 1923), *e. d.* of Sir Charles Watson-Copley, 3rd Bt.; *m.* 1925, Freda Constance, *o. d.* of late Major Sir F. W. B. Cripps, D.S.O.; one *s.* one *d.* *Educ.:* Eton College; Trinity Coll., Cambridge. Served European War, 1914-18 (wounded); War of 1939-45 (wounded, prisoner, but repatriated, D.S.O.). D.L. 1933, J.P. 1934, Leicestershire. *Heir:* *s.* Hon. David Godfrey Bewicke-Copley, 2nd Lieutenant K.R.R.C., [*b.* 29 May 1929; *m.* 1954, Vivian, *y. d.* of H. de L. Penfold, Esher; two *s.* two *d.*]. *Address:* Misterton Hall, near Rugby. *T.:* Lutterworth 15. *Club:* Royal Over-Seas League. [*Died* 21 *Oct.* 1966.

CRONSHAW, Cecil John Turrell, B.Sc., F.R.I.C., F.R.S.E.; F.R.S.A.; M.I.Chem.E.; Hon. D.Sc. (Leeds); F.T.I.; F.S.D.C.; Hon. Associate of Manchester Coll. of Science and Technology; Director, Manchester Ship Canal Co.: District Bank Ltd., Manchester; formerly Pt.-Time Mem. North-Western Gas Bd.; ex-Dep. Chm. and Director British Nylon Spinners, Ltd.; Director (delegate) I.C.I. (General Chemicals) Ltd., 1939-43; Delegate Director, Imperial Chemical (Pharmaceuticals) Ltd.; formerly Director, I.C.I. Ltd.; *b.* 13 June 1889; *s.* of William Robert Cronshaw and Ann Elizabeth Turrell: *m.* 1917, Annie Downham: two *s.* *Educ.:* Grammar School, Bury; Victoria Univ., Manchester. On the Bd. of Management of British Colour Council, 1935-44, Pres., 1945-53. Member Leeds University Clothworkers' Committee, 1932-44; made a Governor of Bury Grammar School, 1930; Vice-Pres. of Soc. of Chemical Industry, 1935-38; Vice-Pres. of Society of Dyers and Colourists, 1934, Pres. 1939-46, Hon. Member, 1947-; Member of the Dyestuffs Industry Development Cttee., 1926-34; mem. of the Court of Governors of the Victoria University of Manchester, and of the Council, 1939-; Prime Warden, Worshipful Company of Dyers, 1949-50; Silver Medallist, R.S.A., 1940; Hinchley Medallist, Brit. Assoc. of Chemists, 1958; Perkin Medallist, Soc. of Dyers and Colourists, 1959. *Publications:* address to Society of Chemical Industry, 1929; Seven Lamps of Chemical Enterprise; In Quest of Colour, S.C.I., Jubilee Lecture, 1934-35; Mather Lecture, 1945; Fifth Dalton Lecture, 1949; various articles in the daily and technical press. *Address:* Alnwick, Prestwich Park, Manchester. *T.:* Prestwich 2654. *Clubs:* Royal Thames Yacht; Clarendon (Manchester). [*Died* 5 *Jan.* 1961.

CROOKENDEN, Col. Arthur, C.B.E. 1939; D.S.O. 1919; *b.* 14 Jan. 1877; *s.* of Colonel H. H. Crookenden, R.A.; *m.* Dorothy Rowlandson; three *s.* one *d.* *Educ.:* Clifton; R.M.C. Commissioned Cheshire Regt., 1897; retired pay, 1932; served S. African War (medal and four clasps); European War (1915 Star, British and Victory medals, Croix de Guerre, despatches six times, Bt. Lt.-Col.); Tactical Instr. at O.C.T.U., 1939-1941. Colonel of The Cheshire Regt., 1930-47. *Publications:* The History of the Cheshire Regiment in the Great War; History of The Cheshire Regiment in the Second World War; Twenty Second Footsteps, 1849-1914. *Address:* 33 Langborough Road, Wokingham, Berks. [*Died* 23 *Dec.* 1962.

CROOKSHANK, 1st Viscount, *cr.* 1956, of Gainsborough; **Harry Frederick Comfort Crookshank,** P.C. 1939; C.H. 1955; M.A. and Hon. D.C.L. (Oxford); High Steward of Westminster since 1960; *b.* 27 May 1893; *o. s.* of late H. M. Crookshank, Cairo, and late Mrs. Crookshank, Pont St., S.W.1, and *g. s.* of Capt. B. Crookshank, 51st (King's Own) Regt. *Educ.:* Eton (King's Scholar); Magdalen Coll., Oxford (2nd Class Hon. Mods.). Served European War, 1914-19; Hampshire Regiment, 1914, transferred to Grenadier Guards, Special Reserve, 1915; demobilised with rank of Capt., 1919; served in France and Salonika (twice wounded, Order of White Eagle, Serbian Gold Medal for Valour); appointed Third Secretary H.M. Diplomatic Service and served in Foreign Office, 1919; Second Secretary and transferred to H.M. Embassy, Constantinople, 1921, and to H.M. Embassy, Washington, 1924; resigned on election to Parliament, 1924; M.P. (U.) Gainsborough, 1924-56; Parliamentary Under-Secretary, Home Office, 1934-35; Secretary for Mines, 1935-39; Financial Secretary to Treasury, 1939-43; Postmaster-General, 1943-45; Minister of Health, 1951-52; Leader of the House of Commons, 1951-55; Lord Privy Seal, 1952-1955. Knight of the Order of St. John of Jerusalem; Jubilee and Coronation Medals. *Heir:* none. *Address:* 51 Pont Street, S.W.1. *T.:* Kensington 3130. *Clubs:* Carlton, Guards, Pratt's. [*Died* 17 *Oct.* 1961 (*ext.*).

CROOME, William Iveson, C.B.E. 1957; Chairman of Cathedral Advisory Committee for England since 1953; Trustee Historic Churches Preservation Trust since 1952; *b.* 23 Nov. 1891; *o. s.* of late Thomas Lancelot Croome, J.P., North Cerney House, Glos., and Mary Stewart Croome, *d.* of late Rev. Robert Duckworth; unmarried. *Educ.:* Malvern; New College, Oxford (M.A.). Chairman: Cirencester Bench, 1943-66; Governors of Barnwood House Registered Mental Hosp., 1938; Managers of Cotswold School, Ashton Keynes (Home Office Approved School), 1944-63; Gloucester Diocesan Advisory Cttee. on Churches, 1944; Committee on Wall Paintings, 1953. Vice-Chm. Standing Joint Cttee. for Gloucestershire, 1947 (subsequently Police Cttee., 1966) until end of 1966. Vice-Chairman Central Council for the Care of Churches, 1943; Chairman, Grants Committee of Historic Churches Preservation Trust, 1964. J.P. Glos. 1927. F.S.A. 1950. *Publications:* articles in Transactions of Bristol and

Gloucestershire Archaeological Soc. *Recreations:* photography, gardening. *Address:* Barton Mill House, Cirencester, Glos. *T.:* Cirencester 367. *Club:* County (Gloucester). [*Died* 29 *April* 1967.

CROPPER, Anthony Charles, T.D. 1945; J.P.; D.L.; Chairman, James Cropper & Co. Ltd. (Papermakers), since 1956; *b.* 27 January 1912; *s.* of James Winstanley Cropper and Marjorie Constance Cropper (*née* Bagot); *m.* 1938, Philippa Mary Gloria Clutterbuck; two *s.* one *d.* (and one *s.* decd.). *Educ.:* Eton; Trinity Coll., Cambridge (B.A.). Captain, Duke of Lancaster's Own Yeomanry, 1939-45. J.P. 1948-, D.L. 1954-, Westmorland; High Sheriff of Westmorland, 1950. Chairman S. Westmorland Rural Dist. Council, 1957-1960; Chm. Westmorland Agric. Exec. Cttee., 1958-65; Mem., I.T.A., 1960-64. Mem. Church Assembly (C. of E.), 1950-60. *Recreations:* shooting, tennis. *Address:* Tolson Hall, Kendal, Westmorland. *T.:* Kendal 2011. *Clubs:* Brooks's, M.C.C. [*Died* 1 *May* 1967.

CROSBY, Very Rev. Ernest H. L.; *see* Lewis-Crosby.

CROSFIELD, Domini, Lady; R.R.C.; Golden Cross of the Order of George I (Greece); Commander of the Order of the Phoenix (Greece); Diploma of Commander of Order of Welfare (Greece); *d.* of Elie M. Elliadi; *m.* 1907, Sir Arthur Crosfield, Bt., G.B.E. Commander of Order of George I (Greece) (*d.* 1938), Liberal M.P. for Warrington, 1906-10. Honorary Adviser during European war on Exhibitions and Art to the Greek Department of Information; Founder and Chairman of Pediki Steghi (Day Nurseries) and of Music for Children in Greece. Member Council, Imperial Society of Teachers of Dancing; President North Islington Infant Welfare Centre; Mem. Grants Cttee. of the National Playing Fields Association; Mem. Exec. of Children's Playground Cttee.; Mem. Exec. of National Association of Maternity and Child Welfare; Mem. Executive and Chm. of Standing Cttees. of Anglo-Hellenic League; Vice-Pres. and Dir. of Lond. Philharmonic Soc.; Vice-Pres. Nat. Playing Fields Assoc., Mem. Grants and Children's Playground Sub-Cttee. Comdt. of two V.A.D. hosps. 1915-1919. *Publication:* Dances of Greece. *Recreations:* music, tennis. *Address:* Witanhurst, 41 Highgate West Hill, N.6. *T.:* Mountview 2686. [*Died* 15 *Jan.* 1963.

CROSFIELD, Lt.-Col. George Rowlandson, C.B.E. 1931; D.S.O. 1916; T.D.; *b.* 29 April 1877; 3rd *s.* of John Crosfield, Warrington; *m.* 1925, Nina Noreen Mary (*d.* 1956), *widow* of Harold Francis Marion-Crawford, and *d.* of late Commander C. W. Wood. *Educ.:* Harrow. Commanded 77th Company Imperial Yeomanry in the South African War (Queen's medal 5 clasps); formerly Deputy Chm. of J. Crosfield & Sons, Warrington; crossed to France, Feb. 1915, as second in command to 1/4th S. Lancs; subsequently commanded 2nd Suffolks and 10th R.W.F. in the field; leg amputated as result of wound at St. Eloi, March 1916; Commissioned in R.A.F. and passed as Observer, 1918; Past National Chm. Brit. Legion; Past Chm. Not Forgotten Assoc., 1953; Officer Legion of Honour; Commander White Lion of Czechoslovakia; Commander of Order of Star of Roumania. *Recreations:* reading, travelling. *Address:* 37 Highgate West Hill, N.6. [*Died* 22 *Aug.* 1962.

CROSS, Sir Alexander, 3rd Bart., *cr.* 1912; Barrister-at-Law, Inner Temple; *b.* 4 April 1880; *o. surv. s.* of Sir Alexander Cross, 1st Bt., and Jessie Mackenzie, 2nd *d.* of Sir Peter Coats of Auchendrane, Ayrshire; *S.* brother, 1947. *Educ.:* Charterhouse; Balliol College, Oxford. *Heir:* none. *Address:* Battleby, Redgorton, Perthshire, Scotland. *T.:* Stanley 255. *Club:* Oxford and Cambridge. [*Died* 12 *May* 1963 (*ext.*).

CROSS, Rev. Dr. Frank Leslie, M.A., D.D., D.Phil. (Oxon); B.Sc. (Lond.); Lady Margaret Professor of Divinity and Canon of Christ Church, Oxford, since 1944; *b.* 22 Jan. 1900; *s.* of late Herbert Francis Cross and late Louisa Georgina Randall; unmarried. *Educ.:* Bournemouth School; Balliol College, Oxford (Natural Science Scholar); Marburg and Freiburg Universities. Hons. in Chemistry (Part I.) with Crystallography, Oxford, 1920; B.Sc., London (2nd Cl. Hons. in Chemistry), 1920; B.A. (Oxon), 1921; Hons. in Theol. (1st Cl.) 1922; Junior Denyer and Johnson Theol. Schol., 1922; Senior Schol., 1922 and 1924; Senior Greek Testament Prize, 1923; Joint Ellerton Essay Prize, 1924; Liddon Student, 1924; Tutor at Ripon Hall, Oxford, 1924-27; M.A. 1925; Chaplain, of Ripon Hall, 1926-27; Deacon, 1925; Priest, 1926; Librarian of Pusey House, Oxford, 1927-44; D.Phil., Oxford, 1930; D.D., Oxford, 1950; Examining Chaplain to Bishop of Bradford, 1933-43; Select Preacher University of Cambridge, 1933 and 1945, Oxford, 1936-38; Oxford University Lecturer in Philosophy of Religion, 1934-42; Wilde Lecturer, in Natural and Comparative Religion, Oxford, 1935-38; Gen. Sec., First, Second, Third, Fourth and Fifth Internat. Confs. on Patristic Studies, Oxford, 1951, 1955, 1959, 1963 and 1967; of Four Gospels Congress, Oxford, 1957; of New Testament Congresses, Oxf., 1961 and 1965. Hon. D.D.: (Aberdeen), 1959; (Bonn), 1960. F.B.A. 1967. *Publications:* Religion and the Reign of Science, 1930; John Henry Newman, 1933; The Tractarians and Roman Catholicism, 1933; The Oxford Movement and the Seventeeth Century, 1933; Anglicanism (with P. E. More) 1935; St. Athanasius' De Incarnatione, 1939; Life of Darwell Stone, 1943; I Peter, 1954; The Early Christian Fathers, 1960; Editor of Huck-Lietzmann, A Synopsis of the First Three Gospels, 1936; Joint Editor of Hastings Rashdall's Principles and Precepts, 1927; of Ideas and Ideals, 1928; and of God and Man, 1930; of St. Cyril of Jerusalem's Lectures on the Christian Sacraments, 1951; of T. Klauzer's Western Liturgy and its History, 1952; of Essays on the Jung Codex, 1955; of Studies in Ephesians, 1956; of A. Baumstark's Comparative Liturgy, 1958; of Studia Patristica, i-ii, 1957; of Oxford Dictionary of the Christian Church, 1957; of Studia Evangelica, 1959, ii-iii, 1964; of Studia Patristica, iii-vi, 1961-62; vii, 1965; ix, 1966; of Studia Evangelica, iv, v, 1968. *Address:* Christ Church, Oxford. *T.:* 43588. [*Died* 30 *Dec.* 1968.

CROSS, Kenneth Mervyn Baskerville, M.A. (Cantab.); Hon. D.C.L. (Durham); Past President R.I.B.A.; F.R.A.I.A.; Architect; *b.* 8 Dec. 1890; *e. s.* of late Alfred W. S. Cross, M.A. (Cantab.), F.R.I.B.A.; unmarried. *Educ.:* Felsted School; Gonville and Caius College, Cambridge. Articled to late A. W. S. Cross; also studied at Cambridge University School of Architecture; started practice, 1919; acted as architect to following Councils and public bodies: Westminster City Council, Marylebone, Fulham, Finsbury, and Deptford Borough Councils, Morecambe and Heysham Council, Bournemouth Council, Newcastle on Type City Council, Islington Borough Council, Epsom Borough Council, Finchley U.D.C., Grocers' Co., Whitgift Foundations, St. John's College, Camb. London Hosp., Commercial Bakery, Plymouth, Café Plymouth, Barclays Bank, Park Lane, W.1, Domestic work, etc. Hon. Fell. Royal Architectural Institute of Canada Hon. Fell. American Institute of Architects; Hon. Fell., New Zealand Institute of Architects. *Publications:* Modern Public Baths,

1938; Swimming Baths, 1928; Practical Notes for Architectural Draughtsmen, 1927; Contributions to technical press on Architectural subjects. *Recreation:* gardening. *Address:* 50 Maddox Street, W.1. *T.:* Mayfair 7016; Greville House, Little Baddow, Chelmsford. *Clubs:* Athenæum, Savile. [*Died* 16 *Jan.* 1968.

CROSS, Mark; *see* Pechey, Archibald T.

CROSS, Rev. Robert Nicol, M.A.; *b.* Hamilton, Scotland, 1883; *m.* 1910, Nellie Reeves; one *s.* two *d.* *Educ.:* Hamilton Academy; Glasgow University; St. Andrews University; Marburg University; Manchester College, Oxford. Graduated with First-Class Honours in Philosophy at Glasgow, 1904, Edward Caird Medallist; Clarke Scholarship in Philosophy; Unitarian Minister at Manchester; Southport; Mill Hill Chapel, Leeds; Rosslyn Hill Chapel, Hampstead; First Presbyterian Church, Belfast; Principal of Manchester College, Oxford, 1938-49; M.A. (*h.c.*) 1939, M.A. (by decree of the house), 1944, Oxon. *Publications:* Socrates, the Man and his Mission; Communion of Man with God; Religious Essays and Articles. *Recreations:* gardening and walking. *Address:* 6 Oakington Avenue, Little Chalfont, Amersham, Bucks. *T.:* Little Chalfont 3216. [*Died* 20 *Sept.* 1970.

CROSS, Rt. Hon. Sir Ronald (Hibbert), 1st Bt., *cr.* 1941; P.C. 1940; K.C.M.G., *cr.* 1955; K.C.V.O., *cr.* 1954; Governor of Tasmania, 1951-58; formerly a Merchant Banker; *b.* 9 May 1896; *s.* of James Carlton Cross; *m.* 1925, Louise Marion, *er. d.* of late Walter Emmott, of Emmott Hall, Colne, Lancs; four *d* (one *s.* decd.). *Educ.:* Eton. Duke of Lancaster's Own Yeomanry and Royal Flying Corps, 1914-18; M.P. (U.) Rossendale, Lancs, 1931-45; Govt. Whip, 1935-37; a Lord of the Treasury, 1937; Vice-Chamberlain of H.M. Household, 1937-38; Parliamentary Sec., Bd. of Trade, 1938-39; Minister of Economic Warfare, 1939-40; Minister of Shipping, 1940-41; High Commissioner in the Commonwealth of Australia for H.M. Government in the United Kingdom of Great Britain and Northern Ireland, 1941-1945; M.P. (C.) Ormskirk Division of Lancashire, 1950-51. Chairman of Public Accounts Committee, 1950-51. Hon. Col. 40th Inf. Bn. (The Derwent Regt.), 1952-58. K.St.J. 1952. [*Died* 3 *June* 1968 (*ext.*).

CROSS BROWN, Lt.-Col. James, D.S.O. 1918; O.B.E. 1961; Director of several Companies; Member, Council of St. Nicholas School for Girls, Hemel Hempstead, Hertfordshire; Co-Founder Anglo-Portuguese Soc., 1939; Chairman to 1967, now Hon. Dep. President; *b.* 3 January 1884; *s.* of Nicol Brown, Glasgow and London; *m.* 1911, Violet Anne (*d.* 1964), *d.* of James Turnbull, Glasgow and London; two *s.* three *d.* *Educ.:* Mill Hill. Associated since 1905 with copper mining industry of the South of Spain and Portugal; European War, 1914-19, Assistant Director of Supplies and Transport, Palestine, 1917-19 (D.S.O., despatches four times). Past Pres. British Overseas Mining Assoc.; Vice-Pres. European Atlantic Group. Member, Court of Govs., Mill Hill Sch., 1925-60. Comdr. of the Order of Industrial Merit, Portugal, 1941; Commander of the Military Order of Christ, Portugal, 1063. *Address:* Waverley Abbey House, Nr. Farnham, Surrey. *T.:* Runfold 2248. *Club:* Old Milhillians. [*Died* 24 *Jan.* 1969.

CROSSLEY, (Joseph) Edward; Editor, The Yorkshire Post, since 1964; *b.* 11 Nov. 1908; *o. c.* of late William and late Annie Crossley, Leeds; *m.* 1935, Evelyn Bell, Leeds; one *s.* two *d.* Weekly newspaper reporter, 1925-29; Daily Express and Scottish Daily Express, 1930; Yorkshire Post reporter, industrial correspondent, 1931-41. Royal Marines (Captain), 1942-46. Yorkshire Post sub-editor, night news editor, night editor, deputy editor, news editor, 1946-64. Director, Yorkshire Post Newspapers, Ltd. *Address:* The Yorkshire Post, Leeds 1. [*Died* 7 *May* 1969.

CROSSWELL, Noel Alfred, C.M.G. 1963; M.B.E. 1959; Commissioner of Police, Jamaica, since 1962; *b.* Jamaica, 29 March 1909; *s.* of late Alfred Noel Crosswell, retd. businessman, and Una, *d.* of late Simon Soutar, J.P.; *m.* 1950, Barbara Ellen, *d.* of late William Thomas Bate and Ellen Bate, Barnstaple, N. Devon; three *d.* *Educ.:* Jamaica College, Jamaica; West Buckland School, Barnstaple, England. Jun. Clerk, Revenue Dept., Jamaica, 1928; 2nd Class Clerk, Colonial Sec.'s Office, 1930-37; Sub Inspector of Police, 1937-39; 3rd Class Inspector, 1939-43; 2nd Class Inspector, 1943-48; Supt. of Police, 1948-52; Asst. Commissioner, 1952-58; Dep. Commissioner, 1958-62. A.D.C. to Governor, 1947-48. Queen's Police Medal, 1959; Colonial Police Medal, 1954; Coronation Medals, 1937 and 1953. O.St.J. *Recreations:* cricket, golf and shooting (member Jamaica shooting team to Bisley, 1939). *Address:* c/o Barclay's Bank (DCO), Harbour Street, Kingston, Jamaica. *Clubs:* Naval and Military; Jamaica, Liguanea and Kingston Cricket (Jamaica). [*Died* 27 *Nov.* 1964.

CROSTHWAITE, Sir William (Henry), Kt., *cr.* 1939; J.P.; French Consular Agent; Chairman, Tees Towing Co., Ltd.; President, British Tugowner's Association. Pres., European Tugowner's Association; *b.* 1 July 1880; *e. s.* of late Thomas Crosthwaite; *m.* 1904, Ada Mary (*d.* 1956), *e. d.* of late Capt. George Elliott; one *s.* two *d.* *Educ.:* Southend School, Middlesbrough. Mayor of Middlesbrough, 1925-26, 1939-43; Past President, Tees-side Chamber of Commerce; Past-Chairman, Tees Conservancy Commission; Freeman, City of London; Liveryman Vintners' Company. Chevalier, Legion of Honour, 1965. *Address:* Cleveland Buildings, Middlesbrough. *T.*; 3273. *Club:* Cleveland (Middlesbrough). [*Died* 13 *May* 1968.

CROUSE, Russel; playwright; *b.* Findlay, O., U.S.A., 20 Feb. 1893; *s.* of Hiram Powers Crouse and Sarah Schumacher; *m.* 1st, 1923, Alison Smith (*d.* 1943); 2nd, 1945, Anna Erskine; one *s.* one *d.* *Educ.:* Public Schools. Began as reporter Cincinnati (O.), Commercial Tribune, 1910; reporter Kansas City Star, Cincinnati Post, New York Globe, New York Mail; columnist New York Evening Post, 1925-31; European War, 1917-18, served U.S. Navy; member Writers' War Board, 1942-46; member board American Theatre Wing; Pres. Authors' League of America, 1943-45; member Council Dramatists' Guild since 1936. *Publications:* Mr. Currier and Mr. Ives, 1930; It seems Like Yesterday, 1931; The American Keepsake, 1932; Murder Won't Out, 1932; (with Anna Crouse) Peter Stuyvesant, 1954; Alexander Hamilton and Aaron Burr; author, libretto, The Gang's All Here, 1931; co-author, libretto, Hold Your Horses, 1933; and, in collaboration with Howard Lindsay: Any thing Goes, 1934; Red, Hot and Blue, 1936; Hooray for What!, 1937: Call Me Madam, 1950; Life With Father, 1939; Strip for Action, 1942; State of The Union (awarded Pulitzer Prize, 1946); Life with Mother, 1948; Remains To Be Seen, 1951; The Prescott Proposals, 1953; The Great Sebastians, 1955; Happy Hunting, 1956; Tall Story, 1959; The Sound of Music, 1959; Mr. President, 1962. Co-producer (with Howard Lindsay): Arsenic and Old Lace, 1940; The Hasty Heart, 1944; Detective Story, 1949; One Bright Day, 1952; The Great Sebastians, 1955; also author of many screen plays. *Address:* 141 East 72nd Street, New York City, U.S.A. *T.:* Butterfield 8 4643. *Clubs:* Players', Dutch Treat (New York). [*Died* 3 *April* 1966.

CROW, Sir Alwyn Douglas, Kt., *cr.* 1944; C.B.E. 1937 (O.B.E. 1918); M.A.; Sc.D., F.Inst.P.; M.R.I.; *b.* London, 10 May 1894; *e. s.* of late John Kent Crow, D.Sc., F.I.C.; *m.* 1st, 1923, Kathleen Christiana (*d.* 1957), *d.* of late N. C. Barraclough; no *c.*; 2nd, 1958, Frances Gore Haynes, Washington, D.C., U.S.A. *Educ.:* Westminster; Queens' College, Camb. Commissioned East Surrey Regiment, 1914; served European War, 1916 (wounded, despatches, O.B.E.); appointed to staff of Proof and Experimental Establishment, Royal Arsenal, 1917; Director of Ballistic Research, Woolwich, 1919-39; Chief Superintendent, Projectile Development, 1939-40; Director and Controller of Projectile Development, 1940-45; Director of Guided Projectiles, Ministry of Supply, 1945-1946; Head of Technical Services, British Joint Services Mission, Washington, U.S.A., 1946-53. Thomas Hawksley Lecturer, 1947. U.S. Medal of Freedom with Bronze Palm, 1948. *Publications:* Author or part-author of a number of scientific papers in Philosophical Transactions of Royal Society, Philosophical Magazine and technical journals. *Recreation:* music. *Address:* 3143 O Street, Washington 7, D.C., U.S.A. *Clubs:* Savage, Buck's. [*Died* 5 *Feb.* 1965.

CROWDEN, Guy Pascoe, O.B.E. 1944; T.D.; D.Sc. (Lond.), M.R.C.P. (Lond.), M.R.C.S. (Eng.); Emeritus Professor of Applied Physiology, University of London, since 1962 (Prof., 1946-62); late Director of Dept. of Applied Physiology, London School of Hygiene and Tropical Medicine; late Hon. Cons. in Applied Physiology to Army; Col., late R.A.M.C. (T.A.); *b.* 17 Nov. 1894; 4th *s.* of late J. T. Crowden, M.A., M.D., Gedney Hill, Lincs.; *m.* 1924, Jean, *d.* of late Edward V. Fleming, C.B.; two *s.* two *d.* *Educ.:* King's School. Peterborough; Univ. Coll., London; Univ. Coll. Hosp. Served European War, 1914-18: commissioned 4th K.O.Y.L.I., Oct. 1914; B.E.F. France, 1915-1918; Intell. Off. 148th Infty. Bde. (despatches); seconded to Special Bde., R.E., 1916-17; Capt. attd. H.Q. 56th (Lond.) Div., 1918. B.Sc. (Lond.), 1921 (1st cl. Hon. Physiol.); M.R.C.S. (Eng.), L.R.C.P. (Lond.), 1925; M.Sc. (Lond.), 1926; D.Sc. (Lond.), 1937; M.R.C.P. (Lond.), 1937; F.R.N.S.; Hon. Sec., Univ. of Lond. Union Soc., 1923; Asst., Dept. of Physiology, U.C.L., 1924; Lectr. in Physiology and Sub-Dean, Faculty of Med. Sciences, U.C.L., 1927-29; Lectr. in Applied Physiology, Lond. Sch. of Hygiene and Trop. Med., 1929; Reader in Industrial Physiology, Univ. of Lond., 1934-45. Commissioned R.A.M.C. (T.A.), 1927; Lt.-Col. O.C. Med. Unit, Univ. of Lond. O.T.C., 1938-1939. Served War of 1939-45: Lt.-Col., Chief Instructor and 2nd i/c. Depot R.A.M.C., 1942-43; Col. O.C. 68 (W.A.) Gen. Hosp., 1944-45. Sec. Nutrition Cttee., M.R.C., 1928-34; Hon. Sec. Research Defence Soc., 1925-45; Editor of the Fight Against Disease, 1925-39; Chm. of Coun., British Assoc. for Physical Training, 1931-35. *Publications:* Muscular Work, Fatigue and Recovery, 1932; chapters in Theory and Practice of Public Health, 1965; papers in medical, scientific and industrial jls. *Recreations:* the garden, local history. *Address:* Wolstenholme, Rectory Lane, Stanmore, Middlesex. *T.:* Grimsdyke 0566. [*Died* 22 *Nov.* 1966.

CROWDER, Sir John Ellenborough, Kt. 1952; *b.* 10 Nov. 1890; *s.* of late A. G. Crowder, J.P., 65 Portland Place, W.1, and Louisa, sister of 6th Baron Ellenborough; *m.* 1918, Florence, *d.* of Alfred R. Petre and *g.d.* of Lady Petre, Hatchwoods, Odiham, Hants; one *s.* two *d.* *Educ.:* Eton; Christ Church, Oxford. Mem. of Lloyds, 1920. M.P. (C.) Finchley Division of Middlesex, 1935-50, Finchley, 1950-Sept. 1959. Parliamentary Private Sec. to A. T. Lennox-Boyd, 1938-40 and 1943-45; to the Chancellor of the Exchequer, 1940. County Council Hants, 1931-46; Fleet U.D.C. 1933-46. Served 1914-19, with Lincolnshire Yeomanry, R.H.G. and on Personal Staff; 1939-45, as Staff Captain and as Army Welfare Officer (unpaid). J.P. Hants, 1942-48. Second (Parliamentary) Church Estates Comr., 1951-1957; Member, Church Assembly, 1956-60. Hon. Freeman, Borough of Finchley, 1960. *Address:* 116 Ashley Gardens, S.W.1. *T.:* Victoria 3901; Charlestown, St. Austell, Cornwall. *Clubs:* Carlton; Royal Fowey Yacht (Fowey). [*Died* 9 *July* 1961.

CROWDY, Mary, C.B.E. 1918; a Serving Sister of Order of St. John of Jerusalem; *d.* of late James Crowdy. Was Deputy Principal Commandant of V.A.D.'s. in France during European War, 1914-18; Secretary Children's Country Holidays Fund, Inc., retired, 1947. *Address:* 43 Beaufort Mansions, Chelsea, S.W.3. [*Died* 16 *Oct.* 1961.

CROWDY, Dame Rachel Eleanor; (Dame Rachel Thornhill), D.B.E., *cr.* 1919; *y. c.* of James Crowdy and Isabel (*née* Fuidge); *m.* 1939, Col. Cudbert Thornhill, C.M.G., D.S.O. (*d.* 1952). *Educ.:* Hyde Park New Coll. Guy's Hosp., 1908; Apothecary's Hall, 1910; Lecturer and Demonstrator National Health Society, 1912-1914; Principal Commandant of V.A.D.'s France and Belgium, 1914-19; despatches; Royal Red Cross, 2nd Class, 1916; 1st Class, 1917; Lady of Grace, 1917; Commander Order of Polonia Restituta, 1922; Hon. Doctor of Laws, Smith College, U.S.A., 1926; Commander of Order of Alphonso XII, 1931; Chief of Social Questions and Opium Traffic Section, League of Nations, 1919-31; Delegate to Conference on Pacific Affairs, Honolulu, 1930; to Conference on Pacific Relations, Shanghai, 1931; International Red Cross Conference, Tokio, 1934; Member of Royal Commission on Private Manufacture of and trading in Arms, 1935-1936; Member of West Indies Royal Commission, 1938-39; Regions' Adviser, Ministry of Information, 1939-46. *Recreations:* study of Far Eastern and International affairs, travelling and reading. *Address:* 35 Duchess of Bedford House, Campden Hill, W.8. *T.:* Western 3398; Sheppards, Outwood, Surrey. *T.:* Smallfield 2005. *Clubs:* V.A.D., Bath, Service Women's, English-Speaking Union. [*Died* 10 *Oct.* 1964.

CROWTHER, Charles, M.A. (Oxon); Ph.D.; 2nd *s.* of Samuel Crowther, of Gildersome, nr. Leeds; *b.* 1876; *m.* 1904, Hilda (*d.* 1950), *d.* of Henry Reed, Stockton-on-Tees; three *s.* one *d.* *Educ.:* Batley Grammar School; Corpus Christi College, Oxford; The Yorkshire College, Leeds; University of Leipzig. Head of Chemical Department, Harris Institute and Lancs. C.C. School of Agriculture, Preston, 1901-3; Lecturer in Agricultural Chemistry, University of Leeds, 1903-13; Professor of Agricultural Chemistry and Head of the Animal Nutrition Research Institute in the University of Leeds, 1913-19; Technical Adviser, Board of Agriculture and Fisheries, 1917-19; Director of Research, Olympia Agricultural Company, Ltd., 1919-22; Principal, Harper-Adams Agricultural College, Newport, Shropshire, 1922-44. Councillor, Surrey County Council, 1949-61; Editor: Journal of the Royal Agricultural Soc.. Journal of Soc. of Dairy Technology, 1948-1960. Educational Adviser to Institute of Corn and Agricultural Merchants. *Publications:* various papers (conjoint and otherwise) in Agricultural and Biochemical Journals, mostly on matters connected with animal nutrition. *Address:* 79 Cheam Road, Ewell, Surrey. *T.:* Ewell 1890. [*Died* 8 *Dec.* 1964.

CROWTHER-SMITH, Vivian Francis; late Comptroller, Guildhall, E.C.2; *b.* 24 Jan. 1875; *y. s.* of Charles Crowther-Smith, Southampton; *m.* Muriel Mary, *e. d.* of late William Henry Jaques; four *d.* Admitted Solicitor, 1899; entered service of the Corporation of London, 1900; Middlesex Yeomanry, 1901-07; Comptroller of Chamber of the City of London and the Bridge House Estates, 1920; retired, 1943; Master of the Worshipful Company of Girdlers, 1930-31. *Recreation:* reading. *Address:* The Littens, Hampstead Norris Berks. [*Died* 13 *April* 1961.

CROZIER, Rt. Rev. John Winthrop, D.D.; retired as Bishop of Tuam Killala and Achonry, and Dean of Achonry (1939-57); *b.* 1879; 2nd *s.* of John Baptist Crozier, late Primate of all Ireland and Archbishop of Armagh, and Alice Isabella, *d.* of Rev. John Winthrop Hackett; *m.* 1910, Bertha Elizabeth, *d.* of C. H. McCall, J.P., Dunida, Banbridge, Co. Down. *Educ.:* Portora Royal School; Trinity College, Dublin. Curate Seapatrick, Banbridge, 1903-05; Naas and Killashee, 1905-07; St. Ann's Dublin, 1907-11; Rector, Celbridge, Co. Kildare, 1911-21; Vicar of St. Ann's, Dublin, 1921-39; Chaplain to Lord Lieutenant, 1917-21; T.C.F. 1915-16 (despatches); Canon of Christ Church Cathedral, Dublin, 1926-34; Archdeacon of Dublin, 1934-39. *Address:* 7 Crannagh Road, Rathfarnham, Dublin. *Clubs:* University, Royal Irish Automobile (Dublin). [*Died* 14 *Feb.* 1966.

CRUICKSHANK, Ernest William Henderson; Regius Professor of Physiology, Marischal College, University of Aberdeen, 1935-58, retired; *b.* Edinburgh, 1888; *s.* of George Hunter and Sarah Henderson Cruickshank; *m.* 1930, Bertha Christina Steventon, A.R.C.M. (London); two *d.* *Educ.:* Marischal College, Aberdeen University; University College, London University; King's College, Cambridge. M.B., Ch.B. Aberdeen, 1910; M.D. (honours), Aberdeen, 1920; D.Sc. London, 1919; Ph.D. Cambridge, 1926; M.R.C.P. Lond., 1926; F.R.S. Edinburgh, 1929; Hon. LL.D. (Aberd.) 1959; Carnegie Research Fellow, Univ. Coll., London, 1912-14; temp. Capt. R.A.M.C., 1915-19; Officer in charge, Prisoners of War Repatriation Commn. to 3rd Bavarian Army Corps Area, 1919; Associate, Physiology, Washington University School of Medicine, St. Louis, U.S.A., 1919-20; Professor, Physiology, Peking Union Medical College, Peking, 1920-24; Rockefeller Foundation Travelling Research Fellow, 1924-26; Professor, Physiology and Biochemistry, Prince of Wales Medical College, Patna, India, 1926-28; Sukhr Raj Ray Reader in Natural Science, the University of Patna, India, 1927; Professor of Physiology, Dalhousie Univ., Halifax, N.S., 1929-35; Mem. National Council of Education, Canada, 1934; Mem. Scientific Advisory Cttee., Department of Health for Scotland, 1944; Nutrition Sub-Committee, 1940-48, Chairman 1944-48. Temporary consultant, World Health Organization, Geneva, 1952, 1953, 1955 and 1964 (S.E.Asia and U.S.S.R.). *Publications:* Practical Biochemistry for Students, 1928; The Value of Scientific Thought in the Advance of Modern Medicine, 1928; Food and Physical Fitness, 1938; Food and Nutrition, 1946, 2nd edn., 1951; Scientific Papers in J. Physiology, Biochemical Journal, Physiological Reviews, etc. *Recreation:* travel. *Address:* Bramblehurst, 113 Anderson Drive, Aberdeen. *T.:* Aberdeen 36422. [*Died* 29 *Dec.* 1964.

CRUICKSHANK, John, C.B.E. 1946; M.D. Glasg.; LL.D. (Aberdeen); Professor of Bacteriology, Aberdeen University 1926-54, Emeritus since Sept. 1954; *b.* 1884; *s.* of George Cruickshank and Alice Hamilton; *m.* Jessie Cromarty Allan (decd.); two *s.* three *d.* *Educ.:* Allan Glen's School and University, Glasgow (M.D. Hons.; Gold Medallist; M.B. Hons.; Ch.B. Hons.; Brunton Memorial Prize). Late Assistant to Professor of Pathology, Glasgow University; Pathologist at Crichton Royal Institution, Dumfries, 1912-20. Served European War, 1914-18, France, 1916-19, o/c Mobile Bacteriological Lab.; Assistant Adviser in Pathology, 3rd Army, 1917; McRobert Research Lecturer in Pathology, 1920, Reader in Bacteriology, 1922, Univ. of Aberdeen; Member: Bacteriology Cttee. of Med. Res. Council, 1935; Cttee. on Laboratory Services, Scotland, 1939; ex-Director Blood Transfusion Services, N.E. Scotland; Mem. of Panel of Consultants and Specialists (Scot.); former Vice-chm. N.E. Reg. Hosp. Bd. and Convener Medical Services Cttee., 1948. Hon. LL.D.: Aberdeen, 1955, Glasgow, 1958. *Publications:* Chapter in System of Bacteriology, Med. Res. Council, 1931; Chapter in Recent Methods in Diagnosis and Treatment of Syphilis; scientific papers on Bacteriological and Pathological subjects. *Recreations:* golf, fishing. *Address:* 46 Gladstone Place, Aberdeen. *T.:* Aberdeen 21038. [*Died* 10 *Oct.* 1966.

CRUICKSHANK, Colonel Martin Melvin, C.I.E. 1942; late I.M.S.; K.St.J. 1958; now retired from active medical work; Deputy Administrative Medical Superintendent, General Hospitals Group, Aberdeen, retired; *b.* Edinburgh, 22 Mar. 1888; *s.* of late George Hunter Cruickshank, Marine Engineer, and of late Sarah Henderson Cruickshank; *m.* 1927, Florence Watson, *d.* of Capt. A. Cruickshank; one *s.* *Educ.:* Robert Gordon's College, Aberdeen; Aberdeen University; Univ. of Munich; Middlesex Hospital, London. B.Sc. 1911; M.B., Ch.B. 1912; George Thomson Research Fellow, 1913-14; served European War, 1914-18, France, Salonika, Palestine; entered I.M.S., 1919; Ophthalmic specialist in Northern and Western Commands, 1921-31; appointments in Madras Presidency, 1931-1940; Professor of Surgery, Madras Medical College, and Senior Surgeon and Supt., General Hospital, Madras, 1934-40; Chief Med. Officer, Delhi Province, 1940; Brigadier and Consultant Surgeon Southern Army, India, 1943; retired, 1946. Member Univ. Court, Delhi Univ.; F.R.S.M.; Member of Ophthalmological Societies, England, India, Egypt. M.D. Honours (Gold Medal), 1925, Ch.M., 1927, Aberdeen; D.O.M.S., London, 1925; F.R.C.S., Edin., 1937; F.A.C.S., 1939; Fellow of International College of Surgeons; F.R.S.E. *Publications:* in British, American, and Indian Medical Journals. *Recreation:* travel. *Address:* Hamewith, 92 Queen's Road, Aberdeen. *T.:* Aberdeen 37759; c/o Glyn, Mills & Co. Kirkland House, Whitehall, S.W.1. [*Died* 10 *Oct.* 1964.

CRUMP, Edwin Samuel, C.I.E. 1936; Indian Service of Engineers, retired; *b.* 6 July 1882; *s.* of late Charles Crump, Wolverhampton; *m.* 1913, Helen Elizabeth, *d.* of late John Jefferis, Croydon; two *s.* Entered Indian Service of Engineers, 1906; retired, 1937. Joined Hydraulic Research Organisation, D.S.I.R., 1949; retired, 1956. *Address:* Blenheim House, Benson-on-Thames, Oxon. [*Died* 5 *March* 1961.

CRUMP, Norman Easedale; retired as City Editor, Sunday Times (1939-60); *b.* 10 Jan. 1896; *s.* of late Charles George Crump, late Principal Assistant Keeper, Public Record Office; *m.* 1927, Kathleen Mary St. Patrick, *d.* of late Prof. T. C. Hodson; two *s.* one *d.* *Educ.:* Winchester College. Middlesex Regt. and R.E. (Signals), 1914-18; Federation of British Industries, 1919-21; Assistant Secretary to Chairman, Westminster Bank, 1921-25; Statistical Correspondent, Financial Times, 1921-39; Member of Staff, Economist Newspaper, 1927-39; Assistant Editor, The Banker, 1930-38;

Editor, Lloyds Bank Monthly Review, 1930-1939; contested (L.) North Bucks, 1929. Fellow Royal Statistical Society. *Publications:* part author of later editions of The A.B.C. of the Foreign Exchanges, 1924-; A First Book of Economics, 1930; By Rail to Victory, 1947; various pamphlets on financial questions. *Recreations:* railways, golf, bridge. *Address:* 20c East Heath Road, N.W.3. *T.:* Hampstead 4964. *Club:* Savile [*Died* 22 *Jan.* 1964.

CRUTCHLEY, Arthur Felton, D.S.O. 1919; *b.* 1883; *s.* of late Commander W. Caius Crutchley, R.D., R.N.R. *Educ.:* Eastman's, Winchester. Royal Navy, 1896-1919; retired Lieut. Commander, 1919; served in China, 1900 (two bars); European War, 1914-19 (despatches, D.S.O.); Mobilised Sept. 1940 and appointed Consular Shipping Adviser at British Consulate General, Lourenço Marques, P.E.A.; reverted to retired list, 1943. *Address:* c/o Barclays Bank, Stanger, Natal, South Africa. [*Died Feb.* 1966.

CRYMBLE, Percival Templeton, M.B., F.R.C.S.Eng.; Hon. F.I.C.S.; Emeritus Professor of Surgery, Queen's University, Belfast, since 1948 (Professor of Surgery, 1933-48); late Examiner in Surgery, London University; *b.* Belfast, 1880; *s.* of George Crymble; *m.* Norah Ireland; one *s.* two *d.* *Educ.:* Academical Institution, Belfast; Queen's Univ., Belfast. Post-graduate study in London and Vienna; B.E.F. France, 1915-1916. *Publications:* Quain's Anatomy, Section on Peritoneum; Current Surgery; articles in medical journals. *Recreations:* golf, music. *Address:* 7 College Gardens, Belfast. *T.:* Belfast 660688. [*Died* 28 *June* 1970.

CUCKNEY, Air Vice-Marshal Ernest John, C.B. 1946; C.B.E. 1943; D.S.C. and Bar, 1917; *b.* 1 Nov. 1896; *s.* of Capt. E. W. Cuckney; *m.* 1920, Lilian, *d.* of J. Williams, Wimbledon; one surviving *s.* *Educ.:* Varndean. Artists' Rifles, 1915; Sub-Lieut. Royal Naval Air Service, 1915 (D.S.C. and Bar); Royal Air Force, 1918; Regular Commission, R.A.F., 1919. Served in India, 1921-1925, Iraq, 1932-34; A.O.C. No. 43 Group Royal Air Force, 1944-45; Chief Maintenance Officer, H.Q., Med. Middle East, 1945-46. Assistant Controller of Supplies (Air), Min. of Supply, 1946-50; retired list, 1950; Director of Planning and Progressing, Min. of Supply, 1950-55. *Recreations:* fishing and gardening. *Address:* 410 Howard House, Dolphin Sq., S.W.1. *T.:* Tate Gallery 3544. [*Died* 8 *Nov.* 1965.

CUDLIPP, Percy; journalist; *b.* Cardiff, 1905; *s.* of William Cudlipp, Cardiff; *m.* 1927, Gwendoline James; one *s.* *Educ.:* Cardiff. Began journalism on South Wales Echo, Cardiff; Reporter on Evening Chronicle, Manchester, and contributor of articles and light verse to London newspapers, 1924-25; dramatic critic and humorous columnist on Sunday News, London, 1925-1929; special writer and film critic, Evening Standard, 1929-31; Assistant Editor, 1931; Editor, 1933; Editorial Manager, Daily Herald, 1938-40, Editor, 1940-53; Columnist, News Chronicle, 1954-56; Editor of New Scientist, from foundation in 1956. A frequent broadcaster in sound and vision programmes. *Publication:* Bouverie Ballads, 1955. *Recreation:* music. *Address:* 11 Falmouth House, Clarendon Place, W.2. *T.:* Ambassador 8323. *Clubs:* Garrick, Press. [*Died* 5 *Nov.* 1962.

CUFF, Maj.-Gen. Brian, C.B. 1945; C.B.E. 1941; *b.* 29 Jan. 1889; *s.* of Robert Cuff, M.D., J.P., Scarborough; *m.* 1923, Elizabeth Constance Louise, *d.* of Rev. W. P. Magee; one *d.* *Educ.:* Malvern; Christ Church, Oxford. Joined Yorkshire Regt., 1910; Captain, Cheshire Regt., 1915; Colonel, 1937; Brigadier, 1940; retired Maj.-Gen. 1945; served European War, 1914-1918 (Greek Military Cross, Bt. Major); in France, 1939-40 (despatches, C.B.E., Officer Legion of Merit, U.S.A.). *Address:* Little Holgate, Kingsland, Leominster, Herefordshire. *T.:* Kingsland 453. *Club:* United Service. [*Died* 12 *March* 1970.

CUFFE, Sir George Eustace, Kt., *cr.* 1946; B.A. (Hons. in Engnr.) (Cantab.); *b.* 15 May 1892; *s.* of late Rev. George Cuffe, Rector of St. John the Baptist, Coventry; *m.* Mabel Greenwood (*d.* 1956); one *s.* two *d.* *Educ.:* Marlborough; Jesus College, Cambridge. Agent and Gen. Manager, Assam Bengal Rly., 1935-40; Gen. Manager, Great Indian Peninsula Rly., 1940-43; Gen. Manager, Bengal Assam Rly., 1943-45; Director-Gen. of Rlys., Calcutta Area, Apr.-Dec. 1945; Gen. Manager, B.B. & C.I. Rly., Dec. 1945-May 1947; Member Indian Railway Enquiry Cttee., 1947-48. *Address:* c/o State Bank of India, 25 Old Broad Street, E.C.2. [*Died* 6 *May* 1962.

CUKE, Sir Hampden Archibald, Kt., *cr.* 1955; C.B.E. 1950 (O.B.E. 1945); *b.* 20 June 1892; *s.* of John Hampden Cuke; *m.* 1917, Isabella Maud, *d.* of Mark Carter. Member of the Legislative Council, Barbados; Member of the Executive Council, Barbados. *Address:* Roslyn, Pine Hill, Barbados. [*Died* 24 *Sept.* 1968.

CULL, Vice-Admiral (acting) Sir Malcolm Giffard Stebbing, K.C.B., *cr.* 1947 (C.B. 1945); C.B.E. 1942 (O.B.E. 1919); M.V.O. 1934; *b.* 7 Mar. 1891; *s.* of late Rev. E. G. Cull, R.N., and Adèle Martel; *m.* 1927, Kathleen Eleanor Forbes; one *s.* *Educ.:* Norwich. Served on the Staffs of Admirals of the Fleet Lord Jellicoe and Sir Charles Madden; Secretary to Admiral of the Fleet Sir Roger Keyes, 1919-31; Dover, 1939-42; Director-General, Supply and Secretariat Branch, Admiralty, 1945-48. *Address:* Hendrick House, Boxford, Colchester. *T.:* Boxford 486. [*Died* 1 *Jan.* 1962.

CULLEN, Mrs. Alice, (Mrs. William Reynolds); M.P. (Lab.) Gorbals Division of Glasgow since Oct. 1948; *d.* of late John McLoughlin; *m.* 1920, Pearce Cullen (decd.); three *d.*; 2nd, 1950, William Reynolds. Member of Glasgow Corporation for 10 years (sub-convener, health committee; convener, Clinical Services and Mental Services; Member of education, housing and transport committees). *Address:* 239 Kennington Rd., S.E.11; 58 Balornock Rd., Glasgow, N. [*Died* 31 *May* 1969.

CULLEN, Rt. Rev. Archibald Howard, D.D.; M.A., B.Sc.; Assistant Bishop of Natal since 1960; *b.* Peckham, 24 Sept. 1887; *s.* of William and Louisa Cullen, of Canterbury; *m.* 1st, 1920, Ivy Gertrude Waters (*d.* 1923), Associate of the Royal Red Cross, S.A.M.N.S., *d.* of Robert Floyd and Isabel Waters, of South Africa; no *c.*; 2nd, 1927, Natalie Beatrice Denoon Stevens, *widow* of Cecil Denoon Stevens of Sezela, Natal, *d.* of Harry Herbert Pepworth and Amy Beatrice Waller of Umzinto, Natal; one *d.* *Educ.:* Simon Langton School, Canterbury; London University; Queens' College, Cambridge. Deacon, 1915; Priest, 1916; Curate of Coalbrookdale, Salop, 1915-1919; temporary Chaplain to the Forces attached to the 1st South African General Hospital, France, 1916-19; Chaplain and Lecturer of Wells Theological College, and Priest-Vicar and Sacrist of Wells Cathedral, 1919-22; Vicar of Umzinto, Natal, 1922-23; Vice-Principal of Leeds Clergy School and Curate of Leeds Parish Church, 1923-24;

Vice-Principal of Bishops' College, Cheshunt, 1924-25; Warden of St. Paul's Theological College, Grahamstown, 1926-31; Bishop of Grahamstown, 1931-59, resigned. Dean of the Province of South Africa, 1951-59. Member of Council, Rhodes Univ. Coll., Grahamstown, 1944-51 (Chairman 1946-48). Hon. Chaplain to H.M. Forces. *Address:* Bishopscote, Park Rynie, Natal, South Africa. *Clubs:* Albany (Grahamstown); Royal Automobile of South Africa.
[*Died* 16 *June* 1968.

CULLINAN, Edward Revill, C.B.E. 1963; M.D., F.R.C.P.; Physician, St. Bartholomew's Hosp., Westminster (Gordon) Hosp. and King Edward VII Hosp. for Officers; Hon. Consulting Physician to the Army and to the Royal Hospital, Chelsea; Member Nuffield Panel of Consultants to the Colonies; Cons. Physician to Woolwich Memorial and Leatherhead Hosps.; Examiner in Medicine to Roy. Coll. of Physicians and to Sheffield University; *b.* 11 June 1901; *o. s.* of late Edward Cullinan, M.D., and May Revill; *m.* 1930, Dorothea Joy, *e. d.* of 1st Baron Horder, G.C.V.O.; three *s.* one *d.* *Educ.:* Downside; Epsom; St. Bartholomew's Hosp. M.R.C.S. (Eng.) L.R.C.P. (Lond.) 1924; M.B., B.S. (Lond.) 1924; M.R.C.P. (Lond.) 1926; M.D. (Lond.) 1926; F.R.C.P. (Lond.) 1934. Late Chief Asst. to a medical unit, Casualty Physn., Sen. Demr. of Morbid Anat. and Asst. Physn. to St. Bartholomew's Hosp. Rose Research, 1932; Cattlin Research Fellow, 1933; Bradshaw Lectr., R.C.P., 1950; Lettsomian Lectures, Med. Soc. of London, 1953. Physician to Luton and Dunstable and Gerrards Cross Hosps. Late examr. in med. in Univs. of London, Liverpool, Witswatersrand, Cape Town and Makerere Coll., Uganda; formerly Hon. editor of Proceedings of Royal Society of Medicine; Member: Association of Physicians, Med. Soc. of London, Brit. Soc. of Gastroenterology, Soc. of Apothecaries; F.R. Soc. Med. Lieut.-Col. R.A.M.C., 1941; Egypt and Syria, 1941-43; Brig., Cons. Physn. to E. Africa Comd., 1944-45. *Publications:* various in medical books and jls., especially concerning diseases of the liver and abdomen. *Recreations:* mountaineering, conjuring, and inland waterways. *Address:* 10 Park Square West, Regent's Park, N.W.1. *T.:* Welbeck 1834. *Club:* Reform.
[*Died* 16 *March* 1965.

CULLIS, Charles Edgar; Master of the Supreme Court, Taxing Department, since 1954; *b.* London, 14 Jan. 1899; *s.* of Charles Edgar Cullis and Martha James; *m.* 1925, Amy Jane George, Woodchurch, Kent. *Educ.:* Hogarth School, Chiswick; City of London College. Served 1916-18, 4th Bn. Scottish Rifles (Cameronians), Instructor, Brigade Signal School, East Linton; Solicitor, 1930; practised as Malkin, Cullis & Co., London, 1934-53. Member of the Law Society. *Recreation:* reading. *Address:* 37 Park Close, Ilchester Place, Kensington, W.14. *T.:* Western 8732.
[*Died* 19 *Oct.* 1964.

CULVERWELL, Cyril Tom; *b.* 22 Oct. 1895; *s* of late T. J. H. Culverwell of Litfield House, Clifton, Bristol, and Louisa Tinn of Begbrooke, Frenchay, near Bristol; *m.* 1919, Muriel Christabel, *d.* of Dr. Fitzwilliam Carter Bristol; one *s* one *d.* *Educ.:* Clifton College; Queens' College, Camb. Army, 1915-1919; Councillor, City of Bristol, 1924-30; M.P. (U.) Bristol West, 1928-45; Member of Public Accounts Committee, 1932-42; of Select Committee on National Expenditure, 1942-45. *Address:* Snapes Manor, Salcombe, S. Devon. *T.:* Salcombe 2884. *Clubs:* Carlton; Royal Western Yacht (Plymouth); Clifton (Bristol).
[*Died* 29 *Oct.* 1963.

CUMMINGS, Edward Estlin, A.B., M.A.; American author and artist; *b.* 14 Oct. 1894. *Educ.:* Harvard University. Has held one-man art shows at the American-British Art Centre, 1944 and 1949, the Rochester Memorial Gallery, 1945, etc. *Publications:* The Enormous Room, 1922 Tulips and Chimneys, 1923; XLI Poems 1925; & (And), 1925; Is 5, 1926; Him 1927; (no title) 1930; CIOPW, 1931; ViVa, 1931; Eimi, 1933; No Thanks, 1935; Tom, 1935; Collected Poems, 1938; 50 Poems, 1940; 1×1, 1944; Anthropos, 1944; Santa Claus, 1946; Khaire, 1950; i (six non lectures), 1953; Poems 1923-1954, 1954; A Miscellany, 1958; 95 Poems, 1958; 100 Selected Poems, 1959; Selected Poems 1923-1958, 1960; 16 Poèmes Enfantins, 1962; 73 Poems (posthumous) 1964. *Address:* 4 Patchin Place, New York, N.Y., U.S.A.
[*Died* 3 *Sept.* 1962.

CUMMINS, Geraldine Dorothy; author; *d.* of late Professor Ashley Cummins, M.D., and Jane Constable; *b.* 1890. *Educ.:* home. *Publications:* The Land They Loved, Fires of Beltane, Irish novels; Variety Show (short stories); The Scripts of Cleophas; Paul in Athens; The Great Days of Ephesus; The Childhood of Jesus; Beyond Human Personality; The Road to Immortality, They Survive (with E. B. Gibbes); When Nero was Dictator; After Pentecost; Healing the Mind (with Dr. Connell); Travellers in Eternity; I Appeal Unto Caesar; The Manhood of Jesus; Dr. E. Œ. Somerville (biography); Unseen Adventures (autobiographical); The Fate of Colonel Fawcett; Mind in Life and Death; Swan on a Black Sea; plays produced: Till Yesterday Comes Again, three Irish plays (with S. R. Day): Broken Faith, Fox and Geese, The Way of the World; two books trans. into four languages; has contributed short stories or articles to periodicals and magazines. *Recreations:* gardening, tennis, music, played in the Irish International Hockey team. *Address:* Woodville, Glanmire, Co. Cork.
[*Died* 24 *Aug.* 1969.

CUNARD, Sir Edward, 5th Bt., *cr.* 1859; *b.* 25 Nov. 1891; *s.* of Sir Gordon Cunard, the Bt., and Edith Mary (*d.* 1927), *d.* of late Col. John Stanley Howard of Ballina Park, Co. Wicklow; *S.* father 1933. *Educ.:* Eton; Cambridge. Entered Diplomatic Service, 1914; served as 3rd Secretary at the British Embassy in St. Petersburg, in Sir F. Lindley's mission to Archangel and at the Peace Conference in Paris; resigned 1919; Private Secretary to Governor of Trinidad, 1940-46. O.St.J. *Heir:* *kinsman:* Henry Palmes Cunard, *b.* 12 Sept. 1909. *Address:* Waverley, Gibbs, St. Peter, Barbados. *Club:* Travellers'.
[*Died* 2 *July* 1962.

CUNDALL, Joseph Leslie, C.M.G. 1960; Q.C. (Jamaica) 1949; President, Jamaica Court of Appeal since 1962; *b.* 22 May 1906; *m.* 1930, Dorothy May Hutchings; no *c.* *Educ.:* Munro Coll., Jamaica; Christ's Coll., Cambridge. Deputy Clerk of the Courts, Jamaica, 1929; Clerk of the Courts, Jamaica, 1933; Resident Magistrate, Jamaica, 1937; Police Magistrate, Sierra Leone, 1939; Resident Magistrate, Jamaica, 1944; Solicitor-General, Jamaica, 1948; Attorney-General of Jamaica, 1952. Has acted as Chief Justice, Jamaica. Chancellor, Diocese of Jamaica, since 1949; Prolocutor, House of Laity, Synod of the West Indies, 1959. *Publications:* (Ed.) Revised Edn. of the Laws of the Turks and Caicos Islands, 1951; (Jt. Ed.) Revised Edn. of the Laws of Jamaica, 1953. *Recreations:* reading and gardening. *Address:* 62 Lady Musgrave Road, Halfway Tree, Jamaica, W.I. *Clubs:* Liguanea, Kingston Cricket, Melbourne Cricket.
[*Died* 28 *March* 1964.

CUNDELL, Edric, C.B.E. 1949; Hon. R.A.M.; F.G.S.M.; composer and conductor; Principal of Guildhall School of

Music and Drama 1938-59; conducted London Philharmonic Orchestra, London Symphony Orchestra, Royal Philharmonic Orchestra, Philharmonia Orchestra, Sadlers Wells Opera, Cape Town Orchestra and B.B.C. Symphony Concerts; *b.* London, 1893; *m.* 1920, Helena, *e. d.* of W. Harding Scott, of Thorpe, Norwich. *Educ.:* Aske's Haberdashers' School. Began musical career as French-horn player; gained scholarship for piano at Trinity College of Music; appointed to teaching staff in 1914 as professor of composition, theory, etc., and examining staff in 1922; took commission in the Army in 1915, and served three years in the Balkans (Serbian Order of White Eagle); won Daily Telegraph prize for string quartet, 1933; conductor of the Westminster Orchestral Society; conductor of the Stock Exchange Orchestral Society, 1924; toured in America and New Zealand in 1925 and S. Africa, in 1934. Chairman of Arts Council Music Panel, 1951-53. Compositions include Symphonic Poem Serbia; Three Orchestral Suites; a Piano Concerto; Symphony; Symphonic Poem Deirdre; Sonnet for Tenor and Orchestra, Our Dead; Three Quartets; Rhapsody for viola and piano; Hymn to Providence, for chorus and orchestra; choral works; Songs, etc. *Address:* Bear House, Ashwell, Herts. *T.:* Ashwell 353.
[*Died* 19 *March* 1961.

CUNLIFFE, 2nd Baron, of Headley, *cr.* 1914; **Rolf Cunliffe;** Chairman of Board, Guy's Hospital; *b.* 13 May 1899; *s.* of 1st Baron and Edith, *d.* of Col. R. T. Boothby, St. Andrews, Fife; *S.* father, 1920; *m.* 1st, 1925, Joan (marriage dissolved, 1952), 2nd *d.* of late Cecil Lubbock; two *s.* two *d.*; 2nd, 1952, Mrs. Kathleen E. Robinson, Woodford Lodge, Trinidad. *Educ.:* Eton; Trinity College, Cambridge. Served as Flt. Sub-Lieut. R.N.A.S. and Lieutenant R.A.F. 1917-1919; re-employed, 1939; Wing Commander R.A.F.V.R. 1942. *Heir:* *s.* Hon. Roger Cunliffe [*b.* 12 Jan. 1932; *m.* 1957, Clemency Ann, *e. d.* of G. B. Hoare, Colville Hall, White Roding, Dunmow, Essex; one *s.* one *d.*]. *Address:* Alscot Lodge, Princes Risborough, Bucks. *T.:* Princes Risborough 531. *Club:* Oxford and Cambridge.
[*Died* 24 *Nov.* 1963.

CUNLIFFE, Sir Cyril (Henley), 8th Bt., *cr.* 1759; *b.* 3 March 1901; *s.* of late Alfred Edward Cunliffe (*s.* of late David Cunliffe, Bengal Civil Service, 3rd *s.* of 4th Bt.), and Agnes (*d.* 1955), *d.* of Dr. J. M. Comley, Calcutta; *S.* cousin, 1949; *m.* 1956, Eileen, *widow* of Charles Clifford, Walton-on-Thames; two *s.* one *d.* *Educ.:* Dulwich Coll.; Faraday House. *Heir:* *s.* David Ellis Cunliffe, *b.* 29 Oct. 1957. *Address:* 17 Gurney Court Road, St. Albans, Herts. [*Died* 12 *Feb.* 1969.

CUNLIFFE, Sir Herbert; *see* Cunliffe, Sir J. H.

CUNLIFFE, Sir John Robert Ellis, Kt., *cr.* 1932; *b.* 4 Mar. 1886; *er. s.* of late Sir Robert Ellis Cunliffe; *m.* 1st, 1915, Gabriella Vaccari; 2nd, 1960, Lynette Rawlinson. *Educ.:* Bradfield College; Magdalen College, Oxford. Called to Bar, Inner Temple, 1911; served R.F.A. 1914-18; resumed practice at the Bar, 1919; Judge, High Court, Rangoon, 1924-34; Judge, High Court, Calcutta, 1934-1937; President Burma Rebellion Tribunal, 1931; Chairman, Board of Trustees, Rangoon University Endowment Fund; Officiating Chief Justice of Burma, 1932 and 1933. *Recreations:* fox-hunting, fly-fishing; Secretary, Pegasus Club, 1919-24. *Address:* Flat 1, Glenside, Manor Road, Sidmouth, Devon.
[*Died* 16 *Jan.* 1967.

CUNLIFFE, Sir (Joseph) Herbert, K.B.E., *cr.* 1946; Kt., *cr.* 1926; Q.C. 1912; *b.* 1 July 1867; 2nd *s.* of late Thomas Cunliffe, J.P., of Bolton, Lancashire, newspaper proprietor; *m.* 1st, 1894, Mary (*d.* 1930), *e. d.* of late Edward Balshaw of Heaton, nr. Bolton; one *s.* one *d.*; 2nd, 1932, Maud (*d.* 1954), 4th *d.* of late Joseph Clegg, J.P., High Crompton, nr. Oldham, Lancashire. Barrister Middle Temple and Lincoln's Inn, 1896; Bencher, Lincoln's Inn, 1919; Treasurer, Lincoln's Inn, 1941; Attorney-General of the Duchy of Lancaster, 1921-46; M.P. (U.) Bolton, 1923-29; a member of the General Council of the Bar, 1914-46 (Vice-Chm. 1931, Chm. 1932-46); a member Joint Committee of the Four Inns of Court since 1929 and Chm., 1933-48; a member of Council of Law Reporting, 1923-48, Vice-Chm. 1936 and Chm., 1942-48; a member of Council of Legal Education, 1920-45; Chairman Essex Quarter Sessions, 1937-46; Chairman of Governors of Brentwood School, 1939-56; Member Lord Chancellor's Committee on County Courts, 1917-19; Chairman Departmental Committee on Supervision of Charities, 1925-27. *Address:* 15 Old Square, Lincoln's Inn, W.C.2. *T.:* Holborn 0745; Hou Hatch, South Weald, nr. Brentwood, Essex. *T.:* Coxtie Green 233.
[*Died* 9 *April* 1963.

CUNLIFFE, Thomas; Chief Registrar in Bankruptcy of the High Court of Justice since 1965; *b.* 27 June 1895; *o. s.* of late Sir Herbert Cunliffe, K.B.E., Q.C.; *m.* 1st, 1924, Laura Margaret (*d.* 1954), *o. d.* of late William Sellers, M.D., Barrister-at-Law, Manchester; 2nd, 1955, Mona Dorothy Marguerite, *widow* of late J. McAlister Ritchie, Mill Hill and Belfast; no *c.* *Educ.:* Monmouth; Balliol Coll., Oxf.; Lincoln's Inn. Served European War, 1914-18, Royal Artillery, France, Salonica. Called to Bar, 1922; practised at Chancery Bar, 1922-1949. Secretary Legal Appointments Committee, Lord Chancellor's Office, 1939-46. Editor of The Solicitor's Journal, 1929-48. A Registrar of the High Court in Bankruptcy, 1949. *Recreations:* fishing and making fishing tackle. *Address:* 6 Engel Park, Mill Hill, N.W.7. *T.:* Finchley 2737. *Clubs:* Flyfishers', Oxford and Cambridge.
[*Died* 7 *May* 1966.

CUNNINGHAM of Hyndhope, 1st Viscount (U.K.), *cr.* 1946; 1st Baron, *cr.* 1945, of Kirkhope; **Adm. of the Fleet Andrew Browne Cunningham,** 1st Bt., *cr.* 1942; K.T. 1945; G.C.B., *cr.* 1941 (K.C.B., *cr.* 1939; C.B. 1934); O.M. 1946; D.S.O. 1915; D.C.L. Oxford; LL.D. Edinburgh, Birmingham, Cambridge, Glasgow, Leeds, Sheffield, St. Andrews; *b.* 1883; *s.* of late Prof. D. J. Cunningham, Dublin and Edinburgh; *m.* 1929, Nona Christine, *d.* of late Horace Byatt, M.A., Midhurst, Sussex; no *c.* *Educ.:* Edinburgh Academy; Stubbington House, Fareham; H.M.S. Britannia. Entered Royal Navy 1898; served European War, 1914-18 (despatches, D.S.O. with two bars); War of 1939-45 (G.C.B.); was President Sub-Commission C Naval Inter-allied Commission of Control; Naval A.D.C. to the King, 1932; Rear-Admiral (D) commanding Destroyer Flotillas, Mediterranean Fleet, 1934-36; Vice-Admiral commanding Battle-Cruiser Squadron and 2nd in Command, Mediterranean, 1937-38; Lord Commissioner of the Admiralty and Deputy Chief of Naval Staff, 1938-39; Commander-in-Chief, Mediterranean, 1939-42; Head of British Admiralty Delegation in Washington, 1942; Admiral, 1941; Naval C.-in-C. Expeditionary Force, North Africa, 1942; C.-in-C. Mediterranean, 1943; Admiral of the Fleet, 1943; First Sea Lord and Chief of Naval Staff, 1943-46. Lord High Commissioner to General Assembly of Church of Scotland, 1950 and 1952; Hon. Freeman: Fishmongers' Company, Company of Shipwrights; Borough of Hove, City of Edinburgh, City of Manchester, City of London, City of Lincoln. Hon. Member the Company of Merchants of Edinburgh; Hon. Bencher Lincoln's Inn; Hon. F.R.C.S.E.; Hon. Member Royal Institution of Naval Architects. Grand Cordon Légion d'Honneur, Médaille Militaire (French); Chief Comdr. Legion of Merit, D.S.M. Army, D.S.M. Navy (U.S.A.); Grand Cordon of Order of George I, Medal of Military Valour (Greek); Grand Cross Netherlands Lion. *Publication:* A Sailor's Odyssey, 1951. *Recreation:* fishing. *Address:* The Palace House, Bishop's Waltham, Hants. *T.:* Bishop's Waltham 2663. *Clubs:* Athenæum, (Hon.) Caledonian, United Hunt, White's, Bath, Flyfishers', United Service, M.C.C., Hurlingham; Royal and Ancient Golf (St. Andrews). [*Died* 12 *June* 1963 (*ext.*).

CUNNINGHAM, Sir Charles Banks, Kt., *cr.* 1933; C.S.I. 1931; *b.* 8 May 1884; *s.* of Dr. John Cunningham, M.B. and C.M., Cambeltown, Argyll; *m.* Grace, *d.* of Hugh Macnish, Campbeltown; one *s.* one *d.* (and one *s.* killed in action, 1940). *Educ.:* Campbeltown Grammar School. Joined the Indian Police Service as probationary Assistant Superintendent of Police, 1904; District Superintendent, 1909; Deputy Commissioner of Police, 1910-15; Commissioner, Corporation of Madras, 1910-1915; Commissioner of Police, Travancore State, 1915-21; Director of Civil Supplies and Controller of Munitions and Member of Legislative Council, Travancore State, 1917-21; King's Police Medal, 1928; Deputy Inspector-General of Police, 1928; Comr. of Police, Madras, 1928; Inspector-General of Police, Madras Presidency, 1930-1938; Indian Police Medal, 1931; retd., 1938; Dep. Chm. and later Chm. Madras and S. Mahratta Railway Co. Ltd., 1938-44; Dep. Controller A.R.P. Bucks County, 1939; Asst. to Regional Comr. Southern Region, 1940; Inspector of Constabulary, Home Office, 1940-45; Vice-Chairman of Committee for the Industrial and Scientific Provision of Housing, 1943-44; Chairman, Animal Feeding Stuffs Committee, Southern Region, 1945-49. Mem. Institute of Bankers in Scotland, 1902; Fellow of Institute of General Managers, 1958; Pres., Taxpayers' Union; a Vice-President of the Free Trade Union and of the Cobden Club. *Publications:* When Steel Met Steel, 1961; The Shining Sword, 1962. *Address:* 93 Iverna Court, W.8. *T.:* Western 6535. *Clubs:* Athenæum, Caledonian. [*Died* 30 *Oct.* 1967.

CUNNINGHAM, Sir George, G.C.I.E., *cr.* 1946 (K.C.I.E., *cr.* 1935 C.I.E. 1925); K.C.S.I., *cr.* 1937 (C.S.I. 1931); O.B.E. 1920; LL.D. (St. Andrews and Edinburgh); *b.* 23 March 1888; *s.* of late James Cunningham, LL.D., St. Andrews; *m.* 1929, Kathleen Mary Adair, Tullow, Co. Carlow. *Educ.:* Fettes College, Edinburgh; Magdalen Coll., Oxford. Entered I.C.S. 1911; served since 1914 on N.W. Frontier, India; Personal Assistant to Chief Commissioner, N.W. Frontier Province, 1915-19; Political Agent, North Waziristan, 1922-23; Counsellor, British Legation, Kabul, 1925-26; Private Secretary to the Viceroy, 1926-31; Member of Executive Council, N.W. Frontier Province, 1932-36, Foreign and Political Dept., Govt. of India; Governor of N.W. Frontier Province, 1937-46 and 1947-48; Rector of St. Andrews University, 1946-49; Hon. Fellow of Magdalen College, Oxford. *Recreations:* shooting, fishing, golf. *Address:* Dykes End, St. Andrews. *Clubs:* Athenæum; New (Edinburgh); Royal and Ancient Golf (St. Andrews). [*Died* 8 *Dec.* 1964.

CUNNINGHAM, Gordon Herriot, C.B.E. 1949; F.R.S. 1950; Director Plant Diseases Division, Department of Scientific and Industrial Research, New Zealand, 1936-57; *b.* 27 Aug. 1892; 2nd *s.* of late J. W. Cunningham and late Helen Donaldson (*née* Heriot); *m.* 1918, Madge Leslie, *d.* of late David McGregor; one *d.* *Educ.:* Victoria University of Wellington, N.Z. B.Sc. 1924; M.Sc. 1926; Ph.D. 1927; D.Sc. 1931. Mycologist, Dept. of Agriculture, 1918; Officer in charge of Plant Protection Services, Plant Research Station, 1928; Delegate to First Imperial Mycological Conference, 1924; to Second, 1929; to Fifth Commonwealth Mycological Conf., 1948. F.R.S.N.Z. 1928 (Hutton Medal, 1934, Hector Medal, 1948); Fellow Aust. and N.Z. Assoc. for the Advancement of Science, 1937. Served European War with N.Z. Infantry Regt., 1914-16; Gallipoli, 1915 (wounded). Coronation Medal, 1937. *Publications:* Fungous Diseases of Fruit-trees in N.Z., 1925; The Rust Fungi of N.Z., 1931; Plant Protection by the Aid of Therapeutants, 1935; The Flying Life of Squadron Leader McGregor, 1936; The Gasteromycetes of Australia and New Zealand, 1944. *Address:* c/o Dept. of Scientific and Industrial Research (Plant Diseases Div.), Auckland, N.Z. *Club:* Northern (Auckland, N.Z.). [*Died* 12 *July* 1962.

CUNNINGHAM, Lt.-Col. John, C.I.E. 1928; F.R.S.E.; I.M.S., retired; *b.* Edinburgh; *s.* of late Prof. D. J. Cunningham, LL.D., D.C.L., F.R.S.; *m.* Bertha Emily Chapman; one *s.* one *d.* *Educ.:* Loretto Sch.; Epsom Coll.; Trinity Coll., Dublin. Entered I.M.S. 1905; Medical Research Dept. of Govt. of India, 1910; Director of the Central Research Institute, Kasauli; Director, King Institute of Preventive Medicine, Madras; Director, Pasteur Institute of India, Kasauli; served Indian North-West Frontier, 1915-16; Medical Superintendent, Astley Ainslie Hospital, Edinburgh, 1929-48. Chairman Board of Management, Astley Ainslie Hosp. and Edenhall and Assoc. Hosps., 1951-59. *Publications:* contributions to scientific journals. *Recreations:* golf, photography. *Address:* 12 Dick Place, Edinburgh. *T.:* Newington 4174. [*Died* 6 *Aug.* 1968.

CUNNINGHAM, Adm. of the Fleet Sir John Henry Dacres, G.C.B., *cr.* 1946 (K.C.B., *cr.* 1941; C.B. 1937); M.V.O. 1924; M.I.E.E. (Hon.); *b.* 1885; *m.* 1910, Dorothy M. (*d.* 1959), *d.* of late G. K. Hannay, Ulverston, Lancs.; one *s.* (and one *s.* killed, 1941, in S/M P33). *Educ.:* Stubbington House; H.M.S. Britannia. Commanded H.M.S. Adventure, 1928-29; Director of Plans Division, Admiralty, 1930-32; commanded H.M.S. Resolution, 1933; A.D.C. to the King, 1935; a Lord Commissioner of the Admiralty, 1936-1938, and Assistant Chief of Naval Staff, 1936-37; Assistant Chief of Naval Staff (Air), 1937-38; and Chief of Naval Air Services, 1938; Vice-Admiral Commanding First Cruiser Squadron, 1938-41 (despatches); a Lord Commissioner of the Admiralty and Chief of Supplies and Transport, 1941-43; C.-in-C., Levant, 1943; C.-in-C. Mediterranean and Allied Naval Commander Mediterranean, 1943-46; First Sea Lord and Chief of Naval Staff, 1946-48; Admiral of the Flee, 1948. Kt. G.C. of Ordeir of St. Olaf (Norway) 1947; Grand Cross (with Swords), Order of George and War Crows 1st Class of Greece 1945; Legion of Merst degree of Chief Com mander (U.S.A.), 1945; Légion d'Honneu Grand Officier and Croix de Guerre, ave Palme (France), 1945: also U.S.A. Campaign Ribbon with Africa Star, 1943; Queen's Medal, S. African War, War Medals, European War, 1914-18; Jubilee (1935) and Coronation (1937 and 1953) Medals; War of 1939-45. *Address:* 52 Westminster Gardens, S.W.1. *T.:* Victoria 9777. *Clubs:* United Service, Naval and Military. [*Died* 13 *Dec.* 1962.

CUNNINGTON, Cecil Willett, M.B., B.C.; retd. Med. practitioner; *b.* 1878; *m.* 1918, Phillis E. Webb; one *d.* *Educ.:* Clifton College; Cambridge; St. Bart's. Served

European War, Capt. R.A.M.C. *Publications:* Feminine Attitudes in the 19th Century, 1935; Englishwomen's Clothing in the 19th Century, 1937; Feminine Figleaves, 1938; Why Women Wear Clothes, 1941; The Perfect Lady, 1948; The Art of English Costume, 1948; (with Mrs. Cunnington) The History of English Underclothes, 1951; English Women's Clothing in the Present Century, 1952; (with Mrs. Cunnington), Handbook of English Mediaeval Costume, 1952; (with Mrs. Cunnington) Handbook of English Costume in 16th Century, 1953; (with Mrs. Cunnington) Handbook of English Costume in 17th Century, 1954; (with Mrs. Cunnington) Handbook of English Costume in 18th Century, 1956; (with Mrs. Cunnington) Handbook of English Costume in 19th Century, 1959; (with Mrs. Cunnington) Dictionary of English Costume 900 A.D.–1900 A.D.; (with Mrs Cunnington) Pictorial History of English Costume, 1960. *Recreation:* the study and collection of English Costume. *Address:* Hillworth, Mersea Avenue, West Mersea, Essex. *T.:* West Mersea 205. [*Died* 21 *Jan.* 1961.

CURCI, Amelita; *see* Galli-Curci.

CURGENVEN, Sir Arthur (Joseph), Kt., *cr.* 1937; J.P., Berkshire; *b.* 24 July 1876; *s.* of J. Brendon Curgenven, M.R.C.S.; *m.* 1903, Florence (*d.* 1948), *d.* of Rev. E. R. Parr; two *s.* *Educ.:* St. Paul's School; New College, Oxford. B.Sc. (Lond.); entered I.C.S. 1898; District Magistrate and Commissioner, Coorg, 1904-11; Deputy Secretary to Government, 1912-14; District Judge, 1915-26; Puisne Judge, High Court of Judicature, Madras; retired, 1936. Trustee, Oxford Preservation Trust, 1945-49. *Address:* Tretawn, Boar's Hill, Oxford. *T.:* Oxford 35256. [*Died* 20 *Nov.* 1965.

CURLE, Richard Henry Parnell; *b.* Melrose, Roxburghshire, 11 March 1883. *Educ.:* Wellington College. Travelled extensively in South America, The West Indies, The United States, Africa (North and South), Europe, The Near East, The Far East, etc. *Publications:* Wanderings; Into the East; Caravansary and Conversation; Oriental Trail; The Atmosphere of Places; Shadows out of the Crowd: Life is a Dream; The Echo of Voices; The One and the Other; Corruption; Who goes Home?; Aspects of George Meredith; Joseph Conrad: a Study; The Last Twelve Years of Joseph Conrad; Joseph Conrad and his Characters; Characters of Dostoevsky: Studies from four novels; Women: an Analytical Study; Reflections on Woman; James Stevens Cox: A Study in Achievement; The Ray Society: A Bibliographical History; Collecting American First Editions; Stamp Collecting: A New Handbook. Edited, Conrad's Last Essays; Conrad to a Friend; Robert Browning and Julia Wedgwood; W. H. Hudson's Letters to R. B. Cunninghame Graham; many introductions to booklets on Thomas Hardy. *Recreations:* travelling, natural history, book collecting. *Address:* West Coker, nr. Yeovil, Somerset. [*Died* 1 *Feb.* 1968.

CURREY, Brig. Henry Percivall C.B.E. 1943; *b.* 30 Jan. 1886; *yr. s.* of Lt.-Col. C. H. Currey, late 4th Dragoon Gds.; *m.* 1916, Hon. Elsie Mabel (*d.* 1965), *er. d.* of 1st Baron Greenway; one *s.* *Educ.:* Bradfield; R.M.C., Sandhurst (Sword of Honour). Cokes Rifles, Frontier Force, 1906-16; Royal Ulster Rifles, 1916-33; p.s.c. 1922-1923; commanded 2nd Bn. Royal Ulster Rifles, 1929-33; Col. 1933; Instructor Senior Officers' School, 1933-36; Brig., Gibraltar, 1936-39; served N.W. Frontier of India, 1908, Mohmand Expedition; action at Kargha (Medal and Clasp); European War, 1914-18; Tochi Valley and Derajat (Bt. Major); War of 1939-45: Norway, 1940: District Comd. South Eastern Comd., 1941-44 (despatches, C.B.E., 1939-45 Star, Defence Medal, Gen. Service Medal); retired, Dec. 1944. *Address:* 30 Modena Road, Hove, Sussex. *T.:* Brighton 36409. [*Died* 29 *Jan.* 1969.

CURRIE, Agnes Jean, C.B.E. 1945; Superintendent W.R.N.S. (retd.); *b.* 30 May 1899; *d.* of late John Currie, 31 Westbourne Gardens, Glasgow, W. *Educ.:* Laurel Bank School, Glasgow; The Mount School, York; also Switzerland. Joined W.R.N.S. 1939. *Address:* 62 Crag Path, Aldeburgh, Suffolk. *T.:* Aldeburgh 2435. [*Died* 17 *Oct.* 1968.

CURRIE, Brig. Douglas Hendrie, C.I.E. 1947; C.B.E. 1942; M.C. 1917; D.C.M. 1917; Meritorious Service Medal, 1917; *b.* 29 May 1892; *s* of William Whitmore Currie, Dover; *m.* 1921, Maud Vernon, K.-I-H. medal (silver), *y. d.* of Col. George Wemyss Anson, I.A.; no *c.* Served European War, 1914-18, in Egypt, Gallipoli, Salonica, Palestine, France, and Belgium, with City of London Yeomanry; joined 18th, afterwards 19th, Lancers (I.A.), 1919; N.W. Frontier and Afghanistan, 1919 and 1936; G.H.Q. India, 1939; Director of Recruiting, G.H.Q., India (Brig.), 1941-44; Military Secretary to Viceroy and Governor-General of India, 1944-48; retired, 1949. Sector Commander, Home Guard, 1952. *Recreations:* polo, tennis, golf, shooting. *Address:* Longwood Barn, Carters Hill, near Sevenoaks, Kent. *T.:* Sevenoaks 61474. *Club:* Wildernesse Country (Seal). [*Died* 25 *Aug.* 1966.

CURRIE, Sir William Crawford, G.B.E. 1947; Kt. 1925; Director, P. & O. Steam Navigation Co. and Director, P. & O. and British India Steam Navigation Companies; Chm., Marine & General Mutual Life Assurance Society; a Dep. Chm. Williams Deacon's Bank; Director: Wm. Cory & Son Ltd.; Suez Finance Co., Marine Insurance Co.; Extraordinary Director, Royal Bank of Scotland; *b.* 4 May 1884; *s.* of late William Currie; *m.* 1914, Ruth Forrest, *d.* of Mr. Dods, Edinburgh; one *s.* (and one *s.* killed in action, 1944). *Educ.:* Glasgow Academy; Fettes Coll., Edinburgh; Cambridge Univ. (B.A.), C.A. (Scotland). Sheriff of Calcutta, 1921-22; President, Bengal Chamber of Commerce, 1924-25; President, Associated Chambers of India, Burma, and Ceylon, 1924-1925; Member Bengal Legislative Council, 1921, 1922, 1924, 1925; Member, Council of State, Government of India, 1925; President, Chamber of Shipping of the United Kingdom, 1929-30; Member, Imperial Shipping Committee, 1927-31; Chairman British Liner Cttee., 1946-48; Director, Liner Division, Ministry of War Transport, 1942-1945; Member Advisory Council, Ministry of War Transport, 1939-45; Member Commonwealth Shipping Cttee.; Trustee National Maritime Museum; Chm. of Hon. Cttee. of Management, Training Ship Worcester, Pres. Seafarers Education Service; High Sheriff of Buckinghamshire, 1946-47; Prime Warden, Shipwright's Co., 1949-50; Hon. Mem. Hon. Co. of Master Mariners; Hon. Capt. R.N.R. Pres., Institute of Marine Engineers, 1945; Member, Executive Committee of British Red Cross Soc. and Order of St. John, 1942-47; Member Prisoners of War Committee of Red Cross, 1943-47. Comdr. Legion of Honour, France, 1953. *Recreations:* riding and shooting. *Address:* Dinton Hall, Aylesbury, Buckinghamshire. *Clubs:* Athenæum, Carlton, Oriental; Bengal (Calcutta). [*Died* 3 *July* 1961.

CURSETJEE, Maj.-Gen. Sir Heerajee Jehangir Manockjee, K.C.I.E., *cr.* 1946; C.S.I. 1943; D.S.O.; *b.* 14 Aug. 1885; *s.* of Jehangir Manockjee Cursetjee, Bombay; unmarried *Educ.:* Gonville and Caius College, Cambridge; London Hospital,

Lieut. I.M.S., 1912; Capt. 1915; Major, 1924; Bt. Lt.-Col. 1931; Col. 1938; Major-Gen., 1941; retired, 1946. K.H.S. 1941. Served European War, 1914-18, Egypt, Gallipoli, Iraq (D.S.O., Servian Order of White Eagle 5th Class, severely wounded, despatches twice); Iraq and Kurdistan, 1919-21; North West Frontier, India, 1922-24; War of 1939-45. *Recreations:* hunting, polo. *Address:* c/o Lloyd's Bank, 6 Pall Mall, S.W.1. *Club:* Hurlingham. [*Died* 26 *July* 1964.

CURTEIS, Admiral Sir Alban Thomas Buckley, K.C.B., *cr.* 1942 (C.B. 1940); *b.* 13 Jan. 1887; 2nd *s.* of late Rev. Thomas Samuel Curteis, Sevenoaks; *m.* 1st, 1915, Essex Helen (*d.* 1940), *d.* of late Cyrus Morrall, Plas Yolyn, Ellesmere, Shropshire; one *s.* one *d.*; 2nd, 1941, Freda, *d.* of late Cyrus Morrall. Rear-Adm. 1938; Vice-Adm. 1941; Commodore R.N. Barracks, Devonport, 1938-40; Rear-Adm. Comdg. 2nd Cruiser Squadron, 1940-41; Vice-Adm. Comdg. 2nd Battle Squadron and 2nd in Command Home Fleet, 1941-42; Senior British Naval Officer, Western Atlantic, 1942-44. Retired List, Dec. 1944; Admiral (ret.), 1945. Served European War, 1914-18; War of 1939-45. *Address:* Plas Yolyn, Ellesmere, Shropshire. [*Died* 27 *Nov.* 1961.

CURTHOYS, Alfred; journalist; proprietor Kingsway Editorial Services; *b.* Bristol. Trained in journalism on Bristol papers. Daily Sketch, 1919 (Editor, 1928-1936); Founder and Editor, The Pilot (Sea), since 1921; Editor, London John, 1949-68. F.J.I. *Address:* 25 Grand Drive S.W.20. *T.:* Liberty 7376. [*Died* 26 *Feb.* 1969.

CURTICE, Harlow H.; Director and member of Financial Policy Committee of General Motors Corporation; Chairman of the Board, Genesee Merchants Bank & Trust Co.; Director of National Bank of Detroit; *b.* Eaton Rapids, Mich., 15 Aug. 1893; *s.* of Marion Joel and Mary Ellen Eckhart Curtice; *m.* 1927, Dorothy Biggs, Sherman, Texas; three *d.* *Educ.:* Eaton Rapids; Ferris Institute, Big Rapids, Mich. Started as bookkeeper at AC Spark Plug, Flint, Mich., 1914; comptroller at AC, 1915; General Manager, 1929; General Manager of Buick, 1933; General Motors Corp.: exec. Vice-Pres., 1948, acting Pres., 1952; President, 1953-58. Graduate Mem. Business Council; Mem. Bd. of Trustees of Connecticut Coll.; Trustee, Clara Elizabeth Maternal Health Fund. Holds honorary doctorates in engineering, law, and commercial science. Commander of Crown, Belgium, 1954; Legion of Honour, France, 1954; Grand Service Cross, Federal Republic of Germany, 1956; Commander of Order of National Economy, France, 1957. *Address:* 1004 Genesee Merchants Bank & Trust Co., Flint, Michigan. *T.:* Cedar 8-3611. *Clubs:* Recess, Detroit, Detroit Athletic, University of Michigan (Detroit); Alfalfa (Washington, D.C.), Eldorado C. C. (Palm Desert, Calif.). Biltmore Forest C. C. (N. Carolina); Flint City, Flint Golf (Flint, Mich.). [*Died* 3 *Nov.* 1962.

CURTIS, Amy, C.B.E. 1946 (M.B.E. 1919); *b.* 4 Feb. 1894; *d.* of George Frederick Wilkinson and Mary Noble Hewson Curtis. *Educ.:* at home, and Belgrave School, Rathmines, Dublin. V.A.D. Clerk, 1915-17, 3rd S.G. Hospital, Oxford; Assistant, later Senior Unit Administrator, Q.M.A.A.C., 1917-20. Partner in Bartels and Curtis, growers, Guernsey, C.I., 1920-30; Sec. and Agent, Chelmsford Div. Unionist Assoc., 1930-39; Superintendent, W.R.N.S., Portsmouth Command, 1939-44; Resettlement Advice Service, Ministry of Labour and National Service, 1945-48; Chief Administrative Officer, Women's Land Army, 1948-50. *Recreation:* gardening. *Address:* Ram Park Cottage, Kilpedder, Co. Wicklow, Ireland. [*Died* 29 *July* 1970.

CURTIS, Squadron Leader Sir Arthur Randolph Wormeley, K.C.V.O. *cr.* 1935 (C.V.O. 1927); C.M.G. 1925; M.C.; J.P.; Leicestershire County Commissioner for Boy Scouts, 1935-57; *b.* Fakenham, Norfolk, 1889; *s.* of late O. S. and Mrs. Curtis. *Educ.:* Eton; Trinity Coll., Camb. (B.A.). Served in 11th Hussars S.R. and was also attached to R.F.C. and Staff during European War, 1914-18; Private Secretary to Admiral of the Fleet Earl Jellicoe whilst Governor-General of New Zealand, 1920-24; Military Secretary to Lord Stonehaven, Governor-General of Australia, 1925-28; Private Secretary to Duke of Gloucester on his World Tour, 1934-1935; served War of 1939-45, in R.A.F.V.R. J.P. and D.L. Leics., 1937; Vice-Lieutenant, Leics., 1961-64. *Address:* The Priory, Knipton, Grantham, Lincs. *T.:* Knipton 238. *Clubs:* Cavalry, M.C.C. [*Died* 1 *April* 1966.

CURTIS, Vice-Adm. Berwick, C.B. 1919; C.M.G. 1920; D.S.O. 1917; Royal Navy, retired; *b.* 9 Oct. 1876; *s.* of late Henry Downing Curtis and Mrs. Curtis, of 63 Eccleston Square, London, and Ferryside, Hamble, S. Hants; *m.* 1st, Mildred Henrietta Constable Curtis (*d.* 1927), *d.* of Frank J. C. Curtis, of Ganarew, Monmouth; one *d.* (and one *d.* decd.); 2nd 1929, Violet Penelope Munro, *widow* of Lt.-Commander George F. Cholmley, R.N. *Educ.:* H.M.S. Britannia. Lieutenant, 1899; Commander, 1911; Captain 1916; Rear-Admiral, 1928; Vice-Adm. 1932; served European War, 1914-18 (despatches, C.B., D.S.O. and bar, C.M.G., Russian Order of St. Stanislas); Baltic, 1919; Rear-Adm. in Charge and Admiral Superintendent, Gibraltar Dockyard, 1929-31; retd. list, 1932. Served War of 1939-45; Commodore of Convoys. *Recreations:* usual. *Address:* Olinda, 4 Western Parade, Emsworth, Hampshire. [*Died* 9 *May* 1965.

CURTIS, Major-General Henry Osborne, C.B. 1940; D.S.O. 1919; M.C. 1917; U.S. D.S.M. 1942; *b.* 18 Nov. 1888; *s.* of Osborne Sargent Curtis and Frances Henrietta Gandy; *m* 1918, Jean Mackenzie, *d.* of late John L. Low, Butterstone, Perthshire; two *s.* (and two *s.* killed in action). *Educ.:* Eton; R.M.C. Sandhurst. Joined 2nd. Bn. K.R.R.C., 1908; served European War 4th Bn. K.R.R.C., France and Salonika; on staff 81st Highland and 30th Irish Brigades and G.S.O. 2, 52nd Lowland Division in Salonika, Palestine, and France (wounded three times, D.S.O., M.C., Brevet Majority, despatches thrice); 4th Bn. K.R.R.C., 1918; Staff College, Quetta, 1920; Staff in Egypt, 1922-26; G.S.O. 2 Staff College, Camberley, 1927-30; 2nd in command 2nd K.R.R.C., 1930; commanded 2nd. Bn. King's Royal Rifle Corps, 1931-34, Officer Commanding, British Troops in Palestine, 1934-36; General Staff Officer, First Grade, Staff College, Camberley, 1936-38; Commander, 3rd Infantry Brigade, 1938-39; G.O.C. 46 Div. 1940 (Dunkirk) and 49 Div. 1940-43 and Iceland, 1940-42; G.O.C. Districts, Salisbury Plain, 1943, Hants and Dorset, 1944, Hants and Aldershot, 1945; retired pay, 1946. Col. Comdt. 1st K.R.R.C., 1946-54; O.C. East Dorset Sector H.G. D.L. Dorset, 1953; Pres. Dorset British Legion, 1953. *Recreations:* shooting, yachting. *Address:* Trokes Coppice, Lychett Minster, Poole, Dorset. *Club:* Naval and Military. [*Died* 28 *Jan.* 1964.

CURTIS, Rt. Rev. John, D.D.; *b.* Dublin, 15 March 1880; *s.* of Thomas Hewson and Margaret Curtis; *m.* 1914, Eda S. Bryan-Brown, M.B., B.S. (Lond.); one *s.* one *d.* (and one *s.* killed on active service, R.A.F., 1943). *Educ.:* Rathmines School; Trinity College, Dublin (B.A. 1902, B.D. 1905, D.D. 1928). Deacon, 1903; priest, 1904; Curate, Christ Church, Leeson Park, Dublin, 1903-6; Member of Dublin University Mission to Fukien, 1909-28 (Funing, Fukien); temporary Chaplain to Forces, 1916-18; Bishop of

Chekiang, 1929-50; Vicar of Wilden, 1950-1957; First Diocesan Bishop consecrated in China under the jurisdiction of the Chung Hwa Sheng Kung Hwei, the branch of the Anglican Communion in China. *Address:* Glendhu, 43 Whitnash Road, Leamington Spa, Warwicks. [*Died* 11 *July* 1962.

CURTIS, Rev. Principal William Alexander, D.Litt., D.D., LL.D., D.Théol.; Professor of Biblical Criticism, Edinburgh University, 1915-46; Dean of Faculty of Divinity, 1928-46; Principal, New College, Edinburgh, 1935-46; retired 1946; *b.* Thurso, Caithness, 17 March 1876; *e. s.* of late John G. Curtis, I.R., Edinburgh; *m.* 1905, Florence, 3rd *d.* of late Robert C. Malseed, Londonderry; two *s.* *Educ.:* George Watson's College and the University, Edinburgh. M.A., with 1st Class Honours in Classics, 1897; travelled in Greece and Italy as Heriot Research Fellow, 1897-98; Member of British School of Archæology at Athens; student of Divinity at Edin. Univ., 1898-1901; Jeffrey Scholarships in Biblical Criticism and in Divinity; B.D., Edin., 1901; studied at Universities of Heidelberg, Leipzig, and Oxford as Pitt Travelling Scholar in Theology, 1901-3; Hon. D.D. (Edin.), 1914; Prof. of Systematic Theology in the University of Aberdeen, 1903-15; Croall Lecturer, 1921; Member of University Court, 1930-34; President of General Presbyterian Alliance, 1933-37; Hon. D. en Théol (Paris, Faculté Protestante), 1933; Hon. D.Theol. (Univ. of Debreczen), 1939; Hon. LL.D., Edin. 1946; Cunningham Lecturer, 1951. *Publications:* A History of Creeds and Confessions of Faith in Christendom and Beyond, 1911; Jesus Christ the Teacher, 1943. *Address:* Waverley Lodge, Melrose, Roxburghshire. *T.:* Melrose 281.
[*Died* 3 *Nov.* 1961.

CURTIS, William Edward, C.B.E. 1967; F.R.S. 1934; D.Sc. (Lond.); A.R.C.S., D.I.C., F.Inst.P.; Professor Emeritus, University of Durham, 1955; *b.* 23 Oct. 1889; *o.s.* of late Charles Curtis, Clacton, Essex; *m.* 1918, Adeline Mary Grace, J.P., 1947, *o. d.* of late Charles Mitchell; one *s.* one *d.* *Educ.:* Owens Sch., London; Imp. Coll. of Science. Demonstrator in Astrophysics, Royal College of Science, 1911-14; served with R.N.D., 1914-1916; Signal Service and Wireless Training Centre, 1916-19; Lecturer in Physics, University of Sheffield, 1919; Reader in Physics, King's Coll., London, 1922; Prof. of Physics, King's Coll., Newcastle upon Tyne, 1926-55. Chm. Jt. Recruiting Bd., Durham Univ., 1939-40; Scientific Adviser, Min. of Home Security, 1940-43. Superintendent of Applied Explosives, Armament Research Department, Min. of Supply, 1943-45; Pres. of Inst. of Physics, 1950-52. Member, Adv. Coun., R.M.C.S., 1952-56, Chm. 1956-58. Senior Scientific Adviser (Northern Region), Civil Defence, 1952-. *Publications:* Papers in Proceedings of the Royal Society, Philosophical Magazine, etc., mainly on Spectroscopy. *Recreation:* music. *Address:* 34 Burdon Terrace, Newcastle upon Tyne 2. *T.:* 81-1 860 [*Died* 6 *May* 1969.

CUSACK, John Winder, C.M.G. 1957; O.B.E. 1947; Administrator, Central Council for the Disabled, and National Secretary, International Society for Rehabilitation of the Disabled, since 1960; *b.* Dublin, 21 November 1907; *e. s.* of late His Honour Judge Cusack, K.C., and late Dora, *d.* of R. Winder; *m.* 1946, Susan Pope; three *s.* one *d.* *Educ.:* Trinity College, Dublin (B.A. hons.); Corpus Christi College, Cambridge (M.A.). Cadet, Colonial Administrative Service, Kenya, 1930; District Officer, 1932; District Commissioner, 1937, Army service with East African Forces in Kenya, Ethiopia and Italian Somaliland, 1940-48; Colonel, 1945. Chief Secretary of Italian Somaliland, 1945, Actg. Chief Administrator, Italian Somaliland, 1948; Sec. for Law and Order, Kenya, 1949; Actg. Provincial Comr., N. Province, Kenya. 1953; Minister for Internal Security and Defence, 1954-59, and Defence Sec., 1955-61. Kenya; M.L.C., Kenya, 1954-59. Chairman of the East Africa Land Forces Organization, 1957-1958; despatches, 1957. Retired from Colonial Service, 1961. *Recreations:* fishing, shooting, reading. *Address:* 8 Norman Road, Hove, Sussex. *T.:* Brighton 47518. *Clubs:* East India and Sports; University (Dublin); Royal Wajir Yacht (Kenya); Beavers (Boston, U.S.A.).
[*Died* 31 *Aug.* 1968.

CUSACK-SMITH, Sir (William Robert) Dermot (Joshua), 6th Bt., *cr.* 1799; M.F.H.; late Capt. 57th (H.C.), Brig., R.A. (T.A.); *b.* 6 Dec. 1907; *s.* of 5th Bt. and Jane (*d.* 1942), *o. d.* of J. M. Jones, 56 Holland Park; *S.* father, 1929; *m.* 1932, Dorothy (who obtained a divorce, 1945), 3rd *d.* of Rev. G. P. K. Winlaw, The Rectory, Houghton Conquest, nr. Bedford; one *d.*; *m.* 1946, A. M. O'Rorke, M.F.H.; one *d.* *Educ.:* Brighton College; Corpus Christi College, Cambridge. *Address:* Bermingham House, Tuam, Co. Galway.
[*Died* 10 *April* 1970 (*ext.*).

CUST, Col. Sir (Lionel George) Archer, Kt. 1959; C.B.E. 1954 (O.B.E. 1939); retired as Sec.-General, Royal Commonwealth Society, 1958; *b.* 6 June 1896; *s.* of Sir Lionel Cust, K.C.V.O., Litt.D., Surveyor of King's Pictures and Works of Art, and Hon. Sybil Lyttelton; *m.* 1925, Margaret Violet Louisa, *d.* of Lt.-Col. H. A. Clowes, Norbury Hall, Ashbourne; one *s.* two *d.* *Educ.:* Eton College. Served European War, 1915-19 in R.F.A. and on Staff (despatches), and later in Germany and Egypt; Palestine Civil Service, 1920-35; A.D.C. to the High Commissioner, 1921-23, and Private Secretary, 1928-31; Secretary of the Bertram-Luke (1921) and Bertram-Young (1925) Commissions on the Jerusalem Orthodox Patriarchate; Seconded as Private Secretary to Governor of Northern Rhodesia, 1932-34; served War of 1939-45 in Military Intelligence and Psychological Warfare (despatches). Officer of the Order of St. John of Jerusalem, 1922. *Address:* Uplands, Fordingbridge, Hants. *T.:* Fordingbridge 2263. *Club:* Travellers'. [*Died* 22 *May* 1962.

CUSTARD, Walter Henry Goss, M.A.; Mus. Doc. (Lambeth); Mus. Bac. Oxon., F.R.C.O., Hon. R.C.M.; formerly Organist and Master of the Music, Liverpool Cathedral, retired 1955; *b.* 7 February 1871; *s.* of Walter and Catherine Goss Custard; *m.* 1903, Millicent Mary Lindridge (*d.* 1961); one *s.* *Educ.:* Private. Organist Christ Church, Blacklands, Hastings, 1889; Holy Trinity Church, Hastings, 1891; St. John's, Lewisham, 1902; St. Saviour's, Ealing, W., 1904; Liverpool Cathedral, 1917; Hon. Organist, Royal Philharmonic Society, 1914-17; Grand Organist of England in the Grand Lodge of English Freemasons, 1928 and 1933; visited America to give Recitals and Lectures at Conference of American Association of Organists, 1928. *Publication:* Communion Service in D. *Address:* 6 Beechfield Road, Trentham, Stoke-on-Trent, Staffs.
[*Died* 6 *July* 1964.

CUTLACK, Colonel William Philip, C.B. 1943; M.A., T.D., D.L., Managing Director, East Anglian Breweries, Forehill Brewery, Ely; *b.* 5 Aug. 1881; *s.* of William Cutlack, of Littleport, and Emily Ann Wilkin; *m.* 1st, 1911, Dora (*d.* 1925), *d.* of Francis J. Dormer; one *d.*; 2nd, 1936, Mrs. Eileen Elsie Hills, *y. d.* of Major J. C. Lewis, Newmarket. *Educ.:* Felsted; Pembroke College, Cambridge. Cambs. Regt.; Chm. Isle of Ely Conservative Assoc.; High Sheriff Cambridgeshire and Huntingdonshire, 1934-35. *Recreations* shooting and golf. *Address:* The Manor, Barton Mills, Bury St. Edmunds. *T.:* Mildenhall 3133. *Club:* Bath. [*Died* 8 May 1965.

CYNAN, *see* Evans-Jones, Sir Albert.

CZACZKES, (Shmuel) Yosef Halevi; *see* Agnon, S. Y. H.

D

d'ABO, Gerard Louis; Director Hambros Bank Ltd.; Director Covent Garden Properties Co. Ltd. and Second Covent Garden Property Co. Ltd.; *b.* 10 October 1884; *e. s.* of Henry William Leonard d'Abo and Emily Francis Burton; *m.* 1st, 1909, Muriel Molesworth Kindersley; two *s.*; 2nd, 1925, Mrs. Violet de Winton Haggie (*née* Morrison). *Educ,:* Abroad. *Recreations:* shooting, golf. *Address:* Coval Court, Sunningdale, Berks. *T.:* Ascot 286; Flat 43, 2 Mansfield Street W.1. *Club:* White's. [*Died* 18 *Jan.* 1962.

D'COSTA, Sir Alfred (Horace), Kt. 1937; Member of Privy Council of Jamaica, 1934-Dec. 1959; *b.* 23 Jan. 1873; *s.* of Daniel Rodriques D'Costa, Jamaica, and Cordelia Margaret Lindo; *m.* 1899, Ethel de Mercado (*d.* 1944), Kingston, Jamaica; one *s.* one *d.* (and one *d.* decd.). *Educ.:* Collegiate and York Castle School, Jamaica. Solicitor of Supreme Court of Judicature of Jamaica, 1894; Registrar of the Supreme Court of Jamaica, 1907-09; Chairman: John Crook Ltd., and Subsidiary Cos.; Lascelles, de Mercado and Co. Ltd., and Subsidiary Cos. Order of Orange Nassau. *Address:* Fort Charles, Constant Spring, Jamaica. *Club:* Jamaica (Kingston). [*Died* 12 *Aug.* 1967.

DACRE, Air Commodore George Bentley, C.B.E. 1941; D.S.O. 1915; R.A.F., retd.; *b.* 22 Mar. 1891; 2nd *s.* of late John Dacre; *m.* 1921, Elizabeth Frances, *d.* of late W. P. Fraser, Johannesburg; (one *s.* killed in action, 1943). *Educ.:* Clifton College. Pilot Aviator's Certificate, No. 162, 1911; Flight Sub-Lieutenant Royal Naval Air Service Aug. 1914; served European War (Gallipoli), 1915 (D.S.O.); 1916, Egypt, prisoner of war in Turkey, Aug. 1916-Nov. 1918; Squadron Leader, 1920; Wing Commander, 1929; Chief of British Air Mission to Greece, 1931-1932; Imperial Defence College, 1933; Group Capt. 1935; Air Attaché, Rome, 1935-37; Commanded No. 25 Group, 1938; Air Commodore, 1938; Advanced Air Striking Force, France, 1939-40; Commanded No. 24 Group, 1940; Commanded 72 Group, 1942; Central Mediterranean Force, 1943-44; Commandant of St. Dunstan's, 1944-48. Vice-Chm. Sussex T. and A.F.A., 1948-55; Pres. Sussex County British Legion, 1948-55; Hon. Air Commodore No. 3618 F.C.U. (Co. of Sussex), R. Aux.A.F., 1958-61. D.L. Sussex, 1951; High Sheriff of Sussex, 1958-1959. Companion of Greek Order of Phœnix. *Address:* The Downings, Bazehill Road, Rottingdean, Sussex. *T.:* Rottingdean 2444. *Club:* R.A.F. [*Died* 4 *Jan.* 1962.

DAGLISH, Eric Fitch, Ph.D., F.Z.S., F.R.M.S., F.R.S.A., A.R.E.; late Capt. R.F.A.; Commissioned R.A.F. 1941; Squadron Leader; Author and Engraver; *b.* London, 29 Aug. 1892; *s.* of James Daglish and Kate Fitch; *m.* 1918, Alice Leslie Mary Archer; two *s.* (twins) one *d.*; *m.* 1933, Esther Lena Rutland; one *s.* one *d.* *Educ.:* Hertford County College; London and Bonn. British Army, 1916-22. Middlesex Imperial Yeomanry and R.F.A.; served in Ireland, Flanders and France; Officer in charge education, Woolwich Garrison, 1918-22; Scientific Correspondent Evening Standard, 1923-25; first book published 1923; first wood engraving, 1924; Member of Society of Wood Engravers, 1924; exhibitions Redfern Gallery, 1925, 1927; wood engravings in permanent collections of British Museum, Victoria and Albert Museum, Art Galleries of Manchester, Liverpool, Antwerp, Metropolitan Museum, New York, Boston, Philadelphia, etc. *Publications:* Woodcuts of British Birds; Our Butterflies and Moths; Our Wild Flowers; Our Birds' Nests and Eggs; Marvels of Plant Life; Book of Garden Animals; Animals in Black and White (6 vols.); Life Story of Birds; Life Story of Beasts; How to see Birds; How to see Plants; A Nature Calendar; How to See Flowers; How to See Beasts; The Dog Owner's Guide; The Book of the Dachshund; Botanical Sections of New Book of Gardening (3 vols.); Name this Bird, 1934; Name this Insect, 1952; The Junior Bird-Watcher, 1936; Birds of the British Isles, 1948; The Dog Breeders Manual, 1951; Enjoying the Country, 1952; The Seaside Nature Book, 1954; The Pet-keeper's Manual, 1958; Dog Breeding, 1962; Translator of and Contributor to: Dogs of the World (Schneider-Leyer), 1964; (part author) The Gardener's Companion; Illustrator of Grey's Fly Fishing; Fabre's Animal Life in Field and Garden; Walton's Complete Angler, and Thoreau's Walden, White's Selborne, Dewar's Game Birds, Nicholson's Birds in England; Hudson's Far Away and Long Ago; Thomas' South Country; Street's Wheat and Chaff, 1951; Editor and Illustrator of the Open Air Library. *Recreations:* Pedigree Animal and Plant Breeding. *Address:* The Old Farmhouse, Darvills Hill, Speen, Aylesbury. *T.:* Hampden Row 219. [*Died* 5 *April* 1966.

DAIN, Sir (Harry) Guy, Kt. 1961; General Medical Practice since 1897; Mem. Council, B.M.A., 1921-60 (Chm., 1942-48); Mem. G.M.C., 1934-61; *b.* 5 Nov. 1870; *s.* of Major and Diana Dain, Four Oaks, Warwicks.; *m.* 1st, 1898, Flora Elizabeth Lewis (*d.* 1934); one *s.* two *d.* (and one *s.* killed in War, 1945); 2nd, 1939, Alice Muriel Hague. *Educ.:* King Edward's School, Five Ways, Birmingham; Birmingham Medical School. M.R.C.S., L.R.C.P., 1893; M.B. Lond., 1894; F.R.C.S. Eng. 1945. Hon. LL.D. Aberdeen, 1939; Hon. M.D. Birmingham, 1944. *Address:* Bournbrook House, Birmingham 29. *T.:* Selly Oak 1772; Highmead, Aberdovey, Merionethshire. *T.:* Aberdovey 326. [*Died* 26 *Feb.* 1966.

DALADIER, Edouard, (Chevalier) Légion d'Honneur, and Croix de Guerre, France; *b.* Carpentras, Vaucluse, 18 Juin 1884; *m.*; two *s.* *Educ.:* Lycée de Lyon (Prof. Edouard Herriot). Formerly: Prof. agrégé d'Histoire et de Géographie (reçu 1er au concours d'agrégation); Maire de Carpentras, Vaucluse, 1912-58; Member of the National Constituent Assembly; Député de Vaucluse, 1919; Ministre des Colonies, 1924; puis Ministre de la Guerre, de l'Instruction Publique, des Travaux Publics: Président du Conseil, Ministre de la Guerre, 1933; Président du Conseil, Ministre des Affaires Etrangères, 1934; Vice-Président du Conseil, Ministre de la Défense Nationale, 1936, Président du Conseil, 1938-40; Ministre des Affaires Etrangères, 1939-40; Ministre de la Défense Nationale et de la Guerre, 1938-40. Grand Cross, Order of St. Michael and St. George (G.C.M.G.) Gt. Britain, 1938. *Publication:* The Defence of France, 1939. *Address:* 9 Place de la Porte-de-Passy, Paris, 16e. [*Died* 10 *Oct.* 1970.

D'ALBIAC, Air Marshal Sir John Henry, K.C.V.O. 1957; K.B.E. 1946; C.B. 1941; D.S.O. 1916; *b.* 28 Jan. 1894; *s.* of late Charles William D'Albiac and late Rhoda Mary Paris; *m.* 1933, Sibyl Mary Owen; one *s.* three *d.* *Educ.:* Seabrook Lodge, Hythe, Kent; Framlingham College.

Commissioned R.M.A., Dec. 1914; seconded R.N.A.S., Feb. 1915; France, 1915-17 (D.S.O.); commissioned in R.A.F., April 1918; entered R.A.F. Staff College, Andover, 1929; Staff College Course at Quetta, India, 1933-34; at Imperial Defence College, 1939; A.O.C., R.A.F. Palestine, 1939; A.O.C. British Forces in Greece, 1940; A.O.C., R.A.F. Iraq, 1941; A.O.C., R.A.F., Ceylon, 1942; A.O.C. Tactical Air Force, 1943-44; Deputy Comdr., Mediterranean Allied Tactical Air Force, 1944; Director-General Personnel, Air Ministry, 1945-46; retired, 1946; Comdt. London Airport, 1947-57; Deputy Chairman of Air Transport Advisory Council, 1957-61. Comdr. Legion of Merit (U.S.A.); Grand Officer Order of Phoenix (Greece); Grand Officer, Order of Orange Nassau (Netherlands). *Rezreations:* golf, tennis, shooting. *Address:* Littlebrook, Burnham Avenue, Beaconsfield, Bucks. [*Died* 20 *Aug.* 1963.

d'ALBUQUERQUE, Nino Pedroso; retd. as Comr. of National Insurance (1948. 1966); *b.* 22 Jan. 1894; *s.* of late Prof. J. P. d'Albuquerque, M.A., F.I.C., F.C.S., and late Beatrice d'Albuquerque; *m.* 1915, Mary, *d.* of late James O'Moran and Mrs. O'Moran, Roscommon, Ireland; one *s.* one *d.* *Educ.:* Harrison College, Barbados; Felstead School; Clare College, Cambridge. B.A. (Cantab.) 1915; Barr., Inner Temple, 1917. Served European War 1914-19 (Inns of Court O.T.C., Westminster Dragoons, King's Shropshire Light Infantry). Past Pres., London Circle, Catenian Assoc. Dep. Umpire under Unemployment Insurance Acts, 1929-48; Dep. Umpire under National Service (Armed Forces) Act, 1940-49; Dep. Umpire under Reinstatement in Civil Employment Act, 1944-49. *Recreation:* riding. *Address:* 10 Edge Hill, Wimbledon, S.W.19. *T.:* Wimbledon 5673. *Clubs:* Oxford and Cambridge; Village (Wimbledon). [*Died* 4 *May* 1969.

DALBY, Maj.-Gen. Thomas Gerald, C.B. 1936; D.S.O. 1917; *b.* 1880; *s.* of late Sir William Bartlett Dalby; *m.* 1917, Lucy Marion (*d.* 1947), *widow* of Louis Carruthers Salkeld, of Holm Hill, Dalston, Cumberland; *m.* 1948, Clarice Violet (she *m.* formerly Brig. T. E. M. Battersby; marriage dissoved). *Educ.:* Eton; R.M.C., Sandhurst. Joined 60th Rifles, 1899; served S. African War, 1901-2 (severely wounded, Queen's medal with five clasps); Somaliland, 1904 (medal with clasp); European War, 1914-18 (twice severely wounded, despatches four times, D.S.O., Brevet Lieut.-Col., Chevalier Legion of Honour, Order of Aviz of Portugal); commanded 2nd Batt. King's Royal Rifle Corps, 1928-31; Commander 3rd Infantry Brigade, 1931-35; retired pay, 1937; Commander 18th Div., Aug.-Dec. 1939. D.L. County of London, 1945-51. *Address:* Crookety South Brent, S. Devon. *T.:* South Brent 2102. *Club:* Army and Navy. [*Died* 14 *March* 1963.

DALE, His Honour Sir Edgar (Thornley), Kt. 1956; retired as County Court Judge; a Divorce Commissioner; Chm. Disciplinary Committee of various Marketing. Boards; Chm. Bucks Q.S., 1959-61; *b.* 25 Mar. 1886; *m.* 1915, Elsie Douglas Bell; one *d.* *Educ.:* privately. Called to Bar, Middle Temple, 1909; practised South-Eastern Circuit and Common Law until apptd. to the Bench; Judge of Birmingham County Court, 1937-46; Lambeth, 1946-47, Bloomsbury, 1947-50, Westminster and Aylesbury, 1950-1959. J.P. Warwick, 1938, Buckingham, 1942; Chm. Departmental Cttee.on Industrial Diseases, 1947; Chm. of Cttee. appointed by Prime Minister, 1949, to advise Govt. as to improved co-relation between Nat. Health Service and various industrial and other health services; member of Standing Cttee. for framing County Court Rules, 1949-59. *Publications:* Editor of County Court Practice, and other legal publications. *Recreations:* music, book collecting and gardening. *Address:* Bakers Close, Long Crendon, Aylesbury, Bucks. *T.:* Long Crendon 264. [*Died* 15 *Dec.* 1966.

DALE, Sir Henry Hallett, O.M., 1944: G.B.E. 1943 (C.B.E. 1919); Kt. 1932; Grand Croix de l'ordre de la Couronne, Belgium, 1949; Pour le mérite, W. Germany, 1955. F.R.S. 1914; M.A.; M.D.; F.R.C.P.; Hon. M.D., Innsbruck, Louvain, Liége, Bruxelles, Utrecht, Paris, Ghent, Graz, Vienna; Hon. LL.D. Toronto, Kingston, Ontario, Edin., Belfast; Hon. D.Sc. Cambridge, Dublin, Durham, Manchester, Oxford, Sheffield, London, Princeton. U.S.A., Western Ontario, McGill (Montreal), Leeds; D.Litt. St. Andrews; Hon. F.R.C.S.; Hon. F.R.C.P. (Ed.); Hon. F.R.S. (Ed.); Hon. F.R.C.O.G.; Hon. Assoc. R.C.V.S.; Hon. Fellow of: Trinity Coll., Cambridge, 1939-; Chemical Soc., 1947; Univ. Coll., London, 1948; Association Orthopædic Surgeons; Hon. Member Royal Soc. of New Zealand 1952; *b.* London, 1875; *s.* of late C. J. Dale; *m.* 1904; two *d.* (one *s.* decd.). *Educ.:* Leys School, Cambridge; Trinity Coll., Cambridge (Scholar, Coutts-Trotter Student); St. Bartholomew's Hospital; George Henry Lewes Student; Sharpey Scholar, University College, London. Director Wellcome Physiological Research Laboratories, 1904-14; Chairman Wellcome Trust, 1936-60; Director of the National Institute for Medical Research, Hampstead, 1928-42; Director of Laboratories of Royal Institution and Fullerian Professor of Chemistry, 1942-30 Sept. 1946; Hon. or Foreign Member of: Roy. Danish Acad., Roy. Swedish Acad., Amer. Acad. Arts and Sci. Boston, U.S.A., Acad. Med. N.Y., Path. Soc. Philadelphia, Amer. Philosoph. Soc. Philadelphia, Coll. Phys. Philadelphia, New York Acad. of Sci., Acad. Med. Washington, Chem. Soc., Pharmaceut. Soc., Roy. Soc. Med. (Pres. 1948-1950), Deutsch. Acad. Naturf. Halle, Deutsch. Pharm. Gesell., Acad. Roy de Méd. Belge, Ind. Acad. Sci., Roy. Soc. Edin., Nat. Acad. Med. Madrid, Soc. de Biol. and Soc. de Thérap. Paris, Soc. Ital. di Biol. Sper., Ind. Assoc. for Cult. Sci. Acad. de Med. Paris, Swiss Acad. Med. Sci., Assn. Chem. and Pharm. Ecuador, Roy. Flemish Acad. Med., Belgium; Associate Member: Roy. Coll. Vet. Surg.; Acad. Roy. de Belgique; Nat. Acad. of Sci., U.S.A.; Nat. Inst. of Sci. India; Soc. de Farmac. y Terapeut. Argentina; Corr. Mem.: Med. Assoc. and Soc. Biol. Argentina, Gesell. d. Aertze and f. inn Med. Vienna. Akad. d. Wissenschaft, Vienna; Roy. Med. Soc. Budapest, R. Accad. Med. Rome, Acad. d. Med. Rumania, Institut Genevois, Geneva, Inst. of Biology. Roy. and Copley Medals, Roy. Society; shared Nobel Prize for Medicine, 1936; U.S.A. Medal of Freedom, with Silver Palm, 1947; Gold Medal of Honour of Canadian Pharmaceutical Manufacturers' Assoc., 1955; Gold Albert Medal, Roy. Soc. of Arts, 1956; Schmiedeberg-Plakette, German Pharmacological Soc., 1962. Mem. General Medical Council, 1927-37; President of Royal Society, 1940-45 (Sec. 1925-35); Member Medical Research Council, 1942-46; Member of Scientific Advisory Cttee. to War Cabinet, 1940-47 (Chm., 1942-47); Advisory Cttee. on Atomic Energy, 1945-57; Mem. Standing Commn. on Museums and Galls., 1946-60; Trustee of Brit. Museum, 1940-63; Pres. Brit. Assoc., 1947; Chm. Radioactive Substances Advisory Cttee., 1949-52; Pres. R.S.M., 1948-1950; Pres. British Council, 1950-55. Hon. Freeman and past Master of Salters' Company; Hon. Freeman Soc. of Apothecaries; Freeman of City of Dundee, 1947. *Publications:* Adventures in Physiology, 1953; An Autumn Gleaning, 1954; numerous articles in medical and scientific journals. *Address:* The Evelyn Nursing Home, Cambridge. *T.:*

Cambridge 53401; The Wellcome Trust, 52 Queen Anne St., W.1. *Club:* Athenæum. [*Died* 23 *July* 1968.

DALEY, Sir Allen; *see* Daley, Sir W. A.

DALEY, Sir Denis Leo, Kt., *cr.* 1941; D.L. Hants; J.P.; *b.* 1 April 1888; *m.* 1931, Margaret Janetta Lewis, *o. d.* of Charles Scott; two *s.* one *d.* *Educ.:* St. Aloysius School, Oxford. Lord Mayor of Portsmouth, 1939-44 and 1950-51. Building Society's Official, retired. Chevalier, Legion of Honour, 1951. *Recreation:* gardening. *Address:* Rockville, 98 Titchfield Rd., Fareham, Hants. [*Died* 17 *Jan.* 1965.

DALEY, Sir (William) Allen, Kt. 1944; *b.* 19 Feb. 1887; *s.* of Dr William Daley; *m.* 1913, Mary Toomey (*d.* 1962); one *s.* one *d.* *Educ.:* Merchant Taylors' School, Crosby; Univ. of Liverpool. B.Sc. London; M.B., Ch.B. Liverpool; D.P.H. Cambridge; M.D. London; F.R.C.P. London; Hon. M.M.S.A.; Hon. LL.D. (Liverpool), 1958. Hon. Member: Liverpool Medical Inst.; Association of Port Health Authorities; British Pædiatric Assoc.; Canadian Public Health Assoc.; Hon. Fellow American Public Health Assoc. M.O.H. Bootle, 1911-20; Blackburn, 1920-25, Hull, 1925-1929; Principal Medical Officer, Public Health Department, L.C.C., 1929-39; M.O.H., L.C.C., 1939-52; A representative of Minister of Health on Central Midwives Board, 1931-49, and on General Nursing Council, 1953-58. Member: Minister of Health's Advisory Cttee. on Civil Nursing Reserve, 1940-48; Medical Research Council's Cttee. on Preventive Medicine, 1940; Minister of Health's Medical Advisory Cttee., 1942-48; N.W. Metropolitan Regional Hospital Bd., 1952-58; Examiner in Public Health University of London, 1939-45; Examiner in Public Health (M.B.) University of Bristol, 1936-1938; Member Rushcliffe Committee on Salaries of Nurses, 1942-48; Member of the Radium Commission, 1944-48; President Society of Medical Officers of Health, 1945-1946 (Chairman of Council, 1948-52, Hon. Fellow, 1952); member of Central Health Services Council, 1948-52; Chm. Standing Mental Health Advisory Committee, 1949-1952; Member of Executive Council for County of London under National Health Services Act, 1948-52; Pres. Central Council for Health Educn., 1958-64; Nat. Assoc. for Maternal and Child Welfare; Vice-Pres. Roy. Soc. of Health, Roy. Inst. of Public Health. Pres., Section of Epidemiology, and State Medicine, Royal Society of Medicine, 1948-49; Vice-Chm., Cttee. of Management, Royal Post-Graduate Med. Sch. of London; Mem. Board of Governors: Bethlem Royal and Maudsley Hospitals, 1948-62; Hammersmith and St. Mark's, Hospital, 1948-63; Hospital for Sick Children, Great Ormond Street, 1948-57 (Vice-Chm., 1955-57); Br. Post Graduate Medical Federation; Mem. Court, School of Hygiene and Tropical Medicine, London; Chairman Chadwick Trustees; President, U.K. Committee for W.H.O.; K.H.P. 1947-50. De Lamar Lecturer, Johns Hopkins Univ., 1952; Associate Health Officer, City of Baltimore, Md., U.S.A., 1952. Presented with Key of City of Washington, D.C., 1952. Nuffield Foundation Visiting Lectr. in Australia, 1953; Croonian Lectr., R.C.P. Lond., 1953. *Publications:* annual reports and contributions to medical periodicals. *Recreations:* walking, motoring. *Address:* 24 Edith Road, W.14. *T.:* 01-603 6204. *Clubs:* Athenæum, Royal Automobile. [*Died* 21 *Feb.* 1969.

DALGLEISH, Wing Comdr. James W. O.; *see* Ogilvy-Dalgleish.

DALGLEISH, Oakley Hedley; Editor and Publisher, The Globe and Mail (Toronto), since 1957; *b.* New Liskeard, Ontario, 29 May 1910; *s.* of Peter O. Dalgleish and Charlotte (*née* Penelton); *m.* 1933, Delsya Griffiths; one *s.* *Educ.:* Toronto University, London School of Economics. Foreign Correspondent for British newspapers in Madrid, Berlin, Geneva and Washington. Joined The Globe and Mail (Toronto), 1935; Dominion Bureau of Information, 1940; Ottawa Corresp., The Globe and Mail, 1941; Editor-in-Chief, 1947; Asst. Publisher, 1952. Launched Overseas Edition of The Globe and Mail, London, 1958 (First for any Canadian newspaper). Trustee, Toronto Gen. Hosp.; Governor, Toronto Univ.; Director, Nat. Heart Foundation. *Recreation:* travel. *Address:* The Globe and Mail, 140 King Street West, Toronto, Ont., Canada. *T.:* Toronto 368-7851; P.O. Box 5, Erindale, Ont., Canada. [*Died* 16 *Aug.* 1963.

DALISON, Maj.-Gen. John Bernard, C.B. 1947; O.B.E. 1940; *b.* 30 March 1898; *s.* of late Dr. Bernard Edward Dalison; *m.* 1929, Eileen Marian, *d.* of late Arthur Fairclough; three *d.* *Educ.* Cheam School; Bradfield College; Staff College. 2nd Lieut. Indian Army, 1916; served 1914-18, German East Africa (wounded); 3rd Afghan War, 1919; Waziristan Campaigns, 1919-20, 1923-24 and 1930; Mahsud Campaign, 1920; Lt.-Col. 1st Punjab Regiment, 1939. War of 1939-45. Egypt, Sudan, Eritrea and India (despatches, O.B.E.); Col. 1940; Brig. 1941; Maj.-Gen. 1944; D.A.G. (India) 1944-1945. Member Armed Forces Pay Cttee. (India), 1946-47; D.Q.M.G. (India), 1947; A.G. (Pakistan), 1947; retd. 1948. Regional Controller, Ministry of Food, 1949-54; Civil Defence Comr., 1954-55. *Address:* North Ridge, The Ridgeway, Tonbridge, Kent. *T.:* Tonbridge 3885. *Club:* United Service. [*Died* 31 *Jan.* 1964.

DALLAS, George, C.B.E. 1946; *b.* Glasgow, 6 Aug. 1878; *s.* of George Dallas and Mary Hay; *m.* 1920; two *s.* *Educ.:* Elementary School; Technical College; London School of Economics. General Secretary I.L.P., Scotland, to 1912; member, Royal Commission on Agriculture; member, Agricultural Wages Board; member, National Council of Agriculture for England; contested Maldon Div., Essex, 1918 and 1922; Roxburgh and Selkirk, 1923 and 1924; M.P. (Lab.) Wellingborough, 1929-31. J.P. Northamptonshire, 1938; Chairman, Northamptonshire Rural Community Council; Chm., River Nene Catchment Board; Chairman, Timber Control Board during War of 1939-1945. *Publications:* Farmer Workers' Greatest Betrayal: An Exposure of the Coalition Government. *Recreations:* music, reading, gardening. [*Died* 4 *Jan.* 1961.

DALMAHOY, Patrick James Edward, C.B. 1952; Principal, Ministry of Transport, since 1960; *b.* Edinburgh, 20 June 1896; *s.* of late J. A. Dalmahoy, M.V.O., W.S. and Frances Marion Henderson; *m.* 1923, Veronica, *d.* of late R. Massingberd Rogers and *widow* of Lieut. L. E. Taylor. *Educ.:* Repton School; Oriel College, Oxford (B.A.). Served European War, 1914-18, in R.F.A. (T.A.) and with Transportation Directorate, France; Captain. Entered Civil Service 1921, as Asst. Commissioner National Savings; Commissioner Northern Region, 1930-35, London Region, 1935-37; transferred to Ministry of Transport, 1938, as Principal; Assistant Secretary, 1943; Under-Sec., Min. of Transport and Civil Aviation, 1948-59, retired 1959, re-employed as Principal, retired 1961. *Address:* 18 Grange Court, Pinehurst, Cambridge. [*Died* 20 *Dec.* 1963.

DALTON, Baron (Life Peer) *cr.* 1960; of Forest and Frith, Co. Palatine of Durham; **Edward Hugh John Neale Dalton,**

P.C. 1940; M.A. Cambridge, D.Sc. Lond.; D.Sc., Sydney; LL.D. Manchester; D.C.L. Durham; M.P. (Lab.), Camberwell (Peckham Div.), 1924-29, Bishop Auckland Div., 1929-31, and 1935-September 1959; *b.* Neath, Glam., 1887; *s.* of late Rev. Canon J. N. Dalton, K.C.V.O., C.M.G.; *m.* 1914, Ruth (M.P. (Lab.), Bishop Auckland Div., Feb.-May 1929), *d.* of late T. Hamilton Fox; one *d.* decd. *Educ.:* Eton; King's College, Cambridge; Winchester Reading Prize, Cambridge, 1909; Hutchinson Research studentship, London School of Economics, 1911-13. Barrister-at-law, Middle Temple, 1914. Hon. Bencher, 1946; served European War 1914-19 (A.S.C. and subsequently R.G.A.), French and Italian Fronts (Italian Medaglio al Valore Militare, 1917); attached to Ministry of Labour for special investigations, 1919; Lecturer London School of Economics, 1919; Sir Ernest Cassel Reader in Commerce, Univ. of London, 1920-25; Reader in Economics, University of London, 1925-36; Hon. Fellow, London School of Economics. Parliamentary Under-Sec., Foreign Office, 1929-31; Minister of Economic Warfare, 1940-42; President of Board of Trade, 1942-45; Chancellor of the Exchequer, 1945-47; Chancellor of the Duchy of Lancaster, 1948-50; Minister of Town and Country Planning, 1950-51; Minister of Local Government and Planning, 1951. Chm. National Executive of Labour Party, 1936-37. Member of Statutory Commission, Cambridge University, 1923; Pres. Ramblers' Association, 1948-50; Master of the Drapers' Company, 1958-59. *Publications:* With British Guns in Italy; Inequality of Incomes in Modern Communities; Principles of Public Finance; The Peace of Nations; Practical Socialism for Britain; Hitler's War; Call Back Yesterday; The Fateful Years; High Tide and After. *Recreations:* travel, trees, walking. *Address:* 185A Ashley Gardens, S.W.1; West Leaze, Aldbourne, Wilts.
[*Died* 13 *Feb.* 1962.

DALTON, Sir Henry, Kt., *cr.* 1956; C.B.E. 1942 (M.B.E. 1937); Assistant Commissioner of Police of the Metropolis, 1946-56; J.P., Middlesex Surrey, Hertford, Essex, Kent, Berks, Buckingham, London, 1946-56; *b.* 27 Feb. 1891; *s.* of late Henry Taylor Dalton, Watton, East Yorks; *m.* 1915, Susan Dalton, Watton, East Yorks; one *s.* one *d.* Joined Metropolitan Police, 1911; retired, 1956; Superintendent 1933; Chief Constable, 1938; seconded Home Office as Police Adviser on A.R.P., 1938; in charge of A.R.P. Department, Metropolitan Police, until outbreak of War of 1939-45; Deputy Assistant Commissioner, 1940; O.St.J., 1942; C.St.J., 1953. Led United Kingdom Police Recruiting Mission to M.E.F.-C.M.F. and Gibraltar Command, 1946. Chm., Public Carriage Drivers, etc., Licensing Cttee. (Metropolitan Area), 1946-56; Member: London and Home Counties Traffic Advisory Committee, 1946-56; London Council of Roy. Soc. for Prevention of Accidents, 1947-56 (elected Vice-Pres., 1949); Traffic Sub-Cttee. of Conf. of Chief Constables, 1946-56; Chm., Management Cttee., Convalescent Police Seaside Home, Hove, 1948-56, Trustee, 1956; Member: Min. of Transport's Cttee. on Road Safety, 1948-56; Nat. Public Safety Cttee., Roy. Soc. for Prevention of Accidents, 1948-1956; Cttee. on Road Layout, Road Research Bd., 1949-56; Road Research Bd., 1950-55; Road Users Cttee., Road Research Bd., 1950-55; Nat. Exec. Cttee. and Nat. Awards Cttee., Roy. Soc. for Prevention of Accidents, 1950-56; London and Home Counties Traffic Advisory Cttee. Special Sub-Cttee. on London Traffic Congestion, 1950; Permanent Internat. Commn. of Road Congresses, 1951 and 1955. Member: Minister of Transport's Working Party on Car Parking in the Inner Area of London, 1953; O.E.E.C. Technical Assistance Mission to U.S.A. to study Traffic Engineering and Control, 1954; Assessor (representing Home Office), Road Research Bd., 1955-56; Chm. Metropolitan Police Canteens Bd., 1955-56. *Recreation:* bowls. *Address:* Yew Trees, 8 Collington Rise, Bexhill-on-Sea, Sussex. *T.:* Cooden 2625. *Club:* Royal Automobile.
[*Died* 10 *Nov.* 1966.

D'ALTON, His Eminence Cardinal John, D.D., D.Litt. Bishop of Meath, (R.C.), 1943-46; Archbishop of Armagh, and Primate of all Ireland (R.C.), since 1946; Cardinal, 1953. Hon. LL.D.: Queen's Univ., Belfast, 1952, Nat. University of Ireland, 1958. *Publications:* Horace and his Age: a study in Historical Background, 1917; Roman Literary Theory and Criticism, A Study in Tendencies, 1931; Selections from St. John Chrysostom, 1940. *Address:* Ara Coeli, Armagh. [*Died* 1 *Feb.* 1963.

DALTON, Lt.-Col. Duncan G.; *see* Grant-Dalton.

DALTON, John Patrick, O.B.E. 1941; M.A., DSc. (St. Andrews), DSc. (C.G.H.); formerly Prof. of Mathematics, Univ. of Witwatersrand, Johannesburg, retired 1946; *b.* Dundalk, Co. Louth, 15 Jan. 1886; *s.* of Michael Dalton Benmore, Athea, Co. Limerick, and Jane Agnes Pye, Ledbury, Herefordshire; *m.* 1910, Christina, *d.* of James Cram, C.A., Dundee, Scotland; three *s.* one *d.* *Educ.:* Universities of St. Andrews, Scotland, and Leiden. Research Scholar and Fellow in Physics, 1906-11; Assistant Lecturer and Demonstrator in Physics, University College, Dundee, 1911-13; Lecturer in Physics and in Applied Mathematics, University College, Stellenbosch, S.A., 1913-14; served War of 1939-45 in East Africa (O.B.E.). *Publications:* Mathematical and Physical papers in Proceedings of Royal Societies and Academies and in mathematical, scientific, and economic journals; Rudiments of Relativity, 1921; An Introduction to Social Insurance, 1934; Symbolic Operators, 1954. *Address:* P.O. St. Winifred's, Natal, S. Africa.
[*Died* 5 *Oct.* 1965.

DALTON, Sir Robert William, Kt., *cr.* 1937; C.M.G. 1928; *b.* 5 April 1882; *s.* of late Rev. Edwin Dalton, D.D., Leeds; *m.* 1912, Louise Bonney, *d.* of late A. L. Bamberger, New York; one *s.* *Educ.:* Leeds Grammar School. Entered Board of Trade, 1900; H.M. Trade Commissioner in New Zealand, 1916-22; H.M. Senior Trade Commissioner in Canada, 1923-24; H.M. Senior Trade Commissioner in Australia, 1924-48; also Economic Adviser to the High Commissioner for the United Kingdom, 1945-1948. *Clubs:* Devonshire, Savage; Australian (Sydney). [*Died* 17 *Jan.* 1961.

DALTON, William Bower, A.R.C.A.; late Principal, Camberwell School of Arts and Crafts; *b.* 29 Feb. 1868; *m.* 1st, Mabel (*d.* 1936), *d.* of H. Plummer, J.P., Manchester; two *d.*; 2nd, 1943, Louise Hoyt, *d.* of Hon. Schuyler Merritt, Stamford, Conn., U.S.A. *Educ.:* Royal College of Art. Member of the Art Workers' Guild. *Publications:* Craftsmanship and Design in Pottery; Notes from a Potter's Diary; Just Clay, etc. *Address:* 298 Ocean Drive East, Stamford, Conn., U.S.A.; c/o Dr. H. M. Bower Alcock, 15 Welbeck House, Wigmore St., W.1.
[*Died* 20 *Oct.* 1965.

DALY, Lieutenant-Colonel Sir Clive Kirkpatrick, Kt., *cr.* 1946; C.S.I. 1943; C.I.E. 1925; Indian Political Service, retired; National Savings Commr., Finance Dept. Government of India; *b.* 3 Apr. 1888. Served European War, 1914-19; Consul for Seistan and Kain, Persia, 1929; Consul-General Khorasan, 1932-36; Resident for Baroda and the Gujarat States, 1939; retired, 1943. *Address:* c/o Lloyds Bank, 6 Pall Mall, S.W.1.
[*Died* 17 *Sept.* 1966.

DALY, Colonel (Hon. Brig.) Louis Dominic, D.S.O. 1916; O.B.E. 1924; late K.O.Y.L.I., Devon, and Leinster Regiments; *b.* Cork, 5 Aug. 1885; *s.* of Maurice Dominic Daly, Cleve Hill, Co. Cork; *m.* 1918, Cora H. (*d.* 1947), *d.* of T. England, Tenby Cottage, Blackrock; one *s.* one *d.* *Educ.:* Downside School, nr. Bath. Served with 4th Royal Munster Fusiliers (Kerry Militia), 1905-7; 2nd Lieut. 2nd Leinster Regt. 1907; Lieut. 1910; Captain, 1915; Major, 1927; joined K.O.Y.L.I. 1929; Lt.-Col. 1932; Col. 1936; served European War, operations in France and Belgium, 1914-18 (despatches five times, Bt. Major, D.S.O.); employed on General Staff, July 1916; 3rd Corps, 1918; Staff College, 1919; Bde. Major, Delhi Bde., 1920; Gen. Staff Officer (II. Grade) Waziristan Force, 1920-23 (despatches twice, O.B.E.); joined Devonshire Regt. 1924; D.A.A. and Q.M.G. 54th E.A. Div. 1925-26; G.S.O. 2, 1927-28; commanded 1st Bn. K.O.Y.L.I. 1932-36; Commander 147th (2nd West Riding) Infantry Brigade T.A., 1936-40; retd., 1940. Hon. Sec. and Treas., Herts Branch S.S.A.F.A., 1948. *Recreations:* cricket, tennis, hockey, golf. *Address:* Leighcroft, Hoddesdon, Herts. *T.:* Hoddesdon 2359. [*Died* 10 *June* 1967.

DALZIEL, Walter Watson, C.I.E. 1944; late I.C.S.; Barrister-at-Law (Gray's Inn); *b.* 5 Oct. 1900; *s.* of Dr. John M. Dalziel; *m.* 1931, Dorothy Dawson; one *d.* *Educ.:* Edinburgh Academy; Corpus Christi College, Oxford. Late Secretary to Govt. of Bihar in Judicial Dept. and Superintendent and Remembrancer of Legal Affairs; Acting Judge, Patna High Court, 1946; retired, 1948. Solicitor's Dept., Board of Trade, 1948-65. *Recreation:* golf. *Address:* 2 Longfield House, Longfield Drive, East Sheen, S.W.14. *Club:* Royal Commonwealth Society. [*Died* 12 *Sept.* 1967.

DAMANT, Captain Guybon Chesney Castell, C.B.E. 1924; *s.* of late Harry Castell Damant and Mary, *d.* of David Wilson of Ballymoney; *m.* 1913, Eleanor May Brook; one *s.* two *d.* Entered Navy, 1895; experimental officer to Admiralty Committee on Deep Water Diving, 1906; later Inspector of Diving; served European War at sea and as an Admiralty Salvage Officer; later in charge of successful operations for recovery of bullion to the value of £5,000,000 from the wreck of the Laurentic. Served War of 1939-45 in Admiralty Salvage Dept. and Overseas. *Publications:* various papers on diving, the natural history of under-water life, compressed air illness, etc. *Address:* Thursford, Cambridge Rd., East Cowes, I. of Wight. *Club:* United Service. [*Died* 29 *June* 1963.

DAMIANO, Most Rev. Celestine Joseph, Titular Archibshop of Nicopolis in Epiro; Apostolic Delegate to Southern Africa, 1952; Archbishop of Camden, N.J., U.S.A. since 1960; *b.* Dunkirk, N.Y., U.S.A.; *s.* of late Vito and Stella Zaccari. *Educ.:* Dunkirk Schools; St. Michael's College, University of Toronto; Urban College, Rome; Apollinaris College, Rome. Ordained, Rome, 1935; Assistant Priest, Niagara Falls, N.Y.; Pastor, Falconer, N.Y.; Official, Sacred Congregation "de Propaganda Fide", 1947, Monsignor, 1949; consecrated Archbishop, 1953. *Address:* 342 Kings Highway, West Haddonfield, New Jersey, U.S.A. [*Died* 2 *Oct.* 1967.

DANE, Clemence (Winifred Ashton), C.B.E. 1953; *b.* Blackheath. *Educ.:* England, Germany, Switzerland; Slade School. *Publications: novels:* Regiment of Women, 1917; First the Blade, 1918; Legend, 1919; Wandering Stars, 1924; The Babyons, 1928; Broome Stages, 1931; The Moon is Feminine, 1938; The Arrogant History of White Ben, 1939; He Brings Great News, 1944; The Flower Girls, 1954; (novels with Helen Simpson) Enter, Sir John, 1929; Printer's Devil, 1930; Re-enter Sir John, 1932; *vol. short stories:* Fate Cries Out, 1935; *omnibus collection:* Recapture, 1932; *anthologies:* The Shelter Book 1939; The Nelson Touch, 1944; *plays:* A Bill of Divorcement, 1921; Will Shakespeare, 1921; The Way Things Happen, 1925; Naboth's Vineyard, 1925; Granite, 1926; Mariners, 1926; Adam's Opera, 1928; Gooseberry Fool (with Helen Simpson), 1930; Wild Decembers, 1932; Come of Age, 1934; Moonlight is Silver, 1934; L'Aiglon (adaptation), 1934; The Happy Hypocrite (adaptation), 1936; Herod and Mariamne, 1938; Cousin Muriel, 1940; Alice in Wonderland (new version), 1943; Call Home the Heart, 1947; Eighty in the Shade, 1958; *essays:* The Women's Side, 1927; Tradition and Hugh Walpole, 1930; *reminiscences:* London has a Garden, 1964. *Address:* c/o Michael Joseph Ltd., 26 Bloomsbury Street, W.C.1. [*Died* 28 *March* 1965.

DANGERFIELD, Roland Edmund; Chairman, 1948-62, and Managing Director, 1933-1962, Temple Press Limited; *b.* 18 June 1897; *s.* of late Edmund and Alice Ada Dangerfield; *m.* 1929, Marjorie, *d.* of late Rev. Edward and Evelyn Page; two *s.* one *d.* *Educ.:* Harrow School. R.F.C. (Special Reserve) and R.A.F. in France, 1916-19. Served on Paper Advisory Committee for Periodical Publications (under Paper Control, Ministry of Supply); Deferment Advisory Committee of Ministry of Labour; and L.D.V. (later Home Guard) during War of 1939-45. Director Temple Press Ltd., 1918; Chairman of Council of Trade and Technical Press, 1938-50; Director George Newnes Ltd., 1953-62; Chairman Petroleum Times Ltd., 1956-62; Chm. St. Bride's Press Ltd., 1959-62. President, Periodical Proprietors Association, 1959-62. Member of Council, Royal Society of Arts, 1958-. Master of Worshipful Company of Coachmakers and Coach Harness Makers, 1953-54. *Recreations:* reading, gardening. *Address:* Hoe Farm, Peaslake, Surrey. *T.:* Abinger 181. *Clubs:* Garrick, Royal Air Force, Royal Automobile. [*Died* 19 *June* 1964.

DANGLOW, Rabbi Jacob, C.M.G. 1956; O.B.E. 1950; V.D. 1929; M.A.; Senior Minister, St. Kilda Hebrew Congregation, 1905-57, Rabbi Emeritus; Senior Jewish Chaplain, Commonwealth Mil. Forces, Aust., since 1942; *b.* 28 Nov. 1880; *s.* of late Michael and Jessie Danglow; *m.* 1st, 1909, May Baruch (decd.); one *s.* two *d.*; 2nd, 1949, Diana Rosen. *Educ.:* Jews' Coll., London; Univ. Coll., London. Jewish Mil. Chaplain, 1908; Vice-Pres., Victorian Deaf School for Children, 1925-; Member: Australian and Victorian Cttees., Red Cross Soc., 1920-40; Melb. Hosp. Sunday Fund Cttee., 1930-; Lord Mayor's Fund Cttee., 1954-. Founded Vict. Jewish Young People's Assoc., 1908, and 3rd St. Kilda Boy Scouts Gp., 1924. Hon. Fell., Jews' Coll., London, 1955; Life Member (1955) Melb. Beth Din (Jewish Eccles. Court). Served as Jewish Chaplain with A.I.F., 1917-19. *Publications:* pamphlets. *Recreations:* golf, bowls. *Address:* 4 Inverleith St., St. Kilda, Vic., Australia. *T.:* L.A. 3124. *Clubs:* Rotary, Naval and Military (Melbourne); Metropolitan Golf (Victoria); City of St. Kilda Bowling. [*Died* 21 *May* 1962.

DANIEL, Thomas Ernest, M.Eng., C.Eng., F.I.E.E., M.I.Mech.E.; Chairman, Joint Industry Board, Electrical Contracting Industry, since 1967; *b.* 9 February 1898; *s.* of late Thomas Daniel, St. Ives, Cornwall; *m.* 1925, Olive (decd.), *d.* of late E. J. Curphey, Isle of Man; one *d.* *Educ.:* Wallasey Gram. Sch.; Liverpool University. Borough Electrical Engr.: Ashton-under-Lyne, 1933-37; Darlington, 1937-48; Dep.

Chm.. N. Eastern Elec. Bd., 1948-53; Dep. Chm., N. Western Elec. Bd., 1953-55; Chairman, North-Western Electricity Bd., 1956-63. *Recreation:* golf. *Address:* 33 Thorngrove Road, Wilmslow, Cheshire. *Club:* Devonshire. [*Died* 11 *Aug.* 1968.

DANIEL-ROPS, Henry, Litt.D.; Commander of the Legion of Honour; Man of Letters; Member of the French Academy; *b.* Êpinal (Vosges), 19Jan. 1901; *s.* of Col. Charles Petiot Daniel-Rops and Odile Grosperrin; *m.* 1924, Madeleine Bouvier. *Educ.:* Universities of Grenoble and Lyon. Professor (agrégé) of the University, 1922. Director of the review Ecclesia, Paris, 1949-; Dr. *h.c.* University of Montreal, Canada. Grand Cross of St. Gregory the Great; Grand Officer of the Order of Christ (Portugal) and Order of Saint Sepulchre. *Publications:* Mort òu est la victoire? (novel), 1932; Histoire sainte, 1943 (Eng. trans., The People of the Bible, 1953); L'Église des Apôtres et des Martyrs, 1948 (Eng. trans., The Church of Apostles and Martyrs, 1960); Jésus en son temps, 1949 (Eng. trans., Jesus in His Time, 1955); Histoire de l'Église du Christ, 1947-60. (Eng. trans., Cathedrals and Crusades, 1957); Missa est, 1953 (Eng. trans., That is the Mass, 1958); L'Église des Temps Barbares (Eng. trans., The Church in the Dark Ages, 1953); The Heroes of God, 1959; La vie quotidenne en Palestine à l'époque du Christ (Eng. trans. by Patrick O'Brian, Daily Life in Palestine at the Time of Christ, 1962). *Address:* 28 Bd. Victor Hugo, Neuilly s/Seine, France. *T.:* Maillot 3081; Tresserve (Savoie), France. *Club:* Union Interalliée (Paris). [*Died* 27 *July* 1965.

DANIELL, John, *b.* 12 Dec. 1878; *s.* of Anthony Frederick Daniell and Joan Meikleham; *m.* 1910, Manora Garfath; one *s.* one *d.* *Educ.:* Clifton, Emmanuel College, Cambridge. Cambridge University XV, 1898-1900; Cambridge University XI, 1899-1901; England XV v. Wales 1899, v. Ireland 1900-1902-4, v. Scotland, 1900-1902-4 (all these as Captain); England Rugby Union Selection Committee, 1913-39 (Chairman, 1932-39); Vice-President Rugby Football Union, 1938-39 and 1939-40, Acting President, 1940-45, President, 1945-47; Somerset County Cricket XI, 1898-1926; Capt. 1908-12 and 1919-26; Hon. Sec. Somerset County C.C., 1932-37 (Pres. 1947-49); England Test Match Selection Committee 1921 v. Australians and 1924 v. S. Africans; Tea Planting in India, 1904-8; Sportsmen's Battalion, Sept. 1914; received Commission as 2nd Lt. R.A.S.C. Nov. 1914; Capt. 1915; Served in France, 1916-19. *Address:* Holway Farm House, Taunton. *T.:* Taunton 3278. *Clubs:* M.C.C., Free Foresters. [*Died* 24 *Jan.* 1963.

DANNREUTHER, Sir Sigmund, Kt., *cr.* 1919; C.B. 1917; *b.* 20 Nov. 1873; 2nd *s.* of Prof. Edward Dannreuther, Windycroft, Hastings; *m.* 1901, Margaret Ethel (*d.* 1954), *d.* of Richard Burbrook; one *d.* (two *s.* decd.). *Educ.:* Eton; Trinity College, Cambridge; B.A. 1895; 1st Division 1st Class Classical Tripos. Entered War Office, 1896; Private Secretary to Sir Evelyn Wood, 1898-1901; went to Ministry of Munitions as Director of Finance, 1915; Controller of Finance and Accounting Officer, Ministry of Munitions, 1917; Joint Sec., 1920; Accounting Officer and Joint Sec., Disposal and Liquidation Commission, 1921-24; Deputy Secretary, Air Ministry, 1923-34; retired 1934. *Recreations:* formerly golf, music. *Address:* Calladown, Stoke Green, Slough, Bucks. *T.:* Slough 22589. [*Died* 5 *April* 1965.

d'ARANYI, Jelly, C.B.E. 1946; violinist; *b.* Budapest; *d.* of Taksony Arany de Hunyadvar and Adrienne Nieviarowicz de Ligenza; unmarried. *Educ.:* Privately in Budapest and at Royal Music Academy there. Began public concert playing at age of 14, when first came to England; since then has played extensively in Europe and the U.S.A. although home is in England and is naturalised British Subject; Ravel, Bartók, Vaughan-Williams and other composers have dedicated works to her; Roman Catholic. *Address:* Via San Carlo 6, Bellosguardo, Firenze, Italy. [*Died* 30 *March* 1966.

DARBHANGA, Maharajadhiraja of, Col. Hon. Dr. Sir Kameshwara Singh, K.C.I.E., *cr.* 1933; LL.D. (Allahabad University) 1937; D.Litt. (Benares Hindu University) 1937; Member of the Parliament of India; *b.* 28 Nov. 1907; *S.* father, Maharajadhiraja Sir Rameshwara Singh Bahadur, G.C.I.E., K.B.E., D.Litt., 1929. Nominated member of the Council of State twice; elected member, since 1937; is head of the Maithil Brahmans in India; is Life President of the Maithil Maha Sabha; Former President: All-India Landholders' Federation; Bengal Landholders' Association; Former Life President of the Bihar Landholders' Association; General President of the Sri Bharat Dharma Mahamandal; a Former Pro-chancellor of Benares Hindu University, a Fellow of Calcutta University and Life Fellow of Patna University; Life Member of Allahabad University and Benares Hindu University Courts; Pro-Chancellor of Kameshwara Singh Sanskrti Vishwa Vidyalaya Darbhanga (for life) and of Mithila Inst. of Postgrad. Studies and Research in Sanskrit learning, Darbhanga. Former President, Bihar Sanskrit Association, and of Bihar Sanskrit Education Reorganisation Committee. Vice-Patron Bihar and Orissa Research Society; Vice-President, Provincial War Board, Bihar; President King George V. Memorial Anti-Tuberculosis Association, Bihar; Trustee Victoria Memorial Hall, Calcutta; Delegate to the two sessions of the Indian Round Table Conference held in London, 1930 and 1931; elected from Bihar as member Constituent Assembly of India, 1946; elected to Council of States from Bihar, 1952-58, re-elected, 1960; Member National Defence Council of Govt. of India; Hon. Col. of 11th Bn. 19 Hyderabad Regt., 1940, and of Bihar Regt. of Indian Army; F.R.S.A. *Recreations:* polo, tennis, and motoring. *Address:* Darbhanga, India; other Palaces at Calcutta, Simla, Allahabad, Benares, Delhi. *T.:* 410. *Clubs:* Hurlingham; Cowdray Park Polo (London); Royal Household Brigade Polo (Windsor); Chelmsford (Delhi and Simla); Royal Calcutta Turf, Calcutta South (Calcutta); Imperial Gymkhana (Delhi); National Sports of India (New Delhi); Darbhanga Rotary. [*Died Oct.* 1962.

DARBISHIRE, Helen, C.B.E. 1955; M.A. Oxon.; Hon. D.Litt. Durham and Lond.; F.B.A. 1947; *b.* 1881; *d.* of Samuel Dukinfield Darbishire, M.D. Oxon. *Educ.:* Girls' High Sch., Oxford; Somerville Coll., Oxford. 1st Cl. Honour School of English Language and Literature, 1903; Visiting Lectr., Royal Holloway College, 1904; Tutor in English, Somerville College, 1908; Univ. Lecturer in English Literature, 1926-31; Principal of Somerville College, Oxford, 1931-45; Visiting Professor, Wellesley College, Mass., U.S.A., 1925-26; Clark Lecturer, Trinity College, Cambridge, 1949. *Publications:* edition of Wordsworth's Poems of 1807; De Quincey's Literary Criticism; edition of the Manuscript of Paradise Lost, Book 1; Early Lives of Milton; edition with E. de Selincourt of Wordsworth's Poetical Works, Vols. III-V; The Poet Wordsworth; editions of Milton's Poetical Works. *Address:* Shepherds How, Grasmere, Westmorland. *T.:* Grasmere 321. [*Died* 11 *March* 1961.

D'ARCY, Lt.-Gen. John Conyers, C.B. 1946; C.B.E. 1942; M.C.; *b.* 12 Feb. 1894; *s.* of late Most Rev. Charles Frederick

D'Arcy, Archbishop of Armagh, Primate of All Ireland; *m.* 1920, Noël Patricia, *d.* of Edward Wakefield, D.L., J.P., Farnagh, Co. Westmeath; one *s.* (and one *s.* decd.). Served European War, 1914-19, in France and Belgium (wounded twice, M.C.; North-West Frontier of India, 1930-31 (wounded); War of 1939-45 (despatches, C.B.E.); commanded 9th Armoured Div., 1942-44; G.O.C. troops in Palestine, 1944-46; retired pay, 1946. *Address:* Clonriff, Oughterard, Co. Galway. *T.:* Oughterard 30. [*Died* 1 *Feb.* 1966.

DARE, Edith Graham, O.B.E. 1948; Hon. Director Human Milk Bank, Queen Charlotte's Hospital; *b.* 1883; British. *Educ.:* Woodville, Pershore, Worcestershire. Matron, Queen Charlotte's Hospital and Associated Districts, 1923-48; Hon. Director of Human Milk Bank (for life), opened the first one in this country in 1938 after visiting America and Canada; one of pioneers of Analgesia for childbirth. Coronation Medal, 1937; 1914-18 War Medal. *Recreations:* music, boating. *Address:* The Friary Cottage, Old Windsor, Berks. [*Died* 8 *Nov.* 1969.

DARKE, Rear-Admiral Reginald Burnard, C.B. 1945; D.S.O. 1918; Royal Navy, retired; *b.* 1885. Served European War, 1914-18 (despatches, D.S.O.); commanded First Submarine Flotilla, Mediterranean, 1927-29; commanded Submarine Depot at Fort Blockhouse, Gosport, 1929-31; commanded H.M.S. Enterprise, 1932-34; Chief of Staff and Maintenance Capt. to Commander-in-Chief, The Nore, 1935-37; Rear-Adm. 1937; retired list, 1937; Served War of 1939-45; Convoy Commodore, 1939; commanded Submarine Depot at Fort Blockhouse, Gosport, Dec. 1939-45. *Address:* 4 Chancellor House, Tunbridge Wells. *T.:* 20840. *Club:* United Service. [*Died* 2 *June* 1962.

DARLEY, Air Commodore Charles Curtis, C.B.E. 1931; A.M.; *b.* Caynton Manor, Salop, 31 July 1890; *s.* of late Captain Charles Edward Darley; *m.* 1925, Hilda, *d.* of late H. P. Stephenson, London (marr. diss., 1949); no *c.*; *m.* Mary Betty. *Educ.:* Dulwich College; R.M.A., Woolwich. 2nd Lieut. R.F.A., 1910; served in India, 1910-14; winner of Officers' Heavy and Middle-weight Boxing Championships, 1911-12; took R.A.C. Flying Certificate No. 591 in 1913; served in France, 1914-15; seconded to R.F.C., 1914; produced first trench map from air photos, 1915; prisoner of war in Germany, 1916-17; Superintendent of Physical Training R.A.F. and Commandant R.A.F. School of P.T., Uxbridge, 1922-25; passed Staff College, Quetta, 1926-27; commanded R.A.F., Kohat, 1929-32; passed Imperial Defence College, 1935; opened and commanded No. 10 Flying Training School, R.A.F., Tern Hill, Shropshire, 1936-37; commanded No. 1 (Indian) Group, Peshawar, 1938; invalided to England, 1939, as result of flying accident and invalided out of R.A.F. Sept. 1939, but re-employed in civilian capacity in Air Ministry. *Address:* Five Ways, 149 Broad St., Birmingham. [*Died* 10 *June* 1962.

DARLING, George Kenneth, C.I.E. 1936; Indian Civil Service retired; *b.* 10 May 1879; *s.* of late Rev. Thos. Darling, Rector of St. Michael, Paternoster Royal, E.C.; *m.* 1st, 1908, Mabel Eleanor (*d.* 1952), *d.* of John Burgess; two *s.* (and one lost in command of submarine Usk, May 1941); *m.* 2nd, 1953, Theodora Mildred, *d.* of C. B. Eustace Ford. *Educ.:* Eton; King's College, Cambridge. Entered Indian Civil Service, 1902; Senior Member, Board of Revenue, U.P., India, 1936-38. *Address:* Dial House, Aldeburgh, Suffolk. *T.:* 295. [*Died* 16 *Jan.* 1964.

DARLING, Sir Malcolm (Lyall), K.C.I.E. 1939 (C.I.E. 1934); Chm. Horace Plunkett Foundation, 1947-58; *b.* 10 Dec. 1880; *s.* of Rev. Thomas Darling and Mildred Ford; *m.* 1909, Jessica (*d.* 1932), *d.* of Lord Low of the Laws, Berwickshire; one *s.* one *d.* (and one *s.* decd.). *Educ.:* Eton; King's Coll., Camb. Joined I.C.S., 1904; Tutor and Guardian to Raja of Dewas (Senior Branch), 1907-08; gazetted for 'valuable services' in India in connection with European War; Registrar, Co-operative Societies, 1927; Chm. Punjab Banking Enquiry Cttee., 1930; Commissioner, Rawalpindi, 1931; Vice-Chancellor, University of the Punjab, 1931 and 1937-38; Chairman, Punjab Land Revenue Committee, 1938; Financial Commissioner Punjab, 1936-39; retired, 1940; Indian Editor, B.B.C., 1940-44; on special duty with the Govt. of India (War Dept.), 1945-46. Chm., Brit. Isles Fed. of Agric. Co-operatives, 1949-51; on special mission for Brit. Council, in Middle East, 1950, Greece, 1951 and Egypt, 1953; for Foreign Office in Yugoslavia, 1951 and Egypt, 1955; for I.L.O. and Government of Pakistan, 1953-54; for Government of Pakistan, 1960. Consultant to Planning Commission, New Delhi, Jan.-April, 1957. Hon. Fellow, King's Coll., Cambridge, 1957. *Publications:* The Punjab Peasant in Prosperity and Debt, 1925; Rusticus Loquitur, 1930; Wisdom and Waste in the Punjab Village, 1934; At Freedom's Door, 1949; Some Aspects of Co-operation in Germany, Italy, Ireland, 1922; Apprentice to Power, 1966. *Address:* 42 Catherine Place, S.W.1. *T.:* Victoria 2720. *Club:* Athenæum. [*Died* 1 *Jan.* 1969.

DARLING, Sir William Young, Kt., *cr.* 1943; C.B.E. 1923; M.C.; D.L., J.P.; F.R.S.E.; LL.D.; Director, Royal Bank of Scotland (1942-57, now extraordinary director); *b.* 8 May 1885; 2nd *s.* of late William Darling, Edinburgh; *m.* 1914, Olive, *e. d.* of late James Simpson, Briar Bank, Bedford. *Educ.:* James Gillespie's School, Daniel Stewart's College, Heriot-Watt Coll., Edinburgh Univ. Trained for business in Edinburgh and London; held variety of appointments in Ceylon and Australia up till 1913; enlisted ranks of the Black Watch, 1914; commissioned France 1915 to Royal Scots; served France, in Black Watch 1915; Salonika, Gallipoli (evacuation), Egypt, 1915-16, with 1st Royal Munster Fusiliers; France, 1917-19, 11th Royal Scots and General List (M.C. and bar, despatches); A.D.C. 1918-19, France, Belgium, Germany; Ireland, 1920-22; resumed business, 1922; T.F. 1930; Member Edinburgh Town Council, 1933; City Treasurer, 1937-1940; Lord Provost of Edinburgh, 1941-44; National Government Candidate, West Lothian, 1937; Chief Air Raid Warden, 1938-39; District Commissioner, S. Eastern Scotland, 1939-41; Chairman, Scottish Council on Industry, 1942-46. M.P. (C.) South Edinburgh, 1945-57, resigned. *Publications:* Private Papers of a Bankrupt Bookseller, 1931; Hades the Ladies, 1933; The Old Mill, 1934; Down but not Out, 1935; Bankrupt Bookseller Speaks Again, 1938; Why I Believe in God; King's Cross to Waverley, 1944; A Book of Days, 1951; So it Looks to Me, 1952; A Westminster Lad (Poems), 1955. *Address:* 6 Rothesay Terrace, Edinburgh. *Clubs:* Scottish Conservative, Royal Scots (Edinburgh), etc. [*Died* 4 *Feb.* 1962.

DART, Rev. John Lovering Campbell; *b.* 30 May 1882; *s.* of John Dart, Bishop of New Westminster and Frances Helen Campbell; *m.* Emelie de Thevos; one *s.* *Educ.:* St. John's College, Oxford. Curate of Christ Church, Clapham, and St. Bartholomew's, Brighton; Assistant Chaplain, St. George's, Paris; Indian Ecclesiastical Establishment, 1911; Senior Presidency Chaplain, Bombay, 1930; Canon of St. Thomas' Cathedral, Bombay, 1930; acting Archdeacon, 1931 and 1933; Bishop's Commissary in charge of the diocese of Bombay, 1933; Chaplain St. George's Church, Paris, from 1934; acting Chaplain, Radley College, 1940; Vicar of St. Margaret's, Oxford, 1943; permission to officiate at: St. Michael and All Angels, Ladbroke Grove, 1945; St. Mary, Pimlico, 1946; diocese of Rochester, 1949-; Chaplain, St. Mary's Abbey, W. Malling, 1948-54. *Publications:* A Short History of St. Thomas' Cathedral, Bombay; The Mysteries of Christ; Peace in Believing; Fullness of Joy; Public School Divinity; An A.B.C. Guide to the Church's Faith and Practice; God's Plan of Salvation; The Old Religion. *Address:* 2 Windsor Court, Brighton Road, Worthing, Sussex. [*Died* 8 *June* 1961.

DARTMOUTH, 8th Earl of, *cr.* 1711; **Humphry Legge,** C.V.O. 1947; D.S.O. 1919; Comdr. R.N. retd.; Baron Dartmouth, 1682; Viscount Lewisham, 1711; *b.* 14 March 1888; 3rd *s.* of 6th Earl of Dartmouth, P.C., G.C.V.O., K.C.B., V.D., T.D.; *S.* brother 1958; *m.* 1923, Roma, *e. d.* of Sir Ernest Horlick, 2nd Bt.; one *s.* one *d.* *Educ.:* H.M.S. Britannia, Dartmouth. D.L. Staffs., 1927-39; Asst. Chief Constable, Staffs., 1928-32; Chief Constable, Berks., 1932-53. Served European War (despatches, D.S.O.). Grand Officer, Order of Orange Nassau, (Netherlands), 1946. *Recreations:* shooting, fishing, cricket, golf. *Heir:* *s.* Viscount Lewisham. *Address:* The Lansdown Grove Hotel, Bath. *Clubs:* Bath, Buck's. [*Died* 16 *Oct.* 1962.

DARVALL, Air Marshal Sir Lawrence, K.C.B. 1956 (C.B. 1945); M.C.; *b.* 24 November 1898; 2nd *s.* of Richard Thomas Darvall, late of Gordon Lodge, Reading; *m.* 1923, Aileen, *d.* of E. Mahony, J.P., Co. Cork, Ireland; one *s.* one *d.* *Educ.:* Dover Coll.; R.M.C. Sandhurst. Commissioned in Green Howards; transf. to R.A.F. 1921, after four years' secondment. Wing Comdr. 1937; Group Capt. 1941; Air Cdre. 1946; Air Vice-Marshal, 1948; Air Marshal, 1956. Dir. of Air Transport Policy and Operations at Air Ministry, 1943-44; commanded No. 46 and 216 Groups in Transport Comd., 1944-46; A.O.C. Air H.Q., Italy, 1946-47; A.O.C. No. 3 Group, Bomber Command, 1947-48; Air Officer i/c Administration, H.Q. Flying Training Command, 1949-50; A.O.C., No. 23 Group, 1950-51; Commandant of the Joint Services Staff College, 1951-53; Commandant, N.A.T.O. Defence College, Paris, Nov. 1953-55; retired 1956. F.R.S.A. *Address:* Russet Cottage, Clifford Manor Road, Guildford, Surrey. *Club:* R.A.F. [*Died* 17 *Nov.* 1968.

DARVIL-SMITH, Major Percy George, C.B.E. 1918; K.St.J.; *b.* 1880; *m.* 1st, 1911, Ethel Kathleen (*d.* 1951), *o. d.* of Thomas Henry Biss, Frome; 2nd, 1954, Iris Muriel, *d.* of late D. R. Wade, Worthing. *Educ.:* Wesley Coll., Dublin. Scottish Horse Yeomanry, South African War; War Office, 1902-9; Captain and Musketry Officer Middlesex Cadet Brigade, 1915-16; Co.-Director Auxiliary Hospitals and V.A.D.'s, Middlesex, 1914-18; Major Commanding Eastern Command Vol. Ambulance Convoy, 1917-20; County Executive Officer, Bucks Jt. Cttee., Order of St. John and B.R.C.S., 1923-52; County Controller Bucks V.A.D.'s, 1923-43; Secretary, St. John Ambulance Brigade, 1912-50. Commissioner, St. John Amb. Bde. Bucks, 1919-52. Hon. Sec. Lindfield Horticultural Society, 1956-. *Address:* East Dormer Flat, Old Place, Lindfield, Sussex. [*Died* 23 *Nov.* 1962.

DARWIN, Bernard, C.B.E. 1937; on the staff of Country Life; *b.* 7 September 1876; *s.* of Sir Francis Darwin, F.R.S.; *m.* 1906, Elinor Mary (*d.* 1954), *d.* of W. T. Monsell; one *s.* two *d.* *Educ.:* Eton; Trinity College, Cambridge. Called to Bar. 1903; was the golf correspondent to The Times for 39 years and is still correspondent of Country Life. Played golf for Cambridge three years (Captain, 1897), eight times for England *v.* Scotland, for Great Britain *v.* America in 1922, and has been twice in semi-final of Amateur Championship; served European War, Lieut. (Acting Major) R.A.O.C., and spent 2½ years in Macedonia. *Publications:* Golf Courses of Great Britain; Tee Shots and Others; Present Day Golf (with George Duncan); Golf, some Hints and Suggestions; A Friendly Round; A Dickens Pilgrimage (reprinted from The Times); Elves and Princesses; Green Memories, 1928; The Tale of Mr. Tootleoo; Tootleoo Two; Mr. Tootleoo and Co.; Ishybushy and Topknot (with Elinor M. Darwin); The English Public School, 1929; Second Shots, 1930; Out of the Rough, 1932; Dickens (Great Lives Series), 1933; W. G. Grace (Great Lives Series), 1934; Playing the Like, 1934; Rubs of the Green, 1936; John Gully and his Times, 1935; Life is Sweet, Brother, 1940; At Odd Moments (anthology), 1941; Pack Clouds Away, 1941; British Clubs, 1943; Golf Between Two Wars, 1944; War on the Line, 1946; Every Idle Dream, 1948; James Braid, 1952; The World that Fred Made, 1955; (Editor) The Dickens Advertiser, 1930. *Recreation:* golf. *Address:* The Dormy House, Rye, Sussex. *Club:* Garrick. [*Died* 18 *Oct.* 1961.

DARWIN, Sir Charles Galton, K.B.E. *cr.* 1942; M.C., M.A., Sc.D., F.R.S.; Hon. Sc.D. (Bristol, Manchester, Delhi, Chicago, California); Hon. LL.D. (St. Andrews and Edinburgh); Hon. Fellow of Christ's College and Trinity College, Cambridge; *b.* 19 December 1887; *s.* of Sir G. H. Darwin; *m.* 1925, Katharine, *d.* of late F. W Pember; four *s.* one *d.* *Educ.:* Marlborough College; Trinity College, Cambridge. Lecturer in Physics, Manchester University, 1910-14; attached R.E. and R.A.F., 1914-18 (actg. Capt.); Lecturer in Mathematics, Christ's College, Cambridge, 1919-1922; Tait Professor of Natural Philosophy, Edinburgh University, 1923-36; Master of Christ's College, Cambridge, 1936-1938; Director of National Physical Laboratory, 1938-49; a Royal Medal of Royal Society, 1935; Member American Philosophical Soc. *Publications:* The New Conceptions of Matter, 1931; The Next Million Years, 1952; various papers in theoretical physics. *Address:* Newnham Grange, Cambridge. *T.:* Cambridge 53910. *Club:* Athenæum. [*Died* 31 *Dec.* 1962.

DARWIN, John Henry, C.I.E. 1932; Indian Civil Service, retired; *b.* 27 Oct. 1884. *Educ.:* Charterhouse; St. John's College, Cambridge. I.C.S., 1908; Magistrate and Collector, United Provinces, 1921; Deputy Secretary to Govt., general branch, 1927-37; Commissioner for Reforms, U.P., 1936-37; retired, 1937. *Address:* Thatched Cottage, Brook Ave., New Milton, Hants. *T.:* 1163. [*Died* 21 *Sept.* 1962.

DASHWOOD, Sir John (Lindsay), 10th Bt., *cr.* 1707; C.V.O. 1952; Premier Bart. of Great Britain; an Extra Gentleman Usher to the Queen since July 1958; retired as Assistant Marshal of the Diplomatic Corps (1933-58); *b.* 25 April 1896; *s.* of 9th Bart. and Ida (*d.* 1945), *d.* of Major W. B. Lindsay; *S.* father, 1908; *m.* 1922, Helen Moira, *d.* of late Lieutenant-Colonel Vernon Eaton, Royal Canadian Horse Artillery; two *s.* one *d.* *Educ.:* Wellington; Magdalen College, Oxford. Served European War, 1914-18, temp. Lieut. 10th Service Bn. Argyll and Sutherland Highlanders, then Major, Tank Corps; Third Secretary in the Diplomatic Service, 1921; Second Secretary 1923; resigned, 1927; Sheriff of Bucks

1934. Served War of 1939-45, A.A.F. and Foreign Service, 1940-45. *Heir:* *s.* Francis John Vernon Hereward [*b.* 7 Aug. 1925; *m.* 1957, Victoria, *d.* of late Baron de Rutzen and of Sheila Baroness de Rutzen who *m.* 2nd, 1947, Lt.-Col. Hon. Randal Plunkett (later 19th Baron Dunsany); one *s.* three *d.*]. *Address:* 10 Cumberland House, Kensington High St., W.8. [*Died* 9 *July* 1966.

DAUNT, Very Rev. Ernest George; Dean of Cork since 1962; *b.* 10 Jan. 1909; 2nd *s.* of Frank Daunt, J.P.; *m.* 1935, Elizabeth Emma Curry McBride, Mod. B.A.; one *s.* three *d.* *Educ.:* Bandon Grammar School; Trinity College, Dublin. Ordained, 1933; Rector of: Balbriggan, 1937-46; Killiney, 1946-50; Zion Church, Rathgar, 1950-53; Vicar of St. Ann's, Dawson St., 1953-62. Asst. Lecturer, Divinity School, Trinity Coll., Dublin, 1949-62. *Publication:* When Thou Prayest, 1945. *Recreation:* gardening. *Address:* The Deanery, Dean St., Cork. *T.:* Cork 20922. [*Died* 1 *Dec.* 1966.

DAVENPORT, Hon. Sir George Arthur, K.B.E., *cr.* 1956; C.M.G. 1953; A.C.S.M., M.I.M.M., M.S.A. Inst. M.M.; *b.* Cheshire, England, 1893; *s.* of Henry Arthur Richard Davenport; *m.* 1919, Violet Bertha, *d.* of H. J. G. Roberts, Kimberley, S. Africa; two *d.* *Educ.:* Camborne School of Mines. Joined Globe and Phoenix Company, 1912. Served European War, 1914-18; 2/6th Royal Sussex Territorials, 1914; 2nd Rhodesia Native Regiment and R.A.F., Egypt, 1917-18. Returned to staff of Globe and Phoenix Mine; later Captain Fred Mine, also Luipaardsvlei Estate and Gold Mining Company, and Manager, New Eland Diamonds Ltd.; rejoined staff of Globe and Phoenix Mine, 1932; General Manager, 1933. President, Chamber of Mines of Rhodesia, 1938-41 and 1944; Member Natural Resources Commission for S. Rhodesia, 1938-39; Member S. Rhodesia Phthisis Board, 1944-45. O.C. Que Que Territorial Co., 1940-44. Elected Member S. Rhodesia Legislative Assembly for Que Que, 1946, re-elected 1948 and returned unopposed, 1954; Minister of Mines, Commerce and Industry, 1946-48; Minister of Mines and Transport, 1948-53; Minister of Mines, Lands and Surveys, S. Rhodesia, 1954-56; resigned 1956; re-appointed Minister for Mines, Lands and Surveys, Jan. 1958; resigned on termination of life of Parliament, June, 1958. *Recreations:* photography and carpentry. *Address:* Bramhall, Steppes Road, Highlands, Salisbury, Rhodesia. *Clubs:* Salisbury, Bulawayo (Rhodesia). [*Died* 17 *Sept.* 1970.

DAVENPORT, Harold, F.R.S. 1940; M.A., Sc.D. (Cambridge); Rouse Ball Professor of Mathematics, Cambridge, and Fellow of Trinity College, Cambridge, since Oct. 1958; *b.* Accrington, 30 Oct. 1907; *s.* of late Percy Davenport and Nancy Barnes; *m.* 1944, Anne Lofthouse, M.A., *y.d.* of J. Lofthouse, Moston, Manchester; two *s.* *Educ.:* Accrington Gram. Sch.; Manchester Univ.; Trinity Coll., Cambridge. Rayleigh Prizeman, 1930; Fellow of Trinity College, Cambridge, 1932-36; Adams Prize, 1941; Berwick Prize of London Mathematical Soc., 1954; Asst. Lectr., Manchester Univ., 1937-41; Prof. of Mathematics, Univ. Coll. of N. Wales, 1941-1945; Astor Prof. of Mathematics in Univ. of London, 1945-58. Visiting Professor at Stanford Univ., California, 1947-48 and Summer Term, 1950; Visiting Professor, University of Michigan, 1962 and 1966; Gauss Professor, Akad. der Wiss., Göttingen, 1966. President London Mathematical Society, 1957-59. Sylvester Medal, Royal Society, 1967. Hon. D.Sc. (Nottingham) 1968. *Publications:* The Higher Arithmetic, 1952; Multiplicative Number Theory, 1967; papers on the theory of numbers in scientific journals. *Recreations:* walking, travel. *Address:* 8 Cranmer Road, Cambridge; Trinity College, Cambridge. [*Died* 9 *June* 1969.

DAVENPORT, Major John Lewes, T.D. 1946; *b.* 13 Oct. 1910; *s.* of late Captain R. T. Hinckes, Foxley, Hereford; *m.* 1933, Louise Aline, *d.* of late Colonel C. J. H. Spence-Colby, C.M.G., D.S.O.; three *s.* Name changed by deed poll. *Educ.:* Malvern; Trinity Hall, Cambridge. Joined Shropshire Yeomanry 1931, Major 1942. Served War of 1939-45, Shropshire Yeomanry and R.A. J.P. Herefordshire, 1946; Dep. Lieutenant Herefordshire, 1948, High Sheriff, 1949. *Address:* Yarsop House, Mansel Lacy, Hereford. *T.:* Bridge Sollars 245. *Club:* M.C.C. [*Died* 2 *June* 1964.

DAVENPORT, Robert Cecil, M.B., B.S. (Lond.); F.R.C.S. (Eng.); Consulting Surgeon, Moorfields Eye Hospital; *b.* Chungking, China, 18 Dec. 1893; *s.* of late C. J. Davenport, F.R.C.S., late Shanghai; *m.* 1928, Helen Elizabeth Mayfield, M.R.C.S., L.R.C.P.; two *s.* one *d.* *Educ.:* Mill Hill School; St. Bartholomew's Hospital. Late House Surgeon, Ophthalmic House Surgeon, Demonstrator of Physiology, St. Bartholomew's Hospital; Moorfields Research Scholar, Royal London Ophthalmic Hospital; Captain R.A.M.C. (S.R.), Mesopotamia, 1917-20; Late Dean of Inst. of Ophthalmology, British Postgraduate Medical Federation of University of London. President: Section of Ophthalmology, Roy. Soc. Med., 1955-57; Ophthalmological Society of the U.K., 1958-60. *Publications:* various papers on ophthalmology. *Address:* 39 Devonshire Place, W.1. *T.:* Welbeck 9701. [*Died* 17 *June* 1961.

DAVENPORT, Vice-Admiral Robert Clutterbuck, C.B. 1936; *b.* 13 Apr. 1882; *s.* of Thomas Marriott and Emily Jemima Davenport; *m.* 1917, Gwladwys Mabel Halahan; one *s.* *Educ.:* H.M.S. Britannia, Dartmouth. Midshipman, 1897; served S. African War, 1899-1900; European War, 1914-19; Captain, 1922; A.D.C. to King George V, 1933-34; Commodore 2 class, R.N. Barracks, Chatham, 1933-35; Rear-Admiral, 1934; Commanding Officer, Coast of Scotland, 1935-37; Vice-Admiral, 1938; retired list, 1938; Commodore of Convoys, 1939-40; Selection Board for Temporary Commissions R.N.V.R., 1941-46. Officier, Légion d'Honneur, 1916. *Address:* Catherington Cottage, Catherington, Nr. Horndean, Hants. *T.:* Horndean 3125. [*Died* 15 *June* 1965.

DAVENTRY, 1st Viscountess, *cr.* 1943; C.B.E. 1918; **Muriel FitzRoy,** Dame of Grace, Order of St. John of Jerusalem; *b.* 8 Aug. 1869; *d.* of late Col. Hon. A. C. H. Douglas Pennant, 2nd *s.* of 1st Lord Penrhyn; *m.* 1891, Capt. Rt. Hon. E. A. FitzRoy, late Speaker of House of Commons (*d.* 1943), 2nd *s.* of 3rd Baron Southampton; two *s.* (and one killed in action, 1915), one *d.* *Heir:* *s.* Capt. Hon. Robert Oliver FitzRoy, R.N., retired [*b.* 1893; *m.* 1916, Grace Zoe, *d.* of late C. H. C. Guinness; five *d.*]. *Address:* 47 Egerton Crescent, S.W.3. *T.:* Kensington 5808. *Club:* V.A.D. [*Died* 8 *July* 1962.

DAVEY, Lt.-Col. James Edgar, D.S.O. 1918; V.D., M.B., M.D.; *b.* 15 May, 1873; *s.* of Robert Davey and Melissa Swartz; *m.* 1904, Jennie E. Flatt; one *s.* one *d.* *Educ.:* Owen Sound Collegiate Institute; Ottawa Normal School; University of Toronto. Taught in Public School for six years; graduated in medicine, 1902 (George Brown Scholarship), University of Toronto; interne in County Hospital, Buffalo, N.Y.; practised in Hamilton, Ont., beginning 1904; Chief School Medical Officer, Board of Education, 1922-34; Asst. M.O.H. of Hamilton, Ont., 1934-40, M.O.H. 1940-46; retired 1946; returned to Gen. Practice, 1947; Med. Officer to Hamilton Dept. of Public Welfare,

1953-58; returned to General Practice. City Alderman and Chairman of Legislation Committee of City Council, 1911, 12, 13, and 14; overseas service as O.C. No. 2 Can. C.C.S. (D.S.O.); President of Hamilton Medical Association, 1920; President International Health Officers' Assoc., 1942-43. Hon. Life Mem. Ontario Medical Assoc., 1962. *Recreations:* lawn bowling, golf, fishing. *Address:* 2 Ray Street S., Hamilton, Ont., Canada. *T.:* JA 2-7224. *Clubs:* Chedoke Golf, Strathcona Lawn Bowling, Lions (Ont.).
[*Died* 14 *July* 1969.

DAVEY, Rev. Principal J(ames) Ernest; Principal of the Presbyterian College, Belfast, since 1942, and Professor (of Church History 1917, of Biblical Literature 1922; of Hebrew and Old Testament 1930, of New Testament Language, Literature and Theology since 1933); *b.* Ballymena, Co. Antrim, 24 June 1890; *s.* of Rev. Charles Davey, B.A., D.D., and Margaret (*née* Beatty); *m.* 1927, Georgiana Eliza O'Neill; one *s.* two *d.* *Educ.:* Methodist College and Campbell College, Belfast; King's College, Cambridge; Edinburgh University; Belfast Presbyterian College. Scholar, R.U.I., 1908; Minor Scholar, 1909, Open Foundation Scholar, 1911-16, King's Coll., Camb.; Fellow of King's Coll., Camb., 1916-22; Classical Tripos Part I, 1st Cl., 1912, Theological Tripos Pt. II, 1st Cl., 1913, Camb. Univ.; B.A. (Cantab.) 1912; M.A. 1916; B.D. (Edin.), 1917; D.D. (hon. causa); St. Andrews, 1928; Edin., 1947; Belfast, 1953; Dublin, 1954. Recognised Teacher, Queen's Univ. Belfast, 1927-. Moderator of Irish Presbyterian Church, 1953-54. *Publications:* Charles Davey, D.D., a Memoir, 1921; Our Faith in God, 1922; The Changing Vesture of the Faith, 1923; The Story of a Hundred Years, 1940; The Jesus of St. John, 1958; various articles. *Recreations:* music, golf. *Address:* 3 College Park, Belfast, Northern Ireland. *T.:* Belfast 26791.
[*Died* 17 *Dec.* 1960.

DAVEY, William Kendall, C.B.E. 1954; *b.* 30 May 1887; *s.* of Richard and Ann Davey; *m.* 1912, Elsie Gann; one *s.* *Educ.:* Merton Court, Sidcup. Business life spent in Metal Industry. Member, London Metal Exchange (Committee 27 years, Vice-Chm. 10 years, Chm. 4 years). F.I.Arb. *Recreation:* cricket. *Address:* The Rosary, Parkside, Cheam, Surrey. *T.:* Vigilant 5909.
[*Died* 27 *June* 1968.

DAVID, Sir Edgeworth (Beresford), K.B.E. 1961; C.M.G. 1954; *b.* 12 June 1908. *Educ.:* St. Edmund's School, Canterbury; Jesus College, Cambridge. Cadet, F.M.S., 1931; Private Sec. to Chief Secretary, 1934; Assistant District Officer, Bukit Mertajam, 1936; Dist. Officer, Pekan, 1938; Sec. to British Resident, Pahang, 1941; Principal Assistant Secretary, Federal Secretariat, 1946; Asst. Malayan Establishment Officer, 1948; Deputy Chief Secretary, Malaya, 1950; Secretary for Defence and Internal Security, 1951; seconded to Colonial Office, 1953; Colonial Secretary, Hong Kong, 1955; seconded as Chief Secretary, Singapore, 1958; Administrator, E. Africa High Commn., 1959; retd., 1962. *Address:* 17 Talbot House, 98 St. Martin's Lane, W.C.2. *Clubs:* East India and Sports, Oxford and Cambridge.
[*Died* 15 *May* 1965.

DAVID, Sir Percival Victor, 2nd Bart., *cr.* 1911; Chairman, Sassoon, J. David and Co., Ltd., Bombay; *b.* 21 July 1892; *s.* of 1st Bt. and Hannah (*d.* 1921) *d.* of Elias David Sassoon; *S.* father, 1926; *m.* 1st, 1913, *c.* Vere Mozelle (marriage dissolved, 1953), *d.* of Aubrey David; one *d.*; 2nd, 1953, Sheila Jane Yorke, *d.* of late Arthur Yorke Hardy, Curator. *Educ.:* Elphinstone College; Bombay University, B.A. D.Lit. London Univ. Officer of the Légion d'Honneur; F.S.A., F.R.A.I., F.R.S.A.; F.R.P.S.L.; Hon. Adviser, 1928-29, National Palace Museums (Peiping); Governor of School of Oriental and African Studies, Univ. of London; Director, International Exhibition of Chinese Art, 1935-36. Donor of Collection in Percival David Foundation of Chinese Art, Univ. of London. *Publications:* in various journals on subjects dealing with Chinese and Japanese art, philately, etc.; Chinese Connoisseurship (posthumous). *Heir:* none. *Address:* 53 Gordon Square, W.C.1. *Clubs:* Athenæum, Royal Societies, White's.
[*Died* 9 *Oct.* 1964 (*ext.*).

DAVIDGE, William Robert, F.R.I.B.A., F.R.I.C.S., Assoc.M.Inst.C.E., M.T.P.I.; Architect and Town Planning Consultant, retired; *s.* of late Henry Thomas Davidge; *m.* 1st, Kathleen (*d.* 1939), *d.* of late John Lane; three *d.*; 2nd, Anne Elphinstone, *y. d.* of late William Kirby. Formerly Housing Commissioner, Ministry of Health for London and Southern Counties; Past President and Member of Council of T.P.I.; Member of Council of The London Society. *Publications:* Regional Planning Reports for West Kent, East Sussex, Berkshire, Hertfordshire, Buckinghamshire, Cambridgeshire, Bedfordshire, etc.; papers for Professional Societies. *Address:* 11 Cambray Court, Cheltenham, Glos.
[*Died* 23 *Dec.* 1961.

DAVIDSON, 1st Viscount, *cr.* 1937, of Little Gaddesden; **John Colin Campbell Davidson,** P.C. 1928; G.C.V.O., *cr.* 1935; C.H. 1923; C.B. 1919; President Hispanic and Luso-Brazilian Councils; President Anglo-Argentine Society; Patron Maida Vale Hospital for Nervous Diseases; *o. s.* of late Sir James Mackenzie Davidson, M.B., C.M.; *b.* Aberdeen, 23 Feb. 1889; *m.* 1919, Frances Joan, Baroness (Life Peeress), *y. d.* of 1st Baron Dickinson, P.C., K.B.E.; two *s.* two *d.* *Educ.:* Westminster; Pembroke College, Cambridge. Called to Bar, Middle Temple, 1913; Private Sec. to Lord Crewe, Sec. of State for Colonies, 1910; to Rt. Hon. L. Harcourt, 1910-15; to Rt. Hon. A. Bonar Law, 1915-16; to Chancellor of Exchequer and Leader of House of Commons, 1916-20; M.P. (U.) Hemel Hempstead Div. of Herts., Nov. 1920-Dec. 1923, and 1924-37; P.P.S. to Leader of House of Commons, Nov. 1920-March 1921; to Rt. Hon. S. Baldwin, Pres. Bd. of Trade, 1921-22; to Mr. Bonar Law, 1922-23; Chancellor, Duchy of Lancaster, 1923-24; Parlty. Sec. to Admiralty, Nov. 1924-27; Chm. Unionist Party, 1927-1930; Chancellor, Duchy of Lancaster, 1931-1937; Hon. Adviser, Commercial Relations, 1940, and Controller of Production, M.O.I., 1941; official tour of S. America, 1942. Chm. Indian States Inquiry Cttee., 1932; Investigator Distressed Areas (W. Cumberland), 1934; Chm. Ordnance Survey Interdeptl. Cttee., 1935; Chm., Goodwill Trade Mission to Iraq, Syria, Lebanon and Cyprus, 1946. Dominican Grand Cross Order of Merit of Duarte, Sanchez and Mella, 1957; Grand Cross, La Orden El Sol, Peru, 1960; Grand Cross, Order of Merit, El Orden de Mayo al merito, Argentina, 1960; Grand Cross, Order Al Merito, Chile. *Recreations:* gardening, motoring, and travel. *Heir:* *s.* Hon. John Andrew Davidson [*b.* 22 Dec. 1928; *m.* 1956, Margaret Birgitta, *o. d.* of Maj.-Gen. C. H. Norton, *q.v.*; four *d.* (including twin *d.*)]. *Address:* Said House, Chiswick Mall, Chiswick, W.4. *T.:* Chiswick 8111 and Chiswick 4342. *Club:* United University.
[*Died* 11 *Dec.* 1970.

DAVIDSON, Maj.-Gen. Alexander Elliott, C.B. 1938; D.S.O. 1916; *b.* 1880; *s.* of late Col. John Davidson, C.B., Indian Army, Mentone and Blackheath; *m.* 1912, Janie (*d.* 1961), *d.* of late Charles MacCall, Blackheath. *Educ.:* Blackheath School;

Royal Military Academy, Woolwich. 1st Commission in Royal Engineers, 1899; Captain, 1908; Major, 1916; Lt.-Col. 1925; Col. 1927; Maj.-Gen., 1936; served South African War (medal with 3 clasps); Secretary Mechanical Transport Committee, War Office, 1910-14; served European War, 1914-18 (despatches, D.S.O., Bt. Lt.-Col.); Chief Inspector R.E. Stores, 1920-24; Deputy Assistant Director of Fortification and Works, 1924-25; Chairman Technical Committee, Mechanical Warfare Board, 1927-31; Assistant Director of Works, War Office, 1931-35; A.D.C. to the King, 1935-1936; Director of Mechanization, War Office, 1936; retired pay, 1940. President, Inst. Mechanical Engineers, 1935; President Diesel Engine Users Assoc., 1950; Col.-Comdt. R.E., 1940. Hon. M.I.Mech.E., M.I.Mar.E. *Address:* 11 The Pryors, Hampstead, N.W.3. *Clubs:* United Service, London Rowing. [*Died* 29 *Jan.* 1962.

DAVIDSON, Sir Andrew, Kt., *cr.* 1946; M.D., F.R.C.P.Ed., F.R.C.S.Ed.; D.P.H., F.R.S.E.; Chairman Advisory Committee on Medical Research in Scotland since 1954; LL.D.; Chief Medical Officer, Dept. of Health for Scotland, 1941-54; *b.* 12 Mar. 1892; *e. s.* of late Charles Davidson, Dalmuir, Dunbartonshire; *m.* 1922, Helen Edith, *e. d.* of late Rev. George Calder, D.D., D.Litt.; two *s*. *Educ.:* Allan Glen's School; University, Glasgow (Hon. LL.D., 1954). Capt. R.A.M.C., 1916-19; Assistant to Regius Professor of Physiology, Glasgow University, 1920-21; Divisional M.O.H., Glasgow, 1921-28; Deputy County M.O.H. and School M.O. Surrey, 1928-36; County M.O.H. and School M.O. Yorkshire (North Riding), 1936-41; K.H.P. 1944-47. Retd. 1954. *Publications:* various in medical and public health journals. *Recreation:* golf. *Address:* Netherby, Stanley, Perthshire. *T.:* Stanley 243. *Club:* New (Edinburgh). [*Died* 13 *March* 1962.

DAVIDSON, Andrew Hope, M.D., F.R.C.P.I., F.R.C.O.G., L.M. (Rotunda); Ex-Master Rotunda Hospital, Dublin; Senior Consulting Obstetrician and Gynæcologist, Rotunda Hospital; Gynæcologist Sir Patrick Dun's Hospital since 1948; Professor of Obstetrics and Gynæcology, Royal College of Surgeons in Ireland since 1926; King's Professor of Midwifery, Trinity College, Dublin; *b.* 29 May 1895; *s.* of John Alexander and Emily Elizabeth Davidson; *m.* 1934, Maureen, *o. d.* of late Dr. Austin Cooper, one *s*. *Educ.:* Academy, Omagh; High School, Dublin; Trinity College, Dublin. M.B., B.Ch., B.A.O., B.A.; Lt. R.A.M.C. Egyptian Expeditionary Force Palestine and Syria, 1917-19; Ext. Maternity Assistant and Assistant Master Rotunda Hospital, 1919-22; travelled in Germany and Austria to medical clinics, 1922; Gynæcologist to Dr. Steevens Hospital, 1924-33; to Royal City of Dublin Hosp., 1940-48. *Publications:* 3 years' work in the Gynæcological Dept. of a General Hospital; Cæsarean Section: Its History and present status; Hysterectomy: a Critical Survey with Report of 200 cases; A Survey of Puerperal Sepsis, etc.; Articles in Butterworth's Medical Encyclopædia. *Recreations:* tennis, golf, squash rackets, hockey, bridge, medical cinematograph films. *Address:* (professional) 44 Fitzwilliam Place, Dublin. *T.:* Dublin 61762; (home) Heidelberg, 17 Ardilea, Dublin 14. *Clubs:* St. Stephen's Green, Fitzwilliam Lawn Tennis (Dublin); Portmarnock Golf (Portmarnock). [*Died* 12 *Feb.* 1967.

DAVIDSON, Professor Charles Findlay, O.B.E. 1953; F.R.S.E.; M.I.M.M.; Professor of Geology, University of St. Andrews, since 1955; *b.* 16 July 1911; *s.* of John Davidson, Monifieth, Scotland; *m.* 1938, Helen McLean Wallace; four *s*. *Educ.:* Morgan Academy, Dundee; University of St. Andrews (B.Sc. 1st Cl. Hons. 1933; D.Sc. 1942). Served with H.M. Geological Survey, 1934-55. In charge of military geology, 1939-42. Chief Geologist to British atomic energy organisations, 1942-1955. F.R.S.E. 1935; F.G.S. London, 1934, S. Africa, 1955, America, 1958, Norway, 1960; Fellow Min. Soc. Amer., 1949; Councillor, Min. Soc., 1942-44 and 1952-54, Roy. Soc. Edin. 1960-66 (Vice-President 1964-1966); M.I.M.M., 1955; Member American Geophys. Un., 1960; Membre Correspondant, Soc. Géol. Belgique, 1958; Hon. Assoc .Editor Economic Geology, 1953-; Vice-Pres. for Europe, Soc. of Economic Geologists, 1955-56, 1957-58; Counsellor for Europe, Internat. Assoc. on Genesis of Ore Deposits, 1967. Distinguished Visiting Lecturer, American Geological Institute, 1963. Lyell Medal, Geol. Soc. Lond., 1965. *Publications:* many papers in scientific jls., principally on geology of mineral deposits. *Recreation:* travel. *Address:* Gowan Park, Cupar, Fife, Scotland. *T.:* Cupar 3290. *Clubs:* Caledonian; Royal and Ancient (St. Andrews). [*Died* 1 *Nov.* 1967.

DAVIDSON, Charles Rundle, F.R.S. 1931; Assistant Astronomer, retired, Royal Observatory, Greenwich; *b.* 28 Feb. 1875; *m.* 1907, Eliza Louisa, *d.* of Benjamin Robert Stanford, Hong Kong; two *s.* two *d. Publications:* Papers in the Monthly Notices and Memoirs of the Royal Astronomical Society. *Address:* 26 Bridgefoot Path, Emsworth, Hampshire. [*Died* 18 *June* 1970.

DAVIDSON, Lieut.-Col. Edward Humphrey, C.B.E. 1919; M.C.; *b.* 19 July 1886; *s.* of George Walter Davidson, 167 Queen's Gate, S.W.; *m.* 1915, Yvonne (*d.* 1955), *y. d.* of late Sir Elwin Palmer, K.C.B., K.C.M.G.; one *s.* one *d. Educ.:* Harrow; Royal Military College, Sandhurst. Joined 2nd Battalion Gordon Highlanders, India, 1906; served European War, Egypt, 1914; France and Belgium, 1915-17 (C.B.E., M.C., 1914-15 Star, Allied and G.S. medals); 3rd Class Order Rising Sun of Japan; appointed Dir. of Intelligence, Air Ministry on formation of R.A.F., 1918-19; Assistant Military Secretary to G.O.C. Egyptian Expeditionary Force, Egypt, 1919-20; retired, 1921; Private Secretary to the Governor of Victoria, 1926-30; Comptroller of the Household and Private Secretary to Governor-General of S. Africa, 1931-33. War of 1939-45, Dep. Director of Intelligence, Air Ministry (Group Captain), 1939-40 (wounded). *Club:* Brooks's. [*Died* 2 *July* 1962.

DAVIDSON, Colonel Sir Jonathan Roberts, Kt., *cr.* 1942. C.M.G. 1915; M.Sc., M.I.C.E.; *b.* 1874. *Educ.:* Victoria University, Liverpool. Served European War of 1914-18 (despatches thrice, C.M.G.); Chief Engineer, Liverpool Corporation Water Works, 1914-34; Chief Engineer, Metropolitan Water Board, 1934-39. Pres. Inst. of Civil Engineers, 1948-49. *Address:* Homefield, Tandridge Lane, Lingfield, Surrey. *Club:* Royal Automobile. [*Died* 21 *June* 1961.

DAVIDSON, Lindsay Gordon, C.B. 1957; retired as Deputy Secretary, Department of Agriculture for Scotland (1953-58); *b.* 17 Oct. 1893; *s.* of Alexander and Margaret Davidson; *m.* 1920, Elizabeth Anderson, *d.* of Tom and Jean Mudie; one *s.* one *d. Educ.:* Royal High School, Edinburgh. Entered Civil Service, Second Division, 1912. Served European War, 1914-18: France and Flanders, Royal Scots Fusiliers and King's Shropshire Light Infantry. Principal, 1938; Assistant Secretary, 1942; Under Secretary, 1952. *Recreation:* golf. *Address:* 13 Lockharton Crescent, Edinburgh 11. *T.:* Craiglockhart 1641. *Club:* Caledonian United Service (Edinburgh). [*Died* 5 *Nov.* 1965.

DAVIDSON, Dame Margaret A., D.B.E., *cr.* 1918; Dame of Grace Order St. John; W.V.S.; *b.* 21 April 1871; *y. d.* of Gen. Hon. Sir Percy and Lady Louisa Feilding; *m.* 1907, Sir Walter E. Davidson, K.C.M.G., late Governor of Newfoundland and New South Wales (*d.* 1923); one *d.* *Educ.:* at home. *Recreation:* stamp collecting. *Address:* 16 Landsown Crescent, Bath, Som. *T.:* Bath 61770.
[*Died* 14 *Oct.* 1964.

DAVIDSON, Maurice, M.A., M.D. Oxon. F.R.C.P. Lond.; Consulting Physician Brompton Hospital for Consumption and Diseases of the Chest; Consulting Physician Miller General Hospital for S.-E. London; Consulting Physician Western Ophthalmic Hospital; late Captain, R.A.M.C., Temp.; *b.* 30 Aug. 1883; *s.* of Alexander Davidson, M.A., M.D. Edin., F.R.C.P. Lond., Emeritus Professor of Pathology, University College, Liverpool, Consulting Physician to the Liverpool Royal Infirmary, and Ellen Alison, *d.* of Lloyd Rayner, Liverpool; *m.* 1913, Gretchen Lucy (*d.* 1963), *y. d.* of Rev. H. Bolton Smith, Vicar of Wymering, Hants.; two *s.* (and one *s.* one *d.* decd.). *Educ.:* Liverpool College; Trinity College, Oxford (2nd class Honours in Final School of Natural Science, Physiology); University College Hospital, London. Served European War in the R.A.M.C. with the Mediterranean Expeditionary Force (Gallipoli, Egypt, Palestine); Medical Registrar and Tutor at St. George's Hospital and subsequently became Physician to the Brompton Hospital; formerly Dean of the Brompton Hospital Medical School (5 years); F.R.S.M. (ex-Pres. Sect. of Medicine, late Hon. Ed. of Proc. Roy. Soc. Med.); late Mem. Thoracic Soc.; Hon. Fell. Royal Institute of Public Health and Hygiene; Hon. Fell. Roy. Soc. Med., 1965; Mem. Horatian Soc.; late Member Association of Physicians of Gt. Britain and Ireland; FitzPatrick Lecturer, Royal College of Physicians, 1952-53. *Publications:* Cancer of Lung and other Intrathoracic Tumours, 1930; A Practical Manual of Diseases of the Chest, 4th Ed. 1954; The Diagnosis and Treatment of Intrathoracic New Growths, 1951; Articles on Diseases of Lung in British Encyclopædia of Medical Practice, 2nd Ed.; Medicine in Oxford—A Historical Romance (FitzPatrick Lectures,) 1953; The Brompton Hospital: The Story of a Great Adventure (jointly with F. G. Rouvray); The Royal Society of Medicine (The Realization of an Ideal), 1805-1955, 1955; (Editor and Contributor) Medical Ethics (a guide to students and practitioners), 1957; Memoirs of a Golden Age, 1958; Destiny and Freewill, 1962; various contributions to Medical Journals. *Recreations:* photography, study of Gothic Church Architecture. *Address:* 32 Bickenhall Mansions, W.1. *T.:* Welbeck 8683. *Club:* United University.
[*Died* 8 *Nov.* 1967.

DAVIDSON, Sir Nigel George, Kt., *cr.* 1930; C.B.E. 1927; B.A.; *b.* 29 October 1873; *s.* of Alexander Davidson, Mugiemoss, Aberdeenshire; *m.* 1912, Iris, *y. d.* of Walter Arrol, Chapelacre, Helensburgh; one *d.* (one *s.* decd.). *Educ.:* Charterhouse; New College, Oxford (Exhibitioner). Called to Bar, Inner Temple, 1899; Member of the Oxford Circuit; Judge of the High Court, Sudan Government, 1907-16; Judicial Adviser, Iraq Government, 1921; Counsellor to the High Commissioner for Iraq, 1923-1924; Legal Secretary Sudan Government, 1926-30; Deputy Chairman Governing Body of Charterhouse School, 1948-60. Order of the Nile (3rd class), 1919 (2nd class), 1930. *Recreations:* fishing, shooting, lawn tennis, represented Oxford, 1896. *Address:* c/o Martin's Bank Ltd., Ludgate Circus, E.C.4. *Club:* Athenæum.
[*Died* 31 *Oct.* 1961.

DAVIDSON, Randall George, M.A. Clare College, Cambridge; *o. s.* of late William Davidson of Muirhouse, Midlothian, and late Charlotte, *o. c.* of John Wood of Hickstead Place, Sussex; *b.* 30 Sept. 1874; *m.* 1st, 1902, Violet Annie (*d.* 1944), *d.* of late Edwin Frend; one *s.* two *d.*; 2nd, 1946, Lydia Mary, *d.* of late F. W. Downie. *Address:* Kemps, Ditchling, Hassocks, Sussex.
[*Died* 5 *July* 1963.

DAVIE, Rt. Rev. C. J. F.; *see* Ferguson-Davie.

DAVIES, Lady; *see* Kennedy, Margaret.

DAVIES, Alice Hollingdrake; *b.* 12 Nov. 1878; *d.* of Rev. Owen Davies and Alice, *d.* of Henry Hollingdrake. *Educ.:* Liverpool, Blackheath and Truro High Schools; Royal Holloway College (Scholar). First Class Honours in the Oxford Final Honours School of English Language and Literature, 1900; Assistant Mistress at West Heath School and Clapham High School, 1901-06; Assistant Lecturer in English at Royal Holloway College and East London College (University of London) 1906-11; Headmistress of Farringtons School, Chislehurst, 1911-39. *Recreations:* reading, walking, travelling. *Address:* New Lodge, Chislehurst, Kent.
[*Died* 28 *Dec.* 1968.

DAVIES, Very Rev. Arthur Whitcliffe, M.A. (Oxon); Hon. D.Litt. (Agra); Dean of Worcester, 1934-49; Dean Emeritus since 1949; *s.* of late Theo. H. Davies, Honolulu; *m.* 1912, Lilian Mabel Birney (*d.* 1961); two *s.* one *d.* *Educ.:* Uppingham School; Univ. College, Oxford. Lecturer St. John's Coll., Agra (Church Missionary Society), 1908-28; Principal 1913-28; Canon of Lucknow, 1917-29; Kaiser-i-Hind Medal (1st class), 1921; Vice-Chancellor, Agra University, 1927; returned England, 1929; Assistant Secretary, Church Assembly Missionary Council, 1929; General Secretary, 1930-35; Hon. Canon Bradford, 1930-34; Select Preacher Oxf. Univ. 1938; Camb. Univ. 1943. *Address:* Evenlode, Cedar Road, Berkhamsted, Herts.
[*Died* 14 *Sept.* 1966.

DAVIES, Arthur William, C.B.E. 1939; late Asst. Secretary, Board of Inland Revenue; *b.* 1878; *s.* of Edwin Davies, Swansea; *m.* 1907, Elsie, *d.* of H. J. Biffen, Cheltenham; one *d.* *Educ.:* Llandovery College; Trinity College, Cambridge. *Address:* 14 Chalton Drive, N.2.
[*Died* 5 *April* 1969.

DAVIES, Cecil Bertrand, C.B.E. 1941; M.I.E.A.; *b.* 20 Nov. 1876; *e. s.* of Sir J. G. Davies; *m.* 1st, 1904, Ruby Alice (*decd.*), *d.* of F. Searl; two *s.*; 2nd, 1943, Ivy Alma, *d.* of J. Hadfield. *Educ.:* Tasmanian University; engineering course Finsbury College, London. Served 4 years Siemens Bros., London; 22 years Engineer for Tramways, Hobart; Consulting Engineer, Hobart; Managing Director Davies Brothers Ltd., Hobart, Publishers of The Mercury, 1931-46; retired, 1946. *Recreations:* golf, fishing, shooting. *Address:* 26 Clare Street, New Town Tasmania. *Club:* (President Athenæum (Hobart).
[*Died* 9 *Dec.* 1960.

DAVIES, Rt. Hon. Clement, P.C. 1947; Q.C. 1926; M.P. (L.) Montgomeryshire since 1929; Leader of Liberal Parliamentary Party, 1945-1956; Hon. Fellow, Trinity Hall, 1950; President of Parliamentary Association for World Government, 1951; Chm. and Trustee of History of Parliament Trust; Bencher of Hon. Society of Lincoln's Inn; *b.* 1884; *y. s.* of Alderman M. Davies, Llanfyllin, Mont.; *m.* 1913, Jano Elizabeth, *e. d.* of Morgan Davies, M.D., F.R.C.S.; one *s.* (and one *s.* decd. one *s.* killed in action, one *d.* killed in action). *Educ.:* Llanfyllin; Trinity Hall, Cambridge (Senior Foundation Scholar); 1st in Preliminary Law exam.; 1st class Law Tripos, Part I. 1906, Part

II. 1907; Law Studentship, Trinity Hall, Cambridge, 1907-11; Law Lecturer, Univ. College of Wales, Aberystwyth, 1908-9; called to Bar, Lincoln's Inn, 1909; prizes in Criminal Law, Constitutional and Real Property; 1st Class and Certificate of Honour in Bar Final, 1909; N. Wales Circuit, 1909-10; transferred to Northern Circuit, 1910; practised in Commercial Court, King's Bench Division and Probate and Admiralty Division; Secretary to Pres. of Probate, Divorce and Admiralty Division, 1918-19; Sec. to Master of Rolls, 1919-23; one of Junior Counsel to the Treasury, 1919-25; founder of Montgomeryshire Society in London; first Chairman of Committee, Pres. 1929-32; a Pres. of Powys Eisteddfod, 1924-39 and 1947, and Royal National Eisteddfod, 1938 and 1939; Member of the Royal Commission on the Despatch of Business at Common Law, 1934-35; Member of the Committee of Inquiry as to B.B.C., 1935; Parliamentary Charity Commissioner, 1936-37; Member of Committee on Third Party Insurance, 1936-37; Chairman of Committee on incidence of Tuberculosis in Wales, 1937-38; Member of Joint Committee of both Houses on Consolidation of Bills, 1936-39, West African Commission, 1938-39, Colonial Empire Marketing, 1937; Chairman Montgomeryshire Quarter Sessions since 1935; Chm. Advisory Committee on Greater London Planning and of the Committee on the method of carrying out the Plan for Greater London, 1945-46. Pres. Welsh Liberal Federation, 1945-1948. Pres. of the Approved Societies of Wales since 1945. Chairman Select Committee on Delegated Legislation, 1953-54; Chairman Select Cttee. on Members' Expenses, 1953-1954; Pres. Cymrodoriaeth Cadair Powys, 1955; Chairman Menorah Parl. Cttee. and presented Menorah on behalf of British Parliament to Knesset, Jerusalem, 1956. President of various literary and agricultural societies. Hon. LL.D. (University of Wales), 1955. *Publications:* Agricultural Law, 1910, 2nd ed., 1919; Finance (1909-10) Act, 1910, 1910; 3rd ed., 1911; Agricultural Holdings Act, 1912, 5th ed., 1934; Law of Auctions and Auctioneers, 1913; various articles. *Address:* Plas Dyffryn, Meifod, Mont. *T.:* Meifod 229; 31 Evelyn Mansions, S.W.1. *T.:* Victoria 8881. *Club:* Reform. [*Died* 23 *March* 1962.

DAVIES, Sir Daniel (Thomas), K.C.V.O., *cr.* 1951 (C.V.O. 1947); M.D., B.Sc. (Wales); F.R.C.P. (London); Extra Physician to the Queen (formerly Physician to King George VI; Physician to H.M. Household; Physician to T.R.H. the Duke and Duchess of York); Honorary Physician: Royal Free Hospital; Hospital of St. John and St. Elizabeth; Emergency Medical Service; London House; Hon. Consulting Physician: Hounslow Hospital, Wood Green and Southgate Hospital; Examiner in Medicine: Royal College of Physicians, Universities of Wales, Edinburgh and Liverpool; *b.* November 1899; *s.* of late Rev. D. Mardy Davies, Pontycymmer, Glam.; *m.* Vera, *o. d.* of J. Percy Clarkson, F.A.I.; two *d.* *Educ.:* Bridgend; University College, Cardiff; Middlesex Hospital. Served European War, as combatant, South Wales Borderers. Hon. Medical Consultant to the Ministry of Supply, 1941-45. Bradshaw Lecturer, R.C.P., 1935; Hunterian Orator, Hunterian Soc., 1950. F.R.S.M.; Member: Exec. Committee, British Empire Cancer Campaign; Assoc. of Physicians; British Soc. of Gastro-Enterologists. Knight Commander of the Order of St. Sylvester, 1953. *Publications:* in various medical journals. *Address:* 36 Wimpole Street, W.1. *T.:* Langham 2777. *Club:* Garrick. [*Died* 18 *May* 1966.

DAVIES, Sir David, Kt. *cr.* 1952; Q.C.; *b.* 14 Sept. 1889; *s.* of late James Davies; *m.* 1925, Margaret Kennedy, *q.v.*; one *s.* two *d.* *Educ.:* Winchester College; New College, Oxford. Home Civil Service, 1913-19; Called to Bar Nov. 1919; K.C. 1935; Q.C. 1952; Judge of County Courts, 1937-47; Commissioner, under National Insurance Acts, 1946-61. *Address:* 180 Oakwood Court, W.14. *T.:* Western 1244. *Club:* Oxford and Cambridge. [*Died* 23 *April* 1964.

DAVIES, David, C.B.E. 1944; Chairman Carmarthen Agricultural Executive Committee (formerly War Agric. Exec. Cttee.), 1939-57, Member of Milk Cttee. since 1950; *b.* 27 February 1877; *s.* of David Davies, Rhiwdywyll, Nr. Carmarthen; *m.* 1907, Sarah (*d.* 1938), *d.* of Evan Davies, Carmarthen; one *d.*; *m.* 1956, Hannah Mary, *d.* of James Jones, Llanelly. *Educ.:* Merchant Venturers School, Bristol; University College of Wales (Aberystwyth). Member of Carmarthen R.D.C., 1921-24. J.P. 1939; C.C. 1924; Chm.: Guardians Cttee., 1930-1931; Roads Cttee., 1933-34; Public Health and General Purposes Cttee., 1935-38; C.A. 1940-49; Chm. County Education Cttee., Mar. 1943-46; Chm. C.C. Mar. 1946-47, Carmarthen. Mem. St. Davids Mental Hospital Cttee., 1929-61, Vice-Chm. 1952-61; Mem. Welsh National Memorial Assoc., 1929-1947; Mem. Alltymynydd Sanatorium House Cttee., 1930-; Governor, County School, 1924- (Chm. 1957-59). *Address:* Uwch-Gwili, Richmond Terrace, Carmarthen. *T.:* 6159. [*Died* 14 *Nov.* 1966.

DAVIES, Professor David Vaughan; Professor of Anatomy, St. Thomas's Hospital Medical School; Director, Arthritis and Rheumatism Council Electron-microscopy Unit; Hon. Consultant, St. Thomas's Hospital; *b.* 28 October 1911; *s.* of Joshua Davies and Mary Emma Ryder, Cemmaes, Mont.; *m.* 1940, Ruby Bertha Ernest; two *s.* one *d.* *Educ.:* Towyn County School; University College and University College Hospital, London. Entrance Exhibitioner, Univ. College, London, 1930, Gold Medallist in Physiology, 1932; Ferriere Scholarship, Univ. Coll. Hosp., London, 1933 and 1934; M.R.C.S., L.R.C.P. (Eng.), 1935 M.B., B.S. (London), 1935; M.A. (Cantab.), 1937; D.Sc. (Lond.), 1961; F.R.C.S. (Eng.), 1963; F.Z.S. Demonstrator in Anatomy Univ. of Cambridge, 1936-39; Lectr. in Anatomy, Univ. of Cambridge, 1939-48; Fellow and Coll. Lectr., St. John's Coll., Cambridge, 1944-48; Sub-dean, St. Thomas's Hosp. Med. Sch., 1958-66; Gresham Prof. of Physic, 1965; Vis. Prof., Auckland Univ., 1966; Hon. M.O., Auckland Hosp. Bd. 1966. Fellow, University College, London, 1956. Arris and Gale Lecturer, Royal Coll. of Surgeons, Eng., 1945; Examiner in Anatomy for Univs. of London, Oxford, Cambridge, St. Andrews, Strathclyde, Khartoum, Melbourne. Member: Coun., Anatomical Soc. (Pres., 1965-67); Cymmrodorion Soc.; London Welsh Assoc.; Heberden Soc.; Hon. Mem. Anatomische Gesellschaft; Governor, St. Thomas's Hospital., 1963-69; President, Montgomeryshire Soc., 1964-65. Editor Jl. of Anatomy, 1960-64. High Sheriff, Montgomeryshire, 1961-62. *Publications:* (Ed.) Gray's Anatomy; Anatomy for Nurses (Joint Author) Synovial Joints; various anatomical and physiological papers relating to joints, teratology, embryology and comparative anatomy. *Recreations:* gardening, shooting. *Address:* 66 Cole Park Road, Twickenham, Middlesex. *T.:* 01-892 1123; Ambleside, Inkpen Common, Berkshire. [*Died* 16 *July* 1969.

DAVIES, Sir (Edward) John, Kt. 1958; Chief Justice of Tanganyika, 1955-60, retired; *b.* 20 Feb. 1898; *s.* of late Dan Davies and of Mary Elizabeth David *m.* 1931, Ada Alberta Carlota de Rodriguez. *Educ.:* Llandovery College and University of Wales. Served European War, 1915-18. Called to Bar, Lincoln's Inn, 1922; practised in London and South Wales Circuit, 1922-27: Crown Counsel. Kenya. 1927;

Senior Crown Counsel, Gold Coast, 1933; Solicitor-General, Trinidad, 1935; Deputy Legal Adviser, F.M.S., 1938; Solicitor-General, Singapore, 1941. Interned at Singapore, 1942-45. Attorney-General, Singapore, 1946-55; member Executive Council and Legislative Council, Singapore; Q.C. (Singapore), 1948. *Recreations:* golf, fishing. *Address:* 20 Howley Place, W.2. *T.:* Paddington 4858. [*Died* 5 *Oct.* 1969.

DAVIES, Eric J. W.; *see* Warlow-Davies.

DAVIES, Evan Thomas, F.R.C.O.; Hon. R.C.M.; Emeritus Director of Music, University College of North Wales, Bangor; Conductor, Adjudicator, Composer, Organist; *b.* Merthyr Tydfil, 10 April 1878; *e. s.* of George and Gwenllian Davies; *m.* 1916, Mary Llewelyn, *y. d.* of D. Williams Jones, J.P. Aberdare, Glam. *Educ.:* privately. Toured U.S.A. as pianist and organist; organist and choirmaster, Christchurch Cyfarthfa, Merthyr Tydfil, 1900-3, Pontmorlais Church, 1903-17; first full-time Director of Music, University College of North Wales, 1920-43, Director Emeritus 1943. Vice-Pres. Welsh Folk Song Society. Member Incorporated Society of Musicians since 1900. Adjudicator: Royal Nat. Eisteddfod fairly regularly, 1915-56, Llangollen International Eisteddfod, 1949-54, many English and Irish Competition Festivals, Canadian Festivals, 1931. Conductor: Royal National Eisteddfod Concerts, 1928 and 1931; Harlech, Caernarvon, Conway, and Anglesey Festivals. Sometime Chief Examiner in Music, Central Welsh Board, and first examiner for School and Higher Certificates; Examiner, Glamorgan County Music Scholarships; Frequent Broadcast Talks. Contributor and Joint Editor, Welsh Methodist Hymnal, 1929; contributor, Church of Wales Hymnal, 1950; Welsh Baptist Hymnal, 1954. Joint arranger and Ed., National Songs of Wales, 1959. *Publications:* Eighteen pianoforte works (1912 onwards); chamber music founded on Welsh Folk Melody; songs, choral works, and about 100 vocal and instrumental arrangements of Folk tunes. Ed. Welsh versions of Bach's St. Matthew Passion, two cantatas and 20 chorales. Various works commissioned by B.B.C. Articles, reviews and commentaries in Welsh Outlook, Y Cerddor, Welsh Folk-Song Journal, and other periodicals. *Recreations:* reading, listening. *Address:* 4 Plasdraw Road, Aberdare, Glam. *T.:* Aberdare 2941. [*Died* 25 *Dec.* 1969.

DAVIES, Francis, D.Sc., M.D., B.S. (London); M.R.C.S., L.R.C.P., F.R.S.E., F.R.C.S., F.R.M.S.; Professor of Anatomy, University of Sheffield, 1935-62, retd. (Emeritus, 1962); Dean of the Faculty of Medicine, Univ. of Sheffield, 1946-47; *b.* 15 Dec. 1897; *s.* of Richard and Ruth Davies; *m.* Gwladys Evelyn, 4th *d.* of David H. and Catherine Thomas, Merthyr Tydfil. *Educ.:* University College, Cardiff; University College Hospital, London. House Physician, Univ. Coll. Hosp. London, 1923; Senior Demonstrator in Anatomy, University College, London, 1924-1930; Reader in Anatomy, King's College, London, 1930-35; Symington Prize for Research in Anatomy, 1932; Hunterian Professor, R.C.S., 1941-42; Arris and Gale Lecturer, R.C.S., 1944-45; Vice-Pres. Anatomical Society of Great Britain and Ireland, 1942-43; Examiner in Anatomy, Universities of Aberdeen, Glasgow, Manchester, Cambridge, Leeds, Sheffield; Battalion Medical Officer, Home Guard (with rank of Major), 1941-42. *Publications:* (Part-editor) Gray's Anatomy, 32nd (centenary) edn. and 33rd edn.; publications of Research, in medical journals. *Recreation:* motoring. *Address:* Glen Usk, 11 Port Rd. West, Barry, Glamorgan, S. Wales. [*Died* 15 *March* 1965.

DAVIES, Hugh Morriston, M.A., M.D., M.Ch. (Cantab.), F.R.C.S.; Ch.M. (Liverpool) Hon.; Hon. LL.D. Wales; Consulting Surgeon, University College Hospital and City of London Hospital for Diseases of the Heart and Lungs; Emeritus Consulting Surgeon, King Edward VII. Welsh National Memorial Association; Consultant to the Royal Navy; Regional Civilian Consultant in Thoracic Surgery to the Royal Air Force; late Clinical Lecturer in Thoracic Surgery, University of Liverpool; late Consultant Adviser in Thoracic Surgery to Liverpool Regional Hospital Board; late Medical Supt. Vale of Clwyd Sanatorium; Dean and Teacher of Practical Surgery, University College Hospital Med. School; Weber-Parkes Prize, 1954; *b.* 1879; *m.* Dorothy, *d.* of late W. L. Courtney, M.A., LL.D.; two *d.* *Educ.:* Winchester College; Trinity College, Cambridge; University College Hospital and Medical School. Surgical Registrar, University College Hospital, 1909; Assistant Surgeon, 1909; Surgeon, 1915. *Publications:* Various papers on surgical subjects, especially in connection with the Surgery of the Chest. *Recreation:* gardening. *Address:* Pen-y-Llwyn, Llanarmon-yn-ial, Denbs. N. Wales. [*Died* 4 *Feb.* 1965.

DAVIES, James H. W.; *see* Wootton-Davies.

DAVIES, Sir John; *see* Davies, Sir E. J.

DAVIES, Very Rev. John Thomas; *b.* 27 Jan. 1881; *e. s.* of Thomas and Elizabeth Davies, of Baileycoch and Sarn Helen, Carmarthenshire; *m.* 1919, Gwenonwy, *e. d.* of late Rt. Rev. John Owen, D.D., Bishop of St. Davids; three *s.* three *d.* *Educ.:* St. Davids College; Jesus College, Oxford. Ordained 1905; Curacies, Talgarth, Brecons., 1905-7, St. Michael's, Aberystwyth, 1907-12; Diocesan Inspector and Minor Canon, St. Davids Cathedral, 1912-20; Vicar of St. Paul's, Llanelly, 1920-37; Vicar of Carmarthen, 1937-41; Examining Chaplain to Bishop of St. Davids, 1919-41; to Archbishop of Wales, 1941; Dean of Bangor, N. Wales, 1941-55; retired; Mem. of Governing and Representative Bodies of the Church in Wales and of the Electoral College. *Recreations:* gardening, delight in an occasional but rather infrequent day's trout fishing. *Address:* Llys Madoc, Llanfairfechan, Caerns. [*Died* 16 *Feb.* 1966.

DAVIES, Joshua David, Q.C. 1939; retired as Stipendiary Magistrate; *b.* 11 Feb. 1889; *o. s.* of Rev. Joshua Davies (*decd.*), late Vicar of Llanllwni, Carmarthenshire; *m.* 1934, Caroline Sybil Amphlett Lewis; one *s.* one *d.* *Educ.:* Llandovery School; St. John's College, Oxford. Called to Bar, Inner Temple, 1919. Recorder of Swansea, 1942-44; Stipendiary Magistrate, N. Glamorgan, 1944-1961. *Recreations:* fishing, shooting. *Address:* Fron, Maesycrugiau, Carms. *Club:* Oxford and Cambridge. [*Died* 3 *Jan.* 1966.

DAVIES, Maj.-Gen. Llewelyn A. E. P.; *see* Price-Davies.

DAVIES, Vice-Admiral Richard Bell, V.C. 1916; C.B. 1939; D.S.O. 1915; *s.* of late William Bell Davies, Croxley Grove, Rickmansworth; *m.* 1920, Mary, *d.* of late Major-General Sir R. A. Kerr Montgomery, K.C.M.G., C.B., D.S.O.; one *s.* one *d.* Served European War, 1914-18 (D.S.O.); Dardanelles, 1915 (despatches twice, V.C., Chevalier Legion of Honour, Croix de Guerre with Palm); in charge of the Air Section of the Naval Staff, 1920-24; Commander H.M.S. Royal Sovereign, Atlantic Fleet, 1924-26; Captain, 1926; Naval Air Section of the Naval Staff at the Admiralty, 1926-28; Flag Captain and Chief Staff Officer to Rear-

Admiral commanding 1st Cruiser Squadron, 1928-30; Liaison Officer for Fleet Air Arm at Air Ministry, 1931-33; commanded H.M.S. Cornwall, 1933-35; R.N. Barracks, Devonport, 1936-38; Rear-Admiral, 1938; Rear-Admiral, Naval Air Stations, 1939-40; retired 1941. *Address:* Dormers, Lee-on-Solent. [*Died* 26 *Feb.* 1966.

DAVIES, Richard Humphrey, C.B., 1913; hon. M.A. (Wales), 1948; *b.* 27 June 1872; *s.* of Richard Davies, Harpenden; *m.* 1907, Mary Elizabeth (*d.* 1960), *d.* of late Humphrey Evans, Ruthin; one *s.* *Educ.:* Medburn Street, London; privately, Private Secretary to Lord Gladstone when chief Opposition Whip, 1899-1905; Private Secretary to Patronage Secretary, Treasury, 1905-16; Clerk to Parliamentary Recruiting Committee, 1914-16; Secretary, Liberal Central Association, 1917-26; Private Secretary to Principal, University College of North Wales, Bangor, 1927-40; Hon. Secretary, Museum of Welsh Antiquities, University Coll. of North Wales, Bangor, 1929-48. *Address:* Wych Cross, Keston, Kent. *T.:* Farnborough, Kent 53212. [*Died* 16 *June* 1970.

DAVIES, Sir Robert (John), Kt. 1961; O.B.E.; solicitor; company director; *b.* 1900; *s.* of John and Anne Davies; *m.* Edith Mary Hayes. *Educ.:* St. George's, Llandudno. Director: Catlin's (North Wales) Ltd.; Catlin's Scarborough Entertainments Ltd.; Llandudno Constitutional Club Ltd.; Llandudno Estates Co. Ltd.; St. George's Hotel, Llandudno, Ltd. and Principality Broadcasts Ltd. Member of Law Society; Member, Solicitors' Benevolent Association; Member, Chester and North Wales Incorporated Law Soc. Chm. Wales and Monmouthshire Conservative and Unionist Assoc., 1958-63, Pres., 1964; Vice-Chm., Nat. Union of Conservative and Unionist Assocs., 1963-. *Recreation:* gardening. *Address:* Trinity Sq., Llandudno, Caerns. *T.:* Llandudno 76271; Sea Breeze, Brynybia Rd., Llandudno, Caerns. *T.:* Llandudno 49346. [*Died* 25 *Feb.* 1967.

DAVIES, Robert (Malcolm Deryck); M.P. (Lab.) Cambridge since 1966; Alderman, Cambridge City Council, since 1964 (City Council, 1954-); *b.* 7 May 1918; *s.* of late Rhys Wilshire Davies, O.B.E., Surveyor, and late Nora Davies; *m.* 1941, Katharine Mary, *d.* of late Rev. Sidney H. Wing, and of Florence Mary Wing; no *c.* *Educ.:* Reading Sch.; London Univ.; Oxford University. Secretary, Univ. of Cambridge Dept. of Applied Economics, 1949-66. Contested (Lab.): Cambridge, 1959, 1964; Cambridgeshire, March 1961. *Recreation:* camping. *Address:* 43 Beaumont Road, Cambridge. *T.:* Cambridge 46456. [*Died* 16 *June* 1967.

DAVIES, Venerable Samuel Morris; Archdeacon of Monmouth, 1940-54; Rector of Penhow with St. Brides, Netherwent, Monmouthshire, 1943-53; of Llandevaud, 1951, Llanvaches, 1948-53; *b.* 1879; *s.* of John Euston and Hannah Davies; *m.* 1911, Ruby Ermyne Rees (*d.* 1962); two *d.* *Educ.:* Privately; Sidney Sussex College, Cambridge (B.A. 1901, M.A. 1905); Wells Theological College. Curate of Corsham, Wilts, 1903-11; Private Chaplain to the Right Hon. Lord Islington, Hartham, Wilts, 1911-13; Rector of Machen, Mon., 1913-1918; Rector of Rogiet, 1919-29; Rural Dean of Netherwent, 1924-29; Vicar of Rumney, 1929-43; Canon of Monmouth, 1935-40. *Address:* Martin's Mead, Shillingstone, Dorset. [*Died* 10 *April* 1963.

DAVIES, Rt. Rev. Stephen Harris, M.A.; *b.* 1883; *s.* of late Rev. J. B. Davies and Susan Anslow; *m.* 1930, (Joan) Edith Nicol, *yr. d.* of late F. F. Cronin, Victoria, Australia; one *s.* *Educ.:* St. John's School, Leatherhead; Hereford Cathedral School; Emmanuel College, Cambridge. Curate St. Matthew's Church, Holbeck, Leeds; Member Charleville Bush Brotherhood, Queensland, 1912-21 (Head, 1917-21); Bishop of Carpentaria, 1922-49. *Address:* 61 Abbotsford Road, Homebush, N.S.W., Australia. [*Died* 29 *Nov.* 1961.

DAVIES, Sydney John, C.B.E. 1959; D.Sc. (Eng.), Ph.D. (Lond.); M.Sc. (Dunelm.); M.I.Mech.E.; Whitworth Exhibitioner; Chm.: Plint and Partners Ltd., engineers, Wokingham; British Internal Combustion Engines Research Inst. Ltd. (B.I.C.E.R.L.); Dean of the R.M.C. of Science, Shrivenham, 1954-62; Prof. of Mechanical Engineering at Univ. of London, King's Coll., 1937-55; *b.* 17 Mar. 1891; *m.* Ida May, *d.* of late H. Owen Davies, Tynemouth; one *s.* *Educ.:* H.M. Dockyard Sch., Portsmouth; Portsmouth Tech. Coll. Inspector of Aircraft Engines, R.A.F. and Air Ministry, 1915-19; Assistant Works Manager, The Clyno Engineering Co., Wolverhampton, 1919-20; Lecturer in Engineering, Armstrong College (University of Durham), Newcastle upon Tyne, 1920-26; Reader in Mechanical Engineering, King's College, London, 1926-36; Member of Court and Senate, Univ. of London, 1949-55. F.K.C. 1951. Chm. Automobile Div. and Member Council Inst.Mech.E., 1953-54. Pres. Whitworth Soc., 1953-54. Pres. J. Inst.E., 1954-55. *Publications:* Heat Pumps and Thermal Compressors, 1949; papers in jls. of various British and foreign engineering socs. *Address:* Mavis Cottage, Wargrave-on-Thames, Berks. *Club:* St. Stephen's. [*Died* 25 *July* 1967.

DAVIES, Dr. William, C.B.E. 1964; D.Sc.; *b.* London, 20 April 1899; *e. s.* of William Davies and Margaret Griffiths; *m.* 1928, Alice Muriel Lewis; one *s.* *Educ.:* Sloane School, Chelsea; Univ. Coll. of Wales. B.Sc. 1923, M.Sc. 1925, D.Sc. 1945. Grassland Agronomist, Welsh Plant Breeding Stn., 1923-28; Plant Geneticist, Palmerston North, N.Z., 1929-31; Empire Grassland Investigator, Empire Marketing Bd., London, 1931-33; Hd. of Dept., Grassland Agronomy, Welsh Plant Breeding Stn., 1933-38; Head of Grassland Survey of England, 1938-40; Asst. Director (to late Sir George Stapledon) of Grassland Improvement Stn., Stratford-on-Avon, 1940-1945, Director, 1945-49; Director, The Grassland Research Inst., Hurley, 1949-64, retd. Director, Hydraumatic Seeding, 1964-67; President, British Grassland Society, 1948 and 1960; Hon. Fellow, Royal Agricultural Society of England, 1963; Hon. Fellow British Grassland Society, 1963; Hon. Life Pres., European Grassland Fedn., 1963. President, Sect. M. (Agric.), British Association for the Advancement of Science, 1960; Hon. Life Mem.: Grassland Soc. Southern Africa, 1966; Spanish Grassland Soc., 1966. Conjecero de Honor (Spain), 1964. Hon. Mem., The Scientific Agric. Soc., Finland, 1968. Hon. D.Sc. New Zealand, 1956. *Publications:* Grasslands of Wales, 1937; Grasslands of the Falkland Islands, 1938; The Grass Crop, 2nd edn., 1960; (Jt. Ed.) Tropical Pastures, 1965; The Hills of Britain, 1969; (with C. L. Skidmore) Pasture Science, 1969; numerous works of scientific nature. *Address:* 51 Gravel Hill, Henley-on-Thames. *T.:* Henley 2966. *Club:* Farmers'. [*Died* 28 *July* 1968.

DAVIES, William John Abbott, O.B.E. 1919; *b.* 21 June 1890; *m.* Margaret Bleecker, *er. d.* of late Major E. G. Waymouth, Royal Artillery, and Mrs. E. G. Waymouth, one *s.* one *d.* *Educ.:* Pembroke Dock Grammar School; R.N.E.C. Keyham; Royal Naval College, Greenwich. Joined Royal Corps Naval Constructors, 1913; served

European War, 1914-18, on staff of Commander-in-Chief Grand Fleet, 1914-19; Constructor, Admiralty, 1929; on Staff of Comdr.-in-Chief, Mediterranean Fleet, 1935-1938; War of 1939-45, Asst. Dir. Warship Production, Admiralty, 1942; Director Merchant Shipbuilding and Repairs, 1949-50. Liveryman of Worshipful Company of Shipwrights, 1951. Captain of England, Royal Navy, Hampshire, and United Services Portsmouth, Rugby Football Teams, 1921, 1922, 23. *Publications:* Rugby Football, 1923; Rugby Football and How to Play it, 1933. *Address:* 109 Cambridge Road, Teddington, Middlesex. *T.:* Teddington Lock 1434. *Club:* United Sports. [*Died* 26 *April* 1967.

DAVIS, Sir Ernest, Kt., *cr.* 1937; Managing Director of Hancock & Co. Ltd., Auckland; *b.* Nelson, N.Z., 17 Feb. 1872; *s.* of late Moss Davis, Auckland, N.Z.; *m.* Marion, *d.* of W. Mitchell, Wellington, N.Z.; one *d.* (one *s.* decd.). *Educ.:* Bishop's School, Nelson; Auckland Grammar School. Mayor of Auckland, 1935-41; Chevalier Legion of Honour, 1938. *Address:* 14 Waterloo Quadrant, Auckland, C.1, New Zealand. [*Died* 16 *Sept.* 1962.

DAVIS, Sir Godfrey, Kt., *cr.* 1941; formerly Chief Judge, Chief Court, Sind; *b.* 23 Oct. 1890; *m.* 1922, Bessie Annie (*d.* 1955), *d.* of late David Ziman, Reefton, New Zealand; two *d.* *Educ.:* University College School; University College, London. Entered Indian Civil Service, 1914. *Address:* 26 Hillway, Holly Lodge Estate, Highgate, N.6; Beresfords, Boughton Monchelsea, Kent. [*Died* 7 *Aug.* 1968.

DAVIS, Herbert John, F.B.A. 1954; M.A., LL.D.; Litt.D.; Reader in Textual Criticism at Oxford University, 1949, Professor, 1956-60, retd.; *b.* 24 May 1893; *s.* of Carter Davis and Martha Ann Sheldon; *m.* 1st, 1922, Gertrud Lucas (*d.* 1928); 2nd, 1930, Gladys Wookey; two *d.* *Educ.:* Oxford. B.A. (Oxon) Hon. School English Language and Literature; M.A. 1919. Served in British Army, 1916-19, gunner R.G.A., later Lt. 301st Battery, B.E.F. Lecturer in English at Leeds, 1920; Assoc. Prof. Univ. Coll., Toronto, 1922-24; Guest Prof. Cologne, 1924-25; Assoc. Prof. Univ. Coll., Toronto, 1925-35; Prof., Univ. Coll., Toronto, 1935-1937; Chm. Dept. of English at Cornell, 1938-40, and Goldwin Smith Prof. of English Lit., 1939-40; President of Smith College, 1940-49. Frederick Ives Carpenter Visiting Professor, Univ. of Chicago, 1937; Vis. Prof., Univ. of Toronto and Columbia Univ., N.Y., 1957; Vis. Prof. Univ. of Minnesota, 1960-1961; Fellowship at Huntington Library, San Marino, California, 1963-64; Visiting Professor, Stanford University, 1964; Brown University, 1964; Folger Library, 1965; Sen. Fell., Clark Lib., Calif., 1966; Member American Academy of Arts and Sciences, 1948. Joint Editor, Oxford Bibliographical Society, 1951-60; General Editor, Oxford English Novels, 1964. Hon. Member, Modern Language Association of America, 1964. President, Malone Society, 1965. Hon. degrees: LL.D.: Amherst, 1940; Queen's, Kingston, Ontario, 1945; Smith, 1949; B.C., 1957; Litt.D., Mount Holyoke, 1949. *Publications:* Swift's View of Poetry, 1931; Challenge to the Intellect, 1941; Stella, A Gentlewoman of the 18th Century, 1942; Satire of Jonathan Swift, 1946; Jonathan Swift, Essays and Studies, 1964; Editor: The Drapier's Letters by Jonathan Swift, 1935; Complete Prose Works of Jonathan Swift (14 vols. 1938-63); Complete Poems of Pope, 1966; Complete Plays of Congreve, 1967; Co-editor, Mechanick Exercises in Printing by Joseph Moxon, 1958; contributions to literary jls. *Address:* Townsend Close, Iffley, Oxford. *T.:* Oxford 78061. *Clubs:* Grolier, Century (New York). [*Died* 28 *March* 1967.

DAVIS, John King, C.B.E. 1964; F.R.G.S.; *b.* London, 1884. *Educ.:* Burford Gram. Sch.; Colet Court. Chief Officer, Nimrod, on Sir Ernest Shackleton's Antarctic Expedition, 1907; Master of Aurora, Australasian Antarctic Expedition, 1911-14; commanded the Ross Sea Relief Expedition of 1916; Murchison Award (1915) of R.G.S. for oceanographical work; Second in Command of the British, Australian, New Zealand, Antarctic Research Expedition, and Master of the Discovery, 1929-30. Director of Navigation for the Commonwealth of Australia, until 1949. *Publications:* With the Aurora in the Antarctic, 1920; Willis Island, a Storm Warning Station in the Coral Sea, 1923; High Latitude: Memoirs of an Antarctic Navigator, 1962. *Recreations:* English literature and the history of deep water ships. *Club:* Melbourne (Melb.). [*Died* 7 *May* 1967.

DAVIS, Rt. Rev. Nathaniel William Newnham; Assistant Bishop of Chichester since 1966; *b.* 17 July 1903; *s.* of William Herbert Davis, M.B.; *m.* 1948, Mary Margaret Coleman, *d.* of late Prebendary Cook, Wells, Somerset. *Educ.:* Harrow School; Merton College, Oxford; Cuddesdon College B.A. 1924; M.A. 1929; Deacon, 1926; Priest, 1927; Curate of Church of Holy Spirit, Beeston Hill, 1926-30; Rector of St. Anne, Sandy Point, St. Kitts, 1931-44; Archdeacon of St. Kitts, 1941-44; Bishop of Antigua, 1944-52; resigned, 1952; Asst. Bishop of Coventry and Rector of Ladbroke, 1952-59; Warden of United Westminster Almshouses, 1959-66; Asst. Bp., dio. London, 1961-66. *Address:* 102 Marine Court, St. Leonards-on-Sea, Sussex. [*Died* 28 *July* 1966.

DAVIS, Sir Robert Henry, Kt., *cr.* 1932; Hon. D.Sc. (Birmingham), 1951; Chairman of Siebe, Gorman and Co., Ltd., whose service he entered, 1882, until 1960, retd.; *b.* London. 6 June 1870; *e. s.* of Robert Davis; *m.* 1900. Margaret (*d.* 1952), 3rd *d.* of William Tyrrell, Kildare; four *s.* two *d.* Inventor of many devices and appliances relating to deep diving, submarine escape, breathing apparatus for use in irrespirable atmosphere, etc.; served on Admiralty Deep Diving Committee. F.R.S.A. (Thomas Gray lectures, 1934). *Publications:* Deep Diving and Submarine Operations; Diving Manual; Breathing in Irrespirable Atmospheres, and at High Altitudes, and Resuscitation; A Brief Personal Record of Siebe, Gorman & Co., 1819. 1957; A few Recollections of an old Lambeth Factory and its Vicinity, etc. *Address:* 19 Randall's Road, Leatherhead, Surrey. [*Died* 29 *March* 1965.

DAVIS, Rushworth Kennard, M.A.; *b.* 2 Mar. 1883; *s.* of late S. Kennard Davis, formerly Underwriter to the London Assurance; *m.* 1909, Maude Agnes (*d.* 1967), *d.* of late J. A. Mack, The Grinstead, Partridge Green, Sussex; two *s.* two *d.* *Educ.:* Bilton Grange Sch.; Rugby Sch. (scholar); Balliol College, Oxford (scholar). Assistant Master, Marlborough College, 1907-13; Headmaster, Woodbridge School, Suffolk, 1914-21; Private, Inns of Court O.T.C., 1918; Headmaster, Birkenhead School, 1921-30; Headmaster of Magdalen College School, Oxford, 1930-44. *Publications:* Translations from Catullus, 1913; The Agamemnon of Æschylus, 1919; Peleus and Thetis, 1924; Diagnosis, a Poem, 1946; Poems, 1967. *Address:* Hafod Bach, Eglwysfach, Machynlleth, Montgomeryshire. *T.:* Glandyfi 215. [*Died* 20 *Jan.* 1969.

DAVISON, Professor Archibald Thompson, Hon.D.Mus.; F.R.C.M.; A.M.; Ph.D.; James Edward Ditson Professor of Music, Harvard University, Cambridge, Mass., U.S.A., 1929-June 1954, Professor Emeritus, 1954; Curator Emeritus, Isham Memorial

Library; *b.* 11 Oct. 1883; *s.* of Archibald Thompson Davison and Lucy Kelley; *m.* 1st, 1926, Dorothy Stanley Starratt (*d.* 1944); 2nd, 1946, Alice Elizabeth Pratt; no *c.* *Educ.:* Boston Latin School; Harvard Univ. Studied organ and composition with Charles Widor in Paris. Harvard Univ.: A.B. 1906, A.M. 1907, Ph.D. 1908; Austin Teaching Fellow of Music, 1909. F.R.C.M. 1931; Hon. Doctor of Music: Williams Coll., 1933; Oxford Univ., 1934; Harvard Univ., 1948. Hon. Doctor of Letters: Washington Univ., 1953; Hon. Doctor of Humane Letters, Temple Univ., 1955. *Publications:* Music Education in America, 1926; Protestant Church Music, 1933; Choral Conducting, 1940; The Technique of Choral Composition, 1945; (with W. Apel) Historical Anthology of Music (2 vols.) Vol. 1, 1946, Vol. 2, 1950; Bach and Handel: Consummation of the Baroque, 1951; Church Music and Reality, 1952. *Address:* (winter) Lexington Road, Lincoln, Mass., U.S.A. *T.:* Clearwater 9-8230; (summer) Brant Rock, Mass., U.S.A. *T.:* Marshfield, Temple 4-8962.
[*Died* 8 *Feb.* 1961.

DAVISON, Professor John Armstrong, T.D. 1944; Professor of Greek Language and Literature, University of Leeds, since 1951; *b.* 23 Sept. 1906; *s.* of H. E. Davison, M.D.; *m.* 1939, Marjorie Richardson, *d.* of H. R. Flower; no *c.* *Educ.:* Haileybury College; Corpus Christi College, Oxford (M.A.). Assistant Lecturer in Greek and Latin, University of Manchester, 1929; Lecturer, 1935; Senior Lecturer, 1950; Secretary, Faculty of Arts, 1946-49; Visiting Professor of Classics, Victoria College, Toronto, 1949-50; Dean of the Faculty of Arts, Leeds Univ., 1953-55; Mem. of the Bd. of Governors of St. Peter's School, York, 1954-. Visiting Prof. of Greek, Trinity Coll., Toronto, 1959-60; Visiting Prof. Tübingen Univ., 1963 and 1965. Churchwarden, St. Michael's Headingley, 1959-66. 2nd Lt. 4th Bn. Northumberland Fusiliers (T.A.), 1927; Lt., 1930; Capt., 1934; Major, 1939; transf. to Cheshire Regt., 1939; Military Assistant Secretary to War Cabinet and G.S.O. 2 in Office of Minister of Defence, 1943-45. U.S. Legion of Merit (Degree of Officer), 1946. *Publications:* contributor to: (Wace & Stubbings) a Companion to Homer, 1962; Encyclopaedia Britannica, (1962, 1964); articles and reviews in learned periodicals. *Address:* 76 St. Michael's Road, Leeds 6. *T.:* Leeds 55695.
[*Died* 28 *Dec.* 1966.

DAVSON, Lieut.-Col. Harry Miller, C.M.G. 1919; D.S.O. 1917; late R.F.A.; *b.* 1872; *s.* of late Sir Henry Davson; *m.* 1910, Hon. Violet St. Clair (*d.* 1957), *d.* of 15th Baron Sinclair; one *s.* *Educ.:* Westminster; R.M.A., Woolwich. Served South African War, 1899-1900 (despatches, Queen's medal and 3 clasps); European War, 1914-19 (despatches six times D.S.O., C.M.G.); retired pay, 1921. Re-employed 1939-45. *Publications:* Napoleon's Marshals; The Story of G Troop, R.H.A.; History of the 35th Division, etc. *Address:* 156 Sloane Street, S.W.1. *T.:* Sloane 3997. *Clubs:* White's, Cavalry. [*Died* 10 *Nov.* 1961.

DAW, Sydney Ernest Henry, C.M.G. 1958; C.B.E. 1953 (O.B.E. 1950; M.B.E. 1941); A.I.E.E.; Foreign Trade Consultant, formerly Counsellor (Commercial) H.M. Embassy, Vienna, from 1948 and Consul-General from 1957; *b.* 22 July 1897; *s.* of late Ernest George and Katherine Daw; *m.* 1925, Corinne Alice (*née* Wahlstad); two *s.* two *d.* *Educ.:* Lower School of John Lyon, Harrow. Served European War in Army, 1914-19: Military Inter-Allied Commission of Control, Germany, 1920-27; with Remington Rand, Germany and France, 1927-37; Home Office, 1937-38; Corpn. of London, Civil Defence, 1938-42; served War of 1939-45, Allied Force H.Q., North Africa and Italy (Lt.-Colonel), 1942-45; Allied Commission, Austria (Colonel), 1945-47. *Recreation:* fishing. *Address:* c/o Lloyds Bank, 6 Pall Mall, S.W.1. *Club:* Reform.
[*Died* 18 *June* 1963.

DAWES, Brigadier Hugh Frank, D.S.O. 1918; M.C.; *b.* 1884; *s.* of late Frank Dawes, 21 Park Crescent, W.; *m.* Adrienne Jean, *y. d.* of late Colonel W. H. Rathborne, R.E.; one *s.* killed in action, 1944. *Educ.:* Harrow School; Staff College. 2nd. Lt., Royal Fusiliers, 1906; Served European War, 1914-18 (despatches, D.S.O., M.C.); commanded 2nd Battalion Royal Fusiliers, 1932-36; A.Q.M.G. Southern Command, 1936-39; served B.E.F. France, 1939-40. *Address:* 26 Campbell Court, Queen's Gate Gardens, S.W.7. *Clubs:* United Service, Royal Automobile.
[*Died* 5 *March* 1965.

DAWNAY, Lt.-Col. Cuthbert Henry, M.C. 1917; farming; *b.* 4 Nov. 1891; *s.* of Hon. Eustace H. and Lady Evelyn de V. Dawnay; *m.* 1921, Marjorie Kathleen, *d.* of Reginald B. Loder; three *d.* *Educ.:* Eton; Trinity College, Cambridge. Served European War, 1914-18, 6th Bn. The Yorkshire Regt., 1914-19. J.P., E.R. Yorks, 1927; D.L., E.R. Yorks, 1942. Home Guard, 1940-45, Battalion Commander. High Sheriff of Yorkshire, 1949-50. *Recreations:* shooting, gardening. *Address:* West Heslerton Hall, Malton, Yorks. *T.:* West Heslerton, 202: 16 Hale House, de Vere Gardens, W.8. *T.:* Western 1394. *Clubs:* Travellers', Bath; Yorkshire (York).
[*Died* 18 *March* 1964.

DAWSON, Sir Benjamin, 1st Bt., *cr.* 1929; J.P.; *b.* Bradford, 20 September 1878; *er. s.* of Joseph Dawson, Bradford; *m.* 1906, Annie Ellen (*d.* 1959), *d.* of Lister Saville, Bradford; one *s.* one *d.* (and two *d.* decd.). *Educ.:* Bradford Grammar School. J.P. West Riding Yorks., 1924; High Sheriff of Yorkshire 1951-52. *Recreation:* yachting. *Heir:* *s.* Lawrence Saville Dawson, *b.* 15 Jan. 1908. *Address:* Nun-Appleton, York.
[*Died* 19 *Sept.* 1966.

DAWSON, Sir Bernard; *see* Dawson, Sir J. B.

DAWSON, Christopher, F.B.A. 1943; M.A.; Professor of Roman Catholic Studies, Harvard University, 1958-62, retd.; *b.* 12 Oct. 1889; *o. s.* of Lt.-Col. H. P. Dawson, Hartlington Hall, Skipton, and Mary Louisa, *e. d.* of Archdeacon Bevan, Hay Castle; *m.* 1916, Valery Mary, *y. d.* of Walter Mills one *s.* two *d.* *Educ.:* Trinity College Oxford. Lecturer in the History of Culture, Univ. Coll., Exeter, 1930-36; Forwood Lecturer in the Philosophy of Religion, Liverpool, 1934; Gifford Lecturer (Edinburgh) 1947 and 1948. *Publications:* The Age of the Gods; The Making of Europe; Progress and Religion; The Spirit of the Oxford Movement; Enquiries into Religion and Culture; Mediæval Religion; The Modern Dilemma; Christianity and the New Age; Religion and the Modern State; Beyond Politics; The Judgement of the Nations, 1943; Religion and Culture, 1948; Religion and the Rise of Western Culture, 1950; Understanding Europe, 1952; Mediæval Essays, 1954; Dynamics of World History, 1957; Movement of World Revolution, 1959; The Historic Reality of Christian Culture, 1960; The Crisis of Western Education, 1961; The Dividing of Christendom, 1965; The Formation of Christendom, 1967. *Address:* Fountain Hill House, Budleigh Salterton, Devon. [*Died* 25 *May* 1970.

DAWSON, Sir (Joseph) Bernard, K.B.E., *cr.* 1948; M.D., F.R.C.S., F.R.C.O.G.; Emeritus Professor of Obstetrics, Univ. of N.Z.; *b.* 8 April 1883; *y. s.* of Joseph Dawson,

Solihull, Warwickshire; *m.* 1909, Norah, *d.* of Richard Lunt, Edgbaston, Birmingham; two *s.* two *d.* *Educ.:* King Edward Sixth School, Birmingham; University of Birmingham; St. Bartholomew's Hospital. Past-Pres. Otago Div., B.M.A.; formerly Examiner for Univ. of N.Z., Roy. Australasian Coll. of Surgeons and R.C.O.G.; Member of Council, R.C.O.G., 1951-52. Past Pres., Otago Branch, Royal Commonwealth Soc. Served European War 1914-18, with R.A.M.C. *Publications:* The History of Medicine, 1912; Midwifery for Nurses, 1952. *Recreation:* gardening. *Address:* 14 Queen Street, Dunedin, New Zealand. *T.:* Dunedin 70.788. *Club:* Dunedin (Dunedin). [*Died* 17 *Aug.* 1965.

DAWSON, Peter; baritone vocalist; *b.* Adelaide, South Australia, 1882; *m.* 1st, 1905, Annie Mortimer, *d.* of late T. J. Noble, stage name Annette George (*d.* 1953); 2nd, 1955, Constance, sister of 1st wife; no *c.* *Educ.:* Pulteney Street Gram. Sch. Came to England 1902; studied under Sir Charles Santley; first appearance Grand Opera Covent Garden, 1909; made first gramophone record, 1904. *Publications:* (Autobiography) Fifty Years of Song, 1951; various songs under the name of J. P. McCall. *Recreations:* painting, gardening. [*Died* 26 *Sept.* 1961.

DAWSON, Warren Royal, O.B.E. 1959; F.R.S.E.; F.R.S.L.; F.S.A.; Hon. Fellow: Imperial College of Science; Medical Society of London; Linnean Society; Hon. Member, Egypt Exploration Society; Membre Associé de l'Institut d'Egypte; Hon. Librarian to the Corporation of Lloyds', 1927-48; Frazer Lecturer, Glasgow, 1936; *b.* Ealing, 13 Oct. 1888; *y. s.* of late Charles R. Dawson; *m.* 1912, Alys Helen, *e. d.* of late Sidney Wood. *Educ.:* St. Paul's School. *Publications:* English Translations of Prof. Capart's Works; Egyptian Mummies, 1924 (with Sir G. Elliot Smith, F.R.S.); The Custom of Couvade, 1929; Magician and Leech, 1929; Clio Medica: The Beginnings, 1930; The Treasures of Lloyd's, 1930; The Bridle of Pegasus, 1930; Life of T. J. Pettigrew, 1931; Marine Underwriting, 1727-42, 1931; Manuscripta Medica, 1932; The Nelson Collection at Lloyd's, 1932; The Frazer Lectures (edited), 1932; Life of Charles Wycliffe Goodwin, 1934; A Leechbook, 1934; Catalogue of Linnean Society MSS., 1934; Life of Sir Grafton Elliot Smith, 1938; The Huxley Papers, 1946; Who Was Who in Egyptology, 1951; The Banks Letters, 1958 (supplements, 1962 and 1965); numerous contribs. on Archæology, Egyptology, and the History of Science to British and foreign scientific journals; contributions to Encyclopædia Britannica. *Address:* Simpson House, Simpson, Bletchley, Bucks. [*Died* 5 *May* 1968.

DAWSON, Warrington; Commander of: French Legion of Honour; Serbian Roy. Order of St. Sava; Gold Medal of Acad. Française; Hon. Citizen of Versailles; Vice-President Société des Americanistes de Paris; contributor to Psychic News; *b.* Charleston (S.C.), 27 September 1878; *s.* of Captain Francis Warrington Dawson (Austin John Reeks), Knight of St. Gregory the Great, of London, and Sarah Fowler Morgan, New Orleans; unmarried. *Educ.:* École Paroissiale St. Thomas d'Aquin, Paris; College of Charleston. Founder and 1st Director, French Bureau United Press of America, 1900-10; War Correspondent in Russia, 1904; Sec.-General of the Assoc. of Foreign Newspaper Correspondents in Paris, 1905-8; Private Secretary to ex-President Theodore Roosevelt in Kenya Colony, 1909; Attaché to U.S. Consulate at Rouen, Jan.-Feb. 1915, in connection with Enemy Prisoners' Camps; Confidential Adviser to the American Ambassador in Paris, 1915-19; engaged on confidential mission work in British, French, and American Army Zones, 1915-18 (seriously injured); Special Attaché, Amer. Embassy Paris, 1917-37; confidential report work; 1937-40 and 1946-(. . . in enemy hands in surveyed diplomatic residence, 1940-44); Deleg. of Amer. Embassy in Paris to Inter-Allied Propaganda Conf. at Paris F.O., March 1918; founder and Chief of Press Bureau of Amer. Embassy in Paris, 1917-26; Dir. French Research Bureau for the Reconstruction of Williamsburg, Colonial Capital of Virginia and Seat of the Royal Governors, undertaken by John D. Rockefeller, jun., 1928-32. *Publications:* The Scar, 1906; The Scourge; Le Nègre aux États Unis; The True Dimension; The Gift of Paul Clermont; The Pyramid; Adventure in the Night (Preface by Joseph Conrad); Les Aventures de Buz et Fury; The Guardian Demons; Et s'il était innocent . . . ?; Le Rapt de la Vierge, 1960; Le Linceul rouge-sang, 1961. Beaumains and other French plays produced in Paris and Versailles, 1936-40; edited with Biographical Introduction, A Confederate Girl's Diary, by Sarah Morgan Dawson; The Speeches of Ambassador Wallace; The War Memoirs of William Graves Sharp, American Ambassador to France, 1914-19; Marthe Richard the Skylark, by Major Georges Ladoux, former Chief of the French Intelligence Service; The Kaiser's Blonde Spy, *idem.* Ed. with Introd. (his father's) Reminiscences of Confederate Service 1861-1865, by Capt. F. W. Dawson. *Address:* 2 Rue de la Paroisse, Versailles (S. et O.), France. [*Died Sept.* 1962.

DAY, Sir (Albert) Cecil, Kt., *cr.* 1932; C.M.G. 1925; C.B.E. 1919; Commander Order of St. John of Jerusalem, 1935; *b.* 9 November 1885; *m.* Clara Katherine (*d.* 1951), *d.* of late William Fisher, Glos. *Educ.:* Northleach Grammar School; privately. Assistant Private Secretary to Governor of New Zealand, 1910-12; Official Secretary to Governors-General of New Zealand, 1912-36; New Zealand Liaison Officer in London for Foreign Affairs, 1936-52; attached to New Zealand Delegations to League of Nations Assembly 1936, Imperial Conference 1937, and United Nations first General Assembly, 1946. *Recreation:* golf. *Address:* 128 Queen's Gate, S.W.7. [*Died* 1 *Jan.* 1963.

DAY, Vice-Adm. Sir Archibald, K.B.E., *cr.* 1954 (C.B.E. 1943); C.B. 1951; D.S.O. 1946; retired; *b.* 19 July 1899; *s.* of late Donald D. Day, F.R.C.S., and Henrietta S. Blaxland; *m.* 1929, Eunice Cassellah Pitt; one *s.* two *d.* *Educ.:* H.M.S. Conway; R.N.C., Dartmouth. During European War saw service in H.M.S. Lowestoft, Britannia, and Courageous as cadet and midshipman, and in the destroyer H.M.S. Welland in Mediterranean as a sub-lieut.; at the end of the war and on completion of courses which included two terms at Cambridge University specialised in Hydrographic surveying; served in H.M.S. Endeavour, Fitzroy, Iroquois, Ormonde, Scott, and at Admty.; Comdr. 1934; Capt. 1940; on the staff of the Flag Officer Commanding Dover, 1939-43; Fleet Hydrographic Officer, E. Indies, 1944-46; Assistant Hydrographer, Admiralty, Whitehall, and in comd. of H.M.S. Dalrymple; Rear-Adm 1949; Flag Officer Commanding British Naval Forces in Germany and Chief British Naval Representative in the Allied Control Commission, 1949-50; Hydrographer of the Navy, 1950-55. Vice-Adm. 1953; retd. 1955. Hydrographic Survey, Lake Nyasa, 1955-56; Co-ordinator of Operations for International Geophysical Year, 1957-58; Acting Conservator, River Mersey, 1961-70; Chairman, Dover Harbour Board, 1965. Hereditary Freeman of City of Norwich, 1920. *Publication:* The Admiralty Hydrographic Service, 1795-1919, 1967. *Address:* 106 Bridge Street, Wye, Ashford, Kent. [*Died* 17 *July* 1970.

DAY, Sir Cecil; *see* Day, Sir A. C.

DAY, Edward Victor Grace, C.M.G. 1952; Malayan Civil Service, retired; *b.* 28 April 1896; *o. s.* of late Victor Grace Day, C.B.E.; *m.* 1939, Dorothy (*d.* 1959), *e. d.* of Captain G. H. Norman, J.P. *Educ.:* Christ's College, Christchurch; Timaru High School, New Zealand. Capt. 2/10 Gurkha Rifles, 1918-21; Malayan Civil Service, 1921-51; Resident Commissioner, Malacca, 1946-47; British Adviser, Kedah, 1947-51. Col., General List, 1943-46. *Recreation:* tennis. *Address:* 2 Valerian, West Parade, Bexhill-on-Sea, Sussex. *T.:* Bexhill 6232.
[*Died* 23 *June* 1968.

DAY, John (Adam); Chairman, Devon County Council, since 1965; Member, Economic Planning Council for the South West, since 1965; *b.* 6 July 1901; *s. s.* of late Herbert Allen Day and Isabella Maud, *d.* of Francis Black, Edinburgh, Publishers; *m.* 1932, Kathleen Emily, *y. d.* of late Harry Hebditch, J.P., The Close, Martock, Somerset; one *s.* one *d.* *Educ.:* Bedales School. Contested (L.) Bury St. Edmunds Div., 1924, Thornbury Div., Gloucester, 1929, Tavistock Div., Devon, 1931, 1935. Elected member of Devon County Council, 1932; County Magistrate for Devon, 1938; County Alderman for Devon, 1947; High Sheriff of Devon, 1949-50. Served War of 1939-45, in Royal Air Force, 1940-44, Flight Lieut.; Deputy Asst. Provost Marshal in charge of Cornwall; invalided out, 1944. Chm. Devon County Children's Cttee., 1948-55; Vice-Chm. Devon Educ. Cttee., 1947-55; Chm. South West Devon Divisional Executive, 1947-48; Chm. Torquay Division Conservative Assoc., 1961-63; Chm. Devon Community Council, 1962; Vice-Chm., Devon C.C., 1955-65 (Chm., Fin. Cttee., 1956-65). Hereditary Freeman of City of Norwich. *Recreations:* yacht racing (Winner Duke of Edinburgh's Cup and Dragon Yacht's National Championship, 1952) and shooting. *Address:* 15 Hertford Street, W.1. *T.:* Grosvenor 5073; Horsford, Middle Warberry Road, Torquay. *T.:* Torquay 3371. *Clubs:* Reform; Exeter and County (Exeter); Royal Torbay Yacht (Torquay).
[*Died* 7 *June* 1966.

DAYNES, His Honour John Norman; Judge of County Courts, 1945-57, retired; Commissioner of Divorce; *b.* 1884; *s.* of late J. W. C. Daynes and Ellen Marion Dawson, Brundall, Norfolk. *Educ.:* Norwich School; Magdalen College, Oxford, M.A., B.C.L. Oxon, 1909 (1st Class Classical Mods., 1st Class Lit. Hum., 1st Class Jurisprudence); Eldon Law Scholar, 1909; Council of Legal Educ. Studentship, 1909; Barstow Law Scholar, 1910. Called to Bar, Lincoln's Inn, 1910; Q.C. 1931; Bencher, Lincoln's Inn, 1935 (Treasurer, 1956); Chm. Central Appeal Tribunal under Coal Act, 1938; Dep. Chm. Norfolk Quarter Sessions, 1939-59; served European War, 1914-18, with R.A.O.C. (in England and France) as private, N.C.O., and ultimately as Lieut. Director of Cement (Ministry of Works), 1942-44. Liveryman of City of London, 1922 (Prime Warden Dyers' Company, 1945-1947); Chairman of St. Mark's Hospital, E.C.1, 1939-48; Vice-Chm. Hammersmith, W. London and St. Mark's Hospitals, 1948-1960; Governor of Norwich School, 1944 (Chairman, 1954); President Old Norvicensian Club, 1947; Pres. Norfolk Branch Oxford Society, 1959; Chairman Bar Library Cttee., 1959. *Publications:* a Short History of the Worshipful Company of Dyers; contributed to Halsbury's Laws of England (Vol. XXI of 1st Edition, Vol. XXIV of 2nd Edition and Vol. XXVIII of 3rd Edition). *Recreations:* billiards, golf, and walking. *Address:* Brundall, Norfolk; 8 Avenue Mansions, N.W.3. *Clubs:* Athenæum, United University, Beefsteak, Eighty; Norfolk (Norwich).
[*Died* 1 *June* 1966.

DEACON, Gerald J. C., *see* Cole-Deacon.

DEALTRY, Lawrence Percival, M.A.; Secretary, Incorporated Association of Preparatory Schools, since 1958; *b.* 8 June 1896; *s.* of P. S. Dealtry, Hoylake, and Marguerettal *d.* of Sir Edward Lawrence, Liverpool; *m.* 1st, 1923, Isabel Rayner (*d.* 1960), two *s.*; 2nd, 1961, Barbara Vise. *Educ.*: Charterhouse; University College, Oxford. R.E. (Territorials), 1914-18, Captain (despatches). Headmaster, Leas School, Hoylake, Cheshire, 1925-44; J.P. Cheshire, 1939-47. Incorp. Association of Prep. Schools: Asst. Sec., 1947-52, Treas. 1952-57. Governor Grey Coat Foundation, 1950-; Schools Broadcasting Council, 1952-57. *Publications:* Teaching of Mathematics, 1945. Jt. Editor, Preparatory Schoolboy and his Education, 1952. *Recreation:* gardening. *Address:* 31 Melbury Court, W.8. *T.:* Western 2072; No. 2, The Village, Moulsford, Berks. *T.:* Cholsey 273. *Clubs:* Bath; Royal Liverpool Golf (Hoylake).
[*Died* 23 *Oct.* 1963.

DEAN, Hon. Sir Arthur, Kt. 1960; Judge Supreme Court of Victoria, Australia, 1949-1965; Chancellor, University of Melbourne, 1954-56; *b.* 25 May 1893; *s.* of J. H. Dean; *m.* 1922, Dorothy M. Bolle; two *d.* *Educ.:* Scotch Coll., Melbourne; Univ. of Melbourne (LL.M.). Hon. LL.D. Melbourne and W. Aust. A.I.F., 1915-19 (active service). Admitted to Victorian Bar, 1919; K.C., 1944. *Publications:* Law of Auctioneers and Estate Agents, 1925; Hire Purchase Law in Australia, 1938; A Multitude of Counsellors: a History of the Bar of Victoria, 1968. *Recreation:* bowls. *Address:* 6 Wilks Avenue, Malvern, Victoria, Australia. *T.:* 50.6798. *Club:* Australian (Melbourne).
[*Died* 25 *Sept.* 1970.

DEAN, Arthur, C.B.E. 1961; retired; *b,* 2 May 1903; *s.* of Walter and Mary Dean, Halifax, Yorks.; *m.* 1st, 1927, Gladys May Bentley; one *s.*; 2nd, 1959, Marion Edith Pollock. *Educ.:* Halifax; City and Guilds Engrg. Coll., Univ. of London. Southern Railway: Civil Engrg. Asst., 1925; Divisional Engr., 1939; Maintenance Engr., 1942; Asst. Chief Civil Engr., 1946; British Railways: Chief Civil Engr., N.E. Region, 1951; Gen. Man., N.E. Region, 1962-66; Chm., N.E. Railway Bd., 1963-66. *Recreations:* gardening, travel. *Address:* Whitewalls, Strensall, York.
[*Died* 14 *Aug.* 1968.

DEAN, Arthur Edis, C.B.E. 1944; M.A., M.Litt. (Dunelm); Order of the Nile, 3rd class, 1920; Warden of Goldsmiths' Coll. (University of London), New Cross, S.E., 1927-50; *b.* Newcastle on Tyne, 8 June 1883; *s.* of Frederick and Margaret Dean; *m.* 1913, Elsie Georgina, *d.* of late W. Musgrave Wood, Leeds; three *s.* *Educ.:* Crossley School, Halifax; Armstrong College, University of Durham. Assistant Master at Preparatory School and at Harvey Grammar School, Folkestone; Assistant Lecturer in Education at Armstrong College; W.E.A. tutor at West Stanley, 1912-13; Professor of Education, University College, Exeter, 1913-19; Lecturer in Methods of Teaching, Army School of Education, Oxford, 1918-19; Inspector under Kent Education Committee, 1919-27; Joint Secretary, Council of Principals of Training Colleges, 1929-33, Chairman, 1940 and 1941; President of Training College Association, 1934; first Chairman, Association of Teachers in Colleges and Departments of Education, 1943; President, 1946-54; ex-Member National Advisory Council, Training and Supply of Teachers; Hon. Liveryman Goldsmiths' Company; Freeman of City of London. *Publications:*

Articles in educational periodicals; part author, The Forge (History of Goldsmiths' College). *Recreations:* dramatic work and walking. *Address:* 38 Kidbrooke Park Road, Blackheath, S.E.3. *T.:* Greenwich 2257. [*Died* 4 *March* 1961.

DEAN, Engineer Rear-Admiral Francis Edward, C.B. 1936; R.N., retired; *b.* 1881. Engineer Capt., 1927; Eng. Rear-Admiral, 1933. On technical and administrative staff of Commander-in-Chief, Portsmouth, 1933-36; retired, 1936. *Address:* Anglesey Hotel, Alverstoke, Hants. [*Died* 1 *March* 1965.

DEAN, Gertrude Mary, C.B.E. 1938; President Blackburn Women's Conservative Association, 1945-56; War work: W.V.S. motoring for A.R.P. sitting casualties, also telephonist work; *b.* 26 Oct. 1878; *d.* of John Dean; *g.d.* of John Dean, J.P., and James Thompson, Mayor of Blackburn. *Educ.:* Blackburn High School; Neuchâtel, Switzerland. Hon. Treasurer Blackburn and Darwen Visiting Society for the Blind; Blind Persons Act Committee, Joint Finance Committee and Relief Committee for the Blind. On Magistrates' retired list, Dec. 1953-; retired from Blackburn Women's Conservative Assoc. after nearly 50 years in office; a Life Member. *Address:* 34 Billinge Ave., Blackburn. *T.:* 5068. [*Died* 10 *July* 1962.

DEAN, Henry Roy, M.A., D.M. Oxon; M.A., M.D. Cantab.; Hon. LL.D., Western Reserve Univ. and Aberdeen Univ.; Hon. D.Sc. Liverpool; F.R.C.P.; Master of Trinity Hall, Cambridge, 1929-54; Professor of Pathology, University of Cambridge, since 1922; Major, R.A.M.C. (T.); Corresp. Fellow in New York Acad. of Medicine, 1947; Hon. Fellow New Coll., 1953; *b.* 1879; *s.* of Joshua Dean, Bournemouth, and Elizabeth, *d.* of Henry MacCormac, M.D., Belfast; *m.* 1908, Irene (*d.* 1959), *d.* of Charles Arthur Wilson; one *s.* one *d.* *Educ.:* Sherborne Sch.; New Coll., Oxf.; Magdalen Coll. (Senior Demy); St. Thomas's Hospital. Research Scholar in Pharmacology of the Salters Company; Medical Registrar, Resident Assistant Physician and Demonstrator of Practical Medicine, St. Thomas's Hospital; Radcliffe Travelling Fellow, University of Oxford; Professor of Pathology and Bacteriology in the University of Sheffield; Professor of Pathology, University of Manchester; Member of Royal Commission on University of Durham, 1934; Vice-Chancellor of the University of Cambridge, 1937-38, 1938-39. Chairman, Council of Imperial Cancer Research Fund, 1941-56. *Publications:* numerous papers on Pathological and Bacteriological subjects. *Recreations:* walking, swimming. *Address:* Department of Pathology, Tennis Court Road, Cambridge. *T.:* Cambridge 58251. *Club:* Bath. [*Died* 13 *Feb.* 1961.

DEANE, Lieut.-Colonel Robert, C.B.E. 1937 (O.B.E. 1918); *b.* 13 June 1879; *s.* of late Henry Deane, Leicester, and Selina Dougherty; *m.* 1906, Honor, *d.* of Samuel McDougall, Manchester; *m.* 1926, Miriam (*d.* 1950), *d.* of Felix Timothy, London; no *c.* *Educ.:* Loughborough; Univ. College, London. South African Constabulary, S. African War; Transvaal Police; 4th Regiment South African Mounted Riflemen; South African Permanent Force (Staff) School of Musketry; Brigade Machine Gun Officer, 1st (Natal) Mounted Brigade, German South-West Africa Campaign, 1914-15; Brigade Machine Gun Officer 1st South African Infantry Brigade, Egypt and France, 1915-16; Commanded 2nd (Reserve) Battalion, South African Infantry, 1917-18 (despatches twice, M.B.E., O.B.E.); Chief of Police, St. Lucia, British West Indies, 1919-22; Deputy Inspector General of Police, Mauritius, 1923; Commissioner of Police ana Superintendent of Prisons, Mauritius, 1926; retired, 1939. Controller, Mauritius Labour Corps, 1940-42; Commandant, Mauritius Police Reserve, 1948-1950. *Address:* c/o Barclays Bank, Smith St., Durban, S. Africa. [*Died* 19 *April* 1969.

DEANS, Harris; Dramatist, Novelist, and Critic; *b.* 10 April 1886; *s.* of W. J. Deans and Kate Harris; *m.* Connie Kay (*d.* 1951); two *s.* one *d.* *Educ.:* Collegiate School, Woolwich. Served in R.F.A., 1914-17, when invalided with wounds; dramatic critic, London Opinion, 1917-39; Illustrated Sporting and Dramatic News, 1925-34; Sunday Graphic, 1921-42; Sunday Dispatch, 1942-44; The Playgoer, 1945-50; Sound, 1945-50; Sunday Dispatch, 1950-57; retired. *Publications: novels:* Business Rivals, 1913; Looking for Trouble, 1914; The Little God and Gladys, 1926; *three-act plays:* Apron Strings, 1922; Husbands are a Problem, 1922; The Rose and the Ring, 1923; The Magic Sword, 1923; Aren't Women Wonderful! 1928; The Call of Youth, 1933. *Recreation:* reading in bed. *Address:* 31 Cambrian Road, Richmond, Surrey. *T.:* Richmond 1013. *Club:* Savage. [*Died* 12 *Feb.* 1961.

DEARDEN, Harold, B.A. Cantab.; late Captain R.A.M.C., M.R.C.S. Eng., L.R.C.P. London; *b.* 13 Dec. 1883; *y. s.* of J. Dearden, Bolton, and Frances Goldsmith; *m.* 1943, Ann Verity, *e. d.* of James Gibson Watt, Doldowlod, Radnorshire; one *s.* three *d.* *Educ.:* Bromsgrove; Gonville and Caius Coll., Cambridge; France; London Hospital. F.R.S.M.; Fellow of Hunterian Society; Member of various scientific Societies; European War, Surgeon in charge Anglo-American Hospital; Medical Officer 3rd Batt. Grenadier Guards (wounded twice); Medical Officer Palace Green Hospital for Officers; Specialises in Psychological Medicine. *Publications:* The Technique of Living, 1924; The Doctor Looks at Life, 1924; A New Way with the Insane, 1923; The Science of Happiness, 1925; Exercise and the Will, 1926; A Wonderful Adventure, 1926; Medicine and Duty, 1928; The Mind of the Murderer, 1930; Such Women are Dangerous, 1933; Queer People, 1933; The Fire Raisers; Death in the Lens; A Confessor of Women, 1934; Devlish, but True; Married Life behind the Scenes; The Wind of Circumstance (an autobiography); Time and Chance (memoirs); several articles on Psychology to various journals. *Plays:* Collision; Interference; Two White Arms; The Flaming Sword; The Siren, 1933; Frail Purposes, 1933; To Kill a Cat (with R. Pertwee), 1939. *Recreations:* motoring, boxing, wrestling, reading. *Address:* Wye Cliff, Hay, Hereford. *T.:* Hay on Wye 17. [*Died* 6 *July* 1962.

DEARING, George Edmund, C.B.E. 1966 (M.B.E. 1950); J.P.; General President, National Union of Hosiery Workers, since 1963; Chairman: East Midlands Economic Planning Council, since 1965; Consultative Council of East Midlands Gas Board since 1967; *b.* 30 Dec. 1911; *s.* of George and Mary Dearing; *m.* 1937, Vera Lois Foster, Hinckley, Leicestershire; one *s.* and *d.* *Educ.:* Elementary Schools. Leicester Dist. Sec., Nat. Union of Hosiery Workers, 1945-1958; Asst. Gen. Sec., 1958-60; Gen. Sec., 1960-63. J.P., Co. Leics., 1952. Hon. M.A., Leicester Univ., 1967. *Recreation:* golf. *Address:* 9 Boyslade Road, Burbage, Hinckley, Leics. *T.:* Leicester 56791. [*Died* 23 *Feb.* 1968.

DEBENHAM, Frank, O.B.E., M.A.Cantab., D.Sc. (Hon.), Perth, W. Australia, Durham and Sydney, N.S.W.; Founder Director (1925-46) of Scott Polar Research Institute; *b.* N.S.W., 1883; *s.* of late Rev. J. W. Debenham and Edith Cleveland; *m.* 1917, Dorothy Lucy, *d.* of late J. T. Lempriere, Melbourne; one *s.* four *d.* *Educ.:* The

King's School, Parramatta; Sydney and Cambridge Univs. Geologist, Scott Antarctic Expedition, 1910-13; Major, 7th Oxford and Bucks Light Infantry, 1914-19; Fellow of Gonville and Caius College, 1919, and Lecturer in Surveying; Tutor of Gonville and Caius College, 1923-28; Reader in Geography 1928; Professor of Geography, Cambridge Univ., 1930-49. *Publications:* Reports on Maps and Surveys, Scott's last Expedition, 1920; Structure and Surface, 1929; The Polar Regions, 1929; Surveying for the Amateur, 1936; Cartographic Exercises, 1936; Astrographics, 1942; Report on the water resources of Central Africa, 1948; Study of an African Swamp, 1952; In the Antarctic, 1952; Kalahari Sand, 1953; The Way to Ilala; Nyasaland, Land of the Lake, 1955; Seven Centuries of Debenhams, 1957; The World is Round, 1958; Antarctica, The Story of a Continent, 1959; Simple Surveying for Farmers, 1959; Discovery and Exploration; Navigation with Alice, 1961; also other papers; formerly Editor, The Polar Record. *Recreation:* gardening. *Address:* Herne Lodge, St. Eligius St., Cambridge. *T.:* Cambridge 54069.
[*Died* 23 *Nov.* 1965.

DEBENHAM, Sir Piers Kenrick, 2nd Bt., *cr.* 1931; *b.* 28 July 1904; *e. s.* of Sir Ernest Ridley Debenham, 1st Bt., and Cecily (*d.* 1950), *d.* of late Rt. Hon. William Kenrick, P.C.; *S.* father 1952; *m.* 1928, Angela Sibell, *d.* of Sir Richard Paget, 2nd Bt.; two *d.* *Educ.:* Eton; Trinity College, Cambridge (B.A.). Served on staff of Economic Advisory Council, 1930-39. (Asst. Sec., 1934-1939); War Cabinet Office, Economic Section, 1939-41; Training Bn., Coldstream Guards, 1941-43; C.C.G. (Dep. Chief, Finance Div.), 1945-47. C.C. Dorset, 1953-. *Heir:* *b.* Gilbert Ridley, *b.* 28 June 1906. *Address:* Blackdown House, Briantspuddle, Dorset. *Club:* Brooks's. [*Died* 14 *Sept.* 1964.

DE BERNOCHI, Francesco; inventor of wireless iconograph and Radiotelestampa; *b.* 1887; *s.* of Cesare and Giustina Sorisio; *m.* 1920, Maria Gariglio; one *s.* Assistente ordinario alla cattedra di Elettrotecnica del Politecnico di Torino; Capo della Sezione Alta Tensione dell' Istituto Elettrotecnico Nazionale Galileo Ferraris di Torino. *Address:* Via Cassini 71, Torino, Italia.
[*Died* 20 *May* 1962.

de BLANK, Most Rev. Joost; Canon of Westminster since 1964; Asst. Bishop, Dio. Southwark, since 1966; Chairman, the Greater London Conciliation Committee since 1966; *b.* 14 Nov. 1908; *y. s.* of Joost de Blank and Louisa Johanna (*née* Quispel), Rotterdam, Holland; unmarried. *Educ.:* Merchant Taylors' Sch.; Queens' Coll., Camb.; Ridley Hall, Cambridge. Deacon, 1931; priest, 1932. B.A., 1930, M.A., 1933. Assistant Curate: Walcot Parish, Bath, 1931-34, Bredon Parish, Worcs., 1934-37. Vicar: Emmanuel, Forest Gate, 1937-41, St. John the Baptist, Greenhill, Harrow, 1948-52; Suffragan Bishop of Stepney, 1952-57; Archbishop of Cape Town, 1957-63, resigned. Chaplain to Forces, 1940-46, Middle East, 1941-44; Senior Chaplain, 1944 (wounded); Commandant Royal Army Chaplains' Dept., Reception Centre and Depot, 1945-46. Assistant Gen. Secretary, Student Christan Mvt., 1946-48. Chaplain sub Prelate Order of St. John in Jerusalem, 1953. Select Preacher; University of Cambridge, 1956 and 1965; University of Oxford, 1964. D.D. Lambeth, 1957. Hon. Fellow, Queens' College, Cambridge, 1961. D.D. Trinity College, Hartford, 1961, Huron College, Ontario, 1963. *Publications:* Is it Nothing to You?, 1953; The Parish in Action, 1954; Saints at Sixty Miles an Hour, 1955; Call of Duty, 1956; Members of Christ, 1956; Uncomfortable Words, 1958; This is Conversion, 1958; A Working Faith, 1960; Out of Africa, 1964. *Recreation:* travel. *Address:* 1 Little Cloister, Westminster Abbey, S.W.1.
[*Died* 1 *Jan.* 1968.

de BRETT, Hon. Brig.-Gen. Harry Simonds, C.B. 1920; C.M.G. 1917; D.S.O. 1898; late R.A.; *b.* 20 Sept. 1870; *s.* of late Major-Gen. Harry de Brett, I.A.; *m.* 1901, Alice Maud (*d.* 1945), 2nd *d.* of late Arthur Davies; one *s.* one *d.* *Educ.:* Clifton; R.M.A., Woolwich. Entered army, 1889; Capt. 1899; Major, 1909; Lt.-Col. 1916; Col. 1919; N.-W. Frontier Campaign with Tochi Field Force, 1897-98 (D.S.O., medal with clasp); S. Africa, 1899-1900 (medal, three clasps); China Expeditionary Force, 1900-1 (medal); operations in Somaliland, 1909-10 (medal with clasp); European War, 1914-18 (despatches, Bt. Lt.-Col., C.M.G., Bt. Col.); Commanded an Air Defence Brigade, 1922-23; Woolwich Garrison and R.A. Depôt, 1923-27; retired pay, 1927. *Address:* Chelveshayes, Clyst Hydon, Cullompton, Devon. [*Died* 25 *Sept.* 1965.

DEBYE, Professor Peter Joseph William; Professor Emeritus of Chemistry, Cornell University, U.S.A., 1950 (Professor, 1940-50); *b.* Maastricht, Holland, 24 March 1884; *m.* 1913, Mathilda Alberer; one *s.* one *d.*; U.S. Citizen since 1946. *Educ.:* Preparatory School, Maastricht; Technische Hochschule, Aachen; Univ. of Munich, Degree in Electrical Engineering, Aachen, 1905; Ph.D. in Physics, Munich, 1908. Asst. in Aachen, 1904-06; Asst. in Munich, 1906-1911; Privatdozent, Munich, 1910-11; Professor of: theoretical Physics, Univ. of Zürich, Switzerland, 1911-12; theoretical Physics, Univ. of Utrecht, Holland, 1912-13; theoretical and experimental Physics, Univ. of Göttingen, Germany, 1913-20; Experimental Physics, Eidgenössische Technische Hochschule, Switzerland, 1920-27; Experimental Physics, Univ. of Leipzig, Germany, 1927-34; Theoretical Physics, Univ. of Berlin, Germany, and Director of Max Planck Institute, Berlin, 1934-39; Doctor Todd Prof. of Chemistry and Head of Chemistry Dept., Cornell Univ., Ithaca, New York, 1940-50; Prof. of Chemistry, Cornell Univ. (resigned as Head of Department), 1950. Extended lecture engagements, during foregoing years, in various Univs. and Insts. of Technology, the Univs. being both in U.S. and in Europe, including Oxford and Cambridge. Member of Academies and Societies all over the world including Royal Institution of Great Britain, and Royal Society, London. Rumford, Lorentz, Franklin, Faraday, Max Planck and Willard Gibbs medals; Nobel Prize in Chemistry (Sweden), 1936; Kendall Award (U.S.), 1957; Nichols Award (U.S.), 1961; Priestley Award, 1963; American Physics Society High-Polymer Physics Prize, 1964; Madison Marshall Award, U.S., 1965; National Medal of Science, 1965, etc. Holds honorary doctorates at Universities in United States and on the Continent, also from Oxford Univ. Comdr., Order of Leopold II, Belgium, 1956. *Publications:* Molecular Structure, etc. Editor of Physikalische Zeitschrift, 1915-40. *Address:* 104 Highgate Road, Ithaca, New York, U.S.A.
[*Died* 2 *Nov.* 1966.

de CAPELL BROOKE, Sir Edward Geoffrey, 6th Bt., *cr.* 1803; C.B.E. 1920 (O.B.E. 1918); *b.* 31 Jan. 1880; 2nd *s.* of Sir Richard Lewis de Capell Brooke, 4th Bt.; *S.* to Baronetcy of brother, Baron Brooke of Oakley, 1944. *Educ.:* Radley; Merton College, Oxford B.A. *Address:* Woodford, Kettering, Northants. *Club:* Travellers'.
[*Died* 6 *Oct.* 1968 (*ext.*).

DECHAMPS, Jules, D. ès L. et Ph.; Grand Officier de l'Ordre de Léopold; Grand Officier de l'Ordre de la Couronne; Chevalier de la Légion d'Honneur; Professor of

French Language and Literature in the University of London (Queen Mary College) 1930-53; Emeritus Professor since 1953; Fellow of Queen Mary College, 1956; *b.* 28 July 1888; *s.* of Pierre Joseph **Dechamps and Honorine Corbier;** *m.* 1917, Veerle Van den Weghe; two *s.* *Educ.:* Athénée Royal of Huy; State University of Liége. Professeur à l'Athénée de jeunes filles de Gand et à l'École normale moyenne, 1911-14; Professeur à l'Institut Français du Royaume Uni, 1917-19; Lecturer, 1917, and Head of the Dept of French Language and Literature, 1924, at East London College, University of London. Late External Examiner for Degrees to Universities of Aberdeen, Glasgow, Leeds, Cambridge, Liverpool, Nottingham and London. Representative in Gt. Britain of Belgian Ministry of Education; Formerly President, The Belgian Institute; Associate member of the Royal Academy of Sciences, Letters and Fine Arts, of Belgium; member Editorial Board of French Studies. *Publications:* numerous papers in Belgian, French and English learned periodicals; Sainte-Beuve et le sillage de Napoléon, 1922; Stendhal et l'Espagne, 1926; Sur la légende de Napoléon, 1931; Chateaubriand en Angleterre, 1934; Benjamin Franklin, 1935; William Hazlitt et Napoléon, 1939; Les Iles Britanniques et la Révolution française, 1949; Les meilleures pages d'Hubert Krains, avec introduction, 1959; Amitiés stendhaliennes en Belgique, 1963. *Recreations:* shooting and travelling. *Address:* Le Prieuré, 2 Rue Pascal Dubois, Amay, Belgium.
[*Died* 2 *Sept.* 1968.

de CRESPIGNY, Air Vice-Marshal Hugh V. C.; *see* Champion de Crespigny.

DEEDES, General Sir Charles Parker, K.C.B. 1935 (C.B. 1919); C.M.G. 1916; D.S.O. 1902; Col. of The King's Own Yorkshire Light Infantry, 1927-47; *b.* 9 Aug. 1879; *s.* of late Rev. Philip Deedes of Little Parndon, Essex; *m.* 1906, Eve Mary, *d.* of late Captain Stanley T. Dean-Pitt, C.B., Royal Navy; one *s.* one *d.* *Educ.:* Winchester College; Royal Military College, Sandhurst. Entered Army, 1899; graduated at the Staff College, Camberley, 1910-11; served South Africa, 1901-02 (despatches, Queen's medal five clasps, D.S.O.); European War, 1914-18 (despatches, Brevet Major, Lieut.-Col. and Colonel, C.B., C.M.G., Legion of Honour, Croix de Guerre, Order of the Crown, Belgium, Distinguished Service Medal, U.S.A.); Col. Commandant 3rd Infantry Brigade, 1926-27; Major-Gen. 1927; Commander 53rd (Welsh) Division T.A., 1928-30; Director of Personal Services, War Office, 1930-33; Lieut.-General, 1933; Military Secretary to Secretary of State for War, 1934-1937; General, 1937; retd. pay, 1937; lately a Commissioner, Royal Hospital, Chelsea; Commander Essex and Suffolk Home Guard, 1940-43. *Address:* Sherwood, Budleigh Salterton, Devon. *Clubs:* United Service, M.C.C., Free Foresters, I Zingari.
[*Died* 9 *March* 1969.

DEEDES, John Gordon, C.M.G. 1948; O.B.E. 1942 (M.B.E. 1918); Brig. (retd.); late Royal Corps of Signals; *b.* 22 March 1892; *s.* of late Gordon Frederic Deedes and of Hon. Alice Fanny Catherine Deedes; *m.* 1st, 1916, Christine Noel (*d.* 1940), *d.* of late Major P. F. Durham, late 10th Hussars, Wingfield, Christchurch, Hants; one *s.*; 2nd, 1942, Louise Ingram, *d.* of late W. J. Crockett, Henderson, Kentucky, U.S.A. *Educ.:* Repton. Served European War, 1914-18, with R.E. Signals, T.F. (M.B.E.); joined R.C.S. as Capt., 1920; retired as Major, 1933. Served War of 1939-1945; rejoined R.C.S., 1939; Dep. Dir. of Signals, W.O., 1943-44; retd. with rank of Brig., 1944; Telecommunications Attaché, British Embassy, Washington, D.C., U.S.A., 1945-47. Officer, American Legion of Merit, 1944. *Recreations:* farming, gardening. *Address:* c/o Barclays Bank (D.C. & O.) Ltd., Bulawayo, Southern Rhodesia. *Clubs:* Farmers'; Bulawayo (Bulawayo).
[*Died* 4 *May* 1962.

DEELEY, Sir Anthony M. M., Bt.; *see* Mallaby-Deeley.

DE FONSEKA, Sir (Deepal) Susanta, Kt. 1954; Ambassador for Ceylon in Japan, since 1955 (Minister, 1953-55); *b.* 25 April 1900; *m.* 1924, Jane Salgado; one *d.* *Educ.:* Downing Coll., Cambridge Univ. M.A., LL.B. Barrister-at-Law, Middle Temple. Chairman, Panadura Urban Council, 1929-30; Member State Council, Ceylon, 1931-47; Deputy Speaker, State Council, Ceylon, 1936-1947; Minister for Ceylon in Burma, 1949-1953. *Recreation:* walking. *Address:* Ceylonese Embassy, Box 1017, Tokyo, Japan; Panadura, Ceylon. *Clubs:* National Liberal; Recreation (Panadura).
[*Died* 17 *March* 1963.

de GALE, Hugh Otway, C.I.E. 1938; Indian Police (retired); *b.* 9 Jan. 1891; *m.* Eileen Nora, *d.* of William Brown, Beckenham, Kent; two *s.* Principal Police Training School, Phillour, 1927; Senior Superintendent of Police, Delhi Province, 1931; Deputy Inspector-General of Police, Punjab, 1933; Inspector-General of Police, North-West Frontier Province, 1935-41; Waziristan campaign, 1940 (despatches). Lieut. Indian Army, 1917-19, and Lt.-Col. Indian Army, 1943-46; served France and Germany. King's Police Medal 1921 and (bar) 1925. *Address:* 30 Wadham Gardens, N.W.3; River Antoine, Grenada, West Indies. *Club:* Royal Commonwealth Society.
[*Died* 5 *May* 1966.

de GAULLE, Général Charles André Joseph Marie; President of the French Republic, 1959-69; President of the "Communauté" (Française); *b.* 22 Nov. 1890; *s.* of Henri de Gaulle and Jeanne Maillot-Delannoy; *m.* 1921, Yvonne Vendroux; one *s.* one *d.* (and one *d.* decd.). *Educ.:* Saint-Cyr Academy. Served as Captain, European War, 1914-18; served War of 1939-45 as General of Brigade, and Commander 4th Armoured Division, 1940; Under-Secretary National Defence, June 1940; Chief of Free French, then President of French National Committee, London and Brazzaville, 1940-1942; President of French Committee of National Liberation, Algiers, 1943; President of Provisional Government of the French Republic and Head Chief of Armies, 1944-46; Founder of "Rassemblement du peuple français", 1947. President of French Government 2 June 1958-8 January 1959. Royal Victorian Chain, 1960. *Publications:* La Discorde chez l'ennemi, 1924; Le fil de l'Epée, 1932; Vers l'Armée de métier, 1934; La France et son Armée, 1938 (Eng. edn., 1945); Discours et Messages, 1947; Mémoires de guerre: l'Appel, Vol. 1, 1954 (Eng. trans., The Call to Honour, 1955); Vol. II, l'Unité, 1956; Vol. III, Le Salut, 1959 (Eng. trans., Salvation, 1960); Mémoires d'Espoir: Le Renouveau, 1958-1962, 1970; L'Effort, 1971; Discours et Messages: vol. I, Pendant la guerre, 1940-1946; vol. II, Dans l'attente, 1946-1958; vol. III, Avec le renouveau, 1958-1962; vol. IV, Pour l'effort, 1962-1965; vol. V, Vers le terme, 1966-1969; all 1970. *Address:* La Boisserie, Colombey-les-Deux-Églises, Haute-Marne, France.
[*Died* 9 *Nov.* 1970.

de GRAND' COMBE, Félix; *see* Boillot. Félix.

de GRUNWALD, Anatole; Author and Film Producer; *b.* St. Petersburg, Russia, 25 Dec. 1910; *s.* of Constantine de Grunwald;

m. 1940, Louise, d. of Carlos de Armada, Lisbon; one s. one d. Educ.: privately; Gonville and Caius College, Cambridge; Sorbonne. Has written either alone or in collaboration the following films: French Without Tears (with Terence Rattigan); Pimpernel Smith; Freedom Radio; Quiet Wedding; Cottage To Let; Jeannie; The First of the Few (with Miles Malleson); Unpublished Story; The Day Will Dawn; Secret Mission; The Demi-Paradise; English Without Tears; The Way to the Stars; While the Sun Shines; Bond Street; The Winslow Boy (the last four with Terence Rattigan); Now Barabbas; Flesh and Blood; The Holly and the Ivy; Innocents in Paris; The Doctor's Dilemma; Libel. Prod. The Demi-Paradise; English Without Tears; The Way to the Stars (won the National Film Award as best British picture made during war years, 1939-1945); While The Sun Shines; Bond Street; The Winslow Boy; Queen of Spades; The Last Days of Dolwyn; Now Barabbas; Flesh and Blood; The Holly and the Ivy; Innocents in Paris; The Doctor's Dilemma; Libel; I Thank a Fool; Come Fly with Me; V.I.P.s; The Yellow Rolls-Royce. *Publications:* two plays. *Recreations:* bookshops and watching football. *Address:* 45 Clarges Street, W.1. *T.:* Grosvenor 6248. *Club:* St. James'. [*Died* 13 *Jan.* 1967.

d'EGVILLE, Sir Howard, K.B.E., *cr.* 1920 (C.B.E. 1918); *e. s.* of late J. Hervet d'Egville and Alice E. Hall. *Educ.: St.* Catherine's College, Camb. Barr., Middle Temple; Hon. Sec. of British-American Parl. Group and Editor of Monthly "Letter from Washington"; for some time one of H.M.'s Treasury Counsel, Midland Circuit; called to Bar of N.S.W. as compliment; Hon. LL.D. Toronto, 1938; travelled widely oversea and made special study of, and lectured upon, Defence and For. Affairs; for some time Hon. Sec. Imp. Co-operation League; Organiser and First Sec. of Empire (now Commonwealth) Parliamentary Association; founded 1920 and edited from then till 1960 Journal of the Parliaments of the Commonwealth and Report on Foreign Affairs; organised visit of Rep. of Dominion Parliaments to Coronation of King George V, visit of Lords and Commons Delegation to Canada, Australia, N.Z., and South Africa, War Visit of Representatives of Dominion Parliaments to United Kingdom, 1916, and Delegations representative of the Parliaments of the Empire for Parliamentary Conferences in S. Africa, 1924; Australia, 1926; Canada, 1928; organised visit of representatives of Overseas Legislatures for Empire Parliamentary Conference in the United Kingdom for Silver Jubilee of King George V, 1935, and again a similar visit and Conference at the Coronation of King George VI, 1937 when, for the first time since the Coronation Feasts in Westminster Hall ceased in the reign of George IV, the King attended a Coronation Luncheon in Westminster Hall to meet representatives of all Parliaments of the Commonwealth; also organised other Parliamentary visits to Newfoundland, Malta, Bermuda, to Colonies in Africa and W. Indies; assisted in organisation of Parliamentary Conference, Ottawa, 1943, when for first time representatives of Commonwealth Parliaments were joined in conf. by a Deleg. representing Congress of U.S.A.; organised: similar Confs. with representatives of U.S.A. Congress in Bermuda 1946, 1948 and 1961, Australia, 1950, Canada, 1952, India, 1957; visit of Reps. of Oversea Legislatures to Commonwealth Parl. Conf. in U.K., 1948; appointed Secretary-General of Commonwealth Parliamentary Association and Editor of its publications, 1949, and held those offices till 1950, when retired through ill-health; organised first meeting of Gen. Council of Commonwealth Parl. Assoc., Ottawa, 1949, subs. annual Council meetings; Commonwealth Parl. Conf., N.Z., 1950, Canada, 1952, Kenya, 1954, India, 1957, Australia, 1959. *Publications:* Parliaments of the Empire; Imperial Defence and Closer Union; The Invasion of England; The Dominions and the War; War Legislation of the Empire; Some Aspects of Imperial Consultation; The Parliamentary System and Commonwealth Unity. *Recreations:* tennis, travelling. *Address:* Palace of Westminster, S.W.1. T.: Whitehall 6240. [*Died* 9 *Jan.* 1965.

de HAVILLAND, Capt. Sir Geoffrey, O.M. 1962; Kt. 1944; C.B.E. 1934; A.F.C. 1919; R.D.I. 1944; aeroplane designer; President, The de Havilland Aircraft of Canada Ltd.; *b.* 1882; *s.* of late Charles de Havilland, Crux Easton, Hants.; *m.* 1907, Louie (*d.* 1949), *d.* of Richard Thomas, Chepstow, Mon.; one *s.* (and two *s.* decd.); *m.* 1951, Joan, *d.* of A. Frith. *Educ.:* St. Edward's Sch., Oxf.; Crystal Palace Engineering Sch. Served European War, 1914-19; technically, with R.F.C. A Vice-Pres. Royal Aero Club, 1943. Hon. F.R.Ae.S. 1953; Hon. Dr.Eng., Univ. of Sheffield, 1955, Hon. Fellow, Soc. of Engineers; Hon. Fellow, Inst. of the Aeronautical Sciences (U.S.A.). Awarded several aviation medals, including Royal Aero Club Gold Medal for outstanding contribution to Aviation and particularly to sporting and private flying, 1963. *Publication:* Sky Fever, 1961. *Relevant Publication:* D. H.: An Outline of de Havilland History, by C. Martin Sharp, 1961. *Address:* Longcote, Tanglewood Close, Stanmore, Middx. *Club:* Royal Aero. [*Died* 21 *May* 1965.

DEHN, Adolf (Arthur), N.A.; Artist, U.S.; *b.* Waterville, Minnesota, U.S.A., 22 Nov. 1895; *s.* of Arthur C. and Emilie Dehn; *m.* 1947, Virginia Engleman. *Educ.:* Minneapolis Art School; Art Students League, N.Y.C. Lived in Europe, mostly Vienna, 7 years; works: in 40 or more American Museums, including Metropolitan Museum, Modern Museum, Whitney Museum, Chicago Art Institution; prints: in British Museum; illustrations: for magazines such as Vanity Fair, Harper's Bazaar, Vogue, Dial, New Masses, Life, Jugend, etc.; 1st prize Chicago Watercolour International, **1942; Guggenheim Fellowship, 1939; 2nd Guggenheim Fell., 1951; 1st prize for Prints, Library of Congress, 1946. *Publications:* Water-colour Painting, 1945; How to Draw and Print Lithographs, 1949; 69 illustrations for selected stories by Guy de Maupassant, 1950; watercolour, gouache, and casein painting, 1955. *Recreations:* sketching, travel. *Address:* c/o Milch Galleries, 21 East 67th Street, N.Y.C. *T.:* AL-5-4208. *Club:* Century Association (N.Y.C.).** [*Died* 19 *May* 1968.

DE LA BERE, Brig. (retired) Sir Ivan, K.C.V.O. 1959 (C.V.O. 1950); C.B. 1957; C.B.E. 1944 (O.B.E. 1934); B.A. (Cantab.); C.St.J. 1950; Secretary, Central Chancery of the Orders of Knighthood, St. James's Palace, 1946-60; Extra Gentleman-Usher to the Queen, since 1961; *b.* 25 April 1893; *s.* of John De La Bere, Battledown Manor, Cheltenham, Glos.; *m.* 1923, Marjorie Minton Haines; (one *d.* decd.). 2nd Lieutenant Dorset Regiment, 1913; Lt.-Col. Dorset Regiment, 1939; Brig., 1941; Acting Maj.-General, 1944. *Foreign decorations* (1946-60): Comdr. Order of Merit (W. Germany); Comdr., Order of Merit (Italy); Officer, Legion of Honour (France); Comdr., Order of White Elephant (Siam); Officer, Order of: Orange (Netherlands); Rafidan (Iraq); Danebrog (Denmark); Christ (Portugal); North Star (Sweden); personal order of Shah of Persia. *Publication:* The Queen's **Orders of Chivalry, 1961. *Address:*** King, **ston House, Corfe Castle, Dorset.** [*Died* 27 *Dec.* 1970.

de la PASTURE, 5th Marquis, **Major Gerard H.**; *see* Pasture.

de LARA, Adelina (Lottie Adelina de Lara Shipwright), O.B.E. 1951; Pianist Composer; retired from playing piano; last broadcast for piano, Wigmore Hall, July 1954; *b.* 23 January 1872; *d.* of George Matthew Tilbury and Anna de Lara; *m.* 1896, Thomas Johnson Shipwright (*decd.*); two *s.* *Educ.:* Frankfurt am Main. Started concert performance in Liverpool, etc., 1878, at age of 6; studied with Fanny Davies, 1885, and Clara Schumann, 1886-91; first appearance at St. James's Hall, 1891; has played continually since. Played Schumann Concerto at Hallé concert in Manchester, 1897, and broadcast same work in 1945; on 74th birthday, played at Nat. Gallery with Dame Myra Hess; many broadcasts, principally of Schumann. During European War, 1914-18, and War of 1939-45 organised War Fund concerts. Compositions include many ballads, two song-cycles, two piano concertos, two suites for String Orchestra, etc. Recorded Schumann's Piano Concerto for World broadcast, with Scottish Orchestra, Glasgow, 1951; Lecture and Recitals in Edinburgh Univ., 1953. Still broadcasting Talks and giving Lectures, 1957. Organises concerts and gives recitals for charities in aid of animals. Television Recital on 82nd birthday. Vice-President Society of Women Musicians. Vice-Pres. of R.S.P.C.A. Woking and district branch. Has recorded a large number of Schumann's Piano works. *Publication: autobiography:* Finale, 1955. *Recreations:* writing, great lover of animals. *Address:* Adelina's Cottage, Woking, Surrey. *Club:* London Musical (Pres.). [*Died* 25 *Nov.* 1961.

de la ROCHE, Mazo; author; *d.* of late Richmond de la Roche and Alberta Lundy, Toronto, Canada. Hon. Dr. of Letters, Toronto Univ.; Mem. Canadian Authors' Assoc.; Rep. Canadian P.E.N. in London. *Publications:* Explorers of the Dawn, 1922; Possession, 1923; Delight, 1926; Jalna, 1927; Low Life and other Plays, 1928; Whiteoaks, 1929 (dramatised 1936); Portrait of a Dog, 1930; Finch's Fortune, 1931; Lark Ascending, 1932; The Master of Jalna, 1933; Beside a Norman Tower, 1934; Young Renny, 1935; Whiteoak Harvest, 1936; The Very House, 1937; Growth of a Man, 1938; The Sacred Bullock, 1939; Whiteoak Heritage, 1940; A Boy in the House, 1941; Wakefield's Course, 1941; The Two Saplings, 1942; The Building of Jalna, 1944; A History of the Port of Quebec, 1944; Return to Jalna, 1949; Mary Wakefield, 1949; Renny's Daughter, 1951; The Whiteoak Brothers, 1954; Variable Winds at Jalna, 1955; The Song of Lambert, 1956; Ringing the Changes (Autobiog.), 1957; Centenary at Jalna, 1958; Bill and Coo, 1958; Morning at Jalna, 1960. *Address:* c/o Macmillan Co., St. Martin's St., W.C.2. [*Died* 12 *July* 1961.

DELME-RADCLIFFE, Sir Ralph (Hubert John), Kt. 1961; J.P. Herts; *b.* 1877; *e. s.* of Rev. Arthur Delmé-Radcliffe and Beatrice, *d.* of Hon. Frederick Dudley Ryder; *m.* 1st, 1912, Countess Néva Ouroussoff; divorced, 1938; 2nd, 1939, Elisabeth Ffennell, *d.* of late Sir Hugh Levick; one *d.* *Educ.:* Eton. Clerk in House of Commons, 1902-6; Pres. North Herts Conservative Assoc. *Address:* Hitchin Priory, Herts. *T.:* Hitchin 2166. *Club:* Turf. [*Died* 23 *Nov.* 1963.

de LOYNES, John Barraclough, C.M.G., 1963; *b.* 4 August 1909; *s.* of Frederic John de Loynes and late Ethel Maud (*née* Plowman); *m.* 1946, Françoise Evelyn Henriette, *d.* of Countess Gabrielle (*née* de Robillard-Cosnac) and late Philippe de Ponthière; one *s.* three *d.* *Educ.:* U.C. Sch.; Gandersheim; Hamburg. Adviser to Central Bank of Ceylon, Colombo, 1952-55; Central Banking Consultant to Ghana Govt., 1956-57; Banking Adviser to Federal Govt. of Nigeria, 1957; Member: E. African Currency Bd., Nairobi, 1960-; W. African Currency Bd., London, 1960-; Chm. Gambia Currency Bd., 1964-; Dir., S. Yemen (formerly S. Arabian) Currency Authority, 1964-; Currency and banking consultant to Govt. of Mauritius, 1965-66; Alternate Governor, I.M.F., for the Gambia, 1967-; Adviser to the Governors of the Bank of England, 1965-. *Publications include:* Report on the Establishment of a Nigerian Central Bank, 1957; The Future of the Currencies of Sierra Leone and the Gambia, 1961; The West African Currency Board, 1912-1962. *Address:* 25 Ave. Rd., Bishop's Stortford, Herts. *T.:* 4576; Campden House, Wells, Norfolk; P.O. Box 3684, Nairobi, Kenya. *T.:* 21161. [*Died* 24 *Aug.* 1969.

del RIEGO, Teresa; British composer; *b.* London, 7 April 1876; *d.* of Miguel and Clara del Riego; *m.* 1908, Francis John Graham Leadbitter (killed in action in France, 1917) of Auckland House, Brondesbury, and Warden, Northumberland; one *s.* *Educ.:* London and Paris. Studied piano and composition in London and Paris, also singing and violin; for all these subjects holds Trinity College Certificates, and the Medal of The Society of Arts for Piano; special subjects: piano, voice technique, and accompanying. Member of Incorporated Society of Musicians and Hon. Vice-Pres. of Society of Women Musicians. Sang and accompanied at War Fund Concerts during European War 1914-18, and War of 1939-45. *Publications:* upwards of 250 musical compositions, including Homing; Oh, Dry those Tears (translated into several languages); Lead Kindly Light; Harvest; Slave Song; Happy Song; Gloria (Song Cycle); Sink red Sun; Thank God for a Garden; To Electra; To Dianeme; Castilian Lament; Herz mein Herz; Allerseelen; Seliger Tod; La Vie est Vaine; Les Larmes; L'Amour; A Star was His Candle; A Garden is a Lovesome Thing; The Madonna's Lullaby; Sleep my Heart; A Southern Night; King Duncan's Daughter; The Three Chariots; The Cherry Tree; Works for Orchestra and Voice: The Unknown Warrior; The King's Song, Three Stuart Songs, etc.; Air in E *b* for Orchestra (arranged for Cello and Piano); Invocation (for solo voice, chorus, and orchestra) performed at her Jubilee Concert, Apr. 1954. Author many lyrics including: O dry those tears, Madonna's Lullaby, Thank God for a Garden, Happy Song. *Recreations:* music, reading, theatre. *Address:* Sycamore, Overstrand, Nr. Cromer, Norfolk. [*Died* 23 *Jan.* 1968.

del TUFO, Sir (Morobo[illegible]) Vincent, K.B.E., *cr.* 1952; C.M.G. 1950; Malayan Delegate on the International Tin Council, 1956 and International Tin Research Council; *b.* 1 April 1901; *s.* of Marchese I. V. del Tufo; *m.* 1935, Katharine Mary Holdsworth; four *s.* one *d.* *Educ.:* Royal College, Colombo; Trinity College, Cambridge (Senior Scholar). B.A. Cantab. 1922 (Wrangler); M.A. 1948; Barrister-at-Law, Inner Temple (Certificate of Honour, 1939). Cadet, Malayan Civil Service, 1923; First Assist. Sec. and Clerk of Councils, Straits Settlements, 1936-38; Dir. of Manpower, 1940; Sec.-Gen. and later Director-Gen., Malayan Dept. of Supply, 1941. Interned by Japanese, 1942-45. Supt. of Census, Malaya, 1946-48; Dep. Comr. for Labour, Federation of Malaya, 1948; Dep. Chief Sec. Fedn. of Malaya, 1949, Chief Sec., Federation of Malaya, 1950-52; Officer Admin. Govt., 1951. *Publication:* Report on the 1947 Malayan Census of Population. *Address:* Chudleigh, Little Gaddesden, Herts. *T.:* Little Gaddesden 2276. *Club:* Athenæum. [*Died* 26 *Nov.* 1961.

DELURY, Justin Sarsfield, Ph.D., F.R.S.C.; late Provincial Geologist Prov. of

Manitoba; *b.* Manilla, Ontario, Canada, 1884; *s.* of Daniel De Lury; *m.* 1921, Paulina Porter Fox, Lower Gagetown, N.B., Canada; no *c.* *Educ.:* Port Perry (Ontario) High School; University of Toronto, B.A.; Assistant in Mineralogy, University of Toronto, 1905-6; Lecturer and Associate Professor of Geology, University of Idaho, 1906-11; Lecturer and Assistant Professor, University of Manitoba, Winnipeg, 1915-1927; Ph.D. University of Minnesota, 1925; Professor of Geology, University of Saskatchewan, 1927-28; Professor and Head, Department of Geology, University of Manitoba, 1928-44; Geological Survey of Canada, 1904, 1923, 1924; Ontario Bureau of Mines, 1906; Province of Manitoba, 1916-1922, 1925, 1926; F.G.S. Am. *Publications:* Bulletins on Mineral Resources of Manitoba; papers on mineral deposits of Manitoba in Canadian Mining Journal and Bulletin of Canadian Institute of Mining and Metallurgy; publications in Canadian Geological Survey Reports and in Geological journals. *Recreations:* canoeing, motoring. *Address:* P.O. Box 22, Uxbridge, Ontario, Canada. *Club:* Winnipeg Scientific. [*Died* 3 *Oct.* 1968.

de MAISTRE, Roy; *see* Maistre Le Roy de.

DE MAULEY, 5th Baron, U.K., *cr.* 1838; **Hubert William Ponsonby;** late Capt. Gloucs. Hussars; *b.* 21 July 1878; *s.* of 4th Baron de Mauley and Hon. Madeleine Emily Augusta Hanbury Tracy (*d.* 1938), 6th *d.* of 2nd Baron Sudeley; *S.* father, 1945; *m.* 1920, Elgiva, *d.* of late Hon. Cospatrick Dundas and Lady Cordeaux; two *s.* two *d.* Served European War, 1914-18 (Légion d'Honneur and Croix de Guerre). *Heir:* *s.* Capt. Hon. Gerald John Ponsonby, R.A. [*b.* 1921. *Educ.:* Eton; Christ Church, Oxford, M.A. Served War of 1939-45 (wounded); *m.* 1954, Mrs. B. A. Collins, *widow* of Lt.-Col. Brian A. Collins, and *d.* of Hon. Charles Douglas]. *Address:* Langford House, Lechlade, Glos. *T.:* Lechlade 210. [*Died* 13 *Sept.* 1962.

de MONTMORENCY, Sir Miles (Fletcher), 17th Bt., *cr.* 1631; R.B.A. 1935, Hon. Librarian R.B.A., 1947; Artist, portrait painter; *b.* 3 March 1893; *s.* of Hervey Lodge de Montmorency and Elizabeth Nicolls, *d.* of Capt. Archibald Fletcher, R.N.; *S.* brother, Sir Angus de Montmorency, 16th Bt., 1959; *m.* 1931, Rachel Marion (*d.* 1961), *d.* of Charles Coverdale Tancock, D.D.; no *c.* *Educ.:* Dover Coll.; The Byam Shaw Sch. of Art; Roy. Academy Schools. Served European War, 1914-18; 2nd Lieut., Kent Cyclist Bn., 1915; Lieut. (Actg. Capt.), Bde. Anti-Gas Officer, 4th Cyclist Brigade, 1917. Exhibitor: Royal Academy; Venice Biennale; Internat. Soc. of Sculptors, Painters and Gravers; Roy. Soc. of Portrait Painters; Roy. Inst. of Oil Painters, etc. Painted portraits for National War Records, 1941. *Publication:* A Short History of Painting in England, 1934. *Heir: cousin* Reginald D'Alton Lodge de Montmorency [*b.* 13 March 1899; *m.* 1928, Dorothy Victoria, *d.* of G. W. Robinson]. *Address:* 45 Rusholme Road, Putney, S.W. 15. *T.:* Putney 6450. [*Died* 22 *Dec.* 1963.

DEMPSEY, General Sir Miles Christopher, G.B.E. 1956 (K.B.E. 1945); K.C.B. 1944 (C.B. 1943); D.S.O. 1940; M.C. 1918; D.L.; p.s.c.; a Director of H. & G. Simonds (Chairman 1953-63); Deputy Chairman, Courage, Barclay & Simonds Ltd., 1961-66; Chairman, Greene, King & Sons Ltd., since 1955; *b.* 15 Dec. 1896; *s.* of late A. F. Dempsey, Hoylake, Cheshire; *m.* 1948, Viola, *y. d.* of Capt. Percy O'Reilly, Colamber, Westmeath. *Educ.:* Shrewsbury; R.M.C., Sandhurst. 2nd Lieutenant, Royal Berkshire Regiment, 1915; served European War, 1916-18 (wounded, despatches, M.C.); Iraq Operations. 1919-20; War of 1939-45 (despatches, D.S.O., C.B., K.C.B., K.B.E.); commanded: 13th Inf. Bde., Dunkirk; 13th Corps, Invasions of Sicily and Italy; Second Army, Invasion of Normandy and N.W. Europe; 14th Army in re-occupation of Singapore and Malaya. C.-in-C. Allied Land Forces, S.E. Asia, 1945-1946; C.-in-C. Middle East, 1946-47; General, 1946. A.D.C. Gen. to the King, 1946-47; retired pay, 1947. C.-in-C. (designate) U.K. Land Forces, 1951-56. Col. Comdt. Corps of Royal Military Police, 1947-1957; Col. The Royal Berkshire Regt., 1947-1956; Col. Comdt. Special Air Service Regt., 1951-60. D.L. Berks., 1950. Chm. Racecourse Betting Control Board, 1947-51. *Address:* Coombe House, Yattendon, Berks. *Clubs:* Turf, Cavalry, Jockey. [*Died* 5 *June* 1969.

DENBIGH, 10th Earl of (*cr.* 1622) and **Desmond,** 9th Earl of (*cr.* 1622); **William Rudolph Stephen Feilding;** J.P.; late Major Coldstream Guards; *b.* 17 Apr. 1912; *s.* of late Viscount Feilding and Imelda (*d.* 1937), *d.* of late F. E. Harding; *S.* grandfather, 1939; *m.* 1940, Verena Barbara, *widow* of Lt.-Col. T. P. Fielding Johnson, *d.* of W. E. Price, Hallgates, Cropston, nr. Leicester; one *s.* one *d.* *Educ.:* Oratory School, Caversham; Christ Church, Oxford. J.P. Warwickshire. *Heir:* *s.* Viscount Feilding. *Address:* Pailton House, Rugby. *T.:* Pailton 236. [*Died* 31 *Dec.* 1966.

DENBY, Elizabeth Marian, Hon. A.R.I.B.A.; F.R.S.A.; sociologist; specialist on low-cost housing; *d.* of Walter Denby, M.D., Bradford, Yorkshire. *Educ.:* privately; Bradford Girls Grammar School; Social Science Dept., London School of Economics. First organising Secretary, the Kensington Housing Trust and the Kensington Housing Assoc.; Organising Chm., first New Homes for Old Exhibition, Olympia, 1932; Leverhulme Research Fellowship into low-cost housing in Europe, 1934-35; collaborated on the design of low-cost estates including Sassoon House, Kensal House, etc.; social surveys, including location of industry, redevelopment of Central areas, etc. Member of Technical Cttee., Nat. Housing and Town Planning Council; Governor of Chelsea College of Science and Technology; was Founder of The Watergate Theatre Ltd. *Publications:* Europe Re-Housed, 1937; collaborated in Our Towns, A Close-up, 1943; Counter-Attack, 1957. *Recreations:* music and the arts. *Address:* 144 High St., Hythe, Kent. *T.:* 66413. [*Died* 3 *Nov.* 1965.

DENCH, William George, C.I.E. 1944; B.A.; B.A.I., Dublin University; late Chief Engineer and Secretary to Govt., Public Works Dept., Irrigation Br., Punjab; *b.* 1 Dec. 1888; *s.* of late George William Dench, Weymouth, Dorset; *m.* Mary Olive Huggard, Milltown, Co. Kerry; one *s.* three *d.* Joined Indian Service of Engineers, 1912; retired, 1943. *Recreation:* painting. *Address:* 32 Wychwood Close, Craigwell, Bognor Regis, Sussex. *T.:* Pagham 2576. [*Died* 19 *April* 1963.

DENEKE, Margaret Clara Adèle; Hon. M.A., Oxford; Hon. Fellow and Choirmaster and Hon Secretary for Philip Maurice Deneke Lecture, Lady Margaret Hall, Oxford; Librarian Oxford Univ. Musical Club and Union; President Oxford Ladies' Musical Society; *b.* 26 Dec. 1882; *yr. d.* of Philip Maurice and Clara Sophie Deneke. *Educ.:* privately. Lecturer on musical subjects in Great Britain and America on behalf of Lady Margaret Hall, St. Hilda's College, St. Anne's College and Oxford University Appeals; lived as nurse, Schweitzer Hospital in West Africa, 1931-32. *Publication:* Ernest Walker, 1950; P.V.M.

Benecke, 1954. *Address:* Gunfield, 19 Norham Gardens, Oxford.
[*Died* 3 *March* 1969.

DENEYS, Commander James Godfrey Wood, D.S.O. 1941; O.B.E. 1942; R.N., retired; Admiralty; 2nd Sea Lord's Office since 1942; *b.* 30 July 1897; *s.* of late J. P. Deneys and Mrs. Myburgh; *m.* 1950, Nora Winifred Mackenzie; two *s.* *Educ.:* Haileybury. Joined R.N., 1915; H.M.S. Shannon, 1916-17; H.M.S. Tormentor, 1918; served in submarines, 1918-31; commanded H.M.S. Vidette, 1932-33; H.M.S. Tyrant, 1935-38; H.M.S. Danae, 1938-39; H.M.S. Vanoc, 1939-42. *Address:* Tigne, St. Catherine's Road, Hayling Island, Hants. *T.:* 77896. [*Died* 25 *Oct.* 1962.

DENHAM, Algernon, J.P.; retired as a Director of Barclays Bank Ltd.; is a Director of Leeds, West Yorks local bd., and Chm. Sheffield local bd.; Bradford Property Trust Ltd. (Chm.); Ealing Tenants Ltd. (Chm.); Glenfield & Kennedy Ltd.; Halifax Building Society Ltd.; J. Blakeborough & Sons Ltd. (Chairman); Sheldon's Ltd.; Trafford Park Dwellings Ltd. (Chm.). *Address:* Priestley Green, Norwood Green, Nr. Halifax, Yorkshire. [*Died* 6 *Nov.* 1961.

DENHAM, Humphrey John, C.B.E. 1946; M.A., D.Sc. (Oxon.), F.Inst.P.; F.I.E.E.; Honorary Colonel; *b.* 15 November 1893; *s.* of late Reverend Canon J. R. Denham and Mary Ramsay Ewart; *m.* 1931, Marjorie, *d.* of late Dr. W. F. Oakeshott, Lydenburg, South Africa; two *s.* one *d.* *Educ.:* Bradfield; Balliol College, Oxford. Served European War, 1914-19, France, 1915-18 (despatches); Captain, R.G.A.; British Cotton Industry Research Association, Didsbury, 1920; Director of Research, Henry Simon, Ltd. (Engineers), Manchester, 1924-28; Technical Adviser, Buckmaster & Moore, Bishopsgate, 1928-30; Director, Institute for Research in Agricultural Engineering, Univ. of Oxford, 1931-37. Served War of 1939-45, June 1939-Sept. 1948, Col. R.A.O.C.: Member Ordnance Board, 1944-51 (Electronics Division); Deputy Chief Inspector (Overseas Division), Electrical and Mechanical Equipment, Ministry of Supply, 1951-52; Group Consultant, A. C. Cossar Ltd., 1953-63. *Publications:* The Skeptical Gardener, 1939; reprint, 1949; many scientific papers and articles, and patents; writes also under pen-name of Humphrey John. *Recreations:* gardening, ornithology, photography. *Address:* c/o Martins Bank Ltd., Carfax, Oxford.
[*Died* 20 *May* 1970.

DENHAM, William Smith; Director of Research, British Silk Research Association, 1921-34; *b.* Glasgow, 1878; 2nd *s.* of Walter Denham, bank agent; *m.* Hilda, *d.* of Thomas Woodhouse; one *s.* one *d.* *Educ.:* Hillhead High School; Royal Technical College; University, Glasgow; University of Jena; Research Fellow, University of St. Andrews; D.Sc. (St. Andrews), B.Sc. (London), F.I.C. Formerly Lecturer in Chemistry, Royal Technical College, Glasgow; University of St. Andrews; St. Mary's Hospital Medical School. *Publications:* Contributions to the Transactions of the Chemical Society. *Address:* 57 Langley Park Rd, Sutton, Surrey. *Club:* Caledonian. [*Died* 1 *June* 1964.

DENNIS, Mrs. A. E. Forbes; *see* Bottome, Phyllis.

DENNIS, Geoffrey Pomeroy, M.A., Oxon.; *b.* Barnstaple, Devon, 20 January 1892; *y. c.* of Austen Dennis, Bradiford House, near Barnstaple, and Annie Handford; *m.* 1st, 1926, Doris Ethel Hall (*d.* 1927); 2nd, 1928, Imogen Christina Rossetti Angeli, great-niece of Dante Gabriel and Christina Rossetti; one *s.* one *d.* *Educ.:* various North Country schools. Articled to Estate Agent and Auctioneer, Walsall, 1907-10; Exeter College, Oxford, 1910-14, First Class Honours in School of Modern History, co-founder of the Oxford Poetry series, Treasurer and Librarian of the Union; Army 1915-20 (B.E.F.; Liaison with French VIIIth Army; then G.H.Q. Cologne), Captain; First Division Civil Service Examination, 1919, passed third in England; eighteen years with League of Nations, Geneva, 1920-37 (Chief Editor and Chief of Document Services); Adviser to International Institute of Agriculture, Rome, 1938-39; Intelligence Corps (Major), 1940-45; Head of Italian Section, B.B.C., 1945-49; B.B.C. special rep. in former Italian Colonies, 1949; The English Editor, U.N.E.S.C.O., 1949-57. *Publications:* Mary Lee, 1922; Harvest in Poland, 1925; Declaration of Love, 1927; The End of the World, 1930 (Hawthornden Prize); Sale by Auction, 1932; Bloody Mary's, 1934; Coronation Commentary, 1937; (General Editor), History of the War of 1939; Till Seven, 1957. Has also written for Punch, Hibbert Journal, New Age, English Review, Time and Tide, North American Review, etc. *Address:* 15 Park Street, Woodstock, Oxford. *Clubs:* Athenæum, United University.
[*Died* 15 *May* 1963.

DENNIS, Maj.-Gen. Meade Edward, C.B. 1945; C.B.E. 1943; D.S.O. 1942; M.C.; Maj.-Gen. Royal Artillery, India, 1946-47; *b.* 6 Aug. 1893; *e. s.* of late Col. M. J. C. Dennis, C.B.; *m.* 1930, Joan Isobel Maud Graham; one *s.* two *d.* *Educ.:* Haileybury; R.M.A., Woolwich. 2nd Lt. Royal Field Artillery, 1913; European War, 1914-18, France, Belgium and Palestine (wounded, M.C., despatches); in Sudan with Egyptian Army, 1920-24; in India on outbreak of war, 1939. Went to Persia commanding Artillery of 6 Indian Division, 1941; Western Desert as Commander Corps Artillery, 30 Corps, 1942, to end of campaign in Sicily (D.S.O. at Alamein, C.B.E. Sicily); Maj.-Gen. Royal Artillery, 21 Army Group B.L.A., 1944-46 (C.B.); retired pay, 1947. Officer, Legion of Honour; Croix de Guerre. *Recreations:* racing, and all field sports. *Address:* Eortgranite, Baltinglass, Co. Wicklow, Eire. *T.:* Baltinglass 8. *Clubs:* Cavalry; Kildare Street (Dublin).
[*Died* 31 *Jan.* 1965.

DENNISTON, Alexander Guthrie, C.M.G. 1941, C.B.E. 1933; late Head of a Dept, in the Foreign Office; *b.* 1 Dec. 1881; *s.* of James Denniston and Agnes Guthrie; *m.* 1917, Dorothy Mary Gilliat; one *s.* one *d.* *Educ.:* Bowdon College, Cheshire; Bonn University; La Sorbonne, Paris. Assistant Master, Merchiston Castle School, 1906-9; R.N.C., Osborne, 1909-14; Admiralty N.I.D., 1914-21; Commander R.N.V.R. 1917; Foreign Office, 1921-45. *Address:* The Rectory, New Milton, Hants.
[*Died* 1 *Jan.* 1961.

DENNY, Barbara Mary (Mrs. Edward Denny), C.B.E. 1920; *b.* 1880; *d.* of Donald William Charles Hood, C.V.O., M.D.; *m.* 1907, Edward H. Marland Denny (*d.* 1941); one *s.* two *d.* Commandant, donor and administrator, Officers' Auxiliary Hospital, Staplefield, during European War. S.S.St.J. Formerly J.P. Sussex. *Address:* The Chantry, Horsham, Sussex.
[*Died* 30 *Nov.* 1965.

DENT, Lt.-Col. John Ralph Congreve, D.S.O. 1918; M.C.; late S. Staffs. Regt. and The Royal Inniskilling Fusiliers; *b.* 25 Feb. 1884; *m.* 1920, Margaret Honor, *yr. d.* of late A. T. Keen and Mrs. Keen, of Harborne Park, Harborne, nr. Birmingham; three *s.* *Educ.:* Bromsgrove School; R.M.C., Sandhurst. Served European War, 1914-19 (D.S.O. and bar, M.C., Croix de Guerre Français); retired pay, 1923; Sheriff of Gloucestershire, 1941. *Address:* Olivers, Painswick, Gloucestershire.
[*Died* 20 *July* 1969.

DENTON-THOMPSON, Merrick Arnold Bardsley; late of H.M. Foreign Service; *b.* 16 May 1888; *e. s.* of late Rt. Rev. James Denton Thompson, D.D., Bishop of Sodor and Man, and late Isabella Suzannah Arnold; adopted by Deed Poll the hyphened name in 1917; *m.* 1919, Carew, 3rd *d.* of A. S. L. Hulett, Durban; two *s.* one *d.* (and one *s.* decd.). *Educ.:* Repton; Emmanuel College, Cambridge, B.A. Served in Civil Service of Southern Rhodesia, 1911-1912; Administrative Officer, Northern Rhodesia, 1912-15; Vice-Consul Elizabethville, Belgian Congo, 1915-23, and at Brussels, 1923-27; Consul at Stockholm, 1927-30; Madrid, 1930-34; Pernambuco, 1934-35; Amsterdam, 1935-38; Oporto, 1938-44; Consul-General, São Paulo, 1944-45; Amsterdam, 1945-48. Coronation Medal, 1937. *Recreations:* golf and tennis. *Address:* Littledown, Sandy Down, Lymington, Hants. [*Died* 23 *Jan.* 1969.

DENYER, Charles Leonard, M.A.; Headmaster, Andover Grammar School, 1929-50; *b.* 15 May 1887. *Educ.:* Portsmouth Grammar School; St. John's College, Cambridge; Class II. in Parts I and II Historical Tripos. Master at Rossall School, 1918-26; Headmaster of Robert May's Grammar School, Odiham, 1926-29. *Address:* Overcross, Shawford, Winchester, Hants. *T.:* Twyford 2212. [*Died* 3 *Dec.* 1969.

de PAULEY, Rt. Rev. William Cecil; Bishop of Cashel and Emly, Waterford and Lismore, since 1958; *b.* Portrush, Co. Antrim, 1893; *s.* of Wm. de Pauley, Banbridge, Co. Down; *m.* 1920, Sara Winifred (*d.* 1947), *d.* of Archdeacon Henry John Johnson; one *s.* *Educ.:* Coleraine Academical Institution; Trinity Coll., Dublin. B.A. (Sen. Moderator and gold medallist in Mental and Moral Philosophy), 1914; B.D., 1919; M.A., 1921; D.D., 1926. Divinity Testimonium, 1916. Deacon, 1917; priest, 1918. Curate-asst. of Enniscorthy, 1917; of Booterstown, 1919; Prof. of Systematic Theology, St. John's Coll., and Canon of St. John's Cathedral, Winnipeg, 1920; Rector of: St. Peter's, Athlone, 1926; St. John's, Sligo, 1930; Prof. of Systematic Theology, Trinity Coll., Toronto, 1932; Rector of: St. Matthias's, Dublin, 1939; Tullow, Carrickmines, Co. Dublin, 1945; Canon of St. Patrick's Cathedral, Dublin, 1945; Dean of St. Patrick's Cathedral, Dublin, 1950-58. Asst. Lecturer in Divinity School, Trinity Coll., Dublin, 1924-54; Examining Chaplain to Archbishop of Dublin, 1944-54; Chaplain to Actors' Church Union, 1939-45; preaching tour in U.S.A. 1955. *Publications:* Punishment Human and Divine, 1925; The Divine in Man, 1931; The Candle of the Lord, 1937. *Address:* Bishopscourt, Waterford, Eire. *Club:* University (Dublin). [*Died* 30 *March* 1968.

DERAMORE, 5th Baron (*cr.* 1885); **Stephen Nicholas de Yarburgh-Bateson,** Bt. 1818; Sqdn. Ldr. R.A.F.V.R. (despatches); *b.* 18 May 1903; *s.* of 4th Baron and Muriel (*d.* 1960), *d.* of late Arthur Duncombe, Sutton Hall, Sutton, York; *S.* father, 1943; *m.* 1929, Nina Marion, (O.B.E. 1956), *e. d.* of late Alastair Macpherson-Grant; one *d.* *Educ.:* Harrow; St. John's College, Cambridge. *Heir-pres.:* *b.* Hon. Richard Arthur de Yarburgh-Bateson [*b.* 9 April 1911; *m.* 1948, Janet Mary Ware; one *d.*]. *Address:* Manor House, Heslington, York. *T.:* York 56158. *Club:* Carlton. [*Died* 23 *Dec.* 1964.

D'ERLANGER, Sir Gerard (John Regis Leo), Kt. 1958; C.B.E. 1943; Chairman: City & International Trust Ltd.; General Consolidated Investment Trust Ltd.; Moorgate Investment Co. Ltd.; Dep. Chm. Provident Mutual Life Association; Director: John Mackintosh & Sons Ltd.; Philip Hill Investment Trust Ltd.; *b.* 1 June 1906; *s.* of late Baron Emile Beaumont d'Erlanger; *m.* 1937, Gladys Sammut; one *s.* two *d.* *Educ.:* Eton. Chartered Accountant, 1933; Partner in Myers & Co. and Member of Stock Exchange, 1935-39; Director of British Airways, 1935-40; Commanding Officer Air Transport Auxiliary, 1939-45; Member of Board of British Overseas Airways Corporation, 1940-46; Managing Director, B.E.A., 1946-47, Chairman, 1947-1949; Member Air Transport Advisory Council, 1952 (Deputy-Chairman 1954), resigned, 1955; Chm. B.O.A.C., 1956-60. *Recreation:* sailing. *Address:* 11 Hyde Park Street, W.2. *Clubs:* Portland, Garrick; Royal Yacht Squadron. [*Died* 15 *Dec.* 1962.

de ROBECK, 6th Baron (of Sweden); **Brig. John Henry Edward de Robeck,** C.B.E. 1945 (M.B.E. 1919); late R.A.; *b.* 10 April 1895; *e. s.* of 5th Baron, of Gowran Grange, Naas, Co. Kildare, and Anne, *d.* of L. W. Alexander, of Straw Hall, Co. Carlow; *S.* father, 1929; *m.* 1940, Katherine, *er. d.* of Lt.-Col. Hugh Simpson, R.A.; two *s.* *Educ.:* Clifton College; R.M.A., Woolwich. Served European War, 1914-18 (despatches, M.B.E.); War of 1939-45 (C.B.E.); retired pay, 1947. *Heir: er. s.* Martin John Michael, *b.* 21 Aug. 1941. *Address:* Gowran Grange, Naas, Co. Kildare, Ireland. *Clubs:* Army and Navy; Kildare Street (Dublin). [*Died* 10 *April* 1965.

de ROTHSCHILD, Anthony (G.); *see* Rothschild.

DERRY, Cyril; Chairman since 1950, and Managing Director since 1930, Ambrose Wilson Ltd.; Chairman: Bassett-Lowke Ltd., since 1932; Stephen Leynham Ltd., since 1942; *b.* 4 Dec. 1895; *o. s.* of Frank Derry; *m.* 1937, Joan Isabel Laura Wright; one *s.* *Educ.:* Manor House, Clapham; Seaford College; Engineering Student, Faraday House, W.C.1. Enlisted in Inns of Court O.T.C., 1915; commissioned A.S.C. (Motor Transport R.E. Signals), 1915; attached R.E., Flanders, 1917 (despatches). On demobilisation, 1919, joined father in firm of Ambrose Wilson Ltd. (of which father was Founder). Freeman of City of London; Liveryman, Worshipful Co. of Horners, 1932 (Master, 1957-58 and Dep. Master, 1958-59); Sheriff for the City of London, 1959-60; Member Court of Common Council for Lime Street Ward, 1963-; Past President Rotary Club of London; Past National Chairman, Institute of Marketing and Sales Management; Chm., Wimbledon, Merton and Malden Sea Cadet Corps (368 Unit); Vice-Pres. and Past Chm. Inst. of Amateur Cinematographers; Mem. Society of Engineers; Mem. Royal Society of St. George. *Recreations:* yachting, photography, tennis, curling. *Address:* Pyms, 1 Neville Avenue, New Malden, Surrey. *T.:* Malden 5669. *Clubs:* City Livery, United Wards, Royal Automobile, City Livery Yacht; Royal Motor Yacht (Sandbanks, Bournemouth). [*Died* 16 *Oct.* 1964.

DERRY, Henry F. H.; *see* Handley-Derry.

DERVILLE, Major Max T.; *see* Teichman-Derville.

de SABATA, Victor; Italian conductor and composer; Supreme Counsellor, La Scala, Milan; Vice-President, St. Cecilia Musical Academy, Rome; *b.* Trieste, 1892; *m.* 1923, Eleonora Rossi Perez; one *s.* one *d.* *Educ.:* Conservatorio, Milan (first prize). Since then he has conducted at the Monte Carlo Opera House, and every season at La Scala, 1929-. Chief compositions include: *Operas:* Il Macigno (later called Driada); Lisistrata; *Symphonic Poems:* Juventus; La Notte Di Platon; Gethsemani; *Ballet:* The Thousand and One Nights. Stage music and vocal music for The Merchant of Venice. His music was first conducted by Toscanini and Richard Strauss. He has conducted orchestras all over Europe and in N. and S. America; among them Salzburg Festival; Bayreuth Festival; London Symphony; London Philharmonic; Philharmonia of Vienna. Has conducted tours of La Scala to Berlin, London, Edinburgh. Golden Medal, Columbus Day; Golden Medal for Culture, 1955; Grand Cross of the Republic, Italy, 1955. *Address:* Via Caroncini 47, Rome, Italy. [*Died* 10 *Dec.* 1967.

de SATGÉ, Lt.-Col. Sir Henry (Valentine Bache), K.C.V.O., *cr.* 1956 (C.V.O. 1931); C.M.G. 1919; D.S.O. 1916; J.P.; Gentleman Usher in Ordinary to the Queen 1952-64 (to King George V, 1927-36, to King Edward VIII, 1936, and to King George VI, 1937-52), Extra Gentleman Usher since 1964; Barrister; *b.* 1874; *o. s.* of late H. de Satgé of Hartfield, Malvern Wells, Worcestershire, and Stratton Manor, Dorset; *m.* 1897, Lorna Mary (*d.* 1948), *d.* of Sir Gerard Smith, K.C.M.G.; one *s.* *Educ.:* Eton. A.D.C. to the Governor of Western Australia, 1896-97; called to Bar, 1906; was in the Dorset and East Surrey Militia and Special Reserve; raised and commanded a Battery (6th Stafford) 3rd N. Midland Brigade, R.F.A., 1911; Lt.-Col, 1916; served European War, 1915-1919 (despatches, D.S.O., C.M.G.); commanded 298th Brigade, R.F.A.; Private Secretary to First Lord of the Admiralty, 1922-24; Ceremonial Secretary, Colonial Office, 1925-31. *Address:* 6 York House, Kensington, W.8. *T.:* Western 8735. *Club:* Carlton. [*Died* 10 *June* 1964.

DE SAUMAREZ, 5th Baron (*cr.* 1831), **James St. Vincent Broke Saumarez,** Bt. 1801; late Captain Scots Guards; *b.* 29 Nov. 1889; *e. s.* of 4th Baron and Jane Anne, O.B.E. (*d.* 1933), *d.* of Capt. Charles A. Vere Broke, R.E.; *S.* father, 1937; *m.* 1914, Gunhild, *y. d.* of Maj.-Gen. V. G. Balck of Sweden, Hon. K.C.M.G.; one *s.* two *d.* (and one *s.* decd.). *Educ.:* Harrow; Trinity College, Cambridge. Served European War, 1914-18 (wounded, 1914); also served as A.D.C. to Air Marshal Viscount Trenchard, 1918; retired, 1919; High Sheriff of Suffolk, 1932. *Heir:* *s.* Hon. James Victor Broke Saumarez [*b.* 1924; *m.* 1953, Joan (Julia) Charlton; two *s.* (twins) one *d.* *Educ.:* Eton; Magdalene Coll., Cambridge. Served War of 1939-45, France and Germany, Life Guards, 1942-45; attached Phantoms, British Army of Occupation, Germany, 1945-47]. *Address:* Springfield Estate, Bredasdorp, Cape Province, S. Africa *Club:* Civil Service (Capetown). [*Died* 16 *Jan.* 1969.

DE SAUSMAREZ, Brig.-Gen. Cecil, C.B. 1923; C.M.G. 1918; D.S.O. 1900; retired; *b.* 29 Sept. 1870; *s.* of Rev. Havilland De Sausmarez and Anne Priaulx Walters; *m.* 1905, Mildred (*d.* 1937), *e. d.* of Rev. J. P. Morgan, Rector of Llandyssil, Montgomery; one *s.* two *d.* *Educ.:* Winchester; R.M.A., Woolwich. Entered Royal Artillery, 1889; Capt. 1899; Major, 1910; Lt.-Col. 1916; Col. 1919; Senior Transport Officer 1st Division and Western District, S.A.F.F., 1900-2; served S. Africa, 1900-2; (despatches twice, Queen's medal with 3 clasps, King's medal with 2 clasps, D.S.O.); Bazar Valley, 1908 (despatches, brevet Major); in command of 2nd Derajat M.B. 1904-9; D.A.A.G., Abbottabad Brigade, 1909-10; General Staff Officer, 2nd Grade, 2nd (Rawalpindi) Division, 1910-13; European War (despatches, Bt. Lt.-Col.); severely wounded while commanding 108 Heavy Battery at the Aisne; at War Office, 1915-20 (Brig.-Gen., 1917-20); commanded No. 1 Pack Arty. Bde., May-Dec. 1920 (mentions thrice, C.M.G., Bt.-Col.); Officer i/c R.G.A. Records, 1921-25; retired pay, 1925. *Address:* Sausmarez Manor, St. Martin's, Guernsey. [*Died* 20 *Aug.* 1966.

de SAUSMAREZ, (Lionel) Maurice, M.A., A.R.A. 1964; R.B.A. 1952; N.E.A.C. 1950; A.R.C.A. 1939; Principal of the Byam Shaw School of Drawing and Painting, London, since 1962; Painter, lecturer and writer on the visual arts; *b.* 20 October 1915; *s.* of C. M. de Sausmarez and Jessie Rose Macdonald (*née* Bamford); *m.* 1st, 1939, Kate Elizabeth Lyons; one *d*; 2nd, 1963, Jane Elizabeth Boswell; two *s.* one *d.* *Educ.:* Christ's Hospital. Royal College of Art, London (Royal Exhibitioner, 1936-1939). Chm. Artists Internat. Assoc., 1946-1948; Head of Dept. of Fine Art, Univ. of Leeds, 1950-59; Pres., Soc. for Educn. through Art (S.E.A.); Mem., Nat. Council for Diplomas in Art and Design, 1968-. Exhibitor: Royal Academy, London Group, R.B.A., N.E.A.C., Leicester Galls., Contemp. Art Soc. and Arts Council. Work in: Victoria and Albert Museum, N.Z. National Gallery, Civic Art Galls. of Leeds, Hull and Bedford; bought by Contemp. Art Soc.; commissioned by Pilgrim Trust (Recording Britain); portraits for Universities, Colleges, Schools and other public bodies. *Publications:* Basic Design: The Dynamics of Visual Form, 1964; Poussin's Orpheus and Eurydice, 1969; articles on visual arts and art education in various journals; broadcasts; reviews in periodicals. *Recreation:* music. *Address:* 16 Leaside Ave., Fortis Green, N.10. *T.:* Tudor 0618. [*Died* 27 *Oct.* 1969.

de SELINCOURT, Aubrey; late English master, Bryanston School; late Headmaster of Clayesmore School; *b.* 7 June 1894; 2nd *s.* of Martin de Sélincourt; *m.* 1919, Irene Rutherford McLeod; two *d.* *Educ.:* Rugby School; University College, Oxford (Classical scholar). War service, 1914-18, in Gallipoli with 7th North Staffs and in France with R.A.F.; Senior Classical Master at the Dragon School, Oxford, 1924-29; Editor of Oxford Magazine, 1927-29. *Publications:* Streams of Ocean, 1922; Family Afloat, 1940; Three Green Bottles, 1941; One Good Tern, 1943; One More Summer, 1944; Six O'clock and After (with Irene de Sélincourt), 1945; Calicut Lends a Hand, 1946; Micky, 1947; Dorset, 1947; Isle of Wight; Capful of Wind; Sailing, 1948; Mr. Oram's Story; Kestrel, 1949; The Raven's Nest, 1949; Odysseus the Wanderer, 1950; The Schoolmaster, 1951; On Reading Poetry, 1952; The Channel Shore, 1953; Six Great Englishmen, 1953; Herodotus (translation), 1954; Cat's Cradle, 1955; Six Great Poets, 1956; Nansen, 1957; Arrian (translation), 1958; Six Great Thinkers, 1958; Six Great Playwrights, 1960; Livy (translation), 1960; The Book of the Sea, 1961; The World of Herodotus, 1962; various literary journalism. *Recreation:* yacht cruising. *Address:* Nutkins, Niton, Ventnor, I.W. *T.:* Niton 300. *Clubs:* Royal Cruising, P.E.N.; Oxford University Authentics. [*Died* 20 *Dec.* 1962.

de SILVA, Rt. Hon. Lucien Macull Dominic, P.C. 1953; Q.C. 1938; Member of the Judicial Committee of the Privy Council; *b.* Ceylon, 25 April 1893; *s.* of G. de Silva; *m.* 1930, Anne C., *d.* of George G. Edwards, Llandrinio, Montgomeryshire; no *c.* *Educ.:* Royal College, Colombo; Trinity College, Kandy; St. John's College, Cambridge. Called to Bar, 1916; Bencher, Gray's Inn, 1953. Solicitor-General, Ceylon, 1931; K.C. Ceylon Bar, 1931; acted as Attorney-Gen., Ceylon, 1932, and as Puisne Judge, 1933; retired from Service of Government of Ceylon, 1934; K.C. Bar of England, 1938; Chairman, Commission to Enquire into Bribery, State Council, Ceylon, 1941-43; Chairman, Commission to enquire into Law relating to Mortgage, Credit Facilities and Protection of Lands of Agriculturists, Ceylon, 1943-45; Chm., Delimitation Commission, Ceylon, 1946; Ceylon Delegate, Commonwealth Conference on Citizenship, 1947; Chm., Commission to enquire into Law Relating to Companies, Ceylon, 1948; Ceylon Delegate, Commonwealth Relations Conference, Canada, 1949. Hon. Fellow St. John's Coll., Cambridge, 1955-. *Address:* Willow Brook, Hassocks, Sussex. [*Died* 28 *Nov.* 1962.

DESMOND, Shaw, D.Litt., F.R.S.A.; sociologist, novelist, dramatist, poet; *b.* Ireland, 19 Jan. 1877; father Irish, mother English; *m.* 1911, Karen Ewald (*d.* 1954), Danish author; one *d.* (one *s.* decd.). *Educ.:* by Irish monks and life. Left school at 15 to go into business in London; later one year's farming, etc., in Ireland; lectured widely in Danish and English throughout Scandinavia, otherwise throughout U.K. and U.S.A.; Sec. and Director of public companies in London before giving up business for literature and journalism in 1909; contested Battersea (Socialist) against John Burns, 1910; sailed round Cape Horn in windjammer and travelled 7000 miles in Africa, 1930-31; trawled to Arctic, 1939; Founder of the International Institute for Psychical Research, 1934; Director of the Sunday Theatre. Hon. D.Litt. (Université Internationale), 1948. *Publications:* Fru Danmark (in Danish), 1917; The Soul of Denmark, 1918; Democracy, 1919; Passion, 1920; My Country; Gods; Labour: the Giant with the Feet of Clay, 1921; Citizenship, 1922; The Drama of Sinn Fein, 1923; The Isle of Ghosts, 1925; Ragnarock, 1926; Echo; London Nights of Long Ago, 1927 (illustrated); Tales of the Little Sisters of Saint Francis (illustrated), 1929; The Love-Diary of a Boy, 1930; Windjammer: The Book of the Horn, 1932; The Story of a Light Lady, 1933; We do not Die, 1934; African Log, 1935; God —?; London Pride, 1936; World-Birth, 1937; Chaos, 1938; Reincarnation for Everyman; After Sudden Death, 1939; Life and Foster Freeman, 1940; You can speak with your Dead, Incarnate Isis, Spiritualism?, 1941; How you live when you Die, 1942; Love after Death; Jesus or Paul?, 1945; Paradise Row (novel), 1946; The Story of Adam Verity (novel), 1947; The Edwardian Story, 1950; Personality and Power, Nathaniel (novel), Psychic Pitfalls, 1950; Pilgrim to Paradise, 1951; Love by the Dark Water (novel), 1952; Adam and Eve, 1954; Irish Moon (novel), 1953; Healing: Psychic and Divine, 1956; God's Englishman, 1956; many of which appeared in U.S. and foreign editions. *Recreations:* music, ju-jutsu, dancing, sailing, fishing, gardening, cricket, tennis. *Address*: Leicester House, 5 Montpelier Row, Twickenham, Middlesex. *T.:* Popesgrove 2664. [*Died* 23 *Dec.* 1960.

de SOISSONS, Louis, C.V.O. 1956; O.B.E. 1918; R.A. 1953 (A.R.A. 1942); F.R.I.B.A. 1923 (A.R.I.B.A. 1918); S.A.D.G., M.T.P.I. 1923; Architectural Town Planner, Welwyn Garden City Development Corporation; *b.* Montreal, Canada, 31 July 1890; *yr. s.* of Count de Soissons; *m.* 1922, Elinor Penrose-Thackwell; three *s.* *Educ.:* Bewshers; privately. Articled to J. H. Eastwood, F.R.I.B.A.; student R.A. Schools and cole des Beaux Arts, Paris; Tite Prizeman, 1912; Jarvis Rome Scholar, 1913. R.I.B.A. Distinction in Town Planning, 1945. Vice Principal, Upper School of the Architectural Association, 1929-1933; Architect, Welwyn Garden City, Herts; Architect for Italy, Imperial War Graves Commn., 1944-; Member Royal Fine Art Commn., 1949-61; Mem. Central Housing Advisory Cttee. and Burt Cttee.; Treas., Roy. Acad. of Arts, and Trustee of the Chantrey Bequest, 1959-. Works include: (as Senior Partner of Louis de Soissons, Peacock, Hodges and Robertson) Welwyn Garden City, Herts, with its houses, industrial and social service buildings, schools, shops, stores, theatre, banks, etc. Factories for Murphy Radio and Ardath Ltd.; Offices for the Royal Exchange Assurance; Churches at Welwyn Garden City and Plymouth. Flats and houses for Duchy of Cornwall, War Office, L.C.C., Plymouth Corporation, St. Marylebone Borough Council and other Boroughs, District Councils and Housing Socs.; Infants, Primary and Secondary Schools in Plymouth, College for Further Education and other schools at Welwyn Garden City, as well as London and Bedford. King George VI Memorial; reinstatement of premises for Leathersellers Company; new building for Royal College of Obstetricians and Gynæcologists; Homes for the retired and aged at Plymouth, Eastbourne, Shenfield and New Malden. Served European War, 1914-19 (despatches, O.B.E., Crown of Italy, Croce di Guerra). *Address:* (business) 3 Park Square Mews, Upper Harley St., N.W.1; Midland Bank Chambers, Welwyn Garden City. *T.:* Welwyn Garden 3806; 12 Baring Crescent, Exeter. *T.:* Exeter 58226; (private) 4 Park Square West, N.W.1. *T.:* Welbeck 9248. *Clubs:* Athenæum, Arts. [*Died* 23 *Sept.* 1962.

de SOYSA, Sir (Lambert) Wilfred (Alexander), Kt., *cr.* 1938; Landed Proprietor; Chairman: De Soysa & Co. Ltd.; De Soysa Estates Ltd.; Mahajana Insurance Ltd.; *b.* 20 Feb. 1884; 7th *s.* of Charles Henry de Soysa, J.P., and Catherine, Lady de Soysa, *widow* of a Knight Bachelor by a special charter; *m.* 1907, Evelyn Johanna Publina Fernando, O.B.E. 1956 (M.B.E. 1950); six *s.* two *d.* *Educ.:* Royal College, Colombo; Royal Agricultural Coll., Cirencester, England (Diploma; Bledisloe Gold Medal, 1962). Twice Acting Mem. of Ceylon Legislative Council; Member of Central Board of Agriculture at Peradeniya, Ceylon; Chairman of Low Country Products Association of Ceylon, 1920 and 1935; Chairman, Agricultural and Industrial Credit Corp. of Ceylon, 1943-49; Pres. Ceylon Chamber of Commerce. Served on the Headmen Commission in 1934; Vice-Pres. Ceylon Cattle Breeders' Assoc.; patron of a number of societies and associations in his ancestral home, Moratuwa; Member Royal Agricultural Society, England; Royal Commonwealth Socy.; India, Pakistan and Ceylon Socy., London. *Recreation:* billiards. *Address:* 25 Barnes Place, Colombo, Ceylon. *T.:* Colombo 95131. *Club:* National Liberal. [*Died* 3 *May* 1968.

de SOYZA, Gunasena, C.M.G. 1954; O.B.E; 1948; High Commissioner for Ceylon in the United Kingdom since 1960; *b.* 20 Dec. 1902; *s.* of late C. A. de Soyza, Inspector of Schools; *m.* 1933, Lavinia Swarnapali Gunasekara; one *s.* two *d.* *Educ.:* Ceylon Univ. Coll.; Jesus Coll., Oxford. Cadet Ceylon C.S., 1926; Asst. Govt. Agent, 1932; Dep. Registrar, 1934, Actg. Registrar, 1938, Co-operative Societies; Comr. of Cooperative Development, 1945; Perm. Sec. Min. of Food and Cooperative Undertakings, 1948; Perm. Sec., Min. of Health, 1951; Chief Planning Comr., 1953. Perm. Sec. Ministry of Defence and External Affairs, Ceylon, 1953. *Recreation:* bridge. *Address:* 21 Addison Road, W.14. *T.:* Park 9833. *Clubs:* Orient (Ceylon); Sinhalese Sports (Ceylon). [*Died* 12 *Oct.* 1961.

de STACPOOLE, 5th Duke (Papal States, *cr.* 1830); **George de Stacpoole,** J.P.; Knight of Malta; Captain, late 3rd Batt. Connaught Rangers; *b.* 8 March 1886; *s.* of 4th Duke de Stacpoole and Pauline (*d.* 1944), *o. c.* of Edward MacEvoy, late M.P. Co. Meath; *S.* father, 1929; *m.* 1915, Eileen Constance, *o. d.* of late James Palmer, Glenlo

Abbey, Galway; two *s.* two *d.* (and one *s.* killed, War of 1939-45). *Educ.:* Downside. *Address:* Tobertynan, Co. Meath. *Club:* Kildare Street (Dublin). [*Died* 3 *April* 1965.

de STEIN, Sir Edward, Kt. 1946; President Gallaher Ltd.; *b.* 16 June 1887; *s.* of Clara Annie and Sigmund Sinauer de Stein; *g.s.* of Baron de Stein. *Educ.:* Eton; Magdalen College, Oxford. Major K.R.R.C., 1914-18; Director of Finance (Raw Materials), Ministry of Supply, 1941-46. Chm., Finance Cttee., British Red Cross Soc., until 1963 (Certificate of Honour Class I). Director, Lazard Bros. & Co. Ltd., 1960-62. *Publication:* Poets in Picardy, 1919. *Recreations:* fishing, shooting. *Address:* Flat 12, 20 Lowndes Square, S.W.1. *T.:* Belgravia 4243; Fulling Mills, Kings Worthy, Hants. *Clubs:* Brooks's, M.C.C. [*Died* 3 *Nov.* 1965.

de TORRENTÉ, Henry; Swiss diplomat; *b.* 5 Nov. 1893; *s.* of Henri de Torrenté, Member of Parliament and President of the Upper Chamber, Switzerland; *m.* 1944, Anne-Marie de Courten; one *d.* *Educ.:* classical schools at Sion and Einsiedeln; Universities of Berne, Basle, and Geneva. Degrees in law, social science, and commercial sciences. Sec. to Delegate of Federal Council for social legislation, 1922; Sec. Federal Dept. of Public Economy, 1923; First Sec. then Counsellor to Swiss Legation, France, 1928-41; on General Staff, Swiss Army, 1929 (Col. 1941); Federal Delegate for trade negotiations with Spain, France, Portugal, U.S.A., Belgium, and Holland, 1942; nominated Minister plenipotentiary, 1945; Swiss Min. to China, 1945-48; Deleg. to Philippine Islands, 1946; Swiss Minister to Court of St. James's, 1948-54; Representative of Swiss Government at Coronation of Queen Elizabeth II, June 1953; Swiss Minister to the United States, 1954-57; Swiss Ambassador to the United States, 1959-60; retd. 1960. Hon. Dr. Polit. Sciences, Univ. of Geneva, 1959. *Address:* Sion, Switzerland. [*Died* 27 *March* 1962.

DEUTSCH, Professor Otto Erich, Dr.Phil. (*h.c.*) Univ. of Tübingen, 1960; *b.* Vienna, 5 Sept. 1883; *s.* of Ignaz Deutsch and Ernestine Gewitsch; *m.* 1917, Johanna Müller (*decd.*); one *s.* one *d.* *Educ.:* Vienna and Graz Universities. University Assitant, 1909-11, bookseller and publisher, 1919-24. Librarian of the Music Collection, A. van Hoboken, 1926-35, all in Vienna; Editor of the British Union Catalogue of Old Music, 1946-50. Served War of 1914-18, Austrian Army, 1915-18 (finally First Lieut.), Prof., 1928; emigrated to England, 1939; naturalized, 1947; returned to Austria, 1952. Vienna Medal of Honour, 1953; Austrian Cross of Honour, 1st Cl., for Science and Art, 1959; Prize of the City of Vienna for his contribution to the Arts, 1966. *Publications:* Franz Schubert, Die Dokumente seines Lebens und Schaffens, 2 vols., Munich, 1913-14; Schubert, A Documentary Life, London, 1948 (German edn., 1964); Schubert, Thematic Catalogue of all his Works, 1951; Handel, A Documentary Life, London, 1955; Schubert, Memoirs by his friends, 1958; Mozart, Die Dokumente seines Lebens, 1961 (English edn., 1965); Mozart und seine Welt in zeitgenössischen Bildern, 1961; Author or Editor of about fifty other books on, or of, Music, Literature, Fine Art and Bibliography, 1905-1965. *Address:* Schwarzenbergplatz 10, Vienna IV. *T.:* 6540853. [*Died* 23 *Nov.* 1967.

DEUTSCHER, Isaac; Author and Lecturer; also Broadcaster and Televiser in various languages; *b.* 3 April 1907; *s.* of Jacob Deutscher and Gustawa Jolles; *m.* 1947, Tamara (*née* Lebenhaft); one *s.* *Educ.:* Cracow. Journalistic work in Polish Press, 1924-39; Mem., Communist Party of Poland and Ed. of Communist periodicals, 1926-32; expelled for leading an anti-Stalinist opposition, 1932; Polish Correspondent in London, 1939. On editorial staff of The Economist, 1942-49; on editorial staff of The Observer (pen-name Peregrine), 1942-47; Roving correspondent in Europe, 1946-47. Dafoe Foundation Lecturer, Canada, 1959. Participant in Washington-Berkeley-New York "Teach-ins" on war in Vietnam, 1965-66. G. M. Trevelyan Lecturer, Cambridge University, 1966-67; Distinguished Vis. Prof., New York State Univ., Harpar Coll., 1967; Vis. Lecturer at many other American univs., 1967. Mem. Tribunal concerned with Internat. War Crimes, 1966-67. Syndicated articles in leading newspapers of Europe, America and Asia. Research on the Trotsky Archives at Harvard Univ., 1950 and 1959. *Publications:* The Moscow Trial, 1936, and many essays and pamphlets published in Polish before 1939; Stalin, A Political Biography, 1949 (new, enlarged editions, 1966, 1967); Soviet Trade Unions, 1950; Russia—What Next (U.S.A.), 1953; Russia after Stalin, 1953; The Prophet Armed, 1954; Heretics and Renegades, 1955; Russia in Transition (U.S.A.), 1957; Tragédie du communisme polonais entre deux guerres, 1958; The Prophet Unarmed, 1959; The Great Contest: Russian and the West, 1960; The Prophet Outcast, 1963; Ironies of History, Essays on Contemporary Communism, 1966; The Unfinished Revolution: Russia 1917-1967 (the G. M. Trevelyan Lectures, delivered Univ. Camb.), 1967; (Editor, and author Introd.) The Age of Permanent Revolution, A Trotsky Anthology, 1964 (U.S.A.); (co-author) The Era of Violence, Vol. XII of New Cambridge Modern History, 1960; contrib. The Socialist Register, 1964 and 1965; contrib. Encyclopædia Britannica and learned journals; The Stalin Myth, 1957; The Great Purges, 1963, serial radio scripts of dramatised historical documentaries. *Posthumous Publications*: The Chinese Cultural Revolution, 1968; The Non-Jewish Jew and other essay (ed. T. Deutscher), 1968; Russia, China and the West (ed. F. Halliday) 1970; Lenin's Childhood, 1970. *Address:* 2A Kidderpore Gdns., N.W.3. *T.:* Swiss Cottage 2873. *Club:* Reform. [*Died* 19 *Aug.* 1967.

de VILLIERS, Maj.-Gen. Isaac Pierre, C.B. 1942; M.C.; Chairman, Union Immigration Selection Board since 1947; *b.* Somerset East, Cape Province, 20 Aug. 1891; *s.* of late Jan S. de Villiers, Cape Town; *m.* 1936, Vivien Patricia, *d.* of late Rupert Marais. *Educ.:* Gill College; South African College School; South African College. Served War of 1939-45, Middle East (C.B.); G.O.C. Coastal Area Command; Commissioner of South African Police; retired, 1945. *Address:* Little Sunlawns, Olifantsfontein, Transvaal, South Africa. [*Died* 11 *Oct.* 1967.

DEVINE, George (Alexander Cassady), C.B.E. 1957; Actor and Producer; Artistic Director, English Stage Company (Royal Court Theatre), 1955-65; *b.* 20 Nov. 1910; *s.* of George Devine and Ruth Cassady; *m.* 1939, Audrey Sophia Harris; one *d.* *Educ.:* Clayesmore School; Wadham Coll., Oxford. Productions: Great Expectations, 1939; The Tempest, 1940; Rebecca, 1940; Bartholomew Fair, 1950; Don Carlos (Verdi), 1951; Eugene Onegin (Tchaikovsky); Volpone, 1952; Romeo and Juliet (Opera, Sutermeister); Taming of the Shrew; King Lear; King John, 1953; A Midsummer Night's Dream; The Taming of the Shrew; Nelson (opera, L. Berkeley); Troilus and Cressida (opera, W. Walton), 1954; The Magic Flute, 1955; King Lear, 1955; The Mulberry Bush, The Crucible, Don Juan, The Death of Satan, The Good Woman of Setzuan, The Country Wife, 1956 (New York, 1957); Nekrassov, Edin. Festival, 1957; lso directed: The Sport of my Mad

Mother; Major Barbara; Live like Pigs; End Game; Cock-a-Doodle Dandy; Rosmersholm; Platonov; August for the People; Happy Days; Exit the King, 1963; Play, 1964. Manager and Producer, London Theatre Studio, 1936-39; Director Old Vic, 1946-51, and founder Young Vic. Served War of 1939-45 (despatches twice). *Recreation:* travel. [*Died* 20 *Jan.* 1966.

de VOIL, Very Rev. Walter Harry, M.A., Ph.D. (Edin.); Dean of Brechin since 1957; Rector of Holy Rood, Carnoustie, since 1949; *b.* 24 May 1893; *e. s.* of late Charles Walter de Voil; *m.* 1940 Mary Winifred, *er. d.* of late Rev. Nathaniel Baxter, Gortnessy, Co. Londonderry; two *s.* (one adopted). *Educ.:* Edinburgh Univ. and Theolog. Coll.; Germany. M.A. 1924, Ph.D. 1936, Edin. Served Army, 1914-20, Herts. Regt.; commnd. (S.R.), P.W.O. W. Yorks. Regt., 1917. Deacon. 1924; Priest. 1925; Asst. Curate, St. Margaret's, Lochee, 1924-27; Chap., St. Ninian's Cath., Perth, 1927-32; Asst. Curate, St. Peter Mancroft, Norwich, 1932-33; Rector: St. John, Pittenweem, 1933-35, St. Margaret, Leven, 1935-42, Fife; Vicar, Holy Trinity, Elsecar, Yorks., 1942-49. *Publications:* Patrick Murray Smythe, Priest, 1935; Old Catholic Eucharistic Worship, 1936, etc. *Recreations:* foreign travel, hill climbing, cycling, antiquarian research. *Address:* Holy Rood Rectory, Carnoustie. Angus, Scotland. [*Died* 9 *Sept.* 1964.

DEVONS, Professor Ely; Professor of Economics, University of London, since 1965; Member (Part-time): of Local Government Commission for England, 1959-65; of Monopolies Commission, since 1966; *b.* 29 July 1913; *s.* of Rev. D. I. Devons; *m.* 1939, Estelle Wine (pianist); two *s.* one *d.* *Educ.:* Hanley High Sch.; Portsmouth Gram. Sch.; North Manchester Municipal High School; Manchester Univ. Manchester Univ.: B.A. Hons. Econ., 1934; Drummond Fraser Res. Fell., 1934-35; M.A.Econ., 1935. Economic Assist., Joint Committee of Cotton Trade Organisations, Manchester, 1935-39; Statistician, Cotton Control, Ministry of Supply, 1939-40; Statistician, Economic Section of War Cabinet Offices and later Chief Statistician Central Statistical Office, 1940-41; Chief Statistician, Director of Statistics, Director-General of Planning, Programmes and Statistics, Ministry of Aircraft Production, 1941-45; Robert Ottley Reader in Applied Economics, Victoria Univ. of Manchester, 1945. Robert Ottley Professor of Applied Economics, Victoria University of Manchester, 1948-59; Professor of Commerce (with special reference to international trade), University of London, at London School of Economics and Political Science, 1959-65. Newmarch Lectr., University College, London, 1954; Member Council, Royal Economic Society, 1956-64; President, Manchester Statistical Society, 1958-59. Harkness Vis. Prof., Johns Hopkins Univ., 1964-1965. *Publications:* Planning in Practice, 1950; (with others) Lessons of the British War Economy, 1951; Introduction to British Economic Statistics, 1956; (with others) The Structure of British Industry, 1958; Essays in Economics, 1961; (with M. Gluckman) Closed Systems and Open Minds, 1964; Papers on Planning and Economic Management, ed. A. Cairncross, 1970 (posthumous). Articles and reviews in Manchester School, Economic Jl., Economica, Lloyds Bank Review. *Recreations:* fell walking, tree felling, looking at pictures, disputing. *Address:* Fairfield, Leigh Hill Rd., Cobham, Surrey. *T.:* Cobham 2208. *Club:* Garrick. [*Died* 28 *Dec.* 1967.

DEW, Sir Harold (Robert), Kt., *cr.* 1955; M.B., B.S., F.R.C.S. 1920; F.R.A.C.S. 1928; Sc.D. Cantab. (Hon.); F.R.C.S. Edin. (Hon.); Professor Surgery, University of Sydney, 1930-1956; Honorary Consulting Surgeon, Royal Prince Alfred Hospital, Sydney; *b.* 1891; *s.* of J. Dew of Melbourne; *m.* 1925, Doreen *d.* of late Norman Lawrance, Melbourne; two *d.* *Educ.:* Scotch College, Melbourne; Ormond College, University of Melbourne. Medical course at Univ.of Melbourne; Resident Surgeon Melbourne Hosp.; four years' war service in France and Palestine, Captain R.A.M.C.; Assistant Director Walter and Eliza Institute of Research, Melbourne, 1923-26; Honorary Surgeon to Out-patients Melbourne Hospital, 1923; Lecturer in Surgery Ormond College, Melbourne; Syme Prizeman, University of Melbourne, 1927; Jacksonian Prizeman, Royal College of Surgeons of England, 1924; Hunterian Prof., Roy. Coll. of Surgeons of England, 1930 and 1953; Sims Commonwealth travelling Professor, 1952-53; President Royal Australasian College of Surgeons, 1954-55. *Publications:* Malignant Disease of the Testicle, 1925; Hydatid Disease, 1928; numerous articles in medical and surgical journals. *Recreations:* fly-fishing, yachting, tennis, field shooting. *Address:* Goombara, Jells Rd., Wheelers Hill, Victoria, Australia. [*Died* 17 *Nov.* 1962.

DEWAR, John, C.B.E. 1938; Retired Colonial Officer; *b.* Alexandra, New Zealand, 10 Dec. 1883; *s.* of late John Dewar and Bethia Bringans; *m.* 1911, Gladys Kathleen Plunkett; one *s.* *Educ.:* New Zealand Univ. Survey Dept., New Zealand, 1901-06; Colonial Survey Service, 1906-38; Surveyor General, Malaya, 1933-38. *Address:* 3 Castle Mount, St. Valerie Road, Bournemouth, Hants. *T.:* Bournemouth 24892. [*Died* 12 *April* 1964.

DEWAR, Vice-Adm. Kenneth Gilbert Balmain, C.B.E. 1919; R.N.; *b.* near Edinburgh, 1879; *s.* of late Dr. Jas. Dewar; *m.* 1914, Gertrude, *y. d.* of late Frederick and Hon. Mrs. Stapleton-Bretherton of the Hall, Rainhill, Lancashire; one *s.* Entered H.M.S. Britannia, 1893; Midshipman, 1895; Lieut. 1900; Commander, 1911; Captain, 1918; awarded Gold Medal of the Royal United Service Institution, 1912; Assistant Director of Plans Division Naval Staff, 1917; Deputy Director Naval Intelligence Division, 1925-27; commanded H.M.S. Royal Oak and Tiger, 1928-29; Rear-Adm. and retired list, 1929; Vice-Adm., retired, 1934. *Publication:* The Navy from Within, 1939. *Address:* The Little House, Charmandean, Worthing, Sussex. *Club:* United Service. [*Died* 8 *Sept.* 1964.

de WATTEVILLE, Lieutenant-Colonel (Hon. Colonel) Herman Gaston, C.B.E. 1919; *b.* 19 Sept. 1875; *e. s.* of A. de Watteville, M.A., M.D., London; *m.* 1914, Hope (*d.* 1960), *o. d.* of C. Calthrop, artist; one *s.* *Educ.:* Westminster; Christ Church, Oxford (Exhibitioner) B.A. Honours, 1898, M.A. 1934. Royal Artillery, 1900-24; p.s.c. 1910; passed Naval War College, 1911; served European War (despatches, Brevet Lieut.-Colonel, C.B.E., Legion of Honour); Military Editor, Royal United Service Institution, 1924-35; i/c Information Branch of the Censorships, 1938; Assistant Master, Lancing College, 1940-41, Mill Hill School, 1942 and 1945; Political Intelligence Department, Foreign Office, 1943-44 (graded Colonel on Staff). *Publications:* Waziristan, 1919-20; Lord Roberts, 1939; Lord Kitchener, 1939; The British Soldier, 1954; numerous articles in daily press and magazines (military and otherwise). *Recreations:* ski-ing, gardening, motor touring abroad, antiquities. [*Died* 31 *Dec.* 1963.

DEWEY, Rt. Rev. Monsignor Edward, C.B.E. 1949; R.N. (retd.); Senior R.C. Chaplain R.N., 1940-50; late Vicar-General (R.C.) R.N.; *b.* 29 Feb. 1884; *e. s.* of John and Mary Dewey. *Educ.:*

Beaconfield College, Plymouth; St. Boniface's College, Plymouth; Colegio Inglés, Valladolid, Spain. Priest, 1907; Priest at Plymouth Cathedral; The Assumption, Torquay; St. Joseph's, Newton Abbot; SS. Michael and Joseph's, Devonport; R.N. Chaplain, 1921; senior R.C. Chaplain, Mediterranean Fleet, H.M.S. Queen Elizabeth, 1931; R.C. Chaplain Boys' Training Establishment, H.M.S. Caledonia, 1937; H.M.S. Pembroke, 1940; H.M.S. President for duty outside the Admiralty, 1943; retired, 1950. *Address:* St. John of God Nursing Home, Abbey Road, Torquay, Devon. [*Died* 27 *Dec.* 1965.

DEWEY, Kenneth Thomas, M.A. (Oxon); *b.* 16 August 1902; *o. s.* of late Samuel Dewey, Oakwood, Selsey, Sussex; unmarried. *Educ.:* Collyer's School; Lincoln College, Oxford, B.A. 1924, M.A. 1930. Senior Science Master at Bloxham, 1925-1940; Housemaster, 1927-39; Officer commanding Officers' Training Corps, 1931-39; Founded the Society of The Friends of Bloxham, afterwards The Bloxham Society, 1931; Second Master, 1937-40; Acting Headmaster, 1939-40; Headmaster of Bloxham School, 1940-52; Member of Headmasters' Conference, 1941-52. *Recreations:* swimming, walking. *Address:* c/o Lloyds Bank, Banbury, Oxon. [*Died* 14 *March* 1961.

DEY, Helen, C.B.E. 1946 (O.B.E. 1937); R.R.C. 1918; Matron and Superintendent of Nursing, St. Bartholomew's Hospital, E.C.1. 1927-49; *b.* 17 April 1888; *d.* of Robert Alexander Dey. *Educ.:* Aberdeen; Berlin. Training as a nurse at St. Bartholomew's Hospital; served in Q.A.I.M.N.S.. 1914-21 (despatches thrice); Assistant Superintendent of Nurses, The Receiving Hospital, Detroit, U.S.A.; Assistant Matron, General Infirmary, Leeds; Life Vice-President: Assoc. of Hosp. Matrons and League of St. Bartholomew's Hospital Nurses; Royal College of Nursing. *Address:* The Old Coastguard Hotel, Bognor Regis, Sussex. *Clubs:* English-Speaking Union, Cowdray. [*Died* 5 *June* 1968.

de ZOUCHE, Dorothy Eva, M.A.; *b.* Dunedin, N.Z., 18 June 1886; *d.* of I. de Zouche, M.D., and Mary English. *Educ.:* Belvedere School (G.P.D.S.T.); Somerville College, Oxford, Lit. Hum. 1909. Assistant and senior classical mistress at Roedean School, 1909-17; King Edward VI High School, Birmingham, 1918-21; Headmistress, High School for Girls, Wolverhampton, Staffs., 1921-48; served on various professional and educational committees, etc.; President, Soroptimist Club of Wolverhampton (Founder), 1936-38; President Headmistresses' Association, 1939-42. *Publications:* Roedean School, 1885-1955, 1955; occasional papers (classical and educational). *Recreations:* walking, climbing, gardening. *Address:* Parkdale, Wolverhampton. *T.:* Wolverhampton 23187. [*Died* 14 *July* 1969.

DIAMOND, George le Boutillier, C.B.E. 1949; M.I.Mech.E.; Chm. West Midlands Gas Board, 1948-61, retd.; *b.* 3 July 1893; *s.* of Arthur W. Diamond; *m.* 1917, Doris Gooding; two *d.* *Educ.:* Wallington; Brighton; privately. Served European War, 1914-18, Essex Regt. and R.F.C. Engineering appts. at Brighton, York, Folkestone, Dover, Rochester, 1920-48; Director of South-Eastern Gas Corp. Ltd. Associated Cos., 1945-1948; Council, Instn. of Gas Engineers, 1939-1943; Pres. Southern Assoc. of Gas Engineers, 1943; Dep. Regional Controller and Regional Controller, Min. of Fuel and Power, South-Eastern Region, 1941-48. Member London and S.E. Regional Bd. for Industry, 1946-48; Chm., Kent Coalfield Joint Council for Production, 1945-48; Member Regional Commissioner's Advisory Council, South-Eastern Region, 1942-45. Dep. Chm., Folkestone Gen. Hosp., 1936-48; Member Kent C.C. Public Health Cttee., 1941-48; Member Medway Conservancy Bd., 1944-48; Chm. The London Cremation Co. Ltd., 1944-58; Mem. Council Birmingham Chamber of Commerce; Mem. B.I.F. Management Cttee., 1954; Mem. Weir Cttee. on Co-operation between Area and Scottish Electricity and Gas Boards, 1958. *Address:* Courtwood, Shorne, Kent. *T.:* Shorne 2278. *Clubs:* Naval and Military; Radnor (Folkestone). [*Died* 8 *Dec.* 1964.

DIBBEN, Major Cecil Reginald, C.B.E. 1955 (O.B.E. 1919); Chairman of Midland Regional Board for Industry since 1951; Chairman of British Bolt, Nut Screw and Rivet Federation; Chairman, Midland Aluminium Ltd.; *b.* 30 August 1885; *s.* of Charles Dibben; *m.* 1916, Emma Helen, *d.* of H. L. O. Grieb; no *c.* *Educ.:* Ashford Grammar School; London University. Dir. of various companies. F.I.I.A. Served European War, 1914-18 (O.B.E.); Major, retired, Royal Leicestershire Regiment. *Address:* The Green House, Tettenhall, Staffs. *Club:* Union (Birmingham). [*Died* 10 *April* 1965.

DICK, Bt. Col. Alan Macdonald, C.B.E. 1936; V.H.S. 1934; I.M.S., retd.; *b.* 30 July 1884; *s.* of late Dr. James Dick, M.D.; *m.* 1915, Muriel Angela, *d.* of late Rev. H. A. Grantham; one *s.* one *d.* *Educ.:* St. Bees School; Edinburgh Univ.; London; Vienna. M.B., Ch.B. Edin. 1st Class Honours, 1906; Resident House Surgeon, Royal Infirmary, Sick Children's Hospital and Chalmers Hospital, Edinburgh; M.R.C.S.; L.R.C.P. London, 1909; F.R.C.S. Eng., 1910; Indian Medical Service, 1909; Professor of Ophthalmology, King Edward Medical College, Lahore, 1922; retired, 1941; Consulting Ear, Nose and Throat Surgeon, Southern Army, Poona, and Adviser G.H.Q., India, 1942-44; Ophthalmic Surgeon, Northern District, Natal, 1944; Chief Medical Officer, Bahawalpur, 1944-48; Montefiore Prize; Fayrer Prize: served European War. Kachin Rising. Burma, Mesopotamia (despatches thrice, Brevet Major, O.B.E.). *Address:* The Old Vicarage, Moulsford, Berks. [*Died* 20 *March* 1970.

DICK, Professor John, B.Sc., Ph.D., M.A., F.I.Mech.E.; Professor of Mechanical Engineering, University of Dundee (formerly Queen's College, Dundee), since 1964; *b.* 6 June 1902; of Scottish parents; *m.* 1935, Elizabeth M. Band (*d.* 1940); one *s.* one *d.*; *m.* 1942, Jean M. Henderson; one *s.* *Educ.:* Waid Acad.; Glasgow Univ. Worked with various engineering firms including Albion Motors and The British Mannesmann Tube Co., 1918-29. Glasgow University, 1924-28 and 1929-30. Muir Bursar; Pendar Scholar and Gold Medallist; Walker Prizeman; George Harvey Prizeman; B.Sc. 1st Class Honours (Electrical Eng. and Mechanical Eng.), 1930; Research Asst., Univ. of Sheffield, 1930-33; Ph.D. 1933; Lecturer, Sheffield Univ., 1933-46; Univ. Demonstrator, Oxford Univ., 1946-50; Donald Pollok Reader in Engineering Science, Oxford Univ., 1950-54; Professor of Civil and Mechanical Engineering, Queen's College, Dundee, 1954-64. *Publications:* papers in various technical journals. *Recreation:* golf. *Address:* University of Dundee, Dundee. [*Died* 3 *Nov.* 1970.

DICK, Brig.-Gen. Robert Nicholas, C.M.G. 1919; D.S.O. 1918; late Royal Sussex Regiment; *b.* 1879; *s.* of late Sir James N. Dick, K.C.B., R.N.; *m.* 1919, Mary Dorothea, *o. d.* of late Robert Melvil Barry Otter-Barry, of Horkesley Hall, Essex; two *s.* (and one *s.* killed in action, 1943). *Educ.:* St. Paul's Sch., R.M.C. Sandhurst; Staff

College, Camberley. Served Somaliland, 1908-10 (despatches, medal and clasp); European War, 1914-18 (despatches, Bt. Lt.-Col., C.M.G., D.S.O.); Commanded Kent and Sussex Territorial Infantry Brigade, 1925-28; General Staff Officer, 1st grade, Western Command, 1928; retired, 1932; Lt.-Col. Home Guard, 1940-45. *Address:* Dee House, Hawkhurst, Kent. *Club:* Royal Commonwealth Society. [*Died* 11 *Aug.* 1967.

DICK, Sir William R., *see* Reid Dick.

DICKEN, Rear-Admiral Edward Bernard Cornish, C.B.E. 1947 (O.B.E. 1925); D.S.C. 1917; Royal Navy; *b.* Plymouth, 18 Jan. 1888; 2nd *s.* of late Admiral Charles G. Dicken; *m.* 1936, Monique, *d.* of Monsieur O'Ryan. Entered Navy, 1902; Commander, 1922; Captain, 1929; A.D.C. to King George VI, 1940; Rear-Adm., 1940; retired; Officer Order of the Redeemer (Greece), 1917; Naval Attaché to France, with headquarters, Paris, 1922-25. Chairman, Shipwrecked Fishermen and Mariners' Society; Assistant-Controller (Admiralty), 1940-46; Grand Officer Order of Orange-Nassau (Netherlands), 1946; Officer Legion of Honour (France), 1948. *Address:* 5 Cresford Road, Fulham, S.W.6. *Club:* United Service. [*Died* 3 *April* 1964.

DICKENS, Admiral Sir Gerald Charles, K.C.V.O., *cr.* 1937; C.B. 1934; C.M.G. 1919; Grand Cross Orange-Nassau; Commander Legion of Merit; Chevalier Légion d'Honneur; *b.* 13 Oct. 1879; 2nd *s.* of late Sir H. F. Dickens, K.C.; *m.* 1915, Kathleen Pearl, *d.* of Col. W. Birch; three *s.* *Educ.:* Beaumont College; Foster's, Stubbington. H.M.S. Britannia, 1894; Lieut. 1902; Commander, 1914; served during European War in H.M.S. Harpy (Dardanelles); Intelligence Division and subsequently as Flag Commander to Commander-in-Chief, Mediterranean; Captain, 1919; Deputy Director Plans Division Admiralty, 1920-22; H.M.S. Carlisle, 1922-24; Captain Auxiliary Patrol, 1925-26; Directing Staff, Imperial Defence College, 1926-29; H.M.S. Repulse, 1929-31; Naval A.D.C. to H.M., 1931-32; Rear-Adm., 1932; Director of Naval Intelligence Division, 1932-1935; Commanded Reserve Fleet, 1935-37; Vice-Admiral, 1936; retired list, 1938; Naval Attaché, Hague, 1940, then Principal Naval Liaison Officer with Allied Navies, subsequently Flag Officer, Tunisia, and then Flag Officer, Netherlands. *Club:* Naval and Military. [*Died* 19 *Nov.* 1962.

DICKINSON, Professor Gladys; Emeritus Professor of French, University of London, since 1963; *b.* 1 November 1895; *o. d.* of Reverend W. Dickinson and Elizabeth Croft. *Educ.:* Reading; Lyons (L. ès L.); London (B.A.); Paris. Assistant Lectr. in French, Univ. of St. Andrews, 1929-1942; Actg. Head of French Dept., Univ. Coll., Dundee, 1942-44; Reader in French, Univ. of London, at Westfield College, 1944-1960; Professor of French in the University of London, at Westfield College, 1961-1963. On Editorial Board of Bibliothèque d'Humanisme et Renaissance. *Publications:* Missions of De La Brosse, 1942; Mission de Beccarie de Pavie de Fourquevaux en Ecosse, 1948; Edition of Fourquevaux's Instructions sur le faict de la guerre, 1954; Du Bellay in Rome, 1960 (publ. Leyden). Articles in Scottish Historical Review, French Studies, Edinburgh Bibliographical Society volumes. Contrib. proc. Scottish Hist. Society. *Recreations:* travel, gardening. *Address:* 58 Denman Drive, N.W.11. [*Died* 6 *Aug.* 1964.

DICKINSON, Professor Henry Douglas; Emeritus Professor of Economics, University of Bristol; *b.* 25 Mar. 1899; *o. s.* of Henry Winram and Edith Dickinson; *m.* 1925, Sylvia (*d.* 1965), *y. d.* of H. G. Sworn, M.D.; two *d.* *Educ.:* King's Coll. Sch., Wimbledon Common; Emmanuel College, Cambridge (Economics Tripos, Part II, 1921; History Tripos, Part II, 1922). Research, London School of Economics, 1922-24; Asst. Lecturer in Economics, 1924, Lecturer in Economic History, 1933, Reader in History of Economic Thought, 1944, Univ. of Leeds (on exchange with Auckland Univ. Coll., N.Z., 1934); Sen. Lectr., Univ. of Bristol, 1947; Prof. of Economics, 1951-64; Temp. Prof. Queen's Univ., Belfast, 1964-65. *Publications:* Institutional Revenue, 1932; Economics of Socialism, 1939; contribs. Economic Jl., Economica, Review of Economic Studies, Sociological Review, etc. *Address:* 18 Little Stoke Road, Bristol 9. *T.:* Bristol 682569. [*Died* 11 *July* 1969.

DICKINSON, Professor W(illiam) Croft, C.B.E. 1963; M.C. 1917; M.A., D.Lit.; Hon. LL.D. (St. Andrews); Sir William Fraser Professor of Scottish History and Palæography in the University of Edinburgh since 1944; Editor of the Scottish Historical Review since 1947; *b.* 1897; *o. s.* of late Rev. William Dickinson and Elizabeth Croft; *m.* 1930, Florence Margery, *e. d.* of late H. M. Tomlinson; two *d.* *Educ.:* Mill Hill; St. Andrews University. Class I, Hons. History (St. Andrews), 1921. D.Lit. (London), 1928. Served in France and Flanders with 45th Coy., M.G.C. (15th Scottish Div.). Librarian of British Library of Political and Economic Science (L.S.E.), 1933-44; Rhind Lecturer in Archæology to Society of Antiquaries of Scotland, 1942; Andrew Lang Lecturer to Univ. of St. Andrews, 1951; Member: Royal Commission on Ancient and Historical Monuments (Scotland); Scottish Records Advisory Council. *Publications:* The Sheriff Court Book of Fife (Scottish History Society), 1928; (in collaboration) The Chronicle of Melrose (facsimile edition), 1936; The Court Book of the Barony of Carnwath (Scottish History Soc.), 1937; The Study of Scottish History, 1944; Borrobil, 1944; The Eildon Tree, 1947; Knox's History of the Reformation in Scotland (ed. 2 vols.), 1949; The Flag from the Isles, 1951; Two Students at St. Andrews, 1711-1716, 1952; The Sweet Singers, 1953; (in collaboration) A Source Book of Scottish History (3 vols.) 1952-54; Early Records of the Burgh of Aberdeen (Scottish Hist. Soc.), 1957; Robert Bruce, 1960; A History of Scotland from the Earliest Times to 1603, 1961; Dark Encounters, 1963; articles and reviews in historical journals. *Address:* 18 Frogston Road West, Edinburgh. *T.:* Fairmilehead 1237. [*Died* 22 *May* 1963.

DICKSON, Charles Gordon; *b.* 28 July 1884; *s.* of James Patrick and Harriet Helen Matilda Dickson; *m.* 1915, Myra Beatrice German; one *s.* one *d.* *Educ.:* Wilsons Grammar School; Kaiserliches Real Gymnasium, Krefeld; Lyon, France. Deputy Alderman; Sheriff of City of London, 1946-47. Governor: Alleyn's College of God's Gift (Dulwich College); Bethlem Royal and Maudsley Hospital; Chairman, 1950, City of London Schools. *Recreations:* county Rugby football player; golf, bowls. *Address:* Ettrick Lodge, Plaistow Lane, Bromley, Kent. *T.:* Ravensbourne 4032. *Club:* City Livery. [*Died* 8 *July* 1963.

DICKSON, John Harold; Q.C. (Scot.) 1949; Hon. Sheriff-Substitute of Ayrshire, 1948; *b.* 6 Sept. 1898; *s.* of late William Dickson, Iron and Steel Manufacturer, and of late Jessie McMeekin Strain; *m.* 1931, Emmeline Edith Gordon, *d.* of late William Thomson, Advocate. M.A., LL.B. Admitted to Scottish Bar, 1924; Sheriff Substitute of Ayrshire at Ayr, 1943-47, retd., 1947. Stipendary and Circuit Magistrate, Bahamas.

Served in Royal Naval Volunteer Reserve, 1916-19 and 1925-43 (V.R.D.), Comdr. R.N.V.R. (retd.). Member, Queen's Body Guard for Scotland (Royal Company of Archers). *Recreations:* fishing, shooting, golf, sailing. *Address:* P.O. Box 194, Suilven, Eastern Road, Nassau, Bahamas. *Clubs:* Lansdowne, Oriental; New (Edinburgh); Honourable Company of Edinburgh Golfers (Muirfield); Senior Golfers' Society; Lyford Cay, East Hill (Nassau, Bahamas). [*Died* 4 *June* 1967.

DIDSBURY, Brian, M.B., Ch.B., D.P.H., D.P.A.; Senior Principal Medical Officer, Department of Education and Science, since 1969; *b.* 27 March 1926; *s.* of Abraham Didsbury and Minnie Elizabeth Walker; *m.* 1952, Dorothy Lewis; three *s.* two *d. Educ.:* Salford Grammar Sch. Miscellaneous hosp. appts., 1950-52; Malayan Med. Service, 1952-55; Asst. M.O.H. Smethwick Co. Borough, 1956-58; Dep. M.O.H. Co. Boroughs of Gt. Yarmouth, 1958-60, and West Ham, 1960-64; S.M.O. Min. of Health, 1964-65; P.M.O., Dept. of Health and Social Security, 1965-69. *Publications:* contrib. Lancet. *Address:* 56 The Charter Road, Woodford Green, Essex. *T.:* 01-504 2718. [*Died* 3 *Sept.* 1970.

DIGBY, 11th Baron (Ire.) *cr.* 1920, 5th Baron (G.B.) *cr.* 1765, **Edward Kenelm Digby,** K.G. 1960; D.S.O. 1919; M.C.; T.D.; Col. late Coldstream Guards; Hon. Col., West Somerset Yeomanry and Dorset Garrison Royal Artillery (formerly Dorset Heavy Bde. and Coast Regiment, R.A.), 1929-60; one of H.M. Body Guard of Hon. Corps of Gentlemen-at-Arms, 1939-62; Lord Lieutenant of Dorset, 1952; *b.* 1 Aug. 1894; *e. s.* of 10th Baron and Beryl, *d.* of Hon. Albert Hood; *S.* father 1920; *m.* 1919, Hon. Pamela Bruce (O.B.E. 1944, J.P., and C.A. Dorset; Senior Commandant A.T.S. Dorset, 1938, Chief Commander A.T.S., 1940-1945), *y. d.* of 2nd Baron Aberdare; one *s.* three *d. Educ.:* Eton; Sandhurst. Served European War, 1914-19 (despatches twice, D.S.O., M.C. and bar, Croix de Guerre); Adjutant, 1st Batt. Coldstream Guards, 1915-1918; Military Secretary to Governor-General and C.-in-C. of Australia (Lord Forster), 1921-23; Assistant Inspector of Infantry, War Office, 1940-42; Inspector of Infantry Training Establishments War Office, 1942-44; President National Pony Soc., 1930-31 and 1952-53; Pres., Bath and West and Southern Counties Soc., 1931-32 and 1950-51; Pres. Hunters' Improvement and National Light Horse Breeding Soc., 1933-1934, and 1955-56; Pres. International Horse Show, 1936-37, 1937-38, and 1938-39; President English Guernsey Cattle Society, 1948-49; Deputy President Royal Agricultural Society of England 1949 and 1950 (President, 1958-59); J.P., C.A., Dorset; Chairman Dorset C.C., 1955-62 (Vice-Chm. 1951-55); Chm. Dorset T. & A.F.A., 1949- (Pres. 1952-). Pres. Brit. Soc. of Animal Production, 1955-56; Brit. Rep. on Council of European Assoc. of Animal Production, 1952-58 (Vice-Pres. 1955-58); Vice-Pres. Internat. Dendrology Union, 1952-62 (Pres. 1962-). M.F.H. Cattistock, 1926-30. V.M.H., 1958. Pres. (Dorset) B.R.C.S.; President (Dorset) Council, Order of St. John. K.St.J. Freeman of City of London. *Heir: s.* Captain Hon. Edward Henry Kenelm Digby, D.L., J.P., late Coldstream Guards, [*b.* 24 July 1924; *m.* 1952, Dione Marian, *yr. d.* of Rear-Admiral Robert St. Vincent Sherbrooke, V.C., C.B., D.S.O.; two *s.* one *d.*]. *Address:* Cerne Abbey, Dorchester, Dorset. *T.:* Cerne Abbas 284. *Clubs:* Guards, Turf, Lansdowne; Kildare Street (Dublin). [*Died* 29 *Jan.* 1964.

DIGBY-BESTE, Capt. Sir Henry Aloysius Bruno, Kt., *cr.* 1945; C.I.E. 1931; O.B.E.; J.P.; R.I.N. retd.; R.N. since 1940; *b.* 5 Nov. 1883; *s.* of Bruno Digby-Beste, *y. s.* of John Richard Digby-Beste of Botleigh Grange, D.L. and Agnes, *d.* of Rev. J. Alleyne, Barbados and Exeter; *m.* 1909, Olave (*d.* 1955), *d.* of Col. Hume-Henderson, I.M.S.; three *s.* two *d.*; *m.* 1958, Miss A. Taylor, 12 First Avenue, Hove. *Educ.:* Stonyhurst Coll. Joined Shaw Saville and Co., sailing ships, 1899; commission Sub-Lieut., R.I.M., 1905; Commander, 1918; Captain, 1928; saw service Persian Gulf Arms Traffic Operations 1910-14; H.M.S. Lawrence, 1914-15; Divisional Naval Transport Officer Central Headquarters to 1921; Command R.I.M.S. Dufferin and Clive, 1923-24; Deputy Port Conservator, Madras, 1925-26; Port Officer, Bombay, 1927; Captain Superintendent, I.M.M.T.S. Dufferin, Bombay, 1927-37; retired, 1938; War of 1939-45; A.R.P. to March 1940; joined R.N. as Temp. Capt.; served with B.E.F. in France, Shetlands, Clyde, India, 1943-45, as Commodore 2nd class; M.W.T. London and Australia as Principal British Sea Transport Officer. Chief Scout's Commissioner, 1947; Chm. Officers' Pension Soc., 1949-; Pres. Nat. Amateur Tobacco Growers' Assoc., 1951-. Chairman Branches Cttee., The Diabetic Assoc. Knight of St. Gregory, 1938. *Publications:* redrafted Marine Transport Regulations. *Address:* c/o National and Grindlay's Bank, 54 Parliament Street, S.W.1; 16 Eaton Gdns., Hove, Sussex. [*Died* 5 *Sept.* 1964.

DIGGLE, Captain Neston William, C.M.G. 1919; R.N., retired; *b.* 1880; *s.* of late Wadham Neston Diggle, of Bratton House, Westbury, Wilts; *m.* 1920, Gladys St. Aubyn, *d.* of late William Collier Angove, and *widow* of Lieut.-Col. Sir Walter Balfour Barttelot, 3rd Bt. Sometime Naval Attaché at Rome; served European War, 1914-19 (despatches, C.M.G.), and 1939-44. *Address:* Tellisford House, Tellisford, Nr. Bath, Somerset. *Club:* Army and Navy. [*Died* 17 *Dec.* 1963.

DILKE, Beaumont A. F.; *see* Fetherston-Dilke.

DILLON, Frederick, M.D. Edinburgh (Gold Medal), 1920; *b.* 14 Mar. 1887; *s.* of F. Baillie Hugh and M. Agnes Lynch Dillon; *m.* 1st, 1911, Ida Mary Sutherland; (one *s.* killed in Italy, 1943); 2nd, 1951, Dorothy Cameron. *Educ.:* St. Bede's Coll., Manchester; Univ. of Edinburgh. Consulting Physician, Dept. of Psychological Medicine, University College Hospital, and Lecturer on Mental Diseases in the Medical School, 1946-52. *Publications:* Contributor to The Neuroses in War, 1940, and to medical journals. *Recreation:* archæology. *Address:* 6 Beaconsfield, 22 Marine Parade, Hythe, Kent. *T.:* Hythe 67019. *Club:* Authors'. [*Died* 8 *May* 1965.

DIMBLEBY, Richard, C.B.E. 1959 (O.B.E. 1945); Broadcaster, Author, Newspaper Director, Editor and Film Producer; *b.* 25 May 1913; *s.* of Frederick J. G. Dimbleby and Gwendoline M. Bolwell; *m.* 1937, Dilys, *d.* of late A. A. Thomas, LL.B., Barrister-at-Law; three *s.* one *d. Educ.:* Glengorse School; Mill Hill School. Learned newspaper work with F. W. Dimbleby & Sons, Ltd., Richmond, Surrey; Editorial Staff, Southern Daily Echo and Hampshire Advertiser, 1933-34; Editorial Staff, later News Ed., Advertiser's Weekly, Fleet Street, 1935-36; appointed first news observer of B.B.C., 1936. Visited many countries for B.B.C., and broadcast reports or commentaries on major news events, including State visits to France and Canada. Became first B.B.C. War Correspondent, Sept. 1939, and went with B.E.F. to France; Chief Corresp. in M.E., Summer 1940, visiting all theatres of war and fourteen countries; entered Berlin with Br. troops, 1945, and was first B.B.C. Corresp. in Berlin during and after Potsdam Conf.; resigned from B.B.C. staff, 1946, but

continued as freelance commentator and broadcaster, particularly on Royal, State, and Governmental occasions. Commentator: for Television at Coronation, in Westminster Abbey, 1953; for Mediterranean Stages of H.M.'s Commonwealth Tour, Spring, 1954; H.M.'s State Visits: Norway, 1965; Sweden, 1956; Paris, 1957; Denmark, 1957; the Netherlands, 1958; and Italy, 1961; The General Election, 1959; State visit of President de Gaulle, 1960; Wedding of Princess Margaret, 1960; Wedding of Princess Alexandra, 1963; Budget Day Programmes, 1963, 1964 and 1965. Funeral of President Kennedy, Washington, 1963. Funeral of Sir Winston Churchill, 1965. First Eurovision relay, 1951, and subseq. regularly for Eurovision; first live television broadcast from Soviet Union, Moscow, May Day, 1961; and Commentator, first live relays from America and Japan. Winner of various National Radio and Television Awards. Television narrator or guide of "Panorama", "London Town", "About Britain", "At Home", "Choice" and (producer of) "Passport" film series, and many television outside broadcasts. Mem. of team in Sound radio "Twenty Questions" for 18 yrs. Contrib. to newspapers and periodicals. Man. Director Times Newspaper Series, Richmond, Surrey, 1954. Chairman and Director, Puritan Films Ltd., 1953, Film Partnership Ltd., 1957; Chairman, Commonwealth Group of Unit Trusts. Member: Authors' Society; Society of Film and Television Arts; Governor of Foudroyant Trust. Hon. Dir., Richmond Theatre; LL.D. (*h.c.*) Sheffield, 1965; F.Inst.D.; F.I.J. *Publications:* The Frontiers are Green, 1943; The Waiting Year, 1944; Storm at the Hook, 1948; Elizabeth Our Queen, 1953. *Recreations:* travelling, sailing. *Address:* c/o Laurence Pollinger Ltd., 18 Maddox Street, W.1. *Clubs:* Beefsteak, Garrick, National Liberal, Lansdowne; Royal Dart Yacht, Little Ship.
[*Died* 22 *Dec.* 1965.

DIMOLINE, Maj.-Gen. William Alfred, C.B. 1947; C.M.G. 1958; C.B.E. 1943 (O.B.E. 1941); D.S.O. 1946; M.C. 1917; retd. Dec. 1953; Secretary, Inter-Parliamentary Union British Group, Palace of Westminster; Secretary for Overseas Organization, Duke of Edinburgh's Award Scheme; late Col. Comd., The King's African Rifles, Northern Rhodesia Regt. and Rhodesian African Rifles; *b.* 6 July 1897; *er. s.* of late Charles Alfred Francis Dimoline, F.C.I.S., Oakwood, Birkenhead; *m.* 1922 Irene Muriel (*d.* 1943), *d.* of A. E. Lawson, C.I.E., Madras; two *d.*; *m.* 1948, Mrs. Rosamond Kathleen Lea, *e. d.* of late H. O. Hobson, Le Touquet, and of Mrs. R. M. M. Hobson, 79 West Kensington Court, W.14. *Educ.:* Birkenhead; Dean Close, Cheltenham. Served European War, 1914-19, with East Surrey Regt. (despatches twice, M.C., Belgian Croix de Guerre, 1914-15 Star, two medals); transferred to Royal Signals, 1920; served in India, 1920-22; Iraq, 1921; West Africa (Nigeria), 1922-28; Staff College, 1933-1934; India, Quetta Earthquake, 1935-1936; N. Rhodesia, 1937, as O.C. Troops; Official M.L.C., N. Rhodesia, 1937-39; War of 1939-45 Abyssinian Campaign including Gondar as Brigade Commander, and Madagascar whole campaign (despatches, O.B.E., C.B.E., D.S.O., Africa Star); Comdr. 11 (E.A.) Div., Burma; G.O.C. East Africa, 1946-48; Commander, Aldershot District 1948-51; U.K. Rep. on Military Staff Cttee U.N., 1951-53. *Recreations:* shooting, golf tennis. *Address:* 10 Lochmore House, Ebury Street, S.W.1. *T.:* Sloane 8891. *Club:* United Service. [*Died* 24 *Nov.* 1965.

DINES, Henry George, geologist; *b.* 20 Oct. 1891; *s.* of Henry Robert and Elizabeth Sarah Dines, late of Chandler's Ford, Hants.; *m.* 1916, Edith Dorothy Connell; one *s.* *Educ.:* Dartford Grammar School; Imperial College of Science and Technology. Served European War, 1914-18, in Royal Naval Division, Gallipoli and 170th Tunnelling Co., R.E., France. Joined H.M. Geological Survey, 1920; District Geologist for South-Western district, 1944; retired, 1956. Bolitho Gold Medal, Roy. Geological Soc. of Cornwall, 1933; Murchison Medal of Geological Soc. of London, 1957. Member of Council: Geological Soc., 1950-54; Mineralogical Soc., 1948-51. *Publications:* Various Geological Survey Sheet Memoirs, The Metalliferous Mining Region of South-West England, 1956 (2 vols.) Mem. Geol. Surv.; contributions to transactions of learned societies and to scientific journals. *Address:* 1 Woodcote Valley Road, Purley, Surrey. *T.:* Uplands 7941. *Club:* Geological Society. [*Died* 21 *March* 1964.

DINESEN, Isak, (pen-name of **Karen Blixen Finecke**); *b.* 17 Apr. 1885; *d.* of Wilhelm Dinesen and Ingeborg Dinesen (*née* Westenholz); *m.* 1914, Baron Bror Blixen Finecke. *Educ.:* at home; in England, France and Switzerland; studied art at Royal Academy of Copenhagen. Ingenio et Arti (Denmark), 1950; Hon. Mem. Amer. Acad. of Arts and Letters and Nat. Inst. of Arts and Letters, New York, 1957; Corresp. Mem. Die bayerische Akad. der schönen Künste, 1957. *Publications:* Seven Gothic Tales, 1934; Out of Africa, 1937 (autobiography); Winter's Tales, 1942; Last Tales, 1957; Anecdotes of Destiny, 1958. *Recreations:* travel, gardening, animals. *Address:* Rungstedlund, Rungsted Kyst, Denmark. [*Died* 7 *Sept.* 1962.

DINGLE, Percival Alfred, C.B.E. 1937; M.R.C.S. Eng., L.R.C.P. Lond.; *b.* 6 Sept. 1881; *s.* of late W. A. Dingle, V.D., M.D.; *m.* 1st, 1909, Norah (*d.* 1920), *d.* of late John Gordon of Ellangowan, Argyllshire; one *s.*; 2nd, 1938, Dorothy Kathleen Thrift. *Educ.:* Merchant Taylors' School; St. Bartholomew's Hospital; London School of Tropical Medicine. Civil Surgeon, 1st London General Base Hospital, 1917; North Borneo Medical Service, 1911-40; Principal Medical Officer, North Borneo, 1918-1940; Member, Legislative Council, North Borneo, 1918-40; member Borneo Planning Unit, 1943-44; Civilian Adviser No. 50 Civil Affairs Unit, 1944-46. Represented North Borneo on League of Nations Eastern Bureau Advisory Council, 1926. North Borneo General Service Medal, 1937. *Address:* Flat No. 6, The Glen, Seaton, Devon. [*Died* 20 *Nov.* 1963.

DISHER, Maurice Willson, F.R.S.L.; Author and Critic; *b.* 10 Jan. 1893; *s.* of T. J. Disher and Emily S. H. Rhodes. *Educ.:* Little education owing to long illness in boyhood. Music-hall critic Standard and Evening Standard, 1911; deputy dramatic critic of the latter, 1912, critic, 1920-21; Music-hall and film critic of Observer, 1927-28; Dramatic critic of Daily Mail, 1933-36; Contributor to The Times and Times Literary Supplement, 1937-53; author of plays: There Remains a Gesture and Joan of Memories (Shaftesbury Theatre, 1920), Rupert's Revenge (Olympia, 1923), Having No Hearts (Mercury, 1934 and tour 1935); designed B.B.C. programmes: Old Music-Halls (1933-35), Theatre Royal, Memory Lane, Theatre Composers, Vanished Theatres, etc.; arranged harlequinades for Players' Theatre pantomimes, from 1940. *Publications:* Clown (novel), 1924; Clowns and Pantomimes (history), 1925; The Cowells in America, 1934; About Nothing Whatever, 1935; The Greatest Show on Earth, 1937; Winkles and Champagne, 1938; Fairs, Circuses and Music-Halls, 1942; The Last Romantic (biography of Sir John Martin-Harvey), 1948; Blood and Thunder (history of melodrama), 1949; Mad Genius (Edmund Kean), 1950; Pleasures of London, 1950; Whiteley Wanton (Shakespeare and

Mary Fytton), 1951; Melodrama, Plots that Thrilled, 1954; Victorian Song, 1955; Pharaoh's Fool-Belzoni, Mummer and Egyptologist, 1957; contr. to Oxford Juvenile Encyclopædia, The Book of the Horse, Quarterly Review, Edinburgh Review, Nineteenth Century, Fortnightly Review, Chambers's Encyclopædia, Encyclopædia Britannica, Enciclopedia dello Spettacolo (Rome), Oxford Companion to the Theatre, etc. *Recreations:* Research into the history of all forms of public amusements. *Address:* Villa Salvador, Campamento de San Roque (Cádiz), Spain. *T.:* Campamento 1219. [*Died* 24 *Nov.* 1969.

DISNEY, Walter E.; Artist; motion picture producer; exec. producer, Walt Disney Productions; *b.* Chicago, 5 Dec. 1901; *s.* of Elias Disney and Flora Call; *m.* 1925, Lillian Marie Bounds, Lewiston, Idaho; two *d.* *Educ.:* Benton School, Kansas City, Mo.; McKinley High School, Chicago, Illinois; Chicago Academy of Fine Arts. Served as a Red Cross Ambulance driver, A.E.F., France, 1917-18. Commercial artist, 1919; cartoonist, Kansas City Film Ad. Co., 1920-22; produced series of seven cartoons for Pictorial Clubs, Inc.; produced the Alice Comedies (a combination of live girl and animated cartoons) for M. J. Winkler, New York, 1923-26; created and produced first 26 Oswald the Rabbit cartoons, 1927; began making Mickey Mouse Cartoons in sound, 1928; released his product through State rights until Feb. 1930 when release transferred to Columbia Pictures, including Silly Symphonies, the first motion pictures to display color. Produced first full-length animation feature in color, Snow White and the Seven Dwarfs, 1938; Pinocchio, Fantasia, 1940; The Reluctant Dragon, Dumbo, 1941; Bambi, Saludos Amigos, 1942; Victory Through Air Power, 1943; The Three Caballeros, 1945; Make Mine Music, Song of the South, 1946; Fun and Fancy Free, 1947; Melody Time, 1948; So Dear To My Heart, Ichabod and Mr. Toad, 1949; Cinderella, Treasure Island, 1950; Alice in Wonderland, 1951; The Story of Robin Hood, 1952; Peter Pan, 1953; The Sword and The Rose, 1953; The Living Desert, 1953; Stormy the Thoroughbred, 1953; 20,000 Leagues Under the Sea, 1954; The Vanishing Prairie, 1954; Lady and the Tramp, 1955; The African Lion, 1955; Davy Crockett, 1955-56; Secrets of Life, 1956; Littlest Outlaw, 1956; The Great Locomotive Chase, 1956; Old Yeller, 1957; Perri, 1957; Davy Crockett and the River Pirates, 1957; Westward Ho!, The Wagons, 1957; The Light in the Forest, 1958; White Wilderness, 1958; Tonka, 1958; Sleeping Beauty, 1959; The Shaggy Dog, 1959; Darby O'Gill and the Little People, 1959; Third Man on the Mountain, 1959; Toby Tyler, Kidnapped, The Sign of Zorro, Pollyanna, Ten Who Dared, Jungle Cat, The Swiss Family Robinson (all 1960); One Hundred and One Dalmatians, The Horse with the Flying Tail, The Absent-Minded Professor, The Parent Trap, Nikki, Wild Dog of the North, Babes in Toyland (all 1961); Moon Pilot, Bon Voyage, Big Red, The Legend of Lobo, In Search of the Castaways, Born to Sing (all 1962); The Three Lives of Thomasina, 1963; The Tiger Walks, 1964; The Moonspinners, 1964; The Monkey's Uncle, That Darn Cat, Mary Poppins, Legend of Young Dick Turpin, Emil and the Detectives (all 1965); Winnie The Pooh and the Honey Tree, The Ugly Dachshund, The Tenderfoot, Lt. Robin Crusoe, U.S.N., The Fighting Prince of Donegal (all 1966). Since 1948, twelve True-Life Adventure pictures (full-length and featurettes) in continuous series of factual nature features. Continuous series of Technicolor featurettes, People and Places. Producer on A.B.C.-T.V. network. Since 1954 TV weekly or nightly shows include: Mickey Mouse Club; Disneyland; Zorro; Walt Disney Presents; Walt Disney's Wonderful World of Color, on N.B.C. Network. In 1955 opened Disneyland, $37,000,000, 160-acre amusement park in Anaheim, Calfornia. Holds over 30 Academy awards and over 900 other awards, citations and university honorariums. *Address:* (office) 500 South Buena Vista St., Burbank, Calif.; (home) Los Angeles. [*Died* 15 *Dec.* 1966.

DITMAS, Lieut.-Colonel Francis Ivan Leslie, D.S.O. 1918; M.C.; Croix d'officier de la Légion d'honneur; French Croix de Guerre avec palme; Croix d'officier de l'Ordre de Léopold, Belgium; Sacred Treasure of Japan, 3rd class; Chartered Engineer; *b.* 12 Aug. 1876; *o. s.* of late Colonel F. F. Ditmas, Royal Artillery, and Isabel, *e. d.* of Rear-Admiral John Adams, R.N.; *m.* 1906, Alice Sarah Louise Nevill (*d.* 1957), *o. d.* of late Maj. Arthur Nevill Hayne, 88th Regt. (Connaught Rangers); two *s.* *Educ.:* privately; France and Germany. Consulting Railway and Mining Engineer; Engineer with the East Indian Rly. Co. Calcutta; served S. African War Machine Gun Commander (medal and two bars); gazetted to the Reserve of Officers, 1902; served European War, 1914-18 (despatches thrice, M.C., D.S.O., 1914 Star with bar, War Medal and Victory Medal with bar). Technical Investigator to Mining Association of Great Britain, 1924-26; during the General Strike, Government Railway Commissioner S.W. Division of England; Technical Adviser to British Delegation Reparation Commission, Paris, on Transportation and Coal, 1920-24; Pres. Upper Silesia Coal Commission and British Member Permanent Delegation, Berlin; (Lt.-Col. R. of O. Durham L.I.); Technical Adviser to Inter-Allied Rhineland High Commission, Coblenz, Germany, 1919-20; Delegate at Health Congress, Brussels, May 1920; Pres. Inter-Allied Railway Sub-Commission, Cologne, 26 Nov. 1918 to Dec. 1919, with British, French, Belgian, and American Members; present at Peace Conference, Versailles, Member Sub-Cttee. on Germany as Expert on German Railways and Coal. Employed Ministry of Food, 1942-43. Founder Mem. Mining Geological and Metallurgical Inst. (M.M.G. & M.) of India; Member Irish Mining and Quarrying Soc. F.G.S., M.I.M.E., A.I.E.E., etc. *Publications:* numerous articles to scientific papers on engineering subjects. *Recreation:* photography. *Address:* 17 Dene Road, Cottingham, Yorkshire. [*Died* 8 *April* 1969.

DIVER, Captain Cyril Roper Pollock, C.B. 1952; C.B.E. 1944; M.A.; F.L.S.; F.R.E.S.; F.R.G.S.; F.Z.S.; *b.* 1892; *s.* of Lt.-Col. T. Diver and Maud Diver; *m.* 1914, Eleanor Joyce, *d.* of Philip Gurdon; one *s.* *Educ.:* Dover College; Trinity College, Oxford. Entered Army, Loyal North Lancashire Regt., 1914; served European War, 1914-18; Adjutant 1st Bn., 1915; France, 1915; invalided, 1918; Assistant Clerkship, House of Commons, 1919; Clerk to Select Committee on National Expenditure, 1939-45; Clerk of Financial Committees, 1945; Clerk of Committees, 1948; Director-General, The Nature Conservancy, 1948-52; Mem. Nature Conservancy, 1953-58; Governing Body, Imperial Coll. of Science and Technology, 1950-60; has carried out researches in genetics, ecology, and animal behaviour. *Publications:* scientific papers in various journals, mostly on genetical and ecological researches. *Address:* Kennel Lane, Frensham, Farnham, Surrey. *Club:* Athenæum. [*Died* 17 *Feb.* 1969.

DIX, Dorothy Knight; *see* Waddy, D. K.

DIXON, Sir Arthur Lewis, Kt., *cr.* 1941; C.B. 1922; C.B.E. 1918; formerly Principal Assistant Under-Secretary of State,

Fire Service Dept., Home Office; retired 1946; *b.* 30 Jan. 1881; *s.* of Rev. Seth Dixon, Wesleyan Minister; *m.* 1909, Marie Price (*d.* 1949). *Educ.:* Kingswood School, Bath; Sidney Sussex College, Cambridge 9th Wrangler, 1902; Home Office, 1903; Private Secretary to Parliamentary Under-Secretary of State, 1908 and to Permanent Under-Secretary, 1910; Member of Royal Commission on Fire Brigades and Fire Prevention, 1920; of Committee on Pay of Prison Officers, 1923; London Traffic Advisory Committee, 1924; and other Committees. Vice-Pres. British and Foreign Bible Soc. *Publication:* Atomic Energy for the Layman. *Address:* Bourne Hall Hotel, Bournemouth, Hants. *Club:* National. [*Died* 14 *Sept.* 1969.

DIXON, Sir Francis Netherwood, Kt., *cr.* 1938; C.B. 1925; Secretary, Exchequer and Audit Department, 1922-44; *b.* Colchester, 28 Sept. 1879; *s.* of E. A. Dixon; *m.* 1907, Olive (*d.* 1965), *d.* of W. W. Daniell; two *s.* one *d.* *Educ.:* Felsted; Gonville and Caius College, Cambridge. [*Died* 5 *Sept.* 1968.

DIXON, Gertrude Caroline, C.B.E. 1920 (O.B.E. 1918); D.Sc.; member of Secretariat of United Nations, 1945-54; *b.* 1886; *d.* of Rev. Seth Dixon, Wesleyan Minister. Secretary Wheat Executive during European War; member of Secretariat of League of Nations, 1919-39; Ministry of Information, 1940-45. *Address:* 87 Broadwalk Court, Palace Gardens Terrace, W.8. [*Died* 21 *March* 1966.

DIXON, Rt. Rev. Horace Henry, C.B.E. 1960; M.A. Cantab.; D.Th. (Australia); Coadjutor Bishop of Brisbane, State of Queensland, 1932-62, retd.; *b.* Cambridge, 1 Aug. 1869; *m.* 1st, 1897, Florence Marie Godbold (*d.* 1932); two *c.*; 2nd, 1936, Enid Rose Morgan-Jones. *Educ.:* Cambridge University. Assistant Curate, Epping; St. Michael's, Walthamstow; St. Margaret's, Ilkley; St. Matthew's, Burnley; Rector of St. Peter's, Southport, Queensland; Headmaster of the Southport School, Queensland, 1901-29; Residentiary Canon St. John's Cathedral, 1929-49; Archdeacon of Brisbane, 1930; Dean, 1931-32. *Address:* Cartref, Dewar Terrace, Sherwood, Brisbane, Queensland. [*Died* 8 *Nov.* 1964.

DIXON, Lieut.-Col. Oscar, T.D.; D.L.; Chairman, Peter Dixon and Son Ltd.; *b.* 20 Apr. 1883; *s.* of Joseph and Mary Hyde Dixon; *m.* 1911, Madeline Nicholson (*d.* 1959); two *s.* three *d.* *Educ.:* Cheltenham; Trinity College, Cambridge, B.A. 5th Lincolns, 1914-18; Commission 1908; resigned 1921; Captain Lincolnshire Shooting VIII since 1908; High Sheriff Lincolnshire 1934-35; Chairman Paper Makers Association Technical Section, 1936-37; President of Grimsby Chamber of Commerce, 1937-38; Officer Comdg. 9th Lindsey Bn. Home Guard, War of 1939-45. D.L. Lincolnshire, 1954. *Recreations:* shooting, swimming, tennis, and photography. Rebuilt Kenwick Hall which was almost destroyed 1944 by enemy action intended for Hull. *Address:* Kenwick Hall, Louth, Lincolnshire. *T.A.:* Dixonia, Grimsby. *T.:* Louth 154 [*Died* 17 *April* 1966.

DIXON, Sir Pierson (John), G.C.M.G. 1957 (K.C.M.G. 1950; C.M.G. 1945); C.B. 1948; Hon. LL.D. (Cambridge); a Director, Westminster Bank, since 1965; *b.* 13 Nov. 1904; *e. s.* of late Pierson John Dixon; *m.* 1928, Alexandra Ismene, *d.* of S. C. Atchley, C.M.G., O.B.E.; one *s.* two *d.* *Educ.:* Bedford; Pembroke Coll., Cambridge. Hon. Fell. Pembroke College, 1949-; Craven Scholar and Porson Prizeman, 1926; 1st cl. hons. in both parts of Classical Tripos; B.A., Craven Student and Fellow of Pembroke, 1927 British School of Archæology at Athens, 1927-28; in residence as Fellow of Pembroke, 1928-29; entered Foreign Office, 1929; M.A. 1932; served at British Embassies at Madrid (1932), Ankara (1936), Rome (1938); transferred to Foreign Office, 1940; served on staff of Resident Minister at Allied Force H.Q., Mediterranean, 1943; Principal Private Secretary to Foreign Sec., 1943-48; Ambassador to Czechoslovakia, 1948-50; Deputy Under Secretary of State, Foreign Office, 1950-54; Permanent Representative of the U.K. to the United Nations, 1954-60; Ambassador to France, 1960-64. *Publications:* Corcyra (Montagu Butler Prize Latin Poem), 1925; The Iberians of Spain, 1939; Farewell, Catullus, 1953; The Glittering Horn, 1958; Pauline: Napoleon's Favourite Sister, 1964; contrib. to Times Literary Supplement, Country Life, etc. *Address:* c/o Foreign Office, S.W.1. [*Died* 22 *April* 1965.

DIXON, Sir Samuel; *see* Gurney-Dixon.

DIXON, Rev. Thomas Harold; Rector of Manaton with North Bovey, Devon, 1940-1957; *s.* of late Thomas Dixon; *b.* Cambridge; *m.* 2nd *d.* of late Major W. Grey, H.M. 60th Foot; one *s.* *Educ.:* Private; Cambridge University. Curate of Lamborn, Berks, and St. Michael's, Headingley, Leeds; Chaplain on the Ecclesiastical Establishment of India, 1907-28; stationed successively at Karachi, Multan, Peshawar, Rawalpindi, and Delhi; was Chaplain at New Delhi for many years; served France, 1915, Mesopotamia, 1916-17, North-West Frontier, 1919-21 (despatches twice); Canon of Lahore, and Rector of Barton Le Cley, Bedford; Vicar of Christ Church, Woburn Square, W.C.1. *Address:* Phœnix House, Hartley Wintney, Hants. [*Died* 12 *Jan.* 1963.

DOBBIE, Lieut.-Gen. Sir William George Sheddon, G.C.M.G. 1942 (C.M.G. 1919); K.C.B. 1941 (C.B. 1930); D.S.O. 1916; Hon. LL.D. (Leeds, Royal Malta); *b.* Madras, 1879; *s.* of late W. H. Dobbie, C.I.E.; *m.* 1904, Sybil (*d.* 1962), *y. d.* of Capt. Orde-Browne, R.A.; one *s.* one *d.* (and one *s.* killed in action). *Educ.:* Charterhouse (Classical Scholar); R.M.A. Woolwich; passed through School of Military Engineering, Chatham. Served S. Africa (medal 5 clasps); served abroad and in Ireland; passed into Staff College, Camberley, 1911; served European War, 1914-18 (Legion of Honour, despatches seven times, D.S.O., Brevet Lieut.-Colonel, Mons ribbon, C.M.G., Officier d'Ordre Léopold, Croix de Guerre, Belgian, Croix de Guerre avec palme, French); Brevet Colonel, 1922; Lieut.-Colonel, 1925; Colonel, 1926; Major-General, 1932; temp. Lieut.-General, 1940; General Staff Officer, 1st grade, War Office, 1926-28; Western Command, 1928; Brigade Commander, Egypt, 1928-32; Inspector of the Royal Engineers, Commander of the Chatham Area, Commandant School of Military Engineering, and O.C., R.E. Depôt, Chatham, 1933-1935; General Officer Commanding Malaya, 1935-39; retired pay, 1939; Governor, Malta, 1940-42; Colonel Commandant R.E., 1940-47. *Publications:* A Very Present Help, 1945; Active Service with Christ, 1948; a few articles in military magazines. *Address:* 89 Coleherne Crt., S.W.5. *Club:* United Service. [*Died* 3 *Oct.* 1964.

DOBBS, Cecil Moore, C.M.G. 1931; O.B.E. 1928, Provincial Commissioner, Kenya Colony, retired; *b.* Cavan, Ireland, 1882; *s.* of late Col. G. C. Dobbs and S. de M. Dobbs; *m.* 1909, Marion Watson Osborne; one *d.* (one *s.* deceased). *Educ.:* St. Columba's Coll., Rathfarnham, Dublin; Trin. Coll., Dublin. Assist. Collector, East African Protectorate, 1906; District Commissioner 1910; Provincial Commissioner, 1925; Formerly Fellow of St. Columba's College,

Rathfarnham; for many years on Board of Governors of Dun's Hospital. Member Royal Dublin Society. *Recreations:* gardening, fishing, tennis. *Address:* 8 Ailesbury Grove, Donnybrook, Dublin 4. *T.:* 692046. [*Died* 5 *July* 1969.

DOBELL, Air Commodore Frederic Osborne Storey, C.B. 1964; C.B.E. 1957; M.A. (Oxon.); *b.* 6 Dec. 1912; *s.* of late Dr. D. C. Dobell; *m.* 1939, Mavis Marjorie, *d.* of late H. Lyon Edwards, Salisbury, S. Rhodesia; one *s.* one *d.* *Educ.:* Stowe; Christ Church, Oxford. Oxford University Air Squadron, 1932-34; Geologist with Aircraft Operating Co. (Johannesburg), 1934-36; Geologist with Geological Survey of S. Rhodesia, 1936-39. Commissioned R.A.F.V.R., 1939; served in East Africa, Middle East and Europe. Permanent Commission in R.A.F., 1945; Group Captain, 1955; Air Commodore, 1960. Station Commander, Binbrook, 1955; Ministry of Defence, 1957; Imperial Defence College, 1959; Asst. Commandant, R.A.F. Staff College, 1960; S.A.S.O. No. 1 (Bomber) Group, 1961; Air Commodore Intelligence (A.), Ministry of Defence, 1964 (Air Ministry, 1963-64). A.M.I.M.M., 1939. Gold Belt (Jtly.), 1938. *Recreation:* sailing. *Address:* Toonagh, Maidens Green, Windsor, Berks. *T.:* Winkfield Row 2561. *Clubs:* Naval and Military; Royal Ocean Racing; Oxford and Cambridge Sailing Society. [*Died* 11 *July* 1965.

DOBELL, Sir William, Kt. 1966; O.B.E. 1965; painter; *b.* Newcastle, N.S.W., 24 Sept. 1899; *s.* of R. Dobell, Newcastle. *Educ.:* Cook's Hill Superior Public School, Newcastle; Julia Ashton School, Sydney (Society of Artists' Travelling Scholarship, 1929); Slade School of Fine Arts, London (prizes for draughtsmanship and painting, 1930). Part-time Art Master, Sydney Technical College. Commissioned to paint Allied Works Council construction work in Northern Territory, War of 1939-45. Exhibitions include: Royal Academy, London; New English Art Club; London Group; (with Margaret Preston) Art Gallery of N.S.W.; Twelve Australian Artists, London; Venice Biennale; Australian Painting, Tate Gallery; (one man) Qantas Gallery, London. Major portraits include: Billy Boy; Prof. John Anderson; Rt. Hon. R. G. Menzies. Archibald Prize: 1943; 1948; 1959; Wynne Prize. Trustee, Sydney National Gallery. *Relevant publication:* J. Gleeson: William Dobell, 1964. *Address:* c/o Hal Missingham Esq., National Art Gallery, Sydney, Australia. [*Died* 14 *May* 1970.

DOBREE, Claude Hatherley, C.B.E. 1929 (O.B.E. 1924); *s.* of late Rev. J. Bonamy Dobree, M.A., West Tilbury, Essex; *m.* 1925, E. Aileen (*d.* 1948), *d.* of Alexander Fraser, M.B., Caistor, Lincs. *Educ.:* Park House School, Gravesend. Associate of Institute of Chartered Accountants, 1902; Northern Rhodesia Civil Service, 1911-33; held following appointments: Auditor, 1913-21; Treasurer, 1921-33; acted as Chief Secretary, 1927-28, and as Governor, 1930. *Address:* 30 Downview Rd., Worthing, Sussex. [*Died* 13 *Dec.* 1960.

DOBSON, Alban Tabor Austin, C.B. 1939; C.V.O. 1932; C.B.E. 1930; Secretary, International Whaling Commission, 1949-59; *b.* 29 June 1885; *y. s.* of late Austin Dobson, LL.D.; *m.* 1st, 1915, Katharine Jean (*d.* 1936), *d.* of late Major R. G. Donaldson-Selby, and *g.d.* of late J. S. Donaldson-Selby, J.P., D.L., of Holy Island, Northumberland; one *s.* one *d.*; 2nd, 1944, Kitty, *twin d.* of Charles Waters, C.B.E., J.P., Herringby Hall, Norfolk. *Educ.:* Clifton College; Emmanuel College, Cambridge. Board of Agriculture and Fisheries, by open competition, 1908; Fisheries Secretary, 1938-46; retired as Under Secretary, 1946; Fisheries Adviser, 1946-54. Hon. President, Internat. Council for the Exploration of the Sea, 1955. Inns of Court O.T.C., 1915; 2nd Lt. Hampshire Regt., West Front (Ypres), 1916; Asst. Director, Agricultural Production, Lieutenant-Colonel (G.H.Q., France), 1918; despatches. Officier, Ordre Mérite Maritime (France); Commander Order of the Dannebrog (Denmark). *Publications:* An Austin Dobson Bibliography, 1925; Austin Dobson. Some Notes, 1929; An Austin Dobson Letter Book, 1935. *Recreations:* played frequently for Cambridge University (not against Oxford) and Blackheath at Rugby football; and in various university trial matches at cricket; Cambridge Crusader Cricket Colours. *Address:* The Elms, Walsham Le Willows, Bury St. Edmunds, Suffolk. *T.:* Walsham Le Willows 258. *Clubs:* M.C.C.; (Hon.) Rowfant (Cleveland). [*Died* 19 *May* 1962.

DOBSON, Frank, C.B.E. 1947; R.A. 1953 (A.R.A. 1942); A.R.B.S. 1938; Sculptor; *b.* London, 18 Nov. 1888; *s.* of Frank Dobson, artist, and Alice Mary Owen; *m.* 1926, Caroline Mary Bussell; one *d.* *Educ.:* Harrow Green School; Leyton Technical; Hospitalfield, Arbroath (Stephens Scholar); City and Guilds School, Kennington. Formerly Professor of Sculpture, Royal College of Art, until July 1953. Worked in studio of Sir William Reynolds; 1st one-man show, drawings, Chenil Galleries, 1914; Member of Group X, Leicester Galleries, 1921; Pres. London Group for 4 years; Exhibitor at: Venice International Exhibition, Tri-national Exhibition; touring exhibition of six European Sculptors in America; International Exhibitions, Stockholm, Paris, Tokio, etc.; works in Tate Gallery, Manchester City Art Gallery, Glasgow Art Gallery, Leeds Art Gallery, etc.; Decorations on Hay's Wharf. *Recreations:* Cinema, walking to studio and talking nonsense. *Address:* 14 Harley Gardens, Kensington, S.W.10. *Club:* Chelsea Arts. [*Died* 22 *July* 1963.

DOBSON, Sir Roy Hardy, Kt. 1945; C.B.E. 1942; J.P.; Hon. F.R.Ae.S.; Director of Hawker Siddeley Group Ltd. (Chairman 1963-67); Chairman of: Hawker Siddeley Canada Ltd.; Kelvin Construction Co. Ltd.; Racair Ltd.; Director: Hawker Siddeley Aviation Ltd.; Dominion Steel and Coal Corp. Ltd. (Chm. 1957-63); Dominion Coal Co. Ltd. (Chm. 1957-63); High Duty Alloys Ltd. (Chm. 1958-63); Mem. Council, Soc. of British Aerospace Companies Ltd. (President 1948-49, 1962-1963); *b.* Horsforth, Yorks, 27 Sept. 1891; *s.* of Horace Dobson and Mary Ann Hardy; *m.* 1916, Annie (*d.* 1954), *d.* of George Smith; one *s.* one *d.* (and one *s.* lost in air accident, 1946). A. V. Roe & Co., Manchester. Engineer, 1914; Works Manager, 1919; Gen. Manager, 1934; Director, 1936; Managing Director, A. V. Roe & Co., 1941; Director, Hawker Siddeley Aircraft Co. Ltd. (name changed to Hawker Siddeley Group Ltd., 1948), 1945, (Vice-Chairman and Managing Director, 1958-63); Pres., A. V. Roe Canada, Ltd., 1945, Chairman, 1951; Director, Canadian Imperial Bank of Commerce, 1955-66. President, Locomotive and Allied Manufacturers Association of Great Britain, 1962. J.P., Ashton-under-Lyne, 1946; Member, Joint Research Council for Manchester Univ. and Chamber of Commerce. Member of Church of England. Conservative. Air League Founders' Medal, 1965. *Recreations:* fishing, shooting, sailing, photography. *Address:* (business) 18 St. James's Sq., S.W.1; Medstead Grange, Medstead, Alton, Hants. *Clubs:* Eccentric, Royal Aero, R.A.F.; Union (Ashton-under-Lyne); Royal Anglesey and York (Toronto); Overseas Bankers'. [*Died* 7 *July* 1968.

DOBSON, Sydney George; formerly Chairman of the Board, The Royal Bank of Canada; *b.* 20 Sept. 1883; *s.* of J. W. Dobson

and Harriett Martell; *m.* 1913, Beatrice, *d.* of S. G. Chambers; one *s.* one *d.* *Educ.:* Sydney Public Schools. Joined The Merchants Bank of Halifax at Sydney, N.S., 1900; transferred to The Royal Bank of Canada, Truro, N.S., 1904; Accountant, Winnipeg, 1906; Asst. Manager, Truro, 1909; Accountant, Toronto, 1910; Manager, Sydney, 1911; Asst. Manager, Montreal, 1915; Manager, Vancouver, 1916; Actg. Supervisor, Winnipeg, 1918; Gen. Inspector at Head Office, 1919; Asst. Gen. Manager, 1922; Gen. Manager, 1934; Dir., 1939; Vice-Pres. and Gen. Manager, 1942; Exec. Vice-Pres., 1945; Pres., 1946. Director of B.C. Power Corp. Ltd., Shawinigan Water & Power Co., and B.C. Electric Co. Ltd.; Formerly Governor of McGill University. *Recreations:* golf, yachting, motoring. *Address:* 1321 Sherbrooke St. West, Montreal, Canada. *Clubs:* Mount Royal, St. James's, Montreal, Royal St. Lawrence Yacht, Mount Bruno Golf and Country, Royal Montreal Golf (Montreal); Rideau (Ottawa).
[*Died* 8 *Aug.* 1969.

DODD, Sir Edward (James), Kt. 1964; C.B.E. 1949; H.M. Chief Inspector of Constabulary for England and Wales, since 1963; *b.* Reading, 19 October 1909; *s.* of late James Dodd; *m.* 1937, Evelyn Mary, *d.* of late Henry James Mackenzie; one *s.* one *d.* *Educ.:* Reading School; H.M.S. Conway. Royal Merchant Navy and Royal Naval Reserve, 1925-31; Metropolitan Police, 1931-41. Metropolitan Police Coll., Hendon, 1934-35. 2nd Asst. Chief Constable, Birmingham, 1941-44, 1st Asst. Chief Constable, 1944-45, Chief Constable, 1945-63. O.St.J. 1960. *Recreations:* general interest in sporting and social activities. *Address:* 15 Stonehill Road, East Sheen, SW.14. *Club:* Junior Army and Navy. [*Died* 16 *Sept.* 1966.

DODD, Norris Edward; *b.* 20 July 1879; of Scottish and German parentage; *m.* 1905, Pauline Ensminger; one *d.* *Educ.:* public schools and Greenwood and Drew Academy, Iowa, U.S.A. Registered Pharmacist. Opened and operated drug stores, Oregon, 1900-07; built and operated rural and city telephone lines, also general store and telephone exchange, Haines, Ore., 1907-12; engaged in livestock feeding under firm name of Coles and Dodd, 1912-33, and owner ranch, since 1912, Haines, Ore. Chairman: Co. Wheat Cttee., Ore., 1933; Co. Corn-Hog Cttee., Ore., 1934; Corn-Hog State Bd. of Control, Ore., 1934-35; Mem. Ore. State Agricultural Conservation Cttee., 1936-37; W. Div. Agric. Adjustment Agency (13 states): Fieldman and Asst. Director, 1938-1939, Director, 1939-43; Chief, Agric. Adjustment Agency (48 states), 1943-46; Under-Sec. of Agriculture, 1946-48; Director-General, Food and Agriculture Organization of the United Nations, 1948-54. Head U.S. deleg.: 2nd session, F.A.O. Conf., Copenhagen, Denmark, 1946; 3rd session, F.A.O. Conf., Geneva, 1947; Chm., U.S. deleg., Internat. Wheat Council, 1948. Hon. Dr. of Humane Letters, Pacific Univ., Forest Grove, Oregon, U.S.A. *Recreations:* fishing, hunting. *Address:* 2730 Wisconsin Avenue, N.W., Washington 7. *Clubs:* Elk's (Baker, Ore., and Washington, D.C.); Cosmos (Washington, D.C.).
[*Died* 23 *June* 1968.

DODDS, Jackson, C.B.E. 1944 (O.B.E. 1919); D.C.L. (hon.); *b.* London, England, 16 Feb. 1881; 3rd *s.* of late Jackson Dodds, Inspector of Inland Revenue, London, and Maria Coath; *m.* 1920, Florence Lydia (*d.* 1951), *d.* of Ebenezer Wood, Catford, Kent; two *s.* two *d.* *Educ.:* City of London School. For four years with Comptoir Nationale d'Escompte de Paris, London Agency; joined the Bank of British North America, 1901; served in branches from Halifax to Vancouver in various capacities; Sec., London, 1913; Assistant Manager, Bank of Montreal, London, 1919; District Superintendent of Manitoba branches, Winnipeg, 1922; Assist. General Manager, Winnipeg, in charge Western branches, 1925; Assistant General Manager, Head Office, Montreal, 1928; Joint General Manager, 1930-42; enlisted as private, 1st Bn. H.A.C. (Inf.), 1914; Lieut. R.A.O.C. 1915; D.A.D.O.S., 59th Division, 1916; Assistant Director of Ordnance Services, 6th Army Corps with rank of Lieut., Colonel, 1918 (despatches four times, Mon. Star, 1914, O.B.E.); President, Canadian Bankers' Association, 1934 and 1935; Director King's Hall School, Compton, Province of Quebec; Hon. President, Boy Scouts' Association of Canada; Order of Bronze Wolf, 1955; Chairman of the Central Council Canadian Red Cross Society, 1941-46; Pres. Canadian Corps of Commissionaires, Montreal Div.; Hon. Consul-General of Greece; Nat. Vice-Pres. Canadian Nat. Inst. for Blind; Silver Jubilee Medal, 1935; Coronation Medals, 1937, 1953; Cross of Commander of Royal Order of Phœnix (Greece), 1948; Officer, Legion of Honour (France), 1950. *Recreation:* golf. *Address:* 706 Victoria Avenue, Westmount, P.Q., Canada. *T.:* HU.1.-7861. *Clubs:* Mount Bruno Country (Montreal); Rideau (Ottawa).
[*Died* 7 *April* 1961.

DODDS, Norman Noel; M.P. (Lab. and Co-op.) Erith and Crayford since 1955 (Dartford, 1945-55); P.P.S. to Secretary of State for Commonwealth Relations, 1964-65; Director, People's Entertainment Society, since 1945; Hon. Secretary, Homeworkers Products Society, for providing work for disabled people; *b.* 25 Dec. 1903; *s.* of late Ambrose Dodds, 55 Oak Av., Dunston-on-Tyne; *m.* 1931, Eva, *d.* of late Frank Pratt, 59 Birkhall Rd., Catford, S.E.9; two *s.* *Educ.:* Dunston-on-Tyne Council School. Served with R.A.F. Mem. Central Adv. Cttee. to Minister of Pensions, 1950-51; P.P.S. to Minister of Labour, May-Oct. 1951. *Address:* 20 Havelock Rd., Dartford, Kent.
[*Died* 23 *Aug.* 1965.

DODGSON, John Arthur; Painter; Member of London Group (President 1950, 1951); *b.* 13 June 1890; *s.* of late Major Heathfield Butler Dodgson, D.S.O., and late Sybil Agnes, *d.* of Honourable John Vivian; *m.* 1st, 1916, Margaret Valentine (*d.* 1952), *d.* of late Howard Pease, Otterburn, Northumberland; one *s.* two *d.*; 2nd, 1955, Agnes, *d.* of Charles Goodchild, Sudbury, Suffolk. *Educ.:* Eton College; University College, Oxford; Slade School of Fine Art. One-man exhibitions: Carfax Gallery; London Artists Assoc.; Beaux Arts Gallery; Works acquired by: Tate Gallery, the Arts Council of G.B. and H.M. Office of Works; also represented in Imperial War Museum. *Recreations:* reading, travelling. *Address:* Hill House, Chelsworth, Ipswich, Suffolk. *T.:* Bildeston 387. [*Died* 10 *Sept.* 1969.

DODSON, Sir Gerald, Kt. 1939; J.P. Kingston Division of Surrey; *b.* 1884; *s.* of late John Dodson, J.P., former Sheriff of Norwich; *m.* 1910, Emily Alice (*d.* 1961), *d.* of late William Chater, Godalming; *m.* 1964, Marjorie Binks Heath, *d.* of late Charles W. Heath, Esher, *Educ.:* Downing College, Cambridge. M.A., LL.M.; served during European War, 1914-18, Lieut. R.N.V.R.; Recorder of Tenterden, 1932-34; Treasury Counsel at Central Criminal Court, 1925-34; Judge of Mayor's and City of London Court, 1934-1937; Recorder of London and High Steward of Southwark, 1937-59; Commissioner, Central Criminal Court, 1959-63; Bencher, Inner Temple, 1938; Hon. Fellow of Downing Coll., Camb., 1945. Order of Menelik (Ethiopia), 1954;

Comendador de Christo (Portugal), 1955; Order of Al Rafidain (Iraq), 1956; Cavaliere Ufficiale, Order of Merit (Italy), 1958; Order of Homayoun (Persia), 1959. *Publications:* (jointly) The Law Relating to Motor Cars; The Road Traffic Act, 1929; article, Mayor's and City of London Court, in Halsbury's Laws of England; "The Fishermen of England" and other lyrics from the light opera "Rebel Maid" (Montague Phillips) and joint author of the book; Consider Your Verdict (Memoirs). *Recreations:* music, fishing. *Address:* Bonchurch Sandown Road, Esher, Surrey. *T.:* Esher 4359. [*Died* 2 *Nov.* 1966.

DODSWORTH, Sir (Leonard) Lumley (Savage), Kt., *cr.* 1953; J.P.; solicitor; *b.* 19 March 1890; *s.* of Leonard Dodsworth, Wheldrake, York, and Ada Lowe, Lincoln; *m.* 1918, Eileen Louise Wilson, Dublin; one *s.* one *d.* *Educ.:* Rugby School; New College, Oxford, Lieut. West Yorks. Regt., 1914-15; invalided out, through wounds, 1916; Admitted solicitor, 1919. Chairman York Conservative Association, 1929-55. J.P. 1936. *Recreations:* (formerly) golf; played for Oxford Univ. *v.* Cambridge Univ., 1912 and 1913. *Address:* 18 St. Peter's Grove, York. *T.:* York 8529. *Club:* Yorkshire (York). [*Died* 16 *Feb.* 1968.

DOHERTY, William David, M.A., M.Ch., F.R.C.S.; Superintendent, Guy's Hospital, 1948-58, retired; Surgeon, Guy's Hospital, 1928-58, retired; *b.* 17 July 1893; *m.* 1922, Annie Ruth Margaret Barker: two *s.* one *d.* *Educ.:* Dulwich Coll.; Cambridge University. M.A., M.Ch. Camb. 1924; F.R.C.S. Eng. 1923. Governor: Alleyn's Coll. of God's Gift; Guy's Hospital; Guy's Hosp. Med. School; Mem. Darenth and Stone Hosp. Management Cttee. *Recreations:* golf, shooting, fishing. *Address:* Forge Cottage, Hogscross Lane, Chipstead, Surrey. *T.:* Downland 4788. *Club:* East India and Sports. [*Died* 31 *March* 1966.

DOLLAN, Sir Patrick Joseph, Kt., *cr.* 1941; LL.D. Glasgow; D.L., J.P. Glasgow; *m.* 1912, Agnes Moir, M.B.E., 1946; one *s.* *Educ.:* St. Bridget's School, Baillieston; Wellshot Academy, Shettleston. Ropeworker; Grocery apprentice; miner in Baillieston, 8 years, and delegate to Lanarkshire Miners' Union; journalist and editor. Member of Glasgow Corporation, 1913-46; Glasgow and Scottish chairman, I.L.P., 1920-31; first winner of St. Mungo Prize for Citizenship, Glasgow, 1939; Lord Provost of Glasgow, 1938-41, prior to which was City Treas. and Convener of several depts.; Sec. and Chm. of Council, Labour Group for 12 years: Chairman Scottish Fuel Efficiency Committee; Director National Industrial Fuel Efficiency Board; Trustee and Manager Savings Bank of Glasgow; Chairman West of Scotland Convalescent Homes, Dunoon; Dir. British European Airways; Chm. Scottish Advisory Council for Civil Aviation; Member of Scottish Aerodromes Board; Chm. East Kilbride New Town Development Corporation; ex-President of the Burns Federation; executive mem. Town and Country Planning Assoc. Legion of Honour; Order of Polonia Restituta, Poland (Civilian). Has travelled in Europe and U.S. studying local government and political organisations. Visited France and America in 1939 and 1950 as the guest of Paris and New York and U.S. govt. *Publications:* books on Democracy, Co-operation, Transport, Housing, Scottish Industries, American Civic and Social Reform Services, Air Raids on London, Robert Burns, and Socialists and Poland. *Address:* 1 Kingsley Avenue, Glasgow, S.2. *T.:* Pollok 0634. [*Died* 30 *Jan.* 1963.

DOLMAN, Alderman Eric Charles, J.P.; Solicitor; *b.* 17 July 1903; *m.* Doreen Mary Bowen Dolman; no *c.* *Educ.:* All Hallows Sch., Honiton. Mem., Cardiff City Coun., 1949; Alderman, 1961; Lord Mayor of Cardiff, 1967-1968; has been Chm., Estates Cttee., and served on Public Works, Finance, Parks, Waterworks and Libraries Committees, Cardiff City Council. J.P. Cardiff. *Recreations:* fishing, gardening; formerly cricket (played for Wales and Mon.; Capt., Cardiff, 1938), hockey, Rugby football. *Address:* Doric House, St. Mellons, Nr. Cardiff. *T.:* 77709. *Clubs:* Cardiff and County (Cardiff); various Sports. [*Died* 6 *June* 1969.

DOMAGK, Professor Gerhard; Dr. med.; Professor, University of Münster (Westphalia), since 1928; Director, Research Laboratories for Experimental Pathology and Bacteriology, Farbenfabriken Bayer Wuppertal-Elberfeld, since 1927; *b.* Lagow, Province of Brandenburg, Germany, 30 Oct. 1895; *m.* 1925, Gertrud Strübe; three *s.* one *d.* *Educ.:* Liegnitz (Silesia); Univs. of Kiel, Greifswald, Münster (Dr. med., Kiel, 1921). Privat-Dozent, Univ. of Greifswald, 1924, Münster, 1925; extra-ordinary Professor, 1928; discovered therapeutic properties of sulphonamides, 1932; research on cancer and tuberculosis; Nobel Prize for Medicine, 1939. *Publications:* Arbeiten über Krebs (cancer), Stoffwechsel, akute Infektionskrankheiten und Tuberkulose, 1923-34; Über Entdeckung der quaternären Ammoniumverbindungen (Zephirol u.a.) zur Desinfektion, 1935; Bericht über chemotherapeutische Verwendung der Sulfonamide, 1935; (Domagk-Hegler) Chemotherapie bakterieller Infektionen, Leipzig, 1939 (3. Auflage 1944); Pathologische Anatomie u. Chemotherapie der Infektionskrankheiten, Stuttgart, 1947; Chemotherapie der Tuberkulose mit dem Thiosemikarbazonen, Stuttgart, 1950; Entdeckung der Heilwirkung des Isonikotinsäurehydrazids (Neoteben) und seiner Derivate zur chemotherapeutischen Behandlung der Tuberkulose, 1950, 1951. *Address:* Wuppertal-Elberfeld, Jägerstrasse 11, Nordrhein-Westfalen, British Zone, Germany. *T.:* Wuppertal 33193. [*Died* 24 *April* 1964.

DON, Rev. Alan Campbell, K.C.V.O. 1948; M.A.; Hon. D.D., St. Andrews, 1932; Dean of Westminster, 1946-59, resigned 1959; Chaplain to the Queen since December 1959; *b.* Broughty Ferry, 3 January 1885; *s.* of Robert Bogle Don and Lucy Flora Campbell; *m.* 1914, Muriel Gwenda McConnel (*d.* 1963). *Educ.:* Rugby Sch.; Magdalen College, Oxford. In business at Dundee, 1908-09; Resident at Oxford House, Bethnal Green, 1909-11; Cuddesdon College, 1911-12; Deacon, 1912; Priest, 1913; Curate of St. Peter's, Redcar, 1912-16; Vicar of Norton-juxta-Malton, Yorks, 1917-21; Provost of St. Paul's Cathedral Church, Dundee, 1921-31, Hon. Canon, 1949-; Chaplain and Secretary to the Archbishop of Canterbury, 1931-41; a Chaplain to the King, 1934-46; Chaplain to the Speaker, House of Commons, 1936-46; Canon of Westminster and Rector of St. Margaret, Westminster, 1941-46; Sub-Dean, 1941-46; Select Preacher, Oxford, 1940-41; Cambridge, 1942; Sub-Prelate, St. John of Jerusalem, 1949-. A Trustee, National Portrait Gallery, 1951-63. Hon. Fell. Magdalen College, Oxford, 1959. Knight Commander, Order of the Phoenix, 1953. *Recreation:* fishing. *Address:* 8 The Precincts, Canterbury, Kent. *T.:* Canterbury 61242. *Clubs:* Athenæum; New (Edinburgh); Royal and Ancient (St. Andrews). [*Died* 3 *May* 1966.

DON, Air Vice-Marshal Francis Percival, O.B.E. 1934; D.L.; R.A.F. retired; *b.* 27 Feb. 1886; *s.* of Robert Bogle Don and Lucy Flora Campbell; *m.* 1930, Angela Jane Birkbeck; two *s.* *Educ.:* Rugby School; Trinity College, Cambridge (M.A.). Qualified Engineer in business until 1914. Commissioned Scottish Horse Yeomanry, 1911; Gallipoli campaign, 1915; transferred R.F.C., 1916; Egypt, France (wounded, P.O.W. 1917); between wars served in Iraq, Egypt, Air Ministry; comd. 33 Squadron, 502 Squadron and Camb. Univ. Air Squadron; Air Attaché, Berlin, 1934-37; Head of Mission to French Air Forces in the field, 1939; A.O.A. British Air Forces in France, 1940 (despatches); A.O.A. Flying Training Comd.; S.A.S.O. Ferry Comd., Canada; invalided, 1942; retired, 1943; Regional Air Liaison Officer, N. Region Civil Defence, 1943-45; Hon. Air Cdre. No. 3620 (Co. of Norfolk) Fighter Control Unit. Gen. Comr. of Income Tax; some time Vice-Chm. Norfolk Territorial Assoc.; D.L. Norfolk, 1950. Fruit Farmer; Chm. Norfolk Fruit Growers' Assoc., 1959. O.St.J.; Legion of Honour (Officer); Croix de Guerre (with palm). *Recreations:* shooting, fishing. *Address:* Elmham House, East Dereham, Norfolk. *T.:* Elmham 262. *Club:* Army and Navy. [*Died* 18 *Sept.* 1964.

DONACHY, Frank, O.B.E. 1959; Part-time Member, British Railways Board, since Nov. 1962 (Deputy Chairman, Scottish Area Board, British Transport Commission, 1959-1962; Part-Time Member, B.T.C., 1959-62); Part-time Mem., Scottish Gas Board, since 1959; *b.* 20 Feb. 1899; *yr. s.* of John Donachy, Glasgow; *m.* 1923, Margaret Spence Hume, *o. d.* of John Hume; one *s.* *Educ.:* Elementary Schools, Glasgow and Edinburgh. Was Railway Signalman for 20 years before becoming full-time official of National Union of Railwaymen, 1941. Pres. of Scottish T.U.C., 1957. *Recreation:* fly fishing. *Address:* Venlaw Bank, Peebles, Scotland. *T.:* Peebles 2373.
[*Died* 1 *Feb.* 1970.

DONALDSON, Comdr. Charles Edward McArthur, V.R.D. 1943; R.C.N.R.; M.P. (C.) Roxburghshire, Selkirkshire and Peeblesshire since 1955 (Roxburgh and Selkirkshire, 1951-55); Selected Member of the Speaker Panel of Chairmen since 1959; Parl. Private Sec. to Lord Advocate for Scotland, 1953-59; *b.* 15 March 1903; *s.* of late Thomas McComb and Fanny Tressidder Hernaman Donaldson, Vancouver, British Columbia; *m.* 1958, Kathleen Bradley; one *d.* *Educ.:* Aberdeen, Dawson and King George High Schools, Vancouver. Joined Royal Canadian Navy (R), 1926; Naval A.D.C. to Lieutenant-Governor of British Columbia, 1936-41; Commanding Officer, Vancouver Div., 1936; R.C.N. Trg. Officer, W. Coast, 1939-41; Fleet Manning Officer, Newfoundland, 1941-42; Executive Officer, H.M.C.S. Stadacona, 1942-44; Canadian Liaison Officer, Portsmouth, 1944-45; Comdg. Officer, H.M.C.S. Niobe, 1945-46; Dep. Head, Canadian Naval Mission, London, 1946-; retd. Dec. 1946. Asst. Sec. Tourist Assoc. of Scotland 1947-51; contested Edinburgh East, 1950; Chm. The Canada Club of Edinburgh, 1947-53 (Hon. Pres. 1953). *Address:* 502 Duncan House, Dolphin Square, S.W.1. *T.:* Victoria 3800 (502 Duncan House). *Club:* Conservative (Edin).
[*Died* 11 *Dec.* 1964.

DONALDSON, Eion Pelly, C.M.G. 1943; M.A.; *b.* 15 April 1896; *o. s.* of late Lieut.-Colonel J. Donaldson, Wisborough Green, Sussex; *m.* 1922, Mary Cecely, *o. d.* of late Lt.-Col. R. M. Helme, D.L., J.P., T.D., Pulborough, Sussex; one *d.* (and one *d.* decd.). *Educ.:* Cheltenham Coll.; Oriel Coll., Oxford (Classical Schol., Dist. Litt. Hum., 1920). 2nd Lt. Rifle Brigade, 1915; served in France with Machine Gun Corps, 1916-19; commanded 35th Machine Gun Coy., 1918-19; served in Inland Revenue, India Office, and Burma Office, 1920-40; Imp. Defence Coll., 1936; Asst. Secretary (Civil), War Cabinet, 1940-43; Secretary-General, European Advisory Commission, 1944-45. Freeman of the City of London; Master, Worshipful Company of Bowyers, 1950-52. Member, Kensington Borough Council (Norland Ward), 1959-62. *Address:* 55 Addison Avenue, W.11 *T.:* Park 5335. *Club:* Union.
[*Died* 13 *Feb.* 1963.

DÖNGES, Dr. Theophilus Ebenhaézer; State President Elect, Republic of South Africa, 1967; *b.* Klerksdorp, Transvaal, 8 March 1898; *s.* of Rt. Rev. T. C. Dönges; *m.* 1926, Billie Schoeman; two *d.* *Educ.:* Robertson; Univs. of Stellenbosch, S. Africa and London; London Sch. of Economics. B.A. (*cum laude*) 1918, M.A. (*cum laude*) 1919, Stellenbosch; Queen Victoria Bursary for overseas study; LL.B. Univ. of S.A., 1922; LL.B. (*cum laude*) Univ. of Lond., 1922; LL.D. (Lond.) 1925. Called to Bar, Middle Temple, 1922. Registrar to Judge President of Orange Free State, 1921; Ed., S.A. Nation, 1924; Co-Ed., Die Burger, 1924-27; resigned to practise at Cape Bar. Legal Adviser, Cape Provincial Admin., 1929-39; K.C. 1939. M.P. for Fauresmith, 1941-48 and for Worcester, 1948-67; Minister of Interior, 1948-1958; Minister of Finance, 1958-67. Leader, S.A. Delegn. to U.N., 1950 and 1951; rep. S.A. at Commonwealth Prime Ministers' Conf., 1951; Cape Leader of Nat. Party, 1954-66. Chancellor, Univ. of Stellenbosch, 1959-. Hon. Ph.D., Stellenbosch, 1959. *Publications:* The Liability of Safe Carriage of Goods in Roman Dutch Law; (with L. de V. van Winsen) Municipal Law. *Recreation:* golf. *Address:* Office of the State President, Pretoria or Cape Town, South Africa. *T.:* Pretoria 743131; Cape Town 27101. [*Died* 10 *Jan.* 1968.

DONNELLY, Harry Hill, C.B. 1963; Secretary, University of Stirling, 1965-70; *b.* 8 July 1909; *o. s.* of late Harry Hill Donnelly, Glasgow; *m.* 1938, Edith McInroy, *o. d.* of late John Ferrie, Edinburgh; no *c.* *Educ.:* Hillhead High School, Glasgow; Glasgow Univ.; Edinburgh Univ. M.A. (Hons.) Glasgow; LL.B. (Distinction) Edinburgh. Historical Dept., H.M. Register House, 1934-40; Scottish Home Dept., 1940-1947; Private Sec. to successive Secretaries of State, 1944-47; Scottish Education Dept., 1947-65. Deputy Secretary, 1959-65. *Recreations:* tennis, riding. *Address:* 2 Airthrey Castle Yard, Stirling. *T.:* Stirling 2327. *Club:* Royal Commonwealth Society.
[*Died* 15 *June* 1969.

DONNITHORNE, Rev. Vyvyan Henry, M.A., M.C.; *b.* 8 Jan. 1886; *s.* of Lt.-Col. E. G. M. Donnithorne, J.P., Royal Scots Greys and Harriet Lucia Alexander, Carlow; *m.* 1919, Gladys Ingram; one *d.* *Educ.:* Christ's Hospital; Clare College, Cambridge; Ridley Hall, Cambridge. Served European War, Hampshire Regt. (wounded, M.C.); Ordained 1919; Missionary in Szechwan, Western China, 1920-49; Chaplain of Downing College, Cambridge, 1928; Archdeacon of Western Szechwan, China, 1935-45; Chaplain, Canary Islands, 1949-53; Director, West China Evangelistic Band, Hong Kong, 1953-. Captured by Chinese brigands with wife and daughter, and held prisoner for a month, 1925. *Address:* 4A Somerset Road, Kowloon Tong, Hong Kong.
[*Died* 12 *Dec.* 1968.

DOODSON, Arthur Thomas, C.B.E. 1956; F.R.S. 1933; Hon. F.R.S.E. 1953; D.Sc.; Dir. of Liverpool Observatory and Tidal Inst. 1946-61, retd.; *b.* 31 Mar. 1890; *s.* of late T. Doodson, Shaw, Lancs.; *m.* 1st, 1919, Margaret Galloway, one *s.*; 2nd, 1933, Elsie Mary Carey. *Educ.:* Rochdale; Liverpool University, B.Sc. 1911; 1st Cl. Hons. 1912; M.Sc. 1914; D.Sc. 1919; Assistant to Professor K. Pearson, University College, 1916-1918; Director ballistic computations, 1918-

1919; Secretary of Tidal Institute, 1919-29; Associate Director of Liverpool Observatory and Tidal Institute, 1929-45; Secretary to British Assoc. Committee on Tides, 1920-30; Hydraulics Research Board, 1947-60; Oceanographical Research Council, 1949-60. Chm. Mean Sea Level Committee; Chairman Committee on Statutes and By-Laws; Chairman Finance Committee, International Union of Geodesy and Geophysics, 1955-60; Mem. Liverpool University Court, 1962-. *Publications:* papers on Electric Waves, Bessel Functions, Statistics, and Tides, published in various journals; Report on London Floods, 1928; Admiralty Method of Tidal Prediction, 1936; Admiralty Manual of Tides, 1942. *Address:* 10 Ingestre Court, Oxton, Birkenhead. *T.:* Claughton 3849.

[*Died* 10 *Jan.* 1968.

DOOLIN, William, M.B., F.R.C.S.I.; Litt.D. *h.c.* (Univ. Dubl.); D.Litt. *h.c.* (N.U.I.); Hon. F.R.C.S. (Eng.) 1955; Surgeon, St Vincent's and Children's Hospitals, Dublin, retired; Professor of History of Medicine University College, Dublin; Editor, Irish Journal of Medical Science and Journal of Irish Medical Assoc.; Mem. Roy. Irish Academy; Fellow and Member of Council, Royal Academy of Medicine, Ireland; Member Irish Medical Registration Council; Member, General Medical Council; Ex-Pres. Royal College of Surgeons, Ireland; Fellow Association of Surgeons, Great Britain and Ireland; Associé-Étranger (*h.c.*) de l'Acad. de Chir, Paris. *b.* Dublin, 19 June 1887; *s.* of Walter G. Doolin, M.A., F.R.I.B.A.; *m.* 1st, Clare, *d.* of M. Kennedy, Dublin; two *s.* three *d.*; 2nd, Maureen, *d.* of Jas. Clinton, Clonmel; two *s.* *Educ.:* Dublin; Paris; London; Berlin. *Publications:* Wayfarers in Medicine, 1948; Dublin's Surgeon-Anatomists (Vicary Lecture, R.C.S., Eng.), 1950; contrib. to Jl. Irish Med. Assoc. *Address:* 2 Fitzwilliam Square, Dublin. *T.:* Dublin 61474. *Club:* The Irish.

[*Died* 14 *April* 1962.

DOPPING-HEPENSTAL, Col. Maxwell Edward, C.B.E. 1919; D.S.O. 1916; 1st K.G.O. Gurkha Rifles, retired; *b.* 7 March 1872; 3rd *s.* of late Col. R. A. Dopping-Hepenstal: unmarried. *Educ.:* King William's College, Isle of Man; R.M.C. Sandhurst. Worcester Regt. 1892; joined Indian Army, 1896; served N.W. Frontier, 1897; Waziristan, 1901; European War, 1914-16 (despatches, D.S.O., Croix de Guerre); Afghan Campaign, 1919 (C.B.E.); Waziristan, 1921-22 (despatches), retired, 1922. *Address:* Duncan, B.C., Canada.

[*Died* 2 *Aug.* 1965.

DORCHESTER, 6th Baron, but 2nd of revised creation of 1899; **Dudley Massey Pigott Carleton;** O.B.E. 1920; J.P.; Bt. Lt.-Col. Reserve of Officers; *b.* 26 Feb. 1876; *o. surv. s.* of Baroness Dorchester and Captain Francis Paynton Pigott, 16th Lancers, of Banbury, Oxon (who assumed the additional name of Carleton) (*d.* 1883); *S.* mother, 1925; *m.* 1911, Hon. Kathleen de Blaquiere, *o. d.* of 6th Baron de Blaquiere; two *d.* Joined 9th Lancers, 1896; served South Africa, 1899-1900 (Queen's medal 2 clasps); commanded Squadron of Mounted Infantry West African Frontier Force; took part in Kano Sokoto campaign (medal with clasps); European War, France, Aug.-Dec. 1914; East Coast, Jan.-Sept 1915; Egypt, Oct. to Jan. 1916; 2nd in Command Derbyshire Yeomanry, Struma Valley, etc., 1916-17; Military Secretary to G.O.C.-in-chief, British Salonika Force, 1917-19 (despatches thrice, Brevet Lt.-Colonel, Croix de Guerre with palm; Serbia, Order of White Eagle with crossed swords; Greece, Order of Saviour Medal for Military Merit with palm); Home Defence Battalion (Hants), 1938; mobilised Aug. 1939; transferred 10th Bn. Royal Berkshire Regt., Company Commander, 1940; Staff Officer to Berkshire County Defence Commander, 1941-42; retired from Army, 1942; joined A.T.C. as Liaison Officer for duration of war. Lord of the Manors of Greywell, Newnham, Nateley, and Scures. *Publications:* Sport: Foxhunting and shooting, 1935; revised shooting section of new edition of Encyclopædia of Sport. *Heir:* none. *Address:* Greywell Hill, Basingstoke, Hants. *Clubs:* Cavalry; Royal Yacht Squadron.

[*Died* 20 *Jan.* 1963 (*ext.*).

DORLING, Captain Henry Taprell, D.S.O. 1918, R.N. (retd.); F.R.Hist.S.; *b.* Duns, Berwickshire, 8 Sept. 1883; 2nd *s.* of late Colonel Francis Dorling, late Royal Sussex Regiment, of Farnborough, Hants; *m.* 1909, Evelyne (*d.* 1968), *d.* of late Roderick MacDonald, Kew, Surrey; one *s.* *Educ.:* H.M.S. Britannia, 1897; served H.M.S. Terrible, South Africa and China, including Relief of Pekin, 1900; European War, 1914-1918, commanding destroyers (despatches, D.S.O.); gold medal from Swedish Government for saving life at sea, 1917; retired, 1929; recalled to Navy, 1939; Ministry of Information and afloat in all types of warships, 1939-42; Staff of C.-in-C. Mediterranean, Dec. 1942-45; a Younger Brother of Trinity House; Member of the Navy Records Society, and of the Society for Nautical Research. R.N. Minewatching Service and Minewatching Service Officer, Port of London, 1954-62. Officer of the Legion of Merit, U.S.A., 1944. *Publications:* Under pseudonym Taffrail, Pincher Martin, O.D.; Michael Bray; Sea Ventures of Britain; Sea Escapes and Adventures; Pirates, 1929; Men o' War, 1929; Kerrell; Endless Story; The Scarlet Stripe, 1932; Dover-Ostend, 1933; The Man from Scapa Flow, 1933; Seventy North, 1934; Second Officer; Swept Channels, 1935; Mid-Atlantic, 1936; Mystery at Milford Haven; Mystery Cruise; Operation M.O.; The Shetland Plan, 1939; The Navy in Action, 1940; Chenies, 1943; Battle of the Atlantic, 1946; Western Mediterranean, 1942-45, 1948; Blue Star Line, 1948; Toby Shad, 1949; The Jade Lizard, 1951; The New Moon, 1952; Eurydice, 1953; Arctic Convoy, 1956; enlarged edns. Ribbons and Medals (first published, 1916), 1956, 1957; other books on naval and nautical subjects; late Naval Correspondent of The Observer; has done considerable broadcasting; written many naval feature programmes for the B.B.C. *Address:* 4A Station Road, Bexhill-on-Sea, Sussex. *T.:* Bexhill 2327. *Clubs:* Army and Navy, Hurlingham; Royal Yacht Squadron.

[*Died* 1 *July* 1968.

DORLING, Vice-Adm. James Wilfred Sussex, C.B. 1941; Director of the Radio Industry Council, 1946-58, retired; *b.* 1889; *s.* of late Col. Francis Dorling, Farnborough, Hants; *m.* 1914, Dorothy Burnett, *d.* of Colonel J. G. Panton, C.M.G. *Educ.:* H.M.S. Britannia. Joined Royal Navy, 1904; Capt. 1928; Rear-Adm., 1939; served European War, 1914-18; Deputy Controller, Admiralty, 1939-41; British Admiralty Supply Representative, Washington, D.C., 1941-44; Flag Officer, Liverpool, 1944-46. M.I.E.E.; M.Brit.I.R.E.; F.R.S.A. A Younger Brother of Trinity House, 1946, Legion of Merit, U.S.A., Degree of Commander, 1946. Hon. Vice-Pres. British Wireless Dinner Club, 1961. *Address:* Shiplands House, Fareham, Hants. *Clubs:* United Service, Royal Cruising; Royal Yacht Squadron (Cowes).

[*Died* 12 *May* 1966.

DORMAN, Brig. Edward Mungo, C.B. 1941; D.S.O. 1918; M.C.; *b.* 11 Mar. 1885; *s.* of late Gen. J. C. Dorman, C.M.G.; *m.* 1911, Georgia Mabel Ingram; one *s.* one *d.* *Educ.:* Bath; Sandhurst. Gazetted to 4th Dragoon Guards, 1905; served European War (despatches, D.S.O., M.C.); commanded 4/7th Dragoon Guards, 1927-31; Brigadier commanding 3rd (Meerut) Cavalry Brigade, India, 1932-

1936; retired pay, 1936; re-employed Brigadier Commander Yorkshire Area, 1940-43; Assistant Chief Constable, War Dept. Constabulary, 1944-46. *Recreation:* sailing. *Address:* Myrtle Lodge, Kinsale, Co. Cork. *T.:* Kinsale 83. *T.A.:* Kinsale. [*Died* 18 *April* 1967.

DORTÉ, Philip Hoghton, O.B.E. 1945; Midlands Controller, Associated TeleVision Ltd., 1956-65; Director, Alpha Television Services (Birmingham) Ltd.; *b.* 28 Oct. 1904; *s.* of late Peter Francis and of Dolores Gertrude (*née* Hoghton) Dorté: *m.* 1935, Evelyn Jon Harper; three *d.* *Educ.:* Downside; Cambridge; Faraday House. Radio Engineer, U.S.A. and Canada, 1926-1929; Recording Engineer, Radio Pictures and Gaumont British Picture Corpn., 1929-1937; Television Outside Broadcasts Manager, B.B.C., 1937-39; Served War, 1939-1946: Signals/Radar Officer, R.A.F.V.R. (Wing Comdr. 1941; Group Capt. 1945, despatches thrice). Head of Television Outside Broadcasts, B.B.C., 1946-49; Head of Television Films, B.B.C., 1949-54; Director of Operations, Independent Television News Ltd., 1955-56. Past-President: Radar Assoc.; Birmingham Publicity Assoc.; Fellow British Kinematograph Soc., M.I.E.E. Television Films: B.B.C. Television Newsreel, 1948-54; Comet over Africa, 1951; Her Peoples Rejoiced, 1953; Christmas Journey, 1953; War in the Air, 1954. *Recreations:* photography, travelling. *Address:* 86 Hampton Lane, Solihull, Warwicks.; 17B Sussex Heights, Brighton. *Club:* Royal Air Force. [*Died* 26 *July* 1970.

DOS PASSOS, John; *b.* 14 Jan. 1896; *s.* of John R. Dos Passos and Lucy Addison Sprigg; *m.* Katharine F. Smith (*d.* 1947); *m.* 1949, Elizabeth Holdridge; one *d.* *Educ.:* Harvard. *Publications:* One Initiation, 1920 (new edn. 1969); Three Soldiers, 1921; A Pushcart at the Curb, 1922; Rosinante to the Road Again, 1922; Streets of Night, 1923; Manhattan Transfer, 1925; Orient Express, 1927; The 42nd Parallel, 1930; Nineteen Nineteen, 1932; In All Countries, 1934; Three Plays, 1934; The Big Money, 1936; USA: Journeys Between Wars, 1938; Adventures of a Young Man, 1939; The Ground we Stand On, 1942; Number One, 1944; State of the Nation, 1944; Tour of Duty, 1946; The Grand Design, 1949; The Prospect Before Us, 1950; Chosen Country, 1951; District of Columbia, 1952; The Head and Heart of Thomas Jefferson, 1955; Most Likely to Succeed, 1955; The Theme is Freedom, 1956; The Men who Made the Nation, 1957; The Great Days, 1959; Prospects of a Golden Age, 1959; Midcentury, 1961; Mr. Wilson's War, 1962; Brazil on the Move, 1963; Occasions and Protests, 1964; (jt.) Lincoln and the Gettysburg Address, 1964; Thomas Jefferson: The Making of a President, 1964; The Shackles of Power, 1966; The Best Times (Memoirs), 1966; World in a Glass, 1966; The Portugal Story, 1970; Easter Island, 1971. *Address:* Westmoreland, VA. 22577, U.S.A. [*Died* 28 *Sept.* 1970.

DOUGHTY-TICHBORNE, Sir Anthony J. H. D.; *see* Tichborne.

DOUGLAS OF KIRTLESIDE, 1st Baron, *cr.* 1948, of Dornock; **Marshal of the Royal Air Force William Sholto Douglas,** G.C.B., *cr.* 1946 (K.C.B., *cr.* 1941; C.B. 1940); M.C., D.F.C.; D.L. London; Chairman of Horizon Travel Associates Ltd., 1964; Hon. Fell. of Lincoln Coll., Oxf., 1941; Hon. Companion, Royal Aeronautical Soc., 1950; Hon. Liveryman Dyers' Company; Liveryman, Guild of Air Pilots and Air Navigators; Vice-Patron, Amateur Athletic Association; *b.* 23 December 1893; *s.* of late Capt. Robert Langton Douglas: *m.* 1st, 1919, May Howard (marriage dissolved, 1932); 2nd, 1933, Joan Leslie (marriage dissolved 1954), *d.* of Col. H. C. Denny, C.B.; 3rd, 1955, Hazel Walker; one *d.* *Educ.:* Tonbridge Sch.; Lincoln Coll., Oxf. (Scholar). Served European War, 1914-18 (despatches thrice, M.C., D.F.C., French Croix de Guerre); commanded Nos. 43 and 84 (Fighter) Sqdns., 1917-18; Chief Pilot, Handley Page Transport Ltd., 1919; returned to R.A.F., 1920; Instructor, Imperial Defence Coll., 1932-35; Dir. of Staff Duties, Air Ministry, 1936-37; Asst. Chief of the Air Staff, 1938-40; Dep. Chief of Air Staff, 1940; Air Officer Commanding-in-Chief, Fighter Command, 1940-42; Air Officer Commanding-in-Chief, Middle East Command, 1943-44; Air Officer Commanding-in-Chief, Coastal Command, 1944-45; Air C.-in-C., British Air Forces of Occupation, Germany, 1945-46; Marshal of the R.A.F., 1946; C.-in-C. and Military Governor, British Zone of Germany, 1946-1947; retired, 1948. Dir., British Overseas Airways Corporation, 1948-49; Chairman, British European Airways, 1949-64; Pres. International Air Transport Assoc., 1956-57. Order of Polonia Restituta, Poland, 2nd Class; Order of the White Lion, of Czecho-Slovakia, 2nd Class; Order of the White Eagle of Yugoslavia with Swords; Chief Commander Legion of Merit, U.S.; Naval Distinguished Service Medal, U.S.; Grand Cross Order of Saint Olaf, Norway; Grand Cross Order of Orange Nassau, Holland; Order of the Phœnix, Greece, degree of Grand Officer (with Swords); Grand Cross Order of Crown, Belgium; Grand Officer Legion of Honour, France; Czecho-Slovak War Cross; Air League Founders' Medal, 1964. *Publications (autobiography):* Years of Combat, 1963 (awarded C. P. Robertson Memorial Trophy, 1963); Years of Command, 1966. *Heir:* none. *Address:* Shepherds Holt, Denham, Bucks. *T.:* 2136. [*Died* 29 *Oct.* 1969 (*ext.*).

DOUGLAS, Claude Gordon, C.M.G. 1919; M.C.; F.R.S. 1922; B.Sc.; D.M.; Hon. Fellow and formerly Fellow and Tutor in Natural Science, St. John's College, Oxford, and Professor of General Metabolism, Oxford University; *b.* 26 Feb. 1882 *s.* of late Claude Douglas, F.R.C.S.; unmarried. *Educ.:* Wellington College; Wyggeston School, Leicester; Magdalen Coll., Oxford; Guy's Hospital. Open Science Exhibition, New College, 1900; Open Science Demyship, Magdalen College, 1900; University Scholarship, Guy's Hospital, 1905; Fellow of St. John's College, 1907; Radcliffe Prize, 1911; Osler Memorial Medal, 1945; temp. Lieut.-Col., R.A.M.C., 1918; served European War, 1914-19 (despatches 4 times, C.M.G., M.C.); Oliver-Sharpey Lecturer, Royal College of Physicians, 1927. *Publications:* Papers on Respiration and kindred physiological subjects in scientific jls. *Recreation:* golf. *Address:* 15 Marston Ferry Rd., Oxford. *Club:* Athenæum. [*Died* 23 *March* 1963.

DOUGLAS, Rt. Rev. Edward, D.D.; Titular Bishop of Botri since 1954; *b.* 26 Aug. 1901; *s.* of Edward Douglas and Sarah Douglas (*née* Drummond). *Educ.:* St. Aloysius College, Glasgow; Blairs College, Aberdeen; St. Peter's College, Glasgow. Ordained, 1924; taught in Blairs College, 1925-40; Parish Priest, Glenboig and Govan, 1940-48; Bishop of Motherwell, (R.C.), 1948-54. *Address:* 58 Castlepark Drive, Fairlie, Ayrshire, [*Died* 13 *June* 1967.

DOUGLAS, Horace (James), Q.C.; *b.* 5 March 1866; 2nd *s.* of Henry William Douglas, Peebles, St. Albans and London. *Educ.:* privately. Called to Bar, Gray's Inn and Middle Temple, 1900. K.C. 1939. Served in ranks of Middlesex Regt., Rifle Volunteers, for 10 years. *Address:* Cloisters, Temple, E.C.4; 62 High Street, Harrow-on-the-Hill. [*Died* 16 *April* 1962.

DOUGLAS, Sir James (Boyd), Kt. 1958; C.B.E. 1945; J.P. Kirkcudbright; Chairman Scottish Milk Board, 1950-62 (Member, 1935-50), retd.; Chairman, Southern Agricultural Executive Committee since 1946; farmer and land valuer; *b.* 27 April 1893; *s.* of late John Douglas and Mary Boyd Crawford; *m.* 1924, Dorothea Napier Dunnachie; one *s.* one *d.* *Educ.:* Glasgow High School. Capt. Lanarkshire Yeomanry. Chairman Kirkcudbright War Agric. Exec. Committee, 1939-46; Chairman, Wallet's Marts Ltd., Castle Douglas. *Recreation:* shooting. *Address:* Barstibly, Castle Douglas. *T.:* Bridge of Dee 209. *Clubs:* Scottish Conservative (Edinburgh); Royal Scottish Automobile (Glasgow).
[*Died* 4 *May* 1964.

DOUGLAS, Sir James Louis Fitzroy Scott, 6th Bart., *cr.* 1786; *b.* 24 Oct. 1930; *s.* of late Capt. George Francis Valentine Scott Douglas and late Lady Blanche Linnie, *d.* of 9th Duke of Beaufort; *S.* great-uncle 1935. *Educ.:* Wellington College. *Recreations:* motor racing and trials driving; shooting and fishing. *Heir:* none. *Address:* Grove House, Sherston, Wilts. *Clubs:* Press, British Racing Drivers'.
[*Died* 16 *July* 1969 (*ext.*).

DOUGLAS, Col. Norman, C.B.E. 1938; T.D., D.L., R.A.; *b.* 20 Oct. 1887; *s.* of Lt.-Col. T. T. Douglas, V.D.; *m.* 1911, Emmie Collingwood Wearmouth; two *s.* one *d.* *Educ.:* Giggleswick School. In business as a Surveyor and Land Agent, retd., 1964; Fellow of Royal Institution of Chartered Surveyors and of Chartered Auctioneers and Estate Agents Inst.; joined Northumberland Hussars, 1906; transferred to Royal Artillery (T.A.), 1909; transferred to R.A.O.C., 1935; re-transferred to R.A., 1940; retired, 1945. *Recreations:* golf, motoring. *Address:* 12 Thornfield Rd., Middlesbrough, Yorks. *T.:* 88494. *Club:* Cleveland (Middlesbrough).
[*Died* 21 *Jan.* 1968.

DOUGLAS, Col. Roderick, C.B.E. 1944; A.F.C.; Chairman of De Havilland Aircraft Co., of S.A. (Pty.) Ltd.; *b.* 5 Dec. 1898; *s.* of Thomas Douglas, Chartered Accountant, Johannesburg; *m.* Dorothy Haggie; one *s.* two *d.* by first wife. *Educ.:* King Edward VII.'s School, Johannesburg. Served European War R.F.C. and R.A.F., mostly in 111 Sqdn. Palestine (A.F.C.). Called up for service with S.A.A.F. Sept. 1939 in rank of Major; Director of Air Personnel and Organisation, South African Air Force 1940; placed on Reserve, Nov. 1944. *Address:* Blair Atholl Farm, P.O. Renos, South Africa. *Club:* Rand (Johannesburg).
[*Died Sept.* 1965.

DOUGLAS-HAMILTON, Lord Malcolm Avendale, O.B.E. 1943; D.F.C. 1944; *b.* 12 November 1909; 3rd *s.* of 13th Duke of Hamilton; *m.* 1st, 1931, Pamela (marriage dissolved, 1952; she *m.* 1962, Sir Tresham Lever, 2nd Bt., *d.* of Lieut.-Col. Hon. Malcolm Bowes Lyon; two *s.* two *d.*; 2nd, 1953, Mrs. Natalie Wales Paine, C.B.E. (Hon.) 1946, *widow* of Edward B. Paine, New York City. *Educ.:* Eton; R.A.F. Coll. R.A.F., 1929-32; Civil Aviation, 1932-39; Auxiliary Air Force, 1932-34; Reserve, 1934-39; served War of 1939-45, R.A.F., 1939-46 (A.T.C. Commandant for Scotland, 1945-46); M.P. (C.) Inverness Division of Ross and Cromarty, 1950-54. Chm. of Charity Organisation Soc., now Family Welfare Assoc., 1938-46, Vice-Pres., 1946-; Governor of Gordonstoun School; Founding Member of Scottish Centre of Outdoor Training, Glenmore Lodge; member of Committee, Central Council of Physical Recreation, Pres. Internat. Flight Centre; Pres. Center Airmotive Corp., Long Island. Member of Royal Company of Archers (Queen's Bodyguard for Scotland). Is interested in Highland development. *Publications:* articles on sport and aviation to various magazines. *Recreations:* mountaineering, sailing, flying. *Address:* 25 Ives Road, Hewlett, Long Island, U.S.A. *T.:* Franklin 4-1067. *Clubs:* Royal Air Force, Royal Aero; Highland (Inverness).
[*Died* 21 *July* 1964.

DOUGLAS-PENNANT, Admiral Hon. Sir Cyril Eustace, K.C.B., *cr.* 1950 (C.B. 1945); C.B.E. 1943; D.S.O. 1944; D.S.C. 1917; *b.* 7 April 1894; *s.* and *heir* of 5th Baron Penrhyn, *q.v.*; *m.* 1st, 1917, Phyllis Constance (who obtained a divorce, 1936), *d.* of late Colonel Oswald Mosley Leigh; one *d.*; 2nd, 1937, Sheila, *d.* of late Stanley Brotherhood, Thornhaugh Hall, Peterborough. *Educ.:* Royal Naval Colleges, Osborne and Dartmouth. Entered Royal Navy, 1907; served European War, 1914-18 (D.S.C.); War of 1939-45 (despatches, C.B.E., D.S.O., C.B., Commander American Legion of Merit, 1945); Commandant Joint Services Staff College, 1947-49; Flag-Officer (Air) Mediterranean, and Second-in-Command, Mediterranean Station, 1948-50; Admiral, British Joint Services Mission in Washington, D.C., 1950-52; C.-in-C., Nore, 1952-53; retired 1953. Officer of French Legion of Honour and Croix de Guerre with Palm, 1948. *Address:* 49 Lowndes Square, S.W.1. *Clubs:* United Service Turf.
[*Died* 3 *April* 1961.

DOVERCOURT, 1st Baron, *cr.* 1954, of Harwich; **Joseph Stanley Holmes,** Kt., *cr.* 1945; *b.* London, 31 Oct. 1878; *m.* 1905, Eva Gertrude, *d.* of Thomas Rowley. *Educ.:* City of London School. Member of the L.C.C., 1910-19; chartered accountant (2nd in Hons., 1901); Chairman, North-West Building Society; Vice-President, Building Societies Association; Trustee of the Portland Club; M.P. (L.) N.E. Derbyshire, Dec. 1918-22; (L. Nat. and C.) Harwich division of Essex, 1935-54. Introduced as a Private Member's Bill the Inheritance (Family Provision) Act, 1938 and the Coast Protection Act, 1939; Member of Order of Merit of Chile. *Recreation:* golf. *Heir:* none. *Address:* 15 Grosvenor Square, W.1; 68 Pall Mall, S.W.1. *Clubs:* Reform, Portland, M.C.C., Hurlingham; Walton Heath; East Devon.
[*Died* 22 *April* 1961 (*ext.*).

DOWBIGGIN, Sir Herbert Layard, Kt., *cr.* 1931; C.M.G. 1926; Knight of Grace, Order of St. John of Jerusalem, 1936; *b.* 1880; *e. s.* of late Reverend R. T. Dowbiggin. *Educ.:* Merchant Taylors' School. Joined Ceylon Police, 1901; Inspector-General, 1913; retired, 1937; on special duty reporting on the Cyprus Police Force, 1926, on the Palestine Police Force, 1930, and on the Northern Rhodesia Police, 1937; has King's Police Medal, Colonial Police Medal and Order of Crown of Belgium. *Address:* Milden, Nr. Ipswich, Suffolk. *T.:* Bildeston 227. *Club:* Alpine.
[*Died* 24 *May* 1966.

DOWDING, 1st Baron, *cr.* 1943, of Bentley Priory; **Air Chief Marshal Hugh Caswall Tremenheere Dowding,** G.C.B., *cr.* 1940 (K.C.B., *cr.* 1933; C.B. 1928); G.C.V.O., *cr.* 1937; C.M.G. 1919; Royal Air Force; *b.* 24 April 1882; *m.* 1st, 1918 (wife *decd.*); one *s.* (one *step d.*); 2nd, 1951, Mrs. Muriel Whiting, Southborough, nr. Tunbridge Wells, *widow* of Pilot Officer Maxwell Whiting (one *step s.*). *Educ.:* Winchester; R.M.A., Woolwich Joined R.A., 1900; Royal Flying Corps, 1914; Royal Air Force, 1918; served European War, 1914-19 (despatches, C.M.G.); Director of Training, Air Ministry, 1926-29; commanded Fighting Area, Air Defence of Great Britain, 1929-30; Air Member for Research and Development of Air Council, 1930-36; Air Officer Commanding-in-Chief Fighter Command, 1936-40; Principal Air A.D.C. to the King, 193'-43; on special duty (under Minister of Aircraft Production) in U.S.A., 1940-41; retired, 1942. President, Battle of Britain Fighter Association, 1958. Awarded Commemorative Medallion by Trans World Airlines, 1960. *Publications:* Many Mansions; Lychgate; The Dark Star. *Heir: s.* Wing Comdr. Hon. Derek Hugh Tremenheere Dowding, R.A.F., Retd. [*b.* 9 Jan. 1919; *m.* 1st, 1940, Joan Myrle (marriage dissolved), *d.* of Donald James Stuart, Nairn; 2nd, 1947, Alison Margaret, *widow* of Major R. W. H. Peebles, B.C.S. (marriage dissolved); two *s.*; 3rd 1961, Odette L. M. S. Hughes, *d.* of Louis Joseph Houles]. *Address:* 1 Calverley Park, Tunbridge Wells, Kent. *T.:* Tunbridge Wells 28812. *Club:* United Service.

[*Died* 15 *Feb.* 1970.

DOWDING, Vice-Admiral (retd.) Sir Arthur Ninian, K.B.E., *cr.* 1945; C.B. 1938; Admiral Superintendent H.M. Dockyard, Devonport, 1938-45; *b.* 4 Jan. 1886; *s.* of A. J. C. Dowding; *m.* 1st, 1915, Kathleen Charlotte Hamilton (*d.* 1961), *d.* of late Capt. J. H. Drummond, 34th Regt. (Border); one *s.* (died of wounds in France, 1940; 2nd, 1964, Penelope Wilhelmina, *o. d.* of late Charles Onslow Master of Flax Bourton, Somerset, and *widow* of John Statter. Joined H.M.S. Britannia from Clifton College, 1900. Legion of Merit (grade of Officer), U.S.A., 1946. *Address:* 69 Wimbledon Hill, S.W.19. *Club:* United Service. [*Died* 26 *Nov.* 1966.

DOWDING, Commodore John Charles Keith, C.B.E. 1942; D.S.O. 1940; R.N.R. retd.; *b.* 1 Nov. 1891; *s.* of late Rev. Charles Dowding; *m.* 1932, Dorothy Waring Evans; one *s.* *Educ.:* Durham and St. Bee's Schools; H.M.S. Conway. Served 4 years in sailing ships; served all 1914-1918 war in 10th Cruiser Squadron and 2nd in Command of Destroyers, Home Station and Mediterranean, until 1919; joined Orient Line, 1919; Staff Commander, 1936; called up for Active Service, Sept. 1939, in Command of H.M.S. Mona's Isle; D.S.O. for Dunkirk Operations; C.B.E. for Cdre. of Convoy P.Q.17. to Archangel, 1942; Captain R.N.R., 1940, Commodore, 1946; retired list, 1946. R.N.R. A.D.C. to the King, 1945-46. *Recreation:* walking. *Address:* Crossways, Crowthorne, Berks. *T.:* 2127

[*Died* 13 *Feb.* 1965.

DOWLER, Lieut.-General Sir Arthur (Arnhold Bullick), K.C.B. 1952; (C.B. 1943); K.B.E. 1946; D.L.; retired; Secretary King George VI Foundation, 1953-60; *b.* 16 July 1895; *e. s.* of late A. E. Dowler; *m.* 1918, Dagmar M. Becker; two *s.* two *d.* *Educ.:* Tonbridge School; R.M.C. Sandhurst. Commissioned East Surrey Regiment, 1914; served European War, 1914-18, France and Flanders (despatches, Croix de Guerre, Brevet Major); Staff College, Camberley, 1931-32; Bt. Lieut. Col. 1935; Directing Staff, Staff College, Camberley, 1937-39; Subst. Lt.-Col. and Command 1st Bn. E. Surrey Regt., July 1939; G.S.O.1 49th (West Riding) Div., Sept. 1939 (despatches, 1940); B.G.S. V Corps; Comd. 2 Inf. Bde. (Brig.) 1940; comd. 38 (Welsh) Div. (Maj.-Gen.) 1942; Maj.-Gen. i/c Administration, Southern Command, 1942-43, and M.E.F., 1944-46; Chief of Staff, British Army of the Rhine, 1946; Dir. of Infantry War Office, 1947-48; G.O.C. East Africa Command, 1948-51. Colonel, the East Surrey Regiment, 1946-54; Deputy Lieutenant of Surrey, 1958. Chairman, Ex-Services War Disabled Help Dept. of Joint Cttee. of St. John and the Red Cross, 1959; a Governor of the Star and Garter Home, Richmond, 1960. Legion of Merit (Officer and Commander), 1947; Chevalier, Legion of Honour, 1947. O.St.J. 1961. *Address:* Long Row, Blechingley, Surrey. *Club:* United Service.

[*Died* 14 *Nov.* 1963.

DOWLING, Vice-Adm. (retd.) Sir Roy (Russell), K.C.V.O. 1963; K.B.E. 1957 (C.B.E. 1953); C.B. 1955; D.S.O. 1945; Australian Secretary to the Queen since 1963; *b.* 28 May 1901; Australian; *m.* 1930, Jess Spencer Blanch; two *s.* three *d.* Roy. Aust. N.C., 1915; specialised as Gunnery Officer, H.M.S. Excellent, 1925; served in: H.M.A.S. Anzac, 1927-28, Australia; H.M.S. Colombo, 1931-32, Mediterranean; H.M.A.S. Canberra, 1933-35, Aust.; in comd. H.M.A.S. Swan, 1937-38, Aust.; Exec. Officer, H.M.S. Naiad, 1939-42, N. Sea and Medit.; Dep. Chief of Naval Staff, Navy Office, Melb., 1943-44; in comd.: H.M.A.S. Hobart, 1944-1946, Pacific; H.M.A.S. Sydney, 1948-50; Second Naval Mem., Navy Office, Melb. (Cdre. 1st cl.), 1950-52; i.d.c. 1953; Flag Officer Comdg. Aust. Fleet, Dec. 1953-1954. Chief of Naval Staff and First Naval Member, Australian Commonwealth Naval Board, 1955-59; Chairman, Chiefs of Staff Committee, Australia, 1959-61, retired, 1961. Commander 1936; Captain 1944; Rear-Adm. 1953, Vice-Adm. 1955. *Recreations:* fishing, golf. *Address:* 91 Empire Circuit, Deakin, Canberra, A.C.T., Australia. *Club:* Naval and Military (Melbourne).

[*Died* 15 *April* 1969.

DOWNE, 10th Viscount (*cr.* 1680), **Richard Dawnay,** O.B.E. 1945; Bt. 1642; Baron Dawnay of Danby (U.K.), *cr.* 1897; *b.* 16 May 1903; *er. s.* of 9th Viscount and Dorothy (*d.* 1957), *o. c.* of late Sir W. ffolkes, 3rd Bt.; *S.* father 1931; *m.* 1928, Margaret Christine, *d.* of late Christian Bahnsen, Passaic, New Jersey; two *s.* *Educ.:* Eton College; R.M.C. Sandhurst. Page of Honour to H.M. the King; Lieut. Grenadier Guards, 1923-26. Served War of 1939-45: Bde. Comdr. 69 Inf. Bde., A.A.G., W. Africa Comd.; Comdr. Sierra Leone and Gambia Area. T.D.; D.L. and J.P., N.R. Yorks. *Recreations:* shooting, fishing. *Heir: s.* Hon. John Christian George Dawnay [*b.* 18 Jan. 1935; *m.* 1965, Alison Diana, *e. d.* of I. F. H. Sconce, Sevenoaks, Kent]. *Address:* Wykeham Abbey, Yorks. *T.A.:* Wykeham. *T.:* Wykeham 204; Danby Lodge, Danby, Yorks. *T.A.:* Danby, Yorks. *T.:* Castleton 224; 22 Down Street, W.1. *T.:* Grosvenor 1976. *Club:* Turf. [*Died* 8 *Dec.* 1965.

DOWNES-SHAW, Sir (Archibald) Havergal, Kt., *cr.* 1952; O.B.E. 1930; Alderman since 1946; *b.* 29 December 1884; *s.* of Rev. Archibald Downes Downes-Shaw and Amy, *d.* of Rev. H. E. Havergal; unmarried. *Educ.:* St. Lawrence, Kent; Liverpool University. B.Eng. 1904, M.Eng. 1911. *Recreation:* fishing. *Address:* 1 Upper Belgrave Road, Bristol, 8. *T.:* Bristol 34993. *Clubs:* Flyfishers', Royal Automobile, Royal Aero; Clifton, Constitutional (Bristol).

[*Died* 4 *Sept.* 1961.

DOWNIE, Sir Harold (Frederick), K.B.E., *cr.* 1951 (O.B.E. 1934); C.M.G. 1939; M.A.; *b.* 26 September 1889; *s.* of Frederick William Downie, Chiswick, and Ada Jane Barnett; *m.* 1918, Margaret Fanny, *d.* of George Saltmarsh Downie; three *s.* *Educ.:* Christ's Hospital; University College, Oxford (Exhibitioner in Classics, 1st Class Hon. Mods., 2nd Class Litt. Hum.). Entered Civil Service (Colonial Office), 1912; Military Service, 1914-18. One of the Crown Agents for the Colonies, 1942; retired 1953. Chairman of West African and East African Currency Boards, 1943-53. *Recreation:* gardening. *Address:* Broadhill Cottage, Ockley Lane, Hassocks, Sussex. *T.:* Burgess Hill 3471.

[*Died* 14 *Jan.* 1966.

DOWNS, Edgar, R.O.I.; Artist; *b.* Birkenhead; *s.* of late William Downs; *m.* 1923, Ella, (*d.* 1949), *d.* of late Insp. Gen. T. R. Pickthorn, R.N.; no c. *Educ.:* Birkenhead School. Artistic

Training at Munich; has exhibited at R.A., R.O.I., etc. *Recreations:* boating, swimming, riding, reading, etc. *Address:* Brix, Mudeford, Christchurch, Hants. *Club:* London Sketch. [*Died* 8 *March* 1963.

DOWSE, Major-General John Cecil Alexander, C.B. 1946; C.B.E. 1942; M.C. (and Bar); M.R.C.O.G.; M.B.; L.M.(Rot.); *b.* 11 Nov. 1891; *s.* of Chancellor J. C. Dowse, Monkstown, County Dublin, Ireland; *m.* 1916 Mary Abigail Todd; one *s.* *Educ.:* Trent College, Derbyshire; Dublin University. Officer in R.A.M.C. since 5 Aug. 1914, retd. 1949; served European War, 1914-18, Western Front; Frontier India, 1919; War of 1939-45, France, North Africa, Italy and Egypt; D.D.G.A.M.S., 1946. Comdt. and Director of Studies, Royal Army Medical College, 1948-49; Col. Comdt. R.A.M.C., 1950-56. C.St.J. 1946. Comdr. Order of the Phœnix (Greece). *Publications:* Contribns. to various journals. *Recreations:* Rugby football (late!), tennis, golf, shooting. *Address:* 48 Combemartin Road, Southfields, S.W.18. *Club:* Coombewood Golf. [*Died* 16 *Aug.* 1964.

DOWSON, Sir Oscar Follett, Kt., *cr.* 1937; C.B.E. 1933 (O.B.E. 1918); Legal Adviser, Home Office, 1933-46; *b.* 23 Oct. 1879; *s.* of late Rev. H. Enfield Dowson; *m.* 1908, Evelyn Tolmé (*d.* 1957), *d.* of late Edmund Kell Blyth. *Educ.:* Rugby; New Coll., Oxford. Barrister-at-law, Inner Temple, 1905; served in France, March 1915-April 1919; Court-Martial Officer, Second Army, 1916-18; D.A.A.G., 5th Army, 1918 (Major); Asst. Legal Adviser, Home Office, 1920; seconded for special duty as Legal Officer in Ireland, 1920-21; gazetted Lt.-Col. 1921; Delegate to Hague Conference on Codification of International Law, 1930. Retired 1946. *Publications:* jt. ed. of Parker on Elections, 1950; joint author of the Law relating to Local Elections, 1950. *Recreation:* gardening. *Address:* Marshwood, Alders Road, Reigate, Surrey. *T.:* Reigate 5868. *Club:* Athenæum. [*Died* 27 *Dec.* 1961.

DOYLE, Edward, O.B.E. 1952; Honorary Editor, Official Report, the Games of the XVIth Olympiad; Director of Publicity, Olympic Games, 1956; Chairman of Press and Publicity Sub-Committee; *b.* Richmond, Victoria, 7 March 1892; *m.* 1917, Olga Marie, *d.* of B. F. Kritz, South Yarra, Melbourne. *Educ.:* private schools. Began as reporter Southern Press Agency covering Federal Parliament for Brisbane, Adelaide, Perth and Tasmania dailies; served European War, A.A.M.C., 1916-18, Italy and France; joined The Argus, Melbourne, 1920; Deputy Chief of Staff, Jan. 1924; Chief of Staff, May 1924; Associate Editor The Australasian, 1929; News Director The Argus, 1936; Editor of The Australasian, 1937; Deputy Managing Editor, The Argus and The Australasian, 1941; Managing Editor, 1942-47; investigated industrial troubles at Newcastle, N.S.W., 1923; represented The Argus with the Commonwealth Industrial Mission to U.S.A., 1927; Staff Capt. Vol. Defence Corps in War of 1939-45 and editor of Home Guard, the official history of the corps. Member: of council of Australian American Assoc., of Exec. of Lord Mayor of Melbourne's Seaside Camps for Country Children; of Exec. (and Chm. of Publications Panel) of Lord Mayor of Melbourne's Cttee. for Olympic Games for Melbourne for 1956; of council of control Boy Scouts Assoc. of Victoria; of council of Royal Agricultural Soc. of Victoria; of council of Empire Youth Movement; of Exec. War Nurses Memorial Centre. Life Mem. Returned Sailors', Soldiers' and Airmen's Imperial League of Australia, 1960. Editor of Three Decades, the History of Victorian State Electricity Commission. Editor-in-Chief, Victorian Govt. Centenary Vols., 1951 *Recreation:* golf. *Address:* Mulutu, Emerald, Victoria, Australia. *Clubs:* Yorick, Kingston Heath, Emerald Legacy, Melbourne Cricket (Melbourne). [*Died* 11 *Sept.* 1965.

DOYLE, Lynn (Leslie Alexander Montgomery); retired; *b.* Downpatrick, Co. Down, 1873; *m.* 1902, Winifred Ratcliffe; three *s.* *Educ.:* Dundalk, Co. Louth. Entered Northern Banking Co., Ltd., at age of sixteen, and remained in one of the Belfast offices for seventeen years (1889-1906); Member of Irish Free State Censorship of Publications Board, Dec. 1936 - Feb. 1937. *Publications:* Ballygullion — Irish short stories, 1908; Mr. Wildridge of the Bank — a novel, 1916; An Ulster Childhood —Irish Essays and Sketches, 1921; Lobster Salad—Irish short stories, 1922; Dear Ducks, Irish short stories, 1925; the plays, Love and Land, Lilac Ribbon, and Turncoats, in separate volumes, 1928; Me and Mr. Murphy, Irish Short Stories, 1930; Rosabelle, Irish Short Stories, 1933; The Spirit of Ireland, travel, 1935; Ballygullion Ballads, verse, 1936; Fiddling Farmer, a novel, 1937; The Shake of the Bag, Irish short stories, 1939; Lilts and Lyrics, verse, 1941; Yesterday Morning, a novel, 1943; A Bowl of Broth, Irish short stories, 1945; Babel Babble, an extravaganza in verse, 1945; Not Too Serious, Essays, 1946; Green Oranges, Irish short stories, 1948; Fiddler's Folly, 3-act play produced Belfast, 1951; Love and Roberta, a novel, 1951; Back to Ballygullion, novel, 1953; The Ballygullion Bus, 1957; contributes fiction to Irish, English and American magazines and papers; lecturer, humorous and literary, broadcaster. *Recreation:* golf. *Address:* Malahide, Co. Dublin. *T.:* 246. [*Died* 13 *Aug.* 1961.

D'OYLY, Sir Charles Hastings, 12th Bart., *cr.* 1663; *b.* 3 July 1898; *s.* of Sir Hadley D'Oyly, 11th Bart. and Beatrice Alice, *d.* of F. B. Clerk, Mysore; *S.* father, 1948. *Heir:* *b.* John Rochfort D'Oyly [*b.* 19 April 1900; *m.* 1930, Kathleen, *e. d.* of Robert Brown Gillespie, Halgolle, Yatiyantota, Ceylon; two *d.* Lt.-Comdr. R.N., 1929.] *Address:* Meads, Mayfield, Sussex. [*Died* 10 *Jan.* 1962.

DRAKE, Sir (Hugh) Garrard Tyrwhitt-, Kt., *cr.* 1936; D.L., J.P.; Hon. F.Z.S. Glasgow and West of Scotland; Hon. F.Z.S. Scotland, C.M.Z.S. New York. C.F.Z.S. of Ireland; Director: Medway Lower Navigation Co.; *b.* 22 May 1881; *o. c.* of late Hugh William Tyrwhitt-Drake, of Amersham, and late Anne, *d.* of Archdeacon Hopper, of Starston, Norfolk; *m.* 1925, Edna Mary Vine. *Educ.:* Charterhouse. Hon. Freeman Borough of Maidstone, 1930-; Mayor (1915-16, 1923-25, 1928-29, 1930-31, 1934-35, 1939-44, 1949-50). High Sheriff of Kent, 1956-57. *Publications:* Beasts and Circuses; My Life with Animals, 1939; The English Circus and Fairground, 1946. *Recreations:* poultry farming and painting inn signs. *Address:* Cobtree Manor, Maidstone, Kent. *T.:* Maidstone 7104. [*Died* 24 *Oct.* 1964.

DRAX, Adm. Hon. Sir Reginald A. R.; *see* Plunkett-Ernle-Erle-Drax.

DRAYSON, Brigadier Fitz-Alan George, C.B.E. 1940; M.C.; *b.* 10 Jan. 1888; *s.* of late Capt. A. F. H. Drayson, R.N. (retd.) and C. F. G. Drayson; *m.* Margaret Gould; one *d.* *Educ.:* Christ's Hospital; R.M.C., Sandhurst. Gazetted 1st Bn. Border Regt., 1906; transferred to Royal Signals, 1921; served in France and Belgium, 1914-1916 (despatches twice, M.C.); Mesopotamia, 1916-17; Afghan War, 1919 (despatches); Waziristan Operations, 1919-21 (despatches) and 1921-24; Operations N.W.F. India, 1930; Palestine, 1936-37; France and Belgium, 1940, to evacuation from Dunkirk

(C.B.E.). Town Councillor, Teignmouth, 1947. *Recreations:* big game shooting, fishing, golf, cricket, stamp collecting. *Address:* Thatch Cottage, Teignmouth, S. Devon. *T.:* 471. [*Died* 16 *April* 1964.

DRAYTON, Harley; *see* Drayton, Harold Charles.

DRAYTON, Harold Charles (Harley Drayton); Chairman: Antofagasta (Chili) & Bolivia Railway Company Ltd.; The British Electric Traction Company Ltd.; Mitchell Cotts Group Ltd.; Provincial Newspapers Ltd.; Director: British Insulated Callender's Cables Ltd.; Consolidated Gold Fields Ltd.; Midland Bank Ltd.; The Standard Bank Ltd., etc. Member Council, Institute of Directors; Treasurer, U.K. Council of European Movement. High Sheriff of Suffolk, 1957. *Address:* 117 Old Broad St., E.C.2; Plumton Hall, Bury St. Edmunds, Suffolk. [*Died* 7 *April* 1966.

DRAYTON, Sir Robert Harry, Kt., *cr.* 1944; C.M.G. 1942; LL.B. (Hons.) Lond.; *b.* 14 April 1892; *s.* of late Harry Godwin Drayton, Exeter, Devon; *m.* 1920, Gertrude Edith, *d.* of late Capt. J. W. Phillips, Sydney, N.S.W.; one *s.* two *d.* *Educ.:* Exeter School. Army, 1914-18; Solicitor, 1918; Treasury Solicitor's Office, 1919-20; Solicitor-General and subsequently Legal Draftsman, Palestine Government, 1920-34; called to Bar, Gray's Inn, 1934; Attorney-General, Tanganyika, 1934-39; Legal Secretary, Ceylon, 1939-42; Chief Secretary, Ceylon, 1942-47; Director, Statutory Publications Office and Ed. of Statutes Revised, 1947-50; Chief Draftsman, Constituent Assembly, Pakistan, 1950-53; Legal Officer, Foreign Compensation, Commission, 1953-55; Chief Draftsman, Government of Jamaica, 1955-58. *Publications:* Revised Edition, Laws of Palestine, 1934; 3rd Edn., Statutes Revised. *Recreations:* tennis, cricket, squash. *Club:* Athenæum. [*Died* 20 *Feb.* 1963.

DRESSEL, Dettmar; violinist; *b.* London, 28 Dec. 1878; 2nd *s.* of late Professor Richard Dressel; *m.* 1907, Amelie, *d.* of Colonel H. Thulstrup, A.D.C. to King Charles XV. of Sweden; one *s.* *Educ.:* St. Paul's School. Studied under August Wilhelmj; made début at the old St. James's Hall, and has toured all over the Continent; founder of the Dettmar Dressel Trio Circle; Silver Jubilee Medal, 1935. *Publication:* Up and Down the Scale. *Address:* 150 Lexham Gardens, W.8. *T.:* Fremantle 8025. [*Died* 25 *Feb.* 1961.

DREW, Air Comdre. Bertie Clephane Hawley, C.M.G. 1918; C.V.O. 1937; C.B.E. 1919; R.A.F. retd.; *b.* 1880; *s.* of late Gen. H. R. Drew, I.A.; *m.* 1907, Edith (*d.* 1964), *d.* of late F. Graham Thomson; one *s.* one *d.* (and one *s.* killed in action, 1940). *Educ.:* Marlborough; Sandhurst. Indian Army, 1898; R.A.F., 1918; served China, 1900 (medal); N.W. Frontier of India, 1901-1902 (medal); Tibet, 1903-4 (medal); European War, 1914-18 (despatches, C.M.G.); retired, 1929; Secretary R.A.F. Display, 1929-37; re-employed A.O.C. 32 Group R.A.F. 1939-40; Lt.-Col. Home Guard. Consultant, Avimo Ltd. (Taunton). *Address:* Montrose, Seaview, I.W. *Club:* United Service. [*Died* 2 *Jan.* 1969.

DREW, Brigadier Francis Greville, C.B.E. 1950 (O.B.E. 1919); *b.* 16 Sept. 1892; *s.* of late A. J. Drew, F.R.C.S., Water Hall, Oxford; *m.* 1923, Sannie Frances, *e. d.* of late Charles Sands, Indian Police; one *s.* one *d.* *Educ.:* Lynams, Oxford; Winchester College; R.M.A. Woolwich. 2nd Lt., Royal Engineers, Dec. 1911. Served European War, 1914-18, France, 1914-15; N.W.F.P., 1916; Iraq, 1917-21. Brevet Major 1919; Brevet Lt.-Col. 1931; Commandant, King George's Own Bengal Sappers and Miners, 1935-38; General Staff, War Office, 1930-34; Member of British Delegation to League of Nations, 1930 and 1931; Staff employment, 1938-46; retired, 1948; Temp. Chief Administrator, Somalia, Apr.-June 1948; Chief Administrator, Eritrea, 1946-51. *Recreations:* rowing, sailing, golf, bridge. *Address:* Winterbrook, Wallingford, Berks. *T.:* Wallingford 3270. *Club:* United Service. [*Died* 17 *Jan.* 1962.

DREWRY, Arthur, C.B.E. 1953; J.P.; Chairman of The Football Association. since 1955; President: Fédération Internationale de Football Association (Vice-Pres., 1946); Lincolnshire Football Association; Lincolnshire Schools' Sports Assoc.; *b.* 3 March 1891; *s.* of William and Agnes Trotter Drewry, Grimsby; *m.* 1919, Ida May, *d.* of J. Wallace Stookes, Grimsby; one *s.* one *d.* *Educ.:* Grimsby Collegiate School. Business activities, Fishing Industry, 1908-1953, retired 1953. Lincolnshire Yeomanry, 1911-19. Served European War of 1914-1918, Western Desert, Palestine; Squadron Quartermaster Sergeant, 1st Lincolnshire Yeomanry (T.D., Efficiency Medal, 4 campaign medals). Organised pre-service training, Blundell Park, Lincs., 1939; a Founder Officer, 195 Sqdn., Air Defence C.C. (later A.T.C.) (Flt. Lieut.), 1939; Head Warden and Chief Fire Guard, N. Lincs., 1940 (Defence Medal); Dir. Humber Frozen Fish Distribution Co., 1941; Member Grimsby Borough Council, 1941; Chm. of Governors, Grimsby Grammar Sch., 1941; Mem. Min. of Labour Rehabilitation Scheme, 1943; Chm. Eng. Soccer Selectors, 1944-52; J.P. Grimsby Borough, 1948; P.M.G.'s Television Advisory Cttee., 1951. Chm., Comité du Terrain, and Juge d'Appel, Olympic Games, 1948, 1952 and 1960. Pres. Football League, 1949. Chevalier, Order of Oaken Crown, Luxembourg, 1959. *Recreations:* comprehensive. *Address:* 1 Eastwood Avenue, Bargate, Grimsby, Lincs. [*Died* 25 *March* 1961.

DRIVER, Professor John Edmund, M.A (Cantab.), Ph.D., M.Sc. (Lond.), F.R.I.C.; Emeritus Professor, University of Hong Kong; *b.* 26 October 1900; *y. s.* of late Frederick Driver, planter, Montserrat, B.W.I., and Mary Eleanor Joyce. *Educ.:* West Buckland School. Lecturer in Chemistry, University College, Nottingham, 1920-1938; University Demonstrator in Chemistry Cambridge, 1938-45; Prof. of Chemistry, Univ. of Hong Kong, 1949-60. General List, 1940; R.E., 1941-45. Editor, Jl. of Chemical Soc., 1946-49. J.P. Hong Kong, 1956-60. *Publications:* (with late A. O. Bentley) Text-book of Pharmaceutical Chemistry, 1925 (latest imp. 1960); (with G. E. Trease) Chemistry of Crude Drugs; researches in J.C.S., J. Amer. Chem. Soc., J. Soc. Chem. Ind., Q.J. Pharm. Pharmacol., Analyst. *Address:* Herne Close, Wherwell, Andover, Hampshire. *Clubs:* Oxford and Cambridge, Savage; The Hong Kong (Hong Kong). [*Died* 27 *March* 1965.

DROOP, John Percival, M.A., F.S.A. 1930; *b.* 4 Oct. 1882; *s.* of Henry Richmond Droop and Clara Baily; *m.* 1916, Ita Bride Molony (*d.* 1957); one *s.* two *d.* *Educ.:* Marlborough College; Trinity College, Cambridge, B.A. 1904; M.A. 1912. Student at British School, Athens, 1905-09, 1911, 1912-14; Excavations at Sparta, in Thessaly, in Melos and in Crete; Camb. Univ. Prendergast Student 1906-07; School Student Brit. School, Athens 1907-08; Assistant in cataloguing collections of Sir M. A. Stein at British Museum 1909-11; Draughtsman to Egypt Exploration Fund's expedition to Abydos, 1911; Wartime: Friends of Foreigners in Distress 1914-15; Lady Roberts' Field Glass Fund, Ministry of Munitions, 1915-17; Admiralty, Secretariat, Military Branch, 1917-21; Charles W. Jones Professor of Classical Archæology, University of Liverpool, 1921-48. Excavations at Lancaster, Bainbridge and Chester, 1927-39; War-time position: Temp. Civil Servant Admiralty, Secretariat (M Branch, 1939-40; Honours and Awards, 1940-45). Joint Editor Annals of Archæology and Anthropology, 1924, Editor, 1934; Joint Editor, 1936-48. *Publications:* Archæological Excavation, 1915; Translation of The Vaulted Tombs of Mesara, by S. Xanthoudides, 1924; The University Press of Liverpool, 1899-1946, 1947; various articles. *Recreations:* golf, bridge, boating, snooker. *Address:* Villa Rose de Mai, Vence, A.M., France. *T.:* Vence 320453. *Club:* University, (Liverpool). [*Died* 26 *Sept.* 1963.

DRUCQUER, His Honour Maurice Nathaniel; *b.* 9 Dec. 1876; *s.* of J. Drucquer; *m.* 1910, Doris Marguerite Levy; (son killed Aug. 1944 in air crash, India) one *d.* *Educ.:* City of London School; London University. M.A., LL.B. Barstow Scholarship at Bar; called to Bar, 1904; Commission in Army, April 1915; demobilised Jan. 1919 (Brevet Major); Commission in the Royal Reserve of Officers, 1919-31; (Bt. Major); Judge of Northampton-Coventry County Court Circuit, 1928-37; Willesden and Brentford, 1937-45, Westminster, 1945-1950. Chairman Midlands Tribunal of Conscientious Objectors. *Publications:* Assistant Editor of Hallech's International Law; various articles for Law Publications. *Recreations:* golf, tennis. *Address:* 138 Latymer Court, Hammersmith Rd., W.6. [*Died* 21 *July* 1970.

DRUMMOND, Vice-Admiral Hon. Edmund Rupert, C.B. 1937; M.V.O. 1922; R.N. retired; *b.* 1884; 3rd *s.* of late Viscount Strathallan; *m.* 1910, Evelyn Butler, *e. d.* of 4th Marquess of Ormonde; (one *s.*, Lieut. R.N., lost in H.M.S. Sickle 1944) two *d.* *Educ.:* H.M.S. Britannia. Lieut., 1906; served as 2nd in command of H.M.S. Caroline, 1914-16, and in H.M.S. Cardiff, 1917-19; Commander, 1918; Captain, 1926; Chief of Staff to Commander-in-Chief, Portsmouth, 1930-32; commanded H.M.S. Delhi, 1932; H.M.S. Despatch, 1933-35 A.D.C. to the King, 1936; Rear-Adm., 1936; commanded N.Z. Station, 1935-38; retired list 1938; Vice-Adm. 1940. Deputy Lieutenant for Ross and Cromarty, 1956-60. *Address:* Upper Queens' Acre, Bolton Road, Windsor, Berks *Club:* United Service. [*Died* 9 *Sept.* 1965.

DRUMMOND, George Henry; *b.* 1883; *s.* of late George James Drummond; *m.* 1st, 1917, Helena Kathleen (*d.* 1933), *o. d.* of T. Grattan Holt; four *d.*; 2nd, 1940, Honora Myrtle, *e. d.* of Lieut.-Colonel Duncan Spiller; one *s.* three *d.* *Educ.:* Harrow; Trinity College, Cambridge. West Kent Yeomanry, 1903-9; Notts R.H.A., 1909-15; served European War with 1st Life Guards (wounded 2nd Battle of Ypres, May 1915); invalided out of the army, 1917; Chairman of Drummond's Branch, Royal Bank of Scotland; High Sheriff of Northampton, 1927. Member House of Keys, 1946-51. Heir general and representative of Aubrey de Vere, 20th and last Earl of Oxford. *Address:* Mount Rule, Isle of Man. *Club:* Buck's (Life Hon.) [Died 12 *Oct.* 1963.

DRUMMOND, Sir James Hamlyn Williams Williams-, 5th Bt. of Hawthornden, *cr.* 1828; Hon. Attaché in Diplomatic Service, 1918-22; J.P. Carmarthenshire and Midlothian; Member Royal Co. of Archers, Queen's Bodyguard for Scotland; *b.* 25 May 1891; *s.* of 4th Bt. and Madeline, *d.* of Sir Andrew Agnew, 8th Bt., *widow* of T. H. Clifton of Lytham Hall; *S.* father, 1913; *m.* 1914, Lady Enid Evelyn Malet Vaughan (*d.* 1958), *o. d.* of 6th Earl of Lisburne. *Educ.:* Eton. 2nd Lt. Yeomanry, 1914-15. *Heir: cousin,* William Hugh Dudley Williams-Drummond, *b.* 13 Feb 1901. *Recreations:* motoring in post-vintage Rolls Royce, and Bentley cars; reading history. *Address:* Hawthornden Castle, Midlothian, Edwinsford, Llandilo, Carmarthenshire. *Clubs:* St. James'; New (Edinburgh). [*Died* 7 *Jan.* 1970.

DRUMMOND, James Montagu Frank, M.A. (Cantab.), F.L.S., F.R.H.S.; Professor (Emeritus), University of Manchester; *b.* 1881, 2nd *s.* of late James Ramsay Drummond, I.C.S.; *m.* 1st, 1906, Agnes Marguerite (*d.* 1923), *d.* of W. B. Ives, Riverside, Saharunpore; no *c.*; 2nd, 1932, Dorothy Marie, *d.* of R. G. Farrant, British East Africa. *Educ.:* King's College, London; Gonville and Caius College, Cambridge. Frank Smart Research Student, Cambridge, 1904-6; Lecturer in Botany, Armstrong College, Newcastle upon Tyne, 1906-9; Lecturer in Plant Physiology, University of Glasgow, 1909-21; First Director of the Scottish Plant-Breeding Station (Scottish Society for Research in Plant Breeding), 1921-25; Regius Professor of Botany, University of Glasgow, 1925-30; Harrison Professor of Botany and Director of Botanical Laboratories, Manchester University, 1930-46. Served European War, 2nd Lieut. and Lieut. 5th Bn. H.L.I., 1915-19; Palestine and France, 1916-1919; O.C. Manchester University Contingent Senior Training Corps, 1932-45 (Bt. Maj. T.A. General List, Acting Lt.-Col., 1941); O.C. 61st (Lancs) Bn. Home Guard, 1941-46. *Publications:* scientific papers and articles. *Recreation:* gardening. *Address:* Greengate, Bradham Lane, Withycombe, Exmouth, Devon. [*Died* 7 *Feb.* 1965.

DRUMMOND, Sir Walter James, Kt., *cr.* 1953; M.Inst.C.E., M.I.Mech.E.; *b.* 14 May 1891; *e. s.* of Reverend W. H. Drummond, D.D.; *m.* 1922, Marjorie (*d.* 1948), *d.* of Ridley Warham; one *s.* one *d.* *Educ.:* Pupil with Harland & Wolff, Belfast; R.N.C., Greenwich. On shipyard staff of Elswick Works, Sir W. G. Armstrong Whitworth & Co. Ltd., 1914-22; joined Ashington Coal Co. Ltd., Newcastle-on-Tyne, 1922; Chief Engineer, 1928; General Works Manager, 1935; Managing Director, 1939. Dep. Chm., N.W. Div. N.C.B., on nationalisation, 1947; Chm. N.W. Div., 1949; Deputy Chairman of the National Coal Board, 1951-1955; Member of: Advisory Council, D.S.I.R., 1944-49; Fuel Research Board. 1944-49, 1950-55; Geological Survey Board, 1946-50 (Chm. 1954-61); Miners' Welfare Commn., 1938-51; Advisory Council on Scientific Policy, 1950-53. D.S.I.R. Council 1956-61. Has served on numerous committees of Mining Association and of Government departments, on matters connected with mining and fuel industries. Hon. D.Sc., Belfast; Hon. D.C.L., Durham. *Publications:* contributions to various technical journals. *Recreations:* travel, motoring, handicrafts, gardening. *Address:* 37 Elmfield Road, Newcastle upon Tyne 3. *Clubs:* Athenæum; Northern Counties (Newcastle upon Tyne). [*Died* 30 *Aug.* 1965.

DRYBURGH, Edward Gelderd, C.B. 1964; M.D.; Chief Medical Officer, Ministry of Pensions and National Insurance, since 1963; *b.* 24 March 1909; *er. s.* of late John Dryburgh and late Elizabeth Griffith Dryburgh (*née* Gelderd). *Educ.:* Manchester Gram. Sch.; Manchester University. M.B., Ch.B. 1934, M.D. 1960, Manchester. Sen. House Surg., Manchester Royal Infirmary, 1934; M.O., Withington Hosp., Manchester, 1935; R.M.O., City Hosp., Stoke-on-Trent, 1937-39; M.O., Min. of Pensions, 1939. Served War of 1939-45, Major R.A.M.C. (despatches). Ministry of Pensions: Sen. M.O., 1948; Principal M.O., 1958; Deputy Chief M.O., 1961. F.R.Soc.Med.; F.R.S.H.; Mem. B.M.A. *Address:* Reedy River, River Avenue, Thames Ditton, Surrey. *T.:* Em-

berbrook 2317. *Clubs:* National Liberal, Royal Commonwealth Society.
[*Died* 26 *March* 1965.

DRYDEN, Sir Noel Percy Hugh, 7th and 10th Bt., *cr.* 1795 and 1733; *b.* 24 Dec. 1910; *s.* of late John Erasmus Skottowe Dryden; *S.* cousin, 1938; *m.* 1941, Rosamund Mary, *e. d.* of late Stephen Scrope and *gr. d.* of Simon Thomas Scrope of Danby; one *s.* *Educ.:* Stowe School. *Heir: s.* John Stephen Gyles Dryden, *b.* 26 September 1943. *Address:* c/o Williams Deacon's Bank Ltd., Old Brompton Rd., S.W.7. [*Died* 23 *March* 1970.

DRYFOOS, Orvil E.; Publisher of The New York Times, since 1961; President since 1957, and Publisher, The New York Times Company; President-Director, The New York Times of Canada Limited, since 1959; also President, Vice-President, or Director of several other companies, since 1944; Director, New York World's Fair 1964-65 Corporation; *b.* 8 Nov. 1912; *s.* of late Jack A. Dryfoos and Florence Levi Dryfoos (now Mrs. Myron G. Lehman), both of U.S.A.; *m.* 1941, Marian Sulzberger; one *s.* two *d.* *Educ.:* Horace Mann School; Dartmouth College (B.A.). With Asiel & Co. (stock brokers), 1934-37; Member New York Stock Exchange, 1937-49; The New York Times: started with this paper, 1942; Asst. to Publisher, 1943-54; Vice-Pres. and Director, 1954-57; President and Director, 1957. Trustee, Dartmouth Coll.; Mem. Bd. Lay Trustees, Fordham University, N.Y.; Trustee and Mem. of Exec. Cttee. The Rockefeller Foundation, etc. Member, The Pilgrims of the U.S.; Sigma Delta Chi, etc. Hon. M.A., Dartmouth College (*in privatim*), 1957; Hon. Dr. of laws, Oberlin College, 1962. *Recreations:* golf, tennis, etc. *Address:* 1010 Fifth Avenue, New York 36, N.Y., U.S.A.; (Summer) Rock Hill, Rockrimmon Road, Stamford, Connecticut. *Clubs:* Dutch Treat (New York); Century Country (White Plains, N.Y.); Century Association; Dartmouth (W. Conn.).
[*Died* 25 *May* 1963.

DRYSDALE, Charles Vickery, C.B. 1932; O.B.E.; D.Sc. (Lond.); M.I.E.E., F.Inst.P., F.C.G.I., M.R.I., F.R.S.E.; President of Malthusian League; Fellow of the Royal Statistical Society; *b.* 1874; *s.* of C. R. Drysdale, M.D., M.R.C.P., F.R.C.S., and Dr. Alice Drysdale-Vickery; *m.* 1898, Bessie Ingman Edwards; one *s.* *Educ.:* privately; Finsbury Tech. Coll.; Central Tech. College, South Kensington. Associate Head of Electrical Engineering and Applied Physics Department, Northampton Institute, 1896-1910; Examiner to Spectacle Makers' Company, 1902-1929; President, Optical Society, 1904; Member of Jury Electrical Section of the St. Louis Exhibition, 1904; Hon. Secretary, Malthusian League, and Editor of the Malthusian, 1907-16; first witness before the National Birth-Rate Commission, 1913; President, International Neo-Malthusian Conferences, London, 1921, and New York, 1925; partner in firm of H. Tinsley & Co., 1916-19; joined Admiralty Experimental Station, Parkston Quay, 1918; Scientific Director, Admiralty Experimental Station, Shandon, 1919-1921; Superintendent, Admiralty Research Laboratory, Teddington, 1921-29; Director of Scientific Research, Admiralty, 1929-34; Member of the Safety in Mines Research Board since 1934; Member of the Board of Managers of the Royal Institution, 1934-36; Duddell Medallist, 1936; Fellow of the Imperial College, 1937; Editor of the Journal of Scientific Instruments, 1927-28; inventor of many scientific instruments. *Publications:* The Foundations of Alternate-Current Theory; The Small Family System; and Electrica Measuring Instruments (with Mr. A. C. Jolley); many pamphlets and papers. *Clubs:* Athenæum, English-Speaking Union.
[*Died* 7 *Feb.* 1961.

DRYSDALE, (George) Russell; Australian artist; Member, Commonwealth Art Advisory Board, since 1962; Director, Pioneer Sugar Mills Ltd.; *b.* Bognor Regis, Sussex, 7 Feb. 1912; *s.* of George Russell Drysdale; *m.* 1st, 1935, Elizabeth (*d.* 1963), *d.* of J. Stephen; one *d.* (one *s.* decd.); 2nd, 1965, Maisie Joyce Purves-Smith. *Educ.:* Grange School, Sussex; Geelong Grammar School, Victoria; George Bell Art Sch., Melbourne; Grosvenor Sch. of Art, London; La Grande Chaumière, Paris. Exhibitions include: Leicester Galleries, 1950, 1958, 1965; N.S.W. Art Gallery, 1960; Queensland Art Gallery, 1961. Represented in permanent collections of Tate Gallery, Metropolitan Museum (N.Y.), National Galls. of Aberdeen, Qld., N.S.W., W. Austr., S. Austr. and Vic., etc. *Publication:* (with Jock Marshall) Journey Among Men, 1962. *Relevant Publication:* Russell Drysdale by Geoffrey Dutton, 1964. *Recreations:* interested in natural history, pre-history, and travelling about the inland of Australia. *Address:* Bouddi Farm, Kilcare Heights, Hardy's Bay, N.S.W., Australia. *Clubs:* Australasian Pioneers (Sydney); North Queensland (Townsville).
Knighthood gazetted, Birthday Honours, 1969. [*Died* 10 *June* 1969.

DRYSDALE, Sir Matthew Watt, Kt., *cr.* 1953; Chairman of Lloyd's, 1949, 1950, 1951, 1952, 1955, 1956; *b.* 27 Nov. 1892; *s.* of late Thomas and Janet Drysdale, Montrose, Scotland; *m.* 1928, Nesta, *d.* of late Hugh Lewis; three *s.* *Educ.:* Stationers' Company's School. Entered Lloyd's 1908; Underwriting Mem. 1919; first served on Cttee. of Lloyd's, 1939; Deputy Chm. of Lloyd's, 1947. Lloyd's Gold Medal, 1952. Director: C. T. Bowring & Co. Ltd.; Barclay's Bank Ltd. Served in European War, 1914-18, with 9th Northumberland Fusiliers. *Address:* 32 Onslow Square, S.W.3. *T.:* Kensington 4202. *Clubs:* City of London, Brooks's. [*Died* 30 *July* 1962.

DRYSDALE, Russell; *see* Drysdale, G. R.

DUBILIER, William; electrical engineer, retired 1960; *b.* New York, 25 July 1888; *s.* of Abraham and Anna Dubilier; *m.*; two *s.* *Educ.:* Technical Institute, New York; Cooper Institute, New York. Awarded the first Gano Dunn Medal, 1955, and the Professional Achievement Citation, 1966, of the Cooper Institute. Technical Director Com. Wireless Tel. and Tel. Co., 1907; Dubilier Electric Syndicate London, England, 1911; Dubilier Condenser Co., Inc., New York, 1916; Dubilier Condenser Co. Ltd., London, 1918; devised system for detecting submarines, as adopted by French and British Governments in 1916; invented first successful substitute for glass Leyden jars, adopted by the U.S., French, British, and other Governments, and now used in practically every Government radio installation in Allied countries; Owner and Inventor of a number of wireless systems of telegraphy and telephony and of high-frequency apparatus, covered by over 500 patents and applications; devised and invented first radio installations for airplane use by British Government in 1912 and for United States Government in 1915; inventions licensed under patents to Dubilier Condenser Co. Ltd., General Electric Co. Ltd. and many leading companies in U.S.A., Canada and Europe; Pres. Radio Patents Corp., N.Y.; Fellow A.I.E.E.; Fellow I.E.R.E.; Mem. World's Soc. Arts; Mem. Société Académique d'Histoire Internationale. Holds many degrees and honours. Was offered, but did not accept, a British knighthood, for work prior to 1914-18. Honorary Medal, Association des Ingenieurs-Docteurs de France, 1949-50; Chevalier Cross of the Legion of Honor and Officer of the French Academy. *Publications:* articles on radio telephony and telegraphy and on wireless apparatus; co-author, Wireless

Telegraph Equipment, 1909. *Address:* c/o Dubilier Condenser Co. Ltd., Victoria Road, North Acton, W.3; 339 Garden Road, Palm Beach, Florida 33480, U.S.A. [*Died* 25 *July* 1969.

DU BOIS, William Edward Burghardt; Writer; *b.* Great Barrington, Massachusetts, 23 Feb. 1868; of Negro, French Huguenot and Dutch descent; *s.* of Alfred Du Bois and Mary Burghardt; *m.* 1896, Nina Gomer (*d.* 1950); one *s.* (one *d.* decd.); *m.* 1951, Shirley Graham. *Educ.:* Public Schools of Great Barrington; Fisk Univ.; Harvard Univ.; Univ. of Berlin A.B. Fisk Univ., 1888; A.B. 1890, A.M. 1891, Ph.D. 1895, Harvard Univ.; LL.D. Howard Univ., 1930; LL.D. Atlanta Univ., 1938; Litt.D., Fisk Univ., 1938; L.H.D. Wilberforce Univ., 1940; L.H.D., Univ. of Sofia, Bulgaria, 1958; Humboldt Univ. (E. Berlin), 1958; Dr. *rer. oec.* Dr. Hist. Science, Charles Univ. (Prague), 1958; Dr. Hist. Science, Lomonovska Univ. of Moscow, 1959. Professor of Greek and Latin, Wilberforce, 1894-96; Asst. Instructor, Univ. of Pennsylvania, 1896-97; Prof. of Economics and History, Atlanta Univ., 1897-1910; Director of Publications, National Assoc. for Advancement of Colored People and Editor of Crisis Magazine, 1910-32; Head of Dept. of Sociology, Atlanta Univ., 1943-44; Vice-Chairman, Council on African Affairs, 1949-54; Editor of Phylon, 1940-44; Editor-in-Chief of Encyclopædia of the Negro, 1933-45; Director, Department of Special Research, National Association for Advancement of Colored People, 1944-48; Director, Secretariat of Ghana Academy of Science and Learning for preparation of an Encyclopædia Africana; Phi Beta Kappa; Fellow of American Association for Advancement of Science; Member of National Institute of Arts and Letters; Corr. Member: German Academy of Sciences, Berlin; Hungarian Academy of Science; Founder of Pan-African Congresses; Internat. Peace Prize, World Peace Council, 1952; Knight Commander of Liberian Order of African Redemption; Lenin International Peace Prize. *Publications:* The Suppression of the African Slave Trade, 1896; The Philadelphia Negro, 1899; Atlanta University Studies, 1897-1911; The Souls of Black Folk, 1903; John Brown, 1909; Quest of the Silver Fleece, 1911; The Negro, 1915; Darkwater, 1920; The Gift of Black Folk, 1924; Dark Princess, 1928; Black Reconstruction, 1935; Black Folk: Then and Now, 1939; Dusk of Dawn, 1940; Color and Democracy: Colonies and Peace, 1945; The World and Africa, 1947; In Battle for Peace—The Story of my Eighty-third Birthday, 1952; The Black Flame: a Trilogy: The Ordeal of Mansart, 1957; Mansart Builds a School, 1959; Worlds of Color, 1961. *Address:* 31 Grace Court, Brooklyn 1, New York, U.S.A. [*Died* 27 *Aug.* 1963.

DUBS, Homer H.; Professor-emeritus of Chinese at Oxford University; Professor, 1947-59; Fellow of Univ. Coll., 1947-59; *b.* 28 March 1892; *s.* of Charles Newton Dubs, D.D., Supt. China Mission of Evangelical Church, Hunan, China, and Emma Matilda Dubs; *m.* 1918, Florence Arnold; one *s.* two *d.*; *m.* 1951, Hon. Grace Dorothy Lowry Lamb (*d.* 1953), *e. d.* of 1st Baron Rochester, C.M.G.; *m.* 1954, Margaret Wilkinson, *widow* of Walter Soothill, *d.* of Alfred and Mary L. Farrar. *Educ.:* Oberlin Preparatory School; Yale University. B.A., Yale, 1914; M.A., Columbia University, 1916; B.D., Union Theological Seminary, 1917; Ph.D., Chicago, 1925; M.A., Oxford, 1947; D.Litt. Oxford, 1958. Missionary, China Mission of Evangelical Ch. in Hunan, China, 1918-24; Instructor in Philosophy, Univ. of Minnesota, 1925-1927; Prof. of Philosophy, Marshall Coll., Huntington, W. Va., 1927-34; Dir. Translation of Chinese Histories Project of American Council of Learned Socs., 1934-37; Actg. Prof. of Philosophy, Duke Univ., 1937-43; Visiting Prof. of Chinese, Columbia Univ., 1944-45; Prof. of Chinese Studies, Kennedy School of Missions, Hartford Seminary Foundation, Hartford, Conn., U.S.A., 1945-1947. Visiting Prof., Univ. of Hawaii, 1962-1963. Stanislas Julien Prize of Académie des Belles-Lettres et Inscriptions, Institut de France, 1947. *Publications:* Hsuntze, the Moulder of Ancient Confucianism, 1927; The Works of Hsuntze, trans. from Chinese, 1928; Rational Induction: An Analysis of the Method of Philosophy and Science, 1930; The History of the Former Han Dynasty, by Pan Ku—critical trans. with annotations, vol. I. 1938, vol. II. 1944, vol. III. 1956; A Roman City in Ancient China, 1957. *Address:* 133A Banbury Rd., Oxford. *T.:* Oxford 59401. [*Died* 16 *Aug.* 1969.

DUCHEMIN, Rt. Rev. Mgr. Charles L. H., M.A.; Rector of Pontifical Beda College, Rome, 1928-61; *b.* Birmingham, 1886. *Educ.:* Cotton Hall, Downside; Trinity College, Cambridge; Beda College, Rome. Admitted Solicitor, 1909; ordained, 1918; Peterborough, 1918; Secretary to Bishop Keating on Special Mission to America, 1918; Woodbridge, 1921; Wandsworth, 1922. Representative, Cardinal Bourne, at Bobbio, 1923; Chaplain to British Delegation at Chicago Congress, 1926; Registrar to Society of Our Lady of Good Counsel (Legal Aid for Poor), 1926; Domestic Prelate, 1928-40; Prot. Apost. ad instar., 1939. *Address:* L.C.M. Convent, Sudbury Hill, Harrow. *Club:* Athenæum. [*Died* 6 *Dec.* 1965.

DUCKWORTH, Francis R. G., C.B.E. 1942; late Senior Chief Inspector, Ministry of Education; *b.* 21 Aug. 1881; *s.* of Henry Duckworth and Mary J. Bennett; *m.* Ethelwyn, *d.* of late Rev. Canon W. C. Compton; no *c.* *Educ.:* Rossall School; Trinity College, Oxford. Assistant Master, Dover College, 1904-5; Cheltenham College, 1905-8; Eton College, 1908-15 and 1920: War service, 1915-19; H.M. Inspector of Schools, 1920. *Publications:* The Cotswolds; Chester. From a Pedagogue's Sketch-Book; Browning Background and Conflict; Swiss Fantasy. *Recreations:* camping, motoring. *Address:* Lebanon, Itchenor, Chichester, Sussex. *Club:* Authors'. [*Died* 21 *Sept.* 1964.

DUDGEON, Major Cecil Randolph, C.B.E. 1951; *b.* 1885; *s.* of late Col. R. F. Dudgeon, C.B.; *m.* 1930, Gladys Mary Marsh. Served European War with King's Own Scottish Borderers; M.P. (L.) Galloway, 1922-24, and 1929-31. Formerly: Chairman, Education Authority for Kirkcudbright; Divisional Food Officer, Eastern Region; Chief Food Officer for Scotland from 1950. *Club:* National Liberal. [*Died* 4 *Nov.* 1970.

DUDGEON, Brig.-Gen. Robert Maxwell, C.B.E. 1944; D.S.O. 1917; M.C.; J.P.; H.M. Inspector of Constabulary for Scotland, 1930-45; *b.* 20 Feb. 1881; *e. s.* of late Col. R. F. Dudgeon, C.B.; *m.* 1907, Kathleen Marion Taylor; no *c.* *Educ.:* Uppingham; Loretto. Joined Cameron Highlanders as 2nd Lieut. 1901; retired with rank of Brigadier-General, 1920; commanded 16th Bn. Royal Warwickshire Regt.; 9th Bn. Black Watch; 1st Bn. Q.O. Cameron Highlanders, and 51st Infantry; Brigadier during European War; served South African War, 1901-2 (Queen's medal 5 clasps); European War, France and Belgium, 1915-19 (1914-15 Star, War medal, Victory medal, M.C., D.S.O., Chev. Legion of Honour, despatches five times); late Hon. Col. 7/9th Bn. (Highlanders) The Royal Scots. *Recreations:* hunting, shooting, golf. *Club:* New (Edinburgh). [*Died* 6 *Nov.* 1962.

DUDLEY, 3rd Earl of (cr. 1860), William Humble Eric Ward, M.C.: T.D.; Baron Ward, 1604; Viscount Ednam, 1860; Major late Q.O.R.R. Staffordshire Yeomanry; formerly: Hon. Col. 51st Midland (Medium) Bde. R.A. (T.A.); Hon. Air Commodore No. 915 Squadron R.A.F.; Lieut. Worcestershire Yeomanry, Major, 10th Royal Hussars, Major, Staffordshire Yeomanry; late Regional Commissioner for Civil Defence No. 9 (Midland) Region; *b.* 30 January 1894; *e. s.* of 2nd Earl and Rachel (*d.* 1920), *y. d.* of Charles Gurney; *S.* father, 1932; *m.* 1st, 1919, Rosemary Millicent, R.R.C. (*d.* 1930), *o. d.* of 4th Duke of Sutherland; two *s.*; 2nd, 1943, Laura, Viscountess Long (marriage dissolved, 1954; she *m.* 3rd, 1960, Michael Temple Canfield, of New York and London), 2nd *d.* of late Honourable Guy Charteris; 3rd, 1961, Princess Grace Radziwill, *d.* of the late Michel Kolin, Dubrovnik, and Mme. Kolin. *Educ.:* Eton; Christ Church, Oxford (M.A.,) Served European War, 1914-18 (M.C., wounded, Chevalier Legion of Honour); M.P. (C.) Hornsey Borough, 1921-24, and Wednesbury, 1931-32; Parliamentary Private Secretary to Under-Secretary of State for India (Earl Winterton, P.C.), 1921-23; President, Society of British Gas Industries, 1926-27; British Iron and Steel Federation, 1935-36; Birmingham Chamber of Commerce, 1937-39; Federation of Chambers of Commerce of the British Empire, 1937-45; British Iron and Steel Institute, 1938-40; ex-Chairman: British Federal Welder and Machine Co. Ltd.; British Iron & Steel Corporation; D.L. Staffordshire, 1927-1966; High Sheriff of Worcestershire, 1930. Officer, Legion of Honour. *Heir: s.* Viscount Ednam. *Address:* Greycliff, Nassau, Bahamas. [*Died* 26 *Dec.* 1969.

DUDLEY, Roland, O.B.E. 1958; A.M.I.C.E.; Vice-President, National Institute of Agricultural Botany, Cambridge; *b.* 5 March 1879; *s.* of W. J. W. Dudley, Gretton, Kettering; *m.* 1908, Mabel Florence (*d.* 1951), *d.* of James A. Michell, Shouldham Hall, Norfolk; one *d.* *Educ.:* Wellingborough; Yorks. Coll., Leeds. Assistant Civil Engineer, Admiralty, 1905-7; High Sheriff, Hampshire, 1941; Chairman Somerville-Barnard Construction Co. Ltd.; Landowner; pioneer mechanised farming. *Recreations:* shooting, fishing. *Address:* Linkenholt Manor, Andover, Hants. *Clubs:* Bath, Farmers'. [*Died* 29 *July* 1964.

DUFF, Charles St. Lawrence; Author and Journalist; *b.* Enniskillen, 7 April 1894. *Educ.:* Portora Royal School. Barrister-at-law, Gray's Inn; served in Merchant Service, 1910-14; in the Army, 1916-19; Interpreter, Portuguese Expiditionary Force (Portuguese Military Medal); British Military Mission, Italy, in the Foreign Office, 1919-36; Press Officer, retired 1936; Literary and Dramatic Correspondent of La Prensa, Buenos Aires, from 1929, of O Estado de Sao Paulo, 1935-38, Lecturer, London Univ., 1937-38; Director, United Editorial, Ltd., 1938-40; Prof. of European Languages, Nanyang Univ., Singapore, 1954-55. *Publications:* Quevedo: Humorous and Satirical Works, 1926 (translated from Spanish). A Handbook on Hanging, 1928; This Human Nature, 1930; Handrail and the Wampus, 1931; James Joyce and the Plain Reader, 1932; Mind Products Ltd. (A Melodrama), 1932; Irish Idyll (A Playlet), 1933; Spanish Front, 1936; Anthropological Report on a London Suburb, 1935; The Truth about Columbus, 1936; Key to Victory: Spain, 1940; No Angel's Wing, 1946; How to Learn a Language, 1947; Ordinary Cats, 1951; Ireland and the Irish, 1952; French for Adults, 1952; England and the English, 1954; English for Adults, 1956; Spanish for Adults, 1956; German for Adults, 1957; Italian for Adults, 1958; Russian for Adults, 1962; A Mysterious People, 1965; Six Days to shake an Empire, 1966; translations from French, Spanish, Portuguese and other languages. Editor: Basis and Essentials series of books on modern languages; contributor to various English and American reviews and magazines. *Recreations:* walking, reading, painting. *Address:* Levally, Monea, Enniskillen, Northern Ireland. [*Died* 15 *Oct.* 1966.

DUFF, Sir James Fitzjames, Kt., cr. 1949; M.A.; M.Ed.; Hon. D.C.L. (Durham); Hon. LL.D. (Aberdeen, Sussex); Lord Lieutenant, County of Durham, since 1964; *b.* 1 Feb. 1898; 2nd *s.* of J. D. Duff, Fellow of Trinity College, Cambridge, and Laura, *d.* of Sir William Lenox-Conyngham, K.C.B. *Educ.:* Winchester; Trinity Coll., Cambridge. Served in Royal Flying Corps, 1916-17; 1st Class, Classical Tripos, 1920; 2nd Class, Economics Tripos, 1921; Assist. Lecturer in Classics, Manchester Univ., 1921; Lecturer in Education, Armstrong Coll., Newcastle-upon-Tyne, 1922; Educational Superintendent, Northumberland County Council, 1925; Senior Lecturer in Education, Manchester Univ., 1927; Sarah Fielden Prof. of Education and Director of the Department of Education, University of Manchester, 1932-37; Warden of the Durham Colleges and alternately Vice-Chancellor and Pro-Vice-Chancellor of Durham University, 1937-1960. Mayor of Durham, 1959-60. A Governor of the B.B.C. 1959-65; Vice-Chairman 1960-65 (Temp. Chairman, 1964). Member of Asquith Commission on Colonial Higher Education, 1943-45; Member of Elliot Commission on Higher Education in West Africa, 1943-45; Member of Government of India's Universities Commission, 1948-49; Vis. Prof., Univ. of Toronto, 1967; Treasurer, University of Sussex. *Publications:* University Government in Canada (with Dr. R. O. Berdahl), 1966; articles in educational and other periodicals. *Address:* Low Middleton Hall, Middleton One-Row, Darlington. *T.:* Dinsdale 245. *Club:* Durham County. [*Died* 24 *April* 1970.

DUFF-GORDON, Sir Douglas (Frederick), 7th Bt., cr. 1813; late Scots Guards; *b.* 12 Sept. 1892; *s.* of Sir Henry William Duff-Gordon, 6th Bt. and Maud Emily (*d.* 1951), *d.* of late Hugh Hammersley; *S.* father 1953; *m.* 1932, Gladys Rosemary (*d.* 1933), *e. d.* of late Col. Vivian Henry, C.B., Oakfield, Hay, Breconshire, and of Mrs. R. Akroyd, Whitelands, Rudford, nr. Gloucester; one *s.* *Educ.:* Radley College, Abingdon, Berks; Exeter Coll., Oxford. Served European War, 1914-18, Lt. Montgomeryshire Yeomanry, and Scots Guards, 1918-19. War of 1939-45, Home Guard. *Recreation:* golf. *Heir: s.* Andrew Cosmo Lewis, *b.* 17 Oct. 1933. *Address:* Harpton Court, Walton, Presteigne, Radnorshire. *T.:* New Radnor 242. *Clubs:* Royal Porthcawl Golf, Kington Golf. [*Died* 15 *March* 1964.

DUFF-SUTHERLAND-DUNBAR, Sir George; *see* Dunbar.

DUFF-SUTHERLAND-DUNBAR, Sir George Cospatrick, 7th Bt., of Hempriggs cr. 1706; D.L.; Barrister-at-law; *b.* 3 Aug. 1906; *o. s.* of Sir George Duff-Sutherland-Dunbar, 6th Bt.; *S.* father, 1962. *Educ.:* Harrow; New College, Oxford. Called to the Bar, Middle Temple, 1931. Served War of 1939-45: London Scottish (Gordons), T.A., transferred R.A., 1939; Hon. Colonel, 1945. D.L. for County of Caithness, 1955. *Heir: kinswoman* Mrs. Leonard James Blake (claiming Baronetcy as Lady Dunbar, of Hempriggs). *Address:* Ackergill Tower, Wick, Caithness. *T.:* Wick 312; 3 New Square, Lincoln's Inn, W.C.2. *T.:* Holborn 5757. *Clubs:* Boodle's, St. James'. [*Died* 4 *Feb.* 1963.

DUFFES, Arthur Paterson, M.C.; Q.C. Scot. 1928; M.A., LL.B.; *b.* 1880; *s.* of George Macpherson Duffes, H.M. Register of Sasines, Edinburgh, and Isabella Paterson (both of Forres, Morayshire). *Educ.:* George Watson's College, Edinburgh; Edinburgh University. Deputy Commissioner under National Insurance Acts, 1948-54. Sheriff of Ayr, 1936, Sheriff of Ayr and Bute, 1946-48. Called to Bar, Inner Temple, 1919; Member of Faculty of Advocates, 1910. *Address:* c/o Clerk of the Faculty, Advocate's Library, Parliament House, Edinburgh. [*Died* 20 *April* 1968.

DUFFY, Hon. Sir Charles L. G.; *see* Gavan-Duffy.

DUGDALE, Rt. Hon. John, P.C. 1949; M.P. (Lab.) West Bromwich since 1941; Minister of State for Colonial Affairs, 1950-1951; *b.* 16 Mar. 1905; *s.* of late Col. Arthur Dugdale, C.M.G., D.S.O., and late Ethel Innes *d.* of Col. John Sherston, D.S.O.; *m.* 1938, Irene Constance Haverson, *gr.-d.* of Rt. Hon. George Lansbury, sometime M.P. (Lab.) Bow and Bromley Div. of Poplar; two *s.* *Educ.:* Wellington College; Christ Church, Oxford. Attaché British Legation, Peking, 1926-1927; Private Secretary to Rt. Hon. C. R. Attlee, M.P., 1931-39. Served War of 1939-1945, in army, 1940-42; Parl. Private Sec. to the Deputy Prime Minister, 1945; Parliamentary and Financial Secretary, Admiralty, 1945-50. Member of L.C.C., 1934-41; contested South Leicester, 1931, Cardiff Central, 1935, York (by-election), 1936; Governor, University of Birmingham; Chairman, Commonwealth Society for the Deaf; Vice-Pres. Assoc. of Municipal Corporations. *Publications:* Contributed Section on The Post Office to Public Enterprise (edited by W. Robson), 1936; edited Speeches of Rt. Hon. C. R. Attlee, M.P., under title The Road to War, 1940; numerous articles. *Recreations:* golf, bridge, sailing. *Address:* House of Commons, S.W.1. [*Died* 12 *March* 1963.

DUGDALE, Sir William (Francis Stratford), 1st Bt., *cr.* 1936; F.S.A.; *b.* 20 Oct. 1872; *e. s.* of W. S. Dugdale (*d.* 1882) of Merevale Hall, and Alice Frances (*d.* 1902), *d.* of Sir Charles Trevelyan, 1st Bart. of Wallington, Northumberland; *m.* 1920, Margaret, 2nd *d.* of late Brig.-Gen. Sir R. G. Gilmour, Bt., C.B., C.V.O., D.S.O.; two *s.* two *d.* *Educ.:* Eton; Balliol College, Oxford. J.P., D.L. Co. Warwick, 1894, High Sheriff, 1911-12; Chairman, Warwickshire C.C., 1934-47, Vice-Lieutenant of Warwickshire, 1939-64; Alderman Warwickshire C.C.; Chairman and Managing Director, Baddesley Collieries Limited; Governor and Trustee of Rugby School; Life Trustee of Shakespeare's Birthplace; Mem. of Trent River Board. *Heir: s.* William Stratford Dugdale, M.C. [*b.* 29 Mar. 1922; *m.* 1952, Lady Belinda Pleydell-Bouverie (*d.* 1961). *d.* of 7th Earl of Radnor, K.G., K.C.V.O.; one *s.* three *d.*]. *Address:* Merevale Hall, Atherstone, Warwicks. *T.:* 3143; 76 Sloane St., S.W.1. *T.:* Belgravia 2467. *Clubs:* Brooks's, White's, Oxford and Cambridge, Roxburghe. [*Died* 18 *April* 1965.

DUGGAN, Alfred Leo; author; *b.* 1903; *er. s.* of late Alfred Hubert Duggan and of late Grace Hinds (by her 2nd marriage Marchioness Curzon of Kedleston); *m.* 1953, Laura, *y. d.* of late St. Quintin Hill; one *s.* *Educ.:* Eton; Balliol College, Oxford. London Irish Rifles (T.A.), 1939-41. *Publications:* Knight with Armour, 1950; Conscience of the King, 1951; The Little Emperors, 1951; Thomas Becket, 1952; The Lady for Ransom, 1953; Leopards and Lilies, 1954; Julius Caesar, 1955; God and My Right, 1955; Winter Quarters, 1956; Devil's Brood, 1957; Three's Company, 1958; He Died Old, 1958; Founding Fathers, 1959; The Cunning of the Dove, 1960; Family Favourites, 1960: The King of Athelney, 1961; Lord Geoffrey's Fancy, 1962; Elephants and Castles, 1963; The Story of the Crusades, 1963; Count Bohemond (posthumous) 1964. *Recreations:* archæology and sight-seeing. *Address:* Old Hill Court, Ross-on-Wye, Herefordshire. *T.:* Ross 2232. *Club:* St. James'. [*Died* 4 *April* 1964.

DUGGAN, George Chester, C.B. 1930; O.B.E. 1918; 2nd *s.* of late George Duggan Ferney, Greystones, Co. Wicklow; *m.* 1912, Elizabeth Gore, *y. d.* of Rev. Robert Blair, Ballinamallard, Co. Fermanagh; one *d.* *Educ.:* The High School, Dublin; Trinity College, Dublin (Classical Scholar). B.A. (T.C.D.) (Senior Moderator and Double Gold Medallist), 1907; M.A. (1910). LL.D. (iure dignitatis), 1946; entered Civil Service, 1908; Admiralty, 1908-10 and 1914-16; Ministry of Shipping, 1917-19; Chief Secretary's Office, Dublin Castle, 1910-14, 1919-21; Assistant Secretary, Ministry of Finance, Belfast, 1922-25; Principal Assist. Secretary, Ministry of Finance, Belfast, 1925; on loan to Ministry of War Transport, London, Sept. 1939-Oct. 1945; Comptroller and Auditor-General for Northern Ireland, Nov. 1945-Oct. 1949. Chevalier, Legion of Honour; Chevalier, Order of Leopold II. *Publications:* The Watchers on Gallipoli: a Poem, 1921; The Stage Irishman, 1937; Northern Ireland—Success or Failure?, 1950; A United Ireland, 1954. *Address:* Gorteen, Mullagh, Kells, Co. Meath. *T.:* Mullagh (Co. Cavan) 17. [*Died* 15 *June* 1969.

DUGUID-McCOMBIE, Colonel William McCombie, D.S.O. 1919; Colonel, retired; *b.* 2 April 1874; *s.* of Peter Duguid-McCombie, Easter Skene and Lynturk, Aberdeenshire, and Cammachmore, Kincardineshire; *m.* 1st, 1903, Helen Emily (*d.* 1903), *d.* of Hon. Walter Courtenay Pepys; 2nd, 1918, Flora Marie (*d.* 1920), *d.* of Sir William Petersen, K.B.E., 80 Portland Place, and Eigg, Scotland; one *d.* *Educ.:* Fettes College, Edinburgh; Trinity College, Oxford (B.A.). Lieut.-Colonel Royal Scots Greys, 1919-23; acting Lieut.-Colonel Royal Scots Greys, 1918-19; served S. African War, 1900-02 (despatches); served European War, 1914-19 (wounded, despatches four times, Brevet Lt.-Col., D.S.O.); retired, 1923. Russian Order of St. Stanislaus, 2nd class. *Recreations:* shooting and golf. *Address:* Easter Skene, Skene, Aberdeenshire. *T.:* Skene 206. *Club:* Royal Northern (Aberdeen). [*Died* 24 *May* 1970.

DUHAMEL, Dr. Georges; Grand-Croix de la Légion d'Honneur, 1960; Man of Letters; Member of the French Academy since 1935; President of l'Alliance française since 1937; President of the National Academy of Medicine since 1960 (Member, 1937-); Member, Academy of Moral and Political Sciences since 1944; Member Academy of Surgery since 1940; Editor and Administrator of daily newspaper, Le Figaro; *b.* Paris, 30 June 1884; *m.* 1909, Blanche Albane-Sistoli; three *s.* *Educ.:* scientific and medical studies (Dr. méd.). Won Prix Goncourt, 1918. Travelled widely. *Publications:* his numerous books include: essays, novels, short stories, poetry, travel, writings on the theatre, etc., translated into many languages; among translations are: News from Havre, 1934; Young Pasquier, 1935; In Sight of the Promised Land, 1935; Salavin, 1936; The Pasquier Chronicles, 1937; In Defence of Letters, 1938; The White War of 1938, 1939; Days of Delight, 1939; Cécile Among the Pasquiers, 1940; Why France Fights, 1940; Suzanne and Joseph Pasquier, 1946; Light on My Days, 1948 (first five vols. of Autobiography, now trans.); Patrice Périot, 1952; Cry Out of the Depths, 1953; Le Japon entre la tradition et l'avenir, 1953; La Turquie nouvelle,

puissance d'Occident, 1954; Refuges de la lecture, 1954; Les Voyageurs de l'esperance, 1954; Archange de l'aventure, 1955; Les Compagnons de l'Apocalypse, 1956; Israël clef de l'Orient, 1957; Problèmes de l'Heure, 1957; Le complexe de Théophile and Voyage au Pérou, 1958; Travail, ô mon seul repos! (1st vol. collection: "Les écrivains juges de leurs œuvres"), 1959; Nouvelles du Sombre Empire, and ed. Mercure Conte philosophique, 1960; Problèmes de Civilisation, 1962. *Address:* 31 rue de Liège, Paris, VIIIe; Valmondois (Seine-et-Oise)
[*Died* 13 *April* 1966.

DUHIG, Sir James (Most Rev. James Duhig), K.C.M.G. 1959 (C.M.G. 1954); *b.* Limerick, 1871. Archbishop of Brisbane (R.C.), since 1917. Went to Qld. at 13; spent several years at Irish College, Rome; priest, 1896; missionary work, Ipswich, Queensland, 1897-1905; R.C. Bishop of Rockhampton, 1905-12; Coadjutor Archbishop of Brisbane, 1912-17. *Address*: Archbishop's House, Brisbane, Australia.
[*Died* 10 *April* 1965.

DUKE, Brigadier Cecil Leonard Basil, C.B. 1951; M.C. 1916 and Bar 1918; p.s.c.; *b.* 27 Nov. 1896. 2nd Lieutenant, Royal Engineers, 1915; Lieutenant, 1917; Captain, 1922; Adjutant, 1930; Major, 1932; Brevet Lieut.-Colonel, 1938; Substantive Lieut.-Colonel, 1939; Colonel, 1940; Brigadier, 1940. Served European War, France and Belgium, 1915-18 (wounded twice, 1914-15 Star, British War Medal, Victory Medal, M.C. and Bar); Adjutant, T.F., 1918-19; D.A.Q.M.G., India, 1936-38; A.A. & Q.M.G., 1940; N.W. European Force, 1940 (despatches); Malaya, 1942 (despatches), 1939-1945 and Pacific Stars, War Medal; retired pay, 1952. *Address:* c/o Standard Bank of South Africa, Nairobi, Kenya.
[*Died* 4 *Nov.* 1963.

DUKE, Hon. Edgar Mortimer, C.B.E. 1962; Speaker, Legislative Council, Trinidad and Tobago, since 1956; *b.* 2 Dec. 1895; 3rd *s.* of late Francis Walter Fitz Arthur Duke and late Rosamond Beatrice Duke; *m.* 1941, Sybillina Eulalie Gamell; one *d.* *Educ.:* Queen's College, British Guiana; City and Guilds Engineering Coll., London; University College, London (Andrews Entrance Schol. in Science, 1913, Joseph Hume Schol. in Jurisprudence, 1914; LL.B. 1916). Barstow Law Scholar in International Law, Jurisprudence, etc., Inns of Court, 1916; Barrister-at-Law, Middle Temple, 1917. British Guiana: Deputy Registrar of Deeds and of the Supreme Court, 1930; Registrar, 1933; Legal Draftsman, 1944; Solicitor-General, 1946; Trinidad and Tobago: Puisne Judge, 1949, retired 1956. *Publication:* Law of Immovable Property in British Guiana, 1922. *Recreation:* motoring. *Address:* Ellerslie Park, Maraval, Trinidad, West Indies. *T.:* Port of Spain 21109.
[*Died April* 1965.

DUKE, Herbert Lyndhurst, O.B.E.; B.A., M.D., B.C. (Cantab.); Sc.D. (Cantab.); D.T.M. and H. (Camb.); Retired as Deputy M.O.H. Cuckfield Urban and Rural and Burgess Hill Urban Councils, 1959; *b.* Lyndhurst, Hants, 31 Aug. 1883; *s.* of late Lt.-Col. Joshua Duke, I.M.S., and late Fanny Harriet Hall; *m.* Marguerite, *d.* of late Robert Collinge, Oldham, Lancs; one *s.* *Educ.:* Eastbourne College; Gonville and Caius College, Cambridge (Scholar); Guy's Hospital. 1st class Nat. Sci. Trip. Cambridge, Part I., 1905; Research Scholar, Protozoology, Heidelberg Univ. 1906; special service on Roy. Society's Sleeping Sickness Comm., 1910-13; Thurston Medal for Research into Tropical Medicine, Gonville and Caius College, Cambridge, 1913-14; Medical Officer, Uganda, 1910; Bacteriologist, 1914; Director of Human Trypanosomiasis Institute, Uganda; retired 1936; active service, East African Campaign, and temp. Captain Uganda Medical Service, 1914-18 (despatches); Chalmers Medal, Royal Society of Tropical Medicine and Hygiene, 1927; President, League of Nations International Commission on Sleeping Sickness, Uganda, 1926-27. *Publications:* papers in medical and other journals. *Recreation:* golf. *Address:* c/o National and Grindlay's Bank Ltd., 13 St. James's Square, S.W.1.
[*Died* 15 *April* 1966.

DUKE, Sir (Robert) Norman, K.B.E., *cr.* 1945; C.B. 1939; D.S.O. 1918; M.C.; *b.* 9 February 1893; *e. s.* of late Robert Whyte Duke and Mrs. Duke, Brechin, Angus; *m.* 1921, Frances Norman, *e. d.* of Arthur Francis Norman-Butler; one *s.* one *d.* *Educ.:* Merchiston Castle School, Edinburgh; Corpus Christi, Oxford. 2nd Lieut. 8th Black Watch, Aug. 1914; served France and Flanders, 1915-18 (D.S.O., M.C., despatches thrice); Staff Captain, General List, 1917; Brigade-Major, 1918; B.A. 1919; entered Civil Service (Scottish Office), 1919; Private Sec. to Under-Secretary for Scotland, 1920-1921; Asst. Sec., 1927-37; Principal Asst. Sec., 1937-39; Secretary Scottish Home Dept., 1939; seconded on outbreak of war for duty as Principal Officer to Regional Commissioner for Scottish Civil Defence Region; additional Deputy Under-Secretary of State, Air Ministry, 1942-43; Joint Dep. Sec., Ministry of Fuel and Power (in charge of Petroleum Div.), 1944-45; resumed duty as Sec. Scottish Home Dept., 1946. Chm. S.E. Scotland Electricity Bd., 1948-55; Dep. Chm., South of Scotland Electricity Bd., 1955-56. *Recreations:* shooting, fishing, golf. *Address:* 30 Regent Terrace, Edinburgh 7. *T.:* 031-556 6533. *Club:* New (Edinburgh).
[*Died* 7 *March* 1969.

DUKE, Winifred; novelist and historian; *b.* Liverpool; *d.* of late Rev. Canon E. St. A. Duke. *Educ.:* privately; Belvedere School, Liverpool. *Publications:* The House of Ogilvy, 1922; The Wild Flame, 1923; The Laird, 1925; Scotland's Heir, 1925; Lord George Murray and the '45, 1927; Tales of Hate, 1927; Madeleine Smith: a Tragi-Comedy, 1928; King of the Highland Hearts, 1929; Continuing City, 1929; Trial of Harold Greenwood (Notable British Trials), 1930; The Drove Road, 1930; Bastard Verdict, 1931; The Dark Hill, 1932; The Sown Wind, 1932; Finale, 1933; These are They, 1933; Six Trials, 1934; Magpie's Hoard, 1934; The Hour Glass, 1934; Stubble, 1935; Skin for Skin, 1935; Crookedshaws, 1936; Long Furrows, 1936; The Stroke of Murder, 1937; Room for a Ghost, 1937; Murder of Mr. Mallabee, 1937; Death and his Sweetheart, 1938; Prince Charles Edward and the '45, 1938; Out of the North, 1939; Trial of Field and Gray (Notable British Trials), 1939; Household Gods, 1939; Counterfeit, 1940; Unjust Jury, 1941; The Shears of Destiny, 1942; Royal Ishmael, 1943; We Owe God a Death, 1944; Funeral March of a Marionette, 1945; The Spider's Web, 1945; Blind Geese, 1946; Seven Women, 1947; The Black Mirror, 1948; Mart of Nations, 1949; Dirge for a Dead Witch, 1949; The Needful Journey, 1950; Trial of Frederick Nodder (Notable British Trials), 1950; Shadows, 1951; Winter Pride, 1952; The Rash Adventurer, 1952; A Web in Childhood, 1953; Lost Cause, 1953; In the Steps of Bonnie Prince Charlie, 1953; The Cherry-Fair, 1954; Second Spring, 1955; My Grim Chamberlain, 1955; The Ship of Fools, 1956: The Dancing of the Fox, 1956. *Recreations:* reading, criminology. *Address:* 19 Hartington Pl., Edinburgh. *T.:* Fountainbridge 1499.
[*Died* 4 *April* 1962.

DUKES, Sir Paul, K.B.E. 1920; author; *b.* 1889; *s.* of late Rev. E. J. and Edith Mary Dukes, B.A.; *m.* 1st, 1922, Margaret Rutherfurd (marriage dissolved, 1929), New York; 2nd. 1959, Diana Fitzgerald, Dublin. *Educ.:* Caterham School; Petrograd Conservatoire.

Member of Anglo-Russian Commission, 1915-1918; representative of same at Foreign Office, 1917; Intelligence Service in Soviet Russia, 1918-20; Special Correspondent of The Times in Eastern Europe, 1921; lectured widely in U.S.A. and Canada; Chm. of British-Continental Press Ltd., 1930-37; during War of 1939-45, visited Finland, Sweden, Holland and France (1940); was a director of Companies making special parts for Ministry of Aircraft Production; lectured extensively on international affairs for Ministry of Information, Royal Institute of International Affairs, Air Ministry and Council for Adult Education in H.M. Forces; series of B.B.C. TV broadcasts on Yoga, 1947-49; extensive lecture tours in India, Australia, S. Africa, New Zealand, 1952-63. *Publications:* Red Dusk and the Morrow, 1922; The Black Horse (with Ropshin-Savinkov), 1926; Ballet Russe (with Nicolas Legat), 1930; The Story of "ST 25", 1938 (republished as Secret Agent ST25, 1949); An Epic of the Gestapo, 1940; Come Hammer, Come Sickle, 1947; The Unending Quest, 1950; Yoga for the Western World, 1953; The Yoga of Health, Youth and Joy, 1960; numerous press and magazine articles. *Address:* c/o Westminster Bank, Piccadilly, W.1. *Clubs:* Royal Automobile, Royal Over-Seas League, Royal Commonwealth Society. [*Died* 27 *Aug.* 1967.

DULLES, Allen Welsh; lawyer, diplomat; *b.* Watertown, N.Y., 7 April 1893; *s.* of Rev. Allen Macy Dulles and Edith Foster; *m.* 1920, Clover Todd; one *s.* two *d.* *Educ.:* Princeton University. B.A., 1914, M.A., 1916; George Washington Univ. LL.B., 1926; Brown Univ. LL.D., 1947; Temple University LL.D., 1952; Columbia University LL.D., 1955; Princeton University LL.D., 195?; George Washington University LL.D., 1959; Boston College LL.D., 1961; University of South Carolina, LL.D., 1962; Williams College, LL.D., 1965. Educational work Allahabad, India, 1914-1915; entered U.S. Diplomatic Service, 1916, and served at Vienna, Berne, American Peace Delegation, Paris, Berlin, 1919; American Commission, Constantinople, 1920; Chief of Division of Near Eastern Affairs, Dept. of State, 1922-26; Deleg. to Intl. Conf. on Arms Traffic, Geneva, Switzerland 1925; member of Deleg. Geneva Disarmament Confs., 1926-27 and 1932 and 1933; resigned from Diplomatic Service, 1926, to take up practice of law with Sullivan and Cromwell, N.Y. City; Dir. Council on For. Relations. War work in Europe with the U.S. Office of Strategic Services, 1942-45. U.S. Central Intelligence Agency: Deputy Director, 1951-1953, Director, 1953-61; resumed law practise with Sullivan & Cromwell, 1962; Member, Presidei Commn. on the assassination of Pres. Kennedy, 1963-64. Presbyterian. Medal of Merit, Medal of Freedom, 1946; Officer of Legion of Honor, 1947; Order of SS. Maurizio e Lazzaro, Italy, 1946; Belgian Cross of Officer of Order of Leopold, 1948. National Security Medal, 1961. *Publications:* Can We Be Neutral? (with Hamilton Fish Armstrong), 1935; Can America Stay Neutral? (with Hamilton Fish Armstrong), 1939; Germany's Underground, 1947; The Craft of Intelligence, 1963; The Secret Surrender, 1966; Great True Spy Stories, 1968. *Address:* (home) 2723 Q St., N.W., Washington 7, D.C., U.S.A. *Clubs:* Century (New York); Metropolitan, Alibi (Washington). [*Died* 30 *Jan.* 1969.

DUMARCHEY, Pierre; *see* MacOrlan, Pierre.

DUMPLETON, Cyril Walter, *b.* 25 June 1897; *s* of late Walter Dumpleton, St. Albans, Herts.; *m.* 1920, Louise, *d.* of Charles Lefevre, Birmingham; three *s.* one *d.* *Educ.:* Elementary Schools and privately. Served 1914-18 R.N.A.S. and R.A.F. St. Albans City Councillor, 1937-50; Alderman, 1946; J.P. (Herts.), 1936-52; Mayor of St. Albans, 1943-44; M.P. (Lab.) for St. Albans Division of Herts, 1945-50. Staff of Colonial Development Corporation, 1950-62. *Recreation:* gardening. *Address:* West View, 230 Sandridge Road, St. Albans, Herts. *T.:* 53849. [*Died Oct.* 1966.

DUNBAR, Sir (Archibald) Edward, 9th Bt. Scot., *cr.* 1700; M.C.; late Major 12th West York Regt.; *b.* 17 Feb. 1889; *g.-g.s.* of 5th Bt., and 2nd *s.* of Lt.-Col. Arbuthnott P. B. S. Dunbar and Catharina Hester, *d.* of John Orred, Ashwicke, Gloucester; *S.* cousin, 8th Bt., 1916; *m.* 1926, Olivia Douglas Sinclair (*d.* 1964), *d.* of Maj.-Gen. Sir Edward May, K.C.B., C.M.G.; two *s.* *Educ.:* Wellington; Pembroke Coll., Cambridge. Served European War, 1914-19 (despatches, M.C.). *Heir:* *s.* Archibald Ranulph Dunbar, *b.* 8 Aug. 1927. *Address:* The Old Manse, Duffus, Elgin. [*Died* 15 *June* 1969.

DUNBAR, Sir Basil D.; *see* Hope-Dunbar.

DUNBAR, Sir Edward, Bt.; *see* Dunbar, Sir A. E.

DUNBAR, Sir George Cospatrick D. S.; *see* Duff-Sutherland-Dunbar.

DUNBAR, Sir George Duff-Sutherland-, of Hempriggs, 6th Bt. (Nova Scotia), *cr.* 1706; *b.* Ackergill Tower, Wick, 29 May 1878; *e. s.* of G. Duff Dunbar and Jane Louisa, *d.* of Lieut.-Colonel James Duff; *S.* grandfather (5th Bt.), 1897; *m.* 1st, 1903, Sibyl Hawtrey (*d.* 1911), *d.* of late Col. C. W. H. Tate; one *s.*; 2nd, 1921, Dorothy Mary Alice (*d.* 1945), *er. d.* of Col. G. G. Hewlett; 3rd, 1956, Dulce, *d.* of Wescombe Joyce. *Educ.:* Harrow; Sandhurst. Queen's Own Cameron Highlanders, 1898; Indian Army, 1902; invalided, 1925; D.A.Q.M.G. (Concentration) A.H.Q., India, 1908-09; Comdt. Lakhimpur Military Police, 1909-14; D.A.A.G., War Office and M.S., India, 1915-16; Abor Expedition, 1911-12 (despatches, King's Police Medal); commanding Escorts Brahmaputra Surveys, 1912-13; served in France and on N.W. Frontier (regimental and staff) during European War, 1914-18; with Indian States Delegation Round Table Conference, 1930-31; special duty, India Office, 1940; War Office lecturer, Army Education, 1941-45. *Publications:* A History of India, 1936, 4th ed. 1951 (German ed., 1937; Italian ed. 1960); India and the Passing of Empire, 1951; Clive; Other Men's Lives; Frontiers, etc.; over 50 broadcasts. *Heir:* *s.* George Cospatrick, *b.* 3 Aug. 1906. *Address:* Windermere, Lake Road, Chandler's Ford, Hants. *T.:* 2612. [*Died* 8 *April* 1962.

DUNBAR, Sir Richard (Fredrick Roberts), K.B.E. 1964 (O.B.E. 1951); C.B. 1962; Permanent Secretary, Ministry of Finance, 1957-65, and Head of Civil Service, 1961-65, Northern Ireland, retd.; *b.* 24 May 1900; *s.* of R. Dunbar, Dublin; *m.* 1927, Elizabeth A. Smith; one *s.* one *d.* *Educ.:* Mountjoy School, Dublin. Cadet College, Quetta, 1918. C.S., Dublin, 1919. Min. of Finance, N.I., 1922; Asst. Sec., Min. of Home Affairs, N.I., 1954. *Address:* 14 Knocklofty Park, Belfast 4, N.I. [*Died* 17 *Oct.* 1965.

DUNBAR, Robert, C.M.G. 1944; M.C.; *b.* 29 June 1895; *s.* of John Peter and Eliza Dunbar, Sheffield; *m.* 1921, Eva Christine, *d.* of Rev. Arthur and Louisa Sowerby. *Educ.:* Central Secondary School, Sheffield; Christ's College, Cambridge. 3rd

Secretary, Diplomatic Service, 1919; 2nd Secretary, 1920; 1st Secretary, 1928; Counsellor, 1940; Head of Treaty Department of Foreign Office until retirement, 1951. Commander of Order of the Star of Ethiopia. *Address:* 74 Grove Park, Camberwell, S.E.5. *Club:* Union Society (Cambridge).
[*Died* 1 *Feb.* 1970.

DUNBAR-NASMITH, Adm. Sir Martin E.; *see* Nasmith.

DUNCALFE, Sir Roger, Kt., *cr.* 1951; President, International Organization for Standardization, 1956-58; Chairman British Glues & Chemicals Ltd., 1946-1957 (Director, 1929-46, Joint Managing Director, 1920-29); *b.* 9 November 1884; *s.* of Alfred Richard and Sarah Elizabeth Duncalfe, Perton, Wolverhampton; *m.* 1912, Irene Frances Beddall; one *d.* *Educ.:* Tettenhall College, Wolverhampton; Nottingham University College. Pres., British Standards Institution, 1953-56 (Vice-President, 1952, Chairman, 1948-52); Pres. International Organization for Standardization (I.S.O.), 1956-58. Federation of British Industries; Vice-President, 1951-; Chairman Technical Legislation Committee, 1947-55. Mem. Grand Council, 1921-; Association of British Chemical Manufacturers: Vice-Pres., 1944-; President, 1941-43; Chairman, 1939-41; Member Council, 1932-; Federation of Gelatine & Glue Manufacturers Ltd.; Pres., 1947-55; Chm., 1938-43; Vice-Chm., 1930-38. Delegate at Joint Anglo-German Industrial Conference, Düsseldorf, 1939; Chm. and Mem. various Advisory Cttees. to Ministries, 1937-; Dep.-Chm., Air Pollution (Beaver) Cttee., 1954-55. F.R.S.H. 1955. Mem. Soc. Chem. Industry. *Address:* Greystones, Western Avenue, Branksome Park, Bournemouth. *T.:* Canford Cliffs 78855. *Clubs:* Junior Carlton, Savage.
[*Died* 15 *April* 1961.

DUNCAN, Col. Sir Alan (Gomme) Gomme-, Kt. 1956; M.C.; F.S.A. Scot.; *b.* 5 July 1893; *o. s.* of late Alfred Edward Duncan and Annie Emily Harriette Barker; assumed by Authority additional surname of Gomme, 1938; *m.* 1919, Mary, *e. d.* of late W. W. Bourne, of Garston Manor, Herts; one *s.* one *d.* *Educ.:* Merchant Taylors' School. Served 1914-19 with London Scottish and Black Watch in France, Belgium and Germany (wounded, despatches twice, M.C.). Served with the Black Watch in India, 1919-27 and 1933-37; Staff Officer Western Command, Quetta, 1923-27, and Northern Command, York, 1929-33; retired, 1937; H.M. Inspector of Prisons for Scotland, 1938-39; recalled to Colours, June 1939; D.A.A.G. War Office, 1939-40; commanded 70th (y.s.) Bn. The Black Watch, 1940-41; attached R.A.F. 1941-42; A.A.G. War Office, 1942-43; commanded 101 Reinforcement Group, 21 Army Group, 1943-1944, and with Second Army in France, Belgium and Holland; retired finally, 1945. M.P. (C.) Perth and Kinross (Perth and E. Perthshire), 1945-September 1959. Member of Royal Company of Archers, Queen's Bodyguard for Scotland, National Trust for Scotland, Society for Preservation of Rural Scotland and Saltire Society. Member N.F.U., Scotland; Vice-Pres. Perthshire Agricultural Society; Pres. Perthshire Musical Festival Assoc. Vice-President, Boy Scouts, Perth District. *Recreations:* gardening, music. *Address:* House of Dunbarney, Bridge of Earn, Perthshire. *T.:* 204.
[*Died* 13 *Dec.* 1963.

DUNCAN, Alexander Mitchell, C.M.G. 1946; Chief Commissioner of Police, State of Victoria, 1937-Dec. 1954, retired; *b.* Dufftown, Scotland, 25 Sept. 1888; *m.* 1917, Elizabeth Ann, *d.* of John MacDonald; one *d.* Joined Metropolitan Police Force, 1910; transferred to C.I.D. 1917; Chief Inspector, 1934-37. O.St.J. *Address:* 45 Dendy Street, Brighton S.5, Victoria, Australia.
[*Died* 1 Sept. 1965.

DUNCAN, Sir (Charles Edgar) Oliver, 3rd Bt., *cr.* 1905; Grand Cross of Merit of Sovereign and Military Order of Malta; Grand Cordon of Royal Order of Saint-Sava with accompanying decorations; *e. s.* of Sir Frederick Duncan, 2nd Bt., and Helen Julia Pfizer, of Brooklyn, New York; *b.* 13 Aug. 1892; *S.* father, 1929; *m.* 1958, Etelka de Vangel. *Educ.:* Harrow; Cambridge. Commission in R.H.G., 1915; Ministry of Munitions, 1917-18. *Heir:* none. *Address:* Villa Beau Desert, Cannes, France; Château Les Crénées, Mies, Vaud, Switzerland.
[*Died* 20 *Sept.* 1964 (*ext.*).

DUNCAN, Very Rev. George Simpson, O.B.E. 1918; Hon. D.D. (Edin.) 1930, (Glasgow) 1951; Hon. D. Théol. (Paris), 1938; Hon. LL.D. (Edin.) 1946, (St. And.) 1955; Prof. of Biblical Criticism, 1919-54 and Principal, 1940-54, of St. Mary's Coll., in the Univ. of St. Andrews; Vice-Chancellor of the University, 1952-53; retired 1954; *b.* 8 March 1884; *er. surv. s.* of late Alexander Duncan, Forfar; *m.* 1929, Muriel, *er. d.* of late James Smith, M.D., Edinburgh; one *s.* *Educ.:* Forfar Academy, Edinburgh University, Trinity College, Cambridge; St. Andrews University, Marburg, Jena, and Heidelberg Universities. M.A., B.D. Edin. (First-Class Honours in Classics, Rhind Classical Scholar, C. B. Black Scholar in Hellenistic Greek, Pitt Club Theological Scholar), M.A. Cantab. (First-Class Classical Tripos, Exhibitioner and Sizar of Trinity College). Ordained to the Ministry of the Church of Scotland, 1915; Presbyterian Chaplain at General H.Q., 1st Echelon, Brit. Armies in France, 1915-19 (despatches twice, O.B.E.); Hon. C.F.; Hon. Prof., Reformed Church Coll., Debrecen, Hungary, 1938, and Budapest, 1946; Pres., Studiorum Novi Testamenti Societas, 1947; Moderator of the General Assembly of the Church of Scotland, 1949; Select Preacher, Univ. of Camb., 1950; Vice-Pres. Brit. Council of Churches, 1952-54; Mem. Board of Scottish National War Memorial, 1949-57; Trustee, Nat. Museum of Antiquities, Scotland; Mem. N.T. Translation Panel, New English Bible; Freedom Cross (Norway), 1947. *Publications:* St. Paul's Ephesian Ministry, 1929; The Epistle of Paul to the Galatians (Moffatt New Testament Commentary), 1934; Jesus, Son of Man (Croall Lectures), 1948. *Address:* 7 Windmill Rd., St. Andrews, Fife. *T.:* St. Andrews 232.
[*Died* 8 *April* 1965.

DUNCAN, Sir Harold (Handasyde), K.C.M.G., *cr.* 1945; Q.C. 1948; *b.* 15 June 1885; *s.* of late A. H. F. Duncan, Lt. Royal Navy. *Educ.:* Eton; Balliol Coll., Oxford (Hons. School of Modern History; M.A.). Qualified in Civil Service Exam. for appointment as Junior Clerk, 1st Class, Foreign Office, 1908; Confidential Sec. to the London Committee, Imperial Ottoman Bank, 1909; on special mission to Constantinople, 1912; served in the Army, 1914-19; Capt. Norfolk Yeomanry; France and Italy; Liaison Officer (Intelligence A) between British G.H.Q. Italy and British Military Mission, Comando Supremo, 1918; called to Bar, Inner Temple, 1919; South-Eastern Circuit; Temp. Legal Assistant, Ministry of Health, 1927; established, 1928; Second Assistant Legal Adviser, 1930-31 and Assistant Legal Adviser, 1931-43 to Dominions Office and Colonial Office (Acting Legal Adviser Dec. 1931-March 1932 and Feb.-July 1933); Legal Adviser to Dominions Office and Colonial Office, 1943-45. Member: British Inst. of International and Comparative Law (Advisory Board, Alternate on Council of Management), Law Advisory Cttee., British Council. Commander, Order of Orange-Nassau, 1955. *Address:* 3 Paper Buildings, Temple, E.C.4. *T.:* City 1920. *Club:* St. James'. [*Died* 2 *Dec.* 1962.

DUNCAN, Maj.-Gen. Henry Clare, C.B. 1931; D.S.O. 1915; O.B.E.; late 9th Gurkha Rifles; *b.* 12 July 1876; *s.* of Lieut.-Gen. John Duncan; *m.* 1st, Edith Irene (*d.* 1918), *e. d.* of late Major-General R. Byng Campbell, C.B.; one *s.*; 2nd, 1924, Gladys Hobart, *widow* of Stuart Vines, M.A. Served European War, 1914-18 (D.S.O., O.B.E., Brevet Lieut.-Colonel); Operations in Kurdistan, 1919-21; Operations N.-W. Frontier, India, 1922-23; A.Q.M.G., Western Command, India, 1925-27; commanded 4th (Quetta) Infantry Brigade, 1928-29; commanded Zhob Independent Brig. Area, 1929-32; Maj.-Gen., 1932; retd. 1933. *Club:* United Service. [*Died* 31 *July* 1961.

DUNCAN, John Douglas Grace; Chairman, Bank of New Zealand since 1965; *b.* 24 January 1899, *s.* of John Gavin Duncan; *m.* 1923, Cecilia Mary, *d.* of P. E. Baldwin; three *s.* *Educ.:* Downside College; Royal Military College, Sandhurst. Served with Imperial Army, 1914-18 War. Joined Levin and Company Limited, 1920; Director, 1938; Managing Director, 1945; Chairman, 1959-63. Director: AMP Society; Meat Export Development Company, Limited; Hutt River Board. *Recreation:* golf. *Address:* 23 Barton Road, Heretaunga, Wellington, New Zealand. [*Died* 5 *July* 1969.

DUNCAN, Joseph Forbes, Hon. LL.D. (Glasg.) 1946; retired Trade Union Secretary; *b.* 3 June 1879; *m.* 1909, Jessie Mabel Saunders; no *c.* *Educ.:* Robert Gordon's College, Aberdeen. Founder and Secretary Scottish Farm Servants Union, 1912-45; Member Agricultural Research Council, 1930-1938 and 1946-52; Chairman Scottish Agricultural Improvement Council, 1951-60. Member Royal Commission: on Housing, Scotland, 1912-17; on Agriculture, 1919-1921; President: International Landworkers Federation, 1924-50; Agricultural Economics Society, 1939-46; Scottish Trade Union Congress, 1926; and numerous other Commissions and Departmental Committees. *Publication:* Agriculture and the Community, 1921. *Address:* Witch Hill, Newburgh, Aberdeenshire. *T.:* Newburgh 271. [*Died* 1 *Dec.* 1964.

DUNCAN, Sir Oliver, Bt.; *see* Duncan, Sir C. E. O., Bt.

DUNCAN, Lt.-Col. Ronald Cardew, C.I.E. 1946; M.V.O. 1929; O.B.E.; late 5th Royal Gurkha Rifles (F.F.); Maj.-Gen. Jodhpur State Forces; *b.* 9 September 1886; *s.* of Lieutenant-General J. Duncan; *m.* 1921, Brenda, *d.* of W. R. Davies, J.P., Camberley; one *d.* (one *s.* died of wounds). *Educ.:* Wellington College; Sandhurst. 2nd Lieut. 5th Gurkha Rifles, 1905; Captain, 1914; Bt. Major, 1918; Major, 1920; Lt.-Col., 1931; Adjutant, 1913-16; served operations on N.W. Frontier, India, 1908 (medal and clasp); European War, 1914-18; Mesopotamia, G.S.O. 3, 13th Division; Bde. Major, 42nd and 7th Infantry Brigades; G.S.O. 2, G.H.Q. (despatches twice, Bt. Major, 1914-15 star, General Service medal, Victory medal); Brigade Major, 68th and 69th Infantry Brigades, Afghanistan, 1919 (clasp); Waziristan, 1919-21 (despatches, O.B.E., two clasps); N.W. Frontier, 1930 (clasp); Assistant Military Secretary, Northern Command, India, 1924-26; Brigade Major, Ambala Brigade, 1926-28; Officer in charge of King's Indian Orderly Officers, 1929 (M.V.O.); attached to Nepalese Mission to England, 1934; Star of Nepal, 3rd class; Commandant Jodhpur State Forces, 1936-47; Hon. Col. 2nd Jodhpur Infantry, 1940-47. Member Chelsea Borough Council, 1949-56. Gold Staff Officer at Coronation, 1953. Has appeared in a number of films including: Three Cases of Murder, Front Page Story, Dangerous Voyage, Storm over the Nile, Touch and Go, Secret Tent, Seven Years in Tibet, Brothers-in-Law, Lucky Jim, North West Frontier, The Trials of Oscar Wilde. *Publications:* Letters of a Soldier to his Son; Some Like the Hills; The Large Sapphire; Tomu from Tibet and other Dog Stories. *Address:* 2 Markham Street, Chelsea, S.W.3. *T.:* Kensington 3560; Rivermead Cottage, Shiplake-on-Thames, Oxon. *T.:* Wargrave 258. [*Died* 30 *June* 1963.

DUNCAN, Hon. Sir Walter Gordon, Kt., *cr.* 1939; M.L.C., for Midland District, S. Australia, 1918-62; President of Legislative Council, 1944-62; Leader Liberal and Country Party in Legislative Council, 1932-44; Pastoralist; *b.* Hughes Park, Watervale, S.A., 10 March 1885; *s.* of late Hon. Sir John Duncan, M.L.C.; *m.* 1909, Bessie G., 2nd *d.* of late A. S. Fotheringham; one *s.* two *d.* *Educ.:* St. Peter's College, Adelaide; Cheltenham College, England. Pres. R. Agric. Soc. of S.A., 1924-25, 1932-50; ex-Director Broken Hill Proprietary Co. Ltd., Australian Iron and Steel, Ltd., and other companies. *Address:* 56 Park Terrace, Parkside, S. Australia; Bank of New South Wales Chambers, 12 King William Street, Adelaide, Australia. *T.:* 51 2679. *Clubs:* Adelaide; Australian (Melbourne.) [*Died* 27 *Aug.* 1963.

DUNCAN, Brigadier William Edmonstone, C.V.O. 1936; D.S.O., M.C.; *b.* 19 March 1890; *s.* of Alexander R. and Frances Duncan; *m.* 1921, Magdalene, *d.* of Colonel H. W. Renny Tailyour, Borrowfield, Forfarshire; two *s.* two *d.* *Educ.:* Cheltenham; R.M.A., Woolwich. Royal Artillery, 1910; European War (despatches four times, D.S.O., M.C. and bar); War of 1939-45 (despatches); Inspector R.A., 1943-45; retired pay, 1946. *Address:* Greenside, Montrose, Angus. *Clubs:* United Service; New (Edinburgh). [*Died* 20 *Dec.* 1969.

DUNCAN-HUGHES, Capt. J. G.; *see* Hughes, Capt. J. G. D.

DUNCAN-JONES, Austin Ernest; Professor of Philosophy, University of Birmingham, since 1951; *b.* Cambridge, 5 August 1908; *e. s.* of late Very Rev. A. S. Duncan-Jones, sometime Dean of Chichester; *m.* 1933, Elsie Elizabeth Phare; one *s.* one *d.* (and one *s.* decd.). *Educ.:* Caius College, Cambridge. Ed. of Analysis, 1933-48. Pres. of Mind Assoc., 1952; Visiting Prof. of Philosophy, Brown Univ., 1954-55; President, Aristotelian Society, 1960-61. *Publications:* Butler's Moral Philosophy, 1952; articles in philosophical jls. *Address:* The University of Birmingham. [*Died* 2 *April* 1967.

DUNCANSON, Sir John (McLean), Kt. 1942; Director of: National Commercial Bank of Scotland, Limited; Grampian Shipyards Ltd.; British Rhodesian Steel Co. (Pte.) Ltd.; Oil and Associated Investment Trust Ltd.; Vice-President and Member of Council Iron and Steel Institute; *b.* 4 Feb. 1897; *s.* of Thomas and Elizabeth McLean Duncanson; *m.* Margaret Black; one *s.* one *d.* Served European War, 1914-18, Queen's Own Royal Glasgow Yeomanry. Director Heavy Steel Products and Deputy Controller of Iron and Steel, 1939-42; Controller of Iron and Steel, 1942-45; Commercial and Technical Director British Iron and Steel Federation, 1945-48; Leader, Anglo-American steel mission (1943) visiting all Dominions, India and U.S.A. U.S. Medal of Freedom, 1947; Commandeur, Luxembourg National Order of

Oaken Crown, 1954. *Recreations:* riding, golf. *Address:* 47 New Church Road, Hove 3, Sussex. *Club:* Caledonian.
[*Died* 25 *July* 1963.

DUNDAS, Lord George Heneage Lawrence; Chairman Hurst Park Syndicate, retired; *b.* 1882; *yr. s.* of late Marquess of Zetland; *m.* 1905, Ivy, *d.* of late Col. Hanley. Served S. Africa, 1901-2; European War, 1914-18; War of 1939-45, R.A.F.V.R., 1940-1946. *Address:* 49 Hallam St., W.1.
[*Died* 30 *Sept.* 1968.

DUNDAS, Sir Henry Matthew, 5th Bt., *cr.* 1898; *b.* 17 May 1937; *o. s.* of Sir Philip Dundas, 4th Bt. and Jean Marian, 3rd *d.* of James A. Hood, Midfield, Lasswade, Midlothian; *S.* father 1952. *Educ.:* Abbotsholme School, Uttoxeter, Staffs. Royal Agricultural College, Cirencester, Glos. *Recreations:* riding, ski-ing, water ski-ing. *Heir: uncle* James Durham, *b.* 31 Aug. 1905. *Address:* c/o British Linen Bank, St. Andrew Square, Edinburgh. *Clubs:* English-Speaking Union, British Ski. [*Died* 24 *June* 1963.

DUNDAS, Lt.-Col. James Colin, D.S.O. 1917; *b.* 6 Jan. 1883; *e. s.* of late Commander Colin Mackenzie Dundas, R.N., and Agnes, *d.* of late Samuel Wauchope, C.B.; *m.* 1912, Kathleen, 4th *d.* of late Lieut.-Col. James Hearn Tarleton, late 54th Regt., and formerly of Rathmacknee, Co. Wexford, and Edith de Sorel, *d.* of late General Reid Browne; no *c.* *Educ.:* Eton; Royal Military Academy, Woolwich. 2nd Lieut., Royal Field Artillery, 1900; Lieut., 1903; Captain, 1913; Major, 1915; Brevet Lieut.-Colonel, 1919; transferred Royal Tank Corps as Major and Bt. Lt.-Col.; Lieut.-Colonel, Royal Tank Corps, 1925; P.S.C.; served European War (despatches twice, D.S.O., Brevet Lieut.-Colonel); D.A.Q.M.G., 6th Division, 1915; Staff Captain, War Office, 1917; Deputy Assistant Director of Artillery, War Office, 1917; 1919; General Staff Officer, 2nd Grade, War Office, 1920-23; D.A.A. and Q.M.G. 51st (Highland) Division, 1924-25; commanded Northern Group, Royal Tank Corps, India, 1925-28; retired pay, 1928; Lt.-Col. R.A. 1939; retired pay, 1941; Vice-Chm., British Hosps. Assoc. and Chm. Scottish Branch until 1948; County Commissioner for Boy Scouts for Perthshire until 1950, Vice-Chm. Scottish Cttee. Boy Scouts Assoc.; Member, Royal Company of Archers (King's Bodyguard for Scotland), 1930; J.P. Perth; D.L. County of Stirling; awarded Naval Gold Medal of R.U.S.I., 1925. *Address:* Ochtertyre, Stirling, Scotland. *Club:* Army and Navy. [*Died* 26 *Aug.* 1966.

DUNDAS, Sir James Durham, 6th Bt., *cr.* 1898; O.B.E. 1958; D.L.; J.P.; *b.* 31 Aug. 1905; 4th *s.* of Sir Henry H. P. Dundas, 3rd Bt., M.V.O., and Lady Beatrix Douglas Home, 2nd *d.* of 12th Earl of Home; *S.* nephew, 1963. *Educ.:* Loretto. D.L. 1958 and J.P. County of Peebles; Member Peeblesshire County Council, 1945-; Convener of County, 1958-. *Heir: b.* Thomas Calderwood Dundas, M.B.E. *Address:* Birkinshaw, Traquair, Innerleithen, Peeblesshire. *Club:* New (Edinburgh).
[*Died* 18 *June* 1967.

DUNDAS, Sir Thomas (Calderwood), 7th Bt. *cr.* 1898; M.B.E. 1945; Director of Barclays Bank Ltd., 1954-67; *b.* 27 November 1906; 5th *s.* of Sir Henry Herbert Philip Dundas, 3rd Bt. of Arniston, and Lady Beatrix Douglas Home, 2nd *d.* of 12th Earl of Home; *S.* brother, Sir James Durham Dundas, 6th Bt., O.B.E., 1967; *m.* 1933, Isabel, *o. d.* of late Charles Goring, Wiston Park, Sussex; two *d.* *Educ.:* Loretto, Musselburgh. Entered Barclays Bank, 1924; a Local Dir. of Barclays Bank, Brighton District, 1935-67. High Sheriff of Sussex, 1959. Major, Scots Guards; served War of 1939-45 (despatches, M.B.E.). *Recreations:* shooting, gardening. *Heir:* none. *Address:* Hammer Hill, Plummers Plain, Horsham, Sussex. *T.:* Handcross 267. *Club:* Guards.
[*Died* 2 *Dec.* 1970.

DUNFIELD, Sir Brian (Edward, Spencer), Kt., *cr.* 1949; Q.C. (Newfoundland); Judge in the Supreme Court of Newfoundland, 1939-63, and District Judge in Admiralty Exchequer Court of Canada, 1949-63; Administrator of the Province on several occasions; *b.* 10 April 1888; *s.* of late Rev. Canon Henry Dunfield, St. John's, Newfoundland, and late Helen Maria Isobel Bremner; *m.* 1918, Sybil Frances Carrington Johnson; two *s.* one *d.* *Educ.:* Bishop Feild College, St. John's, Newfdld.; London University. B.A. 1st Cl. Hons. Philos., 1909; admitted to Newfoundland Bar, 1911; Counsel to Justice Dept., 1928; Secretary for Justice, 1932-39; Chairman various public enquiries and Labour arbitrations, 1939-45; Chairman: Commission of Enquiry on Housing and Town Planning in St. John's, 1942-44; St. John's Housing Corporation, 1944-49; St. John's Town Planning Commission since 1945; Corner Brook Housing Corporation; Nat. Pres. Community Planning Assoc. of Canada, 1953-56. Secretary Rural Reconstruction Cttee., 1935-48; Sec. Defence Cttee., 1938-1939; Chm., St. John's Traffic Commn., 1956; Chm. Commn. of Enquiry into Logging Industry, 1960. *Publications:* ed. of var. Consolidated Statutes, Law Reports, etc. *Recreations:* reading, motoring, fishing. *Address:* Arcady, Waterford Bridge Road, St. John's, Newfoundland. *Club:* City (St. John's, Newfoundland).
[*Died* 19 *March* 1968.

DUNK, Susan S.; *see* Spain-Dunk.

DUNLOP, Rt. Rev. David Colin; retd. as Dean of Lincoln and Canon and Prebendary of Aylesbury in Lincoln Cathedral (1949-64); *b.* 31 July 1897; *s.* of David Jugurtha and Laura Frances Dunlop; *m.* 1935, Mary Geraldine O'Malley; four *s.* *Educ.:* Radley; New College, Oxford. Lieut. 3rd Bn. The Buffs, 1915-19; Assistant Curate S. Mary, Primrose Hill, 1922-27; Domestic Chaplain to Bishop of London, 1927-28; Hon. Chaplain H.M. Legation, Stockholm, 1929; Domestic Chaplain to Bishop of Chichester, 1929-32; Hon. Chaplain, H.M. Embassy, Bagdad, 1932-34; Vicar S. Thomas, Hove, 1934-36; Vicar of Henfield, Sussex, 1936-40; Prebendary of Chichester Cathedral, 1937-1940; Canon Emeritus of Chichester Cathedral, 1940; Provost of S. Mary's Cathedral, Edinburgh, 1940-44; Archbishops' Visitor to R.A.F. Units, 1943-44; Bishop Suffragan of Jarrow, 1944-49; Select Preacher, Cambridge University, 1947; Select Preacher, Oxford Univ., 1950-51, 1961-62. *Publications:* Processions, 1932; Anglican Public Worship, 1953. *Recreation:* music. *Address:* Newhay, Upper Station Rd., Henfield, Sussex. *T.:* Henfield 2053.
[*Died* 23 *Feb.* 1968.

DUNLOP, Ernest McMurchie, M.C.; M.A. (Dunelm); M.D. (Glas.); F.R.S.E.; Emeritus Professor of Bacteriology, Univ. of Durham (1932-59); *b.* 1893; *o. s.* of Thomas Dunlop and Grace McFadyean. *Educ.:* Hutchesons' Grammar School; University of Glasgow. M.B., Ch.B. (Hons.), and Brunton Memorial Prize, 1916; M.D. (Hons.), Bellahouston Gold Medal Thesis, 1930; Captain R.A.M.C. (T.); Assistant to Professor of Pathology, 1919-22. Lecturer in Bacteriology, 1922-32, Univ. of Glasgow; Clinical Pathologist, Western Infirmary, Glasgow, 1919-32; Examiner Univs. of Aberdeen, Birmingham, Edinburgh, etc. *Publications:* Various contributions to scientific journals, etc. *Address:* 21 Racecourse Road, Ayr, Ayrshire.
[*Died* 29 *April* 1969.

DUNLOP, Ven. Maxwell Tulloch; Archdeacon of Aston, Canon Residentiary of Birmingham Cathedral, and Canon Emeritus of Manchester Cathedral since 1955; *b.* 15 Dec. 1898; *s.* of George Alexander Dunlop and Jenny Maine Boyd; *m.* 1933, Stella Louise (*d.* 1961), *d.* of Dr. F. O. Lasbrey, Cairo, and Wethersfield, Essex; two *s.* *Educ.:* Ruthin School; Leeds Gram. Sch.; Hertford College and Ripon Hall, Oxford. Curate: Holy Trinity, Southport, and Alexandria, 1926-30; Lecturer in History, Culham Training Coll., 1930-32; Senior Tutor, Ripon Hall, Oxford, 1932-36; Vicar, West Hendred, Wantage, 1935-38; Director of Social Studies, Mansfield Univ. Settlement, 1936-39; Director, Northumberland and Tyneside Council of Social Service, 1939-48; Director of Religious Education and Hon. Canon of Manchester, 1948-55. *Publications:* responsible for Reports issued by Northumberland and Tyneside Council of Social Service on Infant Mortality, Legal Aid, Care of Deprived Children, and other social questions on Tyneside. Assistant Editor The Modern Churchman, 1932-36. *Recreations:* music, the theatre; swimming, camping abroad. *Address:* 242 Harborne Park Road, Harborne, Birmingham 17. *T.:* Harborne 2000.
[*Died* 2 *Oct.* 1964.

DUNLOP, Sir Robert (William Layard), Kt., *cr.* 1925; C.I.E. 1913; D.S.O. 1917; V.D.; *b.* 19 Aug. 1869; *s.* of late Robert Vetch Dunlop, Vicar of Holy Trinity, Scarborough; *m.* 1919, Irene Lois, *widow* of Capt. Keith Forbes Robertson, Rifle Brigade; two *s.* *Educ.:* Repton. Col. Bombay Volunteer Rifles; D.A.A. and Q.M.G. 1915; temp. Lt.-Col. R.F.A.; Hon. A.D.C. to Governor of Bombay; additional member Bombay Legislative Council; served European War, 1914-17 (despatches, D.S.O.); Solicitor to Govt. of India, 1920; retired, 1927. *Recreations:* M.F.H. Bombay Hunt, 1906-13. *Address:* Croft Lane, Speen, Newbury, Berks. *T.:* Newbury 185.
[*Died* 4 *July* 1962.

DUNLOP, Sir Thomas, 2nd Bt., *cr.* 1916; senior partner of the firm of Thomas Dunlop & Sons, shipowners and Insurance Brokers, Glasgow; *b.* 17 November 1881; *e. s.* of Sir Thomas Dunlop, 1st Bt. and Dorothy Euphemia, *d.* of Peter Mitchell, of Longniddry, East Lothian; *S.* father, 1938; *m.* 1911, Mary Elizabeth, *d.* of late William Beckett, Solicitor, Glasgow; two *s.* one *d.* *Educ.:* Blair Lodge, Stirlingshire. Entered father's firm of Thomas Dunlop & Sons, Glasgow, 1904, and was made a partner in 1911; Member of Committee of Lloyd's Register of Shipping; Income Tax Commissioner; Vice-Commodore Royal Clyde Yacht Club. *Recreations:* yachting, golf, fishing. *Heir:* *s.* Thomas [*b.* 11 Apr. 1912; *m.* 1947, Alison, *y. d.* of late T. A. Smith, Lindsaylands, Biggar; one *s.* two *d.*]. *Address:* 1 Kirklee Gardens, Glasgow, W.2. *T.:* Western 3839. *Clubs:* Western, Royal Scottish Automobile, Art (Glasgow).
[*Died* 8 *March* 1963.

DUNLOP, Sir Thomas Dacre, K.C.M.G., *cr.* 1939 (C.M.G. 1930); *b.* Belfast, 8 Aug. 1883; *s.* of Samuel Dunlop; *m.* 1911, Margaret, *d.* of late Henry Morris, O.B.E., of the Admiralty; one *s.* one *d.* *Educ.:* Campbell College, Belfast; King's College, London. Entered H.M. Consular Service, 1907; served in Egypt, Uruguay, Italy, Dept. of Overseas Trade and New Caledonia; Inspector-General of Consular Establishments, 1923; retired, 1943. *Address:* Claverley Cottage, Chislehurst. *T.:* Imperial 3721. *Club:* Royal Automobile. [*Died* 19 *April* 1963.

DUNMORE, 8th Earl of (*cr.* 1686), **Alexander Edward Murray,** Viscount Fincastle, Lord Murray, 1686; Baron Dunmore (U.K.), 1831; V.C. 1898; D.S.O. 1917; M.V.O. 1906; Maj. 16th Lancers; *b.* 22 Apr. 1871; *s.* of 7th Earl and Lady Gertrude Coke (*d.* 1943), 3rd *d.* of 2nd Earl of Leicester; *S.* father, 1907; *m.* 1904, Lucinda Dorothea, *e. d.* of Horace Kemble, Knock, Isle of Skye; two *d.* (one *s.* killed, 1940). A.D.C. to Viceroy of India, 1895-1897; served Dongola Expedition, 1896 (two medals); served with Guides Cav. in Frontier War, Afghanistan, 1897 (V.C., medal and clasp); served with 6th (Inniskilling) Dragoons and 16th Lancers in South Africa, 1899-1900 (despatches); commanded 31st Batt. Imp. Yeomanry, Fincastle's Horse, in S. African War (medal and four clasps); served European War, 1914-16 (wounded, D.S.O.); Capt. of the Gentlemen-at-Arms, 1924; a Lord-in-Waiting to H.M., 1930-36. *Heir:* *g.s.* Viscount Fincastle. *Publication:* A Frontier Campaign, 1898. *Address:* 23 Sussex Lodge, Sussex Place, W.2. *T.:* Paddington 9115. *Club:* Carlton.
[*Died* 29 *Jan.* 1962.

DUNN, Charles William, C.I.E. 1924; M.A.; *b.* 26 March 1877; *s.* of late Thomas William Dunn. *Educ.:* Bath College; Trinity Coll., Cambridge; Classical Tripos, Part I. 1897, Part II. (B) 1898; Indian Civil Service, 1899; Burma Commission, 1900; joined Co-operative Societies Department, 1911; Registrar of Co-operative Societies, Burma, 1915 and 1919-23; on special duty in Ministry of Education, Local Government, and Public Health, Burma, 1924-27; Financial Commissioner (Transferred Subjects), 1927-32; retired, 1934. *Address:* 18 Avenue Road, Bishop's Stortford, Herts.
[*Died* 16 *Jan.* 1966.

DUNN, James Stormont, C.B.E. 1919; Adviser to South African Press Association 1940; General Manager, Reuter's Agency in South Africa, 1916-40; General Manager, The South African Press Association, 1938-40; Chief Agent of Reuters S. Africa, 1916-40; *b.* Glasgow, 14 May 1879; *s.* of late James Nicol Dunn; *m.* 1st, 1908, Gertrude Esther Kerridge (*d.* 1930); one *d.* (decd.); 2nd, 1931, Harriet Gertrude Impey. *Educ.:* Glasgow, Edinburgh, and London. Came to South Africa to Editorial Department of Reuter's Agency, Cape Town, 1902; South African Editor of Reuter's in London, 1905; Chairman, Cape Town Publicity Association, 1919-26; Chairman, Cape Town Orchestra Advisory Board, 1920; Chairman, Cape Town Orchestra Management Committee, 1921-26; Member, Cape Fishery Advisory Board; established the Cape Town Broadcasting Station, and was Chairman for three years; Transvaal representative of the South African Rugby Bd., 1922-57; Life-Member S. African Railway Advisory Publicity Cttee., 1941; Mem. Govt. Broadcasting Inquiry Commission, 1946-47. *Publication:* (with Romer Robinson) Salt Water Angling in South Africa. *Recreations:* sea angling and gardening. *Address:* Lindertis Cottage, Durbanville, C.P., South Africa. *Clubs:* Civil Service, Olympic, Western Province Cricket (Cape Town).
[*Died* 20 *May* 1965.

DUNN, Peter Douglas Hay, C.M.G. 1946; O.B.E. 1938; *b.* 2 Jan. 1892; 2nd *s.* of Alexander Dunn, Market House, Kilsyth, Scotland; *m.* 1920, Elizabeth Anderson, *d.* of David Shaw, Rosemount, Kilsyth; one *s.* *Educ.:* Allan Glen's School, Glasgow. Customs and Excise, 1911; Ministry of Pensions, 1919; Customs Adviser Newfoundland Govt., 1934; Chm. of Board of Customs, Newfoundland, 1935-37; Ministry of Food, 1939-41; Member of Commission of Govt. of Newfoundland and Commissioner for Natural Resources, 1941-45. Fisheries Secretary, Ministry of Agriculture and Fisheries, 1946-1950; Member of White Fish Authority, 1950-53. Economic Adviser to Hull Fishing Vessel Owners' Association, 1953-55.
[*Died* 3 *Nov.* 1965.

DUNN, Stanley Gerald, M.A. (Oxon); Hon. D.Litt. (Allahabad), F.R.G.S.; late

I.E.S.; *b.* 7 Oct. 1879; *m.* 1930, Marjorie Russell, *d.* of E. C. Windle, Leamington. *Educ.:* King's School, Rochester (King's scholar); Jesus College, Oxford (senior scholar); B.A. Oxford (1902 Hon. Mods. and Lit. Hum.). Educational and literary work (Oxford and Wales) till 1908, when appointed to I.E.S.; Professor of English Literature, Head of the Department of English Studies and Dean of the Faculty of Arts, University of Allahabad; author of A Dear Little Wife and Fancy Dress, produced at the Haymarket and Criterion 1913, 1914; on special duty with General Staff, India, and author of war pamphlets for Central Publicity Board, India; official eyewitness with the Force in Mesopotamia, 1918-19; special correspondent for the Pioneer on N.W. Frontier and Afghanistan, 1919 (Indian Frontier Organisation), and in Kenya, 1922 (letters from Kenya); Lecturer for Oxford University (Extra-mural); Professor of English Language and Literature, University of Witwatersrand, South Africa, 1935. *Publications:* Without Prejudice: Essays in Prose and Verse, 1929; and other volumes, articles, and plays. *Recreations:* mountaineering, travel, etc. *Address:* Alveston Lodge, Alveston, Warwickshire. *Clubs:* East India and Sports; Himalayan (New Delhi). [*Died* 5 *June* 1964.

DUNN, William Norman; retired on pension, 1927; *b.* 9 April 1873; *s.* of late J. W. Dunn, Castle Hill, Newport Road, Stafford; *m.* 1926, Kathleen (*d.* 1951), *yr. d.* of late Rev. A. M. Fosbrooke, Homes of St. Barnabas, Dormans, Surrey; one *s.* (one *d.* decd.). *Educ.:* Shrewsbury; Trinity Coll., Cambridge. Vice-Consul at Bangkok, 1907; Puket, 1911; Consul at Senggora, 1914; Saigon, 1916; employed in Embassy at Washington, end of 1916; Consul-General at Batavia, 1917; Rotterdam, 1921; Cologne, 1924-27. *Address:* Kingsbury Croft, Lyme Regis, Dorset. *T.:* Lyme Regis 230. [*Died* 11 *Feb.* 1961.

DUNNE, Sir Laurence Rivers, Kt. 1948; M.C.; retired as Chief Metropolitan Magistrate (1948-60); Chairman, Berks Quarter Sessions, 1964-66 (Deputy Chairman, 1948-1964); *b.* 1893; *s.* of late Arthur Mountjoy Dunne, K.C.; *m.* 1922, Armorel (*d.* 1967), *d.* of late Col. Herman Le Roy-Lewis, C.B., C.M.G., D.S.O.; one *s.* one *d.* (both decd.). *Educ.:* Eton; Magdalen College, Oxford. *Address:* Kelsall House, Sunninghill, Berks. *T.:* Ascot 23123. *Club:* Garrick. [*Died* 30 *June* 1970.

DUNNE, Philip Russell Rendel; *b.* 28 Feb. 1904; *s.* of late Lt.-Col. Edward Marten Dunne; *m.* 1930, Margaret Ann Walker; two *s.* one *d.*; *m.* 1945, Audrey, *widow* of Bernard Rubin. *Educ.:* Eton; R.M.C., Sandhurst. 11th Hussars, 1924; Royal Horse Guards, 1929-1933; M.P (U.) Stalybridge and Hyde Division of County of Cheshire, 1935-37; Joint-Master of the Warwickshire Hounds, seasons 1932-33, 1933-34 and 1934-35. *Recreations:* hunting, shooting, racing. *Address:* Old Parsonage, East Clandon, Surrey. *T.:* Clandon 193. *Clubs:* Turf, White's. [*Died* 13 *April* 1965.

DUNNETT, George Sinclair, C.M.G. 1954; O.B.E. 1946; Secretary, Commonwealth Economic Committee, since 1946; *b.* 19 March 1906; *e. s.* of late David S. Dunnett, Westerton, Dunbartonshire; unmarried. *Educ.:* Hillhead High School; Glasgow University. Empire Marketing Board, 1927-1933; Imperial Economic Committee, 1933-1939; Ministry of Food, 1939-46. *Recreation:* amateur cinematography. *Address:* 16A Lee Terrace, S.E.3. *T.:* Lee Green 3910. *Club:* Caledonian. [*Died* 5 *July* 1964.

DUNNICLIFF, Rev. Canon Edward Frederick Holwell; Canon Residentiary of Hereford Cathedral since 1960; *b.* 1901; *s.* of Frederick John and Henrietta Woodford Holwell Dunnicliff, Long Eaton, Derbys.; *m.* 1925, Eveline, *d.* of Thomas Edward and Hannah Cunnington, Nottingham; two *s.* two *d.* *Educ.:* Nottingham High School; Worcester College, Oxford; St. Stephen's House, Oxford. Scholar, Worcester Coll., Oxford, 1919; St. Stephen's House, 1924; M.A. 1926. Deacon, 1924; Priest, Southwell, 1925. Service in Diocese of Southwell until 1955; Hon. Canon of Southwell, 1954. Chaplain and Educational Officer, R.A.F.V.R. 1942-45. Director of Training and Examining Chaplain to the Bishop of Hereford, 1959-. *Recreations:* music, philosophy, gardening. *Address:* The Canon's House, Hereford. *T.:* Hereford 5659. [*Died* 30 *Dec.* 1963.

DUNNING, Sir William Leonard, 2nd Bt., *cr.* 1930; *b.* 13 Nov. 1903; *o. c.* of Sir Leonard Dunning, 1st Bt. of Beedinglee, Horsham, Sussex, and Edith Muriel, *d.* of late William Tod; *S.* father, 1941; *m.* 1936, Kathleen Lawrie, *o. c.* of late J. Patrick Cuthbert, M.C., Barclayhills, by Perth; one *s.* one *d.* *Educ.:* Eton; Trinity College, Cambridge. Chartered Mechanical Engineer; A.M.I.Mech.E. Chairman, Executive Committee, Scottish Red Cross. *Recreation:* shooting. *Heir:* *s.* Simon William Patrick, *b.* 14 Dec. 1939. *Address:* Barclayhills, Guildtown, Perth, Scotland. *T.:* Scone 248. [*Died* 10 *Sept.* 1961.

DUNRAVEN and MOUNT-EARL, 6th Earl of, *cr.* 1822, **Richard Southwell Windham Robert Wyndham-Quin,** C.B. 1923; C.B.E. 1921; M.C.; Baron Adare, 1800; Viscount Mountearl, 1816; Viscount Adare, 1822; Bt. 1871; Captain, late 12th Royal Lancers; *b.* 18 May 1887; *er. s.* of 5th Earl and Lady Eva Constance Aline Bourke (*d.* 1940), *d.* of 6th Earl of Mayo; *S.* father, 1952; *m.* 1st, 1915, Helen (who obtained a divorce, 1932; she *d.* 1962), *d.* of John Swire, Hillingdon House, Harlow; 2nd, 1934, Nancy, *d.* of Thomas B. Yuille, of Halifax County, Virginia; one *s.* two *d.* *Educ.:* Winchester; R.M.C., Sandhurst. Served European War, 1914 (wounded, M.C.); Master of the Horse and Military Secretary to Lord-Lieut. of Ireland, 1918-1921; contested (C.) Newcastle upon Tyne Central Division, 1929. *Heir:* *s.* Viscount Adare. *Address:* Kilgobbin, Adare, Co. Limerick; (seat) Adare Manor, Adare, Co. Limerick. *T.:* Adare 18. *Clubs:* Turf, White's, Cavalry, Buck's; Kildare Street (Dublin); Royal Yacht Squadron (Cowes); Travellers' (Paris). [*Died* 28 *Aug.* 1965.

DUNROSSIL, 1st Viscount *cr.* 1959; **William Shepherd Morrison,** P.C. 1936; G.C.M.G. 1959; M.C.; Q.C. 1934; Governor-General of Australia since 1960; *b.* 10 Aug. 1893; *s.* of late John Morrison of Torinturk, Argyll; *m.* Katharine Allison, *d.* of late Rev. William Swan, D.D.; four *s.* *Educ.:* George Watson's College, Edinburgh; Edinburgh Univ. (M.A.). Served in R.F.A. in France 1914-18 (wounded, M.C., despatches thrice, 1914 Star); resigned commission with rank of Captain, 1919; President Edinburgh Univ. Union and Senior President Students' Representative Council, 1920; called to Bar, Inner Temple, 1923; Bencher, 1951. Contested Western Isles Div. of Inverness-shire, 1923 and 1924; M.P. (C.) Cirencester and Tewkesbury Div. of Glos., 1929-Oct. 1959; Mem. Medical Research Council and Industrial Health Research Board, 1931-36; Parliamentary Private Secretary to Attorney-General, 1931-35; Financial Secretary to the Treasury, 1935-36; Recorder of Walsall, 1935-36; Minister of Agriculture and Fisheries, 1936-39; Chancellor of the Duchy of Lancaster, 1939-40; Minister of Food, 1939-40; Postmaster-General, 1940-43; Minister of Town and Country Planning, 1943-45; Speaker of the House of Commons, Oct. 1951-59; Hon. LL.D. (Edinburgh,

Leeds, St. Andrews and London); Hon. F.R.C.S. (Edin.); Hon. M.I.Mun.E. *Publications:* miscellaneous articles and reviews. *Heir: s.* Hon. John William Morrison [*b.* 22 May 1926; *m.* 1951, Mavis Spencer-Payne; two *s.* one *d.*]. *Address:* Government House, Canberra, A.C.T. *Clubs:* Carlton, (Hon.) Oxford and Cambridge, (Hon.) Savage; (Hon.) New (Cheltenham); Cirencester Golf (Pres.); Royal Mid-Surrey Golf. [*Died* 3 *Feb.* 1961.

DUNSTAN, Albert Ernest, D.Sc.; *b.* Sheffield, Jan. 1878; *e. s.* of late Arthur Dunstan; *m.* Louisa Cleaverley (*d.* 1963); one *s.* one *d. Educ.:* Royal Grammar School, Sheffield (Foundation Scholar); Univ. College, Sheffield (Corporation of Sheffield Scholar); studied at Royal College of Science and Univ. College, London. Doctor of Science (London), 1910; Examiner in Petroleum Technology to the Universities of Oxford, London, Birmingham, Sheffield, and Edinburgh; Fellow and late Member of Council of Chemical Society of London; Past Pres. British Association of Chemists; Fellow and Vice-President Royal Institute of Chemistry; Vice-Pres. and Member of Council of Society of Chemical Industry and Past President Institute of Petroleum; late Member of Council of Institute of Fuel; Hon. Chairman of Committee on Petroleum Products, American Society for Testing Materials; late Member of H.M. Fuel Research Board and British National Delegate, World Power Conference; British National Delegate, Second World Petroleum Conference; Chairman Petroleum Committee of the Imperial Institute Mineral Resources Division; late Chief Chemist of the Anglo-Iranian Oil Company and Director, National Oil Refineries, Ltd.; Mem. of General Council British Standards Institution; Member Royal Institution; Redwood Medallist, Institute of Petroleum. *Publications:* Practical Chemistry for Technical Institutes; Organic Chemistry; The Viscosity of Liquids; several text-books on Chemistry; Cantor Lectures on Petroleum, 1928; Gluckstein Lecturer, Royal Inst. of Chemistry, 1931, and Jubilee Memorial Lecturer, Society of Chemical Industry, 1932; many publications on Chemical Research in British and foreign journals; contributor to Encyclopedia Britannica and Thorpe's Dictionary of Applied Chemistry and Managing Editor of Science of Petroleum. *Address:* 2 Luard Rd., Cambridge. *T.:* Cambridge 48997. *Club:* Chemical. [*Died* 6 *Jan.* 1964.

DUNSTAN, Edgar Grieve; Secretary, Friends' Home Service Cttee., 1935-52; Editor of The Wayfarer, Quaker Monthly Journal, 1929-45, incorporating Quaker World Service (1934); Gov. Hollington Park School, St. Leonards-on-Sea, since 1950; *b.* 20 April 1890; *s.* of late Edgar Augustus Dunstan; *m.* 1918, Jessie Florence Bettison; one *s.* one *d. Educ.:* Stationers' Company School and privately. On staff of Methodist Recorder, 1907-16; Public Opinion, 1917-18; in charge of publicity of Friends' (Quaker) War Victims Relief work, 1919-23; visited fields in 1922; established own publicity service, 1920. *Publications:* Quakers and the Religious Quest, 1956. Articles and reviews in Quaker and similar publications. *Recreation:* reading. *Address:* 23 Hartington Grove, Cambridge. *T.:* Cambridge 47482. [*Died* 6 *Dec.* 1963.

DUNSTAN, Victor Joseph, M.A.; Headmaster, Carlisle Grammar School, 1932-62; *b.* 1899; *s.* of Joseph Dunstan, Lincoln; *m.* 1922, Elsie Kathleen, *d.* of W. H. Smith, Lincoln; one *d. Educ.:* Lincoln School; Pembroke College, Cambridge (Major open Scholarship in Classics, 1916). Military training, 1917-18; served European War in France as 2nd Lt. 42nd Siege Battery R.G.A., 1918-19; Pembroke College, Cambridge 1919-21, Porson Prize for Greek Iambics, 1st Class Hon., Classical Tripos, Part I. Beatson Scholar 1920; 2nd Class Hon. Division I, Historical Tripos, Part II 1921; VI. Form Assistant master in Classics, Hereford Cathedral School, 1921-28; Vice-Principal, Liverpool Collegiate School, 1928-32; Flight Lt. in R.A.F.V.R. as C.O. 1862 Squadron (2nd Carlisle) A.T.C. 1943-1944. Lay Reader, Diocese of Carlisle, 1946. Member Carlisle City Council, 1963-. *Address:* 7 Eden Mount, Stanwix, Carlisle. [*Died* 15 *Feb.* 1970.

DUNWOODY, Robert Browne, C.B.E. 1924 (O.B.E. 1920); Secretary Association of British Chambers of Commerce, 1912-46; *b.* 1879; *s.* of late Robert Dunwoody, J.P., Belfast; *m.* 1914, Ethel Fanny (*d.* 1943), *d.* of late John A. Hanna, J.P., of Belfast; one *s.* one *d. Educ.:* Royal Academical Institution, and Campbell College, Belfast. A.M.I.C.E.; F.R.G.S.; F.C.I.S.; past President and Hon. Secretary of Association of Secretaries of British Chambers of Commerce, and a Life Member of International Commission of Permanent Association of International Navigation Congresses, Brussels (Hon. Secretary, London Congress, 1923); trained as civil engineer; Assistant Engineer, Mourne Mountains, Belfast and other water schemes, 1900-3; Engineering Assistant to Royal Commission on London Traffic, 1903-5, and to Advisory Board of Engineers to Royal Commission, 1904-1906; Engineer, Royal Commission on Canals and Waterways, 1906-11; appointed Secretary by Royal Warrant, 1910; Secretary, Government Canal Control Committee, during European War (O.B.E.), and a Member of Ministry of Transport Waterways Committee, 1920-21; Hon. Sec. All-British Delegation to Virginia, May-June 1927; Adviser Economic Consultative Committee League of Nations, 1928, 1929; Secretary, British Preparatory Committee for Imperial Conference, 1930; Secretary to Industrial Advisers to U.K. Delegation Imperial Economic Conference, Ottawa, 1932; Secretary to the Panel of Advisers to the United Kingdom Delegation to the World Monetary and Economic Conference, London, 1933. *Publications:* The Trade Policies and Tariff systems of the British Dominions, Colonies and Protectorates, 1930; Youth's Opportunity, 1928; Chambers of Commerce, Their Constitution and Work, 1935; Reports on the Water Supplies of the "Cross" Canal Routes for the Royal Commission on Canals, Report, Vol. X. 1911 (Cd. 5447); Registration of Business Names, 1961; Economic Requirements for Inland Navigation Transport in the British Isles. *Recreations:* tennis, golf, fishing, painting. *Address:* Runnington, Tadworth, Surrey. *T.:* Tadworth 2030. *Club:* Royal Societies. [*Died* 1 *Jan.* 1966.

DUPUY, Pierre, C.C. (Canada) 1967; C.M.G. 1943; *b.* 9 July 1896; *m.* 1922, Thérèse Ferron; one *s.* one *d. Educ.:* St. Mary's Coll.; Univ. of Montreal, Licencié en droit; Univ. of Paris, L. ès. L.; International Law. Secretary of Canadian Commissioner-General's Office, 1921-29; First Sec. Canadian Legation, Paris, 1928-40; Chargé d'Affaires Belgium Netherlands, France, 1940-43; Chargé d'Affaires to Belgium, the Netherlands, Poland, Czechoslovakia, and Norway; Counsellor of Embassy for Canada in Brussels, 1945; Canadian Ambassador to the Netherlands 1947-52 (Minister, 1945-47); Canadian Ambassador to Italy, 1952-58; Canadian Ambassador to France, 1958-63. Comr.-Gen. of Canadian World Exhibn., 1963-67. Président de la Societé Internationale des Écrivains de Langue Française, Paris. Canada Medal, 1968. *Recreations:* swimming and yachting. *Address:* Résidence Alexandra Palace, Avenue d'Antibes, 06 Cannes, France. [*Died* 21 *May* 1969.

DURDEN, James, R.O.I.; Painter of Portraits, Landscapes and Subject Pictures; *b.* Manchester; *m.* Ruby Valentina, *d.* of late J.

Ellis, Keswick; one *s.* one *d.* *Educ.:* Manchester; Royal College of Art, London. Exhibitor at Royal Academy and Institute of Painters in Oil Colours, also at Manchester, Liverpool, Glasgow and other Galleries; Silver Medal, Paris Salon (Artistes Français), 1927. *Address:* Millbeck Place, Keswick, Cumberland. *T.:* Keswick 2206. [*Died* 9 *Nov.* 1964.

DURHAM, 5th Earl of (*cr.* 1833), **John Frederick Lambton;** Baron Durham, 1828; Viscount Lambton, 1833; Capt. late Northumberland Fusiliers; *b.* 1884; *er. s.* of 4th Earl; *S.* father, 1929; *m.* 1st, 1919, Diana, (*d.* 1924) *o. d.* of Granville Farquhar, of Dalton Hall, Beverley; one *s.*; 2nd, 1931, Hermione, *d.* of late Sir George Bullough, 1st Bt.; one *s.* *Educ.:* Eton. Served European War, 1914-15 (wounded). *Heir: s.* Viscount Lambton. *Address:* Lambton Castle, Fence Houses, Durham; Fenton, Wooler, Northumberland; West Marden Hall, Chichester. *Club:* Jockey (Newmarket). [*Died* 4 *Feb.* 1970.

DURNFORD, Lieutenant-General Cyril Maton Periam, C.B. 1945; C.I.E. 1942; Indian Army (Retired); *b.* 29 September 1891; *s.* of Maton Durnford, Bristol, and Maria Louisa Periam, Bampton, North Devon. *Educ.:* Merchant Venturers School, Bristol. Indian Army from 1914 (Rajputana Rifles); served in France, Mesopotamia, Palestine; N.W. Frontier of India, 1923; Iraq, 1920-22 (Arab Insurrection); N.W. Frontier of India, 1926-30 and 1938 (despatches 4 times); Staff College, Camberley, 1924-25; Naval College, Greenwich, 1930; Imperial Defence College, 1937; Q.M.G. in India 1945-46; retd. 1947. Chinese Order of Cloud and Banner, 1946. *Publications:* Gold Medal Essay of United Service Institution of India, 1926 and 1935. *Address:* c/o Lloyds Bank, 6 Pall Mall, S.W.1. *T.:* (Residence) Bath 63379. *Clubs:* United Service; Bath and County (Bath). [*Died* 21 *March* 1965.

DURNFORD, Hugh George Edmund, M.C.; Fellow King's College, Cambridge; *b.* 4 June 1886; *s.* of late Richard Durnford, C.B., and Beatrice Emma Selby; *m.* 1919, Margaret, *d.* of General Sir William Meiklejohn, K.C.B., K.C.M.G.; two *d.* *Educ.:* Eton (scholar); King's College, Cambridge (Scholar), 1st class Classical Tripos, 1908. In business (India), 1909-15. Served European War, 1914-18, R.F.A., captured and escaped from Germany (M.C.). Bursar, King's College, Cambridge, 1919-35; Joint Hon. Sec., Cambridge Preservation Society, 1928-33. Retired from Cambridge, 1935. R.A.F. Education Officer, 1938-39; R.A.F.V.R. (Intelligence), 1939-46. *Publications:* Tunnellers of Holzminden; Escapers All (part). *Address:* Broadford House, Stratfield Turgis, Basingstoke. *T.:* Turgis Green 265. [*Died* 6 *June* 1965.

DURNFORD, Vice-Adm. (retd.) John Walter, C.B. 1947; *b.* 25 Oct. 1891; *s.* of Richard Durnford, C.B., Hartley Wespall House, Basingstoke; *m.* 1936, Marie de Lancey, *e. d.* of Rupert Greene, Melbourne. *Educ.:* R.N. Colleges, Osborne and Dartmouth. Commander, 1928; Capt. 1935; Imperial Defence College, 1936; Chief Staff Officer, Malta, 1937-39; commanded H.M.S. Suffolk, 1939-40; Second Naval Member, Australian Commonwealth Naval Board, 1941-42; commanded H.M.S. Resolution, 1942-43; Director, R.N. Staff College, 1944; Director of Naval Training, Admiralty, 1945-47; Vice-Adm. retd. 1948. Governor: St. Peter's, St. Paul's and St. Philip's Hospitals, 1950; Star and Garter Home, Richmond, 1952. Mayor of Chelsea, 1962-63; Chm., Chelsea Soc., 1964-. Order of Cloud and Banner (China). *Address:* 12 More's Garden, Cheyne Walk, S.W.3. *T.:* Flaxman 8561. *Clubs:* United Service, M.C.C., Chelsea Arts. [*Died* 7 *Feb.* 1967.

DURRANT, Major-General James Murdoch Archer, C.M.G. 1918; D.S.O. 1917; A.M.F. retired; *b.* Glenelg, South Australia, 17 March 1885; *s.* of Jonathan William Durrant and Margaret Elizabeth Durrant, Adelaide; *m.* 1911, Clara Ellen, *d.* of Henry Birk, Westmead, N.S.W. *Educ.:* private tutor; Adelaide University. Joined permanent staff Australian Military Forces (after eight years' Militia service), 1907; Lieutenant 1910; Captain 1914; Captain and Adjutant 13th Batt. Australian Imperial Force, 1914; landed at Anzac, 1915, and served through Gallipoli campaign; Major, 1915; commanded 13th Batt. for four months (Order of White Eagle of Serbia, 4th Class, with swords, brevet Major in Australian Permanent Forces for services in Gallipoli); served in Egypt and France as Brigade-Major, 4th Australian Infantry Brigade, for eight months; promoted Lt.-Col. and to command 13th Batt. A.I.F. 1916 (despatches five times, D.S.O., C.M.G.); A.A. and Q.M.G. 2nd Australian Division, 1917; A.D.C. to the Governor-General of Australia, 1935; Director of Supplies and Transport, Army Headquarters, Australia, 1935-37; Commander of Field Troops and Base Commandant, 6th Military District Tasmania, 1937-39; G.O.C. Western Command, Australia, 1939-41; G.O.C. Northern Command (Queensland), 1941-43; retired, 1944. *Address:* 15 Jersey Ave., Penshurst, N.S.W. *Club:* Imperial Service (Syd.). [*Died* 18 *Aug.* 1963.

DURST, Alan Lydiat, A.R.A. 1953; Sculptor; *b.* 1883; 2nd *s.* of late Rev. Canon William Durst; *m.* 1918, Clare Butler (*d.* 1967); no *c.* *Educ.:* Marlborough Coll.; Switzerland. Commissioned in R.M.L.I. and served for several years, mainly at sea; left the Service to take up art, and studied at Central School of Arts and Crafts, London, and in Chartres; re-joined Marines for both wars, serving during War of 1939-45 at Admiralty. Started to practise as a sculptor in 1920, working almost entirely as a direct carver in stone, wood and ivory. One-man shows at Leicester Galleries, 1930 and 1935. Taught wood carving at R.C.A., 1925-48 (except war years). Mem. London Group, 1928-51. Represented in Tate Gallery; Glasgow, Manchester, Bradford city galleries; Maritime Museum, Greenwich; Thomas J. Watson Gallery, New York; private collections. Work purchased under terms of the Chantrey Bequest, 1965. Has work on or in many churches and schools, including Canterbury, Winchester, Peterborough, Manchester and Llandaff Cathedrals; R.A.D.A., and Merchant Taylors' Sch. *Publications:* Wood Carving (How-to-do-it series) 1938 (2nd edn. 1948, new revised edn., 1959). *Recreations:* sight-seeing at home and abroad. *Address:* 4 Wychcombe Studios, England's Lane, N.W.3. *T.:* Primrose 0515. [*Died* 22 *Dec.* 1970.

DURWARD, Archibald; Professor of Anatomy, University of Leeds, since 1936; Pro-Vice-Chancellor, University of Leeds, 1959-61; *b.* Denny, Scotland, 6 April 1902; *y. s.* of late Rev. P. C. Durward, M.A., and Elizabeth Wallace Durward; *m.* 1934, Dorothea, *e. d.* of A. E. Westlake, Lagos, Nigeria; one *s.* *Educ.:* Otago Boys' High School, Dunedin, N.Z.; Otago University (Medical Travelling Scholarship); Knox College, Dunedin, N.Z. M.B., Ch.B., 1925, M.D., with distinction, 1930; F.R.S.E.; House Surgeon Public Hospital, Dunedin, N.Z., 1927; Lecturer and Senior Demonstrator of Anatomy and sometime acting-Professor University of Otago, 1927-31; Lecturer in Anatomy and Senior Demonstrator University College, London, 1931-36. Sometime Examiner in Universities of New Zealand, London, Cambridge, Dublin and St. Andrews. *Publications:* various on Comparative Neurology;

The Peripheral Nervous System, in Cunningham's Textbook of Anatomy, 9th Ed.; Vascularity and Patterns of Growth in Biology of Hair Growth, 1958. *Recreation:* angling. *Address:* School of Medicine, Leeds. *Club:* Harrogate Flyfishers'. [*Died* 4 *March* 1964.

DUTHIE, Professor George Ian, Ph.D., D.Litt.; Regius (Chalmers) Professor of English Literature, University of Aberdeen, since 1955; *b.* 9 May 1915; *s.* of Alexander Duthie and Jane Josephine Isabella (*née* Ross); *m.* 1942, Margaret Bruce MacLean, *d.* of Simon MacLean, Beauly, Scotland; one *s.* one *d.* *Educ.:* Inverness Royal Academy; Univ. of Edinburgh. Edinburgh University: M.A. 1937; Ph.D. 1939; D.Litt. 1946; successively Carnegie Research Schol., Senior Schol., and Fellow, 1937-42; Asst. in English Language, 1939-42; Asst. Lecturer, English Language and Literature, Univ. of Bristol, 1943-44; Lectr. in English Literature, Univ. of Edinburgh, 1944-47; Molson Professor of English, McGill Univ., Montreal, Canada, 1947-54. F.R.S.C. 1954. *Publications:* The Bad Quarto of Hamlet, 1941; Shakespeare's King Lear: a Critical Edition, 1949; Elizabethan Shorthand and the First Quarto of King Lear, 1950; Shakespeare, 1951; The New Shakespeare: Romeo and Juliet, King Lear (jt. ed. with J. Dover Wilson), 1955, 1960; (ed.) Papers Mainly Shakespearian, 1964; articles in learned journals. *Address:* Department of English, University of Aberdeen. [*Died* 16 *June* 1967.

du TOIT, F. J.; Chairman: S.A. Oil from Coal Corp., 1951; S.A. Phosphate Development Corp., 1951; Deputy Chairman South African Iron & Steel Corporation; S.A. Steel Sales Co.; Advisory Committee, Development Northern Free State Gold Areas (1946); Union Defence Resources Board; Chancellor University of Potchefstroom; *b.* 25 Aug. 1897; *m.* 1924, Wilhelmina du Plessis; three *d.* *Educ.:* Paarl; Stellenbosch. Senior Economist, Department of Agriculture, Pretoria; S. African Trade Commissioner in London; Official Sec., Office of High Commissioner for Union of South Africa, London, 1938-43; Sec. Union Dept. Commerce and Industries, 1944-49; Professional Adviser, Minister of Economic Affairs, 1949-51; Chm. Council for Development of Natural Resources, 1948-56. *Recreation:* golf. *Address:* P.O. Box 2191, Pretoria, South Africa. *Clubs:* Pretoria, Pretoria Country (Pretoria); Civil Service, City (Cape Town); Rand (Johannesburg). [*Died* 17 *March* 1961.

du TOIT, P. J., F.R.S. 1951; B.A. (Stellenbosch) Ph.D. (Zürich), Dr. Med. Vet. (Berlin); hon. D.Sc. (Stellenbosch, Cape Town, Johannesburg, Utrecht); Hon. LL.D. (Glasgow and Rhodes University, Grahamstown); Hon. Associate R.C.V.S.; Hon. or Corresp. Member of Scientific Societies in France, Belgium, Holland, Britain and South Africa; *b.* Strand, Cape Province, 1888; *s.* of late D. F. du Toit; *m.* 1919, Dorothy Jakeman, Hereford, England; one *s.* three *d.* (one *d.* decd.), *Educ.:* Boys' High Sch., Wellington; Univs. of Stellenbosch, Halle, Berlin and Zürich. Sen. Veterinary Research Officer, 1919; Sub-Director of Veterinary Research and Prof. of Tropical Diseases, Univ. of Pretoria, 1920; Deputy Director, 1921; Director of Veterinary Services and Dean of Veterinary Faculty, 1927-48; Chairman of Senate of University of South Africa, 1924-1926; President S.A. Vet. Medical Assoc., 1924-30; President S.A. Biological Society, 1927; President S.A. Assoc. for the Advancement of Science, 1932; President of Section M of British Assoc. for the Advancement of Science, 1930; President Public Servants Assoc. of S.A., 1934-36; Pres. of African Regional Scientific Conf., Johannesburg, 1949; President South African Council for Scientific and Industrial Research, 1950-52. Chairman Scientific Council for Africa South of the Sahara, 1950-60; Pres., First Federal Science Congress, Salisbury, 1960. Senior Captain Scott Medal for Research in S.A., 1929; South Africa Medal and Grant, 1934; Bernhard Nocht Medal for Tropical Medicine, 1938; Havenga Prize for Medicine of Suid-Afrikaanse Akademie vir Wetenskap en Kuns, 1947; Official Delegate to several Internat. Veterinary and other Confs. in Europe, America, Britain and Australia. *Publications:* (joint) Tropical Diseases of Domestic Animals (in German); many scientific articles. *Recreations:* tennis, motoring. *Address:* S. Africa Council for Scientific and Industrial Research, P.O. Box 395, Pretoria, South Africa. *Club:* Pretoria (Pretoria). [*Died* 13 *Nov.* 1967.

DUTTON, Sir Ernest R.; *see* Rowe-Dutton.

DWYER, Sir John (Patrick), K.C.M.G., *cr.* 1949, Kt., *cr.* 1946; Chief Justice of Western Australia, 1946-59; Lieutenant-Governor of Western Australia and Dependencies, in the Commonwealth of Australia, since 1952; *b.* Gippsland, Australia, 1880; *s.* of Thomas Dwyer and Elizabeth Donaldson; *m.* 1908, Emily Louise Irgens; no *c.* *Educ.:* Geelong Coll.; Melbourne Univ. Admitted to W. Australian Bar, 1904. Served with 44th Australian Infantry, European War, 1914-1918. Puisne Judge of Supreme Court of Western Australia, 1929. K.St.J. (W.A. Commandery, instituted 1947). *Address:* 61 Mount Street, Perth, W. Australia. *Club:* Weld (Perth, W.A.). [*Died* 25 *Aug.* 1966.

DWYER-HAMPTON, Lt.-Col. Bertie Cunynghame, D.S.O. 1917, D.L., J.P.; late Royal Leicestershire Regt.; *b.* 1872; *e. s.* of late Capt. Robt. Hoare Dwyer, R.M.L.I., and Caroline Georgina Thurlow Cunynghame; *m.* 1st, 1906, Beryl (*d.* 1910), *e. d.* of W. Gillman, Rutland House, Southsea; one *s.*; 2nd, 1914, Mary Gwendolen Hampton (*d.* 1946), *e. d.* of late Col. Thomas Lewis Hampton Lewis, of Henllys and Bodior, Anglesey. *Educ.:* privately. Assumed by Royal License the additional name of Hampton, 1915; joined Leicestershire Regt., 1892; served in South Africa, 1899-1902, with Mounted Infantry and on Staff as signalling officer (despatches); European War, 1914-18, on the Staff (Brevet Lt.-Colonel, despatches, D.S.O.); High Sheriff, Anglesey, 1929. *Address:* Cartref, Beaumaris, Anglesey. *T.:* Beaumaris 316. *Clubs:* Army and Navy; Royal Anglesey Yacht (Beaumaris). [*Died* 9 *June* 1967.

DYETT, Sir Gilbert (Joseph Cullen), Kt., *cr.* 1934; C.M.G. 1927; Captain (retired) Australian Military Forces; *b.* Bendigo, 23 June 1891; *s.* of late B. P. Dyett; unmarried. *Educ.:* Marist Bros. Coll., Bendigo. Served European War, A.I.F. (wounded and invalided out, Lone Pine, Gallipoli). Organising Sec. of Vic. State Recruiting Cttee., 1917-18; Member Bd. of Management Aust. War Memorial, 1932-; Dominion Pres. British Empire Service League, 1921-46; Leader Aust. Deleg. to Foundation Conf., Capetown, 1921; to Biennial Confs., London, 1923, 1927 (Chm.), 1937; Melbourne, 1934 (Chm.). Member: Racecourses Licences Board of Victoria, 1931-51; Commonwealth Recruiting Secretariat. Life Gov. St. Vincent's Hosp., Vic., 1926; formerly mem. A.I.F. Canteens Funds Trust, Sir Samuel McCaughey bequest for education of soldiers' children, 1921-1946. Vice-Patron and Hon. Life Member R.S.S.A.I.L.A. (Federal Pres. 1919-46). Hon. Life Mem.: Melb. Racing Club, S. & S. Ex-Imperial Club. *Recreations:* cricket, walking, riding. *Address:* Halcyon, Olinda, Vic., Australia. *Clubs:* Melbourne Cricket, Victoria Racing. [*Died* 19 *Dec.* 1964.

DYKE, Sir Oliver Hamilton Augustus Hart, 8th Bt., *cr.* 1676; M.I.Mech.E.; *b.* 4 Sept. 1885; 3rd *s.* of Rt. Hon. Sir William Hart Dyke, 7th Bt., and Lady Emily Caroline Montagu, *d.* of 7th Earl of Sandwich; *S.* father, 1931; *m.* 1st, 1922, Millicent Zoë (marriage dissolved, 1944), *d.* of Dr. Mayston Bond; two *s.* one *d.*; 2nd, 1945, Mildred Turnour Berens, *widow* of Cecil Berens. *Educ.:* Harrow. Engineering. *Recreation:* tennis. *Heir:* *s.* Derek William Hart Dyke [*b.* 4 Dec. 1924; *m.* 1953, Dorothy Moses, Hamilton, Ont.; one *s.*]. *Address:* Lullingstone Castle, Eynsford, Kent. *T.:* Farningham 2114. [*Died* 9 *July* 1969.

DYNES, Brigadier, Ernest, C.B.E. 1957 (O.B.E. 1941); A.M.I.Mech.E.; late R.A.S.C.; *b.* 30 March 1903; *s.* of late William James Dynes, Bedford; *m.* 1930, Vera Maud, *d.* of A. Warner, Northampton; one *d.* *Educ.:* Bedford Modern; R.M.C. 2nd Lt., R.A.S.C., 1924. Served War of 1939-45; A.D.S. & T. Malaya and S.W. Pacific Commands; A.Q.M.G. Ceylon Army Command; Lt.-Col. 1941 (O.B.E.). Colonel 1946; Brigadier 1951; D.S.T., H.Q., Northern Army Group, 1954-57; A.D.C. to the Queen, 1955-57. Secretary, Ipswich Golf Club; Hon. Sec. Suffolk County Golf Union. *Recreations:* golf, cricket. *Address:* Binnakandy, Colchester Road, Ipswich. [*Died* 21 *June* 1968.

DYNEVOR, 8th Baron (*cr.* 1780). **Charles Arthur Uryan Rhys,** C.B.E. 1962; M.C.; D.L.; J.P.; a Governor of the National Museum of Wales; President of the University College of South Wales since 1960; Chairman, Milford Haven Conservancy Board since 1958; Deputy Chairman Sun Insurance Office and Sun Life Assurance, 1953; Director: Richard Thomas & Baldwins; Sun Alliance Insurance Ltd.; Mem. Welsh Advisory Cttee. on Civil Aviation; *b.* 21 Sept. 1899; *e. s.* of 7th Baron Dynevor and Lady Margaret Child-Villiers (*d.* 1959), *e. d.* of 7th Earl of Jersey; *S.* father 1956; *m.* 1934, Hope Mary Woodbine Soames, *d.* of late Charles W. Parish; one *s.* *Educ.:* Eton; R.M.C., Sandhurst. Formerly Captain Grenadier Guards (Reserve of Officers), employed 1918-20 and 1939-45; served N. Russia, 1919 (M.C., Order of St. Anne of Russia); M.P. (C.) Romford Division of Essex, 1923-29; Guildford Division of Surrey, 1931-35; Parliamentary Private Secretary to the Prime Minister, 1927-29; contested (C.) North Islington, 1945; Chairman, Cities of London and Westminster Conservative Association, 1948-60 (Pres. 1962); Mem. Deptl. Cttee. on Home Grown Timber, 1954. D.L. 1925, J.P. 1931, Carmarthenshire. *Heir:* *s.* Hon. Richard Charles Uryan Rhys [*b.* 19 June 1935; *m.* 1959, Lucy Catherine King, *o. c.* of Sir John Rothenstein, C.B.E.]. *Address:* 76 Eaton Square, S.W.1. *T.:* Belgravia 6507; Dynevor Castle, Llandeilo, Carmarthenshire *T.:* Llandeilo 2169. *Club:* Carlton. [*Died* 15 *Dec.* 1962.

DYSON, Edward Trevor, C.M.G. 1943; *b.* 17 Sept. 1886; *s.* of Edward Alfred Dyson; *m.* 1912, Bertha Kelsey (M.B.E. 1946); one *s.* (one *d.* decd.). *Educ.:* Ruthin Grammar School; U.C.W. Aberystwyth (B.A.); Jesus College, Oxford (B.A.). Entered Ceylon Civil Service, 1910; Government Agent, North Central Province, 1928, Northern Province, 1930, Central Province, Ceylon, 1939-46. *Recreation:* gardening. *Address:* 11 South Dene, Westbury-on-Trym, Bristol. *T.:* Bristol 681195. *Club:* Royal Over-Seas League [*Died* 13 *Dec.* 1969.

DYSON, Sir George, K.C.V.O., *cr.* 1953; Kt., *cr.* 1941; M.A., Mus.D.(Oxon), Hon. LL.D.: Aberdeen, Leeds; F.R.C.M.; Hon. R.A.M.; Hon. F.M.A.; Hon. Fell. Imperial College of Science; *b.* 1883; *m.* Mildred, *d.* of F. W. Atkey; one *s.* one *d.* *Educ.:* Royal College of Music (Scholar). Mendelssohn Travelling Scholar; Director of Music, R.N. College, Osborne, 1908; Marlborough College, 1911; Lt. R. Fusiliers, 1914-1917; Major, R.A.F., 1919-20; Wellington College, 1921-24; Master of Music, Winchester College, 1924-37; Director, Royal College of Music, 1937-52; Alsop Lecturer, Liverpool University, 1926; Cramb Lecturer, Glasgow University, 1927; Northcliffe Lecturer in English Literature, London University, 1946; President, Conference of Educational Associations, 1934; First President, National Federation of Music Societies; Trustee, Carnegie United Kingdom Trust; a Governor of Sadler's Wells; Member of Royal Commission of 1851 Exhibition. Freedom of Winchester, 1963. *Publications:* The New Music; The Progress of Music; Fiddling while Rome burns; Orchestral and Choral Music; In Honour of the City, 1928; The Canterbury Pilgrims, 1931; St. Paul's Voyage, 1933; The Blacksmiths, 1934; Nebuchadnezzar, 1935; Symphony, 1937; Quo Vadis, 1939; Violin Concerto, 1942; Concerto da Camera and Concerto da Chiesa for Strings, 1949; Concerto Leggiero for Piano and Strings, 1951; Sweet Thames run softly, 1954; Agincourt, 1955; Hierusalem, 1956; Let's go a-Maying, 1958; A Xmas Garland, 1959. *Address:* 1 St. James' Terrace, Winchester. *Club:* Athenæum. [*Died* 28 *Sept.* 1964.

E

EADE, Charles (Stanley); Director of Associated Newspapers Ltd. (Daily Mail, etc.) since 1947; an Underwriting Member of Lloyd's; *b.* 10 June 1903; *s.* of Arthur and Alice Eade; *m.* 1941, Vera Manwaring; one *s.* two *d.* Member of Editorial Staffs: Daily Chronicle, Lloyd's Weekly News, 1917-1919; Daily Herald, 1919-22; Daily Mirror, 1922-30; Sunday Pictorial, 1922-24; Observer, 1926-1930; Proprietor, East Ham Echo and South Essex Mail, 1928. World travel, 1930-32. Sports Editor and later Dep. Ed., Sunday Express, 1932-33; Dep. Ed., Sunday Graphic, 1933-36; Dep. Ed., Daily Sketch, 1936-38; Editor, Sunday Dispatch, 1938-57. Radio and film commentator on sports and other subjects, 1932-38; Public Relations Adviser to Adm. Earl Mountbatten, Supreme Allied Comdr. S.E. Asia; organised public relations systems, newspaper and radio services for troops in India, Burma and Ceylon, 1933-34. Mem. Press Council, 1956-57 and 1961-; Mem. Council of Commonwealth Press Union; Director: Associated Rediffusion Ltd., 1957-58; Television Corp. Ltd. (Sydney, Aust.); Empire Printing Ink Co. Ltd.; Taylor Bros. Wharfage Co. Ltd.; Northcliffe Developments Ltd.; Plainpaper Ltd. Comdr. Order of St. Sava (Yugo-Slavia), 1943. *Publications:* Edited into book form War Speeches of Sir (then Mr.) Winston Churchill: The Unrelenting Struggle, 1942; The End of the Beginning, 1943; Onwards to Victory, 1944; The Dawn of Liberation, 1945; Victory, 1946; Secret Session Speeches, 1946. Editor: Churchill by His Contemporaries, 1953. *Recreation:* foreign travel. *Address:* Bleak House, Broadstairs, Kent. *T.:* Thanet 62224. *Clubs:* Carlton, Press. [*Died* 27 *Aug.* 1964.

EADY, Sir (Crawfurd) Wilfrid Griffin, G.C.M.G., *cr.* 1948 (C.M.G. 1932); K.C.B., *cr.* 1942 (C.B. 1934); K.B.E., *cr.* 1939; Director: Richard Thomas and Baldwins; *b.*

Sept. 1890; *s.* of late G. Griffin Eady, M.I.C.E.; *m.* 1915, Elisabeth Margaret (Member of Council, Bedford College; Officier d'Académie), *d.* of late Max Laistner; two *s.* *Educ.:* Clifton Coll.; Jesus Coll., Cambridge (Classical Honours), Hon. Fellow, 1945. Open Civil Service Examination, 1913; Junior Clerk, India Office; Junior Clerk, Home Office, 1914; Private Sec. to Controller, Foreign Trade Dept., 1917; to Sec., Min. of Labour, 1917; to Minister of Labour, 1919; Secretary Industrial Transference Board, 1928; Principal Assistant Secretary Ministry of Labour, 1929-34; Secretary Unemployment Assistance Board, 1934-38; Deputy Under-Secretary of State, Home Office, 1938-40; Deputy Chairman, 1940-41, and Chairman, 1941-42, of Board of Customs and Excise; Joint Second Secretary, Treasury, 1942-52. Director of the Old Vic Trusts and of Glyndebourne Arts Trust; a Governor London School of Economics and of Westminster School. *Recreations:* usual, *Address:* Hill Farm House, Rodmell, Lewes, Sussex. *T.:* Lewes 1568. *Club:* Oxford and Cambridge. [*Died* 9 *Jan.* 1962.

EAGAR, Waldo McGillycuddy, C.B.E. 1945; Secretary-General, National Institute for the Blind, 1928-49; Sec. British Wireless for the Blind Fund, 1930-49; *b.* 17 June 1884; *m.* 1916, Emily Isabel, *d.* of Walter Heald. *Educ.:* Exeter School; Exeter College, Oxford. B.A. 1907; M.A. 1940; Public Schoolmaster and Private Tutor, 1907-12; Sub-Warden, Oxford and Bermondsey Club, 1912-14, Warden, 1919-21; Assistant Director, Central and Borstal Associations, 1914-19; served European War, Lieut. R.F.A., France, 1917-18; Inspector, London Housing Board, 1919-21; Sec. Garden Cities and Town Planning Assoc., 1921-23; Sec. Liberal Land Enquiry, 1923-1927; Gen. Sec. Land and Nation League, 1926-27; Sec. Liberal Industrial Enquiry, 1926-28; Hon. Editor The Boy, 1927-43; Vice-President: British Assoc. of Residential Settlements; Nat. Assoc. of Boys' Clubs; London Federation of Boys' Clubs, Surrey Assoc. of Boys' Clubs; Lucas Tooth Physical Training Institute; Royal Commonwealth Society for the Blind; Hon. Life Member of World Council for Welfare of Blind; Manager, Mayford L.C.C. School; Governor Woolpits School. *Publications:* Unemployment among Boys (with H. A. Secretan), 1925; The Land and the Nation, 1925; Towns and the Land, 1925; The Farmer and his Market (with Sir Francis Acland), 1928; Making Men, 1953; Ewhurst Church, 1959; contributor to: Liberal Points of View, 1927; Britain's Industrial Future, 1928; and to newspapers and magazines on Social Welfare subjects. *Recreations:* gardening and Church architecture. *Address:* c/o Westminster Bank, 21 Golder's Green Rd., N.W.11. [*Died* 2 *Jan.* 1966.

EAGER, Sir Clifden Henry Andrews, K.B.E., *cr.* 1952; Kt., *cr.* 1945; Q.C.; Barrister-at-law; *b.* 14 June 1882; *s.* of late Rev. Clifden Henry Eager, Melbourne, Congregational Minister, and Kate Amelia Andrews; *m.* 1909, Ernestine Isabella May, *d.* of John Campton; four *s.* (one *d.* decd.). *Educ.:* State schools; privately; Melbourne University (LL.M. 1910). Admitted to Victorian Bar, 1911; K.C. 1935; New South Wales Bar, 1939; Minister without Portfolio, Victoria, 1935; Unofficial Leader of Legislative Council, 1937-1943. Member State War Advisory Council, 1940-45; President, Legislative Council of Victoria, 1943-58 (M.L.C., 1930-58); Past Pres., Roy. Soc. of St. George, Melbourne. Life Governor and Past Pres. Trinity Gram. Sch., Kew. Director: Investors Pty. Ltd.; Pearl Assurance Co. Ltd. (Victorian Bd.); Chm. Sir William Angliss Charitable Trust. *Recreations:* golf; formerly rowing. *Address:* 13 Howard Street, Kew, Victoria, Australia. *Club:* Royal Automobile (Victoria). [*Died* 11 *Aug.* 1969.

EALES, Shirley, C.M.G. 1935; C.B.E. 1928 (O.B.E. 1922); *b.* Dewsbury, Yorkshire, 6 June 1883; 2nd *surv. s.* of late Rev. George Eales; *m.* Winifred Anne, *er. d.* of late Hubert J. Roberts, J.P.; one *s.* two *d.* Served South African War, 1899-1902; entered H.M. Colonial Service, 1902; Assistant Imperial Secretary, 1923-1931; Imperial Secretary, 1931-32; Administrative Secretary to High Commissioner for South Africa, 1932-34; member and Deputy Chairman, Rhodesia Railway Commission, 1935-49; retired 1949. *Address:* 2 Mountain View, Beach Road, Fish Hoek, C.P., S. Africa. *Clubs:* Bulawayo (S. Rhodesia); Royal Automobile (S. Africa). [*Died* 29 *Sept.* 1963.

EARDLEY, Joan (Kathleen Harding), R.S.A. 1963 (A.R.S.A. 1956); Artist-painter; *b.* 18 May 1921; *d.* of William Edwin Eardley. *Educ.:* St. Helens, Blackheath London. Glasgow School of Art, 1940-43. Works bought by: Scottish National Gallery of Modern Art, Huddersfield Art Gallery, Arts Council of Great Britain, Glasgow Art Gallery, Birmingham City Art Gallery, Aberdeen Art Gallery, Contemporary Art Society, South London Art Gallery. *Address:* 18 Catterline, Stonehaven, Kincardineshire, Scotland. [*Died* 16 *Aug.* 1963.

EARDLEY-WILMOT, Sir John, 4th Bt., *cr.* 1821; Capt. late 5th Batt. Rifle Brigade; *e. s.* of 3rd Bt. and Mary, 3rd *d.* of David Watts Russell of Biggin, Oundle, Northants; *b.* 14 Oct. 1882; *S.* father, 1896; *m.* 1916, Amabel (*d.* 1961), *d.* of Elverton Chapman, N.Y.; one *d.* *Educ.:* Eton. Served South African War, 1902 (King's Medal and two clasps); European War, 1914-15 (wounded). *Heir:* *nephew* John Assheton Eardley-Wilmot, D.S.C. 1943, Comdr. R.N. [*b.* 2 Jan. 1917; *m.* 1939, Diana Elizabeth, *yr. d.* of Comdr. Aubrey Moore, R.N.; one *s.* one *d.*]. *Address:* 52 Pelham Court, S.W.3. [*Died* 9 *Feb.* 1970.

EARDLEY-WILMOT, May; *b.* 1883; *d.* of late Rear-Admiral Sir S. Eardley-Wilmot. *Educ.:* Heidelberg. Lyric-writer from 1906; Lecturer and Leader of community singing. Member, Performing Right Society. *Publications:* Lyrics of popular songs: Little Grey Home in the West, Rose of My Heart, Coming Home, The Road of Looking Forward, What a Wonderful World it would be; poems: Voice from Dunkirk. *Recreations:* reading, travelling. *Address:* 47 Park Avenue, Bromley, Kent. [*Died* 3 *June* 1970.

EARENGEY, His Honour William George, Q.C. 1931; LL.D., B.A. (Lond.); Senator of University of London, 1950-58; *o. surv. s.* of James and Emma Earengey; *m.* Florence How, B.A. (now J.P. for the County of London and Barrister-at-Law); one *d.* *Educ.:* Cheltenham Grammar School. Solicitor for some years; called to Bar, Middle Temple, 1919 (Certificate of Honour); Recorder of Tewkesbury, 1930-31; of Dudley, 1931-34; Judge of County Courts, Circuit 41 (Clerkenwell), 1934-49. *Publications:* The Law of Hire Purchase, 1938; Editor of 11th Edition (1946) of Mayne on Damages. *Address:* Ashley Rise, Brackendale Road, Camberley, Surrey. *T.:* Camberley 21235. [*Died* 12 *April* 1961.

EARLE, Brig. Eric Greville, D.S.O. 1915; D.L.; Brig. (Retd. Pay) late R.A.; p.s.c.; *b.* 24 Feb. 1893; *s.* of late Lieut. C. A. Earle, R.A.; *m.* 1st, 1918, Noel Downes Martin (from whom he obtained a divorce, 1930); three *s.* (and one *s.* decd.); 2nd, 1931, Diana Mary Harley (*d.* 1964). *Educ.:* Lockers

Park; Wellington Coll.; R.M.A. Woolwich; Staff College, Camberley. Entered Army, 1912; Lieut. 1915; Adjt. 1915; Staff Capt., R.A., 1915; Capt. 1916; Bt. Maj. and Maj. 1931; Bt. Lt.-Col. 1935; Lt.-Col. 1939; Col. 1940; Brig. 1941. Served European War, 1914-18: Mons, Le Cateau (severely wounded, despatches twice, D.S.O.); returned to France 1915 (despatches twice); Somme, 3rd Ypres, St. Quentin, Villers Bretonneux (wounded), Afghan War, 1919 (medal and clasp). S.O., R.A., Eastern Command, 1929; D.A.A.G. 1931; G.S.O. 2, 48 Div., 1934; D.A.A.G., War Office, 1936; C.R.A., 3 Div., 1941; C.C.R.A., 1 Corps, 1942; B.R.A., 1943; C.R.A., Gibraltar, 1944; acting Governor of Gibraltar, Feb.-Mar. 1945. County Councillor, 1949-52; County Scout Comr., 1951-61; Sector Commander, Home Guard, 1952. High Sheriff for Bucks., 1953-54; D.L. Bucks., 1953. Chevalier Order of Leopold and Belgian Croix de Guerre, 1917; 1914 Star, Brit. War Medal, 1919; Italy Star, Defence Medal, British War Medal, 1939-45. *Publications:* has written for Bystander as "Staff Officer"; R.A. Journal as Martin Gale. History of 20th Divisional Artillery, 1914-18. *Recreations:* Master Staff College Draghounds, 1927-28; stalking, shooting. *Address:* Walton Hall, Bletchley, Bucks. *T.:* Milton Keynes 214. *Clubs:* United Services; Roehampton; M.C.C. [*Died* 19 *Oct.* 1965.

EARLE, Sir George Foster, Kt., *cr.* 1954; C.B.E. 1951; President, Associated Portland Cement Manufacturers and British Portland Cement Manufacturers since 1956; *b.* 8 Feb. 1890; *s.* of John Hudson Earle and Alice Bainbridge; *m.* 1931, Margery Schroder. *Educ.:* Harrow; Cambridge. Sec. and Dir., G. & T. Earle Ltd., Hull, 1914. Director: British Portland Cement Mfrs. Ltd., 1922 (Man. Dir. 1937); Associated Portland Cement Mfrs. Ltd., 1921 (Man. Dir. 1937); Chairman, Associated Portland Cement Manufacturers Ltd., 1946-56 (Managing Director, 1946-55). A Vice-Pres. of Institute of Directors. *Recreations:* hunting, shooting, fishing, golf. *Address:* Baggrave Hall, Leicestershire. *T.:* Hungarton 229. *Clubs:* Buck's, White's. [*Died* 11 *Dec.* 1965.

EARNSHAW, Mrs. Harold; *see* Attwell, Mabel Lucie.

EASON, John, M.D. Edin.; F.R.C.P. Edin.; Consulting Physician to the Royal Infirmary, Edinburgh; formerly Examiner in Medicine and Clinical Medicine for the Triple Qualification, Scotland; *b.* Armadale, West Lothian, 18 April 1874; *s.* of John Eason, Leith; *m.* 1909, Christina Joan Wallace, M.A. (*d.* 1950); one *d.* (one *s.* decd.). *Educ.:* Edinburgh University. M.B., C.M. First class Honours, 1896; M.R.C.P. 1899, F.R.C.P. 1902, Edin.; M.D. Edin. (Gold Medal) 1905. Formerly Physician to the Royal Infirmary, Edinburgh; Examiner in Clinical Medicine, Edinburgh Univ.; Senior Lecturer in Clinical Medicine, Edinburgh University; Lecturer in Practice of Physic, School of Medicine of the Royal Colleges, Edinburgh; Physician, Leith Hospital; Medical Referee Commercial Bank of Scotland; Physician, Chalmers Hospital, Edinburgh; Major (ret.) R.A.M.C. (T.); Major 58th Scottish General Hospital, B.E.F. *Publications:* Exophthalmic Goitre, 1927; numerous contributions to medical journals. *Address:* 6 Cumlodden Avenue, Ravelston Dykes, Edinburgh 12. *T.:* Donaldson 3641. [*Died* 31 *Oct.* 1964.

EAST, Charles Frederick Terence, M.A., D.M. (Oxon.), F.R.C.P. (Lond.); retd. as Physician, and Physician-in-Charge Cardiological Department, King's College Hospital; Consulting Physician, Woolwich Memorial Hospital; Medical Officer, National Provident Institution; Examiner in Medicine, R.C.P. and Oxford Univ.; formerly Examiner in Medicine, London Univ.; *b.* 1894; *s.* of C. H. East, M.D., Malvern. *Educ.:* Winchester; Freiburg; Lausanne; New College, Oxford; King's College Hospital. Lieutenant Northamptonshire Regiment; Welch Prize, Oxford University, 1919; Burney Yeo Scholar, King's College Hospital, 1919; Murchison Scholar, Royal College of Physicians, 1922; Member of the Association of Physicians of Great Britain and Ireland and of British Cardiac Society; Radcliffe Travelling Fellow, University College, Oxford, 1924; Fitzpatrick Lecturer, R.C.P., 1956 and 1957. F.R.S.M. *Publications:* Recent Advances in Cardiology, 5th edition (jointly), 1959; Failure of the Heart and Circulation 2nd Ed. 1948; Cardio-Vascular Disease in General Practice, 3rd edit. 1948; Story of Heart Disease, 1958; numerous papers Brit. Heart Jl. *Address:* Gulland, St. Merryn, N. Cornwall. [*Died* 27 *Aug.* 1967.

EASTER, Rev. Canon Arthur John Talbot, M.A.; Retired; *b.* 28 Nov. 1893; *s.* of Arthur Joseph Easter and Alice Bishop; *m.* 1919 Jessica Langford Woodard; two *s.* two *d.* *Educ.:* Dulwich College; St. Catharine's College, Cambridge; Ridley Hall, Cambridge. 2nd Lt. Yorks. Hussars (T.F.), 1915; R.A.S.C. 1915-16; Curate of All Souls, Langham Place, and Resident Chaplain to the Middx. Hosp., 1917-19; Curate of Holy Trinity, Richmond, Surrey, 1919-21; Vicar of St. George's, Tufnell Park, N.7, 1921-1925; St. George's with All Saints, Douglas, 1925-27; St. Paul's Church, Sheffield, 1927-1937; Diocesan Missioner, 1927-42; Proctor in Convocation, Sheffield, 1931-42; Hon. Canon in Sheffield Cathedral, 1934-37; Sen. Chaplain and Precentor, and Canon Residentiary, 1937-42; Chaplain, R.A.F.V.R., 1942-45; Vicar of St. Luke's, Woodside, Croydon, 1945-54; Rector of Lydgate with Ousden, Diocese of St. Edmundsbury and Ipswich, 1954-55; Rector of Icklingham, 1955-1960; Rector of Flax Bourton, 1960-65. Proctor in Convocation, Canterbury, 1947-1950; Hon. Secretary Canterbury Diocesan Conference, 1947-54. *Publications:* Eternal Light, 1922; Sermons, 1931 *Recreations:* golf, riding. *Address:* Flax Bourton Cottage, Well Lane, St. Margarets Bay, Dover, Kent. [*Died* 8 *March* 1969.

EASTHAM, His Honour Sir Tom, Kt., *cr.* 1948; Q.C. 1922; D.L. Surrey, 1953; Senior Official Referee of Supreme Court of Judicature, 1944-54, retired 1954; 3rd *s.* of late James Cook Eastham, Hadfield, Derbyshire; *m.* 1911, Margaret Ernestine, 3rd *d.* of A. E. Smith, J.P., St. Annes-on-Sea, Lancashire; three *s.* two *d.* *Educ.:* Manchester Grammar School; Owens College, Manchester; St. Bart's Hospital; M.B., Ch.B., Victoria University, Manchester, 1902; Resident Medical Officer, Royal Boscombe, West Hants Hospital, 1902; called to Bar, Lincoln's Inn, 1904; Bencher of Lincoln's Inn, 1927, Treasurer, 1948; member of Northern Circuit; Recorder of Oldham, 1924-36; Official Referee of Supreme Court of Judicature, 1936-44; Home Office Enquiry *re* treatment of Borstal Inmate, 1946; Chairman of Royal Corps of Naval Constructors Cttee., 1946. Chairman Admiralty's Manpower Economy Cttee., 1947-48; J.P. Surrey; Deputy Chairman of Surrey Quarter Sessions, 1940-54; Chairman of Dorking Petty Sessions, 1943-54. D.L. Surrey. H.M. Commissioner of Assize, Chester and Wales Circuit, 1948. *Address:* 19 Viceroy Lodge, Hove, Sussex. *T.:* Hove 37371. *Club:* Flyfishers' (Pres. 1953). [*Died* 11 *April* 1967.

EASTON, Hugh; Artist in Stained Glass; Commander R.N.V.R., retd. *Educ.:* Wellington Coll. Studied Art in France and

Italy; Architectural Assoc. London. Chief works: Battle of Britain Memorial and other windows, Westminster Abbey; American Memorial to King George V., and Coronation windows, Winchester Cathedral; South Lancashire Regiment War Memorial, Warrington Parish Church; Naval War Memorial, Chatham Barracks and Portsmouth Dockyard; Windows for the Cathedrals of Ypres, Durban, Canterbury, Exeter, Ely, Brechin, Grahamstown, George and Aklavik, for Romsey Abbey, Clare College, Cambridge, Wellington College Chapel, Clifton College Chapel, Oundle School Chapel, Radley College Chapel, Tonbridge School Chapel, St. Edward's School, Oxford, Wycliffe College, Glos., Kingswood School Chapel, Bath, Bedford Modern School, Rolls Royce Works, Derby, Halifax, Coventry, Bishops Stortford, Hertfordshire County Hall, Dutch Church, Austin Friars, Fishmongers' Hall, Clothworkers' Hall, Inner Temple Hall, Lloyd's, City Temple and Chelsea Parish Church, London, Royal Tank Regt. Memorial, U.S. Air Force Memorial, Elveden, St. Bartholomew's and Westminster Hospitals, Royal Cardiff Infirmary, and for many churches and public buildings. *Address:* 6A Holbein Place, S.W.1. *Clubs:* Brooks's, Arts. [*Died* 15 *Aug.* 1965.

EASTWOOD, Reginald Allen, O.B.E. 1957; LL.D., Barrister-at-law; Professor of English Law, Victoria University of Manchester, 1946–60, now Professor Emeritus; Chairman of Court of Referees for Newton Heath District of Manchester, 1930–54; Joint Chairman, Local Tribunal for Manchester, 1954–63; Chairman Fustian Cutting Wages Council (Gt. Brit)., 1949 56 (Deputy Chairman 1933–49); Deputy Chairman of Cotton Waste Reclamation Wages Council (Great Britain) 1941–58; *b.* 3 April 1893; *e. s.* of late Frederick Allen Eastwood, chemist, Manchester; *m.* 1st, 1920, Elsie Maude, M.A., *y. d.* of J. H. Crompton, Whalley Range, Manchester; no *c.*; 2nd, 1929, Norah Mary, B.Com., Barrister-at-law, *o. d.* of late W. C. Popplewell, M.Sc., A.M.I.C.E., Manchester. *Educ.:* Central High School and Victoria Univ., Manchester. LL.B. 1914; LL.D. 1918; called to Bar, Gray's Inn, 1919; Lecturer in Law, Victoria Univ. of Manchester, 1914–20; Senior Lecturer in Law, 1920–24; Professor of Law, 1924–46; President, Society of Public Teachers of Law, 1934–35; Chm 1936–40, of Lancashire and Cheshire District Committee of Investigation under the Coal Mines Act, 1930; Legal Adviser at the Cotton Control, 1939–47. Hon. Fell., Manchester Medical Soc., 1958. *Publications:* Introduction to Austin's Jurisprudence; The Organisation of a Britannic Partnership; Williams on Real Property (24th ed.); The Austinian Theories of Law and Sovereignty (in collaboration); The Contract of Sale of Goods; Williams and Eastwood on Real Property; Strahan, Equity (6th ed.); articles in periodicals. *Recreations:* fell walking, climbing, riding, fishing. *Address:* 43 King Street, Manchester. *T.:* Blackfriars 6875; Glan y Wern, Llanarmon, D.C., Wrexham. *Clubs:* National Liberal. Rucksack, Reform (Manchester). [*Died* 22 *June* 1964.

EATON, Hon. Herbert Edward; late Lieut. Grenadier Guards; *b.* 12 June 1895; *yr. s.* of 3rd and *heir-pres.* to 4th Baron Cheylesmore, D.S.O.; *m.* 1921, Sheila Ashton Case (who obtained a divorce, 1944), British Columbia; one *d.*; *m.* 1944, Barrie Kinghorn Eaton, *o. d.* of Walter Grey, Edinburgh. Served European War, 1915–16 (wounded). [*Died April* 1962.

EBBUTT, Norman; Journalist; *b.* 1894; *s.* of William Arthur Ebbutt; *m.* 1942, Gladys Holms (*née* Apps). *Educ.:* Willaston School, Nantwich Second correspondent of Morning Leader in Paris in 1911 and 1912. In Russia and Finland, 1913. Joined The Times, 1914; served as Temp. Lieut. R.N.V.R., 1914–19; rejoined The Times, 1919. In Sept. 1925 appointed second correspondent Berlin, and chief correspondent Berlin from 1927 till expulsion from Berlin, 21 Aug. 1937. *Recreation:* gardening. *Address:* 4 Stedham Hall, Midhurst, Sussex. *T.:* Midhurst 628. [*Died* 17 *Oct.* 1968.

EBERLE, George Strachan John Fuller, D.S.O. 1918; T.D.; M.A. (Oxon); Solicitor, retired; *b.* 14 Oct. 1881; *s.* of late James Fuller Eberle and late Florence Mary Strachan; *m.* 1911; two *s.* one *d.* *Educ.:* Clifton College; Trinity College, Oxford. Oxford University Rugby Union XV, 1901 and 1902; Oxford University Water Polo Team, 1901–2; served European War, 1914–1918 (D.S.O., despatches thrice); commanded 475th Field Company R.E., three years, and 5th Bn. the Royal Sussex Regt., one year; retired with rank of Lt.-Col. R.E. (T.); President, Bristol Incorporated Law Society, 1933–34; Major, Home Guard, 1940–45. *Recreation:* golf. *Address:* The Red Lodge, Leigh Woods, Bristol 8. *T.:* 36247. [*Died* 30 *May* 1968.

EBORALL, Sir (Ernest) Arthur, Kt. 1934; C.B.E. 1928; *b.* 6 Aug 1878; 2nd *s.* of Alfred Eborall, St. Leonards-on-Sea; *m.* Hilda M. Jago (*d.* 1960), Plymouth; one *s.* three *d.* Chief Inspector of Taxes, 1932–38; Controller of Rates Division, Ministry of Transport, 1939–41; Principal Asst. Secretary, Board of Trade, 1941–42; member of Inter-Departmental Committee on Income Tax in the Colonies, 1922; Secretary Shipping Taxation Committee, Imperial Economic Conference, 1923. *Recreation:* yachting. *Address:* Little Orchard, Crane Hill, Ipswich, Suffolk. *T.:* Ipswich 54573. [*Died* 7 *April* 1967.

EBRAHIM, Sir Fazulbhoy Currimbhoy; *see* Addenda: II

ECCLES, Adm. (Ret.) Sir John (Arthur Symons), G.C.B. 1958 (K.C.B. 1955; C.B. 1951); K.C.V.O. 1953; C.B.E. 1944; D.L.; *b.* 20 June 1898; *s.* of Arthur Symons Eccles and Anne Jackson; *m.* 1929, Madeleine Cherry Macfarlane; one *s.* *Educ.:* Lancing. Joined Royal Navy, 1916; Commander, 1933; served War of 1939–45 (despatches); Capt., 1939; Rear-Adm., 1949; Vice-Adm., 1952; Adm., 1955; Commodore, R.N. Barracks, Chatham, 1948–49; Flag Officer Commanding Australian Fleet, 1949–51; Admiral Commanding Reserves, 1952; Flag Officer Air (Home), 1953–55; Commander-in-Chief, Home Fleet, and Allied C.-in-C., Eastern Atlantic (N.A.T.O.), 1955–57; retd. 1958. D.L. County of London, 1962. *Address:* Worthy Park, Martyr Worthy, Winchester. *Club:* United Service. [*Died* 1 *March* 1966.

ECCLES, Sir Josiah, Kt. 1957; C.B.E. 1950; M.M. 1917; D.Sc., M.Inst.C.E., F.I.E.E., M.I.Mech.E.; *b.* 29 July 1897; *s.* of Johnston and Mary Anne Eccles; *m.* 1930 Katherine Lillie Gillah Summerson; one *s.* two *d.* *Educ.:* Queen's Univ., Belfast, B.Sc. degree in Engineering with 1st Cl. Honours; D.Sc., 1956. Served European War, 1914–1918 (M.M.). Messrs. Metropolitan-Vickers Electrical Co. Ltd., 1922–28; Edinburgh Corporation Electricity Undertaking, 1928–1944 (Engineer and Manager, 1940–44); City Electrical Engineer and City Lighting Engineer, Liverpool, 1944–48; Chairman, Merseyside and North Wales Electricity Board, 1948–54; Dep. Chm. British Electricity Authority, 1954–57, Electricity Council, 1957–61. Member of Council of Institution of Electrical Engineers, 1945–48, Vice-Pres., 1948–54. Pres., 1954; Mem. of Organising Cttee. of British Electricity Authority, 1947; Pres. Incorporated Municipal Electrical Assoc., 1947–48; Chm. of Council of British Electrical Development Assoc., 1948–1949; President British Electrical Power Convention, 1957. Hon. F.I.E.E. 1967. *Publications:* contributions to proceedings of engineering institutions. *Address:* 21 Sandy Lodge Road, Moor Park, Herts. *T.:* Northwood 25711. [*Died* 14 *Oct.* 1967.

ECCLES, William Henry, F.R.S. 1921; consulting engineer; late Professor of Applied Physics and Electrical Engineering at the City and Guilds of London Technical College, Finsbury, E.C.; late University Reader in Graphics, University College, London; *b.* near Ulverston, Lancashire, 23 Aug. 1875; *m.* Nellie, *d.* of Robert Paterson. *Educ.:* private school; Royal College of Science, London. Associate of the Royal College of Science, 1897; B.Sc. with Honours in Physics, 1898; D.Sc. (London) in Physics, 1901; Fellow of the Imperial College; Vice-Chairman of Commission which planned the Imperial Wireless Stations; late Chairman of British Scientific Instrument Research Association; Past President of Association of Scientific Workers; of Physical Society; of Institute of Physics; of the Institution of Electrical Engineers; of the Radio Society of Great Britain; Pres-d'honneur of the International Scientific Radio Union; Director of Admiralty Electrical Engineering Laboratory, London, 1917 and 1918; Mem. Imperial Wireless Telegraphy Committee, 1919. *Publications:* many contributions to technical and scientific societies and journals, and also Handbook of Wireless Telegraphy and Telephony; Treatise on Continuous Wave Wireless Telegraphy; Wireless (Home University Library). *Recreations:* music, motoring. *Address:* Midway, The Ridings, East Preston, Sussex. *Club:* Athenæum. [*Died* 29 *April* 1966.

ECKERSLEY, Peter Pendleton, M.I.E.E.; F.I.R.E.; Consultant; *b.* La Puebla, Mexico, 1892; *s.* of W. A. Eckersley and Rachel, *d.* of Professor Huxley; *m.* 1st, 1917, Stella (*decd.*), *d.* of J. C. Grove; one *s.* one *d.*; 2nd, 1930, Francis Dorothy Clark, *d.* of Lt.-Col. A. J. Stephen. *Educ.:* Bedales School; Manchester Univ. Apprentice Mather & Platts, Electrical Engineers, 1911; Manchester University, 1912-15; Royal Flying Corps as Wireless Equipment Officer; served in Egypt, Salonika, and France Research Officer and Capt., signals Experimental Establishment, Woolwich, and Wireless Experimental Section, Biggin Hill, 1915-19; Head of Experimental Section of Designs Dept Marconi's Wireless Telegraph Co, 1919-23; Chief Engineer to the British Broadcasting Corporation, 1923-29; Consultant to various Governments, public and private companies. Sometime Vice-Pres. Institute of Radio Engineers, U.S.A.; planned the Regional Scheme, now in operation, for British Broadcasting to give alternative programme service; invited to Australia (1932), where submitted plan for National Broadcasting; pioneer work on Wire Broadcasting particularly for using electric mains for programme distribution. *Publications:* The Power Behind the Microphone, 1941; numerous scientific papers. *Address:* c/o Lloyds Bank, 79 Brompton Road, S.W.3. [*Died* 18 *March* 1963.

ECKHOFF, Nils Lovold Bjarne Victor, M.S., F.R.C.S.; Surgeon Emeritus, Guy's Hospital, and Caterham Hospital; *b.* 18 Aug. 1902; *s.* of F. M. H. Eckhoff, architect, and Louisa Larsen (both Norwegian); *m.* 1931, Audrey Allison; one *s.* one *d.* *Educ.:* Durban High Sch.; Natal Univ. Coll.; Univ. of Cape Town; Guy's Hospital. M.B., B.S. Hons., 1927, M.S. 1928, London; M.R.C.S. Eng., L.R.C.P. Lond., 1923; F.R.C.S. Eng. 1927. House Appointments, Guy's Hosp., 1923-1924; House Surgeon, West London Hosp., 1925; Surgical Registrar, 1926-30. Senior Demonstrator of Anatomy, 1930-33. Guy's Hosp.; Surgeon, St. John's Hosp., Lewisham, 1930-46; Consulting Surgeon, L.C.C., 1930-44; Asst. Surgeon, Guy's Hosp., 1933-46; Surgeon, Cottage Hospital, East Grinstead, 1941-46; Plastic Surgeon, Queen Victoria Hospital, East Grinstead, 1940-1958; Hon. Visiting Surgeon, Johns Hopkins, Baltimore, U.S.A., 1947. Past President Chelsea Clinical Society; Past Pres. Medical Society of London. *Publications:* Aids to Osteology, 1942; various articles in, Encyc. Med. Practice, Guy's Hosp. Reports, Guy's Hosp. Gazette. *Recreations:* golf; Pres. Univ. of London Golf Club; Past Pres. United Hospitals Rifle Club; Past Pres. Medical Golfing Soc. *Address:* 30 Bark Place, Bayswater, W.2. *T.:* 01-229 8551. [*Died* 6 *Nov.* 1969.

EDDIS, Brig. Bruce Lindsay, D.S.O. 1918; late Royal Engineers; *b.* 1883; 2nd *s.* of late William Kearnes Eddis; *m.*; three *d.* *Educ.:* Rugby School; R.M.A., Woolwich; M.A. Cantab. Served European War, 1914-18 (despatches, D.S.O., Brevet); Lt.-Col. 1929; Colonel 1933; Assistant Quartermaster; General, Army Headquarters, India, 1934-38; retired pay, 1938; re-employed, 1939-41. *Address:* Enlin, Assheton Road, Beaconsfield, Bucks. *T.:* Beaconsfield 2121. [*Died* 12 *May* 1966.

EDDOWES, Rev. Canon Edmund Edward, M.A., R.D.; Rector of Kelsale with Carlton, 1931-61; Rural Dean of South Dunwich, 1931; Canon Emeritus of the Diocese of St. Edmundsbury and Ipswich since 1962 (Canon, 1925-62); Private Chaplain to Bishop of St. Edmundsbury and Ipswich, 1930-40; O.C.F. (32 S./L. Regiment R.A.) since 1939; Local Army Welfare Officer since 1941; *b.* 14 March 1871; *s.* of Rev. Edmund Eddowes, Vicar of Hartford, Cheshire, and Louisa Elizabeth Sutton; *m.* 1910, Dorothy Kate (*d.* 1959), *e. d.* of Edward Warner, D.L., J.P., of Quorn Hall, Leicestershire; no *c.* *Educ.:* Marlborough; Jesus College, Cambridge; Leeds Clergy School; Curate of Church and Chapel Brampton, Northants, 1900-09; Rector of Barham, 1909-1929; Rector of Barham with Claydon, 1929-1931; Rural Dean of Claydon, 1914-31; Hon. C.F., 1916-19, 1940-46; Proctor Convocation, 1925-29 and 1936-45. Hon. Chaplain, Government Instructional Centre, Barham, 1926-31; Secretary to St Edmundsbury and Ipswich Diocesan Conference, 1929-61. Member of East Suffolk C.C. Education Committee, 1928; Member Blything Rural District Council, 1931; Chm. of Governors of Leiston Grammar School, 1947-60; Diocesan Pension Officer for Widows of the Clergy, 1928-61. *Recreations:* shooting, fishing, golf. *Address:* Kelsale Place, Saxmundham, Suffolk. *T.:* 15. *Club:* Royal Automobile. [*Died* 5 *July* 1963.

EDDY, Sir (Edward) George, Kt., *cr.* 1947; O.B.E. 1942 (M.B.E. 1918); J.P.; Chemical Manufacturer; *b.* 22 June 1878; *s.* of Edward Eddy, Kidderminster; *m.* 1st, 1905, Florence Wimbury (*d.* 1949); one *s.* one *d.*; 2nd, 1953, Freda Forster, O.B.E. 1964 (M.B.E. 1942), *d.* of T. Foster, Stanley, Co. Durham. *Educ.:* King Charles I School; privately. J.P., Kidderminster 1922; Worcestershire, 1942; former member Worcestershire C.C. Activities in Kidderminster: Town Councillor, 1925, Alderman, 1938, 1955 and 1961, Mayor, 1927, 1928, 1936 and 1937 (Coronation Year); Hon. Freeman, 1951; Chairman of: Income Tax Commissioners since 1931, Governors of Grammar School, Juvenile Employment Committee, 1926-, Savings Cttee. and Trustee Savings Bank, Nursing Assoc., Borough Bench; Past Chm. Finance Cttee. of Town Council; Past Pres. Chamber of Commerce, Rotary Club; Vice-Pres. General Hosp.; Regional Member Nat. Savings for Warwicks, Worcs, Staffs, Salop and Herefordshire, and Member of Nat. Savings Cttee. *Recreation:* tennis. *Address:* The Platts, Kidderminster. *T.:* 2061. *Club:* Junior Carlton. [*Died* 8 *April* 1967.

EDE, Baron James C. C.; *see* Chuter-Ede.

EDELSTEN, Adm. Sir John Hereward, G.C.B., *cr.* 1953 (K.C.B., *cr* 1946; C.B 1944); G.C.V.O., *cr.* 1953; C.B.E. 1941; D.L.; Vice-Admiral of the United Kingdom and Lieutenant of the Admiralty since 1962 (Rear-Adm. of U.K. and of Admty., 1955-62); *b.* 12 May 1891; 3rd *s.* of John J. Edelsten; *m.* 1926, 2nd *d.* of H. V. Masefield; no *c.* *Educ.:* Royal Naval Colleges, Osborne and Dartmouth. Went to sea, 1908; Lieut. 1913; Comdr. 1926; Capt. 1933; Rear-Adm. 1942; Vice-Adm. 1945; Admiral, 1949; served in Grand Fleet in European War; Flag-Lieut. to Admiral Sir A. Thomas Hunt, C.-in-C., S. America Station, 1921-22; Staff Officer to Admiral (then Rear-Admiral) Hon. Sir Hubert Brand, commanding First Light Cruiser Squadron, during World cruise by Special Service Squadron, 1922-24; Imperial Defence College, 1934; Deputy Director of Plans Division, Admiralty, 1938; H.M.S. Shropshire on Trade Routes and as Senior Naval Officer during operations against Italian Somaliland, 1940-1941; Commodore 1st Class and Chief of Staff to Admiral Sir Andrew Cunningham, Commander-in-Chief, Mediterranean Station, 1941-42 (despatches); Lord Commissioner of the Admiralty and Asst. Chief of Naval Staff (U-boat Warfare and Trade), 1942-44. Rear-Admiral (Destroyers) British Pacific Fleet, 1945; Comdg. First Battle Squadron, 1945-1946; 4th Cruiser Squadron, 1946; Lord Comr. of the Admiralty and Vice-Chief of Naval Staff, 1947-49; C.-in-C., Mediterranean Station, 1950-52; Commander-in-Chief, Portsmouth, 1952-54; C.-in-C. Home Station, Designate, 1952-54; Allied Naval Commander-in-Chief, Channel Command, 1952-54; First and Principal Naval A.D.C. to the Queen, 1953-54, retired Nov. 1954. American Legion of Merit, Order of Commander, 1946; Greek Order of Phœnix, Grand Officer, 1947. D.L. Southampton, 1955. *Recreations:* shooting, fishing, tennis, golf. *Address:* Westlands, Liphook, Hants. *T.:* Liphook 2119. *Club:* United Service. [*Died* 10 *Feb.* 1966.

EDEN, Sir Timothy (Calvert), 8th Bt., *cr.* 1672; and 6th Bt., *cr.* 1776; *b.* 3 May 1893; *S.* father, 1915; *s.* of 7th Bt. and Sybil Frances (Lady of Grace, O.B.E.; she died 1945), *d.* of late Sir William Grey, K.C.S.I.; *m.* 1923, Edith Mary, *d.* of Arthur Prendergast; one *s.* four *d.* (and one *d.* decd.) *Educ.:* Eton; Christ Church Oxford. Interned in Germany, 1914-16. Served, European War, 1917-19; Lieut., General List, 1939; Staff Capt., War Office, 1941. *Publications:* Five Dogs and Two More, 1928; The Tribulations of a Baronet, 1933; Durham, 1952. *Heir:* *s.* John Benedict Eden, M.P. *Address:* Fritham House, Lyndhurst, Hants. *T.A.:* Fritham. *T.:* Cadman 2234. [*Died* 13 *May* 1963.

EDENBOROUGH, Eric John Horatio, C.B. 1958; O.B.E. 1946; *b.* 1893; *yr. s.* of Arthur Edenborough and Ada, *d.* of Captain John Barthorp; unmarried. *Educ.:* Weymouth College; Lincoln College, Oxford (M.A.). Served 1914-19 with H.A.C. and Queen's Royal Regt., Belgium, France (wounded 1917); T.A. (General List), 1920-1921; Captain; Clerk in the House of Commons, 1921-58; acting Assistant Serjeant at Arms, 1940-45; Clerk of the Journals, 1953-58. *Publications:* some verse in press and periodicals. *Recreations:* travelling, preferably abroad; mountain walking; golf. *Address:* 1 Chapel Lane, Lower Somersham, Ipswich, Suffolk. *Club:* Athenæum. [*Died* 19 *Jan.* 1965.

EDGEDALE, His Honour Judge Samuel Richards, Q.C.; County Court Judge since 1961; *b.* 23 May 1897; *e. s.* of Samuel Edgedale, Littleton Hall, Cheshire; *m.* 1925, Elaine Blanche, *e. d.* of Maj. A. Hubert Gibbs, Pytte, Clyst St. George, Devon; one *s.* two *d.* *Educ.:* Shrewsbury; Christ Church, Oxford. European War, 1914-18, Lt. R.F.A.; served in France, India and Mesopotamia; called to Bar, 1921. Q.C. 1947. J.P. 1949-52. Special Comr. for the trial of matrimonial causes, 1953. *Recreation:* fishing. *Address:* Field Lodge, Crowthorne, Berks. *T.:* 2374. *Club:* Carlton. [*Died* 5 *April* 1966.

EDGELL, Vice-Admiral Sir John Augustine, K.B.E., *cr.* 1942; C.B. 1936; F.R.S. 1943; Admiralty Representative on the Port of London Authority; *b.* 20 Dec. 1880; *y. s.* of late James Edgell, formerly of Teddington; *m.* 1912, Caroline Elizabeth, *o. d.* of late G. Rodolph, Eastbourne; two *d.* *Educ.:* H.M.S. Britannia. Appointed to command H.M.S. Mutine, Africa Station, 1912, and has since had command of H.M. ships Triton, Hearty, Endeavour (twice), Merlin, and H.M.A.S. Moresby; served in N. Sea and the Dardanelles during the war; Superintendent of Charts, Admiralty, 1917-20 and 1923-25; Assistant Hydrographer, 1928-30 and 1931-32; Hydrographer of the Navy, 1932-45; Acting Conservator of the Mersey, 1945-51; has been in charge of Surveys in China, Australia, Red Sea, Mediterranean, also S. and W. Africa; British Delegate at International Hydrographic Conference in 1919, 1929, 1932, and 1937; awarded O.B.E. for services in command of surveying ships in the war, 1919; Commander, 1915; Captain, 1923; Rear-Adm. 1935; Vice-Adm., 1938; retired list, 1938. *Publications:* Sea Surveys and a few professional papers. *Address:* Highdown Cottage, Worcester Park, Surrey. [*Died* 14 *Nov.* 1962.

EDINGTON, Alexander Robert, C.I.E. 1946; Chief Engineer, South Indian Railway (retired); *b.* 12 Sept. 1895; *s.* of John Edington, Edinburgh, and Barbara Andrea Horsburgh Bolton; *m.* 1925, Esme Marjorie, *d.* of late Roderick Ross, C.V.O., C.B.E., Edinburgh; one *s.* one *d.* *Educ.:* George Watson's College, Heriot-Watt College, Edinburgh. Served European War with Royal Engineers, France, 1917-19. Civil Engineer, South Indian Railway, 1920-1948; Director, Railway Board, Govt. of India, 1944-47. M.I.C.E.; Fell. Permanent Way Inst.; F.R.S.A. *Recreation:* sketching. *Address:* Seton West House, Tranent, East Lothian. [*Died* 8 *Aug.* 1964.

EDINGTON, William Gerald; Director of Midland Bank, Ltd., since May 1956; a Vice-President, Institute of Bankers, London, since 1954; *b.* Liverpool, 2 Feb. 1895; *er. s.* of late Harold Snape Edington and Florence Edington, Liverpool; *m.* 1933, Anne (*d.* 1957), *d.* of late Fred and Mary A. Harrison, Bebington, Cheshire; one *s.* one *d.* *Educ.:* Holt High School, Liverpool. Entered Midland Bank, Liverpool, 1911; Manager, Oldham Branch, 1934; transf. to London, 1937; Joint General Manager, 1945; Chief General Manager, Nov. 1946-March 1956. Fellow Institute of Bankers, London; President, Manchester Institute of Bankers, 1948-1949. Chm. Chief Executive Officers Cttee. of London Clearing Bankers, 1953-54. Served European War, 1914-18, with 9th King's Liverpool Regt. (wounded); invalided out of Army, 1918. Mem. Court of Common Council, City of London. Liveryman of Spectacle-makers' Company. *Recreations:* music, sport, travelling. *Address:* 23 Chelwood House, Gloucester Square, W.2. *T.:* Ambassador 3687. *Clubs:* M.C.C.; Middlesex County Cricket; Surrey County Cricket. [*Died* 28 *June* 1968.

EDMONDS, William Stanley, C.M.G. 1927; O.B.E. 1919 (M.B.E. 1918); *b.* 18 June 1882; *s.* of Charles and Mary E. Edmonds; *m.* 1916, A. Lindo Johnson; two *d.* *Educ.:* Rossall; King's College, Cambridge, B.A.

Mediæval and Modern Languages Tripos; student interpreter in the Levant, 1903; Vice-Consul at Constantinople, 1908; Consul in H.M. Levant Service, 1918; Consul-General at Smyrna, 1923; Counsellor attached to H.M. Embassy, Constantinople; Consul-General at Rabat, 1930-34; at Strasbourg, 1934-38; at Milan, 1938-39; at Genoa, 1939-40; employed in Foreign Office, 1940-47; mem. Brit. Deleg., conference on Tangier, 1945. *Address:* Cock Brig, Glenmore Road, Crowborough, Sussex. [*Died* 14 *Sept.* 1969.

EDMUNDS, Humfrey Henry; Recorder of Bath since 1950; *b.* 29 June 1890; *e. s.* of Lewis Humfrey Edmunds, K.C., D.Sc. and of Ann Margaret, *d.* of Henry Charles Stephens, Cholderton, Wilts.; *m.* 1st, Stella Norman Hanson; one *s.*; 2nd, Beatrice Mary Coleman; two *d.* *Educ.:* Harrow; London University. Barrister-at-Law, Middle Temple, 1915; Bencher, 1947. Served European War, 1914-18, Royal Artillery. Deputy-Chairman, Court of Quarter Sessions, Surrey, 1961-. *Recreations:* shooting, fishing. *Address:* 60 Latymer Court, W.6; 4 Pump Court, Temple, E.C.4. *T.:* Central 3553. *Club:* Carlton. [*Died* 6 *April* 1962.

EDWARD-COLLINS, Maj.-Gen. Charles Edward, C.B. 1937; C.I.E. 1919; Indian Army, retired; High Sheriff of Cornwall, 1955; *b.* 28 May 1881; *s.* of Edward Charles Edward-Collins, D.L. J.P., Trewardale, Cornwall, and Eleanor Mary, *d.* of Lt.-Col. F. Alms; *m.* 1907, Nora Mabel de la Cour (*d.* 1952), *d.* of late Col. R. D. la Cour Corbett, D.S.O.; two *s.* three *d.* *Educ.:* Marlborough; R.M.C. Sandhurst. 2nd Lt. Devon Regt. 1900; transferred to Indian Army, 1909; Bt.-Maj. 1912; Bt.-Lt.-Col. 1924; Col. 1928; Maj.-Gen. 1937; served South Africa, 1900-2; Abor Expedition 1911-12 (despatches, Bt.-Major); European War, 1819, South Persia, 1918-19 (despatches, C.I.E.); A.D.C. to the King, 1935-37; War of 1939-45; retired, 1940. Commanded N. Cornwall Group Home Guard, 1942-45. *Address:* Trewardale, Bilsland, Cornwall. *T.:* Cardinham 226. [*Died* 21 *Nov.* 1967.

EDWARD-COLLINS, Brigadier Gerald, C.I.E. 1938; M.C.; retired; *b.* 23 Feb. 1885; 3rd *s.* of late E. C. Edward-Collins, J.P., Trewardale, Cornwall; *m.* 1920, Muriel Durett, *er. d.* of late Henry Durett Foster, J.P., Polgwin, Bodmin; one *s.* one *d.* *Educ.:* Malvern College. 3rd Bn. (Militia) Duke of Cornwall's L.I., 1905; Prince of Wales Volunteers, 1907; 33rd Queen's Own Light Cavalry (Indian Army) 1909; served European War, 1914-18 (despatches four times); Bde. Major, 4th Cavalry Brigade, 1917-20; G.S.O.2, Tochi Valley, Waziristan, 1921; Bt. Col. 1934; Col. 1934; Brig. 1934; Deputy Director Remounts, India 1930; Director Remounts, India, 1934. U.S.A. and India, 1939-40; Pilot Officer R.A.F.V.R., 1940; Wing Commander, 1941-43. *Address:* Polgwin, Bodmin, Cornwall. [*Died* 25 *March* 1968.

EDWARDS, Arthur John Charles, C.I.E. 1943; F.I.A.; F.R.Econ.S.; F.B.S.; *b.* 24 July 1883; *e. s.* of Arthur John Edwards and Sophie, *d.* of John Honor; *m.* 1905, Violet, *d.* of late James Kirby; one *s.* two *d.* *Educ.:* Aske's Hatcham School. Nat. Debt Office, 1903; Private Secretary to Comptroller-General, 1911; India Office, 1913; Office of High Commissioner for India, 1921; Indian Income Tax Officer, 1924; Treas. Civil Service Housing Assoc. Ltd., 1926; Member of Council Civil Service Statistical and Research Bureau, 1933; Pres. Society of Civil Servants, 1935; Hon. Treas. Roy. Inst. of Public Administration, 1938; President Civil Service Building Society, 1941; Chief Accounting Officer, India House, 1934-46, ret. Defence Medal; Jubilee Medal, 1935; Coronation Medal, 1937. *Recreations:* gardening, cycling music. *Address:* Flawinne, 397 Hanworth Road, Hounslow, Middlesex. *T.:* Hounslow 2180. *Clubs:* Civil Service; Old Askean; Cyclists Touring. [*Died* 26 *July* 1963.

EDWARDS, Lieut.-Col. Cosmo Grant Niven, C.I.E. 1944; Indian Political Service (retired); *b.* 1896; *y. s.* of late Rev. James Edwards, Lossiemouth, Scotland, and Scottish Churches College, Calcutta; *m.* 1930, Emily Evelyn (Kaisar-i-Hind Medal, 1945), *d.* of Dr. E. J. P. Olive, Leamington, Warwickshire; no *c.* *Educ.:* Fettes College; Edinburgh University. Served European War, 1914-19, Highland Light Infantry 1914, France 1915 (wounded); transferred to Indian Army, 1917, Q.V.O. Corps of Guides (Infantry); N.W. Frontier (Afghanistan), 1919; Indian Political Service, 1921; various appts. in N.W. Frontier Province till 1929; Under-Secretary and Deputy Secretary to Govt. of India Foreign and Political Dept., 1930-32; Secretary to Resident in Mysore, 1934-37; Political Agent in Kalat, 1938-40; Political Agent in Bhopal, 1940-42; Resident for Kolhapur and the Deccan States, 1942-44; Resident for the Madras States, 1944-47. *Address:* c/o National and Grindlay's Bank Ltd., 13 St. James's Square, S.W.1. [*Died* 22 *July* 1964.

EDWARDS, Sir David, Kt., *cr.* 1951; *b.* 3 February 1892; *s.* of David Edwards, solicitor, Aberdeen; unmarried. *Educ.:* Aberdeen University (M.A. 1912, LL.B. with distinction, 1914). Member of Scottish Bar; Temp. Officer R.A., 1915-19, serving in Burma, India (N.W. Frontier), German East Africa and Mesopotamia; entered Colonial Service, 1921, holding various posts in Kenya till 1934; Puisne Judge, Supreme Court of Palestine, 1941-47; Chief Justice of Uganda, 1947-52; Relieving President, District Court, Palestine, 1935; President, 1936. Commissioner enquiring into conduct of certain Chiefs, Sierra Leone, 1956-57. Senior Judge, Special Court, Cyprus, 1959-60. *Publication:* Editor, Vol. I Law Reports H.M. Court of Appeal for Eastern Africa, 1934. *Club:* East India and Sports. [*Died* 28 *Feb.* 1966.

EDWARDS, Ebby; Member of National Coal Board, 1946-53, retired; *b.* Chevington, Northumberland, 1884. M.P. (Lab.) Morpeth 1929-31; President Mineworkers, Federation of Great Britain, 1931-32, Secretary, 1932-46. *Address:* 6 South Ridge, Brunton Park, Gosforth, Newcastle upon Tyne 3. [*Died* 6 *July* 1961.

EDWARDS, Edward John Rogers, C.B. 1948; *b* 1 Nov. 1891; *m.* 1st, 1918, Olive Kitty Flack (*d.* 1945); one *d.*; 2nd, 1947, Dorothy Marian Broughton. *Educ.:* Bristol Grammar School; Wadham College, Oxford (Scholar, B.A.). Formerly Under-Secretary, Ministry of Works. *Address:* The White House, Lee Wick, St. Osyth, Essex. [*Died* 10 *April* 1965.

EDWARDS, Frederick Laurence, C.B. 1953; O.B.E. 1942; Under-Secretary for Finance and Accountant-General since 1950, now with Housing and Local Government, previously with Ministry of Health; *b.* 20 March 1903; *o. s.* of late Frederick Lewis Edwards, Middlesbrough; *m.* 1930, Lillian Evelyn, *o. d.* of late J. F. Everitt, Chelmsford; no *c.* *Educ.:* Middlesbrough High School; Jesus College, Oxford; Middle Temple. Open Schol. to Jesus Coll., and State Schol., 1921; first class Hons. Mod. Hist., Oxford, 1925. Entered the Civil Service, Junior Asst. District Auditor, 1925. Transferred to Ministry of Health as Asst. Principal, 1930; Principal, 1935; Asst. Sec., 1945. Called to Bar, Middle Temple, with

Campbell Foster Prize in Criminal Law, 1930. *Publications:* James, First Earl Stanhope: a Biography, 1925; The Parish Councillor's Guide, 7th and 8th Edns., 1946 and 1950. *Recreation:* motoring. *Address:* 84 St. George's Road, Ilford, Essex. *T.:* Valentine 1353. *Club:* Oxford and Cambridge University. [*Died* 17 *July* 1962.

EDWARDS, Geoffrey Richard, O.B.E. 1949; M.A.; Member of Board of Governors, St. John's School, Apethorpe, Northants; *b.* 1891; *s.* of late Richard and of Lucy Edwards; *m.* 1924, Margaret Elizabeth, *e. d.* of 1st Viscount Simon, P.C., G.C.S.I., G.C.V.O.; two *s.* one *d.* *Educ.:* St. Paul's School; St. John's College, Cambridge. Imperial Forest Service of India, 1913; R.F.C. and R.A.F. pilot, 1916-20; Inter-allied Aeronautical Commission of Control to Germany, 1920; assistant to the Secretary, National Physical Laboratory, 1921-25; Secretary of the Royal Society of Medicine, 1925-51. Director, Inst. of Travel Agents, 1951-55. Officer Commanding 1166 Squadron, A.T.C., 1941-43; edited Catholic Medical Guardian, 1938-42. Hon. Fellow Royal Society of Medicine. Officer of Order of Orange Nassau; Military Cross First Class of Czechoslovakia; Commander of Order of Crown, Belgium. *Recreations:* travel, music, theatre. *Address:* 7 Lee Road, Aldeburgh, Suffolk. *T.:* Aldeburgh 374. *Clubs:* Athenæum, Victory Ex-Services. [*Died* 10 *Dec.* 1961.

EDWARDS, Col. Guy Janion, D.S.O. 1919; M.C.; J.P.; late Coldstream Guards; *b.* 1881; *e. s.* of late Arthur J. Edwards of Beech Hill Park, Waltham Abbey, Essex; *m.* 1921, Janet, (*d.* 1940), *o. d.* of late Harold McCorquodale, Forest Hall, Ongar, Essex; two *d.* *Educ.:* Eton; Trinity College, Oxford, M.A. Joined Coldstream Guards, 1904; Capt., 1914; Major, 1919; Lieut.-Col., 1922; Col., 1926; Adjutant 2nd Batt., 1910-13; 4th Batt., 1915-16; Brigade Major, Brigade of Guards, 1919-20; Com. 2nd Battalion, 1922-26: half-pay, 1926; A.A.G., War Office, 1927-30; retired pay, 1930; served European War (despatches twice, M.C., D.S.O., Belgian Croix de Guerre); commanded 4th Battalion (Temp. Lt.-Col.), 1917-19; Re-employed in War of 1939-45 as O.C. Coldstream Guards Regiment and Regimental District, Sept. 1939-May 1941; reverted to retired pay, 1941; one of H.M.'s Hon. Corps of Gentlemen-at-Arms, 1931-51. J.P. Glos., 1933. *Address:* Rockcliff House, Upper Slaughter, Cheltenham, Gloucestershire. *T.:* Stow on the Wold 648. *Club:* Guards. [*Died* 30 *Sept.* 1962.

EDWARDS, Gwilym Arthur, B.A. (Wales), M.A (Oxon); D D. (Edin.); Minister Presbyterian Church of Wales (ordained 1909); *b.* 31 May 1881; *s.* of Rev. Owen Edwards, B.A., Melbourne, Australia, and Mary, *d.* of J. Meyrick Jones, J.P., Dolgelly; *m.* 1917, Mary Nesta, *d.* of Richard Hughes, F.R.C.V.S., Brynoswallt, Oswestry; one *s.* two *d.* *Educ.:* Dolgelly Grammar School; University College of Wales, Aberystwyth; Jesus College, Oxford. B.A. (Honours Classics) University of Wales, 1903; B.A. (Classical Mods., Lit. Hum., Honours Theology) Oxford, 1908; M.A., 1911. Held Pastorates of Zion, Carmarthen, 1908-11; Oswald Road, Oswestry, 1911-17; City Road, Chester, 1917-23; Tabernacle, Bangor, 1923-1928; Lecturer at the Normal College, Bangor, on Religious Instruction, 1923-28, and at Univ. Coll. of Wales, Aberystwyth, 1946-49; Professor at the United Theological College (Welsh Presbyterian) Bala, 1928-39; Principal United Theological Coll. (Welsh Presbyterian) Aberystwyth, 1939-49; retired, 1949; First Sec. of Ministerial Candidates Bd. (N Wales); Davies Lectr., 1933; resigned as Mem. Council and Court of Nat. Library of Wales and of Univ. Coll. of Wales, Aberystwyth, 1957. Founder Pres. of the Aberystwyth Rotary Club, 1948-1949; Hon. D.D. (Edinburgh), 1946; Moderator of Eastern Synod of Presbyterian Church of Wales, 1951-52; Moderator of the Welsh Presbyterian Church General Assembly, 1957-1958. *Publications:* two volumes of Children's Stories in Welsh, 1921, 1928; two volumes in Welsh on the Bible, 1922, 1932; one Welsh volume on the History of Civilisation, 1927; and one on the Kingdom of God and Apocalyptic, 1935; one Welsh volume on History of the Theological College, Bala, 1837-1937, 1937; Editor of Free Churchmanship, 1913, The Leisure of the Adolescent (in Welsh), 1929, and A Syllabus of Religious Instruction in the Schools of Wales, 1945; Christian Doctrine (in Welsh), 1953. *Address:* Faircroft, Queen's Road, Oswestry, Shropshire. *T.:* Oswestry 2624. [*Died* 5 *Oct.* 1963.

EDWARDS, Sir Henry Charles Serrell Priestley, 4th Bart., *cr.* 1866; late Lieut. London Regiment; *b.* 1 Mar. 1893; *s.* of 2nd Bt. (*d.* 1896) and 2nd wife, late Laura Selina, 2nd *d.* of late John Capes Clark; *S.* brother, 1942; *m.* 1st, 1916, Margarita Ethelyn (*d.* 1932), *d.* of late J. B. King Kalvi; 2nd, 1935, Daphne Marjory Hilda, *e. d.* of William George Birt, Kensington, W.; two *s.* *Educ.:* Rossall. *Heir:* *s.* Christopher John Churchill Edwards, *b.* 16 Aug. 1941. *Address:* 47 Redcliffe Gardens, Kensington, S.W.10. *T.:* Flaxman 9247. [*Died* 3 *April* 1963.

EDWARDS, Sir Ifan ab Owen, Kt. 1947; M.A. Wales and Oxon; *b.* 25 July 1895; *s.* of Sir Owen Edwards, M.A., D.Litt.; *m.* 1923, Eirys Mary Lloyd Phillips; two *s.* *Educ.:* Dragon School, Oxford; Grammar Sch., Bala; University Coll. of Wales; Lincoln Coll., Oxford. Founder-Pres., Welsh League of Youth; Pres., Nat. Library of Wales, 1958-67; Vice-President: Soc. for Preservation of Rural Wales; Hon. Soc. of Cymmrodorion; Coleg Harlech. Sometime Dir., Independent Television Wales and the West Ltd. Formerly Member: Court, Univ. of Wales; Court, Nat. Museum of Wales; Council of Wales; Nat. Parks Commn.; Council, Nat. Eisteddfod; Welsh Educn. Adv. Council, Cardiganshire. J.P., 1941-58; High Sheriff, 1950. Hon. LL.D. Wales, 1959. *Publications:* A Catalogue of the Star Chamber Proceedings relating to Wales; Cymru; contribs. to Welsh language magazines. *Address:* Bryneithin, Llanbadarn Road, Aberystwyth, Cardiganshire. *T.:* Aberystwyth 3459. [*Died* 23 *Jan.* 1970.

EDWARDS, Joshua Price, C.B.E. 1952; *b.* 10 May 1898; *o. s.* of J. Price Edwards, Tunstall, Staffs; *m.* 1923, Nancy, *d.* of Dr. B. Wiseman Conway, Manchester; two *s.* *Educ.:* Ellesmere College; Brasenose College, Oxford. B.A. (Oxon.) and Diploma in Forestry (Oxon.) 1923, M.A. (Oxon.) 1946. Private, Artists Rifles, 1916; 2nd Lieut. R.F.C., 1917; Lieut., R.A.F., 1918; served in France and Belgium. Asst. Conservator of Forests, F.M.S., 1924; Conservator, 1937; Dep. Dir. of Forestry, 1947, Director of Forestry, 1950-53, Federation of Malaya. Member, Governing Council, Empire Forestry Assoc., 1951; Chm., F.A.O. Forestry Commission for Asia and the Pacific, 1952. *Publications:* Growth of Malayan Forest Trees, 1930. Editor The Malayan Forester, 1931 and 1947. *Recreations:* cricket, forestry. *Address:* The Croft, Lleaney Road, Ramsey, Isle of Man. [*Died* 21 *Feb.* 1966.

EDWARDS, Sir Lawrence, K.B.E. 1961 (O.B.E. 1950; M.B.E. 1943); Kt. 1946; D.L. Co. Durham; J.P. South Shields; Chairman, North East Coast Ship-repairers Ltd.; Chairman and Managing Director, The Middle Docks and Engineering Co. Ltd., South Shields; *b.* 21 December 1896; *s.* of late J. H. Edwards; *m.* 1921, Dorothy, *d.* of late T. H. Catcheside; two *d.* *Educ.:*

Uppingham School Northumberland Fusiliers and 15th Cavalry Brigade, Egypt, Palestine, Syria. 1914-19; Hon. Col. 439 (Tyne) L.A.A. Regt., R.A. (T.A.), 1947-61. Comd. Officer, 1st Cadet Bn. Durham Light Infantry, 1919-51; Col. Comdt. Durham County A.C.F., 1950-58; Dir. of Merchant Ship Repairs, Admiralty, 1940-45; Pres., Shipbuilding Employers Federation, 1949-50; Mem. of Council, Roy. Inst. of Naval Architects. Freeman and Liveryman of City of London; Member Court of Assistants Worshipful Co. of Shipwrights; Chm., Det Norske Veritas British Cttee. Vice-Pres., Tynemouth Branch, Royal National Lifeboat Institution; Trustee, Uppingham School; President, Rugby Football Union, 1964-65. Commander Order of Orange Nassau (Netherlands), 1948; Commander, Royal Norwegian Order of St. Olav, with star, 1964. *Address:* Culzean Park, Gosforth, Newcastle upon Tyne 3. *T.A.* and *T.:* Gosforth 51908. *Clubs:* Royal Automobile, British Sportsmen's; Sunderland (Sunderland); Durham (Durham). [*Died* 14 *Nov.* 1968.

EDWARDS, Lionel D. R., R.I., R.C.A. 1926; *b.* 9 Nov. 1878; *y. s.* of Dr. James Edwards of Chester and Harriet Maine of Kelso; *m.* 1905, Ethel Ashness Wells; three *s.* one *d.* Artist and press illustrator and writer, chiefly on sporting subjects. *Publications:* (with H. F. Wallace) Hunting and Stalking Deer, 1927; Huntsmen—Past and Present, 1929; My Hunting Sketch Book, 2 vols., 1928 and 1930; Famous Foxhunters, 1932; A Leicester Sketch Book, 1935; Seen from the Saddle, 1936; My Irish Sketch Book, 1938; Horses and Ponies, 1938; Scarlet and Corduroy, 1941; Royal Newmarket, 1944; Getting to Know your Pony, 1947; Reminiscences of a Sporting Artist, 1948; The Fox, 1949; Thy Servant the Horse, 1952; Sportsman's Sketchbook, 1953; (with Frank Meads) They Meet at Eleven, 1956. *Recreation:* fox-hunting. *Address:* Buckholt, West Tytherley, Salisbury, Wilts. *T.:* Broughton 223. *Club:* London Sketch. [*Died* 13 *April* 1966.

EDWARDS, Rev. Maurice Henry, O.B.E. 1928; B.A.; K.H.C.; *b.* 17 May 1886; *s.* of Canon C. Edwards, Hon. Canon of Ripon; *m.* 1918, Edith May Watney; one *d.* *Educ.:* Ripon Grammar School; Queens' College, Cambridge; Leeds Clergy School. Curate of Bedale, 1911-14; Chaplain R.N., 1914-18; Chaplain R.A.F., 1918; served Iraq, 1919-21 and 1930-32; Egypt, 1921-24; Chaplain-in-Chief R.A.F., 1940-44; retired, 1944; Welfare, Rother Vale Collieries, Yorks, 1944-47; Rector of Acton Burnell cum Pitchford, 1948-53; retired 1953. *Recreations:* past: rugger, cricket, hockey; present: salmon and trout fishing. *Address:* Sudgrove Farm, Miserden, Nr. Stroud, Glos. [*Died* 26 *April* 1961.

EDWARDS, Rt. Hon. Ness, P.C. 1947; M.P. (Lab.) Caerphilly Division of Glamorganshire since 1939; *b.* 5 Apr. 1897. *Educ.:* Labour College, London. Started in Pit aged 13 years: Parliamentary Secretary, Ministry of Labour and National Service, 1945-50; Postmaster-General, 1950-51. *Publications:* Industrial Revolution in South Wales; Frost and Chartist Movement in Wales; Workers' Theatre; History of the South Wales Mines; History of South Wales Miners' Federation. *Address:* House of Commons, S.W.1; Danycoed House, Caerphilly, Glamorganshire. *T.:* Caerphilly 3193. [*Died* 3 *May* 1968.

EDWARDS, Admiral Sir Ralph (Alan Bevan), K.C.B. *cr.* 1954 (C.B. 1950) C.B.E. 1943; Royal Navy, retd.; *b.* 31 Mar. 1901 *s.* of Arthur Corbett Edwards; *m.* 1932, Joan le Fowne Hurt; one *s.* one *d.* *Educ.:* Osborne and Dartmouth. Entered Royal Navy, 1914. Served European War of 1914-1918. Midshipman, 1917; Lieut. 1923; Cdr. 1934; Captain, 1939; Rear-Adm. 1948; Vice-Adm. 1952; Adm. 1955. Served War of 1939-45 (despatches 4 times, C.B.E.); Chief of Staff Eastern Fleet and Captain H.M.N.Z.S. Gambia, 1939. A Lord Commissioner of the Admiralty and Assistant Chief of Naval Staff, 1948-50; Flag Officer Second-in-Command, Mediterranean Fleet and Flag Officer (Air) Mediterranean, 1951-52; a Lord Commissioner of the Admiralty, Third Sea Lord and Controller of the Navy, 1953-56; C.-in-C. Mediterranean Station and Allied Forces, Mediterranean, 1957. *Address:* Empshott Lodge, nr. Liss, Hampshire. *T.:* Blackmoor 252. *Club:* United Service. [*Died* 4 *Feb.* 1963.

EDWARDS, Walter James; D.L.; *b.* 1900; *m.* 1919, Catherine, *d.* of Daniel O'Brien, Wapping, E.1; (son died on active service, 1944) one *d.* Formerly a stoker in Royal Navy. Member Stepney Borough Council, 1934-59, Mayor, 1944. M.P. (Lab.) Whitechapel and St. George's Division of Stepney, 1942-50, Stepney, 1950-64; Civil Lord of Admiralty, Aug. 1945-Oct. 1951. D.L., London, 1946. *Address:* 11 Parry House, Wapping, E.1. [*Died* 15 *Oct.* 1964.

EDWARDS, William, M.A. (Camb.); Hon. Litt.D. (Leeds); *b.* 15 July 1874; *s.* of late James Edwards; *m.* 1925, Fanny Spence, *yr. d.* of late James Thomson, Helensburgh. *Educ.:* King Edward's School, Birmingham; Pembroke College, Cambridge (Scholar); First Class Classical Tripos, Parts I. and II. Senior Classical Master, King William's College, Isle of Man, 1897-1900; Bradford Grammar School, 1900-8; Headmaster Heath Grammar School, Halifax, 1908-16; Headmaster, Bradford Grammar School, 1916-36; retired, 1936; President, Incorporated Association of Headmasters, 1929. *Address:* Pentlowe, 270 Hills Road, Cambridge. *T.:* Cambridge 46697. [*Died* 15 *Feb.* 1969.

EDYE, Sir Benjamin Thomas, Kt. 1958; C.B.E. 1957; Hon. Surgeon, Royal Prince Alfred Hospital, Sydney, Australia, since 1928; Hon. Consulting Surgeon, Manly District Hospital, and St. George District Hospital; *b.* Orange, New South Wales, 1884; *s.* of Andrew Edye; *m.* 1919, Jessie McLean (*d.* 1948); *m.* 1955, Katherine Menzies; one *s.* two *d.* *Educ.:* Orange, New South Wales. M.B., Ch.M., 1910; F.R.C.S. 1915; F.R.A.C.S. 1927. R.M.O. Roy. Prince Alfred Hosp., Sydney, 1911. Served as Capt. R.A.M.C., during European War. Hon. Asst. Surgeon, Roy. Prince Alfred Hosp., Sydney, 1920-28. Founder Fellow and Councillor, R.A.C.S., and Mem. N.S.W. State Committee. *Publications:* contrib. to Med. Jl. of Australia. *Recreations:* bowls and golf. *Address:* Craignish, 185 Macquarie St., Sydney, N.S.W., Australia. [*Died* 12 *Oct.* 1962.

EGERTON, Comdr. Hugh Sydney, D.S.C.; Royal Navy (retired); D.L., J.P. East Sussex; *b.* 6 October 1890; *er. surv. s.* of late C. A. Egerton of Mountfield Court and late Lady Mabelle Egerton, *d.* of 1st Earl Brassey; *m.* 1917, Muriel Georgina, *d* of late Beckwith Smith of Aberarder; one *s.* *Educ.:* Royal Naval Colleges, Osborne and Dartmouth. Served in Royal Navy, 1908-1919 and 1939-44. High Sheriff of Sussex, 1925-26. Master East Sussex Foxhounds, 1921-31, 1934-35, and 1943-46. Alderman, East Sussex C.C., 1946-61 (Chm., 1949-52). National Hunt Cttee., 1952; Steward, 1959-1962. *Address:* Mountfield Court, Robertsbridge, Sussex. *T.:* Robertsbridge 442. *Clubs:* United Service, Boodle's. [*Died* 18 *Aug.* 1969.

EGERTON, Sir Philip R. le B. G.; *see* Grey Egerton.

EGERTON - WARBURTON, Geoffrey, D.S.O. 1918; T.D.; D.L.; J.P.; Barrister-at-law, Inner Temple; Architectural Diploma and A.R.I.B.A., 1927; Vice-Lieutenant, Cheshire, 1940; *b.* 18 February 1888; *s.* of late Piers Egerton-Warburton of Arley Hall, Cheshire; *m.* 1927, Hon. Georgiana Mary Dormer, M.B.E. 1943 (*d.* 1955), *e. d.* of 14th Lord Dormer; one *s.* two *d.* *Educ.:* Eton; Christ Church, Oxford; B.A. (1910). Served European War 1914-19 with Cheshire Yeomanry (D.S.O., despatches); Lt.-Col., 1919; Bt. Col. 1925; Hon. Col. 1951. *Address:* Grafton Hall, Malpas, Cheshire. *T.:* Tilston 202. *Clubs:* Bath, Royal Automobile. [*Died* 1 *Aug.* 1961.

EGGAR, James, C.V.O. 1937; C.B.E. 1920 (O.B.E. 1918); *b.* 13 Nov. 1880; *e. s.* of late James Alfred Eggar, Farnham, Surrey; *m.* 1912, Eda Mary (*d.* 1941), *d.* of George Ison, Cambridge; two *s.* *Educ.:* Repton School; Trinity College, Cambridge. Assistant Secretary (Principal Establishment Officer) in H.M. Office of Works, 1917-41; retired, 1941; temp. Administrative Asst., Min. of Supply and Board of Trade, 1941-50. *Address:* Gate House, East Approach Drive, Pittville, Cheltenham. *T.:* Cheltenham 3370. [*Died* 6 *July* 1962.

EGLINTON and WINTON, 17th Earl of (*cr.* 1507); **Archibald William Alexander Montgomerie,** Lord Montgomerie, 1448; Baron Seton and Tranent, 1859; Baron Kilwinning, 1615; Baron Ardrossan (U.K.), 1806; E. of Winton (U.K.), 1859; Hereditary Sheriff of Renfrewshire; D.L. County of Ayr, 1948; V.L. 1953; late Major, Ayrshire Yeomanry T.A.; Member of Royal Coy. of Archers, Queen's Bodyguard for Scotland; *b.* 16 Oct. 1914; *e. s.* of 16th Earl and Lady Beatrice Dalrymple (*d.* 1962), *e. d.* of 11th Earl of Stair; *S.* father, 1945; *m.* 1938, Ursula, *er. d.* of Hon. Ronald Watson, 20 Lyndeoch Place, Edinburgh; one *s.* two *d.* (and one *d.* decd.). *Educ.:* Eton; New College, Oxford. *Heir:* *s.* Lord Montgomerie. *Address:* Monkwood House, By Ayr, Ayrshire. *Clubs:* Cavalry; New (Edinburgh). [*Died* 21 *April* 1966.

EHRENBURG, Ilya, Order of Lenin, 1961; Russian Writer; *b.* 1891. *Educ.:* in Russia. Started literary career at 20; political émigré in France, 1909-17; war correspondent, France, 1914-17; returned to the new Russia, 1917; lived abroad until 1940, mostly in Paris, often returning to study progress of U.S.S.R. Deputy of Supreme Soviet of U.S.S.R. Member, Bureau of World Peace Council. *Publications:* Some 80 novels, volumes of stories and essays, including Julio Jurenito, 1922 (Edn. 1958); The Loves of Jeanne Ney, 1923; A Street in Moscow, The Fall of Paris (Stalin Prize), 1942; The War (short articles), 1943; The Storm, 1949; The Ninth Wave, 1952; The Thaw, 1954; People and Life, 1960 (Eng. trans., 1961); Chekhov, Stendhal and Other Essays (Eng. trans. 1962); The Stormy Life of Laz Roitshvantz (Eng. trans. 1965); *autobiog.:* Childhood and Youth, 1891-1917 (Eng. trans, 1961); First Years of Revolution, 1918-21 (Eng. trans. 1963); Truce 1922-23 (Eng. trans. 1963); Eve of War, 1933-41 (Eng. trans. 1963); War of 1941-45 (Eng. trans. 1964); Post-war Years, 1945-54 (Eng. trans. 1966). *Address:* Rue Gorki 8, Apt. 48, Moscow, U.S.S.R. [*Died* 31 *Aug.* 1967.

EHRLICH, Georg, A.R.A. 1962; R.B.A.; sculptor; Hon. Professor elected by Austrian Government, Vienna, 1956; *b.* 22 February 1897; *s.* of Kurt and Rosa Ehrlich, Vienna; British subject since 1947; *m.* 1930, Bettina Bauer, writer and illustrator of children's books. *Educ.:* Gymnasium, Vienna; Wiener Kunstgewerbeschule, Vienna. Painter, draughtsman, etcher, lithographer until 1927; since then, mainly sculptor. Artist in residence, Columbus Gallery of Fine Arts, Ohio, 1948; teacher, L.C.C., Hammersmith, 1950-51. Has had numerous one-man shows, in Europe and America, from 1920, including several in London from 1938, and West Germany, 1961; Vienna, 1962; Arts Council of Gt. Britain (bronzes) in English towns, incl. Aldeburgh Fest., 1964. Sculptures have been shown in international exhibitions, from 1932, including Venice Biennales, and at the Festival of Britain, 1951. Works (prints, bronzes, etc.) in: British Museum; Victoria and Albert Museum; Tate Gallery; Arts Council of Great Britain; Wakefield City Art Gallery and Museum, York; Tel Aviv Museum of Art, Israel; Metropolitan Museum, New York; and other museums and galleries in U.S.A., and in Vienna, Antwerp, Mannheim, etc. Head of a Horse (bronze) bought by Chantrey Bequest, 1960. Monuments in Public Places: "Pax" (bronze) Memorial, Coventry; Drinking Calf (life-size bronze) Rijksmus. Kröller-Müller, Otterlo, Holland; Old Praying Woman (over-life-size bronze) for old cemetery, marl; The Bombed Child (bronze), Rathaus, Lünen, W. Germany; Standing Boy (life-size bronze) (acquired by Benjamin Britten); Princess Margareth of Hesse and The Rhine (portrait); Prince Ludwig of Hesse and The Rhine (bronze); various bronzes, etc. for County Councils and educational authorities; fountain for Vienna, etc. Silver Tapferkeits Medal, Austria, 1917; Gold Medal, Exposition Internat. des Arts et Techniques, Paris, 1937; Sculpture Award, City of Vienna, 1961. *Relevant publications:* Georg Ehrlich, by Erica Tietze-Conrat (introd. Eric Newton), 1956; Georg Ehrlich Skizzenbuch, 1963. *Recreations:* walking, travelling, reading. *Address:* 22 Palace Gardens Terrace, W.8. *T.:* Bayswater 2948. [*Died* 1 *July* 1966.

EINAUDI, Luigi; *b.* 24 March 1874; *s.* of Lorenzo and Fracchia Einaudi, Placida; *m.* 1903, Ida Pellegrini; three *s.* *Educ.:* University of Turin. Doctor (*hon. causa*) Univ. of Paris, 1951, Univ. of Algiers, 1952; D.C.L. (*h.c.*), Univ. of Trieste, 1952, Univ. of Oxford, 1955, Univ. of Basle, 1956; Univ. of Bologna, 1957; Prof. of Public Finance, Univ. of Turin, 1902-49 and 1955; Professor of Economics, School of Engineering, Turin, 1901-35; Prof. of Public Finance, Bocconi Univ. of Milan, 1904-26. Member of Senate, Kingdom of Italy, 1919-45; Governor, Bank of Italy, 1945-48; Member: Consulta Nazionale, 1945-46; Constituent Assembly, 1946-48; Senate of Italian Republic, April-May 1948 and 1955-; Vice-Premier and Minister of Budget, 1947-1948; President of the Italian Republic, 1948-55. Hon. Pres.: Società Italiana degli Economisti (Turin); Internat. Economic Assoc. (Paris); Vice-Pres. Econ. Hist. Soc. (Cambridge); Member: Accademia Nazionale dei Lincei (Rome); Accademia delle Scienze (Turin); Accademia dei Georgofili (Florence); Accademia delle Scienze dell' Istituto di Bologna; Société d'Économie Politique (Paris); Institut International de Statistique (The Hague); Cobden Club (London); Amer. Philosophical Soc. (Philadelphia); Amer. Acad. of Polit. and Soc. Science (Philadelphia); Econometric Soc. (Chicago); Amer. Economic Assoc.; Amer. Acad. of Arts and Sciences (Boston); Oesterreichische Akademie der Wissenschaften (Vienna); Academia de Ciencias Culturales y Artes (Tucuman). *Publications:* Un principe mercante, 1900; La rendita mineraria, 1901; Studi sugli effetti delle imposte, 1902; Le entrate pubbliche dello stato sabaudo, 1907; Prediche, 1920; Gli ideali di un economista, 1921; Lotte del lavoro, 1924; La terra e l'imposta, 1924; La guerra e il sistema tributario italiano, 1927; Contributo alla ricerca dell' ottima imposta, 1929; Gli effetti economici e sociali della guerra in Italia,

1930; Principi di scienza della finanza, 4th edn., 1948; La guerra e l' unità europea, 1948; Lezioni di politica sociale, 1949; Saggi bibliografici e storici intorno alle dottrine economiche, 1953; Il buongoverno, 1954; Lo scrittoio del Presidente, 1956; Saggi di economia e di finanza, 1958; Director of: La riforma sociale, 1900-36, Rivista di storia economica, 1936-43, Prediche inutili, 1956-. Contributor: La stampa, 1896-1900; Il corriere della sera, 1900-25, 1945-48; Il risorgimento liberale, 1945-48; The Economist (formerly correspondent). *Address:* Dogliani, Cuneo, Italy; Largo Volumnia 1, Rome, Italy.

[*Died* 30 *Oct.* 1961.

EISENHOWER, General Dwight David; President of the United States of America from 20 Jan. 1953 until 20 Jan. 1961; *b.* 14 Oct. 1890; 3rd *s.* of David J. Eisenhower and Ida Elizabeth Stover; *m.* 1916, Mamie Geneva Doud; one *s.* *Educ.:* United States Military Academy, West Point, N.Y. (graduated, 1915). Served with Infantry of U.S Army as a company officer in various staff duties, 1915-17; later instructor in Army Service Schools at Fort Leavenworth, Kansas; in 1918 organised and commanded Camp Colt, for Tank Corps troops; continued with Tank Corps until 1922; Executive Officer of Camp Gaillard, Panama; graduated Command and General Staff School, Fort Leavenworth, Kansas, 1926; with American Battle Monuments Commission, with Headquarters in Paris, 1927; Asst. Executive, Office of Asst. Secretary of War in Washington, 1929-33; drafted the War Department's study and plans for industrial mobilisation; Office of Chief of Staff until 1935; Asst. Military Adviser to Commonwealth of Philippine Islands, 1935-40; served with 15th Inf. in California and Washington State; Chief of Staff: 3rd Division, IX Army Corps, 3rd Army; Assistant Chief of Staff in charge of Operations Div., War Dept., General Staff, Washington, D.C.; command of European Theatre of Operations, 1942; C.-in-C. Allied Forces in North Africa, Nov. 1942-44; Supreme Commander Allied Expeditionary Force in Western Europe, 1944-45; Comdr. American Occupation Zone of Germany, 1945; Chief of Staff U.S. Army, 1945-48; President of Columbia University, New York, 1948 (on leave of absence, 1950, resigned, Nov. 1952). Supreme Commander of the North Atlantic Treaty Forces in Europe, 1950-52. Resigned Commission in Army after nomination as Republican Candidate, 1952; after term of office as President of the United States, Congress unanimously passed bill commissioning him as a General of the Army (without pay and allowances); bill became law, 1961. Republican. Honorary degrees from institutions in the United States and abroad; orders, medals, and decorations from the United States and other governments, including: D.S.M. (U.S.), 1922; D.S.M. (U.S. Navy), 1947; Hon. G.C.B. 1943; Hon. O.M. 1945; LL.D. (Belfast, N. Ire.), 1945; D.C.L. (Oxford, Eng.), 1945; LL.D. (Edinburgh, Scot.), 1946; LL.D. (Cambridge, Eng.) 1946. Pilgrims' Gold Medal, 1963. *Publications:* Crusade in Europe, 1948; Mandate for Change, 1963; The White House Years: Waging Peace, 1956-61, 1965. *Recreations:* golf, bridge, fishing and hunting. *Address:* Gettysburg, Pennsylvania, U.S.A.

[*Died* 28 *March* 1969.

EISENSCHITZ, Professor Robert Karl; retd. as Professor of Theoretical Physics in the University of London, Queen Mary College (1957-65); Emeritus Professor, 1965; *b.* 14 January 1898; *s.* of late Emil Eisenschitz and Felicie Auguste Eisenschitz (*née* Spitzer); *m.* 1948, Eva Regina Therese (*née* Laufer); one *s.* one *d.* *Educ.:* Gram. Sch., Vienna. Univs. of Vienna and Munich; Technical College, Karlsruhe. Employed in industry, Berlin, 1924-27; Research Worker, Kaiser Wilhelm Institute, Berlin-Dahlem, 1924-33; Research Worker, Davy Faraday Laboratory of the Royal Institution, 1933-46; Lecturer, University College, London, 1946-49; Reader in the University of London, Queen Mary College, 1949-56. Dr. phil. Munich, 1924; D.Sc. London, 1952; F.Inst.P. 1949. *Publications:* papers in periodicals such as Zeitschrift für Physik, Proc. Roy. Soc., Science Progress, Phil. Mag., etc., 1926-; Statistical Theory of Irreversible Processes, 1958; Matrix Algebra for Physics Students, 1965. *Recreations:* books, music, the arts—preferably contemporary. *Address:* 22 Chalk Road, E.13. *T.:* 01-476 4059.

[*Died* 15 *July* 1968.

EKINS, Emily Helen, O.B.E. 1934; B.Sc. Hort. (Lond.), N.D.H.; *b.* 9 Nov. 1879; *o. d.* of late A. E. Ekins, F.I.C., J.P., Public Analyst for Herts. *Educ.:* St. Albans High School; Birmingham University; Studley College. Lecturer in Horticulture and allied subjects at Studley College, 1911-22; Acting Warden, 1922-24; Principal Studley Horticultural and Agricultural College, 1924-46. *Publications:* Articles on Outdoor Life. *Recreations:* travel, motoring. *Address:* Combe Cottage, Sandford Orcas, Sherborne, Dorset. *T.:* Corton Denham 291.

[*Died* 4 *June* 1964.

EKWALL, Prof. Bror Oscar Eilert; Emeritus Professor of the English Language in the University of Lund, Sweden; *b.* 1877 *m.*; Dagny (*d.* 1958) *d.* of L. Schmidt Nielsen, Trondheim, Norway. *Educ.:* Univ. of Uppsala. Matric. 1894; Ph.D. 1903; Hon. D.Litt. Oxford, 1939; LL.D. Glasgow, 1951; lectured at King's Coll., London, Nov. 1924, Knight Commander of the Swedish Order of the North Star, 1942; Hon. Corr. Mem. of the English Place-Name Society, 1925; Vice-Pres. since 1926; Fellow of the Royal Swedish Academy of Science, 1935; Corresponding Fellow of the British Academy and of the Prussian Academy of Science, 1937; Fellow of Danish Academy of Science, 1938, Norwegian Academy of Science, 1940, Royal Historical Society (London), 1957; Honorary Fellow of Modern Lang. Assoc. of America, 1949. C.B.E. (Hon.) Great Britain, 1962. *Publications:* Shakspere's Vocabulary, 1903; Dr. John Jones's Practical Phonography, 1907; The Unchanged Plural in English, 1912; Historische neuenglische Laut- und Formenlehre, 1914, 2nd ed. 1922, 3rd. ed. 1956; Old English Dialects, 1917; Scandinavians and Celts, 1918; Place-Names of Lancashire, 1922; English Place-Names in -ing, 1923; English River Names, 1928; Lydgate's Siege of Thebes II (with A. Erdmann), 1930; Studies on English Place and Personal Names, 1931; The Concise Oxford Dictionary of English Place-Names, 1936, 2nd ed., 1940, 3rd ed., 1947, 4th ed. 1960; Studies on English Place-Names, 1936; Early London Personal Names, 1947; (ed.) Two Early London Subsidy Rolls, 1951; Street-names of the City of London, 1954; The Population of Medieval London, 1956, Selected Papers, 1663; articles in the Survey of English Place-Names, Anglia-Beiblatt, Namn och Bygd, etc. *Recreation:* gardening. *Address:* The University, Lund, Sweden. *T.:* Lund 10918.

[*Died* 30 *Nov.* 1964.

ELDER, John Rawson, C.M.G. 1935; M.A. 1902; D.Litt. 1914 (Aberd.); LL.D. (Aberd.) 1943; Professor of History in the University of Otago, Dunedin, New Zealand, 1920-45; Professor Emeritus, 1945; *b.* Gibraltar, 4 Feb. 1880; *s.* of James Elder, Aberdeen; *m.* 1908, Margaret, *d.* of James Mitchell, Aberdeen; two *s.* one *d.* *Educ.:* Robert Gordon's College, Aberdeen; Aberdeen University. M.A. with First Class Honours in English and History, 1902; on staff of Gordon's College, Aberdeen, 1902-20; Caregien

Trust Grantee, 1910-20; Lecturer in Spanish in Robert Gordon's Technical College, Aberdeen, and Lecturer in British History in the University of Aberdeen, 1914-20. *Publications:* The Royal Fishery Companies of the Seventeenth Century, 1912; The Highland Host of 1678, 1914; Spanish Influences in Scottish History 1920; Spanish Composition through Reading, 1923; La Verdad Sospechosa de Alarcón, 1923; Glimpses of Old New Zealand, 1924; The Pioneer Explorers of New Zealand, 1929; New Zealand Gold Seekers and Bushrangers, 1930; The Letters and Journals of Samuel Marsden 1932; Marsden's Lieutenants, 1934; Cambridge History of Empire, Chapter on Early Trading and Exploration in New Zealand, 1934; The New Zealand Book of the Coronation, 1937; The History of the Presbyterian Church of New Zealand, 1940. *Address:* 14 Allandale Road, St Clair, Dunedin, S.W.1, New Zealand. [*Died* 11 *April* 1962.

ELDER, Rear-Admiral William Leslie, C.M.G. 1918; *b.* 1874; *s.* of late Henry Hugh Elder, Stondon Place, Essex; *m.* 1907, Alice Eastlake, *d.* of late Alfred Norman, F.R.I.B.A., J.P., Devonport. Served East Africa, 1896 (despatches); Benin Expedition, 1897 (medal and clasp); European War, 1914-19 (despatches, C.M.G. Officer Legion of Honour, Croix de Guerre with Palm); retired list, 1923. *Address:* 20 Dolphin Court, Craneswater Gardens, Southsea. *T.:* Portsmouth 31576. [*Died* 29 *Oct.* 1961.

ELDERTON, Sir Thomas Howard, K.C.I.E., *cr.* 1943; Kt., *cr.* 1937 Chairman, Calcutta Port Trust, retd. 1947; *b.* London, 28 April 1886; *s.* of late William Alexander Elderton; *m.* 1925, Wilhelmina Sutherland. *Educ.:* Merchant Taylors' School Clare College Cambridge. B.A. (1st Class Mathematical Tripos) 1908, M.A. 1921; Assistant Secretary to Calcutta Port Trust, 1909; Deputy Secretary, 1914; Secretary, 1918; Deputy Chairman, 1924; Chairman, 1932. Special Commissioner for Eastern India and Chairman Railway Priorities Committee, 1942; served European War, 1915-17 2nd Lieut. 3rd Bedfordshire Regt. (Special Reserve); Lieut., 1916 in France with 7th Bedfordshire Regt. (wounded) *Address:* c/o Lloyds Bank, 6 Pall Mall, S.W.1 *Clubs:* Bengal (Calcutta), Tollygunge (Calcutta), Royal Calcutta Turf. [*Died* 14 *Feb.* 1970.

ELDERTON, Sir William Palin, K.B.E., *cr.* 1946 (C.B.E. 1920); Kt., *cr.* 1938; Director, Equitable Life Assurance Society; *b.* 26 June 1877; *s.* of late Wm. Alex. Elderton; *m.* 1920, Enid Muriel, *d.* of George Podmore; one *s.* *Educ.:* Merchant Taylors' School. F.I.A. 1901; F.F.A. 1931; Ph.D. Hon. Oslo, 1938; F.C.I.I. 1940; F.S.G.1955; a Governor of City of London College, since 1920; Corresp. Member of French and Italian Institutes of Actuaries; Actuary of Star Assurance Soc. 1912-13; Actuary and Manager, Equitable Life Assurance Soc., 1913-42, President 1947-53; Statistical Adviser, Ministry of Shipping, 1917-20, Ministries of Shipping and War Transport, 1939-46; Chairman, Life Offices' Assoc., 1927-28; Pres. Institute of Actuaries, 1932-1934; Pres. Insurance Institute of London, 1935-36; Chm. British Insurance Assoc., 1937-38; Chm. White Fish Commission, 1938-39; Pres. Chartered Insurance Institute, 1942-43; Chairman East Indian Railway Co., 1948-53; Chevalier, Legion of Honour, 1920; Gold Medal Institute and Faculty of Actuaries, 1937. *Publications:* Frequency Curves and Correlation; Primer of Statistics; Construction of Mortality Tables; Mortality of Annuitants, 1900-20; Shipping Problems; contributions to scientific journals on actuarial, statistical and genealogical subjects. *Recreations:* walking, sketching. *Address:* 7 Long Park Close, Chesham Bois, Bucks. *T.:* Amersham 437. *Club:* City of London. [*Died* 6 *April* 1962.

ELEY, Rt. Rev. Stanley Albert Hallam, M.A.; Bishop of Gibraltar since 1960; *b.* 31 Aug. 1899; *s.* of late Albert George and Annie Hope Eley; *m.* 1928, Doreen Mabel, *d.* of late Lieut. Herbert and Mabel Bourne. *Educ.:* City of London School; Leeds University; Mirfield. Various curacies; Secretary London Diocesan Fund and Reorganisation Committee, 1934-46; Senior Chaplain to Archbishop of Canterbury, 1946-48; Vicar of Kensington, 1948-60; Rural Dean of Kensington, 1952-60. Asst. Sec., Lambeth Conference, 1948; Member Church Assembly Financial Commission, 1940-43; Proctor in Convocation for Diocese of London, 1949-59; Prebendary of St. Paul's Cathedral, 1944-60. Sub-Prelate, O.St.J., 1960. *Address:* 19 Brunswick Gardens, W.8. *Club:* Athenæum. [*Died* 7 *April* 1970.

ELGIN, 10th Earl of, *cr.* 1633, and **KINCARDINE,** 14th Earl of, *cr.* 1647, **Edward James Bruce,** K.T. 1933; C.M.G. 1919; T.D., C.D., LL.D. (hon.) Glasgow and St. Andrews; Grand Cross Order of Polonia Restituta, 1944; Baron Bruce, 1603; Earl of Kincardine and Baron Bruce of Torry, 1647; Baron Elgin (U.K.), 1949; H.M. Lieutenant, County of Fife, 1935-65; President Fife T.A. Association; Hon. Colonel Elgin Regiment (R.C.A.C.); Captain of Royal Company of Archers, Queen's Body Guard for Scotland; Director, Scottish Amicable Life Assurance Soc.; Past Dir., Royal Bank of Scotland; Vice-President: Building Societies Association; National Trust for Scotland; Scottish Council (Development and Industry); *b.* 8 June 1881; *e. s.* of 9th Earl of Elgin and Lady Constance Carnegie (*d.* 1909), *d.* of 9th Earl of Southesk, K.T.; *S.* father, 1917; *m.* 1921, Honourable Katherine Elizabeth Cochrane, D.B.E., *cr.* 1938, *er. d.* of 1st Baron Cochrane of Cults; three *s.* three *d.* *Educ.:* Eton; Balliol College, Oxford. Formerly Capt. Forfar and Kincardine R.G.A. Militia; Major commanding Highland (Fife) R.G.A.; served European War, 1914-18 (C.M.G.); Zone Adviser Home Guard, 1940-46; Hon. Colonel 357 Medium Regiment, R.A., T.A.; Hon. Colonel 471 H. (M.) AA. Regiment, Forth R.A., T.A.; Hon. Air Commodore 948 Squadron R.A.F.; Lord High Commissioner of Church of Scotland, 1925 and 1926; Chairman, Educational Endowments Commission, Scotland, 1926-36; National Council on Juvenile Employment (Scotland), 1926-46; Fife County Council, 1929-38; Forth Conservancy Board, 1926-55; Member Cttee. of Inquiry, B.B.C., 1949; B.B.C. General Advisory Council, 1952-56; Housing Progress Panel (Scotland); President: Royal Highland and Agricultural Soc., 1949; Scottish-Polish Soc.; Empire Exhibition (Scotland), 1938; Chairman, Land Settlement Assoc., England & Wales, 1933-46; A.D. Labour, 1917; Labour Commandant with rank of Colonel, 1918; Chairman Carnegie United Kingdom Trust, 1923-46; Past Chm. of Governors, Newbattle Abbey Coll. Grand Master Mason Scotland, 1921-24; J.P. Fife. *Heir:* *s.* Lord Bruce. *Address:* Culross Abbey House, Culross, by Dunfermline. *T.:* Newmills 333. *Clubs:* Brooks's, Royal Automobile; Caledonian. [*Died* 27 *Nov.* 1968.

ELIBANK, 3rd Viscount, of Elibank (*cr.* 1911), **Lieut.-Colonel Arthur Cecil Murray,** C.M.G. 1919; D.S.O. 1916; 12th Bt. of Nova Scotia, 1628; 12th Baron Elibank of Ettrick Forest (*cr.* 1643); 4th *s.* of 1st Viscount and 10th Baron Elibank; *b.* 27 Mar. 1879; *S.* brother, 1951; *m.* 1931, Faith Celli Standing (*d.* 1942) (created part of dream daughter in original production of

Dear Brutus, 1917 and in revival 1922, also name part in Peter Pan, 1918). Entered army, 1898; A.D.C. to Lieut.-Governor of Bengal, 1900; served China, 1900 (medal); commanded Mounted Infantry Coy., protecting Sinho-Shanhaikwan Railway, 1901-1902; A.D.C. to G.O.C. 1st Infantry Division, Delhi Manœuvres, 1902; served N.W.F., India, and Chitral, 1903-04; M.P. (L.) Kincardineshire, 1908-23; attended Quebec Tercentenary Celebrations, 1908 (guest of Canadian Govt.) as representing Gen. Hon. James Murray, 1st British Governor of Canada; Parliamentary Private Secretary to Sir Edward Grey, Secretary of State for Foreign Affairs, 1910-14; Member of Special Mission to Foreign Courts to announce King George V.'s accession to the Throne, 1910; passed Bill through House of Commons 1914 to ameliorate conditions of worn-out horse traffic; served European War, France and Belgium, with 2nd King Edward's Horse, 1914-16 (despatches, D.S.O.); Assistant Military Attaché, Washington, 1917 - 18 (C.M.G.); Member of Royal Company of Archers (Queen's Body Guard for Scotland); Director, L.N.E.R., 1923 - 48; Director, Wembley Stadium Ltd., etc. *Publications:* Memorials of Sir Gideon Murray of Elibank and His Times, 1560-1621; Lord Grey of Fallodon, K.G., Quarterly Review, Jan. 1934; The Five Sons of "Bare Betty", 1936; A Modern Marvel, 1938; Master and Brother, 1945; British Foreign Policy between the Two World Wars, 1946; At Close Quarters, 1947; Decisive Battles in History in a Nutshell, 1947; Whatnots, 1947; Corrievreckan, 1949; An Episode in the Spanish War, 1739-1744, 1952. *Heir:* (*to barony and baronetcy only*) *kinsman* James A. F. C. Erskine-Murray. *Address:* Carrington House, W.1. *T.:* Mayfair 0495. *Clubs:* Brooks's; New (Edinburgh). [*Died* 5 *Dec.* 1962 (*Viscountcy ext.*).

ELIOT, Thomas Stearns, O.M. 1948; A.B. and A.M. (Harvard) 1910; Hon. D.Litt. (Oxford); Litt.D. (Cambridge, Harvard, Yale, Princeton, Columbia, Bristol, Leeds, Washington, Rome, Sheffield); LL.D. (Edin., St. Andrews); D. ès L. (Paris, Aix-Marseille, Rennes); D.Phil. (Munich); D.Lit. (Lond.); Nobel Prize for Literature, 1948; Hon. Fellow, Merton College, Oxford, and Magdalene College, Cambridge; Officier de la Légion d'Honneur; President of the London Library since 1952; Foreign Member: Accademia dei Lincei (Rome); Bayer. Akad. der Schönen Künste (Munich); Hon. Member, American Academy-Institute; Director, Faber and Faber, Ltd.; *b.* 1888; *y. s.* of Henry Ware Eliot and Charlotte Chauncy Eliot of St. Louis, U.S.A.; *m.* 1st, Vivienne Haigh (*d.* 1947), *o. d.* of Charles Haigh Haigh-Wood; 2nd, 1957, Esmé Valerie, *o. d.* of James Fletcher, Headingley, Leeds. *Educ.:* Harvard University; University of Paris; Merton College, Oxford. Clark Lecturer, Trinity Coll., Cambridge, 1926; Charles Eliot Norton Prof. of Poetry, Harvard Univ., 1932-33; Pres. Classical Assoc., 1943; late Edit., The Criterion. Hanseatic Goethe Prize, 1954; Dante Gold Medal (Florence), 1959. Hon. Citizen of Dallas, Texas; Hon. Dep. Sheriff of Dallas County. Orden Pour le Mérite (West Germany), 1959; Commandeur Ordre des Arts et des Lettres. *Publications:* The Sacred Wood, 1920; The Use of Poetry and the Use of Criticism, 1933; After Strange Gods, 1934; The Rock, 1934; Elizabethan Essays, 1934; Murder in the Cathedral, 1935; The Family Reunion, 1939; The Idea of a Christian Society, 1939; Practical Cats, 1939; Four Quartets, 1944; What is a Classic?, 1945; Notes Toward the Definition of Culture, 1948; The Cocktail Party, 1950; Poetry and Drama, 1951; Selected Essays, 1951; The Confidential Clerk, 1954; On Poetry and Poets, 1957; The Elder Statesman, 1959; Collected Poems, 1909-62, 1963; *Relevant Publications:* The Making of T. S. Eliot's Plays by E. Martin Browne, 1969; A Student's Guide to the Selected Poems of T. S. Eliot, by B. C. Southam, 1969; T. S. Eliot: A Bibliography, by Donald Gallup, 1969. *Posthumous Publications:* For Lancelot Andrewes: Essays on Style and Order, 1970; The Waste Land: A facsimile and transcript of the original drafts (ed. Valerie Eliot), 1971. *Address:* 24 Russell Square, W.C.1. *Clubs:* Athenæum, Garrick. [*Died* 4 *Jan.* 1965.

EL'KANEMI, Alhaji Sir Umar Ibn Muhammed El'Amin, Shehu of Bornu, K.B.E. 1961 (C.B.E. 1942); C.M.G. 1946; Mem. House of Chiefs, N. Nigeria; *b.* 1873; *s.* of Muhammed El'Amin El'Kanemi; *m.* 1889, Maira Kolo, Shehu of Dikwa, 1917-1937; Shehu of Bornu, 1937. Awarded an honour of Knighthood by President of Niger Republic, 1961. *Address:* Shehu's Palace, Maiduguri, Bornu, N. Nigeria. [*Died* 29 *Dec.* 1967.

ELKINGTON, John St. Clair, M.A., M.D. (Cantab.), F.R.C.P. (London); Physician in charge of the Neurological Department, St. Thomas's Hospital; Physician National Hospital, Queen Square; *y. s.* of late E. A. Elkington, Newport, Shropshire. *Educ.:* Adams' Grammar School, Newport Shropshire; Trinity College, Cambridge (Sen. Scholar); St. Thomas's Hospital. 1st Class Natural Science Tripos Part I, 1924, Part II, 1925; University Scholar and Meade Prizeman, St. Thomas's Hospital; Murchison Scholar, Royal College of Physicians, 1929; Fearnsides Scholar, University of Cambridge, 1932. *Publications:* contributions to neurological literature. *Address:* 60 Montagu Square, W.1. *T.:* Paddington 0433. *Club:* Athenæum. [*Died* 21 *Jan.* 1963.

ELKINS, Major-General William Henry Pferinger, C.B. 1943; C.B.E. 1935; D.S.O. 1918; *b.* Sherbrooke, P.Q., 13 June 1883; *s.* of late A. W. Elkins, Sherbrooke, and Esther Margaret (Breadon); *m.* 1914, Phyllis, *d.* of late Major Charles Short; two *d.* *Educ.:* Bishops College School, Lennoxville, P.Q.; Royal Military College of Canada. Joined Royal Canadian Artillery, 1905; served Canada and India (attached "N" Battery, Royal Horse Artillery, European War, France and Flanders, 1915-18 (D.S.O. and bar, despatches thrice); Staff Officer Artillery, National Defence Headquarters, Ottawa, Ont., 1926-30; Commandant, Royal Military College of Canada, 1930-35; commanded No. 2 Military District, Toronto, 1935-38; Master-General of the Ordnance, Canada, 1938-40; General Officer Commanding in-Chief Atlantic Command, Canada, 1940-43; retd. 1944. K.St.J. *Recreations:* shooting and fishing. *Address:* 3 Emily Street, Kingston, Ontario. *Club:* University (Montreal). [*Died* 20 *Dec.* 1964.

ELLERTON, Sir (Frederick) Cecil, Kt., 1952; Director (formerly Deputy Chairman) Barclays Bank Ltd.; Deputy Chairman Barclays Bank (France) Ltd.; Deputy Chairman, Yorkshire Bank Ltd.; Director: Banque de Commerce; United Dominions Trust; *b.* 8 August 1892; *s.* of late F. G. Ellerton; *m.* 1918, Dorothy Catherine, *d.* of late W. J. Green; two *s.* *Educ.:* Merchant Taylors' Sch. Gen. Man., Barclays Bank Ltd., 1942-50. Dir., Vice-Chm. and Dep. Chm., 1950-58; Pres. Institute of Bankers, 1950-52. *Recreations:* reading, golf and motoring. *Address:* Oriel Lodge, Burkes Road, Beaconsfield, Bucks. *T.:* Beaconsfield 659. *Club:* Reform. [*Died* 20 *Aug.* 1962.

ELLINGFORD, Herbert Frederick, B.Mus. (Oxon), A.R.C.M.; F.R.C.O., Hon. A.R.C.M.; Hon. F.T.C.L.; *b.* London, 1876; *s.* of Arthur William and Priscilla Elizabeth Ellingford, London; *m.* Clara, *d.* of Francis and Caroline Bentley, London; two *d.* *Educ.:*

private; Royal College of Music, London. Organist, St. Andrew's Church, Leytonstone, Essex, 1891-1901; and for Dr. W. G. McNaught's Concerts at Bow and Bromley Institute, London, 1890-1900; Organist and Choirmaster at St. Peter's Parish Church, Carmarthen, South Wales, 1901-06; St. George's Parish Church, Belfast, 1906-13; Organist to Rt. Hon. the Earl of Shaftesbury, Belfast Castle, 1907-13; Organist to the Liverpool Corporation at St. George's Hall, Liverpool, 1913-43; Pres. of the Liverpool Organists' Assoc., 1915-16; Pres. Merseyside Assoc. for Masonic Research, 1942-44; Organ Professor, Trinity College of Music, London, 1944-54; Member of Royal College of Organists Council, 1915-54; has given organ recitals in the most important cities and towns in the United Kingdom; Examiner and Lecturer in Music; Adjudicator at Competitive Festivals. President High Wycombe and District Organists' Association, 1953-1962. *Publications:* songs, part-songs, church music, pianoforte music, and organ primers; Science of Organ Pedalling; various articles in musical jls. *Address:* Merrivale, Sawpit Hill, Hazlemere, High Wycombe, Bucks. *T.:* Holmer Green 3138. [*Died* 19 *May* 1966.

ELLINGTON, Marshal of the Royal Air Force Sir Edward Leonard, G.C.B., *cr.* 1935 (K.C.B., *cr.* 1920; C.B. 1919); C.M.G. 1916; C.B.E. 1919; *b.* 30 Dec. 1877. *Educ.:* Clifton; R.M.A., Woolwich. Served European War, 1914-18 (despatches thrice, Legion of Honour, C.M.G., Bt. Lt.-Col., Bt. Col.); Dir.-General of Supply and Research, Air Ministry, 1919-21 a member of the Air Council, 1918; 1922; Commanded R. Air Force in Middle East, 1922-23; India, 1923-26; Iraq, 1926-28; Air Officer Commanding-in-Chief, Air Defence of Great Britain, 1929-31; Air Member for Personnel on Air Council, 1931-33; Chief of Air Staff, 1933-37; Inspector General of Royal Air Force, 1937-40; Principal Air A.D.C. to the King, 1930-34. *Address:* Scio House, Portsmouth Rd., Putney Heath, S.W.15. *Club:* United Service. [*Died* 13 *June* 1967.

ELLIOT, Major-General Gilbert Minto, C.B. 1949; C.B.E. 1945; D.S.O. 1943; M.C. 1917; D.L.; *b.* 22 May 1897; *s.* of late Colonel R. H. Elliot, M.R.C.S., L.R.C.P., I.M.S., 54 Welbeck St., W.1; *m.* 1922, Margaret, *d.* of late Frank Hinde, M.D., Hook Norton, Oxon; two *s.* one *d.* (and one *s.* decd.). *Educ.:* Cheltenham College; R.M.A., Woolwich. Commissioned, 1915; served European War, 1914-19, with R.A. (despatches, severely wounded). Instr. School of Signals, 1924-26; G.S.O. 3 India, 1933-35; G.S.O. 2 India, 1935-37; Bt. Major, 1934, Major, 1935; Staff Officer R.A. India, 1938; served War of 1939-45. Lt.-Col. 1940; France, 1940; Brig. 1941; C.R.A. Highland Division; Africa and Sicily, 1942-43; C.C.R.A. 12 Corps, 1944; B.G.S. 12 Corps, 1944-45; B.G.S. Scottish Command, 1945-48; Chief of Staff, Western Command, 1948-51; retd. 1951. D.L. Devon, 1964. *Recreations:* outdoor country pursuits and sport. *Address:* Breach, Kilmington, Axminster, Devon. *T.:* Axminster 2132. [*Died* 3 *Jan.* 1969.

ELLIOT, Hubert William Arthur; *b.* 1891; *s.* of late Hon. Arthur R. D. Elliot and Madeleine (*d.* 1906), *d.* of late Sir Charles Lister Ryan, K.C.B.; *m.* 1st, 1919, Mary (*d.* 1945), *d.* of late Hon Sir Langer Owen, C.B.E.; one *s.* one *d.*; 2nd, 1955, Pamela Violet Cathcart, *d.* of P. D. Stirling. Old Kippenross, Dunblane, Perthshire. *Educ.:* Eton; Trinity Coll., Cambridge, (B.A.). Capt. 4th Batt. Wilts. Regt. 1914-19; Land Agent for the Duke of Buccleuch, K.T., 1924-1938, and for Earl Fitzwilliam's Milton Estate, 1938-60. Fellow of Chartered Land Agents' Society (retired). *Address:* Dalliotfield, Muthill, Perthshire. [*Died* 13 *Dec.* 1967.

ELLIOTT, Rt. Rev. Anthony Blacker; *see* Addenda: II.

ELLIOTT, Clarence; Writer; *b.* 1881; *y. s.* of late Joseph John Elliott, Hadley, Herts; *m.* 1911, Phyllis Mary, 3rd *d.* of late Alfred James Eyre, Norwood; two *s.* one *d.* *Educ.:* Giggleswick School. In South Africa fruit farming, 1902-5; established the Six Hills Nursery at Stevenage, 1907; has made numerous plant collecting expeditions, Corsica, 1908; Falkland Islands, 1910; Pyrenees four times, Maritime Alps, Savoy Alps, and Dolomites repeatedly, Majorca, 1926 and 1927; Chili, Patagonia, Juan Fernandez, Tierra del Fuego, Straits of Magellan and Falkland Islands, 1927-28; Chili and the Andes, 1929-30; Cantabrian Alps, 1935; lecture tour in U.S.A., 1931; followed by plant collecting expedition in W. N. America; lecture tour in Sweden, 1934; has introduced and reintroduced to cultivation numerous plants, including Sisyrinchium filifolium, Sisyrinchium odoratissimum, Oxalis enneaphylla rosea, Thymus herba-barona, Verbena tridens, Leucocoryne ixioides odorata, (Glory of the Sun), Verbena corymbosa, Puya alpestris, etc.; retired from Six Hills Nursery, 1946. Victoria Medal of Honour, Royal Horticultural Soc., 1952. *Publications:* Edited Johns' Flowers of the Field, 1907; Rock Garden Plants, 1935; articles on horticultural subjects; regular contributor to Sunday Times, Countryman and Birmingham Post. *Recreations:* gardening, travel, fishing; country club Fox Inn, Broadwell. *Address:* Clematis Cottage, Broadwell, Moreton in Marsh, Glos. *T.:* Stow on the Wold 249. [*Died* 18 *Feb.* 1969.

ELLIOTT, (Colin) Fraser, C.M.G. 1944; Q.C.; (Can.); B.A.Sc.; Law practice, Ottawa; *b.* 7 Oct. 1888; *s.* of William Moore Elliott and Maria Smith; *m.* 1920, Marjorie Sypher; one *s.* one *d.* *Educ.:* Toronto Public School, High School and University of Toronto and Osgoode Hall, Toronto. Law practice, Toronto, Ontario. Overseas in European War, 1914-18 (1st Div., 2nd Brigade, 7th Battery—Artillery). Income Tax administration as Solicitor, Counsel, Asst. Commissioner, Comr. of Income Tax; late Dep. Minister of Nat. Revenue for Taxation; drew fiscal and tax agreements with U.K., U.S.A., and France; salaries controller during War of 1939-45; Canadian Ambassador to Chile, 1946-51; High Commissioner for Canada in Australia, 1951-53. Alternate delegate to 5th Session of General Assembly of the U.N., 1950. *Recreation:* golf. *Address:* 29 Clemow Ave., Ottawa, Canada; (Law Office) 140 Wellington St., Ottawa, Canada. *Clubs:* University, Rotary, Rideau, Canadian, Royal Ottawa Golf (Ottawa). [*Died* 19 *Dec.* 1969.

ELLIOTT, Edward Cassleton, C.B.E. 1955; Chartered Accountant; formerly Senior Partner of Cassleton Elliott and Co., London, Nigeria, Ghana and Sierra Leone; President, City of London College; Governor and Almoner of Christ's Hospital (formerly Chm. of Finance Cttee.); Member of Accountants Advisory Committee to Board of Trade in regard to Companies Act, 1947; Mem. of Catsfield Parish Council, 1963-66; *b.* 17 Mar. 1881; *s.* of Robert Powditch Elliott and Jane Hall; *m.* 1911, Charity May Coleman; two *s.* one *d.* *Educ.:* Christ's Hosp. Incorporated Accountant, 1904 (Hons. Intermediate and Final Exams.); obtained professional experience in South Africa; commenced practice in London, 1917; Controller of Costings, Ministry of Supply, 1904-41; Pres. Soc. of Incorp Acctnts., 1932-1935; Mem. of Hops Reorganisation Commission, 1946; formerly: Chm., Med. Distribn. Cttee., Min. of Health (now dissolved); Pres. Harpenden Auxiliary Hospital and Memorial Nursing Centre; Deputy Chairman, Heritage Craft Schools, Chailey;

Vice-Pres. West India Cttee. Coronation Medal, 1953. *Publications:* Papers on Accountancy subjects. *Recreations:* travel, farming. *Address:* Horns Hill, Catsfield, Battle, Sussex; 4/6 Throgmorton Avenue, E.C.2. *Clubs:* Reform, City of London, West Indian. [*Died* 1 *Aug.* 1967.

ELLIOTT, Frank Herbert, D.L., J.P.; President, Redhill General Hospital; *b.* 6 March 1878; *s.* of Robert Powditch Elliott and Jane Hall; *m.* 1909, Lucy, *d.* of Rev. F. W. Clarke, Frome, Somerset; two *s.* (and one *s.* killed in action, 1944). *Educ.:* Privately. Member of Surrey Council, 1933- (County Alderman, 1942-, Vice-Chm., 1947-1950, Chm., 1950-53); Chm. County Public Health Cttee., 1945-48 (Vice-Chm., 1942-45) Chm. County Central Purchasing Cttee., 1938-45; Chm., County Laundry Cttee., 1939-45; Chm. of South-West Metropolitan Regional Hospital Bd., 1947-53; a Governor of St. Thomas' Hospital, 1947-57; D.L. for County of Surrey; Chairman of Godstone Bench, 1941-53 (J.P. 1933); Mem. Standing Joint Cttee. for Surrey; Ex-chairman and present member of Governing Body, Caterham School; County Council representative on County Councils Assoc., Metropolitan Water Board, and Thames Conservancy, 1952-65. Chm. 450 Sqdn. A.T.C. and former member Surrey T.A. and A.F.A.; formerly member Caterham and Warlingham Urban District Council and Godstone Rural District Council and ex-Chm. of their Finance Cttees.; Chm., Income Tax Comrs., Tandridge, Surrey, Division. Extensive experience in textiles, engineering, insurance and hospital administration. Dir. of United Kingdom Provident Institution, 1935-63; Chm. Finance Cttee., Surrey County Council, 1953-60; Chm. Redhill Group Hospital Management Cttee., 1953-65. *Recreations:* formerly hockey and sailing, now motoring and golf. *Address:* The Larches, Woldingham, Surrey. *T.:* Woldingham 3228; 33 Gracechurch Street, E.C.3. *Club:* National Liberal. [*Died* 11 *June* 1966.

ELLIOTT, Fraser; *see* Elliott, C. F.

ELLIOTT, Sir Ivo D'Oyly, 2nd Bt., *cr.* 1917; *b.* 7 Mar. 1882; *o. s.* of 1st Bt. and Ellen, *d.* of late James Rowe; *S.* father, 1926; *m.* 1911, Margery Helen, *d.* of late Francis Carey, Burgess Hill; two *s.* two *d.* *Educ.:* Harrow; Balliol College, Oxford. Entered Indian Civil Service, 1906; Under Secretary to Government of India, Commerce and Industry Department, 1916; Deputy Commissioner, 1919; Companion of the Order of the Sacred Treasure of Japan, 1920; Secretary to Government, United Provinces, 1925-29; retired 1932; President of Financial Commission of Inquiry, Mauritius, 1931; Franchise Officer, Kashmir State, 1933-1934. *Publication:* Editor Balliol College Register, 1934 and 1952 edns. *Recreations:* French military history; cycling. *Heir:* *s.* Hugh Francis Ivo, O.B.E. 1953 [*b.* 10 Mar. 1913; *m.* 1939, Elizabeth Margaret, *e. d.* of A.G. Phillipson, North Finchley; one *s.* two *d.*]. *Address:* 173 Woodstock Rd., Oxford. [*Died* 18 *Sept.* 1961.

ELLIOTT, Rev. Canon Spencer Hayward, M.A.; D.D.; Canon Emeritus of Sheffield Cathedral, since 1960; *b.* 27 June 1883; *s.* of late Rev. Wm. Hayward Elliott, Vicar of Bramhope, Leeds; *m.* 1914, Hilda Mary (*d.* 1947), *o. d.* of late John William Hawley, Leeds and London; one *s.* two *d.*; *m.* 1949, Sheila Mabel, *d.* of late Lt.-Comdr. Frederick Elliott, R.N., Nanaimo, British Columbia. *Educ.:* Ripon School; Leeds University (De Grey Exhibitioner and University Prize for English Essay); Victoria University of Manchester (Honours English language and literature); Ripon Clergy College. English and Divinity Master, Ripon School, 1904-6; Curate, St. Simon's, Leeds, 1906-10; St. James's, Barrow-in-Furness, 1910-11; Diocesan Missioner of Manchester, 1911-16; Missioner to troops, England and France, 1914-16; Vicar of St. Paul's, Sheffield, and Diocesan Missioner of Sheffield, 1916-27; Vicar and Rural Dean of Mansfield, 1927-30; Vicar of Bolton, 1930-33; Rector of Warrington, 1933-38; Rural Dean of Winwick, 1935-38; member of Mission of Help to India, 1922-23; Hon. Canon of Sheffield, 1922; of Southwell, 1929; of Manchester, 1930; Canon Diocesan of Liverpool, 1933-38; M.A. Manchester, 1906, Leeds, 1927; Dean Starr Lecturer and Hon. D.D. Trinity College, Toronto, 1939; Dean of British Columbia and Rector of Christ Church Cathedral, Victoria, B.C., 1938-48; also Examining Chaplain to Bishop of British Columbia and Prolocutor to the Provincial Synod of British Columbia. Mem. of Examining Bd. of Univ. of Manitoba, 1948-54; Exam. Chap. to Archbishop of Rupert's Land, 1948-56; Prof. St. John's College, Winnipeg, 1948-56. Professor of Liturgics and Practical Theology, Emmanuel College, Saskatoon, 1956-60; Reviewer for Sheffield Daily Telegraph, 1916-1937; Reviewer for The Winnipeg Free Press. Founder Chairman of Leeds Boy Scouts, 1908; Founder President, Mansfield Rotary Club, 1928. Was a pioneer of broadcasting Church services, Aug. 1923; Oxford Univ. Extension Lecturer, 1925. Preached annual Shakespeare sermon at Stratford-on-Avon, 1935. Fellow of Ancient Monuments Soc., London, 1957. Patron, The Churches' Fellowship for Psychical and Spiritual Studies, 1963. *Publications:* The Message of a Mission, 1913; The Gospel of the Father, 1922; A Missioner Abroad, 1923; Religion and Dramatic Art, 1927; The Romance of Marriage, 1929; The Romance of Death, 1931; The Missing Link, 1934; When Trouble Comes, 1939; Members of Christ 1946; various pamphlets, reviews, and literary articles. *Address:* 1007 13t Avenue, S.W., Calgary, Alberta, Canada. [*Died* 27 *Dec.* 1967

ELLIOTT, Thomas Renton, C.B.E. 1919; D.S.O. 1918; F.R.S. 1913; M.A., M.D F.R.C.P.; Colonel A.M.S.; Consulting Physician to University College Hospital; Professor Emeritus of Medicine, London University *b.* 11 Oct. 1877; *e. s.* of A. W. Elliott, Spring field House, Willington, Co. Durham; *m.* 1918 Martha, *d.* of A. K. M'Cosh, Cairnhill, Airdrie Lanarkshire; three *s.* two *d.* *Educ.:* Durham School; Trinity College, Cambridge; Doub first class in Natural Science Tripos, 1900 George Henry Lewes student in Physiology 1904; Fellow of Clare College; Trustee Beit Memorial Fellowships for Medical Research Consulting Physician, British Armies in France, 1914-19 (despatches twice). Member of Medical Research Council (under Committee of Privy Council), 1920-26, 1927-31 1939-43; Member Inter-Departmental Com mittee (Goodenough) on Medical Schools, 1942; Hon. Fellow Trinity College, Cambridge, 1947; Accadem. Onor. R. Accad. Med. di Roma. *Publications:* Physiological papers on the Supra-renal Glands and on the Innerva tion of the Viscera; and medical papers on Gunshot Wounds of the Chest. *Address* Broughton Place, Broughton, Peeblesshire. *T.:* Broughton 234. *Club:* Athenæum. [*Died* 4 *March* 1961.

ELLIOTT-BINNS, Rev. Leonard E.; *see* Binns.

ELLIS, Arthur Isaac, C.B.E. 1949; M.A., F.S.A.; late Superintendent Reading Room and Keeper in Dept. of Printed Books, British Museum; *b.* 4 Oct. 1883; *s.* of late John Ellis, Hampstead. *Educ.:* University College School; St. John's College, Cambridge (Scholar); 1st Class, Classical Tripos. Entered British Museum, 1909; Inns of Court O.T.C.; Royal Fusiliers; a/Capt. attached H.Q. 99th Infantry (2nd Light)

Brigade; retd. 1948. *Publications:* Mallarmé in English verse (introduction by G. Turquet-Milnes), 1927. *Address:* Newlands, Bay Road, Freshwater, I.W. *Club:* Athenæum. [*Died* 1 *Feb.* 1963.

ELLIS, Arthur Thomas; Writer and Journalist; Financial Consultant associated with J. B. Were & Son, Melbourne; *b.* Charleville, Queensland, 24 May 1892; 2nd *s.* of T. J. Ellis and C. J. Ruegg; *m.* 1914, Annie, 3rd *d.* of J. E. Shepherd, Mt. Morgan, Queensland; two *s.* one *d.* *Educ.:* State Schools and Brisbane Grammar School. Journalist, Brisbane, 1909-17; Secretary to Premier and Secretary to Imperial Meat Board, Queensland, 1917-20; Special Writer Melbourne Age, 1920-24; Editor, Melbourne Leader, 1924-32; with J. B. Were & Son, Melbourne, 1933-42 and 1950-54; Executive Asst. to Director of Aircraft Production in Australia, 1942-45; General Manager, Overseas Corporation (Australia) Ltd., 1945-47. *Publications:* various short stories and articles; Editor, J. B. Were & Son publications, 1935-42 and 1948-54; The House of Were, 1839-1954, 1954 (Melbourne). *Recreation:* angling. *Address:* 375 Collins Street, Melbourne; Lyndon Street, Elsternwick, Melbourne, Australia. [*Died* 27 *June* 1964.

ELLIS, Sir Arthur (William Mickle), Kt., *cr.* 1953; O.B.E. 1917; B.A. M.D. (Tor.), M.A., D.M. (Oxford); F.R.C.P. (London); Hon. LL.D. (Toronto); Consulting Physician London Hospital; Consulting Physician Radcliffe Infirmary, Oxford; *e. s.* of late William Hodgson Ellis, Prof. of Chemistry, Univ. of Toronto; *m.* 1922, Winfred (*d.* 1965), *d.* of late Sir William Foot Mitchell; one *s.* *Educ.:* Upper Canada Coll. and Univ. of Toronto. Formerly Fellow in Pathological Chemistry, Univ. of Toronto, Demonstrator in Pathology, Western Reserve, Univ. Cleveland, Ohio; Assistant Resident Physician, Hospital of the Rockefeller Institute, New York; Prof. of Medicine, University of London; Director of the Medical Unit, and Physician to the London Hospital, 1924-43; Adviser in Medicine, Ministry of Health Regions 3 and 4, 1941-42; Director of research in industrial diseases, M.R.C., 1942-43; Regius Prof. of Medicine, Univ. of Oxford, 1943-48, Emeritus since 1948. Croonian Lecturer, 1941, Moxon Medallist, 1951, Roy. Coll. Physicians. Member of Royal Commission on Population. Major C.A.M.C.; served European War, 1914-19 (despatches four times, O.B.E.): Assistant Adviser in Pathology, 4th Army B.E.F. *Publications:* in medical and scientific journals. *Address:* Bedford House, Chiswick Mall, W.4. *Club:* Athenæum. [*Died* 20 *May* 1966.

ELLIS, Colonel Clarence Isidore C.M.G. 1918; T.D.; M.D., C.M. Aberdeen, L.S.A. London; Royal Medico-Psychological Certificate, Gt. Britain and Ire.; late Member Chapter-General of Ven. Order of the Hospital of St. John of Jerusalem; late Army Medical Service (T.A.); late Senior Assistant County Controller for St. John V.A.D.'s for County of Devon; late Commissioner No. IX. District St. John Ambulance Brigade; Member British Medical Assoc. for 52 years; *b.* Hayle, Cornwall, 22 Aug. 1871; *s.* of J. F. Ellis, Hayle, Cornwall; *m.* 1904, Margaret, *o. c.* of John Edwards; two *d.* (and one *d.* decd.). *Educ.:* Probus School, Cornwall; Aberdeen University; St. Thomas's Hosp., London; Coombe Lying-in-Hospital Dublin. General Practice, London, 1896-1904; Dartmouth, 1904-7; School Medical Officer, Torquay, 1908-14; served European War in the R.A.M.C. (T.A.) as Staff Officer for Voluntary Aid Organisations, Southern Command, 1914-15; as C.O. of the 46 (1/1 Wessex) Casualty Clearing Station, 1915-19; and C.O. 41 Stationary Hospital, 1919 (despatches twice, C.M.G.); D.A.D.M.S. 43rd (The Wessex) Division, 1920-22; late Surgeon-in-Chief St. John Ambulance Bde.; late Inspecting Officer on Staff of Chief Commissioner, St. John Ambulance Brigade; Lecturer and Examiner St. John Ambulance Association and British Red Cross Society; author of The V.A.D. Emergency Hospital; Knight St. John of the Venerable Order of the Hospital of St. John of Jerusalem in the British Realm. Vice-Pres. British Legion (Torquay Branch); Vice-Pres. Torquay Navy and Army Veterans' Association. 12 decorations and medals. *Recreations:* golf, gardening, Freemasonry, botany. *Address:* Grey House, Old Torwood Road, Torquay, S. Devon. *T.:* Torquay 22709. *T.A.:* Colonel Ellis, Torquay. *Clubs:* Aberdeen University (Aberdeen); Torquay Golf (Torquay). [*Died* 19 *Nov.* 1961.

ELLIS, Colin Dare Bernard, C.B.E. 1955; M.C., M.A., F.S.A.; Director, Leicester Real Property Co. Ltd.; *b.* 1895; *s.* of late Bernard Ellis, J.P.; *m.* 1922, Ethel V. Clarke; two *d.* *Educ.:* Bootham School; King's College, Cambridge. Served 1915-18, Leicestershire R.H.A. (M.C., despatches). Director of Home Grown Cereals, Ministry of Food, 1941-44. *Publications:* Mournful Numbers, verses and epigrams, 1932; History in Leicester, 1948; Leicestershire and the Quorn Hunt, 1951. *Address:* 2 The Manor House, Bringhurst, Market Harborough, Leics. *T.:* Rockingham 397. *Club:* Leicestershire. [*Died* 4 *July* 1969.

ELLIS, Gerald Edward Harold, B.A. Oxon; Headmaster, Whitgift School, Croydon, 1939-46, retd.; *b.* 17 Dec. 1878; *s.* of Edward Ellis, M.D., University College Hospital, London; *m.* 1909, Gladys Magdalen, 2nd *d.* of late Rev. S. J. Rowton, M.A.; Mus.Doc.; no *c.* *Educ.:* Epsom College; Lincoln Coll., Oxford. Master at Epsom College, Felstead School, and Bradfield College, 1901-03; Whitgift School, 1903. *Recreations:* music, ornithology. *Address:* 5 Lismore Road, Croydon. [*Died* 7 *Aug.* 1967.

ELLIS, Major Lionel Frederic, C.V.O. 1937; C.B.E. 1930; D.S.O. 1919; M.C.; Engaged on Official History of Second World War; *b.* 1885; *m.* 1916, Jane Richmond (*d.* 1958); one *s.* one *d.* Served European War, 1914-19, in Welsh Guards (despatches, D.S.O., M.C.); Gen. Sec., National Council of Social Service (Incorporated), 1919-37; Secretary National Fitness Council, 1937-39; rejoined Welsh Guards on outbreak of war, 1939. *Publications:* Welsh Guards at War; Official Histories of the War: France and Flanders, 1939-40, and Victory in the West, 1944-45: Vol. I, the Battle of Normandy. *Address:* Lansdowne House, Harlington, Middlesex. *T.:* 01-759 9577. [*Died* 19 *Oct.* 1970.

ELLIS, Malcolm Henry; *see* Addenda: II.

ELLIS, Mary Baxter, C.B.E. 1942; T.D. 1951; *b.* 12 Nov. 1892; *d.* of late Sir Joseph Baxter Ellis and Lady Ellis (*née* Taylor), Newcastle upon Tyne. *Educ.:* Central High Sch., Newcastle upon Tyne; Univ. Coll. London. Joined F.A.N.Y. Corps, 1915, and served in France and Belgium until 1919 (1915 Star, Victory and General Service medals, Médaille de la Reine Elizabeth, Chevalier, Ordre de Leopold II); Comdt. F.A.N.Y. 1932; Member of Advisory Council A.T.S., 1938; Service in A.T.S., 1939-45; Senior Controller and Deputy Director A.T.S. (War Office), 1943-45. Demobilised Aug. 1945; resumed command of F.A.N.Y. Corps. 1946; retired, 1947. C.C. (Bellingham district) Northumberland, 1949-52; Member, R.D.C. Jubilee, Coronation, Long Service Medals, American Bronze Star Medal, 1946. *Publications:* with Ethel Boileau) Challenge to Destiny (novel); several short stories. *Address:* The Low

Lands, West Woodburn, Hexham, Northumberland. *Club:* F.A.N.Y. Regimental. [*Died* 12 *April* 1968.

ELLIS, Brigadier Richard Stanley, C.B.E. 1941 (O.B.E. 1918); M.C.; retired; *b.* 1884; *er. s.* of R. H. Ellis, J.P., Eastbourne; *m.* 1914, Margaret Sneyd, *d.* of Col. J. R. Colvin, Indian Army; one *s.* one *d.* (and one *s.* decd.). *Educ.:* Wellington College; Royal Military Academy, Woolwich. 2nd Lt., 1904; served in R.H.A.; served European War, 1914-18 (wounded, despatches, M.C.); Brigadier, 1936; Merseyside A.A. defences war of 1939-45; retired, 1941. *Address:* Old Mill House, Sturminster Newton, Dorset. *T.:* 52. *Club:* United Service. [*Died* 12 *Jan.* 1962.

ELLIS, Richard White Bernard, O.B.E. 1945; M.A., M.D., F.R.C.P., F.R.C.P.E.; F.R.S.E.; Professor Emeritus of Child Life and Health, University of Edinburgh; formerly Physician i/c Children's Dept., Guy's Hospital, London; *b.* 25 August 1902; *s.* of Bernard Ellis, J.P., and Isabel Clare Ellis; *m.* 1941, Audrey Eva Russell, M.B.; one *s.* one *d.* *Educ.:* Leighton Park Sch.; King's Coll., Camb.; St. Thomas's Hosp., London. Research Fell. in Pediatrics, Harvard Med. School, 1928-29. Editor, Archives of Disease in Childhood, 1939-50. Pres. of British Pædiatric Assoc., 1965-66; Past Pres., Scottish Pædiatric Soc.; Hon. Fellow, American Academy of Pediatrics; Hon. Member: American Pediatric Society; Canadian Pædiatric Society; Polish Pædiatric Society; Turkish National Pædiatric Association; Aegean Medical Society; Burma Medical Assoc.; Membre corresp. Soc. de Pédiatrie de Paris; Blackader Lectr., Canadian Med. Assoc., 1952; Blackfan Lectr., Harvard, 1957; Member, Scottish Health Services Council, 1949-52. Mem. Advisory Committee Medical Research (Scotland), 1954-57; War Service: Wing Commander, R.A.F.V.R., 1940-45, served North Africa, Italy, Belgium; Adviser in Medicine, Mediterranean Allied Air Force (despatches). *Publications:* Disease in Infancy and Childhood, 1951, 1956, 1960, 1963, 1965; Health in childhood, 1960; contribs. to British Encyclopædia Medical Practice (1951), British Surgical Practice (1948), Chambers's Encyclopædia (1950), and various medical journals. Ed. and part author, Child Health and Development, 1947, 1956, 1962, 1966. *Recreations:* foreign travel. *Address:* Glebe House, Hawridge, Berkhamsted, Herts. *Club:* Athenæum. [*Died* 15 *Sept.* 1966.

ELLIS, Thomas Iorwerth, O.B.E. 1968; M.A. (Wales *et* Oxon.); on staff of Classics Department, University College of Wales, Aberystwyth, 1941-46; *b.* 19 December 1899; *s.* of Thomas Edward Ellis, M.P. for Merioneth (1886-99) and Annie, *d.* of R. J. Davies, J.P., Cwrt-mawr, Llangeitho, Cards.; *m* Mary Headley, M.A.; one *s* one *d.* *Educ.:* Westminster School (King's Scholar); Univ. Coll. of Wales, Aberystwyth; Jesus College, Oxford. Assistant Master, Cardiff High School for Boys, 1924-28; Asst. Lecturer in Classics, University College, Swansea, 1928-30; Headmaster, County School, Rhyl, 1930-40; Lecturer in Classics, St. David's College, Lampeter, 1940-41. High Sheriff of Cardiganshire, 1944-45. Hon. Secretary, Undeb Cymru Fydd (the New Wales Union), 1941-66; Mem. of Court and Council: Univ. College of Wales; National Library of Wales; Member of Court of Univ. of Wales; Member of Governing Body, Representative Body, and Coll. of Episcopal Electors, Church in Wales; Hon. Treas., Council of Churches for Wales, 1961-66; one of the Editors of the Welsh Book Club, 1943-1945; Warden, Guild of Graduates of the Univ. of Wales, 1943-47. Hon. LL.D. Wales, 1967. *Publications:* The Development of Higher Education in Wales, 1935; Life of Thomas Edward Ellis (Vol. I), 1944, (Vol. II), 1948; Crwydro Ceredigion, 1952; T. C. Edwards letters (ed.) 1952, 1953; Crwydro Meirionnydd, 1954; Ym Mêr Fy Esgyrn, 1955; Crwydro Maldwyn, 1957; Crwydro Mynwy, 1958; Crwydro Sir y Fflint, 1959; Life of J. H. Davies, 1963; Dilyn Llwybrau, 1967; Life of Ellis Jones Griffith, 1969; contributions to Dictionary of Welsh Biography; articles and reviews in Barn, Yr Efrydydd, Y Llenor, Journal of Education, etc. *Address:* 4 Laura Place, Aberystwyth. *T.:* Aberystwyth 7171. [*Died* 20 *April* 1970.

ELLISTON, Julian Clement Peter, C.B. 1965; T.D. 1946; Parliamentary Counsel, since 1955; *b.* 16 May 1911; 3rd *s.* of Sir George S. Elliston, M.C. and Lady (Alice Louise) Elliston (*née* Causton); *m.* 1948, Nora Joyce, *d.* of Stanley Leverton; one *s.* two *d.* *Educ.:* Westminster (King's Scholar); Trinity College, Cambridge (Open and Triplett Exhib.). B.A. (Cantab.) 1932. Harmsworth Law Scholar, Middle Temple, 1932. Called to the Bar, Middle Temple, Nov. 1934; practised at Chancery Bar until 1939. Commissioned R.A. (T.A.), 1932. War service 1939-45, mainly in General Staff appts. (Intelligence or Air), including war course at Staff Coll. and finishing as G.S.O. 2 of Carrier-Borne Army Liaison sect. in H.M.S. Victorious, Brit. Pacific Fleet, 1944-1945. Joined Office of Parliamentary Counsel, 1945. *Recreations:* acting, reading, mild walking, and doing nothing. *Address:* 53 Temple Fortune Hill. N.W.11. *T.:* 01-458 3015. *Club:* Oxford and Cambridge. [*Died* 4 *March* 1970.

ELMAN, Mischa; violinist; *b.* Talnoi, Russia, 20 Jan. 1891; of Russian parentage; *m.* 1925, Helen Frances Katten, San Francisco. *Educ.:* Odessa under Fidelmann; Imperial Conservatoire, Petrograd; Studied under Professor Leopold Auer in Petrograd. First appeared, 1904, in Berlin; London, 1905; New York 1908. *Address:* c/o S. A. Gorlinsky Ltd. 35 Dover Street, W.1. [*Died* 5 *April* 1967.

ELMHIRST, Dorothy Whitney; Trustee, Dartington Hall Trust; *b.* Washington, D.C., 1887; *y. c.* of late Flora Payne and William C. Whitney; *m.* 1st, 1911, Willard Straight (*d.* War of 1914-18); two *s.* one *d.*; 2nd, 1925, Leonard Knight Elmhirst; one *s.* one *d.* *Educ.:* Private Schools in New York. Active in social and eductaional work. Hon. LL.D. (Exeter), 1963. *Recreations:* gardening, drama and the arts. *Address:* Dartington Hall, Totnes, Devon. [*Died* 14 *Dec.* 1968.

ELMSLIE, Christiana Deanes, C.B.E 1919; R.R.C.; late Matron Queen Alexandra's Imperial Military Nursing Service; *b.* 1869; *d.* of late Benjamin Elmslie, Carinton, Kemnay, Aberdeen. Served European War, 1914-15 (C.B.E., R.R.C.). *Address:* The Convent of the Holy Cross, Findon, Nr. Worthing, Sussex. [*Died* 9 *July* 1961.

ELMSLIE, Rev. William Alexander Leslie, M.A., D.D. Cantab.; Hon. D.D. (Aberdeen and Edinburgh); Emeritus Professor of Hebrew and Old Testament Literature (1922-54) (and Principal, 1935) in Westminster Coll., Cambridge; *b.* London, 1885; *s.* of late Rev. Prof. W. G. Elmslie, D.D.; *m.* Edith Clare (*d.* 1935), *y. d.* of late E. Shufflebotham, Barnt Green. *Educ.:* Leys School; Christ's Coll. and Westminster Coll., Cambridge; 1st Class in Classics and in Semitic Languages at Cambridge Univ.; Tyrwhitt Hebrew (University) Scholar, 1909; Examiner for Oriental Languages Tripos; and for Theological Tripos, Camb.; Fellow of Christ's Coll., Cambridge, 1911-17; Minister of St. John's Presbyterian Church, Kensington, 1917-22. *Publications:* Aboda Zara, or The Mishna on Idolatry (Texts and Studies), 1911; Isaiah xl-lxvi. (Revised Version for Schools), 1914; Chronicles i. and ii. (Cambridge Bible for Schools and Colleges), 1916; Studies in Life from Jewish Proverbs, 1917; Five Great Subjects (Broadcast Addresses), 1943; How came our Faith, 1948; Chronicles i. and ii. (The Interpreter's Bible), 1954. *Recreation:* golf. *Address:* 8 Aubrey Walk, Kensington, W.8. [*Died* 15 *Nov.* 1965.

ELPHINSTONE of Glack, Sir Alexander Logie, 10th Bart. of Logie Elphinstone and Nova Scotia, *cr.* 1701; *b.* 8 Mar. 1880; *e. s.* of John Elphinston, H.E.I.C.S., Bombay, and Emma Eliza, 2nd *d.* of George R. Betham; *m.* 1st, 1911, Agnes Gertrude Blanche Durell (*d.* 1961), *e. d.* of Capt. T. E. Charles King, West Yorkshire Regt.; 2nd, 1962, Mrs. Muriel Eileen Patterson Sayles, *widow* of James Patterson Sayles, N. Ireland and 2nd *d.* of late John MacComish, N. Ire.; proved his right (as 10th Bt.), 1927 (title had remained dormant since death of 4th Bt. in 1743); claimant, Barony of New Glasgow, Nova Scotia, 1625. Entered Army (Univ. candidate, Pembroke College, Cambridge), 1899; retired 1930; served South African War, 1899-1902 (Queen's medal 6 bars, King's medal 2 bars); European War, 1914-19 (Star, Victory and Allies medals); War of 1939-45, attached to B.R.C. Coronation Medals (1902 and 1937), Silver Jubilee (1935); Freeman of City of London; Liveryman of Needle Makers' Company. *Heir: nephew* John Elphinston [*b.* 12 Aug. 1924; *m.* 1953, Margaret Doreen, *e. d.* of Edric Tasker, Cheltenham; four *s.*]. *Address:* Kingsway, 5 Bath Road, Worthing, Sussex. *Club:* Royal Over-Seas League. [*Died* 16 *Dec.* 1970.

ELPHINSTONE, Kenneth Vaughan M.A.; *b.* 11 Jan. 1878; *s.* of late Sir Howard Elphinstone, 3rd Bart. *Educ.:* Wellington; Trinity College, Cambridge. Served South Africa, 1900; entered Civil Service, Nigeria, 1902; retired, 1921. *Recreation:* yachting. *Address:* Artillery Mansions, Westminster, S.W.1. *Clubs:* Athenæum, Union; Royal Corinthian Yacht. [*Died* 10 *Feb.* 1963.

ELPHINSTONE, Sir Lancelot (Henry), Kt. 1931; *b.* 2 Sept. 1879; *y. s.* of Sir Howard Elphinstone, 3rd Bt.; *m.* 1913, Jane Edith (*d.* 1959), *y. d.* of R. Jarvie Jamieson, Edinburgh. *Educ.:* Eton; Trinity Coll., Cambridge, M.A. Barrister; Attorney-General of British Honduras, 1913; Solicitor-Gen. of Trinidad, 1919; Attorney-Gen. of Tanganyika Territory, 1921; Attorney-General of Ceylon, 1924; Chief Justice of F.M.S., 1929-32; retired 1932; Chm. of a Pensions Appeal Tribunal, 1943, retd. 1954. *Publications:* The Conveyancers' Year Book; Guide to the War Damage Act; and Covenants affecting land. *Address:* The Beeches, Bank, nr. Lyndhurst. *T.:* Lyndhurst 2672; 15 Old Square, Lincoln's Inn, W.C.2. *Clubs:* Union, Royal Cruising, Bar Yacht. [*Died* 11 *Oct.* 1965.

ELPHINSTONE, Rev. Maurice Curteis, M.A.; Canon Emeritus of Wakefield since 1933; *b.* 27 Jan. 1874; 4th *s.* of Sir Howard Warburton Elphinstone 3rd Bt.; *m.* 1908, Christiana Georgiana, *d.* of late H. H. Almond, Hon. LL.D. Glasgow, Headmaster of Loretto School; three *s.* one *d.* *Educ.:* Trinity College, Cambridge; Ridley Hall; student under Bishop Westcott at Auckland Castle. Deacon, 1898; Priest, 1899; Curate of Bishop Wearmouth, 1898-1901; Mission Curate of St. Andrew's Cathedral, Sydney, N.S.W., and Greek Lecturer at Moore Theological College, 1901-2; Priest in Charge of St. Cyprian's Church, Adelaide, and Warden of St. Barnabas' Theological College, 1902-3; Vicar of Eynsford, 1906-1917; Vicar of Sowerby Bridge, 1917-33; Hon. Canon of Wakefield, 1927-33; Rector of Southchurch, 1933-41. *Publications:* War and the Gospel of Christ, 1915; The Gospel Apologetic, 1927. *Address:* South Park Lodge West, South Park, Sevenoaks, Kent. *Club:* Athenæum. [*Died* 14 *May* 1969.

ELSEY, Rt. Rev. William Edward, D.D.; *b.* 4 July 1880; *s.* of late William Edward Elsey; *m.* 1921, Cecilia Sarah, *y. d.* of late Kenneth McLean, of Langwell Station, North-West Australia, and Mrs. L. J. McLean; one *s.* *Educ.:* King Edward VI. Grammar School, Louth, Lincs; Lincoln College, Oxford; Cuddesdon Theological College. Deacon, 1904; Priest, 1905; Assistant Curate, St. Faith's, Stepney, 1904-1908; Priest in Charge, St. Faith's, 1908-14; Member of the Bush Brotherhood of St. Boniface, Diocese of Bunbury, Western Australia, 1914; Warden of the Brotherhood, 1915-19; Bishop of Kalgoorlie, 1919-1950; Chaplain to the Australian Forces, 1941-44 (E.D.). *Address:* 1A Longroyd Street, Mt. Lawley, Western Australia. [*Died* 25 *Sept.* 1966.

ELVEY, Maurice; Producer and Director of Films; Honorary Life Member of Directors Section of Association of Cinematograph Technicians; *b.* Darlington, Yorkshire, 11 November 1887; *m.* 1st, Philippa Preston (marriage dissolved); 2nd, Isobel Elsom (marriage dissolved). *Educ.:* St. Marks, Chelsea. Stage Director New York and London prior to 1913. Became a motion picture director in 1913. Has since produced and directed 300 or more pictures among which are: Wreck of the Birkenhead, Hound of the Baskervilles, When Knights were Bold, Mlle. from Armentières, Quinneys, School for Scandal, Water Gypsies, Lost Chord, Wandering Jew, Clairvoyant, Man in the Mirror, This Week of Grace, Sally in our Alley, Soldiers of the King, Transatlantic Tunnel, Melody and Romance, Who Goes Next?; The Return of the Frog; Sons of the Sea; Lost on the Western Front; deviser and director For Freedom and The Battle of the River Plate; during the war years co-directed amongst other films with the late Leslie Howard in The Gentle Sex, and directed The Lamp Still Burns, under auspices of Ministry of Health; Director of Stefan Zweig's Beware of Pity. Member; National Council Noise Abatement Society; Council Moving Picture Museum Association; B.B.C. TV; B.B.C. (Home Service); TV and Radio in U.S.A. *Recreations:* music, ballet. *Club:* Savage. [*Died* 28 *Aug.* 1967.

ELVIN, Ven. John Elijah; Archdeacon of West Ham since 1958; Vicar of St. Michael's, Gidea Park, Romford, 1938-58; Hon. Canon of Chelmsford Cathedral since 1947; Director for Church Schools, Diocese of Chelmsford, since 1955; *b.* 8 Aug. 1900; *s.* of Elijah Elvin; *m.* Hannah Elizabeth D. Hancock. *Educ.:* Brincliffe Coll.; Univ. of Sheffield. Deacon, 1927; Priest, 1928. Curate of All Saints, Forest Gate, 1927-31; Curate, Squirrels Heath, in charge of St. Michael's, Gidea Park, 1931-33; Minister of St. Michael's, Gidea Park, 1933-38. Hon. Chaplain to Bishop of Chelmsford, 1948-58. *Address:* 30 Links Ave., Gidea Park, Romford, Essex. [*Died* 25 *Oct.* 1964.

ELWES, Lieut.-Col. Frederick Fenn, C.I.E. 1911; M.D.; *b.* 3 May 1875; *m.* 1905, Mary Aline, O.B.E., *d.* of E. J. Firth; one *d.* First Physician Government General Hospital; Professor of Medicine and Principal, Medical College, Madras, 1913-28; retired from I.M.S., 1928. Entered Army, 1900; served China, 1900 (medal and clasp). *Address:* Golden Haze, 20 Aston's Road, Moor Park, Northwood, Middlesex. [*Died* 24 *June* 1962.

ELWES, Sir Richard (Everard Augustine), Kt. 1958; O.B.E. 1944; T.D.; Judge of the High Court of Justice, Queen's Bench Division, 1958-66; retired; a Knight of Malta; Lt.-Col. Northants Yeomanry; *b.* 28 May 1901; 5th *s.* of late Gervase Elwes of Roxby, Lincs, and Billing Hall, Northampton, and of late Lady Winefride Elwes, *d.* of 8th Earl of Denbigh; *m.* 1926, Mary Freya, *e. d.* of Sir Mark Sykes, 6th Bt. of Sledmere; two *s.* three *d.* *Educ.:* The Oratory School; Christ Church, Oxford (B.A., 1923, M.A. 1929). Called to Bar, Inner Temple, 1925, Bencher 1948, served on General Council of the Bar; Standing Counsel to Jockey Club, 1938-50; Recorder of Northampton, 1946-58; Q.C. 1950; Chairman of Quarter Sessions: Rutland, 1946-54; Derbyshire, 1954-58; Bedfordshire, 1957-1958. Commissioned Northants Yeomanry, 1923; T.A.R.O. 1932; Assistant Adjutant September 1939; Staff Captain 69th Infantry Brigade, B.E.F., Oct. 1939; Major, D.A.A.G. Home Counties Area, July 1940; Lt.-Col., A.A.G., War Office, Dec. 1941-July 1945 (O.B.E.); U.S. Bronze Star Medal, 1945. *Publications:* First Poems, 1941; (with Lady Winefride Elwes) Gervase Elwes—Memoir, 1935. *Recreations:* music, letters, the visual arts. *Address:* 5 Paper Buildings, Temple, E.C.4. *T.:* City 6836. *Club:* Cavalry. [*Died* 4 *Sept.* 1968.

ELWIN, Verrier; writer; *b.* 29 Aug. 1902; *s.* of Rt. Rev. Bishop Elwin of Sierra Leone. *Educ.:* Merton Coll., Oxford. Charles Oldham Scholar, 1923; 1st Class Eng. Lit. Finals, 1924; Matthew Arnold Prizeman, 1925; 1st Class Theology Finals, 1926; Junior Denyer and Johnson Scholar, 1927; Vice-Principal of Wycliffe Hall, Oxford, 1926; Chaplain of Merton, 1927; D.Sc. (Oxon.), 1944. Went to India as member of Christa Seva Sangha in 1927, but retired later into lay life and from 1932-46, and again 1949-1953, lived among aboriginal tribesmen in Central Ind., where he founded with Shamrao Hivale settlement for welfare and research on humanitarian lines; became Indian Citizen in 1954. Awarded Padma Bhushan, 1961. F.R.A.I., F. Asiatic Society, F.N.I.; Hon. Ethnographer to Bastar State, 1940; Anthropologist to Government of Orissa, 1944; Deputy-Director, Department of Anthropology, Government of India, 1946-1949; Adviser for Tribal Affairs, N.E. Frontier Agency, 1954; Member, Scheduled Tribes Commission, 1960-61; Wellcome Medal, 1943; Roy Medal, 1945; Rivers Medal, 1948; Annandale Medal, 1952; Campbell Medal, 1960; Dadabhai Naoroji Prize, 1961. *Publications:* Leaves from the Jungle, 1936; The Baiga, 1939; The Agaria, 1942; Muria Murder and Suicide, 1943, Folk-Tales of Mahakoshal, 1944; Folk-Songs of the Maikal Hills, 1944; Folk-Songs of Chhattisgarh, 1946; The Muria and their Ghotul, 1947; Myths of Middle India, 1949; Bondo Highlander, 1950; The Tribal Art of Middle India, 1952; Tribal Myths of Orissa, 1954; The Religion of an Indian Tribe, 1955; A Philosophy for N.E.F.A., 1957; Myths of the North-East Frontier, 1958; The Story of Tata Steel, 1958; The Art of the North-East Frontier of India, 1959; India's North-East Frontier in the 19th Century, 1959; Nagaland, 1961; *Autobiography* (*posthumous*) The Tribal World of Verrier Elwin, 1964. *Recreations:* travel, photography. *Address:* Shridham, Nongthmai, Shillong, India. [*Died* 22 *Feb.* 1964.

ELY, 7th Marquess of, *cr.* 1800; **George Henry Wellington Loftus,** Bt. 1780; Baron Loftus, 1785; Viscount Loftus, 1789; Earl of Ely, 1794; Baron Loftus (U.K.), 1801; *b.* 3 Sept. 1903; *o. s.* of 6th Marquess and Ethel Beatrice Lempriere (*d.* 1927), *y. d.* of late Nigel J. D. Gresley, of Hobart, Tasmania; *S.* father, 1935; *m.* 1928, Thea Margaret Gordon, *d.* of L. Gronvold, Hove; one *d.* (decd.). Middle East, Staff Major 21st Army Group H.Q., B.L.A., 1939-41. *Heir: cousin,* Charles John Tottenham [*b.* 30 May 1913; *m.* 1938, Katherine Elizabeth, *d.* of Lt.-Col. W. H. Craig; three *s.* one *d.*]. *Address:* 21 Grove Court, The Drive, Hove. Sussex. [*Died* 31 *May* 1969.

EMBERTON, Lt.-Col. Sir (John) Wesley, Kt. 1958; D.L. J.P., Cheshire; *b.* 1896; *s.* of John Emberton, O.B.E., J.P., Nantwich, Cheshire; *m.* 1926, Marion Major, Ravenscroft, Cholmondeston, Cheshire; one *d.* *Educ.:* Rydal School, Colwyn Bay, N. Wales. Served European War, 1914-18; 16th Bn. Roy. Welch Fusiliers, 14th Bn. Cheshire Regt., 1st Garrison Bn., Manchester Regt.; served War of 1939-45: 24th Bn. Cheshire Home Guard, Nantwich; Lt.-Col. 1942. J.P. 1941, D.L. 1952, and Chairman of Cheshire County Council, 1952-. *Address:* The Lymes, Audlem, nr. Crewe, Cheshire. *T.:* Audlem 271. [*Died* 10 *Dec.* 1967.

EMERSON, Sir Herbert (William), G.C.I.E., *cr.* 1937 (C.I.E. 1926); K.C.S.I., *cr.* 1933 (C.S.I. 1931); C.B.E. 1923; *b.* 1 June 1881. *Educ.:* Calday Grange Grammar School; Magdalene College, Cambridge, B.A. Entered Indian Civil Service, 1905; Manager, Bashahr State, 1911-14; Superintendent and Settlement Officer, Mandi State, 1915; Assistant Commissioner and Settlement Officer, Punjab, 1917; Deputy Commissioner, 1922; Secretary to Government Finance Department, 1926; Secretary to Govt. of India, Home Dept. 1930-1933; Governor of the Punjab, 1933-38: High Commissioner for Refugees, League of Nations, 1939-46; also Director of Inter-Governmental Committee on Refugees, 1939-47; Hon. Fellow, Magdalene College, Cambridge. *Address:* 2 Knole Paddock, Sevenoaks. *T.:* 52784. *Club:* Athenæum. [*Died* 12 *April* 1962.

EMERSON, Very Rev. Norman David, Ph.D.; Dean of Dublin (Christ Church), since 1961; *b.* 10 July 1900; *yr. s.* of William and Caroline Emerson, Lurgan, Co. Armagh; *m.* 1936, Edna Belinda, *er. d.* of David and Edith Wilson, Annaghmore, Co. Armagh. *Educ.:* Lurgan; Trinity College, Dublin (LL.B., Ph.D.); London University (B.D.). Ordained, 1924; Rector of St. Mary's, Dublin, 1933-61; Canon of Christ Church, 1954-61. M.R.I.A. 1943; Pres. Irish Historical Society, 1960-62. *Publications:* An Account of Archbishop Ussher, 1956; The Church of Ireland and the 1859 Revival, 1959; St. Columba and his Mission, 1963; (jointly) History of Church of Ireland (3 vols., ed. W. A. Phillips), 1933; Editor, The Vocation of John Bale to the Bishohric of Ossory, 1945. *Recreations:* walking, antiquities, listening to music. *Address:* The Chapter House, Christ Church Cathedral, Dublin. *T.:* 78099; 13 Merlyn Park Merrion Road, Dublin. *T.:* 693044. *Club:* University (Dublin). [*Died* 12 *Jan.* 1966.

EMERSON, Sir Ralf (Billing), Kt. 1956; C.I.E. 1946; O.B.E. 1943; M.I.C.E.; M.Inst.T.; M.I.Loco.E.; Col. (retd.); *b.* 3 July 1897; *s.* of Peter Henry Emerson, B.A., M.B. (Cantab.), and Edith Amy Emerson; *m.* 1926, Grace Everard, *d.* of Rev. J. R. Napier; no *c.* *Educ.:* Bradfield College; R.M.A. Woolwich. Joined Indian State Railways, 1927; Gen. Manager Great Indian Peninsula Rly., 1943; Chief Commr. of Rlys., 1946; retired 1947. Served European War, 1914-18; enlisted in R.F.C., 1915; France, 1916; commissioned 2nd Lt. R.E., 1918. War of 1939-45 in U.K., Middle East, Sicily and Italy with Directorate of Movements and Transportation as G.S.O. 1 and Col.; Col., 1946; retired, 1950. Director, Dowsett Group, 1948-53; General Manager, Nigerian Railway, 1953; Chairman, Nigerian Railway Corporation, 1958-60 (Chm. and Gen.

Manager, 1955). Member, London Board, Provincial Insurance, 1960; Chm.: Metropolitan-Cammell Carriage and Wagon Co. Ltd. 1961; Weymanns Ltd., 1963. *Recreation:* sailing (Cdre. Royal Bombay Yacht Club, 1944-45). *Address:* Norton, Hill Street, Hastings, Sussex. *T.:* Hastings 1685. *Clubs:* Army and Navy, Royal Ocean Racing. [*Died* 30 *Jan.* 1965.

EMLYN-JONES, His Honour Hugh; Judge of County Courts, Circuit No. 7 (Birkenhead, Chester, etc.) 1950-65; *b.* 1902; *s.* of Evan and Ellen Jones, Newton-le-Willows; *m.* 1938, Morfudd, *d.* of David Davies, Cardiff; one *s.* *Educ.:* Manchester Grammar School; Manchester University. First Class Hons. in Law, after winning Dauntesey (Univ.) Legal Schol., Vice-Chancellor of Lancaster's Prize and John Peacock Prize. Called to Bar, Middle Temple, 1930. Practised Wales and Chester Circuit and London. Standing Counsel for Post Office on Circuit. Served in R.A.F. in War of 1939-45, first as Intelligence Officer with 604 Sqdn. and later on Air Staff (acting Wing Comdr.). Hon. Sqdn. Leader, R.A.F. Contested (L.) Chorley Div. of Lancs., 1929. Is a J.P. *Address:* Ribbleton House, Newton-le-Willows, Lancs.; 3 Hare Court, Temple, E.C.4. *Clubs:* Reform, National Liberal; Caernarvon Sailing. [*Died* 9 *June* 1970.

EMRYS-EVANS, Paul Vychan; Chairman, Charter Consolidated Ltd., 1965-66; President, British South Africa Company (Dir. 1949; Vice-Pres. 1959); Director: Anglo American Corporation of South Africa, 1950; Barclay's Bank (D.C.O.); Rand Selection Corp., 1960; De Beers Consolidated Mines, 1962; *b.* 1894; *er. s.* of late John Emrys Evans, C.M.G., and late Johanna Margaretha, *d.* of late P. G. Leeb, Wynberg, Cape of Good Hope; *m.* 1928, Evelyn Dorothy (*d.* 1962), *o. d.* of late Colonel Francis Randle Twemlow, D.S.O., Peatswood, Market Drayton; one *d.* *Educ.:* Harrow; King's Coll., Cambridge, M.A. Late Lieut. Suffolk Regt.; served European War, 1914-18: in France, 1916 (wounded); and at Foreign Office, 1917-1918. H.M. Embassy, Washington, 1918-19; F.O., 1919-23. M.P. (C.) S. Derbyshire, 1931-1945; Parl. Private Sec. to the Financial Sec. to War Office, 1940; Parl. Private Sec. to the Sec. of State for Dominion Affairs, 1940-41; Parliamentary Under-Secretary of State for Dominion Affairs, 1942-45; contested (C.) West Leicester 1929, South Derbyshire, 1945. *Address:* 15 Morpeth Mansions, S.W.1. *T.:* Victoria 4783; Peatswood, Market Drayton, Shropshire. *T.:* 2982. *Clubs:* Carlton, Brooks's, Pratt's. [*Died* 26 *Oct.* 1967.

ENEVER, Sir Francis Alfred, Kt. 1955; C.B. 1950; M.C. 1917; *b.* 24 May 1893; *s.* of late Francis Enever; *m.* 1922, Clare Woolley; one *s.* *Educ.:* Christ's College, Cambridge. B.A. (Cantab.), 1919; LL.B. (Cantab.), 1920; M.A., LL.M. (Cantab.), 1925; LL.D. (Lond.), 1929. Entered Civil Service, 1913. Served European War, London Regt. Roy. Fus., Sept. 1914-Jan. 1919. Called to Bar (Gray's Inn), 1921. Treasury Solicitor's Dept., 1922-37; Board of Trade, 1937-38; Legal Adviser, Coal Commission, 1938-46; National Coal Board, Jan.-Apr. 1947; Principal Assistant Solicitor, Treasury Solicitor's Department, 1947-1953; Deputy Treasury Solicitor, 1953-56, retired. Legal Adviser to Crown Estate Commissioners, 1957-61. *Publications:* Bona Vacantia, 1927; History of the Law of Distress, 1931; Coal Act, 1938, 1938; Law of Support in relation to Minerals, 1947. *Recreations:* chess, sailing. *Address:* Further Hanger, Hindhead Road, Haslemere. *T.:* Haslemere 3704. *Club:* Oxford and Cambridge University. [*Died* 17 *Jan.* 1966.

ENGELBACH, His Honour Archibald Frank; *b.* 1 Jan. 1881; *s.* of Francis William Engelbach, Richmond, Surrey; *m.* 1930, Violet Maude, *d.* of Herbert Baddeley, Dinard, France. *Educ.:* Dulwich College. Called to Bar, Middle Temple, 1906, and joined Oxford Circuit, 1906; Judge of Shoreditch County Court, 1940-55, of Windsor County Court on Circuit 36, 1943-55; retired 1955. Served European War, 1915-1919, Middlesex Regiment. Won Public Schools Gymnastic Championship, 1898; won All England Men's Doubles Badminton Championship, 1920; Vice-Pres. Badminton Assoc. of England since 1935; Steward British Boxing Board of Control since 1957. *Recreations:* golf, lawn tennis, squash rackets. *Address:* 54 Wynnstay Gardens, Allen Street, W.8. *T.:* Western 4878. *Clubs:* Union, Roehampton Country. [*Died* 14 *Dec.* 1961.

ENGLAND, Sir Russell, Kt. 1965; C.B.E. 1957 (O.B.E. 1943); J.P.; rancher and business executive, Botswana. Formerly Chief Agricultural Officer, Bechuanaland Government; M.E.C., 1961-63, also M.L.C.; took part in constitutional discussions, 1963. Chairman: Joint and European Advisory Councils; Livestock Advisory Committee. *Address:* c/o P.O. Box 26, Lobatsi, Botswana. [*Died* 13 *Jan.* 1970.

ENGLISH, Alexander Emanuel, C.I.E. 1911; *b.* 1871; *s.* of late Joseph Thomas English, J.P.; *m.* 1904, Frances Hutchinson (*d.* 1944), *d.* of John King, Stratton, Cornwall; two *d.* *Educ.:* Rugby; St. John's College, Cambridge. Entered Indian Civil Service, 1892; Commissioner in Burma, 1917; Director of Recruiting, 1917; retired, 1920. *Address:* 86 Woodstock Road, Oxford. *T.:* Oxford 58667. [*Died* 22 *Oct.* 1962.

ENNES ULRICH, Ruy, LL.D.; economist; Vice-Chairman: Benguela Railway Co.; Ultramarina Insurance Co.; Chairman, Corporation of Credit and Insurance; *b.* 20 April 1883; *s.* of João Henrique and Maria Christina Orta Ennes Ulrich; *m.* 1907, Genoveva de Lima (*d.* 1963); one *d.* (one *s.* decd.). *Educ.:* Coimbra. Prof. Coimbra Univ., 1907; member Board of Portuguese Public Debt Dept., 1911; Director Bank of Portugal, 1914-29; Chairman: of Mozambique Co., 1923; of Portuguese Railway Co., 1925. Ambassador to Court of St. James's, 1933-35 (resigned) and 1950-53. Prof. Lisbon Univ. Chm Portuguese Nat. Navigation Co. 1936-50. Member, Corporative Chamber, 1937-41, 1944-50, 1963; Member, Academy of Sciences, Lisbon; Hon. Chm. Lisbon Geographical Society. North Atlantic Council Deputy for Portugal, 1950-1952. Grand Cross of: Christ of Portugal, St. James of Portugal, Crown of Rumania. *Publications:* Da Bolsa e suas operações, 1906; Do Reporte no Direito Comercial Portugues, 1907; Politica Colonial, 1909. Economia Colonial, 1910, Economia Politica, 1937, 1938, 1940, Transportes, 1941, Repartição, 1943-44, Credito e Consumo, 1945, Produção, 1946, Introdução ao estudo da economica politica, 1947; Cambios, 1946; Circulação, 1947; Commercio, 1948; Salario, 1949, Lucro, 1949. *Address:* 240 Rua Silva, Carvalho, Lisbon, Portugal. *Clubs:* Travellers' United Service Royal Thames Yacht; Turf (Lisbon). [*Died* 20 *June* 1966.

ENNISDALE, 1st Baron, *cr.* 1939, of Grateley; **Maj. Henry Edward Lyons,** 1st Bt., *cr.* 1937; Kt., *cr.* 1933; O.B.E.; *b.* 1878; *s.* of John Edward Lyons; *m.* 1905, Helen, *d.* of Frank Bishop. Served South African War, 1900-02; European War, 1915-19; D.A.Q.M.G., Southern Command, 1918-19. *Recreations:* polo, racing. *Address:* Baynards Park, Cranleigh, Surrey. [*Died* 17 *Aug.* 1963 (*ext.*).

ENNISKILLEN, 5th Earl of (*cr.* 1789) **John Henry Michael Cole,** C.M.G., 1916; Baron Mountflorence, 1760; Viscount Enniskillen, 1776; Baron Grinstead (U.K.), 1815; Lt.-Col. late North Irish Horse; late 7th (Queen's Own) Hussars; *b.* 10 Sept. 1876; *e. surv. s.* of 4th Earl and Charlotte (*d.* 1937), *d.* of Douglas Baird, Closeburn, Dumfriesshire; *S.* father, 1924; *m.* 1st, 1907, Irene Frances (whom he div., 1931; she *d.* 1937), *d.* of A. E. Miller Mundy; three *d.* (one *s.* decd.); 2nd, 1932, Mary Cicely, *d.* of late Hugh Nevill, and *widow* of Major Thomas Syers, R.A. *Educ.:* Eton. Formerly Lieut. 3rd Batt. Royal Enniskillen Fusiliers. Served European War, 1914-16 (despatches, C.M.G.). Owns about 30,300 acres. *Heir*; *n.* David Lowry Cole, M.B.E. *Address:* Florence Court, Enniskillen, Co. Fermanagh [*Died* 19 *Feb.* 1963.

ENOCK Charles Reginald; *b.* 23 Nov. 1868; *s.* of late Arthur H. Enock, of Newton Abbot, Devon; *m.*; two *c.*Engineer, traveller; F.S.E.; sociologist, has spent many years abroad in professional work, and in the investigation of natural resources, especially in North and South America, and of the British Empire; has carried out scientific work for the Governments of Peru and Mexico; has given papers and lectures before the Royal Geographical Society, Royal Society of Arts (Medallist), British Association, Society of Engineers (Premiated), etc.; Member of the Portsmouth Diocesan Conference; Director of the Truth Campaign; Scoutmaster. *Publications:* The Andes and the Amazon, 4th edition; Mexico, 4th edition; An Imperial Commonwealth; America and England; Pioneering and Map-Making for Boy Scouts and Others, 2nd edition; The Tropics, their Resources, People, and Future; The Etymon, The Origin of Man, Language, Religion and Place Names; The True Plan and Science of Life, Industry and a True Money System, Westward Star (1943 onwards), America as I Saw It. *Address:* Oak Tree Cottage, Froxfield, Petersfield. *T.A.:* Enock, Froxfield, Petersfield, Hants. [*Died* 7 *April* 1970.

ERASMUS, Hon. François Christiaan B.A., LL.B.; Ambassador for the Republic of South Africa to Italy since 1961; *b* Merweville, South Africa, 1896. *Educ.:* Worcester High School; University of Cape Town. Taught in Transvaal; subsequently Registrar to Judge-President of the Cape; in practice as Advocate, Cape Town, 1925-27; Assistant Attorney-General, South West Africa, 1927-28; Assistant Organiser of National Party in Cape Province, 1928-30, Chief Secretary, 1930-48; M.P. for Moorreesburg, South Africa, 1933-61; Minister of Defence, 1948-59; Minister of Justice, 1959-1961. *Address:* South African Embassy, Rome, Italy. [*Died* 7 *Jan.* 1967.

ERIKS, Sierd Sint, Hon. K.B.E. 1961 (Hon. O.B.E. 1948); Director: Cryselco Limited; Mullard Limited; Philips Electronic & Associated Industries Ltd. *Address:* Century House, Shaftesbury Avenue, W.C.2. [*Died* 27 *Sept.* 1966.

ERLANGER, Joseph; Emeritus Professor of Physiology, Washington University School of Medicine, St. Louis 10, Mo., U.S.A.; *b.* 5 Jan. 1874; *s.* of Herman Erlanger and Sarah Galinger; *m.* 1906, Aimée Hirstel (decd.); two *d.* (one *s.* decd.). *Educ.:* Univ. of California (B.S.); Johns Hopkins Medical School (M.D.). Resident House Officer, Johns Hopkins Hosp., 1899-1900; Fellow in Pathology, Asst., Instr., Assoc. and Assoc. Prof. Physiology, Johns Hopkins Univ., 1900-6; Prof. Physiology and Head of Dept., Univ. of Wisconsin, 1906-10; Washington University, 1910-1946. Hitchcock Lecturer, Univ. of Calif.; Eldridge Reeves Johnson Lecturer, Univ. of Pennsylvania; Harvey Lecturer, New York (twice). Member National Academy of Sciences; Amer. Philosophical Society; Amer. Physiol. Soc. (President 3 years); Assoc. Amer. Physicians; Leop.-Carol Deutschen Akad. Naturforscher, Halle; Corr. Member Société Philomathique, Paris. Hon. degrees: LL.D. Univ. of Calif. and Johns Hopkins Univ.; Sc.D. Universities of Wisconsin, Pennsylvania, Michigan and Washington (St. Louis); Dr. (Hon.) Brussels. Nobel Award, Physiology and Medicine, 1944. *Publications:* Electrical Signs of Nervous Activity (with H. S. Gasser), 1937; Symposium on the Synapse (with others), 1936, and some 100 scientific papers. *Recreation:* communion with nature. *Address:* 5127 Waterman Ave., St. Louis 8, Mo., U.S.A. [*Died* 7 *Dec.* 1965.

ERNST, Noel Edward, C.M.G. 1946; Government Agent, Central Province, Ceylon, retired; *b.* 25 Dec. 1891, Ceylonese; *m.* 1916, Margaret Henrietta de Vos; one *s.* one *d.* *Educ.:* Royal Coll. and Medical Coll., Colombo, Ceylon. Appointed to Ceylon Civil Service, 1912, and held several appointments in Judicial and Revenue branches of the Service; retired, 1946. *Recreation:* Study of Ceylon history and sport. *Address:* Naystad, The Fort, Matara, Ceylon [*Died* 6 *June* 1965.

ERROCK, Michael Warden; Counsellor, H.M. Diplomatic Service, since 1964; *b.* 4 July 1921, *s.* of Frederick James and Olive Amy Errock; *m.* 1952, Marie Norah Ileana, *d.* of Sir Hugh Stonehewer Bird; one *s.* two *d.* *Educ.:* Abbotsholme Sch.; Ecole des Roches; Peterhouse, Cambridge (Scholar). Served in H.M. Forces, 1941-46: 2nd Lt. 13/18 Royal Hussars (Q.M.O.); later Capt. and Adjt., Hodson's Horse, I.A. H.M. Foreign Service, 1946: Middle East Centre for Arabic Studies; Baghdad; Jedda; Jerusalem; Tehran; Copenhagen; F.O.; U.K. Mission to the United Nations, New York, 1959-61; Kuwait, 1962-64; M.O.D. (Head of Internat. Dept.), 1964-67; Rawalpindi (Economic Counsellor), 1967-70; Middle East Centre, Cambridge Univ., 1970. Member: R.I.I.A.; R.C.A.S. *Recreations:* walking, bridge. *Address:* 1 Park Parade Cambridge. *T.:* Cambridge 58181. *Club:* Travellers'. [*Died* 10 *Dec.* 1970.

ERSKINE, Colonel Sir Arthur (Edward), G.C.V.O., *cr.* 1935 (K.C.V.O., *cr.* 1931; C.V.O. 1926); D.S.O. 1916; late Royal Artillery; Extra Equerry to the Queen since 1952 (to King George VI, 1941-52); Secretary and Registrar of Order of Merit since 1939; *y. s.* of late Sir H. David Erskine, K.C.V.O.; *b.* 1881; *m.* 1921, Rosemary Freda, *e. d.* of late Brig.-Gen. E. W. D. Baird, C.B.E.; two *s.* *Educ.:* Charterhouse; R.M.A., Woolwich. Served European War, 1914-18 (despatches, D.S.O., Bt. Lieut.-Col.); Equerry in-Ordinary to the King, 1919-24; retired pay, 1924; Crown Equerry to the King, 1924-41; Secretary to the Ascot Authority, 1941-46. *Address:* Annfield, Woodside, Coupar-Angus, Perthshire. *T.:* Burrelton 321 [*Died* 24 *July* 1963.

ERSKINE, Maj. Esmé Nourse, C.M.G. 1937; M.C.; *b.* 1885; *s.* of St. Vincent Erskine; *m.*; two *c.* *Educ.:* Diocesan College; S.A. College Law School, South African University, South Africa Forces 1913; King's African Rifles until 1924; served European War, East Africa (M.C.), Military Administration 1919-23 Northern Frontier Kenya; Anglo-Italian Boundary Commission 1925-28; H.M. Consul for Western Abyssinia, 1928-37; served in Italy 1927; returned to Foreign Office, 1939; recalled Army, 1940; served Middle East and India; Political Staff appt. Military Mission to 1944; reverted to Political Service in Middle East, 1944. Made several new Botanical discoveries in Western Abyssinia; contributed specimens to Kew and Edinburgh; F.R.Hort.S.; F.R.E.S. *Recreations:* general sport and games, big game Africa, horticulture special African plants. [*Died* 7 *July* 1962.

ERSKINE, General Sir George (Watkin Eben James), G.C.B. 1955 (K.C.B. 1952; C.B. 1943); K.B.E. 1950; D.S.O. 1942; *b.* 23 August 1899; *s.* of General George Elphinstone Erskine; *m.* 1930, Ruby, d. of Sir Evelyn de la Rue, 2nd Bart.; two *s.* one *d.* *Educ.:* Charterhouse; R.M.C., Sandhurst. 2nd Lt. K.R.R.C., 1918; Capt. 1928; Bt. Maj. 1936; Maj. 1938; Bt. Lt.-Col. 1938; Lt.-Col. 1941; Col. 1941; Maj.-Gen. 1944; Lt.-Gen. 1946; Gen. 1953. Served European War, 1918; War of 1939-45; G.S.O. 1 1st London Div. (T.A.); commanded 2nd K.R.R.C. 69th Inf. Bde.; B.G.S. 13th Corps; commanded 7th Armoured Division; Head S.H.A.E.F. Mission to Belgium; Comd. 43rd Wessex Division; Deputy Chief of Staff C.C.G. (despatches four times, D.S.O., C.B.); G.O.C. Land Forces, Hong Kong, 1946; Dir.-Gen. T.A., 1948-49; G.O.C. British Troops, Egypt and Mediterranean Command, 1949-52; G.O.C.-in-C., Eastern Command, 1952-53; C.-in-C., East Africa Command, 1953-55. A.D.C. General to the Queen, 1955-58. G.O.C.-in-C. Southern Command, 1955-58, retired. Lieutenant-Governor and C.-in-C., Jersey, 1958-63. K.St.J., 1959. Comdr. Legion of Merit (U.S.); Grand Cross of Order of Leopold II (Belgium); Médaille Militaire (Belgium); Commandeur Ordre du Chêne (Luxemburg). *Address:* Cheriton House, South Cheriton, Templecombe, Somerset. *Club:* Naval and Military. [*Died* 29 *Aug.* 1965.

ESHER, 3rd Viscount (*cr.* 1897), Baron 1885; **Oliver Sylvain Baliol Brett,** G.B.E., *cr.* 1955 (M.B.E. 1918); *b.* 23 March 1881; *e. s.* of 2nd Viscount and Eleanor (*d.* 1940), *d.* of M. Van de Weyer, Belgian Minister at the Court of St. James's; *S.* father, 1930; *m.* 1912, Antoinette, *d.* of August Heckscher, New York; one *s.* three *d.* *Educ.:* Eton. Contested Huntingdon (L.), Jan. and Dec. 1910; Assistant Private Secretary (unpaid) to Sec. of State for India (Viscount Morley), 1905-10; entered 16th Batt. Co. of London Regt. (Queen's Westminster Rifles), 1914; attached to the War Office, 1915-19; Trustee of the London Museum; Chairman: Grants Committee of Historic Churches Trust; Friends of the National Libraries; Theatre Advisory Council; Richmond Georgian Theatre Trust; Victorian Society; Council for Coram's Fields; Mem. Executive Committee of the National Trust; Life Pres., Soc. for Protection of Ancient Buildings, 1960; President: Central Sch. of Speech Training and Dramatic Art; Inst. of Recorded Sound; London Society; Vocational Guidance Association; Governor of the Old Vic. Hon. F.R.I.B.A.; F.R.S.L. *Publications:* A Defence of Liberty, 1920; Wellington, 1928. *Heir:* *s.* Col. Hon. Lionel Gordon Baliol Brett, M.A. *Address:* Turville Grange, Henley-on-Thames, Oxon. *T.:* Turville Heath 206; Altamira, Châteauneuf-de-Grasse, A-M., France; Albany, Piccadilly, W.1. *T.:* Regent 0444. *Clubs:* Athenæum, Brooks's, Beefsteak. [*Died* 8 *Oct.* 1963.

ESSEX, 8th Earl of, *cr.* 1661; **Algernon George de Vere Capell,** Baron Capel, 1641; Viscount Malden, 1661; Assistant Superintendent Remount Service; late 2nd Lieut. 7th Hussars, 1902; *b.* 21 Feb. 1884; *o. s.* of 7th Earl of Essex and Eleanor Harriett Maria, *d.* of late W. H. Harford of Oldown House, Almondesbury; *S.* father, 1916; *m.* 1st, 1905, Mary Eveline (who obtained a divorce, 1926; she *d.* 1955); *d.* of late W. R. Stewart Freeman, of the Manor House, Wingrave, Bucks; one *s.*; 2nd, 1926, Mrs. Alys Montgomery Scott-Brown (marriage dissolved, 1950); 3rd, 1950, Mildred Carlson (marriage dissolved, 1957); 4th, 1957, Christine Davis. *Educ:* Eton. *Heir:* *s.* Viscount Malden, T.D. *Address:* Little Cassiobury, Southampton, Bermuda. *Club:* Bath. [*Died* 8 *Dec.* 1966.

ETHERTON, Colonel P. T.; late Royal Garhwal Rifles, Indian Army; *b.* 4 Sept. 1879; *s.* of late J. Humphrey Etherton, Rowlands Castle, Hants. *Educ.:* privately; France. Served in Kitchener's Fighting Scouts, South African War, 1900-2 (medal and four clasps); Northamptonshire Regt. 1903; Indian Army, 1904; travelled in Europe, Asia, Africa, Australia, and America; served European War, in France and Flanders, 1915 (despatches), Egypt and Sinai Peninsula, 1915-1916; Mesopotamia, 1917-18; raised and commanded the Central Bombing and Trench Warfare School at Mhow, India, 1917; sent by H.M. Government on special mission to Central Asia, 1918; H.B.M. Consul-General and Political Resident in Chinese Turkistan, 1918-24, and Additional Assistant Judge of H.B.M. Supreme Court for China; commanded 51st (London) Anti-Aircraft Brigade, London Air Defences, 1924-29; Hon. Organising Secretary of Houston-Mt. Everest Flight, India, 1933; Aerial tour of South America and flew across the Andes and back, 1934; Personal Assist. and Chief Staff Officer to Admiral Sir Edward Evans, London Regional Commissioner, in charge of Civil Defence, 1940-46. Toured Central America, Mexico, Cuba, and West Indies, 1948. Gold Medallist, French Geographical Society. *Publications:* Across the Roof of the World; In the Heart of Asia, 1925; China, the Facts, 1927; Adventures in Five Continents, 1928; The Pacific: a Forecast; Through Europe and the Balkans; Japan: Mistress of the Pacific? 1933; First Over Everest (part author), 1933; Across the Great Deserts, 1948; All Over the World, 1948; Haunts of High Adventure, 1950; Lundy—The Tempestuous Isle, 1954; On Either Side of the Equator, 1954; numerous articles on sport and travel. *Recreations:* motoring, travel, big-game shooting. *Address:* c/o Midland Bank, Princes St., E.C.2. *Clubs:* United Service; Shikar. [*Died* 30 *March* 1963.

EVANS, 1st Baron, *cr.* 1957, of Merthyr Tydfil; **Horace Evans,** G.C.V.O. 1955 (K.C.V.O. 1949); D.Sc.; M.D., F.R.C.P. (London); Hon. F.R.C.S. (England); Hon. F.F.R.; Physician to The Queen since 1952; Physician to London Hospital and Royal Masonic Hospital; Consulting Physician: Royal Buckinghamshire Hospital, Poplar Hospital, King Edward VII Hospital for Officers, King Edward VII Sanatorium, Midhurst; Consulting Physician to the Navy; Medical Consultant to London Transport Executive; *b.* 1 January 1903; *s.* of late Harry Evans, musician, Liverpool, and Edith G. Evans; *m.* 1929, Helen Aldwyth Davies; one *d.* (and one *d.* decd.). *Educ.:* Liverpool College; City of London School; London Hospital Medical School (Scholar). M.R.C.S. (Eng.); L.R.C.P. (Lond.) 1925; M.B., B.S. 1928; M.R.C.P. 1930; M.D. (Lond.) 1930; F.R.C.P. (Lond.) 1938; K.E.D. Payne Scholar in Pathology; Physician to King George VI, 1949-52, and to Queen Mary, 1946-53; late House Physician, House Surgeon and Resident Accoucheur at London Hospital; late Assistant Director Medical Unit. Late Hunterian Prof., Royal Coll. of Surgeons. Croonian Lecturer, R.C.P., 1955; Late Sen. Censor, R.C.P.; Past Pres. Med. Soc., London; Mem. Bd. of Governors, London Hospital, 1962-. Freedom of Merthyr Tydfil, 1962. Hon. F.R.C.S., Hon. F.F.R.; K.St. J. *Publications:* various in med. and scientific jls., especially concerned with high blood pressure and diseases of the kidneys. *Recreations:* travel, cinematography. *Heir:* none. *Address:* 26 Weymouth St., W.1. *T.:* Langham 7700. *Clubs:* Athenæum, Buck's, Garrick, White's. [*Died* 26 *Oct.* 1963 (*ext.*)

EVANS, Arthur; *see* Evans, H. A.

EVANS, Rev. Arthur W.; *see* Wade-Evans.

EVANS, Sir Charles (Arthur) Lovatt, Kt. 1951; F.R.S. 1925; Emeritus Professor of Physiology, University of London, since 1949, and Consultant, War Office, since 1959 (Min. of Supply, 1949-59); Chm. Council Royal Veterinary College, 1949-63; *m.* 1911; two *d.* *Educ.:* Univ. of Birmingham; University College, London; University College Hosp.; Freiburg i/Br. B.Sc. Lond. 1910; Sharpey Scholar, University Coll., London, 1911-17; D.Sc. London, 1913; M.R.C.S., L.R.C.P., 1916; F.R.C.P., 1929; Hon. LL.D. (Birmingham), 1934; Hon. LL D. (London), 1957; Lt.-Major, Royal Army Medical Corps, 1916-18; Professor of Experimental Physiology, Leeds, 1918-19; National Institute for Medical Research, 1919-22; Professor of Physiology, St. Bartholomew's Medical Coll., 1922-26; Jodrell Professor of Physiology, University College, London, 1926-49; National Service, 1939-44. Member of Council and Vice-Pres. Royal Society, 1946-1948; Chairman Military Personnel Research Committee, War Office, 1948-53; Member Medical Research Council, 1947-50. Pres. Physiology Section, Brit. Assoc. for the Advancement of Science, 1928; Sharpey-Schafer Lectr., Edin., 1939; Abrahams Lectr., R.C.P., 1946; Stephen Paget Lectr., Research Defence Soc., 1949; Bayliss-Starling Lectr., Physiol. Soc., 1963; William Dick Memorial Lectr., Edinburgh, 1965. Fellow of Univ. Coll., London; Fellow, Royal Veterinary Coll.; Hon. Member: Biochem. Soc.; Italian Soc. Exp. Biol.; Physiol. Soc.; Soc. Argentina de Biologia; For. Member Royal Physiographical Society, Lund. *Publications:* Recent Advances in Physiology, 1930; Principles of Human Physiology, 12th edn., 1956; papers on Physiology and Biochemistry. *Address:* Hedgemoor Cottage, Winterslow, nr. Salisbury, Wilts. *T.:* Winterslow 225. *Club:* Savage.
[*Died* 29 *Aug.* 1968.

EVANS, Charles Glyn, C.B. 1942; *b.* 13 Nov. 1883; 2nd *s.* of William Evans, C.B.; *m.* 1920, Esther, J.P. (Essex, 1951), *d.* of Philip Scott Stokes; one *s.* two *d.* *Educ.:* Merchant Taylors' School; St. John's College, Oxford. Barrister, Inner Temple, 1910; Civil Service (Insurance Commission), 1912; Air Ministry, 1916-42. *Address:* Rye Mill House, Feering, Colchester.
[*Died* 5 *Feb.* 1961.

EVANS, Rt. Rev. Daniel Ivor, C.B.E. 1952; Bishop in Argentina and Eastern South America, with the Falkland Islands, since 1946; *b.* 5 July 1900; *m.* 1940, Leone Helene Trery. *Educ.:* St. David's College, Lampeter. Served European war, 1916-18 with R.N.V.R. Ordained 1924; Curate of St. John's, Swansea, 1924-27; St. Martin's, Roath, 1927-30; Asst. Chaplain, St. John's, Buenos Aires, 1930-34; Bishop's Chaplain, 1932; Hon. Assoc. Padre of Toc H, 1933; Chaplain of Hurlingham (Arg.), 1936-38; Christ Church, Rio-de-Janeiro, 1938-46; Assistant Bishop, 1939-46. *Address:* Calle 25 De Mayo 282, Buenos Aires, Argentina. *T.A.:* Bishop Evans, Baires.
[*Died* 30 *July* 1962.

EVANS, Sir (David) Emrys, Kt. *cr.* 1952 M.A. (Wales), B.Litt. (Oxon), Hon. LL.D. (Liverpool and Wales); *b.* 1891; *s.* of Rev. T. Valentine Evans, Clydach, Glam.; *m.* Gwenllian Nesta Jones, M.A., Pontypridd; one *s.* one *d.* *Educ.:* Ystalyfera County School; University Coll., Bangor; Jesus College, Oxford (Meyrick Research Scholar); Univ. of Wales Fellowship. Assistant Master at Pentre Secondary School, 1918; Classical Master at Longton High School, 1918; Asst. Lecturer in Classics, Univ. Coll. of North Wales, 1919; first Professor of Classics at Univ. Coll., Swansea, 1921; Principal, University College of North Wales, 1927-58, Vice-Chancellor, Univ. of Wales, 1933-35, 1941-44, 1948-50 and 1954-56; Vice-Pres. and Rector Emeritus, University College, North Wales. Chairman, Central Advisory Council for Education (Wales), 1944-46; Member Royal Commission on University Education in Dundee, 1951-52; Chairman, Schools Broadcasting Council (Wales); Deputy Chairman Local Government Commn. for Wales, 1959-62; Member, Welsh Cttee., Arts Council; Freedom, City of Bangor, 1958; Member University of Wales Court and Academic Board; Member, Welsh Advisory Committee, National Trust. *Publications:* Amserau'r Testament Newydd; New Testament Times; Crefydd a Chymdeithas (Religion and Society); Welsh translations of Plato's Republic and other Dialogues; The University of Wales; (with R. T. Jenkins) Llais Rhyddid (a freedom anthology); philological, literary, and educational articles. *Address:* Talmaen, Bangor, N. Wales.
[*Died* 20 *Feb.* 1966.

EVANS, Edward Victor, O.B.E. 1918; Hon. D.Sc. (Leeds); F.R.I.C.; C.St.J.; *b.* 12 Dec. 1882; *e. s.* of James Edward and Emily Alma Evans; *m.* 1909, Annie, *d.* of T. D. Leng; two *s.* *Educ.:* Westminster City School; King's College, London. Formerly Managing Director, South Metropolitan Gas Co. President Institution of Gas Engineers, 1942-43; First Chairman Gas Research Board, 1939-47; Chairman British Gas Federation, 1944-48; President, Assoc. of British Chemical Manufacturers, 1943-45; Member North Thames Gas Board, 1949-53; President, Coal Tar Research Association, 1948-54; Member, Board of Governors, Guy's Hospital and Medical School, 1945-1959. *Publications:* Cantor Lectures, Royal Society of Arts, 1924; several technical communications particularly on carbonisation of coal. *Address:* 39 Village Way, Dulwich, S.E.21. *Clubs:* Athenæum, Savage.
[*Died* 8 *July* 1964.

EVANS, Einion, O.B.E. 1957; J.P. Merioneth, 1924; *b.* Dolgellau, 9 Oct. 1896; *s.* of late E. W. Evans, J.P.; *m.* 1920, Dilys, *o. d.* of late J. E. Jones (Cemlyn), Cardiff; two *s.* *Educ.:* Dolgellau Grammar School. Private Secretary to Brig.-Gen. Sir Owen Thomas, 1915-16; served with R.W.F. and Cheshire Regt.; in Egyptian operations with R.F.C., 1916-18; R.A.F.V.R. (Group Captain), 1939-1945; ex-Chairman, Dolgellau Urban Council. Representative for Wales, British Council, 1952-61 (retired Nov. 1961). *Recreation:* motoring. *Address:* Ty Gwyn, Braishfield, Romsey, Hants. *T.:* Braishfield 432.
[*Died* 20 *Aug.* 1969.

EVANS, Emlyn Hugh Garner; barrister; *b.* 3 September 1911; *s.* of Henry and Margaret Garner Evans, Llangollen. *Educ.:* Llangollen Grammar School; University College of Wales, Aberystwyth; Gonville and Caius College, Cambridge (M.A., LL.B.). President of the Cambridge Union, 1934. Contested Denbigh Division as a Liberal, 1945. A founder of the World Youth Congress Movement (President Political Section: Geneva, 1936, New York, 1938). Served War of 1939-45, in North Africa and Italy, Squadron Leader. Editor The New Commonwealth, 1935-50; Pres. Union of University Liberal Societies. M.P. (Nat. L.) Denbigh Div. of Denbighshire, 1950-Sept. 1959, Secretary Parliamentary Committee on Atomic Energy. *Address:* Islwyn, Llangollen, Denbighshire. *Club:* National Liberal.
[*Died* 11 *Oct.* 1963.

EVANS, Sir Emrys; *see* Evans, Sir D. E.

EVANS, Ernest; Judge of County Courts, Circuit No. 29 (North Wales), 1942-57, retired; Q.C. 1937; J.P.; *b.* 1885; *s.* of late Evan Evans, Clerk to Cardiganshire County Council; *m.* 1925, Constance Anne, *d.* of late Thomas Lloyd, Havenholme, Hadley Wood, and Mrs. J. T. Lewis; three *s.* *Educ.:* Llandovery College; U.C.W. Aberystwyth; Trinity Hall, Cambridge (B.A., L.L.B.) President of the Union, Cambridge; called to Bar, 1910; S. Wales Circuit; Chairman Cardiganshire and Anglesey Quarter Sessions. Served with the Forces, 1915-18, France, 1917-18; Captain R.A.S.C. 1918; Private Sec. to Rt. Hon. Lloyd George, Nov. 1918-Dec. 1920; M.P. (Liberal) Cardiganshire, 1921-23; Univ. of Wales 1924-42; Mem. of Council of Univ. Coll. of Wales and of Council of National Library of Wales; Vice-President Hon. Soc. of Cymrodorion. *Publications:* Agricultural Law; Agricultural Holdings Act. *Address:* Huanfa, Ceibach, Newquay, Cards. *T.:* Newquay 221; 20 Roumania Crescent, Llandudno. *T.:* 6369. [*Died* 18 *Jan.* 1965.

EVANS, Sir Evelyn Ward, 3rd Bt., *cr.* 1902; *b.* 4 March 1883; 3rd *s.* of 1st Bt., K.C.M.G., M.P. (*d.* 1907), and Marie de Grasse, *d.* of late Hon. Samuel Stevens, State Attorney, Albany, N.Y.; *S.* brother, 1946; *m.* 1909, Primrose Mary (*d.* 1957), *d.* of James Wyld Brown, J.P., Eastrop Grange, Highworth, Wilts. *Educ.:* Harrow; Trinity Coll., Cambridge (B.A. 1905). A.M.I.C.E. 1907. *Heir:* none. *Address:* c/o Mrs. P. K. Angus, 3 St. Bernard's Road, St. Albans, Herts. *T.:* St. Albans 57593. [*Died* 1 *Feb.* 1970 (*ext.*).

EVANS, Major Fisher Henry Freke, D.S.O. 1902; O.B.E.; D.L. Co. Donegal; *b.* 21 April 1868; *o. s.* of late Captain Richard Fisher Evans; *m.* 1892, Marie Louise Evans (*d.* 1955), *e. d.* of late Major A. K. Haslett, R.E.; (two *s.* killed in action). *Educ.:* Rossall; Peterhouse, Cambridge (B.A. 1890). Major Special Reserve, The King's Own Royal Regiment (Lancaster), 1902-8; attached Loyal N. Lancs Regt. 1914-17; served S. Africa, 1900-1901 (despatches, medal 3 clasps, D.S.O.); served until May 1946 as Lieut. R.I.N.V.R. High Sheriff, Co. Donegal, 1911. *Recreation:* sport. *Address:* 5 Mortimer Road, Cambridge. *Club:* United Service. [*Died* 22 *Sept.* 1961.

EVANS, Sir Geoffrey, Kt., *cr.* 1934; C.I.E. 1919; M.A. (Cantab.), Economic Botanist, Royal Botanic Gardens, Kew, 1938-54 (Acting Director, 1941-43); retired, 1954; *b.* 26 June 1883; *s.* of Canon J. D. Evans, Vicar of Walmersley, Lancashire; *m.* 1914, L. Gertrude, *d.* of J. Kirby Rodwell, of Suffolk; two *d.* *Educ.:* Bury; Downing College, Cambridge (Foundation Scholar). Natural Science Tripos, 1904; Diploma of Agriculture, 1905; on the Staff, Cambridge Univ. Agricultural Dept., until 1906; Indian Agricultural Service, 1906-23; Principal, Agricultural Coll., Nagpore, India, 1906-7; Deputy Director Agriculture, C.P., 1907-17; Director of Agriculture, Bengal, 1919-22; Empire Cotton-growing Corporation; attached to the Queensland Government, Australia, as Director of Cotton Culture, 1923-26; Principal, Imperial College of Tropical Agriculture, Trinidad 1927-38; also doing service in Australia, Fiji, and New Guinea; during the War joined the Indian Army Reserve of Officers, seeing service in India and Mesopotamia; attained the rank of Colonel and was demobilised in 1919 with the rank of Lt.-Col.; was Director of Agriculture to the Mesopotamian Ex. Force, 1918-19 (despatches, C.I.E.); Member British Guiana Refugee Commission, 1939; commission on Higher Education in West Africa, 1943-44; Chairman Commission for Settlement in Br. Guiana and Br. Honduras, 1947-48. *Publications:* numerous bulletins and reports on Tropical Agriculture. *Recreations:* gardening and outdoor games *Address:* Little Lowman, Mayfield, Sussex. *Club:* Royal Commonwealth Society. [*Died* 16 *Aug.* 1963.

EVANS, Lt.-Col. Granville P.; *see* Pennefather-Evans.

EVANS, Griffith Ivor, M.A., D.M.Oxon; F.R.C.S.Eng.; D.O.M.S.Lond.; retd.; *b.* 14 Feb. 1889; *o.s.* of Griffith Evans, Dolaugwyn, Rhyl; *m.* 1916, Dilys, *d.* of William Eames, Bangor; no *c.* *Educ.:* Ruthin School; Magdalen College, Oxon; St. George's Hosp., S.W.1. R.A.M.C., S.R., 1914-19; Res. Med. Officer King Edward VII Hosp. for Officers, 1920; Surgical Registrar, St. George's Hosp., 1919; Surgeon Caernarvonshire and Anglesey Infirmary (resigned 1938); Medical Referee County Court, No. 29; President North Wales branch British Medical Assoc., 1941-1942; High Sheriff Caernarvonshire, 1942-43. *Publications:* Essays on Familial Syphilis, 1929 (gold medal Hunterian Society London, Sir Charles Hastings Certificate of Merit, B.M.A.). *Address:* 13B Melbury Road, W.14. *T.:* Western 4637. [*Died* 20 *Sept.* 1966.

EVANS, Sir Guildhaume M.; *see* Myrddin-Evans.

EVANS, (Henry) Arthur; Consultant, Automobile Association, since 1964; *b.* 23 Oct. 1903; 2nd *s.* of Charles and Caroline Evans; *m.* 1929, Kathleen, *d.* of Adolphe and Florence Cottebrune; no *c.* *Educ.:* privately. Joined A.A. Staff, 1920; Establishment Officer, 1945; Chief Establishment Officer, 1946; Asst. Sec., 1950; Dep. Sec. and Controller of Establishment, 1956; Dep. Sec.-Gen. and Dir. of Administration, 1959; Joint Secretary, 1963. *Recreation:* golf. *Address:* Priory House, St. Catherine's, Guildford, Surrey. *T.:* Guildford 5766. *Clubs:* United Service, Green Room; Royal Scottish Automobile (Glasgow). [*Died* 3 *Dec.* 1965.

EVANS, Herbert Edgar; *see* Addenda: II.

EVANS, Illtyd Buller P.; *see* Pole-Evans.

EVANS, John, O.B.E. 1945; J.P. Glamorgan; C.A. (Glamorgan); County Councillor, 1925-55; *b.* 10 Sept. 1875; *m.* 1909, Ellen Parton; one *s.* three *d.* *Educ.:* Park Board School, Cwmparc, Rhondda Valley; Ruskin College (2 yrs.), 1907-8. Started work in coal-mine at 12 years of age, worked as miner for 21 years. After 2 years at Ruskin College, Miners' Agent for Coegnant Lodge, S. Wales Miners' Federation. Elected to Glamorgan County Council in 1913. Served on Royal Commission (Nat. Health Insurance), 1924-25; on Royal Commission (Justices of Peace), 1946. Member of Maesteg U.D.C., 1916-37. Chairman of Glamorgan County Council, 1939-40 (2 yrs.); Chairman Education and Standing Joint (Police) Committees, Glamorgan; Chairman Emergency (Civil Defence Committee) Glamorgan—served throughout war years; Chairman and Leader of Labour Group (Glam. C.C.); M.P. for Ogmore Division of Glamorganshire, 1946-50. *Recreation:* bowls. *Address:* c/o County Hall, Cardiff. [*Died* 18 *April* 1961.

EVANS, John Howell, M.A., D.M., M.Ch. (Oxon), F.R.C.S.; Surgeon to Prince of Wales Hospital, the Cancer Hospital, Invalid Children's Aid Association and Hospitals in Montgomeryshire; Emergency Defence Service, Surgeon in charge of County of Montgomery; Vice.-Pres. Medico-Legal Society; Examiner in Surgery in the University of Oxford; *s.* of Rev. David Evans, Pont Dolanog; *b.* March 1870. *Educ.:* Christ College, Brecon; Oxford Univ. (Science Sch.); St. George's Hospital (numerous prizes). Jacksonian Prize, Royal College of Surgeons, 1913; Hunterian Professor Royal College of Surgeons, 1907, 1915 and 1927; Arris and Gale Lecturer Royal College Surgeons, 1921; Special Commendation and Honorarium for work on Tumours of the Testis, by Council of R.C.S., 1924; Consultant to Welsh Board of Nat. Health; President of the Montgomeryshire Society; High Sheriff County of Montgomeryshire, 1938; Master of Company of Barbers, 1944; Lecturer on Diseases of the

Urogenital System, Prince of Wales Hospital; Mons Star; Home Guard, Major. *Publications:* Diseases of the Breast, Tongue, and Neck; Tumours and Swellings of the Testicle; Tumours and Cancers of the Breast; Gallstones; The Testicle out of place; numerous publications on Operative Surgery, Cancer Cysts, Tumours, and Congenital Intestinal conditions. *Recreations:* football, golf winter sports etc. *Address:* 3 Chalfont Road, Oxford. *T.:* 55108. [*Died* 11 *Oct.* 1962.

EVANS, Rt. Rev. Kenneth Charles, D.D.; Bishop of Ontario, since 1952; *b.* West China, 1903; *s.* of Rev. Albert Edward Evans, missionary, West China; *m.* 1930, Marjorie Agnes Grace, *d.* of William Kerr Mowat, Toronto; three *s.* two *d.* *Educ.:* schools in Chefoo, N. China; University of Toronto; Wycliffe College, Toronto. B.A. 1928, M.A. 1929, Ph.D. 1932, Toronto Univ.; L.Th. 1930, Wycliffe Coll.; Deacon, 1930; Priest, 1931; Curate, 1930-31, Rector, 1931-1933, Lloydtown, Schomberg, Kettleby and Nobleton; Thayer Fell., Amer. Sch. of Oriental Research, Jerusalem, 1932-33; Lectr. and Prof. of Divinity, Trinity Coll., Toronto, 1934-40, B.D. 1939, D.D. 1944; Dean of Divinity, 1940-44; Dean and Rector, Christ Church Cathedral, Montreal, 1944-52. Hon. D.D.: Wycliffe College, Toronto, 1950; Queen's Univ., 1954; Hon. D.C.L. Bishop's Univ., Lennoxville 1951. *Recreation:* golf. *Address:* Main Street, Barrifield Village, Kingston, Ontario, Canada. *T.:* 546-6873. [*Died* 13 *Feb.* 1970.

EVANS, Lewis Noel Vincent, C.B. 1945; D.L.; J.P.; Deputy Chairman Court of Quarter Sessions, Merioneth, 1953-61, retd.; *b.* 27 Dec. 1886; *s.* of late Sir E. Vincent Evans, C.H.; *m.* 1917, Ellinor, *d.* of late Thomas Lawton, Liverpool. *Educ.:* Rossall. Solicitor, 1911; joined Department of Dir. of Public Prosecutions, 1913; late Asst. and Deputy Director of Public Prosecutions, retired Dec. 1948; enlisted Inns of Court O.T.C. Sept. 1914; gazetted to R.W.F.; served 1914-19; in France, Dec. 1915 to Oct. 1918 (wounded). Member of Council, Hon. Society of Cymmrodorion (Vice-Pres. 1949). J.P., Merionethshire; High Sheriff of Merioneth, 1954-55; D.L. Merionethshire, 1954. O.St.J. 1957. *Address:* Gwylfa, Harlech, Merionethshire. *Club:* Royal St. David's (Harlech). [*Died* 9 *Feb.* 1967.

EVANS, Brig.-Gen. Lewis Pugh, V.C. 1917; C.B. 1938, C.M.G. 1919; D.S.O. 1915, Bar 1918; p.s.c.; D.L. Cardiganshire; late The Black Watch; *b.* 3 Jan. 1881; 2nd *s.* of late Sir Griffith Evans, K.C.I.E., and Lady Evans of Lovesgrove, Aberystwyth; *m.* 1918, Dorothea Margaret Seagrave (*d.* 1921), *e. d.* of late John C. Pryse-Rice and late Dame Margaret Pryse-Rice, D.B.E.; (one *s.* decd.) *Educ.:* Eton; Sandhurst. Entered Army, 1899; served S. Africa, 1899-1902; European War, 1914-19 (despatches seven times, D.S.O. and bar, V.C., C.M.G., Order of Leopold and Croix de Guerre); retired, 1938; re-employed as Military Liaison Officer Wales Region H.Q., 1939-41. *Address:* Lovesgrove, Aberystwyth. *Clubs:* Caledonian, Naval and Military. [*Died* 30 *Nov.* 1962.

EVANS, Sir Lincoln, Kt., *cr.* 1953; C.B.E. 1948; Deputy Chairman Iron and Steel Board (part-time since June 1960; full-time, 1953-60); *b.* 18 Sept. 1889; British; *m.* 1911, Marion (*d.* 1964), *d.* of David Fender; one *s.* one *d.* *Educ.:* Swansea Elementary School. General Secretary, The Iron and Steel Trades Confederation, 1946-53; Member of Iron and Steel Board, 1946-48; Member Economic Planning Board, 1949-53; Deputy Chairman, British Productivity Council, 1952-53; Mem. B.B.C. Gen. Advisory Council, 1952-. *Address:* 22 Beverley Drive, Edgware, Mddx. *T.:* 01-204 3802. [*Died* 3 *Aug.* 1970.

EVANS, Lieut.-Colonel Llewelyn, C.M.G. 1919; D.S.O. 1917; R.E. and Royal Corps of Signals; *s.* of late Rev. H. J. Evans; *m.* 1920, Margaret, *er. d.* of late Lieut.-Gen Sir Arthur Sloggett, K.C.B. K.C.M G., K.C.V.O.; three *s.* *Educ.:* Charterhouse; R.M.A., Woolwich. Served S. African War, 1900-1902 (despatches, Queen's medal and six clasps, King's medal and two clasps); European War, 1914-18 (C.M.G., D.S.O., despatches, Bt. Lieut.-Colonel); Chevalier of the Legion of Honour; Chevalier of the Order of the Crown of Belgium; M.I.E.E.; retired from the Army, 1920. *Address:* Kingston Deverill, Warminster, Wilts. [*Died* 16 *Dec.* 1963.

EVANS, Paul V. E.; *see* Emrys-Evans.

EVANS, Dame Regina (Margaret), D.B.E., *cr.* 1936; Chairman London Hostels Association since 1949; *d.* of S. Evans, Dovercourt, Harwich, Essex. *Educ.:* Mayfield; Dresden. Chm. Central Council of Conservative and Unionist Associations, 1934; Chm. Women's Advisory Council, 1934-35; Chief Comdt., A.T.S., 1939-43. *Address:* 6 Cadogan Court, Draycott Ave., S.W.3. [*Died* 2 *Oct.* 1969.

EVANS, Sir Robert Charles, Kt., *cr.* 1929; Chairman, Evans Brothers, Limited; *b.* Dublin, 1 May 1878; *s.* of late Rev. Dr. Evans, Commissioner of National Education, Dublin; *m.* 1911, Dorothea Grace, *d.* of late Charles Albert Baker, London; four *d.* *Educ.:* Methodist College, Belfast. Founder of the City of London Vacation Course in Education, 1922, and of the Year Book of Education, 1932; Vice-President Periodical, Trade Press and Weekly Newspaper Proprietors' Association. *Publications:* Founder of The Teachers' World and numerous other educational journals, including Pictorial Education, Art and Craft Education, Child Education, La France. *Recreation:* gardening. *Address:* Foxborough, Canon Hill, Bray, Berks. *T.:* Maidenhead 4788; Montague House, Russell Square, W.C.1. *T.A.:* Byronitic, London. *T.:* Museum 8521. [*Died* 4 *Dec.* 1961.

EVANS, Maj.-Gen. Roger, C.B. 1941; M.C. 1918; Commander Order of Crown (Belgium), 1932; p.s.c., i.d.c.; *b.* 9 Jan. 1886; *m.* 1st, 1919, Enid Jocelyn (*d.* 1921), *d.* of late Philip L. Agnew; (one *s.* died on active service, 1942); 2nd, 1931, Eileen, *d.* of late Col. Edward Alexander Stanton, C.M.G.; three *s.* Served European War, Mesopotamia, 1917-18 (M.C., despatches); Commanded 5th R. Inniskilling Dragoon Guards, 1929-33; Colonel 5th Royal Inniskilling Dragoon Guards, 1937-47; A.D.C. to King George VI, 1937-38; Maj.-Gen., 1938; Armoured Div. Commander, 1938-40; District Commander; retired pay, 1944. D.L. Somersetshire, 1947; J.P. Somersetshire, 1950; High Sheriff of Somerset, 1955-56; County Alderman, 1957. *Address:* Stocklinch, nr. Ilminster, Somerset. *Club:* Cavalry. [*Died* 22 *Oct.* 1968.

EVANS, Rev. Canon Stanley George; Canon Residentiary and Chancellor of Southwark Cathedral since 1960; Director of Junior Clergy, Diocese of Southwark, 1960; Director of Training, Diocese of Southwark, since 1961; Examining Chaplain to Bishop of Southwark since 1959; *b.* 1912; *s.* of Sidney P. Evans, London; *m.* 1939, Anastasia Nicholson, Bradford; two *d.* *Educ.:* Westminster City Sch.; King's Coll., London; University of Leeds (M.A.); College of the Resurrection, Mirfield. Assistant Curate: St. Stephen, Shepherd's Bush, 1935-1937; St. Clement, Barnsbury, 1937-38; St. Andrew, Plaistow, 1938-42; St. Stephen, Portland Town, 1942-46; Officiating Chaplain, R.A.F., 1943-46; Licensed Preacher, Diocese of London, 1947-55; Extra-Mural

Lecturer, University of Oxford, 1948-55; Lecturer in Social Studies, City Literary Institute; Vicar of Holy Trinity with St. Philip, Dalston, 1955-60. Chaplain, International Circus Clowns Club, 1959. *Publications:* Churches in the U.S.S.R., 1943; East of Stettin-Trieste, 1950; Return to Reality, 1954; A Short History of Bulgaria, 1960; The Church in the Back Streets, 1963; In Evening Dress to Calvary, 1965; The Visual Hope of the Christian Church, 1965; contributions to Archaeologia Cantiana, etc. *Recreations:* ditchcrawling and pubcrawling. *Address:* St. Stephen's Lodge, Hankey Place, S.E.1. [*Died* 11 *Sept.* 1965.

EVANS, Stanley Norman; *b.* 1 Feb. 1898; *s.* of Francis Joseph and Elizabeth Evans, Harborne, Birmingham; *m.* Muriel Kathleen, *d.* of William and late Adeline Birkett, Keswick, Cumberland; one *d.* *Educ.:* Harborne Elementary School. Served European War, 1914-18, with Northumberland Hussars in France and Belgium. Founded Foundry Moulding Sand business of Stanley N. Evans, Ltd. (Birmingham), 1919. Travelled in Europe, the United States and Latin America. M.P. (Lab.) Wednesbury, 1945-56, resigned; Chm. All Party Anglo-South American Parliamentary Group. Leader of Parl. Deleg. to Rhodesia, Nyasaland, Malta and Mauritius, 1951; Member All Party Parl. Deleg. to Soviet Union, 1954. Parliamentary Secretary, Ministry of Food, March-April 1950. *Recreation:* travel. *Address:* Newlands, Fellows Lane, Harborne, Birmingham 17. *T.:* 021-427 0409. *Club:* Golf (Harborne). [*Died* 25 *June* 1970.

EVANS-FREKE, Hon. Ralfe, M.B.E. 1953; *b.* and *heir-pres.* of 10th Baron Carbery; *b.* 23 July 1897; *m.* 1st, 1919, Vera (who obtained a divorce, 1929), *d.* of C. Harrington Moore; one *s.*; 2nd, 1929, Phyllis, *d.* of C. W. Thorpe; one *d.*; 3rd, 1941, Dorothy May, *d.* of H. G. Surrey. *Educ.:* Eton; R.M.C., Sandhurst. Served European War, 1914-18 (wounded, despatches). Major, Rifle Brigade, and A.D.C. 58th London Division; Mil. Sec. to Governor of Burma, 1946-47. *Address:* Rush Beck, Boxford, Suffolk. [*Died* 23 *May* 1969.

EVANS-JONES, Rev. Sir Albert (bardic name Cynan), Kt. 1969; C.B.E. 1949; President of Court of Royal National Eisteddfod of Wales; *b.* Pwllheli, Caernarvonshire, 14 April 1895; *s.* of R. Albert Jones; *m.* 1st, 1921, Ellen J. Jones, Pwllheli; one *s.* one *d.*; 2nd, 1963, Menna M. Jones, Valley, Anglesey. *Educ.:* Pwllheli Primary and Grammar Schs.; University Coll. of North Wales, Bangor. C.E., Salonika, 1916-1918; Pastor of Welsh Presbyterian Church, Penmaenmawr, Caerns, 1920-31; Staff Tutor in Lit. and Drama, Univ. Coll. of N. Wales, Bangor (Extra-Mural Dept.), 1931-1960. Lord Chamberlain's Reader of Welsh Plays, 1931-68. Elected: Recorder and Dir. of Ceremonies to Gorsedd of Welsh Bards and Jt. Sec. of National Eisteddfod Council, 1935; Arch-Druid of Wales (term of 3 yrs, 1949, 2nd term, 1962); Freeman of Pwllheli, 1963. Winner of: National Eisteddfod Silver Crown for Poetry, 1921, 1923, 1931; National Eisteddfod Chair, 1924. Hon. D.Litt., Univ. of Wales, 1961. *Publications:* Telyn y Nos, 1921; Y Tannau Coll., 1922; Caniadau Cynan, 1927; *collected poems*: Cerddi Cynan, 1959; *prose*: Ffarwel Weledig, 1946; *plays*: 12 Welsh plays. *Recreations:* fishing, shooting. *Address:* Penmaen, Menai Bridge, Anglesey. *T.:* Menai Bridge 313. [*Died* 26 *Jan.* 1970.

EVATT, Rt. Hon. Herbert Vere, P.C. 1942; D.Litt., M.A., LL.D. (Syd.); Chief Justice of New South Wales, 1960-62; Leader of the Parliamentary Labour Party, Australia, 1951-60; *b.* East Maitland, N.S.W., 30 April 1894; *s.* of late John Ashmore Hamilton and late Jeanie Sophia Evatt; *m.* 1920, Mary Alice, *o. d.* of late Samuel Fuller Sheffer, Mosman, New South Wales; one *s.* one *d.* *Educ.:* Fort Street High School and St. Andrew's College (scholar), Sydney University (Government bursar), numerous prizes and scholarships at University in mathematics, philosophy, English literature and law; editor, Hermes magazine; President of Undergraduates Association and first undergraduate President of reconstituted University Union; life member Sports Union for services to University sport; B.A. (triple first); M.A. (first) 1917; LL.B. (Univ. Medal), LL.D. (Univ. Medal), 1924; tutor in philosophy at St. Andrew's College and Challis Lecturer in Legal Interpretation at Sydney University; admitted to N.S.W. Bar; M.L.A. (Lab.) Balmain, N.S.W., 1925-1929; 1926, took part in World Migration Conference as delegate of Australian Labour Movement; K.C. 1929; Justice of the High Court of Australia, 1930-40; resigned to contest Federal elections, 1940; Hon. Commonwealth Dir. of Reconstruction Research, 1941; Deputy Prime Minister of Australia, 1946-49; Attorney-General and Minister for External Affairs, 1941-49; M.H.R. (Lab.) Barton, N.S.W., 1949-60. Member, Advisory War Council, 1941-45; Australian War Cabinet, 1941-46; Australian representative in U.K. War Cabinet, 1942 and 1943; leader Aust. war-time missions to Washington, London and N.Z., 1942-43; initiated establishment and became Aust. Member of Pacific War Council, 1942-43; Aust. deleg. to U.N. Conf., San Francisco, 1945; to U.N. Preparatory Commission, London, 1946; Br. Commonwealth Prime Ministers Conf., London, 1946; Aust. rep., and Chm. Policy Cttee., Far Eastern Commission, 1946; leader, Aust. deleg. to Paris Conf. in relation to Italian peace treaty, 1946; Pres., S. Pacific Regional Conf., Canberra, 1947; Pres. British Commonwealth Conference on Japanese Peace Treaty, Canberra, 1947; Chairman U.N. Palestine Commission, 1947. Aust. rep. on U.N. Security Council, Atomic Energy Commn. (inaugural Chairman) and Conventional Armaments Commn. Leader Australian delegation U.N. Gen. Assembly, 1946, 1947; President U.N. Assembly, 1948; Pres. World Federation of U.N.A., 1949-. Hon. LL.D. Univs. of Leeds, Calif., S. Calif., Fordham (N.Y.). Freeman City of Leeds 1943; Scroll of Honour, City of New York, 1945; Freedom of City of Athens 1945, for defending internat. rights of small nations. Hon. Bencher, Middle Temple. Pres. Trustees of N.S.W. Public and Mitchell Libraries; F.R.A.H.S.; Vice-Pres. N.S.W. Cricket Assoc.; Aust. deleg. to Imperial Cricket Conf., 1938. *Publications:* Liberalism in Australia—an historical study, 1919 (awarded Beauchamp Prize, Univ. of Sydney); Conveyancing in N.S.W. (with J. G. Beckenham), 1923; British Dominions as Mandatories, 1934; The King and His Dominion Governors, 1936; Injustice within the Law, 1937; Rum Rebellion (The Overthrow of Governor Bligh by the N.S.W. Corps, 1808), 1938; Australian Labour Leader (biography of W. A. Holman), 1940; Post-War Reconstruction—A Case for Greater Commonwealth Powers, 1943; Australian Foreign Policy, 1945; Australia in World Affairs, 1946; The United Nations, 1949; monographs on history, political science and constitutional law. *Address:* c/o Supreme Court of N.S.W., Sydney, N.S.W., Australia [*Died* 2 *Nov.* 1965.

EVENNETT, Henry Outram, M.A.; Fellow and Praelector in History of Trinity College, Cambridge; University Lecturer in History since 1931; *b.* 15 May 1901; *o. s.* of late Clement Oakeley Clements Evennett and Emilia Julia Outram. *Educ.:* St. Benedict's, Ealing; Downside; Trinity

College, Cambridge. 1st class honours both parts of Historical Tripos, 1922 and 1923; Research Fellow, 1925-29; College Lecturer in History, 1930-55; Tutor, 1945-55. Attached to Foreign Office, 1939-45. Birkbeck Lecturer in Ecclesiastical History (subject: The Counter-Reformation) in Trinity College, Cambridge, 1950-51. Governor of the Oratory School. *Publications:* The Cardinal of Lorraine and the Council of Trent, 1930; The Catholic Schools of England and Wales (Current Problems Series), 1944; Catholics and the Universities (in the English Catholics 1850-1950, ed. Bishop Beck, 1950); contributor to New Cambridge Modern History; articles in a number of historical and Catholic periodicals. *Recreations:* music, piano. *Address:* Trinity College, Cambridge; Ivyville, Aspley Guise, Beds. *Club:* Travellers'. [*Died* 1 *Oct.* 1964.

EVERARD, Bernard, M.A. (Cantab.); M.Inst.C.E.; *b.* 20 April 1879; 2nd *s.* of late John Breedon Everard, M.Inst.C.E., Leicester; *m.* 1909, Florence Julia Fielding, J.P., *e. d.* of late T. Fielding Johnson, J.P., Goscote Hall, Leicestershire; two *s.* one *d.* (and one *s.* decd.). *Educ.:* Trinity College, Cambridge. Civil Engineer; Commission R.E. (Quarrying Coy.), 1917-18; Sheriff of County of Leicester, 1943-44. *Address:* Bardon Hill House, Leicestershire. *T.:* Coalville 2276.
[*Died* 8 *Oct.* 1963.

EVERSHED, 1st Baron, *cr.* 1956, of Stapenhill; **Francis Raymond Evershed,** P.C. 1947; Kt., 1944; F.S.A. 1950; a Lord of Appeal in Ordinary, 1962-65, retd.; a United Kingdom Member of the Permanent Court of Arbitration at The Hague since 1950; Chm. of The Pilgrim Trust, 1960-1965 (Trustee 1952-66); President, Pilgrims (Society of the U.K.), 1962-65; *b.* Burton-on-Trent, 8 August 1899; *s.* of late Frank Evershed and Helen Lowe; *m.* 1928, Joan, *o. d.* of late Hon. Mr. Justice Bennett. *Educ.:* Clifton; Balliol Coll., Oxford. Served European War, 1918-19, R.E., 2nd Lt. (France); B.A. degree, 2nd class Litt. Hum., 1921; Hon. Fellow Balliol Coll., 1947; Hon. LL.D.: Leeds, 1950; Nottingham, Melbourne, Adelaide and New York, 1951; Birmingham, 1953; Southampton, 1955; London, 1956; Columbia, N.Y., 1960; Hon. D.C.L. Oxford, 1955; Hon. D.Litt. Bristol, 1959; Hon. Fell, Nuffield College, Oxford, 1962; Hon. Freeman of Borough of Burton-on-Trent, 1950; Called to Bar, Lincoln's Inn, 1923, K.C. 1933, Bencher, 1938; Treasurer, 1958. Chm. Central Price Regulation Cttee., 6 Grosvenor Gardens, S.W.1, 1939-42; Regional Controller, Nottinghamshire, Derbyshire and Leicestershire coal-producing region, 1942-1944; Judge of Chancery Division, High Court of Justice, 1944-47; a Lord Justice of Appeal, 1947-49; Master of the Rolls, 1949-62. Member of Committee appointed by Minister of Works and Buildings on Compensation and Betterment, 1941; member of Industrial and Export Council appointed by Pres. of Board of Trade, 1941; Chairman Commission on Wages and Conditions of Labour in Cotton Spinning Industry, 1945-46; Chairman of Committees of Enquiry into Dock Wages, 1945, and into prices and production of Textile Machinery, 1946; Chm. Cttee. on Practice and Procedure in Supreme Court, 1947; President of Clifton College, 1951; Member Royal Commn. on Historical Manuscripts (Chm., 1949-62); Member Council of Legal Education, 1953; Chairman Law Advisory Committee, British Council, 1956; Visitor, St. Hilda's College, Oxford, 1962-. Freeman of City of London, 1953; Hon. Member American Academy of Arts and Sciences, 1956. Vice-Pres. Richmond Football Club; Patron, Derbyshire County Cricket Club; Hon. Member All-England Lawn Tennis Club. *Recreations:* usual. *Heir:* none. *Address:* Wormegay Grange, Setch, King's Lynn. *T.:* Watlington 250. *Club:* Garrick.
[*Died* 3 *Oct.* 1966 (*ext.*).

EVERSHED, Rear-Adm. (retd.) Walter, C.B. 1959; D.S.O. 1940; J.P.; *b.* 19 April 1907; 2nd *s.* of late Edward Evershed and Lilian Johnstone, of 48 Handsworth Wood Road, Birmingham; *m.* 1944, Susan Mary, *d.* of Rev. A. R. Browne-Wilkinson; two *s.* three *d.* *Educ.:* R.N.C., Osborne and Dartmouth. In command H.M.S. Gambia, 1954-1956; Director of Operations Division, Admiralty, 1956-57; Admiral Superintendent, Rosyth Dockyard, 1957-60. Chm., Midhurst R.D.C., 1968. J.P. 1961. Hon. Burgess of Dunfermline, 1960. *Address:* Tillington Old Rectory, Nr. Petworth, Sussex. *Club:* United Service.
[*Died* 23 *Aug.* 1969.

EVES, Sir Hubert Heath, Kt., *cr.* 1946; *b.* 10 March 1883; *y. s.* of late William and Emily Eves; *m.* 1913, Gladys Mary Goring; two *s.* one *d.* (and *er. s.* killed on active service N. Africa, 1943). Spent 14 years in Burma and India; occupied post of General Manager in India, Burmah Oil Co. Ltd.; and Representative in India of Anglo-Iranian Oil Co. Ltd.; joined Anglo-Iranian Oil Co. Ltd. in London, 1921, Managing Director, 1924-41; Dep. Chairman, 1941-50; Director, 1950-53; retd., 1953; Chairman of Tanker Tonnage Committee of Petroleum Board, 1940-46; Director, Suez Canal Co. Officer of the Legion of Honour, 1956. *Recreations:* golf, tennis. *Address:* 7 Kingston House North, Prince's Gate, S.W.7. *Club:* Oriental. [*Died* 24 *July* 1961.

EWART, David Shanks, A.R.S.A. 1934; portrait painter; served War of 1939-45, Royal Navy, Lieutenant Commander, R.N.V.R.; *b.* Glasgow, 1901; *m.* 1928; one *s.* two *d.* A year in business preceded entry into the Glasgow School of Art in 1919; later studied in France and Italy; Travelling Scholarship, Glasgow School of Art, 1924; Guthrie Award, Royal Scottish Academy, 1926; Lauder Award, Glasgow Art Club, 1927; has exhibited Royal Academy, Royal Society of British Artists, Royal Scottish Acad., Royal Glasgow Inst., and in other exhibitions in Great Britain, United States and Canada. Pictures in private and public collections: U.S.A.—New York, Detroit and Cincinnati; Canada—Montreal; Australia—Melbourne; London—Imperial War Museum, National Maritime Museum, United Service Club: Edinburgh—City Chambers, Roy. Soc., The Univ., Signet Library, Ch. of Scotland; Glasgow—Corporation Art Galleries, The University, Royal Technical College, Art Club; also in Wolverhampton, Aberdeen, Dundee, Paisley and Greenock. *Address:* 2 Royal Terrace, Glasgow, C.3. *T.:* Douglas 3562. *Clubs:* R.N.V.R.; Glasgow Art (Glasgow).
[*Died* 12 *Oct.* 1965.

EWBANK, Sir Robert Benson, Kt., *cr.* 1941; C.S.I. 1934; C.I.E. 1924; J.P. (Westmorland); I.C.S., retired; *b.* 22 Oct. 1883; *s.* of Rev. J. Ewbank, Bolton Rectory, Cumberland; *m.* Frances Helen Simpson, Caldbeck Rectory; two *s.* *Educ.:* Queen's College, Oxford. Registrar of Co-operative Societies, Bombay Presidency, 1911-19; Deputy Secretary to the Government of India, 1920-24; on duty at India Office and acting Private Secretary to Lord Reading, 1925; Acting Secretary to Government of India, 1926 and 1927; Sec., Bombay Back Bay Enquiry Committee, 1926; representative of Government of India in East Africa, 1927-28; Member, Legislative Council of Bombay, and General Secretary to Government of Bombay, 1929-34; retired from I.C.S. 1936; Member of Commission of

Government of Newfoundland and Commissioner for Natural Resources, 1936-39; Dominions Office, 1939-41; Dir. Brewers' Soc., 1942-47; Chm. Lake District Cttee. of Nat. Trust, 1948-62; Church Assembly, 1950-60; High Sheriff of Westmorland, 1957-58. *Publications:* Public Affairs in Newfoundland, 1939. *Address:* 2 The Abbey Carlisle. *Club:* East India and Sports. [*Died* 2 *Sept.* 1967.

EWER, Colonel George Guy, D.S.O. 1917; T.D.; M.I.E.E.; M.I.Cert.E.; *b.* 5 Nov. 1883; *s.* of G. W. Ewer; *m.* 1936, Hazel Mary, *d.* of B. V. H. Flack; two *s.* *Educ.:* Brighton. With 161st Inf. Brigade throughout European War, Gallipoli, Egypt, Palestine, Syria (despatches, D.S.O., Order of the Nile); commanded 6th Bn. Essex Regt. 1917-1919, 4th Bn. Essex Regt. 1919; 2/22nd Bn. London Regt., 1919; Staff, Cairo Brigade, 1920; City Electrical Engineer, Pietermaritzburg, Natal, 1923-43. Deputy Director-General Technical Services and Commanding Officer Technical Services Corps, S.A. Defence Force, 1940-44; Director, Central Organisation of Technical Training, S. Africa, 1944-49; Liaison Officer, Native Affairs Dept., South Africa, 1949-50; Administrative Officer, Natal Housing Board (Umlazi), 1950-55; Commissioner, Natal Coastal and Northern District, St. John Ambulance Brigade, 1948-57. K.St.J. *Address:* 174 Edmonds Rd., Durban, Natal, S. Africa. [*Died* 6 *Nov.* 1965.

EWERT, Alfred, M.A.; Hon. Litt.D., Leeds; F.B.A.; Emeritus Fellow, Trin. Coll., Oxford; Officier de la Légion d'Honneur; Corr. Fellow of Mediæval Academy of America; Hon. Fell., United Coll., Univ. of Winnipeg; *b.* 14 July 1891; *m.* 1920, Irene Agnes Oldershaw (*d.* 1959); two *d.* *Educ.:* Univ. of Manitoba; St. John's College, Oxford. Rhodes Scholar for Manitoba, 1912; B.A. 1919, M.A. 1920; served European War, 1914-19, Canadian Expeditionary Force (Western Ontario Regt.). Taylorian Lecturer in French, 1921-26; Lecturer in French at Univ. College, 1922-30; Lecturer in French at Jesus College, 1926-30; University Lecturer in French, 1926-30; Professor of the Romance Languages and Fellow of Trinity College, Oxford, 1930-58; Senior Proctor, 1943-44. Delegate of Local Examinations, 1923-59 (Chairman, 1942-59); Curator of Taylor Institution, 1930-57 (Secretary, 1945-51) Member Mixed Commission under Franco-British Cultural Convention, 1950-54. Barry Cerf Memorial Lecturer, Reed College Oregon, 1957; George A. Miller Visiting Lecturer, Univ. of Illinois, 1957; Zaharoff Lecturer, 1958; Lewis Fry Memorial Lecturer, Bristol Univ., 1961; W. B. Hurd Memorial Lecturer, Brandon Univ., 1967; President: Anglo-Norman Text Society, 1958-62; Medieval Soc., 1958-63; Modern Humanities Res. Assoc., 1959. General Editor of French Studies, 1947-65. *Publications:* Gui de Warewic, roman du 13e siècle (Classiques fr. du moyen âge), 1932; The French Language, 1933; Beroul, The Romance of Tristan, 1939; Marie de France, Fables (with R. C. Johnston), 1942; Marie de France, Lais, 1944; Of the Precellence of the French Tongue, 1958; Centenary Essays on Dante; articles and reviews in Modern Language Review, Arthuriana, Medium Aevum, Romania, etc. *Recreations:* golf and music. *Address:* 15 Blandford Ave., Oxford. *T.:* 55276. [*Died* 22 *Oct.* 1969.

EXLEY, J. R. Granville, R.E., A.R.C.A. (Lond.); Painter, Etcher and Engraver; *b.* Great Horton, Bradford, 16 May 1878; 3rd *s.* of late James Exley of Great Horton, and Kelbrook, Yorks.; *m.* 1911, Elizabeth (*d.* 1961), *e. d.* of late Charles Shuttleworth, of Earby; one *d.* *Educ.:* Bradford Grammar School; Skipton Science and Art Schools; Royal College of Art, London. Worked for some time in Paris; first exhibited in 1906; Works in public collections: Print Room, British Museum, Engraving, Victoria and Albert Museum; Cambridge, Fitzwilliam Museum, etc.; Second Master and Deputy Head Master at the Ryland Memorial Municipal School of Art, West Bromwich; Principal of the Cambridge and County School of Arts and Crafts; Headmaster of the City of Hull Municipal School of Art, 1912-19; Senior Drawing Master (Visiting), City of London School, 1928-46. *Publications:* various etchings and drawings. *Recreation:* sketching. *Address:* Sinclairs, Sand Pit Lane, Penn, Bucks. [*Died* 1 *Oct.* 1967.

EXMOUTH, 9th Viscount (*cr.* 1816); **Pownoll Irving Edward Pellew;** Bt. 1796; Baron, 1814; *b.* 28 May 1908; *s.* of 8th Viscount and Frances, *d.* of Alfred W. Edwards; *S.* father, 1951; *m.* 1938, Maria Luisa, Marquesa de Olias (Spain, *cr.* 1652; *S.* 1940), *d.* of Luis de Urquijo, Marques de Amurrio and Marquesa de Zarreal, Madrid; two *s.* two *d.* *Educ.:* Oundle. *Heir:* *s.* Hon. Paul Edward Pellew [*b.* 8 Oct. 1940; *m.* 1964, Maria Krystina, *d.* of late R. Garay, Madrid; one *d.*]. *Address:* Canonteign, Nr. Exeter, Devon. *T.:* Christow 333. [*Died* 2 *Dec.* 1970.

EXON, Charles, M.A.; *b.* 15 May 1862; *s.* of late Charles Exon of Birmingham; *m.* 1st, 1895, Charlotte (*d.* 1933), *d.* of late Charles Townley of Ballingarry, Co. Limerick; 2nd, Ida, *d.* of Alfred Willcox, London. *Educ.:* King Edward's School, Birmingham and Trinity College, Dublin (Senior Moderator in Classics); Lecturer in Greek and Latin in the University of Birmingham, 1901; Examiner to the Welsh Intermediate Board, 1901-2; Professor of Latin in University College, Galway, 1903-16. *Publications:* many papers in classical periodicals, chiefly on Plautine prosody and metric and comparative philology. *Address:* 12 Douglas Road, Southbourne, Bournemouth. [*Died* 20 *Sept.* 1962.

EYRES, Harry Maurice, C.M.G. 1950; H.M. Foreign Service, retired; *b.* 23 November 1898; *s.* of late Sir Harry Eyres, K.C.M.G.; *m.* 1946, Christina, *d.* of late G. M. Edwardes Jones, K.C.; two *s.* *Educ.:* Marlborough; Caius College, Cambridge. Served European War, 1914-18, in Army, 1917-19 (wounded, despatches). Entered Levant Consular Service, 1924; served in Near and Middle East, 1926-38; Foreign Office, 1938-1944; China, 1944-46; Syria, 1946-47; Minister at H.M. Embassy, Ankara, 1948-51; H.M. Consul General, Alexandria, 1951-57; retired, 1957. *Address:* Earl's Hall, Cockfield, Suffolk. *Clubs:* United Service, Royal Automobile. [*Died* 27 *Oct.* 1962.

EYTON, Lt.-Col. and Brevet Col. Charles R.; *see* Morris-Eyton.

EYTON, Frank, Lyric Author and Librettist; *b.* 30 Aug. 1894. *Educ.:* Bexhill. Originally "something in the City"; served overseas with H.M. Forces, 1916-19; wrote lyrics of Nippy (with Arthur Wimperis), Prince Edward Theatre, 1930; The Millionaire Kid, Gaiety, 1931; Nice Goings On (with Douglas Furber), Strand, 1933; Sporting Love (with Desmond Carter), Gaiety, 1934; Twenty to One, Coliseum, 1935; Over She Goes (with Desmond Carter), Saville; Let's raise the Curtain, Victoria Palace, 1936; Crazy Days (with Desmond Carter), Shaftesbury, 1937; Present Arms, Prince of Wales's, 1940; Lady Behave, His Majesty's, 1941; Meet Me Victoria, Victoria Palace, 1944; Sweetheart Mine, Victoria Palace, 1946; Bob's Your Uncle, Saville, 1948. Contributed lyrics to Love Lies, Gaiety; The Co-Optimists; Silver Wings, Dominion; Darling, I love you, Gaiety; Chelsea Follies, Victoria Palace; The Good Companions, His

Majesty's; Pelissier's Follies of 1938, Saville; C. B. Cochran's revue Lights Up, Savoy 1940; Fine and Dandy, Saville, 1942; La-di-da-di-da, Victoria Palace, 1943; The Love Racket, Victoria Palace, 1943; Follow the Girls, His Majesty's, 1945; Together Again, Victoria Palace, 1947; lyrics of numerous talking films, including Sunshine Susie, Marry Me, Tell me To-night, My Song for You, Band Waggon, 1939, Sailors Three, Champagne Charlie, etc.; Author of musical play, She shall have music, Saville, 1934; farcical comedy, Married in Haste (with George Barry), Birmingham, 1937; part author Maritza, Palace, 1938; (with Barry Lupino) Runaway Love, Saville, 1939; part author, Happy Birthday, Manchester, 1940; Wild Rose, Princes, 1942; various revue sketches. *Publications:* In addition to lyrics for musical plays, etc. mentioned above, many popular songs. *Recreations:* cricket, golf, and reading. *Clubs:* Savage, Green Room.
[*Died* 11 *Nov.* 1962.

F

FABER, Sir Geoffrey (Cust), Kt., *cr.* 1954; President of Faber and Faber, Ltd., publishers; Fellow and formerly Estates Bursar of All Souls; F.R.S.L.; *b.* 23 Aug. 1889; 2nd *s.* of Rev. Henry Mitford Faber; *m.* 1920, Enid Eleanor, 3rd *d.* of Sir H. Erle Richards, K.C.S.I., K.C.; two *s.* one *d.* *Educ.:* Rugby School; Christ Church, Oxford (Scholar). First Classes Classical Moderations and Literæ Humaniores; Oxford University Press, 1913-14; 8th Batt. The London Regiment (Post Office Rifles), 1914-19; France and Belgium; Captain, 1916; Fellow of All Souls College, Oxford, 1919; Eldon Law Scholar, 1919; called to Bar, Inner Temple, 1921; Director of Strong & Co. of Romsey, Ltd., 1920-23; Estates Bursar of All Souls, 1923-51; President of Publishers' Association, 1939-41; Chm., National Book League, 1945-47; Chairman of the Radcliffe Trustees, 1951-60. *Publications:* Interflow, 1915; The Valley of Vision, 1917; Elnovia, 1925; The Poetical Works of John Gay, 1926; Oxford Apostles, 1933: A Publisher Speaking, 1934; The Buried Stream (collected poems), 1941; Jowett, 1957. *Address:* Minsted House, Midhurst, Sussex; 24 Russell Square, W.C.1. [*Died* 31 *March* 1961.

FACHIRI, Adila Adrienne Adalbertina Maria; violinist; *b* Budapest; *d.* of Taksony Arányi de Hunyadvár and Adrienne Nieviarowicz de Ligenza; *m.* 1915, Alexander P. Fachiri (*d.* 1939), barrister-at-law; one *d.* *Educ.:* Budapest; Berlin. Won artist's diploma of Royal Hungarian Academy of Music and various scholarships; studied with Hubay at Budapest and afterwards as his only private pupil with Joachim, her great-uncle; played extensively on the Continent and settled in England. *Recreations:* swimming, tennis, reading. [*Died* 15 *Dec.* 1962.

FAGAN, Hon. Henry Allan; Chief Justice of South Africa, 1957-59, retired; Senator, South Africa, since 1962; *b.* 4 April 1889; *s.* of Henry Allan Fagan and Catherina Susanna Fagan (*née* Smith); *m.* 1922, Jessie Theron; three *s.* *Educ.:* Stellenbosch, S.A. (B.A.); London (LL.B.). Barrister-at-Law, Middle Temple, London, 1913. Advocate of Supreme Court, Cape Town, 1914-16, 1921-1938, 1940-43. Asst. Editor, Die Burger, 1916-19. Professor of Law, Univ. of Stellenbosch, 1920; K.C. 1927. Mem. Union Parl., 1933-43; Minister of Education, Social Welfare and Native Affairs in Hertzog-Smuts Cabinet, 1938-39. Judge of Supreme Court, Cape Town, 1943-50. Chairman of Native Laws Commission (which published rep generally known as Fagan Report, on laws affecting Natives), 1946-48. Judge of Court of Appeal, 1950-59. Hon. LL.D. Univ. of Stellenbosch, 1957, University of the Witwatersrand, Johannesburg, 1959. *Publications:* Ninya (a novel), 1956. Shorthand: A New System, 1950. Dramatic works, poems and short stories in Afrikaans. *Recreations:* bowls and chess. *Address:* Keurbos, Primrose Avenue, Claremont, Cape Town, S.A. *T.:* Cape Town 77-7461. *Clubs:* Bloemfontein (Bloemfontein), Here Sewentien (Cape Town). [*Died* 6 *Dec.* 1963.

FAIR, Hon. Sir Arthur; *see* Addenda II.

FAIRBAIRN, William Ronald Dodds, M.A., M.D., D. Psych., F.R.S.E., F.R.A.I.; F.B.Ps.S.; Consultant in Psychological Medicine; Member, British Psycho-Analytical Society; *b.* Edinburgh, 11 Aug. 1889; *s.* of late Thomas Fairbairn and Cecilia Leefe; *m.* 1st, Mary Ann (*d.* 1952), *o. d.* of late Harry More Gordon, of Charleton and Kinnaber, Angus, Scotland; two *s.* one *d*; 2nd, Marion Frances, *d.* of late Capt. H.E.M. Archer, D.S.O., R.N., and of late Mrs. Archer, of Coulston, Wiltshire. *Educ.:* Merchiston Castle School, and Universities, Edinburgh, Manchester, Kiel, Strasbourg, and Paris. Research study of Hellenistic Greek at Edinburgh, Kiel, Strasbourg, and Manchester, 1912-14; Army Service in R.E. and R.G.A. (T.), 1915-18; Edinburgh and Paris Universities (M.B., Ch.B.Edin.), 1919-23; Assistant Physician, Royal Edinburgh Hospital for Mental Diseases, 1923-24; Assistant Physician, Longmore Hospital, Edinburgh, 1926 31; Lecturer in Psychology, Edinburgh University, 1927-35; Medical Psychologist, Jordanburn Nerve Hospital, Edinburgh, and Edinburgh University Psychological Clinic for Children, 1929-34; Lecturer in Psychiatry, Edinburgh University, 1931-32; Visiting Psychiatrist, Carstairs E.M.S. Hospital, Lanarkshire, 1940-41; Consultant Psychiatrist to Min. of Pensions, 1941-1954. *Publications:* Psycho-Analytic Studies of the Personality, 1952; articles on psychological medicine in scientific journals. *Address:* Lochside Cottage, Duddingston Village, Edinburgh 15. *T.:* Abbeyhill 1704. *Clubs:* Authors'; New (Edinburgh).
[*Died* 31 *Dec.* 1964.

FAIRBANK, Sir (Harold Arthur) Thomas, Kt., *cr.* 1946; D.S.O. 1918; O.B.E. 1919; M.B., M.S. (Lond.), F.R.C.S. (Eng.); M.Ch.Orth. (Hon.) (Liverp.); Consulting Surgeon, Hospital for Sick Children, Great Ormond Street; Consulting Orthopædic Surgeon, King's College Hospital; Emeritus Lecturer in Orthopædic Surgery, King's College Hospital Medical School; Emeritus Surgeon, Lord Mayor Treloar's Orthopædic Hospital, Alton; Hon. Fellow Royal Soc. Medicine, late Pres. Sections of Orthopædics and Children's Diseases; Emer. Fellow and Past Pres. of Brit. Orthopædic Assoc.; Member (Vice-Pres. of 1936 congress) of International Soc. of Orthopædic Surgery; Hon. Member French and Scandinavian Orth. Societies, Brit. Pædiat. Assoc., Brit. Assoc. Pædiat. Surgeons, and Deutsche Orthop. Gesell.; Hon. Fellow Italian Soc. of Orthopædics and Traumatology; Corr. Mem. Amer. and Belgian Orth. Societies and Amer. Acad. of Orthopædic Surgeons; late Examiner in Orthopædic Surgery, University of Liverpool; *b.* 28 Mar. 1876; *s.* of late T. Fairbank, M.D., of Windsor; *m.* 1909, Florence Kathleen, *y. d.* of late A. G. Ogilvie; one *s.* two *d.* *Educ.:* Epsom Coll.; Charing Cross Hosp. (Entrance Schol.). Served as Civil Surgeon in S. African War (Queen's medal with 5 clasps); European War (D.S.O., O.B.E., despatches thrice); Temp. Lt.-Col. Assistant Consulting Surgeon, B.S.F.; Lt.-Col. R.A.M.C. (T.) retired; late 3rd City of London Field Ambulance (T.A.). Lady Jones Lecturer, Liverpool Univ. 1929; Robert Jones

Lecturer, Royal College of Surgeons, 1938; Simpson-Smith Lectr., Hosp. for Sick Children, Gt. Ormond St., 1952; late Consultant Adviser on Orthopædics to Ministry of Health for E.M.S.; Hon. Consultant (Orthopædic) to the Army at Home. *Publications:* numerous in medical journals and certain medical textbooks; Atlas of General Affections of the Skeleton, 1951. *Address:* 6M Hyde Park Mansions, Marylebone Road, N.W.1. *T.:* Ambassador 1600. *Club:* Royal Automobile. [*Died* 26 *Feb.* 1961.

FAIRFAX OF CAMERON, 13th Baron, *cr.* 1627; Thomas Brian McKelvie Fairfax; late Lieut. Grenadier Guards (invalided 1945); Representative Peer for Scotland, 1945-63; *b.* 14 May 1923; *er. s.* of 12th Baron and Maud Wishart, *d.* of James McKelvie, Duckyls Park, East Grinstead, Sussex; *S.* father, 1939; *m.* 1951, Sonia, *yr. d.* of late Capt. Cecil Gunston, M.C.; three *s.* one *d.* *Educ.:* Eton. Asst. Conservative Whip, House of Lords, 1947-48; Parliamentary Private Secretary to Lord Woolton, 1951-54; a Lord-in-Waiting, 1954-1957. *Heir: s.* Master of Fairfax. *Address:* Gays House, Holyport, nr. Maidenhead, Berks. *Clubs:* Carlton, Pratt's; Royal Yacht Squadron. [*Died* 8 *April* 1964.

FAIRFAX-LUCY, Capt. Sir (Henry) Montgomerie (Ramsay), 4th Bart., *cr.* 1836; M.C.; D.L. Warwickshire; *b.* 20 Oct. 1896; *e. s.* of 3rd Bt. and Ada Christina, *d.* and *heiress* of H. S. Lucy of Charlecote Park; *S.* father, 1944. *Educ.:* Wellington College; R.M.C., Sandhurst. Served European War, 1914-19 (M.C., despatches thrice); served Arab Rebellion, Iraq, 1920-21; Capt. Rifle Brigade and Argyll and Sutherland Highlanders, 1923; retired, 1925; Intelligence Officer (G.S.), Kenya Defence Force, 1939-41. Has lived chiefly in Kenya since 1925 and farmed at Kaptagat until 1945. In the U.K. he owns property in Warwickshire and Glen Nevis Estate, Fort William, and still owns property in Kenya where he has residences. *Heir: b.* Major Brian Fulke Ramsay- [*b.* 1898; *m.* 1933, Hon. Alice Caroline Helen Buchan, *o. d.* of 1st Baron Tweedsmuir; one *s.* one *d.*]. *Address:* Charlecote Park, Warwick; (Correspondence to Kenya) c/o P.O. Box 257, Mombasa, Kenya, E. Africa. [*Died* 22 *Dec.* 1965.

FAIRHAVEN, 1st Baron, *cr.* 1929 (U.K.) and 1961 (U.K.) (new creation); **Urban Huttleston Rogers Broughton** (granted the Barony which would have been conferred on his father had he lived); D.L. Cambridgeshire, 1937; J.P. 1939; Hon. M.A. (Cantab.), 1950; F.S.A.; *b.* 31 Aug. 1896; *e. s.* of Urban Hanlon Broughton, M.P., of Park Close, Englefield Green (*d.* 1929) and Cara Leland (*d.* 1939), *d.* of late Henry Huttleston Rogers, New York. *Educ.:* Harrow; R.M.C., Sandhurst. Served European War, 1916-18; entered First Life Guards, 1916; retired, 1924; Liaison Commissioner, Red Cross and St. John War Organisation, 1939-45; K.St.J. *Publication:* The Dress of the First Regiment of Life Guards in Three Centuries, 1925. *Heir:* (2nd *cr.*) *b.* Major Hon. Henry Rogers Broughton. *Address:* Anglesey Abbey, Cambridge; Kirtling Tower, Newmarket; Haven House, Aldeburgh, Suffolk; 37 Grosvenor Square, W.1.; Bank Buildings, 16 St. James's Street, S.W.1. *Clubs:* Boodle's, Brooks's, Buck's Carlton, Turf; Royal Yacht Squadron. [*Died* 20 *Aug.* 1966.

FAIRLESS, Benjamin F.; President of United States Steel Corporation, 1938-51, Chairman of the Board, 1951-55, now a Director; *b.* Pigeon Run, Ohio, 3 May 1890; *s.* of David D. Williams; legally adopted by Jacob Fairless, Justus, Ohio, at the age of 5; *m.* 1st, 1912, Jane Blanche Truby (*d.* 1942); one *s.*; 2nd, 1944, Mrs. Hazel Hatfield Sproul, Philadelphia. *Educ.:* Justus, Ohio; Wooster College; Ohio Northern University. Graduated in Civil Engineering, 1913; Hon. D. Eng. 1935; Hon. D.Sc. (Kent State Univ., Kent, O.), 1937; Hon. D.Sc. (Univ. of Pittsburgh), 1943; D.Eng. (Stevens Inst. of Technology), 1943. C. E. Wheeling and Lake Erie Railroad, 1913; C. E. Central Steel Co., Massillon, O., 1913, and successively Mill Supt., Gen. Supt. and Vice-Pres. in Charge of Operations; Vice-Pres. and Gen. Manager Central Alloy Steel, 1926-28, and Pres. and Gen. Manager, 1928-30; Exec. Vice-Pres. Republic Steel Corporation, 1930-1935; Pres. Carnegie-Illinois Steel Corporation, 1935-37; Pres. and Chm. Exec. Cttee. United States Steel Corporation (Delaware), 1937, Chief Admin. Officer since 1938; Director, United States Steel (N.J.), 1937; member Advisory Staff of Maj.-Gen. Levin H. Campbell, Jr., Chief of Ordnance (War Dept.), 1942; member Iron and Steel Industry Advisory Cttee. of War Production Board; Medal for Merit, 1946; Vice-President American Iron and Steel Inst.; member Chamber of Commerce, Pittsburgh and New York. Horatio Alger Award, 1958. *Address:* Ligonier, Pennsylvania. *Clubs:* Duquesne, Fox Chapel, Pittsburgh, Oakmont, Pittsburgh Field (Pittsburgh); Bankers, Cloud, Links, National Golf, Twenty Nine (New York); Chicago (Chicago); Detroit, Detroit Athletic Assoc. (Detroit); Union (Cleveland); Massillon (Massillon, O.); Brookside Country (Canton, O.); Youngstown Country (Youngstown, O.); Pacific Union (San Francisco, Calif.); California (Los Angeles, Calif.). [*Died* 1 *Jan.* 1962.

FAIRLESS, Margaret; solo violinist; *b.* Northumberland, of British parents. *Educ.:* The Meister Schule of Professor O. Sévcik in Vienna (Scholarship). First appeared in London at Royal Albert Hall; since then has played with many famous Conductors including Franz Schalk, Vienna, Sir Henry Wood, Queen's Hall, London, and Sir Thomas Beecham; has toured British Isles, South Africa on four occasions, East Africa and West Indies; specially known as an interpreter of music of Sir Edward Elgar, who conducted his violin concerto for her at several Musical Festivals. During War of 1939-45 and later toured South Africa as concert and Broadcasting soloist; was invited to rep. string solo playing of S.A. at Royal Command concert given in honour of King George VI and Queen Elizabeth during the visit of the British Royal Family to S. Africa, 1947. [*Died* 28 *March* 1968.

FAIRLEY, Sir Andrew Walker, K.B.E. *cr.* 1951; C.M.G. 1946; Chairman and Managing Director Shepparton Preserving Co., Ltd.; *s.* of James Fairley, Grangemouth, Scotland; *m.* Mineta L., *d.* of John Stewart. Member: Australian Canned Fruits Board; Sugar Industry Cttee.; Mayor of Shepparton 4 times. *Address:* Shepparton, Victoria, Australia. [*Died* 15 *April* 1965.

FAIRLEY, Sir Neil Hamilton, K.B.E., *cr.* 1950 (C.B.E. 1941; O.B.E. 1918); F.R.S. 1942; M.D., D.Sc.(Melb.); F.R.C.P.(Lond.); F.R.A.C.P., Hon. F.R.C.P. (Ed.), 1947; Hon. M.D. (Adelaide), 1949; Hon. LL.D. (Melb.), 1951; Hon. D.Sc. (Sydney) 1956; Brig. (Hon.), A.M.F.; *b.* 1891; 3rd *s.* of late James Fairley, Melb.; *m.* 1st, 1919, Violet May Phillips (marr. diss.); one *s.*; 2nd, 1925, Mary Evelyn, *d.* of late H. R. Greaves, Bombay; two *s.* *Educ.:* Scotch College and University, Melbourne. 1st class final honours; David Syme Research Prize and Medal in Science, 1920; Chalmers Memorial Medal for research in tropical medicine, 1931; Richard Pierson Strong Medal, American Foundation of Tropical Med., 1947; Cameron Prize in Therapeutics

(Edin.), 1947; Moxon Medal, R.C.P., 1948; Mary Kingsley Medal, Liverpool, 1949; Manson Medal, Roy. Soc. of Trop. Med. and Hygiene, 1950; James Cook Medal, Roy. Soc. of N.S.W., 1951; Buchanan Medal (for distinguished contributions to control of malaria), Roy. Soc., 1957. Late Consultant in Tropical Diseases; Consulting Physician, Hosp. for Tropical Diseases, London; Tata Prof. of Trop. Med., Bombay; Wellcome Prof. of Trop. Med., University of London, 1946-49. Served Egypt and Palestine, 1916-18; Lieut.-Col. A.M.C. (temporary) (despatches, O.B.E.); Consulting physician, 2nd A.I.F., Middle East, 1940-42 (despatches, C.B.E.); Brigadier, A.M.F.; Director of Medicine, L.H.Q.; Director, L.H.Q. Medical Research Unit, Cairns, experimenting with anti-malarial drugs which led to successful control of malaria in jungle warfare; Chairman, Combined Advisory Committee on Tropical med., Hygiene and Sanitation, H.Q., S.W. Pacific Area; Mem. Med. Res. Council, 1949-51; President Royal Soc. Tropical Med. and Hyg., 1951-53; Hon. Mem. American Soc. of Tropical Medicine, Société Belge de Médecine Tropicale, American Acad. of Tropical Medicine, and United Services Sect., Roy. Soc. Med.; Corresp. Fellow, New York Acad. of Med.; Hon. Mem. Assoc. Clin. Pathologists, 1955; Hon. Tropical Consultant to the Army, 1950-56. Charles Dohme Memorial Lecture, Johns Hopkins Univ., 1946; Croonian Lectures, R.C.P., 1949; Mathison Memorial Lecture, Univ. Melbourne, 1952; McCallum Memorial Lecture, Univ. Sydney, 1952. C.St.J. 1947. *Publications:* various papers on biology, pathology, chemotherapy and tropical medicine. *Address:* Sonning Grove, Sonning, Berks. *T.:* Sonning 3261; 9 Wimpole Mews, W.1. *T.:* Welbeck 0078. *Clubs:* Athenæum, Royal Automobile.
[*Died* 19 *April* 1966.

FAIRLIE, Professor Margaret, LL.D. (St. And.); M.B., Ch.B., F.R.C.O.G.; F.R.C.S.Ed.; Professor of Gynæcology and Midwifery, St. Andrews University, retired 1956. *Address:* 8 Howard Place, St. Andrews. *T.:* 267. [*Died* 12 *July* 1963.

FAIRWEATHER, Sir Charles Edward Stuart, Kt., *cr.* 1944; C.I.E. 1934; M.A.; Hon. Sheriff Substitute (Angus); *b.* 16 January 1889; *s.* of late D. W. Fairweather, 34 Bingham Terrace, Dundee; *m.* Alice Emily, *d.* of late Francis Edwin Kemp, Deputy Inspector-General Indian Police, Bengal, and Kemptown, Brighton; two *d.* *Educ.:* Websters Seminary, Kirriemir; Forfar Academy, Forfar; St. Andrews University. Joined Indian Police, 1909; late Commissioner of Police, Calcutta; retired, 1944. King's Police Medal, 1932. *Recreations:* fishing, shooting, tennis. *Address:* Forester's Croft, Oathlaw, Angus; c/o Lloyds Bank, 6 Pall Mall, S.W.1. [*Died* 12 *Oct.* 1963.

FALCONBRIDGE, John Delatre, Q.C. (Ont.) 1921: M.A., LL.D.; teacher and author; *b.* Toronto, 7 June 1875; *e. s.* of Hon. Sir Glenholme Falconbridge, Chief Justice of the King's Bench (Ontario); *m.* 1st, 1905, Elizabeth Porter Hamilton; 2nd, 1922, Marguerite Thibault. *Educ.:* University College, Toronto. B.A. 1896, M.A. 1902; LL.B. 1904. Called to Ontario Bar, 1899; lecturer Osgoode Hall Law School, 1909; acting Principal, 1923-1924; Dean, 1924-48; (Dean Emeritus, 1954); docteur en droit honoris causa (University of Montreal), 1948; hon. LL.D.: Univ. of Toronto, 1950, Dalhousie Univ. (Halifax, N.S.), 1958; Law Society of Upper Canada, 1960; Secretary, 1918-30, and President, 1930-1934, of the Conference of Commissioners on Uniformity of Legislation in Canada; Chm., Ontario Church Property Commn. under United Church of Canada Act 1925. *Publications:* Banking and Bills of Exchange, 1907 (6th ed. 1956); Sale of Goods, 1921; Negotiable Instruments, 1923; Cases on the Conflict of Laws, 1926, 5th ed. 1949; Cases on Sale of Goods, 1927; (with Sidney E. Smith), Manual of Canadian Business Law, 1930; Essays on the Conflict of Laws, 1947 (2nd ed., 1954); various articles, esp. on conflicts of laws, in legal periodicals. *Address:* 179 Roe Avenue, Toronto 12, Canada. [*Died* 28 *July* 1968.

FALKLAND, 13th Viscount and 13th Lord Cary (*cr.* 1620), **Lucius Plantagenet Cary,** O.B.E. 1919; *b.* 23 Sep. 1880; *e. s.* of 12th Vis. and Mary (*d.* 1920), *d.* of Robert Reade, New York; *S.* father, 1922; *m.* 1904, Ella Louise (*d.* 1954), *e.d.* of E. W. Catford of Brooklyn, Twickenham; three *s.* two *d.* *Educ.:* Eton; Sandhurst. Late Capt. and Bt. Major Grenadier Guards; served throughout the S. African War as 2nd Lieut. 2nd Batt. Grenadier Guards (2 medals and clasps); E. Africa, 1903-5 (medal and clasp); Prison Service, 1910; European War (Legion of Honour, O.B.E.). *Heir:* *s.* Master of Falkland. *Address:* c/o Ellis Peirs & Co., 17 Albemarle St., W.1. [*Died* 24 *July* 1961.

FALLAS, Carl; Writer; *b.* Wakefield, 2 March 1885; *m.* 1912, Florence, *d.* of James Smithies, artist and metal craftsman, Wilmslow; two *d.* *Educ.:* Travel, other people, books. Apprenticed on staffs new Daily Dispatch and Manchester Evening Chronicle, 1900. Joined Ceylon Observer (leader writer at 22), 1907; Tokyo City editor, Japan Advertiser, 1909; Editor's asst., Japan Mail, Yokohama; reporter, San Francisco. Sailor round Cape Horn in windjammer. Served European War, 1914-18; Infantry, France and Belgium (gassed, despatches); Rhineland Occupation; specially appointed to Brigade School of Citizenship, to prepare troops for civil life. Manchester Evening News, 6 years; Evening Standard, 10 years. War of 1939-1945, commanded Royal Pioneer Companies, Orkney, Shetland and Outer Hebrides, rank, Major; flew with Atlantic Patrol as extra-gunner; sailed in Air-Sea Rescue craft. Contributor many sketches (back-pagers), Manchester Guardian and other journals. *Publications: novels:* The Wooden Pillow, 1935; Down the Proud Stream, 1937; Eve With Her Basket, 1951; Saint Mary's Village, 1954; autobiography and travel: The Gate is Open, 1938. *Address:* Lavender Cottage, Weedon Lane, Amersham, Bucks. *T.:* Amersham 1111. [*Died* 23 *May* 1962.

FALMOUTH, 8th Viscount, *cr.* 1720; **Evelyn Hugh Boscawen;** Baron Le Despencer, 1264; Baron Boscawen-Rose, 1720; M.I.Mech.E.; Hon. Fellow, Imperial College of Science and Technology, and Chm. of the College since 1947; past Master, Worshipful Co. of Clockmakers; Member, Metropolitan Water Board; Hon. Member: Instn. of Civil Engineers; Instn. of Gas Engineers; President Internal Combustion Engine Manufacturers Research Assoc.; past Pres. Conjoint Conference of Public Utility Undertakings; past Pres. Gas Research Board; past Chm. Fire Research Board; Hon. Treas. Instn. of Electrical Engineers, 1955-58; Part-time Mem. S.E. Area Electricity Board till 1959; *b.* 5 Aug. 1887; *s.* of 7th Viscount and Kathleen (*d.* 1954), *d.* of 2nd Lord Penrhyn; *S.* father, 1918; *m.* 1915, Mary Margaret Desirée, C.B.E. 1946, *o. d.* of late Hon. Frederick Meynell; three *s.* one *d.* *Educ.:* Eton; Trinity College, Cambridge. Capt. Reserve of Officers, Coldstream Guards; Past Pres. British Electrical Development Assoc.; Past Pres. British Electrical Research Assoc.; Member London County Council (St. George's, Westminster), 1925-31; Alderman, L.C.C., 1932-37; Member London and Home Counties Joint Electricity Authority, 1927-1937; Executive Committee of National Physical Laboratory, 1935-40; Advisory

Council Department of Scientific and Industrial Research, 1936-41; Fuel Research Board, 1936-41; Head of F division R and E dept., Ministry of Home Security, 1941-45; Chairman Government Committee on the production of oil from coal, 1937, and departmental Cttee. on penalties inflicted by marketing boards, 1938. *Heir:* *s.* Hon. George Hugh Boscawen, Capt. Coldstream Guards [*b.* 31 Oct. 1919. *Educ.:* Eton; Trinity College, Cambridge; *m.* 1953, Elizabeth, *d.* of A. H. Browne, West Peckham, Kent; three *s.*]. *Address:* Tregothnan, Truro; 28 Chelsea Sq., S.W.3. *T.:* Flaxman 4272. *Club:* Athenæum.
[*Died* 18 *Feb.* 1962.

FANE, Major Hon. Mountjoy John Charles Wedderburn, T.D.; R.A.S.C.; *b.* 8 Oct. 1900; *s.* of 13th Earl of Westmorland; *m.* 1926, Agatha Isabel Acland Hood; one *s.* one *d.* *Educ.:* Naval Colleges. *Recreations:* shooting, hunting, and motoring. *Address:* The Old Rectory, Careby, Stamford, Lincs. *Club:* Cavalry.
[*Died* 9 *Oct.* 1963.

FANSHAWE, Captain Guy Dalrymple, R.N. (retired). *s.* of late Admiral of the Fleet Sir Arthur Fanshawe, G.C.B., G.C.V.O.; *m.* 1910, Louisa (*d.* 1948), *d.* of Col. Hon. Sir Henry Crichton; three *s.* one *d.* *Educ.:* Twyford School, Winchester; H.M.S. Britannia. Joined Royal Navy as midshipman, 1898; Commander, 1916; Captain, 1927; Boxer Rising, 1900 (medal and clasp, despatches); European War, 1914-18 (medals, mentioned by Admiralty): Naval Inter-Allied Commission of Control in Berlin, 1920-23; retired, 1923; M.P. (U.) West Stirlingshire, 1924-29; Parliamentary Private Secretary to Secretary of State for Dominions and Colonies, 1928-29; served War of 1939-45, at Admiralty and elsewhere. A Vice-President, Royal National Life-Boat Institution, 1947- (mem. Cttee. of Management, 1925-) Chairman Boat and Construction Sub-Cttee., R.N.L.I., 1949-1960. *Address:* Country House Hotel, Crowborough, Sussex. *Clubs:* Carlton; R.Y.S. (Cowes).
[*Died* 19 *June* 1962.

FANSHAWE, Brig. Lionel Arthur, C.B.E. 1931 (O.B.E. 1919); D.S.O. 1916; Indian Army, retired; *b.* 7 March 1874; *s.* of late Sir Arthur U. Fanshawe, K.C.I.E., C.S.I.; *m.* 1906, Eva Pemberton; one *s.* one *d.* *Educ.:* Dulwich College; Pembroke College, Oxford. Joined Royal Artillery, 1900; joined Indian Army Ordnance Corps, 1904; served on North-West Frontier against Mohmands, 1915 (despatches, D.S.O.); Mesopotamia, 1918-20 (despatches, O.B.E.); Director of Ordnance Services in India, 1928-31; retired, 1931. *Recreations:* golf, tennis. *Address:* Newnhams, West End Grove, Farnham, Surrey. *T.:* Farnham 6090.
[*Died* 2 *May* 1962.

FANTHAM, Mrs. H. B.; *see* Porter, Annie.

FARGUS, Brigadier-General Harold, C.B. 1919; C.M.G. 1916; D.S.O. 1900; late Duke of Cornwall's Light Infantry; *b.* 15 Feb. 1873; *s.* of Frederick John Fargus of Clifton, Bristol; *m.* 1899, Alice Gertrude (*d.* 1952), *d.* of J. L. Evans. *Educ.:* Clifton College. Entered Army, 1893; Adjutant, 1900; Captain, 1901; Major, 1912; Lt.-Col. 1916; served South Africa, 1899-1902 (despatches, D.S.O., Queen's medal 4 clasps, King's medal 2 clasps); Brigade Major, Essex Infantry Brigade, 1911; served European War, 1915-19: commanded 1st Bn. Duke of Cornwall's Light Infantry, 1915-16; 125th Inf. Bde. 1916-19; (despatches five times, C.M.G., promoted Bt. Col. 1918, C.B.); retired pay, 1919; Colonel, 1921. *Address:* Cranford Nursing Home, Cranford Avenue, Exmouth, Devon. *T.:* Exmouth 3295.
[*Died* 28 *Dec.* 1962.

FARGUS, Lieutenant-Colonel Nigel (Harry Skinner), D.S.O. 1915; O.B.E. 1918; *b.* 2 July 1881; *s.* of Henry Robert Fargus; *m.* 1915, Lottie (*d.* 1952), *d.* of Wilfred Trimmer; one *s.* *Educ.:* Rugby; Sandhurst. Entered army, 1900; Captain, 1908; Major, 1915; Lieut.-Colonel 1929; served South Africa, 1899-1902 (Queen's medal 3 clasps, King's medal 2 clasps); European War, 1914-19 (wounded, despatches, D.S.O., O.B.E.); command 1st Batt. The Royal Scots, 1929-33; retired pay, 1933; recalled to Army for special work, Feb. 1943; retired again, June 1943; Defence Medal, 1947. *Address:* 26 Kingsburgh Road, Edinburgh 12. *T.:* 61159. *Club:* New (Edinburgh).
[*Died* 4 *March* 1962.

FARJEON, Eleanor; Author; *b.* London, 1881; *d.* of B. L. Farjeon and Margaret (*née* Jefferson). *Educ.:* privately. Published first book, Nursery Rhymes of London Town, 1916; has since written some 80 works, novels, plays, poems, music and books for children. Awarded Carnegie Medal and Hans Andersen International Medal for The Little Bookroom, 1956. Awarded Regina Medal, 1959, for life work for children. At age of 70 was received into the Roman Catholic Church. *Publications include:* Martin Pippin in the Apple Orchard, 1921; A Nursery in the Nineties, 1935, new edn., 1960; Hummingbird, 1936; Martin Pippin in the Daisyfield, 1937; New Book of Days, 1941; Silver Curlew (play), 1948; Silversand and Snow (poems), 1951; The Little Bookroom, 1955; Edward Thomas, The Last Four Years, 1958 (Memoir); (with her brother, Herbert Farjeon) Kings and Queens, 1932; *Plays:* (also jointly): The Two Bouquets, 1936; An Elephant in Arcady, 1938; The Glass Slipper, 1944. *Recreations:* cooking and cats. *Address:* 20 Perrins Walk, Hampstead, N.W.3. *T.:* Hampstead 2429. *Club:* P.E.N.
[*Died* 5 *June* 1965.

FARLEIGH, John, C.B.E. 1949; R.E. 1948; Painter, Engraver, and Illustrator; working as a free-lance artist; *b.* 16 June 1900; *m.* 1926, Elsie Wooden; one *d.* decd. *Educ.:* St. Mary Abbott's School, Kensington. Apprenticed to commercial studio, 1914-18; Army, 1918-19; student at Central School of Art, Southampton Row, 1919-22; Assistant Art Instructor, Rugby School, 1922-25; Head of Book Illustration Department Central School of Arts and Crafts, 1947-48, resigned; Member: Royal Society of Painter-Etchers; Society of Mural Painters: London Group, Wood-Engraving Soc.; Hon. Chm. Crafts Centre of Great Britain, 1950-64, resigned; exhibn. of water-colours and drawings of Shaw's Methuselah, 1938, at Leicester Gallery, and of pastels and water-colours, 1943; one-man exhibition of paintings, engravings and lithographs including drawings of bombed London, travelling provinces for one year, starting at Leicester, 1941; drawing of Buckingham Palace after bombing purchased by War Artists Committee, 1942; exhibition of Pastels of Pilgrim's Progress and water-colours, Lefevre Gallery, 1946; exhibition of Drawings, Batsford Gallery, 1947; exhibitor at R.A. since 1937; designer of posters, textiles, illustrations, advertising; murals for: Tea centre; two New Zealand liners; Government Printing Office, Trinidad; Reynold and Coventry Chain Co.; B.I.C.C.; Café Royal; I.C.I. Moscow Trade Fair, 1961; Heal's Extension, 1962; postage stamp for postcard and letter card. *Publications:* Autobiography, Graven Image, 1940; 15 Craftsmen on Their Crafts (editor); It never Dies, Lectures and Essays, 1946; The Creative Craftsman, 1950; Engraving on Wood, 1954; Design for Applied Decoration in the Crafts, 1959; contributions on Art to numerous periodicals. Illustrations for Bernard Shaw's

Black Girl in Search of God, and Back to Methuselah, D. H. Lawrence, The Man who Died, S. Sitwell's Old-Fashioned Flowers; Ten Histories, Shakespeare. *Recreation:* theatre. *Address:* 36 Belsize Grove, N.W.3. *T.:* Primrose 3905. *Club:* Arts.
[*Died* 30 *March* 1965.

FARLEY, Brig. Edward Lionel, C.B.E. 1942; M.C. 1915; late R.E., retired; *b.* 27 July 1889; *s.* of Francis John Farley, late of P.W.D., Punjab, India, and Catherine Isabella Ede, Plymouth, Devon; *m.* 1st, 1914, Helen Christine (*d.* 1955), *d.* of late Major-General W. W. Pemberton, I.S.C. and Burma Commission; two *s.*; 2nd, 1958, Patricia Peters. *Educ.:* Blundell's School; Royal Military Academy, Woolwich. 2nd Lt. R. E. 1909; Capt. 1914; Major, 1925; Lt.-Col. 1933; Bt. Col. 1935; Colonel, 1936; Brig. 1939; retired, 1942; re-employed, 1942, in rank of Lt.-Col. as C.R.E. Mhow, C.P., India, 1942-46; reverted to retirement with hon. rank of Brig. 1946. Served European War, 1914-18 (despatches, M.C.); C.R.E. Lucknow, 1933-36; Chief Engineer R.A.F. (India), 1936-39; Chief Engineer Eastern Command and Eastern Army, India, 1939-42. *Recreations:* golf, shooting, fishing. *Address:* c/o Lloyds Bank, 6 Pall Mall, S.W.1. *Club:* United Service.
[*Died* 24 *Feb.* 1968.

FARMAN, Air Vice-Marshal Edward Crisp, C.B. 1953; C.B.E. 1944; retired; *b.* 8 Nov. 1897; 2nd *s.* of late Ernest L. Farman, Bayswater, London; *m.* 1920, Mabel Emily Mitchell; one *s.* *Educ.:* privately. Served with 9th London Regt. (Queen Victoria's Rifles), 1914-16; commissioned R.A.F. 1918; Staff College, Andover, 1932; attached R.C.A.F., 1940-42; commanded 16 Maintenance Unit, R.A.F., 1942-43; A.O.C., 56 Wing, 1945; Senior Equipment Staff Officer, Transport Command, 1945-46; S.A.S.O., 40 Group 1947; A.O.C., 42 Group, 1947-49; Director of Equipment (D) Air Min., 1949-1950; S.A.S.O., Maintenance Command, 1951-53; retired, 1953. *Recreation:* golf. *Address:* The Cottage, Curridge, near Newbury, Berks. [*Died* 27 *July* 1966.

FARMAR, Colonel Harold Mynors, C.M.G. 1918; D.S.O. 1915; *b.* 15 June, 1878; *y. s.* of late Major-General William Roberts Farmar, Bedford House, Southampton; *m.* 1907, Violet, *y. d.* of late Sir William B. Dalby; one *s.* two *d.* *Educ.:* I. W. College; Sandhurst. Entered army, 1898; served Khartoum Expedition and Insurrection in Crete, 1898; served with Mounted Infantry S. Africa, 1899-1900 (despatches); C.R.I. North China Field Force, 1901-3; Adjutant Lancashire Fusiliers, 1904-7; Staff Royal Military College, 1907-11; served European War, 1914-18; Staff Captain; Brigade Major, 86th Brigade 29th Division, 1915; took part in the Lancashire Landing, 25 April 1915, on the Gallipoli Peninsula (despatches, D.S.O., wounded); A.A.&Q.M.G. Third Australian Division and 35th British Division; A.Q.M.G. American G.H.Q. and IX. British Army Corps (Bt. Lt.-Col., C.M.G., despatches thrice); served on the Staff of the Inter-Allied Commission in Turkey, 1920-22; Commanded 2nd Bn. Lancashire Fusiliers, 1922-24; N.W. Frontier, India; promoted Colonel, 1924; A.Q.M.G., H.Q., Southern Command India, 1924-26; A.A. and Q.M.G., H.Q. 5th Mhow Division, 1926-28; Officer in charge Infantry Records, N. Midland Area, 1928-32; to Reserve of Officers, 1932. *Recreation:* played cricket and hockey for Sandhurst, 1897. *Address:* Longs Wharf, Yarmouth, Isle of Wight. *T.:* Yarmouth 349. *Club:* Royal Solent Yacht Club. [*Died* 22 *June* 1961.

FARMER, Henry George, M.A., Ph.D., D.Litt., Mus.Doc.; President and Founder Scottish Musicians' Benevolent Fund; *b.* Birr, Ireland, 1882; *s.* of Henry George and Mary Ann Farmer; *m.* *Educ.:* originally for musical profession, but later at Glasgow University; Prizeman in History and Arabic. Carnegie Research Fellow, 1930-33; Weir Memorial Prizeman, 1932; President, Commission of MSS., Congress of Arabian Music, Cairo, 1932; Leverhulme Research Fellow, 1933-35; Cramb Lecturer in Music, Glasgow University, 1934; Professor of Music, Cairo Univ., 1946, but resigned same year. Vice-Pres. Glasgow Univ. Oriental Society. *Publications:* Memoirs of the Royal Artillery Band, 1904; The Rise and Development of Military Music, 1912; The Music and Musical Instruments of the Arab. 1915; The Arabian Influence on Musical Theory, 1925; The Arabic Musical MSS. in the Bodleian Library, 1925; The Influence of Music: from Arabic Sources, 1926; A History of Arabian Music to the XIIIth Century, 1929; Historical Facts for the Arabian Musical Influence, 1930; The Organ of the Ancients: from Eastern Sources, 1931; Studies in Oriental Musical Instruments, 1931; An Old Moorish Lute Tutor, 1933; Al-Fárábi's Arabic-Latin Writings on Music, 1934; New Mozartiana, 1935; Turkish Musical Instruments in the 17th Century, 1937; The Sources of Arabian Music, An Annotated Bibliography, 1939; Maimonides on Listening to Music, 1941; Music: The Priceless Jewel, 1942; Sa'adyah Gaon on the Influence of Music, 1943; The Minstrelsy of the Arabian Nights, 1946; A History of Music in Scotland, 1947; Music Making in the Olden Days; Handel's Kettledrums; Military Music, 1950; Cavaliere Zavertal and the Royal Artillery Band, 1951; Oriental Studies: Mainly Musical, 1953; History of the Royal Artillery Band, 1954; Bernard Shaw's Sister and Her Friends, 1959; contrib. to Legacy of Islam, Encyclopædia of Islam, Survey of Persian Art, Grove's Dictionary of Music, Die Musik in Geschichte und Gegenwart and New Oxford History of Music. *Address:* Empire, Glasgow.
[*Died* 30 *Dec.* 1965.

FARNAN, R. P., M.B., B.Ch., M.A.O., L.M. (Rotunda); late Gynæcologist, Mater Misericordiæ Hospital, Dublin; late Professor of Obstetrics and Gynæcology, National University, Dublin; *b.* Bolton Castle, Moone, Co. Kildare. *Educ.:* St. Vincent's College, Castleknock; Royal University, Ireland. Hon. LL.D. Trinity Coll., Dublin, 1954. *Address:* Bolton Castle, Moon, Co. Kiledare. *T.:* Moone 2.
[*Died* 7 *Jan.* 1962.

FARNDALE, Rev. William Edward, D.D. (Victoria Univ., Toronto); Methodist Minister, Lecturer, Writer; *b.* York, 25 Sept. 1881; *m.* 1910, Florence May Price, Sydenham; one *s.* one *d.* *Educ.:* Hartley-Victoria College, Manchester. Methodist Minister in London (Forest Hill), 1904-09; Oldham, 1909-13; Chester-le-Street, 1913-1918; Birkenhead, 1918-28; Grimsby, 1928-1933; Chairman of Lincoln and Grimsby District of the Methodist Church, 1932-52; Lecturer, Cliff College, Derbyshire, 1952-59; Pres. of Conference of Methodist Church of Great Britain, 1947. Delegate to Methodist Ecumenical Conference in Springfield, Massachusetts, U.S.A., and Visiting Preacher in Toronto (United Church of Canada), Sept.-Oct. 1947. Moderator of Free Church Federal Council, 1949-51. *Publications:* The Spirit Makes Us Free: Elements in Essential Free Churchmanship, 1949; The Secret of Mow Cop: A New Appraisal of the Origins of Primitive Methodism, 1950; The Psalms in New Light, 1956; Mow Cop: After 150 years, 1957; contributor to "Arthur Samuel Peake (1865-1929): Essays in Commemoration", 1959. *Recreations:* walking, reading. *Address:* 11 Springfield Park, Trowbridge, Wiltshire. *T.:* Trowbridge 3495. *Club:* National Liberal. [*Died* 4 *Feb.* 1966.

FARNSWORTH, William Charles, C.B.E. 1957; Practising Surveyor; Senior Partner in firm of Berry Bros. & Bagshaw and J. Toller Eady, Surveyors and Valuers, of Kettering and Market Harborough; Commissioner of Crown Estates, 1956-63; Member of Agricultural Land Commission, 1952-63; Member of Corby Development Corporation, since 1957; *b.* 25 April 1892; 2nd *s.* of William Farnsworth and Hannah Farnsworth (*née* Bower); *m.* 1916, May Wright; one *s.* one *d.* *Educ.:* King Edward VI Sch., Grantham. Served in France (Manchester Regt.), 1916 (despatches). Council, Roy. Instn. of Chartered Surveyors for 4 years (Pres. 1942-43); Pres. Central Assoc. of Agricultural Valuers, 1945-46; Liveryman of Farmers' Company. F.A.I. *Recreation:* golf. *Address:* The Gables Kettering. *T.:* Kettering 2587. *Club:* Constitutional. [*Died* 4 *Nov.* 1964.

FARQUHARSON, Eric L(eslie), M.D., F.R.C.S.Ed., F.R.C.S.Eng.; Surgeon in charge, Roy. Infirmary Edinburgh; Member Council and Examiner, R.C.S., Edinburgh; Member, Council, R.C.S. England; *b.* 13 Dec. 1905; *s.* of W. A. Farquharson, S.S.C. and Agnes N. Cowie; *m.* 1940, Dr. Elizabeth MacWatt, *yr. d.* of late Dr. John MacWatt, Duns, Berwickshire; two *d.* *Educ.:* Edinburgh Academy; University of Edinburgh. Lt.-Col., R.A.M.C., 1939-45; active service in Africa, Ceylon and India. *Publications:* Illustrations of Surgical Treatment, 1939; Textbook of Operative Surgery, 3rd edn., 1965; numerous contributions to Medical and Surgical Journals. *Recreations:* golf, photography. *Address:* 6 Chamberlain Road, Edinburgh 10. [*Died* 8 *Dec.* 1970.

FARRANT, Sir Geoffrey Upcott, Kt., *cr.* 1956; C.B.E. 1945; J.P.; *b.* 22 Nov. 1881; *s.* of Robert Farrant, Growen, Cullompton, Devon; *m.* 1909, Georgina Milne (*d.* 1956), *d.* of Sir John Anderson, G.C.M.G., K.C.B.; two *s.* three *d.* (and one *s.* decd.). *Educ.:* Blundell's School, Tiverton, Devon. Fraser & Co., Exchange and Share Brokers, 1906-21; Chm. Somerset and Wilts. Trustee Savings Bank, 1925-; Somerset C.C., 1926- (Chm. County Finance, 1940-52; Standing Joint Cttee., 1926-, Chairman, 1947-); Governor Blundell's School, 1937-; Vice-Chm., 1955-; Governor Taunton Sch.; Dir. of Arnold & Hancock, 1943-58; F.I.D., 1949; Taunton Div. Conservative Assoc. (1922-47: Hon. Treas., Chairman, Vice-Pres., 1947-56: President). J.P. Somerset, 1939. *Address:* Milligan Hall, Bishop's Hull, Taunton, Somerset. *T.:* Taunton 2415. *Club:* Somerset County (Taunton). [*Died* 15 *Jan.* 1964.

FARRAR, Geraldine; American singer; *b.* Melrose, Mass. 28 Feb. 1882; *d.* of Sydney Farrar and Henrietta Barnes; *m.* 1916, Lou Tellegen (marr. diss. 1923). *Educ.:* New York; Paris; Berlin. Opera singer, Europe, America. Member Metropolitan Opera Co., 1906-22. *Address:* Ridgefield, Conn., U.S.A. [*Died* 11 *March* 1967.

FARREN, Sir William Scott, Kt. *cr.* 1952; C.B. 1943; M.B.E. 1918; F.R.S. 1945; M.A.; M.Inst.Mech.E.; Hon. F.R.Ae.S.; a Consultant to Hawker Siddeley Aviation Ltd., since 1961; *b.* Cambridge, 3 April 1892; *s.* of Wm. Farren; *m.* 1st, 1917, Carol Erica, *d.* of Wm. A. Warrington; one *d.*; 2nd, 1963, Mildred A. Hooke, M.A., O.B.E. *Educ.:* Perse School; Trinity College, Cambridge. In charge of aerodynamic experiment and design, Royal Aircraft Factory, 1915-18; on technical staff of Armstrong Whitworth Aircraft, 1918-20; Univ. Lectr. in Engineering and in Aeronautics, Cambridge, 1920-37; Lecturer on aircraft Structure, Royal Coll. of Science, 1922-31; Fellow of Trinity Coll., Cambridge, 1934-37; Dep. Dir. of Scientific Research, Air Ministry, 1937-39; Deputy Director Research and Development Aircraft, Air Ministry and Ministry of Aircraft Production, 1939-40; Director of Technical Development, Ministry of Aircraft Production, 1940-41; Director, Royal Aircraft Establishment, Farnborough, Hants, 1941-46; Technical Director, Blackburn Aircraft Co. Ltd. 1946-47; Technical Director, A. V. Roe and Co., 1947-61; Director, Hawker Siddeley Aviation Ltd., 1959-61; Director, Hawker Siddeley Nuclear Power Co. Ltd., 1956-1961; formerly Chm., Aircraft Research Assoc.; President Royal Aeronautical Soc., 1953-54. Hon. Dr.Sc. (Manchester); Hon. F.I.Ae.S. (U.S.A.). *Publications:* in Reports and Memoranda of Aeronautical Research Council and proceedings of Royal Society and of Royal Aeronautical Society. *Address:* Crossways Cottage, Kingston, Cambs. *T.:* Comberton 494. [*Died* 3 *July* 1970.

FARRER, 5th Baron, *cr.* 1893; Bt., *cr.* 1883; **Anthony Thomas Farrer;** *b.* 22 April 1910; *s.* of Hon. Noel Maitland Farrer (*d.* 1929), 3rd *s.* of 1st Baron, and of Mabel Elizabeth (*d.* 1947), *d.* of Ralph Elliot, and *widow* of Sir Alexander Mackenzie, K.C.S.I.; *S.* cousin, 1954. *Heir:* none. *Address:* 55 Rothbury Terrace, Heaton, Newcastle upon Tyne. [*Died* 16 *Dec.* 1964 (*ext.*).

FARRER, Rev. Austin (Marsden), D.D.; F.B.A. 1968; Warden of Keble Coll., Oxford, since 1960; *b.* 1 Oct. 1904; *s.* of late Rev. A. J. D. Farrer; *m.* 1937, Katharine Newton; one *d.* *Educ.:* St. Paul's School; Balliol College. Deacon, 1928; Priest, 1929; Asst. Curate, All Saints, Dewsbury, Yorks, 1928-31; Chaplain and Tutor of St. Edmund Hall, Oxford, 1931-35; Fellow and Chaplain, 1935-60, Trinity Coll., Oxford. Mem. Church of England Liturgical Commission, 1962-. Bampton Lectr., 1948. Gifford Lecturer, Edinburgh, 1957. Hon. Fellow, Trinity Coll., Oxford, 1963. *Publications:* Finite and Infinite, 1943; The Glass of Vision, 1948; A Rebirth of Images, 1949; A Study in St. Mark, 1951; The Crown of the Year, 1952; St. Matthew and St. Mark, 1954; Lord I Believe, 1955; The Freedom of the Will, 1958; Said or Sung, 1960; Love Almighty and Ills Unlimited, 1961; Commentary on the Revelation of St. John, 1964; Saving Belief, 1964; The Triple Victory, 1965; A Science of God?, 1966; Faith and Speculation, 1967; (co-author): Infallibility in the Church, 1968. *Recreations:* literature and gardening. *Address:* Keble College, Oxford. *T.:* Oxford 59201. [*Died* 29 *Dec.* 1968.

FARRER, Philip Tonstall, C.B. 1929; *b.* 1887; *s.* of late Capt. Frederick Farrer, Scaleby Hall, Cumberland, and M.M.F., *d.* of late Rev. Francis Chenevix-Trench, D.D. *Educ.:* Wellington College; Neuchâtel. Served European War, 1914-19, attached General Staff (Intelligence), G.H.Q. France, 1918-19; A.D.C. British Military Mission, Albania, 1919-20; Private Secretary to Lord President of the Council, 1922-24; to the Lord Privy Seal and Leader of the House of Lords, 1924-29; to 4th Marquess of Salisbury, 1929-39. *Recreations:* shooting, tennis, and golf. *Address:* Old Knightons Cottage, Dunsfold, nr. Godalming. *Club:* Royal Automobile. [*Died* 20 *Nov.* 1966.

FARRIS, Hon. John Wallace de Beque, Q.C.; D.C.L., LL.D. (British Columbia); Barrister; Member of Senate of Canada since 1937; *b.* 3 Dec. 1878; *s.* of Hon. L. P. and Mary Louise Hay Farris; *m.* 1905, Evlyn F. Keirstead; three *s.* one *d.* *Educ.:* Acadia University; University of Pennsylvania. Attorney-General British Columbia, 1917-22; Past Treasurer Law Society of British Columbia; President Canadian Bar Association, 1937-38; Hon. member: American Bar Assoc.: Van-

couver Bar Assoc.; Hon. Bencher B.C. Law Soc. *Address:* 3351 Granville Street, Vancouver, B.C., Canada. *Clubs:* Union (Victoria); Vancouver (Vancouver); Rideau (Ottawa).
[*Died* 26 *Feb.* 1970.

FARROW, G. Martin; *see* Addenda: II.

FASS, Sir (Herbert) Ernest, K.C.M.G., *cr.* 1935; C.B. 1930; O.B.E. 1981; 4th *s.* of late Adolphus Fass of Chalfont Grange, Chalfont St. Peter, Bucks.; *m.* 1907, Winifred C. C. (*d.* 1966), *e. d.* of late G. H. Neame; three *d.* (one *s.* killed on active service, War of 1939-45). *Educ.:* Rugby; Corpus Christi Coll., Oxford. Barrister 1904; Board of Education, 1909; Treasury, 1915; Financial Secretary, Sudan Government, 1931-34; Public Trustee, 1934-44; Custodian of Enemy Property for England and Wales, 1939-44; Special Constables War Medal; Commendatore of Order of the Crown of Italy; Officier of Order of the Crown of Belgium. *Address:* Foxhill, Inkpen, Berks. *Club:* Oxford and Cambridge.
[*Died* 30 *July* 1969.

FAULKNER, Sir Alfred Edward, Kt., *cr.* 1930; C.B. 1924; C.B.E.; Officer St. John of Jerusalem; Chevalier Legion of Honour; Officer, Crown of Italy; Officer of the Order of St. Sava of Serbia; *b.* 3 July 1882; 3rd *s.* of William Henry Faulkner; *m.* 1910, Florence Edith, *d.* of A. A. Nicoll; one *s.* one *d.* *Educ.:* St. Alban's School; King's College, London. Appointed Transport Department, Admiralty, 1901; Director of Sea Transport, 1920-27; Under-Secretary for Mines and Petroleum, 1927-42; Chairman Traffic Commissioners, Eastern Area, 1943-1951. *Address:* Grove Hotel, 2 Grove Road, Bournemouth. *Died* 15 *July* 1963.

FAULKNER, Rear-Adm. Hugh Webb, C.B. 1951; C.B.E. 1945; D.S.O. 1942; D.L.; retd.; *b.* 13 June 1900; *s.* of late William Cooke Faulkner, Ardcloney, Sunbury, Victoria, Australia; *m.* 1927, Olave Mary, *d.* of Colonel J. H. Younger, Hassendeanburn, Hawick, Roxburghshire; three *s.* *Educ.:* R.N. Colleges, Osborne and Dartmouth. Served European War, 1914-1918; Midshipman, H.M.A.S. Australia, 1916; Sub-Lieut. 1918; Lieut. 1920; Comdr. 1934; Capt. 1940; War of 1939-45 (despatches four times); commanded H.M.S. Edinburgh, 1940-41; landing in N. Africa, 1942, in Sicily, 1943; Dir. of Combined Ops. (Naval), rank of Cdre. 2nd Cl., 1943-45; Chief of Staff to Allied Naval C.-in-C. expeditionary force, rank of Cdre. 1st cl., 1945; commanded H.M.S. Triumph, aircraft carrier, 1945-47; Captain of Royal Naval College, Dartmouth, 1948-49; Rear-Adm. 1949; Flag Off., Malayan Area, 1950-51; placed on retd. list due to ill health, 1952. Fellow of the Woodward Corporation. C.St.J. D.L., 1968, High Sheriff, 1969, Somerset. *Recreations:* hunting, shooting; formerly rifle shooting (rep. Navy 1930). *Address:* The Close, Hatch Beauchamp, Taunton, Somerset. *T.:* Hatch Beauchamp 424. [*Died* 24 *May* 1969.

FAULKNER, William; author; *b.* New Albany, Mississippi, 25 Sept. 1897; *s.* of Murray Charles Faulkner and Maud Butler; *m.* 1929, Estelle Oldham Franklin. *Educ.:* High School, Oxford, Miss.; Univ. of Mississippi. Served with R.A.F., 1918. Nobel prize for literature (1949), 1950. *Publications:* The Marble Faun, 1924; Soldiers' Pay, 1926; Mosquitoes, 1927; Sartoris, 1929; The Sound and the Fury, 1929; As I Lay Dying, 1930; Sanctuary, 1931; These Thirteen, 1931; Idyll in the Desert, 1931; Light in August, 1932; Green Bough (poems), 1933; Doctor Martino and Other Stories, 1934; Absalom, Absalom, 1936; The Unvanquished, 1938; The Wild Palms, 1939; The Hamlet, 1940; Go Down, Moses, 1942; Intruder in The Dust, 1949; Knight's Gambit; Collected Short Stories of William Faulkner, 1951; Requiem for a Nun, (novel) 1953, (play) 1955; A Fable, 1954 (Pulitzer Prize 1955); Faulkner's County, 1955; The Town, 1958; Uncle Willy and Other Stories, 1958; Dr. Martino and other Stories, 1959; New Orleans Sketches, 1959; The Mansion, 1961. Mosquitoes (posthumous), 1964. *Relevant Publication:* My Brother Bill, by John Faulkner, 1964. *Address:* Oxford, Miss., U.S.A. [*Died* 6 *July* 1962.

FAULL, Joseph Horace, B.A., Ph.D., F.R.S.C., F.A.A.Sc.; Professor of Forest Pathology, Emeritus; *b.* L'Anse, Michigan, 3 May 1870; *s.* of James and Catherine Bennetts Faull, of Cornwall, England; *m.* 1903, Annie Bell Sargent, of Pennsylvania; one *s.* one *d.* (and one *d.* decd.). *Educ.:* Toronto; Harvard; Munich University; Teacher of Mathematics and Physics, Albert College, Belleville, 1898-1900; University of Toronto: Lecturer in Botany, 1902-07; Associate Professor of Botany, 1907-18; Professor, 1918-28; Professor of Forest Pathology, Harvard University, 1928-1940. *Publications:* numerous papers on plant cytology, morphology, mycology, and forest pathology in various periodicals. *Address:* 72 Fresh Pond Lane, Cambridge, 38, Mass., U.S.A.
[*Died* 30 *June* 1961.

FAUNCE, Brigadier Bonham, C.B.E. 1923; *b.* 8 Feb. 1872; *s.* of Major B. B. Faunce; *m.* 1899, Edith Maud (*d.* 1949), *d.* of D. Miller, Camden House, Biggleswade; one *s.* Entered Army, 1891; Colonel, 1919; Sofa Campaign, W. Africa, 1893-94; Sierra Leone, 1898-99 (wounded); Ashanti, 1900 (despatches); Aro Expedition, 1901-2 (despatches, Bt. Major); European War, 1914-1919; Col. Comdt. Sierra Leone, 1920-24; retired pay, 1924. *Address:* 7 The Avenue, Alverstoke, Hants. [*Died* 30 *Dec.* 1961.

FAUSSET, Hugh I'Anson, M.A.; Author and Literary Critic; Contributor to The Times, The Times Literary Supplement, The Guardian, The Yorkshire Post, The Listener, The Aryan Path, etc.; *b.* 16 June 1895; 2nd *s.* of Rev. R. T. E. Fausset, Killington, Westmorland; *g. s.* of Canon A. R. Fausset, D.D., York; *m.* 1918, Marjory, 2nd *d.* of late Rev. G. W. Rolfe, Swanton Novers, Norfolk; one *s.* two *d.* *Educ.:* Sedbergh; Corpus Christi Coll., Cambridge; King's Coll., Cambridge (acting choral scholar), Chancellor's Medallist for English Verse. At Foreign Office, 1918; reviewer for The Times Literary Supplement, Manchester Guardian, etc., since 1919; occasional Reader for publishers and other literary work. *Publications:* The Healing of Heaven, 1920; The Spirit of Love: A Sonnet Sequence, 1921; The Condemned: Two Poems of Crisis, 1922; Keats: A Study in Development, 1922; Tennyson: A Modern Portrait, 1923; Studies in Idealism, 1923; Before the Dawn: Poems, 1924; John Donne: A Study in Discord, 1924; Samuel Taylor Coleridge, 1926; Tolstoy: The Inner Drama, 1927; William Cowper, 1928; Tennyson: new and revised edition (Traveller's Library), 1929; The Proving of Psyche, 1929; Minor Poets of the Eighteenth Century (Everyman's Library), 1930; The Modern Dilemma, 1930; The Poems of John Donne, edited (Everyman's Library), 1931; Selected Poems of William Cowper (Everyman's Library), 1931; The Lost Leader, A Study of Wordsworth, 1933; A Modern Prelude, 1933; Selected Letters of John Keats, edited 1938; The Holy Sonnets of John Donne, edited 1939; Whitman, A Study, 1942; Between the Tides, a Novel, 1943; The Last Days, a Novel, 1945; Poets and Pundits, Essays, 1947; Towards Fidelity, 1952; The Flame and the Light, Meanings in Vedanta and Buddhism, 1958; Fruits of Silence, 1963. *Recreations:* gardening, pondering, singing. *Address:* Forge Cottage, Little Walden, Saffron Walden, Essex. *T.A.:* Little Walden, Essex. *T.:* Saffron Walden 2098. [*Died* 4 *Nov.* 1965.

FAWDRY, Reginald Charles, M.A., B.Sc.; late Head of the Military and

Engineering Side, Clifton College; *b.* 5 Nov. 1873; *s.* of John Fawdry, Worcester; *m.* 1911, Edith Langley Lovejoy (*d.* 1951); two *s.* (and one *s.* decd.). *Educ.:* Worcester; Corpus Christi Coll., Camb. (Schol), Wrangler; M.A.; B.Sc. London. *Publications:* Statics; Dynamics; Co-ordinate Geometry; Problem papers in Mathematics; Readable School Mechanics; Polish up your Mathematics; joint-author, Trigonometry; Calculus for Schools; Arithmetic; Algebra for Schools. *Recreations:* sketching, music. *Address:* Otterden Place, Faversham, Kent. *T.:* Eastling 341. [*Died* 15 *Oct.* 1965.

FAWDRY, Air Commodore Thomas, C.B. 1946; C.B.E. 1944 (O.B.E. 1936; M.B.E. 1918); Royal Air Force, retired; *b.* 1891; *e. s.* of late A. Fawdry, Maidenhead; *m.* 1915, Lilly Louise, *d.* of late Francis John Banks, Felixstowe. *Educ.:* Abingdon. Served European War, 1914-19, with Loyal (North Lancashire) Regiment (despatches, M.B.E.); Staff Captain, Middle East, 1918-1922; transferred to R.A.F., 1922; Squadron Leader, 1924; Staff, Iraq, 1926-28; Wing Commander, 1931; Staff, Middle East, 1933-1936; Group Captain, 1938; War of 1939-45, Command of Maintenance Group, Staff, Maintenance Command; Air Commodore, 1942; Staff, Bomber Command, 1942-46 (despatches). *Address:* Sackville Court Farmhouse, Upper Clatford, Andover, Hampshire. *T.:* Andover 3128. [*Died* 4 *July* 1968.

FAWKES, Rear-Adm. George Barney Hamley, C.B. 1954; C.V.O. 1953; C.B.E. 1943; R.N. retd.; *b.* 4 Sept. 1903, *s.* of Alec Hamley and Alice Kate Fawkes, *m.* 1st, 1924, Winifred Joyce Deakin (marriage dissolved); one *s.*; 2nd, 1949, Suzette Flagler, *d.* of late A. C. Watson, New York. *Educ.:* R.N. Colleges Osborne and Dartmouth. Midshipman H.M.S. Queen Elizabeth, 1921; Sub-Lieut. submarines, 1924; Lieut. R.N. Staff College, Greenwich, 1933; Lieut.-Comdr. H.M.S. Nelson, 1934, submarines, 1935; Comdr., staff officer to Admiral, submarines, 1938; comd. 8th S/M Flotilla, 1941; actg. Capt. Brit. Mil. Mission to U.S.S.R. (Black Sea), 1941; Capt. comd. 8th S/M Flotilla, 1942; Chief of Staff to Admiral, Submarines, 1944; Flag Capt. and Chief of Staff, America and West Indies Station, H.M.S. Sheffield, 1946; Director Ops. Div. Admlty., 1949; Commodore, 1st Class, Chief of Staff Home Fleet, H.M.S. Indomitable, Dec. 1951, H.M.S. Vanguard, 1952; Rear-Adm. 1952; Flag Officer Submarines, at Gosport, 1954-Dec. 1955; retired, Feb. 1956. French Legion of Honour and French Croix de Guerre, 1945; American Legion of Merit, 1949. *Recreations:* fishing, gardening. *Address:* c/o Royal Bermuda Yacht Club, Bermuda. *Clubs:* United Hunts; Royal Bermuda Yacht. [*Died* 26 *July* 1967.

FAWKES, Rowland Beattie, D.S.O. 1919; M.A.; M.B., B.Chir. (Cantab.); M.R.C.P. (Lond.); M.R.C.S. (Eng.); L.R.C.P. (Lond.); Consultant Physician; *b.* 1894; *y. s.* of late Wm. Fawkes, Northampton, solicitor; *m.* 1929, Beryl Constance, *e. d.* of Walter Green, Ealing, W. *Educ.:* Northampton; Queens' College, Cambridge (Scholar); Guy's Hospital. B.A. (Cantab.) in Natural Science Tripos. Served European War, 1914-20; T/Capt. in 6th (S.) Bn. Northampton Regt.; service overseas in France and Belgium (wounded twice, despatches, M.C., D.S.O.). *Address:* Beacon Lodge, Cromer, Norfolk. *T.:* Cromer 2089. [*Died* 24 *April* 1965.

FAWKES, Rupert Edward Francis, C.B.E. 1932; retired; *b.* 26 April 1879; *s.* of Francis Fawkes; *m.* 1911, Theodora Adams; three *d.* *Educ.:* Cheltenham College; Yorkshire College, Leeds. Lancashire and Yorkshire Railway, 1897-1907, including pupilage; Sudan Government Railway, 1907-31; retired as Chief Mechanical Engineer, and created C.B.E. for services in the Sudan; was (now retired) A.M.Inst.C.E., M.I.Mech.E. and Member of Institution of Locomotive Engineers. *Recreations:* fishing, gardening, and country pursuits. *Address:* Mallards, Chirton, Devizes, Wilts. *T.A.:* Chirton. *T.:* Chirton 656. [*Died* 11 *Jan.* 1967.

FAY, Charles Ryle, M.A.; D.Sc.; Reader in Economic History, University of Cambridge, 1930, now Reader emeritus; *b.* 13 Jan. 1884; *o. s.* of Charles and Emily Fay; *m.* Alice Quendryth Hartland; three *s.* *Educ.:* Merchant Taylors' School, Crosby; King's College, Cambridge. Research Student at London School of Economics, 1906-8; Fellow and Lecturer of Christ's College, 1908-22; Lieut. (acting Capt.) The Buffs and Machine Gun Corps, 1915-18 (despatches); Senior Proctor of Cambridge University, 1920-21; Professor of Economic History, University of Toronto, 1921-30. *Publications:* King's College; Co-operation at Home and Abroad; Co-partnership in Industry; Life and Labour in 19th Century; Great Britain from Adam Smith to the Present Day, 1928; Youth and Power, 1930; The Corn Laws and Social England, 1932; Imperial Economy, 1934; Co-operation at Home and Abroad, Vol. II, 1939; English Economic History since 1700; Huskisson and his Age, 1951; Palace of Industry 1851, 1951; Round About Industrial Britain, 1830-1860, 1952; Adam Smith and the Scotland of his day, 1956; Life and Labour in Newfoundland, 1956; The World of Adam Smith, 1960. *Address:* 21 Cyprus Park, Belfast. *Clubs:* Royal Commowealth Society, National Liberal. [*Died* 19 *Nov.* 1961.

FAY, Professor Sidney Bradshaw, Litt.D., L.H.D.; Emeritus Prof. of History in Harvard University, Cambridge, Mass.; *b.* Washington, 13 Apr. 1876; *s.* of Edward Allen Fay and Mary Bradshaw; *m.* 1904, Sarah Proctor, Hanover, New Hampshire; three *d.* *Educ.:* Harvard University; University of Paris; University of Berlin. Professor of History at Dartmouth College, 1902-14; Smith College, 1914-29; Harvard Univ., 1929-46; Lecturer at Amherst Coll., Columbia Univ., 1924-28, and Yale Univ., 1946-47; Round Table leader, Williamstown Institute of Politics, 1924. *Publications:* History Syllabus for Secondary Schools, 1904; Records of the Town of Hanover, N.H., 1761-1818, 1905; Origins of the World War, 2 vols., 1928 (foreign editions, 1929-34, paper-back edition, 1966); Rise of Brandenburg-Prussia to 1786, 1937; Editor (with others), Smith College Studies in History, (1915-1929); Editor (with others), American Historical Review, 1924-1930; Editor (with others), Journal of Modern History; Editor (with others) Guide to Historical Literature, 1931; Contributor to American Historical Review, and other periodicals. *Address:* 194 Brattle Street, Cambridge, Mass., U.S.A. *Clubs:* Faculty (Cambridge); Harvard (Boston). [*Died* 29 *Aug.* 1967.

FEARNLEY, Thomas, K.B.E. (Hon.) 1920; Shipowner, Landowner, Director of Companies; *b.* 16 Jan. 1880; *s.* of Thomas Fearnley and Elisabeth Young; *m.* 1911, Benedicte Rustad, *d.* of F. W. Rustad, G.C.V.O. (Hon.); no *c.* *Educ.:* Christiania Kathedralskole, Commercial College, Leipzig. Partner Fearnley & Eger, shipowners, Oslo, 1908-; President Norwegian Chamber of Shipping, 1918-21; Head of Norwegian Shipping Missions to England, 1917 and 1939; Hon. member of International Olympic Committee and Norwegian Jockey Club. *Recreations:* skiing, shooting, fishing, golf. *Address:* Toresplassen, Sollihögda, Norway; town residence: Kristinelundvei 4, Oslo. *Clubs:* St. James'; Norske Selskap

(Oslo); Travellers' (Paris); Knickerbocker (New York). [*Died* 10 *Jan.* 1961.

FEARNSIDES, William George, F.R.S. 1932; M.A.(Cantab.), F.G.S., M.I.M.E.; Professor Emeritus of Geology, University of Sheffield, 1945; Hon. Fellow, Sidney Sussex College, Cambridge, 1946; *b.* Horbury, Yorks. 10 Nov. 1879; *e. s.* of Joshua and Maria Fearnsides; *m.* 1911, Beatrix Mary Adelaide, *d.* of late William Whitehead Watts, F.R.S.; one *d.* *Educ.:* Wheelwright Grammar School, Dewsbury; Sidney Sussex College, Camb. (scholar); West Riding County Major Scholarship, 1895; Harkness University Scholar, 1901; Fellow of Sidney Sussex College, Cambridge, 1904-15; College and Taylor Lecturer in Natural Science at Sidney Sussex College, 1908-13; University Demonstrator in Petrology of Cambridge, 1909-1913; Sorby Professor of Geology, University of Sheffield, 1913-45; Dean of the Faculty of Pure Science, University of Sheffield, 1931-34; Member of Council Royal Society 1936-37; Member of the Council British Association 1935-45; President Section C., Leicester, 1933; Consultant Geologist to West Midlands Division, Nat. Coal Board, 1947-58. Member of Council of the Geological Society of London, 1913-17, 1925-30, 1936-41 and 1943-47, Vice-President, 1938-40, 1945-47, President, 1943-45, Vice-President Midland Institute of Mining Engineers, 1928-32, Hon. Mem., 1958; awarded Murchison Medal of Geological Society, 1932; Lyell Geological Fund, 1906; Council's Gold Medal of the Surveyors' Institution, 1914; Greenwell medal of the North of England Institute of Mining Engineers, 1917; Bessemer Premium of the Society of Engineers, 1917. *Publications:* many papers in scientific and technical journals. *Recreation:* travel. *Address:* 11 Ranmoor Crescent, Sheffield 10.
[*Died* 15 *May* 1968.

FEATHERSTONE, Eric Kellett, C.M.G. 1944; Grand Officer of Order of Leopold II of Belgium, 1947; *b.* 22 July 1896; *y. s.* of Rev. Thomas Featherstone, B.D., Carlisle; unmarried. *Educ.:* Carlisle Grammar School; Queen's College, Oxford (Thomas Exhibitioner, 1915, B.A. 1920). Military Service, 1916-19; Colonial Administrative Service (Nigeria), 1921; Administrative Officer, Class I, 1939. Resident Commissioner, Swaziland, 1942-46. Senior Resident, Nigeria, 1947; Actg. Chief Comr., Northern Provinces, Kaduna, at various times, 1947-49; Commissioner for Nigeria in the United Kingdom, 1950-55; retired, 1955. *Address:* 3 Cator Road, S.E.26. *Club:* Oxford and Cambridge.
[*Died* 3 *Aug.* 1965.

FEATHERSTONE, Henry Walter, O.B.E. 1945; T.D. 1946; J.P. (Staffs.); retired from medical practice; Cons. Anaesthetist, United Birmingham Hosps. (first apptd. 1919); *b.* 5 April 1894; *s.* of late Alderman William Barltrop Featherstone, M.D., J.P., Erdington, Birmingham; *m.* 1918, Margery Eveline, *d.* of George Harston, Newfield Hall, Sheffield; one *s.* three *d.* *Educ.:* King Edward's School, Birmingham; Trinity College, Cambridge; Birmingham University. M.A., M.D. (Camb.), F.F.A.R.C.S., D.A. Served R.A.M.C., European War, 1914-18 and War of 1939-45 (Lieut.-Col.). Formerly Univ Lectr. Anaesthetics, Birm. University. Pres. Birm. Med. Inst., 1952-61; Editor, Birm. Med. Review, 1935-61. Hon. Fellow (founder, first Pres. and trustee) of Assoc. of Anaesthetists, Gt. Brit. and Ire., John Snow Medal. Pres. Y.M.C.A. Birm. area; a Commissioner of Income Tax. LL.D. (Hon.) Edin. 1947; F.F.A.R.C.S. (Hon.) 1962. *Publications:* numerous articles in textbooks and journals on anaesthetics and biography, 1922-. *Recreations:* farming, forestry and country sports. *Address:* Yoxall Lodge, Newchurch, near Burton-on-Trent, Staffordshire. *T.:* Hoar Cross 226. [*Died* 23 *April* 1967.

FECHTELER, Adm. William Morrow, D.S.M. (U.S.N. and Army), with Star; Legion of Merit; Bronze Star; *b.* 6 March 1896; *s.* of Rear-Adm. A. F. Fechteler and Maud Morrow; *m.* 1928, Goldye Stevens; one *d.* *Educ.:* U.S. Naval Academy. Served European War, 1914-18; commissioned ensign, U.S. Navy, 1916; served War of 1939-45 Captain, U.S.N., in charge of Officer assignment, C.O., U.S.S. Indiana, 1943; Rear-Admiral, 1944; Amphibious Group Commander, 7th Amphibious Force, 1944; Commander Battleships and Cruisers, Atlantic Fleet, 1945-46; Vice-Admiral, 1947; Dep. Chief of Naval Operations (Personnel), 1947-1950; Admiral, 1950; C.-in-C., Atlantic Fleet, 1950; Chief of Naval Operations, 1951-53; C.-in-C. Allied Forces Southern Europe, 1953-56. Mem. U.S. Joint Chiefs of Staff, 1951; retired 1956. *Address:* 5169 Watson St., N.W. Washington, D.C., U.S.A. *Clubs:* Army and Navy, Chevy Chase (Washington). [*Died* 4 *July* 1967.

FEETHAM, Hon. Richard, C.M.G. 1924; *b.* Nov. 1874; *s.* of late Rev. William Feetham, Vicar of Penrhos, Raglan, Mon., and Mary, *e. d.* of Ven. Archdeacon William Crawley; *m.* 1920, Leila, *d.* of L. W. Christopher, Ladysmith; one *s.* two *d.* *Educ.:* Marlborough; New College, Oxford. Called to Bar, Inner Temple, 1899; Deputy Town Clerk, Johannesburg, 1902; Town Clerk, 1903-05; Advocate of the Supreme Court, Transvaal; Member Legislative Council, Transvaal, 1907-10; Legal Adviser to High Commissioner for S.A., 1907; Member for Parktown in Legislative Assembly Union of S.A., 1915-23; initiated, and secured acceptance of, legislation provisions for adoption of children; Lt. 1st Batt. Cape Corps, 1916-1919; Chairman Committee on Functions (one of the Southborough Committees on Indian Reforms), 1918-19; King's Counsel, Transvaal, 1919; Judge of Supreme Court of S.A., Transvaal Provincial Div., 1923-30; Chm. of the Irish Boundary Commission, 1924-25; Chm. of Local Government Commission, Kenya Colony, 1926; Adviser to Shanghai Municipal Council, 1930-31; Judge-President of Natal Provincial Div., 1931-39; Chm. Transvaal Asiatic Land Tenure Act Commission, 1932-35; Judge of Appellate Division of Supreme Court of South Africa, 1939-44; Chm. of Witwatersrand Land Titles Commission, 1946-49; Vice-Chancellor Univ. of Witwatersrand, Johannesburg, 1938-1948, Chancellor, 1949-61. Chm., Gov.-Gen.'s National War Fund, 1940-52. Hon. LL.D. Univ. of Witwatersrand, 1949, Univ. of Natal, 1958. *Publication:* Report to Shanghai Municipal Council, 1931. *Address:* Long Barn, 164 Taunton Rd., Pietermaritzburg, Natal, S.A. *Clubs:* Victoria (Pietermaritzburg); Rand (Johannesburg).
[*Died* 5 *Nov.* 1965.

FEHRENBACHER, Right Rev. Bruno, O.S.B., D. Phil.; Abbot of Buckfast, 1939-56; Titular Abbot of Tavistock since 1956; *b.* Mengen, Germany, 27 July 1895. *Educ.:* Buckfast Abbey; College of St. Anselm, Rome. Teaching Philosophy or Theology at Buckfast for some years, Novice-master, 1926-31; taught for one year at Syrian Seminary in Jerusalem and some months at Patriarchal Seminary at Charfe near Beirut. *Address:* St. Mary's Abbey, Buckfast, S. Devon
[*Died* 19 *July* 1965.

FEILDEN, Lieut.-Colonel Randle Montague, C.B.E. 1918; *b.* 17 July 1871; 4th *s.* of late Sir W. L. Feilden, 3rd Bt.; *m.* 1924, Rachel Mary Gordon (*d.* 1933), *o. c.* of late Horace Gordon Lowe; one *s.* one *d.* *Educ.:* Charterhouse; Sandhurst. Joined 52nd Light Infantry, 1892; Adjutant, 1896-1900; Major,

1911; Lt.-Col. 1914; served Mohmand Expedition, 1897 (medal and clasp); Tirah, 1897-98 (clasp); South Africa, 1901-2 (despatches, Queen's medal 4 clasps; joined Egyptian army, 1903; Civil Administrator during construction of Port Sudan, Red Sea, 1905-8, received 4th class Osmanieh at opening of port by Khedive, 1910; Asst. Civil Sec., Sudan Government, 1908-10; Governor and O.C. Bahr-el-Ghazal Province and District, 1910-17; Civil Secretary, Sudan Government, 1917-21; Member, Governor-General's Council; promoted Pasha, 1920; retired, 1921; served Sudan, operations against Nyam-Nyams, 1904-05 (medal and clasp, 4th class Medjidie); commanded operations against Agaakir-Dinkas, 1913 (3rd class Medjidie); received 3rd class Order of Nile, 1915; Nyma Patrol, Sudan, 1917-18 (medal with clasp); 1914-18 general service medal (despatches twice); 2nd class Order of Nile, 1921; Royal Humane Society's silver medal, 1895; retired from the British army, 1913. *Clubs:* Army and Navy, Royal Automobile.
[*Died* 23 *March* 1965.

FELL, John Robert Massey; H.M. Foreign Service, retired; *b.* 20 Mar. 1890; *s.* of late Brig.-Gen. R. B. Fell, C.B., and of Mary (*née* Wheeler); *m.* 1935, Kathleen, *d.* of Thomas Overton; one *s.* two *d.* *Educ.:* Bedford School; Scarborough Coll.; privately. Vice-Consul Casablanca, 1914; Hamburg; Essen; Consul for Transylvania and Roumanian Banat; for Panama and Canal Zone; Chargé d'Affaires, Panama, 1929; Consul, Rosario, 1930; Coronation Medal, 1937; Consul for Sicily and Egadi Islands until evacuated June 1940; with United Kingdom Commercial Corporation until Apr. 1941; Consul, Madrid, May 1941-Apr. 1945; Minister and Consul-General at Asuncion, Paraguay, 1945-49; retired, 1949. *Recreations:* swimming, fishing, travelling, gardening, painting, photography. *Address:* c/o Lloyds Bank, 6 Pall Mall, S.W.1. *Club:* Compleat Angler's Fishing (Eastbourne).
[*Died* 8 *June* 1969.

FELLOWES, Daisy, (Hon. Mrs. Reginald Fellowes); *d.* of 4th Duc Decazes; *m.* 1st, 1910, Prince Jean de Broglie (*d.* 1918); 2nd, 1919, Hon. Reginald Fellowes (*d.* 1953); one *d.* *Publications:* Cats in the Isle of Man, 1929; Les Filles du Diable, 1933; Les Dimanches de la Csse. de Narbonne, 1935. *Address:* 69 Rue de Lille, Paris, France; Donnington Grove, Newbury, Berks.
[*Died* 13 *Dec.* 1962.

FELLOWES, Sir Edward (Abdy), K.C.B., *cr.* 1955 (C.B. 1945); C.M.G. 1953; M.C. 1917; Chairman: General Advisory Council, B.B.C., 1962-67; Council of Hansard Society for Parliamentary Government, 1962-67; *b.* 23 June 1895; *e. s.* of late W. G. Fellowes, barrister-at-law; *m.* 1921, Ella Mary, *d.* of late Lt.-Col. MacRae-Gilstrap, Eilean Donan, Ross-shire; three *d.* *Educ.:* Marlborough College. Served European War, 1914-18, Queen's Royal Regiment, Captain 1917 (despatches, M.C.); Assistant Clerk, House of Commons, 1919; 2nd Clerk-Assistant, 1937-48, Clerk-Assistant, 1948-54, Clerk, 1954-61, retired. F.R.S.A. 1964. *Publications:* Finance of Government (with late J. W. Hills, M.P.), 1931; Sir Thomas Erskine May's Treatise on the Law, Privileges, Proceedings and Usage of Parliament (ed. with T. G. B. Cocks), 1957. *Recreations:* golf, bowls. *Address:* Paddocks, Scole, Norfolk. *T.:* Scole 241. *Clubs:* Athenæum, Oxford and Cambridge, M.C.C.
[*Died* 28 *Dec.* 1970.

FELLOWES, Hon. Mrs. Reginald; *see* Fellowes, Daisy.

FELTON, Sir John Robinson, Kt., *cr.* 1946; O.B.E. 1920; *b.* 28 Feb. 1880; *s.* of George and Isabella Felton, Blyth, Northumberland; *m.* 1906, Dora Jemison, Saltburn, Yorks; (one *d.* decd.). *Educ.:* Gateshead Higher Grade School; King's Coll., Newcastle upon Tyne. Apprenticeship as Mining Engineer at West Stanley Colliery, Durham, and Stobswood Colliery, Northumberland; Certificated Manager of West Stanley Colliery, 1903; Assistant Inspector of Mines, South Staffs District, 1908; Senior Inspector, 1915; Yorkshire and North Midland Division, 1923; Divisional Inspector, 1924; Deputy Chief Inspector of Mines at Headquarters, London, 1937; H.M. Chief Inspector of Mines (Ministry of Fuel and Power), 1942. 1947. Served 1920-21 as Deputy Director of Production under the Coal Controller. *Publications:* Papers on mining subjects in Transactions of Institution of Mining Engineers; Official Reports on Explosions at Bilsthorpe Colliery (1934), Markham Colliery (1937), Barnsley Main Colliery (1942), Manvers Main Colliery (1945), and Harrington (Lowca) Colliery (1947). *Recreations:* music and reading. *Address:* Southerndown, 49 Banstead Road South, Sutton, Surrey. *T.:* Vigilant 0385.
[*Died* 21 *June* 1962.

FELTON, Mrs. Monica; *b.* 23 Sept. 1906; *d.* of Rev. T. Lloyd Page. *Educ.:* Wycombe High School; Grammar School and Univ. Coll., Southampton; London School of Economics. Member of L.C.C., 1937-46; Chm. of L.C.C. Supplies Cttee., 1939-41; Member of Housing and Town Planning Committees. Served in Ministry of Supply, 1941-1942; Clerk, House of Commons, 1942-43. Member of New Towns Committee (Reith Committee); Chairman, Peterlee Development Corp., 1948-49; Chairman Stevenage Development Corp. 1949-51 (Vice-Chm. 1946-48); Labour Member of Hertfordshire C.C. for Buntingford Division, 1946-47 *Publications:* To All the Living, 1945; British War Production and the Consumer (Ministry of Information), 1945: That's Why I Went, 1953; I Meet Rajaji, 1962; A Child Widow's Story, 1966. *Address:* c/o National and Grindlay's Bank, Mount Road, Madras 2, India.
[*Died* 3 *March* 1970.

FENDICK, Rev. Canon George Harold: Canon Residentiary of Gloucester Cathedral since 1948; *b.* 18 Aug. 1883; *s.* of R. G. Fendick, M.R.C.S. *Educ.:* Clifton College; Exeter College, Oxford. Lecturer in Liverpool University, 1906; Librarian of Pusey House, Oxford, 1910-21; Deacon, 1910; Priest, 1911; T.C.F. 1916-17; Hon. C.F. 1921; Assistant Curate, All Saints, Clifton, 1921-32; Minister of S. Anselm, Clifton, 1932-41; Exam. Chaplain to Bishop of Bristol, 1938-46, to Bishop of Worcester, 1947-48; Precentor of Worcester Cathedral, 1942-48. *Recreations:* walking, reading, and music. *Address:* 13 College Green, Gloucester. *T.:* Gloucester 24547.
[*Died* 24 *Dec.* 1962.

FENNELLY, Sir (Reginald), Daniel, Kt., *cr.* 1951; C.B. 1944; *b.* 6 Dec. 1890; *m.* 1918, Florence Keen; one *s.* one *d.* *Educ.:* St. Ignatius College, Stamford Hill; London School of Economics. Commander Order of Orange Nassau (Netherlands), 1947; formerly Under-Secretary, Ministry of Materials; formerly General Manager, National Sulphuric Acid Association. *Address:* 19 Cranmore Way, Muswell Hill, N.10. *T.:* 01-883 3028.
[*Died* 22 *July* 1969.

FENTON, James, C.B.E. 1938; M.D., Ch.B. M.R.C.P., D.P.H.; Past Chairman Medical Insurance Agency; Past President, Soc. of Medical Officers of Health; Vice-President (Chm. of Council, 1935-36), Royal Society of Health; Past Chairman, Central Council for Health Education; Hon. Fellow of Institute of Hygiene; Hon. Fellow of American Public Health Association; Hon. Captain, R.A.M.C. (T.F.); Past-Pres., Medical Defence Union;

Past-President, Kensington Medical Society; *b.* 29 June 1884; *m.* Beatrice Alice, *d.* of William Page, Deddington, Oxfordshire; two *d.* *Educ.:* University of Birmingham (3 Queen's Scholarships and 1 Ingleby Scholarship). Smith Award, Royal Institute of Public Health, 1943. Late Medical Officer of Health, Royal Borough of Kensington; Editor Public Health; a Principal Medical Officer, Min. of Health; Assistant School Medical Officer, Birmingham; Assistant M.O.H., Hampshire; Assistant M.O.H., Southampton; M.O.H. and Police Surgeon, Shrewsbury; Examiner in Public Health, Royal College of Surgeons; Specialist Bacteriologist to British Salonika Forces with Serbian Army; Order of St. Sava; toured Europe, America and Africa studying public health under auspices of League of Nations, Rockefeller Foundation and Royal Sanitary Institute. *Publications:* Sanitary Law and Practice; Sanitary Law; articles on public health in Lord Macmillan's Local Government Law and Administration; contributions to various journals. *Recreation:* golf. *Address:* Quarrylands, Little John's Cross, Exeter. *T.:* Exeter 74387.

[*Died* 9 *March* 1962.

FENWICK, His Honour Christian Bedford, Q.C.; Retired as Judge of County Courts, Circuit No. 3 (1950-61); *b.* London, 15 Sept. 1888; *s.* of Bedford Fenwick, M.D.; *m.* 1915, Mary Beatrice Wait (*d.* 1953), Newcastle upon Tyne; one *s.* (and one *s.* decd.). *Educ.:* Eton; Magdalen Coll., Oxford. Called to Bar, Inner Temple, 1911; practised Newcastle upon Tyne; Recorder of Doncaster, 1933-46; of Halifax 1946-47; of Kingston-upon-Hull, 1947-50; King's Counsel, 1945; Solicitor-General, County Palatine of Durham 1946, Attorney-General, 1947-50. Enlisted Territorial Force 4 Aug. 1914; Capt. Northern Cyclist Bn., 1914; B.E.F. France, 1916-17. Chm. Q.S., Co. Cumb. 1953-63. *Recreations:* fishing, naval and military history. *Address:* 7 Lambton Road, Newcastle upon Tyne 2. *Club:* Athenæum. [*Died* 5 *Oct.* 1969.

FENWICK-PALMER, Lieut.-Colonel Roderick George, C.B.E. 1938; *b.* 30 March 1892; *s.* of Capt. G. Fenwick, Plas Ffroi, Wrexham; unmarried. *Educ.:* Wellington Coll.; New College, Oxford (M.A.). Joined 2nd Life Guards, 1913; European War, 1914-18 (wounded, despatches); Commanded 61st Medium Brigade R.A. (T.A.), 1929-33; Commanded 4th Batt. Royal Welch Fusiliers, 1933-37; War of 1939-45, Commanded for a period 8th and 31st Battalions Royal Welch Fusiliers; contested Eddisbury Division (C.), March and May 1929. Deputy Lieutenant, Co. of Denbigh. *Address:* Cefn Park, Wrexham. *T.:* Wrexham 2323. *Club:* Kildare Street (Dublin).

[*Died* 17 *Oct.* 1968.

FERBER, Edna; writer; *b.* Kalamazoo, Mich.; *d.* of Jacob Charles Ferber and Julia Neumann Ferber. *Educ.:* Public and High Schools, Appleton, Wisconsin. Began as reporter on Appleton Daily Crescent at 17; employed on Milwaukee Journal. *Publications:* Dawn O'Hara, 1911; Buttered Side Down, 1912; Roast Beef Medium, 1913; Personality Plus, 1914; Emma McChesney & Co., 1915; Fanny Herself, 1917; Cheerful—By Request, 1918; Half Portions, 1919; The Girls, 1921; Gigolo, 1922; So Big, 1924; (with George V. Hobart) the comedy, Our Mrs. McChesney; (with George S. Kaufman) the comedy, Minick; Show Boat, 1926; Mother Knows Best, 1927; (with George S. Kaufman) the comedy, The Royal Family, 1928; Cimarron, 1930; American Beauty, 1931; (with George S. Kaufman) the play, Dinner at Eight, 1932; They Brought their Women, 1933; Come and Get It, 1935; (with George S. Kaufman) the comedy, Stage Door, 1936; Nobody's in Town, 1938; A Peculiar Treasure, 1939; Saratoga Trunk (novel), 1941; Great Son, 1944; (with George S. Kaufman) the play, Bravo, 1948; Giant (novel), 1952; Ice Palace (novel), 1958; A Kind of Magic, 1963. *Address:* c/o Doubleday & Co. Inc., 277 Park Ave., New York, N.Y., U.S.A. [*Died* 16 *April* 1968.

FERGUSON, Maj.-Gen. Augustus Klingner, C.M.G. 1952; C.B.E. 1946; retired; *b.* 30 Oct. 1898; *s.* of A. O. Ferguson, Dublin; *m.* 1931, N. L. Ray; two *d.* *Educ.:* Trinity College, Dublin; R.M.C., Sandhurst. Royal Irish Regt. 1916-22, thereafter Royal Leicestershire Regt.; G.S.O. 2 China; G.S.O. 1 Malaya; Director of Intelligence, India; Military Adviser to U.K. Mission, Japan, 1947-52; employed War Office, Aug. 1954-62. *Address:* Fourways, Solefields Road, Sevenoaks, Kent. *T.:* Sevenoaks 52298. [*Died* 25 *Feb.* 1965.

FERGUSON, Sir David Gordon, Kt., *cr.* 1946; M.C. 1916; Managing Director of Wilson Sons & Co. Ltd. 1945-58; Chairman of the British Coal Exporters Federation, 1952; *b.* Cardiff, 15 March 1895; *s.* of John Sinclair Ferguson and Francesca Brukewich; *m.* 1927, Rosemary Lelia Brass; two *s.* one *d.* *Educ.:* Cardiff High School Served European War, 1914-19, with the Buffs (twice wounded, despatches, M.C.); Director of Coal Division, Ministry of War Transport. 1941-45. *Address:* The Chalet, Pilgrims Way, Reigate, Surrey. *T.:* Reigate 43093. [*Died* 26 *Dec.* 1969

FERGUSON, Sir Edward (Brown), Kt., *cr.* 1953; F.C.I.I.; Chairman Phœnix Assurance Co. Ltd., 1958-66 (General Manager, 1939-53; Managing Director, 1953-1955; Deputy Chairman and Managing Director, 1955-57); *b.* 14 August 1892; *er. s.* of late William Ferguson and of Alison Bryson (*née* Thompson); *m.* 1922, Ethel Anderson, 6th *d.* of James Cooper, Philadelphia, U.S.A.; one *s.* one *d.* (and one *s.* decd.). *Educ.:* Lenzie Academy. Employed in insurance business since 1908 in England, Scotland and S. Africa; formerly Chairman London Guarantee & Accident Co. Ltd.; Union Marine & General Insurance Co. Ltd.; Director: Phœnix Assurance Co. of New York; President of Insurance Institute of London, 1943-44; President Chartered Insurance Inst., 1948-49; Hon. Member Insurance Inst. of America, 1948; Chairman, British Insurance Assoc., 1951-53. Served European War 1914-18, in R.A., 3rd Lowland Div. (despatches); War of 1939-45, served on various Govt. (Insurance) Cttees. *Recreation:* golf. *Address:* Blakeney, Golfside, Cheam, Surrey. *T.:* Vigilant 0451. *Clubs:* Boodle's, Pilgrims.

[*Died* 21 *April* 1967.

FERGUSON, Erne Cecil, LL.B., D.L.; Crown Solicitor for Co. Fermanagh since 1949; Deputy Lieutenant for Co. Fermanagh since 1949; *b.* 2 Oct. 1911; *s.* of late James Ferguson, J.P., and Mrs. Ferguson, Sandhill House, Derrygonnelly, Co. Fermanagh. *Educ.:* Methodist College, Belfast; Queen's University, Belfast. LL.B. Queen's University, 1933; Solicitor, 1935. M.P. Enniskillen Division of Co. Fermanagh, 1938-49. *Recreations:* shooting and golf. *Address:* 25 Chanterhill Road, Enniskillen, N. Ireland. *T.:* Enniskillen 2535. *Club:* Fermanagh County (Enniskillen). [*Died* 22 *Aug.* 1968.

FERGUSON, Frederic Sutherland, Hon. M.A. (Oxon.) 1955; Director of Bernard Quaritch Ltd. (Managing Director, 1928-43); *b.* 26 December 1878; *s.* of late William Sutherland Ferguson and Helen Atkin; *m.* 1905, Bessie, *d.* of late Henry Holmes Leonard, Surveyor; one *s.* three *d.* *Educ.:* Grocers' Company's School, and King's College, London. With the firm of Bernard Quaritch since 1897;

President of the Antiquarian Booksellers' Association (International), 1934; Hon. President, Edinburgh Bibliographical Soc., (Pres. 1935-1936; Bibliographical Soc., 1948-50 (gold medal of the Society, 1951). *Publications*: Title-page Borders used in England and Scotland, 1485-1640 (with R. B. McKerrow), 1932; Additions to Title-page Borders, 1485-1640, 1936; A Bibliography of Sir George Mackenzie, 1936. *Recreations*: bibliography and book-collecting. *Address*: The Homestead 10 Avenue Road, Southgate, N.14. *T.*: Palmers Green 4256. [*Died* 4 *May* 1967.

FERGUSON, Sir Gordon; *see* Ferguson, Sir D. G.

FERGUSON, Hon. Sir John Alexander, Kt. 1961; O.B.E. 1957; B.A., LL.B.; Litt.D.; *b.* Invercargill, New Zealand, 1882; *s.* of late Rev. J. Ferguson. *Educ.*: University of Sydney. Judge of New South Wales Industrial Commission, 1936-51, retired. Trustee, Public Library of N.S.W., including Mitchell and Dixson Libraries, 1935-. Fellow of the Australian Historical Society (Pres., 1922 and 1940). *Publications*: Bibliography of Australia, 1784-1850: Vol. I, 1941, Vol. II, 1945, Vol. III, 1951, Vol. IV, 1955; 1851-1901: Vol. V and Vol. VI, 1964; Bibliography of New Hebrides and A History of the Mission Presses (3 pts.), 1917, 1918, 1943, etc. *Address*: 81 Clanville Road, Roseville, New South Wales, Australia. [*Died* 7 *May* 1969.

FERGUSON, Col. John David, C.M.G. 1917; D.S.O. 1900; F.R.G.S., *b.* 24 October 1866; *e. s.* of late David Ferguson of Shanagour, Co. Limerick, and 27 Upper Pembroke Street, Dublin; *m.* Clara (*d.* 1951), *widow* of late Col. E. W. Dawes, Brook House, Cropthorne, Worcester. Entered A.M.S. 1890; served Uganda and East Africa, with Macdonald Expedition, 1897-99 (despatches, D.S.O., 3rd class Brilliant Star of Zanzibar, medal with two clasps); S. Africa, 1900-2 (Queen's medal 3 clasps, King's medal 2 clasps); Somaliland, 1902-4, present at Jibouti (medal and 2 clasps); European War, 1914-18 (despatches three times, C.M.G.); retired 1920. *Address*: Cassala, Murdoch Road, Wokingham, Berks. [*Died* 5 *Oct.* 1961.

FERGUSON-DAVIE, Right Rev. Charles James; *b.* 16 Mar. 1872; *s.* of late Rev. C. R. Ferguson-Davie; *m.* 1st, 1902, Charlotte Elizabeth, M.D., O.B.E. 1927 (*d.* 1943), *d.* of late Prof. Hull, F.R.S.; one *d.* (adopted); 2nd, 1948, Marie Antoinette Jacobine (*d.* 1963), Pietermaritzburg, *widow* of Gilbert Randles, Barrister-at-Law. *Educ.*: Marlborough; Trinity Hall, Camb. (M.A.). Hon. D.D., Leeds Clergy School. Ordained, 1896; Curate of St. Paul, Preston, 1896-1899; Domestic Chaplain to Bishop of Lahore, 1899-1902; S.P.G. Missionary at Rewari, 1902-4 and 1905-7; Rawal Pindi, 1907-9; Bishop of Singapore, 1909-27; Priest in charge Umgeni North, Natal, 1929-1933-; Warden, Anglican Hostel, Fort Hare, S. Africa, 1933-44; Superintendent Indian Mission, Maritzburg, S. Africa, 1944-46. *Recreations*: formerly bowls; shot for England three times in Mackinnon Cup at Bisley, and won the Silver Medal in the King's Prize, 1904. *Address*: 107 Royston Road, Pietermaritzburg, South Africa. [*Died* 11 *Sept.* 1963.

FERGUSSON, Sir (John) Donald (Balfour), G.C.B., *cr.* 1946 (K.C.B., *cr.* 1937; C.B. 1935); Director, Prudential Assurance Company; Agricultural Mortgage Corporation; *b.* 1891; *s.* of Rev. J. M. Fergusson, D.D.; *m.* Phillis Mary, *e. d.* of late C. F. M. Cleverly; two *s.* one *d.* (and one *s.* killed on active service). *Educ.*: Berkhamsted School; Magdalen Coll., Oxford. 1st class Honours History Finals; served European War, 1914-1918; entered Treasury, 1919; Assist. Sec. 1934; Private Secretary to successive Chancellors of the Exchequer, 1920-36: Permanent Secretary of Ministry of Agriculture and Fisheries, 1936-45; Permanent Secretary, of Ministry of Fuel and Power, 1945-52; retired, 1952. *Address*: Ebbesbourne Wake, nr. Salisbury, Wilts. *Club*: Brooks's. [*Died* 4 *March* 1963.

FERGUSSON, Sir Louis (Forbes), K.C.V.O., *cr.* 1945 (C.V.O. 1934); *b.* Edinburgh, 5 Sept. 1878; *s.* of late Sir James Ranken Fergusson, Bt., Spitalhaugh *m.* 1922, Elizabeth Frances Ethel Lewis; one *d.* *Educ.*: Harrow; University College, Oxford, B.A. Entered Duchy Office, 1903; Private Secretary to fourteen Chancellors of the Duchy, 1909-21; Clerk of the Council and Keeper of the Records of the Duchy of Lancaster, 1927-45; Special Constabulary, 1914-18. *Publication*: Harold Gilman, 1919. *Recreations*: books, paintings, and theatres. *Address*: 44 Coombe Lea, Grand Avenue, Hove, Sussex. *Club*: Constitutional. [*Died* 10 *Jan.* 1962.

FERRARO, Rev. Preb. Francis William; a Prebendary of St. Paul's Cathedral since 1945; Vicar of Heston, Middlesex, 1948-1958; Rector of Bethnal Green and Vicar of St. Phillip's, 1939-48; Rural Dean of Bethnal Green, 1944-48; Chaplain to Coopers' Company, 1944; *b.* 21 Nov. 1888; *s.* of Comdr. John Ferraro, (retired) R.N. *Educ.*: The High School (Naval College), Devonport; King's College, B.A. 2nd Honours in Medieval Languages and Theology (1st Class); M.A., B.D., Trinity College, Dublin (King Edward Prizeman); Deacon, 1911; Priest, 1912; Curate, Holy Trinity Mile End, 1911-17 Head of Christ's Hospital Mission, 1917-1920; Priest charge St. Peter's Whitstable, 1921; Vicar of St. Matthew's, Limehouse 1922-27; Vicar of Holy Trinity, Stepney, 1927-29; of St. John's on Bethnal Green, 1929-35; of St. Andrew's, Stoke Newington, 1935-39; Representative of Senate of University of London in E. London, 1924; President Sion College, 1933; Chaplain to Almshouses of Corporation of Trinity House, 1934; Chairman of Governors of Stepney and Bow Educational Foundation, 1938. *Address*: St. Anthony's House, 25 Bow Rd., E.3. *T.*: Advance 1466. *Clubs*: Athenæum, City Livery. [*Died* 8 *March* 1963.

FERRIER, Thomas Archibald, C.B.E. 1919; late Survey of India; *b.* 1877; *s.* of T. H. Ferrier, W.S. Edin.; *m.* 1st, 1905, Constance Emma (*d.* 1938), *d.* of R. Reid and *widow* of A. T. Ricketts; one *d.* decd.; 2nd, 1949, Ethel, *d.* of late William Thomas Stutchbury and *widow* of William Gordon Edwards. Officer-in-Charge of Mathematical Instrument Office, Survey of India, Calcutta, 1914-24; retired, 1924. *Address*: c/o Lloyds Bank, Cox & King's Branch, 6 Pall Mall, S.W.1. [*Died* 16 *May* 1968.

FETHERSTON-DILKE, Beaumont Albany, M.B.E.; Physician and Landowner; J.P. and County Alderman, Co. Warwick; Alderman, Leamington Borough; *b.* 1875; *e. s.* of late T. H. Percival, India Office, and Edith, *d.* of late John Fetherston, of Packwood, Co. Warwick; *m.* Phoebe Stella, *y. d.* of late Rev. Canon Bedford, Sutton Coldfield, Co. Warwick; two *s.* two *d.* *Educ.*: St. John's College, Cambridge; St. George's Hospital. M.A., M.B. and B.Ch.(Cantab.), M.R.C.P.(London). Assumed the name and arms of Fetherston-Dilke by Royal Licence on inheriting the estates of his maternal uncle (Beaumont T. Fetherston Dilke); formerly house surgeon at St. George's Hospital and to the Northampton General Hospital; has been many years in the Colonial Medical Service in Trinidad, Gibraltar and Nigeria; served during the War as Surgeon to the Colonial Hospital, Gibraltar. Mayor of Leamington Spa, 1945-46, Deputy Mayor, 1949, Mayor, 1950-51. *Recreations*: country pursuits. *Address:* Maxstoke Castle, Coleshill, nr. Birmingham. *T.:* Coleshill 3213. *Club:* Union. [*Died* 11 *Jan.* 1968.

FETHERSTONHAUGH, Adm. Hon. Sir H. M.; *see* Meade-Fetherstonhaugh.

FETHERSTONHAUGH, Lt.-Col. Sir Timothy, Kt 1960; O.B.E 1945 T D.; D.L.; J.P.; Vice-Lieutenant of Cumberland since 1960; Chairman, Cumbria Police Authority, since 1967; *b.* 7 Oct. 1899; *s.* of late Lt.-Col. Timothy Fetherstonhaugh, D.S.O., Kirkoswald, Cumberland; *m.* 1933, Anne Gladys, *d.* of late Sir Harry Ross Skinner, Tarland, Aberdeenshire; two *s.* *Educ.:* Wellington; R.M.C., Sandhurst. Commissioned 2nd Lieut. King's Royal Rifle Corps, 1918; Captain, 1928; retired 1929. Served with 5 Queen's Royal Regt., T.A., 1934-40; commanded No. 6 Commando, 1940-42; 2000 Flotilla I.E. and No. 4 Indian I.W.T. Group, 1942-45 (despatches); retired 1948. D.L. Cumberland, 1948, High Sheriff, 1951-52, J.P., 1955; Chairman, Cumberland and Westmorland T.A. Assoc., 1954-62; Chairman, Northern Counties Provincial Area Conservative and Unionist Assoc., 1957-60. Member, Cumberland County Council, 1949-. Alderman, 1961-. *Recreation:* shooting. *Address:* The College, Kirkoswald, Penrith, Cumberland. *T.:* Lazonby 207. *Club:* Army and Navy. [*Died* 9 *Feb.* 1969.

FEVERSHAM, 3rd Earl of, *cr.* 1868; **Charles William Slingsby Duncombe,** D.S.O. 1945; D.L.; Baron Feversham, (U.K.), 1862; Viscount Helmsley, 1868; Hon. Colonel, Queen's Own Yorkshire Yeomanry, T.A., since 1962; *b.* 2 Nov. 1906; *e. s.* of 2nd Earl and Lady Marjorie Greville, *e. d.* of 5th Earl of Warwick (she *m.* 2nd, Sir Gervase Beckett, 1st Bart.); *S.* father, 1916; *m.* 1936, Hon. Anne Dorothy Wood, M.B.E. 1950, *o. d.* of 1st Earl of Halifax, K.G., P.C., O.M., G.C.S.I., G.C.M.G., G.C.I.E., T.D.; one *d.* Lord-in-Waiting, 1934-36; Parliamentary Sec. to Minister of Agriculture and Fisheries, 1936-39. Served War of 1939-45 (D.S.O.). *Heir:* (to Barony only) Charles Antony Peter Duncombe, *b.* 3 Jan. 1945. *Address:* Nawton Tower, Nawton, Yorks. *Clubs:* White's; Yorkshire (York). [*Died* 4 *Sept.* 1963 (*ext.*).

FEW, Brevet Colonel Robert Jebb, D.S.O. 1917; T.D.; formerly Secretary, Territorial Army Rifle Assoc.; *b.* 1876; *s.* of Rev. William Jebb Few; *m.* 1909, Marie Kate Nina Marguerite, *d.* of late R. A. Baxter, Reigate, and Marie, *er. d.* of late Peter de Mauritz, Russian Privy Councillor and Private Sec. to Empress of Russia; one *d.* *Educ.:* Marlborough. Served South African War, Imperial Yeomanry, 1899-1901 (Hon. Capt.). European War, 2-4th Batt. the Queen's Royal Regt.; Lt.-Col., 5th Batt. Queen's Royal Regt., 1920-24. D.L. Surrey, 1922-46. *Recreations:* golf and shooting. *Address:* Burcher Court, Titley, Nr. Kington, Herefordshire. [*Died* 24 *Aug.* 1965.

FICKLIN, Maj.-Gen. H. P. M. B.; *see* Berney-Ficklin.

FIDDES, Sir James Raffan, Kt., *cr.* 1948; C.B.E. 1943; *b.* 16 July 1883; *s.* of John Fiddes and Jane Raffan; *m.* 1917, Constance Mary Dann Gibb; two *s.* *Educ.:* Ferryhill Public School, Aberdeen. Clerk to Great North of Scotland Railway; entered Aberdeen Savings Bank as clerk and rose through grades to position of Actuary; Actuary of Trustee Savings Bank of Glasgow, 1935-48; Vice-President Trustee Savings Banks Association; President, Savings Banks Inst.; Member Scottish Savings Committee. *Recreations:* walking, golf. *Address:* Kilrene, 3 Kaimes Road, Edinburgh, 12. *T.:* Edinburgh, Corstorphine 2119. *Club:* National Liberal. [*Died* 13 *Feb.* 1961.

FIELD, Allan Bertram, M.I.E.E., M.I.Mech.E., F.Am.I.E.E.; retired: *b.* New Barnet, Dec. 1875; *s.* of James John and Sarah S. Field; *m.* 1911, Virginia W. (*d.* 1956), *d.* of Thomas Hall and Caroline M. Pearne of Cincinnati, Ohio; one *s.* two *d.* (and one *d.* decd.). *Educ.:* St. John's College, Cambridge; M.A. (Camb.); B.Sc. (Lond.). Technical training and early engineering experience in London; followed by eleven years in U.S.A., mostly associated with B. A. Behrend; Consulting Engineer, Prof. of Mechanical Engineering and Member Senate of Manchester University, 1914-17; Technical Director of the Admiralty Experimental Station, Shandon, 1918; Consulting Engineer to Metropolitan-Vickers Electrical Co., Ltd., Manchester, 1920-43. *Publications:* articles to scientific societies and technical press in England and U.S.A. *Address:* Tysties, Woolton Hill, Newbury, Berks. *T.:* Highclere 233. [*Died* 1 *Jan.* 1962.

FIELD, Mary, (Mrs. Agnes Mary Hankin), O.B.E. 1951; Children's Programme Consultant to A.B.C. and A.T.V. Television Companies, since 1959; *b.* 24 Feb. 1896; 2nd *d.* of Ernest and Evelyn Lucy Field; *m.* 1944, Gerald Thornton Hankin, T.D., M.A. *Educ.:* Surbiton High School; The Study, Wimbledon; Bedford College for Women, Univ. of London; Inst. of Historical Research, Univ. of London. M.A. (dist. in Commonwealth Hist.) Lond. On leaving College taught History and English. Joined Brit. Instructional Films as Education Manager, 1926, changing to Production Staff as Asst. Editor, 1927; became continuity girl, script writer, editor, asst. director, director; worked on educ., documentary and feature films, but finally concentrated on educ. and documentary; joined Brit. Indep. Producers as Production Manager, 1933; joined Bd. of G.B. Instructional Ltd., 1934; worked on educ. and documentary films and developed use of diagram and instructional film esp. for teaching of history and economics, inaugurated Children's Entertainment Films Div. of G.B. Instructional Ltd., for J. Arthur Rank Organisation, 1944; Examiner, British Board of Film Censors, 1950; Inaugurated, and acted as Exec. Officer of, Children's Film Foundation, 1951. Commonwealth lecture tour of Australia, N.Z. and India, 1954; tour of Canada and U.S.A. as TV and film consultant, 1960. Past President Brit. Fedn. of Business and Professional Women; Perpetual President Emeritus, Internat. Centre of Films for Children, Unesco. Hon. F.R.P.S.; Hon. F.B.K.S.; Hon. F.B.F.A *Publications:* Good Company, A history of the Children's Entertainment film movement in Great Britain, 1944-50; (jointly): Secrets of Nature; Ciné Biology (Penguin); Boys and Girls Book of the Film; See How They Grow (Penguin); articles for educational, technical and instructional publications. *Recreations:* desultory history reading and research; theatre. *Address:* 22 Mill Road, Worthing, Sussex. *T.:* Worthing 48048. [*Died* 23 *Dec.* 1968.

FIELD, Roland Alfred Reginald; Chairman and Director London West End Board, Eagle Star Insurance Co. Ltd., 1932-64; Chairman and Managing Director, Slaters & Bodega Ltd., 1926-54; Chairman and Managing Director., 1931-59: R. E. Jones Ltd.; Piccadilly Hotel, Ltd.; Angel Hotel (Cardiff) Ltd.; Seabank Hotel (Porthcawl) Ltd.; John Allnutt & Co. Ltd.; Star Enterprises Ltd.; Fellow Hotel and Catering Institute; *s.* of Roland Alfred Field, Liverpool; *m.* 1919, Margery, *d.* of late John A. Willis, London. *Educ.:* privately. *Publications:* War Damaged Houses, 1942. Catering: Chambers's Encyclopædia, 1951, 1955, 1962.

Recreations. golf and fishing. *Address:* 4 Denbigh House, Hans Place, S.W.1. *T.:* Kensington 9366. *Clubs:* Constitutional; St. George's Hill Golf (Weybridge). [*Died* 19 *Nov*. 1969.

FIELD, Hon. Winston (Joseph), C.M.G. 1962; M.B.E. 1944: Rhodesian farmer and politician; retired from politics, 1965, as Prime Minister of S. Rhodesia and Minister of the Public Service (1962-64); M.P. for Marandellas, S. Rhodesia, 1962-65; Pres. Rhodesian Front Party in S. Rhodesia,1962-1965; *b*. Bromsgrove, Worcestershire, 6 June 1904; *s*. of J. W. Field; *m*. 1947, Barbara Ann Hayward; three *s*. one *d*. *Educ.:* Bromsgrove School, Worcs. Came to S. Rhodesia, 1921. Pres. Rhodesian Tobacco Association, 1938-40. Served in Rhodesian and British Forces, 1940-45. Major, 6th Durham Light Infantry. Mem., Federal Parliament of Rhodesia and Nyasaland, 1957-62; Leader of the Opposition in the Federal Parliament, 1958-62. Chairman of Governors of Springvale School, Marandellas, 1961-62. *Address:* Karimba Farm, P.O. Box 51, Marandellas, Rhodesia. *T.:* Marandellas 240728. *Clubs:* Salisbury, National (Salisbury, R.): Marandellas (Marandellas, R.). [*Died* 17 *March* 1969.

FILGATE, John V. O. M.; *see* Macartney-Filgate.

FILGATE, Captain Richard Alexander Baillie; *b*. 1877; *s*. of Richard Baillie Henry and Anna Sophia Bolton; changed name to Filgate by deed Poll in 1917; *m*. 1902, Eileen Georgina, *d*. and heiress of William de Salis Filgate, Lissrenney; two *s*. *Educ.:* Brighton College. European War, France, North Irish Hors 1914-18; M.F.H. Louth Foxhounds, 1916 High Sheriff, Co. Louth, 1921. *Recreation* hunting, fishing, shooting. *Address:* Lissrenney, Tallanstown, Dundalk, Co. Louth. *T.A.:* Tallanstown. *T.:* Tallanstown 3. [*Died* 16 *Nov*. 1967.

FILLITER, Douglas Freeland Shute; *b*. 22 May 1884; *o*. *s*. of late Rev. W. D. Filliter; *m*. Agnes (*d*. 1947), *y*. *d*. of late Rittmeister Alfred von Oven, Liegnitz, Silesia; one *d*. (*er*. *s*. killed in action, 1944, *yr*. *s*. decd.). *Educ.:* Marlborough; Keble Coll., Oxford. H.M. Consular Service, 1908; Vice-Consul, 1908; Consul, 1919; Consul-General, 1930; retired, 1944; served Panama, Bergen (Norway), Argentina, Stockholm, Leghorn, Valparaiso, Hamburg, Naples, and at the Foreign Office. Jubilee Medal, 1935; Coronation Medal, 1937. *Address:* Clavell Cottage, 11A, Springfield Road, Parkstone, Poole, Dorset. *T.:* Parkstone 719. [*Died* 26 *Feb*. 1968.

FINCH, Sir Ernest (Frederick), Kt., *cr*. 1951; M.D., M.S. (London); F.R.C.S. (Eng.); Consultant Surgeon, Royal Infirmary, Sheffield; Hon. Lecturer, History of Medicine, University of Sheffield (late Professor of Surgery); Vice - President, R.C.S. (Eng.); Major R.A.M.C. (T.F.); Member: Association of Surgeons of Great Britain, (Pres., 1939-42); Sheffield Medico-Chirurgical Society (President 1931); F.R.Soc. Med. (Pres. of Surgical Section, 1945-47); *b*. 2 Sept. 1884; *s*. of Frederick James Finch; *m*. 1912, Mary Ainsworth; one *s*. *Educ.:* Royal Commercial Travellers' Schools, Hatch End, Mx.; University of Sheffield. Univ. of Sheffield Med. Entrance Schol., 1901; M.B., B.S. (London, Hons. Pathology), 1906; M.D. (Lond.), 1909; M.S. (Lond.), 1913; F.R.C.S. (Eng.), 1911; M.B., Ch.B. (*ad eund*., Sheffield), 1908; D.Sc. (*Honoris Causa* Sheffield), 1952; Hon. F.R.C.S.I., 1959. Formerly Surgical Registrar, Res. Surgical Officer, Casualty Officer, House Surgeon to various depts., 1907-12; Demonstrator of Physiology, Univ. of Sheffield, 1905-1907; Prof. of Surgery, 1934-44, Lecturer in Clinical Surgery, Demonstrator in Physiology, Applied Anatomy and Surgical Pathology, Univ. of Sheffield. Member (Sec. 1926-47) and Pres. of Moynihan Surgical Club; Member Sheffield Town Trust, 1946-. Bradshaw Lecturer, Vicary Lecturer, Hunterian Orator, R.C.S. 1957. *Publications:* Shock (in Surgery of Modern Warfare), 1940; Lettsomian Lectures, Med. Soc. of Lond., 1947; Contrib. to Lancet, B.M.J., Brit. Jl. of Surgery, Proc. Roy. Soc. Med. *Address:* 344 Glossop Rd., Sheffield, 3. *T.:* 26821; Green Farm, Curbar, via Sheffield. *T.:* Grindleford 363. *Club:* Sheffield (Sheffield). [*Died* 16 *Dec*. 1960.

FINCH, George Ingle, M.B.E. 1917; F.R.S. 1938; D.Tech.Chem. (Zürich), F.Inst.P., F.N.I.; Hon. D.Sc. (Brussels); Hon. A.C.G.I.; Professor Emeritus of Applied Physical Chemistry, University of London, since 1952; Director of the National Chemical Laboratory of India, 1952-September 1957, retired; *b*. Orange, New South Wales, 4 August 1888; *e*. *s*. of late C. E. Finch, Chairman of the Land Court of N.S.W.; *m*. 1921, Agnes Isobel Johnston; three *d*. *Educ.:* Wolaroi College, N.S.W.; École de Médecine (Paris); Swiss Federal High School, Zürich; Geneva Univ. Research Chemist at Royal Arsenal, 1912-13; Demonstrator, Imperial Coll., 1913-14; served European War, 1914-19, with R.F.A. and R.A.O.D., France, Egypt, Macedonia (despatches, M.B.E.); Demonstrator, Imperial College, 1919; lecturer (Electro-Chemistry), 1921; Assistant Professor, 1927; Professor of Applied Physical Chemistry in the Univ. of London at Imperial College, 1936-52; Francqui Professor, Brussels, 1937 - 38; Scientific Adviser, Ministry of Home Security, 1941-1945; Pres. Physical Society, 1947-49; Pres. Alpine Club, 1959-61; Fell. Imperial Coll. of Science and Technology, 1962. Mem., 1922 Everest Expedition and led 2nd climbing party to 27,300 ft. Hughes Medal, Royal Soc., 1944; Physical Society Guthrie Lecturer, 1950; Joykissen—Mookerjee Gold Medal, 1957. Commandeur de L'Ordre de Léopold II, 1938; Chevalier de la Légion d'Honneur, 1952. *Publications:* La Diffraction des Electrons et la Structure des Surfaces (Liége), 1938; Scientific Papers in Proc. Roy. Soc., etc.; The Making of a Mountaineer, 1924; articles in Alpine Journal, Jahrbuch des Schweizer Alpen Club, etc. *Recreations:* mountain climbing, yacht cruising, wildfowling. *Address:* Two Trees Farmhouse, Upper Heyford, Oxford. *T.:* Steeple Aston 267. *Clubs:* Alpine, Athenæum. [*Died* 22 *Nov*. 1970.

FINCH, Major John Philip Gordon, O.B.E. 1942; Language Methods Officer, Institute of Army Education, since 1960; *b*. 27 July 1898; *s*. of Arthur Edward Finch and Charlotte Doyne. *Educ.:* Radley; Merton College, Oxford; Trinity Hall, Cambridge. 1st Cl. Modern History, Oxford, 1922. Served European War, 1914-18, Royal Artillery, 1917-19. Entered Levant Consular Service, 1923; served in Middle East, 1925-46; Oriental Secretary, H.M. Legation, Tehran, 1937-41; Counsellor, Foreign Office, 1947-52; retired, 1952; Royal Army Educational Corps, 1953, retired, 1958. *Address:* c/o Barclays Bank Ltd., 27 Regent Street, S.W.1. [*Died* 22 *Jan*. 1965.

FINCH, Col. Sir William H. W.; *see* Wynne Finch.

FINDLATER, Mary; *b*. Lochearnhead, Perthshire, Scotland, 1865; *d*. of Rev. Eric John Findlater. *Educ.:* home. *Publications:* Sonnets and Songs; (Novels) Over the Hills; Betty Musgrave; A Narrow Way; The Rose of Joy; A Blind Bird's Nest; Tents of a Night, 1914; (with J. H. Findlater) Tales that are Told; Crossriggs; Penny Monypenny; Content with

Flies, 1916; Beneath the Visiting Moon, 1923. *Address:* Four Hollies, Comrie, Perthshire. [*Died* 22 *Nov.* 1963.

FINDLAY, Adam Fyfe, M.A., D.D., LL.D.; *b.* 30 May 1869; *s.* of late William Findlay and Catherine Fyfe; *m.* 1898, Jeanie Macdonald; one *s.* two *d.* (and two *s.* decd.). *Educ.:* Aberdeen Grammar School; Aberdeen Univ.; United Presbyterian Divinity Hall, Edinburgh. After post-graduate studies at University of Berlin and at Athens (University and British School of Archaeology) held ministerial charges at Whithorn, 1896-1902; Arbroath, 1903-11; Bristo, Edinburgh, 1911-21; Linlithgow, 1921-24. Served as Chaplain with 2nd Brigade Scottish Horse and with 52nd (Lowland) Division in Egypt and Palestine 1915-17; Professor of Church History and Christian Ethics in Church of Scotland College, Aberdeen, 1924-35; Professor of Christian Ethics and Practical Theology in University of Aberdeen, 1935-47, and Master of Christ's College (C. of S.), Aberdeen, 1937-47. *Publications:* Byways in Early Christian Literature (Kerr Lectures, 1920-21); articles in Hastings' Dictionary of Christ and the Gospels, and Encyclopædia of Religion and Ethics, and in International Standard Bible Encyclopædia, etc. *Address:* 107 High Street, Aberdeen. *T.:* Aberdeen 43555. [*Died* 19 *Jan.* 1962.

FINDLAY, Alexander, C.B.E. 1948; M.A., D.Sc. (Aberd.), Ph.D. (Leipzig), LL.D. (Aberd.), F.R.I.C.; Professor Emeritus of Chemistry, University of Aberdeen; *b.* 24 Sept. 1874; *y. s.* of late William Findlay and Catherine Fyfe; *m.* 1914, Alice Mary, *y. d.* of late Herbert de Rougemont of Lloyd's; two *s.* *Educ.:* Grammar School, Aberdeen; Univs. of Aberdeen and Leipzig; Univ. Coll., London. Interim Lecturer on Organic Chemistry, Univ. of St. Andrews, 1900; Lectr. on Chemistry and Special Lecturer on Physical Chemistry, Univ. of Birmingham, 1902-11; Prof. of Chemistry, University College of Wales, Aberystwyth, 1911-19; Professor of Chemistry, University of Aberdeen, 1919-43; Examiner in Chemistry, Universities of Aberdeen, Durham, (Newcastle), London, Wales, St. Andrews, New Zealand; Member of Council, Royal Institute of Chemistry, 1915-18, 1919-22, 1935-38, 1939-42, Vice-Pres., 1942-43, 1946-49; Pres., 1943-46; Member of Council, Chemical Soc., 1917-20 and 1939-42, Vice-President, 1942-45; Chairman Chemical Council, 1950-53; Vice-President Faraday Society, 1944-47; Member of Council of Management, Macaulay Institute for Soil Research, 1930-60. Visited India and South Africa on behalf of Royal Institute of Chemistry, 1947-48. Thomson Lecturer, United Free Church Coll. Aberdeen, 1915-16; Hurter and Driffield Memorial Lecturer, Royal Photographic Society, 1920; Acting Professor of Chemistry, Stanford University, California, 1925; Member of Sigma Xi, 1925; Liversidge Memorial Lecturer, Sidney, 1938; Editor of Monographs on Inorganic and Physical Chemistry. *Publications:* scientific papers published in the journal of the Chemical Soc. and elsewhere; biographical and general articles, lectures etc.; The Phase Rule and its Applications; Physical Chemistry and its Applications in Medical and Biological Science; Practical Physical Chemistry; Osmotic Pressure; Chemistry in the Service of Man; The Treasures of Coal Tar; Physical Chemistry for Students of Medicine; The Spirit of Chemistry; Introduction to Physical Chemistry; The Teaching of Chemistry in the Universities of Aberdeen; A Hundred Years of Chemistry; General and Inorganic Chemistry; Translation of Ostwald's Principles of Inorganic Chemistry. *Address:* Glenthorne, Lower Camden, Chislehurst, Kent. *Club:* Athenæum. [*Died* 14 *Sept.* 1966.

FINDLAY, Sir Edmund; *see* Findlay, Sir J. E. R.

FINDLAY, Colonel George de Cardonnel Elmsall, V.C. 1919; M.C.; D.L.; R.E.; *b.* 20 Aug. 1889; *s.* of Robert Elmsall Findlay, D.L., of Boturich, Balloch; *m.* 1959, Nellie Constance Barclay Clark, of Connella, Cardross. *Educ.:* Harrow; R.Mo.A., Woolwich. Served European War (V.C. for bravery at Sambre-Oise Canal, 4 November 1918, despatches twice, M.C. and bar); retired pay, 1939; Temporary Col. 1939-40; reverted to retired pay, 1941; re-employed, 1943-45, Italy. County Councillor Dunbartonshire, 1941-64; Deputy Lieutenant, County of Dunbarton, 1957. *Address:* Drumfork House, Helensburgh, Dunbartonshire. [*Died* 26 *June* 1967.

FINDLAY, George Hugo, C.M.G. 1937; *b.* 16 Feb. 1888; 2nd *s.* of late G. H. Findlay, Leeds; *m.* Mary G. B., *d.* of late Rev. R. W. Bury Sanderson. *Educ.:* Repton; Oriel College, Oxford (Honour school Modern History); Senior Resident, Nigeria Colonial Administrative Service, Nigeria, 1911-37; retired. Late County Archivist, Huntingdonshire. Pres. Cambridge Antiquarian Society, 1960-61. *Address:* White Cottage, Stapleford, Cambridge. [*Died* 25 *July* 1966.

FINDLAY, Sir (John) Edmund (Ritchie), 2nd Bt., *cr.* 1925; B.A.; *b.* 14 June 1902; *e. s.* of 1st Bart., and Harriet, D.B.E. *cr.* 1929 (*d.* 1954), *d.* of Sir Jonathan E. Backhouse, 1st Bart.; *S.* father 1930; *m.* 1927, Margaret Jean (marriage dissolved, 1943), *o. d.* of Norval Bantock Graham; two *d.*; *m.* 1947, Mrs. Laura Hawley Elsom, *d.* of Percival Hawley. *Educ.:* Harrow; Balliol College, Oxford. M.P. (U.) Banffshire, 1935-45. Formerly proprietor of the Scotsman. *Heir: b.* Lt.-Col. Roland Lewis Findlay, *q.v.* *Address:* Balcary Tower, Auchencairn, Castle Douglas, Kirkcudbrightshire. *Clubs:* Carlton; New (Edinburgh). [*Died* 6 *Sept.* 1962.

FINECKE, Karen Blixen; *see* Dinesen, Isak.

FINER, Professor Herman; Professor of Political Science, University of Chicago; *b.* 24 February 1898; *s.* of Max Finer, Jassy, Roumania, and Fanny Winer, Hertza, Roumania; *m.* 1926, Sophie, *y. d.* of Paul and Emma Paul, Glebelands, Glebe Place, Stoke Newington; one *d.* *Educ.:* City of London College, and London School of Economics, University of London. B.Sc. Econ. Lond. 1st Class Hons.; Gladstone Memorial Prizeman, 1919; M.Sc. Econ. Lond., 1922; D.Sc. Econ. Lond., 1924; Rockefeller Fellowship, 1924 (to U.S.A.); Rockefeller Fellowship, 1932-33 (to U.S.A., Italy, Central Europe); Lecturer and Reader in Public Administration, London School of Economics, 1920-42; member of Fabian Society Executive; University Extension Lecturer; Examiner, University of London; Director of Research into Administration of Tennessee Valley Authority (1937-38) at invitation of Social Science Research Council of U.S.A.; Member Civil Service Arbitration Tribunal, 1939. Visiting Professor Political Science, University of Chicago, 1935, 1941, 1942; Special Consultant Post-War Reconstruction to International Labour Office, Montreal, Canada, 1942. *Publications:* Foreign Governments at Work, 1922; Representative Government and a Parliament of Industry, 1924; British Civil Service, 1927, second edition, revised and enlarged, 1937; Theory and Practice of Modern Government, 2 vols., 1932; English Local Government, 1933; Mussolini's Italy, 1935; Municipal Trading, 1940; The Major Governments of Modern Europe, 1961; Dulles Over Suez, 1964; articles in Encyclopædia Britannica, etc. *Recreations:* tennis, swimming, carpentry. *Address:* University of Chicago, Chicago, Ill., U.S.A. [*Died* 4 *March* 1969.

FINLAY, Sir George Panton; *see* Addenda: II.

FINLAY-FREUNDLICH, Erwin; formerly Napier Professor of Astronomy at University of St. Andrews; *b.* Biebrich-Wiesbaden, Germany, 29 May 1885; *m.* 1913, Kate Hirschberg; one *s.* one *d.* *Educ.:* Göttingen University (D.phil.). Asst. at Royal Observatory, Berlin, 1910; Director Einstein Institut, Potsdam (which he had created himself), from 1921; left Germany in protest against Nazi Government, 1933, and became Prof. of Astronomy, Istambul (where he created a modern Observatory); Prof. of Astronomy, University of Prague, 1936; Napier Prof. in Astronomy, University of St. Andrews, 1939. *Publications:* Cosmology, 1951; other books (published on the Continent), 1917-37. Many scientific papers. *Address:* Wiesbaden-Biebrich, Volkerstr. 45, Germany. [*Died* 12 *Aug.* 1964.

FINLAYSON, Horace Courtenay Forbes, C.M.G. 1927; *b.* Aberdeen, 20 Jan. 1885; *s.* of late James Finlayson, Aberdeen. *Educ.:* Aberdeen University; M.A. 1905; studied afterwards at the Universities of Marburg, Strasburg, and Paris; post-graduate student, London School of Economics, 1907-1910. Professor of Politics and Public Administration, Chinese Government University, Peking, 1910; Lecturer on Economic Theory and Statistics, Chinese Maritime Customs College, 1911; served in France, 1916-18; Financial Secretary to the Commission Internationale de Ravitaillement in London, Dec. 1918; Private Secretary to Lord Bradbury, G.C.B., British Delegate to the Reparation Commission in Paris, Sept. 1919; British (Financial) member of the Intelligence Service of the Reparations Commission in Berlin, Feb. 1921; Head of the Finance Section of the Delegation of the Committee of Guarantees in Berlin, 1921; Financial Adviser to British Embassy, Berlin, 1923-28; Technical Adviser to Bank of Greece under League of Nations Reconstruction Scheme, 1928-37; Organising Sec. Refugee Emigration Planning Sub-Cttee. of Co-ordinating Cttee. for Refugees, 1938-39; in Financial Intelligence Branch of Ministry of Economic Warfare, 1939-45; Financial Adviser Inter-Governmental Cttee. for Refugees, 1946; Technical Assist. to Sir R. Kindersley and Sir J. Stamp, British Members of the Dawes Committee of Experts, 1924; Knight Commander of the Order of George I of Greece; Commander the Order of the Excellent Crop, China *Address:* 10 St. Matthews Gardens, St Leonards-on-Sea, Sussex. [*Died* 4 *Dec.* 1969.

FINNEGAN, Prof. Thomas; President, Selly Oak Colleges, Birmingham; *b.* 30 May 1901; *s.* of late John M. Finnegan, Belfast; *m.* 1930, Lucy Agnes, *d.* of late David C. Campbell, Londonderry; three *s.* two *d.* *Educ.*: Methodist College, Belfast; Queen's University, Belfast; St. John's College, Cambridge. Irish National Secretary of the Student Christian Movement, 1927; Assistant Master, Campbell College, Belfast; Lecturer in Classics, Magee University College, 1928-30; The Honourable The Irish Society's Professor of Classics, 1930-57 (now Emeritus Professor) and President, 1947-57, Magee Univ. Coll., Londonderry; Principal, St. Catharine's, Cumberland Lodge, Windsor, 1957-58; Member B.B.C. General Advisory Council, 1952-62; Deputy Chairman Board of Governors, Foyle College, 1953-1957; Member of the Executive Committee N.I. Council of Social Service; Past President, Londonderry Rotary Club; Vice-Chairman, N.I. Advisory Council, B.B.C., 1952-57. Member of Committee (under Chairmanship of Lord Coleraine) apptd. 1957, by Minister of Labour N.I. to enquire into Youth Employment Services. Hon. LL.D. (Dublin), 1953. *Publications:* articles in journals of various kinds. *Address:* President's House, Selly Oak Colleges, Birmingham 29. *T.:* Selly Oak 0120. *Club:* Union (Birmingham). [*Died* 11 *Nov.* 1964.

FINNEY, Victor Harold; Formerly Executive Rank Organisation Ltd.; *s.* of John T. Finney, Sunderland; *m.* 1928, Aileen Rose, 4th *d.* of late J. Whiteley-Gallagher, Co. Cork; one *s.* one *d.* *Educ.:* Durham; B.A. 1922, Mod. Hist.; M.A. 1925. M.P. (L.) Hexham Division, 1923-24. *Recreations:* walking, valued friendships. *Address:* 13 Denfield, Tower Hill, Dorking, Surrey. *T.:* Dorking 4269. *Club:* National Liberal. [*Died* 10 *April* 1970.

FINNIGAN, Surg. Rear-Adm. (D) Charles Joseph, C.B. 1960; L.D.S. 1923; Q.H.D.S. 1955; Deputy Director-General Dental Services since 1957; *b.* 3 Apr. 1901; *s.* of Andrew Finnigan, Dundee, Scotland; *m.* 1937, Milifred Kathleen, *d.* of Captain Leslie Dudgeon, Longford, Eire; one *s.* *Educ.:* Harris Academy, Dundee; St. Andrews University. Joined R.N. 1923. Surgeon Commander (D), 1936; Surgeon Captain (D), 1949; Surgeon Rear-Admiral (D), 1957. Served 1939-45 with Royal Navy in U.K., Africa, Italy and Malta. *Address:* c/o Midland Bank, Chatham, Kent. [*Died* 27 *July* 1967.

FINNIS, Sidney Alexander, O.B.E. 1961; E.R.D. 1953; M.Inst.T.; Chairman, British Transport Docks Board since 1967; *b.* 25 Oct. 1908; *yr. s.* of late J. R. Finnis and Mrs. E. F. Finnis, Hassocks, Sx.; *m.* 1936, Joan, *d.* of late Henry Burton, Hessle, E. Yorks; one *d.* *Educ.:* Brighton Coll. Joined L.N.E.R. as Traffic Apprentice, 1927; held various railway and dock positions, including Chief Docks Man., Humber Ports, 1949-56; Chief Docks Man., Southampton, 1956-62; acting Chm. and Gen. Man., Docks Div., B.T.C., 1962; Gen. Man., Brit. Transport Docks Board, 1963-65; Man. Dir., 1965-67. War of 1939-1945: P.O.W. 1942-45 (despatches twice). Col. Eng. and Railway Staff Corps R.E., (T. & AVR.IV). President, Institute of Transport, 1967-68. Vice-Pres., Dock and Harbour Authorities Association. Director: Internat. Cold Storage Co. Ltd. *Publications:* various papers on dock and transport subjects. *Recreation:* gardening. *Address:* 111 Chiltern Court, Baker St., N.W.1. *T.:* Hunter 3830; Sunny Cottage, Bishopstone, nr. Swindon, Wilts. *Club:* Athenæum. [*Died* 4 *July* 1969.

FINZI, Neville Samuel, M.B. Lond., M.R.C.S., L.R.C.P., L.S.A., D.M.R.E. (Camb.); F.F.R. (Hon.); F.A.C.R. (Hon.); Consulting Radiologist to the Radiotherapy and X-ray Diagnostic Depts., St. Bartholomew's Hosp. *b.* 25 June 1881; *s.* of late J. M. Finzi, M.D. *Educ.:* Univ. Coll. School; Univ. College and Hospital. Formerly: Director of X-ray Dept., St. Bartholomew's Hospital; Medical Officer to Electrical Dept., Metropolitan Hosp.; Medical Officer to X-ray Department, German Hospital. Master, Society of Apothecaries, 1955-56. *Publications:* Radium Therapeutics, 1913; various papers on the treatment of cancer by radium and X-rays; also papers on ionic medication. *Recreations:* climbing, gardening, music. *Address:* The Garth, Miles Lane, Cobham, Surrey. *T.:* 2516. *Clubs:* Alpine, Junior Carlton. [*Died* 3 *April* 1968.

FIRTH, James Brierley, C.B.E. 1954; M.Sc.; D.Sc., F.R.I.C.; Director, North-Western Forensic Science Laboratory (Home Office), Preston, 1938-58; now Consultant; *b.* Stockport, 8 July 1888; *s.* of Joshua and Hannah Firth; *m.* Annie M., *y. d.* of James Patton, Heaton, Newcastle upon Tyne; two *d.* *Educ.* Stockport Technical School; Manchester University; Crace-Calvert Scholar, 1909-11; 1st Class Honours in Chemistry, B.Sc., 1912; Dalton Research Scholar, 1912-13; M.Sc. Durham Univ., 1916; D.Sc. Manchester Univ., 1920. Member of Council: Roy. Inst. Chem., 1936-38 and 1941-44; Chem. Soc., 1933-

1935; Vice-Pres. Soc. of Chem. Industry, 1933-36; Pres. Forensic Science Society, 1959-61. Lecturer in Chemistry, Armstrong College, Newcastle upon Tyne, 1914-18; Senior Lecturer in Chemistry, University College, Nottingham, 1919-38. *Publications:* Practical Physical Chemistry, 1915; Physical Chemistry, 1929; Chemistry in the Home, 1929; A Scientist Turns to Crime, 1960. A large number of original papers in scientific, medico-legal, and legal journals, including papers on Forensic Science, Arson, Causes of Fires, etc. *Address:* 35 Lulworth Road, Birkdale, Southport.

[*Died* 24 *July* 1966.

FISCHER, Louis; journalist and author; *b.* Philadelphia, Pa., 29 Feb. 1896; *s.* of David and Shifrah Fischer; *m.* 1922, Bertha Mark; two *s.* *Educ.:* Philadelphia School of Pedagogy. Volunteer in British Army, 1918-20; School Teacher in Philadelphia, 1917; since 1921 American Correspondent in European countries, particularly Russia and Spain, also in India since 1942. Mem., Institute for Advanced Study, Princeton; Mem. faculty Princeton University. *Publications:* Oil Imperialism, 1926; The Soviets in World Affairs, two vols., 1930 (reprinted, 1951, with new introduction by author); Why Recognize Russia ?, 1933; Machines and Men in Russia, 1934; Soviet Journey, 1935; Why Spain Fights On, 1937; Stalin and Hitler, 1940; Men and Politics (An Autobiography), 1941; Dawn of Victory, 1942; A Week with Gandhi, 1942; Empire, 1943; The Great Challenge, 1946; Gandhi and Stalin, 1947; (Ed.) Thirteen Who Fled, Thirteen Autobiographies by Russian Displaced Persons, 1949; (contrib.) The God That Failed, 1950; The Life of Mahatma Gandhi 1950; The Life and Death of Stalin, 1952; Gandhi: his life and message for the world, 1954; This is Our World, 1956; Russia Revisited, 1957; The Story of Indonesia, 1958 (3rd edn. 1960); Russia, America, and the World, 1961; The Life of Lenin, 1964 (winner of National Book Award); (Ed.) The Essential Gandhi, an anthology; Fifty Years of Soviet Communism, an Appraisal, 1968; Russia's Road from Peace to War: Soviet foreign relations, 1917-1941 (vol. 1 of several-volume appraisal), 1969. *Recreations:* swimming, work. *Address:* Woodrow Wilson School, Princeton University, Princeton, N.J., U.S.A.

[*Died* 15 *Jan.* 1970.

FISH, Anne Harriet, (Mrs. Walter Sefton); Artist; *o. d.* of B. Fish, Maidenhead; *m.* 1918, Walter Sefton (*d.* 1952). *Educ.:* London and New School of Art; Paris. Exhib. Roy. Acad.; one-man exhibition Fine Art Society. Drawings for Eve, The Tatler, Punch, Vogue, Vanity Fair, Harper's Bazaar, Cosmopolitan, etc., and U.S.A.; paintings in oils, watercolour; textile designs, several books of drawings; Member Penwith Society of Arts; Fellow C.I.A.D.; Newlyn Soc. of Artists; St. Ives Old Society of Artists. *Recreations:* cats and travel. *Address:* The Digey Studio, St. Ives, Cornwall. *Club:* University Women's.

[*Died* 10 *Oct.* 1964.

FISH, Wallace Wilfrid B.; *see* Blair-Fish.

FISHER, Alfred George Timbrell, M.C.; M.B.; Ch.B.; F.R.C.S.(Eng.); Surgeon, Specialist in Injuries and Diseases of Bones, Joints and Spine; C.St.J.; Fellow of American and of Internat. College of Surgeons; Fellow Roy. Soc. of Medicine; Orthopædic Specialist to Rheumatic Unit, St. Stephen's Hospital and to Charterhouse Rheumatism Clinic; Co-Trustee and Mem. Executive, Empire Rheumatism Council; Corresponding Member of American Academy of Orthopædic Surgeons; *b.* Bristol, 2nd *s.* of late Canon Walter Henry Fisher; *m.* 1st, 1912, Grace (*d.* 1944), *d.* of George Bond, Bridgwater; two *s.* one *d.*; 2nd, 1949, Edith Frances Clive, *widow* of John B. Clive of Birlingham Manor, Pershore, Worcs. *Educ.:* Clifton College; Bristol Medical School; St. Bartholomew's Hospital. M.R.C.S. (Eng.), L.R.C.P. (Lond.), 1911; M.B.Ch.B. (Bristol), 1912. R.A.M.C.(T.), 1915-19 (M.C., direct award, despatches); F.R.C.S. (Eng.), 1919; Asst. Orthopædic dept. St. Barts. Hospital; Asst. Surgical Unit Univ. Coll. Hosp.; Visiting Surgeon Ministry of Pensions Hospital, Orpington; Surgical Specialist, Ministry of Pensions; Surgeon (with charge of out-patients), Dreadnought Hospital, Greenwich; Joint Lecturer in Operative Surgery, London School of Clinical Medicine; Hunterian Prof. of Royal Coll. of Surgeons of England, 1919-20, 1921-22; Vice-Pres. Orthopædic Section B.M.A., Oxford, 1936; Member of Nat. Cttee. on Chronic Rheumatic Diseases (Chairman of Classification Sub-Committee); Medical Member, Medical and Pensions Appeal Tribunals. *Publications:* Internal Derangements of the Knee-Joint, their Pathology and Treatment by Modern Methods, 1924; 2nd edition, 1933; Treatment by Manipulation, 5th edition, 1948; Chronic (Non-Tuberculous) Arthritis, Pathology and Treatment by Modern Methods, 1928; original articles in Medical journals: The Hunterian Lectures, 1921, 1922; etc. *Address:* 138 Harley St., W.1. *T.:* Welbeck 0554.

[*Died* 10 *Oct.* 1967.

FISHER, Arthur B. K.; *see* Knapp-Fisher.

FISHER, Col. Cecil James, C.B.E. 1945 (O.B.E. 1919); D.S.O. 1917; Retired; late Middlesex Regiment and Royal Pioneer Corps; *b.* 1890; *s.* of late James Fisher, Cambridge; *m.* 1923, Alison Newstead-Crick; two *s.* *Educ.:* St. Paul's School. Served India, 1914-16; Mesopotamia, 1916-1919; 2 i/c 1/5th Batt. The Buffs; Staff Captain 55th Ind. Inf. Bde. (despatches twice, D.S.O., O.B.E.); Afghanistan, 1919; D.A.Q.M.G. Peshawar Area; France 1939-1940, i/c Labour No. 1 Base Amn. Depot; Commanded Bn. Beauman Divn. during evacuation (despatches); Home Forces, 1940-41, Group Cmd. Pioneer Corps; Irak and India, 1942-46; A.D. Pioneers and Labour 4 Corps; 15 Indian Corps; D.D. Pioneers and Labour Fourteenth Army; Eastern Command; II Army Group (despatches, C.B.E.); Director Unskilled Labour Supply, Govt. of India, 1944-46; Agent, Bank of England, Newcastle, 1947-1953. *Address:* 15 Kings Road, St. Mawes, Truro, Cornwall.

[*Died* 1 *Sept.* 1961.

FISHER, Major-General Donald Rutherfurd Dacre, C.B. 1945; C.B.E. 1941; D.S.O. 1917; formerly J.P. Wiltshire; *b.* 5 Feb. 1890; *o. s.* of late John Archibald Fisher of Porth Crugmor, Rhydwen, Anglesey; *m.* 1934, Mary Teresa (*d.* 1956), *o. d.* of late C. L. Sansom, C.M.G.; one *s.* one *d.* *Educ.:* Clifton Coll.; R.M.A., Woolwich. Second Lieut. R.F.A., 1909; Bt. Lt.-Col. 1931; Lt.-Col. R.A. 1936; Col. 1938; served in France and Belgium, Aug.-Dec. 1914, and May 1915-Dec. 1917 (despatches thrice, D.S.O.); p.s.c. Director-General, Army, Requirements, War Office, 1942-46; retired pay, 1947. Medal of Freedom with Silver Palm (U.S.A.). *Address:* Porth Crugmor, Rhydwen, Holyhead. *T.:* Llanfaethlu 306. *Club:* Army and Navy.

[*Died* 18 *Dec.* 1962.

FISHER, Admiral Sir Douglas Blake, K.C.B., *cr.* 1947 (C.B. 1945); K.B.E., *cr.* 1946 (C.B.E. 1940); *b.* 23 Oct. 1890; *s.* of late Admiral W. B. Fisher, C.B., and E. L. Chambers; *m.* 1916, Constance, *d.* of Sir William Parker, 2nd Bart., Fareham, Hants; one *s.* (and one *s.* killed, 1948); *m.* 1946, Anne, *d.* of late Mr. and Mrs. Charles McKay; two *s.* *Educ.:* Stubbington House, Fareham; R.N. Coll., Dartmouth. Midshipman, 1907; Lieutenant 1912; served European War,

H.M.S. Iron Duke, 1914-17; H.M.S. Caradoc, 1918-20 (despatches, O.B.E.); Commander, 1925; Captain, 1932; Captain of the Fleet (Home Fleet), 1938-40 (C.B.E.); Commanded H.M.S. Warspite, 1940-42 (despatches); Russia, 1942-44 (C.B.); Rear-Admiral Fleet Train, British Pacific Fleet, 1944-45; Flag Officer, Western Area British Pacific Fleet, 1945; a Lord Commissioner of Admiralty and Fourth Sea Lord, 1945-48; Rear-Adm. 1942; Vice-Adm. 1945; retired 1948; Adm., retd. list, 1949. *Address:* Tile Barn House, Brockenhurst, Hants. *T.:* Brockenhurst 2255. [*Died* 4 *Oct*. 1963.

FISHER, Brig. Sir Gerald (Thomas), K.B.E., *cr*. 1949; C.S.I. 1942; C.I.E. 1938; M.A.(Oxon); late I.A.; late Indian Political Service; *b*. Dehra Dun, India, 27 Aug. 1887; *s*. of late Professor W. R. Fisher of Coopers Hill; *m*. 1st, 1915, Margery, *d*. of late Ralph Hodgkinson, London; one *s*.; 2nd, 1939, Alice Ruth, *d*. of late Brig. Gen. Sir E. Le Marchant, 4th Bt., K.C.B., C.B.E. *Educ.:* Bradfield; Lincoln College, Oxford. 3rd (Q.A.O.) Gurkha Rifles, 1909; served European War in France 1914-15, and in Mesopotamia, 1917-19; Civil Administration, Mesopotamia, 1918-19; Indian Political Service, 1919, North West Frontier, Central India, Baluchistan, Persia, Aden, Kathiawar, Hyderabad, Kapurthala; Resident at Gwalior, 1937-40; Resident in Central India, 1940-42; Military Governor, British Somaliland. 1943-48. *Address:* Cross. Little Torrington, N. Devon. *Clubs:* Army and Navy Lansdowne. [*Died* 6 *Sept*. 1965

FISHER, Sir Godfrey Arthur, K.C.M.G., *cr*. 1945 (C.M.G. 1941); *b*. [illegible] Aug. 1885; *s*. of late Rev. Arthur T. Fisher; *m*. 1925, Geraldine, *d*. of late C. White Mortimer, formerly H.M. Consul at Los Angeles, U.S.A.; two *d*. *Educ.:* St. Peter's School, York: Queen's College, Oxford. Vice-Consul at Baltimore, U.S.A., 1909-12; Santo Domingo, 1912-1920; Consul at Tahiti, 1920-23; Los Angeles, California, 1923-30; Consul-General at Naples, 1930-37; at Antwerp, 1937-40; Consul-General at San Francisco, 1941-45; received Jubilee Medal, 1935; Coronation Medal, 1937. *Publications:* Barbary Legend, 1957, and articles. *Recreation:* historical research. *Address:* Flat 38, The New Metropole, The Leas, Folkestone, Kent. *T.:* Folkestone 53216 [*Died* 22 *Sept*. 1969.

FISHER, James Maxwell McConnell, M.A.; Deputy Chairman, Countryside Commission, since 1968 (Member, 1966, Deputy Chairman, 1967-68, National Parks Commission); *b*. 3 Sept. 1912; *e*. *s*. of late Kenneth Fisher, M.A., Ph.D., Headmaster of Oundle School, and Constance Isabel, *d*. of late James Boyd, Altrincham, Cheshire; *m*. 1936, Margery Lilian Edith, *e*. *d*. of Sir Henry Turner; three *s*. three *d*. *Educ.:* Eton (King's Scholar); Magdalen College, Oxford. Ornithologist, Oxf. Univ. Expedition to Spitsbergen, 1933; winner of Silver Sculls, 1934; Asst. Master, Bishop's Stortford Coll., 1935-36; Asst. Curator, Zoological Society of London, 1936-39; Hon. Sec. Assoc. for Study of Animal Behaviour, 1936-39, Hon. Treas., 1948-53; Hon. Secretary British Trust for Ornithology, 1938-44; Bureau of Animal Population, Oxf. Univ., 1940-43; Edward Grey Institute of Field Ornithology, Oxf. Univ., 1944-46; adviser to and director of various publishing houses, 1947-65; F.R.G.S.; F.L.S.; F.G.S.; F.Z.S.; Corresp. Fell. Amer. Ornithologists' Union; Hon. Mem. Danish Ornithological Soc.; Scientific Fellow, Zoological Soc. of London (Silver Medal, 1969). Chairman Northamptonshire Naturalists' Trust; Formerly Vice-Chairman, Royal Society for Protection of Birds (Gold Medal, 1961) and Brit. Trust for Ornithology (Bernard Tucker Medal, 1966); Member: Brit. Ornithologists' Union (Union Medal, 1968); Brit. Ecological Soc.; Fauna Preservation Soc.; Survival Service Commission of Int. Union Conservation Nature; and of many scientific and natural history societies. Arthur A. Allen Award (Cornell Univ.), 1968. An editor Collins' New Naturalist books, 1942-; chief editor Rathbone Books, 1956; Aldus Books, 1962-65; writer or ed. of radio, television talks and features (Nature Parliament, Birds in Britain, World Zoos, etc.). *Publications:* Birds as Animals, 1939; Watching Birds, 1940; The Birds of Britain, 1942; Birds of the Village, 1943; Bird Recognition, 1947-55; The Fulmar, 1952; Birds of the Field, 1952; A Thousand Geese (with Peter Scott), 1953; Sea Birds (with R. M. Lockley), 1954; A History of Birds, 1954; Adventure of the World, 1954; Rockall, 1956; Wild America (with Roger Peterson), 1956; Adventure of the Sea, 1956 (Boys' Clubs of America Junior Book Award); Shackleton (with Margery Fisher), 1957; Adventure of the Air, 1958; Nature (ed.), 1960; The World of Birds (with Roger Peterson), 1964; The Shell Nature Lovers' Atlas, 1966; The Shell Bird Book, 1967; Zoos of the World, 1967; Thorburn's Birds, 1967; (with The Duke of Edinburgh) Wild Life Crisis, 1970; other books in collab.; many scientific papers in jls.; film scripts. *Recreations:* bird-watching, paleontology, exploring islands, snooker and music. *Address:* Ashton Manor, Northampton NN7 2JL. *T.:* Roade 277. *Clubs:* Athenæum, Savile, Alpine; Leander (Henley). [*Died* 25 *Sept*. 1970.

FISHER, John Cartwright Braddon, C.M.G. 1963; O.B.E. 1957; *b*. 22 Feb. 1911; *s*. of late Arthur Fisher, The Mazry, Tiverton, Devon; *m*. 1948, Ruth Margaret Colyear, *d*. of late Capt. Arthur Colyear Walker; three *s*. *Educ.:* Blundell's School. Served War of 1939-45: Major, R.A.S.C. and Special Forces, Europe and Western Pacific, 1942-46. Sarawak Civil Service, 1932-63; Cadet, 1932; District Officer, 1937; Divisional Resident, 1948; Senior Resident, 1959. Chairman, Kuching Municipal Council, 1954. *Recreation:* feet up. *Address:* Tara, Three Gates, Leigh, Sherborne, Dorset. *Club:* Special Forces. [*Died* 15 *July* 1968.

FISHER, Rt. Rev. Leonard Noel, D.D.; LL.D.; *b*. 14 Dec. 1881; *s*. of late Rev. Henry Fisher, M.A., of Higham-on-the-Hill, Leicestershire; *m*. 1928, Mabel, *d*. of late W. T. Callund, of Rochester, adopted *d*. of late Rev. W. J. Peacey. *Educ.:* Oakham; Sidney Sussex Coll., Cambridge. Curate of St. Paul's, Hull, 1905-8; Sub-Warden of St. Paul's Theological College, Grahamstown, S. Africa, 1909-12; Curate of Queenstown, S. Africa, 1913; Saltburn-by-the-Sea, 1914-15; 1st Vicar of St. Nicholas, Hull, 1915-18; temporary Chaplain to the Forces, 1917-18; 1st Vicar of Grangetown, Yorkshire, 1918-21; Bishop of Lebombo, 1921-28; Bishop of Natal, 1928-51. Hon. Canon of Grahamstown Cathedral. *Address:* Brookshaw, Grahamstown, S. Africa. [*Died* 4 *July* 1963.

FISHER, Prof. Emer. Matthew George, C.B.E. 1954; Q.C. (Scotland) 1938; Hon. LL.D. (Edinburgh), 1959; Professor of Civil Law in the University of Edinburgh, 1938-58; Dean of the Faculty of Law, 1943-58; Counsel to Secretary of State under Private Legislation Procedure (Scotland) Act, 1928-58; Editor, Session Cases, 1960; *b*. Skelmorlie, Ayrshire, 31 March 1888; *s*. of late Rev. R. H. Fisher, D.D., Minister of St. Cuthbert's Parish, Edinburgh, and Margaret Ada, *e*. *d*. of Robert Hutchison, Carlowrie, Kirkliston; *m*. 1920, Margaret, *e*. *d*. of late H. D. Thomas, Cargilfield, Cramond Bridge, Midlothian; three *d*. *Educ.:* Clifton College; Universities of Edinburgh and Göttingen. M.A. Edin., 1910 1st Cl. Hons. Classics; Rhind Class. Scholar;

LL.B. 1913; admitted to Faculty of Advocates, 1913; Sec. to Scottish Ecclesiastical Comrs., 1925-37; Lect. on Administrative Law, Edinburgh Univ., 1932-38; member of Cttee. for Consolidation of Local Government and Public Health Law of Scotland, 1937-39; Chairman of Cttee. for revision and consolidation of statutory enactments applying to Scotland and affecting Local Authorities and Local Govt., 1948; served European War, 1914-19, Capt. 4th Border Regt. Order of Polonia Restituta, 1944. *Address:* 25 Northumberland Street, Edinburgh, 3. *T.:* Waverley 2256. *Clubs:* Caledonian; New (Edinburgh).
[*Died* 24 *Feb.* 1965.

FISHER, Rev. Philip John; Hon. C.F.; *b.* 1883; 2nd *s.* of Jonathan and Elizabeth Fisher; unmarried. *Educ.:* Evesham and Cheltenham Grammar Schools; Hartley College, Manchester. Entered Methodist ministry as probationer, 1905; ordained 1909, Circuit Minister at Cottingham, Hull; Docking, Norfolk; Tarporley, Cheshire; Bootle, Liverpool; Kingston-on-Thames; Middlesbrough; Whitley Bay; Crewe; Teddington. Retired from circuit ministry, 1950. Temporary Chaplain to the Forces, 1915-19, serving in France and Flanders, chiefly with 55th Division. Reviewer and contributor to The Academy, 1911-15; Editor, The Methodist Leader, 1930-32; Co-Editor, The Methodist Times and Leader, 1932-37. *Publications:* Khaki Vignettes, 1917; Figures and Phases of the War, 1919 (privately printed); Porches of Prayer, 1936; Tales of the Golden Company, 1938; The Vigil with God, 1943; The Service of Worship, 1948; Songs of Desire and of Divine Love, 1950; Prayers out of Church, 1958. *Address:* Lindens, York Road, Woking, Surrey. [*Died* 6 *July* 1961.

FISHER, Sir Ronald (Aylmer), Kt. 1952; F.R.S., F.S.S., Sc.D. (Camb.); Hon. D.Sc. (Amer), Harvard, London, Chicago, Leeds); Hon. LL.D. (Calcutta, Glasgow); President of Gonville and Caius College, Cambridge, 1956-59; Arthur Balfour Professor of Genetics, University of Cambridge, 1943-1957, retired; *b.* 17 February 1890; 7th *c.* and 4th *s.* of G. Fisher of Robinson & Fisher, auctioneers, King Street, St. James's; *m.* 1917, Ruth Eileen, *d.* of H. Grattan Guinness, M.D.; two *s.* six *d.* *Educ.:* Harrow; Gonville and Caius, Cambridge. Statistician to Mercantile and General Investment Company, 1913-15: teaching in Public Schools, 1915-19; Rothamsted Experimental Station, Statistical Dept., 1919-33; Galton Prof. of Eugenics, Univ. Coll., London, 1933; Sc.D. 1926; F.R.S. 1929; Weldon medal, 1929; Royal Medal of Royal Soc., 1938; Guy Medal in gold of Royal Statistical Soc., 1946; Darwin Medal of Roy. Soc., 1948; Copley Medal of Roy. Soc., 1955; Hon. Fellow, American Statistical Assoc., 1930; Foreign Hon. Member American Academy of Arts and Sciences, 1934; Foreign Member: Amer. Philosophical Society, 1941; Royal Swedish Acad. of Sciences, 1946; Leopoldina German Academy, 1961; Pontifical Academy of Sciences, 1961; For. Associate, U.S. Nat. Acad. of Science, 1948. Mem. Royal Danish Acad. of Sciences and Letters, 1950. Hon. Mem. Internat. Soc. of Hematology, 1950; Hon. Pres., Internat. Statistical Institute, 1957. *Publications:* Statistical Methods for Research Workers, 1925 (13th edition, 1957); The Genetical Theory of Natural Selection, 1930 (reprint 1958); The Design of Experiments, 1935 (7th Edition, 1960); Statistical Tables (with F. Yates), 1938 (5th edn. 1957); The Theory of Inbreeding, 1949; Contributions to Mathematical Statistics, 1950; Statistical Methods and Scientific Inference, 1956 (2nd ed. 1959); research papers in many British and foreign scientific journals. *Recreation:* experiments on heredity. *Address:* Undelcarra, 58 Lockwood Road, Burnside, Adelaide, S. Australia. *Club:* Savile. [*Died* 29 *July* 1962.

FISHER, Col. Stanley Howe, C.B. 1956; M.C. 1917; T.D.; D.L.; F.R.I.B.A.; Consultant Architect; *b.* 30 Mar. 1891; *er. s.* of Frank J. Fisher; *m.* 1st, 1927, Dorothy (*née* Carey), (decd.); two *s.*; 2nd, 1933, Marjorie Florence (*née* Merrick). *Educ.:* Dulwich. Pupil to F. J. Fisher, F.R.I.B.A.; A.R.I.B.A. 1914; F.R.I.B.A., 1928. Served in France, 1915-19 (despatches five times). Commanded 47 Division Engineers, England, 1923-29; Hon. Col., 1929-58. Served with R.E., 1940-45. Vice-Chm. Co. of London T. & Aux. F. Assoc., 1953-54, Chm., 1954-56. D.L., Co. of London, 1950, now Greater London. *Recreations:* cricket, tennis, riding. *Address:* Parkland, Prideaux Road, Eastbourne, Sussex. *T.:* Eastbourne 26041.
[*Died* 6 *July* 1967.

FISHER PROUT, Margaret, A.R.A. 1948; R.W.S. 1945; R.W.A. 1947; Member of New English Art Club; *d.* of Mark Fisher, R.A.; *m.* John Alexander Prout. *Educ.:* studied under Mark Fisher, R.A., and Prof. Brown at Slade School. Represented in following National Collections: Tate Gallery; British Museum; Ottawa; Melbourne; Dunedin; National Art Gallery, Wellington, N.Z.; Public Museum and Art Gallery, Hastings; painting purchased by Russell-Smith Trust, 1947; Bristol, 1948; National Art Gallery of N.S.W., 1949; painting purchased by The Contemporary Art Society, 1950; work purchased for Preston Art Gallery, 1951. *Address:* 5 Amherst Gardens, Hastings, Sussex. *T.:* Hastings 3624.
[*Died* 9 *Dec.* 1963.

FISK, Sir Ernest (Thomas), Kt. 1937; Hon. M.I.E.E.; Hon. M.Brit.I.R.E.; chartered engineer (Australia); Consultant, Economics Production, Technology; Vice-Pres. R.E.S., London; Vice-Pres. Inst. of Radio Engineers, U.S.A., 1938, now Fellow for Life; Mem. Instn. of Engineers (Australia); Pres. Inst. Radio Engineers (Australia), 1932-37, and 1939-43; now Hon. Life Mem.; Hon. Mem. British Inst. of Radio Engineers; Hon. Mem. Inst. of Electrical Engineers (London); Pres. Internat. Federation of Phonographic Industries, 1948-52; Hon. Corresp. in Electronics, Museum of Technol. and Applied Science, Sydney; Fell. Television Soc.; F.R.S.A., F.I.D.; *b.* Sunbury-on-Thames, 8 Aug. 1886; *s.* of Thomas Harvey Fisk; *m.* 1916, Florence, *d.* of S. Chudleigh; four *s.* *Educ.:* Sunbury-on-Thames; United Kingdom Coll.; Sydney Univ. Joined Marconi Co. in England, 1906; special mission to Arctic, 1909; first visited Australia, 1910; General Manager Amalgamated Wireless, 1913; pioneered Radio, Broadcasting, Beam Wireless, etc. in Australia; conducted research with Marconi and received first direct wireless messages from England to Australia, 1918; first human voice England to Australia, 1924; pioneered first broadcast Australia to England, 1925; Beam Wireless Australia to England, 1927; Radiotelephone Australia to England, 1930. Director of Economic Co-ordination, Commonwealth Govt., also Secretary to Economic Cabinet and Chairman Seaborne Trade Committee, 1939-41; Chairman, N.S.W. State Council of Physical Fitness, 1939; Managing Director Amalgamated Wireless (Australia), 1917-44, Chairman, 1932-44; Managing Director Electric and Musical Industries Ltd., 1945-51; Pres. Royal Commonwealth Society (N.S.W. branch), 1941-45; Past Pres. Royal Philharmonic Society (Sydney); Past Vice-Pres. Australian Air League; Past Chairman Industrial Section R. Soc. of N.S.W. *Address:* P.O. Box 9, Roseville, N.S.W., Australia. *Clubs:* Union (Sydney); Athenæum (Melbourne).
[*Died* 8 *July* 1965.

FISON, Sir (William) Guy, 3rd Bt., *cr.* 1905; M.C.; *b.* 25 Oct. 1890; *y. s.* of Sir Frederick William Fison, 1st Bt. and Isabella (*d.* 1932), *d.* of late Joseph Crossley, Broomfield, Halifax; *S.* brother 1948; *m.* 1914, Gwladys Rees (*d.* 1963), *d.* of John Robert Davies, Treborth, Bangor; two *s.* one *d.* *Educ.:* Eton; New Coll., Oxford (B.A.). Served European War, 1914-18, in R.A. (T.F.) (despatches, M.C.); War of 1939-45, R.O.C., 1942-43. *Heir: s.* Richard Guy Fison, D.S.C., late R.N.V.R. [*b.* 9 Jan. 1917; *m.* 1952, Elyn, *d.* of M. Hartmann, Bordeaux, France; one *s.* one *d.*]. *Address:* Knoyle Place, East Knoyle, Salisbury, Wilts. *T.:* East Knoyle 227. [*Died* 6 *Dec.* 1964.

FITCH, Ven. Edward Arnold, O.B.E. 1918; Prebendary of Compton Bishop in Wells Cathedral; *s.* of late Rev. E. H. Fitch, Vicar of Burgh-by-Sands, Cumberland; *m.* Dorothy, *d.* of late Rev. A. E. Shaw, D.L., Headmaster of Lord Williams School, Thame, Oxford; one *s.* two *d.* *Educ.:* Denstone College; Edinburgh Theological College. Deacon, 1905; Priest, 1906; Curate, St. James, Leith, 1905-10; Chaplain to the Forces, 1910, stations: Woolwich, Curragh, Pretoria, Harrismith, Bloemfontein; B.E.F., 1914-18, C.F. 15th Infantry Brigade, S.C.F. 41st Div., D.A.C.G. XIXth Corps, A.C.G. Havre (despatches twice, O.B.E., Croix de Guerre); since war, C.F. Tank Corps, Bovington and Parkhurst; S.C.F. Marlborough Lines, Aldershot and Gibraltar; S.C.F. Shorncliffe; A.C.G. Malta, Northern Command, Aldershot Command; Hon. Chaplain to the King, 1936. Proctor, Convocation, 1938; Archdeacon of Taunton and Prebendary of Milverton, 1938-1950; Rector of Angersleigh, 1946-54. *Recreations:* Rugby (trials for Scotland). cricket, golf. *Address:* Eden Grove, South Road, Taunton, Somerset. [*Died* 23 *April* 1965.

FITTON, Colonel Sir Charles (Vernon), Kt., *cr.* 1955; O.B.E. 1942; M.C. 1917; Director of Parson & Crosland Ltd., City Wall House, E.C.2, and Middlesbrough since 1936 (Vice-Chairman 1954, Chm. 1960-66); Chairman, Ferndale Warehousing Co. Ltd., Middlesbrough, since 1966; Pres., Inst. of Export, 1958-61; *b.* 13 Nov. 1894; *s.* of Charlie Fitton, Barnsley; *m.* 1920, Kathleen May Rushforth; one *s.* one *d.* *Educ.:* Archbishop Holgate's Grammar School, Barnsley; Technical College, Barnsley. 14 York and Lancaster Regt., Capt., 2/33 Punjabis, I.A., Major, 1914-20; Home Guard, Col. (1941), Sector Commander, 1941-45. Redcar Borough Council, 1945-1949; Foundation Governor, Coatham School, 1946-; Tees Conservancy Comr., 1952-. *Recreations:* fishing, shooting, golf. *Address:* Chestnut Cottage, Hutton Rudby, Yarm, Yorkshire. *T.:* Hutton Rudby 300. *Club:* Cleveland (Middlesbrough). [*Died* 10 *April* 1967.

FITZ ALAN of Derwent, 2nd Viscount, *cr.* 1921, of Derwent; **Henry Edmund Fitzalan-Howard,** O.B.E. 1922; Capt. 11th Hussars, retd.; *b.* 31 Oct. 1883; *o. s.* of 1st Viscount Fitzalan of Derwent, K.G., P.C., G.C.V.O., D.S.O., and Lady Mary Caroline (*d.* 1938), *d.* of 7th Earl of Abingdon; and *c.* and *heir-pres.* of 16th Duke of Norfolk; *S.* father, 1947; *m.* 1922, Joyce (marriage dissolved, 1955; she *m.* 1956, 10th Earl Fitzwilliam), *e. d.* of late Colonel Philip Langdale, O.B.E.; two *d.* *Educ.:* Oratory School, Birmingham; New College, Oxford. Late Assistant Private Secretary to Lord Lieutenant of Ireland; served European War, 1914-18; retired pay, 1926; re-employed Commanding Beaumont College Junior Training Corps, 1941-46. Director Pullman Car Co., and London and Lancashire Insurance Co.; formerly Dep. Chm. of National Bank. *Heir:* none. *Address:* 38 Green St., Park Lane, W.; Shooting Lodge, Derwent, Sheffield. *Clubs:* Turf, M.C.C. [*Died* 17 *May* 1962 (*ext.*).

FitzGERALD, Sir Arthur (Henry Brinsley), 4th Bt. *cr.* 1880; 22nd Kt. of Kerry; *b.* 6 July 1885; *s.* of Sir Maurice FitzGerald, 2nd Bt., C.V.O. and Amelia (*d.* 1947; *d.* of late H. L. Bischoffsheim; *S.* brother 1957; *m.* 1914, Mary Eleanor (*d.* 1967), *d.* of late Capt. Francis Forester; one *s.* one *d.* (and *er. s.* killed, Tunis, 1943). *Educ.:* Harrow. Irish Guards, 1914; invalided, 1916; A.D.C. to F.M. Earl of Ypres, Lord Lieut. and Governor of Ireland, 1917-1918; A.D.C. and Camp Comdt. to Gen. Sir A. Carton de Wiart, V.C., 1939-40; A.D.C. to F.M. Viscount Gort, V.C., Governor of Gibraltar, 1940-41; A.D.C. to Sir Roger Lumley, Governor of Bombay, 1941-42. Served in Merchant Navy, 1942-45. *Heir: s.* George Peter Maurice FitzGerald, M.C., Major Irish Guards, retd. [*b.* 27 Feb. 1917; *m.* 1939, Angela, *d.* of late Capt. James R. Mitchell; one *s.* one *d.*]. *Address:* 225 Almoners House, St. James' Court, Buckingham Gate, S.W.1. *T.:* Victoria 2369. *Clubs:* White's, Buck's; Royal Yacht Squadron; Royal Hibernian; United Service (Dublin). [*Died* 30 *Nov.* 1967.

FITZGERALD, Sir (Adolf) Alexander; *see* Addenda: II.

FITZGERALD, Garrett Ernest, C.M.G. 1965; *b.* 30 June 1894; *s.* of Michael Fitzgerald, Melbourne, Vic.; *m.* 1st, 1915; one *s.*; 2nd, 1931, Maude, *d.* of Eugene de Pelsenaire; one *s.* one *d.* *Educ.:* Victorian State Schs.; Melbourne Univ. Lt. 1st A.I.F., 1916; Lt.-Col. 4th Australian Div., 1942. Councillor, City of Heidelberg (Austr.), 1938-48 and 1950-52; Mayor, 1945-46. Comr., Melb. and Metrop. Bd. of Works, 1945-48. Victorian Div. Councillor, Commonwealth Inst. of Accountants, 1942-52 (State Pres., 1946-48; Australian Pres., 1951-52); Victorian Div. and Gen. Coun., Australian Soc. of Accountants, 1953-66 (Australian Pres., 1955-57; Victorian Pres., 1964-65). Member of Tribunals on salaries and allowances of Victorian State Parliament, 1954 and 1964, Federal Parliament, 1955 and 1959; Chm. Cttee. of Inquiry, Victorian Housing Commn., 1956; Gen. Councillor, Australasian Inst. of Cost Accountants, 1957-66. Lectr. in Accountancy, Univ. of Melb., 1927-47. *Publications:* (jtly.) Holding Companies in Australia and New Zealand, 1946 (5th edn. 1963); (jtly.) Form and Content of Published Financial Statements, 1947 (3rd edn. 1963). *Recreation:* gardening. *Address:* 81 Relowe Cres., Box Hill, Victoria, Australia. *T.:* 89.5928. *Clubs:* Kelvin, Royal Automobile, Melbourne Cricket (all Melbourne); Accountants (Sydney). [*Died* 5 *Oct.* 1970.

FITZGERALD, Canon Maurice Henry; *b.* 21 April 1877; *e. s.* of late Gerald A. R. FitzGerald, K.C.; *m.* 1918, Isla Margaretha Stuart, *d.* of Rev. M. C. Baynes. *Educ.:* Winchester College; New College, Oxford (Scholar), 1st cl. Cl. Mods. 1898, B.A. (2nd cl. Lit. Hum.) 1900, M.A. 1903; Bishops Hostel, Farnham, 1902. Deacon, 1902; Priest, 1903; Curate of Eastleigh, 1902-04; Domestic Chaplain to Bishop of Winchester, 1904-11; Resident Chaplain to Dean of Westminster, 1911-12; Chaplain, Wadham College, Oxford, 1912-16; Perm. to Offic. Dio. Sarum, 1916-19; Rector of Little Somerford, 1919-33; Hon. Canon of Bristol, 1930-33; Examining Chaplain to Bishop of Bristol, 1914-47; Rural Dean of Malmesbury, 1928-33; Canon Residentiary of Bristol, 1933-45; Canon Emeritus, 1945. *Publications:* A Memoir of Herbert Edward Ryle, 1928; The Story of Bristol Cathedral, 1936; editor, Poems of Robert Southey (Oxford Poets), 1909; Letters of Robert Southey, 1912; Southey's Life of Wesley, 1925;

Southey's The Doctor, etc., 1930. *Address:* Asham House, Nynehead, nr. Wellington, Somerset. *T.:* Wellington 2633.
[*Died* 17 *Feb.*. 1963

FITZGERALD, Sir (William) Raymond, Kt., *cr.* 1946; lately General Manager, Bengal Nagpur Railway, Calcutta; *b.* 1890; *s.* of late George Francis FitzGerald, F.R.S.; *m.* 1925, Catherine Geraldine, *d.* of Garrett W. Walker, K.C., of Dublin. *Address:* Rathmichael Lodge, Shankill, Co. Dublin, Ireland. [*Died* 21 *June* 1964.

FitzGIBBON, Brigadier Francis, D.S.O. 1917; Royal Artillery; *b.* Howth, Co. Dublin, 17 Aug. 1883; *s.* of late Lord Justice FitzGibbon; *m.* 1922, Penelope (*d.* 1960), *d.* of late Rev. W. B. Stillman, M.A.; one *s.* one *d.* *Educ.:* Clifton; R.M. Acad., Woolwich. Captain, 1914; Major, 1916; Lieut.-Col., 1932; Col. 1933; served European War, Nyasaland, 1914-15, France, 1916-18 (despatches 3 times, 1914-15 Star, both war medals, Croix de Guerre, D.S.O.); Iraq, 1920 (medal); Commandant, School of Artillery, India, 1934-36; Brigadier R.A. Eastern Command, India, 1936-39; retired pay, 1939; re-employed, 1939; Commandant, School of Artillery, Larkhill, Sept. 1939-Nov. 1942; on Gen. Staff, War Office, 1943-45; finally retired Sept. 1945. U.S. Legion of Merit (Officer). *Recreations:* fishing, garden. *Address:* Penneys, West Bergholt, Essex. *T.:* Fordham 296. *Club:* Army and Navy.
[*Died* 1 *May* 1964.

FITZHERBERT, Sir William, 7th Bt., *cr.* 1784; *b.* 21 Sept. 1874; *s.* of 5th Bt. and Mary Anne (*d.* 1949), *d.* of Edward Arkwright, Warwickshire; *S.* brother, 1934; *m.* 1899, Lady Nora Maitland (*d.* 1958), *d.* of 13th Earl of Lauderdale. *Educ.:* Trinity Hall, Cambridge (M.A.). Sheriff of Derbyshire, 1940. *Heir: nephew* John Richard Frederick FitzHerbert [*b.* 15 Sept. 1913; *m.* 1957, Anne (Astell), *d.* of late H. J. Rees]. *Address:* Tissington Hall, Ashbourne, Derbyshire. [*Died* 8 *Oct.* 1963.

FITZHERBERT-BROCKHOLES, John William, C.B.E. 1952; M.C. 1917; D.L.; Chairman Lancashire County Agricultural Executive Committee, 1942-60; *b.* 23 May 1889; 2nd *s.* of William Joseph Fitzherbert-Brockholes, C.B.E., and Blanche Winifred Mary, 2nd *d.* of late Major-Gen. Hon. Sir Henry Hugh Clifford, V.C., K.C.M.G., C.B.; *m.* 1917, Hon. Eileen Agnes French, *d.* of 4th Baron De Freyne; three *s.* three *d.* (and one *s.* decd.). *Educ.:* The Oratory School; New College, Oxford. Served European War, 1914-18, Duke of Lancaster's Own Yeomanry. C.C. 1937, C.A. 1953, Lancs. D.L. Lancaster, 1958. *Address:* Loft House, Claughton-on-Brock, Garstang, Lancs. *T.:* Brock 255.
[*Died* 21 *July* 1963.

FITZ-PATRICK, Horace James, C.M.G. 1967; C.B.E. 1957; retired; *b.* 4 Aug. 1894; *s.* of James and Patricia Fitz-Patrick; *m.* 1928, Maxine Marshal, San Francisco; one *s.* one *d.* *Educ.:* King Edward VI Sch., Birmingham. Joined Imperial Bank of India; retd. as Dep. Man. Governor, 1938; Dir. of Supply, British Supply Mission, New York, and a British Mem., Combined Production and Resources Bd., Washington, D.C., 1940-45; Secretary-General, Internat. Civil Aviation Conf., Bermuda, 1946; Chm., Currency and Exchange Control Bd., Bermuda, 1949-66; Currency Comr., Bermuda, 1966-. *Recreations:* tennis, golf, gardening. *Address:* Sleepy Hollow, Warwick, Bermuda. *Clubs:* Oriental, East India and Sports; Royal Bermuda Yacht. [*Died* 19 *Aug.* 1967.

FITZPATRICK, Thomas William, C.B.E. 1944 (O.B.E. 1936); D.C.M.; Lt.-Col. (retired pay). Commissioner of Police and Prisons, Eritrea, 1946-50; *m.* Maud J. Wagner (*d.* 1964); two *s.* one *d.* *Educ.:* St. Aldan's Acad., Enniscorthy, Co. Wexford. Enlisted in ranks of 18th Royal Irish Regt.; commissioned and Adjutant 2nd Bn. 1914 (despatches five times and wounded twice, D.C.M., Russian Cross of St. George, French Médaille Militaire and Croix de Guerre); Bt. Major to West Yorkshire Regt. 1919; Provost Marshal, Egypt and Palestine, 1921; retired, 1926, to Egyptian Police of Alexandria and Cairo; Commandant, Suez Canal Police, 1942 with rank of Lewa (Maj.-Gen.) and title of Pasha. Hon. Observer, Egyptian Royal Air Force. Recalled to Regular Army, 1946. Holds fourteen foreign decorations including Knight Comdr. of Order of Phoenix with Swords. *Publication:* Police Instructions, 1937. *Recreations:* golf, shooting, fishing, bridge, cross-country running. *Address:* S.C.I.O. House, Putney Heath, S.W.15. *T.:* Putney 3462. *Club:* Turf (Cairo).
[*Died* 24 *March* 1965.

FLACK, Harvey; Editor of Family Doctor since inception 1950; *b.* 26 Oct. 1912; *s.* of Isaac Flack, general practitioner and May Flack, J.P. (*née* Harris) of Radcliffe, Lancs. *Educ.:* Stand Grammar School; Owen's College, Victoria University of Manchester. M.B., Ch.B., 1934; M.D. (Commend) 1943; Ed., Manch. Univ. Med. Sch. Gazette, 1931-33; Pres. Med. Students Rep. Council, 1933-34; Ho. Surg., Manch. Roy. Infirmary, 1934-35. Sub-editor, British Medical Journal, 1935-47. Major, R.A.M.C., 1939-45; served M.E.F., 1940-45. Thomas Vicary Lectr. of Roy. Coll. Surgeons, 1947; Fellow. Soc. M.O.H.; F.R.S.H.; Member Council, Central Council of Health Educ.; Mem. Faculty of History of Worshipful Soc. of Apothecaries; Mem. Cttees. of Arthritis and Rheumatism Council; Chairman, Editorial Board, Nat. Assoc. for Mental Health; Mem. Harveian Society; Member Amer. Public Health Association; Director, Thatchmel Properties. *Publications:* A Crab was Crushed, 1937; Surgeons All, 1939, Revised 2nd Edn., 1956 (American Title: Story of Surgery); Lawson Tait, 1845-99, a Biography, 1949; Eternal Eve: a complete history of midwifery and gynæcology, 1951, Revised 2nd Edn., 1960; A Doctor's London, 1952. Numerous publications in the lay and magazine press under the pseudonym Harvey Graham. Broadcasting and TV scripts. *Recreations:* medical history and biography. *Address:* Family Doctor House, Chalton St., N.W.1. *T.:* Euston 9721. *Club:* Devonshire.
[*Died* 8 *Sept.* 1966.

FLAGSTAD, Kirsten; Singer; Director of Norwegian State Opera, since 1958; *b.* Harmar, Norway, 12 July 1895; *d.* of Michael Flagstad and Marie Nelsen; *m.* 1st, 1919, Sigurd Hall; one *d.*; 2nd, 1930, Henry Johansen (*d.* 1946). Made début in opera, 1913, at Oslo; has since given concerts and sung in opera in principal cities of Europe, Australia, and U.S. Dido and Aeneas, and Bach Cantatas, Mermaid Theatre, 1952. *Publication:* (autobiography) The Flagstad Manuscript. *Address:* Den Norske Opera, Norway. [*Died* 7 *Dec.* 1962.

FLECK, 1st Baron *cr.* 1961, of Saltcoats; **Alexander Fleck,** K.B.E. 1955; F.R.S. 1955; D.Sc. (Glas.); Chairman Imperial Chemical Industries Ltd., 1953-60 (Dep. Chm., 1951-53); Director, Midland Bank, since 1955; Chairman, International Research & Development Co. Ltd., since 1963; *b.* 11 November 1889; *o. s.* of Robert Fleck and Agnes H. Duncan; *m.* 1917, Isabel M. Kelly (*d.* 1955); no *c.* *Educ.:* Saltcoats Public School; Hillhead High School; Glasgow Univ. Glasgow Univ. staff, 1911-1913; Glasgow Radium Cttee. staff, 1913-17; Castner Kellner staff, 1917-26; Chm. Billingham Div., I.C.I., 1937-45; Director, I.C.I., 1944-51; Chm. Scottish Agric. Industries Ltd., 1947-51; Dep. Chm., African Explosives and Chem. Industries Ltd., 1953-60.

Mem. Council, Durham Colls.; Chm.: Coal Board Organisation Cttee., 1953-55; Prime Minister's Cttee. on Windscale Accident, 1957-58; Adv. Coun. on Research and Development, 1958-65; Nuclear Safety Adv. Cttee., 1960-65; Pres. Brit. Assoc. for the Advancement of Science, 1958; Pres. Soc. of Chemical Industry, 1960-62; Treas. and Vice-President, Royal Society, 1960-68; Pres., Royal Institution, 1963-. Hon. LL.D. (Glas.), 1953; Hon. D.Sc. (Dur.), 1953; Hon. D.Sc. (Oxon.), 1956; Hon. D.Sc. (London), 1957. Hon.D.Sc. (Nott.), 1955; Hon. F.R.F.P.S. (Glasgow) 1958. Hon. F.R.S.E., 1957. *Publications:* commemoration lecture (Bicentenary, Foundation of Chemical Teaching in Glasgow, 1747-1947). Hamilton Castner Memorial Lecture, 1947. Contributions to chemical journals. *Recreations:* walking, hill climbing. *Heir:* none. *Address:* Aberleven, Crathorne, Yarm, N.E. Yorkshire; 100 Roebuck House, Stag Place, Victoria, S.W.1. *T.:* Tate Gallery 3030. *Clubs:* Athenæum, Caledonian.

Died 6 *Aug.* 1968 (*ext.*).

FLEETWOOD-WALKER, Bernard, R.A. 1956 (A.R.A. 1946); R.W.S. 1945 (A.R.W.S. 1940); R.P. 1945; N.E.A.C. 1950; Portrait and Figure Painter; *b.* Birmingham, 1893; *s.* of William Walker and Electra Varley; *m.* 1st, 1920, Marjorie White (*decd.*); two *s.*; 2nd, 1939, Peggy Frazer. *Educ.:* King Edward's Grammar School, Birmingham. Studied Art in Birmingham, London, and Paris; Silver Medal Paris Salon; works purchased by many public galleries in England and abroad; Mural decoration in Chelmsford County Hall. *Recreation:* looking at things. *Address:* 13 Wallgrave Rd., S.W. 5. *T.:* Fremantle 1804. *Club:* Chelsea Arts. [*Died* 30 *Jan.* 1965.

FLEMING, Edward G.; *see* Gibson Fleming.

FLEMING, Colonel Frank, D.S.O. 1918; T.D.; D.L.; *b.* 1876; *s.* of late Sir John Fleming, LL.D., Dalmuinzie, Aberdeenshire; *m.* 1904, Muriel, *d.* of late R. C. J. Lyons, late 43rd Light Infantry; two *s.* one *d.* Served European War in France with Highland Divisional Artillery (despatches, D.S.O.). *Address:* Kippie Lodge, Milltimber, Aberdeenshire. *Club:* Royal Northern (Aberdeen).

[*Died* 3 *Sept.* 1964.

FLEMING, Ian Lancaster; writer; *b.* 28 May 1908; *s.* of late Major Valentine Fleming, M.P., D.S.O., and Evelyn Beatrice Ste. Croix Rose; *m.* 1952, Anne Geraldine (who *m.* 1945, 2nd Viscount Rothermere; marriage dissolved 1952), *widow* of 3rd Baron O'Neill and *e. d.* of Hon. Guy Charteris; one *s.* *Educ.:* Eton; Sandhurst; Munich and Geneva Universities. Reuters, 1929-33; Cull & Co., Merchant Bankers, 1933-35; Rowe & Pitman, Stockbrokers, 1935-39. Served War of 1939-45: Personal Asst. to Dir. of Naval Intelligence (Comdr. R.N.V.R. (Sp.); later Comdr. R.N.V.S.R. (Sp.)). Foreign Manager Kemsley, later Thomson, Newspapers, 1945-1959. Publisher, The Book Collector, 1949-. Order of Dannebrog, 1945. *Publications:* novels (featuring James Bond), 1953-; Thrilling Cities, 1963; The Man with the Golden Gun, 1965 (posthumous). *Relevant Publication:* The Life of Ian Fleming, by John Pearson, 1966. *Recreations:* First Editions, spear fishing, cards, golf. *Address:* 16 Victoria Square, S.W.1; Goldeneye, Oracabessa, Jamaica. *Clubs:* Turf, Boodle's, Portland.

[*Died* 12 *Aug.* 1964.

FLEMING, William Arnot, M.A., LL.B.; Hon. LL.D. Edinburgh; Advocate; *b.* 1879; *s.* of Alexander Fleming, S.S.C., Edinburgh; *m.* 1909, Mollie M'Leod, *d.* of John Adam Bryden, Edinburgh; two *s.* one *d.* *Educ.:* George Watson's College, and University, Edinburgh; University of Paris. Thow Scholar, Lorimer Scholar. Scottish Bar, 1904; Capt. 8th Bn. The Royal Scots, 1915-19; on active service in France, 1917-1918; President of the Pensions Appeal Tribunals for Scotland, 1919-24; Secretary to the University of Edinburgh, 1924-45. member of Edinburgh Univ Court, 1949-52. *Publication:* University Court Ordinances, 1925-47. *Recreation:* golf *Address:* 22 India Street, Edinburgh. *Club:* Caledonian United Service (Edinburgh)

[*Died* 20 *Dec.* 1970.

FLEMING-SANDES, Alfred James Terence, V.C. 1915; Artists' Rifles and late Lieutenant 2nd Battalion East Surrey Regt.; *b.* 24 June 1894; *m.* 1932, Dorothea May, *d.* of William Weeks, Sandown. *Educ.:* Dulwich College Preparatory School; The King's School, Canterbury. Served European War, 1914-19 (V.C. for conspicuous bravery at Hohenzollern Redoubt, Sept. 1915); appointed Education Dept., Sudan Government, 1919; Seconded Political Service, 1924; called to Bar, Gray's Inn, 1927; Province Judge, 1932; Judge of High Court, Sudan, 1935-44; Acting Chief Justice on occasions; Judge Advocate-General, Sudan Defence Force, 1942-44. Chairman, Pensions Appeal Tribunals (under Pensions Appeal Tribunals Act 1943), 1945-58. Order of the Nile, 3rd Class; Member Old Contemptibles Association and Hon. Member, The Royal Society of St. George. *Address:* Redway, Dawlish Road, Teignmouth. [*Died* 24 *May* 1961.

FLENLEY, Ralph, F.R.S.C.; Professor Emeritus of History and formerly Chairman of the Department, University of Toronto; *b.* 2 Jan. 1886; *s.* of George E. Flenley and Mary E. Caton; *m.* 1919, Dulcie Helen Potts (*d.* 1969). *Educ.:* Liverpool University; New College, Oxford. M.A. (Liverpool); B.Litt. (Oxon.); Fellow of University of Liverpool, 1908-10; Lecturer and Assistant-Professor of History, University of Manitoba, 1911-20; served European War, 1915-18, 2nd Lt., Lt., Capt. and Adj. R.F.A., B.E.F. France (despatches twice); Associate Professor in the University of Toronto, 1920-26. *Publications:* Six Town Chronicles of England, 1911; The Register of the Council of the Marches of Wales, 1562-96, 1916; A Sketch of the History of British Artillery to 1815, 1919; Samuel de Champlain, Founder of New France, 1924; Makers of Nineteenth Century Europe, 1927; Dollier de Casson, History of Montreal, trs. and ed. with a life of the author, 1928; Modern Europe and the World, 1931 and later editions; World History: the Growth of Western Civilization (in collaboration) 1935; Essays in Canadian History (editor), 1939. Modern German History, 1953, 1959. *Address:* Summerfield, Parkgate, Cheshire. *T.:* Neston 1593.

[*Died* 21 *March* 1969.

FLETCHER, Surgeon Rear-Admiral (D) Edward Ernest, C.B.E. 1937 (O.B.E. 1920); F.D.S.R.C.S., M.D.S. (Dunelm), L.D.S., R.C.S. (Eng.); retired; *b.* 6 Feb. 1886; *s.* of late W. E. Fletcher; *m.* 1909, Mabel Constance, *d.* of John French, West Mersea; one *s.* one *d.* *Educ.:* London University, Charing Cross and Royal Dental Hospitals, London. L.D.S. 1907; House Surgeon and Demonstrator, Royal Dental Hospital of London, 1907-10; Civil Dental Practice (part time), 1907-10; Civilian Dental Surgeon to Naval Forces, 1910-1914; Temp. Dental Surgeon, R.N.V.R., 1914-20; Surgeon Lieut. (D) Royal Navy 1920; Dental Assistant to Medical Director General of the Navy, 1920; Surgeon Lieut.-Comdr. (D), 1920; Surgeon Comdr. (D), 1921; Surgeon Capt. (D.), 1926; Deputy Director General for the Dental Services of the Royal Navy, 1942; Surgeon Rear-Adm. (D), 1943; Hon. Dental Surgeon to the King, 1945; retired 1946. Officer of the Legion of Honour, 1948. *Address:* 12 Priory Close, Whitchurch, Tavistock, Devon. *T.:* Tavistock 2460. [*Died* 5 *Jan.* 1968.

FLETCHER, Sir (Edward) Lionel, Kt., *cr.* 1915; C.B.E. 1921; Lt.-Col. R.M. (retd.); Commander R.N.R. (Hon.); Captain (retd.) 6th (Rifle) Batt. the King's Regiment (Liverpool); Major Home Guard, 1941; *b.* 24 May 1876; *e. surv. s.* of late Alfred Fletcher, D.L. of Allerton, and Edith, 3rd *d.* of late Captain Thomas Littledale, D.L., Highfield, West Derby; *m.* 1st, 1903, Mary (*d.* 1935), *o. d.* of late Gilbert Thompson Bates; two *d.*; 2nd, 1936, Lubov, *o. c.* of late Basil Schaposchnikoff, Moscow, and *widow* of Captain William Hicks, M.C., The King's Regt. (Liverpool). *Educ.:* Cheam; Eton. Won Silver Medal, Queen's Prize, Bisley, 1898; shot 6 times in Queen's and King's Hundred; shot 12 times for England in Internat. Rifle Matches; Vice-President of National Rifle Association; Vice-Pres.; County of Lancaster Rifle Assoc.; National Small-bore Rifle Association; late Vice-President Internationale de Tir; Hon. Game Warden, Tanzania. Officer Legion of Honour; Officer Order of Crown of Italy; Swedish Shooting Medal of Merit. *Recreations:* shooting, rifle shooting. *Address:* P.O. Box 1510, Himo, Northern Region, Tanzania, East Africa. *Club:* Arusha.
[*Died* 20 *June* 1968.

FLETCHER, Ernest Tertius Decimus, M.A., M.D. Cantab.; F.R.C.P. Lond.; Consulting Physician: Royal Free Hospital; Middlesex Hospital; Queen Mary's Hosp. for the East End and British Legion; Consultant to the Charterhouse Rheumatism Clinic; *b.* London, 26 Oct. 1891; *y. s.* of late Prof. Banister Fletcher, J.P., D.L., F.R.I.B.A.; *m.* 1st, Muriel, *d.* of Francis Laver, Herne Bay and Westgate-on-Sea; two *s.*; 2nd, 1937, Mary Louise Franks, Rectory Farm, Sellindge, Kent. *Educ.:* Wellington Coll.; Magdalene Coll., Camb.; St. Bartholomew's Hospital. Mem. Empire Rheumatism Council; Mem. Heberden Society (President, 1956-57); Consulting Editor, Postgraduate Medical Journal. F.R.Soc.Med. Brigade Machine Gun Officer, 8th Mounted Bde.; Capt., R.A.F. Medical Service; late Physician in charge of a Med. Div., E.M.S., Ministry of Health; Consulting Physician Kent C.C.; Senior House Physician, St. Bartholomew's Hospital. Heberden Lecturer and Medallist in Rheumatism, 1939; William Marsden Travelling Professor, 1953. *Publications:* Medical Disorders of the Locomotor System including the Rheumatic Diseases, 1946, 2nd edn., 1951, etc. Contrib. Jl. of Laboratory and Clinical Medicine, 1956. *Recreations:* riding golf. *Address:* 106 Berkeley Court, Baker Street, N.W.1. *T.:* Welbeck 0359. *Clubs:* Bath, Littlestone Golf (Littlestone-on-Sea).
[*Died* 16 *April* 1961.

FLETCHER, Major Sir Henry L. A., Bt.; *see* Aubrey-Fletcher.

FLETCHER, Sir Lionel; *see* Fletcher, Sir E. L.

FLEURE, Herbert John, F.R.S. 1936; F.S.A.; D.Sc.; M.A.; Hon. LL.D. (Edin. and Wales); Hon. Sc.D. (Bowdoin); Hon. Secretary Geographical Association and Hon. Editor, Geography, 1917-47; Pres. Cambrian Archæological Association, 1924; Section H British Association, 1926; Section E 1932; Association of University Teachers, 1928; Manchester Lit. and Phil. Society, 1940-44; Royal Anthropological Institute, 1945-47; Folk Lore Society, 1947-48; Geographical Association, 1948; Conf. of Corresp. Socs. of British Assoc. for Advancement of Science, 1948; Chm. National Cttee. for Geography, 1948; *b.* Guernsey, 1877; *s.* of John Fleure, Guernsey: *m.* 1910, Hilda, *d.* of late Rev. C. H. Bishop of Guernsey; one *s.* two *d.* *Educ.:* Guernsey; Univ. Coll. of Wales, Aberystwyth; Fellow Univ. of Wales, 1902-1904; Research Student, Univ. of Zürich 1903-04. Prof. of Zoology and Lecturer in Geography, Univ. Coll., Wales, 1910, Prof. of Geography and Anthropology, 1917-30; Professor of Geography, Manchester University, 1930-44; Tallman Visiting Professor, Bowdoin College, Maine, 1944-45; Visiting Professor in Egypt, 1949, 1950. Research and Gold Medals, Royal Scots. Geog. Soc.; Charles P. Daly Medal, American Geog. Soc.; Huxley Medal, Roy. Anthr. Inst.; Victoria Medal, Roy. Geogr. Soc.; J. G. Frazer Memorial Lecturer (Oxford), 1947. Hon. Member Institut d'Egypte. Hon. Corresponding Member: Italian Anthropological Soc., Hungarian Geographical Soc., Société Jersiaise; Hon. Consultative Ed. American Geographical Soc.; Hon. Fell. Royal Geographical Soc.; Commandeur de l'ordre de Leopold (Belgium). *Publications:* Human Geography in W. Europe, 1918; Peoples of Europe, 1922; Races of England and Wales, 1923; The Races of Man, 1927; (with H. J. Peake) The Corridors of Time, 1927 onwards; French Life and its Problems, 1942; A Natural History of Man in Britain, 1951, 2nd edn. 1959; papers in scientific journals. *Address:* Corner House, West Drive, Cheam, Surrey. *T.:* 01-642 8873.
[*Died* 1 *July* 1969.

FLEW, Rev. Robert Newton, D.D. (Oxon); Hon. D.D. (Aberdeen); Principal and Tutor in Systematic and Pastoral Theology, Wesley House, Cambridge, 1937-55, retd.; *b.* Holsworthy, Devon, 25 May 1886; *e. s.* of Rev. Dr. J. Flew, Wesleyan Minister; *m.* 1921, Winifred, *d.* of B. S. Garrard, Luton; one *s.* *Educ.:* Christ's Hospital; Merton College, Oxford (Postmaster); Universities of Marburg and Fribourg. 1st Classes in Classical Moderations, and Honour School of Theology, Oxford; 2nd Class Lit. Hum.; Senior Hall Greek Testament, Senior Septuagint, and Ellerton Theological Essay Prizes; Senior Denyer and Johnson Scholar, 1915; Assistant Tutor at Handsworth College, 1910-13; Minister successively at Winchmore Hill, Clapham, and Muswell Hill, for eleven years; Temp. Chaplain to the Forces in Mesopotamia and Persia, 1918-20; Acting Professor of N.T. Studies, United Theological College, Bangalore, S. India, 1920-21; Greenhalgh Chair of New Testament Language and Lit., Wesley House, Cambridge, 1927-37; Delegate of Methodist Church to Oxford and Edinburgh World Confs., 1937; Assembly of World Council of Churches, Amsterdam, 1948; World Conf. of Faith and Order (Vice-Chm.), Lund, 1952; Chm. of Internat. Theological Commn. on The Church, 1938-52; Fernley-Hartley Lecturer, 1938; Select Preacher, Univ. of Cambridge 1942, 1951; Hulsean Preacher, 1956; Moderator of Free Church Federal Council of England and Wales, 1945-46; President Methodist Conference, 1946-47. Shaffer Lecturer, Yale University, 1947; Cato Lecturer, Gen. Conf. Methodist Church o Australasia, 1948; Louisa Curtis Lecturer, Spurgeon's Coll., London, 1950. *Publications:* The Teaching of the Apostles, 1915; The Forgiveness of Sins, 1916; Editor (with W. R. Maltby), The Manuals of Fellowship, 1917-29; The Idea of Perfection in Christian Theology, 1934; Jesus and His Church, 1938; The Hymns of Charles Wesley, 1953. Editor (with R. E. Davies), The Catholicity of Protestantism, 1950; Editor: The Church, 1951; The Nature of the Church, 1952. *Recreation:* travelling. *Address:* 49 Glisson Rd., Cambridge. *Clubs:* Athenæum, Royal Commonwealth Society.
[*Died* 10 *Sept.* 1962.

FLINT, Sir William Russell, Kt., *cr.* 1947; R.A 1933 (A.R.A. 1924); President of Royal Society of Painters in Water-Colours, 1936-56; Senior Academician Royal Academy, 1956 (formerly Trustee of Royal Academy); *b.* Edinburgh, 4 April 1880; *e. s.*

of late Francis Wighton Flint, artist; *m.* 1905, Sibylle (*d.* 1960), 3rd *d.* of late Fleet Paymaster J. T. Sueter, R.N.; one *s.* *Educ.:* Daniel Stewart's Coll. and Roy. Institution School of Art Edinburgh. Came to London, 1900; on staff of Illustrated London News, 1903-07. R.W.S. 1917 (A.R.W.S. 1914); R.E. 1933 (Hon. Retired Fellow); Member of Royal Scottish Water-Colour Society and numerous other artistic bodies; Silver Medallist, Paris Salon, 1913; regular exhibitor at R.A., R.W.S., and other principal art exhibitions; Retrospective Exhibition, Diploma Gallery, Royal Academy, 1962; represented by works in the British and Victoria and Albert Museums, Fitzwilliam Museum Cambridge, and in more than fifty permanent collections in Great Britain, Canada, U.S.A., Australia, etc.; Hon. Treasurer, Imperial Arts League, 1932-36, Member of Council of the National Trust, 1942-44; Vice-President of the Artists' General Benevolent Institution; administered, with two others, Pilgrim Trust Recording Britain Scheme, 1940-44. Received thanks of Chancellor of the Exchequer, 1946, for aiding Dollar Exchange by sending his works to U.S.A. Served as Lieut R.N.V.R.; with Airship Section, R.N.A.S., 1916-18; as Captain, Royal Air Force, was Admiralty Overseer on H.M. Airship R. 34, later the first aircraft to fly the Atlantic, 1918-19. *Publications:* Drawings, 1950; Models of Propriety, 1951; Herrick, 1955; Minxes Admonished, 1956; Shadows in Arcady, 1965; The Lisping Goddess, 1967; Breakfast in Périgord, 1968; Autobiography, 1970 (posthumous). Illustrations for Riccardi Press limited editions of Malory, Chaucer, Homer, Theocritus, etc.; articles in volumes of the Old Water-Colour Society's Club. *Recreations:* typography, painting out of doors. *Address:* Peel Cottage, 80 Peel Street, W.8. *T.:* 01-727 6561. *Club:* Arts. [*Died* 27 *Dec.* 1969.

FLOREY, Baron *cr.* 1965 (Life Peer); **Howard Walter Florey,** O.M. 1965; Kt. 1944; F.R.S. 1941; F.R.C.P. 1951; M.D., M.A., B.Sc., Ph.D.; Provost of the Queen's College, Oxford, since 1962; Chancellor of the Australian National University since 1965; Professor of Pathology, Oxford Univ., 1935-62; Pres. of the Royal Society, 1960-1965; Fellow of Lincoln College, Oxford (Hon. Fellow, 1962); Hon. Fellow of Gonville and Caius College, Cambridge, and of Magdalen College, Oxford; *s.* of Joseph Florey; *b.* Adelaide, 24 September 1898; *m.* 1st, 1926, Mary Ethel Reed (*d.* 1966); one *s.* one *d.*; 2nd, 1967, Mrs. Margaret Jennings, *d.* of 3rd Baron Cottesloe. *Educ.:* St. Peter's Collegiate School, Adelaide; Adelaide University (M.B., B.S.); Magdalen College, Oxford (M.A., B.Sc.); Ph.D. Cambridge 1927; M.D. Adelaide, 1944). Hon. F.R.A.C.P., 1944; Hon. D.Sc.: Sheffield, 1947, Birmingham, 1949; Nottingham, 1961, London, 1961, Hull, 1963; Wales, 1964; Hon. Sc.D.: Cambridge, 1962; and foreign universities; Hon. LL.D.: Edin.; Glasgow. Rhodes scholarship for S. Australia, 1921; John Lucas Walker Student, Cambridge, 1924; Rockefeller Travelling Fellow in America, 1925; Freedom Research Fell., London Hosp., 1926; Fell. Gonville and Caius Coll., Cambridge, 1926, Hon. Fellow, 1946; Huddersfield Lecturer in Special Pathology, Cambridge, 1927; Joseph Hunter, Professor of Pathology, Univ. of Sheffield, 1931-35; Nuffield Visiting Professor to Australia and New Zealand, 1944. Charles Mickle Fellowship 1944, Univ. of Toronto; Cameron Prize 1945. Univ. of Edinburgh; Lister Medal 1945, Royal College of Surgeons of England; Berzelius Medal in Silver 1945, Swedish Medical Society; Share of Nobel Prize for Medicine, 1945, and of R. L. St. J. Harmsworth Memorial Award, 1946; Albert Gold Medal, Royal Society of Arts, 1946; Medal in Therapeutics, 1946; Worshipful Society of Apothecaries of London: R.S.M. Gold Medal, 1947; U.S.A. Medal of Merit, 1948; Addingham Gold Medal, 1951; Royal Medal, Royal Society, 1951; Copley Medal, Royal Society, 1957; B.M.A. Gold Medal, 1964; Lomonossov Medal, U.S.S.R. Academy of Sciences, 1965 (For. Mem., 1966). Hon. Fellow: R.S.M., 1954; R.C.S. 1961; R.C.O.G., 1963; For. Mem. Amer. Philosophical Soc., 1963; For. Associate, Nat. Acad. of Sciences, U.S.A., 1963; For. Hon. Mem., American Acad. of Arts and Sciences, 1964; For., Hon. or Corresp. Member many foreign Med. Socs., etc. Comdr. Legion of Honour, 1946. Trustee: British Museum, 1967-; Wolfson College, Oxford, 1967-. *Publications:* Contributions to Scientific journals on Physiological and Pathological subjects; Antibiotics, Florey et al., 1949; (ed. and contrib. to) General Pathology (3rd ed.), 1962. *Address:* The Queen's College, Oxford. *Club:* Athenæum. [*Died* 21 *Feb.* 1968.

FLOUD, Bernard Francis Castle; M.P. (Lab.) Acton since 1964; *b.* 22 March 1915; *yr. s.* of late Sir Francis Floud, K.C.B., K.C.S.I., K.C.M.G.; *m.* 1938, Ailsa Craig (*d.* 1967), 2nd *d.* of late Granville Craig; one *s.* two *d.* *Educ.:* Gresham's Sch., Holt; Wadham Coll., Oxf. War Service in Intelligence Corps., 1939-42; Ministry of Information. 1942-45; Board of Trade, latterly as Assistant Secretary, 1945-51. Farming, 1951-55. Executive of Granada Television Ltd., 1955-. Parish Councillor, Kelvedon Hatch, Essex, 1952-61; Councillor, Ongar R.D.C., 1952-1955. Contested (Lab.): Chelmsford, 1955; Hemel Hempstead, 1959. *Address:* 89 Albert Street, N.W.1. *T.:* 01-387 6389. [*Died* 10 *Oct.* 1967.

FLOUD, Sir Francis (Lewis Castle), K.C.B., *cr.* 1921 (C.B. 1918); K.C.S.I. *cr.* 1941; K.C.M.G., *cr.* 1938; D.C.L., Bishops Univ., Canada; J.P. Oxon; *b.* 18 May 1875; *e. s.* of late Rev. H. Castle Floud; *m.* 1909, Phyllis, *d.* of Col Everard A. Ford, Hampstead; one *s.* one *d.* (and one *s.* decd.). *Educ.:* Cranleigh School; King's Coll., London; Barrister, Lincoln's Inn. Hon. Mem. of the Royal Agricultural Society and of the Royal Institution of Chartered Surveyors; Chairman of Governors of Cranleigh School, 1941-57; Pres. of Old Cranleigheian Society; entered Board of Agriculture, 1894; Private Secretary to Sir Thomas Elliott (1904-1905), and to Mr. Ailwyn Fellowes (Lord Ailwyn) (1905), and Lord Carrington (Marquess of Lincolnshire) (1906-1907), as Presidents of the Board of Agriculture; Head of Land Branch, Board of Agriculture, 1907-14; Asst. Secretary, 1914-19; Permanent Secretary, Ministry of Agriculture and Fisheries, 1920-27; Chairman of Board of Customs and Excise, 1927-30; Permanent Secretary, Ministry of Labour, 1930-34; High Commissioner in Canada for U.K., 1934-1938; Chairman: Bengal Land Revenue Commission, 1938-40; Appeal Tribunal for Conscientious Objectors, 1940-46; Road Haulage Central Wages Board, 1941-47; L.C.C. Staff Arbitration Tribunal; Member Nat. Arbitration Tribunal, 1941-51; Chairman Agricultural Wages Board, 1943-47; Governor New England Co. *Publication:* The Ministry of Agriculture and Fisheries, 1927. *Address:* 13 Brunswick Square, Hove, Sussex. *T.:* Hove 772407. *Club:* Athenæum. [*Died* 17 *April* 1965.

FLOWER, Sir Cyril (Thomas), Kt., *cr.* 1946; C.B. 1939; M.A., F.B.A., F.S.A., F.R.Hist.S.; a Historical MSS. Commissioner, 1938-60; Vice-President, Canterbury and York Society; Pipe Roll Society; Selden Soc.; *b.* 31 March 1879; *s.* of Thomas Flower, M.R.C.S.E., Warminster, Wilts, and of Jessie, *d.* of William Pope, Biggleswade, Beds; *m.* 1910, Helen Mary Harding, *d.* of David Thompson, Inspector of Schools, Punjab; one *d.* *Educ.:* Warminster Grammar School; St. Edward's School, Oxford (Scholar); Worcester College, Oxford (Scholar). First Class, Classical Moderations, 1899; Second Class, Lit. Hum. 1901; entered Public Record Office, 1903; played regularly in Middlesex Rugby Union F.C. 1904-06; Hon. Secretary, Canterbury and York Society, 1909-14; Serjeant, Special Constabulary, Bow Street, Aug.-Nov. 1914; Private Secretary to Director of Army Contracts, War Office, 1914-15; 2nd Lieut. R.G.A. 1915; seriously wounded, France, 1916; Lieut. R.G.A. 1917; Private Secretary to Director of Army Contracts, War Office and Ministry of Munitions until demobilization, 1919; Croix de Guerre (avec palme), 1919; Member of Council Society of Antiquaries, 1928-30, 1940-43, Exec. Comm. 1931-35; Vice-President, 1940-44; Secretary of the Public Record Office, 1926-1938; Deputy Keeper of the Public Records, 1938-47; Acting Director of Institute of Historical Research, 1939-44. Silver Jubilee and Coronation Medals. *Publications:* Public Works in Mediæval Law, two vols. for Selden Society; Introduction to the Curia Regis Rolls, for Selden Society; Register of Simon de Gandavo, Bishop of Salisbury, (with M. C. B. Dawes), two vols. for Canterbury and York Society; Curia Regis Rolls of the reign of King John, seven vols.; Henry III, six vols.; Analytical Index of the Acts and Ordinances of the Commonwealth; Articles and reviews on mediæval history. *Address:* 2 Lammas Park Gardens, Ealing, W.5. *T.:* Ealing 4267. [*Died* 10 *Aug.* 1961.

FLOWER, Lt.-Col. Sir Fordham, Kt., *cr.* 1956; O.B.E. 1945; D.L.; Chairman: Executive Council of Royal Shakespeare Theatre, since 1944; Trustees and Guardians of Shakespeare's Birthplace, since 1946; Flower & Sons Ltd., since 1953; Flowers Breweries Ltd., since 1958; *b.* 15 February 1904; *m.* 1934, Hersey Caroline Balfour; two *s.* two *d.* *Educ.:* Winchester; R.M.C., Sandhurst. Commissioned 9th Queen's Royal Lancers, 1924; served in Egypt, Palestine and India, 1924-32; served War of 1939-45 (despatches thrice, O.B.E.), Middle East and N.W. Europe; Major 1940; Lt.-Col. 1944. Governor, Shakespeare Memorial Theatre, 1926; Trustee, Shakespeare's Birthplace, 1940; Director of: Flower & Sons Ltd., 1934; Whitbread & Co. Ltd., 1962. D.L, Warwickshire, 1952. Officer, Order of Orange-Nassau (with Swords), 1945. *Recreations:* ski-ing and travelling. *Address:* The Hill, Stratford-on-Avon. *T.:* Stratford-on-Avon 2434. *Club:* Cavalry. [*Died* 9 *July* 1966.

FLOWER, Sir (Walter) Newman, Kt., *cr.* 1938; President of Cassell & Company, Ltd.; *b.* Fontmell Magna, Dorset, 8 July 1879; *e. s.* of John Walter Flower; *m.* 1st, 1903, Evelyne, *e. d.* of Thomas Readwin of Wells, Norfolk; one *s.*; 2nd, 1943, Bridget, *d.* of James Downes, Coore, Co Clare. *Educ.:* Whitgift. Joined Cassells, 1906; purchased Cassells, 1927. *Publications:* George Frideric Handel, 1923, new and revised edition, 1959; Sir Arthur Sullivan, his Life and Letters (with Herbert Sullivan), 1927; Franz Schubert, 1928, new and revised Ed. 1949; Through My Garden Gate, 1945; Just as it Happened, 1950 *Recreation:* animals. *Address:* Tarrant Keynston House, nr. Blandford, Dorset. *T.:* Blandford 507. *Club:* Devonshire. [*Died* 12 *March* 1964.

FLOYD, Brigadier Sir Henry Robert Kincaid, 5th Bt., *cr.* 1816; C.B. 1945; C.B.E. 1944; D.L.; Member of H.M.'s Body Guard, Hon. Corps of Gentlemen-at-Arms; Lieutenant since 1966; (Standard Bearer, 1963-66); Lord Lieut. of Bucks. since 1961; Joint Master South Oxfordshire Foxhounds, 1957-61; *b.* 7 May 1899; *s.* of Capt. Sir Henry Floyd, 4th Bt. and Edith Anne (*d.* 1955), *y. d.* of Major John Kincaid-Smith, of Polmont House, N.B.; *S.* father, 1915; *m.* 1929, Kathleen, *er. d.* of 1st Baron Gretton, P.C., C.B.E.; two *d.* Served France and Flanders, 1918; Adjt. 15/19 Hussars, 1921-25; A.D.C. to The High Commissioner for Egypt and the Sudan, 1925-26; Equerry to the Duke of Gloucester, 1927. Served in France with 15/19 The King's Royal Hussars, 1940. B.G.S. 8th Corps Normandy, 1944; Chief of Staff, 8th Army, Italy, Oct. 1944-July 1945; Acting Maj.-Gen. 1945; Brigadier, Regular Army Reserve of Officers. Chairman, Royal National Orthopædic Hospital; Executive Cttee., Royal Armoured Corps War Memorial Benevolent Fund; Col. 15/19 The King's Royal Hussars, 1947-57. D.L. Bucks. 1959. Officer, Legion of Merit (America). K.St.J. *Heir:* *b.* John Duckett Floyd [*b.* 1 Nov. 1903; *m.* 1929, Jocelin Evadne Wyldbore, *er. d.* of late Sir Edmund Wyldbore-Smith; two *s.* (and *e. s.* decd.)]. *Address:* Chearsley Hill House, Chearsley, nr. Aylesbury, Bucks. *T.:* Long Crendon 241. *Club:* Cavalry. [*Died* 5 *Nov.* 1968.

FLYNN, Theodore Thomson, M.B.E. 1945; D.Sc.; F.L.S., F.Z.S., M.R.I.A.; Professor of Zoology, Belfast University, 1931-48 (Emeritus Prof., 1948); *b.* Coraki, N.S.W.; *m.* 1908, Marelle (*d.* 1966), 2nd *d.* of late Capt. Young, M.M.; one *d.* (one *s.* decd.) *Educ.:* Training College for Teachers, N.S.W.; University of Sydney. Graduated B.Sc. (Honours) 1906; (University medal for Biology), John Coutts Research Scholarship; D.Sc 1921 (University Medal); Science Master, Newcastle and W Maitland High Schools, 1906; Lecturer in Chemistry and Physics, Newcastle and W Maitland Technical Colleges, 1907; Lecturer, Biology, Univ. of Tasmania, 1909; Ralston Professor of Biology, Univ. of Tasmania, 1911-31; Macleay Research Fellow Linnean Society, N.S.W., 1911; Rockefeller Fellow, 1930-31. Was in charge of the Summer Cruise, Australian Antarctic Expedition, 1912; sole Royal Commissioner, Tasmanian Fisheries, 1915. Chief Casualty Officer (Civil Defence), Belfast, 1940-45. Hon. Fell. Int. Inst. Embr., Utrecht. J.P. (Portland) 1950. Attorney, Errol Flynn's Estates, Jamaica. *Publications:* various papers on Marsupial Embryology and Structure. Tasmanian Fisheries, etc. *Recreations:* gardening, golf. [*Died* 23 *Oct.* 1968.

FLYNN, Rt. Rev. Thomas Edward, Ph.D., M.A.; Bishop of Lancaster (R.C.), since 1939; *b.* Portsmouth, 1880; *e. s.* of Thomas Flynn, Liverpool, and Elizabeth Ann, *d.* of John Swift. *Educ.:* St. Edward's College, Liverpool; Upholland College; Downing College, Cambridge, Nat. Sci. Tripos; Fribourg. Ordained, 1908; Assistant Master, St. Edward's College, 1912-16; St. Edmund's College, Ware, 1917-24; Headmaster, Upholland College, 1924-1928; Professor of Philosophy, 1924-32; Rector of St. Mary's, Chorley, 1932-39; Canon of Liverpool Metropolitan Chapter, 1938; Editor of Clergy Review, 1931-39; Extern Examiner in Philosophy to National University of Ireland, 1930-33. Assistant at the Pontifical Throne, 1958. Order of Francesco di Miranda (Venezuela). *Publications:* The Supernatural Virtues; contributor to the Catholic Encyclopædic Dictionary, pamphlets and articles. *Address:* Bishop's House, Cannon Hill, Lancaster. *T.:* 2231. [*Died* 4 *Nov.* 1961.

FOGARTY, Sir Reginald Francis Graham, Kt. 1966; C.B.E. 1959; Chm. and Man. Dir., Carlton and United Breweries Ltd.; *b.* Normanton, Qld., 24 Nov. 1892; *s.* of James Richard Fogarty; *m.* 1915, Viola, *d.* of late C. W. Brookes; one *s.* two *d.* Served European War, 1914-18 (Lt., Artillery, 1st A.I.F.). Formerly Mercantile Broker and

Manufacturer's Rep., Brisbane and Townsville. Chairman: N. Aust. Breweries Ltd.; Vict. Assoc. Brewers; Aust. Assoc. Brewers; Manufacturers' Bottle Co. of Vic. Pty. Ltd.; Director: James Hood & Co. Pty. Ltd.; Barnes Engineering Pty. Ltd. Founder and First Pres., Cairns Legacy Club; Life Mem., Returned Servicemen's League. *Address:* 66 Clendon Road, Toorak, Vic., Aust. *Clubs:* Athenæum, Naval and Military, Vic. Racing, Vic. Amateur Turf, Melb. Racing (all Melbourne). [*Died* 27 *Feb.* 1967.

FOGGIN, Lancelot Middleton, O.B.E. 1923; M.A. Oxon; *b.* 1876; *e. s.* of late William Foggin, of Northallerton, Yorks; *m.* 1st, Dorothy Aspin (*d.* 1908), *d.* of late James Aspin Heaton, of Pinner, Middlesex; 2nd Margaret Helen (*d.* 1932), *d.* of late Dr. Alfred Kebbell, of Flaxton, Yorks; one *s.* *Educ.:* Bradford Grammar School (Governors' Scholar) Magdalen College, Oxford (Exhibitioner). 2nd Class Hons., Mathematical Moderations, 1897; 2nd Class Hons., Final School of Modern History, 1899; Master at Bridlington School Yorks, 1900-3; served under Crown Colony Government of Transvaal Colony in Education Dept., 1903-7; Inspector of Schools, Southern Rhodesia, 1907-15; acting Director of Education, Southern Rhodesia, July 1915; Director of Education, Southern Rhodesia, 1917-Apr. 1936; Retired 1936; Delegate representing Southern Rhodesia at Imperial Education Conference, London, 1927; King's Silver Jubilee Medal, 1935. *Publications:* Stories from South African History, 9th edition, 1911, The Civic Reader for South Africa, 1912; article on Rhodesia in Oxford Survey of British Empire, 1913. *Address:* Rhodesville, Box 530, Salisbury, Rhodesia. *Club:* Salisbury (Rhodesia). [*Died* 6 *Sept.* 1968.

FOLEY, Sir (Ernest) Julian, Kt., *cr.* 1936; C.B. 1919; *b.* Liverpool, 19 Oct. 1881; *s.* of John George Foley, Liverpool; unmarried. *Educ.:* Liverpool Coll.; London and Liverpool Universities. Class 1 Clerk, Transport Department Admiralty, after open competition, 1907; Assistant Director of Transports, 1915; Director of Military Sea Transport, Admiralty and Ministry of Shipping, 1917; Principal Assist. Under-Secretary, Department of Mines, 1920 1927; Director of Sea Transport, Board of Trade, 1927-29; Under-Secretary in charge of Mercantile Marine Department Board of Trade, 1929-39; Secretary, Ministry of Shipping, 1939-1942; Liaison Officer, Ministry of Supply (Raw Materials), with East African Governor's Conference, 1943; Representative of Ministry of Supply (Raw Materials) in India, 1945; Leather Controller at Board of Trade, 1947-50, Pres. Institute of Marine Engineers, 1938-39 Chevalier, Ordre de la Couronne (Belgium); St. Anne of Russia (2nd class); Officer of the Legion of Honour; Order of the Crown of Italy; Liberty Medal, Denmark. *Publication:* Manual of Psychology. *Recreations:* golf, fencing, walking. *Clubs:* Union, Anchorites; Bengal (Calcutta); Nairobi (Nairobi). [*Died* 18 *Nov.* 1966.

FOLEY, Guy Francis, C.M.G. 1947; O.B.E. 1941; M.C. 1916; *b.* Fordingbridge, Hants, 27 Oct. 1896; *s.* of late Capt. Reginald Edward Foley, 45th Sikhs, I.A.; *m.* 1928, Helen Frances, 2nd *d.* of late Maj. S. C. Ferguson, O.B.E., Brockenhurst, Hants; no *c.* *Educ.:* Elstree School; Wellington College; R.M.A., Woolwich. R.A., 1915-30; served European War, 1915-18, France and Belgium (wounded); India, 1919-20; Egypt and Sudan (with Egyptian Army and Sudan Defence Force), 1920-30; Sudan Civil Service, 1930-46; Director of Stores and Ordnance, Controller General of War Supply, Director of Economics and Trade, Sudan Govt., 1930-46; Bursar, Wellington College, Berks, 1946-57; retired from Army, 1930, with permanent rank of Major. *Address:* Gatehouse, Queen Camel, Yeovil, Somerset. *Club:* United Service. [*Died* 13 *Oct.* 1970.

FOLEY, Sir Julian; *see* Foley, Sir E. J.

FOLEY-PHILIPPS, Sir Richard Foley, 4th Bt. *cr.* 1887; *b.* 24 Aug. 1920; *s.* of late Captain George William Fisher Foley-Philipps (2nd *s.* of 1st Bt.); *S.* cousin (Sir John Erasmus Gwynne Alexander Philipps), 1948. *Educ.:* Freiburg University, Germany. *Heir:* none. [*Died* 4 *Nov.* 1962 (*ext.*).

FOLIGNO, Cesare, M.A.; *b.* Giussano, 1878; *m.* 1st, 1905, Carolina Ponssen (*d.* 1912); 2nd, 1920, Grace Isabel Moore; one *d.* *Educ.:* Accademia Scientifico-Letteraria Milan, Dottore di belle lettere. Came to England to survey Venetian and Italian MSS. 1903; worked in British Museum, 1905-9; elected corresponding member of the R. Deputazione Veneta di Storia Patria, 1908; Taylorian Lecturer in Italian at Oxford, 1909-15; served European War, Isonzo-Piave, 1915-19; Serena Prof. of Italian at Oxford, 1919-1940; Prof. of English, Univ. of Naples, 1940-53, Emeritus Prof. 1954; Ex-Fellow of Magdalen Coll., Oxford. *Publications:* An Italian version and recension of K. Federn's Dante, 1903; La Guerra d'Attila di N. Da Casola (with Prof. G. Bertoni), 1906; Epistole di Lovato de'Lovati e di altri a lui, 1909; Italian Travellers in England and the Beginning of English Literary Influence in Italy during the Eighteenth Century, an Inaugural lecture, 1910; The Story of Padua (Mediæval Towns Series), 1910; Epochs of Italian Literature, 1920; Dante, 1921; Dante: the Poet (British Academy annual Italian Lecture, 1921); The transmission of the Legacy (Legacy of Rome), 1923; Un Poema d'imitazione dantesca sul Savonarola, 1926; Dante, 1928; Latin Thought during the Middle Ages, 1929; Note su Foscolo critico, 1945; transl. Kaputt, by C. Malaparte, 1946; revised and completed transl. of Chaucer's Canterbury Tales, 1946; ed. Vol. X of Foscolo's Opere, 1952, Vol. XI, 1958; contributed translation of seven plays to: Teatro Inglese, 3 vols., 1961 (Milan); odd articles. *Address:* Via A. d'Isernia 31, Naples. [*Died* 8 *Nov.* 1963.

FOLKARD, Charles James; Artist and Author; *b.* 1878; *m.*; one *s.* two *d.* *Educ.:* Colfe's School, Lewisham. Joined Daily Mail Staff as artist; left to become a book illustrator: asked to contribute to Daily Mail, and invented Teddy Tail, 1915. *Publications:* Illustrated: Flint Heart, 1910; Swiss Family Robinson, 1910; Pinocchio, 1911; Grimm's Fairy Tales, 1911; Æsop's Fables, 1912; Arabian Nights, 1913; Jackdaw of Rheims, 1913; Ottoman Wonder Tales, 1915; Mother Goose Nursery Rhymes, 1919; British Fairy and Folk Tales, 1920; Songs from Alice in Wonderland, 1921; Magic Egg, 1922; Granny's Wonderful Chair, 1925; The Troubles of a Gnome, 1928; Land of Nursery Rhyme, 1932; Tales of the Taunus Mountains, 1937; The Princess and the Goblin, 1949; The Princess and Curdie, 1949; The Book of Nonsense, 1956; author of Teddy Tail, a fantastic children's play, produced in London, 1920. *Recreation:* sketching. *Address:* Gowans, Sandy Cross, Heathfield, Sussex. [*Died* 25 *Feb.* 1963.

FOLLEY, Prof. Sydney John, F.R.S. 1951; D.Sc., Ph.D.; Head of Physiology Department, National Institute for Research in Dairying, Shinfield, Berks, since 1945; Research Professor, University of Reading, since 1964; *b.* Swindon, Wilts., 14 Jan. 1906; *s.* of late Thomas John Folley; *m.* 1st, 1935, Madeline, *e. d.* of late Francis James Kerr, barrister-at-law, Altrincham, Cheshire (marriage dissolved, 1947); 2nd, 1947, Mary Lee Muntz, 3rd *d.* of late Canon William Lee Harnett, Wolverton. *Educ.:* Swindon and North Wilts Secondary School; Victoria Univ., Manchester. Mercer Schol. in Chemistry, Univ. of Manc., 1927, Ph.D.

(Manc.) 1931, D.Sc. (Manc.), 1940. Research Asst. to Prof. of Physiology, Manchester Univ., 1929-31. Asst. Lectr. in Biochemistry, Univ. of Liverpool, 1931; staff of National Institute for Research in Dairying since 1932. In charge of biochem. teaching, Roy. Vet Coll., 1943-45. Rockefeller Foundation Research Fellow, Dept. of Anatomy, Yale University, U.S.A., 1938-39; Cantor Lecturer, Royal Society of Arts, 1946; Chairman: Soc. for Endocrinology, 1951-56; A.R.C. Technical Cttee. on Endocrinology, 1952-56; Editorial Bd., Jl. of Endocrinology, 1959-. Member, various committees of Agricultural and Medical Research Councils, 1940-. Corr. Mem. Société de Biologie, Paris, 1955; Professeur à titre étranger Collège de France, 1953. Hon. Dr. Vet. Med., Ghent, 1964. Dale Medal, Soc. for Endocrinology, 1969. *Publications:* Research papers and review articles in various scientific journals, mainly on the physiology and biochemistry of lactation and reproduction. Recherches récentes sur la physiologie et la biochimie de la sécrétion lactée, 1954; The physiology and biochemistry of lactation, 1956. *Recreations:* interests: modern art and classical music. *Address:* 78 Shinfield Road, Reading, Berks. *T.:* Reading 81451.
[*Died* 29 *June* 1970.

FOOT, Arthur Edward, C.B.E. 1948; M.A.; Headmaster, Ottershaw School, 1948-1964, retd.; *b.* 21 June 1901; *s.* of William Henry Foot and Harriet Pearson; *m.* 1935, Sylvia Hartill; one *s.* one *d.* *Educ.:* Winchester; Trin. Coll., Cambridge. Asst. Master, Eton Coll., 1923-34; Headmaster, The Doon School, Dehra Dun, India, 1935-48. Sec., Science Masters' Assoc., 1932-34; Chm. Indian Public Schools Conf., 1943-44. District Gov. Rotary International, 1943-44; Member Commander-in-Chief's Indian Nat. War Academy Cttee., 1945-46. Pres., Surrey County Teachers' Assoc., 1955-56. Has broadcast in India on educational topics, 1936-45. Boy Scouts Assoc., Medal of Merit, 1934; Kaisar-i-Hind Gold Medal, 1946. *Publications:* School Certificate Chemistry, 1930; articles in Spectator. *Recreations:* cricket, tennis, mountaineering. *Address:* Pitter Cottage, Crawley, Winchester, Hants. *T.:* Sparsholt 450. [*Died* 26 *Sept.* 1968.

FOOT, Stephen Henry, D.S.O. 1918; *b.* 1887; *s.* of William Henry Foot. *Educ.:* Eastbourne College; Emmanuel College, Cambridge, M.A. Formerly Capt. and Brevet Major, R.E. (Reserve); served European War, 1914-18 (despatches twice, D.S.O.); Bursar and Housemaster, Eastbourne College, 1920-34; Member Chichester Diocesan Finance Committee; Chm. Sussex Church-Builders Finance Committee, 1930-34; travelled with Moral Re-Armament in Canada, Denmark, Norway, Switzerland, France, and Holland, 1935-39; U.S.A., 1946; Kenya, Uganda, West Africa, Northern Rhodesia, Southern Rhodesia, Nyasaland and South Africa, 1948-58. *Publications:* Tank Tales, 1919; A Housemaster and his Boys, 1928; Three Lives (an autobiography), 1934; Life Began Yesterday, 1935 (Translations in French, German, Swedish, Dutch, Danish, Japanese, Italian, Yugo-Slavian, Bulgarian, Braille); Three Lives and Now, 1937 (also in Dutch); Wisdom from the Desert, Wisdom from the Sea, 1943; Life Begins Today, 1951; Choice for a Continent, 1954; African Tale, 1955 (later filmed); articles in Times, Daily Telegraph, Nineteenth Century, Journal of Education, Journal of Careers. *Address:* 4 Hays Mews, Berkeley Square, W.1; Box 10144, Johannesburg. *Clubs:* Authors', English-Speaking Union; Civil Service (Capetown). [*Died* 24 *June* 1966.

FORBER, Lady; Janet Elizabeth, M.D., D.Sc. (London); J.P.; now retired; formerly engaged in medical research for the Ministry of Health; late Dean of the Household and Social Science Department, King's College for Women, W.8 (now Queen Elizabeth Coll.), *b* 1877; *d.* of late William Ward Lane-Claypon of Boston, Lincolnshire; *m.* 1929, Sir Edward Rodolph Forber, K.C.B., C.B.E. (*d.* 1960). *Educ.:* Home; London (R.F.H.) School of Medicine for Women; University College, London; University Scholar and Gold Medallist, 1902; B.M.A. Research Scholar, 1902-3; also other research scholarships and medical appointments; Lecturer in Physiology and Hygiene, Battersea Polytechnic, 1910-12; same at King's College for Women, 1912; Assistant Medical Inspector L.G.B., 1912-16. *Publications:* Milk and its Hygienic Relations; The Child Welfare Movement; Hygiene of Women and Children; various pamphlets on original research; articles in Nineteenth Century; reports to Ministry of Health etc. *Address:* 1 Lloyds Bank Chambers, Dane Rd., Seaford, Sussex.
[*Died* 17 *July* 1967.

FORBES, His Honour Arthur Harold; former Judge of Birmingham County Court; Governor and LL.M., Birmingham University; *b.* 29 Oct. 1885; *s.* of H. B. Forbes, Solicitor; *m.* 1914, Bertha, *d.* of C. A. Allison, Patent Agent; two *s.* Called to Bar, Middle Temple, 1906; served European War, 1914-1918, Staff Capt., Salonika Army (despatches). Chairman, Northamptonshire Quarter Sessions, 1946-60. *Address:* 30 Gilhams Avenue, Banstead, Surrey. *T.:* Ewell 3897.
[*Died* 15 *April* 1967.

FORBES, Esther; Writer; *d.* of Wm. T. Forbes and Harriette Merrifield, Westboro', Mass., U.S.A.; *m.* 1926, Albert L. Hoskins (divorced 1933). *Educ.:* Bradford Academy; University of Wisconsin. Editorial staff Houghton Mifflin Co., 1920-26, 1942-46; Litt.D. Clark Univ. and Univ. of Maine, 1944; Litt.D., Univ. of Wisconsin, Tufts College, Northeastern Univ., 1949; Pulitzer Prize American History, 1942; John Newberry Medal, 1944; Metro-Goldwyn-Mayer Award, 1948. Member: American Academy of Arts and Sciences; American Antiquarian Society. *Publications:* O Genteel Lady!, 1926; A Mirror for Witches, 1928; Miss Marvel, 1935; Paradise, 1937; Paul Revere and the World He Lived In, 1941; Johnny Tremain, 1943; America's Paul Revere, 1944; The Boston Book, 1947; The Running of the Tide, 1948; Rainbow on the Road, 1954. *Address:* 23 Trowbridge Road, Worcester, Mass., U.S.A. *Club:* Cosmopolitan (N.Y.). [*Died* 12 *Aug.* 1967.

FORBES, (Joan) Rosita; (Mrs. Arthur T. McGrath); Traveller, Lecturer, and Author; F.R.G.S., Hon. Member of French, Royal Italian, Canadian and Royal Antwerp Geographical Societies; *d.* of H. J. Torr of Morton Hall, Swinderley, Lincolnshire; *m.* 1st, Colonel Ronald Forbes (whom she divorced), 3rd *s.* of Colonel Foster Forbes of Rothiemay Castle, Banffshire; 2nd, Colonel Arthur T. McGrath, D.S.O. (*d.* 1962). Extensive travelling in most known countries; expedition to Kufara in Libya, 1920, unvisited by Europeans since Rohlf's unsuccessful expedition of 1879; expedition to unknown Asir, 1922-23; cinema expedition through Abyssinia in 1924-25; drove ambulance in war for Société de Secours aux blessés militaires (2 war medals); 1940-45, Lecturer for War Office, Air Ministry; Canadian Ministry of Supplies and National Council of Education, Canada; Economic League. Gold Medal Royal Antwerp Geographical Society, 1921; Gold Medal French Geographical Society, 1923; Silver Medal Royal Society of Arts, 1924. *Publications:* The Secret of the Sahara-Kufara; Quest, 1922; From Red Sea to Blue Nile; Adventure, 1928; Conflict, 1931; Eight Republics in Search of a Future, 1933; Forbidden Road—Kabul to Samarkand, 1937; India of the Princes, 1939; A Unicorn in the Bahamas,

1939: The Prodigious Caribbean, 1940; Monograph: Position of the Arabs in Art and Literature; Autobiography: Appointment in the Sun, 1949; Biography: Sir Henry Morgan, Pirate and Pioneer, 1948; Islands in the Sun (W. Indies), 1950. *Recreations:* travelling, hunting, exploration connected with Arab countries. *Address:* Clare Cottage, Warwick, Bermuda. [*Died* 30 *June* 1967.

FORBES-ROBERTSON, Jean; Actress; *b.* 16 March 1905; 2nd *d.* of late Sir Johnston and late Lady Forbes-Robertson (Miss Gertrude Elliott); *m.* 1940, André Van Gyseghem, actor and producer; one *d.* *Educ.:* Folkestone; Ascot; France. First went on the stage in South Africa, Australia and New Zealand, 1921-24; London debut in Dancing Mothers, 1925; amongst other plays, has appeared in Berkeley Square, Romeo and Juliet, Twelfth Night, Midsummer Night's Dream, The Dybbuk, Peter Pan (for 9 Christmas seasons), The Constant Nymph, Hedda Gabler, St. Joan, Strange Orchestra, and Time and the Conways; under own management, 1934-35, with The Lady of the Camellias, Mary Rose, The Red Rover's Revenge, The Sea Nymph, Scored for Drums, and As You Desire Me. Produced under joint management, 1940-42, Berkeley Square, The Long Mirror, Twelfth Night, Distant Point. *Publication:* Chowry, 1953. *Address:* 24 Knox Street, W.1. [*Died* 24 *Dec.* 1962.

FORBES-SEMPILL, Comdr. William F.; *see* Sempill, 19th Baron.

FORD, Vice-Admiral Sir Denys Chester, K.C.B., *cr.* 1948 (C.B. 1947); C.B.E., 1942; M.I.Mech.E.; Retired; *b.* 20 Oct. 1890; *s.* of Arthur Ranken Ford; unmarried. *Educ.:* Preparatory School, Sedbergh; R.N.C., Osborne and Dartmouth. Midshipman, 1908; served European War, 1914-18; Cdr. (E), 1926; Capt. (E), 1936; Technical Adviser to 5th Sea Lord, 1938; Director of Aircraft Maintenance and Repair, Admiralty, 1939-40; Fleet Engineer Officer, Home Fleet, 1940-43; Engineer-in-Chief of the Fleet, 1947-50; retired, 1950. *Address:* The Ruff, Beech Lane, Guildown, Guildford. *T.:* Guildford 5560. *Club:* United Service. [*Died* 3 *Oct.* 1967.

FORD, Hon. Frank, D.C.L.; LL.D., retired as Justice of Appeal, Supreme Court of Alberta, Canada (1936-54); *b.* Toronto, 4 March 1873; *s.* of James Ford and Catherine Poole; *m.* 1st, Nora Elizabeth (*d.* 1920), *d.* of William Armour Sampson; two *s.* two *d.*; 2nd, Jane Duff, *d.* of Thomas Kerr, Edinburgh. *Educ.:* Toronto Public Schools; Ontario Academy; Trinity University; Osgoode Hall. Private Secretary and permanent devil to the late D'Alton McCarthy, Q.C., M.P.; called to Bar, Ontario, 1895; Private Sec. successively to Hon. A. S. Hardy, K.C. (Premier and Attorney-General of Ontario), and Hon. Sir John M. Gibson, K.C., (Attorney-General of Ontario); also Law Clerk of Attorney-General's Department; Solicitor to the Treasury, Ontario, 1900-03, resigned to resume practice in Toronto; Deputy Attorney-General of Saskatchewan, 1906; resigned 1910 to take up practice in Edmonton, Alberta; late Bencher Law Society of Saskatchewan; Bencher Law Society of Alberta, 1913-26; Vice-President, 1923, Acting President, 1926; Chancellor of Diocese of Edmonton, 1913-33, and again, 1941-1959; Deputy Prolocutor Synod of Ecclesiastical Province of Rupert's Land, 1942-47; Prof. in Law, Univ. of Alberta, 1923-26; Hon. Prof. since 1926; Chancellor of the University of Alberta, 1941-46; Lt.-Col. Retired List, Canadian Militia; Bachelor of Civil Law, (Medallist), Trinity University, Toronto; Bachelor of Laws (*ad eundum*) University of Saskatchewan; D.C.L. University of Toronto and (*ad eundum*) University of Alberta; LL.D. (h.c.) University of Alberta and Laval University, Quebec, 1946; Officier d'Académie (France) 1948; Hon. Fellow St. John's Coll., Winnipeg, 1954. K.C. Saskatchewan, 1907, Ontario 1910, Alberta, 1913; Justice of Supreme Court, Alberta, 1926-36 (of Appeal), 1936-54. *Address:* 12410-103 Ave., Edmonton, Alberta, Canada. *Club:* Edmonton (Edmonton). [*Died* 21 *March* 1965.

FORD, Brig. Geoffrey Noel, C.B. 1938; D.S.O. 1932; *b.* 25 Dec. 1883; 3rd *s.* of Everard Allen Ford, Eldon Road, Hampstead; *m.* 1915, Katia Gorkhover; one *s.* one *d.* *Educ.:* Westminster School; R.M.C. Sandhurst. Joined 105th Mahratta Light Infantry, 1902; Lt. Col. 1928; Colonel, 1932; served European War, 1914-19; Iraq, 1920-21; Burmah, 1930-32; Mohmand, 1935; Commander Allahabad Brigade Area, 1935-39; A.D.C. 1937-39; retired, 1939. Re-employed, 1940; Comdg. troops Isle of Man, 1940-43; retired, 1943. *Recreations:* usual. *Address:* Flat 8, 3 Palmeira Square, Hove, Sussex. [*Died* 29 *Oct.* 1964.

FORD, Hugh Alexander, C.M.G. 1943; *b.* 26 July 1885; *s.* of late Alexander Ellis Ford; unmarried. Formerly Consul-General at Boston, Mass.; retd., 1944. *Address:* 736 Riverside Drive, New York 31, N.Y., U.S.A. [*Died* 14 *March* 1966.

FORD, Admiral Sir Wilbraham Tennyson Randle, K.C.B., *cr.* 1942 (C.B. 1934); K.B.E., *cr.* 1940; *b.* St. Helier, Jersey, 19 Jan. 1880; *s.* of late Major C. W. Randle Ford, Bath; *m.* 1924, Violet, *d.* of G. Hurry; two *s.* Director of Physical Training, 1924-26; Training Establishment, Shotley, 1926-28; commanded Royal Oak, 1929; Navigation School, 1930-32; Rear-Adm., 1932; commanded H.M. Australian Squadron, 1934-36; Vice-Adm., 1937; Vice-Adm in charge and Adm. Supt., Malta, 1937-40; Flag Officer in Charge Malta, 1940-41; Admiral, 1941; Commander-in-Chief, Rosyth, 1942-44. *Club:* Lansdowne. [*Died* 16 *Jan.* 1964.

FORESTER, Cecil Scott; author; *b.* 27 Aug. 1899; *s.* of George Forester and Sarah Troughton; *m.* Kathleen (marriage dissolved, 1944), *d.* of G. Belcher; two *s.*; *m.* 1947, Dorothy Ellen, *d.* of William Foster. *Educ.:* Dulwich College. *Publications:* many novels, biographies, and books of travel, including: Payment Deferred, Brown on Resolution, Death to the French, The Gun and The Peacemaker, The African Queen, The General, The Happy Return; A Ship of the Line (James Tait Black Memorial Prize for Literature, 1938); Flying Colours; Captain Hornblower, R.N., 1939; The Earthly Paradise, 1940; The Captain from Connecticut, 1941; The Ship, 1943; The Commodore, 1945; Lord Hornblower, 1946; The Sky and The Forest, 1948; Mr. Midshipman Hornblower, 1950; Randall and the River of Time, 1951; Hornblower and the Atropos, 1953; The Nightmare, 1954; The Good Shepherd, 1955; The Naval War of 1812, 1957; Hornblower in the West Indies, 1958; Hunting the Bismarck, 1959; Hornblower and the Hotspur, 1962; The Hornblower Companion, 1964; Long Before Forty (autobiog.), 1967; The Man in the Yellow Raft, 1969 (both posthumous). *Play:* prod. 1934, Nurse Cavell (with C. E. Bechofer Roberts). *Address:* 1066 Park Hills Road, Berkeley 8, California, U.S.A. *Clubs:* Athenæum; Century (U.S.). [*Died* 2 *April* 1966.

FORESTER, Major Hon. Edric Alfred Cecil Weld-; C.V.O. 1950; J.P.; D.L.; late Rifle Brigade; *y. s.* of 5th Baron Forester; *b.* 1880; *m.* 1916, Lady Victoria, *y. d.* of 1st Marquess of Lincolnshire, and *widow* of Nigel W. H. Legge-Bourke. Coldstream Guards; one *s.* two *d.* Served S. African War, 1902; Major, Rifle Brigade, 1915; G.S.O. 2, 1916; retired, 1920. Exon of the King's Bodyguard of the Yeomen of the Guard, 1937-45; Clerk of the Cheque and Adjutant, 1945-50; retired, 1950. *Address:* Laverton House, Broadway, Worcs. *T.:* Stanton, Glos. 3. *Club:* Army and Navy. [*Died* 24 *Sept.* 1963.

FORESTER, Lt.-Comdr. Wolstan B. C. W.; *see* Weld-Forester.

FORGAN, Very Rev. James Rae, M.A., D.D.; Minister of Trinity Church of Scotland, Ayr, 1921-46, retired 1946; *b.* 1876; *s.* of late Thomas Forgan, J.P., Perth; *m.* 1904, Essex Helen (*d.* 1944), *d.* of late Robert Gray, Bothwell; two *s.* three *d.* *Educ.:* Perth Acad.; Univ. of St. Andrews. Minister, St. Andrew's Church, Auchterarder, 1904; Chalmers Church, Uddingston, 1912; West Church, Broughty Ferry, 1918; Convener, Church of Scotland Committee on Colonial Churches, 1929; Convener, Committee on Maintenance of Ministry, 1936; Church of Scotland Special Commissioner to India, 1935; Moderator of Church of Scotland General Assembly, 1940; Chaplain to Highland L.I. in France, 1915-16. *Publications:* Pamphlets and Magazine Articles. *Recreations:* travel, angling, walking. *Address:* 28 Royal Terrace, Edinburgh 7. [*Died* 14 *Dec.* 1966.

FORMAN, Brig. James Francis Robert, C.B. 1947; C.B.E. 1945; D.S.O. 1945; p.s.c.†, f.s.; late I.A.; Director, Andrews & Co. Ltd.; *b.* 15 November 1899; *s.* of late Reverend A. F. E. Forman, Senior Asst. Master, Repton School; *m.* 1932, Pauline, *d.* of Edgar Reed, Minehead; one *s.* *Educ.:* Laleham Preparatory School; Shrewsbury School. Joined Army, May 1918; commissioned in I.A., Kumaon Regt. (formerly 19th Hyderabad Regt.), 1919; Staff Coll., 1933-34; R.A.F. Staff Coll., 1937; War of 1939-45, G.S.O. 2, H.Q.P. & A. District (at outbreak of war); G.S.O. 1, G.H.Q. India, 1941-42; C.O. 2 Kumaon Regt., 1943; G.S.O. 1 26 Indian Division (Burma), 1944; Commander 4 Indian Infantry Bde. (Burma), 1945 (despatches twice, C.B.E., D.S.O.); Chief of Staff (Maj.-Gen.), H.Q. Allied Forces, Netherlands East Indies, 1946 (C.B.). Chief of Staff, 1 India Corps, 1947; Director Military Operations and Intelligence, H.Q. Pakistan Army, 1947; retired 1948. *Address:* 42 Burghley House, Somerset Road, S.W.19. [*Died* 30 *Aug.* 1969.

FORMAN, Rev. Thomas Pears Gordon, M.A.; Hon. Canon of Newcastle; *b.* 27 January 1885; *s.* of Rev. A. F. E. Forman, Repton School, and Eleanor, *y. d.* of Dr. Pears, Head Master of Repton; *m.* 1920, Eleanor Parkin-Moore (*d.* 1964); one *s.* two *d.* (and one *s.* decd.). *Educ.:* Shrewsbury Sch.; Pembroke Coll., Cambridge; Wells Theological College. Curate of Kenilworth, 1908-11; Assistant Master at Shrewsbury School, 1911-16; T.C.F., 1916-19; Curate S. Clement's, York, 1919-20; Chaplain to Duke of Portland, 1920-24; Rector of Bothal, 1924-44; Archdeacon of Lindisfarne and Vicar of Eglingham, 1944-55. *Address:* 27 King's Avenue, Morpeth, Northumberland. *T.:* Morpeth 2535. [*Died* 22 *Nov.* 1965.

FORMBY, George, O.B.E. 1946; Actor (Stage, Films, Radio); *b.* 26 May 1904; *m.* 1924, Beryl Ingham (*d.* 1960); no *c.* *Educ.:* Wigan. Became a Jockey, 1912; had first mount at Lingfield, 1914, age 10 years, weight 3 st. 13 lbs., finished last. Became Music Hall artist, 1921; made first film, 1932; several Royal Command performances, 1938-. *Publications:* 15 songs. *Recreation:* motor cars and motor yacht. *Address:* Beryldene, Promenade, St. Annes-on-Sea, nr. Blackpool. *Clubs:* Royal Automobile; Royal Motor Yacht; Sussex Motor Yacht. [*Died* 6 *March* 1961.

FORREST, Archibald Stevenson; Artist; *b.* Greenwich, 1869; 2nd *s.* of late James Forrest of Yett, Carluke, Lanark; *m.* 1913, Rose Marion, *e. d.* of late Capt. R. J. Hardy Douglas, R.M.L.I. *Educ.:* Roan School, Greenwich; Edinburgh; Westminster School of Art; the City and Guilds Coll.; Edinburgh Art School. *Publications:* Morocco; West Indies; Normandy; Portugal; A Tour through Old Provence; A Tour through South America; South America. *Address:* 15 Beachwood Road, Beaconsfield, Bucks. [*Died* 3 *Jan.* 1963.

FORREST, George; M.P. (Ind. U.U.) Mid-Ulster since May 1956; auctioneer and livestock salesman; *b.* 26 October 1922; *m.*; one *s.* two *d.* Served War of 1939-45, with Royal Engineers. *Address:* House of Commons, S.W.1; Glenholm, Park Avenue, Cookstown, County Tyrone, Northern Ireland. [*Died* 10 *Dec.* 1968.

FORRESTER, Joseph; *b.* 25 Dec. 1871; *m.* 1904, Alice, *d.* of Frederick Forge, Cleethorpes; two *d.* *Educ.:* Grammar Sch., Leek; Technical Inst., Hanley; Manchester. Member Lindsey C.C. 52 years; Vice-Chm. 18 years, Chm. 1946-51; Chm. of Finance Cttee., 28 years. A county magistrate 45 years. Income Tax Commissioner 25 years. *Address:* Haverstoe, Cleethorpes, Lincolnshire. *T.:* Cleethorpes 61047. [*Died* 11 *Nov.* 1967.

FORRESTER-BROWN, Maud (Frances), M.S., M.D. Lond.; Emeritus consultant, Bath and Wessex Orthopædic Hospital, etc.; research on Peripheral Nerve Suture, Wilkie Dept., Edinburgh Univ.; Mem. of International Orthopædic Soc.; Vice-Chairman, Scottish Assoc. of Sport and Medicine; Emeritus Fellow: British Orthopædic Association; Royal Society Med.; *d.* of J. S. Forrester-Brown, M.I.C.E., Consulting Engineer, Government of India. *Educ.:* Bedford High School for Girls. Trained London (R.F.H.) School of Medicine for Women; House Surgeon, Royal Samaritan Hospital, Glasgow; Dundee Royal Infirmary; Liverpool Royal Infirmary: Sheffield Royal Infirmary; Edinburgh Royal Hospital for Sick Children; House-Physician Royal Free Hosp., London; Resident Surgeon, Edinburgh War Hospital, Bangour, 1916-21 (for last 18 months in independent charge of surgical and orthopædic wards); entrance scholarship L.S.M.W.; Gilchrist studentship, Univ. of London; Wm. Gibson Research Scholar, Royal Society of Medicine. Temporary Orthopædic Consultant, Holy Cross Hosp., Transkei, S. Africa, 1958 and 1959. *Publications:* (With Prof. Sir Harold Stiles) Operative Treatment of Peripheral Nerve Injuries; Diagnosis and Treatment of Deformities in Infancy and Early Childhood, 1928; (with Dr. R. Gordon) Paralysis in Children; Paralysis Section in Modern Trends in Orthopædics, 1949; Operative Treatment of Poliomyelitis, R.C.S. Annals, 1947; Paralysis section in Modern Trends in Orthopædics, 1950; Compensation Treatment of T.B. Spines in Orthopædics, 1959; various Orthopædic articles in B.M.J.; British Journal of Surgery; Lancet; Edinburgh Medical Journal; Practitioner; Medical Women's Journal; Royal Free Hospital Magazine; Cripple Journal, Orthopædics, etc. *Recreations:* Life Member Amateur Skating Assoc.; Member A.A.; riding. *Address:* 13 Palmerston Place, Edinburgh 12 [*Died* 12 *Jan.* 1970.

FORSTER, Baroness, G.B.E., *cr.* 1926: **Rachel Cecily,** *d.* of 1st Baron Montagu of Beaulieu; *m.* 1890, 1st Baron Forster (*d.* 1936); two *d.* (two *s.* killed in European War 1914-18). *Address:* Rose Cottage, Milford-on-Sea, Hants. *T.:* 49. [*Died* 12 *April* 1962.

FORSTER, Lt.-Gen. Alfred Leonard, C.B. 1940; D.S.O. 1915; *s.* of Rev. Bennet Forster; *m.* 1918, Gladys, *o. d.* of R. F. Godfrey-Faussett; one *s.* one *d.* *Educ.:* Blackheath School. 2nd Lieut. Royal Marine Artillery, 1903; Capt. 1914; Bt. Major, June 1918; Major, 1924; Bt. Lt.-Col. 1932; Lt.-Col. 1933; Colonel, 1936; Maj.-Gen. 1939; Lt.-Gen. 1941; served European War, 1914-16 (D.S.O., despatches twice); Assistant Director of Naval Intelligence, Admiralty, 1934-36; Commandant, Royal Marines, Chatham, 1937-39; A.D.C. to the King, 1939; Member of Church Assembly, 1940-61. *Address:* Bridge House, Mersham, Kent. [*Died* 5 *July* 1963.

FORSTER, Arnold John, M.B.E. 1919; Trustee Oxford Preservation Trust, 1954-67; Chm., Acland Nursing Home, 1947-57; Past President, O.U.R.C.; *b.* 31 Jan. 1885; *s.* of late James A. Forster, Fernlands, Chertsey; *m.* 1913, Annie Geraldine (*d.* 1967), *d.* of late William Henry Bewley of Rockville, Blackrock, Co. Dublin; one *s.* *Educ.:* Marlborough; Oriel Coll., Oxford. 2nd Class Honours Natural Science (Physics), 1906; B.A., 1906; M.A. 1930; selected for Sudan Political Service, 1906; seconded Finance Department, Sudan Government. 1908; acted Financial Secretary part of 1919-20; Assistant Auditor General, 1921; Assistant Financial Secretary, 1928; Order of Nile 4th Class, 1922; 3rd Class, 1930; retired, 1930; Fellow and Estates Bursar, Magdalen College, Oxford, 1930-40; Member of Council, Lady Margaret Hall, 1931-54, Hon. Treasurer, 1944-51. *Recreations:* shooting and fishing; Oxford University Bisley Team, 1904, 1905 and 1907, Half Blue 1905; Marlborough Nomads Rugby Football team, 1904-8. *Address:* St. Mary's, Jack Straws Lane, Oxford. *T.:* 62609. *Club:* Royal Commonwealth Society. [*Died* 25 *Aug.* 1968.

FORSTER, Edward Morgan, O.M. 1968; C.H. 1953; Hon. Fellow King's Coll., Cambridge, 1946; Hon. LL.D. Aberdeen, 1931; Hon. Litt.D. Liverpool, 1947, Hamilton Coll., U.S.A., 1949, Cambridge, 1950, Nottingham, 1951, Manchester 1954, Leyden Univ., Holland, 1954, Leicester, 1958; Companion, Roy. Society of Literature (C.Litt.), 1961; a Vice-President of the London Library; Hon. Corresponding Member: American Academy of Arts and Letters; Bavarian Academy of Fine Arts; President, Cambridge Humanists; *b.* 1879; *o. s.* of Edward Morgan Llewellyn and Alice Clara Forster. *Educ.:* Tonbridge (day boy); King's Coll., Cambridge. *Publications:* Where Angels Fear to Tread; The Longest Journey; A Room with a View; Howards End; A Passage to India; Collected Short Stories; Introduction and Notes to the Aeneid of Virgil; Alexandria, a History and a Guide (reissued, U.S.A. 1961); Pharos and Pharillon; Introduction and Notes to the Letters of Mrs. Eliza Fay; The Hill of Devi, 1953; Aspects of the Novel; Introduction to the Life of Crabbe; Goldsworthy Lowes Dickinson; Marianne Thornton, a domestic biography, 1956; Abinger Harvest; Two Cheers for Democracy; England's Pleasant Land, a Pageant-Play; Nordic Twilight; Diary for Timothy (film-script); (with Eric Crozier) libretto for Benjamin Britten's opera Billy Budd; Maurice (novel, posthumous) 1971. *Clubs:* Reform; Royal College of Art Common Room. [*Died* 7 *June* 1970.

FORSTER, Major Francis A. A.; *see* Arnold-Forster.

FORSTER, Comdr. Hugh C. A.; *see* Arnold-Forster.

FORSTER, Lancelot, M.A. (London); *b.* 25 June 1882; *s.* of Christopher James Forster and Catherine Menzies; *m.* Gladys Hutchinson, *d.* of Alfred David Jennings; four *d.* *Educ.:* St. John's College, Battersea; Fitzwilliam Hall, Cambridge; University College, Oxford. Assistant Master, Christ Church School, Newcastle upon Tyne; Headmaster, Victoria British School, Hong Kong; Registrar of University, 1925; Professor of Education, 1925-45; President Hong Kong Teachers' Association, 1934-38; Visiting Lecturer to National University of Pekin, 1935, President Hong Kong Rotary Club, 1935-36; Carnegie Foundation Travelling Fellowship, U.S.A., Germany, 1938. Director Dept. of Information, Hong Kong, 1939-41; Chairman Education Committee, Stanley Internment Camp., 1942-45; Mem., Teachers Training Dept., Oxford Univ., 1945-47; Lectr., Oakley Training Coll., Cheltenham, 1947-51; Staff Mem., Teachers Training Dept., Reading Univ., 1951-55. Member, Goodwill Mission to Chiang Kai-Shek, Formosa, 1957. *Publications:* The New Culture in China; Echoes of Hong Kong and Beyond; English Ideals in Education for Chinese Students. *Address:* 7 Bardwell Road, Oxford. *Died* 14 *June* 1968.

FORSYTH, Lieutenant-Colonel Fredrick Richard Gerrard, M.C.; D.L. of City of Aberdeen; *b.* Netherleigh, Leamington, 1882; *s.* of late Lieut.-Colonel F. A. Forsyth, 5th Fusiliers, and late Ellen Sanford, *d.* of late Col. R. Dougal, Ratho, Midlothian. *Educ.:* Sandroyd School; Wellington College. 3rd Scottish Rifle Militia, Northumberland Fusiliers, 1901; 2nd Lieut. 1902; Lieut. Seaforth Highlanders, 1908; Captain Seaforths, 1914; transferred to 4th (R.I.) Dragoon Guards as Captain, 1916; to Royal Corps of Signals, 1920; Lt.-Col. R. Signals, 1926; Comdt. 51st Highland Div. Signals (T.A.), 1923-28; late Hon. Col. 51st (Highland) Divisional Signals, R. C. of S. Served South Africa, 1901-2 (medal, 5 clasps); wounded in derailment of No. 12 Armoured Train, 1901; North West Frontier of India with Seaforth Highlanders, Mohmand, 1908 (medal and clasp); European War, 1914-18, with 4th Dragoon Guards and attached R.E. Signals (despatches twice, wounded thrice, Bt. Major, M.C.); A.D.C. to Commander-in-Chief, Ireland, 1918; late Hon. Col. 51st/52 Scottish Divisional Signal Regt., Royal Signals; re-employed Royal Signals, 1939-40. Awarded Royal Humane Society Bronze Medal for saving life of a soldier, 1905. *Recreations:* racing, steeplechasing, yachting (late Vice-Commodore Royal Torbay Yacht Club), shooting, fishing. *Address:* 8/9 The Quadrant, Coventry, Warwickshire. *Clubs:* Cavalry, Royal Ocean Racing. [*Died* 3 *Sept.* 1962.

FORSYTH, Ian McMillan, C.B. 1952; *b.* 26 May 1892; *s.* of late Robert Forsyth, Kilrenny Anstruther, Fifeshire; *m.* 1st, 1922, Maud (*decd.*), *d.* of late Thomas Mitchell, Blairgowrie; 2nd, 1930, Beryl, *o. d.* of late Basil Davies, Peerscourt, Aspley Guise; no *c.* *Educ.:* Waid Academy, Anstruther; St. Andrews University (M.A., B.Phil.). Served European War, 1914-18, Gallipoli, Palestine, France. Entered Treasury, 1919; Asst. Secretary, Board of Trade, 1936; Principal Asst. Secretary, Ministry of Fuel and Power, 1943; U.K. Delegate to European Coal Organisation, 1946-47; Under Sec., Min. of Fuel and Power, 1946-52. *Recreation:* golf. *Address:* Round Wood, Brasted Chart, near Westerham, Kent. *T.:* Westerham 3479. [*Died* 4 *July* 1969.

FORSYTH, James Alexander, Q.C. (Scot.); M.A., LL.B., B.Sc.; Sheriff Substitute of Lanarkshire at Glasgow since 1964 (at Hamilton, 1961-64); *b.* 27 August 1921; *s.* of late James A. Forsyth, Solicitor, Kelvindale, Glasgow, and Grace Brown; *m.* 1945, Jean Stewart, *d.* of George Woodburn, Langside, Glasgow, and late Christine

Anderson; two *s*. two *d*. *Educ.:* Hillhead High School, Glasgow; Luisengymnasium, Berlin; University of Glasgow. Junior Scientific Officer, Royal Aircraft Establishment. Farnborough, 1942-45. Called to Bar, 1947; Q.C. (Scot.) 1960. *Recreation:* astronomy (Past Pres. Astronomical Soc. of Edinburgh). *Address:* Kenmill House, Hamilton Drive, Bothwell, Lanarkshire. *T.:* Bothwell 2181. *Clubs:* Scottish Liberal (Edinburgh); Rotary (Glasgow). [*Died* 7 *June* 1968.

FORWOOD, Sir Dudley Baines, 2nd Bt., *cr.* 1895; C.M.G. 1919; *b.* 31 May 1875; *e. s.* of Rt. Hon. Sir Arthur Bower Forwood, P.C., 1st Bt., and Lizzie, *d.* of Thomas Baines, Liverpool; *S.* father, 1898; *m.* 1901, Norae Isabella, *e. d.* of late Richard R. Lock.tt, Alexandra Drive, Liverpool; one *s.* *Educ:* Harrow. Formerly Lt.-Col. R. of O.; late commanding 2nd Lancashire R.F.A.; served with B.E.F., R.F.A., 1915-19 (despatches thrice, C.M.G.). Master of the New Forest Buckhounds, 1950-56. *Heir: s.* Dudley Richard Forwood. *Address:* Stoney Cross Lodge, Lyndhurst, Hants. *T.:* Cadnam 2174. [*Died* 22 *Dec.* 1961.

FOSDICK, Rev. Harry Emerson, A.M., D.D., LL.D., S.T.D., Litt.D., L.H.D.; Pastor, Riverside Church New York City, 1926-46; now minister-emeritus; *b.* Buffalo, N.Y., 24 May 1878; *m.* 1904, Florence Allen Whitney, Worcester, Mass.; two *d.* *Educ.:* Colgate University; Columbia Univ.; Union Theological Seminary. Minister of a Parish, Montclair, N.J., 1904-15; Professor of Practical Theology, Union Theological Seminary, New York City, 1915-1946; Preacher, First Presbyterian Church, NewYork, 1919-25; Member Φ.B.K., Δ.Υ., Sons of the American Revolution. *Publications:* The Manhood of the Master; The Assurance of Immortality; The Meaning of Prayer; The Meaning of Faith; The Meaning of Service; Christianity and Progress; Twelve Tests of Character; The Modern Use of the Bible; Adventurous Religion and other Essays; A Pilgrimage to Palestine; As I see Religion; The Hope of the World; The Secret of Victorious Living; The Power to See It Through; Successful Christian Living; A Guide to Understanding the Bible; Living Under Tension, 1941; On Being a Real Person, 1943; A Great Time to be Alive, 1944; On Being Fit to Live With; The Man From Nazareth, As His Contemporaries Saw Him Rufus Jones Speaks To Our Times (An Anthology); Great Voices of the Reformation; A Faith For Tough Times; What is Vital in Religion; The Living of These Days; Riverside Sermons; Dear Mr. Brown. *Address:* Rivermere Apts., Alger Court, Bronxville, N.Y., U.S.A. *Club:* Century (N.Y.). [*Died* 5 *Oct.* 1969.

FOSDICK, Raymond Blaine; President Emeritus of the Rockefeller Foundation (Pres., 1936-48); *b.* Buffalo, New York, 9 June 1883; *s.* of Frank S. and Amie W. Fosdick; *m.* 1936, Elizabeth R. Miner; no *c.* *Educ.:* Princeton University; New York Law School. Assistant Corporation Counsel, City of New York, 1908-10; Commissioner of Accounts, City of New York, 1910-13; Member of Board of Education, City of New York, 1915-16; Chairman of Commission on Training Camp Activities of War and Navy Departments, 1917-18; Civilian Aide to General Pershing in France, 1918-19 (Distinguished Service Medal); Under-Secretary General of the League of Nations, 1919-20; Member of law firm of Curtis, Fosdick and Belknap, 1920-36; Special Consultant to Secretary of War, 1941-45. Grand Officier Légion d'Honneur (France). Hon. LL.D. Univ. of Edinburgh, 1949. Woodrow Wilson Award, Princeton Univ., 1961; Woodrow Wilson Foundation Award, 1963. *Publications:* European Police Systems, 1915; American Police Systems, 1920; The Old Savage in the New Civilization, 1928; The Story of the Rockefeller Foundation, 1952; Within Our Power, 1952; John D. Rockefeller, Jr.: A Portrait, 1956; Chronicle of a Generation 1958; Adventure in Giving: The Story of the General Education Board, 1962. *Address:* 25 East 83rd Street New York City *Club:* Century (New York). [*Died* 5 *Oct.* 1969.

FOSTER, E(rnest) Marshall; Taxing Master of the Supreme Court since 1952; *b.* 6 Sept. 1907; *s.* of Ernest Henry Foster, J.P., The Rookery, Horsforth, nr. Leeds; *m.* 1941, Mrs. Stella Stones, Headingley, Leeds; one step *s.* *Educ.:* Clifton College; Hertford Coll. (Exhibitioner), Oxford (B.A.), 2nd Cl. Hons. Hon. Mods. and Final Honour School of Jurisprudence; Solicitor (Hons.), 1933; Partner in firm of W. J. Cousins Fletcher & Foster, solicitors, Leeds, 1933-43. Member of Management Cttee., Hospital for Women, Leeds, 1935-45; Sec. Yorkshire Regional Council, Nuffield Provincial Hosps. Trust, 1941-45. County Court Registrar and District Registrar of the High Court: Leeds, Barnsley and Pontefract, 1943-45; Cambridge group, 1945-51. Registrar, Willesden County Court, 1951. Hon. Pres., British Limbless Ex-servicemen's Assoc., Cambridge, 1947-51. Member of Herbert Cttee. on hours of work in the Law Courts, 1952-53 *Address:* Flat 1, 1 Palace Gate, Kensington, W.8. *T.:* Knightsbridge 8947. *Clubs:* National Liberal, Kennel. [*Died* 26 *Dec.* 1970.

FOSTER, Sir Frank Savin, Kt., *cr.* 1955; C.B.E. 1946; J.P.; Director Charles S. Foster and Sons, Ltd., Loughton, Essex; *b.* 27 September 1879; *s* of late Charles S. Foster, Loughton, Essex; *m.* 1905, Emily Charlotte (decd.), *d.* of late Charles James Palmer. Westcliff-on-Sea; one *s.* one *d.* *Educ.:* Loughton School. J.P. Essex, 1929; C.C. 1937; Alderman, 1946; Chm. Essex County Council, 1949-52 and 1955-58; Controller Civil Defence, Essex, 1939-45. Member Loughton U.D.C., 1915-33 (Chm. 1922, 1923); Chairman: Chigwell U.D.C., 1933-49; Epping Group Hosp. Management Cttee., 1948-58; Epping Magistrates Court, 1943-55; Essex Standing Jt. Cttee., 1953-; Chm. Essex Magistrates Courts Cttee., 1953-55; Vice-Chm. Chelmsford Diocesan Board of Finance. President Loughton (South) Conservative Assoc.; Life Vice-Pres. Chigwell and Ongar Conservative Assoc. *Recreation:* cricket (now watching). *Address:* Little Acre, 37 Alderton Hill, Loughton, Essex. *T.:* Loughton 3028. [*Died* 2 *June* 1964.

FOSTER, Gordon Bentley, D.L.; late Major Lincolnshire Yeomanry; *b.* 10 June 1885; 3rd *s.* of late Leonard Foster of Kirklington Hall, Notts; *m.* 1st, 1919, Phyllis (*d.* 1938), *e. d.* of Sir Thomas Pilkington, 12th Bt.; one *s.*; 2nd, 1939, Helen, *e. d.* of late Brig.-Gen. Hon. Everard Baring; two *d.* *Educ.:* Uppingham. President of the Hunter's Improvement Society, 1932; late Master Badsworth Hounds and Sinnington Hounds. *Address:* Leysthorpe, Oswaldkirk, Yorks. *T.:* Nunnington 203. *Clubs:* Boodle's, Yorkshire (York). [*Died* 1 *April* 1963.

FOSTER, Rt. Hon. Sir Harry B. H.; *see* Hylton-Foster.

FOSTER, John Stuart, F.R.S.; Ph.D.; F.R.S.C.; D.Sc.; Formerly Rutherford Research Professor of Physics, and Director of Radiation Laboratory, McGill University, Montreal; *b.* 28 May 1890; *s.* of D. E. and Mary Foster; *m.* 1920, Flora, *e. d.* of Dr. L. Curtis, St. John's, Newfoundland; two *s.* *Educ.:* Acadia; Yale. Instructor, Yale University, 1920-21; National Research Fellow, 1921-24; McGill University;

Assistant Professor of Physics, 1924-30; Prof. of Physics, 1930-35; Macdonald Prof. of Physics, 1935-55: Chairman of Department, 1952-55. Scientific liaison Officer between Radiation Laboratory, Mass. Inst. Tech. and N.R.C. Ottawa, 1941-44; Fellow Int. Ed. Board, 1926-27; Visiting Prof. Ohio State Univ., 1931; Levy Medal of Franklin Institute, 1930; member of Council, Am. Physical Soc., 1941-44; Tory Medal, Roy. Soc. Can., 1946; Medal of Freedom, bronze palm, 1947; Pres. Sec. III Roy. Soc. Can., 1948-49; Medal, Canadian Assoc. of Physicists, 1958. *Publications:* Papers chiefly in Roy. Soc. Proc. dealing with effects of electric fields on spectra, analysis of certain stellar spectra; effects of combined electric and magnetic fields; spectrum analysis of biological material; spectral photometry; radar scanners; cyclotron. *Address:* 1065 Creston Road, Berkeley 8, California, U.S.A. [*Died* 9 *Sept.* 1964.

FOSTER, Maj. Percy John, D.S.O. 1919; late The Royal Warwickshire Regiment; *b.* 1873; *s.* of late Major Charles Marshall Foster, 32nd Duke of Cornwall's Light Infantry; *m.* 1904, Eva Beatrice, *d.* of His Hon. J. S. Udal; two *d.* *Educ.:* Wellington College. Served European War, 1914-19 (D.S.O., despatches). *Address:* Capel House, Creffield Road, Colchester. *Club:* Army and Navy. [*Died* 10 *Nov.* 1969.

FOSTER, Philip Stanley; C.M.G. 1953; Surgeon Consultant, Christchurch Hospital, 1914, Hon. Surgeon, 1914-45. *b.* 4 April 1885; *s.* of Robert Foster; *m.* 1914, Florence Chisholm; three *d.* *Educ.:* Otago Boys High School; Otago University. Junior University Scholar, 1903; M.B., Ch.B., Otago University, 1908; F.R.C.S. Eng., 1913; F.R.A.C.S. (Foundation Fellow). Capt. N.Z. Med. Corps., 1914-18. *Recreations:* cricket (rep. Province of Otago, Wellington and Canterbury); golf. *Address:* 395 Papanui Road, Christchurch, N.Z. *T.:* Christchurch 49753. *Club:* Canterbury (Christchurch). [*Died* 20 *March* 1965.

FOSTER, General Sir Richard Foster Carter, K.C.B. 1935 (C.B. 1930); C.M.G. 1919; D.S.O. 1918; *b.* 27 Jan. 1879; *s.* of late Montagu H. Foster, Stubbington House, Fareham, Hants; *m.* 1905, Hilda Mary (*d.* 1959), 2nd *d.* of late Lieut.-Col. C. H. Atchison, Elm House, Fareham; one *s.* *Educ.:* Stubbington House School, Fareham. Entered Royal Marine Artillery, 1897; Lieut. 1898; Captain, 1904; Major, 1915; Lt.-Col. 1924; Bt.-Col. 1928; Col. 1929; Maj.-Gen., 1932; Lt.-Gen. 1934; Gen., 1936; Adjutant, Royal Carmarthen Artillery (Militia), 1905-8; Temporary Major, March 1914; Temp. Lieut.-Col., Aug. 1915-Apr. 1923, whilst holding following appointments; A.A. and Q.M.G. 63rd (Royal Naval Division), till Aug. 1918; A.Q.M.G. 10th Army Corps, Aug. 1918-Feb. 1919; A.Q.M.G. British Army of Rhine, Feb. 1919-April 1923 (despatches four times, Bt. Lieut.-Col., D.S.O., C.M.G.); Staff College, Camberley, 1912-13; also p.s.c. R.N.S. College; A.A.G. Royal Marines, 1928-30; Col. Comdt. Chatham Division R.M. 1930-32; Adjutant-General Royal Marines, 1933-36; retired list, 1936; Col. East Surrey Regt., 1939-46; Hon. Col. Comdt., Chatham Div. R.M., 1941-49. *Address:* 1A, Castle House, Speen, Newbury, Berks. [*Died* 3 *April* 1965.

FOSTER, Brigadier Thomas Francis Vere, C.B.E. 1941; M.C.; *b.* Dundalk, 27 July 1885; *s.* of late J. R. Foster, Co. Tyrone; *m.* 1926, Phyllis, *d.* of late Col. Frederick Treffry; two *s.* *Educ.:* St. Paul's School; Staff College, Camberley. Commissioned Mayo Militia, 1903; Connaught Rangers, 1904; served with W.A.F.F., 1909-13; European War, France, Mesopotamia, and Palestine, 1914-18; Adjutant 1st Connaught Rangers, 1915-16; Staff, 1916-18 (wounded, despatches four times, Brevet Major M.C.); transferred to Royal Sussex Regt., 1921; served N.W. Frontier, India, 1930-31; commanded 1st Royal Sussex Regt., 1932-36; Col. 1935; A.A.G. British Troops in Egypt, 1937-42; Brig. 1942; D.A. & Q.M.G., B.T.E., 1942-45 (despatches twice). Colonel Royal Sussex Regiment, Dec. 1942-53. *Address:* 69 Springfield Road, N.W.8. *T.:* Maida Vale 4507. *Club:* Army and Navy. [*Died* 30 *Jan.* 1967.

FOSTER, Thomas Henry; *b.* 20 Dec. 1888; *y. s.* of late John Dorsett Foster, Manor House, Bloxwich, Staffs.; *m.* 1919, Evelyn Blanche Parry, *e. d.* of late Major H. H. Parry, Harewood Park, Ross-on-Wye; one *d.* (and one *s.* killed in action, Malta, 1942). *Educ.:* King Edward's School. Served European War, Middlesex Regt., 1914-16 (invalided); A.D.C. to Governor of Falkland Islands, 1917; Lieut. R.N.V.R. 1918-19 (despatches); war of 1939-45, Lieut. 11th R.W.F., Aug. 1939-Dec. 1940 (invalided); High Sheriff of Herefordshire, 1942-43; J.P.; travelled extensively in North and South America and the Far East. *Address:* 10 Hatherley Court Road, Cheltenham. *Club:* New (Cheltenham). [*Died* 5 *Feb.* 1970.

FOUHY, David Emmet, C.V.O. 1954; C.B.E. 1946; Official Secretary to the Governor-General, New Zealand, 1936-60; *b.* 25 Sept. 1891; *s.* of late W. Fouhy, Christchurch, N.Z.; unmarried. *Educ.:* Ashburton (N.Z.) High School. Cadet, Post and Telegraph Dept., Wellington, 1908; seconded to Government House, 1918; Official Secretary to Governor-General, 1936. *Recreations:* golf, racing. *Address:* 99 Rosetta Road, Raumati South, Wellington, N.Z. *T.:* Wellington 44-589. *Clubs:* Wellington (N.Z.); Wellington Racing (N.Z.); Paraparaumu Golf (N.Z.). [*Died* 25 *Jan.* 1967.

FOULGER, Robert Edward, C.M.G. 1947; Comr. of Police, Tanganyika, since 1951; *b.* 21 May 1899; *yr. s.* of late H. B. W. Foulger, solicitor, of Hare Court, Temple; *m.* 1931, Beatrice Marion, M.B.E. 1951, *d.* of late Sir Ransford Slater, G.C.M.G., C.B.E.; no *c.* *Educ.:* Wellington College, Berks; Pembroke College, Cambridge. Coldstream Guards, 1918; Straits Settlements Police, 1920-22; Nigeria Police, 1923-1939; Dep. Comr. Gold Coast Police, 1939-1942; Dep. Comr. Nigeria Police, 1942-45; Comr. of Police, Singapore, 1946-50. *Club:* Bath. [*Died* 6 *March* 1969.

FOULIS, Sir Archibald Charles Liston, 12th Bt., *cr.* 1634; *b.* 5 Aug. 1903; *s.* of 11th Bt. and Maria, *d.* of Richard Moore; *s.* father 1936. *Heir:* *cousin*, Ian Primrose [*b.* 1937; *s.* of late Lt.-Col. James Alastair Liston-Foulis, R.A., and Kathleen, *d.* of Lt.-Col. John Moran, late Indian Army]. *Address:* c/o Mrs. Pietersen, P.O. Box 602, Bulawayo, S. Rhodesia. [*Died* 9 *Oct.* 1961.

FOULIS, Douglas Ainslie, D.S.O. 1917; O.B.E. 1944; D.L.; Director, Hunter & Foulis Ltd.; *b.* 24 April 1885; *y. s.* of Thomas Foulis, Librarian, Edinburgh; *m.* 1921, Kathleen Belle, *e. d.* of late Sir Alex. K. Wright, K.B.E.; one *s.* two *d.* *Educ.:* George Watson's College, Edinburgh; Edinburgh Univ. (M.A. 1905). Partner in publishing firm of T. N. Foulis, 1910-20. Served European War, 1914-18 (D.S.O., despatches); Lieut.-Col. Commanding 10th Bn. The Cameronians (Scottish Rifles), 1918-19. Commanded 1st Bn. Edinburgh Home Guard, 1940-44; President, Edinburgh Chamber of Commerce, 1948-50; Chairman Council of Scottish Chambers of Commerce, 1954-56; Chm. Edinburgh Mid and East Lothian Disablement Advisory

Cttee., 1948-55. *Address:* Cuill, Easter Belmont Road, Edinburgh. *Clubs:* Caledonian United Service, Northern (Edinburgh). [*Died* 21 *Dec.* 1969.

FOULKES, General Charles, C.C. (Canada), 1968; C.B. 1945; C.B.E. 1944; D.S.O. 1945; C.D. 1950; Chairman Canadian Chiefs of Staff, 1951-60; *b.* 3 Jan. 1903; *s.* of Charles Foulkes and Jane Augusta Ellis; *m.* 1932, Phyllis May Beck; one *s. Educ.:* University of Western Ontario. LL.D. 1947; D.Sc. Royal Military College 1959. Lieutenant Royal Canadian Regt. 1926, Canadian Permanent Militia; Captain 1930; Staff College, Camberley, 1937-1938; Bde. Major Canadian Inf. Bde., 1939; Lt.-Col. and G.S.O. 1940; Brig. to Comd. Cdn. Inf. Bde. Sept. 1942; Brig. Gen. Staff 1st Cdn. Army, April 1943; Maj.-Gen. 1944; G.O.C. 2nd Canadian Division First Canadian Army, 1944; Commanded Canadian First Corps in Italy and N.W. Europe 1944-45; Chief of Canadian General Staff, 1945-51; General, 1954. Associate Prof. of Strategy, Carleton Univ., 1969-. Commandeur de la Légion d'Honneur and Croix de Guerre avec Palme, France; Grand Officer, Order of Orange Nassau, with Swords, Netherlands; Grande Officier de l'Ordre de la Couronne avec Palme and Croix de Guerre, 1940, avec Palme, Belgium; Comdr. Legion of Merit, U.S.A.; Grand Officer, Military Order of Italy; Grand Cross, Order of George I, Greece. *Recreations:* badminton, fishing. *Address:* 174 Dufferin Road, Ottawa, Canada. [*Died* 12 *Sept.* 1969.

FOULKES, Major-Gen. Charles Howard, C.B. 1927; C.M.G. 1918; D.S.O. 1915; *b.* 1 Feb. 1875; *m.* 1904, Dorothea Fanny (*d.* 1967), *e. d.* of Herbert Oakey; three *s. Educ.:* Bedford Modern Sch. Entered army, 1894; Capt., 1904; Major, 1914; Lt.-Col. 1921; Col., 1924; Maj.-Gen., 1930; served Sierra Leone, 1898-9 (medal with clasp); S. African War, 1899-1900 (Queen's medal 6 clasps); Asst Comr. Anglo-French Boundary Commission, East of Niger, 1902-4; West Africa, 1903 (Kano-Sokoto Campaign, medal with clasp); European War, 1914-18, G.O.C. Special Brigade, and Director of Gas Services, G.H.Q. (despatches, D.S.O., C.M.G., Legion of Honour with French Croix de Guerre, Belgian Commander Ordre de la Couronne and Croix de Guerre, American Distinguished Service Medal, 1914 Star, British War Medal, Victory medal, Comdr. of the Order of the Crown of Italy; Bt. Lt.-Col., 1917, Bt. Col., 1919); India G.S. medal, clasp Waziristan, 1919-20; Coronation Medal, 1937; Deputy Chief Engineer, Southern Command, 1924-26; Chief Engineer Aldershot Command, 1926-30; A.D.C. to the King, 1928; retired pay, 1930; Col. Commandant Royal Engineers, 1937-45. Gold Medal, Institn. of Royal Engineers, 1964. *Publications:* Gas! The Story of the Special Brigade, 1934; Commonsense and A.R.P., 1938. *Recreation:* International Hockey (Scotland), 1907-09, Olympic medal, 1908. *Address:* The Warren, Fitzroy Road, Fleet, Hants. [*Died* 6 *May* 1969.

FOULKES, P. Hedworth, B.Sc., F.E.S.; *b.* 28 Jan. 1871; *o. s.* of A. Foulkes, Hendregyda, Abergele; *m.* Beatrice (*d.* 1957), *e. d.* of G. Gilligan, J.P., of Reading; three *s.* one *d. Educ.:* University College, North Wales; Edinburgh University. Lecturer in Agriculture at University College, Reading (now University of Reading), 1894-1900; Prin. Harper-Adams Agricultural College, Newport, Salop, 1900-22; Past President National Poultry Council; Chairman National Poultry Diploma Examination Board for 33 years. Past Pres. S.P.B.A.; Distinguished Service Award Medal for his long period of service in field of Agricultural Education and Administration, 1954. Coronation Medal, 1937. *Publications:* reports on Agricultural Experiments; articles on Agricultural Subjects; Agricultural Diary. *Address:* Ayshe Court, Horsham, Sussex. *T.:* Horsham 3563. [*Died* 23 *Feb.* 1965.

FOWKES, Maj.-Gen. Charles Christopher, C.B.E. 1938; D.S.O. 1941; M.C.; *b.* 4 Dec. 1894; *s.* of Henry Evett Fowkes and Alice Maud DelaBere; *m.* 1928, Phyllis Margaret Frend. *Educ:* Dulwich College; R.M.C., Sandhurst. 2nd Lieut. South Wales Borderers, 1914; Major, 1934; Lieut.-Col., 1938; Colonel, 1938; acting Maj.-Gen 1941; temp. Maj.-Gen. 1942; served European War, France, Belgium, Egypt, and N. Russia, 1914-1918; Middle East, 1941 (despatches, D.S.O.). Retired pay, 1946. *Recreations:* golf, sailing. *Club:* Army and Navy. [*Died* 1 *July* 1966.

FOWLE, Brig. Francis Ernlé, C.B.E. 1944, M.C. 1918; *b.* 18 June 1893; *s.* of late Col. T. E. Fowle, C.B.E., and late E. V. Fowle; *m.* 1930, M. B. Spillane (*d.* 1966); one *s. Educ.:* Rugby. R.E., Dec. 1912; served European War, France (Aug. 1914), Salonica, Palestine; Egyptian Army, 1919-29; U.K., 1929; retired 1947. High Sheriff of Wiltshire, 1951. *Recreations:* shooting, fishing. *Address:* Charlton Manor, Pewsey, Wilts. *T.:* Upavon 210. [*Died* 22 *June* 1969.

FOX, Rear-Adm. Cecil Henry, C.B. 1918; *b* 27 May 1873; *s.* of late Charles de Bassyn Fox, of Co Sligo, and Emma Penelope, *d.* of Edmund Packe; *m.* 1916, Eleanora Isobel (*d.* 1939), *d.* of J. Somerville; one *d.* Midshipman of H.M.S. Calliope off Apia, Samoa, in the hurricane of March 1889; 1st Lieut. Impregnable, Training Ship, Devonport, 1901-4; Military Staff College, Camberley, during 1911; Captain in Charge, Branch War College, Chatham, 1912-13; in Command 3rd Destroyer Flotilla, 1913-14; in Command of H.M.S. Amphion and 3rd Destroyer Flotilla on outbreak of War; sank German minelayer Königin Louise, 5 Aug 1914; in Command of H.M.S. Undaunted and four destroyers during the action off Texel when four German destroyers were sunk on 18 Oct.; then in Columbine, at Rosyth, for special service; commanding Powerful, Training Establishment, Devonport, 1915; Senior Naval Officer in the Clyde District, 1918-20; Commanding Officer, Kingstown area, 1921-22, retired with rank of Rear-Admiral, 1922. *Recreations:* shooting, golf, fishing, etc. *Address:* Wistaria House, Long Street, Sherborne, Dorset. *T.:* Sherborne 217. [*Died* 2 *April* 1963.

FOX, Sir Cyril Fred, Kt., *cr.* 1935; F.B.A. 1940; F.S.A.; M.R.I.A.; Ph.D. (Cantab.), D.Litt. Wales, h.c. 1947; Hon. Fellow, Magdalene College, Cambridge, 1953; *b.* 1882; *s.* of late C. Fred Fox, F.S.A., of Bursledon, Hants; *m.* 1st, 1916, Olive (*d.* 1932), *d.* of late Rev. A. Congreve-Pridgeon, Vicar of Steyning, Sussex; two *d.*; 2nd, 1933, Aileen Mary, *d.* of W. Scott Henderson, Walton-on-the-Hill, Surrey; three *s. Educ.:* Christ's Hosp.; Cambridge. Supt. Univ. of Cambridge Field Laboratories, 1912-24, and Asst. to Curator of Museum of Archæology and of Ethnology, Cambridge, 1923-24; a Kingsley Bye-Fellow of Magdalene College, 1924; Keeper, Department of Archæology, National Museum of Wales, and Lecturer in Archæology, University College of South Wales and Monmouth, 1925-26; Director, National Museum of Wales, 1926-48; President, Society of Antiquaries of London, 1944-49; President, Council of British Archæology, 1944-49; G. T. Clark Prizeman, Cambrian Archæological Assoc., 1946; Gold Medallist, Soc. of Antiquaries of London, 1952. Sometime Mem., Roy. Commn. on Ancient Monuments in Wales and Monmouthshire, and of Roy. Commn. on Historical Monuments,

England, and Ancient Monuments Board for Wales; Pres., Museums Assoc., 1933-34; Pres., Cambrian Archæological Assoc., 1933; Pres., Prehistoric Soc. of East Anglia, 1933; Member of Exeter Diocesan Cttee. for Care of Churches, 1949-60. *Publications:* The Archæology of the Cambridge Region, 1923, 2nd Edn. 1949; The Personality of Britain, 4th Edn. 1943; A Find of the Early Iron Age, Anglesey, 1946; (with Lord Raglan) Monmouthshire Houses, Part I, 1951, Part II, 1953, Part III, 1954; Offa's Dyke, A Field Survey, 1955; Pattern and Purpose: A Survey of Early Celtic Art in Britain, 1958; Life and Death in the Bronze Age, 1959; papers on archæological subjects. *Address:* 28 St. Leonard's Road, Exeter. [*Died* 15 *Jan.* 1967.

FOX, Hon. Mrs. Eleanor B. W.; *see* Wilson-Fox.

FOX, Harold Munro, F.R.S. 1937; M.A.; Emeritus Professor of Zoology, University of London, 1954; Fellow and Research Associate, Queen Mary College, London University; *b.* London, 28 September 1889; *m.* *Educ.:* Brighton College; Gonville and Caius College, Cambridge. Lecturer in Zoology, Imperial College of Science and Technology, London, 1913-14 and 1919; Officer in A.S.C., London Mounted Brigade, 1914-19; Lecturer in Biology, Government School of Medicine, Cairo, 1919-23; Fellow of Gonville and Caius College, 1920-28; Balfour Student, Cambridge University, 1924-27; leader of zoological expedition to Suez Canal, 1924; Prof. of Zoology, Birmingham University, 1927-41, Bedford College, London Univ., 1941-54. Editor of Biological Reviews, 1926-; Fullerian Professor of Physiology in the Royal Institution, 1953-56; Hon. President: London Natural History Society, 1950-; President, International Union of Biological Sciences, 1950-53. Gold Medallist, Linnean Society of London, 1959. Darwin Medal, Roy. Soc., 1966. Dr. (*h.c.*) University of Bordeaux, 1965. *Publications:* The Nature of Animal Colours (with G. Vevers), 1960; many papers on physiology in relation to ecology of invertebrates in scientific periodicals. *Recreations* natural history, riding. *Address:* 3 Mulberry Court, The Vale, S.W.3. *T.:* Flaxman 5250. [*Died* 29 *Jan.* 1967.

FOX, Sir John, Kt., *cr.* 1943; O.B.E.; *b.* London, 27 May 1882; *s. s.* of late Sir John Charles Fox and Mary Louisa, 2nd *d.* of John Sutherland Valentine, C.E.; *m.* 1st, 1908, Edith Gertrude Olive (*d.* 1940), *yr. d.* of Henry Walt Sharp; one *s.*; 2nd, 1942, Lilian (*d.* 1959), *d.* of John Lawler; 3rd, 1963, Pearl (*née* Gallantry), *widow* of J. F. Shuter. *Educ.:* Trinity College, Glenalmond. Solicitor, 1905; Legal Asst. to Chief Registrar of Friendly Socs., 1905; Asst. Registrar of Friendly Socs., 1912; Dep. Industrial Assurance Comr., 1923; Chief Registrar of Friendly Socs. and Industrial Assce. Comr., 1937-47; Member: Trustee Savings Banks Inspection Cttee., 1928-30, 1950-65; Perm. Consultative Cttee. on Official Statistics, 1926-37; Nat. Savings Cttee., 1937-47; a Comr. under Crown Estates Paving Act, 1851, 1948; Member: Council Trinity Coll., Glenalmond, 1938-48; Public Schools Govng. Bodies Assoc., 1942-48; a Vice-Pres., Bldg. Socs. Assoc. Formerly Director and later Chairman: King's Lynn Docks and Railway Co.; Minworth Metals Ltd.; Britannic Alloys Ltd.; Peerless and Ericson, Ltd. Served European War, 1915-19 (despatches twice, O.B.E.). *Address:* c/o J. U. Fox, Sideways, Whichford, Shipston-on-Stour, Warwicks. *T.:* Long Compton 679. [*Died* 18 *Dec.* 1970.

FOX, Major Sir John St. Vigor, Kt., *cr.* 1939; Resigned as High Steward of Borough of Louth, 1960; landed proprietor; *b.* 1879; *s.* of late Capt. John Wilson Fox, 12th Lancers; *m.* 1st, 1902, Esther M. (*d.* 1905), *d.* of M. Waldo-Sibthorp, Canwick Hall, Lincoln; 2nd, 1909, Sylvia Katherine, *d.* of F. R. Sutton, Canons, Thetford; four *s.* two *d.* *Educ.:* Eton. *Recreations:* racing and all forms of sport. *Address:* Westholme House, Pilton, Shepton Mallet, Somerset. *T.:* Pilton 221. *Club:* Boodle's. [*Died* 2 *July* 1968.

FOX, Sir Lionel (Wray), Kt. 1953; C.B. 1948; M.C.; Visiting Fellow, Institute of Criminology, Cambridge University, since October 1960; Chairman, Council of the Institute for the Study and Treatment of Delinquency, since 1961; *b.* 21 Feb. 1895; *s.* of Sam Fox, Halifax, and Mona Wray; *m.* 1921, Marjorie, *e. d.* of C. H. Horner, Halifax; one *s.* two *d.* *Educ.:* Heath Grammar Sch., Halifax; Hertford College, Oxford. Served European War, 1914-19; Capt., Duke of Wellington's Regt. (M.C., despatches, Belgian Croix de Guerre); Home Office, 1919; Secretary, Prison Commission, 1925-34; Deputy Receiver for Metropolitan Police District, 1934-42; Acting Receiver, 1941-42; Chairman of Prison Commission for England and Wales, 1942-60, retd.; Chm., Central After-Care Assoc., 1949-60. *Publications:* The Modern English Prison, 1934; The English Prison and Borstal Systems, 1952; contribs. to Encyclopædia Britannica, British Journal of Delinquency, etc. *Club:* Royal Commonwealth Society. [*Died* 6 *Oct.* 1961.

FOX, Richard Hodding; *b.* 9 Sept. 1876; 2nd *s.* of William Fox, civil engineer, 5 Victoria Street, and *g.s.* of William Fox of Elfordleigh, near Plymouth; *m.* 1906, Julia Sophia (Sissy) (*d.* 1949), *o. d.* of Lt.-Col. Edward William Evans, late 19th Regiment; one *d.* *Educ.:* Forest School; Bradfield College. Matriculated (First Class) at London University; admitted a solicitor, 1899; practised as a solicitor and Parliamentary agent in Westminster, 1907-27; retired from private practice to become solicitor to the Central Electricity Board on its formation in March 1927; appointed Secretary, as well as Solicitor, in 1929; retired, 1944. *Recreations:* fishing, motoring, gardening. *Address:* Wolverley, Little Bookham, Surrey. *T.:* Bookham 189. [*Died* 24 *March* 1966.

FOX, Sir Sidney (Joseph), Kt., *cr.* 1953; Chartered Surveyor; Partner in firm of Hallett, Fox and White, Chartered Surveyors; Fellow of Royal Institution of Chartered Surveyors since 1909; Fellow of Chartered Auctioneers' and Estate Agents' Institute since 1920; Member of the Common Council, City of London for the Ward of Bread Street since 1941. Sheriff of the City of London, 1952-53. Past Master of the Wheelwrights' Company; Liveryman of the Haberdashers' Company. *Address:* Hallett, Fox and White, Compter House, Wood St., Cheapside, E.C.2; 8 West Hill Court, N.6. *Club:* City Livery (President 1938-39). [*Died* 1 *Dec.* 1962.

FOX, Terence Robert Corelli; Fellow of King's College, Cambridge, since 1941; University Lecturer in Engineering, since 1959; *b.* 2 May 1912; *o. s.* of late C. Fox, London; unmarried. *Educ.:* Regent St. Polytechnic Secondary School; Jesus College, Cambridge. Technical Assistant, I.C.I. Ltd. (Billingham), 1933-37; Demonstrator, Engineering Laboratory, Cambridge, 1937-45; Lecturer, Engineering Lab., Camb., 1945-46; Shell Professor of Chemical Engineering, Univ. of Cambridge, 1946-59. *Address:* King's College, Cambridge. *T.:* 4411. [*Died* 5 *Oct.* 1962.

FOX, Wilfrid S., M.A., M.D., B.C. Cantab., F.R.C.P. Lond.; retired; *s.* of H. F. Fox, Bromborough, Cheshire; *m.* 1900; one *s.*

one *d.* *Educ.:* Marlborough; Trinity Coll., Cambridge. Director of J. & A. Churchill, Publishers; Director of the Royal Insurance London Board; Consulting Physician for Diseases of the Skin, St. George's Hospital and St. John's Hospital, Leicester Square. Late Asst. Physician to Skin Dept., Seamen's Hospital, Greenwich. *Address:* Winkworth Farm, Godalming, Surrey. *T.:* Hascombe 220. *Club:* Oxford and Cambridge. [*Died* 22 *May* 1962.

FOX, William Sherwood, M.A., Ph.D., D.Litt., LL.D., Docteur en Droit, F.R.S.C. 1922; President and Vice-Chancellor, University of Western Ontario, London, Ontario, 1927-47; *b.* Throopsville, N.Y., 17 June 1878; *s.* of Edward Theophilus and Emma Fox, both of Toronto, Ontario; *m.* 1906, Julia McKinnon; two *d.* *Educ.:* Harbord Street Collegiate Institute, Toronto; McMaster University, Toronto; University of Geneva; Johns Hopkins University, Baltimore. Instructor in Classics, Brandon College, Brandon, Manitoba, 1900-09; Fellow in Classical Archæology, Johns Hopkins University, Baltimore, 1909-11; Assistant Professor in Classics, Princeton Univ., Princeton, N.J., 1911-17; Professor of Classics, Western Univ., London, Ontario, 1917-27; Dean of Faculty of Arts, Western Univ., London, 1919-27. Director Royal Botanical Gardens, Hamilton, Ontario. O.St.J. *Publications:* Johns Hopkins Tabellae Defixionum, Baltimore, 1912; The Mythology of Greece and Rome (vol. I in The Mythology of All Races series), Boston, 1916, 1928; Trans. of Greek and Latin passages relating to Zoroaster (Jl. of K. R. Cama, Oriental Inst., Bombay); A Century of Service, London, Ont., 1945; Letters of William Davies, Toronto, 1854-1861, Toronto, 1946; 'T Ain't Runnin' No More, London, Ont., 1946 (fourth impression, 1958 with a sequel 'T Ain't Runnin' No More—Twenty Years After); St. Ignace, Canadian Altar of Martyrdom, Toronto, 1949; The Bruce Beckons, Toronto, 1952 (1962, paperback edn. with appendix, etc.); Silken Lines and Silver Hooks, Toronto, 1954; Sherwood Fox of Western, Toronto, 1964; Contribs. to Trans. Roy. Can. Inst. on Carolinian Native Trees and Shrubs of Ontario (with Dr. James H. Soper), Toronto, 1952, 1953, 1954; numerous articles in classical, botanical and archæological jls. and in literary periodicals. Baptist. *Recreations:* fishing and botanizing. *Address:* 14 Harrison Crescent, London, Ont., Canada. *T.:* General 4-4747. *Clubs:* London, Rotary, London Hunt (all London, Ont.). [*Died* 14 *Aug.* 1967.

FOX-WILLIAMS, Jack, M.C. 1916; Capt. Royal Artillery, retired; *b.* 23 May 1893; *s.* of J. E. Williams and M. A. Heathcote; *m.* 1930, Cecily Beatrice (*d.* 1939), *d.* of Charles James Fox, Pasadena, California; one *d.* (one *s.* decd.). *Educ.:* Kings School, Chester; Queen's College, Oxford (open scholar). Served European War, in Royal Artillery, 1914-19. Hons. Maths. M.A. (Oxon), 1920. American Radiator & Sta. Sanitary Corpn., U.S.A., 1928-34 and 1939; returned to England, Jan. 1940; Adviser to Director of Warship Production, 1942; British Admiralty Delegation, Washington, 1943; independent member heavy and light clothing working parties, 1946 and 1948; Chairman Clothing Development Council, 1950; Founder member and Vice-President Institute of Export. Past-Master, Pattenmakers' Co. *Recreation:* travel. *Address:* 3 Belgrave Place, S.W.1. *T.:* 01-235 4600. *Clubs:* Carlton, Royal Automobile, Anglo-Belgian Union, Hurlingham. [*Died* 27 *June* 1970.

FOXLEE, Richard William, C.M.G. 1953; C.B.E. 1945; M.Inst.C.E.; Consulting Engineer (on own account); also Consultant to Coode and Partners, Consulting Engineers, at 9 Victoria St., S.W.1.; former member Council Inst. C.E.; *b.* 29 May 1885; *s.* of late William T. Foxlee, M.Inst.C.E.; *m.* 1913, Olive Marjorie, *er. d.* of late Francis Robert Flintan, L.D.S.; one *d.* *Educ.:* Westminster School, Engineering Pupilage under late Alexander Ross, M.Inst.C.E.; Engineering Dept., Great Northern Rly., 1906-9; Great Central Rly., 1909-15; Port of London Authority, 1915-21; Deputy Head Engineering Designs Dept., Crown Agents for Oversea Governments and Administrations, 1921; Deputy Chief Engineer (Civil), 1928; Chief Civil Engineer, 1945-49; Engineer-in-Chief, Crown Agents. Engineering Adviser to Secretary of State for Colonies, 1949-54. *Publication:* Hammer Blow Impact on the Main Girders of Railway Bridges (Proceedings of the Institute of Civil Engineers, 1934) for which the Trevithic Premium was awarded. *Address:* Malmsmead, East Horsley, Surrey. *T.:* East Horsley 57. *Club:* St. Stephen's. [*Died* 27 *Nov.* 1961.

FOYLE, William Alfred; Commander, Order of Red Cross of Estonia; Lord of the Manors of Great Bromley, East Donyland, Fordham Hall, Martells Hall, Blamsters Hall; Managing Director of W. and G. Foyle, Ltd.; Director Foyle's Educational, Ltd.; Foyle's Music Co., Ltd.,; Foyle's Lending Libraries, Ltd.; Foyle's Welsh Co., Ltd.; Piena Music Coy.; Founder of Book Clubs; *b.* 4 Mar. 1885; *m.* 1907, Christina Tulloch; two *d.* (and one *s.* decd.). *Educ.:* Owen's School; King's College. First appointment with the late Sir E. Marshall-Hall; at age of 18 began career in partnership with brother, G. S. Foyle, as a bookseller; in 25 years built up the largest bookselling business of its kind in the world, with a stock of 3,000,000 volumes. *Publication:* First Editions and their Values. *Recreations:* rambling, reading, travel. *Address:* Beeleigh Abbey, Maldon, Essex; 121 Charing Cross Rd., W.C.2. *T.A.:* Foylibra Westcent. *T.:* Maldon 133. *Clubs:* Devonshire, Savage. [*Died* 4 *June* 1963.

FRAENKEL, Eduard, M.A. (Oxf.); Dr.phil. (Göttingen); Dr. *h.c.* Freie Universität Berlin-West, Urbino, St. Andrews, Florence; Fribourg (Switzerland); Hon. D.Litt. Oxford; Member Academies of: Bologna, Göttingen, Lund, Munich, Stockholm and Istituto Lombardo (Milan); Honorary member Linguistic Society of America; Freedom of the City of Sarsina (Italy); *b.* Berlin, 17 March 1888; *s.* of late Julius and late Edith Fraenkel; *m.* 1918, Ruth, *y. d.* of Gustav von Velsen; two *s.* one *d.* (and one *d.* decd.). *Educ.:* Askanisches Gymnasium, Berlin; Universities of Berlin, Rome, Göttingen. Assistant Thesaurus linguae Latinae, 1913; Privatdozent, Berlin Univ., 1917; Prof. extraordinarius, Berlin, 1920; Prof. ordinarius, Kiel, 1923; Göttingen, 1928; Freiburg-i.-Br., 1931; Bevan Fellow of Trinity Coll., Cambridge, 1934; Corpus Christi Prof. of Latin, Oxford Univ., 1935-53, Prof. Emer., 1953; Hon. Fell., Corpus Christi Coll., 1953. F.B.A. 1941-64, retd. Kenyon Medal (for Classical Studies) British Academy, 1965. *Publications:* De media et nova comoedia quaest. sel., 1912; Plautinisches im Plautus, 1922; Iktus und Akzent im latein. Sprechvers, 1928; Kolon und Satz, 1932-33; Das Pindargedicht des Horaz, 1933; Rome and Greek Culture, 1935; Aeschylus Agamemnon, 1950; Horace, 1957; Beobachtungen zu Aristophanes, 1962; Zu den Phoenissen des Euripides, 1963; Kleine Beiträge zur Klassischen Philologie, 1964; Noch einmal Kolon und Satz, 1965; Leseproben aus Reden Ciceros und Catos, 1968. *Address:* Corpus Christi College, Oxford. [*Died* 5 *Feb.* 1970.

FRANCE, Rev. Canon Walter Frederick, M.A.; *b.* 15 Feb. 1887; *s.* of George Thornton France, J.P., and Lucy

Stogdon; *m.* 1920, Marjorie Norris; one *s.* two *d.* *Educ.:* Gonville and Caius Coll., Cambridge; Westcott House, Cambridge. Missionary Service in Japan, 1909-25; Oversea Secretary S.P.G., 1928-45; Hon. Canon Canterbury Cathedral, 1941; Hon. Secretary Colonial Bishoprics Fund, 1938-45. Select Preacher Cambridge University, 1941; Oxford University, 1949. Warden, S. Augustine's College, Canterbury, 1945-52; Hon. Fellow 1953. *Publications:* Industrialism in Japan, 1928; Colonial Bishoprics Fund Centenary History, 1941; St. Augustine's, Canterbury, 1952. *Address:* St. Martins Paddock, Canterbury, Kent. [*Died* 18 *Aug.* 1963.

FRANCIS, Herbert William Sidney, C.B. 1938; O.B.E. 1917; *b.* 27 June 1880; *s.* of Philip Francis and Jane Lloyd Jones; *m.* 1907, Hildegard (*d.* 1960), *d.* of Rev. J. F. D. Hoernle; one *s.* two *d.* *Educ.:* Blundell's Sch.; Balliol Coll., Oxf. (Blundell Scholar). Clerk in Local Government Board, 1903; Barrister-at-Law, Inner Temple, 1908; Assistant Secretary, Ministry of Health, 1919; Director of Housing, 1934; Director Local Government Division Ministry of Health, 1936-38; Secretary and Comptroller-General of the National Debt Office, 1938-46 Liberty Cross (Norway), 1948. Reserve Chairman or Chairman Bournemouth, Portsmouth and Southampton Rent Tribunals, 1950-60. *Address:* 1 Milton Lodge, Gillingham, Dorset. *Clubs:* Oxford and Cambridge, M.C.C. [*Died* 23 *Dec.* 1968.

FRANCIS, Hon. Sir Josiah, Kt. 1957; Statesman, Company Director; *b.* 28 March 1890; *s.* of late Henry Alfred Francis and Ada Florence (*née* Hooper); *m.* 1927, Edna Clarke Cribb. *Educ.:* Christian Brothers College, Ipswich, Qld. Served War, C.M.F., A.I.F., 1912-19; M.H.R. (Lib.) Moreton, Qld., 1922-55; Member Royal Commission and various Public Committees, 1923-31; Assistant Minister for Defence and Minister in charge of War Service Homes, 1932-34; Actg. Min. for Repatriation, 1933; Chm. Public Works Cttee., 1937-40; Rural Industries Cttee., 1941-43; Vice-Chm. Standing Cttee. on Broadcasting, 1943-46; Mem. Parl. deleg., Japan, 1948; Min. for the Army, Dec. 1949-Nov. 1955; Min. for Navy, Dec. 1949-May 1951; Actg. Min. for Navy, June-July 1951; Min. for Navy, July 1954-Nov. 1955; Minister and Consul-General for Australia at New York, 1955-61. *Recreations:* golf, tennis, fishing. *Address:* 15 Archer Street, Toowong, Brisbane, Queensland, Australia. *Clubs:* United Services, Anzac, The Brisbane, Constitutional (all Brisbane). [*Died* 22 *Feb.* 1964.

FRANCIS, Richard Henry, C.M.G. 1960; General Secretary of Queensland Dairymen's Organisation, Australia, since 1947; Secretary, Australian Dairy Farmers' Federation and the Australian Dairy Industry Council, since 1960; *b.* 21 July 1897; *s.* of late John George and Elizabeth Francis, Cranbourne, Victoria, Australia; *m.* 1919, Mary, *d.* of late H. I. Richards, Nagambie, Victoria; two *s.* *Educ.:* State Schools and Business Colleges in Victoria. Commonwealth of Australia Public Service, 1913-23, in Postmaster-General's and Income Tax Departments; qualified as Accountant, now Associate, Australian Society of Accountants; dairy farming in Victoria, 1923-36; on staff of Dept. of Agriculture, Victoria, engaged on dairy factory supervision, instructor Werribee School Dairy Technology and war-time dairy industry organisation, 1936-45; with Commonwealth Dairy Produce Equalisation Committee on dairy costs and subsidy distribution, 1945-47; Joint Secretary of Joint Dairy Industry Advisory Committee, 1946-1952. *Recreations:* music, reading and gardening. *Address:* 41 Bryden Street, Windsor N.15, Queensland, Australia. *T.:* Brisbane 57 3772. [*Died* 29 *Jan.* 1961.

FRANCIS-WILLIAMS, Baron *cr.* 1962, of Abinger (Life Peer): **Edward Francis Williams,** C.B.E. 1945; Author and Journalist; *b.* St. Martins, Shropshire, 10 March 1903; *o. s.* of J. E. Williams; *m.* 1926, Jessie M. Hopkin; one *s.* one *d.* *Educ.:* Queen Elizabeth's Grammar School, Middleton, and on the staffs of various newspapers. Editor Daily Herald, 1936-40; Controller of News and Censorship, Ministry of Information, 1941-45; Adviser on Public Relations to the Prime Minister, 1945-47. Regents' Prof., University of Calif., Berkeley, 1961; Kemper Knapp Visiting Professor, Univ. Wisconsin, 1967-. A Governor, B.B.C., January 1951-52. Member, Monopolies Commission on Newspaper Mergers, 1966-. *Publications:* War by Revolution, 1940; Democracy's Last Battle, 1941; Ten Angels Swearing: or Tomorrow's Politics, 1942; No Man Is an Island (novel), 1945; Press, Parliament and People, 1946; The Triple Challenge: The Future of Socialist Britain, 1948; A Provincial Affair (novel); Fifty Years March: The Rise of the Labour Party, 1949; The Richardson Story (novel), 1951; Ernest Bevin: Portrait of a Great Englishman; Magnificent Journey: The Rise of the Trade Unions, 1954; Dangerous Estate: The Anatomy of Newspapers, 1957; A Prime Minister Remembers (with Earl Attlee), 1961; The American Invasion, 1962; A Pattern of Rulers, 1965; The Right to Know: The Rise of the World Press, 1969; Nothing so Strange: an autobiography, 1970. *Recreations:* talking, walking, doing nothing. *Address:* Griffins, Abinger Hammer, Surrey. *T.:* Dorking 730444. *Club:* Reform. [*Died* 5 *June* 1970.

FRANCK, Harry Alverson; *b.* Munger, Michigan, 29 June 1881; *s.* of Charles A. Franck and Lillie E. Wilsey; *m.* 1919, Rachel W. Latta; three *s.* two *d.* *Educ.:* Michigan Univ.; Harvard; Columbia; abroad. Teacher of French, Detroit, Mich., 1903-04; worked way round the world, 1904-1905; Master of Modern Languages, Bellefonte, Pa. 1906; Browning School, New York, 1906-08; Head Modern Language Department, Technical High School, Springfield, Mass., 1908-11; served in Europe as Lieutenant of Cavalry, American E.F., 1917-19; travelled extensively until 1941; Major, U.S. Army Air Corps, 1942-47. Post-graduate studies, Columbia University, 1948-52; Cruise lecturer, South America, 1950, Mediterranean (two tours), 1951; conducted tourist party around world, 1952, to New Zealand, Australia and around Pacific, 1954; travelled by non-aerial public conveyances from Algiers to Cape Town, 1952-53; Cruise lecturer, Caribbean and Mediterranean, 1955, 1956 and 1957; explored Madagascar and East Coast of Africa from Cape Town to Port Said, during winter, 1957-58; explored British Guiana, 1960. Many years lecturing on four continents in three languages. *Publications:* A Vagabond Journey around the World, 1910; Four Months Afoot in Spain, 1911; Zone Policeman 88, 1913; Tramping through Mexico, 1916; Vagabonding down the Andes, 1917; Vagabonding through Changing Germany, 1920; Roaming through the West Indies, 1920; Working North from Patagonia, 1921; Wandering in Northern China, 1923; Glimpses of Japan and Formosa, 1924; Roving through Southern China, 1925; East of Siam, 1926; The Fringe of the Moslem World, 1928; I Discover Greece, 1929; Marco Polo, Jr., 1929 (juvenile); A Scandinavian Summer, 1930; Travels in many Lands: (School Readers) China, The Japanese Empire, 1927, Mexico and Central America, South America, 1928; Foot-Loose in the British Isles, 1933; A Vagabond in Sovietland, 1935; Trailing Cortez through Mexico, 1935; Roaming in Hawaii, 1937; Sky Roaming above two Continents, 1938; The Lure of Alaska, 1939;

Rediscovering South America, 1943. Many magazine articles. *Recreations:* reading, swimming, photography. *Address:* 162 North Sugan Road, New Hope, Pa., U.S.A. *T.:* Volunteer 2-2474. [*Died* 17 *April* 1962.

FRANCK, Professor James, F.R.S. 1964; Emeritus Professor of Physical Chemistry, University of Chicago (Professor 1938-47); Member and Professor, Research Institutes, University of Chicago, 1949; *b.* 26 August 1882; *s.* of Jacob Franck and Rebecca Drucker; *m.* 1907, Ingrid Josephson (*d.* 1942); two *d.*; *m.* 1946, Hertha Sponer. Came to U.S., 1935; began as Assistant in physical laboratory, Univ. of Berlin, 1906, privat docent, 1911-16, Associate Prof. of Physics, 1916-18; Chairman Dept. Physics, Kaiser Wilhelm Institute of Physical Chemistry, 1918-20; Professor and Director Physical Institute, Univ. of Göttingen, 1920-1933; Guest Prof., Univ. of Copenhagen, 1934; Prof. Physics, Johns Hopkins Univ. 1935-38; Hitchcock Professor, Univ. of Calif., 1941; Emeritus Professor, 1947. Nobel Prize in Physics, 1925; Planck Medal, Germ. Phys. Soc.; Rumford Medal, Acad. of Arts and Sciences (Boston). Holds several hon. degrees. Mem. of several acads. including Nat. Acad. of Sciences and Amer. Philosophical Soc., and other learned socs. Jewish religion. *Publications:* Anregung von Quantensprüngen, 1926; also scientific articles on molecular physics, photochemistry and photosynthesis. *Address:* Dept. of Chemistry, University of Chicago, Chicago, Ill., U.S.A.
[*Died* 21 *May* 1964.

FRANK, Leonhard; novelist; Grand Cross of Federal Republic of Germany, 1957; *b.* Würzburg, 4 Sept. 1882; *m.* 3rd, Charlott Frank; one *s.* (of a former marriage). War in Munich, 1904-10, and at other short periods; lived in Berlin, 1910-33, except for 1914-18, when was in Switzerland; left Germany again in 1933 and was in Zürich, London, Paris, New York, and Hollywood until 1950, when returned to Munich. Member: Preussiche Dichterakad., 1927-33; Bavarian Academy of Fine Arts, 1951; Deutsche Akad. der Künste, 1955. Has won many literary prizes. Dr. *h.c.* Humboldt University, Berlin, 1957. Tolstoy Medal from U.S.S.R., 1960. *Publications:* Die Räuberbande (Fontane Prize), 1914; Die Ursache (dramatised 1930), 1915; Der Mensch ist gut (Kleist Prize, 1920), 1917; Der Bürger, 1924; Im letzten Wagen, 1925-26; Das Ochsenfurter Männerquartett, 1927; Karl und Anna (dramatised 1929), 1927-28; Bruder und Schwester, 1929; Hufnägel (play), 1930-31; Von den drei Millionen Drei, 1932; Traumgefährten, 1934-35; Mathilde appeared first in New York, London, Amsterdam), 1947-48; Die Jünger Jesu, 1949; Links wo das Herz ist, 1952; Deutsche Novelle, 1954; Collected Stories, 1957; four plays for the theatre, 1956-58; Collected Plays, 1959-60. Books trans. into many languages. *Recreation:* motoring. *Address:* Tengstrasse 34, Munich 13, Germany. *T.:* 371672. [*Died* 18 *Aug.* 1961.

FRANKAU, Sir Claude (Howard Stanley), Kt., *cr.* 1945; C.B.E. 1919; D.S.O. 1918; M.S. Lond., F.R.C.S. Eng.; Consulting Surgeon, St. George's Hospital; Emeritus Lecturer in Surgery in Medical School; Consulting Surgeon Royal Waterloo Hospital for Children and Woodford Hospital; Consulting Surgeon (non-obstetric) Queen Charlotte's Hospital; Dir. Emergency Medical Service, Ministry of Health, London and Home Counties, 1940-48; Pres., Assoc. of Surgeons of Great Britain, 1937-38; late Examiner in Surgery, University of London and Member of the Court of Examiners of the Royal College of Surgeons; Adviser in Surgery, Ministry of Health; *b.* 11 Feb. 1883; *y. s.* of F. J. Frankau, Barrister-at-law; *m.* 1st, 1914, Edith Lorne (*d.* 1934), 3rd *d.* of F. A. MacDougall, of Rendham; one *s.* one *d.* (and one *s.* decd.); 2nd, 1935, Isabella, M.D. (*d.* 1967), *d.* of late Angus Robertson and *widow* of Gordon Cunningham. *Educ.:* Rugby; St. George's Hospital (Allingham Scholar in Surgery, William Brown Exhibition), Gold Medal, M.S. Exam., Univ. of London. Colonel, A.M.S.; served European War (France), 1915-19, as Surgical Specialist; in command of 2nd London Clearing Station; and for the last part of the war as Consulting Surgeon to 5th Army B.E.F., with temporary rank of Colonel (despatches three times, brevet majority, D.S.O., C.B.E., slightly wounded). *Publications:* Various articles in medical journals. *Recreation:* fishing. *Address:* Ickleton Grange, Ickleton, Saffron Walden, Essex. *T.:* Chrishall 224. *Club:* Athenæum. [*Died* 29 *June* 1967.

FRANKAU, Pamela; novelist, journalist and short-story writer; *b.* 3 Jan. 1908; *d.* of Gilbert Frankau and Dorothea Drummond-Black; *m.* 1945, Marshall Dill, Jr., San Francisco. *Educ.:* P.N.E.U. School, Burgess Hill, Sussex. Served with A.T.S. during War of 1939-45. Received into the Catholic Church, 1942. *Publications:* Marriage of Harlequin, 1927 (first novel); subsequently (among others): The Willow Cabin, 1949; The Offshore Light, 1952; The Winged Horse, 1953; A Wreath for the Enemy, 1954; The Bridge, 1957; Ask Me No More, 1958; Road Through the Woods, 1960; Pen to Paper, 1961; Sing for your Supper, 1963; Slaves of the Lamp, 1965; Over the Mountains, 1967. *Recreations:* travel, cooking, roulette. *Address:* 55 Christchurch Hill, N.W.3. [*Died* 8 *June* 1967.

FRANKFURTER, Felix; Associate Justice of United States Supreme Court, 1939-62; *b.* Vienna (Austria), 15 Nov. 1882; *s.* of Leopold Frankfurter and Emma Winter; *m.* 1919, Marion A. Denman, Longmeadow, Mass. *Educ.:* Public Schools, New York City; College of the City of New York, A.B. 1902; Harvard Law School, LL.B. 1906; D.C.L. Oxford, 1939; LL.D. Amherst College, 1940, Univ. of Chicago, 1953, Harvard Univ., 1956, Brown University, 1960, Yale University, 1961, hon. Master of Bench of Gray's Inn, 1952. Assistant United States Attorney, Southern District, New York, 1906-09; Special Assistant to the Attorney-General, 1909-11; Law Officer, War Department, 1911-14; Byrne Professor of Administrative Law, Harvard University, Cambridge, Mass., 1914-39; Major and Judge Advocate O.R.C. U.S.A.; assistant to the Secretary of War; Counsel to the President's Mediation Commission, 1917-18; Chairman, War Labor Policies Board, 1918; George Eastman Visiting Professor, Oxford University, 1933-34. U.S. Presidential Medal of Freedom, 1963. *Publications:* The Case of Sacco and Vanzetti, 1927; The Business of the Supreme Court (with J. M. Landis), 1928; The Public and Its Government, 1930; The Labor Injunction (with N. Greene), 1930; The Commerce Clause, 1937; Mr. Justice Holmes and the Supreme Court, 1938; Law and Politics, 1939; Of Law and Men, 1956; Felix Frankfurter Reminisces, 1960. *Address:* c/o Supreme Court, Washington, D.C., U.S.A.
[*Died* 22 *Feb.* 1965.

FRANKLIN, Hon. Mrs. Henrietta, C.B.E. 1950; Hon. Secretary, Parents' National Educational Union, since 1890; Vice-President (former Pres.) National Council of Women; on Advisory Cttee. of Liberal Jewish Synagogue of which she is a Founder Member; *b.* London, 9 April 1866; *e. d.* of 1st Baron Swaythling and Ellen Cohen; *m.* 1885, Ernest L. Franklin; three *s.* two *d.* (and one *s.* decd.). Has worked for P.N.E.U. and Nat. Council of Women; lectured on educational and social subjects throughout United Kingdom, and in all the capitals of Europe,

all over Union of South Africa in 1923. and also in United States and Canada. Has attended and spoken at meetings of International Council of Women as delegate for National Council of Women (Gt. Brit.). Founder of: P.N.E.U. Girls' Public School, Overstone, Northampton; Boys' P.N.E.U. Prep. School, Desmoor, Ewhurst; St. Julian's, Estoril, Portugal. *Publications:* pamphlets and articles on Education in many magazines and papers; *relevant publication:* Netta (by Monk Gibbon), 1960. *Recreations:* entertaining children, embroidery, reading, gardening. *Address:* 88 Carlton Hill, N.W.8. *T.:* Maida Vale 9298; Glenalla, Ray, Letterkenny, Co. Donegal, Eire. *Clubs:* Pioneer, Lyceum, National Book League.
[*Died* 7 *Jan.* 1964.

FRANKLIN, Kenneth James, F.R.S. 1955; D.M., B.Ch. M.A. (Oxon); D.Sc. (Lond.); F.R.C.P. (Lond.); Professor Emeritus of Physiology in the University of London; Emeritus Fellow, Oriel College, Oxford; *b.* 25 Nov. 1897; *m.* Ethel Alice, *yr. d.* of Col. R. H. Adamson, C.B.E.; one *d.* *Educ.:* Christ's Hospital; Hertford College, Oxford (Classical Scholar). Royal Field Artillery, France and Belgium, 1917-19; Welsh Memorial Prize, 1920; First Class Honours Animal Physiology, 1921; Demonstrator in Physiology, Oxford, 1921-22; St. Bartholomew's Hospital, 1922-24; Lecturer in Physiology, Brasenose College, 1923-24; Fellow of Oriel College, 1924; Tutor and Librarian, 1931-47; Demonstrator of Pharmacology, Oxford, 1924-38; Radcliffe Travelling Fellow, 1925; Assistant Professor of Physiology, University of Michigan, 1926; Radcliffe Prize, 1933; Dean of the Medical School, Oxford, 1934-38; Acting Dean, 1939-1945; Dean, 1945-46; Assistant Director of the Nuffield Institute for Medical Research, 1935-47; Professor of Physiology of the University of London at St. Bartholomew's Hospital Medical College, 1947-58, retd.; Visiting Professor, Tulane University School of Medicine, Nov. 1951; Visiting Professor of Physiology, University of Illinois, Sept. 1951-June 1952; Oliver-Sharpey Lecturer, R.C.P., 1951; Fellow, Roy. Soc. Med.; Hon. Mem. Harveian Society of London; Hon. Mem. Renal Assoc.; Life Mem. Anatomical Soc. of Gt. Brit. and Ire.; late Pres., now Hon. Member British Society for Research on Ageing; F.R.C.O.G. 1964. Corresp. Mem. Deutsche Gesellschaft für Photographie; Liveryman, Society of Apothecaries of London (Hon. Fell. Faculty of History of Medicine and Pharmacy of the Society), Osler Memorial Medal, Oxford, 1965. *Publications:* A Short History of Physiology, 1933, 2nd edn., 1949. Facsimile edn. and transl. of Richard Lower's De Corde, London, 1669; of De Venarum Ostiolis, 1603, of Hieronymus Fabricius of Aquapendente; A Monograph on Veins, 1937; The Fœtal Circulation, etc., 1944; Studies of the Renal Circulation, 1947; Cardiovascular Studies, 1948; Joseph Barcroft, 1872-1947, 1953; facsimile edition and translation of William Harvey's De Motu Cordis etc., 1628, 1957; facsimile edition and translation of William Harvey's De Circulatione Sanguinis, 1649, 1958; William Harvey, Englishman, 1578-1657, 1961; papers in med. and sci. jls *Address:* Broomfield, the Street, East Preston, Sussex. *T.:* Rustington 3444.
[*Died* 8 *May* 1966.

FRANKLING, Herbert George, C.B.E. 1919; M.R.C.S.; Hon. Consulting Surgeon Harrogate and District General Hospital, Royal Bath Hospital and Ripon Cottage Hospital; Member Association of Surgeons of G.B. and I.; *b.* 1876; *s.* of late George Frankling; *m.* 1st 1906, Florence (*d.* 1917), *d.* of the late Joseph Ashmall; 2nd, 1936, Eleanor Mary, *er. d.* of late George Ashmall. *Educ.:* Combe Down School, Bath; London Hospital. Late House Surgeon London Hospital, St. Mark's Hospital for Diseases of the Rectum, and St. Peter's Hospital for Stone; Surgeon Grand Duchess George of Russia's Hospital and Royal Bath Auxiliary Military Hospital (C.B.E.). *Address:* Skittle Green, Bledlow, Bucks.
[*Died* 5 *Oct.* 1962.

FRANKLYN, Brig. Geoffrey Ernest Warren, D.S.O. 1919; M.C. *b.* 26 Aug. 1889; *s.* of late Lieut.-General Sir William Franklyn, K.C.B.; *m.* Prudence Earle, *e. d.* of David Charles. *Educ.:* Rugby, Entered Army, 1909; Lieut. 1912; Captain, 1915; Major, 1927, Brevet Lieut.-Col. 1931; Lieut.-Col., 1937; Col. 1938; served European War, 1914 (wounded, Brevet Majority, D.S.O., M.C. Belgian Croix de Guerre); Staff College, 1923; served War of 1939-45; retired 1944. *Address:* Birch Common, South Ascot, Berks. *Club:* Army and Navy.
[*Died* 24 *Nov.* 1967.

FRANKLYN, General Sir Harold Edmund, K.C.B., *cr.* 1943 (C.B. 1940); D.S.O. 1918; M.C.; *b.* 28 Nov. 1885; *s.* of late Lt.-General Sir W. E. Franklyn, K.C.B.; *m.* 1913, Monica, *d.* of late Lt.-General Sir H. E. Belfield, K.C.B., K.C.M.G.; one *d.* (one *s.* killed in action, 1944); *m.* 1941, Helen Thompson (*d.* 1959), *d.* of Rev. C. Titterton, B.D. *Educ.:* Rugby; Sandhurst. 1st commission Green Howards, 1905; Captain, 1914; Bt. Major, 1916; Major E. Lancs Regt. and Bt. Lt.-Col. 1925; Lt.-Col. 1930; Col. 1933; Maj.-Gen. 1938; Lt.-Gen. 1941; Gen. 1943; served European War, France and Belgium, 1914-19 (despatches six times, Bt. Major, D.S.O., M.C., French Croix de Guerre); Commanded 1st Batt. The West Yorkshire Regt., 1930-33; G.S.O.(1) Sudan Defence Force, 1933-35; Commandant, Sudan Defence Force, 1935-38; Commander 5th Division, 1938; Comd. 8th Corps on South Coast of England, July 1940-May 1941; General Officer comdg. British Troops in Northern Ireland, 1941-43; C.-in-C. Home Forces, 1943-45; retd. pay, 1945. *Recreations:* golf, bridge. *Club:* Army and Navy.
[*Died* 31 *March* 1963.

FRANKS, Rev. Robert Sleightholme, M.A. Cantab., D.Litt. Oxon, Hon. LL.D., Bristol University, 1928; B.A. London; *b.* 1 April 1871; *s.* of Rev. W. J. Franks, Redcar; *m.* 1902, Katharine Shewell; two *s.* two *d.* *Educ.:* Sir William Turner's Grammar School, Coatham, Redcar; St. John's College, Cambridge; Mansfield College, Oxford. Assistant Lecturer at Mansfield College, Oxford, 1897-1900; Minister of Prenton Congregational Church, Birkenhead, 1900-04; Theological Lecturer, Friends' Settlement for Religious and Social Study, Woodbrooke, Birmingham, 1904-10; Principal Western College, Bristol, 1910-39. *Publications:* The New Testament Doctrines of Man, Sin, and Salvation, 1908; Bible Notes, the Life of Paul, 1909; Bible Notes, the Writings of Paul, 1910; A History of the Doctrine of the Work of Christ in its Ecclesiastical Development, 1918; The Metaphysical Justification of Religion, 1929; The Atonement (Dale Lectures), 1934; The Doctrine of the Trinity, 1953; various articles in Hastings' Dictionary of Christ and the Gospels, Hastings' Dictionary of the Apostolic Church, and Hastings' Encyclopædia of Religion and Ethics. *Address:* Leppington, Winscombe, Somerset. *T.:* Winscombe 2213.
[*Died* 20 *Jan.* 1964.

FRASER OF ALLANDER, 1st Baron *cr.* 1964; **Hugh Fraser,** Bt. *cr.* 1961; D.L.; LL.D.: J.P.; Chairman and Managing Director, House of Fraser Ltd., since 1941; Chairman: George Outram and Co. Ltd., since 1964 (Deputy Chairman, 1959-64); John Barker & Co. Ltd., since 1957; Harrods Ltd., since 1959; Associated Fisheries Ltd., since 1961; Highland Tourist Development Co. Ltd., since 1960; Chm. Highland Tourist

(Cairngorm Development) Ltd., since 1964; National Treasurer, Scottish Conservative and Unionist Party, since 1965; *b.* 15 January 1903; *s.* of late Hugh Fraser and late Emily Florence McGown; *m.* 1931, Katie Hutcheon, *d.* of late Sir Andrew Lewis, LL.D., J.P.; one *s.* one *d.* *Educ.:* Warriston and Glasgow Academy. Magistrate, 1944-45; Hon. Treasurer: Automobile Association, 1951; Films of Scotland, 1955; Chairman Bd. of Governors, Westbourne School for Girls, Glasgow, 1951. Chairman and Managing Director, Scottish and Universal Investments, Ltd., 1948-. Mem. Scottish Tourist Board, 1958; Mem., British National Export Council, 1964. D.L. 1953. Hon. LL.D. St. Andrews Univ., 1962. *Recreations:* farming, horticulture, motoring. *Heir:* *s.* Hon Hugh Fraser [*b.* 18 December 1936; *m.* 1962, Patricia Mary, *e. d.* of John Bowie, Ardsheean, Milngavie]. *Address:* Dineiddwg, Mugdock, Stirlingshire. *T.:* Milngavie 1182. *Clubs:* Junior Carlton; Portland Conservative, Western (Glasgow). [*Died* 6 *Nov.* 1966.

FRASER, Rev. Alexander Garden, C.B.E. 1930; *b.* Tillicoultry, 6 Oct. 1873; *e. s.* of late Sir A. H. L. Fraser, K.C.S.I., LL.D., and Agnes, *d.* of R. Archibald; *m.* Beatrice, *d.* of R. Glass, Craigielea, Whickham; two *s.* three *d.* *Educ.:* Merchiston Castle School, Edinburgh; Trinity College, Oxford, M.A. Worked in Uganda under the Church Missionary Society, 1900-03; ordained, 1914; Principal of Trinity College, Kandy, 1904-24, with War Service in France, 1916-1918, and Indian Village Education Commission, 1920-21; Principal of Prince of Wales Coll., Achimota, Accra, Gold Coast, 1924-35. Warden, Newbattle Abbey College, 1935-39; Principal Friends' College, Jamaica, 1940-43; Chaplain Outward Bound Sea Sch., 1943-45; Assistant Chaplain Gordonstoun School, Elgin, Morayshire, 1946-51. *Publications:* (with Sir Gordon Guggisberg) The Future of the Negro, 1929; Pamphlets on Educational Questions in the East; Reports on Education Commissions, etc. *Recreations:* fishing, walking. *Address:* c/o M.R.A., 45 Berkeley Square, W.1. *Clubs:* Royal Commonwealth Society, Royal Over-Seas League. [*Died* 27 *Jan.* 1962.

FRASER, Sir Angus, Kt. 1962; Solicitor of Inland Revenue since 1956; *b.* 15 January 1909; *yr. s.* of late Andrew Brown Fraser, Tingley Hall, near Wakefield. *Educ.:* Leeds Gram. School; The Queen's College, Oxford. Barrister-at-law of Lincoln's Inn. *Address:* 1 Whitehall Place, S.W.1. *Clubs:* National Liberal; Arts Theatre. [*Died* 7 *Jan.* 1963.

FRASER, Charles Ian, C.B.E. 1962; T.D.; late Major, The Lovat Scouts; *b.* 6 April 1903; *s.* of late Philip Affleck Fraser of Reelig, Inverness-shire, and Augusta Zelia, *e. d.* of William Frederick Webb, of Newstead Abbey, Nottinghamshire; *m.* 1929, Mary Charity, *e. d.* of late Colonel Robert Campbell-Preston, of Ardchattan, Argyll; two *s.* two *d.* *Educ.:* Wellington Coll.; Magdalen Coll., Oxford. M.A. 1932. D.L. and J.P. Inverness-shire; Dingwall Pursuivant of Arms, 1939-1953; Albany Herald, 1953-61; Hon. Col., 540 L.A.A. Regt. R.A. (Lovat Scouts, T.A.), 1953-57; Member Board of Trustees, Nat. Museum of Antiquities of Scotland, 1954. *Address:* Reelig House, Kirkhill, Inverness-shire. *T.:* Drumchardine 208. *Clubs:* Junior Carlton; New (Edinburgh). [*Died* 4 *Aug.* 1963.

FRASER, Duncan, C.B.E. 1950; D.L. 1925; J.P.; LL.D. (Hon.) Aberdeen, 1951; *b.* 25 Oct. 1880; *s.* of Donald Fraser and Jane Macdonald; *m.* 1907, Charlotte Stewart Hastings; two *d.* *Educ.:* Cromdale, Morayshire; Grantown Grammar School. Served apprenticeship as draper, 1899; business, under title of Duncan Fraser (Draper) Aberdeen Ltd., 1912. Chief interests are economics and social problems; Aberdeen Town Council, 1934-51; was twice a magistrate; Lord Provost of Aberdeen and Lord Lieutenant of County of the City of Aberdeen, 1947-1951. Chevalier de la Légion d'Honneur, 1952. *Recreations:* bowls and fishing. *Address:* Braemoray, 6 Woodburn Avenue, Aberdeen. *T.:* Aberdeen 34480. [*Died* 18 *Feb.* 1966.

FRASER, Eric Malcolm, C.B.E. 1946; retired from I.C.I. Ltd., 1958; *b.* 17 November 1896; *y. s.* of late Sir Thomas R. Fraser, M.D., F.R.S., LL.D., Acharacle, Argyllshire, and of Susannah Fraser, *e. d.* of late Ernest Pease, Ledge House, Bembridge, Isle of Wight; no *c.* *Educ.:* Edinburgh Academy; Oriel College, Oxford. Commissioned Seaforth Highlanders, 1915 (despatches); joined Brunner, Mond & Co. Ltd. (now I.C.I.), 1919. Assistant Director-General of Progress and Statistics, War Office, 1939; Director of Investigation and Statistics, War Office, 1940; Director-General of Equipment Production, Ministry of Aircraft Production, 1942; Director-General of Aircraft Production, Ministry of Aircraft Production, 1943. Member Television Advisory Cttee., Oct. 1952-Dec. 1953; Member Council and of Exec. Cttee., Brit. Inst. of Management, 1952-56; Sales Controller, I.C.I. Ltd., 1946-1958; Chm. Plant Protection Ltd., 1954-58; Director of Pan Britannica Industries Ltd., 1954-58. *Recreations:* fishing, horticulture. *Address:* Radnor House, New Street, Henley-on-Thames, Oxon. *T.:* Henley-on-Thames 146. *Clubs:* Union; Phyllis Court (Henley). [*Died* 9 *Dec.* 1960.

FRASER, Sir Francis Richard, Kt., *cr.* 1944; M.A. (Camb.); M.D. (Edin.); F.R.C.P.; F.R.C.P.E.; Hon. LL.D. (Edin.); Director, British Post-graduate Medical Fedn., 1945-60; Prof. Emer. of Medicine, Dep. Vice-Chancellor (1947-49), and Member of Senate, University of London, 1942-60; late Director-General E.M.S. Ministry of Health; Hon. Fellow Royal Society of Medicine; late Prof. of Medicine, British Postgraduate Medical School; late Director Medical Professorial Unit and Physician, St. Bartholomew's Hosp.; *b.* 1885; *s.* of late Sir Thomas R. Fraser, M.D., F.R.S.; *m.* 1919, Mary Claudine Stirling, M.B.E. 1946, *d.* of late Colin Donald; one *s.* *Educ.:* Edinburgh Academy; Christ's College, Cambridge (Exhibitioner and Scholar); Edinburgh University. House Physician, Hospital for Sick Children, Edinburgh; House Physician and House Surgeon, Royal Infirmary, Edinburgh; Assistant in Medicine, Rockefeller Institute for Medical Research, New York; Assistant Physician, Presbyterian Hospital, New York; Assistant in Medicine, Columbia University, New York; served Harvard University Unit and R.A.M.C.; Consulting Physician, British Army of the Rhine; Goulstonian and Croonian Lecturer, Royal College of Physicians; Frederick Price Lecturer, Royal College of Physicians, Edinburgh; Member of Pharmacopœia Commission until 1945; Member of Lancet Commission on Nursing; Abraham Flexner Lecturer, Vanderbilt University, Nashville, Tenn., U.S.A., 1933; Redman Lecturer, McMaster Univ., Ontario, 1956; Harveian Orator, R.C.P., 1960. Hon. Dr. of Laws, London University, 1961. Commander Order of Orange-Nassau. *Publications:* papers in medical and scientific journals. *Recreation:* fishing. *Address:* 9 Melina Court, Grove End Rd., N.W.8. *T.:* Cunningham 5018. *Club:* Athenæum. [*Died* 2 *Oct.* 1964.

FRASER, Rear-Admiral The Hon. George, D.S.O. 1920; *b.* 1887; 2nd *s.* of 18th Lord Saltoun; *m.* 1st, Elizabeth Ida, *o. d.* of J. M. Spencer Stanhope of Cannon Hall, Barnsley, Yorks; one *s.*; 2nd, 1934, Margaret Elizabeth, 2nd *d.* of Reginald Barnes, St. Ermin's, Westminster; two *s.* *Educ.:* H.M.S.

Britannia. Served European War, 1914-19 (despatches, D.S.O.). *Address:* Languedoc, Firgrove, Cape Province, South Africa. *Clubs:* United Service, M.C.C. [*Died* 13 *June* 1970.

FRASER, Henry Ralph, C.M.G. 1952; O.B.E. 1943; Member Central Legislative Assembly, Uganda, 1947-58; Member of Legislative Council, Uganda, 1942-58; Mem. Executive Council, 1954-56; *b.* 1896; *s.* of Henry Fraser, London; *m.* 1920, Ethel, *d.* of J. H. Jones, Pretoria; one *s.* *Educ.*: Grocers' School, London. Served European War, 6th City of London Rifles, France (wounded), 1914-18. President Uganda Chamber of Commerce, 1937, 1951; Founder member, later Vice-Chm., Uganda Electricity Board, 1953-57. *Address:* c/o National Bank of India Ltd., 26 Bishopsgate, E.C.2; P.O. Box 16, Nakuru, Kenya. [*Died* 22 *Sept.* 1963.

FRASER, Air Vice-Marshal Hugh Henry Macleod, C.B. 1943; *b.* 12 Dec. 1895; *s.* of Lt.-Col. J. R. Fraser, C.M.G., Loyal Regt.; *m.* 1924, Hester Elisabeth May, *e. d.* of Col. W. A. Young, R. Scots Fusiliers; one *s.* one *d.* *Educ.*: Pembroke Lodge, Southbourne; Boyne House, Cheltenham College. Entered Royal Flying Corps Special Reserve as pilot, 1915; served in England, Home Defence night flying, 1916; France on Fighters and Bombers, 1917; Permanent Commission as Flight Lt. R.A.F., 1919; subsequently served in India, 1923-1927; p.s.c. 1930; i.d.c. 1935; R.A.F. member of Joint Planning Staff, 1936-39; First Director of Military Co-operation at Air Ministry, 1940; Director-General of Repair and Maintenance, Ministry of Aircraft Production, 1944; retired, 1945. *Recreations:* fishing, shooting, and cricket. *Address:* The Old Rectory, Twyford, Hants. *Club:* R.A.F. [*Died* 16 *Jan.* 1962.

FRASER, Rev. James, M.A.; Minister, Kentish Town, 1948-61, retd.; *b.* London, 1883; Scottish father, Irish mother; *m.* 1911, Madge Silvers Richardson; two *s.* *Educ.*: St. John's College, Cambridge; Westminster Presbyterian College, Cambridge. Ministerial charges:—Liverpool, 1909; Bexhill, 1910; London: Kentish Town, 1914-38; Hammersmith, 1939-43; Superintendent Minister for East London Area, 1943-48. Moderator Presbyterian Church of England, 1938. *Address:* 1 Rochester Terrace, N.W.1. [*Died* 1 *Sept.* 1966.

FRASER, James Duncan, C.V.O. 1961; M.B.E. 1947; Assistant Secretary, Ministry of Technology, since 1965; *b.* 11 January 1915; *e. s.* of late Lieut.-Colonel A. H. Fraser and late Irene (*née* Brown Douglas); *m.* 1943, Margaret, *e. d.* of B. M. Arnold, D.S.O.; two *s.* *Educ.*: Haileybury; Trinity Hall, Cambridge. Indian Civil Service, 1937-47; Principal: Min. of Works, 1947; Commonwealth Relations Office, 1951; First Secretary, Office of U.K. High Commission, Canberra, 1955; Defence Counsellor, Office of U.K. High Commn., Kuala Lumpur, 1958; British Deputy High Commissioner in Western India, 1960-63; Asst. Sec., C.R.O., 1963-64. *Recreations:* golf, music. *Address:* c/o Ministry of Technology, Millbank Tower, Millbank, S.W.1. *Club:* Oxford and Cambridge. [*Died* 22 *Dec.* 1965.

FRASER, Sir Kenneth (Barron), Kt. 1958; C.B.E. 1953; E.D. 1941; M.B. 1921; Ch.M. 1921; M.S. 1939; F.R.A.C.S. 1940; F.A.C.S. 1968; Hon. Consultant Surgeon, Brisbane Children's Hospital, since 1957 (Senior Visiting Surgeon, 1946-57); Hon. Consultant Surgeon, Mater Children's Hosp., Brisbane, since 1951 (Senior Hon. Surgeon, 1947-51); *b.* 28 March 1897; *s.* of Hugh Barron Fraser, M.Inst.C.E., Civil Engineer, Brisbane; *m.* 1929, Patricia, *d.* of P. L. Hart, Barrister, Brisbane; two *s.* two *d.* *Educ.*: Brisbane Boys' Grammar School; Queensland University; St. Andrew's Coll., Sydney University. Specialist Lecturer in Pædiatric Surgery, Univ. of Q'land, 1939-1961. Senior Visiting Surgeon, Brisbane Children's Hospital, 1946-57. Served A.I.F., 1939-46 (despatches); Brigadier (Retd.); Hon. Colonel, R.A.A.M.C., 1957-62. Hon. Surg. to Gov.-Gen., Australia, 1943-46; Hon. Surgeon to King George VI, 1949-52; Hon. Surgeon to the Queen, 1952-54. Chm. Queensland Medical Coordination Cttee., 1943-46; Foundation Member, Red Cross Blood Transfusion Service, Queensland, 1945-. President B.M.A. Queensland, 1952; Chairman State Committee, Royal Australian College of Surgeons, 1955-57; President Australian Pædiatric Association, 1958-59; Mem. of Senate, Univ. of Queensland, 1956-66; Member Council, Australian Nat. Univ., Canberra, 1961-63. Trustee, Gowrie Scholarship Trust Fund, 1960-; Member: Coun., Royal Flying Doctor Service, Queensland, 1957-66; Royal Brisbane Hosp. Bd., 1958-. Hospitaller and Almoner, Priory of St. John in Australia, 1954-; Commissioner St. John Ambulance Brigade, Queensland, 1953-61; Pres., St. John Coun., Queensland, 1966-. Mem., Anti-Cancer Coun., Queensland, 1962-. K.St.J. 1959. *Publications:* Speech Training for Cleft Palate Patients, 1946; various articles on surgical subjects in medical and surgical jls. *Recreations:* fishing, golf. *Address:* Ballow Chambers, Wickham Terr., Brisbane, Queensland, Australia. *T.*: 2.7906. *Clubs:* Queensland, United Service (Brisbane); Royal Queensland Golf. [*Died* 24 *June* 1969.

FRASER, Lindley Macnaghten, O.B.E. 1958; Head of German and Austrian Services, B.B.C., since 1946; *b.* 14 Aug. 1904; *s.* of late Rev. Norman and of Cecilia Craigie Fraser, Edinburgh; *m.* 1st, 1932, Elspet Mackenzie (marr. diss. 1945), *d.* of Dr. Ridley Mackenzie, Montreal; two *d.*; 2nd, 1959, Elizabeth Scott, *d.* of Arthur and Ellen Marks. *Educ.*: George Watson's, Edinburgh; Liverpool Institute High School; Balliol Coll., Oxford (Classical Exhibitioner), 1st class, Honour Mods. 1924, 1st class Literæ Humaniores, 1926, Oxford Union Society: Treasurer, Librarian, President, 1925-26, Procter Visiting Fellow, Princeton University, U.S.A., 1926-27; Eastman Fellow, Brookings School of Economics, Washington, 1927-28; Fellow and Prælector in Economics, The Queen's College, Oxford, 1928-35; Jaffrey Professor of Political Economy, Aberdeen University, 1935; B.B.C. German News Commentator, 1940; M.A. Oxon., 1929; Ph.D., Brookings Institution, U.S.A., 1932. *Publications:* Protection and Free Trade, 1932; Economic Thought and Language, 1937; Germany Between Two Wars, 1944; Propaganda, 1957; Articles in economic and other periodicals; Translations from German. *Recreation:* music. *Address:* 7 Ridgway Gardens, S.W.19. [*Died* 10 *March* 1963.

FRASER, Sir Stuart (Mitford), K.C.S.I., *cr.* 1918 (C.S.I. 1913); C.I.E. 1902; *b.* 2 June 1864; *s.* of late J. D. Fraser, J.P.; *m.* 1888, Constance, C.B.E. 1918 (*d.* 1937), *d.* of late Col. Edwin Maude; two *d.* (and one *s.* decd.). *Educ.*: Blundell's School, Tiverton; Balliol Coll., Oxford. Entered I.C.S., 1884; served in Bombay Presidency as Asst. Collector and Magistrate; Tutor and Governor to Maharaja of Kolhapur, 1889-94; District and Sessions Judge, 1895; Tutor and Governor to Maharaja of Mysore, 1896-1902; Dep. Sec. to Govt. of India (Foreign and Political Dept.), 1903; officiated as Foreign Sec. to Govt. of India, 1904-5; H.M.'s Commissioner to negotiate with China regarding Anglo-Tibetan Convention of 1904; Resident, Mysore, and Chief Commissioner, Coorg, 1905-10; Resident in Kashmir, 1911-1914; Resident at Hyderabad, 1916-19;

retired, 1920; J.P. Hants; C.C. and C.A., 1922-45; President Hants. and Dorset Branch of Royal Commonwealth Society. *Recreations:* shooting and fishing. *Address:* Brook House, Mudeford, Christchurch, Hants. *T.:* Christchurch 51. [*Died* 1 *Dec.* 1963.

FRASER, Brigadier Hon. William, D.S.O. 1918; M.C.; *b.* 1890; *y. s.* of 18th Baron Saltoun; *m.* 1919, Pamela Cynthia, *widow* of Major W. La T. Congreve, V.C., D.S.O., *y. d.* of late Cyril Maude; one *s.* *Educ.:* Charterhouse; Sandhurst. Served with Gordon Highlanders in India and Egypt; European War, 1914-18 (twice wounded, despatches, D.S.O., M.C.); transferred to Grenadier Guards, 1927; Military Attaché, Brussels and the Hague, 1931-35; Commanded 1st Bn. Grenadier Guards, 1937-38; Military Attaché, Paris, 1938-39; War of 1939-45 (wounded); retired pay, 1944. Chief of U.N.N.R.A. Mission in Paris, 1945-1947. *Address:* Clover House, Aldeburgh, Suffolk. *T.:* 172. *Club:* Turf. [*Died* 11 *Nov.* 1964.

FRASER, Major-General William Archibald Kenneth, C.B. 1941; C.B.E. 1922 D.S.O. 1919, M.V.O. 1928; M.C.; *b.* 1886; *s.* of late Col. James Fraser, R.A.M.C.; *m.* 1920, Cicely, *widow* of J H. Bill, Indian Civil Service one *d.* Served European War, 1914-19 (despatches, Bt Major, M.C., D.S.O. and bar) A.Q.M.G., 1919-20; Inspector-General South Persia Rifles, 1920-21; Military Attaché at Kabul, 1922-24; at Tehran, 1924-28; Military Secretary to the Governor of Bengal, 1930-32; General Staff Officer, 1st Grade, Lahore District, 1936-37, Commander Mhow Brigade Area, India, 1937; Divisional Commander, India, 1941; retired, 1941; re-employed until 1945. *Address:* c/o National and Grindlay's Bank, 13 St. James's Square, S.W.1. *Club:* United Hunts. [*Died* 9 *Feb.* 1969.

FRASER, William Henry, W.S.; retd.; Director (Past Chm.), National Guarantee & Suretyship Association Ltd. Retired from firm of Fraser, Stodart & Ballingall, Writers to the Signet, Edinburgh, 1964. *Address:* 27 Learmonth Terrace, Edinburgh. [*Died* 26 *June* 1966.

FRASER, W(illiam) Lionel, C.M.G. 1945; Merchant Banker; Chairman, Banque de Paris et des Pays-Bas Ltd.; formerly Chairman, Helbert, Wagg & Co. Ltd.; Director: Thomas Tilling Ltd. (Chm.); Triarch Corporation Ltd. (Toronto) (Dep. Chm.); Cornhill Insce. Co. (Chm.); Scandinvest Trust Ltd. (Chm.); Pres., Babcock & Wilcox Ltd.; formerly Deputy Chairman: Atlas Assurance Co. Ltd.; Tube Investments Ltd. Liveryman of Fishmongers Company; Trustee of the Tate Gallery; *m.* 1931, Cynthia Elizabeth Walter; two *s.* (one *d.* decd.). Joined London Scottish, January 1914. Served European War, 1914-19, France, Dardanelles, Egypt. Later seconded for special duties with Naval Intelligence Division Admiralty. Served at H.M. Treasury, November 1939-January 1945. Chairman Issuing Houses Assoc., 1946-48; Member Chelsea Borough Council, 1945-50. *Recreations:* golf, writing. *Publication:* (autobiography) All to the Good, 1963. *Address:* 30 Charles St., W.1. *T.:* Hyde Park 4333. *Clubs:* Garrick, St. James', White's, Portland, City of London, Travellers' (Paris). [*Died* 2 *Jan.* 1965.

FRASER-TYTLER, Lieut.-Col. Sir William Kerr, K.B.E., *cr.* 1939; C.M.G. 1933; M.C.; Order of Astor (Afghan), 1932; K.St.J., 1946; Silver Medal of American Red Cross, 1946; Indian Army retired; *b.* 26 Dec. 1886; 2nd *s.* of late James William Fraser-Tytler, Woodhouselee, Midlothian, and late Christian Alice Scott-Kerr; *m.* 1st, Eila Beatrice (*d.* 1951), *d.* of Major Colin McLean, Chief Constable of Inverness-shire; no *c.*; 2nd, 1953, Aileen MacHenry, *d.* of W. Knox Johnston, Berkhamsted. *Educ.:* Charterhouse; Christ Church, Oxford (B.A. 1909). Entered Indian Army, 1910; posted to 25th Cavalry (Frontier Force), 1911; served on N.W.F., India, 1911-17; East Africa, 1917-1918 (M.C.); 3rd Afghan War, 1919; transferred to Foreign and Politicl aDept., 1919; served in various capacities, chiefly on North-West Frontier of India, with H.M.'s Legation at Kabul, Afghanistan, and with Government of India till 1935; transferred temporarily to Diplomatic Service; British Minister to Afghanistan, 1935-41; Chief Delegate of the Mission of the British Red Cross and Order of St. John at Washington, 1943-46. *Publications:* Afghanistan—A Study of Political Developments in Central Asia; articles on Afghanistan in the Encyclopædia Britannica and in Chambers's Encyclopædia; contributor to various periodicals on Central Asian problems. *Recreations:* fishing, gardening, weaving. *Address:* Pilmuir, Haddington, East Lothian. *Clubs:* Cavalry; New (Edinburgh). [*Died* 23 *Aug.* 1963.

FRAZER, Alastair Campbell, C.B.E. 1962; D.Sc. (Lond.); M.D. (Birm.); Ph.D. (Lond.); M.B., B.S. (Lond.); F.R.C.P. (Lond.); Director-General of British Nutrition Foundation; Hon. Consultant on Metabolic Diseases to British Army; President: British Food Manufacturing Industries Research Assoc.; British Industrial Biological Research Assoc.; Member, Agricultural Research Council; Chairman Research Cttee. on Toxic Chemicals; Chm., Joint A.R.C./M.R.C. Food and Nutrition Research Cttee.; Chairman, Safety of drugs Cttee., Department of Health and Social Security; Scientific Adviser to Minister of Agriculture, Fisheries & Food; Member, F.A.O./W.H.O.; Joint Expert Advisory Panel on Food Additives; Chm., Commn. I, Internat. Union of Nutritional Sciences; Chm., Food Section, Internat. Union of Pure and Applied Chemistry; *b.* London, 26 July 1909; 2nd *s.* of Wilson Frazer, O.B.E., lately Asst. Sec. Min. of Health; *m.* 1943, Hilary, *y. d.* of R. E. Garrod, London; three *s.* one *d.* *Educ.:* Lancing (Scholar); St. Mary's Hospital Medical School, London. Lecturer in Physiology and Pharmacology, 1929-42, St. Mary's Hospital Medical School; Acting Professor, 1933, and 1934-35; Sir Halley Stewart Research Fellow, 1937-45; Prof. of Med. Biochemistry and Pharmacology, Univ. of Birmingham, 1943-67; awarded Buckston Browne Prize for 1944 by Harveian Society of London; Cantor Lecturer, Royal Society of Arts, 1948; Randolph West Memorial Lecturer Columbia Univ., N.Y., 1950; Guest lecturer to United Univs. of Sweden, 1950. Still Memorial Lectr., British Paediatric Assoc., 1953; Chm. Cttee. on Medical Health Policy for Uganda, 1955; Oliver Sharpey Lectr. R.C.P., 1956. Mem. of Visiting Faculty, U.S. Army Med. Graduate and Research School, Washington, D.C., 1950; Bernard Dyer Memorial Lectr., Soc. Analysts, 1960; Chm Commission on Research Services in East Africa, 1961; Leverhulme Memorial Lectr., Soc. Chem. Ind., 1962; Sanderson Wells Lectr., Middlesex Hosp. Med. Sch., 1963; Exchange Prof., Acad Med. Sci U.S.S.R., 1963 Bertram Louis Abraham's Lectr., R.C.P., 1964; Frankland Memorial, R.I.C., 1968; Vis. Prof., Dept. of Medicine, Univ. of Ill., 1968. Elected Hon. Foreign mem., Société Gastro-enterologie de Belge and Société Philomathique de Paris, 1948, Royal Flemish Academy of Sciences of Belgium 1953; Member, New York Academy of Sciences, 1960; Hon. Foreign Member: Royal Flemish Acad. of Med. Sci., 1968; Pan Amer. Med. Assoc., 1968. Chevreux Medal, Assoc. Française Tech. Corps Gras, 1969. Commissioned R.A.M.C. T.A., 1933. *Publications:* scientific and medical papers, mainly on fat absorption and metabolism,

the properties of oil/water interfaces and food research and toxicology. *Recreations:* music, photography and travel. *Address:* 28 Montpelier St., S.W.7. *T.:* 01-589 7655. *Clubs:* Athenæum, Savage.
[*Died* 14 *June* 1969.

FRAZER, Sir Thomas, Kt., *cr.* 1947; O.B.E. 1918; F.F.A 1906; Member Council of Foreign Bondholders; *b.* 19 January 1884; *s.* of Thomas Frazer, Edinburgh, and Elizabeth, *d.* of late Thomas Bell; *m.* 1st, 1910, Florence Maude (*d.* 1941), *d.* of late Vincent Slater; one *s.* two *d.*; 2nd, 1942, Ella Strickland (*d.* 1955), *d.* of late Christopher John Mulvany, Roscommon, Ireland. *Educ.:* Daniel Stewart's College, Edinburgh. *Recreations:* golf, gardening. *Address:* Flat 98, Grosvenor House, W.1. *T.:* Grosvenor 6363. *Club:* Carlton.
[*Died* 1 *Aug.* 1969.

FRAZER, William Miller, R.S.A. 1924 (A.R.S.A. 1909); landscape painter; *b.* Scone, Perthshire, 30 September 1864; *s.* of ex-Bailie Frazer, Perth; *m.* Sarah Eleanor, *o. d.* of late James Robertson, M.D., Edinburgh; three *s.* *Educ.:* Perth Academy; Keith Prizeman, R.S.A. Schools; President S.S.A., 1908; exhibits chiefly in Scottish Exhibitions, but also in Munich, Rome, Vienna, London and Paris; holds record for having exhibited for 73 consecutive years at the Royal Scottish Academy. *Principal pictures:* Whispering Reeds; The Braes of Athol; A Highland Pastoral; Rush Cutting in the Fens; The City of Perth. *Recreations:* billiards, yachting. *Address:* 5 Lady Road, Edinburgh 9. *Club:* Scottish Arts.
[*Died* 7 *May* 1961.

FREEMAN, John, D.M. (Oxon); Consultant Bacteriologist; Consulting Director of clinics for Allergic Disorders, St. Mary's Hospital; *b.* Leeds, 19 July 1877; *e. s.* of late J. J. Freeman, C.B.E.; *m.* 1907, Violet Alice Leslie, *e. d.* of Martin Hadden of Binghill, Murtle; three *s.* one *d.* *Educ.:* Charterhouse; Oxford; Paris; Berlin; Vienna. Lance-Corporal 1st Oxfordshire L.I. in Boer War, 1899-1900; Radcliffe Travelling Fellow, Oxford; Inoculation Department, St. Mary's Hospital, since 1904; Lieut.-Colonel in Russian A.M.S. on Bacteriological Mission to Galicia, 1914; Research Laboratory, Boulogne, 1917; Scientific Expert to H.Q., R.A.F., in France, 1918. Vice-pres. Asthma Research Council; Hon. Member British Assoc. of Allergists; Hon. Member British Soc. for Immunology; Member Med. Research Club; Fellow Amer. Acad. of Allergy. *Publications:* Hay-Fever: A Key to the Allergic Disorders, 1950; contributions on Bacteriology, Immunology and Allergy, etc. *Address:* (home) 4L Portman Mansions, W.1. *T.:* Welbeck 2561; (private consulting room) Wright-Fleming Institute, St. Mary's Hospital, Paddington, W.2. *T.:* Paddington 1662 (Ext. 8).
[*Died* 18 *Jan.* 1962.

FREEMAN-ATTWOOD, Harold Augustus, D.S.O. 1943; O.B.E. 1932; M.C. 1917; *b.* 30 December 1897; *s.* of late Major E. Freeman (killed in action March 1916) and late Mrs. K. M. Ffoulkes (*née* Gillespie); *g.s.* of late Prof. E. A. Freeman, Regius Professor of Modern History at Oxford; *m.* 1st, 1921, Jessie (marriage annulled, 1946), *y. d.* of late Hon. W. C. Job, of Newfoundland; two *s.* one *d.*; 2nd, 1951, Marion, *o. d.* of late G. H. Attewell, Fairham House, Ruddington, Notts. *Educ.:* Marlborough College; Royal Military College, Sandhurst. Joined Royal Welch Fusiliers, 1915; served European War, France, Belgium, and Italy (twice wounded, M.C., V.M. and G.S. Medals); Waziristan Campaign, India, 1921-1923 (N.W. Frontier Medal and Clasp); Capt. 1923; T.A. Adjt., 1924-27; Staff College, 1928-30, p.s.c.; comdg. Troops in Cyprus, 1931-32; Greek Rebellion (O.B.E.); G.3 War Office, 1932-34; Bt. Major, 1935: Bde. Major, Khartoum, 1934-36; G.2 50th (N) Div. 1938-40; Bt. Lt.-Col. 1939; Major, 1939; G.1 1940 and Temp. Lt.-Col.; Bde. Comdr. July 1940 and Temp. Brig.; subs. full Colonel, July 1941; Div. Comdr. Nov. 1941 and Acting Maj.-Gen.; Temp. Maj.-Gen. Nov. 1942; served B.N.A.F. 1942-43 (D.S.O., Africa Star, French Légion d'Honneur, Croix de Guerre and U.S.A. Legion of Merit); military service terminated, Oct. 1943. I.C.I. Ltd., 1944-48; Staff Manager, I.C.I. (India) Ltd., 1949-51; Area Representative Conservative Central Board of Finance, East Midlands, 1953. Jubilee Medal, 1937; Coronation Medal, 1938. *Recreations:* hunting, shooting, gardening and stamp collecting. *Address:* Fairham House, Ruddington, Notts. *Clubs:* Naval and Military; Royal Calcutta Turf (Calcutta).
[*Died* 22 *Sept.* 1963.

FREESE-PENNEFATHER, Harold Wilfrid Armine, C.M.G. 1951: *b.* 2 March 1907: *s.* of late Rev. Frederick Edmeston Freese; *m.* 1949, Mary Patricia (marriage dissolved, 1966), *d.* of late Captain W. R. Moore-Bennet; one *d.* *Educ.:* Eton; Balliol College, Oxford. Entered Diplomatic Service as 3rd Secretary, 1930; Washington, 1931-35; 2nd Secretary, 1935; Buenos Aires, 1935-38; Oslo, 1938-1940; Bagdad, 1940-44; Acting 1st Secretary, 1941; Foreign Office, 1944-49; Counsellor, 1948; Rangoon, 1950-51; H.M. Consul-General, Rabat, 1951-56; H.M. Ambassador: Rabat, 1956-57; Luxembourg, 1957-61. *Recreations:* music, travel. *Address:* c/o Hentsch et Cie, rue de la Corraterie 15, Geneva, Switzerland. *Clubs:* Alpine, St. James'; Kildare Street (Dublin),
[*Died* 12 *March* 1967.

FREESTUN, Col. William Humphrey May, C.M.G. 1919; D.S.O. 1917; *b.* 1878; *s.* of M. J. Freestun, Bassett House, Claverton, Bath; *m.* 1904, Emily Mary (*d.* 1953), *d.* of Lt.-Col. Edward Morell, late Essex Regt.; one *d.* decd. *Educ.:* Harrow. Gazetted Somerset L.I., 1896. Served South African War, 1899-1902 (Queen's medal with five clasps, King's medal with two clasps); European War, 1914-1919 (despatches 6 times, D.S.O., Brevet Major, Brevet Lt.-Col., C.M.G., Chevalier Legion of Honour, Croix de Guerre, France); commanded 2nd Oxfordshire and Buckinghamshire L.I. 1924-28; Comdr. 158th (Royal Welch) Inf. Bde., 1930; Comdr. 129th (South Wessex) Infantry Brigade (T.A.), 1931-34; retired, 1934; re-employed, Commandant P.O.W. Camp, 1939-42 (War Medal). *Address:* Bassett House, Claverton, Bath.
[*Died* 15 *July* 1964.

FREETH, Francis Arthur, O.B.E. 1918; F.R.S. 1925; D.Sc., F.R.I.C., F.Inst.P.; F.Inst.F.; M.I.Chem.E.; formerly on Central Staff Dept. Imperial Chemical Industries, now a chemical consultant, 1952; *e. s.* of late E. H. Freeth; *b.* Birkenhead, 2 Jan. 1884; *m.* Ethel, *d.* of late G. N. Warbrick, Silecroft, Cumberland; one *s.* two *d.* *Educ.:* Liverpool University. B.Sc.; with First Class Honours in Chemistry, 1905; M.Sc. 1906; Doctor in the Faculty of Mathematics and Physics, University of Leyden, 1924; D.Sc. (Liverpool) 1924; Capt. Cheshire Regt., T.A.; mobilised outbreak of 1914 War; recalled in connection with the manufacture of munitions; inventor of several important processes in connection with manufacture of explosives; Member of Council Institute (now Royal) of Chemistry, 1921-23; Founder Member Institute of Fuel, served on Council, 1927-1939; Member of Council of Chemical Society, 1925-28, Vice-President, 1931-34; President, British Cast Iron Research Assoc., 1933-36; Member of Council Institution of Chemical Engineers, 1948-51 (Vice-Pres., 1950). Brevet-Major, 1927; resigned commission in T.A., 1927. *Publications:* Publications in various scientific jnls., notably Phil. Trans. Roy. Soc. vol. 222, 1922. *Address:* c/o Martin's Bank Ltd., Tothill Street, Westminster, S.W.1. *Clubs:* Athenæum, Special Forces. [*Died* 15 *July* 1970.

FREKE, Hon. Ralfe E.; *see* Evans-Freke.

FREMANTLE, Francis David Eardley, T.D. 1943; D.L.; J.P.; Lt.-Col. R.A. (T.A.) Retired; Manager, The Hope Marketing Board, since 1946; *b.* 27 May 1906; *o. s.* of lat Sir Francis E. Fremantle, Bedwell Park, Hatfield, Herts.; *m.* 1936, Emmeline, *d.* of late Brig.-Gen. V. W. de Falbe, C.M.G., D.S.O.; three *s.* one *d.* *Educ.:* Eton; Balliol College, Oxford (M.A.). A.C.A. 1931, F.C.A. 1960. Joined Hertfordshire Yeo., 1927. Served B.E.F. France, 1940; A.A. Command, 1940-43; France and Germany, 1944-1945. J.P., 1951, D.L. and High Sheriff, 1959, Hertfordshire. *Address:* Bayford House, near Hertford. *T.:* Bayford 225. *Club:* Boodle's. [*Died* 1 *July* 1968.

FRENCH, Lieut.-Colonel Hon. (Edward) Gerald, D.S.O. 1918; 2nd *s.* of 1st Earl of Ypres; *u.* and *heir-pres.* to 3rd Earl of Ypres; *b.* 11 Dec. 1883; *m.* 1906, Leila (*d.* 1959), *d.* of R. King, J.P.; two *d.* *Educ.:* Wellington College. Joined Cape Colonial Forces, 1904; served during Zulu Rebellion, 1906 (medal); British North Borneo Constabulary, 1910-14 (severely wounded, commended by Government); Adjutant 11th Batt. Yorkshire Regt. 1914; 2nd in cmd. 11th Batt. Cheshire Regt. Sept. 1915, and proceeded to France; served European War in inf. and as Asst. Provost Marshal (des. twice, D.S.O., slightly wounded and gassed, 1917; horse killed, 1918); relinquished commn., 1920; R. of O., The Green Howards; Deputy Gov, Dartmoor Prison, 1921-23; specially employed under Colonial Office to advise Government as to reorganisation of Bahamas Police Force, 1923-24; Gov. of Newcastle Prison, 1924. Expeditionary Force, 1940; Lt.-Col. 1942; retired, 1944. *Publications:* The Life of Field-Marshal Sir John French, First Earl of Ypres, 1931; French Replies to Haig, 1936; edited Some War Diaries, Addresses and Correspondence of Field-Marshal the Earl of Ypres, 1937; Lord Chelmsford and the Zulu War, 1939; John Jorrocks and other characters from the works of Robert Surtees, 1947; The Corner Stone of English Cricket, 1948; Good-bye to Boot and Saddle, 1951; Gordon Pasha of the Sudan, 1958; It's Not Cricket (An Analysis of the Game's Unwritten Laws), 1960; The Kitchener-French Dispute (A Last Word), 1961; The Martyrdom of Admiral Byng, 1961. *Recreations:* cricket (represented Devon in Minor Counties Championship); racing (rode on the flat in Far East); rifle-shooting (rep. Br. N. Borneo in Empire rifle-shooting competition for Daily Mail Cup); squash rackets (rep. M.C.C. in Bath Club Cup Competition and against American touring team; originated old public schoolboys' competition for Londonderry Cup). *Address:* c/o Glyn, Mills & Co (Holt's Branch), Kirkland House, Whitehall, S.W.1. *Clubs:* M.C.C., I Zingari, Free Foresters. [*Died* 17 *Sept.* 1970.

FRENCH, Frederick George, C.B.E. 1944; M.A. (hon.) Oxon 1944; Judge of Alderney, Channel Islands, 1938-47; *b.* 19 Dec. 1889; *s.* of C. A. Turner French, Lowestoft; *m.* 1914, Annie Sarah (*d.* 1955), *e. d.* of late Herbert Smith, Norwich; no *c.* *Educ.:* Norwich Municipal Secondary School; St. John's Coll., Battersea. Middlesex Regiment, 1914; 36th Sikhs, 1914; Burma Military Police, 1917-21; Headmaster, Government High School, Rangoon, Burma, 1922; Inspector of Schools, Burma, 1931; retired from Burma, 1936. H.M. Forces, 1940-45, General Staff, Brigadier. *Publications:* various scholastic. *Recreation:* yachting. *Address:* Val des Portes, Alderney, Channel Isles. [*Died* 4 *Jan.* 1963.

FRENCH, Sir Henry Leon, G.B.E., *cr.* 1946 (K.B.E., *cr.* 1938; O.B.E. 1918); K.C.B., *cr.* 1942 (C.B. 1920); *b.* 1883; 3rd *s.* of late F. E. French, J.P., Southsea, Portsmouth; *m.* 1st, Clare (*d.* 1954), *d.* of late Charles Grimes, F.R.G.S., Southsea; one *d.*; 2nd, 1929, Violet, *d.* of late G. R. Huntley, Streatham. *Educ.:* privately at Southsea; King's Coll. London. Joined Civil Service by open competition; appointed to the Board of Agriculture, 1901; promoted to First Division, 1909; Assist. Sec., 1920-29; Principal Assist. Sec., 1929; Second Secretary Ministry of Agriculture and Fisheries, 1934; seconded to be Director, Food (Defence Plans) Department, 1936-39; Secretary, Ministry of Food, 1939-45; retired Sept. 1945 and from Civil Service, June 1946; Secretary to Lord Milner's Committee on Home Production of Food, 1915; Joint Secretary to Lord Selborne's Committee on Agricultural Policy, 1916-17; General Secretary of Food Production Department, 1917-19; representative of United Kingdom and Canada on the Permanent Committee of the International Institute of Agriculture, Rome, 1930-34; attended Ottawa Conference as Departmental Adviser, 1932; made official visit to Canada and U.S.A. October 1943, to India Aug.-Sept. 1944, and to Australia, New Zealand and South Africa, 1945-1946; Chairman of U.N.E.S.C.O. Co-operating Body on Mass Communications, 1946-53; a British Delegate to 2nd U.N.E.S.C.O. Conf., Mexico City, Nov. 1947, and to 5th Conf., Florence, May-June 1950; Member of Council of Festival of Britain, 1951; first Chairman of Festival Gardens Ltd., resigned March 1951; Director-General of British Film Producers' Assoc., 1946-57, President, 1957-58, retired; Dir. British Commonwealth Film Corporation, Ltd., 1946-58; Chm. of Film Casting Association Ltd., 1947-58. *Address:* 27 Stourcliffe Close, W.1. *T.:* Ambassador 7822. *Club:* Athenaeum. [*Died* 3 *April* 1966.

FRENCH, Rev. Reginald, M.C. 1917; M.A.; *b.* 20 April 1883; *e. s.* of John Reginald French and Mary Elizabeth (*née* Maycock), Coventry, Warwicks; *m.* 1919, Gertrude Emily Mary, *d.* of Canon James Haworth, Durham; two *s.* one *d.* *Educ.:* Rugby School; University College, Durham. M.A. 1912. In business in Coventry (silk dyeing), 1900-06. Ordained, St. Paul's Cathedral, 1910; Asst. Curate, Christ Church, Hampstead; Home Missioner, 1914, first Incumbent, 1921 (on return from Army), Saint Barnabas, Temple Fortune, N.W.11. Chaplain, B.E.F., 1916; Senior Chaplain to the Forces, 1918, 29th Div.; Asst. to the Asst. Chap.-General, Rhine Army, 1919. Vicar of Hounslow, 1926-34; Rector and Rural Dean, Stepney, 1934-45; Hon. Chaplain to the Queen, 1952- (to King George VI, 1941-1952); Rector of Dunstable, 1945-54; Rural Dean of Dunstable, 1950-54; retired 1954; license to officiate in Diocese of Guildford. *Recreations:* formerly rowing, hockey, running, Rugby football; now cycling, gardening, motoring, and walking; music, Free Masonry, and Rotary. *Address:* Court House, Woburn Place, Addlestone, Surrey. *T.:* Weybridge 4178; "Ossco", Lundy Bay, St. Minver, N. Cornwall. *T.:* Trebetherick 2317. *Club:* Authors'. [*Died* 12 *Dec.* 1961.

FRENCH, Reginald Thomas George, C.B.E. 1941 (O.B.E. 1918); M.A. (Cantab.); *b.* 30 Jan. 1881; *s.* of late Thomas French; *m.* 1907, Hilda, (*d.* 1957), *d.* of late Arthur Parke; two *s.* *Educ.:* Central Foundation School, London; St. John's College, Cambridge (Foundation Scholar and Hockin Prizeman for Physics). H.M. Patent Office (Examining Staff), 1903-14; Ministry of Munitions (Inventions Department and Nitrogen Products Research Section), 1915-18; Secretary, Nitrogen Products Committee of Ministry of Munitions, 1917-19; Secretary, Water Power Resources Committee of Board of Trade,

1919-20; Secretary to the Electricity Commissioners from their establishment in 1920 until Jan. 1945. A Governor, Central Foundation Schools, London, 1954-63. *Address:* 302 Tadcaster Road, York.
[*Died* 7 *Nov.* 1965.

FREUNDLICH, Erwin; *see* Finlay-Freundlich.

FREYBERG, 1st Baron, *cr.* 1951, of Wellington, New Zealand, and of Munstead in Co. of Surrey; **Bernard Freyberg,** V.C. 1916, G.C.M.G., *cr.* 1946 (C.M.G. 1919); K.C.B.; *cr.* 1942 (C.B. 1936); K.B.E., *cr.* 1942; D.S.O. 1915; LL.D. (St. Andrews) 1922; D.C.L. (Oxford) 1945; LL.D. (N.Z.) 1952; p.s.c.; Lt.-Gen., late Grenadier Guards; Deputy Constable and Lieut.-Gov. of Windsor Castle since 1953; *b.* London, 1889; *m.* 1922, Barbara (*see* Lady Freyberg); one *s.* *Educ.:* Wellington Coll., N.Z. Served European War, including Dardanelles with Hood Battalion R.N.D., 1914-18; Brigadier, 1917-18, with 29th Division (despatches six times, wounded nine times, D.S.O. and two bars, C.M.G., V.C., Bt. Major, and Bt. Lt.-Col.); Major, 1927; Lt.-Col. 1929; commanded 1st Battalion Manchester Regiment, 1929-31; Col. 1931; Assistant Quartermaster-General, Southern Command, 1931-33; General Staff Officer, 1st Grade, War Office, 1933-34; G.O.C. Salisbury Plain Area, Sept. 1939; G.O.C. New Zealand Forces, Nov. 1939-45; Commander-in-Chief of Allied Forces in Crete, 1941; Third Bar to D.S.O. 1945 (Italy). Governor-General of New Zealand, 1946-52; *Heir:* *s.* Major Hon. Paul Freyberg, M.C., Grenadier Guards [*b.* 27 May 1923; *m.* 1960, Ivry Perronelle Katharine, *o. d.* of Cyril Guild, Aspall Hall, nr. Debenham, Suffolk; two *d.*]. *Address:* The Norman Tower, Windsor Castle. *Clubs:* Carlton, Bath, M.C.C.
[*Died* 4 *July* 1963.

FREYBERG, Captain Geoffrey Herbert, C.B.E. 1940; Royal Navy (retd.); *b.* 8 July 1881; *er. s.* of late H. Freyberg, F.S.I., and Mrs. Freyberg, Gray's Inn Sq.; *m.* 1909, Kathleen May (*d.* 1959), *y. d.* of late H. J. Nicholls, Dolgelly, N. Wales; one *s.* *Educ.:* Dragon School, Oxford; H.M.S. Britannia at Dartmouth. Naval Cadet, 1895; China War medal, 1900, when serving in H.M.S. Undaunted; Lieut. 1902; Commander, 1915; served with Grand Fleet throughout European War in H.M.S. Colossus and Valiant (despatches for services at Jutland); took part in surrender of German Fleet, 1918; King's Harbour Master, Plymouth, 1919-21 (O.B.E. for War Services); Master Attendant, Singapore, and Marine Adviser to Straits Settlements Govt., 1926-36; Capt., retired, 1926; a Younger Brother of Trinity House Corpn., 1921; King George V Jubilee Medal, 1935; C.B.E. for services afloat with Dover Naval Forces, 1939; commanded H.M.S. Hampton, 1939-40; and H.M.S. Ausonia, 1940-42 (despatches); commanded H.M.S. Gosling, 1942-46. *Recreations:* lawn tennis, boat sailing and gardening. *Address:* 19 Broadclose Hill, Bude, N. Cornwall. [*Died* 22 *Sept.* 1966.

FRIEND, Maj.-Gen. Arthur Leslie Irvine, C.B. 1945; C.B.E. 1940 (O.B.E. 1932); M.C.; D.L.; *b.* 1886; *y. s.* of late James Taddy Friend, D.L., J.P., Northdown, Isle of Thanet; *m.* 1914, Phyllis (*d.* 1950), *d.* of Lt.-Col. John Hoystead, Elvington Court, nr. Dover; one *s.* two *d.*; *m.* 1951, Aline Margaret Grant. *Educ.:* Malvern; Oxford. Joined Royal Fusiliers, 1908; transferred 7th Dragoon Guards, 1911; served European War, France, 1914-19 (despatches M.C.); Major 11th Hussars, 1921; commanding, 1928-32; Colonel, 1932; Instr. Senior Officers' School, Sheerness, 1933-34; cmdg. Cav. Bde., Egypt, 1934-38; retired, 1938; re-employed, 1939; cmdg. G.H.Q. Troops, France, 1939: Director of Labour, France, 1939-40; Director of Labour, War Office, 1940-45; Maj.-Gen. 1942; reverted to retired pay, 1945; Col. Comdt. Royal Pioneer Corps, 1945-48. Commander Legion of Merit (American), 1945. D.L. Kent, 1952. *Address:* Southlands, High Halden, Nr. Ashford, Kent. *Club:* Cavalry.
[*Died* 12 *Aug.* 1961.

FRIEND, John Albert Newton; Retired; *b.* 20 July 1881. *Educ.:* King Edward's High School, Birmingham; Birmingham Univ. (scholar). B.Sc. honours, 1902; M.Sc. 1903; Ph.D. Würz. 1908; D.Sc. 1910; Science Master, Watford Grammar Schools, 1903-6; Student at Würzburg Univ. (Carnegie scholar), 1906-8; Head of Chemistry Department at Darlington Tech. Coll., 1908-12; Carnegie Gold Medallist, 1913; Headmaster Victoria Institute Science and Technical Schools, Worcester, 1912-20; Head of Chemistry Dept., Technical College, Birmingham, 1920-46; Hon. Captain, R.E.; Fellow of the Chemical Soc.; Fellow of Royal Institute of Chemistry, 1915; Pres. Oil and Colour Chemists' Assoc., 1922-24; Hon. Member British Association of Chemists. *Publications:* The Theory of Valency, 1909; Introduction to the Chemistry of Paints, 1910; Elementary Domestic Chemistry, 1911; The Corrosion of Iron and Steel, 1911; Chemistry of Linseed Oil, 1917; Chemistry of Combustion, 1922; Cobalt Nickel, and the Elements of the Platinum Group, 1920; Iron and its Compounds, 1921; Iron in Antiquity, 1926; Text-book of Physical Chemistry, Vol. I, 1932, Vol. II, 1935, 2nd edn., 1948; Man and the Chemical Elements, 1951; Numbers, Fun and Facts, 1954; Words, Tricks and Traditions, 1957; Safety in the Laboratory, 1958; Science Data, 1960; Demonology, Sympathetic Magic and Witchcraft, 1961; More Numbers, Fun and Facts, 1961; Still More Numbers, Fun and Facts; Forgotten Birmingham, 1964; Forgotten Aston Manor in Birmingham. General Editor of Text-book of Inorganic Chemistry; author of hundred and fifty research memoirs in scientific jls. *Address:* 134 Church Rd., Moseley, Birmingham 13.
[*Died* 15 *April* 1966.

FRISBY, Major Cyril Hubert, V.C. 1918; Member of London Stock Exchange; *b.* 17 Sept. 1885; 2nd *s.* of late Henry Frisby, Icklesham, Sx.; *m.* 1911, Audrey Ogilvie Grant (*d.* 1960); one *s.* *Educ.:* Haileybury College. Served with Coldstream Guards during European War (V.C., despatches). *Address:* Glenwoods, Guildford, Surrey. *Club:* Worplesdon Golf. [*Died* 10 *Sept.* 1961.

FROOM, Sir Arthur Henry, Kt., *cr.* 1922; *s.* of late Henry Froom; *b.* 15 Jan. 1873; *m.* 1st, 1905, Effie (*d.* 1924), *y. d.* of late Thomas Bryant, F.R.C.S.; 2nd, 1925, Isabel Patricia, *d.* of late R. Manners Downie, Cornbrook, Knutsford. *Educ.:* St. Paul's School. Entered service of P. & O. S.N. Co., 1890 (Superintendent, Bombay, 1912-16); Partner, Mackinnon, Mackenzie & Co., Bombay, 1916-1930; Trustee, Bombay Port, 1912-24; Chairman, Bombay Chamber of Commerce, 1920; member Imperial Legislative Council, India, 1920; member of the Council of State, India, 1921-30; Member, Indian Mercantile Marine Committee, India, 1923-24; Representative of Employers in India at Labour Conference, Geneva, 1926; Member, Reforms Enquiry Committee, India, 1924; Member of Road Development Committee and Chairman Touring Sub-Committee, 1927-28; Member Indian Central Committee, 1928-29; Member, Central Advisory Council Railways, India, 1921-30; J.P. Bombay. *Recreations:* riding, shooting, golf, tennis. *Address:* Pettistree House, Wickham Market, Suffolk. [*Died* 29 *Oct.* 1964.

FROSSARD, Rev. Canon Edward Louis, C.B.E. 1966; M.A. (Univ. Coll., Durham); Dean of the Bailiwick of Guernsey and its dependencies, 1947-67; Commissary to the Bishop of Winchester, 1947-67; Hon. Canon of Winchester Cathedral since 1947; Rector of Saint Sampson, Guernsey, 1918-65; H.C.F.; *b.* 22 Feb. 1887; *s.* of Charles Edward Frossard and Lucie Eugénie Mowat; *m.* 1917, Margery Smith Latta (*d.* 1958); one *s.* one *d.* *Educ.:* privately; Universities of Durham and Paris; Lichfield Theological College. Deacon, 1911, Priest, 1913, Lichfield; Curate of Penkridge, Staffordshire, 1911-14; C.F., Belgium and France, 1914-18 (1914-15 Star); Vice-Dean of Guernsey, 1946; Acting Pres., States of Guernsey, 1953-67; Chm., Bd. of Directors of Elizabeth Coll., Guernsey, 1947-1967; Prov. Gd. Master of Prov. Gd. Lodge of Free Masons of Guernsey and Alderney, 1956; Chm. Guernsey Savings Bank; Sub-Chaplain, Order of St. John of Jerusalem, 1946-; Pres. Guernsey Branch B.R.C.S., 1955-; Chevalier de la Légion d'Honneur; officer d'Académie. *Recreations:* golf, mountaineering and photography. *Address:* Lyndhurst, Les Banques, Saint Sampson, Guernsey, C.I. *Club:* Royal Commonwealth Society. [*Died* 13 *Aug.* 1968.

FROST, Brig.-Gen. Frank Dutton, C.B.E. 1919; M.C., Indian Army, retired; *s.* of late Alfred John Frost, J.P., of Snaresbrook, Essex, and Frances Emma Dutton, Cheshire; *m.* 1912, Elsie Dora Bright (*d.* 1952); one *s.* two *d.*; *m.* 1954, Mrs. Rhoda Collins, *widow* of Edward Collins, Kelvindale. *Educ.:* Forest School. Served South African War in Wiltshire Yeomanry and Cheshire Regt., 1900-02; European War, 1914-18 (despatches five times); Bt. Major, 1918; Bt. Lt.-Col., 1921; Col., 1925; Temp. Brig.-Gen., 1917-20 (M.C., C.B.E.); entered Indian Army, 1915; retired with rank of Hon. Brig.-General, 1930. Missionary N.W. Frontier, India, until 1945. *Publications:* The Appointed Time; Peace and Safety; Darkness before the Dawn; The Muddle in the Middle East; For Such a Time as This. *Address:* Rock Hill, Hunter's Quay, Argyll. *T.:* Dunoon 214. [*Died* 3 *Dec.* 1968.

FROST, Robert; Poetry Consultant to the Library of Congress since 1958; mem. of American Academy of Arts and Letters; member of American Philosophical Society; George Ticknor Fellow in Humanities, Dartmouth College; *b.* San Francisco, 26 March 1874; *s.* of William Prescott Frost, of old New England family, and Belle Moodie, native of Scotland; *m.* 1895, Elinor White; one *s.* three *d.* *Educ.:* Dartmouth and Harvard Colleges. Pulitzer Prize for Poetry four times, 1924, 1931, 1937, 1943, Gold Medal of Poetry Society of America, 1958; Congressional Gold Medal, 1962. Hon. Litt.D. Cambridge University, 1957; Hon. D.Litt. Oxford University, 1957. *Publications:* A Boy's Will, 1913; North of Boston, 1914; Mountain Interval, 1917; New Hampshire, 1923; West Running Brook, 1929; Collected Poems, 1930; Selected Poems, 1937; A Further Range, 1937; Collected Poems, 1939; A Witness Tree, 1943; Complete Poems, 1951; In the Clearing, 1962. *Relevant Publications:* The Letters of Robert Frost to Louis Untermeyer, 1964; Lawrance Thompson: Robert Frost, The Early Years 1874-1915, 1967; Robert Frost, The Years of Triumph 1915-1938, 1971. *Address:* 35 Brewster Street, Cambridge, Mass., U.S.A.; Ripton, Vermont, U.S.A. *Club:* St. Botolph (Boston). [*Died* 29 *Jan.* 1963.

FRUMKIN, Gad, C.B.E. (Hon.) 1941; **Mr. Justice Frumkin;** Puisne Judge, Supreme Court of Palestine, 1920-48; President Israel-Ibero-America Central Inst. for cultural relations with Latin America, Spain and Portugal, 1956; *b.* Jerusalem, 2 August 1887; *s.* of I. B. Frumkin, Editor of Havazelet (earliest Hebrew Newspaper, 1870-1910); *m.* 1909, Anna, *d.* of Aron Eisenberg, founder of Rehovoth; two *s.* two *d.* *Educ.:* Jerusalem; Constantinople Law Faculty. Crown Advocate, Jerusalem, 1915-17; Chief Magistrate, Jerusalem, 1918-20; Member Palestine Committee on Jurisdiction Religious Courts, 1920; Chairman Palestine Committee on Ritual Slaughtering and Burial, 1922; Lecturer Civil Law Palestine Law School, 1919-47; President Society for Jewish Jurisprudence, 1919; Governor Hebrew University of Jerusalem; President Palestine Friends of the Hebrew University; Grand President District Grand Lodge, Palestine, I. O. B'nai-brith, 1942-49; President Palestine Olympic Committee; Chairman, Israel Commission of Enquiry on Education in Immigrant Camps, 1950; President Jerusalem Young Men's and Young Women's Hebrew Assocs. Co-Editor of Havazelet, 1907-9. *Publications:* Hebrew Translation of Mejelleh; The Way of a Judge in Jerusalem (memoirs) (Hebrew), 1955; contributions to Journal of Comparative Legislation *re* Legal Position of Women in Turkey and Egypt (1928) and Disabilities of Women under Jewish Law (1929). *Recreation:* gardening. *Address:* Havazelet House, Jerusalem. *T.:* 3217. [*Died* 18 *March* 1960.

FRY, (Anna) Ruth; *b.* Highgate, 4 Sept. 1878; *y. d.* of late Rt. Hon. Sir Edward Fry, G.C.B. Hon. Treasurer, Boer Home Industries, 1906; first Chairman, Russian Famine Relief Fund, 1921; Hon. Secretary, National Council for the Prevention of War, 1926-27; Hon. Secretary, Friends Relief Committee, which succoured victims of the War in France, Germany, Netherlands, Serbia, Austria, Hungary, Poland, and Russia, all of which fields she visited, 1914-24. *Publications:* Five Songs; From Campian to Lawes; A Quaker Adventure, the Story of Nine Years' Relief Work and Reconstruction, 1926 (trans. into German, 1933, Danish, 1945); Emily Hobhouse, a Memoir, 1929; Quaker Ways, 1933 (trans. into German, 1935; Swedish, 1937); John Bellers, Quaker, Economist and Social Reformer, 1935; The Whirlpool of War, 1939; Victories without Violence, 1939 (trans. into Bulgarian, 1946); Everyman's Affair, 1941; Three Visits to Russia, 1942; Ruth's Gleanings, An Anthology, 1943; and many pamphlets on Peace. *Address:* 48 Clarendon Rd., W.11. *T.:* Park 2545. [*Died* 26 *April* 1962.

FRY, Augustine Sargood, C.I.E. 1944; *b.* 4 Nov. 1890; *s.* of Dr. Edwin Sargood Fry, M.B., C.M., Edinburgh; *m.* 1920, Ella, *d.* of Rev. A. Scott, Albyfield, Wetheral, Cumberland; one *s.* *Educ.:* George Watson's College, Edinburgh; University of Edinburgh (M.B., Ch.B. 1913). Temp. Lt. R.A.M.C. 1915; Lt. I.M.S. 1916; served B.E.F., France, Indian Expeditionary Force D., South Waziristan Field Force, East Persia; Surgical Specialist, Baluchistan District, 1920-23; F.R.C.S. Edin. 1924; Surgical Specialist Peshawar District, 1925-29; Ch.M. Edin. 1930; Civil Surgeon, Punjab, 1931-41; Professor of Operative Surgery, 1942, Principal from Dec. 1944, King Edward Medical College, Lahore; retired, 1947. *Recreations:* photography, golf. *Address:* Wood Grange, Wetheral, near Carlisle. *T.:* Wetheral 274. [*Died* 17 *Jan.* 1962.

FRY, Ruth; *see* Fry, A. R.

FRY, Sir William Kelsey, Kt., *cr.* 1951; C.B.E. 1946; M.C., M.D.S., D.Sc. (McGill), F.D.S., F.R.C.S., Consulting Dental Surgeon, Eastman Dental Hospital (Post-graduate), Gray's Inn Road, W.C.1; Consulting Dental Surgeon Emeritus, Guy's Hospital; Civilian Consultant in Dental Surgery to Royal Air Force and Ministry of Health; *b.* 18 March 1889; *s.* of Edmund Fry; *m.* 1916, Ruby Hannah, 2nd *d.* of John Preston; one *s.* *Educ.:* Hurstpierpoint; Guy's Hospital. M.R.C.S. Eng., L.R.C.P. London, 1912, L.D.S., R.C.S. Eng., 1913, F.R.C.S., 1952. *Publications:* The Dental Treatment of Maxillo-

Facial Injuries (joint) 1942; and Supplement, 1944: Evolution of Oral Surgery, Proc. Roy. Soc. Med. 1951; and papers in medical and dental journals. *Address:* 22 Marina Court Avenue, Bexhill-on-Sea, Sussex. *T.:* Bexhill 4760. [*Died* 26 *Oct.* 1963.

FUAD, Mustafa Ziai, Bey, C.M.G. 1943; *b.* 1888; *s.* of late Mehmed Ziauddin, Mufti of Cyprus; *m.* 1915, Belkis Hilmi; four *s.* two *d.* Called to Bar, Gray's Inn, 1922; Acted Chief Justice, 1937, 1938; Judge, District Court, 1913; Puisne Judge, 1927; Puisne Judge, Gold Coast, 1939; retired, 1945; advocate. *Address:* 9 MacArthur Street, Nicosia, Cyprus. *Club:* Royal Commonwealth Society. [*Died* 17 *Sept.* 1968.

FUDGE, Edward George, C.B. 1946; C.B.E. 1935; O.St.J.; *b.* 5 Jan. 1888; *s.* of Edward Fudge and Beatrice Glover; *m.* 1922, Lilian Bird; one *s.* one *d.* *Educ.:* William Ellis School. Under-Secretary, Ministry of Fuel and Power, until 1947. *Address:* 6 Arden Grove, Harpenden, Herts. *T.:* Harpenden 474. [*Died* 23 *Feb.* 1961.

FULLAGAR, Sir Wilfred (Kelsham), K.B.E., *cr.* 1955; **Hon. Mr. Justice Fullagar;** Justice of High Court of Australia, since 1950; *b.* 16 November 1892; *s.* of Thomas K. Fullagar, Melbourne; *m.* 1st, 1919, Marion, *d.* of F. W. Lovejoy; four *s.*; 2nd, 1942, Mary, *d.* of W. A. Taylor. *Educ.:* Haileybury College, Melbourne; Ormond College, University of Melbourne. B.A., LL.M., University of Melbourne. Served European War, 1914-18, Australian Field Artillery, France. Commenced practice Victorian Bar, 1922; K.C. (Victoria), 1933; Judge of Supreme Court of Victoria, 1945-50. *Recreation:* bowls. *Address:* 34 Sackville St., Kew, Melbourne. *T.:* WY 1491. *Clubs:* Melbourne (Melbourne); Union (Sydney). [*Died* 9 *July* 1961.

FULLER, Lt.-Col. Albert George Hubert, J.P.; I.A., retired; *m.* 1st, Lilian Margaret Couper (*d.* 1955), 2nd, *d* of D. C. Thomson, J.P., D.L., Broughty Ferry, Angus; no *c.*; 2nd, 1960, Mary Morel. European War, 1914-18; Indian Army, 1918-31; 3rd Afghan War, 1919; M.P. (U.) Ardwick, Manchester, 1931-35; 5th Bn. Queen's Own Royal West Kent Regt., 1936-39; Lt.-Col. Commanding 7th Queen's Own Royal West Kent Regt.; retired Dec. 1939. Sevenoaks R.D.C., 1947-56; J.P. Kent, 1950. *Recreation:* thinking. *Address:* Furnace House, Cowden, Kent. *T.:* Cowden 429. [*Died* 27 *July* 1969.

FULLER, Major-General Algernon Clement, C.B.E. 1941 (O.B.E. 1922); A.M.I. E.E.; *b.* 30 Mar. 1885; 3rd *s.* of Sydney Fuller, P.W.D., Ceylon, and Beatrice Mary Dunphy; *m.* 1908, Ione (*d.* 1965), *y. d.* of Fleet Paymaster M. C. Murdoch, R.N.; one *d.* *Educ.:* St. Augustine's, Ramsgate; Bedford; R.M. Academy, Woolwich (Armstrong Medal). 1st Commission R.E., 1904; experimented with Wireless Telegraphy, 1906; erected as a hobby Wireless Station in Bermuda, 1908-1909; designed wireless controlled boat 1909; Wireless Company, Aldershot Command, 1910-11; invented electrical recording of speech and automatic alarm signal for making special call in absence of radio operator, 1912; invented Dynaphone, an instrument to amplify wireless signals before the introduction of thermionic valves, 1913; this led in 1916 to the invention of the Fullerphone, an instrument enabling telephony and telegraphy to be used simultaneously on the same line, but rendering the telegraphy secret; this instrument was widely used in the European War, 1914-18, and is still in use; served European War, 1914-18 (despatches Bt. Major, Cavalier of Order of the Crown of Italy, Chevalier Légion d'Honneur); Experimental Officer, Signals Experimental Establishment, Woolwich, 1916-20; Webber premium for best paper on military applications of electricity, Institution of Electrical Engineers, 1920; Member of Royal Engineer and Signals Board, 1920-33; Bt. Lt.-Col. 1925; Bt. Col. 1926; Chief Inspector, R.E. and Signals Equipment, Woolwich, 1933-1937; Brig. 1938; Deputy Director of Mechanisation (Engineer and Signals), War Office, 1938; Director of Engineer and Signals Equipment, Ministry of Supply, 1940; Maj.-Gen. 1940 (ante-date 1937); Deputy Director-General, Ministry of Supply, 1941; retired, 1941; Deputy Regional Commissioner for Civil Defence, Eastern Region, 1941-45. Princess Mary Medal of Royal Signals Instn., 1966. *Publications:* Hints on Wireless for Amateurs, 1911; and various technical papers. *Recreation:* fishing. *Address:* 2 Douro Terrace, St. Helier, Jersey, C.I. [*Died* 6 *Aug.* 1970.

FULLER, Brig.-Gen. Francis George, C.B. 1919; C.M.G. 1916; late R.E.; *b.* 25 Mar. 1869; *s.* of late George Fuller, M.I.C.E., D.Sc.; *m.* 1910, Anesta Muriel (*d.* 1934), *d.* of late Most Rev. A. G. Edwards, late Archbishop of Wales; two *s.* *Educ.:* Beaumont College; R.M.A., Woolwich. Joined R.E. 1888; Colonel, 1920; served S. Africa, 1899-1902 (despatches, Bt. Major, Queen's medal 4 clasps, King's medal 2 clasps); European War, 1915-18 (wounded, despatches, Bt. Col., C.M.G., C.B., Commander Order of Redeemer, Officer Legion of Honour); retired pay, 1926. *Address:* 42 Elm Park Gardens, S.W.10. *T.:* Flaxman 4276. *Club:* United Service. [*Died* 29 *Oct.* 1961.

FULLER, Francis Matthew, O.B.E. 1952; Chief Engineer and County Surveyor, London County Council, since 1962; *b.* 29 Dec. 1899; *s.* of Capt. E. F. Fuller, and of Dulcie Fuller; *m.* 1928, Phyllis Coward; one *d.* *Educ.:* Tsingtau, China; Shoreham Grammar School; London University. B.Sc. (Eng.) Hons., M.I.C.E., M.I.Struct.E. Engineering pupilage Joseph Westwood & Co. Ltd., Millwall, 1916-21; Engineer with Rendel Palmer & Tritton: London, 1922-28; Calcutta, 1928-31; London, 1931-34; Asst. Divl. Engr., Divl. Engr. and Dep. Chief Engr. (Roads) with L.C.C., 1934-61. *Recreations:* bridge, gardening. *Address:* Corda, Oakwood Close, Chislehurst, Kent. *T.:* Imperial 3929. *Club:* Royal Automobile. [*Died* 22 *Aug.* 1963.

FULLER, Air Commodore Herbert Francis, C.B. 1948; C.B.E. 1945; Royal Air Force, retd.; *b.* 1893; *m.* 1917, Minnie, *d.* of late Henry Hardy Glasgow. Served European War, 1914-18, with London Scottish, Duke of Cornwall's Light Infantry, R.F.C., R.A.F. Group Captain 1939; temp. Air Commodore, 1943; Command Accountant, Technical Training Command, 1944; Senior Service Accountant, R.A.F., 1945-49. Retired, 1949. [*Died* 27 *Jan.* 1967.

FULLER, Maj.-Gen. John Frederick Charles, C.B. 1930; C.B.E. 1926; D.S.O. 1917; late Oxfordshire and Bucks Light Infantry; *b.* 1878; *m.* 1906, Sonia, *d.* of Dr. M. Karnatzki of Warsaw. Served South African War, 1899-1902 (Queen's medal and three clasps, King's medal and two clasps); European War, 1914-18 (despatches, D.S.O. Brevet Lt.-Col., Col., Legion of Honour, Order of Leopold of Belgium, Officier de l'Instruction Publique); Maj.-Gen. 1930; retired pay, 1933. Chesney Memorial Medal (Royal United Service Instn.), 1963. *Publications:* Tanks in the Great War, 1914-18, 1920; The Reformation of War, 1923; Sir John Moore's System of Training, 1925; British Light Infantry in the 18th Century, 1925; The Foundations of the Science of War, 1926; Imperial Defence, 1588-1914, 1926; On Future Warfare, 1928; The Generalship of Ulysses S. Grant, 1929; India in Revolt; The Dragon's Teeth, 1932; War and Western Civilization, 1832-1932, 1932; Generalship: Its Diseases and their Cure, 1933; Grant and Lee: A Study in Personality and Generalship, 1933; Empire Unity and Defence, 1934; The Army in My Time, 1935; Memoirs of an Unconventional Soldier, 1936; The First of the League Wars, 1936; The Last of the Gentlemen's Wars, 1937; Towards Armageddon, 1937; Decisive Battles of the United States, 1942; Decisive Battles, 1939-40; Machine Warfare, 1941; Armoured Warfare, 1943; Watchwords, 1945; Thunderbolts, 1946; Armament and History, 1946; The Second World War, 1948; The Decisive Battles of the Western World and their Influence upon History, Vol. I, 1954, Vol. II, 1955, Vol. III, 1956; The Generalship of Alexander the Great, 1958; The Conduct of War, 1789-1961, 1961; Julius Caesar: Man, Soldier and Tyrant, 1965. *Club:* United Service. [*Died* 10 *Feb.* 1966.

FULLERTON, Admiral Sir Eric John Arthur, K.C.B., *cr.* 1934 (C.B. 1920); D.S.O. 1915; M.A. (hon.) Camb. 1919; *s.* of Admiral Sir J. R. T. Fullerton; *m.* 1908, Hon. Dorothy Sibyl (*d.* 1962), 2nd *d.* of 1st Lord Fisher; one *d.* In command monitors, Severn, Humber, Mersey, during engagement with right flank German Army, off Belgian Coast, Aug. to Nov. 1914 (promoted Captain, Dec. 1914, despatches); in command Inshore Operations against German cruiser Königsberg, Rufigi River, East Africa, 1915 (despatches, D.S.O.); despatches for subsequent operations on coast of G.E.A.: commanded battleship Orion, Grand Fleet, 1916-18; in charge Naval Officers, Cambridge University, 1919-21; Captain of the Fleet, H.M.S. Queen Elizabeth, Atlantic Fleet, Aug. 1921-1923; Commodore Royal Naval Barracks, Chatham, 1923-25; A.D.C. to King George V, 1925; Rear-Admiral, 1926 Naval Secretary to First Lord of the Admiralty, 1927-29; Commander-in-Chief East Indies Station, 1929-32; Vice-Admiral, 1930; Commander-in-Chief, Plymouth, 1932-35; Adm., 1935; retired list, 1936; Commodore, Royal Naval Reserve, 1940,1942-43: served as Vice-Admiral, 1940-42. *Club:* United Service. [*Died* 9 *Nov.* 1962.

FULLERTON, Harold Williams, M.A., M.D. (Aber.), F.R.C.P. (Lond.); F.R.C.P.E.; F.C.Path.; Regius Professor of Medicine, University of Aberdeen, 1948-70; Physician, Aberdeen Royal Infirmary, since 1948; *b.* 20 July 1905; *m.* 1934, Elizabeth Howland Palfrey, Boston, Massachusetts, U.S.A.; two *d.* *Educ.:* Robert Gordon's College, Aberdeen; University of Aberdeen. House Physician, Aberdeen Royal Infirmary, 1931-1932; Asst. in Dept. of Medicine, Univ. of Aberdeen, 1932-33; Rockefeller Medical Fellow and Research Fellow in Medicine, Harvard Univ., U.S.A., 1933-34; Beit Memorial Research Fellow, 1934-37; Lecturer in Medicine, University of Aberdeen, and Physician, Woodend Hospital, Aberdeen, 1937-48; Asst Physician. Aberdeen Royal Infirmary, 1945. Pres. Assoc. of Physicians of G.B. and Ireland, 1969-70. *Publications:* numerous contributions to text-books of Medicine and to medical journals, especially on Diseases of the Blood. *Address:* 83 Fountainhall Road, Aberdeen. *T.:* Aberdeen 26934. [*Died* 14 *July* 1970.

FÜLOP-MILLER, René, author; *b.* Caransebes, Transylvania, 17 March 1891; father of German Protestant ancestry, by profession chemist, mother a descendant from the famous Macedonian family of Brancovitch; *m.* 1916, the Hungarian soprano Heddy Bendiner of the Budapest Opera; no *c.* *Educ.:* High Schools of Vienna; Lausanne; Paris. Studied Pharmaceutical Chemistry, Anatomy, Psychiatry, and afterwards took up journalism; after the war, several journeys to Soviet Russia which led to the publication of Dostoievski's and Tolstoi's posthumous works as well as to Mind and Face of Bolshevism; since then successful literary career; member Authors' Society. *Publications:* Mind and Face of Bolshevism (Engl. transl. 1927); Lenin and Gandhi (Engl. transl. 1928); The Russian Theatre (Engl. transl. 1930); Power and Secret of the Jesuits (Engl. transl. 1930); The Imagination Machine (Engl. transl. 1931); The Unknown Tolstoi (Engl. transl. 1930); The Ochrana (Engl. transl. 1930); Ghandhi, The Holy Man (Engl. transl. 1931); Leaders, Dreamers, and Rebels (Engl. transl. 1935); Leo XIII (German edn. 1935); Katzenmusik (Novel, German edn. 1935); Triumph over Pain (English transl. 1938). *Address:* Wohllebengasse 5, Vienna, Austria. *T.:* U 40.501. [*Died* 7 *May* 1963.

FURBER, Douglas; Director of League of British Dramatists, Performing Right Society, Incorporated Society of Authors (Cinema Committee), Royal General Theatrical Fund, Song Writer's Guild, etc.; *b.* 13 May 1885; *m.* 1909, Elsa Cutler (*d.* 1945); one *s.*; *m.* 1952, Diana Christiansen. *Educ.:* Compton House and abroad. Author and co-author of over seventy musical plays and revues, including Mr. Leslie Henson's Up and Doing, Going Greek, Swing Along, Lucky Break, Nice Goings On; Mr. Jack Buchanan's That's a Good Girl, Stand Up and Sing, Toni, Battling Butler; Mr. Jack Hulbert's and Miss Cicely Courtneidge's The Nine O'clock Revue, The House that Jack Built, also Me and My Girl, A-Z, Shepherd's Pie, Virginia, Wild Oats, Afgar, etc. Author of British films: Jack's the Boy, Soldiers of the King, etc., and contributor to other films for Bing Crosby, Fred Astaire, Lionel Barrymore, Gracie Fields, etc.; many world-famous songs, including The Lambeth Walk, Limehouse Blues, The Bells of St. Mary's, God Send You Back to Me, Fancy our Meeting, Roll away Clouds, etc. *Publications:* Just Another Murder; These Passing Shows; Surely You Can Write a Song; From London and New York; Take No Notice; Favourites of the Stars; My Longest Runs; My Best Sketches; The All-Star Cast, etc. *Recreations:* golf, bridge. *Address:* 8 Wilton St., S.W.1. *Clubs:* Savage, Screenwriters'. [*Died* 19 *Feb.* 1961.

FURNESS, George James Barnard, T.D.; Major, T.A.R.O.; *b.* 29 July 1900; *o. s.* of late G. J. Furness, Roundwood House, Willesden; *m.* 1932, Phyllis Comyn Radford, *d.* of Stephen Radford, Washington, D.C.; two *d.* *Educ.:* Harrow. Pupil to Capt. C. H. Beames, L. & N.W.R. and L.M.S.R., Crewe; Mx. C.C., 1930-46; re-elected 1949; County Alderman, 1952; High Sheriff of Middlesex, 1939-40; served 1940-45; Maj. Brit. Army Staff, Washington, 1941-43; D.A.D.O.S., New York, 1943-45. *Recreation:* gardening. *Address:* Kingsmead, Little Somerford, Wilts. *T.:* Malmesbury 3143. *Club:* Junior Army and Navy. [*Died* 24 *June* 1962.

FURNIVALL, Baroness, *cr.* 1295 (19th in line); **Mary Frances Katherine Dent;** *b.* 27 May 1900; *d.* of 14th Baron Petre and Ethelreda Mary (Audrey), *d.* of Rev. W. R. Clark, D.D., late Prebendary of Wells [abeyance of Barony determined in her favour, 1913]; *m.* 1st, 1920, Captain A. W. S. Agar, *q.v.* (from whom she obtained a divorce, 1932); 2nd, 1932, William H. S. Dent, M.C. (from whom she obtained a divorce, 1944); two *d.* *Co-heiresses: d.* Hon. Rosamond Mary Dent, *b.* 3 June 1933, and *d.* Hon. Patricia Mary [*b.* 4 April 1935; *m.* 1956, Capt. Thomas Hornsby (marr. diss. 1963); one *s.* one *d.*]. *Address:* c/o Messrs. Longbourne, Stevens and Powell, 7 Lincoln's Inn Fields, W.C.2. [*Died* 24 *Dec.* 1968.

FYFE, Sir William Hamilton, Kt., 1942; M.A., Hon. LL.D. (St. Andrews, Aberdeen, Queen's, Dalhousie, University of Western Ontario, and St. Lawrence Univ., N.Y.); Hon. D.Litt., Laval, Quebec; F.R.S.C.; Hon. F.E.I.S.; J.P.; Hon. Fellow, Merton College, Oxford; Principal and Vice-Chancellor of Univ. of Aberdeen, 1936-48;

retired 1948; Officer d'Académie Française; 3rd and *y. s.* of late James Hamilton Fyfe, Barrister-at-law; *b.* 9 July 1878; *m.* Dorothea, *y. d.* of late John Forbes White, LL.D., of Aberdeen and Dundee; two *s.* one *d.* *Educ.:* Fettes College, Edinburgh; Merton College, Oxford. Assistant Master, Radley College, 1901-3; Fellow, Tutor, and Principal of the Postmasters, Merton College, Oxford, 1904-19; Headmaster Christ's Hospital, 1919-30; Principal and Vice-Chancellor of Queen's University, Kingston, Ont., 1930 - 36; Chairman of Scottish Advisory Council on Education, 1942-46; Member of Scottish Advisory Council on Rehabilitation of Offenders; Mem. of Advisory Cttee. on Colonial Colleges. *Publications:* The Minor Works of Tacitus—Translation; The Histories of Tacitus—Translation; Longinus and Aristotle's Poetics (Loeb Series); Aristotle's Art of Poetry. *Address:* 10 St. Germans Place, Blackheath, S.E.3. *T.:* Greenwich 3164. [*Died* 13 *June* 1965.

FYFFE, Rt. Rev. Rollestone Sterritt, D.D.; *b.* 1868; *s.* of W. J. Fyffe, M.D., Deputy-Surgeon-General, Army Medical Dept.; *m.* 1914, Annis Kathleen (*d.* 1963), *d.* of Herbert Hardy, Danehurst, Sussex; two *s.* (and one *s.* killed in action, 1945). *Educ.:* Clifton College; Emmanuel College, Cambridge. Ordained, 1894; Curate, Bishop Wearmouth, 1894-98; St. Agnes, Bristol, 1898-1900; Vicar, 1901-04; S.P.G. Missionary Mandalay, 1904-10; Examining Chaplain to Bishop of Rangoon, 1905-10; Bishop of Rangoon, 1910-28; Vicar of Westfield, Battle, 1928-31. *Address:* Church Cottage, Lindfield, Sussex. [*Died* 3 *April* 1964.

G

GADD, Cyril John, C.B.E. 1955; M.A.; Hon. D.Litt. (Oxon.) 1953; F.B.A. 1940; F.S.A.; Professor of Ancient Semitic Languages and Civilizations, London University, School of Oriental and African Studies, 1955-60 Professor Emeritus, 1961; Hon. Fellow, Brasenose College, Oxford, 1952; *b.* Bath, Somerset, 2 July 1893; *s.* of Samuel Gadd and Elizabeth Caroline Meddick. *Educ.:* King Edward VI School, Bath; Brasenose College, Oxford (Junior and Senior Hulme Scholar). Served European War 1915-18 Worcestershire Regiment and Royal Engineers; appointed Asst., British Museum, 1919; Keeper, Department of Egyptian and Assyrian Antiquities, British Museum, 1948-55; excavations at Ur, 1923-24, Atshanah, 1946, Nimrud, 1952; Hon. Lecturer in Assyriology K.C.L., 1923. *Publications:* The Early Dynasties of Sumer and Akkad, 1921; Cuneiform Texts, parts 36, 38-41, 1921-31; The Fall of Nineveh, 1923; A Sumerian Reading Book, 1924; History and Monuments of Ur, 1929; The Stones of Assyria, 1936; Ideas of Divine Rule (Schweich Lectures of the British Academy), 1948; (with L. Legrain) Ur Excavations, Royal Inscriptions, 1928; (with S. N. Kramer) Ur Excavations, Literary and Religious Texts I, 1963, II, 1966. *Address:* 11 Northgate Avenue, Bury St. Edmunds, Suffolk. [*Died* 2 *Dec.* 1969.

GADDUM, Sir John (Henry), Kt. 1964; F.R.S. 1945; F.R.S.E.; Sc.D., M.R.C.S., L.R.C.P.; *b.* 1900; *s.* of Harry Gaddum, M.A., J.P., The Priory, Bowdon, Cheshire; *m.* 1929, Iris Mary, *d.* of late Sir Sidney Harmer, K.B.E., F.R.S.; three *d.* *Educ.:* Rugby; Trinity Coll., Camb.; Univ. Coll. Hospital. Member of staff of Wellcome Physiological Research Laboratories, 1925; of staff of the National Institute for Medical Research, 1927; Prof. of Pharmacology, Egyptian University, Cairo, 1934; Professor of Pharmacology, University Coll., London, 1935; Professor of Pharmacology, College of the Pharmaceutical Society, London, 1938; Prof. of Materia Medica, Edin. Univ., 1942; Director of the Agricultural Research Council, Institute of Animal Physiology, Babraham, 1958-65. Member of Medical Research Council, 1948-51; Fellow, New York Academy of Science; Membre corresp. de la Société Philomathique de Paris; Mem. Deutsch. Akad. Naturf. Leopoldina; Hon. Mem: Italian Pharmacological Soc.; Sociedad Farmacologia y Terafentica, Argentina; Brit. Pharmacol. Soc.; Biochem. Soc.; Endocrinol. Soc. Ehrenmitgl. Deutsch. Pharmakol. Soc. Hon. LL.D. Edin. 1964. *Publications:* Scientific papers in the Journal of Physiology, Biochemical Journal, Quarterly Journal of Pharmacy, Special reports of the Medical Research Council, Clinical Science, etc., Gefässerweiternde Stoffe der Gewebe, 1935, Pharmacology, 1940. *Recreations:* reading, writing and arithmetic. *Address:* 10 Fendon Close, Cambridge. *Club:* Athenæum. [*Died* 30 *June* 1965.

GADSBY, John, C.B.E. 1925; Grand Officer of the Order of the Crown of Italy; *b.* Alvaston, nr. Derby, June 1884; *s. s.* of late H. F. Gadsby. *Educ.:* Shrewsbury; Inner Temple. Called to Bar, 1909; was in Japan, 1911-41; formerly lecturer in English Law in the Tokyo Imperial University, but resigned his post in 1929; was a Member of the Committee of the League of Nations Association of Japan for the translation of Japanese Laws into English; Legal Adviser, with local rank of Consul, to H.M. Consul-General at Shanghai, 1945-48, when he resigned his office of Consul; Local Legal Adviser to H.M. Embassy and Consular Establishments in China and Taiwan, 1948-54; formerly Legal Adviser to the British and Italian Embassies and the Canadian Legation at Tokyo. *Publications:* Sovereignty over Air-Space; many articles in English and American Legal Publications. *Recreations:* fishing and the study of art. *Address:* Kylemore House, Kylemore, Connemara, Eire. *Club:* Reform. [*Died* 14 *June* 1970.

GAGARIN, Colonel Yuri Alexeyevich; Hero of the Soviet Union; Master of Radio Sport of the Soviet Union; Col., Soviet Air Force; first cosmonaut (having made first cosmic flight); *b.* Gzhatsk district, Smolensk region of Russian Federation, 9 March 1934; *s.* of Alexei Gagarin, collective farmer; *m.* Valentina Ivanova, med. grad.; two *d.* *Educ.:* secondary school, Gzhatsk; vocational sch.; Lyubertsy; industrial college, Saratov (Hons. degree). Took instruction course, Saratov Aero Club, 1955; entered air school, Orenburg, 1955; joined Soviet Air Force, 1957; joined Communist Party, 1960. First man to travel in space, 108 minutes, circling the earth once, in the Vostok (East) spaceship satellite, 12 April 1961. Gold Medal, British Interplanetary Society, and Gold Medal, Amalgamated Union of Foundryworkers, both awarded in Great Britain, which he visited in July, 1961; Diploma and Gold Medal, Internat. Aeronautical Federation, 1961; Galabert Internat. Astronautical Prize (jointly with Col. John Glenn), 1963, etc. *Publication:* Doroga v Kosmos (The Road to the Cosmos), 1969. *Recreation:* interested in sport. *Address:* Scientific Research Inst. of Aviation Medicine, Petrovsky Park, Moscow. [*Died* 27 *March* 1968.

GAINER, Sir Donald St. Clair, G.B.E., *cr.* 1950 (O.B.E. 1934); K.C.M.G., *cr.* 1944 (C.M.G. 1937); *b.* Thrapston, Northants, 18 Oct. 1891; *s.* of Joseph William Gainer, J.P., and Margaret, *d.* of Peter Sinclair, Edinburgh; *m.* 1924, Beatrice Mercedes, *d.* of Oswald A. Hornsby, P.E.I., Canada, and Havana, Cuba; two *s.* *Educ.:* Charterhouse; Germany;

France. Vice-Consul, Narvik, 1915; Vardo, Aug. 1915; Christianssand, 1916; Tromsö, 1919; Bergen, 1920; Havana, 1921; granted local rank of Second Secretary of Legation, 1923; Chargé d'Affaires, Havana, June-Dec. 1923, and April-Oct. 1924; Acting Consul-General, Rotterdam, March-June 1925; Vice-Consul, Munich, 1926-29; established a Consular Post at Breslau, 1929; Consul-General at Mexico, 1931-32; for Bavaria, 1932-38; for Austria, 1938-39; Minister to Venezuela, 1939-44, Ambassador, 1944; Ambassador to Brazil, 1944-47; Ambassador to Poland, 1947-50; Permanent Under-Secretary of State, F.O. (German Sect.), 1950-51, retd. 1951; Chief Executive, International Road Federation (London Office), 1951-57, retired 1957. Chairman Anglo-Brazilian Soc., 1955-64. *Recreations:* reading and bridge. *Address:* 6 Holland Park Mansions, Holland Park Gardens, W.14. [*Died* 30 *July* 1966.

GAITHER, H. Rowan, Jr.; Partner, Draper, Gaither & Anderson, since 1959; *b.* 23 Nov. 1909; *s.* of H. R. and Marguerite Chamberlain Gaither; *m.* 1931, Charlotte Castle Gaither; two *s.* *Educ.:* Univ. of California, Berkeley, Calif.; Univ. of Calif. School of Jurisprudence. Attorney, Farm Credit Administration, 1933-36; Partner, Cooley, Crowley and Gaither, 1937-53. Asst. Dir., Radiation Lab., Mass. Inst. of Technology, 1942-45; Dir., Study for The Ford Foundation, 1948-50; Assoc. Dir. The Ford Foundation, 1951-53; Chairman of Board of Trustees, Oct. 1956-Dec. 1958, The Ford Foundation (Pres. 1953-Sept. 1956). Member Board of Trustees: Rand Corp. (Chm., 1948-58; 1960-); Mitre Corp. (Chm., 1958-1960); Ford Foundation; American Heritage Foundation; World Affairs Council of N. Calif.; Mem. Bd. of Directors: American Heart Assoc.; Hewlett-Packard Corp.; Pacific National Bank of San Francisco. Presidential Certificate of Merit, 1947. Alumnus of The Year, Univ. of Calif., 1959. Hon. Mem. American Bar Foundation. Hon. LL.D., Univ. of California, 1957. *Recreations:* hunting, wood-working. *Address:* 333 Montgomery St., San Francisco, Calif., U.S.A. *T.:* Douglas 2-7828. *Clubs:* Bohemian (San Francisco); University, Century Association (New York); Cosmos (Washington, D.C.). [*Died* 7 *April* 1961.

GAITSKELL, Rt. Hon. Hugh Todd Naylor, P.C. 1947; C.B.E. 1945; M.P. (Lab.) South Leeds since 1945; Leader, Labour Party, since Dec. 1955 (Treasurer 1954-56); Vice-Chairman Labour Party Executive Committee, Oct. 1962; *b.* 9 April 1906; *s.* of Arthur Gaitskell, Indian Civil Service; *m.* 1937, Anna Dora, *d.* of Leon Creditor; two *d.* *Educ.:* Winchester; New College, Oxford (1st Class Hons. Philosophy, Politics and Economics, 1927). Rockefeller Fellow, 1933-34; Head of Department of Political Economy, U.C., London; Reader in Political Economy, Univ. of London, 1938; Prin. Priv. Sec. to Minister of Economic Warfare, 1940-42; Prin. Asst. Sec., Board of Trade, 1942-45; Parl. Sec. Ministry of Fuel and Power, 1946-1947; Minister of Fuel and Power, 1947-50; Minister of State for Economic Affairs, Feb.-Oct. 1950; Chancellor of the Exchequer, 1950-51. Hon. D.C.L. Oxford, 1958. *Publications:* Chartism, 1929; Money and Everyday Life, 1939; The Challenge of Co-existence, 1957. *Relevant Publication:* Hugh Gaitskell, 1906-1963, Ed. W. T. Rodgers, 1963. Contributions to various books and periodicals. *Recreations:* gardening, walking. *Address:* House of Commons, S.W.1. [*Died* 18 *Jan.* 1963.

GALE, Kenneth Frederick; Chartered Municipal Treasurer; General Manager, Stevenage Development Corp., since 1967; *b.* 13 Apr. 1914; *s.* of late Frederick and Kate Leonora Gale, Exeter; *m.* 1937, Olivia Mae Theresa, *d.* of Walter Selby Wood, Barnstaple; one *s.* three *d.* *Educ.:* Hele's, Exeter. Served R.A.F., 1944-46. City Treasurer's Dept., City of Exeter, 1930-48; Internal Auditor, Harlow and Stevenage Devt. Corps., 1948-49; Chief Finance Off., Stevenage Devt. Corp., 1960-67. Co-Founder and Chm., New Towns Cttee. (Registered Trade Union), 1950-55; Chm., Bowes Lyon House Man. Cttee., 1964-67; Hon. Sec., Stevenage Youth Trust, 1967- (Hon. Treas., 1961-67); Mem., Stevenage Licensed Premises Cttee., 1967-; Vice-Pres., Stevenage Sports Coun., 1968-; New Towns rep. on Gen. Purposes Cttee. of Inst. of Municipal Treasurers and Accountants (Metrop. and Home Cos. Br.). *Publications:* papers in technical jls. *Recreations:* sea fishing, motoring, gardening. *Address:* Westwoods, Whitney Drive, Stevenage, Herts. *T.:* Stevenage 51560. [*Died* 12 *Aug.* 1969.

GALE, Sir Laurence George, Kt. 1968; C.B. 1960; O.B.E. 1945; C.Eng.; M.I.Mech.E.; Controller of Royal Ordnance Factories, Min. of Def., Army Dept., 1964-69, retired; *b.* 25 Sept. 1905; *s.* of George Gale; *m.* 1931, Alice May Canvin; one *s.* *Educ.:* Bedford Modern School; Emmanuel College, Cambridge. Mechanical Sciences Tripos 1929, B.A. (Cantab.) 1929. Supt. Royal Ordnance Factory: Kirkby, 1940-45; Swynnerton, 1945-47; Chorley, 1947-50. Director of Filling Factories, 1950-52; Deputy Director-General of Armament Production, 1952-57, Dir.-Gen., 1957-64. *Recreations:* sailing, walking, music. *Address:* 57 Court Road, S.E.9. *T.:* 01-850 7985. *Clubs:* Senior Service; Medway Yacht (Upnor). [*Died* 8 *July* 1969

GALER, Sir (Frederic) Bertram, Kt., 1939; M.A., F.I.A. 1904; D.L., J.P.; Vice-President, England and Wales of Internat. Union of Towns; Mem. of Lloyd's; *b.* 6 Aug. 1873; *m.* 1912, Berthe Elisa, 2nd *d.* of Henri Rieckel, Banker, La Chaux de Fonds, Switzerland; one *d.* *Educ.:* Dulwich Coll., Corpus Christi Coll., Cambridge. Asst. Sec., Norwich Union Life Office, 1910-13; General Manager and Actuary, Eagle Insurance Co., 1914-17; Life Manager Eagle Star Insurance Co., 1917-21; Underwriter Lloyd's, 1919; 24th (Queen's Battn.) London Regt., 2nd Lieut. 1909; Capt. 1914; Adjt. 1915-17; Member for Streatham L.C.C., 1921-49; Chief Whip M.R. Party, 1929-37; Deputy Chairman L.C.C., 1937-38; Mem. Port of London Authority, 1934-49. *Recreation:* golf. *Address:* The Speakers House, Henley-on-Thames. *T.:* Henley 4832. *Club:* Oxford and Cambridge. [*Died* 15 *Oct.* 1968.

GALLACHER, William; *b.* 25 Dec. 1881; *s* of John Gallacher and Mary Sutherland; *m.* 1913, Jean Roy. *Educ.:* Elementary School, Paisley. Socialist Agitator; Chairman of Clyde Workers Committee, 1914-18; Leading member of Communist Party and Communist International since 1920 (President, Communist Party, 1956-63). M.P (Com.) Western Division of Fife, 1935-50. *Publications:* Revolt on the Clyde; The Rolling of the Thunder; The Case for Communism; The Last Memoirs of William Gallacher, 1966 (posthumous); also several pamphlets on current political issues. *Address:* 68 Rowan Street, Paisley. [*Died* 12 *Aug.* 1965.

GALLARATI SCOTTI, Tommaso, Duke of S. Pietro in Galatina, Prince of Molfetta, Marquis of Cerano; Hon. C.M.G.; *b.* Milan, 18 Nov. 1878; *e.s.* of late Duke Giancarlo Gallarati Scotti and of Contessa Luisa Melzi d'Eril; *m.* 1918, Countess Aurelia Cittadella Vigodarzere; three *s.* two *d.* *Educ.:* University of Genoa. Graduated in Law. One of founders of Opera Bonomelli for assistance to Italian emigrants; one of founders of Popular Univ. of Milan; co-editor of review

Rinnovamento, 1906-07, which included as collaborators the most eminent writers and thinkers of that period. Volunteered in European War, 1915-18, and was promoted to Captain for merit; Officer in Alpine Troops, A.D.C. to General Cadorna, 1917-18. Founder with Ferruccio Parri of the anti-Fascist newspaper Il Caffè, 1922-24; in Switzerland as political refugee, 1943-44; Ambassador to Spain, 1945-46; Italian Ambassador to the Court of St. James's, 1947-51; one of founders of Cttee. of Liberation of Milan in July 1943. Silver Medal and two crosses for valour, 1915-18; Chevalier de la Légion d'Honneur; Comdr. Ordre Polonia Restituta; Cavaliere S.M.O. de Malta. *Publications:* Mazzini e il suo idealismo politico e religioso, 1904; Storie dell' amore sacro e dell' amore profano, 1911; Adamo Michiewicz, 1915; La vita di A. Fogazzaro, 1920; Vita di Dante, 1922; Così sia, 1922 (written for E. Duse); Miraluna, 1927; Storie di noi mortali, 1939; La confessione di Flavio Dossi, 1942; essays and articles in principal newspapers and reviews. *Recreation:* fishing. *Heir: e. s.* Giancarlo Gallarati Scotti, *b.* 1920. *Address:* Villa Melzi, Bellagio, Como, Italy; 30 Via Manzoni, Milan
[*Died* 1 *June* 1966.

GALLI-CURCI, Amelita; *b.* Milan, 18 Nov. 1882; *m.* 1st, 1910, Marquis Luigi Curci of Simeri; 2nd, 1921, Homer Samuels, Minneapolis. *Educ.:* Milan Conservatory. Début as Gilda at Costanzi Theatre, Rome, 1910; Chicago Opera Co., 1916-24; Metropolitan Opera Co., N.Y., from 1921, now retired. *Address:* Rancho Santa Fé, California, U.S.A.
[*Died* 26 *Nov.* 1963.

GALLON, William Anthony, B.Sc. M.I.E.E., M.Inst.F., F.R.Econ.S., F.R.S.A.; Chairman, South Wales Electricity Board, 1957-62, retd.; *b.* 27 June 1898; *m.* 1923, Elsie Ness; no *c.* *Educ.:* Rutherford College; King's Coll., Durham Univ. Engineer, Newcastle Elec. Supply, 1921-28; Engineer, Imperial Chemicals, 1928-35; Deputy Borough Engr., Plymouth, 1935-38; Deputy Borough Engr., Southampton, 1938-41; Borough Elec. Engr., Woolwich, 1941-48; Chief Engr., S. Eastern Elec. Bd., 1948-52; Divl. Controller, Merseyside & North Wales Div., 1952-53; Dep. Chm., S. Wales Elec. Bd., 1953-57. O.St.J. *Address:* 149 Lake Road West, Cardiff. *T.:* Cardiff 51623. *Club:* Cardiff and County (Cardiff).
[*Died* 4 *Aug.* 1962.

GALLOP, Constantine, Q.C. 1946; B.C.L. (Oxon); LL.B. (Lond.); *s.* of late Frederick and Marie Gallop, Eton Ave., London, N.W. *Educ.:* University College, London; Balliol College, Oxford. Barrister, Middle Temple, 1914; Bencher 1954. Barstow Law Scholar in International Law; Inns of Court Studentship, University Law Scholarship (London University, 1912); placed first in First Class Honours both in bar final and in final LL.B. Examinations. King Edward VII Memorial Essay Prize, Middle Temple, etc. President Oxford Union Society, 1919. Special Divorce Commissioner, 1953-. Contested (Lab.) Hythe Division of Kent, 1924, South Oxfordshire (Henley Division), 1951. Military Service, 1915-18. *Publications:* miscellaneous writings on Matrimonial Law, etc. *Address:* (Residential) 2 Essex Court, Temple, E.C.4. *Club:* Reform.
[*Died* 19 *April* 1967.

GALLOWAY, Alexander, C.M.G. 1963; M.B.E. 1942; Professor Emeritus, Makerere University College, The University of East Africa, since 1962; *b.* 19 Aug. 1901; *s.* of James Galloway; *m.* 1963, Barbara Geraldine Watkinson. *Educ.:* Fraserburgh Academy; Aberdeen Univ. Professor of Anatomy, Univ. of Saskatchewan, 1927-32; Sen. Lecturer in Anatomy, Univ. of the Witwatersrand, 1932-46; Professor of Anatomy and Dean of Faculty of Medicine, Makerere Univ. College, 1947-62. Visiting Prof. of Anthropology, Univ. of Chicago and Northwestern Univ., 1949. F.R.C.S. (without Examination) 1958; Chairman, Uganda Foundation for the Blind, 1950-62. *Publications:* The Skeletal Remains of Bambadyanalo, 1959; also numerous Anthropological Papers. *Address:* The Lindens, Alresford, Hants. *Club:* United Service.
[*Died* 24 *Sept.* 1965.

GALLWEY, Sir Reginald Frankland Payne-, 5th Bt., *cr.* 1812; *b.* 15 April 1889; *s.* of Wyndham Harry Payne-Gallwey (*d.* 1916), 4th *s.* of 2nd Bt. and Edith Millicent (*d.* 1939), *d.* of late Wainwright Crowe, Ennis, Co. Clare, Ireland; *S.* cousin 1955; *m.* 1912, Rosetta (marriage dissolved), *d.* of Henry Durdle, Reading; one *d.*; *m.* 1956, Dorothy, *d.* of Bertram Henry Madge and *widow* of Stanley Bathurst. *Educ.:* Temple Grove; Lancing: St. Edmund Hall, Oxford. Comp.I.E.E. *Heir: cousin* Philip Payne-Gallwey [*b.* 15 March 1935. *Educ.:* Eton. 2nd Lieut. 11th Hussars]. *Address:* 12 Palace Mansions, W.14. *T.:* Fulham 5778.
[*Died* 12 *Jan.* 1964.

GAMBIER-PARRY, Brigadier Sir Richard, K.C.M.G., *cr.* 1956 (C.M.G. 1945); late Royal Welch Fusiliers; Director of Communications to the Foreign Service since 1947; *b.* 1894; *s.* of late Sidney Gambier-Parry, Cirencester, Glos.; *m.* 1944, Elizabeth Clare, *d.* of Col. H. B. Towse, Royal Scots Greys. *Educ.:* Eton. Served European War, 1914-18, Royal Welch Fusiliers and R.F.C. in France and Belgium (despatches, twice, wounded thrice, 1914-15 star, two medals). Public Relations Dept., B.B.C., 1926-31; attached to Foreign Office since 1938. War of 1939-45, in North-West Europe; Col 1939; Brig. 1942 (1939-45 star, France and Germany stars, Defence and 1939-45 War medals, Order of Polonia Restituta, 2nd class, Order of White Lion of Czechoslovakia, 3rd class). *Address:* Abbots Close, Milton Keynes, Bletchley, Bucks. *T.:* Milton Keynes 215.
[*Died* 19 *June* 1965.

GAME, Henry Clement, C.V.O. 1952 (M.V.O. 1941); O.B.E.; 4th *s.* of late George Beale Game, Barn House, Broadway; *m.* 1913, Annie, *d.* of late Dr. John Appleyard, Bradford, Yorkshire. *Educ.:* Charterhouse; The Slade School of Art; Examiner of Plays, 1936-52; Assistant Examiner, 1930. Served European War, 1914-19. *Address:* c/o Midland Bank Ltd., 25 Wigmore Street, W.1.
[*Died* 28 *May* 1966.

GAMBLE, Brigadier Geoffrey Massey, C.M.G. 1950; O.B.E. 1945; A.D.C. 1949-1950; *b.* 7 Feb. 1896; *s.* of late A. Gamble, Gamston Manor, Retford; *m.* 1938, Diana Holland Robinson; two *s.* *Educ.:* Charterhouse; R.M.C. Sandhurst. Served European War, 1914-18, Sherwood Foresters (wounded twice). Regimental and staff duties, 1919-34; Instructor R.M.C. Sandhurst, 1934-37; Regimental duty, 1937-1938; Officer Commanding 2nd Bn. Sherwood Foresters till wounded and captured near Dunkirk, 1938-40; prisoner of war in Germany, 1940-45; A.A.G., A.G.2, W.O., 1945-47; comdg. Eritrea Dist., 1947-48; Chief Administrator, Somalia, 1948-50; retd. pay, 1950; served with E. Africa High Commission, 1950-52. *Publication:* Simplified Tactical Instruction, 1936. *Recreations:* fishing, golf. *Address:* Little White Cottage, Rotherfield Greys, Henley-on-Thames RG9 4QL. *T.:* Rotherfield Greys 334. *Club:* Army and Navy.
[*Died* 12 *Jan.* 1970.

GAME, Air Vice-Marshal Sir Philip Woolcott, G.C.B., *cr.* 1945 (K.C.B., *cr.* 1924; C.B. 1919); G.C.V.O., *cr.* 1937; G.B.E., *cr.* 1929; K.C.M.G., *cr.* 1935; D.S.O. 1915; *b.* 30 March 1876; *s.* of late George Beale Game, Barn House, Broadway, Wor-

cestershire; *m.* 1908, Gwendolen Margaret, *d.* of the late Francis Hughes-Gibb of Gunville Manor House, Blandford, Dorset; one *s.* one *d.* (and one *s.* died on active service, 1943). *Educ.:* Charterhouse. Entered R.A. 1895; Captain, 1901; Adjutant, 1902-5; Major, 1912; General Staff Officer 3rd and 2nd Grade War Office, 1910-14; won Gold Medal, United Service Inst., 1911; served South Africa, 1901-2 (despatches, Queen's medal 5 clasps); European War, 1914-18 (despatches 6 times, C.B., D.S.O., Brevet Lieut.-Colonel and Col., Order Crown of Italy, Officer Legion of Honour); Director of Training and Organisation Air Ministry, 1919-22; commanded R.A.F. in India, 1923; Air Member for Personnel on Air Council, 1923-28; retired list, 1929; Governor of N.S.W. 1930-35; Commissioner of Metropolitan Police, 1935-45; Grand Officer Legion of Honour; Grand Cross, Order of Leopold II; Grand Cross, Crown of Roumania; Grand Officer of Order of Orange Nassau. *Address:* Blakenhall, Wildernesse Avenue, Sevenoaks. *Club:* Army and Navy.
[*Died* 4 *Feb.* 1961.

GAMLIN, Lionel James, M.A. (Cantab.); Actor, Broadcaster and Author; *b.* 30 April 1903; *y. s.* of late Alderman James Gamlin, J.P., Birkenhead, and of Katharine Clara Charlotte Gamlin; unmarried. *Educ.:* Birkenhead School; Fitzwilliam College, Cambridge University. Formerly: President, Union Society, President, A.D.C., Editor of The Granta, Cambridge. Business in Liverpool, 1922-25; Liverpool Playhouse Company, 1926. Schoolmaster: Birkenhead School, 1927; Bedford School, 1931-33; Dauntsey's School, 1933-35. Actor, London and Provinces, 1936; joined B.B.C. as Announcer, 1936, B.B.C. Staff, 1936-45; free-lance broadcaster and news-reel commentator, 1945. Returned to stage, 1956. *Publications:* Don't Be A-Freud! (with Anthony Gilbert), 1946; You're on The Air, 1947. Contrib. chapter to "The Cambridge Union, 1915-1939", 1953. Entered films, 1961. *Recreations:* listening to music, travelling, conversation. *Address:* c/o Broadcasting House, W.1
[*Died* 16 *Oct.* 1967.

GAMMIE, John, C.M.G. 1942; Vice-President of States Marine Corporation, 1945-66; *b.* Glasgow, 16 Mar. 1896; *s.* of James Alexander Gammie and Jean Cant; *m.* 1938, Frances Kerlin; two *s.* one *d.*; *m.* 1963, Genevieve Louis. *Educ.:* Glasgow University. Manager Liner Department, British Ministry of Shipping, 1915-18; Manager, Freight Department Cunard Steam Ship Co. Ltd., N.Y., 1919-23; Manager, Chicago Office, Cunard Steam Ship Co. Ltd., 1923-25; Asst. General Manager Cunard White Star Ltd. in U.S.A., 1925-39; Deputy Representative British Ministry of War Transport (25 Broadway, New York City), 1939-45. *Recreations:* golf, fishing. *Address:* Horse Hollow Road, Locust Valley, New York, U.S.A. *Clubs:* Whitehall (N.Y.); Creek, Manhasset Bay Yacht (L.I.).
[*Died* 22 *Feb.* 1968.

GAMOW, George, Ph.D.; Professor of Physics, University of Colorado; Member: Royal Danish Academy of Sciences; Nat. Acad. of Sciences of U.S.A.; *b.* Odessa, Russia, 4 March 1904; *s.* of Anthony Gamow and Alexandra Lebedinzeva; *m.* 1931 (divorced 1956); one *s.*; *m.* 1958. *Educ.:* Univ. of Leningrad. Fellow Univ. of Copenhagen, 1928-29; Rockefeller Fellow Cambridge, 1929-30; Master in research Academy of Sciences, Leningrad, 1931-33; Lecturer at Universities of Paris and London, winter 1933-34; Lecturer at Univ. of Michigan, U.S.A., summer 1934; Prof. at George Washington Univ., 1934-56; Vis. Fell., Churchill Coll., Camb., autumn, 1965. *Publications:* Structure of Atomic Nuclei, 1931, 2nd ed. 1937, 3rd ed. 1949; Mr. Tompkins in Wonderland, 1939; The Birth and Death of the Sun, 1940; Biography of the Earth, 1941; Mr. Tompkins explores the Atom, 1943; Atomic Energy in Cosmic and Human Life, 1946; One, two, three . . . infinity, 1947; Creation of The Universe, 1952; Mr. Tompkins Learns the Facts of Life, 1953; The Moon, 1953; Puzzle Math, 1958; Matter, Earth and Sky, 1958 (rev. edn. 1965); Physics: Foundations and Frontiers, 1960; The Atom and Its Nucleus, 1961; Biography of Physics, 1961; Gravity, 1962; A Planet Called Earth, 1963; A Star Called the Sun, 1964; Mr. Tompkins in Paperback, 1965; Thirty Years that Shook Physics, 1966; (with M. Ičas) Mr. Tompkins Inside Himself, 1967; large number of articles on the problems of nuclear physics and astrophysics in scientific journals. *Recreation:* travelling. *Address:* 785-6th St., Boulder, Colorado, 80302, U.S.A. *T.:* 442-3525.
[*Died* 19 *Aug.* 1968.

GANLEY, Mrs. Caroline Selina, C.B.E. 1953; J.P.; *b.* 16 Sept. 1879; *d.* of James and Selina Mary Blumfield; *m.* 1901; two *s.* one *d.* Sec. to School Care Cttee.; Member of many public bodies including Borough and County Councils, and of Co-operative Movement; M.P. (Lab.-Co-op.) Battersea South, 1945-51; Councillor Battersea Borough council, 1953-65; Ex-President London Co-operative Society. J.P. 1920. *Address:* 5 Thirsk Road, S.W.11. [*Died* 31 *Aug.* 1966.

GARÇON, Maurice; Member of the French Academy since 1946; Barrister, Paris; *b.* 25 Nov. 1889; *m.* 1921, Suzanne Grivelle; two *s.* one *d.* *Publications:* La Vie exécrable de Guillemette Babin, 1925; Le Diable, 1926; Vintras, hérésiarque et prophète, 1928; Trois Histoires diaboliques, 1930; Magdeleine de la Croix, abbesse diabolique, 1939; Huysmans inconnu, 1941; Essai sur l'éloquence judiciaire, 1941; Tableau de l'éloquence judiciaire, 1943; Procès sombres, 1950; Louis XVII ou la fausse énigme, 1952; La vie tumultueuse de Maubreuil, 1954; Histoire de la Justice sous la IIIe République (3 vols.), 1957; huit volumes de plaidoyers, 1925-66; Lettre ouverte à la Justice, 1965. *Address:* 10 Rue de l'Éperon, Paris VI, France. *T.:* Danton 46.85.
[*Died* 29 *Dec.* 1967.

GARDEN, Mary, Operatic Soprano; *b.* Aberdeen, Scotland, 20 Feb. 1874; unmarried. Came to America with parents at six; lived at Chicopee, Mass., and Hartford, Conn., family moving to Chicago, 1888; began to learn violin when 6 years of age and played in concert at 12; studied piano several years; took part at 16 in an amateur performance of Trial by Jury, Chicago; went to Paris, 1896; studied voice under Trabadello, Chevalier and Fugere; never took lessons in acting; debut in title rôle of Charpentier's Louise, Opera Comique, Paris, 13 April 1900, as substitute in 3rd act for Mlle. Rioton, who became suddenly ill, and continued in same part for 100 nights; later sang in London and Brussels; début in America in Thais, under Oscar Hammerstein's management, at New York, 25 Nov. 1907, and later appeared as Mélisande in Pelléas and Mélisande and in the title rôle of Salome; sang in Chicago, 5 Nov. 1910, and since has appeared each season with Chicago Grand Opera Co.; General Manager, Chicago Opera, 1921-23. American lecture tours, 1948 and 1954. Has broadcast in Great Britain recently. *Publication:* (with Louis Biancolli) Mary Garden's Story, 1952. *Address:* National Arts Foundation, 342 Madison Avenue, New York City, N.Y., U.S.A.
[*Died* 3 *Jan.* 1967.

GARDINER, Sir Alan (Henderson), Kt. *cr.* 1948; D.Litt.; M.A.; Hon. D.Litt. (Durham), 1952; Hon. Litt.D. (Cambridge), 1956;

F.B.A.; Hon. Fellow of Queen's College, Oxford; President of the Egypt Exploration Soc.; *b.* Eltham, 29 Mar. 1879; *y. s.* of late Henry John Gardiner, Chairman of Bradbury, Greatorex & Co Ltd; *m.* Hedwig, *d.* of late Alexander von Rosen, King's Councillor (Hungary); two *s.* one *d.* *Educ.:* Charterhouse; Sorbonne, Paris; Queen's Coll., Oxford; Laycock Student of Egyptology, Worcester Coll., Oxford, 1906-12; for some years sub-editor of the Hieroglyphic Dictionary of the United German Academies; reader in Egyptology at Manchester University, 1912-14; theory of origin of the alphabet from inscriptions found in Sinai, 1915; Hon. Secretary of the Egypt Exploration Society (formerly Fund) 1917-20; Editor of the Journal of Egyptian Archæology, 1916-21, 1934, and 1941-46; undertook inscriptions in the tomb of Tutankhamun, 1923; Research Professor in Egyptology in the University of Chicago, 1924-34. Assoc. Member of Acad. des Inscriptions et Belles Lettres, Paris, and of Inst. d Egypte; corresp. Mem. of Bavarian, Danish, Prussian and Austrian Acads., and of Oriental Inst. of Prague; For. Member of Philosophical Soc. of America, of the American Academy of Arts and Sciences and of Roy. Netherlands Acad.; Hon. Member of Soc. Asiatique de Paris. *Publications:* The Inscription of Mes, 1905; Die Klagen des Bauern (with Vogelsang), 1908; Die Erzählung des Sinuhe und die Hirtengeschichte, 1909; The Admonitions of an Egyptian Sage, 1909; Egyptian Hieratic Texts, 1911; Theban Ostraca (with J. G. Milne and Sir Herbert Thompson), 1913; Tarkhan I., Memphis V. (with W. M. Flinders Petrie and G. A. Wainwright), 1913; A Topographical Catalogue of the Private Tombs of Thebes (with A. E. P. Weigall), 1913; The Tomb of Amenemhet (with Nina de Garis Davies), 1915; Notes on the Story of Sinuhe, 1916; The Inscriptions of Sinai, Part I. (with T. E. Peet), 1917; The Tomb of Huy, Viceroy of Nubia under Tutankhamen (with Nina de Garis Davies), 1926 Egyptian Grammar, 1927, 3rd edn., 1957; Egyptian Letters to the Dead (with Kurt Sethe), 1928; Late Egyptian Stories, 1932; The Theory of Speech and Language, 1932, 2nd edn., 1951; The Chester Beatty Papyri, No. I, 1931; Hieratic Papyri in the British Museum, Chester Beatty gift, 1935; The Attitude of the Ancient Egyptians to Death and the Dead (Frazer Lecture), 1935; Ancient Egyptian Paintings (with Nina de Garis Davies), 1936; Late-Egyptian Miscellanies 1936; Le Papyrus Léopold II. (with J. Capart), 1939; The Theory of Proper Names, 1940, 2nd edn., 1954; The Wilbour Papyrus, 1941-48; Ancient Egyptian Onomastica, 1947; Ramesside Administrative Documents, 1948; The Ramesseum Papyri, 1955; (with J. Cerny) Hieratic Ostraca, 1957; The Royal Canon of Turin, 1959; The Kadesh Inscriptions of Ramesses II, 1960; Egypt of the Pharaohs, an Introduction, 1961; Tutankhamun's Painted Box (with Nina de Garis Davies), 1962; many articles. *Recreations:* music, travelling, croquet. *Address:* Court Place, Iffley, Oxford. *T.:* Oxford 77401.
[*Died* 19 *Dec.* 1963.

GARDINER, Rt. Hon. James Garfield, P.C. 1947; B.A., LL.D.; *b.* Farquhar, Ont., 30 November 1883; *s.* of James C. and Elizabeth (Brown) Gardiner; *m.* 1917, Violet McEwen (*d.* 1944); one *s.* (and one killed in action), two *d.*; *m.* 1946, Mrs. H. H. Christie, Ottawa. *Educ.:* Normal School, Regina, Sask.; Manitoba Coll., Winnipeg (B.A.). Hon. LL.D. Manitoba, 1926, Ottawa, 1944, Saskatchewan, 1960. Principal of Lemberg Continuation Sch., Saskatchewan, 1911; farming since 1916; elected to Legislature at by-election, 1914, 1917, and at Gen. Election, 1921, 1925; Min. of Highways, Saskatchewan, 1922; Premier of Saskatchewan, 1926, re-elected at Gen. Election, 1929, resigned with his cabinet, Sept. 1929, re-elected at gen. election, 1934; also Minister of Education, 1926-29; Premier of Saskatchewan, July 1934, also Provincial treas.; resigned as Premier; P.C. (Can.) and Minister of Agriculture, 1935; elected to H. of C. at by-election, 1936, re-elected at gen. election, 1940, 1945, 1949, 1953, 1957, defeated, 1958; Minister of Agriculture, 1935-57, served as minister of Nat. War Services, 1940-41. Breeder of Shorthorn Cattle and Yorkshire Hogs on farm at Lemberg, Sask. Member Liberal Party. Member United Church of Canada. Order of Leopold I, Belgium, 1946. *Address:* Lemberg, Sask., Canada.
[*Died* 12 *Jan.* 1962.

GARDINER, Sir Thomas Robert, G.C.B., *cr.* 1954 (K.C.B., *cr.* 1937); G.B.E., *cr.* 1941 (K.B.E., *cr.* 1936); Hon. LL.D. (Edin.); *b.* 8 March 1883; *s.* of late Matthew John Gardiner and Elizabeth Granger; *m.* 1919, Christina Stenhouse. *Educ.:* Lurgan College, Co. Armagh; Royal High School, Edinburgh; Edinburgh University. Entered Post Office, 1906; Private Sec. to Sec. of Post Office, 1913-17; Controller London Postal Service, 1926-34; Dep. Dir.-Gen. Post Office, 1934-36; Dir.-Gen., 1936-45; Sec., Ministry of Home Security, 1939-40; Chm. Stevenage New Town Development Corp., 1947-48; Vice-Chm. and actg. Chm. Nat. Dock Labour Bd., 1949-51; a Government Director of the Anglo-Iranian Oil Company, 1950-53; Member of Royal Commission on Scottish Affairs, 1952-54; Member of Forces Medical and Dental Services Cttee., 1953-56. *Address:* 106 St. Mary Abbots Court, W.14. *T.:* Western 9955. *Club:* Athenæum.
[*Died* 1 *Jan.* 1964.

GARDNER, Lieutenant - Colonel Charles James Hookham, C.B.E. 1919; *s.* of late Captain Gardner, R.N.; *b.* 1875; *m.* 1910, Helen Faith (*d.* 1949), *d.* of Edwin Gray, J.P., Gray's Court, York, and Almyra Gray, J.P., *e. d.* of Albert Vickers. *Educ.:* Christ's Hospital. Trained as an Engineer at the Crystal Palace Engineering College, and afterwards in large engineering works; served in the ranks of the Royal Dragoons during the South African War, 1899-1902 (Queen's medal 6 clasps, King's medal 2 clasps); granted a commission in the Green Howards (Alexandra Princess of Wales' Own Yorkshire Regt.); served with them in India, S. Africa, Egypt; retired, 1913; rejoined 1914, and in 1915 appointed D.A.A.G., afterwards A.A.G. Northern Command; served later as A.A.G. in Mobilisation Directorate, W.O. (C.B.E.); A.M.S., Northern Command, 1940-41; now retired. *Recreations:* shooting, golf. *Address:* Grays Court, York. *T.:* York 2963. *Clubs:* Naval and Military; Yorkshire (York).
[*Died* 4 *Nov.* 1962.

GARDNER, Erle Stanley; author, lawyer, U.S.A.; *b.* 17 July 1889; *s.* of Charles Walter Gardner and Grace Adelma Waugh; *m.* 1912, Natalie Talbert (*d.* 1968); one *d.*; *m.* 1968, Agnes Jean Bethell. *Educ.:* Palo Alto High School. Law offices, E. E. Keech, Ben Geis, Charles & Schneider; Bar Examinations, 1911; Law offices, Oxnard, 1911-16. Pres. Consolidated Sales Co., San Francisco, 1918-20. Practised law, Ventura, California, 1916-45; formerly Pres. Ventura County Bar Association. Co-founder Argosy Magazine's "Court of Last Resort". Member: American Acad. Forensic Sciences; Amer. Bar Assoc.; Amer. Judicature Soc.; California Bar; Paisano Productions; Amer. Soc. of Criminology; Harvard Associates in Police Science; The Law Science Acad. of America; Nat. Sheriff's Assoc.; New Hampshire Medico-Legal Soc.; Acad. of Science Interrogation; Kansas Peace Officers' Assoc.; The Amer. Polygraph Assoc. Hon. alumnus, Kansas City University, 1955; Hon. Dr. of Law, McGeorge College of Law, Sacramento, California, 1956. *Publications:* The

Case of the Velvet Claws, 1934, followed by over 100 published books (under own name and pen-name A. A. Fair); The Court of Last Resort, 1952; *travel books:* The Land of Shorter Shadows, 1947; Neighborhood Frontiers, 1954; Hunting the Desert Whale, 1960: Hovering Over Baja, 1961; The Hidden Heart of Baja, 1962; The Desert is Yours, 1963; The World of Water, 1964; Hunting Lost Mines by Helicopter, 1965; Off the Beaten Track in Baja, 1967; Gypsy Days on the Delta, 1967; Mexico's Magic Square, 1968; Drifting Down the Delta, 1969; Host With the Big Hat, 1969; contributor to Saturday Evening Post, etc. *Address:* Rancho del Paisano, Temecula, Cal., U.S.A. *Clubs:* Adventurers' (N.Y., Chicago), Elks (Hon. Life Mem.), etc. [*Died* 11 *March* 1970.

GARDNER, James Clark Molesworth, C.I.E. 1945; Forest Entomologist, E. African Agricultural and Forestry Research Organisation, 1951-57; *b.* 15 March 1894; *s.* of late J. C. Gardner, M.R.C.S., L.R.C.P., *m.* 1928, Mary Elizabeth Mouritz (marriage dissolved, 1947); one *s.* one *d.* *Educ.:* Brighton College; Imperial College of Science; Cambridge University. A.R.C.S.; D.I.C.; Diploma in Forestry, Camb. Univ. Served European War with Dorsetshire Regt. and Machine Gun Corps, 1914-19. Carnegie Research Scholar in U.S.A., 1920-21. Indian Forest Service, 1922-49; Forest Entomologist: Forest Research Inst., Dehra Dun, U.P., 1922-49; Kenya, 1949-57. *Publications:* technical papers in scientific jls. *Address:* c/o Glyn, Mills & Co., Kirkland House, Whitehall, S.W.1. *Club:* Public Schools. [*Died* 7 *March* 1970.

GARDNER, Robert Cotton Bruce, O.B.E. 1955; Secretary, Royal Forestry Society of England and Wales, 1935-59; *b.* 3 Dec. 1889; *s.* of late Philip Thomas Gardner, D.L., J.P., Conington Hall, Cambs., late 14th Regt., and Emily Elizabeth Calland; *m.* 1916, Olive Muriel Winifred, *d.* of Lt. Col. W. P. Holmes, Ballingrawn, Kings Co., Ireland; two *s.* *Educ.:* Oundle; Caius College, Cambridge (B.A. 1911). Employed under Ministry of Agriculture at S.E. Agricultural College, Wye, Kent, on investigating certain sheep diseases, 1911-12; in charge of Marquis of Bute's Natural History Museum, Isle of Bute, 1912-14; Army service, 1914-21, R.G.A. (T.F.); in France 3 years with 51st (Highland) Division and H.Q. X Army Corps, transferred to Royal Army Ordnance Corps, Temp. Captain (despatches); with Anglo-Persian Oil Company's subsidiaries in England and France, 1922-28; has broadcast several talks on trees and shrubs, and timber subjects from B.B.C. *Publications:* Parasitic gastritis in sheep and cattle, 1912; Preservative treatment of Farm and Estate Timber, 1933; has contributed articles to London papers and journals on arboriculture, topography and bagpipe music. *Recreations:* gardening, topography, photography. *Address:* 45 Crondal Lane, Farnham, Surrey. [*Died* 5 *July* 1964.

GARIOCH, Lord (Master of Mar); **David Charles of Mar;** *b.* 10 Aug. 1944; *o. s.* and *heir* of 30th Earl of Mar. *Educ.:* Marlborough. *Recreation:* fishing. *Address:* 6 Dalrymple Crescent, Newington, Edinburgh. [*Died* 8 *Jan.* 1967.

GARMONSWAY, Prof. George Norman, M.A. (Cantab.), F.S.A., F.R.Hist.S.; Professor Emeritus of English Language, University of London, 1965 (Professor 1956); Fellow of King's College; *b.* 6 May 1898; *o. s.* of Robert Garmonsway and Elizabeth Haswell, Hartlepool, County Durham; *m.* 1929, Doris Patricia, *er. d.* of George Webster, Porth, Wales; one *d.* *Educ.:* Henry Smith School, Hartlepool; St. Catharine's College, Cambridge. Lieut. R.G.A., 1917. Scholar of St. Catharine's Coll., 1919; English Tripos (1st Cl. Hons.), B.A. 1921; M.A. 1924. Asst. Lecturer, Univ. Coll. of Wales, Aberystwyth, 1921-30; Lecturer, King's Coll., Univ. of London, 1930; Pres. Viking Soc. for Northern Research, London, 1936; Mem. Advisory Cttee. for the Promotion of Scandinavian Studies, 1938-66; Dep. Priority Officer, Min. of Food, 1939-45; University Reader in English, King's College, 1946; Chairman Board of Studies in English, University of London, 1950-52; Visiting Professor of English: University of California (Los Angeles), 1955; University of N. Carolina (Chapel Hill), 1962; University of Toronto, 1965-67. *Publications:* An Early Norse Reader, 1928; Aelfric's Colloquy, 1939; The Anglo-Saxon Chronicle, 1954 (Everyman edn.); Canute and his Empire, 1965; The Penguin English Dictionary, 1965; various papers and reviews in learned jls. *Recreations:* music, cricket, motoring. *Address:* Gages, Faygate, Horsham, Sussex. *T.:* Faygate 327. [*Died* 27 *Feb.* 1967.

GARNER, Frederic Horace, O.B.E. 1943; Medal of Freedom, Silver Palm (U.S.A.), 1947; Ph.D.; M.I.Mech.E., M.I.Chem.E., F.R.I.C., F.Inst. Fuel, F.S.A.; Professor and Director of Chemical Engineering Department, Univ. of Birmingham, 1942-61, Emeritus Professor since 1961; Chairman, Fire Research Board, since 1961; *b.* 1 Aug. 1893; *s.* of William Garner, Wymeswold, Loughborough; unmarried. *Educ.:* Market Bosworth Grammar School; University of Birmingham (1851 Exhibition Research Scholar); University of Pittsburgh. Chemist Royal Aircraft Establishment, Farnborough; Fellow Mellon Institute of Industrial Research, Univ. of Pittsburgh; Chief Chemist, Agwi Petroleum Corporation, Fawley, 1921-1928; Chief Chemist, Anglo-American Oil Company, 1928-35; Director of Research, Esso European Laboratories, 1935-42; Chairman, Water Pollution Research Board, 1956-1961; Chairman Fire Research Board, 1961-. Hon. Fellow: Institute of Petroleum (Past Pres.); Inst. Gas Engineers; Inst. Sewage Purification. Redwood Medallist (Inst. Pet.). Melchett Medallist (Inst. Fuel), Reynolds Medallist (Inst. Chem. Eng.). Hon. Mem. foreign societies. *Publications:* Chem. Engineering Subjects, fuels and their combustion, viscosity problems; Editor, English Delftware, 1948. *Address:* 10 Far Street, Wymeswold Loughborough. [*Died* 19 *Sept.* 1964

GARNER, John Nance, *b.* 22 Nov. 1868; *s.* of John N. and Sarah Garner; *m.* 1896, *Educ.:* Vanderbilt University, University of the South, Tenn., U.S.A. Barrister 1890; Member Texas House of Representatives 1898-1902; Member United States Congress 1903-33; Speaker of House of Representatives, U.S.A., 1931-33. Democrat. Vice-President of U.S.A., 1933-37 and 1937-41 *Address:* Uvalde, Texas, U.S.A. [*Died* 7 *Nov.* 1967

GARNETT, William James; land owner in Lancashire; D.L., J.P. Lancs County Councillor, 1931, County Alderman 1949; *b.* July 1878; *s.* of William Garnett, High Sheriff of Lancashire, 1879; *g. s.* of William James Garnett, M.P. for Lancaster, 1857-64; unmarried. *Educ.:* Eton; Christ Church, Oxford. Diplomatic Service, 1902; served in Constantinople, 1903-05; Peking, 1905-08; travelled across Mongolia for 9 months in 1908, Roumania 1909; St. Petersburg, 1909-11; Teheran, 1911-14; Sofia, 1915 (left on rupture of relations with the Allies); Athens, 1916; Tangier, 1917; Buenos Aires, 1918-19; resigned, 1920; High Sheriff, Lancs. 1937 and, for a 2nd time, 1941. Coronation Medals, 1937 and 1953. *Recreations:* everything connected with country life; chief interest local government.

Address: 2 Hill House, Quernmore Park, Lancaster. *T.:* Caton 314. [*Died* 22 *Oct.* 1965.

GARNIER, Colonel (Hon. Brig.) Alan Parry, C.B. 1939; M.B.E.; M.C.; *b.* 9 Aug. 1886; *s.* of Commander Keppel Garnier, R.N.; *m.* 1914, Hilda de B. d'Arcy; two *s.* (and one *s.* decd.). *Educ.:* Uppingham; Royal Military College, Sandhurst. 2/Lt. Northumberland Fusiliers, 1906; served European War, 1914-18 (wounded, despatches, 1914-15 Star, General Service and Victory Medals, M.B.E., M.C., Karageorge of Serbia IV Class with Swords); p.s.c.; commanded 2nd Bn. Royal Northumberland Fusiliers, 1933-36; Assistant Adjutant General War Office, 1936-39; Commander Welsh Area and N. Wales Area, 1939-41; Commander Border Sub-District, 1941-44; retired, 1944. A.D.C. to the King, 1939-44. *Club:* United Service. [*Died* 27 *June* 1963.

GARNIER, Rt. Rev. Mark R. C.; *see* Carpenter-Garnier.

GARNIER, Lt.-Col. Walter Keppel, O.B.E.; *b.* 6 March 1882; *y. s.* of late Rev. Canon Thomas Parry Garnier, M.A., *s.* of Dean of Lincoln and late Hon. Louisa Vernon Warren, *d.* of 5th Baron Vernon. *Educ.:* Haileybury College. Royal Marines, 1901; Royal Naval School of Physical Training, Portsmouth (Staff Officer), 1912-14; Superintendent of Physical Training, Royal Marines, 1914; retired, 1923; Director of the Incorporated Lucas-Tooth Boys' Training Fund Ltd., 1923-39, 1946-52. Superintendent, R.N. School of Physical Training, Portsmouth, 1945-46. *Recreations:* cricket, fencing, motoring. *Club:* United Service. [*Died* 6 *May* 1969.

GARRETT, Sir (Arthur) Wilfrid, K.B.E., *cr.* 1955; Kt., *cr.* 1942; B.Sc.; *b.* 8 Jan. 1880; British. Colonel (Territorial Army) retired; served European War, 1914-1918; H.M. Chief Inspector of Factories, 1939-46. First Principal of Y.M.C.A. College for Adults, Kingsgate, Kent, 1946-50. Chairman, Industrial Injuries Advisory Council, Ministry of Pensions and National Insurance 1946-55. *Address:* The Mulberry Tree, Broadstairs, Kent. *T.:* Thanet 61398. [*Died* 9 *June* 1967.

GARRETT, John Walter Percy, Headmaster of Bristol Grammar School, 1943-1960; *b.* 30 May 1902; *o. c.* of late P. E. T. Garrett and late F. E. Garrett; unmarried, *Educ.:* Trowbridge High School; Exeter College, Oxford. Asst. Master at Victoria College, Jersey, C.I., R.N. College, Dartmouth, Crypt School, Gloucester; Head of English Department, Whitgift School, Croydon; First Headmaster of Raynes Park County School, 1935-42; Page Travelling Scholarship to U.S.A., 1934. Gov. Royal Shakespeare Theatre, Stratford-upon-Avon; Smith-Mundt Fellowship, U.S.A., 1952. Hon. D.Litt. Univ. of Bristol, 1960. *Publications:* The Poet's Tongue (with W. H. Auden), 1935; Chapters on the Secondary School, in Manhood in the Making, 1939, and on Drama in Schools in The Universities and the Theatre, 1952; (ed.) Talking of Shakespeare, 1954; More Talking of Shakespeare, 1959; contrib. to Sunday Times, Observer, Times Literary and Educational Supplements, Atlantic Monthly, etc. *Recreations:* gardening, ornithology, and the theatre. *Address:* 2 St. Aubyn's Avenue, Wimbledon, S.W.19. *T.:* Wimbledon 0910. [*Died* 23 *Dec.* 1966.

GARRETT, Sir Wilfrid; *see* Garrett, Sir A. W.

GARRETT, William, Q.C. (Scotland) 1936; Sheriff-Substitute of the Lothians and Peebles at Edinburgh, 1948-60, retired 1960; (of Ayrshire at Ayr, 1940-48); *b.* 1890; *s.* of late George Garrett, iron and steel manufacturer, Coatbridge; *m.* 1915, Mary, *d.* of late D. C. McNaught; one *s.* one *d.* *Educ.:* Fettes College; Cambridge University (B.A., LL.B.) Glasgow University (LL.B.). Admitted to Faculty of Advocates, 1914; in practice as advocate from 1918; Junior Counsel to Admiralty in Scotland, 1934-36; Lecturer in International Private Law, Edinburgh University; Novelist. *Publications:* The Secret of the Hills, 1921; Friday to Monday; Dr. Ricardo; The Multitude; The Professional Guest; From Dusk till Dawn; The Man in the Mirror, 1931, etc. *Recreation:* golf. *Address:* 21 Blackford Road, Edinburgh. *T.:* Newington 2905. *Clubs:* New (Edinburgh); Royal Scottish Automobile (Glasgow). [*Died* 17 *Oct.* 1967.

GARROD, Air Chief Marshal Sir (Alfred) Guy (Roland), G.B.E., *cr.* 1948 (O.B.E. 1932); K.C.B., *cr.* 1943 (C.B. 1941); M.C.; D.F.C.; Hon. LL.D. Aberdeen; Hon. Fellow of Univ. Coll., Oxford; Mem. Advisory Panel, Official Military Histories of the War, 1949; Director Regis Property Co., 1949, and Humphreys Ltd., 1950-64; Chairman Malkay Investments Ltd., 1954; *b.* 13 April 1891; 3rd *s.* of H. B. Garrod, Barrister-at-law, Hampstead; *m.* 1st, 1918, Cicely Evelyn, A.R.R.C. (despatches) (*d.* 1960), *d.* of John Bray; one *s.* one *d.*; 2nd, 1961, Mrs. Doris Baker, *widow* of Samuel J. Baker, Malvern, Worcs. *Educ.:* Bradfield Coll. (Class. Schol.); Univ. Coll., Oxf. (Class Schol.). M.A. (Oxon.); Oxford *v.* Cambridge Cross Country, 1911; Oxford *v.* Cambridge Rifle Shooting, 1911, 1912, 1913; Second Lt. Leicestershire Regiment, Aug. 1914 (M.C.); joined Royal Flying Corps, Aug. 1915; Lt.-Col. 1918; D.F.C. 1919; Squadron Leader R.A.F. 1919; Air Vice-Marshal, 1939; Air Marshal, 1945; Air Chief Marshal, 1946; Royal Naval Staff College, 1921-22; Directing Staff, R.A.F. Staff College, 1923-27; Chief Instructor Oxford Univ. Air Squadron, 1928-30; R.A.F. Headquarters, Iraq, 1931-32; Imperial Defence College, 1933; Deputy Director of Organization, Air Ministry, 1934-36; A.O.C. Armament Group, 1937; Director of Equipment, Air Ministry, 1938-40; Air Member for Training on Air Council, 1940-43; Deputy A.O.C.-in.-C, India, May-Oct. 1943, Deputy Allied Air C.-in-C. S.E. Asia, Oct. 1943-Feb. 1945; C.-in-C. Royal Air Force, Mediterranean and Middle East, March-Nov. 1945; Permanent R.A.F. Representative, Military Staff Committee United Nations, Dec. 1945-May 1948; and Head of the R.A.F. Delegation, Washington, U.S.A., March 1946-May 1948; retired from active list, 1948. *Recreations:* rifle shooting (English XX, and British Team to Australia and S. Africa, 1920-21), music, violin playing. *Address:* Lea, Sling Lane, Malvern, Worcs. *Clubs:* United Service, Leander. [*Died* 3 *Jan.* 1965.

GARROD, Dorothy Annie Elizabeth, C.B.E. 1965; M.A. (Cantab.); D.Sc. (Oxon.); Hon. D.Sc. (Pa.); Hon. Docteur-ès-Sciences (Poitiers); Hon. Docteur-ès-Lettres (Toulouse); F.B.A., 1952; F.S.A.; F.R.A.I.; Associate Member, Société d'Anthropologie de Paris; *b.* 5 May 1892; *d.* of late Sir Archibald Garrod, K.C.M.G., F.R.S. *Educ.:* Privately; Newnham Coll., Camb. (Mary Ewart Travelling Scholar, 1922-23); Oxford. Excavated pre-historic rock shelter at Gibraltar, 1925-26; Member of Internat. Commn. to investigate the Glozel finds, 1927; Director: Joint Expedn. of Sladen Memorial Fund and Amer. Sch. of Prehistoric Research to S. Kurdistan, 1928; Joint Expedn. of British Sch. of Archæology in Jerusalem and Amer. Sch. of Prehistoric Research to excavate caves of Wady al Mughara, Mt. Carmel, 1929-1934; Excavations in Bulgaria, 1938; (with S. C. de St. Mathurin) Excavation of Magdalenian Rock Shelter at Angles-sur-l'Anglin,

1948-68; Excavations in Lebanon, 1958-64; Research Fellow, Newnham Coll., 1929-32; Leverhulme Research Fellow, 1934; Pres., Section H, British Association, 1936; Disney Professor of Archæology, Univ. of Cambridge, 1939-52; Section Officer W.A.A.F., 1942-45; Reckitt Lecturer, British Acad., 1957; Huxley Memorial Lectr., Royal Anthropological Inst., 1962. Huxley Medal for 1962. Gold Medal of Soc. of Antiquaries, 1968. *Publications:* The Upper Palæolithic Age in Britain, 1926; Excavation of a Mousterian Rock Shelter at Devil's Tower, Gibraltar (with L. H. Dudley Buxton), 1928; The Palæolithic of Southern Kurdistan, 1930; (with D. M. A. Bate) The Stone Age of Mt. Carmel, 1937; Excavation in the Cave of Bacho Kiro, N.E. Bulgaria, 1939; (with Diana Kirkbride) Excavation of the Abri Zumoffen, Adlun, South Lebanon, 1961; papers in various archæological journals. *Address:* Chamtoine, Villebois-Lavalette (Charente), France. *Club:* University Women's.
[*Died* 18 *Dec.* 1968.

GARROD, Air Chief Marshal Sir Guy; *see* Garrod, Air Chief Marshal Sir A. G. R.

GARROD, William Henry Edward, C.I.E. 1946; Chief Engineer, retired; *b.* 10 May 1892; *s.* of late H. W. Garrod; *m.* 1921, Kate, *d.* of late Vavasour Robert Shrigley. *Educ.:* St. Paul's School, London. Served European War, 1914-19, Royal Marines and Royal Engineers; Indian Service of Engineers, 1919-49; Chief Engineer, Bombay Presidency, 1944-49; under Colonial Office, Chief Engineer, Waterworks Department, Barbados, W.I., 1949-59. Freeman of City of London, 1953. *Address:* c/o Lloyds Bank, 6 Pall Mall, S.W.1. [*Died* 4 *Feb.* 1967.

GARROW, Alexander; M.P. (Lab.) Pollok Division of Glasgow since 1964; Co-operative Insurance Society Agent; *b.* 12 March 1923; *s.* of late William Garrow, Glasgow; *m.* 1955, Flora Wilson, *d.* of J. B. Mackay, Paisley; one *s.* *Educ.:* Queen's Park Secondary School, Glasgow; N.C.L.C. Joined Labour Party, 1946; Branch Chairman, Union of Shop, Distributive and Allied Workers; Councillor, Govanhill Ward, Glasgow, 1954-57, Pollokshaws Ward, 1960-. Chairman, Municipal Transport Cttee., Glasgow; Magistrate and J.P., Glasgow, 1960-63. *Address:* 45 Titwood Road, Glasgow, S.1. *T.:* Langside 9007. [*Died* 16 *Dec.* 1966.

GARSIA, Lt.-Col. Herbert George Anderson, C.B.E. 1919; D.S.O. 1902; *b.* 6 Feb. 1871; *m.* 1919, Myra, *d.* of late Sir George Fottrell, K.C.B., and *widow* of F. Mooney. Entered E. Surrey Regt. 1892; transferred A.S.C. 1894; served with Egyptian Army in Soudan, 1898-9 (British and Khedive's medals); S. Africa, 1899-1902 (despatches twice, Queen's medal 5 clasps, King's medal 2 clasps, D.S.O.); served with Egyptian Army, 1904-25; Order of the Nile, 2nd class. *Club:* United Service.
[*Died* 23 *Jan.* 1965.

GARSIA, Lieut.-Col. Willoughby Clive, D.S.O. 1918; M.C. 1915; p.s.c.; *s.* of Capt. C. Garsia, Bengal Staff Corps; *b.* Nelson, N.Z., 22 Feb. 1881. *Educ.:* N.Z. Entered Army, 1900; retired pay, 1920. South African War, 1901-2 (Queen's Medal and five clasps); Language Officer, Japan (attached Japanese Army), 1908-10; served European War, 1914-18; organised and served as Chief Staff Officer, British Adriatic Mission, 1915; O.C. British Mission with R. Serbian Army, 1916; G.S.O. 1 54th Div. 1917; G.S.O. 1 53rd Div. 1918; Acting Chief of Staff, British Forces in Egypt, 1919 (D.S.O., M.C., Servian White Eagle, 3rd class, Order of Nile, 3rd class, despatches 3 times). *Publications:* (under pseudonym, Guy Cottar) Tenacity, 1927; A Key to Victory, 1940; Planning the War, 1941. *Address:* Villa Le Lavandou, Vence, A-M, France. *Clubs:* Athenæum, Army and Navy.
[*Died* 4 *Jan.* 1961.

GARSON, Alexander Denis, C.M.G. 1954; *b.* 5 December, 1904; *s.* of W. R. J. Garson, Birsay, Orkney, and Bebington, Cheshire; *m.* 1934, Brenda Valerie, *d.* of G. B. Richards, St. Keverne, Cornwall. *Educ.:* Epsom College; Magdalene College, Cambridge. Colonial Administrative Service, Nigeria, 1928-33; Colonial Office 1933-62. *Recreation:* fishing. *Address:* Abbey House, Sutton Montis, Nr Yeovil, Somerset. *T.:* Corton Denham 268. *Club:* Oxford and Cambridge.
[*Died* 23 *Dec.* 1968.

GARSTIN, Charles Fortescue, C.M.G. 1930; O.B.E. 1928; *b.* 14 April 1880; *s.* of John Henry Garstin C.S.I.; *m.* 1919, Carol Mary, *d.* of Paul King, Commissioner of Chinese Maritime Customs (marriage dissolved 1939); one *s.* *Educ.*: Sherborne. Student Interpreter in China, 1901; Assessor in the Mixed Court at Shanghai, 1910-16; called to Bar, Middle Temple, 1917; held temp. commission in the Chinese Labour Corps in France, 1917-18; Vice-Consul, 1918; one of H.M. Consuls in China, 1922; Consul-General, Harbin, 1930-35; retired, 1935; served in H. G., 1940-44. *Club:* Reform.
[*Died* 7 *June* 1969.

GARTON, Lieut.-Colonel James Archibald, C.B.E. 1958; M.C., J.P.; Former Vice-Lieutenant of Somerset; *b.* Shepton Mallet, Somerset, 18 April 1891; *s.* of Major J. W. Garton; *m.* 1915, Dora Marjorie, *d.* of J. P. A. Cuvelier; one *d.* (and one *d.* decd.). *Educ.:* Eton College. Served European War, Flanders, 1914-18; and in War of 1939-45, British Isles, N. Africa and Italy, 1940-45; now managing own Estate; Ecclesiastical and Civil County Work; Master Emeritus, Somerset Guild of Craftsmen; High Sheriff, Somerset, 1937. *Publications:* The Guest; The Bowman; Glowing Embers from a Somerset Hearth. *Recreations:* work in iron and wood, writing, shooting. *Address:* The Manor House, Pylle, Shepton Mallet, Somerset. *T.A.* and *T.:* Ditcheat 292. *Club:* Cavalry. [*Died* 20 *Dec.* 1969.

GASCOIGNE, Sir Alvary Douglas Frederick, G.B.E., *cr.* 1953; K.C.M.G., *cr.* 1948 (C.M.G. 1942); *b.* 6 August 1893; *m.* 1st, 1916, Sylvia (*decd.*), *d.* of General Wilbur Wilder, United States Army; one *d.* (and one *s.* killed in action, 1944); 2nd, 1935, Lorna Priscilla, O.B.E. 1934 *d.* of late Edmund E. Leatham. *Educ.:* Eton. Served European War, 1914-18 with 6th Dragoons and Coldstream Guards (despatches); temp. clerk in Foreign Office, 1919; Third Secretary in Diplomatic Service, 1921; Second Secretary, 1925; First Secretary, 1933; Counsellor, 1941; Consul-General for Tangier Zone and the Spanish Protectorate of Morocco, 1939-44; British Political Representative in Hungary, with rank of Minister, 1945-46; United Kingdom Political Representative, Japan, with rank of Ambassador, 1946-51; Ambassador to the U.S.S.R., 1951-53; retired 1953. *Recreations:* reading, walking. *Address:* 66 The Bishops Avenue, N.2; Lotherton, Aberford, Yorks. *Clubs:* Carlton, Guards, United Service, Royal Automobile.
[*Died* 18 *April* 1970.

GASKELL, Lady Constance M.; *see* Milnes Gaskell.

GASKING, Mrs. Ella Hudson, O.B.E. 1948; Member of B.T.C. Hotels and Catering Services since 1954; Director of Westwick Products, Westwick, Norfolk, since 1953; *m.* C. T. Gasking, M.D.; no *c.* *Educ.:* Sheffield. Chairman, Batchelor's Peas, Sheffield, for 30 years; retired 1948; part-time mem. Hotels Exec., B.T.C., 1948-50;

full-time mem., 1950-53; Chairman Fruit and Vegetable Canners, 1939-45; Mem. Central Price Regulations Cttee., Board of Trade, 1944-48. Member Brit. Federation of Business and Professional Women. *Recreations:* golf, racing and travel. *Address:* Beauséjour, Spencer Rd., Ryde, I.O.W. *T.:* Ryde 3586; 181 Chiltern Court, Baker St., N.W.1. [*Died* 17 *Dec.* 1966.

GASS, Sir Neville (Archibald), K.B.E. 1958 (C.B.E. 1953); M.C.; Chairman (1957-1960), Managing Director (1930-60), The British Petroleum Co. Ltd.; *b.* 1893; *s.* of late Horace and Gertrude Gass. *Educ.:* Tonbridge Sch.; McGill Univ., Montreal. Served European War, 1914-19, as Capt. R.F.A. and R.H.A. (M.C., Belgian Croix de Guerre). *Address:* 28 Kingston House, Prince's Gate, S.W.7. *Clubs:* Bath, Royal Thames Yacht, City of London. [*Died* 23 *Sept.* 1965.

GASSER, Herbert Spencer; Director Emeritus of The Rockefeller Institute for Medical Research; *b.* 5 July 1888; *s.* of Herman Gasser and Jane Elizabeth Griswold; unmarried. *Educ.:* Univ. of Wisconsin (A.B. and A.M.); Johns Hopkins University (M.D.). Prof. Pharmacology, Washington Univ., 1921-31; Prof. Physiology, Cornell Medical College, 1931-35; Director The Rockefeller Institute for Medical Research, 1935-53; Johnson Foundation Lecturer, University of Pennsylvania, 1936; Hon. LL.D. Washington University, St. Louis and Johns Hopkins University; Hon. D.Sc. Harvard, Oxford, Pennsylvania, Rochester, Wisconsin, Columbia and Rockefeller Institute; Doctor Honoris Causa, Université Libre de Bruxelles, 1949; Hon. Doctor of Medicine, Université Catholique de Louvain, 1949; Docteur (*h.c.*) Université de Paris, 1953. Nobel Prize, Physiology and Medicine, 1944; Kober Medal Assoc. of Am. Physicians, 1954. Fell. American Academy of Arts and Sciences; Foreign Member: Royal Swedish Academy of Sciences; Finnish Academy of Science; The Royal Society (London); Hon. Foreign Member Académie Royale de Médecine de Belgique; Hon. F.R.S.E.; Corr. Member Société Philomathique and Accademia delle Scienze dell' Istituto di Bologna; Member National Academy of Sciences, Philosophical Soc., Assoc. of American Physicians, and American Physiological Soc.; Hon. Member Physiological Soc. (Britain) and Asociación Médica Argentina; President Board of Dirs., Russell Sage Institute of Pathology. *Publications:* Electrical Signs of Nervous Activity (with J. Erlanger), 1937; Papers on Neurophysiology in Scientific Journals. *Address:* Rockefeller Institute for Medical Research, 66th St. and York Ave., New York. *Clubs:* Century (New York); Quadrangle (Chicago). [*Died* 11 *May* 1963.

GATEHOUSE, Maj.-Gen. Alexander Hugh, D.S.O. 1941 and Bar 1942; M.C. 1917 and Bar 1918; *b.* 20 May 1895. *Educ.:* private; Roy. Military Coll., Sandhurst. Commanded Tank Bn. in European War, 1914-1918; commanding Tank Bn. at outbreak of war, sailed for France, Sept. 1939; 2nd i/c 7th Armoured Bde., 1940-41; Brigadier, 1941, in command. 4th Armoured Bde., 7th Armoured Div.; Acting Maj.-Gen. in comd. 10th Armoured Div., 8th Army, M.E.F., 1942; Temp. Maj.-Gen. 1943; British Army Attaché in Moscow, 1946-47; A.D.C. to the King, 1946-48; Maj.-Gen. 1947; retired pay, 1947. Legion of Merit (U.S.). *Recreations:* boxing, swimming, Rugby, cricket, ski-ing, golf, tennis. *Address:* Flat 2, Kingsmead, Gower Road, Weybridge, Surrey. [*Died* 21 *Aug.* 1964.

GATER, Sir George Henry, G.C.M.G. 1944 (C.M.G. 1918); K.C.B. 1941; Kt. 1936; D.S.O. 1916 and Bar 1917; Fellow of Winchester College since 1936 (Warden 1951-59); Hon. Fellow, New College; Hon. Fell. Roy. Coll. of Music; co-opted Mem. Oxon Education Committee; *b.* 1886; *s.* of late W.H. Gater, Winslowe House, Westend, Southampton; *m.* 1926, Irene, M.B.E. 1946, *er. d.* of late Bowyer Nichols, Lawford Hall, Manningtree; one *s.* *Educ.:* Winchester; New College, Oxford; 2nd Class Honours, Modern History; Diploma in Education. Oxfordshire Education Cttee., 1911-1912; Assistant Director of Education for Nottinghamshire, 1912-14; Director of Education, Lancashire County Council, 1919-24; Education Officer, London County Council, 1924-1933; Clerk of the Council, 1933-39; Permanent Under-Secretary of State for the Colonies, 1939-47; seconded as Joint Secretary Ministry of Home Security, 1939-40; Secretary, Ministry of Supply, 1940 and Secretary, Ministry of Home Security, 1940-42. Formerly Chm. (until 1961): Special Overseas Appointments Committee; Member, Oxford University Building and Works Committee. Served European War, Gallipoli, Egypt, France (despatches four times, twice wounded, C.M.G., D.S.O. and bar, Commander Legion of Honour, Croix de Guerre). *Address:* The Barn House, Church Handborough, Oxon. *Club:* Athenaeum. [*Died* 14 *Jan.* 1963.

GATES, Edward, O.B.E., M.D. (London); M.R.C.P.(Lond.); M.D.(Florence); Consulting Physician, Italian Hospital, London; *s.* of Philip Chasemore Gates, K.C., Recorder of Brighton, Judge of County Courts; *m.* 1st, Mary (*d.* 1931), *d.* of Major-General Charles Fowler, R.E.; two *s.*; 2nd, 1935, Dora, *d.* of late David Kenning. *Educ.:* Westminster School; University College; St. Thomas's Hospital. Civil Surgeon with Egyptian Army, 1900-2; practised in Florence, Italy, 1905-14; B.E.F. 1914-19; Consulting Physician, B.E.F., Italy; Lt.-Col. R.A.M.C., retired; late Medical Officer, Westminster School; late Senior Member Egyptian Medical Commission London Board. *Address:* Lake Rising, Lake, Salisbury, Wilts. [*Died* 19 *July* 1965.

GATES, Horace Frederick Alfred, C.M.G. 1959; M.B.E. 1943; H.M. Ambassador to Paraguay since 1959; *b.* London, 25 Sept. 1903; *s.* of John Frederick and Annie Gates; *m.* 1936, Astrid Ingegerd Andersson; no *c.* *Educ.:* London University and privately. Entered Foreign Office, 1919; Second Secretary and Vice-Consul at Lima, 1938; Control Commission for Germany, 1945; First Secretary, Guatemala, 1946, and at Washington, 1947; Ambassador and Consul-Gen. to Nicaragua, 1954. Special Ambassador to Inauguration of Luis Somoza Debayle as Pres. of Nicaragua, May 1957. Life Fellow Royal Geographical Society, London. *Recreations:* swimming, travel. *Address:* British Embassy, Asunción, Paraguay. *Clubs:* Royal Automobile, Canning, Travellers'. [*Died* 23 *June* 1962.

GATES, R(eginald) Ruggles, F.R.S. 1931; M.A. (Mt. Allison), B.Sc. (McGill), Ph.D. (Chicago); D.Sc. (London); LL.D. (Mt. Allison); F.L.S.; F.R.A.I.; F.R.M.S.; biologist, botanist, geneticist, anthropologist; Professor of Botany, University of London (King's College), 1921-42; Emeritus Professor, 1943; Fellow of King's College, London; *b.* 1 May 1882; *s.* of A. B. Gates, Middleton, Nova Scotia and Elizabeth Ruggles; *m.* 1955, Mrs. Laura Greer (*née* Nowotny), Texas. *Educ.:* Mt. Allison Univ.; McGill; Univ. of Chicago. Scholarships at Marine Biological Laboratory, Wood's Hole, Mass., 1904-08; Demonstrator in Botany, McGill Univ., 1905; Senior Fellow, Univ. of Chicago, 1906-08; Asst., 1909; Research at Missouri Botanical Gdns., 1910-11; Lecturer in Biology, St. Thomas's Hosp., London, 1912-14; Mendel Medal, 1911; Huxley Medal and Prize, Imperial Coll. of Science, London, 1913; Consultative Council Eugenics Soc.; Roy. Anthropological Institute, Council, 1927-33, 1935-37; Council, Linnean Soc., 1928-32, Vice-Pres., 1931-32; Council Royal Microscopical Soc., Sec., 1928-30, Pres., 1930-32, Hon. Fellow, 1951; Society Experimental Biology, Secretary, 1923-28; Royal Society Arts; Advisory Council, Monarchist League; Lecturer in Cytology, Bedford College, London, 1912, 1914; and on Heredity in Relation to Cytology, Oxford University, 1914; Associate Professor in Zoology, Univ. of California, 1915-16; Instructor in aerial gunnery, R.A.F., 1917-18; Reader in Botany, University of London (King's College), 1919-1921: Amazon Expedition, 1925; Russian travels to inspect plant breeding stations, 1926; Canadian Arctic Expedition, 1928, South Africa, 1929; delegate from Brit. Assoc. and American Assoc. to Indian Science Congress, Calcutta, 1937; De Lamar Lectures at Johns Hopkins University on Human Heredity and Society, 1932; Lecture tour in American Univs., 1940-42; Lowell Lectures on Human Heredity, 1944; Research Fellow in Biology, Harvard Univ., 1946-50; an Hon. Pres. of 7th Internat. Botanical congress, Stockholm, 1950 and of 8th Botanical Congress, Paris, 1954; Cuban Expedition, 1952; Mexico, 1953; Study of Ainu and racial genetics in Japan, 1954; anthropological studies in S. Africa, Kenya, Uganda, 1955; Australia, New Guinea, N.Z., 1958; India, 1959; Far East, 1960; Anthropological Studies in Iran, 1961; Guest of Indian Statistical Institute, 1961-62. Research in Anthropology, Harvard Univ.; Hon. Mem. Botanical Soc., Japan; Life Mem. British Inst. of Biology; Mem. Ancient Monuments Soc.; Bd. of Regents, Mount Allison Univ., 1951-58; Assoc. Mem., Assoc. for Research in Nervous and Mental Disease. *Publications:* numerous memoirs in botany, cytology, genetics, and anthropology; The Mutation Factor in Evolution, 1915; Mutations and Evolution, 1921; Heredity and Eugenics, 1923, Russian edition, 1925; A Botanist in the Amazon Valley, 1927; Heredity in Man, 1929; Human Genetics, 2 vols., 1946; Human Ancestry, 1947; Pedigrees of Negro families, 1949; Racial Genetics, 1962. *Recreation:* travelling. *Address:* 46 Lincoln House, Basil St., S.W.3. *Club:* Athenæum. [*Died* 12 *Aug.* 1962.

GATHORNE-HARDY, Lady Isobel, D.C.V.O., *cr.* 1945; *b.* 20 Sept. 1875; *d.* of 16th Earl of Derby; *m.* 1898, late General Hon. Sir Francis Gathorne-Hardy, G.C.B., G.C.V.O., C.M.G., D.S.O.; one *d.* *Address:* 3 Wellington Court, S.W.1. *T.:* Kensington 9035. [*Died* 30 *Dec.* 1963.

GATTIE, Vernon Rodney Montagu, C.B.E. 1919; J.P.; *b.* 29 May 1885; *e. s.* of late Walter Montagu Gattie and Catherine Anne, *d.* of late Rev. T. R. Drake; *m.* 1st, 1928, Dorothy Mary Leach (*née* Freshwater) (*d.* 1930); 2nd, 1933, Marguerite Lesley Harris; one *s.* *Educ.:* Tonbridge School; Worcester College, Oxford, M.A. 1912. Called to Bar, Lincoln's Inn, 1911; Western Circuit; Treasury Counsel at Middlesex Sessions, 1920; Metropolitan Police Magistrate, 1925-28; Major and D.A.A.G., Headquarters Staff, 1917; Member of the Military Delegation to the Peace Conference, 1919; Member of the Committee of Enquiry into Breaches of the Laws of War, 1920. Dep. Chm. Surrey Quarter Sessions, 1956. J.P. Middlesex, 1949, Surrey, 1955. Chairman of Council, London Academy of Music and Dramatic Art, 1952-63. *Address:* Pullington House, Benenden, Kent. *T.:* Benenden 603. *Club:* United University. [*Died* 23 *May* 1966.

GAUNTLETT, Sir (Mager) Frederic, K.C.I.E., *cr.* 1929 (C.I.E. 1915); K.B.E., *cr.* 1922 (C.B.E. 1918); *b.* 12 Oct. 1873; *s.* of Charles Augustus and Maria Anne Gauntlett; *m.* 1898, Sophie Gertrude (*d.* 1958), *d.* of W. J. Weller; two *s.* two *d.* *Educ.:* Dulwich College; Emmanuel College, Cambridge. Passed into the Indian Civil Service, 1891; arrived in India, 1893; joined the Behar Settlement, 1894; Assistant Settlement Officer in charge Saran district, 1895; joined Indian Finance Department, 1897; Accountant-General of the United Provinces, 1904; Burma, 1906; Bengal, 1909; Accountant-General for Railways, 1910; Comptroller and Auditor-General of India, 1912. On vacating that appointment in 1914 went on leave, and helped temporarily at the Admiralty during 1915-17; Comptroller and Auditor-General of India, 1918; retired, 1929; Finance Minister, Patiala State, 1930-36. *Publication:* An Introduction to Indian Government Audit. *Address:* c/o Lloyds Bank, Haslemere, Surrey. [*Died* 25 *Jan.* 1964.

GAVAN-DUFFY, Hon. Sir Charles Leonard, Kt., *cr.* 1952; Justice of Supreme Court of Victoria, Australia, since 1933; *b.* 15 June 1882; *s.* of late Sir Frank Gavan-Duffy, K.C.M.G., P.C. and Ellen Torr; *m.* 1919, Mary Marjorie Alexa Back. *Educ.:* St. Ignatius, Sydney, N.S.W.; Xavier College, Melbourne, Vic.; Trinity College, University of Melbourne. Admitted to practice at Victorian Bar, 1908. Served European War, 1914-18, A.I.F. Artillery, 1915-19; Major, 1918. *Address:* Cliveden Mansions, East Melbourne, Vic., Australia. *Clubs:* Melbourne, Roy. Melb. Golf. [*Died* 12 *Aug.* 1961.

GAVIN, Sir William, Kt., *cr.* 1942; C.B.E. 1920; Director: Strutt and Parker (Farms) Ltd.; Lord Rayleigh's Farms Inc. and other companies; Chairman of Trustees, Lord Wandsworth College, 1944-65; *b.* 31 May 1886; *m.* 1911, Lilian M. T. Forteath (*d.* 1968), *d.* of late W. E. Hilliard and *step-d.* of late Col. F. W. H. Forteath of Newton, Morayshire; two *s.* *Educ.:* Uppingham; Trinity College, Cambridge. M.A. and Agricultural Diploma; represented Cambridge at athletics and cross-country running; served R.N.V.R. (auxiliary patrol), sub-Lieutenant, 1916; Lieutenant, 1917; Director of Flax Production, 1918; Director of Land Reclamation, Ministry of Agriculture, 1919; with I.C.I. (Agric. Dept.), 1928-51; Chairman Jamaica Banana Commission, 1936; Chief Agricultural Adviser to Ministry of Agriculture, 1939-47; Chairman, Scottish Agricultural Industries Ltd., 1951-56; Mem. Royal Commission on Scottish Affairs 1952-1954. *Publication:* Ninety Years of Family Farming, 1967. *Address:* Flat 2, Letchworth Hall Hotel, Letchworth, Herts. *Clubs:* United University, Beefsteak, Farmers'. [*Died* 4 *June* 1968.

GAWSWORTH, John; (Terence Ian Fytton Armstrong); Poet, Bibliographer; *b.* Kensington, 29 June 1912; *m.* 1955, Doreen Emily Ada Downie (*née* Rowley) *Educ.:* Merchant Taylors' School. With London Publishers. Freeman of City of London and of Merchant Taylors' Company, 1935; Co-ordinator of Neo-Georgian lyric poetry movement, 1937; F.R.S.L. 1938 (Benson Medal, 1939); Founder-Ed. of The English Digest, 1939-41. Served War of 1939-45, R.A.F. (in ranks), 1941; as Sergeant on Algerian, Tunisian, Sicilian, and Italian Campaigns and in Middle East, and, as officer, in India, 1942-45; Flying Officer, 1946. Délégué Général de la Société des Écrivains de l'Afrique du Nord, Tunis, 1943; elected to Salamander Soc. of Poets, Cairo, 1944; Lecturer, Roy. Asiatic Soc. of Bengal, 1945; Editor of Literary Digest, 1946-49; Editor of The Poetry Review, 1948-52; Acting Editor, of Enquiry, 1949; London Editor of The English Digest, 1957-58; British Editor of Ellery Queen's Mystery Magazine 1958; London Archivist, Brandaris Insurance Co.

Ltd. (Amsterdam), 1960. *Publications:* Poems, 1930-32, 1933; New Poems, 1939; The Mind of Man, 1940; Marlow Hill, 1941; Legacy to Love, 1943; Snow and Sand, 1945; Blow No Bugles, 1945; Collected Poems, 1948; prose and bibliography: Above the River, 1931; Backwaters, 1932; Apes, Japes and Hitlerism: an Essay on P. Wyndham Lewis, 1932; Ten Contemporaries (2 series), 1932 and 1933; Annotations on Some Minor Writings of T. E. Lawrence, 1935; (with M. P. Shiel) The Invisible Voices, 1935; The Dowson Legend, 1939; Letters in French Barbary, 1948; editor of some sixty verse collections and volumes of prose. *Address:* Flat 116, 6 Campden Houses, Peel Street, W.8.

[*Died* 23 *Sept.* 1970.

GEDDES, Irvine Campbell; Director: Anderson, Green & Co. Ltd.; Orient Underwriting Co. Ltd.; O.U.C. Investment Co. Ltd.; *b.* 9 July 1882; *m.* 1911, Dorothy Jefford Fowler; three *s.* *Address:* 42 Arlington House, Arlington Street, S.W.1. *Clubs:* City of London; Union (Sydney).

[*Died* 18 *May* 1962.

GEDDIE, John Liddell, M.A., Chevalier de la Légion d'Honneur (1936); Officier d'Académie (1932); ex-Dir. and Editor, W. & R. Chambers, Ltd.; Member of Scottish Advisory Cttee., British Council; *b.* Edin., 27 Nov. 1881; 3rd *s.* of late John Geddie of The Scotsman; *m.* Agnes Mary Muller (*d.* 1938), Cape Town. *Educ.:* Daniel Stewart's College, Edinburgh; Edinburgh University. M.A. (1st Class Honours in English), 1903; Lecteur d'Anglais at University of Lyons, 1903-4, and at Sorbonne, Paris, 1905-6; Assistant Editor, Cape Times, Cape Town, 1906-10; Chief Assistant Editor, New Encyclopædia, 1911-12; Assistant Editor, Everyman, 1913-14; Assistant Editor, then Editor, Chambers's Journal, 1915-47. Hon. Gen. Sec., Franco-Scottish Society, 1928-45; President, Scottish P.E.N., 1938-44. *Publications:* Articles in Chambers's Encyclopædia, and in periodicals. *Recreation:* golf. *Address:* 21 Falcon Gardens, Edinburgh. *T.:* Morningside 6634. *Club:* Royal Scots (Edinburgh).

[*Died* 15 *March* 1969.

GEDYE, George Eric Rowe, M.B.E. 1946; Vienna Correspondent of Radio Free Europe and Special Correspondent of The Guardian in Vienna 1956-61; *b.* Clevedon, Som., 27 May 1890; *e. s.* of late George E. Gedye, Clifton; *m.* 1st, 1922, Elisabeth Bremer, Cologne (decd.); no *c.*; 2nd, 1948, Alice Lepper, Vienna; one *s.* *Educ.:* Clarence School, Weston-super-Mare; Queen's College, Taunton; Matriculated London University. Spent pre-war years collecting reject slips for articles and fiction; Gazetted Aug. 1914 from London University O.T.C., to 12 Batt. The Glos. Regt.; served with Batt. Western Front from Nov. 1915; Asst. Staff-Captain; wounded Somme, Sept. 1916; Instructor, Officer-cadet Batt.; Intelligence Corps, France, May 1918-Nov. 1918 (despatches); attached Cavalry during advance from Armistice Line to Germany; on G.H.Q. Staff, Cologne, British Military Governor's Staff, and Inter-Allied Rhineland High Commission, Cologne, 1919-22; The Times Correspondent, 1922; The Times special correspondent in Rhineland and Ruhr, 1922-25; went Vienna, 1925; Central European Correspondent of The Times, 1925-26, of the Daily Express, 1926-28, and of the Daily Telegraph, 1929-39; on New York Times Central European Staff since 1929; expelled from Vienna on annexation of Austria by Nazi Germany; moved headquarters to Prague, March 1938; left Czechoslovakia, March 1939, after annexation by Nazi Germany, to avoid arrest under Gestapo warrant; Moscow correspondent of the New York Times, 1939-40; Turkey Correspondent, 1940-41; employed on Special Military Duties in Middle East, 1941-45; Daily Herald Correspondent for Central Europe, Vienna, 1945-50; Observer, 1950-52; Manchester Guardian Correspondent for Central and S.-E. Europe, 1953-54; Head of Evaluation, Radio Free Europe, Munich, 1954; F.J.I., etc. Lectr. on Central European and Iron Curtain Countries. *Publications:* A Wayfarer in Austria, 1928, fourth edn., 1931, continental edn., 1948; The Revolver Republic, 1930—also German translation; Heirs to the Habsburgs, 1932; Fallen Bastions (American Ed., Betrayal in Central Europe), 1939 (Austrian Edition, Die Bastionen Fielen, 1948); We Saw it Happen (part author), 1939; translation: of George London's Red Russia, 1928; of Das Oesterreichbuch (The Book of Austria), 1949; (part author) Fodor's Modern Guide to Austria, 1953; Introducing Austria, 1955; articles Rhineland and Ruhr in Encyclopædia Britannica, 13th edition; and many articles. *Recreations:* reading, swimming, sun-basking, gardening, irritating the conventional. *Address:* Crownhill, Ensleigh, Lansdown, Bath. *T.:* Bath 2261. *Club:* Special Forces.

[*Died* 21 *March* 1970.

GEE, Harry Percy, C.B.E. 1953 (O.B.E. 1941); J.P.; Chairman of Stead and Simpson, Ltd., since 1924; *b.* 30 March 1874; 2nd *s.* of late H. Simpson Gee, Knighton Frith, Leicester; *m.* 1st, 1901, Augustine Flora (*d.* 1919), *d.* of late Robert Pagett; one *s.* three *d.*; 2nd, 1922, Mary Elinor (*d.* 1962), *d.* of late John Edward Stocks, D.D., Archdeacon of Leicester and Canon of Peterborough. *Educ.:* Oakham School. President of Leicester Chamber of Commerce, 1925-27; President, Leicester Literary and Philosophical Soc., 1932-33; Chairman, Leicester Univ. Coll. Council, 1945-57; Pro-Chancellor, University of Leicester; High Sheriff of Leicestershire, 1942. Hon. Freeman City of Leicester, 1950. Hon. LL.D. (Leicester), 1958. *Recreation:* gardening. *Address:* Birnam House, Ratcliffe Road, Leicester. *T.:* Leicester 75321.

[*Died* 23 *Feb.* 1962.

GEEN, Burnard; Practice, Consulting and Chartered Civil Engineer, since 1910; *b.* 30 July 1882; *s.* of John and Sarah Geen; *m.* 1906, Evelyne May Brown; no *c.* *Educ.:* Private Boarding School; Whitgift Grammar School; Crystal Palace Engineering School. Engineer to: Cathedrals of Liverpool, 1935, Guildford, 1936 and Cairo, 1935; New Bodleian Library, 1937; New University Library, Cambridge, 1932; Guildhall Reconstruction, 1952; Peterborough Town Hall, 1928; Worthing Municipal Buildings, 1933. Over 600 structures in Great Britain, Ireland, S. America, Africa, New Zealand and Australia. Declined offer of O.B.E., 1961. *Publications:* Continuous Beams in Reinforced Concrete, 1913; two papers in Proceedings of Institution of Civil Engineers. *Address:* 30 Lushington Road, Eastbourne, Sussex. *T.:* Eastbourne 6220.

[*Died* 16 *March* 1966.

GELL, William Charles Coleman, C.B. 1944; D.S.O. 1918; M.C., T.D., D.L.; M.A., LL.B. (Cantab.): Solicitor practising at Birmingham since 1919; *b.* 10 July 1888; *s.* of William James Gell, Cora Lyn, Solihull, Warwickshire; *m.* 1923, Edith Maud, *d.* of F. W. Gosling; one *s.* three *d.* *Educ.:* Malvern College; Caius College, Cambridge. Articled in Birmingham and London, 1913; passed Solicitors' Final Examination with honours; Solicitor in London, Jan. 1914-Aug. 1914; served European War, England, France, Italy, Aug. 1914-April 1919 (despatches, D.S.O. and bar, M.C., Bt. Major, Italian silver medal for valour); Air Vice-Marshal late A.A.F.; A.O.C. Balloon Command, 1944-45. *Address:* 87 Cornwall

Street, Birmingham 3. *T.:* Central 7878. *Club:* Union (Birmingham)
[*Died* 16 *May* 1969.

GELL, William John, C.B.E. 1939; Chairman and Managing Director Monarch Film Corpn. Ltd., and Monarch Productions Ltd.; *b.* 23 July 1893; *e. s.* of late William Thomas and late Sarah Gell; *m.* 1919, Helen Clara Jennings (*d.* 1959); two *s. Educ.:* Technical Coll., East Ham. Mem. Court of Assistants, Worshipful Company of Gold and Silver Wyre Drawers of the City of London, 1953. *Address:* 6 Hall Road, St. John's Wood N.W.8. *Club:* Royal Automobile.
[*Died* 28 *June* 1961.

GELSTHORPE, Rt. Rev. (Alfred) Morris; Asst. Bishop in diocese of Southwell, since 1952; D.D., L.Th.; D.S.O. 1917; *b.* 26 Feb. 1892; *s.* of John Gelsthorpe and Annie Kendall; *m.* 1949, Elfrida, 3rd *d.* of late Rev. G. F. Whidborne and of Mrs. Whidborne, Hammerwood, E. Grinstead, Sussex. *Educ.:* King's School, Canterbury; Hatfield College, Durham University. Enlisted in Artists' Rifles, Sept. 1914; commissioned to Durham Light Infantry 8th Battn. (T.F.), Oct. 1914; served in France May 1915-Sept. 1916, and April 1917-Sept. 1917; Mesopotamia, Sept. 1917-Jan. 1919 (D.S.O., despatches twice); Deacon, 1919; Priest, 1920; Curate at St. Gabriel's, Sunderland, to 1922; C.M.S. Missionary on Staff of C.M.S. Training College, Awka, Southern Nigeria, 1923; Principal of above Coll., 1926-33; Assistant Bishop to Bishop on the Niger, 1933-1938; Assistant Bishop to the Bishop in Egypt and the Sudan, 1938-45; 1st Bishop in the Sudan, 1945-52; Rector of Bingham, Notts., 1952-63. Hon. D.D. Durham, 1933. *Recreations:* special interest in all athletics, played for Blackheath Club, 1911 and 1912, played for Durham County Rugby, 1913-14 and 1919-20-1921; Captain Durham County, 1920. *Address:* Ashleigh, 31 Church Street, Southwell, Notts. [*Died* 22 *Aug.* 1968.

GENEE-ISITT, Dame Adeline, D.B.E., *cr.* 1950; C.D. 1953 (Commander of the Dannebrog); M.I.etA., B.M.I.; Hon. D.Mus. London; Founder-Pres. of The Royal Academy of Dancing, 1920-54; Member of Council Anglo-Danish Society; *b.* Hinnerup, near Aarhus, Denmark, 6 January 1878; *d.* of Peter Jensen, Aarhus; *m.* 1910, Frank S. N. Isitt, R.D. (*d.* 1939); no *c. Educ.:* Aarhus. First public appearance at age 10 Christiania; première danseuse, Stadt Theatre, Stettin, at age 15; Imperial Opera, Berlin, at age 17; première danseuse Royal Opera Munich, at 18; came to London at 19; appeared as guest-artiste, 1902, at Royal Theatre, Copenhagen; remained ten years in London; went to America, 1908; took her own company to America, 1912; visited Australia and New Zealand, 1913; retired from the stage, 1914; reappeared for charity several times during the war, during which she was a V.A.D. at St. Dunstan's; has Orders of Ingenii et Arti, and Gold Medal of Merit of 1st Class with Crown, Denmark; King Christian X Medal of Liberty. *Address:* Hyde Park Hotel, S.W.1. *Club:* Danish.
[*Died* 23 *April* 1970.

GENTLE, Francis Steward, C.B.E. 1955; Chairman Greyhound Racing Association Trust Ltd.; Chairman White City Stadium Ltd., Harringay Arena Ltd., etc.; *b.* 24 June 1894; *s.* of late Sir William Gentle; *m.* 1920, Louise, *d.* of late George H. Richmond, Rochester, N.Y., U.S.A.; three *d. Educ.:* privately. Solicitor, 1919. U.S.A. 1920, Paper-making and Conversion; returned, 1926, on formation of the Greyhound Racing Association as Assistant Managing Director; President of National Greyhound Racing Soc. and Member of Board of Control; Chairman Canine Cttee., Council Member and Member of Exec. Cttee., Animal Health Trust; Member Assoc., Member Cttee., The Dogs' Home, Battersea; Vice-Chairman Assoc. for Protection of Copyright in Sport. Served European War, 1914-19, in Sussex Yeomanry, Lieutenant, Egypt and Palestine. *Recreations:* golf, shooting. *Address:* 4 Grand Avenue, Hove, Sussex. *T.:* Hove 31445. *Clubs:* Carlton, Portland, Royal Wimbledon; Royal and Ancient (St. Andrews). [*Died* 26 *Sept.* 1962.

GENTLE, Sir Frederick (William), Kt., 1947; Q.C. 1948; Judge Advocate General of H.M. Forces, 1955-62, retd. (Vice-Judge Advocate Gen., 1952-54); Comr. of Assize, 1948, 1949 and 1950; Dep. Chairman West Kent Q.S., 1948-59; one of H.M. Commissioners of Duke of York's Royal Military School, 1955-62; *b.* 12 July 1892; *er. s.* of late Sir William Gentle; *m.* 1927, Ursula Willmer (*d.* 1965), *d.* of late C. Percival White, M.V.O.; one *s. Educ.:* Queens' Coll., Camb. (M.A.; Hon. Fellow). Called to Bar, 1919; South-Eastern Circuit; Recorder of Margate, 1935-36; Puisne Judge, High Court of Judicature, Madras, 1936-41; Puisne Judge, High Court of Judicature, Calcutta, 1941-47; Chief Justice of Madras, 1947-48; Mem. of General Council of the Bar, 1921-26 and 1935-36; Pres. Rewa Commn. of Enquiry, 1942-43. Served European War, 1914-19, First Life Guards, France and Flanders; retired 1919, Capt. *Publication:* contributor to title Royal Forces in Halsbury's Laws of England (Simonds edn.). *Recreations:* shooting, fishing. *Address:* Flat 4, 8 Cleveland Square, W.2. *T.:* Ambassador 9516; 6 Adelaide Mansions, Hove 3. *T.:* Hove 30544. *Clubs:* Carlton, United Service; Hove; Pilgrims; Royal Calcutta Turf (Calcutta). [*Died* 24 *Feb.* 1966.

GEOGHEGAN, Colonel Norman Meredith, C.B. 1929; D.S.O.; retired; *b.* 7 Sept. 1876; 5th *s.* of Stannus Geoghegan, of Glenageary, Co. Dublin; *m.* Georgina Sancton (*d.* 1949), *d.* of Charles Scammell, of St. John, New Brunswick; no *c. Educ.:* Galway Grammar School; Rugby; R.M.C., Sandhurst. Entered I.A. 1897, First Commission, 1896; Served European War, 1914-19 (despatches 6 times, wounded twice, Bt. Lieut.-Col.); Colonel 1921; retd., 1929. King's India Police Medal, 1910 (awarded, 1913). *Address:* Rake's Holt, Cove, Tiverton, Devon. *T.:* Bampton 329. [*Died* 28 *Sept.* 1962.

GEORGE, Daniel, (*pseudonym of* D. G. Bunting); author and critic; *b.* 20 Jan. 1890; *e. s.* of Daniel Taylor and Emily Bunting; *m.* 1914, Mary Margaret, *d.* of Rev. John Whittle; one *s.* F.R.S.L. *Publications:* Tomorrow Will Be Different, 1932; Lunch, 1933; A National Gallery, 1933; The English in Love, 1934; Holiday, 1934; Roughage, 1935; Pictures and Rhymes, 1936; A Peck of Troubles, 1936; Pick and Choose, 1936; All in a Maze, 1938; Alphabetical Order, 1950; Lonely Pleasures, 1954; A Book of Anecdotes, 1957; A Book of Characters, 1959; The Anatomy of Love, 1962; The Perpetual Pessimist, 1963; An Eclectic A.B.C., 1964; Edited with Introduction, Finishing Touches by Augustus John, 1964. *Recreations:* reading and writing. *Address:* c/o John Bunting, Barrie and Rockliff, 2 Clement's Inn, W.C.2. *T.:* Chancery 9171. *Club:* Garrick.
[*Died* 2 *Oct.* 1967.

GEORGE, Hugh Shaw, C.I.E. 1945; Indian Forest Service, retired; *b.* 29 Jan. 1892; *s.* of late Edward Monson George; *m.* 1935, Joan, *d.* of J. F. Stokes; two *s.* one *d. Educ.:* Sexey's School, Bruton; Magdalen College, Oxford. Entered Indian Forest Service, 1915; Chief Conservator of Forests, Central Provinces and Berar, 1943;

retired, 1947. *Address:* Redroofs, Gorse Close, Farnham, Surrey. *T.:* Farnham 4456. [*Died* 26 *Nov.* 1967.

GEORGE, Air Vice-Marshal Sir Robert Allingham, K.C.M.G. 1958; K.C.V.O. 1954; K.B.E. 1952 (C.B.E. 1944); C.B. 1948; M.C.; p.s.a.; Director: Bank of Adelaide; Australian Estates Co.; Governor of S. Australia, 1953-60; *b.* 25 July 1896; *s.* of William George, Invergordon, Scotland; *m.* 1927, Sybil Elizabeth Baldwin, D.St.J., *d.* of A. R. Baldwin, Caythorpe; three *s.* one *d.* Seaforth and Gordon Highlanders, 1914-15, France; R.F.C. 1916-18, France; R.A.F., 1919-; India N.W.F., 1919-24; Staff, Cadet Coll., Cranwell, 1924-30. R.A.F. Staff Coll., 1931; Senior Air Staff Officer, Singapore, 1934-37; Air Attaché, Turkey, Greece and R.A.F. Middle East, 1939-44; A.O.C. Iraq and Persia, 1944-45; Air Attaché, Paris, 1945-1952; retd., 1952. Hon. Col. S.A. Scottish Regt.; Hon. Air Cdre. Royal Australian Air Force. Pres. St. John's Ambulance Bde., No. 1 (Prince of Wales's) District; K.St.J. 1953. Commandeur Légion d'Honneur, France, 1952; Order of King George I, Greece, 1942. *Recreations:* polo, painting, and fishing. *Address:* 6 Campden House Close, W.8; Holme Farm House, Rowlands Castle, Hants. *Clubs:* White's, R.A.F., Royal Aero. [*Died* 13 *Sept.* 1967.

GEPP, Maj.-Gen. Sir (Ernest) Cyril, K.B.E., *cr.* 1946; C.B. 1937; D.S.O. 1916 and bar, 1917; *b.* 7 July 1879; *s.* of late Rev. H. J. Gepp, for many years Vicar of Adderbury, Oxon; *m.* Evelyn Marion (*d.* 1940), *y. d.* of late Lieut.-Colonel G. Wilbraham Northey, J.P., D.L., of Ashley Manor, Box; no *c.*; *m.* 1944, Katie, *d.* of George Deeley, Alvechurch, Worcs. and widow of Brigadier H. C. Harrison. *Educ.:* Marlborough College. Entered Army, 1901; retired, 1911; served South African War, 1900 (Queen's medal 3 clasps); Somaliland, 1909-1910 (despatches); re-gazetted, 1917; served European War (despatches five times, D.S.O. and bar, Bt. Lt.-Col., Legion of Honour); commanded 4th (Quetta) Infantry Brigade, 1929-30; Brig. Gen. Staff, Western Command India, 1930-32; Comdt. Small Arms School, 1932-36; Maj.-Gen., 1935; Maj.-Gen. in charge of Administration, Northern Command, 1937-41; retired pay, 1941; Director of Prisoners of War, 1941-1945; Legion of Merit Degree of Commander, 1946. *Address:* Chelsea Cottage, North Road, Bath. *T.:* Bath 5117. [*Died* 28 *Feb.* 1964.

GERARD, Amelia Louise, F.R.G.S., Novelist and Traveller; *b.* 1878. *Educ.:* Nottingham High School. First novel The Golden Centipede, 1910; Author of 23 novels, most of which have been published not only in Gt. Britain and the Empire, but also in America, Norway, Sweden, Denmark, Holland, France, Spain and Hungary; has also done travel articles, short stories, film and serial work for England, America and France. *Recreations:* travelling, walking. *Address:* c/o Mills and Boon, 50 Grafton Way, W.1. [*Died* 5 *Nov.* 1970.

GERBRANDY, Professor Doctor Pieter S.; Minister of State, The Netherlands, since 1955; President Council for Restoration of Civil Rights; President of Broadcasting Board, The Hague; *b.* in Goengamieden, Friesland, 13 April 1885; *m.* Hendrina Elizabeth Sikkel; two *s.* one *d.* *Educ.:* Gymnasium (boarding school) Zetten; Free Univ. of Amsterdam. Barrister, 1911-1930; in the Army as reserve-officer, 1914-18; Member, Provincial Government Friesland, 1920-30; Professor of Commercial Law and International Law at the Free Univ. of Amsterdam, 1930-39; Minister of Justice 1939-42, 1945 (ad interim); Prime Minister of the Netherlands, 1940-45; also Minister for Colonies, 1941-42; Minister for Co-ordination of Warfare of the Kingdom of the Netherlands, 1942-45. Member of Parliament, 1948; Member of Parliament, 1954. *Publications:* het Heimstättenrecht, 1911; de overeenkomst van Londen, 1924; de Strijd voor nieuwe Maatschappij vormen, 1927; Het religieus socialisme, 1928; Het vraagstuk van den Radio-omroep, 1934; Het Burgerlijk Wetboek en het Administratief Recht, 1938; National and International Stability (Taylorian Lecture), 1944; Indonesia, 1950: De scheuring van het Rijk, 1951. *Recreation:* mountaineering. *Address:* Kanaalweg 113c, Scheveningen. Holland. *T.:* 555614; (Office) van Stolkweg 21, Scheveningen. [*Died* 7 *Sept.* 1961.

GERHARD, Roberto Juan René, C.B.E. 1967; composer; *b.* Valls, Tarragona, 1896; *s.* of late Robert Gerhard; *m.* 1930, Poldi, *d.* of Franz Feichtegger, Vienna. *Educ.:* Munich Conservatoire; pupil of Pedrell; Preussische Akademie der Künste (Schoenberg Master Class). Prof. of Music, Barcelona, 1930; Head of Music Dept., Biblioteca de Catalunya, 1931-38; Member: Consell de la Música de la Generalitat, 1932-38; Consejo Central de la Música, Spanish Republican Govt., 1937-38. Hon. Fellow, University College, Cambridge. Compositions include: symphonies (4th, New York, 1967), concertos, opera: The Duenna (Sheridan); The Plague (Camus); chamber music, songs. Hon. Mus.D. Cambridge, 1968. Awarded Composer of the Year Award, 1969. *Recreation:* conversation. *Address:* 14 Madingley Road, Cambridge. [*Died* 5 *Jan.* 1970.

GERHARDT, Elena; Concert Singer; *b.* Leipzig, 1883; *m.* 1932, Dr. F. Kohl. *Educ.:* Leipzig Conservatory. Made début Leipzig, 1903; London, 1906; New York, 1912; taught at Guildhall School of Music, London, Feb. and March, 1934; now teaching privately. *Publication:* Recital (autobiography), 1953. *Address:* 53 Redington Road, N.W.3. *T.:* Hampstead 2421. [*Died* 11 *Jan.* 1961.

GERRARD, Sir (Albert) Denis, Kt., *cr.* 1953; M.A., LL.B. (Cantab.); *b.* 27 May 1903; *yr. s.* of Samuel and Ruth Gerrard, Southport; *m.* 1927, Hilda Goodwin Jones; one *s.* *Educ.:* Merchant Taylors' School, Crosby; Gonville and Caius College, Cambridge. Called to Bar, Gray's Inn, 1927; Q.C. 1945; Bencher, 1948; Recorder of Salford, 1945-48; Judge of the Salford Hundred Court of Record, 1948-53; Judge of Appeal, Isle of Man, 1950-53; Judge of the High Court of Justice, Queen's Bench Division, 1953-56; retired 1956. Treasurer, Gray's Inn, 1964, Vice-Treasurer, 1965. *Recreations:* music, books and gardening. *Address:* c/o National Provincial Bank Ltd., 26 Trinity Street, Cambridge. [*Died* 23 *Jan.* 1965.

GERRARD, Charles Robert, A.R.C.A., R.B.A., R.O.I., F.R.S.A.; J.P.; painter; Ex-Director Sir J. J. School of Art, Bombay; Ex-Member of Board of Trustees, Prince of Wales Museum, Bombay; Ex-Chairman, Higher Art Examinations throughout India; *s.* of John Thomas Gerrard, Lancaster; *m.* Doris Warne. *Educ.:* Antwerp. Early training Lancaster School of Art; Royal College of Art, London, 1915-20; A.R.C.A.; studied art in France, Belgium and Italy; Exhibitor R.A.; one-man exhibition, London, 1927, 1929, and 1931; work exhibited in New York, Montreal, Toronto, Winnipeg, Vancouver; painting purchased for the Birmingham City Art Gallery; two works purchased for the private collection of Lord Ivor Spencer Churchill; one man show, French Gallery, London, 1933; Portrait of Mrs. Mollison (Amy Johnson) purchased by Lord Wakefield and presented to Hull Art Gallery; painting purchased by the Contemporary Art Society.

Publications: paintings reproduced in colour for the Studio and Colour Magazine; specialised in oriental art; pub. set of pictorial charts dealing with Hindu and Muslim Painting, Sculpture and Architecture, and research work in Hindu mythology. *Recreation:* travel. *Address:* Tirainia, Slade Oak, Denham, Buckinghamshire. [*Died* 4 *June* 1964.

GERRARD, Sir Denis; *see* Gerrard, Sir A. D.

GERRARD, Air Commodore Eugene Louis, C.M.G. 1919; D.S.O. 1916; *b.* Dublin, 14 July 1881; *y. s.* of late Thomas Gerrard; *m.* 1922, Phyllis Louisa Ball, 4th *d.* of late Edward Stone. Joined Royal Marines, 1900; Captain, 1911; Brevet Major, 1914; temp. Lieut.-Col. 1914; Air Commodore, 1923; Commanding Forces in Palestine, 1924-27; retired 1929. Chevalier Order of Leopold, Belgium, 1917. *Address:* Centre Cliff Lodge, Southwold, Suffolk. [*Died* 7 *Feb.* 1963.

GESELL, Arnold, M.D., Ph.D., Sc.D.; Research Consultant, Gesell Institute of Child Development, 1950 60; Director Emeritus, Clinic of Child Development, Yale University, School of Medicine (Director, 1911-48); Professor of Child Hygiene, Yale School of Medicine, 1915-48; *b.* Alma, Wisconsin, 21 June 1880; *s.* of Gerhard Gesell and Christine Giesen; *m.* 1909, Beatrice Chandler; one *s.* one *d.* *Educ.:* State Normal Sch., Stevens Point, Wisconsin, B.Ph., Univ. of Wisconsin, 1903; Sc.D. 1953; Ph.D. Clark Univ., 1906, Sc.D. 1930; M.D., Yale, 1915; Teacher Dept. of Psych., Los Angeles State Normal Sch., 1908-10; Asst. Prof. Education, Yale, 1911-15; assoc. several years in school of special training in Psychology and Pedagogy, for defective children, summers N.Y. Univ.; established, 1911, and Dir. Yale Psycho-Clinic (Clinic of Child Development, Yale Sch. of Med.); school psychologist Conn. State Bd. Educn., 1915-19; Mem. Conn. Commn. on Child Welfare, 1919-21; established Photographic Research and Film Library at Yale, 1925, produced scientific and educational motion pictures since 1930 (Yale Films on Child Devel.—silent and sound—distributed by Encyclopædia Britannica Films, Inc.); Medical film, Embryology of Human Behavior, Med. Film Inst.; Consulting Editor, Journal of Genetic Psych., since 1926; Attending Pediatrician, New Haven Hospital, 1928-48; Research Associate, Harvard Pediatric Study, 1948-1952; Fellow, National Academy of Sciences; Fellow A.A.A.S. and many other Societies; Member White House Conf. on Child Health and Protection, White House Conference on Children in a Democracy; Member Nat. Research Council, 1937-40; Pres. Amer. Acad. for Cerebral Palsy, 1952. *Publications:* The Normal Child and Primary Education (with wife), 1912; The Pre-School Child from the Standpoint of Public Hygiene and Education, 1923; The Mental Growth of the Pre-School Child, 1925; Infancy and Human Growth, 1928; An Atlas of Infant Behavior (2 vols. in collab.), 1934; Infant Behavior—Its Genesis and Growth (with H. Thompson), 1934; How a Baby Grows, 1936 and 1945; Feeding Behaviour of Infants (with F. Ilg), 1937; The Psychology of Early Growth (with H. Thompson), 1938; The First Five Years, 1940; Wolf Child and Human Child, 1941; Developmental Diagnosis (with C. S. Amatruda), 1941, 1947; Infant and Child in the Culture of Today (with F. Ilg), 1943; The Embryology of Behavior, 1945; The Child from Five to Ten (with F. Ilg), 1946; Studies in Child Development, 1948; Vision: Its Development in Infant and Child, 1949; Infant Development: The Embryology of Early Behaviour, 1952; Youth: The years from ten to sixteen, 1956. *Recreations:* sailing, biography. *Address:* 185 Edwards Street, New Haven, Conn., U.S.A. *T.:* 7-2567. *Clubs:* Graduates (New Haven); Yale (New York City). [*Died* 29 *May* 1961.

GEYER, Albertus Lourens; Director of Die Nasionale Pers Limited; *b.* 11 Aug. 1894; *s.* of late C. F. Geyer; *m.* 1921, Anna Elizabeth Joubert; one *d.* *Educ.:* Somerset East, Grahamstown, Stellenbosch and Berlin. Asst. Editor, Die Burger, Cape Town, 1923, Editor, 1924-45; Editor-in-Chief, publications of the Nasionale Pers Company, 1945-1950; High Commissioner in London for the Union of S. Africa, 1950-54. Hon. Life-Pres., S.A. Bureau for Racial Affairs (Sabra). Ph.D. (*h.c.*), Univ. of Stellenbosch. *Publications:* Das wirtschaftliche System der Niederländischen Ostindischen Kompanie am Kap der Guten Hoffnung, 1785-1795, 1923; Die Stellenbosse Gemeente in die Agtiende Eeu, 1926. *Recreation:* cultivation of South African succulent plants. *Address:* Weltevreden, Box 14, Barrydale, C.P., South Africa. [*Died* 13 *Dec.* 1969.

GEYL, Pieter, Lit.D. (Leyden); Emeritus Professor, University of Utrecht, since 1958; *b.* Dordrecht, 15 December 1887; *s.* of Dr. Arie Geyl and Ada, *d.* of W. F. van Erp Taalman Kip; *m.* 1st, 1911, Maria Cornelia van Slooten (*d.* 1933); one *s.* one *d.*; 2nd, 1934, Garberlina Kremer. *Educ.:* The Hague Gymnasium; Leyden University. With a travelling scholarship to Italy, 1911; Master at Schiedam Gymnasium, 1912; came to London at the end of 1913 as Correspondent of the Nieuwe Rotterdamsche Courant; resigned 1919 on being appointed to the newly founded Chair of Dutch Studies in the University of London; in 1924 title changed into Professor of Dutch History and Institutions; resigned 1935; Professor of Modern History, Univ. of Utrecht, 1936-58; 7 Oct. 1940 arrested as hostage, spent thirteen months in Buchenwald, then over two years in various internment camps in Holland, released 14 Feb. 1944; 28 Nov. 1942 dismissed by Reichskommissar from professorship on ground of suspect "general mentality," restored after liberation of Holland. F.R.Hist.S. (1921), Corresp. Member (1951); Hon. Mem.: Amer. Hist. Assoc., 1957; Amer. Acad. of Arts and Sciences, 1958; Corr. Fell. Brit. Acad., 1961; May 1941 elected member of Royal Academy at Amsterdam, not confirmed by Reichskommissar, confirmed by Queen after liberation of Holland; Inst. for Advanced Study, Princeton, New Jersey, U.S.A., Sept.-Dec. 1949; Smith College, Mass., U.S.A. (as W. A. Neilson Research Professor), Feb.-June 1952; Terry Lectr., Yale Univ., 1954, Stanford University (summer), Harvard University (fall semester) 1957; G. M. Trevelyan Lectr., Camb., 1963. Netherlands State Prize for Literature, 1958; Macvane Prize, Harvard University, 1966 (for distinguished contributions to European historiography; first award), 1966. Hon. awards: LL.D., St. Andrews Univ., 1958; D.Litt. (Oxford and Harvard Univs., 1959); Order pour le mérite (Germany), 1959; C.B.E., 1959. *Publications:* Christofforo Suriano, Resident van Venetie in Den Haag 1616-23, 1913; Holland and Belgium, their Common History and their Relations, three lectures, 1920; Willem IV. en Engeland tot 1748 (vrede van Aken), 1924; A beautiful Play of Lancelot of Denmark, and the Tale of Beatrice, both translated from the Middle Dutch, in The Dutch Library, 1924 and 1927; De Groot-Nederlandsche Gedachte, I., 1925, II, 1930; Geschiedenis van de Nederlandsche Stam, I., 1930, II., 1934, III., 1937, 2nd ed. in two vols., 1948 and 1949; co-founder and co-editor of the periodical Leiding, 1930-31, and Nederlandsche Historiebladen, 1938; The Revolt of the Netherlands, 1555-1609, 1932 (several printings); The Netherlands Divided, 1609-1648, 1936; Oranje en Stuart, 1641-72,

1939; Nederland en de oorlog, December 1939; collected sonnets written during internment (a number had appeared clandestinely, 1944,) 1945 (selection republished, Het leven wint altoos, 1958); Napoleon, For and Against, 1944 (translated from Dutch, 1958); Tochten en Toernooien, 1950; Reacties, 1952; Historicus in de tyd, 1954; essays on Ranke, Macaulay, Carlyle, Michelet, Toynbee, American Civil War, Netherlands History, etc., all now to be found in Debates with Historians, 1955 (American paperback edition, 1958, English, 1961, further printings); Use and Abuse of History (Terry Lectures, Yale), 1955; Studies en Strydschriften, essays on Netherlands History, 1958; Encounters in History, U.S. 1961 (Engl., 1963); History of the Low Countries, Episodes and Problems (G. M. Trevelyan Lectures), 1964; articles in the Encyclopædia Britannica and in Dutch, Flemish, English, American and German reviews. *Address:* Willem Barentzstraat 5, Utrecht, Netherlands. *T.:* 18617.

[*Died* 31 *Dec.* 1966.

GHOSE, Hemendra Prasad; Author and Journalist; *s.* of Girindra Prasad Ghose, Zeminder; *b.* Chaugachha, Bengal, 24 Sept. 1876; *m.* Manorama, *d.* of Mr. Kar. *Educ.:* Calcutta Presidency College; B.A. 1899. Member Institute of Journalists, London; was a member of the Press Deputation to Mesopotamia, 1917; representative of the Vernacular Press of Bengal in the Indian Press Delegation to the Western Front, 1918. Lecturer, Calcutta University (Dept. of Journalism). *Publications:* Bipatnik, Adhapatan, Premerjoy, Nagapasa, Premmarichica, Mritumilan, Adristachakra, Asru, Indian National Congress, New Germany, Tusanal, Press and Press Laws in India, The Famine of 1770, The Newspaper in India, etc. *Address:* 12/10 Goa Bagan Street, Calcutta (6), India. [*Died* 16 *Feb.* 1962.

GHOSE, Sir Sarat Kumar, Kt., *cr.* 1938; M.A.; Chairman of Advisory Bd., W. Bengal Govt., from 1951; *b.* 3 July 1879; 3rd *s.* of late Tarini Kumar Ghose, Inspector General of Registration, Bengal; *m.* Belle, *d.* of B. De, Indian Civil Service; one *s.* one *d.* *Educ.:* Presidency College, Calcutta (B.A. with 1st Class Honours); Trinity College, Cambridge; Inner Temple. Tripos in History, Mental and Moral Science, M.A. (Cantab.); I.C.S. Examination, 1903; served in Bengal and Behar, District and Sessions Judge, 1911; acting Judge, 1928, Puisne Judge, 1929-39, Calcutta; Chief Justice, Jaipur, 1943-46, and again, 1948-50; Jammu and Kashmir, 1946-48. *Recreations:* lawn tennis, running, walking. *Address:* 4 Moira St. Calcutta. *Clubs:* Calcutta, Royal Calcutta Turf, Lake (Culcutta).

[*Died* 8 *Jan.* 1963.

GIACOMETTI, Alberto; sculptor and painter; *b.* Stampa, Grisons, 10 October 1901; *s.* of Giovanni Giacometti, painter, and Annette (*née* Stampa); *m.* 1949, Annette Arm, Geneva. *Educ.:* École des Arts et Métiers, Geneva; Rome and Paris. First one-man exhibition, Galerie Pierre Colle, 1933; subsequent exhibitions in New York, Paris, London, etc.; retrospective exhibitions, Solomon R. Guggenheim Museum, New York, 1955; Museum of Modern Art, New York, 1965; Tate Gallery, London, 1965. Works represented in Tate Gallery, Baltimore Museum of Art, New York Museum of Modern Art, and principal modern art museums in France, Italy and Switzerland. *Address:* c/o Federal Academy of Fine Art, Berne, Switzerland. [*Died* 11 *Jan.* 1966.

GIBBINS, Joseph; *b.* Toxteth, 1888; *s.* of George Gibbins, Liverpool; *m.* 1912, Sarah Beatrice, *d.* of George William Hugill; two *s.* two *d.* *Educ.:* St. Thomas C.E. Schools; Evening Tutorial Classes Liverpool Univ. M.P. (Lab.) West Toxteth Div. of Liverpool, 1924-31 and 1935-50. Served European War in Royal Naval Reserve; 1915-19; J.P. Liverpool, 1924. *Address:* 8 Hargreaves Road, Sefton Park, Liverpool.

[*Died* 26 *Aug.* 1965.

GIBBS, Major Arthur Hamilton, M.C.; author; *y. c.* of Henry James Gibbs and Helen Hamilton; *m.* 1919, Jeannette, *d.* of Benjamin Phillips, lawyer, of Boston, Mass., U.S.A.; no *c.* *Educ.:* Collège de St. Malo; St. John's College, Oxford. Started writing at Oxford; edited and founded there The Tuesday Review, a weekly; went on the stage for two years in the U.S.A. and wrote two novels at the same time; enlisted as private in 21st Lancers, Sept. 1914; received commission in R.F.A., 1915; demobilised as Major, M.C., 1919; naturalized in U.S.A., 1926. F.I.A.L. *Publications:* The Compleat Oxford Man (sketches); Cheadle and Son (novel); Rowlandson's Oxford history; The Hour of Conflict (novel); The Persistent Lovers (novel); Bluebottles (verse); Gunfodder (war biography); Soundings (novel); Labels (novel); Harness (novel); Chances (novel); Undertow (novel); Rivers Glide On, 1934 (novel); The Need We Have, 1936 (novel); The Young Prince, 1938; A Half-Inch of Candle, 1939; Way of Life, 1947; One touch of France, 1953; Obedience to the Moon (novel), 1956. *Recreations:* golf, music. *Address:* The Highlands, Middleboro, Mass., U.S.A. *Club:* St. Botolph (Boston, Mass.).

[*Died* 24 *May* 1964.

GIBBS, George Howard, C.M.G. 1944; M.C.; Gold Coast Administrative Service; retired; *b.* 1889; *m.* 1st, 1915, Katharine Stella (*d.* 1956), *d.* of F. Brierley; *m.* 2nd. 1957, Hildegard, *d.* of F. Flügel, Hanover. European War, 1914-19 (despatches), 1st Canadian Division and Royal Dublin Fusiliers (Spec. Res.). Gold Coast Administrative Service, 1920 Chief Commissioner Northern Territories, 1942-46. *Address:* 22 Beit Road, Murambi Umtali, Rhodesia. *Club:* Umtali.

[*Died* 11 *June* 1969.

GIBBS, John Herbert, F.R.C.S. Ed., L.R.C.P., L.D.S. Ed.; *b.* London, 1872; *s.* of James Gibbs, of Somerset House; *m.* 1906, Aimée Eveline Mills, M.A., B.Sc., M.B. Ch.B.; one *s.* *Educ.:* Nelson College; Otago University, N.Z.; Edinburgh and London. Hon. Surgeon Dentist to H.M. in Scotland, 1922-31; Consulting Dental Surgeon, Royal Infirmary, Edinburgh; Ex-President Scottish Society of Anæsthetists. *Address:* 2 Ranui Road, Remuera, Auckland, S.E.2, New Zealand. [*Died* 30 *Dec.* 1962.

GIBBS, Brigadier Lancelot Merivale, C.V.O. 1937; D.S.O. 1919; M.C.; one of H.M.'s Hon. Corps of Gentlemen-at-Arms, 1939-60; *b.* 23 Dec. 1889; *s.* of late Antony Gibbs of Tyntesfield, Bristol; *m.* 1st, 1929, Hon. Marjory Florence Maxwell (*d.* 1939), *e. d.* of 11th Baron Farnham, D.S.O.; one *s.*; 2nd, 1942, Diana Primrose (marriage annulled, 1945), *y. d.* of Percy Quilter. *Educ.:* Eton. Joined Coldstream Guards, 1910; served European War, 1914-18 (D.S.O., M.C. and bar, despatches four times); A.D.C. to Lord Rawlinson, C.-in-C., India, 1922-25; commanded 1st Batt. Coldstream Guards, 1930-1934; A.A.G., War Office, 1934-38; retired pay, 1938; Brigadier in charge of Administration, London District; reverted to retired pay, 1945; recalled War Office in connection with Victory March, Jan.-July 1946; reverted to retired pay, 1946. *Recreations:* hunting, polo, shooting. *Address:* Flat 4, 1 Sloane Court East, S.W.3. *Clubs:* Guards, Turf, St. James'. [*Died* 8 *Dec.* 1966.

GIBBS, Very Rev. Michael McCausland; Dean of Chester since 1954; *b.* 1 Sept. 1900; *s.* of Rev. Reginald Gibbs and Lucia (*née* McCausland); *m.* 1926, Edith Marjorie, *d.* of John Spenser Ward and Beatrix (*née* Dunbar);

three *s.* two *d.* *Educ.:* **Lancing Coll.; Keble Coll., Oxford; Cuddesdon Coll. B.A. 1922, M.A. 1927; Deacon, 1925; Priest, 1926, Diocese of Southwark; Curate of St. Mary, Putney, 1925-28; Asst. Priest, Cathedral Church, Salisbury, S. Rhodesia, 1928-36; Sub-Dean, 1934-36; Chaplain to Bishop of S. Rhodesia, 1929; Rector of Bulawayo, 1936-42; Archdeacon of Matabeleland, 1936-42; Rector of St. Saviour, Claremont, Cape Town, 1942-48; Canon of St. George's Cathedral, Capetown, 1946-48; Dean and Rector of St. George's Cathedral, and Archdeacon of Capetown, 1948-54. *Address:* The Deanery, Chester. *T.:* 25920. [*Died* 27 *July* 1962.

GIBBS, Sir Philip, K.B.E., *cr.* 1920; Chevalier de la Légion d'Honneur; author and journalist; *s.* of Henry Gibbs, of the Board of Education, and Helen Hamilton; *b.* 1 May 1877; *m.* 1898, Agnes (*d.* 1939), *d.* of Rev. W. J. Rowland; one *s.* *Educ.:* privately. At twenty-one years of age became one of the editors of Cassell and Company; editor of Tillotson's Literary Syndicate, 1901; entered journalism, 1902; and acted successively as a literary editor of the Daily Mail, the Daily Chronicle, and the Tribune, afterwards becoming special correspondent and descriptive writer on the Daily Chronicle, etc.; Editor of The Review of Reviews, 1921-22; War correspondent with the Bulgarian army, 1912; with the French and Belgian armies, 1914; with the British armies in the Field, 1915-18. *Publications: novels:* The Individualist; The Spirit of Revolt; The Street of Adventure; Intellectual Mansions, S.W., Oliver's Kind Women; Helen of Lancaster Gate; A Master of Life; The Custody of the Child; Back to Life, 1920; Venetian Lovers, 1922; The Middle of the Road, 1922; Heirs Apparent, 1923; Little Novels of Nowadays, 1924; The Reckless Lady, 1925; Unchanging Quest, 1925; Young Anarchy, 1926; Out of the Ruins, 1927; The Age of Reason; Darkened Rooms, 1929; The Hidden City, 1930; The Wings of Adventure, 1930; The Winding Lane, 1931; The Golden Years, 1931; The Anxious Days, 1932; The Cross of Peace, 1933; Paradise for Sale, 1934; Blood Relations, 1935; Cities of Refuge, 1936; Great Argument, 1938; This Nettle Danger, 1939; Broken Pledges, 1939; Sons of the Others, 1940; The Amazing Summer, 1941; The Long Alert, 1941; The Interpreter, 1943; The Battle Within, 1944; Through the Storm, 1945; The Hopeful Heart, 1947; Behind the Curtain, 1948; Both Your Houses, 1949; Thine Enemy, 1950; The Spoils of Time, 1951; The Cloud Above the Green, 1952; Called Back, 1953; Lady of the Yellow River, 1953; No Price for Freedom, 1954; The Ambassador's Wife, 1956; The Healing Touch, 1957; The Curtains of Yesterday, 1958; One of the Crowd, 1959; The Wheel of Fortune, 1960; His Lordship, 1961; The Law-Breakers, 1963 (posthumous); *historical:* Founders of the Empire; The Romance of Empire; Men and Women of the French Revolution; George Villiers, 1st Duke of Buckingham; King's Favourite; Adventures of War with Cross and Crescent; The Soul of the War; The Battles of the Somme; From Bapaume to Passchendaele; Open Warfare; The Way to Victory; Realities of War; The Hope of Europe; People of Destiny; Since Then, 1930; Ways of Escape, 1933; European Journey, 1934; England Speaks, 1935; Ordeal in England, 1937; Across the Frontiers, 1938; America Speaks, 1942; The Journalist's London, 1952; The New Elizabethans; How Now, England?, 1959; The Riddle of a Changing World, 1960; *essays:* Knowledge is Power; Facts and Ideas; The Eighth Year; The New Man; Adventures in Journalism, 1923; Ten Years After, 1924; The Day after To-morrow, 1928; *autobiography:* The Pageant of the Years, 1947; Crowded Company, 1949; Life's Adventure, 1958. *Address:* Shamley Green, Surrey. *Club:* Reform. [*Died* 10 *March* 1962.

GIBBS, Lieut.-Colonel William, C.V.O. 1948; one of the Exons of the King's bodyguard of Yeomen of the Guard, 1926-47; *b.* 1877; 3rd *s.* of late Antony Gibbs of Tyntesfield, Somerset, D.L.; *m.* 1911, Ruby Mabel, 5th *d.* of late Henry Brassey of Preston Hall, Kent, M.P.; two *d.* *Educ.:* Eton; Magdalen College, Oxford. Served in South African War, 1901-2; European War, 1914-1918 (Croix de Guerre); late Lieut.-Col. 7th Hussars. *Address:* The Severalls, Hatherop, Cirencester, Glos. *T.:* Coln St. Aldwyns 214. *Clubs:* St. James', Cavalry. [*Died* 25 *Jan.* 1963.

GIBBS-SMITH, Very Rev. Oswin Harvard, C.B.E. 1961; Dean of Winchester, 1961-69; *b.* 15 Nov. 1901; *e.s.* of late Dr. E. G. Gibbs-Smith; *m.* 1949, Nora, *yr. d.* of late Harry Gregg, Esher; one *s.* one *d.* *Educ.:* Westminster School; King's College and Clare College (Choral Scholar and Beck Exhibitioner), Cambridge; Cuddesdon College. B.A. 1922; M.A. 1927; Deacon, 1924; Priest, 1925; Asst. Master, Harrow School, 1925-27; Curate of St. Margaret's, Ilkley, Yorks, 1927-31; built and became first Vicar of John Keble Church, Mill Hill, 1932-41; Rector of Christchurch, St. Marylebone, with St. John's Wood Chapel, 1941-47; Archdeacon of London and Canon Residentiary of St. Paul's Cathedral, 1947-61. Commissary of Archbishop of Quebec, 1942-60, of Bishop of Christchurch, N.Z., 1951-61, and of Archbishop of New Zealand, 1948-51. Senior Officiating Chaplain (R.A.F.) to personnel of Air Ministry, 1944-47; Hon. Visitation Chaplain to Bishop of London, 1947, Examining Chaplain, 1948-61; Select Preacher, Univ. of Cambridge, 1950; Hon. Chaplain to The Pilgrims since 1951; Chaplain Order of St. John, 1952, Sub-Prelate, 1962. Freeman of City of London, 1953. Sub Dean of Order of British Empire, 1957-1961. Hon. Chap. Merchant Taylors' Co., 1958-59. Chapter Treasurer of St. Paul's Cathedral, 1960-61. *Publication:* Message for a Mission, 1957. *Address:* Tudor Cottage, Church Lane, King's Worthy, Winchester, Hants. *Club:* Athenæum. [*Died* 26 *Sept.* 1969.

GIBSON, Hon. Lord; Robert Gibson, F.R.S. (Edin.); M.A., B.Sc., LL.B. Hons. (Glasgow); Chairman Scottish Land Court, 1941-April 1965; *b.* 20 April 1886; *m.* 1913, Elizabeth Campbell (*d.* 1959), *d.* of late William Atkinson; two *s.* one *d.* *Educ.:* Hamilton Acad.; Glasgow Univ. Cunninghame Gold Medallist in Mathematics, Donaldson Scholar in Chemistry, Major Young Bursar in Arts and Law, Metcalfe Bursar in Science, Stewart Bursar and Prizeman in Law; Secretary (1909) and President (1910) Students' Representative Council, Glasgow Univ. Lecturer, Applied Electricity, Hamilton Technical School, 1911; Royal Garrison Artillery (S.R.) 1915; Capt., Technical Trng. Staff, Scottish Command; Mem. Faculty of Advocates, 1918; Senior Advocate-Depute, 1929-31; Q.C. 1931. Member, Scottish Churchmen's Commission to U.S.A. and Canada, 1923; travelling on investigations from Boston to San Francisco, Victoria, Vancouver, Montreal. M.P. Greenock, 1936-41; Member: The Grotius Society, 1940; British Society for the History of Science, 1950-63; Philosophy of Science Group, 1950-63; Hon. Pres. Glasgow Univ. Law Society, 1942-43; Extraordinary Mem., Scots Law Society of Edinburgh Univ., 1946. Council, Roy. Scottish Soc. of Arts, 1953-55; Scot. Artists' Benevolent Assoc., 1954-63. *Publications:* Report of the Scottish Churchmen's Commission to U.S.A. and Canada, 1923 (in part); Law of Trade Unions and Trade Disputes (to Encyclopædia of the Laws of Scotland), 1933;

numerous articles on legal, scientific, religious and literary subjects. *Recreations:* chess, travel. *Address:* Shawburn, 443 Lanark Road, Juniper Green, Midlothian. *T.:* Edinburgh Colinton 2022. Caledonian 3595. *Clubs:* Royal Over-Seas League; Scottish Arts, Murrayfield Golf (Edinburgh); Royal Scottish Automobile (Glasgow). [*Died* 9 *April* 1965.

GIBSON, Sir Basil; *see* Gibson, Sir E. B.

GIBSON, Sir Christopher Herbert, 2nd Bt., *cr.* 1931; resigned in 1950-51, as Partner in firm of Gibson Brothers to take up radiesthesia having become a member of the British Society of Dowsers; Member of British Ornithologists' Union; *b.* 1897; *e. s.* of Sir Herbert Gibson, 1st Bt., and Madeleine Jessie, *d.* of late Rev. W. J. Savell, LL.M. (Cantab.) of St. Clement Danes: *S.* father, 1934; *m.* 1919, Dorothy Edith Orme, *d.* of Maj. W. D. Bruce, Vancouver, B.C.; two *s.* *Educ.:* Eton; R.M.A., Woolwich. Served in France with R.F.A. as 2nd Lieut. Oct. 1916-July 1917; and with Y Battery, R.H.A., April-Aug. 1918; resigned commission with rank of Lieut. 1919; farmed in Argentine, 1919-28; appointed to town office in Buenos Aires, 1929. *Publications:* Gran Chaco Calling, 1934; Chunga Tales, 1937; Enchanted Trails, 1948. *Recreations:* shooting, fishing, ornithology. *Heir:* *e. s.* Christopher Herbert [*b.* 2 Feb. 1921. Served with Canadian Forces, 1940-45]. *Address:* (temp.) Eduardo VII 1238, Hurlingham, F.C.N.G.S.M., Buenos Aires. *Clubs:* Ex-Service, Hurlingham (Buenos Aires). [*Died* 20 *July* 1962.

GIBSON, Clement William Osmund, C.B.E. 1944; *b.* 17 Nov. 1878; *s.* of late Jasper Gibson. *Educ.:* Ushaw College, near Durham. Asst. District Auditor, Local Government Board, 1915-19; Asst. Principal, Ministry of Health, 1920; District Auditor, 1921-26; Inspector of Audit, 1926-1936; Deputy Chief Inspector of Audit, 1936-38; Chief Inspector of Audit, 1938-47. *Address:* 3 Avonmore Mansions, W.14. [*Died* 23 *April* 1963.

GIBSON, Sir (Ernest) Basil, Kt., *cr.* 1941; C.B.E. 1951; J.P.; LL.D.; Member of War Works Commission, since 1943; *b.* 1877; 2nd *s.* of George T. Gibson, York; *m.* 1914, Edith M. (*d.* 1945), 4th *d.* of Jesse James Davis, Redditch, Worcestershire; no *c.* *Educ.:* Manor School, York. Solicitor, 1908. 43 years in Local Govt. service; Deputy Town Clerk, Sheffield, 1913; Town Clerk, 1931; retired, 1942. J.P. for Sheffield City, 1942-53; Chm. Sheffield Regional Hospital Board, 1948-56. LL.D. (*h.c.*) Sheffield, 1956. *Address:* 16 Gladstone Road, Sheffield 10. *T.:* 32182. [*Died* 10 *Feb.* 1962.

GIBSON, Hon. Sir Frank (Ernest), Kt., *cr.* 1948; M.L.C. for Western Australia, 1942-1956, retired; Pharmaceutical Chemist; *b.* Egerton, 17 July 1879; *s.* of A. Gibson, Egerton, Vic.; *m.* 1910, Jean, *d.* of J. Ella; one *s.* one *d.* *Educ.:* Grenville Coll. and School of Mines, Ballarat, Vic. Mayor of Leonora, W.A., 1912-14; M.L.A. for Freemantle, 1921-24; Mayor of Fremantle, 1919-23 and 1926-51. *Address:* High St., Fremantle, W.A. [*Died* 31 *Dec.* 1965.

GIBSON, Harold, M.C., M.A.; Lecturer; *b.* 7 Aug. 1884; *o. s.* of Alexander Loonie Gibson of Birmingham; *m.* 1927, Mary Isabelle, *er. d.* of J. R. Kemys Warneford, Warneford Place, Wilts; one *s.* *Educ.:* Hartlebury Sch.; Fitzwilliam Hall, Camb. B.A. 1906; M.A. 1909; served in European War, 1914-1919 (despatches twice, M.C.); General Director of World Service Exhibition, 1919-1920; Lecturer and Administrator of European Student Relief in France, Germany, Austria, Czechoslovakia and Poland, General Director of University Relief in Russia, 1921-1922; Commissioner for League of Nations Intellectual Commission in Russia, 1922; Appeal Director of University College, Southampton, Royal South Hants Hospital and Royal Hampshire County Hospital; General Director of Merchant Navy Week, 1937; Deputy Director of Supplies and Chief Disposals Officer for the International Board for non-Intervention in Spain, 1938-39; granted a Royal Licence to recruit British Volunteers for service in Finland, Feb. 1940; Director of Finnish Aid Bureau, 1940-41; Deputy Regional Information Officer, Midland Region, 1941-42; Special Mission to West African Colonies for Ministry of Information, 1943-44; National Staff Lecturer for the Ministry of Information, 1943-45; Special Mission to Germany for Central Office of Information, 1947; National Lecturer for Central Office of Information, 1945-52. *Publications:* Laughter in Russia, and various papers on International Affairs. *Recreations:* riding and driving. *Address:* Crumpets, Lytchett-Matravers, nr. Poole, Dorset. *T.:* Lytchett Minster 341. [*Died* 9 *Nov.* 1961.

GIBSON, Sir (Horace) Stephen, Kt., *cr.* 1956; C.B.E. 1947; M.A., M.I.Mech.E., F.Inst.Pet.; Director, The Chartered Bank, and Farmer; Chairman: Southwell Diocesan Board of Finance; Permanent Council of the World Petroleum Congress; Member Council of Industrial Welfare Society; *b.* 12 May 1897; *o. s.* of late George Gibson, Rempstone, nr. Loughborough; *m.* 1927, Jessie Wilhelmina Blyth, A.R.R.C., *y. d.* of late Prof. James Blyth, M.A., LL.D., F.R.S.E. of Glasgow. *Educ.:* High Pavement School, Nottingham; Emmanuel College, Cambridge. Served European War, 1915-19, 1st Bn. York & Lancaster Regt., France, Egypt, Salonika; Captain (despatches). Production Engineer with Anglo-Iranian Oil Co. Ltd., in South Persia, 1922-45; General Fields Manager, Anglo-Iranian Oil Co. Ltd., 1945-1948; Managing Director Iraq Petroleum Co. Ltd. and Associated Companies, 1950-1957; Director, Chartered Bank, 1958. President Institute of Petroleum, 1952-54. Redwood Medal, 1947; Cadman Medal, 1961; Carl Engler Medal, Deutsche Gesellschaft für Mineralölwissenschaft und Kohlechemie e.V., 1961. K.St.J. 1956. Officer, Legion of Honour, 1956. *Address:* The Manor Farm, Halam, near Newark, Notts. *T.:* Southwell 2223. *Clubs:* Athenæum, Farmers', Oriental. [*Died* 4 *Nov.* 1963.

GIBSON, John Gibson, C.B. 1946; M.A., B.Sc., F.R.S.E. 1941; *b.* 3 Sept. 1889; *s.* of John Gibson, Edinburgh; *m.* 1st, 1916, Edith Auld (*d.* 1956); two *s.*; 2nd, 1957, Marion Margaret Neil (*née* Reoch). *Educ.:* George Watson's Coll., Edinburgh; Edinburgh Univ. Higher Div. Civil Service (H.M. Office of Works), 1913; London Regt. and R.E., 1914-19; Air Ministry, 1919-47; Director of Home Civil Aviation (Air Ministry), 1938-39; Director of Accounts, Air Ministry, 1943-44; retired, 1947. *Address:* 43 Pentland Terrace, Edinburgh. *T.:* 031-447 4587. [*Died* 13 *June* 1970.

GIBSON, Rev. John Paul S. R., M.A., F.I.A.; *s.* of Rev. W. Gibson; *m.* K. M. Armitage (*d.* 1962); one *s.* two *d.* *Educ.:* Kingswood Sch., Bath; Sidney Sussex Coll., Cambridge (scholar). Burney and Harness Prizes; Clerk in Holy Orders, 1906; C.M.S. Missionary in Ceylon, 1908-27; Principal of the Training Colony, Peradeniya, 1914-27; Principal of Ridley Hall, Cambridge, 1927-45; Diocesan Missioner, Kampala, Uganda, 1945-49; retired, 1949. Examining Chaplain to the Bishop of Ripon, 1928-1934, to the Bishop of Uganda, 1953; Select Preacher, Cambridge University, 1929, 1934 and 1942; Chm. of the Anglican Evangelical Group Movement, 1933; Member of the Arch bishop's Council on Foreign Relations; Mem

ber of the Executive of the Bureau of Inter-Church Aid. *Publications:* Shakespeare's Use of the Supernatural; articles in The International Review of Missions; Unmerited suffering in relation to Atonement. *Address* c/o Rectory House, Bedale, Yorks.
[*Died* 22 *Nov.* 1964.

GIBSON, Sir Kenneth Lloyd, 2nd Bt., *cr.* 1926: *b.* 11 May 1888; *s.* of Sir Herbert Gibson, 1st Bt., and Lilian, *d.* of Lt.-Col. Iltid Thomas; *S.* father 1932; *m.* 1914, Mary Edith, *d.* of late Algernon Leveson Elwes, J.P., of Cecily Hill, Cirencester; two *d.* Served European War, 1914-19, also served 1940-45. *Heir: b.* Ackroyd Herbert [*b.* 5 Aug. 1893; *m.* 1918, Maud Lilian, *d.* of Dr. Arnold, Forest Hill; two *s.* two *d.*]. *Address:* 5 Gateways, Chelsea, London, S.W.3. [*Died* 14 *May* 1967.

GIBSON, Myra Macindoe, C.B.E. (Mrs. E. H. Gibson); *b.* 26 May 1886; 3rd *d.* of W. M. Dunlop, M.D.; *m.* 1908, Edward Hotham Gibson. *Educ.:* Private tuition; Frances Mary Buss Schools. Hon. General Manager The Central Depot (Princess Beatrice's), 1916-19 Honorary Administrator, League of Remembrance (1914 19), 1919 39; Hon Gen. Organiser Chislehurst Hospital Supply Depot, 1939-47; Hon. Administrator, League of Remembrance (1914-1945), 1949-. *Address:* 270 St. James' Court, S.W.1. [*Died* 26 *June* 1966.

GIBSON, Rt. Rev. Percival William, C.B.E. 1960; *b.* 26 Aug. 1893; B.D. 1917; B.A. 1922; B.D. (Hons.) 1924; University of London. Deacon, 1917; Priest, 1918, Jamaica; Curate of Golden Grove, Jamaica, 1918-19; St. George's, Kingston, 1919; Headmaster Kingston College, Jamaica, 1925-56; Hon. Canon of Jamaica Cathedral, 1939; Exam. Chaplain to Bishop of Jamaica, 1946; Suffragan Bishop of Kingston, 1947-1955; Bishop of Jamaica, 1955-67; retired, 1967. Hon. D.D. Montreal, 1957. *Address:* 3 Oxford Road, Kingston 5, Jamaica.
[*Died* 3 *April* 1970.

GIBSON, Maj.-Gen. Ralph Burgess, C.B. 1946; C.B.E. 1944; V.D.; Q.C. 1933; *b.* 15 Sept. 1894; *s.* of Thomas A. Gibson, Q.C., Toronto, and Margaret B. Burgess; *m.* 1924, Doris S., *d.* of Charles L. Benedict; one *d.* *Educ.:* Upper Canada Coll., Univ. of Toronto (B.A.); Osgoode Hall, Toronto. Served in European War, 1914-19, Lt. Canadian Infantry, Capt. Canadian Engineers, France, Belgium and Germany. Continued service in Queen's Own Rifles of Canada, 1920-37; commanded Regt. with rank of Col., 1935-37. Called to Bar of Ontario, 1920. Served again, 1940-46; Dir. of Milit. Operations and Intelligence, 1941; Assistant Chief of the General Staff (Brig.), 1942-44; Vice-Chief of the Gen. Staff, Canadian Army, with rank of Maj.-Gen., 1944-46; Commissioner of Penitentiaries for the Dominion of Canada, Dept. of Justice, Ottawa, 1946-60; Special Adviser to the Minister of Justice on Correctional Planning, 1960-62; retired, 1962. Hon. LL.D. (Queen's Univ.), 1953; President, American Prison Assoc., 1953. *Recreations:* golf, gardening. *Address:* 476 Wilbrod St., Ottawa, Canada. *Clubs:* Rideau, Royal Ottawa Golf (Ottawa); Royal Canadian Military Institute (Toronto).
[*Died* 3 *Aug.* 1962.

GIBSON, Raymond Evelyn, C.S.I. 1936; C.I.E. 1924; Indian Civil Service, retired; *b.* 10 Oct. 1878; *s.* of late Edward Gibson; *m.* 1st, 1925, Mrs. Effie Kerr Gordon (*d.* 1926); 2nd, 1927, Mrs. Greta Twiss (*d.* 1950), Kaisar-i Hind Gold Medal, 1935. *Educ.:* Winchester; New Coll., Oxford. Entered I.C.S., 1901; Private Sec. to Governor of Bombay, 1912-14; Collector and District Magistrate, 1923-31; Comr. in Sind, 1931; Revenue Commissioner for Sind, 1936; retd. 1937. *Address:* Wykeham, Lymington, Hants.
[*Died* 2 *March* 1969.

GIBSON, Sir Stephen; *see* Gibson, Sir H. S.

GIBSON, Wilfrid; *b.* 2 Oct. 1878. *Publications:* Poetry - Stonefolds, 1907; Daily Bread, 1910; Fires, 1912; Thoroughfares, 1914; Borderlands, 1914; Battle, 1915; Friends, 1916; Livelihood, 1917; Whin, 1918; Home, 1920; Neighbours, 1920; Krindlesyke, 1922; Kestrel Edge, and other plays, 1924; I Heard a Sailor, 1925; Sixty-Three Poems: A Selection, 1926; Collected Poems (1905-1925), 1926; The Golden Room, 1928; Hazards, 1930; Highland Dawn, 1932; Islands, 1932; Fuel, 1934; Coming and Going, 1938; The Alert, 1941; Challenge, 1942; The Searchlights, 1943; The Outpost, 1944; Solway Ford and other Poems: a Selection, 1945; Coldknuckles, 1947; Within Four Walls, 1950. *Address:* Cricket Green, Queen's Road, Weybridge, Surrey. [*Died* 26 *May* 1962.

GIBSON, Lieut.-Colonel William, D.S.O. 1918; O.B.E. 1944; M.C. 1916; late Senior Partner in the firm of Knight, Frank & Rutley; *b.* 19 January 1887; *e. s.* of late John Gibson and Mrs. Elizabeth Gibson, Edinburgh; *m.* 1st 1917, Vera Nina, *d.* of late Frederick Snowden, Hampstead; two *d.*; 2nd, 1948, Winifred Joan Bates, *d.* of late J. G. Stapleton, Oxford. *Educ.:* Watson's Coll., Edinburgh. Cadet H.M.S. Conway, 1902-04. Served in Merchant Service in Sail and later in Steam; Navigating Officer until 1910; served European War, 1914-18; Commanded 10th Bn. West Yorkshire Regiment (despatches, M.C., D.S.O.); F.R.I.C.S. *Address:* Harewood, Great Missenden, Bucks. *Club:* Oriental.
[*Died* 22 *Dec.* 1969.

GIBSON-CRAIG-CARMICHAEL, Sir (Archibald Henry) William, 14th Bt., *cr.* 1702 (Gibson Carmichael) and 7th Bt., *cr.* 1831; Capt. 16th/5th Lancers; *b.* 28 March 1917; *s.* of Sir Eardley Gibson-Craig-Carmichael, 13th Bt., and Emily Ellen, *d.* of Henry Rummel; *S.* father 1939; *m.* 1941, Rosemary Anita, *d.* of H. Crew; two *s.* *Heir: s.* David Peter William Gibson-Craig-Carmichael, *b.* 21 July 1946. *Address:* 15 The Close, Salisbury, Wilts.
[*Died* 1 *Dec.* 1969.

GIBSON FLEMING, Edward; J.P. (Hants) 1941; *b.* 15 Nov. 1885; *s.* of John Gibson Fleming, C.A., of Glasgow, and Marjory Corbet Alexander; *m.* 1921, Margaret Eveline Paterson (*d.* 1956); no *c.* *Educ.:* Clifton College; Elizabeth College, Guernsey. Entered East India Merchants business, 1904; in Burma, 1908-25; Member of Legislative Assembly, India, 1924-25, representing European Constituency of Burma; retired, 1925. Chairman Winchester R.D.C., 1932-40. Held commission in 1st V. Bn. H.L.I., 1904-8 and in I.A.R.O., 1917-1923; saw active service in Mesopotamia, Persia, and Kurdistan, 1918-20 (despatches twice); commanded 1024 Company (Burma) M.T., R.A.S.C.; High Sheriff, Hampshire, 1942. Member of Southampton University Court. *Address:* Wyke Croft, Winchester, Hants. *T.:* 4300. *Clubs:* Oriental; Hampshire (Winchester). [*Died* 27 *Dec.* 1962.

GIDNEY, Sir Claude Henry, K.C.I.E., *cr.* 1942 (C.I.E. 1932); C.S.I. 1937 I.C.S., retired; *b.* 23 Nov. 1887; *m.* 1920, Muriel Katharine (Kaiser-i-Hind Medal), *d.* of Lt.-Col. H. F. Shairp, O.B.E.; one *s.* *Educ.:* Haileybury Coll.; Hertford Coll., Oxford; Univ. Coll., London. Entered I.C.S. 1911; Sec. to Chief Comr N.W. Frontier Province, 1928-32; Member Executive Council, N.W. Frontier Province, 1932-33, and 1936-37; Acting Resident at Hyderabad, April to Oct. 1937; Resident at Hyderabad, 1938-42; retired, 1944. *Address:* Edgefield, Hartley Wintney, Hants.
[*Died* 3 *Oct.* 1968.

GIFFARD, General Sir George James, G.C.B., *cr.* 1944 (K.C.B., *cr.* 1941; C.B. 1938); D.S.O. 1917; *b.* 27 Sept. 1886; *s.* of George Campbell Giffard, Englefield Green; *m.* 1915, Evelyn Norah (*d.* 1964), *d.* of Richard Margerison, Winchester; one *d.* Served East Africa, 1913-14 (medal and clasp); European War, 1914-18 (wounded, despatches four times, Bt. Major, Bt. Lt.-Col., D.S.O., French Croix de Guerre, Order of Aviz of Portugal); General Staff Officer, 1st Grade, 2nd Division, 1933-36; Inspector-General Royal West African Frontier Force and King's African Rifles, 1936-38; Inspector-General African Colonial Forces, 1938-39; Military Secretary to Secretary of State for War, War Office, 1939; G.O.C. the British Forces in Palestine and Transjordan, 1940; G.O.C. West Africa, 1940; G.O.C.-in-C., 1941; G.O.C.-in-C. Eastern Army, India, 1943; C.-in-C. 11th Army Group in S.-E. Asia, 1943-44; retired pay, 1946. Col. Comdt. Royal West African Frontier Force, The King's African Rifles and the Northern Rhodesia Regt., 1945-54; Col. of The Queen's Royal Regiment, 1945-1954: A.D.C. General to the King, 1943-46. *Address:* Broadview, Andover Road, Winchester, Hants. [*Died* 17 *Nov.* 1964.

GIFFEN, Edmund, D.Sc. (Eng.) and Ph.D. London; M.Sc. (Eng.), Belfast; M.I.Mech.E.; Professor of Civil and Mechanical Engineering in University of London, Queen Mary College, 1945-59; Professor of Mechanical Engineering since 1959; *b.* 1 Jan. 1902; *s.* of late Samuel Giffen; *m.* 1928, Anna Elizabeth Henderson; two *d.* *Educ.:* Masonic School, Dublin; Queen's Univ., Belfast. Harland & Wolff Ltd., Belfast, 1918-27; Lecturer, and later Reader, in Mechanical Engineering, King's College, Univ. of London, 1927-40; Director of Research, Institution of Automobile Engineers, 1940-45. *Publications:* (with A. Murasezew) Atomisation of Fuel Sprays; Papers on Mechanical Engineering subjects to Institution of Mechanical Engineers, Institution of Automobile Engineers, Society of Automotive Engineers (U.S.A.), and in various technical journals. *Address:* Queen Mary College Mile End Road, E.1. *T.:* Advance 4811. [*Died* 2 *July* 1963.

GIFFORD, 5th Baron, *cr.* 1824; **Charles Maurice Elton Gifford;** Commander Royal Navy; Chairman, Challis & Benson, Ltd.; a Director of E. Wood Ltd., of B.E.T. Omnibus Services and Credit Card Facilities Club Ltd.; *b.* Boothby Pagnell, Lincolnshire, 4 March 1899; *s.* of late Lieutenant-Colonel Hon. Maurice R. Gifford, C.M.G., 4th *s.* of 2nd Baron, and Marguerite Thorold (*d.* 1958); *S.* uncle 1937; *m.* 1939, Ellice Margaret, *d.* of late Arthur Wigram Allen, Merioola, Woollahra, Sydney, Australia; one *s.* *Educ.:* St. David's School, Reigate; Royal Naval Colleges, Osborne and Dartmouth. Served European War at sea, Midshipman and Sub. Lieut., 1914-18; H.M.S. London, Mediterranean, Gallipoli Landing, Italy; H.M.S. Repulse, North Sea; various destroyers North Sea and Baltic, Russia, 1919; transferred to Royal Air Force, 1923, as Flight Lieutenant and served until 1930; went to Australia as A.D.C. to Governor of N.S.W., 1930; Organising Secretary of Royal Prince Alfred Hospital, Sydney, N.S.W., 1935-36; returned to England, 1936; returned to Active List for War of 1939-45 (despatches for Service in N. African Waters, 1942). *Recreations:* shooting, golf, etc. *Heir:* *s.* Hon. Anthony Maurice Gifford [*b.* 1 May 1940. *Educ.:* Winchester; King's College, Cambridge (scholar)]. *Address:* 8 Hanover Square, W.1. *T.A.:* Chalbenco Wesdo London; Mackenzies, Tilford, nr. Farnham, Surrey; 1 Barton Street, S.W.1. *Clubs:* Boodle's; Union (Sydney). [*Died* 16 *April* 1961.

GIFFORD, Walter Sherman; former U.S. Ambassador to Great Britain, 1950-53; *b.* Salem, Mass., 10 Jan. 1885; *s.* of Nathan Poole Gifford and Harriet Maria Spinney; *m.* 1st, 1916, Florence Pitman (decd.), Brooklyn, N.Y.; one *s.* (and one *s.* decd.); 2nd, 1944, Augustine Lloyd Perry. *Educ.:* Harvard (A.B. *cum laude*). Asst. Sec. and Asst. Treas. Western Electric Co., N.Y., 1905-08; Chief Statistician, American Telephone and Telegraph Co., 1911-16: V.P., 1919-23; Exec. V.P., 1923-25; Pres., 1925-48; Chm., 1948-50; Hon. Chm., 1950-. Trustee: Carnegie Instn. of Washington, D.C., (Vice-Pres.) Grand Central Art Galls., Metropolitan Museum of Art, Fund for Advancement of Education; Hon. Chm. and Trustee, Community Service Soc. of N.Y., etc. Mem. Exec. Cttee., Pilgrim Soc. of U.S.; Prior to Dec. 1950, served as Director of: American Telephone and Telegraph Co.; First Nat. Bank of N.Y.; U.S. Steel; Greater New York Fund, Inc.; also served as Chm, etc., on many public bodies. Incorporator, Grand Central Art Galleries, 1920; Member Bd. of Overseers, Harvard Univ., 1930-36. 1944-50. Served early in 1916 as Supervising Dir. of Cttee. on Industrial Preparedness of Naval Consulting Bd.: Exec. Dir. U.S. Council of Nat. Defense and Advisory Commn., Washington, D.C., Dec. 1916-Nov. 1918; Sec., U.S. Representation on Inter-Allied Munitions Council, Paris, July-Sept. 1918. Member, War Resources Board, Aug.-Nov. 1939; Chm. Industry Advisory Cttee., Bd. of War Communications, 1941-47. Nat. Chm., Amer. Red Cross, 1943 War Fund Campaign. Mem. War Finance Cttee. for N.Y. State, 1941-50. Hon. Bencher, Middle Temple (Eng.). Member American Philosophical Society; Fellow: American Assoc. for Advancement of Science, American Statistical Assoc., etc. Holds several hon. doctorates. Gold Medallist, Nat. Inst. of Social Sciences, 1938; Vermilye Medal, Franklin Inst., 1943; awarded Medal for Merit by President of U.S., 1946. *Publications:* Does Business Want Scholars?. 1928; Pensions, Charity and Old Age, 1930; Can Prosperity Be Managed?, 1930. *Address:* (home) North Castle, N.Y. (P.O. Greenwich, Conn.), U.S.A.; (office) 195 Broadway, New York 7, N.Y. *Clubs:* University, Harvard, Links, National Arts, Recess, River (New York). [*Died* 7 *May* 1966.

GILBERT, Brig. Leonard, C.I.E. 1943; M.C.; *b.* Farnsfield, Notts., 16 Feb. 1889; *m.* 1919, Reiniera (decd.), *d.* of J. and G. Davison, Alnwick; one *s.* decd. *Educ.:* Gram. Sch., Southwell; Univ. Coll., Nottingham (B.A. Lond.); Staff Coll., Quetta. Served European War, 1914-18 (P.O.W., wounded, despatches, M.C.): Sherwood Foresters, Britain and France, comdg. 10th Bn. 1917 (Actg. Lt.-Col.); Royal Inniskilling Fusiliers, Gallipoli and India; Baluch and Punjab Regts., I.A. (Staff). Bt. Maj. 1930; N.W. Frontier, 1930, 1934-36; comdg. 5/10 Baluch Regt., Mohmand Ops., 1936 (despatches, Bt. Lt.-Col.); Comdg. 10/16 Punjab Regt., 1937-38. Asst. Comdt., Indian Mil. Acad., 1938-40 (Bt. Col.); Founder and Comdt., Officers' Trng. Sch., Bangalore, 1940-43 (Brig., C.I.E.); retd. 1943. Re-employed as Chief of Staff, Hyderabad State Forces, 1943-47; Organizer and Inspector, Hyderabad State Civic Guard, 1947-48. Asst. Civil Defence Officer, Northumberland, 1950-53. *Address:* c/o National and Grindlay's Bank Ltd., 13 St. James's Square, S.W.1. [*Died* 11 March 1966.

GILBERT, Admiral Thomas Drummond, C.B. 1918; *b.* 1870. Member of Committee to inquire into Disciplinary Matters of the Navy, 1912 (Legion of Honour); naval A.D.C. to the King, 1921-22; commanded 2nd Light Cruiser Squadron, 1923-25; retired list, 1927; Adm., retired, 1931. Assumed name of

Gilbert by Royal Licence, 1920. *Address:* Taynton House, Taynton, near Burford, Oxon. *T.A.:* Burford. *T.:* Burford 2125. *Club:* United Service. [*Died* 24 *Jan.* 1962.

GILBERT, William Gladstone, C.B.E. 1938; I.S.O. 1934; *b.* 22 Oct. 1877; 2nd *s.* of Thomas Philip and Sarah Ann Gilbert, Brixton Hill, London; *m.* 1920, Lucy Elizabeth Vair; two *s.* *Educ.:* London Church and Council Schools; courses at King's College, London. Entered General Post Office, 1897, following short service in Admiralty; engaged mainly on International Postal relations; Member of British Delegations to International Postal congresses, Madrid, 1920, Stockholm, 1924, London, 1929, Cairo, 1934; Deputy Comptroller and Accountant-General of the Post Office, 1933-38; Chief Accountant, Ministry of Information, 1940-43; Finance Officer, Postal and Telegraph Censorship Dept., 1943-44. *Recreation:* gardening. *Address:* Ranmore, Hawks Hill, Fetcham, Leatherhead, Surrey. *T.:* Leatherhead 2000. [*Died* 4 *June* 1964.

GILBERT-CARTER, Humphrey, M.A. (Cantab.), M.B., Ch.B. (Edin.); Hon. A.L.S.; retd.; *b.* 19 Oct. 1884; 2nd *s.* of late Sir Gilbert Thomas Gilbert-Carter, K.C.M.G.; *m.* 1914, Dorine Nanette, 4th *d.* of late W. C. Beloe, Bristol; four *d.* *Educ.:* Tonbridge; Edinburgh; Marburg; Trinity College, Cambridge. Economic Botanist to Botanical Survey, India, 1913-21; Director Cambridge University Botanic Garden, 1921-50; and University Lecturer in Botany, 1930-50; retired 1950. *Publications:* Genera of British Plants; Descriptive Labels for Botanic Gardens; Catkin-bearing Plants; British Trees and Shrubs; Glossary of the British Flora. *Address:* Thatches, Holcombe, Dawlish, S. Devon. *T.:* Dawlish 2361. [*Died* 4 *Jan.* 1969.

GILBERTSON, Rev. Canon Arthur Deane, C.B. 1937; O.B.E. 1935; Canon Emeritus of Worcester, 1953; *b.* 31 Aug. 1883; *s.* of Richard Deane and Mary Gilbertson; *m.* 1914 Janet Elsie, *d.* of late General W. F. Howard Stafford, C.B.; two *d.* *Educ.:* Blundell's, Oswestry; Keble College, Oxford; Wells Theological College. Curate at Boston, Lincs, 1906-9; Chaplain R.N. 1909; served in H.M.S. Tiger, Battle Cruiser Squadron during European War; The Chaplain of the Fleet, and Archdeacon for the Navy, 1935-38; Hon. Chaplain to the King, 1935-38; retired list, 1938; Resident Chaplain, Royal Merchant Navy School, 1938-39; Vicar of West Hoathley, 1939-40; Warden of Royal Merchant Navy School, 1940-41; Vicar of Kempsey, 1941-48. Hon. Canon of Worcester, 1951-53; Chaplain of S. Oswald's Hosp., Worcester, 1948-53. Chaplain of St. Hugh's College, Oxford, 1954. *Address:* 29 Latimer Road, Headington, Oxford. *T.:* Oxford 61682. *Club:* Oxford Union Society. [*Died* 30 *Jan.* 1964.

GILCHRIST, Archibald Daniel, V.D., M.A., B.C.E.; retd.; *b.* Kew, Victoria, 14 Apr. 1877; *s.* of Archibald Gilchrist, M.A., LL.B., Insp.-Gen. of Schools, Victoria; *m.* 1906, S. E., *d.* of S. S. Topp, M.A., LL.B., Barrister; four *s.* one *d.* *Educ.:* Xavier Coll., Melbourne; Ormond College; Melbourne University. Instructor, Engineering Dept., Melbourne Technical Coll.; Prof. of Engineering, Ballarat School of Mines; Prof. of Mathematics, R.M. Coll. of Australia, Duntroon, until Sept. 1938; temp. R.M.C. 1941-47. Major (ret.) Commonwealth Military Forces. *Address:* 17 Tasmania Circle, Canberra, A.C.T., Australia. *T.:* X2657. [*Died* 22 *March* 1964.

GILCHRIST, Sir James A(lbert), Kt., *cr.* 1953; Q.C., M.A., LL.B.; Sheriff of the Lothians and Sheriff of Chancery in Scotland, 1951-60; *b.* 16 June 1884; *s.* of late James Gilchrist, D.L., Shipbuilder and Engineer, Glasgow; *m.* 1914, Alice Mitchell; one *s.* *Educ.:* Parkhurst School, Buxton; Glasgow Univ. Admitted Faculty of Advocates, 1910; Q.C. (Scot.), 1934; served as Sub-Lt. and Lt. R.N.V.R. Auxiliary Patrol during European War; Sheriff-Substitute of the Lothians and Peebles at Edinburgh, 1938-51. *Recreations:* angling, golf, billiards. *Address:* 30 Great King Street, Edinburgh. *T.:* Waverley 2912. *Clubs:* Northern, Royal Burgess Golf (Edinburgh); Gullane Golf. [*Died* 28 *Jan.* 1965.

GILDERSLEEVE, Virginia Crocheron; Dean Emeritus of Barnard College, Columbia University, since 1947; Hon. Vice-Chairman, Near East College Association; Hon. Member: Bd. of Directors, Reid Hall, Paris; Board of Trustees, American College for Girls, Istanbul, Turkey; Board of Trustees, Institute of International Education; *b.* 3 October 1877; *d.* of Henry Alger Gildersleeve and Virginia Crocheron. *Educ.:* Barnard College (A.B.); Columbia University (A.M. 1900, Ph.D. 1908). Teaching in English Department, Barnard College, 1900-11; Professor of English and Dean of Barnard College, 1911-47; Past President International Federation of University Women, 1924-26, 1936-39; Member, Nat. Cttee. of U.S.A. on International Intellectual Cooperation, 1926; Past Member, Judicial Council of State of New York, 1935-1941; Chm. Advisory Council of Women's Reserve, U.S. Navy, 1942; Delegate of United States to United Nations Conference on International Organization, 1945. Hon. degrees: Litt.D. Columbia, 1929; L.H.D. Smith, 1936; LL.D. Rutgers, 1916; Mount Holyoke, 1937; Western Reserve, 1938; Goucher, 1941; Mills, 1945; Univ. of Pennsylvania, 1945; Princeton, 1947. Numerous other educational awards and decorations. Chevalier de la Légion d'Honneur (France), 1947. *Publications:* Government Regulation of the Elizabethan Drama, 1908; Many a Good Crusade, 1954; A Hoard for Winter, 1962; contributions to various journals. *Address:* Bedford, N.Y., U.S.A. *Clubs:* Women's University, Cosmopolitan (New York). [*Died* 7 *July* 1965.

GILES, Carl P.; *see* Prausnitz Giles.

GILES, Major-General Edward Douglas, C.B. 1932; C.M.G. 1919; D.S.O. 1916; late I.A.; *b.* 13 Oct. 1879; *s.* of late Edward Giles, C.I.E.; *m.* 1915, Eileen Graham *o. c.* of late C. G. Dingwall-Fordyce and Mrs. J. F. Barry, and *g.d.* of late Lt.-General Sir John Dingwall-Fordyce, K.C.B. *Educ.:* Marlborough College; R.M.C., Sandhurst. Entered 1st King's Shropshire Light Infantry, 1899; transferred to Indian Army (35th Scinde Horse), 1901; passed Staff College, Quetta, 1912; served European War in France, Nov. 1914-Jan. 1918 (Bt. Lieut.-Col., D.S.O., despatches four times); G.S.O.1 of British Military Mission in U.S. America, Jan.-Nov. 1918 (C.M.G. and American D.S.M.): transferred to K.G.O. Central India Horse, 1920; Instructor Staff College, Quetta, 1921-24; commanded 3rd (Meerut) and 4th (Secunderabad) Cavalry Brigades, 1925-29; Director of Military Operations, A.H.Q. India, Feb. 1930 to Jan. 1931; Maj.-Gen. 1931; Major-General Cavalry in India, 1931-35; A.D.C. to the King, 1930; retired 1935. *Address:* c/o Westminster Bank, Piccadilly, W.1. *Club:* United Service. [*Died* 26 *Sept.* 1966.

GILES, George Henry, O.B.E. 1955; Secretary and Director of Examinations, British Optical Association, since 1942; Secretary, Association of Optical Practitioners, since 1948; *b.* 23 Aug. 1904; *s.* of G. E. Giles and Emma L. O'Brien; *m.* 1927, Kathleen Joan Clemens (*d.* 1962); two *d.*; *m.* 1964, Ivy Parnum. *Educ.:* St. Matthew's, N.W.1; Northampton College, London (Science Exhibitioner). Consultant H.M.S. Worcester, 1934-; Sen. Refractionist, Orthoptist and Lectr., London Refraction Hosp., 1936-50; Mem. Bd. of Management, 1939-; Mem. Council, Brit. Opt. Assoc., 1936-42; Pres. Internat. Optical League, 1954-; Chm. Optical Whitley Council (N.H.S.), 1948; Mem. N.H.S. Standing Ophth. Adv. Cttee., 1948-; Hon. Sec. Jt. Cttee. Ophth. Opts., 1942-; Mem. Gen. Optical Council, 1959. Editor of Brit. Jl. Physiol. Optics, 1951-; Ophthalmic Optician, 1960. F.S.M.C. 1926, F.B.O.A. 1928, (Hons.) Fell. 1932, D.Orth., 1939, F.I.E.S. 1945; Barrister at Law, Lincoln's Inn, 1949, Ernest Aves Medal, 1949; M.R.I. 1950, F.A.A.O. 1952, City of Paris Silver Medal, 1959, F.R.S.H. 1960; Mem. Coun., Royal Soc. of Health, 1965. Hon. Mem. or Fell. of several home and overseas Optical Assocs. *Publications:* A Manual of Practical Orthoptics, 1938; The Practice of Orthoptics, 1943; The Ophthalmic Services under the National Health Service Act, 1953; The Principles and Practice of Refraction, 1960 (2nd Edn., 1964). Many papers and monographs. *Recreations:* writing, travel, golf. *Address:* 65 Brook Street, W.1. *T.:* Mayfair 3382; 189 Watford Road, Harrow. *Club:* National Liberal. [*Died* 26 *Sept.* 1965.

GILES, John Laurent; Managing Director, Laurent Giles & Partners Ltd., Lymington, Hants., since 1927; *b.* 22 June 1901; *s.* of Leonard Thomason Giles, F.R.C.S. and Janet Elizabeth (*née* Whitwell); *m.* 1929, Elizabeth Constance Alice Falconar; two *s.* one *d.* *Educ.:* Bramcote, Scarborough; Winchester Coll.; Magdalene Coll., Cambridge. R.D.I. (Naval Architecture), 1951. *Publications:* contribs. to yachting jls. *Recreation:* sailing. *Address:* Normandy Mead, Woodside, Lymington, Hampshire. *T.:* Lymington 3160. *Clubs:* Royal Ocean Racing; Royal Lymington Yacht; etc. [*Died* 20 *Feb.* 1969.

GILES, Lieut.-Col. Sir Oswald (Bissill), Kt., *cr.* 1955; D.L.; Chairman of Holland County Council, Lincolnshire, 1945-63, retd.; *b.* 11 Apr. 1888; *s.* of Dr. Oswald Giles, Sleaford, Lincs.; *m.* 1st, 1914, Lucy Annie (*d.* 1960), *d.* of late Mr. and Mrs. Arthur Stuart, Birkdale, Lancs.; one *s.* one *d.* (and *yr. s.* killed at Tobruk, 1942); 2nd, 1963, Rosalind Hendrick. *Educ.:* Epsom Coll. Admitted Solicitor, 1911; Senior Partner, Millington, Simpsons & Giles, Boston, Lincs., retd. 1967. 2nd Lieut. R.F.A. (T.), 1911; Major, 1918; served European War, 1914-19, France and Belgium, and as Lt.-Colonel Home Guard, 1940-45. C.C. 1913-67; C.A. 1933, Chm. of Coun., 1945-63, Holland, Lincs.; D.L. Lincs. 1947; High Sheriff, Lincs., 1951. *Address:* Clare House, 5 Burton Close, Boston, Lincs. *T.:* Boston 2316. [*Died* 4 *Aug.* 1970.

GILL, Conrad; Emeritus Professor of History, the University of Hull; Hon. D.Litt. (Hull) 1957; *b.* Redhill, Surrey, 1883; 4th *s.* of Joseph J. Gill; *m.* 1921, Jeanette *d.* of Arthur Priestman, J.P., Bradford, Yorks; two *s.* one *d.* *Educ.:* Ackworth School; Univ. of Leeds (Litt.D. 1923); King's Coll., Cambridge (B.A. 1910; M.A. 1920). Asst. Lectr. in Victoria University, Manchester, 1911; Lecturer in Economic History in Queen's University, Belfast, 1913; War service in Friends' Ambulance Unit. Reader in Constitutional History, University of Birmingham, 1920; Leverhulme Research Fellowship, 1935. *Publications:* The Naval Mutinies of 1797, 1913; National Power and Prosperity, 1916; Government and People 1921, 3rd edition 1933; The Rise of the Irish Linen Industry, 1925; Studies in Midland History, 1930; (with Sir Charles Grant Robertson) A Short History of Birmingham, 1938; (with Asa Briggs) A History of Birmingham 1952; Merchants and Mariners of the Eighteenth Century, 1961; articles and reviews in periodicals. *Recreations:* gardening, music. *Address:* Storth, Milnthorpe, Westmorland. *T.:* Milnthorpe 3212. [*Died* 10 *March* 1968.

GILL, Colonel Gordon Harry, C.M.G. 1919; D.S.O. 1917; late R.A.S.C.; *b.* 1882; *m.* Doris; one *s.* Served European War, 1914-18 (despatches, D.S.O., Bt. Col., Order of Aviz of Portugal); Officer Commanding, R.A.S.C. Colchester, 1930-32; A.Q.M.G., Scottish Command, 1932-34; Assistant Director of Supplies and Transport, Eastern Command, 1934-38; A.D.C. to the King, 1936-38; retired pay, 1938. [*Died* 16 *Sept.* 1962.

GILL, Commodore (2nd Class) Sir Roy, K.B.E., *cr.* 1945 (C.B.E. 1943); R.D. 1921; R.N.R. retd.; *b.* Philadephia, U.S.A. 19 Feb. 1887; *s.* of Mason Gill, dentist, and British subject; *m.* 1914, Ivy Gwendolen Taylor, Kingston-on-Thames; one *s.* one *d.* *Educ.:* Shoreham Grammar School; H.M.S. Worcester. Served with Geo. Milne & Company as apprentice in the Barques Inverneill and Inverness, 1908; 2nd mate of Inveresk; served in command of South Metropolitan Gas Company's Steamers, 1920-39; Commodore of Ocean Convoys, 1940-45; (despatches), 1944; Naval Officer in Charge (Tyne Area), 1945-46, until demobilised; Commodore 2nd Class retired, 1946. Joined R.N.R. 1905; served European War, 4½ years in command, 1914-19 (R.D.); Lt. Comdr. R.N.R. 1923; Comdr. 1930; Captain, 1935; called up for service in R.N. 1939; A.D.C. to the King, 1941-42; retired as Capt. R.N.R. 1942; formerly River Superintendent South Eastern Gas Board, Metropolitan Division. Vice-Pres. The Royal Naval Assoc.; Pres. Assoc. of Old Worcesters. Master of Clipper Ship Cutty Sark, 1957-65; now Captain Commodore (Hon.); Governor of Cutty Sark Society. *Recreation:* gardening. *Address:* 3 Liskeard Gardens, Blackheath, S.E.3. *T.:* Greenwich 2031. [*Died* 13 *Oct.* 1967.

GILLESPIE, Thomas Haining, F.R.S.E., M.B.O.U., F.Z.S., Secretary to the Zoological Society of Scotland and Director of the Scottish National Zoological Park, 1913-50; *b.* Dumfries, 3 Oct. 1876; *s.* of Thomas Haining Gillespie and Julia Ann Satchell; *m.* 1920, Mary Elizabeth Gamble. *Educ.:* Private schools; Edinburgh University. Qualified as Solicitor, 1899; was instrumental in founding The Zoological Society of Scotland, 1909; Hon. Secretary thereof until 1913, when the Society was incorporated by Royal Charter. Vice-Pres. of Roy. Zoological Soc. of Scotland; Hon. Member of Roy. Zool. Soc. of Ireland; Corr. Member of New York Zool. Soc.; Hon. Vice-Pres. of Edinburgh Scientific Film Soc. *Publications:* Zoo Ways and Whys; More Zoo Ways; A Book of King Penguins; Is it Cruel?—A Study of the Condition of Captive and Performing Animals; Zoo Tales; The Way of a Serpent; Zoo-Man Talks; More Zoo Tales; Our Friends the Spiders; The Story of the Edinburgh Zoo; numerous magazine and newspaper articles on popular aspects of animal life and behaviour. *Recreations:* reading, writing, music, photography. *Address:* 8 William St., Edinburgh 3. *Club:* Scottish Arts (Edin.). [*Died* 3 *Aug.* 1967.

GILLESPY, Rev. Francis Roebuck, M.A.; *b.* 16 Aug. 1880; Hon. Canon of Gloucester since 1951; 7th *s.* of late John Roebuck Gillespy of The Postern, Tonbridge, Kent; *m.* 1st, 1909, Edith May, *d.* of late Frederic Truman Wiltshire of The Manse, Addiscombe, Surrey; (one *s* killed on active service, 1941) three *d.* (and one *d.* decd.); 2nd, 1923, Ellen Rose, *widow* of E. Cecil W. Hicks-Austin,

M.A., B.C.L., J.P. *Educ.:* Whitgift; Hatfield College, Durham University. Planter in West Indies, 1899-1903; Deacon, 1907; Priest, 1908; Curate of Great Stanmore, 1907-9; Rector of Ayr cum Brandon, N. Queensland, 1909-12; Curate, St. John's, Southend, 1912-13; Vicar of Alvanley, Cheshire, 1913-16; Indian Ecclesiastical Establishment, 1916; Chaplain XI. Brigade Marri Field Force, 1918; Head Master, Bishop Cotton School, Simla, 1918-22; Head Master, The King's School, Gloucester and Minor Canon, Gloucester Cathedral, 1922-30; Precentor of Gloucester Cathedral, 1926-30; Hon. Minor Canon Gloucester Cathedral, 1930; Rector of Ashleworth, Gloucester, 1931-51; Rural Dean of Gloucester, 1935-41. *Recreations:* shooting, gardening. *Address:* Ashleworth Manor, Gloucester. *T.:* Hartpury 232. [*Died* 9 *March* 1962.

GILLETT, Charles William; Managing Director, 1929-67, Vice-Chairman, 1959-67, Cadbury Bros. Ltd.; Managing Director, 1929-67, Vice-Chairman, 1964-67, British Cocoa & Chocolate Co. Ltd.; *b.* 21 April 1901; *s.* of late Charles Edwin Gillett; *m.* 1926, Doreen Southall; one *s.* three *d.* *Educ.:* Leighton Park Sch., Reading. Hon. Treas., Birmingham and Midland Hosps. for Women, 1935-48. Chm. and Treas., Coun., Selly Oak Colleges, 1949-; Life Governor, University of Birmingham, 1950. Member: Birmingham Regional Hospital Board; Birmingham (Selly Oak) Hospital Management Committee. *Recreations:* farming fishing and golf. *Address:* Heanor, Rednal, Birmingham. *T.:* Rubery 3505. [*Died* 25 *Oct.* 1968.

GILLIAM, Laurence Duval, O.B.E. 1946; Head of Features, B.B.C. since 1947; *b.* London, 4 March 1907; *e. s.* of Ernest William Gilliam and Beatrice Bishop; *m.* 1940, Marianne Helweg (marriage dissolved); three *s.* one *d.* *Educ.:* City of London School; Peterhouse, Cambridge. Worked first with Gramophone Co. in various capacities, and later, as free-lance journalist, actor and producer; joined ed. staff of Radio Times, 1932, transferred to Drama Dept., B.B.C., 1933, and worked on development of special feature programmes. Responsible for B.B.C.'s world-wide Christmas Day programme since 1933. *Publication:* B.B.C. Features, 1950. *Recreations:* golf and cooking. *Address:* 5 St. George's Terrace, N.W.1. *T.:* Primrose 2540. *Club:* Savile. [*Died* 15 *Nov.* 1964.

GILLIAT, Algernon Earle, C.I.E. 1928; *b.* 1 Jan. 1884; *s.* of late George Henry Gilliat, Manchester; *m.* 1917, Hazel M. G. (*d.* 1961), *d.* of late Major F. Gordon Alexander, I.A.; two *s.* one *d.* *Educ.:* Manchester Grammar School; Wadham College, Oxford. Entered I.C.S. (Burma), 1908; Under-Secretary Govt. of India, 1916-19; Secretary Indian Sugar Committee, 1919-21; Secretary to the Govt. of Burma, Finance Dept., 1927-29; Commissioner, Arakan Division, Akyab, Burma 1932-33; Member, Burma Retrenchment Committee, 1933-34; Commissioner, Irrawaddy Division, Bassein, Burma, 1935-38; Financial Commissioner, Rangoon, Burma, 1939-42; retired, 1943. *Address:* Faulkland Lodge, Ferndown, Dorset. *T.:* Ferndown 3523. [*Died* 25 *May* 1970.

GILLICK, Mary, O.B.E. 1953; Sculptor; *d.* of Thomas Tutin, Nottingham; *m.* 1905, Ernest Gillick, A.R.A. (*d.* 1951). Studied sculpture at Royal College of Art. Work includes: Effigy of the Queen for the coinage and for Official medals; Royal Tour Medal; bronze bas-relief portraits of Sir Henry Dale, O.M. for Wellcome Foundation and of Victor Heal for Bank of England; bronze portrait memorials to Sir William Bragg, O.M., in Chiddingfold Church, Surrey; to Sir James Molteno, in Parliament House, S. Africa; to Frederic Anstruther Cardew, in English Church in Paris; to Kathleen Ferrier in University College Hospital, London; to Margaret Babington in Canterbury Cathedral; and other memorials in London and in Cambridge. Medals for the Royal Mint, the Royal Society, the Physical Society, etc. *Recreation:* painting. *Address:* Moravian Close, 381 King's Road, Chelsea, S.W.10. *T.:* Flaxman 6454. [*Died* 27 *Jan.* 1965.

GILLITT, Lt.-Col. William, C.I.E. 1916; M.D., M.R.C.S., L.R.C.P.; D.P.H.; *b.* 26 Dec. 1879; *s.* of Charles Gillitt, Stanwick, Northants; *m.* 1925, Helen Julia (*d.* 1954), *d.* of F. B. Osborne, Malvern House, Blockley, Worcs. *Educ.:* Wellingborough; Middlesex Hospital; late House Physician there; entered I.M.S. 1904; Jail Dept. 1907; military employment again, 1914; served Indian Frontier, 1914-15; Mesopotamia, 1915-17 (despatches, C.I.E.); N. Persia, 1918-19 (despatches); late Inspector-Gen. of Prisons, Bihar and Orissa, India; retired, 1926. *Address:* Flat 2, 26 Arlington Road, Eastbourne, Sussex. [*Died* 1 *Dec.* 1962.

GILMORE, Dame Mary, D.B.E. *cr.* 1937; Writer; *b.* Australia 1865; *d.* of Donal Cameron, Locheil, Scotland; *m.* 1897, William Alexander Gilmore (*decd.*), Burnside, Victoria, Australia. *Educ.:* Wagga, N.S.W. Helped found the New Australia Colony in Paraguay, S. America; Journalist in Sydney for fifty years; associated with much public work. *Publications:* Verse: Married and other Verses; The Tale of Tiddley Winks (Children's verse); The Passionate Heart; The Tilted Cart; The Wild Swan; The Rue Tree; Under the Wilgas; Battlefields; The Disinherited; Selected Verse, Fourteen Men; Verses for Children. Prose: Hound of the Road; Old Days Old Ways; More Recollections; The Worker Cook Book. *Recreations:* none outstanding. *Club:* Lyceum (Sydney, Australia). [*Died* 3 *Dec.* 1962.

GILMOUR, Lady Susan, D.B.E., *cr.* 1936; *b.* 1870, 2nd *d.* of 6th Earl Beauchamp; *m.* 1889, Sir Robert Gordon Gilmour, 1st Bt., C.B., C.V.O., D.S.O. (*d.* 1939); one *s.* three *d.* *Address:* 21 Cadogan Gardens, S.W.3. *T.:* Sloane 0502. [*Died* 28 *Jan.* 1962.

GINGELL, Overy Francis; a Deputy Secretary, Ministry of Transport, since 1966; *b.* 4 Dec. 1916; *e. s.* of Francis John and Nora Mildred Gingell, Hilmarton, Wilts; *m.* 1940, Lena Parker (marr. diss. 1951), one *d*; *m.* 1951 Muriel Christine, *y. d.* of Frederick and Mabel Gayes. *Educ.:* Commonweal Gram. Sch., Swindon, Wilts; London Sch. of Economics and Political Science. Army service in War of 1939-45. Entered Home Civil Service (Administrative Class), Min. of Transport, 1947. Principal Private Secretary: to Min. of Transport (Rt. Hon. Alfred Barnes, M.P.) 1951, and to successive Ministers of Transport to 1953. Joint Prin. Private Sec. to successive Ministers of Transport and Civil Aviation, 1953-57; Asst. Sec., 1957; Sec., Special Advisory Group on British Transport Commn. (Chm., Sir Ivan Stedeford, K.B.E.), 1960; Under Secretary, Ministry of Transport, 1962-66. *Recreations:* fell walking, fishing. *Address:* Cator Lodge, South Row, Blackheath, S.E.3. *T.:* Lee Green 6747. *Club:* United Service. [*Died* 20 *April* 1966.

GINSBERG, Morris, F.B.A. 1953; M.A.; D.Lit. (London); LL.D. (Glasgow); LL.D. (Nottingham); Fellow of University College, London; Martin White Professor of Sociology in the University of London, London School of Economics, 1929-54; Emeritus Professor, 1954; *b.* 14 May 1889; *m.* 1931, Ethel Street (*d.* 1962). *Educ.:* University College, London (John Stuart Mill Scholar, Martin White Scholar and Research Student). Lecturer in Philosophy at University College,

London, 1914-23; Frazer Lecturer, 1944; Conway Memorial Lecturer, 1952; Clarke Hall Lecturer, 1953; Huxley Memorial Lecture and Medal, 1953; Herbert Spencer Lecture, Oxford, 1958. Hon. Fellow, L.S.E. President, Aristotelian Society, 1942-1943; Past Editor of British Journal Soc. and Soc. Rev. *Publications:* The Psychology of Society, 1921 (9th edn., revd., 1964); Studies in Sociology, 1932; Sociology, 1934; Moral Progress, 1944; The Idea of Progress: A Revaluation, 1953; Reason and Experience in Ethics (Auguste Comte Lecture, 1956); Essays on Sociology and Social Philosophy: Vol. 1, On the Diversity of Morals; Vol. 2, Reason and Unreason in Society, 1956; Vol. 3, Evolution and Progress, 1961; Nationalism; a Re-appraisal, 1961; (Ed.) Law and Opinion in England in the Twentieth Century, 1959; The Material Culture and Social Institutions of the Simpler Peoples, 1915 (jt. author); L. T. Hobhouse: His Life and work (jt. author), 1931; On Justice in Society, 1965; papers in sociological and psychological jls. and in Proc. of the Aristotelian Society. *Address:* 5 Millfield Lane, N.6. *T.:* 01-340 5809. *Club:* Athenæum. [*Died* 31 *Aug.* 1970.

GINWALA, Sir Padamji Pestonji, Kt., *cr.* 1927; Director and Adviser, Indian Iron and Steel Co., Ltd., Calcutta (also on London Board), and Indian Standard Wagon Co. Ltd.; India Steamship Co. Ltd.; *b.* Ankleshwar, Nov. 1875; 2nd *s.* of late Pestonji N. Ginwala; *m.* 1918, Frenny Bezonji; one *s.* *Educ.:* Government High School, Ahmedabad; Trinity Hall, Cambridge. Historical Tripos, 1897; Called to Bar Lincoln's Inn, 1899; Advocate High Court of Bombay, 1899; Acting Professor, History and Economics, Elphinstone Coll., Bombay, 1900; Advocate Chief Court of Lower Burma, 1905; Editor Burma Law Times, 1907-10; Mem. Rangoon Municipal Cttee., 1911-23; Assistant Government Advocate, Burma, 1915; Assistant Secretary Legislative Department, Burma, and Secretary to the Burma Legislative Council, 1916; on special duty to draft the Rangoon Municipal Bill and the Rangoon Development Bill, 1917; Vice-President, Rangoon Municipal Committee, 1918-22; Deputy Legal Remembrancer, Burma, 1919; resigned, 1920; Member Legislative Assembly, India (Burma General Const.), 1921-23; Governing Director, Rangoon Daily News, 1921-23; Member Burma Reforms Committee, 1921; Chief Whip Democratic Party, 1921-23; President Rangoon Municipal Corporation, 1922 and 1923; Member Indian Tariff Board, 1923-30; President, 1926-30; resigned, 1930; Delegate Imperial Conference 1930; Indian Round Table Conference, 1931; Ottawa Conference, 1932; World Monetary and Economic Conference, 1933; President, Indian Air Force Pilot Selection Board, 1940 and 1941; Chairman Iron and Steel (Major) Panel, Govt of India, 1945; Chairman Calcutta Terminal Facilities Cttee., Govt. of India, 1947. *Address:* 12 Mission Row, Calcutta. *Clubs:* National Liberal; Royal Calcutta Turf; Calcutta (Calcutta); Royal Western Indian Turf (Bombay). [*Died* 18 *April* 1962.

GIRDWOOD, Maj.-Gen. Sir Eric Stanley, K.B.E., *cr.* 1935; C.B. 1918; C.M.G. 1919; late Cameronians; *b.* 1876; *y. s.* of late John Girdwood of Prospect House, Carrickfergus, and Binstead, Isle of Wight; *m.* 1st, 1907, Flora (d. 1916); 2nd *d.* of Kenneth Mathieson; one *s.*; 2nd, 1919, Hilda (*d.* 1959), *y. d.* of Kenneth Mathieson, 50 Princes Gate, S.W.; one *s.* 2nd Lt. The Cameronians (Scottish Rifles), 1899; Served S. African War, 1899-1902 (despatches, Queen's medal four clasps, King's medal two clasps); European War, 1914-18 (despatches 9 times, C.B., Brevets of Lt.-Col. and Col., O. Legion of Honour, Croix de Guerre, Order of Nile); commanded 156th Infantry Brigade, Egypt and Palestine, 1916; 74th (Yeo.) Division, Palestine and France, 1916-18; Brigade Commander 9th Infantry Brigade and Southern Area, 1919-23; Brigade Com., Military Forces in Iraq, 1924-25 (Medal); Maj.-Gen., 1925; G.O.C. Bombay District, 1926-27; Colonel, The Cameronians (Scottish Rifles), 1927-45; Commandant Royal Military College, 1927-31; G.O.C. Northern Ireland District, 1931-35, retired pay, 1935. Chief Gold Staff Officer at Coronation, 1937. *Club:* Army and Navy. [*Died* 24 *May* 1963.

GIRI de TERAMALA di FOGLIANO, Count Piero Mariano; Lord of the Carpinetae, *cr.* 964; Lord of Teramala, *cr.* 1072; Lord of Fogliano, *cr.* 1159; Lord of Cervia and of Bertinoro, *cr.* 1249; Duke of Spoleto, *cr.* 1254; Count of Romagna, *cr.* 1254; Count of Fogliano, *cr.* 1747; Count of the Holy Roman Empire, *cr.* 1747; Count of Teramala, *cr.* 1755; Knight Comdr. of the Order of Saint Maurice and Saint Lazarus; Research Engineer; *b.* 23 Nov. 1885; 3rd *s.* of late Antonio Nazzareno Giri, 5th Count of Teramala and Elena Antoniadi; *m.* 1909, Marie-Therese Elisabeth, *o. d.* of late Adolphe de Coucy, Paris; one *d.* *Educ.:* Regio Istituto di Scienze Sociali, Florence; École Libre des Sciences Politiques, École de Droit, and École du Louvre, Paris. *Address:* Lillibrooke Manor, Cox Green, Berks. [*Died* 7 *Nov.* 1962.

GIRLING, James Lawrence, C.B. 1958; retired; *b.* Buckminster, Rutlandshire, 8 July 1901; *s.* of Robert James Girling, F.S.I. and Jessie Laura Sadd. *Educ.:* Eastward Ho! College, Felixstowe; Ipswich Secondary School; Queen Mary Coll., London Univ. (Drapers' Scholar). B.Sc. (Hons.), 1921; called to Bar, Gray's Inn, 1950. Joined Examining Staff Patent Office, 1921. Served in R.A.F.V.R., 1939-45; relinquished commission with rank of Sqdn. Leader. Comptroller-General of Patents, Designs and Trade Marks, 1954-58. *Address:* The Hook, 1 Rosebery Road, Felixstowe, Suffolk. *T.:* Felixstowe 2401. [*Died* 26 *Oct.* 1969.

GIVEN, Ernest Cranstoun, C.B.E. 1920; M.Inst.C.E., M.I.Mech.E., M.Inst.N.A.; Past President of Liverpool Engineering Society; *b.* 11 Nov. 1870; *s.* of late John Given of Aigburth Lodge, Liverpool; *m.* Winifred (*d.* 1955), *e. d.* of R. Currie, J.P., M.D., of Oakcraig, Skelmorlie; two *d.* *Educ.:* Harrow; Univ. Coll., Liverpool. Cape Government Railways, 1890; Wm. Cramp & Sons, Philadelphia, 1892; Priestman & Co., Philadelphia, 1894; Flannery & Given, Ltd., Consulting Engineers, 1897-1917; Hon. Sec, Liverpool Munitions of War Committee, 1915-17; Director of Airship Production, Admiralty, 1917-19; Director General of Factories, Ministry of Munitions, 1919-20; Manager Slough Trading Co., 1920-22; Chairman of Appeal Tribunal of Assistance Board, 1935-46; Member of Social Welfare Cttee., L.C.C. 1930-52; Referee Min. of Health Evacuation Assessments, 1939-46; Member of Governing Bodies of South-East Technical Coll., of Wandsworth Technical Coll., of Distributive Trades Tech. Coll., and of Putney group of Hospitals. Member of Advisory Cttee., National Insurance; National Assistance: Member Streatham Ratepayers Assoc.; Past Hon. Treasurer Streatham Conservative Association; Civil Defence Warden. *Publications:* various papers to Engineering Socs. *Recreation:* motoring. *Address:* 16 Polworth Road, S.W.16 *T.:* Streatham 0815. *Club:* Royal Automobile. [*Died* 16 *May* 1961.

GLADSTONE, Sir Albert Charles, 5th Bt., *cr.* 1846; M.B.E. 1919; Constable of Flint Castle since 1935; late Capt., I.A.; D.L., Flint; lately senior partner Ogilvy, Gillanders & Co., East India merchants; *b.* 28 Oct. 1886; *s.* of late Rev. Stephen Edward Gladstone and Annie Crosthwaite, *d.* of late Charles Bowman Wilson, surgeon; *S.* cousin, 1945. *Educ.:* Eton; Christ Church, Oxford,

M.A. Served European War, 1914-18 (despatches, M.B.E.). Dir., Bank of England, 1924-47. Past Chm., Income Tax City of London Commissioners for General Purposes. *Heir:* *b.* Charles Andrew Gladstone, *q.v.* *Address:* 56 Marsham Court, S.W.1. *T.:* Victoria 8181. [*Died* 2 *March* 1967.

GLADSTONE, Charles Andrew; *b.* 28 Oct. 1888; *s.* of Rev. Stephen E. Gladstone and Annie Crosthwaite Wilson and *b.* of Sir Albert Gladstone, 5th Bt. (*d.* 1967); *m.* 1925, Isla Margaret, *d.* of late Sir W. Erskine Crum; four *s.* two *d.* *Educ.:* Eton; Christ Church, Oxford. Assistant Master, Eton College, 1912-46. Served European War with Intelligence Corps and Royal Flying Corps in France and Belgium, 1914-15 (prisoner of war); D.L. Flintshire, 1929, V.L. 1948; High Sheriff of Flintshire, 1951. Officier d'Académie, 1939. *Recreations:* rowing, birds, and gardening. *Address:* Hawarden Castle, Deeside, Flintshire. *Club:* Leander. [*Died* 28 *April* 1968.

[*Proved his claim to the baronetcy* (*cr. 1846*), *on the death of his brother, but did not use the title.*

GLANVILLE, Harold James Abbott, J.P.; President, National Liberal Club; Chairman, 1944-63; Trustee and Vice-Pres. since 1947; *b.* 26 June 1884; *e. s.* of late Harold J. Glanville, M.P., J.P.; *m.* 1926, Hilda Evelyn Boyd; three *d.* *Educ.:* Aske's School, Hatcham. Member of War Pensions Cttee., 1918; Mem. London County Council, 1919-22 (Progressive); J.P. Co. London, 1925; Mem. Children's Court Panel, 1927-1932; Mem. London Ministry of Information Cttee., 1940-45; Chm. London Standing Joint Cttee. of Quarter Sessions, 1949-59; Mem. Bench, Blackheath, 1925- (Vice-Chm. 1939-52; Chm. 1952-59); A former Vice-Chm. London Licensing Planning Cttee.; Mem. London Magistrates Court Cttee., from inception; Mem. Lord Chancellor's Advisory Cttee. for J.P.'s, 1928-50. Formerly Hon. Sec., Chm. and Pres. of London Liberal Fedn. and many constituency offices; President, Liberal Party, 1959-60. *Publications:* various political memoranda. *Recreations:* chess, lawn tennis. *Address:* 26 Dartmouth Row, Blackheath, S.E.10. *T.:* Tideway 1916. *Club:* National Liberal. [*Died* 21 *Feb.* 1966.

GLASGOW, 8th Earl of (*cr.* 1703), **Patrick James Boyle,** D.S.O. 1915; D.L. Co. Ayr; Baron Boyle, 1699; Viscount Kelburn, 1703; Baron Fairlie (U.K.), *cr.* 1897; Captain R.N., retd.; *b.* 18 June 1874; *s.* of 7th Earl and Dorothea, *d.* of Sir Edward Hunter-Blair, 4th Bt.; *S.* father, 1915; *m.* 1906, Hyacinthe Mary, *d.* of late W. A. Bell, of Pendell Court, Bletchingley; one *s.* two *d.* Lieut. R.N. 1897; Commander, 1909; served European War, 1914-19 (despatches, D.S.O.); retired as Captain, R.N., June 1919; Lieut., Royal Company of Archers, Queen's Body Guard for Scotland; retd. 1955. D.L. Ayrshire since 1942 (formerly V.L.), and ex-convener of the County Council. *Heir:* *s.* Viscount Kelburn, C.B. *Address:* Kelburn Castle, Fairlie, Ayrshire. *T.:* Fairlie 204. *Clubs:* United Service; New (Edinburgh). [*Died* 14 *Dec.* 1963.

GLASGOW, Raymond C. R.; *see* Robertson-Glasgow.

GLASS, George William; *b.* 1877; *o. surv. s.* of late George William Glass, Dartmouth; *m.* Helen (*d.* 1950), *y. d.* of late John Nevill Dumbrill, Eastbourne; one *d.* Director of Thames Grit and Aggregates Ltd., and subsidiary companies, 1933-49. Financial Editor of Sunday News, 1931; City Editor Daily Chronicle, 1925-30; City Editor Glasgow Herald, 1912-25; Assistant City Editor of the Morning Post, 1907-12; Financial Correspondent of Glasgow Chamber of Commerce Journal, 1916-28, Edinburgh Chamber of Commerce Journal, 1918-28; London Correspondent New York Annalist, 1915-17. *Recreations:* travelling, motoring. *Address:* Commercial Bank of Scotland, 60-62 Lombard Street, E.C.3. [*Died* 11 *Nov.* 1967.

GLASS, William Mervyn, R.S.A., 1959 (A.R.S.A., 1934); *b.* 1885; *m.* 1917, Sadie, *d.* of William Roberts, Dunmurry, Co. Antrim; one *d.* *Educ.:* Aberdeen School of Art, R.S.A. Life School, Paris and Italy. President Society of Scottish Artists, 1930-33. *Address:* 38 Drummond Place, Edinburgh. *T.:* Edinburgh Waverley 2879. *Club:* Scottish Arts (Edinburgh). [*Died* 14 *Aug.* 1965.

GLASSEY, Alec Ewart, J.P.; Chief Commissioner of Reconstruction of Congregational Union, 1942-57; *b.* Normanton, Yorkshire, 29 December 1887; *s.* of late Reverend William Glassey and late Elizabeth Glassey; *m.* 1910, Mary Eleanor Longbottom; three *d.* *Educ.:* Penistone Grammar School. Served European War, 1914-18 (despatches); Member of Council of Congregational Union of England and Wales; contested East Dorset, 1924; M.P. (L.) East Dorset, 1929-31; a Lord Commissioner of the Treasury, 1931; Chairman: Congregational Union of England and Wales, 1941-42 (Co.-Treas., 1953-57); Commonwealth Missionary Soc., 1945-47, 1961-62; Dir. of Congregational Insurance Co. Ltd. Collected over £500,000 for re-building bombed churches. J.P., Poole, Dorset. *Recreation:* gardening. *Address:* The Homestead, Penn Hill Avenue, Parkstone, Dorset. *T.:* Parkstone 286. *Clubs:* National Liberal, Eighty. [*Died* 26 *June* 1970.

GLENAVY, 2nd Baron, *cr.* 1921, of Milltown; **Charles Henry Gordon Campbell,** Bt., *cr.* 1916; *b.* 22 Oct. 1885; *er. s.* of 1st Baron and Emily, 2nd *d.* of John MacCullagh, R.M., and *niece* of late James MacCullagh, Fellow and Professor of Mathematics, Trinity College, Dublin; *S.* father, 1931; *m.* 1912, Beatrice Moss, *d.* of William Elvery, Rothbury, Foxrock, Co. Dublin; two *s.* *Educ.:* Charterhouse; R.M.A., Woolwich. Lt. R.E. 1905-10; Barrister, Gray's Inn, 1911 (Cert. of Honour); King's Inns, 1919; Asst. Controller Ministry of Munitions, 1915-18; Secretary, Irish Dept., Ministry of Labour, 1919-22; Dept. of Industry and Commerce, 1922-32; Director Bank of Ireland and Central Bank of Ireland; Chairman Hibernian Insurance Co. and Property Loan and Investment Co.; Director British and Irish Steam Packet Co., Cyril Lord Carpets Ltd., and other companies. *Heir:* *s.* Hon. Patrick Gordon Campbell, *b.* 6 June 1913. *Address:* Rockall, Sandycove, Co. Dublin. [*Died* 30 *July* 1963.

GLENDAY, Sir Vincent Goncalves, K.C.M.G., *cr.* 1942 (C.M.G. 1937); O.B.E. 1929; *b.* 11 Feb. 1891; *s.* of Alexander Glenday; *m.* 1939, Elizabeth Mary Bader, *e. d.* of late Sir Jacob Barth, C.B.E.; three *s.* *Educ.:* St. Bees School, Cumberland; Wadham College, Oxford. M.A. Oxon; 2nd Class Honours Natural Science (Geology); Diploma Forestry; entered Colonial Administrative Service, 1913; posted to East Africa Protectorate, 1913, afterwards called Kenya Colony; Mission to Abyssinia, 1927-28 (O.B.E.); Senior District Commissioner, and Officer-in-Charge, Northern Frontier, Jan. 1934; Provincial Commissioner, Dec. 1934; Governor and Commander-in-Chief of Somaliland Protectorate, 1939-42; Colonial Office, 1942-43; British Agent in Eastern Aden Protectorate and Resident Adviser Hadramaut States, 1944-45; British Resident, Zanzibar, 1946-51; retired from Colonial Administrative Service. Speaker of E. African Central Legislative Assembly, Sept. 1953-Dec. 1961, resigned. F.G.S. Order of Brilliant Star of Zanzibar, 1st Cl., 1951. *Publications:* geological papers (with

Dr. John Parkinson, D.Sc.). *Recreations:* fishing, shooting, cricket, golf. *Address:* 61 Krantzview Road, Kloof P O. Natal, South Africa. [*Died* 30 *April* 1970.

GLENDYNE, 2nd Baron, of Sanquhar, Dumfries, *cr.* 1922; Bt., *cr.* 1914; **John Nivison;** *b.* 14 March 1878; *er. surv. s.* of 1st Baron and Jane (*d.* 1918), *d.* of John Wightman, Sanquhar; *S.* father 1930; *m.* 1920, Ivy May Rose; one *s.* three *d.* *Educ.:* Harrow. *Recreation:* shooting. *Heir:* *s.* Hon. Robert Nivison, Lt. Grenadier Guards [*b.* 27 Oct. 1926; *m.* 1953, Elizabeth, *yr. d.* of late Sir Cecil Armitage, C.B.E.; one *s.* two *d.*]. *Address:* Herontye, East Grinstead, Sx. *T.:* East Grinstead 23096; 47 Grosvenor Square, W.1. *T.:* Mayfair 1015; Aultmore, Nethy Bridge, Invernessshire. *T.:* 210. *Clubs:* Carlton, Bath. [*Died* 28 *Jan.* 1967.

GLENN, Air Vice-Marshal Robert William Lowry, C.B. 1960; C.B.E. 1957; retired; *b.* 11 July 1901; *s.* of Rev. William Glenn; *m.* 1938, Mary Britten, *d.* of Sir James Donald, C.S.I., C.I.E., LL.D. *Educ.:* Foyle Coll., Londonderry; Dublin University. Director of Postings (B.), Air Ministry, 1953-56; A.O.C. Records Office, Gloucester, 1956-58; Dir.-Gen. of Personal Services, Air Ministry, 1958-60; retd. 1960. *Recreations:* sailing, golf. *Address:* Owls' Roost, Gillham Wood Road Bexhill-on-Sea, Sussex. *T.:* Cooden 2325. *Club:* R.A.F. [*Died* 7 *April* 1970.

GLENNY, Alexander Thomas, F.R.S. 1944; B.Sc.; Immunologist; lately Wellcome Physiological Research Laboratories, Beckenham, Kent; *b.* 18 Sept. 1882; *s.* of Thomas Armstrong Glenny; *m.* 1910, Emma Blanche Lilian Gibbs; one *s.* one *d.* (and one *s.* decd.). *Educ.:* Alleyns School, Dulwich. Jenner Medal Royal Soc. Med. 1953; Addingham Medal, 1953. *Publications:* numerous articles on immunology in various scientific journals. *Address:* c/o 12 Gatesden Road, Fetcham, Leatherhead, Surrey. [*Died* 5 *Oct.* 1965.

GLENNY, William James, C.B.E. 1934; *b.* Nov. 14, 1873; *s.* of Thomas Armstrong Glenny and Elizabeth Forman; *m.* 1905, Jessie Reid MacLeish; one *d.* *Educ.:* Wilson's Grammar School; London Univ., B.A. Inspector General Dept. of Overseas Trade 1925-29; Commercial Counsellor, H.M. Legation, Stockholm 1929-34. *Publications:* Reports on Economic Conditions in Sweden, Feb. 1930 and April 1932. *Address:* Westholme, Laton Road Hastings. *T.:* Hastings 2884. [*Died* 6 *Aug.* 1963.

GLOVER, Maj.-Gen. Sir Guy de Courcy, K.B.E., *cr.* 1944; C.B. 1941; D.S.O. 1918; *b.* 1887; *s.* of late Colonel R. F. B. Glover, D.S.O.; *m.* 1918, Vera Phœbe, *d.* of Rev. T. M. Bell-Salter; one *s.* two *d.* *Educ.:* Cheltenham; Sandhurst. Served European War, 1914-18 (despatches six times, Bt. Major, Bt. Lt.-Col., D.S.O., M.C., 1914 Star, Portuguese Order of Aviz, 2nd class, Italian Silver Medal for military valour, two medals); commanded 2nd Battalion The South Staffordshire Regt. 1931-34; A.A.G. War Office, 1934-38; Comdr., Bombay District, India, 1939-40; Director of Recruiting and Organization 1940; Deputy Adjutant-General (B), 1940-46; retired pay, 1946. Col. of S. Staffs. Regt., 1946-55. *Clubs:* Army and Navy; Royal Yacht Squadron (Cowes) [*Died* 30 *April* 1967.

GLOVER, Sir Harold Matthew, Kt., *cr.* 1942; *b.* 29 Oct. 1885; *s.* of George Henry Glover, Worcester, and Hester Amy, *d.* of Charles Mason Collins, Napleton House, Worcs.; *m.* Mildred Ethel (*d.* 1961), *d.* of Alderman H. C. Gardner, J.P., Ombersley, Worcestershire; two *s.* one *d.* *Educ.:* Worcester Royal Grammar School; Magdalen Coll., Oxford (Mathematical Demy)-1st Cl. Mathematical Mods. 1906; 1st Cl; Hons. School of Natural Science, 1907. Diploma of Forestry, 1908. Indian Forest Service, 1908; Political Assistant to Superintendent Hill States, Simla, 1914; officiated as Conservator 1925, confirmed 1933; Chief Conservator of Forests, Punjab, 1939-43; retired, 1943; employed on special duty by Punjab and Baluchistan Govts. 1944; Director Forest Management Allied Control Commission for Germany (British Section), Jan.-March 1945; Forest Adviser Allied Commission for Austria (British Element), 1945-46. Toured and lectured on Soil Conservation on behalf of British Council, in Brazil, Peru, Columbia, Jamaica, Cuba, Mexico, 1950, and in Tanganyika, Kenya and the Middle East, 1952. *Publications:* Soil Erosion (Oxford pamphlets on Indian Affairs, 1944); Soil Erosion in the Punjab, 1945; numerous technical articles. *Recreations:* fishing and shooting. *Address:* Uphampton, Ombersley, Worcestershire *T.:* Ombersley 292. [*Died* 22 *Dec.* 1961.

GLOVER, James Alison, C.B.E. 1941 (O.B.E. 1919); M.D. (Camb.), F.R.C.P. (London) D.P.H.; late Senior M.O., Board of Education; Deputy Senior Medical Officer, Ministry of Health; *b.* 21 Feb. 1876; *s.* of late James Grey Glover, M.D.; *m.* Katharine, *d.* of Charles Pierce Merriam; three *s.* (and one *s.* decd.). *Educ.:* St. Paul's School; St. John's Coll., Cambridge; Guy's Hospital. Served S. African War, C.I.V., 1900; European War, R.A.M.C., 1914-19, Malta, France, Officer in charge cerebro-spinal fever laboratory, London (O.B.E.); Milroy Lecturer, Roy. Coll. of Physicians, 1930; late Lecturer in Physic Gresham Coll.; Jenner Medal and Hon. Fellowship, 1951, Roy. Soc. Med., ex-President, Section of Epidemiology. Hon. Freeman, City of London. *Publications:* Official Reports to Medical Research Council and Ministry of Health, and papers on Cerebro-spinal Fever, Incidence of Rheumatic Diseases, Acute Rheumatism and Heart Disease, Chronic Arthritis, Dysentery, nasopharyngeal infections, tonsillectomy, purification of the water of swimming baths, etc. *Address:* Merriam's, Gravel Path, Berkhamsted, Herts. [*Died* 17 *Sept.* 1963.

GLOVER, Major-General Malcolm; C.B. 1947; O.B.E. 1942; retired; *b.* 25 July 1897; *m.* Jean, *d.* of late Col. J. Will, R.A.M.C.; two *s.* one *d.* *Educ.:* Birkenhead School; Staff College. Served European War, 1914-19, with South Lancashire Regiment; transferred Indian Army; 14 Punjab Regiment. War of 1939-45, A.M.G.O. G.H.Q. India, 1940; B.G.S. H.Q. North Western Army, 1941; Commander 3 Indian Infantry Brigade, 1943; Director of Organization G.H.Q. India (Maj.-Gen.) 1944; Deputy Adjutant General, 1946; retired 1948. *Address:* 5 The Lawn, Budleigh Salterton, Devon. [*Died* 26 *Nov.* 1970.

GLUNICKE, Major-General R. C. A.; R.M. retired; D.L.; *b.* 6 March 1886; *m.* 1933, Mrs. Gammell, *d.* of Joseph Miller and *widow* of Kensington Gammell, Bedford. *Educ.:* Bedford School. 2nd Lieut. Royal Marine Light Infantry, 1904; Capt. 1915; Major, Royal Marines, 1927; Lt.-Col. 1934; Colonel, 1935; Brigadier, 1939; Major-General, 1940; war service, in H.M. Fleet to 1916; East African Expeditionary Force, 1916-17 (despatches), Adjutant Divisional Artillery and Staff Captain, R.A., G.H.Q.; Adjutant, Chatham Division, 1918-22; Qualified Naval Staff College, 1923; Brigade Major, Chatham Division, 1930-33; Commandant, Plymouth Division. Royal Marines, 1939-41; A.D.C. to the King, 1939-40; retired list, 1941; D.L. Beds. 1953. *Address:* 33

Conduit Road, Bedford. *T.:* Bedford 2026. *Club:* United Service. [*Died* 20 *Oct.* 1963.

GLYN, Sir Francis Maurice Grosvenor, K.C.M.G. 1954; Director: Bank of London and South America, Ltd.; Glyn, Mills & Co. (late Chairman); formerly Dep. Chm. of Advisory Council of Exports Credits Guarantee Department, Board of Trade; J.P. Herts; *b.* August 1901; *s.* of Maurice G. C. Glyn and Hon. Maud Grosvenor; *Heir-pres.* to 5th Baron Wolverton; *m.* 1st, 1926, Jane, *d.* of William Perkins, Seattle, U.S.A. one *s.* one *d.*; 2nd, 1941, Mary Elspeth Milln (*d.* 1966). *Educ.:* Eton. *Recreations:* shooting, fishing. *Address:* Hole Farm, Albury, Much Hadham, Herts. *T.:* Albury 209. *Club:* Boodle's. [*Died* 15 *Dec.* 1969.

GLYNN, Air Commodore Arthur Samuel, C.B.E. 1940; M.B., Ch.B.; late Principal Medical Officer, Fighter Command, Royal Air Force; *b.* 29 June 1885; *s.* of late Major Martin Glynn, M.B.E., late The Seaforth Highlanders; *m.* 1st, 1925, Helen Moya (*d.* 1946), *d.* of late Thomas Lennard-Charles; no *c.* 2nd, 1948, Evelyn Dorothy, *d.* of late William Henry Pulleine; no *c.* *Educ.:* Dover College; George Watson's College, Edinburgh; Edinburgh University. Joined R.A.M.C. 1914, served throughout European War, 1914-19, in France, Italy and Salonica (despatches twice), transferred to R.A.F. 1918; Principal Medical Officer, Royal Air Force, Middle East, and Iraq; K.H.S. 1938-42; retired list, 1942. *Publications:* A Chapter on the Transport of Casualties by Air in Organisation, Strategy and Tactics of the Army Medical Services in War, by Lieut.-Colonel T. B. Nicholls, R.A.M.C. *Address:* P.O. Box 322, Malindi, Kenya. [*Died* 15 *April* 1967.

GOBLE, Leslie Herbert, C.M.G. 1953; retired, 1961; *b.* 10 August 1901; *s.* of late James Blackley and Phoebe Elizabeth Goble, Lydd, Kent; *m.* 1921, Lilian Miriam (*d.* 1963), *d.* of late John and Louisa Greenwood Pinder Hague Cunningham, Liverpool; one *s.* (one *d.* decd.). *Educ.:* King's School, Canterbury; Royal Military College, Sandhurst. Entered Army, 1920; joined 1st Bn., The Worcestershire Regt., 124th Baluchistan Rifles, 1922; apptd. Administrative Officer, Nigeria, 1924; Senior District Officer, 1943; Resident, 1945; Senior Resident, 1947; Secretary, Northern Provinces, 1947; Administrative Secretary to the Government of Nigeria, 1952. Acting Chief Secretary to Government and Governor's Deputy on various occasions. Member: International Tin Council representing the Government of the Federation of Nigeria, 1955-61, International Tin Research Council, 1957-61. *Address:* 45A, Earl's Avenue, Folkestone, Kent. *T.:* Folkestone 54875. [*Died* 31 *July* 1969.

GODDARD, Thomas Herbert, C.B.E. 1941; B.A.; M.B.; Medical Practitioner, Hobart, 1919-45; Director of Tuberculosis, Tasmania (retired); Consular Agent for France in Tasmania (retired); Hon. M.O. Tasmanian Sanatorium, 25 yrs.; Officer-in-charge, Hobart Chest Clinic, 8 yrs.; Captain A.A.M.C., 1917-19; *b.* 26 March 1885; *s.* of Alfred Russell Goddard, born Rye, England, and Eliza, born Enniskillen, Ireland; *m.* 1916, Dagmar Charlotte Jones (decd.); one *d.* *Educ.:* Maitland High Sch., N.S.W.; Sydney University, B.A. 1904, M.B. 1914. Assistant Medical Officer Mt. Bischoff Mine, Tasmania, 1914; Medical Superintendent Hobart General Hospital, 1915-17; Medical Officer Claremont Military Camp, Tasmania, 1917-18; Officer in charge Tasmanian Quarantine Station, 1919; visited England, Europe, America in 1935 for study of Pulmonary Tuberculosis. President Alliance Française, Hobart, 1925-. Former President Tasmanian Branch of B.M.A. K.St.J. 1944; Chevalier, Légion d'Honneur, 1952. *Publications*: Report on Investigation of Tuberculosis in Wives and Dependants of Tuberculous Ex-soldiers, 1944; Control of Tuberculosis in Tasmania, 1945. *Recreation*: tennis. *Address*: Villa Waratah, Rond Point, Terre Adélie, St. Raphael, Var, France. *Club:* Tasmanian. [*Died* 17 *Feb.* 1967.

GODFREY, Walter Hindes, C.B.E. 1950; F.S.A., (V.P., 1947-51); F.R.I.B.A., Architect and Author; Director, National Buildings Record, 1941-60; *b.* 1881; *e. s.* of Walter Scott Godfrey and Gertrude Annie Rendall; *m.* Gertrude Mary (*d.* 1955), 2nd *d.* of Alexander Grayston Warren; one *s.* three *d.* *Educ.:* Whitgift School. Member of Royal Commission on Historical Monuments (England) and Advisory Cttee. to the Minister of Housing and Local Government; Member of Councils of: Sussex Archæological Soc., 1922-56 (V.P. 1951- President 1957); Sussex Record Society, 1924-56 (Chairman, 1934-1956, V.P. 1957-); London Soc.; Georgian Gp.; V.P. and Hon. Editor of the London Topographical Soc., 1928-58; Hon. Editor of The London Survey Cttee., etc. Hon. V. P. of the Royal Archæological Institute, Hon. Secretary, 1928-31; V.P. Council of British Archæology, 1952-54; Trustee of the London Museum and Sir John Soane's Museum and Historic Churches Preservation Trust. Commenced architectural practice, 1905; R.I.B.A. Silver Medallist (Essay), 1906. Consulting Architect, Beverley Minster, 1953-59. Works include (besides new bldgs.) the rebuilding of Crosby Hall at Chelsea, Memorial Chapel, Eton College, the restoration of a number of ancient buildings (Burford Priory, Sudeley and Herstmonceux Castles, Old Surrey Hall, Temple Church, London, Dorchester Abbey, Chelsea Old Church, etc.) and the planning of gardens; devised a system of Service Heraldry for recording service in the European War. *Publications:* The Life of George Devey, 1907; A History of Architecture in London, 1911 (new ed. 1962); The English Staircase, 1911; The Parish of Chelsea, 1909-27; (with Sir A. W. Clapham), Some Famous Buildings and their Story, 1913; Gardens in the Making, 1914; The Story of Architecture in England, 1931; Our Building Inheritance, 1944; The Church of St. Bride, Fleet Street, 1944; The English Almshouse, 1955; Guides to Sussex churches; (edited) The Book of John Rowe, and Sussex (Medieval) Wills for the Sussex Record Society; (Ed.) Colsoni's Guide de Londres (1693); etc.; contributor to architectural and archæological journals. *Recreations:* architectural and topographical research. *Address:* 81 The Causeway, Steventon, Abingdon Berks. *T.:* Steventon 265. [*Died* 16 *Sept.* 1961.

GODFREY, His Eminence Cardinal William, D.D. (Greg.), Ph.D.; Archbishop of Westminster since 1956; *b.* Liverpool, 1889; *y. s.* of George Godfrey and Maria Garvey. *Educ.:* Ushaw College, Durham; Venerable English College, Rome. Took Doctor's Degree in Philosophy at Gregorian University, Rome, 1913; Priest, 1916; took Doctor's Degree in Theology at Gregorian University, Rome, in a Solemn Public Defension (Public Act), 1917; attached to parish of St. Michael, West Derby Road, Liverpool E. as curate, 1917-19; Professor of Classics at Ushaw College, Durham, 1919-1920; of Philosophy, 1920-28; of Dogmatic Theology, 1928-30; Rector of the Venerable English College, Rome, 1930-38; Domestic Prelate of His Holiness Pope Pius XI, 1930; member of Supreme Council of the Propaganda Fidei; accompanied Cardinal Lépicier as member of the Papal Legation to Malta, 1935; Hon. Canon of Collegiate Church of St. Lawrence, Vittoriosa, Malta 1935;

Counsellor of the Papal Mission, for Coronation of King George VI, 1937; Papal Visitor of Seminaries and Ecclesiastical Colleges in England, Wales, and Malta, 1938; Apostolic Delegate to Great Britain, Malta, Gibraltar, 1938-54; to Bermuda, 1953-54; Titular Archbishop of Cius, 1938-53; Archbishop of Liverpool, 1953-56; Chargé d'Affaires for the Holy See to the Polish Republic, 1943; Assistant at Pontifical Throne, 1953. Exarch to Ukrainians in England and Wales, 1957-. Created a Cardinal, Dec. 1958; Holds Order of Polonia Restituta; Bailiff Grand Cross of Honour and Devotion, of the Sovereign Order of Malta, 1958; Grand Officer of Order of the Holy Sepulchre, 1951. *Publications:* two books of spiritual conferences: The Young Apostle and God and Ourselves; various articles in Catholic periodicals. *Recreation:* music. *Address:* Archbishop's House, Westminster, S.W.1. *Club:* Athenæum. [*Died* 22 *Jan.* 1963.

GODFREY-FAUSSETT, Brig. Bryan Trevor, C.B. 1945; D.S.O. 1944; O.B.E. 1940; M.C. 1917; *b.* 28 Nov. 1896; *s.* of Richard Fermor Godfrey-Faussett; *m.* 1925, Katherine Monica, *d.* of J. H. Paterson, Harviestoun House, Gorebridge, Midlothian; one *s.* one *d.* *Educ.:* R.N. College, Osborne; Wellington College; R.M.A., Woolwich; Jesus College, Cambridge. Commissioned R.E. 1915; European War, France and Flanders, 1915-18 (despatches); Major, 1932; Brevet Lieut.-Col. 1938; Col. 1941; Brig. 1941; Operations in France and Belgium, 1940; N. Africa and Italy, 1943-45 (despatches); Chief Engineer 8th Army, 1944; Chief Engineer 15th Army Group, 1945; Commandant School of Military Engineering, 1946-48. A.D.C. to the King, 1946. Bronze Star Medal (U.S.A.). *Address:* The Old Rectory, Badlesmere, Near Faversham, Kent. [*Died* 17 *Dec.* 1970.

GODSALL, Walter Douglas, C.M.G. 1949; Consultant to Messrs. Preece, Cardew and Rider, Consulting Engineers, Westminster since 1957; *b.* 26 January 1901; *er. s.* of Walter Godsall and Fanny Mary Chinn; *m.* 1926, Anne Jane, *er. d.* of John Macdonald; three *d.* *Educ.:* Bromsgrove School; Worcester College, Oxford. Cadet, Ceylon Civil Service, 1923; various administrative appointments, 1924-33; temporarily attached Colonial Office, 1933-34; Controller of Establishments, General Treasury, Ceylon, 1935; Asst. Chief Sec. and Sec., Public Services Commission, 1939; Chief Censor, Ceylon, Sept. 1939; Controller of Establishments, General Treasury, Ceylon, 1940, Controller Finance and Supply, 1942; Controller Finance and Accounts, British Military Admin. Malaya, with rank of Brig., 1945; Financial Sec., Malayan Union, 1946; Financial Sec., Federation of Malaya, 1948; Member, East African and Somaliland Protectorate Salaries Commissions, 1953; Chm. Civil Service Commn., Kenya, 1954-55; conducted Salaries Review, Hong Kong; enquiry into organisation of Electricity Corp. of Nigeria and Salaries Commn., Barbados, 1956. *Recreations:* golf and billiards. *Address:* Tregaron, New Park Road, Cranleigh, Surrey. *T.:* 598. *Club:* East India and Sports. [*Died* 16 *Oct.* 1964.

GODWIN-AUSTEN, General Sir Alfred Reade, K.C.S.I., *cr.* 1946; C.B. 1941; O.B.E.; M.C.; *b.* 17 April 1889; 2nd *s.* of late Lt.-Col. A. G. Godwin-Austen, 24th and 89th Regiments. *Educ.:* St. Lawrence College, Ramsgate; R.M.C., Sandhurst. Joined S. Wales Borderers, 1909; served in European War, Gallipoli and Mesopotamia, 1915-19, on Staff 40th Inf. Bde. and 13th Div. (despatches twice, M.C., O.B.E.); Staff College, Camberley, 1923-25; Staff appointments War Office, R.M.C. Sandhurst and Egypt; Commanded 2nd Bn. D.C.L.I., 1936-37; employed with Brit. Mil. Mission to Egyptian Army, 1937-38; Commanded 14th Inf. Bde. in Palestine Rebellion, 1938-39 (despatches); Major-General 1939; Commanded 8th Division, 1939; served in E. Africa and Abyssinia (C.B.) and Libya; War Office, 1943-45; Q.M.G. India Command New Delhi, 1945; Principal Administrative Officer, India Command, New Delhi, 1945-46; Lt.-Gen. 1946; General 1946; retired pay, 1947. Chairman South-Western Div., N.C.B., 1946-48. Col. S. Wales Borderers, 1950-54; Hon. Col. 2nd Bn. The Monmouthshire Regt., 1950-54. *Publications:* The Staff and The Staff College, 1927; various articles in Military Journals. *Recreation:* tennis. *Address:* Ladye Place, Hurley, nr. Maidenhead, Berks. *T.:* Hurley 250. [*Died* 20 *March* 1963.

GOFF, Captain Reginald Stannus, C.B.E. 1946; D.S.O. 1918; late R.N.; *b.* 27 Feb. 1882; 2nd *s.* of late Lt.-Col. Trevor Goff; *m.* 1918, Vera Colville (*d.* 1963), *widow* of Col. A. D. Geddes, The Buffs. Entered H.M.S. Britannia, 1896; Midshipman, 1897; Sub-Lt. 1901; Lieut. 1903; Comm. 1916; retired list, 1922; Capt., retired, 1927; Russian Order of St. Anne with crossed swords, 1916; King Haakon VII Liberty Cross (Norwegian), 1947. *Address:* Chillaway Lodge, Crondall, Hants. *Clubs:* Naval and Military; Royal Yacht Squadron (Cowes). [*Died* 12 *Nov.* 1965.

GOLDHAWK, Rev. Ira G.; Minister Winchmore Hill Methodist Church; *b.* Kimbton, Hertfordshire; *s.* of George Goldhawk; *m.* Mary Elisabeth, *o. d.* of Arthur A. Armstrong, Kimpton, Herts.; one *s.* *Educ.:* Richmond College. Superintendent Minister Albert Hall Mission, Nottingham, 1918-26; West London Mission, Kingsway Hall, 1926. *Recreation:* golf. *Address:* 53 Church Hill, N.21. [*Died* 21 *Aug.* 1967.

GOLDIE, Archibald Hayman Robertson, C.B.E. 1951; D.Sc.; F.R.S.E.; Deputy Director, Meteorological Office, Air Ministry, until 1953; *b.* 1888; *s.* of late Rev. Andrew Goldie, M.A., Glenisla, Angus; *m.* 1st, 1928, Marion Nairne (*d.* 1948), *d.* of late James Wilson, Dalkeith; no *c.*; 2nd, 1952, Helen, *d.* of late Percy Carruthers, Sandford, Devon. *Educ.:* Harris Academy, Dundee; University of St. Andrews; St. John's College, Cambridge. Wrangler, Mathematical Tripos, 1913; served European War, 1915-19 (despatches twice), temp. Major R.E. *Publications:* Papers in the Proc. and Trans. Royal Society of Edinburgh; Journal of Royal Meteorological Society, and in Memoirs of Meteorological Office, London. *Address:* 3 Laurelhill Place, Stirling. *T.:* Stirling 3859. [*Died* 24 *Jan.* 1964.

GOLDIE, Sir Noel Barré, Kt., *cr.* 1945; Q.C. 1928; Recorder of Burnley, 1929-35, of Manchester, 1935-56; *b.* 26 Dec. 1882; *o. c.* of late John Henry Goldie, of Southfields, Lillington, Leamington; *m.* 1911, Effie Agnes Graham, 2nd *d.* of late Charles Graham Rowe, of Alscott, Aigburth, Liverpool; two *d.* *Educ.:* Rugby; Trinity College, Cambridge. B.A., LL.B. 1904; called to Bar, Inner Temple 1905; Bencher, 1935; Reader, 1958; joined Northern Circuit; Commr. of Assize, South Eastern Circuit, 1947; Divorce Commr., 1947-1948. Member General Council of the Bar, 1932-1946; M.P. (C.) Warrington, 1931-45; Chairman United Club, 1935, 1936 and 1937; served European War in France and Belgium as Staff Captain Royal Artillery, 57th (West Lancs) Division (despatches); contested (C.) Warrington, 1929 and 1945. *Recreations:* golf, riding. *Address:* 7 Metropole Court, Folkestone, Kent. *T.:* Folkestone 54435; 3 Dr. Johnson's Buildings, Temple, E.C.4. [*Died* 4 *June* 1964.

GOLDING, Rev. Harry, C.B.E. 1940 (O.B.E. 1927); Brig. (ret.); *b.* 7 April 1889;

m. 1st, 1914, Ada Maud Spears (*d.* 1942); two *d.*; 2nd, 1961, Dame (Cecilie) Monica Johnson (*see* Dame Monica Golding). *Educ.:* Privately. In commerce as Chartered Secretary prior to war of 1914-18; enlisted ranks Devonshire Regt., 1916; Lieut., Royal Army Pay Corps, 1918; Captain, 1919; Major and Staff Paymaster, 1924; Lieut.-Colonel, 1929; Colonel and Chief Paymaster, 1937; served with Army of Occupation in Germany (O.B.E.) 1925-29. Served War of 1939-45 (despatches, C.B.E.); Brigadier, 1941. Army of Occupation, Germany, 1945-1947; retired from Army, 1949; Assistant Director of Expenditure, C.C.G., 1949-50; Deacon, 1952; Priest, 1953; Asst. Curate, St. Edyth's Church, Sea Mills, Bristol, 1952-1960. Was in Port Macquarie, New South Wales, during 1961. *Address:* 9 Sandford Court, 32 Belle Vue Road, Southbourne, Bournemouth *T.:* 44122. *Club:* United Service. [*Died* 30 *July* 1969.

GOLDSBROUGH, George Ridsdale, C.B.E. 1948; F.R.S. 1929; D.Sc. (Dunelm); F.R.A.S.; Professor of Mathematics, King's College, Newcastle on Tyne, in the University of Durham, 1928-48, emeritus since 1948; *b.* 19 May 1881; *s.* of late George Ridsdale Goldsbrough; *m.* Jennie, *d.* of late William Shotton; three *d.* *Educ.:* Bede School, Sunderland; Armstrong College, Newcastle on Tyne. Senior Mathematical Master, County School, Jarrow on Tyne, 1905; Lecturer in Applied Mathematics at Armstrong College, 1919; Reader in Dynamical Astronomy, 1922; Member of Senate of University of Durham, 1925-29, and 1933-49; Mem. Court of Univ. of Durham, 1937-61; Junior Proctor of University of Durham, 1929; Senior Proctor, 1931; Dean of the Faculty of Science, 1934-36; Dean of Faculty of Arts, 1936-38; Sub-Rector of King's College, Newcastle on Tyne, 1942-47; Member of Nat. Oceanographic Council, 1950-; Vice-Pres. Newcastle Lit. and Phil. Soc., 1954-. *Publications:* Papers in the Proceedings of the London Mathematical Society and in the Transactions and Proceedings of the Royal Society on problems of dynamical astronomy. *Address:* 49 Graham Park Road, Gosforth, Newcastle upon Tyne 3. [*Died* 26 *May* 1963.

GOLDSMITH, Frank, O.B.E.; T.D.; *b.* 1878; *m.* 1928; two *s.* *Educ.:* Magdalen Coll. Oxf. (M.A.), Honours in Law. Called to Bar, Inner Temple 1902; Mem. of Westminster City Coun. 1903-7; L.C.C. for South St. Pancras, 1904-10; was Whip of Municipal Reform Party. M.P. (C.) Stowmarket Division of Suffolk, 1910-18, Major in Suffolk Yeomanry; French Legion of Honour. *Address:* 1 Rue Scribe, Paris *Clubs:* St. James', Carlton, Buck's; Travellers (Paris). [*Died* 14 *Feb.* 1967.

GOLDSWORTHY, Captain Ivan Ernest Goodman, R.D.; R.N.R. retired; formerly Commodore of the Orient Line; *b.* 8 May 1894; *s.* of John and Ellen Goldsworthy; *m.* 1924, Enid Picton Thomas; one *s.* one *d.* *Educ.:* Jersey Modern School. Commenced sea career in a sailing ship, 1909; joined R.N.R., 1915; served European War, 1914-18 as Sub-Lieut. and Lieut. with Grand Fleet, until 1918; then in Baltic Sea, 1919; joined Orient Line, 1921. Took part in evacuation Norway and St. Nazaire, 1940; Commodore of Convoys 1941-45. *Recreation:* gardening. *Address:* Highmead, Steeple Lane, St. Ives, Cornwall. *T.:* St. Ives 5969. [*Died* 10 *June* 1970.

GOLLA, Frederick Lucian, O.B.E. 1919; F.R.C.P., M.B.Oxon; late Dir. of Burden Neurological Clinic (1939-); late Prof. of Pathology of Mental Disorders, University of London; late Director Central Pathological Laboratory for Research in Mental Diseases; late Physician St. George's Hospital; Physician Hospital for Paralysis and Epilepsy; Hon. Director Maudsley Hospital Medical School, University of London; President neurological section R. Soc. Med., 1934; Psychiatrical Section R. Soc. Med., 1940; Electro-encephalographic Soc., 1949; Soc. Study of Addiction, 1949; Hon. Member Royal Medical Psychological Soc., 1949; *b.* London, 1878; *s.* of Lucien Golla; *m.* 1st, 1908, Thérèse d'Haussaire; one *d.*; 2nd, 1919, Yvonne Ray (*d.* 1963). *Educ.:* Tonbridge Sch.; Magdalen College, Oxford. From 1905 has been engaged in research work in Neurology; joined B.E.F. as Lieut., 4 Aug. 1914; served with 2nd Division in France (despatches); subsequently on various War Office Committees; delivered Croonian Lectures, 1921; Maudsley Lecture, 1937. *Publications:* numerous Medical, Psychological and Physiological Publications. *Address:* Newlands, Frenchay, near Bristol. *T.:* Bristol 655977. [*Died* 6 *Feb.* 1968.

GOLLAN, Herbert Roy, D.S.O. 1919; M.C. 1918; *b.* 29 Aug. 1892; *s.* of Robert Harper Gollan and Harriet Wilson; *m.* 1920; no *c.* *Educ.:* Central School, Bendigo. Served with Hamilton Spectator and Geelong Advertiser; enlisted with Australian Imperial Force, Oct. 1914; served till Nov. 1919; Adjutant 54th Infantry Batt., Staff Captain 15th Infantry Brigade, and later Brigade Major (D.S.O., M.C., wounded, despatches thrice); Manager Victorian Government Tourist Bureau, 1923-28; Manager, The Argus and The Australasian, 1928-1937; Australian Government Trade Commissioner in India, 1939. Delegate to Eastern Group Supply Conference, 1941; Australian Member Eastern Group Supply Council, 1943-45; Senior Australian Government Trade Commissioner in India and Burma, 1945-49; High Commissioner for Australia in India, 1949-52; now retd. *Recreations:* bowls, trout fishing, horse riding. *Address:* Kings Road, Emerald, Victoria, Australia. *Club:* Upway-Tecoma Bowling. [*Died* 28 *March* 1968.

GOLLANCZ, Sir Victor, Kt. 1965; Publisher and Writer; President of Victor Gollancz, Ltd.; *b.* London, 9 April 1893; *s.* of Alexander Gollancz and Nellie Michaelson; *m.* 1919, Ruth Lowy; five *d.* *Educ.:* St. Paul's School; Oxford (Scholar of New College; Chancellor's Prize for Latin Prose). Taught at Repton, 1916-17; inaugurated with D. C. Somervell Civics Class and Political Education. Managing Director of Ernest Benn Ltd. (successful large-scale "paper-backs"), 1920-28; founded Victor Gollancz Ltd., 1928. When Japan attacked China, became Chairman of China Campaign Cttee.; subsequently devoted major attention, as publisher, pamphleteer and speaker, and through Left Book Club, to exposure of Nazism and attempt to halt Hitler without war; helped to found The National Cttee. for Rescue from Nazi Terror (Chm. late Archbishop Temple), 1941; organised "Save Europe Now" for relief of starvation in Germany and elsewhere, 1945; visited Germany, 1946, 1947; founded "Assoc. for World Peace", now "War on Want", 1951; as Chm., Jewish Soc. for Human Service, organised relief work for Arabs during Arab-Israel war, and later for Arab refugees in Gaza strip. Governor, Hebrew University of Jerusalem, 1944-52; Alternate Governor, 1952-64; Chairman, National Campaign for the Abolition of Capital Punishment, 1955-56, Jt. Chm., 1960-64, Chm., 1964-. Hon. LL.D., Dublin; Dr. jur. *h.c.*, Frankfurt, Peace Prize of West German book trade 1960. Glorious Star of China; Grand Cross of Order of Merit of Federal Republic of Germany; Goethe Medal. *Publications:* Our Threatened Values; Shall our Children Live or Die?; The Devil's Repertoire; The Case of Adolf Eichmann; Journey towards Music; *The Ring* at Bayreuth and Some Thoughts on Operatic Production;

autobiography: My Dear Timothy; More for Timothy; *anthologies:* A Year of Grace; From Darkness to Light; The New Year of Grace, 1961; God of a Hundred Names (with Barbara Greene), 1962; Reminiscences of Affection, 1968 (posthumous). Many pamphlets. Edited paper-back series The World Today (himself contributing Industrial Ideals), 1920-; published The Brown Book of the Hitler Terror, 1933. *Recreations:* listening to music, arguing, travelling, playing poorish bridge. *Address:* 90 Eaton Place, S.W.1. [*Died* 8 *Feb.* 1967.

GOMME-DUNCAN, Col. Sir Alan G.; *see* Duncan, Col. Sir A. G. G.

GOMPERTZ, Frank P. V.; *see* Vincent-Gompertz.

GONZALEZ-LLUBERA, Ignacio Miguel, M.A. (Belfast); Dr. en L. (Madrid); Emeritus Professor of Spanish, Queen's Univ. of Belfast; *b.* Barcelona, 1893; *e. s.* of late Don Leoncio González Llopis, Barcelona, and Doña Clotilde Llubera y Blanch; *m.* 1921, Jeanne Georgette Montrouge; two *d.* *Educ.:* Colegio del Sdo. Corazón, Barcelona; Univs. of Barcelona, Madrid, and Paris. Lic. en Filosofía y Letras, Barcelona; Premio Extraordinario and Premio Rivadeneira of Faculty of Philosophy, Barcelona Univ.; Doctorate at Univ. of Madrid; Research Scholar at Centro de Estudios Históricos, Madrid, and at École des Hautes Études at the Sorbonne. Musgrave Professor of Spanish Language and Literature (1926-60), Dean of the Faculty of Arts (1941-44 and 1954-56), Queen's Univ. of Belfast; visiting professor in Medieval Literature, Univs. of Barcelona and Toronto; past Examiner in Spanish, Univs. of Oxford, Cambridge, Birmingham, Manchester, Liverpool, Sheffield, Edinburgh, Glasgow, and various other bodies; Corresp. Member of Hispanic Society of America, Real Academia de Buenas Letras, and Institut d'Estudis Catalans (Barcelona). *Publications:* Los Viajes de Benjamin de Tudela, 1918; Nebrija, Gramática de la Lengua Castellana, 1926; Ibn Sabara, Llibre d'Ensenyaments, 1931; Coplas de Yoçef: A Medieval Spanish Poem, 1935; Santob de Carrión, Proverbios Morales (a critical edition), 1947; Contributions to the Butlleti de la Biblioteca de Catalunya, Estudis Universitaris Catalans, Medium Aevum, Revue Hispanique, Hispanic Review, Romance Philology, Enciclopedia Hispano-Americana (Espasa-Calpe), New Chambers's Encyclopædia, etc. *Address:* 227 Chesterton Road, Cambridge. *T.:* 53600. [*Died* 19 *March* 1962.

GOOCH, Brian Sherlock, D.S.O. 1945, T.D.; D.L.; *b.* 1 Aug. 1904; 2nd *s.* of Sir Thomas Vere Sherlock Gooch, 10th Bt. (*d.* 1946), of Benacre Hall, Suffolk, and Lady Gooch (*d.* 1932); *m.* 1935, Monica Mary, *o. c.* of late N. A. Heywood, Glevering Park, Wickham Market, Suffolk; two *s.* two *d.* *Educ.:* privately; Caius Coll., Cambridge. Commanded Loyal Suffolk Hussars (55 Anti-Tank Regt., R.A., T.A.), 1944-49 (despatches, D.S.O.). Director British Red Cross Soc. Co. Suffolk, 1957 (Dep. Dir., 1955-57); J.P. Suffolk, 1954; High Sheriff, Suffolk, 1956; D.L. Suffolk, 1958. *Recreation:* hunting (Joint Master Norwich Staghounds, 1946, Master, 1962). *Address:* Tannington Hall Woodbridge, Suffolk. *T.:* Worlingworth 226. *Club:* Boodle's. [*Died* 15 *April* 1968.

GOOCH, Alderman Edwin George, C.B.E. 1944; M.P. (Lab.) Northern Norfolk since 1945; J.P., C.A., Norfolk; Journalist; President of the National Union of Agricultural Workers, since 1928; *b.* 15 January 1889; *y. s.* of late Simon Gooch, Wymondham, Norfolk; *m.* 1st, 1914, Ethel (*d.* 1953), *yr. d.* of late C. D. Banham, Wymondham, Norfolk; one *s.*; 2nd, 1960, Mary Agatha, *y. d.* of late W. Curl, Norwich. *Educ.:* Duke Street, Municipal Secondary School, Norwich. Started life as a blacksmith, later served in the printing trade; until election to Parliament was Chief Sub-Editor Norwich Mercury series of newspapers. Vice-Chm. Norfolk County Council and Norfolk Education Committee; Member Min. of Agriculture's Smallholdings Advisory Council; Member of Council Royal Agricultural Soc.; Vice-Chm. Agricultural Apprenticeship Council. *Recreations:* public, social, and political work. *Address:* Rydal Mount, Wymondham, Norfolk. *T.:* Wymondham, 3179. [*Died* 2 *Aug.* 1964.

GOOCH, George Peabody, O.M. 1963; C.H. 1939; Hon. Fellow of Trinity College, Cambridge; Hon. D.Litt. (Oxford and Durham), F.B.A.; *b.* 1873; *s.* of C. C. Gooch and Mary Blake; *m.* 1903, Sophie Else Schön; two *s.* *Educ.:* King's Coll., London; Trinity Coll., Camb. Studied in Berlin and Paris; M.P. (L., Bath, 1906-10; contested Bath, 1910; Reading, 1913; President of the Historical Association, 1922-25; President of the National Peace Council, 1933-36; President of English Goethe Society; Chairman of the Sir Richard Stapley Educational Trust. *Publications:* English Democratic Ideas in the 17th Century; Annals of Politics and Culture; History of our Time; History and Historians in the Nineteenth Century; Life of Charles, Third Earl Stanhope; Political Ideas from Bacon to Halifax; Germany and the French Revolution; Life of Lord Courtney; Nationalism; History of Modern Europe, 1878-1919; Franco-German Relations, 1871-1914; Germany; The Later Correspondence of Lord John Russell; Recent Revelations of European Diplomacy; Studies in Modern History; Before the War, 2 vols.; Studies in Diplomacy and Statecraft; Courts and Cabinets; Frederick the Great: Studies in German History; Maria Theresa and other Studies; Catherine the Great and other Studies; Louis XV; Under Six Reigns; The Second Empire; French Profiles: Prophets and Pioneers; Historical Surveys and Portraits; contributor to the Cambridge Modern History; editor, Contemporary Review, 1911-1960; joint editor: Cambridge History of British Foreign Policy; British Documents on the Origins of the War, 1898-1914. *Address:* Upway Corner Chalfont St. Peter, Bucks. [*Died* 31 *Aug.* 1968.

GOODALL, Sir Stanley Vernon, K.C.B., *cr.* 1938 (C.B. 1937); O.B.E. 1934; *b.* 1883; *s.* of late Samuel and Eliza Goodall; *m.* 1908, Helen (*d.* 1953), *d.* of late C. W. Phillips, Plymouth. *Educ.:* Owens School, Islington; Royal Naval Engineering Coll., Devonport; Roy. Naval Coll., Greenwich. Royal Corps of Naval Constructors, 1907, retired 1945; Instructor in Naval Architecture, Royal Naval College, 1914-15; Constructor Commander, R.N., 1917-19; Director of Naval Construction, Admiralty, 1936-44; Asst. Controller (Warship Production) 1942-1945; American Navy Cross; Charles Parsons Memorial Medal, 1941; An Hon. Vice-Pres. Roy. Instn. of Naval Architects; Past Prime Warden Company of Shipwrights; M.Inst.C.E. *Recreations:* croquet and gardening. *Address:* 50 Lyford Road, S.W.18. *T.:* Vandyke 8566. *Clubs:* Athenæum, United Service. [*Died* 24 *Feb.* 1965.

GOODCHILD, George: Author and Playwright; *b.* Kingston-on Thames, 1888; *s.* of George William Goodchild; *m.* 1913, Dora Mary Hill; one *s.* two *d.* Started as Publisher; associated with J. M. Dent and Sons, Jarrolds, Allen and Unwin; later, musical critic, Outlook, Saturday Review; served European War, commissioned R.G.A., 1916 wounded and gassed at Messines, 1917; invalided from Army, 1918; took up authorship as full-time job. *Publications:* Death on the Centre Court; Knock and Come In; The Triumph of McLean; Captain Sinister; Mountain Gold; Rainbow; Road to Marrakesh; The Splendid Crime; Hurricane

Tex; Tall Timber; The Black Orchid; The Monster of Grammont; Ace High; The Rain on the Roof; The Alaskan; Steve; The Yellow Hybiscus; The Freeze-Out; Quest of Nigel Rix; Colorado Jim, Trooper O'Neill; Jack O'Lantern; Rough Going; The Eye of Abu; The Isle of Hate; McLean Takes Charge Captain Crash Mushalong; No Exit; McLean Excels, and over 100 other novels. *Recreations:* tennis, golf, fishing. *Address:* Willow Cottage, Tilehouse Rd., Guildford, Surrey. *T.:* Guildford 2555. *Club:* Savage.
[*Died* 25 *March* 1969.

GOODCHILD, Norman Walter, C.B.E. 1961; Executive Director, Securicor (Midlands) Ltd., since 1967; *b.* 17 Mar. 1901; *s.* of Walter Goodchild, Bournemouth; *m.* 1928, Nancy Kathleen, *e. d.* of G. Fowler, Oxford; one *s.* *Educ.:* Bournemouth Municipal Gram. School. Served R.A.F., 1918-19. Electrical Engineer, 1919-22; Oxford City Police, 1922-1939 (Deputy Chief Constable, 1936-39); Chief Constable: Barrow-in-Furness, 1940-1944; Wolverhampton, 1944-66; West Midlands Constabulary, 1966-67. President, Wolverhampton and District Spastics Soc. O.St.J., 1952; Queen's Police Medal, 1955. *Recreations:* photography, gardening. *Address:* 38 Meadow Road, Wolverhampton. *Club:* St. John House. [*Died* 4 *May* 1970.

GOODEN, Rev. Malcolm Cecil Whitridge; Archdeacon of Adelaide, 1957-65, retd.; Archdeacon (Actg.) of Eyre Peninsula since 1962; *b.* Norwood, S. Australia, 10 July 1894; 4th *s.* of Henry Alfred Gooden, Norwood; *m.* 1925, Clare, *d.* of Edwin Measday, Glenelg, S. Australia. *Educ.:* Norwood Public School. S. Australian Public Service, 1910-23. Engaged in commercial activities, 1924-25. Ordained Deacon, 1927; Priest, 1928; Priest-in-Charge, Kaniva, Diocese of Ballarat, Victoria, 1928-30; Vicar of Linton, 1930-32; Vicar of Dimboola, 1932-34; Vicar of Port Fairy, 1934-36; Rector of Balaklava, Diocese of Adelaide, S. Australia, 1936-39; Rector of Strathalbyn, 1939-44; Organising Chaplain, Bishop's Home Mission Society, 1944-55; Rector, Henley Beach, 1955-62. Chaplain, A.M.F., 1941-46; Canon of Adelaide, 1948-57; Archdeacon of Strathalbyn 1953-57. National Vice-President, Australia, Church of England Boys' Society, 1965. Medal of Merit (Boy Scouts), 1939. *Recreations:* youth work, Boy Scouts and Church of England Boys' Society. *Address:* 4 Canning Street, Glenelg North, South Australia 5045, Australia. *T.:* 95.2657.
[*Died* 19 *May* 1969.

GOODFELLOW, Col. Napier George Barras, C.I.E. 1919; Indian Army, retired; *b.* 1878; *s.* of Col. George Ritso Goodfellow, C.I.E., I.S.C.; *m.* 1908, Aileen, (*d.* 1958), *d.* of H. C. Gompertz, Bedford; one *s.* (one *d.* decd.). *Educ.:* Bedford School; R.M.C., Sandhurst. Served European War, 1914-19 (wounded, despatches four times, Bt. Lt.-Col., C.I.E.); Kurdistan. 1919. Defence Medal, War of 1939-45, War Service and Special Constable. *Address:* c/o National and Grindlay's Bank, 54 Parliament Street, S.W.1; 40 Linden Rd., Bedford.
[*Died* 10 *Feb.* 1963.

GOODHART, Sir Ernest Frederic, 2nd Bt., *cr.* 1911; Barrister-at-law; *b.* 12 Aug. 1880; *e. s.* of 1st Bt. and Emma Sandford, *d.* of W. Bennett, J.P., of Ashgrove, Herefordshire; *S.* father, 1916; *m.* 1906, France; Evelyn (*d.* 1953), *d.* of M. F. Armstrongs one *d.* *Educ.:* Westminster, Merton College, Oxford; M.A. Called to Bar, Inner Temple, 1904; Western Circuit, Hants. *Heir: nephew,* John Gordon Goodhart, M.B., B.S., M.A. [*b.* 14 Dec. 1916; *m.* 1944, Margaret Mary Eileen, *d.* of late Morgan Morgan, Cray, Breconshire; one *s.* (*b.* 15 Dec. 1948), one *d.* *Educ.:* Rugby; Trinity Hall, Cambridge. Served War of 1939-45; R.N.V.R., 1942-45]. *Address:* 157 Ashley Gardens, S.W.1. *T.:* Victoria 3562. [*Died* 13 *Jan.* 1961.

GOODHART, Leander M.; *see* McCormick-Goodhart.

GOODLET, Brian Laidlaw, O.B.E. 1944; M.A., Sc.D. (Cambridge); M.I.Mech.E., M.I.E.E.; Managing Director, Brush Electrical Engineering Co., since 1957; Director Hawker Siddeley Industries and Hawker Siddeley Brush Turbines Ltd.; *b.* St. Petersburg (Russia), 13 March 1903; *s.* of late Charles William Goodlet and Agnes Mary Laidlaw; *m.* 1932, Norah, 2nd *d.* of late Rev. T. E. McCormick, Vicar of Broadclyst, Devon; two *s.* two *d.* *Educ.:* in Russia; Sheffield Univ.; St. John's College, Cambridge. Engineering training with Vickers Ltd., Sheffield and Metropolitan-Vickers Elec. Co., Ltd., Manchester, 1919-24; Technical Assistant and later Research Engineer, Metropolitan-Vickers Elec. Co., 1924-30; Research Engineer M.V.E. Co., 1932-36; Professor of Electrical Engineering, University of Birmingham, 1939-40; Temp. Comdr. S. A. Naval Force, 1941-46, serving on Africa and East Indies Stations and at Admiralty (O.B.E.); Professor of Electrical Engineering, University of Cape Town, South Africa, 1937-39 and 1940-50; Head, Engineering Research and Development Division. Atomic Energy Research Establishment, Harwell, 1950-56. Awarded Thomas Hawksley Gold Medal by Institution of Mechanical Engineers; Kelvin and Overseas Premiums by Institution of Electrical Engineers; Trevithick Premium by Institution of Civil Engineers. Chairman Naval Educ. Advisory Cttee., Admiralty, 1952. *Publications:* one book and various Technical and Scientific Papers. *Recreation:* rock-climbing. *Address:* Essex Lodge, Chaveney Rd., Quorn, Leics. *Clubs:* Athenæum, R.N.V.R.
[*Died* 27 *Oct.* 1961.

GOODMAN, Reginald Ernest, C.B.E. 1938; retired; *b.* 1886; *s.* of Herbert Alfred Goodman, architect, Newport, Mon., and Johannesburg; *m.* Doris Inyoni, 2nd *d.* of H. J. Roberts, J.P., Johannesburg; one *s.* (and *er. s.* presumed killed in action with R.A.F., 1944, Belgium) one *d.* *Educ.:* Bellevue, Queenstown; Fawcetts Academy, Cork, Ireland. Architecture, 1903-06; banking 1907-10; accountancy since 1911; accountant, Basutoland Government, 1916-27; financial secretary, Bechuanaland Protectorate, 1927-34; Auditor for Basutoland, the Bechuanaland Protectorate and Swaziland, 1934-47. *Recreation:* bowls. *Address:* Mirca, 36 Hillside Road, Fish Hoek, Cape Province, S. Africa. *T.:* 85861. [*Died* 25 *March* 1968.

GOODMAN, Sir Victor Martin Reeves, K.C.B. 1959 (C.B. 1951); O.B.E. 1946; M.C. 1919; Clerk of the Parliaments, 1959-63 (retd.); a Trustee of the British Museum, 1949-63; a Trustee of the Natural History Museum since 1963; *b.* 14 February 1899; *s.* of late George Henry Goodman and Mary Alice Reeves; *m.* 1st, 1928, Julian Morrell (marriage dissolved, 1946); two *s.* one *s.*; 2nd, 1948, Anstice Crawley. *Educ.:* Eton Coll. Served European War with Coldstream Guards in France and Germany, 1918-19; Intelligence Officer, 2nd Guards Brigade, 1919. Clerk in office of the Clerk of the Parliaments, 1920; Judicial Taxing Officer of the House of Lords, 1934; Principal Clerk of the Judicial Office, 1946; Reading Clerk and Clerk of Outdoor Committees, 1949; Clerk-Assistant of the Parliaments, 1953. Chief A.R.P. and Security Officer of the Palace of Westminster, 1941-45. *Address:* 32 Onslow Square, S.W.7.
[*Died* 29 *Sept.* 1967.

GOODMAN, Vyvian Edwin, M.B.E. 1950. J.P. for Bedfordshire; *b.* 13 Feb. 1889; *s.* of Frederick William Goodman, Kew Gardens,

Surrey, and Kate Edwards; *m.* 1922, Cissie Mary, *d.* of William Solomon Goodyear, London; one *s.* *Educ.:* Christ's Hosp. High Sheriff for Bedfordshire, 1942; J.P. 1925, D.L. County of Beds.. 1935-45; Chairman Beds. Territorial Army Association 1936-43; Chairman Beds. Education Committee, 1935-46; County Comdt., Beds. Special Constabulary. Liveryman of Stationers' Company, Renter Warden, 1943-1944; Mem. Roy. Instn.; Fell. Instn. of Works Managers. *Recreations:* book collecting and photography. *Address:* c/o National Provincial Bank Ltd., 94 Moorgate, E.C.2. *Clubs:* Devonshire, City Livery; Norfolk (Norwich). [*Died* 12 *April* 1961.

GOODMAN, Sir William George Toop, Kt., *cr.* 1932; M.Inst.C.E., M.I.E.E., M.I.E. (Aust.); Chief Engineer and General Manager Municipal Tramways Trust, Adelaide 1907-50, retired, 1950; Member Council Adelaide Univ., 1913-53; Chm. Finance Cttee. of University, 1936-53; *b.* 1872; *s.* of late W. H. Goodman, St. Peters, Kent; *m.* 1893, *d.* of T. Atreed; two *s.* four *d.* *Educ.:* St. George's College, Kent. Assistant Engineer Tramways Construction Branch, Public Works Dept., Sydney, N.S.W., 1897-1902; designing and supervising engineer, Dunedin City Corp., for Elec. Tramways system and hydro-electric power scheme, 1902-7; consulted by N.Z. Govt. 1903-6, South Aust. Govt. 1909, and Tasmanian Govt. 1911, *re* electric railway schemes; Chm. South Aust. Advisory Committee of Inst.C.E. London; Past President South Aust. Inst. of Engnrs. (1914). Member Royal Commission on Auckland Transport, 1928; Member special committee appointed by Commonwealth Govt. and Govts. of N.S.W., Victoria and South Aust. to inquire into the Hume Reservoir, 1929; Chm. of Royal Commission on South Aust. Railways, 1931; Commonwealth Rep. at World Power Conference held in Scandinavia, 1933; Chm. Birkenhead Bascule Bridge Technical Advisory Committee, 1936-1941; Member South Aust. Traffic Laws Committee since 1935; Chm. South Aust. Housing Trust, 1937-45; Technical Director South Aust. Portland Cement Co. Ltd., retired 1955 (Chairman, 1944-53); Director South Australian Branch of Commercial Union Assurance Co. Ltd., retired 1955; Member Council of South Australian Zoological Society; Member special committee appointed by Commonwealth Government to advise regarding its participation in the New York (1939) Exhibition; Director Transport Committee of Civil Defence Council of South Australia, 1939-45; visited N.Z. to advise Dunedin City Corporation on the future transport services, 1944; visited Launceston, Tas., to advise City Corporation on future transport services, 1945; Peter Nichol Russell Memorial Medal, 1945, Inst. of Engineers, Australia. *Address:* 108 Buxton Street, North Adelaide South Australia. *Club:* Adelaide. [*Died* 4 *Feb.* 1961.

GOODRICH, Henry E., J.P.; *b.* 6 Apr. 1887; *s.* of late Edward Goodrich; *m* 1911. Julia Murphy; two *s.* two *d.* *Educ.:* Balham Grammar School. Royal Navy; Metropolitan Police; Solicitor's Clerk. M.P. (Lab.) North Hackney, 1945-50. *Address:* 257 Evering Road, Hackney. E.5. *T.:* Amherst 1597. [*Died* 13 *April* 1961.

GOODRIDGE, Major Edwin, D.S.O. 1940; M.B.E. 1953; Royal Army Medical Corps, 1920-58, retired; Civil Servant, 1958; *b.* 7 April 1903; *m.* 1931, Maria Gale (*née* Newton); one *s.* (and one *s.* decd.). *Educ.:* Battersea Grammar School. *Address:* 7 Heathfield Court, Fleet Road, Fleet, Hants. *T.:* Fleet 6787. [*Died* 3 *April* 1969.

GOODWIN, Aubrey, O.B.E.; M.D.; B.S. Lond.; F.R.C.S. Eng. and Edin.; L.R.C.P. Lond.; Retd. as: Obstetric Surgeon, Westminster Hospital; Surg., Chelsea Hosp. for Women; Gynæcologist, Prince of Wales's General Hospital, N.14; Examiner to Universities of Cambridge, London and Central Midwives Board; *b.* 4 Sept. 1889; *y. s.* of late Professor Alfred Goodwin, M.A.Oxon., sometime Fellow of Balliol College, Oxford, and of late Sara Simmons, Coventry; *m.* 1915, Elsa Mary (*decd.*), *y. c.* of late John Rudhall, Grays, Essex; one *d.*; *m.* 1939, Lilian, *y. d.* of late Robert Roberts, Penycae, Wrexham, Denbighshire; three *d.* (one *s.* decd.). *Educ.:* University College School; Univ. College, London; Univ. Coll. Hospital, London. Hosp. appointments till 1914; served European War, R.A.M.C., 1914-19, at home, Salonika and Malta; Staff Officer to D.M.S., Malta Command with local rank of Major; retired with rank of Captain (O.B.E.); since the war has specialised in Obstetrics and Gynæcology, studying in Dublin and Edinburgh. *Publications:* (Joint) Sex Ethics: The Principles and Practice of Contraception, Abortion and Sterilization, 1934; Contributor: Midwifery, and Diseases of Women, by Ten Teachers; The Health of the Married Woman, Journal of State Medicine, 1936. *Recreations:* fishing, shooting, big-game hunting and photography. *Address:* Ern Fechan, Grange Road, Llangollen, Denbighshire. [*Died* 18 *Aug.* 1964.

GOODWIN, Engineer-Rear-Adm. Frank Rheuben, D.S.O. 1917; *b.* 23 Sept. 1875; *m.* 1st, 1901, Sybilla (*d.* 1942), *d.* of John Hutchinson, Hexham, Northumb.; two *s.* one *d.* (and one *s.* decd.); *m.* 2nd, 1950, Violet Vaux, *widow* of George Curwen Mumford. Served H.M.S. Trafalgar, Cretan Insurrection, 1897; in H.M.S. Terrible, South African War, 1899-1900 (Queen's medal and Natal clasp); China (Boxer) War, 1900 (medal); European War, Belgian and French Front, 1914-15; British Adriatic Squadron, 1915-18 (despatches, D.S.O., Italian Silver Medal for military valour, Chevalier Legion of Honour); Engineer Officer on staff of Adm. Comdg. Coast Guard and Reserves, 1911-15 and 1919-1922; Engr. Capt. of H.M.S. Hood, 1922-24, and during her Empire World Cruise, 1923-1924; Engr.-Inspector of Naval Gun Mountings at Woolwich Arsenal, 1925-27; retd. list, 1929; Lieut.-Colonel Commanding 18th Co. of London H.G., 1940-42. Governor of Public Schools, Voluntary Aided Grammar Schools and other educational foundations; Vice-Chm., British Home and Hospital for Incurables; Chairman, Assoc. of Governing Bodies of London Aided Grammar Schools, 1950-63. *Address:* 21 Carson Rd., West Dulwich, S.E.21. *T.:* Gipsy Hill 2710. [*Died* 9 *March* 1966.

GOODWIN, Sir Stuart (Coldwell), Kt., *cr.* 1953; D.L.; J.P.; Chairman of various companies, estate owner; *b.* 19 April 1886; *m.* 1909. *Educ.:* Retford Grammar School. Lord High Steward of Retford; Town Trustee of Sheffield; D.L. Nottinghamshire, 1958. Hon. LL.D. Sheffield Univ. K.St.J. *Recreation:* golf. *Address:* 406A Fulwood Road, Sheffield 10. *T.:* Sheffield 31079; Hexgreave Park, Newark, Nottinghamshire. *T.:* Farnsfield 208. [*Died* 6 *June* 1969.

GOODWIN, Lieut.-Colonel Thomas Frederick, D.S.O. 1940; T.D.; R.E.; Manager; *b.* 4 Dec. 1904; *m.* 1933, Lucia Vera May Pike; three *d.* *Educ.:* Durban, Natal. Engineer. *Recreation:* shooting, Kent County Champion (small bore), 1935. *Address:* Formerly of Leagrave, Luton; latterly in South Africa. [*Died* 18 *July* 1965.

GOOLD, Sir George Ignatius, 6th Bt. *cr.* 1801; *b.* 29 April 1903; *s.* of Sir George Patrick Goold, 5th Bt. and Mary, *d.* of Nicholas Browne; *S.* father, 1954; *m.* 1923, Rhoda, *d.* of Albert Benn, Port Pirie, S.

Australia; two *s*. *Heir:* *s*. George Leonard Goold [*b*. 26 Aug. 1923; *m*. 1945, Joy Cecelia, *d*. of William Cutler, Melbourne; one *s*. four *d*.]. *Address:* 30 Balmoral Road, Solomon Town, Port Pirie, S. Australia.
[*Died* 26 *April* 1967.

GOOSMAN, Hon. Sir (William) Stanley, Kt. 1965; retired from New Zealand Parliament, Dec. 1963; *b*. 2 July 1890; *s*. of George and Eliza Goosman, Mangere; *m*. 1912, Margaret Boyd; one *s*. *Educ.:* Mangere Public School. Farmwork and share-milking, 1903; started farming on own, 1911; carrying and road construction, 1921; retired from carrying and contracting, 1940. Entered Parliament, Member for Waikato, 1938; later Member for Piako and Waipa; Minister for Works, Electricity and Transport, 1949-57; Minister for Works and Electricity, 1960-63; retired Dec. 1963. *Recreations:* golf and racing. *Address:* 402 Thames St., Morrinsville, N.Z. *T.:* 7298. *Club:* Town and Country (Morrinsville).
[*Died* 10 *June* 1969.

GOOSSENS, Sir Eugene; Kt. 1955; F.R.C.M., A.R.C.M.; Conductor and Composer; *b*. London, 26 May 1893; *s*. of late Eugène Goossens (formerly conductor of the Carl Rosa Opera Co.) and Annie, *d*. of Aynsley Cook, operatic basso; *m*. 1st, 1919, Dorothy Millar, *d*. of late Frederick C. Smith Dodsworth; three *d*.; 2nd, 1930, Janet Lewis; two *d*.; 3rd, 1947, Marjorie Fetter Foulkrod. *Educ.:* Bruges Conservatoire; Liverpool Coll. of Music; Royal Coll. of Music, London (Liverpool Scholarship, 1907), studying with Rivarde (violin), Dykes (piano), Dr. Wood (harmony), Sir Chas. Stanford (composition). Began as violinist Queen's Hall Orchestra, London, 1911; Served as conductor various opera Companies, including Beecham Opera Co. (1916), British Nat. Opera Co., also Covent Garden Opera seasons and guest conductor London Symphony, Philharmonic, Albert Hall and Provincial orchestras, Royal Choral Society, Diaghileff Russian Ballet, Handel Society (London); went to United States 1923, as conductor Rochester (New York) Philharmonic Orchestra, continuing 8 years; conductor Cincinnati Symphony Orchestra, 1931-47; musical director Cincinnati May Festival, 1931, 1933, 1935, 1937, 1939 1941, 1943, 1946; resident conductor Sydney Symphony Orchestra and director New South Wales Conservatorium of Music, 1947-56. Has appeared as guest conductor symphony orchestras—New York, Boston, Philadelphia, San Francisco, Detroit, etc.; Composer (operas) Judith, Don Juan (Covent Garden, 1929 and 1937); The Apocalypse (oratorio); (orchestra) Two symphonies, Sinfonietta, Concertino, etc.; also chamber music, songs, piano music, etc. Chevalier of the Legion of Honour. *Publications:* comprise orchestral, instrumental, and vocal music; "Overture and Beginners" (Autobiography), 1951. *Address:* 76 Hamilton Terrace, St John's Wood, N.W.8. *Club:* Savage (London). [*Died* 13 *June* 1962.

GORDON, Alexander, C.I.E. 1938; Chief Engineer and Secretary to Government, Sind (retd.); *b*. 15 June 1886; *s*. of John Gordon and Elizabeth Russell; *m*. 1926, Muriel Annie Houlden; two *s*. one *d*. *Educ.:* Allan Glen's School; Glasgow University. After practical Training, joined P.W.D. India, 1909; posted to Sind and was there entire service, except for a period as Under Secretary, P.W.D., Bombay, 1920-23; retired, 1941. Provost of Helensburgh, 1952-55; Convener of Dunbartonshire, 1955-58. *Recreations:* golf, shooting, reading. *Address:* Woodville, Helensburgh, Scotland
[*Died* 17 *March* 1965.

GORDON, Lieutenant-Colonel Rt. Hon. Sir Alexander (Robert Gisborne), P.C. (N. Ireland) 1951; G.B.E. 1965 (C.B.E. 1949); D.S.O. 1918; D.L.; *b*. 28 July 1882; *e*. *s*. of A. H. Gordon, D.L., of Florida Manor and Delamont, Co. Down; *m*. 1914, Dorothea (*d*. 1962), *o*. *d*. of late Robert Gordon, Tulley Lodge, Kildare; no *c*. *Educ.:* Rugby; Royal Military College, Sandhurst. The Royal Irish Regiment, 1901; Served European War, 1914-1918; severely wounded at Le Cateau, 26th Aug. 1914; subsequently served on the staffs of 40th and 51st Divisions and VII Army Corps (D.S.O., promoted Bt. Lt.-Col., despatches five times, awarded Croix de Guerre); retired with the rank of Lt.-Col., 1923; Recommissioned as Major, 1940-42; H.Q. Staff N.I.D.; M.P. (U.) East Down, Parliament of Northern Ireland, 1929-49; Minister in the Northern Ireland Senate, 1951-61, Speaker, 1961-64. President Royal Ulster Agricultural Soc., 1952-64. *Address:* Delamont, Killyleigh, Co. Down. *Club:* Kildare Street (Dublin).
[*Died* 23 *April* 1967.

GORDON, Sir (Archibald) Douglas, Kt. 1943; C.I.E. 1934; D.L.; *b*. 14 Apr. 1888; *s*. of Alfred Ernest Gordon and Ada Marion Fellows; *m*. 1912, Aileene Marie Oliver; three *s*. two *d*. *Educ.:* Bedford School. Passed competitive examination into the Indian Police and appointed Assistant Superintendent of Police at Dacca in Bengal, 1907; Superintendent of Police, 1915; Assistant Inspector General, 1919; Principal Police Training College, Bengal, 1921; Deputy Commissioner of Police, Calcutta City, 1927; Deputy Inspector General of Police, Bengal, 1931; Officiating Commissioner of Police, Calcutta, 1935; Inspector General of Police, Bengal, 1938-42; Civil Security Adviser to G.O.C.-in-C. Eastern Command, India, and XIV Army, 1942-45; Dir.-Gen. of Enforcement, Bengal, 1945-46; retired from India, 1946; Chief of Brit. Police Mission, Colombia, 1948-1952. Vice-Pres. Beds. Assoc. of Boys' Clubs; Chm. of Governors, Harpur Trust; President Old Bedfordians Club; D.L. County of Bedford, 1957; High Sheriff, Bedfordshire, 1959. King's Police Medal, 1931; O.St.J. 1941; Grand Officer of Military Order of Merit (Antonio Narino), 1951; Colombia Police Badge for Distinguished Service, 1951. *Address:* Buttercups, Biddenham, Beds. *Club:* East India and Sports
[*Died* 21 *Sept*. 1966.

GORDON, Crawford, O.B.E. 1946; President, Gordon Enterprises Ltd., Canada; President and General Manager, A. V. Roe Canada Limited, 1951; President and Chairman of Exec. Committee, Dominion Steel and Coal Corp. Ltd.; Director: Canadian Liquid Air Co. Ltd., Montreal; Dominion Coal Co. Ltd., Montreal; Hawker Siddeley Group Ltd., London, Eng.; Nova Scotia Steel and Coal Co. Ltd., Montreal; Superior Propane Ltd., Toronto; Thor Industries Ltd., Toronto; Truscon Steel Co. of Canada Ltd., Montreal; Union Acceptance Corp. Ltd., Toronto; *b*. Winnipeg, Man., 26 Dec. 1914; *s*. of late Crawford Gordon and Ethel Fortune; *m*. 1937, Mary Marjorie, *d*. of John Tearney; one *s*. two *d*. *Educ.:* Appleby College, Oakville, Ont.; McGill University, Montreal (B.Com.). Dir.-General of Organization and Asst. Co-ordinator of Production, Dept. of Munitions and Supply, 1941-45; then Dir.-Gen. of Industrial Conversion, Dept. of Reconstruction and Supply (O.B.E.). President and Director, English Electric Co. of Canada Ltd., St. Catherines, Ont., and Exec. Vice-Pres., John Inglis Co. Ltd., Toronto, Ont., 1947; on loan to Federal Govt. as Co-ordinator of Defence Production, Feb.-Oct. 1951; resigned from English Electric Co., John Inglis Co., and associated companies, on joining A. V. Roe Canada Ltd. Trustee Quetico Foundation; Hon. Chm. Bd. of Governors, Queensway Gen. Hospital. Member Newcomen Society. Holds hon. degree of LL.D. Protestant.

Recreations: golf, squash, badminton. *Address:* 789 Lexington Avenue, Westmount, P.Q., Canada. *Clubs:* Toronto, Toronto Golf, Granite, Badminton and Racquet, York (Toronto); Rideau (Ottawa); Wings (New York). [*Died* 26 *Jan.* 1967.

GORDON, Donald, C.C. (Canada) 1968; C.M.G. 1944; LL.D.; President and Chief Executive Officer, British Newfoundland Corporation Ltd.; Chairman, Churchill Falls (Labrador) Corporation Ltd., since 1967; *b.* Old Meldrum, Scotland, 11 Dec. 1901; *s.* of John Gordon and Margaret L. Watt; *m.* 1st, 1926. Maisie Barter (*d.* 1950); two *s.*; 2nd, 1953, Norma Hobbs; one *s.* *Educ.:* public schools, Scotland and Canada. Bank of Nova Scotia, Toronto, Ont. 1916-35; Secretary, Bank of Canada, 1935; Deputy Governor, Bank of Canada, 1938; Chm. (alternate) Foreign Exchange Control Board, 1939; Chm., Wartime Prices & Trade Board, 1941, on loan, returning to the Bank of Canada, 1947; Director of the Industrial Development Bank, 1944-49; Exec. Director, Internat. Bank for Reconstruction and Development, 1948; retired from Bank of Canada, 31 Dec. 1949; Chm. and Pres., Canadian National Railways, 1950-66; Dir., Air Canada, 1950-66; Director: Bank of Montreal; Canadian Enterprise Development Corp. Ltd.; Canadian Investment Fund Ltd.; Canadian Fund Inc.; Hudson's Bay Co.; Rio Algom Mines Ltd.; British Newfoundland Corpn. Ltd.; Churchill Falls (Labrador) Corpn. Ltd.; Royal Trust Mortgage Corpn.; RCA Victor Co. Ltd.; Royal Trust Co. Hon. D.C.L., Bishop's Univ., 1958; Hon. LL.D.: Queen's Univ., 1947; Univ. of Western Ontario, 1952; McGill Univ., 1965; Univ. of Waterloo, 1966; Hon. D.Sc. C(om)., University of Moncton, 1966. K.G.St.J. 1958. Presbyterian. *Address:* (home) 172 Edgehill Road, Westmount, Montreal 6, P.Q., Canada; (business) 1980 Sherbrooke Street West, Montreal, P.Q. *Clubs:* St. James's, Mount Royal (Montreal); Toronto (Toronto). [*Died* 3 *May* 1969.

GORDON, Sir Douglas; *see* Gordon, Sir A. D.

GORDON, Sir Douglas F.; *see* Duff-Gordon.

GORDON, Col. Esme C. W.C.; *see* Conway-Gordon.

GORDON, Lt.-Col. Evelyn Boscawen, C.M.G. 1919; D.S.O. 1916; late Northumberland Fusiliers; *b.* 6 Oct 1877; *s.* of late Charles William Gordon, Wincombe Park Shaftesbury; *m.* Martha Florence, *d.* of late Dr. Wheldon, Mauritius. *Educ.:* Stubbington House, Fareham. Served South African War, 1900-02 (Queen's medal and clasp, King's medal and two clasps); N.-W. Frontier of India, 1907-08 (medal and clasp); European War, 1914-18 (despatches five times, Bts. Maj. and Lt.-Col., C M G., D S O). *Address:* Westhayes, Rockbourne, Hants. *Club:* United Servic . [*Died* 27 *Oct.* 1963.

GORDON, Col. George Hamilton, C.M.G. 1919; D.S.O. 1918; *b.* 1875; *s.* of late Col. James Henry Gordon, C.B., D.S.O., Indian Army; *m.* 1908, Mary Louise Stanley, *d.* of H. Stanley Parsons; one *s.* two *d.* Served European War, 1914-19 (despatches, D.S.O., C.M.G.). *Address:* c/o Barclays Bank, 61 Old Christchurch Road, Bournemouth. [*Died* 9 *May* 1961.

GORDON, Capt. Sir Henry Robert, Kt., *cr.* 1944; D.S.C.; formerly Commodore Captain, Shaw Savill & Albion Co. Ltd., retired; *b.* 1886; *s.* of Francis Thomas Gordon; *m.* 1914, Alice Maud Elliott. Joined Shaw Savill & Albion Co. Ltd., 1910; received first command in 1919, commanded the Wairangi, 1942; commanded The Dominion Monarch, 1943-51; retired, 1951. [*Died* 11 *Dec.* 1969.

GORDON, Herbert Ford, C.M.G. 1946; retired; *b.* 10 June 1882; *s.* of Rev. John A. Gordon, D.D., and Margaret Ann Ford; *m.* 1922, Alice May Brock; one *s.* one *d.* *Educ.:* St. John High School. Served in France, European War, 1914-18, Canadian Field Artillery; Superintendent The Soldier Settlement Board of Canada, 1922-35; Department of Finance, 1935-39; Director Farmers' Creditors' Arrangement Act, Administrator Municipal Improvement Assistance Act; Administrative Officer, Department of National Defence, since 1939; Assistant Deputy Minister; late Deputy Minister of National Defence for Air (Canada); retired, 1947; Member National War Labour Board, Inspection Board of U.K. and Canada, and Inventions Board of Canada; Vice-President of Supervisory Board of the British Commonwealth Air Training Plan. *Address:* 312 Daly Ave., Ottawa. *T.:* 3-7664. *Club:* Rideau (Ottawa). [*Died* 26 *April* 1963.

GORDON, Rt. Hon. John Fawcett, P.C. Northern Ireland; Chairman National Assistance Board, N. Ireland, 1943-56, retired; *b.* Belfast, 1879; *s.* of late Wm. Jas. Gordon and Margaret Fawcett Gordon; *m.*; one *d.* M.P. (U.) Antrim, Northern Ireland Parliament, 1921-29, Carrick Division, 1929-43; Parliamentary Secretary, Ministry of Labour, 1921-38; Minister of Labour for Northern Ireland, 1938-43. *Address:* Innisfayle Park, Belfast. *T.:* 77200. [*Died* 21 *June* 1965.

GORDON, Richard J., Hon. M.A. (Leeds, 1936), F.L.A.; *b.* 18 July 1881; *s.* of John Gordon and Margaret Creer; *m.* 1911, Blodwen, *d.* of Lewis Gill; two *s.* *Educ.:* Oxford Street School, Swansea. Assistant, Swansea Public Library; Chief Librarian, Rochdale, 1911-14; Chief Librarian and Curator, Rochdale, 1914-21; Chief Librarian, Sheffield, 1921-27; City Librarian, Leeds, 1927 46; Fellow of Library Association, 1914; Member of Library Association Council since 1925, Chm., 1936-37, Vice-Pres., 1938-45; Pres., 1947; Hon. Fellow, 1949; Chm. Yorkshire Regional Library System, 1935-45; Hon. Sec. Leeds Information Committee, Ministry of Information, 1939-45; Member Yorkshire Archæological Society Council, 1944-45. Visited Canada and United States on invitation of Carnegie Corporation of New York, 1934; Organiser of Edward Stott Memorial Exhibition and Edwin Waugh Centenary Exhibition and various art exhibitions. *Publications:* Editor of the Leeds What to Read pamphlets. *Recreation:* reading. *Address:* 2 Shelley Court, Parkleys, Ham Common, Richmond, Surrey. [*Died* 14 *Sept.* 1966.

GORDON, Rupert Montgomery, O.B.E. 1958; M.D., Sc.D., F.R.C.P., D.T.H., D.T.M.; retired as Dutton and Walter Myers Professor of Entomology and Parasitology, University of Liverpool, October 1958; *b* Dublin, 1893; *s.* of late Dr. S. T. Gordon, Surgeon to the Royal Irish Constabulary; *m.* Dr. Joycelyn Cronin Lowe; two *s* *Educ.:* privately; Trinity Coll., Dublin. Late Capt. R A M C., Salonica, 1916-19; Research Assistant, Liverpool School of Tropical Medicine's Laboratory at Manaos on the Amazon, 1920 and 1921, Professor of Tropical Diseases of Africa, University of Liverpool; Director Sir A L. Jones Research Laboratory, Freetown, Sierra Leone, 1930-37; Chalmers Memorial Gold Medal, 1937; Mary Kingsley Medal, 1958 President Royal Society of Tropical Medicine and Hygiene, 1955-57. *Publications:* Scientific papers in various Journals; Co-editor, Annals of Tropical Medicine and Parasitology. *Recreations:* various. *Address:*

Arcadia, 3 North Road, Grassendale Park, Liverpool 19. [*Died* 26 *July* 1961.

GORDON, Dr. William Smith, C.B.E. 1948; Director, Agricultural Research Council, Institute for Research on Animal Diseases, Compton, Berks., 1942-67; *b.* 1902; *s.* of Robert Gordon, Pollokshields, Glasgow; *m.* 1st, 1934, Mary Leone (*d.* 1956), *d.* of J. Findlay Porter, Edinburgh; one *d.*: 2nd, 1959, Elizabeth Webster, *d.* of Percy C. Greaves, Wakefield, Yorks; one *step s.* one *step d.* (decd.). Obtained M.R.C.V.S. Glas., 1923; Ph.D. Edin., 1934. Veterinary Officer, Min. of Agric., 1923-26; Research Officer, Wellcome Physiological Research Laboratories, Beckenham, Kent, 1926-30; Chief Bacteriologist, Moredun Inst., Edin., 1930-42. Contributed to investigation of diseases in farm animals and devised vaccines, now in general use, for prevention of certain diseases in sheep. F.R.S.E. 1938. *Publications:* in scientific jls. from 1926. *Recreations:* golf, tennis, shooting, fishing; Goring and Streatley Golf (Pres. 1962-67; Life Mem., 1967). *Address:* Handsmooth House, Ipsden, Oxon. *T.:* Checkendon 491. *Club:* Farmers'. [*Died* 20 *Oct.* 1967.

GORDON-SMITH, Frederic, Q.C. (Trinidad), 1934; *b.* 23 April 1886; *s.* of Walter Leopold Smith, solicitor, Dudley, Worcs, and Mary Elizabeth Beach; *m.* 1918, Elsie, *d.* of George Foster, Wassell Wood, Bewdley, Worcs; three *s.* *Educ.:* Bromsgrove School. Admitted solicitor, 1909; practised to 1913; Legal Dept., Livingstone, N. Rhodesia, under B.S.A. Co. administration, 1913; War service, German S.-W. and German E. African campaigns, with N. Rhodesia Police, 1915-18; Barrister-at-Law, Inner Temple, 1921; Assistant Legal Adviser and Public Prosecutor, N. Rhodesia, 1918-24; Assistant Attorney-General, 1924-26; Solicitor-General, Kenya, 1926-27; Attorney-General, N. Rhodesia, 1927-32; Attorney-General, Trinidad, 1932-35; Puisne Judge, Straits Settlements, 1935-41; acting Judge of Appeal for Malaya, 1939 and again 1940; Chief Justice of Palestine, 1941-43; Chm. Pensions Appeal Tribunals, 1945-48; Puisne Judge (Temp.) Singapore, June 1948, and acting Chief Justice; Chm. Public Services Commn., 1950-52; retired. *Publications:* Revised Editions of the Laws of N. Rhodesia, 1930. *Recreation:* golf: winner Rhodesian Golf Championship four times; Trinidad Golf Championship, 1934 and 1935 *Address:* Chelmer, 2 Merdon Avenue, Chandler's Ford, Hants. [*Died* 14 *Aug.* 1967.

GORE, Sir Ralph St. George Claude, 10th Bt., *cr.* 1621; late Major 2nd County of London Yeomanry; *b.* 12 May 1877; *S.* father, 1887; *m.* 1st, 1905, Elsie Vaughan (*d.* 1942), 2nd *d.* of late Henry Tully Grigg and Mrs. Grigg of Queensberry House, Richmond; one *s.*; 2nd, 1943, Mrs. Algernon Turnor, *widow* of Lt.-Col. A. C. Turnor, Royal Horse Guards. *Educ.:* Eton. Late Lt. Royal Dragoons. *Heir: s.* Lt.-Col. Ralph St. George Brian, Royal Dragoons [*b.* 31 May 1908; *m.* 1947, Phyllis Gabrielle, *o. d.* of M. van der Porten, New Rochelle, New York; one *d.*]. *Clubs:* Cavalry, Turf; Royal Yacht Squadron (Commodore). [*Died* 27 *March* 1961.

GORE-BROWNE, Colonel Sir Eric, Kt., 1948; D.S.O. 1918; O.B.E. 1939; T.D. 1925; Director: Glyn, Mills & Co. Provident Mutual Assurance Association (Chairman until 1963); Chairman, Oakham Sch.; Gov., Uppingham Sch.; Chm. of Trustees, Commonwealth War Graves Commission; *b.* 2 Oct. 1885; *s.* of late Spencer Gore-Browne of Rowledge, Farnham, Surrey; *m.* 1912, Mary Imogen, *d.* of late Rt. Hon. Charles Booth; two *s.* two *d.* *Educ.:* Malvern; Worcester Coll., Oxford (M.A.). Barrister-at-law; served European War, 1914-18 (despatches, D.S.O., Croix de Guerre); Lt.-Col. Cmdg. Leicestershire Yeomanry, 1933-1938; Col. 1939; on Staff, 1939-41; Controller of Rubber, 1943-44; A.D.C. to the King (Additional), 1938-48; Member of Royal Commission on Betting, 1949. High Sheriff, Rutland, 1957. *Address:* Glaston House, Uppingham, Rutland. *Clubs:* Brooks's, M.C.C. [*Died* 28 *May* 1964.

GORE-BROWNE, Lt.-Col. Sir Stewart, Kt., *cr.* 1945; D.S.O. 1917; late R.F.A.; *b.* 1883; *e. s.* of late Sir Francis Gore-Browne, K.C.; *m.* 1927, Lorna (marriage dissolved, 1950), *d.* of late Prof. Goldman, F.R.S.; two *d.* *Educ.:* Harrow; R.M.A., Woolwich. Assistant Comr. Anglo-Belgian Boundary Commission, 1911-14; served European War, 1914-18 (D.S.O., Bt. Lt.-Col., despatches, Chevalier of the Order of the Aviz, Order of St. Iago del Espada); M.L.C. and M.E.C., Northern Rhodesia, 1935-1951 resigned 1951. *Address:* Shiwa, Ngandu, Zambia. *Club:* Army and Navy. [*Died* 4 *Aug.* 1967.

GORELL, 3rd Baron, *cr.* 1909; **Ronald Gorell Barnes,** C.B.E. 1919 (O.B.E. 1918); M.C. 1917; M.A.; Hon. R.W.S.; Author; Colonel; Hon. Fellow, Royal Society of Teachers; Hon. Member N.U.T.; President, Royal Literary Fund; *b.* 16 April 1884; 2nd *s.* of 1st Baron and Mary Humpston, *d.* of T. Mitchell of West Arthurlie; *S.* brother, 1917; *m.* 1922, Elizabeth (*d.* 1954), *e. d.* of late Alexander N. Radcliffe; two *s.* one *d.* *Educ.:* Winchester; Harrow; Balliol College, Oxford. Barr. 1909; on the editorial staff of The Times, 1910-15; Capt. and Adjutant 7th Battalion The Rifle Brigade, 1915-16; Major, General Staff, 1917; as Deputy Director of Staff Duties (Education) at the War Office, 1918-20, founded Roy. Army Educational Corps; Pres., National Council for combating Venereal Diseases, 1920-1922; Under-Secretary of State for Air, July 1921-Oct. 1922. Chairman: King's College Hospital, 1929-33; Committees on Art and Industry, 1932; Control of Private Flying, etc., 1933-34 and 1938-39; Teachers' Registration Council 1922-35 (Pres. Royal Society of Teachers, 1929-35); Society of Authors, 1928-35; Royal Aero Club, 1933-36 and 1944-46; Prime Minister's Cttee. on Carlton House Terrace and other references, 1933-41; Prime Minister's Cttee. on Regent's Park Terraces, 1946. Editor of Cornhill Magazine, 1933-39. Coy. Cmdr., West Sussex Home Guard, 1940-45; Chairman, Refugee Children Movement, 1939-1948. Chm., Bd. of Governors, Dulwich College and Alleyn's School, 1949-59. Lay Reader C. of E., specially licensed for Chichester, Southwark and London dioceses, 1956-60. *Publications:* He walked in Light, 1954; One Man ... Many Parts, 1956; many volumes of poetry, fact, fiction, and religion. *Heir: s.* Hon. Timothy John Radcliffe Barnes [*b* 2 Aug. 1927; *m.* 1954, Joan Marion, *yr. d* of John Collins, Moseley, Birmingham]. *Address:* Tiplands, Burpham, Arundel, Sussex. *Clubs:* Oxford and Cambridge, Royal Aero. [*Died* 2 *May* 1963.

GORER, Peter Alfred, F.R.S. 1960; D.Sc. Lond.; M.R.C.P. Lond.; Reader in Experimental Pathology, Guy's Hospital Medical School, since 1948 (designate Professor of Immunology from 1961); *b.* 14 April 1907; *s.* of late Edgar Gorer and late Rachel Alice Cohen; *m.* 1st, 1941, Gertrude Kahler (*d.* 1945); 2nd, 1947, Elizabeth Bruce Keucher; one *s.* one *d.* *Educ.:* Golden Parsonage School; Charterhouse. Guy's Hosp. Med. School, 1924-32. B.Sc. 1929; D.Sc. Lond. 1940; M.R.C.P. Lond. 1950. Research Asst., Dept. of Genetics, Univ. Coll., 1933-34; Lister Inst., 1934-40; Actg. morbid histologist and haematologist, Guy's Hosp., 1940-46; Sen. research Fellow, Roscoe Jackson Lab., Bar Harbor, Maine, 1946-1947. *Publications:* contrib. to learned journals on tissue transplantation, leukaemia and other aspects of cancer research. *Recreations:* natural history, fishing, shooting. *Address:* 3 Fairway Close, Wildwood Rd., N.W.11. *T.:* Meadway 2459. *Club:* East India and Sports. [*Died* 11 *May* 1961.

GORMAN, Sir William, Kt., *cr.* 1950; **Hon. Mr. Justice Gorman;** Judge of the High Court of Justice Queen's Bench Division since 1950; *s.* of William Gorman, Wigan, Lancashire. *Educ.:* Wigan Grammar School. Barr., Middle Temple, 1921; K.C. 1932; Bencher, Middle Temple, 1938; Northern Circuit. European War, served in Royal Artillery: France, Belgium, and Italy, 7th Division; contested Royton Division of Lancashire, 1922, 1923 and 1924; M.P. (L.) Royton Division of Lancashire, 1923-24. Recorder of Wigan, 1934-48; of Liverpool, 1948-50. R.A.F.V.R. 1940-44; Wing Commander, Assistant Judge Adv. General, 1942-44. Pres., Caterham School, 1953-. Treasurer Middle Temple, 1959. Hon. Freeman of Wigan, 1954. Hon. LL.D. (Manchester) 1957. *Address:* 32 Kensington Court, W.8. *T.:* Western 1971. [*Died* 21 *Dec.* 1964.

GOSFORD, 6th Earl of, *cr.* 1806; **Archibald Alexander John Stanley Acheson,** O.B.E. 1946; Bt. of Nova Scotia, 1628; Baron Gosford, 1776; Viscount Gosford, 1785; Baron Worlingham (U.K.) 1835; Baron Acheson (U.K.) 1847; Group-Captain, Royal Air Force, retired, 1955; Chairman: British Universities' Sports Federation; British Road Federation; Vice-Pres. R.A.F. Assoc.; Pres., Vocational Guidance Assoc.; *b.* 14 Jan. 1911; *er. s.* of 5th Earl of Gosford, M.C., and Mildred (*d.* 1965), *d.* of John Ridgely Carter, Baltimore, U.S.A.; *S.* father 1954; *m.* 1st, 1935, Francesca Augusta (marriage dissolved, 1960), *er. d.* of Francesco Cagiati, New York; one *s.* two *d.*; 2nd, 1960, Cynthia Margaret Delius, *widow* of Maj. J. P. Delius, 13th/18th Royal Hussars. *Educ.:* Harrow; Trinity College, Cambridge (M.A.). Commnd., R.A.F., 1932. Assistant Air Attaché, British Embassy, Paris, 1938-40; C.O. 613 (City of Manchester) Royal Auxiliary Squadron, 1941-1942; Chief Instructor Cambridge Univ. Air Squadron, 1946-48. Parliamentary Secretary, Ministry of Defence, 1956-57; Joint Parliamentary Under-Secretary of State for Foreign Affairs, 1957-58; Assistant to and Spokesman in House of Lords for Minister of Transport and Civil Aviation, 1958-59; Lord-in-Waiting to the Queen, 1958-59; Foreign Affairs Adviser to Richard Thomas & Baldwins Ltd., 1960-64. Mem. Council of British Olympic Association; Officer of Legion of Honour; U.S. Bronze Star Medal. *Recreations:* athletics, cricket, golf, aviation, motoring, wine, etc.; Inter-Public Schools Athletics Champion: 880 yards, 1929. *Heir: s.* Viscount Acheson. *Address:* Heath Cottage, Heathway, Camberley, Surrey. *Clubs:* St. James', White's, R.A.F., M.C.C., Pitt, Hawks, Achilles, Alveston (Cambridge); Travellers' (Paris) [*Died* 17 *Feb.* 1966.

GOSLING, Major William Richard, C.M.G. 1946; O.B.E. 1918; *b.* 12 April 1891; *o. s.* of late Francis William and Winifred Mary Gosling; *m.* 1929, Eveline Margaret, *o. d.* of late A. C. Macintosh, Llandaff, Glam.; one *d.* *Educ.:* Sutton Valence School; Selwyn College, Cambridge (B.A.). Military Service 1914-19, with Welch Regt. and S. W. Borderers in France, the Balkans and Turkey (despatches twice, O.B.E., 1914-15 Star and War and Victory Medals); Demobilized in rank of Major. Colonial Administrative Service, 1920, as Asst. Dist. Commissioner, Gold Coast Colony; Dist. Commissioner 1924; Provincial Commissioner 1942; Acting Chief Commissioner 1945; retired, 1946. Coronation Medal. *Address:* Heronshaw, Ightham, Kent. [*Died* 5 *Aug.* 1968.

GOSS, His Honour Judge (William) Alan (Belcher); Judge of County Courts since 1961; Deputy Chairman East Riding Quarter Sessions since 1956; Deputy Chairman West Riding Quarter Sessions since 1957; *b.* 3 December 1908; *s.* of William Louis Goss, St. Paul's Priory, St. Leonards-on-Sea, Sussex; *m.* 1941, Yvonne, *d.* of V. F. Samuelson, 24 Iverna Court, Kensington; two *s.* one *d.* *Educ.:* Charterhouse; Trinity Hall, Cambridge. B.A. 1930. Barrister, Inner Temple, 1933; joined N.E. Circuit, 1934. Served War of 1939-45, in the Army: North Africa, 1942; Italy, 1944; demobilized with rank of Major. Recorder of Pontefract, 1957-58; Recorder of Doncaster, 1958-61. *Recreations:* gardening, walking. *Address:* 34A Rutland Drive, Harrogate, Yorks. *T.:* Harrogate 4494; 39 Park Square, Leeds 1. *T.:* Leeds 26633. *Club:* Leeds (Leeds). [*Died* 23 *July* 1963.

GOSS-CUSTARD, Walter Henry; *see* Custard.

GOSSE, Laura Sylvia, R.B.A. 1929; R.E. 1936; F.R.S.A.; Painter and Engraver; *b.* 1881; *yr. d.* of late Sir Edmund Gosse, C.B. Silver Medal R.B.A., 1931. Paintings and prints acquired by the British Museum Print Room, Victoria and Albert Museum, Nat. Portrait Gallery, Tate Gallery (Millbank); Fitzwilliam Museum (Cambridge); also by Sheffield, Liverpool, Gloucester, Leeds, Stoke-on-Trent, Manchester, Salford, Oldham, Glasgow, Aberdeen, Johannesburg, Pietermaritzburg, Rugby, Temple Newsam, Plymouth, Portsmouth, Northampton, Hastings, Harrogate, Worthing, Bath, Hertford, and York Art Galleries; Salesian School (Burwash), Leicester, Bristol, Eastbourne, Contemporary Arts Soc., Stoneyhurst College. *Address:* 335 Old London Road, Ore, Hastings, Sussex. [*Died* 6 *June* 1968.

GOTT, Sir Charles (Henry), Kt., *cr.* 1930; *b.* 1866; *e. s.* of Charles Gott, Bradford, Yorks.; *m.* 1903, Annie (*d.* 1960), *d.* of William Docksey, Bradford; no *c.* *Educ.:* private schools. In practice as Civil Engineer and Surveyor, Yorks. from 1887; entered Government Service, 1909; Chief Valuer to Board of Inland Revenue, 1927-31; retired and resumed private practice at Westminster and Bradford, 1931-37; Official Arbitrator, Acquisition of Land Act, 1937-40; M.Inst.C.E.; Fellow and Vice-President Royal Institution of Chartered Surveyors; Vice-Pres. of International Federation of Surveyors. *Publications:* Text Books and Papers on professional subjects. *Recreation:* music. *Address:* Ghyll Court, Ilkley, Yorks. [*Died* 11 *Sept.* 1965.

GOUGE, Sir Arthur, Kt., *cr.* 1948; B.Sc., M.I.Mech.E., Hon. F.R.Ae.S., F.I.Ae.S. (U.S.A.); formerly Vice-Chairman and Chief Executive Saunders-Roe Ltd.; *b.* 3 July 1890; *s.* of George Gouge, J.P., C.C., and Elizabeth Gouge, Northfleet, Kent; *m.* 1918, Margaret Ellen Cook (*d.* 1940); one *s.* one *d.* *Educ.:* C. of E. School, Northfleet; Gravesend Technical School; Woolwich Polytechnic. Joined firm of Short Brothers Ltd., Rochester, in 1915 as a mechanic; from 1920 onwards did research work in connection with flying boat hull form and metal aircraft; Chief Designer, 1926, and from that date until 1943 responsible for all aircraft design of Short Brothers, Ltd., who produced such craft as Singapore, Calcutta, Kent, Valetta, Sarafand, Empire Boat, Sunderland, Golden Hind, Stirling, Shetland, and in conjunction with late Major Mayo, the Mayo Composite; General Manager 1929; Vice-Chairman, 1939-43; resigned from Short Bros. in 1943 and joined Saunders-Roe Ltd.

Pres. of Royal Aeronautical Soc. 1942-43, 1943-44; Pres. Soc. of British Aircraft Constructors, 1945-46; Dep. Pres., 1946-47 and 1947-48. Wilbur Wright Memorial Lecturer, 1948. Freeman of the City of Rochester, 1937; British Gold Medal for Aeronautics, 1937; Musick Memorial Trophy, 1939. *Publications:* several papers and lectures on the design and construction of flying boats. *Recreations:* horology, photography. *Address:* Wootton House, Wootton, Isle of Wight. *T.:* Wootton Bridge 132. *Clubs:* Royal Aero, Royal Automobile.
[*Died* 14 *Oct.* 1962.

GOUGH, Herbert John, C.B. 1942; M.B.E. 1919; F.R.S. 1933; D.Sc., Ph.D.; M.I.Mech.E.; Engineer-in-Chief, Unilever Ltd., 1945-55; *b.* 26 April 1890; *s.* of Henry James Gough and Mary Anne Gillis; *m.* 1918, Sybil Holmes; one *s.* one *d.* *Educ.:* University College School; London Univ. Apprenticeship to Vickers Ltd., 1909-13; Scientific Staff of National Physical Laboratory, 1914; Superintendent, Engineering Dept. National Physical Laboratory, Teddington, 1930-38; Director of Scientific Research, War Office, 1938; Director-General Scientific Research and Development, Ministry of Supply, 1942-45; served with R.E. in France and Belgium 1914-18; commanded Signal Section, 1916-19; Army of Occupation till demobilised, 1919 (despatches twice, awarded Commission in the Field, 1916); Cantor Lecturer to Royal Society of Arts, 1928; Autumn Lecturer to Institute of Metals, 1932; Edgar Marburg Lecturer to Amer. Soc. Test Materials, 1933; Keith Lecturer to Royal Scottish Society of Arts, 1938; Wilbur Wright Memorial Lecturer to Royal Aeronautical Society, 1938; Thomas Hawksley Lecturer to Institution of Mechanical Engineers, 1946; Pres. Inst. of Mechanical Engineers, 1949. *Publications:* Fatigue of Metals; 87 papers on Engineering Subjects in Proc. Royal Society, Phil. Trans. Royal Soc., Proc. Inst. Mechanical Engineers, Proc. Inst. Civil Engineers, Journal Institute of Metals, Philosophical Magazine, Faraday Soc., Journal Iron and Steel Institute, Journal Royal Institution, etc. *Recreation:* golf. *Address:* Upland, Grand Crescent, Rottingdean, Sussex.
[*Died* 1 *June* 1965.

GOUGH, General Sir Hubert (de la Poer), G.C.B., *cr.* 1937 (K.C.B., *cr.* 1916); G.C.M.G., *cr.* 1919; K.C.V.O., *cr.* 1917; *b.* 12 Aug. 1870; *e. s.* of late Sir Charles John Stanley Gough, G.C.B., V.C., and Harriette A. De la Poer, of Gurteen le Poer, co. Waterford; *m.* 1898, Louisa Nora (*d.* 1951), *d.* of Maj.-Gen. H. C. Lewes; four *d.* *Educ.:* Eton; R.M.C., Sandhurst. Joined 16th Lancers, 1889, served Tirah Expedition, 1897-98 (medal and two clasps); South African War, 1899-1902 (despatches, Queen's Medal and five clasps, severely wounded, King's Medal and two clasps, Bt. Lt.-Col.); Professor, Staff College, 1904-06; European War, in France and Flanders, 1914-1918; General, commanded 5th Army, Battles: Pozières, Thiepval, Beaumont-Hamel, operations on the Ancre, Langemark, and St. Quentin (G.C.M.G., K.C.V.O., promoted Lt.-Gen., despatches, K.C.B., Grand Officier Légion d'Honneur, Order of the White Eagle of Russia with swords, Order of Leopold of Belgium, Croix de Guerre); commanded 16th Lancers, 1907-11; 3rd Cavalry Brigade, 1914; 2nd Cavalry Division and 7th Division, 1915; I. Army Corps, 1916; V. Army, 1916-18; Chief Allied Mission Baltic, 1919; retired pay, with rank of General, 1922; Colonel of 16th/5th Lancers, 1936-43; Col. and Zone Comdr. Home Guard; resigned 1942; formerly Chm. Siemens Bros., Director Caxton Electric Development, and other companies. *Publications:* The Fifth Army, 1931; Soldiering On (memoirs), 1954. *Address:* 14 St. Mary Abbots Court, W.14. *Club:* Cavalry.
[*Died* 18 *March* 1963.

GOURELLI, Princess; *see* Rubenstein, Helena.

GOURLAY, Brig. Kenneth Ian, D.S.O. 1919; O.B.E. 1945; M.C. 1915; *e. s.* of WilliamFrederick Gourlay, B.Sc.; *b.* 1891; *m.* 1917, Victoria, *y. d.* of Basil H. M. Oldrini, Newark, Notts; two *s.* one *d.* *Educ.:* Merchiston Castle, Edinburgh; R.M.A., Woolwich. Served European War, Royal Engineers, 1914-19 (despatches, D.S.O., M.C.); War of 1939-45 (O.B.E.); retired pay, 1946. Served C.C.G., 1946-52. *Address:* 16A Sutherland Avenue, Bexhill-on-Sea, Sussex.
[*Died* 14 *March* 1970.

GOWER, Sir (Robert) Patrick (Malcolm), K.B.E., *cr.* 1924; C.B. 1922; C.V.O. 1923; President of Charles F. Higham Ltd., since 1956 (Chairman, 1939-56); *b.* 18 Aug. 1887; *yr. s.* of late Captain Erasmus Gower of Castle Malgwyn, Llechryd, Pembrokeshire; *m.* 1st, 1913, Nancy (*d.* 1940), *d.* of late Joseph Barkley; one *d.* (one *s.* decd.); 2nd, 1941, H. Margaret, *d.* of late F. G. Hawdon, Berkhamsted. *Educ.:* Marlborough; Emmanuel College, Cambridge (Scholar). 1st Class Classical Tripos, 1909; entered Inland Revenue Dept. by open competition (Class I.), 1910; transferred to Treasury, 1919; Assistant Private Secretary to Chancellor of the Exchequer (the late Rt. Hon. A. Bonar Law), 1917-18; Private Sec. to Rt. Hon. Austen Chamberlain as Chancellor of the Exchequer and as Lord Privy Seal, 1919-22; Private Secretary to successive Prime Ministers (late Rt. Hon. A. Bonar Law, Rt. Hon. J. Ramsay MacDonald, and Rt. Hon. Stanley Baldwin), 1922-28; Chief Publicity Officer, Conservative and Unionist Central Office, 1929-39; Freeman of City of London. *Recreation:* golf. *Address:* Kilgerran, Wargrave Road, Henley, Oxon. *Club:* Farmers' (Chm. 1948).
[*Died* 31 *Aug.* 1964.

GOWERS, Sir Ernest Arthur, G.C.B., *cr.* 1953 (K.C.B., *cr.* 1928; C.B. 1917); G.B.E., *cr.* 1945 (K.B.E., *cr.* 1926); M.A.; Hon. D.Litt. Manchester; Hon. A.R.I.B.A.; Hon. Fellow of Clare College, Cambridge; *b.* 1880; *y. s.* of Sir William R. Gowers, M.D., F.R.S., London, and Mary, *d.* of Frederick Baines, Leeds; *m.* 1905, Constance, M.B.E. 1946 (*d.* 1952), *d.* of Thomas Macgregor Greer, D.L., of Ballymoney, Co. Antrim; one *s.* two *d.* *Educ.:* Rugby; Clare College, Cambridge (scholar); (First Class Classical Tripos). Entered Civil Service (Inland Revenue), 1903; transferred to India Office, 1904; Barrister, Inner Temple, 1906; Private Secretary to successive Under-Secretaries of State for India, 1907-11; Principal Private Sec. to Chancellor of the Exchequer (Rt. Hon. D. Lloyd George), 1911-12; Chief Inspector National Health Insurance Commission, 1912-17; attached to Foreign Office, 1914-17; Secretary to the Civil Service Arbitration Board, 1917-1919, and Director of Production Coal Mines Dept. 1919-20; Permanent Under-Secretary for Mines, 1920-27; Chm. of Board of Inland Revenue, 1927-30; Chm. of Coal Mines Reorganisation Commission, 1930-35; Chm. of Coal Commission, 1938-46; Regional Commissioner for Civil Defence London Region, 1939-45; Chm. of Cttee. on admission of women to the Foreign Service, 1945; Chm of Committee on Shops Acts, etc., 1946; Chm. of Cttee. on the Preservation of Historic Houses, 1949; Chairman: St. Felix School, Southwold, 1934-47; Harlow Development Corp., 1947-50; Royal Commission on Capital Punishment, 1949-53; Committee on Foot-and-Mouth Disease, 1952-53; Chm. National Hospitals for Nervous Diseases, 1948-57; Pres. English Assoc., 1956-57; Gentleman Usher of the Purple Rod of the Order of the British Empire, 1952-60. Freeman of Royal Borough of Kingston-on-Thames. Chevalier of the Order of the Crown of Belgium, 1918. *Publications:*

Plain Words: a Guide to the Use of English, 1948; ABC of Plain Words, 1951; The Complete Plain Words, 1954; A Life for a Life? The Problem of Capital Punishment, 1956. Editor, Fowler's Modern English Usage, 1965. *Address:* Rondle Wood, Liphook, Hants. *T.:* Rogate 51. *Clubs:* Athenæum, Brooks's. [*Died* 16 *April* 1966.

GRACE, Sir Gilbert; *see* Grace, Sir O. G.

GRACE, Rev. Canon Harold Myers, C.B.E. 1950; M.A.; *b.* 28 Dec. 1888; *s.* of George F. and Caroline Grace; *m.* 1920, Enid Mary Dundas Harford; two *s.* one *d.* *Educ.:* Trent College; Queens' College and Ridley Hall, Cambridge. College Missioner at Queen's College Mission, Rotherhithe, 1911-12; Curate, Holy Trinity, Hull, 1912-1914; Uganda in educational work, 1914-1934; Hon. Canon of St. Paul's Cathedral, Namirembe, Kampala, Uganda; Principal, Achimota College, Gold Coast, 1935-40; Secretary, Conference of Missionary Societies in Great Britain and Ireland, 1940-50; war service in German East Africa, 1917-19 (despatches). *Address:* The Old School, Kimmeridge, Wareham, Dorset. *T.:* Kimmeridge 200. *Club:* Royal Commonwealth Society. [*Died* 30 *May* 1967.

GRACE, Leo Bernard Aloysius, C.M.G. 1966; M.R.C.V.S., D.V.S.M., F.R.S.H.; Chief Adviser on Meat Inspection, Ministry of Agriculture, Fisheries and Food, 1954-1968; *b.* 21 June 1903; 3rd *s.* of Hugh and Mary Anne Grace; *m.* 1928, Mary Dowdall; three *s.* one *d.* (and one *s.* decd.). *Educ.:* St. Aloysius Coll., Glasgow; Glasgow Veterinary Coll.; Royal (Dick) Veterinary Coll., Edinburgh. Asst. in gen. veterinary practice, 1924-26; organised meat inspection in Chile, 1927-29; Lectr. in Pathology, Glasgow Veterinary Coll., 1929-30; County Veterinary Officer, Derbyshire, 1930-32; Veterinary Officer and Chief Meat Inspector: Cardiff, 1932-34; Smithfield Market, London, 1934-1940; Chief Adviser on Meat Inspection, Min. of Food, 1940-54. Benjamin Ward Richardson Lectr., R.S.H., 1958. *Publications:* contribs. to various veterinary and public health jls. *Recreations:* golf, bowls. *Address:* Flat 56, Lynden Hyrst, Addiscombe Road, E. Croydon, Surrey. *T.:* Addiscombe 7528. *Clubs:* City Livery, Civil Service. [*Died* 20 *Aug.* 1969.

GRACE, Sir (Oliver) Gilbert, Kt., *cr.* 1953; C.I.E. 1945; O.B.E. 1934; Inspector-General of Police, Karachi, Pakistan, 1951-1956; *b.* 1896, *s.* of Charles Sebastian Grace, Fairfield, Tring, Hertfordshire. *Educ.:* Berkhamsted School. Served European War, 1914: Captain and Adjutant, Green Howards, Staff Captain and Brigade Major, 189th Infantry Brigade. Entered Indian Police, 1920; Commandant N.W. Frontier, Constabulary, 1937-47; Inspector-General of Police, N.W.F.P., Pakistan, 1947-51. Afghan War, 1919 (despatches); Ahmedzai Salient operations, 1940 (despatches). *Recreation:* walking. *Address:* Dormehls Drift, George, Cape Province, S. Africa. *T.:* George 674 *Club:* East India and Sports.
[*Died* 23 *Jan.* 1968.

GRACE, Rear-Admiral Walter Keir Campbell, C.B.E. 1942; *b.* 18 June 1890; 3rd *s.* of Rev. George and Caroline Grace; *m.* 1917, Edith Gwendolen Elizabeth, *o. d.* of Dr. John and Edith Kyffin; two *s.* three *d.* *Educ.:* Gresham's School, Holt. Entered Navy, 1907; Paymaster Capt. 1939; Rear-Admiral (S) (acting), 1944; retired, 1946; Secretary to Rear-Admiral, Pacific, 1917-19; Empire Cruise of the Special Service Squadron, 1923-24; Secretary to Naval Personnel Committee, 1925-27; to Commodore, Hong Kong, 1930-32; to Rear-Admiral, Gibraltar, 1933-34; to Fifth Sea Lord, 1936-38; Fleet Accountant Officer, Home Fleet, 1939-42; Command Supply Officer, Portsmouth, 1943-45. *Recreation:* gardening. *Address:* Penrhyn, 20 Bury Rd., Alverstoke, Hants. *T.:* Gosport 80083. *Club:* Nuffield United Services Officers (Portsmouth). [*Died* 7 *March* 1964.

GRACE, Wilfrid Arnold, M.A.; Headmaster of Queen Elizabeth Grammar School, Wakefield, 1939-55, retired; *b.* 26 April 1895; *s.* of Charles Millar Grace and Louisa Gertrude Brown; *m.* 1924; three *d.* *Educ.:* The Leys School, Cambridge; The Queen's College, Oxford: 2nd Cl. Hon. Sch. Modern Hist., O.U.A.C. Blue. Teaching Lindisfarne College, Westcliff, 1913-14; served European War, 1914-19, on active service, 1915-19, Captain, The Border Regt.; University, 1919-22. Teaching: St. Bees School, Cumberland, 1922-23; Bembridge School, I.W., 1924-29; Headmaster, Halesowen Grammar School, 1929-39. *Recreations:* walking, tennis, music, literature, etc. *Address:* Lindisfarne, 12 Great Headland Road, Paignton, Devon. *Club:* English-Speaking Union.
[*Died* 25 *July* 1964.

GRACEY, Gen. Sir Douglas David, K.C.B. *cr.* 1951 (C.B. 1945); K.C.I.E., *cr.* 1947; C.B.E. 1945 (O.B.E. 1943); M.C. 1917, and bar 1918; *b.* 3 Sept. 1894; *s.* of H. K. Gracey, C.B.E., I.C.S., and M. A. Gracey, M.B.E.; *m.* 1931, K. C. M. O'B. Spring; one *s.* one *d.* *Educ.:* Blundell's; R.M.C., Sandhurst. 2nd Lt. I.A., 1914; served in France, 1915, with 2nd Royal Munster Fusiliers, and in Iraq, Palestine, Syria, Egypt, 1916-20, with 1/1st K.G.O. Gurkha Rifles (twice wounded, M.C. and bar); Instructor, R.M.C., Sandhurst, 1925-27; Student, Staff College, Quetta, 1928-29; G.S.O. 2 G.H.Q. (India), 1930-34; G.S.O. 2 Western Command, 1936-37; B.G.S. Western Command, 1938; Brevets of Major and Lt.-Col.; Commandant 2/3rd Q.A.O. Gurkha Rifles, 1939-40; N.W.F. operations, 1939; served War of 1939-45 (despatches thrice); Assistant Commandant (Colonel) Staff College, Quetta, 1940-41; Commander 17th Ind. Inf. Bde. (Brigadier), 1941-1942, Iraq and Syria (O.B.E., despatches); Commander 20th Indian Division, 1942-46 - Battles of Imphal (C.B.E.), Mandalay, Irrawaddy and Rangoon (C.B.); Comd. Allied Land Forces, French Indo-China, 1945-46; created Citoyen d'Honneur of town of Saigon, 1946; Grand Cross Royal Order of Cambodia, 1945; Commander Legion of Honour, and Croix de Guerre avec palme, 1950. Offg. G.O. C.-in-C. Northern Command, India, 1946; Commander 1st Indian Corps, 1946-1947; Chief of Staff, Pakistan Army, 1947-1948; Commander-in-Chief, Pakistan Army, 1948-51; retd. Chairman, Royal Hospital and Home for Incurables, Putney, 1960-. *Recreations:* shooting, fishing. *Address:* The Grange, Hook Heath, Woking, Surrey. *T.:* Woking 3375. *Clubs:* United Service, M.C.C. [*Died* 5 *June* 1964.

GRADWELL, Leo Joseph Anthony, D.S.C. 1942; M.A. Oxon; Metropolitan Magistrate Gt. Marlborough St. Magistrates' Court, 1961-67 (Thames Court, 1950-61); retd. 1967; *b.* 28 July 1899; *s.* of Joseph Gradwell, solicitor; *m.* 1940, Jean Ormonde Adamson; two *s.* two *d.* *Educ.:* Stonyhurst Coll.; Balliol Coll., Oxford (Exhib.). Called to Bar, Inner Temple, 1925. Northern Circuit. Served European War, 1917-18, as Midshipman, R.N.V.R.; War of 1939-45, R.N.V.R. (D.S.C.); served at sea in command of H.M.S. Ayrshire and other anti-submarine vessels in Western Approaches. *Recreation:* sailing. *Address:* B7 Shirley Towers, Vane Hill Rd., Torquay. *T.:* Torquay 27439. *Clubs:* Royal Ocean Racing, Royal Torbay Yacht.
[*Died* 9 *Nov.* 1969.

GRAEME, Sir Egerton H. M. H., Bt.; *see* Hamond-Graeme.

GRAFTON, 10th Duke of (*cr.* 1675); **Captain Charles Alfred Euston FitzRoy;** Earl of Euston, Viscount Ipswich; J.P. W. Suffolk; D.L. Suffolk; late Royal Welch Fusiliers; *b.* 4 June 1892; *s.* of late Rev. Lord Charles Edward FitzRoy, 4th *s.* of 7th Duke, and late Hon. Ismay Mary Helen Augusta FitzRoy, *d.* of 3rd Baron Southampton; *S.* cousin, 1936; *m.* 1st, 1918, Lady Doreen Maria Josepha Sydney Buxton (*d.* 1923), *d.* of 1st Earl Buxton; one *s.* (and one killed in action, 1944) one *d.*; 2nd, 1924, Lucy Eleanor (*d.* 1943), *d.* of late Sir George Stapylton Barnes, K.C.B., K.C.S.I.; one *s.* (and one *s.* decd.); 3rd, 1944, Mrs. Rita Currie, *d.* of late J. S. Carr-Ellison. *Educ.:* Wellington College; R.M.C., Sandhurst. Joined R.W.F. in Quetta, 1911; France, 1914; A.D.C. and Comptroller to Lord Buxton, Governor General South Africa, 1917-20; Retired from Army, 1921; Farmed at Coney Weston, Suffolk, 1921-27; Agent to Owen Hugh Smith, Langham, Oakham, Rutland, 1927-36. *Heir:* *s.* Earl of Euston. *Address:* Euston Hall, Thetford, Norfolk. *T.A.:* Euston Suffolk. *T.:* Thetford 3282. [*Died* 11 *Nov.* 1970.

GRAHAM, Captain Alan Crosland, F.S.A., B.A.; *b.* 2 Aug. 1896; *s.* of late Sir Crosland Graham and late Marah Bond Graham; *m.* 1st, 1939, Marion (marriage dissolved, 1948), *o. c.* of M. C. du Plessis, Capetown; two *d.*; 2nd, 1953, Marie Antoinette Louise Pavluc; one *s.* one *d.* *Educ.:* Rugby; Trinity College, Oxford. B.A. (Oxon) Honours in History; 2nd Lt. Q.O. Cameron Highlanders, 1915; served European War, France, 1916-17; N. Russia, 1918-19 (3rd cl. Order of St. Anne, with crossed swords; Private Sec. to 1st Earl of Balfour, 1925-29; contested Denbigh Div., 1929, Darwen, 1931; Private Secretary to Viscount Hailsham, as Leader of House of Lords, 1932-35; M.P. (U.) Wirral Division of Cheshire, 1935-45; Chairman, Anglo-Polish Parliamentary Committee; Polonia Restituta, 3rd Class; formerly member Viscount Mersey's Committee for the Preservation of Antiquities of Cyprus. *Recreations:* shooting, archæology, foreign travel. *Address:* Plas Llanychan, nr. Ruthin, N. Wales. *T.:* Ruthin 141; 14 Lansdowne Road, Wimbledon, S.W.20. [*Died* 10 *May* 1964.

GRAHAM, Lt.-Col. Charles Percy, C.B.E. 1919; D.S.O. 1915; late Welsh Regiment; *b.* 12 July 1881; *m.* 1910, Doris (*d.* 1960), *d.* of Francis Nalder, East Keal, Lincolnshire; two *s.* one *d.* Entered army, 1900; Indian army, 1901; Welsh Regiment, 1913; retired, 1920. Served European War (despatches, C.B.E., D.S.O.). *Address:* Hunter's Lodge, Monkleigh, Bideford, Devon. [*Died* 12 *April* 1961.

GRAHAM, Sir Clarence (Johnston), 1st Bt., *cr.* 1964; Kt. 1952; President, Ulster Unionist Council, 1963-64 (Chm., Standing Committee, 1947-63, retd.); Director, John Graham (Dromore) Ltd., Engineering Contractors since 1955; *b.* 8 May 1900; *s.* of John Graham, J.P.; *m.* 1935, Margaret Christina Moodie (*d.* 1954); one *s.* *Educ.:* Banbridge Academy; Queen's University, Belfast. B.Sc., Q.U.B., 1919. Partner in John Graham, Engineering Contractors, 1924; Chairman: Dromore Urban Council, 1928-32; Iveagh Unionist Assoc., 1935-65 (Pres., 1965-); Exec. Committee, Ulster Unionist Council, 1946-49. *Recreations:* golf and shooting. *Heir:* *s.* John Moodie Graham, *b.* 3 April 1938. *Address:* Dromore House, Dromore, Co. Down, N. Ireland. *T.:* Dromore 318. [*Died* 22 *Dec.* 1966.

GRAHAM, Rt. Rev. Eric; in charge of Matterdale, Parish of Greystoke, Cumberland, since 1959; *b.* 1888; *s.* of late Venerable Malcolm Graham, Archdeacon of Stoke-on-Trent; *m.* 1919, Phyllis Norton, *d.* of late Maj.-Gen. C. R. Buckle, C.B., C.M.G., D.S.O.; four *s.* two *d.* *Educ.:* Cheltenham; Oriel College, Oxford; Wells Theological College. Vice-Principal Salisbury Theological College, 1914-19; Fellow and Dean of Oriel College, Oxford, 1919-25; Rector of Boyton-cum-Sherrington, Wilts, 1925-1929; Principal of Cuddesdon College and Vicar of Cuddesdon, 1929-44; Rural Dean of Cuddesdon, 1943-44; Bishop of Brechin, 1944-59. Select Preacher, Oxford University, 1930-31. Hon. D.D. St. Andrews, 1954. *Publication:* Waymarks of the Passion, 1961. *Address:* Matterdale Vicarage, Penrith, Cumberland. *T.:* Glenridding 301. [*Died* 18 *Jan.* 1964.

GRAHAM, Very Rev. George Frederick, M.A.; *b.* 1877; *e. s.* of late Rev. Chancellor G. R. Graham; *m.* 1904, Mirabel Eileen, *e. d.* of late W. Perry Odlum, J.P., Huntington, Portarlington; three *s.* two *d.* *Educ.:* Perse School, Cambridge; Dublin University. Senior Moderator and Gold Medallist, Exptal. Science, 1898; Curate, New Ross, 1900-02; St. Mary's, Dublin, 1902-03; Diocesan Inspector of Schools, Dublin, Glendalough and Kildare, 1903-09; Rector of Monasterevan and Nurney, nr. Kildare, 1909-38; 1st Canon of Kildare 1923-28; Precentor of Kildare, 1928-38; Dean of Kildare, 1938-52; Select Preacher, Dublin University, 1930 and 1942. *Recreation:* golf. *Address:* Dunmore, Proby Sq., Blackrock, Co. Dublin. *T.:* Dunleary 81703. *Club:* Royal Dublin Society (Dublin). [*Died* 24 *Feb.* 1962.

GRAHAM, Hamilton M. H.; *see* Howgrave-Graham.

GRAHAM, Harold, C.I.E. 1932; Indian Civil Service, retired; *b.* 26 April 1889; *er. s.* of late Thomas Lightfoot Hatton Graham, Liscard, Cheshire; *m.* 1916, Gwendolen Irene, *d.* of Charles Frederick Burgess, Littlecourt, Sevenoaks, Kent; one *s.* one *d.* *Educ.:* Manchester Grammar School; Merton College, Oxford. B.A. with 1st class honours Literae Humaniores, 1912; M.A. 1919; appointed to Indian Civil Service, 1912; Assistant Magistrate and Collector, Bengal, 1913; Indian Army Reserve of Officers attached 9th Gurkha Rifles, 1915-19; wounded in action at Beit Aiessa, Mesopotamia, 24 April 1916; Supervising Officer, Kali Bahadur Regiment Nepalese Contingent, 1918; released from army service with rank of Captain, 1919; District and Sessions Judge, Bengal, 1919-22; District Magistrate and Collector, Bengal, 1923-27; Private Secretary to Governor of Bengal, 1927-30; District Magistrate and Collector, Mymensingh, Bengal, 1931-1932; Officiating Commissioner Dacca Division, Bengal, 1933-34; Secretary, Education Department, Government of Bengal, 1935-36; Commissioner Presidency Division, Bengal, 1937-40; retired, 1942; Company Commander Bicester Company Home Guard, 1940-42. *Recreation:* riding. *Address:* Langleys, Launton, near Bicester, Oxon. *T.:* Bicester 164. *Club:* United University. [*Died* 30 *Nov.* 1963.

GRAHAM, Major Henry Archibald Roger; late Grenadier Guards; *b.* 21 Dec. 1892; *s.* of late Major Henry Graham and late Ellen, C.B.E. (*née* Peel; she *m.* 2nd, 1908, the first and last Baron Askwith); *m.* 1927, Margaret, *d.* of 1st Baron Roborough; one *s.* four *d.* *Educ.:* Radley; Trinity Coll., Cambridge (B.A. 1920). Joined Gren. Gds., Aug. 1914; served European War, 1914-18, Reserve of Officers; attached Foreign Office as King's Foreign Service Messenger; served War of 1939-45; has travelled Europe, Africa, and America; contested (C.) West Bromwich, 1924. *Recreations:* fishing, shooting, golf. *Address:* 21 Old Court Mansions, Kensington, W.8. *T.:* Western 7740; Old Mill House, Micheldever, Hants. *Club:* Guards. [*Died* 25 *Feb.* 1970.

GRAHAM, Rev. Henry Burrans, S.T.D. Vicar of Blackawton, Devon, since 1961; Archdeacon of Richmond and Canon Residentiary of Ripon, 1954-61; *b.* 1909; *s.* of Henry Graham, Lockwood, Yorks. *Educ.:* King James' Grammar School, Almondbury: Durham University (Diploma in Biblical Studies). Dr. of Sacred Theology, Ripon Coll., Wisconsin, 1960. Ordained 1939; Curate of Hitcham, and Chaplain R.A.F. Station, Wattisham, 1939-41; Dioc. Sec., St. Edmundsbury and Ipswich, 1941-54; Sec. Dioc. Bd. of Finance, Pastoral Cttee., Dioc. Bd. of Dilapidations, Dioc. Bd. of Patronage, etc.; Editor Diocesan Year Book for 10 years; Hon. Chaplain to Bishop of St. Edmundsbury, 1945-54; Hon. Canon of Baldwin, Abbott, in St. Edmundsbury Cathedral, 1947-54; Surrogate 1945-54; Chaplain to High Sheriffs of Suffolk, 1949-50 and 1952-53; Hon. Chaplain, St. Felix School, 1948-50; Mem. Church Information Bd. and its Exec. Cttee., 1948-59; Governor, Ipswich School, 1948-54; Mem. Church Assembly, 1947-61; Proctor in Canterbury Convocation, 1947-54; Ex-officio in York Convocation, 1954-61; Member Ipswich Country Borough Education Cttee. (Chm. Sub.-Cttees., 1948-54); Chm. Ripon Diocesan Moral Welfare Assoc., 1954-61; Chm. G.F.S. Central Finance Committee, 1953-59; Hon. Treasurer, G.F.S. 1960; Trustee of Lord Grimthorpe's Charity, 1954; Member Governing Body of Corp. of Church House, Westminster, 1956; one of the Church Commissioners for England, 1958-; Member, Church Assembly Legislative Cttee., 1958. Chm. Ripon Diocesan Missionary Council, 1959; Mem. Management Cttee. of Church Information Office, 1959; Mem. Cathedrals Commission, 1959; Mem. C. of E. Central Bd. of Finance, 1961; Mem. Kingsbridge R.D.C., 1962-. Press Officer to the Bishop of Exeter, 1962. *Publications:* Prayers in War-time, Church Assembly Commentary; Anglican Correspondent to the Guardian; Venture (Editor). *Recreations:* church music, walking. *Address:* Blackawton Vicarage, Nr. Totnes, Devon. [*Died* 4 *July* 1963.

GRAHAM, James, C.B.E. 1920; *b.* 1870; *s.* of late James Graham, Stirling, and Jane (*née* Buckley) of Lima, Peru; *m.* 1898, Louisa Edith (*d.* 1957), *e. d.* of Robert Rule; two *s.* one *d.* (and one *s.* killed in action, 1940). *Educ.:* Charterhouse; Glasgow University. Commercial Assistant Ministry of Shipping, 1917-19. Formerly Director of Ker Bolton & Co. Ltd., East India Merchants, London. *Address:* Oakside, Wheeler Avenue, Oxted, Surrey. *T.:* Oxted 2599. [*Died* 15 *March* 1961.

GRAHAM, Rev. John D.; *see* Graham, Rev. Jonathan J. D.

GRAHAM, Sir John Gibson, Kt. 1946; M.C.; Director Galbraith Pembroke & Co. Ltd.; Underwriting Member of Lloyd's; *b.* 1896; *s.* of late John C. Graham; *m.* 1931, Jessie Enid, *d.* of Edmund Risoliere Burrell; one *s.* *Educ.:* Glasgow Academy. Deputy Director of Commercial Services, 1940-42. Representative of Ministry of War Transport in Mediterranean, 1942-45. Served European War, 1914-18, with Royal Scots Fusiliers (M.C.). *Recreations:* golf, shooting. *Address:* Bankside House, 107 Leadenhall Street, E.C.3; Seascape, Botany Close, Rustington, Sussex. *Club:* Conservative (Glasgow). [*Died* 5 *May* 1964.

GRAHAM, Rev. (Jonathan) John Drummond, M.A.; Father Superior of the Community of the Resurrection, Mirfield, since 1958. *Educ.:* Trinity Coll., Cambridge; Coll. of the Resurrection, Mirfield. B.A. 1933, M.A. 1937, Camb. Deacon, 1937; Priest, 1938. Curate of St. John the Evangelist, Middlesbrough, 1937-43; Licensed to Officiate, Diocese of Wakefield, 1943-55; Warden, Hostel of the Resurrection, 1950-1955; Proctor in Convocation, Ripon, 1951-1955; Principal, Codrington Coll., Island and Diocese of Barbados, 1955-57; Prior of St. Mary Magdalen, Barbados, 1957-58. *Address:* House of the Resurrection, Mirfield, Yorks. [*Died* 22 *Aug.* 1965.

GRAHAM, Brigadier Lancelot Cecil Torbock, C.I.E. 1945; M.C. 1917; retired Indian Army; *b.* 1890; *s.* of Col. Henry Graham, 16th Lancers, Mossley Vale House, Mossley Hill, Lancs. *Educ.:* Charterhouse; R.M.C., Sandhurst. Joined 9th Hodson's Horse, I.A., 1910. Served European War, 1914-19, France and Palestine (M.C., despatches twice). Bt. Lt.-Col., 1932; Colonel, 1937; Brig., 1940; Area Comd., India, 1940; Director of Organization, G.H.Q., India, 1941; D.A.G. Persia and Iraq Command, 1942 (despatches twice, C.I.E.). A.D.C. to the King, 1942-46; retired, 1946; p.s.c. Camberley, 1926. *Address:* The Red House, Windsor, Berks. *T.:* 61533. *Club:* United Service. [*Died* 20 *Nov.* 1962.

GRAHAM, Air Vice-Marshal Ronald, C.B. 1943; C.B.E. 1942; D.S.O. 1917; D.S.C. and Bar; D.F.C.; p.s.a., i.d.c.; J.P.; Lord Lieut. of Bute since 1963; *b.* 19 July 1896; *s.* of late William Graham, Yokohama; *m.* 1918, Phyllis (Nancy), *o. d.* of late Henry E. Farmer, M.B.E., F.R.I.B.A.; two *d.* *Educ.:* private; St. Joseph's Coll., Yokohama; Castle Douglas Acad., Scotland. Served European War, 1915-18 (despatches, D.S.C. and bar, D.S.O., D.F.C., Croix de Guerre avec Palme (France), Order of the Crown (Belgium)); **Waziristan, 1919; Iraq, 1930;** Army **Staff College, Quetta, 1922-23; Air Ministry, 1923-26; Directing Staff, R.A.F. Staff** College, 1926-29; O.C. R.A.F. Station, **Kenley, 1929-30; in charge Intelligence, Air H.Q., Iraq, 1930-33; Air Ministry, 1934-36; Imperial Defence College, 1936-37; S.A.S.O.** Armament Group, 1937; **Asst. Cdt. R.A.F. Staff College, 1937-38; Staff Imperial** Defence **College, 1939; Deputy** S.A.S.O. **Fighter Command, 1939; Air Mission North Africa, Dec. 1939 and Jan. 1940; S.A.**S.O. **Flying Training and A.O.A. Technical Training Commands, 1940;** A.O.A. Bomber Command, 1941-42; Air Officer, and Air Chief of Staff, H.Q. Combined Operations, 1943; A.O.C. West Africa, 1944; **Comdt. R.A.F. Staff Coll., 1945-46; A.O.C., R.A.F. Mission to Australia and N.Z., and member of Joint Chiefs of Staff Organization, Australia, 1946-48; retired, 1948;** Commandant, **Scottish Police College, 1949-57. D.L. Bute, 1961, J.P. Bute, 1961. Comdr. Legion of Honour (Fr.), 1949. Hon. Spahi 2nd Class, Algeria, 1940. *Recreations:* golf and sketching. *Address:* Woodside Cottage, Sannox, Isle of Arran, Scotland. *T.:* Corrie 207.** [*Died* 23 *June* 1967.

GRAHAM, Rose, C.B.E. 1939; M.A.; **D.Litt.; F.S.A.;** F.R.Hist.S.; Hon. Gen. Editor, Canterbury and York Soc., 1924-58; *b.* 1875; *d.* of late W. Edgar Graham and Jane, *d.* of Thomas Newton. *Educ.:* Notting Hill High Sch.; Somerville Coll., Oxford. Oxford Honours School of Modern History, Class II, 1897; B.A. and M.A. 1920; D.Litt. 1929; Hon. Fellow of Somerville College, 1933; Member Roy. Commission on Historical Monuments, 1934-63; Pres. British Archæological Assoc., 1945-51. *Publications:* St. Gilbert of Sempringham and the Gilbertines, 1901; An Abbot of Vézelay, 1918; The Chantry Certificates and the Edwardian Inventories of Church Goods of Oxfordshire (Oxfordshire Record Society), 1919; English Ecclesiastical Studies, 1929; A Picture Book of the Life of St. Anthony the Abbot (Roxburghe Club), 1937; The Register of Archbishop Winchelsey (Canterbury and York Society); various contributions to historical and archæological publications. *Address:* 29 Ladbroke Grove, W.11. *Club:* University Women's. [*Died* 29 *July* 1963.

GRAHAM, Sydney, C.B.E. 1920; Managing Director of Harris and Graham Ltd., 52 Lime Street, E.C.3. Underwriting Member of Lloyd's; *b.* 1879; *s.* of James Graham, Longtown and Carlisle; *m.* 1907, Madeleine, *d.* of Alfred Bell, J.P., Newcastle upon Tyne. Served European War, 1914-18, in R.N. Representative of British Ministry of Shipping for Italy and Western Mediterranean, 1918-20. Order of Crown of Italy (Cav.). *Address:* 76 Harley House, N.W.1. *T.:* Welbeck 3226; Three Decks, Itchenor, Chichester, Sussex. *Clubs:* Bath, Royal Thames Yacht, Royal London Yacht; Royal Corinthian Yacht; Lloyd's Yacht; Wentworth (Virginia Water). [*Died* 3 *May* 1966.

GRAHAM, Thomas Ottiwell, M.C., M.D. D.P.H., F.R.C.S.I., Member of Council (Past Pres.) Royal Coll. of Surgeons in Ireland; Consulting Surgeon for Throat, Nose, and Ear to Roy. City of Dublin Hosp., and to Roy. Victoria Eye and Ear Hosp., Dublin; Consulting Aural Surgeon to Dr. Steevens Hospital; Consulting Aural Surgeon, Min. of Pensions Hosp., Dublin; Consulting Surgeon for Nose, Ear and Throat, Monkstown Hospital and St. Ultan's Hospital; Past President Royal Academy of Medicine in Ireland; *b.* 25 Jan. 1883 2nd *s.* of Christopher Graham, M.A; *m.* 1st, 1918, Susan Eva (*d.* 1926), *d.* of Canon C. LL. Sanctuary, Sherborne; one *d.*; 2nd 1931, May Gertrude, *d.* of George Griffin, Dublin. *Educ.*: Cambridge; Trinity College, Dublin (Medical Scholar, Senior Moderator). Vienna, Heidelberg and Freiburg. Gold Medallist Natural Science, M.B., B.Ch. (Stip. Cond.); Bennett Surgical Prizeman and Special Travelling Surgical Prizeman; B.A.O. Dublin University, 1906; D.P.H. Dublin University, 1908; ex-House-Surgeon, Sir Patrick Dun's Hospital, Dublin; ex-House-Surgeon Royal Victoria Eye and Ear Hospital, Dublin; Ex-Surgeon for Ear, Nose and Throat, National Children's Hospital; ex-Laryngologist to Richmond, Whitworth, and Hardwicke Hospitals, Dublin; ex Demonstrator in Zoology, Physiology, Anatomy, Pathology, and Surgery T.C.D., Past President of Dublin University Biological Association; Major, R.A.M.C. (S.R.) *Publications:* papers to medical journals *Recreations:* tennis, gardening, golf, farming. *Address:* 61 Fitzwilliam Square, Dublin 2 *T.*: Dublin 62054; Montrose, 51 Merrion Road, Dublin 4. *T.:* 692846. [*Died* 19 *March* 1966.

GRAHAM BROWN, Thomas, F.R.S 1927; D.Sc., M.D.; Prof. of Physiology, Univ of Wales, 1920-47; retired 1947; *e. s.* of late Dr J. J. Graham-Brown, Edinburgh. *Educ.:* Edinburgh Academy; Universities of Edinburgh and Strasbourg. Muirhead Demonstrator of Physiology, University of Glasgow, 1907; Carnegie Fellow, working in Physiology Dept. University of Liverpool, 1910; Lecturer in Experimental Physiology, University of Manchester, 1913; served European War, 1915-19; from 1916-19 British Salonika Force, with 26th Division, British units attached to Royal Serbian Army, and finally in charge Neurological Department of the British Salonika Force. Editor of The Alpine Journal, 1948. *Publications:* Brenva, 1944; (with Sir Gavin De Beer) The First Ascent of Mont Blanc, 1957; Papers on Physiology of Nervous System. *Recreations:* sailing, climbing. *Address:* 20 Manor Place, Edinburgh. *Clubs:* Athenæum, Alpine; New, Royal Forth Yacht (Edinburgh). [*Died* 28 *Oct.* 1965.

GRAINGER, Percy Aldridge; pianist and composer; *b.* Melbourne, Australia, 1882; *s.* of John and Rose Grainger; father well-known architect and engineer; *m.* 1928, Ella Viola Strom, Swedish Poet, Composer and Painter. *Educ.:* Frankfurt-a-Main. Studied music with his mother in Australia till the age of ten, and then went to Germany; came to London when 18 years old, and since then has given many hundreds of concerts in Europe, America, Russia, South Africa, and Australasia; received several Royal Commands. *Publications:* British Folk-music Settings (30 numbers); Room-music Tit-bits (3 numbers); Kipling Settings (18 numbers); Father and Daughter, dance-ballad for chorus and orchestra; several songs and piano pieces; Journal of the Folksong Society, No. 12; Marching Song of Democracy for chorus, organ, and orchestra; English Dance for organ and orchestra; Hillsongs I. and II. for large chamber-music. *Recreations:* long distance walking, study of languages (Scandinavian, old Icelandic, Dutch, Maori, Polynesian), and phonetics; collection of British folksongs and sea-chanties and native music (Polynesian, African, Australian, etc.). *Address:* 7 Cromwell Place, White Plains, N.Y., U.S.A. [*Died* 20 *Feb.* 1961.

GRANT, Sir (Albert) William, Kt. *cr.* 1955; C.B.E. 1946; Chairman, Engineering Employers' West of England Association, 1938-60; *b.* 6 February 1891; *s.* of William Edwards Grant and Ellen Maria Grant; *m.* 1916, Vera Gertrude Hubbard (*d.* 1964); twin *d.* Entered engineering industry, 1910; with The Bristol Aeroplane Co. Ltd., until 1938. *Recreations:* riding, golf. *Address:* Edymead, 30 Clarence Road South, Weston-super-Mare. *T.:* Weston-super-Mare 1259. [*Died* 9 *Nov.* 1965.

GRANT, Capt. Alexander, C.B.E. 1927; D.S.C.; R.N., retired; *b.* 1872; *s.* of Arthur John Grant, Elgin; *m.* 1895, Margaret, *d.* of Duncan Phimister, Elgin. Served European War, 1914-19 (specially promoted Lieut., despatches, D.S.C.); retired list, 1927; Capt., retired, 1942. *Address:* 23 Westbourne Avenue, Emsworth, Hants. [*Died* 4 *May* 1961.

GRANT, Air Marshal Sir Andrew, K.B.E., *cr.* 1946 (C.B.E. 1942; M.B.E. 1919); C.B. 1945; R.A.F. (retd.); *b.* 1890; *m.* 1916, Elsie, *o. d.* of late George Crowther, Bradford. *Educ.:* Edinburgh University (M.B., Ch.B. 1913). D.P.H. Camb. 1918; served European War, 1915-19 (wounded, despatches, M.B.E.); Deputy Director-General of Medical Services, Air Ministry, 1937-42; Principal Medical Officer, Bomber Command, 1942-44; P.M.O. Air Command South-East Asia, 1945; Air Marshal, 1946; Director-General of R.A.F. Medical Services, Air Ministry 1946-48; Hon. Surgeon to the King, 1942-48; retired, 1948; Pres. Eastbourne Div. B.R.C.S., 1952. K.St.J. 1946. *Address:* Stanton Prior Lodge, Meads, Eastbourne, Sx. *T.:* Eastbourne 23766. [*Died* 7 *May* 1967.

GRANT, Rev. (Arthur) Rowland (Harry), C.V.O. 1926 (M.V.O. 1918); D.D., 1924; M.A., 1908; Chaplain to King George VI, 1926-52 and to the Queen since 1952; *b.* 28 Jan. 1882; *s.* of late Rev. Prebendary Grant of Wells Cathedral; *m.* 1908, Hon. Margaret (*d.* 1948), *d.* of late Col. Hon. L. P. Dawnay and Lady Victoria Dawnay (Maid of Honour to Queen Alexandra, 1905-8); one *s.* two *d.* *Educ.:* Monkton Combe School, Bath; Oxford University. Curate of Walcot, Bath, 1905-8; Rector of Great Warley, Essex, 1908-12; Rector of Sandringham and Domestic Chaplain to King George V., 1912-26; Hon. Domestic Chap. to Queen Alexandra; Librarian at Sandringham, 1912-26; Canon Residentiary in Norwich Cathedral, 1926-36; Vice-Dean, 1934-36; Rector of Walcot, Bath, 1936-41; Vicar of Holy Trinity, Southwell, 1941; Rural Dean of Southwell, 1943; Vicar of Scalby, 1944-49; Rural Dean of Scarborough, 1947; Rector of Wingfield, Wilts., 1949-52. C.F., B.E.F., 1916 and

1918; Senior C.F., 43rd Wessex Div. T.A., 1938-40; Senior Chaplain to Netley Hosp., 1940. *Recreation:* motoring. *Address:* 86 Pepys Road, Wimbledon, S.W.20. *T.:* Wimbledon 3954. [*Died* 24 *Oct.* 1961.

GRANT, Charles Frederick, C.S.I. 1937; I.C.S. (retired); *b.* 30 Sept. 1878; *s.* of Rev. Dr. C. M. Grant, St. Mark's, Dundee. Asst. Commissioner I.C.S., Burma, 1901; served in Indian Army, 1915-19; posts held, Chief Secretary to Government, Commissioner, Chairman of the Rangoon Development Trust, Financial Commissioner; Chm. of the Public Service Commission, Burma, 1937-39; Dep.-Chm. and Chm. Cttee. of Management, Dr. Barnardo's Homes, 1950-1956. *Address:* Palais Ausonia, Menton, A.M., France. *Club:* East India and Sports. [*Died* 25 *Jan.* 1966.

GRANT, Prof. Douglas B.; *see* Grant, Prof. W. D. B.

GRANT, Sir Duncan Alexander, 13th Bt., *cr.* 1688; *b.* 16 Dec. 1928; *s.* of late Alexander Lovett Grant; *S.* grandfather, 1937; *m.* 1949, Joan Penelope, *d.* of Capt. Sir Denzil Cope, 14th Bt.; three *s.* two *d.* *Educ.:* Gordonstoun School. *Heir:* *s.* Patrick Alexander Benedict, *b.* 5 Feb. 1953. *Address:* Polmailly House, Drumnadrochit, Inverness-shire. *T.:* Drumnadrochit 257. [*Died* 25 *March* 1961.

GRANT, Sir Francis Cullen, 12th Bt., *cr.* 1705; Capt. R.E.; *b.* 5 Oct. 1914; *s.* of 10th Bt. and Evelyn, *y. d.* of late Collingwood L. Wood, of Freeland, Perthshire; *S.* brother, 1944; *m.* 1953, Jean Margherita, *d.* of Captain Humphrey Tollemache, R.N., London, S.W.3; three *s.* two *d.* *Educ.:* Stowe. Served War of 1939-45 (despatches). *Heir:* *s.* Archibald, *b.* 2 September 1954. *Address:* House of Monymusk, Aberdeenshire. *Clubs:* St. James'; Royal Northern (Aberdeen). [*Died* 31 *Aug.* 1966.

GRANT, Francis Henry Symons, C.B.E. 1942; *b.* 18 Sept. 1883; *s.* of George and Mary Elizabeth Grant, Wimbledon; *m.* 1910, Alice Maude May (*d.* 1950), *d.* of Samuel Broadhurst, Stoke-on-Trent. *Educ.:* Westminster City School; St. John's College, Cambridge. Entered Secretary's Office, the Post Office, 1907; Private Secretary to Permanent Secretary, Sir Alexander King, 1912; Member of Gt. Britain's delegation International Telegraph Conference of Paris, 1925; Assistant Secretary, 1927; Regional Director Home Counties Region, Post Office, 1939; Controller-General, Posts and Telecommunications Branch, Control Commission for Germany (British Element), 1945-46. *Recreations:* travel, motoring, cycling, archæology. *Address:* 7 Ashley Lane, N.W.4. *T.:* Sunnyhill 2468. [*Died* 5 *Dec.* 1963.

GRANT, Dr. Ian Dingwall, C.B.E. 1960; Fellow College of General Practitioners since 1959 (President, 1956-59); Chairman, British Medical Association, since 1961; *b.* 6 June 1891; *e. s.* of Rev. Evan Grant and Jessie Dingwall; *m.* 1925, Gertrude Pearson; one *s.* *Educ.:* Bellahouston Acad.; Glasgow Univ. M.B., Ch.B. 1913; House Surgeon, Victoria Infirmary, 1914. Served European War, 1914-18, I.M.S., 1914-20 (despatches), retired, 1920; Major, 3rd Bn. Home Guard, Glasgow, 1940-45. Gen. Practice in Glasgow, 1920-. Mem. Gen. Med. Council, 1950-; Vice-Pres. B.M.A. (Chm. Representative Body, 1954-1957; Chm. Internat. Relations Cttee., 1957-); Fellow Australian Coll. of Gen. Practitioners, 1959. McKenzie Lecturer, 1957. M.D. (Hon.) Birmingham, 1958. *Publications:* contrib. to medical journals. *Recreations:* travel, fishing. *Address:* 74 St. Andrews Drive, Glasgow, S.1. *T.:* Ibrox 0986. *Clubs:* Royal Over-Seas League; Royal Scottish Automobile (Glasgow). [*Died* 17 *April* 1962.

GRANT, Colonel John Duncan, V.C. 1904; C.B. 1929; D.S.O. 1922; Indian Army, retired; *b.* 28 Dec. 1877; *o. s.* of Col. Suene Grant, R.E.; *m.* 1907, Kathleen, *o. d.* of late Col. Sir Peter J. Freyer, K.C.B.; one *s.* one *d.* *Educ.:* Cheltenham. Entered army, 1898; served Tibet, 1903-04 (wounded, despatches, V.C.); Persian Gulf, 1915-16 (wounded, despatches); France and Belgium, 1917; Mesopotamia, 1918; Afghanistan, 1919 (despatches); Waziristan, 1920-21 (despatches D.S.O.); A.A.G., A.H.Q., India, 1925-28; Deputy Director of Auxiliary and Territorial Forces in India, 1928-29; retired, 1929; Col. of 10th Gurkha Rifles, 1934-47. *Address:* 116 Cranmer Court, Sloane Avenue, S.W.3. *T.:* Kensington 4779. *Club:* United Service. [*Died* 20 *Feb.* 1967.

GRANT, John Peter, of Rothiemurchus; C.B. 1948; M.C.; T.D.; M.A. (Oxon); LL.B. (Edin.); D.L.; J.P., Advocate; Sheriff-Substitute of Inverness, Elgin and Nairn, at Inverness, 1927-56; *b.* 24 June 1885; *e. s.* of late J. P. Grant of Rothiemurchus and Edith M. Brewster Macpherson; *m.* 1913, Gertrude Margaret, *d.* of late Rev. W. H. A. and late Lady Cornelia Truell of Clonmannon, Rathnew, Co. Wicklow; one *s.* two *d.* *Educ.:* Cargilfield; Winchester; Magdalen Coll., Oxford. Advocate, 1913; Sheriff-Substitute of Caithness, Orkney and Zetland, at Lerwick, 1922; Vice-Lieut. Inverness-shire, 1939-63; Lt.-Col., and Bt. Col., Lovat Scouts; European War, Gallipoli, Egypt, Macedonia, France, 1914-18 (despatches three times, M.C.). *Address:* Aviemore, Scotland. *Club:* Highland (Inverness). [*Died* 23 *Aug.* 1963.

GRANT, Prof. Sir Kerr, Kt., *cr.* 1947; President South Australian School of Mines and Industries, 1942-59; Professor of Physics, Adelaide University, 1911-48, Professor Emeritus since 1948; *b.* Melbourne, 1878; *m.*; three *s.* *Educ.:* Univ. of Melbourne. Was Lecturer in Physics, School of Mines, Ballarat, and Melbourne University; invented, with Dr. Steele, a wonderfully fine method of weighing. *Address:* 56 Fourth Avenue, St Peters, Adelaide, S. Australia. [*Died* 13 *Oct.* 1967.

GRANT, Colonel Maurice Harold; *s.* of Maurice and Frances Grant; *m.* Muriel, *d.* of C. Jorgensen; one *s.* *Educ.:* Harrow; Royal Military College, Sandhurst. Entered Devon Regt., 1892; served with Regt. and on Staff throughout S. African War, of which he wrote most of Official History (present at 7 major actions and many minor affairs); D.A.A.G. at War Office, 1902-08; Commanded a Battalion in European War, 1914-1918, in France and on Staff until 1920; Staff appointment on H.G. during War of 1939-45. *Publications:* The Makers of Black Basaltes; Chronological History of Old English Landscape Painters; a Dictionary of Old English Landscape Painters; Dictionary of old British Etchers; Dictionary of Old British Sculptors; The Marbles, Granites, etc. of the World; also 6 works on the Old Flower-Painters, Catalogue of British Medals; under pseudonym, *Linesman:* Words by an Eye-witness; The Mechanism of War; under pseudonym, *Scolopax:* A Book of The Snipe; contributed to magazines, notably Blackwood's, Baily's, United Service, Burlington, New English, Contemporary, Spectator, Connoisseur; Country Life; owns extensive Collections of Old English Landscapes, Granites and Marbles, and frequent lender of the same to public Exhibitions in many cities. *Address:* c/o Lloyds Bank, 6 Pall Mall, S.W.1. [*Died* 17 *Feb.* 1962.

GRANT, Neil Forbes, C.B.E. 1918; M.A.; late London Editor of Cape Times, Natal Mercury, Rand Daily Mail, and Sunday Times of Johannesburg; *b.* Forres, Morayshire, 1882; *s.* of James Grant; *m.* Nancy Elizabeth Puckett (*d.* 1954). *Educ.:* Edinburgh Univ.; Brasenose Coll., Oxford (scholar). Joined staff of Morning Post, 1907; Foreign Editor, 1918 to 1925; Editor, Wireless and Cable Section, Ministry of Information; officer of the Order of Crown of Belgium Commander of Order of Dannebrog. *Publications:* Possessions, Getting Mother Married, A Valuable Rival, Thy Name is Woman, Petticoat Influence, The Nelson Touch, Dusty Ermine, and other plays; edited Willy Nicky Letters. *Recreation:* motoring. *Address:* Flat 2, 6 Third Avenue, Hove, Sussex. *Clubs:* Royal Automobile; Royal Commonwealth Society (Sussex Branch). [*Died* 24 *Dec.* 1970.

GRANT, Rev. Rowland; *see* Grant, Rev. A. R. H.

GRANT, Sir William; *see* Grant, Sir A. W.

GRANT, Prof. (William) Douglas (Beattie); Professor of American Literature, University of Leeds, since 1960; *b.* Newcastle upon Tyne, 3 Feb. 1921; *s.* of late Alexander Grant and Elizabeth McAlister Reid; *m.* Stella Joan, *e. d.* of late E. R. Appleton and Margaret Deacon; one *d.* *Educ.:* Royal Grammar School, Newcastle upon Tyne; Merton College, Oxford, 1939-41, 1945-46. B.A. 1941, M.A. 1946, D.Phil. 1950. Captain, 41st R.M. Commando. Lectr. in English Literature, Edinburgh Univ., 1946-48; Associate Professor of English Literature, Toronto Univ., 1948-1958; Nuffield Travelling Fellow in the Humanities, 1953-54; Editor, University of Toronto Quarterly, 1955-60; Professor of English Literature, Toronto Univ., 1958-60; visiting Professor of English, Leiden Univ., 1959; Chairman, Governor-General's Cttee. for Literary Awards, 1959-60. Brooks Fellow, Univ. of Queensland, 1964. F.R.S.L. 1957. *Publications:* (Ed.) Sir Walter Scott's Private Letters of the Seventeenth Century, 1947; The Fuel of the Fire, 1950; (Ed.) Selected Works of Sterne, 1950; James Thomson, Poet of the Seasons, 1951; (Ed.) Selected Works of Dryden, 1952; Poetical Works of Charles Churchill, 1956; The Phanseys of William Cavendish, Marquis of Newcastle, 1956; Margaret the First, a Biography of Margaret Cavendish, Duchess of Newcastle, 1957; Mark Twain, 1962; The Cock Lane Ghost, 1965; Purpose and Place, 1965; articles and reviews in several periodicals and jls. *Recreations:* travel, gardening. *Address:* Manna Ash, 228 High Street, Boston Spa, Yorks. *T.:* Boston Spa 2258. *Club:* Athenæum. [*Died* 1 *Feb.* 1969.

GRANT-DALTON, Lt.-Col. Duncan, C.M.G. 1919; D.S.O. 1917; late West Yorkshire Regiment; *b.* 1881; *m.* 1919, Gwavas May (*d.* 1955), *e. d.* of late S. Spry; one *s.* one *d.* Served S. African War, 1900-2 (Queen's medal and three clasps, King's medal and two clasps); European War, 1914-17 (despatches twice, C.M.G., D.S.O.); retd. pay, 1923; late Mem. Truro R.D.C.; late C.C. Cornwall (resigned); J.P. *Address:* c/o National Provincial Bank, Tiverton, Devon. [*Died* 10 *Feb.* 1969.

GRANTHAM, Vincent Alpe; Chairman of the Chartered Bank, 1940-67; and Director of Companies; *b.* 17 April 1889; 2nd *s.* of Col. Charles Fulford Grantham and Margaret Rosalind, *d.* of John Pretheroe Alpe; *m.* 1919, Margaret Violet Grantham, *o. d.* of William Henry Crowe, I.C.S., Judge of High Court, Bombay, and Violet Mary Bashall, *d.* of Col. Charles Caldwell Grantham; six *s.* (two *d.* decd.). *Educ.:* Elizabeth College, Guernsey, C.I. Joined firm of Forbes Forbes Campbell & Co. Ltd., Bombay, 1910 (Partner 1924); Director of Public Companies in India. Indian Defence Force, 1916-19. Member, Cotton Contracts Board, 1919; Member Cttee. Bombay Chamber of Commerce, 1919, Dep. Chm., 1921 and 1924, Pres., 1925. Vice-Pres. Assoc. Chambers of Commerce of India, Burma and Ceylon, 1925; Director E. India Cotton Assoc. Ltd., 1921, Dep. Chm., 1923-1924; Member: Central Cotton Cttee., 1921; Indian Central Cotton Cttee., 1923-26; First Vice-Pres., 1923; Legislative Council, Bombay, 1923-24; Bd. of Trustees, Port of Bombay, 1924-25. Director Imperial Bank of India, 1924; J.P. Bombay, 1925; retired from India, 1926. Board of Management, London Chest Hospital, 1927-48, Chairman, 1948; Board of Governors, Hospital for Diseases of the Chest, 1948; Visitor, King Edward's Hospital Fund, 1944-51; Chairman, The Guernsey Society, 1950-52. Chm. Bd. of Govs., London Clinic, 1966-. First Pres. Overseas Bankers' Club. *Recreation:* sailing. *Address:* St. Clere's Hall, St. Osyth, Essex. *Clubs:* Bath; Royal Yacht Squadron (Cowes); Royal Bombay Yacht. [*Died* 1 *Aug.* 1968.

GRANVILLE, Countess, (Rose Constance Leveson-Gower), G.C.V.O., *cr.* 1953 (D.C.V.O., *cr.* 1945); LL.D.; *b.* 6 May 1890; *d.* of 14th Earl of Strathmore and Kinghorne, K.G., K.T., G.C.V.O.; *m.* 1916 (as Lady Rose Bowes-Lyon), 4th Earl Granville, K.G., K.C.V.O., C.B., D.S.O. (*d.* 1953); one *s.* (*see* 5th Earl Granville) one *d.* Hon. LL.D. Belfast; Freeman of Belfast and Larne; C.St.J. *Address:* Pearsie, Kirriemuir, Angus. [*Died* 17 *Nov.* 1967.

GRANVILLE-SHARP, Gilbert; *see* Sharp.

GRATTON, Norman Murray Gladstone, C.B.E. 1952; B.A. (Melbourne), B.A. (Adelaide); Dip. Ed.; first Headmaster, Scotch College, Adelaide, 1919-51, retd.; *b.* 21 July 1886; *s.* of Joseph Gladstone Gratton and Annie Cay Carlin; *m.* 1912, Jeannie Gordon Tweedie; two *s.* (one *d.* decd.). *Educ.:* Privately; Univ. of Melbourne; Teachers' College, Univ. of Melbourne. Asst. Master at various schools, including St. Peter's Coll., Adelaide, till 1918; Chief Commissioner of the Boy Scouts Assoc. (S.A. Section), 1929-31; Member of Institute of Associated Teachers, 1933-34; Member of the Public Examinations Committee, University of Adelaide, 1922-51; Chairman Headmasters' Assoc. of S.A.; Member of the English Headmasters' Conference and the Australian Headmasters' Conference. *Address:* 22 George St., Hawthorn, S. Australia. *T.:* U 5055. [*Died* 1 *Jan.* 1965.

GRAUER, Albert Edward; Chairman, British Columbia Power Corporation, since 1961; Chairman, British Columbia Electric Company Ltd. since 1961 (President since 1946); Chancellor, University of British Columbia, since 1957; *b.* Eburne, B.C., 21 January 1906; *s.* of John Jacob and Mary Neth Grauer, Germany; *m.* 1933, Shirley Woodward; three *s.* three *d.* *Educ.:* King Edward High School; University of British Columbia; Univ. of California (Ph.D.); Oxford Univ. Lawyer, E. P. Davis & Co., Vancouver, 1930; Lecturer in Economics, Univ. of Toronto, 1931; Asst. Prof., Dept. of Social Science, Univ. of Toronto, 1935; Prof. of Social Science and Director of Dept., Univ. of Toronto, 1937; Gen. Sec., British Columbia Electric Co. Ltd., Vancouver, 1939; Executive Vice-Pres., Brit. Columbia Power Corp. Ltd., 1944. Member, Royal Commission on Canada's Economic Prospects, 1957-59; Expert with Royal Commission on Dominion-Provincial Relations. Hon. LL.D., Univ. of British Columbia, 1958. *Publications:* Labour Legislation, 1939; Public Health, 1939; Public

Assistance and Social Insurance, 1939; Housing, 1939. *Recreations:* swimming, riding, music. *Address:* 3390 The Crescent, Vancouver 9, B.C. *T.:* Regent 3-8035. *Clubs:* Vancouver, Capilano Golf and Country, Royal Vancouver Yacht, University (Vancouver); Union (Victoria); Mount Royal (Montreal). [*Died* 29 *July* 1961.

GRAUL, Isidore, C.B. 1953; O.B.E. 1941; Under-Secretary, Ministry of Food, 1947-55, retd.; *b.* 14 July 1894; *m.* 1925. *Educ.:* Strand School, King's Coll., London; London School of Economics and Political Science. Reparations Commission, Berlin, 1923-30; Empire Marketing Board, 1931-34; Imperial Economic Cttee., 1934-35; Market Supply Committee, 1935-36; Food (Defence Plans) Dept., 1936-39; Ministry of Food, 1939-55. B.Sc. (Econ.) 1st Class Hons., 1921. President, Students' Union London School of Economics, 1922. *Address:* Villa Merry, Coxyde-Bains, Belgium. *T.:* Coxyde 212, 57. *Club:* Danish. [*Died* 28 *Feb.* 1962.

GRAVES, 7th Baron (*cr.* 1794); **Henry Algernon Claud Graves;** *b.* 3 Oct. 1877; *s.* of late Claude Thomas Graves; *S.* cousin 1937; *m.* 1909, Vera Blanche Neville (whom he divorced, 1922), *d.* of late Alfred Neville Snepp; one *s.* Served European War, 1914-19. *Heir: s.* Hon. Peter (George Wellesley) Graves. *Address:* Kensington Close, W.8. [*Died* 6 *Nov.* 1963.

GRAVES, Marjorie; *d.* of late William Graves, J.P., Newells, Horsham, Sussex. *Educ.:* Privately; Château de Dieudonne, Bornel, France. Archives Research Bibliothèque Nationale and Archives Nationales, Paris; Foreign Office during the War; Paris Peace Conference, 1919; Secretary, Intelligence Department, Home Office, 1919-20; Historical Research; Borough Councillor, Holborn, 1928-34; M.P. (C.) South Hackney, 1931-1935; Chairman Metropolitan Area of National Union of Conservative and Unionist Associations, 1936-37; British Government Delegate XVII. Assembly League of Nations. C.C. Dorset. *Publications:* Quelques Pièces relatives à la vie de Louis, duc d'Orléans; Deux Inventaires du Moyen Age, etc. *Recreations:* historical research, observing birds, music. *Address:* Cocknowle, Wareham, Dorset. [*Died* 17 *Nov.* 1961.

GRAY, Sir Alexander, Kt., *cr.* 1947; C.B.E. 1939; M.A.; Hon. LL.D. (Aberdeen; St. Andrews; St. Francis Xavier, N.S.; Edinburgh); Professor Emeritus of Political Economy, University of Edinburgh, since 1956; *b.* 6 Jan. 1882; 3rd *s.* of late J. Y. Gray, Dundee and Letham, Angus; *m.* 1909, Alice Gunn; one *s.* three *d.* *Educ.:* Dundee High School; Universities of Edinburgh, Göttingen, Paris. 1st Class Mathematics (Edin.), 1902; 1st Class Economic Science, 1905; Local Government Board, 1905-1909; Colonial Office 1909-12; Insurance Commission, 1912-19; Insurance Department of Ministry of Health, 1919-21; Jaffrey Professor of Political Economy, University of Aberdeen, 1921-34; Professor of Political Economy and Mercantile Law, University of Edinburgh, 1935-56; at various times External Examiner in Economics, Universities of Edinburgh, Glasgow, St. Andrews, etc.; awarded Peddie Steele prize of 100 guineas on occasion of Quincentenary Celebrations at St. Andrews, 1911. Member, or Chairman, of Government Commissions, Committees, Courts of Enquiry, Advisory Councils, etc., 1922-55; also concerned with: Scottish Central Library; Schools Broadcasting Council; Fulbright Commission (G.B.). President, Section F. British Association, 1949. *Publications:* The Scottish Staple at Veere (with the late Professor Davidson), 1909; Three pamphlets on the first War: The True Pastime, The Upright Sheaf, The New Leviathan, 1915; Some Aspects of National Health Insurance, 1923; Family Endowment, 1927; The Development of Economic Doctrine, 1931; Robert Burns, an Address, 1944; The Socialist Tradition, 1946; Adam Smith (an Historical Assoc. pamphlet), 1948; A Timorous Civility: A Scots Miscellany, 1966; various translations including the works of Dr. Grelling, viz.: J'accuse, 1915; The Crime (3 vols.), 1917-18; Belgian Documents, 1919. Poetry: Songs and Ballads chiefly from Heine, 1920; Any Man's Life, 1924; Poems (a Broadsheet), 1925; Gossip, 1928; Songs from Heine, for Schumann's Dichterliebe, 1928; Arrows, 1932; Selected Poems, 1948; Sir Halewyn, 1949; Four-and-Forty (Danish Ballads) 1954; Historical Ballads of Denmark, 1958. *Address:* 8 Abbotsford Park, Edinburgh 10. *T.:* Edinburgh Morningside 6027. [*Died* 17 *Feb.* 1968.

GRAY, Sir Alexander (George), Kt. 1941; late Manager, Bank of India, Ltd., Bombay; Vice-President, Indian Institute of Bankers; *b.* 1 March 1884; *s.* of late A. G. Gray, Macclesfield and Fraserburgh; *m.* 1922, Dulce Muriel Fanny Wild; one *s.* (one *d.* decd.). *Educ.:* Macclesfield Grammar School. Parrs Bank Ltd., Manchester and District; arrived India 1905; entered service of Bank of India Ltd., 1908; retired, 1943; Sheriff of Bombay, 1937; Dir. Asian Ltd., London, and Agent in London Bombay Gas Co. Ltd.; Chm. Executive Council Berkshire National Health Service Act, 1947-54. Grand Commander Cross Order of Polonia Restituta, 1945, for services to Polish Relief, India, 1939-43. *Address:* Leyfields, Ashampstead, Berks. *T.:* Yattendon 241. *Clubs:* Oriental, East India and Sports; Berkshire (Reading), South Berks (Newbury). [*Died* 26 *Oct.* 1968.

GRAY, Sir Archibald (Montague Henry), K.C.V.O. 1959; Kt., 1946; C.B.E. 1919; M.D., B.S. (Lond.); F.R.C.P. (Lond.); F.R.C.S. (Eng.); Cons. Physician, Univ. Coll. Hosp.; Consulting Physician for Diseases of the Skin, Hosp. for Sick Children, Great Ormond Street; Consulting Dermatologist to Goldie Leigh Hosp.; Hon. Consulting Dermatologist R.A.F.; *b.* Ottery St. Mary, Devon, 1880; *s.* of late Frederick A. Gray, M.R.C.S.; *m.* 1917, Elsie, R.R.C., *y. d.* of late F. B. Cooper, Newcastle, Staffs; one *s.* one *d.* *Educ.:* Cheltenham College; University College and Hospital; University of Bern. M.B. (Lond.) Honours, 1903; B.S. (Honours), 1904; M.D. (University Medal), 1905; F.R.C.S. 1908; F.R.C.P. 1918; Fellow Univ. Coll., London, 1908; Member General Medical Council, 1950-52; Member Court (1947-58) and Senate (1929-50), Univ. of London, Deputy Vice-Chancellor, 1938-39; Dean of Faculty of Medicine, 1932-36; Dean, Univ. College Hosp. Medical School, 1926-35; Adviser in Dermatology to the Min. of Health, 1948-62; Chm., Distribution Cttee., King Edward's Hospital Fund for London, 1948-59; Chm. Board of Management, London School of Hygiene and Tropical Medicine, 1951-61. Member of Govt. Cttee. on Medical Services of the Navy, Army and Air Force, 1931-33; of Inter-departmental Committee on the Organisation of Medical Schools, 1942-44; Malcolm Morris Lecturer, 1945; Harveian Orator, R.C.P., 1951; Prosser White Orator, 1954; Hon. Fellow R.S.M., President 1940-42, Hon. Secretary 1919-24, Hon. Treas. 1926-32; Past Pres. Section of Dermatology; Pres. British Assoc. of Dermatology, 1938-39; Pres. 10th Internat. Congress of Dermatology, London, 1952. Pres. Cheltonian Soc., 1950-51; Hon. Fellow, School of Pharmacy, London Univ.; Hon. Mem.: Polish Acad. of Science and Letters; Am. Dermatological Assoc.; Spanish Acad. of Dermatology; Yugoslav Assoc. of Dermatologiss; Australian, Austrian, Canadian, Berlin, French, German and Israeli Dermatological Socs., and Soc for Investigative Dermatology; Corr. Mem. Argentine, Danish, Hungarian, Polish, and Swedish Dermatological Socs.; formerly Lt.-Colonel R.A.M.C. (T.A.); T.D.; attached to General Staff at War Office, 1914, 1918; Consulting Dermatologist Army Zone, B.E.F., 1918-19 (despatches). Hon. LL.D. (Lond.), 1958. *Publications:* papers on medical subjects. *Address:* 7 Alvanley Gardens, N.W.6. *Club:* Athenæum. [*Died* 13 *Oct.* 1967.

GRAY, Colonel Arthur Claypon Horner, O.B.E. 1919; late R.A.M.C.; *b.* 12 April 1878; *s.* of late Rev. John D. Gray, vicar of Nayland; *m.* Dorothy M., *d.* of Rev. J. Denham, late Canon of Rochester; two *s.* one *d.* *Educ.:* Malvern College; Guy's Hospital. Lieut. R.A.M.C., 1903; Member of Royal Society's Sleeping Sickness Commission, Uganda, 1904-1906; in charge Sleeping Sickness Extended Investigation, Uganda, 1906-9; Attached Pasteur Institute, Tunis, 1912; Assistant Professor, R.A. Medical College, 1914; in charge Princess Christian Mobile Laboratory B.E.F., France, 1915-16; O.C. No. 37 C.C.S. B.E.F., France, 1916-1918, prisoner of war, Germany, 1918 (despatches twice, 1914-15 Star, O.B.E.); Waziristan, 1921-24 (Medal and Clasp); A.D.P. British Forces in Turkey, 1922-23; Professor R.A.M. College, 1926-30; Brevet Colonel, 1929; Colonel, 1930; Director of Pathology, War Office, 1930-32; Director and Professor of Pathology, Royal Army Medical College, 1932-34; K.H.S. 1932; retired pay, 1934; re-employed in Army in rank of Major, 1941; 1939-45 Star, Atlantic Star, War Medal. *Address:* Stour Fields, Nayland, nr. Colchester. *T.:* Nayland 252. [*Died* 28 *April* 1963.

GRAY, Ethel, C.B.E. 1919; R.R.C.; *b.* Melbourne; *d.* of Samuel Gray, Ireland, and Amelia Gray, England. *Educ.:* Public State School and Presbyterian Ladies' College, Melbourne. Training Melbourne Hospital (Sister and House Matron); Matron, Infectious Diseases Hospital: Assistant Matron, Melbourne Hospital; Matron, Perth Public Hospital and Infectious Hospital, Perth, two years, then enlisted; served 1915; started Harefield Hospital in Middlesex; to France, 1916, in charge as Matron No. 2 Australian General Hospital, there until after Armistice; closed the Hospital; returned to England; stationed at Sutton Veny, 1919-20; Matron and Lady Superintendent, Epworth Hospital, Melbourne; retired 1939; now doing social service work, Red Cross, etc. *Address:* Tay Bank, 754 Canterbury Road, Surrey Hills, E.10, Melbourne, Australia. *Clubs:* Lyceum, Returned Army Nurses, Melbourne. [*Died* 22 *July* 1962.

GRAY, Harold St. George, O.B.E. 1949; M.A., F.S.A., F.M.A.; *b.* in The Close, Lichfield, 15 Jan. 1872; *m.* 1899, Florence Harriett Young. Formerly Director of archæological excavations for the British Association and other Societies and Committees. Received his scientific training with General Pitt-Rivers, 1888-99; Sec. and Librarian, 1901-49, President 1951-52, of the Somerset Archæological and Natural History Soc.; Keeper of the Somerset County Museum, 1901-49; Pres. South-Western Naturalists' Union, 1945-47. *Publications:* Excavations at Arbor Low Stone Circle, Derbyshire, 1903; Memoir of General Pitt-Rivers, D.C.L., F.R.S., and Index to his Works, 1905; The Stone Circles of East Cornwall, 1908; Excavations at Wick Barrow, Somerset, 1908; Reports on the Meare Lake Village, Ham Hill (Som.), Maumbury Rings, Kingsdown Camp, Battlegore (Williton), Warham Camp (Norfolk), Combe Beacon (nr. Chard), and Burrow Mump (Som.), 1908-39; The Yeovil Gold Torc, 1909; The Avebury Excavations, 1908-22, 1934; joint author of The Glastonbury Lake Village, vol. i. 1911, vol. ii. 1917, and of The Meare Lake Village, vol. i. 1948, vol. ii. 1953; author of numerous papers in various transactions on archæological excavations in England. *Address:* The Treasurer's House, Martock, Somerset. *T.:* Martock 3288. [*Died* 28 *Feb.* 1963.

GRAY, James, C.B.E. 1942; M.I.C.E.; Director Union Castle Mail Steamship Co. Limited, 1950-55 (Chief Superintendent Engineer, 1915-25 and 1935-53); *b.* 1877; *s.* of late John Gray, Edinburgh; *m.* 1916, Dorothy Eileen, *d.* of Albert Hunt, C.B.E.; two *d.* B.Sc. Bristol University. Chief Supt. Engineer, Canadian Pacific Steamships, 1913-15; General Manager, Harland & Wolff's Works, London, Liverpool, and Southampton, 1925-35; Director Harland & Wolff's, 1929-35. *Address:* 31 Barton Court Avenue, Barton-on-Sea, Hampshire. [*Died* 20 *Jan.* 1968.

GRAY, James Andrew; Managing Director of Southern Africa and African World; *b.* 16 August 1890; *m.* 1920, Vera Frances (*d.* 1962), *d.* of John Tiernen, Dublin; two *s.* one *d.* (and one *s.* killed in action). Served formerly on The Scotsman and The Times; editor, Pretoria News, 1924-32; editor, South Africa, 1934-62; special correspondent at Imperial Economic Conference, Ottawa, 1932; accredited correspondent on royal tour of Belgian Congo, 1955; France and Flanders, 1915-18 (Royal Scots); Parliamentary Company of Home Guard, 1940-45. Chevalier, Order of the Lion, Belgium, 1953; Prix de Journalisme Colonial (Ghent), 1956. *Publications:* South Africa and Rhodesia To-day, 1937; New South Africa, 1949; (ed.) Rhodesia and Nyasaland, 1957; (ed.) South Africa To-Day, 1960. *Address:* 112 Worple Road, Wimbledon, S.W.19. [*Died* 2 *April* 1966.

GRAY, Sir John (Milner), Kt., *cr.* 1944; M.A. (Cantab.); F.R.G.S.; *b.* 7 July 1889; *s.* of Arthur Gray, late Master of Jesus College, Cambridge; unmarried. *Educ.:* Perse School, Cambridge King's College, Cambridge. Articled to a firm of solicitors, 1911-1914; served with 8th Bn. (T.F.) Sherwood Foresters, European War, 1914-18 (twice wounded), demobilised with rank of Capt. Solicitor, 1923, and called to bar, Gray's Inn, 1932. Asst. District Commissioner, Uganda, 1920-24; District Magistrate, Uganda, 1924-1933; Acting Solicitor-General, Uganda, 1929, and Acting Judge, Uganda, 1933; Judge of Supreme Court, Gambia, 1934-42; Acting Governor of the Gambia, 1935 and 1940; Chief Justice, Zanzibar, 1943-1952. *Publications:* History of the Perse School, Cambridge. 1921; Biographical Notes on the Mayors of Cambridge, 1921; The School of Pythagoras, 1932; A History of the Gambia 1940; The British in Mombasa, 1824-1826, 1958; Early Portuguese Missionaries in East Africa, 1960; History of Zanzibar from The Middle Ages to 1856, 1962; contributions to various periodicals on East and West African History. *Address:* 34 Highsett, Hills Road, Cambridge. *Club:* Royal Commonwealth Society. [*Died* 15 *Jan.* 1970.

GRAY, Joseph Alexander, O.B.E., B.Sc. (Melbourne), D.Sc. (Manchester), F.R.S.C. 1922; F.R.S. 1932; Hon. LL.D. (Queen's); Emeritus Professor of Physics, Queen's University, Ontario; *b.* 7 Feb. 1884; 3rd *s.* of late James Gray; *m.* 1919, Elizabeth Watson. *Educ.:* Univ. High School, Ormond Coll., Univ. of Melbourne; Imperial College of Science and Technology, London; University of Manchester, 1851 Exhibition Scholar, 1909-12; Lecturer, Assistant and Associate Professor, McGill University, Montreal, 1912-1924; Chown Research Prof. of Physics, Queen's Univ., Kingston, Ontario, 1924-52;

retd. 1952; Mem. National Research Council of Canada, 1942-48. Awarded 1st Medal of the Canadian Assoc. of Physicists for achievement in Physics, 1956. Overseas service, mainly in Sound Ranging, 1915-19 (despatches, O.B.E., Captain R.E.), retired, 1952. *Publications:* Various scientific papers in the Proceedings of the Royal Society, Philosophical Magazine, Transactions of the Royal Society of Canada and Canadian Journal of Research, on radioactivity and X-rays. *Recreation:* golf. *Club:* Sesame. [*Died* 5 *March* 1966.

GRAY, Leonard Thomas Miller, J.P., B.Sc., Ph.D., A.R.I.C.; Chairman and Managing Director, Miller & Co. Ltd., Ironfounders, 1945-61 (retired); Member of the Monopolies Commission, 1956-64; *b.* 31 Aug. 1893; *er. s.* of Robert Smith Gray, farmer, Duddingston, Midlothian; *m.* 1st, 1915, Mary Rachel Scott; three *d.*: 2nd, 1946, Alison Logan Mack. *Educ.:* Merchiston Castle and Haileybury; Birmingham and London (King's College) Universities. Capt., Royal Scots, 1914-17. Research Worker and Asst. Lecturer in Chemistry, King's College, London, 1921-28; Exec. Director, Welwyn Garden City Ltd., 1928-34, Gen. Manager 1935, Director 1935-48. Temp. Principal, Board of Trade, 1941: Temp. Asst. Secretary, 1941-45. Member: Linoleum Industry Working Party, 1946-47; Schuster Cttee. on Qualifications of Town Planners, 1948-50; Glenrothes New Town Corp., 1948-53; Advisory Cttee., Dept. of Health, Scotland, 1949. Chm., Scottish Liberal Party, 1948-51; Pres., Edinburgh Chamber of Commerce and Manufactures, 1956-58; Director, Friends Provident and Century Life Office, 1955-64. *Recreations:* reading and travelling. *Address:* 6 Eton Terrace, Edinburgh 4. *T.:* Dean 6281. *Clubs:* Athenæum; New (Edinburgh).
[*Died* 4 *Aug.* 1969.

GRAY, Louis Harold, Ph.D.; F.R.S. 1961; Nuffield Fellow and Director, British Empire Cancer Campaign Research Unit in Radiobiology, Mount Vernon Hosp., Northwood, since 1953; *b.* 10 Nov. 1905; *s.* of Harry and Amy Gray; *m.* 1932, Frieda Marjory Picot; two *s.* *Educ.:* Christ's Hosp.; Trin. Coll., Cambridge. Rouse Ball Research Student under Lord Rutherford, Cavendish Laboratory, 1927-30; Fellow of Trin. Coll., Camb., 1930-34; Prophit Scholar, R.C.S., 1934-1939. Senior Physicist, Mount Vernon Hosp., 1934-47; Sen. Physicist, then Dep. Dir., M.R.C. Radiotherapeutic Res. Unit, Hammersmith Hosp., 1947-53. Sylvanus Thompson Memorial Lectr., Brit. Inst. of Radiology, 1953. Guest Lectr. at many confs. and instns. throughout the World, on radiology and radiobiology, 1933-. Chairman Hospital Physicists Association, 1946-1947; President British Inst. of Radiology, 1950; Councillor, Radiation Research Soc., 1955-59; Chm. Assoc. for Radiation Research, 1959-60; Pres. Internat. Congress of Radiation Research, 1962 (Chm. Organising Cttee., 1960-62). Member: M.R.C. Protection Cttee.; Statutory Cttee. of Min. of Health Protection Service; W.H.O. Expert Advisory Panel on Radiation; Internat. Cttee. on Radiological Protection; Univ. of London Special Adv. Bd. in Biophysics, etc. Advances in Med. and Biolog. Physics. Hon. Mem. Amer. Radium Society. Barclay Medal, Brit. Inst. Radiol., 1960, etc. Hon. D.Sc. Leeds, 1962; Bertner Award, 1964. *Publications:* in nuclear and radiological physics and in radiobiology, ref. radiotherapy of cancer and hazards associated with use of ionising radiations. *Address:* 5 St. Mary's Ave., Northwood, Mx. *T.:* 22102; B.E.C.C. Research Unit in Radiobiology, Mt. Vernon Hospital, Northwood, Mx. *T.:* 26111. [*Died* 9 *July* 1965.

GRAY, Theodore Grant, C.M.G. 1938; M.B., Ch.B., F.R.A.C.P.; M.P.C.; *b.* Aberdeen, 31 Jan. 1884; *s.* of Henry and Helen Gray; *m.* 1914, Catherine, *d.* of David Sutherland, Torphins, Aberdeen; three *s.* three *d.* *Educ.:* Aberdeen Grammar School; University of Aberdeen. House Surgeon and House Physician Royal Hospital for Sick Children, Aberdeen, 1907; Assistant Physician, Kingseat Mental Hospital, 1908-11; Assistant Medical Officer New Zealand Mental Hospitals, 1911; Medical Superintendent Nelson Mental Hospital, 1922; Director-General of Mental Hospitals, New Zealand, 1927-47; retired, 1947; now consultant psychiatrist, Wellington. *Publications:* Treatment of Mental Deficiency, 1927; Post Epileptic Automatism as a defence in murder cases, Jl. of Mental Science, 1932; The Very Error of the Moon, 1959. *Recreations:* motoring, gardening. *Address:* 20 Izard Rd., Khandallah, N.Z. *Club:* Wellington. [*Died* 8 *Sept.* 1964.

GRAZEBROOK, Henry Broome Durley, Q.C. 1939; Barrister-at-law; *b.* 6 June 1884; *er. s.* of late Henry Durley Grazebrook, Barrister-at-law; *m.* 1917, Ethel Gertrude (*d.* 1945), *er. d.* of late Arthur Sydney Westmore, Bournemouth; one *d.*; *m.* 1946, Florence Gertrude, *d.* of Arthur Baldwin. *Educ.:* Tonbridge School; St. John's College, Oxford (M.A.). Called to Bar, Gray's Inn and Middle Temple, 1908; Bencher of Gray's Inn, 1945; Treasurer of Gray's Inn, 1960; served European War, 1916-19, R.F.C. and R.A.F. Special Divorce Commissioner, 1946-1957; Recorder of Penzance, 1940-56. *Recreations:* golf, gardening, farming. *Address:* Francis Taylor Building, Temple, E.C.4. *T.A.:* 35 Temple. *T.:* Central 9942; Fieldings, Golden Avenue, Angmering-on-Sea, Sussex. *T.:* Rustington 6822.
[*Died* 25 *March* 1969.

GRAZEBROOK, Brigadier Tom Neville, C.B.E. 1945; D.S.O. 1943; D.L.; retd., 1958; *b.* 12 July 1904; *s.* of Tom Grazebrook, Stourbridge, Worcs.; *m.* 1937, Marion Betty (*née* Asplin); one *s.* two *d.* *Educ.:* Shrewsbury School; R.M.C. Sandhurst. Commissioned 1924; served West Africa, 1932-1933; Staff College, Camberley, 1938-39; served War of 1939-45 (D.S.O., C.B.E.): France, North Africa, Sicily, Italy, N.W. Europe; Control Commission for Germany, 1945-47; Malaya, 1947-49. D.L. Gloucestershire, 1965. U.S. Legion of Merit (Officer Cl.), 1945. *Recreations:* genealogy and gardening. *Address:* Sheepscombe House, Sheepscombe, Nr. Stroud, Gloucestershire.
[*Died* 24 *Aug.* 1967.

GREATHED, Rear-Admiral Bernard Wilberforce, C.B. 1946; M.I.Mech.E.; *b.* 5 Nov. 1891; *s.* of late Edward Archer Greathed, of Winnipeg, Manitoba, Canada, and Chandlersford, Hants., and Janet Georgiana Greathed; *m.* 1928, Beatrix Mary, *d.* of Mark George Davidson, Ruchill, Guildford, Surrey; no *c.* *Educ.:* Downs School, Clifton, Bristol; R.N. Colleges, Osborne and Dartmouth. Joined R.N. College, Osborne, 1904; Midshipman H.M.S. Shannon, 1909; Lieut. 1913; Lieut. (E) 1914; Lt.-Comdr. (E) 1921; Comdr. (E) 1926; Capt. (E) 1937; Rear-Adm. (E) 1944. Served European War, 1914-18, in Channel Fleet, Grand Fleet, and Harwich Force; Service in Admiralty, 1939-1946. *Recreations:* golf, fishing, boat sailing. *Address:* c/o Bank of Montreal, 9 Waterloo Place, London, S.W.1.
[*Died* 19 *June* 1961.

GREAVES, Sir John Brownson, Kt. 1946; C.B.E. 1941; Director, Ransomes, Sims & Jefferies Ltd., Ipswich; formerly Managing Director, Davey, Paxman & Co. Ltd., Colchester; Hon. Adviser, Greaves Cotton & Co. Ltd., Bombay (Chairman, 1921-47); Member, Ipswich District Cttee. Eastern Regional Board for Industry, since 1957; Member, Essex C.C., since 1958; *b.* 20 July 1900; *s.* of Herbert Rufus Greaves, Bombay;

m. 1927, Doris Io, *d.* of late Frank Clifton, Boyne House, Bournemouth; two *d.* *Educ.:* Harrow; Trinity Hall, Cambridge. C.I.Mech.E. 1947. Sheriff of Bombay, 1945; Member, Legislative Council, Bombay, 1932-36; Member, Legislative Assembly, Bombay, 1937-40; Chairman, Bombay Education Soc., 1930-47. Chief Controller (Hon.), Raw Materials and Stores, Cotton Textiles, Govt. of India, 1943-45. Mem. Bishop of Chelmsford's Commission to examine the financial needs and resources of the diocese, 1952. *Address:* 171 Lexden Road, Colchester, Essex. *T.:* Colchester 4867. *Clubs:* Oriental; Royal Bombay Yacht, Willingdon Sports (Bombay). [*Died* 22 *Dec.* 1965.

GREEN, Brig.-General Arthur Frank Umfreville, C.M.G. 1919; D.S.O. 1917; retired pay; H.G. Volunteer, 1940; Bn. Commander, 1941; Private, 1943; *b.* 20 Aug. 1878; *s.* of late Col. A. O. Green, R.E., and A. Buckle; *m.* 1933, Annie Livingstone (*d.* 1954), *d.* of A. L. Bruce, Edinburgh. *Educ.:* Haileybury; R.M.A., Woolwich. First commission, 1897; served South African War (Queen's medal 3 clasps, King's medal 2 clasps); European War, 1914-1918 (1914 Star, War Medal, Victory Medal, C.M.G., D.S.O., Brevet of Lieut.-Col. and Col.; despatches six times; Officer Legion of Honour and Croix de Guerre, France; Officer Order of Leopold, Croix de Guerre, Belgium; Officer SS. Maurice and Lazarus (twice) and Croce di Guerra, Italian; Military Order of Aviz, 1st class, Portuguese; Distinguished Service Medal, U.S.A.); went to Belgium as Capt. of 112 Battery, R.G.A., with 7th Division, 1914; D.A.Q.M.G. 3rd Division, and A.Q.M.G. XI. Corps, 1915; D.A. and Q.M.G. XI. Corps, with rank of Brig.-Gen., Nov. 1916 to Armistice; on Armistice Commission, Nov. 1918-Aug. 1919, as Chief of Staff, British Mission; Col. on the Staff i/c Administration, Malta, and Member of Nominated Council, 1920-24. Member, Association of Sussex Artists, 1950. *Publications:* As Down of Thistle 1904; The Countermine, 1905; Landscape Sketching for Military Purposes; Home Guard Pocket Book (W.S.H.G.), 1940; Evening Tattoo, 1941; Rifle Shooting Questions Answered, 1944. *Recreations:* rifle shooting; Cadet Trophy, Bisley, 1893; Haileybury VIII., 1894; won fencing for R.M.A. *v.* Sandhurst, 1896; cricket, golf, billiards, shooting, and sketching. *Address:* Blue Cedar, Roundabout, Pulborough, Sussex. *T.:* W. Chiltington 2148. *Club:* West Sussex Golf. [*Died* 20 *Apr.* 1964.

GREEN, Frederick Charles, M.C.; M.A. (St. And.); M.A. (Cantab.); Dr. phil. (Cologne); Docteur de l'Univ. de Paris; Emeritus Professor of French Literature, University of Edinburgh; former Fellow of Magdalene Coll., Cambridge; *b.* Aberdeen, 25 Feb. 1891; *o. s.* of James Green and Jessie Isobel Mathieson; *m.* 1916, Mary Balairdie, *o. d.* of Alexander Gilchrist, Dundee; two *s.* two *d.* *Educ.:* Harris Academy, Dundee; Univs. of St. Andrews, Paris, and Cologne. First Class Mod. Langs., 1913; Tyndale-Bruce Scholarship, 1913; Carnegie Research Scholarship, 1914. Served European War, 1914-18, in Artillery, Trench Mortars, and Intelligence Corps. Served in R.A.R.O., War of 1939-45, as G.S.O. 3 and for special duty. Lecturer, Armstrong Coll., Univ. of Durham, 1920-21; Assist. Prof. University of Manitoba, 1921-25; Professor, University of Rochester N.Y., 1925-26; Professor of French at University College, University of Toronto, 1926-35; Drapers Professor of French, Cambridge University, 1935-51; Prof. of French Literature, Univ. of Edinburgh, 1951-61. Docteur *h.c.* de l'Univ. de Rennes; Docteur *h.c.* de l'Université de Grenoble; Officier de l'Instruction Publique; Chevalier de la Légion d'Honneur; Officier de la Couronne de Belgique. *Publications:* Robert Ferguson's Anteil an der Literatur Schottlands, 1920; La Peinture des Mœurs dans le Roman français de 1715 à 1761, 1924; French Novelists from the Renaissance to the Revolution, 1928; Eighteenth Century France, Six Essays, 1929; French Novelists from the Revolution to Proust, 1931; Minuet: A Critical Survey of French and English Literary Ideas in the Eighteenth Century, 1935; Stendhal, 1939; The Mind of Proust, 1949; Rousseau and the idea of Progress (Zaharoff Lecture), 1950; Jean-Jacques Rousseau, 1955; edited Everyman Molière, Salammbo, 19th and 20th Century French Short Stories; Le Rouge et le Noir; ed. Diderot's writings on the Theatre, 1936; ed. Duclos: Considérations sur les Moeurs, 1939; ed. Rousseau: Discours sur l'inégalité, 1941; contrib. Free France and England, 1941; ed. Prévost, Manon Lescaut, 1942; Maupassant, Quinze Contes, 1943; La Rochefoucauld, Maximes; Maupassant, Choix de contes, 1945; Anthologie des conteurs du XIXe siècle, 1951; Voltaire, Choix de contes, 1951; The Ancien Régime: Manual of French Institutions, 1958; articles to learned periodicals. *Address:* 12 North Park Terrace, Edinburgh 4. [*Died* 23 *March* 1964.

GREEN, George Norman, Chairman, North Eastern Electricity Board, since 1961 (Dep. Chm. 1957-60); *b.* 1906; *s.* of late George Ernest and late Ellen Green; *m.* 1933, Olive Taylor Killey, *d.* of late Alfred Edward and late Ann Taylor Killey; one *s.* Trained with St. Helen's Electricity Undertaking, subseq. with Brit. Insulated Cable Co. Ltd., and Croydon Elec. Undertaking. City Electrical Engr. and Manager, Peterborough, 1944-48; Chief Engr., Eastern Elec. Bd., 1948-57. Mem. Elec. Supply Res Council, 1955-58; Mem. Electricity Council, 1961. Mem. various Cttees. of Electrical Res. Assoc.; Leader, Brit. Delegn. on Electric Power Cables, to Commonwealth Standards Conf., India, 1957, etc. Vice-Chm., N. Eastern Centre, I.E.E., 1960-61; Mem. Council, Electrical Devel. Assoc., 1961. Vice-Chm., 1963-. Mem., Northern Regional Council of C.B.I., 1965. C.Eng., F.I.E.E., F.B.I.M., F.R.Econ.S. *Recreations:* outdoor sports. *Address:* 34 Reid Park Road, Jesmond, Newcastle upon Tyne 2. *T.:* (business) Newcastle 27520, (private) Newcastle 81-1565. [*Died* 6 *Jan.* 1968.

GREEN, Professor Harry Norman; Mackintosh Professor of Experimental Pathology and Cancer Research, University of Leeds, since 1965 (Prof. of Experimental Pathology, 1954-65); Director of Cancer Research, Univs. of Leeds and Sheffield, since 1954; Consultant in Cancer Research and Human Pathology, Leeds General Infirmary; Consultant in Cancer Chemo-therapy, Leeds Regional Hospitals Board; *b.* 21 September 1903; *s.* of Harry Green and Beatrice Holmshaw; *m.* 1940, Cecilia Merina Whitworth; one *s.* one *d.* *Educ.:* Sheffield University. M.B., Ch.B., Sheffield, 1924; B.Sc. (1st Class), 1925; Clinical Assistant Royal Infirmary, Sheffield and Research Assistant, Dept. of Pharmacology, Univ. of Sheffield, 1926-33. M.Sc., 1926, M.D., 1927; M.A. (Camb.), 1934; Lecturer in Pathology, Univ. of Cambridge, 1933-35; Professor of Pathology, Univ. of Sheffield, 1935-53. Lt.-Col., R.A.M.C., O.C. British Traumatic Shock Unit, 1945-46. *Publications:* Biological Actions of the Adenine Nucleotides, 1950; numerous articles in medical and scientific journals. *Recreations:* climbing, gardening, antique furniture; "Those things do best please me that befall preposterously". *Address:* Lumby Hall, South Milford, nr. Leeds. *T.:* South Milford 205 [*Died* 16 *May* 1967.

GREEN, Hon. Sir Kenneth; *see* Green, Hon. Sir R. K.

GREEN, Leonard, C.B. 1937; C.B.E. 1959 (M.B.E. 1946); M.C., T.D., D.L. (Lancs);

b. 1890; *s.* of late Roger Green, Whalley, Lancashire. *Educ.:* Bromsgrove School, Worcestershire. Joined 4th East Lancashire Regt. 1910; served European War, 1914-19; Colonel 1934; Lancs. County Council, 1946; Alderman, 1956; Chairman C.D. Committee; High Sheriff, County Palatine of Lancashire, 1954-55. *Recreations:* played for Lancashire County Cricket Club, 1922-28 (Captain 1926, 1927, 1928); played for Lancashire Hockey Club, 1920-21. *Address:* Manor House, Whalley, Lancashire. *T.:* 2221. *Club:* M.C.C. [*Died* 2 *March* 1963.

GREEN, Captain Leonard Henry, C.B.E. 1949; M.A. (Oxon) 1910; Chairman, Save the Children Fund, 1947-56; Chairman, Yugoslav Society of Great Britain, 1937-56; *b.* 8 Oct. 1885; *s.* of John Theodore Green, Normanton-le-Heath, Ashby-de-la-Zouche, and of Florence Anne Frances Christian, Knaresborough. *Educ.:* Birkenhead School; St. John's College, Oxford. Diplomé in Education. Tutor at Saltley College, Birmingham, 1910-14, and Asst. to Professor of Philosophy at Birmingham University. Lieutenant, Royal Warwickshire Regt., 1910; Capt., 1915; (home despatches twice); retired, 1918. Adviser in labour matters to the Flour Milling Industry, 1918-50, and Secretary Flour Milling National Joint Industrial Council, 1919-50. *Address:* 6 The Hermitage, Richmond, Surrey. *T.:* Richmond 1655. *Club:* Reform. [*Died* 13 *April* 1966.

GREEN, Rev. Canon Peter; Canon Residentiary of Manchester, 1912-56, Canon Emeritus since 1956; *b.* Southampton, Jan. 1871; *s.* of late Henry George Green, solicitor, of Southampton, and Elizabeth Sophia Saintsbury. *Educ.:* Cranleigh School; St. John's College, Foundation Scholar, 3rd Class Math. Tripos, 1st Class 2nd Pt. Moral Science Tripos, Cambridge; B.A. 1893; M.A. 1902; Hon. D.D. (Manc.) 1936; President Cambridge Union Soc., 1893. Curate of Church of Lady Margaret, 1894; Leeds, 1898; Rector of Sacred Trinity, Salford, 1902; St. Philip's, Salford, 1911-50. Select Preacher before the Universities of Cambridge, 1912, 1915, 1927, 1930, and 1937 and Oxford, 1913-14, and 1937-38; Examining Chaplain to the Bishop of Manchester, 1910-19; Lecturer in Pastoral Theology, Cambridge, 1914, King's College, London, 1914 and Durham, 1935; Hon. Chaplain to the King, 1914-1950; Member of the Mission of Help to S. Africa, 1904; offered Bishopric of Lincoln, 1919, and refused. Freedom of City of Salford, 1944. *Publications:* How to Deal with Lads, 1910; How to deal with Men, 1911; Studies in Popular Theology, 1913; Studies in the Devotional Life, 1913; Teaching for Lads, 1914; Studies in the Cross, 1914; The Town Parson, 1919; The Problem of Evil, 1920; Personal Religion and Public Righteousness, 1923; Betting and Gambling, 1924; Our Lord and Saviour, 1928; Parochial Missions To-day, 1928; Our Heavenly Father, 1930; The Problem of Right Conduct, 1931; The Holy Ghost, 1933; The Profession of a Christian, 1933; Watchers by the Cross, 1934; This Holy Fellowship, 1935; The Man of God, 1935; Progress in Prayer, 1936; This Our Pilgrimage, 1936; Some Gospel Scenes and Characters, 1937; The Problem of Art, 1937; The Christian Man, 1937; Our Great High Priest, 1939; The Gospel Story, 1939; The Devotional use of the Bible, 1939; The Path of Life, 1940; Manchester Cathedral Intercessions (3 series), 1940-43; The Seven Golden Candlesticks, 1943; The Great Commandment, 1946; Good Friday Victory, 1948; Fishers of Men, 1954. *Address:* 14 Upper Cleminson Street, Salford, 3. *T.:* Blackfriars 4945. [*Died* 17 *Nov.* 1961.

GREEN, P(hilip) M(arion) Kirby, C.M.G. 1960; attached War Office, 1942-64, retd.; *b.* Nyasaland, 16 Sept. 1905; *s.* of William Cardwell Kirby Green, C.M.G., Chief Provincial Comr., Nyasaland; *m.* 1929, Naomi Beatrice Nina, *d.* of Col. A. C. T. Veasey; one *d.* *Educ.:* Nautical College, Pangbourne; Christ's College, Cambridge. Active Service as Midshipman, R.N.R., 1st Destroyer Flotilla, during League of Nations intervention in Græco-Turkish War, 1922; Merchant Navy, (obtained 2nd Mate's Ticket), 1923-25. Member of the Metropolitan Police 1931-41; Member of first opening term, Metropolitan Police College, Hendon, 1934. *Recreation:* painting (Mem. Pastel Society; exhibited Royal Acad., Royal Inst. Painters in Oil and at Gibraltar, Jamaica, Trinidad, Hong Kong, Singapore, Accra, Cyprus, etc.). *Address:* Coombe House, North Wootton, Somerset. [*Died* 25 *April* 1969.

GREEN, Hon. Sir (Richard) Kenneth, K.B.E. 1957; Puisne Judge, Supreme Court of Tasmania, since 1950; *b.* 3 Dec. 1907; *s.* of E. A. W. Green and Florence Green; unmarried. *Educ.:* Hutchins School, Hobart; University of Tasmania. LL.B. 1932, Univ. of Tasmania. Captain, Australian Army Legal Corps, 1942. Member of Legislative Council of Tasmania, 1946-50. *Recreation:* golf. *Address:* 15A Brisbane Street, Launceston, Tasmania. *Clubs:* Tasmanian (Hobart); Launceston, Northern (Launceston). [*Died* 19 *March* 1961.

GREEN, Thomas Farrimond; Headmaster, Bootham School, York, 1944-61, retd.; *b.* 29 April 1899; *s.* of Charles and Jane Green; *m.* 1924, Jessie Doris Leonard (*d.* 1948); one *s.* (and one *s.* decd.); *m.* 1950, Lucy (Jane) Cahill. *Educ.:* Up Holland Grammar School; Liverpool and Sheffield Univs. Asst. Master Royds Hall School, Huddersfield, 1922-28; Headmaster Stramongate School, Kendal, 1928-32; Headmaster Leominster Grammar School, 1932-1944. Chairman, Joseph Rowntree Memorial Trust, 1963-. *Publication:* Preparation for Worship (Swarthmere Lecture), 1952. *Recreations:* fell walking, golf. *Address:* The Chapel House, Thornton-le-Dale, Pickering, Yorks. *T.:* Thornton-le-Dale 230. [*Died* 6 *Oct.* 1966.

GREEN-ARMYTAGE, Lieut.-Col. Vivian Bartley, I.M.S. (ret.); on Gynecological and Obstetric staff of British Post-Graduate Hospital, Hammersmith; late Professor of Obstetrics and Gynecology, Medical Coll., and Surgeon to Eden Hosp. for Women, Calcutta; *b.* 14 Aug. 1882; *s.* of A. Green-Armytage, Clifton, and Thick Hollins, Yorks; married. *Educ.:* Clifton Coll.; Univ. of Bristol and Royal Infirmary; Paris. M.D., F.R.C.P., F.R.C.S., F R.C.O.G. Lond.; late Examiner in Midwifery and Gynecology, Camb. Univ. Dublin, and Conjoint. Exam. Board of England; late F.R.S.M. (Pres. obstetrical section); formerly Vice-Pres. R.C.O.G.; served European War, 1914-18 (Mons Star; despatches thrice; Croix d'Officier, Legion of Honour, Order of White Eagle of Serbia with crossed swords); Montefiore Surgical Medallist, R.A.M. College; many resident and house surgeon appointments in England and Calcutta. Hon. F.I.C.S. *Publications:* Labour Room Clinics, 1912; Tropical Gynecology and Tropical Midwifery, 2 vols. 1929 and 1936; Management and Treatment of Diseases of Children in India, 6th edition; many contributions to journals of surgery obstetrics and gynecology. *Recreations:* riding, bridge. *Address:* 40 Harley Street, W.1. *Clubs:* Athenæum, Oriental, East India and Sports Reform. [*Died* 11 *April* 1961.

GREEN-PRICE, Sir John, 4th Bt., *cr.* 1874; *b.* 26 August 1908; *s.* of John Powell Green-Price (*d.* 1926); *S.* uncle, Major Sir Robert Henry Green-Price, 1962; *m.* 1st, 1938, Irene Marian (*d.* 1955), *e. d.* of Major Sir (Ernest) Guy (Richard) Lloyd, 1st Bt., D.S.O. one *s.* one *d.*; 2nd, 1956, Jean Chalmers, *d.* of David Low Stark, Arbroath, and *widow* of Thomas Scott, Arbroath. *Educ.:* Cheltenham; Gonville and Caius College, Cambridge (B.A.). Served War of 1939-45. Formerly Staff Captain, R.A. *Recreations:* shooting, fishing. *Heir:* *s.* Robert John Green-Price, 2nd Lt. R.A.S.C., *b.* 22 Oct. 1940. *Address:* Gwernaffel, Knighton, Radnorshire; Corrymeela, Craigendoran, Dunbartonshire. [*Died* 30 *Sept.* 1964.

GREEN-PRICE, Major Sir Robert Henry, 3rd Bt., *cr.* 1874; *b.* 6 Jan. 1872; *s* of 2nd Bt. and Clara, *d.* of Rev. T. Powell, Dorestone Rectory, Herefordshire; *S.* father, 1909; *m.* 1906, Lucile (*d.* 1961), *e. d.* of Frederick G. Potter, New York; one adopted *s.* Temp. Commn. 1st/1 Montgomeryshire Yeo.; served S. African War with Shropshire Imperial Yeo., 1900-1; European War, 1914-18; Dep. Assistant Quartermaster-General, Jan. 1918; High Sheriff of Radnorshire, 1930; J.P., D.L. Radnorshire; late Joint Master of Teme Valley Foxhounds; owns about 4000 acres. *Heir: n.* Capt. John Green-Price, R.A. [*b.* 26 Aug. 1908; *m.* 1938, Irene Marian (*d.* 1955), *e. d.* of Maj. Sir Guy Lloyd, Bt., D.S.O.; one *s.* one *d.*; *m.* 1956, Jean Chalmers Scott. *Educ.:* Cheltenham; Caius Coll., Camb.]. *Address:* Gwernaffel, Knighton, Radnorshire. *T.:* Knighton 80. *Clubs:* Boodle's, M.C.C., English-Speaking Union. [*Died* 2 *Oct.* 1962.

GREEN-WILKINSON, Most Rev. Francis Oliver, C.B.E. 1958; M.C. 1943; M.A.; Archbishop of Central Africa since 1962 and Bishop of Zambia since Oct. 1964 (Northern Rhodesia, 1951-64, name of diocese changed); *b.* 7 May 1913; *e. s.* of late Reverend Lumley Green-Wilkinson and of late Myfanwy, *o. d.* of Sir Francis Edwards, 1st and last Baronet. *Educ.:* Eton; Magdalen College, Oxford; Westcott House, Cambridge. B.A. 1937, M.A. 1946. Deacon, 1946; priest, 1947; Curate of St. Mary, Southampton, Diocese of Winchester, 1946-1950; Pretoria Diocese, 1950-51. Served with King's Royal Rifle Corps, 1939-45. Middle East (wounded, M.C.), Italy and Normandy; Major. *Recreations:* riding and walking. *Address:* Bishop's Lodge, Box 183, Lusaka, Zambia. *T.:* Lusaka 62391. [*Died* 26 *Aug.* 1970.

GREENBANK, Percy; author and lyric writer; Director of the Performing Right Society; *b.* Bayswater, 24 Jan. 1878; *y. s.* of Richard Hewetson and Mary Greenbank; *m.* 1902, Alice Henrietta Dillman (*d.* 1962), *y. d.* of Edward Dillman Pyne; one *d.* Studied for the law but never practised; started contrib. to Punch, 1897, and also wrote occasionally for Sketch and the Tatler; on the death of his elder brother, Harry Greenbank, in 1899, came under the notice of Mr. George Edwardes and ever since has written for the stage. *Publications:* has written lyrics, either alone or in collaboration for the following amongst other plays—Messenger Boy; Toreador; Orchid; The Spring Chicken; Our Miss Gibbs; San Toy; A Country Girl; The Cingalee; The Little Michus; Three Little Maids; Lady Madcap; Earl and the Girl; Blue Moon; Veronique; My Lady Molly; The Belle of Brittany; Quaker Girl; Dancing Mistress; Girl from Utah; After the Girl; To-Night's the Night; Tina; Vanity Fair; High Jinks; The Boy; The Kiss Call; The Girl for the Boy; My Nieces (book and lyrics); The Street Singer; Yvonne (book and lyrics); Her Ladyship (book and lyrics); Cupid and the Cutlets; The Three Cruisers (Cantata). *Recreations:* gardening, photography, tennis. *Address:* 17 The Cloisters, Rickmansworth, Herts. *Club:* Green Room. [*Died* 8 *Dec.* 1968.

GREENBERG, Leopold, B.A.; LL.B.; K.C. 1924; Judge of the Appellate Division, 1943-55, retired; Judge Pres. of the Supreme Court of S.A., Transvaal Provincial Division, since 1938, Puisne Judge since 1924; *b.* 21 Mar. 1885, Calvinia, C.P.; *s.* of late Samuel Bernard Greenberg; *m.* 1913, Jennie Braun; two *s.* *Educ.:* Grey Coll., Bloemfontein; S.A. Coll., Cape Town. Honours degree (B.A.) of the Univ. of the Cape of Good Hope; six years in solicitor's office in Johannesburg; commenced to practise at Bar in Johannesburg, 1911. Hon. LL.D.: Univ. of Cape Town; Witwatersrand Univ.; Hon. D.Jur., Hebrew Univ. of Jerusalem. *Recreation:* golf. *Address:* 7 Rock Ridge Road, Parktown, Johannesburg. *Clubs:* Bloemfontein, Glendower Golf, Rand (Johannesburg). [*Died* 12 *Sept.* 1964.

GREENE, Sir Edward Allan, 3rd Bt., *cr.* 1900; M.C.; T.D.; *b.* 12 Sept. 1882; 2nd *s.* of late Sir Walter Greene, Bt.; *S.* brother, 1947; *m.* 1948, Monica, *d.* of late Sir Paul Makins, Bt., and *widow* of Major Francis Lowsley-Williams. *Educ.:* Eton; Oxford. Served with Suffolk Yeomanry in Gallipoli, 1915, and on the Staff in France, 1916 to end of War (despatches, M.C., 1914-15 Star); Controller to H.E. General Lord Byng of Vimy, Governor-General of Canada, 1921. *Heir:* none. *Address:* Wickham House, Newbury, Berks. *T.:* Boxford 231. *Clubs:* Turf; Royal Yacht Squadron (Cowes). [*Died* 26 *Dec.* 1966 (*ext.*).

GREENE, Eric Gordon; singer; conductor; organist; pianist; lecturer; adjudicator; *b.* London 8 Feb. 1904; *s.* of Harry Greene, Somersham, Hunts., and Isabel Wallace, Hamilton, Lanark; *m.* 1952, Kathleen Mary Cheselden. *Educ.:* Winchester Cathedral Sch., Roy. Acad. of Music (scholar). First professional engagement, singing, 1926; Queen's Hall (direction, Sir Henry Wood) Promenade Concerts from 1928. All principal Festivals: Three Choirs, Edinburgh, Leith Hill, etc. Organist, St. Peter's, Gt. Windmill St., W., 1922-25; Conductor and Chorus Master of Westminster Bank Music and Operatic Society, 1933-36. President of London Bach Society, 1946-. Toured Central Europe, U.S.A., Canada, 1936, 1937; Germany (Amer. and Brit. Zones), 1947; Holland, 1952. Reg. Officer for Yorks area (war period), 1941-44, C.E.M.A. (now Arts Council of Gt. Britain); Member of Worshipful Company of Musicians; Founder and Director of Pro Canto Singers, Choir of registered blind persons. F.R.A.M. *Recreations:* music, walking. *Address:* 81 Westbourne Terrace, Hyde Park, W.2. *T.:* Paddington 6435. [*Died* 6 *Dec.* 1966.

GREENFIELD, Sir Henry Challen, Kt., *cr.* 1944; C.S.I. 1941; C.I.E. 1934; B.A.; J.P.; *b.* 8 Dec. 1885; *s.* of Joseph Henry Greenfield and Alice Brain; *m.* 1916, Helen Eva Macmillan; one *d.* *Educ.:* Lancing College; Pembroke College, Oxford. I.C.S. 1910; retired Nov. 1945; re-employed as Adviser until Dec. 1945. *Address:* Steyning, Sussex. [*Died* 14 *Sept.* 1967.

GREENHAM, Alfred Howard, C.M.G. 1959; *b.* Quorn, S. Australia, 21 Mar. 1895; *s.* of late George and Caroline Greenham; *m.* 1922, Adelaide Plant, Manchester; three *d.* *Educ.:* Muirden Coll., Adelaide; Univ. of Adelaide. Joined South Australian Public Service, 1910; served European War, 1916-18, 1st A.I.F., France; Secretary S.A. Dept. of Agriculture, 1938-46; served War of 1939-45 (despatches): R.A.A.F., 1941-45; Western Desert, Tripolitania and Italy, Middle East Staff Coll., 1943; Asst. Trade Commissioner, London, 1950-53, Agent General and Trade Commissioner for S. Australia, 1953-61. *Recreations:* swimming, gardening. *Address:* c/o Bank of Adelaide, 11 Leadenhall St., E.C.3. *Club:* Savage. [*Died* 25 *Nov.* 1966.

GREENHILL, 1st Baron, *cr.* 1950, of Townhead; **Ernest Greenhill** O.B.E. 1947; J.P.; *b.* 23 April 1887; *s.* of late Maurice Greenhill and of Sophia Greenhill; *m.* 1914, Ida Goodman; two *s.* one *d.* *Educ.:*

privately. Town Councillor, Glasgow Corporation, 1932- (formerly De.. Chairman, Senior Magistrate, City Treasurer, etc.). Clyde Navigation Trust, 1935; Convener, Law and Parliamentary Bills Cttee.; Chairman, Glasgow Savings Cttee.; Member, Scottish Savings Cttee.; Deputy Traffic Commissioner (Scottish Area); Gen. Commissioner, Inland Revenue (Chm., Glasgow District); Member: Advisory Council on Education in Scotland; Local Government Man-Power Cttee. (Scotland); Interdepartmental Cttee. on Rating of Site Values; Educational Endowments Cttee. (Scotland); Min. of Labour and Nat. Service Advisory Council on Relationship between Employment in Forces and Civilian Life; Chairman: Exec. Cttee., Newbattle Abbey Residential College; W.E.A. (Scottish Council); Vice-Chairman: Glasgow University Extra-Mural Cttee.; Scottish Institute of Adult Education; Director, Glasgow Citizens' Theatre, Ltd.; Governor, Glasgow and West of Scotland Commercial College. Trustee National Museum of Antiquities, Scotland, since 1954. *Heir: s.* Hon. Stanley E. Greenhill, M.D., D.P.H., *b.* 17 July 1917. *Address:* 68 Glencairn Drive, Glasgow, S.1. *T.:* Pollokshields 0129. [*Died* 18 *Feb.* 1967.

GREENWAY, 2nd Baron, *cr.* 1927, of Stanbridge Earls; **Charles Kelvynge Greenway,** Bt., *cr.* 1919; *b.* 24 Mar 1888; *s* of Charles, 1st Baron Greenway, and Mabel, *d.* of Edwin Augustine Tower; *S.* father 1934; *m.* 1916, Eileen Constance, *d* of late Major-General Sir Harry Triscott Brooking, K.C.B., K.C.S.I., K.C.M.G.; two *s. Educ.:* Charterhouse; Sandhurst. Joined 68th Durham Light Infantry, 1907; Indian Army, 1908; 26th K.G.O. Light Cavalry; served Mesopotamia, 1914-15 (despatches); Aden Field Force, 1915-16 (despatches); Military Secretary to Governor of Bombay and Commandant Bombay Body Guard, 1917-1918; retired, 1920. *Heir: er. s* Major Hon Charles Paul Greenway, Parachute Regt. [*b.* 31 Jan. 1917; *m.* 1939, Cordelia Mary, *yr. d.* of Major Humfrey Campbell Stephen, Pleasaunce Court, East Grinstead; three *s.*]. *Address:* 12 Orange Grove Drive, Salisbury, S. Rhodesia. [*Died* 30 *April* 1963.

GREENWAY, Maj.-Gen. Charles William, C.B. 1955; C.B.E. 1953; late R.A.M.C.; retired, 1957; *b.* 2 Oct. 1900; *s.* of Dr. C. M. Greenway; *m.* 1924, C. Beryl Mabel Dearman; one *s.* one *d.*; *m.* 1957, J. C. M. Campbell. *Educ.:* Epsom Coll., Epsom. Commissioned, R.A.M.C. as Lieutenant, 1924; Major-General, 1953; Dep. Dir. of Medical Services, H.Q. Northern Command, York, 1953-57. *Recreations:* reading, hunting, polo, shooting, motoring, tennis, golf. *Address:* Elmhurst, Newark Street, Greenock, Renfrewshire. [*Died* 13 *Jan.* 1968.

GREENWAY, John Dee, C.M.G. 1948; *b.* 28 Mar. 1896; *s.* of Davenham Greenway, Darwen, Lancs, and Ethel Constance Osborne; unmarried. *Educ.:* Tonbridge School; Magdalen College, Oxford. Served European War, Rifle Brigade, 1915-19; Third Secretary at Rome, 1920; subsequently served in Turkey, Czechoslovakia, U.S.S.R., Brazil, Sweden, Roumania, China, Hungary and Persia; Minister to Panama, 1946-50; Minister and Consul-General to Iceland, 1950-53. *Publication:* Fish, Fowl and Foreign Lands, 1950. *Address:* Simmonds Court, Earls Court Gardens, S.W.5. *Club:* Pratt's.
[*Died* 16 *March* 1967.

GREENWELL, Colonel Thomas George, T.D. 1944; *b.* 18 Dec. 1894; *o. s.* of late T. W. Greenwell, Sunderland; *m.* 1918, Mabel Winifred, *er. d.* of late T. H. Catcheside, J.P., Newcastle on Tyne; one *s.* one *d. Educ.:* Gresham's School, Holt; King's College, Durham University. M.P. (Nat. C.) for the Hartlepools, 1943-45; J.P. and D.L. for County of Durham; High Sheriff, County Palatine of Durham, 1951-52; Director: T. W. Greenwell & Co. Ltd.; Moor Engineering and Pipe Works Ltd. *Recreation:* salmon fishing. *Address:* Whitburn Hall, Sunderland; Thornley Cottage, Tow Law, Bishop Auckland. *Club:* Carlton. [*Died* 15 *Nov.* 1967.

GREENWELL, Colonel William Basil, C.B.E. 1929; D.S.O. 1918; D.L. 1938; *b.* 29 Oct. 1881; 2nd *s.* of Alan and Isabella Augusta Greenwell. *Educ.:* Durham School. Joined 1st Durham Light Infantry, 1901; Capt. 1914; Lt.-Col. 1931; Col. 1933; served S. African War, 1901-2 (medal 3 clasps); European War, 1914-18 (D.S.O.); with Nigeria Regiment, 1924; Commandant, 1925-29; commanded 1st Batt. Durham Light Infantry, 1931-33; Commander 151st (Durham Light Infantry) Brigade T.A., 1933-37; retired pay, 1937. *Recreations:* cricket, shooting. *Address:* Greenwell Ford, Lanchester, Durham.
Died 6 *Nov.* 1964.

GREENWOOD, Viscountess, D.B.E. *cr.* 1922 (C.B.E. 1920); O.St.J. 1942; **Margery Greenwood**; *b.* 20 Dec. 1886; *d.* of late Walter Spencer, Fownhope Court, Herefordshire, formerly Codicote, Herts, and Anne Elizabeth, *d.* of Robert S. Hudson; *m* 1911, Hamar Greenwood, M.P., later 1st Viscount Greenwood, P.C., K.C., LL.D. (*d.* 1948); two *s.* two *d. Educ.:* Eversley; Folkestone; Italy. Former Treasurer, Consultative Cttee. of Women's Organizations. First woman apptd. to Bd. of Governors on founding of Bonar Law Memorial Coll., Ashridge; first Chairman Women's Section, Comrades of the Great War (later British Legion); Chairman Ladies' Carlton, 1932-1937; Chairman London Penny-a-Week Fund, 1941-45. *Recreations:* painting and sculpture. *Address:* 13 Kingston House East, Princes Gate, S.W.7. *T.:* Knightsbridge 0320. *Club:* Naval and Military
[*Died* 24 *April* 1968.

GREENWOOD, Henry Harold, F.R.C.S., M.B., B.S., M.B.Ch.B.; retd. 1960; *b.* Halifax, 17 Sept. 1873; *s.* of Thomas Greenwood; *m.* Bertha Wagstaffe Hogg (*d.* 1959), Skipton-in-Craven; one *d. Educ.:* Skipton Grammar School; Leeds University, Gold and Silver Medallist; McGill Prizeman in Surgery. Capt. R.A.M.C. (T.) with charge of Surgical Beds, East Leeds War Hospital, 1915-19; Hon. Surgeon Leeds Public Dispensary, 1920; Specialist Surgeon Ministry of Pensions, Orthopædic Hospital, Beckett Park, Leeds, 1920; Hon. Surgeon to Victoria Hospital, Swindon, 1922-28; Surgeon G.W.R. Accident Hospital, Swindon, 1922-39; Hon. Consulting Surgeon to Stratton Infirmary, to the British Legion, etc.; Surgeon to Three Counties Emergency War Hosp., Arlesey, Beds., Sept. 1939-40; Fellow Association of Surgeons of Great Britain and Ireland; Member International Society of Surgery; Consulting Surgeon to Ministry of Pensions, 1943-45-48. *Publications:* Kohler's Disease of the Tarsal Scaphoid, Lancet, 1923; Lengthening of the Tendo Achillis, Brit. Journal of Surgery, 1923; Menace of Appendicitis, Lancet, 1929; Cardiospasm, Brit. Med. Journal, 1928; Removal of Non-malignant Tumours of the Breast, Lancet, 1930; Massive Enlargement of the Breast, Lancet, Jan. 1932; Reconstruction of Forearm after loss of Radius, Brit. Journ. Surgery, Vol. XX, 1932; Anatomy of Approach to the Abdomen, Post-graduate Medical Journal, Oct. 1936. *Recreations:* painting, book illustration; swimming. *Address:* 2 Brookfield, West Hill, Highgate, N.6. *T.:* Mountview 7511. [*Died* 9 *June* 1962.

GREENWOOD, Sir James (Mantle), Kt. 1962; C.B.E. 1956; J.P.; Chairman, James

M. Greenwood Advertising Ltd.; Chairman and Managing Director, Greenwood Developments Ltd.; Greenwood Properties Ltd.; *b.* 22 Jan. 1902; *s.* of James Greenwood, Camberwell, London. *Educ.:* St. Matthew's Church School, Denmark Hill. Contested (C.) Southwark: 1945, 1948, 1950, 1951, 1955, and 1959. Gov., Guy's Hospital; Secretary-General: Council of European Municipalities; Council of Commonwealth Municipalities; Mem. Exec. Cttee., British Council of European Movement; Mem. Cttee. United Europe Assoc. Co-Founder, Local Government Educational Trust. J.P., Co. London, 1946; Alderman, L.C.C., 1955-1965. *Address:* Greenwood House, Salisbury Court, Fleet Street, E.C.4. *T.:* Fleet Street 8274; Astoria, Garrick Lawn, Hampton, Middlesex. *T.:* Molesey 3206. *Clubs:* City Livery, United Wards. [*Died* 5 *Dec.* 1969.

GREENWOOD, John French, C.B. 1953; *b.* 13 May 1904; *s.* of Frederic Greenwood; *m.* 1937, Margaret, *d.* of Charles Dean; two *s.* one *d.* *Educ.:* Bradford Grammar School; Corpus Christi College, Oxford. Post Office, 1927-41; War Damage Commn., 1941-54; Director Inland Telecommunications, Post Office, 1954-56. *Address:* 11 Priory Way, Gerrards Cross, Bucks. [*Died* 15 *Sept.* 1968.

GREEVES, R(eginald) Affleck, B.A., M.B., B.S., F.R.C.S., Consulting Ophthalmic Surgeon, Middlesex Hospital; Consulting Surgeon, formerly Curator and Pathologist, Royal London Ophthalmic Hospital (Moorfields); Ophthalmic Surgeon, St. Saviour's Hospital, Osnaburgh Street, London, N.W.; *b.* 1878; *s.* of T. M. Greeves, Strandtown, Co. Down, N. Ireland; *m.* 1908, Sarah (*d.* 1954), *d.* of late Leonard Acutt, Natal; two *s.* one *d.* *Educ.:* privately; Queen's College, Belfast; University College, London; Guy's Hospital. Fellow, Royal Society of Medicine; late President of Ophthalmological Society of the United Kingdom; Montgomery Lecturer Royal College of Surgeons, Dublin 1935; Lecturer in the Department of Ophthalmology Oxford University, late Examiner Ophthalmology, Conjoint Board, London. *Publications:* papers on Ophthalmological subjects in various medical periodicals. *Address:* The Bungalow, Crapstone, Yelverton, S. Devon. [*Died* 4 *Oct.* 1966.

GREGG, Dr. Edward Andrew; Chairman, Council of British Medical Association, 1949-1956; Direct Representative G.M.C. 1942-1961; Treasurer, G.M.C.; Chairman Representative Body, British Medical Association, 1948-49; *b.* 28 Dec. 1881; 2nd *s.* of late Edward Gregg, Schoolmaster, Belfast Model School, and Elizabeth Delap; *m.* 1910, Mary Tell (decd.), *e. d.* of Duncan McCallum Smith; one *s.* one *d.* (and one *d.* decd.). *Educ.:* Ward's School, Bangor, Co. Down; Model School, Belfast; Methodist College, Belfast; Marlborough College, Dublin; R.C.S. Ireland. Schoolmaster, Londonderry Model School, 1901-03; qualified L.R.C.P.I., L.R.C.S.I. and L.M., L.M. Rotunda, 1909. Held Hospital and medical appts. in Dublin, Belfast, London, etc. Police Surgeon, Metropolitan Police; Hon. Lecturer in health subjects, Working Men's College, London; Lecturer and examiner, St. John's Amb. Assoc., B.R.C.S. and L.C.C.; Clin. Asst., Central London Nose, Throat and Ear Hosp., Royal Eye Hosp., Southwark, St. Paul's Hosp. for Skin and Genito-Urinary Diseases. Served R.A.M.C.(T.), European War, 1914-18. J.P. Co. London; Mayor of St. Pancras (Alderman 18 years); Chm. St. Pancras Board of Guardians, 1925-26. Liveryman of Society of Apothecaries and Worshipful Co. of Basket Makers; Freeman of City of London. Chairman London Insurance; Member Central Health Services Council, Min. of Health; Medical referee, Min. of Health and Min. of Labour. U.K. rep., British Commonwealth Med. Assoc. and World Med. Assoc., 1947-56. F.R.Soc.Med., F.R.S.A.; Fell. Tuberculosis Soc.; etc. Hon. degrees: M.D. Liverp., 1950; M.D. Dublin, 1952; LL.D. Tor., 1955. Gold medallist, B.M.A., 1951. *Publications:* various papers and contribs. to med. jls. *Recreations:* reading, drama, music. *Address:* 47 Wembley Park Drive, Wembley, Middlesex. *T.:* Wembley 1336. *Club:* Royal Automobile. [*Died* 7 *June* 1969.

GREGG, Most Rev. John Allen Fitzgerald, C.H. 1957; Archbishop of Armagh, and Primate of All Ireland, 1939-59, retd.; *b.* 4 July 1873; *s.* of late Rev. J. R. Gregg, Vicar of St. Nicholas', Deptford; *m.* 1st, 1902, Anna Alicia (*d.* 1945), *d.* of late F. M. Jennings, Brookfield, Cork; two *d.*; 2nd, 1947, Lesley Alexandra, *d.* of Very Rev. T. J. McEndoo, Dean of Armagh. *Educ.:* Bedford School; Christ's College, Cambridge. 1st Classical Scholar; Stewart of Rannoch Scholarship, Camb., 1894; 1st Class, Classical Tripos, Part i., 1894; 1st Class, Part ii., 1895; Hulsean Prize, 1896; B.A. 1894; M.A. 1897; B.D. 1909; D.D. 1929 (B.D. *ad eundem*, T.C.D. 1911); D.D. 1913 (T.C.D.); Hon. Fellow Christ's College, Cambridge, 1934; Curate of Ballymena, 1896; Cork Cathedral, 1899; Incumbent of Blackrock, Cork, 1906; Canon of St. Patrick's Cathedral, Dublin, 1912; Chaplain to the Lord Lieutenant, 1912; Examining Chaplain to the Archbishop of Dublin, 1913; Archbishop King's Professor of Divinity, Trinity College, Dublin, 1911-15; Bishop of Ossory, Ferns, and Leighlin, 1915-20; Archbishop of Dublin, 1920-38. M.R.I.A. 1914; Select Preacher, Cambridge, 1916, 1930, 1936; Select Preacher, Oxford, 1946, 1947. *Publications:* Decian Persecution, 1897; Epistle of St. Clement of Rome, 1899; Commentary of Origen on the Epistle to the Ephesians (in Journal Theological Studies), 1900; Book of Wisdom, Cambridge Bible for Schools, 1909; Additions to Esther (in Charles' Apocrypha and Pseudepigrapha of the Old Testament), 1913. *Address:* The Woodhouse, Rostrevor, Co. Down. *Clubs:* Athenæum; University (Dublin). [*Died* 2 *May* 1961.

GREGG, Sir Norman McAlister, Kt., *cr.* 1953; M.C.; M.B., Ch.M.; F.R.A.C.S. 1932; F.R.C.O.G. 1953; F.R.A.C.P. 1953; Hon. Cons. Ophth. Surgeon, Royal Prince Alfred Hospital, Sydney, and Royal Alexandra Hospital for Children, Sydney; *m.* 1923, Haidee Margaret Carson; two *d.* M.B., Ch.M. Sydney, 1915; D.O.M.S. Eng. 1922. M.D. (Hon.) Melb., 1952; D.Sc. (Hon.): Syd., 1952; Australian National University, 1958. *Publication:* contrib. to Trans. Ophthal. Soc. Austr. *Address:* 193 Macquarie Street, Sydney, N.S.W. *Clubs:* Australian, Royal Sydney Golf (Sydney). [*Died* 27 *July* 1966.

GREGORY, Frederick Gugenheim, F.R.S. 1940; A.R.C.S.; D.Sc.; Professor of Plant Physiology, Imperial College of Science and Technology, 1937-58, Emeritus Professor, 1959; *b.* London, 22 December 1893. *Educ.:* Dame Alice Owen's School; Imperial College of Science. Engaged in research in Institute of Plant Physiology, at Horticultural Research Station, Cheshunt, Rothamsted Experimental Station and Imperial College of Science. For. Assoc. Nat. Acad. Sci., U.S.A., 1956. Royal Medal of Royal Society, 1957. *Publications:* Various scientific papers in botanical journals. *Recreation:* music. *Address:* 8A Worsley Road, Hampstead, N.W.3. *T.:* Hampstead 1727. *Club:* Athenæum. [*Died* 27 *Nov.* 1961

GREGORY, Joshua C., B.Sc. (Lond.), F.R.I.C.; Hon. Lecturer in History of Science, University of Leeds; Membre Correspondant de l'Académie internationale d'histoire des Sciences; *b.* 25 Feb. 1875; *s.* of Rev. James Gregory of Thornton, Bradford. *Educ.:* Craigmount House School, Edinburgh; Edinburgh University; Yorkshire College. School teaching, analytical practice in Glasgow, war work at Leeds Univ., 1915-18; on staff of Univ. of Leeds, 1919; Lecturer in Chemistry, Univ. of Leeds; retired 1936. *Publications:* Articles in scientific, philosophical and other journals; The Nature of Laughter, 1924; Vol. III., pt. ii. of Friend's Text Book of Inorganic Chemistry (with Mrs. Burr), 1926; The Scientific Achievements of Sir Humphry Davy, 1930; a Short History of Atomism from Democritus to Bohr, 1931; Combustion from Heracleitos to Lavoisier, 1934. *Recreations:* walking, reading; formerly cricket and tennis. [*Died* 28 *July* 1964.

GREGORY, Padraic; poet, dramatist, folklorist; architect; F.R.I.B.A.; M.R.I.A.I.; M.I.Struct.E.; M.R.San.I.; F.R.S.A.; Member of the Roy. Ulster Society of Architects; has designed many ecclesiastical buildings in Ireland and new Cathedral of Christ the King, Johannesburg, S. Africa; *b.* Belfast, Sept. 1886; *e. s.* of late Patrick K. Gregory, of Durango, Colorado, and Hannah Mary, *y. d.* of late Patrick Downey, of Craigbilly, Ballymena, Co. Antrim; *m.* 1st, 1917, Madeline (*d.* 1920), 3rd *d.* of late Hugh Crothers, Belfast; 2nd, Sara, *e. d.* of John MacKeown, of Burren, Ballynahinch, Co. Down; five *s.* five *d.* *Educ.:* U.S.A.; and by the Christian Brothers and private tutors in Ireland. LL.D., N.U.I., 1942; Fellow of the Roy. Soc. of Literature, 1930; Vice-Pres. of the Catholic Poetry Soc. of England; Literary Editor of the Catholic Monthly Review, 1926-27; connected from its inception till 1916 with the Ulster Literary Theatre; contributor of prose and verse to periodicals; is represented in many modern anthologies; some of his historical ballads have been, since 1916, set forth in Irish School Texts and have been done into Danish; greatly interested in the revival of mediæval Mystery and Miracle plays in England and Ireland; has lectured on balladry to learned societies in England, Ireland; lectured in 1950 in all principal American cities from New York through to Chicago and Notre Dame. Rep. Falls Div. Belfast City Council, 1946-49; member of B.B.C. Advisory Council for N. Ireland; J.P. County of the City of Belfast. *Publications: verse:* The Ulster Folk, 1912; Old-World Ballads, 1913; Love-Sonnets, 1914; Ireland: A Song of Hope, 1917; Ulster Songs and Ballads, 1920; Selected National Ballads (for use in Schools), 1933; Complete Collected Ballads, 1935; Complete Ulster Ballads, 1959; Ed. vols.: Modern Anglo-Irish Verse, 1914; the Poems of Sean MacEntee, 1917; *criticism:* Poets of The Insurrection (with Rev. George O'Neill, M.A., S.J., Prof. Arthur Clery and others), 1918; When Painting was in Glory, 1941; *sacred drama:* Bethlehem: A Nativity Play, 1928; The Coming of the Magi, 1931 (with a Preface by H. E. Cardinal MacRory, Archbishop of Armagh), 1931; Calvary; A Play for Passiontide; *folk song:* The Anglo-Irish Folk Songs of Padraic Gregory—vol. i. with settings by the late Dr. Charles Wood, 1931; vol. ii. with settings by Carl G. Hardebeck, 1935. *Recreations*: chess, angling, motoring, the study of the origins of balladry, and collecting old Irish peasant songs and tunes. *Address:* 5 Crescent Gdns., University Road, Belfast 7; Marlborough Park Central, Malone Road, Belfast 9. *T.:* 26548 and 669204. *Club:* Co. Antrim Yacht (Whitehead). [*Died* 9 *June* 1962.

GREGORY, Sir Theodore, Kt., *cr.* 1942; D.Sc. (Econ.) Lond.; sometime British member of the Currency Committee, Bank of Greece, and Financial Adviser to British Economic Mission to Greece; *b.* London, 10 Sept. 1890; *m.* 1st, 1917 (marriage dissolved, 1951); no *c.*; 2nd, 1952, Mme. Iphigenia Toumba, *widow* of Admiral Nikola Toumba, R.H.N. *Educ.:* Owens' School, Islington; Stuttgart; London School of Economics; Assistant and Lecturer, London School of Economics, 1913-19; Cassel Reader in International Trade, 1920; Acting Professor of Economics at Univ. Coll., Nottingham, 1915-1916; some-time Member of Council, R.Econ.S. Dean of the Faculty of Economics, Univ. of London, 1927-30; Pres., Section F of British Assoc., 1930; Senator of the University, 1928-30; Newmarch Lecturer, University College, 1929; Member, Macmillan Committee on Industry and Finance, 1929-31; Economic Adviser, Niemeyer Mission to Australia and New Zealand, 1930; Sir E. Cassel Professor of Economics in the University of London, 1927-37; Economic Adviser to Govt. of India, 1938-46; Member, Irish Free State Banking Commission, 1934-1937; Chairman, Foodgrains Policy Committee (India), 1943; Professor of Social Economics in the University of Manchester, 1930-32; Examiner in the Universities of London, Cambridge, Oxford, Edinburgh, etc. Hon. Fellow, London School of Economics, 1958. Comdr., Order of George 1st (Greece); Comdr. Austrian Order of Merit. *Publications:* Tariffs, a Study in Method; Foreign Exchange, before, during, and after the War; Present Position of Banking in America; The Return to Gold; First Year of the Gold Standard; The Practical Working of the Federal Reserve System in the U.S.; Introduction to Tooke and Newmarch's History of Prices; Select Statutes, Documents and Reports relating to British Banking; The Gold Standard and its Future, 1932; Gold, Unemployment, and Capitalism, 1933; The Westminster Bank Through a Century, 1936; India on the Eve of the Third Five-Year Plan, 1960; Ernst Oppenheimer and the Economic Development of Southern Africa, 1962; joint editor, Ricardo's Notes on Malthus and various official publications. *Club:* Reform. [*Died* 24 *Dec.* 1970.

GREGORY, William King; *see* Addenda: II.

GREIG, John Russell, C.B.E. 1946; Ph.D., M.R.C.V.S., F.R.S.E.; Director, Animal Diseases Research Institute, Moredun, Edinburgh, 1930-54; Hon. Research Professor in Animal Pathology, Royal (Dick) Veterinary College; *b.* Sept. 1889; *s.* of William C. Greig, Leith; *m.* 1915, Margaret McDougal Christie, *d.* of Alexander Smart, Leith; two *s.* *Educ.:* Royal High School and Royal (Dick) Veterinary College, Edinburgh. Professor of Medicine and Materia Medica, Royal (Dick) Veterinary College, Edinburgh, 1919-30; Scientific Secretary, Scottish Board of Research in Veterinary Science, 1935-50; Official Consultant Adviser to Scottish Veterinary Investigation Officer Service, 1947-54. Neill Gold Medal, Roy. Soc. of Edin., 1952; member of several Government Committees concerned with Animal Health; Hon. Member American Veterinary Medical Association, 1955; Correspondant Etranger de l'Académie d'Agriculture de France; Socio Correspondiente de la Sociedad Veterinaria de Zootecnia, Spain; served in Veterinary Department, City of Glasgow, and on Veterinary Staff, Ministry of Agriculture; Captain late R.A.V.C. *Publications:* editor, Wallis Hoare's Veterinary Materia Medica and Therapeutics (4th, 5th, and 6th editions); Editor, 4th and 5th English editions, Hutyra and Marek's Special Pathology and Therapeutics; The Shepherd's Guide, 1951, 2nd edn. 1956, 3rd edn. 1958; The Etiology of Milk Fever (jointly); The Nature of Lambing Sickness. *Recreations:* fishing, gardening. *Address:* Wedderlie, Kirk Brae, Liberton, Edinburgh. [*Died* 1 *May* 1963.

GREIG, John Young Thomson; *b.* Ch'ang Ch'un, Manchuria, 1891; *e. s.* of late Dr. James A. Greig; *m.* 1916, Margaret Theresa, 2nd *d.* of William Thomson of Inverurie, Aberdeen, and Glasgow; one *s.* one *d.* *Educ.:* Greenock Collegiate School; Glasgow Academy; Glasgow University. M.A., 1913; D.Litt. 1924; Journalist, 1913-14; temp. Capt., Northumberland Fusiliers and Staff, 1914-19; Registrar and Sec. of Examinations, Armstrong Coll., Newcastle on Tyne, in the University of Durham, 1919-31; Prof. of English language and Literature, Univ. of the Witwatersrand, Johannesburg, 1932-51; Professor of English Language and Literature, Otago University, Dunedin, N.Z., 1952-1956; Carnegie Visiting Prof. of English at Vanderbilt University, Nashville, Tennessee, 1930; Organiser, Army Educational Services for the Transvaal, 1943-45. *Publications:* The Psychology of Laughter and Comedy, 1923; The Fighting Instinct (a translation from the French of Pierre Bovet), 1923; Breaking Priscian's Head (To-day and To-morrow Series). 1928; David Hume: a Biography (James Tait Black Memorial Prize), 1931; The Letters of David Hume, 1932; Language at Work. 1943; Structure and Meaning, 1950; Thackeray: A Reconsideration, 1950. Under pseudonym of John Carruthers: *novels:* The Virgin Wife, 1925; Adam's Daughter, 1926; A Man Beset, 1927; Lothian Cameron, 1928; *criticism:* Scheherazade, or the Future of the English Novel (To-day and To-morrow Series), 1927. *Recreations:* tennis, skating, swimming. *Address:* Poplar Avenue, Bonza Bay, East London, South Africa. [*Died* 13 *Feb.* 1963.

GRENFELL, Rt. Hon. David Rhys, P.C. 1951; C.B.E. 1935; J.P.; *b.* Penrheol, near Swansea, Wales, 27 June 1881; father a coal miner; *m.* 1905, Beatrice Morgan; one *d.* Went to work underground at twelve years, and continued until he was thirty-five; undertook studies in mining and allied subjects and qualified as colliery manager; appointed miners' agent, 1916. M.P. (Lab.) Gower Div. of Glam., July 1922-Sept. 1959. Member: Forestry Commn., 1929-42; Royal Commn. on Safety in Mines, 1936; Welsh Land Settlement Commn., 1936-56; Secretary for Mines, 1940-42; Chairman Welsh Tourist Board, 1948; "Father of the House of Commons", 1953-1959. Chevalier de la Légion d'Honneur, 1953. LL.D. Univ. of Wales, 1958. *Address:* Carnglas Road, Sketty, Glam.
[*Died* 21 *Nov.* 1968.

GRENSTED, Rev. Canon Laurence William; Examining Chaplain to the Bishop of Gloucester; Canon Emeritus of Liverpool Cathedral since 1942; Professor Emeritus, Oxford, since 1950; Fellow Emeritus of Oriel College, Oxford, since 1951; *b.* Blundellsands, Lancashire, 6 Dec. 1884; *e. s.* of Canon F. F. Grensted; *m.* 1923, Norah Frances, *d.* of Herbert Knott, J.P., Wilmslow; two *s.* *Educ.:* Merchant Taylors' School, Crosby, Liverpool; University College, Oxford (Maths. Scholar). 1st Class Mods., 1905; 2nd Class Maths. Finals, 1906; 2nd Class Lit. Hum., 1908; B.A., 1906; Aubrey Moore Student, 1908; Egerton Hall Scholar, Manchester, 1908-10; M.A. and Manchester B.D., 1910; Oxford B.D., 1922; D.D. 1931; Vice-Principal of Egerton Hall, 1910-15; Temporary Chaplain to the Forces 1915-19; Principal of Egerton Hall, 1919-24; Lecturer in History of Doctrine, Manchester University, 1919-24; Fellow, Chaplain and Lecturer of University College, Oxford, 1924-30; Nolloth Professor of the Philosophy of the Christian Religion, Oxford, 1930-50; Secretary of Faculty of Theology, Manchester, 1923-24; Chairman of the Anglican Fellowship, 1922-27; Member: Archbishops' Commission on Doctrine, 1923-38, Archbishops' Committee of Doctors and Clergy since 1926, Archbishops Commission on the Ministry of Women, 1932, Archbishops' Commission on Divine Healing, 1955; Select Preacher, Oxford, 1927; Examiner in the Hon. School of Theology, Oxford, 1927-29 and 1947-49; University Lecturer in Psychology of Religion, Oxford, 1928-30; Bampton Lecturer, 1930; Lecturer in Pastoral Theology, Cambridge, 1932; Hulsean Preacher, Cambridge, 1932; Fellow of Royal Entomological Society, 1928; Fellow of British Psychological Society, 1945; Canon Theologian of Liverpool Cathedral, 1930-41. *Publications:* Introduction to the Books of the New Testament (with Archdeacon Allen), 1913; A Short History of the Doctrine of the Atonement, 1920; The Making of Character, 1928; The Atonement in History and in Life (editor), 1929; Psychology and God, 1930; The Person of Christ, 1933; Religion, Fact or Fancy, 1936; This Business of Living, 1939; Jesus and our Need, 1941; The Psychology of Religion, 1952; Contributor to Dictionary of the Apostolic Church, 1912; The Inner Life, 1924; Psychology and the Church, 1925; The Natural History of the Oxford District, 1926; The Study of Theology, 1939; Federal Union, 1940, etc. *Recreations:* sketching, gardening, natural science. *Address:* 9 Shepherds Way Cirencester, Glos. *T.:* 910.
[*Died* 18 *March* 1964.

GRENVILLE, Lt.-Col. Hon. Thomas G. B. M.; *see* Morgan-Grenville.

GRESHAM COOKE, Roger; *see* Cooke, R. G.

GRETTON, Mary Sturge, J.P., B.Litt., Oxon; F.R.Hist.S.; author; Visiting Justice of Oxford Prison, 1924-36; only woman Appointed Member of the Agricultural Wages Board Committee for Oxfordshire, 1918-22; *d.* of late Marshal Sturge, J.P., and Anne, *d.* of Francis Burke, Puisne Judge and Loan Commissioner of Montserrat, West Indies; *widow* of Richard Henry Gretton, M.A., late demy of Magdalen College, Oxford, author of A Modern History of the English People, etc. *Publications:* A Corner of the Cotswolds through the Nineteenth Century; A Calendar of the War; Burford, Past and Present; Some English Rural Problems; The Writings and Life of George Meredith, A Centenary Study, for Oxford and Harvard University Presses; Crumplin'; Oxfordshire Justices in the 17th Century; Rue and Rosemary; Re-Cognitions; contributor to many English Reviews. *Address:* Montserrat, 37 Norham Road, Oxford. *T.:* Oxford 57394. *Club:* University Women's. [*Died* 15 *Aug.* 1961.

GREW, Joseph Clark; *b.* 27 May 1880; *s.* of Edward Sturgis Grew and Annie Crawford Clark; *m.* 1905, Alice de Vermandois Perry; four *d.* *Educ.:* Groton School; Harvard Univ. Clerk, American Consulate-General, Cairo, 1904; Dep. Consul-General, Cairo, 1904-6; 3rd Sec. American Embassy, Mexico City, 1906-7; St. Petersburg, 1907-8; 2nd Sec. Embassy, Berlin, 1908-11; Sec. Embassy, Vienna, 1911-12; Sec. Embassy, Berlin, 1912-16; Counsellor, Embassy, Berlin, 1917; Counsellor Embassy and Chargé d'Affaires at time of break of diplomatic relations with Austria-Hungary, Vienna, 1917; Acting Chief, Division of Western European Affairs, Dept. of State, 1917-18; Secretary-General, American Commission to Negotiate Peace, 1919; Minister to Denmark, 1920; Minister to Switzerland, 1921; Am. rep. Conference on Near Eastern Affairs, Lausanne, 1922-23; negotiated and signed treaty with Turkey, 6 Aug. 1923; unofficial rep. with Temporary Mixed Commission of League of Nations for Control of Traffic in Arms, Geneva and Paris, 1924; Under-Secretary of State, 1924-27; Ambassador to Turkey, 1927-32; Ambassador to Japan, 1932-41; Special Assistant to the Secretary of State, 1942-44; Director Office of Far Eastern Affairs, Dept. of State, 1944; Under-Secretary of State, U.S.A., 1944-45. *Publications:* Sport and Travel in the Far East, 1910; Report from Tokyo, 1942; Ten Years in Japan, 1944; Turbulent Era: A Diplomatic Record of Forty Years, 1952. *Address:*

Manchester, Mass., U.S.A. *Clubs:* Metropolitan, Harvard, Chevy Chase, Burning Tree, Alibi (Washington); Somerset, Harvard (Boston); Brook Coffee House, Harvard, Century (New York)
Died 25 May 1965.

GREY, 5th Earl, *cr.* 1806; **Charles Robert Grey,** Bt. 1746; Baron Grey, 1801; Viscount Howick, 1806; *b.* 15 Dec. 1879; *s.* of 4th Earl and Alice (*d.* 1944), 3rd *d.* of Robert Stayner Holford, M.P., Westonbirt, Gloucestershire; *S.* father, 1917; *m.* 1906, Lady Mabel Laura Georgina Palmer, C.B.E. (*d.* 1958), *d.* of 2nd Earl of Selborne; one *d.* Late 2nd Lieut. 1st Life Guards; contested (C.) Central Bradford, 1910; served European War, 1914-18. Owns about 3,000 acres. *Heir: cousin* Richard Fleming George Charles Grey, *b.* 5 March 1939. *Address:* Howick Hall, Alnwick, Northumberland. [*Died 2 April* 1963.

GREY DE RUTHYN, 25th Baron, *cr.* 1324; **John Lancelot Butler-Bowdon;** J.P. Derbyshire; *b* 1883. *o. c.* of Lancelot George Butler-Bowdon and Hon. Ella Cecily Mary, *e. d.* of late Augustus Wykeham Clifton and Bertha Lelgarde, 22nd Baroness Grey de Ruthyn (*d.* 1887); *S.* 1939. *Educ.:* Mount St Mary's College, Spinkhill; Oak View, Hathersage. President of League against Cruel Sports; Hon. Treasurer of Anti-Vivisection Society. *Heir:* none. *Address:* Barlborough House, Chesterfield. [*Died 24 Oct.* 1963 (*ext.*).

GREY, Maj.-Gen. Wulff Henry, C.B. 1917; C.M.G. 1918; late R.E.; *m.* 1917, Alix, *d.* of late Charles Lenox Simpson, Senior Commissioner of Customs, China; one *s.* (and one *s.*, Capt. Grenadier Guards, killed in Normandy, 1944). Served European War, Mesopotamia, 1916-18 (C.B.); Italy (C.M G.); attached Serbian Army, 1915 (Order of White Eagle); Italian Order of S.S. Maurice and Lazarus; Officer of Order of Orange-Nassau, 1948 (Netherlands).
[*Died 24 Nov.* 1961.

GREY EGERTON, Sir Philip Reginald le Belward, 14th Bt., *cr.* 1617; D.L., J.P. Cheshire; landowner; *b.* 3 Sept. 1885; *s.* of Colonel Caledon Egerton and Caroline, *d.* of Rev. Reginald Southwell Smith; *S.* cousin 1945; *m.* 1st, 1916, Dorothy Aveys Balguy (*d.* 1952); two *s.* one *d.*, 2nd, 1961, Mrs. Kathleen Dickson, Lulworth Cove. *Educ.:* Repton. Sudan Civil Service; High Sheriff of Cheshire, 1941; Hon. Col. 521 L.A.A. Regt. T.A. R.A., 1947; President British Casting Assoc., 1948. *Recreations:* fishing, shooting. *Heir: s.* Philip John Caledon, [*b.* 1920; *m.* 1952, Margaret Voase, *widow* of Squadron Leader Robert A. Ullman, R.A.F., and *er. d.* of late Rowland Rank and of Mrs. Rank, Wick Cottage, Aldwick, West Sussex]. *Address:* Stafford House, Dorchester, Dorset. *T.:* Dorchester 1036. *Clubs:* Boodle's, Pratt's, St. James'.
[*Died 9 June* 1962.

GRIBBLE, Bernard Finegan, R.B.C.; S.M.A.; *b.* S. Kensington, 10 May 1872; *s.* of Herbert A. K. Gribble, M.R.I.B.A. (architect of Brompton Oratory, etc.); *m.* Eleanor Mabel, *d.* of Philip Edward Clunn, the founder of the London Shipping Conference. Worked with his father at architecture during the erection of the present Brompton Oratory façade; studied drawing at South Kensington Art Schools; has exhibited at the Royal Academy for the past thirty years, and at the Paris Salon since 1905 (Mention d'Honourable, 1907); works purchased for the Plymouth Museum (Art Gallery, permanent collection); Preston Museum and Art Gallery, and Bristol Museum and Art Gallery, also United States Naval Academy, Annapolis and Rhode Island Naval College, U.S.A; has illustrated works of various authors, including Sir Arthur Conan Doyle; was special artist to Black and White during the Fashoda trouble, Hispano-American War, etc.; present at the surrender of the German Fleet and the sinking of the German Fleet; is marine painter to the Shipwrights' Company and hon. Freeman of the Company. *Address:* 3 Springfield Crescent, Parkstone, Dorset. *T.:* Parkstone 1358. *Club:* Savage. [*Died 21 Feb.* 1962.

GRIDLEY, 1st Baron, *cr.* 1955; **Arnold Babb Gridley,** K.B.E., *cr.* 1920; M.I.E.E.; Consulting Engineer and Company Director; *b.* 16 July 1878; *s.* of late Edward Gridley; *m.* 1905, Mabel (*d.* 1955), *d.* of Oliver Hudson, Fakenham, Norfolk; one *s.* three *d.* (and one *s.* deceased). *Educ.:* Bristol Grammar School; Clifton Laboratories. For many years engaged in the administration and direction of various Electric Supply and Manufacturing Undertakings at home and overseas; during European War, 1916-19, was Controller of Electric Power Supply at the Ministry of Munitions, and Chairman of various War-Cabinet sub-committees; Pres. British Assoc. of Chambers of Commerce, 1946-48. Chm. Conservative Members' Cttee. (House of Commons), 1946-51; Member of Supreme Court Cttee. on Practice and Procedure of the High Courts, 1947-53; for many years Government nominated member, Pigs Marketing Board; M.P. (U.) Stockport, 1935-50; M.P. (C.) South Division of Stockport, 1950-55. *Heir: s.* Hon. Arnold Hudson Gridley [*b.* 26 May 1906; *m.* Edna Lesley Winifred, *d.* of late L. R. Wheen of Shanghai and Penselwood, Somerset; one *s.* three *d.*]. *Address:* Lye Green, Chesham, Bucks. *T.:* Chesham 8321. *Clubs:* Carlton, Devonshire. [*Died 27 July* 1965.

GRIDLEY, John Crandon, C.B.E. 1945; Chairman, Mobil Oil Co. Ltd. since 1949; Director: Powell Duffryn Ltd.; Morice Tozer & Beck Ltd., and other Companies; *b.* 28 May 1904; *o. s.* of late William Joseph Gridley and late Mary Ellen (*née* Michell); *m* 1933, Joan Marion, *er. d.* of late Sir Herbert Merrett; two *s.* *Educ.:* Queen's College, Taunton. Joint Chairman of North African Joint Economic Mission, 1943-44; Economic Adviser to British Ambassador in Paris, 1944-45; Chm. European Coal Organisation, 1945; Marketing Member, Nat. Coal Board. 1946-1948; Mem. University Grants Cttee., 1954-1963; Pres. Inst. of Petroleum, 1962-64; Mem. Marshall Aid Commemoration Commn., 1959-66; Mem. Court of London University, 1962-; Governor, Westminster Hospital, 1962-; Mem. Council, Westminster Med. Sch., 1965-. Hon. LL.D., London, 1967. *Address:* 71 Melbury Court, W.8. *T.:* Western 8305; Cwrt-yr-Ala, Nr. Dinas Powis, Glam. *T.:* Dinas Powis 3177. *Clubs:* Brooks's; Cardiff and County (Cardiff). [*Died 25 Nov.* 1968.

GRIER, Lynda, C.B.E. 1951; M.A. (Oxon); Hon. LL.D. (Cantab), 1953; Principal Lady Margaret Hall, Oxford, 1921-45; Hon. Fellow Lady Margaret Hall; *o. d.* of late Rev. R. M. Grier, Vicar of Hednesford, Rural Dean of Rugeley and Preb. of Lichfield; *b.* May 1880. *Educ.:* Home; Newnham Coll., Cambridge. Economics tripos Part I. 1907, Part II. 1908. Acting Head Economics Department, Leeds University during absence of Professor of Economics on war service, 1915-19; Sometime Fellow and Lectr. at Newnham Coll., Cambridge; Member Consultative Cttee., Bd. of Educ., 1924-38; Pres. Economics Section British Assoc., 1925; Member Hebdomadal Council, Oxford, 1926-1945; Member Archbishops Commission on Religious Education, 1927-29; Faculty Fellow of Nuffield College, 1944-45; Pres. Education Section of British Association, 1946; British Council rep. in China, 1948-50. Apptd. Mem. of Wages Councils until 1948. *Publications:* Life of Winifred Mercier, 1937; Investigations into substitution of men by

women in industry during the war, published by authority of the British Association, 1919-1921; Achievement in Education, the work of Michael Sadler, 1885-1935, 1952; various articles and reviews in the Economic Journal and other papers. *Address:* Flat 10, 29 Bramham Gardens, S.W.5. *Clubs:* University Women's, Oxford and Cambridge.
[*Died* 21 *Aug.* 1967.

GRIERSON, John, C.B.E. 1954; Public Accountant and Company Director; Chairman of Directors: Bank of New Zealand; Mason Bros. Ltd.; Associated Engineering N.Z., Ltd.; C. & A. Odlin Timber & Hardware Co. Ltd.; Wisemans, Ltd.; John Henderson Ltd.; Director, Union Steam Ship Co. Ltd., and other companies; *b.* 16 July 1898; *s.* of John Cresswell Grierson and Susan Grierson; *m.* 1924, Lillias Christie; three *s.* *Educ.:* Auckland Grammar School; Auckland University. Chm. Auckland Hosp. Bd., 1947-59. Chancellor in New Zealand of Most Venerable Order of St. John, 1961. K.St.J. *Recreations:* golf, fishing, racing. *Address:* 130 St. Stephens Avenue, Parnell, Auckland, New Zealand. *Clubs:* Northern, Auckland, Wellington (all in New Zealand).
[*Died* 27 *Aug.* 1964.

GRIERSON, Philip F. H.; *see* Hamilton-Grierson.

GRIEVE, Lt.-Col. Angus A. M.; *see* Macfarlane-Grieve.

GRIEVE, William, C.I.E. 1938; M.A., B.Sc.; Joint Sec. to Govt. Education Dept., Bombay, from 1939; *b.* 21 March, 1885; *m.* 1920, Agnes Sutherland (*d.* 1952). one *s.* one *d.* Joined Indian Educational Service, 1914. Director of Public Instruction, Bombay, 1936-39; War Service, Indian Army, N.-W. Frontier, Palestine, Syria, Turkey. *Address:* 13 Rothesay Place, Edinburgh 3. *T.:* Edinburgh Caledonian 6326. *Club:* Caledonian United Service (Edinburgh). [*Died* 15 *Dec.* 1967.

GRIFFIN, Alan Francis Rathbone, C.M.G. 1964; Senior Resident, Sarawak, since 1962; *b.* 1911; *s.* of late Rev. Thomas Noel Rathbone Griffin; *m.* 1957, Monica, *d.* of Leslie Best, Hull. *Educ.:* St. John's, Leatherhead; Selwyn College, Cambridge. Interned, 1942-45. Administrative Cadet, Sarawak, 1934; District Officer, 1939; Resident, 1955; Administrative Officer, 1955. *Address:* The Residency, Sibu, Sarawak. *Club:* Travellers'.
[*Died* 7 *Sept.* 1965.

GRIFFIN, Alexander, J.P.; *b.* 5 July 1883; *s.* of Joseph and Janet Griffin, Dumfriesshire, Scotland; *m.* 1913, Edith Marjorie (*née* Lovell): one *s.* two *d.* *Educ.:* Wallace Hall Academy, Dumfriesshire. Liverpool City Council: elected to Edge Hill Ward, 1928, re-elected, 1929, 1932-35 and 1938; apptd. Alderman, 1942; Lord Mayor of Liverpool, 1954-55. J.P. Liverpool, 1941. Member of Health Committee, and of Liverpool Show Special Committee. *Address:* 45 Glendyke Road, Allerton, Liverpool 18. *T.:* Allerton 1202. [*Died* 18 *Dec.* 1966.

GRIFFIN, Sir Arthur (Cecil), K.C.I.E., *cr.* 1946; K.B.E., *cr.* 1954 (O.B.E., 1919); Kt., *cr.* 1943; B.Eng.; *b.* 30 Mar. 1888; *s.* of late H. W. Griffin, J.P.; *m.* 1914, Beryl Kathleen Dillon, *d.* of J.D. Flynn, C.I.E.; one *s.* one *d.* *Educ.:* privately; Liverpool Univ. Went to India in 1911 and posted as Asst. Eng. North-Western Railway. Employed on survey and construction and open line works until 1914. Being commissioned in the Royal Reserve Engineers recalled to military duty in 1914. War Service until 1919; War Office, 1919-20. Services lent to Iraq as Deputy Director of Rlys. and later Director; returned to India in 1925; Executive Engr. and on special duty in connection with Rly. working of the Karachi Port; Deputy Agent N W Rly.; and later Divisional Supt., Secretary Railway Board, Govt. of India; General Manager North-Western Railway, India, 1940-44; Chief Commissioner of Railways, India, 1944-46; Member, Viceroy's Executive Council, Aug.-Oct. 1945; Resident Director and General manager Rhodesia Railways, 1947; Chairman Rhodesia Railways, 1953-1954; Adviser on Economic Development to the High Commissioner for Basutoland, the Bechuanaland Protectorate and Swaziland, 1956-60. K.St.J. *Address:* Nutbourne Ridge, Pulborough, Sussex. *T.:* West Chiltington 2314. *Club:* East India and Sports. [*Died* 28 *Jan.* 1970.

GRIFFIN, Sir Cecil L.; *see* Griffin, Sir L. C. L.

GRIFFIN, Sir Charles James, Kt., *cr.* 1923; Q.C. Ireland 1920; *b.* 1875; *y. s.* of late John Griffin, Solicitor, and Clerk of the Peace for Mayo, and Anna M., *d.* of Henry de Burgh Daly, Cooloney, Co. Galway; *m.* Aileen Mary (*d.* 1954), *o. c.* of late John Fanning, Solicitor, Kilkenny; one *s.* two *d.* *Educ.:* Catholic Univ. School, Dublin; Belvedere College (S.J.), Dublin; University College, Dublin. Ex-Scholar, Exhibitioner and B.A. (Hons.), Royal University, Ireland; Chancellor's Gold Medallist. Called to Irish Bar, 1898; went Connaught Circuit; Crown Prosecutor, B.C.A. Protectorate—now Nyasaland Protectorate, 1901; Attorney-General, 1905; Judge of High Court, 1906; Attorney-General, Gibraltar, 1914-19; Chief Justice, Leeward Islands, 1919-21; Chief Justice, Uganda Protectorate, 1921-32; retired, 1932. *Publications:* Revised and Consolidated Laws of Nyasaland, 1913; Revised Statutes of the Presidency of Montserrat (Leeward Islands), 1921; Revised Statutes of the Presidency of Antigua (Leeward Islands), 1921, and Uganda, 1923. *Address:* Deepdene, Aldeburgh, Suffolk. *Clubs:* Savile; Stephen's Green (Dublin).
[*Died* 3 *Jan.* 1962.

GRIFFIN, Sir Herbert John Gordon, Kt. 1957; C.B.E. 1938; Secretary, Council for the Preservation of Rural England, 1926-65; *b.* 16 Dec. 1889; *s.* of Michael John Griffin; *m.* 1914, Meredyth Rose (*d.* 1960), *o. d.* of late Brig.-Gen. F. B. Matthews, C.B., D.S.O.; five *d.* *Educ.:* Lancing Coll. Served European War, Western Front, 1914-20, as Capt. 3rd Battn. Duke of Wellington's West Riding Regt. (twice wounded, despatches); and as Capt. Infantry, 1941-1942; is an Hon. A.R.I.B.A. and an Hon. A.T.P.I.; a National Park Comr., 1955-66. Member of Council of National Playing Fields Assoc. and National Council of Social Service. Van Tienhoven Prize, Rheinische-Friedrich-Wilhelms-University, Bonn, 1961. *Recreations:* fishing and books. *Address:* Kelbarrow, Grasmere, Westmorland. *T. A.* and *T.:* Grasmere 325. [*Died* 3 *March* 1969.

GRIFFIN, Sir (Lancelot) Cecil Lepel, Kt., *cr.* 1947; C.S.I. 1946; C.I.E. 1942; J.P.; M.A.; *b.* 5 Jan. 1900; *s.* of late Sir Lepel Henry Griffin, K.C.S.I. *Educ.:* Wellington College; Christ Church, Oxford. Served in the Household Brigade Officers' Cadet Bn., 1918; entered Indian Civil Service, 1923; retired, 1947. C.C. (Middlesex), 1955-61. J.P. Middlesex, 1960. *Address:* Riverside Cottage, Sunbury-on-Thames, Middlesex. *T.:* Sunbury-on-Thames 3402. *Club:* Travellers'.
[*Died* 28 *May* 1964.

GRIFFITH, Alan Arnold, C.B.E. 1948; F.R.S. 1941; aeronautical engineer; research consultant, Rolls-Royce, Ltd. (having retd. as Chief Scientist to Company); *b.* 1893; *s.* of late George Chetwynd Griffith; *m.* 1925, Constance Vera, *d.* of R. T. Falkner, Farnborough, Hants. *Educ.:* Liverpool University. B.Eng. 1914; M.Eng. 1917; D.Eng. 1921. Louis Bréquet Memorial

Trophy, 1963. *Address:* Dovercourt, Alexandra Rd., Farnborough, Hants; Highfield Lawn, Derby. [*Died* 11 *Oct.* 1963.

GRIFFITH, His Honour Frank Kingsley, M.C.; County Court Judge, Circuit No. 16 (Hull, etc.), 1940-56, retd.; Chairman East Riding Quarter Sessions, 1947-56; *b.* 1889; *s.* of late Colonel Frank Griffith, V.D., and Mrs. Griffith, Bromley, Kent; *m.* 1st, 1924, Eleanor (*d.* 1954), *o. d.* of late Sir Robert Bruce, C.B.; one *d.*; 2nd, 1955, Margaret Winifred, *widow* of H. Louch. *Educ.:* Marlborough; Balliol Coll., Oxf., Williams History Exhibitioner, M.A. Pres. Oxford Union Soc., 1912; Barrister-at-law, Inner Temple and North-Eastern Circuit; Recorder of Richmond, Yorks, 1932-40; served in France with 1st Gloucester and 2nd Lincoln Regts., Dec. 1914-18 (M.C.); contested Bromley, Kent, 1922, 1923 and 1924; M.P. (L.) Middlesbrough West, 1928-40; Parliamentary Private Secretary to the Home Secretary, 1931-32; Past-master, Plasterers Company, *Recreation:* chess. *Address:* 9 Esplanade Crescent, Scarborough. *Club:* National Liberal. [*Died* 25 *Sept.* 1962.

GRIFFITH, Lt.-Col. Sir Ralph Edwin Hotchkin, K.C.S.I., *cr.* 1932; Kt., *cr.* 1932; C.I.E. 1917; *b.* 4 Mar. 1882. Deputy Commissioner Peshawar, 1924; Resident Waziristan, 1929-31; Chief Commissioner, N.W. Frontier Province, 1931-32; Governor of N.W. Frontier Province and Agent to Gov.-General, Tribal Areas, 1932-37. *Address:* Little Corsley, Great Barton, Bury St. Edmunds Suffolk *T.:* Gt. Barton 52. [*Died* 11 *Dec.* 1963.

GRIFFITH-JONES, Rev. William; Chairman Congregational Union of England and Wales (May 1958-May 1959); *b.* Deiniolen, N. Wales, 2 Nov. 1895; *m.* 1925, Annie Kathleen (*née* Speakman); one *s.* one *d.* *Educ.:* Lancashire College; Manchester University. Served in Salonica, 1916-19. Theological training, 1919-24. Minister of: Freemantle Congregational Church, Southampton, 1924-36; Emmanuel Church, West Wickham, Kent, 1936-51. Moderator, Wales and Monmouth Province, Congregational Union of England and Wales, 1951-. Pres., Hampshire Free Church Federation, 1931; Chairman: Kent Congregational Assoc., 1945; London Congregational Union, 1949. *Recreation:* golf. *Address:* 16 Llwyn-y-Grant Road, Cardiff. *T.:* Cardiff 44755. *Club:* National Liberal. [*Died* 10 *July* 1961.

GRIFFITHS, Albert Edward; General Secretary, Associated Society of Locomotive Engineers and Firemen, since 1963; *b.* 21 May 1908; *s.* of George Griffiths and Martha (*née* Bates); *m.* 1928, Clare Bucknall; one *d.* *Educ.:* Wolverhampton Secondary School. L.M.S. Region Sectional Council No. 2, 1943. Secretary, L.M.R. Sectional Council No. 2, 1950. A.S.L.E.F.: Irish Officer, 1956; Organising Secretary, 1958; Assistant General Secretary, 1959. Mem. General Council, T.U.C., 1963; Special Member, National Board for Prices and Incomes, 1965. *Recreations:* tennis, football, boxing. *Address:* 24 Beverley Gardens, Stanmore, Middlesex. *T.:* Harrow 3825 [*Died* 13 *Feb.* 1970.

GRIFFITHS, David Nathaniel, B.Sc., M.I.Mech.E.; *b.* Caemawr, Manordeilo, Carmarthenshire; *s.* of John and Elizabeth Griffiths; *m.* Beatrice Ann Cleminson, Tynemouth; one *d.* *Educ.:* Llandovery College. Engineering pupil Guest, Keen & Nettlefold, Ltd., Dowlais Works, 1898-1904; Assistant Engineer Cammell, Laird & Co., Workington Works, 1904-7; Head of Engineering Dept., Darlington Technical College, 1907-13; Principal Verdin Technical School, Northwich, 1913-21; Principal Wandsworth Technical College, 1921-46. Pres. Assoc. of Principals in Technical Institutions, 1940 and 1941. *Recreations:* golf, fishing. *Address:* 21 Manor Way, Onslow Village, Guildford. [*Died* 6 *Dec.* 1961.

GRIFFITHS, Ezer, O.B.E. 1950; F.R.S.; F.Inst.P.; Hon. M.Inst.R.; D.Sc.; *b.* 28 Nov. 1888. *Educ.:* Univ. College, Cardiff. Formerly Fellow of Univ. of Wales. Past-Pres. Institute of Refrigeration and Chm. Research Committee. Member General Board National Physical Laboratory. Vice-Pres. Inst. of Engineers in Charge. Hon. Pres. Institut International Du Froid. Past Pres. International Commission II, transfer of heat, thermal properties of materials, instrumentation, insulating materials, of the Institut, and member of Technical Board; Vice-Chm. Governing Body, Twickenham Technical College. Formerly Senior Principal Scientific Officer, Physics Div., National Physical Laboratory, Teddington; retd. Nov. 1953. *Publications:* Methods of Measuring Temperatures. Pyrometry, Papers in scientific journals; Reports dealing with Refrigeration, published by H.M. Stationery Office. Consulting editor Refrigeration Principles and Practice (publ. Geo. Newnes), 1951. *Address:* 18 The Grove, Teddington. *T.:* Teddington Lock 3508. [*Died* 14 *Feb.* 1962.

GRIFFITHS, Brigadier Felix A. V.; *see* Copland-Griffiths.

GRIFFITHS, Lieut.-General Francis Home, O.B.E. 1946; D.L. Hampshire; J.P. Winchester; *b.* 11 Feb. 1877; *s.* of Richard S. P. Griffiths, R.N., Inspector-General of Hospitals and Fleets; *m.* 1916, Everilda (*d.* 1956), *d.* of Comm. E. G. F. Law; one *s.* two *d.* *Educ.:* Portsmouth Grammar School. 2nd Lieut. R.M., 1895, served European War, 1914-19; Naval Intelligence Officer, Colombo, 1911-14; G.S.O.1 Singapore, 1916-19; G.S.O.1 Hongkong, 1919-20; D.N.I. Melbourne, 1921-23; A.D.N.I. Admiralty, 1923-26; commanding Chatham Div. R.M., 1928-30; A.D.C. to the King, 1929; Winchester City Council, 1934-47; Alderman 1944; Hampshire County Council, 1937-46; Mayor of Winchester, 1938-45; Hampshire County A.R.P. Controller, 1938-44; Central Valuation Committee, 1945-48; Hampshire Valuation Panel, 1950-54; Pres. Hampshire Field Club, 1955-57. Chm. Winchester Branch, Trustee Savings Bank, 1949-50. Hon. Freedom of Winchester, 1953. *Address:* 2 Beaufort Rd., Winchester. *T.:* 4765. [*Died* 21 *April* 1961.

GRIFFITHS, Sir Hugh (Ernest), Kt., *cr.* 1949; C.B.E. 1945; M.S.; F.R.C.S.; late Surgical Director, Albert Dock Hosp., Accident and Rehabilitation Service; Hon. Consulting Surgeon, Min. of Supply, etc.; *b.* 10 March 1891; *s.* of T. L. and S. A. Griffiths; *m.* 1918, Doris Eirene, *d.* of W. H. and Elizabeth James; one *s.* one *d.* *Educ.:* Univ. of Wales; St. Bartholomew's Hosp. Surg. Probationer, R.N.V.R., 1914-15, invalided; Surg., First London General Hosp., 1916-18 (despatches); Demonstrator Anatomy, St. Bartholomew's Hospital, 1916-26; Chief Assistant (Surgical), St. Bartholomew's Hospital, 1919-22; Hunterian Professor, Royal College of Surgeons, 1922 and 1943, Arris and Gale Lecturer, 1923, Luther Holden Research Scholar in Surgery, 1918; Surgeon Seamen's Hospital Society since 1920; Consulting Surgeon, Hertford County Hospital, Wimbledon Hospital and Potters Bar Hospital. Late Assistant Surgeon, All Saints Hospital for Genito-Urinary Diseases. *Publications:* Diseases of Spleen, Diseases of Gall Bladder and Pancreas in Gask and Wilson's System of Surgery, 1920; Injury and Incapacity, 1935; Treatment of the Injured Workman (Hunterian Lecture R.C.S.), 1943; The Surgeon in Industry (McKenzie Lecture), 1949. *Recreations:* golf, fishing. *Address:* 90 Harley Street, W.1. *T.:* Welbeck 3261; Woodside, Gillham Wood Road, Cooden, Sussex. *T.:* Cooden 3004. [*Died* 16 *May* 1961.

GRIFFITHS, Air Commodore John Swire, C.B. 1948; C.B.E. 1944; *b.* 19 June 1894; 2nd *s.* of William Griffiths and Edith Swire, Pembrey and Cardigan, South Wales; *m.* 1923, Beryl Irene, *d.* of Sidney H. Thomas, Neath, S. Wales; two *d.* *Educ.:* privately; County Technical Coll., Carmarthenshire; University of London. Served European War, 1914-18, Royal Fusiliers and Welch Regiment, 1914-21; Suvla Bay, 1915; Gallipoli, 1915 (wounded); Palestine and Western Desert, 1916-20 (wounded); Actg. Staff Captain 159 Bde., 1919; Corps of Military Accountants, War Office, 1920-21. Transferred R.A.F., 1922; Iraq, 1926-28; Command Accountant; Aden, 1936-38, Army Co-operation Command, 1940-42, India and South East Asia, 1942-45, Technical Training Command, 1945-48; Senr. Service Accountant, Air Ministry, 1948-50; Director of Personal Services (B) Air Ministry, 1951-52; retired 1952. 2nd Lieut., 1914; Lieut., 1915; Capt., 1916; Sqdn. Leader, 1928; Wing Comdr., 1937; Group Capt., 1940; Air Commodore, 1943. *Publication:* The Odd Hint, 1944. *Recreations:* golf, tennis, fishing, gardening, free-lance journalism. *Address:* Waterwynch, Amersham-on-the-Hill, Bucks. *T.:* Amersham 629. *Clubs:* Junior Army and Navy, Royal Over-Seas League. [*Died* 2 *Aug.* 1969.

GRIGG, Rt. Hon. Sir (Percy) James, P.C. 1942; K.C.B., *cr.* 1932; K.C.S.I., *cr.* 1936; Director: of Imperial Tobacco Company since 1947; of Prudential Assurance Company since 1948; of National Provincial Bank, since 1949 (Dep. Chm. since 1957); of Distillers Company since 1950; Chairman of Bass, Mitchells & Butlers, since 1961; *b.* Exmouth, 16 Dec. 1890; *e. s.* of Frank Alfred Grigg; *m.* 1919, Gertrude Charlotte, *y. d.* of Rev. G. F. Hough; no *c.* *Educ.:* Bournemouth School; St. John's College, Cambridge (Hon. Fellow, 1943), Wrangler, Mathematical Tripos; appointed to Treasury, 1913; served R.G.A., 1915-18; Principal Private Sec. to successive Chancellors of the Exchequer, 1921-30; Chairman, Board of Customs and Excise, 1930; Chairman, Board of Inland Revenue, 1930-34; Finance Member of Government of India, 1934-39; Permanent Under-Secretary of State for War, 1939-42; Secretary of State for War, 1942-45; Hon. LL.D. (Bristol), 1946; Hon. Bencher, Middle Temple, 1954; M.P. (Nat.) East Cardiff, 1942-45; British Executive Director, International Bank for Reconstruction and Development, 1946-47. *Publication:* Prejudice and Judgment. *Address:* A15 Albany, W.1. *Club:* Athenæum. [*Died* 5 *May* 1964.

GRIMM, Stanley, R.P., R.O.I.; *b.* London, 2 June 1891; British; *m.* 1913, Masha Oulpé; two *s.* *Educ.:* Riga, Russia. Arts School, Riga, 1910-13, Munich, 1913-14. During European War, 1914-18, was prisoner in Germany. Exhibited Germany, Venice, France, America. Pres. National Society (Painters, Sculptors, Gravers, Potters); Pres. Artists of Chelsea. War of 1939-45: Special Constable until 1941, then Lieut. R.N.V.R. until 1946. *Recreation:* painting. *Address:* 1 Beaufort Street, Chelsea, S.W.3. *T.:* Flaxman 4089. *Club:* Chelsea Arts. [*Died* 16 *Feb.* 1966.

GRIMSHAW, Most Rev. Francis Joseph D.D.; Archbishop of Birmingham (R.C.), since 1954; *b.* 6 Oct. 1901; *s.* of Joseph Grimshaw and Sarah Theresa Handley. *Educ.:* Dr. Morgan's School, Bridgwater; St. Brendan's College Boarding House, later transferred to Prior Park College, Bath; Ven. English College, Rome. Degree in theology; priest, 1926; Asst. Priest, Holy Rood, Swindon, 1926-32; Parish Priest, St. Joseph's, Fishponds, 1932-46; St. Mary's, Julian Rd., Bath, 1946-47; Diocesan Inspector of Schools for Clifton Diocese, 1934-47; Bishop of Plymouth, 1947-54; translated to Birmingham, 1954. *Address:* Archbishop's House, 6 Norfolk Road, Edgbaston, Birmingham 15. *T.:* Edgbaston 0564. [*Died* 22 *March* 1965.

GRIMTHORPE, 3rd Baron, *cr.* 1886; **Ralph William Ernest Beckett,** T.D.; Chairman, Troydale Industries Ltd.; *s.* of 2nd Baron Grimthorpe and Lucy Tracy, *d.* of W. P. Lee, New York (*d.* 1891); *b.* 3rd May 1891; *S.* father, 1917; *m.* 1914, Mary (who obt. a divorce 1945; she *d.* 1962); *d.* of Col. Archdale, late 12th Lancers; two *s.* one *d.*; *m.* Angela (*née* Courage); one *s.* *Educ.:* Eton; Oxford. Hon. Lt.-Col., Yorkshire Hussars; Master Middleton Fox Hounds, 1921-27 and 1932-39; served European War, France, 1915-17 (despatches); War of 1939-1945, Italy (despatches). *Recreations:* fox hunting, flying, winter sports. *Heir:* *s.* Brig. Hon. Christopher John Beckett, O.B.E. *Address:* Easthorpe Hall, Malton, Yorks. *Clubs:* Turf, White's; Yorkshire (York). [*Died* 22 *Feb.* 1963.

GRIMWADE, Geoffrey Holt, C.M.G. 1960; Member Board of Commonwealth Bank since 1951; Chairman: Drug Houses of Australia Ltd.; Carba Dry Ice (Australia) Pty. Ltd.; Wrightcel Pty. Ltd.; *b.* Melbourne, 19 Sept. 1902; *s.* of E. N. Grimwade, Melbourne; *m.* 1931, Mary Lavender, *d.* of L. Stuart; four *d.* *Educ.:* Melbourne Grammar School; Trinity College, Melbourne University (B.Sc.); Emmanuel College, Cambridge University (M.A.). Director: Courtauld's (Australia) Ltd.; Commonwealth Industrial Gases Ltd.; D.H.A. (Vic.) Pty. Ltd.; Victoria Insurance Co. Ltd.; Lincoln Stuart Pty. Ltd.; A.M.P. Soc., Cuming Smith & Co. Pty Ltd. Investigated manufacture of optical glass in U.S.A. on behalf of Ministry of Munitions, 1941. President, Walter and Eliza Hall Inst. of Research. *Recreations:* golf (Blue, Cambridge, 1925, 1926, 1927; Capt. Cambridge, 1927), shooting and fishing. *Address:* 34 Irving Road, Toorak, Victoria, Australia. *Clubs:* Melbourne, Australian, Union; Royal Melbourne Golf. [*Died* 22 *Feb.* 1961.

GRINLING, Brigadier Edward Johns, D.S.O. 1919; M.C.; T.D.; D.L. Lincolnshire; Director, Lee and Grinling, Ltd., Maltsters, Grantham; *b.* Burton-on-Trent, 13 March 1889; *e. s.* of late Edward Grinling, St. Catherines, Grantham; *m.* 1st, 1915, Helen Mary (*d.* 1933), *d.* of late R. P. Cafferata, Harrowby House, Grantham; one *d.*; 2nd, 1935, Paula (*d.* 1944), *d.* of late Ernest Pelgrims, Antwerp; one *d.*; 3rd, 1945, Margaret, *d.* of late Claude Harrison, Grantham; one *d.* *Educ.:* Yarlett Hall, Stafford; Haileybury College. Gazetted 2nd Lieut. 4th Batt. Lincolnshire Regiment, 1910; served European War, 1914-19, France, 1915-19, with 46th North Midland Division; Staff Capt. 138 Infantry Brigade, Feb. 1917; Brigade-Major 139 Infantry Brigade, Aug. 1917 (despatches thrice); Major 4th Batt. Lincolnshire Regt., 1929; Bt. Lt.-Col. 1930; Lt.-Colonel, 1933; commanded 4th Bn. Lincolns. Regt. T.A., 1933-37; Col. 1937; commanded 138 Inf. Bde., 1939-40. *Address:* Friston Cottage, Nr. Saxmundham, Suffolk. *T.:* Snape 204. [*Died* 27 *June* 1963.

GRISWOLD, A(lfred) Whitney; President Yale University since 1950; *b.* Morristown, New Jersey, 27 Oct. 1906; *s.* of Harold Ely Griswold and Elsie M. Whitney; *m.* 1930, Mary Morgan, *d.* of John H. and Augusta Archbald Brooks; one *s.* three *d.* *Educ.:* Hotchkiss School; Yale University.

B.A. 1929, Ph.D. 1933; Guggenheim Fellowship, 1942 and 1945; Instructor, History, 1933-36; Research Asst., International Relations, 1935-38; Asst. Prof., Govt. and International Relations, 1938-42; Assoc. Prof., 1942-45; Assoc. Prof.: of Polit. Sci., 1945-46, of Hist., 1946-47; Prof., History, 1947-50; Director: U.S. Army Specialized Training Program, Foreign Area and Language Studies, Yale, 1942-45; U.S. Army Civil Affairs Training School, Yale, 1943-45. Trustee the Hotchkiss School; Trustee, Carnegie Foundation for the Advancement of Teaching. Hon. Degrees: LL.D.: Harvard and Princeton, 1950, Columbia Univ. 1954, Brown Univ., 1954; Univ. of Pennsylvania, 1956; Wesleyan, Conn., 1956; Johns Hopkins, 1959; L.H.D. Trinity (Connecticut) College, 1950; Litt.D. Jewish Theological Seminary of America, 1951. Officer, Legion of Honour (French), 1953; German Commander's Cross, 1960. *Publications:* The Far Eastern Policy of the United States, 1938; Farming and Democracy, 1948 and 1952; Essays on Education, 1954; In the University Tradition, 1957; Liberal Education and the Democratic Ideal, 1959. *Address:* (office) Yale University, New Haven, Connecticut, U.S.A.; (home) 43 Hillhouse Avenue, New Haven, Connecticut, U.S.A. *T.:* STate 7-3131, ext. 2635.
[*Died* 19 *April* 1963.

GROGAN, Brig.-Gen. George William St. George, V.C 1918; C.B 1919; C.M.G. 1916; D.S.O. 1917 and Bar, 1918; Col. Worcestershire Regt., 1938-45; *b.* 1 Sept. 1875; *e. s.* of Brig.-Gen. E. G. Grogan, C.B, C.B.E.; *m.* 1920, Ethel Gladys, *e. d.* of John Elger; two *s.* *Educ.:* United Services College, Westward Ho!; Royal Military College, Sandhurst. Served Sierra Leone, 1898 (medal with clasp); W. Africa, 1898-99 (clasp); European War, 1914-18 (despatches, C.B., C.M.G., D.S.O. and Bar, Bt.-Col., V.C.); commanded 23rd Infantry Brigade, France, and 1st Brigade Russian Relief Force; retired pay, 1926; Gentleman-at Arms H.M.'s Bodyguard, 1933-45. *Recreations:* golf and reading books. *Address:* Silverdene, Sunningdale, Berks. *T.:* Ascot 419. *Club:* United Service. [*Died* 3 *Jan.* 1962.

**GROPIUS, Prof. Emeritus Dr. (e. h.) Walter; Architect; Professor of Architecture, 1937-52, and Chairman of the Department of Architecture, Graduate School of Design, Harvard University, 1938-52, Professor Emeritus since 1952; *b.* 18 May 1883; *s.* of Walter Adolf Gropius, Architect, Berlin and Manon Scharnweber; *m.* 1923, Ilse Frank; one *d.* *Educ.:* Technische Hochschule, Munich. Studied architecture in Univs. of Charlottenburg-Berlin and Munich, 1903-07. Started work in office of Peter Behrens, German architect; served in the army 3½ years from 1914; Director of Grand Ducal Academy of Arts, Weimar, 1919, and Grand Ducal Saxon School of Applied Arts, Weimar, which he fused under name Staatliches Bauhaus; the Bauhaus moved to Dessau, 1925; resumed practice in Berlin as private architect, 1928; private architect in London in partnership with Maxwell Fry, 1934-37; with Marcel Breuer, 1937-40. Hon. degrees: Dr. Ingenieur (Technische Hochschule, Hannover), 1929; A. M. Harvard, 1942; D.Sc. Western Reserve Univ. 1951; Dr. of Arts, Harvard, 1953; Dr. of Architecture, N. Carolina State Coll. of Agriculture and Engineering, 1953; D.Sc., Sydney, 1954; Dr. Univ. of Brazil, Rio de Janeiro, 1955; Dr. of Humane Letters, Columbia University, New York, 1961, Williams College, 1963; Dr. of Fine Arts Pratt Institute, New York, 1961; Dr. Phil. (*h.c.*) Freie Universität, Berlin. 1963, Vice-President of Congrès Internationaux de'Architecture Moderne, 1929-57; Member Comité Permanent des Architectes; Hon. Mem.. R.I.B.A., London, 1937; Vice-Pres. Inst. of Sociology, London, 1937; F.A.A.S. 1944; Partnership The Architects Collaborative, Cambridge, Mass., 1946; Hon. R.D.I., London; R.S.A. London, 1946; Hon. F.S.I.A., London, 1950; F.A.I.A. 1954 (Mem. 1938). Hon. Senator, Hochschule für bildende Künste, Berlin, 1962. Mem. Nat. Inst. of Arts and Letters; Mem. and corresp. mem. numerous foreign architectural socs., etc.; Gold Medal of Honor, Architectural League of New York, 1951; Grand Prix Internat. d'Architecture, São Paulo, Brazil, 1953; Hanseatic Goethe Prize of Univ. of Hamburg, 1956; Royal Gold Medal, R.I.B.A. London, 1956; Gold Medal, Amer. Inst. of Architects, 1959; Grand Prix of Architecture, Germany, 1960; Gold Albert Medal R.S.A., London, 1961; Goethe Prize, Frankfurt A/M, Germany, 1961; Kaufmann Internat. Design Award, 1961; Cornelius Gurlitt Medal, German Acad. for City and Regional Planning, 1962. Hon. R.A. 1967; Assoc. Nat. Acad. of Design, N.Y., 1967. Hon. Degrees: Stonehill Coll., Mass., 1967; Univ. of Illinois (Urbana-Champaign), 1968; Univ. of Brit. Columbia, 1968. Grand Cross of Merit with Star, of Federal Republic of Germany, 1958. *Publications:* Staatliches Bauhaus, 1923; Internationale Architektur, 1925; Bauhaus Bauten, 1930; The New Architecture and the Bauhaus, 1935; The Bauhaus, 1919-28, 1938; Rebuilding our communities, 1946; Scope of Total Architecture, 1955; Apollo in der Demokratie, 1967; contrib. articles on architecture, planning, housing, industrial design, etc. *Recreations:* swimming, riding. *Address:* Baker Bridge Road, Lincoln, Mass., 01773, U.S.A.; The Architects Collaborative, 46 Brattle St., Cambridge, Mass., 02138, U.S.A. *T.:* 868-4200. *Club:* Harvard (N.Y.C.).
[*Died* 5 *July* 1969.

GROSE-HODGE, Humfrey, M.A.; Headmaster of Bedford School, 1928-51; *b.* 4 April 1891; *e. s.* of Edward Grose-Hodge, late Rector and Canon of Birmingham, and Florence, *d.* of Col. J. T. Smith, R.E., F.R.S.; *m.* 1921, Pamela, *d.* of W. H. Moresby, C.B.E., LL.B.; two *s.* *Educ.:* Marlborough College; Pembroke College, Cambridge (Scholar). 1st Class Classical Tripos and Pres. of the Union, 1913; passed into Indian Civil Service, 1914; served as Assistant Magistrate and Collector, Bengal; Commissioned in Indian Army Reserve of Officers, 1916; served with Q.V.O. Corps of Guides on N.W. Frontier of India and in Mesopotamia, Palestine, and Syria; invalided out of I.C.S., 1920; Asst. Master of Charterhouse, 1920-28; F.S.A. 1946. *Publications:* Four Speeches of Cicero translated into English, Loeb Classical Library, 1927; Murder at Larinum, 1932; (in collaboration) Verses in Sicily, 1935; Roman Panorama, 1944; A Case of High Treason, 1956. *Address:* The Grange, Woolton Hill, Newbury, Berkshire. *T.:* Highclere 222. *Club:* Athenæum.
[*Died* 7 *Jan.* 1962.

GROSS, Richard Oliver, C.M.G. 1938; F.R.B.S.; Chairman, Associated Art Society of N.Z.; Mem. Cttee. to advise on Post Primary Educn. in N.Z.; Past President, Auckland Society of Arts; Past Chairman, McKelvie Trust Bd. (resigned, 1956); *b.* 1882; *s.* of George Gross, Barrow-in-Furness, England; *m.* 1912, Ethel Jane Bailey; one *s.* (and two *s.* decd.). *Educ.:* Barrow-in-Furness Grammar School. London and Provincial Studios seven years; South Africa, Sculpture on Public Buildings, 1910-1914; six years' farming in N.Z. 1914-20; completed many works of sculpture including sculpture for Wellington Citizen War Memorial, National Memorial, Wellington, Auckland Memorial, Invercargill, Dunedin, Cambridge, Auckland Grammar School, Memorials. Decorative Sculpture; Domain Gates, Auckland, The Harry Holland Memorial,

Wellington, Sculpture on Monument to the Maori People, on Maungakiekie. Designed and executed monument to M. J. Savage, 1st Labour Premier, N.Z., Bastion Point, Auckland; sculpture for Trevor Davis Fountain; Matamata Memorial Shrine; Memorial Bronze figure of Rev. Shirley Baker of Samoa; Sculpture for Teachers' Trg. Coll., Auckland, N.Z.; sculptured marble panel, Dunedin Medical School. *Recreation:* trout fishing. *Address:* 27 Evelyn Rd., Howick, New Zealand. [*Died* 27 *Dec.* 1964.

GROSSMITH, Caryll Archibald, C.M.G. 1953; O.B.E. 1945; Colonial Service, retired; *b.* 28 April 1895; *s.* of late George Grossmith (School-master); *m.* 1920, Dorothy Irene (*d.* 1942), *d.* of late Horace Hickling; *m.* 1943, Sandra, *d.* of Maj. E. M. Allan-Hallett; one *s.* *Educ.:* London Univ.; Germany. Served European War, 1914-19: Lt.; Mesopotamia, Persia (despatches); attached British Mission, Prague, 1919. Enemy Debts Dept., Board of Trade, London and Berlin, 1920-26; entered Colonial Office, 1926; Asst. Principal, 1934; Private Secretary to Parliamentary Under-Secretary of State, 1937; Principal. 1937; Asst. Secretary, 1946. Administrative Secretary, Development and Welfare Organisation in the West Indies, Barbados 1950-1956, ret. 1956. Acted as Comptroller Devel. and Welfare, W. Indies, and British Co-Chairman Caribbean Commn., 1953 and 1955; Admin. Asst. to Lt.-Gov. of Malta, 1958-59 Member, Commission of Inquiry on the disturbances in Zanzibar, 1961; Member, Salaries Commission, Fiji, 1963-64. *Recreations:* riding, amateur dramatics, and foreign travel. *Address:* Pineridge, Longdown Rd., Farnham, Surrey. *Club:* Royal Commonwealth Society. [*Died* 22 *June* 1964.

GROSVENOR, Gilbert Hovey, LL.D., Litt.D., Sc.D.; Chairman of the Board of Trustees, National Geographic Society, Washington, D.C., U.S.A.; Editor-in-Chief, National Geographic Magazine, 1903-54 (Asst. Editor, 1899-1900, Managing Editor, 1900-02); Nat. Geographic Soc.: President, 1920-54; Director, 1899-1919 (during these periods members increased from 900 to 2,150,000); Chairman Bd. of Trustees, 1954; *b.* Constantinople, 28 Oct. 1875; *s.* of Edwin A. Grosvenor, LL.D., Litt.D., and Lilian H. (*née* Waters); *m.* 1900, Elsie May (*d.* 1964); *e. d.* of late Dr. Alexander Graham Bell; one *s.* five *d.* (and one *s.* decd.). *Educ.:* Robert Coll., Constantinople; Worcester (Mass.) Acad.; Amherst Coll. (A.B. *magna cum laude*, A.M., Litt.D.). LL.D. Georgetown Univ. 1921, William and Mary College, Williamsburg, Virginia, 1930, Lafayette College, 1938; Univ. of Alaska, 1957; Sc.D., S. Dakota State School of Mines, 1935, George Washington Univ., 1952; Litt.D., Univ. of Maryland 1938, Univ. of Miami, 1944. Gold medals and other geographical awards. Officer Legion of Honour, France; Comdr., Order of St. Olav, Norway; Comdr., Order of Leopold II, Belgium. U.S. Navy Distinguished Public Service Award, 1953. *Publications:* Historical summary of polar exploration for Peary's The North Pole, 1910; Young Russia, 1914; The Land of the Best, 1916; Flags of the World (with Byron McCandless), 1917 (with W. J. Showalter), 1934; The Hawaiian Islands, 1924; Discovery and Exploration, 1924; A Maryland Pilgrimage, 1927; The National Geographic Society and its Magazine, 1936, 1941, 1948, 1952, 1957; Maps for Victory, 1942; The Map Services of The National Geographic Society, 1947; We Followed Peary to the Pole, 1953; numerous articles for magazines; Assoc. Editor Proceedings 8th International Geographic Congress, 1905; Scientific Report of Ziegler Polar Exped. of 1905-1906; Editor: Scenes from Every Land, 1907; 2nd series, 1909; 3rd series, 1912; 4th series, 1917; Book of Birds (with Alexander Wetmore), 1937; 2nd edn., 1939. *Recreations:* sailing, travel by air. *Address:* (home) Wild Acres, 5400 Grosvenor Lane, Bethesda 14, Maryland, U.S.A.; (summer) Baddeck, N.S.; (office) National Geographic Society, Washington, D.C. *Clubs:* Chevy Chase, Cosmos (Pres., 1922), National Press, Overseas Writers, English-speaking Union (Washington); Explorer's, Cruising of America (New York); Bath, Biscayne Bay Yacht (Miami); Bras d'Or Yacht, Baddeck, N.S., Northern Yacht, No. Sydney, N.S. [*Died* 4 *Feb.* 1966.

GROSVENOR, John Ernest, M.B.E. 1939; Governor King Charles I School, Kidderminster; Governor, Kidderminster Coll. for Further Education; *b.* 1 Nov. 1887; 4th but *o. surv. s.* of late George William Grosvenor, D.L., J.P., Mayor of Kidderminster, 1882, 1892, and 1897, High Sheriff of Worcestershire, 1896, Broome House, Worcs., and Emily Anne, *d.* of Herbert Mountford Holmes, Derby; *m.* 1915, Margery Gertrude, 2nd *d.* of late Edmund Ernest Bentall, J.P., Heybridge, Essex; three *d.* *Educ.:* Harrow. Theological Studies in 1946 at St. John's Coll., Durham. Chairman and Managing Director Woodward, Grosvenor & Co. Ltd., Carpet Manufacturers, 1923-46. Reader in Diocese of Worcester, 1938-47; deacon, 1947; priest, 1948; Mayor of Kidderminster, 1926 (3rd successive generation); J.P. Kidderminster, 1937; High Sheriff of Worcestershire, 1939. Joined, 1905, 1st Volunteer Battalion (afterwards 7th (T.F.) Bn.) Worcestershire Regiment; Major 1917; T.D. 1920; retired 1920; served in France and Flanders 1915, 1916, attached Machine Gun Corps and commanded 181st Brig. M.G. Company in Palestine, 1917, 1918, present at Capture of Jerusalem (despatches); Observer Corps, 1939-40; Major, 10th Worcestershire Bn., Home Guard, 1940-45. *Recreations:* hunting and climbing. *Address:* New Wood, Blakedown, nr. Kidderminster, Worcestershire. *T.:* Blakedown 367 *Clubs:* Alpine, Travellers'. [*Died* 4 *Feb.* 1963.

GROSVENOR, Vernon William, C.B.E. 1955; J.P.; retired as Secretary Trustees of Barber Institute of Fine Arts, 1959; Chairman Birmingham Regional Hospitals Board, 1951-57; *b.* 30 March 1889; *s.* of late William John and Amy Grosvenor; *m.* 1st, 1911, Marie Tennant; two *d.*; 2nd, 1928, Ada Marion Randlesome; two *d.* *Educ.:* St. Mary's Higher Grade School, Balham; Univ. of Birmingham (LL.B., Hons.). Soc. of Incorporated Accountants (Fell., Hons. Int. and Final, 1920); Fell. Inst. of Chartered Accountants, 1958. Birmingham City Council, 1936-45; Chm. Public Health Cttee., 1938-45; Chm., Birmingham Hosp. Saturday Fund, 1942-61; Founder Mem., Bd. of Governors, Birmingham Accident Hosp., 1941-48 (Chm. 1945-48); Birmingham R.H.B., 1947-57; Bd. of Governors, United Birmingham Hosp., 1947-57; Chm. Birmingham (Dudley Rd.) Group Hosp. Management Cttee., 1948-51; Independent Chm., Birmingham Area Fish Distribution Cttee., 1940-45; Gen. Nursing Council for England and Wales, 1950-58. Birmingham Home Guard (Lt.-Col.), 1940-45. *Recreations:* many social activities. *Address:* Birchland, Melville Street, Sandown, Isle of Wight. *T.:* Sandown 324. *Clubs:* Midland, Edgbaston Golf (Birmingham). [*Died* 18 *July* 1961.

GROUT, Reginald George; Chairman, The General Steam Navigation Co. Ltd., since 1958; Director, Peninsular and Oriental Steam Navigation Co. since 1959; *b.* 5 Aug. 1901; *m.* 1926, Doris Newman; one *s.* *Educ.:* Christ's College, Finchley. Joined The General Steam Navigation Co. Ltd., 1919; served in Ostend, Havre, Paris, Antwerp; Secretary, 1941; Director, 1947; Vice-Chairman, 1954. Pres. Chamber of

Shipping of the U.K. 1962, 1963 (Vice-Pres.); Chm. Hon. Cttee. of Management, The Thames Nautical Training College, H.M.S. Worcester; Chm. Royal Alfred Merchant Seamen's Society; Hon. Treasurer: British Ship Adoption Society; Seafarers' Education Service. *Address:* 8 Lawrence Court, Mill Hill, N.W.7. *T.:* Mill Hill 4411. [*Died* 28 *Dec.* 1963.

GROVE, Professor Alfred John; Professor Emeritus of Zoology in the University of London, since 1950; *b.* 29 Jan. 1888; *s.* of Alfred James and Martha Jane Grove; *m.* 1st 1918, Agnes Clarissa Ayrton; one *s.*; 2nd, 1931, Winifred May Westwood. *Educ.:* Univs. of Birmingham and Cambridge. B.Sc. (Birm.), 1907; M.Sc. 1908; D.Sc. 1919; B.A. (Cantab.), 1920; M.A. 1926. Piddock Scholar, 1904-07; Research Scholar, Univ. Birmingham, 1908-10; 1851 Exhibition Research Scholar, Univ. Cambridge, 1910-11; Indian Agric. Service, 1911-15; Lecturer Univ. Birmingham, 1916; served European War, 1916-19, Lieut. (Unattached List); Lecturer in Zoology University Sheffield, 1919-29; Queen Mary College, University of London, 1929; Reader, 1934; Professor, 1947. *Publications:* (with R. H. Whitehouse) Series of Dissection Manuals: Frog, 1930; Rabbit, 1933; Dogfish, 1936; Earthworm, 1943; Crayfish, 1947; Cockroach, 1949; Manual of Practical Chordate Embryology, 1957; (with G. E. Newell) Animal Biology, 1942; original papers in Journ. of Parasitology, Indian Agric. Journ. Quart., Journ. Micro. Sci., Ann. Mag. Nat. Hist., etc. *Recreations:* reading and gardening. *Address:* 7 Redcliffe Road, St. Mary Church, Torquay, Devon. *T.:* Torquay 88713. [*Died* 5 *June* 1962.

GROVE, Sir Gerald, 3rd Bart., *cr.* 1874; J.P.; Director of Film Research; *b.* 18 Dec. 1886; *e. s.* of Sir Walter Grove, 2nd Bt., and Lady Grove, *d.* of Lt.-Gen. Pitt Rivers and Hon. Mrs. Pitt Rivers; *S.* father, 1932; unmarried. *Educ.:* Sherborne School; privately abroad in France and Germany. Joined British South Africa Police, Rhodesia, 1911; Rhodesia Native Regiment, 1915; 1st King's African Rifles as Lieut., 1917; served German South West and East Africa, 1915-17; acted as extra A.D.C. to Earl Buxton, Governor-General, Union of South Africa, 1918; invalided on pension from Army, 1919; Foreign Office, 1920; Private Secretary to Earl of Stradbroke, Governor of Victoria, Australia, 1922; Technical Adviser Motion Pictures (Hollywood), 1924-33. *Publications:* Editor, Rhodesia Defence Force Journal, 1914-15. *Recreations:* reading, riding, and researching. *Heir:* *n.* Walter Philip, *b.* 18 March 1927. *Address:* Sedgehill Manor, Shaftesbury, Dorset. *T.A.:* Grove, Semley. *T.:* Shaftesbury 2468. *Club:* Brooks's. [*Died* 3 *March* 1962.

GROVE, Colonel Thomas Thackeray, C.M.G. 1919; D.S.O. 1917; late R.E.; *b.* 1879; *s.* of late Rev. W. H. Grove. Served European War, 1914-19 (despatches, D.S.O. and bar, Bt. Lieut.-Colonel, Officer of Legion of Honour, French Croix de Guerre); Chief Engineer, Territorial Army Air Defence Formations, 1929-33; retired pay, 1933. [*Died* 29 *Oct.* 1965.

GROVE-WHITE, Lt.-Gen. Sir Maurice Fitzgibbon, K.B.E., *cr.* 1945; C.B. 1941; D.S.O. 1917; *b.* 1887; *s.* of Col. James Grove-White, C.M.G., J.P., D.L., Kilbyrne, Doneraile, Co. Cork; *m.* 1919, Bernice Agnes, *d.* of D. F. W. Parlane; one *s.* (and one killed in action, 1940). *Educ.:* Wellington Coll.; R.M.A., Woolwich. 2nd Lt., R.E. 1907; Served European War, 1914-1919 (despatches, D.S.O., O.B.E., Bt. Major; Legion of Honour); Bt. Lt.-Col. 1928, and 1939-45 (C.B., K.B.E.); Maj.-Gen., 1938; Comd. 2nd A.A. Div., 1939 and 2nd A.A. Corps, 1940; Dumbarton Oaks conversations, 1944; also served in West Indies and Malaya; retd. 1945, with hon. rank of Lt.-Gen.; Col. Comdt. R.E. 1946-53. *Address:* c/o Lloyds Bank, Ltd., Waterloo Place, S.W.1. *Club:* Army and Navy. [*Died* 3 *April* 1965.

GRUMELL, Ernest Sydney, C.B.E. 1943; D.Sc.; F.R.S.A.; formerly Chairman Fuel Efficiency Committee (member of Industrial Consumer Council and Scientific Advisory Council), Ministry of Fuel and Power; *b.* Jan. 1885; *s.* of Ernest E. Grumell, London; *m.* 1911, Katharine Wyman Stern, Bangor, Maine, U.S.A.; one *d.* *Educ.:* Tonbridge; Univs. of Leipzig and Geneva. Late Head of Fuel Economy Dept. of Imperial Chemical Industries. Melchett medallist, Institute of Fuel. *Publications:* many in this country and the United States. *Recreations:* Past: Rugby, ski-ing; squash, tennis. *Address:* Red Tiles, 2 Home Farm Close, Thames Ditton, Surrey. *T.:* Emberbrook 3210. [*Died* 12 *Nov.* 1962.

GRUNDY, Sir Claude (Herbert), Kt. 1966; Master of the Supreme Court, Queen's Bench Division, 1947-65; Senior Master and Queen's Remembrancer, 1962-65; *b.* 9 Feb. 1891; 2nd *s.* of Rev. George William Grundy, sometime Vicar of Chobham, Surrey; *m.* 1st, Alice Marjorie Upjohn (marr. diss.); three *s.* one *d.*; 2nd, Kathleen Dorothy (Barbara) Wadge. *Educ.:* Hillstone, Malvern. Served European War (Aug. 4th) 1914-19, in Royal Highlanders of Montreal, 1st Canadian Div. until Nov. 1915; commissioned 6th Bedfordshire Regt. (wounded, Somme, Nov. 1916); Staff Capt., Southern Command, H.Q. Staff, 1918. Called to Bar, Gray's Inn, 1920 (Arden Prizeman). Contested (C.) Leigh, Lancs, Gen. Elect., 1929, and W. Walthamstow. Gen. Elect., 1931. Served War, 1939-44, Major, D.A.A.G. (Legal), G.H.Q., Home Forces, Adviser on Martial Law and War Zone Courts. Member, General Council of the Bar, 1945-46. Served on Evershed Cttee. on Practice and Procedure in Supreme Court, 1951-53. *Recreations:* numerous. *Address:* 117 Latymer Court, W.6. [*Died* 31 *May* 1967.

GUDGEON, Stanley Herbert, C.B.E. 1941; *b.* Rio de Janeiro, Brazil, 7 April 1896; *s.* of Gustavus Gudgeon and Corinne Nathan; *m.* 1928, Amy Cranmer, *e. c.* of late Sir George Kenrick, K.B.E.; one *d.* *Educ.:* Hurst Court, Ore, Sussex; Cheltenham College. Interned in Germany 1914-18. Vice-Consul at Rio de Janeiro, Dunkirk, Iquique, Lisbon and Buenos Aires at various dates; Consul at Oporto, 1934; at Lille, 1936; prisoner in enemy hands, May 1940-Nov. 1942; Consul-General at Lisbon, 1944; at São Paulo, 1945-48; Ambassador to Dominican Republic, 1951-54 (Minister, 1948-51): Special Ambassador for the Inauguration of General Hector Trujillo as President of the Dominican Republic in 1952; retired 1954. *Address:* Rua Almeida Brandão 13 (2.D), Lisbon, Portugal. *Clubs:* Public Schools; Incogniti / Cryptics / Forty / Romany / Royal British (Lisbon). [*Died* 25 *May* 1966.

GUGGENHEIM, Professor Edward Armand, F.R.S. 1946; M.A., Sc.D. (Cantab.); F.R.I.C.; Professor of Chemistry, Reading University, 1946-66; *b.* 11 August 1901; *s.* of Armand Guggenheim, Swiss Consul in Manchester; *m.* 1934, Simone Ganzin (*d.* 1954); *m.* 1955, Ruth Helen (Peggy) Aitken (*née* Clarke), *widow* of Major Charles Fleming Aitken, M.C.; no *c.* *Educ.:* Charterhouse; Gonville and Caius College, Cambridge. Studied under Professors R. H. Fowler (Cambridge), J. N. Brönsted (Copenhagen) and N. Bjerrum (Copenhagen). Teaching posts at Danish Royal Agric. College. 1928-29; Stanford

University, California, 1932-33; Reading University, 1933-35; London University, 1936-39. Scientific Staff of Admiralty, 1939-1944; Staff of Montreal Laboratory of Atomic Energy, 1944-46. Member, Royal Danish Academy of Sciences. *Publications:* Modern Thermodynamics, 1933; Statistical Thermodynamics (with R. H. Fowler), 1939; Thermodynamics for Chemists and Physicists, 1949; Mixtures, 1952; Physico-Chemical Calculations (with J. E. Prue), 1954; Boltzmann's Distribution Law, 1955; Elements of the Kinetic Theory of Gases, 1960; Applications of Statistical Mechanics, 1965; Elements of Chemical Thermodynamics, 1966; Special Relativity, 1967. Over 100 papers in various journals. *Address:* Selborne, Peppard Road, Caversham, Reading. *T.:* Reading 72316; Pier House, Salen, Isle of Mull. *T.:* Aros 16. *Club:* Royal Automobile. [*Died* 9 *Aug.* 1970.

GUGGISBERG, Lady Decima M.; *see* Moore-Guggisberg.

GUILD, David Alexander, M.A., LL.B.; Sheriff Substitute of Inverness, Moray, Nairn and Ross & Cromarty, at Elgin, since 1955; *b.* 16 Sept. 1884; *s.* of Alexander Guild, W.S., Edinburgh, and Margaret Arnott Macmeikan; *m.* 1915, Maggie Clark Ritchie; one *s.* one *d.* *Educ.:* Edinburgh Academy (Dux); Edinburgh University. Called to Scots Bar, 1909; Counsel for the Crown as Ultimus Hæres, 1925-28; Junior Counsel for the Board of Trade, 1928-33; Sheriff Substitute; of Lanarkshire, at Airdrie, 1933-1937, at Glasgow, 1937-55; of Inverness and Moray, at Elgin, 1955. Lieut. R.F.A. European War (wounded). *Publications:* The Law of Arbitration in Scotland; legal articles in technical legal publications. *Recreations:* golf (Blue, Edinburgh University), motoring, fishing. *Address:* Deansford, Bishopmill, Elgin. *Clubs:* Scottish Conservative (Edinburgh); Royal Scottish Automobile (Glasgow). [*Died* 26 *May* 1961.

GUILLAUME, Rev. Alfred, M.A., D.D. Oxon; Professor of Arabic, School of Oriental and African Studies, and Head of the Dept. of the Near and Middle East, Univ. of London, 1947-55; Professor Emeritus, 1955; Visiting Professor, Leeds Univ., 1958-59; *b.* 8 Nov. 1888; *s.* of late Alfred Guillaume; *m.* 1916, Margaret Woodfield, *o. d.* of late Rev. W. O. Leadbitter, D.C.L., Rector of West Walton, Norfolk, two *s.* two *d.* *Educ.:* Wadham College, Oxford (Exhibitioner). Pusey and Ellerton Hebrew Scholarship; Houghton Syriac Prize; First-Class Honours, School of Oriental Languages, 1913; Hall and Houghton Septuagint Prize; Junior Kennicott Hebrew Scholarship; Private, Royal Fusiliers, 1914; Lieut., Lancashire Fusiliers, 1915; served in France and Egypt, Captain on the staff of High Commissioner (despatches); Liddon Theological Student, 1919; Denyer and Johnson Scholar, 1920; Curate and Hebrew Lecturer, Cuddesdon College, 1919, and Lecturer in Old Testament, King's College, London; Professor of Hebrew and Oriental Languages in the University of Durham, 1920-30; Rector of St. Mary-le-Bow with St. Mary-the-Less, Durham, 1922-30; Censor of University College, 1929-30; Principal of Culham College, Abingdon, 1930-45; Hon. Asst. Keeper of the Public Record, 1941-44; Prof. of Arabic, American University of Beirut, 1944-45; Davidson Prof. of Old Testament Studies, Univ. of London, 1945-47; Examining Chaplain to Bishop of Oxford, 1937-46; Bampton Lecturer for 1938; Fellow of King's College, London, 1947. Member of the Arab Academy of Damascus, 1949, and of the Arab Academy of Baghdad, 1950; Select Preacher, Cambridge, 1955; Visiting Professor of Arabic, Princeton University, New Jersey, 1955-57; Fellow, School of Oriental and African Studies, 1955. *Publications:* The Traditions of Islam, 1924; The Influence of Judaism on Islam, 1927; Al Shahrastani's Nihayatu-l-iqdam fi'ilmi-l-Kalam, 1931; Prophecy and Divination, 1938; Islam, 1954 (Arabic, Italian and Spanish trans.); The Life of Muhammad, 1955; New Light on the Life of Muhammad, 1960; Co-editor (with Bishop Gore) of the O.T. and Apocrypha in New Commentary on Holy Scripture, including the Apocrypha, and author of several articles therein, 1928; The Legacy of Islam (with Sir Thomas Arnold), 1931; contributor to the Encyclopædia of Islam. *Recreation:* walking. *Address:* High View, Streatley, Berks. *T.:* Goring 2290. *Club:* Athenæum. [*Died* 30 *Nov.* 1965.

GUISE, Sir Anselm (William Edward), 6th Bt., *cr.* 1783; late Captain Royal Gloucestershire Hussars; *b.* 18 Sept. 1888; *o. surv. s.* of 5th Bt. and Ada Caroline (*d.* 1945), *d.* of late O. E. Coope, M.P., Rochetts, Brentwood; *S.* father, 1920; *m.* 1924, Margaret, *d.* of late Sir James Grant, 1st Bt.; two *s.* one *d.* *Educ.:* Eton. Patron of one living; formerly J.P. Co. Gloucester; High Sheriff, 1926; owns about 1400 acres. *Heir:* *s.* Capt. John Grant Guise, late 3rd Hussars, *b.* 15 Dec. 1927. *Address:* Elmore Court, near Gloucester. *Club:* M.C.C. [*Died* 12 *Sept.* 1970.

GUNN, Alistair Livingston, V.R.D., M.D. (Wales), F.R.C.S. (Edin.), F.R.C.O.G., Consulting Obstetrician, Lewisham and Bromley, Kent, Hospitals; Consulting Gynæcologist to numerous hospitals and public authorities; *b.* 14 Feb. 1903; *s.* of George H. Gunn and Mary Tait; *m.* 1930, Sibyl Marian Thomas, *d.* of late Lt.-Col. G. C. Thomas, D.S.O., O.B.E.; two *s.* one *d.* *Educ.:* Cardiff High School; Univs. of Wales and Edinburgh. Chairman Cardiff Medical Students Club; resident hospital appointments at Cardiff Royal Infirmary, Redhill Hospital, Edgware and Mile End Hospital; Obstetrician and Gynæcologist, St. Mary's, Mayday and Borough Hosps., Croydon, 1933-36. Served War of 1939-45, Surgeon Comdr. R.N.V.R.; M.O. i/c R.N. hosp., Duncraig, Scotland, 1940-43; Surgical Specialist R.N. Hosp., Durban and H.M.S. Westcliff. Lectr. and Examr. Central Midwives Bd.; Examr. in Obst. and Gynæc. for Lond. Univ. M.B., B.S.; to conjoint Examining Bd. in Eng. and for Membership of R.C.O.G.; Mem. Ct. of Assts. of Worshipful Soc. of Apothecaries of London; Hon. Librarian and Mem. Council of R.C.O.G.; James Young Simpson Orator, 1967; F.R.Soc.Med. (Vice-President, Sect. of Obst. and Gynæc.); Fellow and Member, Council, Hunterian Soc.; Hunterian Orator, 1968. Rep. of Roy. Coll. on S.E. Reg. Cttee. of Brit. Postgrad. Med. Fedn.; Chm. Maternity Liaison Cttees. for Lewisham and Bromley; Past Pres.; W. Kent Medico-Chirurgical Soc.; New Cross Med. Soc.; Sec. Gynæcolog. Sect., B.M.A. Meeting, 1952. Freeman of City of London; Conservator of Chislehurst Common; Chairman Chislehurst Playing Fields Association. *Publications:* Treatment of Uterine Hæmorrhage, 1942; articles and clinical reports, mainly obstetrical. *Recreations:* travel, book-collecting. *Address:* 82 Harley Street, W.1. *T.:* 01-580 4357; 9 Holbrook House, Chislehurst, Kent. *T.:* 01-467 1625. *Clubs:* Athenæum; Chislehurst Golf; Gynæcological Travellers'. [*Died* 18 *Nov.* 1970.

GUNN, Herbert Smith; *b.* Gravesend, Kent, 3 April 1904; *yr. s.* of late Herbert Gunn, and Alice Gunn; *m.* 1927, Ann Charlotte Thomson (decd.); two *s.*; *m.* 1944, Olive Melville Brown; two *s.* Trained as reporter, Kent Messenger, 1920-25; Sub-editor Straits Times, Singapore, 1925; Manchester Evening News, 1926-28; Evening News, London, 1929; Evening

Standard sub-editor, 1931, news editor, 1933-1936; editor Daily Express, Manchester, 1936-38; asst. editor Daily Express, London, 1938-42, managing editor, 1943-44; Editor Evening Standard, London, 1944-50; publisher, 1951: Managing Editor, Daily Mail, London, 1952-53; Editor of the Daily Sketch, Oct. 1953-Dec. 1959; of the Sunday Dispatch, Dec. 1959 when it merged with the Sunday Express, 1961; resigned from Associated Newspapers Group (ill-health), 1962. President, Institute of Journalists, 1958-59. *Address:* The Coachhouse, Somerset Road, Wimbledon Common, S.W.19. *Clubs:* Press, Savage. [*Died* 2 *March* 1962.

GUNN, Sir James, Kt. 1963; R.A. 1961 (A.R.A. 1953); R.P. 1945; LL.D.; portrait painter; President Royal Society of Portrait Painters since 1953; *b.* 30 June 1893; *s.* of Richard Gunn and Thomasina Munro; *m.* 1929, Pauline (*d.* 1950), *d.* of A. P. Miller; one *s.* one *d.* Studied Glasgow Sch. of Art; Acad. Julien, Paris; Spain. Served European War, 1914-18, enlisted Artists' Rifles; commissioned 10th Scottish Rifles, 15th Div. Pictures in Nat. Portrait Gallery, Glasgow, Dundee, Rochdale, Preston, Bradford; best known works: Conversation Piece, Hilaire Belloc, G. K. Chesterton and Maurice Baring, 1932, Delius, 1933, H.M. King George VI, Pauline in the Yellow Dress, F.M. Sir B. L. Montgomery (France), 1944, H.M. The Queen, 1946, Conversation Piece at the Royal Lodge, Windsor Great Park, 1950; State Portrait of H.M. the Queen, 1953-54. Hon. LL.D.: Manchester, 1945; Glasgow, 1963. Gold Medal, Paris Salon, 1939. *Address:* 7 Kidderpore Ave., N.W.3. *T.:* Hampstead 5919. *Clubs:* Arts, Athenæum, Beefsteak, Garrick, Savage, White's. [*Died* 30 *Dec.* 1964.

GUNN, Major-Gen. John Alexander, C.M.G. 1918; D.S.O. 1917; *b* 1873; *s.* of Donald Gunn, Toronto; *m.* 1st, 1903, Isabella Elliott Montgomery, B.A. (*d.* 1925); two *s.* two *d.*; 2nd, 1929, Mrs. Helen Wellington Parsons (*née* Housser). *Educ.:* Toronto Schools. Served European War 1914-19, with Canadian army corps; recruited and commanded 24 battalion Victoria Rifles, Montreal, 1914-17; Brig.-Gen.; 1918 (despatches D.S.O., C.M.G., two medals) Commanded 6th Infantry brigade, Toronto, 1920-21; G.O.C. military district No. 2, Toronto, 1919; Col. Comdt Queen's Own Rifles of Canada, 1920-21; Major-Gen., 1937. Hon. Member, Royal Canadian Military Institute. Engaged in Insurance business. *Address:* 3 Rosedale Road, Toronto 5, Canada. *Clubs:* Royal Commonwealth Society, Farmers'; National (Toronto); (Life Member) Royal Canadian Yacht [*Died* 15 *May* 1966.

GUNNING, Sir (Orlando) Peter, Kt. 1959; C.M.G. 1956; *b.* 1 October 1908; *s.* of late Brigadier-General O. G. Gunning, C.M.G., D.S.O.; *m.* 1940, Patricia Mary, *d.* of Capt. D. P. O'Connor, M.C.; two *d.* *Educ.:* Haileybury Coll.; Trinity Coll., Cambridge (M.A.). Nigerian Administrative Service, 1931-40. Served R.A.F. (Ft.-Lt.), 1941-45. Nigerian Admin. Service, 1946-58; Deputy Governor, Eastern Nigeria, 1956-58; Chairman Public and Police Service Commissions, Uganda, 1959-62; Dep. Sec. King Edward's Hospital Fund for London, 1962-. *Recreations:* tennis, shooting. *Address:* c/o National & Grindlay's Bank, 13 St. James's Square, S.W.1; 68a Chelsea Square, S.W.3. *T.:* Flaxman 1858. *Club:* Leander. *Died* 4 *Nov.* 1964.

GUNSON, Sir James Henry, Kt., cr. 1924; C.M.G. 1922; C.B.E. 1919; seed, grain and produce merchant; (retired): Director New Zealand Insurance Co. Ltd. (late Chm.); Chairman Auckland Gas Company Ltd.; *b.* Auckland N.Z., of English parents, 1877; *m.* 1st, 1905, Jessie, O.B.E., *d* of Jas. Wiseman; two *s.* one *d.*; 2nd, 1959, Margaret May Ryan, formerly of Thames, N.Z. *Educ.:* Auckland Grammar School. President Auckland Chamber of Commerce, 1910; Chairman Auckland Harbour Board, 1911-1915; Mayor of Auckland, 1915-25; O.B.E. 1918. *Address:* Rydal Mount, Panmure, Auckland, E.2, N.Z. *Club:* Northern (Auckland). [*Died* 12 *May* 1963.

GUNTER, Sir Geoffrey (Campbell), Kt. 1961; C.B.E. 1954 (O.B.E. 1951); *b.* 30 Apr. 1879; *s.* of late Thomas Moreau Gunter and Eliza Heslop Campbell; *m.* 1903, Florence Madeline, *d.* of Rev. J. E. Miller, Stewart Town, Jamaica; one *s.* two *d.* *Educ.:* Kingston Collegiate School, Jamaica. Chief Accountant, Ja. Govt. Railway and an Alderman of Kingston and St. Andrew Corp., 1943-47 (Dep. Mayor, 1944-46, Mayor 1946 and 1947); Trade Controller and Competent Authority, 1948, and Commissioner for Parochial Govt., Parish of St. Catherine; Mem. Incorp. Lay Body of Church of England in Jamaica; Chm. Nuttall Memorial Hosp.; Chm. Victoria League in Jamaica for 21 years (Pres. 1960-). Appointed to act as Governor of Jamaica and its Dependencies 14th June-13th Oct. 1960. European War, 1914-18, as Lieut. Jamaica Reserve Regt.; Chief A.R.P. Warden and Competent Authority, St. Andrew, 1939-44. Honble. Custos Rotulorum parish of St. Andrew, Jamaica, 1958-. *Recreations:* horticulture, orchid culture, stamp collecting. *Address:* 6 East Kings House Road, Liguanea, Kingston 6, Jamaica, West Indies. *Club:* Melbourne Cricket (Kingston, Jamaica). [*Died* 17 *Sept.* 1961.

GUNTHER, John; Writer; *b.* Chicago, Illinois, U.S.A., 30 August 1901; *s.* of Eugene McClellan Gunther and Lisette Schoeninger; *m.* 1927, Frances Fineman (marriage dissolved, 1944; she *d.* 1964); (one *s.*, *d.* 1947); 2nd, 1948, Jane Perry Vandercook; one *s.* *Educ.:* Univ. of Chicago (Ph.B.). Began journalism with Chicago Daily News, 1922; asst. London correspondent, 1924-26; variously correspondent in Paris, Berlin, Rome, Scandinavia, Near East, Geneva, Spain, Moscow, 1926-30; correspondent in Vienna and the Balkans, 1930-35; chief correspondent in London, 1935-36; resigned from Chicago Daily News, 1936, to devote self to writing; travelled widely in India, China, Japan, 1937-38; covered outbreak of war in London, Sept.-Oct. 1939; visited all twenty of Latin American Republics, 1940-41; war correspondent in London, 1941; attached to Gen. Eisenhower's headquarters and to British 8th Army, invasion of Sicily, 1943. Commentator on international affairs for Blue Network, New York, 1942-45; travelled in Central and E. Europe, 1948, for New York Herald Tribune and Look Magazine; took trip to Japan and around the world, during 1950: visited 31 countries in Africa, 1952-53; revisited South America, Far East, North Africa, Eastern Europe, various trips, 1955-69. *Publications:* Inside Europe, 1936 (repeatedly revised and republished); Inside Asia, 1939 (revised, 1942); The High Cost of Hitler, 1939; Inside Latin America, 1941; D-Day, 1944; The Troubled Midnight, 1945; Inside U.S.A., 1947; Death Be Not Proud, 1949; Behind the Curtain, 1949; Roosevelt in Retrospect, 1950; The Riddle of MacArthur, 1951; Eisenhower, 1952; Alexander the Great, 1953; Inside Africa, 1955; (jointly) Days to Remember: America 1945-55, 1957; Inside Russia Today, 1958; Julius Caesar, 1959; Taken at the Flood, 1960: Inside Europe Today, 1961; A Fragment of Autobiography, 1962; The Lost City, 1964; Procession, 1965; Inside South America, 1966; Chicago Revisited, 1967; Twelve Cities, 1969; Quatrain, 1970. Contributor to British, American, and Continental periodicals. *Address:* 1 East End Ave., New York, City, U.S.A. [*Died* 29 *May* 1970.

GURNELL, Engineer Rear-Admiral Thompson, C.B. 1933; *b.* 1878. Served European War, 1914-19. Engineer Rear-Adm. 1930; Extra Naval Assistant to Second Sea Lord for Engineering personnel duties, 1933-34; retired list, 1934; recalled, 1939; Admiralty Regional Officer, London and South-Eastern Regions, 1940-45. *Address:* 9 Cousins Grove, Southsea, Hants.
Died 20 *May* 1965.

GURNEY, Sir Hugh, K.C.M.G., *cr.* 1935 (C.M.G. 1918); M.V.O. 1913; *b.* 4 February 1878; 3rd *s.* of John Gurney, of Sprowston Hall, Norfolk (*d.* 1887); *m.* 1911, Mariota, *e. d.* of late Rt. Hon. Sir Lancelot D. Carnegie, G.C.V.O., K.C.M.G., and *g.d.* of 9th Earl of Southesk; two *s.* three *d.* (and one *s.* decd.). *Educ.:* Eton; Trinity College, Oxford. Diplomatic Service, 1901; served at Vienna, Washington, The Hague, Paris, Berlin, Copenhagen, Brussels, Tokyo, Madrid, Tangier and Rio de Janeiro; Minister to Denmark, 1933-35; Ambassador to Brazil, 1935-39. Retired from Diplomatic Service, 1940. A Director, National Provident Instn., 1944-59; a Governor, London Hosp., 1945-58; Chm., Incorp. Church Building Soc., 1951-54 and 1955-61; Chm., Metropolitan Drinking Fountain and Cattle Trough Assoc., 1947-64. Served in 5 Berks Bn. Home Guard, 1940-44; J.P. Berks. 1942-46; Member of Berkshire County Council, 1941-46. Knight Grand Cross, Order of Dannebrog (Denmark). *Address:* 1 Sloane Gardens, S.W.1. *T.:* Sloane 4257. *Clubs:* Brooks's, Turf; Norfolk (Norwich).
[*Died* 7 *March* 1968.

GURNEY, Quintin Edward, T.D., D.L.; Local Director at Norwich of Barclays Bank Ltd. (formerly Director); *b.* 20 Feb 1883; *s.* of late R. H. J. Gurney, Northrepps Hall, Norwich; *m.* 1911, Emily Ada Pleasance, *d.* of late A. W. Ruggles-Brise, Spains Hall, Essex; two *s.* two *d.* (and two *s.* decd.). *Educ.:* Harrow; Trinity College, Cambridge. B.A. 1904 (Camb.) subsequently entering Bank. Served European War, 1914-19, with Norfolk Yeomanry; Major, 1914. High Sheriff of Norfolk, 1932; D.L. Norfolk, 1935. *Address:* Bawdeswell Hall, East Dereham, Norfolk. *T.:* Bawdeswell 224
[*Died* 30 *June* 1968.

GURNEY-DIXON, Sir Samuel, Kt. 1942; M.A., M.D. (Cantab.); J.P.; Senior Pro-Chancellor, 1952-66 (Chairman of Council, 1952-57) University of Southampton (formerly a Vice-President (Chairman of Council, 1936-52) University College, Southampton); (Pres., 1946-47, 1947-48) Assoc. of Educn. Cttees.; a Vice-Pres. County Councils' Assoc., 1952-64 and of Nat. Foundation for Educational Research, since 1947; *b.* 6 July 1878; *s.* of late John Dixon and Harriet Edith, *d.* of Thomas Gurney; adopted additional surname Gurney by Deed Poll, 1911; *m.* 1918, Hilda, *d.* of late Professor J. H. Poynting, F.R.S., J.P., and *widow* of Capt. John Chamberlain, M.C., Birmingham; two *d.* (and one *d.* decd.). *Educ.:* Leys School; Trinity College, Cambridge. Camb. Univ. Swimming Teams, 1900-1901; Pres. C.U.S.C. 1902. St. Bartholomew's Hosp., London. M.R.C.S. (Eng.), L.R.C.P. (Lond.). Served European War, 1914-17, with 19th Field Ambulance, France, Capt. R.A.M.C. (despatches twice). J.P. (Hants), 1926. Member Hampshire County Council, 1923; Alderman, 1928-65; Vice-Chm., 1938-48; Chairman, Hampshire Education Cttee., 1929-47; Chairman, Educ. Cttee. of County Councils Assoc., 1937-48; Chairman, Central Advisory Council for Education (England), 1948-56; Chairman Southern Regional Council for Further Education, 1947-52; Vice-Chm. Nat. Advisory Council on Education for Industry and Commerce, 1948-51; President, Union of Educational Institutions, 1951; Founder Member, British Ship Adoption Society, 1936 (Vice-Pres. 1962) and of Association of Agriculture; Chairman Hampshire Rivers Board of Conservators, 1938-50; Member Burnham Committee, 1933-53; a Director, Nat. Camps Corp. (Camps Act, 1939), 1939, Chm. Bd., 1949-58; Governor: Leys School, Cambridge (and Rep. on G.B.A.), 1942-56; Ottershaw School, Surrey, etc. Hon. LL.D. (Southampton). *Publication:* The Transmutation of Bacteria, 1919. *Recreation:* fishing. *Address:* Aldermoor, Stoney Cross, Lyndhurst, Hants. *T.:* Cadnam 2227. *Clubs:* Athenæum, Oxford and Cambridge.
[*Died* 30 *April* 1970.

GURNEY-SALTER, Emma, M.A., Litt.D. (Dublin); *b.* 1875; *o. d.* of late William Henry Gurney Salter, The Official Shorthand Writer to the Houses of Parliament; unmarried. *Educ.:* Notting Hill High School; Girton College, Cambridge (Class. Tripos, 1896). *Publications:* Franciscan Legends in Italian Art; Nature in Italian Art; Tudor England through Venetian Eyes translations of The Legend of the Three Companions and Bonaventura's Life of St. Francis (Temple Classics); The Coming of the Friars Minor to England and Germany; Nicholas of Cusa's The Vision of God articles and verses in various reviews, etc. *Address:* 43 Cadogan Place, S.W.1. *Club:* University Women's.
[*Died* 27 *March* 1967.

GUTHRIE, Hon. Lord; Henry Wallace Guthrie; Senator of the College of Justice in Scotland since 1949; *b.* 20 Oct. 1903; *e. s.* of Rev. W. A. Guthrie, T.D., D.D., Fountainbridge Church, Edinburgh, Lieut.-Colonel Army Education Corps, and Agnes Gilmour Rattray; *m.* 1934, Jeannie Hendry Rutherford, M.A., *d.* of T. H. Rutherford, Auldearn; one *s.* one *d.* *Educ.:* Broughton School, Edinburgh; Edinburgh University. M.A. (Edin.) 1st Class Hons. English, 1923; LL.B. (Edin.) with distinction, 1925; Vans Dunlop Scholar, Public Law, 1926; Advocate, Scottish Bar, 1927; Liberal Candidate, Dunbartonshire, 1929; Pres., Scottish League of Young Liberals, 1928-32; Lecturer in Scots Law, Edinburgh Univ., 1935-38; Advocate Depute, 1940-45; Home Advocate Depute, 1945-48; K.C. (Scot.) 1946; Sheriff of Ayr and Bute, 1948. Commissioner, War Damage Commission and Member of Central Land Board, 1947-49; Chairman, Scottish Nurses' Salaries Cttee., 1947; Keeper of Advocates' Library, 1948; Chairman of Cttee. of Inquiry into Tenure of Shops and Business Premises in Scotland, 1948-49; Chairman: Scottish Central Probation Council, 1950-65; Scottish Leases Cttee., 1951; Scottish Cttee. on Legal Aid in Criminal Proceedings, 1957-60. Pres., Scottish Italian Circle. *Publications:* Ed.: Our Scottish Sea Fisheries, 1929; Ed.: Scots Law Times, Sheriff Court Reports, 1928-36. *Recreations:* books, chess. *Address:* Medwynbrae, West Linton, Peeblesshire. *T.:* West Linton 287. [*Died* 11 *March* 1970.

GUTTERY, Sir Norman (Arthur), K.B.E., *cr.* 1951; C.B. 1947; *b.* 4 July 1889; *s.* of Rev. A. T. Guttery, D.D., Methodist Minister; *m.* 1920, Elsie Crankshaw, M.A.; two *d.* *Educ.:* Elmfield College, York; King's College, London. Joined Civil Service, 1910; served in Ministries of Education and of National Health, Insurance Commission, Ministry of Shipping, Board of Trade and Ministry of Transport. Under-Secretary, Ministry of Transport, 1946-48; Deputy Secretary, 1948-54. Officer Order of Leopold (Belgium); Chev. Order of St. Olav (Norway). *Address:* 17 The Chilterns, Brighton Rd., Sutton, Surrey. *T.:* Vigilant 2913.
[*Died* 23 *April* 1962.

GUTTRIDGE, George Herbert, M.A. (Cantab.); Emeritus Sather Professor of

History, University of California, since 1965; *b.* Hull, 6 Aug. 1898; *o. s.* of Frederick W. H. Guttridge and Eleanor Cowley Guttridge (*née* Peace); *m.* 1928, Eleanor, *d.* of F. J. Mann, M.D., Poughkeepsie, N.Y. *Educ.:* Nottingham High Sch.; St. John's Coll., Cambridge (scholar). 2nd Lt. R.G.A., 1917-18; Prince Consort Prizeman, Cambridge, 1922; Lecturer in British Empire History for Board of Military Studies, 1921-22, and for Economics Tripos, 1923-24; Choate Memorial Fellow of Harvard University, 1922-23; Assistant Professor of Modern History, University of California, 1925; Associate Professor, 1931; Professor of English History, 1942; Sather Professor of History, 1958-65. *Publications:* Colonial Policy of William III, 1922 (new edn. 1966); David Hartley, M.P., 1926; American Correspondence of a Bristol Merchant, 1934; English Whiggism and the American Revolution, 1942 (new edn. 1966); Early Career of Lord Rockingham, 1952; Correspondence of Edmund Burke, Vol. III, 1961. *Recreations:* gardening, music. *Address:* P.O. Box 6345, Carmel, California, 93921, U.S.A. [*Died* 7 *Jan.* 1969.

GUY, William Henry. Formerly Member London County Council for South Poplar and of Poplar Borough Council. M.P. (Lab.) South Poplar, 1942-50. *Address:* 2 East India Buildings, Saltwell Street, Poplar, E.14. [*Died* 1 *Aug.* 1968.

GWALIOR, Ruler of; H.H. Maharaja, Mukhtar-ul-Mulk, Azim-ul-Iqtidar, Rafi-us-Shan, Wala Shikoh, Mohatashim - i - Dauran, Umdat - ul - Umra, Maharajadhiraj, Hisam-us-Saltanat, Lt.-Gen. Sir George Jiwaji Rao Scindia, Alijah Bahadur, G.C.S.I. 1946; G.C.I.E. 1941; Shrinath, Mansur-i-Zaman, Fidwi - i - Hazrat - i - Malik - i - Moazzam - i - Rafi-ud-Darjat-i-Inglistan; *b.* Gwalior, 26 June 1916; *s.* of His late Highness Maharaja Sir Madhav Rao Scindia and Her late Highness Maharani Gajra Raja Scindia; *m.* Kumari Lekha Divyeshwari Devi; one *s.* four *d.* *Educ.:* privately, under distinguished tutors; attended Inter. Arts, Victoria Coll., Gwalior; Settlement and Revenue trg. at Lyallpur, Punjab; Admin. trg. at Bombay and Bangalore; Mil. trg. at Poona. King George V was his godfather. Salute: 21 guns hereditary. Associate Knight, Order of St. John of Jerusalem, 1937; Vice-Pres. East India Assoc., 1937; Capt. 1941; Major, 1943; Lt.-Col. 1944; Maj.-Gen. 1945; Lt.-Gen. 1946. *Recreations:* motoring, shooting (big game), riding, tennis, polo, reading. *Heir:* *s.* Prince Madhav Rao Scindia. *Address:* Jai Vilas Palace, Gwalior, India; Madhav Vilas, Shivpuri, Gwalior State, India. *T.A.:* Scindia, Gwalior. [*Died* 16 *July* 1961.

GWATKIN, Major-General Sir Frederick, Kt., *cr.* 1942; C.B. 1938; D.S.O. 1919; M.C.; Indian Army (retired); *b.* 1885; *s.* of Col. F. S. Gwatkin, C.B.; *m.* 1920, Lydia Winifred, 2nd *d.* of late Colonel E. C. Stanton, R.E.; one *d.* (two *s.* killed in action, Burma, 1945). *Educ.:* Clifton College, R.M.C. Sandhurst, i.d.c. Served European War, 1914-19 (despatches, D.S.O., M.C., Belgian Croix de Guerre); Bt. Lt.-Col. 1927; Lt.-Col. 1929; Colonel, 1934; Major-Gen. 1938; Commander 2nd (Sialkot) Cavalry Brigade, 1934-38; Military Adviser-in-Chief to Indian States Forces, 1939; retired, 1943. *Address:* c/o National and Grindlay's Bank Ltd., 13 St. James's Square, S.W.1. [*Died* 20 *April* 1969.

GWYNN, Major-Gen. Sir Charles William, K.C.B., *cr.* 1931 (C.B. 1918); C.M.G. 1903; D.S.O. 1894; *b.* Ramelton, County Donegal, 4 Feb. 1870; 3rd *s.* of Rev. John Gwynn, D.D., Regius Professor of Divinity, Trinity College, Dublin, and Lucy Josephine, *d.* of William Smith O'Brien, Cahirmoyle, Co. Limerick; *m.* 1904, Mary (*d.* 1951), widow of Lieut. Lowry Armstrong, R.N. *Educ.:* St. Columba's College, Rathfarnham, Dublin; R.M.A. Woolwich; Staff College, Camberley. 2nd Lieut. R.E. 1889; Lieutenant, R.E. 1891; Captain, R.E. and Brevet Major, 1900; Director Military Art, Royal Military College, Duntroon, Australia, 1911-14; served Sofa Expedition, Sierra Leone, West Africa, 1893-94 (wounded, despatches, Brevet Major, D.S.O.); European War, 1914-18 (despatches, Bt. Lieut.-Col. and Bt. Col., C.B.; Belgian Croix de Guerre, 1918; Officier Legion of Honour, 1919); Maj.-Gen. 1925; A.D.C. to the King, 1923-24; Commandant, Staff College, Camberley, 1926-30; retired pay, 1931; C.M.G. for services in delimiting Sudan-Abyssinian Frontier; R.G.S. Peake Fund Medal, 1909. *Publication:* Imperial Policing, 1934. *Address:* c/o Lloyds Bank Ltd., Cox's and King's Branch, 6 Pall Mall, S.W.1. [*Died* 12 *Feb.* 1963.

GWYNN, Rev. Robert Malcolm, B.D.; *b.* Ramelton, Co. Donegal, 26 April 1877; *s.* of Rev. John Gwynn, D.D.; *m.* 1914, Eileen Gertrude, M.B., of Trinity Coll., Dublin, and *d.* of Rev. William Glenn, B.A., of Altadesert Rectory, Pomeroy, Co. Tyrone; two *s.* four *d.* *Educ.:* St. Columba's College, Rathfarnham; Trinity Coll., Dublin (1st Scholarship, 1896; Classical Studentship, Large Gold Medals in Classics and Modern Literature, 1898; 1st Theological Exhibition, 1902; Fellowship, 1906-57; Tutorship, 1907; Chaplain, 1911-18); Professor of Biblical Greek, 1916; Professor of Hebrew, 1920-37; also formerly: acting Warden, St. Columba's College, 1909. Vice-Provost of Trinity College, Dublin, 1942-43, Senior Lecturer, 1944-1950, Senior Tutor, 1950-52; Senior Dean, 1952-53; Hon. Fell., Trinity Coll., Dublin, 1957. *Publications:* Amos, in the Revised Version for Schools, 1928. *Recreation:* gardening. *Address:* Botanic House, Lansdowne Road, Dublin. [*Died* 10 *June* 1962.

GWYNNE-VAUGHAN, Dame Helen Charlotte Isabella, G.B.E. (civil), *cr.* 1929 (D.B.E. (mil.), *cr.* 1919; C.B.E. (mil.), 1918); D.Sc. (Lond.), Hon. LL.D. (Glasgow), F.L.S., etc.; Fellow of King's College, London; Fellow of Birkbeck College; Professor Emeritus, University of London; *b.* 21 January 1879; *e. d.* of Capt. Hon. A. H. D. Fraser (Scots Guards); *m.* 1911, Professor D. T. Gwynne-Vaughan (*d.* 1915). *Educ.:* Cheltenham Ladies' College; King's College, University of London. Carter Medallist, King's College, 1902; B.Sc. (Lond.), 1904; D.Sc. (Lond.), 1907; Head of Department of Botany, Birkbeck College, London, 1909-17; during the European War Chief Controller Queen Mary's Army Auxiliary Corps British Armies in France, from formation in Feb. 1917 till Sept. 1918 (despatches, C.B.E.); Commandant Women's Royal Air Force, Sept. 1918-Dec. 1919 (D.B.E.); returned to University of London, January 1920; Professor of Botany in the University of London and Head of the Dept. of Botany, Birkbeck Coll., Univ. of London, 1921-39 and 1941-44; Director, Auxiliary Territorial Service with rank of chief controller, 1939-41; Trail medal of Linnean Society for researches on protoplasm, 1920; Member of Royal Commission on Food Prices, 1924; President of Section K., British Assoc., 1928; President of British Mycological Soc., 1928. Life Vice-President and Hon. Mem. of Council, Royal Air Forces Association; Vice-Pres. and Mem. Council W.R.A.C. Assoc. *Publications:* Fungi 1922; Structure and Development of the Fungi, 1927, 1937 (jointly with Dr. B. Barnes); Service with the Army, 1942; The Junior Leader, 1943; scientific papers, chiefly on cytology and mycology, in the Annals of Botany and elsewhere. *Relevant Publication:* A Heroine in Her Time, by

Molly Izzard. *Address:* Sussexdown, Storrington, West Sussex. *Club:* Service Women's. [*Died* 26 *Aug.* 1967.

GWYTHER, Reginald Duncan, C.B.E. 1954; M.C. 1917; Consultant to Coode & Partners, Consulting Civil Engineers; *b.* 15 March 1887; *s.* of late R. F. Gwyther; *m.* 1921, Dorothy Wilberforce Gwyther; two *s.* *Educ.:* Ripon School, Yorkshire; Manchester University. Posts in Argentine, Johore, Jersey, Grimsby, Singapore. Partner of firm Coode, Wilson, Mitchell & Vaughan-Lee, 1936 (now Coode & Partners) responsible with partners for design and construction of Kut Barrage, bridges over River Tigris and other rivers in Iraq, Habbaniyah Flood Relief Scheme, harbour and port works in Freetown, Lagos, Mtwara, Dar es Salaam, Mombasa, Colombo, Singapore, Port Swettenham, Bahrain and Barbadoes, also dams etc. in Ceylon Hydro-Electric scheme. Mem. Panel of Civil Engineers under Reservoirs (Safety Provisions) Act, 1930; Mem. Departmental Committee on Coastal Flooding, 1953-54. Served in Royal Engineers, 1914-1919 (despatches, M.C.); commanded No. 148 Army Troops Co. R.E. Lieut.-Col. Engr. & Railway Staff Corps, R.E. (T.A.). Past Pres. Brit. Sect. Société des Ingénieurs Civils de France. The Institution of Civil Engineers, Telford Premium, 1910, 1929, 1959; U.S.A. Medal of Freedom (Silver Palm), 1945. *Recreation:* golf. *Address:* 2 Victoria St., Westminster, S.W.1. *T.:* Abbey 1889, 2794, 2795; Dalmahoy, Kettlewell Hill, Woking, Surrey. *T.:* Woking 60663. [*Died* 26 *Nov.* 1965.

H

HAAGNER, Alwin Karl, Hon. D.Sc., F.Z.S.; Honorary Member British Ornithologists' Union; Hon. Corr. Fellow American Ornithologists' Union, etc.; ex-Vice-President S.A. Biological Society; ex-President Wild Life Protection Society of S. Africa; *b.* Hankey, East Cape Province, 1 June 1880; *s.* of late S. Haagner; *m.* 1910, J. A. Moll of Volksrust (*d.* 1922); one *s.* one *d.*; 1946, Gwen Allen, Maritzburg. *Educ.:* Private tuition. Clerk, Dynamite Company, before Boer War; served in S.A. Constabulary two years (S.A. medal and 3 clasps); Chief Clerk, Stores Department, Dynamite Factory Modderfontein, 1902-8; temporary assistant Transvaal Museum, 8 months; transferred to Zoological Gardens, Pretoria, as assistant to the late Director, 1909; Asst. and Director National Zoological Gardens of S. Africa, 1909-26; took up zoology as a hobby at the age of 16, ornithology being speciality; founded S.A. Ornithologists' Union in 1904 and was Secretary Treasurer (afterwards also Editor of Journal) till the amalgamation with the Biological Society, 1916. *Publications:* Sketches of S.A. Bird Life; Short Manual of S.A. Mammals; Check list of S.A. Birds and numerous papers on birds in the Ibis and Journal of S.A. Ornithologists' Union; also papers on mammalogy and preservation of game in various journals and magazines. *Recreations:* motoring, singing (choir). *Address:* 71 Boshoff Street, Pietermaritzburg, Natal, S. Africa. [*Died* 15 *Sept.* 1962.

HACKETT, Francis; author; *b.* Kilkenny, 21 Jan. 1883; *s.* of John Byrne Hackett, M.D., and Bridget Doheny; *m.* 1918, Signe Toksvig Denmark; no *c.* *Educ.:* Clongowes Wood College, Co. Kildare. Went to New York, 1901; worked in law office, magazine office, was paymaster's yeoman on school ship, worked in railroad office, as tutor, in department store, as editorial writer and literary critic; Resident of Hull-House Settlement, Chicago, 1905-6; Founded Chicago Evening Post Friday Literary Review, 1909; Co-Editor New Republic, 1914-22; Special correspondent New York World, 1920-23; Left New York for Denmark, England, Italy and France, 1922; Returned to Ireland, 1927; because of censor banning The Green Lion, left Ireland, 1937. Lived in Denmark, 1937-39; Book Critic, New York Times, 1944-45; Member National Institute of Arts and Letters) U.S.A. Received Liberty Medal from King Christian X of Denmark, 1946. *Publications:* Horizons, a book of criticism, 1918; Ireland, a study in nationalism, 1918; The Invisible Censor, 1921; The Story of the Irish Nation, 1922; That Nice Young Couple, a novel, 1924; Henry the Eighth, 1929; Francis the First, 1934; The Green Lion, a novel, 1935; Queen Anne Boleyn, 1939; I Chose Denmark, 1940; What 'Mein Kampf' Means to America; 1941; The Senator's Last Night, a novel, 1943 On Judging Books in General and in Particular, 1947. *Address:* Skovriderstien 6, Holte, Denmark. [*Died* 25 *April* 1962.

HACKETT, Walter William, C.B.E. 1944; J.P.; F.R.Ae.S.; F.R.S.A.; First President, 1960, formerly Chairman Accles & Pollock Ltd.; *b.* 29 May 1874; *s.* of Thomas and Catherine Hackett; *m.* 1897; three *s.* one *d.* *Educ.:* Dudley Road School, Birmingham. With Accles & Pollock Ltd. since company came into existence. *Recreations:* golf, bowls. *Address:* Ravenhurst, Beeches Road, West Bromwich, Staffs. *T.:* West Bromwich 0453. [*Died* 12 *April* 1964.

HACKING, Sir John, Kt., *cr.* 1949; *b.* 16 December 1888; *s.* of late William Edward Hacking and late Martha Birtwistle; *m.* 1917, Janet Stewart Scott, *d.* of Alexander Stewart and Elizabeth Scott; one *s.* one *d.* *Educ.:* Burnley Grammar School; Leeds Technical Institute; Leeds University. Newcastle-upon-Tyne Electric Supply Co. Ltd., 1908-1913; various engineering posts with Messrs. Merz & McLellan, Consulting Engineers, Newcastle, 1913-15; Buenos Aires, 1915-23; London, South Africa, and Bombay, 1923-33; Newcastle, 1933-34. Central Electricity Board, Deputy Chief Engineer, 1934-44, and Chief Engineer, 1944-1947; Deputy Chairman (Operations), British Electricity Authority, 1948-53. Consulting Engineer, Merz & McLellan, 1954-66. Vice-President Institution of Electrical Engineers, 1946-51; President, 1951-52; Hon. Member, 1962. *Recreation:* golf. *Address:* Ockley House, Wrotham Kent. *T.:* Borough Green 2552. *Club:* Reform. [*Died* 29 *Sept.* 1969.

HADDON, Sir Richard (Walker), Kt. 1951; C.B.E. 1944; Past Chairman and Managing Director, Farmer and Stockbreeder Publications Ltd.; Chairman: Associated Iliffe Press, 1960-64; Kelly-Iliffe Holdings, 1960-64; Cornwall Press Ltd., 1960; *b.* 28 October 1893; *s.* of Richard Walker Haddon, Norwich; *m.* 1921, Helen Anita, *d.* of James Frederick Fisher Cox, Birkenhead. *Educ.:* Norwich; Brighton. Chairman: Red Cross Agriculture Fund, 1940-46; Ministry of Agriculture's Publicity Advisory Cttee., 1939-51; Min. of Agriculture's Working Party on Publicity 1951-56; Min. of Agriculture's Advisory Cttee. on Farming Publicity, 1956-1958. Chairman, Farmers' Club, 1946; Senior Warden Farmers' Company, 1948-53, Master, 1953-54. Founder (first Chairman 1945, Fellow 1946, President 1953) Guild of Agricultural Journalists; Chm. Livestock Export Group, 1946-48; Govt. Delegate World's Poultry Congress, Cleveland, 1939; Official Delegate, Primary Producers' Conference, Sydney 1938; Chairman: Patrons' Council World Ploughing Organisation, 1958; National Exhibition Cage Birds; Past Chm., International

Poultry Show; President National Council of Aviculture; Festival Chm. Newsvendors' Benevolent Instn. ("Old Ben"), 1961-62, Vice-Chm., 1967-. *Address:* Wensleydale, Broomhall Lane, Sunningdale, Surrey. *T.:* Ascot 22988. [*Died* 25 *Dec.* 1967.

HADFIELD, Charles Frederick, M.B.E., M.A., M.D. (Camb.), D.A.; F.F.A., R.C.S.; Consulting Anæsthetist to St. Bartholomew's Hosp. and to Prince of Wales's Gen. Hosp.; Chairman Anæsthetics Committee of M.R.C. and R.S.M.; Ex-President Section of Anæsthetics R.S.M.; Ex-President Fell and Rock Club of English Lake District; *b.* Birkenhead, 17 June 1875; *s.* of late G. H. Hadfield, J.P., of Moraston, Ross, Herefordshire; *m.* 1906, Wine-Field (*d.* 1960), *d.* of late Alex. W. MacDougall, Barrister-at-law; two *s.* one *d.* *Educ.:* The Leys School, Cambridge; Trinity College, Cambridge (Major Scholar); Natural Science Tripos Pt. I. Class 1, Pt. II. Class 1; St. Bartholomew's Hospital (Shuter Scholar). After some years devoted to educational and scientific work at Cambridge and the Marine Biological Station at Naples, devoted himself to medicine; later went into general practice at Malvern and in London; during European War, 1914-18, was attached to the City of London Military Hospital and other hospitals; late Anæsthetist to E.M.S.; subsequently devoted himself entirely to anæsthetics. *Publication:* Practical Anæsthetics, 1923, 2nd edition 1931. *Recreation:* mountaineering. *Address:* Strouds, Ashampstead Common, Pangbourne, Berks. *T.:* Yattendon 394. *Club:* Alpine. [*Died* 15 *June* 1965.

HADFIELD, Geoffrey, M.D. (Lond.), F.R.C.P. (Lond.); F.R.C.S. (Eng.); **Mem. Bd. of Trustees, Hunterian Collection, Roy. Coll. of Surgeons of England since 1954; Cons. Pathologist to St. Bartholomew's Hospital, 1956; *b.* 1889; *e. s.* of James H. Hadfield, Manchester; *m.* 1918, Eileen, *d.* of William Irvine, Co. Fermanagh; two *s.* one *d* *Educ.:* St. Bartholomew's Hosp. M.B., B.S (London), 1911; M.D. (University Gold Medal), 1913; F.R.C.P. (Lond.), 1932; F.R.C.S. (Eng.), 1954; House Physician St. Bartholomew's Hospital; Capt. R.A.M.C. (Specialist in Pathology) 5 years, 1914-19; Overseas service—France and Gallipoli, 3 yrs. engaged in practice and teaching of Pathology since 1914; Professor of Pathology, University of London and Pathologist Royal Free Hospital, 1928-33; Professor of Pathology, Bristol University, 1933-34; lately Professor of Pathology, University of London; Pathologist, St. Bartholomew's Hospital, 1935-48; lately Sir Wm. Collins Professor of Pathology and Dean, Institute of Basic Medical Sciences, Royal College of Surgeons of England; Director of Clinico-pathological Research, Imperial Cancer Research Fund 1954-61. Consultant Pathologist to the Army, 1935-54** *Publications:* **Recent Advances in Pathology, ed. 6th edn., 1953. On Neuropathology, Pathology of Tumour Formation and Cardiac Infections, in Pathological and Medical Journals.** *Address:* 11 Rupert Close, Henley-on-Thames, Oxon. [*Died* 9 *Jan.* 1968.

HADFIELD, James Arthur, M.A. (Oxon.); M.B., Ch.B (Edin.); late Lecturer in Psychopathology and Mental Hygiene, London Univ. (1931-58); Consultant in psychological medicine since 1920; *b.* 11 Nov. 1882; 2nd *s.* of late Rev. James Hadfield Loyalty Isles, South Pacific; *m.* Grace Sherwood Calver M.B.; three *s* *Educ.:* Eltham Coll; Mansfield Coll. and Queen's Coll, Oxford; Edinburgh University. Demonstrator in Anatomy 1916. House Surgeon and House Physician, Royal Infirmary Edinburgh; Surgeon R.N., 1916-18; Neurologist, Royal Naval College Chatham; Medical Officer, R.A.M.C.; Neurologist Ashhurst Neurological Hospital Oxford, 1918-20, Lecturer Birmingham University Psychotherapy, 1920; Chairman British Psychological Society, Medical Section, 1929; Secretary and Member of Committee, 1921-34; Lieut.-Col. R.A.M.C., Officer, i/c Division, 1940-41. Past Pres Philosophical Soc. of England English Pres. Internat. Assoc. for Study of Hypnosis. *Publications:* Psychology and Morals 1920; The Psychology of Power, 1933; Psychology and Mental Health, 1950; Mental Health and the Psychoneuroses, 1952; Dreams and Nightmares, 1954; Childhood and Adolescence; contributions to medical journals. *Recreations:* sailing, swimming. *Address:* Whithurst Park, Kirdford, W. Sussex. *Clubs:* Royal Society of Medicine, Little Ship, Dell Quay Sailing. [*Died* 4 *Sept.* 1967.

HADOW, Lt.-Col. Arthur Lovell, C.M.G. 1916; late The Norfolk Regiment; *b.* 1877; *y. s.* of late Rev. J. L. G. Hadow; *m.* 1916, Adela Maude (*d.* 1963), *e. d.* of late Colonel E. R. Bayly, D.L. of Ballyarthur, Woodenbridge, Co. Wicklow; one *s.* (and one *s.* killed, R.A.F., 1943). *Educ.:* Repton; Oriel College, Oxford Served with 1st Batt. Norfolk Regt. in India, 1898-1904; Waziristan Expedition, 1901-2 (medal with clasp); Tibet Expedition, 1903-4; action at Niani; operations in and around Gyantse; march to Lhasa (despatches, medal with clasp); S. Africa, 1905; attached Egyptian Army, 1906-15, during which time served under the Sudan Civil Administration (4th Class Order of the Nile); European War, joined the Mediterranean Expeditionary Force as Staff Captain, 88th Brigade, 29th Division, Aug. 1915; Brigade Major, 34th Brigade, 11th Division, Nov. 1915; served through both evacuations of Gallipoli, afterwards in France, 1916-17; commanded Newfoundland Regiment Gallipoli and France (despatches thrice, C.M.G.); commanded 2nd Bn. Norfolk Regiment, 1922-25; retired, 1926. *Address:* Kester, Highlands Park, Chudleigh, Newton Abbot, Devon. *Club:* United Service. [*Died* 19 *April* 1968.

HADOW, Sir Raymond Patrick, Kt., *cr.* 1934; C.I.E. 1925; A.M.Inst.C.E.; *b.* 26 March 1879; *s.* of Reginald Townshend Hadow, Newcastle; *m.* 1912, Dora Chalmers Kennedy; one *s.* one *d.* *Educ.:* Sedbergh School; R.I.E. College, Coopers Hill. Assistant Engineer in P.W.D., Punjab, 1900; Executive Engineer, 1908; Under-Secretary to Govt., Punjab, P.W.D., 1914-19; Deputy Secretary to Govt. of India, P.W.D., 1920-22; Superintending Engineer, 1921; Chief Engineer, 1927; President, Central Board of Irrigation, India, 1932, 1933; retired 1934; Fife County Council, 1935-42; Fife and Kinross Agricultural Wages Committee, 1937-39; Ministry of Works, Edinburgh, 1942-45. *Address:* Coates House, Lower Largo, Fife. *T.A.* and *T.:* Upper Largo 249. [*Died* 19 *Feb.* 1962.

HADOW, Sir Robert (Henry), K.B.E. 1953; C.M.G. 1946; M.C.; retired; *b.* 13 Aug. 1895; *s.* of Cecil Macdonald Hadow and Margaret Campbell Baines; *m.* 1925, Elizabeth Lindsay Lomax Wood; one *s.* one *d.* *Educ.:* Harrow Sch. Pte. London Scottish, 1914, 2nd Lt.-Capt. 1915-18; 3rd A. & S. Highlanders, attached 1st Seaforth Highlanders, France, Mesopotamia, Palestine (despatches, M.C.). 3rd Sec. H.M. Diplomatic Service, 1919; Washington, 1919, 1920; Tehran, 1921-25; Ankara, 1925-28; 1st Sec. 1928; Ottawa, 1928-31; Vienna, 1931-34; Prague, 1934-37; F.O., 1937-39; Buenos Aires, 1940-44; Counsellor, Washington and Adviser to U.K. Delegation to U.N., 1944-48; Consul-General for S. California and Arizona, 1948; Consul-General, N. California, Nevada and Hawaii, 1954-57; retired, Dec. 1957. *Address:* c/o Bank of Montreal, 47 Threadneedle St., E.C.2. [*Died* 13 *Jan.* 1963.

HAGGARD, Sir Godfrey Digby Napier, K.C.M.G., *cr.* 1943 (C.M.G. 1934); C.V.O.,

1939; O.B.E. 1918; *b.* 6 Feb. 1884; 3rd *s.* of late Alfred Haggard, Indian Civil Service; *m.* 1910, Georgianna, *d.* of Hubert Ruel, Quebec; two *d.* (one *s.* decd.). Entered Consular Service; Vice-Consul, Central America, 1908; Paris, 1914; Chargé d'Affaires, Bolivia, 1915; Havana, 1921; Consul-General, Brazil, 1924; Chicago, 1928-32; Paris, 1932-38; Consul-General at New York, 1938-44; retired; Director, American Forces Liaison Division, Ministry of Information, 1944-45. *Address:* Broomfield, Chelmsford, Essex. *T.:* Broomfield 227. [*Died* 3 *April* 1969.

HAGGARD, Lilias (Margitson) Rider, M.B.E. 1919; *b.* 9 Dec. 1892; *y. d.* of late Sir Henry Rider Haggard, K.B.E., and Marianna Louisa Haggard, Ditchingham, Norfolk. *Educ.:* privately; St. Felix School, Southwold. *Publications:* I Walked By Night (edited), 1935; The Rabbit Skin Cap (edited), 1939; Norfolk Life (with Henry Williamson), 1943; Norfolk Notebook, 1947; Country Scrapbook, 1950; The Cloak that I Left, 1951. *Recreations:* gardening, nature study. *Address:* Ditchingham House, Nr. Bungay, Suffolk. *T.:* Bungay 2011 [*Died* 9 *Jan.* 1968.

HAHN, Prof. Dr. Otto; Hon. Pres. Max-Planck-Gesellschaft (former Kaiser-Wilhelm-Gesellschaft), Göttingen, since 1960; *b.* Frankfurt-am-Main, 8 March 1879; *m.* 1913, Edith Junghans; one *s.* *Educ.:* Frankfurt; Marburg (Dr. 1901); Munich. Assistant, 1902-4; London, Univ. College with Sir William Ramsay, Winter 1904-5; Montreal, McGill Univ. with Prof. Ernest Rutherford, Winter 1905-6; Privatdozent, University of Berlin, 1907; Professor, 1910; Member Kaiser Wilh. Institute of Chemistry, 1912; Direktor Kaiser Wilhelm Institut für Chemie, Berlin-Dahlem, 1928; Pres. Max-Planck-Gesellschaft (former Kaiser-Wilhelm-Gesellschaft), 1946-60. Nobel Prize for Chemistry (for 1944), 1945. Grand Cross of the Order of Merit of the Federal Republic of Germany, 1959. Mem. Order of Pour le mérite (Friedensklasse) of the Federal Republic of Germany, 1952. Hon. Fell., Univ. Coll., London, 1968. *Publications:* Radioactivity, pure and applied Radiochemistry, artificial radioactive elements, fission of uranium, 1939; Vom Radiothor zur Uranspaltung, 1962; Otto Hahn: A Scientific Autobiography, 1966. *Address:* Bunsenstrasse 10, and Gervinusstr. 5, Göttingen, Germany. [*Died* 28 *July* 1968.

HAIGH, Frank Fraser, C.I.E. 1944; Indian Service of Engineers (Retired); *b.* 4 Feb. 1891; *m.* 1919, Charlotte Greated; one *s.* two *d.* *Educ.:* Knaresborough Grammar School; Queen's College, Galway. Scholar, R.U.I.; B.Sc., B.E., 1912; appointed to Indian Service of Engineers, 1913; Chief Engineer and Secretary to Govt. of the Punjab, P.W.D. Irrigation Branch, 1941; Pres., Irrigation Development Commission, Iraq, 1946-49. Commissioned 1915, demobilised with rank of Capt. 1919. Consultant to Haigh, Zinn & Associates, 1958-; M.Cons.E., M.I.C.E. *Publication:* Emerson Barrage, Proc. Inst. C.E., 1940. *Address:* c/o National and Grindlay's Bank, 13 St. James's Square, S.W.1. [*Died* 27 *Jan.* 1970.

HAIGH, Rt. Rev. Mervyn George, D.D., M.A.; Hon. C.F.; Chaplain and Sub-Prelate, Order of St. John of Jerusalem; Member of Snowdonia National Park Joint Advisory Cttee. and Caernarvonshire National Park Planning Cttee. since 1953; Merioneth National Park Planning Cttee., since 1958; Council of Clifton Coll., 1944-61; *b.* London, 14 Sept. 1887; *o. s.* of late Rev. Canon W. E. Haigh. *Educ.:* Clifton; New Coll., Oxf.; Ellerton Prize, 1912. Curate of Holy Trinity, E. Finchley, 1911-14; St. Peter, Cranley Gardens, 1914-16; temp. C.F. 1916-19 (despatches); Chaplain and Lecturer, Ordination Test School, Knutsford, 1919-24; Examining Chaplain to the Bishop of Llandaff, 1920-24; Resident Chaplain and Private Secretary to Archbishop (Davidson) of Canterbury, 1924-28; Principal Chaplain and Private Secretary to Archbishop (Lang) of Canterbury, 1928-31; Six Preacher in Canterbury Cathedral, 1929; Chaplain to the King, 1929-31; Assistant Secretary, Lambeth Conference, 1930; Secretary, Lambeth Conference, 1948; Bishop of Coventry, 1931-42; Bishop of Winchester and ex-officio Prelate of Most Noble Order of the Garter, 1942-52, resigned. *Address:* Argoed, Dolgellau, Merioneth. *T.:* Dolgellau 366. *Club:* Athenæum. [*Died* 20 *May* 1962.

HAILEY, 1st Baron, *cr.* 1936, of Shahpur, Pakistan, and Newport Pagnell, Bucks; **William Malcolm Hailey,** P.C. 1949; O.M. 1956; G.C.S.I., *cr.* 1932 (K.C.S.I., *cr.* 1922; C.S.I. 1915); G.C.M.G., *cr.* 1939; G.C.I.E., *cr.* 1928 (C.I.E. 1911); M.A.; *b.* 15 Feb. 1872; *s.* of Hammett Hailey, M.R.C.S., Newport Pagnell, Bucks; *m.* 1896, Andreina (*d.* 1939), F.R.G.S., and Lady of Grace of St. John of Jerusalem, *d.* of Count Hannibale Balzani, Italy. *Educ.:* Merchant Taylors' School; Corpus Christi College, Oxford (Scholar); 1st Class Moderations, 1st Class Litt. Hum. Indian Civil Service, 1895; Colonisation Officer, Jhelum Canal Colony, 1902; Chief Comr., Delhi, 1912-18; Major, late Indian Defence Force, 1912-1918. Member of Exec. Coun. of Governor-General, in Finance and Home Departments, 1919-24; Governor of the Punjab, 1924-28; Governor of the United Provinces, 1928-30 and 1931-1934; Director, African Research Survey, 1935-38; Member of Permanent Mandates Commission, League of Nations, 1935-39; Chm. Air Defence Cttee., 1937-38; Chm. Cttee. for Co-ordination of Work on Refugees, 1938-39; Hd. of Economic Mission to Belgian Congo, 1940-41; Chm. Governing body of School of Oriental and African Studies, 1941-45, and of International African Institute, 1945-47; Pres. Royal Central Asian Soc., 1943-47; Chm. Colonial Research Cttee., 1943-48; President Research Defence Society, 1945-54; Chm. London Association of Boy Scouts, 1943-48; Dep. Chm., Royal African Soc., 1949-59; Chm. I.C.S. (Ret.) Assoc., 1946-58; Mem. Senate, London Univ., 1946-48; Freeman of City of London, 1957. Pres. E.I. Assoc., 1951-54; Mem. Gen. Advisory Council, B.B.C., 1953-56; Mem. Rhodes Trust, 1946-66; Assoc. member Institut Roy. Coloniale Belge and Académie des Sciences Coloniales, Paris; Hon. Fellow Roy. Soc. of Tropical Med.; K.St.J.; Hon. Fellow Corpus Christi Coll, Oxford, 1925; D.Litt. (Lahore), 1928; D.Laws (Allahabad) 1933, (Lucknow) 1934; Hon. D.Litt. (Bristol), 1935; Hon. Visiting Fellow, Nuffield Coll., Oxford, 1939-47; Hon. D.C.L. (Camb.) 1939, (Oxon.) 1941, (Toronto) 1943, (Witwatersrand) 1946, (London) 1953; Hon. Doctorate (Leiden), 1948. Hon. LL.D. Sheffield, 1955. Hon. Fellow, School of Oriental and African Studies, 1956. Grand Cross of the Order of Public Instruction (Portugal), 1947. *Publications:* An African Survey, 1938 (revised, 1956); Romanes lecture, Oxford, 1941: Britain and her Dependencies, 1943; Future of Colonial Peoples, 1943; Great Britain, India and the Colonial Dependencies in the Post-War World, 1943; Native Administration in the British African Territories, 1951; (four Vols.) Native Administration in the High Commission Territories, South Africa, 1953; Republic of South Africa and the High Commission Territories, 1963. *Address:* 2 Ross Court, Putney Hill, S.W.15. *Club:* Athenæum. [*Died* 1 *June* 1969 (*ext.*).

HAINES, Professor F(rederick) Merlin, Ph.D., D.Sc.; Professor of Botany, Queen Mary College (University of London) 1950-1958 (retired); Professor Emeritus since

1958; *b.* 8 July 1898; *s.* of Frederick Haselfoot Haines, D.P.H., M.R.C.S., L.R.C.P., Winfrith, Dorset, and Eva Mary Haines; *m.* 1931, Ethel Millington; one *d.* *Educ.:* Exeter School, Exeter; Queen Mary College, London. Degrees (Lond.): B.Sc. 1919, Ph.D. 1925, D.Sc. 1939. Queen Mary College: Lecturer, 1919, Reader, 1945, in Plant Physiology. *Publications:* Tone and Colour in Landscape Painting, 1955; contributions on plant physiological topics, especially plant water relations, to botanical journals, etc. *Recreations:* painting, music, photography, cinematography, polyphonic recording, mechanical work. *Address:* Mayfield House, Blissford, Fordingbridge, Hants. *T.:* Fordingbridge 3383. [*Died* 29 *Dec.* 1963.

HAINS, Charles Brazier, C.B.E. 1941; *b.* 5 June 1882; *s.* of late Lieut. J. G. Hains, R.N.; *m.* 1905, Alice Eliza Hill; four *d.* *Educ.:* William Knight's School, Gillingham, Kent; H.M. Dockyard School, Chatham. Royal Dockyard Apprentice, H.M. Dockyard, Chatham, 1897; Writer, H.M. Dockyard, Chatham and Admiralty, 1904-14; Third Grade Clerk, Admiralty, 1914; Assist. Naval Store Officer, Admiralty, 1915; Deputy Naval Store Officer, Admiralty, 1917; Naval Store Officer, Admiralty, 1931; Member British Naval Advisory Mission to Govt. of Chile, 1931; Commander of Order of Al Merito, 1931; Superintending Naval Store Officer, Eastern Mediterranean, 1936; Asst. Director of Supply, Home Office, 1936; Director of Supply and Transport, Home Office, 1938-47. *Recreation:* golf. *Address:* 23 Bedford Rd., Horsham. [*Died* 26 *Aug.* 1962.

HAIR, Gilbert; Assistant Director, Prison Department, Home Office, since 1960; *b.* 13 May 1899; *s.* of Edwin Hair and Henrietta Hay; *m.* 1927, Lucy Scholes; one *s.* one *d.* *Educ.:* Felsted; Pembroke Coll., Oxford. Dep. Gov. of H.M. Borstal Institution, Rochester, 1923; Deputy Governor of H.M. Prisons: Wandsworth, 1926; Durham, 1926; Wakefield, 1927; Liverpool, 1931; Wormwood Scrubs, 1933; Governor H.M. Prisons: Cardiff, 1936; Lewes, 1939; Camp Hill, 1941; Stafford, 1943; Sudbury, 1948; Manchester, 1949; Wormwood Scrubs, 1956. *Recreation:* gardening. *Address:* 6 Hall Road, N.W.8. *T.:* Cunningham 0471. *Club:* Union. [*Died* 5 *March* 1965.

HAIRE OF WHITEABBEY, Baron *cr.* 1965 (Life Peer); **John Edwin Haire;** *b.* 14 Nov. 1908; *yr. s.* of late John Haire and of M. Haire, Portadown, Co. Armagh; *m.* 1939, Suzanne Elizabeth Kemeny, Ph.D., B.Litt., *er. d.* of Dr. Eugene Kemeny, London; two *s.* *Educ.:* Queen's University, Belfast; London. M.A. 1st Cl. Hons. English Literature, 1934; B.A. Modern History and Economics, 1931; Diploma in Education, 1931; Licentiate, Guildhall School of Music and Drama, London, 1934. School teacher and Ministry of Information and Forces Lecturer. Theatrical Producer. Joined Royal Air Force, 1941; served with Coastal Command as Operations Officer; on staff of Air Officer Commanding, 19 Group, Plymouth, 1942; Air Liaison Officer to the Admiralty, 1943; Air Historian, Air Ministry, London, 1945-46. M.P. (Lab.) Wycombe Division of Bucks, 1945-51; P.P.S. to Under-Sec. for the Dominions, 1946-47; to Financial Sec. to Treasury, 1950-51; Leader of Parl. Deleg. to Hungary, Apr. 1946; Mem. of Parl. Delegns. to France, 1946, and Berlin, 1948. Lecture Tour in U.S.A., Autumn, 1947; played leading rôle in parl. film, Servant of the People, 1947. Chairman: Harelands Ltd.; Hill Estates Ltd. *Publications:* various articles and papers on political and international affairs. *Recreations:* hockey, tennis, golf, theatre, and travel. *Address:* 3 Cheyne Gardens, Chelsea, S.W.3. *Clubs:* Reform, Royal Air Force, English-Speaking Union. [*Died* 7 *Oct.* 1966.

HAKE, Guy Donne Gordon, R.W.A.; F.R.I.B.A. (Retd.); Hon. M.A. Bristol; Principal, Royal West of England Academy School of Architecture, Bristol, 1922-52; *b.* 1887; *s.* of late George Gordon Hake and Mary Rose Donisthorpe Donne; *m.* 1924, Elizabeth Forbes, *er. d.* of late Sir Robert W. Burnet, K.C.V.O., M.D.; one *s.* *Educ.:* Christ's Hospital; Geneva; Architectural Association Schools, London. Articled to Col. Sir Robert Edis, C.B., F.R.I.B.A.; R.I.B.A. Athens Bursary 1930; President Bristol Society of Architects, 1936-38; Past Member of Boards of Architectural Education of R.I.B.A., and Architects Registration Council; Chairman of Advisory Panel of Architects to the Corporation of Bristol; Member: Bishop of Bristol's Commission on City Churches, 1938-39; Bristol Diocesan Reorganisation Cttee. 1945-52 (Chm. Bristol Diocesan Advisory Cttee.); Chm. of Min. of Health Housing Medal Awards Cttee., Western Region, 1950-51; Mem. Ministry of Works and Buildings Panel of Architects for Air Raid Damage to Buildings of Historic Interest, 1941-46; Consultant Architect to the National Trust for certain properties; a Vice-Pres. Bristol Civic Society; Mem. Advisory Panel (Western Region), Historic Churches Preservative Trust; Mem. Advisory Panel of Architects, Dartmoor National Park Committee. Executed Works: rebuilding the Victoria Rooms, the University of Bristol Union (in collaboration); Domestic Buildings and Ecclesiastical work in the West of England; served European War, Trooper 2nd King Edward's Horse, Aug. 1914; 2nd Lt. 1st Wilts Regt. 1914; severely wounded at Hooge, June 1915; invalided out of the Army, Dec. 1916; Lieut. R.A.F., Air Construction Service, 1918. *Publication:* Architectural Drawing (in collaboration), 1930. *Recreations:* fly fishing, sketching. *Address:* Stotehayes, Yarcombe, Honiton, Devon. *T.:* Stockland 200. *Club:* Bristol Savages (Bristol) (Pres. 1931, 1939, 1940). [*Died* 22 *Nov.* 1964.

HALAHAN, Air Vice-Marshal Frederick Crosby, C.M.G. 1919; C.B.E. 1923; D.S.O. 1918; M.V.O. 1907; *s.* of late Col. S. H. Halahan, Chiddingfold and Hannah (*née* Engham); *m.* 1905, Eve Muriel, *e. d.* of late James Grimble Groves, D.L., J.P., Cheshire; one *s.* (*er. s.* killed, 1941) one *d.* *Educ.:* Dulwich Coll.; R.N. Coll., Eltham; H.M.S. Britannia. Entered Navy, 1896; Lt., 1900; Wing Capt. R.N.A.S., 1917; Temp. Col. and Lt.-Col., R.A.F., April 1918; served European War, 1914-18 (prom. Wing Capt., D.S.O., Legion of Honour, Order of Crown of Belgium; Belgian Croix de Guerre); Dir. of Aeronautical Inspection, 1922-23; Director of Technical Development, Air Ministry, 1924-26; Air Vice-Marshal, 1927; Commandant, R.A.F. Cadet Coll., Cranwell, 1926-29; retired list, 1930; recalled active service, 1939-44; Chairman R.A.F. Rifle Association since 1929; D.L. Lincolnshire, 1937-50. *Address:* The Glebe House, Bramshott, Liphook, Hants. *T.:* Liphook 3124; The Glebe, Maughold, I. of M. *Club:* United Sports. [*Died* 17 *Oct.* 1965.

HALAHAN, Group Captain John Crosby, C.B.E. 1919; A.F.C.; late R. Dublin Fusiliers and R.A.F.; *b.* 1878; *s.* of late Col. Samuel Handy Halahan, Sydenhurst, Chiddingfold. *Educ.:* Dulwich College. Served South African War, 1899-1900; European War, 1914-19 (despatches, C.B.E., A.F.C.); War of 1939-45, R.A.F. and Colonial Office. *Address:* Huntly, Bishopsteignton, S. Devon. [*Died* 22 *Feb.* 1967.

HALDANE, John Burdon Sanderson, F.R.S. 1932; author; Head of Genetics and Biometry Laboratory, Government of Orissa, since 1962; *b.* 5 Nov. 1892; *s.* of late J. S. Haldane, C.H., F.R.S.; *m.* 1926, Charlotte Franken (marr. diss. 1945); *m.* 1945 Helen

Spurway. *Educ.:* Oxford Preparatory Sch.; Eton; New Coll., Oxford (M.A.). Served in Black Watch (France and Iraq), 1914-19, Capt. 1915; Fellow of New College, 1919-1922 (Hon. Fellow, 1961); Reader in Biochemistry, Cambridge University, 1922-32; Fullerian Professor of Physiology, Royal Institution, 1930-32; Professor of Genetics, London University, 1933-37; Professor of Biometry, London University, 1937-57; subsequently Research Professor, Indian Statistical Institute from which he resigned, 1961. Corresponding Member Société de Biologie, 1928; Pres., Genetical Soc., 1932-1936; Chevalier, Légion d'Honneur, 1937; Chm., Editorial Bd. of Daily Worker, 1940-1949; Hon. Mem., Moscow Acad. of Sciences, 1942; Corresp. member: Deutsche Akademie der Wissenschaften zu Berlin, 1950; National Institute of Sciences of India, 1953; Royal Danish Academy of Sciences, 1956; Hon. D.Sc. Gröningen, 1946; Hon. D.Sc. Oxford, 1961; D. de l'Univ. Paris, 1949; LL.D. Edinburgh, 1956; Darwin Medal of Royal Soc., 1953; Darwin-Wallace Commemorative Medal, Linnean Soc., 1958; Kimber Medal, Nat. Acad. of Sciences, Washington, 1961; Feltrinelli Prize, Accademia dei Lincei, 1961. *Publications:* numerous papers in scientific jls.; Daedalus, 1924; Callinicus, 1925; Possible Worlds, 1927; Animal Biology (with J. S. Huxley), 1927; Science and Ethics, 1928; Enzymes, 1930; The Inequality of Man, 1932; The Causes of Evolution, 1933; Fact and Faith, 1934; My Friend Mr. Leakey, 1937; Heredity and Politics, 1938; A.R.P., 1938; The Marxist Philosophy and the Sciences, 1938; Science and Everyday Life, 1939; Keeping Cool, 1939; Science in Peace and War, 1940; New Paths in Genetics, 1941; A Banned Broadcast, 1947; Science Advances, 1947; Everything has a history, 1951; The Biochemistry of Genetics, 1953. *Recreation:* swimming. *Address:* Genetics and Biometry Laboratory, Government of Orissa, Bhubaneswar, Orissa, India.
[*Died* 1 *Dec.* 1964.

HALDANE, John Rodger, M.A., LL.B.; Advocate; Sheriff-Substitute, retired; *b.* Bishopton, Renfrewshire, 7 May 1882; *s.* of late T. Frederick Haldane, Chemical Manufacturer, Paisley; *m.* 1909, Bessie Young Laughland (*d.* 1962), *d.* of late William Paterson, Biggarford, Newarthill, Lanarks.; two *s.* one *d.* *Educ.:* Hillhead High School, Glasgow; Glasgow University. Called to Scottish Bar, 1904; Interim Sheriff-Substitute, Portree, 1911; Rothesay, 1914-15; Dingwall, 1920; Sheriff-Substitute of Ross, Cromarty and Sutherland at Stornoway, 1921-27, of Ayrshire at Ayr, 1927-33, of Lanarkshire at Glasgow, 1933-43; 2nd Lt., R.A.S.C. 1915; served 22nd Division Train, Salonika Force; retired Capt. 1919; Chairman 3rd Scottish Pensions Appeal Tribunal, 1921. *Publications:* Article on Defamation in Encyclopædia of the Laws of Scotland; Gravitation — a Simplified Theory of Relativity, The Monist, Oct. 1925; Cosmic Mechanics and the Atom, 1965; With All Thy Mind, 1967 (posthumous). *Address:* 1 Devonshire Gardens, Glasgow, W.2. *T.:* Western 2001. [*Died* 12 *Feb.* 1967.

HALE, Arthur James, B.Sc.(Lond.); Chemist (retd.); *b.* 25 Jan. 1877; *m.* 1st, 1907, Gertrude Ann (*d.* 1945); 2nd, 1947, Winifred F. E. Clifford (*d.* 1966). *Educ.:* Manor House Sch., Clapham; S.-Western Polytechnic. Demonstrator, Chemical Department Borough Polytechnic, 1903-6; Lecturer in Chemistry and Physics, Waterford Technical Institute, 1906-10; Lecturer, Dept. of Applied Chemistry, City and Guilds' Technical College, Finsbury, 1910-17; Chief Assistant, 1918-21; Professor of Applied Chemistry, City and Guilds' Technical College Finsbury, 1921-26. *Publications:* Practical Chemistry for Engineering Students; The Synthetic Use of Metals in Organic Chemistry; The Applications of Electrolysis in Chemical Industry; The Manufacture of Chemicals by Electrolyis; Modern Chemistry, Pure and Applied. *Address:* c/o Lloyds Bank Ltd., Terminus Road, Eastbourne, Sussex.
[*Died* 26 *Aug.* 1970.

HALE, Sir William Edward, Kt. 1958; C.B.E. 1950; Chairman, New Zealand Dairy Board, 1938-57; *b.* Thames, Auckland, New Zealand, 1883; *s.* of Eugene Hale; *m.* 1914, Margaret Isabel Plummer; three *s.* three *d.* *Educ.:* Parawai, Thames, N.Z. Formerly Member: Horahia Drainage Board; N.Z. Meat Board. Director, N.Z. Dairy Co., 1921-; Chm. Auckland Farmers' Freezing Co., 1940-. Chm. Thames Hospital Board; Member Hauraki Plains City Council, New Zealand. *Address:* Kopuarahi R.D., Hauraki Plains, North Island, New Zealand.
[*Died* 15 *Sept.* 1967.

HALKYARD, Colonel Alfred, C.B. 1956; M.C. 1918; T.D. 1936; D.L.; Chairman, Leicester No. 1 Hospital Management Committee, 1957-63; *b.* 18 November 1892; *s.* of Dr. Alfred Lees Halkyard, M.R.C.S., L.R.C.P., L.M., and Emma Halkyard, Oldham and Leicester; *m.* 1922, Constance Mary West Walton, Chilwell Manor, Notts.; three *s.* one *d.* *Educ.:* Oundle School. Qualified as solicitor (1st cl. Hons.), 1916. Comd. as 2nd Lt. 4th Bn. Leicestershire Regt. 1916; served France and Belgium with 8th Bn., 1916-18. LL.B. London 1919. Mem. T. & A.F.A. for Leicestershire (later Leics. and Rutland), 1925-57 (Chm. 1948-1957). O.C. 4th Bn. Leics. Regt., 1930-36; Bt.-Col., 1934; served War of 1939-45, in England, 1940-41. D.L. (Leics.) 1941; Leicester City Council, 1938, Alderman, 1949, High Bailiff, 1954-55; Lord Mayor of Leicester, May 1956-57. *Recreation:* shooting. *Address:* Upperlands, Narborough, Nr. Leicester. *Club:* Leicestershire (Leicester).
[*Died* 7 *Aug.* 1964.

HALL, 1st Viscount, *cr.* 1946, of Cynon Valley; **George Henry Hall,** P.C. 1942; *b.* Penrhiwceiber, Glamorganshire, Dec. 1881; *s.* of George and Ann Hall; *m.* 1st, 1910, Margaret Jones (*d.* 1941); one *s.* (and one killed on active service); 2nd, 1964, Alice Martha Walker. *Educ.:* Penrhiwceiber Elementary School. Commenced work at the Penrikyber colliery at 12 years of age; continued to work as a collier until appointed checkweigher in 1911; continued to act as checkweigher Local Agent at the South Wales Miners' Federation until elected to Parliament in 1922; M.P. (Lab.) Aberdare Division of Merthyr Tydfil, 1922-46; Civil Lord of the Admiralty, 1929-31; Parliamentary Under-Secretary of State, Colonial Office, 1940-42; Financial Secretary to the Admiralty, 1942-1943; Parliamentary Under-Secretary of State for Foreign Affairs, 1943-45; Secretary of State for the Colonies, 1945-46; First Lord of the Admiralty, 1946-51, retd. Dep. Leader, House of Lords, 1947-51. Mem Mountain Ash Council and Educ. Committee for 18 years; passed through the Chair of both bodies; Governor, Cardiff University; J.P. 1925, D.L. 1953, Glamorganshire. Hon. LL.D. Birmingham Univ. and Univ. of Wales. *Heir:* *s.* Hon. (William George) Leonard Hall [*b.* 1913; *m.* 1st, 1935, Joan Margaret, *d.* of William Griffiths, Coedeley; two *d.*, 2nd, 1963, Constance Gathorne Hardy]. *Address:* House of Lords, S.W.1; Germains Lodge, Chesham, Bucks. *T.:* Chesham 3800; Penrhiwceiber, Glam. [*Died* 8 *Nov.* 1965.

HALL, Rev. Charles Albert, F.R.M.S.; Minister of the New Church (retired); author and lecturer; *b.* Eastfield, near Peterborough, 11 July 1872; *s.* of Henry James Hall and Christiana Littlejohns; *m.* 1896, Annie Unwin, Sheffield; two *s.* *Educ.:* Deacon's School, Peterborough; New Church College, London. Travelled in North America, 1888-91; settled in Sheffield in commercial work, 1891-96; entered New Church Ministry, 1896; Pastorates at Hull, Bristol, Paisley, Southport, and Argyle Square, London, 1896-1935; engaged in editorial and journalistic work from age of 18; commenced book-writing in 1902. *Publications:* Art of Being Happy; Art of Being Healthy; Art of Being Successful; Art of Remembering; The Manly Life; The Divinity that shapes our Ends; The Open Book of Nature; Wild Flowers and their Wonderful Ways; Romance of the Rocks; Pond-Life; How to Use the Microscope; Common British Beetles; The Isle of Arran; Plant-Life; They do not Die; Bees, Wasps, and Ants; Trees; Birds Eggs and Nests; The Lordship of Jesus; The Conquest of Care; a Programme for Life; The Blessed Way; The Friendliness of Things; Pocket Book of British Birds; Pocket Book of British Wild Flowers; Pocket Book of British Butterflies and Moths; Pocket Book of British Birds' Eggs and Nests; Wild Flowers in their Haunts, etc. *Recreations:* Nature-study, photography, gardening. *Address:* Gables, Sleepy Hollow, nr. Storrington, Sussex. *T.:* Storrington 2847. [*Died* 27 *Aug.* 1965.

HALL, Lieut.-Colonel Sir Douglas (Montgomery Bernard), 2nd Bt., *cr.* 1919; D.S.O. 1918; late Coldstream Guards; *b.* 30 Dec. 1891; *o. c.* of Sir D. B. Hall, 1st Bt., and Caroline (*d.* 1941), *o. d.* of T. J. Montgomery, of Larchmont Manor, New York State; *S.* father, 1923; *m.* 1st, 1915, Mary (from whom he obtained a divorce, 1923), *d.* of Capt. W. A. Grant, late 13th Hussars; one *d.*; 2nd, 1925, Nancie Walton (who obtained a divorce, 1950), *o. d.* of late J. Edward Mellor, C.B.; one *s.*; 3rd, 1951, Diana Joan (she *m.* 1st, 1929, 4th Baron Romilly, from whom she obtained a divorce, 1944), *o. d.* of 4th Baron Sackville, K.B.E. *Educ.:* Eton; R.M.C., Sandhurst. Served European War, 1914-19 (wounded twice, despatches thrice, D.S.O.); retired pay, 1931. Raised Home Guard in Argyll, 1940; Zone Commander, 1940-43. *Heir:* *s.* John Bernard [*b.* 20 March 1932; *m.* 1957, Delia Mary, *d.* of late Lt.-Col. J. A. Innes and of Mrs. E. J. de Lotbinière, Horringer Manor, Bury St. Edmunds; one *s.* one *d.*]. *Address:* 9 Hertford Street, W.1. *Clubs:* Carlton, Pratt's. [*Died* 30 *Aug.* 1962.

HALL, Brigadier Edward George, C.B. 1938; C.I.E. 1919; p.s c.; *b.* 13 Sept. 1882; *s.* of Rev. Edward Stephenson Hall, M.A., Bombay, Ecclesiastical Estabt.; *m.* 1912, Elinor Brodrick, *d.* of Col. W. S. Birdwood, late Indian Army; two *s.* one *d.* *Educ.:* Sherborne; R.M C., Sandhurst. Served European War, 1914-19 (despatches, C.I E., Order of Kara George, Serbia, with Swords); Staff College, Quetta, 1919-20; Lieut.-Col. 1926; Bt. Col. 1929; Col. 1930; A.A.G Northern Command, India, 1930-34; Commander, Ambala Brigade Area, India, 1934-38; retired, 1938; re-employed, 1939-46. *Address:* The Old Rectory, St. James, Shaftesbury, Dorset. *T.:* Shaftesbury 2003. *Club:* United Service.
[*Died* 20 *Dec.* 1968.

HALL, Captain Geoffrey Fowler, C.I.E. 1935; M.C.; late Chief Engineer and Secretary to Govt., Public Works Dept., Bihar, India; retired 1943; *b.* 9 Mar. 1888; *s.* of Perceval Ledger Hall and Margaret Fowler; *m.* 1910, Nellie Kate Pidduck; one *s.* *Educ.:* Marlborough; London University. Appointed to Public Works Department, India, 1911; Irrigation, 1911-14; European War, 1915-18, France and Salonika; served with 17th Fd. Coy. R.E.; commanded 126th A. T Coy. R.E. and 426th Fd. Coy. R.E. (wounded, M.C., despatches); P.W.D. India, Irrigation, 1919-22; Roads and Buildings from 1923; C.I.E. for services in connection with Bihar Earthquake of 1934. *Publications:* The Guru's Ring; Moths round the Flame; The Dragon and the Twisted Stick; (with Mrs Joan Sanders) D'Artagnan: The Ultimate Musketeer. *Address:* Greenhills, Drumconrath, Navan, Co. Meath, Ireland; c/o State Bank of India, 14/18 Gresham St., E.C.2.
[*Died* 8 *Aug.* 1970.

HALL, Rt. Rev. (George) Noel (Lankester); *b.* 25 December 1891; *s.* of George Hall, Baldock, Herts; unmarried. *Educ.:* Bedford School; St. John's College, Cambridge; Bishop's College, Cheshunt. 1st Cl. Class. Tripos pt. I, 1913, pt. II, 1914; 1st. Cl. Theol. Tripos pt. II, 1915; B.A. 1913; Lightfoot Scholar, 1916; M.A. 1918; deacon, 1917; priest, 1918; Curate, Christ Church, Luton, 1917; Vice-Principal, Ely Theological College, 1919-25; S.P.G. Missionary, Chota Nagpur, 1925-36; Bishop of Chota Nagpur, 1936-57; Fellow of St. Augustine's, Canterbury, July 1957-Apr. 1960. *Publication:* The Seven Root Sins, 1936. *Recreation:* idle conversation. *Address:* The Homes of St. Barnabas, Dormans, Lingfield, Surrey. [*Died* 12 *May* 1962.

HALL, Major Harold Wesley, O.B.E. 1952; M.C.; retired; *b.* 27 Nov. 1888; *s.* of Thomas Skarratt and Jane Hall; *m.* 1914, Doris Goodall Clegg; no *c.* *Educ.:* Eton; R.M.C. Sandhurst. Joined Queens Bays, 1908; served with regiment, 1914-16, G.S.O. 3 2nd Cavalry Division, 1916-18; G.S.O.2. Cavalry Corps, 1918; retired from army, 1920; since date director of public companies; travelled extensively Sudan, India, Polynesia, America and Australia. Served War of 1939-45, Wing-Commander Auxiliary Air Force, 1939-43. *Recreations:* big game hunting, shooting, yachting, marine biological research. *Address:* Downton Fields, nr. Lymington, Hants. *Clubs:* Cavalry; Royal Yacht Squadron (Cowes); Royal Lymington Yacht. [*Died* 20 *Nov.* 1964.

HALL, Herbert Austen, F.R.I.B.A., Consulting Architect; *b.* 1881; *y. s.* of Reverend Arthur Hall; *m.* 1st, 1912, Marjorie Bitter (*d.* 1927); one *s.* one *d.*; 2nd, 1933, Countess Claire Seyssel d'Aix; one *s.* *Educ.:* privately. Godwin Bursar R.I.B.A., 1919; past President of the Architectural Association. Recent architectural work: Bankers Clearing House; Institute of Bankers; rebuilding Clothworkers' Hall; Carpenters' Hall; the reconstruction of the Fishmongers' Hall; extensions Drapers' Hall. *Address:* 55 Whitfield St., W.1. *Clubs:* Garrick, City of London. [*Died* 19 *Feb.* 1968.

HALL, Sir Herbert Hall, K.C.M.G., *cr.* 1938 (C.M.G. 1930); B.A. Cantab.; *b.* 19 Jan. 1879; *m.* 1915, Lucy, *y. d.* of late Sir Robert J. Kennedy, K.C.M.G.; one *s.* three *d.* *Educ.:* Chigwell School, Essex; Jesus College, Cambridge. Entered Consular Service, 1906, Vice-Consul at Buenos Aires, 1907, at Monte Video, 1908, at Paris, 1911; Consul at Loanda, Portuguese West Africa, 1913; at Malaga, 1919; Consul-General at Lourenço Marques, Portuguese East Africa, 1921; an Inspector-General of H.M. Consulates, 1923; retired 1939. *Address:* Hertcombe, 62 Ashley Rd., Walton-on-Thames, Surrey. *T.:* Walton-on-Thames 27094. *Clubs:* Athenæum, Royal Over-Seas League; Effra Conservative (Brixton). [*Died* 5 *April* 1964.

HALL, John, O.B.E. 1964; Chief Secretary, R.S.P.C.A., since 1957; *b.* Tynemouth, 1 Sept. 1915; *s.* of Percy and Margaret Hall; *m.* 1942, Yolanda Clotilda Elizabeth (*née* Carbonero); two *s.* *Educ.:* Shrewsbury School. Admitted Solicitor, 1938; private practice, 1938-39. Served War of 1939-45: Royal Artillery, U.K., France and Germany (Major); demobilised, 1946. Unilever, 1946-1948; Legal Secretary, R.S.P.C.A., 1948-56. *Recreations:* walking, reading. *Address:* 103 Edgewarebury Lane, Edgware, Middlesex. *T.:* Stonegrove 6577. *Club:* Royal Automobile. [*Died* 14 *Feb.* 1966.

HALL, Rear-Adm. John Talbot Savignac, C.I.E. 1944; *b.* 30 Nov. 1896; 3rd *s.* of late Dr. Wm. Hamilton Hall, F.S.A.; *m.* 1933, Agnes Maud, *d.* of late Arthur Sherren, Iver Heath, Bucks; one *d.* (one *s.* decd.). *Educ.:* Elstow School, Bedford; Training Ship Mersey. Midshipman, 1914; Actg. Rear-Admiral, 1947; Rear-Admiral, 1950; Chief of Staff to Flag Officer commanding R.I.N. 1941 (Commodore 2nd class); Senior Naval Staff Officer, India Office, and R.I.N. Liaison Officer, 1944-46; Captain H.M.S. Achilles, 1947; Flag Officer Commanding (later Comdr.-in-Chief), R.I.N. 1947-48; Flag Officer Commanding R.I.N. Squadron, 1948-49. Civil Defence Officer, N.E. Essex, 1951-59. *Address:* c/o Westminster Bank, 173 Victoria St., S.W.1. [*Died* 21 *Jan.* 1964.

HALL, Julian Dudley, C.M.G. 1946; *b.* 12 March 1887; *s.* of late Edwin T. Hall, V.P.R.I.B.A.; *m.* 1923, Olive Margaret Jane (*d.* 1956), *d.* of late William Leach, Dublin; two *d.* *Educ.:* Dulwich Coll.; New Coll., Oxford. Entered Malayan Civil Service, 1910; British Adviser, Kedah, Malaya, 1932; retired, 1946. *Address:* Abbey Lea Cottage, Stonegate, Wadhurst, Sussex. *T.:* Ticehurst 221. [*Died* 17 *Feb.* 1961.

HALL, Professor Kenneth Ronald Lambert; Professor of Psychology, University of Bristol, since 1959; *b.* 21 July 1917; *s.* of K. L. Hall; *m.* 1941, Pauline Sophie Assinder; no *c.* *Educ.:* Cheltenham College; Brasenose College, Oxford. M.A. ((Oxford) 1946; D.Phil. (Oxford) 1949. Lecturer in Psychology, University of Bristol, and Head of Department of Experimental and Clinical Psychology, Bristol Mental Hospital, 1949-54; Professor of Psychology, University of Cape Town, S. Africa, 1955-59; Fellow, Center for Advanced Study in the Behavioural Sciences, California, 1962-63. Served War, Middle East, Germany, 1940-45; Captain, Royal Artillery, later Staff. *Publications:* Scientific papers on experimental psychopathology, animal behaviour, and the natural history of African monkeys. *Recreations:* tennis, golf, gardening, literature. *Address:* Department of Psychology, University of Bristol, Bristol 8. *T.:* Bristol 24161. [*Died* 14 *July* 1965.

HALL, Rt. Rev. Noel; *see* Hall, Rt. Rev. G. N. L.

HALL, Col. Ralph Ellis Carr-, C.I.E. 1917 Indian Army, retired; late Military Accounts Dept. Military Accountant General, Simla; *b.* 30 Oct. 1873; *m.* Agnes Alexander, *d.* of Lieut.-Col. W. L. Lane, R.A.M.C.; one *s.* 2nd Lt. Durham L.I. 1894; Capt. Indian Army, 1903; Major, 1912; Lt.-Col. 1920; Col. 1922; served Tirah, 1897-98 (medal, two clasps); European War, 1914-17 (despatches, C.I.E.; Mons Medal, 1914; British War Medal, 1914-19; Victory Medal, 1918; mentioned Gazette of India, 21 Sept. 1918; Com.-in-Chief's despatch, 1919); retired, 1923. *Address:* Astor House, 127 Princess Road, Bournemouth. [*Died* 31 *Jan.* 1963.

HALL, Air Marshal Sir Robert H. C.; *see* Clark-Hall.

HALL, Sir Roger Evans, Kt., *cr.* 1937; C.B.E. 1955; *b.* 16 April 1883, *s.* of Frederic Evans and Helen Elizabeth Hall; *m.* 1944, Adelaide Gladys (M.B.E. 1947), *d.* of late Dr. Dudley C. Trott, Pembroke, Bermuda. *Educ.:* Winchester; New College, Oxford, Called to Bar, Inner Temple, 1908; asst. District Commissioner, Gold Coast, 1910; Crown Counsel 1914; Senior Crown Counsel, 1915; Circuit Judge Ashanti and Northern Territories of Gold Coast, 1918; Puisne Judge, Gold Coast, 1921; Judge of the High Court, Northern Rhodesia, 1931; Acting Governor, 1934; Chief Justice, Uganda, 1935-37 Chief Justice, Federated Malay States, 1938-39. *Recreation:* gardening *Address:* Lulworth, Bermuda. [*Died* 6 *Feb.* 1969.

HALL, Ronald Acott, C.B.E. 1946; *b.* Burton Joyce, Nottinghamshire, 24 May 1892; *s.* of late J. E. Hall. Fought in France 1915-18 in European War. Formerly H.M. Consul-General, Canton, and Member H.M. Diplomatic and Consular Service, and later Secretary, Economic League for European Co-operation (British Section). *Publications:* Frederick the Great's Seven Years War; Studies in Napoleonic Strategy; Eminent Authorities on China; The Official Pocket Guide to China; Lame Ducks (a play); (with Prof. Whymant) 3000 Commonest Chinese Terms. *Address:* 8 Chapel Hill, Lewes, Sussex. *T.:* Lewes 4941. *Clubs:* National Liberal, Royal Automobile. [*Died* 21 *March* 1966.

HALL, Stewart S.; *see* Scott Hall.

HALL, Thomas Donald Horn, C.M.G. 1939; LL.B. (N.Z.); *b.* 4 Oct. 1885 (of English parentage); *s.* of J. H. Hall, Accountant, and Mary Brown; *m.* 1922, Annie Catherine, *d.* of late Prof. Hugh Mackenzie, C.M.G. *Educ.:* Wanganui Collegiate School; Wellington College; Victoria University College. Entered service of N.Z. Govt. in Dept. of Agriculture, attaining position of Senior Clerk and Legal Officer; Asst. Law Draftsman, 1921; Clerk of the House of Representatives, 1930-45; retired 1945; Past Pres., N.Z. Library Assoc. and Hon. Life Member; Past Member of Committee of Management, National Art Gallery; served European War with N.Z.E.F., 1915-19. *Publications:* Captain Joseph Nias and the Treaty of Waitangi, 1938; Contributor to N.Z. Affairs, 1929, to Legal Status of Aliens in Pacific Countries, 1937, and to Cyclopaedia of the Social Sciences. *Recreations:* reading, gardening. *Address:* 3 Braithwaite St., Wellington W.3, N.Z. [*Died* 28 *Dec.* 1970.

HALL, Dr. Wilfrid John, C.M.G. 1951; M.C. 1917; D.Sc., Ph.D., A.R.C.S.; Director Commonwealth Institute of Entomology, 1946-58, retd.; *b.* 13 Dec. 1892; British; *m.* 1923, Marjorie Mary Hall (*née* Dewe) (*d.* 1961); one *s.* two *d.* *Educ.:* St. Pauls Sch., W. Kensington (Sen. Sch.); Imperial College of Science and Technology, South Kensington. 1st XV Rugby, St. Pauls School. Served European War, 1914-19, in the Army; in France and Belgium, in Machine Gun Corps, 1916-19; demobilised with rank of Major. Ministry of Agriculture, Cairo, Egypt, in Entomological Section 1919-26, holding a post as Senior Entomologist on retirement. On the staff of British South Africa Company, S. Rhodesia, 1927-42 Entomologist, 1927-30, Director, Mazoe Citrus Experimental Station, 1930-33, Supt. Mazoe Citrus Estate, 1933-42. Commonwealth Institute of Entomology; Senior Entomologist, 1943-44, Asst. Director, 1944-1946, Director, 1946-58. A.R.C.S. 1914; Ph.D. (Lond.), 1927; D.Sc. (Lond.), 1930. *Publications:* entomological papers in various jls. dealing with taxonomy and applied entomology. *Recreations:* gardening and wireless. *Address:* Green Hedges, The Forebury Sawbridgeworth, Herts. *T.:* Sawbridgeworth 3380. *Clubs:* Farmers', Royal Over-Seas League; Salisbury (Southern Rhodesia). [*Died* 13 *Jan.* 1965.

HALL, Rt. Hon. William Glenvil, P.C. 1947; M.P. (Lab.) Colne Valley Div. of Yorks since 1939; barrister-at-law; *b.* Almeley, Herefordshire, 1887; *s.* of William George and Elizabeth Hall, Almeley; *m.* 1921, Rachel (*d.* 1950), *d.* of Rev. Bury Sanderson; one *s.* one *d.* Brit. representative U.N. Assembly, 1945, 1946, 1948; Final Assembly, League of Nations, 1946; Paris Peace Conf., 1946; Consultative Assembly, Strasbourg, 1950, 1951. 1952. Served European War, 1914-18, The Buffs, later attached Tank Corps (wounded once, despatches); M.P. (Lab.) Portsmouth Central, 1929-31. Financial

Secretary to the Treasury, 1945-50; Chairman Parliamentary Labour Party 1950 and 1951. *Address:* House of Commons, S.W.1. [*Died* 13 *Oct.* 1962.

HALL CAINE, Gordon Ralph, C.B.E. 1920; Officier Légion d'Honneur; late Government representative on the Cinematograph Advisory Cttee.; Director, Second Broadmount Trust, Ltd.; Director of South African Board Mills Ltd. and companies manufacturing paper or wood-pulp in England, United States, and Canada; *b.* 16 Aug. 1884; *s.* of late Sir Hall Caine, C.H., K.B.E.; *m.* (wife *d.* 1948); one *s.* one *d.*; *m.* 1949, Dorothy Sara, *e. d.* of late J. T. Hornsby-Sample and of Mrs. Howard Tripp. *Educ.:* King William's Coll., Isle of Man. Left school at age of about 15 to enter the printing and paper trade; served his apprenticeship in England and America, ultimately becoming Director of Ballantyne, Hanson & Co., Ltd., of Edinburgh and London; during European War, 1914-18, served whole time voluntarily first as Chief Technical Adviser on Paper to Ministry of Munitions and later to other Government Departments, in addition was Chairman or Vice-Chairman of about 14 departmental or other Committees under the Government dealing with paper, and in 1918 appointed Deputy Controller of Paper till end of control, when served as Vice-Chairman of Paper Restrictions Department till end of 1919; M.P. (C.) East Dorset, 1922-29 and 1931-45 when he retired; has been associated from time to time with publications of several important books for charity, including The Queen's Xmas Carol, Queen Alexandra's Xmas Gift Book, King Albert's Book, etc. *Publications:* Articles on Papermaking and Wood-pulp Manufacture. *Recreations:* golf, shooting, fishing, and motoring. *Address:* Suffolk House, 117 Park Lane, W.1; Greeba Castle, Isle of Man. *Clubs:* Carlton; Temple Golf (Maidenhead); Metropolitan (New York); Canada (Montreal). [*Died* 5 *March* 1962.

HALLAM, Sir Clement Thornton, Kt. 1948; Retired as Solicitor to the General Post Office, October 1953; *m.* 1915, Irene, *d.* of Rev. J. W. Faraday; two *s.* Entered Solicitors' Department, General Post Office, 1915; Solicitor to the G.P.O., 1943-53. During War of 1939-45, seconded for Special work at Imperial Defence College. *Address:* 43 Elm Park Court, Pinner, Middlesex. *T.:* Pinner 1046. [*Died* 17 *March* 1965.

HALLETT, Harold Foster, M.A., D.Litt. (Edinburgh); Professor Emeritus of Philosophy in the University of London; *b.* 1886. *Educ.:* Brighton; Varndean School and Technical College. Engineering pupil in works and shipyard of Messrs. Yarrow and Co. at Poplar, 1904-8; King's Prizeman in Applied Mechanics and in Steam, 1904; University of London (Inter. B.Sc. (Engineering), 1906); University of Edinburgh (Medallist in Logic, 1910; in Moral Philosophy, 1911 and 1912; in Metaphysics, 1912; M.A. with First Class Honours in Mental Philosophy, 1912; Bruce of Grangehill Prizeman in Metaphysics, 1912; Vans Dunlop Scholar in Logic, 1912; Rhind Philosophical Scholar, 1914; Hamilton Philosophical Fellow, 1915; D.Litt., 1930). University of Edinburgh: Lecturer in Logic and Assistant in Logic and Metaphysics, 1912-16; Assistant in Moral Philosophy, 1915-16; University of Leeds: Asst. Lecturer in Philosophy, 1919-1922; Lecturer in Philosophy, 1922-31; Professor of Philosophy in Univ. of London, King's College, 1931-51; sometime examiner in Philosophy in the Universities of Edinburgh, Glasgow, etc.; British Secretary of Societas Spinozana, 1929-35; Chairman of Board of Philosophical Studies, University of London, 1935-45; Chm. Board of Internal Examiners in Philosophy, Univ. of London, 1943-51; Member of Delegacy of King's College, University of London, 1944-49. F.R.S.A. *Publications:* Aeternitas, A Spinozistic Study, 1930; Benedict de Spinoza, The Elements of His Philosophy, 1957; Creation, Emanation, and Salvation, A Spinozistic Study, 1962 (The Hague); articles and reviews in various philosophical journals and encyclopædias, British and foreign. *Address:* Blue Waters, St. Agnes, Cornwall. *T.:* St. Agnes 587. [*Died* 24 *April* 1966.

HALLETT, Sir Hugh Imbert Periam, Kt., *cr.* 1939; M.C.; *b.* 12 Dec. 1886; *s.* of Forbes Ernest Hallett and E. S. Imbert-Terry; *m.* 1921, Winifred Sydney Spalding; one *d.* *Educ.:* Westminster; Christ Church, Oxford (M.A.). President, Oxford Union Society, 1908; Hon. Sec. Junior Imperial League, 1910-39; called to Bar, Inner Temple, 1911; served European War, 1914-1919; K.C. 1936; Recorder of Newcastle upon Tyne, 1938-39; Bencher of Inner Temple, 1939; Assistant of Haberdashers' Company, 1939; Judge of the High Court of Justice, Queen's Bench Division, 1939-57, resigned. Electoral Boundaries Comr. for Brit. Guiana, 1960. Reader of Inner Temple 1963, Treasurer, 1964. *Address:* 60 Wynnstay Gardens, Kensington, W.8. *Club:* Garrick. [*Died* 8 *Sept.* 1967.

HALLETT, Leslie C. H.; *see* Hughes-Hallett.

HALLETT, Sir Maurice Garnier, G.C.I.E., *cr.* 1943 (C.I.E. 1930); K.C.S.I., *cr.* 1937 (C.S.I. 1934); K.St.J.; *b.* 28 Oct. 1883; *y. s.* of late Rev. J. T. Hallett; *m.* Gladys, Kaisar-i-Hind Gold Medal, 1941, C.St.J., *d.* of late H. C. Veasey; one *s.* (and one killed in action). *Educ.:* Winchester College; New College, Oxford. Joined I.C.S., 1907; Magistrate and Collector, 1916; Secretary to Government of Bihar, 1920-24; Officiating Commissioner, 1929; Chief Secretary, Bihar and Orissa, 1930-32; Secretary to Government of India in the Home Dept., 1932-36; Governor of Bihar, 1937-39; Governor of United Provinces, 1939-Dec. 1945. *Address:* Ashdene, St. Giles' Hill, Winchester, Hampshire. *T.:* Winchester 4784. *Club:* Athenæum. [*Died* 30 *May* 1969.

HALLIDAY, J.; Organiser and Lecturer in Handwork to the Education Committees, City and County of Oxford, retired. *Publications:* Bookbinding as a Handwork Subject; Handwork and Rural Industries; Handwork for Juniors; Handwork for Seniors; Simple Upholstery for Schools; Making Musical Pipes; Ideas for the Woodwork Room; Bookcraft and Bookbinding. *Address:* 31 King's Rd., Berkhamsted, Herts. [*Died* 21 *Nov.* 1962.

HALLIDAY, General Sir Lewis Stratford Tollemache, V.C.; K.C.B., *cr.* 1930 (C.B. 1913); late R.M.; Hon. Col. Comdt. Plymouth Division, Royal Marines, since 1930; *b.* 14 May 1870; *e. s.* of late Lt.-Col. Stratford C. Halliday, R.A.; *m.* 1st, 1908, Florence Clara (*d.* 1909), *o. d.* of late Brig.-Gen. W. Budgen, D.S.O.; one *s.*; 2nd, 1916, Violet (*d.* 1949), *d.* of Maj. Victor Blake, Hayling Island, Hants; one *s.* one *d.* Royal Marines, 1889; Capt. 1898; Bt. Major, 1900; Maj. 1908; Col. 1920; Col.-Comdt. 1923; Maj.-Gen. 1925; Lt.-Gen. 1927; General, 1928; served China, 1900 (dangerously wounded, despatches, Brevet Major, medal with clasp, V.C.). Passed Staff College, 1906; Commander of a Company of Gentlemen Cadets, R.M.C., Sandhurst (G.S.O. 2nd grade), 1908-11; Staff of R.N. War College, 1912; G.S.O.2 (Army) Malta, 1914; G.S.O.1 (Army) England and France, 1915-1916; G.S.O.1 Admiralty (Plans Division) 1917-1918; R.M. A.D.C. to the King; Adjutant-General Royal Marines, 1927-30; retired 1930; Gentleman Usher to the Sword of State, 1933-1946. D.L., Devon, 1936. *Address:* 23 Rose Hill, Dorking, Surrey. [*Died* 9 *March* 1966.

HALLIDAY, Sir William Reginald, Kt., *cr.* 1946; M.A., B.Litt.; Hon. LL.D. Glasgow; Hon. D.Phil. (Thessalonica); Officer of Legion of Honour; *b.* Belize, British Honduras, 26 Sept. 1886; *s.* of Charles Reginald Hoffmeister; took the name of Halliday, 1905; *m.* 1918, Edith Hilda, *y. d.* of late Professor W. Macneile Dixon; four *s.* *Educ.:* Winchester (Scholar); New College, Oxford (Classical Scholar); 1st class Lit. Hum., 1908; Charles Oldham Prize, 1910; Craven Fellow, 1909; studied also at Berlin University and as student of the British School at Athens. Has taken part in excavation and travel in the Levant; Lecturer on Greek History and Archæology in the University of Glasgow, 1911-14; Rathbone Professor of Ancient History in the University of Liverpool, 1914-28; Principal of King's College, London, 1928-52; Deputy Vice-Chancellor of the University of London, 1932-33; Chm. of Collegiate Council, 1932-34 and 1944-46; Member of the Court of the University of London, 1933-51; Chairman of the National Froebel Union, 1936-43. Lieut. R.N.V.R. and Intelligence Officer in Crete, 1916-18 (Chevalier of the Order of the Redeemer (Greek), 1918, despatches). *Publications:* Greek Divination, 1913; (with R. M. Dawkins) Modern Greek in Asia Minor, 1916; Lectures on the History of Roman Religion, 1922; The Growth of the City State, 1923; Folklore Studies, Ancient and Modern, 1924; The Pagan Background of Early Christianity, 1925; Greek and Roman Folklore, 1927; Introduction to Penzer-Tawney, The Ocean of Story, vol. viii. 1927; The Greek Questions of Plutarch, 1928; Indo-European Folk-Tales and Greek Legend, 1933; Sir Thomas Cockaine, a Short Treatise of Hunting, 1932; (with T. W. Allen and E. E. Sikes) The Homeric Hymns, 1936; contributions to The Cambridge Ancient History, Encyclopædia Britannica, Folklore, Journal of the Gypsy Lore Society, and to various classical periodicals. *Address:* 25 Chepstow Villas, W.11. *Club:* Athenæum. [*Died* 25 *Nov.* 1966.

HALLOWES, Frederick; Chief Officer of Greater London Council Parks Department since 1964; *b.* 17 Dec. 1907; *e. s.* of Charles Henry and Annie Hallowes; *m.* 1938, Kathleen, *yr. d.* of Francis Henry and Ellen Roper; one *s.* one *d.* *Educ.:* North Darley County Sch.; Manchester Coll. of Art; Dept. of Civil Engineering, Nottingham University. Trained at James Smith's, Darley Dale, Derbyshire; Technical Asst., Kettering Corporation, 1938; Superintendent of Parks, Dukinfield Corporation, 1939; Superintendent of Parks and Estates, City of Nottingham, 1941-56; Director of Parks, City of Nottingham, 1956-63; Chief Officer of L.C.C. Parks Department, 1964. Member: Exec., London and S.E. Sports Council; Royal Musical Association. Liveryman, Musicians Company; Mem., Guild of Freemen of City of London. *Publications:* The Newstead Abbey Collection of Trees and Shrubs, 1953; articles to technical journals. *Recreations:* all forms of outdoor sport, gardening, music, reading. *Address:* 10 Hillmont Road, Hinchley Wood, Esher, Surrey. *T.:* 01-398 2991. [*Died* 12 *Dec.* 1968.

HALLS, Arthur Norman, (Michael), M.B.E. 1945; T.D.; Principal Private Secretary to the Prime Minister since 1966; *b.* 6 Oct. 1915; *s.* of Sidney and Clara Halls; *m.* 1941, Marjorie Claysmith. *Educ.:* Stationers' Company School; King's College, London. Entered H.M. Customs and Excise, 1936; Inland Revenue, 1939. Commissioned R.A. (T.A.) 1937. Embodied service, 1939-1946: B.E.F., 1939-40; Staff Coll., Camberley, 1942; B.E.F., 1944; Lt.-Col., H.Q. British Troops, Berlin, 1945. Board of Trade, 1947: Private Sec. to Pres. of Bd. of Trade, 1948-50; Asst. Sec., 1955; Regional Controller for Midland Region, 1955. Imperial Defence College, 1962. Under-Sec., Bd. of Trade, 1965; Deputy Sec., 1969. *Address:* 56 Cardigan Street, Lambeth, S.E.11. *Club:* Army and Navy. [*Died* 3 *April* 1970.

HALLSTROM, Sir Edward John Lees, Kt. 1952; Hon. Life Director Taronga Park Zoological Trust, Sydney; benefactor and member of Board of Directors, Royal Prince Alfred Hospital, Sydney; benefactor Hallstrom Institute of Cardiology, Royal Prince Alfred Hospital; Advisory Mem., Internat. Union against Cancer; Mem. Management Committee and benefactor Hallstrom Cancer Research and Treatment Clinic, Sydney Hospital; *b.* New South Wales, 25 Sept. 1886; *s.* of William C. Hallstrom, London; *m.* 1st, 1912, Margaret E., *d.* of Douglas Jaffrey, Qld.; one *s.* three *d.*; 2nd, 1969, Mabel Maguire, *d.* of Arthur McElhone, Sydney. *Educ.:* State public schools. Governing Director Hallstroms Pty. Ltd., Refrigerator Mfrs. and Engrs. Hon. Fellow, Zool. Soc. of London. Life Member and Fellow, Roy. Zool. Soc. N.S.W. Member Roy. Hist. Soc.; Hon. Fellow, North of England Zool. Soc. *Address:* Hallstroms Pty. Ltd., 462 Willoughby Rd., Willoughby, N.S.W.; 1 Coolawin Road, Northbridge, N.S.W., Australia. *Club:* Explorers' (New York). [*Died* 27 *Feb.* 1970.

HALLWORTH, Albert; *b.* 5 Jan. 1898; *m.*; one *d.* *Educ.:* Elementary School. Worked in a cotton mill; served H.M. Forces throughout European War, 1914-18; entered railway service, 1919; successively engine cleaner, fireman and spare driver, London, Midland & Scottish Railway, 1919-38; Organising Secretary, A.S.L.E. & F., 1938-1948; Acting Assistant General Secretary, 1948-56; General Secretary of Associated Society of Locomotive Engineers and Firemen (A.S.L.E. & F.), 1956-60; Member of General Council of the T.U.C., 1955-60. Member of Labour Party. Ex-Editor Locomotive Journal (monthly publication of A.S.L.E. & F.). *Address:* 29 Cardinal Road, Eastcote, Ruislip, Mddx. [*Died* 18 *April* 1962.

HALSE, Most Rev. Reginald Charles, K.B.E. 1962; Archbishop of Brisbane since 1943; *b.* Luton, Beds., 16 June 1881; 3rd *s.* of late James John and Gulielma Halse; unmarried. *Educ.:* St. Paul's School; Brasenose College, Oxford; Kelham Theological College. Assistant Priest, St. Saviour's, Poplar, 1906-11; Priest in charge of St. Nicholas, Blackwell, 1911-12; Warden of the Brotherhood of St. Barnabas, 1913-25; Headmaster of All Souls School, 1920-25; Canon of Townsville Cathedral, 1921; Bishop of Riverina, 1925-43. Hon. Fell. Brasenose Coll., Oxford, 1960. *Recreation:* gardening. *Address:* Bishopsbourne, Brisbane, Australia. [*Died* 9 *Aug.* 1962.

HALSE, Colonel Stanley Clarence; C.M.G. 1918; late Royal Artillery; Director Waite and Son, Ltd., *b.* 14 Jan. 1872; *s.* of Richard Clarence Halse, Inverness Terrace, W.; Solicitor; Alderman, City of ondon; *m.* Edith Mary, M.B.E. (*d.* 1946), *d.* of J. H. Smalpage, The Firs, East Sheen; one *s.* one *d* *Educ.:* Harrow; Royal Military Academy, Woolwich. 2nd Lieut. R.A. 1891; Lieut. 1894; Capt. 1899; Major, 1912; Bt. Lt.-Col. 1915; Lt.-Col. 1917; Bt.-Col. 1919; served European War in department of M.G.O. and in Ministry of Munitions (despatches twice, C.M.G., Bt. Lt.-Col., Bt.-Col., Legion of Honour, Order of the Crown, Belgium); Staff Employment in the branch of the M.G.O., 1899-1900; 1901-7; 1908-12; 1914-15; Ministry of Munitions 1915-20; passed advanced class Ordnance College, 1901; retired pay, 1920. *Recreations:* bridge, gardening. *Address:* 286 Earls Court Road, S.W.5. *T.:* Fremantle 0080. *Club:* United Service. [*Died* 10 *March* 1961.

HALSEY, Captain Sir Thomas Edgar, 3rd Bt., *cr.* 1920; D.S.O. 1940; J.P.; Royal Navy, retired; Vice-Lieutenant, County of Hertford, since 1957; *b.* 28 November 1898; *er. s.* of Sir Walter Johnston Halsey, 2nd Bt., O.B.E., and late Agnes Marion, *d.* of William Macalpine Leny; *S.* father, 1950; *m.* 1926, Jean Margaret Palmer, *e. d.* of Captain Bertram Willes Dayrell Brooke (Tuan Muda of Sarawak); one *s.* one *d.* *Educ.:* Eton. Joined Royal Navy, 1916; served European War, 1916-19; Commander, 1933; Captain, 1939; War of 1939-46; Commanded: 16th Destroyer Flotilla, 1939-41, H.M.S. St. George, 1942-1943, H.M.S. King George V, 1943-45; Commodore R.N. Air Station, Lee on Solent, 1945; retired list, 1946. D.L. Herts., 1948; J.P. 1950; C.C. 1953. *Heir: s.* John Walter Brooke Halsey, *b.* 26 Dec. 1933. *Address:* The Golden Parsonage, Hemel Hempstead, Herts. *T.:* Markyate 315. [*Died* 30 *Aug.* 1970.

HAM, Very Rev. Herbert, M.A. Oxon.; Vicar of All Saints Cathedral Church, Derby, 1925-38; Provost, 1931-38, Provost Emeritus since 1938; *m.* 1914, Hilda Annie (*d.* 1958), *e.d.* of Sir Alfred Seal Haslam, Breadsall Priory, Derbyshire; one *s.* (and one *s.* decd.). *Educ.:* St. John Baptist College, Frome; Worcester Coll., Oxford (2nd Class Modern History, 1899); M.A. 1916; F.R.C.O. 1898. Curate of Wormley, Herts, 1900-3; of Chelmsford, 1903-10; Vicar of St. James', Derby, 1910-18; Wirksworth, Derbyshire, 1917-25; Rector of Carsington, 1920-25; Priest-in-Charge of Alderwasley, 1922-25; Hon. Canon of Bakewell in Southwell Cathedral, 1924-28; Hon. Canon of Derby, 1928-1938; Rural Dean of Derby, 1931-38. Warden of Retreat House, Ambergate, 1926-30; Priest-in-charge of Dethick, Lea and Holloway (war-time), 1939-43. *Publications:* My Pilgrimage to Jerusalem, 1961; Church Music: Te Deum, Benedicite; Musical Sketches for pianoforte, etc. *Recreations:* music, archæology. *Address:* Wood End, Cromford, Matlock, Derbyshire. *T.:* 217. *Clubs:* Oxford and Cambridge; County (Derby). [*Died* 2 *Dec.* 1964.

HAMBLING, Capt. Sir (Herbert) Guy (Musgrave), 2nd Bart., *cr.* 1924; late Canadian Infantry; solicitor; farmer; Director of Lewis Berger and Sons Ltd.; Chairman of Directors, National Test; *b.* 12 Aug. 1883; *o. surv. s.* of Sir Herbert Hambling, 1st Bt., and Thirza, *d.* of W. G. Twigg, solicitor, Dunstable; *S.* father 1932; *m.* 1911, Olive Margaret Gordon, *d.* of late Mr. and Mrs. Edwin Carter, Leeds; one *s.* two *d.* Admitted Solicitor, 1907; Partner in Durrant Cooper & Hambling. *Heir: s.* Herbert Hugh Hambling [employed with B.O.A.C., Renton, Washington, U.S.A.; *b.* 3 August 1919; *m.* 1950, Anne Page, *er. d.* of late Judge Hugo Oswald Seattle, U.S.A.; one *s.* Served War of 1939-45, in R.A.F.]. *Address:* Rookery Park, Yoxford, Suffolk. *T.:* Yoxford 310. *Club:* Carlton [*Died* 13 *Feb.* 1966.

HAMBLY, Wilfrid Dyson, D.Sc.; *b.* Clayton, Yorkshire, 1886; *s.* of Rev. J. W. Hambly of Liskeard, Cornwall, pastor of Clayton Baptist Church, and Jane, *d.* of Rev. Eli Dyson, pastor of Rishworth Baptist Church, Yorks; *m.* Annie E. Larkin, Leytonstone, London. *Educ.:* Sheffield Central Secondary School; Hartley College, Southampton; Board of Education's Certificate, Distinctions in Theory and Practice of Teaching, Licentiate of College Preceptors, Honours and first place, Biology, 1907-9; Jesus College, Oxford (1912), Oxford Diploma in Anthropology; B Sc. research degree in Anthropology; Wellcome Expedition to the Sudan, 1913-14; served in R.N.D. with Hawke Batt. in Gallipoli, and with Howe Batt. in France, 1914-19; Research Investigator for Industrial Fatigue Research Board, 1919-22; Lecturer in Biology, West Ham Municipal College, 1922-26; Leader of Rawson-Field Museum ethnological expedition to Angola and Nigeria, 1929-30; D.Sc. (Oxford), 1936; Curator of African Ethnology, Chicago Natural History Museum; retired, 1953. *Publications:* Joint Research for Industrial Fatigue Research Board; Tests of Physical Efficiency; Atmospheric Conditions in Boot Factories. Individual Publications: Native Races of British Empire, 3 books, 1920; History of Tattooing, 1925; Origins of Education, 1926; Tribal Dancing and Social Development, 1926; African Ethnology, a guide to Field Museum Collections, 1930; Serpent Worship in Africa, 1931; With a Motor Truck in West Africa, 1931; The Ovimbundu of Angola, 1934; Culture Areas of Nigeria, 1935; Primitive Hunters of Australia, 1936; Skeletal Material from San José, British Honduras, 1937; Source Book for African Anthropology, 1937; Anthropometry of the Ovimbundu, 1938; Craniometry of New Guinea, 1940; Craniometry of Ambrym, 1946; Cranial Capacities, 1947; Clever Hands of African Negroes, 1947; Jamba, 1947; Talking Animals, 1949; Bibliography of African Anthropology (1937-1949), 1952; Desert Boy, 1957. *Recreations:* sailing, swimming, bridge. *Address:* 1635 Hyde Park Blvd., Chicago 15, Illinois, U.S.A. [*Died* 18 *July* 1962.

HAMBRO, Sir Charles Jocelyn, K.B.E., *cr.* 1941; M.C.; Chairman, Hambros Bank Ltd.; Pres., Union Corporation; Chm., Bay Hall Trust Ltd.; Director: Bank of England; British South Africa Company; Cable & Wireless (Holding) Ltd.; Globe Telegraph and Trust Ltd.; *b.* London, 1897; *e. s.* of late Sir Eric Hambro, K.B.E.; *m.* 1st, Pamela (*d.* 1932), *d.* of late J. D. Cobbold and late Lady Evelyn Cobbold; one *s.* three *d.*; 2nd, 1936, Dorothy, *d.* of late Alexander Mackay, Glencruitten, Oban; one *d.* *Educ.:* Eton. Coldstream Guards, European War, 1915-19; Sheriff of County of London, 1933; D.L. City of London; Col., General Staff War Office, 1940-43; U.K. Member Combined Raw Materials Board and Head of British Raw Materials Mission, Washington, 1944-45. *Address:* Hambros Bank, 41 Bishopsgate, E.C.2; 72 North Gate, Regents Park, N.W.8; Dixton Manor, Gotherington, Glos. *Clubs:* Turf, White's. [*Died* 28 *Aug.* 1963.

HAMBRO, John Henry, C.M.G. 1944; Chairman since 1963 (Dep. Chm. 1963, Man. Dir., 1931-63), Hambros Bank Ltd.; Director, John Dickinson and Co. Ltd.; *b.* 7 July 1904; *s.* of late Henry Charles Hambro and late Edith Gertrude Bonsor; *m.* 1st, 1930, Elizabeth Theresa de Knoop; one *s.* one *d.*; 2nd, 1947, Linnet, *o. d.* of late Major E. M. Lafone. *Educ.:* Eton. *Address:* The Hyde, nr. Luton, Beds. *T.:* Harpenden 2191. *Club:* Turf. [*Died* 4 *Dec.* 1965.

HAMBRO, Ronald Olaf; Chairman Hambros Bank Ltd. since 1933; *b.* 1 Dec. 1885; *s.* of Everard Hambro and Gertrude Mary Stuart; *m.* 1917, Winifred Martin Smith (*d.* 1932); three *s.* *Educ.:* Eton College; Trinity College, Cambridge. Entered father's business, C. J. Hambro & Son, 1908; served in Coldstream Guards during European War, 1914-18, and discharged with rank of Captain; member of Board of London Assurance, 1914, Governor 1934-59. J.P. County of Kent; High Sheriff County of Sussex, 1931; Hon. Colonel 139th Regiment, Royal Artillery. *Address:* 68 Pall Mall, S.W.1. *T.:* Whitehall 0173; Linton Park, Linton, Kent; Logan House, Port Logan, nr. Stranraer, Wigtownshire. *Club:* White's. [*Died* 25 *April* 1961.

HAMER, Sir George (Frederick), Kt., *cr.* 1955; C.B.E. 1948; Lord Lieutenant of Montgomeryshire and Custos Rotulorum 1950-60; *b.* 1885; *s.* of late Edward and Martha Hamer, Summerfield Park, Llanidloes, Montgomeryshire; *m.* 1920, Sybil Dorothy (High Sheriff of Montgomeryshire, 1958), 3rd *d.* of late Dr. John Vaughan-Owen, M.R.C.S., L.R.C.P., M.O.H., and of Mrs. Vaughan-Owen, Castle House, Llanidloes; one *d.* (and one *d.* decd.). *Educ:* Llanidloes Grammar School. Joined firm of Edward Hamer & Co., Llanidloes, 1902; became sole proprietor of firm of T. Pryce Hamer, Leather Manufacturers, Llanidloes, 1919, and became Chm. of Dirs. upon firm becoming Ltd. Company, 1946; retired, 1954. Member Borough Council of Llanidloes, 1919-63; Mayor on eleven occasions; Alderman, 1932-63; Hon. Freeman of Borough, 1948. Montgomery C.C., 1929 (Chm. 1951-54 and 1956-58); Alderman, 1949; Chairman Montgomeryshire Education Committee, 1947-51; Member of Council for Wales and Monmouthshire, 1949-53 and 1956-1959; Chm. Wales Gas Consultative Council, and Mem. of Wales Gas Board, 1949-58; Member of Central Advisory Council for Educ. (Wales), 1945-49; Member of B.B.C. Advisory Council for Wales, 1946-1949. J.P. Montgomeryshire, 1932; Chairman Llanidloes Borough and Upper Petty Sessional Benches, 1950-60; High Sheriff of Montgomeryshire, 1949. County President Venerable Order of St. John, 1951-; C.St.J. *Address:* Summerfield Park, Llanidloes, Montgomeryshire. *T.:* Llanidloes 298. *Club:* National Liberal. [*Died* 3 *Feb.* 1965.

HAMILTON, (Anthony Walter) Patrick; novelist and playwright; *b.* Hassocks, Sx., 17 Mar. 1904; *s.* of Bernard Hamilton; *m.* 1st, 1930, Lois M. Martin; 2nd, 1954, Lady Ursula Winifred Stewart. *Educ.:* Westminster. *Publications:* Monday Morning, 1923; Craven House, 1926; Twopence Coloured, 1928; The Midnight Bell, 1929; Rope, a play, 1929; The Siege of Pleasure, 1932; The Plains of Cement, 1934; Twenty Thousand Streets under the Sky, 1935; Impromptu in Moribundia, 1939; Gas Light, a play, 1939; Money with Menaces and To the Public Danger, two radio plays, 1939; Hangover Square, 1941; The Duke in Darkness, a play, 1942; The Governess, a play, 1945; The Slaves of Solitude, 1947; The West Pier, 1951; Mr. Stimpson and Mr. Gorse, 1953; The Man Upstairs, 1954; Unknown Assailant, 1955. *Recreation:* golf. *Club:* Savile.
[*Died* 23 *Sept.* 1962.

HAMILTON, Lt.-Col. Arthur Francis, C.I.E. 1930; M.B., F.R.C.S.; F.C.O.G.; Indian Medical Service (retd.); late Professor of Midwifery and Gynæcology, Grant Medical College, Bombay; *b.* 1880; *s.* of T. S. Hamilton, I.C.S.; *m.* 1905, Winifred May Kilner; no *c.* *Educ.:* Prior Park College, Bath; St. Bartholomew's Hospital. Entered I.M.S., 1905; Staff Surgeon, Poona; Surgeon to His Excellency Governor of Bombay; Civil Surgeon, Poona; war service, 1914-18; retired, 1935. *Publications:* Enteric Fever in Infancy, I.M. Gazette; Surgical Experience in Poona, I.M. Gazette. *Recreations:* music, gardening. *Address:* Eastlands, Ashley Rise, Walton-on-Thames. *T.:* Walton 20626.
[*Died* 10 *May* 1965.

HAMILTON, Charles (Harold St. John); *see* Richards, Frank (pen-name).

HAMILTON, Rt. Rev. Eric Knightley Chetwode, K.C.V.O., *cr.* 1955; Dean of Windsor since 1944; a domestic chaplain to the Queen since 1952 (to King George VI, 1944-52); Registrar of the Most Noble Order of the Garter since 1944; *b.* 1890; *s.* of late Rev. C. Chetwode Hamilton; *m.* 1915, Jessie, *d.* of late Sir Walter Cassels; one *s.* (*yr. s.* killed in action in Italy, 1943) two *d.* *Educ.:* Bradfield; University College, Oxford. Deacon, 1913; Priest, 1914; in charge of S. John's, Wilton Road, S.W., 1918-25; Vicar of Chiswick, 1925-29; Vicar of S. Paul's, Knightsbridge, 1929-40; Bishop Suffragan of Shrewsbury, 1940-44; Rector of Edgmond, 1940-44; Proctor in Convocation from 1931. *Recreation:* golf. *Address:* The Deanery, Windsor Castle. *T.:* Windsor 561. *Clubs:* Athenæum; Vincent's (Oxford).
[*Died* 21 *May* 1962.

HAMILTON, Eric Ronald, C.B.E., 1954; M.A. (Camb.); B.Sc. (Lond.); Principal, Borough Road College, Isleworth, 1932-61; *b.* 1893; *e. s.* of John George Hamilton, lecturer at the Froebel Educational Institute and elsewhere, and of Bessie Hamilton; *m.* 1924, Alice Janet, *e. d.* of Frederick and Helena Wood; two *d.* *Educ.:* Clapham High School for Boys; University College, London; Trinity College, Cambridge (Exhibitioner). Instructor Lieut. R.N. 1916-20; taught in schools, Yorkshire and London, 1920-22; lecturer in Education, University College of N. Wales, Bangor, 1922-32; Examiner for the Civil Service Commission, etc.; Hon. Sec., Council of Principals of Training Colleges, 1934-42; Chairman of Governors, Isleworth Grammar School; Member of Heston and Isleworth Education Committee; Squadron Leader R.A.F.V.R., 1942-44. Chm. of Assoc. of Teachers in Colleges and Depts. of Education, 1950; Member of Council, Coll. of Preceptors, 1952; Member of Nat. Advisory Council on Training and Supply of Teachers, 1953; Chairman of Committee of Principals, University of London Institute of Education, 1952-54. *Publications:* The Art of Interrogation, 1929; Fundamental Geometry, 1935; Geometry and Trigonometry (London Mathematical Series), 1939; Air Navigation (Nelson's Aeroscience Manuals), 1942; The Teacher on the Threshold, 1946; Mathematics for Living, 1953; Go Ahead Arithmetic, 1957; numerous articles on psychology, mathematics and education. *Recreations:* walking, reading, etc. *Address:* 34 St. Mary's Crescent, Osterley, Middlesex. *T.:* Isleworth 5546. [*Died* 3 *May* 1967.

HAMILTON, Sir George Rostrevor, Kt., *cr.* 1951; poet, writer and civil servant; F.R.S.L. (Vice-President); President, Society of Civil Service Authors; *b.* London, 11 April 1888; *s.* of Rev. C. Chetwode Hamilton; *m.* 1918, Marion Hermine, *d.* of Rev. W. L. S. Coghlan; one *s.* *Educ.:* Bradfield; Exeter College, Oxford (Classical Scholar, 1st class Hon. Mods., 1909; 1st class Litt. Hum., 1911). Entered Inland Revenue Department, 1912; Private Secretary to Chairman of Board of Inland Revenue, 1913; Secretary to Committee on National Debt and Taxation, 1926; an Assistant Secretary to Board of Inland Revenue, 1929; a Special Commissioner of Income Tax, 1934; Presiding Special Commissioner, 1950-53. *Publications:* (verse) Escape and Fantasy, 1918; Pieces of Eight, 1923; The Making, 1926; Epigrams, 1928; Light in Six Moods, 1930; John Lord, Satirist, 1934; Unknown Lovers, 1935; Memoir, 1887-1937, 1938; The Sober War, 1940; Apollyon, 1941; Death in April, 1944; Selected Poems and Epigrams, 1945; Crazy Gaunt, 1946; The Inner Room, 1947; The Carved Stone, 1952; The Russian Sister, 1954; Collected Poems and Epigrams, 1958; Landscape of the Mind, 1963; (anthologies) The Soul of Wit, 1924; The Latin Portrait, 1929; The Greek Portrait, 1934; Wit's Looking-Glass, 1934; Landmarks (with John Arlott), 1943; James Hurnard, 1946; (prose) Bergson and Future Philosophy, 1921; Poetry and Contemplation, 1937; The World to Come, 1939; Hero or Fool, 1944; The Tell-Tale Article, 1949; Guides and Marshals, 1956; Walter Savage Landor (British Council series), 1960; English Verse Epigram, 1965; Rapids of Time, 1965. *Address:* 5/8 The Paragon, Blackheath, S.E.3. *T.:* Lee Green 3618. *Club:* Athenæum. [*Died* 1 *May* 1967.

HAMILTON, Professor Henry, M.A., D.Litt.; Jaffrey Professor of Political Economy, University of Aberdeen, since 1945; *b.* 2 March 1896; 3rd *s.* of late Thomas Hamilton and Elizabeth Currie, Islay and Fairlie, Ayrshire; *m.* 1929, Agnes Shanks, Uddingston, Lanarkshire; two *s.* one *d.* *Educ.:* Dunoon Grammar School; Glasgow University. Glasgow Univ.: M.A. 1919, Gladstone Memorial Prize in Econ., 1919, Clark Scholar in Econ., 1919-20. Lecturer in Social Science, Selly Oak Colls., Birmingham, 1920-21; Ext. Lecturer in Economics, Birmingham Univ., 1921-25; D.Litt. (Glas.), 1925; Smart Memorial Prize for Research, Glasgow, 1925. Lecturer in Economic History, Aberdeen Univ., 1925-45. Examiner in Econ. Hist., Univ. of Edin., 1933-36; Examiner in Polit. Econ., Univ. of St. Andrews, 1946-50; Dean, Scottish Univ. Summer School, 1955-. Chairman of Aberdeen Local Employment Cttee., and of four Wages Councils; Member: Jute Working Party, 1946-48; Cttee. of Investigation for Scotland (Agricultural Marketing Act), 1950; Scottish Records Advisory Council; Education Cttee. of Aberdeen Town Council, 1954-. *Publications:* English Brass and Copper Industries, 1926; Industrial Revolution in Scotland, 1932. Economic Evolution of Scotland (Hist. Assoc. pamphlet), 1933; Monymusk Papers (Scottish Hist. Soc.), 1945; Life and Labour on an Aberdeenshire Estate (Spalding Club), 1946; History of the Homeland, 1947; White Fish Industry of Aberdeen and the Granite Industry in Further Studies in Industrial Organization, ed. Fogarty, 1948. Editor: County of Aberdeen; County of Banff (Third Statistical Account of Scotland), 1960; An Economic History of Scotland in the Eighteenth Century, 1963. *Address:* 33 Hazledene Road, Aberdeen. *T.:* Aberdeen 36221. [*Died* 4 *May* 1964.

HAMILTON, Rear-Admiral Hugh Dundas, retired; *b.* 16 Aug. 1882; *e. s.* of His Honour Judge Hugh Montgomerie Hamilton, Sydney, New South Wales; *m.* Marion Edith, *d.* of Lt.-General J. Cloete, I.A., Guernsey; one *d.* *Educ.:* Saundersons, Cheltenham; H.M.S. Britannia. Joined R.N. 1897; served in European War, 1914-1918; Captain, 1920; second Naval Member, New Zealand Naval Board, 1922-1924; Asst. Director of Naval Equipment, Admiralty, 1926-28; Supt. Sheerness Dockyard, 1930-32; A.D.C. to the King, 1932; Rear-Admiral, 1933; retired, 1933; was employed as Commodore of Convoy in 1939. J.P. 1946, D.L. 1952, Bucks. *Recreations:* shooting, etc. *Address:* The Limes, Haddenham, Aylesbury, Bucks. *T.:* Haddenham (Bucks) 356. *Club:* United Service. [*Died* 29 *Nov.* 1963.

HAMILTON, Surgeon Rear-Admiral James, C.B. 1955; C.B.E. 1949; M.A. (Oxon.) 1955; R.N. retd.; Director of Postgraduate Medical Studies, Oxford, 1955-60, retd.; *b.* 29 Oct. 1899; *s.* of Robert Hamilton, Strathaven, Lanarkshire; *m.* 1941, Helen Johnston Allan, Mauchline, Ayrshire; one *d.* *Educ.:* Kilmarnock Academy; Glasgow University. Flying Officer, R.F.C., 1917-19. M.B., Ch.B. Glasgow, 1923. Entered R.N., 1923; R.N. Hospital, Haslar, 1937-42; H.M.S. King George V, 1942-44; R.N. Auxiliary Hospitals, Kingseat and Sydney, 1945-46; Asst. to Medical Director-General, 1946-51; Dep. Med. Dir.-Gen., 1951-52; Surgeon Rear-Adm., 1952; Medical Officer i/c R.N. Hospital, Haslar, 1952-55. Q.H.S., 1952-55. O.St.J. 1951. *Address:* 40 Midton Road, Prestwick, Ayrshire. [*Died* 7 *Jan.* 1964.

HAMILTON, Kismet Leland Brewer, C.I.E. 1934; I.C.S., retired; *b.* 13 Aug. 1883; *s.* of William Robarts Hamilton and Lilian Brewer; *m.* 1913, Madeleine Ruth Dennys; two *s.* *Educ.:* Tonbridge School; St. John's College, Cambridge. Joined Indian Civil Service, 1907; posted to Central Provinces as Assistant Commissioner; Under-Secretary, 1910-13; Settlement Officer, Seoni, 1915-20; Deputy Commissioner; Political Agent Chhattisgarh Feudatory States, 1925-28; Officiating Commissioner Chhattisgarh Division, 1928-34; confirmed as Commissioner, 1933; retired, 1936. *Recreations:* shooting, fishing, golf, tennis. *Address:* Ladymead, Convent Road, Sidmouth, Devon. [*Died* 16 *April* 1966.

HAMILTON, Lord Malcolm A. D.; *see* Douglas-Hamilton.

HAMILTON, Mary Agnes, C.B.E. 1949; *e. d.* of late Robert Adamson, Professor of Logic, Glasgow University. *Educ.:* Glasgow Girls' High School; Newnham College, Cambridge. M.P. (Lab.) Blackburn, 1929-31; late Parliamentary Private Sec., P.M.G.; Member, British Delegation, League of Nations Assembly, 1929, 1930; Royal Commission on Civil Service, 1929-31; Governor of British Broadcasting Corporation, 1933-1937; Alderman L.C.C., 1937-40; temp. civil servant, 1940-52. *Publications:* Junior History of Rome; Greek Legends; Ancient Rome; etc.; *novels:* Less than the Dust; Yes; Dead Yesterday; Full Circle; The Last Fortnight; Follow my Leader; Follys Hand-book; Special Providence; Murder in the House of Commons, 1931; Life Sentence, 1935; *biographies:* Margaret Bondfield, J. Ramsay MacDonald, Mary Macarthur; Carlyle (Travellers' Library); Sidney and Beatrice Webb, 1933; Newnham, 1936; Arthur Henderson, 1938; Women at Work, 1941; Remembering My Good Friends, 1944; Up-hill All the Way, 1953. *Recreations:* walking, sketching, listening to music. *Address:* 62 Beaufort Mansions, Chelsea, S.W.3. *T.:* Flaxman 0546. [*Died* 10 *Feb.* 1966.

HAMILTON, Patrick; *see* Hamilton, A. W. P.

HAMILTON, Sir (Thomas) Sydney (Percival), 6th and 4th Bt.; *cr.* 1776 and 1819; *b.* 1 Apr. 1881; *S.* brother 1939; *m.* 1920, Bertha Muriel (*d.* 1961), *d.* of J. R. King, Singleton Park, Kendal; one *s.* *Heir:* *s.* Edward Sydney, *b.* 14 Apr. 1925. *Address:* The Cottage, Lavant, Sussex. *T.:* Chichester 7414. [*Died* 26 *Feb.* 1966.

HAMILTON, Major-General William Ralston Duncan, C.B. 1954; O.B.E. 1940; retired; *b.* Campbeltown, Argyllshire, 17 Oct. 1895; *s.* of late Duncan Hamilton of Lamlash, Isle of Arran, Scotland, and late Jessie Wright Ralston, Paisley; *m.* 1st, 1923, Florence May Taylor (*d.* 1942); one *s.*; 2nd, 1956, Joyce C. Clark, *d.* of late John Clark and Mrs. L. M. Clark, Birmingham. *Educ.:* High School, Glasgow; University of Glasgow. M.B., Ch.B. (Hons.) 1918; M.D. 1951. Commissioned Royal Army Medical Corps as Lieut. 1918; Capt. 1919; Maj. 1930; Lt.-Col. 1944; Col. 1948; Brig. 1951; Maj.-Gen. 1953. Served European War, 1914-18; War of 1939-45: Malta, W. Africa; Consulting Physician, M.E.L.F., 1948-50. Q.H.P. 1952-55 (K.H.P. 1951-52); Director of Medicine and Consulting Physician to the Army 1951-55. retired 1955. *Recreation:* golf *Address:* 10 King's Drive, Edgeware, Middx. *T.;* 01-9588646. [*Died* 5 *Oct.* 1969.

HAMILTON-GRIERSON, Philip Francis; Sheriff Substitute of Inverness, Elgin and Nairn, 1936-55; *b.* Edinburgh, 15 April 1883; *e. s.* of Sir P. J. Hamilton-Grierson, LL.D.; *m.* 1928, Margaret, *d.* of J. G. Bartholomew, LL.D.; one *s.* three *d.* *Educ.:* Edinburgh Academy; Trinity College, Oxford, B.A. Scottish Bar; served European War, 1914-19, Captain 5th R.S.F., Staff Captain; District

Judge, Sudan, 1919; Judge of High Court, Advocate General, Sudan Government; retired 1933. *Recreation:* fishing. *Address:* 4 Pentland Road, Edinburgh 13. *Club:* New (Edinburgh). [*Died* 19 *Feb.* 1963.

HAMILTON HARDING, George Trevor, C.I.E. 1931; Secretary to the Governors and Bursar of Kings College Sch., Wimbledon, 1949-67; *b.* Kandy, Ceylon, 18 June 1895; *s.* of A. J. Hamilton Harding; *m.* 1930, Anne Gregg Waterhouse; two *s.* one *d.* *Educ.:* Haileybury College. Indian Police, Punjab, 1915; served European War, 1916-19, N.W. Frontier, and Palestine, attached 15th (Ludhiana) Sikhs; Senior Superintendent of Police, Lahore, 1929, Officer on Special Duty reorganizing the Bikaner State Police, 1934-37; Home Minister, Bikaner State, 1937; Deputy Inspector-Gen., Amballa, 1941; Inspector-Gen. of Police, Patiala State, 1944-46; Deputy Inspector-General, Lahore, Jan.-Aug. 1947. *Recreation:* gardening. *Address:* 7 Devas Road, S.W.20. [*Died* 10 *Sept.* 1967.

HAMILTON-MONTGOMERY, Sir Basil P. R., Bt.; *see* Montgomery.

HAMMARSKJÖLD, Dag (Hjalmar Agne Carl); Secretary-General of the United Nations since 1953; *b.* Jönköping, Sweden, 1905; *s.* of late Hjalmar L. Hammarskjöld and Agnes (*née* Almquist); unmarried. *Educ.:* Uppsala University (Bachelor of Laws); Stockholm University (Dr. Phil.). Asst. Prof. in Polit. Econ., Stockholm Univ., 1933; Sec. to Commn. on Unemployment, 1930-34; Sec. in Sveriges Riksbank (Bank of Sweden), 1935; Under-Sec. of State to Min. of Finance, 1936-45; Chm. Sveriges Riksbank, 1941-48; Envoy Extraordinary and Financial Adviser to Min. for Foreign Affairs, 1946-49; Under-Sec. of State in Min. for Foreign Affairs, 1949-51; Minister of State, 1951-53; Swedish Deleg. at Paris Conf. Econ. Co-op., 1947 and 1948; Deleg. to O.E.E.C., Uniscan and Council of Europe, 1948-53; Vice-Chm. in O.E.E.C. Exec. Cttee., 1948-49; Deleg. at negotiations with Gt. Britain, U.S.A. and other countries, 1944-48; Delegate of Sweden to General Assembly of United Nations, 1949 and 1951-53; Vice-Chm. Swedish Touring Club, 1950; Chm. Swedish Mountaineers Club, 1945-52; Member. Swedish Academy, 1954. Nobel Peace Prize, 1961. Holds several hon. degrees. *Relevant Publication:* Dag Hammarskjöld, by Joseph P. Lash, 1962. Markings (autobiog.) trans. W. H. Auden and Leif Sjöberg, 1964 (*posthumous*). *Address:* Stockholm, Sweden; United Nations, New York City, U.S.A. [*Died* 17 *Sept.* 1961.

HAMMERSLEY, Samuel Schofield; Chairman of cotton-spinning and other industrial companies; Member of Lloyd's; *b.* 1892; *s.* of late John Schofield Hammersley, cotton spinner; *m.* 1919, Kate Wakley; five *d.* *Educ.:* King's College, Cambridge. Joined the Army from the University; served as a subaltern with the East Lancashire Regiment in Gallipoli; in France with the Tank Corps (Captain); M.P. (U.) Stockport, 1924-35; M.P. (U.) East Willesden, 1938-45; Parliamentary Private Secretary to Financial Secretary to Treasury, 1927; Textile Mission to India, 1933; rejoined Army, 1939; work for Ministry of Supply on Tanks, 1940-43. Chm. Parliamentary Palestine Cttee., 1943-45; Exec. Chm., Anglo-Israel Association, 1951-63; Chm. General Comrs. Income Tax Division of Lower Pevensey, 1961-. *Publications:* Industrial Leadership, 1925; various articles on industrial and economic subjects. *Recreation:* gardening. *Address:* Saxon Court, Uckfield, Sussex. *T.:* Buxted 2285; 6 Lennox Garden Mews, S.W.1. *T.:* Knightsbridge 4562. *Clubs:* Carlton, Brooks's; St. James's (Manchester). [*Died* 28 *March* 1965.

HAMMERSLEY-SMITH, Ralph Henry, C.B.E. 1922 (O.B.E. 1918); Lt.-Col., retired; *b.* 7 June 1880; *s.* of R. E. H. Smith, Mall House, Cahir; *m.* Magdalene Frances, *d.* of Henry MacDowell, Oatlands Park, Weybridge: five *d.* (and one *d.* decd.). *Educ.:* St. Edward's School, Oxford. Entered Army through the Imperial Yeo., 1900; transferred to 14th Bengal Lancers, I.A., 1905; transferred to 11th Sikh Regt. 1922; served S. African War, 1900-2; European War, 1914-18 (O.B.E.); Waziristan, 1920-23 (C.B.E., Brevet Lieut.-Col., 1924); commanded 2/11th Sikh Regt. (Ludhiana Sikhs), 1925-29; retired, 1930. *Address:* 30 Stirling Rd., Bournemouth, Hants. *T.:* Winton 2393. [*Died* 18 *Nov.* 1964.

HAMMERTON, Colonel George Herbert Leonard, C.M.G. 1918; D.S.O. 1917; Col. (Retd.); late R.A.M.C.; K.St.J.; *b.* 1875. Served European War, 1914-18 (despatches four times, C.M.G., D.S.O., T.D.); retired 1927. Late O.C. 5th Cavalry Field Ambulance; County Surgeon St. John Ambulance Bde., North Western Area. *Address:* Beechwood, 57 Esplanade, Hornsea, E. Yorks. *T.:* Hornsea 408. [*Died* 4 *Aug.* 1961.

HAMMETT, (Samuel) Dashiell; Writer since 1922; *b.* 27 May 1894; *s.* of Richard Thomas and Annie Dashiell Hammett; *m.* 1920, Josephine Annas Dolan (marriage dissolved, 1937); two *d.* *Educ.:* United States Public Schools. Successively messenger boy, clerk, stevedore, private detective, advertising manager, etc. from 1908. European War, 1914-18, enlisted in U.S. Army and served 1918-19; War of 1939-45, in U.S. Army, 1942-45. *Publications:* Red Harvest, 1929; The Dain Curse, 1929; The Maltese Falcon, 1930; The Glass Key, 1931; The Thin Man, 1934; The Dashiell Hammett Omnibus, 1950. *Recreations:* shooting and fishing. *Address:* 63 East 82nd Street, New York 28, U.S.A. *T.:* Rhinelander 4-4328. [*Died* 10 *Jan.* 1961.

HAMMICK, Dalziel Llewellyn, M.A. D.Sc. (Oxon); F.R.S. 1952; Fellow, 1921-52, and Tutor, 1923-52, Oriel College, Emeritus Fellow, 1952, Oxford; Vice-Provost, 1946-1949; Univ. Demonstrator in Chemistry; Aldrichian Praelector in Chemistry, 1949-52; *b.* 8 March 1887; *s.* of late Llewellyn Sidney Herbert Hammick; *m.* 1910, Phillippa Tilbrook; one *s.* two *d.* *Educ.:* Whitgift School; Magdalen Coll., Oxford (Demy). 1st Class Nat. Sci. (Chemistry), 1909; Univ. of Munich, 1909-10; Schoolmaster, Gresham's School, Holt, 1910-18; Winchester Coll., 1918-21; Leverhulme Research Fellow. 1933-34; Member of the Hebdomadal Council, 1940-47. *Publications:* Introduction to Organic Chemistry, 1920; papers in Journal of Chemical Society and elsewhere. *Recreation:* fly-fishing. *Address:* Oriel College, Oxford. [*Died* 17 *Oct.* 1966.

HAMMICK, Sir George Frederick, 4th Bt., *cr.* 1834; late Agent to Lord Clifford of Chudleigh Estates in Somerset, Warwickshire, Bucks, Devon, and Cornwall; *b.* 24 Sept. 1885; *er. s.* of late Vice-Admiral R. F. Hammick and Grace Caroline, *d.* of William Longman; *S.* uncle, 1927; *m.* 1925, Mary Adeliza, *d.* of late Lt.-Col. Henry Welch-Thornton, Newton Abbot; one *s.* *Educ.:* Farnborough; Dartmouth. Royal Navy; retired, 1902; rejoined Aug. 1914; served Royal Naval Division during War. *Recreations:* hunting, shooting, cricket. *Heir:* *s.* Stephen George [*b.* 27 Dec. 1926; *m.* 1953, Gillian Elizabeth, *yr. d.* of Major Inchbald, Wraxall Manor, Dorchester; two *s.* one *d.*]. *Address:* Green, Hayes, Kilmington, Axminster, Devon. *T.:* Axminster 3206. [*Died* 12 *April* 1964.

HAMMOND, Arthur H. K.; *see* Knighton-Hammond.

HAMMOND, Dennis; Assistant Under-Secretary of State, Ministry of Defence, since 1964; *b.* 11 March 1913; *o. c.* of late Herbert Hammond, Oulton, Yorks; *m.* 1939, Edith, *o. d.* of late Harry Humphreys Jones; no *c.* *Educ.:* Normanton Grammar School; Christ Church, Oxford (Scholar, Dixon Scholar and Gladstone Exhibitioner). 1st Cl. Final Hons. School of Modern History, 1934; Curzon Prize, 1935. Asst. Principal, War Office, 1936; Asst. Under-Secretary of State, War Office, 1963. *Address:* Dorters, Linersh Wood, Bramley, Guildford, Surrey. *T.:* Bramley 3383. [*Died* 25 *Aug.* 1969.

HAMMOND, Sir John, Kt. 1960; C.B.E. 1949; F.R.S. 1933; M.A.; Hon. D.Sc. (Iowa, Durham, Leeds); Hon. D.Ag. (Vienna, Louvain, Copenhagen, Cracow); Fellow of Downing College, Cambridge, 1936-54; Honorary Fellow, 1954; *b.* 23 February 1889; *s.* of Burrell Hammond and Janette Louise Aldis; *m.* 1916, Frances Mercy Goulder; two *s.* *Educ.:* Gresham's School, Holt; Edward VI Middle School, Norwich; Downing College, Cambridge. Agricultural Research Scholar, Ministry of Agriculture, 1912-14; Captain 7th Battalion Norfolk Regiment, 1914-18; Staff Captain 201st Brigade, 1917-18; Inspector, Live Stock Branch, Ministry of Agriculture and Fisheries, 1919; Research Physiologist, Animal Nutrition Institute, School of Agriculture University of Cambridge, 1920; reported to Empire Marketing Board on Problem of Tropical Cattle-breeding in West Indies, 1930; Superintendent Animal Research Station, Cambridge, 1931; Guest Professor of Animal Production and Physiology, Iowa State Coll., Ames, Iowa, U.S.A., 1932; Guest Professor, Ibadan Univ., Nigeria, 1964; reported to C.A.P. on Meat Production in Argentine, 1936; reported to D.S.I.R. New Zealand and C.S.I.R. Australia on Animal Production, 1938; served on Livestock Cttee. of Post-War Allied Rehabilitation Council and U.N.N.R.A. 1942-45, and Meat Boards New Zealand and Australia, 1958; reported to S. African Meat Control Board, 1948; reported to F.A O. on Animal Production, Bombay, 1956, Sudan, 1957; Advisory Cttee., Southern Rhodesia, 1961-62; formerly Reader in Agricultural Physiology, Cambridge University, retired 1954; Hon. Fell. R.A.S.E. 1956; Hon. Associate, R.C.V.S. 1959; Foreign Mem. Roy. Swedish Acad. Agriculture, Acad. Nac. Agron. y Vet Buenos Aires; Czechoslovakian Academy of Agriculture; Acad. d'Agric. de France. Commander Order Orange-Nassau, 1946; Commenda al Merito della Repubblica Italiana, 1954. *Publications:* Reproduction in the Rabbit, 1925; Reproduction in the Cow, 1927; Growth and the Development of Mutton Qualities in the Sheep, 1932; Farm Animals, 1940; Physiology of Farm Animals, 1954; Handbuch der Tierzüchtung, 1958; many papers on fertility, growth, milk, and meat production. *Recreation:* travel. *Address:* 1 Luard Road, Cambridge. *Club:* Farmers'. [*Died* 25 *Aug.* 1964.

HAMMOND, Rt. Rev. Lempriere Durell; Bishop of Stafford, 1939-58, resigned; *b.* 14 Aug. 1881; *s.* of Rev. Vavasour Fitz-Hammond Hammond and Caroline Annie Webb; *m.* 1918, Ethel Anne Godden (*d.* 1954); one *s.* one *d.* *Educ.:* St. Augustine's School, Dewsbury; The Academy, Greenock. Commercial career until 1907; Lincoln Theological College, 1907-09; D.D. (Lambeth), 1948; Curate St. John's, Chatham, 1909-14; St. James, Tunbridge Wells, 1914-18; Vicar St. Mary the Virgin, Strood, Kent, 1918-25; Dartford, Kent, Parish Church, 1925-30; Vicar and Rural Dean of Walsall, 1930-34; Canon Residentiary of Lichfield Cathedral, 1934-Dec. 1954; Prebendary of Offley in Lichfield Cathedral and Treasurer of the Cathedral, 1936; Prebendary of Tachbrook in Lichfield Cathedral, 1955-58. *Address:* 23 The Close, Lichfield. *T.:* Lichfield 3337. [*Died* 5 *Jan.* 1965.

HAMMOND, Lucy Barbara; *b.* July 1873; *y. d.* of Rev. E. H. Bradby, D.D., formerly Head Master of Haileybury College; *m.* 1901, J. L. Hammond (*d.* 1949). *Educ.:* St. Leonards School, St. Andrews; Lady Margaret Hall, Oxford (Scholar), 1st class Classical Moderations; 1st class Lit. Hum. 1896; Hon. Fellow Lady Margaret Hall; Hon. D Litt. Oxon 1933. *Publications:* Joint-author with her husband, The Village Labourer; The Town Labourer; The Skilled Labourer; Lord Shaftesbury; The Rise of Modern Industry; The Age of the Chartists; James Stansfeld; The Bleak Age; articles in the Economic Journal. *Address:* Oatfield, Piccotts End, Hemel Hempstead *T.:* Boxmoor 316. [*Died* 14 *Nov.* 1961.

HAMMOND, Ven. Thomas Chatterton, M.A., T.C.D.; Th.D.; Rector, St. Philip's Church, Church Hill, Sydney; Principal, Moore Theological College, Sydney 1936-54; Canon St. Andrews Cathedral, Sydney, 1939; Archdeacon, Sydney, 1949 (without territorial jurisdiction); Lecturer Divinity Studies, University of Sydney, 1942; *b.* 20 Feb. 1877; *s.* of Colman Mark Hammond and Elizabeth Sarjeant; *m.* 1906, Margaret McNay; three *s.* one *d.* *Educ.:* Elementary School; Private Tuition; Trinity College, Dublin. Curate and Rector, St. Kevin's Church, Dublin, 1903-19; Dublin Superintendent Irish Church Missions, 1919-31; General Superintendent Irish Church Missions, 1931-36. *Publications:* Authority in the Church, 1921; Concerning Penal Laws, 1930; In Understanding be Men, 1936; Perfect Freedom, 1938; The One Hundred Texts, 1938; Fading Light, 1942; Age-Long Questions, 1942; Reasoning Faith, 1944; Anselm, Abelard and Wickcliffe in History of Evangelical doctrine of Holy Communion; The New Creation, 1953; Contributor to Protestant Dictionary, new edition. *Address:* St. Philip's Rectory, Church Hill, Sydney, N.S.W. *T.:* BU 1071. [*Died* 16 *Nov.* 1961.

HAMMOND, Walter R.; Sqdn. Ldr. R.A.F.V.R.; *b.* Dover, 19 June 1903; *m.* 1947, Sybil Ness-Harvey, Durban, S.A.; one *s.* one *d.* *Educ.:* Cirencester Grammar School. Company Director, 1937. Played cricket for Gloucestershire, amateur, 1920, professional, 1923-37, amateur since 1938. Capt. of Gloucestershire County C.C., 1939-1947. Played for England from 1925; Captain, 1938-39-45-47. Completed 100 Hundreds in 1935; made 13 Hundreds in 1933 and in 1937; scored 1028 runs May 7-28, 1927. *Publications:* Cricket my Destiny, 1946; Cricket my World, 1947. *Address:* c/o Messrs. Richardson, Sadler & Co., 17 Clarges St., Piccadilly, W.1 [*Died* 1 *July* 1965.

HAMOND-GRAEME, Sir Egerton Hood Murray, 5th Bt., *cr.* 1783; T.D.; *b.* 23 May 1877; *e. s.* of 4th Bt. and Evelyn (*d.* 1937), *d.* of R. B. Lawes, Old Park, Dover; *S.* father, 1920; *m.* 1st, 1921, Mrs. Preston (*d.* 1952), *d.* of Wm. Leatham, J.P. of Acaster, Yorks; 2nd, 1953, *widow* of Major Herbert Musker, Rushford Hall, Norfolk and Bembridge Lodge, I.O.W. *Educ.:* Winchester; Trinity College, Cambridge. Major Hampshire Carabiniers; served European War Hampshire Yeomanry and 76th Brigade R.F.A.; Home Guard, 1940. *Heir:* none. *Recreations:* hunting, shooting, yachting, fishing. *Address:* Rushford Hall, Thetford, Norfolk. *T.:* 2272. *Clubs:* Brooks's, St. James' [*Died* 8 *Nov.* 1969 (*ext.*).

HAMPDEN, 4th Viscount *cr* 1884; Baron Dacre *cr.* 1307; **Thomas Henry Brand,**

C.M.G. 1943; Chairman since 1965, Managing Director since 1931, Lazard Brothers & Co. Ltd.; late Lieutenant Rifle Brigade; *b.* 30 March 1900; *e. s.* of 3rd Viscount Hampden, G.C.V.O., K.C.B., C.M.G.; *S.* father 1958; *m.* 1923, Leila, *d.* of late Lieut.-Colonel Frank Seely, Ramsdale Park, Notts; two *d.* (co-heiresses to the Barony of Dacre). Chief Executive Officer on British side of Combined Production and Resources Board in Washington, 1942-44; Chairman of Supplies for Liberated Areas (Official) Committee, 1944-45. Chairman, Issuing Houses Association, 1953 and 1954. *Heir:* (to Viscountcy): *b.* Hon. David Francis Brand. *Address:* Mill Court, Alton, Hants. *T.:* Bentley 3125; 53, Fursecroft, George St., W.1. *T.:* Paddington 8602. [*Died* 17 *Oct.* 1965.

HAMPSON, Sir Cyril Aubrey Charles, 12th Bt., *cr.* 1642, of Taplow, Co. Buckingham; *b.* 18 March 1909; *s.* of late Charles Seymour Hampson, *b.* of 10th Bt.; *S.* cousin, 1939. *Educ.:* Oratory School, Caversham. Lord of the Manor and Lay Rector of Thurnham Parish, Kent. *Heir:* none. *Address:* c/o British P.O., Tangier, Morocco. [*Died* 13 *Nov.* 1969 (*ext.*).

HAMPTON, 4th Baron (*cr.* 1874), **Herbert Stuart Pakington,** Bt. 1846; C.B.E. 1962; *b.* 15 May 1883; *s.* of 3rd Baron and Evelyn Nina Frances, *d.* of Sir George Baker, 3rd Bt.; *S.* father, 1906. *Educ.:* Wellington; R.M.C. Sandhurst. Formerly Lieut., Rifle Bde., and Major Worcs. Yeomanry. *Heir:* *bro.* Hon. Humphrey Arthur Pakington, O.B.E. *Publications:* Scouting Sketches, 1925. *Address:* Old Stables, 125 Strawberry Vale, Twickenham. [*Died* 30 *Oct.* 1962.

HAMPTON, Lt.-Col. Bertie Cunynghame; *see* Dwyer-Hampton.

HANAFIN, Lieut.-Colonel John Berchmans, T C.I E. 1919; F.R.C.S.I.; D.P.H.; D.M. and H. (Camb.); retired; *b.* 10 Aug. 1882; 2nd *s.* of late James Hanafin, M.D.; *m.* 1926, Rosamond Sidney (*d.* 1968), of Blyth, Northumberland; one *d.* *Educ.:* Dublin. Entered Royal Army Medical Corps as subaltern, 1907; served Aldershot, Ireland; in India since 1910; entered Indian Medical Service, 1914; served European War, Aden Hinterland, 1914-16; Mesopotamia, E African Campaign, 1917-18; East Persian Field Force, 1918-20 (despatches thrice, C.I.E.); Afghan War, 1919; retired 1936; re-employed 1939; retired 1945; served Channel Isles and Home Forces till Sept. 1945. *Address:* Alpha Lodge, Dooks, Glenbeigh, Co. Kerry; c/o Glyn, Mills, Holt's Branch, Whitehall, S.W.1. *Clubs:* Army and Navy, Royal Commonwealth Society. [*Died* 25 *Aug.* 1970.

HANBURY, Brig.-Gen. Philip Lewis, C.M.G. 1919; D.S.O. 1915; late the King's Shropshire Light Infantry; *b.* 1879; 3rd *s.* of late Capel Hanbury and Catherine Sophia Hanbury; *m.* 1st, 1905, Jess, *d.* of W. G. Allan; three *d.* (one *s.* killed in action 1945, Sqdn. Ldr. R.A.F., D.F.C. and bar); 2nd, Vanda, *d.* of late F. W. Wood. *Educ.:* Eastbourne College. Entered Army, 1899; Major, 1915; Brigadier-General, 1919-20; Lt.-Col. 1923; Col. 1925; served South African War, 1899-1902 (Queen's medal and four clasps, King's medal and two clasps); European War, 1914-18 (despatches, D.S.O., C.M.G., Order of SS. Maurice and Lazarus, Italy); Order of the Redeemer (Greece), and White Eagle (Serbia); Legion of Honour (France), Croix de Guerre, Military Cross (Greek); Assist. Director of Territorial Army, War Office, 1929-32; Commander 141st (5th London) Infantry Brigade T.A., 1932-36; A.D.C. to the King, 1932-36; retired pay, 1936. *Address:* Coopers, Laughton, Lewes, Sussex. *T.:* Ripe 225 [*Died* 2 *March* 1966.

HANBURY-WILLIAMS, Sir John (Coldbrook), Kt., 1950; C.V.O. 1956; Chairman, Courtaulds Ltd., 1946-62, retired; Director, Bank of England, 1936-63; one of H.M.'s Lieuts. for City of London since 1936; a Gentleman Usher to King George V, 1931, to King Edward VIII, 1936, and to King George VI, 1937-46, Extra Gentleman Usher to King George VI, 1946-52, and to the Queen since 1952; *b.* 1892; *s.* of late Maj.-Gen. Sir John Hanbury-Williams, G.C.V.O., K.C.B., C.M.G.; *m.* 1928, Princess Zenaida Cantacuzene; one *s.* two *d.* *Educ.:* Wellington College. High Sheriff of the County of London, 1943 and 1958. *Address:* 7 Princes Gate, S.W.7. *Club:* Turf. [*Died* 10 *Aug.* 1965.

HANCOCK, Anthony John, (Tony Hancock); Actor; Film and Television Comedian; *b.* Birmingham, 12 May 1924; *s.* of John and Lucy Lilian Hancock; *m.* 1950, Cicely Romanis (marriage dissolved, 1965); *m.* 1965, Freddie Ross. *Educ.:* Durlston Court, Swanage; Bradfield Coll., Reading. Served War of 1939-45; R.A.F. 1942; toured with R.A.F. Gang Show; demobilized 1946. Windmill Theatre, London, 1948. Played Tutor to Archie Andrews in Educating Archie, B.B.C., 1951-53; Hancock's Half Hour, B.B.C., 1954- (televised, 1956-60, concluding with résumé The Best of Hancock); 'Hancock' B.B.C. TV Series, 1961; ITV Series 'Hancock', 1963. Has also appeared in pantomime and variety. *Films:* The Rebel, 1961; The Punch and Judy Man, 1963; The Wrong Box, 1966. Television Award, Comedian of the Year, 1959, 1960. *Recreations:* reading, travel, cricket. *Address:* c/o Delfont-Grade Agency, 235 Regent St., W.1. [*Died* 25 *June* 1968.

HANCOCK, Sir Henry (Drummond), G.C.B. 1962 (K.C.B. 1950); K.B.E. 1947; C.M.G. 1942; *b.* Sheffield, Yorks, 17 Sept. 1895; *o. s.* of Percy G. Hancock; *m.* 1926, Elizabeth, *d.* of Captain H. Toop, R.N.(E.) (retired); one *s.* one *d.* *Educ.:* Haileybury; Exeter Coll., Oxford. Chairman: Local Govt. Commn. (Eng.); N.E.D.C.; Phosphate and Sugar Confectionery Industry; Director: Booker Bros., McConnell & Co.; Yorkshire Insurance Co. Served European War, 1915-18, 2/5 Sherwood Foresters and Intelligence Corps; entered Home C.S., 1920; served Min. of Labour; Office of the Lord Privy Seal; National Assistance Bd.; Home Office and Ministry of Home Security; Sec.-General, British Purchasing Commission and British Raw Materials Mission, U.S.A., 1941-1942; Dep. Sec. Ministry of Supply, 1942-1945; Dep. Sec. Min. of Nat. Insurance, 1945-48, Permanent Sec., 1949-51; Permanent Secretary, Ministry of Food, 1951-55; Chairman, Board of Inland Revenue, 1955-1958, retired. *Address:* 69 Courtfield Gardens, S.W.5. *T.:* Frobisher 3939. *Club:* Oxford and Cambridge University. [*Died* 24 *July* 1965.

HANCOCK, Kingsley Montague, C.B.E. 1962; Director of Scottish Prison and Borstal Services 1950-61, retired; *b.* 5 April 1899; *m.* 1923, Hilda Maysie (*née* Glenn); one *d.* *Educ.:* Bristol Grammar School; Exeter College, Oxford (Scholar). Lieut. Somerset Light Infantry 1917; Assistant Auditor, Exchequer and Audit Department, 1919, Auditor, 1922; Private Secretary to the Comptroller and Auditor General, 1926-1928; Secretary, Scottish Physical Training and Recreation Grants Cttee., 1938; Principal, Scottish Home Dept., 1939, Asst. Sec. 1948. *Recreations:* hockey goalkeeping for thirty years and now watching hockey goalkeepers; economic and political history; philately; needlework tapestry. *Address:* 16 Chester Street, Edinburgh 3. *T.:* 031-225 8159. [*Died* 13 *Sept.* 1969.

HANCOCK, Tony; *see* Hancock, A. J.

HAND, The Hon. Learned; United States Circuit Judge for Second Circuit, retired; *b.* 27 Jan. 1872; *s.* of Samuel Hand and Lydia Coit (*née* Learned); *m.* 1902, Frances Amelia Fincke; three *d. Educ.:* Albany Academy, Albany, N.Y.; Harvard (A.B. 1893); Harvard Law School (LL.B. 1896). Practised law: in Albany for six years, in New York, Nov. 1902-April 1909, when became U.S. District Judge for Southern District of New York; Circuit Judge from Dec. 1924; retired, 1951. Hon. LL.D.: Columbia Univ., 1930; Yale Univ., 1931; Pennsylvania Univ. 1933; Amherst 1938; Dartmouth 1938; Harvard 1939; Princeton, 1947; New School of Social Research 1950; New York Univ. 1951; Cambridge (England) 1952; State of New York Univ., 1952; Univ. of Chicago, 1952; Washington Univ., St. Louis Missouri, 1953; Yeshiva Univ., N.Y., 1953; Wesleyan Univ., 1957. *Publications:* articles in legal magazines; collection of papers and addresses under title The Spirit of Liberty, 1952. *Recreations:* travel and reading; in younger days did considerable walking; tried golf and tennis. *Address:* 142 East 65th St., New York, N.Y. *T.:* Rhinelander 5488. *Clubs:* Athenæum; Century, Harvard (New York City). [*Died* 18 *Aug.* 1961.

HANDLEY, William Sampson, Consulting Surgeon Middlesex Hospital; late Vice-President of R.C.S., England, President Section of Surgery, Royal Society of Medicine and Medical Director Bournemouth Municipal Cancer Clinic; formerly Hunterian Professor of Surgery and Pathology in the Royal College of Surgeons of England and Capt. R.A.M.C.(T.); M.D., M.S. (Lond.); F.R.C.S. (Eng.); Hon. Fellow Amer. Coll. of Surgeons and Med. Society of London; Hon. Fellow Royal Society of Medicine; Foreign Member Academy of Medicine of Rome and of Royal Flemish Acad. of Medicine; *m.* 1908, Muriel, *d.* of late Rev. Clayton Rigby of Great Yarmouth; four *s.* one *d. Publications:* papers and lectures on the surgery of the abdomen and of tumours; Cancer of the Breast and its Operative Treatment, 1906 (translated into French, 1909), second edition, 1922; The Genesis of Cancer, 1932. *Address:* 35A Welbeck Street, W.1. *T.:* Welbeck 4737; Waveney House, St. Olaves, Nr. Gt. Yarmouth, Norfolk. *T.:* Fritton 258. [*Died* 18 *March* 1962.

HANDLEY-DERRY, Henry Forster, C.B.E. 1932; *b.* 20 July 1879; *s.* of late John D. Derry and late Edith F. Handley; *m.* 1908, Beatrice M. Hopkins (*d.* 1949), *e. d.* of Arthur Hopkins, R.W.S.; one *s.* Entered Consular Service, China, 1901; called to Bar, Middle Temple, 1910; Consul-General, Chungking, 1927-30; acting Consul-General, Tsinanfu, 1930-31; Consul-General, Yunnanfu, Yunnan, 1932-33; Consul-Gen., Tsingtao, Shantung, 1934; retired, 1939; Jubilee Medal; Coronation Medal. *Recreations:* gardening, walking. *Address:* Garsdale, Emsworth, Hants. *T.:* Emsworth 2316. *Club:* Royal Automobile. [*Died* 23 *July* 1966.

HANDLEY PAGE, Sir Frederick; *see* Page, Sir F. H.

HANKEY, 1st Baron, *cr.* 1939, of The Chart; **Maurice Pascal Alers Hankey,** P.C. 1939; G.C.B., *cr.* 1919 (K.C.B., *cr.* 1916; C.B. 1912); G.C.M.G., *cr.* 1929; G.C.V.O. *cr.* 1934; LL.D. (Hon.) Birmingham, Edinburgh, and Cambridge; D.C.L. (Hon.) Oxford; F.R.S. 1942; *b.* 1 April 1877; 3rd *s.* of late Robert Alers Hankey of S. Australia and Brighton; *m.* 1903, Adeline, *d.* of A. de Smidt, formerly Surveyor General of Cape Colony; three *s.* one *d. Educ.:* Rugby. Joined Royal Marine Artillery, 1895; served in H.M.S. Ramillies, flagship and 2nd flagship, Mediterranean, 1899-1901; Naval Intelligence Dept., 1902-1906; Capt. 1912; Lt.-Col., Nov. 1914; Col. retired, 1929; Assistant Secretary, Committee of Imperial Defence, 1908; Secretary: Committee Imperial Defence, 1912-38; War Cabinet, 1916, Imperial War Cabinet, 1917-18; Cabinet, 1919-38, and Clerk of the Privy Council, 1923-38; Minister without Portfolio in War Cabinet, 1939-40; Chancellor of the Duchy of Lancaster, 1940-41; Paymaster-Gen., 1941-42. Sec. Gen. Imperial Conf., 1921, 1923, 1926, 1930 and 1937; a Director: Suez Canal Company, 1938-39 and 1945-; Royal Insurance Co., 1938-39 and 1942-; Jorehaut Tea Co., 1945-; Nile Insurance Co. (Cairo), 1947-. Member of Permanent Mandates Commission, Geneva, 1939; Chairman of: Scientific Advisory Cttee. and Engineering Advisory Cttee. 1941-42; Technical Personnel Cttee. 1941-52; Interdepartmental Cttee. on Further Education and Training; Cttee. on Higher Appointments, 1943; Cttee. on Imperial Agricultural Bureaux, 1943; Cttee. on Television, 1943; and Colonia Products Research Council, 1943-53; Hon. M.I.E.E. 1943; Member of Minister of Supply's Advisory Council on Scientific Research and Technical Development, 1947-1949; Colonial Research Council, 1949-53. British Secretary Peace Conference, 1919; Washington Conference, 1921; Genoa Conference, 1922; London International Conference on Reparations, 1924; Secretary-General, Hague Conference, 1929-30, London Naval Conference, 1930, and Lausanne Conference, 1932. Member of Governing Body of Rugby School, 1925-46. Romanes Lecturer (Oxford), 1951. Adviser to Japanese Ambassador on visit of H.R.H. the Crown Prince of Japan, 1953; Grand Officer, Legion of Honour, 1951; Grand Cross of the Crown of Italy, 1920; Grand Cross of the Crown of Belgium, 1921; Japanese Order of the Rising Sun, First Class, 1955; Assoc. Mem. French Académie de Marine, 1956. *Publications:* Government Control in War, 1945; Diplomacy by Conference, 1946; Politics, Trials and Errors, 1949; The Supreme Command, 1914-18, 1961; Forewords to Major-General F. S. G. Piggott's Broken Thread, 1950, and Mr. R. T. Paget's Manstein, 1951, and Postscript to Viscount Maugham's U.N.O. and War Crimes, 1951 and F. T. P. Veale's Crimes Discreetly Veiled; The Supreme Control at the Paris Peace Conference, 1919, 1963 (*posthumous*). *Heir: s.* Hon. Sir Robert Maurice Alers Hankey, K.C.M.G., K.C.V.O. *Address:* Highstead, Limpsfield, Surrey. *Clubs:* Athenæum, United Service. [*Died* 26 *Jan.* 1963.

HANKEY, Richard Lyons A.; *see* Alers Hankey.

HANN, Edmund Lawrence, *b.* 19 Aug. 1881; *s.* of Edmund Mills Hann and Mary Brown; *m.* 1907, Mary Alice Redwood; four *d. Educ.:* Haileybury. Gold medallist South Wales Institute of Engineers; past Chm. Monmouthshire and South Wales Coalowners Association. Past Chm. of Powell Duffryn Ltd. *Address:* Tregarth, Creigiau, nr. Cardiff. *T.:* Pentyrch 358. *Club:* Cardiff and County (Cardiff). [*Died* 10 *Aug.* 1968.

HANNAN, Albert James, C.M.G. 1946; Q.C. (Aust.); Chairman, Metropolitan Transport Advisory Council since 1956; Acting Judge of the Supreme Court of South Australia, in 1954, 1955, and 1956; formerly Crown Solicitor and Solicitor for Railways, South Australia; Member of Council of University of Adelaide since 1939; Warden of the Senate of the University; *b.* Port Pirie, S. Australia, 27 July 1887; *m.* 1st, 1919, Elizabeth Mary Catherine Rzeszkowski (*d.* 1922); 2nd, 1927, Una Victoria Measday; two *d. Educ.:* Sacred Heart College, Semaphore; Adelaide University. B.A. hons. 1909, LL.B. 1912, M.A. 1914. Called to Bar,

South Australia, 1913. K.C., S. Aust., 1935. Decoration "Pro Ecclesia et Pontifice" 1952: Papal knighthood of St. Sylvester (K.S.S.) 1955. *Publications:* Local Court Practice, 1934; Summary Procedure of Justices, 1957 (3rd edn.); Life of Chief Justice Way, 1960. *Recreation:* bowls. *Address:* 19 Robe Terrace, Medindie, South Australia. *Club:* Adelaide (Adelaide). [*Died* 1 *Jan.* 1965.

HANNAY, Sir Hugh Augustus Macnish, Kt. 1934; V.D.; Col. Auxiliary Force of India; retd. as Director Chinnor Industries Ltd.; *b.* 14 May 1878; *s.* of Henry Eric Sutherland Hannay and Maria Josephine Hughesden; *m.* 1903, Reine, (*d.* 1952), *d.* of Richard Rowe, Horsham. *Educ.:* Oundle. Arrived in India 1897; engaged in mica mining; manager of F. F. Chrestien and Co's Mica Mines, 1900; Assistant Traffic Superintendent, East Indian Railway, 1906; General Traffic Manager, 1923; on special duty reorganising and amalgamating the East Indian and Oudh and Rohilkhand Railways, 1924-25; Chief Operating Superintendent, 1925; Member of Railway Board, Government of India, 1929-32; General Manager, Eastern Bengal Railway, 1932; General Manager, East Indian Railway, 1933-36, retd.; Pres. Indian Railway Conf. Assoc., 1933. *Recreations:* shooting, and fishing. *Address:* c/o Lloyds Bank, 6 Pall Mall, S.W.1. *Clubs:* Oriental; Royal Thames Yacht. [*Died* 12 *March* 1962.

HANNAY, Rt. Rev. Thomas, D.D.; *b.* 10 June 1887; *y. s.* of John Hannay and Martha Johnstone. *Educ.:* University of Liverpool B.A., 1907; Queens' College, Cambridge, B.A. 1910; M.A. 1914; Hon. Fellow, 1952; D.D. Lambeth, 1954. Ordained, 1910; Curate of Holmfirth, 1910-14; Universities' Mission to Central Africa, Diocese of Nyasaland, 1914-27; Community of the Resurrection, Mirfield, 1927-42; Principal, College of the Resurrection, 1933-40; Bishop of Argyll and The Isles, 1942-62; Primus of the Episcopal Church in Scotland, 1952-62. *Address:* House of The Resurrection, Mirfield, Yorks. *T.:* Mirfield 3318. [*Died* 31 *Jan.* 1970.

HANNAY, Sir Walter Fergusson (Leisrinck), Kt., *cr.* 1951; Consulting Physician to Hospital Saturday Fund; Knight Chirurgeon to Knights of the Round Table; Medical Consultant to Open Way Clinic; Fellow of Royal Society of Medicine; Fellow of Hunterian Society (on council); Past Pres. Chelsea Clinical Soc.; Mem. Med. Soc. of London; Mem. Harveian Soc.; Mem. Osler Club (Med. writing); Clinical Assistant (Senior Hospital Medical Officer) West End Hospital for Neurology and Neurosurgery; Clinical Assistant St. Mary's Hospital; Divisional Surgeon St. John Ambulance Brigade, London (Prince of Wales's) District; *b.* London, 22 November 1904; *s.* of David Fergusson Hannay; *m.* Doris Leslie; no *c.* *Educ.:* Berkhamsted School; Guy's Hospital. M.R.C.S. (Eng.), L.R.C.P. (Lond.); Resident M.O., Horton General Hosp., Banbury, 1928; Clinical Asst. Lambeth Hosp., 1928; Princess Beatrice Hosp., 1930-35; Nat. Heart Hosp., 1938-48; Prof. Pembry Prize, Guy's Hosp. Physical Soc., 1925. Pres. East Herts Liberal Assoc. Pres. Herts Beekeepers' Assoc. Chm., Noise Abatement Soc., 1959-60. Vice-Pres. National Pure Water Association. *Publications:* contrib. to Medical Science, on Acme Vulgaris, Physiology of Sleep, Diesel Fumes, Cancer of Lung, Noise as a Health Hazard, etc. *Recreations:* fishing, gardening, chess. *Address:* 55 Harley St., W.1. *T.:* Langham 2422. *Clubs:* Flyfishers', Royal Automobile. [*Died* 14 *Aug.* 1961.

HANNAYS, Sir (Leonard) Courtenay, Kt. 1957; Q.C. (Trinidad) 1937; Minister without Portfolio, Trinidad; Barrister; *b.* Trinidad, 3 May 1892; *s.* of George Samuel and Sarah Ann Hannays; *m.* Victoria Delfina (*née* Gonzalez); four *s.* five *d.* *Educ.:* Tunapuna E.C. School; Queen's Royal College; Trinidad Scholar, Gray's Inn. Qualified Bar Finals, 1913 (Certificate of Honour). Vice-Chairman Trinidad Bar Association; Member: Standing Closer Assoc.; Cttee. on West Indian Fedn.; Charter Member, University College of the West Indies; Chancellor of the Anglican Diocese. Chairman: Ne Plus Ultra Arbitration Commn.; Rent Assessment Bd., 1941-47, and many other Govt. bds.; Legislative Council, 1943-56; Executive Council, 1946-56. Delegate, Trinidad Delegations, 1946-55. Trinidad Chef de Mission, First Pan-American Games and British Empire Games, 1954. *Address:* 19 St. Vincent St., Port of Spain, Trinidad, W.I. *Clubs:* Queen's Park Cricket, Arima and Union Park Race Maple (Trinidad). [*Died* 10 *June* 1964.

HANNON, Sir Patrick Joseph Henry, Kt., 1936; Vice-President, Commonwealth-Industries Association and of F.B.I.; Dep. Chm. Sheffields Ltd.; late Deputy Chairman Birmingham Small Arms Group of Companies and Daimler Company; late Director James Booth & Co. Ltd.: Member Dollar Exports Council; President: Aston Villa Football Club; Midland Assoc. of Building Societies; Past President: Ideal Benefit Soc.; Birmingham Boys' and Girls' Union; Soc. of Commercial Accts.; Mem. Court of Governors, Birmingham Univ.; Governor John Fisher School; Vice-President and Member Council, Birmingham Chamber of Commerce; late Member Post Office Advisory Council; Vice-President Royal Eye Hospital, S.E.1; Hon. Treasurer, Apostleship of the Sea; late Public Morality Council; Chairman Political Committee Constitutional Club, 1927-36. Chairman of Club, 1936-55, Vice-Pres.. 1955-; late Chm. Political Cttee. Carlton Club; *m.* 1st, 1894, Mary (*d.* 1928), *d.* of Thomas Wynne, Castlebar; 2nd, 1931, Amy Hilda Gordon (*d.* 1960), *d.* of late James Barrett. *Educ.:* Royal College of Science; Royal University of Ireland. Actively engaged in the promotion of agricultural co-operation among Irish farmers, 1896-1904; Assistant Secretary and subsequently Chief Organiser, Irish Agricultural Organisation Society; awarded Diploma of Royal Agricultural Society of England, 1899; Director, Irish Agricultural Wholesale Society, 1901-4; reported on agriculture in various countries, 1902-7; visited the United States and Canada on behalf of Irish Industrial Movement, 1904; Director of Agricultural Organisation to the Government of Cape Colony, 1905-9; J.P. for all the districts of Cape Colony, 1907-9; contested (U.) East Bristol, 1910; Vice-President, Grand Council, Tariff Reform League, 1910-14; Member General Council National Service League, 1911-15; Member Navy League Executive, 1910-11 and 1918; General Secretary of the Navy League, and Editor of The Navy, 1911-18; Founder and Hon. Sec. Navy League Overseas Relief Fund and Navy League Education Fund, 1916-18; Director British Commonwealth Union, 1918-1925. M.P. (U.) Birmingham (Moseley), Mar. 1921-Feb. 1950; Hon. Secretary, Industrial Group in the House of Commons, 1921-29; Member Estimates Cttee., House of Commons, 1921-38; National Whitley Council Civil Service, 1922-29; First Gen. Sec. and Joint Founder of the Comrades of the Great War; Joint Hon. Sec. Imperial Exhibition, 1915; F.R.G.S., F.S.S., F.R.E.S., F.R.Econ.S.; F.R.S.A. (medal, 1910); Hon. Sec. National Aerial Defence Association, 1912-15; Chairman, Central Committee, Boys' Naval Brigade, 1911-20; ex-Chairman, National Council of Inland Waterways; Master of the Worshipful Company of Pattenmakers, 1930-31 and 1931-32; President: Industrial

Transport Association, 1927-37; Institute of Export, 1939-43; British and Latin-American Chamber of Commerce, 1935-53 (now Hon. Vice-Pres.); Vice-Pres. Nat. Assoc. of Brit. Manufacturers (Pres. 1935-53); Member Executive Committee British Empire Exhibition, Wembley, 1924 and 1925; Past President, Central Chamber of Agriculture. *Address:* 9 Campbell Court, 1-10 Queen's Gate Gardens, S.W.7. *T.:* Knightsbridge 9894. *Clubs:* Carlton, Coningsby, Constitutional; Moseley Golf, Conservative, Midland Conservative (President, 1922-29), (Birmingham). [*Died* 10 *Jan.* 1963.

HANSON, Rev. Preb. Richard, M.A., B.D.; Fellow of King's Coll., London; *b.* 1 March 1880; *s.* of late Alfred Hanson, York; *m.* Esther, *d.* of late Edward Dickenson, Stockton-on-Tees; no *c.* *Educ.:* privately; Queen's Coll., Oxford. Curate, St. Mark, Camberwell, 1903-8; St. Albans Cathedral, 1908-11; Putney, 1911-16; T.C.F. 1917-19 (despatches); Chaplain and Tutor, King's College, London, 1919-24; Vicar of St. Botolph Without, 1924-32; Lecturer and Tutor since 1924; Select Preacher, University of Oxford, 1924-25; Dean of King's College, 1932-45; Examining Chaplain to Bishop of Southwark, 1932-46, and to the Bishop of London, 1946-56. Hon. Chaplain to Bishop of Gloucester, 1934-46; Prebendary of Caddington Major in St. Paul's, 1935-57 (Prebendary Emeritus, 1957). *Address:* 49 Eglinton Road, Chingford, E.4. *Club:* Athenæum. [*Died* 14 *Aug.* 1963.

HAPPELL, Sir Alexander John, Kt., *cr.* 1942; O.B.E. 1925; J.P.; *b.* 13 June 1887; *e. s.* of late W. A. Happell, I.C.S., Ayr, Scotland; *m.* 1930, Doris, *d.* of W. Parbury, Toorak, Melbourne, Victoria; three *s.* *Educ.:* Tonbridge School. Joined Indian Police, 1907; served as Asst. and District Supt. of Police, Deputy Commissioner Madras City, Supt. Special Branch C.I.D., Deputy Inspector-General, Commissioner of Police and Inspector-General of Police, Madras; retired, 1942. Served European War, 1916-19, attached to Indian Army. *Recreations:* hunting (M.F.H. Madras Hunt, 1928-29), fishing, shooting, golf. *Address:* 15 Tintern Avenue, Toorak, Victoria, Australia. *Club:* East India and Sports. [*Died* 8 *Jan.* 1968.

HARBACH, Otto A., M.A., Playwright, *b.* Salt Lake City, 18 Aug. 1873; *s.* of Adolf Hauerbach and Sena Olsen; *m.* 1918, Eloise Smith; two *s.* *Educ.:* Knox Coll., Galesburg; Columbia Univ.. Prof. of English at Whitman Coll., Wash., 1895-1901; Member, Phi Gamma Delta; engaged in advertising work and on staffs of N.Y. newspapers, 1902-10; amongst many other plays wrote (with W. A. McGuire Kid Boots, 1923; (with Frank Mandel and Irving Cæsar) No, No, Nanette, 1924; (with Oscar Hammerstein 2nd) Rose Marie, 1924; (with Oscar Hammerstein 2nd and Frank Mandel) The Desert Song, 1926; (with Oscar Hammerstein 2nd) Good Boy, 1928; (with Irving Cæsar) Nina Rosa, 1929; subsequently engaged in motion picture work with Warner Bros, 1930-31, collaborating with Jerome Kern. Wrote the Cat and the Fiddle, 1931; Roberta, 1933; The Forbidden Melody, 1936. *Recreations:* golf, riding, driving. *Address:* c/o A.S.C.A.P., 575 Madison Ave., New York, N.Y., U.S.A. *Clubs:* Lambs', Larchmont Yacht (New York). [*Died* 24 *Jan.* 1963.

HARCOURT, Sir John R.; *see* Harcourt, Sir R. J. R.

HARCOURT, Sir (Robert) John (Rolston). Kt. 1957; J.P.; Alderman, Belfast City Council; firm of F. E. Harcourt & Co. Ltd., coal importers. M.P. (N. Ire.) Woodvale Div. of Belfast, 1950-55; Member of N. Ireland Senate, 1955. Lord Mayor of Belfast, 1955. J.P. Belfast; High Sheriff, Belfast, 1949. Fell. of Inst. of Directors. *Address:* 47 High Street, Belfast; 60 Malone Road, Belfast 9. [*Died* 25 *Aug.* 1969.

HARCOURT, Robert Vernon; *b.* 7 May 1878; *s.* of late Rt. Hon. Sir W. Harcourt, M.P., leader of the House of Commons, and Elizabeth (*d.* 1928), *d.* of J. L. Motley, United States Minister in London, author of The Dutch Republic; *m.* 1911, Margorie, *d.* of late W. S. Cunard; one *d.* *Educ.:* Eton; Trinity College, Cambridge, Honours History Tripos; Clerk Foreign Office, 1900-6; M.P. (L.) Montrose Burghs, 1908-18; Lieut. R.N.V.R., 1914-18; Pilot Officer, R.A.F.V.R., Feb. 1939; Flight Lieut. Aug. 1939. *Publications:* An Angel Unawares, comedy, 3 acts, Terry's, 1905; A Question of Age, comedy, 3 acts (Court), 1906. *Address:* 9 Headfort Place, S.W.1; Malwood, Lyndhurst. *Clubs:* Turf, M.C.C., Roy. Lymington Yacht. [*Died* 8 *Sept.* 1962.

HARCOURT-SMITH, Air Vice-Marshal Gilbert, C.B. 1946; C.B.E. 1941; M.V.O. 1937; R.A.F.; *b.* 7 May 1901; *m.* 1931, Monica, *d.* of late Ernest Edwin Beare, C.B.E.; two *s.* Commissioned R.A.F. 1920; active service Kurdistan, 1922-23; Southern Desert, 1928; Group Captain, 1940; Air Commodore. 1942. Qualified R.A.F. Staff College, 1935; Gp. Capt. (Ops.) No. 11 Gp. Fighter Comd. throughout Battle of Britain; S.A.S.O., H.Q., A.C.S.E.A., 1945; Director of Organisation, Air Min., 1946-48; A.O.C. No. 12 Group Fighter Command, 1948-51; Head of the United Kingdom Service Liaison Staff, Australia, 1951-53; Commandant, School of Land-Air Warfare, Old Sarum, 1953-55, retired. *Address:* Sonamarg, Little Kingshill, Great Missenden, Bucks. [*Died* 16 *Dec.* 1968.

HARCUS, Rev. A(ndrew) Drummond, O.B.E. 1952; M.A., D.D.; *b.* 3 Dec. 1885; *s.* of Rev. William Harcus, M.A.; *m.* 1922, Veira, *d.* of Rev. Alex. Spark, Church of Scotland; one *d.* *Educ.:* Wesley College, Sheffield; Glasgow University; Westminster College, Cambridge. Ordained, 1911; Minister of Presbyterian Church in Malaya, 1915, in Ealing, 1923; Moderator of Presbyterian Church of England, 1944; General Secretary, Presbyterian Church of England, 1945-52; Moderator of Free Church Federal Council of England and Wales, 1951; Vice-President, British Council of Churches, 1958-1960. Hon. D.D. Glasgow, 1945. *Publications:* contrib. to Expository Times. *Recreation:* music. *Address:* 33 Crediton Hill, N.W.6. *T.:* Hampstead 4934. *Club:* Athenæum. [*Died* 10 *May* 1964.

HARDAKER, Benjamin Rigby, C.I.E. 1947; *b.* 27 Nov. 1890; *s.* of Robert Hardaker; *m.* 1st, Janet Robinson; one *s.* two *d.* (and one *s.* decd.). 2nd, Agnes Halliwell. *Educ.:* Bacup Central School; Newchurch Grammar School; Rochdale Secondary School. Officer, Customs & Excise, 1911; Surveyor, 1930; Inspector, 1936; Collector, Hull, 1945; Senior Adviser, Central Excises, Central Board of Revenue, India, 1945; Supt. Inspector, Customs and Excise, 1948; Deputy Chief Inspector, Customs and Excise, 1949-52, retired. *Recreations:* music, gardening. *Address:* 64 Portland St., Southport, Lancs. [*Died* 5 *Feb.* 1961.

HARDCASTLE, Mary; Principal of Charlotte Mason College, Sept. 1955-July 1962, retd.; *b.* 24 Sept. 1901; *d.* of late Ven. E. H. Hardcastle. *Educ.:* privately; Charlotte Mason College, Ambleside (teaching certificate). Oxford Diploma in Theology. On staff of: Burgess Hill P.N.E.U. School, 1922-1923; Charlotte Mason College, 1923-38; Vice-Principal, Charlotte Mason Coll., 1938-1942; Warden, Social Service Centre, Woodlands, nr. Doncaster, 1942-45; Sec. to Bishop of Sheffield and Tutor in Adult Religious Education, Diocese of Sheffield, 1945-53; Warden of Whirlow Grange, Diocesan Conference House, Sheffield, 1953-55. Member of Church Assembly (C. of E.), 1950-2., *Address:* St. Monica's, Westbury-on-Trym, Bristol. *Club:* Royal Commonwealth Society. [*Died* 7 *Nov.* 1964.

HARDCASTLE, Monica Alice, S.Th.; Member of Church Assembly, since 1946. *b.* 6 Nov. 1904; *d.* of late Ven. Edward Hoare Hardcastle, Archdeacon of Canterbury, and late Hon. Alice Hardcastle, *d.* of 1st Viscount Goschen. *Educ.:* privately; St. Katharine's School, Wantage; Training College, St. Christopher's College, Blackheath. Gained Lambeth Diploma in Theology, 1931; Asst. Adviser in Religious Education, Chichester Diocese, 1931-47; Assistant Adult Education Officer, Church of England Council for Education, 1947-48; Principal, St. Christopher's College, Blackheath, S.E.3 (Church of England Theological College for Women training for work in Religious Education), 1948-63. Retired, 1964. *Address:* 1 Selbourne House, Chatham Place, Brighton 1. *Club:* Royal Commonwealth Society. [*Died* 14 *Sept.* 1966.

HARDIE, Steven James Lindsay, D.S.O. 1917; Hon. LL.D. Edinburgh, 1944; Hon. LL.D. St. Andrews, 1964; *b.* Paisley 1885; *s.* of late John Hardie, M.A., Paisley; *m.* Maie (*d.* 1939), *d.* of late D. H. Nicolson, Kirkcaldy. *Educ.:* Paisley Grammar School; Glasgow University. Served European War, 1914-19, with 6th Argyll and Sutherland Highlanders and 51st (Highland) Division; commanded 51st (Highland) Bn. Machine Gun Corps in France, Belgium, and Germany (despatches thrice, D.S.O.). Has travelled extensively in the British Commonwealth. Dep. Chm. The King Haakon Fund for Relief in Norway; King Haakon VII Liberty Cross, 1947. Chm. Jute Working Party, 1946-47; Independent Member (apptd. by Pres. of Bd. of Trade), Cinematograph Films Council, 1948; Member: Exec. Cttee. of Scottish Council (Development and Industry); Special Cttee. of Inquiry into Scottish Revenue and Expenditure (apptd. by Sec. of State for Scotland), 1950; British Transport Commn., 1950; Chairman Iron and Steel Corporation of Great Britain, 1950-52; ex-Chm. The British Oxygen Co. Ltd., and associated companies. *Address:* Ballathie Perthshire. *Clubs:* United Service; New (Edinburgh); Western (Glasgow). [*Died* 22 *July* 1969.

HARDIMAN, John Percy, C.B.E. 1919; I.C.S. (retired); *s.* of late George James Hardiman, Kidderminster; *b.* 1874; *m.* 1903, Gertrude Percival Smith (*d.*1953); one *d.* (and one *d.* decd.). *Educ.:* Malvern Coll.; Oriel Coll., Oxford (1st cl. Classical Moderations); Lincoln's Inn. B.A., 1897; entered Indian Civil Service, 1897; Asst. Comr., Burma, 1897; Deputy Accountant-General, Bengal, 1903; Burma 1903; Dep. Comr., Burma, 1910 Comr., Tenasserim Div., Burma, 1920; Chairman, Government of India Committee on Deck Passengers, 1921; Controller of Munitions, Custodian of Enemy Property, and Liquidator of Hostile Firms, Burma, during European War; retired, 1923. *Publications:* (with Sir J George Scott, K.C.I.E.) The Upper Burma Gazetteer; Report on Regular Settlement of the Lower Chindwin District, 1909; Gazetteer of Lower Chindwin District, 1912. *Recreation:* ornithology. *Address:* Hyrons Cottage, Woodside Rd., Amersham. *T.:* Amersham 367. [*Died* 5 *April* 1964.

HARDING, George Frederick Morris, O.B.E. 1950; R.H.A.; *b.* 1874; *s.* of J. J. Harding, Surveyor, Stevenage, Herts, and Sarah Ann, sister of late Harry Bates, A.R.A.; *m.* 1895, Ellen (*d.* 1942), *d.* of James Wheeldon, of Fir Close, Claydon, Oxon; one *d.* *Educ.:* Stevenage Gram. Sch. A pupil of late Harry Bates, A.R.A., John M. Swan, R.A., and Herbert Hampton; elected a member of Royal Society of British Sculptors, 1912; served in France as a Corporal in Royal Engineers, wounded at Ypres, 1917; a Member of the Society of Animal Painters, 1921; Mem. of Royal Ulster Acad. of Arts, 1931, Pres. 1947. Hon. M.A., Queen's Univ, Belfast, 1958. *Principal Works:* Memorial to late Hussey Packe at Prestwold; Memorial to Kenneth, son of Sir Henry and Lady Vansittart-Neale of Bisham Abbey, Bucks; War Memorial at Eastergate, near Chichester; The Capitals of the Nave of Belfast Cathedral; Tomb of 7th Marquess of Londonderry, Mountstewart, Co. Down, N.I., 1952. *Address:* The Studio, 104 Church Road, Holywood, Co. Down, N. Ireland. *T.:* Holywood 3033. [*Died* 15 *Jan.* 1964.

HARDING, George Trevor H.; *see* Hamilton Harding.

HARDING, Lt.-Colonel Maynard Ffolliott, C.M.G. 1918; Indian Army, retired; *b.* Tullamaine Castle, Fethard, Ireland; *s.* of late Henry Maynard Harding; *m.* 1893, Violet (*d.* 1956), *d.* of late Major F. Blumberg, 17th Lancers; no *c.* *Educ.:* abroad. Royal Marine Light Infantry, 1888-93; Indian Army, 1893-20; Commandant 69th Punjabis, 1913-18; served Egypt, 1914-15; Gallipoli, 1915, France, 1915; Aden, 1916-18 (despatches thrice, C.M.G.). Elected People's Deputy, States of Guernsey, 1928; Education Council; Board of Health; Police Cttee.; Housing and Food Exec. Officer, Chelmsford, 1939; Fire Guard, 1940. Journalist. *Address:* Box 17, Doonside, Natal, S. Africa. [*Died* 30 *Dec.* 1961.

HARDINGE, Sir Charles Edmund, 5th Bt., *cr.* 1801; *b.* 15 Nov. 1878; *s.* of 4th Bt. and Evelyn, *d.* of late Maj.-Gen. Maberly, C.B.; *S.* father 1924. *Educ.:* Harrow; Trinity College, Cambridge. *Heir:* *kinsman* Robert Hardinge [*b.* 3 Dec. 1887; *m.* 1st, 1911, Emma Vera (marriage dissolved, 1938), *d.* of Charles Arnold; one *s.* one *d.*; 2nd, 1947, Mrs. Nellie May Houser]. *Address:* 139 Holland Park Avenue, W.11. [*Died* 20 *Oct.* 1968.

HARDMAN, Rev. Oscar, D.D.; Priest-in-charge of Monksilver with Elworthy since 1959; Fellow of King's College, London, 1938; *b.* 30 Aug. 1880; *s.* of late Thomas Hardman, Canterbury; *m.* 1st, 1903, Anne Hunter Fairweather (*d.* 1958); two *s.*; 2nd, 1959, Beatrice Doreen Pearce. *Educ.:* Simon Langton School, Canterbury; University of London, B.A. 1901; B.D. 1909; B.D. (Hons.) 1912; M.A. 1916; D.D. 1923. Ordained, 1906; Assist. Curate of St. Peter, Rochester, 1906-7; Minor Canon of Rochester Cathedral, 1907-13; Sacrist, 1907-11; Precentor, 1911-1913; Master of the Choir School and Librarian to the Chapter, 1909-13; Diocesan Warden of the Society of Sacred Study, 1911-1913; Chaplain of Alleyn's College of God's Gift at Dulwich, 1913-30; Warden of the Rochester and Southwark Diocesan Deaconess Institution, 1916-26; Hon. Chaplain to the Mothers' Union, 1925-30; Hon. Canon of Southwark, 1927-30; Rector of Chislehurst, 1930-36; Professor of Pastoral and Liturgical Theology, King's College, London, 1932-1944; Warden of King's College Theological Hall, 1936-44; Chaplain of St. Monica's Home, Westbury-on-Trym, Bristol, 1944-48; Vicar of Christ Church, Lancaster Gate, W.2, 1948-57; Rural Dean of Paddington, 1950-1956; Prebendary of St. Paul's Cathedral, 1952-59; Prof. of Divinity, Gresham Coll., 1958-62. Examining Chaplain to Bishop of London, 1937-56. *Publications:* The Ideals of Asceticism, 1924; editor of Psychology and the Church, 1925, and of Confirmation (Practical), 1927; A Companion to the 1928

Prayer-Book, 1929; The Christian Life, its Standards and Discipline, 1932; The Resurrection of the Body (White Lectures), 1934; A History of Christian Worship, 1936; The Christian Doctrine of Grace, 1937; Announcing the Psalms and Lessons, 1939; A Prayer Book for 1949, 1946; "But I am a Catholic," 1958. *Address:* Ealdland Cottage, Monksilver, Taunton, Som.
[*Died* 19 *Feb.* 1964.

HARDMAN-JONES, Vice-Admiral Everard John, C.B. 1935; O.B.E. 1920; *b.* 1881; *s.* of late R. J. Hardman-Jones, Woodlands, Binfield, Berks, and Florence Lambert; *m.* 1921, Lilian Ursula, *d.* of late Col. Sir Arthur Pendarves Vivian, K.C.B., V.D., D.L., and *widow* of Captain W. M. Parker, Rifle Brigade; no *c.* *Educ.:* H.M.S. Britannia. Joined Royal Navy, 1897; Commander, 1916; Captain, 1921; served European War, 1914-19; commanded Erebus, special entry cadets training ship, 1927-29; aircraft carriers Furious and Courageous, 1929-1930; Boys' Training Establishment, Shotley and S.N.O., Harwich, 1931-33; A.D.C. to the King, 1932; Rear-Admiral, 1933; Commanding Officer, Coast of Scotland, 1933-35; Vice-Adm., 1937; retired list, 1937; recalled Senior Naval Officer Newhaven Sub-Command, 1942-44. *Address:* Northend House, Hursley, Hants. *T.:* Hursley 254. *Clubs:* United Service, Royal Automobile. [*Died* 28 *June* 1962.

HARDWICKE, Sir Cedric Webster, Kt. 1934; actor; *b.* Lye, Worcs. 1893; *s.* of Edwin Webster Hardwicke and Jessie Masterson; *m.* 1st, Helena (marr. diss.; she *died* 1959), *d.* of Percy Pickard and Jennie Skelton; one *s.* 2nd, Mary Scott (marr. diss.) one *s.* *Educ.:* Bridgnorth. Intended for medical profession; failed to qualify. Came to London and studied at the Royal Academy of Dramatic Art; first appearance on the stage at Lyceum in The Monk and the Woman; after a variety of small parts joined the F. R. Benson Shakespearian Company and toured South Africa; on return to England in 1915 obtained commission in Army and served in France from 1915-22; was the last British Officer to leave war zone; intended to give up stage, but chance meeting with Sir Barry Jackson led to joining the Birmingham Repertory Company and playing a large variety of parts; came to London with this Company early in 1924, and appeared at the Court Theatre in Shaw's Back to Methuselah and as Churdles Ash in The Farmer's Wife; has since played Cæsar in Cæsar and Cleopatra, Richard Varwell in Yellow Sands, Captain Andy in the Show Boat, King Magnus in The Apple Cart, Edward Moulton-Barrett in The Barretts of Wimpole Street; Captain Shotover in Heartbreak House, and Aubrey, the Burglar, in Too True to be Good; Dr. Haggett in The Late Christopher Bean; Prince Mikail Alexandrovich Ouratieff, in Tovarich, 1935-36; Canon Skerritt in Shadow and Substance, New York, 1937-38; Creon, in Antigone, New York, 1946; joined Old Vic Co.—: Toby Belch, Twelfth Night; Dr. Faustus; Gaev, Cherry Orchard. Was principal lead in Malvern Festivals of 1929, 1930, 1931, and 1932. Awarded Delia Austrian Medal by Drama League of New York, 1937-38. Enacted the name parts in the silent film of Nelson; the talking film of Dreyfus; and has also played in The Rome Express, Nell Gwynn, Jew Süss, Bella Donna, Peg of Old Drury, Things to Come, Tudor Rose, Laburnum Grove, The Moon is Down, On Borrowed Time, Wilson, The Winslow Boy, The White Tower, Rommel—Desert Fox, Botany Bay, Helen of Troy, Richard III, The Power and the Prize, The Story of Mankind. Rede Lecturer, Cambridge, 1936. *Publications:* Let's Pretend: Recollections and Reflections of a Lucky Actor, 1932; A Victorian in Orbit: as told to James Brough, 1962; has written many articles on the stage for newspapers. *Club:* Garrick. [*Died* 6 *Aug.* 1964.

HARDY, Rt. Rev. Alexander Ogilvy, D.D., M.A.; Assistant Bishop of Bradford, 1948-57; Vicar of Gargrave-in-Craven, 1948-1957; Hon. Canon of Bradford, 1949-57; *b.* 1891; *s.* of late W. J. Hardy, R.M.; *m.* 1935, Ruth, *d.* of late W. P. Bocock; two *s.* three *d.* B.A. 1914, M.A. 1917, Senior Moderator, 1914, Trinity College, Dublin. D.D. (*jure dig.*) 1938; Deacon, 1915; priest, 1917; Curate of Templemore, Derry, 1915-17; Missionary, Dublin University Mission at Hazaribagh, 1917-35; Head of Dublin University Mission, 1926-35; S.P.G. Missionary at Murhu, 1935-37; Bishop of Nagpur, 1937-48. *Address:* 70 Kimberley Road, Cambridge. *T.:* Cambridge 59867.
[*Died* 14 *Sept.* 1970.

HARDY, Hon. Arthur Charles, P.C. Canada, 1930; K.C. 1934; B.A., LL B; *b.* Brantford, Ont., Canada, 3 Dec. 1872; *s.* of Hon. Arthur S. Hardy, K.C., LL.D, sometime Prime Minister of Ontario, and Mary Morrison, *d.* of Hon. Jos. Curran Morrison, Judge of Appeal, Supreme Court of Ontario; *m.* 1904, Dorothy (*d.* 1949), *d.* of Hon. George T. Fulford, Senator of Canada; one *s.* one *d.* (and one *s.* decd.) *Educ.:* Upper Canada Coll., Toronto; Univ. of Toronto; Osgoode Hall. Called to Bar of Ontario (Osgoode Hall), 1898; practised law for some years, but giving up active practice, engaged extensively in agricultural pursuits, chiefly the breeding of high class cattle; interested in public affairs; appointed to the Senate, 1922; Speaker of Senate of Canada, 1930; Honorary Lieutenant-Colonel Governor-General's Foot Guards, 1931-51. Trustee Nat. Sanitarium Assoc. of Canada; Dir. of Toronto General Trusts Corporation. *Address:* Thornton Cliff, Brockville, Canada; Avondale, Brockville, Ontario. *Clubs:* Royal Canadian Yacht, Toronto (Toronto); Rideau, Royal Golf, University (Ottawa); Montreal Reform (Montreal); Brockville, Brockville Country and Golf (Brockville). [*Died* 13 *March* 1962.

HARDY, Major Eric John, D.S.O. 1917; Royal Scots Greys, 1905-25; *b.* 1884; *y. s.* of Sir Reginald Hardy, 2nd Bt. *Educ.:* Eton. D.L., J.P. Staffordshire; 2nd Lieut. 4th North Staffordshire Regt., 1903; served European War, France and Flanders, Aug. 1914-Nov. 1917, April 1918-Nov. 1918 (despatches, D.S.O.); Co-opted member Staffordshire T.A. Assoc., 1927-44 and 1947-53; Chairman Standing Joint Committee of Staffordshire, 1936-47; Deputy Chairman of Quarter Sessions, Staffordshire, 1939-1956; Dep. Chm. Appeal Cttee., 1939-59; Alderman 1943-52, Vice-Chairman 1941-1943, Chairman 1943-46, of Staffordshire County Council, and its representative on Midland Regional Council for Civil Defence, 1939-45; Chairman Staffs County Licensing Cttee., 1948-56; Chairman, Lichfield Diocesan Board of Finance, 1955-60, Vice-Chairman, 1960-; Member House of Laity of Church Assembly, 1951-62. Pres. Burton and Dist. Br. Old Contemptibles Assoc. since its formation in 1925. *Address:* Holland House, Barton-under-Needwood, Burton-on-Trent. *T.:* Barton-under-Needwood 273.
[*Died* 10 *Dec.* 1965.

HARDY, Professor Evan A., M.S.; Hon. Dr. of Laws, Univ. of Saskatchewan, 1957; United Nations Programme for provision of Operational, Executive and Administrative personnel (OPEX), Ceylon; Technical Training Inst., Amparai; Prof. of Agricultural Engineering, Univ. of Saskatchewan, retd.; *b.* 1890; Naturalized Canadian; *m.* 1917, Lois Hicks; three *d.* *Educ.:* Iowa State Coll. Member: Amer. Soc. of Agricultural Engineers; Soc. of Automotive Engineers; Automobile Assoc. of Ceylon; Agricultural Inst. of Canada; Saskatchewan Institute of Agrologists; Fellow Agricultural Institute of Canada, 1949. Member of High School Board, City of Saskatoon, for eighteen

years, Chairman, 1941-46. *Publications:* The Automobile and Farm Lighting Plant Storage Battery; Gasoline Engine Ignition; Maintenance and Overhaul of the Farm Tractor; Engine Fuels; Engine Lubrication; Maintenance and Operation of Tillage Machinery; Grain Binder Adjustments; Header and Header Barge for Grain Harvesting; Seed Cleaning on the Farm; The Tractor Sweep; Water and Disposal Systems for Homes in Rural Saskatchewan; Farm Shop Work; Harvesting Malting Barley; Tractor Data from Nebraska Tests; Selection of Farm Power; Servicing the Automobile for Winter Driving; Draft Data; Welders and Welding for the Farm Shop; Grain Storage Problems; Land Clearing, etc. *Recreations:* Rugby football (on Board of Governors of Canadian Rugby Union), boys' work camps. *Address:* Technical Training Institute, Amparai, Ceylon.
[*Died* 4 *Dec.* 1963.

HARDY, Lady Isabel G.; *see* Gathorne-Hardy.

HARDY, Thomas Lionel, M.A., M.D., F.R.C.P.; formerly Consulting Physician United Birmingham Hospitals; *b.* 15 April 1887; *s.* of late Rev. Thomas Barker Hardy, Narborough Rectory, Leicester, and Edith Hassell; *m.* 1st, 1916, Elizabeth Clark Ritchie (*d.* 1952); three *s.* one *d.*; 2nd, 1954, Margaret Askham. *Educ.:* Radley Coll. (Class. Schol.); Selwyn Coll., Camb.; Middx. Hosp. Hons. Degree, Science Tripos, Camb., Univ. Entrance Schol. and Senior Broderip Schol., Middlesex Hosp.; Examiner Royal College of Physicians, 1950; Croonian Lecturer, Royal College of Physicians, 1944; President British Society of Gastroenterology, 1948; President Selwyn College Association, 1949-50; President Birmingham Graduates Club, 1951-52. *Publications:* various contributions to medical journals; Croonian Lectures; Order and Disorder in Large Intestine, Lancet, 1945. *Recreation:* gardening. *Address:* St. Mary's, Alfrick, Worcester. *T.:* Suckley 218. *Clubs:* Church House (Worcester), The Club (Malvern).
[*Died* 16 *May* 1969.

HARE, Dorothy Christian, C.B.E. 1919; M.D., F.R.C.P.; retired; late Physician Royal Free Hospital and Elizabeth Garrett Anderson Hospital; *d.* of late Edward Hare, C.S.I., Inspector-General of Hospitals. *Educ.:* Cheltenham Ladies' College; London School of Medicine for Women. Qualified 1905; Hospital appointments, 1906-10; general practice in Cambridge, 1910-16; attached R.A.M.C. Service in Malta, 1916-17; served in Women's Royal Naval Service as Medical Director, 1918-19. *Publications:* in medical journals. *Address:* c/o Coutts and Co., 440 Strand, W.C.2.
[*Died* 19 *Nov.* 1967.

HARE, Edgar James, C.B.E. 1948; *b.* 28 June 1884; *y. s.* of late Rev. E. M. Hare, Rector of Little Dunham, Norfolk; *m.* 1913, Suzanne, *d.* of late Leopold Bezineau, Bordeaux: one *s.* two *d.* *Educ.:* Marlborough. Called to Bar, Lincoln's Inn, 1911; served in Queen's R.W. Surrey and Bedfordshire Regiments, 1916-18; Official Solicitor to Queen Anne's Bounty, 1925-35; Asst. Secretary, 1935-42; Secretary, 1942-48; Treasurer, 1945-48. Member of Legal Board of Church Assembly, 1944-60. *Recreation:* Entomology. *Address:* Harrow Place, Pinden, Dartford, Kent. *T.:* Longfield 2212.
[*Died* 23 *Feb.* 1969.

HARE, Major-General James Francis, C.B. 1945; D.S.O. 1940; *b.* 26 March 1897; *e. s.* of late Major-General Sir Steuart Hare, K.C.M.G., C.B.; *m.* 1st, 1935, Diana Eleanor Woodroffe (*d.* 1940); two *d.*; 2nd, 1945, Eileen Knowles; one *d.* *Educ.:* Malvern; Royal Military College, Sandhurst. 2nd Lt. King's Royal Rifle Corps, 1915; served European War, 1915-18 (despatches); Adjt., 1920-23; Staff College, 1928-29; called to Bar, Inner Temple, 1933; Colonel, 1940; Temp. Maj.-Gen. 1944; retired pay, 1946, with hon. rank of Maj.-Gen. Research Secretary, King George's Jubilee Trust, 1949-56; Assistant Secretary, 1956-60; Secretary, Atlantic College (U.K.) Ltd. and Service by Youth Trust Ltd., 1960-1963. *Address:* 35 Ovington Street, S.W.3. *Clubs:* Naval and Military, Hurlingham.
[*Died* 28 *Aug.* 1970.

HARE, Kenneth, M.A.; F.R.S.L.; F.A.M.S.; *b.* 1888; 2nd *s.* of Alfred Thomas Hare, M.A. Oxon, late Principal, Law Courts Branch of Dept. of the Treasury; *m.* 1926, Mary, *d.* of H. J. Lee-Bennett of the Colonial Service; one *d.* (by former marriage). *Educ.:* St. Paul's School; abroad; Wadham College, Oxford; 2nd Honours, School of English Language and Literature. Commission, 2nd Lieut. 25th London Regiment, Sept. 1914; Lieut. 1915; Liaison Officer attached Belgian Army, Ypres, 1918; Curator of Photographs, Imperial War Museum, at the opening of that department. Poets' Club Gold Medallist, 1925; Lewis K. Lewis Gold Medallist, verse, 1933; Winner Sunday Times prize for best trans. of a sonnet by Philippe Desportes (1546-1606), 1949. *Publications: verse:* Green Fields; Three Poems; Sir Gawayne and the Green Knight, 2nd Ed.; New Poems; The Ballad of Sir John Philpot; Nymphs and Rivers; *prose:* Guide to Bruges (5th ed.); London's Latin Quarter; Our Cockney Ancestors; The Archer's Anthology; Roads and Vagabonds; Gloucestershire (English Counties series); No Quarrel with Fate (Autobiography), 1946; The Last Secrets of the Earth (from the French); contributor to reviews, etc. *Recreations:* picture galleries, music. *Address:* Three Beeches, Bussage, near Stroud, Glos. *T.:* Brimscombe 2385. *Clubs:* Authors'; St. Sebastian (Archery), (Bruge
[*Died* 4 *Jan.* 1962.

HARE, Prof. Hon. Richard Gilbert; Professor of Russian Literature, London University; *b.* 5 Sept. 1907; *s.* of 4th Earl of Listowel; *m.* 1936, Dora] Gordine. *Educ.:* Balliol College, Oxford; abroad. Laming Fellow, Queen's College, Oxford, 1929; Secretary, H.M. Diplomatic Service, 1930; served in Foreign Publicity Dept., Ministry of Information, 1939-46. Rockefeller Foundation Fellow of Hoover Institute, Stanford University, California, 1947; Visiting Professor in Slavic Studies, University of Indiana, U.S.A., 1959. *Publications:* Russian Literature from Pushkin to the Present Day, 1947; Pioneers of Russian Social Thought, 1951; Portraits of Russian Personalities between Reform and Revolution, 1959; Maxim Gorky: Romantic Realist and Conservative Revolutionary, 1962; The Art and Artists of Russia, 1965; also translations of selected novels and stories of Turgenev and Ivan Bunin, and contrib. to Encyclopædia Britannica, Collier's Encyclopædia, The Slavonic Review, American Russian Review, History Today, American Slavic Review, The Connoisseur, etc. *Recreation:* gardening. *Address:* School of Slavonic Studies, London University, Malet Street, W.C.1. [*Died* 14 *Sept.* 1966.

HARES, Ven. Archdeacon Walter P., M.B.E., B.A.; *b.* 12 April 1877; *m.* 1906; two *s.* *Educ.:* King's Lynn; C.M. College, Islington; Durham University. C.M.S. Missionary, 1903; Principal and Warden, Divinity School, Lahore, 1912; Examining Chaplain to Bishop of Lahore, 1916; C.M.S. Missionary in charge Gojra, Panjab, 1917-40; Hon. Canon of Lahore Cathedral, 1929; Staff Major, G.H.Q., Simla, for Soldiers' Welfare Work, 1940; Archdeacon of Sind, 1946; Rector of Somerton, Oxon, 1950. *Publications:* Church History

of First Six Centuries in Persian Urdu, 2nd edition; The Call from the Land of the Five Rivers; An English-Panjabi Dictionary; Jangal Vichch Mangal, the Story of the Gojra Mission in the Chenab Colony, Panjab, 1934; Reviser of Book of Common Prayer in Persian Panjabi, Roman Panjabi, and Gurmukhi; Gojra, the story of a Canal Colony; The Doctrine of the Church of Rome (In Persian-Urdu), 1936; The Teaching and Practice of the Church of Rome in India, 1936, 3rd ed.; The Blessed Virgin Mary and Mariolatry (4th ed.), 1936; Some Claims of the Church of Rome Examined, 2nd ed. 1939; The One Holy Catholic and Apostolic Church, 2nd ed. 1939; A Collection of 900 Panjabi Proverbs, 1940; A History of the Christian Church of the First Six Centuries (2nd Ed.). (English and Persian Urdu). *Address:* College of St. Mark, Audley End, Saffron Walden, Essex.
[*Died* 17 *Sept.* 1962.

HARFORD, Sir (George) Arthur, 2nd Bt., *cr.* 1934; Lt.-Col.; Director Cater Brightwen & Co. Ltd., 38 Lombard St., E.C.3; *b.* 29 Dec. 1897; *s.* of Sir John Charles Harford, 1st Bt., and Blanche, *d.* of Rt. Hon. Henry Cecil Raikes; *S.* father 1934; *m.* 1931, Anstice Marion, *y. d.* of Sir Alfred Tritton, 2nd Bt.; two *s.* one *d.* *Educ.:* Harrow; Sandhurst. With 21st (E. of I.) Lancers, 1917-23; served with 17/21st Lancers and General Staff 1940-45. J.P. Hampshire 1953; formerly J.P., D.L., Cards., High Sheriff, 1938-39. *Heir:* *s.* John Timothy Harford [*b.* 6 July 1932; *m.* 1962, Carolyn, *d.* of Brig. Guy John de Wette Mullens, O.B.E.; one *s.* one *d.*]. *Address:* Lockeridge Down, Marlborough, Wilts. *T.:* Lockeridge 244. [*Died* 18 *Dec.* 1967.

HARGREAVES, Professor George Ronald, O.B.E. 1946; M.Sc.; M.R.C.S., L.R.C.P.; F.R.C.P. (Edin.), F.B.Ps.S.; Nuffield Professor of Psychiatry and Head of Department of Psychiatry, Leeds University, since 1955; Hon. Consultant Psychiatrist, Leeds General Infirmary and Leeds Regional Hosp. Board; *b.* 14 July 1908; *s.* of James Arthur Hargreaves and Ada Jubb; *m.* 1933, Eva Chrystobel Gladys Byrde, M.B., B.Ch. (Cantab.), D.A. (*d.* 1962); four *d.* *Educ.:* Mill Hill Sch.; Univ. Coll. Lond.; Univ. Coll. Hosp. Med. School. M.R.C.S. (Eng.), L.R C.P. (Lond.) 1933; M.Sc. Leeds 1957; M.R.C.P. (Edin.) 1959, F.R.C.P.E. 1962. Clinical Assistant, Dept. of Psychological Medicine. Univ. Coll. Hosp., London; Asst. M.O., Hill End Hosp. for Mental and Nervous Diseases; M.O., The Cassell Hosp.; Asst. Physician, Tavistock Clinic. Served War, 1940-45: Lt.-Col. R.A.M.C.; Command Psychiatrist, Northern Command; Psychiatrist to Directorate of Selection of Personnel; Asst. Dir., Directorate of Army Psychiatry. Chief Medical Officer, Unilever Ltd., 1945-48; Chief of Mental Health section, W.H.O. and Secretary, W.H.O. Expert Cttees. on Mental Health, Alcoholism, and Psychiatric Nursing, 1948-55. Heath Clark Lecturer, London Univ., 1957; Bertram Roberts Memorial Lecturer, Yale Univ., 1961. Fellow, Brit. Psychological Soc.; Corresp. Fell., Amer. Psychiatric Assoc.; Corresp. Mem. Société Suisse de Psychiatrie. *Publications:* Psychiatry and the Public Health, 1958; contribs. to professional jls., and publications of the World Health Organisation. *Address:* The University, Leeds 2. *Club:* Savile. [*Died* 17 *Dec.* 1962.

HARGREAVES, Sir Thomas, Kt. 1960; retired; Chairman, Lancashire County Council, Highways and Bridges; Chairman, Lancashire Rivers Board; *b.* 27 Jan. 1889; *m.* 1913, Alice Elizabeth Hodgkinson; one *d.* *Educ.:* Wheelton. *Recreations:* all forms of sport. *Address:* Harwood, Church Road, Leyland, Lancs. *T.:* Leyland 21136.
[*Died* 22 *March* 1966.

HARISINGHJI, Lt.-Gen. Shri Sir, G.C.S.I., *cr.* 1933; G.C.I.E., *cr.* 1929 (K.C.I.E., *cr.* 1918); G.C.V.O., *cr.* 1946 (K.C.V.O., *cr.* 1922); *b.* 1895. *Educ.:* Mayo College, Ajmer; Imperial Cadet Corps, Dehra Dun. Hon. Lt.-Gen. in the British Army; a Representative of India to War Cabinet, 1944. Formerly Ruler of Jammu and Kashmir, but the Crown Prince assumed active reign, 1949, and was elected head of state, 1952. Chancellor, Ben Hindu University, 1943; Hon. LL.D. Punjab and Ben Hindu Univs. *Address:* c/o University of the Panjab, Lahore, Pakistan. [*Died* 26 *April* 1961.

HARKER, Gordon; Actor (on Stage and Screen); *b.* 7 Aug. 1885; *s.* of Joseph and Sarah Harker; *m.* 1938, Christine Barry (*d* 1964). *Educ.:* Ramsey Grammar School. First London appearance in Ellen Terry's revival of Much Ado About Nothing, Imperial Theatre, 1903; with Oscar Asche and Lily Brayton, 1904-13; war service with 8th Hants. Regt., invalided out 1919; among subsequent parts, Batouch in Garden of Allah, 1920, the Sergeant in Quality Street, 1921, Jefferson Davis in Robert E. Lee, 1923, Hackitt in The Ringer, 1926. Walker in Major Barbara, 1929, Hillcott in The Calendar, 1929, Totty in The Case of The Frightened Lady, 1931, Cheatle in Hyde Park Corner, 1934, The Frog, The Phantom Light, Number Six, Saloon Bar, Once a Crook, Warn that Man, Acacia Avenue, 1943, The Poltergeist, 1946, Doolittle in Pygmalion, 1951, Small Hotel, 1955; commenced film career in The Ring, 1927. *Recreations:* reading, walking music, photography *Club:* Savage. [*Died* 2 *March* 1967.

HARKNESS, Sir Joseph Welsh Park, Kt., *cr.* 1956; C.M.G. 1941; O.B.E. 1935; B.Sc.; M.B., Ch.B.; D.P.H.; Medical Adviser to Comptroller for Development and Welfare in West Indies since 1946; *b.* 1890; *s.* of late John Harkness of Rosneath, Dunbartonshire; *m.* 1920, Florence Margaret, *d.* of Frederick Furniss, Rockferry; one *s.* one *d.* (and one *s.* killed in action 1943). *Educ.:* Glasgow Academy; Glasgow University. M.A. 1910; M.B., Ch.B., 1914; B.Sc. 1923; D.P.H. 1928; R.A.M.C. S.R. 1914; European War, 1914-19 (despatches twice); C.St.J.; Senior Medical Officer, Palestine, 1920; Deputy Director, Department of Health, 1930; Director of Medical Services, Gold Coast, 1939-42; Director of Medical Services, Nigeria, 1942-46. *Recreation:* yachting. *Address:* c/o Comptroller for Development and Welfare for the West Indies, Barbados; c/o Glyn, Mills & Co., Kirkland House, Whitehall, S.W.1. *Club:* Royal Commonwealth Society.
[*Died* 15 *Dec.* 1962.

HARLECH, 4th Baron, *cr.* 1876; **William George Arthur Ormsby-Gore;** K.G. 1948; P.C. 1927; G.C.M.G., *cr.* 1938; Lord-Lieutenant Merionethshire. 1938-57; Constable of Harlech Castle since 1938; Constable of Caernarvon Castle, 1946-63; an Elected Trustee of British Museum, 1937; a Trustee of the National Gallery, 1927-34 and 1936-41; a Trustee of Tate Gallery, 1931-38 and 1945-1953; Pro-Chancellor of Univ. of Wales, 1945-57; Director: Bank of West Africa (late Chm.); Midland Bank Ltd. (late Chm.); *b.* 11 April 1885; *s.* of 3rd Baron and Lady Margaret Ethel Gordon (*d.* 1950), *d.* of 10th Marquess of Huntly; *S.* father 1938; *m.* 1913, Lady Beatrice Cecil (D.C.V.O. 1947), *d.* of 4th Marquess of Salisbury, K.G., G.C.V.O.; two *s.* three *d.* *Educ.:* Eton; New College, Oxford; B.A., 1908, Hon. Fellow of New Coll., Oxford, 1936; Hon. D.C.L. Oxf., 1937; Hon. LL.D. Univ. of Wales, 1947; F.S.A.; Lieut. Aug. 1914; Capt. Mar. 1915; Staff Capt., May 1915; Active Service in Egypt; Intelligence Officer, Arab Bureau, Oct. 1916; M.P. (U.) Denbigh Dis-

trict, 1910-18, and for Stafford, Dec. 1918-38; Parliamentary Private Secretary to Viscount Milner, and Assistant Secretary, War Cabinet, 1917-18; Assistant Political Officer in Palestine, 1918; Under-Secretary of State for the Colonies, 1922-24 and Nov. 1924-29; Postmaster-General, 1931; First Commissioner of Works, 1931-36; Secretary of State for the Colonies, 1936-38; North-East Regional Commissioner for Civil Defence, Sept. 1939-March 1940; High Commissioner for the United Kingdom in the Union of South Africa and High Commissioner for Basutoland, Bechuanaland, and Swaziland, 1941-1944; Member of the British Delegation to the Peace Conference (Middle Eastern Section), 1919; British official representative on the Permanent Mandates Commission of the League of Nations; member of the Colonial Office Mission to the British West Indies, 1921-22; Chairman East African Parliamentary Commission, 1924; visited British West African Colonies, 1926, and Malaya and Ceylon, 1928; Chairman of the Advisory Council of the Victoria and Albert Museum, 1933; Pres. of the National Museum of Wales, 1937; Ex-Chm. Standing Commission on Museums and Galleries; Chairman Governing Body of the School of Oriental Studies, London University, 1938-41. *Publications:* Florentine Sculptors of the Fifteenth Century, 1930; Guide to the Mantegna Cartoons at Hampton Court, 1935; Guides to the Ancient Monuments of England three vols. *Heir:* s. Rt. Hon. Sir (William) David Ormsby Gore, P.C., K.C.M.G. *Address:* 14 Ladbroke Rd., W.11; Glyn, Talsarnau, Merionethshire.
[*Died* 14 *Feb.* 1964.

HARLOW, Frederick James, O.B.E. 1956; Ph.D., B.Sc., F.Inst.P., A.R.C.Sc., D.I.C.; Hon. Member and Past President, Association of Principals of Technical Institutions; Past Chairman of Council, Association of Technical Institutions; Chairman, Examinations Board. Member, Council, Executive, Policy and Overseas Committees, City and Guilds of London Institute; Hon. Sec., Canterbury and District Branch, Gideons International; Member: Executive Cttee., Sudan United Mission; Governing Body, Simon Langton Schs., Canterbury; Canterbury Technical Coll.; Visitor, General Optical Council; Past Member: Burnham Technical Committee; Council of Overseas Colls. of Arts, Science and Technology; Advisory Committee on Education in the Colonies, Colonial Office; *b.* Whitstable, Kent. *Educ.:* Simon Langton School, Canterbury; Imperial College of Science and Technology. Lectr. in Physics and subsequently Head of Department of Mathematics and Physics, Sir John Cass Technical Coll., 1909-20; in charge of X-Ray and Electromedical Supplies, Army Medical Dept., War Office, 1915-1919; Principal, Municipal Technical Coll., Blackburn, 1921-25; Principal, Wigan and District Mining and Technical Coll., 1925-28; Principal, Chelsea Polytechnic, 1928-49; Assistant Educational Adviser for Technical Education, to Sec. of State for the Colonies, 1950-56. Has undertaken Commissions on Technical Education in East, West and Central Africa, B.W.I., Brit. Territories in Mediterranean and Far East; also the South Seas for the S. Pacific Commission and Govt. of Fiji. *Publications:* Original Researches on Thermal Expansion of Mercury and Fused silica, X-Rays, etc.; joint Author of Technical College Buildings: their Planning and Equipment; Reports to Sec. of State and to various Colonial Govts. on Development Projects in Trade Training, Technical Education, and Colleges of Arts, Science and Technology. *Address:* Tresco 67 St. Swithins Road, Tankerton. Kent. *T.:* Whitstable 4788. [*Died* 22 *Oct.* 1965.

HARLOW, Vincent Todd, C.M.G. 1952; M.A. D.Litt.; Beit Professor of the History of the British Commonwealth, Fellow of Balliol College, Oxford, since 1948; *b.* 14 Aug. 1898; *s.* of late Rev. Vincent Harlow and Esther Agnes Todd; *m.* 1924, Margretta, *d.* of late J. Cory Badcock, J.P., Yarm, Yorks. *Educ.:* Durham School; Brasenose College, Oxford. Temporary commission, Royal Field Artillery, 1917-19 (despatches); Assistant Lecturer in Modern History, University College, Southampton, 1923-26; lecturer, 1926-27; Keeper of Rhodes House Library, Oxf., 1928-38; Beit Lecturer in Colonial History, Oxford, 1930-35; Min. of Information, 1939-45; Rhodes Professor of Imperial History, University of London, King's College, 1938-48. Chairman History and Administration Cttee. of the Colonial Social Science Research Council; Commr. for Constitutional Reform in British Guiana, 1950-1951; Constitutional Consultant, Sudan Govt., 1951-52; Crown Member of Governing Body of School of Oriental and African Studies, London University; a Vice-President of Royal Commonwealth Society; Mem. Bd. of Governors, Commonwealth Inst., 1958-. Corresponding Member Indian Historical Records Commission, 1958; Anglican Mem. Brit. Council of Churches, 1958. *Publications:* Voyages of Capt. Jackson, 1923; West Indies and Guiana, 1623-1667, 1924; History of Barbados, 1927; Christopher Codrington, 1928; critical edition of Ralegh's Discoverie of Guiana, 1928; Ralegh's Last Voyage, 1932; contributions to the Cambridge History of the British Empire; The Historian and British Colonial History (inaugural lecture), 1951; Founding of the Second British Empire, 1763-93, vol. I, 1952; New Continents and Changing Values, vol. II, 1965 (posthumous); British Colonial Developments, 1774-1834; Select Documents (with A. F. Madden), 1953; joint editor with Dr. J. A. Williamson of the Pioneer Histories. *Address:* Fir Tree House, Old Marston, Oxon. *T.:* Oxford 43872. *Club:* Athenæum. [*Died* 6 *Dec.* 1961

HARMAN, Lieut.-General Sir (Antony Ernest) Wentworth, K.C.B. *cr.* 1934 (C.B. 1919); D.S.O. 1916; *b.* 1872; *s.* of late Rev. Canon Samuel Thomas Harman, Chancellor of Cork, of Rathcormac, Co. Cork; *m.* 1902, Dorothy Ricardo (*d.* 1957). *Educ.:* privately. Served European War, 1914-18 (despatches, D.S.O., Brevet Lieut.-Col. and Col., Legion of Honour, Croix de Guerre, C.B.); Commandant Cavalry School, Netheravon; Commanded 1st Cavalry Brigade, Aldershot, 1920-24; A.D.C. to H.M., 1923-28; Colonel on the Staff in Charge of Administration, Northern Command, 1924-26; Comdt. Equitation School and Inspector of Cavalry 1926-30; Col. Queen's Bays, 1930-45; Comd. 1st Div. Aldershot, 1930-34; ret. 1934. *Club:* Cavalry. [*Died* 26 *Sept.* 1961.

HARMAN, Rt. Hon. Sir Charles Eustace, Kt. 1947; **Rt. Hon. Lord Justice Harman;** P.C., 1959; a Lord Justice of Appeal, since 1959; *b.* 22 Nov. 1894; *e. surv. s.* of John E. Harman and Ethel Frances Birch; *m.* 1924, Helen Sarah Le Roy Lewis; two *s.* *Educ.:* Eton (scholar); King's College, Cambridge (scholar). Served in war with Middlesex Regt. (Prisoner); called to Bar, Lincoln's Inn, 1921. K.C. 1935; Judge of the High Court of Justice, Chancery Div., 1947-59. Treas., Lincoln's Inn, 1959-. *Recreations:* fishing, shooting. *Address:* Tully-Louisburgh, Co. Mayo; 6 Stone Buildings, Lincoln's Inn, W.C.2. *Club:* United University. [*Died* 14 *Nov.* 1970.

HARMAN, Lt.-Gen. Sir Wentworth; *see* Harman, Lt.-Gen. Sir A. E. W.

HARMER, Florence Elizabeth, M.A., Litt.D. (Camb.); B.A. (Lond.); F.B.A.; F.S.A.; F.R.Hist.Soc.; Hon. Fellow, Girton College, Cambridge, since 1957; *er. d.* of late Horace Alfred Harmer and Harriett Frances (*née* Butler). *Educ.:* City of London School for Girls; Girton College, Cambridge

(Scholar). Lecturer in English Language and Literature, Manchester Univ., 1920-49, Senior Lecturer, 1949-55, Reader in Anglo-Saxon, 1955-57, retired. Pres. of Viking Soc. for Northern Research, 1948-51. Sir Israel Gollancz Memorial Prize (British Academy), 1957. Hon. Litt.D. (Manchester), 1964. *Publications:* English Historical Documents of the Ninth and Tenth Centuries, 1914; (with E. Classen) An Anglo-Saxon Chronicle, 1926; Anglo-Saxon Charters and the Historian (Rylands Bulletin), 1938; Chipping and Market (H. M. Chadwick Memorial Studies), 1950; The English Contribution to the Epistolary Usages of early Scandinavian Kings (Saga-Book of the Viking Society), 1950; Anglo-Saxon Writs, 1952; A Bromfield and a Coventry Writ of King Edward the Confessor (B. Dickins volume), 1960. *Recreations:* travel, gardening. *Address:* 80 Cecil Park, Pinner, Middlesex. *T.:* Pinner 6870. [*Died* 5 *Aug.* 1967.

HARMER, William Douglas, M.A., M.B., M.C. (Cantab.), F.R.C.S.; Consulting Surgeon, Throat Department St. Bartholomew's Hospital; Consulting Surgeon, Mt. Vernon Hospital; *b.* 25 Aug. 1873; *m.* 1906, May (*d.* 1954), *d.* of late John Hedley, M.D.; three *s.* *Educ.:* Uppingham; King's Coll., Cambridge. Late Asst. Surgeon and Warden, St. Bartholomew's Hospital; Surgeon to the Metropolitan Hospital. *Publications:* Operations upon the Larynx and Trachea; clinical papers on diseases of the throat and nose. *Address:* Red Willows, Littlestone-on-Sea, Kent. *T.:* New Romney 2328. [*Died* 24 *Oct.* 1962.

HARMSWORTH, Sir Alfred Leicester St. Barbe, 2nd Bt., *cr.* 1918; *b.* 26 Nov. 1892; *s.* of Sir Leicester Harmsworth, 1st Bt., and Annie, *e. d.* of late Thomas Scott of Clapham and Cornard, Suffolk; *S.* father, 1937; *m.* 1936, Margaret Florence Ivy Hall (marriage dissolved, 1939). *Educ.:* Westminster; Christ Church, Oxford, B.A. Served European War, 1914-19, Lt. Gloucestershire Regt., Capt. General List. Chairman, Retford & Gainsborough Times Co. Ltd. *Heir:* *b.* Geoffrey Harmsworth. *Address:* Manor House, Bexhill, Sussex. [*Died* 1 *March* 1962.

HARMSWORTH, (Perceval) Anthony (Thomas Hildebrand), Q.C. 1965; Barrister-at-Law; Deputy Chairman West Sussex Quarter Sessions since 1961; *b.* 29 December 1907; 4th *s.* of Sir Hildebrand Aubrey Harmsworth, 1st Bt.; *m.* 1st, 1930, Pansy Nina, *d.* of late Maj. W. G. Chambers, Edinburgh; 2nd 1961, Marie Dorothy, *d.* of Robert Henry Miller, Jersey. *Educ.:* Harrow School; Merton College, Oxford. Called to the Bar Middle Temple, 1936, Bencher, 1961. South-Eastern Circuit. *Address:* 1 King's Bench Walk, Temple, E.C.4. *T.:* City 7751; The Cottage, Withdean Avenue, Brighton 5, Sussex. *Club:* Garrick. [*Died* 27 *March* 1968.

HARNETT, Air Commodore (retired) Edward St. Clair, C.B.E. 1937 (O.B.E. 1918); *b.* 25 March 1881; *s.* of William O'Sullivan Harnett; *m.* 1st, 191, Dorothy. Grace, *d.* of Colonel Henry Waring, R.A.; one *s.*; 2nd, 1927, Eleanor Neale (*d.* 1958), *d.* of Robert Tailford. *Educ.:* Repton. Barrister, Grays Inn, 1904; enlisted 1914; Capt. in Black Watch in France and Flanders; Staff Captain 21st Infty. Brigade in Retreat of Fifth Army, 1918 (despatches); Legal Officer to R.A.F. in Cologne, 1918-19; Appointed Office of Judge Advocate General, 1923; Deputy Judge Advocate General in Baghdad, 1925-27; and for British Troops in Middle East, Cairo, 1927-29; Head of Legal Branch R.A.F., 1932; Air Force Deputy of Judge Advocate General of the Forces, 1939-45; Director of the German Courts Martial Control Branch of the Control Commission for Germany, 194-46. *Publications:* Text book on Law of Mortgages, 1909; has published several novels. *Address:* Hillstone, Osborne Road, Shanklin, I.W. [*Died* 30 *Dec.* 1964.

HARPER, Sir Kenneth Brand, Kt., *cr.* 1936; retired as Chairman, The Burmah Oil Company Ltd. (1948-57); *b.* 1891; *s.* of James Harper, M.D., 25 Rosary Gardens, S.W.7; *m.* 1929, Kate Donaldson, *d.* of Peter Donaldson Haggart, Adelaide, S. Australia; two *s.* one *d.* *Educ.:* Uppingham. Served European War, 1914-18, with Royal Marines. Represented Europeans in Burma at Burma Round Table Conference in London, 1931-32; Delegate from Burma to Joint Parliamentary Committee on Indian Constitutional Reform, 1933. *Address:* 169 Queen's Gate, S.W.7. *Club:* Oriental. [*Died* 21 *Jan.* 1961.

HARPER, His Honour Judge Norman; Judge of County Courts, Circuit 16, since 1958; *b.* 20 May 1904; *s.* of late James Harper, Idle, Bradford; *m.* 1931, Iris Irene, *d.* of late W. W. Rawson, Capetown; one *s.* two *d.* *Educ.:* Silcoates School, Wakefield; Magdalen College, Oxford. Called to Bar, Inner Temple, 1927. R.A.F.V.R. Sept. 1939-Feb. 1945; Squadron Leader, 1940-45. Recorder of Richmond, 1944-1951, of Doncaster, 1955-57, of Bradford, 1957-58. *Address:* Whin Brow, Cloughton, Scarborough. [*Died* 25 *Aug.* 1967.

HARPOLE, James; *see* Abraham, James Johnston.

HARRAGIN, Sir Walter, Kt., *cr.* 1945; C.M.G. 1941; Q.C. (Kenya); Judge of Court of Appeal for Basutoland, Bechuanaland and Swaziland, since 1956; President of Court, 1966; Dir. of various Companies; *b.* 23 Dec. 1890; *s.* of William Campbell Harragin and Mary Isabella Austin; *m.* 1919; one *s.* two *d.* (and one *s.* decd.). *Educ.:* Berkhamsted School; Gray's Inn. Called to Bar, 1912; Private Practice, Trinidad, 1912; joined Army, 1915; served in France, Major Royal Field Artillery; Magistrate, Trinidad, 1919; Crown Counsel, Trinidad, 1923; Attorney-General, Nyasaland, 1927; on several occasions acted as Judge between 1927 and 1933; acted as Chief Secretary, Kenya, 1938 and 1939; acting Governor, 1939; Attorney-General, Kenya, 1933-44; Chief Justice of the Gold Coast, 1944-48; Legal Adviser to the High Commissioner and Chief Justice High Commission Territories, 1948-52; President, West African Court of Appeal, 1946-48. *Recreations:* bridge, bowls. *Club:* Rand (Johannesburg). [*Died* 26 *June* 1966.

HARRAP, Walter Godfrey; Chairman: George G. Harrap & Co. Ltd., Publishers; The Holborn Property Co. Ltd.; *b.* 21 July 1894; *s.* of George Godfrey Harrap and Christina Mary (*née* Steward); *m.* 1920, Ivy Alice (*née* Wallace); one *s.* *Educ.:* Southend-on-Sea Technical School. Entered printing for instruction with Ballantyne & Co. Ltd., London, 1911; joined family business, 1913. Served European War, 1914-18, 5½ years in Armed Forces; joined Queen's Westminster Rifles, active service in France and Mesopotamia; commissioned, Machine Gun Corps (despatches). Rejoined Harrap's, 1920, as Secretary of Company; director, 1923; Managing Director, 1950. Pres. Publishers' Assoc., 1941-43; Founder of Publishers' Publicity Circle and British Publishers' Guild Ltd.; Chairman of various liaison cttees. with Govt., 1939-45. *Recreation:* golf. *Address:* Daleside, Banstead Road, Banstead, Surrey. *T.:* Ewell 3086. *Clubs:* City Livery, R.N.V.R. [*Died* 16 *April* 1967.

HARRINGTON, Vice-Admiral Sir (Wilfred) Hastings, K.B.E. 1963 (C.B.E. 1957); C.B. 1962; D.S.O. 1942; Retired as Chief of Naval Staff, Commonwealth of Australia, 1962-65; *b.* 17 May 1906; *s.* of H. E. Harrington, Barrister-at-Law, Sydney, Australia; *m.* 1945, Agnes Janet, *d.* of Legh Winser, *q.v.*; two *s.* two *d.* *Educ.:* Wychbury Preparatory School; Royal Australian Naval College. Midshipman, 1924; Captain, 1947; Rear-Admiral, 1957; Flag Officer Commanding the Australian Fleet, Dec. 1959-62; Vice-Admiral, 1962. *Recreations:* fishing, golf. *Address:* 24 Melbourne Avenue, Canberra, Australia. *T.:* 7-1694. *Clubs:* Naval and Military (Melbourne); Australian (Sydney); Commonwealth (Canberra). [*Died* 17 *Dec.* 1965.

HARRIS, Sir Douglas Gordon, K.B.E., 1942; C.S.I. 1932; C.I.E. 1925; *b.* 19 Oct. 1883; *s.* of late Arthur Harris, Ilkley, Yorks; *m.* 1908, Alice (*d.* 1953), *d.* of late Spencer Ackroyd, Bradford, Yorks; one *s.* *Educ.:* Rugby; Zürich. Asst. and Executive Engineer, Indian Public Works Department, 1907-15; Under-Secretary to Government of United Provinces, 1915; Under-Secretary to Government of India, 1916-19; Assistant Inspector-General of Irrigation in India, 1920-22; Deputy Secretary to Government of India, 1922-25; Consulting Engineer to the Government of India, 1925-32; Member Orissa Flood Committee, 1928; Member Bengal Irrigation Committee, 1930; Member, Sind Financial Enquiry Committee, 1931; Member, Bombay Reorganization Committee, 1932; Tana River Expedition, Kenya, 1934; Irrigation Adviser to the Government of Palestine, 1935; Commissioner on Special Duty and Member Executive Council of Palestine, 1936-44; Chairman Palestine War Supply Board, 1940-43; Reconstruction Commr. Palestine, 1943; Development Commr. in Cyprus, 1945; on special duty in Colonial Office, 1945-47; Development Commissioner and M.L.C. Uganda, 1947-50. Chairman, East African Agricultural and Fisheries Research Council, 1953-55; Development Consultant, Uganda, 1950-62; Member, Uganda Electricity Bd., 1951-63. *Publication:* Irrigation in India. *Address:* Makongi Farm, Hoey's Bridge, Kenya. [*Died* 4 *June* 1967.

HARRIS, Rev. Canon George Herbert, M.A.; Rector and Rural Dean of Rothbury, 1935-55, retired; Hon. Canon of Newcastle, 1942-55, Canon Emeritus, 1955; Hon. Canon of Worcester, 1936, Canon Emeritus, 1941; *b.* 14 February 1885; *s.* of Frederick George and Lucy Anne Harris, Ellacombe, Torquay; *m.* Lavinia Nina Lansdell; one *s.* one *d.* *Educ.:* private; Collège Jean Bart, Dunkerque; Fitzwilliam Hall, Cambridge. Curate of St. Andrew's, Plymouth, 1914-16; T.C.F. 1916-19 (despatches); Vice-Principal, Ridley Hall, 1919-23; Editorial Secretary, Church Missionary Society, 1926-30; Principal of King William's College, Isle of Man, 1930-35; Hon. C.F., 1919; O.C.F. 1942; Theo. Trip. pt. i, 1st cl. (dist. in N.T.), Theo. Trip. pt. ii, 1st cl.; Carus Prize (Jun., 1913); Carus Prize (Sen., 1914); Scholefield Prize, 1914; Crosse Scholar, 1913; Wordsworth Student, 1913; Select Preacher, Cambridge, 1919, 1921; Examining Chaplain to: Bishop of Bradford, 1920-31; Bishop of Truro, 1919-23; Bishop of Sodor and Man, 1928-42; Bishop of Oxford, 1924-1925; Bishop of Worcester, 1931-41; Bishop of Newcastle, 1935-41 and 1945-55; Central Advisory Council for the Training of the Ministry, 1926-30; Joint Editor The Church Overseas, 1928-30. *Publications:* Vernon Faithfull Storr —A Memoir; Contributor to The Inner Life, 1925; The Call For Christian Unity, 1930. *Address:* Hyde Abbey House Hotel, Winchester. *T.:* Winchester 4557. [*Died* 25 *March* 1968.

HARRIS, Henry Albert, M.A., M.D. (Pathology), D.Sc., M.B., B.S. (Hons.), M.R.C.S., M.R.C.P., Hon. D.Sc. (Univ. of Wales); F.R.C.S.(Eng.): late Prof. of Anatomy, Univ. of Khartoum, 1952, Cairo, 1951; Prof. Emeritus and Fellow of St. John's College Camb.; *b.* 13 Sept. 1886; *s.* of late Henry Harris, Rhymney, Mon.; *m.* 1912, Margaret, *d.* of late Llewellyn Webb, Hay; two *s.* three *d.* *Educ.:* Abermorlais and Secondary Schools, Merthyr Tydfil; University College, Cardiff; University College Hosp. Med. School, London. Demonstrator, Assistant Professor, Curator of the Anatomical Museum, Lecturer in Surgical Anatomy, University College, London, 1918-31; Assistant to Child Welfare Clinic, 1921-31; Assistant to the Medical Unit, University College Hospital, 1927-31; Professor of Clinical Anatomy, University College and University College Hospital, 1931-34; Hunterian Professor, Royal College of Surgeons; Bucknill Scholar, Gold Medallist in Anatomy and Physiology, Cluff Prizeman, Fellowes Gold Medal in Clinical Medicine, University College Hospital Medical School; Ernest Hart Memorial Fellow, B.M.A., 1921-23; Rockefeller Foundation Fellow, 1925-1926; Arris and Gale Lecturer, Royal College of Surgeons, 1929 and 1943; Wm. Julius Mickle Fellowship for Research, 1929; Symington Prize Anatomical Research, 1929; Alvarenga Prize, Philadelphia, 1930; Fellow of University College, London, 1932; Life Member Society of Radiographers; Member of Board of Examiners, Royal College of Surgeons and University of London. *Publications:* Bone Growth in Health and Disease, 1933; various anatomical and medical papers relating to Bone Growth, Growth in Children, Radiology, Embryology, Physical Anthropology, and Teratology. *Recreations:* travel, walking, gardening. *Address:* 5 Selwyn Gardens, Cambridge. [*Died* 10 *Sept.* 1968.

HARRIS, Air Vice-Marshal (Retd.) Jack Harris, C.B. 1953; C.B.E. 1946; *b.* 4 Nov. 1903; *s.* of late A. Harris, J.P.; *m.* 1937, Edytha Maud Boddington, *d.* of late Major C. L. H. Dickinson, D.S.O., Droitwich; one *s.* *Educ:* Scotch Coll., Melbourne, Australia. Gen. Duties Branch R.A.F., 1926; transf. 7th Rajput Regt., I.A., 1930; returned R.A.F. 1937; Air Ministry G.D. 2 and F.O. 3, 1940; joined R.A.F. Regt. on formation, 1942; Command Defence Officer, Air Command, S.E. Asia, 1942 (despatches); Chief Instructor, R.A.F. Regt. Depot, 1946; Group Captain, 1947; Deputy Director of Ground Defence, Air Ministry, 1948; Director, 1951; Air Commodore, 1951; Senior Ground Defence Staff Officer, Middle East Air Force, 1953; Director of Ground Defence, Air Ministry, 1955-59; Commandant-General, Royal Air Force Regiment, 1959-61; retired, 1961. *Recreation:* sailing. *Address:* Maytone, Highfields, East Horsley, Surrey. *Clubs:* United Service; R.A.F. Yacht (Hamble). [*Died* 9 *July* 1963.

HARRIS, John Edward, C.B.E. 1961; F.R.S. 1956; M.A.; Ph.D.; Vice-Chancellor and Professor of Animal Biology, University of Bristol, since 1966; *b.* 15 Sept. 1910; *s.* of late John Henry Harris and Annie Fisher; *m.* 1935, Elsie Mae Hutcheon, Cleveland, Ohio, U.S.A.; two *d.* *Educ.:* City School, Lincoln; Christ's College, Cambridge (Scholar). Commonwealth Fund Fellow (Columbia Univ. U.S.A.), 1933-35; Messel Research Fellow of Royal Society, 1937-40; Investigator on Fouling of Ships to Marine Corrosion Sub-Cttee. of Iron & Steel Inst., 1941-44 (later a Sub-Cttee. of The British Iron and Steel Research Assoc.), Chm., 1945-1948; Prof. of Zoology, Univ. of Bristol, 1944-1965; Deputy Vice-Chancellor, 1965-66. Member: Advisory Committee on Fisheries, 1953-65, Dep. Chm., 1964-65; Water Pollution Research Bd., 1955-58; (Fleck) Adv. Cttee. on Nuclear Safety, 1960-65; (Hale) Cttee. on Univ. Teaching Methods; Council Roy. Soc., 1960-62; Commonwealth Scholarships Commn., 1962-64, 1965-; Agricl. Research Council, 1962-; Natural Environment Research Council, 1965-68; Committee of Award, Harkness Fellowships,

1967- ; Vice-Chm., United Bristol Hosps., Bd., 1966-. Governor, Bristol Old Vic Trust, 1967-. *Publications:* papers on physical structure of protoplasm, hydrodynamics of fish locomotion, fossil fishes, fouling of ships in various British and American scientific journals, 1932 onwards. *Address:* Pine Trees, Camp Lane, Clapton in Gordano, Somerset. *T.:* Nailsea 2540. *Clubs:* Athenæum, English-Speaking Union.
[*Died* 24 *June* 1968.

HARRIS, John Henry, B.A.; *b.* 10 Sept. 1875; 2nd *s.* of James Harris, F.C.A.; *m.* 1905, Gladys Edith, *d.* of E. Meredith Hardy; three *s.* two *d.* *Educ.:* St. Paul's School (Foundation Scholar); Merton College, Oxford (Classical Postmaster). Called to Bar, Inner Temple, 1900; joined Western Circuit; Recorder of Portsmouth, 1927-28; Metropolitan Magistrate, 1928; Metropolitan Magistrate, Thames Police Court, 1930-45; Member of Departmental Committee on Adoption Societies and Agencies, 1936-37. *Recreation:* gardening. *Address:* Ardnardeen, Woking, Surrey. *T.:* Woking 293. *Club:* Athenæum.
[*Died* 18 *March* 1962.

HARRIS, Brigadier Lawrence Anstie, C.B.E. 1945; D.S.O. 1937; M.C.; retd. *b.* 1896; *e. s.* of A. H. Harris, formerly Commissioner, Chinese Maritime Customs Service; *m.* 1924, Dorothy Mary (*d.* 1962), *e. d.* of F. A. England, Hibernian Bank, Dublin; no *c.*; *m.* 1965, Mrs. Marjorie S. Bayley. *Educ.:* Tonbridge School; R.M.A., Woolwich. Commissioned Royal Artillery, 1915. Served European War, B.E.F. (France), 1915-1918 (M.C.); N.W.F. India, 1919, 1920-21, 1922: Waziristan 1937 (despatches twice D.S.O.); Burma (C.B.E.). Retd., 1948. *Recreation:* fishing. *Address:* King's Thursday, Denmead, Hants. *T.:* Waterlooville 3465. [*Died* 19 *Jan.* 1970.

HARRIS, Mary Kathleen, C.B.E. 1941; R.R.C. 1940; *b.* 19 June 1885; *d.* of late David Barclay, Belfast; *m.* 1942, Capt. St. George Eyre Harris, O.B.E., M.D., R.A.M.C. (*d.* 1945). *Educ.:* privately. Q.A.I.M.N.S., 1914; served European War of 1914-18 (despatches); A.R.R.C. 1919; Matron, 1934; Principal Matron, 1939; served War of 1939-45 (despatches), Mediterranean Stations; Principal Matron, Middle East, 1940; Principal Matron Middle East, 1942; retired from the Q.A.I.M.N.S., 1942. *Address:* Fairfax Cottage, Church Circle, Farnborough, Hants. [*Died* 25 *Aug.* 1968.

HARRIS, Noel Gordon, F.R.C.P.; Retd. as Physician for Psychological Medicine (now Hon. Cons. Physician in Psychol. Med.) The Middlesex Hospital (1938-59), and Lectr. in Psychol. Med., The Middlesex Hospital Medical School; *b.* 20 Dec. 1897; *s.* of late Sir Alexander Harris, K.C.M.G., C.B., C.V.O. and late Lady Harris, D.St.J.; *m.* 1923, Hon. Thelma Kitson, *d.* of 2nd Baron Airedale; one *s.* three *d.* *Educ.:* St. Peter's College, Westminster; St. Thomas's Hospital; London University. D.P.M. 1928; M.D. 1933; F.R.C.P. Lond. 1941. Clinical Asst., Dermatological Dept., St. Thomas's Hosp., 1923; Asst. Medical Officer, Springfield Hosp., 1923-35; Chief Asst., Dept. of Psychological Medicine, St. Thomas's Hosp., 1930; Physician-in-charge, Woodside Hosp., 1935-48. Civilian Consultant in Psychological Medicine to Royal Navy, May-Sept., 1939. Examiner: in Psychological Medicine, London Univ., 1938; for Gaskell Gold Medal, Royal Medico-Psychological Assoc.; in Psychological Medicine, R.C.P., 1948-52. Pres. Roy. Medico-Psychological Assoc., 1954-55 (Hon. Mem. 1959-); President of the Psychiatric Section of The Roy. Soc. Med., Oct. 1960. *Publications:* (with Gordon and Rees) An Introduction to Psychological Medicine. 1936; Modern Psychotherapy, 1938; (Ed.) Modern Trends in Psychological Medicine; contrib. to Lancet, Journal of Mental Science, The Urologic and Cutaneous Review of America. *Recreations:* gardening, fishing. *Address:* The Cottage, Ford, Wiveliscombe, Som. *T.:* Wiveliscombe 244.
[*Died* 20 *Oct.* 1963.

HARRIS, Norman Charles, C.M.G. 1949; D.S.O. 1918; M.C. 1916; Chm. Commissioners, Victorian Railways, Australia, 1940-1950; retd.; *b.* 10 April 1887; *s.* of Charles Joseph Harris and Isabella (*née* McKay); *m.* 1912, Rita May Wilson Moss; no *c.* *Educ.:* Scotch College, Melbourne, Australia; McGill University, Montreal, Canada. Special Apprentice, Canadian Pacific Railway, 1909-1911, Inspector of Piece Work, 1911; Asst. Engineer, Hydro-Electric Power Co., Tasmania, 1911-12; Draughtsman, Victorian Railways, 1913. Served European War, 1914-18, Lieut. and Capt., Australian Engineers, A.I.F., 1915; Major, 1916; Lieut.-Col., 1919; General Staff, 1926. Asst. Chief Mechanical Engineer, Vic. Railways, 1922, Chief Mechanical Engineer, 1928, Commissioner, 1933. *Recreation:* tennis. *Address:* Talahena, Park St., Brighton, Victoria, Australia. *Clubs:* Naval and Military, Legacy (Melbourne). [*Died* 3 *May* 1963.

HARRIS, Sir Sidney West, Kt., *cr.* 1946; C.B. 1916; C.V.O. 1918; formerly Assistant Under Secretary of State, Home Office; Pres. British Board of Film Censors, 1947-60; *b.* 1876; *m.* Emily Mary (*d.* 1940), *d.* of George David Wilson, Darlington; one *s.* three *d.* (and one *s.* killed 1940). *Educ.:* St. Paul's School; Queen's College, Oxford. Entered Home Office, 1903; Private Secretary to successive Home Secretaries, 1909-19; Assistant Secretary in charge of Children's Branch, 1919-34; Chairman of the Committee on the Social Services in Courts of Summary Jurisdiction, 1936; British representative on the Permanent Advisory Committee of the League of Nations for Social Questions, 1921-1939; British Representative on the Social Commission, United Nations, 1946; Chairman of Cttee. on Marriage Guidance, 1947; a Governor of King's College School. *Address:* 4 Highbury Road, Wimbledon Common, S.W.19. *T.:* Wimbledon 2682. *Club:* United University.
[*Died* 9 *July* 1962.

HARRISON, Alick Robin Walsham, C.B.E. 1950 (O.B.E. 1943); Warden of Merton College, Oxford, since 1963 (Fellow and Tutor in Ancient History, 1950-63; Senior Tutor, 1952, Domestic Bursar, 1954-1959); *b.* 15 November 1900; *s.* of late Rev. A. L. and late Ethel Harrison; *m.* 1932, Margaret Edith, *e. d.* of Sir David Ross; three *s.* one *d.* *Educ.:* Haileybury College; Merton College, Oxford. Asst. Master, Westminster School, 1923-30; Fellow, Tutor, and Principal of Postmasters, Merton College, 1930; Ministry of Food, 1940; Private Secretary to the Minister, 1941-43; Under-Secretary 1948-50. Joint Editor, Classical Quarterly, 1957-62. Hon. Fellow: St. Cross Coll., 1966; Wolfson Coll., 1967. *Publication:* The Law of Athens, 1967. *Address:* Merton College, Oxford. *T.:* 49651. *Club:* Oxford and Cambridge.
[*Died* 18 *May* 1969.

HARRISON, Beatrice; Cellist; *b.* Roorkee, N W P, India; *d.* of Col J H C Harrison, R.E. At ten years of age won Senior Gold Medal of Associated Board, at eleven became an exhibitor at Royal College of Music; at fourteen a scholar there, under W E Whitehouse; studied with Hugo Becker and at Hochschule, Berlin; won the Felix Mendelssohn Prize, being the first 'cellist and the youngest student to do so; made her *début* as a soloist at Bechstein Saal, Berlin. Toured

Europe and America. Made broadcasts for the B.B.C. from the early days of Savoy Hill. *Address:* Hollesley Farm Smallfield, Surrey. [*Died* 10 *March* 1965.

HARRISON, Cecil Stanley, C.M.G. 1954; O.B.E. 1951; Bailiff of Jersey, Channel Islands, since Nov. 1961 (Dep. Bailiff, 1958-1961); *b.* 17 November 1902; *yr. s.* of late Arthur Harrison, Rocqueberg, Samarès, Jersey, C.I.; *m.* 1927, Evelyn Jeanie, *o. d.* of late Thomas Dixon Reid, Bangor, Co. Down; one *d. Educ.:* Victoria College, Jersey. Admitted to Bar of Royal Court of Jersey, 1925; called to English Bar, Middle Temple, 1925. Solicitor General, Jersey, 1936; Attorney General, Jersey, 1948-58. *Recreations:* golf, fishing. *Address:* St. Clair, Pontac, Jersey, C.I. *T.:* Central 1676. *Club:* United Sports. [*Died* 14 *April* 1962.

HARRISON, Major George, M.C. 1917, and Bar, 1918; Chairman London Press Exchange Ltd. since 1940; *b.* 14 Jan. 1885; *e. s.* of Henry and Helena Harrison; unmarried. *Educ.:* Urmston School. Served European War, 1914-18, in H.M. Forces, 1914-20, in France, Egypt, Palestine, Syria, Mesopotamia (Second in Command). London Press Exchange Ltd.: Secretary, 1921; Director, 1923; Managing Director, 1930. *Publications:* (with F. C. Mitchell) The Home Market, since 1936. *Recreations:* golf, gardening, stamp collecting. *Address:* Merrywood, Deepdene Wood, Dorking, Surrey. *T.:* Dorking 2482. *Club:* Royal Automobile. [*Died* 26 *July* 1961.

HARRISON, Brigadier-General George Hyde, D.S.O. 1917; *b.* Forton, Gosport, 24 Sept 1877; *s.* of late Captain George Hyde Harrison, 55th Regt.; *m.* 1917, Mabel (*d.* 1959), *e. d.* of late John Parker Norfolk of Harewood, Leeds. *Educ.:* United Services College, Westward Ho! Joined 1st Batt. The Border Regt as 2nd Lt. from 3rd Militia Batt. 1899; served South African War, 1899-1902 (despatches, Queen's medal with 5 clasps, King's medal with 2 clasps); Europaen War 1914-18 served in Gallipoli and France; Commanded 11th Royal Sussex Regt. 1916-1917, 62nd Batt Machine Gun Corps 1917-18, 155 Inf. Bde. 1918-19; Brig Gen 1918 despatches, 1914-15 Star, British War Medal, Victory, Medal, D.S.O., Legion of Honour, French Croix de Guerre, Brevet Lieut.-Colonel); commanded 1st Batt. Border Regt. 1923-27; Col 1927; Commanded Poona Brigade Area 1928-1931; 132nd (Middlesex and Kent) Infantry Brigade, T.A., 1931-34; retired pay, 1934. Colonel of Border Regt. 1936-47. *Address:* c/o Lloyds Bank, Ltd., Guildford, Surrey. *Club:* United Service. [*Died* 11 *March* 1965.

HARRISON, John William H.; *see* Heslop-Harrison.

HARRISON, Julius Allan Greenway, Hon. R.A.M.; F.T.C.L.; F.B.S.M.; conductor and composer; *b.* Stourport, 26 March 1885; *e. s.* of Walter H. and Henriette Harrison; *m.* 1st, 1913, Mary Eddison, Eastbourne; one *d.*; 2nd, 1929, Dorothy Helen Day, Baldock; one *s. Educ.:* Queen Elizabeth's School, Hartlebury; Birmingham, under Sir Granville Bantock. Conducted for some years in Sir Thomas Beecham's Opera Co., and British National Opera Co., Royal Opera House, Covent Garden; co-conductor with Sir Landon Ronald, Scottish Orchestra; Musical Director to Hastings Corporation, 1930-40; late Conductor Handel Society, London; late Musical Director, Opera Class, Royal Academy of Music and Professor of Composition, Royal Academy of Music; Conductor of many Symphony Concerts, B.B.C., London Philharmonic Orchestra, London Symphony Orchestra, Hallé Orchestra, Liverpool Philharmonic Orchestra, etc.; Director of Elgar Festival, Malvern 1947; Member of Corporation of Trinity College of Music, London, etc. *Works:* Mass in C and Requiem Mass, 1957, for solo voices, chorus, organ and orchestra; Missa Liturgica for unaccompanied voices; Requiem of Archangels; Worcestershire suite; Blessed Damozel; Rhapsody for Baritone Voice and Orchestra; Cornish Sketches and Autumn Landscape for String Orchestra; Rhapsody, Bredon Hill, for Violin and Orchestra; Radio Operetta, A Fantasy of Flowers; Incidental Music to Radio Plays; Troubadour Suite for Strings, Horns and Harp; Sonata for Viola and Piano; many choral works, songs, part-songs, pianoforte, organ, instrumental pieces, and chamber music. *Publications:* Brahms and his Four Symphonies; Contributor to the Musical Companion, the New Musical Educator and Antonin Dvořák, His Achievement. *Address:* The Greenwood, Ox Lane, Harpenden, Herts. *T.:* Harpenden 2478. [*Died* 5 *April* 1963.

HARRISON, Colonel Lawrence Whitaker, C.B. 1946; D.S.O. 1915; M.B., Ch.B. (Glasg. 1897); F.R.C.P.E.; Hon. Mem. (President, 1923-25 and 1938-42) Med. Soc. Study of Venereal Diseases; Corr. Member American Dermatological Association; Hon. Member: American V.D. Association; Danish French and Japanese Socs. Dermat. and Syphilogr.; F.R.S.M.; *b.* 2 April 1876; *y. s.* of late Jonathan A. Harrison, M.D., J.P., Haslingden, Lancashire; *m.* 1905, Mabel Alice, *y. d.* of late Colonel E. J. Fairland, A.M.S.; two *s.* two *d. Educ.:* Manchester Grammar Sch. (Schol.); Glasgow Univ.; Royal Army Medical Coll. Entered army, 1899; Captain, 1902; Major, 1911; Lieutenant Col. 1915; Hon. Physician to the King and Bt. Col. 1917; retired, 1919; served S. African War, 1899-1902 (despatches, Queen's medal 4 clasps, King's medal 2 clasps); European War, 1914-18 (despatches twice, D.S.O., Mons star); Ed. 1925-42, Brit. Journal of Venereal Diseases; late Chairman, Venereologists Group, Cttee.; B.M.A., 1948-54; late Vice-Pres. Union Internationale contre le Péril Vénérien. Adviser on Venereal Diseases, Ministry of Health, 1919-46. Wm. Freeman Snow Medal, Amer. Soc. Hyg Ass. (for Dist. Services to Humanity), 1946. Late Hon. Consultant on Venereal Diseases. British Post-Graduate Medical School. *Publications:* The Diagnosis and Treatment of Venereal Diseases in General Practice, 4th ed., 1931; A Manual of Venereal Diseases for Students, 1920; The Modern Diagnosis and Treatment of Syphilis, Chancroid, and Gonorrhœa, 1924; Venereal Disease Guide for Practitioners working under Provisions of Circulars of Ministry of Health, 2226 and Dept. of Health for Scotland No. 50/1941; part author of Gonococcal Infections; Manual of Venereal Diseases by Officers of the R.A.M.C.; and A System of Syphilis by D'Arcy Power and J. Keogh Murphy; articles in Med. Res. Council's System of Bacteriology, Choyce's System of Surgery, and Price's Practice of Medicine, 5th edition, 1936; in British Encyclopædia of Medical Practice, in Dictionary of Practical Medicine, and Oxford Index of Therapeutics: in Bulletin of Hygiene, and 13th ed. new vols. Encyclopædia Britannica; numerous (150) articles on bacteriology and V.D., medical journals since 1904. *Address:* 6 Wilton Court, 59 Eccleston Square, S.W.1. *T.:* Victoria 7435. [*Died* 9 *May* 1964.

HARRISON, Brigadier Thomas Carleton, C.B.E. 1945; T.D. 1949; D.L. Middx., 1947; J.P. County of Berkshire, 1950; Chairman and Man. Dir., Gillette Industries Ltd., 1958 (Deputy Chairman and Man. Dir., 1946-58); Director and Vice-President, The Gillette Company, Boston, U.S.A., 1948-59; *b.* 1896; *s.* of late Stanley Carleton Harrison, Tyn-y-Rhos Hall, nr. Chirk, N. Wales; *m.* 1924, Mary Anne Peabody, *d.* of late James Riddle, Norfolk, Va., U.S.A.; one *s.* one *d.* *Educ.:* Denstone College, Staffordshire. Served in European War, 1914-19, with R.A. (T.F.); War of 1939-45, rejoined R.A. (T.A.), 1939, Major; Lt.-Col., 1940; Brig. 1942. *Recreation:* golf. *Address:* Wittenham Court, Monterey Drive, Constantia, Cape Province, S. Africa. [*Died* 27 *July* 1962.

HARRISON-WALLACE, Captain Henry Steuart Macnaghten, D.S.O. 1940; Royal Navy; *s.* of late Hon. James Harrison, Hordley Estate and Custos of St. Thomas, Jamaica, and Caroline, *d.* of Major-General R. H. Page; *m.* 1923, Eileen Constantia (*d.* 1944), *d.* of Sir Henry McCallum, G.C.M.G.; one *d.*; *m.* 1946, Barbara, *widow* of Capt. Frank Belville and *d.* of late Herbert Stourton. *Educ.:* H.M.S. Britannia, Dartmouth; R.N. College, Greenwich. Went to sea as Midshipman in 1899; served throughout European War, 1914-18, as Gunnery Commander H.M.S. Emperor of India, and in command of H.M.S. Caledon, Grand Fleet (despatches); retired as Captain, R.N., in 1923; Director of several public companies; rejoined Navy, 1939; Norwegian Expeditionary Force, 1940 (D.S.O.); Captain H.M.S. Quebec, 1941-42; Headquarters Staff Combined operations and Admiralty Naval Staff, 1942-44; Invasion of Normandy, 1944, Captain of Landing Barges; reverted to retired list R.N. 1945. *Recreations:* shooting, salmon fishing, and golf. *Address:* 23 Carlyle Sq., S.W.3. *T.:* Flaxman 9589; Fort George Estate, Annotto Bay, Jamaica. *Clubs:* Carlton, City of London, Royal Thames Yacht; Royal Yacht Squadron; Swinley Forest Golf. [*Died* 24 *June* 1963.

HARROP, Angus John, M.A., Litt.D. (N.Z.), Ph.D. (Camb.); Editor, The New Zealand News (London); *b.* Hokitika, N.Z., 7 March 1900; *s.* of A. N. Harrop, Lands and Survey Department; *m.* Hilda Mary, *d.* of J. A. Valentine, O.B.E., B.A., former Senior Inspector of Schools, Taranaki, N.Z.; one *s.* one *d.* *Educ.:* Waitaki School; Canterbury University College, N.Z.; Gonville and Caius College, Cambridge; Senior Scholar in History, University of N.Z., 1921; M.A., 1st Class Honours in History, 1922; joined staff of The Press, Christchurch, 1921; entered Caius College, 1923; Ph.D., 1925; Editorial Department, Daily Mail (London), 1925-28; founded The New Zealand News (London), 1927; Representative in England of the University of New Zealand, 1931-43; Member of Executive Council of Universities Bureau of the British Empire, 1931-44; News Editor, Sydney Daily Mirror Cable Service, 1941-49; editor, 1949-53; Member R.I.I.A. *Publications:* The Romance of Westland, 1923; England and New Zealand, 1926; The Amazing Career of Edward Gibbon Wakefield, 1928; Touring in New Zealand, 1935; England and the Maori Wars, 1937; My New Zealand, 1939; New Zealand after Five Wars, 1947; new edn. The Long White Cloud by W. Pember Reeves, with additional chapters, 1950; Contributor to the Cambridge History of the British Empire. *Address:* 72E Church Rd., Richmond, Surrey. [*Died* 10 *Aug.* 1963.

HARROP, Wilfrid Orrell, C.M.G. 1954; retired; *b.* 29 July 1893; *s.* of late Robert Harrop and Miriam (*née* Orrell); *m.* 1917, Alexandra Evelyn Olive Johnson (*d.* 1966); one *d.* *Educ.:* St. Margaret's and Teachers' Training Coll., Manchester; London Univ. Admiralty Secretariat, 1913-38; Sub-Lieut. R.N.V.R., 1917-18; Air Ministry, Civil Aviation Dept., 1938-39, Personnel Dept. 1939-40; Min. of Aircraft Production, 1940-1944; Dir. of Finance and Administration, Brit. Air Commn. and Brit. Supply Office, Washington, D.C., U.S.A., 1944-46; Min. of Supply, 1946-47; seconded to Treasury, 1947; transferred to Foreign Office, 1947; retired Dec. 1954, re-employed, 1955-58. Coronation Medal, 1953. *Recreations:* orchid growing, photography, music. *Address:* Inglewood, 42 Sutton Lane, Banstead, Surrey. *T.:* Burgh Heath 56030. [*Died* 15 *March* 1969.

HARROWING, Lt.-Col. Wilkinson Wilberforce, D.S.O. 1940; J.P.; late The Duke of Cornwall's Light Infantry; *b.* 5 September 1898; *s.* of late Sir John Harrowing; *m.* 1926, Ruth Elspeth Moubray. *Educ.:* Rugby School; Clare College, Cambridge; R.M.C., Sandhurst. J.P. 1950-. Served European War, France, Italy, 1917-18; Iraq, 1920-21; N.W.F.P., 1934-35; B.E.F., 1940 (despatches, D.S.O.); N. Africa 8th Army, 1943; R.A.F. Levies (Iraq), 1943-46. *Recreations:* ski-ing and sailing. *Address:* Boyke Manor, Ottinge, Elham, Kent. *T.:* Lyminge 87178. *Club:* United Service. [*Died* 6 *Dec.* 1967.

HART, Bernard, C.B.E. 1945; M.D., F.R.C.P. (Lond.); Fellow of University College, London; Consulting Physician Psychological Medicine, University College Hospital, London; Consulting Physician in Psychiatry, National Hosp., Queen Square, London; Consultant Adviser to Ministry of Health; *b.* 24 March 1879; *m.* 1912, Mabel Spark (*d.* 1958). *Educ.:* Univ. Coll. School, Coll. and Hosp. Formerly Lecturer in Psychiatry, Univ. Coll. Hosp. Medical School; Lecturer on Psychopathology, Maudsley Hosp.; Lecturer at Maghull Military Hosp.; Physician to the Special Hosp. for Officers, Palace Green, Hon. Consultant in Mental Diseases to London Military Hospitals; Examiner in Psychiatry University of Cambridge; Goulstonian Lecturer Royal College of Physicians, London. *Publications:* Psychopathology; The Psychology of Insanity; various papers on medical and psychological subjects. *Recreations:* history and biography. *Address:* 67 Pashley Rd., Eastbourne, Sussex. *T.:* Eastbourne 2067. *Club:* Athenæum. [*Died* 16 *March* 1966.

HART, Sir Bruce, Bt.; *see* Hart, Sir E. B.

HART, Cecil Augustus, C.M.G. 1958; T.D., D.Sc. (Eng.) Lond., Ph.D. (Lond.); F.I.C.E., F.I.Mech.E., F.R.I.C.S., M.I.Struct.E.; Fellow of University College, London University; Hon. Lieut.-Colonel R.E.; Leader, U.K. Colombo Plan Mission to advise Govt. of Singapore on technological education, 1964; Consultant: to S.E.A.T.O., Bangkok on post-graduate engineering training, 1964; in Technology to Open University, 1969; *b.* 4 November 1902; *s.* of late Edwin A. Hart, Dover; *m.* 1928, Elsie Hilda Boddington, *d.* of late William Jordan, Surbiton, Surrey. *Educ.:* Dover Grammar School; University College, London. Dover Engineering Works, 1919-20; Kitchener Schol., 1920; B.Sc. (Eng.) Lond. 1st Cl. Hons. and Dip. in Civil and Municipal Eng. (U.C.L.) with distinction, 1923; Asst. Engineer on various public works schemes, 1923-26; Asst. in Municipal Engineering and Surveying, U.C. London; Asst. Lecturer, Lecturer; Sen. Lecturer, Consultant in Development Schemes and Surveys, 1936; M.Sc. (Eng.) Lond., 1933; Ph.D. Lond. for thesis on Air Survey, 1939; D.Sc. (Eng.) Lond. 1950. Appointed Tutor in Engineering at College of Estate Management, London, 1939; served War of 1939-1945; mobilised with T.A. (U.L.O.T.C.); B.E.F., France, with 13th (Field Survey) Coy. Sept. 1939, subsequently G.H.Q. till May 1940; served in War Office, Air Ministry, Middle East and S.E. Asia; was in charge of Air Survey Research during considerable part of War and was responsible for devel. of application of radar to air survey (awarded

Murchison Grant of R. Geog. Soc., 1946); demobilised with rank of Hon. Lt.-Col. R.E., 1946 (T.D.). Prof. of Surveying and Photogrammetry, Univ. of London (Univ. Coll.), 1946-50 (first chair in this country); Comd. Univ. of Lond. U.T.C. (T.A.), 1949-50; Vice-Chancellor Univ. of Roorkee, U.P., India, 1950-53; Rector and Principal, Nigerian College of Arts, Science and Technology, 1954-60; Director, London Master Builders Association, 1960-63. Hon. Lieutenant-Colonel N.C.C. (India) 1950. Member: Expert Commission to R. Tech. University, Stockholm, 1946; Air Photography Research Committee, Ministry of Supply, 1946-50; Joint Advisory Survey Board, Air Survey Sub-Committee, 1946-50; Board of Management Association for Planning and Regional Development, 1946-1950; Council of Royal Institution of Chartered Surveyors, 1947-50; Council Institute of Navigation, 1948; Editorial Board International Society of Photogrammetry; Scientific Council for Africa, 1958; Corresp. Member International Assoc. of Geodesy; Survey Cttee. R. Geog. Soc., 1946-50. Pres. Institn. of Surveyors (India), 1952-53; Member: Eng. Research Coun. (India), 1950; Civil Eng. Research Cttee. (India), 1950; Building Research Cttee. (India), 1950. Council, Lord Kitchener Nat. Memorial Fund, 1966. *Publications:* Principles of Road Engineering, 1936; Air Photography applied to Surveying, 1940. Surveying from Air Photographs fixed by Remote Radar Control (first two papers presented on this subject), Royal Soc. Empire Scientific Conf., 1946; various papers on civil engineering and surveying subjects on technical journals. F.I.N. 1949. *Address:* The Old Greyhound, Akeley, Buckingham. *T.:* Lillingstone Dayrell 260. *Club:* Athenæum.

[*Died* 27 *July* 1970.

HART, Sir (Edgar) Bruce, 2nd Bt., *cr.* 1893; *b.* 8 July 1873; *o. s.* of 1st Bart. and Hester Jane, *e. d.* of Alexander Bredon, M.D., Portadown; *S.* father, 1911; *m.* 1894, Caroline Moore (*d.* 1938), *o. d.* of late William Moore Gillson, of Hove, Sussex. *Educ.:* Harrow; University Coll., Oxford. Formerly Commissioner in England of Chinese Customs. Blue Button, Third Class, China; Double Dragon, Second Division, Third Class, China. *Heir: g. s.* Robert [*b.* 4 Aug. 1918; *o. s.* of Robert Bruce Hart (*d.* 1933) and Annie Irene (*d.* 1927), *d.* of late Henry Matthews]. *Address:* 35 Draycott Place, S.W.3. [*Died* 4 *Feb.* 1963.

HART, Brigadier-General Sir Herbert Ernest, K.B.E., *cr.* 1935; C.B. 1919; C.M.G. 1918; D.S.O. 1915; V.D.; barrister and solicitor; *b.* 1882; *s.* of late William Hart of Carterton, New Zealand; *m.* 1903, Minnie Eleanor, 2nd *d.* of Roger Z. Renall of Wairarapa, New Zealand; one *s.* two *d.* Served S. African War, 1902, with New Zealand Forces (Queen's medal 2 clasps); in Dardanelles and France, European War, 1914-18 (despatches five times, D.S.O., C.M.G., C.B., Croix de Guerre); Lieutenant-Colonel, 1915; Brigadier-General, 1917; retired list, 1930; Administrator of Western Samoa, 1931-35; Chief Administrative Officer, Imperial War Graves Commission, Eastern District, 1936-43. Served as Asst. Director at G.H.Q., Middle East, 1940-42. *Address:* Masterton, N.Z.

[*Died March* 1968.

HART, Ivor Blashka, O.B.E., Ph.D., B.Sc.; Group Captain, Royal Air Force (retd.); *b.* London, 14 July 1889; 2nd *s.* of Isaac Blashka Hart; *m.* Deborah Anidjar, *e. d.* of Samuel Anidjar Romain; one *s.* *Educ.:* Earlsmead; Queen Mary College; University College (University of London). Resident Science Master, St. George's School, Eastbourne, 1910-11; Physics Master, Tavistock Grammar School, 1911-13; Head of Science Department, Leamington College, 1913-20; Lecturer in Physics, Leamington Technical School, 1913-1920; War Service in Italy, Mesopotamia, and India, Lieut. R.G.A. 1915-19. R.A.F. Education Service, 1920-49; Principal Deputy Director of Educational Services, Air Ministry, 1945-49. Secretary Insignia Awards Committee, City and Guilds of London Institute, 1950-58. *Publications:* A Student's Heat, 1914; Experimental Statics, 1915; Makers of Science, 1923; Aeronautical Science (with W. Laidler), 1924; Mechanical Investigations of Leonardo da Vinci, 1924; Introduction to Physical Science, 1925; Elementary Heat, 1926; The Great Physicists, 1927; The Great Engineers, 1928; Introduction to Advanced Heat, 1928; James Watt and the History of the Steam Engine, 1949; Introduction to Mechanics, 1961: The World of Leonardo da Vinci, 1961; Leonardo da Vinci, Pathfinder, 1962; various Essays and Studies on the History of Science in Monist, The Open Court, Nature, Journal of the Royal Aeronautical Society, Scientia, Aryan Path, etc. *Address:* Lynwood, Rosemary Lane, Thorpe, Surrey. *T.:* Egham 3442.

[*Died* 28 *Oct.* 1962.

HART, Moss; Playright; *b.* 24 Oct. 1904; *m.* 1946, Kitty Carlisle; one *s.* one *d.* *Educ.:* New York City Public Schools. *Plays:* Merrily We Roll Along; The American Way; Once in a Lifetime; The Man Who Came to Dinner; George Washington Slept Here; You Can't Take It With You; The Fabulous Invalid; As Thousands Cheer; Face the Music; Lady in the Dark; Winged Victory; Jubilee; Christopher Blake; Light up the Sky; The Climate of Eden; My Fair Lady (Director); Camelot (Director). *Films:* Gentlemen's Agreement; Hans Christian Andersen; A Star is Born; Prince of Players. *Publication:* Act One: An Autobiography, 1960. *Recreations:* croquet and swimming. *Address:* 1185 Park Avenue, New York City, N.Y., U.S.A. *Club:* Lambs (New York City).

[*Died* 20 *Dec.* 1961.

HART, Sir Robert, 3rd Bt., *cr.* 1893; *b.* 4 August 1918; *s.* of late Robert Bruce Hart and late Annie Irene, *d.* of Henry Matthews; *S.* grandfather, Sir (Edgar) Bruce Hart, 2nd Bt., 1963. *Educ.:* abroad; University College, Oxford. *Heir:* none. *Address:* 20 Hyde Park Place, W.2.

[*Died* 15 *Oct.* 1970 (*ext.*).

HART, Siriol; *see* Hugh-Jones, Siriol.

HARTFORD, Rev. Canon Richard Randall; Chancellor of St. Patrick's Cathedral, Dublin, since 1957; Regius Professor of Divinity in Dublin University since 1957; *b.* 21 Sept. 1904; *y. s.* of late James Hartford, and late Martha Foster, Fordville, Abbeyleix, Queen's Co., Ireland; *m.* 1943, Diana Mary, *er. d.* of Most Rev. Arthur W. Barton, *q.v.* *Educ.:* Kilkenny College; Mountjoy School; Trinity College, Dublin Univ. First Sizarship in Mathematics and Junior Exhibitioner; First Class Honours in Mathematics and Mental and Moral Science, 1924; Hons. in Experimental Science, 1924; First Class Honours and Prize in Mental and Moral Science, 1925, and Senior Exhibition, 1925; Scholar of the House, 1926; Divinity Composition Prize and first Downes Prize for Written Composition, 1927; First Class Moderatorship, Large Gold Medal and Moderatorship Exhibition, 1927; Auditor of the Coll. Theological Soc., 1927; B.A. 1927; M.A. 1931; B.D. 1936; D.D. 1948; 1st Downes Prize for Extempore Speaking, Robert King Memorial Prize and Divinity Testimonium (2nd Class), 1928; President and Medallist of University Philosophical Society, 1928-29; Curate Assistant of SS. Philip and James, Booterstown, 1928-31; Minor Canon of St. Patrick's Cathedral, Dublin, 1930-35; Curate Assistant, Christ Church, Leeson Park, 1931;

Honor Lecturer and Examiner in Mental and Moral Science, Trinity College, Dublin, since 1931; Dean of Residence, 1931-35; Assistant Lecturer to Regius Professor of Divinity, 1931; Acting Archbishop King's Professor, 1935-36; Examining Chaplain to Bishop of Ossory (Dr. Day), 1935-38; Examining Chaplain to Archbishop of Armagh (Dr. Day) April-Sept. 1938, Private Chaplain to the Bishop of Derry; 1951-58; Examining Chaplain to the Bishop of Cork, 1952; Member of Faith and Order Commission of the World Council of Churches; Member of General Synod of Church of Ireland, 1946; M.R.I.A., 1946; Archbishop King's Professor of Divinity in Dublin University, 1936-57; Canon of St. Patrick's Cathedral Dublin (Prebendary of Maynooth), 1945-57; Select Preacher, Cambridge, 1957. *Publications:* Godfrey Day: Missionary, Pastor and Primate, 1940; John Scotus Erigena, a Great Irishman, 1943; Edward Synge (1691 1762), Fellow and Bishop, 1947; various articles and reviews. *Recreations:* Rugby football and golf. *Address:* Trinity College, Dublin; Zion Lodge, Zion Road, Rathgar, Dublin. *T.:* Dublin, 906970. *Clubs:* Friendly Brothers of St. Patrick (Dublin) Island (Golf), Wanderers F.C. [*Died* 7 *Aug.* 1962.

HARTGILL, Major-General William Clavering, C.B. 1945; O.B.E. 1940; M.C. 1917; K.H.S., 1944-47; *b.* 1 Jan. 1888; *s.* of late William Henry Hartgill, Cannon Heath, Dannevirke, New Zealand; *m.* 1922, Katherine Robertson Lowe (*d.* 1967); one *s.* two *d. Educ.:* Wanganui Collegiate School; Otago University, Dunedin; London Hospital. M.R.C.S., L.R.C.P. 1914; Lieutenant, R.A.M.C. 1914; Captain 1918; Major, 1926; Bt. Lt.-Col. 1934; Lt.-Col. 1939; Col. Nov. 1941; Brig. Aug 1941; Maj.-Gen. 1943. Served European War, 1914-18 (despatches, M.C. and Bar, Médaille de la Reconnaissance en argent); Somaliland Campaign, 1920 (Af. gen. service medal with Somaliland clasp); War of 1939-45 (despatches, O.B.E., C.B., Commander, Legion of Merit, U.S.A.). C.St.J. Chairman of War Office Committee on Reorganization of Medical Services in the Field, 1942; retired pay. 1947; now resident in N.Z. *Address:* c/o Glyn, Mills & Co. (Holt's Branch), Whitehall, S W 1. [*Died* 26 *April* 1968.

HARTIGAN, Lieut.-Gen. Sir James Andrew, K.C.B., *cr.* 1935 (C.B. 1933); C M G. 1918; D S.O. 1916, M B; D.Ch.; late R.A.M.C.; *b* 1876; *s.* of late J. T. Hartigan Crean Lodge, Bruff, Co. Limerick; *m.* 1920, Marion Helena, *o. d.* of late H. C. Smith, Knock, Co. Down one *d. Educ.:* Trinity College, Dublin; Durham University, M.B., B.S. Entered R.A.M.C. 1899; Lt.-Col 1917 Col. 1927; Maj.-Gen 1930; Lt.-Gen. 1934; served South African War, 1900-2 (Queen's medal and three clasps, King's medal and two clasps); European War, 1914-18 (despatches, D S O, C M G., Bt. Col.); Dep. Director Medical Services Aldershot Com., 1930-34; Director-General Army Medical Services, War Office, 1934-38; retired pay, 1938; C.St.J.; Col. Comdt. R.A.M.C., 1941-46; late Pres. British Legion, Ireland (Southern) Area. *Address:* 8 Eglinton Park, Dun Laoghaire, Co. Dublin. *Club:* Royal Irish Yacht (Dun Laoghaire). [*Died* 12 *Oct.* 1962.

HARTILL, Ven. Percy; Rector and Archdeacon of Stoke-on-Trent, 1935-55; Archdeacon Emeritus, 1955; Prebendary of Ufton Decani in Lichfield Cathedral, 1935-1956; President of Anglican Pacifist Fellowship since 1939; *b.* Willenhall, Staffs, 10 Feb. 1892; *y. s.* of late Dr. John T. Hartill; *m.* 1956, May Allen, Pool Hill, Newent. *Educ.:* privately; New Coll., Oxon.; Cuddesdon Theological Coll. 2nd Cl. Honour Moderations, 1912; 2nd Class Litteræ Humaniores, 1914; 1st Class Honour Theology, 1915; Hall Greek Testament Prize, 1915; Ellerton Essay Prize. 1916; Fereday Fellowship of S. John's, 1921-28; B.A., 1914; M.A., 1917; B.D., 1927; Deacon, 1916; Priest, 1917; Assistant Curate, Christ Church, West Bromwich, 1916-20; Domestic Chaplain to the Bishop of Lichfield, and Lecturer at Lichfield Theological College, 1920-25; Vice-Principal, Lichfield Theological College, 1925-30; Vicar and Rural Dean of West Bromwich, 1930-35; Examining Chaplain to Bishop of Lichfield, 1930-55; Proctor in Convocation for Diocese of Lichfield, 1931-55; Pro-Prolocutor of Lower House of Convocation of Canterbury, 1955-1956. *Publications:* Faith and Truth (with Rev. F. H. Brabant), 1926; The Necessity of Redemption, 1927; Pacifism and Christian Commonsense, 1938; Revealing Christ, 1939; Article XXXVII and War, 1946; The Unity of God, 1952; War, Communism, and the Christian Faith, 1954; contributor to The Christian Life, 1932; Editor of Into the Way of Peace, 1941; of On Earth Peace, 1944; contributor to Steps to Christian Understanding. *Address:* Pool Hill, Newent, Glos. [*Died* 2 *Dec.* 1964.

HARTING, Pieter, D.Lit. (Utrecht); *b.* 15 Jan. 1892; *m.* 1919, Cornelia Nobel; two *s.* one *d. Educ.:* Univ. of Utrecht. Reader in Dutch, University of London (University and Bedford Colleges), 1919; Reader in Dutch Language and Literature, Head of Department, University of London, 1924; Lecturer in Dutch at the Taylor Institution Oxford, 1924-25; Professor of English Language and Literature, University, Groningen, 1925; Professor of English Language and Literature, University of Amsterdam, 1937-62. *Publications:* Selections from the Baudhayana Grhya-Parisistasutra, 1923; Engelse Taalstudie aan Engelse Universiteiten, 1925 *Address:* Ruimzicht 12, Amsterdam 18, Holland. [*Died* 11 *Aug.* 1970.

HARTLEY, Lieut.-Col. (Hon. Col.) Donald Reginald Cavendish, C.I.E., 1946, C.B.E. 1936; D.S.O. 1918; E.D.; late Partner Killick, Nixon and Co.; *b.* 4 Mar. 1893; *s* of late Arthur Meigh Hartley and Charlotte Helena Pratt; *m.* 1928, Grace Sara (*d.* 1934), *d.* of late J. H. Hardie; no *c.*; *m.* 1939, Mary McCulloch, *widow* of R. P Scott; no *c.* European War, 1914-1918, 4th and 7th Divisions, R.F.A., Major 35th Battery R.F.A., 1918-19 (D.S.O., Despatches); Major, 11th Field Battery Auxiliary Force, India, 1919; Lieut.-Col., Commanding 5th Field Brigade (Bombay), Indian Auxiliary Force, 1924; Commandant, The Bombay Contingent, Indian Auxiliary Force, 1933; Commandant Bombay Civic Guards, 1940-45; Additional A.D.C. to King George V, 1935; to King Edward VIII, 1936; to King George VI, 1937; Hon. Colonel on appointment to H.E. the Viceroy, 1931. *Recreation:* golf. *Address:* Mockbeggars, Fittleworth, W. Sussex. *Club:* East India and Sports. [*Died* 25 *March* 1970.

HARTLEY, Frederic St. Aubyn, C.B.E. 1952; A.C.G.I.; Keeper, Science Museum, South Kensington, retired 1957; *b.* 1896; *e. s.* of Rev. R. S. Hartley, R.N., and Georgina St. Aubyn; *m.* 1917, Dorothy, *d.* of Dr. William Dewsnap; four *s. Educ.:* Imperial Service College; City and Guilds (Eng.) Coll. Entered Royal Navy in 1914; entered Science Museum, 1920; Board of Trade, 1940-47. *Recreations:* painting, bee-keeping. *Address:* The Grange, Hillside Horsham, Sussex. [*Died* 4 *Aug.* 1969

HARTWELL, Major-General John Redmond, C.B. 1941; D.S.O. 1916; *b.* 7 May 1887; *s.* of Sydney Charles Elphinstone Hartwell; *m.* 1st, 1911, Nina Oliver (marriage dissolved, 1921), *d.* of General G. F. W. St. John; one *d.*; 2nd, 1929, Hazel Hay (*d.* 1945), *yr. d.* of Sir John Benton, K.C.I.E., *widow* of Captain Liston, I.A.; one *s.*; 3rd, 1946, Edith Elizabeth, *d.* of lat F. W. Frosdyke. *Educ.:* Radley; R.M.C., Sandhurst. 1st

Commission, 1906; joined 89th Royal Irish Fusiliers; joined 1/4th P.W.O. Gurkha Rifles, 1907; served continuously with them until 1928, when he was transferred to 1st Batt. 2nd K.E.O. Gurkha Rifles (the Sirmoor Rifles). European War, France and Belgium, Gallipoli, Egypt, N.W. India, Baluchistan (wounded, despatches, D.S.O.); A.H.Q., India, 1919-24; D.A.A.G. Shanghai Defence Force, 1927; Major, 1921; Lt.-Col. 1930; Col. 1934; Maj.-Gen. 1941; commanded 1st Bn. 18th Royal Garhwal Rifles, 1930-34; Instructor Senior Officers School, Belgaum, 1935-38; Brigadier Commanding Sind Brigade Area, Karachi, 1938; Maj.-Gen. 1941, Commander Kohat District, N.W.F.P.; retired 1943. *Recreations:* represented Radley at cricket, rackets, and fives, and R.M.C. at these and hockey; Army Lawn Tennis VI., 1926; and won Indian Army Lawn Tennis Singles, 1924 and 1925 and doubles 1925 and 1926. *Address:* c/o National and Grindlay's Bank Ltd., 13 St James's Square, S.W.1. [*Died* 19 *Sept.* 1970.

HARVEY OF TASBURGH, 1st Baron (U.K.), *cr.* 1954, of Tasburgh, Norfolk; **Oliver Charles Harvey,** 4th Bt. *cr.* 1868; G.C.M.G. 1948 (K.C.M.G. 1946; C.M.G. 1937); G.C.V.O. 1950; C.B. 1944; *b.* 26 November 1893; *yr. s.* of late Sir Charles Harvey, 2nd Bart., Rainthorpe Hall, Norwich; *m.* 1920, Maud Annora, *er. d.* of late Arthur Watkin Williams-Wynn, Coed-y-Maen, Meifod, Mont.; two *s.* *Educ.:* Malvern; Trinity College, Cambridge, B.A. Served European War, 1914-18, in France, Egypt, and Palestine (despatches); entered Foreign Office, 1919; Second Secretary, 1920; appointed to Rome, 1922; transferred to Foreign Office, 1925; First Secretary, 1926; transferred to Athens, 1929; to Paris, 1931; Counsellor and Principal Private Secretary to Secretary of State for Foreign Affairs, 1936-39; Envoy Extraordinary and Minister Plenipotentiary at Paris, 1940; P.P.S. to Secretary of State for Foreign Affairs, 1941-43; an Assistant Under-Secretary of State, Foreign Office, 1943-46; Deputy Under-Secretary of State (Political), 1946-47; Ambassador to France, 1948-54; retired 1954. A Trustee of the Wallace Collection, 1955-; a Governor of St. Mary's Hosp., 1956-58; a Member of Reviewing Cttee. on Export of Works of Art, 1959-1964. Chm. Franco-British Soc., 1956-63; Vice-Pres. British Cttee. Alliance Française. Grand Cross, Legion of Honour. Grand Cross, Ordre National du Mérite. *Heir:* *s.* Hon. Peter Charles Oliver Harvey [*b.* 28 Jan. 1921; *m.* 1957, Penelope Anne, *yr. d.* of Lt.-Col. Sir William Makins, 3rd Bt., *q.v.*; two *d.*; served War of 1939-45]. *Address:* 32 Onslow Square, S.W.7. *Club:* Brooks's. [*Died* 29 *Nov.* 1968.

HARVEY, Sir (Charles) Malcolm B.; *see* Barclay-Harvey.

HARVEY, Maj.-Gen. Sir Charles Offley, Kt., 1946; C.B. 1941; C.V.O. 1922; C.B.E. 1922; M.C. and Bar; LL.D. (Hon.); Chief Steward of Hampton Court Palace since 1962; *b.* 16 July 1888; *s.* of late Prebendary F. Clyde Harvey, Vicar of Hailsham, Sx.; *m.* 1931, Lily Millicent, *yr. d.* of late Maj.-Gen. H. L. Pritchard, C.B., C.M.G., D.S.O.; two *s.* one *d.* *Educ.:* Marlborough; R.M.C., Sandhurst. Commn., 1908; attached Highland Light Infantry; joined Central India Horse, 1909; served with Egyptian Expeditionary Force, 1914-18; A.D.C. to Duke of Connaught during his Indian tour, 1921; Assistant Military Secretary to Prince of Wales during his Indian tour, 1921-22; passed Staff College, 1922; Military Secretary to the Viceroy, 1926-31; Commandant, Central India Horse, 1933-36; commanded Indian Contingent at Coronation of King George VI, 1937; G.S.O.1. Meerut District, 1936-39; Comd. Wana Brigade, 1939-40; Comd. 8 Ind. Div., 1940-42; Military Adviser-in-Chief, Indian States Forces, 1943-1946; retd., 1946; Colonel Central India Horse, 1945-52; Asst. Managing Director, A. Guinness, Son & Co. Ltd., 1946-61. *Address:* Wilderness House, Hampton Court Palace, East Molesey, Surrey. *T.:* Teddington Lock 4643. *Club:* Cavalry. [*Died* 11 *Oct.* 1969.

HARVEY, Cyril Pearce, Q.C. 1950; *b.* 14 October 1900; 2nd *s.* of late Sir Ernest Maes Harvey, K.B.E. and late Blanche Harvey (*née* Pogson); *m.* 1924, Kathleen Nina (*d.* 1954), *y. d.* of late Alfred Darley, D.L., Dublin; one *s.* one *d.* *Educ.:* Dragon School, Oxford; Rugby; Brasenose Coll., Oxford. B.A. (Jurisprudence, 1st cl. hons.), 1922; B.C.L. (1st cl.), 1923; Vinerian Scholar, 1923. Called to the Bar, Inner Temple, 1923, Bencher, 1958. Civil Defence, 1939-40; War Office, 1940-43; British Council, 1943-45; Director, Administrative Tribunals Control Branch, Legal Div., C.C.G., 1945-46. Legal Assessor to General Medical Council and to Dental Board of U.K. (now Gen. Dental Council), 1947-; Dep. Chm., Beds. County Q.S., 1950-. A Governor of the Dragon School (Chm. 1958-66); Member: Air Transport Licensing Board; 1960-; Criminal Injuries Compensation Board, 1966-; Chm., Medical Appeals Tribunal, 1966-. Chm. Barristers' Benevolent Association, 1962-. Member British Council. *Publications:* Solon, or The Price of Justice, 1931; (with late Sir T. Willes Chitty, Bt., and A. T. Denning) Smith's Leading Cases (13th edn.), 1929; The Advocate's Devil, 1958; articles in legal and other periodicals. *Recreations:* fishing, golf, gardening. *Address:* 2 Crown Office Row, Temple, E.C.4. *T.:* City 6807; 4 Paper Buildings, Temple, E.C.4. *T.:* Central 3420. *Club:* United University. [*Died* 3 *Jan.* 1968.

HARVEY, Capt. Edward M.; *see* Murray-Harvey.

HARVEY, Air Vice-Marshal Sir George David, K.B.E. 1957 (C.B.E. 1943); C.B. 1953; D.F.C. 1934; p.s.a.; *b.* 1905; 2nd *s.* of late Maj.-Gen. David Harvey; *m.* 1939, Barbara Isabel Daphne, *d.* of late Arthur Knowles; one *s.* three *d.* *Educ.:* Westminster. Joined R.A.F., 1924; retired 1958. *Address:* Woodcutters Lodge, Over Worton, Middle Barton, Oxon. *T.:* Great Tew 285. *Club:* R.A.F. [*Died* 24 *Feb.* 1969.

HARVEY, Henry, C.B.E. 1958 (O.B.E. 1952); Director of Accounts, Air Ministry, 1954-60; *b.* 20 June 1899; *s.* of late Charles Henry Garnet Harvey; *m.* 1923, Mabel Catherine Cox; one *s.* one *d.* *Educ.:* St. Dunstan's College, Catford. Entered Civil Service, 1914. Served European War, R.N.V.R. Joined Air Ministry, 1919. War of 1939-45: Deputy Financial Adviser, Govt. of India, G.H.Q. India. Asst. Sec., Air Ministry, 1953. *Recreations:* gardening, motoring. *Address:* 7 Sandstone Court, Sandgate Rd., Folkestone, Kent. *T.:* Folkestone 55034. *Clubs:* Royal Commonwealth Society; North Foreland Golf. [*Died* 13 *May* 1965.

HARVEY, Hildebrand Wolfe, C.B.E. 1958; F.R.S. 1945; Sc.D.; formerly on scientific staff of Marine Biological Assoc. of the U.K., 1921-58; *b.* 31 Dec. 1887; *m.* 1923, Elsie Marguerite, *d.* of late H. Sanders; *m.* 1933, Marjorie Joan, *d.* of late J. Sargeant; one *s.* *Educ.:* Gresham's School, Holt; Downing Coll., Cambridge. Alexander Agassiz Medal, Nat. Acad. Science, New York, 1952. *Publications:* Biological Chemistry and Physics of Sea Water, 1927 (Moscow 1933); The Chemistry and Biology of Sea Water, 1945 (Paris, 1949); Chemistry and

Fertility of Sea Waters, 1956; scientific papers relating to the fertility of the sea. *Address:* Southern House, 123 Furzehatt Rd., Plymstock, Plymouth, South Devon. [*Died* 26 *Nov.* 1970.

HARVEY, John Wilfred; Emeritus Professor of Philosophy, Leeds University; *b.* 16 Feb. 1889; *y. s.* of William Harvey, Leeds; *m.* 1924, Phyllis Mabel, *d.* of C. B. Bishop. *Educ.:* Bootham School, York; Rugby School; Balliol College, Oxford. Professor of Philosophy, Armstrong College, Newcastle on Tyne, 1927-1932; University of Leeds, 1932-54. *Publications:* joint author of Competition, 1912 and Christianity and the Present Moral Unrest, 1926; The Naturalness of Religion, 1929; Poems, 1924; translated Rudolph Otto's Das Heilige (The Idea of the Holy), 1923; The Salt and the Leaven, 1947. Edited: John Henry Muirhead, 1942. *Address:* 8A Claremont Road, Headingley. Leeds. *Club:* National Liberal. [*Died* 14 *Nov.* 1967.

HARVEY, Sir Robert (James Paterson), K.B.E. 1960; C.B. 1949; M.A.; Vice-Chairman, Management Committee, Printing and Allied Trades Research Association since 1964; *b.* 28 July 1904; *s.* of late Reverend Thomas Harvey, M.A.; *m.* 1934, Margaret Mitchell; two *s.* one *d.* *Educ.:* Daniel Stewart's College, Edinburgh; Edinburgh University. M.A. 1st Class Hons. History (Edinburgh), 1926. Assistant Principal, G.P.O., 1926; Chief Supt., London Postal Service, 1934; Imperial Defence Coll., 1935; Principal, Treasury, 1936; Private Sec., Minister of Food, 1940; Asst. Sec., Treasury, 1941; Under-Sec., Treasury, 1946; Regional Director, Home Counties Region, G.P.O., 1947; Director of Inland Telecommunications, G.P.O., 1949-54; Director of Radio and Accommodation, G.P.O., 1954-55; Dep. Director-General, General Post Office, 1955-1964. *Recreation:* golf. *Address:* Airlie, 41 Cornwall Road, Cheam, Sutton, Surrey. *T.:* Vigilant 3874. *Club:* Royal Automobile. [*Died* 8 *July* 1965.

HARVEY, Rt. Rev. Thomas Arnold, D.D.; *b.* 17 Apr. 1878; *s.* of Rev. Alfred Thomas Harvey and Ida Susette Weguelin; *m.* Isabel Kathleen, *d.* of Rev. F. R. Burrows; three *s.* two *d.* *Educ.:* St. Oswald's College, Ellesmere; Trinity College, Dublin. Deacon, 1903; Priest, 1904; Curate of St. Stephen's, Dublin, 1903-08; Rector of Lissadell, Sligo, 1908-12; Portrush, Antrim, 1912-16; of Booterstown, Dublin, 1916-33; Canon of St. Patrick's, Dublin, 1930-33; Dean of St. Patrick's, Dublin, 1933-35; Professor of Pastoral Theology, Trinity College, Dublin, 1929-34; Bishop of Cashel and Waterford, 1935-58. *Address:* 1 Dartry Road, Dublin, Ireland. [*Died* 25 *Dec.* 1966.

HARWOOD, Sir Edmund (George), K.B.E., *cr.* 1956; C.B. 1948; *e. s.* of late E. T. Harwood, Shrewsbury; *m.* 1921, Ruth (*d.* 1964), *e. d.* of late A. G. Freeman; two *d.* Civil Service, 1921; Paymaster-General's Office, 1921-39; Ministry of Food, 1939-46; Civilian Director, Imperial Defence College, 1947; Ministry of Food, 1948-55; Deputy Secretary, Ministry of Agriculture, Fisheries and Food, 1953-59. Appointed Member, Milk Marketing Board, 1959-; Chairman, National Cold Stores (Management) Ltd. *Address:* King's Ride, Alfriston, Sussex. *Clubs:* Union, Royal Commonwealth Society. [*Died* 10 *Dec.* 1964.

HARWOOD, Henry Cecil; Journalist; *b.* 21 Oct. 1893; *o. s.* of Henry Harwood, of Boston, Lincs.; *m.* 1919, Dorothy Blackledge. *Educ.:* Shrewsbury; Balliol College, Oxford (Exhibitioner) 2nd Lit. Hum. 1915. Called to the Bar, 1922. *Publications:* Judgment Eve, short stories; contributed to Encyclopædia Britannica, Quarterly, 19th Century, etc. *Recreation:* walking. *Address:* 293 Woodstock Road, Oxford. [*Died* 6 *Oct.* 1964.

HASELTINE, Herbert, N.A.; Hon. M.A. Harvard; Chevalier Légion d'Honneur; For. Mem. Académie des Beaux Arts, 1956; Nat. Inst. of Arts and Letters, U.S.A.; Nat. Sculpture Soc., U.S.A.; Sculptor; *b.* Rome, 10 April 1877; *s.* of late William Stanley Haseltine and Helen Marshall; *m.* 1911, Madeleine Keith; one *s.* one *d.* *Educ.:* Collegio Romano, Rome; Class of 1899, Harvard; studied drawing: Royal Academy; Munich; Rome; Paris. Pupil of late Aimé Morot. First exhibited in Paris Salon, 1906, and subsequently at Royal Acad. London, and Internat. Exhibns. in Vienna, Liverpool, Venice, Rome, Brussels, Ghent; also at Walker Art Gallery, Liverpool and Roy. Glasgow Inst. of Fine Arts. Commanded by King Edward VII to execute bronze of his charger, Kildare, 1908; attached to American Embassy in Paris, 1914-16; Capt., Engr. Corps, U.S. Army, 1918-19; organised Camouflage Section of American Army in France; one-man shows in Paris, 1920, 1925, 1955; London, 1914, 1921, 1925, 1930, 1953; U.S.A., 1934, 1936 and 1940-45. Monuments: Cavalry Club War Memorial: "The Empty Saddle," 1924; equestrian monuments of Jam Shri Rawalji, and of Prince Ranjitsinjhi, India, 1934; monument of Man O'War, Lexington, U.S.A., 1948; equestrian monument of Field Marshal Sir John Dill, Washington, D.C., 1950; equestrian statue of George Washington, for Washington, D.C., 1959; commissioned to make statue of Auriole for Queen Elizabeth II, presented Buckingham Palace. Other works are represented in following museums and galls.: In England: Tate Gallery, Imperial War Museum, Eton College Art Museum; in France: Musée de l'Art Moderne; in New York: Metropolitan Museum of Art, Museum of the Hispanic Society of America, Whitney Museum of American Art, Museum of the National Institute of Arts and Letters; in Chicago: (Field Museum) "The British Champion Animals" (twenty statues in bronze, marble and stone of British Champions: horses, cattle, sheep and pigs); also in Philadelphia Museum of Art; Fogg Art Museum, Harvard Univ.; Yale University Art Gallery, etc. Bronzes of famous race-horses include: Spearmint, Mumtaz Mahal, Sergeant Murphy, Easter Hero, Fox Hunter, Bois Roussel, etc. *Address:* 20 Impasse Raffet, rue Raffet, Paris XVIe; *T.A.:* Haseltine, Paris. *T.:* Auteuil 95-19; (Studios): 4 rue du Docteur Blanche, Paris XVIe. *T.:* Auteuil 84-91; 200 Central Park South, New York 19, U.S.A. *T.:* Circle 6-7047. *Clubs:* Buck's (London); Polo de Paris, Travellers; University (Paris); Century (New York). [*Died* 8 *Jan.* 1962.

HASKARD, Brigadier-General John McDougall, C.M.G. 1919; D.S.O. 1917; *b.* Florence, 27 Nov. 1877; *s.* of W. T. Haskard, Florence; *m.* 1911, Alicia Isabel (*d.* 1960), *d.* of S. Newburgh Hutchins, of Ardnagashel, Bantry, Ireland; one *s.* *Educ.:* Blairlodge, Stirlingshire. Joined R. Dublin Fusiliers, 1897; served S. African War, and took part in the engagements at Talana Hill, Colenso, Spion Kop, Vaal Krantz, and Pieter's Hill (wounded, despatches, Queen's medal 6 clasps, King's medal 2 clasps); operations in the Aden Hinterland, 1903; served in the Egyptian Army, 1908-11; passed Staff College, 1914; European War 1914-18, and served in France, Salonika and Egypt; amongst other engagements was present at the Battles of the Somme and Ancre, Ypres, 1917, Cambrai and St. Quentin (despatches five times, D.S.O., C.M.G., Bt. Lt.-Col.); served successively as Staff Capt. of a Brigade; Brigade-Major; Gen. Staff Officer 2nd Grade of a Division and Corps; Gen. Staff Officer 1st Grade of a Division; Brig-Gen. Gen. Staff; Gen. Staff Officer 1st

Grade, Staff College, Camberley, 1919-20; commanded 1st East Yorkshire Regt., 1923 27; Colonel on the Staff and G.S.O. 1st Grade Shanghai Defence Force and China Command, 1927-30; Assistant Adj.-Gen., Aldershot, 1930-31; retired pay, 1932. *Recreations*: shooting, fishing. *Address:* Tragariff, Bantry, Co. Cork. *T.:* Bantry 74.
[*Died* 26 *Aug.* 1967.

HASLAM, Hon. Lt.-Col. Sir (Robert) Humphrey, Kt., *cr.* 1955; O.B.E. 1944; *b.* 30 May 1882; *s.* of Thomas and Eleanor Eliza Haslam; *m.* 1911, Marian, 2nd *d.* of late Vice-Adm. O. P. Tudor, C.V.O. *Educ.:* Shrewsbury School. Served European War, 1914-1919 (severely wounded, 1918); J.P. Hertfordshire, 1925; County Council, Hertfordshire, since 1922; County Alderman, 1940; High Sheriff of Hertfordshire, 1934; D.L. Hertfordshire, 1936; Vice-Chairman, Thames Conservancy Board, 1949-60; Chm. Eastern Provincial Area Conservative Assoc., 1952-56. *Address:* Cross Oak, Berkhamsted, Herts. *T.:* Berkhamsted 14. *Club:* Carlton.
[*Died* 22 *Dec.* 1962.

HASSALL, Christopher Vernon; Author; *b.* 24 March 1912; *s.* of late John Hassall, R.I., R.W.A., and late Constance Brooke-Webb; *m.* 1938, Evelyn, *d.* of late Eustace Chapman; one *s.* one *d.* *Educ.:* St. Michael's Coll., Tenbury Wells; Brighton Coll.; Wadham Coll., Oxford. Played Romeo in John Gielgud's production for the O.U.D.S., 1932; toured Egypt and Australia with Nicholas Hannen, 1933; played in Henry VIII, Old Vic, and joined Ivor Novello's company, 1934; left stage; wrote lyrics for Ivor Novello, 1935-49; Glamorous Night, Careless Rapture, Crest of the Wave, The Dancing Years, Arc de Triomphe, King's Rhapsody; produced and acted in his own Devil's Dyke at Oxford Festival, 1937; composed music for production of his Christ's Comet, Canterbury Festival, 1938; Radio Series in Five parts, The Story of George Frideric Handel, 1949; adapted Barrie's Quality Street, as a musical play (Dear Miss Phoebe), Phœnix, 1950; The Great Endeavour, drama for the Empire Day Movement, Drury Lane, 1948; The Player King (verse drama), Edinburgh Festival, 1952. Director of Voice, Old Vic Theatre School, 1947-49; Poetry Editor, B.B.C. Third Programme, 1950; played Ishak in Hassan, 1947; Antonio in the Duchess of Malfi, 1941, for the B.B.C.; Poetry Reader for the Apollo Society, 1946-. A.C. Benson Medal and Hawthornden Prize, 1939; Councillor and Fellow R.S.L.; Director of the Performing Right Society; Governor of The London Academy of Music and Dramatic Art; Mem. Arts Council Poetry Panel, 1951-53. Joined R.A., June 1940; commissioned March 1941; trans. Army Educational Corps, 1942; demobilised as Staff Major War Office, 1946. Founded Stratford Annual Poetry Festival, 1954. *Original librettos for Opera:* (for Anthony Hopkins) The Man from Tuscany, Canterbury Festival, 1951; (for Franz Reizenstein) Anna Kraus (Radio Opera), 1952; (for William Walton) Troilus and Cressida, 1954; (for Arthur Bliss) Tobias and the Angel, 1960. *Original texts for Cantatas:* The Rainbow (for Festival of Britain), 1951; (with Thomas Wood) Yggdrasil, Bryanston Summer School, 1951; (with Wilfrid Mellers) Voices of Night, 1952; Genesis, 1958. *English versions of Opera:* Dvořák's Rusalka, Rimsky-Korsakov's Kitesh, Donizetti's Il Campanello, Bartok's Bluebeard's Castle, Lehar's The Merry Widow, The Land of Smiles, and Johann Strauss's Fledermaus (these last three for the Sadler's Wells Opera Company). *Publications:* Poems of Two Years, 1935; Devil's Dyke, 1936; Christ's Comet, 1937; Penthesperon, 1938; Crisis, 1939; S.O.S. Ludlow, 1941; The Timeless Quest, 1948; The Slow Night, 1949; Words by Request, 1952; Out of the Whirlwind, The Player King, 1953; The Red Leaf (Poems), 1957. Edited The ABCA Song Book for the War Office, 1944; (Ed. with Introd.) The Prose of Rupert Brooke, 1956; Edward Marsh, Patron of the Arts, A Biography, 1959; *Posthumous Publications:* Rupert Brooke, 1964; Ambrosia and Small Beer, 1964. *Address:* Tonford Manor, Canterbury, Kent. *T.:* Canterbury 2524. *Club:* Savile.
[*Died* 25 *April* 1963.

HASTINGS, Somerville, M.B., M.S. (Lond.), F.R.C.S. (Eng.); Alderman L.C.C. 1946; Cons. Surgeon and Lecturer to Ear and Throat Dept., Middlesex Hospital; *b.* Warminster, Wilts, 1878; *s.* of Rev. H. G. Hastings, M.A.; *m.* Bessie (*d.* 1958), 4th *d.* of W. C. Tuke, architect, Manchester. *Educ.:* Wycliffe Coll., Stonehouse, Glos.; Univ. Coll. (Gold and Silver Medallist in Botany); Middlesex Hospital (Entrance Scholar and Governor's Prizeman). Late Demonstrator of Physiology; Cancer Research Scholar; House-Surgeon, Casualty Surgical Officer, and Surgical Registrar, Middlesex Hospital; late Assistant-Surgeon East London Hospital for Children; late Assist.-Surgeon, London Throat Hospital; late President Otological Section of Royal Society of Medicine; M.P. (Lab.) Reading, 1923-24, and 1929-31; (Lab.) Barking, 1945-September, 1959, Freeman of Barking, 1960. Member L.C.C. for Mile End, 1932-46; Chairman of Hospitals and Medical Services Committee, L.C.C., 1934-44; Chairman L.C.C. 1944-45; late President Socialist Medical Association; late Member N.E. Metropolitan Regional Hosp. Bd. *Publications:* numerous medical and surgical papers; Summer Flowers of the High Alps; Alpine Plants at Home; First Aid for the Trenches, etc. *Recreations:* plants, photography, mountains. *Address:* Brackenfell, Kingwood, Oxon. *T.:* Rotherfield Greys 342. [*Died* 7 *July* 1967.

HASZARD, Colonel Gerald Fenwick, C.B.E. 1943; D.S.O.; D.L., J.P. Staffs; Royal Marines (retired); *b.* 22 October 1894; *o. s.* of Captain H. F. Haszard, Royal Navy; *m.* 1928, Dyonese Rosamond, *o. d.* of Captain W. S. B. Levett, D.L., J.P., Milford Hall, Stafford; two *s.* *Educ.:* Haileybury. Joined Royal Marine Artillery, 1914; served France and Belgium, 1914-18 (O.B.E., D.S.C. and bar, Royal Humane Society's medal, Croix de Guerre); served Anti-Aircraft and Experimental Depts. and retired, 1934; recalled for service at outbreak of War, 1939. High Sheriff of Staffordshire, 1952. *Recreations:* shooting, carpentering and engineering. *Address:* Milford Hall, Stafford. *T.:* Stafford 61001.
[*Died* 4 *Feb.* 1967.

HATCH, George Washington, C.I.E. 1927; *b.* 1872; *s.* of Henry Hatch; *m.* 1908, Jessie (*d.* 1934), *d.* of Henry Harrison; three *d.* (and one *s.* decd.). *Educ.:* St. Paul's School; Balliol College, Oxford. Passed into the I.C.S., 1891; Assistant Collector in the Bombay Presidency, 1893; Acted as Under-Secretary to Govt., 1899 and 1904; Collector of Kaira, 1905; of Bombay, 1906; acted as Chairman Bombay Improvement Trust, 1914; Additional Member of the Legislative Council, 1914; Collector of Poona, 1915; Chairman Bombay Port Trust, 1918; Commissioner Central Division, Bombay Presidency, 1922; Member of the Council of State, Delhi, 1928; Member of the Executive Council of the Bombay Government (temporary), 1928; retired from the I.C.S. 1928. *Recreation:* golf. *Address:* Little Cobbetts, Farnham, Surrey. [*Died* 7 *Feb.* 1963.

HATCHARD, Caroline, (Caroline Langford), F.R.A.M.; *b.* Portsmouth, 12 October 1883; *m.* Robert S. Langford, I.S.O.; two *s.* *Educ.:* Royal Academy of Music, London. Campbell Clarke Scholarship.

1903; Rutson Memorial Prize, 1904; Melba Prize, 1905; A.R.A.M. 1907; début Covent Garden as Dew Fairy in Hansel and Gretel, 1906; sang in Italian and other Grand Opera seasons at Covent Garden, 1906-8; in later opera created the parts of Tilburina in Stanford's opera, The Critic, produced in 1915; and Madam Herz in Mozart's Impressario at its revival in London, 1910; best known rôles in opera are the Queen of Night Magic Flute), Sophie (Rosenkavalier) Eva (Meistersinger), and the Doll (Tales of Hoffman); has sung in Oratorio and Concerts for the principal Societies and Festivals. In Oratorio the renderings of The Messiah and The Creation are the best known; formerly: Professor of Singing at Royal Academy of Music; Adjudicator at Singing Festivals, etc. *Recreation:* gardening. *Address:* 66 Belsize Park Gardens, N.W.3. *T.* Primrose Hill 0032. *Club:* R.A.M. [*Died* 7 *Jan.* 1970.

HATHERTON, 5th Baron (*cr.* 1835), **Edward Thomas Walhouse Littleton,** R.N. (retired); *b.* 13 Aug. 1900; *s.* of 4th Baron; *S.* father 1944; *m.* 1st, 1925, Ida Guendolen (marriage dissolved, 1951), *d.* of Robin Legge; two *d.*; 2nd, 1952, Mrs. Kathleen May Westendarp, *o. d.* of late Clarence Ernest Orlando Whitechurch and of Mrs. Whitechurch. Served European War, 1914-18, and War of 1939-45. Conservative Whip, House of Lords, 1946-49; D.L. Staffordshire. *Heir: b* Hon. John Walter Stuart Littleton [*b.* 9 Aug. 1906; *m.* 1932, Nora Evelyn (*d.* 1955), *d.* of R. C. Smith, Edgbaston; one *d.*]. *Address:* Hatherton Hall, Cannock, Staffs. *Clubs:* Carlton, Naval and Military. [*Died* 13 *Nov.* 1969.

HATTON, Sir Ronald George, Kt.; *cr.* 1949; C.B.E. 1934, F.R.S. 1944; M.A., D.Sc. (Hort.) 1936; Director of East Malling Research Station, 1918 retired 1949; late Consultant Director, Commonwealth Bureau of Horticulture and Plantation Crops, East Malling; *b.* 6 July 1886, *s.* of late Ernest Hatton, Inner Temple, and Amy, *d.* of late William Pearson, K.C.; *m.* 1914, Hannah Rachel, *d.* of late Henry Rigden, Ashford, Kent; one *s.* *Educ.:* Brighton College, Exeter School; Balliol College, Oxford. S.E. Agricultural Coll., Wye. On staff Horticultural Dept., S.E. Agricultural Coll., Wye; acting Director Wye Coll. Fruit Experimental Station, East Malling 1914-18; investigating wages and conditions of employment in Lincolnshire for Agricultural Wages Board; Member Adult Education Committee of Ministry of Reconstruction, 1917-19; Vice-Chairman and lecturer Kent Federation of Workers Educational Association; Travelling Research Fellowship to U.S.A., 1923; Masters Memorial Lecturer, awarded Victoria Medal of Honour by Royal Horticultural Society, 1930, tour of horticultural regions and research institutes of the Empire on behalf of the Empire Marketing Board, 1930-31; visited S. African fruit growing areas at invitation of Union Govt., 1936, Ridley Medal from Company of Fruiterers, 1936; Hon. Fell. Wye Coll.; Foreign Member, R. Acad. of Agriculture, Sweden, 1926; Hon. Member, N.Z. Institute of Horticulture, 1930; Hon. D.Ag. Univ. of S. Clement, Sofia, 1939; a Vice-Pres. R. Hort. S., 1952; Hon. Fell. R.A.S.E., 1955. *Publications:* numerous papers dealing with research in horticultural science and practical fruit growing in periodicals; (Ed.) Folk of the Furrow (by Christopher Holdenby), 1913. *Address:* Sleightholme, Benenden, Nr. Cranbrook, Kent. *T.:* Benenden 634. [*Died* 11 *Nov.* 1965.

HAUGH, Hon. Kevin O'Hanrahan; Judge of the Supreme Court, Eire, since 1961; *b.* 17 Nov. 1901; *s.* of late Professor John Joseph Haugh author of Haugh's Higher Arithmetic, and late Kathleen O'Hanrahan; *m.* 1941, Brenda *d.* of John A. Cullen, Solicitor, Dublin; five *s.* *Educ.:* Belvedere and Blackrock Colleges, Dublin. Graduate of National University, Dublin; called to Irish Bar, 1925; called to the Inner Bar, 1939; Attorney-General, Eire, 1940-42; Judge of the High Court, Eire, 1942-61. *Recreation:* golf. *Address:* 79 Ailesbury Road, Dublin. *T.:* Dublin 84182 [*Died* 5 *April* 1969.

HAULTAIN, Herbert Edward Terrick; Professor of Mining Engineering, University of Toronto, 1908, now Professor Emeritus; *b.* Brighton, England, 1869; *y. s.* of late Major-General F. M. Haultain; *m.* Muriel Frances Cronyn; one *d.* *Educ.:* University of Toronto; Freiberg. Mining Engineer in Ireland, Bohemia, South Africa, Western United States, and Canada; Randolph Bruce Gold Medal, 1936. *Address:* University of Toronto, Toronto 5, Canada. *Club:* National (Toronto). [*Died* 19 *Sept.* 1961.

HAVELOCK, Sir Thomas (Henry), Kt. *cr.* 1951; F.R.S. 1914; M.A., D.Sc., Hon. M.I.N.A.; Corr. Mem. Acad. Sci. Paris; Hon. Fellow of St. John's College, Cambridge; formerly Professor of Mathematics, King's College, Newcastle, and Director of the Department; Sub-Rector of King's College, 1937-42; *b.* Newcastle upon Tyne, 1877; *s.* of late Michael Havelock; unmarried. *Educ.:* Armstrong College, University of Durham; St. John's College, Cambridge. Vice-Principal of Armstrong College, 1933-37. Smith's Prizeman, Isaac Newton Student, and Fellow of St. John's College, Cambridge. William Froude Gold Medal, 1956. Hon. D.C.L. Durham 1958; Hon. D.Sc., Hamburg, 1960. *Publications:* various papers published by the Roy. Soc. and other learned societies. *Address:* 8 Westfield Drive, Gosforth, Newcastle upon Tyne. *T.:* Gosforth 52393. *Club:* Athenæum. [*Died* 1 *Aug.* 1968.

HAVILAND, Rev. Edmund Arthur; B.A. 1896; M.A. 1901; *b.* 10 May 1874; *s.* of late Rev. A. C. Haviland, Senior Fellow, St. John's College, Cambridge; *m.* 1st, 1915, Irene Margaret (*d.* 1916), *d.* of late Col. Cardwell; 2nd, 1922, Vivienne, *yr. d.* of Selwyn Brown, Kimberley, S. Africa; two *s.* (and one *s.* decd.). *Educ.:* Wellington; King's College, Cambridge; Wells Theological Coll. Ordained 1899; Curate of St. Hilda, Darlington, 1899-1903; Selly Oak, 1904-9; Vicar, 1909-15; Archdeacon of Kimberley, 1915-22; Rector o Brightling, 1922-31; Rector of Heene, Worthing 1931-47. *Address:* Great Wishford, Salisbury, Wilts. *T.:* Stapleford 247. *Club:* Royal Over-Seas League [*Died* 4 *Aug.* 1966.

HAWARD, Edwin, O.B.E. 1953; Journalist; *b.* Bungay, 9 Oct. 1884; *e. s.* of late Frederic Haward and Jane Fanny Botwright; *m.* 1st; two *s.* one *d.*; 2nd, Isabel Winter (*d.* 1955); 3rd, 1955, Muriel, *widow* of C. L. Page. *Educ.:* Bungay Grammar, Stamford and Reading Schools; King's College, London. Joined Civil and Military Gazette, Lahore, 1909; Manager, 1916-20; Correspondent of the Pioneer and The Times (London) at the Headquarters of the Government of India, 1921-25; Editor of the Pioneer, Allahabad, 1926-28; Information Officer, India Office, 1928-30; Editor North China Daily News, Shanghai, 1930-38; on staff of Information Section of League of Nations Secretariat, 1939; Adviser on India Affairs Far Eastern Bureau, British Ministry of Information (Singapore), 1940-1941; Secretary, India, Pakistan and Burma Association, 1942-53; Liveryman of Stationers' and Newspaper Makers' Company (City of London); F.J.I. *Publications:* The Last Rebellion; Manchurian Medley; A Picture of India. *Address:* 31 Stone Close, Worthing. *T.:* Swandean 1950. *Club:* Royal Over-Seas League. [*Died* 11 *Dec.* 1961.

HAWES, Charles George, C.I.E. 1939; Hydrological and Irrigation Consultant; M.C.; B.Sc. (Lond.); A.C.G.I.; M.Inst.C.E.; Indian Service of Engineers (retd.); *b.* 7 March 1890; *s.* of Charles Anley Hawes; *m.* 1922, Marion Terrick Sworder; two *d.* Entered Indian Service of Engineers, 1912; served European War, 1915-19; late Chief Engineer and Sec. to Govt. of Sind, P.W.D.; served as Brig. Works of Services, E.-in-C.'s Branch G.H.Q. India Comd., 1943-45. *Address:* Spriggsmoor, South Brent, Devon. *T.:* S. Brent 3287. [*Died* 30 *Dec.* 1963.

HAWES, Sir Richard Brunel, Kt. 1957; C.M.G. 1949; M.B. Lond., F.R.C.P. Lond., D.T.M. and H. Lond.; Hon. M.D. Malaya; former Consulting Physician to Colonial Office; former Professor of Medicine, King Edward VII College of Medicine, Singapore; *b.* Tarapaca, Chile, 1893; *s.* of late Dr. F. Brunel Hawes; *m.* K. A. (*d.* 1958), *d.* of late M. O'Neill, Galway; two *s.* (and eldest son killed in action, Burma, 1944). *Educ.:* Stonyhurst; St. Thomas's Hospital. Served European War in Royal Engineers, Aug. 1914-Sept. 1915; Retreat from Mons, Aisne, 1st and 2nd Battle Ypres (despatches, Mons Star); later Captain R.A.M.C. in Mesopotamian Campaign till 1919; joined Colonial Service, 1922 *Address:* c/o National & Grindlay's Bank, 13 St. James's Square, S.W.1. [*Died* 30 *Dec.* 1964.

HAWES, Sir Ronald N.; *see* Nesbitt-Hawes.

HAWKE, Sir (Edward) Anthony, Kt., *cr.* 1954; Barrister-at-Law; Recorder of London, since Nov. 1959; President, London Cornish Association, since 1946; *b.* 26 July 1895; *s.* of late Hon. Mr. Justice Hawke; *m.* 1931, Evelyn Audrey Lee Davies; one *d.* *Educ.:* Charterhouse; Magdalen College, Oxford. Called to Bar, 1920; Bencher, Middle Temple, 1942; Master Treasurer, 1962. Member of Western Circuit and Devon Sessions; Junior Prosecuting Counsel at Central Criminal Court, 1932; Third Senior Prosecuting Counsel, 1937, 2nd Senior, 1942, Senior Prosecuting Counsel for Crown, 1945-50; Recorder of Bath, 1939-50; Deputy Chairman County of Hertford Quarter Sessions, 1940-50; Chairman County of London Quarter Sessions, 1950-54; Common Serjeant of the City of London, 1954-59. Mem. Standing Cttee. on Criminal Law Revision, 1959-. *Publications:* Editor, Roscoe's Criminal Evidence, 15th Edition. *Recreation:* golf. *Address:* 143 Cranmer Court, Sloane Avenue, S.W.3. *Club:* United University. [*Died* 25 *Sept.* 1964.

HAWKES, Lieut.-Col. Corlis St. Leger Gillman, C.M.G. 1919; D.S.O. 1917; late R.F.A.; *b.* 23 Mar. 1871; *s.* of late Corliss Hawkes, Lackaroo House, and Carhue, Co. Cork, and Jane Cotter Williamson, *d.* of Rev. W. C. Williamson, Vicar of Christ Church, Cork; *m.* 1907, Eleanor Muriel, *e. d.* of late Major E. H. Pares, of Hopwell Hall, Derbyshire; (*s.* Pilot Officer R.A.F.V.R. killed on Active Service, Middle East, 22 Oct. 1942), one *d.* *Educ.:* privately. Joined R.A. from Militia, 1893; served South African War, Nov. 1899 to May 1901 (Queen's medal and 6 clasps); European War in France, 1914-19 (despatches 4 times, D.S.O., C.M.G., 1914 Star, French Croix-de-Guerre); promoted Temp. Lt.-Col. 1915, and Substantive, 1916; retired pay, 1921. D.L. Pembrokeshire, 1951. *Address:* Milton House, Tenby. [*Died* 4 *May* 1963.

HAWKES, Rt. Rev. Frederick Ochterloney Taylor; *b.* 22 November 1878; *s.* of John Devonshire Hawkes, J.P. of Kilcrea, Co. Cork, and Emma Taylor of Clontough, Co. Kerry. *Educ.:* Magdalen College, Oxford; Wells Theological College. Assistant Curate of St. Mary's, Portsea, 1903-11; Vicar of Aldershot, 1911-19; Rural Dean of Aldershot; Senior Chaplain of Guards Division, 1919; Rector of Lambeth, 1919-27; Archdeacon of Southwark, 1927-52; Bishop Suffragan of Kingston on-Thames, 1927-52; resigned 1952. *Recreations:* golf, travelling. *Address:* Kilcrea, Barrow Green Rd., Oxted, Surrey. *T.:* Oxted 3729. [*Died* 26 *Jan.* 1966

HAWKES, Ven. Leonard Stephen, T.D. 1951; Archdeacon of Lindisfarne, Hon. Canon of Newcastle, and Vicar of Eglingham, since 1960; *b.* 5 Oct. 1907; *s.* of Dr. James Leonard Hawkes, M.D., Wallasey, Cheshire; *m.* 1939, Josephine Mary Pearce Hubbard; three *s.* one *d.* *Educ.:* Oakham Sch.; Emmanuel Coll., Camb.; Cuddesdon Theol. College. Deacon, 1931; Priest 1932, Southwark; Curate of St. And. Catford, 1931-34; Vice-Principal, Dorchester Miss. Coll., 1934-1938; Curate of St. John Divine, Kennington, 1938-46. C.F., T.A., 1939-57. Vicar of Oxton, 1946-50; Canon of Sacrista in Southwell Minster, 1946-50, Treas., 1948-50; Dioc. Dir of Educn. 1946-50; Rector of Blechingley, 1950-60; Hon. Canon of Southwark, 1957-60. Proctor in Convocation, Southwell, 1948-50 and Southwark, 1959-60; Member: Ch. Assembly, Standing Cttee., Bd. of Educn. and Schools Council (Vice-Chm.). *Publication:* There's an Answer Somewhere (Jt., with Canon Marcus Knight), 1953. *Address:* Eglingham Vicarage, Alnwick, Northumberland. *T.:* Powburn 250. *Club:* United University. [*Died* 3 *Aug.* 1969.

HAWKES, Captain William Arthur, C.B.E. 1935; R.D., A.D.C., R.N.R. (retired); *b.* 3 June 1881; *s.* of Alderman Richard Hawkes, J.P., and Anne Hawkes; *m.* 1917, Eileen Fanny, *d.* of W. W. Woodman, Old Town House, Stratford-on-Avon; no *c.* *Educ.:* K.E.S. Grammar School, Stratford-on-Avon; H.M.S. Conway. Entered Merchant Navy, 1898; Obtained Extra Master's certificate, 1905; Joined Cunard Steamship Coy's service, 1905; Captain, 1922; retired from Cunard White Star, Dec. 1945; served European War, 1914-19; Captain R.N.R. active list, 1928; A.D.C. to King George V. 1934-36; retired list, 1936; Marine Representative for Johnson and Phillips Ltd., Electrical Engineers and Cable Makers, Columbia House, Aldwych, W.C.2, 1946-50; Member Hon. Co. of Master Mariners. *Address:* Flat One, 10 Grassington Road, Eastbourne. *T.:* 5905. *Club:* English-Speaking Union [*Died* 23 *March* 1962.

HAWKESWORTH, Geoffrey, C.M.G. 1956; *b.* 18 April 1904; *s.* of late Rev. J. Hawkesworth, Ambleside, Westmorland; *m.* 1949, Kathleen Mary Pullom; one *s.* *Educ.:* St. Bees School, Cumberland; The Queen's College, Oxford (B.A.). Appointed to Sudan Political Service, 1926; Deputy Governor, Kordofan Province, Sudan, 1945; Governor Kordofan Province, Sudan, 1950-54; Head of Sudan Service Resettlement Bureau, 1954-end of Jan. 1956; Chairman of the Federal Public Service Commission, Nigeria, 1956-61. Order of the Nile (fourth class), 1939. *Recreations:* golf and gardening. *Address:* The Spring, Stanford Dingley Nr. Bradfield, Berks. [*Died* 1 *Aug.* 1969.

HAWKESWORTH, Rear-Admiral Richard Arthur, C.B. 1946; O.B.E. 1919; *b.* 1890; *o. s.* of late John Hawkesworth, Forest, Mountrath, Queen's Co., Ireland; *m.* 1949, Mrs. Violet Esmé Feild. Joined Royal Navy, 1908. Served War of 1914-18 and 1939-45 (despatches, 1942). *Address:* Rofford House, Yarmouth, Isle of Wight. *Clubs:* Royal Western Yacht Club of England (Plymouth); Royal Solent Yacht. [*Died* 22 *June* 1968.

HAWKINS, Brian Charles Keith, C.M.G. 1952; O.B.E. 1946; retired; *b.* 22 Aug. 1900; *s.* of Arthur Vernon Hawkins, C.I.E., and Lilian Celia Hawkins; *m.* 1928, Gladys Helen Johnstone. *Educ.:* St. Paul's School, London; Hertford College, Oxford (B.A.). Cadet officer, Hong Kong Civil Service, 1924; Hong Kong, 1925; various administrative posts, 1927-40; Labour Officer, 1940-41; interned by Japanese, 1941-45; Secretary, Chinese Affairs and Labour (H.K. Military Administration, 1945-46); Adviser U.K. Delegation 29th I.L.O. Conference, 1946. Cadet Officer, Class I, 1946. Commissioner of Labour, Hong Kong, 1947. Member Executive Council, Hong Kong, 1947; Secretary for Chinese Affairs and *ex-officio* Member of Executive and Legislative Councils, 1955-58; retired, 1958. A Member, Salaries Commission, Hong Kong, 1959. *Recreations:* cricket, walking. *Address:* c/o National and Grindlay's Bank Ltd., 54 Parliament Street, S.W.1. [*Died* 5 *June* 1962.

HAWKINS, Maj.-Gen. Edward Brian Barkley, D.S.O. 1918; O.B.E. 1931; *s.* of late Edward Hawkins, J.P., D.L., White Lodge, Wrecclesham, Surrey; *m.* Anne, *d.* of G. Debayser, 12 rue Cortambert, Paris; one *s.* one *d.* *Educ.:* Winchester College; Sandhurst. Joined West Yorkshire Regt., 1909; Capt., 1914; Temp. Major, 1916; Temp. Lt.-Col., 1918; Bt.-Major, 1919; Major, 1926; Lt.-Col. 1936; Col. 1939; Temp. Maj.-Gen. 1941; served in Uganda, British East Africa, German East Africa, Portuguese East Africa, Nyasaland, Northern Rhodesia, 1912-19; H.B.M.'s Consul for South-western Ethiopia, 1920-22; Local Lt.-Col. commanding 1st Batt. The King's African Rifles, Zomba, Nyasaland, 1926-31; commanded 2nd Battalion The West Yorkshire Regiment, 1936-39; Brigade Comm., 1939; Maj.-Gen., 1940; retired pay, 1946. *Recreations:* shooting and golf. *Address:* Villa Dormy Two, Allée des Amazones, Avenue du Golf, Le Touquet, P. de C., France. *T.:* Le Touquet 759. *Clubs:* Army and Navy; Phyllis Court (Henley). [*Died* 7 *June* 1966.

HAWKINS, Herbert Leader, F.R.S. 1937; F.G.S.; D.Sc.; Professor of Geology, University of Reading, 1920-52, Emeritus since 1952; *b.* Reading, 1887; *m.* 1912 (wife *d.* 1953); two *s.* one *d.*; *m.* 1955, Sibyl Marion Hampton. *Educ.:* Reading School; Kendal; Manchester University. (1st Mark Stirrup Research Scholar in Palæontology). Lecturer in Geology at Univ. Coll., Reading, 1909; Awarded moiety of Lyell Geological Fund (Geological Soc). 1921; Lyell Medal, 1940; President: Cotteswold Field Club, 1929-31; South Eastern Union of Scientific Societies, 1934, 1958; Geological Section of British Assoc., 1936, and London Geologists' Assoc., 1938; Geological Soc. of London, 1941 and 1942; Consulting Geologist, Thames Valley Water Board, 1961. President Palæontographical Society, 1943-66; elected Hon. Member, 1966. *Publications:* Invertebrate Palæontology, 1920; many papers and memoirs (chiefly on Fossil Echinoidea) in Phil. Trans. Royal Soc., Proc. Zool. Soc., Quart. Journ. Geol. Soc., and Geological Magazine, etc. *Recreation:* music. *Address:* 63 Tilehurst Road, Reading, Berks. [*Died* 29 *Dec.* 1968.

HAWKINS, Ven. John Stanley, M.A. (Dunelm); Archdeacon of Totnes and Canon Residentiary of Exeter Cathedral since 1962; *b.* 30 June 1903; *s.* of Charles Hawkins, Liverpool; *m.* 1935, Elsie, *d.* of John Briggs, Liverpool; three *s.* *Educ.:* The Holt School, Liverpool; St. Chad's College, Durham, Curate of St. Stephen's, Liverpool, 1933; Rector of Dalwallinu, W.A., 1938; Rector of S. Perth, W.A., 1941; Exam. Chap. to Archbp. of Perth, 1943-45. Chaplain R.A.A.F., 1942-45. Curate of Wolborough, Newton Abbot. 1945-49. Vicar of Withycombe Raleigh, 1949-62. Rural Dean of Aylesbeare, 1953-57. *Address:* 15 The Close, Exeter. [*Died* 23 *Aug.* 1965.

HAWKSLEY, Dorothy Webster, R.I.; Painter, in tempera and water colour, of Portraits and subject pictures; *b.* 1884; *d.* of T. P. Hawksley and Maria S. Walters, London. *Educ.:* Royal Academy Schools (silver medal and Landseer Scholar). Exhibited at Royal Academy, 1909; represented in Walker Art Gallery, Liverpool, Birmingham, Oldham, Brighton, Bristol, National Gallery of Canada, and Bedford; silver medal at Salon, 1931. Illustrated : The Gospel of St. Luke (entitled The Story of Jesus). *Address:* 31 Queen's Gate Terrace, S.W.7. [*Died* 1 *July* 1970.

HAWKSLEY, Brig.-General Randal Plunkett Taylor, C.M.G. 1919; D.S.O. 1918; *b.* 1870; *s.* of late James Taylor Hawksley of Caldy Island, Pembrokeshire; *m.* 1900, Kate Marjorie (*d.* 1941), *d.* of late Bowen Pottinger Woosnam, D.L., of Tyn-y-Graig, Breconshire; two *d.* *Educ.:* Harrow. Served in the Royal Engineers in the British Isles, India, South Africa, Gallipoli, Egypt, Palestine, Syria, and Asia Minor; served in the army of the Union of South Africa during the Boer rebellion of 1914 and the Campaign in German South-West Africa; served in the Public Works Department of India, 1896-97; War Medals, etc.; North-West Frontier India, 1897-8 (medal and clasp); South African War, 1900-2 (Queen's medal and two clasps. King's medal and two clasps); European War, 1914-18 (despatches, C.M.G., D.S.O., Order of the White Eagle, Order of the Nile, 1914-15 Star, British War Medal, Victory Medal); Chief Engineer 21st Corps, 1917-1919; Chief Engineer, Palestine, 1919-20; Chief Engineer, Gibraltar, 1923-26; retired pay, 1926; D.L., Co. Brecon. *Address:* Bronllys Castle, Talgarth, Breconshire. *T.:* Talgarth 216. [*Died* 13 *May* 1961.

HAWTREY, Brigadier Henry Courtenay, C.M.G. 1918; D.S.O. 1916; *b.* 29 June 1882; 5th *s.* of late Rev. H. C. Hawtrey, Rector of Nursling, nr. Southampton; *m.* 1st, 1907, Emily Mildred (*d.* 1960), *e. d.* of late F. C. Gough; two *d.*; 2nd, 1961, Mrs. J. P. J. Vera Westby, *widow* of Capt. E. H. H. Westby, Welch Regt. *Educ.:* Uppingham; R.M.A., Woolwich. Entered army (R.E.), 1900; Capt. 1910; temp. Major, 1915; temp. Lt.-Col. 1916; Lt.-Col. 1921; Col. 1921; was 3 years in West Africa and 12 years in India with R.E.; served European War, 1914-18 (D.S.O., C.M.G., Bt. Lt.-Col.); Afghan War, 1919 (despatches); passed out Staff College, Quetta, Sept. 1920; transferred from R.E. into Royal Corps of Signals, 1920; Commandant Signal Training Centre, India, 1925; Signal-Officer-in-Chief A.H.Q., India (Brigadier), 1926-30; Chief Signal Officer, Aldershot Command, 1930-34; A.D.C. to the King, 1931-34; retired 1934; re-employed as Brigadier, Sept. 1939; reverted to retired pay, 1942. *Recreations:* won 5-mile race in Olympic games at Athens, 1906; cross-country runner; won 10-mile championship, L.A.C., and many other races; equalled mile record. *Address:* Middlewood, Fleet, Hants. *T.:* 652. [*Died* 16 *Nov.* 1961.

HAY, Sir Bache McEvers Athole, 11th Bt. *cr.* 1635; *b.* 24 Sept. 1892; *s.* of Athole Stanhope Hay (*d.* 1933) (3rd *s.* of 8th Bt.) and Caroline Margaret (*d.* 1943), *y. d.* of Sir Edward Cunard, 2nd Bt.; *S.* cousin, 1965; *m.* 1918, Judith Mimi, *widow* of Captain Alfred Spencer Mason Summers, and *d.* of Captain Davies Bryan Poole; (one *s.* died on active service, 1941). *Educ.:* Eton. Lt.-Col. late 19th Hussars; served European War, 1914-19 and War of 1939-45. Member, Royal Company of Archers, Queen's Body Guard for Scotland. D.L. Peebles-shire. *Address:* Crookston, Peebles. [*Died* 2 *April* 1966.

HAY, Sir Duncan Edwyn, 10th Bt., *cr.* 1635; *b.* 25 Sept. 1882; *o. s.* of 9th Bt. and Anne, *d.* of Sir R. J. M. Napier, 9th Bt.; *m.* 1st, 1905, Lavinia Mary (*d.* 1958), *d.* of Wallace C. Houstoun; 2nd, 1958, Isobel Rose, *e. d.* of late Sir Alexander Walker, K.B.E., Piersland, Troon. *Educ.:* Eton. *S.* father, 1895. Late Lt. 3rd Royal Scots; served European War, 1914-18, Royal Naval Division and Personal Staff; J.P., D.L., County of Peeblesshire; Lieutenant Queen's Bodyguard for Scotland; owns about 6000 acres. *Heir: cousin* Lt.-Col. Bache McEvers Athole Hay, *b.* 24 Sept. 1892. *Address:* Haystoun, Peebles, Scotland. *Club:* New (Edinburgh).
[*Died* 7 *Dec.* 1965.

HAY, Sir John George, Kt., *cr.* 1939; Chairman of United Sua Betong Rubber Estates, Ltd.; Director of Mercantile Bank Ltd. (formerly Deputy Chairman); Chairman and Dir. of other Rubber and Palm Oil Cos.; *b.* 1 Feb. 1883; *s.* of Peter Hay, Aberdeen; *m.* 1910, Constance Maye (*d.* 1959), *d.* of Thomas Leveritt, Bath; one *s.* two *d.* *Educ.:* privately. East India Merchant; Chm. Rubber Growers' Assoc. 1930-31; President Assoc. of British Malaya, 1936-37. *Recreations:* golf, fishing. *Address:* Hawthorndene, Westcott, Surrey. *T.:* Westcott 190. *Clubs:* Caledonian, Gresham, Singapore, etc.
[*Died* 26 *May* 1964.

HAY, of Seaton, **Major Malcolm Vivian;** D.L., J.P.; *b.* 1881; *m.* 1st, 1902, Florence Erlington; two *s.* three *d.*; 2nd, 1956, Alice Ivy, *widow* of Walter Edward Moncrieff Paterson, Tilliefoure, and *d.* of Herbert John Wigmore, Perth, Western Australia. Late Major 3rd Battalion Gordon Highlanders; served European War; Royal Company of Archers. K.St.J. (Hon.) LL.D. (Aberdeen). *Publications:* Wounded and a Prisoner of War; A Chain of Error in Scottish History; The Blairs Papers; The Jesuits and the Popish Plot; Winston Churchill and James II; The Enigma of James II; The Foot of Pride (U.S.A.), republished, 1960, as Europe and the Jews; Failure in the Far East, 1956; Prince in Captivity: Antoine Philip D'Orleans, Duc de Montpensier (1775-1807), 1960; How to Pass the Time, 1961; The Prejudices of Pascal, 1962. *Address:* 21 Rubislaw Den North, Aberdeen.
[*Died* 27 *Dec.* 1962.

HAY, Brig. Ronald Bruce, D.S.O. 1918; late R.A.; *b.* 1887; *m.*; one *d.* Served European War, 1914-18 (D.S.O., despatches four times, Bt. Lt.-Col., four medals). Retd., 1947. *Recreations:* tennis, golf, travelling. *Address:* 9 Strathearn Place, W.2. *T.:* Paddington 4521.
[*Died* 27 *May* 1961.

HAY, Lieut.-Colonel Sir (William) Rupert, K.C.M.G., *cr.* 1952; K.C.I.E., *cr.* 1947 (C.I.E. 1934); C.S.I. 1943; late Indian Army and Indian Political Service; *b.* 16 December 1893; *s.* of William Alfred Edward Hay and Louisa Tucker; *m.* 1925, Sybil Ethel, *d.* of late Sir Stewart and Lady Abram, Reading; three *s.* two *d.* *Educ.:* Bradfield; Univ. Coll., Oxford. Served European War in Mesopotamia; entered Political Dept., Government of India, 1920; Political Agent, South Waziristan, 1924-28; Assistant Commissioner or Joint Deputy Commissioner, Mardan, 1928-31; Political Agent, Malakand, 1931-33; Counsellor Brit. Legation, Kabul, 1933; Deputy Secretary to the Government of India in the External Affairs Dept., 1936-40; Resident in Waziristan, 1940-41; Resident in the Persian Gulf, 1941-42; Revenue and Judicial Commissioner, Baluchistan, 1942-43; Agent to the Governor-General, Resident and Chief Commissioner in Baluchistan, 1943-46; Political Resident in the Persian Gulf, 1946-53; retired, 1953. Member Dorset County Council, 1955-61. *Publications:* Two Years in Kurdistan, 1921; The Persian Gulf States, 1959; few articles in the Royal Geographical and Royal Central Asian Society Journals. *Recreation:* fishing. *Address:* Hillfield, 181 Dorchester Road, Weymouth, Dorset. *T.:* Weymouth 2584. *Club:* Challoner.
[*Died* 3 *April* 1962.

HAYCOCK, Alexander Wilkinson, *b.* Cataraqui, Ontario, Canada, 1882; *s.* of J. L. Haycock; *m.* Elsie, *d.* of George and Elizabeth Pierce. *Educ.:* Cataraqui School; Kingston Collegiate Institute; Queen's University; Called to the Bar, Gray's Inn; Organising Secretary of Manchester Norman Angell League; Foreign Policy Committee before War; Ex-President Manchester and Salford Independent Labour Party Federation; contested Winchester, 1922; M.P. (Lab.), W. Salford, 1923-24 and 1929-31. *Address:* Tarporley, Cheshire.
[*Died* 15 *Dec.* 1970.

HAYCRAFT, John Berry, M.C., M.B. (Edin.), F.R.C.S.(Eng.); Consulting Surgeon; *b.* Edinburgh, 1888; *s.* of John Berry Haycraft and Charlotte Isobel Stacpoole; *m.* 1921, Gertrude Kaye (*d.* 1967); four *d.* *Educ.:* Cardiff High School; Edinburgh Univ. M.B., Ch.B.; France, 1914-18; Major R.A.M.C.; Surgical Specialist No. 1 C.C.S. (M.C., despatches); Consulting Surgeon, Cardiff, 1920; Hon. Surgeon, Cardiff Royal Infirmary; Hon. Surgeon, Prince of Wales Hospital, Cardiff and Glan Ely Tuberculosis Hospital, Cardiff; Consulting Surgeon, Chepstow, Caerphilly, Maesteg and Bridgend Hospitals and Ministry of Pensions; formerly Assist., Surgical Unit, Welsh National School of Medicine. *Publications:* Articles in British Medical Journal and Lancet. *Recreations:* golf, fishing, shooting. *Address:* 9 Windsor House, Westgate Street, Cardiff. *T.:* Cardiff 33334. *Clubs:* Cardiff and County (Cardiff); Glamorganshire Golf (Penarth); Royal Porthcawl Golf (Porthcawl); British Tunny (Scarborough); Bristol Channel Yacht (Mumbles). [*Died* 6 *Feb.* 1969.

HAYDN WILLIAMS, Benjamin, Ph.D.; Director of Education, Co. Flint, since 1942; *b.* Rhosllanerchrugog, Denbighs., 9 Oct. 1902; *m.* 1932, Sarah; one *s.* one *d.* *Educ.:* Ruabon Grammar School; University of Liverpool (B.Sc., Ph.D.). Research, D.S.I.R., 1927-31; Chem. Lectr., Denbighs. Tech. Coll., Wrexham, 1931-38; Deputy Director of Education, Co. Flint, 1938-42. Mem. Coun. Univ. of Wales, 1952; Chm. Coun. R. Nat. Eisteddfod of Wales, 1961-64; Chm., Wales (West and Nth.) TV, 1962-63. *Recreation:* music. *Address:* Pen-Lon, Hendy, Mold, Flints. *T.:* Mold 483. [*Died* 29 *May* 1965.

HAYDON, Dame Anne, D.B.E. 1951 (C.B.E. 1948); R.R.C.; Q.A.R.A.N.C. (retd.) Col. Comdt. Q.A.R.A.N.C., Dec. 1954-June 1956; *b.* 29 Oct. 1892; *m.* 1960, Dr. Leonard John Haydon, T.D. *Educ.:* London and Berlin. Professional Training, Royal Free Hospital, 1918-22. Joined Q.A.I.M.N.S., 1923. Service in: China, 1927-29; India, 1932-38; France, 1939-40; M.E., 1940-43; War Office, 1943-46; G.H.Q. India, 1946-48; Brigadier Q.A.R.A.N.C.; Matron-in-Chief and Director of Army Nursing Services, 1948-52; retired 1952. *Recreations:* reading, gardening. *Address:* Hollamby's, Speldhurst, Nr. Tunbridge Wells, Kent. *T.:* Speldhurst 76. *Clubs:* Royal Over-Seas League, Oxford and Cambridge.
[*Died* 17 *March* 1966.

HAYDON, Major-General Joseph Charles, C.B. 1948; D.S.O. 1940 and bar 1942; O.B.E.; *b.* 1899; *s.* of late Frank Knowles Haydon; *m.* 1926, Florence (*d.* 1957), *d.* of late John Stephen Keogh, Chicago, U.S.A.: one *d.* *Educ.:* Downside; R.M.C. Sandhurst. Served European War. 1914-19 (despatches); 2nd Lieutenant Irish Guards, 1917. Military Assistant to Secretary of State for War, 1938. Lieutenant-Colonel Commanding 2nd battalion of the Irish Guards, 1939; Brigadier, 1941 (commanding Commandos, 1940-42); Colonel, 1942; Vice-Chief of Combined Operations Staff, 1942; Comd. 1st Guard Bde., Italy, 1944; Brit. Jt. Services Mission, Washington, D.C., 1944-1945; Brit. Army Rep., Jt. Chiefs of Staff, Australia, 1946-47; Chief Intelligence Div., Control Commn., Germany, 1948-50; Major-General, 1944; retired pay, 1951. Served: in Foreign Office, 1951-58; with F. G. Miles Ltd. and Beagle Aircraft Ltd. at Shoreham-by-Sea, Sussex, 1958-68. Chevalier Legion of Honour (France); Officer Legion of Merit (U.S.A.). *Address:* College Cottage, Winson, Nr. Cirencester, Glos *Club:* Royal Aero. [*Died* 8 *Nov.* 1970.

HAYES, Carlton Joseph Huntley; *b.* Afton, New York, 16 May 1882; *s.* of Philetus A. Hayes, M.D., and Permelia Huntley Hayes; *m.* 1920, Evelyn Carroll; one *s.* one *d.* *Educ.:* Columbia University, New York. Connected officially with Columbia University since 1907 as Lecturer in History, 1907-10; Assistant Professor, 1910-15; Associate Prof., 1915-19; Professor, 1919-50; (American Ambassador to Spain, 1942-45); acting Prof. of History, Univ. of Chicago, 1911; Univ. of California, 1917-1923; Johns Hopkins University, 1930; Stanford University, 1941; Michigan State, 1954; served European War as Captain, U.S. Army, Military Intelligence Division, General Staff, 1918-19; Major, Officers' Reserve Corps, 1928-33. Knight of Malta; Grand Cross, Order of Alfonso el Sabio. *Publications:* Sources relating to the Germanic Invasions, 1909; British Social Politics, 1913; Political and Social History of Modern Europe (2 vols.), 1916, 2nd ed. 1924; Brief History of Great War, 1920; Essays on Nationalism, 1926; France, a Nation of Patriots, 1930; Historical Evolution of Modern Nationalism, 1931; Political and Cultural History of Modern Europe, 2 Vols. 1932-1936, new ed., 1939; A Generation of Materialism, 1871-1900, 1941; Wartime Mission in Spain, 1942-45, 1945; United States and Spain, 1951; Modern and Contemporary Europe, 2 vols., 1953; Nationalism as a Religion, 1960; History of Western Civilization, 1962. Editor: Social and Economic Studies of Post-War France, 7 vols., 1929-31. *Address:* Jericho Farm, Afton, N.Y. *Died* 3 *Sept.* 1964.

HAYGARTH, Colonel Sir Joseph Henry, Kt. 1959; C.B.E. 1956; Deputy-Chairman, Greater London Council, 1964-1967 (elected 1964); *b.* 1892; *s.* of Joseph D. Haygarth; *m.* 1922, Elizabeth Jane, *d.* of Andrew Yule, Calcutta. Chm., Hendon North Conservative and Unionist Assoc. and of Northern Area of Home Counties; Mem., Nat. Exec. and Gen. Purposes Committee of Conservative Party. Colonel, King's Liverpool Regiment and Royal Army Service Corps. C.A. Middx., 1955-65 (Chm. C.C., 1961-62); High Sheriff of Middlesex, 1963. *Address:* Braeside, 44 Manor Park Gardens Edgware, Middlesex. [*Died* 9 *Jan.* 1969.

HAYLEY, Frederic Austin, M.A., D.C.L. (Oxon); Q.C. (Ceylon) 1927; retired; *b.* 1881; 3rd *s.* of late Charles P. Hayley, Galle, Ceylon, and of Glen Eyre, Bassett, Southampton; *m.* 1915, Kathleen Douglas, *e. d.* of late Gilbert Francis Traill, Tunbridge Wells; two *s.* one *d.* *Educ.:* Elizabeth College, Guernsey; Exeter College, Oxford (Scholar). Called to the Bar, Middle Temple, 1906; 1st Class and Certificate of Honour in Final Examination; 2nd Class B.C.L. Oxford, 1906; admitted Advocate of Supreme Court of Ceylon, 1906; Asst. Reader, Council of Legal Education, Ceylon, 1909-15; Member of Council of Legal Education; acting European Urban Member of Legislative Council of Ceylon, 1919-20; Pres. European Assoc. of Ceylon, 1920-21; D.C.L. (Oxon), 1924; deferment officer of Man-Power Board, Southampton, under Ministry of Labour and Nat. Service, 1942-43; retired from practice, 1950. *Publications:* Truths and Untruths, 1909; The Laws and Customs of the Sinhalese, 1923. *Recreations:* cox of Exeter College Eight, 1903-04, and of O.U.B.C. Trial Eight, 1903. *Address:* Gilletts, Smarden, Kent. *T.:* Smarden 224. *Clubs:* Leander; Colombo (Ceylon). [*Died* 15 *Oct.* 1968.

HAYMAN, Sir (Cecil George) Graham, Kt. 1954; retired as Chm. The Distillers Company Ltd. (1958-63), and as Chm., British Plaster Board (Holdings) Ltd. (1956-65); *b.* 1 Apr. 1893; *s.* of Charles Henry Hayman; *m.* 1918, Elsie Lilian Leggett (*d.* 1950); one *s.* one *d.* *Educ.:* London. Served European War, 7th London Regiment, 47th Division; Director of various industrial Companies, 1927-; Chairman, B.T.R. Industries Ltd., 1952-60; Chairman, Assoc. of Brit. Chemical Manufacturers, 1950-53; President, Federation of British Industries, 1955-57. *Recreation:* golf. *Address:* Larchside, Larch Avenue, Sunninghill, Berks. *T.:* Ascot 615. [*Died* 10 *March* 1966.

HAYMAN, Frank Harold; M.P. (Lab.) Falmouth and Camborne Division of Cornwall since 1950; Parliamentary Private Secretary to Mr. Hugh Gaitskell, Leader of the Opposition, Nov. 1959-Dec. 1963; *b.* 12 Dec. 1894; *s.* of Frank Edward and Catherine Hayman, Truro; *m.* 1920, Amelia Vaughan, *d.* of George Turner, Newquay, Cornwall; no *c.* *Educ.:* Primary School, Truro; Truro Technical School (evening classes). Joined clerical staff of Cornwall County Council, 1913; District Education Officer of the Redruth Education Dist. of Administrative County of Cornwall, 1920. Contested (Lab.) Camborne Division of Cornwall, 1945. President of Cornwall Federation of Divisional Labour Parties. Has held various offices in National Assoc. of Local Government Officers, 1928-49. Mem. Court of Referees for Private Bills. Delegate to Inter-Parliamentary Union conference, 1952-; Member parliamentary delegations to: W. Germany, 1955; Jersey, 1956; Finland, 1961. *Recreations:* gardening, bird-watching. *Address:* 8 West Park, Redruth, Cornwall. *T.:* Redruth 738. [*Died* 4 *Feb.* 1966.

HAYNES, Alwyn Sidney, C.M.G. 1934; O.B.E. 1950; J.P. County of Warwick; Malayan Civil Service, retd.; Chairman Warwick County Magistrates' Bench, retd. 1953. Deputy Chairman Warwick County Agricultural Executive Committee, retd. 1955; member Warwickshire Agricultural Wages Committee since 1940; Past Vice-President Royal Empire Society; *b.* 22 Oct. 1878; *y. s.* of late H. S. Haynes of Warwick and New Place, Upminster, and of Caroline Henrietta, *d.* of Henry S. Illingworth, Surgeon Apothecary to Queen Adelaide; *m.* 1911, Susanna (*d.* 1947), *o. c.* of late H. Legler, LL.D., Asst. Librarian at Windsor Castle; one *s.* two *d.* *Educ.:* Haileybury. Malayan Civil Service from 1901; held following posts acting or substantively: Secretary to High Commissioner for Malay States, 1920; Secretary for Agriculture, Straits Settlements and F.M.S., and Director of Food Production, 1922; British Resident, Pahang, 1924 and 1926; British Resident, Perak, 1925; British Adviser, Kedah, 1925; represented Malaya at Imperial Agricultural Research Conference, London, 1927; Member of Lord Lovat's Committee on Colonial Agricultural Service, 1927; Secretary for Postal Affairs, Straits Settlements and Federated Malay States, 1928; Controller of Labour, Malaya; British Adviser, Kelantan, Malay States, 1930; Colonial Secretary and Member

Executive and Legislative Councils, Straits Settlements, 1933; Lecturer on Malay and on Far Eastern Countries at Oxford for Colonial Administrative Service Course, 1935-40; Hon. Life Fellow Royal Colonial Institute (now Roy. Commonwealth Soc.), 1916, Mem. of its Council, 1934 and 1939-54; toured Asia as Chairman of a League of Nations Commission on Rural Hygiene in the Far East in 1936; External Expert on Board of Advisers in Malay, University of London, since 1937, and member of Panel of Additional Lecturers in Malay at School for Oriental and African Studies; Delegate to Intergovernmental Conference of Eastern Nations on Rural Hygiene, Java, 1937; contributed to and attended International Geographical Conference, Amsterdam, 1938. *Publications:* various reports and papers on colonial administrative subjects and for League of Nations and World Health Organisation. *Recreations:* riding, cricket, polo. *Address:* 9 Lansdowne Circus, Leamington Spa. *T.:* Leamington Spa 24792. [*Died* 9 *May* 1963.

HAYTER, 2nd Baron, *cr.* 1927, of Chislehurst, Kent; **Charles Archibald Chubb,** 2nd Bt., *cr.* 1900; a Managing Director of Chubb and Son's Lock & Safe Co., Ltd., 1898 - 1948; President, Planet Building Society; *b.* Chislehurst, Kent, 11 Nov. 1871; *e. s.* of 1st Baron Hayter and Sarah Vanner (*d.* 1940), *o. d.* of Charles Early, J.P., Witney, Oxon; *S.* father 1946; *m.* 1st, 1898, Mary (*d.* 1948), *d.* of J. F. Haworth, J.P., of Manchester; two *s.*; 2nd, 1949, Margaret Alison, *d.* of John Gimson Pickard, Leicester. *Educ.:* Leys School, Cambridge. Member, Court of Common Council, City of London, Castle Baynard Ward, 1919-64; Upper Bailiff of Weavers' Company, 1922, 1936 and 1950. Governor of Leys School, 1928. *Heir:* *s.* Hon. George Charles Hayter Chubb. *Address:* 24 Kingston House South, Ennismore Gardens, S.W.7. *T.:* Kensington 5613; Old Housing Witney, Oxon. *Clubs:* Carlton, Constitutional. [*Died* 3 *March* 1967.

HAYTER HAMES, Sir George Colvile, Kt. 1957; C.B.E. 1941; M.A.; D.L., J.P.; Vice-Chairman, Westward Television Ltd., since 1960; Director Barclays Bank Ltd.; *b.* 18 July 1898; *e. s.* of late Colvile George Hayter Hames, J.P.; *m.* 1950, Anne Longfield, *d.* of Mrs. Neville Flower, Castle Mary, Cloyne, Co. Cork; three *d.* *Educ.:* Winchester; Christ Ch., Oxf. Served with 1st Life Guards, 1916-19 and with R. Devon Yeo.; Chm. Devon War Agricultural Cttee., 1939-1947; Sheriff of Devonshire, 1943; Chm. Devon C.C., 1955-65. *Address:* Chagford House, Chagford, Devon. *T.:* Chagford 3153. *Club:* Cavalry. [*Died* 21 *Oct.* 1968.

HAYWARD, Arthur Lawrence, Editor and Author; *b.* Croydon, Surrey, 1885; *s.* of late William Ralph Hayward; *m.* Margaret Bisset; one *d.* Chief Editor, Cassell & Co. *Publications:* Londoniana; Days of Dickens; Dickens Encyclopedia; Book of Pirates; Book of Explorers; Indiscretions of a Prefect of Police; Colloquial Italian; Memoirs of Madame du Barry; Treason; The Traveller in Italy; A Book of Kings and Queens. Edited Johnson's Pirates, Smith's Lives of the Highwaymen, Ward's London Spy, Tom Brown's Amusements Serious and Comical, Lives of Criminals, English Rogues; translated various French and Italian works; English and Italian dictionaries. Broadcast talks. *Address:* Cherry Bounce, Jordans, near Beaconsfield, Bucks. [*Died* 27 *July* 1967.

HAYWARD, Frederick Edward Godfrey; Director, Midland Bank Ltd. and Midland Bank Executor and Trustee Company since 1958 (Chief General-Manager 1956-58, retired); Director Belfast Banking Co. Ltd.; *b.* 10 September 1893; *s.* of Edward Godfrey and Eleanor Matilda Hayward; *m.* 1925, Elsie Mary, *y. d.* of William and Margaret Matthews; two *d.* *Educ.:* Acton County School. Entered Midland Bank Ltd., London, 1909; Asst. Gen. Manager, 1941, Joint Gen. Manager, 1951. Served European War, 1914-19, 2nd London Regt. (Royal Fusiliers), Queen's Westminster Rifles (wounded twice, M.M.); commissioned K.R.R.C.; Middle East, France and Belgium. Liveryman, Worshipful Company of Masons. *Recreations:* reading and gardening. *Address:* Eversley, 8 Bournwell Close, Cockfosters, Herts. *T.:* Barnet 8211. *Club:* Constitutional. [*Died* 14 *Dec.* 1961.

HAYWARD, Ian Dudley, C.M.G. 1964; M.B.E. 1943; Chairman since 1954, Managing Director since 1936, John Martin & Co. Ltd., Adelaide; Mem. of Principal Board and Chairman of South Australia Branch, Australian Mutual Provident Society; Director: Adelaide Chemical and Fertilizer Co. Ltd.; Executor Trustee & Agency Co. of S.A. Ltd.; S.A. Insurance Co. Ltd.; Advisory Board, Elder Smith Goldsbrough Mort Ltd. (S.A. Branch); *b.* Adelaide, 9 December 1899; *s.* of A. D. Hayward; *m.* 1928, Agnes, *d.* of late Hon. Sir William Irvine, G.C.M.G.; two *s.* *Educ.:* Collegiate School of St. Peter, Adelaide; Jesus College, Cambridge. Served War of 1939-45: 2nd A.I.F.; Major, 2/10 Bn., N. Africa, S.W. Pacific, N.W. Europe; D.A.Q.M.G., New Guinea Force (M.B.E.); D.A.Q.M.G., 1st British Corps, British Liberation Army; G.2 Ops., 1st Australian Army, New Guinea (despatches twice). *Recreation:* golf. *Address:* Rust Hall, Mitcham, South Australia. *Clubs:* East India and Sports; Hawks (Cambridge); Adelaide, Royal Adelaide Golf (Adelaide); Melbourne (Melbourne); Union (Sydney). [*Died* 20 *Nov.* 1964.

HAYWARD, John (Davy), C.B.E. 1953; *b.* London, 2 Feb. 1905; *yr. s.* of late John Arthur Hayward, M.D., F.R.C.S., M.R.C.P., and Rosamond Grace Rolleston. *Educ.:* Gresham's School; France; King's College, Cambridge (M.A.). Chevalier de la Légion d'Honneur, 1953. Editorial adviser to the Cresset Press; Editorial Dir., The Book Collector; Vice-Pres. Bibliographical Soc. Hon. Foreign Corresp. Member, Grolier Club, New York. Hon. Mem. Assoc. Internat. de Bibliophilie, Paris. *Publications: edited:* Collected Works Earl of Rochester, 1926; Poetry and Prose of Donne, 1929; Letters of St. Evremond, 1932; Swift's Gulliver's Travels, etc., 1934, and Swift's Selected Prose, 1949; *anthologies:* 19th Century Poetry, 1932; Silver Tongues, 1937; Love's Helicon, 1940; T. S. Eliot, Points of View, 1941; 17th Century Poetry, 1948; Dr. Johnson, 1948; Donne (Penguin Poets), 1950; T. S. Eliot, Selected Prose (Penguin), 1952; Penguin Book of English Verse, 1956; Herrick (Penguin Poets), 1961; Oxford Book of 19th Century Verse, 1964; *biography:* Charles II, 1933; *bibliography:* Catalogue of Swift Exhibition, 1945; Catalogue of English Poetry Exhibition, 1947 (revised and illustrated edn., 1950). *Address:* 19 Carlyle Mansions, Cheyne Walk, Chelsea, S.W.3. [*Died* 17 *Sept.* 1965.

HAYWARD, Sir Maurice Henry Weston, K.C.S.I., *cr.* 1925; Kt., *cr.* 1923; LL.B. (Cantab.). Barrister-at-law; I.C.S.; retired, 1926; J.P.; Member of Church Assembly, 1935; Vice-Chairman, Bucks Quarter Sessions, 1938; *b.* 2 June 1868; *s* of late Robert Baldwin Hayward, F.R.S., House Master, The Park, Harrow; *m.* Alice Christine, *d.* of His Honour the late Judge William Barber, Q.C. of Derbyshire; one *s.* three *d.* *Educ.:* Harrow School; St. John's Coll., Cambridge. Entered

I.C.S. 1888; called to the Bar, 1909; served as Asst. Collector and Under-Secretary, Bombay; Judicial Assistant Political Agent, Kathiawar; District Judge and Secretary Legal Department, Bombay; Judicial Commissioner, Sind; Puisne Judge of the Bombay High Court, 1918; Member of the Executive Council of the Governor of Bombay, 1921-26. *Address:* Wade Hill House, Totton, Hants. [*Died* 31 *Aug.* 1964.

HAYWARD, Lt.-Col. Reginald Frederick Johnson, V.C. 1918; M.C. 1916 (Bar 1917); (late the Wiltshire Regiment); *b.* East Griqualand, South Africa; *e. s.* of late F. J. Hayward, Limpley Stoke, Bath; *m.* 1938, Linda, *d.* of late Charles Brice Bowen. *Educ.:* Hilton College, Natal. Represented Natal v. England, Rugby Football, 1911, Middlesex and Rosslyn Park, 1912-14. Commissioned Wiltshire Regiment, 1914. Served European War, France, 1914-1918. Adjt. 1st Bn. the Wiltshire Regiment, 1919-21, Dublin; served with the Regiment in Egypt and Palestine; retired pay, 1935. Recalled 1939; served 1939-45, C.R.A.S.C., A.A. Command. Commandant, P.O.W. Camps, 1945-47; B.B.C. Publications Dept., 1947-52; Games Manager, The Hurlingham Club, 1952-67. *Address:* 7 Ormonde Gate, S.W.3. *T.:* Flaxman 4621. [*Died* 17 *Jan.* 1970.

HAYWARD, Richard Frederick, M.C.; Q.C. 1936; *b.* 22 Mar. 1879; *s.* of C. J. and H. S. Hayward; *m.* 1912, Mabel Whitaker (*d.* 1956); one *s.* *Educ.:* H.M.S. Worcester. Entered Merchant Navy, 1895; Lieut. R.N.R., 1904; called to Bar, Inner Temple, 1908; Bencher, 1943; retired, 1961. Lieut. 22nd London Regiment, T.A., 1912. Served European War: commanded Machine Gun School at Bisley, 1915, and M.G. Units in France, 1916-17 (M.C., despatches); served with Military Mission in U.S.A. and later with R.N. Division in France. *Address:* Swafield, North Walsham, Norwich. *T.:* North Walsham 3206. [*Died* 8 *Feb.* 1962.

HAYWARD, Sidney Pascoe, Q.C. 1946; M.C. 1917; B.A.; Barrister-at-law; *b.* 2 Sept. 1896; *e. s.* of late Albert Edward Hayward, Rector of Emley, nr. Wakefield, Yorks (1901-35); *m.* 1926, Irene Dorothy, *e. d.* of Otho Hall, Tonbridge, Kent; one *s.* two *d.* *Educ.:* Queen Elizabeth's Grammar School, Wakefield; Jesus College, Oxford (Exhibitioner). Served European War, 1914-19 with 7th (D. of W.) West Riding Regt., reached rank of Capt. (M.C.); Jesus College, Oxford, 1919-22; 1st cl. hons. Maths. Moderations, 1920; 2nd cl. hons. Jurisprudence Finals, 1922; called to Bar, Middle Temple, 1923. *Publications:* Law of Town and Country Planning, 1933; Law of Housing, 1937. *Recreations:* croquet, chess. *Address:* New Court, Temple, E.C.4. *T.:* Central 2670; Clatford Manor, Andover, Hants. *Club:* Reform. [*Died* 11 *Feb.* 1961.

HAYWOOD, Colonel Austin Hubert Wightwick, C.M.G. 1919; C.B.E. 1923; D.S.O. 1915; Military Knight of Windsor; late R.A.; *y. s.* of late Lt.-Col. Wightwick Haywood; *m.* Isabella Rosamond (*d.* 1960); *o. d.* of late Canon Henry Walters, R.D.; one *s.* *Educ.:* Abroad; Royal Military Academy, Woolwich. Served in India, the Mediterranean, and W. Africa; employed with W. African Frontier Force; Kwale-Ishan Operations, S. Nigeria; during European War, 1914-18, commanded a Field Column in Kamerun and served on Western Front (Bt. Lt.-Col., wounded thrice, despatches, 1914-15 Star, C.M.G., D.S.O., Croix de Guerre, Legion of Honour (Croix d'Officer)); Asst. Dir. of Recruiting, War Office, 1916 (temp. Col.); attached Gen. Staff, War Office, 1919. Inspector-General West African Frontier Force (temp. Col. on Staff) Col. 1922; Comdr. R.A., 55th West Lancs. Division T.A. (Col.); Special Comr. Soc. of Preservation of Fauna of Empire, 1931. Dep Asst. Censor, London Area, 1939-40; Comdg. Home Guard of Ordnance Factories, 1941-42; Examiner 1st Grade Traveller's Censorship, Min. of Information, 1943; Welfare Officer, Hertfordshire, 1944-46. Defence Medal, War of 1939-45. *Publications:* English-Hausa Vocabulary of 1000 Words in Everyday Use; Through Timbuctoo and across the Great Sahara; Sport and Service in Africa, 1926; (jt. author) History of the Royal West African Frontier Force, 1964. *Address:* 10 Lower Ward, Windsor Castle. *T.:* Windsor 789. *Club:* United Service. [*Died* 28 *March* 1965.

HEAD, Leslie Charles B.; *see* Broughton-Head.

HEADLAM, Lieut.-Col. Rt. Hon. Sir Cuthbert Morley, 1st Bt., *cr.* 1935; P.C. 1945; D.S.O. 1918; O.B.E. 1919; T.D. 1926; *b.* 1876; *m.* 1904, Georgina Beatrice, C.B.E. 1929, *d.* of late George Baden Crawley. *Educ.:* King's School, Canterbury; Magdalen College, Oxford (Demy). Barrister, Inner Temple, 1906; Bedfordshire Yeomanry, 1910-26; served European War, 1914-18, G.S.O.1, 1918 (despatches, D.S.O., O.B.E.); Clerk in the House of Lords, 1897-24; M.P. (C.) Barnard Castle, 1924-29, and 1931-35, North Newcastle, 1940-52; Parliamentary and Financial Sec. to the Admiralty, 1926-29; Parliamentary Sec. to the Ministry of Pensions, 1931-32; Parliamentary Secretary, Ministry of Transport, 1932-1934; is a D.L., County Councillor, 1931-39, and J.P. for County of Durham. Chairman: Northern Counties Conservative Area, 1937-1946; National Union of Conservative and Unionist Associations, 1941. *Publications:* The History of the Guards Division; Knight Reluctant, 1934, etc.; (with A. Duff Cooper) House of Lords or Senate?, 1932; Editor of the Army Quarterly, 1920-42. *Address:* 19 Camden Crescent, Bath. *T.:* Bath 4445. *Club:* Travellers'. [*Died* 27 *Feb.* 1964 (*ext*).

HEADLEY, 6th Baron, *cr.* 1797; **Rowland Patrick John George Allanson-Winn,** 12th Baronet of Nostell, Yorkshire, 1660; 6th Baronet of Little Warley, Essex, 1796; Temp. Lt. R.N.R.; late Flight Lt. R.A.F.V.R.; *b.* 22 May 1901; *e. s.* of 5th Baron and Teresa (*d.* 1919), *y. d.* of late W. H. Johnson, formerly governor of Leh and Jumoo; *S.* father, 1935; *m.* 1936, Edith Jane, *y. d.* of late Rev. George Dods. *Heir:* *b.* Hon. Charles Rowland Allanson-Winn [*b.* 1902; *m.* 1927, Hilda May, *d.* of Thomas Wells Thorpe; one *s.* three *d.*]. *Address:* Glendarroch, Kirkcowan, Wigtownshire. *T.:* Kirkcowan 249. *Club:* Public Schools. [*Died* 17 *Dec.* 1969.

HEALD, Nora Shackleton; journalist Entered journalism in 1918, as Women's Page Editor of the Sunday Despatch; has been Dramatic Critic, Daily Mail, London Columnist on Daily Chronicle, Woman's Page Editor, Daily Herald, and Editor, The Queen and subsequently of The Lady, until 1954. *Address:* The Chantry House, Steyning, Sussex. [*Died* 5 *April* 1961.

HEALE, Lt.-Col. Robert John Wingfield, C.I.E. 1930; O.B.E. 1917; M.A.; *b.* Addington, Kent, 24 Sept. 1876; *s.* of Rev. J. Newton Heale; *m.* 1st, 1906, Alice Isabel, *d.* of late James Hope, I.C.S.; one *s.* one *d.*; 2nd, 1922, Ethel J. R., *d.* of late David Scott of Alyth, Blairgowrie; 3rd, 1926, Muriel Trestrail, *d.* of Brigadier-General H. Palmer, Ashleigh, Worthing. *Educ.:* King's School, Canterbury; Trinity College, Cambridge. B.A., 1899; M.A., 1924; commissioned 2nd Batt. South Staffordshire Regt., 1900; transfer to Indian Army, 46 Punjabis, 1902; Political Department of Government of India, 1903; served European War, 1914-18; Afghan War, 1919; served in N.W.F.P., 1906-24; Commissioner, Ajmer-Merwara, 1925; Resident, Gwalior, 1928;

Resident, Waziristan, 1929; Offg. Chief Commissioner, N.W.F.P., 1929; Agent to the Governor-General in Central India, 1929-31; retired 1931. *Recreations:* hunting, golf, tennis, shooting. *Address:* 20 Hyde Park Place, W.2. *T.:*Ambassador 0894. *Club:* United Service.
[*Died* 4 *March* 1962.

HEALY, Cahir; M.P. (N.) Northern Ireland Parliament, 1925-65, when he retired; *b.* 2 Dec. 1877; *s.* of a small farmer in Co. Donegal; *m.* 1897, Catherine (*d.* 1940); two *s.* one *d.* Member, Committee of Ulster Folk Museum. Was interned by the Northern Government, 22 May 1922 to 11 February 1924, without charge, and only released when the matter was raised at Westminster; interned by British Government, 1941-1942, in Brixton Jail. M.P. (Irish Nat.) Fermanagh and South Tyrone, 1924-31 and 1950-55. *Publications:* A Volume of Verse, many short stories of Irish life, as well as articles on national and political matters. *Recreation:* reading. *Address:* Enniskillen, Ireland. *T.A.:* Healy, Enniskillen. *T.:* 2439 Enniskillen. [*Died* 8 *Feb.* 1970.

HEALY, Daniel, C.I.E. 1937; *b.* 22 Aug. 1884; *s.* of late J. J. Healy, Cobh, Co. Cork; unmarried. *Educ.:* Presentation Brothers' College, Cork. Joined Indian Police, 1904; Officiated in 1924, 1927, and 1930, as Commissioner of Police, Bombay; Inspector-General of Police, Sind, 1936-39; retired 1939. *Address:* c/o National and Grindlay's Bank Ltd., 54 Parliament Street, S.W.1.
[*Died* 20 *April* 1962.

HEARLE, Francis Trounson, C.B.E. 1950; F.R.Ae.S.; retired 1956; *b.* 12 Sept. 1886; *s.* of James Hearle; *m.* 1914, I. F. J. de Havilland (*d.* 1953); one *s.* *Educ.:* Trevethan Grammar School, Falmouth. Aircraft experimental work with Capt. de Havilland, 1908; Balloon Factory, Farnborough, 1911-13; Works Manager, Vickers Ltd. Aviation, 1913-17; Experimental Manager, Aircraft Manufacturing Co., 1917-1921; The de Havilland Aircraft Co., 1921-1951, Works Manager, Managing Director; Chairman, 1950-54. *Recreations:* no speciality. *Address:* Shepherds, Bushey Heath, Herts. *Club:* Royal Aero.
[*Died* 1 *Sept.* 1965.

HEARN, John Whitcombe, C.S.I. 1945; C.I.E. 1941; late I.C.S., Financial Commissioner, Punjab; *b.* 27 November 1885; *s.* of late John and Ada E. Hearn, late of Awsland, Exeter; *m.* 1912, Dorothy, *d.* of late Col. H. James, C.B.; three *s.* *Educ.:* Blundell's School, Tiverton; Sidney Sussex Coll., Camb., B.A., LL.B. Entered I.C.S., 1910; retd., 1945; re-employed by Pakistan Govt. as Development Commr., West Punjab, 1947-50. *Address:* Coolinge Lodge, Folkestone. *T.:* Folkestone 2587.
[*Died* 10 *May* 1968.

HEARNE, Sir Hector, Kt., *cr.* 1946; *b.* 23 Feb. 1892; *s.* of late Samuel Hearne and Edith Alice, *d.* of late Robert William Butterfield; *m.* Winifred (*d.* 1959), *d.* of late Ernest Combridge; two *s.* Barrister-at-law of Lincoln's Inn; joined Colonial Service as an Asst. District Commissioner, Uganda, 1916, and after holding the appointments of first class Magistrate, District Magistrate, Senior Magistrate and Acting Puisne Judge, was appointed as Puisne Judge, Tanganyika, in 1933; acted as Chief Justice in 1935 and 1936; Puisne Justice, Ceylon, 1936; Chief Justice of Jamaica, 1945-51; Chief Justice, Kenya, 1951-54; retired 1954. Appeal Justice, West African Court of Appeal, 1954-55; Acting Pres. West African Court of Appeal, 1958. *Address:* 23 Riverview Gardens, Barnes, S.W.13. [*Died* 31 *Dec.* 1962.

HEARSON, Air Commodore John Glanville, C.B. 1919; C.B.E. 1924; D.S.O. 1916; late R.E. and R.A.F.; *b.* 5 Aug. 1883; *s.* of late Professor T. A. Hearson; *m.* Winifred Maude, *y. d.* of G. Shaw of Syston, Leicesters.; one *s.* one *d.* 2nd Lieut. R.E. 1902; Captain R.E. 1913; Major, R.E. 1917; Flight Commander, R.F.C. 1915; Squadron Commander, R.F.C., 1915; Wing Commander, R.F.C., 1916; Brigadier-General, R.F.C., 1917; Air Commodore, R.A.F., 1923. Employed on Cross River, S. Nigeria Boundary Commission, 1905-6; Niger-Chad Boundary Commission, 1906-8; Superintendent of Roads, Gold Coast Colony, 1910-12. Served European War, 1914-18 (despatches 4 times, D.S.O., St. Anne 3rd class, Brevet Major 1917). Director of Training, R.A.F., Air Ministry, 1918; retired list, 1927; Air Officer Commanding No. 30 (Balloon Barrage) Group, 1937-39.
[*Died* 9 *Jan.* 1964.

HEATH, Ambrose; Culinary Journalist, Author and Broadcaster; *b.* 7 February 1891; regular contributor to The Guardian, Daily Mirror, etc.; Cookery Correspondent of Morning Post, 1931-37; Cookery Correspondent of the periodical, The Queen, 1938-64; Author Daily Mirror Patsy Cookery Strip, 1946-53. *Publications:* Good Food, 1932; Good Food on the Aga, 1933; More Good Food, 1933; The Book of the Onion, 1933; Good Savouries, 1934; Good Potato Dishes, 1935; Good Soup, 1935; News Chronicle Cookery Book, 1936; (with D. D. Cottington-Taylor) National Mark Calendar of Cooking, 1936; Dining Out, 1936; Good Sweets, 1937; Country Life Cookery Book, 1937; (with C. H. Middleton) From Garden to Kitchen, 1937; Vegetable Dishes and Salads, 1938; Good Drinks, 1939; Ed. and Trans. Madame Prunier's Fish Cookery Book, 1938; Open Sesame, 1939 (reprinted as Good Dishes from Tinned Food); From Creel to Kitchen, 1939; American Dishes for English Tables, 1939; Savoury Snacks, 1939; Cooking in War Time, 1939; Good Food without Meat, 1940; Good Breakfasts, 1940; Meat Dishes without Joints, 1940; What's left in the Larder, 1940; Good Fish Dishes, 1940; Kitchen Front Recipes, 1941; More Kitchen Front Recipes, 1941; War Time Recipes, 1941; Good Food for Children, 1941; How to Cook in War Time, 1941; New Dishes for Old, 1942; Good Food in War Time, 1942; Cooking for One, 1942; There's Time for a Meal, 1942; Simple Salads, 1943; Simple American Dishes, 1943; Good Cheese Dishes, 1943; Vegetables for Victory, 1944; The Good Cook in Wartime, 1944; Good Cooking on Rings, 1946; What's Wrong with the Cooking, 1947; Good Puddings and Pies, 1947; Good Sweets and Ices, 1947; Good Jams, Preserves and Pickles, 1947; Good Cakes, Bread and Biscuits, 1948; The Book of Sauces, 1948; Good Sandwiches and Picnic Dishes, 1949; Good Salads, 1949; Good Vegetables, 1949; Good Food Again, 1950; Fare Wisely and Well, 1951; Pig-Curing & Cooking, 1952; Good Egg Dishes, 1952; Small Meat Dishes, 1953; Good Poultry and Game, 1953; Home made Wines, 1953; Biscuits and American Cookies, 1953; Dishes without Meat, 1953; Herbs in the kitchen, 1953; Kitchen Table Talk, 1953; Children's Party Fare, 1954; Herrings, Bloaters and Kippers, 1954; Good Cooking with Yeast, 1955; Small Cheese Dishes, 1955; Ambrose Heath's Honey Cookery, 1956; Home Cookery, 1956; English Cheeses of the North, 1956; Soups and Soup Garnishes, 1957; Casserole and Chafing Dish, 1958; (Ed.) With a Jug of Wine, by Morrison Wood, 1958; (Trans.) The Art and Magic of Cookery, by Raymond Oliver, 1959; Learn to cook by Pictures, 1960; The Queen Cookery Book, 1960; Hay Box Cookery 1961; The Birds Eye Book of Britain's Favourite Recipes, 1964; Meat, 1968. *Recreation:* reading. *Address:* Holmbury St. Mary, Nr. Dorking, Surrey. [*Died* 31 *May* 1969.

HEATH, Archie Edward, M.A.; Emeritus Professor, University of Wales; *b.* 1887; *s.* of late Edward Heath, Hasland Derbyshire; *m.* Florence Emily, *d.* of late Mansell Powell, Hendon; one *s.* *Educ.:* Hasland School; Chesterfield Grammar School; Nottingham High School; Trinity College, Cambridge; Arnold Gerstenberg Studentship in Philosophy, 1912; Master at Oundle and Bedales; Lecturer in Education, University of Manchester, 1919; Senior Lecturer, University of Liverpool, 1921-25; Professor of Philosophy, University College, Swansea, 1925-52. *Publications:* books and articles on education, scientific methodology and philosophy. *Recreations:* walking and talking. *Address:* 2 Devon Terrace, Swansea, W. [*Died* 18 *May* 1961.

HEATH, Col. George Noah, C.B.E. 1944; D.S.O. 1918; J.P.; *b.* Macclesfield, 23 June 1881; *s.* of late George Henry Heath, J.P., Macclesfield, and Fanny, *d.* of late Capt. Wheeler, Fleetwood; *m.* 1909, Kate Lisette, *y. d.* of William Smale, J.P., C.C., Macclesfield; three *d.* *Educ.:* Macclesfield Grammar School; Uppingham. Served European War, 1914-18, Gallipoli, Egypt, Palestine, and Syria (despatches, D.S.O. and bar); Colonel, 1927; Commander 125th (Lancashire Fusiliers) Infantry Brigade, 1929-1930; retired from T.A. 1930. *Recreations:* hunting, shooting, fishing. *Address:* The Grey House, Ivy Lane, Macclesfield. *T.A.:* Heath, Macclesfield. *T.:* Macclesfield 2897. *Club:* Royal Automobile. [*Died* 23 *April* 1967.

HEATHCOTE, Rt. Rev. Sir Francis Cooke Caulfeild, 9th Bt., *cr.* 1733; L.Th.; D.D.; *b.* 20 Apr. 1868; *S.* cousin, 1937; *m.* 1901, Evelyn Margaret (*d.* 1957), *d.* of J. F. Smith, K.C., Rosedale, Toronto. *Educ.:* Trinity Coll., Toronto. Ordained, 1891; Incumbent of Mission of King and Vaughan, 1891-95; Curate of St. Simon, Toronto, 1895-1896; Rector of St. Clement, 1896-1905; All Saints, Winnipeg, 1905-13; Archdeacon of Vancouver, 1913-40; Bishop of New Westminster, 1941-50; retired, 1950. Prolocutor of the Provincial Synod of British Columbia, 1920; re-elected, 1935; Prolocutor of General Synod Canadian Church, 1927-34. *Heir:* *half-b.*, Leonard Vyvyan [*b.* 7 Sept. 1885; *m.* 1923, Joyce Kathleen, *d.* of B. P. Willis, Calcutta; one *s.* one *d.*]. *Address:* 1507 W. 12th Ave., Vancouver, British Columbia. [*Died* 11 *Sept.* 1961.

HEATHCOTE, Sir Leonard (Vyvyan), 10th Bt., *cr.* 1733; retired; *b.* 7 Sept. 1885; *s.* of Rev. G. V. Heathcote (*d.* 1890; 3rd *s.* of 5th Bt.) and Mrs. M. H. Gourlay (*d.* 1938); *S.* half-brother, Rt. Rev. Sir Francis Cooke Caulfeild Heathcote, D.D., 9th Bt., 1961; *m.* 1903, Joyce Kathleen Willis; one *s.* one *d.* *Educ.:* Wellington College; Clare College, Cambridge. Engaged by Asiatic Petroleum Co., 1908, and worked for them, retiring as General Manager in India of Burmah-Shell, 1935. Is in remainder to Earldom of Macclesfield. *Heir:* *s.* Michael Perryman Heathcote [*b.* 7 Aug. 1927; *m.* 1956, Victoria Wilford; one *s.* one *d.*]. *Address:* Mayborne, Pilley, Lymington, Hants. *T.:* Lymington 2817. [*Died* 24 *June* 1963.

HEATHCOTE, Robert Evelyn Manners, D.S.O. 1918; landowner; *b.* 4 Sept 1884; *s.* of Robert Heathcote, of Lobthorpe and Manton; *m.* 1st, 1912, Edith Millicent (who obtained a divorce, 1922), *d.* of W. Walton, of Horsley Priory, Glos; one *s.* one *d.*; 2nd, 1922, Nesta, *d.* of late Evan Hanbury Braunston Manor, Oakham; one *d.* *Educ.:* Eton. Served European War, 1914-18 (Lieut.-Colonel, D.S.O., despatches four times); served as Major R.A., 1940-41; Sheriff of Rutland, 1936. *Recreations:* hunting and shooting. *Address:* Manton Hall, Oakham, Rutland. *T.:* Manton 212. *Club:* White's. [*Died* 17 *July* 1970.

HEATHCOTE-SMITH, Sir Clifford (Edward), K.B.E. 1943 (C.B.E. 1930; O.B.E. 1918); C.M.G. 1936; Vice-Chairman: Migration Council, 1950-55; Refugees Defence Cttee.; Commonwealth Unity Group; *b.* 26 Mar. 1883; *s.* of late Rev. Heathcote Smith, Vicar of Princetown; *m.* 1909, Elaine, *d.* of John R. Spiegelthal de Fonton, Cannes; one *s.* two *d.* *Educ.:* Brighton College; Pembroke College, Cambridge. Student Interpreter in Levant Consular Service, 1903; served at Uskub, Smyrna, and Dedeagatch; Intelligence Officer in the Aegean, 1915-18; hon. temporary Commander, R.N.V.R., 1918-19; on staff of British High Commission at Constantinople, 1919; at Foreign Office, 1920-22; Consul in Albania (Durazzo), 1921-22; Casablanca, Morocco, 1922-24; Consul-General, Alexandria, 1924-1943; retired, 1943; Representative in Italy of Inter-Governmental Committee on Refugees, 1944-45. *Address:* Duckings, Blackboys, Uckfield, Sussex. *T.:* Framfield 314. *Club:* Royal Automobile. [*Died* 3 *Jan.* 1963.

HEATHCOTE-WILLIAMS, Harold; Q.C. 1949; Recorder of Tiverton, 1947-51; *b.* 19 Sept. 1896; 9th *s.* of Joseph Ellis Williams and Martha Amelia Heathcote, Abbotsfield, Chester; *m.* 1940, Margaret Julian, *d.* of Rev. E. C. Henley; one *s.* one *d.* *Educ.:* The King's School, Chester; Brasenose College, Oxford (Hulme Scholar). Hons. Jurisprudence, 1922; Editor, Isis, 1922-23. Served European War, 1914-19, in R.A. Called to Bar, Inner Temple, 1923; Master of the Bench of The Inner Temple, 1957, legal member, of Council of Town Planning Inst. *Publications:* (with others) (Ed.) Foà's General Law of Landlord and Tenant, 8th edition; various legal works. *Recreations:* travel and book collecting. *Address* 47 Hurlingham Court, S.W.6; 11 King's Bench Walk, Temple, E.C.4. *Club:* Hurlingham. [*Died* 15 *Aug.* 1964.

HEATON, Sir Herbert Henniker, K.C.M.G. 1937 (C.M.G. 1928); B.A.; *b.* 1880; 3rd *s.* of Sir John Henniker-Heaton, 1st Bt.; *m.* 1st, 1909, Phœbe Angele Susan (*d.* 1922), *d.* of Lindsey Talbot Crosbie of Ardfert Abbey, Co. Kerry; one *s.* two *d.* (and one *s.* decd.); 2nd, 1926, Helena Iris (*d.* 1927), *d.* of Sir Henry McCallum, G.C.M.G.; one *s.*; 3rd, 1947, Mrs. Gladys Going, 45 Crompton Court, S.W.3, *widow* of Col. George Going and *d.* of late Col. Claud Francis. *Educ.:* Eton; New Coll., Oxon. Entered Colonial Service, 1902; Cadet, Fiji, 1902; Magistrate, 1906; Assist. Native Commissr., 1906; Assist. Colonial Secretary, Mauritius, 1913; Colonial Secretary, Gambia, 1917; Falkland Islands, 1921-25; Bermuda, 1925-29; received in 1929 grant of £500 from Colonial Parliament for signal services rendered to Colony; Colonial Secretary, Cyprus, 1929-34; Governor and Commander-in-Chief of Falkland Islands, 1935-41; has acted as Colonial Secretary, Mauritius, for two years, as Governor of the Gambia, the Falkland Islands, and Cyprus for one year each. *Address:* 14 Palmeira Court, Hove, Sx. [*Died* 24 *Jan.* 1961.

HEATON, Sir John Henniker, 2nd Bt., *cr.* 1912; *s.* of 1st Bt. and Rose, *e. d.* of Samuel Bennett, N.S. Wales; *b.* 19 April 1877; *S.* father, 1914; *m.* 1902, Hon. Catherine Mary Sermonda Burrell (*d.* 1958), *o. s. c.* of 5th and last Baron Gwydyr; three *s.* one *d.* *Educ.:* Eton. Served with 10th Batt. Imp. Yeomanry, S. African war 1900-01 (medal with three clasps); European War with 8th Australian Light Horse, 1914; Captain, Welsh Horse, 1916. *Heir:* *s.* John Victor Peregrine [*b.* 10 Feb. 1903; *m.* 1st, 1927, Gladys (marriage dissolved, 1937), *d.* of P. E. Tyson, Alnwick, Northumberland; two *d.*; *m.* 2nd, 1948, Margaret Patricia Wright; one *s.* one *d.*] *Club:* Royal Thames Yacht. [*Died* 21 *Feb.* 1963.

HEATON, Raymond H.; *see* Henniker-Heaton.

HEATON-ARMSTRONG, Sir John Dunamace, Kt., *cr* 1953; M.V.O. 1937; Clarenceux King of Arms since 1956; Captain (retired) I.A.R.; XXth Roya Deccan Horse; Squadron Leader (retd.) R.A.F.V.R.; Barrister-at-law; *b.* 21 Feb. 1888; 2nd *s.* of late William Charles Heaton-Armstrong, J.P., F.R.A.S., F.R.G.S., M.P. for Sudbury, Lord of the Manor of Roscrea, Ireland, and late Bertha Maximiliana, Baroness Zois; *m.* 1919, Suzanne Laura, 2nd *d.* of late M. Béchet de Balan of Sedan and Les Rosiers, Ardennes, France, and *widow* of late 2nd Lieut. J. R. G. Whitehead, R.F.C.; one *s.* two *d.* and one *step d.* *Educ.:* Eton; Trinity Hall, Cambridge, M.A. Called to Bar, Inner Temple, 1912. Served in European War in France and Palestine, 1914-1918; also served 1939-44 (England and France). Colonial Office, 1920-21; Rouge Dragon Pursuivant of Arms, 1922-26; Chester Herald, 1926-56. Order of the Eagle of Albania, 5th class *Address:* 46 Carlisle Mansions, S.W.1. *Club:* Boodle's.
[*Died* 27 *Aug.* 1967.

HEBDEN, George Brentnall, C.M.G. 1941; A.M.I.E.E.; *b.* 22 Jan. 1886; *m.* 1918, Mabel Woollaston, *d.* of W. Balfour Clarke; one *d.* *Educ.:* Bedford School. Entered Colonial Service as telegraph construction superintending engineer in Nigeria, 1909; Engineer-in-chief, Nigeria, 1921; Postmaster-General, 1928; Postmaster-General of Kenya, Uganda and Tanganyika, 1936-45; Chief Censor, East Africa, 1939-1945; retired from Colonial Service, Dec. 1945; Area Director, London, Ministry of Works, 1947; retired. Served with Cameroons Expeditionary Force, 1914-16, as Director of Posts and Telegraphs. *Address:* Old Orchard, Buxted, Sussex. [*Died* 28 *April* 1968.

HEDGES, Brigadier Killingworth Michael Fentham, C.B.E. 1946 (O.B.E. 1922); D.S.O. 1917; M.A.; F.I.Mech.E.; late R.A.S.C.; *b.* 29 Sept. 1890; *o. s.* of Killingworth Richard Hedges and Emily Margaret Bourne (*née* Royds); *m.* 1930, Lucy Dorothy (*d.* 1962), *er. d.* of late Charles Napier Curling. *Educ.:* Charterhouse; Trinity College, Cambridge. B.A., 1911; M.A., 1916; commissioned R.A.S.C., 1911; served European War, France, August 1914 to end of War (D.S.O., despatches thrice); Egyptian Army and Sudan Defence Force, 1922-27; to R. of O. 1927; Sudan Government Railways and Steamers as Director of Mechanical Transport, 1927; Assistant General Manager, Sudan Government Railways, 1927-32. Recalled to the Army 1939; Acting Lieut.-Col. 1939, Temp. Lt.-Col. 1940; Acting Col. 1940; Temp. Brigadier, 1942; Assistant Director of Mechanisation, 1939; Director of Mechanisation, Ministry of Supply, 1942-45; Brigadier (retired 1945). *Address:* Wedhampton Cottage, nr. Devizes, Wilts. *T.:* Chirton 202. *Club:* United Service.
[*Died* 27 *May* 1969.

HEDGES, Robert Yorke; Legal Assistant, Lord Chancellor's Office (Council on Tribunals), since 1961; *b.* 6 August 1903; *s.* of late James Hedges, London; *m.* 1st, 1929; two *d.*; 2nd, Dora, *d.* of late Hon. O. F. Ricketts. *Educ.:* Central High School and Victoria University, Manchester. LL.M., LL.D., Manchester; LL.D. Qld.; Diploma in Internat. Law, Geneva. Called to Bar, Gray's Inn, 1928; admitted to Queensland Roll of Barristers, 1936; Laura Spelman Rockefeller Memorial Fellow, Harvard Univ., 1926-27; Switzerland, 1927-28; Lectr. in Law, Manchester Univ., 1925-31, Sen. Lecturer, 1931-36; Prof. of Law and Dean of Law School, Queensland Univ., 1936-1945. Formerly Law Examiner, Univs. of London, Liverpool and New Zealand. Confidential duties, Dept. of Army, Commonwealth of Australia, 1941-45. Legal Staff Officer (Acting Major) British Military Administration (Brit. Borneo), 1945-46. Actg. Chief Justice of North Borneo, 1949; Chief Justice of Sarawak and Judge of Appeal, Brunei, 1946-51; Member Supreme Council, Sarawak, 1946-49; Chm. Social Welfare Council, Sarawak, 1950; Ed. Sarawak Law Reports, 1946-51. Law Revision Commissioner (Brunei), 1951-52; Puisne Judge, Supreme Court, Nigeria, 1952-55; High Court Judge, Western Nigeria, 1955-59; Chief Justice of Western Nigeria, 1959-1960. Member (later Chm.), Judicial Service Commn., 1958-60. Engaged on survey of criminal justice in Africa for Brit. Inst. of Internat. and Comparative Law, 1962-. *Publications:* Legal History of Trade Unionism (joint), 1930; Law Relating to Restraint of Trade, 1932; International Organization, 1935; Laws of Sarawak (6 vols. prepared as Commissioner); Laws of Brunei; Introduction to Nigerian Criminal Law, 1962; contrib. to various legal journals. *Recreations:* travel, chess problems. *Address:* c/o Williams Deacon's Bank Ltd., 155 High Street, Southampton. *Club:* Masonic (Kuching).
[*Died* 29 *May* 1963.

HEENEY, Arnold Danford Patrick, C.C. (Canada) 1968; Q.C. (Can.), M.A., B.C.L., LL.D.; Chairman, Canadian Section, Internat. Jt. Commission (Canada and U.S.) since 1962; Canadian Chairman, Perm. Jt. Board on Defence (Canada and U.S.), since 1967; *b.* 5 Apr. 1902; *s.* of late Rev. Canon Bertal Heeney and late Eva Marjorie Holland; *m.* 1931, Margaret Yuile, Montreal; one *s.* one *d.* *Educ.:* St. John's Coll. Sch., Winnipeg; Univ. of Manitoba; St. John's Coll., Oxford (Rhodes Scholar, Mod. Hist.); McGill Univ. (Law). M.A. (Manitoba and Oxford); B.C.L. (McGill). Admitted to Bar of Quebec, 1929; practised law in Montreal, 1929-38; Sessional Lecturer, Faculty of Law, McGill Univ., 1934-38. Principal Secretary to Prime Minister, Oct. 1938; Clerk of Privy Council and Secretary to Cabinet, 1940; K.C. (Dominion), 1941; Under-Secretary of State for External Affairs, 1949. Ambassador and Permanent Representative of Canada to the North Atlantic Council and to the Organization for European Economic Co-operation, Paris, 1952; Canadian Ambassador to the U.S., 1953-57; Chm. of the C.S. Commission of Canada, 1957-59; Canadian Ambassador to the United States, 1959-62. Member, Board of Govs. McGill Univ. Hon. LL.D.: British Columbia, 1948; Manitoba, 1950; Franklin and Marshall Coll., 1954; Michigan State Univ., 1955; Kenyon Coll., 1955; Univ. of Rhode Island, 1960; McGill Univ., 1961; Alberta Univ., 1967; Hon. D.C.L. St. John's Coll., Winnipeg, 1966. *Recreations:* golf and ski-ing. *Address:* (office) 850 Burnside Bldg., 151 Slater St. Ottawa 4, Canada; (home) 428 Buena Vista Rd., Rockcliffe, Ontario, Canada. *Clubs:* Rideau, Royal Ottawa Golf, Country, (Ottawa); University (Montreal). [*Died* 20 *Dec.* 1970.

HEITNER, H. Jesse; Editor of The Sphere 1926-60; Editor of Britannia and Eve, from its foundation in 1929 until 1957; retired, 1961, as Director of Illustrated Newspapers Ltd., and of British National Newspapers Ltd.; *b.* Long Buckby, Northamptonshire, 24 Nov. 1893; *e. s.* of Adolph Heitner, London. Assisted in the reorganisation of the Graphic as acting editor, 1927; was supervisory editor of the weekly Britannia until its amalgamation with Eve and subsequent production as a monthly magazine; Editorial Director: the Sporting and Dramatic News, 1934; The Tatler, 1957-1958; The Sketch, 1958-59. Served three years in France during European War, 1914-1918; has held pilot's "A" Licence. *Publications:* various articles in The Sphere and other journals; dramatic criticism, etc. *Recreations:* chess book-binding, flying. *Address:* 21 Carlisle Mansions. S.W.1. *T.:* Victoria 1932. [*Died* 21 *Jan.* 1965.

HELFRICH, Admiral Conrad Emile Lambert, K.C.B. (Hon.) 1942; Royal Netherlands Navy (retd.); *b.* 11 Oct. 1886; *s.* of A. J. Helfrich, Surgeon-Col., Royal Neth. Indian Army, and B. Steyns, Limburg, Holland; *m.* 1919, A. C. Gieben, Middelburg, Holland; two *s.* two *d.* *Educ.:* Naval Academy, Den Helder Naval Base, Holland. Naval cadet, 1903; Cdr. 1930; Capt. 1934; Rear-Admiral, 1938; Vice-Admiral, 1940; Admiral 1945; Naval Staff, The Hague, 1920; Naval War College, The Hague, 1922-27; in command Destroyer Piet Hein, N.E.I., 1927-30; Asst. Chief of Staff and Chief of Staff Naval Dept., Batavia, Java, 1930-33; in command H.M. Training Ship Hertog Hendrik and training squadron, Baltic Sea, European waters, 1934-35; as Commodore in command of N.E.I. squadron at sea, in Flagship Sumatra, 1936-37; Director of Naval War College, The Hague, 1938-39; Commander-in-Chief Neth. Naval Forces in the East, 1939-42; Commander-in-Chief Allied Naval Forces in the Neth. East Indies, Feb. 1942; Commander-in-Chief of the Netherlands Forces in the East, 1942; Delegate U.N.O. Conf., San Francisco, 1945; Netherlands rep. Japanese surrender, Tokyo Bay, Sept. 1945; C.-in-C. Royal Neth. Navy, 1945-48; retired, 1948. *Publications:* Memoirs, 1939-48 (two vols.); 1950 (ed. Elseviers), many in the Elseviers Weekblad, the Marineblad (Periodical for the Royal Neth. Navy) and in some other Dutch magazines and papers. *Address:* The Hague, 44 Louis Couperusplein, Holland. [*Died* 20 *Sept.* 1962.

HELM, Sir (Alexander) Knox, G.B.E., *cr.* 1953 (C.B.E. 1932; O.B.E. 1924); K.C.M.G., *cr.* 1949 (C.M.G. 1945); *b.* 24 March 1893; *s.* of William Hunter Helm, Kirkgunzeon, Dumfries, and Annie Clark; *m.* 1st, 1922, Grace Little (*d.* 1925); 2nd, 1931, Isabel, *o. d.* of late Walter G. Marsh, J.P. Cardiff; one *s.* two *d.* *Educ.:* Dumfries Academy; King's College, Cambridge. Entered Civil Service and employed in Foreign Office, 1912; 2nd Lieut., Royal Field Artillery, 1917; served in Palestine; Vice-Consul in Levant Consular Service, 1919; Vice-Consul at Salonica, 1920; 3rd Dragoman at Constantinople, 1920; 2nd Secretary attached to H.M.'s Embassy at Ankara, 1927; promoted H.M.'s Consul and transferred to Foreign Office, 1930; H.M.'s Consul at Addis Ababa, 1937-39; Counsellor at Washington, 1939-42; Counsellor, British Embassy, Ankara, 1942-46; British Political Representative in Hungary, 1946-47; Minister, 1947-49; Minister to Israel, 1949-51; British Ambassador to Turkey, 1951-54; Governor-General of the Sudan, 1955-56. *Recreations:* golf, gardening. *Address:* The Old Rectory, Tewin, Herts *T.:* Tewin 220. *Club:* Brooks's. [*Died* 7 *March* 1964.

HELMORE, Hon. Air Commodore William, C.B.E. 1942; Ph.D., M.Sc. (Cantab.); F.C.S.; F.R.Ae.S.; Director General Aluminium Development Association, 1946, and Director C. C. Wakefield & Co. Ltd.; *b.* 1 March 1894; *m.* 1939, Enid Sylvia, *d.* of Henry Edward Capes, J.P., Stowcroft, Chislehurst, Kent. *Educ.:* Blundell's School; R.M.A., Woolwich; Christ's College, Cambridge. Served with R.F.C. in France, 1916, and later with R.A.F.; Groves prize for Aeronautical Research, 1931; carried out refuelling in air experiments, and record attempt with Sir Alan Cobham, 1934; Wing Commander, 1935. Broadcast Schneider Races, R.A.F. Displays, and official air events since 1926; R.A.F. War Commentator, 1941-1943; broadcast eye-witness description of Invasion from a Mitchell bomber, D-Day, 1944; M.P. (C.) Watford Div. of Herts, 1943-1945. Inventor of various industrial processes and apparatus used in aircraft. Asst. Scientific Adviser of Chief of Air Staff, 1939; Technical Adviser, Ministry of Aircraft Production, 1941-45; member of the Brabazon Cttee. on Civil Aviation, 1943-45; Chm. of Civil Aviation Cttee. on Certification of Aircraft and Vice-Chm. of Cttee. on Recruitment and Licensing of Civil Aviation personnel, 1947-48; Parliamentary and Scientific Cttee., 1953. *Publications:* Cavalry of the Air, 1917; Air Commentary, 1942; numerous scientific works on fuels, engines, and aeronautical subjects. *Recreations:* fishing and sailing. *Address:* Shotover, Coombe Hill, Surrey. *Clubs:* Athenæum, R.A.F. [*Died* 18 *Jan.* 1964.

HELY, Air Vice-Marshal William Lloyd; *see* Addenda: II.

HELY-HUTCHINSON, Maurice Robert, M.C.; *b.* 22 May 1887; 3rd *s.* of Rt. Hon. Sir Walter Francis Hely-Hutchinson, G.C.M.G.; *m.* 1920, Melita, *d.* of late Admiral Sir Colin Keppel, G.C.V.O., K.C.I.E., C.B., D.S.O.; two *s.* four *d.* *Educ.:* Eton (K.S.); Balliol College, Oxford. Served European War, 1915-18, Irish Guards; G.S.O. 3 Guards Division (M.C., despatches). M.P. (U.) Hastings, 1937-45. *Publication:* Capitalism?. *Recreations:* golf, shooting. *Clubs:* Carlton, Beefsteak. [*Died* 11 *Feb.* 1961.

HEMBRY, Henry William McQuitty; Member (for matters relating to finance) National Coal Board since 1957; *b.* 27 April 1903; *s.* of Henry Robert Hembry and Jessie Mappin Hembry; *m.* 1929, Dorothy (*née* Griffith); one *s.* two *d.* *Educ.:* Methodist College, Belfast; Liverpool College, Liverpool. Chief Accountant, Belfast Omnibus Co. Ltd., 1926-28; Sec. Low Temperature Carbonisation Ltd., 1928-39; War service, 1939-45: Scotland, West Africa, Middle East, Germany; Lt.-Col. R.A.; Dep.-Chm. (British) Coal Control, Germany, 1945-50; National Coal Board (Finance Director), 1950-55, Dep.-Chm. 1955-57, Northern Division. Fellow Inst. of Chartered Accountants, England and Wales. *Address:* 40 Ovington Square, S.W.3. *T.:* Kensington 0425. *Club:* Roehampton. [*Died* 1 *Feb.* 1961.

HEMINGWAY, Ernest; Writer and War Correspondent; *b.* Oak Park, Illinois, U.S.A., 21 July 1898; *m.*; one *s.*; *m.*; two *s.*; *m.* Mary Welsh. *Educ.:* Abroad. *Publications:* Three Stories and Ten Poems; In our Time; The Torrents of Spring; The Sun also Rises (published in England as Fiesta); Men Without Women; A Farewell to Arms; Death in the Afternoon; Winner Take Nothing; Green Hills of Africa; To Have and Have Not; The Fifth Column and the First Forty-Nine Stories; For Whom the Bell Tolls; Across the River and Into the Trees; The Old Man and the Sea (Pulitzer Prize, 1953); The Snows of Kilimanjaro; A Moveable Feast, 1964 (posthumous); Islands in the Stream (novel, 1970, posthumous). Award of Merit, American Academy of Arts and Letters, 1954; Nobel Prize for Literature, 1954. *Relevant Publications:* Hemingway, by Stewart Sanderson, 1961; Hemingway, by Ted Kiley, 1965; Great Hemingway: The Life Story, by Carlos Baker, 1969. *Recreations:* reading, fishing, shooting. *Address:* c/o Guaranty Trust Company of New York, 4 Place de la Concorde, Paris. *T.A.:* Garritus, Paris; (residence) Finca Vigia San Francisco de Paula, Cuba. *Clubs:* Players (New York); International Yacht, Vedado Tennis, Club de Cazadores Del Cerro (Havana). [*Died* 2 *July* 1961.

HEMINGWAY, Sir William, Kt. 1965; J.P.; *b.* Leeds, 21 January 1880. Alderman 1926, Leeds; Lord Mayor of Leeds, 1934-35. Knighted for political and public services in

Leeds. J.P. 1930; Freeman of Leeds, 1956. *Address:* 48 Ring Road, Middleton, Leeds 10. [*Died* 30 *May* 1967.

HEMMANT, George, C.M.G. 1929; *s.* of late William Hemmant, Bulimba, Sevenoaks, Kent; *b.* 1880; *m.* 1925, Gladys Evelyn, *d.* of the late Edward Knight, Oaklands, St. Leonards; one *s.* *Educ.:* Tonbridge School; Pembroke College, Cambridge. 1st Mathematical Tripos, 1902; entered Malayan Civil Service; Under-Secretary of Straits Settlements, 1924; acted as Colonial Secretary, 1928-29; Chie. Secretary to the Government of Nigeria, 1930-34; Officer Administering the Govt. of Nigeria, Nov. 1930-June 1931; retired 1934. [*Died* 31 *Dec.* 1964.

HEMMING, (Arthur) Francis, C.M.G. 1938; C.B.E. 1923; Secretary International Commission on Zoological Nomenclature, 1936-58; *b.* 9 Feb. 1893; *e. s.* of late Arthur George Hemming; *m.* 1st, 1924, Vera Murray (marriage dissolved 1933); one *s.*; 2nd, 1947, Margaret Frances Waley Joseph, *e. d.* of late Francis George Joseph; two *d.* *Educ.:* Rugby; Corpus Christi Coll., Oxford. 2nd Lt. 3rd Bn. Duke of Wellington's Regt., Aug. 1914; transferred to 2nd Batt., Dec. 1914; served British Expeditionary Force, France, 1914-16; Captain, 1916; severely wounded July 1916; retired on account of wounds. Dec. 1918; appointed to Home Civil Service and assigned to the Treasury, Dec. 1919; Assistant Private Secretary to the Chancellor of the Exchequer (Rt. Hon. J. Austen Chamberlain, M.P.), Jan.-Nov. 1920; Principal Private Secretary to the Chief Secretary for Ireland (Rt. Hon. Sir Hamar Greenwood, Bart., K.C., M.P.), 1920-22; Acting Principal, Irish Branch, Home Office and Colonial Office, 1922-24; Principal Private Secretary to Rt. Hon. J. R. Clynes, M.P., Lord Privy Seal and Deputy Leader of the House of Commons, Jan.-Nov. 1924; Acting Principal, Mercantile Marine Department, Board of Trade, 1924-25; Asst. Sec. to Committee of Civil Research, 1925-30, and to Economic Advisory Council, 1930; Secretary, Economic Advisory Council, 1930-39; Principal Asst. Sec. War Cabinet Offices, 1939-41; Administrative Head, Economic Section, War Cabinet Secretariat, 1939-40, and Central Statistical Office, 1941; Principal Officer, No. 6 Civil Defence Region, 1941; Principal Asst. Sec. (Fire Guard), Ministry of Home Security, 1941-44; Director of Petrol Rationing, Ministry of Fuel and Power, 1944-45; Principal Assistant Secretary (Economics and Statistics), Ministry of Fuel and Power, 1945-46, and Under-Secretary, 1946-53; Joint Sec., Imperial Cttee. on Economic Consultation and Co-operation, 1933; Secretary to Spanish Non-Intervention Committee, 1936-39, and to Spanish Non-Intervention Board, 1937-39; Special Mission to General Franco, 1938; Treasurer, Royal Entomological Society of London, 1929-39. *Publications:* The Generic Names of the Holarctic Butterflies, 1934; Hübner, 1937; Annotationes Lepidopterologicae, 1960; papers on entomological subjects. *Address:* 28 Park Village East, Regent's Park, N.W.1. *T.:* Euston 7733. [*Died* 22 *Feb.* 1964.

HENCH, Dr. Philip Showalter, M.D., M.S.; (Hon.)Sc.D., (Hon.)LL.D.; physician; Staff Consultant and Head of Dept. of Rheumatic Diseases, Mayo Clinic, since 1926; Professor of Medicine, Univ. of Minnesota (Mayo Foundation), since 1947; *b.* Pittsburgh, Pa., 28 Feb. 1896; *s.* of Jacob Bixler Hench, Litt.D., and Clara John (*née* Showalter); *m.* 1927, Mary Genevieve Kahler; two *s.* two *d.* *Educ.:* Preparatory Schools; Lafayette Coll. (A.B., 1916, Hon. Sc.D. 1940); School of Medicine, Univ. of Pittsburgh (M.D. 1920); Univ. of Minnesota (M.S. 1931); Univ. of Freiburg, Germany; Ludwig-Maximilians-Universität, Munich. Several hon. degrees. Mayo Foundation: Fellow, 1921-23, 1st Asst. in Med. 1923-25, Assoc. in Div. of Med., 1925. Univ. of Minnesota: Instructor, 1928-32; Asst. Prof., 1932-35; Assoc. Prof., 1935-47. Military Service: Medical Enlisted Reserve Corps 1917-19; War of 1939-45, Lt.-Col. U.S. Med. Corps, 1942; Col. 1945; discharged 1946; expert civilian consultant to Surgeon-General of U.S. Army, 1946-. Vice-Pres., Kahler Corp., Rochester, Minn. Fellow Amer. Med. Assoc., Amer. Coll. Physicians, etc.; Chm. and Member of many cttees. and assocs.; Hon. Member Roy. Soc. Med., Heberden Soc. (Heberden medal, 1942), London, and of other societies. Chief Ed., Annual Rheumatism Reviews (Amer. Rheumatism Assoc.), 1932-1948; Assoc. Editor, Annals of the Rheumatic Diseases (London). Nobel Prize for Medicine (joint), 1950, and recipient of many other awards both American and foreign. Republican. Presbyterian. *Recreations:* music, photography, medical history, tennis. *Publications:* articles to Med. Jls. *Address:* (home) 517 4th St.. S.W., Rochester, Minn., U.S.A.; (office) Mayo Clinic, Rochester, Minn. [*Died* 31 *March* 1965.

HENDERSON, Sir Alan Gerald Russell, Kt., *cr.* 1945; M.A.; Additional Judge of the Calcutta High Court, 1933-37, a permanent Puisne Judge, 1937, retired 1946; *b.* 22 March 1886; *s.* of Rev. Canon Alexander Henderson and Gertrude Harrison; *m.* 1922, Joan Margaret Takle; one *s.* *Educ.:* Westminster School; Christ Church, Oxford. 2nd Class Hon. Moderations, 2nd Class Lit. Hum. Selected for Indian Civil Service, 1909; Posted to Eastern Bengal and Assam, 1910; Posted to Bengal, 1912; Confirmed as District and Sessions Judge, 1922; Secretary to Government of Bengal and Legal Remembrancer, 1932. *Address:* c/o Lloyd's Bank, 6 Pall Mall, S.W.1. [*Died* 17 *May* 1963.

HENDERSON, Andrew Graham, R.S.A. 1953 (A.R.S.A. 1943); F.R.I.B.A.; President, Royal Institute of British Architects, June 1950-52; *b.* Auckland, N.Z., 1882; *s.* of William Nisbet Henderson and Elizabeth Black Graham; *m.* 1919, Agnes Garrett Sclanders; one *d.* *Educ.:* Allan Glen's School; Royal Technical College and School of Art, Glasgow. Apprenticeship with Macwhannell & Rogerson, Glasgow, 1898-1903; Asst. with Honeyman, Keppie & Mackintosh, Glasgow, 1903-13; Arthur Cates Prizeman, 1911; Partner in firm of John Keppie & Henderson, Glasgow, 1913. Served European War, 1914-18, Lt. Glasgow Highlanders, 1915, France (wounded); War Dept. Valuer, 1917-20; resumed practice, 1920; War of 1939-45. Quartering Commandant, West Scotland District, Lt.-Col.; resumed practice, 1945. President Glasgow Institute of Architects, 1933-34; President Royal Incorporation of Architects in Scotland, 1946-47. Member Royal Fine Art Commission for Scotland. *Recreations:* sketching, golf. *Address:* (office) 21 Woodside Place, Glasgow, C.3. *T.:* Douglas 7821; (home) 96 Sprinkell Avenue, Glasgow, S.1. *Club:* Art (Glasgow). [*Died* 21 *Nov.* 1963.

HENDERSON, Archibald, M.A., Ph.D. (Univ. of N. Carolina, Univ. of Chicago); D.C.L. (Hon. University of the South); LL.D. (Hon. Tulane Univ., Hon. Coll. of William and Mary); Litt.D. (Hon. Oglethorpe Univ., Hon. Catawba Coll.; Hon. Univ. of N. Carolina); Emeritus Professor of Mathematics, Univ. of North Carolina; *b.* Salisbury, North Carolina, 17 June 1877; *s.* of John Steele Henderson and Elizabeth Brownrigg Cain; *m.* 1st, 1903, Minna Curtis Bynum; two *s.* three *d.*; *m.* 1957, Lucile Kelling. *Educ.:* Church (Episcopal) High School, Salisbury; University of North Carolina; Univ. of Chicago; Cambridge Univ.; Univ. of Berlin; The Sorbonne. Instructor in Mathematics, Univ., North Carolina, 1898; became in turn Associate Prof. of Mathematics,

Professor of Pure Mathematics, Head Department of Mathematics, 1920; Kenan Professor of Mathematics, 1925; prosecuted research work in Relativity at Cambridge University, England, at the University of Berlin, 1923-24; Southern University Exchange Lecturer at University of Virginia, 1925-26; late Head Department and Kenan Prof. of Mathematics, Univ. of North Carolina; retired, 1948. Pres. The Shaw Soc. of America, Inc; Vice-Pres. The Shaw Soc., London; F.R.S.L.; Member: Soc. Colonial Wars; Soc. of Amer. Historians; etc. *Publications:* The Size of the Universe; The Twenty-Seven Lines upon the Cubic Surface; The Teaching of Geometry; Number, and the Fundamental Laws of Algebra; Relativity, a Romance of Science; The Theory of Relativity (in collaboration); The New World of the Atom; A Classic Problem in Euclidean Geometry; Chapter on Mathematics in Roads to Knowledge; and numerous scientific periodical publications; Interpreters of Life, and the Modern Spirit; Mark Twain; George Bernard Shaw: his Life and Work; William James (trans. from Emile Boutroux, with his wife, Barbara Henderson); European Dramatists; O. Henry; The Changing Drama; The Star of Empire; The Conquest of the Old Southwest; Dr. Thomas Walker and the Loyal Company of Virginia; Washington's Southern Tour; Washington the Traveller; Table-Talk of G.B.S. (German translation: Tischgespraeche mit Bernard Shaw); Is Bernard Shaw a Dramatist?; Contemporary Immortals; Bernard Shaw; Playboy and Prophet; The Episcopal Church in Orange County, N.C.; Old Homes and Gardens of North Carolina; The Old North State and the New (2 vols.); The Campus of the First State University; Cradle of Liberty; George Bernard Shaw: Man of the Century; and innumerable periodical publications in American, English, and Continental magazines. Editor: Modern Drama and Opera, II.; A False Saint (De Curel); The Prince of Parthia (Thomas Godfrey); Pioneering a People's Theatre. *Recreations:* lawn tennis, swimming, wild game shooting; varying scientific, literary and historical pursuits; public lecturing. *Address:* 721 E Franklin St., Chapel Hill, N.C., U.S.A. [*Died* 6 *Dec.* 1963.

HENDERSON, Archibald; *b.* 15 Jan. 1886; *s.* of an Innkeeper, Straiton Inn, Midlothian; *m.* 1912, Emma Maud Lettin; one *s.* three *d.* *Educ.:* Simpsons Acad. Edinburgh; London School Board, City of London Coll. Clerk in various London offices, 1901-13; L.C.C. Tramways Dept., 1913-15; Trade Union Official, 1915-31; Chm. Traffic Commn., Scotland, 1931-48; Member of Road Transport Executive from its inception in 1948 (renamed Road Haulage Executive, 1949). Member Board of Management, British Road Services of British Transport Commission, 1953-56, retired. *Recreations:* reading, arguing, gardening. *Address:* Liberton, Green Lane, Bovingdon, Herts. *T.:* Bovingdon 2392. [*Died* 20 *Oct.* 1962.

HENDERSON, Charles Lamond, Q.C. 1943; J.P. Herts.; *b.* 12 April 1896; 2nd *s.* of William and Elizabeth Henderson, Auchenblae, Kincardineshire; *m.* 1922, Rose, *o. d.* of Canon R. C. F. Scott; one *s.* one *d.* *Educ.:* Edinburgh University. Served with Gordon Highlanders and Bedfordshire Regt., European War, 1914-18; M.A. (Edin.), 1919; called to Bar, Middle Temple, 1920; Member of Midland circuit; Recorder of Newark, 1943-45; Recorder of Warwick, 1945-49; Chairman Beds. Quarter Sessions, 1946-56; Recorder of Bedford, 1949-63. *Address:* Tilsworth House, nr. Leighton Buzzard. *T.:* Hockliffe 230. [*Died* 16 *Jan.* 1966.

HENDERSON, Sir David Kennedy, Kt. 1947; M.B., Ch.B., M.D., F.R.C.P. (Ed., Glasg., Lond.); LL.D.; Hon. M.D. (N.U.I.); Hon. F.R.S.M.; Hon. F.R.M.S. (Edin.); Hon. D.Sc. (McGill); Professor Emeritus of Psychiatry, University of Edinburgh; late Physician-Superintendent, Roy. Edin. Hosp. for Nervous and Mental Disease; late Physician-Consultant in Psychiatry, Edinburgh Royal Infirmary; *b.* Dumfries, Scotland, 24 April, 1884; *m.* Margaret, *d.* of late Dr. William Mabon of Ward's Island, N.Y.; three *d.* *Educ.:* Royal High School, Edinburgh; Edinburgh University; New York, Baltimore, Munich. Late Major R.A.M.C. Formerly Physician-Superintendent, Royal Mental Hospital, Glasgow; Lecturer in Psychological Medicine, Univ. of Glasgow; Hon. Consulting Physician, Western Infirmary, Glasgow; Senior Resident Physician Henry Phipps Psychiatric Clinic, Johns Hopkins Hospital, Baltimore; Assistant Physician, Royal Edinburgh Asylum; Assistant Physician, Psychiatric Institute, Manhattan State Hospital, New York; Assistant, Royal Psychiatric Clinic, Munich; Assistant, Pathological Laboratory of the London County Council Asylum, Claybury; Clinical Assistant, Royal Infirmary, Edinburgh; Clinical Assistant, Royal Edinburgh Asylum. Past President Psychiatry section R.S.M.; Pres. R.M.P.A. 1946-47; Pres. Roy. Coll. of Physicians, Edin., 1950-51; Morison Lectures, Mental Diseases, Royal Coll. of Physicians, Edinburgh, 1931; Norman Kerr Memorial Lectures, 1936; Salmon Memorial Lectures, New York, 1938; Maudsley Lecturer, 1938; Hon. Fell., Spanish Nat. Assoc. of Forensic Med., 1962. *Publications:* A Textbook of Psychiatry for Students and Practitioners (with R. D. Gillespie, M.D.), 1927; Social Psychiatry; Mind and Medicine; Affective Reaction Types, Psychopathic States; Evolution of Psychiatry in Scotland, 1964. *Address:* 11 Braid Mount, Edinburgh. [*Died* 20 *April* 1965.

HENDERSON, David Willis Wilson; C.B. 1957; F.R.S. 1959; D.Sc., Ph.D.; **Formerly Director of the Microbiological Research Establishment, Ministry of Defence;** *b.* **23 July 1903**; *s.* of late John and Mary Henderson, Glasgow; *m.* 1st, 1930, Beatrice Mary Davenport (*d.* 1952), *d.* of Sir Westcott Abell, K.B.E.; 2nd, 1953, Emily Helen, *d.* of D. Theodore Kelly, New York; no *c.* *Educ.:* Hamilton Academy; Glasgow University. B.Sc. Glasgow, 1926, M.Sc. Durham 1930, Ph.D. London 1934, D.Sc. London 1941. Lecturer in Bacteriology, King's Coll., Univ. of Durham, 1926-31; Carnegie Research Fellow, 1931-32, Beit Memorial Research Fellow, 1932-35, Lister Inst. of Preventive Medicine. Member of Scientific Staff, Lister Inst., 1935-46. Medal of Freedom, Bronze Palm (U.S.A.), 1946. *Publications:* papers on immunology and diseases of the respiratory tract. *Recreations:* gardening and fishing. *Address:* Swaynes Living, Great Durnford, Salisbury, Wilts. *Club:* Athenæum. [*Died* 16 *Aug.* 1968.

HENDERSON, Frank Young, C.B.E. 1951; D.Sc.; D.I.C.; Director, Forest Products Research Laboratory, D.S.I.R., 1945-60; *b.* 13 October 1894; *s.* of Frank Young Henderson, F.S.A.A., Glasgow, and Catherine Moody Cuthbert; *m.* 1932, Elizabeth Douglas, *d.* of late J. Douglas Pringle, Hawick, Scotland; two *d.* *Educ.:* High School of Glasgow; Glasgow University. Supt. of Detonator Dept., Nobels Explosives Co., 1915-18; Geological Survey of Nigeria, 1919-21; Plant Physiologist, Imperial College of Science, 1921-31; Lecturer in Timber Technology, Imperial College, 1931-44; Reader in Timber Technology, University of London, and Professor of Timber Technology, Imperial College, 1944; Director of Biological Studies, Sir John Cass Institute, 1932-39; Supt. of Examinations in Biology Pharmaceutical Society, 1928-45. Pest Infestation Laboratory, D.S.I.R., 1939-44.

Publications: Timber—its Properties, Pests and Preservation: scientific papers. *Recreations:* music, gardening. *Address:* School House, Upton Pyne, Nr. Exeter, Devon. *T.:* Stoke Canon 339
[*Died* 9 *April* 1966.

HENDERSON, Hector Bruce; Consul-General, Dakar, 1945-51; *b.* 1 Apr. 1895; *m.* 1928, Ida Elizabeth Margaret Murphy, Brisbane, Queensland; no *c.* Served European War, 1914-19, Northumberland Hussars, France and Belgium (despatches). Student Interpreter, Siam Consular Service, 1920. Various appts., including Bangkok, Saigon, Surabaya, Nakawn Lampang, Senggora, Batavia, Medan; Consul, Medan, Sumatra, 1933-39. Consul-General, Saigon, Dec. 1939-1941; seconded to N.I.D. Admiralty, 1942-45; appointed H.M. Minister, Monrovia, but did not proceed; retd. 1951. *Recreations:* shooting, riding, fishing. *Address:* c/o Foreign Office, S.W.1. *Club:* Royal Automobile.
[*Died* 1 *Feb.* 1962.

HENDERSON, Henry Ludwig, O.B.E. 1920; Emeritus Fellow of New College, Oxford; *b.* 4 July 1880; *s.* of Henry William Henderson and Louisa Augusta Schneider. *Educ.:* Highgate School; Westminster; Christ Church, Oxford. First Class Classical Moderations, First Class Literæ Humaniores, Craven Scholar, Chancellor's Prize for Latin Verse, Gaisford Prize for Greek Verse, Chancellor's Prize for Latin Essay; First Division Clerk in the Admiralty (Secretary's Department), 1904; Fellow and Lecturer of New Coll., 1905; Tutor, 1910; during European War, 1914-18, served as Lieut. 12th Batt. Worcestershire Regt., as Lieut. 1st Garrison Batt. Devonshire Regt. in Egypt, in the Censorship Department of the War Office, and finally as Censor at Singapore (Captain graded as G.S.O.2); granted rank of Captain after demobilisation; held several offices at New College, including that of Dean (1919-34); served in Postal Censorship, 1939-1940, and in Admiralty as Personal Assistant to Deputy Secretary, 1942-45. Governor of the Harpur Trust, Bedford, 1935-0; President, of the New College Society, 1950, 1951. *Address:* 1 Staverton Road, Oxford; New College, Oxford. *Clubs:* Athenæum, Royal Automobile.
[*Died* 26 *Dec.* 1963.

HENDERSON, Rev. Professor Ian; Professor of Systematic Theology, University of Glasgow, since 1948; *b.* 1910; *s.* of late Alexander Henderson and Elizabeth Gaudie, Edinburgh; *m.* 1947 Kathrine, *d.* of late W. A. Macartney, M.I.C.E., Edin.: one *s.* one *d.* *Educ.:* George Watson's College; Oban High School; Universities of Edinburgh, Zürich and Basel. Edinburgh Univ.: M.A. (1st Cl. Hons., Mental Philosophy), 1933, B.D. (Distinction, Systematic Theol.), 1936; D.D. 1954: Bruce of Grangehill Scholar in Philosophy and Senior Cunningham Fellow in Theology. Ordained to Ministry of Church of Scotland, 1938: translated to Kilmany, 1942; Moderator of Presbytery of Glasgow, 1967. External Examiner in Theology: St. Andrews Univ., 1945-48, 1966-69; Queen's Univ., Belfast, 1950; Aberdeen Univ., 1951; Manchester Univ., 1954. *Publications:* Can Two Walk Together?, 1948; Myth in the New Testament, 1952; Rudolf Bultmann, 1965; Power Without Glory, 1967; (Joint-Translation) Barth, Knowledge of God and Service of God, 1938; Lüthi, In Time of Earthquake, 1939; various theological articles. *Recreations:* gardening. *Address:* Kirkland, Campsie Glen, Nr. Glasgow. *T.:* Lennoxtown 545.
[*Died* 8 *April* 1969.

HENDERSON, Sir James, K.B.E. 1938 (C.B.E. 1928); *b.* 1882; Chairman Cucirini Cantoni Coats, Milan (Italy); Chairman, Banca d'America e/d'Italia, Milan (Italy); Vice-Chm., Cotonificio Vittorio Olcese, Milan (Italy); Director, Banca Vonwiller, Milan (Italy); late President British Chamber of Commerce for Italy; retired as Director, J. and P. Coats, Ltd., and Managing Director, The Central Agency, Ltd., Glasgow. *Address:* (home) Via Marchiondi 3, Milan, Italy.
[*Died* 2 *April* 1967.

HENDERSON, James; Company Director; D.L. for County Borough of Belfast; Barrister-at-law; *b.* 1889; *e. surv. s.* of late Sir James Henderson, D.L., and late Lady Henderson, Belfast. *Educ.:* Methodist College, Belfast; Dublin University (M.A.). Called to Irish Bar, 1911; entered journalism 1912, and for year or so was acting Editor of Dublin Daily Express; served European War, 1914-18, in R.A.S.C.; editorial staff Belfast News-Letter, 1919-28; Director, Belfast News-Letter Ltd., since 1928; Deleg. to Imperial Press Conf., Canada, 1920; President Newspaper Soc., 1936-37; Director, Press Assoc. Ltd., 1935-47 (Chairman 1940 and 1945); Director, Reuters Ltd., 1936-41; Trustee, Reuters Ltd., 1943; Chairman of Trustees, 1960-; Director, Portsmouth & Sunderland Newspapers Ltd., since 1946; Chm. Joint Advisory Council of British Golf Unions, 1926 and 1934; Pres. Golfing Union of Ireland, 1946 and 1947; Member of Senate, Queen's Univ. of Belfast; Pres. Trinity Coll. (Dublin) Assoc. of Northern Ireland, 1946-48. *Address:* 36 Windsor Park, Belfast. *T.:* Belfast 667353. *Club:* Ulster (Belfast).
[*Died* 30 *July* 1963.

HENDERSON, John, F.R.S.E., F.C.I.I., *b.* 23 Jan. 1883; *e. s.* of late Charles Henderson, Dundee and London; *m.* 1907, Elsie Catherine (died 1947); *er. d.* of late Frederick Johnson Jones, Civil Servant; one *s.* one *d.* *Educ.:* Bancroft's; F.C.I.I. (Rutter prizeman), 1914. Hand-in-Hand Fire and Life Insurance Society, 1899-1910; Commercial Union Assurance Company, Ltd., 1910-20; Edinburgh Assurance Company, Limited, 1920-43 (Manager and Secretary, 1927-43). Past President, Insurance Society of Edinburgh; Gazetted to K.O.Y.L.I., 1917; served with 2/4th East Yorks, Bermuda, 1917-19. *Publications:* Thorns and Mary-Lilies (poems), 1949; technical and other essays and sketches; (with J. E. Matthews) Profits Insurance, 1923. *Recreations:* walking, reading. *Address:* 48 India Street, Edinburgh 3. *T.:* Caledonian 6472.
[*Died* 10 *May* 1965.

HENDERSON, John Scott, Q.C. 1945; Recorder of Portsmouth, 1945-62; *b.* 28 September 1895. *Educ.:* Airdrie Academy; London Univ., B.Sc. (Econ.) 1st class hons. Served European War, 1914-19, Royal Dublin Fusiliers and R.A.S.C. (despatches, wounded twice). Ministry of Health, 1920-27; Sec. British Delegation, International Sanitary Conference, Paris, 1926; Sec. Inter-Departmental Committee Optical Practitioners Bill, 1927; Barrister, Inner Temple, 1927; Bencher, Inner Temple, 1952. Recorder of Bridgwater, 1944. Chairman, Cttee. on Cruelty to Wild Animals and Humane Traps Awards Panel; Broadmoor Inquiry Cttee., Evans Inquiry; Member Myxomatosis Advisory Cttee. *Address:* 2 Mitre Court Buildings, Temple, E.C.4; Sutton Mandeville, Salisbury. *T.:* Central 2246. *Clubs:* Union, Bath.
[*Died* 5 *Nov.* 1964.

HENDERSON, Comdr. Oscar, C.V.O. 1935; C.B.E. 1925; D.S.O. 1918; late Royal Navy; President, Century Newspapers Ltd., Belfast; *b.* 7 Oct. 1891; 3rd *s.* of late Sir James Henderson, D.L.; *m.* 1920, Alicia Mary, *d.* of late R. B. Henry, D.L., Belfast; two *s.* *Educ.:* Bradfield College, Berkshire; R.N. Colleges, Osborne and Dartmouth. European War, China, 1914-Jan. 1915; Gallipoli, 1915-16 (despatches thrice); Grand Fleet, 1916-18; Zeebrugge (despatches, D.S.O., Croix de Guerre), in command of destroyers till

1922; retired list, 1922. Comptroller to the Governor of Northern Ireland (the Duke of Abercorn and Earl Granville), 1923-47. Vice-Pres. and Mem. Cttee. of Management R.N.L.I. and Chairman Belfast Branch. *Address:* Glenburn House, Dunmurry, Co. Antrim. *T.:* Dunmurry 3369. *Club:* Ulster (Belfast). [*Died* 3 *Aug.* 1969.

HENDERSON, Major-General Patrick Hagart, C.B. 1934; D.S.O. 1916; K.H.P. 1930; *b.* 17 Feb. 1876; *y. s.* of late Wm. Henderson of Lawton, Perthshire; *m.* 1904, Alice Ethel (*d.* 1957), *d.* of late General Charles Thompson, and *g. d.* of late Admiral J. Thompson, Longparish, Hants; no *c. Educ.:* Dollar Academy; Edinburgh University. Lieut. R.A.M.C., 1900; served in India, Africa, Arabia, 1901-6; India, 1928-30; Capt. 1903; Major, 1911; Lt.-Col. 1917; Brevet-Colonel, 1925; Col. 1928; Major-Gen. 1931; served European War, 1914-19; Embarkation Staff Southampton, 1914; with 7th Division in France, 1914-15; with 28th Division in Egypt and Macedonia, 1915-17; with 27th Division in Macedonia, South Russia, and Trans-Caspia, 1917-19 (despatches four times, D.S.O. Bt. Lt.-Col.); retired pay, 1935. *Publications:* various. *Recreations:* ski-ing, pig-sticking, hunting, fishing, shooting, golf, etc. *Address:* c/o Glyn, Mills & Co., Kirkland House, Whitehall, S.W.1. *Clubs:* Army and Navy, Edinburgh University of London, Ski of Great Britain. [*Died* 18 *July* 1968.

HENDERSON, Robert Candlish, Q.C. (Scot.) 1921; M.A., LL.D.; Professor of Scots Law, University of Edinburgh, 1922-1947; *b.* 1874; *s.* of Rev. Archibald Henderson, D.D.; *m.* Frances Josephine Moinet; one *s.* two *d. Address:* 422 Lanark Road, Colinton, Edinburgh 13. *T.:* 88301. *Club:* New (Edinburgh). [*Died* 8 *March* 1964.

HENDERSON, Capt. Thomas M. S. M.; *see* Milne Henderson.

HENDERSON, Lieut.-Col. Sir Vivian Leonard, Kt., *cr.* 1927; M.C.; *s.* of Francis Henderson, J.P., shipowner, Glasgow, and Alice, *d.* of late Sir C. F. Hamond, M.P.; *b.* Liverpool, 6 Oct. 1884; *m.* 1913, Eileen Marjorie, *y. d.* of late Brig.-Gen. G. W. Dowell, C.M.G., C.B.E.; three *d. Educ.:* Uppingham; Sandhurst. Entered Army, Loyal North Lancashire Regt., 1904; Capt., Special Reserve, 1914; Major and D.A.A.G., 1918; Lt.-Col. commanding 3rd Loyal Regiment, 1921-39; A.D.C. and Private Secretary to Sir Cavendish Boyle, Governor of Mauritius, 1909-11; served European War, 1914-18 (M.C., 1914 Star, despatches); M.P. (U.) Tradeston Division of Glasgow, Dec. 1918-22; M.P. (C.) Bootle, 1924-29; Chelmsford Division, Essex, 1931-35; Parliamentary Private Secretary to Sir J. Craig, M.P., at Pensions Ministry, 1919; Parliamentary Under-Secretary of State, Home Office, and Representative Office of Works, House of Commons, 1927-29; Member of Royal Commission on Fire Prevention, 1921; Hon. Sec. King's Roll National Council, 1922-27; was Chairman of Estimates Committee, House of Commons, 6 years; Chairman of Committees under the Home Office dealing with Factories, Fire, and Juvenile Delinquency; Chairman Visiting Justices Conference, 7 years; Pres. Home Office Schools Managers Assoc. 13 years; sometime Chm. Hampstead and Lambeth Juvenile Courts. Chairman Fire Service Commission, 1939, and Fire Service Research Trust, 1940-60; J.P. County of London, 1934; D.L. 1937; Dep. Chm. Marylebone and N. Paddington Rent Tribunal, 1949-52; Chm. Domestic Proceedings Court, Hampstead Petty Sessions, 1937-59. *Address:* 14 Kidderpore Gardens, Hampstead, N.W.3. *Club:* United Service [*Died* 3 *Feb.* 1965.

HENDERSON-SCOTT, Lieut.-Colonel Archibald Malcolm, C.B.E. 1920; M.A., B.C.L.; *b.* 16 Jan. 1882; *s.* of late Charles Henderson-Scott, F.J.I., Barrister-at-law; *m.* 1917, Grace Kathleen, *d.* of late George Mackern, M.D., of Buenos Ayres and Eastbourne; no *c. Educ.:* Westminster School; Exeter College, Oxford; Middle Temple, and Staff College, Camberley. Called to Bar, Middle Temple, 1905; gazetted from the Queen's Westminster Rifles to a Commission in the Royal Inniskilling Fusiliers, 1905; served with that Regiment at home and abroad till joining the Staff College, Camberley, of which he is a graduate, 1914; has travelled extensively in Russia: Lieutenant, 1907; Captain, 1914; European War, 1914-18, served as G.S.O. 3rd Grade 48th (South Midland) Division; D.A.A. and Q.M.G., 1st Corps, France; D.A.A.G. 1st Army, France; A.A.G. War Office with temporary rank of Lieut.-Col. (C.B.E., Bt. Major, Bt. Lieut. Col. on promotion to Major, despatches); retired pay, 1922. Farming in Argentina until 1959 (temporarily employed British Embassy, Buenos Aires, 1939-42). Rowed several years in the Exeter College eight and for the Thames Rowing Club at Henley and other regattas. *Recreations:* formerly rowing, motoring, country pursuits. *Address:* Flat 96, Kingsway Court, Hove 3, Sussex. *Club:* Bath. [*Died* 4 *March* 1967.

HENDERSON-STEWART, Sir James, 1st Bt. *cr.* 1957, of Callumshill; M.P. (Liberal Unionist), East Fife, since 1933; Sessional Chm. Liberal National Parliamentary Party, 1945; *b.* Crieff, 6 Dec. 1897; *s.* of late Matthew Deas Stewart and late Isabella Niven Todd; officially recognised in the surname of Henderson-Stewart and the designation of Callumshill by warrant of Lord Lyon, 1957; *m.* 1940, Anna Margaret (Peggy), *d.* of Sir Bernard Greenwell, 2nd Bt.; one *s.* one *d. Educ.:* Morrison's Acad., Crieff; Edinburgh Univ., B.Com. 1922, M.A. (Hons. Economics), 1923. Served in Royal Artillery, European War, 1916-19 (wounded); retired Captain, Reserve of Officers; Territorial service, 1921-25; served R.A. Sept. 1940-June 1941; contested (L.) Leicester East, 1923, Derby, 1924, Dundee, 1929. Joint Parl. Under-Sec. of State for Scotland, 1952-57. Hon. Vice-Pres. Trustees Savings Banks Association; Member Management Cttee. of Shipwrecked Fishermen and Mariners Roy. Benevolent Society. *Recreation:* Scottish country pursuits. *Heir: s.* David James Henderson-Stewart, *b.* 3 July 1941. *Address:* 10 Edwardes Square, W.8. *T.:* Western 5569. *Clubs:* New, Scottish Liberal (Edinburgh); Royal and Ancient (St. Andrews). [*Died* 3 *Sept.* 1961.

HENDRIE, Professor Donald Stewart; Principal West of Scotland Agricultural College, and Professor of Agriculture, University of Glasgow, since 1954; *b.* 31 March 1909; *s.* of John Hendrie, Solicitor, Galston, and Mary Hendrie (*née* Stewart); *m.* 1939, Janet Margaret Forrest, *d.* of W. F. Valentine, Architect, Kilmarnock; one *s. Educ.:* Galston; Kilmarnock Academy; Glasgow Univ.: Trinity Coll., Camb.: Ontario Agricultural Coll., Guelph. B.Sc. in Agric. (First Cl. Hons.) 1930 and 1935 (Glasgow); N.D.A. and N.D.D. 1930; Dip. Agric. Sci. 1931 (Cantab.); B.Sc. in Estate Management, 1949 (London). Asst. Lectr., West of Scotland Agricultural Coll., 1932-36; Dist. Lectr. in Agriculture, Leeds Univ., 1936-40; County Agricultural Exec. Officer, N.R. Yorks (Min. of Agriculture), 1940-49; Agricultural Adviser to High Commissioner for the U.K. in New Zealand, 1949-54. Member of Cttee. of Enquiry into Horticultural Marketing, 1955, Grassland Utilisation, 1957 and Agricultural Graduates, 1962; Governor: Scottish Horticultural Research Inst.; Grassland Research Inst.; Chairman, Hebridean Bulb Growers Ltd.; Member: Scottish Milk Records Assoc.; Scottish Agricultural Improvement Council; Scottish Livestock Records Advisory Cttee.; West Scotland Regional Advisory Cttee. on Forestry. *Recreation:* golf. *Address:* 116 Terregles Ave., Glasgow, S.1. *T.:* Pollok 4682. *Clubs:* Farmers'; Roy. Scottish Automobile (Glas.). [*Died* 16 *June* 1965.

HENDRY, William Edward Russell; Sheriff-Substitute of Dumfries and Galloway at Dumfries, 1952-65; *b.* 19 Nov. 1911; 7th *s.* of late John Wilson Hendry, Solicitor, Glasgow; *m.* 1948, Margaret McNeill, *d.* of late Henry Gair; two *s.* one *d.* *Educ.:* Glasgow High School; University of Glasgow. Admitted to Faculty of Advocates, 1940. Served War of 1939-45 in R.A.F.V.R. *Publication:* Joint Editor, Walton on Husband and Wife, 3rd Edn., 1952. *Recreations:* curling, golf, fishing, shooting. *Address:* Lochanhead House, Lochfoot, by Dumfries. *T.:* Lochfoot 291. *Clubs:* Caledonian, United Services (Edinburgh). [*Died* 18 *March* 1965.

HENEAGE, 3rd Baron, *cr.* 1896; **Rev. Thomas Robert Heneage;** *b.* 24 July 1877; 3rd but *o. surv. s.* of 1st Baron Heneage (*d.* 1922) and Lady Eleanor Cecilia Hare (*d.* 1924), *d.* of 2nd Earl of Listowel; *S.* brother 1954. *Educ.:* Trinity Hall, Cambridge (B.A.). Deacon 1903; Priest 1905; Curate of Spalding, Lincs., 1903-06; British Columbia from 1907 to present time. Chaplain to Bishop of British Columbia, 1912-17; formerly Chaplain to 5th Regiment Royal Canadian Garrison Artillery and Cadets; Executive Commissioner for Boy Scouts Association, British Columbia. *Heir:* none. *Address:* 777 Burrard Street, Vancouver 1, British Columbia, Canada. [*Died* 19 *Feb.* 1967 (*ext.*).

HENLEY, 6th Baron (Ireland), *cr.* 1799; **Francis Robert Eden,** Baron Northington (U.K.), *cr.* 1885; J.P.; *b.* 11 April 1877; 4th *s.* of 3rd Lord Henley; *S. half-brother,* 1925; *m.* 1913, Lady Dorothy Howard, 3rd *d.* of 9th Earl of Carlisle; two *s.* three *d.* *Educ.:* Harrow; Oxford. Lieut. in Royal Naval Division in Dardanelles. Chairman Northants County Council, 1944-49. *Recreations:* lawn tennis, and Natural History. *Heir:* *s.* Hon. Michael Francis Eden. *Address:* Watford Court, Rugby. *T.:* Long-Buckley 204. *Club:* Brooks's. [*Died* 21 *April* 1962.

HENLEY, Vice-Adm. Joseph Charles Walrond, C.B. 1925; *b.* 12 Sep. 1879; *o. s.* of late Joseph Arthur Henley, 82nd Regt., and Kate Isabella, 2nd *d.* of late Colonel James William Graves, 18th Royal Irish; *m.* 1902, Esmé Gordon, *y. d.* of late Colonel Aylmer Spicer Cameron, V.C., C.B., 72nd Highlanders; four *s.* one *d.* Served European War, 1914-19 despatches twice); Vice-Adm. 1932; retd. 1932. D.L. and J.P. Kent. *Address:* c/o National Provincial Bank, Trafalgar Square Branch S.W.1. *Club:* United Service. [*Died* 9 *Jan.* 1968.

HENN, Colonel William Francis, C.B.E. 1955; M.V.O. 1946; retired as Chief Constable of Gloucestershire (1937-59): *b.* 1892; *er. s.* of Francis Blackburne Henn, R.M., J.P., Paradise, Ennis, Co. Clare, Ireland; *m.* 1915, Geraldine Frances, *y. d.* of T. G. Stacpoole Mahon, D.L., Corbally, Quin, Co. Clare; two *s.* one *d.* *Educ.:* Aldenham School; Magdalene Coll., Cambridge. Served European War, 1914-19: Roy. Munster Fusiliers (wounded, despatches). Egyptian Civil Service and Police, 1920-37; Commandant, Alexandria City Police, 1930-37. King's Police Medal. Comdr., Nile and Ismail, Egypt; Phœnix, Greece; Crown of Italy, 1925-37; C.St.J. *Recreations:* fishing and motoring. *Address:* 1 Rothsay Mansions, Albert Road, Cheltenham, Glos. *Clubs:* East India and Sports; New (Cheltenham). [*Died* 27 *April* 1964.

HENNESSY, Hon. Sir Alfred (Theodore), K.B.E., *cr.* 1923; Government nominated Senator of Union of S.A. Parliament since 1939; *b.* 1875; 2nd *s.* of J. Hennessy of Ballymacorrig, Co. Cork; *m.* Margaret Isabella (*d.* 1960), 2nd *d.* of Donald Moodie, J.P. (the younger of Melsetter), of Grootvader's Bosch, S.A.; three *s.* four *d.* *Educ.:* privately. Chief Agent, Unionist Party of South Africa, 1911-21; Chairman and Founder of Royal Automobile Club of S.A.; Director of various companies. *Recreations:* motoring, golf. *Address:* St. John's House, Wynberg, S. Africa. *Clubs:* Royal Automobile; Civil Service, City, Royal Automobile of S.A., Royal Cape Golf, Cape, S.A. [*Died* 27 *Nov.* 1963.

HENNIKER-HEATON, Raymond, F.S.A.; *b.* London, 1874; Art Consultant; Director Phillimore Ives Memorial Gallery, Stellenbosch, since 1950; *m.* Faith, *o. d.* of late Commander William Henniker Heaton, Royal Navy, Plas Heaton, North Wales; one *s.* one *d.* *Educ.:* privately. Two years on stage; studied painting, Acad. Délécluse, Paris, and history of art, especially primitive art; active in writing and lecturing, and assembling art objects for public and private galleries; went to Canada 1909, U.S.A. 1912. Appointed Director of Hackley Art Gallery, Michigan, and formed a collection of early and modern paintings; resigned, 1916; Director Worcester Art Museum, Massachusetts, 1918-25, then Foreign Adviser until 1933; had charge of British Government Exhibition of War Paintings and Drawings, and its presentation in chief cities of U.S.A., 1919-20; Member Consultative Cttee., Burlington Magazine; Director Newspaper Features Ltd. since 1932; Editor, You, Magazine of Practical Psychology, 1938-39; Home Guard, 1941; Chm. Henniker-Heaton Pro. Ltd. Engineers, 1941-1946; Hon. Librarian, British Social Hygiene Council, 1942. *Publications:* Inaugural Catalogue of Hackley Gallery; The Goal, a war play in two acts; a series of articles on Armenia for the British Govt., 1916; Catalogue of Early and Modern Painting in Worcester Art Museum, 1923; Monograph on Titian, 1926; Perplexes and Complexes, 1936; Sexes and Sevens, 1937; Drifting with Direction, 1941; Preservation of Old Paintings, 1947; Catalogue, Phillimore Ives Memorial Collection, 1951; contributes to Burlington Magazine, International Studio, etc., on primitive general art subjects and psychology. Assumed name of Henniker-Heaton in lieu of Wyer, 1923. *Recreations:* poetry, and observing human reactions, including own. *Address:* Phillimore House, Stellenbosch, S. Africa. *Club:* Royal Automobile. [*Died* 15 *April* 1963.

HENNING, Walter Bruno, F.B.A. 1954; Ph.D.; Professor of Iranian Studies, Univ. of California, Berkeley, since 1961; Chairman, Executive Council, Corpus Inscriptionum Iranicarum, since 1954; *b.* 26 August 1908; *m.* 1937, Maria Polotsky; one *d.* *Educ.:* University of Göttingen. Asst. to Concordance of Islamic Tradition (Leyden), 1930; Ph.D. (summa cum laude), Göttingen, 1931; Editor of Manichæan manuscripts for the Prussian Acad. of Science and Learning (Berlin), 1932; Parsee Community's Lecturer in Iranian Studies (School of Oriental Studies, London), 1936; visiting Professor of Indo-Iranian, Columbia University, 1946; Reader in Central Asian Studies, University of London, 1947; Professor of Central Asian Studies in the University of London, 1948-61. Ratanbai Katrak Lecturer, Oxford, 1949; Southern Persia (on invitation of Iranian Government), 1950; Head of the Department of the Near and Middle East, School of Oriental and African Studies, 1958-61 Member, Inst. for Advanced Study, Princeton, New Jersey, 1956; Member, Royal Danish Academy,

Corresp. Member: Deutsche Akademie der Wissenschaften (Berlin); School of Oriental and African Studies. *Publications:* The Verb in Middle Persian (German), 1933; A Manichæan Prayer and Confession Book (German), 1937; Sogdica, 1940; Zoroaster—politician or witchdoctor?, 1951; (ed.) Middle Iranian Manichæan Texts, 3 parts, 1932-34; The Inscription of Sar-Mashhad, 1955; The Inscription of Naqš-i Rustam, 1957; (ed.) A Locust's Leg, 1962; Minor Inscriptions of Kartir, 1963; articles in Bulletin of the School of Oriental Studies, Journal of the Royal Asiatic Soc., Transactions of Philological Soc., Orientalia, Asia Major, etc. *Recreations:* numismatics, chess. *Address:* 7 Eton Court, Berkeley, Calif. 94705, U.S.A. *T.:* 415-658-6362. [*Died* 8 *Jan.* 1967.

HENRIOT, Emile; Grand Officier, Légion d'Honneur; Croix de Guerre, France; Member of the French Academy; author and journalist; *b.* 3 March 1889; *m.* Germaine Gounod; two *s.* *Educ.:* École Fénélon; Lycée Condorcet. Literary Critic, "Le Temps", 1911-42. Literary Critic, "Le Monde". President Alliance Française. *Publications:* Aricie Brun ou les Vertus Bourgeoises, 1924; Le Diable à l'Hôtel, 1919; Les Occasions Perdues, 1931; Le Livre de mon Père, 1938; La Rose de Bratislava, 1948; Les Fils de la Louve, 1950; Au Bord du Temps, 1958; On n'est pas perdu sur la Terre, 1960, etc. *Recreations:* country, hunting, travelling. *Address:* 10 rue Daubigny, Paris. [*Died* 14 *April* 1961.

HENRIQUES, Sir Basil L. Q., Kt., *cr.* 1955; C.B.E. 1948; M.A., J.P.; *b.* 17 Oct. 1890; *s.* of David Q. and Agnes C. Henriques; *m.* 1916, Rose L. Loewe. *Educ.:* Harrow; University College, Oxford. Founded Oxford and St. George's Club, 1914, which developed into Bernhard Baron St. George's Jewish Settlement; Warden until 1947. Served 3rd Bn. Buffs; seconded in 1915 to the Tank Corps (Capt., Italian Silver Medal, despatches twice); Vice-Chm. National Association Boys' Clubs; Chairman of the East London Juvenile Court, 1936-55; Pres. London Federation of Boys' Clubs; President British Diabetic Assoc. *Publications:* Club Leadership, 1933; The Indiscretions of a Warden, 1937; So You're being Called Up, 1947; The Indiscretions of a Magistrate, 1950; Club Leadership To-day, 1950. Fratres, club boys in uniform, 1951; The Home Menders, The Prevention of Unhappiness in Children, 1955. Pamphlets on Judaism, Juvenile Delinquency, and Boys' Clubs. *Recreation:* travelling. *Address:* Berner Street, E.1. *T.:* Royal 5526. *Club:* Reform. [*Died* 2 *Dec.* 1961.

HENRIQUES, Colonel Robert David Quixano, M.B.E. 1943; farmer and writer; *b.* 11 December 1905; *s.* of late Julian Quixano Henriques and of Margaret Beddington; *m.* 1928, Vivien Doris, *d.* of Major W. H. and Hon. Mrs. Levy; two *s.* two *d.* *Educ.:* Lockers Park; Rugby; New College, Oxford (B.A.). Joined Royal Artillery, 1926, and served in Egypt and Sudan, retiring 1933; Territorial Army, 1934-1939; served War of 1939-45 in Royal Artillery, Commandos, and Combined Operations Headquarters (U.S. Silver Star, U.S. Bronze Star). Cavendish Lecturer, 1961. *Publications:* Death by Moonlight, 1938; No Arms No Armour, 1939 (British Empire prize and International prize for literature); Capt. Smith and Company, 1943; The Journey Home, 1944; Through the Valley (James Tait Black Memorial prize), 1950; The Cotswolds, 1950; A Stranger Here, 1953; Red over Green, 1955; 100 Hours to Suez, 1957; Marcus Samuel, First Viscount Bearsted, 1960; Sir Robert Waley Cohen, 1966. *Recreation:* fishing. *Address:* Winson Mill Farm, Winson, Cirencester, Glos. *T.:* Fossebridge 234. *Clubs:* Garrick, Cavalry, Savile. [*Died* 22 *Jan.* 1967.

HENRY, Sir David, Kt., *cr.* 1954; Chairman, New Zealand Forest Products Ltd., Penrose, Auckland, since 1936 (Managing Director, 1938); *b.* 24 Nov. 1888; *s.* of Robert Henry, Upperlands, Londonderry, Ireland, and Agnes Stevenson, Kirkintilloch, Scotland; *m.* Dorothy M. Osborne; one *d.* *Educ.:* Heriot-Watt, Edinburgh. Arrived in New Zealand, 1907; since then associated with metal industry and utilisation of exotic timbers; founded Sheet Metal Co., D. Henry & Co. Ltd., 1920; Past President: N.Z. Manufacturers Fedn.; Auckland Rotary Club; Auckland Y.M.C.A.; Past Member, Auckland City Council. *Recreations:* bowls, golf. *Address:* 23 Stilwell Road, Mount Albert, Auckland, New Zealand. *T.:* 84-522. *Club:* Northern (Auckland). [*Died* 20 *Aug.* 1963.

HENRY, Prof. Robert Francis Jack, F.R.C.S.I., Professor of Clinical Surgery, Trinity College, Dublin, 1953-67; Surgeon, Royal City of Dublin Hospital and National Children's Hospital, Dublin; *b.* 18 Feb. 1902; *s.* of R. G. N. Henry; *m.* Stella Christine, *d.* of William Ross. *Educ.:* St. Stephen's Green School, Dublin; Trinity College, Dublin. B.A., M.B., B.Ch., B.A.O., Dublin, 1924; F.R.C.S.I. 1927. Second Assistant, Department of Physiology, Trinity College, Dublin, 1923; House Surgeon, Ancoats Hospital, Manchester, 1925; Professor of Surgery, Royal College of Surgeons in Ireland, 1938-53. Fellow, Royal Academy of Medicine in Ireland; Senior Fellow: Association of Surgeons of Great Britain and Ireland; Society of Thoracic Surgeons of Great Britain and Ireland (Pres., 1963). *Publications:* papers on surgical subjects in Irish Journal of Medical Science, etc. *Recreations:* sailing, fishing, golf. *Address:* Matchbox, Mount Anville Road, Dundrum, Co. Dublin. [*Died* 28 *Aug.* 1970.

HENSON, John; *b.* 3 April 1879; *s.* of Geo. Thomas and Hannah Henson; *m.* 1906, Mary Ellen Bridgeman (decd.); two *d.* *Educ.:* Kirkella Church School, East Yorks. Began work in wholesale drapery, City of London. Held Secretaryships British Socialist Party, 1912-14; gen. sec. Hull Trades Council, 1921-29; sec. Humber Dist. Nat. Transport Workers' Fed., 1921-24; Area Trade Group Sec. Passenger and Commercial Groups, East Coast Transport and Gen. Workers' Union, 1920-44; member Road Haulage Wages Board until 1944, etc. Served European War, 1914-18, 10th Bn. East Yorks. Regt., Egypt and France. Lord Mayor of Kingston upon Hull, 1949-50; Deputy Lord Mayor, 1950-51; Alderman Hull City Council, 1929-. Hon. Mem., Area D, Municipal Passenger Transport Assoc., (Chm., 1959-60). *Recreations:* gardening and reading good literature. *Address:* 1 Calvert Road, Kingston upon Hull. *T.:* 53357. *Club:* Hull Cricket (Hon.). [*Died* 12 *Dec.* 1969.

HEPBURN, Sir John K. T., 5th Bt.; *see* Buchan-Hepburn.

HEPBURN, William Andrew Hardie, C.B. 1957; retired as Under Secretary, National Assistance Board (1950-58); *b.* 26 April 1898; *s.* of William and Mary Hepburn, Moffat, Dumfriesshire; *m.* 1930, Marion Margaret Rae; one *d.* *Educ.:* Dumfries Acad.; Edinburgh Univ. Scottish Board of Health, 1922: Unemployment Assistance Board: Carlisle, Dec. 1934, Dundee, Jan. 1936, Headquarters, Dec. 1937; Ministry of National Insurance, 1944. *Address:* 21 Fairmile Avenue, Edinburgh 10. *T.:* Fairmilehead 1230. [*Died* 6 *May* 1965.

HEPENSTAL, Col. M. E. D.; *see* Dopping-Hepenstal.

HERBERT, Sir Charles Gordon, K.C.I.E., *cr.* 1947 (C.I.E. 1939); C.S.I. 1944; *b.* 28 Feb. 1893; *s.* of Edward Herbert, Highgate. *Educ.:* Merchant Taylors' School; Wadham College, Oxford. Served European War, 1914-18, Middx. Regt. 1914-19 (despatches). Joined Indian Civil Service, 1920; Indian Political Department, 1938; resident Hyderabad, 1946. *Address:* c/o National and Grindlay's Bank Ltd., 13 St. James's Square, S.W.1. *Clubs:* Athenæum, East India and Sports. [*Died* 4 *April* 1970.

HERBERT, Sir Edward (Dave Asher), Kt., *cr.* 1951; O.B.E. 1919; Croix de Guerre (France), 1918; formerly Chairman: William Hollins & Co. Ltd.; Short Bros. and Harland Ltd.; Director: Midland Bank Ltd.; Northern Assurance Co. Ltd.; and other public cos.; *b.* 12 Feb. 1892; *y. s.* of M. H. and Amelia Herbert; *m.* 1920, Jean Sybil Ingram, *d.* of Peter Davis, Pietermaritzburg, Natal; one *s.* one *d.* *Educ.:* King's College, Cambridge. M.A. (Cantab.); M.I.C.E.; M.I.Mech.E.; M.I.E.E.; F.I.I.A.; served European War, 1914-18; enlisted H.A.C., 1914; B.E.F., France, 1914-19; commissioned, R.A., 1915; IX Corps Staff, 1918-19 (wounded thrice, despatches thrice). Engaged in railway, bridge and other civil and mechanical engineering constructional work in South Africa, 1919-26. Engaged in reorganising the administration, production and distribution methods of a number of public companies in a variety of widely differing industries, 1927-39. Director-General Fabricated Building, Ministry of Aircraft Production, 1944-45. Member of Postmaster General's Television Advisory Committee; Member, Grand Council, F.B.I.; Chairman: Governing Body, Loughborough College of Technology; Member: Western Hemisphere Exports Council; Robbins Cttee. on Higher Education; Central Council of Economic League; Minister of Power's Committee on Co-operation between Area and Scottish Electricity and Gas Boards, 1958; Dollar Exports Council Mission to Canada, 1958. Freeman of the City of London. High Sheriff of Nottinghamshire, 1959-1960. *Address:* 20 Albert Court, Kensington Gore, S.W.7. *T.:* Knightsbridge 3141. *Clubs:* Brooks's, Carlton, Devonshire, Royal Automobile; Bankers (New York); Rand (Johannesburg). [*Died* 28 *April* 1963.

HERBERT, Rt. Rev. Percy Mark; K.C.V.O. 1954; D.D.; Clerk of the Closet to the Queen, 1952-63 (to King George VI, 1942-52); 2nd *s.* of late Major-General Hon. William Henry Herbert and Sybella Augusta, *d.* of late Mark Milbank; *b.* Shrewsbury, 24 April 1885; *m.* 1922, Hon. Elaine Orde-Powlett, *d.* of 5th Baron Bolton; three *s.* one *d.* *Educ.:* Rugby; Trinity College, Cambridge. Deacon, 1908; Priest, 1909; Curate of Rugby, 1908-15; Vicar of St. George's, Camberwell, and Warden of the Trinity Cambridge Mission, 1916-22; Rural Dean of Camberwell, 1918-22; Bishop Suffragan of Kingston-on-Thames, 1922-26; Bishop of Blackburn, 1926-42; Bishop of Norwich, 1942-59. Chaplain to the King, 1921; Chaplain and Sub-Prelate, Order of St. John of Jerusalem, 1939; Hereditary Freeman borough of Shrewsbury. *Address:* Virginia Water Cottage, The Great Park, Ascot, Berks. *T.:* Ascot 21952. *Club:* United University. [*Died* 22 *Jan.* 1968.

HERBERT, Sydney, M.A.; J.P.; Lecturer in History from 1928, and International Politics from 1919, University College of Wales, Aberystwyth; retired, 1951; *b.* London, 1886; *m.* 1909, Ellen Mary Hatherill; one *s.* *Publications:* Modern Europe, 1789-1914, 1916; Nationality and its Problems, 1920; Fall of Feudalism in France, 1921; The French Revolution, 1923; (with C. K. Webster) The League of Nations in Theory and Practice, 1933. *Recreations:* none. *Address:* 7 Marine Terrace, Aberystwyth. *T.:* Aberystwyth 7164. [*Died* 17 *Dec.* 1967.

HERBST, Major John Frederick, C.B.E. 1919; King's Jubilee Medal; retired Secretary of Department for Native Affairs, Union of S. Africa; *b.* 1873; *s.* of H. W. Herbst. Anglo-Boer War and European War Medals. *Clubs:* Civil Service, Royal Automobile (Cape Town). [*Died* 1 *Feb.* 1961.

HERCHENRODER, (Marie Ferdinand) Philippe, C.M.G. 1960; C.B.E. 1952; British Judge, Supreme Restitution Court, Herford, Germany, since 1957 and British Member of Arbitral Tribunal and Mixed Commn. for the Agreement on German External Debts since Sept. 1961; *b.* 1 Jan. 1893; 2nd *s.* of late Sir Alfred Herchenroder, K.C. and Lady Herchenroder (*née* Vinton); *m.* 1916, Millicent Louisa Dick (*d.* 1967); two *d.* *Educ.:* Royal College, Mauritius; University of London; Christ Church, Oxford. Inns of Court Studentship; Barrister, Middle Temple, 1914; first place in open competitive exam. for Home and Indian Civil Services, 1915; LL.B Hons. and Univ. Schol. (London), 1916. I.C.S. 1916-31; Docteur en Droit, Paris, 1936; Temp. Government Dept., England, 1939-44; C.C.G. 1944-55. British Judge, Supreme Restitution Court for Berlin, 1955-57. Coronation Medal, 1953. *Publications:* contrib. to Journal of former Society of Comparative Legislation. *Recreations:* books, music, languages. *Address:* Supreme Restitution Court, 2nd Division, Herford (Westfalen), Germany. *T.:* Herford (Germany) 2974. *Club:* Royal Commonwealth Society. [*Died* 1 *Sept.* 1968.

HERON, Colonel Sir George Wykeham, Kt., *cr.* 1944; C.M.G. 1938; C.B.E. 1926 (O.B.E. 1919); D.S.O. 1916; R.A.M.C. retired; M.R.C.S. Eng., L.R.C.P. Lond.; *b.* 16 Oct. 1880; *m.* 1910, Elsa Burch (*d.* 1962); one *s.* one *d.* *Educ.:* Rugby; Westminster Hospital. House Physician and Assistant House Surgeon, Westminster Hospital, 1904-1905; R.A.M.C. 1905; seconded for service with Egyptian Govt. 1908; E.E.F. 1914; Major, 1915; Temp. Lt.-Col. 11 June 1917; Temp. Col. 1918; retired with rank of Col. 1923; Director of Medical Services, Government of Palestine, 1920-44; Controller of Medical Supplies, Palestine, 1939-45; Controller of Supplies, Palestine, 1939-41; Reconstruction Commissioner, Palestine, 1944-45; Official Member of Executive Council, Palestine, 1942. Order of the Nile, 1919; Knight of Grace of the Order of St. John of Jerusalem in England, 1926. *Address:* Three Chimneys, Linton, nr. Maidstone. *T.:* Maidstone 83423. *Club:* Constitutional. [*Died* 22 *July* 1963.

HERRICK, Frederick Charles; painter and designer; engaged on experimental research into the relationship between impression and design; Fellow British Institute of Industrial Art; Member Art Workers' Guild and Fellow Society of Industrial Artists: N.R.D.; *b.* Mountsorrel, Leicestershire, 20 Sept. 1887; *y. s.* of Thomas Herrick, Mountsorrel; *m.* 1931, Lily, *y. d.* of William Ray, Basingstoke; one *s.* *Educ.:* Alderman Newton's School, Leicester; Leicester College of Arts and Crafts (Mulready Prize); the Royal College of Art; gained Royal Exhibition tenable at the Royal College of Art, 1908; awarded Travelling Scholarship in painting, 1912; served with the Grenadier Guards, 1914-19 (severely wounded at Hulluch, 1915); poster and commercial designer with the Baynard Press, 1919-26; awarded Diploma at the International Exhibition of Decorative Art, Italy, 1923; awarded Grand Prix at the International

Exhibition of Modern Decorative and Industrial Art, Paris, 1925; formerly Instructor of Drawing at Royal College of Art; Instructor of Drawing and Illustrative Design at Sir John Cass Technical Institute; Instructor of drawing, painting, composition, and anatomy in action at Brighton College of Art; Examiner in Drawing and Painting for East Midlands Educational Union; Professional Inspector (Board of Education) in Illustrative Design; Professional Examiner (Board of Education) in Pictorial Design; Chief Professional Examiner (Board of Education) in Industrial Design; Assessor for Diploma (Scottish Education Department) in Industrial Design. *Principal Works:* Mural decorations at Plymouth, Southampton, Reading, and Brighton; many posters, chiefly for London Underground Railways, Royal Mail Steam Packet Co., L.C.C., and Empire Marketing Board; numerous commercial devices, including the Wembley Lion and the emblem Truth in Advertising, for the International Advertising Convention. *Recreations:* rowing and sailing. *Address:* 44 Selborne Road, Hove 3. [*Died* 29 *June* 1970.

HERRIDGE, Major Hon. William Duncan, P.C. Canada 1931; D.S.O. 1919; M.C.; Q.C.; B.A.; *b.* Ottawa, 18 Sept. 1888; *s.* of Very Rev. William Thomas Herridge, D.D., and Marjorie Duncan, both British; *m.* 1st, 1916, Rose (*d.* 1925), *d.* of Andrew W. Fleck and Gertrude Booth, Ottawa; 2nd, 1931, Mildred Mariann (*d.* 1938), *d.* of H. J. Bennett and Henrietta Stiles; one *s.* *Educ.:* Ottawa Public School; Collegiate Institute; Univ.of Toronto (B.A. 1909); Osgoode Hall. Served European War, 1915-19 in France (despatches twice, M.C. and Bar, D.S.O.); Canadian Minister to the United States, 1931-35. At outbreak of war declared for total war. In the general election of March 1940, was defeated in the Constituency of Kindersley (candidate for universal conscription). *Address:* Rox. Apts., Ottawa, Ontario. [*Died* 21 *Sept.* 1961.

HERRING, Maj. Alfred Cecil, V.C. 1918; F.C.A.; a partner in the firm of Laing and Cruickshank, stockbrokers, 1925-61; *b.* 26 Oct. 1888; *s.* of George Edward Herring; *m.* *Educ.:* Tottenham County School. Served Articles under Daniel Steuart Fripp, F.C.A.; Chartered Accountant, 1912; Acting Paymaster, A.P.D. at Chatham Pay Office, 1914-1916; joined A.S.C.; went to France, Nov. 1916; attached 6th Batt. Northampton Regt., 1917 (V.C. at Jussy, 22 March 1918; captured and repatriated); assumed duty at War Office and promoted Major, 1919; relinquished commission, 1922; a partner in the firm of Evans, Fripp, Deed & Co., chartered accountants, 1920-25; admitted as member of Stock Exchange, May 1925. *Recreations:* golf; Captain of School at cricket and football; Captain of Old Boys at football. *Address:* Oatlands Park Hotel, Weybridge, Surrey. *T.:* Weybridge 4242. *Club:* Gresham. [*Died* 10 *Aug.* 1966.

HERRING, Percy Theodore, M.D. (Edin.), LL.D. (St. Andrews), F.R.C.P.E., F.R.S.E.; Professor Emeritus, St. Andrews University; *b.* Yorkshire, 1872; *s.* of Edward and Mary Herring, late of South Elmsall, Yorkshire, and Alford, New Zealand; *m.* Mary Marshall, *e. d.* of Thomas Callender, J.P., Edinburgh; four *d.* *Educ.:* Christ's College, Christchurch, New Zealand; Otago and Edinburgh Universities. Formerly Lecturer on Histology and Assistant to the Physiology Department, University of Edinburgh; Murchison Memorial Scholar in Clinical Medicine, 1897; Chrichton Research Scholar in Pathology, 1898; Goodsir Memorial Fellow in Anatomy and Physiology, University of Edinburgh, 1899; President of the Royal Medical Society, 1898-99; Chandos Professor of Physiology, University of St. Andrews, 1908-48; Dean of the Faculty of Science, 1921-39. Vice-President, St. Leonard's and St. Katharine's Schools; Chairman of Council, 1930-47, and Hon. Treasurer, 1928-49. *Publications:* papers in physiological journals, etc. *Address:* 16 Hepburn Gardens, St. Andrews, Fife. *Club:* Royal and Ancient Golf (St. Andrews). [*Died* 24 *Oct.* 1967.

HERSCHELL, Charles Richard, C.B.E. 1941; Officer Order of St. John of Jerusalem; J.P.; Chairman of Directors, Herschell's Pty. Ltd., Documentary Film Producers, Melbourne, 1912-49; appointed Consultant for Life upon retirement, 1949; *b.* 20 Sept. 1877; *s.* of Richard Herschell, Scotsman, and Jessie Wilson, Australian; *m.* 1900, Grace Watkins, Seymour; two *d.* *Educ.:* Camp Hill School and High School, Bendigo. Managing Director, British Dominion Films, Ltd., 1927-28, Director, 1929-53; Foundation Member The Great Ocean Road Trust, 1917, Hon. Managing Director, 1930 - 33, President, 1933 - 55; Foundation Member The Flying Doctor services of Australia, Victorian Section, President, 1936-38, Vice-President, 1938-1940; Member of Red Cross Society (Victorian Division), St. John Ambulance Association, and Appeals Committee, Anti-Cancer Council until 1952. *Recreation:* social service. *Address:* Blue Haze, 71 Alexandra Avenue, South Yarra, S.E.1, Victoria, Australia. *T.:* BM 1347. *Club:* Commercial Travellers' (Melbourne). [*Died* 25 *May* 1962.

HERTER, Christian Archibald; Special Representative for Trade Negotiations, since Dec. 1962; *b.* Paris, France, 28 March 1895, of American parents; *s.* of Albert Herter and Adele McGinnis; *m.* 1917, Mary Caroline Pratt, Brooklyn, N.Y.; three *s.* one *d.* *Educ.:* École Alsatienne, Paris; Browning School, N.Y.C.; Harvard Univ. (A.B., *cum laude*). Attaché, Amer. Emb., Berlin, 1916-1917; Special Asst. Dept. of State, 1917-18; Sec., Amer. Commn. to Negotiate Peace, Paris, 1918-19; Asst. to Sec. of Commerce (Herbert Hoover), 1919-24; Exec. Sec., Eur. Relief Council, 1920-21. Editor, The Independent, 1924-28; Associate Ed., The Sportsman, Boston, Mass., 1927-36; Lectr. on Internat. Relations, Harvard Univ., 1929-1930; Rep. in Mass. Legislature, 1931-43; Speaker, Mass. House, 1939-43; Mem. Mass. House of Reps., 78th-82nd Congresses, Mass. Tenth Dist., 1943-53; Governor, Commonwealth of Mass., 1953-57; Under-Secretary of State, 1957-59; Secretary of State, Apr. 1959-20 Jan. 1961); Chairman, Atlantic Council of the U.S., Inc., 1961-62. Former Director, Commission for Relief of Belgium Educational Foundation; President Board of Trustees, Foreign Service Educational Foundation; Advisor on International Affairs, and Hon. Trustee, Johns Hopkins Univ.; Trustee World Peace Foundn.; Trustee Boston Library Society; Mem. Internat. Cttee. Y.M.C.A.; Overseer, Harvard Univ., 1940-44 and 1950-56. Medal of Freedom, U.S.A., 1961, etc. Has Hon. degrees from various univs. and colls. Holds several foreign orders. *Publication:* Toward an Atlantic Community, 1963. *Address:* (Residence) 3108 P Street, N.W. Washington, D.C., U.S.A.; (Office) Executive Office Building, Washington 25, D.C., U.S.A. [*Died* 30 *Dec.* 1966.

HESLOP-HARRISON, John William, F.R.S. 1928; F.R.S.E. 1921; D.Sc.; Emeritus Professor of Botany, University of Newcastle upon Tyne (formerly King's Coll., Univ. of Durham); Reader in Genetics, 1925; Sen. Research Fellow, 1946-49; *b.* 1881; *o. s.* of George Heslop-Harrison, Birtley, Co. Durham; *m.* 1906, Christian Watson, *d.* of Capt. John Watson Henderson, Leith; two *s.* one *d.* *Educ.:* Rutherford Coll., Newcastle upon Tyne; Armstrong Coll. (Univ. of Durham),

Newcastle upon Tyne. Graduated with distinction in Chemistry, 1903; Science Master, Middlesbrough High School, 1905-1917; M.Sc., 1916; D.Sc., 1917; Research Worker, 1917-23; Lecturer in Zoology, Armstrong College, 1919-27; Secretary, Univ. of Durham Schools Examinations Board, 1940-50; Vice-President, Sect. D, British Association, 1925, Section K, 1949; Council, Royal Society of Edinburgh, 1942-1945, 1949-52, Vice-President, 1945-48; President of Northern Naturalists' Union, 1946 and 1957-58. *Publications:* papers in scientific journals; Editor of Vasculum and of Trans. of Northern Naturalists' Union. *Recreation:* fieldwork. *Address:* Gavarnie, 1 Ruskin Road, Birtley, Co. Durham.
[*Died* 23 *Jan.* 1967.

HESS, Dame Myra, D.B.E., *cr.* 1941 (C.B.E. 1936); Pianist; British parentage. *Educ.:* Royal Academy of Music (Fellow and Associate); professor, Tobias Matthay. Concert tours in England, Holland, France, Germany, Austria, Hungary, Canada, America, etc.; started 1939, and organised the series of lunch-hour concerts at the National Gallery; Gold Medal of Royal Philharmonic Soc., 1941; Cobbett Gold Medal, 1944. Hon. LL.D.: Manchester Univ. 1945, St. Andrews Univ. 1946. Leeds Univ. 1951; Hon. D.Mus. Durham Univ. and Univ. of London, 1946, Cambridge Univ., 1949; Hon. D.Litt. Univ. of Reading, 1947. Commander, Order of Orange-Nassau (Holland). *Address:* 23 Cavendish Close, N.W.8. *T.:* Cunningham 8806.
[*Died* 25 *Nov.* 1965.

HESS, Victor F(rancis), Ph.D., Sc.D. h.c., M.vet. D.h.c.; Prof. of Physics, Fordham University, New York City, since 1938; *b.* Castle of Waldstein (Styria) in Austria, 24 June 1883; *s.* of Vincens Hess and Serafine v. Grosshauer-Waldstaett; *m.* 1920, Mary Berta Breisky; *m.* 1955, Elizabeth (*née* Hoencke). *Educ.:* University of Graz; Vienna. Dr.phil. 1906, University of Graz; Lecturer in Medical Physics, Veterinary Acad. of Vienna, 1908-1920; Lecturer (Privatdozent) for Physics, University of Vienna, 1910-20; Associate Professor of Experimental Physics, University of Graz, 1920-25; Director of Research Dept. U.S. Radium Corp. New York, U.S.A., 1921-23; Professor of Experimental Physics, University of Graz, 1925-31; Professor of Experimental Physics and Director of Institut für Strahlenforschung University of Innsbruck, 1931-37; Professor of Physics and Director of Physical Institute, Univ. of Graz (Austria), 1937-38; Life Member of the Academy of Science, Vienna; Member of Pontifical Acad. of Science, 1961; Ernst Abbé Prize in Physics, 1932; Nobel Prize in Physics (together with C. D. Anderson), 1936. *Publications:* The Electrical Conductivity of the Atmosphere, 1928; The Ionisation Balance of the Atmosphere, 1933; Cosmic Radiation and its Biological Effects (with J. Eugster), Zurich, 1940, new revised edn., New York, 1949; about 130 papers in various journals. *Recreation:* motoring. *Address:* 20 William Street, Mount Vernon, N.Y., U.S.A.
[*Died* 17 *Dec.* 1964.

HESSE, Hermann; Author, Bookseller; *b.* 2 July 1877; *s.* of Johannes Hesse and Maria Gundert; *m.* 1904, Maria Bernoulli (divorced, 1923); three *s.*; *m.* 1931, Ninon Auslaender. *Educ.:* Basel, Calw, Tübingen. Seminar Maulbronn, Gymnasium Cannstadt; Nobel Prize for Lit., 1946; Goethe Prize, 1946. *Publications:* Gedichte, 1903; Peter Camenzind, 1904 (Eng. trans. 1961); Unterm Rad, 1906 (Eng. trans. 1956); Gertrud, 1910 (Eng. trans. 1955); Rosshalde, 1914; Knulp, 1915; Demian, 1919 (Eng. trans. 1923); Siddhartha, 1922 (Eng. trans. 1954); Kurgast, 1925; Der Steppenwolf, 1927 (Eng. trans. 1929); Narziss und Goldmund, 1930 (Eng. trans. 1959); Die Morgenlandfahrt, 1932 (The Journey to the East, Eng. Trans. 1956); Fabulierbuch, 1935; Betrachtungen; Die Gedichte, 1942; Das Glasperlenspiel, 1943 (Magister Ludi, Eng. trans. 1949); Krieg und Frieden, 1946; Spaete Prosa, 1951; Briefe, 1951; Beschwoerungen, 1955. *Address:* Montagnola, nr. Lugano, Switzerland.
[*Died* 9 *Aug.* 1962.

HETHERINGTON, Sir Hector (James Wright), G.B.E. 1962 (K.B.E. 1948); Kt. 1936; D.L. for County of Glasgow; M.A.; LL.D.: Glas., Liverpool, St. Andrews, Sheffield, Wales, Princeton, Cambridge, London, Edinburgh, Belfast, Tufts (U.S.A.), Exeter, British Columbia, Hull, Aberdeen; Litt.D.: McGill, Laval; L.H.D.: Wooster (Ohio); Hon. A.R.I.B.A.: Hon. F.R.C.P.S. (Glasgow); F.K.C.; Hon. F.E.I.S.; Hon. F.R.C.O.G.; Principal and Vice-Chancellor of University of Glasgow, 1936-61; *b.* Cowdenbeath, Fifeshire, 1888; *e. s.* of late Thomas Hetherington, J.P., Tillicoultry; *m.* 1914, Mary Ethel Alison Reid, M.A.; two *s.* *Educ.:* Dollar Academy; Univ. of Glasgow, 1905-10; Merton College, Oxford, 1912. Lecturer in Moral Philosophy, Univ. of Glasgow, 1910-14; Lecturer in Philosophy, Univ. of Sheffield, 1914-15; Professor of Logic and Philosophy, Univ. Coll., Cardiff, 1915-20; Principal and Professor of Philosophy, Univ. Coll., Exeter, 1920-24; Professor of Moral Philosophy, Univ. of Glasgow, 1924-27; Vice-Chancellor of Liverpool Univ., 1927-36. Chairman Cttee. of Vice-Chancellors and Principals, 1943-47, 1949-52; Chairman, Commonwealth Univs.' Grants Cttee., 1946-1964; Vice-Chm. Central Advisory Council in Adult Education in H.M. Forces, 1942-48; Intelligence Div. Min. of Labour, 1918-19; Secretariat, Internat. Labour Conference (League of Nations), Washington, D.C., 1919; appointed Member and Chairman of certain Trade Boards, 1930-40; Mem. Royal Commn. on Unemployment Insurance, 1930-32; Chairman, Board of Enquiry into Wages Agreement in Cotton Manufacture, 1935 and 1937, and Royal Commission on Workmen's Compensation, 1939; Member, National Arbitration Tribunal, 1940-48; Mem. of Industrial Disputes Tribunal, 1948-59; Chm. Departmental Cttee. on Hosp. Policy in Scotland, 1942; Pres. National Institute of Social and Economic Research, 1942-45; Pres. Scottish Council of Social Service, 1945-49; President Section L, British Assoc., 1951; Chairman: Cttee. of Award, Commonwealth Fund Fellowships, 1951-56; Commn. on Roy. Univ. of Malta, 1957; Life Trustee of Carnegie U.K. Trust; Member, Carnegie Trust for the Universities of Scotland; Chm. Advisory Committee, Leverhulme Research Fellowship Scheme, 1933-58; Vice-Chairman of Managing Trustees, Nuffield Foundation; Chm. Roy. Fine Art Commn. for Scotland, 1957-64; Chm. Sch. Broadcasting Council for Scotland, 1961-. Howland Memorial Prize (Yale), 1958. Hon. Freeman of City of Glasgow, 1961; Dunning Lectr., Queen's Univ. Kingston, Ont., 1962. *Publications:* Social Purpose, 1918 (with J. H. Muirhead); International Labour Legislation, 1920; The Life and Letters of Sir Henry Jones, 1924; The British Experiment in Democracy, 1962; contributions to periodicals, etc. *Recreation:* golf. *Address:* 27 Cramond Road North, Edinburgh 4. *T.:* Davidson's Mains 2431. *Clubs:* Athenæum; Bruntsfield (Edinburgh); Art, Literary, Royal Scottish Automobile; Glasgow Golf (Glasgow).
[*Died* 15 *Jan.* 1965.

HETT, Major Francis Paget, M.B.E. 1943; D.L.; J.P.; *s.* of Hon. John Roland Hett, Attorney-General British Columbia, and Letitia, *d.* of Capt. Thomas Sibbald, R.N., D.L.; *m.* 1904, Alice Helena Talbot (*d.* 1943), *d.* of Joseph Cliff, D.L., Scawby, Lincs; no *c.*; *m.* 1947, Gladys Maud, *d.* of late Frank Belton, B.Sc., and *widow* of D. B. Drake, F.C.A. *Educ.:* Upper Canada College. Served European War, 1914-18, with R.N.V.R. as Lieutenant and Hon. Lieutenant-Commander; Vice-

President Preston Hall Tuberculosis Settlement; Chm. training ship Stork; Director and Past Chm. British Legion Poppy Factory; Member Nat. Exec. Council British Legion; Min. of Pensions Central Advisory Committee, 1921-26, and of Govt. Standing Joint Cttee. on ex-Servicemen's Questions since 1921; National Vice-President, British Legion. C.A. Surrey. High Sheriff, 1944 and 1951. Lay Assessor for Dioceses of Canterbury and Guildford. *Publications:* The Memoirs of Susan Sibbald (1783-1812), 1926; The Memoirs of Sir Robert Sibbald (1641-1722), 1932; Georgina, a type study of early settlement and church building in Upper Canada, 1939. *Recreations:* flyfishing, sailing, golf, bibliography. *Address:* Eildon Hall, Sutton West, Ontario, Canada. *Club:* Oriental. [*Died* 17 *Oct.* 1966.

HEVESY, George de, Ph.D. (Hon.); D.Sc. (Hon.); Sc.D. (Hon.); M.D. (Hon.); D.iur. (Hon.); Professor, University of Freiburg, from 1926; Associate of the Institute for Research in Organic Chemistry, University of Stockholm, from 1943; and of the Institute of Theoretical Physics, Copenhagen, from 1920; *b.* 1 Aug. 1885; *s.* of Louis de Hevesy and Baroness Eugeny Schosberger; *m.* 1924, Pia Riis; one *s.* three *d.* Hon. Fellow: Roy. Institution; Chemical Soc., London, Helsingfors and Tokyo; German Bunsen Society and Physiol. Society; Society Nuclear Med.; Brit. Inst. Radiology; Member: Swedish Acad. Sci.; Foreign Mem. Royal Society, and Member of 12 other scientific Academies; 13 Hon. degrees; obtained Canizzaro Prize from the Academy of Sciences at Rome, 1929; 1943 Nobel Prize for Chemistry, awarded, 1944; Copley Medal, 1949; Faraday Medal, 1950; Bailey Medal, 1951; Sylvanus Thompson Medal, 1955; Niels Bohr Medal, 1961; Rosenberger Medal, Chicago University, 1961. United Nations Atoms for Peace Award, 1959. German O.M., 1957. *Publications:* Manual of Radioactivity (Oxford); Propriétés du Hafnium (Copenhagen); Seltene Erden und Atombau (Berlin); Radioactive Indicators (New York); Adventures in Radioisotope Research (London); numerous papers in Nature and other periodicals. *Address:* Stockholm Högskola, 2 Sandasgaten, Stockholm; 18 N. Mälarstrand. Stockholm. *T.:* 542844. [*Died* 5 *July* 1966.

HEWART, 2nd Viscount, *cr.* 1940, of Bury, in County of Lancaster; Baron (*cr.* 1922); **Hugh Vaughan Hewart;** *b.* 11 Nov. 1896; 2nd *s.* of 1st Viscount and Sara Wood, *e. d.* of J. Hacking Riley, Bury; *S.* father 1943. *Educ.:* Manchester Grammar School; St. Paul's School; University College, Oxford. Invalided since European War, 1918. *Heir:* none. [*Died* 23 *July* 1964 (*ext.*).

HEWAT, Air Commodore Harry Aitken, C.B.E. 1943; Retd.; *b.* 17 Sept. 1888; *s.* of late Richard G. Hewat, Edinburgh; *m.* 1932, Hon. Victoria Esmé, *o. d.* of 6th Baron Erskine and *sister* of 16th Earl of Buchan; no *c.* *Educ.:* Cargilfield; Loretto; abroad; Edinburgh University. Principal Medical Officer British Forces in Iraq, 1938-40; Flying Training Command, 1940-45; retired Sept. 1945. Medical Adviser, British Red Cross Society, 1948-58. *Recreations:* outdoor; music. *Address:* 34 Bryanston Square, W1H 7LQ. *T.:* 01-262 0589. [*Died* 4 *April* 1970.

HEWER, Maj.-Gen. Reginald Kingscote, C.B. 1945; C.B.E. 1942 (O.B.E. 1940); M.C. 1917; (Retd.); *b.* 24 Oct. 1892; *s.* of late R. T. Hewer, Down Ampney, Cirencester, Glos.; *m.* 1925, Elizabeth Ivan Leslie, *d.* of Col. L. Findlay of Craigellachie, Banffshire; two *s.* one *d.* *Educ.:* Haileybury; Oxford (B.A.). Served European War in R.A. 1914-18 (despatches, M.C.); transferred to 7th Dragoon Guards, 1921, and to 7th Hussars, 1923; Major 1935; Col. 1942; Acting Brig. 1940; Acting Maj.-Gen. 1942; Temp. Maj.-Gen. 1943. Served War of 1939-45 (despatches four times, O.B.E., C.B.E., C.B.). Deputy Director General, European Central Inland Transport Organisation, 1945-47. *Recreations:* hunting, shooting. *Address:* Bleeke House, Marston Meysey, Cricklade, Wilts. *T.:* Kempsford 237. *Club:* United Hunts. [*Died* 15 *Nov.* 1970.

HEWETT, Captain Gilbert George Pearse, C.B.E. 1941; R.N.; *b.* 10 March 1880; 2nd *s.* of G. E. Hewett, late of Charlton Kings, Gloucestershire; *m.* 1911, Margaret Pearse, *o. d.* of late F. T. Depree, J.P., Exeter; four *d.* *Educ.:* Clifton College. Cadet H.M.S. Britannia, 1894; Midshipman H.M.S. Fox, Cape Station, Sierra Leone Rebellion, 1898 (medal and clasp, Sierra Leone); specialised in Navigation; Lieutenant, 1902; Commander, 1914; H.M.S. Hercules, Grand Fleet, 1913-16; H.M.S. Courageous, 1916-19 (1914 Star, War and Victory medals, despatches); commanded H.M.S. Odin and Senior Naval Officer in the final operations against the Mad Mullah, 1919-1920 (medal and clasp, Somaliland, despatches); Captain, 1919; H.M.S. Greenwich, Atlantic Fleet, 1920-22; retired, 1922. Commanded H.M.S. Laconia, armed merchant cruiser, in North Atlantic, 1939-41 (1939-45 Star, Atlantic Star); H.M.S. Eaglet and Maintenance Captain, Liverpool, 1941-46 (Defence Medal). Member of Bridge-Blean R.D.C. in Kent for many years; Chairman Canterbury Div. Conservative and Unionist Assoc., 1947-49. *Recreation:* gardening. *Address:* 5 Kent House, Folkestone. *T.:* 51904. [*Died* 28 *July* 1966.

HEWETT, Capt. Robert Roy Scott, C.B.E. 1958; Common Councillor for Billingsgate, 1934; Alderman of Ward of Billingsgate, 1946-57, resigned (after deciding in 1956 not to go forward to Mayoralty, having been elected one of two to do so, September 1955); Sheriff, City of London, 1942-43; Managing Director of Hewett & Co. Ltd., the Hewett Fishing Co. Ltd., Fylde Engineers, Ltd., and other Fishing Companies at London, Brixham, Fleetwood and Lowestoft; *b.* 29 May 1886; *s.* of Robert Muirhead Hewett, J.P., Chairman of Becontree Bench, and Alice Minna Scott; *m.* 1st, 1911, Clare Lindsell Allard (*d.* 1945), Ilford; no *c.*; 2nd, 1946, Ella Bonell, Bradford. *Educ.:* Forest School, Essex; Charterhouse. Vice-Pres. Fleetwood Fishing Vessels Owners' Assoc.; Dir. British Trawlers' Federation; at Guildhall served on Port Health (Past Chm.), Streets, Civil Defence, and General Purposes Cttees. Joined a Mercantile Marine Fleet Auxiliary as Mate, 1914; transferring to Army, was Supply Landing Officer at Rouen, Adjutant of 36th Divisional Train, commanded 2nd Cavalry Mobile Limber Column, served with G.H.Q., and ended war as a lectr. F.R.San.I.; Past Master of Fletchers' Company, Renter Warden (1951); Member of Court, Watermen and Lightermen's Company; Amateur Figure Skating Champion of Great Britain five times; was first Chairman of Ice and Roller Committees, Nat. Skating Assoc., which systematised Dancing on Skates. *Recreations:* yachting, skating, and squash. *Address:* 11 St. Mary-at-Hill, E.C.3; 117 Marine Parade, Leigh, Essex. *T.A.:* Hewett, Billingsgate, London. *T.:* Mansion House 7725; 3106-3107 and 8989. *Clubs:* City Livery, United Wards, Royal Thames Yacht; Royal Corinthian Yacht (Burnham-on-Crouch); Royal Skating, etc. [*Died* 23 *May* 1967.

HEWLETT, Brig.-Gen. Ernest, C.M.G. 1919; D.S.O. 1916; O.B.E. 1924; late Devon Regt.; *b.* 1879; *s.* of W. H. Hewlett, Standish. Served European War, 1914-17 (despatches,

D.S.O., Bt. Lt.-Col.); Lt.-Col. 1926; Col 1929; retired pay, 1933. *Address:* c/o Lloyds Bank, Ltd., 6 Pall Mall, S.W.1. [*Died* 1 *Jan.* 1965.

HEWSON, Hon. Mrs. (Anne Elizabeth Mary Llywelyn); *b.* 17 April 1902; *d.* of Herbert Clark, 2nd Baron Merthyr, and Elizabeth Anna Couchman; *m.* 1941, Brig. Arthur George Hewson, *s.* of Capt. G. Hewson, D.L., of Dromahaire, Co. Leitrim; one *s.* Joint Master South Pembrokeshire Foxhounds, 1929-32; Master, 1932-33; Master Monmouthshire Foxhounds, 1933-37. *Address:* Attyflin, Patrickswell, Co. Limerick, Ireland. *T.:* Patrickswell 8. [*Died* 7 *Feb.* 1963.

HEYDEMAN, Major-General C. A., C.B. 1941; M.C.; *b.* 16 Aug. 1889; *s.* of late Lt.-Col. H. E. Heydeman and of Henriette de G. Ligneau; divorced; no *c.*; *m.* 1941, Leona (*d.* 1949), *e. d.* of Capt. A. Whitney, Wenderholm, Sarisbury, Hampshire, and of Australia. *Educ.:* Temple Grove; Harrow. Joined Queen's Bays, 1909; served European War, 1914-19 (despatches, M.C., Legion of Honour); Col., 1932; A.A. and Q.M.G. 1st Div. 1933; Brigadier Cmdr. 2nd Cavalry Brigade, 1935; War of 1939-45 (despatches, C.B.); Commander Presidency and Assam District, Calcutta, 1939-41; Divisional Commander, 1941-43; Cmdr. No. 1 District C.M.F., 1943; retd. pay, 1946. *Recreations:* shooting, polo (Pres. Army Polo Assoc. 1939), hunting, racing. *Address:* c/o Westminster Bank, Doncaster. *Clubs:* Cavalry, Royal Automobile. [*Died* 2 *Nov.* 1967.

HEYMAN, Major-General George Douglas Gordon Dufferin, C.B. 1955; C.B.E. 1945 (M.B.E. 1941); Chief, Hampshire Area Road Safety Unit, since 1963; *b.* Edin., 13 May 1905; *s.* of Col. A. A. I. Heyman, D.S.O., and Mrs. Heyman (*née* Wood), Shanganagh Castle, Shankill, Co. Dublin; *m.* 1935, Patricia, *d.* of Atkin Lee Marsh, Formby, Lancs; four *d.* *Educ.:* King's Sch., Canterbury; R.M.C. Sandhurst. Staff Coll., 1938; Imperial Defence Coll., 1950. Director of Plans, G.H.Q., Middle East, 1942-44; Brig. G.S. S.H.A.E.F., 1944-45; Deputy Chief Internal Affairs and Communications Division, Control Commission, Germany, 1946; Brig. G.S. (Chief of Staff), British Joint Services Mission, Washington, 1947-50. Brig. i/c Admin. H.Q. 1 Corps (Germany), 1951-53; Chief of Staff, G.H.Q. East Africa, 1953-1955; Chief of Staff, H.Q. Southern Command, 1956-59, retired. Colonel, The King's Regiment (Manchester and Liverpool), 1962. Officer Legion of Merit, U.S.A., 1945; Chevalier Legion of Honour, France, 1945; Croix de Guerre, France, with star (1943), with Palme (1945). *Address:* Mead House, Appleshaw (Nr. Andover, Hants). *T.:* Weyhill 408. *Club:* Buck's. [*Died* 18 *May* 1965.

HEYROVSKÝ, Prof. Jaroslav, D.Sc., Ph.D.; Czechoslovak Academician, 1952; Order of the Republic, 1955, 1960; Director emer. of the Polarographic Institute, Czechoslovak Acad. of Sciences, 1950-63; *b.* 20 Dec. 1890; *s.* of Leopold H. and Clara (*née* Hanlová); *m.* 1926, Marie Koránová; one *s.* one *d.* *Educ.:* University College, London; Prague University. Demonstrator, University College, London, 1913; Assistant, Chemistry Department, Charles University, Prague, 1920; Lecturer, 1922; Assistant Professor, 1924; Professor of Physical Chemistry, 1926-54. Carnegie Visiting Professor, University of California, U.S.A., 1933. Inventor of polarography. Awarded Czechoslovak State Prize, 1951; Nobel Prize for Chemistry, 1959. Golden Plaquet of Czechoslovak Acad. of Sciences, 1962; Dr.chem.Sci., Univ. of Warsaw, 1950; Hon. Dr.rer.nat., Technische Hochschule, Dresden, 1955; Hon. Dr.rer.nat., Univ., Paris, 1960; Hon. Dr.med., Univ. Vienna, 1965; Hon. Dr.chem.Sc., Charles Univ., Prague, 1965; Hon. Dr.Phil.nat., J. W. Goethe Univ., Frankfurt/Main, 1966. Fellow, Univ. Coll. London, 1927; Hon. Member: Amer. Acad. of Arts and Sciences, Boston, Mass., 1933; Hungarian Acad. of Science, 1955; Indian Acad. of Science, 1962; For. Mem., Roy. Soc., London, 1965. *Publications:* Application of the Polarographic Method in Practical Chemistry, 1933; Polarographie, 1941; Oscillographic Polarography, 1943, 1960; Polarographisches Praktikum, 1948, 1960; Principles of Polarography, 1962, 1965; Joint Editor, Collection of Czechoslovak Chemical Communications, 1929-48. *Address:* The Jaroslav Heyrovský Polarographic Institute of the Czechoslovak Academy of Sciences, Vlasska 9, Prague 1, Czechoslovakia. [*Died* 27 *March* 1967.

HEYS, John, C.B.E. 1942; Town Clerk, Sheffield, since 1943; *b.* 13 Jan. 1899; *e. s.* of John Heys; *m.* 1926, Nora James; one *s.* one *d.* *Educ.:* King Edward's Grammar School, Birmingham. Deputy Town Clerk: Ilkeston, 1924-25, Ipswich, 1925-27, Rochdale, 1927-31; Chief Asst. Solicitor, Manchester, 1931-38; Deputy Town Clerk, Sheffield, 1938-43. *Recreation:* golf. *Address:* 27 Taptonville Road, Sheffield 10. *T.:* Sheffield 60479. *Club:* National Liberal. [*Died* 7 *April* 1963.

HEYSEN, Sir Hans, Kt. 1959; O.B.E. 1945; Artist; *b.* Hamburg, 8 October 1877; *s.* of Louis Heysen; *m.* 1904, Selma (*née* Bartels) (*d.* 1962); three *s.* one *d.* (and two *d.* decd.). Studied art in Adelaide, Paris and Italy. Has exhibited in Paris, Adelaide, Sydney, Melbourne and Brisbane. Has paintings in many public galleries in Australia and New Zealand. Trustee of National Gallery of Sth. Australia. *Publications:* Watercolours and Drawings, 1952 (publ. Australia). Relevant contribs. to Art in Australia, 1920-, on his work. *Recreation:* gardening. *Address:* Hahndorf, South Australia. [*Died* 2 *July* 1968.

HEYWOOD, Valentine; journalist and author; *b.* West Wickham, Kent, 14 Feb. 1891; *m.* 1915, cousin Jennie (*d.* 1960), 2nd *d.* of late Richard Edmundson of Fenton and Longton, Staffordshire; one *s.* Managing Editor Yorkshire Observer, 1919; Editor Sheffield Independent, 1920-25; an Assistant Editor Star, 1926-30; Managing Editor, The Sunday News, 1930-32; News Editor, The Sunday Times, 1933-44; Assist. Editor, 1944-46; Deputy Editor, 1946-50; Managing Editor, 1950-55; Associate Editor, 1956-59. *Publications:* Re-Building Europe, 1942; British Titles, 1951; articles, Titles of Honour, Courtesy Titles, Precedence in Chambers's Encyclopædia. *Address:* Birch Hanger, Chalfont St. Giles, Bucks. *T.:* Chalfont St. Giles 2256. [*Died* 2 *Jan.* 1963.

HEZLET, Lieut.-Col. Charles Owen, D.S.O. 1918; *b.* 1891; *s.* of late Lt.-Col. R. J. Hezlet, R.A., of Boovagh, Aghadowey, Co. Londonderry; retired; *m.* 1920, Anni Maitland (*d.* 1931), *d.* of James Stuart, Somerset, Coleraine, Ireland; one *s.* one *d.* Served European War, 1914-18 (despatches thrice, D.S.O.); rejoined Army, Sept. 1939-43, as Major Royal Artillery. *Recreations:* golf, was runner-up in amateur championship, 1914; won Irish Golf Championship, 1920; runner-up in Welsh Open Championship and Irish Open Championship, 1923; went to America as Member of Walker Golf Team for Great Britain, 1924; St. George's Gold Vase, 1926; played for Great Britain *v.* America, Walker Cup, 1926; won Irish Open Championship, 1926; runner-up in Irish Open Championship, 1925; Member of British Golf Team to South Africa, 1927-28; went to America and member of Walker Cup Team, 1928; won Irish Open Amateur, 1929; captained Irish Golf Team, 1921-30 (8 times); Non-Playing Capt., 1948-49-50-51-52-53; Captain British Team, South Africa, 1952. *Address:*

Wilmshurst, Fletching, Sussex. *Clubs:* Devonshire; Ulster (Belfast); Royal and Ancient (St. Andrews), etc. [*Died* 22 *Nov.* 1965.

HEZLET, Maj.-Gen. Robert Knox, C.B. 1935; C.B.E. 1919; D.S.O. 1916; D.L.; late R.A.; M.R.C.V.S.; *b.* Dungannon, Co. Tyrone, 21 Dec. 1879; *s.* of Lt.-Col. R. J. Hezlet, R.A., of Bovagh, Aghadowey, Co. Londonderry; *m.* 1909, Josepha Dorothy Arter; one *s.* two *d.* *Educ.:* Clifton College; R.M. Academy, Woolwich. 2nd Lieut. 1898; Captain, 1907; passed Advanced Class Ordnance College, 1907; Instructor in Artillery Ordnance College, 1908-10; Major, 1914; Lt.-Col. 1921; Col. 1923; Maj.-Gen. 1934; served France and Mesopotamia, 1915-16 (despatches twice, D.S.O.); Bt. Lt.-Col. 1918; Member Ordnance Committee, 1916-20; Superintendent External Ballistics, Ordnance Committee, 1920-24; Chief Superintendent, Research Dept., 1924-28; Commandant Military Coll. of Science 1928-30; Director of Artillery, War Office, 1930-34. Deputy Master-General of Ordnance, India, 1935-38 and Director of Artillery, 1934-38; retired pay, 1938; Area Officer, Ministry of Supply, Northern Ireland, 1940-41. *Publications:* Nomography, 1913; Papers on Ballistics in R.A. Journal and Journal United States Artillery. *Address:* Bovagh, Aghadowey, Co. Londonderry. *Club:* Army and Navy. [*Died* 14 *Jan.* 1963.

HEZLETT, James, C.I.E. 1928; I.C.S.; *b.* 26 June 1875; *s.* of late I. Hezlett, Coleraine; *m.* 1902, Mary Kathleen (*d.* 1949), *d.* of late Captain Good, R.I.M., Port Officer, Chittagong; one *s.* two d. *Educ.:* Coleraine; Queen's College, Galway; University College, London. Entered I.C.S. 1898; Deputy Commissioner, Assam, 1912; Superintendent, Lushai Hills, 1912-17; Deputy Commissioner, Sylhet, 1917-20; Commissioner of Excise, 1921-22; Officiating Commissioner, 1923; Commissioner, Surma Valley and Hill Division, Assam, 1927; Member, Legislative Assembly, 1923-34; Chief Government Whip, 1932-34; retired, 1934. Chairman, Assam Public Service Commission, 1937-40. *Address:* c/o National Bank of India, 2 Bishopsgate, E.C.2. [*Died* 17 *Sept.* 1963.

HIBBERT, John Geoffrey, C.M.G. 1949; M.C. 1916; *b.* 23 April 1890; *s.* of late John Hibbert; *m.* 1922, Joyce, *d.* of late R. B. Brierley; two *d.* *Educ.:* Clifton College; Balliol College, Oxford. Served European War, 1914-18, Artists' Rifles; 15th (Scottish) Division, B.E.F. (despatches); Board of Trade, 1920-29; Colonial Office, 1929-52. Seconded to Petroleum Division, Ministry of Fuel and Power, 1943-46. *Address:* Stane Street Cottage, Watersfield, Pulborough, Sussex. [*Died* 5 *March* 1968.

HIBBERT, Brigadier Oswald Yates, D.S.O. 1916; M.C.; late The Queen's Own Royal West Kent Regt.; *b.* 26 Jan. 1882; *s.* of late P. J. Hibbert, D.L., Hampsfield, Grange over Sands, Lancs; *m.* 1st, 1914, Violet Marion Watson (*d.* 1935), *d.* of late Sir William Pike, K.C.M.G., D.S.O.; two *s.*; 2nd, 1939, Dorothea Anne, *d.* of late William Boyd, Oakley, Holywood, Co. Down. *Educ.:* Shrewsbury; R.M.C. Sandhurst. Served South African War, 1902 (Queen's medal with three clasps); Mesopotamia, 1915-16 (wounded, despatches, D.S.O., M.C., prisoner); Commander 132nd (Surrey and Kent) Infantry Brigade, T.A., 1934-38; retired pay, 1938. *Address:* Woodcroft, Haverthwaite, Ulverston, Lancs. *T.:* Newby Bridge 256. *Club:* Army and Navy. [*Died* 4 *July* 1966.

HIBBERT, Hon. Wilfrid H.; *see* Holland-Hibbert.

HICKES, Maj.-Gen. Lancelot Daryl, C.B. 1941; O.B.E.; M.C.; *b.* 30 May 1884; *m.* 1915, Vera Newbury (decd.); one *s.*; *m.* 1962, E. Halford (Holly) Black. *Educ.:* Blundell's; St. Albans; Bedford; R.M.A., Woolwich. 2nd Lt. Royal Artillery, 1903; Capt., 1914; Major, 1918; Bt. Lt.-Col., 1928; Lt.-Col., 1933; Col., 1936; Maj.-Gen., 1938; served European War, 1914-18 (despatches four times, Bt. Major, O.B.E., M.C.); retired pay, 1942. *Recreation:* golf. *Address:* c/o Lloyds Bank (Cox and King's Branch), 6 Pall Mall, S.W.1. *Club:* Army and Navy. [*Died* 4 *Oct.* 1965.

HICKIN, Welton, F.R.A.M., F.R.C.O.; Professor of the Pianoforte and Examiner; Royal Academy of Music, from 1924; also, Examiner, Royal Schools of Music; *b.* 16 Sept. 1876; *s.* of Charles Hickin and F. M. Welton; *m.* 1904, Elizabeth Poole (*d.* 1949); one *s.* one *d.* *Educ.:* Royal Academy of Music Gained Highest Awards of the R.A.M. in three subjects, also Robert Cock's Prize for Pianoforte Playing and Charles Mortimer Prize for Composition; Appointed Assistant to the Principal, 1899; Director of the Accompaniment Class, 1911; served European War, in the Buffs and Scottish Rifles, 1916-1918; elected Chairman of the Music Teachers association, 1932; Chairman of the London Musical Competition Festival, 1934; Pianoforte Adjudicator at the London and Provincial Festivals. *Publications:* Pianoforte Accompaniment (Novello's Primers); Two Pianoforte Suites. *Recreations:* reading, motoring, gardening. *Address:* 113 Brighton Road, Sutton, Surrey. *T.:* Vigilant 1344. [*Died* 3 *May* 1968.

HICKLING, Vice-Admiral Harold, C.B. 1948; C.B.E. 1944; D.S.O. 1941; Vice-Adm. retd.; *b.* 1892; *m.* 1920, Gwynneth Emily, *d.* of David Tennant, Glenconner, Kenilworth, S. Africa; (one *s.* killed in action) one *d.* *Educ.:* Bradfield College; R.N. Colleges Osborne and Dartmouth. Joined R.N. 1905; served European War, 1914-19, present at Battles of Coronel and Falkland Islands; Captain, 1935-; recapture of Berbera, 1941 (D.S.O.); Member Admiralty Delegation, Washington, 1942-43; on staff of Admiral Sir B. Ramsay planning "Mulberry" artificial harbours for invasion of Normandy; Naval Officer-in-Charge of "Mulberry B", Arromanches, Normandy, June-Aug. 1944 (C.B.E.) A.D.C. to the King, 1944; Rear-Adm. 1945; Rear-Adm., Training Battleships, Home Fleet, 1946-47; retired list, 1948. *Publications:* Freshwater Admiral, 1960; One Minute of Time, 1965; Sailor at Sea, 1965. *Address:* Turangi, N.Z. *Club:* United Service. [*Died* 12 *Nov.* 1969.

HICKS, Brig. Philip Hugh Whitby, C.B.E. 1945; D.S.O. 1940 (Bar 1943); M.C.; *b.* 25 September 1895; *s.* of Dr. Philip Hicks and Beatrice Whitby, novelist; *m.* 1927, Patty, *d.* of late Brigadier L. A. Fanshawe, C.B.E., D.S.O.; one *s.* one *d.* *Educ.:* Winchester Coll. Commissioned 1914; served European War, 1914-18 (M.C., despatches twice, wounded); many years in India; served as A.D.C. at Karachi, 1924-26; Staff Captain, Guernsey, 1933-36; War of 1939-45; commanded Bn. in Battle of Dunkirk; Sicily, 1st Airborne Div., 1942-44; commanded Air Landing Brigade at Arnhem (D.S.O. and Bar, C.B.E.); served with International Refugee Organization, 1948-52, as Regional Comr. in Germany and with Nat. Playing Fields Assoc., in London, 1955-61. *Recreations:* shooting, gardening. *Address:* Swampton Cottage, Brackley Avenue, Hartley Wintney, Hampshire. [*Died* 8 *Oct.* 1967.

HICKS-BEACH, Lady Victoria Alexandrina; *y. d.* of 1st Earl St. Aldwyn; *b.* 1879. *Publication:* Life of Sir Michael Hicks-Beach, 1932. *Address:* Fittleton Manor, Netheravon, Wilts. *T.:* Netheravon 228. [*Died* 29 *April* 1963.

HIGGINS, Brigadier-General Charles Graeme, C.M.G. 1919; D.S.O. 1916; late Oxfordshire Light Infantry; *b.* 12 Aug. 1879; *e. s.* of late Capt. C. C. Higgins, 13th Hussars, of Boycott Manor, Buckingham; *m.* 1909, Algitha (*d.* 1940), *d.* of Capt. John Howard; one *s.* one *d.* *Educ.:* Charterhouse. Entered army, 1899; Capt. 1909; Maj., 1915; Bt. Lt.-Col. 1 Jan. 1917; Brig.-Gen. 21 Apr. 1917; Lt.-Col. 1924; served S. African War (Queen's and King's medals); European War, 1914-18 (wounded, despatches, D.S.O. and bar), C.M.G., Bt. Lt.-Col.; retired pay, 1924; re-employed, 1939; D.L. Berks. *Address:* Badbury Hill, Faringdon, Berks. *T.:* Faringdon 3162. *Clubs:* United Service, Army and Navy. [*Died* 15 *March* 1961.

HIGGINS, Thomas Twistington, O.B.E., M.B., Ch.B. (Vict.), F.R.C.S.; Consulting Surgeon, Hospital for Children, Great Ormond Street, W.C., etc.; retired; *b.* Bolton, Lancs, 1887; *s.* of Rev. T. Twistington Higgins, M.A., LL.B. (T.C.D.), late Vicar of Congleton, Cheshire; *m.* Jessie, *d.* of Thomas Ingram, B.A., Melrose, Scotland; two *s.* four *d.* *Educ.:* Pocklington Sch. (Foundation Scholar); Manchester Univ. (Cheshire C.C. Entrance Scholarship). Jones' Exhibitioner and Medallist, Anatomy, Surgery, Pathology, etc.; Dumville Surgical Prizeman, Turner Medical Scholar and Medallist; graduated M.B., Ch.B. (Honours), Distinction in Medicine, Forensic Medicine and Midwifery; House Surgeon and Casualty Officer, Manchester Royal Infirmary; House Surgeon and Medical Superintendent, Hospital for Sick Children, Great Ormond Street; R.A.M.C. 4½ years O.A.S. France, Surgical Specialist, etc. (despatches, O.B.E., and rank of Major); consulting surgical practice; Consulting Surgeon Hosp. for Sick Children, Northwood War Memorial Hospital, Wood Green and Southgate Hospital; late Royal Northern Hospital. Late Member Court of Examiners Royal Coll. of Surgeons, etc. Robert Campbell Memorial Orator, Belfast; Hon. Mem. Brit. Paediatric Assoc.: Hon. Pres. and Yorkhill lecturer, Brit. Assoc. of Paediatric Surgeons. *Publications:* The Urology of Childhood: Great Ormond Street, 1852-1952; papers and monographs on various surgical subjects. *Recreations:* fishing, ornithology. *Address:* Old School House, Great Mongeham, Deal. *T.:* Deal 1629. *Club:* Savage. [*Died* 3 *July* 1966.

HIGGINSON, Charles James, C.B.E. 1920 (O.B.E. 1918); Barrister-at-law; at present associated with the United Baltic Corporation; Hon. Freeman of Met. Borough of Hampstead; *b.* 1871; *s.* of late Charles Frederick Higginson; unmarried. *Educ.:* privately. Called to Bar, Inner Temple, 1896; practised on common law side; for some years Secretary to the Home and Foreign Produce Exchange; proceeded abroad on invitation of Government to take part in negotiations in connection with Blockade, 1916; Secretary to Restriction of Enemy's Supplies Department, subsequently becoming Director of the Department. Knight of the Royal Order of the Dannebrog, 1947. *Publication:* Manual on Sale of Food and Drugs Acts. *Recreations:* golf, billiards, chess. *Address:* 54 Crediton Hill, N.W.. *T.:* Hampstead 7069. *Club:* Royal Societies. [*Died* 28 *March* 1964.

HIGGS, Walter Frank; Founder and formerly Chairman, of Higgs Motors, Ltd., Witton, Birmingham 6; *b* 7 Apr. 1886; *s.* of late Charles Higgs, Kidderminster; *m.* 1921, Cecilia Elizabeth, *d.* of J. S. Yeoman; two *s.* *Educ.:* Birmingham Technical School. Member of Institution of Electrical Engineers; served with Gen. Electric Co., Ltd., British Thomson-Houston Co., Ltd., Electric Construction Co., Ltd., and others; Pres. of Birmingham Chamber of Commerce, 1948; Life Governor of Univ. of Birmingham; Member of Birmingham City Council (Edgbaston Ward), 1934-37; M.P. (U.) West Birmingham 1937-1945; introduced Leasehold Property (Repairs) Act in the House of Commons, 1938; Hall-Marking of Foreign Plate Act, 1939. Member of House of Commons Select Committee on National Expenditure, 1939-43. *Recreation:* farming. *Address:* Nuthurst Grange, Hockley Heath, Solihull, Warwickshire. *T.:* Lapworth 219. *Clubs:* Carlton, Conservative, Union (Birmingham). [*Died* 8 *Aug.* 1961.

HIGHTON, Mark Edward; Commander R.N. retired; *b.* 1888; *e. s.* of late R. E. Highton, Rogerscale, Cockermouth; *m.* 1914, Norma Winifred, *y. d.* of late Dr. Speirs, Cleator; one *s.* *Educ.:* Bradfield. Joined H.M.S. Britannia, 1902; served European War, 1914-18, in Grand Fleet and at Gallipoli; invalided from R.N., 1918; served War of 1939-45, at Admiralty and with R.A.F. J.P. Cumberland, 1934. Chairman of Directors, Jennings Bros. Ltd. High Sheriff of Cumberland, 1948-49. D.L. Cumberland, 1952. *Recreations:* fishing and shooting. *Address:* Dunthwaite, Cockermouth. [*Died* 14 *Nov.* 1966.

HILBERY, Rt. Hon. Sir Malcolm, P.C. 1959; Kt. 1935; Judge of High Court of Justice, King's Bench Division, 1935-1962, retd.; *b.* 14 July 1883; *s.* of Henry Hilbery, 4 South Square, Gray's Inn; *m.* 1915, Dorothy Violet Agnes, *d.* of Lt.-Col. St. John Christophers, D.S.O.; no *c.* *Educ.:* University College School. Certif. of Honour Council of Legal Educ.; Arden Scholar, Gray's Inn; Barrister, Gray's Inn, 1907; Bencher, 1927; K.C. 1928; Recorder of Margate, 1927-35; Chm. Berks Quarter Sessions, 1946-63; Mem. of Council of Legal Education and Board of Studies; Chairman Roy. Masonic Hosp. *Publication:* Duty and Art in Advocacy. *Recreation:* gardening. *Address:* 5 Gray's Inn Sq., W.C.1. *Clubs:* Royal Thames Yacht, Garrick. [*Died* 18 *Sept.* 1965.

HILDITCH, Thomas Percy, C.B.E. 1952; F.R.S. 1942; D.Sc.(Lond.); F.C.I.C.; Emeritus Professor, University of Liverpool, 1951; Campbell Brown Professor of Industrial Chemistry, 1926-51; *b.* 22 April 1886; *s.* of Thomas and Priscilla Hilditch; *m.* 1929, Eva, *d.* of John Richardson; three *d*; *m.* 1952, Margery, *d.* of George Davies. *Educ.:* Owen's School, Islington; University College, London; Universities of Jena and Geneva. 1851 Exhibition Research Scholar, 1908-11; research chemist to J. Crosfield and Sons Ltd., soap and chemical manufacturers, 1911-25; served on councils of Institute of Chemistry, Chemical Society, Society of Chemical Industry. *Publications:* History of Chemistry; Third Year Course of Organic Chemistry; Industrial Fats and Waxes; Catalytic Processes in Applied Chemistry; Chemical Constitution of the Natural Fats; articles on Catalysis and on Fatty Oils in Thorpe's Dictionary of Applied Chemistry and on Chemie der Fette and Fett-Hydrierung in Hefter-Schönfeld's Technologie der Fette; Contributions in scientific journals, especially on organic sulphur-compounds (1907-1911), Optical Activity (1908-12), Catalytic Action (1919-25), and the Constitution and Properties of Fats and their derivatives (1924-). *Recreations:* gardening, walking. *Address:* 107 Shrewsbury Road, Birkenhead. *T.:* Claughton 3224. [*Died* 9 *Aug.* 1965.

HILDYARD, General Sir Reginald John Thoroton, K.C.B. *cr.* 1936 (C.B. 1928); C.M.G. 1917; D.S.O. 1915; *b.* 11 Dec. 1876; 3rd *s.* of late Gen. Sir H. J. T. Hildyard; *m.* 1911, Muriel, *d.* of Sir H. Cosmo Bonsor, 1st Bart.; one *s.* Entered Army, 1896; Capt., 1904; Major 1915; Col., 1919; Maj.-Gen., 1929; Lt.-Gen., 1934; Gen. 1938; employed with S.A. Constabulary, 1900-3; A.D.C. to Lieut.-General, South Africa, 1904-5; to G.O.C., Africa, 1905-8; General Staff Officer, 3rd grade War Office, 1911-13; Brigade-Major, S. Command, 1913-14; p.s.c.; served South Africa, 1899-1902 (Queen's medal 4 clasps, King's medal 2 clasps); European

War, 1914-18 (despatches seven times, D.S.O., Bt. Lieut.-Col., C.M.G., Bt. Col.); Brigade Commander 2nd Rhine Brigade, 1928-29; Commander 43rd (Wessex) Division T.A. 1930-34; Governor and Commander-in-Chief, Bermuda, 1936-39; retired pay, 1939. *Address:* South Hartfield House, Coleman's Hatch, Sussex. [*Died* 29 *Sept.* 1965.

HILES, Sir Herbert, Kt., *cr.* 1937; M.B.E.; J.P.; Chairman: Welsh Regional Council for the Blind; Welsh Association of Boys' Clubs; *b.* Wellington, Somerset, 1881; *m.* 1903, Elizabeth Ethel Thompson (*d.* 1952); two *s.*; *m.* 1961, Elsie Rose Rhodes. *Educ.:* Wellington British School. Lord Mayor of Cardiff, 1936-37. *Address:* 8 Cherry Tree Gardens, Bexhill-on-Sea, Sussex. [*Died* 18 *Nov.* 1968.

HILKEN, Captain Thomas John Norman, D.S.O. 1940 (and Bar 1944); Royal Navy, retired; Warden, University Centre, Cambridge, since 1967; Secretary of Department of Engineering, University of Cambridge, 1954-67; Fellow of University College, Cambridge, 1965-68; Vice-President, 1966-68; *b.* 23 April 1901: *s.* of Thomas Henry Hilken and Anne (*née* Hitchman); *m.* 1933, Edith Barkley, *e. d.* of Rev. Canon Herbert Dudley Lampen, M.A.; three *s.* *Educ.:* Merchant Taylors' Sch.; R.N.C. Keyham. Commanded destroyers, 1934-37; Admiralty, N.I.D., 1937-39; lent R.A.N. as Commander, H.M.A.S. Sydney, 1939-41 (D.S.O.); Naval Staff, Cairo and Algiers, 1941-43; commanded H.M. Escort Carrier Emperor, 1943-44 (Bar to D.S.O., despatches twice); Naval air staff S.E.A.C., 1945; R.N.A.S. Eglinton, 1946-47; Imperial Defence College, 1948; commanded H.M.S. Mauritius (Flag Ship, East Indies Fleet), 1949-50; Deputy Director of Naval Intelligence, 1951-53, retired 1954. M.A. (Cantab.), 1957. *Publication:* Engineering at Cambridge University, 1783-1965, 1967. *Address:* 56 Highsett, Hills Road, Cambridge. *T.:* 56371. [*Died* 14 *July* 1969.

HILL OF WIVENHOE, Baron *cr.* 1967 (Life Peer), of Wivenhoe; **Edward James Hill**; President, The Amalgamated Society of Boilermakers, Shipwrights, Blacksmiths and Structural Workers, 1963-65; *b.* London, 20 Aug. 1899. *Educ.:* Council Sch. Served European War, 1914-18, R.M. Engineers. Joined United Society of Boilermakers, 1916; subseq. Shop Steward, Branch Sec., Branch Chm., London Dist. Organizer. Formerly Chm. London Dist. Cttee. (10 years); General Sec., United Soc. of Boilermakers, 1948-63. Confederation of Shipbuilding and Engineering Unions; Member General Council, Trades Union Congress, 1948-65, retd. (Chm. 1961, Vice-Chairman 1962); Member: Central Training Council, 1965-66; British Egg Marketing Board, 1966-. *Recreation:* gardening. *Address:* 4 Clifton Terrace, Wivenhoe, Essex. [*Died* 14 *Dec.* 1969.

HILL, Rt. Rev. Alfred Thomas, C.M.G. 1961; M.B.E. 1951; *b.* 2 Nov. 1901. Deacon 1938; Priest 1939; Head Master, Sen. Boys' Sch., Pawa, Melanesia, 1938-54; Bishop of Melanesia, 1954-67. *Address:* c/o Bishop of New Guinea, Port Moresby, New Guinea. [*Died* 27 *Aug.* 1969.

HILL, Lieut.-Col. Arthur Hardie, C.B. 1947; M.C. 1918; *b.* 1887; *yr. s.* of late Thomas N. Hill, I.M., F.S.I., Glasgow; *m.* Georgina V. A., 3rd *d.* of late George Gibson, J.P., Halkerton, Carnoustie, Angus. Served European War, 1914-19 (despatches twice, M.C., Greek Military Cross) 4th Highland (Mountain) Bde. R.G.A., T.A. *Address:* 40 Kelvinside Gardens, Glasgow, N.W. *T.:* Maryhill 1395. [*Died* 6 *Feb.* 1963.

HILL, Douglas Rowland Holdsworth; Director, City of London Brewery and Investment Trust Ltd. and other Companies; *b.* 20 Oct. 1904; *e. s.* of Horace Rowland and Elizabeth H. Hill; *m.* 1933, Agnes Margaret Douglas; three *d.* *Educ.:* Malvern Coll.; Trinity Coll., Cambridge (M.A.). Served War of 1939-45, France and N. Africa, with R.A.S.C. and on H.Q. Staff, Malta. Mem. Court of Common Council, for Dowgate Ward, 1947; Alderman, City of London for Queenhithe Ward, 1960; elected Sheriff, City of London, 1966; one of H.M. Lieutenants for City of London. Chairman: Bridge House Estates Cttee., 1953 and 1958; City Schools Cttee., 1956 and 1957. Trustee, Rowland Hill Benevolent Fund; Mem., Visiting Cttee., Holloway Prison (Dep. Chm. 1963-65); Mem. Council, Boy Scouts Assoc. and Chm. Camp Sites Board, Boy Scout H.Q.; Past Master Leathersellers Company; Mem. Court, Painter Stainers Company. *Address:* Woodside, Cranham, Nr. Gloucester. *T.:* Painswick 3146. *Clubs:* United Service, Junior Carlton, City Livery. [*Died* 16 *Oct.* 1966.

HILL, Edward John; Chief General Manager, Lloyds Bank Ltd., 1953-60, retired; Chairman, Property Holding and Investment Trust since 1961 (Director, 1960-); Director: National Bank of New Zealand, since 1958; Bowmaker Ltd., since 1958; Lloyds Bank Ltd., since 1960; *b.* 27 October 1897; 2nd *s.* of J. W. Hill; *m.* 1924, Joyce Mary Owen (*d.* 1951); two *s.* one *d.*; *m.* 1953, Gertrude Sylvia Frank. Entered the service of Lloyds Bank, 1915. *Address:* Inwood, Croham Manor Road, South Croydon. *T.:* Croydon 7607. [*Died* 2 *Jan.* 1965.

HILL, Brigadier Ernest Frederick John, D.S.O. 1919; M.C.; *b.* 6 Aug. 1879; *e. s.* of late Ernest George Hill; *m.* 1929, Edeline Botelier Marjorie Bellingham, *y. d.* of late Bellingham Arthur Somerville. *Educ.:* St. Paul's School; R.M.A., Woolwich. Entered army, Royal Engineers, 1898; K.G.O. Bengal Sappers and Miners, India, 1901-26; served Waziristan, 1901-2 (medal and clasp); Tibet, 1903-4 (medal); European War, 1914-18, France and Flanders, Mesopotamia and Palestine; C.R.E. 7th Indian Division, 1917-19 (despatches six times, Bt. Lieut.-Colonel, D.S.O., M.C., 1914 Star and clasp, War medal, Victory medal); Order of Nile, 4th Class; Commandant K.G.O., Bengal Sappers and Miners, 1922-26; Bt. Colonel, 1926; Brigadier, Royal Engineers, General Staff, Army Headquarters, India, 1927-31; retired 1933; Home Office and Ministry of Home Security, 1937-49. *Recreations:* polo, shooting. *Address:* c/o Lloyds Bank Ltd., 6 Pall Mall, S.W.1. *Clubs:* United Service, M.C.C. [*Died* 19 *Nov.* 1962.

HILL, Ernest Saphir, C.B. 1946; Under-Secretary, Ministry of Housing and Local Government, until retirement in 1952 (Town and Country Planning, 1946-51; Local Govt. and Planning, 1951); *b.* 1891. *Address:* Geneffe, 125 Woodcote Valley Rd., Purley, Surrey. [*Died* 3 *March* 1967.

HILL, James Meechan; *b.* 1899. *Educ.:* Bellshill Public School. Elected to Musselburgh Town Council, 1945, and to Midlothian County Council, 1946. Chairman, for five years, Member for eleven years, Musselburgh ward Labour Party. M.P. (Lab.) Midlothian, 1959-66. A miner. *Address:* 46 Windsor Park Terrace, Musselburgh, Midlothian. [*Died* 22 *Dec.* 1966.

HILL, Levi Clement, C.B.E. 1935; M.A., F.C.I.S.; *b.* 26 May 1883; *s.* of late William Hill, Bolton, Lancs, and Ellen Dickinson; *m.* 1911, Mary Josephine Browne (*d.* 1933); one *s.* three *d.* Finance Dept. Bolton Corporation, 1901-9; General Sec., National Association of Local Government Officers, 1909-43; Founder and Member of Council of

Institute of Public Administration until 1943; Member of Permanent Bureau of International Union of Local Authorities and Hon. Sec. Gen. and Director, International Union of Local Authorities, 1942-45; was three years Member of Consultative Council of Ministry of Health on N.H.I.; Member of International Committee on Teaching and Training for Public Administration; Spelman Travelling Fellowship to America, 1936; Special Comr. for Colonial Office in W. Indies and E. Africa, 1943-45, Singapore, 1951; Lecture tour for British Council in West African territories, 1948; Head of the Sub-department of Public and Social Administration, Univ. College, Exeter, 1946-54; United Nations Organization lecturer on municipal administration, Fundaçao Getulio Vargas, Rio de Janeiro, Brazil, 1954-55; Senior Administrative Officer, Local Government Reorganisation, British Guiana, 1956-57; Tutor in charge of Special Training Course in Local Government for Overseas Officers, 1959-, Queen Elizabeth House, St. Giles, Oxford. Presented with Key to Washington, D.C., U.S.A., 1959. LL.D. (Hon.) S.W. University, Texas, U.S.A., 1944. *Publications:* The Local Government Officer; contributed to Municipal Press of many countries; articles in A Century of Municipal Progress, 1835-1935, and The British Civil Servant. *Recreation:* gardening. *Clubs:* National Liberal, Royal Automobile. [*Died* 4 *Sept.* 1961.

HILL, Martin Spencer, C.B.E. 1950; *b.* 30 Nov. 1893; *e. s.* of late Sir Leonard Hill, F.R.S.; *m.* 1921, Bertha Erwine Lancaster; one *s.* two *d.* *Educ.:* Merchant Taylors' School. Hon. Member of Liverpool Steam Ship Owners' Association and of Council of Chamber of Shipping. Director, Maritime Insurance Co. Ltd., 1949. *Address:* 35 Stanley Road, Hoylake, Cheshire. *T.:* Hoylake 3143.

[*Died* 11 *Jan.* 1968.

HILL, Maurice Neville, F.R.S. 1962; M.A., Ph.D.; Fellow since 1949, King's College, Cambridge; Reader in Marine Geophysics, Department of Geodesy and Geophysics, Cambridge University, since 1965; *b.* 29 May 1919; *yr. s.* of Professor A. V. Hill, C.H., O.B.E., F.R.S.; *m.* 1944, Philippa, *d.* of A. D. Pass, O.B.E.; two *s.* three *d.* *Educ.:* Highgate School; King's Coll., Cambridge (1938-39 and 1946). Experimental Officer, Admiralty Scientific Service, 1939-45; served in Anti-Submarine Establishment, 1939-41; Sweeping Div., Mine Design Dept., 1941-45. Asst. in Research, Dept. of Geodesy and Geophysics, 1949-53; University Demonstrator, 1953-54; Asst. Dir. of Research, 1954-65; Dir. of Studies in Natural Sciences, 1961-65. Leader of numerous geophysical sea-going expeditions, 1947-. Charles Chree Medal and Award of Physical Society, 1963. *Publications:* Papers on marine geophysics in scientific journals; General Editor, The Sea, Vols. 1, 2 and 3, 1962-63. *Recreations:* shooting, walking, croquet. *Address:* 11 Chaucer Road, Cambridge. *T.:* 50885.; Rushay, Wootton Fitzpaine, Charmouth, Bridport, Dorset. *T.:* Charmouth 289. *Club:* United University.

[*Died* 11 *Jan.* 1966.

HILL, Oliver, M.B.E. 1952; F.R.I.B.A.; F.R.S.A.; F.I.L.A.; *b.* 15 June 1887; *s.* of William Neave Hill. *Educ.:* Uppingham. Apprenticed to firm of builders and worked in the shops, afterwards articled pupil to late William Flockhart, F.R.I.B.A.; served European War, 1914-18; in London Scottish; designer of many houses in England, Scotland, Ireland and France. Architect of the Exhibition of British Industrial Art, 1933, British Government Pavilion, Paris, 1937 and the Cotswold Tradition for the Festival of Britain, 1951. Member of the Council for Art and Industry, 1933-38. *Publications:* several volumes of illustrated books. *Recreations:* foreign travel and country pursuits. *Address:* Daneway House, Sapperton, Gloucestershire. *T.:* Frampton Mansell 232. *Club:* Bath.

[*Died* 29 *April* 1968.

HILL, Sir Quintin; *see* Hill, Sir T. St. Q.

HILL, Ralph William, C.B.E. 1951; J.P. Dorset; M.A. (Oxon.); Headmaster of Hardye's School, Dorchester, 1927-55; *b.* 5 May 1893; *s.* of William and Edith Margaret Hill; *m.* 1st, 1920, Lucy Rosa Turner (*d.* 1937); one *d.*; 2nd, 1940, Ann Evans. *Educ.:* City of Oxford High School; St. John's Coll., Oxford, 3rd class, Lit. Hum. Assist. Master, Wyggeston Grammar School, Leicester, 1915-1919; Classical Master, Royal Grammar School, Worcester, 1919-26; Ex-Member Headmasters' Conference and Incorporated Association of Headmasters, President, 1949. *Recreations:* cricket and golf. *Address:* South Ridge, Sutton Poyntz, Nr Weymouth. *T.:* Preston 3213. [*Died* 8 *Feb.* 1966.

HILL, Maj.-Gen. Robert C. C.; *see* Cottrell-Hill.

HILL, Robert Hughes, C.I.E. 1946; *b.* 5 Nov. 1892; *m.* 1922, Ida May Hayes, Kaisar-i-Hind; one *s.* one *d.* *Educ.:* Christ's College, Cambridge (Kitchener, Rhodes Scholar). Went to New South Wales, Australia, 1910, studied wet and dry farming; joined A.I.F., 1915; overseas in 1915; Cambridge, 1918-20; Deputy Director of Agriculture, Indian Agricultural Service-1920; D.D.A. Economics and Marketing, 1934-43; Director of Agriculture, Central Provinces and Berar, 1943-47. *Recreations:* travel, photography. *Address:* 22 Nash Street, Glen Iris, Melbourne, Australia. *Club:* Royal Commonwealth Society.

[*Died* 15 *Feb.* 1963.

HILL, Rowland, M.D., M.R.C.P. London; Consultant Physician, Roy. Belfast Hosp. for Sick Children; *b.* 1883; *s.* of Squire Hill and Sarah Birtwistle; *m.* 1916, Gertrude Langridge; no *c.* *Educ.:* Privately; Queen's University, Belfast. M.B., B.Ch. 1907; Surgeon-Lieutenant R.N. 1915-19; travelled in Russia, China, Japan, Canada, U.S.A. and various European Countries, 1902-12. *Publications:* Contributions to:—British Medical Journal, Medical Press and Circular, Ulster Medical Journal. *Recreations:* travel, golf, contract bridge. *Address:* 6 Mountpleasant, Stranmillis Road, Belfast. *T.:* Belfast 666040. [*Died* 19 *Aug.* 1962.

HILL, Brigadier Rowland Clement Ridley, D.S.O., late Chief Engineer Southern Command, India; *b.* 3 Sept. 1879; *s.* of late Major-General Charles Rowland Hill. *Educ.:* Clifton College; R.M.A., Woolwich. Commission in Royal Engineers, 1899; served Aden Hinterland, 1904; European War (Brevet Major, D.S.O., despatches thrice); retired 1935; Col. Q.V.O. Madras Sappers and Miners, 1943; Col. Comdt. Corps of Royal Indian Engineers, 1946. *Recreations:* racing, shooting. *Club:* Naval and Military. [*Died* 7 *Oct.* 1967.

HILL, Sir Sidney (Pearson), Kt. 1965; B.E.M. 1964; retired; *b.* 30 March 1900; *s.* of late Edward and Mary Jane Hill; *m.* 1920, Sarah Ann Fenton; three *s.* *Educ.:* County schools, Nottingham. Served European War as Private, Sherwood Foresters, 1915-19 (War Medal, Victory Medal); Irish Rebellion, 1916; France, 1916-18: Germany, 1919. Member, British Esperanto Association, 1930. Member, Nottingham Corpn., 1945, Alderman, 1958; Sheriff of Nottingham, 1959-60, Lord Mayor, 1962-63. *Recreations:* gardening, cycling, swimming. *Address:* 12

Ewell Road, Wollaton, Nottingham. *T.:* 283528 [*Died* 28 *Sept.* 1968.

HILL, Sydney, O.B.E. 1968; General Secretary of National Union of Public Employees, 1962-67, retired; *b.* 29 Oct. 1902; *s.* of William and Clara Hill; *m.* 1944, Constance Crew; no *c.* *Educ.:* Dudley Intermediate School. Left school and started as an apprentice engineer at age of 14. Pres., Dudley and Dist. Trades Council, 1928-35; Councillor, Tipton Borough Council, 1937-47; County Magistrate. Joined staff of Nat. Union of Public Employees, as Midlands organiser, 1935; apptd. Nat. Officer, 1945, Chief National Officer, 1960, Asst. Gen. Sec., 1962. *Recreation:* cricket. *Address:* Wynton, Brookside, Cradley, Malvern, Worcs. [*Died* 17 *Aug.* 1968.

HILL, Thomas Rowland, F.R.C.P.; consulting neurologist; *b.* 14 Jan. 1903; *s.* of Thomas Holt and Eleanor Jane Hill, Gravesend, Kent; *m.* 1942, Janet Sybil Cumming, S.R.N.; no *c.* *Educ.:* privately; Guy's Hospital Medical School, University of London. M.D.(Lond.) 1929, F.R.C.P.(Lond.) 1950. Physician, West End Hospital for Neurology and Neurosurgery, London, W.1, 1930; neurologist, Royal Eye Hosp. (King's Coll. Hosp.), 1932; neurologist to Southend General Hosp., 1932; neurologist, King George Hosp., Ilford, 1946. Chairman: Central Consultants and Specialists Cttee., B.M.A., 1950; Thames Hospital Management Cttee. *Publications:* Editor: Contributions to Clinical Practice, 1936; Treatment of Some Common Diseases, 1938; articles in medical journals. *Recreation:* sailing. *Address:* 14 Wimpole Street, W.1. *T.:* Langham 1711. *Clubs:* Reform National Liberal. [*Died* 14 *April* 1967.

HILL, Sir (Thomas St.) Quintin, K.C.M.G., *cr.* 1939 (C.M.G. 1935); O.B.E. 1926; *b.* 1889; *s.* of late R. A. St. Quintin Hill; *m.* 1921, Mary Paolina, *d.* of late Hon. H. A. Lawrence; four *d.* Entered Board of Trade, 1912, and served in various grades there and in other Departments. *Address:* 17 Wynnstay Gardens, Allen St., W.8. [*Died* 19 *June* 1963.

HILL, Eng. Rear-Admiral Walter S.; *see* Scott-Hill.

HILLS, Sir Reginald (Playfair), Kt., *cr.* 1952; O.B.E. 1919; M.C.; Recorder of Winchester, 1925-54; Barrister-at-law; *b.* 1877; *y. s.* of late O. L. Hills, solicitor, 15 John Street, Bedford Row, W.C.; *m.* 1933, Edith Angela, 2nd *d.* of late Eric M. Carter. *Educ.:* Malvern; St. John's College, Oxford. Called to Bar, 1903, Bencher, 1935, Inner Temple. Served Board of Education, Whitehall, 1903-6; Capt. 6th K.O.S.B.; Major, D.A.A.G. Fourth, Second, and Rhine Armies, 1914-19 (O.B.E., M.C., despatches four times). Junior Counsel to Inland Revenue, 1919-57. *Recreations:* formerly fishing, and walking. *Address:* 37 Cottesmore Court, W.8. *Clubs:* Athenæum, Travellers', Hampshire (Winchester). [*Died* 23 *Feb.* 1967.

HILTON, Reginald, M.A., M.D. (Cantab.); F.R.C.P.; Consulting Physician St. Thomas's Hospital; *b.* 1895; *s.* of Philip Hilton; *m.* 1925, Gwen (*see* Gwen Hilton), *d.* of Micaiah J. M. Hill; one *d.* *Educ.:* Merchant Taylors' School, Crosby; Corpus Christi College, Cambridge (Scholar); St. Bartholomew's Hospital, London (Scholar, gold medal for Clinical Medicine); Paris and Frankfurt. Beit Research Fellow, 1922; Copeman Medallist; Assistant Physician and Assistant Director of Medical Unit St. Bartholomew's Hosp. *Publications:* Physiological Principles in Treatment (8th Edition) (with Sir Walter Langdon Brown); Editor (with Sir Robert Hutchison) Index of Treatment, 13th Ed.; various papers in scientific journals on the Heart and the Lungs. *Recreations:* music and painting. *Address:* 8 Elm Tree Rd., N.W.8. [*Died* 13 *Feb.* 1969.

HINCHLIFFE, William A. S.; *see* Simpson-Hinchliffe.

HINCKS, Hon. Sir Cecil Stephen, Kt. 1960; Minister of Lands, Repatriation and Irrigation, State of South Australia, since 1946; M.H.A., for Yorke Peninsula, S.A., since 1941; *b.* 18 Feb. 1894; *m.* 1935, E. M. Staples; one *s.* one *d.* *Educ.:* St. Peter's School Collegiate. Flour milling and wheat industry until 1914. War Service, 1914-19 (10 Bn., Gallipoli and France; wounded). Corn Agencies and Cereal growing, 1919-41. *Recreations:* (younger days) cricket, swimming, football, tennis, etc. *Address:* 28 Alexander St., Largs Bay, South Australia. *T.:* JX 6429. [*Died* 1 *Jan.* 1963.

HINDE, Brig. Harold Montague, C.B. 1951; C.B.E. 1943 (O.B.E. 1919); retd.; *b.* 24 Aug. 1895; *s.* of late Col. W. H. Hinde, Heathcote, Crowthorne, Berks; unmarried. *Educ.:* Wellington Coll.; Blundell's; R.M.C. Sandhurst. Served European War, 1914-1918, with R.A.S.C. (despatches), and in War of 1939-45 (despatches four times, Norway, N. Africa, Italy, N.W. Europe); Lt.-Col. 1939; Brig. 1948; A.D.C. to the King, 1947-50; retired, 1950. Chevalier Légion d'Honneur; Croix de Guerre avec Palme; Bronze Star (U.S.A.); Officer of Legion of Merit (U.S.A.); Commander of Order of Couronne de Chêne (Luxembourg). *Address:* Villa Elstino, Santa Margherita, Ligure, Italy. *Club:* Army and Navy. [*Died* 16 *Nov.* 1965.

HINDLE, Wilfrid Hope; Consultant to the United Nations since 1964; *b.* Barrow-in-Furness, 12 Dec. 1903; *s.* of Isaiah Hindle and Janet Hope; *m.* 1st, 1929, Annette (marriage dissolved 1946), *d.* of Eugene and Geraldine Zeiss, San Diego, California; two *d.*; 2nd, 1948, Eilanna, *d.* of Sidney and Eileen Bent, Southold, Long Island. *Educ.:* Municipal Gram. Sch., Barrow-in-Furness; St. Edmund Hall, Oxford; the Sorbonne, Paris. Leader-writer, Yorkshire Post, 1926; Editorial Staff of the Times, 1927-33; The Londoner and Literary Editor of Evening Standard, 1934-36; Leader-writer, Morning Post, 1936-37; Editor of the Review of Reviews, 1933-36; attached to H.B.M. Legation, Prague, 1938-39; Second Secretary, H.B.M. Legation, Budapest, 1939-41; First Secretary, H.B.M. Legation, Teheran, 1941-1943; Editor of Britain, 1943-45; Special Assistant to U.S. rep. of Anglo-Iranian Oil Company, 1945-46; United Nations Officer, 1947-64. *Publications:* Cartoon History of the Disarmament Conference, 1934; Portrait of a Newspaper, 1937; Foreign Correspondent, 1939; A Guide to Writing for the United Nations, 1965. *Recreation:* travel. *Address:* Mill Road, New Canaan, Conn., U.S.A. *Clubs:* Athenæum; Lotos (New York). [*Died* 31 *May* 1967.

HINDLIP, 4th Baron, *cr.* 1886; **Charles Samuel Victor Allsopp,** Bart. 1880; Major, R.A.S.C. (despatches); *b.* 5 Nov. 1906; *e. s.* of 3rd Baron and Agatha (*d.* 1962), 2nd *d.* of late John C. Thynne; *S.* father, 1931; *m.* 1939, Hansina Elfrida Cecilia Harris (Tulla Karr); two *d.* *Educ.* Eton. *Heir:* *b.* Major Hon. Henry Richard Allsopp, Coldstream Guards [*b.* 1 July 1912; *m.* 1939, Cecily Valentine Jane, *d.* of late Lt.-Col. Malcolm Borwick, D.S.O.; two *s.* one *d.*]. *Address:* Botches, Wivelsfield Green, Haywards Heath, Sussex. *T.:* Wivelsfield Green 266. [*Died* 30 *March* 1966.

HINDEMITH, Paul; composer and violist; Professor of Musical Theory, University of Zürich, since 1952; *b.* Hanau, Germany, 16 Nov. 1895. *Educ.:* Frankfurt-am-Main, under Arnold Mendelssohn and Bernhard Sekles. Concertmeister of Orchestra, Frankfurt Opera House, 1915; Professor of Composition, Berlin Hochschule, 1927; formerly Professor of Music, Yale University. Member German Academy, 1927, but officially condemned for composing un-German works. Works include: Sancta Susanna; Cardillac; Hin und Zurück; Mathis der Maler; Neues vom Tage; Damon, Herodiade, Four Temperaments; Nobilissima Visione; Symphony in E♭; The Perpetual (Oratorio); When Lilacs Last in the Dooryard Bloomed (an American Requiem); Cupid and Psyche, Symphonia Serena, Symphonic Metamorphosis, Piano Concerto, Violin Concerto, Cello Concerto, Clarinet Concerto; Schwanendreher (for Viola and Orchestra); Ludus Tonalis; Marienleben: The Harmony of the World; The Long Christmas Dinner (Opera), etc. Hon. D.Mus. (Oxford) 1954. Balzan Prize, 1963. *Publications:* The Craft of Musical Compositions (2 vols.); Traditional Harmony; Elementary Training; A Composer's World; Johann Sebastian Bach. *Address:* Department of Music, University of Zürich, Switzerland. [*Died* 28 *Dec.* 1963.

HINDUS, Maurice Gerschon; journalist and author; *b.* Russia, 27 Feb. 1891; *s.* of Jacob Hindus and Sarah Gendelisvitch. *Educ.:* Colgate Univ. (B.S. 1915, M.S. 1916, D.Litt. 1931); Harvard. Left Russia for America, 1905; has revisited Russia frequently since 1923. *Publications:* The Russian Peasant and Revolution, 1920; Broken Earth, 1926; Humanity Uprooted, 1929; Red Bread, 1931; The Great Offensive, 1933; Moscow Skies, 1936; Green Worlds, 1938; We Shall Live Again, 1939; To Sing With The Angels, 1941; Hitler Cannot Conquer Russia, 1941; Russia and Japan, 1942; Mother Russia, 1943; The Cossacks, 1946; In Search of a Future, 1949; House Without a Roof, 1962. *Recreations:* walking, swimming, gardening. *Club:* City (New York). [*Died* 8 *July* 1969.

HINE, Montague Leonard, M.D.Lond.; F.R.C.S. Eng.; retired Consulting Surgeon, Moorfields Eye Hospital, Charing Cross Hospital and Miller General Hospital; *b.* Leytonstone, 24 Jan. 1883; *s.* of Dr. A. Leonard Hine and Helen Hine; *m.* 1924, Jennette M. Robertson, Alva, Clackmannanshire; one *s.* one *d.* *Educ.:* Rydal School; Middlesex Hospital (Scholar). House Physician, House Surgeon and Casualty Medical Officer, Middlesex Hospital, 1906-7; Broderip Scholar, Leopold Hudson and Governor's prizeman; Medical Officer Eastern Extension Cable Co. Singapore and Cocos I, 1909-10; House Surgeon Royal Westminster Ophthalmic Hospital, 1912-1913; Surgeon, 1915; Capt. R.A.M.C. (Eye Specialist), 1916-19; Ophthalmic Specialist Ministry of Pensions, 1919-23; Ophthalmic Surgeon, Miller General Hospital, 1919-34. Past-Pres. Ophthalmic Section, R.S.M.; *Publications:* papers in medical journals. Editor VIIth-Xth Eds. May and Worth's Diseases of the Eye, 1949, etc. *Address:* 9 Kirkwick Avenue, Harpenden, Herts. *T.:* 2148. [*Died* 2 *Dec.* 1967.

HINGSTON, Lieut.-Colonel Clayton Alexander Francis, C.I.E. 1925; O.B.E. 1919; I.M.S., retd.; *b.* 6 May 1877; *s.* of Col. C. W. J. Hingston, late I.S.C.; *m.* 1908, Gladys Violet Scroggie; two *s.* one *d.* *Educ.:* private; Middlesex Hospital; London University. Late Principal Medical College, Madras; Superintendent and Senior Obstetric and Gynaecological Surgeon, Government Hospital for Women and Children, Madras; Professor of Midwifery, Medical College, Madras; retired 1932: Officer of the Order of St. John of Jerusalem *Publications:* several in Medical Journals on Eclampsia and Amenorrhoea. *Address:* Aglis, Flushing, Falmouth, Cornwall. *T.:* Flushing 486 [*Died* 17 *Sept.* 1969.

HINGSTON, Major Richard William George, M.C., I.M.S.; *b.* 1887; *s.* of Rev. R. E. H. Hingston, Felhampton, Merton: *m.* 1926, Mary Siggins Kennedy, Ashford, Middlesex; one *s.* two *d.* *Educ.:* Merchant Taylors' School; University College, Cork. Qualified in Medicine with First Class Honours, M.B., B.Ch., B.A.O., National University, Ireland, 1910; Blaney Scholar; entered Indian Medical Service, 1910, retired, 1927; served as Naturalist to Indo-Russian Pamir Triangulation Expedition, 1913; war service in East Africa, France, Mesopotamia, 1914-18 (M.C., despatches twice); Commanded military hospitals, 1918-24; Medical Officer and Naturalist, Mount Everest Expedition, 1924; made physiological investigations into effects of high altitudes on human body; Surgeon-Naturalist, Indian Marine Survey, 1925-27; Second-in-Command, Oxford University Expedition to Greenland, 1928; Organiser and Leader of Oxford University Expedition to British Guiana, 1929; conducted Mission to Northern Rhodesia, Nyasaland, Tanganyika, Kenya, Uganda, to investigate methods for preserving their indigenous fauna, 1930; F.Z.S., F.R.E.S., F.L.S., F.R.G.S. *Publications:* A Naturalist in Himalaya, 1920; A Naturalist in Hindustan, 1923; Nature at the Desert's Edge, 1925; Scientific Chapters in the Fight for Everest, 1925; Problems of Instinct and Intelligence, 1928; A Naturalist in the Guiana Forest, 1932; The Meaning of Animal Colour and Adornment, 1933; Darwin, 1934; numerous papers on natural history in scientific journals and Govt. publications. *Address:* c/o Lloyds Bank, Ltd., Cox & King's Branch, 6 Pall Mall, S.W.1. *Club:* Alpine. [*Died* 5 *Aug.* 1966.

HINSHELWOOD, Sir Cyril (Norman), O.M. 1960; Kt. 1948; F.R.S. 1929; M.A., D.Sc. (Oxon); Hon. D.C.L. (Oxon); Hon. Sc.D. (Dublin, Cambridge); Hon. D.Sc. (Lond., Leeds, Sheffield, Bristol, Hull, Wales, Ottawa, Southampton, City Univ.); Sen. Research Fell., Imperial Coll. of Science and Technology, since 1964; Dr. Lee's Professor of Chemistry, Univ. of Oxford, 1937-64; Hon. Fellow of Trinity Coll., Balliol Coll., Exeter Coll., and St. Catherine's Coll.; Delegate, Clarendon Press; Nobel laureate, 1956; Pres., British Assoc., 1964; *b.* London, 19 June 1897; *o. s.* of late Norman Macmillan Hinshelwood; unmarried. *Educ.:* Westminster City Sch.; Balliol Coll., Oxford. Fellow of Balliol Coll., 1920-21; Fellow and Tutor of Trinity College, Oxford, 1921-37; Pres. Chemical Soc., 1946-48; Foreign Sec., Royal Soc., 1950-55; Pres., Royal Soc., 1955-60; Trustee, British Museum, 1963; Chm. of Coun., Queen Elizabeth Coll., London Univ., 1964-. Foreign member: Accademia Nazionale dei Lincei, Rome; Accademia dei XL, Rome; Real Academia de Ciencias, Madrid; U.S.S.R. Academy of Sciences; U.S. National Academy of Sciences; American Academy of Arts and Sciences; Pontifical Academy of Sciences, 1961. Grande Ufficiale dell' ordine al Merito della Repubblica Italiana, 1956. *Publications:* Kinetics of Chemical Change, 1926, 4th edit., 1940; Thermodynamics for Students of Chemistry, 1926; The Reaction between Hydrogen and Oxygen (with A. T. Williamson), 1934; The Chemical Kinetics of the Bacterial Cell, 1946; The Structure of Physical Chemistry, 1951; Growth, Function and Regulation in Bacterial Cells (with A. C. R. Dean), 1966; papers in Proceedings of Royal Society and other scientific journals. *Address:* Imperial College, S.W.7. *Club:* Athenæum. [*Died* 9 *Oct.* 1967.

HINTON, Captain Eric Perceval, D.S.O. 1940; M.V.O. (4th cl.) 1934;

Royal Navy; retired; *b.* 26 July 1902; *s.* of late Lt.-Col. G. B. Hinton, C.M.G., R.A.; *m.* 1934, Kathleen Doreen Nita, *d.* of late Lt.-Col. N. Sinclair, D.S.O., R.A.; no *c.* *Educ.:* R.N. Colleges, Osborne and Dartmouth. Served War of 1939-45 (D.S.O. and Bar). Order of the Red Banner (U.S.S.R.), 1942. *Address:* Hazelbury Bryan, Sturminster Newton, Dorset. *T.:* Hazelbury Bryan 294. [*Died* 30 *March* 1970.

HINTON, Martin Alister Campbell, F.R.S. 1934; F.L.S., F.G.S., F.Z.S., F.R.S.A.; *b.* 29 June 1883; *m.* 1949, Dina Portway Dobson, J.P., Litt.D., M.A., F.S.A., Wrington, Som. Volunteer worker British Museum (N.H.) from 1910; Assist. 1921; Deputy Keeper, 1927; Keeper of Zoology, 1936-45; has made special study of living and fossil rodents and of the Pleistocene geology of Southern Britain; has given much attention to economic problems connected with whaling, rats and mice, vole plagues, and the musk rat in Great Britain and Western Europe; reported on Barrett-Hamilton's researches on whales in South Georgia to the Colonial Office, 1915; collected an entire school of 127 whales of a rare species, the False Killer (Pseudorca crassidens) stranded in the Dornoch Firth, Oct. 1927; has studied many hoaxes including the Loch Ness Monster. Since 1945 devoted to mathematics and astro-navigation; two round voyages in M.V. City of Manchester to South Africa and India, experimenting with aircraft instruments, 1955-56. *Publications:* a long series of papers, from 1899 onwards, on geology, palaeontology, and zoology; several books on the same subjects; for the British Museum (N.H.): Rats and Mice as enemies of Mankind (Economic Guide No. 8) and a Monograph of Voles and Lemmings, Living and Extinct. *Address:* Glaisters, Wrington, nr. Bristol. *T.:* Wrington 327. [*Died* 3 *Oct.* 1961.

HIORNS, Frederick Robert, F.S.A. 1929; F.R.I.B.A. 1921; R.I.B.A., Dis.T.P.; Architect (retd.), Antiquary and Author; *b.* 1876; *s.* of Thomas Frederick Hiorns, Warwick; *m.* Janie Beatrice Mary Pitcher; two *s.* *Educ.:* S. Devon. Godwin Bursar and Travelling Student, R.I.B.A.; Member of Hellenic and Roman Societies, Classical Association, Art Workers' Guild, etc.; for many years a Senior Member of Architectural Staff of L.C.C.; Deputy Chief Architect, 1935; Architect to the L.C.C. and Superintending Architect of Metropolitan Buildings, 1939-41; works in architecture for L.C.C. include S.E. London Technical Institute; Weights and Measures Office, Euston Road; a considerable number of Hospital units and extensions, including rebuilding of N. Eastern Hospital at Tottenham; many schemes for Working Class Housing; and the Extension of London County Hall, east of the original building; Member of Departmental Committee on Hospital Standards, 1930-33; served on a number of Committees of R.I.B.A.; Board of Architectural Education (sometime External Examiner), and other bodies; Member of Council National Buildings Record; Cttee. of Society for the Protection of Ancient Buildings; Consultative Panel, Ministry of Works and Buildings, 1941-43; Town and Country Planning Advisory Cttee., Min. of Health, etc. *Publications:* Town-Building in History, 1956; various essays and papers on Architecture and Art Criticism, etc. *Recreations:* travel, pastel painting, and book collecting. *Address:* The Red House, Yelverton, S. Devon. *Club:* Reform. [*Died* 15 *Jan.* 1961.

HIPWELL, Ven. Richard Senior, O.B.E. 1919; M.A.; B.D.; Archdeacon of Meath, since 1940; Rector of Ardbraccan, 1928; in charge of Donaghpatrick and Kilshine, 1954, and Castletown-Kilpatrick, 1958; *b.* 1881; *s.* of Abraham and Ellen Hipwell; *m.* 1921, Elizabeth, *d.* of Rev. John Preston; one *s.* two *d.* *Educ.:* Patrician School, Mountrath; University of the Cape of Good Hope; Trinity College, Dublin. Carson Biblical Prize T.C.D., 1912; Divinity Testimonium (1st Class), 1913; M.A. and B.D., 1916; Deacon, 1912; Priest, 1913; Curate of St. Peter's, Drogheda, 1912-15; Temporary Chaplain to the Forces, Gallipoli, France, Egypt, and Mesopotamia, 1915-20 (despatches, O.B.E.); Hon. Chaplain to the Forces, 1920; Curate in Charge of Oldcastle, 1920-23; Incumbent of Kilskyre with Killalon, 1923-26; Rector of Navan, 1926-54: Rural Dean of Upper Kells, 1932-58; Examining Chaplain to the Bishop of Meath since 1934; Prebendary of Tipper in St. Patrick's Cathedral, Dublin, 1935-40; Private Chaplain to the Bishop of Meath, 1937-45; Member of General Synod of Church of Ireland; Select Preacher, Trinity College, Dublin, 1939. *Address:* Donaghpatrick Rectory, Navan, Co. Meath. *T.:* Navan 65. *Club:* Friendly Brothers (Dublin). [*Died* 22 *Feb.* 1962.

HISCOX, Ralph, C.B.E. 1969 (O.B.E. 1943); Partner, Roberts & Hiscox; *b.* 1 April 1907; *s.* of late Ralph Hiscox and late Margaret Sturrock Scrymgeour; *m.* 1937, Louisa, *e. d.* of late Hugh Boal; one *s.* two *d.* *Educ.:* Cranleigh Sch. Entered Lloyd's, 1925. Joined 600 City of London Sqdn. A.A.F., 1929. Served War of 1939-45: Group Capt., O.B.E., despatches twice. First served on Cttee. of Lloyd's, 1956; Dep.-Chm., 1959; Chm., 1967, 1968. Cttee. of Lloyd's Under-writers' Fire & Non-Marine Assoc., 1950-; Dep.-Chm., 1954; Chm., 1955, 1956. Cttee. of Lloyd's Register of Shipping. *Recreation:* golf. *Address:* Scott's Farm, Scott's Grove Road, Chobham, Surrey. *T.:* Chobham 8526. *Clubs:* R.A.F.; New Zealand Golf. [*Died* 6 *May* 1970.

HISLOP, Thomas Charles Atkinson, C.M.G. 1935; Barrister-at-Law; *b.* Wellington, New Zealand, 30 November 1888; *s.* of late Hon. Thomas William Hislop and Annie Simpson Hislop; *m.* 1921, Ailsa Craig Dalhousie, *o. d.* of J. W. E. Dalhousie Ramsay, Christchurch, N.Z.; one *d.* *Educ.:* Wellington Coll. (N.Z.); Caius College, Cambridge. Called to Bar, Inner Temple, 1911; joined firm Brandon, Hislop and Brandon; (now Brandon, Ward and Watts), Barristers and Solicitors, Wellington, N.Z.; elected Wellington City Council 1913; resigned 1914 on joining N.Z. Expeditionary Force, European War; served Wellington Regiment Egypt, Gallipoli, France (twice wounded, Rank Captain); returned N.Z. 1920 and resumed practice; re-elected Wellington City Council 1927; Mayor of Wellington, 1931-44, Past President Wellington District Law Society; Chm. of Directors N.Z. Centennial Exhibition, held in N.Z., 1940. High Commissioner for New Zealand, to Canada, 1950-57; Past Chm. N.Z. Bd. of Directors, Royal Exchange Assurance. *Recreations:* fishing, shooting, golf, riding. *Address:* 33 Salamanca Road, Wellington, W.1, N.Z. *Club:* Wellington (N.Z.). [*Died* 21 *June* 1965.

HITCHENS, Harry Butler, O.B.E. 1944; T.D. 1949; M.A.; Headmaster, Solihull School, Warwickshire, since 1947; *b.* 21 April 1910; *o. s.* of late Frank Hitchens and Kate Butler, Gravesend, Kent; unmarried. *Educ.:* Bushey; Cambridge (M.A.). Scholar, St. Catharine's Coll., 1928; 1st Class Hons., Mod. Langs. Tripos, 1931. Asst. Lectr., Univ. of Rostock, Germany, 1933; Sixth Form Master, Clifton College, 1934-39, 1946-47; Lay Reader. War Service, 1939-1946, North Africa, Italy, Austria (despatches), Brigadier. Hon. Doctorate Philology, Rostock. Officer, U.S. Legion of Merit; French Croix de Guerre (Palme). *Recreations:* climbing, spelaeology. *Address:* The Headmaster's House, Solihull, Warwicks. *Clubs:* English-Speaking Union, Royal Automobile. [*Died* 21 *Aug.* 1963.

HITCHINS, Captain Henry Luxmoore, C.B.E. 1937; Royal Navy, retired; *b.* 23 Jan. 1885; *s.* of Charles W. M. Hitchins, late Fellow of Sidney Sussex College, Cambridge, and Adeline Mary Luxmoore, Bryn Asaph, St. Asaph. *Educ.:* Felsted: H.M.S. Britannia. Cadet, 1899; Midshipman, 1901; Lieutenant, 1905, qualified in torpedo; served battle of Jutland in H.M.S. Thunderer; Commander, 1917; retired with rank of Captain, 1931; Director of Admiralty Compass Observatory, Ditton Park, Slough, 1928-1948; Member of Royal Institution; Fellow of Roy. Astronomical Society. *Publications:* Canterbury Tales: Chaucer for present-day readers, 1946; From Lodestone to Gyro-Compass, 1952; contributed to Brassey's Naval Annual and the Naval Review. *Address:* 44 Crag Path, Aldeburgh, Suffolk. [*Died* 24 *July* 1961.

HIVES, 1st Baron, *cr.* 1950, of Duffield; **Ernest Walter Hives,** C.H. 1943; M.B.E. 1920; D.Sc., LL.D.; retired as Chairman Rolls Royce Ltd.; as Chairman Industrial Development Board for Malta; also as Chm., Nat. Council for Technological Awards; *b.* Reading, 21 Apr. 1886; *m.* 1913, Gertrude Ethel Warwick (*d.* 1961); four *s.* three *d.* *Educ.:* Redlands Sch., Reading. Joined Rolls Royce, Ltd. in 1908 and retd. in 1957; formerly Dir. Rotol Ltd. Gold Medal, Roy. Aeronautical Soc. 1955. Hon. D.Sc. Nottingham, 1949; Hon. LL.D. Cambridge, 1951; Hon. D.Sc. (Eng.) London, 1958. *Recreations:* golf, fishing. *Heir:* *s.* Hon. John Warwick Hives [*b.* 26 Nov. 1913; *m.* 1937]. *Address:* Hazeldene, Duffield, Derbyshire. *T.A.:* Hives, Duffield. *T.:* Duffield 2369. *Club:* Derbyshire (Derby). [*Died* 24 *April* 1965.

HOARE, Brig.-Gen. Cuthbert Gurney, C.M.G. 1918; C.B.E. 1919; late R.A.F.; Indian Army, retired; *b.* 1883 served European War, 1914-19 (despatches, C.M.G., C.B.E.); retired, 1923. *Address:* White Cottage, E. Bradenham, Thetford, Norfolk. *T.:* Shipdham 341. [*Died* 31 *Jan.* 1969.

HOARE, Sir Edward O'Bryen, 7th Bt., *cr.* 1784; *b.* 29 April 1898; *s.* of 6th Bt. and Mabel (*d.* 1916), *d.* of Major O'Bryen Taylor; *S.* father, 1933; *m.* 1932, Nina, *er. d.* of late Charles Nugent Hope-Wallace, M.B.E.; one *s.* one *d.* *Educ.:* Charterhouse. Served in the Army 1916-19 and 1940-45 (Major R.A.S.C.). *Heir:* *s.* Timothy Edward Charles Hoare [*b.* 11 Nov. 1934; *m.* 1969, Felicity Anne, *o. d.* of Peter Boddington]. *Address:* 61 Flask Walk, Hampstead, N.W.3. *Club:* Public Schools. [*Died* 4 *Dec.* 1969.

HOARE, Henry Noel, D.S.O. 1916; O.B.E. 1917; Director of Central & Western Development Co., Ltd., Hadfields (Merton) Ltd., and several other companies; *b.* 3 May 1877; *s.* of Gerard Noel Hoare and Lucy Cotterill; *m.* 1909, Sybil Margaret Mappin (*d.* 1954); one *d.* *Educ.:* Dulwich. Business till 1914; R.N.V.R. Sub-Lieut., 1914-15; Army 1915-18 (despatches, D.S.O., O.B.E.); business since 1918. *Recreations:* golf, sailing. *Address:* 28 Melbury Ct., W.8. *T.:* Western 5004. *Club:* Royal Thames Yacht. [*Died* 27 *Jan.* 1962.

HOARE, Michael Richard; Recorder of Bournemouth since 1964; *b.* 23 Jan. 1903; *s.* of late Arthur Richard Hoare and late Anne Elizabeth Mary Hoare. *Educ.:* Uppingham School; Oriel College, Oxford. Called to the Bar, 1926. Served War of 1940-45, Lincolnshire Regt. and R.A., in N.W. Europe (despatches). Bencher of Gray's Inn, 1959. A Deputy Chairman, Middlesex Quarter Sessions, 1963-65. Recorder of Andover, 1962-64. *Recreations:* music, gardening. *Address:* 3 Pump Court, Temple, E.C.4. *T.:* Central 4411: (home) 23 Nottingham Road, South Croydon. *Club:* Hampshire (Winchester). [*Died* 20 *Feb.* 1970.

HOBART, Brig. James Wilfred Lang Stanley, C.B.E. 1945; D.S.O. 1919; M.C.; p.s.c.; *b.* 28 April 1890; *s.* of R. T. Hobart, I.C.S., and Janet, *d.* of Charles Stanley, Roughan Park, Ireland; *m.* 1914, Kathleen, *d.* of Commander Fell-White, Springfort Hall, Mallow, Co. Cork; one *d.* *Educ.:* Temple Grove; Charterhouse; R.M.C., Sandhurst. Joined North Staffordshire Regiment, 1908; Shorncliffe, Ireland, 1911-14; served European War, 1914-19, in France, Belgium, and Germany (wounded, despatches six times, Brevet Major, Belgian War Cross, French War Cross, 1914 star and clasp, B.W. medal, Victory medal, D.S.O., M.C.); Adjutant, 1914-15; Captain, 1915; Brevet Major, 1917; Substantive Major, 1925; Staff Captain, France, 1916; G.S.O. 3, France, 1916; Brigade Major, France, 1916-17; G.S.O. 2, France (temp. Major), 1917-19; Brigade Major, Irish Command, 1919; Staff College, Camberley, 1920; G.S.O. 3, Eastern Command, 1921; Brigade Major, Aldershot Command, 1921-23; D.A.A. and Q.M.G., Western Command, 1923-25; G.S.O. 2, Army H.Q. India, 1926-27; Brigade Major, India, 1927; D.A.G., Western Command, 1928-30; O.C. Depôt, Lichfield, 1930-33; Brevet Lt.-Col., 1931; Lt.-Col., 1933; Commanded 1st Bn. N. Staffordshire Regt., 1933-36; Col., 1934; Instructor Senior Officers' School, Sheerness, 1936-39; Commander (temp. Brigadier) Infantry Brigade, T.A., 1939; Brigadier, General Staff, H.Q. Troops, Sudan, 1941-42; Commander Glasgow Area, 1942-1945; served War of 1939-45 in West Africa, the Western Desert, Cyprus, and the Sudan; retired pay, 1945. *Address:* Overmore, Burley, Ringwood, Hants. [*Died* 10 *March* 1970.

HOBBS, Sir John (Berry), (Jack); Kt., *cr.* 1953; retired professional cricketer; *b.* Cambridge, 16 Dec. 1882. Played for Cambridgeshire, 1904; for Surrey, 1905-35; for England, 1907-30; captained England against Australia at Manchester, 1926; made 3636 runs, including 12 hundreds, in test matches against Australia; in 1925 scored 16 hundreds, this record was beaten by Dennis Compton, 1947; made 197 hundreds in first-class cricket, a record; in 1926 made 316 for Surrey *v.* Middlesex, the highest individual score at Lord's. *Publications:* Cricket for Beginners, 1922; My Cricket Memories, 1924; Between the Wickets, 1926; Playing for England! My Test Cricket Story, 1931; The Fight for the Ashes, 1932-33, 1933; My Life Story, 1935. *Address:* 23 Furze Croft, Furze Hill, Hove 2, Sussex. [*Died* 21 *Dec.* 1963.

HOBHOUSE, Sir Arthur Lawrence, Kt., *cr.* 1942; Hon. F.R.I.B.A. 1948; J.P., C.C., M.A., Pro-Chancellor, Bristol University, since 1947, *b.* 15 Feb. 1886; 2nd *s.* of late Rt. Hon. Henry Hobhouse and Margaret, 7th *d.* of Richard Potter; *m.* 1919, Konradin Huth, *e. d.* of late Rt. Hon. F. H. Jackson and Annabel Clare, *d.* of late Sir Mountstuart Grant Duff, G.C.S.I.; two *s.* three *d.* *Educ.:* Eton; St. Andrews Univ.; Trinity College, Cambridge (Nat. Science Tripos). Admitted Solicitor, 1911, and practised in London till outbreak of War; Sec. East Coast Raids Committee, 1914-15; served in B.E.F. (21st Div.), 1915-19, Staff Capt.; farmed in Sussex and Somerset 1919 onwards; M.P. (L.) Wells, 1923-24 and candidate General Elections 1922, 1924 and 1929; elected Somerset County Council 1925, Alderman 1934, Chm. Public Health Committee, 1933-38; Vice-Chairman Somerset County Council, 1937-1940, Chm. 1940-47; President County Councils Association (England and Wales), 1951-53 (Chm. 1946-50); Chairman of Bath Town-planning Committee, South Western Joint Vagrancy Committee, and of various secondary Schools and public bodies. Chairman: Rural Housing Committee (Min.

of Health) 1942-47 (Third and Fourth Reports); National Parks Committee (Min. T. and C. Planning), 1945-47; Footpaths and Access to the Countryside Committee, 1946-1947. *Address:* Hadspen House, Castle Cary, Somerset. *T.:* Castle Cary 200. *Club:* Athenæum. [*Died* 20 *Jan.* 1965.

HOBHOUSE, Sir John (Richard), Kt. 1946; M.C. 1917; J.P. Liverpool, 1929-57; *b.* 27 Feb. 1893; 3rd *s.* of Rt. Hon. Henry and Margaret Hobhouse, Hadspen, Somerset; *m.* 1926, Catherine Stewart Brown, Liverpool; two *s.* two *d.* (and one *s.* decd.). *Educ.:* Eton (King's Schol.); New Coll., Oxford. Capt. R.G.A., 1917-19; partner Alfred Holt and Co., Shipowners, 1920-57; Chm. Royal Insurance and Liverpool & London & Globe Insurance Companies, 1954-56; Chm. General Council of British Shipping, 1942-43; Chm. Liverpool S.S. Owners Assocn., 1941-43; Chm.: Nat. Assoc. of Port Employers, 1948-1950; Employers Assoc., Port of Liverpool, 1947-54; Pro-Chancellor Univ. of Liverpool, 1948-57; Dep. Regional Commissioner, N.W. Region, 1939-40; Reg. Shipping Repr. N.W., Min. War Transport, 1941-45; Member Royal Commission on Population, 1944-49; Chm. S.W. Regional Museum Service, 1959. Hon. LL.D. Liverpool Univ., 1958. Commander of Order of Oranje Nassau, 1951. *Recreation:* gardening. *Address:* Glebe Court, West Monkton, nr. Taunton, Somerset. *T.:* West Monkton 224. *Clubs:* Brooks's, Bath. [*Died* 9 *May* 1961.

HOBSON, Baron *cr.* 1963 (Life Peer), of Brent, Co. Mddx.; **Charles Rider Hobson;** a Lord-in-Waiting to the Queen since Oct. 1964; is a power station engineer; *b.* 1904; *m.* 1933, Doris Mary Spink, *d.* of F. Spink Butcher; one *d.* Member of Amalgamated Engineering Union for 30 years; Member Willesden Borough Council, 1931, later Alderman. M.P. (Lab.) Wembley North, 1945-50, Keighley, 1950-Sept. 1959. Asst. Postmaster-General, 1947-51. Vice-Chairman, Joint East Africa Board, 1955-58, and 1964-65. *Address:* 115 Dewsbury Road, Willesden, N.W.10. *Club:* National Trade Union. [*Died* 17 *Feb.* 1966.

HOBSON, Frederick Greig, D.S.O. 1916; M.A. (Oxon); D.M., B.Ch. (Oxon); F.R.C.P. (Lond.); M.R.C.S. (Eng.); Honorary Consulting Physician, Radcliffe Infirmary and County Hospital, Oxford; *m.* Audrey Gotch (*d.* 1959); one *s.* two *d.* *Educ.:* Westminster, New College, Oxford. Served European War 1914-17 (D.S.O.). During thirty hours he continually organised parties for water and bomb-carrying, and also for carrying the wounded. *Publication:* What is Scarlet Fever for the Clinician, Lancet, Feb. 1936; Medical Practice in Residential Schools, 1938. *Address:* 112 Banbury Road, Oxford. *T.:* Oxford 57307. [*Died* 26 *June* 1961.

HOBSON, Lieut.-Col. Gerald Walton, C.MG. 1919; D.S.O. 1915; late XII (Prince of Wales's Royal) Lancers; *b.* 20 June 1873; *e. s.* of late Richard Hobson, D.L., J.P., of The Marfords Bromborough, Cheshire; *m.* 1908, Winifred Hilda (*d.* 1957), *d.* of late J. Gardiner Muir, D.L., J.P., of Farmingwoods Hall, Thrapston, Northants; two *s.* one *d.* *Educ.:* Harrow; Sandhurst. Entered army, 1892; Major, 1906; retired, 1908; served S. African War, 1899-1901 (despatches, Queen's medal 7 clasps); European War, 1914-19 (despatches twice, D.S.O., C.M.G.); J.P. Northamptonshire. Former Chairman J. Kershaw Ltd., Cotton Spinners, Ashton-u.-Lyne. *Publications:* Some XII R. Lancers; The Story of The XII R. Lancers. *Address:* The Manor House, Wappenham, Towcester, Northants. *T.:* Blakesley 218. *Club:* Cavalry. [*Died* 6 *Sept.* 1962

HOBSON, Harry Roy, D.S.O. 1918; Past Chairman Parry Murray & Co. Ltd. Served European War, 1914-18 (despatches four times, D.S.O.); Greek Order of Military Merit. *Address:* 88 St. James's Street, S.W.1. *Clubs:* Carlton, Bath. [*Died* 30 *Oct.* 1965.

HOBSON, Sir Henry (Arthur), K.B.E., *cr.* 1952 (C.B.E. 1944; M.B.E. 1929); *b.* 28 Aug. 1893; *s.* of A. J. Hobson, O.B.E.; *m.* 1920, Marianne Audrey Scott (*d.* 1965); one *d.* *Educ.:* Whitgift Middle. Vice-Consul, Tangier, 1919; served: Barcelona, Vigo, Caracas (Chargé d'Affaires, 1925 and 1926); Ghent, Lille, La Paz (Chargé d'Affaires, 1931), Lima (Chargé d'Affaires, 1932), Baltimore, and Riga; Consul-General, Havana, 1940-45, Barcelona, 1945-50, New York, 1951-53; retired, 1954. *Address:* 21 Scarsdale Villas, W.8. *T.:* Western 5090. [*Died* 4 *Feb.* 1968.

HOBSON, Rt. Hon. Sir John (Gardiner Sumner), P.C. 1963; Kt. 1962; O.B.E. 1945; T.D. 1948; Q.C. 1957; J.P. 1954; M.P. (C.) Warwick and Leamington since March 1957; *b.* 18 April 1912; *s.* of late Col. Gerald Walton Hobson, C.M.G., D.S.O.; *m.* 1939, Beryl Marjorie, *d.* of A. Stuart Johnson, Henshall Hall, Congleton, Cheshire; three *d.* *Educ.:* Harrow (Head of School); Brasenose College, Oxford (Scholar); Inner Temple (Entrance Scholar). Called to the Bar, 1938. Served War of 1939-45: Northamptonshire Yeo.; France and Belgium, 1940; N. Africa (1st Army), 1942; Lt.-Col. and A.Q.M.G. (despatches), 1943; A.Q.M.G., H.Q. 21 Army Group, 1944-45. Chm. Rutland Q.S. 1954-62; Dep. Chm. 1957-58, Chm. 1958-62, Beds. Q.S.; Recorder of Northampton, 1958-62; Parl. Priv. Sec. to Minister of State for Commonwealth Relations, 1959-61; Solicitor-General, Feb.-July 1962; Attorney-General, 1962-64. Member: Royal Commission on the Police, 1960; Home Secretary's Advisory Cttee. on Treatment of Offenders, 1960; Governor, Harrow School, 1962. *Recreations:* field sports, and fine arts. *Address:* 28 Hereford Square, S.W.7. *T.:* Fremantle 0144; 1 Harcourt Buildings, Temple, E.C.4. *T.:* Central 3731. *Clubs:* Cavalry, Pratt's. [*Died* 4 *Dec.* 1967.

HOBSON, Sir Oscar (Rudolf), Kt. 1955; M.A.; Chairman: Association of Unit Trust Managers; Commonwealth Unit Trust Fund (Managers) Ltd.; A.E. and G. Unit Trust (Managers); Member, Court of Governors, London School of Economics and Political Science; Member, Council of Royal Economic Society; *b.* 15 March 1886; *s.* of late Professor Ernest William Hobson, F.R.S.; *m.* 1910, Frances Josephine, *d.* of late Charles Milner Atkinson, Stipendiary Magistrate at Leeds. *Educ.:* Aldenham; King's College, Cambridge. First Class Classical Tripos, 1907; Junior Optime Mathematical Tripos, 1908; entered the London Joint-Stock Bank, 1910; Financial Editor of the Manchester Guardian, 1920-29; Editor-in-Chief of the Financial News, 1929-1934; City Editor of the News Chronicle, 1935-59. *Publications:* How the City Works, 1938; Does Money Matter?, 1942; Can We Afford It?, 1943; Talks with a Banker, 1944; A Hundred Years of the Halifax, 1953. *Address:* Penbury End, Penn, Bucks. *T.:* Penn 2241. *Club:* Reform. [*Died* 18 *June* 1961.

HOBSON, Sir Patrick, Kt. 1961; Chairman and Managing Director, Executive Services Ltd., since 1964; Chairman, Geo. F. Huggins & Co. Ltd.; Director: Colonial Life Insurance Co. Ltd.; Federation Chemicals Ltd.; Halliburton Tucker Ltd.; Senator of the Parliament of Trinidad and Tobago, since 1961; *b.* 10 July 1909; *s.*

of Leonard Manning Hobson and Dorothy (*née* Carrington); *m.* 1934, Dora Agatha (*née* de Barry); one *d.* *Educ.:* Queen's Royal College, Trinidad. Trinidad Leaseholds Ltd., 1927; Trinidad Consolidated Oilfields Ltd., 1936; Nat. Mining Corp. Ltd. group of companies, 1945. Pres., The Petroleum Assoc. of Trinidad, 1954-64. *Recreations:* boating and fishing. *Address:* (private) Maple Manor, Sunset Drive, Bayshore, Trinidad, W.I. *T.:* 637-4338; (office) P.O. Box 375, Port-of-Spain, Trinidad, W.I. *T.:* 34398. *Clubs:* West Indian; Union, Yacht, Country (Trinidad). [*Died* 30 *July* 1970.

HOBSON, Sidney; business and company director; Lord Mayor of Nottingham, 1954-1955; *b.* 29 Sept. 1887; *s.* of James and Mary A. Hobson; *m.* 1919, Hilda Mary (*née* Scanlan) (*d.* 1965); one *s.* one *d.* *Educ.:* Nottingham. President: Nottingham City Business Club, 1927-28; Nottingham Rotary Club, 1931-32; National Wood Box & Packing Makers Federation, 1943-44; Chairman, Joint Industrial Council Wood Box & Packing Makers Federation, 1943-44. Councillor, Nottingham City, 1943; Alderman, 1957-58. Sheriff of Nottingham, 1951-52. *Recreation:* fishing. *Address:* 9A Villiers Road, Woodthorpe, Nottingham. *T.:* 65437. *Club:* Nottingham Borough. [*Died* 18 *July* 1970.

HODDER-WILLIAMS, Ralph Wilfred, M.C., M.A. (Oxon. and Columbia, N.Y.); Lieutenant-Colonel (Home Guard); Publisher; President, Matthew Hodder Ltd.; Chairman, The Lancet, Ltd., University of London Press Ltd.; Director: English Universities Press, Ltd.; Brockhampton Press Ltd.; *b.* 31 Jan. 1890; *y. s.* of late John and Mary Williams, Bromley Common, and *g.s.* of Matthew Henry Hodder; *m.* 1917, Marjorie, *e. d.* of late Arthur Glazebrook, Toronto; two *s.* three *d.* *Educ.:* Westminster; Christ Church, Oxford. Lecturer and Associate Professor of Modern History, University of Toronto, 1911-1923; Captain P.P.C.L.I., 1915-18 (M.C. 1916); 54th Kent (Chislehurst) Battalion H.G., 1940-45 (Lt.-Colonel comdg., 1943-45); joined brothers as Director of Hodder and Stoughton, Ltd., 1923 (Chairman, 1947-60). President of Publishers' Association, 1953-55. *Publication:* Princess Patricia's Canadian Light Infantry, 1914-1918, 1923. *Address:* St. Paul's House, Warwick Square, E.C.4; Duddings, Dunster, Somerset. *Club:* Union. [*Died* 11 *July* 1961.

HODGE, Lieut.-Colonel Edward Humfrey Vere, C.I.E. 1938; M.D. (Cantab.), F.R.C.P. (Lond.); Indian Medical Service (retd.); Physician Consultant in Tropical Diseases to Royal Infirmary, Edinburgh, 1939-1950; Senior Physician, Unit for Tropical Diseases, Edinburgh, 1945-50; *b.* 28 Aug. 1883; *s.* of late Rev. Edward Vere Hodge; *m.* 1921, Barbara, *d.* of late Lt.-Gen. Sir Alfred Bingley, K.C.I.E., C.B.; one *d.* *Educ.:* Oakham; Clare College, Cambridge; St. George's Hospital. Indian Medical Service, 1909-38; served European War, 1914-18 (despatches); Professor of Medicine, Medical Coll., Calcutta, 1934-38; formerly Lecturer, Diseases of Tropical Climates, University of Edinburgh, (1939). F.R.S.M.; Fellow Royal Society of Tropical Medicine and Hygiene (Pres. Edinburgh Branch, 1946-51); Hon. Fellow State Medical Faculty of Bengal. *Publications:* Birch's Management and Medical Treatment of Children in India and the Tropics; contribution on Nursing in the Tropics to Alan Moncrieff's Nursing and Diseases of Sick Children, 3rd, 4th, and 5th ed. *Address:* The Little Causey, Cranleigh, Surrey. *T.:* Cranleigh 396. [*Died* 27 *April* 1968.

HODGE, Humfrey G.; *see* Grose-Hodge.

HODGEN, Maj.-Gen. Gordon West, C.B. 1943; O.B.E. 1921; I.A. (retd.); Col. Comdt. of R.I.A.S.C. since 1945; *b.* 2 February 1894; *m.* 1949, Amy Jane Roper-Robinson; one *s.* one *d.* 2nd Lieutenant Indian Army, 1914; D.D.S. & T., 1939-1941; D.S.T., 1941-45; M.G.A. (Central Command), 1945-46; Dir.-Gen. Lands, Hirings and Disposals; Pres. Claims Commission (India), 1946-47; retired 1947. *Club:* Army and Navy. [*Died* 29 *Feb.* 1968.

HODGES, Kenneth Henry; Chairman, Welsh Board of Health, since 1958; *b.* 15 Jan. 1915; *s.* of late Alfred Henry and Winifred May Hodges; *m.* 1940, Beatrice Alice Greenwood; one *s.* two *d.* *Educ.:* Cardiff High School. Ministry of Health, 1933-57; Principal Regional Officer, 1951-1953; Assistant Secretary, 1953-57. War of 1939-45; Intelligence Corps, 1942-46; commissioned, 1944; served U.K. and in France and Germany. Fellow Royal Horticultural Society. *Recreations:* cricket, gardening, golf. *Address:* Holly Bank, Mill Rd., Llanishen, Cardiff. *T.:* Cardiff 53717. *Club:* Cardiff and County (Cardiff). [*Died* 21 *Feb.* 1961.

HODGSON, Herbert Henry, M.A. (Camb.), B.Sc.(London), Ph.D.(Heidelberg), F.S.D.C., F.R.I.C.; Head of Departments of General Chemistry and Colour Chemistry, Huddersfield Technical College, 1918-48; retired; *b.* Bradford, 7 Mar. 1883; *o. s.* of late Henry Hodgson, Director of Bradford Co-operative Society and Director of Co-operative Printing Society, Manchester; *m.* Annie, *e. d.* of late T. W. Procter, Bradford; one *d.* *Educ.:* Bradford Grammar School; Trinity College, Cambridge (Major Scholar); The Zürich Polytechnic; The University of Heidelberg. Natural Sciences Tripos, Parts I. and II., 1903-4; Mathematical Tripos, 1905; Wiltshire Prize, 1903; Lecturer and Research Chemist, Bradford Technical College, 1908-1912; Head of Chemical Dept., Northern Polytechnic, London, N., 1912-15; Chief Chemist for Brotherton & Co. Ltd., at their Birmingham and Stourton works, 1915-18; Examiner for London Univ., 1912-15, 1940; Examiner for Civil Service Comms., 1913-39; Examiner for L.C.C., 1927, 1951-53; Assessor for West Riding County Council, 1932-56; General Member Council, Roy. Inst. of Chem., 1927-30, 1931-34, 1938-41, 1942-45, 1946-49, 1950-53, 1954-57, 1958-61; Vice-Pres., 1934-37; formerly Member: Colour Index Editorial Panel; Advisory Cttee. on Advanced Chemistry, Yorkshire Council for Further Education; Publication and Fastness Cttees. of Soc. of Dyers and Colourists; Chairman City and Guilds Advisory Committee on Dyeing of Textiles, and Mem. Consultative Cttee. for Textile Subjects; delivered many Public Lectures, 3rd Brotherton Memorial Lectr., 1950; nine patents for dye-stuffs and intermediates; Dyers' Gold Medal for Research, 1925-26, 1929-30; Gold Medal Soc. of Dyers and Colourists, 1947 (and Bar 1958); Vice-Pres. Soc. of Dyers and Colourists, 1948-51. *Publications:* 376 scientific papers; *translations:*—Enamelling on Iron and Steel, Grünwald, 1909; Technology of Iron Enamelling and Tinning, Grünwald, 1912; Raw Materials of the Enamel Industry, Grünwald, 1914; Celluloid, by Masselon, Roberts & Cillard, 1912; The Chemistry of the Colloids, Pöschl 1910. *Recreations:* gardening, languages. *Address:* Clowde, 48 St. Thomas' Road, St. Annes-on-the-Sea, Lancs. *T.:* St. Annes 21665. [*Died* 5 *Dec.* 1967.

HODGSON, Rev. Leonard, D.D.; S.T.D.; Hon. D.C.L.; *b.* London, 24 October 1889; *s.* of Walter Hodgson, late official Shorthand Writer to the Houses of Lords and Commons, and Lillias Emma *d.* of

William Shaw, of Wolsingham, Co. Durham; *m.* 1920, Ethel Margaret du Plat (*d.* 1960), *d.* of Rev. Charles Frederick Archer, late Rector of Moy, Co. Tyrone; one *s.* one *d.* *Educ.:* St. Paul's School; Hertford College, Oxford. 2nd class Class Mods., 1st class Lit. Hum. 1st class Theology: St. Michael's College, Llandaff. Curate of St. Mark's Church, Portsmouth, 1913-14; Vice-Principal of St. Edmund Hall, Oxford, 1914-19; Official Fellow and Dean of Divinity, Magdalen College, Oxford, 1919-25; Professor of Christian Apologetics, The General Theological Seminary, New York, 1925-31; Residentiary Canon of Winchester Cathedral 1931-38; Regius Professor of Moral and Pastoral Theology and Canon of Christ Church, Oxford, 1938-44; Regius Professor of Divinity and Canon of Christ Church, Oxford, 1944-58; Warden of William Temple College, Rugby, 1954-66. Examining Chaplain to the Bishop of Lichfield, 1917-25; Theological Secretary to the Commission on Faith and Order of the World Council of Churches, 1933-52. Hon. Fellow: St. Edmund Hall, Oxford, 1944; Selwyn Coll., Cambridge, 1957; Emeritus Student, Christ Church, Oxford, 1959. *Publications:* The Place of Reason in Christian Apologetic, 1925 And was made Man, 1928; Essays in Christian Philosophy, 1930; Eugenics, 1933; The Lord's Prayer 1934; Democracy and Dictatorship in the Light of Christian Faith, 1935; The Grace of God in Faith and Philosophy, 1936; This War and the Christian, 1939; The Christian Idea of Liberty, 1941; Towards a Christian Philosophy, 1942; The Doctrine of the Trinity, 1943; Theology in an Age of Science, 1944; The Doctrine of the Church, 1946; Biblical Theology and the Sovereignty of God, 1947; Christian Faith and Practice, 1950; The Doctrine of the Atonement, 1951; For Faith and Freedom 1956; Church and Sacraments in Divided Christendom, 1959; The Bible and the Training of the Clergy, 1963; Sex and Christian Freedom, 1967; Joint Editor with G. R. Driver of Nestorius; The Bazaar of Heracleides, 1925. *Recreations*: reading, walking. *Address:* 34 Newbold Terrace, Leamington Spa, Warwickshire. *T.:* Leamington Spa 23619. [*Died* 15 *July* 1969.

HODGSON, Sir Mark, Kt., *cr.* 1945; O.B.E. 1938; Hon. D.C.L.; J.P., Northumberland; *b.* 19 Nov. 1880; *s.* of Joshua Hodgson, Shipbuilder and Lydia Hodgson; *m.* 1900, Elizabeth Jane, *d.* of Henry and Mary Davis; one *s.* two *d.* *Educ.:* Diamond Hall, Sunderland; Technical College, Sunderland. Apprentice Boilermaker: passed through all offices in The United Society of Boilermakers, etc. Technical Adviser to Admiralty, 1916-1918. Serving on following Government Committees: National Production Advisory Council for Industry, 1945-65; Chairman Northern Regional Board for Industry, 1949-65; Chairman of Appeals Tribunal (National Assistance Board), 1935-56; Mem. of Cttee. reviewing Admiralty Organisation. Dir. North-Eastern Housing Assoc., 1935-; Chm. of Dirs. Co-operative Printing Society Ltd. (Newcastle Branch); Council Member, King's College, Newcastle, Univ. of Durham; Member, Court of Univ. of Newcastle upon Tyne; Panel member of Industrial Disputes Tribunal (Min. of Labour and Nat. Service), 1938-56; one of Managers of Newcastle Savings Bank; Past Member Board of Governors of United Newcastle upon Tyne Hospitals; Trustee, Hospital of Saint Mary the Virgin, 1957-62; Secretary T.U.C. Northern Regional Advisory Committee; Assessor under Armed Forces Act and Reinstatement in Civil Employment Tribunals; Mem. N.E. Area Board, B.T.C., 1955-57. President of Confederation of Shipbuilding and Engineering Unions, 1943-45 and 1947-48; General Sec., The United Society of Boilermakers, and Iron & Steel Shipbuilders, 1936-48, and Member of Exec. Council, 1913-36; Member cttee. on organisation of Nat. Coal Board, 1948. Hon. D.C.L. (Durham Univ.), 1950. *Recreations:* horticulture, bowling. *Address:* Bellfield, 31 Kenton Road, Gosforth, Newcastle upon Tyne 3. [*Died* 17 *Oct.* 1967.

HODGSON, Professor Norman, F.R.C.S.; Emeritus Professor of Surgery, University of Durham (King's College, Newcastle upon Tyne); Honorary Consultant Surgeon, Royal Victoria Infirmary, Newcastle upon Tyne; Hon. Consultant Surgeon, Ingham Infirmary, South Shields; *b.* 19 April 1891; *s.* of late Cuthbert Hodgson, Sunderland; *m.* 1st, 1922, Bessie (*d.* 1943), *d.* of J. E. Mellodew, Oldham; one *s.* two *d.*; 2nd, 1945, Violet Ann, *d.* of Thomas Dixon, Tynemouth. *Educ.:* Argyle House School, Sunderland; University of Durham. M.B., B.S. 1912; M.S. 1921; F.R.C.S. (Edin.), 1921; F.R.C.S. (Eng. *ad eundem*) 1949; Major, R.A.M.C. (T.), 1915-19 (Salonika); Royal Victoria Infirmary, Newcastle upon Tyne; Surgical Registrar, 1914. Asst. Surgeon, 1922, Surgeon, 1929; Professor of Surgery, Univ. of Durham, 1954-56; President: Newcastle and Northern Counties Med. Soc., 1950; North of England Surgical Soc., 1952; North of England Branch B.M.A., 1937; Assoc. Surgeons of Gt. Brit. and Ireland, 1957. *Publications:* various contributions to medical Jls. *Recreations:* angling, bowling. *Address:* 31 Crossway, Newcastle upon Tyne 2. [*Died* 30 *Aug.* 1963.

HODGSON, Patrick Kirkman, C.M.G. 1926; C.V.O. 1927; O.B.E. 1918; *b.* 4 July 1884; *s.* of late R. K. Hodgson and late Lady Norah Hodgson. *Educ.:* Radley College; Trinity College, Oxford (M.A.). Clerk in the House of Lords, 1908-14; served European War, 1914-18, Suffolk Yeomanry; Asst. Military Secretary to G.O.C. 3rd Army, B.E.F. (despatches, O.B.E.); Private Secretary and Comptroller to Governor-General of Canada, 1922-25; Private Secretary to Duke of York, 1926-33. *Address:* 36 Ashley Gardens, S.W.1. *T.:* Tate Gallery 0965. *Club:* Athenæum. [*Died* 13 *April* 1963.

HODGSON, Ralph; poet; *b.* 1871. Polignac Prize, 1914. Lecturer in English Studies, Imperial University, Sendai, Japan, 1924-38. Order of the Rising Sun, 1938; Annual Award of National Institute of Arts and Letters (U.S.A.), 1946; Queen's Gold Medal, 1954. *Publications* include: Last Blackbird; The Bull; A Song of Honour; The Skylark; Poems. *Address:* c/o Macmillan & Co. Ltd., St. Martin's Street, W.C.2. [*Died* 3 *Nov.* 1962.

HODGSON, William Archer, L.D.S., R.C.S. Eng.; Guy's Hosp.; retired; late Hon. Dental Surgeon to Hampstead Gen. and North-West London Hospital; late Staff Demonstrator Guy's Dental Sch.; *b.* June 1887; 2nd *s.* of late Frederick Hodgson and Caroline Elizabeth; *m.* 1st, Gladys Martha (*d.* 1932), *d.* of late George Hyde; one *s.* three *d.*; 2nd, Hildegard, *d.* of August Bredendich; one *s.* *Educ.:* Wilson's Grammar School. *Publication:* Chronic Suppurative Periodontitis (Norman Bennett's Dental Surgery). *Recreations:* golf, motoring. *Address:* Breden House, Torrington Close, Claygate, Surrey. *T.:* Esher 62916. [*Died* 18 *July* 1965.

HODSON, Rt. Rev. Augustine John, M.A.; Bishop of Tewkesbury, 1938-55; Canon of Gloucester since 1934; *b.* 6 May 1879; *s.* of John Humphris and Annie Hodson; unmarried. *Educ.:* Lichfield Grammar School (King Edward VI); Bridgnorth Grammar School; Christ Church, Oxford (Careswell Exhibitioner). 3rd Class Modern History; Law Society Final Exam.; S. Stephens House, Oxford; deacon, 1906; priest, 1908; Curate All Saints', Cheltenham, 1906-11; Assistant Missioner, Gloucester Diocesan Mission, 1911-15; Curate-in-

Charge, Leckhampton, 1915-21; temp. Chaplain to the Forces, 1918-20; Vicar of Chalford, 1921-24; Vicar of Wotton-under-Edge, 1924-34. Archdeacon of Gloucester, 1938-48. *Address:* 86 Kingsholm Road, Gloucester. *T.:* Gloucester 23323.
[*Died* 28 *Jan.* 1961.

HOENIG, Rose, C.B.E. 1930; *m.* 1939, Laszlo Hoenig (marriage dissolved, 1954). Legal Adviser, Nat. Council for Civil Liberties. Was Personal Private Secretary to J. Ramsay MacDonald when he was Prime Minister, 1929-35; continued in that capacity when he was Lord President of the Council, 1935-37; Member of Official Delegation which accompanied Prime Minister to the United States and Canada. Oct. 1929; Member of Home Office Women's Advisory Council of Women's Voluntary Services for Civil Defence; F.Z.S.; Jubilee Medal, 1935; Coronation Medal, 1937. *Publications:* contributions to Women's Newspaper on Women's National Service. *Recreations:* music, reading, theatre, walking. *Address:* 50 South Audley Street W.1. *T.:* Grosvenor 2913. [*Died* 13 *April* 1966.

HOEY, Robert Alexander; Member of the Citizenship Commission, 1949; *b.* Enniskillen, 12 Sept. 1883; *s.* of Alexander Hoey and Jane Beatty; *m.* 1917, Violet Ena, *d.* of Wm. Brett, Dugald, Manitoba. *Educ.:* Wesley and Manitoba Colleges, Winnipeg. Came to Canada, 1909; pioneer worker in farmers' movement; Provincial Director, 1915; Field Secretary, 1919-21; represented Springfield in the House of Commons, 1921-1925; Minister of Education, Province of Manitoba, 1927-36; retired from politics to take part in organization of Western Wheat Pools; Director of Indian Affairs, 1945-48; Executive Director United Nations Appeal for Children (Canadian division), 1949-51; party politics Progressive; religion, United Church of Canada. *Address:* 750 Parkdale Avenue, Ottawa, Ont., Canada.
[*Died* 15 *Nov.* 1965.

HOFSTADTER, Richard; De Witt Clinton Professor of American History, Columbia University, U.S.A., from July 1960; *b.* 6 Aug. 1916; *s.* of Emil A. Hofstadter and Katherine Hill Hofstadter; *m.* 1st, 1936, Felice Swados (*d.* 1945); one *s.*; 2nd, 1947, Beatrice Kevitt; one *d.* *Educ.:* University of Buffalo; Columbia University. B.A. Univ. of Buffalo, 1937; Ph.D. Columbia Univ., 1942. Wm. Bayard Cutting Travelling Fellow, Columbia Univ., 1941-42; Asst. Professor of History, Univ. of Maryland, 1942-46; Assistant Professor of History, Columbia Univ., 1946-50; Assoc. Prof., 1950-52; Professor, 1952-59. When in Britain: Commonwealth Lecturer in American History, University Coll., London, 1955; Fulbright Conference in American Studies, University Coll., Oxford, 1955; Pitt Professor of American History and Institutions, Cambridge, 1958-59; Herbert Spencer Lecture, Oxford Univ., 1963. Mem. Amer. Academy of Arts and Sciences; Mem. Amer. Philosophical Society. Beveridge Memorial Award of Amer. Historical Assoc., 1942; Pulitzer Prize for History, 1956. *Publications:* Social Darwinism in American Thought, 1944, revised edn., 1955; The American Political Tradition, 1948; (with C. D. Hardy) The Development and Scope of Higher Education in the U.S., 1952; The Age of Reform, 1955; (with W. P. Metzger) The Development of Academic Freedom in the U.S., 1955; Great Issues in American History, 1958; The American Republic, 1959; (with Wilson Smith) American Higher Education: A Documentary History, 1961; Anti-intellectualism in American Life, 1963 (Pulitzer Prize, 1964, etc.); The Progressive Movement, 1963; The Paranoid Style in American Politics, 1965; The Progressive Historians: Turner, Beard, Parrington, 1968; The Idea of a Party System, 1969; American Violence: A Documentary History, 1970. *Address:* Department of History, Columbia University, New York 27, N.Y., U.S.A. [*Died* 24 *Oct.* 1970.

HOGAN, Hon. Edmond John; M.L.A., Warrenheip and Grenville, Victoria, 1913-43; *b.* Wallace, near Ballarat, 12 Dec. 1884; *s.* of late Jeremiah Hogan; *m.* 1917, Molly Conroy; three *s.* *Educ.:* Springbank, Victoria. Farming and road making; timber worker; 1903-12, worked in the Western Australian Goldfields timber industry; Chairman of the Firewood Workers Delegates in the timber dispute at Kalgoorlie in 1911; Secretary of the Kurrawang Timber Workers' Union in 1912; President of the Victorian Branch of the Australian Labour Party in 1922; member of the Central Executive of the Australian Labour Party for 16 years; Minister for Railways, Minister for Agriculture, and Minister for Markets in 1924; Leader of the Victorian State Parliamentary Labour Party, 1926-32; Premier, Treasurer, and Minister of Markets, Victoria, 1927-28 and 1929-32; rep. Victoria at 1927 and 1931 Premiers' Conferences; visited Europe, Britain, Ireland, and America, 1932; during his absence from Victoria was excluded from the Labour Party by the Central Executive of the Labour Party, because he refused to obey their dictation to oppose the re-enactment of the Premiers' Plan. Minister of Agriculture and Mines, Victoria, 1935-43; Chairman Soil Conservation Board of Victoria, 1945-50. *Publications:* Profiteering; Unemployment Relief; Co-ordination of Transport; Beneficial Results in Victoria following the adoption of the Premiers' Plan; What's Wrong with Australia, 1953; The Pro Communist Split in the Australian Labor Party, 1955; Facts everyone should know about Communism, and the Dictatorship of the Proletariat, 1956. *Recreations:* in youth—weight putting, hammer throwing, caber tossing. *Address:* 11 Lyndock Avenue, East St. Kilda, Melbourne, Australia. [*Died* 23 *Aug.* 1964.

HOGARTH, William David, O.B.E. 1941; M.A.; Secretary to the Athlone Press of University of London since 1949; *b.* 6 Nov. 1901; *s.* of late D. G. Hogarth, Fellow of Magdalen College, Oxford; *m.* 1936, Grace, *d.* of late J. Weston Allen, Newton Highlands, Mass., U.S.A.; one *s.* one *d.* *Educ.:* Winchester; Balliol College, Oxford. Assistant, Oxford Univ. Press, 1924-35; Asst. Sec., Nat. Council of Social Service, 1935-39; Gen. Sec., London Council of Social Service, 1939-43; Sec., Council of British Societies for Relief Abroad, 1943-47; Clerk of the Court, Univ. of London, 1948-49. *Address:* Flat 55, 59 Weymouth St., W.1. *Club:* United University. [*Died* 29 *Sept.* 1965.

HOGBIN, Henry Cairn, J.P.; *b.* 16 Nov. 1880; *s.* of late Thomas Parker Hogbin of Tilmanston, Kent; *m.* 1st, 1905 (wife *d.* 1940); two *s.* four *d*; 2nd, 1955, Jessie McKenzie Sutherland: *Educ.:* Montague House School; privately. Chairman of The Allied Guano and Chemica Co. Ltd.; M.P. (L.) North Battersea, 1923-24; during the War organised agricultural production, and was Chairman of Home Counties Claims Commission for Ministry of Food. *Recreations:* cricket, lawn tennis, golf (founded the Magistrates Golfing Society, 1938). *Address:* Westwood, Elgin Road, Bournemouth, Hants. *T.:* Westbourne 61474; *Club:* 1900. [*Died* 13 *June* 1966.

HOGG, Sir Anthony H. L.; *see* Lindsay-Hogg.

HOGG, Maj.-Gen. Douglas McArthur, C.B.E. 1940; M.C.; *b.* Cheltenham, Glos., 23 Sept. 1888; *s.* of late Maj.-Gen. G. C. Hogg, C.B.; *m.* 1921, Eithne Geraldine, *d.* of late R. W. W. Littledale, K.C., Dublin; one *d.*

Educ.: Cheltenham College; R.M.A., Woolwich. 2/Lt. R.E., 1906; served European War, 1914-19, in Egypt, Mesopotamia and Siberia (despatches thrice, M.C., 1914-15 Star, British War and Victory Medals); War of 1939-45, in Norway, 1940 (despatches), and U.K. (C.B.E., 1939-45 Star, Defence and War Medals). Staff College, Quetta, 1922-23, p.s.c.; Brevet Lt.-Col., 1931; Brig. i/c Administration, Anti-Aircraft Command, 1938-40; Maj.-Gen. i/c Administration, Northern Command, 1941; retired, 1942; joined the John Lewis Partnership, Ltd., 1942; General Manager, Peter Jones, 1943-45. *Publications:* professional, economic, etc. in Service and other magazines and journals. *Recreations:* ski-ing, gardening. *Address:* Dixgate, Benenden, Cranbrook, Kent. *Clubs:* United Service, Ski Club of Great Britain; Kandahar Ski.

[*Died* 11 *Sept.* 1965.

HOGG, William Edward, C.B.E. 1941; A.R.C.S. M.Inst.C.E.; F.R.S.A.; *b.* 21 Oct. 1880; *m.* 1917, Harriet Gladys Tring; two *s.* two *d.* *Educ.:* City of London School; Royal College of Science, London. Engineering Apprentice, James Simpson and Co. (now Worthington Simpson), Ltd., 1897; Draughtsman, Brush Electrical Engineering Co., Ltd., 1903; Whitworth and Royal Exhibitioner, 1903; Whitworth Scholar, 1906; Assistant Engineering Inspector for Indian State Railways, 1907; Engineering Inspector, Crown Agents for the Colonies, 1910; Assistant Engineer, 1919; Deputy Head, Engineering Inspection Department, 1920; Chief Inspecting Engineer, Crown Agents for the Colonies, 1934-45; retired. *Address:* Silver Poplars, Maddox Park, Little Bookham, Leatherhead.

[*Died* 2 *March* 1968.

HOGG, Lt.-Col. Willoughby Lugard, D.S.O. 1921; J.P. (Hants) 1936; Indian Army, retired; *b.* 29 Dec. 1881; *s.* of late Major-Gen. George Crawford Hogg, C.B.; *m.* 1924, Esmé Genoveva, 4th *d.* of late John Helps Starey, Milton Ernest Hall, Beds. *Educ.:* Cheltenham College; R.M.C. Sandhurst. Received commission, 1900; served World War, 1914-19 (Egypt, Mesopotamia, and Persian Gulf); Waziristan, 1919-21 (wounded, despatches, D.S.O.); retired, 1930. Bronze Medal for gallantry in saving life at sea in Persian Gulf, 1923. *Address:* Wilverley, Sandy Way, Cobham, Surrey. *T.:* Oxshott 2447. [*Died* 20 *Jan.* 1969.

HOGGARTH, Arthur Henry Graham, M.A., F.R.Hist.S.; *b.* 31 Oct. 1882; *s.* of Arthur Hoggarth, F.S.I., and Henrietta Steele. *Educ.:* Kendal Grammar School; Keble College, Oxford. 2nd Class Honours Modern History; Assistant Master Sir Roger Manwood's School, Sandwich, 1906-10; Bootham School, York, 1911; Churcher's College, 1911-27; Headmaster, Churcher's College, 1927-46; has contributed drawings to Punch and other magazines; exhibitor at Royal Academy, R.B.A., etc.; Member of Lake Artists' Society. *Recreations:* gardening, sketching. *Address:* Elph Howe, Staveley, Westmorland. *T.:* Staveley 334

[*Died* 27 *Feb.* 1964.

HOGGATT, William, R.I.; R.B.C.; *b.* Lancaster, 1880; *s.* of James Hoggatt and Margaret Stalker; *m.* 1907, Dazine, *d.* of late William Archer of Ashwells; no *c.* *Educ.:* Lancaster; Julian's Academy, Paris. Started professional career in 1903; went to reside in Isle of Man in 1907; many of his Manx landscapes have passed into public collections, of which the chief official purchases are by National Gallery of Australia, Melbourne and the city of Adelaide; Diploma work in the Royal Institute Galleries; represented by works purchased by Corporation Art Galleries of Liverpool, Manchester, Oldham, Preston, Rochdale, Lancaster, Douglas, Wolverhampton, Lady Leverhulme Gallery, and Brighton; and in the Town Halls of Lancaster, Stretford, and Douglas, I. of Man; designed the T. E. Brown memorial window in Manx National Museum. Works in private collections in America, Canada, S. Africa, Australia, India and China. Two Manx Landscapes presented to King George and Queen Elizabeth by Borough of Douglas, Isle of Man, 1945. Works in other Royal Collections. Pres. Preservation of the Manx Countryside Soc. *Recreations:* chess and walking. *Address:* Darragh, Port Erin, I. of Man. *T.:* Port Erin 3132. *Club:* Ellan Vannin (Douglas, I. of Man).

[*Died* 4 *June* 1961.

HOGSHAW, Brigadier (retired) John Harold, C.B. 1948; M.C.; late Infantry; *b.* 15 January 1896. 2nd Lieutenant Northumberland Fusiliers, 1914; Lieutenant, 1915; Captain, 1920; Major, Royal Northumberland Fusiliers, 1934; Lieut.-Colonel, 1938. Served European War, 1914-18, France and Belgium (wounded, 1914-15 Star, British War and Victory Medals, M.C.); Palestine, 1936-39 (despatches medal and clasp); War of 1939-45 (despatches). *Address:* Hill House, Eversley, Hants.

[*Died* 23 *March* 1968.

HOLBECH, Lt.-Col. Laurence, C.V.O. 1947; D.S.O. 1918; O.B.E. 1936; M.C. 1918; Military Knight of Windsor, 1953; *b.* 1888; *s.* of late Canon Hugh Holbech, Farnborough, Warwickshire, and of Ada Lloyd; *m.* 1943, Betty, *e. d.* of late S. C. Clayton; one *s.* Joined Grenadier Guards, 1916; served European War, 1916-19 (despatches); A.D.C. to Governors of Ceylon and Kenya Colony, 1921-31; Private Secretary and A.D.C. to High Commissioner for U.K. in Union of S. Africa, 1931-35; A.D.C. to Governor of S. Rhodesia, 1935-36; Comptroller to Gov.-Gen. S. Africa, 1936-37; Comptroller to Governor of Southern Rhodesia, 1937-47. O.St.J. *Address:* 18 Lower Ward, Windsor Castle. *Club:* Guards. [*Died* 12 *Oct.* 1963.

HOLBEIN, Arthur Montague, C.B.E. 1949; Director: D. & C. and William Press, Ltd. since 1949; Newton Chambers & Co. Ltd. since 1950; Ransomes & Rapier Ltd., 1958-69; *b.* 9 September 1897; *s.* of Montague A. Holbein and Constance, 2nd *d.* of William Fairley; unmarried. *Educ.:* City and Guilds College; Imperial College, London University. Served European War, 1914-18, Captain R.A., 1915-19 (wounded). B.Sc., 1921; A.C.G.I., 1921; D.I.C., 1922; F.C.G.I., 1947; M.I.C.E., 1950. Asst. Engineer, Perry & Co. (Bow) Ltd., 1923-24; Agent: Charles Brand & Son, 1924-26; Perry & Co., 1926-29; Sir John Wolfe Barry & Partners, 1929-32; Chm., 1944, and Vice-Pres., 1945-56; Pres., 1956-58, of Fedn. of Civil Engineering Contractors; Nat. Advisory Council and Payment-by-Results Cttee., Ministry of Works, 1941-46; Baillieu Cttee. on Management, 1946; various Retail Wages Commissions, 1946; City and Guilds of London Institute: Chm. Technology Cttee., 1945-58, Chm. Educational Policy Cttee., 1959-; Mem. Council, British Inst. of Management, 1947-; Building Research Bd., 1947-51; Advisory Cttee. on Research, Min. of Works, 1946-; member of Cttee. of Inquiry into unofficial stoppages in the London Docks, 1951. Director Demolition and Construction Co. Ltd., 1932-58, retd. Deleg. City and Guild's College, 1944 (Chm. 1955-); Chm. City and Guilds of London Institute, 1962- (Vice-Pres. 1958-); Gov. Imperial Coll., 1953, Hon. Fell. Imperial Coll., 1954. Dep. Chm. Central Advisory Cttee. and of U.K. Cttee. of Commonwealth Technical Training Week, 1960-61. F.R.S.A. 1963. *Recreations:* sailing and swimming. *Clubs:* Union, Royal Thames Yacht, Beefsteak.

[*Died* 8 *Feb.* 1970.

HOLDEN, Arthur; M.A., B.Sc.; Headmaster of Queen Elizabeth's Grammar School, Blackburn, 1919-47; *b.* 8 Nov. 1881; *s.* of Atherton Holden, Lower Darwen, and Alice Duerden; *m.* 1911, Bertha, *d.* of John Holden, Kearsley, Lancs; two *s.* *Educ.:* Queen Elizabeth's Grammar School, Blackburn; Queens' College, Cambridge (Scholar). B.A., 1903, Math. Tripos. (Sen. Opt.), M.A., 1907; B.Sc. London, 1913; Math. Master Friar's School, Bangor, N. Wales, 1903-04; Tutor, St. Mark's Training College, Chelsea, S.W., 1904-1907; Tutor and Asst. Lecturer, University of Sheffield, 1907-19; Examiner in Maths. Joint Matric. Board, Northern Universities, 1913-1919; Bristol Univ. Sch. Cert., 1919-21, and General School Exam. Univ. of London, 1922-38; O.C. Sheffield University, O.T.C., rank of Captain. *Recreations:* rowing, fives, tennis, mountaineering. *Address:* Manor House, Much Wenlock, Shropshire. *T.:* 352.

[*Died* 24 *Dec.* 1964.

HOLDEN, Sir Harry Cassie, 2nd Bt., *cr.* 1909; *s.* of 1st Bt. and Annie, *y. d.* of William Cassie, late of Aberdeen; *b.* 20 Oct. 1877: *S.* father, 1919; *m.* 1905, Edith Ross, (*d.* 1965), *d.* of late John Pryor. *Educ.:* Trinity Hall, Cambridge. (B.A., LL.B.). Barrister-at-law of the Inner Temple, 1901. *Heir:* none. *Address:* 27 Poultry, E.C.2.

[*Died* 1 *Dec.* 1965 (*ext.*).

HOLDEN, Henry Smith, C.B.E. 1958; D.Sc., F.R.S.E., F.L.S.; Retd. as Forensic Science Adviser to Home Office, (1951-58); *b.* Castleton, Lancs, 30 Nov. 1887; *m.* 1917; one *s.* one *d.* *Educ.:* Victoria Univ. Manchester. Late Lectr. in Botany, Univ. Coll., Nottingham; Bacteriologist, Royal Naval Hosp., Plymouth; Professor of Botany, University College, Nottingham; Director of the Forensic Science Laboratory (East Midlands Area) Nottingham; Director Metropolitan Police Laboratory, New Scotland Yard, S.W.1, 1946-51. *Publications:* Original Papers in Annals of Botany, Journal of the Linnean Society and elsewhere; Section of A Text Book of Pharmacy, by A. O. Bentley; articles dealing with the scientific aspects of criminal investigation in Police Journal and elsewhere; the section of Hans Gross, Criminal Investigation, (4th Edn.), dealing with rôle of the expert in criminal case work. *Address:* Spinney Hill, Welcomes Rd., Kenley, Surrey. *T.:* Uplands 9019.

[*Died* 16 *May* 1963.

HOLDEN, Sir Isaac Holden, 5th Bt., *cr.* 1893; J.P. for County Palatine of Lancaster, appointed in 1909 (now on Retired list); *b.* 8 July 1867; *er. s.* of Edward Holden (*d.* 1913; *bro.* of 2nd Bt.), and Maria Elizabeth (*d.* 1932), *d.* of Peter Wood, M.D., Southport, Lancs.; *S.* to baronetcy of 3rd Baron Holden, 1951; *m.* 1st, 1905, Marian (*d.* 1908), *d.* of Peter Keevney; 2nd, 1913, Alice Edna, *d.* of George F. Byrom; two *s.* three *d.* *Educ.:* The Leys School and Christ's Coll., Cambridge. *Heir:* *s.* Edward Holden, M.R.C.S., L.R.C.P., D.A., F.F.A. [*b.* 8 Oct. 1916; *m.*, 1942, Frances Joan, *e. d.* of John Spark, J.P., Stockton on Tees; (two adopted *s.*)]. *Address:* Fisher Field, Portinscale, Keswick, Cumberland. *T.:* 433.

[*Died* 5 *Jan.* 1962.

HOLDER, Sir Frank Wilfred, Kt. 1957; C.M.G. 1955; *b.* 1 July 1897; *s.* of Samuel Sedgrove and Helena Augusta Holder; *m.* 1937, Beryl Acourt Seale; no *c.* *Educ.:* Harrison College, Barbados; Codrington College, Barbados; University of Durham (M.A.). Called to Bar, Middle Temple, 1924. Barbados: admitted to practice at Bar, 1924; M.H.A., 1930-41; Member Exec. Cttee., 1933-41; Mem. Education Bd., 1930-44; Solicitor-Gen., 1936; Judge of Assistant Court of Appeal, 1942; Comr St. John Ambulance Brigade, 1942. Solicitor-General of British Guiana, 1944; Attorney-General, British Guiana, 1946-55; Chief Justice, British Guiana, 1955-59. K.C., British Guiana, 1946; Chancellor of Diocese of Guiana, 1946-59; Registrar of Province of the West Indies, 1949-59; Chm. Georgetown Planning Comrs., 1946; Pres., Georgetown Y.M.C.A., 1946-58; Chm. Youth Advisory Commn., 1957-59. C.St.J. 1965 (O.St.J. 1944). *Address:* c/o Registrar, Supreme Court, Bridgetown, Barbados, West Indies.

[*Died* 15 *June* 1967.

HOLDERNESS, Sir Ernest William Elsmie, 2nd Bt., *cr.* 1920; C.B.E. 1950; *b.* 13 March 1890; *s.* of 1st Bt. and Lucy Shepherd (*d.* 1948), *d.* of G. R. Elsmie, I.C.S. C.S.I.; *S.* father, 1924; *m.* 1926, Emily Carlton (*d.* 1950), *y. d.* of late Frederick McQuade, Sydney, N.S.W.; one *s.* one *d.* *Educ.:* Summerfields, Oxford; Radley Coll. (Exhibition); private tuition; Corpus Christi Coll., Oxford. Late Assistant Secretary, Home Office, Whitehall. *Recreation:* golf (Walton Heath); golf amateur champion 1922 and 1924, and Surrey county amateur champion, 1925. *Heir:* *s.* Richard William Holderness [*b.* 30 Nov. 1927; *m.* 1953, Pamela, *d.* of Eric Chapman, Maseru, Basutoland; two *s.* one *d.*]. *Address:* Verno West, Roeshot Hill, Christchurch, Hants.

[*Died* 23 *Aug.* 1968.

HOLDICH, Brigadier-General Harold Adrian, D.S.O. 1916; Indian army, retired; *b.* 20 March 1874; *e. s.* of late Sir T. H. Holdich, K.C.M.G., K.C.I.E., C.B.; *m.* 1910, Gertrude Elizabeth, *d.* of William Brooke, Honley, Yorks.; one *s.* two *d.* 2nd Lieut. Cameronians, 1894; Lieut. Indian Army, 1897; Major, 1912; Bt. Lieut.-Col. 1915; Col. 1919; served Tirah, 1897-98 (medal, clasp); European War, 1914-18 (despatches, D.S.O.); retired, 1922. D.L. 1948, N. Riding, Yorks. *Address:* Brandsby, York.

[*Died* 11 *March* 1964.

HOLDSWORTH, Sir Frank (Wild), Kt., 1968; M.A. (Cantab.), M.B., M.Chir., F.R.C.S.Eng.; Senior Orthopædic Surgeon Royal Infirmary, Sheffield, since 1937; *b.* 22 Sept. 1904; 2nd *s.* of John William Holdsworth and Elizabeth Denison, Bradford; *m.* 1932, Marjorie Lund, Shipley, Yorks.; one *s.* one *d.* *Educ.:* Bradford Gram. Sch.; Downing Coll., Camb. (Exhibnr.). Sen. Scholar, House Surgeon and House Physician, St. George's Hosp.; Emeritus Professor Associate, Univ. Dept. of Orthopædics, Univ. of Sheffield, and Cons. Orthopædic Surgeon, United Sheffield Hosps. Mem. Council Roy. Coll of Surgeons of England (Vice-Pres., 1969); Fellow, Br. Orthopædic Assoc. (Past Pres.); Corresp. Member, Orthopædic Association; Hon. Fellow: Amer. Acad. of Orthopædic Surgeons; Spanish Orthopædic Assoc. Hon. F.A.C.S. *Publications:* papers and chapters in surgical med. jls. *Address:* 84 Stumperlowe Hall Road, Sheffield 10. *Clubs:* United University; Sheffield (Sheffield).

[*Died* 11 *Dec.* 1969.

HOLFORD, Lt.-Col. Cecil Francis Lovell, D.S.O. 1940; Royal Marines; *b.* 8 July 1900; *s.* of Herbert Frank Stanley Holford and Fanny Elizabeth Lovell; *m.* 1930, Aileen Margery Rees; one *d.*; *m.* 1949, Mrs. Lucy Lillian Berg, Dunrobin, East Beach, Selsey, Sussex. *Educ.:* Westminster. Probationary 2nd Lieut. 1919; Lieut. 1923; Captain, 1930; Major, 1939; 16 years of service spent in H.M. Ships; one year in Fleet Air Arm (Pilot); remainder at Royal Marine Divisions (1939-45 Star, Africa Star, Sicily and Defence and General Service Medals); lately on Staff of Commander-in-Chief, Portsmouth; retired 1948, with rank and pension of a Lt.-Col. *Recreations:*

hockey, tennis, squash, etc. *Address:* Pax, The Bridgeway, Selsey, Sussex. *T.:* Selsey 2080. *Club:* Royal Naval (Portsmouth).
[*Died* 15 *June* 1963.

HOLLAND, Sir Alfred (Herbert), Kt., *cr.* 1947; *b.* 15 July 1878; 2nd *s.* of William and Frances Amelia Holland; *m.* 1st, 1907, Bertha Eleanor Parrock (*d.* 1938); one *s.* three *d.* (one *s. d.* 1942 in air operations); 2nd, 1941, Mary Coysh, *widow* (*d.* 1957); 3rd, 1959, Margaret Evelyn Trehearne, *widow.* *Educ.:* privately. Admitted Solicitor, 1904, Hons. Certificate; Partner in firm of Corbin, Greener and Cook, Solicitors, London, until 1928; Master of Supreme Court of Judicature (Chancery Division), 1928-50; Chief Master (Chancery Division), 1936-50; retired 1950. *Recreations:* gardening, golf. *Address:* Collingwood Grange, Portsmouth Road, Camberley, Surrey. [*Died* 13 *March* 1968.

HOLLAND, Sir Eardley Lancelot, Kt., *cr.* 1947; M.D., B.S. (Lond.), F.R.C.S. (Eng.), F.R.C.P. (Lond.), F.R.C.O.G.; Hon. LL.D. (Birm. and Leeds), Hon. M.D. (Dublin), Hon. F.R.C.S. (Edinburgh), Hon. M.M.S.A.; Hon. Fellow Roy. Soc. Med. and Amer. Gynæcological Soc.; corresp. mem. French and German Gynæcol. Socs.; Hon. Fellow: Royal Medical Society, Budapest; Gynæcological Society of Brazil; Fellow King's College, London; Consulting Gynæcologist London Hospital, City of London Maternity Hospital; *b.* 29 Oct. 1879; *e. s.* of Reverend W. L. Holland, Rector of Puttenham, and Edith, *e. d.* of Canon E. R. Eardley-Wilmot; *m* 1st, 1913, Dorothy (*d.* 1951), *e. d.* of Dr. Henry Colgate Eastbourne; three *d.*; 2nd, 1952, Olivia, *d.* of late L. L. Constable, J.P.. *Educ.:* Merchiston Castle; King's Coll. and Hosp., London (Warneford Entrance and four other schols., Warneford Medal). Univ. of Berlin; first-class honours at M.B. and Gold Medal at M.D. Examination, University of London; Assistant Obstetric Surgeon to King's College Hospital, 1914-16; Gynæcologist to London Hospital and lecturer in Medical School, 1916-46; adviser, Min. of Health, in Obstets., 1937-40 (on evacuation of pregnant women from London, 1939; on nomenclature of diseases); in charge of Obstet. Emergency Service in Herts and E. Anglia, and Temp. Obstet. Consultant to Herts C.C., 1939-43; Mem. Roy. Commn. on Population (Med. and Biol. Cttee.); Mem. Central Midwives' Board, 1934-39; Mem. Council of King Edward's Hosp. Fund (Chm. Radium Cttee.). Examiner in Gynæcol. in most British Universities; in Nat. Univ., Eire; in Univ. of Cairo; in Kitchener Med. Sch., Khartum. Pres. Royal College of Obstetricians and Gynæcologists, 1943-46; Pres. of 12th British Congress of Obstetrics and Gynæcology, London, 1949. Late Editor of Journal of Obstetrics and Gynæcology of British Empire. Temporary Captain Royal Army Medical Corps, and employed as Surgical Specialist in France, 1916-19. *Publications:* Manual of Obstetrics (with Dr. T. W. Eden), ninth ed. 1937; Report to Ministry of Health on the Causation of Still-birth, 1922; Princess Charlotte of Wales, a triple obstetric tragedy, 1951; various papers in Brit. and Amer. Med. Jls. Editor, British Obstetric Practice, 1955. *Address:* The Dower House, West Dean, Chichester. *T.:* Singleton 218. *Club:* Brooks's.
[*Died* 21 *July* 1967.

HOLLAND, Sir (Edward) Milner, K.C.V.O. 1965; Kt. 1959; C.B.E. 1945; Q.C. 1948; B.C.L., M.A.; Barrister-at-Law; Attorney-General of the Duchy of Lancaster and Attorney and Serjeant within the County Palatine since 1951; *b.* 8 September 1902; *s.* of late Sir Edward John Holland, D.L., J.P., and of Lady (Selina) Holland; *m.* 1929, Elinor Doreen Leslie-Jones; two *s.* *Educ.:* Charterhouse; Hertford College, Oxford. Junior and Senior Scholar, Gordon Whitbread prize (classics), Talbot Gold Medallist (classics), Classical Leaving Exhib., Charterhouse; Classical Scholar, Hertford Coll., Oxf., 1921; Hons. degrees in Lit. Hum. and Law, and Hons. B.C.L. Profumo prizeman, Inner Temple; Certificate of Honour, Bar Exam., 1926; Asst. Reader in Equity, Council of Legal Educ., 1931, Reader in Equity, 1935. Served War of 1939-45, 2nd Lt., R.A.S.C., 1939; Dep. Dir. of Personal Services, W.O. (Brig.), 1943. Chairman of General Council of the Bar, 1957-58, 1962-63. Elected Mem. of the Pilgrims, 1957; Mem. of Council on Tribunals, 1958-62; Vice-Chm., Inns of Court Executive Council, 1962; Chm., London Rented Housing Survey, 1963. Hon. Fell., Hertford Coll., Oxford, 1968. Kt. Cdr., Isabel la Catolica, 1968. *Recreation:* golf. *Address:* (home) 8 Grand Ave. Mansions, Hove, Sx. *T.:* Brighton 733434; 7 New Square, Lincoln's Inn, W.C.2. *T.:* Holborn 1266, 1267. *Club:* Brighton and Hove Golf.
[*Died* 2 *Nov.* 1969.

HOLLAND, Sir George (William Frederick), K.B.E. 1961 (C.B.E. 1938); Kt. 1953; M.M. 1917; Chairman Discharged Servicemen's Employment Board of Victoria; Commr. State Savings Bank of Victoria (Chm. of Commissioners, 1959); Member Commonwealth of Australia Government Immigration Planning Council; National President (Hon.) R.S.S. & A.I.L.A., 1950-1961, and Chairman of Trustees, Victorian Branch thereof (various Trusts); *b.* 5 January 1897; *s.* of late William Henry Vernon Holland and late Amy Louisa Holland (*née* Vernon); *m.* 1919, May Hollingworth; one *s.* four *d.* State President (Hon.) (Vic.), R.S.S.A.I.L.A., 1929-51; representative R.S.S.A.I.L.A., British Empire Service League Confs.: Australia, 1934; London, 1937, 1951, 1953, 1955, Australia, 1958, London, 1960; leader of delegs., 1951, 1953, 1955, 1960, Chm. Conf. 1958. Chm. R.S.L. War Veterans Homes Trust of Victoria; Vice-Chairman Sailors, Soldiers' Widows and Widowed Mothers' Trust Fund of Victoria; Chairman Florence Nightingale Trust (Vic.). Trustee Shrine of Remembrance, Victoria; Mem. Council, Lord Mayor's Fund, Vic.; Chm., Patriotic Funds Council of Vic. *Address:* Albert St., E. Malvern, Vic., Aust. *Clubs:* Athenæum (Melbourne), R.A.C. of Vic., C.T.C. of Vic. (also Melb.); R.A.C. of Australia (Sydney). [*Died* 14 *June* 1962.

HOLLAND, Sir Henry Tristram, Kt., *cr.* 1936; C.I.E. 1929; M.B., Ch.B., F.R.C.S.E.; I.A. retired, in charge of Quetta Mission Hospital, Baluchistan; *b.* The College, Durham, 12 Feb. 1875; 2nd *s.* of late Canon W. L. Holland; *m.* 1910, Florence Ethel Tunbridge; two *s.*; one *d.* *Educ.:* Loretto School; Edinburgh University, M.B., Ch.B. 1899; distinction in second and final Professional Examinations; Medallist in Anatomy and Prizeman in Surgery; F.R.C.S.E. 1907; Kaiser-i-Hind Silver Medal, 1910; Gold Medal, 1925, Bar, 1931; Silver Jubilee Medal, 1935; Coronation Medal, 1937; during the War acted as Civil Surgeon at Sibi and Hyderabad, Sindh, and then as Chief Medical Officer, Baluchistan; Lt.-Col. I.A.R.O. 1928. Lawrence of Arabia Memorial Medal, 1949; Ramon Magsaysay Award (given in Manilla), 1960; Award of Sitárá-i-Khidmat (Pakistan), 1961; Hon. Mem. Section of Ophthalmology, of Royal Society of Medicine, 1961-; Hon. Mem. Oxford Ophthalmology Congress, 1961-. *Publications:* Frontier Doctor, 1958; joint author Text-book on Cataract; article in Br. Journ. of Ophthalmology, 1949. *Recreations:* salmon and trout fishing. *Address:* 4A The Fairfield, Farnham, Surrey. *Clubs:* Royal Over-Seas League; Fettesian Lorettonian.
[*Died* 19 *Sept.* 1965.

HOLLAND, Rt. Rev. Herbert St. Barbe, M.A.; *b.* 15 Oct. 1882; *s.* of Canon W. L. Holland of Cornhill-on-Tweed, *g.s.* of Canon H. B. Tristram Durham; *m.* Milly (*d.* 1965), *d.* of J. McIntyre, Newcastle on Tyne; two *s.* one *d.* *Educ.:* Durham Sch.; Univ. Coll. Oxford (Exhibitioner); 2nd Class Classical Moderations; 1st Class Final School of Modern History, B.A. In India, 1905-6; Bishop's Hostel, Farnham, Surrey, 1907; Curate of Jesmond Parish Church, Newcastle on Tyne, 1908-12; Vicar of St. Luke's Newcastle on Tyne, 1912-17; Metropolitan Secretary, Church Missionary Society, 1917-1920; T.C.F. served in France, 1918-19. Home Secretary, Church Missionary Society, 1920-24; Canon and Sub-Dean of Coventry Cathedral; Vicar of St. Michael's, Coventry, R. D. of Coventry, 1924-29; Archdeacon of Warwick, 1929-36; Rector of Hampton Lucy, 1929-36; Examining Chaplain to Bishop of Coventry, 1924-29; Chief Commissary to the Bishop of Victoria, Hong Kong, 1920-36; Bishop of Wellington, N.Z., 1936-46; Dean of Norwich, 1946-52. *Recreations:* gardening, motoring. *Address:* The Cottage of Killiemore, Aros, Isle of Mull, Argyll. *T.:* Aros 43. [*Died* 9 *June* 1966.

HOLLAND, Leonard Duncan, C.B.E. 1920; 2nd *s.* of late Rev. H. W. Holland; *b.* 16 Jan. 1874; *m.* 1st, 1903, Gertrude Mary (*d.* 1926), *e. d.* of late John Conacher, 69 Westbourne Terrace, W.; 2nd, 1927, Florence Kate, *d.* of late John Stabb, Norfolk Square, W. *Educ.:* Kingswood School, Bath; Merton College, Oxford (Classical Exhibitioner). Appointed to Higher Division Clerkship in the War Office, 1896; Confidential Clerk to the Accountant-General, 1899; Resident Clerk, 1900-3; Assistant Principal Clerk, 1903; Principal Clerk, 1918; an Assistant Secretary in War Office, 1920-34. *Address:* 10 Vallance Road, Hove, Sussex. *T.:* Hove 34822. [*Died* 17 *March* 1964.

HOLLAND, Sir Milner; *see* Holland, Sir E. M.

HOLLAND, Sir Robert (Erskine), K.C.I.E., *cr.* 1925 (C.I.E. 1917); C.S.I. 1921; C.V.O. 1922; V.D. 1920; M.A.; I.C.S. (retired) 1st Class of the Order of the Crown of Siam; 1936; Barrister-at-law, 1930; *b.* London, 29 June 1873; 2nd *s.* of late Sir T. Erskine Holland, K.C.; *m.* 1910, Anne, *e. d.* of Francis E. Crow. *Educ.:* Winchester (scholar); Oriel College, Oxford (scholar). Entered I.C.S. 1895; Secretary, Board of Revenue, Madras, 1903; served Foreign Department of Government of India Secretariat, 1904-8; Political Agent and H.B.M.'s Consul at Muscat, 1908-10; Political Agent, Eastern States, Rajputana, 1911-13; Deputy Secretary, Govt. of India, 1914; on political duty with Mesopotamia Field Force, 1915 and 1917 (despatches); Officiating Political Secretary to the Government of India, 1919; A.G.G. in Rajputana, 1920-25; Member of the India Council, 1925-31; Judicial Adviser to Siamese Government, 1933-36. Chm. Canadian Drama Award, 1938-59. Has lectured extensively in U.S. and Canada on India and the Far East. *Publications:* Japan's Flying Start in the Pacific; Post-War Pacific, and many magazine articles. *Address:* 1131 Beach Drive, Victoria, B.C., Canada. *Club:* Athenæum. [*Died* 30 *Sept.* 1965.

HOLLAND, Robert Wolstenholme, O.B.E.; Governor of Pitman's College; Barrister-at-law; of the Middle Temple, 1908; *b.* Romiley, Cheshire, 21 March 1880; 2nd *s.* of George Holland, J.P., Blackpool; *m.* 1st, 1903, Annie Glover, *d* of J. Code, Manchester; 2nd, 1911, Bertha (*d.* 1957), *d.* of F. Mills, Manchester; three *s.* one *d.*; 3rd, 1958, Helen Josephine Bate, Willingdon, Sussex. *Educ.:* Victoria Univ. Manchester. B.Sc. First Class; M.Sc. in Chemistry, 1902; LL.B. First Class Honours, 1905; Certificate of Honour, Bar Final, 1907; called to Bar, Middle Temple, 1908; M.A. in Economics; Dauntesey Legal Scholar of the Manchester University; Doctor of Laws of the Manchester University, 1914; Headmaster of St. Margaret's Junior Boys' School, Whalley Range, Manchester, 1905-7; Lecturer in Legal and Commercial subjects to the Manchester Education Authority, 1907-13; Director of Studies Pitman's Schools, 1913-15; Principal, Technical College, Newport, Mon., 1915-19; Hon. Military Service (Civil Liabilities) Commissioner for Monmouth, 1916-18; Vice-Chairman Newport (Mon.) War Pensions Committee, 1919; Chairman Employment Sub-Committee of the Joint Disablement (War Pensions) Committee, South Wales and Monmouthshire, 1919; Member of City of London Employment Cttee., 1920-35; Former Chm. Bd. of Management Royal Masonic Institute for Boys; Vice-Chm. Board of Governors, Royal Normal College for the Blind; Past Chm. Council, Royal Society of Arts. *Publications:* The Law Relating to the Child, 1915; Articles on Debentures, Pitman's Secretaries Dictionary; The Law of Contract, 1920; Business Statistics, 1921; Partnership Law and Accounts, 1920, Adversis Major, The Story of the British Red Cross Educational Books scheme in Prisoner of War Camps, 1939-45, etc. *Address:* 1 Coventry Court, Pevensey Garden, Worthing, Sussex. *Club:* Authors'. [*Died* 22 *May* 1962.

HOLLAND, Rt. Hon. Sir Sidney George, P.C. 1950; G.C.B. 1957; C.H. 1951; M.P. (Nat.) Fendalton, N.Z.; *b.* Greendale, Canterbury, N.Z., 18 Oct. 1893; *s.* of Henry Holland, formerly Mayor of Christchurch, and M.P. for Christchurch North; *m.* 1920, Florence Beatrice Drayton; two *s.* two *d.* *Educ.:* West Christchurch District High School. Began work in hardware firm in Christchurch, and in 1912 entered his father's engineering business. Enlisted for overseas service in 1915 and served with N.Z.E.F. in France, where held commn. as Artillery Officer; contracted severe illness at Messines. After war entered business with his brother and formed Midland Engineering Co., Christchurch. For 3 years Chairman Christchurch Citizen's Assoc., Vice-Pres. Canterbury Chamber of Commerce, 3 years Pres. Canterbury Employers' Assoc. and Pres. Christchurch Businessmen's Club. Entered Parl. as Nat. Party Member for Christchurch North, 1935; re-elected 1938 and 1943; in 1946, name of electorate was changed to Fendalton, for which dist. he was re-elected, 1946, 1949, 1951 and 1954; Leader of Opposition, 1940-49; Minister of Finance, 1949-54; Minister of Police, 1954-56; Minister without Portfolio, New Zealand, Sept.-Dec. 1957; Prime Minister of New Zealand, and in charge of Legislative Department, Dec. 1949-Sept. 1957. Selector and Manager of New Zealand Hockey Team which toured Australia, 1932; Life Member Hockey Assoc. Owns Greta Paddock Farm in North Canterbury, where he breeds Romney sheep and Black Polled Angus Cattle. *Recreations:* golf, gardening, fishing. *Address:* 11 Stowe Hill, Wellington, N.Z. *Clubs:* Canterbury (Christchurch); Wellington, Wellesley (Wellington). [*Died* 4 *Aug.* 1961.

HOLLAND, Vyvyan Beresford, O.B.E. 1918; F.R.S.L.; Writer; *b.* 3 Nov. 1886; 2nd *s.* of Oscar Wilde; *m.* 1943, Thelma, *er. d.* of Frank Besant, Melbourne, Australia; one *s.* *Educ.:* Neuenheim; Monaco; Stonyhurst College; Trinity Hall, Cambridge (B.A.). Called to the Bar and practised as a barrister until outbreak of war, 1914, when he joined the Army, first in Interpreters Corps, later in R.F.A., apptd. to Staff of 3rd Corps, 1916 (despatches four times, O.B.E.). Spent the period between the wars in travelling and literary activities. War of

1939-45, foreign service of B.B.C. and Sergeant in the Home Guard. Since the War has worked at intervals as historical adviser on various films at Pinewood and Shepperton. *Publications:* The Mediaeval Courts of Love, 1927; On Bores, 1935; Son of Oscar Wilde, 1954; Hand-Coloured Fashion Plates, 1955; Oscar Wilde: a Pictorial Biography, 1960; Goya: a Pictorial Biography, 1961; Time Remembered, after Père Lachaise, 1966; Drink and be Merry, 1967; An Explosion of Limericks, 1967; Writing a Book and Similar Papers, 1968. Many translations into English from French, Spanish, Italian and German from 1923 onwards; many short stories. Numerous contributions to periodicals on a large number of subjects, mostly Gastronomy and Wine. *Recreations:* conversation, philology, chess and golf. *Address:* 5c The Boltons, S.W.10. *T.:* Fremantle 2913. *Clubs:* Beefsteak, Saintsbury, Omar Khayyam, Odd Volumes, Chelsea Arts (hon.). [*Died* 10 *Oct.* 1967.

HOLLAND-HIBBERT, Hon. Wilfrid; Estates Bursar, Merton College, Oxford, since 1932; Member: Bullingdon R.D.C., 1932 (Chairman 1938-43); Council of Land Agents' Society (President 1946-47); General Claims Tribunal, 1948; Governor, Royal Agricultural College, Cirencester; *b.* 4 Jan. 1893; *yr. s.* of 3rd Viscount Knutsford, and Ellen, *d.* of Sir Wilfrid Lawson, 2nd Bt.; *m*, Audrey, *d.* of Mark Fenwick, Abbotswood, Stow-on-the-Wold, Glos; one *s.* two *d.* *Educ.:* Eton; Trinity College, Cambridge. Land Agent for several small properties in Berkshire and Sussex. 1920-23; served in Herts Yeomanry, 1912-18; in Egypt and on Viceroy of India's staff as A.D.C., 1916-18; 399th Battery R.A. (T.A.) Oxfordshire Yeomanry, 1926-32; retired with rank of Captain; Land Agent, New College, Oxford, 1923-57; Land Agent, Oxford Preservation Trust, 1926-54. J.P. 1946-57. *Address:* Grove House, Beckley, Oxford. T.A.; Beckley, Oxford. *T.:* Stanton St. John 202. *Club:* Boodle's. [*Died* 18 *Feb.* 1961.

HOLLELY, Sir Arthur Newton, Kt. 1938; J.P.; *m.* 1931, Florence, *d.* of Capt. Charles Rippon; one *s.* (decd.). Past President of Drapers' Chamber of Trade of Great Britain and Ireland. *Address:* Yalta, Hartley, Plymouth. *T.:* Plymouth 65504. *Club:* Royal Automobile. [*Died* 17 *April* 1961.

HOLLIDAY, Major Lionel Brook, O.B.E. 1918; T.D. 1917; J.P. West Riding, Yorks; Master York and Ainsty (North) Hounds since 1937; *b.* 1880; *s.* of late Thomas Holliday, J.P., Lunnclough Hall, Huddersfield, Yorks. *Educ.:* Uppingham; Bonn Univ. Joined 5th Bn. Duke of Wellington's Regt., 1898, and served European War, 1914-1919 (despatches); Master Derwent Hounds, 1918-22; Badsworth Hounds, 1922-31; Grove Hounds, 1932-37; Fellow of the Chemical Society; Governing Director, L. B. Holliday & Co., Ltd. President Yorkshire Agricultural Society, 1931; High Sheriff of Yorkshire, 1943. *Address:* Copgrove Hall, Burton Leonard, Yorks; Kirkburton, Yorks; Sunnyside, Park Lane, Newmarket; Cleaboy Stud, Mullingar, Westmeath, Ireland. *Clubs:* Royal Societies; Jockey (Newmarket); Yorkshire (York). [*Died* 17 *Dec.* 1965.

HOLLINGSWORTH, John Ernest; Conductor at Royal Opera House for Covent Garden Opera and Sadler's Wells Ballet Companies since 1950; Musical Director for Films; Principal Conductor, Tunbridge Wells Symphony Orchestra, since 1942; *b.* 20 March 1916; *s.* of Alfred Ernest and Edith Elizabeth Hollingsworth; unmarried. *Educ.:* Bradfield Coll., Berks.; Guildhall Sch. of Music, London. First conducted London Symphony Orchestra, 1937; Associate conductor R.A.F. Symphony Orchestra, 1940-45, travelling in England, America, 1944-45, Potsdam Conf., 1945. Appearances as guest conductor with Liverpool Philharmonic, City of Birmingham and B.B.C. Symphony Orchestras, 1945 and 1946; Danish State Radio Orchestra in Copenhagen, 1947. Associate Musical Director to J. Arthur Rank Organisation, 1946-49; Associate Conductor Henry Wood Promenade Concerts, 1949-1959; Conductor, Sadler's Wells Ballet Company, 1950-54. Musical Director: Films Division, Central Office of Information, 1947-52; Cinemascope film of Royal Tour, Flight of the White Heron, 1954; conducted at Royal Command Film Performances, 1949 and 1952; First conducted at Royal Opera House, Covent Garden, 1948. Sadler's Wells Ballet: Conductor, U.S. and Canada, 1950-51, Lisbon, Oporto and Berlin, 1952, U.S. and Canada, 1953-54; Holland Festival and Edinburgh Festival; also extended Continental Tocr. including La Scala, Milan, 1954; Guest conductor Radio Eireann Symphony Orchestra, Sadler's Wells Ballet Co. (Edin. Festival), and Royal Choral Society, 1956. Conductor, University of London Orchestra, 1955-57; Guest Conductor, Royal Ballet, 1961. Advisory Cttee. World Record Club, 1961-. *Publications:* contrib. various musical jls, *Recreations:* sailing and ski-ing. *Address:* 239 Latymer Court, W.6. *Club:* Savile. [*Died* 29 *Dec.* 1963.

HOLLINGWORTH, Professor Sydney Ewart, M.A. (Cantab.); D.Sc. (Lond.); F.G.S.; Yates-Goldsmid Professor of Geology at University College, London University, since 1946; *b.* 7 Nov. 1899; *m.* Anne Mary Lamb; two *s.* *Educ.;* Northampton School; Clare College, Cambridge. 1st Cl. Hons. Nat. Sci. Trip. Pt. 1, 1920; 1st Cl. Hons. Nat. Sci. Trip. Pt. II, 1921; Harkness University Scholar (Geology), 1921; Geologist, H.M. Geological Survey, 1921. *Publications:* Geological Survey Maps and Memoirs; scientific papers on glacial geology, geomorphology, gypsum, ironstone, etc. in various journals; Current Research in Norway and Chile. *Address:* University College, Gower St., W.C.1. *T.:* Uplands 0752. *Club:* Athenæum. [*Died* 23 *June* 1966.

HOLLINS, Arthur, C.B.E. 1949; J.P.; formerly Vice-Chairman, Stoke-on-Trent Hospital Management Committee; General Secretary National Society of Pottery Workers, 1910-47 (retd.); *b.* 19 Sept. 1876; *s.* of William and Caroline Hollins, Burslem, Staffs; *m.* 1900, Ann, *d.* of George and Elizabeth Sturgess, Wolstanton, Staffs; one *s.* one *d.* *Educ.:* St. Paul's Church School, Burslem; Wedgwood Institute, Burslem. First Class Certificates, Honours Grade, Pottery and Advanced Chemistry, of City and Guilds Examination; M.P. (Lab.) Hanley, 1928-31 and 1935-45; Past Member of Postmaster General's Advisory Committee; Ex-Chairman, National Council of the Pottery Industry; Member of the Board of Trade Advisory Council, 1924-27; Member of Home Office Departmental Committee on Compensation for Silicosis in the Pottery Industry, 1927-28; Member of Board of Trade Committees under the Safeguarding of Industries Act; Member of Home Office Departmental Cttee. on the Employment of Prisoners. Lord Mayor, City of Stoke upon Trent, 1933-34. Freeman of the City of Stoke-on-Trent. Fellow of Royal Society of Arts; Trustee of the Silicosis and Asbestosis Medical Expenses Fund. *Publication:* Improperly Pugged Clay Transactions of the Ceramic Society of Great Britain, 1924. *Recreations:* bowls, reading. *Address:* Eastbourne Villa, 2 Eastbourne Road, Hanley, Stoke-on-Trent. [*Died April* 1962.

HOLLINS, Frank, C.B. 1960; General Manager, Covent Garden Market Authority, since 1961; *b.* 19 June 1907; unmarried.

Educ.: Winchester College; Trinity College, Cambridge. Teaching, 1931-36; Asst. Secretary, Devon County Education Committee, 1936-39; H.M. Inspector of Schools (H.M.I.), June 1939; transferred to Ministry of Food on loan, November 1939; on loan to Control Commission for Germany, as Director-General of Food and Agriculture, 1944-46; Under-Secretary, 1950; Min. of Agriculture, Fisheries and Food, 1955-61. *Recreations:* music, folk dancing, travel, real tennis, cricket, golf, sailing. *Address:* 38A Abercorn Place, N.W.8. *T.:* Cunningham 2813. *Club:* Travellers'.
[*Died* 28 *Feb* 1967.

HOLLINS, Sir Frank Hubert, 3rd Bt., *cr.* 1907; *b.* 31 Oct. 1877; 2nd *s.* of Sir Frank Hollins, 1st Bt., and Dora Emily Susan, O.B.E., 3rd *d.* of Caleb Cox; *S.* brother, 1938. *Educ.:* Horris Hill; Eton College; Magdalen College, Oxford. Director (retired) Horrockses Crewdson & Co., Ltd., Preston, Manchester, London. *Recreations:* cricket, football. *Heir:* none. *Address:* c/o Barclays Bank Ltd., 1 Pall Mall East, S.W.1. *Club:* East India and Sports. [*Died* 31 *Jan.* 1963 (*ext.*).

HOLLINS, Samuel Thomas, C.I.E. 1931; *b.* 6 Oct. 1881; 2nd *s.* of late Samuel Hollins, Dingle, Co. Kerry and Blackrock, Co. Cork; *m.* Ethel, *y. d.* of Thomas Sheffield, Montenotte, Cork; three *d.* *Educ.:* Christian College and Queen's University, Cork. Entered Indian Police, 1902; served as Assistant Superintendent Police in various districts; Assistant to D.I.G., C.I.D., 1908; Assistant to the Inspector-General in 1911; Inspector-General of Police, Tonk State, 1915-18; King's Police Medal, 1918; Superintendent of Police, Agra, 1918-20; Judicial Member and Vice-President, Tonk State Council, 1921-25; Superintendent Police, Allahabad, 1926; Deputy Inspector-General, 1928; Inspector-General of Police, U.P., 1931-35; apptd. Dir.-Gen., Police and Jail, Hyderabad, 1935; Police Adviser to group of Indian States, 1942-45. *Publications:* The Criminal Tribes of the United Provinces; The Gaurakshani Movement in the United Provinces; Tonk State Police Regulations; Tonk State Criminal and Civil Court Manual; No Ten Commandments; Life in the Indian Police. *Recreations:* tennis, golf. *Address:* Flat 1, Pier View, Stanley Mount, Ramsey, Isle of Man.
[*Died* 17 *Aug.* 1965.

HOLLIS, Sir (Alfred) Claud, G.C.M.G., *cr.* 1934 (K.C.M.G., *cr.* 1927; C.M.G. 1911); C.B.E. 1919; *b.* 12 May 1874; 2nd *s.* of late George Hollis of the Inner Temple and West Worthing, and Susannah, *d.* of Francis Smith, of Highgate and Widdington, Essex; *m.* 1910, Enid Mabel (*d.* 1939), *y. d.* of late Valentine I. R. Longman, C.C., of Highgate; (one *s.* killed in action 1941) two *d.* *Educ.:* privately; Switzerland and Germany. Assistant Collector, East Africa Protectorate, 1897; Collector, 1900; Acting British Vice-Consul for German East Africa, 1900-1; Sec. to the Administration, East Africa Protectorate, 1902; Sec. for Native Affairs and Member of Legislative Council, 1907-12; Colonial Secretary, Sierra Leone, 1912-16; Secretary to the Provisional Administration, German East Africa, 1916-19; Chief Secretary, Tanganyika Territory, 1919-24; British Resident in Zanzibar, 1924-30; Governor and C.-in-C. of Trinidad and Tobago, 1930-36; Representative of Colonies on Imperial Communications Advisory Cttee. (later the Commonwealth Communications Council), 1936-47; Actg. Chm., 1945-46; attended Bermuda Telecommunications Conf., 1945; Chairman Civil Defence Joint Cttee. for N.W. Essex, 1938-45; a Past Master of Leathersellers' Co.; Dir., Trinidad Petroleum Development Co., 1944-51; J.P. Essex; served Uganda Mutiny, 1897-98; Jubaland Expedition (African General Service Medal, Jubaland clasp); Nandi Expedition, 1905-6 (clasp); 1st class Order of the Brilliant Star, Zanzibar, 1929; King George V. Jubilee Medal. *Publications:* The Masai, their Language and Folklore, 1905; The Nandi, their Language and Folklore, 1909; A Brief History of Trinidad under the Spanish Crown, 1941; various articles and pamphlets. *Address:* Widdington, nr. Saffron Walden, Essex. *Clubs:* Athenæum, East India and Sports.
[*Died* 22 *Nov.* 1961.

HOLLIS, Sir Leslie Chasemore, K.C.B., *cr.* 1951 (C.B. 1943); K.B.E., *cr.* 1946 (C.B.E. 1942); company director and author; *b.* 9 February 1897; *s.* of late Canon C. J. Hollis, M.A.; *m.* 1922, Rose May Fraser; no *c.* *Educ.:* St. Lawrence College, Ramsgate. Joined R.M.L.I. as a Probationary 2nd Lt. 1914; Grand Fleet and Harwich Force, 1915-19; Capt. R.M. 1922; Naval Staff Course, 1927-28; Staff of C.-in-C. Africa Station, 1929-32; Admiralty (Plans Division), 1932-36; Major, 1935; Assistant Secretary, Committee of Imperial Defence, 1936; Bt. Lt.-Col. 1937; Acting Col. Commandant (temp. Brig.), 1941; Acting Maj.-Gen. 1943; Colonel, 1946; Senior Asst. Sec. in office of War Cabinet, 1939-1946; Major-General, Acting Lieut.-General, 1947; Lieut.-General, 1949; General, 1951; Chief Staff Officer to Minister of Defence, also Deputy Secretary (Military) of the Cabinet, 1947-49; retd. 1952; Commandant General, Royal Marines, 1949-52. Mem. Inst. of Directors. Commander Legion of Merit (U.S.A.). *Publications:* One Marine's Tale, 1956; War at the Top, 1959; The Captain General, 1961. *Address:* Birchlands, Haywards Heath, Sx. *T.:* 955. *Club:* East India and Sports. [*Died* 9 *Aug.* 1963.

HOLLOWAY, Baliol; actor; *b.* Brentwood, Essex, 28 Feb. 1883. *Educ.:* Denstone College. Toured for some years in various classical and modern rep. companies, joining the Benson Company, 1907; Liverpool Rep. Theatre, 1912; Granville Barker Rep. Co., St. James's Theatre, 1913, and Savoy Theatre, 1914. Subsequent London engagements under Arthur Bourchier, Matheson Lang, Julia Neilson and Fred Terry. Leading parts in several Stratford-on-Avon Festivals. Leading man at Old Vic, 1925-28. Own production of Richard III, playing Richard, New Theatre, 1930. Other London röles include: Long John Silver, Undershaft (Major Barbara), Hook and Darling (Peter Pan), Cassius (all star Julius Caesar), His Majesty's, 1932; replaced Gerald du Maurier, in Diplomacy, Prince's; Dick Phenyl (Sweet Lavender), 1933. Acted many parts with late Phoenix Society. Played in Oedipus Rex, Pilgrims Progress, Fairy Queen, Opera House Covent Gdn. Produced and acted in Sydney Carroll's revivals of Old Comedies and Restoration plays at Ambassadors Theatre. *Address:* 36 Thayer Street, Manchester Sq., W.1. *T.:* Welbeck 5338. [*Died* 15 *April* 1967.

HOLLOWAY, Rt. Hon. Edward James, P.C. 1950; *b.* Hobart, Tasmania, 1880; *m.*; one *s.* one *d.* *Educ.:* private boys' school; Workers Education Assoc. Labour Colleges. Member of the Joint Committee on Public Works, 1929-31; Assistant Minister for Industry, Council of Scientific and Industrial Research Development, and Assistant to the Treasury, 1931; Member of the Australian Delegation to the International Labour Organization of the League of Nations, 1923; Past Pres. Victorian and Federal Labour Parties; Member House of Representatives (Labour Party), Australia, for Melbourne Ports, Victoria, 1931-51 (M.H.R. for Flinders, 1929-31); Minister for Health and Social Services in the First Curtin Government; Minister for Labour and National Service in the Second Curtin Government; Minister for

Labour and Nat. Service in Forde Govt. and First and Second Chifley Govts. Actg. Prime Minister during Mr. Chifley's absence abroad; retired, 1951. *Address:* Federal Members' Rooms, Melbourne, Vic. [*Died* 3 *Dec*. 1967.

HOLLOWAY, Sir Ernest, K.C.B., *cr.* 1944 (C.B. 1941); O.B.E. 1919; M.Inst. C.E.; *b.* 24 April 1887; 2nd *s.* of late E. Holloway; *m.* 1911, Doris Irene, *s. d.* of late George Wood, Warley, Birmingham; two *d.* *Educ.:* King Edward VI. School, Birmingham; Birmingham Technical College. Local Govt. Services, 1908-15; European War, 1915-19, served in R.F.C. and R.A.F., demobilised rank of Major (O.B.E.); entered Civil Service, 1919; Air Ministry works Directorate, 1919-47; Director-General of Works, Air Ministry, 1940-47; retired, 1947. *Address:* 10 Lichfield Court, Pevensey Garden, Worthing, Sx. *T.:* Worthing 30752. [*Died* 27 *Feb*. 1961.

HOLLOWAY, Leonard Cloudesley; *b.* 20 Aug. 1885; *s.* of Frederick Henry Cloudesley and Charlotte Holloway; *m.* 1911, Clare Alix Whitworth McGowan; one *s.* two *d.* *Educ.:* Grove House School, Highgate. Admitted a Solicitor, 1909; 2nd Lieut. and Lieut. Worcestershire Regt., 1917; Capt., 1918; Adjutant, 15th (T.W.) Batt. Worcestershire Regiment, 1917-18. A Master of the Supreme Court (Chancery Division), 1935-57; retired 1957. *Address:* Staceys, Ledborough Lane, Beaconsfield, Bucks. *T.:* Beaconsfield 75. [*Died* 5 *April* 1966.

HOLMAN, Professor Bernard Welpton, O.B.E.; Chevalier of Order of the Crown of Belgium; Order of Mareef (2nd cl.), Egypt; Matthey Prize for Original Research; Sir Robert Hadfield Travelling Scholarship; Gold Medal and Diploma of French National Bureau of Scientific Research, 1938; Associate R.S.M., M.Inst.M.M., M.Inst.Chem.E., Hon. M.Inst.Fire E.; *s.* of late H. Holman, Topsham, Devon. *Educ.:* Leys School, Cambridge; Birkbeck College and Royal School of Mines. Mining S. Wales, 1909; S. Africa, 1910-13 and 1925-26; Reader in Mining, Univ. of Lond., 1933-44; Professor of Mining and Metallurgy, Univ. of Cairo, 1944-52; Professor of Mining, Univ. of Panjab, Pakistan. Visited 17 countries on technical work. Royal Engineers, 1914-1919 (France 3 years, despatches, Capt.); Anglo-French Ambulance Corps, 1939-40. Vice-Pres. Parliamentary and Scientific Committee; Member of Brentford and Chiswick Borough Council 1936-44; Member War Cabinet, Engineering Advisory Committee, 1941-44. President Mining and Petroleum Assoc. of Egypt, 1947-49. *Publications:* original research on magnetic separation, heat disintegration of rocks, dielectric properties of minerals, etc. *Recreations:* Committees. *Address:* 104 Pall Mall, S.W.1. *Clubs:* Reform; Punjab (Lahore). [*Died* 16 *Feb*. 1964.

HOLMES, Arthur, F.R.S. 1942; D.Sc., A.R.C.S., F.R.S.E., M.R.I.A., F.G.S.; Regius Professor of Geology, Univ. of Edinburgh, 1943-Sept. 1956, Professor Emeritus since 1956; *b.* Hebburn-on-Tyne, 14 Jan. 1890; *m.* 1st, 1914, Margaret Howe (*d.* 1938); one *s.*; 2nd, 1939, Doris Livesey Reynolds. *Educ.:* Imperial College of Science and Technology, London. Explorer in Mozambique, 1911-12; Demonstrator in Geology, Imperial College, 1912-21; Chief Geologist Yomah Oil Co. Ltd., Burma, 1921-24; Prof. of Geology, Durham Colleges, University of Durham, 1924-43; Exchange-Professor, Basel Univ., 1930; Lowell Lecturer, Harvard Univ., 1932; Correspondent of Geological Society of America, 1936; Corresp. Member, 1946, Hon. Mem. 1956, Geological Soc. of Belgium; Hon. Member Belgian Soc. of Geology, 1947; Foreign Member Royal Swedish Academy of Sciences, 1947; Foreign Member Royal Academy of Sciences of Amsterdam, 1947; For. Member Geol. Soc. Stockholm, 1952; For. Member Acad. of Sciences, Institute of France, 1955; Wollaston Medal, Geological Society London, 1956; Penrose Medal, Geol. Society Amer., 1956; Fellow of Imperial College, 1959; Hon. LL.D. (Edinburgh), 1960. Vetlesen Prize and Medal, 1964; Makdougall Brisbane Medal, Roy. Soc. Edinburgh, 1965. *Publications:* The Age of the Earth, 1913, 1927, 1931, and 1937; The Nomenclature of Petrology, 1920 and 1928; Petrographic Methods and Calculations, 1921 and 1930; Petrology of the Bufumbira Volcanoes, 1937; Principles of Physical Geology, 1944 (re-written edition, 1965); 130 scientific papers. *Recreation:* music. *Address:* 6 Albany, 20 St. John's Ave., Putney, S.W.15. [*Died* 20 *Sept*. 1965.

HOLMES, Commander Gerard (Robert Addison), C.M.G. 1919; O.B.E. 1918; R.N.V.R.(retired); *s.* of late Sir G. C. V. Holmes, K.C.B., K.C.V.O.; *b.* 31 Aug. 1881; unmarried. *Educ.:* Wellington College; Glasgow University D.Sc. Apprenticed to Fairfield Shipbuilding and Engineering Co., Govan, 1900-06; Naval Architect, 1906; Lecturer in Naval Architecture and Marine Engineering, Glasgow University, 1908; Assistant Naval Architect to Cunard Co. 1912; formed and commanded Sea Scouts with 2nd Baron Inverclyde as Pres., 1908; on outbreak of War, 1914, commission as Lieut. R.N.V.R.; Lieut.-Commander, 1915; Commander, 1916; transferred to R.A.F. (Lieut.-Colonel), 1918; served afloat at Raid on Cuxhaven, Christmas 1914, and on Belgian Coast, 1915 (1914-15 medal); Captain Supt. of the National Nautical School, Portishead, 1924-27; Headmaster, Ship School, Redhill, 1929-35. Inaugurated the Peebles Highland Boys, 1949-. *Publications:* The Idiot Teacher; several short literary articles in public press and elsewhere. *Recreations:* exploration, sketching. *Address:* Kerfield Cottage, Peebles, Scotland. *T.:* Peebles 2264. *Club:* R.N.V.R. [*Died* 1 *Dec*. 1963.

HOLMES, Sir Gordon (Morgan), Kt., *cr.* 1951; C.M.G. 1917; C.B.E. 1919; F.R.S. 1933; B.A., M.D., D.Sc. Hon. (Dubl.), D.C.L. Hon. (Durham), LL.D. Hon. (Edin.), F.R.C.P.; Consulting Physician to National Hospital for Nervous Diseases, to Charing Cross Hospital, and to the Royal London Ophthalmic Hospital; late Consulting Neurologist, B.E.F.; *e. s.* of late Gordon Holmes, Dellin House, Castlebellingham, Ireland; *m.* 1918, Rosalie (*d.* 1963), L.R.C.P., M.R.C.S., *d.* of late Brigade Surgeon W. Jobson, A.M.D.; three *d.* *Educ.:* Dublin University; Berlin; Frankfurt-am-Main. Medical Scholar and Medical Travelling Prizeman, Trinity College, Dublin; Assistant, Neurological Department of the Senckenberg Institute, Frankfurt-am-Main; Resident Medical Officer, National Hospital for the Paralysed and Epileptic; Director Nervous Diseases Research Fund; Assistant Physician and Neurologist to the Seaman's Hospital, Greenwich; served European War, 1914-18 (C.M.G.); President, 2nd International Neurological Congress, 1935. *Publications:* various articles on the Anatomy, Physiology, and Pathology of the Nervous System, and on nervous diseases. *Address:* Sirmoor, Shortheath Road, Farnham, Surrey. [*Died* 29 *Dec*. 1965.

HOLMES, Professor James Macdonald, B.Sc., Ph.D.; F.R.S.G.S., F.R.G.S.; Professor of Geography, University of Sydney; *b.* Scotland, 26 Feb. 1896; *m.* 1929; two *s.* *Educ.:* Glasgow University. *Publications:* Geographic Basis of Government; Soil Erosion in Australia and New Zealand; The Murray Valley; articles in British and Australian scientific journals. *Recreations:* surfing, bush walking, tennis, motoring. *Address:* University of Sydney, N.S.W. [*Died* 28 *Aug*. 1966.

HOLMES, Rev. John Haynes; Minister, The Community Church, New York City, U.S.A., 1907-49, retired as Minister Emeritus; *b.* 29 Nov. 1879; *s.* of Marcus Morton Holmes and Alice F. Haynes; *m.* 1904, Madeleine H. Baker; one *s.* one *d.* *Educ.:* Harvard College; Harvard Divinity School. A.B. (summa cum laude) Harvard Coll., 1902; S.T.B. Harvard Divinity School, 1904; Minister. Third Religious Soc., Dorchester, Mass., 1904-07; Chairman, General Unitarian Conf., 1915-17; Pres. Free Religious Assoc., 1914-19; Vice-Pres. Nat. Assoc. for Advancement of Colored People since 1909; Director, American Civil Liberties Union since 1917 (Chm. Board of Directors, 1939-49); Chm. City Affairs Cttee. of New York, 1929-38, active in campaign for ousting of Mayor Walker; on special mission to Palestine for Jews, 1929; Gottheil Medal for service to Jews, 1933; annual Ingersoll Lecture on Immortality at Harvard Univ., 1946; left Unitarianism and became Indep., 1919; mem. Phi Beta Kappa; D.D., Jewish Inst. of Religion, 1930; St. Lawrence Univ., 1931; Meadville Theol. Sch., 1935; Litt.D., Univ. of Benares (Ind.), 1947; Hum. D., Rollins Coll., 1951. *Publications:* The Revolutionary Function of the Modern Church, 1912; Marriage and Divorce, 1913; Is Death the End?, 1915; New Wars for Old, 1916; Religion for Today, 1917; The Life and Letters of Robert Collyer (2 vols.), 1917; Readings from Great Authors, 1918; The Grail of Life, 1919; Is Violence the Way Out?, 1920; New Churches for Old, 1922; Patriotism is Not Enough, 1925; Palestine Today and Tomorrow, 1929; The Heart of Scott's Poetry, 1932; A Sensible Man's View of Religion, 1933; If This Be Treason (play with Reginald Lawrence), produced by N.Y. Theatre Guild, 1935; Through Gentile Eyes, 1938; Rethinking Religion, 1938; Out of Darkness, 1942; The Second Christmas, 1943; The Affirmation of Immortality, 1947; My Gandhi, 1953; I Speak for Myself, an Autobiography, 1959; The Collected Hymns of J. H. H., 1960; sermons in Annual Community Church Pulpit Series; magazine articles and book reviews; contributor, Am. Dictionary of Nat. Biography; writer of hymns accepted by church hymnals in U.S., England, and Japan. *Recreations:* reading and travelling (England, Europe, Russia, Near East, Far East). *Address:* Ten Park Avenue, New York, 16, New York, U.S.A. *T.:* Murray Hill 8-4983.
[*Died* 3 *April* 1964.

HOLMES, Hon. Julius Cecil, C.B.E. (Hon.) 1943; D.S.M.(U.S.), Officer Legion of Merit, U.S. Army; U.S. Diplomatic Agent; U.S. Ambassador to Iran since 1961; *b.* 24 April 1899; *s.* of James Reuben Holmes and Lou Jane (*née* Trussell); *m.* 1932, Henrietta Allen; two *s.* one *d.* *Educ.:* University of Kansas. Served in cavalry and infantry, National Guard and Reserve, 8 years; Major, U.S. Army, 1942; Brig.-Gen., 1943. In Insurance business, 1923-25; entered U.S. Foreign Service, 1925; served various posts abroad, 1925-34; Asst. Chief, Div. of Protocol Internal Confs., Dept. of State, 1934-37; Sec.-Gen. Inter-American Conf., Rio de Janeiro, 1935; Sec. "I'm Alone" Arbitration Commn., 1936; Vice-Pres. N.Y. World's Fair, 1937-40; Pres., Gen. Mills, Brazil, 1941-42, Director 1942-; served as Asst. Sec. of State, resigned 1945; Vice-Pres. Trans-Continental Western Air, Inc., 1945; Pres. Taca Airways, S. America, 1946; U.S. Foreign Service Officer, 1948; Minister, American Embassy, London, 1948-53. Minister Plenipotentiary of the U.S.A., Tangier, 1955-56; Special Assistant to Secretary of State, for N.A.T.O. affairs, 1956-59; U.S. Consul-General, Hong Kong, 1959-61. Officer French Legion of Honour, Croix de Guerre with Palm; Comdr. Crown of Yugoslavia; Comdr. Order of Phoenix, Greece, etc. *Recreation:* golf. *Address:* c/o State Department, Washington, D.C., U.S.A. *Clubs:* White's; Halfway House (Rio de Janeiro); Metropolitan, Chevy Chase (Washington, D.C.).
[*Died* 13 *July* 1968.

HOLMES, Sir Leonard (Stanistreet), Kt. *cr.* 1951; Sole Partner, Miller Taylor & Holmes, Solicitors, Liverpool, since 1911; *b.* 8 Jan. 1884; *s.* of Isaac and Isabel Stanistreet Holmes; unmarried. *Educ.:* Liverpool College; Liverpool University. Law Society Scholarship, 1904; Liverpool University: LL.B. (Hons.), 1905, LL.M. (Hons.), 1906; Law. Soc. Honoursman, 1906; admitted Solicitor, 1907. Referee, Landlord and Tenant Act, 1927-54. President, Incorporated Law Society of Liverpool, 1930; J.P. 1933; Member of Supreme Court Rule Cttee., 1939-60; Clerk of the Peace, Liverpool, 1940-49; President of the Law Society, 1950; Joint Pres., Internat. Bar Assoc., 1950; Member of Magistrates' Courts Rule Cttee., 1952-60; Mem. Departmental Cttee., on Central Criminal Court for Lancashire, 1953. *Recreations:* bridge, racing, gardening. *Address:* Ellel House, Mossley Hill, Liverpool 18. *T.:* Allerton 1368. *Club:* Liverpool Cricket (Liverpool).
[*Died* 9 *March* 1961.

HOLMES, Sir Maurice Gerald, G.B.E. *cr.* 1946 (O.B.E. 1919); K.C.B., *cr.* 1938 (C.B. 1929); *b.* 1885; *o. surv. s.* of late Edmond G. A. Holmes; *m.* 1917, Ivy, *o. d.* of late Brig.-Gen. F. P. S. Dunsford, D.S.O.; two *d.* *Educ.:* Wellington College; Balliol College, Oxford. First Class Honours School of Jurisprudence, 1908; called to Bar, 1909; entered Board of Education, 1909; Director of Establishments, 1923-26; Principal Assistant Secretary, 1926-31; Deputy Secretary, 1931-37; Permanent Secretary, 1937-45; ex-mem. of Court of Univ. of London; Chm. East African Salaries Commission, 1947; Chm. Caribbean Public Services Unification Commission, 1948; Chm. Lord Chancellor's Cttee. on Office of Public Trustee, 1954. Served European War, France and Egypt, 1914-19; Lieut.-Col. 1917 (despatches twice, 1914 Star, O.B.E., Order of the Nile). *Publications:* Some Bibliographical Notes on the Novels of George Bernard Shaw, 1929; An Introduction to the Bibliography of Captain Cook, 1936; Captain James Cook, a Bibliographical Excursion. *Address:* 7 Sloane Street, S.W.1. *T.:* Belgravia 2272. *Club:* Oxford and Cambridge.
[*Died* 4 *April* 1964.

HOLMES, Lt.-Gen. Sir William George, K.B.E., *cr.* 1944; C.B. 1938; D.S.O. 1917; *b.* 1892; *s.* of late Dr. Reid Holmes, Aberdeen; *m.* Yvonne Dorine De Bourbon. Joined Royal Welch Fusiliers; served European War, 1914-18 (despatches four times, D.S.O. with bar, Brevets Major and Lt.-Col., Italian silver medal for valour); Waziristan, 1921 (medal with two clasps); commanded 2nd Bn. The East Lancashire Regt.; Col. 1933; General Staff Officer, 1st Grade, Northern Command, 1934-35; Commander 8th Infantry Brigade, 1935-37; Major-General, 1937; Commander, 42nd (East Lancashire) Division, T.A., 1938; Lt.-Gen. 1940; served Middle East (K.B.E.); retired pay, 1945. Order of Phoenix, Class II (Greece), 1944; Pologna Restituta, Class II (Poland), 1945. *Address:* P.O. Tumacacori, Arizona, U.S.A. [*Died* 1969.

HOLROYD-REECE, John; Knight Commander of the Crown of Italy; Member Royal Institution of Great Britain; Director, Musée Ethnographique du Trocadéro, Paris; Managing Director, Pegasus Press; Editions des Bibliothèques Nationales de France; Chairman and Managing Director of the Publishing Holding Company, controlling Albatross & Tauchnitz Editions; Underwriting Member of Lloyd's; *b.* 30 April

1897; *s.* of late M. H. Reece and Lucy Mabel Pigott; *m.* Jeanne de Brouckère (*d.* 1945); *m.* 1960, Gitta, *o. d.* of Otto Erich Deutsch. *Educ.:* Stancliffe Hall, Matlock; Repton. After entering King's Coll., Camb., failed to go into residence to serve in Egyptian Expeditionary Force with the Dorset Yeomanry and on the staff of 5th Cavalry Brigade and 5th Cavalry Division; Military Governor of Zahle and Moallaka, 1918; Journalist, special correspondent of Christian Science Monitor; contributor to Westminster Gazette, New Statesman, The Nation, Athenæum, etc., 1919; appointed official expert on Collotype to the First International Mixed Arbitral Tribunal, 1920; Founded The Pegasus Press, 1927, in Paris; Director of Pantheon Casa Editrice, Florence, 1930; Founded The Albatross Continental Library, 1931. Took over control of the Tauchnitz Editions in 1934. While in Paris, Director of banking and insurance firms. *Publications:* Translated: Count Andrassy; Vincent van Gogh, Degas, Cézanne, Spanish Journey (by J. Meler-Graefe), Travel Diary of a Philosopher (by Count Keyserling), The Soul of China, etc. *Recreations:* riding, swimming, collecting. *Address:* The Keep, Chilham Castle, Kent. *Clubs:* Royal Automobile; Travellers' (Paris).
[*Died* 7 *March* 1969.

HOLT, Charles, C.B.E. 1961; Managing Director, Thos. Cook and Son Ltd. and subsidiary companies, since 1959; Chairman: Hernu Peron and Stockwell Ltd.; England and Perrott's Ltd.; *b.* 4 September 1899; *y. s.* of late Fredrich Holt; *m.* 1928, Gretchen Doering; one *d.* Served with Middlesex Regt., European War, 1914-18. Joined Thos. Cook and Son as trainee, 1920; following posts abroad, appointed general management of company, 1940. Mem. Inst. of Travel Agents (M.T.A.I.). Cavaliere Ufficiale. Order of Merit of Republic of Italy. *Publications:* many technical papers on travel and the tourist industry. *Recreation:* travel. *Address:* 10 Mayfair Place. W.1. *T.:* Grosvenor 4000. [*Died* 5 *Jan.* 1966.

HOLT, Sir Edward, 2nd Bt., *cr.* 1916; *b.* 16 April 1883; *o. surv. s.* of 1st Bt. and Elizabeth (*d.* 1934), *d.* of Joseph Brooks, Cheetham, Manchester; *S.* father, 1928; *m.* 1931, Margaret, *y. d.* of T. S. Lupton, Runswick, Cheadle Hulme, Cheshire. *Heir:* none. *Address:* Holmacre, Alderley, Cheshire.
[*Died* 3 *Nov.* 1968 (*ext.*).

HOLT, Rt. Hon. Harold Edward, P.C. 1953; C.H. 1967; Prime Minister, Commonwealth of Australia, since 1966; M. H. R. for Higgins, Victoria, since 1949 (Fawkner, Victoria, 1935-49); solicitor since 1933; Principal of Holt, Newman and Holt, solicitors, 178 Collins St., Melbourne; *b.* Sydney, Aust., 5 Aug. 1908; *s.* of late Thomas James and late Olive M. Holt, Melbourne; *m.* 1946, Mrs. Zara Fell, *d.* of late Sydney Dickins; three *step-s.* *Educ.:* Wesley Coll., Melb.; Queen's Coll., Univ. of Melbourne (LL.B.). Actg. Min. for Air, 1940; enlisted A.I.F., 1940, but recalled to take Ministerial post, Commonwealth of Australia; Minister: for Labour and Nat. Service, 1940-41; for Immigration, 1949-56; for Labour and National Service, 1949-58; Treasurer, 1958-1966; Dep. Leader of the Liberal Party and Leader of the House of Representatives, 1956-66; Member Australian Delegation to Commonwealth Parliamentary Conference, London, 1948; Leader Australian Deleg. to Commonwealth Parl. Conf., Wellington, 1950, Ottawa (presided), 1952, Nairobi (presided), 1954, Canberra, 1959. Chm. Gen. Council Commonwealth Parl. Assoc. 1952-55. Leader Austr. Deleg. to I.L.O. Conf., Geneva, 1957, elected President; Member Boards of Governors, International Bank for Reconstruction and Development, International Monetary Fund and International Finance Corporation, 1959-65 (Chairman, 1960, these international institutions). Leader Australian Delegation, Manila Summit Conference, 1966. Member Royal Commonwealth Society. Hon. Dr. of Laws, Seoul Nat. Univ., 1967. *Recreations:* spear fishing, racing and golf. *Address:* Prime Minister's Lodge, Canberra, A.C.T. *Clubs:* Athenæum, Melbourne, V.R.C., V.A.T.C., M.V.R.C. (all Australian).
[*Died* 17 *Dec.* 1968.

HOLT, James, C.B.E. 1964 (O.B.E. 1941); Director of Prison Administration, Prison Dept., Home Office, 1960-64, retd.; *b.* 30 March 1899; *s.* of Harry and Annie Holt, Denton, Lancs.; *m.* Dora, *o.d.* of Herbert and Annie Hartley, Denton, Lancs.; one *s.* two *d.* *Educ.:* Ashton Grammar School; Victoria Univ., Manchester. H.M. Borstal Institutions: Housemaster, Feltham, 1923; Deputy-Governor, Portland, 1926; Governor, Portland, 1928; Governor, Feltham, 1930; Governor, H.M. Prison, Wormwood Scrubs, 1938; Governor, H.M. Prison, Liverpool, 1939; Asst. Comr., Prison Commn., 1943. Director of Prison Administration, Prison Commn., 1960. *Recreation:* reading. *Address:* 39 Thistledene, Hampton Court Way, East Molesey, Surrey. *T.:* Emberbrook 3486. [*Died* 22 *July* 1965.

HOLT, John Alphonse, M.B.E. 1945; President, John Holt & Co. (Liverpool) Ltd., since 1967 (Chairman, 1949-67); *b.* 27 Aug. 1906; *s.* of Robert Longstaff Holt and Lucy Ellen Holt (*née* Juvet); *m.* 1937, Pamela Esther (*née* Holt); two *d.* (one *s.* decd.). *Educ.:* Radley; Merton Coll., Oxf. Served in R.A., T.A., 1938-45; West Africa Colonial Office (G.S.O. 2), France, Belgium, Germany (M.B.E., T.D., despatches). Director, Cunard Steamship Co. Ltd.. *Address:* The Old House, Odiham, Hants. [*Died* 8 *Oct.* 1968.

HOLT, Lawrence Durning; retired shipowner; partner in Alfred Holt & Co., 1908-53; *b.* Liverpool, 27 Nov. 1882; *s.* of Robert Durning Holt and Lawrencina Potter; *m.* Evelyn, *o. d.* of late Dr. L. P. Jacks; three *s.* one *d.* *Educ.:* Lockers Park; Winchester. Served with Alfred Booth & Co., 1900-4; with Alfred Holt & Co., 1904-7; City Councillor for Liverpool, 1913-32; Lord Mayor, 1929-30; Chairman Liverpool Local Employment Committee, 1918-29; Member of Prime Minister's Modern Languages Committee, 1918; Blanesburgh Unemployment Insurance Committee, 1927; Coal Mines Reorganisation Commission, 1931; Imperial Communications Inquiry Committee, 1931; Chairman Liverpool Steam Ship Owners Association, 1935; Lord Fleming Tribunal, 1938; Trustee of the National Maritime Museum, 1937-44; Joint Founder with Kurt Hahn of Outward Bound Sea School, 1941; Chairman, Liverpool Institute High School and Blackburne House Girls' School, Management Committee H.M.S. Conway and of Outward Bound Sea School, resigned June 1953. J.P. Liverpool, 1918-53. *Address:* Farmore, Dewsall, Hereford.
[*Died* 5 *Feb.* 1961.

HOME, Gordon Cochrane, F.S.A. Scot.; author and artist; *b.* London, 25 July 1878; *y. s.* of late Erskine Sandilands Home of West Reston, Berwickshire; member, Art Workers' Guild, Roy. Archæological Inst. and Roy. Instn.; *m.* 1926, Violet (*d.* 1944), *o. d.* of late William C. N. Chapman, of Heppington, Canterbury; one *s.* one *d.* Edited magazine page Morning Herald, 1900; art editor of The Tatler, 1901; art editor of The King, 1902-3; exhibitor at the Royal Academy; Major R.A.S.C., 1914-20, France and N. Africa. Vice Pres. Border Area of British Legion, 1949. Has travelled much in North Africa and throughout the British Empire. Hon. Mem. Mark Twain Society, Kirkwood, Missouri, 1963 *Publications:* Farnham and its Surroundings, 1900; Epsom, its History and its Surroundings, 1902; What to see in England, 1903; Yorkshire, coast and moorland scenes, 1904; The Evolution of an English Town, 1905; Normandy; Yorkshire Dales and Fells, 1906; Yorkshire Vales and Wolds; Along the Rivieras of France and Italy, 1908—all illustrated by the author; The Motor Routes of England, 1909: of France, 1910; The Romance of London, 1910; Through Yorkshire, 1922; Roman York, 1924; Through East Anglia, Through the Chilterns, 1925; Roman London, 1926, 1948; Mediæval London, Roman Britain, Edinburgh, 1927; Canterbury of our Grandfathers, 1928; The Charm of Surrey, 1929; Old London Bridge, 1931; York Minster, 1936, 1947; Cyprus Then and Now, 1960; Editor of Dent's Cathedral Series; has illustrated and edited numerous historical and topographical works. *Recreations:* archæological rambles in country or English Lake District. *Address:* Malt House Cottage, Little Bognor, Fittleworth, near Pulborough, Sussex. *T.:* Fittleworth 260. *Club:* Authors'. [*Died* 13 *Dec.* 1969.

HOME, Sir John Hepburn Milne, Kt., *cr.* 1935; D.L., J.P.; *b.* 20 Oct. 1876; *s.* of Col. David Milne Home, of Wedderburn, and Jane, *d.* of late Sir T. Buchan Hepburn, Bart.; *m.* 1907, Mary Adelaide, *d.* of Colonel Hon. Fitzwilliam Elliot; three *s.* *Educ.:* Privately. *Address:* Elibank, Walkerburn, Scotland. *T.:* Walkerburn 245. *Club:* New (Edinburgh). [*Died* 28 *April* 1963.

HONE, Rt. Rev. Campbell Richard, M.A. (Oxon), D.D. (Lambeth); Hon. Fellow Wadham College, 1939; *b.* 13 Sept. 1873; *s.* of late Rev. Evelyn J. Hone; *m.* Emily Maude, *d.* of late F. P. Weaver, M.D.; one *s.* two *d.* *Educ.:* Blackheath School; Wadham College, Oxford (Exhibitioner); Leeds Clergy School. Ordained, 1898; Curate of Holy Trinity, Habergham-Eaves, 1898-1902; Domestic Chaplain to Bishop of Wakefield, 1902-5; Vice-Principal Leeds Clergy School, 1905-9; Vicar of Mt. Pellon 1909-15, of Brighouse, 1916-20; Hon. Canon of Wakefield, 1918-20; Examining Chaplain to the Bishop of Wakefield, 1907-28; Rector of Whitby, 1920-30; Proctor in Convocation, 1925-30; Prebendary and Canon of York, 1926-30; Bishop Suffragan of Pontefract, 1931-38; Archdeacon of Pontefract and Canon of Wakefield, 1931-38; Bishop of Wakefield, 1938-45. *Publication:* Life of Dr. John Radcliffe, 1652-1714, 1950. *Address:* 2 Belbroughton Road, Oxford. *T.:* 58864. [*Died* 16 *May* 1967.

HONOUR, Benjamin, C.B. 1947; M.C. 1918; U.K. representative on panel of arbitrators established by International Convention, concerning Carriage of Goods by Rail, 1952 (C.I.M.) and International Convention concerning carriage of Passengers and Luggage by Rail, 1952 (CIV), 1956; *b.* 4 June 1888; *o. s.* of late Emanuel Nison Honour and Pauline Hamburg; *m.* 1920, Alice, *y. d.* of late Emile Delfosse, Valenciennes, and Henriette Génard; one *s.* *Educ.:* City of London School; Univ. Coll., London. LL.B. 1910; called to Bar, Middle Temple, 1910, and joined Western Circuit; commissioned R. of O., R.H. and R.F.A., 1913; served European War, 1914-18, with B.E.F., 1915-1918 (M.C.); entered Government Service, 1919; Dep. Administrator of Hungarian and Bulgarian Property, 1921; Senior British Govt. Agent at Anglo-German, Anglo-Austrian Anglo-Hungarian and Anglo-Bulgarian Mixed Arbitral Tribunals, 1923; entered Solicitors' Dept., Board of Trade, 1935; Asst. Solicitor to Board, 1938; Solicitor to Ministry of Shipping, 1939; Principal Assistant Solicitor, office of H.M. Procurator-General and Treasury Solicitor (Ministry of Transport Branch), 1944; Head of Highway Law Consolidation Branch, Ministry of Transport and Civil Aviation, 1953-58. *Address:* Chandos House, 46 New Cavendish St., W.1. *T.:* Welbeck 5155. *Club:* Royal Societies. [*Died* 6 *Feb.* 1961.

HOOD, Hon. Dorothy Violet; *b.* 4 Sept. 1877; *d.* of 4th Viscount Hood and Edith, *d.* of A. Ward. *Publications:* Looking Back to London, 1933; The Admiral's Hood, 1942; London is Invincible, 1946. *Address:* Little Water Farm, Stogursey, Bridgwater, Somerset. [*Died* 28 *Jan.* 1965.

HOOD, James Reaney, C.B.E. 1949; Legal Adviser, Ministry of Food, 1946-54, and Principal Assistant Solicitor, Department of H.M. Treasury Solicitor, retired; *b.* 4 May 1888; 4th *s* of late Henry George Hood: *m.* 1927, Elsie Mary (*d.* 1968), *d.* of late Rev. G. H. Streeten; one *d.* *Educ.:* Woodbridge School; Pembroke College, Oxford. M.A. Oxford. Barrister-at-Law, Middle Temple, 1927. Served in Indian Civil Service, 1912-1932, finishing as Collector and District Magistrate, Karachi, 1930-32; practice at the Bar, 1933-40; Ministry of Aircraft Production, 1940-42; Treasury Solicitor's Dept., 1942-54. *Recreations:* history, arm-chair travel, music, gardening. *Address:* Kolaba, Deneside, East Dean, Eastbourne, Sussex. *T.:* East Dean 3188. [*Died* 31 *July* 1968.

HOOD, Rev. Dr. John Chas. Fulton; *b.* 2 December 1884; *s.* of late Reverend John Fulton and Christina duPlat Hood; *m.* 1920, Helen Patuffa Kennedy-Fraser (collector and singer of Songs of the Hebrides); two *d.* (one *s.* killed in North Africa, 1943). *Educ.:* St. John's, Leatherhead; Christ's College, Cambridge (Tancred Student). B.A. (Class and Theol. Hons.) 1905, M.A. 1909; Durham B.D., 1922; D.D. 1943; Curate of Nottingham Parish Church, 1907-11; Leeds Parish Church, 1911-15; C.F. (B.E.F.), 1915-18; Vicar of St. Barnabas, Leeds, 1917-23; Garstang, 1923-32; on Lancs Education Comm. and dio. Inspector of Schools; Rector of Keighley, 1932-45; Rector of Nuneham Courtenay, 1945-47; Rector of Moulton (Suffolk) and Kennett (Cambs.), 1947-56; Canon in Bradford Cathedral, Rural Dean of Craven, Surrogate, Chaplain to High Sheriff of Yorks (Sir Prince Prince-Smith, Bt.). Chaplain to T.A. 1915-45; T.D. 1939; Chief Chaplain British Forces in Norway, 1940, Iceland, 1940-41; Dep. Asst. Chaplain-Gen., 1942-44. Founder and Editor of The Midnight Sun (Troops' newspaper in Norway and Iceland). Knight of the Icelandic Order of the Falcon, 1949. *Publications:* An Account of St. Mary's Church, Nottingham, 1910; An Account of Garstang Parish Church, 1929; An Account of Keighley Parish Church, 1936; A Soldier's Breastplate, 1939; Icelandic Church Saga, 1946; Contributor to The Times, Yorkshire Post, etc. *Recreations:* antiquarian, gardening, fishing, climbing. *Address:* Battel Lodge, Battle, Sussex. *T.:* Battle 384. [*Died* 19 *Dec.* 1964.

HOOKE, Samuel Henry, M.A. Oxon, Hon. D.D. Glasgow; Hon. D.Th. Upsala; B.D. London; F.S.A.; Professor Emeritus of Old Testament Studies, University of London; *m.* 1946, B. E. Wyatt. *Educ.:* St. Mark's School, Windsor; Jesus Coll., Oxford. Flavelle Associate Prof. of Oriental Languages and Literature at Victoria Coll., Univ. of Toronto. Pres. of Folklore Society, 1936-37; Pres. of Society for Old Testament Studies, 1951. British Academy Bronze Medal for Bib. Studies, 1948. Speaker's Lectr., Univ. of Oxford, 1956-61. Hon. Fellow, Jesus College, Oxford, 1964. *Publications:* Christ and the Kingdom of God; Christianity in the Making; New Year's Day; Myth and Ritual; The Labyrinth; Schweich Lectures for 1935; In the Beginning; What is the Bible?; The Kingdom of God in the Experience of Jesus; Babylonian and Assyrian Religion; The Siege Perilous; Translation of the Bible into Basic English; Myth, Ritual and Kingship; Translation of Samaria; The Capital of the Kingdom of Israel; Alpha and

Omega; Middle Eastern Mythology; The Resurrection of Christ as History and Experience, 1966; contributions to Hastings' Dictionary of Apostolic Christianity, Expository Times, etc. *Address:* Westbrook Cottage, Buckland, Faringdon, Berks. [*Died* 17 *Jan.* 1968.

HOOPER, Sir Frederic (Collins), 1st Bt. *cr.* 1962; Kt. 1956; Managing Director, Schweppes Group of Companies; *b.* 19 July 1892; *o. s.* of Frederick Stephen Hooper, Bruton, Somerset; *m.* 1st, Eglantine Irene, *d.* of Thomas Bland; one *s.* one *d.*; 2nd, Prudence Avery, *d.* of Basil Wenham; one *d. Educ.:* Sexeys School, Bruton; University College, London (B.Sc.). Commissioned Dorset Regt., 1914-19; Camp Commandant and A.D.C. to Gen. Sir Reginald Pinney, Commanding 33rd Division, 1917-18; Ionian Bank, Athens, 1919-21; Lewis's Ltd., 1922-42; Director of Lewis's Ltd., and associated companies, 1934-42; Joint Managing Director, 1940-42. Director of Political Research Centre, 1942-44; Director of Business Training, Ministry of Labour and National Service, 1945-46; Member of Committee of Enquiry into Organisation of the R.A.F., 1954; Dep. Chm. of Committee on Servicing Aspects of R.A.F., 1955; Member of Committee on Employment of National Servicemen in the U.K., 1956; Chm. Advisory Bd., to Regular Forces Resettlement Service, Min. of Labour and National Service, 1957-60; Adviser on Recruiting to Minister of Defence, 1960-; Governor Ashridge Trust since 1958; Chairman Royal Academy of Dancing; Chairman of Finance Cttee., Royal College of Nursing. Fellow, University College, London, 1957. *Recreation:* not working at week-ends. *Heir: s.* Anthony Robin Maurice Hooper, *b.* 26 Oct. 1918. *Address:* 5 Clive House, Connaught Place, W.2. *T.:* Ambassador 0946; The Dandy, Tenterden, Kent. *T.:* Tenterden 173. *Club:* Savile. [*Died* 4 *Oct.* 1963.

HOOPER, Sydney Ernest, O.B.E. 1949; B.A. (Durham); M.A. (London); late Director of Studies and Editor of Philosophy (the Journal of the Royal Institute of Philosophy); *b.* Petersfield, Hampshire, 24 May 1880; 2nd *s.* of late Thomas Hooper of Lyss and Martha Matilda, *d.* of Francis Hood Withers of Westbury; *m.* 1915, Frances Gramina Brine, *d.* of Admiral Lindesay Brine; one *s.* one *d. Educ.:* University College, Durham; University College, London. Master at Bournemouth School, 1907-08; General Secretary to Bristol Civic League, 1910; extra-mural Tutor in Philosophy, London University, 1919-23; concerned in the founding of the British Institute of Philosophy, 1925. *Publications:* Editor of The Deeper Causes of the War and its issues, 1940; various articles in British Journal of Psychology, Psyche, the Hibbert Journal; Studies of Whitehead's Organic Philosophy published in Philosophy, 1941-45. *Recreation:* cricket. *Address:* Redlayne, Cookham Dean, Berks. *T:* Marlow 2535. [*Died* 4 *Feb.* 1966.

HOOTON, Maj.-Gen. Alfred, C.I.E. 1923; Indian Medical Service, retired; *b.* Manchester, 1870; *s.* of late Jonathan Hooton, Manchester; *m.* 1925, Agnes Dora, *d.* of F. H. Warden, Indian Police (retired); one *d. Educ.:* Manchester Grammar School; The Owens College, Manchester. L.R.C.P. Lond., M.R.C.S. Eng. 1893. Served Mohmand and Tirah Expeditions, 1897-98; Bushire Force, 1918-19. *Address:* 10 Milton Road, Bournemouth, Hants. [*Died* 29 *May* 1967.

HOOVER, Herbert: *b.* West Branch, Iowa, 10 Aug. 1874; *s.* of Jesse C. Hoover and Hulda Randall Minthorn; *m.* 1899, Lou Henry (*d.* 1944); two *s. Educ.:* A.B., 1895, Stanford University, California, as Engineer Hon. Degrees from 85 Universities in U.S. and abroad; 108 Medals from American and foreign organizations and societies; Honorary citizen of various European cities; Professional work in mines, railroads, metallurgical works in U.S., Mexico, Canada, Australia, Italy, Gt. Britain, S. Africa, India, China, Russia, etc.; Chairman, American Relief Committee, London, 1914-15; Chairman of Commission for Relief in Belgium, 1915-19; Food Administrator for the United States, Member War Trade Council, etc., 1917-19; Chairman United States Grain Corporation, United States Sugar Equalisation Board, Inter-allied Food Council; Supreme Economic Council, European Coal Council; Director of various economic measures in Europe during the Armistice; Secretary of Commerce, United States, 1921-1928; President of the United States, 1929-1933. At request of President Truman undertook coordination of world food supplies of 38 countries, Mar. 1946; at request of President Truman undertook a study of econ. situation in Germany and Austria, 1947; Chm. Comm. on Orgn. Exec. Branch of Govt., 1947-49; Chm. Second Comm. on Organization of Exec. Branch of Govt., 1953-55; guest of Federal Republic of Germany at request of Chancellor Adenauer, 1954; Special envoy of President Eisenhower to Brussels Exhibition, 1958. Member Advisory Board World Bank Reconstruction and Development. Trustee of various educational and scientific institutions. Chm. Belgian-American Educational Foundation, American Children's Fund, Boys Clubs of America, Finnish-Relief Fund, Inc. *Publications:* Agricola de Re Metallica (joint trans. with Mrs. Hoover); American Individualism, 1922; The Challenge to Liberty, 1934; American Road, 8 vols., 1933-1961; America's First Crusade, 1941; The Problems of Lasting Peace, 1942. The Memoirs of Herbert Hoover: (English edns.) vol. i, Years of Adventure, 1874-1920, 1952; vol. ii, The Cabinet and Presidency, 1953; vol. iii, The Great Depression; The Ordeal of Woodrow Wilson, 1955; An American Epic, 3 vols., 1959-61. *Address:* Waldorf Astoria Towers, New York, U.S.A. *Clubs:* University (New York); Bohemian (San Francisco). [*Died* 20 *Oct.* 1964.

HOOVER, Herbert Clark, Jr.; Consulting Engineer, 1930-54 and since 1957; Consultant to Secretary of State since 1957; *b.* 4 Aug. 1903; *s.* of late Herbert Hoover, *q.v.*; *m.* 1925, Margaret Watson; one *s.* two *d. Educ.:* Stanford University (B.A.); Harvard Business Sch. (M.B.A.). Mining Engineer, 1925; member research staff, Harvard Business Sch. 1928-29; Communications Engineer, Western Air Express, 1929-31; Transcontinental & Western Air (TWA), Inc., 1931-34; Teaching Fell., California Inst. Technology, 1934-35; Pres. United Geophysical Co., Inc., 1935-52 (Chm. Bd., 1952-1954); Pres. Consolidated Engineering Corp., 1936-46; Consultant to Governments of Venezuela, Iran, Brazil, Peru, etc., 1940-53; Special Adviser to Secretary of State, 1953; Under Secretary of State, U.S.A., 1954-57; Director of many companies. Holds many hon. degrees in American Univs. Decorated by governments of Venezuela, Chile and Peru. *Address:* Suite 1230, Statler Center Building, 900 Wilshire Boulevard, Los Angeles, Calif. *Clubs:* University (New York); Bohemian (San Francisco); California (Los Angeles); Metropolitan, Chevy Chase (Washington). [*Died* 9 *July* 1969.

HOPE, Adrian James Robert, C.I.E. 1922; *b.* 1874; *m.* 1913, Jessie Newall (*d.* 1950), *d.* of late David McLellan and *widow* of Major D. J. Welsh; one *s. Educ.:* Royal Indian Engineering College, Coopers Hill. Entered Indian Service of Engineers, 1897; Chief Engineer, Public Works Dept., Burma, 1921; retired, 1928. *Address:* 23 Ann Street, Edinburgh. [*Died* 8 *March* 1963.

HOPE, Lord Charles (Melbourne); D.L. County of West Lothian; *b.* 20 Feb. 1892; 2nd *s.* of 1st Marquess of Linlithgow, P.C., K.T., G.C.M.G., G.C.V.O. *Educ.:* Eton. Late Bn. Commander, 1st West Lothian Bn. Home Guard; late Captain Lothian and Border Horse Yeomanry; late 2nd Lieut. 1st Life Guards. *Address:* Sunning House, Sunningdale, Ascot, Berks. *Club:* Buck's. [*Died* 11 *June* 1962.

HOPE, Admiral Herbert Willes Webley, C.B. 1917; C.V.O. 1925; D.S.O. 1919; D.L., J.P. County of Cardigan; *y. s.* of late Rear-Admiral Charles Webley Hope; *b.* 26 May 1878; *m.* 1905, Katherine (*d.* 1966), *y. d.* of Rev. Francis Kewley, M.A., B.A.; one *s.* one *d.* (and one *d.* decd.). Entered Navy, 1892; Lieut. for Experimental Duties, Excellent, 1905-9; Comdr. of Prince of Wales Coronation Review, 1911 (medal); of King Edward VII. occupation of Scutari, 1913; on Staff of War College, 1913; War Staff Officer, 1914; commanded H.M.S. Dartmouth in the operations in the Adriatic, 1918; commanded H.M.S. Repulse during visit of Prince of Wales to South Africa, 1925 (C.V.O.); a Naval A.D.C. to the King, 1926; Rear-Adm., 1926; President of Ordnance Committee, Royal Arsenal, Woolwich, 1928-31; Vice-Adm. 1931; retired list, 1931; Adm., retired, 1936. *Address:* Glanhelyg, Llechryd, Cardiganshire. *T.:* Llechryd 302. *Club:* United Service. [*Died* 26 *April* 1968.

HOPE, Brig.-Gen. John Frederic Roundell, C.B.E. 1922; D.S.O. 1916; *b.* 14 Aug. 1883; *s.* of late H. J. Hope, J.P., of Preston House, nr. Basingstoke. *Educ.:* Winchester; R.M.C., Sandhurst. 1st K.R. Rifles, 1902; served European War (despatches four times, wounded thrice, D.S.O.).; Bt. Lt.-Col. 1919; Lt.-Col. 1928; temp. Brig.-Gen. 50th Infantry Brigade, Sep. 1918; commanded Royal Tank Corps Depot, 1928-32; Col. 1932; Commander 129th (South Wessex) Infantry Brigade T.A., 1934-37; A.D.C. to the King, 1934-38; retired pay, 1938; comdg. 3rd Bn. Hants Home Guard, 1940-45; Welfare Officer, North Hants, 1939-45; County Army Welfare Officer, Hants, 1946-58. *Publications:* Winchester College Notions, Vols. I and II, 1910; A Short History of the Royal Tank Corps, 4 edns., 1930-36; A History of Hunting in Hampshire, 1950. *Address:* Preston Grange, Basingstoke, Hants. *T.A.:* Preston Candover. *Club:* Hampshire (Winchester). [*Died* 26 *July* 1970.

HOPE, Hon. Richard Frederick, O.B.E. 1963; *b.* Dec. 1901; Regional Information Officer, Quebec City, 1956-63; *s.* of 1st Baron Rankeillour, P.C.; *m.* 1938, Helen, *yr. d.* of Alfred Lambart; two *s.* one *d.* *Educ.:* Oratory Sch.; Christ Church, Oxford. Asst. Master, Oratory School, Caversham, 1930-1931; Second Master, 1931-34; Headmaster, 1934-38; at Ministry of Information, 1939-1945; appointed Commonwealth Relations Office, 1946. *Recreation:* mountaineering. *Address:* Rookery Farm House, Kettleburgh, Woodbridge, Suffolk. *Clubs:* Travellers', Alpine. [*Died* 9 *May* 1964.

HOPE-DUNBAR, Sir Basil (Douglas), 7th Bt. *cr.* 1664; *b.* 16 Feb. 1907; *o. s.* of Major Sir Charles Dunbar Hope-Dunbar, 6th Bt. and late Lady Hope-Dunbar; *S.* father, 1958; *m.* 1st, 1932, Evelyn Diana (marriage dissolved in Scottish courts, 1937), *e. d.* of late Colonel G. I. Fraser, C.M.G., D.S.O., Q.O. Cameron Highlanders; 2nd, 1940, Edith Maude Maclaren, *e. d.* of late Malcolm Cross, and late Mrs. Cross; one *s.* *Educ.:* Eton; R.M.C. 2nd Lieut., Q.O. Cameron Highlanders, 1926; Captain, 1936; Major, 1942. Served in War of 1939-45. *Heir: s.* David Hope-Dunbar, *b.* 13 July 1941. *Address:* Senwick House, Kirkcudbright. *T.:* Borgue 237. *Club:* Army and Navy. [*Died* 21 *July* 1961.

HOPE-MORLEY, Captain Hon. Claude Hope; late Grenadiers Guards; High Sheriff of County of London, 1938; *y. s.* of 1st and *b.* and *heir-pres.* to 2nd Baron Hollenden; *b.* 5 June 1887; *m.* 1911, Lady Dorothy Edith Isabel, *e. d.* of 7th Earl of Buckinghamshire; one *s.* three *d.* *Address:* The Mount, Pinkneys Green, Maidenhead, Berks. *T.:* Marlow 2097. [*Died* 8 *April* 1968.

HOPE SIMPSON, Sir John; *see* Simpson.

HOPEWELL-ASH, Edwin Lancelot; *see* Ash, E. L. H.

HOPKINS, Major Adrian Edmund, M.C. 1916; Royal Artillery (retired); Alderman, City of Bath, since 1945; *b.* Portlemouth, Devon, 8 Oct. 1894; *e. s.* of John Edric Murray Hopkins, formerly of Tidmarsh Manor, Berkshire; *m.* 1925, Brenda Hannah, *y. d.* of Frank Fairclough, Kensington, London; one *d.* *Educ.:* Clifton College, R.A. (Regular Army), 1915-26 (M.C., severely wounded); recalled War, 1941-46, Major, R.A. Staff. Entered Bath City Council, 1930; Alderman, 1945; Mayor of Bath, 1937-38, 1938-39, 1953-54. Chm. Bath Conservative Assoc., 1933-36. Governor, The Royal School for Daughters of Officers of the Army, Bath, 1955. Mem. Jury Nat. Philatelic Exhibition, America, 1949; Chairman Philatelic Congress of Great Britain, 1935, 1940, 1960; Chairman Executive Cttee. Philatelic Congress of Great Britain, 1947-52; Vice-Pres. and Past Pres. (now Hon. Ed. of Bulletin), The Postal History Society. Has travelled in Europe, India, Africa, United States, Canada, B.W.I. Roll of Distinguished Philatelists, 1947; President, The Sette of Odd Volumes, 1953 *Publications:* A History of Wreck Covers (2nd edn.), 1948; (with H. E. Lobdell, U.S.A.) Hong Kong and the Treaty Ports—Postal History and Postal Markings, 1949; many articles on philatelic and Postal History subjects. *Recreations:* ornithology, 18th-century history and architecture. *Address:* Ormonde House, Sion Hill, Bath, Somerset. *T.:* Bath 4775. *Club:* Cavalry. [*Died* 1 *March* 1967.

HOPKINS, Gerard Walter Sturgis; Translator and Critic; *b.* 12 Apr. 1892; *s.* of Everard Hopkins and Amy Sichel; *m.* 1949, Babette Johanna, *widow* of Peter Cornwallis, and *d.* of Ernest and Helena Stern. *Educ.:* Marlborough College; Balliol College, Oxford (Williams Exhibitioner). President of the O.U.D.S., 1913; Second in Greats, 1914; commissioned as 2/Lt. in 2/5 R. Warwickshire Regiment, 1914; served European War in France; seconded in 1916 to command 182 Trench Mortar Battery (M.C.); prisoner of war 22 March 1918 to end of war. Served with Oxford University Press, London, 1920-57, first as Publicity Manager, and later, as Editorial Adviser. Chevalier de la Légion d'Honneur, 1951. *Publications:* A City in the Foreground; An Unknown Quantity; The Friend of Antæus; Seeing's Believing; Something Attempted; An Angel in the Room; Nor Fish nor Flesh; *trans.:* vols. vii-xxvii of Men of Good Will by Jules Romains, Novels of François Mauriac, Flaubert's Madame Bovary, Proust's Jean Santeuil, Letters to Antoine Bibesco, and Miscellanea, Rousseau's Contrat Social, Stories by Maupassant, Zola's l'Assommoir, Lélia, Olympio, Three Musketeers, Life of Sir Alexander Fleming by André Maurois, and many other books from the French; reviews and broadcasts. *Address:* 13 Montagu Place, W.1. *T.:* Ambassador 6515. *Club:* Garrick. [*Died* 20 *March* 1961.

HOPKINS, The Very Rev. Noel Thomas; Provost Emeritus since 1962 (Provost of Wakefield Cathedral and Vicar of Wakefield, 1933-62); *b.* 8 January 1892;

s. of Arthur Hopkins, York; *m.* 1922, Patricia Mary, 2nd *d.* of William Richardson of Guisborough and Sandsend, Yorkshire; two *d.* *Educ.:* Archbishop Holgate's School, York; Clare College, Cambridge (Scholar); Cuddesdon College. Curate of Whitby, 1915-17; Chaplain in the Army and the Air Force. 1917-19; Chaplain of Cuddesdon College. 1919-22; Rector of Churchill, Oxon, 1922-25; Minor Canon and Sacrist of St. Paul's Cathedral, 1925-33; Inspector of Schools, Diocese of London, 1926-33; Assistant Hospitaller, St. Bartholomew's Hospital, 1928-33; Editor of the Quarterly Intercession Paper, 1931-60; Hon. Secretary, Candidates' Five-Shilling Fund, 1931-60; Church Commissioner, 1950-62. Hon. Freeman, City of Wakefield, 1958. *Address:* 22 Harlow Oval, Harrogate, Yorkshire. [*Died* 26 *July* 1969.

HOPKINS, Professor Reginald Haydn, D.Sc., F.R.I.C.; Professor of Brewing and Applied Biochemistry, University of Birmingham, 1931-56, retd.; Director of Research Institute of Brewing, 1934-51; *b.* Birmingham 13 Feb. 1891; *s.* of Albert H. Hopkins, Birmingham; *m.* 1st, 1918, Ruth (whom he divorced, 1933), *d.* of James Storer, Birmingham; one *s.*; 2nd, 1953, Phyllis May, *d.* of Alderman Walter T. Harrison, Sutton Coldfield. *Educ.:* King Edward's Grammar Sch., Five Ways, Birmingham; Univ. of Birmingham, D.Sc. Chief Asst. to Public Analysts to the County of Warwick, 1911-17; Lectr. in Brewing and Fermentation Dept., Univ. of Birmingham, 1918-20; Research on Natural Food Products in connection with Food Conservation during both wars; Lecturer in Biochemistry and Head of the Dept. of Brewing, Heriot-Watt College, Edinburgh, 1920-31; Fellow of Institute of Chemistry (Branch E, Analysis of Food and Drugs, 1918), former member of Council; formerly Fellow of Chemical Soc. *Publications:* Text Book, Biochemistry Applied to Malting and Brewing, 1937; Many scientific papers in Biochemical Journal, Journal of Institute of Brewing, Thorpe's Dictionary of Applied Chemistry, and other scientific and technical journals. *Recreation:* music. *Address:* 12 Curzon Court, Portarlington Rd., Bournemouth, Hants. [*Died* 20 *Sept.* 1965.

HOPKINSON, Austin; *b.* 1879; 3rd *s.* of late Sir Alfred Hopkinson, K.C.; unmarried. Served as Lieut. Imperial Yeomanry, S. Africa, 1900; 2nd Lt. The Royal Dragoons, European War, 1914-16; Private The Royal Dragoons, 1918; Lieut. Fleet Air Arm, 1940; M.P. Prestwich, unopposed, 1918; M.P. (Ind.) Mossley Division of Lancs, Dec. 1918-29 and 1931-45. J.P. Lancashire. *Publications:* The Hope of the Workers, 1923; Religio Militis, 1927. *Address:* 23 Carlton House Terrace, S.W.1. *Club:* Athenæum. [*Died* 2 *Sept.* 1962.

HORAN, Henry Edward, C.B. 1947; D.S.C. 1914; Rear-Admiral (retd.); *b.* 12 Aug. 1890; *s.* of John Horan, M.I.C.E., Newcastle West, Co. Limerick; *m.* 1916, Ruth, *e. d.* of Rev. H. Bidwell, Michel Troy; one *d.* *Educ.:* Stubbington House, Fareham. Joined H.M.S. Britannia, 1905; served in destroyers, European War, 1914-18; Commander, 1924; Captain, 1930; Rear-Admiral, 1941; commanded H.M.S. Coventry, 1931-1935; i.d.c. (staff), 1935-37; commanded H.M.S. Barham, 1937-38; chief of naval staff, New Zealand, 1938-40; commanded H.M.S. Leander, 1940-41; Combined Operations Headquarters, 1941-43; Rear-Admiral comdg. Combined Operational Bases (Western Approaches), 1943-46. *Address:* St. Anne's Cottage, Shedfield, Southampton. *Club:* United Service. [*Died* 15 *Aug.* 1961.

HORE-RUTHVEN, Col. Hon. Malise; *see* Ruthven, Col. Hon. C. M. H.

HORGAN, John Joseph; LL.D (h.c.), N.U.I. 1952; Solicitor since 1902; Coroner County Cork since 1914; Belgian Consul at Cork since 1929; *b.* 26 April 1881; *e.s.* of M. J. Horgan, Clanloughlin, Cork; *m.* 1st, 1908, Mary Katherine (*d.* 1920), *e. d.* of Sir B. C. A. Windle, F.R.S.; two *s.* one *d.*; 2nd, 1923, Mary, *e. d.* of Walter Brind, Madras; one *s.* one *d.* *Educ.:* Clongowes Wood College; Queen's College, Cork. Gold Medallist Incorporated Law Society of Ireland, 1901; held inquest on Lusitania victims, 10 May 1915; Member of Council of Incorporated Law Society of Ireland, 1921-50; President, Southern Law Assoc., 1928, 1934, 1955; Chm. Cork Harbour Commissioners, 1924-25, 1949-61; Chairman Cork Public Library Committee, 1924-28; member of Rules Committee for Irish Circuit Courts under Courts of Justice Act, 1924-41; Chm. Irish Free State Liquor Commission, 1925 and 1929; member of Town Tenants Commission, 1927; President: Cork Literary and Scientific Assoc., 1928-31; Cork Arts Society, 1963; Cork Incorporated Chamber of Commerce and Shipping, 1936-38; Barrington Lecturer on Economics, 1943-44; Chairman: Robertson, Ledlie, Ferguson and Co., Ltd., Belfast and Cork, since 1928; Carrigaline Pottery Co. Ltd.; Director: Verolme Cork Dockyard Ltd.; Ranks (Ireland) Ltd. Chevalier of Order of Leopold II (Belgium), 1956; Officer of the Order of the Crown (Belgium,) 1965. *Publications:* Great Catholic Laymen, 1908; Home Rule — A Critical Consideration, 1911; The Complete Grammar of Anarchy, 1918 (2nd edition, 1920); The Cork City Management Act—its Origin, Provisions, and Application, 1929; Parnell to Pearse; Recollections and Reflections, 1948; numerous articles on Legal, Economic, and Political Matters. *Recreation:* painting. *Address:* Lacaduv, Cork. *T.A.:* Horgan, Solicitor, Cork *T.:* Cork 41720. *Clubs:* Cork, City and County (Cork). [*Died* 21 *July* 1967.

HORN, David Bayne; Professor of Modern History, University of Edinburgh since 1954; *b.* 9 July 1901; *er. s.* of James Adam Bayne Horn, S.S.C., and Lilias Wilson Mossman; *m.* 1929, Barbara Mary, *yr. d.* of William Scott, J.P., Blaydon-on-Tyne, Co. Durham; two *d.* *Educ.:* Edinburgh Institution; Edinburgh University. M.A. 1st cl. hons. (history) Edin. Univ., 1922; Kirkpatrick Scholar, 1922-23; Assistant in History, 1923-27, Lecturer in History, 1927-54, Edinburgh Univ.; D.Litt. (Edin.) 1929; Professor of History (temp.), Hull University College, 1935-36. President of Historical Association of Scotland, 1956-59; Hon. President of Edinburgh W.E.A. *Publications:* A History of Europe, 1871-1920, 1927; Sir Charles Hanbury Williams and European Diplomacy, 1930; British Diplomatic Representatives 1689-1789, 1932; Scottish Diplomatists 1689-1789, 1944; British Public Opinion and the First Partition of Poland, 1945; ed. English Historical Documents, 1714-1783 (Vol. X) (with Mary Ransome), 1958; British Diplomatic Service, 1689-1789, 1961; Frederick the Great and the Rise of Prussia, 1964; Short History of the University of Edinburgh, 1556-1889, 1967; Great Britain and Europe in the Eighteenth Century, 1967; articles and reviews in English Historical Review, etc. *Address:* 8 Pentland Avenue, Edinburgh 13. *T.:* Edinburgh Colinton 2146. [*Died* 7 *Aug.* 1969.

HORNBY, Charles Windham L. P.; *see* Penrhyn-Hornby.

HORNBY, Rt. Rev. Hugh Leycester, M.C. 1916; M.A.; *b.* 20 Nov. 1888; *e. s.* of late Ven. Phipps John Hornby, Archdeacon of Lancaster; *m.* 1921, Katharine Rebecca May, *d.* of C. G. May, 49 Lincoln's Inn Fields; four *s.* *Educ.:* Rugby School; Balliol College, Oxford. Curate of St. Anne's-on-Sea, 1913-14; Chaplain to the Forces, 1914-1919 (M.C.); Vicar of S. Michael's on Wyre, 1919-30. Hon. Canon of Manchester, 1937-

1945; Rector of Bury, 1930-53; Suffragan Bishop of Hulme, 1945-53. *Address:* Grabbist House, Dunster, Somerset.
[*Died* 24 *March* 1965.

HORNE, (Charles) Kenneth; *b.* 27 February 1907; *s.* of Rev. C. Silvester Horne and Hon. Mrs. Katherine Maria Horne; *m.* 1945, Mrs. Marjorie Mallinson Thomas, *widow* of Lieut. George Ambler Thomas. *Educ.:* St. George's, Harpenden; Magdalene College, Cambridge. Joined Triplex from Cambridge, 1928. Served War of 1939-45, A.A.F.; reached rank Wing-Comdr. Frequent broadcaster: Much Binding in the Marsh, Twenty Questions, Beyond our Ken, Round the Horne, etc. *Recreations:* golf, tennis, squash. *Address:* 110 Albert Hall Mansions, S.W.7. *T.:* Knightsbridge 1297. *Club:* Royal Automobile.
[*Died* 14 *Feb.* 1969.

HORNER, Arthur Lewis; General Secretary National Union of Mine Workers, 1946-1959, retired; *b.* 5 April 1894; *m.* 1916, Ethel Mary Merrick; three *d.* *Educ.:* Merthyr Elementary Schools. Miners' Agent, 1933; President, South Wales Miners, 1936-46. Freedom of Merthyr Tydfil, 1959. *Publications:* One Mineworkers' Union, 1926; Coal and Communism, 1928; Constitution for One Miners' Union; Incorrigible Rebel, 1960, etc. *Recreations:* reading, gardening. *Address:* 21 Eversley Avenue, Wembley Park, Mx. *T.:* Arnold 1537.
[*Died* 4 *Sept.* 1968.

HORNIMAN, Laurence Ivan, Q.C. 1947; M.A. (Oxon); *b.* 22 Jan. 1893; *surv. s.* of late Emslie John Horniman and late Laura Isabel Plomer; *m.* 1923, Lucile le Brun de DuPlessis Milne, *o. d.* of late Alfred Milne Gossage, C.B.E., F.R.C.P.; one *s.* one *d.* *Educ.:* Rugby School; Exeter College, Oxford. Served in infantry, European War, 1914-18, B.E.F.; enlisted Aug. 1914; commission, 1915; Captain 17th Service Bn. (Football) Middlesex Regt. (wounded), 1916; called to Bar, Inner Temple, 1918, *in absentia* while serving with B.E.F.; after demobilisation practised in London. *Publication:* edited 13th edition, Wharton's Law Lexicon, 1925. *Recreation:* fly fishing. *Address:* Limbury, Salway Ash, Nr. Bridport, Dorset. *T.:* Bridport 2487. *Club:* Athenæum.
[*Died* 25 *March* 1963.

HORNYOLD-STRICKLAND, Hon. Mary Constance Elizabeth Christina, C.B.E. 1952 (M.B.E. 1919); J.P.; *b.* 4 June 1896; *e. d.* of 1st and last Baron Strickland, G.C.M.G. (*d.* 1940), and 1st wife, Lady Edeline Sackville (*d.* 1918), *d.* of 7th Earl De La Warr; *m.* 1920, Henry Hornyold; one *s.* one *d.* *Educ.:* privately. Served in W.R.N.S., European War, 1917-19 (M.B.E.). Chm. Westmorland Women Unionists, 1929-1933; Chm., 1934-36, Pres., 1937-42, N.W. Area Women Conservatives; Chm. Women's Advisory Cttee. of Conserv. Nat. Union, 1942-1945; Chm. Nat. Union of Conserv. & Unionist Assocs., 1947-48, and for many years mem. Party Exec. Pres. Kendal and Dist. Guild of Service, 1936-37, and of Kendal Women's Employment Cttee. at Min. of Labour and Nat. Service, 1940-45; J.P. Westmorland, 1942; mem. Standing Joint Cttee. and Chm. Probation Cttee., of County Council; Westmorland Co. Organiser, W.V.S., 1940-45, and 1951-59. For many years Nat. Vice-Pres. British Legion, Women's section, N.W. Area. *Address:* Sizergh Castle, nr. Kendal, Westmorland. *T.:* Sedgwick 203. *Club:* Lansdowne. [*Died* 18 *Jan.* 1970.

HORRABIN, James Francis; Journalist and Artist; *b.* Peterborough, 1 Nov. 1884; *e. s.* of James Woodhouse Horrabin, Sheffield, and Mary Pinney, Stamford, Lincolnshire; *m.* Winifred Batho (marriage dissolved); *m.* 1948, Margaret V. McWilliams. *Educ.:* Stamford (Lincs) School; Sheffield School of Art. Originally metal-work designer; Staff Artist, Sheffield Telegraph, 1906-09; Art Editor, Yorkshire Telegraph and Star, 1909-11; London News Chronicle and Star Staff, 1911-60; Evening News, 1960-; rifleman, Queen's Westminster Rifles, 1917-18; M.P. (Lab.) Peterborough division, 1929-31; Television News Map series, 1939, 1946-49; Chairman, Fabian Colonial Bureau, 1945-1950; Columnist, Socialist Commentary. *Publications:* 31 Japhet and Happy Annuals (1921-52); Dot and Carrie; An Outline of Economic Geography, 1923 (revised and largely rewritten), 1942; Working-Class Education, 1924; (with Hilda Trevelyan) Sir Japhet of The Ark, and other children's plays, 1923-26; The Plebs Atlas, 1926; A Short History of the British Empire, 1929, revised, 1946; An Atlas of Current Affairs, 1934; How Empires Grow, 1935; An Atlas of European History, 1935; The Opening-Up of the World, 1936; Atlas of Empire, 1937; an Atlas-History of the Second Great War (10 vols.), 1940-47; Atlas of Post-War Problems, 1943; contributor to Fabian Colonial Essays, 1944; Penguin Atlas of the U.S.S.R., 1945; Atlas of Africa, 1960; illustrated H. G. Wells' Outline of History, 1919-20 (revised, 1950, 1959); Lancelot Hogben's Mathematics for the Million and Science for the Citizen, 1936-38; and Nehru's Glimpses of World History, 1942. *Address:* 16 Endersleigh Gardens, Hendon, N.W.4. *Club:* Savile.
[*Died* 2 *March* 1962.

HORSBRUGH, Baroness *cr.* 1959 (Life Peeress); **Florence Horsbrugh,** P.C. 1945; G.B.E. 1954 (C.B.E. 1939; M.B.E. 1920); *d.* of late Henry Moncrieff Horsbrugh, C.A., Edinburgh. *Educ.:* Lansdowne House, Edinburgh; St. Hilda's, Folkestone. M.B.E. for work in canteens and national kitchens, 1916-18; M.P. (C.) Dundee, 1931-45; Parliamentary Secretary, Ministry of Health, 1939-45; Parliamentary Secretary to Ministry of Food, June 1945; M.P. (C.) Moss Side Div. of Manchester, March 1950-59. Minister of Education, 1951 - Oct. 1954. Delegate to Council of Europe and Western European Union, 1955-60. Doctor of Letters, Mills College, California, 1945; Hon. F.R.C.S.Edin. 1946; Hon. LL.D. Edinburgh Univ., 1947. *Address:* 21 Marsham Court, S.W.1. *T.:* Victoria 8181; 4 Merchiston Crescent, Edinburgh 10. *T.:* Fountainbridge 1185. [*Died* 6 *Dec.* 1969.

HORSMAN, Sir Henry, Kt. 1939; M.C.; *b.* 1887; *s.* of late Albert Francis Horsman; *m.* 1923, Dorothy Richardson (marriage dissolved, 1950); two *s.*; 2nd 1950, Mrs. Beryl Harris, *d.* of Dr. W. A. Salmond. Pres. Upper India Chamber of Commerce, 1936-38. Chairman, Swadeshi Cotton Mills, Cawnpore. Served European War, 1914-18 (M.C. and Bar). *Address:* c/o Barclays Bank (D.C.O.), Adderley St., Cape Town, South Africa; Shaw Park, Pembroke, Bermuda. *Club:* Devonshire.
[*Died* 11 *Aug.* 1966.

HORT, Professor Greta, R. of Dbg.; Prof. of English Literature, University of Aarhus, Denmark, since 1957; Ph.D. (Cantab); *b.* 25 May 1903; *d.* of late Vilhelm Hjort, Astronomer Royal, Magnetic Observatory, Denmark, and late Anne Margrethe (*née* Ulrich). *Educ.:* N. Zahle's Skole; University of Copenhagen (M.A.). Research student, Newnham College Cambridge, 1929-1931. Asst. Lectr., Univ. of Copenhagen, 1928-29; Pfeiffer Research Fellow, Girton Coll., Camb., 1931-34; Supervisor, Newnham Coll., 1930-35, 1937-38; Subwarden, Univ. House, Birmingham, 1936-37; Principal, Univ. Women's Coll., Univ. of Melbourne, Australia, 1938-47; travel and studies on the Continent, 1946-57. Gold Medal, Univ. of

Copenhagen, 1925: Gamble Prize, Girton College, 1936; Tagea Brandt Prize, Denmark, 1965. *Publications:* Sense and Thought: A Study in Mysticism, 1936; Piers Plowman and Contemporary Religious Thought, 1938; Mamre: Translation of Essays by Martin Buber with Introduction and Notes, 1945; Two Poems, 1946; An Anthology of Australian Literature (with A. Salling), 1966; articles in learned journals. *Recreations:* Comparative Religion; music. *Address:* Fortegaarden 2, Risskov, Denmark. *T.:* Aarhus 177452. [*Died* 19 *Aug.* 1967.

HORTON, Percy Frederick, M.A.; R.B.A.; A.R.C.A.; Painter and Draughtsman; Ruskin Master of Drawing, University of Oxford, 1949-64; *b.* Brighton, 8 March 1897; *s.* of Percy Horton and Ellen Batchelor; *m.* 1921, Lydia Sargent Smith; one *d.* *Educ.:* Brighton Municipal Secondary Sch.; Brighton Coll. of Art; Central Sch. of Arts and Crafts; Roy. Coll. of Art (Roy. Exhibn.). Asst. Art Master, Rugby School, 1920-22; A.R.C.A. with distinction, 1924; Art Master, Bishops Stortford Coll., 1925-30; Art Classes Working Men's College, 1926-36; Instructor in Painting Sch., Roy. Coll. of Art, 1930-49. Examiner in Fine Arts, Univ. of Reading, 1949-57, 1960-65; M.A. Oxford, 1949; Extraordinary Member, Senior Common Room, New College, Oxford, 1949. Paintings and drawing shown at exhibns. including United Artists', National War Pictures, 100 British Painters' (America), Arts Council Travelling Exhibns., Roy. Acad., New English Art Club and in many London and provincial galleries. Works represented in permanent collections of: Tate Gallery, National Portrait Gallery, Ashmolean Museum, FitzWilliam Museum, City Art Galleries of Sheffield, Leeds, Huddersfield, Carlisle, Eastbourne. During War of 1939-45 drew portraits for National War Records; portraits drawn and painted for various colleges at Oxford and Cambridge, The English Association, etc. *Publications:* contribs. to Architectural Review, Art Work, The Studio. *Recreations:* music and travel. *Address:* The Broads, Southover, High Street, Lewes, Sussex. *T.:* Lewes 2687. *Club:* Athenæum. [*Died* 4 *Nov.* 1970.

HORTON, Ralph Albert, C.I.E. 1928; I.P.S.; retired; *b.* 5 October 1885; *y. s.* of A. Horton, of Olton, Warwickshire; *m.* 1913, Mabel St. Aubyn Wemyss (*d.* 1965), *d.* of J. D. Young, United Provinces, India, and Culdaff, Ireland; two *d.* *Educ.:* King Edward VI's Sch., Birmingham; privately. Entered the Indian (Imperial) Police as Assistant District Superintendent, 1906; Special Duty King-Emperor's Durbar, 1911; District Superintendent of Police, Jhansi, 1913; Cawnpore, 1915; Captain, 1/131 Infantry, 1918; District Superintendent of Police, Bareilly, 1922; Officer in Charge, Investigation Branch, United Provinces C.I.D., and Assistant to the Deputy-Inspector-General of Police, 1924; on special duty Kakori Revolutionary Conspiracy Case, 1925-1927; on special duty Central Intelligence Bureau, Govt. of India, 1928; Deputy Inspector-General, 1932; Inspector-General of Police, United Provinces, 1935; Minister of Police, Holkar State, Central India, 1941; Deputy Prime Minister, 1943; Prime Minister to H.H. the Maharaja Holkar of Indore, 1947. *Address* Tamarisks, Rock, N. Cornwall. [*Died* 2 *Oct.* 1969.

HOSIE, Ian, F.J.I.; Editor, Liverpool Daily Post, 1947-68; *b.* 8 April 1905; *s.* of David Stewart and Jean Hosie, Douglas, I.O.M.; *m.* 1929, Annie Muriel, *d.* of John and Annie Chadwick, Douglas I.O.M.; one *s.* *Educ.:* Douglas High Sch.; Merchant Service. Entered journalism on Manx weekly, after several years in Merchant Navy as apprentice, 1927. After English provincial experience, Chief Sub-Editor, Glasgow Evg. News, 1933-36; Day Chief Sub-Editor, Daily Sketch, 1936-37; Sub-Editor, London Evg. News, 1937-41; Chief Sub-Editor, Sunday Graphic, 1941-42; Asst. Editor, 1942-47. Chairman, British Guild of Newspaper Editors, N.W. Region, 1963-64. *Recreations:* golf, motoring, foreign travel. *Address:* Upover, Higher Street, Dittisham, Dartmouth, S. Devon. *Club:* Rotary (Liverpool). [*Died* 15 *Aug.* 1970.

HOSIER, Arthur Julius, O.B.E. 1949; Hon. LL.D. Cambridge 1951; farmer and engineer; *b.* 16 Oct. 1877; *s.* of Joshua and Sarah Hosier; *m.* 1st, 1901, Ruth Smith (decd.); one *s.* two *d.* (and one *s.* one *d.* decd.); 2nd, Florence Joyce (*née* Orchard); one *d.* *Educ.:* Bradford-on Avon Gram. Sch. Engaged in farming until 1904, in engineering, 1904-10, in farming again since 1910 and also in engineering since 1922. Inventor of Hosier Open Air Milking Bail. R.A.S.E. Silver Medals, 1928, 1929 and 1934. *Publication:* Hosier Farming System, 1951. *Address:* Wexcombe House, Marlborough, Wilts. *T.:* Oxenwood 229. [*Died* 3 *April* 1963.

HOSKING, Paymaster Rear-Admiral Richard Bosustow, C.B. 1924; retired; *b.* 23 Sept. 1869; *y. s.* of Rev. Henry Hosking, B.A., of Syleham Vicarage, Scole; *m.* Elizabeth Susan (*d.* 1958), *d.* of Edmund Boyle of Bermuda; no *c.* *Educ.:* Llandaff Cathedral School; Probus School. Entered Royal Navy, 1886; retired, 1924; served on board H.M.S. Britannia during European War, and afterwards held position of first Port Accountant Officer, Devonport. *Address:* Greenbank, Crown Hill, S. Devon. *T.:* Plymouth 71762. [*Died* 23 *Nov.* 1962.

HOSSIE, Major David Neil, D.S.O. 1919; Q.C.; barrister and solicitor; *b.* 27 Dec. 1890; *s.* of David Walker Hossie and Sarah Crone; *m.* Mary Gordon Stuart; one *s.* two *d.* *Educ.:* University of Saskatchewan; B.A.; Rhodes Scholar (Alberta and Sask.), 1912; New College, Oxford, B.A., M.A.; Inner Temple. K.E.H. to Dec. 1914; R.F.A. to Feb. 1919, France and Salonika, temp. Major acting Lt. Col. (1914-15 star, D.S.O., Serbian White Eagle 4th Class with Swords, despatches thrice); Major R.F.A. Canadian Militia, m.s.c.; Past Chairman of Board of Vancouver General Hospital; practice of law, Vancouver, B.C., since 1919. *Recreations:* golf, shooting. *Address:* 1030 West Georgia, Vancouver, 5, B.C. *T.A.:* Damarell. *T.:* Mutual 5-8521; Walnut 2-8241. *Clubs:* Union (Victoria); Vancouver (Vancouver); Capilano Golf (B.C.). [*Died* 31 *May* 1962.

HOTHAM, 7th Baron *cr.* 1797; 17th Bt. 1621; **Henry Frederick Hotham,** C.B.E. 1958; late Major Grenadier Guards; D.L. East Riding of Yorkshire; Honorary Colonel 440 L.A.A. Regt., R.A. (T.A.), 1938-57; *b.* 13 Aug. 1899; *s.* of late Captain Henry Edward Hotham, late the Cameronians (Scottish Rifles), and Ethel Lindsay, *d.* of Collingwood Lindsay Wood, of Freeland; *S. cousin,* 1923; *m.* 1937, Lady Letitia Sibell Winifred Cecil, *er. d.* of 5th Marquess of Exeter, K.G.; three *s.* *Educ.:* Winchester; Sandhurst. Owns about 19,000 acres. *Heir:* *s.* Hon. Henry Durand Hotham, *b.* 3 May 1940. *Address:* Dalton Hall, Dalton Holme, Beverley, Yorkshire. *Clubs:* Carlton, Guards; Yorkshire (York). [*Died* 18 *Nov.* 1967

HOTHAM, Admiral Sir Alan Geoffrey, K.C.M.G., *cr.* 1938; C.B. 1923; Gentleman Usher of the Blue Rod in Order of St. Michael and St. George, 1934-59; *b.* 3 Oct. 1876; *o. surv. s.* of late Admiral of the Fleet Sir Charles F. Hotham, G.C.B., G.C.V.O. Retired, 1929; Member of Port of London Authority, 1929-56. *Address:* 65 Ashley Gardens, S.W.1. *T.:* Victoria 1497. [*Died* 10 *July* 1965.

HOTHFIELD, 3rd Baron, *cr.* 1881, **Henry Hastings Sackville Thanet Tufton,** Bt. 1851; Lt.-Col. (retd.) 15th Hussars; *b.* 16 March 1897; *er. s.* of 2nd Baron and Lady Ierne Hastings (*d.* 1935), *d.* of 13th Earl of Huntingdon; *S.* father 1953; *m.* 1918, Dorothy, *d.* of late William George Raphael, 9 Connaught Place, W.1. and Castle Hill, Englefield Green. *Educ.:* Eton. Served European War, 1914-19; Lieut. 15th/19th Hussars, 1917. Assistant Director of Public Relations, Home Forces, 1942. *Heir: cousin* Thomas Sackville Tufton, *b.* 20 July 1916. *Address:* Castle Hill, Englefield Green, Surrey; (seats) Appleby Castle, Westmorland; Skipton Castle, Yorkshire. *Club:* Turf. [*Died* 20 *Aug.* 1961.

HOTINE, Brigadier Martin, C.M.G., 1949; C.B.E. 1945; Surveys Adviser and Director of Overseas (Geodetic and Topographic) Surveys, Department of Technical Co-operation, 1961-63: with United States Coast and Geodetic Survey and Institute of Earth Sciences, Washington D.C. and Boulder, Colorado, 1963-68; *b.* 17 June 1898; *s.* of Frederick Martyn Hotine; *m.* 1924, Kate Pearson; three *d. Educ.:* Southend High Schools; Woolwich; Magdalene Coll., Cambridge. Commnd. R.E., 1917; European War, 1914-18, Regimental service in Persia, Iraq, India; Research Officer, Air Survey Cttee., 1925-28; G.S.O.3 and G.S.O.2 War Office, 1928-31; Survey of Malta and Gozo; Survey of 30th Meridian Arc in Central Africa, 1931-33; in charge of Map Publication Div., Triangulation and Levelling Div., Ordnance Survey, 1933-39: served War of 1939-45 in France, Belgium, East Africa, Greece; Director of Military Surveys, War Office, 1941-46; retired pay, 1949; Director of Overseas Surveys and Survey Adviser, Colonial Office, 1946-61. Founder's Medallist, Roy. Geographical Soc.; Gold Medallist, Instn. of Royal Engineers; President's Medallist, Photogrammetric Soc. Officer, Legion of Merit (U.S.A.). *Publications:* Surveying from Air Photographs, 1931; numerous monographs on air survey and geodesy. *Recreations:* golf, philately. *Address:* 44 Highpoint, Heath Rd., Weybridge, Surrey. [*Died* 12 *Nov.* 1968.

HOUGH, William; retired member of H.M. Foreign Service; *b.* 9 Sept. 1884; *e. s.* late P. J. Hough, Manchester; *m.* 1st, Kathleen Margaret Altintop; one *s.*; 2nd, 1925, Hortense, *e. d.* of late Louis Rocher, Chinese Customs Service; one *s.* one *d. Educ.:* The Hulme Grammar School, Manchester; abroad. Student Interpreter, Levant Consular Service, 1904; Probationer Course, Pembroke College, Cambridge; served at Smyrna, 1907-09; Dardanelles, 1908; Salonica, 1909; Uskub, 1910-11; Jaffa, 1912; Jerusalem, 1914; served during War in Gallipoli and Palestine Campaigns (Captain), also at New York (special duty), 1918-22, at Department of Overseas Trade (head of Eastern Section); Consul, Port Said, 1922; Aleppo, 1924; Athens, 1928; Consul-General at Constantinople, 1930; Commercial Sec. British Legation, Prague, 1937-39; Commercial Counsellor, British Embassy in Spain, 1939-40; British Commercial Agent, Jerusalem, 1940; retired from H.M. Foreign Service, 1944; Dep. Controller of Light Industries, Palestine, 1945-46. *Publication:* A song cycle of 6 sonnets from E. H. R. Altounyan's Ornament of Honour. *Recreation:* music. *Address:* Rest Harrow, Holt, Wimborne, Dorset. *T.:* Wimborne 766. [*Died* 26 *Feb.* 1962.

HOUGHTON, Claude; *see* Oldfield, C. H.

HOULDSWORTH, Brig. Sir Henry (Walter), K.B.E. 1960; D.S.O. 1940 (Bar 1942); M.C.; T.D.; Lord Lieutenant of Moray since 1943; one of H.M.'s Body Guard of Hon. Corps of Gentlemen-at-Arms since 1939; Chairman Glenlivet and Glengrant Distilleries Ltd.; Member: Scottish Hospital Endowments Research Trust; Council on Tribunals; Director: Coltness Iron Co. Ltd.; Outward Bound Moray Sea School; Gordonstoun Schools Ltd.; *b.* 28 Jan. 1896; *yr. s.* of late James Hamilton Houldsworth, Castlebank, Lanark; *m.* 1921, Katharine, *d.* of late G. S. and Lady Laura Douglas, Edenhall, Kelso; two *d.* (one *s.* decd.). *Educ.:* Eton; R.M.C., Sandhurst. Joined Seaforth Hglndrs., 1915; served European War, 1915-18 (despatches, twice wounded, M.C.); War of 1939-45, commanded 4 Bn. B.E.F., France, 1940 (wounded, D.S.O.); Brigade Commander 51 (Highland) Div., 1941-43, including Middle East, 1942 (Bar to D.S.O.); Commandant, School of Infantry, 1943-44. Hon. Col. 11th (T.A.) Bn. Seaforth Highlanders, 1948-56. C.St.J. 1958. *Address:* Dallas Lodge, Forres, Scotland. *T.:* Dallas 205. *Clubs:* United Service, M.C.C., Buck's (Life Hon. Mem.); New (Edinburgh). [*Died* 9 *Oct.* 1963.

HOUNSELL, Major-General Harold Arthur, C.B. 1951; C.B.E. 1943; late R.A.; late Comdg. 3rd Anti-Aircraft Group; *b.* 31 March 1897. Served European War, 1914-18, in France and Belgium (wounded, British War Medal and Victory Medal); 2nd Lieut., Royal Artillery, 1916; Lieut., 1918; Captain, 1929; North-West Frontier of India, 1930-31 (medal with clasp); North-West Frontier of India (Mohmand), 1933 (clasp); Instructor in Gunnery, 1935-38; Major, 1938. Instructor in Gunnery, 1938-1940; War of 1939-45, in Tunisia and Italy (despatches twice, C.B.E.); acting Lieut.-Col., 1940-41; temp. Lieut.-Col., 1941; Maj.-Gen., 1949; retired, 1952. Bronze Star (U.S.), 1945. *Club:* Naval and Military. [*Died* 14 *March* 1970.

HOUSTOUN-BOSWALL, Major Sir Gordon, 6th Bt., *cr.* 1836; *b.* 15 March 1887; *s.* of Colonel Thomas Alford Houstoun-Boswall-Preston (*d.* 1918), and Alice Mary (*d.* 1916), *o. d.* of William Cunard; *S.* cousin (Sir Thomas Randolph Houstoun-Boswall) 1953; *m.* 1916, Daisy, *d.* of Edwin Copeland Waller, Yarmouth; two *s. Educ.:* Marlborough. Served European War, 1914-18, with 1st Life Guards, France and Belgium. *Heir:* Thomas Houstoun-Boswall [*b.* 13 Feb. 1919; *m.* 1945, Margaret, *d.* of George Bullen-Smith, Summerdale, Hailsham; one *s.* one *d.* Served War of 1939-45, Pilot-Officer R.A.F.V.R.]. *Address:* Tootenhill, Church Lane, Southwick, Sussex. *T.:* Southwick 3041. *Club:* English-Speaking Union. [*Died* 28 *Feb.* 1961.

HOW, Right Rev. John Charles Halland; D.D. (Hon.) Glasgow, 1943; Canon Emeritus of Chichester, 1940; *s.* of late Charles How, Forest Hill, Kent, and late Elizabeth Halland; *m.* 1st, 1925, Naomi Junie Katherine (*d.* 1938), *d.* of late Rev. S. M. Reynolds, Burnmoor, Co. Durham; one *s.* one *d.*; 2nd, 1939, Barbara, *d.* of late Dr. A. M. Collcutt, Brighton. *Educ.:* Christchurch Cathedral Choir School, Oxford; Pocklington School; St. John's Coll., Camb. (Scholar); Ely Theological Coll. B.A. (2nd Class Oriental Languages Tripos)1903; 1st Class Theological Tripos, Part ii, 1904; Stewart of Rannoch Hebrew Scholarship (University Hebrew Prize), 1901; Tyrrwhit Hebrew Scholar, Mason Hebrew Prize, 1904; M.A. 1907. Deacon, 1905; Priest, 1906; Wellington College Mission, Walworth, 1905-06; Hebrew Lecturer, St. John's College, Cambridge, 1906-20; Precentor (and Hebrew Lecturer, 1907-13) Trinity College, Cambridge, 1907-20; Superior of the Oratory of the Good Shepherd, 1913-24; Warden of the Oratory House, Cambridge, 1920-24; Manchester Diocesan Missioner, 1924-26; Rector of Liverpool 1926-35; Examining Chaplain to the Bishop of Liverpool, 1930-35; Canon Residentiary, 1931-35; Rural Dean of Liverpool North,

1930-35; Vicar and Rural Dean of Brighton, 1935-38; Rector of West Blatchington, 1935-38, Canon and Prebendary of Waltham (Chichester), 1935; Examining Chaplain to Bishop of Southwark, 1908-11, to Bishop of Winchester, 1911-24; C.F. 1915-19; Hon. Canon of Liverpool, 1927-31: Chaplain to the King, 1933-38. Bishop of Glasgow and Galloway, 1938-52; Primus of the Scottish Church, 1946-52, retd.; Licensed Preacher Dioc. of Bath and Wells (in charge of the Parishes of Blackford and Compton Pauncefoot), 1952-55, retd. *Publications:* Joel and Amos (Cambridge Bible for Schools), 1910: The Sung Eucharist, 1920; Contributor to the New Commentary, 1928; Christian and Churchman, 1930; Personal Discipleship and the Way of Prayer, 1931; The Venture of Christian Marriage, 1938; Faith and Fellowship, 1950. *Recreations:* walking and odd jobs. *Address:* 17 The Droveway, Hove 4, Sussex. *T.:* Brighton 59876.
[*Died* 22 *May* 1961.

HOWARD, Sir Algar (Henry Stafford), K.C.B., *cr.* 1951 (C.B. 1937); K.C.V.O., *cr.* 1944 (C.V.O. 1935); M.C., T.D., J.P. and D.L. County of Gloucester; An Extra Gentleman Usher to the Queen since 1952 (to King George VI, 1950-52); Barrister-at-law, Inner Temple; Major Royal Gloucestershire Hussars Yeo.; *b.* 7 Aug. 1880; *s.* of late Sir E. Stafford Howard (*d.* 1916); *m.* 1921, Hon. Violet Ethel Vandeleur (*d.* 1960), *e. d.* and co-heir of 1st Baron Knaresborough, and *widow* of Captain A. M. Vandeleur; two *d. Educ.:* Harrow. Served European War (M.C.); Rouge Dragon Pursuivant of Arms; Windsor Herald, 1919-31; Norroy King of Arms and Principal Herald of the North Part of England, 1931-43, Norroy and Ulster King of Arms, 1943-44; Garter Principal King of Arms, 1944-50; Genealogist, Order of the Bath, 1946-50. *Recreation:* fishing. *Address:* Greystoke, Penrith, Cumberland. *T.:* Greystoke 275. *Clubs:* Travellers', Pratt's.
[*Died* 14 *Feb.* 1970.

HOWARD, Andrée; choreographer; dancer; *b.* 3 Oct. 1910. Studied under Marie Rambert. First stage appearance, Duke of York's, 1929, in Jew Süss; an original member of the Ballet Club, 1930 (Façade, Le Spectre de la Rose, etc.); joined de Basil's Ballet Russe de Monte Carlo, 1933; devised dances for productions from 1933 (Savile, Birmingham Repertory, Old Vic, etc.). Went to New York, 1939, to join Ballet Theatre as solo dancer and choreographer. Produced La Fête Etrange for London Ballet, Arts Theatre, London, 1940. Costumes, décor and choreography for ballet Assembly Ball, Sadler's Wells, 1946; Costumes and choreography for A Mirror for Witches, Covent Garden, 1952; Veneziana, Covent Garden, 1953; décor and choreography La Belle Dame sans Merci, Covent Garden, 1959; choreography for Sadler's Wells Production of Merry England, 1960. Made debut on stage of Royal Opera House, as the "Ashton" ugly sister (Cinderella) during Christmas season 1960. Catharsis, for the Masque Ballet Club, for 1st performance on 22nd July 1961; décor and costumes for London Ballet's Fair Maid, Lyceum Theatre, Edinburgh, 1961; prod. Death and the Maiden, Assembly Ball, and Les Barricades Mysterieuses, for Turkish Ballet, at opera, Ankara, 1962; designed costumes and sets for Turkish Ballet prod. of The Sleeping Beauty, 1963; Choreography for The Tempest, London Dance Theatre and New Lyric, Hammersmith, 1964; revised Barricade and Veneziana for London Dance Theatre, at Vaudeville Theatre, London; also rehearsed Death and the Maiden for Scapino Ballet, Amsterdam. 1965. *Address:* 1 Nugent Terrace, N.W.8.
[*Died* 18 *April* 1968.

HOWARD, Lieut.-General Sir Geoffrey Weston, K.C.B., *cr.* 1938 (C.B. 1932); C.M.G. 1919; D.S.O. 1902; *b.* 14 Dec. 1876; 3rd *s.* of Henry Howard of Stone Ho., Worcester; *m.* 1905, Meta Minnia Gregory (*d.* 1949). Entered army, 1897; served South Africa, 1899-1902 (despatches twice, Queen's medal six clasps, King's medal two clasps, D.S.O.); European War, 1914-18 (despatches seven times, C.M.G., Bt. Col.); Brigade Commander 9th Infantry Brigade, 1927-31; Maj.-Gen. in charge of Administration, Eastern Command, 1931-34; Commander of 5th Div., 1934-37; retired pay, 1938; a Comdr., 1940. Colonel the Essex Regt., 1935-47. *Address:* Bishops Down, Tunbridge Wells. *Club:* United Service.
[*Died* 3 *Oct.* 1966.

HOWARD, G(eorge) Wren, M.A., M.C.; Chairman: Jonathan Cape Ltd.; A. W. Bain & Co. Ltd.; Director: Book Centre Ltd.; The Australasian Publishing Co. (Pty.); Duralin Products Ltd.; *b.* 24 March 1893; *s.* of late Frank G. and Feona Howard, Hampstead; *m.* 1915, Eileen Swinburne-Hanham (*d.* 1959); one *s.* one *d. Educ.:* Marlborough College; Trinity College, Cambridge. Served with King's Royal Rifle Corps, 1914-19, in France, Belgium, and Italy; joint founder of firm of Jonathan Cape as a partnership, 1921; Treasurer The Publishers Association 1935-37; Treasurer International Publishers Congress, London, 1936; President The Publishers Association, 1937-39, Vice-President 1939-40. *Recreations:* gardening, photography. *Address:* 3 Hampstead Way, N.W.11. *T.:* 01-455 6360. *Club:* Garrick.
[*Died* 28 *July* 1968.

HOWARD, Sir (Harold Walter) Seymour, 1st Bt., *cr.* 1955; Kt. 1955; J.P.; late Lieutenant, City of London; Senior Partner in Stockbroking Firm of Charles Stanley and Co.; *b.* April 1888; *s.* of William A. Howard, Glos.; *m.* 1915, Edith M. (*d.* 1962), *d.* of Edward Turner, Warminster, Wilts; one *s.* (and one *s.* decd.). *Educ.:* privately, Switzerland. Contested (Nat.) Barnsley, Yorks, 1938; gave services to Ministry of Aircraft Production in 1941 and served on a number of Government Committees, including the War Cabinet Committee for Allied Supplies; Alderman and Sheriff of City of London, 1944-45; Lord Mayor of London, 1954-55. *Recreation:* ski-ing. *Heir: s.* (Hamilton) Edward de Coucey Howard [*b.* 29 Oct. 1915; *m.* 1943, Elizabeth Howarth (*née* Ludlow); two *s.*]. *Address:* 104 Whitelands House, King's Road, S.W.3.
[*Died* 15 *April* 1967.

HOWARD, Sir Harry, (Henry Rudolph), K.B.E. 1963; Kt. 1961; Lord Mayor of Perth, W. Australia, 1955-64; Chairman, British Empire and Commonwealth Games, Perth, W.A., 1962; Consul for Finland in W.A. since 1954; *b.* Sale, Cheshire, 20 April 1890; *s.* of Frederic Joseph Howard and Mary Jane Howard (*née* Harris); *m.* 1920, Thelma May Tilburn; two *s. Educ.:* Manchester Technical Sch. Employed Accountants Office Gas Dept., Manch. Corp., 1904-12; Thomas A. Edison Ltd., Sydney, N.S.W., 1912-24; Man. Dir., Wyper Howard Ltd., Perth, W.A., 1924-56; retired, 1956. Chm. Congregational Union of W. Aust., 1936-1938; President: Perth Chamber of Commerce and of Federated Chambers of W.A., 1942-43; Royal Automobile Club of W.A., 1944-46; Royal Over-Seas League (W.A.), 1967. Companion Institution Radio Engineers (Aust.), 1940; Fellow, Corporation Consulting Accountants (Aust.), 1940; Life member, Sportsmen's Assoc. of Aust., 1965. Freedom of Cities of Detroit (1961), San Francisco and Kansas City (1963). J.P. 1936. *Recreations:* music and golf. *Address:* Ferry Court, Esplanade, South Perth, Western Australia. *T.:* 67.1198. *Club:* Weld (Perth, W.A.).
[*Died* 11 *Aug.* 1970.

HOWARD, Major Sir Henry (George), Kt., *cr.* 1939; C.I.E. 1935; M.C.; M.I.E.E.; M.Inst. C.E.; Retired Consulting Civil and Electrical Engineer; *b.* 5 Oct. 1883; *s.* of Henry Thomas Howard and Harriet Kate Gutsell; *m.* 1920, Olga Alexandra Weston; no *c.* *Educ.:* University of California, U.S.A. Hydro-Electric Engineer since 1905; Associated as Engineer with large hydro-electric systems in North and South America and India; with Hants Yeomanry during South African War (Queen's Medal and five bars); served European War, R.F.A., Major, France, Mesopotamia, 1915-19 (despatches, M.C.); C I E. 1935 for services to Madras Government; Member American Society Civil Engineers. *Recreations:* golf, shooting. *Address:* c/o English Rooms, Funchal, Madeira; San Martinho, Funchal. *Club:* Oriental. [*Died* 2 *Aug.* 1968.

HOWARD, Sir Herbert; *see* Howard, Sir S. H.

HOWARD, Sir John Curtois, Kt., *cr.* 1942; Chairman, Police Council for Great Britain, 1953-57, retired; *b.* Spalding, 15 January 1887; *s.* of late Fitzalan Howard, Holyrood House, Spalding; *m.* 1912, North Carey, *d.* of late Capt. John Lakes; one *s.* three *d.* *Educ.:* Uppingham; Clare Coll., Cambridge (Exhibitioner). B.A. 1909; Barrister-at-Law, Inner Temple, 1913; served European War, 1915-1920; Brigade Trench Mortar, Officer, 177th Brigade, 59th Div.; Staff Captain British Troops France and Flanders, 1919-20; Pres. District Court, Cyprus, 1920-24; Attorney-General, Cyprus, 1924-26; Solicitor-General, Nigeria, 1926-33; K.C., Gold Coast, 1934; Attorney-General of the Gold Coast, 1933-1936; Attorney-General, Ceylon, 1936; K.C., Ceylon, 1936; Legal Secretary, Ceylon, 1936-1939; Acting Governor, Ceylon, July 1946-Feb. 1947 and July 1947-Aug. 1947; Chief Justice of Ceylon, 1939-49. *Publication:* Joint Edition, Laws of Cyprus, 1924. *Recreation:* golf. *Address:* 19 Denton Road, Meads, Eastbourne, Sussex. *Club:* East India and Sports. [*Died* 19 *Nov.* 1970.

HOWARD, Peter D.; Author and Farmer; *b.* 20 Dec. 1908; *s.* of E. Cecil Howard and Evangeline Bohm; *m.* 1932, Doris Metaxa, Ithaca; two *s.* one *d.* *Educ.:* Mill Hill School; Oxford University. Articled Godden, Holme and Ward, 1932-33; Political Columnist, Express Newspapers Ltd., 1933-1941; farming, 1937-. Member N.F.U. Liveryman Worshipful Company of Wheelwrights, 1937-; Member of Court, 1961-. Hon. Senator of the State of Mississippi. Freedom of the City of Atlanta, Ga. *Publications:* Innocent Men, 1941; Fighters Ever, 1942; Ideas Have Legs, 1945; That Man Frank Buchman, 1946; Men on Trial, 1946; The World Rebuilt, 1951; Remaking Men, 1954; Effective Statesmanship, 1955; America Needs an Ideology, 1957; Frank Buchman's Secret, 1961; Britain and the Beast, 1963; Design for Dedication, 1964; Beaverbrook: A Study of Max the Unknown, 1964; *plays:* The Real News, 1953; The Dictators' Slippers, 1953; The Boss, 1953; We Are Tomorrow, 1954; The Vanishing Island, 1955; Rumpelsnits, 1956; The Man Who Would Not Die, 1957; Miracle in the Sun, 1959; Pickle Hill, 1959; The Hurricane, 1960; The Ladder, 1960; Music at Midnight, 1962; Space is so Startling, 1962; Through the Garden Wall, 1963; The Diplomats, 1963; Mr. Brown Comes Down the Hill, 1964; Give a Dog a Bone, 1964; Happy Death-day, 1965; *Film plays:* Music at Midnight; The Voice of the Hurricane; The Dictator's Slippers; Give a Dog a Bone; Mr. Brown Comes Down the Hill. *Recreations:* human nature; formerly winter sports (Member of British Bobsleigh team that broke World Record at Cortina d'Ampezzo, World's Championship, 1939); Rugby football (Oxford Univ. *v.* Camb. Univ., 1930 and 1931; capped eight times for England, 1930, 1931, and captained England, 1931). *Address:* Hill Farm, Brent Eleigh, Sudbury, Suffolk. *T.:* Lavenham 296. [*Died* 25 *Feb.* 1965.

HOWARD, Roy Wilson; President, Scripps-Howard Newspapers, 1922-52; Chm. and Dir., Exec. Cttee., from 1953; retired as Editor of New York World-Telegram and Sun, Sept. 1960, continuing as President to May 1962 and (present) Director; Chm. and Dir., Exec. Cttee., E. W. Scripps Co.; *b.* 1 Jan. 1883; *s.* of William A. Howard and Elizabeth Wilson; *m.* 1909, Margaret Rohe; one *s.* one *d.* *Educ.:* Manual Training High Sch., Indianapolis, Indiana. Reporter Indianapolis News, 1902; successively sports editor Indianapolis Star, asst. telegraph editor St. Louis Post-Dispatch, news editor Cincinnati Post; New York corr. Scripps-McRae League, 1906; New York mgr. Publishers' Press Assoc., 1906; became New York mgr. United Press Assocs., 1907 (when it took over Publishers' Press Assoc.); president and general manager, Jan. 1912-21; chm. bd., same assoc., Jan. 1921-37; chm. bd. and business dir. of Newspaper Enterprise Association and all Scripps-McRae (now Scripps-Howard) newspapers, 1921-36; assumed editorial direction of above-named properties, in association with Robert P. Scripps, 1922; negotiated purchase of New York World, Feb. 1931, New York Sun, Jan. 1950, combining same with New York Telegram as New York World-Telegram and Sun. Chm., Midtown Advisory Board, Chemical Bank, N.Y. Trust Co.; Director: Pan-American World Airways; Deafness Research Foundation; Boys' Clubs of America; Mem., Bd. of Trustees, Foundation Josée et René de Chambrun (for preservation of La Grange, Lafayette's home). Dir., New York World's Fair Co., 1964-65. Hon. LL.D. Indiana Univ., 1954. Mason 33°. *Address:* 200 Park Avenue, New York, N.Y., 10017, U.S.A. *T.:* Tn 7-5000. *Clubs:* Sky, Sigma Delta Chi, American Soc. of Newspaper Editors, Dutch Treat, Artists and Writers (N.Y.C.); Silurians; Bohemian (San Francisco). [*Died* 21 *Nov.* 1964.

HOWARD, Sir Seymour; *see* Howard, Sir H. W. S.

HOWARD, Sir (Stanley) Herbert, Kt., *cr.* 1943; Retired as Secretary, Commonwealth Agricultural Bureaux, (1946-60); *b.* 17 April 1888; *s.* of late Major Walter Howard, D.S.O.; *m.* 1st, 1913, Mary Anne Fergusson (*d.* 1915); 2nd, 1918, Kathleen Muriel Kavanagh (divorced 1924); one *s.*; 3rd, 1937, Florence Kathleen (*née* Turner), *widow* of James Mackay, Duntanlich, Perth; one *s.* *Educ.:* St. George's Sch., Bulawayo; Exeter College, Oxford, Rhodes Scholar, B.A. (Hons. Natural Science), Diploma of Forestry. Imperial Forest Service, 1911; Imperial Silviculturist, 1919-26: Inspector-General of Forests to Government of pre-partition India and President of Forest Research Institute, 1940-46. Represented pre-partition India, Rome International Forestry Conference, 1926, Empire Forestry Conference, Australia, 1928, Stockholm International Forestry Conference, 1929, Food and Agriculture Organisation Conference, Quebec, 1945; represented Commonwealth Agricultural Bureaux Empire Forestry Conf., 1947; F.A.O. U.N. Korean Relief Administration mission to South Korea, 1952; F.A.O. assignment to Iran, 1955. *Publications:* Forest Pocket Book, 1927, 5th ed. 1943; and many others on Forestry. *Recreations:* cricket, football, boxing, ski-ing, shooting, fishing—nowadays only fishing. [*Died* 23 *Dec.* 1968.

HOWARD, William Reginald; *b.* 10 June 1879; 2nd *s.* of late Alderman

John Howard, J.P., Bootle, Lancs. and Aberfeldy, Scotland, and of Emma Howard (*née* Muncaster); *m.* 1902, Alice Marian (*d.* 1944), *e. d.* of late G. E. Trevor-Roper, Richmond House, Mold; one *s.* decd. *Educ.:* Bootle College; The King's School, Chester. Joined family business of Howard Brothers of Liverpool and London, 1899; in 1908 director of Dey Time Registers Ltd., and since 1914 legal adviser to their successors I.B.M. United Kingdom Ltd., formerly International Time Recording Co. Ltd. Called to Bar, Middle Temple, 1911 (J. S. Taylor Common Law Prize at final exam. 1910); joined Northern Circuit and practised in Liverpool. Lieut. King's (6th) Liverpool Regt. Nov. 1914; Capt. 1916; seconded to War Office as Military Representative to Essex Appeal Tribunal, 1916. Practised in London after war until appointed Stipendiary Magistrate, East Ham, 1935; Metropolitan Magistrate (Greenwich and Woolwich), 1939-49; retired 1949. J.P. for Surrey and Member Appeals Cttee. of Surrey Quarter Sessions, 1949-54. Chairman Southwark Diocesan, C.E.T.S. Home Office Approved Boys' Shelter Home Cttee. (renamed Ellison House, 1959), 1946-; Member General Cttee., London Assoc., for the Blind, 1948-59, and Finance Cttee., 1951 (Vice-Pres. and resigned. 1960). Member: Metropolitan Magistrates Dining Club, 1939; Surrey Magistrates Club, 1949; Middlesex and Surrey Society, 1953. *Recreations:* golf, bowls (Pres. Rowledge Bowling Club, 1956; Life Mem. 1960; a Vice-Pres. The Paddington Bowling and Sports Club, 1956). *Address:* 19a North Gate, Regents Park, N.W.8. *T.:* Primrose 2185; Ellerslie House, Rowledge, Surrey. *T.:* Frensham 3185. *Clubs:* Carlton; The Three Counties (Haslemere).
[*Died* 17 *Feb.* 1966.

HOWARD-VYSE, Major-General Sir Richard Granville Hylton, K.C.M.G., *cr.* 1935 (C.M.G. 1918); D.S.O. 1915; Vice-Lieutenant of Buckinghamshire since 1957; Colonel, Royal Horse Guards, since 1951; *b.* 27 June 1883; *s.* of late H. H. Howard Vyse; *m.* 1925, Hermione, *d.* of Saxham Drury and *widow* of Hon. Arthur Coke, 2nd *s.* of 3rd Earl of Leicester. Entered army, 1902; Adjt., 1907-1910; Capt. 1908; Lt.-Col. commanding R.H.G., 1922-26; Col. 1926; Maj.-Gen. 1933; employed with Canadian Forces, 1913; served European War, 1914-17, as Brigade-Major 5th Cavalry Brigade, and Chief Staff Officer 5th Cavalry Division; in Palestine, 1917-18 (temp. Brig.-Gen.), as Chief Staff Officer, Desert Mounted Corps, and G.O.C. 10th Cavalry Brigade (despatches, Bt. Major and Lt.-Col., D.S.O., C.M.G.); Commanded the Cairo Cavalry Brigade 1928-30; Inspector of Cavalry, 1930-34; Chief of Staff to Duke of Gloucester on visit to Australia and New Zealand, 1934-1935; retired pay, 1935; Head of Military Mission with French High Command, 1939-40; Chairman, P.O.W. Dept. Red Cross and St. John, 1941-45; Chairman, British Legion, 1950-1953, Pres. 1958-62. Sheriff of Buckinghamshire, 1938. *Address:* Stoke Place, Slough, Bucks. *T.:* Slough 22277. [*Died* 5 *Dec.* 1962.

HOWARD-WILLIAMS, W., C.B.E. 1920; *b.* Monmouthshire, 1879; *o. s.* of late Sir Thomas Williams. Entered the London and North-Western Railway as Cadet, 1896; Assistant General Manager, 1917; Director Inland Transport Ministry of Munitions, 1915-18; Attended Labour Conference at Washington, 1919; General Manager Central Argentine Railway, 1920-26, Deputy Chairman, 1930, Chairman, 1931-44. *Address:* 34 Ennismore Gardens, S.W.7.
[*Died* 21 *Jan.* 1962.

HOWARTH, Harry; J.P.; M.P. (Lab.) Wellingborough since 1964; *b.* 3 Aug. 1916; *s.* of late Robert and Annie Howarth; *m.* 1945, Kathleen Marion Rayner; no *c.* *Educ.:* Crompton House School, Shaw, Lancs. Railway Clerk, 1934-64. J.P., Gore Div. of Middlesex, 1957-65, Gore Div. of Middx. Area of Greater London, 1965-. Served with R.A.F., 1940-46. *Address:* 2 Kenwood Drive, Rickmansworth, Herts. *T.:* Rickmansworth 76167.
[*Died* 8 *Aug.* 1969.

HOWARTH, Walter Goldie, M.A., M.B., B.C. (Camb.), F.R.C.S.Eng.; retired as Consulting Surgeon, Ear, Nose, and Throat Dept., St. Thomas's Hosp.; *b.* 1879; *y. s.* of J. E. Howarth, Prestwich; *m.* 1915, Esther Mary, *y. d.* of late Halsey Ricardo, F.R.I.B.A.; three *s.* one *d.* *Educ.:* Shrewsbury School; King's College, Cambridge; St. Thomas's Hospital. Has spent a considerable time at the universities of Vienna, Freiburg i. B., and Berlin, and has since then practised in London as an ear and throat specialist; has been Hunterian Professor of Surgery at the Royal College of Surgeons; President of the Laryngological section of the Royal Society of Medicine and Semon Lecturer at the University of London; is an Examiner at London University and the Royal College of Surgeons; Chairman of the St. Dunstan's Medical Advisory Committee and member of Executive Council. *Publications:* articles and papers relating to the surgery of the ear, nose and throat; editor of the Journal of Laryngology and Otology, 25 years. *Recreations:* riding, hunting, farming, was captain of the Cambridge University Golf Team, 1901. *Address:* Ingrams Farm, Wisborough Green, Sussex. *T.:* Wisborough Green 395. *Club:* Boodle's.
[*Died* 29 *April* 1962.

HOWDEN, Capt. Harry Leslie, C.B.E. 1940; R.A.N.; retired; *b.* 4 July 1896; *s.* of Patrick Grieve Howden, of Edinburgh, Scotland, and Wellington, New Zealand, and Mary Elizabeth Niblett, of Devon, England; *m.* 1931, Vanda Mary Sanders Fiske; three *s.* *Educ.:* Wellington Coll., N.Z. Midshipman, 1915; Lieutenant, 1919; Commander, 1931; Captain, 1938; served British Embassy, Tokio, 1927-28; Naval Intelligence Division, Admiralty, 1937-38; O.B.E. for services in Yangtze River, China, 1930-32; C.B.E. for services as Senior Naval Officer conducting the evacuation of British Somaliland 1940; despatches, Java Sea, 1942. A.D.C. to King George VI, 1951-52. Naval Officer in Charge, Western Australia, retd. Life Governor: N.S.W. Soc. for Crippled Children; Bush Nursing Hosp., Vic.; Benevolent Society of New South Wales. *Recreation:* hunting. *Address:* The Quarterdeck, Applecross, Western Australia. *T.:* MJ 1344. *Clubs:* United Service, United Hunts; Weld, West Australian Hunt (Perth, W.A.)
[*Died* 16 *Feb.* 1969.

HOWE, 5th Earl (*cr.* 1821), **Francis Richard Henry Penn Curzon,** P.C. 1929; C.B.E. 1924; Baron Howe, 1788; Baron Curzon, 1794; Viscount Curzon, 1802; a Commodore in the Naval Reserve; V.D.; *b.* 1 May 1884; *s.* of 4th Earl and Lady Georgina Elizabeth Spencer-Churchill (*d.* 1906), *d.* of 7th Duke of Marlborough; *S.* father 1929; *m.* 1st, 1907, Mary (marr. diss. 1937; *d.* 1962), *d.* of late Colonel Hon. Montagu Curzon of Garatshay, Loughborough; one *s.* one *d*; 2nd, 1937, Joyce Mary McLean Jack (from whom he obtained a divorce, 1943); one *d.*; 3rd, 1944, Sybil Boyter, *o. c.* of late Capt. Francis Johnson, Palmeira Sq., Hove, Sussex; one *d.* *Educ.:* Eton; Christ Church, Oxford. Served in command of Howe Battalion R.N.D. in Belgium, and H.M.S. Queen Elizabeth, 1914-1919; M.P. (C.) South Battersea, 1918-29; A.D.C. to King, 1925-28; Lond. Whip, Unionist Central Office, 1927; Patron of eight livings; Premier and Perpetual Govr. and Trustee of King William IV Naval Asylum; Chm. Roy. Nat. Life-Boat Instn., 1956-. *Heir:* *s.* Viscount Curzon, C.B.E. *Address:* 32 Curzon Street, W.1. *T.:* Grosvenor 2320; Penn House, Amersham, Bucks;

Penn House Farm, Penn, Bucks. *T.:* Penn 25 and 67; Hatchets, Penn, Bucks. *T.:* Penn 3229. *Clubs:* Turf, Carlton, 1900, Royal Automobile, British Racing Drivers'. [*Died* 26 *July* 1964.

HOWE, Air Commodore Thomas Edward Barham, C.B.E. 1936; A.F.C. and bar; *b.* 4 Sept. 1886; *s.* of Thomas Scrope Howe, J.P., and Frances Mary Howe; *m.* 1939, Mary, *widow* of Wing Commander Wilfrid R. Dyke Acland, D.F.C., A.F.C.; one *s.* *Educ.:* Bilton Grange; Dover College. Served in A.I.F., 1914-15 (wounded at Anzac Cove); entered R.N.A.S., 1916; flying instructor at Cranwell, 1916-17; served in France, 1918-19, with 18 Sqdn., R.A.F. permanent commission in R.A.F. as Flight-Lt Group Capt., 1933; Air Cdre., 1937; R.A.F Staff Coll., 1924-25; Fleet Air Arm, H.M.S. Furious, 1925-28; 203 (F.B.) Sqdn., Basra, 1929-1930; Directorate of Training, 1931-33; Extra Air A.D.C. to King George V., 1934-35; Air Attaché British Embassy, Washington, 1935-37; Senior Air Staff Officer No. 12 Group, Royal Air Force, 1937-38; commanded No. 17 Group, 1938-41 (despatches); retired list, 1941; employed on Aircrew Reception duties, 1941-48. *Address:* Little Orchard, Hill Brow, Liss Hants. *T.:* Liss 2253. *Club:* Royal Air Force. [*Died* 2 *Jan.* 1970.

HOWELL, Maj.-Gen. Frederick Duke Gwynne, C.B. 1939; D.S.O. 1917; M.C., R.A.M.C.; D.L., J.P. Radnorshire; *b.* 1881; *s.* of late Major Marmaduke G. Howell, Llanelwedd Hall, Radnorshire; *m.* 1912, Gertrude, *d.* of late J. A. Sinclair, Barrister-at-law, Lahore; one *s.* one *d.* *Educ.:* privately; St. Thomas's Hospital, London. M.R.C.S (Eng.) and L.R.C.P. (Lond.), 1905; D.P.H. (College of Surgeons, England), 1914; joined R.A.M.C., 1906; Capt. 1909; Major, 1918; Brevet Lt.-Col., 1919; Lt.-Col. 1930; Bt.-Col. 1930; Col. 1934; Maj.-Gen. 1937; served European War, 1914-18 (despatches five times M.C., D.S.O.); (temp.) Deputy Director Gen., A.M.S. War Office, 1933-34; Deputy Director of Medical Services Army Headquarters, India 1934-37; Deputy Director of Medical Services Aldershot Command, 1937-41; Hon. Surgeon to the King, 1930-41; retired pay, 1941 High Sheriff County of Radnor, 1945. *Recreations:* golf, etc. *Address:* Dol-y-ffin, Llanelwedd, Builth Wells, Radnorshire, Wales *Club:* Army and Navy. [*Died* 25 *Jan.* 1967.

HOWELLS, Rt. Rev. Adelakun Williamson, O.B.E. 1952; M.A., B.D. (Dunelm); Bishop of Lagos since 1955; *b.* 17 Sept. 1905; *m.* 1931, Aduke-Daniel (*d.* 1961). *Educ.:* C.M.S. Gram. Sch.; King's Coll., Lagos. Tutor, C.M.S. Training Coll., Awka, 1928-33; Pastor, St. Bartholomew's, Enugu, 1934-35; Vice-Prin., Fourah Bay Coll., Freetown, Sierra Leone, 1938-43; Pastor, St. John's, Aroloya, Lagos, 1943-51; Canon Residentiary, Cathedral Church, Lagos, 1944, Provost, Cathedral Church, Lagos, 1951; Asst. Bishop of Lagos, 1952. *Publication:* Directions for Holy Communion. *Recreation:* tennis. *Address:* Bishopscourt, Lagos. *T.:* 20416. *Clubs:* Royal Commonwealth Society; Lagos Dining (Lagos). [*Died* 7 *March* 1963.

HOWES, Arthur Burnaby; Bexhill representative on Sussex County Committee of National Register of Archives; *b* 15 Feb. 1879; *y. s.* of late Major-General F. A. Howes, R.E., and late Emily A. J. Fladgate; *m.* 1st, 1912, Mabel A. C. Neighbour; one *d.*; 2nd, 1937, Marjorie, *widow* of Eng. R.-Adm. Cory Sanders, C.B., D.S.O. *Educ.:* Dulwich Coll. Articled to and became a Fellow of the Chartered Surveyors' Institution; called to Bar, Middle Temple, 1906; practised in London, and on Western Circuit; Conveyancer, Uganda Protectorate, 1916; Magistrate, 1917; acted there as Judge on several occasions, and in 1921 as Attorney-General; Puisne Judge Gold Coast, 1924; acted as Chief Justice, Gold Coast, in 1927 and 1928; Puisne Judge, Straits Settlements, 1933; acted as Chief Justice, Straits Settlements and later of Federated Malay States in 1937; retired 1941; Councillor, Bexhill Borough Council, 1945-54. *Publications:* (with R. Parry) Law of Easements, 1910; editor Macer's Dilapidations, 1911; and Law of Fixtures, 1912. *Recreation:* gardening. *Address:* 27 Buckhurst Road, Bexhill-on-Sea, Sussex. *T:* Bexhill 1032. [*Died* 18 *Dec.* 1963.

HOWES, Brig. Sidney Gerald, D.S.O. 1919; M.C.; *s.* of late J. G. Howes, 48 Porchester Terrace, W.2, and Kings Cliffe, Northants; *m.* Muriel Vida Hay; one *s.* two *d.* *Educ.:* Harrow; Christ Church, Oxford. Served 21st (E. of I.) Lancers, 1907, 1921; 1st The Royal Dragoons, 1922-29; commanded 1st King's Dragoon Guards, 1929-33; European War, France, 1914-18 (D.S.O., despatches thrice, M.C.). Commander 6th Cavalry Brigade, T.A., 1934-38; re-employed War of 1939-45; Colonel 1st King's Dragoon Guards, 1945-53. *Address:* Lyneal Lodge, Ellesmere, Shropshire. *T.:* Bettisfield 226. *Clubs:* Cavalry, Royal Automobile, M.C.C. [*Died* 13 *Dec.* 1961.

HOWGRAVE-GRAHAM, Hamilton Maurice, C.B.E. 1929; Secretary to the Metropolitan Police, 1927-46; *b.* 21 April 1882. *Educ.:* Felsted School. Customs and Excise Department, 1901-14; served as Captain in the 1/9th Battn. Hampshire Regiment in India and Siberia, 1914-19; Principal in the Treasury, 1920-27. *Publications:* Light and Shade at Scotland Yard, 1947; The Metropolitan Police at War, 1948. *Address:* 6 Spanish Place, W.1. *T.:* Welbeck 2121 *Clubs:* Beefsteak, Travellers'. [*Died* 17 *Nov.* 1963.

HOWITT, Cecil; *see* Howitt, T. C.

HOWITT, Charles Roberts, C.M.G. 1957; retired from Malaya; *b.* 5 November 1894; *s.* of J. G. and Mary Howitt, Carlisle, Cumberland; *m.* 1920, E. Vera, *d.* of R. Rhodes, J.P., Kendal, Westmorland; two *d.* *Educ.:* Carlisle Grammar School; Queen's College, Oxford. Army Service: Royal Fusiliers, 1914-16; Border Regt., 1916-19. B.A. Oxon., 1920; Malayan Civil Service, 1920-50; British Adviser, Perlis, 1935-37; Malayan Establishment Officer, 1938; Under-Sec. Straits Settlements Govt., 1940; Actg. Chief Secretary, 1948; re-appointed Malaya, 1951; Chm. Public Service Board, 1954-57, Dept. Chm. Public Services Commn. also Mem. Judicial and Legal, Police & Railway Service Commns. from 1957-62 (all in Fedn. of Malaya), retd., 1963. *Address:* Holmcroft, Colborne Rd., Guernsey. [*Died* 23 *Dec.* 1969.

HOWITT, Sir Harold (Gibson,) G.B.E. 1946; Kt. 1937; D.S.O. 1918; M.C.; D.C.L.; LL.D.; D.L.; J.P. 1942 (City of London); Chartered Accountant; Partner in Peat, Marwick, Mitchell & Co., 11 Ironmonger Lane, E.C.2, 1911-61; *b.* Nottingham 5 Oct. 1886; *s.* of Arthur Gibson Howitt, Burland, Magdala Rd., Nottingham; *m.* 1917, Dorothy Wentworth (*d.* 1968), *d.* of William Henry Radford, Woodlands, Sherwood, Nottingham; one *s.* three *d.* *Educ.:* Uppingham (Chm. Trustees, 1949-67). Served European War, 1914-18 (despatches four times, M.C., D.S.O.); Capt. The Green Howards (Yorks) Regt.; Mem. of Council of Institute of Chartered Accountants, 1932-61 (Pres. 1945-46); of Toynbee Hall and of East End Hostels, 1922-51; Advising Accountant to Lord Cave's Commission to Rhodesia, 1920; Chm. of British North Borneo Committee, 1926; Member Lord Bridgeman's Committee to investigate British Legion, 1930; Council of Officers' Assoc. and Benevolent

Committee of British Legion, 1932-51; Reorganisation Commission for Pigs and Pig Products, 1932; Reorganisation Commission for Fat Stock, 1933; Agricultural Marketing Facilities Cttee., 1943-66; of Cattle Industry (Emergency) Cttee., 1934; Livestock Commission. 1937; London Civil Airports Cttee., 1939; Air Council, 1939-1946; Air Supply Bd., M.A.P., 1940-43; Council of N.A.A.F.I., 1940-46; Joint Hops Cttee., 1941-67 (Chm. 1952-67); Colonial Economic Advisory Cttee., 1943-46; Wool Marketing Cttee., 1944-45; Coal Owners Compensation Tribunal, 1946; Mem. Tribunal to assess value of colliers' houses, 1953; Mem. Courts of Inquiry into Engineering and Shipbuilding disputes, 1954; Chm. Air Training Corps, Board of Finance, 1940-46; Commissioner to Southern Africa to advise Governments concerning possible acquisition of Rhodesian Railways, 1945; Chairman and Dep. Chm. B.O.A.C., 1943-48; Dir., The United Services Trustee, 1944-66 (Chm. 1952-1966); Chm. of Building Materials Board, 1942-43; Financial Adviser to Ministry of Works (Building Materials), 1943-45; Hon. Treas.: N.S.P.C.C., 1948-52; Chairman of Hampstead Bench, 1950-58; President Sixth Internat. Congress on Accounting, London, 1952; Master Merchant Taylors' Company, 1952-53; Chm. Pig Production Breeding Policy Cttee., 1954; Chm. Commn. of Enquiry on powers of Crown over unpatented inventions, Bd. of Trade, 1955. Apptd. by Minister of Transport to enquire into allegations concerning purchasing procedure of British Transport Commn., 1957; Mem. Council on Productivity, Prices and Incomes, 1957-60; Mem. Cttee. to enquire into financial Structure of Colonial Development Corp., 1959. Hon. D.C.L. Oxford, 1953; Hon. Mem. former Soc. of Incorp. Accountants, 1953; Hon. LL.D. Nottingham Univ., 1958. *Address:* 1 Cressy House, Queen's Ride, Barnes, S.W.13. *T.:* 01-789 3715. *Clubs:* Athenæum, Carlton, Gresham. [*Died* 30 *Nov*. 1969.

HOWITT, (Thomas) Cecil, D.S.O. 1919; O.B.E. 1949; F.R.I.B.A.; Architect and Surveyor; *b*. 1889; *s*. of late J. C. Howitt of Hucknall, Notts.; *m*. 1918, Irene Adelaide, *d*. of late W. Woolley; one *d*. *Educ.:* Nottingham High School; Arch. Assoc. London; travels in Italy, Greece, and Germany, France and America. Associate R.I.B.A. 1912; Fellow 1931, Vice-Pres. 1944-46; bronze medallist in architectural design, 1911 and 1913; Designer Nottingham Town Hall, 1929; Birmingham Civic Centre, 1935; Newport Civic Centre, 1936; Winner Yeovil Civic Centre Design, 1938; R.I.B.A. bronze Medals for Buildings, 1933, 1936 and 1953; Deputy Commissioner War Damage Commission, 1941; temporary Commission in Leicestershire Regiment, Oct. 1914; Temporary Major, Oct. 1916; Temporary Lieut.-Col. commanding 8th Batt. Leicester Regiment, 1917 (despatches thrice, D.S.O., Légion d'Honneur). *Address:* Orston, Notts. *T.:* Whatton 360; St. Andrew's House, Nottingham. *T.:* 65052, 3. *Clubs:* Arts, Savage; Borough (Nottingham); Conservative (Birmingham). [*Died* 3 *Sept*. 1968.

HOWLETT, Reginald, C.B. 1957; Under-Secretary, Ministry of Education, and Department of Education and Science, since 1951; *b*. 4 Sept. 1908; *s*. of late Alfred Reginald and Caroline Louisa Howlett; *m*. 1936, Leila, *er. d*. of Amedeo Cagna, Milan, Italy; two *s*. *Educ.:* Tonbridge School; St. John's College, Oxford. 1st cl. Hon. Mods., 1929; 1st cl. Lit. Hum., 1931. Entered Board of Education, 1933. *Address:* Heathdene, Pennington Road, Southborough, Tunbridge Wells, Kent. *T.:* Tunbridge Wells 28327. [*Died* 23 *Feb*. 1969.

HOWORTH, Sir Rupert Beswicke, K.C.M.G., *cr*. 1933 (C.M.G. 1931); K.C.V.O., *cr*. 1942; C.B. 1926; F.S.A.; J.P. 1942; *b*. 13 July 1880; 2nd *s*. of late Sir Henry H. Howorth, K.C.I.E., F.R.S.; *m*. 1907, Evelyne Maria, *o. c*. of late William Roope Ellicott, Oporto; one *s*. three *d*. *Educ.:* St. Paul's School; New College, Oxford. Barrister-at-law, Inner Temple, 1903; entered Board of Education, 1908; transferred to Treasury, 1915; seconded to Cabinet Office, 1919; transferred to Cabinet Office, 1930, on appointment as Deputy Secretary to the Cabinet; Administrative Secretary, Imperial Conferences, 1923, 1926, 1930, and 1937; Sec., U.K. Delegation, Imperial Economic Conference, Ottawa, 1932, and Monetary and Economic Conference, London, 1933; Deputy Secretary to the Cabinet, 1930-42; Clerk of the Privy Council, 1938-42; Secretary of Commissions to the Lord Chancellor, 1945-48. *Address:* The Manor House, Edenbridge, Kent. *T.:* Edenbridge 3185. [*Died* 3 *Jan*. 1964.

HOWSON, Brig. Geoffrey, C.I.E. 1919; M.C. 1915; *b*. 14 Aug. 1883; 3rd *s*. of late Ven. Archdeacon G. J. Howson; *m*. 1911, Evelyn (*d*. 1935), 3rd *d*. of Andrew Murray; two *s*. two *d*.; *m*. 1945, Grizel Baird Smith. *Educ.:* Uppingham; R.M. College, Sandhurst. 2nd Lieut. Unattached List, Indian Army, 1903; 4th Cavalry, 1904-22; 2nd Royal Lancers (Gardner's Horse), 1922-28; Lt.-Col. 1929; retired from Indian Army, 1932; served European War, France and Mesopotamia (despatches twice, M.C., C.I.E.); Temp. Lt.-Col. as Commandant M.G.T.C. India, 1917-20; guardian to the Maharaja of Dumraon, 1922-25; Assistant English Master, Mayo College, Ajmer, 1927-35; Vice-Principal, Mayo College, 1935-38. Guardian to the heir to H.H. the Maharaol of Baria State, 1938-40; re-employed, July 1940; Admin.-Comdt., Deolali, 1941; Temp. Brig. 1942, comdg. Deolali Area; retired, 1943, rank of Hon. Brig.; re-employed, May 1944, as Services Resettlement Liaison Officer, Rajputana and Central India; retired Nov. 1945. *Recreation:* gardening. *Address:* Llys Cyngar, Morfa Bychan, Portmadoc, N. Wales. *T.:* Portmadoc 2274. [*Died* 16 *Oct*. 1961.

HUBBACK, Vice-Adm. Sir (Arthur) Gordon Voules, K.B.E. 1957 (C.B.E. 1944); C.B. 1953; *b*. 11 Sept. 1902; *s*. of late Brig.-Gen. A. B. Hubback, C.M.G., D.S.O. and of late Mrs. M. Hubback, *d*. of late Sir Gordon Voules; *m*. 1st, 1930, Elizabeth Pearson Rogers (*d*. 1949); one *s*.; 2nd, 1949, Sheila Mary Roberton. *Educ.:* R.N. College, Osborne and Dartmouth. Commander, 1936; Captain, Coastal Forces Mediterranean, 1942-1943; Chief Staff Officer, Force J, Normandy, 1944; Jt. Planning Staff, Cabinet Offices, 1944-45; Captain H.M.S. Glasgow, 1946-47; Commodore Superintendent, Malta, 1947-50; Commodore R.N. Barracks, Lee, 1950-51; Rear-Adm. 1951; Admiral Superintendent H.M. Dockyard, Portsmouth, 1951-1954; Vice-Adm., 1954; Dir. of Dockyards, Admiralty, 1954-57; a Lord Commissioner of the Admiralty and Fourth Sea Lord, Admiralty, 1958; Managing Director, Dockyard, Malta, 1958-59. French Croix de Guerre, 1940. O.St.J. 1949. *Recreation:* gardening. *Address:* Pound Mead, Burley, Ringwood, Hants. [*Died* 25 *Aug*. 1970.

HUBBACK, Sir John (Austen), K.C.S.I., *cr*. 1936 (C.S.I. 1933); *b*. 27 Feb. 1878; *m*. 1906, Bridget Alington Royds, Kaisar-i-Hind Gold Medal, 1939 (*d*. 1964). *Educ.:* Winchester; King's Coll., Cambridge. Entered I.C.S. 1902; Member of Executive Council, Bihar and Orissa, 1935-36; Governor of Orissa, 1936-41; retired, 1941; Adviser to Secretary of State for India, 1942-47. *Address:* 1 Normans, Norman Road, Winchester, Hants. *Club:* Athenæum. [*Died* 8 *May* 1968.

HUBBARD, Percival Cyril; retired; *b.* Southend-on-Sea, 6 April 1902; *s.* of late Chalton Hubbard, J.P., and late Elizabeth Mary Hubbard; *m.* 1930, Alice Schlaepfer; one *s.* one *d.* *Educ.:* Mill Hill School; Gonville and Caius College, Cambridge. Called to the Bar, Inner Temple, 1925. Administrative Service, Brit. Solomon Islands Protectorate, 1928; Chief Magistrate and Legal Adviser, 1930; transferred to Palestine as Chief Magistrate, 1934; Relieving President, District Courts, 1941; President, 1945; Puisne Judge, Palestine, 1947-49, Nigeria, 1949-55; Judge of High Court of Lagos, Nigeria, 1955-58. Senior Mem. British Interplanetary Soc.; Mem. Howard League; Justice. *Address:* 20 Fitz-George Av., W.14. *T.:* Fulham 5846. *Club:* Royal Commonwealth Society. [*Died* 3 *Sept.* 1961.

HUBBARD, Thomas Frederick; Mem. Kirkcaldy Town Council; *b.* 1898; *s.* of late F. J. Hubbard, Kirkcaldy; *m.* 1922, Jessie, *d.* of T. Cooper, Dysart; two *s.* M.P. (Lab.), Kirkcaldy, 1944-Sept. 1959. *Address:* 80 Normand Road, Dysart, Fife. [*Died* 7 *Jan.* 1961.

HUDD, Walter; actor and producer; Drama Director Central School of Speech and Drama; *b.* 20 Feb. 1898; *s.* of Frederick John Hudd and Alice Maria Humberstone. *Educ.:* various schools. Began stage career, 1919, after serving three years as Lt. R.F.A.; toured England with Tod Slaughter Melo-Drama Co. and Fred Terry Co.; toured with Courtneidge Repertory, India, Africa, China, etc.; London début with Reandean Co., St. Martin's Theatre, 1922. Since then, major rôles include: Private Meek in Too True To Be Good; Sir Broadfoot Basham in On the Rocks; Tesman in Hedda Gabler; Charleston in Thunder Rock; Trovimov in The Cherry Orchard; Dauphin in St. Joan; Malvolio, Capulet, Antonio (Merchant of Venice), Stratford-on-Avon, 1947; Polonius, Old Vic, 1949; Kuligin in The Three Sisters, 1950; Dr. Bonfant in The Waltz of the Toreadors, 1956-57. Major productions: Dr. Faustus, Richard II, Twelfth Night, Stratford-on-Avon, 1946-47; Titus Andronicus, Comedy of Errors, Old Vic, 1957; Midsummer Night's Dream, The Cherry Orchard, National Theatre of Iceland, 1957. During 1942-45 toured own Company for C.E.M.A. (Classical Plays) in Industrial Hostels, Camps, etc. Old Vic Company: 1959-60 season and subsequent tour of England and Russia, 1961-62 season. *Recreations:* various. *Address;* 76A South Hill Park, Hampstead, N.W.3. *T.:* Hampstead 1732. [*Died* 20 *Jan.* 1963.

HUDLESTON, Lt.-Gen. John Wallace, C.B. 1935; late Royal Marines; *b.* 22 Feb. 1880; *s.* of Lt.-Col. Wilfred Hudleston, Madras Staff Corps, and Louisa Emma Jellicoe; *m.* 1911, Winifred Shadwell de Winton Randall; one *s.* *Educ.:* Wellington College. Joined Royal Marine Artillery, 1898; served European War, 1914-18, Brevet Lieut.-Col. 1918; Colonel Commandant Plymouth Division, Royal Marines, 1933-36; A.D.C. to the King, 1934-36; retired list, 1938. *Recreation:* fishing. *Address:* Porch House, West Alvington, Kingsbridge, S. Devon. *Club:* United Service. [*Died* 28 *Jan.* 1961.

HUDSON, Arthur Cyril, M.A., M.D., B.C., (Cantab.), F.R.C.S. Eng.; retd.; Consulting Surgeon, Moorfields Eye Hosp.; Consulting Ophthalmic Surg. St. Thomas's Hospital; Ex-Pres. Ophthalmological Section, Royal Society of Medicine; Ex-Vice-Pres. Ophthalmological Society, United Kingdom; *b.* 30 Nov. 1875; of late Rev. Albert Hudson, Bingley, Yorks. *Educ.:* Rugby School; Trinity College, Cambridge; St. Thomas's Hospital (University Scholar). *Publications:* various medical publications, chiefly in ophthalmological periodicals. *Recreation:* country life. *Address:* c/o National Provincial Bank Ltd., 291B, Oxford St., W.1. [*Died* 13 *May* 1962.

HUDSON, Colonel Arthur Ross, C.M.G. 1919; D.S.O. 1917; *b.* 3 Jan. 1876; 2nd *s.* of John Hudson and Elisabeth (*née* Thomson), of Yokohama, Japan. *Educ.:* Eastbourne College; Royal Military Academy, Woolwich. Joined R.A. 1896; Captain, R.F.A., 1902; Major, 1914; Lt.-Col. 1916; Colonel, 1921; retired pay, 1933; served European War, 1914-19 (twice wounded, despatches thrice, D.S.O., C.M.G., Mons Star); apptd. on the field, by Regimental Order, to rank of Corporal in 32nd Regt. of French Inf., 3 May 1915; Croix de Guerre with palm, 1916; Order of Nile, 3rd Class, 1919; Order of St. Vladimir, 3rd Class (with swords), 1920. *Address:* Carlston, Camberley. *T.:* Camberley 71. *Club:* Army and Navy. [*Died* 19 *Dec.* 1963.

HUDSON, Hon. Sir Edward (Herbert), Kt. 1965; Justice of Supreme Court of Victoria, since 1950; *b.* 10 Sept. 1898; *s.* of William and Florence Maud Hudson; *m.* 1923; one *s.* (one *d.* decd.). *Educ.:* University of Melbourne. LL.M. 1921. Admitted as Barrister and Solicitor of Supreme Court of Victoria, 1922; K.C. 1939. Judge Advocate General of R.A.A.F. (with rank of Group Captain), 1942-44. *Recreations:* golf, trout fishing, bowls. *Address:* 26 Christowel Street, Camberwell, Victoria, Australia. *T.:* 29.4995. *Club:* Melbourne (Melbourne, Victoria). [*Died* 15 *Dec.* 1966.

HUDSON, James Hindle; Secretary, National Temperance Federation and Parliamentary Temperance Group; *b.* Flixton, Lancs, 1881; *s.* of late James Hudson, schoolmaster, Flixton, Lancs, and Elizabeth Hindle; *m.* 1913, Nancy Horsfield (*d.* 1958), of Barnoldswick, Yorks; no *c.* *Educ.:* Elementary School at Flixton; Manchester Univ. M.A., Cobden Prize and Cobden Club Prize; teacher in an Elementary School, Manchester, 1903-7; Master in Salford Secondary School for Boys, 1907-16; M.P. (Lab.) Huddersfield, 1923-31, Ealing (West), 1945-50, (North) 1950-55; Private Parliamentary Secretary to the Rt. Hon. Philip Snowden, M.P., when Chancellor of the Exchequer, 1924 and 1929-31; and also to the President of the Board of Trade, 1951. *Address:* 14C The Oval, Kennington, S.E.11. *T.:* Reliance 3757. [*Died* 10 *Jan.* 1962.

HUDSON, Lady; (Mary Elizabeth), G.B.E., *cr.* 1918; R.R.C.; *e. d.* of late Robert Milner, Kidlington, Oxford, and St. Vincent, West Indies; *m.* 1st, 1888, 1st Viscount Northcliffe (*d.* 1922); 2nd, 1923, Sir Robert Arundell Hudson, G.B.E. (*d.* 1927). Vice-Patron, London Hospital; Vice-Patron Westminster Hospital; Vice-Chairman Personal Service League; Chm., Friends of Poor Disabled Soldiers Needlework Industry. Lady of Grace, Order of St. John of Jerusalem. *Address:* Huntersdale, Virginia Water, Surrey. *T.:* Egham 2088. [*Died* 30 *July* 1963.

HUDSON, Rt. Rev. Noel Baring, D.S.O. 1919; M.C.; D.D. (Lambeth), 1940; Hon. D.D. (Durham), 1950; D.D. (*h.c.*) Cambridge, 1957; *b.* 18 Dec. 1893; 6th *s.* of late Rev. T. W. Hudson, Vicar of Wendover; unmarried. *Educ.:* St. Edward's School, Oxford; Christ's College, Cambridge (Tancred Student); Westcott House, Cambridge. Joined Royal Berkshire Regiment, Sept. 1914; served European War, Lt.-Col. commanding 8th Royal Berks Regiment (despatches twice, D.S.O. and Bar, M.C. and Bar); Deacon, 1920; Priest, 1921; Assistant Priest, Christ Church, Leeds, 1921-22; Vicar of Christ Church, Leeds, 1922-26; Vicar of St. John's, Newcastle upon Tyne, 1926-31; Bishop of Labuan and Sarawak, 1931-38; Secretary of S.P.G., 1938-41; Hon. Canon and Assistant Bishop of St. Albans, 1939-41; Bishop of Newcastle, 1941-56; Bishop of Ely, 1957-63. Select Preacher: Univ. of Cambridge, 1937, 1950, and 1957; Oxford, 1941 and 1958. *Address:* 3, Stuart Tower, 105 Maida Vale, W.9. *Club:* Athenæum. [*Died* 5 *Oct.* 1970.

HUDSON, Professor Robert George Spencer, F.R.S. 1961; Professor of Geology and Mineralogy at Trinity College in the University of Dublin, since 1961; *b.* 17 Nov. 1895; *e. s.* of Robert Spencer Hudson, Mayor and first Freeman of Rugby; *m.* 1st, Dorothy Wayman Francis; one *s.* two *d.*; 2nd, Jane Naden Airey; three *s.* one *d. Educ.:* Lower School of Lawrence Sheriffe, Rugby; Univ. Coll. London. B.Sc. (1st Hons.) 1920, M.Sc. 1922, D.Sc. (Lond.) 1929; M.A. (Dubl.) 1964. Univ. of London Scholar in Geology, 1919-20; Morris Prize, 1919. Served European War (France); 1st Artists' Rifles and 2nd R. War. Regiment, 1915-18 (despatches). Demonstrator in Geology, U.C. London, 1920-1922; Asst. Lectr., Lectr. and Prof. of Geology, Univ. of Leeds, 1922-40; Research Fell., Univ. of Leeds, 1940-42; Cons. Geologist (Petroleum Explorn. in Gt. Brit.), 1942-1945; Geologist and Palæontologist, Iraq Petroleum Co., 1946-58; Field parties, Kurdistan, N. Iraq, 1949 and 1950, and Oman Mts., Arabia, 1951 and 1952; Iveagh Research Fellow in Geology, Trinity College, Dublin, 1960-61. Hon. Lecturer in Geology, 1947-58, and Research Associate, 1958-62, at U.C. London: Chairman Geological Conservation Council, 1957-59; Board of Studies in Geology, Univ. of London, 1948-1963; Examr. in Geology, Univs. of Oxford, London, Liverpool and Birmingham. Foulerton Award, Geologists' Assoc., 1945. Geol. Society, Wollaston Award, 1931; Murchison Medal, 1958. President: Yorks. Geolog. Soc., 1941-42; Palæontolog. Assoc., 1957-1959; Liverpool Geolog. Soc., 1960-61; Irish Geolog. Assoc., 1964- ; Member Royal Irish Academy, 1962; Fellow University College, London, 1962. Membre d'Honneur, Société belge de Géologie et Paléontologie, 1959. *Publications:* contrib. on Stratigraphy and Palæontology (of Upper Palæozoic and Mesozoic) in scientific jls. *Address:* Trinity College, Dublin, Ireland. [*Died* 29 *Dec.* 1965.

HUDSON, Hon. Sir Robert James, K.C.M.G., *cr.* 1950 (C.M.G. 1938); Kt., *cr.* 1944; M.C. 1917; K.C. 1923; *b.* Mossel Bay, Cape Colony, 15 May 1885; *s.* of George Matthews Hudson and Rosa Crozier; *m.* 1st, 1920, Constance de Beer (*d.* 1925); no *c.*; 2nd, 1928, Milicent Bruce, *d.* of George Sutherland; one *s.* one *d. Educ.:* Diocesan Coll., Rondebosch; Caius Coll., Cambridge. Called to Bar, Middle Temple, 1909; practised as barrister at Bulawayo, 1910-14; served in 1st Rhodesia Regt., S.W. Africa, 1914-15; R.F.C. and R.A.F. as pilot, 1915-18; Squadron Commander, 1917; retired with rank of Major after armistice; returned Rhodesia, 1919; Attorney-General and Minister of Defence, Southern Rhodesia, 1923-33; Minister of Justice and Defence, 1933; Judge, High Court of Southern Rhodesia, 1933-1942; Chief Justice of Southern Rhodesia, 1943-50. Chairman Rhodesian Board of Standard Bank of South Africa, 1957-62. *Recreation:* gardening. *Address:* P.O. Box H.G. 81, Highland, Salisbury, S. Rhodesia. *Clubs:* Salisbury, Bulawayo (S. Rhodesia). [*Died* 17 *June* 1963.

HUDSON, R(upert) Vaughan, F.R.C.S.; Consulting Surgeon; Honorary Consultant Surgeon Middlesex Hospital and Surgeon Emergency Medical Service; Lecturer in Surgery, Middlesex Hospital; Consulting Surgeon to Connaught Hospital, Walthamstow, and to St. Saviour's Hospital; Consulting Surgeon Royal Wanstead Orphanage; Examiner in Surgery, Univ. of London and Cambridge; Member: Penicillin Therapeutic Trials Cttee., Streptomycin Clinical Trials Cttee.; Internat. Soc. of Surgery; M.R.C.; F.R.S.M.; Medical Society, London; Fellow Assoc. of Surgeons of Great Britain and Ireland; *b.* Jan. 1895; *s.* of late J. Wasdale Hudson, M.R.C.S., L.R.C.P., and Helen, *d.* of late Cedric Vaughan; *m.* 1929, Esmé, *d.* of Gladstone Wilson; one *s.* two *d. Educ.:* Epsom College; Middlesex Hospital Medical School. Prosector of Anatomy; House Surgeonship and Registrarship, Middlesex Hospital; late Clinical Asst. St. Mark's Hospital, Med. Off. Special Depts., Clinical Research and Crausaz Memorial Cancer Research Scholar, Middlesex Hospital; Non-Commissioned 1914-1915, Commissioned, 1915-19, Hertfordshire Yeomanry and Cavalry Reserve; Member Anæsthetic Committee, M.R.C. *Publications:* Herniae, Handfield-Jones and Porritt's Essentials of Modern Surgery, 1938. Contributions to Brit. Jl. Surg., Mddx. Hosp. Archives, B.M.J., Lancet, etc. *Address:* 18 Wimpole Street, W.1; 19 Tufton Court, Tufton Street, S.W.1. [*Died* 10 *Sept.* 1967.

HUDSON, Sidney Rowland, T.D. 1939; M.A.; F.R.G.S.; Headmaster, Alleyn's School, 1945-63, retired; *b.* 15 June 1897; *s.* of late Sidney Robert Hudson and Charlotte Rowland; *m.* 1942, Mary Barbara Beaumont, *d.* of late A. E. Farrow; one *d. Educ.:* Emanuel School; Clare College, Cambridge. Served European War, 1915-19, Lieut. Royal Fusiliers (wounded, 1917); War of 1939-45, 1939-40, Major. Assistant Master, Alleyn's School, 1926-45. President, Alleyn Old Boys' Club. *Recreations:* country and gardening. *Address:* 14 Dulwich Village, S.E.21. *T.:* Gipsy Hill 0695. [*Died* 15 *Aug.* 1966.

HUDSON, Walter Richard Austen, C.B.E. 1962; *b.* 8 Dec. 1894; *s.* of Walter Hudson; *m.* 1917, Marion Hyde; one *s.* two *d. Educ.:* Hymer's Coll., Hull; Ashville Coll., Harrogate. Sheriff of Kingston upon Hull, 1946-47. Served European War, East Yorks Regt. and R.A.S.C., 1914-17. M.P. (C.) Kingston upon Hull (North), 1950-Sept. 1959. *Recreations:* gardening and photography. *Address:* 21 Kappara Court, St. Julian's, Malta G.C. [*Died* 21 *Aug.* 1970.

HUDSON, Lt.-Col. William, C.B.E. 1932; M.C. 1917; *b.* 1880; *s.* of William and Mary Hudson; *m.* Adele Joan, *d.* of late F. W. Badcock; one *d. Educ.:* privately; King's College, London. Served S. African War, 1900-1902 (Queen's medal and two clasps, King's medal and two clasps); Controller's Staff, Central Telegraphs, London, 1902; Deputy Postmaster-General, Northern Nigeria, 1912; served European War, 1914-18; Officer in charge Civil Telegraphs, Occupied Enemy Administration, Palestine, 1919; Postmaster-General, Palestine, 1920-37; Member of Advisory Council to Palestine Government, 1926-37. *Address:* 8c Suffolk House, Cheltenham. *T.:* Cheltenham 23185. [*Died* 28 *March* 1967.

HUDSON-WILLIAMS, Thomas, M.A., D.Lit.; Emeritus Professor of Greek in the University College of North Wales, Bangor; *b.* Caernarvon, 4 Feb. 1873; *s.* of late R. Williams, Castle Square, Caernarvon; *m.* 1905, Gwladys, B.A., *d.* of late W. Prichard Williams, Cae'r Onnen, Bangor; two *s.* one *d. Educ.:* Friars School and University College, Bangor; University of Greifswald; B.A. London University, 1894; M.A. 1895, in Classics, French and Celtic; D.Lit. 1911. Asst. Lectr. in French and German at Univ. Coll., Bangor, 1896-98, in Classics, 1900-4; Prof. of Greek, 1904-40. Hon. D.Litt. (Wales), 1956. *Publications:* The Elegies of Theognis, 1910; Early Greek Elegy, 1926; Welsh Handbook to New Testament Greek, 1926; Y Groegiaid Gynt, 1932; A Short Introduction to the Study of Comparative Grammar,

1935; A Grammar of Old Persian, with a Reader, 1936; numerous Welsh translations, especially from the French and Russian; articles and reviews in Die Celtische Zeitschrift, Modern Language Monthly, American Journal of Philology, The Classical Quarterly, The Classical Review, The Journal of Hellenic Studies, Russian Studies; articles in Welsh periodicals; a history of Polish Lit. in Welsh, 1954. *Recreation:* learning new languages, especially Slavonic. *Address:* 94c Banbury Road, Oxford. [*Died* 12 *April* 1961.

HUFFAM, Major James Palmer, V.C. 1918; Duke of Wellington's Regiment; *b.* 31 March 1897; *y. s.* of late E. V. Huffam, Berwick-on-Tweed; *m.* 1935, Marian, *d.* of late Leonard William Huffam, Cloughton, Yorks; one *s.* one *d.* Served European War, 1915-18 (V.C.); employed under Air Ministry, 1922-26; with Royal W.A.F.F., 1927-33; Assistant Provost Marshal France, 1940 (despatches); retired Aug. 1945. *Address:* 58 Silverston Way, Stanmore, Middx. *Club:* Royal Air Force. [*Died* 16 *Feb.* 1968.

HUGGETT, Prof. Arthur St. George Joseph McCarthy, D.Sc., Ph.D., M.B., B.S. (Lond.); F.R.S. 1958; F.R.C.O.G. 1960; F.R.S.E. 1965; Consulting Physiologist, Agricultural Research Council Inst. of Animal Disease Research, Moredun, Edinburgh, 1964-68; *b.* 1897; *s.* of late Arthur Henry Richard Huggett, Wimbledon; *m.* 1st, 1923, Marguerite Mary, *d.* of late Archibald Potter Head; one *s.* one *d.*; 2nd, 1938, Esther M., D.Sc., M.R.C.P. (*d.* 1960), *d.* of late Dr. Arthur Killick; two *d.*; 3rd, 1962, Helen, *d.* of late George Kemp Archbold (*see* Prof. Helen Kemp Porter). *Educ.:* Wimbledon College; City of London School; St. Thomas's Hospital Medical School (Senior Entrance Science Scholar and Musgrove Scholar). Beit Memorial Medical Research Fellow, 1921; Demonstrator of Physiology, St. Thomas's Hospital 1919-30; Lecturer in Physiology and Pharmacology, School of Medicine, Leeds, 1930-31; Reader in Pharmacology University of Leeds, 1931-1935; Head of the Department of Physiology, St. Mary's Hospital Medical School, W.2; Professor of Physiology, University of London, 1935-64; Visiting Lecturer, Obstetrics, Johns Hopkins University and Research Fellow, Carnegie Institute of Embryology, Baltimore, 1953-54; De Lee Lecturer, Univ. of Chicago, 1953; Claude Bernard Lecture, Sorbonne, 1955; Merck Anniv. Lecture, Univ. of W. Ontario, London, 1961. R.A.M.C.; Medical Officer Archangel, 1919; Commander Order of the Nile. *Publications:* scientific and medical papers in British and foreign journals. *Recreation:* growing old. *Address:* 75 Greenbank Crescent, South Morningside, Edinburgh 10. *T.:* 031-447 2542. *Clubs:* Athenæum, Lansdowne. [*Died* 21 *July* 1968.

HUGGINS, Lt.-Col. Henry William, D.S.O. 1914; M.C. 1916; D.L. Warwickshire; *b.* 26 Oct. 1891; *s.* of late Henry Huggins, 36 Orchard Ct., Portman Sq., W.1; *m.* 1923, Elizabeth Edith Cadbury (*d.* 1959), *d.* of Arnold Butler, J.P., Malvern; four *s.* *Educ.:* Rugby; Trinity College, Cambridge, B.A. Entered army, 1912; served European War, 1914-18 (despatches five times, D.S.O., Brevet Major, 1919); retired 1920 with rank of Major; recalled from Regular Reserve, 1939; commanded 120th Field Regiment, Royal Artillery, 1939-42 and 35th Signal Training Regt. Royal Artillery, 1942-45. *Recreations:* shooting and archery. *Address:* The Grange, Berkswell, Warwickshire. *T.:* Berkswell 3251. *Club:* Cavalry. [*Died* 22 *April* 1965.

HUGH-JONES, Llewelyn Arthur, O.B.E. 1929; *b.* Wrexham, North Wales, 18 May 1888; *e. s.* of late Llewelyn Hugh-Jones C.B.E., Wrexham, North Wales; *m.* 1st, 1914, Dulcibella, *d.* of late Robert H. H. Eden, Heytesbury, Wilts.; two *d.*; 2nd, 1925, Hildred, (*d.* 1938), *d.* of late Herbert G. Steele, Guildford; two *s.* one *d.*; 3rd, 1939, Pamela, *d.* of Mrs. Masefield, Grey Gables, Thurlestone, S. Devon; one *s.* *Educ.:* Rugby (Scholar); St. John's College, Oxford (Scholar). Entered Egyptian Ministry of Finance, 1912; political officer Egyptian Expeditionary Force, 1919; Controller-General of Budget, 1921; Financial Sec. to the Financial Adviser of the Egyptian Government, 1922; Delegate of Great Britain on the International Financial Commission of Greece, 1936-46; Deputy Commissioner in Greece of British Red Cross Society, Mar.-April 1941; Economic Adviser of Spears' Mission to Syria and the Lebanons, Oct.-Dec. 1941; Financial Adviser (Greece Mission) U.N.R.R.A., Sept. 1944-Jan. 1945. Grand Officer of Order of the Nile. *Address:* The Knapp, Watchett's Drive, Camberley, Surrey. *Club:* Leander. [*Died* 8 *Jan.* 1970.

HUGH-JONES, Siriol (Mary Aprille), (Siriol Hart); free-lance journalist since 1955; *b.* 19 April 1924; *er. d.* of late Major P. Hugh-Jones, R.T.R., and Violet Helen Mary, *née* Hughes; *m.* 1951, Derek Osborne Hart; one *d.* *Educ.:* St. Paul's Girls' School; Cheltenham Ladies' College; Somerville College, Oxford. Inter-Services Topographical Department, 1944-45; free-lanced (contrib. to New Statesman and Tribune), also joined B.B.C. Feature Department, 1946-47; Features Editor, Vogue, 1947-55. Now free-lances: Sunday Times; Punch; book critic, the Tatler. Occasional broadcaster. *Address:* 33 Addison Avenue, W.11. *T.:* Park 8905. [*Died* 11 *March* 1964.

HUGHES, Brig. Archibald Cecil, C.B.E. 1944; T.D. 1925; B.Sc.; M.Inst.C.E.; D.L.; County Surveyor of Hampshire, 1933-57; *b* 19 April 1886; *m.* 1911, Florence Isobel Hall; one *d.* *Educ.:* Ascham House School, Reading; Weymouth College; London Univ. Articled to F. W. Albury, Consulting Engineer, Reading, 1906; with various Contractors, 1909-12; Chief Engineering Assistant, Berkshire C.C., 1912; Deputy County Surveyor, Norfolk, 1923; Deputy County Surveyor, Hampshire, 1925. D.L. Hampshire. Royal Berkshire Regiment (4th Bn.), 1905; Bt. Major, 1925; Lieut.-Colonel and Commanding Bn. 1934-1938; Bt. Colonel 1937; Colonel, Brig. 145 South Midland Brigade, 1938 Served European War, 1914-19, in France and Belgium (despatches, 1914-15 star, 2 medals); War of 1939-45, Commander 145 Brigade in France and Belgium (1939-43 star); G.S.O. 1 North Midland District, 1940; G.S.O. 1 West Riding District, 1941. *Publications:* (joint) Tar Roads; Asphalt Roads, 1938 (Roadmakers' Library); various pamphlets and articles on engineering subjects. *Recreations:* golf, walking, ornithology. *Address:* 40 Cheriton Road, Winchester. *T.:* Winchester 4006. *Clubs:* Royal Automobile; Hampshire (Winchester). [*Died* 2 *June* 1961.

HUGHES, Collingwood; *b.* Chatham, 31 Jan. 1872; *o. s.* of late William Collingwood Hughes, Plymouth, and Fanny Agnes, *d.* of Lieut.-Col. James Fynmore, Royal Marines; *m.* 1899, Lilian, *d.* of John Crocker, Plymouth; two *d.* *Educ.:* Plymouth Grammar School; King's College, London. Political Organizer, Lecturer; Private Political Secretary, Sir Abe Bailey, 1909-10; Lecturer, Cape Town Branch Navy League, 1904-14; Paymaster C.C.D., R.N.V.R., 1905-09; Principal, Civil Service College, Cape Town, 1901-09; Private, South West African Expeditionary Force, 1914-15; Paymaster Lieut.-Commander, R.N.V.R., 1915-1919; Lecturer Publicity Department, Daily Mail, 1922-23; contested Peckham as Independent Conservative, 1918 ; M.P. (C.) Peckham Division of Camberwell, 1922-24 ; seconded Address in reply to King's Speech 13 Feb. 1923 ; Member Select Committee, Betting Tax ; Local Legislation Committee, Nationality Married Women Committee ; Manager Daily Express Centre of Public Opinion, 1942-43 ; General Secretary Council of Retail Distributors, 1943-45. *Publication :* Bets and the Betting Tax, 1927. *Recreation :* walking. [*Died* 25 *March* 1963.

HUGHES, David Arthur, C.B.E. 1964 ; Chief Engineer, Ministry of Health, 1960-1968 ; *b.* 5 Feb. 1905 ; *o. s.* of Rev. Thomas Hughes and Margaret Davies-Evans ; *m.* 1937, Irene Phyllis Manning. *Educ.:* Dolgelley Grammar School ; Battersea Institute of Technology. London County Council, 1931-43 ; Dept. of Health for Scotland Inspectorate, 1943-47 ; Ministries of Health, and of Housing and Local Government Inspectorate, 1947-60. C.Eng., F.I.Mech.E. *Recreations:* gardening, travel. *Address:* Copse Edge, Courtenay Road, Winchester, Hants. *T.:* 5788. [*Died* 29 *Oct.* 1968.

HUGHES, Donald Wynn, J.P.; Headmaster of Rydal School, Colwyn Bay, N. Wales, since 1946 ; *b.* 1911; *s.* of late Rev. Dr. H. Maldwyn Hughes ; unmarried. *Educ. :* The Perse School ; Emmanuel College, Cambridge (Scholar, 1st Class English Tripos). Senior English Master at the Leys School, Cambridge, 1935-46 ; Housemaster, 1939-1946 ; commissioned 1st Perthshire Bn. Home Guard. J.P. Denbighshire. *Publications:* The Public Schools and the Future, 1942 ; Some Educational Foundations, 1945 ; Reason and Imagination, 1949 ; What Kind of Education ?, 1957 ; The Apostle's Creed, 1960 ; The Changing Background of Modern Youth, 1963 ; A Layman's View, 1964 ; (with P. M. Heywood, composer) The Batsman's Bride, etc. ; contributor to : The Assistant Master Speaks, 1937 ; Under Thirty Speaks for Christ, 1939. *Recreations:* normal. *Address:* Rydal School, Colwyn Bay, N. Wales. *T.:* Colwyn Bay 2063. *Club:* The Union Society (Cambridge). [*Died* 12 *Aug.* 1967.

HUGHES, Edward, M.A. ; Professor of History in the University of Durham since 1939 ; *b.* 11 Nov. 1899 ; 2nd *s.* of late William and Mary Hughes, Red Hall, Betley, Crewe ; *m.* 1923, Sarah, *d.* of late Edward and S. C. Hughes of Newtown, Mont., two *s.* one *d. Educ.:* Orme Boys' School, Newcastle, Staffs. ; Manchester Univ. Wireless Telegraphist, R.N.V.R., 1917-18 ; Assistant Lecturer, Queen's University, Belfast, 1922-1927 ; Lecturer in Modern History and Senior Lecturer in History, The University, Manchester, 1927-39. *Publications :* Studies in Administration and Finance, 1558-1825, 1934 ; North Country Life in the Eighteenth Century, vol. I 1952 ; vol. II 1965 ; (ed.) Letters of Spencer Cowper, Dean of Durham, 1746-1774, 1956 ; (ed.) Private Correspondence of Admiral Lord Collingwood, 1957 ; (ed.) Diaries and Correspondence of James Losh (2 vols.), 1962-63 ; (ed.) Fleming-Senhouse Papers, 1962 ; and articles in English Historical Review, History, etc. B.B.C. talks. *Address:* Manor House, Shincliffe, Durham ; Ty Llan, Llanfyhangel-y-Pennant, Merioneth. [*Died* 3 *July* 1965.

HUGHES, Prof. Edward David, F.R.S. 1949 ; Ph.D. (Wales), D.Sc. (Lond.) ; F.R.I.C. ; Professor of Chemistry, University of London, University College, since 1948 ; Director of Chemistry Laboratories since 1961 ; *b.* 18 June 1906 ; *y. s.* of late Hugh and Ann Hughes, Ynysgain, Criccieth ; *m.* 1934, Ray Fortune Christina, M.A., Ph.D., *o. d.* of late Rev. Ll. Davies, Brecon ; one *d. Educ.:* Portmadoc Grammar School ; Univ. Coll. of North Wales, Bangor ; University College, London ; B.Sc. (1st Cl. Hons.), Wales, 1927 ; Diploma in Secondary Education and Board of Education Certificate, 1928 ; Ph.D., Wales, 1930 ; M.Sc., London, 1932 ; D.Sc., London, 1936. Fellow of the University of Wales, 1931 ; Ramsay Memorial Fellow, 1936 ; Meldola Medallist, Royal Institute of Chemistry, 1936. Tilden Lecturer, Chemical Society, 1945. Lecturer, University College, London, 1937-43 ; Professor of Chemistry, Univ. Coll. of North Wales, Bangor, 1943-48, and Dean of the Faculty of Science, 1946-48. Fell. Univ. Coll., Lond. Hon. Sec. of Chemical Society, 1950-56. Vice-President, 1956-59 ; Chairman Joint Library Cttee., 1959-. Hon. Sec. Chemical Council, 1953-55 ; Chm. Board of Studies in Chemistry and Chemical Industries, Univ. of London, 1955-60 ; Mem. Council, Roy. Inst. of Chemistry, 1961-. Dean of the Faculty of Science, University College, 1958-61 ; Governor of Northern Polytechnic, 1950-60 ; Hon. Sec. Ramsay Memorial Fellowships Trust, 1949-61, and Chairman of Advisory Council since 1961. *Publications:* scientific papers, mainly in the Journal of the Chemical Society. *Address:* University College, Gower St., W.C.1; 39 Taunton Way, Stanmore, Mx. *T.:* Wordsworth 6040. *Club:* Savage. [*Died* 30 *June* 1963.

HUGHES, Emrys ; M.P. (Lab.) South Ayrshire Division of Ayrshire and Bute since 1946 ; *b.* 10 July 1894 ; *m.* 1924, Nan (*d.* 1947), *d.* of Keir Hardie, M.P. *Educ.:* Abercynon Council School ; Mountain Ash Secondary School : City of Leeds Training College. Editor of Forward, 1931-46. *Publications:* Keir Hardie, 1950, new edn. 1957 ; Winston Churchill in War and Peace, 1950 ; Pilgrim's Progress in Russia, 1957 ; Macmillan : portrait of a politician, 1962 ; Sir Alec Douglas-Home, 1964 ; Parliament and Mumbo-Jumbo, 1966 ; The Prince, the Crown and the Cash, 1969 ; Sidney Silverman : rebel in Parliament, 1970 (posthumous) ; many Socialist and anti-war pamphlets. *Address:* Lochnorris, Cumnock, Ayrshire, Scotland. *T.:* Cumnock 2234. [*Died* 18 *Oct.* 1969.

HUGHES, Very Rev. Frederick Llewelyn, C.B. 1949 ; C.B.E. 1943 ; M.C. ; T.D. 1948 ; M.A. ; Dean of Ripon since 1951 ; *b.* 12 July 1894 ; *s.* of Rev. Canon Llewelyn R. Hughes, Rector of Llandudno (Canon of Bangor) ; *m.* 1925, Dorothy Mackenzie Mead ; two *d. Educ.:* Christ's Hospital ; Jesus College, Oxford. European War, 1914-18, in King's (Liverpool) Regiment and on General Staff ; ordained, 1922 ; Curate Holy Trinity, Brompton, 1922-30 ; Vicar of St. Stephen's, Paddington, 1930-38 ; Vicar of Mansfield, Notts, 1938-46 ; C.F. (T.A.), 1935-1939 ; Senior C.F. 1939-42 ; A.C.G., Eighth Army, 1942-44 ; D.C.G., 21 Army Group, 1944 ; Chaplain-General to the Forces, 1944-1951 ; Hon. Canon of Southwell, 1944-48, and of Canterbury Cathedral, 1948-51 ; K.H.C. 1944-52 ; Chaplain to King George VI, 1946-52. *Recreations:* travel, tennis, golf, sailing. *Address:* The Deanery, Ripon, Yorks. *T.:* Ripon 3615. *Club:* Cavalry. [*Died* 4 *June* 1967.

HUGHES, Hector, Q.C. 1932 ; M.P. (Lab.) Aberdeen, North, since 1945 ; *s.* of Alexander Wilson Hughes and Elizabeth Anne Hughes ; *m.* ; two *d.* ; *m.* 1966, Mrs. Elsa Lilian Riley. *Educ.:* Diocesan School (Boy Chorister, St. Ann's Church) and St. Andrew's College, Dublin ; Dublin University. Called to Irish Bar at King's Inns, 1915, and English Bar, Gray's Inn, 1923 ; K.C. Ireland, 1927 ; K.C. England, 1932 ; Member of Middle Temple, 1932. Mem. Ghana Bar ; Mem. Nat. Union of General and Municipal Workers ; Mem. Nat. Union of Seamen ; Mem. Board of Church Army ; Pres. Nat. Council for Promotion of

Education in Swimming. A Founder: of Socialist Party of Ireland, 1918, and Irish Co-operative Labour Press Ltd.; James Connolly Labour College, 1920. Committee Mem. British-American Parliamentary Group; Mem. Parliamentary Delegations to Nigeria, 1957, Malta and Gibraltar, 1957; Mem. Commonwealth Parl. Delegation to Canada, 1952. Contested (Lab.) N.W. Camberwell, 1931 and 1935. Has visited Russia (1931) and numerous European, American and African countries. *Publications:* Select Cases in Registration of Title in Ireland; The Increase of Rent and Mortgage Interest (Restrictions) Act, 1920; The Rent Restrictions Acts 1920-1923 (annotated with decided Cases); The Betting Acts and Duties with decided Cases; The Land Acts 1923 to 1927 (with notes of decided cases); National Sovereignty and Judicial Autonomy in the British Commonwealth of Nations; The Landlord and Tenant Act 1931 (fully annotated with decided Cases); The Law Relating to Road Users Rights, Liabilities and Insurance (Foreword by Rt. Hon. Lord Atkin, a Lord of Appeal in Ordinary); Reinstatement in Civil Employment (Foreword by Rt. Hon. George Isaacs, M.P., then Minister of Labour and National Service); diverse articles, poems and broadcasts. *Recreations:* foreign travel, swimming, riding. *Address:* 1 Garden Court, Temple, E.C.4. *T.:* 01-236 1491; Marine Gate, Brighton. *Clubs:* Devonshire National Sporting, Royal Automobile; Regency Society (Brighton); Aberdeen, Sandy Cove, Highgate and Brighton Swimming Clubs; Hove and Brighton Cruising. [*Died* 23 *June* 1970.

HUGHES, Maj.-Gen. Ivor Thomas Percival (gazetted K.C.V.O. 1962, but did not receive accolade), C.B. 1944; C.B.E. 1951; D.S.O. 1940; M.C.; D.L. Surrey; Serjeant at Arms, The House of Commons, since 1957; Member: Surrey T. and A.F.A. (Chm. 1947-49); House Cttee. Westminster Hosp.; *b.* 21 Dec. 1897; *s.* of late Rev. F. G. Hughes, M.A., Rector of Slinfold, Sx.; *m.* 1923, Eileen Dora, *d.* of Walter G. Fladgate, Hill, Slinfold; one *s.* three *d.* *Educ.:* Wellington College; Royal Military College, Camberley. 2nd Lieut. Queen's Royal Regt. 1916; served European War, 1916-18 (M.C. despatches); N.W. Frontier, 1920-21 (despatches); Adjt. 2nd Bn. Queen's Royal Regt., India and Sudan, 1925-28; Staff College, Camberley, 1929-30; Staff Officer R.A., Scottish Command, 1932-34; Brigade Major, 12th Infantry Brigade (Dover), 1934-35; Assistant Serjeant at Arms, House of Commons, 1935-1939; commanded: 4th Bn. Queen's Royal Regiment (T.A.), 1937-39; 1/6th Bn. Queen's Royal Regt., 1939-40; 219 Brigade 1940, 131 (Queen's) Brigade, 1941; 44th (Home Counties) Div., 1942; 25 Corps, 1943; Military Liaison, Greece, Jugoslavia and Albania, 1944-45 (despatches, Greek M.C. 1st Class), F.R.G.S.; F.R.S.A.; Member R.I.I.A. Air Ministry "A" Licence, 1929. Dep. Serjeant at Arms, The House of Commons, 1940-56. *Address:* Flushings Meadow, Great Bookham, Surrey. *T.:* Bookham 3020. *Clubs:* Army and Navy, Little Ship. [*Died* 16 *Aug.* 1962.

HUGHES, John David Ivor, M.A., B.C.L., Professor of Law, Univ. of Leeds, 1919-51; retd.; Barrister-at-law; *b.* Nottingham, 12 Nov. 1885; *s.* of John Bowen Hughes, J.P., Nottingham; *m.* 1920, Dorothy, *d.* of Ernest Lingford, J.P., Cotherstone, Yorks; two *s.* *Educ.:* High School, Nottingham; University College of Wales, Aberystwyth; Balliol College, Oxford. Studentship of the Council of Legal Education; called to Bar, Middle Temple, 1910; Vinerian Scholar University of Oxford; Senior Demy of Magdalen College, Oxford; Lecturer University College of Wales, Aberystwyth, 1910-11; served European War, 1915-19, with Friends Ambulance Unit; Chairman of Trade Boards, 1920-28; President of Society of Public Teachers of Law, 1931-32; Member of Lord Chancellor's Committee on Legal Education. *Publications:* The Law of Transport by Rail; occasional contributions to Law Reviews. *Recreations:* golf, motoring, etc. *Address:* Bugeilyn, Borth, Cards. [*Died* 23 *Jan.* 1969.

HUGHES, Capt. John Grant Duncan-, M.V.O. 1920; M.C.; member Commonwealth House of Representatives, 1922-28 and also 1940-43; *b.* 1882; *s.* of late Hon. Sir John James Duncan; *m.* 1910, Gertrude Rosalie, *d.* of Brig.-Gen. George Henry Dean, Truro, South Australia. *Educ.:* St. Peter's College, Adelaide; Cheltenham College; Trinity College, Cambridge, LL.B. Called to Bar, Inner Temple, 1907; served European War, 1915-19 (M.C., Belgian Croix de Guerre); attached to Staff of Prince of Wales during his tour of Australia, 1920 (M.V.O.); Commonwealth Senator for South Australia, 1932-38. *Address:* 20 Robe Terrace, Medindie, S.A. [*Died* 13 *Aug.* 1962.

HUGHES, Reginald R. M.; *see* Meyric Hughes.

HUGHES, Ven. Richard; Archdeacon of Bangor, 1947-57, retired; Rector of Llangelynin, 1948-56, retired; *b.* 1881 *Educ.:* University of London (B.A.); Cuddesdon College. Deacon, St. Asaph for Bangor, 1904; Priest, Bangor, 1905; Curate of Llanbeblig with Caernarvon, 1904-15; Curate-in-charge of Conv. district of Dolgarrog, 1919-23; Vicar of Dolwyddelen, 1923-30; Rector of Machynlleth, 1930-34; Vicar of Holyhead, 1934-48; Canon of Bangor and Surrogate, 1931-47; Rural Dean of Talybolion and Llifon, 1934-47. Served as Temp. Chaplain to the Forces, 1915-19; Hon. C.F., 1919. *Address:* Gwynant, Criccieth, Caerns. *T.:* 133. [*Died* 26 *Oct.* 1962.

HUGHES, Sir Richard Edgar, 13th Bt., *cr.* 1773; *b.* 8 June 1897; *s.* of late Hubert Edgar Hughes (6th *s.* of 9th Bt.) and late Mary Charlotte Harrison; *S.* uncle 1951; *m.* 1927, Angela Lilian Adelaide (*d.* 1967), *e. d.* of late Maj. Albert Julian Pell, J.P., D.L.; one *s.* one *d.*; *m.* 1967, Jessica Broomhall. *Educ.:* Uppingham. Served European War, 1914-19, in 2nd Artists' Rifles. *Recreations:* shooting, fishing, golf, billiards, snooker. *Heir:* *s.* David Collingwood Hughes [*b.* 29 Dec. 1936; *m.* 1964, Rosemary Ann, *o. d.* of Rev. John Pain, Framfield Vicarage, Uckfield; two *s.*]. *Address:* Rivelin Cottage, Hollow Meadows, nr. Sheffield. *Clubs:* Sheffield (Sheffield); West Suffolk County (Bury St. Edmunds). [*Died* 29 *Aug.* 1970.

HUGHES, Sydney Herbert George, C.B. 1939; C.B.E. 1918; *b.* 14 July 1879; *e. s.* of late George Charles Hughes, of Folkestone; *m.* 1902, Leonora Louise (*d.* 1955), *o. d.* of late John J. Carnon of Southsea; one *d.* *Educ.:* Alleyn's School, Dulwich; Univ. Coll., London. B.A. London, 1898. Chairman Sutton Dwellings Trust. Entered Admiralty, 1899; Secretary to Admiral Superintendent, Gibraltar, 1904-9; National Health Insurance Commission, 1912; Ministry of Shipping, 1918; Accountant-General, Ministry of Shipping, 1920; Ministry of Health, 1927; Principal Assistant Secretary for Finance and Accountant-General, Ministry of Health, to 1939. Financial Director, Disabled Persons Employment Corporation, 1945-48. *Recreations:* motoring, golf. *Address:* Rose Leigh, 25 George V Avenue, West Worthing, Sussex. *T.:* Worthing 845. *Club:* Reform. [*Died* 13 *Oct.* 1962.

HUGHES, Hon. Sir Wilfrid (Selwyn) Kent, K.B.E. 1957 (O.B.E. 1946); M.V.O. 1934; M.C. 1916; E.D. 1946; M.H.R. for Chisholm, Vic., Australia, since 1949; Chm.

Organising Cttee. Olympic Games, 1950-56; President: Victorian A.A.A., since 1957; Australian Nat. Ski Federation, 1959-62; Victorian Olympic Council since 1950; *b.* E. Melbourne, 12 June 1895; *s.* of Dr. Wilfrid Kent Hughes; *m.* 1923, Edith, *d.* of Robert C. Kerr, Montclair, N.J., U.S.A.; three *d.* *Educ.:* Trinity Gram. Sch., Kew; Melbourne Gram. Sch.; Christ Church, Oxford. Served War, 1914-19 (despatches 4 times, M.C.); Maj. 8th A.L.H., 1916. Rhodes Schol., B.A. Hons. Hist., M.A. 1961. M.L.A. Kew, Vic., 1927-49; Hon. Minister, 1931-33; Minister: for Labour and Transport, 1934-35; for Transport and Education, 1947; for Transport and Elec. Undertakings, also Dep. Premier, Vic., 1948-49; Commonwealth Minister for Interior and Works, 1951-56; Chm. Foreign Affairs Committee, 1956-61. Aust. Envoy to China (Taiwan) in May 1966; Aust. Rep., Asian Peoples Anti-Communist League, Taipei, 1967. Major D.A.Q.M.G., Headquarters, 8th Div. A.I.F., 1940; Malaya, 1941; Lt.-Col. 1941; Col. 1942; P.O.W. 3½ yrs., 1942-; despatches, 1946. Director: Ramsay Ware Publishing Pty. Ltd., Melb.: Ramsay Catalogue Service. Hon. LL.D. China Academy, 1967. *Publications:* Modern Crusaders, 1918; Slaves of the Samurai, 1946. *Recreations:* gardening, ski-ing (was Captain Oxford Team); formerly: athletics (rep. Aust. Olympic Games, 1920; Brit. Empire *v.* U.S.A., 1920; Eng. *v.* France, 1920; Manager Aust. Team for Empire Games, 1938; Chef de Mission, Australian Commonwealth Games, 1962; ½ blue O.U.A.C.); lacrosse (½ blue O.U.). *Address:* 4 Selborne Road, Kew, Victoria, Australia. *Club:* Naval and Military (Melbourne).
[*Died* 30 *July* 1970.

HUGHES-HALLETT, Leslie Charles, C.M.G. 1947; O.B.E. 1941; *b.* 2 Dec. 1887; *e. s.* of Charles Frederick Hughes-Hallett, M.A., Brooke Place, Ashford, Kent, and Josephine Laura Hamilton, Ballymacoll, Co. Meath, Ireland; *m.* 1917, Violet Mary, *e. surv. d.* of Lieut.-Col. Arthur Gray Tidy; one *s.* one *d.* *Educ.:* private schools; London University; tutors in France and Germany. Mechanical and Consulting Engineer in Argentina and England until 1914; joined Electrical Engineers (T.) and R.E. (T.) and was released for service as Inspector of Munitions (London Division) until the end of the war; entered Consular Service, 1919; Vice-Consul at Chicago, 1919-22; Vice-Consul Aarhus, Denmark, 1922, Galatz 1922, Munich 1924; Acting Consul-General, Munich, 1924, 1925, 1926; Consul at Santiago de Cuba, 1926; in charge of the Legation at Havana each year, 1926-1929; at Detroit, 1931-39; Consul and Commercial Secretary with rank of 2nd Secretary at Copenhagen, 1939; evacuated from Denmark on the occupation of that country by the Germans, 1940; transferred to Guatemala with rank of 1st Secretary, 1940; Minister Resident at Quito, 1941-43; Minister, 1943-45; Minister in Guatemala, 1946-47; retired, 1948. *Recreations:* motoring, gardening. *Address:* 17 First Avenue, Bexhill-on-Sea, Sussex. [*Died* 5 *Aug.* 1966.

HUGHES-MORGAN, Sir John Vernon, 2nd Bt., *cr.* 1925; *b.* 12 Aug. 1900; *e. s.* of Major Sir David Hughes-Morgan, 1st Bt., and Blanche Elizabeth Wedge (*d.* 1965), *e. d.* of James Buckley; *S.* father 1941; *m.* 1923, Lucie Margaret, *o. c.* of Thomas Parry Jones-Parry, Llwyn Onn, Wrexham, North Wales; two *s.* (and one *s.* decd.). *Educ.:* Malvern College. *Heir:* *s.* Lt.-Col. David John Hughes-Morgan, M.B.E., Army Legal Services [*b.* 11 Oct. 1925; *m.* Isabel Jean, *o. d.* of J. M. Lindsay, of Annan, Dumfriesshire; three *s.* Served Royal Navy (retd.)]. *Address:* The Old Rectory, Mordiford, Hereford. *T.:* Holme Lacy 256.
Died 13 *Jan.* 1969.

HUGILL, Rear-Adm. Réné Charles, C.B. 1944; M.V.O. 1916; O.B.E. 1919; *b.* 1883; *s.* of C. R. and H. K. Hugill, Beverley, Yorks; *m.* 1915, Winifred Fleming, *d.* of Rev. H. Backwell, R.N., R.N. Hospital, Haslar; two *s.* one *d.* *Educ.:* Beverley Grammar School. Entered Royal Naval Engineering College, 1900; qualified as French Interpreter, 1908; and Italian Interpreter, 1928; served European War, 1914-18 (M.V.O.); Royal Yacht, 1911-14; H.M.S. Calliope, 1915; H.M.S. Renown, 1916-20; H.M.S. Cardiff, Mediterranean Fleet, 1926; Chief Engineer, Hong Kong, 1932-36; Engineer Rear-Admiral, 1936; Engineer Manager, Malta Dockyard, 1936-38; A.D.C. to the King, 1936; retired list, 1938; Technical Director of Portuguese Naval Arsenal at Alfeite Lisbon, 1938-40; recalled to service, 1941, and employed i/c Engineering Repairs to H.M. Ships in Clyde Area, 1941-46; replaced on retired list, 1946. Chairman of Council of Society of Yorkshiremen in London and of Yorkshire Society, 1952-53. *Address:* 1 The Hermitage, Lewisham Hill, S.E.13. *T.:* Lee Green 4632. [*Died* 11 *Feb.* 1962.

HUISH, Sir Raymond (Douglas), Kt., *cr.* 1953, C.B.E. 1937; State President Returned Sailors, Soldiers, and Airmen's Imperial League of Australia (R.S.S.A.I.L.A.), 1930-1967; *b.* 7 Dec. 1898; *s.* of Edward William Huish, Rockhampton, Qld.; *m.* 1921, Hilda May Weber; two *d.* *Educ.:* England; U.S.A. R.S.S.A.I.L.A. activities: State Councillor, 1927-28; State Treas., 1928-29; State Pres., Qld. Br., 1930-67; Member State Repatriation Bd., 1932-50; Austr. Deleg. to 7th and 9th B.E.S.L. Conf., London, etc. Served European War from 1915 to Armistice with 5th Aust. Light Horse Regt. and 2nd Signal Troop (wounded). Honorary Work, War of 1939-45: Organised R.S.L. Vol. Defence Corps in Qld., and when it was taken over by Dept. of Army was apptd. Liaison Officer with rank of Hon. Capt.; Chm. or Member various Cttees., etc. Chairman, Cribb & Foote Ltd., Ipswich; Director several companies. Visited Europe to investigate and report to Commonwealth Government on Australian Migration activities overseas, 1951. *Address:* 103 Riverpark, Watson Esplanade, Surfers Paradise, Qld., Australia. *T.:* 7.6364. *Clubs:* Masonic, Legacy, Royal Automobile of Queensland (Brisbane).
[*Died* 26 *Jan.* 1970.

HULBERT, Claude Noel; Actor; *b.* 25 Dec. 1900; *s.* of Dr. H. H. Hulbert; *m.* 1924, Enid, *d.* of late Col. Philip Trevor, C.B.E.; two *d.* *Educ.:* King's College, Chatham; Caius College, Cambridge. Musical Comedy dancing parts in various West End Productions, 1924-27; then Radio with Enid Trevor and Those Four Chaps; filming with All English Film Companies (one of these films, Bull-Dog Jack, being made with brother Jack Hulbert) until Jan. 1939; returned to stage, appearing in Worth a Million at Saville Theatre; Somewhere in England, with Will Hay, Lyric Theatre, Oct. 1940; on tour with the Hulbert Follies with Jack Hulbert and Cicely Courtneidge, 1941; on tour for E.N.S.A. with revue Glad to Meet You, with Enid Trevor, 1942; toured Music Halls with Enid Trevor for Jack Hylton in Road Show with Florence Desmond, 1942; Vivien Budd in Panama Hattie at Piccadilly Theatre, 1943-44; made The Dummy Talks film for British National, 1942; My Learned Friend with Will Hay for Ealing Studios, 1943; toured Belgium and Holland to play to troops with Enid Trevor, Oct. 1944; West and East Africa, 1945. Filmed in London Town with Sid Field, 1945-46; played The Cowardly Lion in The Wizard of Oz at Winter Garden and Saville Theatres, Dec. 1946-April 1947; did series of Overseas Broadcasts with Tommy Trinder called Tommy Get Your Fun. Broadcast every week with Enid Trevor in Here's Wishing You Well Hospital Programme, April 1946. Xmas 1947-48 pantomime Dick Whittington (with Enid Trevor); in Hulbert Follies (series on Television, with his brother Jack), 1948; in Revue, Sauce Tartare, Cambridge Theatre, 1949; in series on air "I Haven't A Clue", 1949; on air in Variety Bandbox, with Enid Trevor, 1949; since April 1950, Guest Artist with Enid Trevor to various Repertory Cos. in British Isles, appearing in The Chiltern Hundreds, See How They Run, and Queen Elizabeth Slept Here; Series, on television children's hour, Claude Clutter, 1951; tour with Enid Trevor, for the Love of Mike, 1951; Cinderella, Tchaikovski music pantomime at Malvern, with Enid Trevor, 1951-52; tour with Enid Trevor, Nothing but the Truth, 1952; tour with Sonnie Hale and Enid Trevor, Not A Clue (for Roy Limbert of Festival Theatre, Malvern), 1953; tour with Enid Trevor (presented by Roy Limbert), Not A Clue, and Chiltern Hundreds, Cape Town, S.A., Jan.-March 1954; continued tour of Not A Clue, with Sonnie Hale, in England, Spring (Television, Aug.), 1954; tour, with Enid Trevor, Pardon My Claws, 1955; in revival of Where The Rainbow Ends, Coliseum, Dec. 1956; Let 'Em Eat Cake, Cambridge Theatre, May 1959. Also broadcasts with Enid Trevor. *Publications:* Radio numbers for Jack Payne; Hats on the Side of your Head, Keep it Under Your Hat; Lyrics. *Address:* 5 Sydney Place, S.W.7. [*Died* 22 *Jan.* 1964.

HULL, Surgeon Rear-Adm. Herbert Richard Barnes, C.B. 1947; K.H.S. 1946; *b.* 1886; *e. s.* of Joseph Hull and Annie Barnes; *m.* 1st, 1914, Angela Dorothea (*d.* 1941), *d.* of Col. Versturme-Bunbury; one *d.*; 2nd, 1953, Mrs. Mary Isobel Ogilvie, *d.* of Alexander Duffus. *Educ.:* Bath Coll.; Bristol Univ.; Middlesex Hosp. M.R.C.S. (Eng.), L.R.C.P. (Lond.), 1910; Casualty Officer and Anæsthetist, Metropolitan Hospital, London; A.M.O. Three Counties Asylum, Arlesly; Surgical Registrar, Royal Victoria Infirmary, Newcastle; joined R.N., 1911; European War, 1914-18, German New Guinea, North Sea, Gallipoli, Palestine (despatches); lent R.A.F., served with them in France and was P.M.O. R.A.F. Scotland; wrecked in H.M.S. Raleigh off Labrador, 1921; F.M.O. North America and West Indies: G.U. Specialist Hospital Ship Maine, Chatham and Haslar Hospitals; Surgical Specialist Bermuda, Chatham, and Haslar Hospitals; in charge Bermuda Naval Hospital, and R.N. Hospital, Kingseat, Aberdeen; late Surgeon Rear-Admiral i/c Royal Naval Hospital, Haslar; retired list, 1946. *Publications:* various articles on surgical subjects in medical journals. *Recreations:* hockey for the Navy and Devon, cricket for the Navy. *Clubs:* Public Schools, M.C.C.; Royal Navy (Portsmouth). [*Died* 31 *May* 1970.

HULL, Sir Percy Clarke, Kt., *cr.* 1947; Mus. Doc., F.R.C.O., L.R.A.M.; Hon. A.R.C.M.; Hon. R.A.M.; Organist and Master of the Choristers, Hereford Cathedral, 1918-49, now Emeritus; Conductor of the Three Choirs Festival, Hereford, 1921, 1924, 1927, 1930, 1933, 1936, 1946, and 1949; the Choral and Orchestral Societies; Vice-Pres. Royal College of Organists, 1948; Adjudicator at Principal Festivals in Great Brit. and Canada; Fellow St. Michael's Coll., Tenbury; Examiner to Associated Board, Roy. Schools of Music; visited Canada as such, 1940, Malta, 1948, Canada and West Indies, 1950, New Zealand, 1951 and South Africa, 1954; 2nd *s.* of late Henry James and Prudence Hull; *m.* 1922, Mary Elizabeth Hake; two *s.* *Educ.:* Hereford Cathedral School. Articled to late Dr. G. R. Sinclair, 1894; Assistant Organist, Hereford Cathedral, 1896-1914; interned as prisoner of war in Germany, 1914-18: Sub-Canon of Hereford Cathedral, 1904. *Address:* Vaga House, Lynch Road, Farnham, Surrey. [*Died* 31 *Aug.* 1968.

HULME TAYLOR, Colonel J(ack), O.B.E. 1946; *b.* Ceylon 11 Dec. 1894; *s.* of late George Herbert Taylor and late Mary Florence-Hulme; *m.* 1928, Vere Frances, *d.* of late Lt.-Gen. Sir Edwin Atkinson, K.C.B., K.B.E., C.M.G., C.I.E.; one *d.* *Educ.:* Aldenham; R.M.C. Sandhurst. Commissioned 1914; attached Royal Sussex Regt., 1914; posted to XI K.E.O. Lancers (Probyn's Horse), (present designation Probyn's Horse 5th K.E.O. Lancers); A.D.C. to Lord Birdwood, C.-in-C. in India, 1925; Senior A.D.C. to Lord Halifax, Viceroy of India, 1926-28; officiated as Comptroller for 6 months; Asst. Military Secretary to Gen. Sir Robert Cassels, G.O.C. in C. Northern Command, India, 1930-34. During War of 1939-45 raised, and was first Commandant for 4 years, of Indian Armoured Corps Tank School; retired, 1946; Marshal of the City of London, 1938-57; Common Cryer and Serjeant-at-Arms, 1957-58; Swordbearer, 1958-59; O.St.J. 1953. *Recreations:* polo, squash, fishing, golf, shooting. *Address:* Inwoods, Lower Knaphill, Woking. *T.:* Brookwood 3186. *Clubs:* Cavalry; Worplesdon Golf (Captain, 1947). [*Died* 3 *Nov.* 1970.

HUME, Sir (Hubert) Nutcombe, K.B.E., *cr.* 1956 (C.B.E. 1946); M.C.; Hon. President: Charterhouse Group Ltd.; Associated British Maltsters Ltd.; Chairman: Charterhouse Investment Trust Ltd.; Currys Ltd.; Yeoman Investment Trust Ltd.; Director: Associated Book Publishers Ltd.; Metropolitan Estate and Property Corporation Ltd.; Slough Estates Ltd.; The Bank of Montreal; Charterhouse Group Canada Ltd.; African Finance Corp. Ltd.; *b.* 4 Sept. 1893; *s.* of Frederic Nutcombe Hume and Caroline Mary Walton; *m.* 1927, Anne, *o. d.* of late Donald Campbell and Charlotte Forbes. *Educ.:* Westminster School; Royal Military College, Sandhurst. Gazetted to Royal Scots, September 1912, but resigned November 1912 to seek fortune in Canada. Rejoined regular army (Hampshire Regt.) Sept. 1914; European war, 1914-18 (despatches, M.C.); resigned, 1919, to enter the City. Director of Finance (commercial), Ministry of Supply, 1940-45. Chairman, Colonial Development Corporation, 1959-60 (Deputy Chairman, 1953-59); Chairman, National Film Finance Corp., 1956-64. Past Vice-President, F.B.I. (now C.B.I.); Chairman, London Adv. Bd. of Salvation Army; Gov., English-Speaking Union; British Correspondent National Industrial Conference Board of America, and Councillor, 1966-. *Recreations:* fishing, shooting, golf. *Address:* Flat 27, 7 Princes Gate, S.W.7. *T.:* Kensington 0605. *Clubs:* Carlton, Lansdowne; Mount Royal (Montreal); York (Toronto); Swinley Forest Golf (Ascot). [*Died* 22 *Dec.* 1967.

HUME-ROTHERY, Professor William, O.B.E. 1951; F.R.S. 1937; M.A.; (Oxon.); Ph.D. (London); D.Sc. (Oxon.); Hon. D.Sc. (Manchester); Hon. D.Met. (Sheffield); Professor Emeritus, Oxford; first Isaac Wolfson Prof. of Metallurgy, Oxford, 1958-66; St. Edmund Hall Professorial Fellow, 1958-66, Hon. Fellow, 1966; Fellow, Imperial Coll. of Science and Technology, since 1963; Hon. Lecturer in the University of Sheffield; *b.* 15 May 1899; *s.* of Joseph Hume Hume-Rothery and Ellen Maria Carter; *m.* 1931, Elizabeth Alice Fea; one *d.* *Educ.:* Cheltenham College; Royal Military Academy, Woolwich; Magdalen College, Oxford (Demyship in Natural Science, 1st Class Natural Science, Chemistry); Royal School of Mines; Magdalen College, Oxford. Senior Demyship, 1925; Armourers' and Brasiers'

Company Research Fellowship in Metallurgy, 1929; Royal Soc. Warren Research Fellow, 1932-42 and 1943-55; Fellow of Magdalen College, Oxford, 1938-43; Lecturer in Metallurgical Chemistry, Oxford, 1938-55; George Kelley Reader in Metallurgy, Oxford, 1955-58; Sir George Beilby Memorial Award, 1934. American Institute of Mining and Metallurgical Engineers Annual Lecturer, 1946. Institute of Metals Platinum Medal, 1949; Franklin Institute, Francis J. Clamer Medal, 1949; Royal Netherlands Acad., Roozeboom Gold Medal, 1950; Luigi Losana Prize Medal, Italy, 1955; Hon. Life Member American Society for Metals, 1957; Hon. Mem. Institute of Metals, 1960; Membre d'Honneur, Société Française de Métallurgie, 1962. *Publications:* The Metallic State, 1932; The Structure of Metals and Alloys, 1936 (2nd, 3rd and 4th Editions with G. V. Raynor, 1944, 1954, 1962, 5th Edn. with R. E. Smallman and C. W. Haworth, 1968); Atomic Theory for Students of Metallurgy, 1946 (2nd revised Edition 1952, 3rd Edition 1960); Electrons, Atoms, Metals and Alloys, 1948, 1963; Metallurgical Equilibrium Diagrams (with J. W. Christian and W. B. Pearson), 1952; Elements of Structural Metallurgy, 1961; The Structure of Alloys of Iron: An Elementary Introduction, 1965. Papers in Proceedings and Transactions of Royal Society, Journal of Institute of Metals and elsewhere. *Recreations:* painting and fishing. *Address:* Cherry Orchard, Abberbury Road, Iffley, Oxford. [*Died* 27 *Sept.* 1968.

HUMFREY, Lieut.-Col. Richard Edmond, C.M.G. 1919; *b.* 1881; *s.* of late Col. B. G. Humfrey, R.A., and Mrs Humfrey, Bethlehem, S. Africa, and Cavancor, Donegal; *m.* 1926, Isabel Norah Stewart (*d.* 1951), 3rd *d.* of Horace Holt and late Adeline Holt, of Strawberry Hill and Lyme Regis, and *g.d.* of late Rev. Edward Arthur Litton, M.A., Rector of Naunton, Glos. Served France and East Africa, 1914-19 (C.M.G.). *Address:* P.O. Box 2729, Mombasa, Kenya. [*Died* 2 *Sept.* 1962.

HUMPHREY, George, M.A. (Oxon), Ph.D. (Harvard); F.R.S.C. 1942; Emeritus Professor, 1956; Professor in Psychology, University of Oxford, 1947-56, and Director of the Institute of Experimental Psychology, 1948-56; *b.* 17 July 1889; *m.* 1st, 1918, Muriel (*d.* 1955), *d.* of late George Miller; one *d.*; 2nd, 1956, Berta Hochberger, M.B.E., *d.* of late Max Wolpert. *Educ.:* Queen Elizabeth's School, Faversham; All Souls College, Oxford (Bible Clerk); Leipzig (Cassel Scholar); Harvard (Townsend Scholar). Tutor in Latin and Greek Borough Rd. Coll., 1915; Prof. of Classics, Univ. of St. Francis Xavier, Antigonish, Nova Scotia, 1916-18; Assistant Professor of Psychology, Wesleyan University, Middletown, Conn., 1920-24; Special Lecturer on Education, Harvard, 1924; Charlton Prof. of Philosophy, Queen's University, Kingston, Ontario, 1924-47; Sec. Canadian Psychological Association 1938-42, President 1942-44, Hon. Pres., 1944-45; Chm. (Military) Test Research Cttee., Canadian Psychological Assoc., 1942-1946; Member Canadian Social Science Research Council, 1942-44; Member Civilian Advisory Cttee., Canadian Directorate of Personnel Selection (Army), 1943-45; Regional Rep. for Canada, Council of American Psychological Association, 1945-48; Dominion Fellow, St. John's College, Cambridge, 1947; Fellow of Magdalen College, Oxford, 1947-56. Hon. Life Fellow, British, American and Canadian Psychological Associations. *Publications:* The Story of Man's Mind, 1923, 1932, 1937; Trans. of Itard's The Wild Boy of Aveyron (with Muriel Miller Humphrey), 1932, 1962; The Nature of Learning, 1933; Directed Thinking, 1948; Thinking: an introduction to its experimental psychology, 1951, 1963; Ed., Psychology Through Experiment, 1963; Ed. (with Michael Argyle), Social Psychology Through Experiment, 1962; The Chemistry of Thinking (with R. V. Coxon), 1963; contributed to Warren's Dictionary of Psychology, Encyclopædia Americana and Encyclopædia Britannica; chapter on Thought in Boring, Langfeld and Weld's Psychology; papers in scientific and other journals; also two novels. *Address:* 52 Sherlock Close, Cambridge. *T.:* Cambridge 58779. [*Died* 24 *April* 1966.

HUMPHREY, George Magoffin; Director, National Steel Corporation, U.S.A. (on resuming business after holding political office in U.S. Treasury); *b.* 8 Mar. 1890; *s.* of Watts S. Humphrey and Caroline Magoffin; *m.* 1913, Pamela Stark; one *s.* two *d.* (and one *s.* decd.). *Educ.:* Univ. of Michigan (LL.B.). Practised law with Humphrey, Grant & Humphrey, Saginaw, 1912-17; The M. A. Hanna Co., Cleveland, Ohio; Gen. Counsel, 1917-20; Partner, 1920-22; Vice-Pres., 1922-25; Exec. Vice-Pres., 1925-29; Pres., 1929-52; Chm., 1952; Dir. many subsidiary and affiliated cos. Formerly, Chm. Pittsburgh Consolidation Coal Co. Secretary of U.S. Treasury, Eisenhower Administration, 1953-57. Holds several hon. degrees. *Address:* Holiday Hill Farm, Mentor, Ohio 44060, U.S.A. *Clubs:* Union, Tavern, Chagrin Valley Hunt, Kirtland Country, Fifty (Cleveland); Links (N.Y.); Duquesne (Pittsburgh); Detroit; Glen Arven Country (Thomasville, Ga.); Kitchi Gammi (Duluth, Minn.). [*Died* 20 *Jan.* 1970.

HUMPHREYS, Gordon Noel, M.A., M.R.C.S., L.R.C.P.; diploma, R.G.S., in surveying, cartography, etc.; *s.* of late Noël A. Humphreys I.S.O., F.S.S.; *m.* 1934, Marion, *o. d.* of late J. Bradshaw White, M.D., M.Ch.; two *s.* one *d.* *Educ.:* Epsom College; Cambridge University. Helped to construct and learnt to fly on previously untested experimental single-seater aeroplanes, May 1912; commissioned in R.F.C. (S.R.), 1913; Central Flying School, 1913; transferred from S.R. to regular R.F.C. (Military Wing), 1914; service with B.E.F. in France; Lieut. 1914; started in St. Omer first Lewis-gun school, making first modifications of Lewis-gun for adaption as an air arm (despatches); shot down for third time by enemy anti-aircraft guns, and made prisoner, 1915; Capt. 1915; repatriated, 1919; returned to flying duties in various units until 1920, when lent by Air Ministry for staff appointment in Geographical Section, General Staff, War Office, for design of series of international aeronautical maps; passed to reserve, 1923; retired, 1927. *Expeditions:* economic botanic expedition in Mexico, having as a result first cultivation, in India, of the linaloe tree, 1910; first ascent of Pico Mayor, highest point of Popocatepetl, 1911; first flights over Ruwenzori and six expeditions on foot to unexplored regions of the mountains, ascent of the six snow mountains and of subsidiary peaks, including first ascents, first crossing of the massif via the snows and first penetration into Northern and Southern plateaux, collection of undescribed species of plants, mapping of previously unexplored headwaters of eight rivers and some twenty lakes first seen from the air, location of legendary Fountain of the Nile of Herodotus, 1926, 1931-32; Murchison Grant, R.G.S., for Ruwenzori expeditions, 1932; Oxford Univ. Ellesmereland Expedition, 1934-35; Mount Everest Expedition, 1936. *Publications:* papers, before British Association, R.G.S., Alpine Club, etc. *Address:* c/o Royal Geographical Society, S.W.7. [*Died* 11 *March* 1966.

HUMPHREYS, Hubert; J.P.; Managing Director Midland Fan Co. Ltd. since 1912; *b.* 14 July 1878; *s.* of George H.

Humphreys: *m.* 1st; one *s.* (and one *s.* decd.); 2nd, 1927, Gertrude Greenwood (*d.* 1952). *Educ.:* King Edward's Gram. Sch., Aston. Started life as a blacksmith; on the stage, 1903-6; Midland Representative, 1906-1912. Chm., Birmingham Borough Labour Party, 1936-39; mem. Fabian Soc. and for some years member Nat. Exec.; contested Ladywood as a Parl. candidate, 1935; elected to City Council for Northfield, 1937; alderman 1945 and chm. Water Cttee.; city magistrate, 1942; Lord Mayor of Birmingham, 1949-50; Dep. Mayor of Birmingham, 1950-51. Vice-Pres. Shaw Society. *Recreations:* the theatre, tennis. *Address:* 78 Cambridge Rd., King's Heath. Birmingham 14. *T.:* 021-444 2346. [*Died* 4 *Oct.* 1967.

HUMPHRIES, Rev. Canon James Henry; Residentiary Canon of St. Albans and Chaplain of Mid-Herts. Group of Hospitals since 1960; *b.* 23 Jan. 1890; *s.* of James Humphries and Sarah Humphries, formerly Turner; *m.* 1917, Florence Elsie Louisa Heaps, Exeter; one *s.* one *d.* *Educ.:* Birmingham College of Art; Leeds University; College of the Resurrection, Mirfield, Yorks. Ordained Deacon, 1914; Priest, 1915; Assistant Curate: St. Jude's, Peckham, Southwark, 1914-19; St. Margaret's, Plumstead, Southwark, 1919-24; Vicar, St. Andrew's, Battersea, 1924-31; Hon. Chaplain, Battersea Gen. Hosp., 1924-31; Vicar, Ch. of Holy Spirit, Clapham, 1931-39; Hon. Chaplain, S. London Hosp. for Women, 1931-1939; Rector of Digswell and Rural Dean of Welwyn, 1939-43; Rector of Bushey, 1943-1960. Hon. Canon of St. Albans, 1952-60. Chairman St. Albans Dio. Advisory Committee, 1955. *Recreations:* painting, architecture, fishing. *Address:* 25 Worley Road, St. Albans, Herts. *T.:* St. Albans 50383. [*Died* 20 *May* 1962.

HUNGARTON, 1st Baron, *cr.* 1951, of Hungarton; **Archibald Crawford;** farmer; managing director Crawford, Prince & Johnson, agricultural equipment makers; *b.* 12 Sept. 1890; *s.* of Robert and Ruth Crawford, Highfields Farm, Lowesby, Leics.; *m.* 1914, Jean (*d.* 1966), *d.* of David Johnstone, Linkins, Castle Douglas; one *d.* (one *s.* killed in action, 1945). *Educ.:* Wyggeston Gram. Sch., Leicester. Formerly Chairman of National Farmers' Union. Member Leics. C.C., 1936-46. Contested (Lab.) Melton Mowbray, July 1945 and February 1950. *Address:* Crawford, Prince and Johnson, Syston, Leicestershire; The Manor House, Hungarton, Leicester. *Clubs:* National, Farmers'. [*Died* 14 *June* 1966 (*ext.*).

HUNGERFORD, Sir (Alexander) Wilson, Kt., *cr.* 1929; Senate, Northern Ireland, 1948-57; 2nd *s.* of John and Susan Hungerford; *m.* 1927, Joan Hooper, *o. d.* of Lt.-Col. W. Hooper Pinches; one *s.* one *d.* *Educ.:* Model School, Belfast. Joined the staff of the Unionist Party in Belfast, 1912; took a conspicuous part in the organisation of many historic events in Ulster history; Secretary of the Ulster Unionist Council, 1921-41; Chief Unionist Agent, Northern Ireland, 1921-41; M.P. Oldpark Div. of Belfast, Parliament of Northern Ireland, 1929-45; Assistant Parliamentary Secretary to Ministry of Finance, 1933-41; Parliamentary Secretary, Ministry of Commerce, 1941-43; Ministry of Home Affairs, 1943-44; Ministry of Health and Local Government, 1944; Chief Government Whip, 1944-45. *Recreations:* cricket, football, golf. *Address:* Dragons, Loughton, Essex. *Club:* Ulster Reform (Belfast). [*Died* 19 *Jan.* 1969.

HUNT, Alan Henderson, D.M., M.Ch., M.A. (Oxon.); F.R.C.S.; Senior Surgeon, St. Bartholomew's Hospital; and Surgeon, The Royal Marsden Hospital; *b.* Nov. 1908; *s.* of late Edmund Henderson Hunt, Farnham; *m.* 1940, Ethel Muriel Chandler; two *s.* three *d.* *Educ.:* Charterhouse (Leaving Science Exhib.); Balliol College, Oxford (Theodore Williams Schol.): St. Bartholomew's Hosp. (Luther Holden Research Schol.). Hunterian Professor, 1954, Jacksonian Prize Winner, 1957, Member of Council, 1965, and Mem. Court of Examiners (Chm. 1966), Royal Coll. of Surgeons Eng.; Fellow Association of Surgeons of Great Britain and Ireland; F.Roy.Soc.Med. (Pres. Sect. of Proctology, 1959-60); Mem. British Soc. of Gastro-Enterology; Corresp. Mem. French Gastro-Enterological Soc. Served War of 1939-45, E.M.S. Surgeon; surgical specialist, R.A.M.C. and S.M.O. Special Service Brigade (Commandos). *Publications:* Portal Hypertension, 1958; chapters and articles in scientific journals on wound healing, the surgery of the digestive tract, liver, spleen, upper jaw. *Recreation:* travel. *Address:* 149 Harley Street, W.1. *T.:* 01-935 4444; 38 Hamilton Terrace, St. John's Wood, N.W.8. *T.:* Cunningham 9123. *Club:* Royal Automobile. [*Died* 4 *July* 1970.

HUNT, Cecil Arthur, M.A., LL.B.; R.W.S. 1925 (Vice-Pres., R.W.S. 1930-33); Barrister, Inner Temple; *b.* Torquay, 1873; *s.* of late A. R. Hunt, M.A., F.G.S., F.L.S.; *m.* Phyllis Clara (*d.* 1964), *d.* of Edgar Lucas; one *s.* *Educ.:* Winchester; Trinity College, Cambridge. On election as A.R.W.S. in 1919 ceased to practise at the Bar; R.B.A., 1914-1924. Water colours in permanent collections: British Museum, Victoria and Albert Museum, Leighton House, Trinity Coll., Cambridge, Royal Geographical Society, Alpine Club, Corporation Galleries at Glasgow, Manchester, Newcastle, Liverpool, Huddersfield, Hull, Eastbourne, Leeds, Oldham, Preston, Northampton, Torquay, Stoke-on-Trent, Bury, Bradford, Sheffield, Rochdale, Newport (Mon.), and Fitzwilliam Museum, Cambridge, Ashmolean Museum, Oxford; public galleries, Johannesburg, Melbourne, Pietermaritzburg, Sydney, and Vancouver; Exhibitor, oils and water-colours at R.A.; illustrator of Dartmoor Novels (Widecombe edition) by Eden Phillpotts; employed at the Home Office, 1916-19, first in connection with the Irish prisoners interned in England after the Sinn Fein Rebellion, and subsequently assisting Home Office Committee for Employment of Conscientious Objectors. *Publications:* Tudor on Charities, 4th ed.; Bunyan on Life Assurance, 4th ed.; contributor of titles, Charities, Boundaries, Friendly Societies, etc., to Halsbury's Laws of England; and of many conveyancing precedents to Encyclopædia of Forms; Stories of English Artists (with Randall Davies); articles on Baxter prints in Connoisseur Magazine; six articles on Watercolour Technique in The Artist, 1936; Sketching in the Alps, Alpine Journal, 1940; Improvement of Trout Streams, Field, 1940. *Address:* Mallord House, Old Church Street, Chelsea, S.W.3. *T.:* Flaxman 0443; Foxworthy, Manaton, Newton Abbot, S. Devon. *T.:* Manaton 310. *Club:* Athenæum. [*Died* 5 *Aug.* 1965.

HUNT, Colonel John Philip, T.D.; *b.* 27 April 1907; 2nd *s.* of late John Edwin Hunt, Hope, Derbyshire; *m.* 1935, Jean Margaret, *o. d.* of C. A. Nicholson, Sheffield; three *s.* one *d.* *Educ.:* Malvern Coll. Director: Cooper & Turner Ltd.; Philblack Ltd.; Wellington Tube Holdings Ltd.; Midland Bank Ltd.; Newton, Chambers and Co. Ltd.; Eagle Star Insurance Co. Ltd. (South Yorkshire). Chairman, The Sheffield Amateur Sports Club Ltd.; A Town Trustee of Sheffield; Master of Company of Cutlers in Hallamshire (Sheffield), 1948-49; J.P. Sheffield, 1951-54. A Governor of Malvern College. Served Hallamshire Battalion (T.A.) York and Lancaster Regiment, 1927-40; Norway,

Iceland, 1940; Home Guard, 1941-45; re-formed Hallamshire Bn. and commanded, 1946-49; Bt.-Col. 1949; reformed Sheffield Bn. Home Guard, 1951 and resigned 1953. Hon. Col. The Hallamshire Bn. (Territorial), T. & A.V.R., 1965. *Recreation:* fishing. *Address:* Holme Hall, Bakewell, Derbyshire; Beauregard, Flamboro' Head, East Yorks. *Club:* Sheffield (Sheffield).

[*Died* 9 *July* 1970.

HUNT, Martita; actress, stage and films; *b.* Argentina, 30 Jan. 1900; *d.* of Alfred Hunt and Marta Burnett. *Educ.:* Queenwood, Eastbourne. First stage appearance, with Liverpool Repertory Company, 1921; first London appearance for Stage Society, Kingsway Theatre, 1923; subsequently played frequently in West End. Parts include: Mrs. Linden in A Doll's House, Playhouse, 1925; (after joining Old Vic Company Sept. 1929): Nurse, in Romeo and Juliet; Portia, in Merchant of Venice; The Queen, in Richard II; Helena; Portia, in Julius Cæsar; Rosalind; Queen Elizabeth, in the Dark Lady of the Sonnets; Lady Macbeth; The Queen, in Hamlet, etc.; Edith Gunter, in Autumn Crocus, Lyric, 1931; Masha, in The Seagull, New, 1936; Emilia, in Othello, Old Vic, 1938; Mrs. Cheveley, in An Ideal Husband, Westminster, 1943; Countess Aurelia, in The Mad Woman of Chailliot, New York, and on tour, Dec. 1948-50; The Grand Duchess in The Sleeping Prince, 1953; Angelica in Hotel Paradiso, 1956. Entered films, 1933, in I was a Spy, and has played many parts including that of Miss Haversham in Great Expectations. *Address:* 7 Primrose Hill Studios, Fitzroy Road, N.W.1.

[*Died* 13 *June* 1969.

HUNT, Sir Reuben (James), Kt., *cr.* 1953; Life President, R. Hunt & Co. Ltd., Earls Colne, 1968 (Chairman, 1947-67; Managing Director, 1927-67); (until 1965) Deputy Chairman and Director, Ransomes, Sims & Jefferies Ltd., Ipswich (Chairman 1951-1963); *b.* 21 September 1888; *s.* of Reuben Hunt and Elizabeth Culf; *m.* 1914, Dudley Ethel Grimwood Goodchild; four *d.* *Educ.:* Earls Colne Grammar School; Forest School, Walthamstow. *Address:* Bearcroft, Earls Colne, Essex. *T.:* Earls Colne 228.

[*Died* 22 *Jan.* 1970.

HUNT, Sir William Edgar, Kt., *cr.* 1938; C.M.G. 1934; C.B.E. 1929; *b.* Apr. 1883; 3rd *s.* of late Rev. O. Hunt, Budbrooke, Warwick; *m.* 1938, Mrs. Margaret Batty, *d.* of late Sir John Harbottle. *Educ.:* Warwick School; Selwyn College, Cambridge; B.A. Appointed to Nigerian Civil Service as Assistant District Commissioner, 1909; District Officer, 1917; Resident, 1924; Senior Resident, 1929; Chief Commissioner Southern Provinces, Nigeria, 1935-38; Acting Governor, 1938; retired 1939. *Address:* Blackbirds, Fleet, Hants. *T.* Fleet 6244.

[*Died* 10 *Dec.* 1969.

HUNTER, Albert Edward; M.P. (Lab.) Feltham, 1955-66; *b.* 1900; *s.* of Alfred and Evelyn Hunter. Sales representative; President of the National Union of Shop Assistants, 1936-37; National Treasurer, 1938-44. Member of Holborn Board of Guardians, 1925-30; Member of Holborn Borough Council, 1928-34; St. Pancras Borough Council, 1945-53, Alderman. J.P. County of London, 1951. Contested (Lab.) Spelthorne Division of Middlesex, 1951. Served European War, 1914-18. *Address:* c/o House of Commons, S.W.1

[*Died* 6 *April* 1969.

HUNTER, Andrew, C.B.E. 1946; M.A., B.Sc., M.B.(Edin.), F.R.C.P.Glasg., F.R.S.C.; Associate, Research Institute, Hospital for Sick Children, Toronto, 1947-66; Emeritus Professor of Pathological Chemistry, University of Toronto; *b.* Edinburgh, 1876; *s.* of late James Hunter and Janet Heggie; *m.* 1908, Janet Arthur. *Educ.:* George Heriot's Hosp. School, Edinburgh; Universities of Edinburgh, Berlin, and Heidelberg. House Physician, Royal Edinburgh Infirmary; Assistant in Physiology, Universities of Edinburgh and Leeds; Assistant Professor of Biochemistry, Cornell University, U.S.A., 1908-14; Biochemist, U.S. Public Health Service, 1914-15; Professor of Pathological Chemistry, University of Toronto, 1915-19; Professor of Biochemistry, University of Toronto, 1919-29; Gardiner Professor of Physiological Chemistry, Glasgow University, 1929-35; Dean of the Faculty of Medicine, Glasgow University, 1930-35; Prof. of Pathological Chemistry, 1935-47, and Dean of the School of Graduate Studies, Univ. of Toronto, 1945-47; Captain, C.A.M.C., 1916-19. *Publications:* Monograph on Creatine and Creatinine, 1928; papers in Journal of Biological Chemistry, Biochemical Journal, and other scientific periodicals. *Address:* 2 Sultan Street, Toronto, Canada. *T.:* 923-3660. *Club:* York (Toronto).

[*Died* 11 *July* 1969.

HUNTER, Sir Ellis, G.B.E. 1961; Kt. 1948; Chairman since 1948 (Managing Director, 1938-61), Dorman Long & Co. Ltd.; Chairman: British Structural Steel Co. Ltd.; Cleveland Trust Ltd., Redpath Brown & Co. Ltd., Tees Side Bridge & Engineering Works Ltd.; Director: Darlington & Simpson Rolling Mills Ltd., Dorman Long (Africa) Ltd., Dorman Long (Rhodesia) Ltd., Royal Exchange Assurance; *b.* 18 Feb. 1892; *yr. s.* of William Hunter, Great Ayton, Yorkshire; *m.* 1918, Winifred Grace Steed; two *d.* *Educ.:* privately. A.C.A. 1914; F.C.A. 1927; partner in W. B. Peat & Co. (later Peat, Marwick, Mitchell & Co.), 1922, general partner, 1928; joined Board of Dorman Long & Co. Ltd., as Deputy Chairman 1938. First Chairman British Steel Producers' Conference, 1945-46; President British Iron & Steel Federation, 1945-53, and took leading part in formulation of Iron & Steel Industry's Plan of Development, submitted in Dec. 1945, and later approved by Govt. and published as a White Paper in May 1946 (Ref. No. Cmd. 6811). *Recreations:* country life and travel. *Address:* Howden Gate, Northallerton, Yorks. *Club:* East India and Sports. [*Died* 21 *Sept.* 1961.

HUNTER, Air Commodore Henry John Francis, C.B.E. 1941; M.C.; late R.A.F.; *b.* 29 December 1893; *s.* of late Henry Charles Vicars Hunter and Hon. Mrs. Florence Louise Hunter (*née* Dormer); *m.* 1935, Kathleen Witts; one *s.* one *d.*; *m.* 1949, Kathleen Kirkpatrick, *d.* of late Mr. Justice Morice and of Mrs. Morice, 34 Queen's Gate, S.W.7. *Educ.:* Eton; R.M.C., Sandhurst. Rifle Brigade, 1913; wounded, 1915; seconded to R.F.C. autumn 1915; transferred to R.A.F. on formation; served in France with Rifle Brigade and R.F.C.; since served in Germany (army of occupation), China and Iraq; War of 1939-45 in Bomber Command till Jan. 1942, then Singapore, Sumatra, Java, India and Ceylon; retired 1946. *Address:* Little Warham, Beaford, North Devon. *Club:* R.A.F.

[*Died* 12 *Sept.* 1966.

HUNTER, Brigadier Henry Noel Alexander, D.S.O. 1918; late the Queen's Royal Regt.; *b.* 1881; *m.* 1912, Meta, 2nd *d.* of late A. G. Steel, K.C., and Mrs. Steel, of 12 Cleveland Gardens, W.; one *s.* one *d.* *Educ.:* Temple Grove; Haileybury College. Served South African War, 1899-1902 (Queen's medal and three clasps, King's medal and two clasps); European War, 1914-18 (despatches, D.S.O., Bt. Lt.-Col.); A.Q.M.G. Southern Command, India, 1931-34; Commander 11th Infantry Brigade, 1934-37; retired, 1937. *Ad-*

dress: 10 Carlyle Mansions, Cheyne Walk, S.W.3. *T.:* Flaxman 8868. *Club:* Army and Navy. [*Died* 8 *Nov.* 1964.

HUNTER, Col. Sir Herbert Patrick, Kt., *cr.* 1946; C.B. 1951; C.B.E. 1932 (O.B.E. 1919); D.L.; Chief Constable of Staffs., 1929-1950; *b.* abroad, 1880; *s.* of W. Hunter, Norwich, *m.* 1914, Eleanor Isac, Norwich; one *d.* (one *s.* killed on active service). *Educ.:* abroad. Served S. African War, 1899-1902 (wounded at Modder River); served in Malay States as Assistant Supt. of Chandu and Assistant Commissioner of Police 1903-14; European War, 1914-19 (wounded twice, despatches twice); Major, 1916; Brevet Lt.-Col., 1928; commanded Stafford Battery R.A. (T.), 1921-1929; Asst. Chief Constable of Staffordshire, 1919-29; Chm. Staffs. Territorial Army Assoc., 1946-51; ex-Mem. T.A. Advisory Cttee., Council of T. & A.F.A.; Hon. Col. 666 L.A.A./S.L. Regt., Roy. Artillery, 1947-51; King's Police Medal, 1939. Headed Govt. Police Mission to India and Far East, 1946. *Publications:* a number of short stories, dealing mainly with crime and adventure, for magazines; book on Gunnery, 1917. *Recreations:* shooting, golf. *Address:* Sentosa, Brocton, Stafford. *T.:* Stafford 61195. *Clubs:* Royal Automobile, Junior Army and Navy, [*Died* 2 *April* 1968.

HUNTER, James de Graaff., C.I.E. **1933; F.R.S. 1935; M.A., Sc.D., F.Inst.P., F.R.A.S., F.R.G.S., Hon. M.I.R.E., Hon. M.R.I.C.S., Hon. F.I.S.Aust.; Consulting Geodesist;** *b.* 11 Sept. 1881; *s.* of James and Sarah Jane Pierrepont Hunter; *m.* 1st, Ruby Julia Strachey; one *s.*; 2nd, 1929, Gwendoline Maud Henville, 3rd *d.* of Colonel G. H. Davis; one *d.* *Educ.:* King's School, Chester; Pembroke College, Cambridge (senior scholar). 12th Wrangler Math. Tripos, 1903; 1st Class Mechanical Science Tripos, 1904; Master at Harrow School, 1904; Private Secretary and Scientific Assistant to Lord Kelvin, 1904-05; Assistant, National Physical Laboratory, 1905-07; joined Survey of India, 1907, Deputy Superintendent, 1920, Superintendent, 1926; Director of the Geodetic Branch, 1927-1932; served European War and after in Iraq and Kurdistan. Leverhulme Research Fellow, 1936-38. Joint British delegate 6th Pacific Science Congress, San Francisco, 1939. P.O.W., 1941-42; Assistant Surveyor-General (Delhi), Jan.-July 1943; Dir. of War Research, Survey of India, 1943-46. Visiting lecturer, South African Universities, Mar.-June 1950. Pres. d'Honneur International Association of Geodesy. *Publications:* Atmospheric Refraction, 1913; Earth's Axes and Triangulation, 1918 (Prof. Papers 14, 16 of Survey of India); Articles Geodesy, Ency. Brit. 12th and 13th editions; Articles Refraction, and Gravity Survey in Dict. of Applied Physics; Geodetic Reports of the Survey of India, Vols. I-VIII.; various papers; Trans. and Proc. R.S. Bulletin Geodesique. *Address:* 7 Beaconsfield Road, Mosman, N.S.W., Australia.
[*Died* 3 *Feb.* 1967.

HUNTER, Rt. Rev. John; Bishop of George since 1951; *b.* 16 Feb. 1897; *s.* of late William George Hunter, C.B.E.; *m.* 1927, Philippa Dora Mary, *d.* of late Alfred Hugh Mead and of Mrs. Mead, Elwell Manor, Weymouth; one *s.* two *d.* *Educ.:* Keble Coll., Oxford. Curate of Harrow Parish Church, 1922-24, of Holy Trinity, Weymouth, 1924-1927, and of St. Paul's, Rondebosch, Cape Town, 1927-30; Rector of St. Augustine's, O'okiep, Namaqualand, 1930-33; Rector of St. Mary's, Stellenbosch, Cape, 1933-40; Canon of Bloemfontein and Rector of the Cathedral Parish, 1940-43; Bishop of Kimberley and Kuruman, 1943-51. Coronation Medal, 1953. *Address:* Bishop's Lea, George, C.P., S. Africa. *T.:* 95.
[*Died* 27 *Dec.* 1965.

HUNTER, Sir John Adams, K.C.M.G., *cr.* 1942 (C.M.G. 1940); B.A. (Cantab.); C.St.J.; *b.* 30 October 1890; *s.* of late John Main Hunter and Mrs. Janet Vardy, Wylam, Northumberland; *m.* 1931, Catherine Gladys (Kathleen), *d.* of late Geo. William Greener. *Educ.:* Royal Grammar School, Newcastle on Tyne; St. John's Coll., Cambridge. Entered Colonial Administrative Service as Eastern Cadet after competitive examination, 1914; has held various appointments in Malayan Civil Service, including Malayan Establishment Officer, 1933, Acting Under-Secretary, Straits Settlements, 1935, and Acting Colonial Secretary, 1936; Lieutenant-Governor of Malta, 1938-40; Governor and Commander-in-Chief of British Honduras, 1940-47. *Address:* Strange Cottage, Dunsfold, nr. Godalming, Surrey. *T.:* Dunsfold 320. *Club:* East India and Sports. [*Died* 17 *Nov.* 1962.

HUNTER, John George, C.M.G. 1957; B.Sc., M.B., Ch.M.; *b.* 19 Sept. 1888; *s.* of late William Fyfe Hunter, Tillicoultry, Scotland, and Ellen Jane Hunter, Sydney, Aust.; *m.* 1916, Clarice Mary Hunter; four *s.* one *d.* *Educ.:* Fort Street High School; Sydney University. B.Sc. 1909, Hons. Biology and Geology; M.B. Hons. 1915. Chief Biologist, Australasian Antarctic Expedition, 1911-14; Assistant Physician, Sydney Hospital, 1923-1929; Lecturer, Medical Ethics, Sydney University, 1943-; Medical Secretary, New South Wales Branch, B.M.A., 1929-62. Gen. Sec., Fed. Council of B.M.A. in Australia, 1933-61; Gen. Sec., Aust. Med. Assoc., 1962; Mem. Council, World Med. Assoc., 1960-; Chm., Aust. Council of Social Service, 1962-. Gold Medal of B.M.A. in Aust., 1956. Served Aust. Army Medical Corps: Captain, 1916-1918; Major, 1941-43. *Recreations:* gardening, fishing. *Address:* 4 Korokan Rd., Lilli Pilli, Sydney, N.S.W. *Club:* Antarctic (Australian Section). [*Died* 27 *Dec.* 1964.

HUNTER, Sir Summers, Kt. 1943; J.P. Wallsend; retired as Managing Director of Richardsons, Westgarth & Co. Ltd., 1955; Hon. President North Eastern Marine Engineering Co. Ltd.; Chairman, Pass Engineering Ltd.; *b.* 1890; *s.* of late Summers Hunter, C.B.E., and late Dora Elizabeth Hunter; *m.* 1915, Aline, *d.* of late Dr. Arthur Charles Adams Lovegrove, Settle, Yorkshire; three *s.* *Educ.:* Oundle; King's College, Newcastle upon Tyne. Royal Naval Engineer Officer, 1915-18. Was first Chairman National Association of Marine Enginebuilders. Hon. Vice-Pres. Royal Institution of Naval Architects; M.I.Mech.E.; Hon. Vice-Pres. Institute of Marine Engineers, Fellow and Past President N.E.C. Inst. of Engineers and Shipbuilders; formerly Mem. of General Committee, Lloyd's Register of Shipping; Council British Shipbuilding Research Assoc.; Regional Director of Admiralty Merchant Shipbuilding and Repairs for N.E. Area, 1940-46. *Publications:* papers before various Technical Institutions. *Recreations:* fishing and shooting. *Address:* Redwayes, Adderstone Crescent, Jesmond, Newcastle upon Tyne 2. *T.:* Newcastle 81-3384.
[*Died* 25 *March* 1963.

HUNTER, Lt.-Col. Thomas, C.I.E., 1923; I.M.S.; retired; *b.* 1873; *s.* of Thomas Hunter, Kilmarnock; *m.* Jessie Catanach (*d.* 1960), *d.* of Adam A. Haig, Innerleithen; two *s.* four *d.* *Educ.:* Kilmarnock Academy; Glasgow Univ. M.A. 1892; B.Sc. (1st Hons.) 1895; M.B., Ch.B. (1st Hons.) 1897; M.D. 1907. Entered I.M.S. 1898; served with China Exped. Force, 1900-1; Civil Surgeon United Provinces, 1902; Civil Surgeon, Lucknow, and Professor of Obstetrics and Gynæcology, University of Lucknow; retired, 1928. *Address:* 2 Mill Road, Eastbourne. *T.:* Eastbourne 2199.
[*Died* 5 *May* 1965.

HUNTER, William, R.O.I.; *b.* Glasgow; *s.* of William Hunter and Jane Kay. Studied under Prof. M. Greiffenhagen, and Prof. Paul Artôt, Brussels; assisted Prof. M. Greiffenhagen, and Prof. R. Anning Bell, with mural paintings; travelled extensively in Europe, studying in the chief cities. Exhibited in Paris Salon, Royal Academy, Royal Scottish Academy, Royal Institute of Oil-Painters, other Exhibitions in Great Britain, also in Canada, United States of America, and South Africa; *work purchased:* Oriental Poppies, by Caird Bequest, Greenock; The Bubble, by Glasgow Corporation, etc. *Address:* Rigside, Iain Road, Bearsden, Glasgow. *Club:* Art (Glasgow). [*Died* 29 *March* 1967.

HUNTING, (Gerald) Lindsay, A.E.A.; F.Z.S.; Director (formerly Chairman) Hunting Group, Shipping, Oil, Aviation, Survey, Industrial and Engineering Companies; *b.* 28 March 1891; *s.* of Charles Samuel Hunting, Shipowner, and Agnes Mona Hunting; *m.* 1924, Ruth Pyman; three *s. Educ.:* Loretto. *Recreations:* fishing, gardening. *Address:* Norwich House, 4 Dunraven St., W.1. *Clubs:* R.A.F., M.C.C. [*Died* 4 *Sept.* 1966.

HUNTINGFIELD, 5th Baron (*cr.* 1796), **William Charles Arcedeckne Vanneck,** Bt. 1751; K.C.M.G., *cr.* 1934; late Captain 13th Hussars; *b.* Gatton, Queensland, Australia, 3 Jan. 1883; *e. s.* of late Hon. W. A. Vanneck, The Cupola, Leiston, Suffolk, 2nd *s.* of 3rd Baron and Mary, *d.* of late William Armstrong, of Toowoomba, Queensland; *S.* uncle, 1915; *m.* 1st, 1912, Margaret Eleanor (*d.* 1943), *o. d.* of late Ernest Crosby of Grasmere, Rhinebeck, New York; two *s.* two *d.*; 2nd, 1944, Muriel (*d.* 1953), (who *m.* 1905, Baron Eltisley, *d.* 1942), *o. c.* of late Col. Jemmett Duke, 17th Lancers. M.P. (U.) Eye Division of Suffolk, 1923-29; Parliamentary Private Secretary to the President of the Board of Trade, 1927-29; Governor of State of Victoria, 1934-39; Acting Governor-General of Australia, March-Sept. 1938; appointed Governor of Southern Rhodesia, 1942, but did not take up appointment owing to ill-health; Hon. Air Commodore No. 21 City of Melbourne Squadron, R.A.A.F.; Col. comdg. 58th Bn. London Home Guard. *Heir:* *s.* Hon. Gerard Charles Arcedeckne Vanneck [*b.* 29 May 1915; *m.* 1941, Janetta Lois, *er. d.* of Commander R. H. Errington, Tostock Old Hall, Bury St. Edmunds, and 122 Marsham Court, S.W.1; one *s.* three *d.*]. *Address:* 54 Wilsbury Road, Hove, Sussex. *Clubs:* Brooks's, Cavalry. [*Died* 20 *Nov.* 1969.

HUNTON, Gen. Sir Thomas Lionel, K.C.B., *cr.* 1944 (C.B. 1941); M.V.O. 1927; O.B.E. 1918; *b.* 30 October 1885; *s.* of Theodore Hunton; *m.* 1919, Margaret M. F., *d.* of Lt.-Col. W. H. Steele, late R.A.M.C.; one *s.* (one *d.* decd.). *Educ.:* Clifton Coll. Joined Royal Marines, 1903; Capt. 1914; Bt. Major, 1919; Major, 1924; Bt. Lt.-Col. 1931; Lt.-Col. 1933; Bt. Col. 1935; Col. 1936; Maj.-Gen. 1940; Lt.-Gen. 1943; Gen. 1945; served European War, 1914-18, including Battle of Jutland (despatches twice, Chevalier Légion d'Honneur, Star of Roumania, Chevalier); A.A.G. Royal Marines, H.Q., 1935-1938; Commanded Portsmouth Div., Royal Marines, 1938-41; Commandant General Royal Marines, 1943-46; retired list, 1946; A.D.C. to the King, 1939-40; interpreter in Japanese. *Address:* Belvedere, Lympstone, Near Exmouth, South Devon. *T.:* Exmouth 3141. [*Died* 20 *April* 1970.

HURD, Baron, *cr.* 1964 (Life Peer), of Newbury; **Anthony Richard Hurd,** Kt. 1959; farmer; Chairman Westbourne Park Building Society; Thames Valley Eggs Ltd.; English Farms Ltd.; Director: Falkland Islands Co., Scottish Australian Co., Massey-Ferguson Holdings, Fisons Fertilizers, Muar River Rubber Co.; Mem. South Midlands Cttee., Lloyds Bank Ltd.; *b.* 2 May 1901; *s.* of late Sir Percy Hurd; *m.* 1928, Stephanie, *e. d.* of late E. M. Corner, F.R.C.S.; two *s.* (and one *s.* decd.). *Educ.:* Marlborough; Pembroke Coll., Camb., M.A. Farming in Wiltshire since 1926. Farm Editor of The Field 1924-27; series of farming talks B.B.C., 1937, 1938 and 1939; Agricultural Correspondent The Times, 1932-58. M.P. (C.) Newbury Div., of Berks, 1945-64. Visited Tanganyika 1948, to study groundnut scheme, and N.Z. and Australia, 1950, as a member of Commonwealth Parliamentary delegn.; first Member of the U.K. House of Commons to visit the Falkland Islands, 1956; Chairman Conservative Agriculture and Food Cttee. in House of Commons, 1951-64; Vice-Pres. of Royal Agricultural Society of England; President, Farmers' Club, 1951; Member of Council of N.F.U., 1936-40, representing Wiltshire; Asst. Agricultural Adviser, Min. of Agriculture, 1939-45 and Minister's Liaison Officer for South Western Counties. Fellow Institute of Journalists; Chairman Guild of Agricultural Journalists, 1954, President, 1965; Deputy President, Royal Agricultural Society of the Commonwealth, 1965. *Publication:* A Farmer in Whitehall, 1951. *Address:* Winterbourne Holt, Newbury, Berks. *T.A.* and *T.:* Chieveley 220. *Clubs:* United University, Carlton, Farmers'. [*Died* 12 *Feb.* 1966.

HURLEY, Captain Frank; (James Francis) O.B.E. 1941; *s.* of E. Harrison Hurley; *b.* 1890; *m.* T., *d.* of Col. Leighton, Calcutta. *Educ.:* Sydney University. Explorer Author, Film Producer; accompanied Sir Douglas Mawson on the Australian Antarctic Expedition, 1911-14, and sledged to South Magnetic Pole; on Staff Sir Ernest Shackleton's Trans-Imperial Antarctic Expedition, 1914-17; Official War Photographer, A.I.F.; traveller and explorer New Guinea and Central Australia; made first Australian Pioneer flight, Sydney to Athens, 1928; Member British Australian New Zealand Antarctic Research Expedition First Cruise S.Y. Discovery, 1929-30; Member second cruise B.A.N.Z. Expedition, 1930-31; Official War Corres. and Commentator with A.I.F. for Australian Broadcasting Commission, 1940; Official War Photographer A.I.F., Middle East, 1941-44; Official Photographer to British M.O.I. doing Documentary Films, 1945-46, in Middle East. *Publications:* Pearls and Savages, 1924; Argonauts of the South, 1926; Snowdrift and Shellfire, 1940; Sydney Today, 1948; The Holy City, 1948; Shackleton's Argonauts, 1948; Glorious Queensland, 1949; Blue Mountains, 1951; New South Wales, 1952; Tasmania, 1953; Western Australia, 1953; Australia, 1955; Victoria, 1956. *Address:* Stonehenge, Edgecliffe Boulevarde, Collaroy Plateau, Sydney, Australia. [*Died Jan.* 1962.

HURNDALL, Brig. Frank Brereton M.C.; *b.* 1883; *o. s.* of Watkin F. Hurndall, Eastbourne; *m.* 1911, Madine (*d.* 1965), *e. d.* of Brig.-Gen. F. Waldron, C.B.; one *s.* (and one *s.* decd.); *m.* 1966, Gwendolyne Margaret Marina Bonsall. *Educ.:* Charterhouse; Royal Military College, Sandhurst. 2nd Lieut. 20th Hussars, 1903; Lieut., 1906; Capt., 1911; Major, 1915; transferred to 14th Hussars as second in command, 1921; Commanded 14th/20th King's Hussars, 1925-1929; 5th Cavalry Brigade T.A. 1929-31; 2nd Cavalry Brigade, 1931-35; served European War, 1914-18, in Egypt, Gallipoli, France, and Belgium (M.C., despatches twice); Officer of the Order of St. John of Jerusalem, 1925; A.D.C. to the King, 1935-1936; retired pay, 1936; Colonel of 14th/20th King's Hussars, 1937-47; Brig., General Staff, Southern Command, 1939-40; retired, 1943. *Recreation:* fishing. *Address:* Vane Cliff, Vane Hill Road, Torquay, Devon. *Club:* Cavalry. [*Died* 14 *Jan.* 1968.

HURST, Sir Cecil (James Barrington), G.C.M.G. 1926 (K.C.M.G. 1924); K.C.B. 1920; LL.M.; Hon. LL.D.: Cambridge and Edinburgh; Judge of the Permanent Court of International Justice at The Hague, 1929-46; President, 1934-36; British Member of Permanent Court of Arbitration at The Hague, 1929-50; Chairman of the United Nations War Crimes Commission, 1943-44; *b.* 28 Oct. 1870; *y. s.* of late R. H. Hurst, of Horsham Park, Sussex, and Barrington Grove, Gloucestershire; *m.* 1901, Sibyl (*d.* 1947), *d.* of late Sir Lumley Smith; two *s.* one *d.* *Educ.:* Westminster; Trinity Coll., Cambridge. Called to Bar, Middle Temple, 1893; Junior Counsel to Post Office on S.E. Circuit, 1901-2; Asst. Legal Adviser to Foreign Office, 1902-18; Legal Adviser to Foreign Office, 1918-29; K.C. 1913, Q.C. 1952; Bencher of the Middle Temple, 1922, Treasurer, 1940. *Address:* South Grove, Horsham, Sussex. *T.:* 3457. *Club:* Athenæum. *Died* 27 *March* 1963.

HURST, Christopher Salkeld, C.B. 1929; O.B.E. 1919; *b.* 1886; 2nd *s.* of Peter Hurst, Beckenham, and Janet, *d.* of Henry Hicks, Weybridge; *m.* 1st, 1914; one *s.* two *d.*; 2nd, 1930, Joan Elizabeth Glanvill, *d.* of Arthur Willis, Beckenham. *Educ.:* Uppingham (Scholar); Exeter College, Oxford (Exhibitioner). B.A. 1909 (2nd class Law); M.A. 1912; Barrister, Inner Temple, 1910; entered Public Trustee Office, 1911; transferred to Ministry of Munitions, 1915; to Ministry of Labour, 1919; to Coal Control Dept., 1919; Sec. of Royal Commn. on Coal Industry, 1925; Principal Asst. Secretary, Mines Department, Board of Trade, and Secretary Coal Mines Reorganisation Commission, 1930-38; Sec. and Controller, Coal Commission, 1938-47; retired. *Address:* Kingsbury, Deepdene Avenue, Dorking. [*Died* 18 *Dec.* 1963.

HURST, Fannie; novelist; *b.* Hamilton, Ohio; *o. c.* of Samuel Hurst and Rose Koppel; *m.* Jacques S. Danielson (*d.* 1952). *Educ.:* Washington University, St. Louis Mo. (A.B.). Took graduate work, Columbia Univ. Besides literary career, she has also been active in civic and intellectual fields. has lectured and travelled extensively. Formerly: Pres. Authors' Guild of America; Vice-Pres. Authors' League of America; Chairman Women's National Housing Commission; Member National Advisory Committee to the Work Projects Administration; Member Speakers Bureau of Office of Civil Defense; Chm. Committee on Workman's Compensation for Household Employees; Member New York Mayor's Cttee. on Unity; Board of Directors of the United Neighbourhood Houses; Board of Trustees of the Heckscher Foundation; Associate Trustee Russell Sage Coll.; U.S. delegate, by presidential appt., to U.N. World Health Assembly, Geneva; visited Israel at invitation of Israeli Government. Honorary degrees: D.Litt.: Washington University; Fairleigh Dickinson University. *Publications: novels:* Stardust; Lummox; Appassionata; A President is Born; Five and Ten; Back Street; Imitation of Life; Anitra's Dance; Great Laughter; Lonely Parade; Hallelujah; Hands of Veronica; Anywoman; Man With One Head; Family!; God Must Be Sad; Fool—Be Still; Lonely is Only a Word. *autobiography:* Anatomy of Me; *vols. of short stories incl.:* Just Around the Corner; Humoresque; Every Soul hath its Song; Gaslight Sonatas; The Vertical City; Song of Life; Procession; We are Ten; all of these have been translated into numerous languages: *also in book-form:* No Food with my Meals; *plays:* Back Street; Humoresque; Back Pay; Land of the Free; It is to Laugh. These and many others have been made into motion pictures of which outstanding successes are: Humoresque; Lummox; Back Street; Imitation of Life; Symphony of Six Million; Four Daughters. *Address:* 1 West 67th Street, New York 23, N.Y., U.S.A. [*Died* 23 *Feb.* 1968.

HURST, Frank Arnold; President, Samuel Osborn & Co., Ltd., Sheffield, since 1966; Chairman and Managing Director, Anglo-Swiss Aluminium Co. Ltd., Sheffield; Chairman, Star Aluminium Co., Ltd., Wolverhampton; Chairman or Director of various other engineering and steel cos.; *b.* 28 June 1883; *s.* of Harry Marland Hurst and Florence Hurst, *née* Greaves; *m.* 1905, Nellie Mackinder Cottam; four *s.* *Educ.:* Secondary School and Sheffield University. During War of 1939-45, Member: Armour and Bullet Proof Plate Cttee.; Technical Cttee. on Tank and Aircraft Armour; Advisory Cttee. on Alloy Steels. Member: Iron and Steel Institute; Soc. of Engineers and Metallurgists; Founder Member of Sheffield Metallurgical Assoc. Freeman of Company of Cutlers in Hallamshire. Formerly: Vice-Pres. Sheffield and District Engineering Trades Employers' Association; President of Sheffield Chamber of Commerce, 1955-56; Pres. Sheffield and District Rollers' and Tilters' Assoc., 1945-46; Chairman Technical Cttee. of High Speed Steel Assoc., 1946-52. *Publications:* various articles in newspapers and magazines. *Recreations:* gardening and reading. *Address:* 24 Whiteley Wood Road, Sheffield 11. *T.:* Sheffield 31649. [*Died* 13 *April* 1967.

HURT, Captain Henry Albert le Fowne, C.M.G. 1919; R.N. retd.; *b.* 5 Sept. 1881; 3rd *s.* of Albert Hurt, D.L., Alderwasley, Derbyshire, and Castern Hall, Staffs; *m.* 1906, Mabel Alleyne (*d.* 1964), *e. d.* of W. de B. Jessop, Overton Hall, Derbyshire; one *s.* three *d.* *Educ.:* Ludgrove, New Barnet; H.M.S. Britannia. Midshipman, 1897; served in H.M.S. Victorious on China Station; Lieut. 1901; retired, 1911; served again July 1914 to 8 Feb. 1919; promoted to Commander R.N. and to Acting Captain R.N.; served in command of squadron mine-sweepers, North Sea, and later in same capacity in White Sea; and in command of all ice-breakers, mine-sweepers, etc., in White Sea; was present at occupation of Archangel (C.M.G.); served in 1939-45 War, Royal Navy, and retired again in 1945. *Address:* Castern Hall, Ashbourne, Derbyshire. [*Died* 12 *Jan.* 1969.

HURWITZ, Alter Max; Recorder of Halifax since 1957; *b.* 27 June 1899; *s.* of Hirsh Hurwitz (Rabbi) and Hannah Lily Hurwitz; *m.* 1925, Dora Rebecca Cohen; one *s.* two *d.* *Educ.:* Central High School, Leeds; University of London (LL.B. Hons.). Barrister-at-Law (Certificate of Honour), 1924. Chm. Medical Appeal Tribunal under National Insurance (Industrial Injuries) Act. *Recreations:* literature, bridge. *Address:* 12 Bentcliffe Drive, Leeds 17. *T.:* 683366. [*Died* 20 *Oct.* 1970.

HUSAIN, Dr. Zakir, M.A., Ph.D.; President of India, since 1967; *b.* Hyderabad-Deccan, 8 Feb. 1897; *m.* 1915, Shahjehan Begum; two *d.* *Educ.:* Islamia High School, Etawah (U.P.); Mohammedan Anglo-Oriental Coll., Aligarh; Berlin University. Vice-Chancellor: Jamia Millia Islamia, Delhi, 1926-48; Aligarh Muslim University, 1948-1956; Chancellor, Delhi Univ., 1962-67. Pres., Hindustani Talimi Sangh of Sevagram, 1938-1950; Mem., U.N.E.S.C.O. Exec. Bd., Paris, 1956-58; Gov. of Bihar, 1957-62; Vice-Pres. of India, and Chm., Rajya Sabha, 1962-67. Member: Univ. Educn. Commn., 1948-49; Indian Press Commn., 1952-54; Educational Reorganisation Cttee. of Bihar, Madhya Pradesh, Uttar Pradesh; Univ. Grants Commn., until 1957. Chairman: Basic National Educational Cttee., 1937; World Univ. Service, Geneva, 1955-57; Central Bd. of Secondary Educn., until 1957; Internat. Students Service (India Cttee.), until 1955.

Padma Vibhushan award, India, 1954; Bharat Ratna award, India, 1963. D.Litt. (*h.c.*): Aligarh; Allahabad; Budapest; Cairo; Calcutta; Delhi; Madurai; Malaysia; Michigan. *Publications:* The Dynamic University, 1965; Capitalism: An Essay in Understanding, 1967; Educational Discourses (in Urdu); Shiksha (in Hindi); Principles of Educational Reconstruction (Patel Memorial Lectures), 1958; Scope and Method of Economics (Hindustani Acad. Lectures); Ethics and the State (Mavalankar Memorial Lectures), 1960; translations into Urdu of Plato's Republic, 1967, List's National System of Economics and Cannan's Elements of Economics; Abbo Khan Ki Bakri and other Stories (Urdu). *Recreations:* gardening; collection of rocks, fossils and minerals. *Address:* Rashtrapati Bhavan, New Delhi, India. [*Died* 3 *May* 1969.

HUSKINSON, Air Cdre. Patrick, C.B.E. 1942; M.C. and bar; *b.* 17 Mar. 1897; *s.* of Col. Charles John Huskinson, O.B.E., T.D.; *m.* 1940; one *d.* (of a previous marriage). *Educ.:* Harrow; R.M.C., Sandhurst. Served European War, 1914-18, with R.F.C., then R.A.F.; Group Captain 1937; Air Commodore, 1940; V.P. Ordn. Board, Woolwich Arsenal, 1939; Director Armament Development, Ministry Aircraft Production, 1940; retired, 1946. Officer Legion of Merit (U.S.A.), 1945. *Publication:* Vision Ahead, 1949. *Address:* 58 Princes Court, Knightsbridge, S.W.3. *Club:* Bath. [*Died* 24 *Nov.* 1966.

HUSSEY, Christopher Edward Clive, C.B.E. 1956; M.A.; F.S.A.; Hon. A.R.I.B.A.; Hon. A.I.L.A.; Architectural Historian; *b.* 1899; *s.* of late Major W. C. Hussey, C.V.O., 2nd *s.* of Edward Hussey, Scotney Castle, Kent; *m.* 1936, Elizabeth Maud, *d.* of late Major P. Kerr Smiley. *Educ.:* Eton; Christ Church, Oxford. 2nd Lieut. R.F.A. 1919; Architectural Adviser, Country Life, 1930-64; Editor, 1933-40; Chm. Executive Committee, Exhibition of Industrial Art, 1933. Corr. Member Amer. Soc. of Landscape Architects; Member: Treasury Cttee. on Export of Works of Art of Nat. Importance, 1950-52; Roy. Commn. on Historical Monuments (England), 1960-67; Historic Buildings Council (England); Pres., Society of Architectural Historians, 1964-66; Chairman, Rochester Diocesan Advisory Cttee. Pres., Sussex Cattle Soc., 1962. High Sheriff of Kent, 1963. *Publications:* Eton College, 1922; Petworth House, 1926; Garden Ornament (with Gertrude Jekyll), 1927; The Picturesque, 1927; The Architecture of Vanburgh and his school (with H. Avray Tipping), 1928; Tait McKenzie, Sculptor of Youth, 1930; Architecture of Sir Robert Lorimer, 1931; Introductory chapters, Buckingham Palace, by H. Clifford Smith, 1931; Clarence House, 1949; The Life of Sir Edwin Lutyens, 1950; Country Houses open to the Public, 1951; English Country Houses: Early Georgian, 1955; Mid Georgian, 1956; Late Georgian, 1958; English Gardens and Landscapes 1700-1750, 1967. *Recreation:* country life. *Address:* Scotney Castle, Lamberhurst, Kent. *T.:* Lamberhurst 306. *Club:* Garrick. [*Died* 20 *March* 1970.

HUSTON, Major-Gen. (Retd.) John, C.B. 1958; retd. as Consulting Surgeon to the Army and Director of Surgery, The War Office (1954-59); Q.H.S. 1954-59; *b.* 6 July 1901; *s.* of S. Huston, Ballykeel, Holywood, County Down, and Sara (*née* Graham); *m.* 1929, Winton, *d.* of E. Barnard, Longstock Manor, Stockbridge, Hampshire; two *s.* three *d.* (and one *s.* decd.). *Educ.:* Sullivan School; Queen's University, Belfast; The London Hospital; Edinburgh Royal Infirmary. M.B., B.Ch., 1923; F.R.C.S.Ed. 1947. Lt. R.A.M.C. 1924. Served War of 1939-45: B.E.F. and Malaya. Lt.-Col. 1946; Brig. 1954; Maj.-Gen. 1956. *Publications:* contrib. to surgical journals. *Recreation:* travel. *Address:* c/o Glyn, Mills & Co., Kirkland House, Whitehall, S.W.1. [*Died* 16 *Nov.* 1969.

HUTCHINGS, Capt. John Fenwick, C.B.E. 1944 (O.B.E. 1928); D.S.O. 1919; R.N. retd.; *b.* 17 May 1885; *s.* of C. R. and Lizetta Mary Hutchings; *m.* 1st, 1913, Dorothy, *d.* of James Kennedy, Dundee; two *s.* one *d.* (and one *s.* lost at sea, 1940); 2nd, 1940, Olive, *d.* of Dr. Keith Welsh, Southsea; no *c.* *Educ.:* H.M.S. Britannia. H.M. Submarine Service, 1905; Home Fleet, 1910; returned to Submarines, 1913. Served European War, in command Submarines (D.S.O.). In command, Reserve K class submarines, Rosyth, 1919-20; apptd. Experimental Comd. on staff of Rear-Adm. Submarines (comd. K.14, 1920-22); exclusive experimental work with models, 1922-34 (O.B.E.). Retd. as Capt., 1934. Advising on submarines in Greece, 1934-35; Commercial experience, 1934-39. Comd. Contraband Control station, Falmouth, 1939-40; employed on Coast Defence, Western Approaches, June-Dec. 1940; Naval Officer i/c Lamlash, 1940-42; Admty., 1942-43; Victory (for special service), 1943, and Comd. Naval Force Pluto, 1943-46; comd. Force Pluto for invasion of Normandy (C.B.E.); retd. 1946. Founded The Atlantic Charter Brotherhood, 1954. *Publication:* The Chart of the Threefold Path to World Recovery (with Guide to same), 1950. *Address:* c/o National Provincial Bank, Shaftesbury, Dorset. [*Died* 20 *Sept.* 1968.

HUTCHINSON, Professor Arthur Cyril William, D.D.S., M.D.S., F.D.S., F.R.S.E.; Professor of Dental Surgery and Director of Dental Studies, University of Edinburgh, 1951-58; Superintendent Edinburgh Dental Hosp. and Cons. Dental Surgeon to S.E. Regional Hosp. Bd., Scot., 1951-58; Cons. Dent. Surg. to Royal Navy since 1940; Mem. Nat. Panel of Specialists since 1948; Mem. Dental Council, R.C.S., Edin. since 1953; Mem. Gen. Dental Council, 1956-59; Assessor to University Grants Cttee., 1958-; Pres. Odonto-Chirurgical Soc. of Scotland, 1958-1959. Vis. Prof. in Diagnosis in Dental Sch. of Northwestern Univ., Chicago, since 1958; Pres. East of Scotland branch of British Dental Association, 1959; External Examiner to R.F.P.S. Glas.; Examiner R.C.S., Edin.; *b.* 26 July 1889; *s.* of Rev. Edward William Roberts Hutchinson, Vicar of St. John's, Oldham, Lancs, and Annie Lowater Hutchinson; *m.* 1918, Dorothy Mary Orme. *Educ.:* Univs. of Manchester and Pennsylvania. Univ. of Manchester: L.D.S., B.D.S. 1912; M.D.S. (Commend.), 1929. Univ. of the Witwatersrand: D.D.S. 1934; F.R.S.E. 1934; F.D.S., R.C.S. Edin., 1951; F.D.S., R.C.P.S.Glas. 1967; D.D.S. (*h.c.*) Edin. Awarded Travelling Scholarship to University of Pennsylvania, U.S.A., by Dental Hospital of Manchester, 1912; Demonstrator in Operative Dental Surgery and in Porcelain and Gold Inlays, Dental Hospital of Manchester, 1913-23; Hon. Dental Surgeon, Oldham Royal Inf., 1913-1933, and Dental Hosp. of Manch., 1920-33; Lectr. in Dental Prosthetics and Dental Mechanics, Univ. of Manchester, 1925-33; Postgrad. Lectr. to Dental Bd. of U.K., 1931; Mem. Adv. Cttee. to Educ. and Research Cttee. of Dental Bd., 1932; Dean of Edin. Dent. Hosp. and Sch., 1934-51; Mem. Scottish Central Dent. War Cttee., 1938-45; Mem. Scottish Central Med. War Cttee., 1938-45. Mem. Interdepartmental Cttee. on Dentistry (Teviot Cttee.), 1943-45; Mem. Dental Curriculum Cttee. of G.M.C., 1948-52. Formerly Ext. Examr. to Univs. of Manchester, Liverpool, Leeds, Glasgow, Durham. Member: Brit. Dental Assoc.; Sect. Odontology, Roy. Soc. of Med.; Odonto-Chirurgical Soc. of Scotland; Internat. Dental Federation; Brit. Inst. of Radiology; Brit. Soc. of Dental Radiologists; Nutrition Soc.; Chicago Br. of Internat. Soc. for Dental Research; Roy. Soc. of Arts. *Publications:* some observations on Cast and Swaged Dental Plates (with Prof. F. C. Thompson), 1932; Dental and Oral X-ray Diagnosis, 1954. Also numerous articles in scientific journals. *Address:* 12 Glencairn Crescent, Edinburgh 12. *T.:* Edinburgh Donaldson 5586. *Club:* Scottish Conservative. [*Died* 16 *Dec.* 1969.

HUTCHINSON, Rev. Canon Frederick William; Canon Emeritus of Lincoln since 1949; *b.* 7 August 1870; *s.* of late Rev. W. H. Hutchinson, Rector of Welney; *m.* 1900, Phoebe, *d.* of Canon Elliott; four *s.* (and one *s.* died of wounds, Middle East, 1942) three *d.* *Educ.:* Haileybury College, Keble Coll., Oxford (Classical Scholar). 2nd Class Hon. Mods. 1891. 2nd Class Lit. Hum. 1893; B.A. 1893; M.A. 1895; Deacon, 1894; Priest, 1895; Assistant Curate of Gainsborough Parish Church, 1894-97; St. Martin's, Scarborough, 1897; Vice-Principal of Ely Theological College, 1897-1900; Vicar of St. John's, Gainsboro', 1900-12; Holbeach, 1912-1936; Rector of Fleet, Lincs, 1936-46; Rural Dean of East Elloe, 1915-46; Prebendary of Welton Rivall in Lincoln Minster, 1919-49. *Recreation:* lawn tennis. *Address:* 42 Greevegate, Hunstanton, Norfolk. [*Died* 17 *Jan.* 1964.

HUTCHINSON, M. R.; *see* Hely-Hutchinson.

HUTCHINSON, William H.; *b.* Manchester; *m.*; one *s.* one *d.* *Educ.:* Elementary and Secondary Schools. Executive Council of Amalgamated Engineering Union, 1913-30; President, 1930-33; retired, 1943; Executive Council of Labour Party, 1914; Chairman, 1920; Member of L.C.C., 1925-30; contested Bolton, 1924; Organiser for Industrial Orthopædic Society for South Wales, 1944; retired, 1946. *Recreation:* golf. *Address:* 3 Chapel Row, St. Mellons, Cardiff. [*Died* 19 *May* 1965.

HUTCHISON, Lieutenant-General Sir Balfour Oliphant, K.B.E., *cr.* 1946 (C.B.E. 1940); C.B. 1941; *b.* 12 Feb. 1889; *s.* of late Alexander Hutchison, Braehead, Kirkcaldy, and *y. b.* of Lord Hutchison of Montrose, P.C., K.C.M.G., C.B., D.S.O.; *m.* 1920, Audrey, *e. d.* of late Herbert Jervis-White-Jervis; one *s.* (and one killed in action 1942, one died of wounds 1945) two *d.* *Educ.:* Bilton Grange; Uppingham. 2nd Lt. R.A. (S.R.), 1909; 2nd Lt. 7th Q.O. Hussars, 1911; Capt. 1918; Maj. 10th Royal Hussars, 1930; Lt.-Col. 1935; commanded 10th Royal Hussars, 1935-37; Col. 1937; Brig. 1938; Maj.-Gen. 1941; Temp. Lt.-Gen. 1945; passed through Staff College, Camberley, in 1923-24; D.A.Q.M.G., China, 1927; D.A. and Q.M.G. Eastern Command, 1928-1929; A.A. and Q.M.G. 1st Armoured Division, 1937; Brigadier i/c Administration, Palestine, 1938-39; Deputy Q.M.G., Middle East, 1940-42; G.O.C. Sudan and Eritrea, 1942-43; Q.M.G., India, 1944-45; served European War, 1916-18, in Mesopotamia (despatches four times); Palestine Rebellion, 1938-39, (despatches, C.B.E.); War of 1939-45 (despatches five times, C.B.); retired pay, 1945. *Address:* Rendham Court, nr. Saxmundham, Suffolk. *Club:* Cavalry. [*Died* 26 *April* 1967.

HUTCHISON, Sir John Colville, K.B.E., 1951; *b.* 16 Oct. 1890; *s.* of John D. Hutchison; *m.* 1919, Dora Winifred Evans; one *s.* one *d.* *Educ.:* Malvern; Gonville and Caius College, Cambridge. Student Interpreter, China, 1915; Commercial Secretary, 1930; transferred to Hong Kong and held appointment of H.M. Trade Commissioner, 1938; Minister (Commercial) in China, 1948; H.M. Chargé d'Affaires at Peking until 1951; retired, 1951. *Address:* Bullaceton, Saltwood, Hythe, Kent. *Clubs:* Athenæum, Junior Carlton. [*Died* 11 *July* 1965.

HUTCHISON, Sir William Oliphant, Kt. 1953; President Royal Society of Portrait Painters, since 1965; R.P. 1948; R.S.A. 1943 (A.R.S.A. 1937); President Royal Scottish Academy, 1950-59; Hon. R.A.; Hon. LL.D. Edinburgh 1956; Director Glasgow School of Art, 1933-43; *b.* 2 July 1889; 4th *s.* of late H. W. Hutchison, Kinloch, Collessie, Fife; *m.* Margery, *y. d.* of late E. A. Walton, P.R.S.W., R.S.A.; two *s.* one *d.* *Educ.:* Rugby; Edinburgh College of Art; Paris. Served in Royal Artillery, European War, 1914-18. Portrait and landscape painter; represented in Scottish Modern Arts, Glasgow Corporation and Paisley Collections; Hon. Mention Paris Salon, 1930, Gold Medal 1961. Portraits include: H.M. The Queen; H.R.H. Prince Philip, Duke of Edinburgh; the late Viscount Ruffside as Speaker of the House of Commons; the Lord Parker, Lord Chief Justice of England; the Marquis of Aberdeen and Temair. *Address:* 30 Oakwood Court, W.14. *T.:* 01-603 6806. *Clubs:* Arts, Savage. [*Died* 5 *Feb.* 1970.

HUTTON, Edward; Man of Letters; Cavaliere of the Order of the Crown of Italy, 1917; Commendatore of the Order of Merit of the Republic of Italy, 1959; Medaglia culturale d'Oro, Italy, 1965; a Member of the Council of the British Institute of Florence, 1918-54; Member of Cardinal Hinsley's Advisory Committee for Decoration of Westminster Cathedral; British Academy Gold Medallist (Italian), 1924; *b.* London, 12 April 1875; *s.* of J. E. Hutton, of London and Sheffield; *m.* 1898, Charlotte (*d.*1960) *e. d.* of G. R. Miles; one *s.* *Educ.:* Highgate Sch.; Blundell's Sch., Tiverton. A.B. in R.N.A.S., 1915; entered F.O., 1916; in Italy for F.O., 1916-17; lent to Italian F.O. at Baron Sonnino's request, 1917-18. One of founders of British Inst., Florence, 1917; associated with late Arthur Serena in founding Professorships in Italian at Oxford and Cambridge, 1918. Wrote descriptive chapters in Brit. Intelligence Zone Handbks. for Italy (19 vols.), 1943-44. Has studied especially Italian history, literature and art. Designed the Cosmati mosaic pavements in Westminster Cathedral, 1940, and Buckfast Abbey, 1942-43 and 1944-45. *Publications:* Frederic Uvedale: A Romance, 1901; Italy and the Italians, 1902; Studies in the Lives of the Saints, 1902; The Cities of Umbria, 1905; The Cities of Spain, 1906; Sigismondo Malatesta, 1906; Florence and Northern Tuscany, 1907; Country Walks about Florence, 1908; edited Denistoun's Dukes of Urbino, 3 vols., 1908; and Crowe and Cavalcaselle's History of Painting in Italy, 3 vols., 1908-09; In Unknown Tuscany, 1909; Giovanni Boccaccio, 1909; Rome, 1909; Siena and Southern Tuscany, 1910; Venice and Venetia, 1911; Highways and Byways in Somerset, 1912; Milan and Lombardy, 1912; Ravenna, 1913; The Cities of Romagna and the Marches, 1913; England of My Heart, 1914; Naples and Southern Italy, 1914; Attila and the Huns, 1915; Highways and Byways in Wiltshire, 1917; The Pageant of Venice, 1921; Pietro Aretino, 1922; delivered the Italian Lecture before the British Academy, 1922; The Sienese School in the National Gallery, 1925; The Mastiff of Rimini, 1925; Cities of Sicily, 1926; The Franciscans in England, 1926; The Valley of Arno, 1927; A Glimpse of Greece, 1928; A Note on Theocritus, 1929; Highways and Byways in Gloucestershire, 1932; Life of Christ in the Old Italian Masters, 1935; Catholicism and English Literature, 1942; Rome (7th enlarged edn.),

1950; The Cosmati, the Roman Marble Craftsmen, 1950; Florence, 1952; Assisi and Umbria Revisited, 1953; Venice and Venetia (4th enlarged edn.), 1954; Siena and Southern Tuscany (4th enlarged edn.), 1955; Highways and Byways in Somerset (6th revised edn.), 1955; Naples and Campania Revisited, 1958. Editor Anglo-Italian Review, 1918-19. *Address:* 114 Clifton Hill, St. John's Wood, N.W.8. *T.:* Maida Vale 1747. [*Died* 20 *Aug.* 1969.

HUTTON, John Henry, C.I.E. 1920; D.Sc.; *b.* 1885; *s.* of Rev. Joseph Henry Hutton; *m.* 1st, 1920, Stella (*d.* 1944), *d.* of late Rev. Rhys Bishop; two *s.* one *d.*; *m.* 2nd, 1946, Maureen Margaret, *d.* of late Henry Osborne O'Reilly. *Educ.:* Chigwell School; Worcester College, Oxford. Entered I.C.S., 1909; retired, 1936. William Wyse Professor of Social Anthropology, Cambridge, 1937-50; Hon. Fellow of St. Catharine's Coll., Camb., 1951. Sheriff of Radnorshire, 1943; Ex-President Roy. Anthropological Inst. (Rivers Memorial Medal, 1929); Folklore Society; Asiatic Society of Bengal (Fellow; Annandale Memorial Medal, 1937); Hon. Member Anthropologische Gesellschaft of Vienna; Silver Medal, Royal Society of Arts, 1932; Frazer Lecturer, Oxford, 1938. *Publications:* The Angami Nagas, 1921; The Sema Nagas, 1922; Report on the Census of India, 1933; Caste in India, 1946; Pictures at St. Catharine's College, 1950. *Address:* New Radnor, Presteign, Radnorshire. *T.:* New Radnor 228. [*Died* 23 *May* 1968.

HUTTON, Sir Maurice (Inglis), Kt., *cr.* 1948; C.M.G. 1944; Managing-Director, Anglo-Australian Corporation (Pty.) Ltd. Melbourne, since June 1955; Chairman: London Australia Investment Co. Ltd.; Power Cables of Aust. Pty. Ltd.; Food Machinery (Aust.) Ltd.; Director: Borg-Warner (Aust.) Ltd.; Vickers (Aust.) Ltd.; Bryant & May Pty. Ltd.; Glaxo-Allenbury's (Aust.) Pty. Ltd.; North British & Mercantile Insurance Co. Ltd. (Australasian Board); Allied Mills Ltd.; Australian United Acceptance Pty. Ltd.; United Discount Co. of Aust. Pty. Ltd.; *b.* 3 August 1904; *s.* of late Reverend John Alexander Hutton, M.A., D.D., and of late Margaret Johnstone Cameron Hutton; *m.* 1934, Vera Louise Müller. *Educ.:* Kelvinside Academy, Glasgow; Glasgow University (M.A.); Balliol College, Oxford (B.A.); Yale University, New Haven, Conn., U.S.A. (Commonwealth Fellow). With Buckmaster & Moore, Stockbrokers, and O. T. Falk & Co., London, 1929-39; joined Ministry of Food as Temp. Civil Servant, July 1939; Member of British Food Mission in North America since its inception in March 1941; Head of Mission, 1944-48; Head of British Supply Office in U.S.A., 1947-48; British Member: Combined Food Bd., 1944-46; Internat. Emergency Food Council, 1946-48; Internat. Wheat Council, 1944-48; U.K. Exec. Director (Alternate) of Internat. Bank for Reconstruction and Development, 1946-1947; Member British Trade Mission to Argentina, Dec. 1947-Feb. 1948; Head of Internat. Bank and F.A.O. Mission to Uruguay, 1950-51; Chairman Cttee. on Tax-Paid Stocks, 1952-53; formerly Dir.: Glaxo Laboratories Ltd.; North British & Mercantile Insurance Co. Ltd.; Colonial Development Corp. (Mem. Bd.). Officer, Order of Leopold, 1948. *Address:* Greenways, Terrara Rd., Vermont, Vic., Australia. *T.:* BM 9772; (Business) Anglo-Australian Corp. Pty. Ltd., 406 Collins St., Melbourne, C.1. *T.:* 67-5108. *Clubs:* Reform; Melbourne, Athenæum (Melb.); Union (Sydney). [*Died* 1 *May* 1970.

HUTTON, Robert Salmon, D.Sc. (Manc.); M.A. (Cantab.): Fellow of Clare College since 1936; on Court of Goldsmiths' Company since 1936; Vice-President, City and Guilds of London Institute since 1950; Hon. Fellow, Imperial College of Science and Technology, 1952; *b.* 28 Nov. 1876; *s.* of J. E. Hutton of London and Sheffield; *m.* 1912, Sibyl M., *d.* of late Sir Arthur Schuster, F.R.S.; one *s.* one *d.* *Educ.:* Blundell's School, Tiverton; Owens Coll., Manchester; Leipsic and Paris Universities. Electric furnace research with late Professor Moissan in Paris; Lecturer in Electro-Metallurgy at Manchester University, 1900-1908; invented method of producing fused silica; in family silver business in Sheffield, 1908-1921; Director of the British Non-Ferrous Metals Research Association, 1921-32; Member of Council, Institute of Metals, 1909-1935; Platinum Medallist, 1958; one of founders of A.S.L.I.B., 1924; Professor of Metallurgy, Cambridge University, 1931-42; Vice-Pres. and Gov., Bedales School, 1949-62. *Publications:* Recollections of a Technologist, 1964 (Supplement, 1966); scientific and technical papers in Phil. Trans. Royal Soc., Trans. Faraday Soc., Journal Institute of Metals, Research, etc. *Address:* 1 Chaucer Road, Cambridge. *T.:* Cambridge 53126. [*Died* 5 *Aug.* 1970.

HUTTON, Samuel King, M.D., Ch.B. (Manch.); D.Obst.R.C.O.G., F.R.G.S.; Fellow American Geog. Soc.; Hon. Editorial Sec. of Moravian Missions (5-7 Muswell Hill, N.10); Member Executive Council, Evangelical Alliance; Hon. Life Member British Red Cross Society; *b.* Kilkeel, Co. Down, 26 Nov. 1877; *s.* of Rev. Robert Hutton; *m.* Mary, *d.* of Henry Lintott, Chiddingfold, Surrey. *Educ.:* Fulneck School; Manchester Grammar School; Victoria University, Manchester (Owens College). House Physician and House Surgeon, Ancoats Hospital, Manchester, 1901-02; Moravian Mission Hosp., Okak, Labrador, 1903-08 and 1911-13; in practice at Poole, 1914-28 and Orpington, 1935-51; temp. Captain R.A.M.C. (France), 1917-19; Surgeon and Gynæcologist, Cornelia and East Dorset Hosp., Poole, 1919-28. *Publications:* Among the Eskimos of Labrador, 1912; By Eskimo Dog-sled and Kayak, 1919; Health Conditions and Disease Incidence among the Eskimos of Labrador, 1925; An Eskimo Village, 1929; By Patience and the Word, 1935; A Shepherd in the Snow, 1936; The Household Doctor, 1938; The Moravians in Labrador (The Common Weal, Sept. 1925); Health in Northern Labrador (The World's Health, Feb. 1927); The Labrador Eskimo and his Problems (Hospital Social Service, 1928). *Recreations:* music, photography, bees. *Address:* 169 Burnham Road, Highbridge, Somerset. *T.:* Highbridge 403. *Clubs:* M.C.C., Rotary. [*Died* 11 *May* 1961.

HUXHAM, Harold James, C.M.G. 1936; *b.* 6 Sept. 1889; *s.* of John Huxham and Ellen Burdick; *m.* 1st, Helen Maude Gilbert; no *c.*; 2nd, Millicent Ferguson. *Educ.:* Christ's Hospital. Board of Inland Revenue, 1907-29; Income Tax Adviser to Ceylon Government, 1929-31; Commissioner of Income Tax, Estate Duty and Stamps, Ceylon, 1932-34; Financial Secretary, Ceylon, 1934-45; retired, 1945; Chairman Gal Oya Development Board, Ceylon, 1949-; retired 1952. *Recreations:* yachting, fishing. *Address:* Rocklyn 30 Clarke Avenue, Hobart, Tasmania. [*Died* 28 *Jan.* 1961.

HUXLEY, Aldous (Leonard); writer; Companion, Royal Society of Literature (C. Lit.), 1962; *b.* 26 July 1894; 3rd *s.* of late Leonard Huxley and Julia Arnold; *m.* 1919, Maria Nys (*d.* 1955); one *s.*; *m.* 1956, Laura Archers. *Educ.:* Eton; Balliol College, Oxford. Worked on the editorial staff of the Athenæum, 1919-20; dramatic critic of Westminster Gazette, 1920-21. *Publications:* The Burning Wheel, 1916; The Defeat of Youth, 1918; Limbo, 1920; Leda, 1920; Crome Yellow, 1921; Mortal Coils, 1922; On the

Margin, 1923; Antic Hay, 1923; Little Mexican, 1924; Those Barren Leaves, 1925; Along the Road, 1925; Two or Three Graces, 1926; Jesting Pilate, 1926; Proper Studies, 1927; Point Counter Point, 1928; Do What You Will, 1929; Brief Candles, 1930; The World of Light, 1931; The Cicadas, 1931; Music at Night, 1931; Brave New World, 1932: Texts and Pretexts, 1932; Beyond the Mexique Bay, 1934; Eyeless in Gaza, 1936; The Olive Tree and Other Essays, 1936; Ends and Means, 1937; After Many a Summer, 1939 (James Tait Black Memorial Prize for 1940); Grey Eminence, 1941; The Art of Seeing, 1942; Time Must Have a Stop, 1944; The Perennial Philosophy, 1946; Science, Liberty and Peace, 1947; Ape and Essence, 1948; Themes and Variations, 1950; The Devils of London, 1952; The Doors of Perception, 1954; The Genius and the Goddess, 1955; Heaven and Hell, 1956; Adonis and the Alphabet, 1956; Collected Short Stories, 1957; Brave New World Revisited, 1958; Collected Essays, 1960; Island, 1962; Literature and Science, 1963. (Editor) The Letters of D. H. Lawrence, 1932. *Relevant Publications:* Aldous Huxley; a Literary Study, by John Atkins, 1956; Aldous Huxley 1894-1963 (memorial volume), 1965; Aldous Huxley: a Study of the Major Novels, by Peter Bowering, 1968; The Letters of Aldous Huxley (ed. Grover Smith), 1969; Laurence Brander: Aldous Huxley, a Critical Study, 1970. *Recreation:* reading. *Club:* Athenæum. [*Died* 22 *Nov.* 1963.

HYDE, Donald Frizell; corporation and estate lawyer, New York, since 1932; Hon. Vice-President of Johnson Society, Lichfield; Hon. Fellow, Pembroke College, Oxford; *b.* 17 April 1909; *s.* of late Wilby Grimes Hyde and Helen May Frizell; *m.* 1939, Mary Morley Crapo. *Educ.:* Ohio State University (A.B.); Harvard Law School (LL.B.) (Hon. Lit.) Trinity Coll., Hartford, Conn. Partner Browne, Hyde & Dickerson, Counsellors-at-law, N.Y.C.; Director, Constable & Company Ltd., London. Lieutenant-Comdr. U.S.N.R., 1943-46. Mem. Bd. of Governors, Johnson House, Gough Square, London; Mem. Johnson Club, London; Mem. Roxburghe Club, London; Mem. Committee for Amer. Friends of Bodleian Library, Oxford; Past Pres. Bibliographical Soc. of Amer.; President, Keats-Shelley-Assoc. of Amer.; Dir. Shakespeare Assoc. of Amer.; Past Pres., Grolier Club, New York; Mem. Club of Odd Volumes, Boston; Mem. Philobiblon Club, Philadelphia; Mem. Advisory Bds. of Yale Edn. of Private Papers of James Boswell and Yale Edn. of Works of Samuel Johnson; Mem. Harvard Visiting Cttees. for the Univ. Libraries and English Dept.; Mem. Council of Friends of Princeton Univ. Library; Member Chicago Univ. Visiting Committee for Department of Humanities; Trustee, Pierpont Morgan Library; Trustee: American-Scandinavian Foundation; Yale Library Associates; New York Public Library; New York Genealogical and Biographical Soc.; Vice-Pres. and Dir., Master Drawings Assoc. Inc. *Publications:* (with Mary C. Hyde and E. L. McAdam, Jun.) Johnson's Diaries, Journals and Annals, 1958. *Recreations:* book collecting, travel. *Address:* (business) 61 Broadway, New York 6, N.Y. *T.:* Whitehall 3-7000; (residences) Four Oaks Farm, R.F.D. 3, Somerville, N.J. *T.:* Randolph 5-0966; 30 Sutton Place, New York 22, N.Y. *T.:* Murray Hill 8-2084. *Clubs:* Knickerbocker, Century Association (New York); Essex Fox Hounds (Far Hills, N.J.). [*Died* 5 *Feb.* 1966.

HYDE, Lady; (Marion Féoderovna Louise), D.C.V.O. 1961 (C.V.O. 1945); Woman of the Bedchamber to Queen Elizabeth the Queen Mother, 1937-61, Extra Woman of the Bedchamber since 1961; *b.* 23 Aug. 1900; *er. d.* of 4th Baron Wolverton; *m.* 1932, Lord Hyde (*d.* 1935), *e. s.* and *heir* of 6th Earl of Clarendon, K.G., P.C., G.C.M.G., G.C.V.O.; one *s.* one *d.* *Address:* Freckenham House, Bury St. Edmunds, Suffolk. *T.A.:* Freckenham, Suffolk. *T.:* Isleham 281. [*Died* 13 *Dec.* 1970.

HYDE, Sir Robert Robertson, K.B.E., *cr.* 1949; M.V.O. 1932; Founder and lately Director, Industrial Welfare Society; *b.* London, 7 Sept. 1878; *s.* of Robert Mettam Hyde and Marjory Robertson; *m.* 1917, Eileen Ruth, *d.* of Dr. G. Parker, Cuckfield; (son missing from air operation, Oct. 1943) one *d.* *Educ.:* privately; King's College, London. Business, 1893-1901; Deacon, 1903; Priest, 1904; Curate S. Saviour's, Hoxton, 1903-7; Head Maurice Hostel, Hoxton, 1907-16; Vicar of S. Mary's, Hoxton, and Chaplain, Royal London Ophthalmic Hospital, 1912-16; resigned living and other ecclesiastical offices at urgent behest of Archbishop Lang in order to foster industrial welfare work. Welfare Department, Ministry of Munitions, 1916-18. Compelled by ecclesiastical authorities to relinquish clerical orders on appointment as K.B.E., 1949. Member: I.L.O. Cttee. on Workers' Spare Time, Industrial Medical Services Cttee., London Dock Unrest Enquiry; Chm. Ministry of Agriculture School Harvest Camps Committee; Veterinary Surgeons Act Cttee. *Publications:* The Boy: in Industry and Leisure; The Camp Book, being some account of the Duke of York's Camp; articles and pamphlets on Industrial Relations. *Recreations:* gardening, fishing. *Address:* Glevering, Beech Rd., Haslemere. [*Died* 31 *Aug.* 1967.

HYDE-LEES, Rev. Harold Montagu, M.A.; *b.* 1890; *s.* of late William Gilbert Hyde-Lees; *m.* 1921, Ada Gwynne Younghughes (*d.* 1943). *Educ.:* Eton; Wadham College, Oxford; Wells Theological College. B.A. and M.A., Oxford, 1917. Deacon, 1920; Priest, 1921; Curate of S. Luke's, Derby, 1920-23; Assistant Chaplain at S. John's, Mentone, and Acting Chaplain at S. Mark's, Florence, 1923-24; Curate of Falmouth, 1924-27; Vicar of East with West Looe, 1927-37; Archdeacon of Portsmouth, 1937-45; Examining Chaplain to the Bishop of Portsmouth, 1937-45; Editor of the Portsmouth Diocesan News, 1941-45. Permission to officiate in Diocese of Salisbury, 1946-52. Permission to officiate at Milborne Port, Diocese of Bath and Wells, 1946-50; Curate of Milborne Port and Goathill, 1950-52: Rector of Withycombe, 1952, with Rodhuish, 1954-62. *Recreations:* gardening and archæology. *Address:* Barnica, Parkhouse Road, Minehead, Somerset. *T.:* Minehead 501. [*Died* 14 *June* 1963.

HYDERABAD, Nizam of, H.E.H. Asaf Jah, Muzaffar-ul-Mulk-Wal-Mumilak, Nizam-ul-Mulk, Nizam ud Daula Nawab Mir Sir Usman Ali Khan Bahadur, Fateh Jung, G.C.S.I. 1911; G.B.E. 1917; *b.* 1886; *S.* 1911. Has retired from active public life. Granted title of "Faithful Ally of The British Government" and hereditary style of His Exalted Highness, 1918; Royal Victorian Chain, 1946; Hon. Gen. in the Army. Formerly Chancellor of Aligarh Univ.; Rajpramukh of Hyderabad from 1950. *Heir:* *s.* Prince of Berar. *Address:* Hyderabad, Deccan, India. [*Died* 24 *Feb.* 1967.

HYLAND, Major-General Frederick Gordon, C.B. 1942; M.C.; *b.* 8 Feb. 1888; *s.* of late A. Y. Hyland; *m.* 1st, 1918, Mary Amelia (*d.* 1919), *d.* of late Surgeon-Major W. Jobson; 2nd, 1922, Teresa Frances Nicol, *d.* of late G. R. Gould. *Educ.:* Marlborough. 2nd Lieut. R.E., 1909; served European War, 1914-19 (despatches five times, Bt. Major, M.C.); Commander R.E. Singapore, 1931-34;

Bt. Colonel, 1934; Commander R.E. 3rd Division, 1935-36; Brigade Comdr. A.A. Command T.A., 1936-39; Division Comdr., 1939; Chief of Staff and Deputy Commander of the Fortress, Gibraltar, 1942-44; retired pay, 1946. *Recreation:* golf. *Address:* Camrie, Maple Avenue, Cooden, Sussex. *T.:* Cooden, 2965. *Club:* United Service. [*Died* 16 *April* 1962.

HYLAND, Hon. Sir Herbert John Thornhill, Kt 1952; Leader, Country Party, Vic., since 1955; Minister of Transport, Prices and State Development, 1950-52. Chm. Latrobe Valley Development Advisory Committee. M.L.A. for Gippsland South, 1929-. Formerly Chief Secretary, Vic.; Minister of Labor and Decentralisation, 1947-1948; Minister for Transport, 1938-43; Hon. Minister, June 1936-Apr 1938. *Address:* Parliament House, Melbourne Vic., Aust. [*Died* 18 *March* 1970.

HYLTON, 4th Baron, *cr.* 1866; **Lt.-Col. William George Hervey Jolliffe;** late Coldstream Guards; Lord Lieutenant of Somerset since 1949; Member of Somerset C.C. since 1937; Alderman, 1948; *b.* 2 Dec. 1898; *e. s.* of 3rd Baron and Lady Alice Adeliza Hervey (*d.* 1962), *d.* of 3rd Marquess of Bristol; *S.* father 1945; *m.* 1931, Lady Perdita Asquith, *d.* of late Raymond Asquith; two *s.* one *d.* *Educ.:* Eton College; Sandhurst. Served in both wars against Germany; in France and Germany, 1918. A.D.C. to Governor-General of Canada, 1921-23; Adjutant, Eton College Officers' Training Corps and Staff Captain O.T.C. Camps, 1928-30; retired, 1931; Brigade Major, 142nd Infantry Brigade, 47th Division, T.A., 1931-36; D.A.Q.M.G. H.Q. London District, 1939-41; A.Q.M.G. War Office 1942; Commanded Training Bn. Coldstream Guards, 1943. J.P. Somerset. K.J.St.J. *Heir:* *er. s.* Hon. Raymond Hervey, Jolliffe, A.L.A.S. [*b.* 13 June 1932; *m.* 1966, Joanne de Bertodano; one *s.* *Educ.:* Eton College (King's Scholar); Trinity College, Oxford. (M.A.). Lieut. R. of O. Coldstream Guards]. *Address:* Ammerdown, Radstock, Bath. *Clubs:* Turf, M.C.C. [*Died* 14 *Nov.* 1967.

HYLTON, Jack; Impresario; Chairman and Managing Director, Jack Hylton Ltd.; Chairman and Director, Piccadilly Theatre Ltd.; Director, T. W. W. Ltd.; *b.* 2 July 1892; *s.* of George Hylton and Mary (*née* Greenhalgh); *m.* 1922, Florence Parkinson (*d.* 1957); one *s.* two *d.*; 1963, Beverley Prowse. *Educ.:* Higher Grade School, Bolton, Lancashire. Started professional career at age of 10 as singing "mill boy"; first engagement as pianist and vocalist in a Pierrot Troupe, Rhyl, 1905; subseq. conductor for musical comedies, pantomimes and ballet. Formed own band, 1922, and with it he toured Europe and America for many years. Pioneer in modern gramophone recording; has made numerous records. Began managerial activities at London Palladium with Life Begins at Oxford Circus, 1935; took over London Philharmonic Orchestra, 1940; revived Peter Pan and presented the play annually for 8 years; was exclusive impresario for Beniamino Gigli and Maurice Chevalier; as a West End theatre manager and impresario, has presented over 100 productions including: Lady Behave, Irene, Duet for Two Hands, The Merry Widow, No Room At The Inn, Circus for two seasons, Kiss Me Kate, Call Me Madam, Paint Your Wagon, Ingrid Bergman in Joan At The Stake, Salad Days, Kismet, La Plume de ma Tante, The Roses are Real, Camelot, and all the post-war Crazy Gang shows. President of the Lancastrian Assoc.; Citizen and Baker of London. Officier de l'Instruction Publique; Chevalier de la Légion d'Honneur, 1932. *Recreations:* race-horse owner and breeder; golf, motoring, music and cricket. *Address:* Jack Hylton Ltd., Adelphi Theatre, Strand, W.C.2. *T.:* Temple Bar 1166. *Clubs:* Savage, Victoria, Royal Automobile; Newmarket. [*Died* 29 *Jan.* 1965.

HYLTON-FOSTER, Rt. Hon. Sir Harry (Braustyn Hylton), P.C. 1957; Kt. 1954; Q.C. 1947; M.P. (C.) Cities of London and Westminster from Oct. 1959; Speaker of the House of Commons from October 1959; *b.* 10 April 1905; *o. s.* of late H. B. H. Hylton-Foster, Barrister-at-Law, Old Dene, nr. Dorking; *m.* 1931, Hon. Audrey Pellew Clifton Brown, *d.* of late Viscount Ruffside, P.C.; no *c.* *Educ.:* Eton; Magdalen College, Oxford. Legal Secretary to late Lord Finlay at Permanent Court of International Justice, 1928; called to Bar, 1928; Recorder of Richmond, 1940-1944; of Huddersfield, 1944-50; of Kingston-upon-Hull, 1950-Oct. 1954. M.P. (C.) York, 1950-Sept. 1959. Solicitor-General, Oct. 1954-59. Chancellor of Diocese of Ripon, 1947-54; of Durham, 1948-54. Intelligence R.A.F.V.R. 1940; served Deputy Judge Advocate, North Africa and Italy, 1942-45; contested (Nat. Con.) Shipley Division, 1945. Hon. LL.D. Leeds Univ., 1962. *Recreations:* travel, golf, fishing. *Clubs:* Athenæum, Buck's, Oxford and Cambridge. [*Died* 2 *Sept.* 1965.

HYNDLEY, 1st Viscount, *cr.* 1948, of Meads; **John Scott Hindley,** Baron, *cr.* 1931; Bt., *cr.* 1927; G.B.E., *cr.* 1939; Kt., *cr.* 1921; Cross of Chevalier of the Crown of Italy; Commander of the Légion d'Honneur; American Medal of Freedom with palm leaf, 1947; *b.* 24 Oct. 1883; *s.* of late Rev. Wm. Talbot Hindley, M.A., of Eastbourne; *m.* 1909, Vera, *er. d.* of late James Westoll, J.P., of Coniscliffe Hall, Darlington, Co. Durham; two *d.* *Educ.:* Weymouth College. Member of Coal Controller's Export Advisory Committee, 1917-1918; Commercial Adviser, Mines Department, 1918-38 and 1939-42; Controller-General Ministry of Fuel and Power, 1942-43; Director, Bank of England, 1931-45; Chairman, Stephenson Clarke Ltd., 1938-46; a Managing Director of Powell Duffryn Ltd., 1931-46; Chairman, Maris Export and Trading Co. Ltd., 1938-46; Chairman Finance Corporation for Industry, Ltd., 1945-46; Chairman, London Committee of the Combined Production and Resources Board, 1943-1946; Chairman of the National Coal Board, 1946-51; Alderman Ward of Tower, 1924-30; Member of the Committee on Industry and Trade, 1924-29. Master of Clothworkers Company, 1953-54. LL.D. (Hon.) Leeds. *Heir:* none. *Address:* Meads Cottage, Rondle Wood, nr. Liphook, Hants. [*Died* 5 *Jan.* 1963 (*ext.*).

HYNE, Sir Ragnar, Kt., *cr.* 1956; *b.* 16 Feb. 1893; *s.* of Harald Oscar Hein, Kongsberg, Norway; *m.* 1st, 1920, Dorothy Harpur, *d.* of Mr. Justice Woolcock, Supreme Court, Queensland; 2nd, 1930, Effie Harris, *d.* of J. Harris, Adelaide; no *c.* *Educ.:* S. Brisbane Tech. High Sch.; Queensland Univ. (B.A.). Barrister-at-Law, Qld., 1924; called to English Bar (Gray's Inn), 1950. Military duty, 1916-17, and 1943-44 (Major). Director of Education, Tonga, 1920. Chief Magistrate and Legal Adviser Brit. Solomon Is. (on secondment), 1929. Director of Education and Sec. to Premier, Tonga, 1932-36, also Chief Police Magistrate, Tonga, 1933-36; Sec. to Premier, Chief Police Magistrate, Judge of Land Court and Chief Justice, Tonga, 1936-38; Resident Magistrate and Assistant Legal Adviser, W. Pacific High Commission (on secondment), Fiji, 1942-1943; Chief Magistrate, Legal Adviser, and Judicial Commissioner, British Solomon Islands, 1938-44. Sierra Leone: Solicitor-Gen., 1944; Attorney-Gen., 1945;

Actg. Governor and Actg. C.-in-C., 1948. Puisne Judge, Gold Coast, Nov. 1948. Chief Justice Fiji, 1953-58, retired. Re-employed as Acting Chief Justice and later Senior Puisne Judge, Cyprus, July 1958-Jan. 1959, and as Stipendiary Magistrate, Coroner, Public Trustee and Judge of Court of First Instance, Gibraltar, Oct. 1959-Oct. 1961. *Recreation:* golf. *Address:* 11 High St., Lavenham, Nr. Sudbury, Suffolk. *Club:* Roy. Commonwealth Soc. [*Died* 4 *Oct.* 1966.

HYNES, Capt. William Bayard, C.B.E. 1943; D.S.O. 1920; R.N., retired; *b.* 1889; *s.* of late William Hynes; *m.* 1928, Sylvia Geraldine, *d.* of Gerald Yeo, Aldsworth House, nr. Emsworth. Served Sea of Marmora, 1920 (D.S.O.); Director of Naval Intelligence, Royal Canadian Navy, 1931-33; retired list, 1935; called to Bar (Inner Temple), 1938; Officer U.S. Legion of Merit, 1945; has bronze medal of Royal Humane Society. *Club:* United Service. [*Died* 2 *March* 1968.

I

IBBERSON, Dora, C.B.E. 1948; M.A.; Social Welfare Adviser to Comptroller for Development and Welfare in the British West Indies, 1945-55; retired; *b.* 23 Nov. 1890; *d.* of Joseph Ibberson. *Educ.:* Redland High School, Bristol; St. Hugh's College, Oxford. Entered Trade Boards Inspectorate of Ministry of Labour, 1917; transferred to Assistance Board as Special Enquiry Officer, 1934-45; Social Welfare Officer of Trinidad, 1943. *Publication:* Our Towns, 1943. *Recreation:* travel. *Address:* Hathersage, Oare, Marlborough, Wilts. *Club:* University Women's. [*Died* 17 *May* 1962.

IBERT, Jacques; French musician; *b.* Paris, 1890; *m.* Rosette Jean-Vebero one *s.* one *d.* *Educ.:* University and Conservatoire, Paris. Winner of the first Grand Prix de Rome for music, 1919; Member Higher Council of Nat. Conservatoire; Director of the French Academy (Villa Medici), Rome; Administrator of Théâtres Lyriques Nationaux, France, 1955-56. Served European War, 1914-18 and War of 1939-45. *Publications:* La Ballade de la Geôle de Reading, 1920; Escales, 1922; Les Rencontres, 1924; Angélique, 1926; Divertissement, 1928; Persée et Andromaque, 1929; Le Roi d'Yvetot, 1930; Suite symphonique, 1931; Gonzague, 1932; Diane de Poitiers, 1934; Don Quichotte, 1936; concertos for flute and saxophone, 1933 and 1935; (with A. Honegger) L'Aiglon, 1937; Le Chevalier errant, 1937; Capriccio, 1938; Ouverture de fête, 1940; Quatuor à cordes, 1942; Suite élisabéthaine, 1942; Barbe-Bleue, 1943; Trio for violin, cello and harp, 1944; Antoine et Cléopâtre, 1945; Les Amours de Jupiter, 1946; Étude-Caprice for solo cello, 1948; Symphonie concertante, with solo oboe, 1949-50; Triumph of Chastity, 1950; Caprilena for solo violin, 1951; Invitation to the Dance, 1952; Louisville-Concert, 1953; Broo and Tiss, 1954; Bacchanal, 1957. *Address:* 30 Avenue d'Eylau, Paris XVI, France. [*Died* 6 *Feb.* 1962.

IDDESLEIGH, 3rd Earl of (U.K.) (*cr.* 1885); **Henry Stafford Northcote;** Bt. 1641; Visc. St. Cyres, 1885; *b.* 19 Nov. 1901; *s.* of late Preb. the Hon. John Stafford Northcote, Hon. Chaplain to H.M., 3rd *s.* of 1st Earl, and Hilda Cardew, 2nd *d.* of late Very Rev. F. W. Farrar; *S.* uncle, 1927; *m.* 1930, Elizabeth, *er. d.* of late F. S. A. Lowndes and late Marie Belloc; two *s.* two *d.* *Educ.:* Rugby; Magdalen College, Oxford, B.A. 1923, M.A. 1927. Served in Welsh Guards, 1939-46. *Heir:* *s.* Viscount St. Cyres. *Address:* Pynes, Exeter. [*Died* 16 *Feb.* 1970.

IDUN, Sir Samuel O. Q.; *see* Quashie-Idun.

IEVERS, Maj.-Gen. Osburne, C.B. 1937; D.S.O. 1917; M.B. London, M.R.C.S.; L.R.C.P. Lond.; late R.A.M.C.; 3rd *s.* of late Dr. Eyre Ievers, Tonbridge, Kent; *m.* Norah (*d.* 1950), *d.* of late Pierce Ryan, Rosebank, S. Africa; one *d.* *Educ.:* Tonbridge School; St. Mary's Hospital, London. Joined R.A.M.C. 1903; Major, 1915; Brevet Lt.-Col. 1919; Lt.-Col. 1926; Col. 1931; Maj.-Gen. 1934; served in South Africa, 1904-11; India, 1924-29; went to France with Expeditionary Force, Aug. 1914 (D.S.O.); to Salonica and Army of the Black Sea, 1917-19 (Greek Order for Military Merit); Deputy Director of Medical Services, Southern Command, 1934-38; Hon. Surgeon to the King, 1935-38; Colonel Commandant R.A.M.C., 1945-47. Retired pay, 1938. *Address:* c/o Glyn, Mills & Co., Kirkland House, Whitehall, S.W.1. [*Died* 19 *Feb.* 1963.

IKRAMULLAH, Mohammad, Hilal-i-Pakistan, 1958; Chairman of the Commonwealth Economic Committee since 1961; *b.* 1903; *s.* of Khan Bahadur H.M. Wilayatullah; *m.* 1933, Shaista, *d.* of late Sir Hassan Suhrawardy, O.B.E., J.P.; one *s.* three *d.* *Educ.:* Allahabad and Nagpur Universities; Trinity College, Cambridge. Joined Indian Civil Service, 1927; Officer on special duty in C.P., 1927-33; Under-Secretary, Govt. of India, Min. of Industry and Labour, 1933; Dep. Sec. 1933-36; Sec. Coal Mining Cttee., 1936-37; Indian Trade Comr. in U.K. 1937-39; Adviser and Sec., 24th and 25th I.L.O. Confs., and Dep. Sec. Supply Dept., Govt. of India, 1940-44; Joint Sec. Supply Dept. 1944-45; Adviser and Secretary to Prep. Commission of U.N. and to first session of General Assembly of U.N., 1945-1946; Member Indian Coalfields Committee, 1946; Joint Sec. Min. of Transport and later Ministry of Commerce; Deleg. to Internat. Trade Conf., Geneva, 1947; Mem. partition Cttee. on India, and Sec., Min. of Commerce, Information & Broadcasting, Commonwealth Relations and Foreign Affairs of provisional Govt. of Pakistan; after partition of India, served as Sec. for Foreign Affairs and Commonwealth Relations, Govt. of Pakistan, 1947-51; High Comr. of Pakistan in Canada, 1952-53; Ambassador of Pakistan in France, 1953-55; High Commissioner for Pakistan in the U.K., 1955-59, and Minister for Pakistan in Lisbon, 1957-60; Sec. to Ministry of Foreign Affairs, 1959-61. Delegate to six Commonwealth Prime Ministers' Conferences, London; Pakistan alternate deleg. Commonwealth Foreign Ministers' Conf., Colombo, 1950; negotiated first Trade agreement with India, following devaluation of Indian rupee, 1951; Mem. confs. on Suez, and Pakistan's observer at Suez Canal Users' Assoc. Conf., London, 1956. C.I.E. 1946; Grand Cross, Military Order of Christ, Portugal, 1959; K.C.M.G. (Hon.), 1961. *Recreations:* fishing, shooting, gardening. *Address:* Marlborough House, Pall Mall, S.W.1. *Club:* Athenæum. [*Died* 12 *Sept.* 1963.

ILCHESTER, 7th Earl of, *cr.* 1756; **Edward Henry Charles James Fox-Strangways,** D.L.; Baron Ilchester and Strangways, 1741; Baron Ilchester and Stavordale, Baron Redlynch (G.B.) 1747; late Royal Horse Guards; *b.* 1 Oct. 1905; *er. s.* of 6th Earl of Ilchester, G.B.E., F.S.A., and Lady Helen Vane-Tempest Stewart (*d.* 1956), *o. d.* of 6th Marquess of Londonderry; *S.* father 1959; *m.* 1931, Helen Elizabeth, twin *d.* of late Capt. Hon. Cyril Ward, M.V.O., R.N.; one *d.* (and two *s.* decd.). *Educ.:* Eton; Christ Church, Oxford. Entered Army, 1929; resigned commission, 1931. Captain R. of O., Royal Horse Guards. D.L. Dorset, 1957. *Heir:* *c.* Walter Angelo

Fox-Strangways [*b.* 1887; *m.* 1916, Laure Georgine Emilie, *d.* of late E. G. Mazaraki, two *s.* *Educ.:* Eton; Christ Church, Oxford. Served War of 1939-45, Capt. Royal Horse Gds.]. *Address:* 9 Cottesmore Gardens, W.8. *T.:* Western 7340; Melbury House, Dorchester, Dorset. *Clubs:* Turf, White's, Brooks's. [*Died* 21 *Aug.* 1964.

ILCHESTER, 8th Earl of, *cr.* 1756; **Walter Angelo Fox-Strangways;** Baron Ilchester and Strangways, 1741; Baron Ilchester and Stavordale, Baron Redlynch, 1747; retired; *b.* 24 Sept. 1887; *s.* of late Maurice Walter Fox-Strangways, C.S.I., and late Louisa Blanche (*née* Phillips); *S.* kinsman, 1964; *m.* 1916, Laure Georgine Emilie, *d.* of late Evanghelos Georgios Mazaraki, sometime Treasurer of Suez Canal Company, at Suez; two *s.* one *d.* (and one *d.* decd.). *Educ.:* Charterhouse (Scholar); Pembroke College, Cambridge (Exhibitioner). B.A. Hons. 1911. Levant Consular Service, 1910-1923; subsequently: in Business; Gen. Sec., Rotary Club of London; Languages Tutor. Served European War, 1916 (Intelligence), and War of 1939-45 (Infantry). *Publications:* various articles in Nineteenth Century and other jls. *Recreations:* football (unfortunately no longer a participant); languages. *Heir:* *s.* Lord Stavordale. *Address:* 1 Bronshill Court, Bronshill Road, Torquay, Devon. *T.:* Torquay 39473. [*Died* 4 *Oct.* 1970.

ILES, Colonel Frederic Arthur, C.B.E. 1922; D.S.O. 1916; *b.* 1874; *s.* of Capt. A. I. Iles, B.S.C., Osmanthorpe, Laleham; *m.* 1906, Clara, *d.* of H. E. Karl von Grabmayr-Angerheim, Member of the Austrian Upper House; one *s.* two *d.* Served European War, 1914-18 (despatches five times, D.S.O., Bt. Lieutenant-Colonel); Home Guard, 1940-44; retired pay. *Address:* Villa Waldeck, Innsbruck-Mühlau, Austria. [*Died* 18 *July* 1966.

ILLING, Professor Vincent C., F.R.S. 1945; M.A. (Cantab.); Hon. A.R.S.M., F.G.S., F.Inst.Pet., M.I.M.M.; Emeritus Professor of Oil Technology, Imperial College of Science and Technology; Fellow of Imperial College of Science and Technology, 1958; *m.* Frances Jean; one *s.* four *d.* *Address:* V. C. Illing & Partners, Cuddington Croft, Ewell Road, Cheam, Surrey. *T.:* Ewell 0911; The Beeches, 24 The Avenue, Cheam, Surrey. *T.:* 01-642 0380. [*Died* 16 *May* 1969.

ILSLEY, Rt. Hon. James Lorimer, P.C. 1946; P.C. Canada 1935; Q.C. 1928; Lawyer; Chief Justice of Nova Scotia, since 1950; *b.* Somerset, Nova Scotia, 3 Jan. 1894; *s.* of Randal Byron Ilsley and Catherine Caldwell; *m.* 1919, Evelyn Wilhelmina Smith. two *d.* *Educ.:* Acadia University, Wolfville, N.S. (B.A.); Dalhousie University, Halifax, N.S. (LL.B.). Called to bar of Nova Scotia, 1916; Member of Royal Commission on Price Spreads and Mass Buying, 1934-35; Minister of National Revenue, Canada, 1935-1940; M.P. 1926-48; Minister of Finance, 1940-46; Minister of Justice and Attorney-General, Canada, 1946-48. *Address:* Halifax, Nova Scotia, Canada. *Club:* Halifax (Halifax, N.S.). [*Died* 14 *Jan.* 1967.

IMBERT-TERRY, Captain Frederic B.; *see* Terry, Capt. F.B.I.

IMBERT-TERRY, Lt.-Col. Sir Henry Bouhier, 2nd Bt., *cr.* 1917; D.S.O. 1919; M.C.; late R.A.; D.L. Devon; *e. s.* of Sir Henry Imbert-Terry, 1st Bt.; *b.* 10 Feb. 1885; *m.* 1910, Mildred Dorothy, O.St.J., *o.d.* of late Brig.-Gen. E. M. Flint, R.A.; one *s.* three *d.* Served European War, 1914-18 (despatches, D.S.O., M.C.); retired, 1938; High Sheriff of Devonshire, 1948-49; K.St.J. *Heir:* *s.* Edward Henry Bouhier, M.C., Major Coldstream Guards [*b.* 28 Jan. 1920; *m.* 1944, Jean, 2nd *d.* of Stanley Garton, Danesfield, Marlow, Buckinghamshire; two *s.* two *d.*]. *Address:* Keeper's Lodge, Strete Ralegh, Whimple, Devon. [*Died* 9 *Oct.* 1962.

INCHIQUIN, 16th Baron, *cr.* 1543; **Donough Edward Foster O'Brien,** Bt. 1686; *b.* 5 Jan. 1897; *e. s.* of 15th Baron and Ethel Jane (*d.* 1940), *e. d.* and *co-heir* of late Johnstone J. Foster, Moor Park, Ludlow; *S.* father, 1929; *m.* 1921, Hon. Anne Thesiger, 2nd *d.* of 1st Viscount Chelmsford; two *d.* *Educ.:* Eton; R.M.C., Sandhurst; Magdalen College, Oxford. Served in the Rifle Brigade, 1916-21; A.D.C. to Viceroy of India, 1919-20; Capt. London Rifle Brigade, 1939-42. *Heir:* *b.* Maj. Hon. Phaedrig Lucius Ambrose O'Brien, Rifle Brigade [*b.* 4 April 1900; *m.* 1945, Vera Maud, *d.* of late Rev. C. S. Winter. Served War of 1939-45 (wounded, despatches].) *Address:* Thomond House, Dromoland, Newmarket-on-Fergus, Co. Clare. *Clubs:* Naval and Military; Kildare Street (Dublin). [*Died* 19 *Oct.* 1968.

INCZE, Jenő; Ambassador of Hungarian People's Republic to the Court of St. James's since 1963; *b.* 1901; *m.* Gizella Merk; two *d.* *Educ.:* Budapest Techn. Univ. (Engr.). Asst. Lectr., Budapest Techn. Univ., and Engr., Ganz Works, 1926-45; subseq. Chief Engr.; Dep. Dir., 1945-48; Dep. Dir., Nikex (heavy machinery, shipbuilding and diesel engines trading corp.), 1949-53; Dept. Head, Min. of Foreign Trade, 1954-55; Dep. Minister of Foreign Trade, 1955-57; Minister of Foreign Trade, 1957-63. Gold and Silver Medals, Order of Merit for Labour; Gold Medal, Order of Merit of Red Banner for Labour. *Address:* 35 Eaton Place, S.W.1. *T.:* 01-235 4048. [*Died* 4 *May* 1969.

INDORE, Maj.-Gen. H.H. Maharaja of, Maharajadhiraj Raj Rajeshwar Sawai Shree Yeshwant Rao Holkar Bahadur, G.C.I.E., *cr.* 1935; LL.D.; Senior Up-Rajpramukh (Vice-Pres.) of United State of Gwalior, Indore and Malwa (Madhya Bharat), May 1948-Nov. 1956; *b.* 6 Sept. 1908; *s.* of H. H. Tukoji Rao Holkar (who abdicated as Maharaja of Indore); *S.* 1926; *m.* 1924, Sanyogitabai (*d.* 1937), *d.* of the Chief of Kagal Junior (Kolhapur); one *d.*; *m.* 1943, Fay Crane; one *s.* *Educ.:* England, 1920-23; Christ Church, Oxford, 1926-29. Assumed full ruling powers, 1930; has a salute of 21 guns within his territories and 19 outside; invited delegate to the Round Table Conference, 1931; State has an area of 9902 sq. miles; population 1,513,966. *Recreations:* tennis and shikar. *Heir:* (by Gazette Extraordinary, 1950), *d.* Usha Raje Holkar, *b.* 1933. *Address:* Indore, Madhya Pradesh. [*Died* 5 *Dec.* 1961.

INGALL, Douglas Heber, O.B.E. 1966; D.Sc., F.R.I.C., F.Inst.P.; Principal of Borough Polytechnic, 1934-56; Director of the National College for Heating, Ventilating, Refrigeration and Fan Engineering, 1948-56; retired 1956; *b.* 14 June 1891; *s.* of George H. Ingall, J.P. Birmingham; *m.* 1929, Nellie H., *d.* of J. R. Winpenny, Middlesbrough; two *s.* *Educ.:* King Edward's High School, Birmingham; University of Birmingham. Metallurgist to Patent Shaft and Axletree Co., Ltd., Wednesbury, Staffs, 1913-1916; Commissioned services with H.M. Forces, Royal Engineers, 1915-19; Senior Lecturer, Department of Metallurgy, University of Birmingham, 1919-21; Principal and Head of the Department of Metallurgy, The Staffordshire County Technical College, Wednesbury, 1921-28; Principal Constantine Technical College, Middlesbrough, 1928-31; Assistant Director British Non-Ferrous Metals Research Association, 1931-33; President Staffordshire Iron and Steel Institute, 1926-27. Hon. M.I.H.V.E. *Publications:*

contrib.: Institute of Metals; Iron and Steel Institute; Institute of British Foundrymen. *Recreation:* music. *Address:* Gosfield Hall, Halstead, Essex. [*Died* 5 *Feb.* 1968.

INGE, Mrs. W. F.; (Mary Caroline); Dame of Justice of the Order of St. John of Jerusalem; a Director of Oakeley's Quarries Co.; Master of the Atherstone Hounds, 1914-20; *d.* of late W. E. Oakeley and Hon. Mrs. Oakeley, and *widow* of W. F. Inge of Thorpe Constantine, Staffordshire; one *d.* (and two *d.* decd.). *Recreations:* hunting, farming, gardening, needlework. *Address:* Cliff House, Atherstone, Warwickshire. *T.:* Twycross 280. [*Died* 20 *Nov.* 1961.

INGHAM, Albert Edward, F.R.S. 1945; M.A.; Emeritus Reader in Mathematical Analysis, Cambridge, since 1967; Fellow of King's College, Cambridge, since 1930; *b.* 3 April 1900; *s.* of late A. E. Ingham and late Mrs. Ingham; *m.* 1932, Rose Marie Tupper-Carey; two *s.* *Educ.:* Stafford Grammar School; Trinity College, Cambridge. Fellow of Trinity College, Cambridge, 1922-28; 1851 Exhibition Senior Studentship, 1922-24; Reader in Mathematical Analysis, University of Leeds, 1926-30; University Lecturer in Mathematics, Cambridge, 1930-53; Cayley Lectr., 1951-53; Reader in Mathematical Analysis, Cambridge, 1953-67; Vis. Prof., Tata Inst. of Fundamental Research, Bombay, 1962. *Publications:* The Distribution of Prime Numbers, 1932 (reprint, 1964); papers in mathematical journals. *Address:* King's College, Cambridge; 14 Millington Road, Cambridge. [*Died* 6 *Sept.* 1967.

INGLE, Rt. Rev. George Ernest, M.A.; Bishop Suffragan of Willesden, since 1956; *b.* 21 Oct. 1895; *s.* of Rev. G. H. N. Ingle, Rector of Wells, Norfolk; *m.* 1922, Mary Frederick, *d.* of late H. P. Frederick, Burgh Hall, Burgh Castle, Great Yarmouth; two *s.* one *d.* *Educ.:* Felsted School; Jesus College, Cambridge; Bishop's College, Cheshunt. Rustat Scholarship, Jesus Coll., Camb., 1914; served European War, 1914-18, war service, the Royal Norfolk Regt., 1915-19; Deacon, 1922; Priest, 1923, Dio. Liverpool; Assistant Master, Liverpool Coll., 1921-24; also curacies in Liverpool, 1922-24; Asst. Curate, St. Peter's, Cranley Gardens, S.W.7, 1924-26; Asst. Master, Felsted School, Essex, 1926-44, House-master, 1929-44; Vicar of S. John's, Greenhill, Harrow, 1944-47; Principal Chaplain, Control Commission for Germany, and Rural Dean of the British Zone of Germany, 1947-49; Bishop of Fulham, 1949-55. *Address:* 58 Chiltern Court, Baker Street, N.W.1. *T.:* Welbeck 4984. [*Died* 10 *June* 1964.

INGLEBY, 1st Viscount, *cr.* 1955, of Snilesworth; **Osbert Peake,** P.C. 1943; Chairman Board of Governors, St. George's Hospital; *b.* 30 December, 1897; *s.* of late G. H. Peake; *m.* 1922, Lady Joan Capell, *d.* of 7th Earl of Essex; one *s.* three *d.* *Educ.:* Eton; Royal Military College, Sandhurst; Christ Church, Oxford, M.A. Lieutenant Coldstream Guards, 1916-19; Barrister, Inner Temple, 1923; Major Notts (Sherwood Rangers) Yeomanry. M.P. (C.) North-East Leeds, May-Dec. 1955 (North Leeds, 1929-1955); Parliamentary Under-Secretary of State, Home Office, 1939-44; Financial Secretary to Treasury, 1944-45; Chairman, Public Accounts Cttee., 1945-48; Minister of Pensions and National Insurance, 1953-55 (of National Insurance, 1951). *Heir:* *s.* Hon. Martin Raymond Peake [*b.* 30 May 1926; *m.* 1952, Susan, *d.* of Russell Landale, Ewell Manor, West Farleigh, Kent; one *s.* four *d.*]. *Address:* 36 Kingston House, Princes Gate, S.W.7; Snilesworth, Osmotherley, Northallerton, Yorks. *Clubs:* Brooks's, Carlton. [*Died* 11 *Oct.* 1966.

INGLEBY MACKENZIE, Surg. Vice-Adm. Sir (Kenneth) Alexander, K.B.E., *cr.* 1953; C.B. 1951; Assistant Managing Director, Arthur Guinness, Son, & Co. Ltd., since 1956; *b.* 19 August 1892; *er.* and *o. surv. s.* of K. W. Ingleby Mackenzie, M.R.C.S., L.R.C.P., Lansdowne House, Ryde, I. of W.; *m.* 1929, Violetta Constance Maria, *yr. d.* of late His Honour Judge Longstaffe and Lady Tindal Atkinson (by her first marriage); one *s.* one *d.* *Educ.:* Repton; Trinity College, Oxford; St. Bartholomew's Hospital, E.C.1. B.A. 1914, B.M., B.Ch., Oxon, 1916; M.R.C.S. Eng., L.R.C.P. Lond., 1917. Willett Medal for operative surgery, St. Bartholomew's Hosp., 1916. Joined R.N. Medical Service, 1916; served European War, 1916-18, Grand Fleet; served War of 1939-1945; Atlantic and Mediterranean and Eastern Fleet (Fleet Medical Officer); Senior Medical Officer, Medical Section, R.N. Hospital, Haslar, 1944-47; Medical Officer-in-charge, R.N. Hospital, Chatham, 1948-52. Surg. Capt. 1942; K.H.P. 1948; Surg. Rear-Adm. 1948; Surg. Vice-Adm. 1952; Q.H.P. 1952-56; Medical Dir.-Gen. of the Navy, 1952-56; retired 1956. K.St.J. 1956. *Recreations:* cricket, lawn tennis, golf. *Address:* 22 South Terrace, Thurloe Square, S.W.7. *T.:* Kensington 8081. *Clubs:* White's, Union, M.C.C.; All England Lawn Tennis (Wimbledon); Vincent's (Oxford). [*Died* 17 *Jan.* 1961.

INGLIS, Air Vice-Marshal Francis Frederic, C.B. 1946; C.B.E. 1944; D.L.; *b.* 22 June 1899, *s.* of Alfred Markham and Ernestine Inglis; *m.* 1927, Vera Helen Turner; two *d.* *Educ.:* Rugby; R.M.C., Sandhurst. 2nd Bn. D.C.L.I., 1918-21; seconded R.A.F., 1921-25; transferred R.A.F., 1925; graduated R.A.F. Staff College, 1936; Air Staff, Air Ministry, 1937-45; Asst. Chief of the Air Staff (Intelligence), 1942-45; A.O.C. No. 23 Gp. R.A.F., 1945-47; S.A.S.O., H.Q. Air Command, Far East, 1947-49; Senior Air Staff Officer, Flying Training Command, 1949-52; retired at own request, 1952. D.L. Kent, 1957-. *Address:* Gayshaws, Ide Hill, Sevenoaks, Kent. [*Died* 25 *Sept.* 1969.

INGLIS, Rev. George John, M.A.; Prebendary Emeritus of St. Paul's Cathedral (Prebendary, 1954-59); *b.* 11 Feb. 1900; *s.* of George Inglis, S.S.C., J.P., and Alexa Marion Orr; unmarried. *Educ.:* Edinburgh Acad.; Univ. Coll., Oxford; Cuddesdon Theological Coll. Temporary 2nd Lieut. R.F.A., 1919; B.A., 2nd Class Honours in Modern History, 1922; Diploma in Theology (with distinction), 1923; Ellerton Theological Essay Prize, 1925; M.A. 1926; Ordained 1925; Curate of St. Gabriel's, Warwick Square, 1925-27, Chaplain of Bishops' College, Cheshunt, 1927-29; Vice-Principal, 1929-33; Warden of Stephenson Hall, University of Sheffield, 1933-39; Warden of St. Anselm Hall, University of Manchester, 1939-48; Priest-in-charge of St. Lawrence Jewry, City of London, 1948-54; Vicar of St. Botolph without Aldersgate, City of London, and Dir. of Clerical Studies, Diocese of London 1954-57. Examining Chaplain to Bishop of London, 1948-61; Chaplain of the Ironmongers' Co., 1956-57. *Publications:* articles in the religious journals. *Recreations:* walking and swimming. *Address:* Imperial Hotel, Devonshire Place, Eastbourne, Sussex. [*Died* 2 *June* 1965.

INGLIS, Lt.-Col. John, C.M.G. 1919; D.S.O. 1918; late Queen's Own Cameron Highlanders; *s.* of James T. Inglis, The Hirsel, St. Andrews; *b.* 28 June 1882; *m.* 1918, Helen Jean, *d.* of late Lt.-Col. C. A. Logan; one *s.* one *d.* *Educ.:* Winchester; Royal Military College, Sandhurst. 2nd Lieut., H.L.I., 1901; Captain, 1912; Major, 1916; Lt.-Col. 1930; Adjutant, 1st H.L.I., 1911; served European War (twice wounded, twice despatches, D.S.O., C.M.G.); commanded 17th H.L.I., July 1917 to Feb. 1918; 5th Q.O. Cameron Highlanders, March

1918 to Feb. 1919; Transferred to 20th Cameron Highlanders, 1919; p.s.c., 1921; retired pay, 1930; Mem. Royal Co. of Archers, The Queen's Bodyguard for Scotland. Capt. Royal and Ancient Golf Club, 1953. *Recreation:* golf. *Address:* Grangemuir, Pittenweem, Fife. *T.:* Pittenweem 213. *Clubs:* Army and Navy, Brooks's. [*Died* 27 *Feb.* 1967.

INGLIS, Lindsay Merritt, C.B. 1948; C.B.E. 1944; D.S.O. 1942 (Bar 1943); M.C.; V.D.; E.D.; retired; *b.* 16 May 1894; *s.* of James Hunter Inglis, Barrister and Solicitor, Timaru, New Zealand; *m.* 1919; two *d.* *Educ.:* Waitaki, Oamara, N.Z.; Otago University. Served European War, 1914-18, with N.Z.E.F. in Mediterranean Theatre, France, Flanders and Germany, in N.Z. Rifle Bde. and N.Z. Machine Gun Corps; War of 1939-45 with 2 N.Z.E.F.; Cmd. 27 N.Z. (M.G.) Bn., 1940; Comd. 4 N.Z. Inf. Bde. (Egypt, W. Desert, Crete and Syria, 1940-42); Comd. 4 N.Z. Armd. Bde. (Egypt and Italy, 1943-44); Temp. Comd. 2 N.Z. Div. for periods in 1942 and 1943; served in peace-time with N.Z. Territorial Force (1st Bn. Canterbury Regt.). Practised as a Barrister and Solicitor of Supreme Court of N.Z., 1920-39; Chief Judge and President of Court of Appeal, Control Commission Supreme Court, Germany, 1947-1950. Maj.-Gen., N.Z. Forces, retd. *Address:* 18 Young St., Hamilton, N.Z. [*Died* 17 *March* 1966.

INGLIS, Sir Robert John Mathison, Kt. 1947; C.I.E. 1944; T.D.; D.L.; M.Inst.C.E.; M.Inst.T.; F.R.S.E.; late Lieutenant-Colonel Eng. and Railway Staff Corps, Royal Engineers; *b.* 5 May 1881; *s.* of late James C. Inglis, Slafarquhar, Stirlingshire and Tantah, Peebles; *m.* 1923, Barbara Selkirk, *d.* of John Sommerville, Queen Sq., Glasgow; one *s.* one *d.* *Educ.:* Bonnington Park; Edinburgh University, Engineering pupilage, 1900, with Engineer-in-Chief N.B.R., thereafter holding various offices in that Coy.; Deputy Chief Engineer Rlys., Ministry of Transport, 1919; Chief Engineer Rlys., Ministry of Transport, 1921; Permanent Way Engineer, L.N.E.R., London, 1929; Chief Assistant Construction, 1932; Asst. Chief Engineer, 1935; Chief Engineer Southern Area L.N.E.R., 1937; Divisional General Manager, Scotland, L.N.E.R., 1941; sent by Govt. on mission to India to report on Rlys., 1943-44; Chief of Transport over Railways, Roads, Inland Waters, Ports and Shipping in British Zone, 1945-47, thereafter Chief of Transport over Combined British and American Zones in Germany, 1949. Chairman: Glasgow and District Transport Cttee., 1949-51; Investigating Cttee. Rhodesian Rlys., 1954-55. Mem. Exec. Cttee. Scottish Council, Member of Institution of Civil Engineers, Member Institute of Transport. D.L., Dunbartonshire, 1957. Vice-Chm., Royal Scottish Auto Club. *Publications:* technical papers to Institutions and Societies. *Address:* Lynton, Helensburgh, Dunbartonshire. *T.:* Helensburgh 198. *Club:* New (Edinburgh). [*Died* 23 *June* 1962.

INGOLD, Sir Christopher (Kelk), Kt. 1958; F.R.S. 1924; D.Sc. (London); Hon. D.Sc. (Leeds, Sheffield, Southampton, Oxford, McMaster Univs. and N.U.I.); Hon. Sc.D. (Dublin); Hon. PhD. (Oslo); Hon. Dr. Faculty of Science (Bologna, Paris, and Montpellier); A.R.C.S., F.I.C.; Professor of Chemistry, University of London, University College, since 1930; Director of Chemistry Laboratories, 1937-61, since when Emeritus Professor and Special Lecturer; *b.* 1893; *s.* of William Kelk Ingold and Harriet Walker Newcomb, Forest Gate, London; *m.* Edith Hilda, *d.* of T. S. Usherwood, Finchley; one *s.* two *d.* *Educ.:* Univ. Coll., Southampton; Imperial Coll. of Science and Technology, London. Research Chemist Cassel Cyanide Company, Limited, 1918-20; Lecturer in Chemistry, Imperial College of Science and Technology, 1920-24; Professor of Organic Chemistry, University of Leeds, 1924-30. Visiting Lecturer, Stanford University, U.S.A., 1932; Reilly, Glidden, Davis, American Cyanamide, and 3 M Lectr. respectively at Univs. of Notre Dame, Illinois, Kansas, Connecticut, and Minnesota, U.S.A.; Redman Lecturer, McMaster University, Canada, 1957. Corresp. member of Roy. Acad. of Sciences of Spain, 1948; Hon. Counsellor for Higher Scientific Investigations in Spain; Hon. For. Mem. of: Weizmann Inst., Israel; New York Acad. of Science; Amer. Acad. of Arts and Sciences, 1958; Hon. Fell., Univ. Coll., London, 1964; Fell., Imperial Coll. of Sci. and Techn., London; Foreign Academician, Bologna Academy of Science, 1965. Baker Lecturer, Cornell University, U.S.A., 1950; President of the Chemical Society, 1952-54. Meldola Medal, Royal Inst. Chem., 1922; Davy Medal of Royal Society, 1946; Longstaff Medal of Chemical Society, 1951; Royal Medal of Roy. Soc., 1952; Faraday Medal of Chemical Society, 1962; James Flack Norris Award for Physical Organic Chemistry, 1965. *Publications:* Structure and Mechanism in Organic Chemistry, 1953 (2nd edn. 1969) (U.S.); Introduction to Structure in Organic Chemistry, 1956. Scientific papers published mainly in the Journal of the Chemical Society, since 1915. *Address:* 12 Handel Close, Edgware, Mddx.; University College, Gower St., W.C.1. *Club:* Athenæum. [*Died* 8 *Dec.* 1970.

INGRAM, Ven. Arthur J. W.; *see* Winnington-Ingram.

INGRAM, Sir Bruce (Stirling), Kt. 1950; O.B.E. 1918; M.C. 1917; D.Litt.; Officer of Legion of Honour; F.S.A.; Editor Illustrated London News since 1900; Hon. Vice-Pres. Soc. for Nautical Research; Hon. Keeper of drawings, Fitzwilliam Museum, Cambridge; Hon. Adviser on pictures and drawings, Nat. Maritime Museum, Greenwich; late editor of Sketch; Chm. of Illustrated London News and Sketch, Ltd.; Director of Illustrated Sporting and Dramatic News, Ltd., and Pres. (lately Dir.), Illustrated Newspapers, Ltd.; 2nd *s.* of Sir W. J. Ingram Bt., and *g.s.* of Herbert Ingram, founder of the Illustrated London News; *b.* 1877; *m.* 1st, 1904, Amy (*d.* 1947), *d.* of John Foy; one *d.*; 2nd, Lily (*d.* 1962), *d.* of Sydney Grundy. *Educ.:* Winchester; Trinity Coll., Oxford (B.A.). Took honours in Law. Late Lt. in East Kent Yeomanry. Served in R.G.A. on French front during European War, 1916-19 (despatches thrice, M.C., O.B.E.). Donor of Battle of Britain Roll of Honour in the Royal Air Force Chapel, Westminster Abbey. Hon. D.Litt., Oxford, 1960. *Publication:* (Editor) Three Sea Journals of Stuart Times, 1936. *Recreation:* collecting old master drawings. *Address:* 9 North Terrace, S.W. 3; Great Pednor, Bucks. *T.:* Great Missenden 2155. *Club:* Athenæum. [*Died* 8 *Jan.* 1963.

INGRAM, Archibald Kenneth; author; Vice-Chairman of National Peace Council; Barrister; *b.* 1882; *o. s.* of late Archibald Brown Ingram. *Educ.:* Charterhouse. Commenced career as journalist; called to Bar, Inner Temple, 1909; served European War in France, 1915-18, Lieut. R.A. (despatches); contributor of Special Literary Work for War Office, 1916-18; Ministry of Labour, 1919-22; Secretary of Grants Committee, Appointments Department, 1920; founded and edited Green Quarterly, 1924; edited the Police Journal, 1929. *Publications:* The Symbolic Island, 1924; England at the Flood Tide, 1925; The Changing Order, 1925; The Man who was Lonely, 1926; Why I Believe, 1927; Out of Darkness, 1927; Has the Church Failed?, 1929;

The Steep Steps, 1931; The Church of Tomorrow, 1932; John Keble, 1933: Death Comes at Night, 1933; Modern Thought on Trial, 1933; Midsummer Sanity; It is Expedient, 1935; The Coming Civilization, 1936; Basil Jellicoe, 1936; Christianity, Right or Left? 1937; The Ambart Trial, 1938; Towards Christianity, 1939; Sex Morality Tomorrow, 1940; The Night is Far Spent, 1941; Return of Yesterday, 1942; Taken at the Flood, 1943; The Premier tells the Truth, 1944; Years of Crisis (1919-45), 1946; Communist challenge, 1948; Christianity, Communism and Society, 1951; Easter Journey, 1952; Storm in a Sanctuary, 1954; History of the Cold War, 1955; Is Christianity Credible?, 1964. *Address:* 31 Queen's Gate Terrace, S.W.7. *T.:* Knightsbridge 8639. *Club:* Reform.
[*Died* 28 *June* 1965.

INGRAM-JOHNSON, Rev. Rowland Theodore, M.A.; *b.* Radwell Rectory, Herts, 30 July 1877; *m.* 1914, Edith Gertrude, *d.* of G. J. Dawson of Canada, formerly of Birkenhead; two *s.* two *d.* *Educ.:* St. Edmund's School, Canterbury; Selwyn College, Cambridge; Wells Theological College. Curate of Milnsbridge, Huddersfield; St. Luke's, Maidenhead; St. Andrew's, Blagdon, Somerset; sent to Canada in 1911 by S.P.G. to work under the Bishop of Calgary, in Alberta; successively Rector of St. George's, Fort Saskatchewan, St. Luke's, South Edmonton, St. Faith's, Edmonton; became senior Canon of the Diocese of Edmonton; Rector of St. George's Parish, Grenada, B.W.I., Archdeacon of Grenada and Hon. Canon (St. Anselm) St. Vincent Cathedral, 1922-27; Rector of St. John's Church, Barbados, 1927-1928; Vicar of Kimpton, Herts, 1928-48; retired. Rural Dean of Welwyn, 1935-40. Chaplain, Rowley Bristow Orthopædic Hosp., Pyrford, 1954-57, retired. *Recreation:* gardening. *Address:* Grand Anse, Queen's Road, Bisley, Woking, Surrey.
[*Died* 12 *Aug.* 1964.

INNES, Sir Charles Alexander, K.B.E., 1953; ex-Director: Mercantile Bank Ltd., Linggi Plantations Ltd.; *b.* 10 Jan. 1902; *e. s.* of late Sir Charles Innes; *m.* 1930; Daphne, *y. d.* of late J. W. Nunn; two *s.* one *d.* *Educ.:* Haileybury College. Joined Best & Co. Ltd., Madras, 1922; Andrew Yule & Co. Ltd., Calcutta, 1931 (Chairman, 1950-1953); Member Indian Coalfields Committee, 1946; President: Bengal Chamber of Commerce and Industry, 1952-53; Associated Chambers of Commerce of India, 1952-1953. *Address:* Dorsetts, Grassy Lane, Sevenoaks. *Clubs:* M.C.C., Oriental; Bengal (Calcutta).
[*Died* 15 *Nov.* 1963.

INNES, Professor Donald Esme, M.C. 1918; M.A.; Hon. LL.D.; Professor of Geology, University of St. Andrews, 1936-54, retired; Emeritus Professor since 1955; *b.* 22 Nov. 1888; British; *m.* 1925, Lilian Grace Isaacson; one *s.* *Educ.:* Oxford Preparatory School; Repton; Univ. College, Oxford. B.A. (Oxon), 1st Cl. Hons. in Geology, 1911; Burdett-Coutts Scholar, Univ. Coll., Oxford, 1911-13; Asst. Lecturer, Bristol, 1913-14. Served European War, Royal Engineers, Despatch Rider, 1914-15, Lieut., 1915-19, France and Salonica (despatches). Asst. Lecturer, Bristol, 1919-20; Lecturer, St. Andrews, 1920-26, Reader, 1926-36. F.R.S.E. 1936; F.G.Soc., 1943. Hon. LL.D. St. Andrews Univ., 1955. *Recreations:* gardening; formerly hockey: represented Oxford University (1911) and Scotland (1922-23-24). *Address:* Ashmount, Ashmount Road, Grange-over-Sands, Lancs.
[*Died* 28 *May* 1961.

INNES, John, C.B. 1942; *b.* 11 Dec. 1888; *s.* of David T. and Jessie Cameron Innes; *m.* 1916, Violet Inglis (*d.* 1932); one *s.*; 2nd, 1932, Ethel May Currie. *Educ.:* Royal High Sch. and Heriot-Watt Coll., Edinburgh. B.Sc. London; Pupil Civil Engineering Burgh Engineer, Edinburgh; entered Post Office Engineering Department, 1913; seconded to African Government as adviser on Automatic Telephony, 1929-30; Asst. Engineer-in-Chief, Post Office, 1935; Asst. Sec., 1936; Principal Asst. Sec., 1939; Director of Telecommunications, 1940; Director Services, Ministry of Fuel and Power, 1942, Deputy Secretary, 1945; Managing Director Cable and Wireless, 1947-50; Director Telegraph Construction and Maintenance Co., 1950-59. *Recreation:* golf. *Address:* 38 Barrie House, Lancaster Gate, W.2. *Club:* Athenæum.
[*Died* 16 *Aug.* 1961.

INNES, Sir Peter David, Kt., *cr.* 1944; C.B.E. 1936; M.A. (Edin.); Hon. LL.D. (Edin.); B.A. (Cantab.); B.Sc., D.Sc. (Edin.); *b.* 22 Feb. 1881; *m.* 1909, Maybelle Annie Stewart, *d.* of James Wright, Edinburgh; one *s.* one *d.* *Educ.:* Perth Academy; Edinburgh University; Trinity College, Cambridge; Heidelberg University. Assistant Demonstrator in Physics at Edinburgh University, 1902-3, Maclaren Mathematical Fellow, Baxter Physical Science Scholar, Carnegie Research Scholar, 1851 Exhibition Scholar; Assistant Prof. in Department of Physics and Electrical Engineering, Heriot-Watt College, Edinburgh, 1908-10; Head of Physics Dept., 1910-12; Principal Assistant to Education Officer, London County Council; in charge of Technology and Continuation Schools Branch, 1912-19; Chief Education Officer, Birmingham, 1919-46; Director of National Foundation for Educational Research in England and Wales, 1947-50. Pres., Association of Directors and Secretaries for Education, 1925; Educational Adviser H.M. Prison, Birmingham; Member of National Advisory Council for England and Wales for Extension and Development of Facilities for Physical Training and Recreation; Member of Burnham Cttee.; Member of Univ. Grants Cttee.; Chairman of Education Cttee. of Assoc. of Municipal Corporations; Exec. Cttee. of Assoc. of Education Cttees., 1940-46; Central Advisory Cttee. for Certification of Teachers; Secondary Schools Examination Council; Juvenile Organisation Cttee. of Board of Education; Executive Cttee. of National Assoc. of Boys' Clubs; Council of the Nat. Playing Fields Association; Chairman of West Midlands Area Council and Member of Central Council for Broadcast Adult Education; Mem. St. Andrews Univ. Statutory Commn.; Bd. of Management, Edinburgh Northern Hospitals; Education Board of Edinburgh Merchant Company. *Publications:* Scientific papers. *Address:* 24 Moorland Court, Melville Road, Edgbaston, Birmingham. *Clubs:* Caledonian; Union (Birmingham).
[*Died* 11 *Dec.* 1961.

IREDELL, Air Vice-Marshal Sir Alfred William, K.B.E., *cr.* 1937; C.B. 1936; M.R.C.S., L.R.C.P.; *b.* 10 May 1879; *s.* of Colonel J. S. Iredell, Bombay Staff Corps; *m.* 1921, Marjorie, *d.* of Robert Scholefield, Dublin; one *d.* *Educ.:* Whitgift; Guy's Hospital. Surgeon, Royal Navy, 1903; Surgeon Commander, 1917; served in Great War, 1914-18; transferred to Royal Air Force, 1918; Wing Commander, 1919; Group Captain, 1926; Air Commodore, 1934; Air Vice-Marshal, 1936; Deputy Director of R.A.F. Medical Services, 1921-26; P.M.O., R.A.F., Inland Area, 1932-35; Hon. Physician to the King, 1934-38; Director of R.A.F. Medical Services, Air Ministry, 1935-38; retired list, 1938. *Address:* Dormers, Old Odiham Rd., Alton, Hants. *T.:* Alton 3380.
[*Died* 29 *Dec.* 1967.

IREDELL, Charles Edward; Consulting Surgeon to Actino-Therapeutic Department, Guy's Hospital; *b.* 1877; *e. s.* of late Colonel J. S. Iredell, Bombay Staff Corps; *m.* Isobel Hilda (*d.* 1960), *d.* of late Harry Farnall of

Auckland, New Zealand; two *s.* two *d.* *Publications:* Colour and Cancer; various medical articles. *Address:* 2 Fairways, Dyke Road, Brighton 5, Sussex. [*Died* 30 *Jan.* 1961.

IRELAND, John, Mus.D. Dunelm (hon.); F.R.C.O., F.R.C.M., Hon. R.A.M; composer; *b.* 13 August 1879; *s.* of late Alex. Ireland, editor of the Manchester Examiner, author of The Booklover's Enchiridion, etc., and of late Annie E. Ireland, author of works on Jane Welsh Carlyle; *m.* 1927, Dorothy Phillips. *Educ.:* Leeds Grammar School; privately. Student and Composition Scholar R.C.M., London. Professor of Composition, R.C.M., London, 1923-39; Examiner to the Associated Board of the Royal Schools of Music, London, 1923-39. *Publications:* (principal) *orchestra:* The Forgotten Rite, 1915; Symphonic Rhapsody, Mai-Dun, 1921; Concerto for Piano and Orchestra, 1930; Legend, piano and orchestra, 1934; A London Overture, 1936; These Things Shall Be, chorus and orchestra, 1937; Concertino Pastorale, string orchestra, 1939; Epic March, 1942; Overture, Satyricon, 1946; *chamber music,* Sextet for clarinet, horn and string quartet, 1898; (pianoforte, violin, 'cello): Phantasy Trio, 1908; Trio No. II. in one movement, 1917; Trio No. III, 1938; (violin and pianoforte) Sonata No. I, 1909; Sonata No. II, 1917; ('cello and pianoforte) Sonata, 1923; Fantasy-Sonata (clarinet and piano), 1943; *piano music:* Decorations (three pieces), 1913; Rhapsody, 1915; Four Preludes, 1918; London Pieces (three pieces), 1919; Sonata, 1920; Prelude in E flat, 1924; Sonatina, 1928; Ballade, 1930; Green Ways (three pieces), 1936; Three Pastels, 1941; Sarnia: an Island Sequence (three pieces), 1941; and many other pieces; *song cycles* (voice and piano): Songs of a Wayfarer (five songs), 1908; Marigold (three songs), 1913; Mother and Child (seven songs), 1919; The Land of Lost Content (six songs), 1922; Five Songs to Poems of Thomas Hardy, 1925; We'll to the woods no more (two songs, one piano piece), 1926; Songs Sacred and Profane (six songs), 1933; Five Songs to Sixteenth-century Poems, 1935; *voice and piano:* Sea Fever, 1912; Two Songs, 1917; Earth's Call (Sylvan Rhapsody), 1918; Three Songs, 1919; about fifty other songs to poems by Hardy, Housman, Masefield, Symons, and others; *church music:* Vexilla Regis, hymn for chorus, soli, two trumpets, three trombones and organ (1898, publ. 1961); Service in F, 1907; Office of Holy Communion in C, 1914; Service in C, 1942; Motet: Greater Love Hath No Man, 1912; Anthem: Ex ore innocentium, 1941; *organ:* Elegiac Romance, 1901; Sursum Corda, Alla Marcia, 1909; Meditation, 1958; works for brass and military bands, and music for the film The Overlanders. *Address:* c/o Midland Bank, 315 Fulham Road, S.W.10. *Club:* Chelsea Arts. [*Died* 12 *June* 1962.

IRONSIDE, Redvers Nowell, F.R.C.P.; Hon. Cons. Physician to: Charing Cross Hospital; Maida Vale Hospital for Nervous Diseases; West London Hospital; Physician, Royal Scottish Corporation; *b.* 1899; 2nd *s.* of late W. Dalton Ironside, civil engineer. *Educ.:* Aberdeen Grammar School; University of Aberdeen. M.B., Ch.B., 1st Class Hons. (Aberd.) 1922; M.R.C.P. (Lond.) 1925; F.R.C.P. (Lond.) 1936; Murray Scholar and Gold Medal, 1922. After graduating in medicine was Resident at Westminster Hospital, then at National Hospital, Queen Sq.; Registrar to Neurological Department, Guy's Hospital, 1927-32. Served European War, 1914-18, in R.A., 1917-18; War of 1939-45, in R.A.F.V.R., 1939-45; Consultant Neurologist (overseas) to R.A.F.; Air Commodore, 1944. Member, Board of Registration of Med. Auxiliaries. Examiner in Neurology to Conjoint Bd., 1950; Mem. Inst. of Neurology, and formerly Adviser on Studies, Maida Vale Hosp., 1951. F.R.Soc.Med. (Pres. Neurolog. Sect. 1956); Mem. Assoc. Brit. Neurologists; Mem. English Ceramic Circle; Master, Worshipful Society of Apothecaries, 1963-64; F.R.S.A. 1964. O.St.J. 1932. *Publications:* Section on Neurology in Savill's System of Clinical Medicine, 14th edn., 1964; (joint) Aviation Neuropsychiatry, 1945; and papers on neurological subjects in scientific journals. *Recreation:* ceramics. *Address:* 5 Wyndham House, 24 Bryanston Square, W.1. *T.:* Ambassador 0939. *Club:* Athenæum. [*Died* 18 *July* 1968.

IRONSIDE, Robin; Painter and Writer; *b.* 10 July 1912; *s.* of Dr. R. W. Ironside and of Mrs. Ironside (*née* Cunliffe; she *m.* 2nd, A. R. Williamson); unmarried. *Educ.:* 2 Elvaston Place; Courtauld Institute; abroad. Asst. Keeper, the Tate Gallery, 1937-46; Asst. Secretary, Contemporary Art Soc., 1938-45; Secretary, Massey Cttee. on the National and Tate Galleries, 1945; Member of Cttee. of Contemporary Art Soc., 1946-52. Exhibits at the Jeffress Gallery, London, and at Messrs. Durlacher, New York. Pictures acquired for Tate Gallery; Contemporary Art Society; City of Leicester Art Gallery. Décors: Rosenkavalier, Covent Garden, 1948; (with Christopher Ironside): Sylvia, Covent Garden, 1952; Midsummer Night's Dream, Edin. Festival, 1954; La Sylphide, Sadler's Wells, 1960. *Publications:* Wilson Steer, 1944; The Pre-Raphaelites, 1948; British Painting since 1939, 1948; David Jones, 1948; (trans. from French of E. and J. de Goncourt) XVIII Century French Painters, 1949. *Recreations:* none. *Address:* 40 Clarendon Street, Westminster, S.W.1. [*Died* 2 *Nov.* 1965.

IRVINE, Brig.-Gen. Alfred Ernest, C.B. 1919; C.M.G. 1918; D.S.O. 1916; *b.* 28 Sep. 1876; *s.* of late John Irvine; *m.* 1920, Katharine Helen, *e. d.* of late Lieut.-Gen. H. M. C. W. Graham, C.M.G.; three *s.* two *d.* Entered Army through Militia, 1897; Captain, 1903; Major, 1915; Temp. Lt.-Col., 1916; Lt.-Col., 1923; Col., 1927 (dated 1921); half pay, 1927; commanded 147th (West Riding) Infantry Brigade T.A. 1928-29; retired pay, 1929, with hon. rank of Brig.-General; served European War, 1914-18 (despatches, D.S.O. and bar, C.B., C.M.G., Bt. Lieut.-Colonel, Officier Ordre de Léopold, Croix de Guerre, Belgium). *Address:* Under the Hill House, Wotton-under-Edge, Gloucestershire. *T.:* Wotton-under-Edge 2267. [*Died* 7 *Jan.* 1962.

IRVINE, Captain Charles Alexander Lindsay, C.V.O. 1938 (M.V.O. 1917); O.B.E. 1920; Extra Gentleman Usher to the Queen since 1952 (to King George VI, 1946-1952); *b.* 1876; *s.* of late Duncan Irvine, Edinburgh; *m.* 1919, Ivy, *d.* of late Josiah Lindfield. *Educ.:* Lancing. Served South African War, 1900-2 (Queen's medal and three clasps, King's medal and two clasps); S. Nigeria, 1905-06 (severely wounded, and subsequently disabled, medal and clasp); Adjutant and Musketry Instructor Wellington College Cadet Corps, 1907-8; in attendance on Prince Danilo of Montenegro at coronation of King George V., 1910; Coronation Medal; to Canada with Sir Robert Baden-Powell (each Province) to inaugurate Boy Scouts of Canada, 1910; General Staff Officer, Imperial General Staff, 1914-18; Liaison Officer between Chief of Imperial General Staff and the King, also Keeper of the King's War Maps, 1914-18; Private Secretary (unpaid) to the Under-Secretary of State for War, 1919-20 (O.B.E., M.V.O.); Gentleman Usher to Kings George V., Edward VIII., and George VI. Raised and commanded Southwater Home Guard, 1940-41. *Address:* Cripplegate House, Southwater, Sussex. *T.:* Southwater 236. *Club:* United Service. [*Died* 11 *May* 1965.

IRVINE, Colonel Francis Stephen, C.M.G. 1918; D.S.O. 1915; M.B.; retd.; *b.* 26 Dec. 1873; *s.* of late Rev. Canon Richard Irvine, D.D., Belfast. Entered army, 1899; Capt. 1902; Maj., 1911; Lt.-Col. 1916; Bt.-Col. 1924; Colonel, 1927; retired, 1930; employed with Transvaal Volunteers, 1906-1909; served South Africa, 1899-1902 (Queen's medal 4 clasps, King's medal 2 clasps); European War, 1914-18 (prisoner (escaped), wounded, despatches, C.M.G. 1914 Star, D.S.O.). Has held the following appointments: D.D.M.S. Northern Command; A.D.M.S. London District; O.C. Cambridge Hospital, Aldershot; O.C. Brit. Station Hosp., Rawalpindi; A.D.M.S. Aldershot Command, H.Q.; A.D.M.S. A.H.Q., India; Comdt. R.A.M.C. Training Establishment, and O.C. R.A.M.C. Depot. War of 1939-45; re-employed, 1940-46, Commandant and Director of Studies, R.A. Medical College, Actg. Major-Gen. (Defence and Victory Medals). Hon. Surgeon to Viceroy of India, 1922-25. *Address:* c/o Glyn, Mills & Co., Whitehall, S.W.1. [*Died* 3 *July* 1962.

IRVINE, William Fergusson, M.A., F.S.A.; *b.* 1869; 2nd *s.* of James Irvine of Claughton, Cheshire, African merchant; *m.* 1897, Lilian (*d.* 1950), 3rd *d.* of late T. C. Davies-Colley, M.A., of Higher Broughton; five *s.* one *d.* *Educ.:* Birkenhead School. Trained in firm of James Irvine and Co., Liverpool; Hon. Secretary and General Editor of the Record Society of Lancashire and Cheshire, 1895-1909; Hon. Sec. and General Editor of Historic Society of Lancashire and Cheshire, 1902-10; Hon. Sec. Local History School, Liverpool University, 1903-10; Hon. M.A. Liverpool University, 1909; Local Secretary for Cheshire for Society of Antiquaries, since 1909, and for N. Wales since 1930; High Sheriff of Merionethshire, 1933-34. *Publications:* Parish Registers of Bidston, Co. Cest., 1893; Notes on the History of Bidston, 1894; West Kirby 300 years ago, 1895; Notes on the Churches of Wirral, 1896; Liverpool in the Reign of Charles II., 1899; Parish Registers of Overchurch, Co. Cest., 1900; The Hollands of Mobberley, 1902; Notes on the Old Halls of Wirral, 1903; A Short History of Rivington, Co. Lanc, 1904; The Colleys of Churton Heath, 1931; in addition to being General Editor has specially edited 15 vols. of the Record Society and is author of various articles in the Transactions of the Hist. Soc., the Chester Arch. Soc., and British Arch. Assoc.; author of several articles in the Supplement to 9th edition of the Encyclopædia Britannica and in the 10th edition. *Address:* Bryn Llwyn, Corwen, Merioneth. *T.:* Corwen 53. [*Died* 4 *March* 1962.

IRVING, Sir Miles, Kt., *cr.* 1934; C.I.E. 1926; O.B.E.; M.A. Oxford; F.R.G.S.; I.C.S. retired; *b.* Singapore, 21 Aug. 1876; *s.* of Charles John Irving, C.M.G., Auditor General, Straits Settlements, and Mary Jane Tompkins; *m.* 1st, 1901, Gertrude Edith Clarke; one *d.*; 2nd, 1916, Margaret Mary Crick (Kaisar-i-Hind Gold Medal, 1935, Officer of Order of St. John of Jerusalem, 1935; she died 1946); three *d.*; 3rd, 1947, Dr. Emily Elspeth Grace, *d.* of late Canon William Baillie, Dublin. *Educ.:* Blundell's School; Balliol Coll., Oxford. First class Hon. Mods.; 1st class Lit. Hum., Oxford I.C.S. 1899; Deputy Commissioner, Montgomery, 1905-6, and 1909-13; Amritsar, 1907-8, and 1919; Attock, 1919-22; Senior Sec., Financial Commissioners, Punjab, 1914-17; Financial Secy., Punjab, 1922-26; Commissioner, Lahore, 1927; and Ambala, 1929-31; Secretary Reforms, 1928; Financial Commissioner Punjab, 1931-34; Acting Revenue Member Punjab Government, 1934; retired, 1935; served European War, A.A.G., A.H.Q., India, 1917, A.A.G., South. Command, 1918 (O.B.E., despatches); retired, rank Lieut. Col.; O.C. Punjab Rifles, A.F.I., 1927-29; Officer of Order of St. John of Jerusalem, 1932. *Publications:* A Catalogue of Christian Monuments in the Punjab; The Irvings of Newton. *Address:* Culmore, Burton Bradstock, Dorset. *T.:* Burton Bradstock 218. [*Died* 24 *June* 1962.

IRVING, Robert Lock Graham; Writer on Mountaineering; Retired Schoolmaster; *b.* 17 Feb. 1877; *s.* of Rev. Robert Irving; *m.* 1908, Oriane Sophy Tyndale (*d.* 1966); two *s.* one *d.* *Educ.:* Liverpool Coll.; Winchester College (Scholar); New College, Oxford (Scholar). Abroad, 1899-1900; First Class Maths. Moderations, 1897; Second Class Maths. Finals, 1900; Asst. Master, Winchester Coll., 1900-9, House-master 1909-1937. Winchester City Council, 1921-31, 1935-47, Alderman 1947-52. *Publications:* Romance of Mountaineering, 1934; The Mountain Way (Anthology), 1938; The Alps, 1939; Ten Great Mountains, 1940; The Mountains Shall Bring Peace, 1947; A History of British Mountaineering, 1955. *Recreations:* mountaineering, formerly cricket (Winchester Cricket XI, 1895, 1896). *Address:* Park House Nursing Home, Park Road, Winchester, Hants. *Clubs:* Alpine (Cttee. 1919, Vice-Pres. 1940, Hon. Mem. 1958), Free Foresters. [*Died* 10 *April* 1969.

IRVING, Sir Stanley Gordon, K.B.E., *cr.* 1947; C.M.G. 1934; Director of Natural Healing Ltd., Champneys; *b.* 5 November 1886; *s.* of Charles Frederick Irving; *m.* 1920, Irene Hazel, M.B.E., *d.* of late Allan Bruce Maclean, C.M.G.; two *d.* (and one *d.* decd.). Entered Consular Service by competitive examination, 1913; Vice-Consul and Acting Consul-General at Valparaiso, 1913-19; Commercial Secretary of Embassy (grade III) at Madrid, 1920-22; Consul and Commercial Secretary (grade II) at Lisbon, 1922-28; Commercial Secretary (grade I) at Rio de Janeiro, 1928-31; Commercial Counsellor, Buenos Aires, 1931-39; Commercial Counsellor at H.M. Embassy, Paris, 1939-40; Secretary-General of Willingdon Mission to South America, 1940; Commercial Counsellor, British Embassy, Madrid, 1941-42 (Head of Economic Dept.); Economic Adviser, British Embassy, Lisbon, 1942-43 (Chairman, Anglo-American Economic Committee); Envoy Extraordinary and Minister Plenipotentiary to Panama and Costa Rica and Consul General for Panama Canal Zone, 1943-46; British Delegate at 2nd International Coffee Conference at Sao Paulo, Brazil, 1931. *Publications:* Economic Reports, on various Latin countries. *Recreations:* boxing, swimming, riding and most games. *Address:* Well Place, Ipsden, Oxon. *T.:* Checkendon 216. *Club:* Travellers'. [*Died* 16 *May* 1970.

IRVING, William John, J.P.; Member Middlesex County Council since 1936 (Chairman 1948); *b.* 1 April 1892; *s.* of Annie and Robert Irving; *m.* 1917, Martha Cowley Strong; no *c.* *Educ.:* Workington Secondary School; W.E.A. courses on Local Govt., Economics and Industrial History. Trade Union Organiser, 1917-27; Political Organiser, 1927-45; M.P. (Lab.) North Tottenham, Dec. 1945-Feb. 1950, (Lab.-Co-op.) Wood Green, 1950-55. Formerly Member Lee Conservancy Catchment Board (Chm. 1948). Hon. Freedom of Borough of Tottenham, 1958. *Publications:* many articles in Co-operative Press. *Recreations:* walking, theatre. *Address:* 12 Kimberley Road, N.17. *T.:* Tottenham 2334. *Club:* Tottenham Trades. [*Died* 15 *March* 1967.

IRWIN, Joseph Boyd, C.S.I. 1947; C.I.E. 1942; D.S.O. 1919; M.C.; *b.* 6 March 1895; *s.* of Joseph Irwin and Ellen Boyd; *m.* 1927, Helen Monica Clark (*d.* 1945); one *s.* two *d.* (and one *s.* decd.). *Educ.:* Trinity College, Dublin. Served European War, 1915-19; B.A., T.C.D. 1919; Indian Civil

Service, 1920-47. *Address:* White House, West Ashling, Chichester.
[*Died* 23 *Sept.* 1968.

IRWIN, Cyril James, C.S.I. 1930; C.I.E. 1922; V.D.; late Commissioner, Central Provinces; *b.* Dublin, 4 Jan. 1881; *y. s.* of late Colonel Richard Irwin of Rathmoyle, Co. Roscommon; *m.* 1923, May, *e. d.* of Stephen Grehan, D.L., of Clonmeen, Co. Cork; one *d.* *Educ.:* Stonyhurst; Wadham College, Oxford. Joined the Indian Civil Service (Central Provinces Commission), 1904; served World War, 1918, Indian Army Reserve of Officers attached 2nd Lancers (despatches); late Col., Nagpur Regiment, Indian Auxiliary Force. Hon. Sec., I.S.P.C.C. Dublin Branch. *Recreation:* golf, *Address:* The Glen, Greystones, Co. Wicklow.
[*Died* 7 *May* 1962.

IRWIN, Leighton Francis, C.M.G. 1952; architect, Leighton Irwin & Company, 406 Collins St., Melbourne; *b.* 1892; *s.* of Edward H. Irwin, Hagley, Tasmania and Helen Mary, *d.* of Maj.-Gen. Downes; *m.* 1916, Freda Gwendolyn; one *d.* *Educ.:* Haileybury College; Melbourne University; Architectural Association, London. Served European War, 1914-18. President Royal Victorian Institute of Architects, 1932-34. Founded Building Industry Congress of Australia; Director Melbourne University Atelier, 1921-50; President Royal Melbourne Technical College, 1946-48; Member Councils of various educational and Research bodies. F.R.I.B.A.; (life) F.R.A.I.A. *Publications:* has contributed extensively to professional and lay press, mainly on architectural and building subjects. *Recreation:* golf. *Address:* 406 Collins St., Melbourne, Australia. *T.:* M.U. 7724. *Clubs:* Savage, T. Square (Melbourne); University (Sydney). [*Died* 4 *Aug.* 1962.

IRWIN, Margaret; Writer; *d.* of late Andrew Clarke Irwin; *m.* 1929, John Robert Monsell, artist. *Educ.:* Clifton; Oxford. *Publications: fiction:* Still She Wished for Company, 1924; These Mortals, 1925; Knock 4 Times, 1927; Fire Down Below, 1928; *one-act play and short stories:* Madame Fears the Dark, 1935; Mrs. Oliver Cromwell, 1940; Bloodstock, 1953; *historical novels:* None so Pretty, 1930; Royal Flush (the story of Minette), 1932; The Proud Servant (the story of Montrose), 1934; The Stranger Prince (the story of Rupert of the Rhine), 1937; The Bride (the story of Louise and Montrose), 1939; The Gay Galliard (the love story of Mary Queen of Scots), 1941; The Story of Elizabeth Tudor (Young Bess, 1944; Elizabeth, Captive Princess, 1948; Elizabeth and the Prince of Spain, 1953); *biography:* That Great Lucifer: a portrait of Sir Walter Raleigh, 1960. *Address:* c/o Chatto and Windus, 40-42 William IV Street, W.C.2. [*Died* 11 *Dec.* 1967.

IRWIN, Sir Samuel (Thompson), Kt. 1957; C.B.E. 1947; M.B. 1902; M.Ch. 1906; F.R.C.S.Ed. 1909; D.L.; M.P. N. Ireland since 1948; Vice-Chairman, General Health Services Board, N. Ireland, since 1948; *b.* 3 July 1877; *s.* of John Irwin, Bovally, Limavady, Co. Derry, N. Ire.; *m.* 1911, Mary Jemima, *d.* of Abraham Sinclair, J.P., Newry, Co. Down, N. Ire.; three *s.* two *d.* *Educ.:* Foyle College, Londonderry. Graduated Medicine, Queen's Univ., Belfast, 1902; House Surgeon: Roy. Victoria Hosp., Belfast, 1902-03; St. Peter's Hosp., London, 1904; Surgeon: Ulster Hosp. for Children and Women, Belfast, 1912-30; Roy. Victoria Hosp., Belfast, 1918-45. Capt., R.A.M.C., 1914-18. Consultant Surgeon, British Troops in N. Ireland, 1939-45. Extern Examiner in Surgery, Dublin Univ. Vice-Pres. Brit. Orthopædic Assoc.; Pres. Ulster Medical Soc.; Pres., B.M.A., N. Ire. Br.; Pres., Orthop. Sect., B.M.A., 1937; Clinical Lecturer in Surgery, Queen's University. *Publications:* Surgical sections in Whitla's Dictionary of Treatment, 1919. Various publications in medical journals, over forty in all. *Recreations:* Rugby football (Irish International, 1900-03), cricket, golf. *Address:* 14 Lennoxvale, Malone Road, Belfast. *T.:* Belfast 660111. *Clubs:* Constitutional; Ulster (Belfast). [*Died* 21 *June* 1961.

IRWIN, Major-Gen. Stephen Fenemore, C.B. 1947; C.B.E. 1944; late Indian Army; Assistant Under-Secretary of State, Home Office, retired 1960; *b.* 29 September 1895; *s.* of late Captain Stephen Irwin; *m.* 1921, Dorothy Ina, *d.* of Lt.-Col. F. O. N. Mell, C.I.E., I.M.S.; one *s.* one *d.* *Educ.:* Tiffins, Kingston. European War, 1914-18, served with London Irish Rifles, 1914; 1st Bn. East Surrey Regt., 1915-18; 1st Punjab Regt., 1918-40; Bde. Comd., **1941-42; Chief of Staff to Comdr. 14th Army, Burma, 1943-44; Commandant Staff College, Quetta, 1945-46; Deputy Chief of General** Staff, India, 1947; retired 1948. *Address:* 43 Queensberry House, Richmond, Surrey.
[*Died* 9 *Dec.* 1964.

ISAACS, Dr. Alick, F.R.S. 1966; Head of Laboratory for Research on Interferon, National Institute for Medical Research, since 1964; *b.* 17 July 1921; *s.* of Louis and Rosine Isaacs; *m.* 1949, Susanna Foss; two *s.* one *d.* *Educ.:* Pollokshields Sec. Sch., Glasgow; Medical Sch., Glasgow. M.B., Ch.B. 1944; M.D. (hons.) 1954. Rockefeller Travelling Fellowship, Walter and Eliza Hall Inst. of Medical Research, Melbourne, 1948-50. Member of Scientific Staff, National Inst. for Medical Research, 1950-. Hon. M.D., Catholic Univ. of Louvain, Belgium, 1962. *Publications:* contribs. to jls. on virology, viral interference and interferon. *Recreations:* chess, music. *Address:* 1 Hollycroft Avenue, Hampstead, N.W.3.
[*Died* 26 *Jan.* 1967.

ISITT, Dame Adeline G.; *see* Genée-Isitt.

ISMAY, 1st Baron, *cr.* 1947, of Wormington; **General Hastings Lionel Ismay,** K.G. 1957; P.C. 1951; G.C.B. 1946 (K.C.B. 1940; C.B. 1931); C.H. 1945; D.S.O. 1920; D.L.; Hon. LL.D. (Q.U.B.), 1951, Bristol 1952, Cambridge 1957; Governor of Sutton's Hospital in Charterhouse; Hon. Freeman, Borough of Cheltenham, 1951: *b.* 1887; *yr. s.* of late Sir Stanley Ismay, K.C.S.I.; *m.* 1921, Laura Kathleen, *o. d.* of late H. G. Clegg, of Wormington Grange, Broadway, Worcestershire; three *d.* *Educ.:* Charterhouse; R.M.C., Sandhurst. First commission, 1905; joined 21st Cavalry (Frontier Force), 1907; Captain, 1914; Brevet Major, 1918; Brevet Lieut.-Colonel, 1928; Lieut.-Col., 1931; Colonel, 1932; Major-General, 1939; Lieut.-Gen., 1942; General, 1944; served N.W. Frontier of India, 1908; operations in Somaliland, 1914-20 (despatches twice, Brevet majority, D.S.O.). Staff College, Quetta, 1922; D.A.Q.M.G. Army Headquarters, India, 1923; R.A.F. Staff College, Andover, 1924; Army Headquarters, India, 1925; Assist. Secretary, Committee of Imperial Defence, 1926-30; Military Secretary to Lord Willingdon, Viceroy of India, 1931-33; G.S.O. 1st Grade, War Office, 1933-36; Deputy Sec. Committee of Imperial Defence, 1936-38; Secretary, Committee of Imperial Defence, 1938; Chief of Staff to Minister of Defence (Mr. Winston Churchill), 1940-45; Deputy Sec. (Military) to War Cabinet, 1940-45; Additional Sec. (Military) of the Cabinet, 1945; Chief of Staff to Earl Mountbatten of Burma, last Viceroy of India, March-Nov. 1947; Chm. of Council, 1951 Festival of Britain, 1948-51; Sec. of State for Commonwealth Relations, 1951-52; Secretary-General of North Atlantic Treaty Organization, 1952-57; Vice-Chairman of North Atlantic Council, 1952-56, Chairman of

North Atlantic Council, 1956-57. Chairman, Royal National Inst. for the Blind, 1946-1952, President, 1952-64. Formerly Director: Portals Ltd.; Lloyds Bank Ltd.; Commercial Union Assurance Co. Ltd.; Ashanti Goldfields Corp. Ltd.; Bibiani (1927) Ltd. Grand Officer, Legion of Honour (France); Commander, U.S Legion of Merit; K.St.J. *Publication:* The Memoirs of General the Lord Ismay, 1960. *Address:* Wormington Grange, Broadway, Worcestershire. *T.:* Stanton (Glos.) 205. *Clubs:* White's, Buck's, United Hunts. [*Died* 17 *Dec.* 1965 (*ext.*).

IVEAGH, 2nd Earl of (*cr.* 1919); **Rupert Edward Cecil Lee Guinness,** K.G. 1955; C.B. 1911; C.M.G. 1901; Viscount Elveden, *cr.* 1919; Viscount Iveagh (*cr.* 1905), Baron (*cr.* 1891); Baronet, 1885; F.R.S., 1964; Chm., Arthur Guinness, Son & Co., 1927-62; Chancellor Dublin Univ., 1927-63; D.L. Suffolk and Surrey, and a Lieut. of the City of London; Captain, retired, Royal Naval Volunteer Reserve; *b.* London, 29 March 1874; *e. s.* of 1st Earl and Adelaide (*d.* 1916), *d.* of late Richard Samuel Guinness, M.P., Deepwell, Co. Dublin; *S.* father, 1927; *m.* 1903, Lady Gwendolen Onslow, C.B.E. (*d.* 1966), *e. d.* of 4th Earl of Onslow; (son killed on active service, 8 Feb. 1945) three *d.* *Educ.:* Eton; Trinity College, Cambridge. LL.D. (T.C.D.), D.Sc. (Reading), LL.D. (N.U.I.). Won Eton School Sculling, 1892; rowed in Eton Eight, 1893, which won Ladies Plate at Henley; won Diamond Sculls at Henley, 1895; won Diamond and Wingfield Sculls, 1896; served in South Africa with Irish Hospital, 1900; M.P (U.) Haggerston, Shoreditch, 1908-10; M.P. (U.) South-East Essex, 1912-18; Southend-on-Sea, 1918-27; Member London County Council, 1904-10, and London Education Committee, 1911-13. *Recreations:* yachting, rowing, shooting. *Heir: g.s.* Viscount Elveden. *Address:* Pyrford Court, Woking; Elveden, Suffolk. *Clubs:* Leander, Carlton; Royal Yacht Squadron (Cowes). [*Died* 14 *Sept.* 1967.

IVEAGH, Countess of; (Gwendolen), C.B.E. 1920; *e. d.* of 4th Earl of Onslow; *m.* 1903, 2nd Earl of Iveagh, K.G. C.B., C.M.G.; (son killed on active service, 8 Feb. 1945) three *d.* M.P. (C.) Southend, 1927-35. *Address:* Pyrford Court, Woking; Elveden, Suffolk. [*Died* 16 *Feb.* 1966.

IVIMEY, John William, D.Mus. (Oxon), F.R.C.O., A.R.C.M.; *b.* 1868; *s.* of Joseph Ivimey, London; *m.* 1st, 1893, Mabel, *d.* of Francis Cancellor, Stock Exchange, London; one *s.* one *d.*; 2nd, 1947, Irene, *d.* of Rufus Glew, Market Rasen. *Educ.:* Herne Bay College, Kent. Won Exhibition for composition, Guildhall School of Music, 1886; F.R.C.O., 1890; A.R.C.M. (composition), 1896; B.Mus. Oxon, 1911; D.Mus., 1916; Asst. Organist, Wellington College, 1888; Harrow, 1890; Head of Musical Dept., Chelsea Polytechnic, 1896-1902; Organist, Dulwich Coll., 1906; Director of Music and Organist, Cheltenham Coll., 1915; Marlborough Coll., 1919, retd. 1933; Organist, Grand Lodge of Freemasons, 1911 (Craft, Royal Arch, and Mark); P.G.D. 1936; Hon. R.C.M., 1933; Member Royal Philharmonic Academy, Rome; Lecturer in Music, L.C.C.; Examiner for Associated Board Royal Schools of Music; Member of Council, Three Arts Club; Judge in Musical Festivals at Stratford, Isle of Man, Southport, Weybridge, etc.; Organist, St. Peter's, Norbiton, 1883-90; St. Paul's, Onslow Square, 1891-1906; All Souls, Langham Place, 1934-38; Llandaff Cathedral, 1941-1942. *Publications:* Church and Chamber Music, Educational Works; Songs; etc.; composer of opera, The Rose of Lancaster, and operettas; Fairy Genesta; Y'lang, Y'lang; Lady Lawyer; White Blackbird; Marie Tanner; Red Rider; New Dean; Paying the Piper; 'Varsity B.C.; Reading Party; Honorary Degree; Socialist: The Vegetarians; Was it the Lobster ?; Cheerio! Cambridge; Reconstruction; On Zephyr's Wings; Witch of the Wood; Headmistress. Orchestral Works: Symphony in C—; Prelude and Fugue; Nursery Rhymes Suite; cantata. Alexander's Feast, etc.; Marlborough College Hymn Book; Marlborough College Songs; The True Story of the Three Blind Mice; Boys and Music; contributed to Strand. Cassell's, and other magazines. *Recreations:* building, gardening. *Address:* Hillside, Bath Road, Marlborough, Wilts. *Club:* Savage. [*Died* 16 *April* 1961.

IWI, Edward Frank; Solicitor; *b.* 28 Nov. 1904; *s.* of late Joseph Iwi; *m.* 1931, Esther Sacker; two *s.* *Educ.:* John Bright Grammar School, Llandudno. Admitted a Solicitor, 1927 (Hons.); Examiner, for the Law Society, 1938-62; Member No. 1 (London) Legal Aid Area Committee, 1963; Livery of Worshipful Company of Paviors, 1938, and City of London Solicitors Company, 1945; Mem. Council Anglo-Jewish Assoc., 1946; served as Fireman: Hendon Fire Brigade, 1938-41; National Fire Service, 1941-45. Legal Adviser National Tithe Payers Association; gave evidence Royal Commission on Tithe Rent Charge, 1934; Chairman Exec. of Petition to Admit Women to House of Lords, 1947; Council of Christians and Jews, 1948. Associate Mem., Irish Peers Assoc., 1964. *Publications:* Joint Editor: Stephens Commentaries of Laws of England, 20th Edn., Vol. I, and 21st Edn., Vol. III. The Yearly Practice of Supreme Court; contributor: Encyclopaedia Court Forms; Grotius Society's Publications; A Plea for an Imperial Privy Council and Judicial Committee, 1937; The Evolution of the Commonwealth since the Statute of Westminster, 1951; Laws and Flaws, 1956. Contributions to Law Journal, Modern Law Review, Time and Tide. *Recreations:* Constitutional problems and journalist. *Address:* 5 Meadway, N.W.11. *T.:* Speedwell 7839. [*Died* 6 *June* 1966.

IZAT, Sir (James) Rennie, Kt., *cr.* 1943; B.Sc. (Edin.); *b.* Dollar, Scotland, 18 Aug. 1886; *s.* of Alexander Izat, C.I.E.; *m.* 1923, Eva Mary Steen Cairns; one *s.* one *d.* *Educ.:* Dollar Academy; Edinburgh Univ. Civil Engineer, Bengal and North Western Rly. and Rohilkund and Kumaon Rly.; Deputy Agent Rohilkund and Kumaon Rly., 1937-38; Chief Engineer B. & N. W. and R. & K. Rlys., 1938-41; Agent and General Manager, 1941-42; General Manager Oudh and Tirhut Railway, 1942-44; retired in 1944 from Indian Railways. *Recreations:* captained Edinburgh Univ. Rugby XV. in 1909-10, also got Blue for athletics. *Address:* Balliliesk, Muckhart, Dollar, Scotland. *T.A.:* Balliliesk Muckhart. *T.:* Muckhart 11. [*Died* 30 *June* 1962.

IZAT, John, C.I.E. 1918; Assoc. M.Inst.C.E.; late Agent, Assam Bengal Railway; *b.* 17 July 1879; *s.* of Alexander Izat, C.I.E., of Balliliesk, Dollar, Scotland. *Educ.:* Dollar Academy; Cooper's Hill. Served European War (Mesopotamia), 1917-18 (despatches, C.I.E.). *Address:* Ardmorag, Victoria Terrace, Crieff, Perthshire. [*Died* 13 *Oct.* 1966.

IZAT, Sir Rennie; *see* Izat, Sir J. R.

J

JACK, Brigadier-General James Lochhead, D.S.O. 1917; late The Cameronians (Scottish Rifles); *b.* 1880; *er. s.* of late Peter Jack, Paisley; *m.* 1923, Jeanette Lucy Vickers, *o. d.* of late T. W. Watson,

W.S., Neilsland, Hamilton; two *s.* *Educ.:* Merchiston Castle Sch., Edinburgh. Served S. African War, 1901-2 with 1st Argyll and Sutherland Highlanders and Scottish Horse (Queen's medal with five clasps, despatches); European War, 1914-19, commanded 2/W. Yorks Regt.; 1st Cameronians, and 28th Infantry Brigade, 9th (Scottish) Div. (wounded, despatches twice, D.S.O. with bar, Legion of Honour, Bt. Lt.-Col., Croix de Guerre, Belgium); Bt. Col. 1929; retired with hon. rank of Brig.-Gen. 1921, commanded 5/6th Argyll and Sutherland Highlanders (T.A.), 1925-29 and Argyll and Sutherland Brigade, T.A., 1929-33; A.D.C. to the King, 1931-41; raised and commanded Market Harborough Bn. Home Guard, 1940; commanded Harborough-Bosworth Group, Home Guard, 1940-41. J.P. 1928-55; D.L. Leicestershire, 1935. *Address:* The Old House, Kibworth, Leicestershire. *Club:* United Service. [*Died* 22 *Dec.* 1962.

JACK, Sir Robert Ernest, Kt., *cr.* 1937; *s.* of late Robert Jack, Kilkenny, and Annie, *d.* of Thomas Humphries; *m.* 1912, Bertha Innerarity (*d.* 1954), *d.* of John Shallcross of Capenhurst Grange, Cheshire; two *s.* (and one *s.* killed on active service, 1943). *Educ.:* Queen's College, Cork; Christ Church, Oxford. Entered Indian Civil Service, 1902; went out to India as Assistant Magistrate; Assistant Magistrate and Collector, Bengal, 1902; District Magistrate and Collector, 1908; District and Sessions Judge, 1910; Puisne Judge of the High Court, Calcutta, 1928-38; Coronation Medal, 1937 and 1953. *Recreations:* reading and gardening. *Address:* Bramerton, West Byfleet, Surrey. *T.:* Byfleet 43123. *Club:* East India and Sports. [*Died* 26 *Jan.* 1962.

JACKLIN, Air Vice-Marshal Edward Ward Seymour, C.B. 1961; C.B.E. 1958 (O.B.E. 1953); A.F.C.; Managing Director, Hawker Siddeley International (Pty.) Ltd.; Director, Ardrox Chemicals (Pty.) Ltd.; *b.* 24 Nov. 1917; *s.* of Seymour Jacklin; *m.* 1940, Dorothy Alida, *d.* of late A. A. Haarhoff; one *s.* one *d.* *Educ.:* Cranleigh School, England. Went to Rhodesia, 1936. Served War of 1939-45 (A.F.C.). Formerly C.A.S., Fedn. of Rhodesia and Nyasaland and A.O.C., Royal Rhodesian Air Force, 1949-61; Air Vice-Marshal, 1958; retd., 1961. Associate F.R.Ae.S. F.Inst.D. *Address:* Box 7105, Johannesburg, S.A. *Clubs:* Rand, Inanda (S.A.). [*Died* 11 *July* 1969.

JACKS, Maurice Leonard, M.A.; Director of Dept. of Education, Oxford University, 1938-57; Director, Oxford University Institute of Education, 1951-57; *s.* of late Dr. L. P. Jacks; *g.s.* of Stopford Brooke; *b.* Liverpool, 1894; *m.* Emily, *d.* of late Henry P. Greg. *Educ.:* Dragon School, Oxford; Bradfield College, Berks; Balliol College, Oxford. 1st Class Classical Honour Moderations, 1914; Goldsmiths' Company Exhibitioner, 1914; 2nd Lieutenant, 13th King's Royal Rifle Corps, Nov. 1914; served in France till wounded, Nov. 1914; subsequently as Instructor in No. 4 Officer Cadet Batt.; Acting Captain; M.A. (Oxford), May 1919; Fellow, Tutor and Dean, Wadham College, Oxford, 1919-22; Poor Law Guardian, 1920-22; Headmaster, Mill Hill School, 1922-37 and 1943-1944. *Publications:* Contribution to The Headmaster Speaks, 1936; Education as a Social Factor, 1937; Physical Education, 1938; God in Education, 1939; Total Education, 1946; Modern Trends in Education, 1949; The Education of Good Men, 1955. *Recreations:* walking, gardening, cricket. *Address:* The Four Winds, Pitch Hill, Ewhurst, Surrey. [*Died* 24 *Jan.* 1964.

JACKS, Thomas Lavington, C.B.E. 1925; *b.* 19 Nov. 1884; *s.* of Richard Harry Jacks and Selina Jacks; *m.* 1929, Elsie Sheridan Stevens (*d.* 1966). *Educ.:* Wellingborough Gram. Sch. *Recreation:* motoring. *Address:* Meadow Lake, Sandown Avenue, Esher, Surrey. *T.:* Claygate 2860. *Club:* East India and Sports. [*Died* 13 *Dec.* 1966.

JACKSON OF BURNLEY, Baron *cr.* 1967 (Life Peer), of Burnley; **Willis Jackson,** Kt. 1958; F.R.S. 1953; D.Sc., D.Phil., F.I.Mech.E., F.Inst.P.; Professor of Electrical Engineering, Imperial College of Science and Technology, 1946-53, and 1961-67, Pro Rector since October 1967; *b.* 29 October 1904; *s.* of Herbert Jackson, Thompson Park, Burnley; *m.* 1938, Mary Elizabeth, *d.* of Robert Oliphant Boswall, D.Sc.; two *d.* *Educ.:* Grammar School, Burnley; Victoria Univ., Manchester. Lectr. in Electrical Engineering, Technical Coll., Bradford, 1926-1929; Coll. Apprentice, Metropolitan Vickers Electrical Co., and Industrial Bursar, 1851 Exhibition Commn., 1929-30; Univ. Lectr. in Electrical Engineering, Coll. of Technology, Manchester, 1930-33; Lectr. and Tutor in Engineering Science, Exeter and The Queen's Colleges, Oxford Univ., 1933-1936; Research Engineer, Metropolitan Vickers Electrical Co., 1936-38; Prof. of Electrotechnics, Victoria Univ. of Manchester, 1938-46. Director of Research and Education, Associated Electrical Industries (Manchester) Ltd., 1953-61. President: I.E.E., 1959-60; Assoc. of Supervising Electrical Engineers, 1961-63; Brit. Assoc. for Commercial and Industrial Education, 1961-; British Assoc. for the Advancement of Science, 1966-67; Assoc. of Technical Instns., 1968-; Electrical Res. Assoc., 1969-70. Vice-Pres., Univ. of Manchester Inst. of Science and Technology, 1962-. Chairman: Min. of Educn. Cttee. on Supply and Training of Technical Teachers, 1956-57; F.B.I. Research Cttee., 1958-60; Governing Body, Salford Royal Technical Coll., 1958-62; Television Adv. Cttee., 1962-; Scientific Manpower Cttee., 1963-64; Cttee. on Manpower Resources for Science and Technology, 1964-. Member: Radio Research Board, D.S.I.R., 1944-48, 1950-54; Central Adv. Council for England, Min. of Education, 1945-48; Scientific Adv. Council, Min. of Supply, 1947-54; Engineering Adv. Cttee., B.B.C., 1948-53, 1961-; Cttee. of Selection, Commonwealth Fund Fellowships, 1951-54; Royal Commn. on Civil Service, 1953-55; U.G.C., 1955-65; Council for Technological Awards, Min. of Education, 1955-65; Lord President's Cttee. on Management of Research, 1958-60; Adv. Council on Scientific Policy, 1961-64; Central Training Council, Min. of Labour, 1964-; Adv. Council for Technical Education for Overseas Countries, 1962-; Council for Scientific Policy, 1964-. Part-time Member, S. Eastern Electricity Board, 1962-. Fellow, Imperial College, London. Hon. F.I.E.E.; Hon. F.C.G.I. Hon. Senior Fell., R.C.A. Hon. Dr. Sc. Tech., Zürich; Hon. D.Sc.: Bristol; Dublin; City of London; Salford; Hon. D.Eng., Sheffield; Hon. LL.D.: Aberdeen; Leeds; Dundee; Hon. D.Tech., Bradford. *Address:* Imperial College of Science and Technology, London, S.W.7. *Club:* Royal Society. [*Died* 17 *Feb.* 1970.

JACKSON, Sir Barry Vincent, Kt., *cr.* 1925; Hon. M.A. (Birm.), Hon. LL.D. (St. A.); Hon. D.Litt. (Birm., Manchester); theatre director, dramatic author; *b.* Birmingham, 6 September 1879; 2nd *s.* of George and Jane Jackson, Birmingham. Founder of the Pilgrim Players, 1907; founder and governing dir. of Birmingham Repertory Theatre, 1913; served in the Royal Navy, 1914-18. Took over Court Theatre, 1924 and Kingsway Theatre, 1925; provided the annual productions at the Malvern Summer Festivals, 1929-37; Director of Stratford-upon-Avon Festival for 1946 and 1947 and of the Shakespeare Memorial Theatre, 1946-48. A Governor of the Old Vic., Sadler's Wells and of Shakespeare Memorial Theatre,

Stratford-upon-Avon; a Director of the Royal Opera House, Covent Garden, 1949-55; awarded Gold Medal of the Birmingham Civic Society, 1922; Hon. Freedom of the City of Birmingham, 1955. *Publications:* Fifinella (with Basil Dean), 1911; Ser Taldo's Bride (with John Drinkwater), 1911; The Christmas Party, 1913; The Marvellous History of Saint Bernard (translated from French of Henri Ghéon), 1925; The Marriage of Figaro (new adaptation, 1926); He Who Gets Slapped (from the Russian, with Gertrude Schurhoff), 1926; Demos, King and Slave (trans. from the French of Henri Ghéon), 1931; The Theatre and Civil Life, 1922; recent plays include: Too Clever by Half (from the Russian of Griboyedev), 1944; Doctor's Delight (trans. and adapted from Molière's Le Malade Imaginaire), 1945; Jonathan Wild (adapted from Henry Fielding's novel), 1948; The Bears of Bay-Rum (operetta, trans. and adapted from Eugène Scribe's L'Ours et le Pacha, with music by Offenbach); Love in a Labyrinth (trans. from Les Prétendants of Charles Bertin), 1949; Emmy (adapted from Edmée by P.-A. Bréal), 1952. *Recreations:* travelling and painting. *Address:* Repertory Theatre, Birmingham. [*Died* 3 *April* 1961.

JACKSON, Lt.-Col. Basil A.; *see* Archer-Jackson.

JACKSON, Brigadier Cecil Vivian Staveley, C.I.E. 1942; C.B.E. 1935; late R.E.; *b.* 4 Jan. 1887; *s.* of late Major-General Sir Louis Charles Jackson, K.B.E., C.B., C.M.G.; *m.* 1915, Margaret Jean, *d.* of Lieut.-Colonel Charles Davidson, I.A.; two *s.* two *d.* *Educ.:* Clifton College; R.M.A., Woolwich. Served European War (despatches, 1914-15 star, medal, victory medal, Croix de Guerre, Order of St. Anne of Russia); Operations in Waziristan, 1937 (despatches, medal), C.B.E. for roadwork in Waziristan, 1932-33; retired, 1943. Member of Society for Nautical Research. *Address:* Burnside, Aboyne, Aberdeenshire. *Clubs:* United Service; Royal Northern (Aberdeen). [*Died* 14 *Nov.* 1964.

JACKSON, Rev. Canon Cyril; Canon Residentiary and Precentor of Salisbury Cathedral, 1947-68, Canon Emeritus, 1969; *b.* 2 August 1897; *s.* of late Charles William and Mrs. Jackson, Leamington Spa; *m.* 1929, Frances Eleanor Coles; one *d.* *Educ.:* Warwick Sch. Royal College of Music, 1915. Served Royal Naval Air Service, 1916-18. College of the Resurrection, Mirfield, 1919-23. Curate of Ellesmere, Salop, 1923-26; Succentor of Southwark Cathedral, 1926-28; Sub-Chanter of York Minster, 1928-44; Vicar of Aldborough, 1944-47. *Recreations:* music, cricket. *Address:* Little Mainards, Stuckton, Fordingbridge, Hants. *T.:* Fordingbridge 3525. [*Died* 16 *Sept.* 1969.

JACKSON, Sir Edward St. John, K.C.M.G., *cr.* 1943; K.B.E., *cr.* 1941 (O.B.E. 1918); Kt., *cr.* 1933; K.C. (Ceylon), 1929; *b.* 14 Oct. 1886; 2nd *s.* of late Sir Henry Moore Jackson, G.C.M.G.; *m.* 1929, Audrey, 2nd *d.* of P. T. Butler, Rosebank, Cape Town; two *s.* *Educ.:* Stonyhurst and Beaumont Colleges; Brasenose College, Oxford. B.A., Law, 1908. Called to Bar, Inner Temple, 1910; Legal Adviser to the Government of the Gambia, 1912; Attorney-General, Nyasaland Protectorate, 1918; Judge of the High Court, Nyasaland Protectorate, 1920; Attorney-General, Tanganyika Territory, 1924-29; Attorney-General, Ceylon, 1929-1936; retired 1936. Legal Sec. to Govt. of Malta, 1937-40; Lieut.-Governor of Malta, 1940-43; Chief Justice of Cyprus, 1943-51; retired, 1951; Judge of Supreme Court, later Chief Judge, British Zone of Germany, 1953; U.K. Member of Mixed Board to review sentences for war crimes in Germany, 1955-57; U.K. Member of Mixed Cttee. in connexion with deconcentration of German coal and steel industries, 1959-60. *Address:* Flat 2, 14 Onslow Square, S.W.7. *T.:* Knightsbridge 2221. [*Died* 29 *Aug.* 1961.

JACKSON, Rt. Rev. Vibert; Vicar of South Ascot, Berks, since 1940; Hon. Assistant Bishop of Oxford since 1951; *b.* London, 1874; *s.* of Thomas and Ann Jackson, late of The Manor House, Brentwood, Essex, and of Brentwood, Ilfracombe; *m.* 1926, Dorothy Frances, M.B.E. (*d.* 1938), *d.* of Walter and Frances Anne Watson; one *s.* *Educ.:* City of London School; Keble Coll., Oxford. B.A. 1899; M.A. 1903; B.D. and D.D., 1924; Assistant Curate of St. Matthews, Newcastle upon Tyne, 1899-1903; Priest of Oxford Mission to Calcutta, 1903-5; Curate in charge of the Mission of the Holy Spirit, Newcastle upon Tyne, 1906-13; Vicar of St. Michael and St. George, Fulwell, Middlesex, 1913-19; Archdeacon in Central America and Rector of St. Mark, Limon, Costa Rica, 1919-27; Assistant Bishop of Honduras, 1921-27; Examining Chaplain to Bishop of Honduras, 1923; Archdeacon of Grenada and Rector of St. George's, Grenada, B.W.I., 1927-30; Bishop of the Windward Islands, 1930-36; Dean of the Cathedral Church, 1930-36; Rector of Astbury, 1936-40; Commissary of Bishop of the Windward Islands since 1936. *Address:* The Vicarage, South Ascot, Berks. [*Died* 19 *Jan.* 1963.

JACKSON, Prof. William Alexander; Professor of Bibliography, Harvard College Library, since 1943; Librarian, Houghton Library, since 1956; *b.* 25 July 1905; *s.* of Charles Wilfred and Alice Mary Fleming Jackson; *m.* 1929, Dorothy Judd; one *s.* *Educ.:* Williams College. A.B. 1927. Cataloguer: Chapin Library, Williams Coll., 1924-30; Carl H. Pforzheimer Library, 1930-1938; Associate Prof. of Bibliography, Harvard College Library, 1938-43; Asst. Librarian, College Library, 1938-56. F.S.A.; Fellow, American Acad. Arts and Sciences, etc. Hon. A.M., Williams College, 1938; Hon. L.H.D., Harvard Univ., 1962; Hon. D.Litt., Oxford Univ., 1964. *Publications:* The Carl H. Pforzheimer Library, English Literature, 1475-1700, 1940; (Ed.) Stationers' Court-Book, 1603-1640, 1957; numerous contribs. to bibliographical jls., etc. *Address:* (home) 1 Waterhouse Street, Cambridge, Mass., U.S.A. *T.:* KI 7-1529; (office) The Houghton Library, Cambridge, Mass., U.S.A. *T.:* UN 8-7600, ext. 2440. *Clubs:* Athenaeum, Roxburghe; Century, Grolier (New York); Odd Volumes, Tavern (Boston). [*Died* 18 *Oct.* 1964.

JACKSON, Rear-Adm. (retired) William Lindsay, D.S.O. 1918; *b.* 1889; *s.* of late W. M. Jackson; *m.* 1918, Evelyn (*d.* 1956), *d.* of late W. O. Gilchrist; two *d.* *Educ.:* H.M.S. Britannia. Entered Navy, 1904; Comdr., 1923; Capt., 1929; Rear-Adm., 1940; Served in Chilean Navy, 1926-1928 and 1930-32; British Naval Attaché in Turkey, 1942-46; A.D.C. to the King, 1939-40; Control Commission, Germany, 1947-49; served European War, 1914-1918 (despatches, D.S.O., Chevalier Star of Roumania, Belgian Croix de Guerre); Chilean Order of Merit, 1928. Asst. County Comr., Sea Scouts, Hampshire, 1951-57. *Address:* Soberton Mill, Swanmore, Hants. *T.:* Wickham (Hants) 3118. *Club:* United Service. [*Died* 12 *Aug.* 1962.

JACOB, Sir George H. L.; *see* Lloyd-Jacob.

JACOB, John Hier, C.B.E. 1936; *b.* 20 Feb. 1884; *s.* of Hier Jacob and Katie Jane Mason; *m.* 1st, 1915, Alice Mortimer (*d.* 1921); one *s.* two *d.*; 2nd, 1924, Marjorie Langford. *Educ.:* St. Paul's School; Lincoln College, Oxford. B.A. 1905, Honours in Law School; Admitted Solicitor, 1909; Entered Public Trustee Office, 1909; Assistant Public Trustee, 1924-44. *Re-*

creation: golf. *Address:* Chaddesley Manor, Chaddesley Glen, Canford Cliffs, Dorset. [*Died* 19 *Feb.* 1964.

JACOB, Naomi; Writer; *b.* 1 July 1884 *Educ.:* Middlesbrough High School and in the world in general. Teacher in a Church of England school in Middlesbrough; Manager and secretary to Marguerite Broadfoote, the variety artiste; Officer in the Women's Legion; in charge as Supervisor of a munition factory; sanatorium, and illness; no work; the stage offered an opening; for eleven years the stage and the Labour Party (has now become a member of the Conservative Party) occupied her time. Had previously been a suffragist; health decided that must live out of England; lived in Italy; complete health. Again an officer in the Women's Legion, 1939; did 10 months' Welfare for E.N.S.A. in Italy, returned U.K. June 1944, back as P.R.O. E.N.S.A. Jan. 1945. Writes two novels a year, articles on cookery, and keeps Pekinese dogs. *Religion:* Catholic. *Recreations:* work — writing novels — telling people how to cook; working for the animals' cause; never takes exercise; lectures on the theatre, literature. *Address:* Casa Micki, Sirmione, Provincia di Brescia, Italy. *Club:* Sesame Imperial [*Died* 27 *Aug.* 1964.

JACOBSSON, Per; Chairman of the Executive Board and Managing Director of the International Monetary Fund, 1956-63; *b.* Tanum, Sweden, 5 Feb. 1894; *s.* of Carl Julius Jacobsson and Emma Christina Mellander; *m.* 1921, Violet Mary Nye, Farnham, Surrey; three *d. Educ.:* High School, Vaesteraas; Uppsala University. Lectr. in Economics, High School of Forestry, Stockholm, 1918-20; Mem. Economic and Financial Section of Secretariat of League of Nations, 1920-28; Secretary-General to Economic Defence Council, Stockholm, 1929-30; Economic Advisor and Head of Economic Dept. of Bank for International Settlements in Basle, 1931-56. Mem. Irish Banking Commn., 1934-38. Ahrends Prize, Swedish Acad. of Science, 1938. For. Mem. Amer. Philosophical Soc., 1957. Lord Stamp Memorial Lecturer, London University, 1959; Jayne Lectures, Amer. Philosophical Soc. and Pennsylvania Univ., Philadelphia, 1961. World Trade Award (given by Metrop. Washington Bd. of Trade) for 1960. Hon. LL.D.: Trinity Coll., Dublin, 1938; Gettysburg Coll., Pa., 1946; Uppsala Univ., Sweden, 1953; Columbia Univ., N.Y., 1958; Doctor Rerum Politicarum, Basle Univ., Switzerland, 1949. Holds decorations from: Sweden (1932 and 1944). Rumania (1938), Finland (1945), Belgium (1950), Italy (1952), Netherlands (1955). *Publications:* Postwar Economic Problems, 1918; Some Monetary Problems, National and International, 1958; The Market Economy in the World of Today, 1961; pamphlets, and leading articles in Skandinaviska Bankers Quarterly, 1946-56; ed. The Bank for International Settlements' Annual Reports, 1932-56, etc.; (under pseud. Peter Oldfield, with Vernon Bartlett): The Death of a Diplomat, 1927; The Alchemy Murder Case, 1929. *Recreations:* golf and skating; omnivorous reading. *Address:* Sheraton Park Hotel, Washington, D.C., U.S.A. *T.:* Columbia 5.2000. *Clubs:* Political Economy; Merchants (Stockholm); Chevy Chase, The 1925 F. Street (Washington, D.C.). [*Died* 5 *May* 1963.

JACOMB, Rear-Admiral Humphrey Benson, C.B.E. 1943; R.N.; *s.* of late Reginald Benson Jacomb, 72 Courtfield Gdns., S.W.5; *b.* 27 June 1891; *m.* Ruby Gilkes (*née* Tattersall) (*d.* 1953). *Educ.:* R.N. Colleges, Osborne and Dartmouth. Served European War, 1914-18, H.M.S. Dublin, Gallipoli and later service in Adriatic; Executive Officer of H.M.S. Obedient, Battle of Jutland; later commanded H.M Ships P.37, Liberty and Ambuscade. R.N. College, Dartmouth, afterwards H.M.S. Southampton (East Indies), R.N. Barracks, Chatham; Executive Officer H.M.S. Curlew (West Indies); Cdr. 1926; Training Cdr. R.N. Barracks, Devonport, H.M.S. Resolution, Admiralty, and R.N. College, Dartmouth, 1931-33; Capt. 1933; commanded H.M.S. Londonderry as Senior Naval Officer, Red Sea, 1935-37; Naval Assistant to Admiral Commanding Reserves, 1938-39; commanded H.M. Ships Royal Sovereign, Blenheim, and Nelson, 1939-43; Commodore, R.N. Barracks, Portsmouth (H.M.S. Victory), 1943; Deputy Admiral Commanding Reserves, 1945-46; Rear-Admiral (retd.) 1946. *Address:* 3 Pembroke Chambers, Penny St., Portsmouth, Hants. *Club:* United Service. [*Died* 10 *March* 1969.

JACQUES, (Thomas) Reginald, C.B.E. 1954; D.Mus. Cantuar.; M.A., B.Mus., Oxon; F.R.C.M.; sometime Fellow of Queen's College, Oxford; Director of Music to the Bach Choir, London, 1932-60; Founder and Conductor of the Jacques Orchestra; *b.* 13 Jan. 1894; *s.* of Thomas and Sarah Anne Jacques; *m.* 1929; one *s. Educ.:* The Grammar School, Ashby-de-la-Zouche; Queen's College, Oxford. During European War, 1914-18, served in the West Yorkshire Regt. (2nd Batt.) in France and Flanders; organist of SS. Philip and James Church, Oxford, 1918-22; Director of Music and Conductor of Eglesfield Musical Society Concerts, Queen's College, Oxford, 1926-36; Conductor of Oxford Harmonic Society, 1923-30; Conductor of Oxford Orchestral Society, 1930-1936: Fellow of Queen's College, Oxford, 1933; Fellow and Member of Board of Professors, Royal College of Music, 1937; Director of Music in the University of Reading, 1937-38; Music Adviser to the L.C.C., 1936-1942; first Director of Music to C.E.M.A. (now Arts Council of Great Britain), 1940-1945; Silver Medal Royal Society of Arts, 1945; Elected Fellow, 1946; conducted B.B.C. Orchestra and all established Symphony Orchestras in Great Britain; conducted at all principal Festivals in England and Wales. Directed and lectured in conducting at vacation Schools and Short Courses for many years, also at Rural Schools of Conducting (National Council of Social Service). With the Jacques Orchestra has given concerts throughout British Isles, also N. Ireland and Germany, and at Internat. Festival of Music, Edinburgh. *Publications:* Voice Training and Conducting in Schools, 1934; The Thirty Song Book, 1939; The Forty Song Book, 1941; The Oxford S.A.B. Song Book, 1951; The Oxford S.A.B. Carol Book, 1960; (with David Willcocks) Carols for Choirs, 1961; *music:* carols, songs, choral and orchestral arrangements. *Address:* Manna Wood Farm, Stackyard Green, Monks Eleigh, Ipswich, Suffolk. [*Died* 2 *June* 1969.

JAEGER, Werner W., Ph.D. (Berlin), Hon. D.Theol. (Tübingen), Hon.Litt.D. (Manchester, Cambridge and Harvard), Hon. Dr. Phil. (Athens, Salonica), L.H.D. (Kenyon); Univ. Prof. emeritus, Harvard Univ., Cambridge (Mass.); *b.* Lobberich, Rhineland, Germany, 30 July 1888; *s.* of Karl Jaeger, owner of a factory, and Helene Birschel; *m.* 1st, Dora Dammholz (deceased); two *s.* one *d.*; 2nd, 1931, Ruth Heinitz; one *d. Educ.:* Gymnasium Thomaeum at Kempen, Rhineland; Univs. of Marburg and Berlin. Privat-Docent at Univ. of Berlin, 1913; Professor of Greek Language and Literature, Univ. of Bâle, Switzerland, 1914; Professor of Classical Philology, University of Kiel (Germany), 1915-21; Professor of Classical Philology, University of Berlin, 1921-36; Edward Olson Professor of Greek, and Professor of Ancient Philosophy, University of Chicago, 1936-39; Sather Prof. of Classical Literature, University of California at

Berkeley, 1934; Gifford Lecturer, University of St. Andrews, Scotland, 1936; Member of numerous Academies of Sciences. International Prize of Philosophy, Accademia dei Lincei, Rome, 1955. Commander's Cross, Order of the Redeemer, Greece, 1928; Ehrenmedaille der Notgemeinschaft der deutschen Wissenschaft, 1930; Order Pour le Mérite, Germany, 1955; Comdr.'s Cross, Order of King George, Greece, 1957. *Publications:* Emendationum Aristotelearum Specimen, 1912; Studien zur Entstehungsgeschichte der Metaphysik des Aristoteles, 1912; Nemesios von Emesa, 1914; Aristoteles de animalium motione et incessu, 1913; Gregorii Nysseni Opera Vol. I-II, 1921, 2nd edn. 1960; Vol. VIII, 1, 1952, Vol. III, 1, 1957, Vol. VIII, 2, 1959, Vol. VI, 1960, Vol. V, 1961; Aristoteles Grundlegung einer Geschichte seiner Entwicklung, 1923, English Edition, 1934, 2nd edition, 1947; Paideia, Die Formung des Griechischen Menschen, 1933; 2nd edition, 1935; Paideia, The Ideals of Greek Culture, 3 vols., 1939, 1943, 1944, 3rd edn., 1948; Humanistische Reden und Vorträge, 1937, 2nd enlarged edn., 1960; Demosthenes, Origin and Growth of his Policies, 1938; Diokles von Karystos, Die griechische Medizin und die Schule des Aristoteles, 1938; Humanism and Theology, 1943; The Theology of the Early Greek Philosophers, 1947, German edition 1953; Two rediscovered works of Ancient Christian Literature, 1953; Aristotle's Metaphysica, 1957; Scripta Minora, vols. I-II, 1960; Editor of: Neue Philologische Untersuchungen, Vol. 1-11, 1925-37; Die Antike, Vol. 1-12, 1925-36; Co-editor of Gnomon, 1925-1933; Das Problem des Klassischen, 1931. *Address:* 43 Bailey Road, Watertown, Massachusetts, U.S.A. [*Died* 19 *Oct.* 1961.

JAGOE, Rt. Rev. John Arthur, C.B. 1949; C.B.E. 1946; M.A.; D.D. *h.c.*; Rector of Schull, Diocese of Cork, since 1956; *b.* 2 Jan. 1889; *e. s.* of A. Jagoe, J.P., Schull, Co. Cork, Ireland; *m.* 1919, Janet, *er. d.* of Dr. W. E. Flewett, late Bishop of Cork, Cloyne and Ross; no *c.* *Educ.:* Cork; Trinity College, Dublin. Ordained, 1912; C.F., 1918-23; Chaplain, R.A.F., 1923; Asst. Chaplain-in-Chief, R.A.F., 1939, Chaplain-in-Chief, 1944-1949; rel. rank Air Vice-Marshal, 1946. K.H.C. 1943-49. Bishop of Bermuda, 1949-1955, resigned. *Recreations:* rowing, shooting, yachting. *Address:* The Rectory, Schull, Co. Cork, Eire. *Club:* R.A.F. [*Died* 16 *Oct.* 1962.

JAMES, Hon. Sir Claude (Ernest Weymouth), Kt., 1941; M.E.C., State of Tasmania; Fellow Australian Soc. of Accountants; Fellow Australian Institute of Secretaries. Formerly City Treasurer and Accountant of Launceston, Tasmania (resigned 1918); company director; Member of Tasmanian Parliament, 1925-37; Chief Secretary, Minister for Mines and Minister for Railways, 1928-34; Chairman of the Economic Case for Tasmania Committee, 1933-35 (Govt. appointment); Agent General for Tasmania in London, 1937-50; Alderman of Launceston, 1920-28; Mayor, 1924; Pres. Launceston Chamber of Commerce, 1924-25; Pres. Rotary Club of Launceston, 1927, of London, 1942. Freeman of London; Hon. Freeman of Launceston, Cornwall (England); Liveryman of Butchers' Company. *Address:* 48 Frankland St., Launceston, Tasmania. [*Died* 27 *Aug.* 1961.

JAIPUR, Maharaja of, Lieut.-General H.H. Saramad-i-Rajahai Hindustan Raj Rajendra Shri Maharajadhiraj Sir Sawai Man Singh Bahadur, G.C.S.I., *cr.* 1947; G.C.I.E., *cr.* 1935; LL.D. Agra Univ. 1944; thirty-ninth Ruler of Indian State of Jaipur and head of the Kachhawa clan of Rajputs; *b.* 21 Aug. 1911; adopted *s.* of Lt.-Gen. Maharaja Sir Sawai Madho Singh Bahadur, G.C.S.I., G.C.I.E., G.B.E., LL.D., whom he succeeded, 1922; assumed full Ruling Powers, 1931; *m.* 1st, 1924, *sister* of Air V.-M. Sir Umed Singh Bahadur, G.C.S.I., G.C.I.E., K.C.V.O., Maharaja of Jodhpur; 2nd, 1932, *d.* of Sir Sumer Singh, Maharaja of Jodhpur; 3rd, 1940, *yr. sister* of Maharaja of Cooch Behar; four *s.* one *d.* *Educ.:* Mayo College, Ajmer; Royal Military Academy, Woolwich. Hon. Lt.-Gen. in Indian Army; Hon. Col. 61 Cav. and Raj. Rifles (Sawai Man Guards). Commissioned in H.M.'s Life Guards, 1939; served War of 1939-45; attended Staff College Course at Quetta, 1943; Entitled to permanent salute of 17 guns and local salute of 19; celebrated Silver Jubilee of reign, 1947. Hereditary Mem. of Ct. of Benares Hindu Univ.; President: Gen. Coun., Mayo Coll., Ajmer, until 1965; Indian Polo Assoc. (until 1961); Trustee Victoria Memorial, Calcutta; Mem. Gen. Council of King Edward Hosp. and Med. Sch., Indore. Patron of: Indian Gymkhana Club, London; National Horse Breeding and Show Society, Delhi; Cricket Club of India Ltd.; Aero Club of India and Burmah; Jaipur Med. Association; Vice-Patron of Royal Indian Navy Benevolent Assoc., New Delhi; Life Member and Vice-Pres. Indian Rifle Club, England; Founder Member, Internat. Club of India. Rajpramukh of Rajasthan, 1949-56. Elected Member, Rajya Sabha, 1962. Ambassador of India in Spain, 1965. *Recreations:* international polo (took his team to England, 1933, where it set up a record by winning all open tournaments and led Indian Polo Team which won Gold Cup at Deauville, 1957), tennis, shooting, and flying. *Address:* Rajmahal Palace, Jaipur, Rajasthan, India. *Clubs:* Guards, Cavalry, White's, Buck's, Hurlingham, Roehampton; Jaipur Ashok; Ootacamund (Nilgiris); Willingdon Sports, O.I.A.A. (Bombay). [*Died* 24 *June* 1970.

JAMES, David Gwilym, M.A., F.R.S.L.; Hon. LL.D.: Mount Allison, Brown; Hon. D.Litt. (Wales); Hon. Litt.D. (Southampton); Hon. Docteur de l'Univ. de Dijon; Fellow of University College, London; *b.* Griffithstown, Mon., 25 Sept. 1905; *s.* of Alfred James and Margaret Ann Morgan, Fishguard, Pembrokeshire; *m.* 1st, 1931, Dilys Margaret Cledwyn (*d.* 1965); one *s.* three *d.*; 2nd, 1967, Gwynneth Chegwidden. *Educ.:* West Monmouth Sch., Pontypool; University College, Aberystwyth; University College, London; Trinity College, Cambridge. Warden of Merthyr Settlement, 1930-34; Extra-Mural Tutor in Worcester, Univ. of Birmingham, 1934-37; Lecturer in English, Univ. Coll., Cardiff, 1937-41; Temp. Principal, Board of Trade, 1941; Winterstoke Professor of English, Univ. of Bristol, 1942-52; Dean of Faculty of Arts, 1949-52; Vice-Chancellor, Univ. of Southampton, 1952-1965. Chm. Univ. Council for Adult Educn., 1955-58; Mem., Academic Planning Board, University of Essex, 1961-65; Chm. Min. of Education State Studentships Selection Cttee., 1962-65. Gregynog Lectr., Univ. Coll. of Wales, Aberystwyth, 1959; Lord Northcliffe Lectr., Univ. Coll. London, 1965; Vis. Prof. of English, Yale Univ. 1965-1966; Vis. Prof., Univ. of Calif. (Santa Cruz), 1967; Riddell Lectr., Univ. of Newcastle, 1968; Ballard Matthews Lecturer, University College of North Wales, Bangor, 1968. *Publications:* Scepticism and Poetry, 1937; The Romantic Comedy, 1948; The Life of Reason, 1949; Warton Lecture, British Academy, 1950: Wordsworth and Tennyson; Byron Foundation Lecture, Univ. of Nottingham, 1951: Byron and Shelley; The Dream of Learning, 1951; (ed.) The Universities and the Theatre, 1952; Matthew Arnold and the Decline of English Romanticism, 1961; The Dream of Prospero, 1967. *Address:* 17 Elm Tree Avenue, Aberystwyth, Cardiganshire. *Clubs:* Athenæum, English-Speaking Union. [*Died* 10 *Dec.* 1968.

JAMES, Sir David J(ohn), Kt. 1959; Hon. LL.D. Univ. of Wales, 1957; Company Director; Underwriter of Lloyd's; Member of Gorsedd, 1965; *b.* 13 May 1887; *s.* of John and Catherine James; *m.* 1924, Grace Lily (*d.* 1963), *d.* of Ashley Stevens, Davington Hall, Faversham; no *c.* *Educ.:* St. John's College, Ystrad Meurig, Cardiganshire. Entered Grain business, 1904. Commenced building Super Cinemas, 1918, and sold eight to Mr. J. A. Rank (now Lord Rank), 1936, retaining only Studios One and Two, Oxford Street, W.1. Closely connected with Welsh affairs. Freedom of Aberystwyth, 1965. Founder of Catherine and Lady Grace James Foundn. of approx. £1,200,000, and John and Rhys Thomas James Foundn. of £300,000. Has also given £200,000 to the Church in Wales, £100,000 to St. David's Coll., Lampeter, over £160,000 to the Welsh and English Presbyterians, over £140,000 to the Welsh and English Congregationalists, and over £270,000 to the village of Pontrhydfendigaid. Has also given over a million pounds amongst various instns. incl. Colleges, Church Societies, Universities, Dr. Barnardo's Homes, Welsh League of Youth, Evangelical Movement, The Welsh Eisteddfodau, Social Centres, Homes for the Aged, World Refugee Movement, Freedom from Hunger Campaign, Nat. Playing Fields Assoc., Imperial Cancer Research Fund, and scores of other worthy causes. Offered the Baptists, Congregationalists and Presbyterians of Wales £250,000 if they would unite. *Recreations:* shooting and fishing. *Address:* Sutton Hall, Barcombe, Sussex; 225 Oxford Street, W.1. [*Died* 7 *March* 1967.

JAMES, Ven. Denis; Archdeacon Emeritus of Exeter Cathedral since 1959; Archdeacon of Barnstaple, 1946-58; Rector of Tawstock, N. Devon, 1948-58; *b.* 3 May 1895; *s.* of late Francis James and late Mary Ann James, Northam; *m.* 1942, Madeline Gertrude Keir Moilliet; two *s.* *Educ.:* Cirencester Grammar School; Salisbury Theological College. Served Indian Army, attached to Gen. Staff, European War, 1914-18. Ordained, 1923; curate: Carisbrooke, I.O.W., 1923-26; St. Mary's, Portsea, 1926-29; Vicar of St. Matthew's, Gosport, 1930-37; Vicar and Rural Dean of Retford, Notts., 1937-45; Vicar of Barnstaple Parish Church, 1945-48. *Recreations:* gardening and music. *Address:* Bankside, Crock Lane, Bridport, Dorset. *T.:* 2086. [*Died* 28 *July* 1965.

JAMES, Frank; *see* Cooper, Gary.

JAMES, George William Blomfield, C.B.E. 1944; M.C.; Hon. Consulting Psychiatrist, St. Mary's Hospital, W.2; Honorary consulting Psychiatrist, Queen Charlotte's Hospital, W.6; Vice-President, the Lebanon Hosp. for Nervous Diseases; late Hon. Consultant in Psychiatry to the Army; *e. s.* of late Rev. G. H. James; *m.* Marie Magdeleine *d.* of late Henry Augeard and Madame Augeard, C.B.E., Chateau de Coudavid, near Poitiers, France; two *s.* *Educ.:* Tettenhall College; St. Mary's Hospital (Entrance Scholar in Natural Science). M.B., B.S., 1912; M.D. London, 1914; D.P.M. Lond., 1921; late Physician to Hayes Park Nursing Home; late Psychiatrist to St. Mary's Hosp., London, and teacher in Psychiatry, St. Mary's Medical School, Univ. of London; Capt. R.A.M.C. in European War, 1914-18 (despatches, M.C. and bar); late Temp. Brig., R.A.M.C., War of 1939-45; Consultant in Psychiatry to M.E.F., 1940-43 (despatches, C.B.E.); Consultant in Psychiatry to the Army at Home, 1943-45; late Examiner in Mental Diseases and Psychology, Univ. of London and Royal Colleges of London and England; F.R.S.M. (late Pres., Section of Psychiatry); Member Roy. Medico-Psychological Association; Hon. Member Société Médico-Psychologique de France and Société de Médecine Mentale de Belgique. *Publications:* Articles on Mental Disease in medical journals. *Recreation:* yachting. *Address:* 57 Wykeham Rd., Hastings, Sx. [*Died* 12 *Oct.* 1968.

JAMES, Mrs. Helena C. R.; *see* Romanné-James.

JAMES, Ivor Benjamin Hugh, C.B.E. 1953; Past Professor of Violoncello and Chamber Music, Royal College of Music; *b.* 12 Oct 1882; *m.* 1928, Helen Just; one *d.* *Educ.:* Emanuel School, Wandsworth Common, S.W.; Royal College of Music. Formerly Musical Dir. Summer School of Chamber Music, founded in 1929. F.R.C.M.; Hon. Member Royal Academy of Music. *Address:* 65 Clarendon Road, W.11. *T.:* Park 5134. [*Died* 28 *Feb.* 1963.

JAMES, John Egbert, F.R.S.A., F.C.I.S., LL.B.; Solicitor; *b.* 29 March 1876; *s.* of Wm. Warwick James; *m.* 1909, Kathleen Lois, *d.* of Edward William Sweet; two *s.* three *d.* *Educ.:* Wellingborough School. Sec. Imperial Chemical Industries, Ltd., 1929-4; Vice-President Trade Marks Patents and Designs Federation; Board of Trade Trade Marks Committee, 1933; British Government Delegate, London Congress, 1934, for revision of International Industrial Property Convention; Minister of Health's River Pollution and Town and Country Planning Advisory Cttees. (retired 1938) and Statutory Central Advisory Water Cttee. (retd. 1946); Executive Cttee. of Society of Comparative Legislation; Internat. Law Assoc. *Publication:* Commercial Arbitration under British Law, 1936. *Address:* Bishops Hull House, Taunton, Somerset. *T.:* Taunton 81121. *Clubs:* Alpine, Athenæum. [*Died* 7 *Aug.* 1965.

JAMES, Sir John Ernest, Kt., *cr.* 1949; Hon. Pres. (retd. Chairman) Lancashire Steel Corp. Ltd., Bewsey Road, Warrington; Chairman: Lancashire Steel Manufacturing Co. Ltd. Lancashire and Corby Steel Manufacturing Co. Ltd.; Whitecross Co. Ltd.; Whitecross Co. (Canada) Ltd.; Pearson & Knowles Engineering Co. Ltd.; Rylands Bros. Ltd. *Address:* c/o Lancashire Steel Corporation Ltd., Bewsey Road, Warrington, Lancashire. [*Died* 3 *June* 1963.

JAMES, Very Rev. John Gwynno; Dean of Brecon since 1964; Vicar of St. Mary's, Brecon and Battle, since 1964; *b.* 7 Sept. 1912; *m.* 1947, Mary David; one *s.* one *d.* *Educ.:* Keble Coll., Oxf. B.A. 1934; deacon 1936; priest 1937; M.A. 1938. Warden, St. Tello's Hall, 1940-45; Examining Chaplain to Bishop of Llandaff, 1944-; Lecturer, St. Michael's College, Llandaff, 1945-49; Minor Canon of Llandaff Cathedral, 1946-49; Vicar of Roath, 1949-55; Archdeacon of Llandaff, 1953-64. *Address:* The Deanery, Brecon, S. Wales. *T.:* Brecon 310. [*Died* 18 *Feb.* 1967.

JAMES, Lt.-Col. Ralph Ernest Haweis, C.M.G. 1917; C.B.E. 1919; D.S.O. 1918; now retired from business; late the Loyal Regt. *b.* 31 Oct. 1875; *e. surv. s.* of late Lieut.-Colonel W. H. James, Royal Engineers, and Mabel Caunter, *o. d.* of late Rev. George Akehurst; *m.* Louise Enders (*d.* 1944), *o. d.* of C. W. Brega, 2816 Michigan Avenue Chicago; one *s.* two *d.* *Educ.:* Eton College. 2nd Lieut. Loyal North Lancashire Regt., 1895; Captain the Chinese Regt., 1899; Boxer Campaign, 1900; Captain Loyal North Lancashire Regt., 1901; Instructor, Royal Military College, 1902-6; Staff College, 1906-8; War Office 1908-16; Staff Captain, 1908-11; Assist. Adj.-General and Brevet-Major, 1911-12; General Staff Officer, Second Grade, 1912; General Staff Officer, First Grade, 1914; Brevet Lieut.-Col. 1915; G.H.Q., Home Forces, 1916; G.S.O.1 in France, June 1916 to Nov. 1916; Assistant Director-Gen. of Transportation, 1916-18; lent to the

Admiralty for special service as Director of Organisation Civil Eng. in Chief's Depart., 1918-19; China Medal, 1900; the European War, British and International Medals; King Edward VII Coronation Decoration. *Recreations:* shooting, fishing *Address:* The Old House, 132 Skippack Pike, Fort Washington, Pennsylvania, U.S.A. *Clubs:* United Service, Flyfishers'; Chicago (Chicago).
[*Died* 25 *Dec.* 1964.

JAMES, Reginald H. L. L.; *see* Langford-James.

JAMES, Reginald William, F.R.S. 1955; Hon. D.Sc. (Univ. of Witwatersrand); Professorof Physics, University of Cape Town, 1937-56; Vice-Chancellor and Acting Principal, 1956-57; Prof. Emeritus, 1957; *b.* 9 Jan. 1891; *s.* of late William George James, Paddington; *m.* 1936, Anne, *o. d.* of late John Watson, Rochdale; two *s.* one *d.* *Educ.:* The Polytechnic, Regent Street; City of London School; St. John's College, Cambridge. Physicist to Sir Ernest Shackleton's Antarctic Expedition, 1914-16; served European War with Sound Ranging Section, Royal Engineers, 1917 - 19; Lecturer in Physics, 1919-34, and Reader in Experimental Physics, 1934-37, Univ. of Manchester; President: Manchester Literary and Philosophical Society, 1935-37; Royal Society of South Africa, 1950-53. *Publications:* X Ray Crystallography, 1930; The Optical Principles of the Diffraction of X-rays, 1948; various papers in Scientific Journals on experimental physics and crystallography. *Address:* Brandreth, 5 Mulvihal Rd., Rondebosch, Cape Province, South Africa.
[*Died* 7 *July* 1964.

JAMES, Richard Bush, Q.C. 1939; *b.* 27 Sept. 1889; *s.* of late Alfred B. James, North Petherton, Somerset; *m.* 1926, José Margaret, *d.* of late Sir George Donaldson; no c. *Educ.:* Harrow; Christ Church, Oxford. Called to Bar Inner Temple, 1919; Bencher, 1946; served European War, 1914-18, France, 1915-18 (despatches, wounded); Captain, Royal Horse Guards. *Address:* 1019 Kings House, St. James's Court, S.W.1. *T.:* 01-834 6907. *Club:* Buck's.
[*Died* 20 *June* 1970.

JAMES, Thomas Maurice, M.A.; J.P., Kent; Headmaster, Sutton Valence School, 1932-50; retired, 1950; *b.* 14 Dec. 1890; *s.* of Thomas James and Mary Alice Beatrice Hughes; *m.* 1915, Hilda Joan Castle; two *s.* one *d.* *Educ.:* Clifton College; Emmanuel College, Cambridge. Sutton Valence School, 1913. *Address:* St. Michael's Cottage, Benenden, Kent. *T.:* Benenden 3110.
[*Died* 15 *June* 1962.

JAMES, Vice-Admiral Thomas Norman, C.B. 1931; M.V.O. 1924; Royal Navy; 4th *s.* of late W. E. A. James, J.P., Barrock Park, Cumberland; *b.* 1878; *m.* 1918, Katherine Mary, *d.* of C. E. Stewart, M.A.; one *s.* one *d.* *Educ.:* Clifton College; Stubbington, Fareham. Entered Navy, 1893; Lieut. 1901; Commander, 1913; Capt. 1917; Rear-Adm. 1929; Vice-Adm. 1934; General African medal and clasp, Somaliland, 1904; served European War, 1914-18; Jutland (Order of St. Stanislaus, 2nd Class with swords); Flag-Captain H.M.A.S. Australia, 1918-19; Flag-Captain H.M.S. Cardiff, 1919-21; Captain H.M.S. President, 1921-23; Flag-Captain and Chief of Staff Reserve Fleet, 1923-24; Captain of the Fleet, H.M.S. Revenge, Atlantic Fleet, 1925-27; Flag-Captain H.M.S. Warspite and H.M.S. Queen Elizabeth, 1927-28; Rear-Admiral in charge and Admiral Superintendent Gibraltar, 1931-33; retired list, 1934. *Address:* Wheltones, Seer Green, Bucks. *Club:* United Service.
[*Died* 25 *Sept.* 1965.

JAMES, William Warwick, O.B.E.; F.R.C.S. Eng.; L.R.C.P. (Lond.); F.D.S., R.C.S. (Hon.) Eng.; M.Ch. (Birm.) Hon.; Hon. Member Staff, Birmingham Univ.; Emeritus Consultant Dental Surgeon to the Middlesex Hospital; Consulting Dental Surgeon, Great Ormond Street Hospital for Sick Children and Royal Dental Hospital (an Annual Warwick James Lecture estab. at Roy. Dental Hosp., 1960); late Member of the Army Advisory Committee on Maxillo-facial Injuries; *b.* 20 September 1874; *e. s.* of Warwick James, Wellingborough; *m.* 1903, Ada Louisa Mary (*d.* 1948), *o. c.* of L. Froude, Calne; six *s.* one *d.* *Educ.:* Wellingborough School; Middlesex Hospital; Royal Dental Hospital. Late Lecturer and Dental Surgeon, Royal Dental Hospital, London; F.R.S.M.; F.Z.S.; Mem. Geological Association; Hon. Mem. Anatomical Soc.; Royal College of Surgeons John Tomes Prize, 1922-24. *Publications:* The Jaws and Teeth of Primates, 1960; numerous publications in medical and dental literature; contrib. Trans. Zool. Soc.; article in T. E. Lawrence, by his friends. *Recreations:* mountaineering, golf, music, chess. *Address:* The Limes. Curry Rivel, Langport, Somerset. *Clubs:* Athenæum, Alpine.
[*Died* 14 *Sept.* 1965.

JAMESON, Cecil Stuart; *b.* 1883; *s.* of J. S. Jameson. *Educ.:* Wellington College, New Zealand. Left N.Z. at age of 20 to study art in London; worked at Lambeth, Kensington, and Royal Academy Schools, won scholarship at Allan-Fraser Art College, Arbroath, Scotland; Member Royal Society of Portrait Painters and exhibitor at Academy, Salon and other exhibitions. *Recreation:* sketching in water colour. *Club:* Chelsea Arts.
[*Deceased.*

JAMESON, Brigadier Frank Robert Wordsworth, D.S.O. 1918; M.C.; *b.* 24 March 1893; *s.* of late Frank Wordsworth Jameson, Aston Hall, North Ferriby and Seaton House, E. Yorks, and late Ethel M. M. Jameson, *d.* of late A. S. Ayre, Hessle, E. Yorks; *m.* 1921, Violet, *d.* of late Henry FitzGibbon, M.D., F.R.C.P.I.; one *s.* one *d.* *Educ.:* Uppingham (Allin Exhibitioner); Emmanuel College, Cambridge (Sizar, Soley Scholar, M.A.). Honourable Artillery Company, 1914-16, and, to date, as Veteran Member; Royal Engineers (Signal Service), 1916 - 19; Captain; served in France, Flanders, and Italy with 1st Bn. H.A.C. and 23rd Divisional Signal Company R.E., 1915-18; Fiume, 1919 (D.S.O., M.C. with two bars, despatches twice); Egyptian Civil Service, 1919; Inspector Egyptian Ministry of Finance; Assistant Private Secretary (Appointments) to the Secretary of State for the Colonies, 1928; Assistant Principal Colonial Office, 1931; Assistant Secretary Development Commission, 1934; Assistant Secretary Agricultural Research Council, 1934; Assistant Sec. Min. of Agriculture and Fisheries, 1949; Min. Agriculture, Fisheries and Food, 1954. Secretary Committee on the Agricultural Colleges, 1954. Retired from Home Civil Service, 1955. Senior Instructor, National Coal Board, teaching English to Hungarian Miners, 1957. Recommissioned from Officers Emergency Reserve, Royal Corps of Signals, 1939; Captain, 1940; Major, 1941; Lieut.-Colonel, 1942; Colonel, 1942; Brigadier 1946; served 18 Div. Sigs., U.K., 1939-41, 6 and 70 Div. Sigs., Egypt, Syria, Tobruk, Eighth Army in Western Desert, 1941-42; Deputy Chief Sec., Occupied Enemy Territory Administration, Eritrea, 1942; Chief Sec., British Military Administration, Eritrea, 1942-43; Chief Civil Affairs Staff Officer, East Africa Command (Mil. Admin of Somalia, Brit. Somaliland and Reserved Areas of Ethiopia), 1943-47; Deputy Chief Civil Affairs Officer, G.H.Q., M.E.L.F. (Mil. admin. of Tripolitania, Cyrenaica, Eritrea, Somalia, Brit. Somaliland and Reserved

Areas of Ethiopia), 1947-48; D.C.C.A.O., War Office, 1948. F.R.S.A. Member of Council, Housing Association for Officers' Families. *Address:* Oakridge, Limpsfield, Oxted, Surrey. *T.:* Oxted 4160. *Club:* Civil Service. [*Died* 8 *May* 1965.

JAMESON, James Alexander, C.B.E. 1927; formerly Director, Anglo-Iranian Oil Co.; *b.* 1885; *s.* of John Jameson, Glasgow; *m.* 1925, Jean Wilson, *d.* of George Fenning, Cheltenham; one *d.* *Educ.:* Allan Glen's School, Glasgow. *Address:* 5 Temple Gardens, Moor Park, Rickmansworth, Herts. *Clubs:* East India and Sports, Royal Thames Yacht. [*Died* 17 *Jan.* 1961.

JAMESON, Rear-Admiral Sir William Scarlett, K.B.E., *cr.* 1951 (C.B.E. 1964); C.B. 1951; retd.; *b.* Drogheda, Ireland, 3 Sept. 1899; *s.* of William Bellingham Jameson and Evelyn Constance Scarlett-Campbell; *m.* 1924, Elizabeth Mary, *d.* of William Fisher, Hudshaw House, Hexham; one *d.* *Educ.:* Royal Naval Colleges, Osborne and Dartmouth; Royal Naval Engineering College, Keyham. H.M.S. Canada, Grand Fleet, 1915-17; H.M.S. Venturous, Minelaying Destroyer, 1917-1919; specialised in Engineering, 1919; service in submarines, including H.M. Submarines K14, X1, and Thames, 1923-35; Commander, 1931; H.M.S. Ark Royal, 1939-40 (despatches); Assistant Naval Attaché, Washington, 1941-43; Captain, 1942; Naval Aviation, 1943-52; Staff of Flag Officer, Naval Air Pacific, 1944-46; Rear-Admiral, 1948; Rear-Admiral Reserve Aircraft, 1948-52; retired 1952. Contested (Nat. L. and C.) North Norfolk Parliamentary division, 1955. *Publications:* Ark Royal, 1939-41, 1957; The Wandering Albatross, 1958; The Fleet that Jack built, 1962; Submariners V.C., 1963; The Most Formidable Thing, 1965. *Recreations:* fishing, ski-ing and bird-watching. *Address:* Ham Cross, Ham, Nr. Marlborough, Wilts. *T.:* Inkpen 247. *Clubs:* United Service; Kildare Street (Dublin).
[*Died* 14 *Nov.* 1966.

JAMESON, Sir (William) Wilson, G.B.E., *cr.* 1949; K.C.B., *cr.* 1943; Kt., *cr.* 1939; M.A., M.D., F.R.C.P., D.P.H.; Barrister-at-law; Hon. LL.D. (Aberdeen, Manchester, Wales, Belfast, Toronto); Hon. D.Hy. Durham; Hon. F.R.C.P. (Canada) and F.R.C.O.G.; Hon. Sc.D. (Camb.); U.S.A. Medal of Freedom with gold palms; Hon. Fellow: Soc. Med. Officers of Health; American Public Health Association; New York Academy of Medicine; Foreign Correspondent (Hygiene), Académie de Médicine; *b.* 12 May 1885; *s.* of late John Wilson Jameson, Perth; *m.* 1st, 1916, Pauline (*d.* 1958), *d.* of J. P. Helm; two *d.*; 2nd, 1959, Constance, *d.* of Dr. H. Dobie. *Educ.:* Aberdeen Grammar School and Aberdeen University; University College, London. Assistant and Lecturer, Department of Hygiene, Univ. College, London, 1914; M.O.H., Finchley and Borough of Hornsey; Lecturer on Public Health and Preventive Medicine, Guy's Hospital Medical School; Dean and Prof. of Public Health, London School of Hygiene and Tropical Medicine (Univ. of London); Medical Adviser to Secretary for the Colonies, 1940; Member Medical Research Council, 1940-44; Chief Medical Officer of Min. of Health and Min. of Educn., 1940-50; medical adviser to King Edward's Hosp. Fund for London, 1950-60. Harveian Orator, R.C.P., 1942; Buchanan Medallist, Roy. Soc., 1942; Bisset Hawkins Medallist, R.C.P., 1950; Crown Nominee, General Medical Council, 1942-47; K.H.P. 1947-50; Master Soc. Apothecaries, 1952-53. Captain R.A.M.C.; Specialist Sanitary Officer, England, France, and Italy. *Publications:* Synopsis of Hygiene (with G. S. Parkinson); official reports and various medical articles. *Address:* 6 Palace Mansions, W.14. *Club:* Athenæum. [*Died* 18 *Oct.* 1962.

JAMIESON, Stanley Wyndham, C.B.E. 1919; LL.D.; *b.* 1885; *er. s.* of late John Donaldson Jamieson, Greenock; *m.* 1st, 1908, Muriel Cartmel Whiteley (marriage dissolved, 1949; she *d.* 1952), *er. d.* of 1st Baron Marchamley; one *s.* two *d.* (and one *d.* decd.); 2nd, 1950, Anne, *widow* of Thomas Adam-Evans, Deal. *Educ.:* Charterhouse. Director: Duttons Blackburn Brewery, and all subsidiary Cos., 1908-1963 (Chm., 1940-63); Ashley Courtenay, Ltd.; County Councillor Gloucestershire, 1919-1922; served Gloucestershire Regiment, 1914-1915; Private Secretary (unpaid) to Deputy Secretary of State for War, 1916-19; Assistant to Controller of Inspection of Munitions, 1919. *Recreations:* golf, photography. *Address:* White Lodge, Kingsdown, Deal. *T.:* Kingsdown (Deal) 442. *Club:* Junior Carlton.
[*Died* 26 *April* 1970.

JANE, Professor Frank William; Professor of Botany in University of London, at Royal Holloway College, since 1949; *b.* April 1901; *e. s.* of J. W. Jane, London; *m.* 1929, Grace Irene Ruth, 3rd *d.* of E. J. W. Chinnery, New Barnet; one *d.* *Educ.:* Queen Elizabeth's Grammar School, Barnet; University of London (Birkbeck College). Assistant Lecturer in Botany, 1929-32, Lecturer in Botany, 1932-45, Reader in Botany, 1945-49, University College, London. *Publications:* The Structure of Wood, 1956, 1962; numerous papers, chiefly on Freshwater Algae and Botanical Aspects of Wood in scientific journals. *Recreations:* ornithology, gardening. *Address:* Highfield, Englefield Green, Surrey. *T.:* Egham 3066.
[*Died* 6 *May* 1963.

JARDINE, Sir John, 2nd Bt., *cr.* 1919; O.B.E. 1943; T.D.; C.St.J.; Chairman, Local Board Royal Insurance Co.; Director: John Jardine Ltd.; Midland Machine Trust Ltd., and other Cos.; *b.* 3 Oct. 1884; *s.* of Sir Ernest Jardine, 1st Bart., and Ada Jane Fletcher; *S.* father, 1947; unmarried. Served European War, 1914-18. Lt.-Col., R.E. (Signals); J.P., Nottingham; High Sheriff of Notts., 1932-33. Dep. Red Cross Comr. for Middle East, 1940-43. *Heir:* none. *Address:* Monks Place, Charlton Horethorne, Sherborne, Dorset. *T.:* Corton Denham 253; Pier Terrace, West Bay, Dorset. *T.:* Bridport 2405. *Clubs:* Carlton, Royal Automobile; Savage; Royal Channel Islands Yacht. [*Died* 1 *Aug.* 1965 (*ext.*).

JARDINE, Captain Sir John William Buchanan-, 3rd Bt., *cr.* 1885; J.P Dumfriesshire; Royal Horse Guards; *b.* 7 Mar. 1900; *s.* of 2nd Bt. and Ethel Mary, O.B.E. (*d.* 1952), *d.* of Benjamin Piercy, Marchwiel Hall, Wrexham, and Macomer, Sardinia; *S.* father, 1927; *m.* 1st, 1921, Jean (who obtained a divorce, 1944), *yr. d.* of late Lord Ernest Hamilton; one *s.*; 2nd, 1944, Prudence A., *d.* of W. Haggie, Knayton, Thirsk; one *s.* one *d.* M.F.H. Dumfriesshire hounds, 1921-. Jt. Master New Forest Buckhounds, 1936-38; Member of the Royal Body Guard for Scotland; 2nd Lt. Royal Horse Guards, 1940; Capt. 1942. *Publication:* Hounds of the World, 1937. *Heir:* *s.* Major Andrew Rupert John Buchanan-Jardine, M.C. 1945, R.H.G. [*b.* 2 Feb. 1923; *m.* 1950, Jane Fiona, 2nd *d.* of Sir Charles Edmonstone, 6th Bt.; one *s.* one *d.*]. *Address:* Castle Milk, Lockerbie, Dumfriesshire; Moulin de la Mourachonne, Mouans Sartoux, Alpes Maritimes, France.
[*Died* 5 *Nov.* 1969

JARRATT, Sir William Smith, Kt., *cr.* 1929; *b.* Bradford, 28 June 1871; *s.* of J. W. Jarratt, J.P.; *m.* Isabel A. (*d.* 1956), *widow* of E. R. Durant; two *d.* *Educ.:* Bradford; Royal College of Science, South Kensington;

Trinity College, Cambridge (Scholar). First Class Natural Science Tripos; 1st Class Mathematical Tripos; Barrister, Middle Temple; Comptroller-General of Patents, Designs, and Trade Marks, and Comptroller, Industrial Property Department, Board of Trade, 1926; retired, 1932; Secretary Trade Marks, Patents, and Designs Federation, 1932-57, retired, 1957. British Delegate at the Rome Conference, 1928, for revision of the Berne Copyright Convention, and at the London Conference, 1934, for revision of the International Convention for the Protection of Industrial Property. *Address:* 36 Regent's Park Road, N.W.1. *T.:* Primrose 9996. [*Died* 23 *March* 1966.

JARRELL, Randall; author; Teacher at Woman's College of University of North Carolina at Greensboro, U.S.A., 1947-51, 1953-56 and again since 1958; *b.* 6 May 1914; *s.* of Owen Jarrell and Anna Campbell Jarrell; *m.* 1952, Mary von Schrader. *Educ.:* Vanderbilt University. Teacher at: Kenyon College, 1937-39; University of Texas, 1939-42; Sarah Lawrence Coll., 1946-47; Princeton Univ., 1951-52; Univ. of Illinois, 1953; Consultant in Poetry to the Library of Congress, U.S.A., 1956-58. Literary Editor of Nation, 1946-47. Served with U.S. Army Air Force, 1942-46. Mem., Nat. Inst. of Arts and Letters, 1960-. A Chancellor, American Acad. of Poets. *Publications:* Blood for a Stranger, 1942; Little Friend, Little Friend, 1945; Losses, 1948; The Seven-League Crutches, 1951; Poetry and the Age, 1953; Pictures from an Institution, 1954; Selected Poems, 1955; The Woman at the Washington Zoo, 1960 (Nat. Book Award, 1961); A Sad Heart at the Supermarket (essays), 1962; The Gingerbread Rabbit (for children), 1963; The Lost World (poems). *Recreations:* music, tennis, sports cars. *Address:* 5706 S. Lake Drive, Greensboro, N.C., U.S.A. [*Died* 14 *Oct.* 1965.

JARRETT, Sir Francis M. K.; *see* Kerr-Jarrett.

JARVIE, John Gibson; Founder, and Chairman from its beginning in 1919, of United Dominions Trust Ltd. and the UDT Group of companies until 1963 when he retired from the Chair and became President; *b.* Carluke, Scotland, 29 Oct. 1883; 2nd *s.* of late John Jarvie, J.P., Carluke; *m.* Ethel Mary Patricia, *d.* of late Col. M. C. Rowland, C.M.G., Johannesburg, S. Africa; one *s.* three *d.* *Educ.:* studied Law in Scotland, and Art in Glasgow, London and on the Continent. Gave up Art and went into Commerce, becoming Sec. to prominent City financier; went to U.S.A. where he lived for several years and joined staff of the, then, largest Bank in New York; travelled extensively in America and Canada. Read Law in London and became Barrister-at-Law (Middle Temple); travelled in Commonwealth and other countries incl. Russia and Middle East. Owns the Loch Dee and Talnotrie Estates, Kirkcudbrightshire and Glenvernoch, Wigtownshire, Scotland, and farms in Scotland and Suffolk; breeds pedigreed livestock. Regional Port Director under Min. of War Transport, 1941-42. High Sheriff of Suffolk, 1951-52. Liveryman of City of London; Burgess of Glasgow; Mem. Royal Order of Scotland; Lord of Manors of Gedding and of Haughley. *Recreations:* shooting, fishing, painting. *Address:* 9 Hyde Park Gate, S.W.7. *T.:* Knightsbridge 1107; Gedding Hall, Nr. Bury St. Edmunds, Suffolk. *T.:* Rattlesden 253; Cardristan, Wigtownshire. *T.:* Newton-Stewart 60. *Clubs:* Junior Carlton, Devonshire, Caledonian, City of London, Hurlingham; Palatine (Liverpool); Bankers (New York). [*Died* 29 *Dec.* 1964.

JARVIS, Sir (Arnold) Adrian, 2nd Bt., *cr.* 1922; M.A., F.C.A.; Chairman: Goldfields of Mysore & General Exploration Ltd.; J. & A. Churchill Ltd.; J. Jarvis & Sons Ltd.; Jarvis Property Co.; Armstrong Whitworth Metal Industries Ltd.; Director: Tor Investment Trust; National Employers Mutual Association Ltd.; National Employers Life Co.; *b.* 25 Oct. 1904; *s.* of Sir John Jarvis, 1st Bt., and Bessie (*d.* 1956), 3rd *d.* of Edwin Woodfield, Enfield; *S.* father, 1950; *m.* 1935, Joan Mary (from whom he obtained a divorce, 1945), *d.* of Cecil F. Brightman, Hampstead, N.W. *Educ.:* Malvern; Pembroke College, Cambridge. Served War of 1939-45 in Middle East, 1940-45 (despatches); Lt.-Col. R.A.O.C. High Sheriff of Surrey, 1950-51. *Heir:* none. *Address:* Admiral's Walk, Pirbright, Surrey. *T.:* Brookwood 2282. *Clubs:* Junior Carlton, Junior Army and Navy; Royal Thames Yacht. [*Died* 21 *Jan.* 1965 (*ext.*).

JARVIS, Very Rev. Ernest David, M.A., D.D.; *b.* 28 Feb. 1888; *s.* of William Jarvis and Isabella Warden; *m.* 1921, Clara Lois, *d.* of Rev. John Reid, Inverness; three *s.* (and one *s.* killed in action, I.A.). *Educ.:* Univ. of St. Andrews; New Coll., Edinburgh. Served in R.F.A., Capt., 1915-19. Minister in: Penicuik, Midlothian, 1920-24; London, 1924-1929; Minister of Wellington Church, Glasgow, 1929-58; Moderator of the General Assembly of the Church of Scotland, 1954-55. Hon. D.D. St. Andrews, 1943; Hon. D.D. Glasgow, 1952. *Publications:* More than Conquerors (Sermons), 1935; "If Any Man Minister" (Warrack Lectures on Preaching, 1950). 1951. *Recreations:* golf, motoring. *Address:* Kingsmuir, Earlsferry, Elie, Fife. *T.:* Elie 165. [*Died* 21 *Jan.* 1964.

JARVIS, Sir John Layton, Kt. 1967; Trainer since 1914; *b.* 28 Dec. 1887; *s.* of William Arthur Jarvis; *m.* 1914, Ethel Edina Leader; one *d.* *Educ.:* Cranleigh School, Surrey. Jockey, 1903-09. Trained Derby winners: Blue Peter, 1939; Ocean Swell, 1944; trained winners of 9 Classic races; headed winning list of Trainers, 1939, 1951 and 1953. *Posthumous Publication:* They're off (autobiog.), 1969. *Recreations:* shooting and cricket. *Address:* Park Lodge, Newmarket, Suffolk. *T.:* Newmarket 2914. *Clubs:* East India and Sports; Subscription Rooms (Newmarket). [*Died* 19 *Dec.* 1968.

JASPERS, Karl, Dr. med.; Professor of Philosophy, Univ. of Basel, 1948-61, Emer. 1961; *b.* 23 Feb. 1883; *s.* of Karl Jaspers, Bank Manager, and Henriette Tantzen; *m.* 1910, Gertrud Mayor. *Educ.:* Humanistisches Gymnasium, Oldenburg; Univs. of Heidelberg, Munich, Berlin, Göttingen. Univ. of Heidelberg: Privat-Dozent, 1913; Professor, 1920-48 (dismissed by the national-socialist government, 1937, reinstated, 1945). Corresp. Member, Heidelberg Academy of Sciences; Honorary Member, Society of German Neurologists and Psychiatrists; Foreign or Corresp. Mem., etc. of several foreign socs. Holds hon. doctorates: Lausanne; Heidelberg; Gent; Paris; Basel. Goethe Prize (Frankfurt), 1947; Friedenspreis des Deutschen Buchhandels, 1958; Erasmus Prize, 1959, etc. *Publications:* Allgemeine Psychopathologie, 1913, 8th edn., 1965; Psychologie der Weltanschauungen, 1919, 5th edn., 1960; Die geistige Situation der Zeit, 1931, 11th edn., 1965; Philosophie (3 vols.), 1931, 3rd edn., 1966; Vernunft und Existenz, 1935, 3rd edn., 1960 Nietzsche, 1936, 3rd edn., 1950; Descartes, 1937, 4th edn., 1966; Existenzphilosophie, 1938, 3rd edn., 1964; Die Schuldfrage, 1946, 4th edn., 1947; Von der Wahrheit, 1947, 2nd edn., 1958; Der Philosophische Glaube, 1948, 5th edn. 1963; Vom Ursprung und Ziel der Geschichte, 1949, 5th edn., 1963; Einführung in die Philosophie, 1950, 10th edn., 1965; Vernunft und Widervernunft in unserer Zeit, 1950, 2nd edn., 1952; Rechenschaft und Ausblick, 1951, 2nd edn., 1958;

Schelling, 1955; Die grossen Philosophen, 1957, 2nd edn., 1959; Philosophie und Weit, 1958, 2nd edn., 1963; die Atombombe und die Zunkunft des Menschen, 1958, 5th edn., 1962; Freiheit und Wiedervereinigung, 1960; Der philosophische Glaube angesichts der Offenbarung, 1962, 2nd edn., 1963; Gesammelte Schriften zur Psychopathologie, 1963; Nikolaus Cusanus, 1964; Kleine Schule des Philosophischen Denkens, 1965 3rd edn., 1967; Wohin treibt die Bundesrepublik?, 1966, 7th edn., 1967; Antwort, 1967; Schicksal und Wille, 1967. Many of his works have been trans. into other languages. *Address:* Austrasse 126, Basel, Switzerland. [*Died* 25 *Feb.* 1969.

JAY, Thomas; member of the staff of Punch since 1917; *b.* 2 Sep. 1887; *m.* Grace Margaret, *e. d.* of John Russell Dun, Douglas, Lanarkshire. *Educ.:* Elementary School and Public Libraries. Drifted into career at office desk; preferred literary career, so drifted out again, 1913; wrote the By the Way column on London Globe for a while; for short period on literary staff Western Daily Press, was later mistaken for a journalist, so left, 1917; President of National Union of Journalists, 1921-22. *Publications:* Knight Errants of Mercy, 1913; The Seaside Guyed, 1920; Believe Me, 1921; Flashlights, 1922; Old Jim Nasium, 1923; Says Mr. Mivvens; Encyclopædia of Fads and Fallacies, 1956. *Plays:* The Man at the Window, 1924; Concerning Mr. Conway, 1925; (joint), A Mixed Foursome, 1926. *Recreations:* failing to catch fish, and listening-in to golfers. *Address:* Bristol Road, Portishead, Somerset. *Club:* Press. [*Died* 19 *Feb.* 1962.

JAYASUNDERA, Sir Ukwatte, K.C.M.G., *cr.* 1955; K.B.E., *cr.* 1953 (C.B.E. 1950); Kt., *cr.* 1951; Q.C.; J.P.; Member of Senate, Ceylon, since 1948; Hon. General Secretary of The United National Party since 1948; Acting Minister of Justice, 1950, 1955 and 1956; *b.* Kalutara, 18 Dec. 1896; *s.* of Don Simon Jayasundera; *m.* Lilian Pusumbawathie Kalupahana (decd.); two *d.* *Educ.:* Nanodaya Coll., Kalutara; Sri Sumangala Coll., Panadura. Enrolled as Proctor of Supreme Court of Ceylon, 1920; Member Urban Council, Kalutara, 1923-37; Vice-Chairman, 1930-31; Chairman, 1932-1934; J.P. 1934, Western Province; Actg. Magistrate and Addtl. District Judge, Kalutara, 1936; Advocate, 1937; called to English Bar, Lincoln's Inn, 1949; K.C. (Ceylon), 1949. *Address:* Lileena, 126 Havelock Road, Colombo, Ceylon. [*Died* 1 *Aug.* 1962.

JEANNERET, Charles-Edouard; *see* Le Corbusier.

JEANNERET, Prof. François Charles Archile; Chancellor of the University of Toronto, 1959-65; Professor Emeritus, and Principal Emeritus of University College, University of Toronto, 1959; *b.* 18 Nov. 1890; *s.* of late Louis Alfred Jeanneret and Phoebe S. Jeanneret; *m.* 1913, Evelyn Frances, *d.* of Dr. Walter W. Geikie; one *s.* (and one *s.* killed on active service, 1945). *Educ.:* Public School, Elmira, Ont.; Collegiate Inst. Kitchener, Ont.; Univ. of Toronto; Univ. of Chicago; Sorbonne, Paris. Head of Dept. of Mod. Langs., Upper Canada Coll., Toronto, Ont. 1912-13; Lectr. in French, Univ. Coll. Toronto, 1913-21; Asst. Prof., 1921-26; Prof. 1926-59; Chm. of Div. I, Sch. of Grad. Studies, Univ. of Toronto, 1947-51; Head of Dept. of French, 1927-59; Principal of Univ. Coll., 1951-59. Principal of Oral French Course, in Quebec, for Ont. Dept. of Educn., 1924-47; Pres. of Ont. Mod. Lang. Assoc.; Hon. degrees: D. ès L. Laval, 1938; Montreal, 1957; LL.D. McMaster, 1956; D.Litt. Newfoundland, 1963. Officier d'Académie, 1948; Medal, Government of France, 1959; Médaille Chauveau of Royal Soc. of Canada, 1960. Canadian delegate to Commonwealth Education Conference, Oxford 1959, Delhi, India 1962, Ottawa 1965. *Publications:* numerous text-books, including Cours Primaire de Français, 1940; Cours Moyen, 1942; Le Français Vivant, 1957. Articles on the Literature and Language of French Canada. *Address:* University of Toronto, Toronto, Canada. *Clubs:* Faculty, York, Canadian, Empire (all in Toronto). [*Died* 15 *Jan.* 1967.

JEANS, Allan; Director, Liverpool Daily Post and Echo, Ltd., C. Tinling and Co. Ltd.; *b.* 1877; *e. s.* of late Sir Alexander Jeans. *Educ.:* Birkenhead School; Rossall. Past Chairman of Press Assocn., and twice Pres. of Newspaper Society; was an original member of Reuters Trust. Hon. LL.D. Liverpool University. J.P. Liverpool. *Address:* Delavor, Noctorum, Birkenhead. *T.:* Claughton (Birkenhead) 6000. *Clubs:* Press (London); Press, Exchange (Liverpool). [*Died* 25 *Oct.* 1961.

JEANS, Major Thomas Kilvington, M.C. 1917; land owner, farmer; *b.* 11 Jan. 1885; *s.* of late H. W. Jeans, Sutton Veny and Knighton Manor, Broadchalke; *m.* 1914, Ethel (*d.* 1959), *d.* of late John Stevens, Broadchalke; two *s.* *Educ.:* privately. Commission R.H.A. (T.F.), 1909; pioneering, S. America, 1910-14; served European War with R.H.A., 1914-19; Major 1916; retd., 1921. Formerly Director of Lloyds Bank Ltd. (and Chairman of Salisbury committee). *Recreations:* hunting, shooting. *Address:* Chalke Pyt House, Broadchalke, Salisbury, Wilts. *T.:* Broadchalke 207. *Club:* Farmers'. [*Died* 6 *June* 1962.

JEFFCOAT, Colonel Algernon Cautley, C.B. 1919; C.M.G. 1916; D.S.O. 1900; late Royal Fusiliers; *b.* 14 Aug. 1877; *y. s.* of late Deputy Surgeon-General J. H. Jeffcoat; *m.* 1st, 1906, Mabel (*d.* 1907), *e. d.* of late William Burrows; 2nd, 1910, Ethel, *d.* of J. R. Temperley; 3rd, 1928, L. L. Daphne, *d.* of late William Edward Stirling Napier; one *d.* *Educ.:* Rugby; R.M.C., Sandhurst. Entered Roy. Inniskilling Fusiliers, 1897; promoted into Royal Fusiliers, 1901; served South Africa, 1899-1902 (despatches twice, Queen's medal 5 clasps, King's medal 2 clasps, D.S.O.); present at battles of Colenso, Spion Kop, Val Krantz, Peter's Hill, and Bergendal; served with 10th Soudanese, Egyptian Army, 1904-6; European War, 1914-18 (despatches five times, Legion of Honour, Croix de Chevalier, C.M.G., Bt. Lt.-Col., C.B., Belgian Croix de Guerre; Mesopotamia Rebellion 1920-21 (Bt. Col.); Embarkation Commandant, Southampton, 1927-31; retd. pay, 1931. *Address:* c/o Lloyds Bank, Ltd., 6 Pall Mall, S.W.1. [*Died* 10 *Dec.* 1963.

JEFFERIS, (Hon.) Maj.-Gen. Sir Millis Rowland, K.B.E., *cr.* 1945 (C.B.E. 1942); M.C. 1923; retd.; *b.* 9 Jan. 1899; *s.* of Rowland John Jefferis; *m.* 1925, Ruth Carolyne Wakefield; three *s.* *Educ.:* Tonbridge School; Royal Military Academy. Joined Royal Engineers, 1918; India, N.W.F.P., 1920-36; commanding 1st Field Squadron R.E., 1937-39; Norway, 1941 (despatches, Norwegian Military Medal); Ministry of Supply, 1942-45; Dep. Engineer-in-Chief, India, 1946; Engineer-in-Chief, Pakistan (with temp. rank of Maj.-Gen.), 1947-50; reverted to Brig., 1950; Chief Superintendent Mil. Engineering Experimental Establishment, 1950-53. A.D.C. to King George VI, 1951-52, to the Queen, 1952-53. *Recreations:* yachting, squash rackets, hunting. *Address:* Fletchers, Bosham, Sussex. *Club:* Royal Ocean Racing. [*Died* 5 *Sept.* 1963.

JEFFERSON, Sir Geoffrey, Kt., *cr.* 1950; C.B.E. 1943; F.R.S. 1947; M.S. (Lond.), F.R.C.S.; F.R.C.P.; Emeritus Professor of Neuro-Surgery, University of Manchester; Consultant Adviser in Neuro-Surgery, Ministry of Health; Cons. Neurological Surgeon, Manchester Royal Infirmary; *b.* 10 April 1886; *s.* of Arthur John Jefferson, M.D.; *m.* Gertrude, *e. d.* of A. C. Flumerfelt, Vict., B.C.; two *s.* one *d.* *Educ.:* Manchester Grammar School; Manchester University. Renshaw Exhibitioner in Physiology; Univ. Prize in Anatomy, London University; Gold Medal at examination for Master of Surgery, London Univ. Surgical Specialist, B.E.F.; sometime Hunterian Professor, Royal College of Surgeons; Saville Orator, 1932; late Examiner in Surgery, Cambridge and Sheffield Univs.; late Hon. Surgeon to the National Hospital, Queen Square, W.C.; Fellow (late President) Assoc. of Surgeons; Hon. Fellow Royal Society of Medicine; Corresponding Member Acad. de Chir., Paris; Hon. Member, American Neurological Assoc., Harvey Cushing Soc., Congress of Neurological Surgeons (U.S.A.), Amer. Acad. Neurosurgery, Canadian Neurological Soc.; Indian Neurological Soc.; Swedish Medical Assoc., Nederlandsche Neuro-chirurgische Studiekring, Nordisk Neurokirurgish Förening, Wiener Gesellsch. d. Aertzen; Mem. Med. Research Council of Privy Council, 1948-52; Chm. Clinical Research Bd., M.R.C., 1953-59. Lister Medallist, Roy. Coll. Surgeons, 1948. Hon. M.Ch. (Dublin) 1948; Hon. LL.D. (Glas., Manchester), Hon. F.R.F.P.S.(G.), Hon. F.R.C.S.I., Hon. F.R.C.S.E.; Hon. F.R.C.S. (Australia); Hon. Fell. Amer. Coll. Surg.; Hon. Mem. Acad. Real das Sciencias, Lisboa, 1956; Hon. Sc.D. (Camb.) 1957; Hon. D.Sc. (Birmingham), 1960; President, First Internat. Congress, Neurological Surgery, Brussels, 1957; Purser Lectr., 1949. Macewen, Marnoch, Cavendish, Godlee, Martin, Balfour, Sherrington, Bowman, Ludwig Mond and Sir Victor Horsley Memorial Lectr. Doyne Medal, 1945; Lister Medal, 1949; Bowman Medal, 1953; Hughlings Jackson Medal, 1955; Fedor Krause Medal, Deutsch. Gesellschaft Neuro-chirurg. Founder Mem. twice President, Society British Neurological Surgeons; President, First International Neurosurgical Congress, Brussels, 1957. *Publications:* Surgery of the Brain, Carson's Operative Surgery; Selected Papers, 1960; numerous papers on neurosurgical and general surgical subjects; Selected papers, 1959. *Recreation:* fishing. *Address:* High Bank, Didsbury, Manchester. *T.:* Didsbury 3677. *Clubs:* Athenæum; Union (Manchester). [*Died* 29 *Jan.* 1961.

JEFFERSON, Rt. Rev. Robert; Bishop of Ottawa, 1939-54, retired; *b.* 11 July 1881; *s.* of Robert Samuel Jefferson and Amelia J. Gardiner; *m.* 1st, 1910, Edith B. Strong; one *d.*; 2nd, 1930, Helen M. Morris. *Educ.:* Belfast, Ireland. Assistant Master Broadway National School, Belfast, Ireland, 1898-1901; Principal of St. Simons Church School, Belfast, Ireland, 1902-06; Math. and Science Master, Westwood Ho!, Edmonton, Alberta, 1906-07; Curate All Saints' Church, Edmonton, Canada, 1907-09; Rector of Christ Church, Edmonton, 1909-12; Incumbent of Montague, Diocese of Ottawa, 1914-16; Rector of Church of the Ascension, Ottawa, 1916-27; Rector St. Matthew's Church, Ottawa, 1927-39; Examining Chaplain to Bishop of Ottawa, 1922-39; Rural Dean of Ottawa, 1923-29; Canon of Christ Church Cathedral, Ottawa, 1926-39; B.A., R.U.I., 1906; B.D. 1915; D.D. 1939 St. John's College, Winnipeg; D.D. Trinity College, Toronto, 1940; D.C.L. Bishop's University, Lennoxville. *Recreations:* boating; P.M. of A.F. and A.M. (Masonic); member of Grand Lodge of Ontario, member of Perfection, Rose Croix and Consistory of Scottish Rite Masons. *Address:* Carp, Ontario, Canada. [*Died* 1 *Jan.* 1968.

JEFFREY, Very Rev. Dr. George Johnstone; Minister Emeritus of Sherbrooke-St. Gilbert's Church, Glasgow, since 1951; *b.* Alloa, Clackmannanshire, 19 Dec. 1881; *s.* of late Archd. Jeffrey; *m.* 1910, Christian (*d.* 1956), *d.* of J. D. Cuthbertson, Glasgow; two *s.* two *d.* *Educ.:* Alloa Acad.; Glasgow University. M.A. 1903; B.D. 1907; Hon. D.D. 1945. Charges in Stewarton, 1908-15; Kirkcudbright, 1915-20; Kilmarnock, 1920-1928; Helensburgh, 1928-37; Glasgow, 1937-51. McNeil Fraser Lecturer in Homiletics, Glasgow University, 1940-45; Warrack Lecturer in Homiletics, 1947-48. Moderator of General Assembly of Church of Scotland, 1952-53. Served European War, 1914-18, in the Scottish Churches Huts. *Publications:* Christian Intimacies, 1940; Christian Resources, 1943; This Grace, wherein we stand, 1948; Editor of The Sacramental Table, 1954; numerous articles in Expository Times, etc. *Recreation:* golf. *Address:* 123 Moss Side Road, Glasgow, S.1. *T.:* Langside 3814. *Club:* Glasgow Theological. [*Died* 18 *March* 1961.

JEFFRIES, Hon. Sir Shirley Williams, Kt., *cr.* 1953; LL.B.; *b.* 28 Feb. 1886; *s.* of William and Mercie Jeffries; *m.* 1st, 1914, Catherine Emma Padman; 2nd, 1935, Berta Marion Saint; one *s.* one *d.* *Educ.:* Prince Alfred College, Adelaide; Adelaide University. Bachelor of Laws, Adelaide University, 1908; Admitted to Bar, 1909. M.P. South Australia, 1927-30, 1933-44 and 1947-53; Attorney-General, Min. of Education, Minister of Industry and Employment in State of South Australia, 1933-44. Trustee, Savings Bank of S.A.; Director: R. J. Finlayson Ltd.; Gillingham & Co. Ltd. *Address:* Pirie Street, Adelaide. [*Died* 13 *Sept.* 1963.

JEFFRIES, Brig. William Francis, C.B.E. 1945; D.S.O. 1918; B.A.; Secretary of Junior Carlton Club, 1938-58, retired; *b.* 1891; *o. s.* of William Carey Jeffries, M.D., of Coolcarron, Co. Cork, and Maud Grace Kennedy of Ballinamultina, Co. Waterford; *m.* 1920, Leila, *er. d.* of Francis Downing of Ballyvelly, Tralee, Co. Kerry; one *s.* *Educ.:* Downside; Trinity College, Cambridge. Travelled in East, 1912-13; 2nd Lieut. Royal Dublin Fusiliers (S.R.), Aug. 1914; served European War, 1914-18, France (wounded battles of Ypres, 1915 and Somme, 1916, despatches twice, D.S.O.); Major, 1917; Secretary H.M. Legation to Vatican, Rome, 1919-20; Intelligence Staff, Dublin and Horse Guards, 1920 and 1921; Major R. of Officers, 1922; Administrative Officer Southern Nigeria, 1923-27; Maj., Gen. Staff, 1938; Col., Gen. Staff, Special Employment, 1940; Brig. C.M.F., 1943. Officer, American Legion of Merit, 1945. *Publication:* Two Undergraduates in the East, 1914. *Address:* Broomfield House, Sunningdale, Berks. *T.:* Ascot 21253. *Club:* Junior Carlton. [*Died* 12 *July* 1969.

JEHANGHIR, Sir Cowasjee, 2nd Bt., *cr.* 1908; G.B.E., *cr.* 1944 (O.B.E. 1918); K.C.I.E., *cr.* 1927 (C.I.E. 1920); J.P.; *b.* 16 Feb. 1879; *s.* of Sir Cowasjee Jehanghir, 1st Bt.; *S.* father, 1934; *m.* 1911, Hilla Hormarji, M.B.E., Kaiser-i-Hind Gold Medal and Bar, *g.d.* of Sir Jamsetjee Jejeebhoy, Bt.; one *s.* one *d.* *Educ.:* St. Xavier's College, Bombay; St. John's College, Cambridge; B.A. 1900. Member of the Bombay Corporation, 1904-21; Chairman of the Standing Committee, 1914-15; Member of the Bombay Improvement Trust; President Bombay Municipal Corporation, 1919-20; Hon. Secretary War Loan Committee, 1917-18; non official member of the Legislative Council, Bombay; Acting Member of the Government of Bombay, in charge of the Revenue Department (6 Dec. 1921-15 July 1922); Member of the Government of Bombay, in charge of the General Department, 1923-28; Member of the Legislative Assembly (Central) elected by City of Bombay, 1930-47; Delegate Round Table Conferences, 1930-31-32;

Delegate World Economic Conference, 1933; represented Central Legislature, Empire Parliamentary Conference, London, 1935; President of National Liberal Federation of India, 1936-37; one of India's representatives at Coronation, 1937: Chairman in the firm of Cowasjee Jehangir & Co (Private) Ltd.; elected President of Parsi Punchayet. *Heir: s.* Hirjee Cowasjee, *b.* 1 Nov. 1915. *Address:* Readymoney House, Malabar Hill, Bombay, India. *Clubs:* St. James'; Ripon, Orient, Willingdon (Bombay). [*Died* 17 *Oct.* 1962.

JEJEEBHOY, Sir Jamsetjee, 6th Bt., *cr.* 1857; B.A. (Cantab.); J.P.; Merchant and Company Director; *b.* 10 May 1909; *s.* of Sir Jamsetjee Jejeebhoy, 5th Bart., K.C.S.I., and Serenebai, *d.* of Jalbhoy A. Sett; *S.* father, 1931, assuming present name in lieu of Cowasji; *m.* 1951, Soonoo, *d.* of Hormusji F. Commissariat, Bombay; three *d. Educ.:* Cathedral and John Connon High School, Bombay; Gonville and Caius Coll., Cambridge. Director: Bombay Dyeing & Mfg. Co. Ltd.; Bombay Burmah Trading Corp. Ltd.; Central Bank of India Ltd., and several other joint stock companies; Chairman: Sir Jamsetjee Jejeebhoy Charity Funds; Sir J. J. Parsee Benevolent Institution; Sir J. J. School of Arts; N. M. Wadia Charities; Bombay Panjrapole and other charitable institutions and educational trusts. Member Bombay Municipal Corp., 1934-35; Dist. Scout Comr., Bombay, 1934; Provincial Scout Comr., Bombay Presidency, 1937; Hon. Presidency Magistrate until 1958. Trustee, Parsee Punchayet Funds & Properties, 1938-48; Trustee, Willingdon Sports Club; one of founders of Progressive Group, Bombay, 1936-39. *Address:* Sett Minar, Peddar Road, Bombay; 372 Koregaon Park, Poona. [*Died* 24 *Sept.* 1968.

JELLICOE, Brigadier-General Richard Carey, C.B.E. 1919; D.S.O. 1918; *b.* 1875; *m.* Sophia Mary, *d.* of late Bt. Colonel F. Howard, R.A.; one *s. Educ.:* Portora and Trinity Coll., Dublin, B.A. 1898; Hon. LL.D., 1919. Univ. Commission in Army, 1900; Adj. A.S.C. (Regular Army), 1905-7; passed London School of Economics, 1908; Adjutant T.F., 1911-14; Staff Captain, War Office, 1914; Deputy Assistant Director, War Office, 1915; A.Q.M.G., 1916; Director of Labour (Temp. Brigadier-General), 1917-20; Assistant Director of Supplies and Transport, Egypt. 1926-30; served S. African War, 1901-2 (medal and four clasps); with G.H.Q. Mediterranean and Egyptian Expeditionary Forces during the European War (despatches five times, Bt. of Lt.-Col., D.S.O., C.B.E., White Eagle of Serbia with swords, Order of the Nile); retired pay, 1930. *Address:* Abbotts Ann, Andover; Hampshire. *T.:* Abbotts Ann 265. [*Died* 16 *March* 1962.

JENKIN, Thomas James, C.B.E. 1950; D.Sc.; Professor-Emeritus, University of Wales; *b.* 8 Jan. 1885; *yr. s.* of David and Sarah Alice Jenkin, Budloy, Henry's Mote Parish, Pembrokeshire; *m.* 1919, Kate Laura, *yr. d.* of James and Maria Griffiths, Lletycaru, nr. Carmarthen; two *s. Educ.:* private and Univ. Coll. of Wales, Aberystwyth. First Agricultural Organiser for Brecon and Radnor, 1914-15; Adviser in Agricultural Botany for North Wales Province at Univ. Coll. of North Wales, Bangor, 1915-19; Adviser in Agricultural Botany, Univ. Coll. of Wales, Aberystwyth, 1919-20; Senior Research Officer, Welsh Plant Breeding Station, U.C.W., Aberystwyth, 1920-1940, Assistant Director, 1940-42, Director, and Professor of Agricultural Botany, U.C.W., Aberystwyth, 1942-50; Consultant Director, Commonwealth Agricultural Bureau for Pastures and Field Crops, 1942-50; Pres. Welsh Black Cattle Soc., 1950-51; Vice-Chm., Council of Nat. Inst. of Agricultural Botany, Cambridge, 1952, 1953; Chairman, 1954, 1955-; Member of N.I.A.B. Council, 1942-; Vice-Pres., 1957-; Hon. Member Swedish Seed Assoc., 1961-; Life Governor of University College of Wales, Aberystwyth (Member of Council, 1956-); Hon. Life Vice-President, Royal Welsh Agricultural Soc., 1957-. First Sir Bryner Jones Gold Medallist, Roy. Welsh Agricultural Soc., 1957. *Publications:* papers and articles in Journal of Genetics and other periodicals; articles in Handbuch der Pflanzenzüchtung, 2nd edn., Vol. IV, 1959. *Address:* Rhoslwyn, Iorwerth Ave., Aberystwyth. *T.:* Aberystwyth 500. *Club:* Farmers'. [*Died* 7 *Nov.* 1965.

JENKINS, Baron (Life-Peer) *cr.* 1959; **David Llewelyn Jenkins,** P.C. 1949; Kt. 1947; a Lord of Appeal in Ordinary, 1959-63, retd.; *b.* Exmouth, S. Devon, 8 Apr. 1899; 3rd *s.* of late Sir John Lewis Jenkins, K.C.S.I., I.C.S., and late Florence Mildred Jenkins; unmarried. *Educ.:* Charterhouse (Scholar); Balliol College, Oxford (Domus Exhibitioner, 1916). Served European War, 12th (S) Bn. Rifle Bde., B.E.F., France, 1918-19; at Oxford, 1919-22; 2nd Craven Scholarship and prox. acc. Ireland Scholarship, 1919; prox. acc. Hertford Scholarship, 1920; 1st Class Honour Mods. Classics, 1920; 2nd Class Greats, 1922; M.A. Oxon; called to Bar, Lincoln's Inn, 1923 (Bencher 1945); K.C. 1938; Temp. Commission, R.A.S.C., 1940 1945; Attorney-General of Duchy of Lancaster, 1946-47; Judge High Court of Justice, Chancery Division, 1947-49; a Lord Justice of Appeal, 1949-59. Hon. Fellow, Balliol Coll., Oxford, 1950. A Governor of Sutton's Hosp. in Charterhouse, 1953-65. *Address:* 24 Ashley Gardens, S.W.1. [*Died* 21 *July* 1969.

JENKINS, Douglas; U.S. diplomat, retired; *b.* on a plantation in South Carolina, 6th Feb. 1880; *s.* of James Joseph Jenkins and Cecile Swinton; *m.* 1st, 1905, Charlotte Keith Furman (*d.* 1915), Charleston, South Carolina; one *s.* one *d.*; 2nd, 1918, Lucia Lesesne Dean, Greenville, South Carolina. *Educ.:* Porter Military Academy, Charleston, S.C. Studied law and admitted to Bar of South Carolina, 1901, but did not practise; entered United States Foreign Service, 1908, as Vice-Consul at Halifax, Nova Scotia; subsequently served at various posts in Europe and Asia, including Consulates General at Canton and Shanghai, China, Hong Kong, and Berlin, Germany; as American Consul at Riga, Russia, during war, was in charge of British interests for some time; Consul-General, 1921; Consul General in London, 1937-39; Minister of U.S.A. to Bolivia, 1939-41; retd. 1942. *Recreations:* shooting and fishing. *Address:* 2257 Central Ave., Augusta, Georgia, U.S.A. [*Died* 18 *Dec.* 1961.

JENKINS, Robert Thomas, C.B.E. 1956; Hon. LL.D (Wales), 1956; D.Litt. (Wales), 1939; M.A. (Cantab), 1909; F.S.A.; Professor of Welsh History, 1945-48 (Head of the Department, 1930), University College of North Wales, Bangor; Warden of Guild of Graduates of the University of Wales, 1940-43; Medallist of Hon. Soc. of Cymmrodorion, 1953; *b.* Liverpool, 31 August 1881; *m.* 1st, 1907, Mary Davies (*d.* 1946), Aberystwyth; 2nd, 1947, Myfanwy Wyn Williams, Aberdare. *Educ.:* Bala Grammar School; University College of Wales, Aberystwyth; Trinity College, Cambridge. Assistant Master, Llandysul County School; Brecon County School; Cardiff High School for Boys (Senior History Master, 1917-30). *Publications:* Hanes Cymru yn y Ddeunawfed Ganrif (A History of Wales in the Eighteenth Century), 1928; Yr Apêl at Hanes (The Appeal to History), 1930; Hanes Cymru yn y xix Ganrif, Vol. I. (1789-1843), 1933; The Moravian Brethren in North Wales, 1938; contributor to History of

Caermarthenshire, Vol. II., 1939; Orinda, 1943; (with Helen M. Ramage) The History of the Hon. Society of Cymmrodorion, 1952; Edrych yn ôl (autobiography), 1968; other books and papers, mostly in Welsh; Joint Editor, University of Wales Bibliography of Welsh History, 1931; Editor of Cymmrodorion Dictionary of Welsh Biography (Welsh Edn.), 1953, (English Edn.), 1959; contrib. to Encyclopædia Britannica, 1955. *Recreations:* travel, study of architecture. *Address:* Rhuddallt, Siliwen Road, Bangor, Caerns. *T.:* 3473.

[*Died* 11 *Nov.* 1969.

JENKINS, Romilly James Heald, M.A.; F.S.A.; Professor of Byzantine History and Director of Studies, Harvard University Dumbarton Oaks Research Library and Collection, Washington, D.C., U.S.A., since 1960; Member of Managing Committee, American School of Classical Studies, and Sub-Committee for Gennadius Library, Athens; Corresponding Member German Archæological Institute, Berlin; *b.* 10 Feb. 1907; *m.* 1932, Juliette Céline Haegler; two *s.* *Educ.:* The Leys School; Cambridge University; Davies Univ. Scholar (Classics), 1928; Chancellor's Classical Medallist, 1929. Studied at British School of Archæology at Athens, 1930-34; Lewis-Gibson Lectr. in Modern Greek, Cambridge Univ., 1936-46; Foreign Office, 1939-45; Koraës Professor of Modern and Byzantine Greek, University of London, King's College, 1946-60; and Hon. Lecturer in Classical Archæology, King's College, 1950-60. *Publications:* Dedalica, a Study of Dorian Plastic Art in the VIIth Cent. B.C., 1935; Dionysios Solomós, 1940; Perachora: The Terracottas, 1940; (with G. Moravcsik) Constantini Porphyrogeniti De Administrando Imperio, 1949; Ed. and part-author of Commentary to De Administrando Imperio, 1962; The Dilessi Murders, 1961; Byzantium and Byzantinism, 1963; Byzantium: The Imperial Centuries A.D. 610-1071, 1966. *Address:* 1703 Thirty-second Street, Washington, D.C. 20007, U.S.A. *T.:* ADams 2-3101; 8 Rose Walk, Radlett, Herts. *T.:* Radlett 5580. *Club:* Athenæum.

[*Died* 30 *Sept.* 1969.

JENKINS, Sir William (Albert), Kt., *cr.* 1938; Principal of Wm. A. Jenkins & Co., Swansea, Wholesale Coal and Coke Factors; Shipbroker; *b.* Swansea; *s.* of Daniel and Elizabeth Ann Jenkins; *m.* 1906, Beatrice (*d.* 1967), *d.* of Frederick and Elizabeth Tyler, Pirbright, Surrey. M.P. (N.L.) Counties of Breconshire and Radnorshire, 1922-24; J.P. Co. Glamorgan, 1928; Ex-Chairman, Bench of Magistrates, Gower Petty Sessional Division; Member Swansea Borough Council, 1927-54; Mayor, 1947-1949. Pres. and Custodian Trustee, S.W. Wales Savings Bank; President: Roy. Welsh Agric. Soc., 1949; Swansea and Central Wales Adult Deaf and Dumb Mission; also Deaf and Dumb Regional Association for Wales; Swansea Business Club; Borough of Swansea Order of St. John Council. F.I.C.S. K.St.J.; Knight Class 1, Order of Dannebrog (Denmark), 1933; Gold Cross Royal Order George I (Greece), 1938; Chevalier de la Légion d'Honneur (France), 1949. *Address:* Redhill, Gower Road, Swansea. *T.A.:* Business, Swansea. *T.:* 22218. [*Died* 23 *Oct.* 1968.

JENKINSON, Sir (Charles) Hilary, Kt., *cr.* 1949; C.B.E. 1943; M.A., LL.D. (Aberdeen), F.S.A.; Hon. Fellow, Univ. Coll., London; Mem. Royal Commission on Historical MSS.; Hon. Vice-Pres. Conseil Internat. des Archives, Vice-Pres. British Records Association; President Society of Archivists, Surrey Record Society and Surrey Archæological Soc.; Vice-Pres. (Pres. 1954-55) Jewish Hist. Soc. of England; Mem. Records and Ancient Monuments Committee, Surrey C.C., and Records Committee, West Sussex C.C.; Hon. Member Indian Historical MSS. Commission; *y. s.* of William Wilberforce Jenkinson; *m.* 1910, Alice Violet (*d.* 1960), *d.* of Andrew Knox Rickards. *Educ.:* Dulwich Coll.; Pembroke College, Cambridge. 1st class Classical Tripos, 1904; Civil Service Examination, 1905; Public Record Office, 1906; Maitland Lecturer, Cambridge, 1911-35, 1938, and 1949; Lecturer, London School of Economics, 1913; served as Captain R.G.A. in France and Belgium, 1916-18; General Staff (Education), 1918-20; Lecturer, King's College and Univ. Coll., London, 1920-25; Reader in Diplomatic and Archives, University of London, 1925-47; Hon. Secretary, British Records Association from foundation (1932) to 1947; Hon. Sec. and Editor, Surrey Archæological Society, 1909-24. Acted as Adviser on Archives to War Office, 1943-45, and spent some months in Italy, 1944, to organise work of Protection of Italian Archives; similar work for Western Germany and Austria, 1944-45; visited Nuremberg to advise on Archives of Tribunal, 1946; Deputy Keeper of the Records and Keeper of the Land Revenue Records, 1947-54; Mem. of Cttee. of Expert Archivists (U.N.E.S.C.O.), Paris, 1948; reported on Archives to Govt. of Malta, 1944, and Jamaica, 1950. *Publications:* Court Hand Illustrated (with C. Johnson), 1915; Palæography and the Study of Court Hand, 1915; Financial Records of the Reign of King John (in Magna Carta Commem. Essays), 1917; 133, the War Service of a Siege Battery, 1919; Manual of Archive Administration, 1922 (new edition 1937); The Later Court Hands in England, 1927; Calendar of the Plea Rolls of the Exchequer of the Jews, 1929; Select Pleas in the Exchequer, 1932; British Section of International Guide to Archives (Inst. Intern'le de Coop'n Intellectuelle), 1934; Italian Archives during the War and at its close (with H. E. Bell), 1947; Brit. Rec. Assoc. Memoranda Nos. 1-10 (1940-1948), etc.; The English Archivist, a New Profession (Inaugural Lecture at Univ. Coll. Lond.), 1948; Introduction to Pub. Rec. Off. Catalogue of Exhibition of Treaties, 1948; Guide to the Pub. Records, Part I, 1949; Domesday Re-bound, 1954; Guide to Seals in the Pub. Rec. Off., 1954. Article on Great Seal (Roy. Soc. Arts Medal), 1953; other articles in English Historical Review; History; Archæologia; Antiquaries' Journal; Bibl. Soc. Transactions; American Archivist; Archivalische Zeitschrift, Archivum, etc. *Address:* Arun House, Horsham, Sussex. *T.:* 5672. *Club:* Athenæum.

[*Died* 5 *March* 1961.

JENNINGS, Sir Ivor; *see* Jennings, Sir W. I.

JENNINGS, Sir Roland, Kt., *cr.* 1954; F.C.A., J.P.; chartered accountant; J.P. Co. Durham; *b.* 1894; *m.* 1919, Hannah H., *d.* of John T. Peacock, Sunderland; two *s.* two *d.* M.P. (U.) Sedgefield Div. of Durham, 1931-35; Hallam Div. of Sheffield, 1939-59. *Address:* 28 Thornhill Terrace, Sunderland, Co. Durham. *T.:* 56006. *Club:* Sunderland. [*Died* 5 *Dec.* 1968.

JENNINGS, Sir (William) Ivor, K.B.E. 1955; Kt. 1948; Q.C. 1949; Litt.D. (Cantab.); LL.D. (Lond.); Hon. LL.D. (Univs. of Bristol, Southampton, Ceylon, Leeds, Belfast, Hong Kong, Manchester); Hon. Docteur (Paris); F.B.A.; Master, Trinity Hall, Camb., since 1954; Downing Professor of the Laws of England, Univ. of Cambridge, since Oct. 1962; *b.* 16 May 1903; *s.* of late William and Eleanor J. Jennings; *m.* 1928, Helena Konsalik; two *d.* *Educ.:* Queen Elizabeth's Hospital; Bristol Grammar School; St. Catharine's College, Cambridge (Hon. Fellow, 1950-). Whewell Scholar, 1926; Holt Scholar of Gray's Inn, 1925; Barstow Scholar, 1926; Certificate of Honour and Studentship,

1928; called to Bar, 1928; Lecturer in Law, University of Leeds, 1925-29; Lecturer in English Law, London School of Economics, 1929-30; Reader in English Law in the Univ. of London, 1930-40; Professor of Political Science, University of British Columbia, 1938-39; Principal, Ceylon University College, 1940-42; Waynflete Lecturer, Magdalen College, Oxford, 1948-49; Visiting Professor, Australian Nat. Univ., 1950. Deputy Civil Defence Commissioner, Ceylon, 1942-45; Chm., Ceylon War Publicity Cttee., 1942-45; Vice-Chancellor, Univ. of Ceylon, 1942-55. Chairman, Ceylon Social Services Commission, 1944-46; Member, Commission on University Education in Malaya, 1947; Member, Commission on the Ceylon Constitution, 1948; President Inter-Univ. Bd. of India, 1949-50; Constitutional Adviser and Chief Draftsman, Pakistan, 1954-55; Chm. Royal Commn. on Common Land, 1955-58; Mem. Malayan Constitutional Commn., 1956-57; Chm. Roy. Univ. of Malta, Commn., 1957-61; Vice-Chancellor, Univ. of Cambridge, 1961-63. Master of the Bench of Gray's Inn, 1958. Nepalese Order of Right Hand of Gurkha (First Class), 1959. *Publications:* The Poor Law Code, 1930, 2nd ed. 1937; Principles of Local Government Law, 1931, 3rd ed. 1947; Law relating to Town and Country Planning, 1932, 2nd ed. 1946; The Law and the Constitution, 1933, 5th ed. 1959; Law relating to Local Authorities, 1933; Parliamentary Reform, 1934; Law of Housing, 1935, 2nd ed. 1936; Cabinet Government, 1936, 3rd ed. 1958; Law of Public Health, 1936; Parliament, 1939, 2nd ed. 1958; Constitutional Laws of the Commonwealth, 3rd ed. 1956; Law of Food and Drugs (jt.), 1939; A Federation for Western Europe, 1940; British Constitution, 4th ed. 1961; The Economy of Ceylon, 1948, 2nd ed. 1951; The Constitution of Ceylon, 1950, 3rd ed. 1953; The Commonwealth in Asia, 1951; Some Characteristics of the Indian Constitution, 1954; The Approach to Self-Government, 1956; The Queen's Government, 1954; Constitutional Problems in Pakistan, 1957; Problems of the New Commonwealth, 1958; Das Britische Regierungsystem, 1958; Party Politics, Vol. I, 1960, Vols. II 1961, III, 1962. *Recreation:* books. *Address:* The Lodge, Trinity Hall, Cambridge. *T.:* Cambridge 52396. *Club:* United University. [*Died* 19 *Dec.* 1965.

JENSEN, Sir John Klunder, Kt., *cr.* 1950; O.B.E. 1938; retired from Service of Commonwealth Government, Australia; Company Director; *b.* 20 March 1884; *s.* of Thomas Henry and Margaret Jensen, Bendigo, Vic.; *m.* 1911, Maria Ruby, *d.* of G. S. Gordon, Sydney, N.S.W.; one *s.* three *d.* (and one *s.* decd.). *Educ.:* St. Kilians School, Bendigo (to 11 years, but thereafter self-educated). Telegraph Messenger, Postal Dept., 1897; in Mil. Ordnance Dept., 1900-1906; in Central Defence Admin., 1906; sent to U.S.A. for trg. munitions admin., 1910; Accountant Govt. Small Arms Factory, 1911; Senior Clerk, Central Defence Admin., 1914; sent to U.S.A. and England for further trg. in munitions organisation as Sec. Austr. Arsenal, 1918; remained in England until 1921 in charge matters relating to Munitions Supply; Sec. Munitions Supply Bd. in Australia, 1921 (Chm. Defence Contract Bd. for Army, Navy and Air Force supplies, 1923-39); Member Munitions Supply Bd., 1936; Controller of Munitions Supply, 1937-1939; Asst. Sec., Depts. of Supply and of Munitions, 1939-41; Sec., Dept. of Munitions (later Dept. of Supply and Development), 1942-49; retired from Commonwealth Public Service, 1949. Chm. Secondary Industries Commn., 1943-50; Member Immigration Planning Council, 1949-60; Fellow (1929) and Life Mem. (1949) Australasian Inst. of Cost Accountants; Fellow and Life Mem. (1966), Australian Soc. of Accountants; Fell. Australian Inst. of Management, 1953; Fell. Inst. of Directors, 1960. *Recreations:* reading, writing, wandering in the remote places of the bush and mountains. *Address:* 31 Chrystobel Crescent, Hawthorn, Victoria 3122, Australia. [*Died* 20 *Feb.* 1970.

JEPHSON, Brigadier Maurice Denham, C.B.E. 1940; *b.* 28 May 1890; *y. s.* of late Jermy F. Jephson; *m.* 1922, Eileen May, *y. d.* of late Thomas Gallaher, J.P., Belfast; no *c.* *Educ.:* King's School, Canterbury. Norfolk Regt. 1911-33; 5th Royal Norfolk Regt. T.A., 1934-39; Colonel (temp. Brig.) T.A. 1939, retired, 1950. *Recreations:* fishing and shooting. *Address:* Mallow Castle, Co. Cork. *T.:* Mallow 21469. *Clubs:* Army and Navy; Kildare Street (Dublin). [*Died* 24 *March* 1968.

JERICHOW, Herbert Peter Andreas, Commander (1st cl.) of the Dannebrog, 1960; Hon. K.B.E. 1956; Director Tuborg Breweries, Copenhagen; *b.* 4 July 1889; *er. s.* of P. A. Jerichow and Dagmar J., *née* Thiedemann; *m.* 1926, Eva J. (*née* Dessau) (marriage dissolved); one *s.* one *d.*; *m.* 1941, Grethe J. (*née* Bjerregaard); one *s.* one *d.* *Educ.:* Metropolitan School, Copenhagen; University of Copenhagen. Bachelor of Law, 1913. Bankers L. Behrens and Söhne, Hamburg, 1914; London City and Midland Bank, Ltd., 1914-15; British Bank of Northern Commerce Ltd., 1915-21; Continental and Overseas Trading Co. Ltd., Paris, 1921-25; Managing Director, Gyldendal Publishing Co. Ltd., Copenhagen, 1925-31; joined management The United Breweries, Copenhagen, 1931; Man. Dir. 1937-59; Chairman, Danish Brewers Assoc., 1946-1959; Chairman State Export Guarantee Committee, 1947-59; President, Danish British Society; chairman and member of several industrial and cultural bodies. Mem. F.R.S.A. Commander, Order of Wasa, Sweden, Order of St. Olav, Norway; Officer of the Legion of Honour, France, etc. *Recreation:* Art collecting. *Address:* Hellerupلund Alle 15, Hellerup, Denmark. *T.:* Hellerup 4315. *Clubs:* Special Forces, Danish. [*Died* 17 *Aug.* 1967.

JERRAM, Lieut.-Col. Charles Frederic, C.M.G. 1919; D.S.O. 1917; Lt.-Col., Royal Marines; recalled for service, 1940; *b* 13 Nov. 1882; *s.* of C. S. Jerram, M.A., and M. F., *d.* of E. Knight of Pap Castle, Cumberland; *m.* 1912, Sibyl V. G. (*d.* 1953), *d.* of Dr. J. G. O'Neill, Auckland, N.Z.; one *s.* (and one killed on active service, 1944) two *d.* *Educ.:* Hillside, Godalming. 2nd Lt. R.M.L.I. 1901; Lieut. 1903; posted to Plymouth Division; served in H.M.S. Hogue and Suffolk in Mediterranean under late Earl Beatty; H.M.S. Astraea and Flora in China (received thanks of Admiralty for reconnaissance work in China); Capt. 1912; served European War: H.M.S. Euryalus in North Sea until Nov. 1914; Staff Capt. Royal Marines Brigade, Dec. 1914; Brigade Major, June 1915; served in the action of Kum Kaleh, Feb. 1915; landed Gallipoli 26 April 1915, and served during whole campaign with R. Naval Division (despatches); to France, May 1916; Brig. Maj. 190th Inf. Bde. July 1916; served with R.N. Division at the Battle of the Ancre (D.S.O., despatches); G.S.O. (2) 31st Division, 1917 (despatches twice); G.S.O. (1) 46th Division, 1918 (C.M.G., despatches); retired list, 1929. *Recreation:* small boat sailing. *Address:* Pengwedhen, Helford, Helston, Cornwall. *T.:* Manaccan 215 [*Died* 12 *Jan.* 1969.

JERROLD, Douglas; Author and Publisher; formerly Chairman, Eyre and Spottiswoode (Publishers) Ltd.; Director, Eyre and Spottiswoode Ltd., etc.; *b.* Scarborough, 3 August 1893; *s.* of S. D. Jerrold; *m.* 1919, Eleanor, *d.* of Henry Arnold. *Educ.:* Westminster; New Coll., Oxford (Mod. Hist. Schol.). Served with the R.N. Div., Gallipoli and France; Ministry of Food, 1918-20; Treasury, 1920-23. Ed. English Review, 1930-36; Ed., New English Review, 1945-1950. *Publications:* The Royal Naval Division; The War on Land, 1914-18; England, 1935; They that Take the Sword, 1936; Georgian Adventure, 1937; The Necessity of Freedom, 1938; Britain and Europe, 1900-40, 1941; An Introduction to the History of England, 1949; England, Past, Present and Future, 1950; The Lie about the West, 1956; *novels:* The Truth about Quex; Storm over Europe. *Address:* 130 Marsham Court, Marsham St., S.W.1. *Clubs:* Athenæum, Garrick, Authors', Pratt's. [*Died* 21 *July* 1964.

JERVIS, Col. Herbert Swynfen, M.C.; Hon. R.C.M.; *b.* 14 April 1878; 2nd *s.* of late Col. W. S. Jervis; *m.* 1907, Marie T. Donlea (*d.* 1935); (one *s.* Capt. J. S. Jervis, S. Staffs. Regt. killed in action Normandy 1944) two *d.* *Educ.:* Oxford Military College; R.M.C. Sandhurst. Joined Royal Munster Fusiliers, 1898; commanded 2nd Batt., 1919-22; served on the staff in Lancashire, A.H.Q. India and Quetta, India; Colonel, 1923; served S. African War, 1899-1902; European War, 1914-1918 (M.C.); Chevalier of the Order of the Crown of Roumania; Commanded 125th Lancashire Fusilier Bde. (T.A.), 1930-31; Commandant Royal Military School of Music, Kneller Hall, 1931-35; retired pay, 1935; Pres. Officers' Dinner Club Royal Munster Fusiliers; Pres. Old Comrades Association R.M.F.; Hon. Vice-Pres. British Red Cross Society (Hon. Life Member), Surrey. Distinguished War Service Certificate, B.R.C.S. *Publications:* The 2nd Munsters in France; A Regimental Calendar. *Recreations:* music, gardening, and golf. *Address:* Munster, Tilford, Farnham, Surrey. [*Died* 4 *Sept.* 1965.

JERVIS, John Johnstone, M.D., D.P.H.; Emer. Professor of Public Health, Leeds Univ., since 1947; M.O.H., City of Leeds and Professor of Public Health, University of Leeds, 1919-47; retired 1947; Member Examining Boards, General Nursing Council and F.R.S.H.; *b.* Stobo, Peeblesshire, 1882; *s.* of late Andrew Jervis, schoolmaster, Stobo, and Katherine Anderson Johnstone, Moffat, Dumfriesshire; *m.* Dr. Agnes Wright Andrew, M.A., M.B., Ch.B.; three *s.* one *d.* *Educ.:* Peebles Boro and County High School; Edinburgh Univ.; U.C., London. Held various resident appointments in hospitals in England; Asst. M.O.H. and Asst. School Medical Officer, Croydon; Asst. Medical Officer for Maternity and Child Welfare in Leeds, 1915; Deputy M.O.H., 1917; member of Central Midwives Board, 1921-31; External Examiner in Public Health, Universities of Sheffield, 1926-1930 and 1936-39, Edinburgh, 1930-33, Birmingham, 1938-40, Durham, 1947-49, and Leeds, 1948-50; External Examiner in Hygiene for the Yorkshire Training Colleges, 1939-41; F.R.S.H., 1926, Member of its Council; Member Central Medical War Committee, and Sec. Local Med. War Cttee., 1942-48; Pres. Soc. of Medical Officers of Health, 1946-47; Vice-Pres. Soc. of Medical Officers of Health, 1947-50; Vice-Pres. National Smoke Abatement Soc.; Regional Medical Officer, Ministry of Health; retired 1952; Chairman Leeds Division B.M.A.; Chairman of Hosp. Management Committee, No. 22 (Group B), Leeds; Medical Referee, Leeds Crematorium. *Publications:* Annual Reports of the City of Leeds, 1916-45; papers to medical journals. *Recreations:* golf, gardening. *Address:* 45 The Crescent, Adel, Leeds 16. *T.:* Leeds 678927. [*Died* 9 *April* 1969.

JESPER, Col. Norman McKay, D.S.O. 1940; O.B.E. 1941; M.C.; E.R.D.; retired as Chief Officer of Police, British Transport Commission (1956-58); *b.* York, 21 June 1896; *s.* of Charles Jesper, Gen. Goods Manager, North Eastern Railway; *m.* Evelyn Veronica Alexander; one *d.* *Educ.:* Oundle. Served Grenadier Guards, 1915-18 (wounded twice, despatches, M.C.). Joined N.E. Railway as traffic apprentice and held various appointments. Joined Supplementary Reserve, 1925, and went to France as dep. asst. Director of Docks, 1939. Joined H.Q. Staff, 1940; Director of Northern Ports during evacuation through Dunkirk (D.S.O.); held the following appointments: A.Q.M.G. Movements, N. Ireland, Greece (O.B.E.); Canal Area, Egypt, A.Q.M.F. Movements and Transportation, Suez and Sudan; Col. Movements and Transportation, W. Africa and N. Africa (despatches). Demobilised (with rank of Col.) 1945. Returned to L.N.E.R. *Recreation:* golf. *Address:* 17 Chatsmore Crescent, Goring-by-Sea, Sussex. *T.:* Goring-by-Sea 43485. *Club:* English-Speaking Union. [*Died* 9 *Sept.* 1968.

JESSOP, Frederic Hubert; solicitor; *b.* 7 April 1882; *s.* of late Joe Jessop; *m.* 1913, Dorothy May (*d.* 1959), *d.* of Samuel Watson; one *s.* two *d.* *Educ.:* Huddersfield Coll.; Yorkshire College, Leeds (at that time a constituent college of Victoria University, Manchester). Admitted solicitor, 1904. Council Law Soc., 1933-67; President: West Wales Law Society, 1932-35 and 1939-58; Associated Law Societies of Wales, 1939-55; Law Society, 1954-55. *Recreations:* travel, reading and motoring. *Address:* Nantcaerio Hall, Llanbadarnfawr, Aberystwyth. *T.:* Aberystwyth 3532. *Club:* National Liberal. [*Died* 12 *March* 1969.

JEWSON, Dorothy; *b.* 1884; *d.* of Alderman George Jewson, J.P.; *m.* 1936, R. Tanner Smith (*d.* 1939); *m.* 1945, Campbell Stephen, M.P. (*d.* 1947). *Educ.:* Norwich High School; Girton College, Cambridge, B.A., M.P. (Lab.) Norwich, 1923-24; Member of National Administrative Council of I.L.P., 1925-35; Member of Norwich City Council, 1927-36. *Address:* Riverdene Cottage, 49 Low Road, Lower Hellesdon, Norwich, Norfolk. [*Died* 29 *Feb.* 1964.

JEWSON, Percy William, J.P.; retired as Chairman and Director of Jewson and Sons Limited, Timber Importers, and Co., 1962; *b.* 16 February 1881; *s.* of John William Jewson, Norwich; *m.* 1908, Ethel Marion, *d.* of Edward Boardman, F.R.I.B.A.; two *s.* one *d.* *Educ.:* Privately. M.P. (L.Nat.) for Great Yarmouth, 1941-45; Lord Mayor of Norwich, 1934-35; Pres. Norwich Chamber of Commerce, 1940-46; held a Commn. in European War, 1914-18 in Worcestershire Regt. and served in France and Belgium (wounded); interested in Religious Education and work among young people; Pres. Westhill Training Coll., 1944-1947. *Recreations:* lawn tennis, represented Norfolk for many years; formerly Chm. and now an Hon. Life Vice-Pres. of L.T.A. *Address:* Horsford Hall, Norwich. *T.A.:* Jewson, Norwich. *T.:* St. Faith's 248. *Clubs:* Reform, Lansdowne, All England Lawn Tennis; Norfolk (Norwich). [*Died* 18 *April* 1962.

JIVANJEE, Sir Yusufali Alibhai Karimjee, Kt. 1958; *b.* Zanzibar, 1882; *m.*; four *s.* five *d.* Spent early life in Zanzibar; subsequently came to Tanganyika and became a Senior Director of Karimjee Jivanjee group of companies; has travelled extensively in Europe, India and the Far East. Founder of the Yusufali Charitable Trust, 1943. Holds Brilliant Star of Zanzibar and Turkish decorations. *Address:* P.O. Box 51, Dar es Salaam, Tanzania. [*Died* 17 *March* 1966.

JOBLING, Geoffrey Lionel; Hon. Mr. Justice Jobling; Judge of High Court of

Lagos and Southern Cameroons, 1955-57, retd.; *b.* 24 Oct. 1889; *m.* 1945, Jane Kindness. *Educ.:* Australia and South Africa, Barrister-at-Law, Gray's Inn, 1926. Colonial Legal Service since 1915. Served European War, in South Africa and German South-West Africa, 1914-15; R.A.F., 1917-19. *Recreations:* golf, fishing. *Club:* Royal Commonwealth Society. [*Died* 22 *Sept.* 1965.

JOHN XXIII, His Holiness Pope, Angelo Giuseppe Roncalli, D.D.; elected Pontiff of the Roman Catholic Church October 1958; *b.* Sotto il Monte, near Bergamo, Italy, 25 November 1881. Studied at diocesan seminary, Bergamo, and in Rome (degree in Theology). Ordained, 1904; Secretary to the Bishop of Bergamo, 1905-1914 and 1918-21; Army Chaplain during European War, 1914-18; in charge of reorganisation of work for Propagation of the Faith in Rome, 1921-25; consecrated Titular Archbishop of Areopoli, 1925; Apostolic Visitor, later Delegate, in Bulgaria, 1923-34; Apostolic Delegate in Athens and Turkey, 1934-44; Apostolic Nuncio in France, 1945-1953; Permanent Observer of the Holy See to U.N.E.S.C.O., 1952; created a Cardinal, 1953; Patriarch of Venice, 1953-58. Balzan Peace Prize, 1963; U.S. Presidential Medal of Freedom, 1963 (posthumous). *Posthumous Publication:* Journal of a Soul: the Diary of Pope John XXIII, trans. Dorothy White, 1965. *Address:* The Vatican. [*Died* 3 *June* 1963.

JOHN, Augustus E., O.M. 1942; R.A. 1928 (A.R.A. 1921); LL.D., Cardiff, 1933; Member, New English Art Club; Fellow of University College, London; President, Gypsy Lore Society, 1937; President, Society of Mural Painters; *b.* 1878. Trustee of Tate Gallery, 1933-41; resigned from R.A., Royal Cambrian Academy, and Royal Society of Portrait Painters, 1938; re-elected R.A. 1940; R.P., 1939 (President, 1948-53). Exhibition, Diploma Gallery, Royal Academy, 1954. Associé, Académie Royale de Belgique, 1946; Hon. Member, London Group. Freeman of Tenby, 1959. *Publications:* Chiaroscuro, 1952; Finishing Touches, 1964 (posthumous). *Address:* Fryern Court, Fordingbridge, Hants. *T.:* Fordingbridge 2273. *Clubs:* Savage (Hon. Member), St. James', Chelsea Arts. [*Died* 31 *Oct.* 1961.

JOHNS, Charles Rowland; Hon. Consultant on dogs and road safety to Royal Society for the Prevention of Accidents, 1947; Secretary National Canine Defence League, 1909-1946; then became campaign Director to League; Journalist and Author; *b.* Holyhead, 1882; *s.* of late R. J. Johns, Journalist, Bahama House, Holyhead; *m.* 1909, Jessie, *y. d.* of Henry Harvey, Leicester; one *s.* one *d.* *Educ.:* Holyhead and Liverpool. Several years on Welsh newspapers; British Delegate to American Humane Convention, San Francisco, 1932, Washington, 1935; and St. Louis, 1938; Hon. Vice-Pres., American Humane Education Soc. Awarded Silver Meritorious Service (Queen's) Medal, R.S.P.C.A. 1935, Argus Medal, National Canine Defence League, 1947. *Publications:* Mind You; Aberdeen Mac; Dog Stealing; Dogs You'd like to Meet; Pitiful story of Performing Animals; Let Dogs Delight; Puppies, All Sorts of Dogs; Let's Talk of Dogs; Lucky Dogs; So you Like Dogs; Rowland Johns Dog Book, 1933; Every Dog Its Day, 1934; Jock, King George's Pony, 1936; Dogs for Profit, 1937; 250 Questions answered about Dogs, 1944; Dog-owners' Treasury, 1947; and many articles in leading journals; *Editor*, Our Friend the Dog Series (38 books on breeds), 1932-59. *Recreations:* gardening, walking. *Address:* 8 Waverley Road, Bognor Regis, Sussex. *Clubs:* Rotary; 40 Years Humane Service (U.S.A.). [*Died* 29 *March* 1961.

JOHNS, Horace John, C.B. 1948; M.B.E. 1933; Member White Fish Authority since 1953; *b.* 18 Feb. 1890; *m.* 1919, Esmeralda Murray; one *s.* one *d.* *Educ.:* Latymer Upper School, Hammersmith. Secretary of several Committees and Commissions; Minister's Private Secretary, 1937-1938; formerly Under-Secretary, Ministry of Agriculture and Fisheries; Fisheries Secretary, 1950-52. *Publication:* Fertilisers and Feeding Stuffs Act, 1926, 1928. *Address:* Windyridge, Ninfield Rd., Bexhill, Sussex. *T.:* Ninfield 326. [*Died* 8 *Jan.* 1961.

JOHNS, John Francis, C.M.G. 1931; *b.* 20 Nov. 1885; *s.* of late Rev. Thomas Johns, Manor Owen, Pembrokeshire; *m.* 1921, Nora Lettice, *o. c.* of late C. G. Liddle; one *s.* Entered the Far Eastern Consular Service as a Student Interpreter in Siam, 1907; a second class assistant, 1909; a first class assistant with local rank of Vice-Consul, 1911; has acted at various consular posts in Siam and Indo-China; Vice-Consul at Puket, 1914; Consul at Senggora, 1921; H.B.M. Consul General and first Secretary of Legation, Bangkok, Siam, 1924; acted as Chargé d'Affaires at Bangkok in each year, 1924-32; retired, 1933. *Address:* St. Giles, Uzmaston Road, Haverfordwest, Pembs. *T.:* Haverfordwest 2837. [*Died* 30 *July* 1967.

JOHNS, Captain William Earl; retired; *b.* 5 Feb. 1893; *s.* of William Richard Eastman Johns, Hertford. *Educ.:* Hertford Grammar School. Entered Army, 1913; served European War, 1914-18, Middle East; transferred R.F.C., 1916, and served continuously on flying duties home and abroad until 1930 when retired to take up aviation journalism. Founder Editor Popular Flying, 1932, and Flying, 1935; gave up both in 1939 to lecture to air cadets and develop a British-type character for advanced juvenile fiction, who became well known as "Biggles", of whose exploits more than 80 books have been published (trans. into 17 languages). During War of 1939-45 worked for M.O.I. *Publications:* Fighting Planes and Aces, 1932; The Air V.C.s, 1934; Milestones of Aviation, 1935. and 200 fiction books with aviation background; many short stories (adult) for British and American publications (some dramatised and broadcast). *Recreations:* travel, salmon fishing, shooting. *Address:* Park House, Hampton Court. *T.:* Teddington Lock 2511. [*Died* 21 *June* 1968.

JOHNSON, Charles, C.B.E. 1951; M.A. (Oxon); F.B.A. 1934; F.S.A. 1920 (Vice-Pres. 1938-41); F.R.Hist.S. (Hon. Vice-Pres. 1943); *b.* Newcastle on Tyne, 2 May 1870; *s.* of Edmund White Johnson, timber merchant, and Elizabeth Hannah Herring; *m.* 1907, Mabel Catherine Rudd (*d.* 1947); no *c.*; *m.* 1950, Violet Margaret, *e. d.* of late Arthur Mutrie Shepherd, Boar's Hill, Oxford. *Educ.:* Giggleswick School; Trinity College, Oxford. Junior Clerk in Public Record Office, 1893; retired 1930; recalled Dec. 1941; retired again 1946; was Asst. Keeper of the Public Records (first class). Lent to War Office, 1917-18. Concerned since 1913 in the scheme for an international dictionary of Medieval Latin and joint sec., 1924-34, of committee appointed by British Academy for that purpose; joint secretary and afterwards a Vice-Pres. (1951), of Canterbury and York Society. *Publications:* Domesday Book; Norfolk (in Victoria County History: Norfolk, vol. II.) (with J. H. Round), tr. and ed., 1906; Richard FitzNeale: De Necessariis Observantiis Scaccarii dialogus (with A. Hughes and C. G. Crump), ed. 1902; English Court Hand, 1066-1500 (with C. H. Jenkinson), 1915; Medieval Latin Word-List (with J. H. Baxter), 1934; Dialogus de Scaccario, tr. and ed., 1950; Registrum Hamonis Hethe, ed., 1914-48; Regesta Regum Anglo-Normannorum, Vol. II (with Prof. H. A.

Cronne), 1956; trans. Nicholas Oresme's De Moneta (with other tracts on coinage), 1956; trans. Hugh the Chantor's History of the See of York, 1066-1127, 1960, etc. *Address:* Gloucester House, 13A Downshire Hill, N.W.3. *T.:* Hampstead 2648. *Club:* Athenæum. [*Died* 5 *Nov.* 1961.

JOHNSON, Charles William Heaton; Extra Mural Lecturer in History of Art, University of London, since 1934; *b.* 5 April 1896; *s.* of William Ernest Johnson and Barbara Keymer Heaton; *m.* 1951, Margaret Brimley Johnson. *Educ.:* Private tuition; Fitzwilliam Hall, Cambridge; B.A., Cambridge University, 1920; M.A., 1927. Official Lecturer, National Gallery, 1930-62; has lectured at the Courtauld Inst. of Art; asst. sec. to the Exhibition of British Art, Burlington House, 1933, and as editor of the catalogue of the said exhibition, 1933 and 1934 *Publications:* English Painting from the Seventh Century to the Present Day, 1932; A Short Account of British Painting, 1934; The Growth of Twelve Masterpieces, 1947; The Language of Painting, 1949; Memlinc, 1954. *Address:* 9 Pembridge Crescent, W.11. [*Died* 30 *Oct.* 1964.

JOHNSON, Professor Daniel Cowan, M.A.; F.I.Mech.E.; Engineering Consultant; Professor of Industrial Technology, University of Bradford, since 1967 (Visiting Professor in Fibres and Materials Engineering, 1966-67); *b.* 25 August 1915; *s.* of Herbert H. and Emily M. Johnson; *m.* 1942, Vera Olive Roston; one *s.* *Educ.:* Mill Hill School; King's College, Cambridge. Rolls-Royce Ltd., Derby, 1937-1946; Engineering Dept., Cambridge University, 1947-55; Sec., Faculty Bd. of Engineering, Camb., 1954-55; Prof. of Mechanical Engineering, Univ. of Leeds, 1956-62; Professor of Mechanics, Cambridge University, 1962-64; Fellow of Trinity Hall, 1954-55, 1962-64. Chairman, Applied Mechanics Group of Institution of Mechanical Engineers, 1962-64. *Publications:* (with Professor R. E. D. Bishop) Vibration Analysis Tables, 1957; The Mechanics of Vibration, 1960; Editor, Engineering Design (trans. from German), 1963; papers on vibration and gearing. *Address:* 19 Shaw Lane, Leeds 6. *T.:* Leeds 53752. [*Died* 9 *June* 1969.

JOHNSON, Sir Ernest (James), Kt., *cr.* 1937; Managing Director in Johnson Bros. (Hanley) Ltd., Stoke-on-Trent, Earthenware Manufacturers; *b.* 1881; 3rd *s.* of Robert L. and Sarah Johnson, Butterton Hall, Newcastle, Staffs.; *m.* 1906, Anna Shepard, *e. d.* of Alfred Boote, East Orange New Jersey, U.S.A.; three *s.* one *d.* *Educ.:* Rugby School. President N. Staffs Royal Infirmary, 1927-31 and 1945-48; Pres. Stone Conservative and Unionist Assoc., 1933-53; Pres. Stafford and Stone Conservative and Unionist Assoc.; Pres. North Staffordshire Political Union, 1936-52; Pres. Staffordshire Potteries Manufacturers Federation, 1934-46; J.P. Staffordshire. *Recreations:* cricket, golf, shooting. *Address:* Altona, Stone, Staffs. *T.:* 54. *Club:* Carlton. [*Died* 21 *Dec.* 1962.

JOHNSON, Guy Francis, C.B.E. 1945; M.A.; Past Chm., Air Registration Board; *s.* of A. A. Johnson, Sunderland; *m.* Enid, *d.* of T. B. Kittel, Hampstead; two *s.* two *d.* *Educ.:* Gresham's School; King's College, Cambridge. Called to Bar, Inner Temple, 1920; Member of Ministry of Transport Road Safety Committee, 1934; of Delevigne Cttee. on Rehabilitation, 1937. Served European War, 1914-18 (despatches twice); Major, R.A., 1918. *Address:* 29 Morpeth Mansions, Westminster, S.W.1. [*Died* 18 *Feb.* 1969.

JOHNSON, Engineer Rear-Adm. Harry Herbert, D.S.O. 1919; *s.* of F. J. B. Johnson, of Great Yarmouth; *b.* 7 Nov. 1875; *m.* 1921, Mabel Selina, *d.* of Isaac A. Mack, J.P., of Bootle, nr. Liverpool. Served European War, 1914-19 (D.S.O.); Naval A.D.C. to the King, 1927-28; retired list, 1928; served in War appointment, 1941-45. *Address:* Hartsfield Manor Hotel, Betchworth, Surrey. *T.:* Betchworth 3185. [*Died* 26 *Oct.* 1961.

JOHNSON, Sir Henry Allen Beaumont, 5th Bt., *cr.* 1818; *b.* 3 Jan. 1887; *s.* of Brig.-Gen. Sir H. A. W. Johnson, 4th Bt.; *S.* father 1944; *m.* 1917, Dorothy Nora, *y. d.* of late M. C. Gurney, C.M.G., M.V.O.; two *d.* *Educ.:* Uppingham; R.M.C. Sandhurst. Commissioned I.A. 1905; Capt. 1914; Major, 1920; Lt.-Col. 1931. Served European War, France, 1914-16; Aden Field Force, 1916-18; Afghan War, 1919 (medal with clasp); retired, 1937; in France with Pioneer Corps, 1940, in re-employment (Mons Star, British G.S. and Allied Victory Medals, 1939-43 Star). King's Foreign Service Messenger, 1942-51; retired, 1951. Jubilee and Coronation Medals. *Heir:* *cousin*, Victor Philipse Hill, *b.* 1905. *Address:* c/o National and Grindlay's Bank Ltd., 13 St. James's Square, S.W.1. [*Died* 24 *July* 1965

JOHNSON, Herschel V.; United States diplomat; retired May 1953; *b.* 3 May 1894; *s.* of William White Johnson and Arabella Kenan Horne; unmarried. *Educ.:* University of North Carolina; Harvard University Law School. B.A. (Univ. of North Carolina), 1916; LL.D., 1947. Lieut. and Capt. Infantry U.S. Army, 1917-19, overseas service (France); entered U.S. Foreign Service, 1920, and advanced through grades to that of Ambassador, 1946. 1920-34: Served at Berne, Sofia, Mexico City, Tegucigalpa (Honduras), and Dept. of State, Washington, D.C. First Sec. and Counsellor U.S. Embassy, London, 1934-41, with rank of Minister from 1941; Del. Int. Conf. on Whaling, London, 1937; Del. (and Chm. Am. Del.) Int. Confs. on Whaling, London, 1938 and 1939; U.S. Del. Meetings Int. Sugar Council, London, 1937-41. U.S. Minister to Sweden, 1941-46; dep. U.S. rep. on Security Council, U.N., 1946-48; acting U.S. rep. to U.N. and on Security Council U.N., 1946-47; alt. United States rep., special session on Palestine, General Assembly, U.N., N.Y., 1947; U.S. rep., 2nd session of General Assembly, U.N., N.Y., 1947; U.S. Ambassador to Brazil, 1948-53; Mem. N. Carolina State Constitutional Commn., 1957-59. *Address:* 1235 King's Drive, Charlotte 7, North Carolina, U.S.A. *Clubs:* Metropolitan (Washington); The Brook (New York). [*Died* 16 *April* 1966.

JOHNSON, Very Rev. Hewlett, M.A., B.Sc., D.D.; Dean of Canterbury, 1931-63; *b.* 1874; *s.* of C. H. Johnson, late of Upton Grange, Macclesfield, and Rosa, *d.* of Alfred Hewlett, D.D.; *m.* 1st, Mary (*d.* 1931), *d.* of Fred. Taylor, Broughton Park, Manchester; 2nd, 1938, Nowell Mary, *d.* of late Rev. G. Z. Edwards, Liverpool; two *d.* *Educ.:* King Edward's School, Macclesfield; Victoria University, B.Sc. (took Geological prize, 1894; Assoc. M.I.C.E., 1898-1902); Wadham College, Oxford, 1900, hons. in Theology. D.D. Oxford, 1924; Hon. D.Th. Prague Huss Faculty, 1947; Hon. D.Ph. Humbolt University, Berlin, 1960. Deacon, 1905; priest, 1906; Vicar of St. Margaret's, Altrincham, 1908; Examining Chap. to Bishops of Chester, 1913-24; Dean of Manchester, 1924-31; Hon. Canon of Chester Cathedral, 1919; Select Preacher before the University of Cambridge, 1921, 1926 Assize Sermon, Oxford, 1924; Rural Dean of Bowden, 1922; Proctor in Convocation, 1922; Founder and Proprietor of the Interpreter, and Editor, 1905-24. *Publications:* The Socialist Sixth of the World,

22nd ed. (translated into some 24 languages); Soviet Strength, 3rd ed.; Soviet Success, 1947; China's New Creative Age, 1953; Eastern Europe in the Socialist World, 1954; Christians and Communism: 14 sermons preached in Canterbury Cathedral, 1955-56, 1956; The Upsurge of China, 1961; articles and editorials in the Interpreter and other magazines. *Address:* The Red House, 24 New Street, St. Dunstan's, Canterbury, Kent. [*Died* 22 *Oct.* 1966.

JOHNSON, Major Hugh Spencer, C.B.E. 1920; T.D.; F.R.G.S.; retired; late Hon. Secretary, Advisory Committee, Army Savings Association and Hon. Sec. R.A.F. Savings Association; *s.* of late Matthew Johnson, Travancore, South India; unmarried. *Educ.:* King Edward VI Grammar School, Birmingham. Formerly Secretary, City of London Maternity Hospital, Fellow Chartered Institute of Secretaries; Freeman of the City of London; served European War, 1914-16. *Club:* Junior Army and Navy. [*Died* 15 *Dec.* 1962.

JOHNSON, Louis Arthur; lawyer, U.S.; *b.* 10 Jan. 1891; *s.* of Marcellus A. and Katherine Leftwich (*née* Arthur); *m.* 1920, Ruth F. Maxwell; two *d.* *Educ.:* University of Virginia (LL.B.). Began practice at Clarksburg, West Virginia, 1912; member Steptoe and Johnson, Clarksburg and Charleston, W. Va. and Washington, D.C.; Director: Union Nat. Bank, Community Savings and Loan Co. (Clarksburg). Civilian aide to Sec. of War, State of W. Va., 1933; mem. Federal Advisory Council of U.S. Employment Service under Dept. of Labor; apptd. by President Asst. Sec. of War, 1937, and served until 1940; personal rep. of President in India, March - Dec. 1942; Secretary of Defense, U.S.A., 1949-50. Served European War, 1917-18, Captain, Infantry, overseas for one year; Lieutenant-Colonel Inf. Res.; Commander Légion d'Honneur. Member W. Va. House of Representatives, 1917 (Chm. Judiciary Cttee.; majority floor leader). Nat. Comdr. Am. Legion, 1932-33. Deleg. to Dem. Nat. Conv., 1924; National Chairman Dem. Advisory Cttee.; Chairman of Finance Cttee. of Democratic National Cttee., 1948; Hon. Degrees: Salem, 1938; Kenyon, 1939; West Virginia Univ., 1949; Creighton (Nebraska), 1949; Villanova (Pa.), 1949; Marietta (Ohio), 1949; Pennsylvania Military (Pa.), 1950. Medal for Merit, awarded by the President. *Recreations:* golf, Chinese antiques, gardening. *Address:* Union National Bank Building, Clarksburg, West Virginia, U.S.A. *Clubs:* Metropolitan, Army and Navy, Burning Tree, Chevy Chase 1925 "F" Street (Washington); Rotary (ex-Pres.), Clarksburg Country (Clarksburg); University, Metropolitan, Midday, Drug and Chemical, Recess (New York City); Bohemian (San Francisco). [*Died* 24 *April* 1966.

JOHNSON, Sir Philip Bulmer, Kt., *cr.* 1948; Dep. Chairman, R. and W. Hawthorn, Leslie & Co. Ltd., Newcastle on Tyne; *b.* Hong Kong, 12 Nov. 1887; *s.* of late Alfred Bulmer Johnson, Woodlands, Guildford; *m.* 1921, Janet, *d.* of late Sir Herbert B. Rowell, K.B.E.; one *s.* two *d.* *Educ.:* Marlborough; Trinity College, Cambridge. 1st class Hons. Mechanical Sciences Tripos, 1909. Pres. of Engineering and Allied Employers Nat. Federation, 1946-48; Member of Govt. Shipbuilding Mission to S. America, 1946. *Recreation:* fishing. *Address:* Redesmouth House, Bellingham, Hexham, Northumberland. *T.:* Bellingham 213. *Club:* Flyfishers'. [*Died* 12 *June* 1964.

JOHNSON, Rev. Rowland T. I.; *see* Ingram-Johnson.

JOHNSON, Seymour Shepherd; Chief Accountant and Secretary National Discount Company Ltd., retired 1939; *b.* 21 April 1875; *s.* of William and Marie Johnson; *m.* 1900, Bertha Ayton Innes (*d.* 1958); one *s.* *Educ.:* Grocers' Company School. With Midland Bank Ltd., 1891-1900; entered National Discount Co., 1900. *Address:* Rosemar, 48 York Road, Cheam, Surrey. *T.:* Vigilant 6766. [*Died* 9 *April* 1962.

JOHNSON, Stanley W.; *see* Webb-Johnson.

JOHNSON, Rev. Wilfrid Harry Cowper; retired; *b.* 24 Feb. 1879; *s.* of late Canon W. Cowper Johnson, Rector of Yaxham, Norfolk; *m.* Ethel Mary Langdon, B.A., S.Th., Ryde, I.W., S.P.G. Missionary, Burma; two *d.* *Educ.:* Chigwell School; Trinity College, Cambridge. Curate S. Columba's, Stratford, E., 1902-4; Yaxham, Norfolk, 1904-6; Thorpe Hamlet, Norwich, 1906-8; Chaplain, Indian Ecclesiastical Establishment, Diocese of Rangoon, 1909-30; Archdeacon of Rangoon and Bishop's Commissary, 1923-30; Rector of Dickleburgh, Norfolk, 1930-47. *Address:* 4 Harraton House, Exning, W. Suffolk. [*Died* 12 *July* 1967.

JOHNSTON, Carruthers Melvill, C.M.G. 1953; *b.* 27 Aug. 1909; *e. s.* of Leslie Darrell Johnston and Elaine Hudson; *m.* 1936, Barbara Mary, *yr. d.* of George and Gertrude Bonnor; one *s.* one *d.* *Educ.:* Shrewsbury School; Brasenose College, Oxford (B.A.). Appointed Cadet, Colonial Administrative Service, Kenya, 1933; Provincial Commissioner, 1951; Minister for African Affairs and Community Development, Kenya, 1957-1960. *Address:* Gothic Cottage, Bishops Cleeve, Gloucestershire. *Clubs:* Oxford University Boat (Pres., 1931-32); Leander. [*Died* 13 *Nov.* 1970.

JOHNSTON, Rt. Rev. Francis Featherstonhaugh, C.B.E. 1944; M.A.; H.C.F.; Assistant Bishop of Guildford, since 1961; Hon. Canon of Guildford Cathedral since 1961; *b.* 21 Apr. 1891; *s.* of Walter Mowbray Johnston and Fanny Louise Dunne; *m.* 1919, Gladys Katie Head; (son killed 3 Jan. 1945) one *d.* *Educ.:* Ramsgate; Hatfield Coll., Durham Univ. (B.A.) Deacon, 1914; licensed to All Saints, Fishponds, Bristol; Priest, 1915; Temporary Chaplain to Forces, 1915; France, attached 17th Division, 1916; Salonika, attached 60th Division, 1916; Palestine, attached 60th Division, 1917-18; Chaplain of Port Said, 1919-33; Hon. Canon of All Saints Cathedral, Cairo, 1930; Archdeacon in Egypt, 1932-52; Sub-Dean, All Saints Cathedral, Cairo, 1933-47; Senior Chaplain of Alexandria, 1947-52; Bishop in Egypt, 1952-58; Vicar of Ewshott, Hampshire, 1958-63. War of 1939-45 (despatches, C.B.E.). Hon. M.A. Durham, 1957. *Recreation:* golf. *Address:* Annandale, Busbridge Lane, Godalming, Surrey. *Club:* National. [*Died* 17 *Sept.* 1963.

JOHNSTON, Hugh Anthony Stephen, C.M.G. 1959; O.B.E. 1954; D.F.C. 1942 and Bar 1944; Clerk to the City Parochial Foundation since 1965; *b.* 7 December 1913; *s.* of James Johnston, Indian Civil Service; *m.* 1942, Berrice Jacqueline (*née* Lincoln); one *s.* one *d.* *Educ.:* King's Sch., Canterbury; Brasenose Coll., Oxford (M.A.). H.M.O.C.S., 1936-61 (Dep. Gov. of the Northern Region of Nigeria, 1960); Director, Overseas Services Resettlement Bureau. 1961-65. R.A.F.V.R., 1940-45. *Publications:* (as A Fighter Pilot) Tattered Battlements, 1943; (as Hugh Sturton) Zomo the Rabbit, 1966; (under own name) A Selection of Hausa Stories, 1966; The Fulani Empire of Sokoto, 1967. *Address:* 40 Middleway, N.W.11. *Club:* East India and Sports. [*Died* 9 *Dec.* 1967.

JOHNSTON, Right Hon. Thomas, P.C. 1931; C.H. 1953; LL.D.; F.E.I.S.; Hon. F.R.C.S.Ed.; Journalist; formerly Chairman, North of Scotland Hydro Electric Board; Scottish Tourist Board (formerly Chairman until 1959); President Scottish History Society, 1950-52; ex-officio Mem., British Electricity Authority, 1947-48; Pres., British Electrical Development Association, 1958-60; Chancellor of Aberdeen Univ. since 1951; *b.* Kirkintilloch, Dunbartonshire, 1881; *m.*; two *d.* *Educ.:* Lairdsland Public School, Kirkintilloch; Lenzie Academy, Glasgow University; M.P. (Lab.) West Stirlingshire, 1922-24; Dundee (by-election), 1924-29; West Stirlingshire, 1929-31 and 1935-45; Parliamentary Under-Secretary for Scotland, 1929-31; Lord Privy Seal, 1931; Secretary of State for Scotland, 1941-45; Regional Commissioner for Scottish Civil Defence Region, 1939-41; Chairman Scottish National Forestry Commissioners, 1945-48; Founder and for 27 years Editor of the Forward; Member Education Authority, Dunbartonshire, for 2 years; Member Town Council, Kirkintilloch, 8 years; senior Magistrate; Convener Finance Committee, and first Chairman Municipal Bank; initiated many municipal schemes; public speaker on financial and historical questions; contested by-election Dunbartonshire, 1932. Member, Board of Governors of B.B.C., National Governor for Scotland, and Chairman, Broadcasting Council for Scotland, 1955-56. Dir., Indep. TV Authority in N.E. Scot., 1960-. *Publications:* Our Noble Families; History of the Working Classes in Scotland; The Financiers and the Nation; Old Kirkintilloch; Memories; numerous pamphlets. *Recreations:* angling, swimming, historical research. *Address:* Caledon, Lynn Drive, Milngavie, Scotland. [*Died* 5 *Sept.* 1965.

JOHNSTON, Sir William (Wallace Stewart), Kt. 1960; C.B.E. 1941; D.S.O. 1917; M.C. 1916; E.D.; M.D.; F.R.A.C.P.; Consulting Physician, Royal Melbourne Hospital, since 1948; *b.* 21 Dec. 1887; *s.* of Judge W. E. Johnston, Melbourne, and Clara Jane Wallace, Morrisons, Victoria; *m.* 1923, Jessie Mary (O.B.E.), *d.* of Brig.-Gen. W. J. Clark; two *s.* *Educ.:* Melbourne Church of England Grammar School; Trinity College, University of Melbourne. M.D. 1921. Served European War, 1914-18; A.I.F., A.A.M.C., 1915-18 (despatches, M.C., D.S.O.). Served War of 1939-45: A.I.F., A.A.M.C., 1939-43; Brig. D.D.M.S. 1 Aust. Corps (despatches, C.B.E.). Chairman: Melbourne Medical Post Graduate Committee, 1956-; Brit. Med. Insce. Co. of Vic.; a Vice-Pres., R.A.C.P., 1958-60; Mem. Council, Univ. of Melbourne, 1961-, Pres. Grad. Union, 1958-61. Chief Comr., S.J.A.B. (Aust.), 1957-; K.St.J. *Recreation:* golf. *Address:* 16 Stradbroke Avenue, Toorak, Melbourne S.E.2, Victoria, Australia. *T.:* 24 1566. *Clubs:* Oriental (London); Melbourne, Naval and Military (Melbourne). [*Died* 21 *Aug.* 1962.

JOHNSTONE, Hilda, M.A., Litt.D.; Prof. Emeritus of History in University of London since 1948; Hon. Consultant on Ecclesiastitical Archives to Records Cttee., W. Sussex County Council, 1951; *b.* 4 Jan. 1882; *d.* of late Herbert Alison Johnstone, Stockport, and Sarah Anne (*née* Brocklehurst). *Educ.:* Manchester High School for Girls; University of Manchester. B.A. (Hons. Hist.), 1903; Univ. and Jones Fellow in History, 1904; M.A. 1906; Litt.D. 1940; Assistant Lecturer in History, University of Manchester, 1906-13; Editorial Section, War Trade Intelligence Department, 1916-19; Reader in History, Univ. of London, 1913-22; Professor of History, Univ. of London (Royal Holloway College), 1922-42; Hon. Archivist to Bishop of Chichester, 1942-51. *Publications:* Jt. Editor of State Trials in the Reign of Edward I. (Royal Hist. Soc.), 1905; Archbishop Pecham and the Council of Lambeth (in Essays presented to T. F. Tout), 1925; the Queen's Household (in Chapters in Mediæval Administrative History), 1930; Letters of Edward Prince of Wales, 1304-05 (Roxburghe Club), 1931; The Queen's Exchequer under the three Edwards (in Historical Essays in honour of James Tait), 1933; new ed. of Tout, Place of Edward II. in History, 1936; The Queens' Household (in The English Government at Work, 1327-36), Mediæval Academy of America, 1940; Edward of Carnarvon, 1946; Churchwardens' Presentments, 2 volumes (Sussex Record Society), 1948; Annales Gandenses (Medieval Classics, Nelson), 1951; also contributor to Handbook of British Chronology (Royal Hist. Soc.), 1939, Dictionary of English Church History, 3rd edn., 1948, the English Historical Review, Contemporary Review and various other periodicals. *Address:* St. Francis Nursing Home, Littlehampton, Sussex. [*Died* 25 *June* 1961.

JOHNSTONE, Robert William, C.B.E. 1920; M.A., M.D.; Hon. LL.D. (Edin.); F.R.C.S. Edin., M.R.C.P. Edin., F.R.C.O.G., F.R.S.E.; Emeritus Prof. of Midwifery and Diseases of Women, Univ. of Edinburgh; Consulting Obstetrician and Gynæcologist, Royal Infirmary, Edinburgh; Hon. Fellow: Edinburgh Obst. Soc., American Association of Obstetricians and Gynæcologists; Glasgow Obstetrical and Gynæcological Society; Manchester Medical Society; York Medical Society; *b.* 1879; *m.* Jean (*d.* 1960), *d.* of late George Alexander Gibson, LL.D., M.D., F.R.C.P.E., Edinburgh; two *s.* two *d.* *Educ.:* George Watson's Coll., and Univ., Edinburgh. M.B., Ch.B. (Hons.), 1903. President, Royal Medical Society, 1904-5; studied in Vienna and Prague, 1906; assistant to Professor of Midwifery and Diseases of Women, University of Edinburgh, 1906-1919; Surgeon-in-charge, Royal Victoria Red Cross Hospital, 1914-16; Temp. Lieut., R.A.M.C., Surgical Specialist, 1917, in France; Deputy Commissioner, Medical Services (H.Q.) and later Commissioner (H.Q.), Ministry of National Service, London, 1918-19; Lecturer on Midwifery and Gynæcology, School of Medicine of Royal Colleges, 1919-26; Chairman Central Midwives Board for Scotland, 1937-53. *Publications:* William Smellie, The Master of British Midwifery, 1952; (Ed.) Historical Review of British Obstetrics and Gynæcology, 1800-1950, 1954; Textbook of Midwifery, 21st edn.; The Midwife's Textbook, 8th edn. *Address:* 53 Murrayfield Gardens, Edinburgh 12. *T.:* 031-337 2870. [*Died* 27 *Nov.* 1969.

JOHNSTONE, Very Rev. Thomas McGimpsey, B.A., D.D.; *b.* 1876; *s.* of J. H. Johnstone; *m.* 1908, Emily Isobelle McClement; one *s.* *Educ.:* Queen's University and Assembly's College, Belfast. Graduate Royal Univ. of Ireland and Doctor in Divinity Presbyterian Theological Faculty in Ireland; Dufferin Medallist for Oratory and sometime Pres. Queen's Univ. Literary and Scientific Society; Senior Minister of Newington Presbyterian Church, Belfast. Ex-Moderator, Presbyterian Church in Ireland. *Publications:* Ulstermen: their Fight for Fortune, Faith and Freedom; The Crisis in Industry, 1930; These Fifty Years, 1926; Food for the Reformer, 1930; The Vintage of Memory, 1942; Where the Foxglove Glows, 1946; Sunset Soliloquy, 1956. *Recreation:* none. *Address:* Mahee Island, Comber, Co. Down. [*Died* 21 *Aug.* 1961.

JOICEY, 3rd Baron, *cr.* 1906; **Col. Hugh Edward Joicey,** Bt., *cr.* 1893; D.S.O. 1919; J.P.; Chairman, Albyn S.S. Co.; *b.* Durham, 21 Nov. 1881; 2nd *s.* of 1st Baron Joicey; *S.* brother 1940; *m.* 1921, Joan, *y. d.* of 4th Earl of Durham; one *s.* (and *er. s.* died of wounds, Salerno, 1943). *Educ.:* Harrow. Served in the Northumberland

Fusiliers Militia, 1899; gazetted to 14th Hussars, 1900; served South African War, 1900-2 (Queen's medal and 3 clasps); Adjutant 14th Hussars, 1905-8; served with 2nd Life Guards in France, 1914-15; commanded 1st Batt. Suffolk Regt., 1915-18; bringing the 14th Hussars home from Mesopotamia, 1919; High Sheriff of Northumberland, 1933; has the Order of the Redeemer of Greece, 2nd Class; patron of one living. *Recreations*: shooting, hunting. *Heir*: *s.* Hon. Michael Edward Joicey, Capt. Coldstream Guards [*b.* 28 Feb. 1925; *m.* 1952, Elisabeth Marion, *y. d.* of Lt.-Col. Hon Ian Leslie Melville; two *s.* one *d.*]. *Address*: Etal Manor, Ford, Berwick-on-Tweed. *T.*: Crookham 205. *Clubs*: Cavalry, Bath. [*Died* 14 *Oct.* 1966.

JOLLIFFE, John Edward Austin; Emeritus Fellow of Keble College, Oxford; *b.* Southampton, 1891; *s.* of Austin and Ellen Jolliffe. *Educ.*: Weymouth College; Keble College, Oxford. 1st Class Final School of Modern History, 1914; Assistant Master, St. Bees School, 1914-18; Tutor of Keble College, Oxford, 1919; University Lecturer in Medieval English History, 1930-38; Prof. of English Literature in Federal Univ. of Rio de Janeiro, 1941; Director of the British Institute of Santos, Brazil, 1942-45. Fellow, 1930-54 and Sub-Warden, 1937-54, of Keble College, Oxford. F.R.Hist.Soc. *Publications*: Pre-Feudal England: the Jutes, 1933; A Constitutional History of Medieval England, 1937; Angevin Kingship, 1955; articles in various historical periodicals. *Address*: Vila Torralta, Lagos, Algarve, Portugal. *T.*: Lagos 248. *Club*: Royal British (Lisbon). [*Died* 13 *Jan.* 1964.

JOLLY, Lieut.-Gen. Sir Gordon Gray, K.C.I.E., *cr.* 1941 (C.I.E. 1919); K.St.J. 1944; M.B., Ch.B., D.P.H., D.T.M. and H.; *s.* of late Rev. James Jolly, West Port Church, Edinburgh; *m.* 1st, 1920, May Wilson Forster; one *s.* one *d.*; 2nd, Doreen Marion Stamper; one *s.* one *d.* *Educ.*: Watson's College, Edinburgh; Edinburgh University. M.B., Ch.B. 1907; entered Indian Medical Service, 1908; served European War Aug. 1914 till termination throughout the operations in East Africa (despatches, C.I.E.); Medical Officer of Health, Imperial Delhi, 1921; Asst. Director of Public Health, Burma, 1922-27; Director of Public Health, Burma, 1928-33; Dep. Director-General, Indian Medical Service, 1933-36; Public Health Commissioner, Govt. of India, 1935-36; Secretary-General National Association for Prevention of Tuberculosis, 1936-37; Inspector-General of Civil Hospitals, Punjab, 1937-39; Director-General, I.M.S., 1939-43; K.H.P. 1939-1943; retired, 1943; Hon. Lt.-Gen. Chief Commissioner, Indian Red Cross War Organisation, 1943-46; K.I.H. gold, 1946; Grand Cordon Chinese Order of the Cloud and Banner, 1947. Fellow Royal Institute of Public Health; Fellow Royal Numismatic Soc. *Publications*: various contributions to the medical Press. *Recreation*: golf. *Club*: Civil Service (Cape Town). [*Died* 1 *March* 1962.

JOLLY, James, C.M.G. 1955; C.B.E. 1946; R.D. 1939; *b.* 8 Aug. 1902; *o. s.* of James Jolly, Bolton, Lancs.; *m.* 1946, Elizabeth Maude Witchell, Hong Kong; one *s.* *Educ.*: Bolton Municipal School, Lancs.; Cadet Ship, H.M.S. Conway. Merchant Navy, 1918-27; Nigerian Marine, 1927-39; Director of Marine, Hong Kong, 1940-57; H.M. Oversea Civil Service, 1927-57; retired. Extra Master's Certificate of Competency, 1926; Younger Brother of Trinity House, 1946. *Address*: 21B Austen Road, Guildford, Surrey. *Club*: Skäl (Hong Kong). [*Died* 19 *Aug.* 1968.

JOLLY, Rear-Admiral Sir William E. H., K.C.B., *cr.* 1944 (C.B. 1943); *b.* 11 Sept. 1887; *s.* of late Dr. R. W. Jolly; *m.* 1915, Frances Winifred, *d.* of Martin Odam; no *c.* *Educ.*: privately, abroad. Royal Navy since 1905; Paymaster Director-General and Director-General (S), Admiralty, 1942-45. *Recreation*: gardening. *Address*: Orchardleigh, Cookham Dean, Berks. *T.*: Marlow 93. *Club*: Army and Navy. [*Died* 12 *Jan.* 1961.

JONES, Rev. Sir Albert E. (bardic name Cynan); *see* Evans-Jones.

JONES, Arnold Hugh Martin; Professor of Ancient History, Cambridge University, since 1951; Fellow of Jesus College since 1951; *b.* 9 March 1904; *s.* of late John Arthur Jones, C.I.E.; *m.* 1927, Freda Katharine Mackrell; two *s.* one *d.* *Educ.*: Cheltenham College; New College, Oxford (Hon. Fell. 1968). LL.D. (Cantab.), 1965; D.D. (Oxon.), 1966. Fellow of All Souls College, 1926-46; Excavation (Constantinople and Jerash), 1927-29; Reader in Ancient History in the Egyptian University, Cairo, 1929-34; Lecturer in Ancient History, at Wadham College, 1939-46; Professor of Ancient History, University College, London, 1946-51. Ministry of Labour and War Office (military intelligence), 1941-45; F.B.A. 1947; President of Roman Society, 1952-55; F.S.A. 1957, Corresponding Member of the Institut d'Égypte, 1965. Hon. L.H.D. Chicago, 1969. *Publications*: Articles in the Journals of Roman Studies and of Egyptian Archæology, Economic History Review, Past and Present, Cambridge Hist. Jl., Jls. of Theological Studies and of Ecclesiastical History, Historia, etc.; A History of Abyssinia (in collaboration with Elizabeth Monroe), 1935; The Cities of the Eastern Roman Provinces, 1937; The Herods of Judæa, 1938; The Greek City from Alexander to Justinian, 1940; Constantine and the Conversion of Europe, 1949; Documents illustrating the reigns of Augustus and Tiberius (in collaboration with Dr. V. Ehrenberg), 1949; Ancient Economic History, 1948; The Athens of Demosthenes, 1952; Athenian Democracy, 1957; Studies in Roman Government and Law, 1960; The Later Roman Empire, 1964; Sparta, 1966; (Ed.) A History of Rome Through the Fifth Century: vol. 1, The Republic, 1968. *Recreation*: walking. *Address*: Fen Ditton Hall, Fen Ditton, Cambs. *T.*: Teversham 3214. [*Died* 9 *April* 1970.

JONES, Rt. Hon. Arthur Creech, P.C. 1946; *b.* 1891; *m.* 1920, Violet May Tidman. Formerly National Secretary, Transport and General Workers Union, 1919-29; Organising Secretary, Workers Travel Association, 1929-1939. Contested Heywood and Radcliffe Division of Lancashire, 1929. M.P. (Lab.) Shipley Division of Yorkshire, 1935-50, Wakefield, 1954-64. Parly. Private Sec. to Mr. Ernest Bevin, Minister of Labour and National Service, 1940-45; Parliamentary Under-Secretary of State, Colonial Office, 1945-46; Secretary of State for the Colonies, 1946-50. Vice-Pres. of National Federation of Professional Workers, 1929-30; Hon. Sec. of Camberwell Trades Council and Borough Labour Party, 1913-22; Executive Member of London Labour Party, 1921-28; Executive Member Fabian Society; Vice-Pres. W.E.A.; Governor of Ruskin Coll., Oxford, since 1923; Treasurer, Workers' Travel Assoc.; formerly Vice-Chm. of British Inst. of Adult Education; formerly Pres. of International Federation of Commercial Employees; Member Colonial Office Educ. Advisory Cttee., 1936-45; Chairman, Fabian Colonial Bureau and formerly of Labour Party Imperial Advisory Cttee.; former Councillor of R.I.I.A.; Vice-Chm. of Higher Education Commission to West Africa, 1943-1944; Chm. British Council of Pacific Relations, 1952-54. Delegate Internat. Pacific Relations, Canada, U.S.A., India; Governor Queen Elizabeth House, Oxford; Treas. and Counc., Commonwealth Parl Assoc.; Vice-President, Anti-Slavery Soc.; Exec. Mem. Africa Bureau; Vice-Pres. Royal Commonwealth Soc. U.K. delegate to U.N., 1946 and 1947-48. Travelled extensively in British colonies. Introduced Access to Mountains Act, 1939. Treas. Pit Ponies Protection Soc. Former Mem. of Southern Electricity Bd. and of B.B.C. Advisory Council. Member of Metropolitan Water Board, 1924-1930 and 1934-36. Executive of British Council; Executive, Travel Assoc. of Great Britain and National Film Council. Director: Marchon Products; Solway Chemicals; Trustee Municipal Mutual Insurance Ltd. *Publications:* Trade Unionism To-day; The Ruhr; Fabian Colonial Essays, and colonial pamphlets and articles. *Address:* 3 Stirling Mansions, Canfield Gardens, N.W.6. [*Died* 23 *Oct.* 1964.

JONES, Hon. Sir Austin Ellis Lloyd, Kt. 1945; M.C.; retired; Judge High Court, King's Bench Division, 1948-61 (Probate, Divorce and Admiralty Div., 1945-48); *b.* 27 April 1884; *s.* of late Rev. T. E. Jones, Rector of Hope, Flintshire. *Educ.:* Haileybury; Liverpool Univ. (LL.B.; Hon. LL.D., 1951). Barrister, Inner Temple, 1907, Bencher, 1945. Served European War, 1914-18, with R.F.A. (M.C., despatches twice); Conservative candidate, Carnarvon Boroughs, 1910 and 1923, and Flintshire, 1922; County Court Judge, Circuit No. 50 (Sussex), 1931-39; Additional Judge at Westminster County Court and Judge, Circuit No. 34 (Uxbridge), 1939-43; Judge of Westminster County Court, 1943-45; Chairman of Tithe Arrears Investigation Committee, 1937-39; Chm. Cttee. on County Court Procedure, 1947-49; Chm. Flintshire Quarter Sessions, 1948, 1961. *Clubs:* Athenæum, Travellers'. [*Died* 31 *March* 1967.

JONES, Austin Ernest D.; *see* Duncan-Jones.

JONES, Sir Bertram (Hyde), K.B.E., *cr.* 1920; *b.* 9 Jan. 1879; *e. s.* of E. I. Jones; *m.* 1905, Constance Elizabeth, *d.* of W. J. Renshaw; two *s.* one *d.* *Educ.:* privately. Member of Council of Welfare, Air Training Corps, and Chairman of Chairmen's Advisory Cttee. and of Local Cttee.; Member A.T.C. Cttee. Surrey T. & A.F.A., and of Exec. Cttee. of Air League of British Empire; of Mechanical Transport Board, War Office, of Weir Cttee., and of various other Committees. Served South Africa (medal with three clasps); travelled extensively in Canada, the West Indies and South Africa. During European War, 1914-1918, Civil Assistant, unpaid, to Controller-General of Equipment, Air Ministry; devoted his time to National Service, and was responsible for bringing about the reorganisation of the commercial side of the War Office, 1917; at the request of Lord Rothermere undertook, together with Sir Arthur C. Roberts, the organisation of the finance and other arrangements for the amalgamation of the R.N.A.S. and R.F.C. into the new Royal Air Force (this work included the creation of a Finance Department of the new Ministry); appointed Adviser to the Finance Department. Hon. Member Air Cadet League of Canada; Member Council, Air League of British Empire; Hon. Fellow Royal Microscopical Society. *Publications:* contributions to daily papers, principally on Finance and Political Economy. *Recreations:* various and varying; microscopy, Fellow of Royal Microscopical Society. *Address:* Sunset, Rhodes Drive, Kirstenbosch, Cape Town, S. Africa. *T.:* 7-4066. *Clubs:* Danish, Knights of the Round Table, Norwegian, Junior Carlton; South African Turf; Cape Microscopical Association.; Cape Natural History; Quekett Microscopical (Life Member); Western Prov. Sports. [*Died* 14 *Oct.* 1961.

JONES, Sir Clement Wakefield, Kt. *cr* 1946; C.B. 1919; M.A.; *b.* 26 June 1880; *y. s.* of Rev. Canon W. Jones, Vicar of Burneside Westmorland, and Margaret, *d.* of John Cropper; *m.* 1911, Enid, *e. d.* of Trevor Griffith Boscawen of Trevalyn Hall, Rossett, N. Wales; two *s.* one *d.* *Educ.:* Haileybury; Trin. Coll., Camb. B.A. 1902; Edited Granta, 1901; Dir. of Alfred Booth & Co. Ltd., and Sea Insurance Co. Ltd.; entered 4th Bn. Roy. Welch Fusiliers, 1914; Capt. 1915; served in European War, Dardanelles Campaign, 1915; Secretary to Lord Curzon's Shipping Control Committee; accompanied Mr. Runciman to Anglo-Italian Conference, Pallanza, Aug. 1916; an Assist. Sec. to the War Cabinet; Secretary, British Empire Delegation, Peace Conference, Paris, 1919; Vice-Chairman of Technical Personnel Cttee., 1941-50; Member of Radio Board, 1942-45; Member of Committee on Higher Appointments (appointed by Minister of Labour) and Chairman of Sub-Committee, 1943; Member of Interdepartmental Committee on Further Education and Training, 1943; Chairman of Council of Roy. Institute of Internat. Affairs, 1948-53; Mem. of Bd. of Brit. Overseas Airways Corp., 1946-54; Chairman of Commonwealth Shipping Cttee., 1947-63; a Governor and Almoner of Christ's Hospital; Member of Council of Bedford College for Women; Life Gov. of Haileybury and Pres. of Old Haileyburian Soc., 1951-52; formerly Member of Cambridge University Appointments Board. *Publications:* British Merchant Shipping, 1922; Pioneer Shipowners, 1935, Vol. II., 1939; Sea Trading and Sea Training, 1936; A Tour in Westmorland, 1948; Walks in North Westmorland, 1955; Chief Officer in China, 1955; John Bolton of Storrs, 1959. *Address:* Trevalyn Hall, Rossett, N. Wales. *Club:* Athenæum. [*Died* 29 *Oct.* 1963.

JONES, Sir Cyril (Edgar), K.C.I.E., *cr.* 1944; (C.I.E. 1937); C.S.I. 1941; Chairman, Commonwealth Trust Ltd., since 1961 (Dir., 1952); *b.* 29 Dec. 1891; *s.* of Henry Charles Jones, London; *m.* 1925, Irene Lilian, *d.* of late Mrs. J. Hill, Exmouth, S. Devon; one *s.* one *d.* *Educ.:* Jesus Coll., Cambridge. Indian Civil Service, 1914; military duty in India, 1917-19; Secretary to the Government of Madras, Finance Dept., 1934-39; Secretary to the Government of India Finance Dept., 1939-47; Asst. Under Sec. of State, Foreign Office (German Section), 1947-50. Member: Overseas Food Corp., 1950-52; Chancellor's Purchase Tax (Valuation) Committee, 1952-53; United Nations Committee of Financial Experts, 1953. Chairman, Indian Steelworks Construction Co. Ltd., 1955-67; Dir., Mercantile Bank Ltd., 1952-1966 (Dep. Chm., 1954-66; Mem., London Adv. Cttee., 1966-68). *Address:* Dalveen, Wych Hill Way, Woking, Surrey. *T.:* Woking 60685. *Club:* Oriental. [*Died* 21 *June* 1970.

JONES, Lieut.-Col. Sir Cyril Vivian, Kt., *cr.* 1947; C.B.E. 1919; Vice-President Federation of British Industries; Director Eagle Star Insurance Co. Ltd. (Kent Board) *b.* 1882; *s.* of John W. Jones; *m.* 1928, Olive Louise Targett. Served European War, 1914-19 (despatches four times, C.B.E.). President Food Manufacturers' Federation, 1944-46, Vice-President, 1955-; Member, Govt. Industrial Mission to Pakistan, 1950. *Address:* Summerhayes, Hythe, Kent. *T.:* Hythe 67048. [*Died* 2 *Sept.* 1961.

JONES, Daniel, M.A.; Professor Emeritus of Phonetics in the University of London, 1949; *b.* 12 September 1881; *s.* of Daniel Jones, Barrister, one of the founders of the All England Tennis Club, and Viola, *d.* of Richard Carte, musician (flautist, instrument designer), sister of Richard D'Oyly Carte; *m.* 1911, Cyrille, *d.* of Henri Motte of Bourg-la-Reine, nr. Paris, artist; one *d.* (one *s.* decd.).

Educ.: Ludgrove (preparatory school); Radley; University Coll. School (Cook prize for mathematics); King's College, Cambridge; B.A. 1903 (sen. optime); M.A. 1907. Called to Bar, Lincoln's Inn, 1907; Lectr. in Phonetics, University College, London, 1907; Reader, 1914; Professor, 1921-49; Asst. Sec. International Phonetic Assoc., 1907-27, Sec., 1928-50; Pres., 1950; Pres. Simplified Spelling Soc., 1946; Corr. Mem. German Acad. of Sciences, Berlin, 1950; Hon Mem. Royal Irish Acad., 1957; has lectured at Paris, Geneva, Zürich, Berlin, Cologne, Bonn, Göttingen, Bremen, Hamburg, Marburg, Rotterdam, Copenhagen, Gothenburg, Stockholm, Upsala, Madras, Bombay, Lahore, New York, Northampton (U.S.A.). Dr. Phil. *h.c.* (Zürich), 1936; Hon. LL.D., Edin., 1958. *Publications:* The Phoneme, its Nature and Use, 2nd edn., 1962; Outline of English Phonetics, 9th edn., 1960; English Pronouncing Dictionary, 12th edn., 1966; The Pronunciation of English, 4th edn., 1958; Phonetic Readings in English, 1956; Intonation Curves, 1900; The Tones of Sechuana Nouns, 1927; The Problem of a National Script for India, 1942; Linguaphone records of Cardinal Vowels, 1956; Concrete and Abstract Sounds; Dhe Fonetik Aspekt ov Speling Reform; (with E. M. Stéphan) Gramophone Course of Colloquial French; (with H. S. Perera) A Colloquial Sinhalese Reader; (with Kwing Tong Woo) A Cantonese Phonetic Reader; (with S. T. Plaatje) A Sechuana Phonetic Reader; Assistant Editor of Le Maître Phonétique, 1907-40, Editor, 1941-50. *Recreations:* phonetics, music (especially Bach). *Address:* 3 Marsham Way, Gerrards Cross, Bucks. *T.:* Gerrards Cross 83490 [*Died* 4 *Dec.* 1967.

JONES, David Thomas; railway signalman; Member Pontypridd Urban District Council; Chairman East Glamorganshire Planning Committee; Chairman S. Wales Advisory Planning Cttee. M.P. (Lab.) The Hartlepools, 1945-Sept. 1959. Member of Council of Europe, 1955-57, and Vice-Chairman of its Municipal and Regional Affairs Committee; Member of W.E.U. Assembly (Cttee. on Defence Questions and Armaments), 1956-57. *Address:* 65 Charlbert Court, Regent's Park, N.W.8. [*Died* 4 *April* 1963.

JONES, Sir Edgar (Rees), K.B.E., *cr.* 1918; Barrister-at-law; *b.* Cwmaman, Aberdare, 27 Aug. 1878; *e. s.* of Rev. Morgan Humphrey Jones, Baptist Minister; *m.* 1919, May, *d.* of George Brackley, Harringay; one *s.* one *d.* *Educ.:* University College, Cardiff. M.A. University of Wales; called to Bar, Gray's Inn, 1912; Lecturer on English Literature; M.P. (L.) Merthyr-Tydfil, 1910-15, and Merthyr Division, Dec. 1918-22; Controller Priority Department, Ministry of Munitions, 1915-18; Chairman Welsh Consultative Council of Health, 1920-22; Chairman National Food Canning Council; President World Trade Alliance Assoc. *Publications:* The Meaning of Literature; The Art of the Orator; Selected Speeches. *Address:* Gwyndy, Monkmead Lane, Roundabouts, Sussex. [*Died* 16 *June* 1962.

JONES, Sir Edward R.; *see* Redmayne-Jones.

JONES, Edward Taylor, D.Sc. (Lond.); Hon. D.Sc. (Wales); LL.D. (Glasgow); F.Inst.P.; Emeritus Professor of Natural Philosophy in the University of Glasgow; *b.* Denbigh, 24 Dec. 1872; *m.* 1913, Kathleen Gladys, *e. d.* of late Captain N. P. Stewart, J.P., Bangor; one *s.* one *d.* *Educ.:* University College, Bangor; University of Berlin. B.Sc. (Lond.) 1892, 1st Class Hons. with Scholarship marks in Physics, 2nd Class Hons. 1st on list in Mathematics; 1851 Exhibition Scholar; formerly Professor of Physics in the University College of North Wales, Bangor; President Royal Philosophical Society of Glasgow, 1937-40. *Publications:* Papers on magnetic stress, magnetic deformation, electrical oscillations, the singing arc, the induction-coil, the Tesla coil, the high-tension magneto, electric spark ignition, valve-generated oscillations, diffraction of cathode rays, structure of celluloid films, a quantum theory of electrostatic and magnetic energy, the vibratory doublet theory of the photon, dispersion theory for photons, reflexion and refraction of photons, Aeolian tones, theory of line spectra. Books: Theory of the Induction Coil, 1921; Induction Coil Theory and Applications, 1932. *Address:* 5 Wellswood Park, Torquay, Devon. *T.:* 4124. [*Died* 25 *Sept.* 1961.

JONES, Ernest W.; *see* Whitley-Jones.

JONES, Vice-Adm. Everard J. H.; *see* Hardman-Jones.

JONES, Sir E. Wynne C.; *see* Cemlyn-Jones.

JONES, Frank, B.A. (Lond.); Second Master, King Edward's School, Aston, Birmingham (retired); *b.* 7 Jan. 1873; *s.* of late Edward Jones; unmarried. *Educ.:* King Edward's School, Aston, Birmingham; Mason College, Birmingham. Lecturer in Anglo-Saxon and English Literature, Midland Institute; Lecturer, City of London Vacation Course in Education; President North Midlands R.F.U. *Publications:* Oral Latin Reader; A First English Course; A New English Course (2 vols.); A New English Composition; Brummagem English; A Schoolmaster Looks Back; How we Speak; Grammar and Smiles; (Joint) First and Second Latin Courses; First Latin Grammar; Editor of The Golden Books of English Verse (6 vols.); The Silver Books of English Verse (2 vols.); Shakespeare's Tempest. *Recreations:* golf, Rugby football. *Address:* 16 Livingstone Road, Handsworth, Birmingham 20. *T.:* Birchfield 4355. *Clubs:* Cosmopolitan, Press (Birmingham). [*Died* 10 *April* 1961.

JONES, Hon. Frederick; retd. as N.Z. High Commissioner in Australia (1958-61); *b.* 16 November 1884; *s.* of Charles and Jessie Jones; *m.* 1910, Jessie Agnes Hudson; three *s.* *Educ.:* Albany Street, Dunedin; Normal School, Christchurch. Apprenticed Boot Trade, 1898; Labour Member of Parliament, Dunedin South, 1931-51; Postmaster General and Minister of Defence in Labour Govt., 1935-40; Minister of Defence and War Pensions, 1945-49. Formerly Mem. City Council and various local bodies; a Mem. of Labour Movement for many years. *Address:* 43 Surrey Street, Dunedin, New Zealand. [*Died* 25 *May* 1966.

JONES, Frederick Theodore, C.I.E. 1931; M.V.O. 1911; V.D.; Works Directorate Air Ministry, since 1951; *b.* 30 July 1885; *m.* 1st, 1912, May Saunders (marriage dissolved, 1935); one *s.* one *d.*; 2nd, 1935, Doris May Milne, *d.* of George Elsey Mason; one *d.* *Educ.:* Rugby; London University. Entered Indian Service of Engineers, 1907; Exec. Engineer, U.P., 1917-20; Exec. Engineer, Imperial Works, Govt. of India, 1920-25; Supt. Engineer, P.W.D. Delhi, 1925; Actg. Chief Engineer, Government of India, during part of 1933. Kaisar-i-Hind gold medal, 1936. Chief Engineer, Govt. of India, 1938-40; Consulting Engineer with Govt. of India, 1940-42; H.M. Forces, 1942-1947 (local rank Brig., substantive rank Col., on retirement); Allied Control Commn., Germany, Principal Control Officer, 1948-49. *Address:* 37 Wessex Gardens, N.W.11. *T.:* Meadway 1780. *Club:* East India and Sports. [*Died* 25 *July* 1968.

JONES, George Arthur, C.M.G. 1950; O.B.E. 1934; Principal, Colonial Office, since 1920; *b.* 11 March 1889; 4th *s.* of late Charles E. Jones; unmarried. *Educ.:* Owen's School, Islington. Civil Servant. Entered Colonial Office as a Second Division Clerk, 1907; appointed Second Class Clerk, 1919. *Recreation:* bowls. *Address:* c/o Midland Bank Ltd., Cambridge Circus Branch, 138 Shaftesbury Avenue, W.C.2. [*Died* 6 *March* 1962.

JONES, Very Rev. Herbert Arthur; Dean of Manchester, 1954-63, now Emeritus; *m.* 1st, 1919, Lily Scattergood; one *s.* one *d.*; *m.* 2nd, 1964, Florence Marjorie Green. *Educ.:* Birmingham University (Scholar, B.Sc. 1913); Lichfield Theological College. Provost and Vicar of Leicester, 1938-54. M.A. (*h.c.*) Manchester, 1958. *Publications:* Prayer and Purpose; Evangelism and the Laity. *Address:* Rossall, Higher Ainsworth Rd., Radcliffe, Manchester. [*Died* 17 *Feb.* 1969.

JONES, His Honour Hugh; *see* Emlyn-Jones.

JONES, Isaac, M.B.E. 1949; N.D.A., N.D.D.; Principal of Madryn Cas le Farm School, Caernarvonshire, 1922-48; *b.* Beiliglas, Cwmgors, Glam., 6 Sept. 1883; *s.* of John and Elizabeth Jones; *m.* 1923, Bronwen Agnes Hannah James; one *s.* *Educ.:* County School, Ystalyfera; University College, Cardiff; West of Scotland Agricultural College, Glasgow; British Dairy Institute, Reading. Lecturer in Book-keeping at the University College, Cardiff, 1914-17; Agricultural Officer in Glamorgan, 1918-19; Chief Agricultural Officer for the Breconshire County Council, 1919-22; Agricultural Organiser for Caernarvonshire, 1922-48, retired. *Recreations:* reading and motoring. *Address:* Llywel, Nefyn, Pwllheli, Caernarvonshire, N. Wales. *T.:* Nevin 496. [*Died* 3 *April* 1968.

JONES, Jack, C.B.E. 1948; Author and Playwright since 1934; *b.* 24 Nov. 1884; *e. s.* of David and Sarah Ann Jones; *m.* 1st, 1908, Laura Grimes Evans; two *s.* one *d.* (and two *s.* decd.); 2nd, 1954 Gladys Morgan. *Educ.:* St. David's Elementary School, Merthyr Tydfil, Glamorgan. Miner for 27 years from age of twelve, 1896-1923. Trades Union Official, 1923-28; contested Neath Constituency (L.), 1929. Served European War, 1914-18, in Welch Regt. Two lecture tours in America and European battlefronts during War of 1939-45. *Publications: autobiography:* Unfinished Journey, 1937; Me and mine, 1946; Give Me Back My Heart 1950; *Plays:* Land of My Fathers, 1937; Rhondda Roundabout, 1939; Transatlantic Episode, 1947; *novels:* Rhondda Roundabout, 1934; Black Parade, 1935; Bidden to the Feast, 1938; Off to Philadelphia in the Morning, 1947; Some Trust in Chariots, 1948; River Out of Eden, 1951; Lily of the Valley, 1952; Lucky Lear, 1952; Time and the Business, 1953; Choral Symphony, 1955; *biography:* The Man David, 1944. *Address:* 57 Pen-y-dre, Rhiwbina, Cardiff. [*Died* 7 *May* 1970.

JONES, Sir James, Kt., *cr.* 1946; C.I.E. 1942; Director James Finlay & Co. Limited; *b.* 23 Sept. 1895; *s.* of T. A. Jones and Annie Runciman; *m.* 1934, Margaret E. Watson; no *c.* *Educ.:* George Watson's College, Edinburgh. *Recreation:* golf. *Address:* 22 West Nile Street, Glasgow. *Club:* Oriental. [*Died* 28 *May* 1962.

JONES, James W. W.; *see* Webb-Jones.

JONES, John Henry; M.P. (Lab.) Rotherham since 1950 (Bolton Division, Lancashire, 1945-50); *b.* 26 Oct. 1894; *m.* 1919, Olive Archer (*d.* 1957); four *s.* two *d.*; *m.* 1958, Mabel Graham, Shildon, nr. Bishop Auckland. *Educ.:* Port Talbot Central Sch., Rotherham; Elementary School; W.E.A. Course, Bangor University. 1914-19, R.Q.M. Sergeant, Imperial Camel Corps, East Riding Yorks. Yeomanry. 1913-14 and 1919-45, Lancashire Steel Corporation, employed as steel smelter. Local Government, 1921-36. T.U.C. Delegate to America, 1943-44. Joint Parliamentary Secretary, Ministry of Supply, 1947-50. *Publication:* America as I Saw It (on behalf of War Production Board of America). *Recreations:* gardening, fishing, cricket and swimming. *Address:* Braemar, 17 Holcroft Lane, Culcheth, Nr. Warrington. *T.:* Culcheth 3170. [*Died* 31 *Oct.* 1962.

JONES, John L.; *see* Lees-Jones.

JONES, Dame Katharine Henrietta, D.B.E., *cr.* 1942; R.R.C. 1941 (and Bar 1944); *b.* 3 Feb. 1888; 3rd *d.* of late S. S. Jones, Bengal Civil Service. *Educ.:* Highfield School, Beccles; Bad Neuenahr, Germany. Trained at St. Bartholomew's Hospital, London, 1913-17; joined Q.A.I.M.N.S. in 1917 and served in France; mentioned in despatches, 1937 (Palestine); Principal Matron, War Office, 1938; Senior Principal Matron, B.E.F., Sept. 1939; Matron-in-Chief, 1940-44; retired, 1944. *Recreation:* reading. *Address:* c/o Barclays Bank Ltd., Beccles, Suffolk. *Club:* United Nursing Services. [*Died* 29 *Dec.* 1967.

JONES, Sir Lawrence Evelyn, 5th Bt., *cr.* 1831; M.C.; T.D.; F.R.S.L.; Barrister, Inner Temple; *b.* 6 April 1885; *e. surv. s.* of Sir Lawrence Jones, 4th Bart. and 1st wife, Evelyn Mary Bevan (*d.* 1912); *S.* father 1954; *m.* 1912, Lady Evelyn Grey, *y. d.* of 4th Earl Grey; three *d.* (and two *d.* decd.). *Educ.:* Eton; Balliol College, Oxford (1st Class Mod. Hist.); President O.U.B.C. Major in Bedfordshire Yeomanry (retired). With Helbert, Wagg & Co. Ltd., 1914-45. *Publications:* You and the Peace (with G. B. Shirlaw); The Bishop and the Cobbler; Jesus: Discoverer and Genius; Beyond Belief; A la Carte; Stings and Honey; A Victorian Boyhood; An Edwardian Youth; Georgian Afternoon I forgot to tell You: The Bishop's Aunt; Trepidation in Downing Street; Father Lascaut Hits Back. *Heir: nephew* Christopher Lawrence Jones, *b.* 19 January 1940. *Address:* 14 Wellington Court, St. John's Wood, N.W.8. *T.:* 01-722 1390. *Clubs* Travellers', Beefsteak. [*Died* 6 *Sept.* 1969

JONES, Sir Lewis, Kt., *cr.*1944; J.P.; LL.D. Secretary, The South Wales Siemens Steel Association, North Hill, 2 St. James Cres., Swansea, 1917-61; *b.* Brynamman, 1884; *e. s.* of Evan Jones; *m.* 1911, Alice Maude, *d.* of Frederick Willis, Bath; one *s.* (*yr. s.* killed in India on Service, 1947). *Educ.:* Ammanford; University College, Reading. Served as schoolmaster at Reading for five years; resigned to enter political work; on the outbreak of War, served in the Ministry of Munitions, becoming secretary of the Priority Department; M.P. (L. Nat.) Swansea West Division, 1931-45; Parliamentary Charity Commissioner, 1937-45; Senior Vice-President and Member of the Council and Court of Governors of the University College of Swansea and of the Court of Governors of the University of Wales; appointed by the Minister of Health 1933 as the representative of Wales on the National Health Insurance Joint Committee. J.P. Swansea Borough, 1934-; mem. B.B.C. Gen. Advisory Council, 1952. Hon. LL.D. University of Wales, 1954. *Publications:* miscellaneous articles and papers on economic and industrial questions. *Address:* 32 Harford Court, Sketty, Swansea. *T.:* Swansea 25217. *Club:* National Liberal. [*Died* 10 *Dec.* 1968.

JONES, Lionel; *see* Powys-Jones.

JONES, Llewelyn A. H.-; *see* Hugh-Jones.

JONES, Dame Mary L(atchford) Kingsmill, D.B.E. 1958 (C.B.E. 1949; O.B.E. 1938); M.A. h.c. (Manchester), 1943; *d.* of late Percival and late Margaret Jones, Orwell Park, Dublin; unmarried. *Educ.:* Alexandra College, Dublin. J.P., 1920; elected to Manchester City Council, 1921; Alderman, 1938-66, Hon. Alderman, 1967; Lord Mayor of Manchester, 1947-49; Hon. Freeman of Manchester, 1956; served on following Committees; Education (Chairman 1939-42), Public Health (Chairman 1929-32), Libraries (Chm.), War Memorial (Chm. 1945-51). Ex-Member Lancs. Mental Hosps. Bd. (now part of general health service); Member of Curtis Cttee. on Care of Children, 1944-45; Member of Royal Commission on Justices of the Peace, 1945-47. During War of 1939-45, Regional Officer Central Hosp. Supply Service Red Cross War Organisation. *Address:* 9 Neston Avenue, Withington, Manchester 20. *T.:* Didsbury 5033. *Club:* Soroptimist (Manchester). [*Died* 2 *April* 1968.

JONES, Owen Thomas, F.R.S.; M.A. (Cantab.); D.Sc. (Wales); Emeritus Professor of Geology, Cambridge; *b.* 16 April 1878; *m.*; one *s.* one *d.* (and one *s.* decd.). *Educ.:* Pencader Grammar School; Univ. Coll. of Wales, Aberystwyth (Keeling Natural Science Scholar); Trinity College, Cambridge (Exhibitioner). 1st Class Nat. Sci. Trip. Pt. I. 1902, and Wiltshire Prizeman (Geology and Mineralogy); 1st Class Nat. Sci. Trip. Pt. II. 1903; Harkness Prizeman (Geology), 1904; Sedgwick Essay Prize (Geology), 1910; served on H.M. Geological Survey, 1903-10, surveying parts of Western Carmarthenshire and Pembrokeshire coalfields; Professor of Geology, Aberystwyth, 1910-19; Manchester University, 1919-30; Woodwardian Professor of Geology, Cambridge, 1930-43; Fellow of the Geological and Mineralogical Societies; President 1936-38 and 1950-51, and Foreign Secretary Geological Soc. until 1944; Corresp. of the Geological Society of America and of Palæontological Soc.; Hon. Mem. Société Belge de Géologie. Lyell Medal, Geol. Soc., 1926; Wollaston Medal, Geological Society, 1945; Royal Medal, Royal Society, 1956. Hon. LL.D., Wales. *Publications:* The Mining District of Cardiganshire and West Montgomeryshire; also numerous others on: The Geology of Wales; Geophysics; continental shelves; geology of parts of N. America; Palæontology; igneous intrusions, etc. *Address:* 73 Barton Road, Cambridge. *T.:* 52090. [*Died* 5 *May* 1967.

JONES, Parry (William John), O.B.E. 1962; Hon. A.R.C.M., F.G.S.M.; F.T.C.L.; Principal Tenor, Royal Opera House, Covent Garden, until 1955 when joined Managerial Staff of the Royal Opera House; Professor: Guildhall School of Music; Trinity College of Music; adjudicator; *b.* Blaina, Monmouthshire, 14 February 1891; *s.* of John Rees Jones and Mary Jones (*née* Parry); *m.* 1917, Hilda Dorothy Morris, Cirencester, Glos.; one *s.* *Educ.:* privately; Roy. Coll. of Music; Germany; Italy. Toured U.S.A. and Canada, 1913-15; survivor of torpedoing of Lusitania, May 1915. Served European War, 1914-18, in R.G.A. Principal Tenor D'Oyly Carte, Carl Rosa, Beecham and British National Opera Companies. Has sung in 19 International seasons at Royal Opera House; 27 consecutive seasons of Henry Wood promenade concerts; opera in U.S.A. and most European countries; 70 operas and over 80 oratorios; also all principal festivals, including International Contemporary Festivals, and for choral and orchestral societies since 1920; Amsterdam, Copenhagen and Oslo Festivals since 1945. Principal Tenor chosen for Beethoven Centenary Festival, 1927, Schubert Centenary Festival, 1928; Tenor chosen for bi-centenary Festival performance Messiah (Handel), 1942; soloist at Dedication of Unknown Warrior's Tomb at Westminster Abbey; Member Coronation Choir, 1953, also at Coronation of King George VI. Has been broadcasting since 1923. Member: Royal Philharmonic Soc., 1951, Management Cttee., 1953; Council Incorporated Soc. of Musicians. Liveryman, Worshipful Company of Musicians. *Publications:* musical journalism. *Recreations:* reading, wine tasting, watching cricket and Rugby football. *Address:* 185 Old Brompton Rd., S.W.5. *T.:* Fremantle 4777. *Clubs:* Savage, Chelsea Arts, London Sketch, M.C.C. [*Died* 26 *Dec.* 1963.

JONES, Professor Percy Mansell, M.A.; Professor Emeritus of Manchester University; *b.* 11 April 1889; *s.* of Arnaud Johnson Jones, house decorator, Carmarthen; unmarried. *Educ.:* Queen Elizabeth Grammar School, Carmarthen; University College, Aberystwyth; Balliol College, Oxford. M.A. (Wales) 1913; B.Litt. (Oxon.) 1920; M.A. (Cantab.), 1937; M.A. (Manchester), 1954; D.Litt., *h.c.* (Wales), 1960. Professor of Modern French Literature in the University of Manchester, 1951-56. *Publications:* Emile Verhaeren, 1920; Tradition and Barbarism, 1930; French Introspectives, 1937; Background of Modern French Poetry, 1951; Baudelaire, 1951; Modern French Verse: an Anthology, 1953; Racine and Tragic Poetry (trans.), 1955; Emile Verhaeren (Essay), 1957; (ed.) The Oxford Book of French Verse, 1957; The Assault on French Literature (Essays), 1963; A Book of French Verse (ed. with G. Richardson), 1964. Articles and reviews in Cambridge Jl., French Studies, Modern Language Review, Universities Review, Universities Quarterly, etc. *Recreation:* travel. *Address:* Oak House, Carmarthen.

[*Died* 24 *Jan.* 1968.

JONES, Sir Pryce V. P., Bt.; *see* Pryce-Jones.

JONES, Sir Roderick, K.B.E. 1918; formerly Principal Proprietor of Reuters; Member of Councils of Royal Institute of International Affairs (1927-55) and of The Commonwealth Press Union; Chm. Governing Council, Roedean School; *b.* 1877; *s.* of late Roderick Patrick Jones, Manchester, and Christina, 2nd *d.* of late William Gibb, Kilmarnock; *m.* 1920, Enid Bagnold, writer, *o. d.* of late Col. Arthur Bagnold, C.B., C.M.G.; three *s.* one *d.* An assistant Reuter correspondent in South Africa, 1895; a correspondent, 1900; Reuter's South African editor in London, 1902; in charge of Reuter's in South and Central Africa, Cape Town, 1905; succeeded Baron Herbert de Reuter (*s.* of the founder) in control of the organisation, 1915; Chm. and Managing Dir., 1919-41; in charge of cable and wireless propaganda, 1916-18, when appointed Chief Executive and Dir. of Propaganda in newly-established Ministry of Information; Member Advisory Council, Ministry of Information, 1939; to safeguard Reuter's in the national interest, converted the Company in 1916 into a private Trust at a cost of over half a million sterling; became Principal Proprietor in 1919, and concluded negotiations in 1926 with the Press Association for transfer of Reuters by stages to the British newspapers as a body; retired, 1941, when this process was completed and control was vested in Trustees representing equally London and Provincial newspapers. Delegate to the Imperial Press Conferences in London, 1909, Ottawa 1920, London 1930, Cape Town 1935, London 1946, 1957, and to Internat. Press Conferences, Stockholm, 1923, Warsaw, 1926; Geneva, 1927; also Commonwealth Conference, Royal

Institute of International Affairs, London, 1945. A British delegate to Congress of Europe at The Hague, 1948. Frequent travels British Empire, European countries, Far East, North America, and two journeys round world. Chairman of Marlborough-Windham Club, 1943-52. Legion of Honour; Knight Commander of the Order of the Saviour (Greece); First Class of the Order of the Brilliant Jade (China); Grand Officer of the Order of the Crown of Italy. *Publications:* A Life in Reuters, 1951; articles in the Nineteenth Century and other Periodicals; many lectures and addresses on Internat. Affairs and journalism. *Recreations:* formerly hunting (sometime Master of the Cape Hounds), riding and ski-ing. *Address:* 29 Hyde Park Gate, S.W.7; Rottingdean, Sussex. *Clubs:* Brooks's, Travellers', Beefsteak, Garrick; Civil Service (Cape Town).
[*Died* 23 *Jan.* 1962.

JONES, Maj.-Gen. Roderick Idrisyn, C.B. 1947; C.B.E. 1946 (O.B.E. 1943); D.L.; I.A. (retd.); County Civil Defence Officer, Glos. C.C., 1951-61; *b.* Welshpool, 4 Oct. 1895; *y. s.* of late Rev. John Idrisyn Jones; *m.* 1927, Mollie Audrey, *yr. d.* of late William Lewis Macgregor; no *c.* *Educ.:* Cardiff High School; Manchester University. Studied Electrical Engineering. Served European War, 1914-18, R.E. (in ranks); commissioned 3rd Bn. S. Wales Borderers, 1915; 4th Bn. Gallipoli and Mesopotamia, 1915-18. Transferred I.A. as regular officer in 88th Carnatic Infantry, and when regt. disbanded transferred to R.I.A.S.C. War of 1939-45, with 10th Ind. Inf. Div. as Comdr. R.I.A.S.C. and A.A., and Q.M.G., Iraq, Syria, Persia, Egypt and Libya (despatches, O.B.E.). G.H.Q. India, D.D.S.T., 1943-45; D.A. and Q.M.G. 33rd Ind. Corps in Burma, 1945 until defeat of Japanese Forces; D.A. and Q.M.G. 12th Army and Burma Command, 1945-46 (C.B.E.); Dir. of Supplies and Transport, India, and Head of R.I.A.S.C. (with rank of Maj.-Gen.), 1946-47. C.C. Gloucestershire, 1961-64. D.L. Gloucestershire, 1963. *Recreations:* golf, fishing, horticulture. *Address:* Gun House, Bowbridge, Stroud, Glos. *T.:* Stroud 4766. [*Died* 10 *July* 1970.

JONES, Comdr. Ronald L.; *see* Langton-Jones.

JONES, Ronald O. L. A.; *see* Armstrong-Jones.

JONES, Stanley Wilson, C.M.G. 1939; *b.* 1 July 1888; *y. s.* of late David Jones, Manchester; *m.* 1919, Esther Olive Hartley; one *s.* two *d.* *Educ.:* Hulme Grammar School; Manchester University. Entered Malayan Civil Service, 1911; Under Secretary to F.M.S. Government, 1935; British Resident, Selangor, 1937; Colonial Secretary, Straits Settlements, 1940-42; Officer Administering the Government of the S.S. and High Commissioner of the Malay States, 1940. *Address:* 6 Boscombe Cliff Rd., Bournemouth.
[*Died* 17 *Jan.* 1962.

JONES, Thomas Boughton B.; *see* Bovell-Jones.

JONES, Sir Vincent Strickland, K.B.E., *cr.* 1941 (O.B.E. 1918); *b.* 15 Feb. 1874; *s.* of late Canon Jones, Burneside, Westmorland; *m.* 1910, Mary, *d.* of late Colonel Joscelyn Fitzroy Bagot, M.P., Levens Hall, Kendal; one *s.* one *d.* *Educ.:* Haileybury College. Played Rugger for Westmorland County, 1893, 1894, Capt. 1895; 2nd V.B. Border Regt., 1900; 4th Border Regt., European War, 1914-19; Lt.-Col. A.A. and Q.M.G. Peshawar Division; Afghan War, 1919 (O.B.E. despatches twice); Hon. Lt.-Col. Newfoundland Militia, 1940-1945. Went to Newfoundland, 1910, as Mill Manager of Paper Mill at Grand Falls and has been connected with its progress and expansion ever since. 1912-45: Vice-Pres. and Managing Director, Anglo-Newfoundland Development Co. Ltd., Pres. Anglo-Newfoundland Steamship Co. Ltd., Director Terra Nova Properties Ltd., Gaspesia Sulphite Co. Ltd., Vice-Chairman Newfoundland Forest Fire Patrol. *Recreations:* cricket, lawn tennis, golf. *Address:* Brae House, Willingdon, Eastbourne, Sussex. *T.:* Eastbourne 52387. *Clubs:* English-Speaking Union; Devonshire (Eastbourne); Sussex Cricket (Hove). [*Died* 1 *May* 1967.

JONES, Sir Walter Benton, 2nd Bt., *cr.* 1919; LL.D. M.A.; President and Director, United Steel Cos., Ltd., since 1962 (Chairman, 1928-1962); Director, Appleby-Frodingham Steel Co.; *b.* 26 Sept. 1880; *s.* of Sir Frederick Jones, 1st Bt., and Annie Elizabeth (*d.* 1893), *d.* of Walter Benton; *S.* father, 1936; *m.* 1907, Lily Marguerite (*d.* 1938), *d.* of late James Dixon Fawcett; one *s.* two *d.* *Educ.:* Repton; Trinity College, Cambridge. *Heir: s.* Peter Fawcett Benton Jones, O.B.E. 1945 [*b.* 9 Jan. 1911; *m.* 1936, Nancy, *o. c.* of late Warley Pickering; one *s.* one *d.*] *Address:* Irnham Hall, Grantham. *T.:* Corby Glen 212.
[*Died* 5 *Dec.* 1967.

JONES, Sir William, Kt., *cr.* 1949; C.B.E. 1941; Deputy-Chairman, Denbighshire Quarter Sessions, 1953; part-time Director, South-Western Regional Coal Board since 1949; *b.* 27 June 1888; *s.* of Hugh and Mary Jones; *m.* 1917, Charlotte Maud (*d.* 1932), *d.* of Jos. Dykins; *m.* 1942, Ellen, *d.* of Henry Bennett; two *d.* *Educ.:* Llanrwst and Denbigh. Solicitor, 1922; Clerk of the Peace, Denbighshire, 1930-1949; Regional Controller, Wales, Ministry of Fuel and Power, 1942-45. Member of Royal Commission on Capital Punishment, 1949; part-time Director, Wales Gas Board, 1948-59; Chairman, Re-Development and Government Administration Panels, Council of Wales (resigned 1959). *Address:* Hafod, Ruthin, Denbighshire. *T.:* Ruthin 96.
[*Died* 7 *June* 1961.

JONES, Rev. William G.; *see* Griffith-Jones.

JONES, William Henry Samuel, F.B.A. 1944; Litt.D.; once Pres. of St. Catharine's Coll., Cambridge; *b.* Birmingham, 1876; *s.* of Samuel John Jones, Birmingham; *m.* 1911, Norah Mary Kathleen, *e. d.* of Rev. Dr. Elliott, Shortlands, Kent; one *d.* *Educ.:* King Edward's School, Birmingham; Selwyn Coll., Cambridge. Tutor, York Training College, Classical Master at Stonyhurst College, and Classical Master at Perse School, Cambridge, where he co-operated with Dr. W. H. D. Rouse in applying the Direct Method to the teaching of Latin and Greek, 1902-22; Fellow of St. Catharine's College, Cambridge 1908 (retired, 1943), Bursar, 1919-1933, Hon. Fellow, 1943; Corr. Member of Royal Society of Medicine since 1923; Leverhulme Research Fellow, 1938. *Publications:* editions of Eutropius and of Cornelius Nepos; Latin Teaching; Malaria; Malaria and Greek History; Dea Febris; Greek Morality; The Moral Standpoint of Euripides; Remember; Via Nova; How we Learn; Scientific Method in Schools; Disciplina; What did Jesus mean?; Pausanias (Loeb translation); Hippocrates (Loeb translation); Hippocrates and the *Corpus Hippocraticum* (British Academy publication); The Doctor's Oath; History of St. Catharine's College; Anonymus Londinensis: Philosophy and Medicine in Ancient Greece; The Story of St. Catharine's College, Cambridge, 1951; Pliny's Natural History, Vol. VI, 1951, Vol. VII, 1957 (Loeb Classical Library); articles in learned and scientific journals. *Address:* 28 Millington Road, Cambridge. *T.:* Cambridge 50061. [*Died* 4 *Feb.* 1963.

JONES, William Morris, M.A. (Cantab.), M.Sc. (Wales); F.Inst.P.; retired; *b.* 15 Mar. 1889; *e. s.* of late J. Jones, B.A., Headmaster, Georgetown Schools, Tredegar, Mon.; *m.* Gertrude, *d.* of late Walter Lewis, Pen-y-bryn, Bryn Road, Swansea; one *d.* *Educ.:* University College, Bangor (Prizeman in Mathematics, First Class Hons. in Physics); Emmanuel College, Cambridge (Open Research Exhibitioner). In turn Research Student and Research Fellow of the University of Wales; holder of the University of Cambridge Certificate for Research in Physics; served European War, 1914-18, as Captain, Royal Air Force (Naval Branch); Senior Lecturer in Physics, University College of North Wales, Bangor, 1919-21; Senior Lecturer in Physics, University College, Swansea, 1921-31; Director of Education, Rhondda Urban Dist. Council and Educ. Officer, Rhondda Excepted District (Educ. Act 1944), 1932-54. *Publications:* papers on Electrical Resistance of Nickel in Magnetic Fields; Frictional Electricity on Insulators and Metals; The Most Effective Primary Capacity for Tesla Coils; X-rays and Crystal Structure; an X-ray investigation of Copper-Magnesium Alloys; The Crystal Structures of the Copper-Antimony Alloys; X-ray investigations of Lead-Antimony, Lead-Bismuth, Tin-Bismuth, Tin-Antimony and Bismuth Antimony systems of Alloys. *Address:* Pinnerwood, Parkhouse Road, Minehead, Somerset. *T.:* Minehead 249. [*Died* 19 *Jan.* 1963.

JONES, William Richard, C.B.E. 1948; D.Sc. (Lond.), D.I.C., M.Inst.M.M.; Professor Emeritus of the University of London and of the Imperial College of Science and Technology in Mining Geology and late Dean of Royal School of Mines; Past-Pres. and Gold Medallist, Inst. of Mining and Metallurgy, London; *b.* 8 Jan. 1880; *s.* of Henry and Elizabeth Jones; *m.* 1916, Mary Janet, *d.* of late Capt. D. Roberts; one *s.* *Educ.:* Royal College of Science and Royal School of Mines, London. Chief Asst. Geologist and Acting Govt. Geologist, Federated Malay States and Straits Settlements; Managing Director in the East, High Speed Steel Alloys Mining Co.; Consulting Mining Geologist; Lecturer and Asst. Prof. in Mining Geology, Royal School of Mines; Fell., Imp. Coll. of Science and Technology. *Publications:* Tinfields of the World, 1925; German-English Geological Terminology, 1931; Silicotic Lungs: The Minerals they Contain, 1933; Lead and Zinc Mineral Resources of Great Britain, 1940; Minerals in Industry, 1943; memoirs and papers dealing with ore deposits; General Editor of Murby's German-English Scientific Terminologies. *Address:* 64 Gerard Road, Barnes, S.W.13. *T.:* 01-748 2211. *Club:* Athenæum. [*Died* 9 *June* 1970.

JOPSON, Norman Brooke, M.A. Cambridge; Professor of Comparative Philology, University of Cambridge, 1937-55; Professor Emeritus, 1955; Fellow of St. John's College, Cambridge, since 1937; *b.* Leeds, 20 Jan. 1890; unmarried. *Educ.:* Merchant Taylors' School, Crosby; St. John's College, Cambridge (Scholar). Modern and Mediæval Languages Tripos, and Oriental Languages Tripos, 1912 and 1913; War Office, 1914-1919; Admiralty, 1919-20; 1st Division Civil Servant, Foreign Office, 1920-23; Reader in Comparative Slavonic Philology, Univ. of London, 1923-36, Professor, 1936-37. War Service, 1939-45: Head of Uncommon Languages Department of Postal and Telegraphic Censorship. *Publications:* (with S. C. Boyanus) Spoken Russian; contributions to Encyclopædias and learned publications chiefly on Slavonic and Eastern European Languages. *Recreation:* cycling. *Address:* St. John's College, Cambridge. [*Died* 13 *Jan.* 1969.

JORDAN, Humfrey Robertson, M.A.; Author; *b.* 1885; English; *m.* 1921, Margery James; one *s.* *Educ.:* Bedford; Pembroke College, Cambridge; Sorbonne, Paris. Served with Devonshire Regt. in France and Flanders, 1914-18; travelled widely. *Publications:* The Commander Shall . . .; Sea Way Only; Ship by Herself; Anchor Comes Back; Tide Still Flowing; This Island Demands; Decency of Hate; Day Without Evening; Landfall Then Departure; From Such Freedoms; Blue Water Dwelling; Overdue—Arrived; The Islander; A Valley Decides; Only a Real Jonah; No One Way; No Charts For The Job; Found At Sea; Spoiling For Mischief; Broken Link Holds; Finished with Engines; Not so Easy, etc. *Recreation:* travelling. *Address:* Riccardsdown, Abbotsham, Bideford, N. Devon. *Club:* Oxford and Cambridge. [*Died* 24 *Oct.* 1963.

JORDAN, Louis Arnold, C.B.E. 1948; D.Sc. (London); A.R.C.S.; D.I.C.; F.R.I.C.; M.I.Chem.E.; Member (co-opted), Senate of London University, since 1958; *b.* 23 Sept. 1892; *s.* of late Richard M. Jordan, Leicester; *m.* 1916, Marjorie Rossiter, *d.* of late Weston Aplin, Yeovil; two *d.* *Educ.:* Univ. of London; Roy. Coll. of Science. Scientific Adviser to State of Bhopal, Central India, 1923-26; Director, Research Assoc., Brit. Paint, Colour and Varnish Manufacturers, 1926-59; Prof. of Chemistry, Royal Acad. of Arts, 1958-62; Vice-Pres. and Chm. of Council, Soc. of Chemical Industry, 1952-; Soc. Medallist, 1953; Pres. Oil and Colour Chemists' Association, 1947-48, first Foundation Lecturer, 1963. Member Surrey County Council, 1946-58. Member Pakistan Science Commission, 1959. Mattiello Memorial Lectr., Washington, U.S.A., 1961. Chevalier, Crown of Italy, 1918. *Publications:* Report on Lac to Government of India, Indian Lac Cess Cttee., 1956; Report to the Government of the Federation of Malaya on the Industrial Research Project, 1960. Many papers in scientific and tech. jls. *Address:* Oakhill Drive, Surbiton, Surrey. *T.:* Elmbridge 2405. *Club:* Athenæum. [*Died* 1 *Dec.* 1964.

JORDAN, Lt.-Col. Richard Price, C.M.G. 1916; D.S.O. 1901; late Commanding 2nd Batt. Gloucester Regt.; *b.* 2 Nov. 1869; *m.* 1933, Mary Lilian Gerrish (*d.* 1941), Penn, Bucks. Entered Army, 1889; Captain, 1899; Major, 1910; served S. Africa, 1900-2 (despatches, Queen's medal 4 clasps, King's medal 2 clasps, D.S.O.); European War, 1914-18 (C.M.G.); Bt. Lt.-Col. 1918; retired pay, 1922. *Club:* Army and Navy. [*Died* 22 *Oct.* 1963.

JORY, Norman Adams, B.Sc. (Univ. of N.Z.); F.R.C.S. (Eng.); retired; formerly Consulting Ear, Nose, Throat Surgeon, St. Bartholomew's Hosp., London; *b.* Lawrence, N.Z., 27 July 1896; *s.* of late Rev. J. D. Jory; *m.* 1930, Daphne Forster; two *s.* three *d.* *Educ.:* Auckland Grammar School; Auckland University College, N.Z. (Junior and Senior University Scholar); St. Bartholomew's Hospital and College, London (Treasurer's Prize in Anatomy, Junior Schol. Anatomy and Physiology, Brackenbury Surgical Scholar). Demonstrator of Anatomy, Aural Surgeon, St. Bart's Hospital; late Vice-President and Secretary, Section of Otology, Roy. Soc. Med. Served European War, 1914-1918, as Lieut. N.Z. Rifle Brigade. *Publications:* Meningitis of Otitic Origin, Proc. Roy. Soc. Med., 1935; Acute Otitis Media (Post-graduate Med. Journal, 1938). *Recreations:* swimming, gardening, rifle shooting. *Address:* Highmead, Tilford, Farnham, Surrey. *T.:* Elstead 3157. [*Died* 28 *Dec.* 1965.

JOSE, Sir Ivan Bede; *see* Addenda: II.

JOSLIN, Prof. David Maelgwyn; Professor of Economic History since 1965, and Fellow of Pembroke College since 1951, Cambridge University; *b.* 29 Apr. 1925; *yr. s.* of James John and Mary Joslin; *m.* 1969, Mary M. P. Kidston, *d.* of Col. Richard Kidston, Helensburgh. *Educ.:* Barry County Sch.; St. John's Coll., Cambridge (Scholar). Served in R.N., Sub-Lieut. (Sp.) R.N.V.R., 1943-46. First Cl. Hist. Tripos, Parts I and II, 1947 and 1948; Strathcona Studentship, 1949-1951; Fellow of Pembroke College, 1951; Director of Studies in History, 1952-65; Assistant Tutor, 1958-62; Senior Tutor, 1962-65; University Assistant Lecturer and Lecturer in History, 1954-65. Editor: Jl. of Latin American Studies; Cambridge Latin American Studies. *Publications:* A Century of Banking in Latin America, 1963. Contributor to Studies in the Industrial Revolution, Ed. L. S. Pressnell, 1960. *Recreations:* tennis, travel. *Address:* Court House, Selwyn Gardens, Cambridge. *T.:* Cambridge 57304. *Club:* Oxford and Cambridge University. [*Died* 15 *Oct.* 1970.

JOUBERT DE LA FERTE, Air Chief Marshal Sir Philip Bennet, K.C.B., *cr.* 1938 (C.B. 1936); C.M.G. 1919; D.S.O. 1917; *m.* 1915, Marjorie Denison (marr. diss., 1948), *y. d.* of late F. J. Hall, Bellevue, Sheffield; two *d.*; *m.* 1948, Joan Catherine Cripps, C.St.J. *Educ.:* Elstree; Harrow; Woolwich. R.F.A. 1907; seconded R.F.C. 1913; served in France from Aug. 1914; Egypt, 1916-17 Italy, 1917-18 (Order of SS. Maurice and Lazarus, Cavaliere, 1918; Croce di Guerra, 1918; despatches six times); R.A.F. Instructor at Imperial Defence College, 1927-29; Commanded No. 23 Group, Inland Area, 1929 30; Commandant Royal Air Force Staff College, Andover, 1930-34; Air Officer Commanding Fighting Area, 1934-36; Air Officer Commanding-in-Chief, Coastal Command R.A.F., 1936-37; Air Officer Commanding Royal Air Force, India 1937-39; Assistant Chief of Air Staff; Air Chief Marshal, 1941; Officer Commanding-in-Chief, Coastal Command, 1941-43; an Inspector-General of the Royal Air Force, 1943; retired and re-employed, 1943; Deputy Chief of Staff, for Information and Civil Affairs, S.E.A.C., 1943-45; reverted to retired list, 1945; Director of Public Relations, Air Ministry, 1946-47; reverted to retired list, 1947. Commander Legion of Merit, U.S.A.; Knight Grand Cross of Orange Nassau, with Swords. *Publications:* The Fated Sky, 1952; The Third Service, 1955; Rocket, 1956; Birds and Fishes, 1960; Look at Aeroplanes, 1960; The Forgotten Ones, 1961; Fun and Games, 1964. *Address:* 43 Blomfield Road, W.9. [*Died* 21 *Jan.* 1965.

JOURDAIN, Lt.-Col. Henry Francis Newdigate, C.M.G. 1916; F.R.G.S.; F.R.S.A.I.; O.St.J., 1928; Life Governor Universal Beneficent Society, 1922; Hon. Secretary and Hon. Treasurer The Connaught Rangers Regimental Association, 1912-14 and 1922-63; President, 1942; F.A.G.S. 1926; Great Gold Medal of the Institut Historique et Héraldique de France, 1934; Pres. Oxford Philatelic Society, 1930, Vice-Pres., 1937, Pres., 1938, Life Mem., 1959; Hon. Treasurer and Vice-President St. John Ambulance Association, Oxfordshire County Centre, 1926-46; President League of Mercy, Dover, 1918-28; Vice-President League of Mercy for Oxfordshire, 1918-46; Vice-President Commonwealth Irish Association 1943; Member Hakluyt Society; Corr. Mem. Mil. Soc. of Ireland; *b.* 27 March 1872; 4th *s.* of late Rev. F. Jourdain, M.A., R.D.; *m.* 1st, 1908, Molly (*d.* 1920), 2nd *d.* of late Henry O'Farrell, Portumna; no *c.*; 2nd, 1923, Mary Mackintosh (*d.* 1963), *o. d.* of late J. Maclennan, Portree. *Educ.:* Derby Sch.; R.M.C., Sandhurst. 2nd Lieut. 1st Batt. The Connaught Rangers (88th). 1893; Capt. 1900; Major, 1912; Lt.-Col. (temp.), 1914; Subst. Lt.-Col. 1920. S. African War, 1899-1902, Colenso, Spion Kop, Relief of Ladysmith, etc. (Queen's medal 5 clasps, King's medal 2 clasps); European War, 1914-18; raised and comd. 5th Batt.; then comd. 29th Inf. Bde., Gallipoli, Aug.-Sept. 1915; Salonika, 1915; Serbia and Bulgaria, 1916 (despatches, C.M.G.); France and Belgium, 1917, Messines, 3rd Ypres, etc.; comd. 6th Batt. The Connaught Rangers and 16th Batt. R.W.F.; also served in Egypt (1914-15 Star, General Service Medal, and Victory Medal and Palm); comd. 3rd Batt. The Connaught Rangers, 19 Jan. 1918-3 April 1919; commanded 2nd Bn. The Connaught Rangers in Upper Silesia, 1921-22; retired pay 1922; Order of Mercy, 1923, bar, 1932; La Croix de la Reconnaissance, Yougoslave, 1938. *Publications:* A History of the Mess Plate of the 88th Connaught Rangers, 1904; A Record of the 5th Service Battalion The Connaught Rangers, 1916; a History of the 1st Battalion the Connaught Rangers, 1793-1922, 1924; Some Regimental Medals of the 88th and 94th Regiments, 1923; History of 2nd, 3rd, 4th, 5th, and 6th Battalions of the Connaught Rangers, in vols. ii. and iii., 1927 and 1928; Medals and Decorations of the Connaught Rangers, 1933; Ranging Memories, 1934; The Natal Campaign, 1899-1900, 1948; Editor of The Ranger, 1912-14 and 1922-1962. *Recreations:* The Regimental Association (which he founded in 1912); tennis and gardening. *Address:* Fyfield Lodge, Fyfield Road, Oxford. *T.:* Oxford 57789. *Club:* Army and Navy (Life Member).
[*Died* 29 *Jan.* 1968.

JOWITT, Harold, C.M.G. 1945; B.A., M.Ed., Dip.Ed. (S. Africa); Senior Lecturer in Education and Native Administration. Roma University College, Basutoland, since 1950; *b.* 1893. *Educ.:* Univ. College, Southampton. Headmaster Edendale Training Coll., Natal, 1913; Inspector of Schools, Natal, 1918; Director of Native Education, Southern Rhodesia, 1924; Director of Native Development, 1929; Director of Education and Member of Legislative and Executive Councils, Uganda, 1934-45; Director of Education, Bechuanaland, 1945-50. *Publications:* Principles of Education for African Teachers; Suggested Methods for African Schools. *Address:* University College, Roma, Basutoland, S. Africa. [*Died* 1963.

JOYCE, Archibald; Waltz Composer; *b.* Belgravia, 1873; married. *Educ.:* Paddington. Started life as a chorister, afterwards became a pianist, specializing in dance music; started Archibald Joyce's Orchestra, and attended a very large number of functions; toured as Conductor with Ellen Terry, 1909; since 1914 has largely devoted time to composing; first English Waltz Composer to have Compositions published on the Continent. *Publications: Waltzes:* Chanson de mon Cœur; Songe d'Automne; Vision of Salome; Sweet Memories; Vision d'Amour; Remembrance; Love and Life; Thousand Kisses; Dreaming; When the Birds began to Sing; Passing of Salome; Charming; Always Gay; Maiden's Blush; Entrancing; Love's Mystery; L'Automne; Acushla; Blue; Paradise; Dreams of You; Bohemia; Just a Memory; Militaire; Song of the River (for B.B.C.); Violetta; Première Danseuse; I Could Dance For Ever With You; Trottie True (Rank film). Musical Comedy, Toto with Merlin Morgan, 1916; One Night of Love; Let All the World go by; Dream of the Ball; Sleeping Water; Re-in-carnation-of-Salome; Sweet William; Musical Comedy, Gabrielle; Caravan; Suite; Alpine Climbers; Skating on the Ice; Danse de Ballet; Iris; A Night in Vienna; A River Dream; Romance; Novelty Dance; Tangle Toes; Novelty, Bangkollerdy, Lambeth Way; Waltz Militaire, Victorious (dedicated by kind permission, to Rt. Hon.

Winston Churchill); Grand Ensemble; Homage to the R.A.F.; Tango; Fidelity; Grand Waltz Imperial; Café Colette, Polka; Tales of Joyce (selection); Spanish Tambourine Dance; Concert-Polka, Xylophone Solo, Vienna Café; Military Band Tarantella; Vocal Concert Waltz; Waltz of my Dreams; Neapolitan Tambourine Dance; Polka; Frou Frou; Irish Dance novelty; Mickey's Birthday; Violoncello Solo; Spanish Bolero; The Modern Girls Parade; *Songs:* I'm Skipper of a Submarine, God's Greatest Gift, The Rogue of the Road, Awake, The Morning Light, Dreams of Bohemia, Friends dear to Me, The Modern Girl; *Marches:* The Palace Guard, The Recruit, Queen's Guard, Colour Sergeant, The Old Grenadier, Royal Standard, American March, The Coon Drum Major, Royal Parade, Hiking to Brighton, Ceremonial March Britannica, Wedding Bells. *Recreation:* motoring. *Address:* Kya, 75 Langley Park Road, Sutton, Surrey. *T.:* Vigilant 4682. [*Died* 22 *March* 1963.

JOYCE, Rt. Rev. Edward Michael; Bishop of Christchurch, N.Z. (R.C.), since 1950; *b.* 26 June 1907. *Educ.:* Holy Cross College, Mosgiel, New Zealand. Assistant Priest at St. Teresa's Church, Riccarton. Major Chaplain, second N.Z.E.F. overseas. Parish Priest of Our Lady of Victories Church, Sockburn. *Address:* Cathedral of the Blessed Sacrament, Christchurch, New Zealand. *T.:* 33.808. [*Died* 28 *Jan.* 1964.

JOYCE, Lieut.-Col. Pierce Charles, C.B.E. 1920; D.S.O. 1918; late S. Staffs. Regt. and The Connaught Rangers; late Military Adviser to the Iraq Government; *o. surv. s.* of Pierce J. Joyce, D.L., of Mervue, Galway, Ireland; *m.* 1921, Colin, *o.d.* of late Maj.-Gen. R. H. Murray, C.B., C.M.G. *Educ.:* Beaumont College, Old Windsor. Joined 1st Battalion The Connaught Rangers, 1900; served South African War, 1900-1902 (severely wounded, Queen's medal with 3 clasps, King's medal with 2 clasps); attached Egyptian Army, 1907-16 (Egyptian medal and clasp, 4th Class Order of the Medjidieh, 4th Class Order of the Nile); served European War, 1915-18; Gallipoli, Egyptian Expeditionary Force (Brevet Lt.-Col., C.B.E., D.S.O., Croix d'Officier Legion of Honour, Arabian Order of the Nahda, 2nd Class); retired pay, 1932. *Address:* Firtrees, Crowthorne, Berks. *Club:* Army and Navy. [*Died* 1 *Feb.* 1965.

JUDD, Harold Godfrey, C.B.E. 1918; C.A.; of Mann, Judd & Co., chartered accountants, London; *b.* Wuchang, China, 14 Dec. 1878; *s.* of Charles Henry Judd, Missionary, China; *m.* 1st, Constance Zoë, *e. d.* of Wm. H. Hoyte, architect, Nottingham; one *s.* four *d.*; 2nd, 1922, Elizabeth Miller, *e. d.* of Andrew Dodds Fairbairn, Hampstead. *Educ.:* The Collegiate School, Chefoo. Articled to John Mann & Son, C.A., Glasgow and London, 1894; assumed partner, 1905; entered Ministry of Munitions, 1915; Deputy Director of Accounts (National Factories), 1916; Director of Contract Finance, 1917; Deputy Controller of Contracts, 1917; on honorary service in Ministry of Supply, as Controller of Salvage, 1939-41, and as Director of Salvage and Recovery (General), 1941-46; resumed professional practice as Senior partner of his firm, 1946. Mayor of Hampstead, 1951-53. *Publications:* Colliery Accounts (joint author); Oncost; other booklets on cost accounts. *Recreations:* golf, painting. *Address:* 7 Bell Moor, Hampstead Heath, N.W.3. *T.:* Hampstead 0132; 8 Fredericks Place, E.C.2. *T.:* Metropolitan 8613. [*Died* 5 *Jan.* 1961.

JUIN, Alphonse Pierre; Maréchal de France; Hon. G.C.B. 1944; Grand Croix de la Légion d'Honneur; Médaille Militaire; D.S.M. and Chief Commander, U.S. Legion of Merit; *b.* 16 December 1888; *m.* 1928, Cécile Bonnefoy; two *s.* *Educ.:* Lycées Constantine and Alger; École Spéciale Militaire de Saint-Cyr. Moroccan campaign, 1912-14; Lt. and Capt., 1914-18 (severely wounded); Rif campaign, 1925; Brig.-Gen., Chief of Staff, North African Forces, 1938; G.O.C. 15th Motorised Div., Northern France, 1939; prisoner of Germans, 1940; released, 1941; C.-in-C., North African Forces, Nov. 1941; C.-in-C., French Forces, Tunisian campaign, 1942-43; C.-in-C. French Expeditionary Corps, Italy, 1943; Battles of Belvedere and Garigliano; Chief of General Staff, French Armed Forces, 1944-47; Resident-General in Morocco, 1947-51; C.-in-C. Allied Land Forces, Central Europe, 1951-53; Commander-in-Chief, Allied Forces, Central Europe, 1953-1956. Received Marshal's baton, 1952. Member of French Academy, 1953. *Publications:* Le Maghreb en feu, 1957; L'Europe en question, 1958; Mémoires, 1959-1960; Je suis soldat, 1960; C'étaient nos frères, 1962; La Campagne d'Italie, 1962; Trois siècles d'obéissance militaire, 1963; La France en Algérie, 1963; La brigade marocaine à la bataille de la Marne, 1964. *Recreations:* bridge, hunting, fishing, riding. *Address:* 26 Avenue Kléber, Paris 16e, France. [*Died* 27 *Jan.* 1967.

JUKES HUGHES, Captain Edward Glyn de Styrap, C.B.E. 1940; Royal Navy; *b.* 10 May 1883; *s.* of late Comdr. R. Jukes Hughes, R.N., Whiddon, nr. Newton Abbot, Devon; *m.* 1928, Dorothy Noel, twin *d.* of late Maurice Turner, Ashe House, Hants; one *s.* twin *d.* *Educ.:* R.N. School, Lee on the Solent; H.M.S. Britannia. Went to sea, 1898; qualified as a Gunnery Lieutenant; served during European War, H.M.S. Minotaur and as Commander of H.M.S. Glorious; retired in 1928. Served War of 1939-45, as Principal Sea Transport Officer (with rank of Commodore 2nd class) at Southampton, 1939-40 (responsible for dispatch of Expeditionary Force to France); at Dover for Dunkirk evacuation, 1940 (C.B.E.); Principal Sea Transport Officer for Clyde and Scottish Ports, 1940-46. Chevalier of Legion of Honour; Imperial Russian Order of St. Anne with crossed swords. *Address:* Stourbridge House, Milton-on-Stour, Gillingham, Dorset. [*Died* 21 *May* 1966.

JULER, Frank Anderson, C.V.O. 1947; M.A., M.B., B.Ch., F.R.C.S.; Col. late R.A.M.C.; Extra Surgeon-Oculist to Her Majesty's Household since 1952; Consulting Surgeon, Moorfields Eye Hospital, E.C.1; Consulting Ophthalmic Surgeon, St. Mary's Hospital, W.2; Mem. Council, Roy. Medical Benevolent Fund; *b.* 22 Aug. 1880; *s.* of Henry Juler, F.R.C.S., and Amy M. C. Juler 23 Cavendish Square, W.1.; *m.* Mabel, *d.* of Stanes Chamberlayne of Witherley Hall, Atherstone; one *s.* four *d.* *Educ.:* St. Paul's School; Trinity College, Cambridge (1st Cl. Nat. Sci. Tripos, Pt. I); St. Mary's Hosp. Paddington (entrance Univ. Scholar); subsequently Ophthalmic Surgeon: Queen Elizabeth Hosp. for Children, Shadwell, Central London Ophthalmic Hosp., the London Lock Hosps., the Hosp. of St. Luke (Clergy Nursing Home), St. John's School, Leatherhead; Queen Charlotte's Maternity Hospital; Royal Society of Musicians. Served European War of 1914-19: Ophthalmic Surgeon Specialist; Capt. Royal Army Medical Corps, 1916-1919; Cons. Ophthalmologist, B.E.F., France, 1939-40. Surgeon-Oculist to King George VI's Household, 1936-52. Pres., Ophthalmological Soc. of U.K., 1948-50; Pres. Ophthalmic Section, R.S.M., 1942-44; Vice-Pres. Faculty of Ophthalmologists, 1946-47. *Publications:* contribs. to medical jls., B.M.J., British Jl. of Ophthalmology, The Ophthalmoscope. *Address:* 36 Harley House, Marylebone Road, N.W.1. *T.:* Welbeck 7442. *Club:* Oxford and Cambridge University. [*Died* 7 *Feb.* 1962.

JUNG, Carl Gustav, M.D., LL.D., D.Sc., D.Litt.; Dr. ès lettres; Hon. F.R.S.M.; Professor ordinarius of Medical Psychology at University of Basle, 1944; Professor of Psychology at the Federal Polytechnical Univ., Zürich, 1933-41; physician for nervous and mental diseases since 1909; *b.* 26 July 1875; father, philologist and clergyman; *m.* 1903, Emma (*d.* 1955); one *s.* four *d.* *Educ.:* Bâle (Medical Degree); psychological studies in Paris. Physician at the Psychiatric Clinic of the University of Zürich, 1900-9; Lecturer on Psychiatry at the University, 1905-13. Hon. degrees include: LL.D.: Clark Univ., U.S.A., 1909; Fordham Univ., U.S.A., 1920; Univ. of Calcutta, 1938; D.Sc.: Harvard Univ., 1936; Univ. of Allahabad, India, 1937; Oxford Univ., 1938; D.Litt.: Benares Hindu Univ., 1937; Univ. of Geneva, 1945. Hon. Associate, Kaiserlich Deutschen Akademie der Naturforscher, 1934; Hon. F.R.Soc.Med. Lond., 1939; Hon. Mem. Roy. Medico-Psychological Assoc., 1952. *Publications:* Psychology of Dementia Præcox, 1906; The Theory of Psychoanalysis, 1916; Studies in Word Association, 1916; Collected papers on Analytical Psychology, 1917; Psychological Types, 1923; Contributions to Analytical Psychology, 1928; The Secret of the Golden Flower (with Richard Wilhelm), 1930; Modern Man in Search of a Soul, 1933; Psychology and Religion, 1938; Essays on Contemporary Events, 1947; (with C. Kerényi) Introduction to a Science of Mythology, 1951; The Undiscovered Self, 1958; Flying Saucers, 1959; *Collected Works* (English): Vol. 1, Psychiatric Studies; Vol. 5, Symbols of Transformation; Vol. 7, Two Essays on Analytical Psychology; Vol. 8, The Structure and Dynamics of the Psyche; Vol. 9, I, The Archetypes and the Collective Unconscious; Vol. 9, II, Aion: Researches into the Phenomenology of the Self; Vol. 11, Psychology and Religion; Vol. 12, Psychology and Alchemy; Vol. 16, The Practice of Psychotherapy; Vol. 17, The Development of Personality. *Relevant Publication:* C. G. Jung, by E. A. Bennett, 1961. *Recreations:* sailing, researches about Primitive Psychology in North Kenya, 1925-26, and other voyages. *Address:* (private) Seestrasse 228, Kuesnacht-Zürich, Switzerland; C. G. Jung Institute, Zürich, Switzerland.

[*Died* 6 *June* 1961.

JURY, Colonel Edward Cotton, C.M.G. 1919; M.C.; *b.* 20 Oct. 1881; *s.* of late Charles Cotton Jury, of Aultmore, Tunbridge Wells; *m.* 1st, 1906, Edith Mary (*d.* 1930), *e. d.* of late E. Ralph Dodsworth, J.P., York; one *s.* (one *d.* decd.); 2nd, 1932, Dorothy Rose, *y.d.* of late E. R. Dodsworth, J.P., York. *Educ.:* Rugby; Royal Military College, Sandhurst. Entered Army as 2nd Lieut. 18th Hussars, 1900; served S. Africa, 1901-2 (Queen's medal with 5 clasps); European War, 1914-18 (despatches thrice, C.M.G., M.C., Legion of Honour, Croix de Guerre, Order of the Crown of Belgium, American Distinguished Service Medal); commanded 18th Queen Mary's Own Royal Hussars, 1919-22; G.S.O.1 Poona District, 1922-26; A.A.G. Egypt, 1927-29; retired pay, 1929. *Address:* Clonmore, Foxrock, Co. Dublin. *Club:* Cavalry.

[*Died* 1 *Jan.* 1966.

K

KAHLE, Paul Ernest, Dr.phil., Lic.theol.; F.B.A. 1948; Professor Emeritus, Bonn University, 1939; Hon. Professor, Münster University, 1953; *b.* Hohenstein, E. Prussia, 21 Jan. 1875; *s.* of late Ernest Kahle, D.D., Professor, and late Bertha (*née* Schmidt), Danzig; *m.* 1917, Marie (*née* Gisevius) (*d.* 1948); four *s.* (and three *s.* decd.). *Educ.:* Univs. of Marburg, Halle, Berlin; German Pastor (Cairo, Egypt, 1903-08); Asst., German Archæol. Inst., Jerusalem, 1909-10; Dozent, Halle University, 1909-14. Ord. Professor Oriental Languages, Giessen Univ., 1914-23. Hon. D.Theol., Giessen, 1923; Prof., Dir. of Orient. Inst., Bonn Univ. 1923-1939; emigrated to England, Apr. 1939; Mem. Hon. Société Asiatique, Paris, 1935; Hon. D.Litt. Oxford, 1939; Hon. Mem., Soc. for O.T. Study, 1939; Hon. D.D. Aberdeen, 1940; D. of Heb. Letters (*h.c.*) New York, 1944; Hon. Mem., Soc. of Biblical Literature and Exegesis, America, 1941; Corr. Mem.: Berlin Acad., 1947; Leipzig Acad., 1958; For. Assoc., Roy. Belgian Acad., 1947. Consejero de Honor, Consejo Superior de Investigaciones Cientificas, Madrid, 1951; Hon. Mem., Deutsche Morganländische Gesellschaft, 1952; Corr. Mem., Higher Inst. of Coptic Studies, Cairo, 1954; Burkitt Medal, Brit. Acad. (for Biblical Studies), 1954; Hon. Mem., Franz Delitzsch Gesellsch, Münster, 1958; Hon. Fellow, School of Oriental and African Studies, Univ. of London, 1960. Royal Prussian Order of Crown, 1906; Comdr. Order of Merit, Federal Republic of Germany, 1955. *Publications:* Masoreten des Ostens, 1913; Masoreten des Westens, I, II, 1927, 1930; Biblia Hebraica, ed. R. Kittel, Textum Masoreticum curavit P. Kahle, 1937; Volkserzählungen aus Palästina (with Hans Schmidt), I, II, 1918, 1930; Piri Reis, Bahriye, 1926; Der Leuchtturm von Alexandria, 1930; Die Chronik des Ibn Iyas (with Dr. Mohamed Mostafa), 1931, 1932, 1935; Die verschollene Columbuskarte von 1498, 1933; The Cairo Geniza Schweich Lectures of the British Academy 1941, London, 1947, 2nd edn., Oxford, 1959, German Trans. (Berlin) 1962; Die hebräischen Handschriften aus der Höhle, 1951; Der hebräische Bibeltext seit Franz Delitzsch, 1960; Presentation Volumes: Studien zur Geschichte und Kultur des Nahen und Fernen Orients, Leiden, 1935; Opera Minora (Leiden), 1956. *Address:* Graf Recke Strasse 17, Düsseldorf, Germany.

[*Died* 24 *Sept.* 1964.

KAISER, Henry J.; Industrialist, Builder and Founder of Hospitals, U.S.A.; *b.* Sprout Brook, N.Y., 9 May 1882; *s.* of Francis J. Kaiser and Mary Yops; *m.* 1st, 1907, Bessie Hannah Fosburgh (*d.* 1951); one *s.* (and one *s.* *decd.*); 2nd, 1951, Alyce Chester. Engaged in highway construction, British Columbia, Washington, California, Cuba, 1914-30; Mississippi Levee, 1927-1930, pipe-line projects in South-west, 1930-1933; Chairman exec. cttee. of Six Companies, Inc. (contractors for constrn. of Boulder Dam), 1931; Pres. and Chm. exec. com. Bridge Builders, Inc., 1933; organizer and Pres. Columbia Construction Co., Consolidated Builders, Inc.; Manager of seven shipyards on Pacific Coast during War of 1939-45; Nat. Chm., Victory Clothing Collection, 1945-46. Chairman of Board, Kaiser Industries Corporation; "Kaiser Family of Industries" include (besides Kaiser Industries Corp., parent company) Kaiser Aerospace & Electronics Corp.; Kaiser Broadcasting Corp.; Kaiser Hawaii-Kai Development Co.; Kaiser 'Jeep' Corp.; (operates) Kaiser Engineers Division; Nat. Pres., Associated General Contractors of America; Member: Newcomen Soc. of North America; Beta Gamma Sigma Business Fraternity, etc. La Salle medal, 1944; Cunningham Award, 1954, and many other awards, 1960-. Founder, with Mrs. Kaiser, of Permanente Foundn., 1948 (Chm. Trustees, 1948-), now Kaiser Foundn., sponsors prepaid health plan; also Cal. Rehabilitation Centers. Holds hon. degree from univs. and colls. Episcopalian. Chevalier, Legion of Honour.

Address: Kaiser Center, 300 Lakeside Drive, Oakland, Calif. 94604, U.S.A. *Clubs:* Saints and Sinners (New York); Commonwealth (Calif.); Press (San Francisco); Automobile Old Timers; Waialae Country (Honolulu); Elks (Everett, Washington).
[*Died* 24 *Aug.* 1967.

KAISER SHAMSHER JANG BAHADUR RANA, H.H. Commanding-General Sir, First Class Star of Nepal, 1920; 1st Class Gurkha Right Hand, 1935; Grand Officer Legion of Honour, 1934; G.B.E. (Hon.) *cr.* 1927 (K.B.E. (Hon.), *cr.* 1924); Defence Minister, Nepal, since 1951; Senior Commanding General of Nepalese Army, 1948; *b.* Thapathali, 8 Jan. 1892; 3rd *s.* of late Maharaja of Nepal, Sir Chandra Shamsher Jang Bahadur Rana, G.C.B., G.C.S.I., G.C.M.G., G.C.V.O., D.C.L., and H.H. Bada Maharani Loka Bhakta Laxmi Devi (*d.* 1905); *m.* 1st, 1904, H.R.H. The Princess Royal of Nepal; 2nd, 1943, Krishna Chandra Kumari of Bajura; four *s.* five *d.* *Educ.:* private tuition; Singha Durbar School, and Durbar High School. Accompanied father on state visit to Europe, 1908; in charge of reception on King George V.'s visit to Nepal, 1911; led second contingent to India, 1915-16 (British War Medal, K.B.E.); Director-General Dept. of Commerce (Foreign Imports), 1907-39; Director-Gen. of Museum, 1928-39; Director-Gen. of Archæology (Lumbini Excavations), 1931-39; Director-Gen. Foreign Affairs, 1932-37; Commanding-Gen. Southern Command and Q.M.G., Nepalese Army, 1934-45; Nepalese Ambassador in London, 1947-48; Pres. of Prince of Wales' Nepal Visit Committee and in charge shikar arrangements, 1920-21; Chairman of Kathmandu Municipality and Water-works and Rotary Judge, Supreme Court of Appeal, 1922-30; Senior Member Reorganization Board and Legislative and Administrative Council, 1930-32; Earthquake, Jubilee, and Long Service Medals. *Publications:* trans. Vikramorvashi into Nepali, 1924. *Recreations:* archælogical, historical and literary research, gardening and shikar. *Address:* Kaiser Mahal, Kathmandu, Nepal.
[*Died* 7 *June* 1964.

KALMUS, Herbert Thomas, B.S., Ph.D., Dr. Eng.; Exec. and Chem. Engineer; Director, Stanford Research Inst.; President and General Manager, Technicolor Corp., and Technicolor, Inc.; Hon. Chm. Société Technicolor, Paris; *b.* Chelsea, Mass., 9 Nov. 1881; *s.* of Benjamin G. Kalmus and Ada Isabella Gurney; *m.* 1st, 1902, Natalie Mabelle Dunfee (marriage dissolved, 1921); no *c.*; 2nd, 1949, Eleanore King. *Educ.:* Massachusetts Institute of Technology (B.S. 1904); University of Zürich (Ph.D. 1906). Principal, University School, San Francisco, Cal., 1904-05; Grad. Fellow, Mass. Inst. Technology, studying in Europe, 1905-1906; Instr. 1907-08, Research Associate, 1908-10, Mass. Inst. Technology; Prof. Physics, 1910-12, Prof. Electro-Chemistry and Metallurgy, 1913-15, Queen's Univ., Kingston, Ont.; Dir. Research Lab. of Electro-chemistry and Metallurgy, Canadian Government, 1913-15; Member American Inst. Chem. Engineers, American Physical Soc., Soc. of Motion Picture and Television Engineers (New York), Acad. of Motion Picture Arts and Sciences (Hollywood, Calif.). *Publications:* about 50 articles to technical journals. *Recreation:* golf. *Address:* Centerville, Cape Cod, Massachusetts; 671 Siena Way, Bel Air, Los Angeles, California; 30 Rockefeller Plaza, New York, N.Y.; 6311 Romaine St., Hollywood, California, U.S.A. *Clubs:* Wianno (Wianno, Mass.); Oyster Harbors (Osterville, Mass.); Algonquin (Boston); Masquers (Hollywood); Los Angeles Country, Bel Air Country (Los Angeles); Union League, Motion Picture Pioneers (New York). [*Died* 11 *July* 1963.

KANDEL, Isaac Leon; Professor Emeritus, Teachers College, Columbia University, since 1946; Professor emeritus, University of Manchester, since 1950; *b.* Romania, 22 Jan. 1881; *s.* of Abraham and Fanny Kandel, Manchester; *m.* 1915, Jessie S. Davis (*d.* 1949), Manchester; one *s.* one *d.* *Educ.:* Manchester Grammar School; University of Manchester; Columbia University. Asst. Classical Master, Royal Academical Institution, Belfast, 1906-08; Asst. Editor, Monroe's Cyclopedia of Education, 1909-13; Lecturer, 1913-23, Professor, 1923-46, Teachers College, Columbia University. Staff Member, Carnegie Foundation for the Advancement of Teaching, 1914-23; Simon Research Fellow, Univ. of Manchester, 1947-48; Professor of American Studies, University of Manchester, 1948-50; Staff member, Nat. Cttee. for a free Europe, New York, 1952-. Litt.D. Univ. of Melbourne, 1938; LL.D. Univ. of North Carolina, 1946. Chevalier, Légion d'Honneur, 1937. *Publications:* History of Secondary Education, 1930; Comparative Education, 1933; Conflicting Theories of Education, 1938; Cult of Uncertainty, 1943; Intellectual Co-operation, National and International, 1944; The New Era in Education, 1955; American Education in the Twentieth Century, 1957; William Chandler Bagley: Stalwart Educator, 1961. (ed.) Educational Yearbook, 1924-44; (ed.) School and Society 1946-53; Universities Quarterly, 1948-49, etc.; contrib. to Times Educational Supplement, Journal of Education, Universities Quarterly, American Scholar, Educational Forum, etc. *Address:* Woodside Ave., Westport, Conn., U.S.A.
[*Died* 14 *June* 1965.

KANTHACK, Francis Edgar, C.M.G. 1917; D.Sc.; M.Inst.C.E.; M.I.Mech.E.; F.R.S (S.A.); Consulting Engineer; late Director of Irrigation, Union of South Africa; *b.* Liverpool, 15 Jan. 1872; *m.* 1899, Rosa Higham (*d.* 1947); one *d.* *Educ.:* Liverpool College; Germany; R.I.E. College, Coopers Hill. India P.W.D., 1894-1906; went to S. Africa, 1906. *Address:* Escom House, Rissik Street, Johannesburg, S. Africa. [*Died* 3 *Oct.* 1961.

KAPP, Reginald Otto, B.Sc. (Eng.) Birmingham; M.I.E.E., Pender Professor of Electrical Engineering, University College, 1935-50 (now Emeritus Professor); Dean of the Faculty of Engineering and Member of Senate, University of London, 1946-50; apptd., 1950, Consultant to Kennedy & Donkin, Consulting Engineers; *b.* Brentwood, Essex, 2 Aug. 1885; *s.* of Gisbert Kapp, late Prof. of Electrical Engineering at the Univ. of Birmingham; *m.* 1932, Dorothy M. Wilkins, B.Sc., M.B., B.S. (*d.* 1966); one *s.* one *d.* *Educ.:* School in Germany; Univ. of Birmingham. With Brown, Boveri & Co. of Baden, Switzerland, employed on electric traction work, 1909-13; with exception of the war years assistant to Kennedy and Donkin, consulting engineers, and responsible to them for the design and supervision of various work on railway electrification, electric power stations, and transmission and distribution networks, incl. British Grid system, 1913-35; Mem. Council of Middlesex Hospital Medical School; Governor Northampton College of Advanced Technology and Chairman of its Academic Advisory Cttee.; Founder: Presentation of Technical Information Discussion Group; Occam Soc.; served European war as sniper and scout, and later as an officer in the R.E. *Publications:* Science versus Materialism; The Presentation of Technical Information; Mind, Life and Body; Facts and Faith (The Dual Nature of Reality); Towards a Unified Cosmology; Revised the late Dr. Gisbert Kapp's book on Transformers; Edited Pitman's series on Electrical Transmission and Distribution; Numerous papers to the Institution of Electrical Engineers and other learned bodies, and articles in the technical press. *Recreations:* music, gardening. *Address:* Gardole, Stanhope Rd., Croydon, Surrey. *T.:* Croydon 6711. *Club:* Athenæum. [*Died* 20 *Feb.* 1966.

KARLOFF, Boris (William Henry Pratt); Actor (stage and film); *b.* Dulwich, England, 23 Nov. 1887; *s.* of Edward Pratt and Eliza Sara Millard; *m.* 1928, Dorothy Stine; one *d.*; *m.* 1946, Evelyn Helmore. *Educ.:* Merchant Taylors' School, London; Uppingham School. Began stage career in U.S., 1910; has acted successfully in films since 1920; *later films include:* Secret Life of Walter Mitty, Unconquered, Personal Column, Strange Door, Voodoo Island, Isle of the Dead, Haunted Strangler, Doctor from Seven Dials, Frankenstein The Mummy, The Terror, The Venetian Affair, The Sorcerers, Blind Man's Bluff, The Sniper, House of Evil, Snake People, Fear Chamber, Crimson Altar, Incredible Invasion. *TV Series:* Colonel March of Scotland Yard; Thriller; Out of this World. Appeared on New York stage in: Arsenic and Old Lace, Linden Tree, Shop at Sly Corner, Peter Pan, The Lark. *Publications:* (Ed.) Tales of Terror (anthology), 1943; (Ed.) And the Darkness Falls (anthology), 1946. *Recreations:* cricket, Rugby. *Address:* 25 Gilbert Street, W.1. [*Died* 2 *Feb.* 1969.

KARNEY, Rt. Rev. Arthur Baillie Lumsdaine, D.D.; *b.* Isle of Wight, 14 Sept. 1874; *s.* of Rev. Gilbert Sparshott Karney; *m.* Georgina Maude Bessie Fielding (*d.* 1956); three *s.* four *d.* *Educ.:* Haileybury; Trinity Coll., Cambridge. Asst. Chaplain, Missions to Seamen, Sunderland, 1897-98; Chaplain, Missions to Seamen, San Francisco, 1899-1903; Rector, Woolpit, Suffolk, 1903-6; Chaplain, Missions to Seamen in Buenos Aires, 1906-14; Hon. Canon, St. John's Pro-Cathedral, 1910-14; Chaplain, R.N. 1914-17; T.C.F. 1918-19; Prisoner of War, 1918; Oxford Diocesan Missioner, 1919-22; Bishop of Johannesburg, 1922-33; Suffragan Bishop of Southampton and Residentiary Canon of Winchester, 1933-43; Chaplain of Marlborough College, 1943-44; Rector of Blendworth, 1944-49. *Publications:* Studies in the Character of Christ; In Other Men's Shoes; The Divine Gardener; The Father and his Sons; God in the Bible; Saying Better Prayers; An Ambassador in Chains. *Address:* 2 Houndean Rise, Lewes, Sussex. *Club:* United University. [*Died* 8 *Dec.* 1963.

KARVE, Dattatreya Gopal, M.A. (Bombay); Executive Director, Homi Bhabha Fellowship Council; *b.* 24 December 1898; *s.* of Karve, Gopal Balkrishna and Gopikabai; *m.* 1924, Sumatibai, *d.* of Mr. Khare; four *s.* one *d.* *Educ.:* New English School and Fergusson College, Poona. Cobden Medallist, 1921; Wedderburn Schol., 1923; Lieutenant and sometime Acting Adjutant Univ. Training Corps, 1924-28; Prof. of Economics and Politics, Fergusson Coll., 1923-43; Principal: Willingdon Coll., Sangli, 1935-40; B.M. College of Commerce, 1943-49; Sec., Descan Educ. Soc., Poona, 1940-44; Sec. and Asst. Comdt. Poona, Civic Guards, 1940-45; Pres., Indian Economic Association, 1945; Chairman: Bombay Administrative Inquiry Committee, 1947-; Bombay Minimum Wage Committee (Tanneries and Oil), 1950; Madhya Bharat Co-operative Planning Cttee., 1952; Executive Editor, Bombay District Gazeteers (Revision), 1949-52; Mem., Bombay Local Bd. of Reserve Bank of India, 1952; Director, Programme Evaluation, Planning Commission, 1952-55; Dir., Indian Inst. of Public Administration, 1954-55. Chm. Village and Small-Scale Industries (2nd Five Year Plan) Cttee., 1955. Pres., Indian Agricultural Economics Conf., 1956; Pres. Indian Sociological Conference, 1960. Dir. Life Insurance Corp., 1957-60; Vice-Chancellor, Univ. of Poona, 1959-61; President, Indian Society of Agricultural Economics; Deputy Governor, Reserve Bank of India; Chm., Agricultural Refinance Corporation, 1962-1964; Vice-Chm., State Bank of India, 1959-1962; Member Finance Commission, 1964-1965; Chairman, I.C.A. Co-operative Principles Commission, 1965-66; Special consultant on Agrarian Reform, U.N. and F.A.O. Hon. Fellow Institute of Social Sciences, Hague. Has frequently contrib. to the press on political, economic, and constitutional matters. *Publications:* two Marathi books on Principles of Economics and Indian Economic Problems, 1927, 1929; Federations, a Study in Comparative Politics, 1933; Indian Federal Finance, 1929; Geneva and Indian Labour, 1931; Economic Conditions of the Deccan at the advent of British Rule; Parliamentary Govt., 1934; Poverty and Population in India, 1936; Democracy and Capitalism, 1936; Unemployment Insurance in India, 1937; The New Indian Constitution, Prospects and Principles, 1940; Historical and Economic Studies (Edited), 1941; Ranade, the Prophet of Liberated India, 1942; Progress in Economics, 1946; Population Planning in India, 1948; Public Administration in a Democracy, 1950; Administrative Implications of Planning, 1956; Rural Development, 1957. *Recreation:* light reading. *Address:* Suyog, Poona, 4, India. *Club:* Radio (Bombay). [*Died* 28 *Dec.* 1967.

KATCHEN, Julius; Concert pianist; *b.* U.S.A., 15 Aug. 1926; *m.* 1956, Arlette Patoux; one *s.* *Educ.:* Haverford Coll., U.S.A. Grad. 1945 (Philos. and English Lit.). First concert with Philadelphia Orchestra and Ormandy, 1937; European debut, at U.N.E.S.C.O. Festival, Paris, 1946. Subseq. concert tours in all the continents. First pianist to play the complete piano works of Brahms in 4 recitals, in all the capitals of the world. Has made numerous recordings. *Recreation:* collecting Japanese Netsukes. *Address:* 3 bis Avenue Franco-Russe, Paris 7, France. *T.:* 4685078. [*Died* 29 *April* 1969.

KATER, Hon. Sir Norman (William), Kt., *cr.* 1929; M.B., Ch.M., J.P.; served as M.L.C., N.S.W., 32 years; grazier; Governing Director of H. E. Kater & Son, Pty. Ltd., of Warren, N.S.W., Merino Ram Breeders; Director of Grazcos Co-operative Ltd., Globe Worsted Mills, Peko-Wallsend Investments Ltd.; Mem. Bd. of Reference of The Liverpool and London and Globe Insc. Co., Ltd.; Life Governor of Royal Prince Alfred Hospital, Sydney; *b.* Pennant Hills, N.S.W., 1874; *s.* of late Hon. Henry Edward Kater, M.L.C., and Mary Eliza *d.* of William Forster; *m.* 1st, 1901, Jean Gaerloch (*d.* 1931), *d.* of late William Henry Mackenzie; four *s.* two *d.*; 2nd, 1938, Mary, *d* of late L. A. B. Wade. *Educ.:* All Saints College, Bathurst; Sydney Grammar School and Sydney University. First year Renwick Scholarship and Professor Haswell's prize for Biology; passed with honours each succeeding year; resident Medical Officer at Prince Alfred Hospital for one year; took up pastoral pursuits, 1904; President of The Graziers' Association of N.S.W. for three years and member of the Executive of that body for 35 years. Served European War, 2 years with French Army Medical Service; 2 years R.A.M.C. Home Service; retd. with rank of Major. Chevalier de la Légion d'Honneur; Médaille de la Reconnaissance Française. *Recreations:* bowls; formerly rowing (University blue). *Address:* 9 Wellington Street, Woollahra, N.S.W., Australia. *Clubs:* Junior Carlton; Australian (Sydney); Queensland (Brisbane); Royal Sydney Golf. [*Died* 18 *Aug.* 1965.

KAUFMAN, George S.; Playwright; *b.* 16 Nov. 1889; *s.* of Joseph S. Kaufman and Nettie (Schamberg) Myers; *m.* 1917, Beatrice Bakrow; one *d.*; *m.* 1949, Leueen MacGrath. *Educ.:* Pittsburgh High School. Newspaper reporter and dramatic writer, New York, 1912-30; co-author following plays and musical shows: Someone in the House, 1918; Jacques Deval, 1919; Dulcy, 1921; To the Ladies, 1922; The Forty-niners, 1922; Merton of the Movies, 1922; Helen of Troy, N.Y. (musical), 1923; Be Yourself (musical), 1924; Beggar on Horseback, 1924; The Cocoanuts (musical), 1925; The Butter and Egg Man, 1925; Minick, 1926; The Good Fellow, 1926; Strike Up the Band (musical), 1927; Animal Crackers (musical), 1928; The Royal Family, 1928; June Moon, 1929; The Bandwagon (musical), 1930; Once in a Lifetime, 1930; The Channel Road, 1930; Eldorado, 1931; Of Thee I Sing (musical), 1931; Dinner at Eight, 1932; Let 'Em Eat Cake (musical), 1933; The Dark Tower, 1933; Merrily We Roll Along, 1934; Bring on the Girls, 1934; (with Edna Ferber), Theatre Royal, 1934; First Lady, 1935; Stage Door, 1936; You Can't Take it With You, 1936; I'd Rather be Right (musical), 1937; The Fabulous Invalid, 1938; The American Way, 1938; The Man Who Came to Dinner, 1939; George Washington Slept Here, 1940; The Land is Bright, 1941; The Late George Apley, 1944; Hollywood Pinafore (musical), 1945; Park Avenue (musical), 1946; Bravo, 1948; The Small Hours, 1951; Fancy Meeting You Again, 1952; The Solid Gold Cadillac, 1953; Silk Stockings (musical), 1954. *Address:* 1035 Park Av., New York, N.Y., U.S.A. [*Died* 2 *June* 1961.

KAULA, Sir Ganga, Kt., *cr.* 1944; C.I.E. 1930; B.A.; Assoc. K.G.St.J., 1946; Patron, Indian Council for Child Welfare (formerly Hon. Treasurer); *b.* 9 May 1877; *s.* of Pundit Tikarama Kaula; *m.* 1896, Bhagyabbari (*decd.*), *d.* of Pundit Lalita Pershad Wanchoo; one *s.* two *d.* *Educ.:* Central Model School, Lahore; Govt. College, Lahore; Punjab University, Lahore (B.A. 1896). Joined Indian Finance Dept. 1896; retired, 1932; Chief Minister Jind State, 1936-43, Musheer-i-Khas, 1944-46. *Recreation:* social service (honorary). *Address:* 7 Sikandra Road, New Delhi, India. [*Died July* 1970.

KAVAN, Anna; writer of short stories, literary criticism, essays, novels. *Publications:* Asylum Piece, 1940; Change the Name, 1941; I am Lazarus, 1945; The House of Sleep, 1947; The Horse's Tale (with K. T. Bluth), 1950; A Scarcity of Love, 1956; Eagles' Nest, 1957; A Bright Green Field, 1958; Who are You?, 1963; Ice, 1967. *Address:* 19A Hillsleigh Road, W.8. [*Died* 5 *Dec.* 1968.

KAVANAGH, Patrick; poet; Television Columnist (on the Telefis Eireann-Radio-Eireann weekly), since 1962; *b.* 1905; *s.* of James and Bridget Kavanagh; *m.* 1967, Katherine Moloney. *Educ.:* local school. Small farmer to 1939; then went to live in Dublin; wrote a gossip column, 1942-1944; newspaper film critic, 1945-49; illness, 1949-55; Edited Review, Kavanagh's Weekly, 1952; travel, 1956-57; extra-mural Lecturer, U.C., Dublin, 1957; Columnist for farmers' newspaper, 1958-62. *Publications:* Ploughman and Other Poems, 1936; The Green Fool, stage-Irish autobiography, 1938; The Great Hunger (poem), 1942; A Soul For Sale and Other Poems, 1947; Tarry Flynn (novel), 1948; Come Dance with Kitty Stobling and other poems, 1960; Self Portrait, 1962; Collected Poems, 1964; Selected Prose, 1966. *Recreation:* racing. *Address:* Inniskeen, Dundalk, Republic of Ireland. *T.:* Inniskeen 23. [*Died* 30 *Nov.* 1967.

KAY, Arthur William, O.B.E. 1962; Chairman: Newcastle Regional Hospital Board, since 1968; Northern Arts Association, since 1967; People's Theatre Arts Group Ltd., since 1962; *b.* 2 March 1904; *s.* of William Arthur Kay and Margaret Emma Kay; *m.* 1933, Alison Beatrice Fraser; two *s.* one *d.* *Educ.:* Ackworth Sch.; University Coll., London. B.Sc. 1926. Scott & Turner Ltd.: Industrial Chemist, 1926; Dir. of Production, 1942; after amalgamation, Dir., Sterling Winthrop Group Ltd.; Man. Dir., Winthrop Laboratories Ltd., 1956; retd., 1969. *Recreations:* theatre (acting and producing); gardening, swimming, natural history. *Address:* 16 Jesmond Park Court, Newcastle upon Tyne NE7 7BW. *T.:* 812408; Springwell House, Steel, Hexhamshire, Northumberland. *T.:* Slaley 309. [*Died* 18 *March* 1970.

KAY, Sir James Reid, Kt., *cr.* 1939; *b.* 20 Feb. 1885; *s.* of James Kay and Elizabeth Margaret Morton, Glasgow; *m.* 1915, Marguerite Landles Law (*d.* 1961), Glasgow; two *s.* two *d.* *Educ.:* Kelvinside Academy, Glasgow. With James Finlay & Co., Ltd., Calcutta, 1906-40; served European War, R.F.A. in France, 1917-18; President, Imperial Bank of India (Bengal Circle), 1933-1934, 1935-36, 1939-40, Pres., Associated Chambers of Commerce of India, 1937-38; President, Bengal Chamber of Commerce, 1937-38; member, Council of State, India, 1937-38. *Address:* Blair Lodge, Ayr. *Club:* Oriental. [*Died* 1 *Nov.* 1965.

KAY, Katharine Cameron, R.E. 1964 (A.R.E. 1920); R.S.W.; F.R.S.A. 1950; painter and etcher; *b.* Glasgow; *d.* of Rev. Robert and Margaret Cameron; *m.* 1928, Arthur Kay, H.R.S.A. (*d.* 1939), but retains maiden name professionally. *Educ.:* Glasgow Sch. of Art; Paris; Calarossi's Studio. Exhibited at Roy. Acad., Roy. Scottish Academy, Royal Glasgow Institute, Berlin, Liverpool, Venice, Leipzig, Munich, Turin, etc.; works purchased by: Scottish Modern Arts Association; Corporations of Liverpool and Leeds; Glasgow Corp., for Kelvingrove Art Gallery. Collection of etchings purchased by Library of Congress, Washington, U.S.A.; represented by etchings in the British Museum Print Room, and by water-colour drawings in the Tate Gallery and Victoria and Albert Museum; Books illustrated: Flowers I Love, Haunting Edinburgh, Where the Bee Sucks; Iain, The Happy Puppy, etc. Corr. Mem. International Institute of Arts and Letters, 1957. *Address:* 8 Henderland Road, Edinburgh, 12. *T.:* 61695. *Clubs:* Ladies' Caledonian (Edinburgh); Lady Artists' (Glasgow). [*Died* 21 *Aug.* 1965.

KAYE, Sir Lister L., Bt.; *see* Lister-Kaye.

KEAN, Oscar; *b.* 25 Oct. 1875. *Educ.:* New College, Eastbourne; Trinity College, Cambridge. Called to Bar Inner Temple, 1901; served European War in France with 8th Divisional Train, 1917-19. Senior and Chief Registrar of Supreme Court of Judicature in Bankruptcy and Companies Winding Up, 1947, retired 1949. *Recreations:* reading, bridge and watching cricket. *Address:* 12 Wythburn Court, Seymour Place, W.1. *T.:* Paddington 7982. *Club:* Oxford and Cambridge. [*Died* 10 *Feb.* 1961.

KEARNEY, Elfric Wells Chalmers, F.R.S.A.; F.R.E.S.; M.I.Struct.E.; Honorary Technical Advisor to the Agent-General for Victoria, Australia Corps Diplomatique; Engineer and Managing Director of Kearney High-Speed Tube Railway Co. Ltd. and Kearney Railway Construction Co. Ltd.; *b.* Geelong, Australia, 3 Feb. 1881; *s.* of Rev. A. W. Kearney, M.A., Cambridge and Adelaide; *m.* 1924, Dorothy Leigh. *Educ.:* privately in Australia and England. Inventor of Kearney High-Speed Railway; railway motor wheel, stepless subway station, gas switch, etc.; developed an improved system of construction for tube railways which greatly reduces cost; exhibited a working model of his system, 1908, subsequently tested and approved of by the Board of Trade when it attained a speed of over 20 miles an hour, a pace never before equalled with a model railway of similar size; exhibited improved models at Crystal Palace, 1910, the Royal Institution, 1910; London Louvre, 1912; Olympia, 1913; Society of Engineers, 1919; built a full-size car and promoted a tube railway to be built on the Kearney system between North and South Shields, 1926, for which a Provisional Order was granted by the Ministry of Transport, 1927. *Publications:* Rapid Transit in the Future; High Speed Railways; Erone—a story in economics. *Recreation:* travel. *Address:* Wendouree, Burgh Heath, Surrey, *T.:* Burgh Heath 53622. [*Died* 15 *April* 1966.

KEARNS, Sir (Henry Ward) Lionel, Kt., *cr.* 1946; C.B.E. 1941; B.A.; Chairman and Managing Director H. W. Kearns and Co. Ltd., Broadheath, near Manchester; *b.* 1 Dec. 1891; *y.s.* of late Henry Ward Kearns, B.Sc., J.P., Boothroyd, Brooklands, Manchester. *Educ.:* Rugby; Christ's College, Cambridge. Served European War, 1914-19, Capt. R.A. (despatches, Belgian Croix de Guerre); Member, Ministry of Supply Mission to India, 1940-41. Pres. Machine Tool Trades Association, 1943-45; Chairman Eastern Group Requirements Committee, Ministry of Supply, 1942-45; Director-General Production Services, Min. of Supply, 1945-46; Chm. Council and Executive Cttee. Production Engineering Research Assoc. of Great Britain, 1947-59. *Address:* The Crossways, Groby Road, Altrincham, Cheshire. *T.A.:* Kearns Altrincham. *T.:* Altrincham 3284. *Clubs:* International Sportsmen's; Clarendon (Manchester). [*Died* 4 *Nov.* 1962.

KEARNS, Rev. John Willis, M.A.; retired; *s.* of late James Kearns, Roscommon; *m.* Edith Williams, *d.* of late T. R. Williams, Southsea; four *s.* two *d.* (and three *s.* decd.). *Educ.:* private; Wadham College, Oxford. Assistant Master, Yarmouth Coll., 1882; Headmaster, Lyttelton Grammar School, Malvern, 1883-94; B.A. London University, 1888; B.A. Wadham College, Oxford, 1891; ordained to curacy at the Priory Church, Malvern, 1893; Headmaster, Monkton Combe Junior School, 1895; Headmaster, Monkton Combe School, 1900-26; now Governor, Monkton Combe School; Vicar of Almeley, 1927-46. *Address:* 14 The Lees, Malvern. [*Died* 30 *Oct.* 1962.

KEARNS, Sir Lionel; *see* Kearns, Sir H. W. L.

KEATING, Brig. Harold John Buckler; *see* Addenda: II.

KEATINGE, Gerald Francis, C.I.E. 1911; *b.* March 1872; 4th *s.* of late Maurice Keatinge; *m.* Marion (*d.* 1934), *d.* of J. S. Cotton; one *s.* one *d.* *Educ.:* Sherborne School; Balliol College, Oxford. Entered Indian Civil Service, 1894; served in Revenue Department, Bombay Presidency, 1894-1904; Under-Secretary to Government, 1904-7; Director of Agriculture, 1907-21; Member of the Legislative Council, Bombay, 1916; retired from Indian Civil Service, 1921. *Publications:* Rural Economy in the Bombay Deccan; Agricultural Progress in Western India. *Address:* Teffont, Salisbury, Wilts. [*Died* 6 *Feb.* 1965.

KEATINGE, Richard Herbert; retired as Puisne Judge in the Uganda Protectorate (1955-67); *b.* 25 April 1911; *s.* of William Maybury Keatinge and Alice (*née* Kenny); *m.* 1938, Mary, 3rd *d.* of Major J. D. Leonard, O.B.E.; two *s.* two *d.* *Educ.:* Avoca School; Portora Royal School; Dublin University. Barrister-at-law, Gray's Inn, 1933; Deputy Registrar, High Court, Tanganyika, 1937; served King's African Rifles, 1939-43; Resident Magistrate, Kenya, 1944; Acting Puisne Judge, 1949; Judge, Somaliland Protectorate, 1950. *Recreation:* golf. *Address:* Castlemartyr, Co. Cork, Eire. *Clubs:* Nairobi; Kampala. [*Died* 12 *Jan.* 1968.

KEAY, Sir John, Kt. 1950; F.C.A.; President, English China Clays Ltd. (Chm., 1947-63); Director, English Clays Lovering Pochin & Co. Ltd. (Man. Dir.. 1937-60; Chm., 1953-63); *b.* 31 March 1894; *s.* of John Keay and Alice (*née* Allman); *m.* 1917, Agnes Cooper; one *s.* two *d.* Served European War, 1915-18, Civil Service Rifles. Admitted Assoc. Member of Institute of Chartered Accountants, 1921; Partner in the firm of Bourner, Bullock & Co., Chartered Accountants, St. Austell, 1924-28; Director and Secretary, English China Clays Ltd., 1928; Asst. Managing Director, English Clays Lovering Pochin & Co. Ltd., 1932. *Recreations:* golf and beekeeping. *Address:* Little Cosgarne, Truro Road, St. Austell, Cornwall. *T.:* St. Austell 2968. [*Died* 20 *Aug.* 1964.

KEEFE, Sir Ronald (Barry), Kt. 1958; *b.* 31 July 1901; *s.* of William Edgar Keefe, solicitor, Norwich; *m.* 1925, Joyce Margaret, *d.* of John Youngs, Norwich; one *s.* two *d.* *Educ.:* King Edward VI School, Norwich. Admitted as Solicitor, 1924; Notary Public, 1956. Director: Norwich Building Soc., since 1953; Norwich Union Insurance Socs., and Leadenhall-Sterling Investments Ltd., since 1960. Chapter Clerk of Norwich Cathedral, 1955. *Address:* (Home) Boyton House, Ipswich Road, Norwich. *T.:* Norwich 53330; (Office) Opie House, Castle Meadow, Norwich. *T.:* Norwich 23241. *Clubs:* United Service; Norfolk, Royal Norwich Golf (Norwich); Royal West Norfolk Golf (Brancaster). [*Died* 6 *May* 1967

KEELING, Thomas, C.B.E. 1952; Chairman: Liverpool Regional Hospital Board, 1947-59; Board of Governors, United Liverpool Hospitals, 1950-59; *b.* 14 Aug. 1882; British; *m.* (wife decd.); *m.* 1953, Eva Rigby, widow. *Educ.:* Church of England School, Liverpool. Early years uneventful. Trade Union official, 1919-; Member of management of Royal Southern Hospital, Liverpool. 1932-; Chairman, 1942-; J.P. Liverpool, 1936-; Hon. M.A. (Liverpool Univ.) 1950. *Recreation:* ballroom dancing. *Address:* 1 Gladstone Avenue, Liverpool 16. [*Died* 24 *June* 1963.

KEESEY, Walter Monckton, O.B.E.; M.C.; A.R.C.A.; Hon. F.I.B.D.; Hon. Vice-President, R.B.S.A.; architect and etcher; *b.* 16 June 1887; *s.* of Rev. G. W. Keesey; *m.* J. H. Swinglehurst (*d.* 1963), Kendal, Westmorland; one *d.* *Educ.:* Caterham; St. Olave's; Royal Coll. of Art. Architectural Assoc. Staff, 1913-25; Brit. Institution Scholar; served Royal Engineers, 1914-1919 (Major, M.C.). Lately H.M.I. Ministry of Educn. Hon. Life Member, B.F.C.A.A.; President, Cheltenham Group, 1961. *Principal Works:* Caterham Memorial Hall, etc., various domestic jobs. *Publications:* Architectural Drawing; various papers, etc. *Recreation:* golf. *Address:* Yew Tree Cottage, Epperstone, Notts. *T.:* Lowdham 2545. *Club:* Chelsea Arts. [*Died* 4 *Dec.* 1970.

KEESING, Felix Maxwell, M.A., Litt.D.; Professor of Anthropology, Stanford University, California, from 1943; *b.* Penang, S.S., 5 Jan. 1902; *s.* of Joshua C. Keesing and Ethel, *d.* of William L. Beaumont, Auckland, N.Z.; *m.* 1928, Margaret Marie, *d.* of Frederick Martin, Auckland, N.Z.; two *s.* *Educ.:* Grammar School and University, Auckland (Univ. Scholar); first class honours in Education; diploma in journalism; fellow of the Rockefeller Foundation at Yale

and Chicago Universities, U.S.A.; advanced research at London School of Economics; doctor of literature, University of New Zealand, 1933. Director of Research on Pacific dependencies, Institute of Pacific Relations, 1930-34, studying in the Orient and the South Sea Islands; Prof. of Anthropology, Univ. of Hawaii, 1934-43; on leave with Office of Strategic Services, Washington, D.C., 1942-43; Assoc. Director, Stanford School of Naval Administration, 1946-48; Executive Head, Dept. of Sociology and Anthropology, 1948-56; Executive Head, Dept. of Anthropology, 1956-; U.S. Senior Commissioner, South Pacific Commission, 1948-57. *Publications:* The Changing Maori, 1928; Maori Progress on the East Coast, 1929; Dependencies and Native Peoples of the Pacific, 1931; Modern Samoa, 1934; Taming Philippine Headhunters, 1934; The Filipinos: A Nation in the Making, 1935; Hawaiian Homesteading on Molokai (Hawaii), 1936; Education in Pacific Countries, 1937; The Menomini Indians of Wisconsin, 1939; The South Seas in the Modern World, 1941; Native Peoples of the Pacific World, 1945; (co-author) Farmers of the World, 1945; (co-author) The Science of Man in the World Crisis, 1945; (co-author) Specialised Studies in Polynesian Anthropology, 1947; (ed.) Handbook of the Trust Territory of the Pacific Islands, 1948; The Pacific Island Peoples in the Postwar World, 1950; Social Anthropology in Polynesia, 1953; Culture Change: an analysis and bibliography of anthropological sources, 1953; Elite Communication in Samoa, A Study of leadership, 1956; (co-author) Social Anthropology and Industry, 1957; Cultural Anthropology: The Science of Custom, 1958; Field Guide to Oceania, 1959; Ethnohistory of Northern Luzon, 1962; various papers. *Recreations:* tennis, swimming, walking. *Address:* 744 Frenchman's Road, Stanford University, California, U.S.A.
[*Died* 1961.

KEFAUVER, Estes; United States Senator since 1948; *b.* 26 July 1903; *s.* of Robert Cooke Kefauver and Phredonia (*née* Estes); *m.* 1935, Nancy Patterson Pigott, Glasgow, Scotland; one *s.* three *d.* *Educ.:* Elementary schools of Madisonville, Tenn.; University of Tennessee, Knoxville; Yale Univ., New Haven. Attorney, 1927-39. Comr. of Finance and Taxation (4 mths.); resigned to run for House of Representatives, U.S. Congress, and elected; tenure of office began 1939. Delegate to N.A.T.O. Parliamentarians' Conference. Chairman, U.S. Delegation, 1961. Democratic Nominee for Vice-Presidency of U.S., 1956. Vice-Pres. American Delegn. to Atlantic Congress, 1959. *Publications:* 20th Century Congress, 1947; Crime in America, 1951. Contributions to American Bar Assoc. Journal, Tennessee Law Review, Amer. Assoc. of Political Science Jl. and numerous leading magazines. *Address:* Senate Office Buildings, Washington, D.C., U.S.A.
[*Died* 10 *Aug.* 1963.

KEFLEGZI, Gabre-Mascal; Ambassador of Ethiopia to the Court of St. James's since 1966; *b.* Ethiopia, 1917; *m.*; two *s.* two *d.* Dir. of Educn., 1935; Dept. Sec., Gen. Min. of The Pen, 1941-42; Dir. of Govt. Printing Works, 1943; Chief of Cabinet (rank, Dir.-Gen.), Min. of Interior, 1944-47; Dir.-Gen., Amer. Affairs Dept., Min. of For. Affairs, 1947; Alt. Deleg. and Sec. to Ethiopia Delegn., U.N. Conf., N.Y., 1947; Rep., U.N. Conf., N.Y., 1948-49; Mem. Ethiopian Delegn., African Defence Conf., Nairobi, 1951; Deleg. to 7th Session of U.N. Gen. Assembly, 1952; Envoy and Minister to: India, 1952; Sweden, 1954; Ambassador to Yugoslavia, 1956; Deleg. to 12th Session of U.N. Gen. Assembly, 1957; Ambassador to U.A.R., 1958; Minister of State, Min. of Educn. and Fine Arts, 1961-66. Holds foreign orders, incl. Grand Cordon and Grand Officer, Star of Ethiopia. *Address:* Imperial Ethiopian Embassy, 17 Prince's Gate, S.W.7.
[*Died* 8 *Dec.* 1969.

KEILIN, Dr. David, F.R.S. 1926; Quick Professor of Biology, Cambridge Univ., 1931-1952. *Educ.:* Magdalene College, Cambridge. M.A. Royal Medal of Royal Society, 1939; Copley Medal of Royal Society, 1951. Assoc. For. Mem. Acad. des Sciences, Paris, 1955. *Address:* c/o Molteno Institute, Cambridge.
[*Died* 27 *Feb.* 1963.

KEITH OF AVONHOLM, Baron (Life Peer), *cr.* 1953, of Saint Bernard's in the City of Edinburgh; **James Keith,** P.C. 1953; a Lord of Appeal in Ordinary, 1953-61; Honorary Master of the Bench, Inner Temple, since 1953; *b.* 20 May 1886; *e. s.* of Sir Henry Shanks Keith, G.B.E.; *m.* 1915, Jean Maitland, *d.* of Andrew Bennet, solicitor, Arbroath; one *s.* two *d.* *Educ.:* Hamilton Acad.; Glasgow Univ. M.A. (1st class Hons. History, 1906; LL.B. 1908; Hon. LL.D., Glasgow, 1948; admitted to Faculty of Advocates, 1911; K.C. 1926; Dean of the Faculty of Advocates, 1936-37; a Senator of the College of Justice in Scotland, 1937-53. Military service, 1914-19; commission, Seaforth Highlanders (10th and 8th Service Battns.); France, 1916; attached Egyptian Army, 1917; served under Sudan Government, 1917-19; Trustee National Library of Scotland, 1925-1937; Standing Counsel to Convention of Royal Burghs of Scotland, 1934-37; Scottish Youth Hostels Association: Hon. President, 1957-; Chm. Nat. Exec., 1948; Chm. Edinburgh District, 1938-48; Pres. Edinburgh District, 1951-; President, Scottish Council for National Parks, 1942-54; Chairman, Edinburgh Branch British Red Cross Society, 1942-54; Pres. St. George's School for Girls, Edinburgh, 1942-54; Chairman, Departmental Committee on Poor Law in Scotland, 1935-38; Member Scottish Advisory Council on Physical Training and Recreation and Chm. Edinburgh Region, 1938-39; Chairman: Scottish Youth Advisory Committee to Secretary of State, 1942-46; Chairman Scottish Central Probation Council, 1943-49; Mem. Roy. Commn. on Marriage and Divorce, 1951-55. President, The Holdsworth Club, 1956-57; Chm. Committee on Scottish Record Office regarding accommodation, 1961-63. *Publications:* Editor and contributor to various legal publications. *Recreations:* formerly golf, curling, swimming, walking; now reading. *Address:* 32 India Street, Edinburgh. *Clubs:* Bath; New (Edinburgh).
[*Died* 29 *June* 1964.

KEITH, Alexander Milne; Landowner and Farmer; *b.* 1886; *s.* of late James Keith, West Barsham Hall, Fakenham, Norfolk; *m.* 1920, Daphne Eyre, *d.* of J. C. Straker, Stagshaw House, Corbridge on Tyne; four *d.* (one *s.* decd.). *Educ.:* privately. European War, 1914-19, Derbyshire Yeomanry; Capt. retd. High Sheriff of Northumberland, 1949-50. *Recreations:* hunting, racing, tennis. *Address:* Chesters, Humshaugh, Hexham. *T.:* Humshaugh 203. *Clubs:* Bath; Northern Counties (Newcastle upon Tyne). [*Died* 10 *June* 1967.

KEITH, Edward John, Q.C. (Scot.) 1949; Sheriff-Substitute of the Lothians and Peebles at Edinburgh, since 1960; *b.* 17 April 1908; *s.* of late Peter Keith, solicitor, Thurso, and late Catherine Jamesina Swanson Bruce; *m.* 1942, Isobel Galloway Shearer; two *s.* one *d.* *Educ.:* Thurso; George Watson's School, Edinburgh; Edinburgh University. Called to the Bar, 1932. Sheriff-Substitute of Stirling, Dunbarton and Clackmannan at Falkirk, 1956-60. *Address:* 50 Gamekeepers' Road, Edinburgh 4.
[*Died* 16 *Sept.* 1968.

KEKEWICH, Rear-Admiral Piers Keane, C.B. 1946; retired; *b.* 23 Jan. 1889; *s.* of Charles Granville Kekewich and Mary Marion Mackintosh; *m.* 1st, 1916 (marriage dissolved); one *s.* two *d.*; 2nd, 1940. *Educ.:* Cheam, Surrey. Royal Navy. Citizen and Merchant Taylor. Served European War, 1914-18, Battle Cruiser Fleet (H.M.S. Galatea and Cardiff); War of 1939-45, Northern Patrol, Coastal Forces, Malta Dockyard. *Address:* 24 Thorney Court, Palace Gate, W.8. *Club:* Naval and Military.
[*Died* 5 *Oct.* 1967.

KELLER, Prof. Adolf, Dr. theol., D.D.; Titular Professor Emeritus, Univ. of Zurich; *b.* Rüdlingen, nr. Schaffhausen, Switzerland, 7 Feb. 1872; *m.* Tina Jenny, Glaris; two *s.* three *d.* *Educ.:* College of Schaffhausen; Universities of Basle, Berlin, and Geneva. Pastor and teacher at the German and Swiss Evangelical Church at Cairo, and member of a scientific expedition to the monastery of S. Catherine on Mt. Sinai, 1896-99; Pastor in Burg-Stein a/R., 1899-1904; Pastor in Geneva at the Auditoire John Knox's Chapel), 1904-9; Pastor at St. Peter's Church in Zürich, 1909-24; Secretary of the Swiss Church Federation; General Secretary of the European Central Office for Inter-church aid; European delegate of the American Federal Council of Churches, 1924; one of the secretaries of the Universal Conference of the Churches on Life and Work, 1925; Gen. co-ord. Sec. of the International Christian Social Institute at Geneva 1927-1932; Hon. Professor at the Universities of Geneva, Debrecen and the Academy of Pápa (Hungary); Vice-President of the World Alliance of Reformed Churches holding the Presbyterian system; a Vice-Chairman of the World's Sunday School Assoc.; Director the Ecumenical Theological Seminar; Consultant World Council Churches; Hon. Rector centennial of University of Dubuque, Iowa, 1952; D.D. Geneva, Yale, Edinburgh; LL.D. Heidelberg College, Tiffin; Hon. Lecturer of the Universal Council on Life and Work Stone Lectureship, Princeton Seminary; Beckley Lectureship; Carew Lectures, Hartford; Lowell Lectures, Boston; Moore Lectures, San Francisco; Earl Lectures, Berkeley. Member Swiss-Brit. Soc.; Soc. of cultural relations with U.S.A.; Advisory Cttee. of Inst. for foreign studies. *Publications:* Eine Sinai-Fahrt, 1900; Eine Philosophie des Lebens (Henri Bergson), 1914; Dynamis, Formen u. Kräfte des amerikanischen Protestantismus, 1925; Protestant Europe (with George Stewart), 1927; Die Kirchen und der Friede, 1928; Die Fortsetzungsarbeit der Stockholmer Weltkirchenkonferenz, 1928; Die sozialen Programme der Kirchen, 1929; Xenos Auf der Schwelle, 1929; Weg der dialektischen Theologie durch die Kirchliche Welt, Eng. Translation: Karl Barth and Christian Unity, 1933; Vom unbekannten Gott, 1932; Von Geist und Liebe, 1933; Religion and the European Mind, 1934; Church and State on the European Continent, 1936; Five Minutes to Twelve, 1938; Am Fusse des Leuchtturms, 1940; Christian Europe To-day, 1942; Amerikanisches Christentum heute, 1945; Zeitwende, 1945. *Address:* Siriusstrasse 10, Zürich 44. *Clubs:* P.E.N.; Psychological (Zürich). [*Died* 10 *Feb.* 1963.

KELLER, Helen Adams; Counselor on National and International Relations, American Foundation for the Blind, Inc.; and the American Foundation for Overseas Blind, Inc.; *b.* Tuscambia, Ala., 27 June 1880; *d.* of Capt. Arthur H. Keller and Katherine (*née* Adams); deaf and blind since age of 19 months as result of illness. *Educ.:* under direction of Anne Sullivan Macy, 1887-1936; Radcliffe College (A.B. *cum laude* 1904). On behalf of the blind has lectured in numerous countries all over the world. Member Trustees, American Hall of Fame and National Institute of Arts and Letters. Holds numerous awards for achievement, and for work in relief of the handicapped. In 1957 a television programme called The Miracle Worker gave the story of Helen Keller's first meeting with her teacher; expanded version, Broadway, 1959, Royalty, London, 1961, motion picture, 1962. Hon. degrees: Dr. of Humane Letters, Temple University, 1931; LL.D.; Glasgow, 1932, Witwatersrand, 1951; Doctor of Letters, Delhi, 1955; Doctor of Medicine, Free Univ. of Berlin, 1955; Doctor of Laws, Harvard, 1955. Order of St. Sava, Yugoslavia, 1931; Roosevelt Medal, 1936; Chevalier of French Legion of Honour, 1952; Medal of Merit, Lebanon, 1952; Award of Southern Cross, Brazil, 1953; Order of Sacred Treasure, Japan, Class, III, 1955; Order of the Golden Heart, Philippines, 1955. *Publications:* Story of My Life, 1902; Optimism (an essay), 1903; The World I Live In, 1908; The Song of the Stone Wall, 1910; Out of the Dark, 1913; My Religion, 1927; Midstream—My Later Life, 1930; Helen Keller's Journal, 1938; Let Us Have Faith, 1941; Teacher, Anne Sullivan Macy, 1956; The Open Door, 1957. *Relevant publications:* Helen Keller: Sketch for a Portrait, by Van Wyck Brooks, 1956; Helen Keller by J. W. and Anne Tibble, 1957. *Address:* c/o American Foundation for the Blind Inc., 15 West 16th St., New York 11. [*Died* 1 *June* 1968.

KELLETT, Sir Henry de Castres, 4th Baronet (U.K. of Lota, *cr.* 1801); *b.* 2 Oct. 1882; *e. s.* of 3rd Baronet and Joan R. M., 2nd *d.* of William Harrison of Richmond, Victoria; *S.* father, 1924; *m.* 1905, Rubie Septima, 7th *d.* of Easton Johnston; one *s.* one *d.* *Heir:* *s.* Henry de Castres, *b.* 3 June 1914. *Address:* 6 Matong Street, Gordon, N.S.W., Australia. [*Died* 25 *July* 1966.

KELLETT, Sir Henry de Castres, 5th Bt. *cr.* 1801; *b.* 3 June 1914; *s.* of Sir Henry de Castres Kellett, 4th Bt. and Rubie Septima, 7th *d.* of Easton Johnston; *S.* father 1966; *m.* 1952, Ida Mary Grace-Weaver; no *c.* *Heir: kinsman,* Stanley Everard Kellett [*b.* 1911; *m.* 1938, Audrey Margaret Phillips; one *s.* one *d.*]. [*Died* 6 *Aug.* 1966.

KELLY, Brigadier Edward Henry, D.S.O. 1916; M.C.; late R.E.; J.P.; *b.* 29 July 1883; *s.* of late Maj.-Gen. F. H. Kelly; C.B., C.M.G.; *m.* 1918, Helen Beatrice (*d.* 1953), *y. d.* of late P. G. Heyworth, Yew Tree, West Derby, and *widow* of Major Carson, R.A. *Educ.:* R.M.A., Woolwich (Sword of Honour); commissioned Royal Engineers, 1902; served N.W. Frontier of India Mohmand Expedition, 1908 (medal and clasp); Adjutant, 1st K.G.O., Sappers and Miners, 1909-12; 3rd Field Coy. S. and M. France, 1914 (severely wounded hand grenade Festubert, Nov. 1914, M.C.); 5th Field Squadron, R.E., 1915; G.S.O. 3, 4th Cavalry Division, 1916; Brigade-Major, 8th Infantry Brigade (D.S.O.); G.S.O. 2, 7th Corps; G.S.O. 1, 5th Army (Bt. Lt.-Col., despatches seven times), Staff College, Camberley, 1919; Chief Instructor, School of Military Engineering, 1922; Bt.-Col. 1926; G.S.O. 1st London Div. (T.A.), 1926; Imperial Defence College, 1928; Deputy Director Military Intelligence, A.H.Q., India, 1929-32; Brigadier, General Staff, British Troops in Egypt, 1932-36; retired 1936. *Publications:* articles in Encyclopædia Britannica on Fortifications, Field Engineering and Military Mining. *Address:* Dane Cottage, Bratton, Westbury, Wilts. *Club:* Army and Navy [*Died* 21 *Dec.* 1963.

KELLY, Dame Elisabeth (Hariott), D.B.E., *cr.* 1953 (C.B.E. 1920; O.B.E. 1918; M.B.E. 1917); J.P.; Hon. Organiser Portsmouth Social Service Council since 1939; Divisional President, Portsmouth, British Red Cross Society; Chairman Portsmouth and District War Pensions

Committee; *y. d.* of late Lieut.-Col. H. Holdsworth Kelly, R.M.A., and Elisabeth, *d.* of John Collum, Bellevue, County Fermanagh. Engaged in social work; Hon. Secretary Portsmouth Services Committee National Relief Fund, 1914-16, and Portsmouth War Pensions Committee, 1916-20; Member Special Grants Committee, Ministry of Pensions, 1917-26; Member Departmental Committee of Inquiry, Ministry of Pensions, 1920-1921; Member Central Advisory Committee, Ministry of Pensions, since 1921; Member Departmental Committee of Inquiry, Offences against Young Persons, Home Office, 1924-25; Member Home Office Committee on Street Offences, 1927; Member of the Home Office Committee of Inquiry into Imprisonment for Debt, 1933-34; Chairman Juvenile Court, 1933-50; Child Welfare Committees and Committees under Ministry of Labour, etc.; appointed by Royal Warrant Member of the Executive, Royal Patriotic Fund Corporation, 1923-60; Hon. Organiser, Visiting Justices Conference, Home Office, 1926-46; J.P. 1920. Coronation Medals, 1937 and 1953, and Defence Medals. *Address:* 2 Solent Gate, Southsea. *T.:* Portsmouth 31753. *Club:* Naval and Military (Lady Assoc. Mem.).

[*Died* 30 *March* 1962.

KELLY, John William, C.I.E. 1934; B.A.; *b.* 28 Sept. 1885; *s.* of T. O'D. Kelly, Newry, Co. Down; *m.* 1914, Nina Viola Angell. *Educ.:* Campbell College, Belfast; Trinity College, Dublin. Appointed to Indian Finance Dept. (enrolled list), 1910; Officiating Deputy Controller of Currency, Calcutta, 1925, Bombay, 1926; Controller of Currency, Calcutta, 1935; ex-officio Director of Reserve Bank of India; retired. Lieut. R.A.P.C., 1940-45. *Address.* Cooleen, Clonallon, Warrenpoint, Co. Down. *T.:* Warrenpoint 2233. *Club:* Oriental.

[*Died* 9 *March* 1966.

KELLY, Sir Patrick Aloysius, Kt., *cr.* 1930; C.I.E. 1926; late Indian Police Service; *b.* 14 July 1880; *m.* 1908, Elizabeth (*d.* 1965), *d.* of James O'Callaghan, Dublin. Joined Indian Police Service, 1902; Superintendent of Police, 1912; Commissioner of Police, Bombay, 1922-33; retired 1933; King's Police Medal, 1921; bar to Police Medal, 1931. *Address:* 80 Ernle Road, Wimbledon, S.W.20. [*Died* 13 *Feb.* 1966.

KELLY, Air Vice-Marshal Thomas James, C.B.E. 1945; M.C. 1917; M.A.; M.D., B.Ch.; R.A.F.M.S., retired; *b.* 18 April 1890; *s.* of late John Kelly, J.P., The Hall, Killarney, Co. Kerry; *m.* 1920, Kathleen, *d.* of late Charles Knox, Union Lodge, Dungannon, Co. Tyrone; one *s.* one *d.* *Educ.:* Clongowes Wood; Trinity College, Dublin (M.A., M.D., B.Ch., 1913). Served in R.A.M.C., European War 1914-18, France, Flanders and Italy (promoted Major, M.C., Order of St. Stanislaus, Russia, Médaille d'Honneur, France, despatches); Arnott Gold Medal, 1915; transferred R.A.F. 1918; Air Commodore, 1941; Air Vice-Marshal, 1944. P.M.O. Palestine, 1930-34; P.M.O. Bomber Command, 1941-1942 (despatches); P.M.O. North Africa, 1943; P.M.O. Mediterranean and Middle East, 1944-46 (Commander, Legion of Merit, U.S.A., 1945); K.H.S. 1945-47; retired list, 1947. *Publications:* various scientific papers. *Recreations:* golf and ski-ing. *Address:* Southview, Pevensey Road, Worthing, Sussex. [*Died* 25 *May* 1967.

KELLY, Colonel Tom, C.M.G. 1917; *b.* 1869. Served European War, 1914-18 (despatches, C.M.G.). Colonel Royal Engineers (Postal Section) and in Surveyor's Department General Post Office. *Address:* 128 Dorset Road, Bexhill-on-Sea.

[*Died* 10 *Aug.* 1965.

KELSEY, Vice-Adm. Marcel Harcourt Attwood, C.B. 1948; D.S.C. 1918; R.N. retired; *b.* 21 February 1894; *s.* of Edward Frederick Kelsey, solicitor; *m.* 1922, Lilian Vera. *Educ.:* Eastman's, Winchester; Osborne; Dartmouth. Served H.M. Ships: Good Hope, Monmouth, Hampshire, Triumph, Defender, 1914; Obdurate, 1916; Valentine, 1917; Warwick, 1918; Warspite, 1921; Espiegle, 1922; Repulse, 1925; Australia, 1928; Vivid, 1930; Admiralty, 1932; London (Comdr.), 1934; Admiralty, 1937; Naiad (Capt.), 1940; Commodore Freetown, 1942; Warspite (Capt.), 1944; Commodore Royal Naval Barracks, Chatham, 1945; Flag Officer Malta (R.A.), 1946-48; retired, 1949. *Address:* 41 Wynnstay Gdns., W.8. *Club:* United Service. [*Died* 27 *Aug.* 1964.

KEMBALL, Christopher Gurdon, C.M.G. 1952; C.V.O. 1958; *b.* 24 Oct. 1899; *o. surv. s.* of late Lt.-Col. C. A. Kemball, C.I.E.; *m.* 1928, Norma Sinnickson Grey, Philadelphia, U.S.A.; one *s.* one *d.* *Educ.:* Charterhouse; Trinity College, Cambridge. Served in Welsh Guards, 1918-19. Vice-Consul: Zürich, 1925-26; Philadelphia, 1926-30; Santiago, 1930-33; Naples, 1934-37; Consul at New York, 1937-40; Chargé d'Affaires ad interim and Consul at Tegucigalpa, 1940-44; Consul at Oporto, 1944-47; Counsellor, Foreign Office, 1948-56; Consul-General, Amsterdam, 1956-60, retired. *Address:* 22 Clarendon Street, S.W.1; West Sunnedon House, Coggeshall, Essex.

[*Died* 7 *Sept.* 1969.

KEMMIS BETTY, Vice-Admiral Arthur, D.S.O. 1917; *b.* 1877; *s.* of late Col. Joshua Frederic Kemmis Betty; *m.* 1911, Ethel Beatrix Mary Ellen Agar; one *s.* Served European War, 1914-18 (despatches, D.S.O.); Rear-Adm. and retired list, 1929; Vice-Adm., retired, 1934. *Address:* Framfield, Seaford, Sussex. *T.:* Seaford 2400. [*Died* 11 *May* 1961.

KEMP-WELCH, Margaret, A.R.E. 1901; artist; *d.* of late Stanley Kemp-Welch. *Educ.:* Kensington High School. Studied art under Sir Hubert von Herkomer, R.A., and Sir Frank Short; has exhibited at Royal Academy, Royal Institute of Water Colours, Liverpool, Manchester, Paris Salon, etc. *Address:* St. Elizabeth Nursing Home, 18 West Drive, Brighton, Sussex.

[*Died* 15 *Jan.* 1968.

KEMPTHORNE, Rt. Rev. Leonard Stanley, C.B.E. 1953; D.D.; Bishop in Polynesia, 1923-62, retd.; *b.* Nelson, N.Z., 2 Aug. 1886; *s.* of Archdeacon Kempthorne, Brightwater, N.Z.; *m.* 1931, Ruth Beall, California. *Educ.:* Queen's College, Oxford (M.A.); University College, London. Ordained in St. Paul's Cathedral, London, 1914; for 18 months worked at Zaria in Northern Nigeria; Chaplain to Bishop of Lichfield, 1916-20; Chaplain at Ipoh, Federated Malay States in Diocese of Singapore, 1920-22. D.D. Lambeth, 1958. *Address:* Clarke St., Suva, Fiji.

[*Died* 25 *July* 1963.

KEMPTON, Charles Leslie, C.B.E. 1919; *m.* 1940, Monica, *yr. d.* of Col. H. S. Jervis, M.C. Served European War, 1914-19 (despatches, C.B.E., Legion of Honour); retired as Lieut.-Col., 1920. *Address:* 79 Stanhope Mews East, Queen's Gate, S.W.7.

[*Died* 18 *April* 1965.

KEMSLEY, 1st Viscount, *cr.* 1945, of Dropmore; 1st Baron, *cr.* 1936, of Farnham Royal; **James Gomer Berry,** 1st Bt., *cr.* 1928; G.B.E. 1959; *b.* Merthyr Tydfil, Wales, 1883; *s.* of late John Mathias Berry, J.P., and Mary Anne Berry; *m.* 1st, 1907, Mary Lilian (*d.* 1928) *d.* of Horace George Holmes, J.P., Brondesbury Park: four *s.* one *d.* (and one *s.* decd. and one *s.* killed in action, 1944); 2nd, 1931, Edith (O.B.E. 1953; O.St.J.; Comdr. Order of Phœnix, Greece; Comdr. Legion of Honour), *d.* of E. N. Merandon du Plessis, of Constance, Flacq, Mauritius. Chairman, Kemsley Newspapers, Ltd., 1937-59. Editor in Chief Sunday Times, 1937-59. Reuters Trustee 1941- (Chairman 1951-59). Hon. LL.D. Manchester Univ. and Univ. of Wales; Pres. Univ. College of South Wales and Monmouthshire, 1945-50; Chm., Infants Hosp., 1922-37; King Edward VII Hosp., Windsor, 1933-37; President: Merthyr Gen. Hosp., 1928-49; Football Assoc. of Wales, 1946-60; British Gliding Assoc., 1947-61 (Vice-Pres., 1962-); Founder Kemsley Flying Trust, 1947. J.P. Bucks., 1927; High Sheriff of Buckinghamshire, 1929; Master, Spectaclemakers' Co., 1934-36; Conservative; Hon. Col. R.A.S.C., 1939-48; K.St.J. 1944; Officer Legion of Honour (France); Grand Cross of George I (Greece); Commander Order of Crown of Belgium. *Publication:* Kemsley Manual of Journalism. *Heir:* *s.* Hon. (Geoffrey) Lionel Berry. *Address:* 54 South Street, W.1. *T.:* Grosvenor 1336; Dropmore, Bucks. *T.:* Bourne End 880. *Clubs:* Athenæum, Carlton; Royal Yacht Squadron (Cowes). [*Died* 6 *Feb.* 1968.

KENCHINGTON, Brigadier Arthur George, C.B.E. 1943; M.C.; p.s.c.; *b.* 29 Dec. 1890; *s.* of G. Kenchington, Hythe, Kent; *m.* 1919, Lucy, *d.* of A. D. C. Danks, Hucclecote, Glos.; two *s.* two *d.* *Educ.:* Folkestone Grammar School; Univ. of London. The Buffs, 1914-17; R. Tank Regiment, 1917-38; Colonel 1939; served European War, 1914-19 (M.C., Croix de Guerre, Bt. Major), N.-W. Frontier, 1930-1931; Bt. Lieutenant-Colonel, 1934; War Office, 1940. D.D.S.D., A.F.V.; Egypt and N. Africa, 1942-43 (C.B.E.); Staff appts.: Rhine Army, U.K., India, International Saar Force, War Office; Commanded: Rhine Tank Co., 7 R. Tanks, 21 and 24 Armoured Brigades; D.M.T. C.M.F.; retired, 1946; British Resident, Göttingen, 1948-57. *Recreation:* music. *Address:* West Bank, Crondall, Farnham, Surrey. [*Died* 13 *Oct.* 1966.

KENDAL, Sir Norman, Kt., *cr.* 1937; C.B.E. 1927; *b.* 1880; 2nd *s.* of late T. Herbert Kendal, Cheadle, Cheshire; *m.* 1913, Ruth Milner, *d.* of late John R. Oliver, Bowden, Cheshire; one *s.* two *d.* *Educ.:* Rossall; Oriel College, Oxford. B.A.; called to Bar, Inner Temple, 1906; served European War, 1914-18, 5th Cheshire Regiment (wounded 1916), attached Ministry of National Service, 1917; Deputy Assistant Commissioner, C.I.D., New Scotland Yard, 1918-28; Assistant Commissioner, 1928-45; Chairman Bucks Quarter Sessions Appeal Cttee., 1950-55. *Recreations:* cricket, tennis, shooting, gardening. *Address:* Roughwood Barns, Chalfont St. Giles, Bucks. *Club:* United University. [*Died* 8 *March* 1966.

KENDALL, Anthony Colin, C.B.E. (O.B.E. 1946); H.M. Consul-General, Mogadishu, Somalia, 1957-60, retired; *b.* 12 Apr. 1898; *s.* of Edmund E. Kendall and Margaret (*née* McDowall); *m.* 1919, Mila Todorova; one *d.* *Educ.:* Cotton College; Beaupreau (France). Served European War in R.W. Fusiliers, France, 1916-18; Brit. Mil. Mission, Bulgaria, 1918-20; Brit. Vice-Consul, Burgas, Bulgaria, 1920-35; British Vice-Consul, Galatz, Roumania, 1935; British Consul, Constantza, Roumania, 1939; served on staff at G.H.Q., Cairo, 1941-44 (despatches) and on Mil. Mission, Bucharest, 1944-46 (Lt.-Col.); Head of Consular Section, British Legation, Bucharest, 1946-48; British Consul: Beira, Mozambique, 1948-50; Venice, 1951-57. Knight of Holy Redeemer (Greece), 1919. *Recreations:* tennis, swimming. *Address:* 15 Dealtry Road, S.W.15. *T.:* Putney 7500. [*Died* 20 *June* 1967.

KENDALL, Henry, A.F.C. 1918; Actor Producer; Television Producer since 1957; *b.* 28 May 1897; *s.* of William Kendall and Rebecca Nathan. *Educ.:* City of London School. Started in theatrical profession in 1914 playing several Shakespearean parts at Old Vic. Served European War, 1918-19, in R.A.F., as Capt., until 1919. Returned to stage and made first big success in French Leave, 1920. Other outstanding successes in: Havoc, A Murder has been Arranged, East of Suez, The Flying Fool (also in the film of the play), The Ghost Train, Someone at the Door, Room for Two, Rise Above It, On Monday Next, Angels in Love, à La Carte, Aunt Edwina (title role) and numerous other revues, including the famous "Sweet and Low" series at the Ambassadors, 1944-48. Producer of several well-known plays including: Other Peoples' Houses, This Was a Woman, The Shop at Sly Corner, See How They Run and On Monday Next; Macadam and Eve, Aldwych; Where the Rainbow Ends, Stoll; The Happy Family, Duchess (also played lead); Down Came a Blackbird, Savoy; Meet a Body, Duke of York's; The Lion in the Lighthouse (also played lead), Embassy Theatre; You too can have a Body, Victoria Palace; Let Them Eat Cake, Cambridge Theatre; Watch it Sailor, Aldwych; Pools Paradise, Phœnix; One for the Pot, Whitehall, etc. Has appeared in numerous films since 1931. Television plays, etc.; producer of programmes for the B.B.C. and Independent Television. *Publication:* (autobiography) I Remember Romano's, 1960. *Recreations:* music and writing. *Address:* Wetherall Lodge, Well Rd., Hampstead, N.W.3. *Club:* Green Room. [*Died* 9 *June* 1962.

KENDALL, Rev. Henry Ewing, O.B.E.; V.D.; M.A.; *b.* 11 Nov. 1888; *s.* of Francis Henry Kendall. *Educ.:* Shrewsbury School; Pembroke Coll., Cambridge. Assistant Master at Rossall, 1912-13; Shrewsbury School, 1913-25; Superintendent, Shrewsbury School Mission, 1914-16; Chaplain, R.N., 1916-19; Hon. Chaplain, R.N.V.R., 1919-39. Housemaster, Shrewsbury, 1921-25; Warden St. Edward's School, Oxford, 1925-54; Rector, St. Mary Arches, Exeter, 1955-61; Director of training of Ordination Candidates, Diocese of Exeter, 1957-61. *Recreation:* golf. *Address:* Brackenhill, Cotswold Road, Cumnor Hill, Oxford. *T.:* Cumnor 2750. [*Died* 26 *April* 1963.

KENDALL, Mrs. John; *see* Sowerby, Katherine G.

KENDALL, Major-General Roy, C.B.E. 1943; (Retired List); Chartered Electrical Engineer; *b.* 1 Nov. 1897; *s.* of late Joseph and Margaret Kendall; *m.* 1925, Maude Edith, *y. d.* of late George Williams, Queenstown, Tasmania; no *c.* *Educ.:* Royal Military College of Australia. Served European War with Australian Signals in Belgium, 1918-19; War of 1939-45, Greece 1941 (despatches); Middle East, 1941-42; C.S.O. 1st Aust. Corps and New Guinea Force (Papuan Campaign), 1942-43 (C.B.E.); G.S.O. (Signals), Aust. Military Mission, and U.S. War Dept., Washington D.C. 1943-45; Commdr.: Central Signal Training Depot, 1946-47; Army Technical School, 1947-50; 11th Infantry Brigade, 1950-51; G.O.C. Central Command, 1951-52; Hon. Col. Royal Aust. Sigs. and Col. Comdt., Royal Aust. Sigs. 1952-63; Director of Recruiting, Aust. Defence Services, 1953-58, Hon. A.D.C. to H.E. the Governor General of Australia, 1949-51. President Australian Hockey Association, 1956; Vice-President,

Fédération Internationale de Hockey, 1956-1960; A.M.I.E.E.; Fellow of Institution of Radio Engineers (Australia). *Address:* Box 593, G.P.O., Sydney, Australia. *Clubs:* Naval and Military (Melbourne); Imperial Service, The Lakes Golf (Sydney).
[*Died* 22 *Oct.* 1963.

KENDREW, Hubert, C.B. 1949; *b.* 10 February 1894; *s.* of John Kendrew, Oulston Hall, Oulston, York; *m.* 1922, Eva, *d.* of I. Spencer, Harrogate; one *s.* one *d.* *Educ.:* Archbishop Holgate's School, York. Entered Civil Service, 1912; R.A.S.C. and Connaught Rangers, 1914-19; Ministry of Labour, 1919; Director of Establishments, Min. of Economic Warfare, 1940-42; Asst. Secretary, Min. of Labour, 1942-43; Director of Establishments, Min. of Town and Country Planning, 1943-45; Director of Establishments, Min. of Works, 1945-56; Deputy Secretary, Ministry of Works, 1956-59. *Recreations:* farming, bridge. *Address:* The Croft, Welburn, York. *T.:* Whitwell-on-the-Hill 244. *Clubs:* Reform; Yorkshire (York).
[*Died* 10 *Oct.* 1966.

KENDREW, Wilfrid George, M.A.; formerly Reader in Climatology, University of Oxford. *Educ.:* Mountjoy School, Dublin; St. Catherine's Society, Oxford. Served European War, 1914-18, and War of 1939-45 (R.N.V.R.). Visiting Professor, University of British Columbia; Service for Defence Research Board, and Meteorological Division of Dept. of Transport, Canada, 1950-54. *Publications:* The Climates of the Continents, 5th ed., 1961; Climatology, 2nd ed., 1957; The Climate of Central Canada (in collaboration), 1955; The Climate of British Columbia and the Yukon Territory, 1956, etc. *Recreations:* travelling, ski-ing, skating. *Address:* c/o Barclays Bank, High St., Oxford.
[*Died* 4 *April* 1962.

KENNAN, Thomas Brereton, C.B.E. 1943; M.C.; *b.* 3 Feb. 1891; *er. s.* of late Thomas Ponsonby King and Emily Charlotte Kennan; *m.* 1st, 1914, Dorothy Margaret (*decd.*), and 2nd, 1918, Brenda Boyd, both *d.* of late Rev. Charles A. and Helen Dutton, Lothersdale, Yorks; three *s.* three *d.* *Educ.:* Colet Court Prep. School, London; Worcester Cathedral King's School. Clerk Basutoland Civil Service, 1910; Sub-Inspector of Police (Lieut.), 1912; Inspector of Police (Capt.), 1919; Asst. District Commissioner (Administrative Service), 1927; District Commissioner, 1929; First Asst. Sec. 1938; Deputy Resident Commissioner and Govt. Sec. of Basutoland, 1942-48; retired, 1948 2nd Lt. with Royal Welch Fusiliers in France, 1918. *Address:* 2 Adylinn, Gilchrist Rd., Salisbury, Rhodesia.
[*Died* 28 *Aug.* 1965.

KENNARD, Sir Lawrence (Ury Charles), 2nd Bt., *cr.* 1891; *b.* 6 Feb. 1912; *s.* of Sir Coleridge Kennard, 1st Bt. and Dorothy Katharine, *o. c.* of late Sir George Head Barclay, K.C.S.I., K.C.M.G.; *S.* father, 1948; *m.* 1940, Joan Perschke (*d.* 1964). *Educ.:* Eton. *Heir:* *b.* Lt. Col. George Arnold Ford Kennard, 4th Hussars [*b.* 27 Apr. 1915; *m.* 1940, Cecilia Violet Cokayne, *o. d.* of Major Cecil John Cokayne Maunsell].
[*Died* 3 *May* 1967.

KENNEDY, Rev. Archibald Cowan, D.D.; Regius Professor of Hebrew and Semitic Languages, University of Aberdeen, since 1932; *b.* Old Aberdeen, 2 March 1892; *o. s.* of late Rev. Professor A. R. S. Kennedy; *m.* 1923, Janet Amy, *e. d.* of Rev. James Lumsden, D.D., of Ratho, Midlothian. *Educ.:* George Watson's College, and University of Edinburgh, M.A. 1914, B.D. 1921, D.D. 1944. Vans Dunlop Scholar in Semitic Languages, 1919-21, Examiner in Hebrew, etc., for B.D. Degree Edinburgh, 1926-30; External Examiner for B.D., Univ. of Edinburgh, Glasgow, and Belfast, 1925-29, 1933-36, 1936-39; Jun. O.T.C. 1908-10. Sen. O.T.C. (Arty.), 1910-14, 103rd and 100th Batteries R.F.A. and "N" R.H.A.; served European War, France and Salonika, 1914-19, Liaison Officer with 1st Hellenic Division; Capt., 1918; Minister of Church of Scotland at Arbirlot, Angus, 1923-28, and St. Enoch's-Hogganfield, Glasgow, 1928-32. Hon. LL.D. Aberdeen University, 1963. *Address:* 47 Queen's Road, Aberdeen.
[*Died* 1 *March* 1966.

KENNEDY, Aubrey Leo, M.C.; Publicist; *b.* 6 Feb. 1885; *s.* of Sir John Kennedy, K.C.M.G., of H.M. Diplomatic Service; *m.* 1921, Sylvia Meysey-Thompson; three *d.* *Educ.:* Harrow; Magdalen College, Oxford. Joined staff of The Times, 1910; Correspondent in Paris and the Balkans, 1911-14; served European War, 1914-19; K.O.Y.L.I., Intelligence Corps, Scots Guards (M.C., despatches, Croce di Guerra); rejoined Times, 1919-42; Diplomatic Correspondent, European Division, B.B.C., 1942-45. *Publications:* Old Diplomacy and New; From Salisbury to Lloyd George, 1922; Britain Faces Germany, 1937; Salisbury (1830-1903); Portrait of a Statesman, 1953; (Ed.) My Dear Duchess, 1956. *Address:* 24 Hans Place, S.W.1. *Clubs:* Travellers', M.C.C.
[*Died* 8 *Dec.* 1965.

KENNEDY, Sir Donald; *see* Mackenzie-Kennedy, Sir H. C. D. C.

KENNEDY, Henry Albert; *b.* 1877; *s.* of late Henry George Kennedy, Barrister; *m.* 1910, Maud Mary, *d.* of Edward Brooks; one *d.* *Educ.:* Cheltenham College (Scholar), Worcester College, Oxford (Exhibitioner). Lit. Hum. (Hon.) 2nd class 1900; Fed. Malay States Civil Service, 1900; District Officer, Kuantan, Pahang, 1906; transferred to Board of Education, England, 1908; Secretary to Advisory Council, Victoria and Albert Museum, 1910; Deputy Keeper, Victoria and Albert Museum, 1923; Keeper Victoria and Albert Museum, S.W.7, 1926-38; retired, 1938. *Publications:* Early English Portrait Miniatures in the Collection of the Duke of Buccleuch (Studio special number, 1917); Catalogue of the Travelling Collection of Leaves and Cuttings from Illuminated MSS. (Victoria and Albert Museum, 1924); Local Museums: Notes on their Building and Conduct, 1938. *Recreation:* golf. *Address:* 1 Little Anglesey Road, Alverstoke, Gosport, Hants. *T.:* Gosport 81894.
[*Died* 5 *March* 1965.

KENNEDY, John Fitzgerald; President of the United States of America since 20 Jan. 1961; *b.* Brookline, Massachusetts, U.S.A., 29 May 1917; *s.* of Joseph Patrick Kennedy, *q.v.*; *m.* 1953, Jacqueline Lee Bouvier; one *s.* one *d.* (and one *s.* decd.). *Educ.:* Harvard University, U.S.A. (B.Sc.). Served with United States Navy, 1941-45 (Navy and Marine Corps medal, Purple Heart). Correspondent of the International News Service, 1945. Member, House of Representatives, United States, 1947-53; Senator from Massachusetts, 1953-60. U.S. Presidential Medal of Freedom, 1963 (posthumous). Is a Democrat. *Publications:* Why England Slept, 1940; Profiles in Courage, 1956 (Pulitzer Prize for biography, 1957); The Strategy of Peace, 1960; A Nation of Immigrants, 1963. *Relevant publications:* A. M. Schlesinger, A Thousand Days, 1965; T. Sorensen, Kennedy, 1966; P. Salinger, With Kennedy, 1966; W. Manchester, Death of a President, 1967. *Address:* The White House, Washington, D.C., U.S.A.
[*Died* 22 *Nov.* 1963.

KENNEDY, Maj.-Gen. Sir John Noble, G.C.M.G., *cr.* 1953 (K.C.M.G., *cr.* 1952); K.C.V.O., *cr.* 1947; K.B.E. *cr.* 1945; C.B. 1942; M.C.; Chairman: Rosehill Arts Trust; Outward Bound Mountain School, Ullswater; Yehudi Menuhin School; *b.* 31 Aug. 1893; *e. s.* of late Rev. James Russell Kennedy and Sarah Maude Noble;

m. 1st, 1926, Isabella Rosamond Georgiana (*d.* 1941), *e. d.* of late Col. Lord John Joicey-Cecil; three *s.* two *d.*; 2nd, 1942, Catherine (*d.* 1969), *o. d.* of late Major John Gurney Fordham. *Educ.:* Stranraer; R. M. Academy, Woolwich, 1915. Entered Royal Navy, 1911. Transferred to Royal Artillery, 1915; Capt. 1927; Bt. Major, 1930; Bt. Lt.-Col. 1934; Major, 1936; Bt. Col. 1938; Col. 1938; Acting Maj.-Gen. 1940; Maj.-Gen. 1941; served European War, 1914-18, in Royal Navy Aug. 1914-Jan. 1915; 1915-18, France, Flanders, and Egypt, in Royal Artillery, and on Staff of the Australian Corps as Reconnaissance Officer and Brigade Major (M.C., despatches); S. Russian Campaign, 1919-20 (despatches); in Turkey, 1920; from 1922 to 1937 served with Royal Artillery in England and Egypt as Battery Commander and Brigade Major R.A. 3rd Division, on General Staff, War Office, and as Instructor Staff College; Imp. Defence College, 1938; Deputy Director of Military Operations, 1938; Director of Plans, 1939; Commander, R.A., 52nd Division, France, 1940; Brigadier General Staff, Northern Ireland, 1940; Director of Military Operations, War Office, 1940-43; Asst. C.I.G.S. (Ops. and Intelligence), 1943-45; retired, 1946. Colonel Comdt. Royal Artillery, 1948-58. Governor of Southern Rhodesia, 1946-54. Chairman: Central African Council, 1946-53; Central African Defence Cttee., 1950-53; Inter-governmental Conf. on Federation of Rhodesias and Nyasaland, 1951; Chairman, National Convention of Southern Rhodesia, 1960; Freeman of Cities of Salisbury and Bulawayo; K.St.J. Knight Commander of the Commandery of the Order of St. John in Central Africa, 1952-53; Mem. Royal Co. of Archers (Queen's Body Guard for Scotland); Knight of Polish Order of Polonia Restituta, 1944; Grand Cross of the Order of the Crown (Belgium), 1946; Croix de Guerre (Belgium), 1946; Commander, White Lion (Czechoslovakia), 1947. *Publications:* The Business of War, 1957. Numerous articles on biographical, military subjects, sport, and ornithology. *Recreations:* salmon and trout fishing, ornithology, etc. *Address:* Broxmouth House, Dunbar, East Lothian. *T.:* Dunbar 3211. *Clubs:* Travellers', Pratt's. [*Died* 15 *June* 1970.

KENNEDY, Sir John Ralph Bayly, 4th Bt., *cr.* 1836; *b.* 9 Apr. 1896; *e. s.* of 3rd Bt. and Maude, *d.* of Sir James Macaulay Higginson; *S.* father, 1923; unmarried. *Educ.:* Uppingham; R.M.A., Woolwich. Lieut. R.F.A., 1916-20 (Reg.); Lieut. R.A., 1940-42; farming about 500 acres. *Heir:* *b.* James Edward Kennedy, *b.* 1898. *Address:* Johnstown Kennedy, Rathcoole, Co. Dublin. *T.:* Celbridge 289203. [*Died* 9 *Aug.* 1968.

KENNEDY, Joseph Patrick; *b.* Boston, 6 Sept. 1888; *s.* of Patrick J. Kennedy and Mary Hickey; *m.* 1914, Rose Fitzgerald, Boston, Mass.; one *s.* (and *e. s.*, Joseph P. Kennedy, Jr., killed in action, 1944; President John F. Kennedy, assassinated, 1963; Senator Robert F. Kennedy, assassinated, 1968) four *d.* (and 2nd *d.*, Kathleen, Marchioness of Hartington, decd.). *Educ.:* Boston Latin Sch.; A.B. Harvard, 1912; hon. LL.D. Nat. Univ. of Ireland (Dublin), 1938, Univs. of Edinburgh, Manchester, Liverpool, Bristol, and Cambridge, 1939; also hon. degree from Catholic Univ., Oglethorpe Univ., Notre Dame Univ. and from Colby College, 1946. Bank Examiner for Mass., 1912-14; Pres. Columbia Trust Co., Boston, 1914-17; Asst. Gen. Manager, Fore River (Mass.) Plant of Bethlehem Shipbuilding Corporation, 1917-1919; Manager, Hayden, Stone Co., investment bankers, Boston branch, 1919-24; Pres. and Chairman, Board of Directors Film Booking Offices of America, 1926-29, and of Pathé Exchange, Inc., 1928-1930; corporation finance, 1930-34; Chairman, Securities Exchange Commission, 1934-35; and of U.S. Maritime Commission, 1937; Ambassador of the United States to Court of St. James's, 1937-41. Chm. Special Cttee. Relative to Establishing Dept. of Commerce in Mass.; Trustee Notre Dame Univ.; Member Commission on Organisation of Exec. Branch of Federal Govt., 1947; appointed to new Commission, 1953. Democrat. Catholic. Knight of Malta, and Grand Knight of Pius IX; Knight of Equestrian Order of Holy Sepulchre, 1946; Grand Cross Order of Leopold II (Belgium), 1959. *Publications:* numerous magazine and newspaper articles. *Address:* North Ocean Boulevard, Palm Beach, Florida, U.S.A. [*Died* 18 *Nov.* 1969.

KENNEDY, Margaret; (Lady Davies), F.R.S.L.; writer; *er. d.* of Charles Moore Kennedy, Barrister-at-law; *m.* 1925, David Davies (later Sir David Davies, Q.C.; *d.* 1964); one *s.* two *d.* *Educ.:* Cheltenham; Somerville College, Oxford. *Publications:* A Century of Revolution, 1922; The Ladies of Lyndon, 1923; The Constant Nymph, 1924; (with Basil Dean) Play of The Constant Nymph, 1926; Red Sky at Morning, 1927; (with Basil Dean) Come with Me (play), 1928; The Fool of the Family, 1930; Return I dare not, 1931; A Long Time Ago, 1932; Escape Me Never (play), 1933; Together and Apart, 1936; (with Gregory Ratoff) Autumn (play), 1937; The Midas Touch, 1938; The Feast, 1950; Jane Austen (biography), 1950 (English Novelists Series); Lucy Carmichael (Book Society Choice), 1951; Troy Chimneys (James Tait Black Award) 1953; The Oracles, 1955; The Heroes of Clone, 1957; The Outlaws on Parnassus, 1958; A Night in Cold Harbour, 1960; The Forgotten Smile, 1961; Not in the Calendar, 1964. *Address:* c/o Curtis Brown, Ltd., 13 King Street, W.C.2. [*Died* 31 *July* 1967.

KENNEDY, Milward; *see* Burge, Milward R. K.

KENNEDY, Myles Storr Nigel; *b.* 12 Oct. 1889; *e. s.* of late Myles Kennedy, J.P., D.L., of Stone Cross, Ulverston; *m.* 1946, Dorothy Emerson-Millington. *Educ.:* Harrow; Trinity College, Cambridge. Called to Bar, Inner Temple, 1920; M.P. (U.) Lonsdale Division, Co. Lancaster, Nov. 1922-Dec. 1923; Lancashire County Council, 1922-41, Alderman, 1927-41. Major (retired) 3rd Batt. The Border Regt. (despatches). *Address:* Hill Foot, Ulverston, Lancs. *Club:* Royal Automobile. [*Died* 19 *Jan.* 1964.

KENNEDY, Robert Francis; Senator for New York, U.S.A., since 1965; *b.* Boston, Mass., 20 November 1925; third *s.* of Joseph Patrick Kennedy *q.v.*; *m.* 1950, Ethel Skakel; seven *s.* three *d.* *Educ.:* Milton Academy, Mass.; Harvard University (B.A.); University of Virginia Law School (LL.B.). U.S. Naval Reserve, 1944-46 (seaman); War correspondent in Palestine for the Boston Post, 1948. Admitted to Massachusetts State Bar, 1951; admitted to practise before U.S. Supreme Court, 1955; Attorney, Criminal Div., U.S. Dept. of Justice, 1951-52; Manager, electoral campaign for J. F. Kennedy as Senator, 1952; Asst. Counsel, Senate Permanent Sub-cttee. on Investigations, 1953, Chief Counsel to Democratic Minority, 1954, Chief Counsel and Staff Director, 1955-59; Asst. Counsel, Hoover Commn., 1953-54; Chief Counsel, Senate Select Cttee. on Improper Activities in Labor or Management Field, 1957-59; Manager, Presidential election campaign for J. F. Kennedy, 1960; Attorney-General of the U.S.A., 1961-64. Is a Democrat. Holds awards and Hon. Degrees. *Publications:* The Enemy Within, 1960 (U.S.A.); Just Friends and Brave Enemies, 1962; The Pursuit of Justice, 1964; *Posthumous Publication:* 13 Days: The Cuban

Missile Crisis, October 1962, 1969. *Recreations:* ski-ing, sailing, touch football, riding. *Address:* 870 United Nations Plaza, New York, N.Y., U.S.A. [*Died* 6 *June* 1968.

KENNEDY of Knockgray, Lt.-Col. William Hew Clark-, V.C. 1919; C.M.G. 1918; D.S.O. 1916; late Canadian Expeditionary Force; *b.* 1879; *s.* of late A. W. M. Clark-Kennedy, of Knockgray; *m.* 1914, Kate, *d.* of late Robert Reford, Montreal. Served South Africa, 1900-2; European War (severely wounded, C.M.G., D.S.O. and bar, V.C., Croix de Guerre). *Address:* Knockgray, Carsphairn, Galloway, Scotland. [*Died* 26 *Oct.* 1961.

KENNEDY, William Paul McClure, Litt.D., Dr. en Droit, LL.D.; F.R.S.C. 1935; Professor Emeritus of Law and Dean Emeritus of the Faculty of the School of Law, University of Toronto, since 1949; Fellow of St. John's College, Cambridge, 1949; Member of the Canadian Bar Association; Legal Adviser: to Royal Commission on Dominion-Provincial Relations, 1937-38; to Prime Minister and Attorney-Gen. of Ont. at Dominion-Provincial Conf. on Canadian Constitutional Law, 1950-51; Member Attorney-General's Committee on B.N.A. Act, 1935; Expert Witness before the Special Committee of the House of Commons on the revision of the B.N.A. Act, 1935; External Examiner, Faculty of Law, University of Melbourne, 1931-32; Member of and Draughtsman to the Committee of the Govt. of Canada on the Law of Nationality, 1928-1929; appointed by Govt. of Canada to prepare a confidential report on workings of Law of Nationality, 1930; Canadian Legal Corresp. for S. African Law Times, 1932-37; Goldwin Smith Lectr. in Constitutional Law, Cornell Univ., 1926-27; Kirby Foundation Lectr. on Comparative Law Lafayette Coll., 1930-31; Assoc. Prof. of Modern History and Special Lecturer on Federal Law, Univ. of Toronto, 1914-26; Prof. of Law and Dean of Faculty of Law, Univ. of Toronto, 1926-49; Member Canadian Delegation, British Commonwealth Relations Conference, Toronto, 1933; Editor (and Founder) of University of Toronto Law Journal, 1935-49; Legal Adviser to Committee which drafted the Constitution of the I.F.S.; Emeritus Member of Soc. of Public Teachers of Law, 1949; *b.* 1879; *m.* Pauline Simpson, of Hamilton, Ontario; two *s.* two *d.* *Educ.:* privately; Paris; Vienna; Berlin; Trinity College, Dublin. Graduated with 1st Class Honours and Senior Moderatorship and Gold Medal, M.A., LL.B., and proceeded Litt.D.; Vice-Chancellor's Prizeman in English prose; Dr. en Droit, Montreal, 1939; LL.D. Toronto, 1953. *Publications:* The Elizabethan Interpretations; Life of Archbishop Parker; Studies in Tudor History; The Development and Law of the Canadian Constitution; Documents of the Canadian Constitution, 1713-1926; Visitation Articles and Injunctions, 1535-1575 (3 vols. with Dr. W. H. Frere); The Nature of Canadian Federalism; Elizabethan Administration—An Essay in Law and Politics (3 vols.); Ed. (revised and new edn.) Baldwin, Lafontaine and Hincks (Stephen Leacock); Life of Lord Elgin; Short Treatise on Canadian Constitutional Law (with late A. H. F. Lefroy); The Laws of Quebec, 1767-71; Theories of Law and the Constitutional Law of the British Empire; The Law and Custom of Reservation, 1549-1661; The Law of Nationality; Statutes, Treaties and Documents of Canadian Constitution; The Law of the Taxing-Power in Canada (with D. C. Wells); Some Aspects in the Theories and Workings of Constitutional Law; The Right to Trade; An Essay in the Law of Torts (with J. Finkelman); Essays in Constitutional Law; The Law and Custom of the South African Constitution (with H. J. Schlosberg); Cambridge History of the British Empire (ed. vol. vi., Canada; contributor to the leading legal and juristic Reviews. *Recreations:* fly-fishing, canoeing, billiards. *Address:* 77 Spadina Road, Toronto, Ontario, Canada; Faculty of Law, University of Toronto; Narrow Waters, Beaver Lake, Kearney, Ontario. *T.:* WA2-6978, Midway WA3-6611. *Club:* Faculty Union (Toronto). [*Died* 12 *Aug.* 1963.

KENNEDY-COOKE, Brian, C.B.E. 1953; M.C. 1918, and Bar, 1918; Vice-President, Council Royal Over-Seas League; *b.* 22 Oct. 1894; *s.* of late Rev. George Kennedy-Cooke; *m.* 1925, Annette Rae, *d.* of Dr. A. W. Cooke; two *s.* one *d.* *Educ.:* St. Edward's School (Scholar) and Worcester College, Oxford (Senior Exhibitioner and Goldsmith and Ewelme Exhibitioner). Served European War, 1914-18, in Ox. and Bucks. Lt. Inf. and on staff; Major and acting Lt.-Col., 1918. Joined Sudan Political Service, 1920; Asst. Dist. Commissioner successively in Kordofan and Red Sea Provinces; Dist. Commissioner Gedaref (Kassala Province), 1928; Dep. Governor Kassala Province, 1931; Asst. Civil Sec., 1934; Governor Kassala Province, 1935-41. War of 1939-45, recommissioned with rank of Brigadier and appointed Military Administrator, Eritrea, 1941-42; despatches 1942; special duties, Sudan Govt., 1942-43; Controller Arts and Sciences Div., British Council, 1943-50; British Council Representative in Italy, 1950-56; Course Organizer, Oversea Service, 1957-63. Order of the Nile 3rd Class (Egypt), 1936; Coronation Medal, 1937; Officer of Legion of Merit (U.S.A.), 1946; Coronation Medal, 1953; Gold Medal Benmeriti della Cultura (Italy) 1958. *Publications:* The Trees of Kassala Province (Sudan), 1944; King Arthur of Britain, 1946; Sir Lancelot du Lake, 1951; The Holy Grail, 1953; The Quest of the Beast, 1957; occasional articles in various journals. *Club:* Royal Over-Seas League. [*Died* 13 *June* 1963.

KENNEDY-COX, Sir Reginald Kennedy, Kt., *cr.* 1930; C.B.E. 1944; J.P.; Founder of the Dockland Settlements; *s.* of late Reginald Cox of Brockley and Weston, Somerset, and Ada Harriette, *d.* of late Aeneas Sage Kennedy, Dornoch, Sutherlandshire; unmarried. *Educ.:* Temple Grove School; Malvern College; Hertford College, Oxford. Went in for literature and wrote many plays which were produced in London and the provinces, notably the Chetwynd Affair, at the Royalty Theatre, 1904, at the Coliseum, 1906; Mary Stuart for Mrs. Brown-Potter and the Marriage Brokers for Mrs. Langtry; in 1905 joined the Malvern Mission in Canning Town E.16, and in later years remodelled it, founding the Dockland Settlement there, 1918, and branch Dockland Settlements at Millwall, Bristol, Rotherhithe, Southampton, Stratford, E., Dagenham and Plymouth; served European War, going overseas Aug. 1914; held a Commission in the 3rd Hampshire Regt. and was attached later to the 3rd K.R.R.C. and served at 27th Div. H.Q. (despatches); Col. Southern Command Army Welfare Officer, 1940-46; Chairman, Salisbury Arts Theatre Board, etc.; a Governor of Malvern College. *Publications:* Reginald Kennedy-Cox: An Autobiography, 1931; The Happiest Man; Through the Dock Gates, 1939; Dockland Saga, 1955; various plays, short stories and articles dealing with social and spiritual problems. *Recreations:* the theatre, travel, criminology, gardening and building. *Address:* The Close, Salisbury, Wilts. *Clubs:* Garrick, Royal Automobile. [*Died* 27 *July* 1966.

KENNY, Brigadier Vincent Raymond, C.B. 1944; M.B.E. 1919; *b.* 21

Feb. 1882; *s.* of William Kenny, J.P.; *m.* 1925, Margaret (*d.* 1966), *d.* of James Barton, Carr House, Chorley, Lancs. *Educ.:* Blackrock College; Royal University of Ireland. Called to Irish Bar, 1909; Director of Army Postal Services, 1940-44; invalided from Army, 1944. *Address:* Rathenree, Foxrock, Co. Dublin. [*Died* 3 *Dec.* 1966.

KENSINGTON, Brig. Edgar Claude, C.B.E. 1924; D.S.O. 1919; M.C.; p.s.c.; retired; *b.* 2 June 1879; *s.* of late Col. E. Kensington, R.A.; *m.* 1st, 1907, Katherine Damer, *d.* of Dr. R. Dawson; one *s.* one *d.*; 2nd, 1928, Jane Doris Shrapnell-Smith (*d.* 1965); 3rd, 1966, Dorothy Joan Stollery, *d.* of Arthur George Candler Stollery. *Educ.:* Bedford School; Royal Military College, Sandhurst. Indian Army (130th K.G.O. Baluchis), 1898; served operations in the Aden Hinterland, 1902-04; European War, 1914-18, France, Mesopotamia, Palestine to 1920 (despatches, M.C., D.S.O.); Waziristan, 1921-26 (despatches, C.B.E.); retd. 1927. *Address:* Hollow Dene East, Frensham, Farnham, Surrey. *T.:* Frensham 2676. [*Died* 19 *July* 1967.

KENSWOOD, 1st Baron, *cr.* 1951, of St. Marylebone; **Ernest Albert Whitfield;** *b.* 15 Sept. 1887; *m.* 1st, 1920, Madeline Howard (*d.* 1961); one *s.* one *d.*; 2nd, 1962, Mrs. Catherine Chilver-Stainer. *Educ.:* University College School, London; University Vienna; University London. Entered City, 1906; English Correspondent in Vienna, 1907-9; lost sight, 1909, and studied music, taking London and Vienna diplomas; professional violinist in Vienna until 1914 when returned to London; toured Britain and the Continent as concert violinist; ordered to rest, 1923; after tour to Ceylon, India and E. Africa, studied at London School of Economics; B.Sc., 1926, Ph.D., 1928; returned to concert platform until 1935; retired owing to damaged hand. Elected to Council Nat. Inst. for Blind, 1928, Hon. Jt. Treas., 1931-39; deputation to France and Germany to study Blind employment conditions, 1930; delegate to World Conference on Blind, New York, 1931; Vice-Chm. Jt. Cttee. on Educ. of Blind, 1932-36; Member Governing Bodies of various organisations dealing with blind welfare. Contested (Lab.) St. Marylebone, 1931, S. Bucks, 1935; L.C.C. candidate, N. Paddington, 1937; co-opted on to Educ. Cttee., L.C.C., 1934-39. In France at outbreak of war, 1939, until 1941, thence to Canada via Portugal as unable to return to England; research worker New York Inst. for the Blind, 1941-42; Supervisor of Musical Research and Rehabilitation worker for blind ex-service men at Cdn. Nat. Inst. for Blind, Toronto, also lecturer on music, Port Hope, 1942-46; Management Cttee.: Schools for deaf and blind; Friern Mental Hosp.; Chm. Camberwell Hospitals Group, 1951-54; lectr. at various times on social and political subjects; Pres. Nat. Fed. of Blind, 1951-55 (Hon. Vice-Pres. 1955). Vice-Pres. Pembs. Community Council; Mem. Pembrokeshire Old Peoples' Welfare Cttee., 1956; Governor, B.B.C., 1946-50. *Publications:* Gabriel Bonnot de Mably, 1928; contrib. to Columbia Encyc. of Political Science and various technical periodicals on the blind. *Recreations:* reading; music; theatre. *Heir: s.* Hon. John Michael Howard Whitfield [*b.* 6 April 1930; *m.* 1951, Deirdre Anna Louise, *d.* of Colin Malcolm Methven, of Mains of Megginch, Perthshire; four *s.*]. *Address:* Roch Castle, Pembs. *T.:* Camrose 282; Villa les Terrasses, Cavalaire-sur-Mer, Var, France. [*Died* 21 *April* 1963.

KENT, Charles Kenneth Stafford; professional name Keneth Kent; Actor (retd.), Author, Producer; *b.* 20 April 1892; *s.* of Charles Henry Kent and Beatrice, *d.* of Sir John Fox-Turner. *Educ.:* Eastbourne College; abroad. First appeared at the Comedy Theatre, London, 1912; has played in over fifty West End productions, including original production of St. Joan; made a hit in The Constant Nymph as Jacob Birnbaum, 1926; Napoleon, in St. Helena, 1936; Beethoven in Muted Strings, Daly's Theatre, 1936; played lead in To Have and To Hold, Haymarket Theatre, 1937; starred in The Shop at Sly Corner, St. Martin's Theatre; known as a delineator of foreign and dialect parts; author of The Cheat, Blue Sky Beyond (plays), was in management at the Royalty Theatre, 1929; also has produced several plays; graduated at the R.A.D.A., 1912, and has since become a teacher there; made several Films taking part of Hanaud in an A.E.W. Mason series of Detective Films; played in several Television plays, including The Shop at Sly Corner. *Recreations:* bridge, swimming, reading, theatre-going. *Address:* 8 Dorset Court, Dorset St., W.1. *T.:* Welbeck 4601. [*Died* 17 *Nov.* 1963.

KENT, Rev. Harry Arnold, B.A., M.A., D.D.; LL.D.; F.R.S.A.; Principal Emeritus, Queen's Theological College, Kingston, and Professor Emeritus, Old Testament Literature; *b.* Truro, N.S., 12 May 1880; *s.* of John Harvey Kent and Sarah McCully; *m.* 1907, Edith Sutherland (*d.* 1953), *d.* of R. D. Fraser, R.N.; four *s.* two *d.*; *m.* 1954, Violet Emily Posselwhite. *Educ.:* Public Schools, Nova Scotia; Dalhousie University, Halifax; Presbyterian College, Halifax; Marburg; Berlin. Lecturer in Old Testament in Presbyterian College, Halifax, 1908; Professor, 1910; Dean, 1914; Professor of Old Testament Literature, Presbyterian College, Halifax, N.S., 1910-26; Principal Queen's Theological College, 1926-52; commanded a company of Nova Scotia Highlanders, 1916-17; Chaplain in Overseas Military Forces of Canada, 1917-19; E.D. 1936; Asst. Prin. Chaplain in Canadian Active Service Force (Overseas), 1939-40. *Recreation:* golf. *Address:* 78 Traymoor Ave., Kingston, Ontario, Canada. *T.:* Liberty 6-9873. [*Died* 4 *Jan.* 1962.

KENT, Keneth; *see* Kent, C. K. S.

KENT, Percy Horace Braund, O.B.E. M.C.; Captain late Scots Guards; M.A. (Oxon), of Lincoln's Inn, Barrister-at-law; *b.* 11 Sept. 1876; *e. s.* of Horace Kent, of Lincoln's Inn, Barrister-at-law; *m.* 1901, Anna Mary (*d.* 1957), *y. d.* of late Rev. Henry Kingdon Simcox, M.A., Lord of the Manor of Harborne, and formerly Rector of Ewelme, Oxfordshire; two *s.* one *d.* *Educ.:* Rugby; Corpus Christi College, Oxford. Called to Bar, 1900; practising in Consular Courts at Tientsin, 1901-41; formerly Legal Adviser at Peking to Ministries of Finance and Communications, Chinese Government Salt Administration and Chinese Government Peping-Liaoning Railway Administration; Legal Adviser, British Municipal Council, Tientsin; Kailan Mining Administration, etc.; served European War; Guards' Division, in France Oct. 1916 to June 1918 (acting-Major attached Guards' Machine-gun Regiment); attached Staff United States 27th (New York) Division in France, June to Aug. 1918; passed Staff Course Machine Guns, Grantham; Commanded North China British Volunteers, 1920-1921. Formerly Chairman: China Association, Tientsin Branch, Associated British Committee, Tientsin British Committee of Information, and of Public Trusts for Tientsin British Municipal Loans, Pensions, Schools, and Recreation grounds. Member British and Chinese Commission (1927) appointed to consider future administration British Concession, Tientsin. Evacuated from occupied China, 1942; attached Treasury

Solicitor's Dept., 1943-46 (War Crimes); returned China, engaged in negotiations with Chinese Liquidation Commission, 1946-47, in connection with implementation of Treaty with China so far as concerns British Concession at Tientsin. *Publications:* Railway Enterprise in China, 1907; The Passing of the Manchus, 1912; The Twentieth Century in the Far East, 1937. *Recreation:* golf. *Address:* Clavering, Cooden, Sussex. *T.:* Cooden 3907. *Clubs:* National Liberal, Third Guards; Cooden Beach Golf. [*Died* 2 *Jan.* 1963.

KENT, William Richard Gladstone; London guide and lecturer since 1915; *b.* 27 Oct. 1884; *s.* of Richard Kent (Master Printer) and Janet Jackson; *m.* 1912, Edith Bryon (*d.* 1957); two *s.* one *d.* *Educ.:* Larkhall Lane and South Lambeth Road Board Schools; Battersea Polytechnic. Publishers' Assistant (Hutchinson and Co.), 1898; Clerk in printing office of Kent and Matthews, Ltd., Wandsworth Road, 1899-1901; Boy Clerk H.M. Treasury and H.M. Office of Works, 1901-4; entered service of L.C.C., 1904; transferred from its Solicitor's Department to Solicitor's Department of London Passenger Transport Board, 1933; seconded to L.C.C. 1941; pensioned by L.P.T.B. 1943; obtained Honours in London History from London Univ. 1914; lost almost all library, files, notebooks, lantern slides, etc., through enemy action, 1941; F.S.A. 1948. *Publications:* With Dickens in the Borough, 1927; Dickens and Religion, 1930; London for Everyman, 1931, revised (post-blitz) edition, 1947; London for Heretics, 1932; George Inn, Southwark, 1932; London for Shakespeare Lovers, 1935; London for Dickens Lovers, 1936; Encyclopædia of London, 1937 (revised edition, 1951); The Testament of a Victorian Youth, 1938; London Worthies, 1939; London for the Curious, 1947; The Lost Treasures of London, 1947; My Lord Mayor, 1947; Fifty Years a Cricket Watcher, 1947; Lift up your Heads, 1948; Mine Host London, 1949; London for the Literary Pilgrim, 1949; Let's all go on the Thames, 1950; London for Americans, 1950; Look at London, 1950; John Burns, Labour's Lost Leader, 1950; Walks in London, 1951; London Mystery and Mythology, 1952; London in the News, 1954; contrib. articles on London to Chambers's Encyc. and Encyc. Americana. *Recreations:* watching cricket, reading. *Address:* 76 Brodrick Road, S.W.17. *Clubs:* Surrey County Cricket, Pepys. [*Died* 9 *May* 1963.

KENT-LEMON, Brig. Arthur Leslie, C.B.E. 1940; York and Lancaster Regt.; retired; *b.* 30 Nov. 1889; *er. s.* of Lieut.-Col. W. Kent-Lemon; *m.* 1914, Muriel Wanklyn (*d.* 1965); two *d.* *Educ.:* Tonbridge Sch. 2nd Lt. York and Lanc. Regt., 1913; Lt.-Col. commanding 1st York and Lanc. Regt., 1938; served in France and Macedonia, 1915-18 (despatches, 4 Class Order of Nile, 3 war medals, Sudan Medal with two clasps); served in France and Norway, 1939-40, also N. Africa, Italy, Burma, Java (despatches five times, C.B.E.); Brigadier, 1940; King's African Rifles, 1923-29. O.St.J. 1951. Officer of Legion of Merit of U.S.A., Africa Star, 1st Army Clasp. *Recreations:* fishing, shooting, golf. *Address:* Carclew, Sheringham, Norfolk. [*Died* 13 *July* 1970.

KENYON, Arthur William, C.B.E. 1946; F.R.I.B.A.; Dis. T.P.; M.T.P.I.; Architect; *s.* of William Padley Kenyon, Sheffield; *m.* 1911, Alice Williams (*d.* 1965); one *s.* *Educ.:* Sheffield. Articled to Architecture in Sheffield; carried on practice as Architect in London; Member Town Planning Institute; Past President Architectural Association, 1941 and 1942; Past Vice-President Royal Institute of British Architects. *Publications:* Site Planning in Practice, 1927; Building Roundabout, 1960; Series of articles, on building topics, to journals. *Recreations:* travel, sketching, writing. *Address:* 60 Albion Gate, W.2. *T.:* Ambassador 9852; The Studio, Strathmore Gardens, W.8. *T.:* Park 2092. [*Died* 2 *Jan.* 1969.

KENYON, Joseph, F.R.S. 1936; D.Sc.; F.R.I.C.; *b.* 8 Apr. 1885; *e. s.* of late Lawrence Kenyon, Blackburn; *m.* 1917, Winifride, *y. d.* of late Cornelius Foley, County Cork; one *d.* Lecturer in Chemistry, Blackburn Technical Coll., 1907-14; Research Chemist, Medical Research Association, Leeds University, 1915-16; Research Chemist, British Dyestuffs Corporation, Oxford University, 1916-20; Head of Department of Chemistry, Battersea Polytechnic, 1920-50; Part-time Supervisor of Research, Battersea Coll. of Technology, 1950-. Visiting Professor of Chemistry: University of Alexandria, 1950-1951; 1951-52; University of Kansas, 1954-55; Riley Lecturer, University of Notre Dame, Indiana, 1955. Vice-Pres. of Chem. Soc. *Publications:* numerous in Journals of Chemical and Faraday Socs. dealing mainly with optically active compounds, and the mechanism of organic reactions. *Recreation:* golf. *Address:* 21 Sandy Lane, Petersham, Surrey. *T.:* Richmond 3697. [*Died* 12 *Nov.* 1961.

KENYON-SLANEY, Major Robert Orlando Rodolph, D.L., J.P.; Major Grenadier Guards (retd.); *b.* 1892; *o. s.* of late Col. Right Hon. William Slaney Kenyon-Slaney, M.P., and Lady Mabel Selina, *e. d.* of 3rd Earl of Bradford; *m.* 1st, 1917, Lady Mary Hamilton (from whom he obtained a divorce, 1930; she *m.* 2nd, 1930, Sir John Gilmour, 2nd Bt.), *e. d.* of 3rd Duke of Abercorn; one *s.* one *d.* (and one *d.* decd.); 2nd, 1931, Nesta (*d.* 1947), *d.* of Sir George Forestier-Walker, 3rd Bt.; one *s.* *Educ.:* Eton; Christ Church, Oxford. Served European War, 1914 (wounded) and in War of 1939-45. High Sheriff of Shropshire, 1935. *Address:* Hatton Grange, Shifnal, Shropshire. *T.:* Shifnal 415. *Club:* Guards. [*Died* 14 *Jan.* 1965.

KENYON-SLANEY, Sybil Agnes, C.V.O. 1947; Lady-in-Waiting to the late Princess Royal, 1923-47, Extra Lady-in-Waiting, 1947-62; *b.* 1888; *d.* of late Col. the Rt. Hon. W. Kenyon-Slaney, P.C., M.P., and Lady Mabel Selina (*d.* 1933), *d.* of 3rd Earl of Bradford. *Address:* The Old Vicarage, Shawbury, Shrewsbury. [*Died* 10 *June* 1970.

KEOGH, Most Rev. Thomas; Titular Bishop of Turretamallensis, since 1967; *b.* Gurteen, Co. Kilkenny, 1884. Bishop of Kildare and Leighlin, 1936-67. *Address:* Braganza, Carlow. *T.:* Carlow 41137. [*Died* 22 *May* 1969.

KEOWN, Eric Oliver Dilworth; Writer; Staff of Punch (Eric); *b.* 2 July 1904; *y. s.* of late Robert Keown and Sarah White; *m.* 1931, Cicely, 3rd *d.* of late H. A. Ritchie; one *s.* one *d.* *Educ.:* Highgate School; Pembroke College, Cambridge (Second Class, English Tripos); Grenoble. Wrote for the Granta. Joined Editorial Staff of Punch, 1928; Part Dramatic Critic, 1932-1940; Dramatic Critic since 1945; Parliamentary Correspondent, 1933-40; R.A.F.V.R. 1940-45. Wrote the story on which René Clair's first English film, The Ghost Goes West, was based. Mem. Arts Council Drama Panel. Occasional broadcaster. *Publications:* The Complete Dog's Dudgeon; Peggy Ashcroft; Margaret Rutherford. *Recreations:* fishing, boules, and snuff. Owns about 1·627 acres. *Address:* Stringer's Barn, Worplesdon, Surrey. *T.:* Guildford 3912. *Clubs:* Garrick, Royal Automobile. [*Died* 15 *Feb.* 1963.

KEPPEL, Captain Hon. Rupert Oswald Derek; late Coldstream Guards; *b.* 27 July 1886; 3rd *s.* of Colonel 8th Earl of Albemarle; *m* 1919, Violet, *o. d.* of Sir Humphrey de Trafford, 3rd Bt. *Educ.:* Eton College; R.M C., Sandhurst. Joined Coldstream Guards, 1906; Captain, 191 ; served European War, France and Flanders, Aug. 1914, wounded and taken prisoner at Battle of Landrecies, 25 Aug. 1914 (Mons Star). *Recreations:* country pursuits. *Address:* Keepings Barn, Ringwood, Hants. *T.:* Ringwood 2239. [*Died* 7 *May* 1964.

KER, Major-General Charles Arthur, C.B. 1926; C.M.G. 1916; C.B.E. 1919; D.S.O. 1900; *b.* 18 Apr. 1875; *s.* of late C. Buchanan Ker of Clifton; *m.* 1906, Blanche (*d.* 1955), *d.* of Charles Bewes of Gnaton Hall, Yealmpton, Devon; one *s.* one *d.* *Educ.:* Clifton College; Royal Military Academy, Woolwich. Entered Royal Artillery, 1895; served Northern Nigeria, 1898-99 (despatches twice, medal with clasp, D.S.O.); South Africa, 1899-1901 (despatches, Queen's medal six clasps); Adjutant, R.G.A. Plymouth, 1902-05; Instructor, R.M. College, Camberley, 1906-09; Student at Staff College, Camberley, 1910-11; D.A.A. and Q.M.G. South-Western Coast Defences, 1912-14; General Staff Officer 2nd Grade, R.M. College, Kingston, Canada, 1914; Brigade Major 21st Divisional Artillery, 1914-15; G.S.O. 2nd Grade, 2nd Canadian Division, 1915; G.S.O. 1st Grade 2nd Canadian Division, 63rd (R.N.) Division, and L. of C. Area, 1916-17; Bt. Lt.-Col. 1917; Brig.-Gen. Gen. Staff (Head of British Mission with Portuguese Corps), 1917-19 (Bt. Col. 1918, despatches four times, Grand Officer of Portuguese Orders of Aviz and Christo); Company Commander, R.M.C., Camberley, 1919-20; G.S.O. 1st Grade, War Office, 1920-23; Col.-Commandant R.A. (Heavy) Southern Command, 1923-26; Col.-Comdt. R.A. Southern Command, 1926-27; Maj.-Gen. 1927; G.O.C. Territorial Army Air Defence Formations, 1928-31; Commander 3rd Indian Division and Meerut District, 1931-34; retired pay, 1934; Colonel Commandant R.A., 1939-45. *Address:* Duloe, Hockering Road, Woking, Surrey. [*Died* 24 *Jan.* 1962.

KER, James Campbell, C.S.I. 1928; C.I.E. 1924; I.C.S., retired; *b.* 1878; *s.* of Rev. William Lee Ker, Kilwinning, Ayrshire; *m.* 1925, Mary Katherine, *y. d.* of William Brown, of Rhuallan, Giffnock, Renfrewshire. *Educ.:* Irvine Academy; Glasgow University, M.A. First class Hons. in Mathematics, Eglinton Fellowship, Caius College, Cambridge, B.A. Entered I.C.S. 1901; Personal Assistant to the Director of Criminal Intelligence, 1907; on special duty in A.H.Q., Simla, 1914-17; Collector and District Magistrate of Kaira, 1918; Secretary to Government of Bombay, General and Educational Department, 1920-23; Private Secretary to the Governor of Bombay, 1924-29; M.P. (U.) West Stirlingshire, 1931-35. *Address:* Maimhor, West Kilbride, Ayrshire. *Club:* Royal Scottish Automobile (Glasgow). [*Died* 28 *Dec.* 1961.

KER, Mrs. Phyllis de Burgh; *see* Lett, Phyllis.

KERBY, Air Vice-Marshal Harold Spencer, C.B. 1943; D.S.C.; A.F.C.; Commander Legion of Merit (U.S.A.); *b.* Hamilton, Canada, 14 May 1893; *s.* of Rev. Dr. G. W. Kerby, M.A., LL.D.; *m.* 1921, Muriel Finch Roberts; one *s.* one *d.* *Educ.:* Univ. of Toronto. Commissioned in Royal Naval Air Service, 1915; served in Gallipoli and France, 1914-18; attended first course R.A.F. staff college. Served India, 1923-29, Air Ministry 1929-34, Singapore 1935; Air Attaché H.B.M. Embassy, China, 1936-39; served with Advanced Air striking Force in France, 1939-40; R.A.F. H.Q. Northern Ireland, 1941-42; A.O.C. R.A.F. East Africa, 1943-44; Air Officer i/c Administration, Coastal Command, 1944-46; retired, 1946. *Address:* Les Rotondes, Bd. Jardin-Exotique, Monaco. *Club:* International Sportsmen's. [*Died* 8 *June* 1963.

KERMACK, William Ogilvy, F.R.S. 1944; M.A., D.Sc., LL.D.; F.R.I.C.; Emeritus Professor of Biological Chemistry, and Senior Research Fellow, University of Aberdeen; *b.* Kirriemuir, Angus, 26 April 1898; *s.* of William Kermack; *m.* 1925, Esábeletta Raimunda Blázquez; one *s.* *Educ.:* Webster's Seminary, Kirriemuir; Aberdeen University. M.A., B.Sc. 1918; served in Royal Air Force; carried out research work at Oxford under Prof. W. H. Perkin, 1919-21; in charge of the Chemical Dept. of the Research Laboratory, Royal College of Physicians, Edinburgh, 1921-48; Prof. of Biological Chemistry, Univ. of Aberdeen, 1949-68 (Dean of Faculty of Science, 1961-64). Ferguson Scholar in Mathematics, 1919; met with laboratory accident during research resulting in loss of eyesight, June 1924; Fellow of the Royal Society of Edinburgh, 1924; D.Sc. Aberdeen University, 1925; awarded Freeland Barbour prize by the College of Physicians, Edinburgh, 1925; awarded the Macdougall Brisbane prize by the Royal Society, Edinburgh, for research work in chemistry, 1929; LL.D. (Hon.) St. Andrews, 1937. *Publications:* The Stuff We're Made of (joint), 1938; various scientific papers, chiefly on organic and medical chemistry, published in the Journal of the Chemical Society, Biochemical Journal and elsewhere. *Address:* Beechwood, Bieldside, Aberdeenshire. *T.:* Aberdeen 47881. [*Died* 20 *July* 1970.

KEROUAC, Jack, (Jean-Louis); author; *b.* Lowell, Mass., 12 March 1922; *s.* of Leo Alcide Kerouac, printer, and Gabrielle (*née* LeVesque); *m.* 1944 (marr. diss.); *m.* 1950 (marr. diss.); *m.* 1966, Stella Sampas. *Educ.:* parochial sch.; Horace Mann School, New York; Columbia College. Served in U.S. Navy and Merchant Marine. Spent many years travelling in N. and Central America, Europe and N. Africa. *Publications:* The Town and the City, 1950; On the Road, 1957; The Dharma Bums, 1958; The Subterraneans, 1958; Doctor Sax, 1959; Maggie Cassidy, 1959; Mexico City Blues (poems), 1959; Tristessa, 1960; Lonesome Traveler, 1960; Visions of Cody, 1960; Scripture of the Golden Eternity (philosophy), 1960; Book of Dreams, 1961; Big Sur, 1962; Visions of Gerard, 1963; Desolation Angels, 1965; Satori in Paris, 1966; Vanity of Dulvoz, 1968. *Address:* The Sterling Lord Agency, 75 East 55th St., New York 22, N.Y., U.S.A. [*Died* 21 *Oct.* 1969.

KERR, James Lennox; Author; *b.* 1 July 1899; *s.* of John Kerr and Sarah Mathers; *m.* 1932, Elizabeth Lamorna, *e. d.* of late S. J. Lamorna Birch; one *s.* *Educ.:* North School, Paisley. R.N.V.R. 1915-19 and 1942-46; Mercantile Marine, 1919-29 and 1939-42. *Publications:* Wavy Navy; Touching the Adventures; The Great Storm; Biography: Sir Wilfred Grenfell; Backdoor Guest; The Eager Years (Autobiography). Author of Boys' Books as Peter Dawlish. *Recreation:* yachting. *Address:* Lamorna, nr. Penzance, Cornwall. [*Died* 11 *March* 1963.

KERR, Col. Rowan S. R.; *see* Rait Kerr.

KERR-JARRETT, Sir Francis Moncreiff, Kt. 1965; *b.* Trelawny, Jamaica, 27 Aug. 1885; *s.* of Herbert Jarrett Kerr, Custos of Trelawny, and Henrietta Theresa Vidal; *m.* 1909, Adela Isabel Clerk; two *s.*

four *d.* *Educ.:* Bedford Modern Sch., Bedford, England. Hon. M.L.C., Jamaica, 1919-1921 (resigned). Manager and Owner Barnett Estates, 1910; Chairman, Rose Hall Ltd., 1960; Chairman, Jamaica Sugar Manufacturers' Association, 1930-45. Custos Rotulorum for St. James, Jamaica, 1933-65. Religion: Anglican; promoter of moral re-armament. *Recreations:* reading, public affairs; Life Pres., Montego Bay Cricket Club. *Address:* Catherine Hall, Montego Bay, Jamaica, W.I. *T.:* 2382. *Clubs:* Caledonian (London); Liguanea, Jamaica (Jamaica). [*Died* 13 *Dec.* 1968.

KERSH, Gerald; author and journalist; *b.* Teddington-on-Thames, 6 Aug. 1911; *e. s.* of H. L. Kersh and Leah Miller; *m.* 1938, Alice Thompson Rostron (marr. diss., 1943), *d.* of Nellie and Robert Rostron, Darwen, Lancs.; *m.* 1943, Claire Alyne (marr. diss., 1955), *d.* of Helen and Lucien Pacaud, Quebec; *m.* 1955, Florence, *d.* of Lisa and Morris Sochis, Philadelphia. Is a refugee from "the Welfare State"; became citizen of U.S.A., 1959. *Educ.:* The Polytechnic, Regent Street. Got his living in a dozen different ways while learning to write; achieved publication first in 1935—a novel, withdrawn because of several libel suits. Joined Coldstream Guards, 1940: transferred for special duties, 1942. War correspondent for The People, 1943; a script writer, Army Film Unit, 1943; specialist, Films Division Ministry of Information, 1943-44; under contract to M.G.M. as film writer. Accredited to S.H.A.E.F. in 1944. Chief feature-writer for The People, 1941-45 (under pseudonym Piers England); is known, unbeknown to many readers, under five other noms-de-plume and anonymities. *Publications:* Jews without Jehovah, 1935; Men Are So Ardent, 1936; Night And The City, 1937; I Got References, 1938; They Die With Their Boots Clean, 1941; The Nine Lives of Bill Nelson, 1941; The Dead Look On, 1942; Brain And Ten Fingers, 1943; Faces In A Dusty Picture, 1943; The Horrible Dummy, 1944; An Ape, A Dog, and A Serpent, 1945; The Weak and The Strong, 1945; Neither Man Nor Dog, 1946; Clean, Bright and Slightly Oiled, 1946; Sad Road to the Sea, 1947; Prelude to a Certain Midnight, 1947 (first published in U.S.A.); The Song of the Flea, 1948; Clock Without Hands, 1949; Jack of Swords, 1950; The 1000 Deaths of Mr. Small, 1951; The Brazen Bull, 1952; The Great Wash, 1953; The Brighton Monster, 1953; The Guttersnipe, 1954; Men Without Bones, 1955; Fowlers End, 1958; On An Odd Note, 1958 (U.S.); The Ugly Face of Love, 1960; The Terribly Wild Flowers, 1962; More Than Once Upon a Time, 1964; A Long Cool Day in Hell, 1965; The Hospitality of Miss Tolliver, 1965; The Angel and the Cuckoo, 1966. Some thousands of stories, film and television scripts, articles and some poetry, incl. A Soldier—His Prayer, etc. *Relevant Publications:* The Best of Gerald Kersh, 1960; The Implacable Hunter, 1961. *Recreation:* none, and has no clubs. *Address:* c/o Joan Daves, 145 East 49th St., N.Y.C., N.Y., U.S.A. [*Died* 5 *Nov.* 1968.

KERSHAW, 1st Baron, *cr.* 1947, of Prestwich, in the County Palatine of Lancaster; **Fred Kershaw;** O.B.E. 1931; J.P.; Deputy Speaker, House of Lords; Governor, Westminster Hospital; Chairman: Gordon Hospital; Marie Curie Memorial; *b.* 6 Nov. 1881; *s.* of John Joseph Kershaw, Prestwich; *m.* 1903, Frances Edith Wigmore (*d.* 1960); four *s.* *Educ.:* Church of England National School, Prestwich. President National Association of Trade Union Approved Societies, 1924-26; Chairman Courts of Referees (Unemployment Insurance Act), 1927-47; a Lord-in-Waiting to King George VI, 1949-51; during War of 1939-45, Chm. Military Service (Hardship) Cttees., Appeal Boards (Essential Work Orders). *Heir:* *s.* Hon. Herbert Kershaw, *b.* 21 Aug. 1904. *Address:* 27 Runnymede, Courtlands, Richmond, Surrey. *T.:* Richmond 0915. [*Died* 5 *Feb.* 1961.

KERSHAW, 2nd Baron, *cr.* 1947, of Prestwich; **Herbert Kershaw;** *b.* 21 Aug. 1904; *e. s.* of 1st Baron and Frances Edith Wigmore (*d.* 1960); *S.* father, 1961; *m.* 1933, Cissie Burness Smyth. Served War (commissioned R.N.V.R.), 1942-46. *Heir:* *b.* Hon. Edward Aubrey Kershaw [*b.* 29 Aug. 1906; *m.* 1935, Katharine Dorothea Staines; one *s.* one *d.*]. *Address:* 33 Burdenshott Ave., Richmond, Surrey. [*Died* 18 *July* 1961.

KERSHAW, 3rd Baron, *cr.* 1947, of Prestwich; **Edward Aubrey Kershaw;** *b.* 29 Aug. 1906; 2nd *s.* of 1st Baron and Frances Edith Wigmore (*d.* 1960); *S.* brother, 1961; *m.* 1935, Katharine Dorothea, *d.* of Charles Harry Staines, Clapham; one *s.* one *d.* *Educ.:* Friern Barnet Gram. Sch. *Heir:* *s.* Hon. Edward John Kershaw, *b.* 12 May 1936. *Address:* 478 Upper Richmond Rd. West, Richmond, Sy. *T.:* Prospect 3686. [*Died* 22 *Feb.* 1962.

KERSHAW, Harold Slaney, C.B.E. 1944; Solicitor; *b.* 9 March 1882; 3rd *s.* of James Kershaw, Manchester; *m.* 1913, Pleasance, *d.* of Sir Edward Holt, 1st Bt., C.B.E.; one *s.* (and two killed in War of 1939-45). *Educ.:* Bilton Grange; Rugby. Solicitor, 1906; Solicitor, Manchester; Director, Bridgewater Estates; Director, Williams Deacons Bank, 1940-64 (Dep. Chm. 1950-61); Director, Yates Castle Brewery, and Joseph Holt; Chm. North West Regional Price Regulation Cttee., Board of Trade, 1940-47; Hon. Sec. Manchester Tennis and Racquet Club, 1908-48, Pres. 1938-50; Member Committee of Tennis and Rackets Association, 1921-. *Recreation:* gardening. *Address:* Endon Hall, Macclesfield, Cheshire. *T.:* Bollington 3161. *Clubs:* Royal Automobile; St. James's (Manchester). [*Died* 17 *April* 1969.

KERWIN, Hon. Patrick, P.C. (Canada) 1954; Chief Justice of Canada since 1954; *b.* 25 Oct. 1889; *s.* of Patrick Kerwin and Ellen Gavin; *m.* 1917, Georgina Mary, *d.* of George Mace and Bridget Ryan; two *s.* one *d.* (and one *s.* decd.). *Educ.:* Sarnia (Ont.). Separate and Collegiate Schools; Osgoode Hall, Toronto, Ont. Read law with Hanna, Le Sueur and Price, Sarnia, W. M. Douglas, K.C. and F. E. Hodgins, K.C.; called to the Bar of Ontario, 1911, K.C. 1928; practised law in Guelph, Ontario, in partnership with Hon. Hugh Guthrie, K.C.; Member Ontario Parole Board, 1932; Justice of Supreme Court of Ontario, 1932; Justice Supreme Court of Canada, 1935; Member Board of Regents, Ottawa University; Chairman, Lay Advisory Board, St. Patrick's College, Ottawa. Holds several Hon. degrees in Law. *Recreation:* bridge. *Address:* Chief Justice's Chambers, Supreme Court, Ottawa, Ont., Canada; 177 Wilbrod, Ottawa, Canada. *Club:* Rideau. [*Died* 2 *Feb.* 1963.

KETCHUM, Philip A. C., M.A., B.Paed., LL.D.; Special Assistant to the President, University of Toronto; *b.* 20 July 1899; *s.* of Jay Ketchum and Margaret Jane Davidson; *m.* 1924, Ottilie Ann Marion Ormsby; three *s.* three *d.* *Educ.:* The Model School, Toronto; Trinity College School, Port Hope; Trinity College, Toronto; Emmanuel College, Cambridge. Pres., Univ. of Toronto Rugby Club, 1921-22; Sec., Canadian Inter-Collegiate Rugby Union, 1921-22. Asst. master, Lakefield Preparatory School, 1916-17; Royal Air Force, 1918-19; Pilot, 1918, Flying in England; Assistant Master Upper Canada College, Toronto, 1923-24; Trinity College School, Port Hope, 1924-27; St. Mark's

School, Southboro', Mass., U.S.A., 1929-33; Headmaster Trinity College School, 1933-62. *Address:* Fairmount, Port Hope, Ontario, Canada. *T.:* 2058. *Clubs:* University (Toronto); Zeta Psi Fraternity. [*Died* 21 *July* 1964.

KETTLE, Sir Russell, Kt., *cr.* 1947; formerly Senior Partner of Deloitte, Plender, Griffiths & Co., Chartered Accountants, 5 London Wall Buildings, E.C.2; *b.* 30 Jan. 1887; *s.* of late John Kettle, Forest Gate, Essex, and Jane Russell; *m.* 1913, Ethel, *d.* of late W. S. Drake; three *s.* one *d.* *Educ.:* Tonbridge School. Member: Company Law Amendment Cttee., 1943-45; Red Cross Stores Cttee., 1940-45; Accountancy Advisory Committee on the Companies Acts (Chm. 1948-55); Transport Arbitration Tribunal, 1947-48; Tithe Redemption Commission, 1940-60; Council of Inst. of Chartered Accountants in England and Wales, 1940-55 (Pres. 1949); Rural Housing Cttee., 1936-40; Cttee. to consider a new Queen's Hall, 1954-1955. *Address:* Greenbriar, St. John's, Woking, Surrey. *T.:* Woking 2839. *Club:* Gresham. [*Died* 20 *June* 1968.

KETTON-CREMER, Robert Wyndham, F.B.A. 1968; M.A., F.S.A.; F.R.S.L.; Author; *b.* 2 May 1906; *s.* of late Wyndham Cremer Ketton-Cremer and Emily, *d.* of late Robert Bayly, Torr, Plymouth. *Educ.:* Harrow; Balliol Coll., Oxf. (Exhibnr.). J.P. (Norfolk), 1934 (Chm. of North Erpingham Bench, 1948-66); Major, East Norfolk Home Guard, 1941-45; High Sheriff of Norfolk, 1951; a Trustee of National Portrait Gall., 1958-; Rede Lecturer, Cambridge University, 1957; Warton Lecturer, Brit. Acad., 1959; Lamont Memorial Lecturer, Yale University, 1960; President, Johnson Society of Lichfield, 1961-62; a Governor, Gresham's School, Holt, 1957-67. Fellow-Commoner, Christ's College, Cambridge, 1966-. Hon. Litt.D. East Anglia, 1969. *Publications:* The Early Life and Diaries of William Windham, 1930; Thomas Gray (Great Lives), 1935; Horace Walpole, 1940; Norfolk Portraits, 1944; A Norfolk Gallery, 1948; Country Neighbourhood, 1951; Thomas Gray, 1955 (James Tait Black Memorial Prize and W. H. Heinemann Foundation award); Norfolk Assembly, 1957; Matthew Prior (Rede Lecture), 1957; Lapidary Verse (Warton Lecture), 1960; Forty Norfolk Essays, 1961; Felbrigg: The Story of a House, 1962; Norfolk in the Civil War, 1969. *Recreation:* forestry. *Address:* Felbrigg Hall, Norwich. *T.:* West Runton 444. *Clubs:* Athenæum, Beefsteak; Norfolk (Norwich). [*Died* 12 *Dec.* 1969.

KEY, Alderman Rt. Hon. Charles William, P.C. 1947; M.P. (Lab.) Poplar since 1950 (Bow and Bromley Division of Poplar, 1940-50); Regional Commissioner for London Civil Defence Region, 1941-45; Parliamentary Secretary, Ministry of Health, 1945-47; Minister of Works, 1947-50. *Address:* Little Chantry, Gerrards Cross, Bucks. [*Died* 6 *Dec.* 1964.

KEYES, Frances Parkinson, (Mrs. Henry Wilder Keyes); author; *b.* 21 July 1885; *d.* of John Henry Wheeler and Louise Fuller Johnson; *m.* 1904, Henry Wilder Keyes (*d.* 1938); three *s.* *Educ.:* private schools, Boston, Switzerland, Berlin (Germany). Litt.D., George Washington University, 1921, Bates College, Lewiston, Maine, 1934. Dr. of Humane Letters, Univ. of New Hampshire, 1951. Started writing as a child, but made no attempt to secure publication until 1918 when first magazine article appeared in Atlantic Monthly. Since then has been a frequent contributor to leading periodicals in U.S., Latin America and England. Associate Editor Good Housekeeping 1923-36, making a trip around the world as its representative 1925-26, a trip through South America, 1929-30, also eight trips to Europe and one to Persia, 1931. Edited National Historical Magazine, 1937-1939. On staff Our Lady of the Lake College, San Antonio, Texas, 1941. Has lectured on many subjects and travelled in many parts of the globe. At one time took active part in private theatricals and has worked in many philanthropic and patriotic causes and lived largely in political circles, both at home and abroad from 1917-36, during which time her late husband was Governor of the State of New Hampshire, 1917-19, and afterwards, 1919-36, United States Senator from New Hampshire. Siena Medal, 1946; Diploma of Amis de Saumur, 1948; Medal of Honor, Gen. Council of the Seine, 1950; Silver Medal of French Recognition, 1951; Order of Isabella the Catholic, 1958; Legion of Honour, 1962. *Publications:* The Old Gray Homestead, 1919; The Career of David Noble, 1921; Letters from a Senator's Wife, 1924; Queen Anne's Lace, 1930; Silver Seas and Golden Cities; Lady Blanche Farm, 1931; Senator Marlowe's Daughter, 1933; The Safe Bridge, 1934; The Happy Wanderer, 1935; Honor Bright, 1936; Written In Heaven; Capital Kaleidoscope, 1937; Parts Unknown, 1938; The Great Tradition, 1939; Along A Little Way; The Sublime Shepherdess; Fielding's Folly; Grace of Guadalupe, 1941; All That Glitters, 1941; Crescent Carnival, 1942; Also The Hills, 1943; The River Road, 1946; Vail d'Alvery, 1947; Came a Cavalier, 1948; Once on Esplanade, 1949; Dinner at Antoine's, 1949; All This is Louisiana, 1950; St. Teresa of Lisieux, 1950; Joy Street, 1951; Steamboat Gothic, 1952 The Cost of a Best Seller, 1953; Larry Vincent, 1953; The Royal Box 1954; The Frances Parkinson Keyes Cookbook, 1955; St. Anne: Grandmother of Our Saviour, 1955; Blue Camellia, 1957; The Land of Stones and Saints 1957; The Gold Slippers, 1958; The Letter from Spain, 1959; Frances Parkinson Keyes' Christmas Gift, 1959; Mother Cabrini: Missionary to the World, 1959; Third Mystic of Avila, 1960; Roses in December, 1960; The Chess Players, 1960; The Rose and the Lily, 1961; Madame Castel's Lodger, 1963; Three Ways of Love, 1964; The Restless Lady and Other Stories, 1964; The Explorer, 1965; I, the King, 1966; Tongues of Fire, 1966; The Heritage, 1968. *Recreations:* collects fans, dolls, maps, costumes, crucifixes; plays bridge; enjoys dramatics, music, motoring. *Address:* Pine Grove Farm, North Haverhill, New Hampshire, U.S.A. *T.:* P.G.F.—North Haverhill 7-5441; 1113 Chartres Street, New Orleans, La. *T.:* 523-7257. *Clubs:* Orleans (New Orleans); Sulgrave (Washington). [*Died* 3 *July* 1970.

KEYES, Mrs. Henry Wilder; *see* Keyes, Frances Parkinson.

KIDNER, Brigadier William Elworthy, C.I.E. 1937; M.C.; late R.E.; *b.* 16 Nov. 1884; *s.* of John Kidner, Dodhill, Taunton, and Emily Jane Elworthy; *m.* 1914, Aimée Margery Aldridge George (*d.* 1969); two *s.* one *d.* (and two *s.* decd.). *Educ.:* Sherborne; R.M.A. Woolwich. Second Lieut. R.E., 1902; Col., 1932; Chief Signal Officer, India, 1919; Chief Engineer, India, 1936; retired, 1939; served European War, 1915-18, France and Belgium (despatches, M.C.). *Address:* Fylde Court, Huntingdon Road, Cambridge. *Club:* United Service. [*Died* 1 *Sept.* 1969.

KIDSON, Fenn, C.B.E. 1921; F.C.A.; senior partner in W. H. Kidson, Son & Co., Chartered Accountants: *b.* 1874; *e. s.* of William Henry Kidson, F.C.A., M.L.S.B., and Charlotte Anne Emily Fenn; *m.* 1900, Gertrude Florence, *yr. d.* of Frank Stanley Price, Surveyor, of London; one *d.* *Educ.:* Merchant Taylors' School. Auditor, St. Paul's Cathedral, since

1900; Statutory Auditor, Ely Cathedral, 1917-1956; Assistant Adviser on Costs of Production, Admiralty, 1917; on the Staff of Accountant-General of the Navy, 1917-19; Adviser on Costs, Ministry of Shipping, 1919-21; and to Mercantile Marine Department, Board of Trade, subsequently; on the Livery of the Worshipful Company of Merchant Taylors; Master of Worshipful Company of Parish Clerks, 1943; Provincial Grand Master of Mark Master Masons, Middlesex, 1953-. *Recreations:* gardening, photography. *Address:* The Hermitage, 116 Dollis Hill Lane, N.W.2. *T.:* Gladstone 1323; 31 Great Queen Street, W.C.2.
[*Died* 6 *March* 1965.

KILBURN, John Maurice, C.B.E. 1937; Dir. Makum (Assam) Tea Coy., Ltd., Dekhari Tea Company, Ltd., Namdang Tea Co. Ltd., Eastern Assam Tea Company, Ltd., Amgoorie Tea Estates Ltd., Badulipar Tea Co. Ltd., Rajah Alli Tea Estates Ltd., Balijan Tea Co. Ltd.; *b.* 13 Jan. 1885; *s.* of John and Sarah Jane Kilburn, late of Meltham, Huddersfield; *m.* 1920, Doris Mellor, *d.* of G. E. Clementson, St. Anne's-on-Sea; two *d.* Chairman, Assam Branch Indian Tea Association, 1931-36. *Address:* Dirok, Woodbridge, Suffolk. *T.:* Woodbridge 403. *Clubs:* Oriental, City of London.
[*Died* 1 *April* 1965.

KILLEARN, 1st Baron, *cr.* 1943, of Killearn; **Miles Wedderburn Lampson,** P.C. 1941; G.C.M.G., *cr.* 1937 (K.C.M.G., *cr.* 1927; C.M.G. 1922); C.B. 1926; M.V.O. 1906; *b.* 24 Aug. 1880; 2nd *s.* of late Norman George Lampson and Helen Agnes, 4th *d.* of Peter Blackburn, M.P., of Killearn, Stirling; *m.* 1st, 1912, Rachel Mary Hele (*d.* 1930), *y. d.* of late Wm. Wilton Phipps; one *s.* two *d.*; 2nd, 1934, Jacqueline Aldine Lesley, *o. d.* of Aldo Castellani, one *s.* two *d.* *Educ.:* Eton. Entered Foreign Office, 1903; Secretary to Garter Mission, Japan, 1906; 2nd Secretary, Tokyo, 1908-10; Sofia, 1911; 1st Secretary, Peking, 1916; Acting British High Commissioner in Siberia, 1920; British Minister to China 1926-33; High Commissioner for Egypt and the Sudan, 1934-36; British Ambassador to Egypt and High Commissioner for the Sudan 1936-46; Special Commissioner in South-East Asia, 1946-48; 3rd class Rising Sun; 3rd class Sacred Treasure. *Recreations:* shooting, fishing. *Heir:* *s.* Major Hon. Graham Curtis Lampson, late Scots Guards [*b.* 28 Oct. 1919; *m.* 1946, Nadine Marie Cathryn, *o. d.* of late Vice-Adm. C. H. Pilcher, D.S.O.; two *d.*]. *Address:* Haremere Hall, Etchingham, Sussex; Dorchester Hotel, W.1. *Club:* Travellers'. [*Died* 18 *Sept.* 1964.

KILLICK, Sir Anthony Bernard, K.B.E. 1961; C.M.G. 1950; B.Sc. (Lond.); *b.* Eastbourne, Sx., 1901. *Educ.:* Eastbourne Coll.; Wye Coll. (Univ. of London), Kent. Diploma in Agriculture, Wye College. Agricultural Officer, Uganda, 1924; Senior Agricultural Officer, 1924-36; Deputy Director of Agriculture, Trinidad, 1936; Tanganyika Territory, 1939; Kenya, 1941; Director of Agriculture, Uganda, 1947-51; Professor of Agriculture, Imperial College of Tropical Agriculture, Trinidad, 1952-56; Minister of Natural Resources, Uganda, 1956-61. *Address:* Eastover, Avon Castle Drive, Ringwood, Hants. [*Died* 23 *May* 1966.

KILMOREY, 4th Earl of, *cr.* 1822; **Francis Charles Adalbert Henry Needham,** P.C. (N.I.) 1936; O.B.E. 1936; Viscount Kilmorey, 1625; Viscount Newry and Mourne, 1822 (Ire.); Representative Peer for Ireland; Captain R.N.V.R., retired; H.M. Lieutenant for Co. Down, 1949-59; *b.* 26 Nov. 1883; *s.* of 3rd Earl and Ellen, 2nd *d.* of late Edward Holmes Baldock, M.P., Shrewsbury; *S.* father, 1915; *m.* 1920, Lady Norah Hastings, 2nd *d.* of 14th Earl of Huntingdon; two *d.* *Educ.:* Eton. Late Captain 1st Life Guards; resigned, 1911; rejoined, 1914; served European War, 1914-1915; Commanded Ulster Division R.N.V.R. 1930-40. High Sheriff of County Down, 1913; D.L. and J.P. for County of Down. Owns pictures by Gainsborough, Kneller, Cuyp, Both, Berghem, Boucher. *Recreations:* shooting, fishing, yachting. *Heir:* *n.* Francis Jack Richard Patrick Needham, late Major Grenadier Guards [*b.* 4 Oct. 1915; *m.* 1941, Helen Bridget, *d.* of Sir Lionel Lawson Faudel-Phillips, 3rd Bt.; three *s.*]. *Address:* Mourne Park, Newry, Co. Down. *T.:* Kilkeel 227. *Clubs:* Turf; Ulster (Belfast).
[*Died* 11 *Jan.* 1961.

KILMUIR, 1st Earl of, *cr.* 1962; **David Patrick Maxwell Fyfe,** P.C. 1945; G.C.V.O. 1953; Kt. 1942; Viscount Kilmuir, 1954; Baron Fyfe of Dornoch, 1962; Lord High Chancellor of Great Britain, Oct. 1954-July 1962; Hon. Fellow of Balliol College, Oxford, 1954; Hon. R.C.A., 1955; Hon. F.R.C.S.E., 1955; *b.* 29 May 1900; *s.* of late W. T. Fyfe and Isabella, *d.* of late David Campbell of Tordarroch, Dornoch, Sutherland; *m.* 1925, Sylvia, D.B.E. 1957, *d.* of W. R. Harrison, Liverpool; two *d.* (one *d.* decd.). *Educ.:* George Watson's College, Edinburgh; Balliol College, Oxford (M.A.). Served Scots Guards, 1918-19; on staff of British Commonwealth Union, 1921-22; called to Bar (Gray's Inn), 1922; Bencher, 1936; Treasurer, 1949; practised on Northern Circuit (Liverpool), 1922-34; Q.C. 1934. Contested Wigan (Conservative), 1924; Conservative candidate Spen Valley 1927, but withdrew on Sir J. Simon undertaking Indian commission; M.P. (C.) Liverpool, West Derby Div., 1935-54. Member of the General Council of the Bar, 1936; Recorder of Oldham, 1936-42; Major and Deputy Judge Advocate, J.A.G.'s Office, 1940; Solicitor-General, 1942-45; Attorney-General, 1945; Deputy Chief Prosecutor, Trial of Nazi War Criminals, Nuremberg, 1945-46; Chairman, Conservative Party Committee on Post-War Reconstruction, 1943; Conservative member of Council of Europe, Strasbourg, 1949; President Nat. Union of Conservative and Unionist Assocs., 1950; Home Secretary and Minister for Welsh Affairs, 1951-54; Deputy Chairman, Liverpool Constitutional Association, 1934-(Pres. 1952). President, British Standards Institution, 1963-. Visitor of St. Antony's College, Oxford, 1953. Hon. D.C.L. Oxford, 1953. Hon. LL.D.: Liverpool, 1947; Manitoba, 1954; Edinburgh, 1955; Wales, 1955; St. Andrews, 1956; Chicago, George Washington, Columbia and Ottawa Universities, 1960. Hon. Member: Canadian Bar Association, 1954; American Bar Association, 1954; New York Bar Association, 1954. Rector of St. Andrews Univ., 1955-58. Pres., Highland Society of London, 1963-66. Chairman: Malta Round Table Conference, 1955; Conference of Privy Councillors on security procedures, 1956; Joint Select Cttee. on House of Lords Reform, 1962; Thomson Foundation, 1962-. Trustee: Wolfson Foundation, 1962-; National Police Fund, 1965-. Chm. Plessey Company, 1962-. Pres., Electrical Development Assoc., 1963-1964; 1st Pres. Bar Assoc. for Commerce, Finance and Industry, 1965-. Chm. Commonwealth Scholarship Commn. in the U.K., 1963-. *Publications:* Monopoly, 1948; Political Adventure, 1964; and introds. to legal books. *Heir:* none. *Address:* Hardings, Withyham, Sx. *T.:* Hartfield 364; 33 Whitehall Court, S.W.1. *T.:* Whitehall 3160. *Clubs:* Carlton; Royal and Ancient.
[*Died* 27 *Jan.* 1967 (*ext.*).

KILNER, T(homas) Pomfret, C.B.E. 1946; M.A., D.M. (Oxf.); M.B., Ch.B. (Manch.); M.B., B.S. (Lond.); M.R.C.S., L.R.C.P. (Lond.), F.R.C.S. (Eng.); Emeritus

Nuffield Professor of Plastic Surgery, Oxford University; Emeritus Fellow, St. John's College, Oxford; Consulting Plastic Surgeon: Queen Mary's Hospital, Roehampton; Ministry of Health; St. Dunstan's; Hon. Cons. Plastic Surgeon: Queen Elizabeth Hosp. for Children, London; Hosp. for Tropical Diseases, London; Manchester Royal Infirmary; Lord Mayor Treloar Hospital, Alton; St. Thomas's Hospital, London; United Oxford Hospitals. Fellow: Royal Society Medicine, Lond.; Hon. Fellow Amer. Assoc. of Plastic Surgeons; Corresp. Mem. Amer. Soc. of Plastic and Reconstructive Surgery; For. Mem. Turkish Med. Soc.; Hon. Member: Greek Stomatological Soc.; Scandinavian Society of Plastic Surgeons; Assoc. Plastic Surgeons of Southern Africa. Governor Central School of Speech and Drama, London; Hon. Fell., Coll. of Speech Therapists, Lond.; *b.* 17 Sept. 1890; *s.* of late Thomas Kilner and late Mary Pomfret; *m.* 1st, 1915, Olive Mary Brown; (one *s.* decd.); 2nd, 1926, Florence Mary Brennan (*née* O'Neill); two *s.* *Educ.:* Queen Elizabeth's Grammar School, Blackburn; University of Manchester (Dauntesey Scholar and Sidney Renshaw Exhibitioner, Medals in Anatomy and Physiology, Distinction in Surgery and Pathology). Demonstrator of Anatomy, University of Manchester, 1912-14; Senior House Surgeon, Manchester Royal Infirmary, 1914; served European War, Captain R.A.M.C. (T.F.) Surgeon to No. 64 C.C.S. 1915; Surgical Specialist No. 4 Gen. Hosp. B.E.F. 1918; Plastic Surgeon Queen Mary's Hosp. for Face and Jaw Injuries, Sidcup, 1919; Surgeon, Royal Albert Dock Hosp., 1921; Senior Surgeon, Hosp. for Tropical Diseases, Endsleigh Gardens, 1924; Cons. Plastic Surg., Lord Mayor Treloar Hospital, Alton, 1931; Plastic Surgeon, St. Andrew's Hospital, Dollis Hill, 1931; East London Hospital for Children, 1932; St. Thomas's Hospital, 1934; Manchester Royal Infirmary, 1935; Manchester & Salford Hospital for Skin Diseases; Duchess of York Hospital for Babies, Manch., 1936; Dental Hospital of Manch.; Birm. United Hosps., 1937; O. i/c Plastic Surg. Div., Min. of Pensions; Hon. Cons. Plastic Surg., Carms, C.C., 1939; Nuffield Prof. of Plastic Surgery, Oxford Univ., 1945; Director, Depts. Plastic Surg.: Churchill Hosp., Oxford (United Oxford Hosps.), 1945; Stoke Mandeville Hosp., Aylesbury (Min. of Pensions, 1943; Oxf. Reg. Hosp. Bd., 1951); Hon. Cons. in Plastic Surgery to the Army, 1952-55. Hunterian Prof. R.C.S., 1935. Pres. Brit. Assoc. of Plastic Surgeons, 1948 and 1955. *Publications:* Plastic Surgery, Hare Lip and Cleft Palate, Ogilvie's Recent Advances Surgery, 1928; Hare Lip and Cleft Palate, Parsons and Barling's Diseases of Infancy and Childhood, 1933 and 1954; Plastic Surgery, Maingot's Post-Graduate Surgery, 1937; Wounds of the Face and Jaws, Hamilton Bailey's Surgery of Modern Warfare, 1941, etc. *Recreations:* photography, gardening. *Address:* Rutland House, 41 Davenant Road, Oxford. *T.:* Oxford 55127.

[*Died* 2 *July* 1964.

KILPATRICK, Florence Antoinette; novelist and playwright; *b.* Peterborough; *d.* of late George Wharton, Calvert; *m.* James Kilpatrick, former editor of London Evening Standard; two *d.* *Educ.:* privately. France. Studied art and music; wrote tragedies and was a general failure; finally took seriously to writing humour; contributions to Punch and the London and American magazines. *Publications: plays:* Virginia's Husband; Wild Cat Hetty; Getting George Married; Murder Without Tears; Uneasy Living; *novels:* Our Elizabeth; Educating Ernestine; Our Elizabeth Again; Sunshine Street; Virginia's Husband; Red Dust; Camilla in a Caravan; Wildfire Hetty; Hetty Married; Hetty's Son; Rift Valley; The Return of Our Elizabeth; Paradise Ltd.; Illicit; Oh, Joy; White Man Black Man; The Eldest Miss Grimmett; Our Elizabeth in America; Six Marriages; What a Liberty; Within Four Walls; Elizabeth in Africa; Men are just Marvellous; Elizabeth in Wartime; Elizabeth to the Rescue; Gentlemen should Marry; Elizabeth the Sleuth: Elizabeth finds the Body; *films:* Virginia's Husband; Wild Cat Hetty; *radio plays:* The Tiger's Spring; The Colonel's Secret; Nine O'Clock; Our Elizabeth; Cabin No. 3; Leave it to Lomax, and others. *Recreations:* writing humour, travelling, going to the theatre. *Address:* 17 Bede House, Manor Fields, Putney Hill, S.W.15. *T.:* Putney 3826. *Club:* P.E.N.

[*Died* 1 *Jan.* 1968.

KIMBALL, LeRoy Elwood; Vice-Chancellor, New York University, 1945-56, Emeritus, 1956; *b.* Flint, Michigan, 31 Oct. 1888; *s.* of Gustavus Sylvester Kimball and Marie Guy; *m.* 1914, Gipsy Robinson; no *c.* *Educ.:* Albion Coll., Michigan (A.B. 1910, Hon. LL.D. 1935); New York University (A.M. 1917, Hon. LL.D. 1956). City editor Albion Evening Recorder, 1910-11; Asst. Bursar, New York University, 1911-1920; Bursar, 1920-25, Comptroller, 1925-45; Pres. Amer. Scenic and Historic Preservation Soc., 1933-41; Pres. Bibliographical Soc. of America, 1948-50; Pres. Assoc. of American Colleges, 1951-52; Pres. New York Historical Soc., 1956-61; elected Trustee and Hon. Pres. for Life, 1962. Held trusteeships. Pres. Mod. Lang. Assoc. of Amer., 1954. *Publications:* Alcuin, 1935; also numerous monographs, 1935-48 (U.S.A.). *Address:* Buckberg Mountain, Tomkins Cove-on-Hudson, Rockland County, N.Y., U.S.A. *T.:* Stony Point 6-2765. *Clubs:* Century, Grolier, Quill (U.S.A.); Athenæum (London).

[*Died* 27 *Nov.* 1962.

KIMBELL, Rev. Ralph Raymond, M.A., Mus.Bac.; Curate, Ledbury Parish Church since 1950; *b.* 12 June 1884; *s.* of Peter Eaton Kimbell, Boughton, Northampton, and Fanny Priscilla Tucker; *m.* 1st, 1916, Anna Emmeline (*d.* 1946), *d.* of Thomas Winsor, Blagdon House, Paignton; 2nd, 1949, Audrey, *d.* of Bernard Wragg, Thorpe House Rise, Sheffield. *Educ.:* Culham Training College; Non-Collegiate, Oxford. Assistant Master in Elementary Schools, Northampton and Oxford; Lecturer in Music, Instructor in Physical Training, Asst. Lecturer in Education, Culham Training College, 1920; Lecturer in Education, Culham Training College, 1925; Vice-Principal, Lecturer in Education, Lecturer in Music and Speech Training, Bede College, Durham, 1927; Organist St. Paul's Church, Northampton, 1906-9; St. John the Evangelist Church, Oxford, 1910-12; St. Andrew's Church, Oxford, 1912-16; Conductor, Durham University Choral Soc., 1927-30; Principal, Sheffield City Training College, 1932-49. Ordained, 1950. *Publications:* A few songs. *Recreations:* music, reading, cricket (played for Northants C.C. and Oxfordshire C.C.), golf. *Address:* Ankerdine, South Parade, Ledbury, Herefordshire.

[*Died* 4 *Aug.* 1964.

KIMBERLEY, Paul, C.B.E. 1944 (O.B.E. 1921); **A.R.P.S.; *b.* Langley, near Birmingham; two *s.* three *d.* Assistant Manager to** Church Army Lantern Department, 1905; joined Frank Brockliss, 1909; founded Imperial Film Co. 1913; supervised production of Ivanhoe, biggest British production of that time; became associated with Hepworth Picture Plays, 1917; Director, Sales and Distribution Manager; Managing Director, Hepworth Film Service, Ltd., until 1924; in 1916 founded scheme for training disabled ex-Service men as operators, afterwards taken over by National Kinema Trades Advisory Committee; technical adviser to Committee; Man. Dir. of National Screen Service Ltd., and N.S.S. Productions Ltd., retired, 1945; Dir. of Army Kinematography to War Office, 1940-44. F.Z.S., resigned, 1945; Fellow Society Motion Picture Engineers; Governor of British Film Institute, 1940-43. *Address:* St. Martin's, Freshwater Bay, Isle of Wight. [*Died* 3 *Nov.* 1964.

KIMMINS, Captain Anthony, O.B.E. 1946; R.N. (retd.); Film Producer and Director; Author and Playwright; *b.* 10 Nov. 1901; *s.* of late Dr. Charles William Kimmins and late Dame Grace Kimmins, D.B.E.; *m.* 1928, Elizabeth Hodges; one *s.* one *d.* *Educ.:* R.N.C., Osborne and Dartmouth. Served European War, 1914-18, in H.M.S. Marlborough; later specialised as naval pilot on formation of Fleet Air Arm, retired 1932 with rank of Lt.-Cdr. to take up play-writing and film direction. *Wrote:* While Parents Sleep (produced at Royalty Theatre), 1932; Night Club Queen (Playhouse), and Chase the Ace (Westminster and Daly's). Wrote and directed number of films for Fox-British and other companies, including most of George Formby successes. War of 1939-45, duties with Director of Naval Intelligence; gave many B.B.C. commentaries on Naval Operations in various theatres of war; Chief of Naval Information, British Pacific Fleet, 1945-46; produced and directed Mine Own Executioner, 1947; directed: Bonnie Prince Charlie, 1948; Flesh and Blood, 1950; produced and directed: Mr. Denning Drives North, 1951; Who Goes There!, 1952; The Captain's Paradise, 1953; Aunt Clara, 1954; Smiley, 1956; Smiley Gets A Gun, 1958. *Publications:* While Parents Sleep (play), 1932; The Amorous Prawn (play), 1960; (film), 1962; *books:* It is Upon the Navy, 1944; Half-Time, 1947; Lugs O'Leary, 1960. *Recreations:* golf, tennis, ski-ing. *Address:* Acres Gate, Hurstpierpoint, Sussex. *T.:* Hurstpierpoint 2367. *Club:* Garrick. [*Died* 19 *May* 1964.

KING, Sir Alexander (William), 6th Bt. *cr.* 1815; *b.* 25 Nov. 1892; *s.* of late Robert Ebenezer King, Deal, Kent (brother of Sir George Adolphus King, 5th Bt.) and late Margaret Dempster; *S.* uncle 1954; *m.* 1924, Dorothy Alice, *d.* of Henry William Champion, Park Road, Sittingbourne, Kent; one *s.* *Educ.:* Herne Bay College; Borden College. Served European War, 1914-19, with Royal Navy; War of 1939-45, with Civil Defence. *Heir:* *s.* Peter Alexander King [*b.* 13 Nov. 1928; *m.* 1957, Jean Margaret, *d.* of Christopher Thomas Cavell; one *s.* one *d.* *Educ.:* Cliftonville College; Cranbrook School]. *Address:* Charlestown, 365 London Road, Deal, Kent. [*Died* 7 *April* 1969.

KING, Sir Archibald John, Kt., *cr.* 1944; **Hon. Mr. Justice King;** I.C.S. retd.; Puisne Judge, High Court of Judicature, Madras, 1934-45; *b.* 1887; *s.* of Rev. E. G. King; *m.* 1915, Mary Annette Halliwell; no *c.* *Educ.:* Liverpool College; Lincoln College, Oxford. Entered Indian Civil Service, 1910. *Address:* Shepherd's Hey, Old Camp Road, Eastbourne, Sussex. *T.:* 5723. [*Died* 10 *March* 1961.

KING, Sir (Arthur) Henry (William), K.B.E., *cr.* 1949 (C.B.E. 1939; O.B.E. 1932); *b.* 2 July 1889; *e. s.* of late Arthur Thomas King and Agnes Hutchison Reid; *m.* 1919, Marjorie (*d.* 1962), *d.* of late Francis Young, Washington, D.C.; one *s.* Entered Consular service; Vice-Consul Washington, Chicago, and New Orleans; H.B.M. Consul and Chargé d'Affaires, Honduras, 1924-27; H.B.M. Consul Lisbon and Commercial Secretary to Embassy, 1928; Consul-General, 1940-44; Minister (Commercial), Rio de Janeiro, 1946-51; (Commercial Counsellor, 1944); retired, 1951. Managing Director, Industrias Elétricas e Musicais Fábrica Odeon S.A., 1951-54. Overseas Director, Timor Oil Ltd., Sydney, Australia; Director, Cia. dos Petroleos de Timor, Lisbon. *Recreations:* music, fishing. *Address:* Av. Duque de Loulé 47, 3 Lisbon. *T.:* 59137. *Club:* Canning. [*Died* 13 *March* 1966.

KING, Lieut.-Gen. Sir Charles John Stuart, K.B.E., *cr.* 1945 (C.B.E. 1939; O.B.E. 1920); C.B. 1943; *b.* 13 Oct. 1890; *m.* 1920, Kathleen Margaret, *d.* of Col. T. W. Rudd; three *s.* *Educ.:* Felsted School; R.M.A., Woolwich. 2nd Lt. R.E. 1910; Capt. 1916; Major 1926; Bt. Lt.-Col. 1931; Lt.-Col. 1933; Colonel, 1937; Major-General, 1941; served European War, 1914-18 (despatches); Afghanistan, 1919 (O.B.E.); Engineer-in-Chief, War Office, 1941-44; Special Mission, India and S.E.A.C., 1944; retired 1946 with hon. rank of Lt.-Gen. Col. Comdt. R.E., 1946-56. *Address:* Walsham-le-Willows, Suffolk. *Club:* Army and Navy. [*Died* 7 *Jan.* 1967.

KING, Earl Judson, B.A., M.A., Ph.D., D.Sc.; M.D. (hon. Oslo; Iceland); F.R.I.C.; Professor of Chemical Pathology in Univ. of London at Postgraduate Medical School since 1944; Chairman, Dept. of Pathology, since 1957; Consultant in Biochemistry, R.A.M.C., since 1950; *b.* 19 May 1901; *s.* of Reverend Charles W. and Charlotte Stark King; *m.* 1927, Hazel Marion Keith; two *d.* *Educ.:* Brandon Coll.; McMaster Univ.; Univ. of Toronto, Canada; Lister Institute, London; University of Munich, Germany. Bursar Nat. Research Council of Canada, 1924; Fellow, 1925; Research Associate Banting Institute, Demonstrator in Pathological Chemistry, Univ. of Toronto, 1927-31; Asst. Prof. of Med. Research, Univ. of Toronto and Director of Biochemical Section, Banting Institute, 1931-34; Sec., Canadian Biochemical Soc., 1930-34; Reader in Pathological Chemistry, Br. Postgraduate Med. School, London, 1934-44; James Page Rutherford Fellow, Univ. of Toronto, 1939; Sector Chemical Pathologist, E.M.S., 1939-45; Consultant in Chemical Pathology, R.A.M.C.; Consultant R.A.M.C., India (actg. rank Brig.), 1945; Subdean of British Postgrad. Medical School, 1944-: Member International Silicosis Conf., 1938, and Corr. Mem. in Industrial Hygiene of I.L.O., 1938-50; Hon. Member: American Assoc. Clinical Chemists; Toronto Biochemical and Biophysical Soc.; Canadian Physiological Society; Canadian Society of Clinical Chemistry; Chairman Cttee. on Clin. Chem., Int. U. Pure and Applied Chem. 1951-59 (Pres. Biological Section, 1959-); Chairman International Federation of Clinical Chem., 1952-60, and of Brit. Assoc. Clin. Biochem., 1953-55, Pres. 1956-58; Sec. Bd. of Studies in Biochemistry, Univ. of London, 1943-46, Chm. 1951-55; Chm. Central Acad. Council, Brit. Postgrad. Med. Fedn., 1952-55; Member Editorial Board, Biochemical Journal, 1942-46; Chairman, 1946-52; Chm. Cttee. Biochem. Soc. 1957-59; Member Lister Institute, 1953-; President British Occup. Hyg. Society, 1954-55; Member of University of London boards, of Medical Research Council cttees. on several subjects, and of Biochemical Soc. Cttees. McIntyre Res. Foundation lect., Canada, 1951; Kettle Mem. lect., 1954; Walter Estell-Lee lect., Philadelphia, 1954; adviser on silicosis, S.A., 1955; Hon. Consultant, S. Africa Council of Scientific and Industrial Research, 1956-; Chadwick lect., 1955. Brit. Rep. Med. Research Cttee. of the High Authority, European Coal and Steel Community. *Publications:* Microanalysis in Medical Biochemistry; Chronic Pulmonary Diseases in South Wales Coal Miners: Experimental Studies: Biochemical Disorders in Human Disease; A Symposium on Industrial Pulmonary Diseases; Biochemists' Handbook; papers in med. and scientific jls. on silicosis, phosphatase, analysis and other biochemical, medical and pathological subjects in Br. and Amer. scientific journals. *Address:* 2 Sunnydene, Bridgewater Road, Wembley, Middlesex. *T.:* Wembley 1812. *Club:* Savage. [*Died* 31 *Oct.* 1962.

KING, Engineer Rear-Adm. Frank Victor, C.B.E. 1942; *b.* 18 Sept. 1889; *e. s.* of late William King, Maidstone; *m.* 1914, Marjorie, *er. d.* of late H. A. Merry and of Mrs. L. F. Seale, Parkstone, Dorset; two *s.* (and one *s.* decd.). *Educ.:* Strand School; King's College, London; R.N.E.C. Keyham. R.N.C. Greenwich, 1909-12; Engr. Comdr. 1923; Eng. Capt. 1934; Engr. Rear-Adm., 1940; Deputy Engineer-in-Chief of the Fleet, 1943-47; retired, 1947. *Recreation:* golf. *Address:* Greenhill Cottage, Wealden Way, Little Common, Bexhill-on-Sea. [*Died* 21 *July* 1961.

KING, George Edward Fenton, C.V.O. 1947 (M.V.O. 1942); *b.* Pernambuco, Brazil, 10 June 1887; *s.* of late Robert George King, London, and Pernambuco, Brazil; *m.* 1912, Constance Mary, *d.* of late John Bamber, Medstead, Hants; one *d.* *Educ.:* privately. Served European War, 1914-18, with R.F.A. as Lieut. in France, Belgium, and Italy, 1916-1919; Inspector in Metropolitan Special Constabulary, 1937-46; Secretary Coutts & Co. (Bankers), 440 Strand, W.C.2, 1949-52; retired. *Recreations:* badminton, tennis. *Address:* c/o Coutts & Co., 440 Strand, W.C.2; Sentosa, Upper West Drive, Ferring, Sussex. *T.:* Goring By Sea 42060. [*Died* 12 *Feb.* 1962.

KING, Lt.-Col. Harold Holmes, C.I.E. 1934; M.B., B.S.; M.R.I.; I.M.S. (retd.); *b.* 1884; *s.* of A. R. King; *m.* 1919, Lilian, *d.* of G. W. Outhwaite, Norton-on-Tees. *Educ.:* Tollington Park College; St. Bartholomew's Hospital. Joined I.M.S., 1909; served Mesopotamia, 1914-16; East Africa, 1916-19; Director the King Institute, Guindy, 1926-34; retired 1936; attached Inter Services Research Bureau, 1940-44. *Publications:* The Expectation of the Relative Prevalance of Plasmodial Species and other papers in the Indian Journal of Medical Research. *Address:* The White House, Loudhams Wood Lane, Chalfont St. Giles, Bucks. *T.:* Little Chalfont 2194. [*Died* 21 *Oct.* 1961.

KING, Sir Henry W.; *see* King, Sir A. H. W.

KING, Most Rev. John Henry; Bishop of Portsmouth (R.C.), since 1941; *b.* Wardour, Wilts., 16 Sept. 1880; *s.* of John Frederick King and Mary Lucy Darley. *Educ.:* Woolhampton; English College, Rome. Secretary to R.C. Bishop of Portsmouth, 1910-23; Auxiliary R.C. Bishop of Portsmouth, 1938-41; Personal title of Archbishop, 1954. *Address:* 29 Jewry Street, Winchester. *T.:* Winchester 2804. [*Died* 23 *March* 1965.

KING, Professor Kenneth Charles, M.A. (Oxon.), Ph.D. (Lond.); Professor of German, King's College, London, since 1965; *b.* 5 Sept. 1911; *s.* of Charles Henry and Maud Ann King; *m.* 1953, Zoë Lenore Russell; no *c.* *Educ.:* City of London School; Oriel College, Oxford; Univ. College, London. Ph.D. (Lond.) 1938, M.A. (Oxon.) 1956. Lektor, Univ. of Basel, 1935-1936; Lektor, Univ. of Giessen, 1936-39. Served War of 1939-45: R.A., 1940-42; Intelligence Corps, 1942-46. Lecturer and Senior Lecturer, Univ. of Manchester, 1946-1952; Senior Lecturer, Univ. of Nottingham, 1952-59, Professor 1959-65. *Publications:* Das Lied vom Hürnen Seyfrid, 1958; Das Lied von Herzog Ernst, 1959; articles in learned journals. *Address:* 52 Stoke Rd., Leighton Buzzard, Beds. *Club:* Swiss Alpine (Basel). [*Died* 3 *Nov.* 1970.

KING, Martin Luther, Jr., D.D., Ph.D.; Pastor, Baptist Church, Alabama, U.S.A., since 1954; *b.* Atlanta, 15 Jan. 1929; *s.* of Martin Luther King and Alberta (*née* Williams); *m.* 1953, Coretta Scott; one *s.* one *d.* *Educ.:* Morehouse College (A.B.); Crozier Theological Seminary (B.D.); Boston University (Ph.D.). Pres., Montgomery Improvement Association; Founder and Leader, Southern Christian Leadership Council; Member, National Association for Advancement of Coloured Peoples. Has numerous awards for leadership of Montgomery movement. Holds honorary doctorates. Nobel Peace Prize, 1964. *Publications:* Stride Towards Freedom, 1958; Strength to Love, 1964; Why We Can't Wait, 1964; Chaos or Community, 1968; *Relevant Publication*: My Life with Martin Luther King, Jr., by Coretta King, 1969. Contributions to periodicals. *Address:* 454 Dexter Avenue, Montgomery, Alabama, U.S.A. [*Died* 4 *April* 1968.

KING, Sir Norman, K.C.M.G., *cr.* 1937 (C.M.G., 1926); *b.* 6 Dec. 1880; *s.* of Rev. Norman King, Vicar of Luddenden, Yorks; *m.* 1930, Mona, *d.* of late Ernest Dutton, British Vice-Consul, Hayti; one *s.* two *d.* *Educ.:* King's School, Worcester (King's Scholar); Sidney Sussex College, Cambridge (Scholar); Honours Degree Classical Tripos, 1903. Consular service since 1907; Consul-General, Mexico City, 1920-26; Chargé d'Affaires en titre at Mexico City, 28 Aug.-10 Dec. 1925; Consul-General Barcelona, 1926-38; Consul-General Marseilles, 1938-40; retired from Consular Service, 1940. *Address:* Pomaret, Ash, Canterbury, Kent. [*Died* 28 *April* 1963.

KING, Rear-Adm. Richard Matthew, D.S.O. 1918; R.N retired; *b.* 2 Nov. 1883; *s.* of late Colonel C. R. King (50th Regt.); *m.* Milly Frances Beatrice (*d.* 1944), *d.* of Charles Bewes of Gnaton Hall, Yealmpton, Devon; two *s.*; *m.* 1946, Katherine Margaret (*d.* 1968), *d.* of late T. C. Sheppard, Bryn Glas, Newbridge, Mon. *Educ.:* Stubbington House, Fareham; H.M.S. Britannia. Entered Navy, 1898; Lieut., 1904; Commander, 1916; Capt. 1922; Rear-Adm. 1934; served European War, 1914-18, in Grand Fleet Destroyer Flotillas (D.S.O.); Chief Staff Officer to Rear-Admiral (D) Mediterranean Fleet, 1924-1926; Assistant Director, Mobilization Department of Admiralty, 1928-30; Captain of Dockyard, Devonport, and Deputy Superintendent, 1930-32; Captain of H.M.S. Iron Duke, 1932-1933; commanded H.M.S. Cardiff, and Senior Officer Reserve Fleet, the Nore, 1933-35; A.D.C. to the King, 1934; retired list, 1934; Flag Officer-in-Charge Belfast, Aug. 1939-Oct. 1942; Commodore of Convoys, 1943-45; reverted to retired list, Aug. 1945. *Address:* c/o Westminster Bank, 8 The Strand, Torquay, Devon. [*Died* 15 *Dec.* 1969.

KING, William Bernard Robinson, O.B.E. M.C.; F.R.S. 1949; M.A., Sc.D.; Hon. D.Sc. (Lille University and Rennes University); Woodwardian Professor of Geology, Cambridge Univ., 1943-55; Yates Goldsmid Prof. of Geology at Univ. College, London Univ., 1931; *b.* 12 Nov. 1889; *m.* Margaret Amy Passingham; two *d.* *Educ.:* Uppingham School; Jesus College, Cambridge. Joined the Geological Survey of Great Britain, 1912; Assistant to the Woodwardian Professor in the University of Cambridge, 1920-31; Fellow of Jesus College, 1920; of Magdalene College, Cambridge, since 1922. President Geological Society of London, 1953-55. *Address:* Worton, Askrigg, Leyburn, N. Yorkshire. *T.:* Bainbridge 309. [*Died* 23 *Jan.* 1963.

KING, William Cyril Campbell, C.M.G. 1943; *b.* 24 August 1891; *s.* of late Captain W. H. King, late 12th Royal Lancers; *m.* 1921, Lois, *d.* of late Harry Cater, Torquay; one *s.* one *d.* *Educ.:* Cranbrook School. Ceylon Police, 1912; on war service, England, Ireland, and France, 1917-19; Chief Commandant of Police and Inspector of Prisons, Cyprus, 1933; Deputy Commissioner of Police, Nigeria, 1937; Commissioner of Police, Nigeria, 1941-47; Deputy Chief, British Police and Prisons Mission to Greece, 1948-50; Local Commandant, Cyprus Special Constabulary, 1952-57. King's Police Medal, 1937; Colonial Police Medal, 1942; O.St.J. 1945. *Address:* Kyrenia, Cyprus. *T.:* Kyrenia 350. *Club:* East India and Sports. [*Died* 25 *April* 1963.

KING-HALL, Baron *cr.* 1966 (Life Peer), of Headley; **William Stephen Richard King-Hall;** Kt., *cr.* 1954; Royal Navy, retired, 1929; a Director of the United Kingdom Provident Institution; *b.* 21 Jan. 1893; *e. s.* of late Admiral Sir George King-Hall, K.C.B., C.V.O.; *m.* Kathleen Spencer (*d.* 1963); three *d. Educ.:* Lausanne; Osborne; Dartmouth. Served in H.M.S. Southampton with Grand Fleet, 1914-17; then with 11th S/M Flotilla; Admiralty naval staff, 1919-20; awarded the Gold Medal of the R.U.S.I., 1919; R.N. Staff Coll., 1920-21; China Squadron, 1921-23; Staff College, Camberley, 1924; Intelligence Officer, Mediterranean Fleet, 1925-26; Atlantic Fleet, 1927-28; Admiralty Naval Staff, 1928-29; M.P. (Ind. Nat.) for Ormskirk Division of Lancashire, 1939-44. Served War of 1939-45 in Min. of Aircraft Production and Min. of Fuel and Power. Founded K-H News-Letter Service in 1936. Founded the Hansard Society for Parliamentary Govt., 1944. Hon. Dir. and Chm. of Council, 1944-1962, Pres. 1963. Radio and TV Commentator on current events. *Publications:* political and historical: A Naval Lieut., 1914-18; Western Civilisation and the Far East; Imperial Defence; The China of To-day; Letters to Hilary, 1928; Hilary Growing Up; The War at Sea, 1914-18; Our Own Times, 2 vols., 1935; Total Victory, 1941; Britain's Third Chance, 1943; My Naval Life, 1952; History in Hansard (with Ann Dewar), 1952; The Communist Conspiracy, 1953; Defence in the Nuclear Age, 1958; Common Sense in Defence, 1960; Men of Destiny, 1960; Our Times, 1900-1960, 1961; Power Politics in the Nuclear age, 1962; has written plays. *Recreation:* fishing. *Address:* The Penthouse, 162 Buckingham Palace Rd., S.W.1. *T.:* Sloane 5432. *Club:* Athenæum. [*Died* 2 *June* 1966.

KINGDON, Sir Donald, Kt., *cr.* 1931; M.A., LL.B.; *b.* Florence, Italy, 24 Nov. 1883; *s.* of late Walter Kingdon; *m.* 1914, Kathleen, *e. d.* of late Charles E. Moody; one *d.* (one *s.* decd. and *er. d.* killed on active service 1941). *Educ.:* Eastbourne College; St. John's Coll. Cambridge. Called to Bar, Inner Temple, 1905; Legal Assistant and Inspector of Schools, the Gambia, 1907; Member of Executive and Legislative Councils; Acting Colonial Secretary, the Gambia, 1912; Attorney-General, Uganda, 1912; Acting Chief Justice, Uganda, 1917 and 1918; Attorney-General, the Gold Coast, 1918; Member of Executive and Legislative Councils; Acting Colonial Secretary, the Gold Coast, 1919; Commissioner for the preparation of the Revised Edition of the Laws of the Gold Coast, 1920; Attorney-General, Nigeria, 1921-29; Member of Executive and Legislative Councils; Commissioner for the preparation of the Revised Edition of the Laws of Nigeria, 1923; K.C., Nigeria, 1925; Acting Chief Secretary to the Government, Nigeria, 1928 and 1929; Chief Justice of Nigeria, 1929-46; President of the West African Court of Appeal, 1936-46; Comr. for Revised Edn., Laws of Tanganyika, 1947, of Kenya, 1948, of Uganda, 1951, of British Guiana, 1953, of Gambia, 1955, of Nyasaland, 1957, of the Federation of Nigeria, 1958; Chairman Committee appointed by E. African High Commission to enquire into causes of failure of K.A.G. and other vaccines prepared at Kabete, 1949; Sole Comr. to enquire into riots in Uganda, 1949; Chm. Commn. to enquire into explosion at Mulago, 1951. *Address:* 8 Old Camp Road, Eastbourne, Sussex. *Club:* East India and Sports. [*Died* 17 *Dec.* 1961.

KINGHAM, Sir Robert Dixon, Kt., *cr.* 1945; C.B.E. 1939; Secretary, National Savings Committee, 1937-46; *b.* 13 Nov. 1883; *o. s.* of late R. D. Kingham, J.P., Farnham, Surrey; *m.* 1910, Millicent (*d.* 1941), *d.* of J. W. Proctor, J.P., York; one *s.* one *d. Educ.:* Charterhouse; Wadham College, Oxford. Called to Bar, Inner Temple, 1912. *Address:* Five Winds, Lewes, Sussex. [*Died* 27 *Oct.* 1966.

KINGSALE, 34th Baron, *cr.* 1189 (by some reckonings 29th Baron); **Michael William Robert de Courcy,** D.S.O. 1917; Baron Courcy and Baron of Ringrone, 1181; Premier Baron of Ireland; late Corps of Sikh Pioneers; *b.* 26 Sept. 1882; *o. s.* of 33rd (by some reckonings 28th) Baron and Emily (*d.* 1926), *d.* of William Sinclair de Courcy; *S.* father, 1931; *m.* 1st, 1906, Constance Mary Rancé (*d.* 1946), *d.* of late Maj.-Gen. Sir T. P. Woodhouse, K.C.M.G., C.B.; two *d.* (and two *s.* and two *d.* decd.); 2nd, 1947, Ruth (from whom he obtained a divorce, 1957), *d.* of H. T. Holmes, O.B.E.; one *d. Educ.:* Dulwich Coll.; Kelly Coll., Tavistock; Sandhurst. Joined Connaught Rangers, 1902; Indian Army, 1904; Lt.-Col. 1927; served Tibet, 1904; Abor Expedition, 1911-1912 (despatches); European War, 1915-18 (D.S.O., despatches three times); Serbian Order of the White Eagle, 5th Class, with Swords; Marri Operations, 1918 (despatches) N.W.F. Force against Afghans, 1919 (despatches twice); Waziristan, 1922; retired, 1931. *Heir: g. s.* John de Courcy (posthumous), *b.* 27 January 1941. *Address:* c/o Lloyds Bank, Newton Abbot, Devon. [*Died* 7 *Nov.* 1969.

KINGSBURY, Allan Neave, J.P.; B.Sc. (Eng.); M.D., B.S., M.R.C.S., L.R.C.P., D.P.H., D.T.M. & H.; Mem. Coll. Pathologists Austr.; retired; *b.* 22 Nov. 1888; *s.* of William George Kingsbury and Elizabeth Neave; *m.* Lucienne Alexis; one *s.* one *d. Educ.:* Bancrofts School; Middlesex Hospital. Assistant Pathologist, Middlesex Hospital. Pathologist, City of London Maternity Hospital; acting Government Pathologist, Penang; Pathologist, Institute for Medical Research, F.M.S.; Professor of Bacteriology, Singapore Medical College; Director, Institute for Medical Research, F.M.S.; late Government Pathologist, W. Australia; North Persia Forces Memorial Medal, 1927; sometime Lt. R.F.A. *Publications:* The Pathogenicity of the Diphtheria Group of Bacilli, Lancet, 1922; A Note on the Alleged Deterioration of Insulin in the Tropics, Lancet, 1925; Local and General Defences against Infection and the Effect on them of Vitamin Deficiency, British Journal of Experimental Pathology, 1924; Some Investigations of Malarial Fevers, Trans. Roy. Soc. of Trop. Med. and Hyg., 1926-27; The Serum Prophylaxis of Measles, Journal of Hygiene, 1927; On Canine Anti-Rabies Vaccination in Malaya, Malayan Medical Journal, 1927; On Occupational Cancer, with special reference to the industries of Malaya, Malayan Medical Journal, 1927; A Nutritional Survey of the F.M.S., Bull. I.M.R., F.M.S., 1940 and 1941. *Recreations:* golf, fishing. *Address:* 73 Cooper St., Mandurah, Western Australia. [*Died* 21 *Oct.* 1965.

KINGSLEY, Brigadier Harold (Evelyn William Bell), C.I.E. 1939; D.S.O. 1917; late 4th The Prince of Wales's Own Gurkha Rifles; *b.* 1885; *s.* of late Col, W. H. B. Kingsley, C.B., the Hampshire Regt., and late Mrs Kingsley, River View, Nenagh, Co. Tipperary; *m.* 1926, Hon. Olive Kitson (*d.* 1964), *d.* of 1st Baron Airedale. *Educ.:* Bedford Modern School; Sandhurst. Served in Mesopotamia, 1916-18 (despatches, D.S.O.); Balkans, 1918; Russia, and Trans Caspia, 1919; Black Sea and Turkey, 1919-20; Waziristan, 1921-24 (despatches); Col. 1933; Deputy Military Secretary, Army Headquarters, India, 1933 - 36; Commandant, Indian Military Academy, 1936-39; A.D.C. to the King, 1938-1939; retired, 1939. *Address:* Warnford House, Warnford, Hampshire. *T.:* West Meon 363. *Club:* Army and Navy. [*Died* 15 *April* 1970.

KINGSTONE, Brigadier James Joseph, C.B.E. 1954; D.S.O. 1919; Bar to D.S.O. 1941; M.C.; Colonel The Queen's Bays, 1945-54; *o. s.* of late W. J. Kingstone, of Milton, Wiltshire; *m.* Dorothy Constance, *d.* of late Colonel E. G. Hardy, C.M.G., D.L.; one *s.* one *d.* *Educ.:* Sherborne School; R.M.C., Sandhurst. Commander 5th Cavalry Brigade T.A., 1936-38; Commandant School of Equitation, 1938; A.D.C. to the King, 1944-45; retired pay, 1945. D.L. Wiltshire, 1953. Knight Commander of Order of Orange Nassau, 1946. *Address:* Green Fields, Upton Lovel, Warminster, Wilts. *Club:* Cavalry. [*Died* 20 *Sept.* 1966.

KINNEAR, Her Honour Helen Alice; retired as County Court Judge for the County of Haldimand (Province of Ontario, Canada), (1943-62); Apptd. Mem., Minister's Advisory Council on the Treatment of the Offender; *b.* 1894; *d.* of Louis Kinnear, M.A., and Elizabeth Eleanor Thomson Kinnear. *Educ.:* Port Colborne Public School; Welland High School; University of Toronto; Osgoode Hall Law School. B.A. Univ. Coll., Univ. of Toronto, 1917; graduated from Osgoode Hall and called to Bar, Ontario, 1920; K.C. 1934 (first woman in Commonwealth to take silk); apptd. County Court Judge, 1943 (first woman County Court Judge in Commonwealth). Mem. Senate of Univ. of Toronto, 1944-52. Mem. Roy. Commissions: to inquire and report upon proposed amendment of criminal law of Canada relating to defence of insanity, 1954; to inquire into amendment of criminal law of Canada relating to criminal sexual psychopaths, 1954. Hon. Mem., Kappa Beta Pi International Legal Sorority, 1944; Hon. Mem. Nat. Assoc. of Women Lawyers (U.S.A.), 1945; Hon. Doctor of Laws, Univ. of Toronto, 1953 (100th anniversary of founding of University College). John Howard Society of Ontario Medal and Citation for Distinguished Humanitarian Service, 1966. *Publication:* contrib. to Canadian Bar Review. *Address:* 487 Sugarloaf Street, Port Colborne, Ontario, Canada. *T.:* Temple 835-1586, Area code 416. [*Died* 25 *April* 1970.

KINSMAN, Colonel Gerald Richard Vivian, C.M.G. 1919; D.S.O. 1915; late R.A.; *b.* 18 May 1876; *s.* of late Col. H. J. Kinsman, R.A., of Antron Hill, Penryn, Cornwall; *m.* 1st, 1916, Dorothy (*d.* 1957), *d.* of Arthur Whitaker; one *s.* one *d.*; 2nd, 1957, Winifred Marion Noel, *d.* of late Charles Hoare. Entered R.A., 1896; Captain, 1902; Adjutant, 1904-07; Major, 1912; employed with West African Frontier Force, 1901-02; Adjutant T.F., 1909-12; European War, 1914-17; Chief Instructor in Gunnery, 1918-19 (despatches twice, D.S.O., C.M.G.); attached Chilean Army, 1921; Chilean Order of Merit; Military Attaché, Chile and Brazil, 1923-27; retired pay, 1928. Vickers Armstrong Staff, 1928-45. *Address:* Little Thorbens, Greensted, Ongar, Essex. *T.:* North Weald 248. [*Died* 20 *Aug.* 1963.

KINTORE, 11th Earl of (*cr.* 1677), **Arthur George Keith - Falconer;** Lord Falconer, 1647; Lord Keith of Inverurie, 1677 (Scot.); Lord Kintore, 1838 (U.K.); Captain, late Scots Guards; *b.* 5 Jan. 1879; 2nd *s.* of 10th Earl and Lady Sydney Charlotte Montagu (*d.* 1932), *d.* of 6th Duke of Manchester; *S.* father, 1930; *m.* 1937, Helena, Duchess of Manchester, *d.* of late Eugene Zimmerman, U.S.A. *Educ.:* Eton. Lieut. 3rd Cameron Highlanders, 1899; Scots Guards, 1899 - 1903; served South Africa, 1900 - 2; (Reserve) Scots Guards, European War, 1914-1918. *Heir: sister,* Sydney, Viscountess Stonehaven. *Address:* Keith Hall, Inverurie, Aberdeenshire. *Club:* Carlton. [*Died* 25 *May* 1966.

KINVIG, Prof. Robert Henry, M.A.; Emeritus Prof. of Geography Univ. of Birmingham (Prof. 1948-58); *b.* 19 July 1893; *s.* of James Kinvig, Isle of Man; *m.* 1923, Hilda M., *d.* of Thomas H. Gelling, Isle of Man. *Educ.:* Oulton School, Liverpool; University of Liverpool (M.A.). Lecturer in Geography, Univ. of Liverpool, 1919-24; Reader in Geography, Univ. of Birmingham, 1924-48. Travelled in many parts of South America, South and East Africa, India as well as Europe. Smith-Mundt and Fulbright Fellow, United States, 1952. President, Sect. E (Geography) Brit. Assoc., 1953 (Liverpool Meeting); Pres., Inst. of British Geographers, 1957. Hon. F.R.G.S. 1967. *Publications:* History of the Isle of Man (3rd Edn. 1968); The West Midlands (in Great Britain: Geographical Essays), 1962; Domesday Geography of Warwickshire (in Domesday Geog. of Midland England), 1954. Contrib. to Chambers's Encyclopædia (articles on South and Middle America); also to Geography and Geographical Journal. *Address:* 36 Oakfield Road, Selly Park, Birmingham 29. *T.:* 021-472 1206. [*Died* 24 *May* 1969.

KIRBY, Major-General Stanley Woodburn, C.B. 1943; C.M.G. 1947; C.I.E. 1940; O.B.E. 1927; M.C. and bar; Military Historian, 1950; *b.* 13 February 1895; *s.* of late Sir Woodburn Kirby; *m.* 1st, 1924, Rosabel Gell (*d.* 1954); one *s.*; 2nd, 1955, Mrs. Joan Catherine. *Educ.:* Charterhouse. 2nd Lt. R.E. 1914; served European War, 1914-18, France, Macedonia (despatches, M.C. and Bar); Singapore, 1923-26; Staff College, 1928-30; War Office, 1931-34; Imperial Defence College, 1936; Col. 1936; Major-General, 1941; Deputy Master-General of the Ordnance, G.H.Q., India, 1940-41; D.S.D. India, 1941-42; D.C.G.S. India, 1942-43: Director of Civil Affairs, War Office, 1943-44; Deputy Chief of Staff, Control Commission for Germany, 1945; retired, 1947. Grand Officer Order of Orange Nassau, with Swords (Netherlands); Comdr. Legion of Merit (U.S.A.); Comdr. Order of the Crown (Belgium). *Publication:* The War Against Japan (with others), Vol. I 1957, Vol. II 1958, Vol. III 1962, Vol. IV 1965. *Recreation:* golf. *Address:* Quains, Minchinhampton, Glos. *Club:* United Service. [*Died* 19 *July* 1968.

KIRK, Admiral Alan (Goodrich), U.S.N. (retd.); Hon. K.C.B. 1944 (Hon. C.B. 1943); D.S.M. (U.S.), 1944, 1950; Legion of Merit, 1943, 1945; *b.* 30 October 1888; *s.* of William T. and Harriet Goodrich Kirk; *m.* 1918, Lydia Chapin; one *s.* two *d.* *Educ.:* U.S. Naval Acad. Graduated U.S. Naval Acad., 1909; served afloat various stations, including Asiatic during Sun Yat Sen revolution; served European War, 1914-18, proof experimental officer Naval Proving Grounds; specialist naval gunnery; Capt. destroyer and light cruiser; staff operations officer, U.S. Fleet, 1937-39; War of 1939-45, Naval Attaché, London, 1939-41; Director of Naval Intelligence, 1941; Escort N. Atlantic, 1941-1942; Rear-Adm. Chief of Staff, U.S. Naval H.Q., London, 1942; Comdr. U.S. Atlantic Fleet Amphibious Forces, 1943; Assault Group, Sicily invasion, 1943; Comdr. U.S. Assault Force, Normandy invasion, 1944; Vice-Adm., Comdr. Naval Forces, France, 1944-45; Actg. Allied Naval Comdr.

Expeditionary Force, 1945; Member General Board 1945-46; retd. (voluntarily), 1946, with rank of Admiral. U.S. Ambassador to Belgium, and Minister to Luxembourg, 1946-1949; U.S. Ambassador, Moscow, 1949-1952; U.S. Ambassador, Taipei, Taiwan, 1962-63. Chief U.S. Deleg. U.N. special cttee. on Balkans, 1947-48. Hon. Comdr. Légion d'Honneur, 1945, and Croix de Guerre avec Palme (France); Gr. Comdr. Order of Leopold, 1949, Order of the Crown of Belgium, 1945, and Croix de Guerre (Belgium); Gr. Comdr. de la Couronne de Chêne, and Croix de Guerre, 1949 (Luxembourg). *Publications:* articles on ballistics, proc. U.S. Naval Institute. *Recreations:* golf, shooting, gardening. *Address:* 1 West 72nd St., New York 23, N.Y., U.S.A. *Clubs:* Chevy Chase, Metropolitan, Army and Navy, Alibi (Washington); Ends of Earth, Lotos, Century (N.Y.). [*Died* 15 *Oct.* 1963.

KIRK, Lucy Phoebe; *b.* 7 June 1890; *d.* of Ralph Robert Scott and Charlotte Mary Mather; *m.* 1917, Leslie Kirk. *Educ.:* Bath High School; Somerville College, Oxford. M.A. 1922; Sheffield Univ. Teaching Diploma, 1st Class, 1914; Assistant Mistress Liverpool Coll. for Girls, Huyton, 1914-16; Censor's Office London, 1917-18; Asst. Mistress Redland H.S., Bristol, 1918-24; Headmistress, Derby High School, 1925-32; Headmistress Leeds Girls' High School, 1933-49; retired, 1949. *Address:* Brantwood, Chalford Hill, Glos. [*Died* 22 *Aug.* 1961.

KIRK, Rev. Preb. Paul Thomas Radford-Rowe, M.A.; C.F.; Founder and General Director, Industrial Christian Fellowship, 1918-54, retired, Vice-President since 1961; *e. s.* of Thomas and Emilie Radford-Rowe Kirk, Dublin; *m.* Louisa, *e. d.* of late Rev. J. Seaver, B.D., Vicar of Bonchurch, Isle of Wight; one *d.* (and one *d.* decd.). *Educ.:* Wesley and Trinity Colleges, Dublin. Deacon, 1902; Priest, 1903; Curate of Berrieu, 1902-04; St. Mary, Dublin, 1904-06; St. Matthew, Surbiton, 1906-07; Walcot St. Swithin, 1907-09; Vicar of St. Mary Magdalene, Peckham, 1909-15; Vicar, Christ Church, Westminster, 1922-53; Priest-in-charge of St. Peter's, Eaton Square, 1941-53; Rural Dean of Westminster, 1941-1952. Prebendary of Harleston in St. Paul's Cathedral, 1942-54, Prebendary Emeritus since 1954. *Publications:* Re-discovered Message of Christ; The True Lent; The True Advent; Housing; Ideals in Politics; The Kingdom of God or The Kingdom of Mammon?; Communism; Fascism; The Christian Attitude to the State; The Movement Christwards, etc.; contributor to Christianity and the Crisis; The Best Book in the World; Revolutionary Christianity. *Recreations:* golf, motoring, walking, riding. *Address:* Flat 1, 11 Third Avenue, Hove, Sussex. [*Died* 16 *Sept.* 1962.

KIRKE, Percy St. George, M.A. (Cantab.), M.Inst.C.E., M.I.Mech.E.; Proprietor P. Kirke & Co., Research Engineers; *s.* of late Colonel St. George M. Kirke, C.B.E., and Mrs. Kirke, M.B.E.; *m.* 1904, Alice (*d.* 1959), *d.* of Sir James Gibson-Craig, 3rd Bt.; three *s.* (one *d.* decd.). *Educ.:* St. Peter's, York; Trinity Coll., Cambridge, Honours degree in Mechanical Sciences Tripos; Member of the Senate of Cambridge University. Pupil Willans & Robinson, Rugby, and Bruce Peebles & Co., Ltd., Edinburgh; engaged by Bramwell & Harris in erection of Scottish Central Electric Power Station, Bonnybridge, Scotland, subsequently Engineer-in-charge; Chief Engineer British American Tobacco Co., Ltd., at Bristol; Assistant Engineer, Avonside Engine Co., Bristol; Managing Director Bonecourt Waste Heat Boiler Co., Ltd.; Consulting Engineer, Bristol Aeroplane Co., Ltd.; Founder, Consulting Engineer and Director of Spencer-Bonecourt, Ltd.; inventor and patentee of the Spencer Bonecourt Patent Waste-heat and Gas-fired Boilers, manufactured at home and abroad by the Babcock and Wilcox and other Companies; inventor and patentee of improved Spencer-Hopwood Patent Water-tube Boilers, manufactured by Robert Stevenson and Co., Ltd.; Consulting Engineer to Cochran and Co. (Annan), Ltd., 1934-40; inventor of Kirke Patent Sinuflo Gas-Fired, Waste Heat and Super-Economic Steam boilers manufactured by Cochran & Co. Annan Ltd.; inventor of the Sinuflo Patent Superheaters; inventor of Sinuflo Patent Air Heaters used in H.M. Navy, etc.; read papers before the annual meeting of the Society of Chemical Industry in 1920, before the West of Scotland Iron and Steel Institute in 1921, on Efficient Steam Generation, again in 1935 on Heat Transmission in some Steam Boilers and before the Liverpool Society of Engineers in 1937. *Publications:* Various. *Address:* 4 Boscombe Cliff Road, Bournemouth, Hants. *T.:* Bournemouth 36791. [*Died* 20 *Feb.* 1966.

KIRKLAND, Rev. Canon Thomas James, B.Sc.; F.C.S., F.R.I.C., A.K.C.; Vicar of Rustington, 1941-61; Hon. Canon Ely Cathedral, 1927; Fellow of King's College, London, 1933; *b.* Wakefield, 5 Jan. 1884; *s.* of late Alfred and Kate Kirkland; unmarried. *Educ.:* Westminster; King's College, London. Assistant Master at King's School, Ely, 1906; Deacon, 1911; Priest, 1912; Headmaster of The King's School, Ely, 1918-41; Member of Ely Urban District Council, 1919-37 and 1940-41; Chairman, 1931-37. *Recreations:* cricket, Association football, motoring. *Address:* St. Ovin's, Rustington, near Littlehampton. *T.:* Rustington 95. *Club:* Royal Societies. [*Died* 5 *March* 1965.

KIRKMAN, Major-General John Mather, C.B. 1949; C.B.E. 1944; Retd. Commissioner-in-Chief, St. John Ambulance Brigade (Dec. 1956-Aug. 1962); *b.* 5 May 1898; *yr. s.* of J. P. Kirkman, J.P., of Bedford; unmarried. *Educ.:* Westminster (King's Scholar); R.M.A., Woolwich. Gazetted to R.A., 1917; served European War, France and Belgium, 1917-18 (British War and Victory medals); Maj.-Gen. 1949; Staff Coll., Quetta, 1933-34; D.D.M.I., War Office, 1942; B.G.S. Southern Command, 1944; B.G.S. Greece, 1945 (despatches); Chief of Staff, Palestine, 1947 (despatches); Chief of Staff, Far East Land Forces, 1948-1950 (despatches); Chief of the Intelligence Division, Germany, 1950-54. Retired, 1954. Liveryman of the Worshipful Company of Coachmakers and Coach Harness Makers. Colonel Comdt., R.A., 1957-63; F.R.G.S.; K.St.J. 1957. Commander Order of George I with swords (Greece). *Recreations:* golf, music. *Address:* c/o Lloyds Bank, 6 Pall Mall, S.W.1. *Clubs:* Army and Navy, Royal Commonwealth Society. [*Died* 14 *Oct.* 1964.

KIRKPATRICK, Sir Ivone (Augustine), G.C.B. 1956 (K.C.B. 1951); G.C.M.G. 1953 (K.C.M.G. 1948; C.M.G. 1939); Chm. of the National Bank since 1963; British President of Channel Tunnel Study Group since 1958; *er. s.* of late Col. Ivone Kirkpatrick, C.B.E.; *m.* 1929, Violet Caulfeild Cottell, M.B.E.; one *s.* one *d.* *Educ.:* Downside. Served European War, 1914-18 (wounded, despatches twice, Belgian Croix de Guerre); entered Diplomatic Service, 1919; Third Sec. at Rio de Janeiro; transferred to Foreign Office, 1920; Second Sec., 1921; First Sec., 1928; 1st Sec., Brit. Embassy, Rome, 1930-32; Chargé d'Affaires, Vatican, 1932-33; 1st Secretary, British Embassy, Berlin, 1933-38; Director of Foreign Div., Ministry of Information, 1940; Counsellor of

Embassy, 1941; Controller (European Services) B.B.C., 1941; Dep. Comr. (Civil) C.C.G. (British Element), 1944; Assistant Under-Sec. of State, Foreign Office, 1945; Deputy Under-Sec., 1948; Permanent Under-Secretary, F.O. (German Section), 1949: U.K. High Commissioner for Germany, 1950-53; Permanent Under-Secretary of State, Foreign Office, 1953-57, retd. Chm. Independent Television Authority, 1957-62. *Publication:* The Inner Circle, 1959; Mussolini, Study of a Demagogue, 1964 (posthumous). *Address:* Donacomper, Celbridge, Co. Kildare, Eire. *T.:* Celbridge 221; 160 Cranmer Court, S.W.3. *Clubs:* St. James'; Kildare St. (Dublin).
[*Died* 25 *May* 1964.

KIRKWOOD, 2nd Baron, *cr.* 1951, of Bearsden; **David Kirkwood;** *b.* 15 October 1903; *s.* of 1st Baron Kirkwood, P.C., of Bearsden, Dunbartonshire; *S.* father 1955; *m.* 1931, Eileen Grace, *d.* of Thomas Henry Boalch, of Pill, nr. Bristol; two *s.* *Educ.:* Royal Technical College, Glasgow. Deputy Controller Non-Ferrous Metals, 1941-45. Director, several industrial cos. Vice-President: Inst. of Metals; Nat. Sulphuric Acid Assoc. Ltd. Hon. Treas., The Chest & Heart Assoc. *Heir:* *er. s.* Hon. David Harvie Kirkwood [*b.* 24 Nov. 1931; M.A., Ph.D.; *m.* 1965, Judith Rosalie, *d.* of late John Hunt, Leeds; two *d.*]. *Address:* Norval, 54 Mayfield Avenue, Orpington, Kent. *T.:* Orpington 21154. *Club:* Caledonian. [*Died* 9 *March* 1970.

KIRWAN, Lt.-Col. Ernest William O'Gorman, C.I.E. 1939; Indian Medical Service, retired; *b.* 18 May 1887; *s.* of Patrick Joseph and Ellen O'Gorman Kirwan; *m.* 1927, Mary Dorothy Therkelsen; two *s.* *Educ.:* Belvedere College and University College, Dublin. M.B., B.Ch., B.A.O. (R.U.I.), 1909; M.Sc., N.U.I., 1919; F.R.C.S.I., 1920; M.D. (N.U.I.), 1938. Entered Indian Medical Service, 1910; served European War, France, 1914-15; Mesopotamia, 1916-19; N.W.F. India, 1917 (despatches twice); retired, 1944. Jubilee Medal, 1935; Coronation Medal, 1937. *Publications:* Diabetic Cataract, Brit. Journal of Ophthalmology, 1933; Primary Glaucoma—A Symptom Complex of Epidemic Dropsy, Archives of Ophthalmology, 1934; Epidemic Superficial Punctate Keratitis in Bengal, Folia Ophthalmologica Orientale; Orbital Teratomata, Brit. Journal of Ophthalmology, 1935; The Etiology of Chronic Primary Glaucoma, Brit. Journal of Ophthalmology, 1936, etc. *Recreations:* golf and bowls. *Address:* Route 2, Box 80, Franciscan Way, Carmel, California, U.S.A. *Clubs:* Oriental; Old Capital (Carmel, Cal.) [*Died* 17 *Oct.* 1965.

KIRWAN, Geoffrey Dugdale, C.B. 1945; C.M.G. 1954; M.C. 1918; *b.* 17 Oct. 1896; *s.* of late G. R. Kirwan, South Shields; *m.* 1st, 1929, Mary, *d.* of R. A. Morrow (marr. diss., 1948); two *s.* one *d.*; 2nd, 1950, Diana *e. d.* of late Dr. R. L. E. Downer. *Educ.:* South Shields High Sch.; Repton; Univ. College, Oxford. Commissioned Royal Garrison Artillery, 1915; served in France, 1915-1918; Staff Captain V. Corps Heavy Artillery, 1918; entered Home office, 1919; assistant secretary to Royal Commission on Police Powers and Procedure, 1928-29; secretary of Committee of Inquiry into London Motor Coach Services, 1932; A.R.P. Dept. of Home Office, 1935-39; Ministry of Home Security, 1939-45; Home Office, 1945; Control Office for Germany and Austria, 1945-47; Foreign Office (German Section), 1947-54. Secretary and Comptroller General, National Debt Office, 1954-61. A Vice-Pres., Trustee Savings Banks Association, 1961-. Coronation Medal, 1953. *Address:* Old Hall, 39 Nargate Street, Littlebourne, Canterbury, Kent. *T.:* Littlebourne 383.
[*Died* 11 *Nov.* 1970.

KISCH, Barthold Schlesinger, C.I.E., 1926; I.C.S., retired; *b.* 25 Oct. 1882; *s.* of late Henry Joseph Kisch, 24 Chepstow Villas, W.11; *m.* 1906, Madeleine Louise Claire (*d.* 1956), *d.* of late Henri Josef Bernard-Antony of Douai; no *c.* *Educ.:* St. Paul's School; Exeter College, Oxford, B.A. Entered I.C.S. 1905; Secretary to Joint Committee of the House of Lords and House of Commons to enquire into the Organisation and Methods of the Central Prisoners of War Committee, 1917; Controller Local Clearing Office (Enemy Debts) and Administrator of Austrian and Hungarian Property in India, 1920-28; Judge, Chief Court of Oudh, Lucknow, 1931-33; Puisne Judge, High Court of Judicature, Allahabad, 1933-35. *Recreation:* malacology. *Address:* 38 Boulevard Thiers, St. Jean-de-Luz, B.P., France. [*Died* 25 *Dec.* 1961.

KISCH, Sir Cecil, K.C.I.E., *cr.* 1932; C.B. 1919; *b.* 1884; *e. s.* of late H. M. Kisch, C.S.I.; *m.* 1st, 1912, Myra (*d.* 1919), *y. d.* of late Marcus N. Adler; one *s.* (and one *s.*, Oliver, killed in action, 1943 and one *d.* decd.); 2nd, 1922, Rebekah Grace, *d.* of late L. Joseph. *Educ.:* Clifton; Trinity Coll., Oxford. 1st Class Honour Mods. 1905 and Lit. Hum. 1907. Chairman, Trinity College, Oxford, Society, 1954-56; President, Old Cliftonian Society, 1955-57. Entered Secretary's Office, Gen. Post Office, 1907; apptd. to India Office, 1908; Private Sec. to Permanent Under-Secretary of State, 1911, to Parliamentary Under-Secretary of State in addition, 1915; Private Secretary to Secretary of State for India, 1917, in which capacity accompanied Rt. Hon. E. S. Montagu, Sec. of State, to India, 1917-18, and to Paris, Peace Conference, 1919; Secretary, Financial Dept., India Office, 1921-33; Assistant Under-Secretary of State for India, 1933-43; Deputy Under-Secretary of State for India, 1943-46; on deputation as Director-General, Petroleum Department, 1939-42; then on special duty in Petroleum Warfare Department, retired 1946. Mem. Exec. Cttee. of United Kingdom Council of European movement (Economic League for European Co-operation); Delegate, Hague Conference, 1953; Westminster Conference, 1954; Brussels Conference, 1960. Assistant Secretary to British Empire Delegation, Paris, 1919; Sec. to Indian Currency Cttee. 1919; Member Preparatory Commission of Experts, Geneva, for Monetary and Economic Conf.; of Indian Deleg. to above, 1933; British rep., Internat. Cttee. on Tangier Finances, 1937; Member, Supervisory Financial Commission, League of Nations, 1938-46, and Board of Liquidation (Vice-Chm.), 1946; Contributions Cttee., U.N., 1946-47; Currency Cttee., Bank of Greece, 1949. Member: Court of Governors, London School of Economics; Governing Body of School of Oriental Studies (Hon. Treas., 1946-61), Hon. Fellow, 1961. *Publications:* The Portuguese Bank Note Case, 1932; Central Banks (4th ed. 1932), (with Miss W. A. Elkin); The Waggon of Life (verse trans. of Russian poems), 1947; Alexander Blok: Prophet of Revolution (Study of life and work of Russian poet), 1960; contributions to The International Gold Problem, 1931, and to Press. *Address:* 21 Pembroke Sq., W.8. *Club:* Reform.
[*Died* 20 *Oct.* 1961.

KITCHEN, Percy Inman, O.B.E. 1942; B.Sc.; A.M.I.E.E.; *b.* 8 Dec. 1883; *s.* of late Charles and Elizabeth Kitchen, Keighley, Yorks; *m.* Elizabeth, *d.* of late John and Jane Green, Bingley, Yorks; one *s.* one *d.* *Educ.:* Keighley Technical Coll.; Bradford Technical Coll.; London Univ. Assistant Master, Keighley Grammar School, 1907-08; Ossett, Yorks, Grammar School, 1908-12; Principal, Bingley, Yorks, Technical School, 1912-14; Principal, Batley Technical College, 1914-19; Chairman of Council of Association of Technical Institutions 1933; Principal, Rugby Coll. of Technology and Arts and Organiser of Further Education, Rugby, 1919-47; retired, 1947. *Publications:* From Learning to Earning; contributions to various educational journals. *Recreation:* music. *Address:* 51 Ladbrook Road, Solihull, Warwickshire. [*Died* 1 *Jan.* 1963.

KITCHIN, Clifford Henry Benn; Writer; *b* 17 Oct. 1895; *er. s.* of late Clifford Kitchin. *Educ.:* Clifton; Exeter College, Oxford (Scholar). Served European War in France, 1916-18; called to Bar, Lincoln's Inn, 1924. *Publications:* Streamers Waving, 1925; Mr. Balcony, 1927; Death of My Aunt, 1929; The Sensitive One, 1931; Crime at Christmas, 1934; Olive E., 1937; Birthday Party, 1938; Death of His Uncle, 1939; The Auction Sale, 1949; The Cornish Fox, 1949; Jumping Joan, 1954; The Secret River, 1956; Ten Pollitt Place, 1957; The Book of Life, 1960. *Address:* 11 Abbotts, Kings Road, Brighton 1, Sussex. [*Died* 2 *April* 1967.

KITTOE, Lt.-Col. Montagu Francis Markham Sloane, O.B.E. 1918; T.D.; D.L.; London Stock Exchange, retired; *s.* of Capt. Markham Robinson Kittoe, late 106th Regt. (Durham L. Infantry); *m.* 1899, Blanche (*d.* 1951), *d.* of J. G. Scott, Southport; one *s.* *Educ.:* private. High Sheriff, County of Middlesex, 1932-33; served European War, 1914-18, Lt.-Col. Commanding 1/10 London Regt.; Member C. of Essex Territ. Army Association, 1907-13; C. of Middlesex Territ. Army and Air Force Assoc., 1924-47; Middlesex County Council, 1922-46; Vice-Chairman C.C., 1943-46; Alderman, 1933-46; President, Harrow Conservative Association, 1935-48. *Recreation:* fishing. *Address:* 1 Copland Ave., Wembley Park, Middx. [*Died* 25 *May* 1967.

KLAESTAD, Helge, LL.D.; Norwegian Jurist; President of the International Court of Justice, 1958-61; *b.* 6 Dec. 1885; Norwegian; *s.* of Lt.-Col. and Mme. Klaestad; *m.* Lalla Richter. Legal Adviser, Reparations Commn., Austrian Section, 1920-21; Pres. Anglo-German Mixed Arbitral Tribunal, 1925-31; Member, Permanent Ct. of Arbitration, The Hague; Judge of Supreme Ct., Norway, 1931-46; Judge of Internat. Ct. of Justice, The Hague, 1946-61. Member, Norwegian Acad. of Sciences. *Publications:* On Salvage, 1917; Liability of Shipowners, 1920; Landslott, 1922; Exoneration in Charter Parties, 1924. *Address:* Rosenborgg 5, Oslo, Norway. [*Died* 23 *May* 1965.

KLECZKOWSKI, Alfred Alexander Peter, M.D. (Cracow), Ph.D. (London); F.R.S. 1962; Biochemist, Department of Plant Pathology, Rothamsted Experimental Station, Harpenden, Herts, since 1946; *b.* 4 Dec. 1908; *s.* of Alfred and Isabella Kleczkowski; *m.* 1932, Janina Helen Mirzynski; one *d.* *Educ.:* Cracow University, Cracow, Poland. Worked at Rothamsted Experimental Station, Harpenden, Herts, from 1939, at first as a voluntary worker (schols. and grants); Beit Memorial Res. Fellow, 1943-45; on staff of Rothamsted Experimental Station, 1946-; Sen. Principal Scientific Officer, 1961. *Publications:* articles in various scientific jls. *Recreations:* various. *Address:* 7 Grasmere Avenue, Harpenden, Herts *T.:* Harpenden 4252. [*Died* 27 *Nov.* 1970.

KLINCK, Leonard Sylvanus; President Emeritus, Univ. of British Columbia, Canada, 1944; *b.* 20 Jan. 1877; *s.* of T. W. and Catherine Klinck; *m.* 1st, 1904, Mary Alice Macdougall (*d.* 1939); one *s.*; 2nd, 1941, Elizabeth B. Abernethy. *Educ.:* Ontario Agricultural College, Guelph, Canada; Iowa State Coll. B.S.A. (Toronto) 1903; M.S.A. (Iowa State College), 1905; D.Sc. (Iowa State College), 1920, (British Columbia), 1944; LL.D. (Western Ontario), 1924; F.R.S.C. 1942; F.A.I.C. 1922. Lectr. Iowa State Coll., 1904; in charge of Cereal Husbandry Department Macdonald College, 1905-07; Professor of Cereal Husbandry, Macdonald College, 1907-14; Professor of Agronomy and Dean, Faculty of Agriculture, The Univ. of British Columbia, 1914-19; President University of British Columbia, Canada, 1919-44; Officer, Order of Agricultural Merit, 1928; Officier de l'Instruction Publique, 1931. United Church of Canada. *Address:* 2627 Marine Drive, West Vancouver, B.C., Canada. [*Died* 27 *March* 1969.

KLINGHOFFER, Clara; painter; *b.* Szezerzec, near Lemberg, Austria, 1900; *d.* of S. Klinghoffer and Anna Stark; *m.* 1926, Joseph Willem Ferdinand Stoppelman, an American author and journalist of Dutch birth; one *s.* one *d.* *Educ.:* Slade Sch., University College, London; Central School of Arts and Crafts. First exhibition of drawings and paintings at Hampstead Art Gallery; subsequent one-man shows in Leicester Galleries, Redfern Gallery (1923, 1926, 1932 and 1938); Royal Glasgow Institute of the Fine Arts, 1962; Royal Academy, London, 1933, 1962; Scottish Academy, 1963. Also exhibited repeatedly in other London Galleries and in numerous provincial shows. Had works at numerous New English Art Club Exhibitions; Women's International Exhibitions; Whitechapel Art Gallery; Contemp. Portrait Soc., London, 1961, 1963; Royal Society of Portrait Painters, 1964, 1966, 1968. Three one-man shows in Amsterdam and The Hague. Also exhibited in: Stockholm, Paris, Venice (Bi-Annual), Toronto, New York; Wildenstein Gallery, London, 1947, 1961, 1963; one-man shows at 460 Park Avenue Gallery, 1941, New School for Social Research, 1951; Juster Gallery, New York, 1958; Fairleigh Dickinson Univ., Rutherford, N.J., 1968. Connected with, Pittsburgh (U.S.A.—Carnegie International). Member of New English Art Club; Board Member, Artists' Equity, New York, 1953, re-elected on Board, 1956, 1957. Works in permanent collections: Tate Gallery (bought by Chantry Bequest from Royal Academy Exhibition, 1933), Manchester Art Gallery, The Art Gallery and Industrial Museum, Aberdeen, Stoke-on-Trent Museum, British Museum (Print Room), Victoria and Albert Museum (Print Room), Brisbane Art Gallery, Contemporary Art Society; also in many private collections in England, France, Holland, Mexico, Canada and America. *Recreations:* music and literature. *Address:* (studio) 800 Riverside Drive, New York 10032, U.S.A. *T.:* Wadsworth 7-3220. [*Died* 18 *Nov.* 1970.

KNAPP, Marion Domville, C.B.E. 1926; R.R.C.; *b.* 1870; *d.* of late Rev. John Harvey Knapp, M.A., R.N. Chief Lady Superintendent, Queen Alexandra's Military Nursing Service for India, 1923-26; served S. Africa, 1901-2; European War, 1914-18 (R.R.C.); Afghanistan, 1919; Waziristan, 1919-20. *Address:* 23 Manor Road, Bexhill-on-Sea, Sussex. [*Died* 4 *Oct.* 1963.

KNAPP-FISHER, Arthur Bedford, M.V.O. 1959; F.R.I.B.A.; F.S.A.; Hon. A.R.C.A.; F.R.S.A.; Architect (Chartered and Registered), 9 Gower St., W.C.1; *b.* 15 Mar. 1888; *s.* of George Arthur and Louisa Hawes Knapp-Fisher; *m.* Heather Florence Mary, *d.* of Dr. Edward Philip, Redcliffe Gdns.; one *s.* one *d.* *Educ.:* Radley; Architectural Assoc. School. In private practice since 1912; Architectural Association, Hon. Treas. 1929-30, Pres. 1930-31. 1931-32; Member Architects' Registration Council of the United Kingdom; Chairman Board of Architectural Education, 1946-47; Professor of Architecture Royal College of Art, 1933-43; Vice-Pres., R.I.B.A., 1948-49, 1949-50; Member Executive Committee Council for the

Preservation of Rural England, 1926-1935; Chairman Artists Guild, 1923-26; Member of Council British School at Rome; Hon. Associate Institute of Landscape Architects; Temp. Sec. Royal Fine Art Commission, 1944-48; Member St. Edmundsbury and Ipswich Diocese Advisory Committee. Divisional Officer R.E. 1914-15; Captain 18th Bn. London Regt., 1915-17; R.A.F. 1917-19; Major R.E. D.C.R.E. 1939-43. *Principal Works:* Onslow village, Surrey; country houses, rectories, and vicarages; George V Garden of Remembrance, Windsor; buildings and work at Keble College, Oxford; Radley College (with H. I. Merriman); Westminster School; Stowe; Framlingham College; St. George's School, Windsor Castle; Haileybury and Imperial Service College; Kent County Ophthalmic Hospital; Dockhead House, S.E.1; Cottages and Control Rooms, S.W. England Electricity Scheme; Churches at Ewell, Stoneleigh, Crawley, Orpington, Chatham, etc.; Chapel Royal, Savoy; schools, etc., in Kent and Yorkshire, with Gollins Melvin Ward & partners; Consulting Architect, Allied Schools (until 1940) and Bow Church. *Publications:* Illustrated Oxford Renowned; various articles and reviews on architecture and topography. *Recreations:* tennis, painting. *Address:* The Flying Chariot, Hadleigh, Ipswich, Suffolk. *Clubs:* Athenæum, Architecture.
[*Died* 26 *June* 1965.

KNIGHT, Arthur Harold John, M.A.; Fellow and Praelector, Trinity Coll., Cambridge; Reader in German, Cambridge University, since 1957; *b.* 8 April 1903; *s.* of William Arthur Knight and Mary Frances Ferguson-Davie; *m.* 1928, Ella Dutton; one *s.* one *d.* *Educ.:* Marlborough College; Trinity College, Cambridge. English Lector at Leipzig Univ., 1925-27; Asst. Master, Stowe School, 1927; Reader in German, Aberdeen University, 1929-30; Univ. Lecturer in German, Cambridge Univ., 1930-57; Director of Scandinavian Studies, Camb., 1946-50; Chairman Faculty Board of Modern and Medieval Languages, Cambridge, 1954 - 57. Chevalier of the Royal Order of the North Star, Sweden, 1954. *Publications:* Some Aspects of the Life and Work of Nietzsche, 1933; Heinrich Julius, Duke of Brunswick, 1948; Georg Büchner, 1951; articles in critical journals. *Recreations:* mountaineering, ski-ing, sailing. *Address:* Trinity College, Cambridge; Camusantallen, Arisaig, Inverness-shire.
[*Died* 14 *Sept.* 1963.

KNIGHT, Professor (Arthur) Rex; Anderson Professor of Psychology in University of Aberdeen since 1947; *b.* 9 May 1903; *o. c.* of late Arthur Knight and Mary Horsnell; *m.* 1936, Margaret Kennedy, *o. c.* of E. P. Horsey, Harlow, Essex; no *c.* *Educ.:* Sydney University; Trinity College, Cambridge. First Class Hons. in Philosophy, Univ. Medallist, Muscio Prizeman, Woolley Travelling Scholar, Univ. of Sydney, 1923; First Class Moral Sciences Tripos, Scholar, Hooper Prizeman, Trinity Coll., Cambridge, 1925; Asst. to Director, Co-Editor of The Human Factor, Nat. Institute of Industrial Psychology, 1925-28; Lecturer in Psychology and Philosophy, Univ. of St. Andrews, 1928-1929; Anderson Lecturer in Psychology, Univ. of Aberdeen, 1929-43; A.A.G., Selection of personnel, Scientific Branch, War Office, 1943-45; Reader in Psychology, Univ. of Aberdeen, 1945-47; Visiting Lecturer in Univ. of Sydney, 1935; Fellow of Br. Psychological Soc., 1942; Pres. Scottish Branch of Br. Psychological Soc., 1943; Pres. Psychological Section of the British Assoc., 1948; Pres. British Psychological Soc., 1953-54; Member of Council of Industrial Welfare Soc., Technical Advisory Board, Nat. Institute of Industrial Psychology, and various other boards and cttees. *Publications:* (with C. S. Myers and others) Industrial Psychology, 1928; Intelligence and Intelligence Tests, 1st ed. 1933, 5th ed. 1950; (with M. K. Knight) A Modern Introduction to Psychology, 1948, 6th edn. 1959; (with others) Education in a Changing World, 1951; Incentives, 1951; (with others) Studies in Education 7, 1955; numerous contributions to psychological and other scientific periodicals. *Recreations:* reading, travel, swimming, bridge. *Address:* Hope House, Bucksburn, Aberdeenshire. *T.:* Bucksburn 113. *Club:* Authors'.
[*Died* 12 *March* 1963.

KNIGHT, Harold, R.A. 1937 (A.R.A. 1928); Member of the National Portrait Society; Member of the Royal Portrait Society; *b.* 27 Jan. 1874; *s.* of Wm. Knight, architect, Nottingham; *m.* 1903 (*see* Dame Laura Knight). *Educ.:* Nottingham High School. Student at Nottingham School of Art and with Jean Paul Laurens and Benjamin Constant, Paris; gold, silver, and bronze medals, Science and Art Department, South Kensington; South Kensington Local Scholarship; British Institute Scholarship, 1895; 2nd Medal, Salon, 1925; Pictures in the permanent collection at Leeds, Rochdale, Preston, Newcastle, Brisbane, Capetown, New Zealand, Nottingham, Manchester, Merthyr Tydfil; Picture in Tate Gallery, Millbank, diploma gallery, Burlington House, Welsh National Museum, Municipal Gallery, Perth, Australia. *Recreation:* fishing. *Address:* 16 Langford Place, St. John's Wood, N.W.8. *Club:* Arts. [*Died* 3 *Oct.* 1961.

KNIGHT, Jackson; *see* Knight, W. F. J.

KNIGHT, Dame Laura, D.B.E., *cr.* 1929; R.A., 1936 (A.R.A. 1927); R.W.S. 1928; R.E. 1932; Hon. Member Royal Portrait Soc. (Hon. R.P.) 1960; Hon. LL.D., St. Andrews Univ., 1931; Hon. D. Litt., Nottingham Univ., 1951; *b.* Long Eaton, 1877; *d.* of Charles Johnson; *m.* 1903, Harold Knight, R.A. q.v. 1961). *Educ.:* Brincliffe, Nottingham; St. Quentin, France. Studied Art at Nottingham School of Art; gold, silver, and bronze medals, South Kensington and Princess of Wales scholarship; hon. mention Carnegie Institute, Pittsburg, 1912; gold medal, San Francisco, 1915; 2nd Medal, Olympia Sports Exhibition, Amsterdam, 1928; Hon. Mention, Paris Salon, 1928; exhibited first in Royal Academy in 1903; retrospective exhibition, Diploma Gallery, R.A., 1965; represented Diploma Gallery, R.A., Tate Gallery, British Museum and Victoria and Albert Museum, Imperial War Museum, and in many Public Museums in the Brit. Isles, Colonies and Abroad. *Publications:* Oil Paint and Grease Paint, 1936; A Proper Circus Omie, 1962; The Magic of a Line, 1965. *Address:* 16 Langford Place, N.W.8. *Clubs:* Arts, Chelsea Arts. [*Died* 7 *July* 1970.

KNIGHT, Percy, M.B.E. 1951; Assistant General Secretary, National Union of Seamen, 1955-56 (National Organiser, 1942-55); retd.; Vice-Chm. Labour Party; *b.* 16 Apr. 1891; *m.* 1933, Elizabeth Johnson; one *s.* *Educ.:* Crindau Sch., Newport, Mon. Served European War, 1914-18, Tenth Cruiser Squadron. Worked with J. Havelock Wilson, M.P., in setting up National Maritime Board, 1917. Elected to National Executive Committee of Labour Party, 1945. *Recreations:* all sports, gardening, theatre. *Address:* 683 Haslucks Green Road, Majors Green, Nr. Shirley, Warwicks. *T.:* 021-474 4486.
[*Died* 31 *Dec.* 1968.

KNIGHT, Professor Rex; *see* Knight, Professor A. R.

KNIGHT, W(illiam) F(rancis) Jackson; Reader in Classical Literature, Univ. of Exeter, 1942-Sept. 1961, retired; *b.* 20 October 1895; *s.* of George Knight and Caroline Louisa Jackson; unmarried. *Educ.:*

Dulwich Coll.; Hertford Coll., Oxford (Open Schol., Classics). In residence, Hertford Coll., Oxf., 1914-15. Served European War in France, R.E. Signals, as motor-cyclist Despatch Rider, 1915-17; Commnd. Officer, 1917-20 (wounded). Taught at Banstead Hall, Banstead, and Henley House, Frant, 1920; in residence at Hertford College, Oxford, 1920-22; Lit. Hum. 1922; Henley House, 1922-25; All Saints' Sch., Bloxham, 1925-35; Bt. Maj. T.A.R.O., 1932; temp. Lectr. Univ. of St. Andrews. 1935. Asst. Lectr., 1936, Lectr., 1937, Reader, 1942, Univ. Coll., Exeter; founded and comd. U.C., Exeter, O.T.C., 1937; Mil. Rep. Exeter Jt. Recruiting Bd. and Mem. Interviewing Bd., 1939-40. Foundation Cttee. Mem. and first Hon. Sec., 1943, Pres. 1949-50, The Virgil Soc.; F.R.S.L. 1945, Hon. Life Mem. Internat. Mark Twain Soc., 1946; Vice-Pres. of Review "Erasmus", Basel, 1949; Cttee. of Direction of Review "Orpheus", Catania, 1953, and co-director, "Le Parole e le Idee", Naples, 1959; Visiting Lectr.: Univ. of the Witwatersrand, Johannesburg, 1950; Univ. of Catania, 1961. Chm., Exeter Br. The Churches' Fellowship for Psychical and Spiritual Studies, 1960. *Publications:* Vergil's Troy, 1932; Cumaean Gates, 1936; Accentual Symmetry in Vergil, 1939; Roman Vergil, 1944 (rev. and enl. version for Penguin Classics, 1966); Poetic Inspiration, An Approach to Vergil, 1946; St. Augustine's De Musica, A Synopsis, 1949; Vergil, Selections, 1949; Virgil's Aeneid, a translation (Penguin Classics), 1956. Director, The Pelican Classical Dictionary (not completed). Contrib. to The Oxford Classical Dictionary, Collier's Encyclopædia, and to numerous classical jls., periodicals, etc. *Posthumous publications:* Vergil: Epic and Anthropology, 1967; Many-Minded Homer, 1968; Elysion: on ancient Greek and Roman beliefs concerning a life after death, 1970. *Recreations:* gardening; formerly motor-cycling, riding, shooting, golf. *Address:* Caroline House, Streatham Rise, Exeter. *T.:* Exeter 59432. [*Died* 4 *Dec.* 1964.

KNIGHT DIX, D.; *see* Waddy, D. K.

KNIGHTON-HAMMOND, Arthur Henry, Hon. R.O.I.; Hon. Mem. R.I.; Hon. Mem. Pastel Society; late Mem. R.S.W. and the Société Internationale d'Aquarellistes, Paris; life Member of American Watercolor Society, New York; *b.* Arnold, Nottinghamshire, 18 Sept. 1875. *Educ.:* Nottingham School of Art; Westminster School of Art; Paris. Works in: National Portrait Gallery (life sized oil of Edward Johnston; chalk drawing also etching from life of Sir Frank Brangwyn; life sized oil of Prof. T. Pomfret Kilner); Musée de Jeu de Paume, Paris; Belgrade Museum; Auckland Art Gallery; National Gallery of South Africa; Glasgow, Edinburgh, Manchester, Aberdeen, Dundee, Rochdale and Newport (Mon.), Art Galleries and galleries in America; exhibited R.W.S. Galleries, London, 1959; one-man shows in London, Paris, Florence, Sydney, N.S.W. and Boston, U.S.A. During European War, 1914-18, made many drawings of munition plants for British Govt.; painted a series of thirty oil paintings of views on big chemical plant in Michigan, U.S.A., 1920. Has lived in Italy and in France for many years. *Address:* Higher Farm, Seaborough, Beaminster, Dorset. *T.:* Broadwindsor 206.

KNITTEL, John Herman Emanuel; author and dramatist; *b.* Dharwar, Bombay Province, 24 Mar. 1891; *s.* of the Very Rev. William Herman Knittel and Anna Schultze-Bodmer; *m.* 1915, Frances Rose White-Bridger; one *s.* two *d.* *Educ.:* Bâle; Zürich. Studied Philosophy; resided in England, 1910-18; travelled intermittently Europe and Africa; held financial post in the City; managed theatre with M. Moscovitch, 1921; writes in English and German; Schiller Prize-Winner. Member, Inner Council, Pan Europa Union. *Publications:* Aaron West; A Traveller in the Night; Into the Abyss (dramatised and filmed as Therèse Etienne); Nile-Gold; Midnight People (dramatised, as Protectorate); The Torch, in four acts (Apollo Theatre, London, 1921); Cyprus Wine; The Commandant; Via Mala (dramatised and twice filmed); Doctor Ibrahim (filmed); Power for Sale; Socrates (drama); Terra Magna; Jean-Michel, Arietta; La Rochelle (drama). *Recreations:* golf, riding, fishing. *Address:* Römersteig, Maienfeld, 7304 Grisons, Switzerland. *Clubs:* International P.E.N., Royal Automobile. [*Died* 26 *April* 1970.

KNOLLYS, 2nd Viscount, *cr.* 1911; **Edward George William Tyrwhitt Knollys,** Baron of Caversham, *cr.* 1902; G.C.M.G., *cr.* 1952 (K.C.M.G. *cr.* 1941); M.B.E., D.F.C.; Chairman: The Employers' Liability Assurance Corporation Ltd., 1955 (Managing Director, 1933-41, and 1947-54); Northern and Employers' Assurance Co.; Director: International Nickel Co. of Canada Ltd.; Barclays Bank Ltd.; Chairman, Council of Royal Air Force Benevolent Fund; Chairman, Arthritis and Rheumatism Council for Research in Great Britain and the Commonwealth; Mem. Council, King Edward VII Hospital; Trustee, Churchill Coll., Cambridge; Trustee, United States Churchill Foundation; Mem., Advisory Cttee., International Nickel Co. (Mond); *b.* 16 Jan. 1895; *e. s.* of 1st Viscount Knollys and Hon. Ardyn Mary Tyrwhitt (*d.* 1922), *d.* of Sir H. Tyrwhitt, 3rd Bt., and Baroness Berners; *S.* father 1924; *m.* 1928, Margaret, *o. d.* of Sir Stuart Coats, 2nd Bt.; one *s.* one *d.* *Educ.:* Harrow; New Coll., Oxford. Page of Honour to King Edward, 1904-1910; to King George, 1910-11; served European War, 1914-18, 16th London Regt. and R.A.F. (M.B.E., D.F.C.); Local Dir., Cape Town, Barclays Bank (Dominion, Colonial and Overseas), 1929-32; Deputy Commissioner, South Eastern Civil Defence Region, 1939-41; Governor and Commander-in-Chief of Bermuda, 1941-43; Chairman, British Overseas Airways Corporation, 1943-1947; United Kingdom representative on International Materials Conference, Washington, and Minister, British Embassy, Washington, responsible for raw materials, 1951-52. Chairman: Vickers Ltd., 1956-1962; English Steel Corporation, 1959-65. F.R.S.A. 1962. *Heir:* *s.* Hon. David Francis Dudley Knollys [*b.* 12 June 1931; *m.* 1959, Hon. Sheelin Maxwell, *d.* of late Lt.-Colonel Hon. Somerset Maxwell and late Mrs. Remington Hobbs; two *s.* one *d.*]. *Address:* Gavelacre, Longparish, Andover, Hants. *T.:* Longparish 323; 20 Laxford House, Cundy Street, S.W.1. *T.:* Sloane 2616. *Club:* White's. [*Died* 3 *Dec.* 1966.

KNOTT, Frank Alexander, M.D., B.S. (Lond.), F.R.C.P. (Lond.), M.R.C.S., D.P.H., A.R.C.Sc.; Consultant Emeritus in Clinical Pathology and Bacteriology, Guy's, Wimbledon and Putney Hospitals; Member, Hospital Management Committee, Metropol. group 3; formerly Reader in Pathology, University of London; War Service in R.N. Hospitals and H.M.S. Achilles; *b.* London, 1889; *o. s* of John D.A Knott; *m.* 1916, Dorothy, *o. d.* of Grosvenor Thomas; two *d.* *Educ.:* privately; London University and Guy's Hospital. *Address:* Guy's Hospital, S.E.1. *T.:* Hop 1654; 46 Bathgate Road, Wimbledon Common, S.W.19. *T.:* Wimbledon 1464. *Clubs:* Athenæum, Roehampton; Royal Wimbledon Golf. [*Died* 12 *Jan.* 1962.

KNOWLES, Rt. Rev. Edwin Hubert, D.D., LL.B., F.R.G.S.; *b.* 7 June 1874; *s.* of Edwin Knowles and Martha Jane Bassett; *m.* 1898, Violet Dora Mary Mapleton; one *s.*

Educ.: Burton School, England; University of Manitoba. Deacon, 1905; Priest, 1906; Incumbent of Buffalo Lake, Sask., 1905-09; of Kamsack, Sask., 1909-11; Secretary of Synod, 1911-35; Hon. Canon of Qu'Appelle, 1914; Archdeacon of Qu'Appelle, 1918; Chaplain to the Royal Canadian Mounted Police, 1917-56, retd. Bishop of Qu'Appelle, 1935-50. *Recreations:* photography and astronomy. *Address:* 2344 Quebec Street, Regina, Sask., Canada. [*Died* 27 *Oct.* 1962.

KNOWLES, Rear-Adm. George Herbert, D.S.O. 1918; R.N., retd.; *b.* 20 Nov. 1881; *s.* of G. H. Knowles, Gomersal; *m.* 1st, Winnefred Gladys (*d.* 1937), *d.* of E. Millar, Rossie Castle, Montrose; one *d.*; 2nd, Mrs. Olga Mills, *d.* of Vincent Frisby. Served European War, 1914-1918 (despatches, D.S.O.); retired list, 1933; served as Commodore 2nd Class R.N.R. during War of 1939-45. *Address:* c/o Admiralty, S.W.1. *Club:* United Service. [*Died* 1 *April* 1961.

KNOX, Maj.-Gen. Sir Alfred William Fortescue, K.C.B., *cr.* 1919 (C.B. 1917); C.M.G. 1918; late Indian Army; *b.* 30 Oct. 1870; *s.* of late Vesey Knox of Shimnah, Newcastle, Co. Down; *m.* 1915, Edith Mary, (*d.* 1959), *d.* of late Colonel F. J. Colin Halkett and *widow* of Richard Boyle. *Educ.:* St. Columba's College, Rathfarnham; Dublin; R.M.C., Sandhurst. Joined R. Irish Rifles, 1891; 58th Vaughan's Rifles, Indian Army, 1898; A.D.C. to Earl Curzon, 1899-1900, and 1902-03; Staff College, Camberley, 1904-5; General Staff, War Office, 1908-11; Military Attaché Petrograd Embassy, 1911-18. Served N.W. Frontier, India (Mahsud-Waziris), 1901-02 (despatches, medal with clasp); European War, with Russian forces, 1914-17; Chief of British Military Mission to Siberia, 1918-20; retired, 1920; M.P. (C.) Wycombe Division of Buckinghamshire, 1924-45; holds Orders of St. Stanislaus (1st Class), St. Vladimir (3rd Class), St. Anne (2nd Class), all of Russia; Commandeur of Legion of Honour and Croix de Guerre with Palms of France, Order of the Crown of Italy, Croix de Guerre of Czecho-Slovakia, and Japanese Order of Rising Sun (2nd Class). *Publication:* With the Russian Army, 1914-1917. *Address:* Binfield House, Binfield, Berks. *Clubs:* Carlton, United Service. [*Died* 9 *March* 1964.

KNOX, John Crawford, C.B.E. 1941; M.B.; B.Sc.; D.P.H.; Late Administrative Medical Officer, North-Eastern Regional Hospital Board, National Health Service, retired; *b.* 1891; *s.* of late John Knox, Oakbank, Shandon, Dunbartonshire; *m.* 1930, Dora Winifred, *d.* of John William McConnell, Heathcote, Harrogate. *Educ.:* Glasgow High School; Universities of Glasgow and Leeds. B.Sc. 1913, M.B. and Ch.B. 1915; D.P.H. Leeds, 1933; formerly Medical Superintendent, Aberdeen Royal Infirmary; Med. Sup. Min. of Pensions Hospitals, Glasgow, Liverpool, and Leeds; Hon. Adviser Hospital organisation, Dept. of Health, Scotland; Lieut.-Col. (retd.) R.A.M.C. (T.A.); Officer Comdg. 1st Scottish Gen. Hospital, 1937-38; served European War, 1915-19, France, Salonica, and N.W. Persia. *Publications:* Papers (jointly) in Journal of Pathology and Bacteriology, 1934, 1935. *Address:* Lorndale, Milltimber, Aberdeenshire. *Clubs:* Junior Army and Navy; Royal Northern (Aberdeen). [*Died* 22 *Aug.* 1964.

KNOX, Sir Robert Uchtred Eyre, K.C.B., *cr.* 1953; K.C.V.O., *cr.* 1937 (C.V.O. 1933); D.S.O. 1916; *b.* 1889; *e. s.* of late Alexander Knox; *m.* 1924, Dorothy Margaret, *y. d.* of late James Duke Hill, D.L., of Terlings, Harlow, Essex. *Educ.:* Dulwich; St. John's College, Cambridge, Exhibitioner; B.A. (Natural Science Tripos), 1911. War Office, 1912-14; Captain late The Suffolk Regiment, 8th Bn., 1914-16 (D.S.O., despatches, severely wounded); attached Staff, War Office, 1918-1919; H.M. Treasury, 1920; Private Secretary to Permanent Secretary of H.M. Treasury, 1928-39; Sec. Coronation Commission and Cttees., 1936-37 and 1952-53; Secretary, Political Honours Scrutiny Committee, since 1939. *Address:* 153 Cranmer Court, S.W.3. *Clubs:* Athenæum, Oxford and Cambridge. [*Died* 15 *Oct.* 1965.

KNOX, Walter Ernest, C.M.G. 1955; M.M. 1916; *b.* 8 October 1894; *s.* of late William James Knox, of Streatham; *m.* 1st, 1925, Clare Langdon (marriage dissolved); 2nd, 1946, Evelyn Bradford (*née* Goudge); one *s.* (one *step s.* one *step d.*). *Educ.:* St. George's College, London; London School of Economics, University of Lond. (Hons. B.Sc.Econ.). Foreign Office, 1914; National Insurance Audit Dept., 1914. Served European War, 1915-18: Queen's Westminster Rifles (wounded 1916; invalided 1918). Ministry of Pensions, 1922-1927; Empire Marketing Board, 1927-33; Imperial Economic Cttee., 1933-35; Customs and Excise, 1935-39. Lieut. 6th Surrey Home Guard, 1940-44. Secretary and Establishment Officer, Export Credits Guarantee Dept., 1950-58, retired. *Recreation:* reading history and biography. *Address:* Southfields, Bates Lane, Weston Turville, Bucks. *T.:* Stoke Mandeville 3547. [*Died* 28 *June* 1970.

KNOX-SHAW, Harold, M.A.; D.Sc. Oxon. F.R.A.S.; F.R.Met.Soc.; *b.* 1885; *e. s.* of late C. T. Knox-Shaw; *m.* 1938, May, *o. d.* of Robert Weir; one *s.* *Educ.:* Wellington College (Mathematical Scholar); Trinity College, Camb. (Major Scholar); Sheepshanks Exhibitioner; Sixth Wrangler, 1907. Assist. Helwan Observatory, 1908-13; Director, 1913-1924; also Director of the Meteorological Service of Egypt and the Sudan, 1918-24; Order of the Nile, 4th class, 1917; 3rd class, 1926; President of the Royal Astronomical Society, 1931-33; Radcliffe Observer (Oxford and then Pretoria), 1924-50; David Gill Medal, 1956. *Publications:* papers on astronomical subjects. *Address:* Elgin, Cape Province, South Africa. [*Died* 11 *April* 1970.

KNYVETT, Rt. Rev. Carey Frederick, O.B.E.; M.A.; *b.* Birmingham 13 Oct. 1885; *s.* of late Seymour Henry Knyvett, I.S.O., Deputy Chief Inspector of Factories, and Margaret Louisa Smith; *m.* 1918, Mary Geraldine, *o. d.* of late Rt. Rev. L. H. Burrows. *Educ.:* Rugby School; Trinity College, Oxford; Wells Theological College. Curate at Petworth, Sussex, 1911-14; Domestic Chaplain to the Bishop of Sheffield, 1914-19; Temporary Chaplain to Forces, 1916-19; Hon. Chaplain to the Forces, 1919 (despatches, O.B.E.); Vicar of Benwell, Newcastle on Tyne, 1919-34; Diocesan Secretary of the Diocese of Newcastle, 1935-1936; Archdeacon of Northampton and Canon Residentiary of Peterborough, 1936-1941; Hon. Chaplain to Bishop of Sheffield, 1919-39; Hon. Chaplain to Bishop of Newcastle, 1928-35; Hon. Canon of Newcastle, 1932; Suffragan Bishop of Selby, 1941-62. *Recreation:* gardening. *Address:* Cobblers, East Shalford Lane, Guildford, Surrey. *Club:* Yorkshire (York). [*Died* 9 *June* 1967.

KOCH, Dr. Lauge; Consulting Geologist for Greenland Ministry; *b.* 5 July 1892; *s.* of Parson Carl Koch and Elizabeth Knauer; *m.* 1st, 1924, Birgit Kewenter (*d.* 1933), Journalist, Stockholm; 2nd, 1937, Ulla Richert, Stockholm; 3rd, 1944, Edith Nielsen. *Educ.:* University of Copenhagen. Undergraduate, 1911; mag. scient. 1920; Ph.D. 1929; travelled in West Greenland, 1913; cartographer and geologist on the 2nd Thule Expedition to Melville Bay and the north coast of Greenland, 1916-18; Chief of the bi-centenary Jubilee Expedition north

around Greenland, 1920-23 (the Danish Gold Medal of Merit; the Swedish Vega-Medal, 1924; the English Patrons' Medal, 1927; Danish Hans Egede Medal, 1927; the German Ritter Medal, 1928, French Gaùdy Medal, 1929, Charles P. Daly Medal, 1930), French Roquette Medal, 1933; Mary Clark Thompson Medal, 1949; Hon. and Corresponding Member of many Geographical Societies; lectures at American Universities, 1924-25; at Polish Universities, 1926; Chief of the Geological Government Expeditions to East Greenland, 1926-27, 1929 and 1930, and to West Greenland, 1928; Leader of the Danish Three-year Expedition to East Greenland, 1931-34; Leader of the Danish Geological Expedition to East Greenland, 1936-39; Leader of airplane expedition to Peary Land, 1938; Comdr. of the Danebrog, Cl. I (Denmark), 1962, Silver Cross of Danebrog, Danish Silver Medal of Merit with inscription; Rink Medal (Denmark), 1961; Commander of the Nordstiernen (Swedish); Officer of the French Legion of Honour; Commander of the Finnish White Rose; Officier de l'instruction publique. Dr. *h.c.* (Basel), 1960. *Publications:* articles on Arctic Geology in geographical journals; Report on the Danish Bicentenary Jubilee Expedition north of Greenland, 1920-23, 1926; Contributions to the Glaciology of North Greenland, 1928; the Geology of East Greenland, 1929; Stratigraphy of Greenland, 1929; Map of North Greenland, 1932; Survey of North Greenland, 1940; The East Greenland Ice, 1945; Report on the expeditions to Central East Greenland, 1926-39, Parts I, II and III; New East Greenland Expeditions, from 1947-58. *Address:* Christians Brygge 24, Copenhagen V.
[*Died* 7 *June* 1964.

KODÁLY, Zoltán, Doctor Phil.; *b.* 16 Dec. 1882; *s.* of Frigyes Kodály and Paulina Jalovetzky; *m.* 1910; *m.* 1959, Sarolta Péczely. *Educ.:* Middle schools, Nagyszombat; Univ., Music-High Sch., Budapest; Berlin; Paris. Prof. of Theory and Composition Roy. High Sch. of Music, Liszt Ferenc, 1907-42. Pres. of Hungarian Arts Council, 1945-49 (when it was abolished); Pres. Hungarian Academy of Science, 1946-49 (elected for 3 years). Pres. Internat. Folk Music Coun., 1961. Hon. D.Mus.: Oxford, 1960; Toronto, 1966. Hon. Mem. American Academy of Arts and Letters, 1963. Royal Philharmonic Society's Gold Medal, 1967. *Publications:* musical compositions, as Psalmus Hungaricus, 1923; Nyári est, 1929; Marosszéki táncok, 1929; Galántal táncok, 1933; Te Deum, 1936; Felszállott a páva, Variations for Orchestra, 1939; Concerto for Orchestra, 1940; Missa Brevis, 1944; Tombeau des Martyrs, 1945; Zrinyi's Hymn, 1955; Symphony, 1961; Cantata; The Music Makers, 1964; Sonatas, Quartets, Songs, Piano pieces, Choruses for children, male, mixed voices; Opera Háry János, 1926; Székely Fonó (Engl. Spinnery), 1932; Cinka Panna, incid. music, 1948. *Books:* Transylvanian Folksongs (with B. Bartók), 1921; Folksongs from Nagyszalonta 1924; A Magyar Népzene, 1937 (3rd rev. edn., 1952; German edn., 1956; English edn. 1959); Editor: Corpus Musicae Pop. Hung. (A Magyar Népzene Tára), Vol. I, 1951, Vol. II, 1953, Vol. III, 1955, Vol. IV, 1958; Vol. V, 1966; articles in Reviews. *Address:* Népköztársaság út 89, Budapest VI. *T.:* 428-448.
[*Died* 6 *March* 1967.

KOENIG, Général d'Armée Marie-Pierre, C.B. (Hon.) 1946; D.S.O.; Député du Bas-Rhin, 1951, re-elected to National Assembly, France, 1956; Member of the Institute (Académie des Sciences Morales et Politiques), 1951; *b.* Caen, France, 10 Oct. 1898. *Educ.:* Collège Sainte-Marie, Caen; Lycée Malherbe, Caen (Bachelor's degree). Sous-Lieut. 1918; Lieut. 1920; Capitaine, 1932; Commandant, 1940; Lieut.-Col., 1940; Colonel, 1943; Général de Corps d'Armée, 1944; Général d'Armée, 1946. Campaigns: Erythrée, 1941; Libye, Bir-Hacheim, 1942; Tunisie, 1943; Commandant Supérieur, French Forces in Great Britain; Délégué Militaire, Comité Français de la Liberation Nationale, with the Supreme Allied Commander, and Commandant, French Forces of the Interior, 1944; Gouverneur Militaire du Paris, 1944-45; Commandant en Chef Français, in Germany, 1945-49; Inspecteur, Land, Sea and Air Forces in N. Africa, 1949-51; Vice-Président, Conseil Supérieur de la Guerre, 1950-51; Président de la Commission de la Défense Nationale, National Assembly of France, 1951, 1952, 1953, 1954; Minister of National Defence and of the Armed Forces, June-Aug. 1954, and Feb.-Oct. 1955. *Decorations:* Grand' Croix de la Légion d'Honneur, Croix de la Libération, Médaille Militaire. *Address:* 3 rue Ernest-Hébert, Paris 16e.
[*Died* 2 *Sept.* 1970.

KOHAN, Robert Mendel; H.B.M. Consular Service, retired; *b.* 8 June 1883; *e. s.* of M. Kohan of Galatz; *m.* 1937, Cecile Ethel (*d.* 1964), *d.* of Edward James Rose, New Orleans. *Educ.:* Manchester Grammar School; Gonville and Caius College, Cambridge. B.A. (Modern Language Tripos). Entered Consular Service, 1907; served at Zanzibar, Genoa, Port-au-Prince, Stettin, Leipzig, Bremen, and Quito; Chargé d'Affaires and Consul-General, Quito, Ecuador, 1926-33; Consul-General, New Orleans, 1933-37; Consul-General, Buenos Aires, 1937; retired, 1943. *Recreation:* golf. *Address:* Heather Cottage, Beacon Hill, Hindhead, Surrey. *Club:* St. James'.
[*Died* 8 *Aug.* 1967.

KONSTAM, Geoffrey Lawrence Samuel, M.D., F.R.C.P. Lond.; Consultant Physician and Physician in charge Cardiographic Dept., West London Hospital; Lecturer in Medicine West London Hospital Medical School; Consultant Physician London Jewish Hospital with charge electrocardiographic dept.; Consulting Physician East Ham Memorial Hospital and Bearsted Maternity Hospital; *b.* 23 Nov. 1899; 3rd *s.* of Rudolph and Emily Konstam; *m.* 1928, Helen Lorna, *o. d.* of Frederick W. Dunn, O.B.E., B.A., B.Sc., Barrister-at-Law; two *s.* one *d.* *Educ.:* Westminster Sch.; King's College, King's College Hospital Medical School, London. House Physician: Hampstead Gen. Hospital, 1924; Paddington Green Children's Hospital, 1925; House Surgeon, King's College Hospital, 1923-24; Medical First Assistant and Registrar, London Hospital, 1927-30; Medical Registrar, West London Hospital, 1930-32. Officer Cadet R.E. (Signals), 1918. Temp. Lt.-Col. R.A.M.C., 1940-45; Officer i/c Medical Divisions 43rd, 63rd General Hospitals. Examiner in Medicine, Cairo University, 1945; Examiner in Medicine Conjoint Board of England, 1951-55; Past-Pres. West London Medico-Chirurgical Society; F.R.Soc.Med.; Fellow Medical Soc. of London; Member Brit. Cardiac Society. *Publications:* contributions to medical journals, etc. *Recreations:* sculpting, tennis. *Address:* 40 Harley St., W.1. *T.:* Langham 1011; 6 Wildwood Rise, N.W.11. *T.:* Speedwell 9228.
[*Died* 27 *Feb.* 1962.

KORSAH, Sir (Kobina) Arku, K.B.E. 1960 (C.B.E. 1944; O.B.E. 1937); Kt. 1955; first Chief Justice of the Republic of Ghana, 1960-63, retd.; *b.* 3 April 1894; *s.* of Robert Marmaduke Korsah and Dinah, *d.* of Charles Gardiner; *m.* 1923, Kate Ethel Amanuah, *d.* of James Bannerman Hyde; one *s.* four *d.* *Educ.:* Methodist High School and Fourah Bay College, Sierra Leone; Universities of London and Durham. B.A. 1915; B.C.L. Dunelm 1917; LL.B. London 1919; M.A. 1943; D.C.L. 1944. Called to the Bar, Middle Temple, 1919. M.L.C., Gold Coast, 1928-40; M.E.C., Gold Coast, 1942-45; Commission on Higher

Education for W. Africa, 1943-45; Puisne Judge, Gold Coast, 1945-56; Justice of Appeal, West African Court of Appeal, 1956; Chief Justice of Gold Coast, April 1956-March 1957; Chief Justice of Ghana, March 1957-June 1960. Actg. Governor-General of Ghana, May-Nov. 1957. Member: Board of Education, Ghana; Central Advisory Committee, Ghana; Chairman: University Council, University College, Ghana; Council of Legal Education, Ghana, 1958-. Hon. Fellow, Educational Institute of Scotland. *Recreation:* golf. *Address:* The Retreat, Cape Coast, Ghana. [*Died* 25 *Jan.* 1967.

KREISLER, Fritz; violinist; *b.* Vienna, 2 Feb. 1875; *m.* 1901, H. Lies, U.S.A. *Educ.:* Vienna Conservatoire under Hellmesberger (gold medal, 1st prize); Paris, under Massert (1st prize and Prix de Rome). Toured through United States; spent four years at College and two at University; first appearance in London, 1902; Captain in the Austrian Army; served Austro-Russian War, 1914 (wounded); Hon. LL.D. (Glasgow); Grand Officer, Belgian Order Leopold II, Star of Roumania, Greek Order of George I; Commander, Swedish Order of Wasa, French Legion of Honour, Portuguese Order of St. Jago, etc. *Play:* Sissy, 1932. *Address:* 435 E. 52nd Street, New York 22, N.Y., U.S.A. [*Died* 29 *Jan.* 1962.

KRISHNAMA CHARIAR, Sir Vangal Thiruvenkatachari, K.C.S.I., *cr.* 1946; K.C.I.E., *cr.* 1936 (C.I.E. 1926); Kt., *cr.* 1933; Rao Bahadur, 1921; Member, Council of States, since Aug. 1961; *b.* Vangal, Trichinopoly District, S. India, 8 Feb. 1881; *m.* 1896; three *s.* two *d.* *Educ.:* Presidency College, Madras; Law College, Madras. Entered service as Deputy Collector Madras Service, 1903; Chief Revenue Officer, Cochin State, 1908-11; Asst. Secretary Board of Revenue and Under-Sec. to Government; Officer on special duty, Southborough Committee, 1918-19; Trustee Vizianagram Raj, 1919-22; Collector of Ramnad, 1923-1924; Secretary to Government Law Department Madras, 1924; Diwan Baroda State, 1927-1944; Prime Minister Jaipur State, 1946-1949; a delegate to the First Indian Round Table Conference in London, 1930-31; Member of the Sub-Committee No. II. (Provincial Constitution) of Conference; also a member of the Sub-Committee No. VIII. (Services); acted as a delegate to the Second Indian Round Table Conference in London, 1931; Member of the Federal Structure Committee; acted as delegate to the Third Round Table Conference, 1932; Member Federal Finance Sub-Committee, 1931-32; a delegate to the Joint Parliamentary Select Committee, 1933; Delegate to Assembly of League of Nations, 1934 and 1936; attended Coronation of King George VI, 1937; Adviser to Indian Delegation to Imperial Conference, 1937; Chairman, Committee of Ministers, Chamber of Princes, 1941-44; Vice-Pres. of Constituent Assembly of India, 1947. Delegate to United Nations Conference on International Organisation, San Francisco, 1945; to Preparatory Commission and first session of first General Assembly of U.N., London, Nov. 1945-Feb. 1946; Mem. sterling balances' deleg. to England, June-July 1948; Chm. Indian States' Finances Enquiry Cttee., 1948-49; Chairman, Indian Fiscal Commn., 1949; Mem. Planning Commn., 1950, (Dep. Chm., 1953-60). *Publications:* speeches; Community Development in India, 1958 (revised, 1962); Planning in India, 1961; Fundamentals of Planning in India, 1962. *Recreations:* tennis, billiards. *Address:* Lloyd Road, Madras, India; New Delhi, India. *Clubs:* National Liberal; Cosmopolitan (Madras). [*Died* 13 *Feb.* 1964.

KRISHNAN, Sir Kariamanikkam Srinivasa, Kt., *cr.* 1946; Padma Bhushan, 1954; F.R.S. 1940; D.Sc. (Madras); D.Sc. Hon. (Allahabad, Delhi, Lucknow, Calcutta, Jadavpur); LL.D. Hon. Banaras; For. Assoc., Nat. Acad. Sci., Washington, 1956; F.R.S.A. 1951; F.Inst.P., Lond., 1933; F.I.M., Lond., 1946; Hon. Fell., Instn. Telecom. Engineers, 1955; Hon. Mem. Indian Inst. Metals, 1957; Hon. Mem. Operational Research Club, 1957; Meml Council of Honour, Soc. for Visiting Scientists, 1960; Director National Physica. Laboratory of India, since 1947; National Professor since 1958; Hon. Visiting Prof., Delhi Univ., since 1958; Hon. Prof., Ind. Assoc. Cultivation of Science, since 1958; Pres. Nat. Institute of Sciences of India, 1953-54; Pres. Nat. Acad. of Sciences, India, 1945-46; Founder Pres. Bharathi Tamil Sangam; Pres. Delhi Tamil Sangam; Vice-Pres. Indian Acad. of Sciences, 1939-47; Vice-Pres. Indian Assoc. for the Cultivation of Science, 1945-49 and 1953-56; Vice-Pres. Indian Standards Institution, 1953-55; Pres. Physics Section Indian Science Congress, 1939-40; General Pres. Indian Science Congress, 1948-1949; Chm., Bd. of Res. in Nuclear Science since 1955; Mem. Indian Atomic Energy Commn. since 1948; Mem. Scientific Advisory Cttee., to Cabinet, since 1956; First President Indian Society of Theoretical and Applied Mechanics, 1955-57; Pres. Inst. Metals, India, 1957 and 1958; Chm. Radio Research Cttee. since 1950; Mem. Gov. Body C.S.I.R., since 1956; Mem. Board of Scientific and Industrial Research, since 1942; Bd. of Engineering Research, since 1953; Mem. Central Adv. Bd. Educn., 1956-; Mem. Standing Bd. Astronomy, 1956-; Vice-Pres., Internat. Council of Scientific Unions since 1955, and of Internat. Union of Pure and Applied Physics, 1951-57; Mem. Exec. Cttee. Internat. Union Crystallography, 1951-54; Mem. Internat. Commission of Weights and Measures, 1958-; Chm. Scientific Advisory Cttee., Unesco, 1955; Chm. Unesco Ed. Cttee., Modern Research Trends in Natural Sciences, 1960; Mem. Universities Grants Commission, 1957-; Chairman Indian National Cttee., Internat. Geophys. Year since 1955; Mem. Central Council Sanskrit Education, 1958-; Chm. Sci. Sub-Cttee. for Cooperation with Unesco; India's Representative Pan-Indian Ocean Sci. Assoc., 1957-; Life Mem. Senate Roorkee Univ., 1951-; *b.* Watrap, S. India, 4 Dec 1898; *e. s.* of Kariamanikkam Srinivasa Iyengar; *m.* Srimati Lakshmi; two *s.* four *d.* *Educ.:* Hindu High Schools at Watrap and at Srivilliputtur; American College, Madura; Christian Coll., Madras; University College of Science, Calcutta. Demonstrator in Chemistry at Madras Christian College for nearly two years; Research Associate at Indian Association for the Cultivation of Science, 1923-28; Reader in Physics, University of Dacca, 1928-33; Mahendralal Sircar Research Prof. of Theoretical and Experimental Physics at Indian Assoc. for the Cultivation of Science, 1933-42; Prof. and Head of Dept. of Physics, Univ. of Allahabad, 1942-47. Liége Univ. Medal, 1937; Krishnarajendra Jubilee Gold Medal, 1941; Bhatnagar Memorial Award, 1959. Special Univ. lectures at: Calcutta, Madras, Patna, Benares Hindu, Baroda; Convocation Address: Aligarh, Patna, Mysore, Punjab, and Jadavpur Univs.; Sardar Patel Memorial Lectures, A.I.R., 1956; Sir Thomas Holland Memorial Lecture, Mining, Geol. Metal. Inst. of India, 1957. Delegate to several International scientific conferences; Guest of Honour, Nat. Academy of Sciences, U.S.A., 1955; Internat. Tele-Communications Union, 1959; Mem. Bd. of Trustees, I.C.S.U. Financial Bd., 1959-; Editorial Advisory Bd., I.C.S.U. Review, 1958-. *Publications:* scientific papers in Trans. and Proc. Royal Society, and in other scientific journals, on optics (collaborated with Sir C. V. Raman in the discovery of the Raman Effect), magnetism, and physics and chemistry of solids, particularly of metals. *Recreations:* Tamil and Sanskrit classics.

Address: National Physical Laboratory, New Delhi 12. [*Died* 14 *June* 1961.

KRONBERGER, Hans, C.B.E. 1966 (O.B.E. 1957); F.R.S. 1965; Ph.D.; Member for Reactor Development, United Kingdom Atomic Energy Authority, since 1969; *b.* 28 July 1920; *s.* of Norbert and Olga Kronberger; *m.* 1951, Joan Kronberger (*née* Iliffe) (*d.* 1962); one step-*s.* two *d.* *Educ.:* King's College, Univ. of Durham; Univ. of Birmingham. B.Sc. 1944 (Durham); Ph.D. 1948 (Birmingham); F.Inst.P. 1955. Joined war-time Atomic Energy Team ("Tube Alloys"), 1944; A.E.R.E., Harwell, 1946; joined Industrial Group of Atomic Energy Dept., 1951; Head of U.K.A.E.A. Diffusion Plant Laboratories, Capenhurst, 1953; Chief Physicist, U.K.A.E.A. (Industrial Group), Risley, 1956; Director of Research and Development, U.K.A.E.A. (Dev. & Eng. Group), 1958-60; Deputy Managing Director, U.K.A.E.A. (Reactor Group), 1960-1964, Scientist-in-Chief, 1964-68. Leverhulme Medal, Royal Soc., 1969. *Publications:* various papers on Isotope Separation, Reactor Technology, and Desalination. *Recreations:* music, mountaineering, skiing. *Address:* 3 Smith's Lawn, Holly Road South, Wilmslow, Cheshire. *T.:* Wilmslow 27897. *Club:* Athenæum. [*Died* 29 *Sept.* 1970.

KRUG, Julius A.; Chairman, Brookside Mills, Inc. and Volunteer Asphalt Co., Knoxville, Tennessee; Washington, D.C., New York City; *b.* 23 November 1907; *s.* of J. J. Krug and Emma Korfmacher; *m.* 1926, Margaret Dean; one *s.* one *d.* *Educ.:* University of Wisconsin. A.B. 1929, A.M. 1930. Research statistician, Wisconsin Telephone Co., 1930 and 1931; chief, depreciation section, Wisconsin Public Service Commn., 1932-35; public utilities expert, Federal Communications Commn., 1936-37; technical director, Kentucky Public Service Commn., 1937; with Tennessee Valley Authority as chief power planning engineer, 1938, chief power engineer, 1939-40, and power manager, 1941. Served with War Production Board on loan from T.V.A., 1941-44; held following positions in Office of Production Management and War Production Board: Chief, Power Branch; Dep. Dir. Gen. for Priority Control; Dep. Dir. Gen. for Distribution; Program Vice-Chm. and Dir., Office of War Utilities. Served, 1941-45; on active duty in U.S. Navy, April-Aug. 1944, as Lt. Comdr. U.S.N.R. Actg. Chm., War Production Board, Aug. 1944, Chm., Sept. 1944-Nov. 1945. Secretary of the Interior, U.S., 1946-1949; resigned, Dec. 1949. Leader, U.N. Flood and Water Control Mission to Pakistan, 1956-57. *Address:* (home) 2900 44th Street, N.W. Washington 16, D.C., U.S.A.; (business) 444 Madison Ave., New York City. *T.:* Plaza 5-3400. *Clubs:* Army and Navy, National Press (Washington, D.C.); Metropolitan (N.Y. City). [*Died* 26 *March* 1970.

KUHN, Professor Dr. Richard; Director of the Kaiser-Wilhelm-Institut (since 1950, Max-Planck-Institut) für Medizinische Forschung, Heidelberg, since 1937; *b.* Vienna, 3 December 1900; *s.* of Hofrat Richard Clemens Kuhn, engineer, and Angelika (*née* Rodler); *m.* 1928, Daisy Hartmann; two *s.* four *d.* *Educ.:* Universities of Vienna and Munich. Study of chemistry, Univ. Vienna, 1918-19; Univ. Munich, 1919-22; Doctor degree, 1922. Priv. Dozent Univ. Munich, 1925; Professor for general and analytical chemistry at the Eidgenössische Technische Hochschule, Zürich, 1926; Honorarprof. at Univ. Heidelberg; director of Institut für Chemie am Kaiser-Wilhelm-Institut für Medizinische Forschung, Heidelberg, 1928; ord. Prof. für Biochemie, Univ. Heidelberg, 1950; Vice-Pres. Max-Planck-Gesellschaft, 1955. Nobel Prize for 1938, but unable to take it up. Pour le Mérite für Wissenschaften und Künste, 1958; Dr. h.c., Vienna Univ., 1960, Technische Hochschule, Munich, 1960. *Address:* Heidelberg, Wilckensstrasse 41, Germany. *T.:* Heidelberg 41928. [*Died* 1 *Aug.* 1967.

KUWAIT, Emir of; H.H. Shaikh Abdullah as-Salim as-Sabah; *b.* 1895; *e. s.* of Salim Mubarak as-Sabah, Ruler, 1917-21; *S.* cousin, Ahmed al-Jabir as-Sabah, 1950; *m.*; three *s.* Holds honorary British orders and other foreign decorations. *Recreations:* literature and history. *Address:* Sha'ab Palace, Kuwait, Arabia. [*Died* 24 *Nov.* 1965.

KYD, James Gray, C.B.E. 1942; F.F.A., F.R.S.E.; Chairman Scots Ancestry Research Council; *b.* 9 Aug. 1882; *s.* of Thomas Kyd, Actuary; *m.* 1912, Marjorie Amey Chalmers; two *s.* one *d.* *Educ.:* Aberdeen Grammar School. Actuary to Irish Insurance Commission, 1912-21; Actuary in Scotland, 1921-26; Principal Actuary Government Actuary's Dept., 1926-37; Registrar-General for Scotland, 1937-48; President of Faculty of Actuaries, 1944-46, Ex-Pres., Scottish Rights of Way Society. *Publications:* Scottish Population Statistics (Scottish History Society); Drove Roads and Bridle Paths around Braemar, and contributions to Actuarial and Statistical Journals and Mountaineering Literature. *Recreations:* walking and trout fishing. *Address:* Danny House, Hurstpierpoint, Hassocks, Sussex. *T.:* Hurstpierpoint 2494. *Club:* Scottish Arts. [*Died* 25 *June* 1968.

KYLE, William Galloway; Editor the Poetry Review for 38 years; Knight of the Order of the Redeemer (Greece); *b.* 1875; *s.* of a Yorkshire farmer. *Educ.:* privately. Journalist, lecturer, examiner in verse-speaking, and publisher; founder of The Poetry Society (Incorporated); co-founder and editor of The Northern Counties Magazine, Travel, and Vision. *Publications:* various anthologies as editor. *Address:* 21 Earls Court Square, S.W.5. *T.:* Fremantle 0598. [*Died* 25 *May* 1967.

KYNE, Most Rev. John Anthony; Bishop of Meath (R.C.), since 1947; *b.* 4 Nov. 1904; *s.* of John Kyne and Mary Clancy. *Educ.:* St. Finian's College, Mullingar; Irish College, Rome. Teacher, St. Finian's College, Mullingar, 1928-30; Vice-Rector, Irish College, Rome, 1930-47. *Address:* Bishop's House, Mullingar, Co. Westmeath, Eire. [*Died* 23 *Dec.* 1966.

L

LABARTHE, André; Founder and Editor of monthly review, Constellation, 1948-64; Editor, Science et Vie (monthly review); *b.* 26 January 1902. *Educ.:* Sorbonne. Docteur-ès-Sciences-Physiques; conscription military service at Physical Research Laboratory, Air Ministry, 1927-1928; Acting Asst. to Laboratory of Physical Mechanics, 1931; Asst. 1934; Scientific collaborator to Dept. of Research, Air Ministry; Laureate of Soc. of Civil Engineers of France (Prix Merville 1934); mission to England, 1934, Cambridge National Physical Laboratory, Ricardo Laboratory, Industrial Laboratories; mission to Germany for study of Diesel Engines, 1934; tour of the leading Technical Laboratories of United States; D.Sc. (Physics with full honours); Private Sec. to Technical Director of Under-Secretary's Dept. for Air; Director of National Establishment of Research and Technical

Experiment; Director of Bellevue Group of Laboratories: Laureate of Institut de France; Plumey Prize for Mechanics; left France, June 1940; Director-General of French Armament and Scientific Research at General de Gaulle's Headquarters till Sept. 1940; Founder and Editor of monthly review La France Libre, Nov. 1940; Foreign Scientific Correspondent of France-Soir; Secretary of Information in North Africa, 1943. Editor of Tricolor (monthly magazine), New York, 1943-45. *Publications:* La France devant la Guerre, 1938; La vérité sur la bombe atomique, 1946; La Vie commence Demain, 1947; papers and reports on engineering subjects. *Recreation:* painting. *Address:* 48 Avenue de New York, Paris 16. [*Died* 12 *Nov.* 1967.

LABIA, Princess Ida; 2nd *d.* of Sir Joseph Benjamin Robinson, 1st Bt., and Lady (Elizabeth) Robinson; *m.* 1921, Prince Natale Labia (*d.* 1936), 1st Royal Minister Plenipotentiary for Italy in the Union of S. Africa; two *s.* *Educ.:* England; Continent. *Recreations:* greatly interested in works of art and owns one of the finest private collections of old masters in the world, pictures collected by her late father, Sir Joseph Robinson. *Address:* Hawthornden, Wynberg, South Africa; The Fort, Muizenberg, South Africa. [*Died* 6 *March* 1961.

LACEY, Alfred Travers, C.M.G. 1944; O.B.E. 1936; *b.* 1892; *s.* of late R. L. Lacey, Castlepark House, Exmouth, Devon; *m.* 1927, Dorothy Kathleen, *d.* of late J. A. Van der Byl, Irene, Transvaal. *Educ.*. King Edward VI. Grammar School, Norwich; King's College, Cambridge (M.A.). Served European War, 1914-19, with Bedfordshire Regt. and Machine Gun Corps; invalided, 1919, with rank of Major. Entered Colonial Service 1924 as Superintendent of Education, Tanganyika Territory; Director of Education, Nyasaland Protectorate, 1930, Director of Education, Kenya, 1939-44; Member of Kenya Legislative Council, 1939-1944; retired from Colonial Service, 1944, now resident in S. Africa. *Address:* Nyumbani, St. James Road, St. James, The Cape, South Africa. [*Died* 22 *April* 1966.

LACEY, Sir Ralph (Wilfred), K.B.E., *cr.* 1954; Kt., *cr.* 1948; Vice-Chairman, Fine Spinners & Doublers Ltd.; *b.* 23 Mar. 1900; *s.* of William James Lacey and Mary (*née* Morgan); *m.* 1926, Hilda Mabel (*d.* 1963), *d.* of Herbert Jesse and Emma Gauntlett; no *c.* *Educ.:* Latymer Upper Sch.; Queens' Coll., Cambridge. Learning cotton spinning, 1922-1925; managing cotton mills, 1925-27; Secretary, Joint Committee of Cotton Trade Organisations, 1928-39; Secretary, Cotton Control, 1939-45; Cotton Controller, 1945-1948; Director Yarn Spinners' Association, 1948-51; Chairman, Raw Cotton Commission, 1951-54. President, Manchester Statistical Society, 1953. *Publication:* Cotton's War Effort (paper to Manchester Statistical Soc.). 1946. *Recreation:* snooker. *Address:* c/o Fine Spinners & Doublers Ltd, Michael House, Longridge Place, Manchester 4. *T.:* Blackfriars 8686. *Clubs:* Reform, Press (Manchester); Old Hall (Liverpool). [*Died* 13 *Jan.* 1965.

LACY, Sir Maurice John Pierce, 2nd Bt., *cr.* 1921; Lieutenant (retired), The Life Guards; *b.* 2 April 1900; *s.* of Sir Pierce Thomas Lacy, 1st Bt. and Ethel Maud (*d.* 1955), *d.* of late James Finucane Draper; *S.* father 1956; *m.* 1st, 1932, Primrose Russell-Roberts (marr. diss., 1939); one *d.*; 2nd, 1940, Nansi Jean, *d.* of late Myrddin Evans; two s. one *d.* *Educ.:* The Oratory School, Edgbaston, nr. Birmingham; Royal Military College, Sandhurst. Lieutenant, The Life Guards, 1919-24. Flight-Lieut., R.A.F.V.R., 1940-43. *Recreations:* shooting, cricket, golf. *Heir:* *s.* Hugh Maurice Pierce Lacy, *b.* 3 Sept. 1943. *Address:* Orchard Hill House, Bideford, Devon. *T.:* Bideford 73. *Club:* M.C.C. [*Died* 22 *April* 1965.

LA DELL, Edwin, A.R.A. 1969; R.B.A. 1950; artist (painter and lithographer); Senior Tutor, Royal College of Art, since 1948; *b.* 7 Jan. 1914; *s.* of Thomas La Dell and Ellen La Dell (*née* Boardman); *m.* 1939, Joan Josephine Kohn; one *s.* *Educ.:* South Grove, Rotherham; Royal College of Art (A.R.C.A., Fellow). Civil Camouflage, 1939-43; Army Camouflage, 1943-46. *Publication:* Your Book of Landscape Drawing, 1961. *Recreations:* croquet, boules. *Address:* StocksHouse, Grafty Green, Maidstone, Kent. *T.:* Maidstone 787206. *Club:* Chelsea Arts. [*Died* 27 *June* 1970.

LA FARGE, Oliver; Commendation Medal, U.S., 1945; Legion of Merit, U.S., 1946; Writer; *b.* New York City, 19 Dec. 1901; *s.* of C. Grant La Farge and Florence Bayard Lockwood; *m.* 1st, 1929, Wanden E. Mathews (marriage dissolved); one *s.* one *d.*; 2nd, 1939, Consuelo Otille C. de Baca; one *s.* (one *d.* decd.). *Educ.:* Groton School, Harvard (A.M.). Peabody Museum (Harvard) Archæological Expeditions, Arizona, 1921-22-24; Hemenway Fellow in Anthropology, 1925-26; Tulane Univ., Dept. of Middle American Research, Expedns. to Mexico and Guatemala, 1926-28; Columbia Univ. Expedn. to Guatemala, 1932. Fellow: Am. Assoc. for Advancement of Science, 1938; Am. Anthropological Assoc., 1947; Am. Acad. of Arts and Sciences (Boston), 1953; Mem. Am. Inst. of Arts and Letters, 1957; Pres. Assoc. on Amer. Indian Affairs, 1932-41 and 1948-. Military service, 1942-46 (retd. as Lt.-Col.). Pulitzer Prize, fiction, 1929; O. Henry Prize, short story, 1931. Hon. A.M., Brown Univ., 1932. *Publications:* Laughing Boy, 1929; Sparks Fly Upward, 1931; Long Pennant, 1933; All the Young Men, 1935; The Enemy Gods, 1937; As Long as the Grass shall Grow, 1941; The Copper Pot, 1942; Raw Material, 1945; The Eagle in the Egg, 1949; Cochise of Arizona, 1953; Behind the Mountains, 1956; The Mother Ditch, 1954; Pictorial History of the American Indian, 1956; A Pause in the Desert, 1957; Sante Fe, 1960; *scientific:* The Year Bearer's People, 1933; Santa Eulalia, 1947; various scientific papers. Numerous short stories and articles. *Recreations:* camping, fishing. *Address:* 647 College St., Santa Fe, New Mexico, U.S.A. *T.:* 3-8377. *Clubs:* Century, Coffee House (New York City); Quien Sabe (Santa Fe). [*Died* 2 *Aug.* 1963.

LA FONTAINE, Lt.-Col. Sydney Hubert, D.S.O. 1918; O.B.E. 1930; M.C. 1917; late Provincial Commissioner Administrative Service, Kenya Colony; *b.* 2 Dec. 1885; *s.* of late S. J. W. La Fontaine, Moda, Constantinople; *m.* 1930, Honor, *d.* of Dr. H. M. Stewart, Dyffryn, Dulwich; three *d.* *Educ.:* Uppingham; Caius Coll., Camb. (schol. and exhibn.). Entered Administrative Service, Kenya Colony, 1910; joined E. African forces during war (M.C., D.S.O., despatches); acting Chief Native Commissioner, 1933, 1934, 1935, 1937, and 1939; retired, 1940; joined East African Forces, 1941-44, rank Lt.-Col.; served in Somaliland, Abyssinia and Egypt. Regional Director U.N.R.R.A., Western Greece, 1944-47. Hon. Citizen of three Greek cities, 1945-46. Rejoined Kenya Administration and still serving on Advisory Cttee. for Mau-Mau Detainees and other cttees. *Recreations:* tennis and fishing. *Club:* Public Schools. [*Died* 25 *Jan.* 1964.

LA FORCE, Auguste de Caumont, Duc de; Member of French Academy since 1925; *b.* 1878; *s.* of late Bertrand de Caumont, Duc de la Force and late Blanche de Maillé; *m.* 1908, Marie Thérèse de Noailles; two *s.* two *d.* Officier de la Légion d'Honneur; Commandeur de l'Ordre de Pie IX; Grand Croix de l'ordre de Saint-Silvestre. *Publications:* L'Architresorier Le Brun, gouverneur de la Hollande; Lauzun, un courtisan du Grand Roi; Le Grand Conti; Curiosités historiques; Le Maréchal de la Force; La Vie Amoureuse de la Grande Mademoiselle; Comédies sanglantes, drames intimes; Dames d'autrefois; Femmes fortes; Chateaubriand au travail; Histoire et portraits; Histoire et portraits (deuxième série); Histoire et portraits (troisième série); Histoire du Cardinal de Richelieu, tomes III - VII (avec Gabriel Hanotaux); Richelieu (en un volume avec Gabriel Hanotaux); La Grande Mademoiselle; En suivant nos pères; Devant l'echafaud; Le Beau Passé: I, De Bayard au Roi Soleil; II, De Colbert à Marat; Le dernier amoureux de Madame de Genlis; Journal de J. P. Viennet avec introduction et présentation; Louis XIV et sa Cour; Amours et usages de jadis; Dix siècles d'histoire de France: Les Caumont La Force; La fin de la douceur de vivre. *Address:* Château de St. Aubin (par Fresnay sur Sarthe), Sarthe, France; 10bis avenue de la Grande Armée, Paris XVIIe. *Clubs:* Jockey, Comité France - Amerique (Paris). [*Died* 4 *Oct.* 1961.

LAGOS, Oba of; H.H. Sir Adeniji-Adele II, K.B.E. 1962 (C.B.E. 1956); Paramount Chief of Lagos; Vice-President of the Senate (Federal Upper House); President, Lagos Town Council. Formerly Revenue Official, Asst. Treasurer, Kano, Northern Region. Visited Britain, 1961. Is Chief Muslim of Lagos. *Address:* The Iga, Lagos, Nigeria. [*Died* 12 *July* 1964.

LAIDLAW, Sir George, Kt., *cr.* 1952; O.B.E. 1943; Chairman, George G. Kirk, Ltd., Glass Merchants and Glaziers, Glasgow, and Branches, 1935-68; Hon. Vice-Pres. Scottish Council of Social Service (a member since inception, 1943; Chm. 1949-54); Member: Glasgow Council for Community Service (Chm. 1932-50); Scottish Housing Advisory Cttee., 1936-48 (Vice-Chm., 1944-46; Chm., 1946-48); *b.* Sept. 1883; *s.* of late James Laidlaw, Master Plasterer, Ecclefechan, and late Janet Gass; *m.* 1st, Mary Greenhorne (*d.* 1955), *d.* of late George G. Kirk, Paisley; one *s.*; 2nd, 1957, Elizabeth Henderson, *d.* of late John N. Haran, Paisley. *Educ.:* Hoddam Public Sch.; Edinburgh Univ. (M.A., B.Sc.). Dir. of Studies, Glasgow and West of Scotland Commercial Coll., 1912-14. Served European War, 1914-18, Argyll and Sutherland Highlanders. Glass Merchant, 1919-21; Executive positions with Shell Mex, and Scottish Oils and Shell Mex, 1921 - 48, being Branch Manager in Scotland for 23 years till retired in 1948. Chm., B.B.C. Appeals Advisory Cttee. (Scotland), 1950-55; Chm. National Assistance Advisory Cttee. for Renfrewshire, 1955-64. Hon. F.E.I.S. *Address:* Windyhaugh, Knockbuckle Road, Kilmacolm, Renfrewshire. *T.:* 3230. [*Died* 13 *Sept.* 1969.

LAIDLAW, Robert; Chairman, Clydesdale Bank Ltd.; Director: Midland Bank Ltd.; J. and P. Coats, Patons and Baldwin Ltd.; *b.* 24 February 1897; *s.* of Rt. Hon. Thomas Kennedy Laidlaw and Elizabeth Balfour Clark; *m.* 1923, Kathleen Marion, *d.* of Charles F. Garrard, Tysoe, Warwickshire; three *s.* *Educ.:* Cargilfield, Midlothian; Uppingham; Sandhurst. Entered Army, 1916; Lieut., Royal Scots Greys, 1916-23; served European War, 1916-1918 (wounded). Joined J. & P. Coats Ltd., 1923, Director, 1938, Chm., 1946-60. *Recreations:* hunting, racing, fishing, yachting. *Address:* Somerton, Castleknock, Co. Dublin. *T.:* Dublin 343030. *Clubs:* Cavalry, Kildare Street (Dublin); Western (Glasgow); Royal Yacht Squadron. [*Died* 26 *April* 1964.

LAING, Col. Stanley van Buren, C.I.E. 1938; D.S.O. 1919; M.C.; Indian Army, retired; *b.* 21 April 1884; *m.* Dorothy Hall; two *s.* Served European War (Mesopotamia), 1914-16 (despatches, D.S.O., M.C.); Lt.-Col. 1929; Col. 1933; commanded 3rd Batt. 1st Punjab Regt., 1929-33; retired 1938. *Address:* Yateley, Hants. [*Died* 16 *May* 1962.

LAIRD, Sir Patrick (Ramsay), K.B.E., *cr.* 1953; Kt., *cr.* 1941; C.B. 1936; *b.* 13 Jan. 1888; *e. s.* of late T. P. Laird, Prof. of Accountancy, Edinburgh Univ.; *m.* 1913, Mary (*d.* 1966), *d.* of late J. F. B. Sharpe, Christ's Hosp., Hertford; one *d.* *Educ.:* Edinburgh Acad.; Pembroke Coll., Cambridge. Entered Civil Service (Scottish Office) 1912; Principal, 1919; Assistant Secretary, 1921; Secretary to Department of Agriculture for Scotland, 1934-53. *Address:* 38 Park Avenue, Bedford, Beds. *Clubs:* Royal Commonwealth Society; Caledonian United Service (Edinburgh). [*Died* 29 *June* 1967.

LAIRD, William, C.B.E. 1920; J.P.; L.R.C.P. & L.R.C.S. Ed.; late Surgeon Out-Patients, Royal Infirmary, Glasgow; *b.* 18 Nov. 1881; *s.* of Robert Laird, of Larkhall, Scotland; *m.* Mary, *d.* of Robert Mulholland, merchant, Glasgow; one *s.* one *d.* *Educ.:* St. Mungo's College, Anderson's College and University, Glasgow. Late Demonstrator of Anatomy and Botany, St. Mungo's College; Assistant to Prof. of Surgery (St. Mungo Chair), University of Glasgow; Lieut. R.A.M.C., Surgical Specialist, 48th General Hospital, Salonica; Surgeon in Charge Orthopædic Institute and Limbs (Artificial) Repair Depôt, Glasgow, under Ministry of Pensions; Visiting Surgeon, Bellahouston Hospital, Shakespeare Hospital, and Springburn Red Cross Hospital, Glasgow. *Publications:* Reports on treatment of discharged soldiers in Glasgow and South-West of Scotland. *Recreations:* shooting, fishing, motoring. *Address:* 1 Rosslyn Terrace, Helensburgh, Scotland. *Club:* Royal Scottish Automobile. [*Died* 10 *Aug.* 1962.

LAKE, Norman C.; Honorary Consulting Surgeon, Charing Cross Hospital; Consulting Surgeon, Queen's Hospital for Children; Emeritus Consulting Surgeon, Bolingbroke Hosp.; Member Court of Examiners, R.C.S.; Senior Examiner in Surgery, University of London; External Examiner in Surgery, Victoria University, Manchester; *b.* July 1888; *s.* of Nicholas O. Lake, Plymouth; *m.* 1928, Dorothy, *d.* of late T. J. Rees, C.B.E.; one *d.* *Educ.:* Charing Cross Hosp.; University of London. M.D. (Gold Medal), M.S., D.Sc.(Lond.), F.R.C.S.(Eng.), late Major R.A.M.C., Fellow Royal Society of Medicine; Consulting Surgeon, Hendon District Hospital; West Herts Hospital; Emeritus Lecturer in Surgery, Charing Cross Hospital. *Publications:* Lectures to Chiropodists, 1925; a Text-Book of Surgical Anat. and Phys., 1934; The Foot and its Disorders, 4th Ed., 1951; The Use of Suction in Surgery, Lancet, 1924; Partial Gastrectomy, a review of 320 cases, B.M.J., 1937; Precision in Spinal Anaesthesia, Lancet, 1938; The Effects of Cold upon the Tissues, Lancet, 1917; The Aftermath of Gastrectomy, B.M.J., 1948, Spinal anaesthesia, the present position, Lancet, 1958 Tattooing in the service of surgery, B.M.J., 1958; The Huxley Lecture, 1961, etc. *Address:* Grimsdyke, Potten End, Berkhamsted, Herts. *T.:* Berkhamsted 438. [*Died* 5 *April* 1966.

LALLY, Miss Gwen, O.B.E. 1954; Pageant Master, Play Producer, Lecturer; *d.* of late Rev. Jocelyn Henry Speck, M.A. Oxon, Hon. Canon of St. Albans and Rosalie, *d.* of Alexander Dalrymple, *g.g.d.* of late Captain Edmund Lally, 4th Dragoon Guards, Grimston Park, Yorks. *Educ.:* at home. Pageant Master and Play Producer

acted in Shakespearian and other plays under management of Sir Herbert Tree at His Majesty's Theatre and at Old Vic 1914-19; Pageants Produced—West Kent 1924, Nutfield 1925, Shere 1926, Rillington 1927, Chobham 1928, Ashdown Forest 1929, Warwick 1930, Tewkesbury 1931, Battle Abbey 1932, Runnymede 1934; The Pageant of England, Langley Park, Bucks, 1935; Historical Ice Festival, Earls Court, 1938; The Pageant of Birmingham, 1938; Churt Pageant, 1942; Tudor Pageant, (Churt), 1943; Judgment of Chelmsford (Pageant Play), Scala Theatre, 1947; Greatness of England (Churt), 1947; Dudley Castle, 1951; Malvern Pageant, 1951; Pageant of Poole, 1952. Director and Producer of Repertory Theatres (Little Theatre, Leeds 1931 and Palace Theatre, Westcliff on Sea 1933); Produced plays by Coward, Lonsdale, Barrie, Galsworthy, Arnold Bennett, Hugh Walpole, Van Druten, J. B. Priestley, etc., also produced many Shakespearian plays, and the classics; Adjudicator for Shakespearean and Drama Festivals; Lecturer on Shakespeare, The Drama, Repertory Theatres, The Modern Stage, etc; Laurel Chaplet presented by Poets Club. *Publications:* Behind the Veil and other Poems; Flaming Youth and other Poems; Part author of The Street of Many Arches; Contributor to magazines on Pageantry and Dramatic work. *Recreation:* writing poetry. *Address:* c/o Barclays Bank, 4 Vere Street, Cavendish Square, W.1.
[*Died* 14 *April* 1963.

LAMB, Frank de Villiers, C.B.E. 1918; *b.* Hunters Hill, N.S.W., 17 Nov. 1880; *y. s.* of John de Villiers Lamb; *m.* 1920, Florence Eadith Milner (*d.* 1944), *d.* of late Edward Milner Stephen, Sydney; *m.* 1945. Irene Lydia, *d.* of late H. J. Grummitt, Hornsea, Yorks. *Educ.:* Sydney C. of E. Grammar School. Was for 17 years on the staff of Dalgety & Co. Ltd.; selected for service overseas with the Australian Red Cross Society, 1915; Served in Malta, Egypt, and England (C.B.E.); Private Secretary to Sir Walter Davidson, K.C.M.G., Governor of N.S.W., 1919-21; Organizing Secretary of St. Luke's (C. of E.) Hospital, 1921-26; Secretary, N.S.W. Homes for Incurables, 1929-37. *Address:* 17 Wallaroy Road, Double Bay, N.S.W. [*Died* 17 *May* 1962.

LAMB, Sir Walter Rangeley Maitland, K.C.V.O., *cr.* 1943 (C.V.O. 1933; M.V.O. 1925); M.A.; Secretary of the Royal Academy of Arts, 1913-51; *b.* 1882; 2nd *s.* of late Sir Horace Lamb, LL.D., F.R.S.; *m.* 1927, Rose, *d.* of Samuel Brooks, of Chicago. *Educ.:* Manchester Grammar School, Trinity College, Cambridge. Classical Tripos, Part I., 1903: Part II. (Greek Philosophy), 1905; B.A. 1905, M.A. 1908; editor of Cambridge Review, 1905-06; Fellow of Trinity College, 1907-13; Classical Lecturer at Newnham College, 1905-07; King's, 1909-11; Emmanuel, 1909-13; Girton, 1911-13; Assist. Master, Clifton Coll., Bristol, 1907-09; Sec. of Camb. Philological Soc., 1910-13; Belgian Medal of King Albert for War Services, 1920; Comdr. Legion of Honour, 1950 (Officer, 1933); Silver Jubilee Medal, 1935; Coronation Medal, 1937. *Publications:* Clio Enthroned: a study of prose-form in Thucydides, 1914; The Discourses of Sir Joshua Reynolds, 1924; The Royal Academy, 1935, 2nd ed. 1951. Trans. of Plato's Dialogues and Orations of Lysias in the Loeb Classical Library. *Address:* The Red Cottage, Eastbury Ave., Northwood, Mx. *T.:* 1189. *Club:* Athenæum.
[*Died* 27 *March* 1961.

LAMBE, Philip Agnew, R.P. 1939; N.S. 1952-62; Gold Medallist, Paris Salon: Portrait Painter since 1914; *b.* 23 February 1897; 2nd *s.* of John Lawrence Lambe, M.A., F.S.A., author, and Mina Marguerite Edwina (*née* de Laune), *o. c.* of Alice, *d.* and *heiress* of Joseph-Ferdinand Boissard de Boisdenier, painter, poet, musician and dilettante; *m.* 1955, Zoë Violetta (*née* Lane), N.Z. *Educ.:* Westminster Sch. and Trinity Hall, Cambridge. Studied under the late Charles Buchel, 1914, subsequently under Charles Simpson, 1923-25; and Arthur Hayward, 1925-26; worked at Heatherleys Art School, 1934, and then under Bernard Adams. Served throughout European War, 1914-18, chiefly in Tenth Cruiser Squadron; rejoined Navy in War of 1939-45. Has lived on the Continent a great deal, also travelled to United States, Canada, South Africa, and New Zealand, etc. *Recreations:* cycling, chess, Greek coins (F.R.N.S.). *Address:* 13B Addison Crescent, W.14. *T.:* Western 3571; Studio 8, South Bolton Gardens, S.W.5. *T.:* Fremantle 2912 (Studio).
[*Died* 28 *Dec.* 1968.

LAMBERT, Bertram, O.B.E., M.A., D.Sc.; Fellow Emeritus of Merton Coll., Oxford, Tutor, 1920-47; Aldrichian Praelector in Chemistry in the University of Oxford, 1920-47; Curator University Chest, 1940-52; *b.* 21 Sept. 1881; *s.* of James Wilcock Lambert; *m.* 1908, Sylvia, *yr. d.* of William Dewe, Longworth, Berkshire; one *s.* one *d.* *Educ.:* Giggleswick School; Merton College, Oxford. 1st Class Final Honour School of Natural Science (Chemistry) 1903: served European War, Major R.E. (despatches twice, O.B.E.). *Publications:* Various papers in the Philosophical Transactions and Proceedings of the Royal Society, the Journal of the Chemical Society and elsewhere. *Recreations:* golf, motoring. *Address:* 1 Mansfield Rd., Oxford. *T.:* Oxford 44019.
[*Died* 1 *July* 1963.

LAMBERT, Engineer Rear-Adm. Charles William, C.B. 1946; *b.* 23 Sept. 1891; *s.* of W. E. Lambert, Bristol; *m.* 1916, Muriel, *d.* of J. C. Nicholson, London; one *s.* two *d.* *Educ.:* Bristol Grammar School; R.N.E. Coll., Devonport. Joined R.N. 1906; served in European War, 1914-1918; Engineer Capt. 1936; Engineer Rear-Adm. 1943; retired list 1946. *Recreation:* gardening. *Address:* Totnell House, Leigh, Sherborne, Dorset. *Club:* Army and Navy.
[*Died* 19 *Sept.* 1961.

LAMBERT, Rear-Admiral Sir David Sidney, K.C.B., *cr.* 1941 (C.B. 1939); O.B.E.; *b.* 2 March 1885; *s.* of Major-General William Lambert, C.B.; *m.* 1920, Dorothy Campbell, *d.* of F. W. Jones, Victoria, B.C.; no *c.* *Educ.:* Dover College. Royal Navy, 1903; served European War, 1914-19; Paymaster Captain, 1934; Paymaster Rear Admiral, 1939; Paymaster Director General, Admiralty, 1939-1942; Retired List, 1942; Ministry of Supply (Directorate of Economy), 1942-44. *Address:* Pilgrim's Hill, Merstham, Surrey. *T.:* Merstham 327. *Club:* Naval and Military.
[*Died* 15 *May* 1966.

LAMBERT, Maurice, R.A. 1952 (A.R.A., 1941); F.R.B.S. (1938-48, resigned and was re-elected 1951); Sculptor; *b.* 1901; *s.* of George Washington Lambert, A.R.A., and Amelia Beatrice Absell; *m.* Olga Marie Stuart Morrison. *Educ.:* privately. *Address:* 42 Peel Street, W.8. *Club:* Athenaeum.
[*Died* 17 *Aug.* 1964.

LAMBIE, Charles George, M.C., M.D., Gold Medal; F.R.C.P.Ed., F.R.S.E., F.R.A.C.P.; Emeritus Professor of Medicine, University of Sydney, since 1957; (Professor, 1930-56); formerly Assistant Physician, Royal Infirmary, Edinburgh, Lecturer in Clinical Medicine Edinburgh University, and Lecturer in Medicine, School of Medicine of Royal Colleges, Edinburgh; *b.* Trinidad, B.W.I., 24 July 1891; *s.* of Lieut.-Col. George Lambie, M.B.E.; *m.* 1925, Eliza Anne, *d.* of late William Gandy Walton, F.F.A., President of the Faculty of Actuaries, Edinburgh; two *d.* *Educ.:* Stanley House, Bridge of Allan;

Edinburgh University. Matriculated, 1909; M.B., Ch.B. 1914; Resident Physician, Royal Infirmary, Edinburgh, 1914-15; President, Royal Medical Society, 1914-15; Murchison Scholarship in Clinical Medicine, Oct. 1915; Commission, R.A.M.C. (Lieut. and later Captain); served in Mesopotamia, India, and France; Lecturer in Pharmacology, Edinburgh University, 1919-22; Beit Memorial Fellow, 1923-26; Lister Fellowship, 1928. *Publications:* Clinical Diagnostic Methods, 1948; papers in medical journals. *Recreations:* golf, tennis, skating. *Address:* 30 Churchill Crescent, Cammeray, Sydney, Australia.
[*Died* 28 *Aug.* 1961.

LAMBURN, Richmal Crompton, (Richmal Crompton), B.A. London (Classics 2nd class honours); *b.* 15 Nov. 1890; 2nd *d.* of Rev. E. J. S. Lamburn, Bury, Lancs. *Educ.:* S. Elphin's School, Darley Dale; Royal Holloway College. Senior Classical Mistress at S. Elphin's, Darley Dale, 1915-1917; Senior Classical Mistress at Bromley High School for Girls (G.P.D S.), 1917-24. *Publications:* TheInnermost Room; The Hidden Light; Anne Morrison; The Wildings, David Wilding, The Thorn Bush (a Trilogy); The House; Leadon Hill; Millicent Dorrington; Roofs Off; The Four Graces; Abbots' End; A Monstrous Regiment; Mist; The Middle Things; Sugar and Spice; Ladies First; Blue Flames; The Silver Birch; Naomi Godstone; Portrait of a Family; The Odyssey of Euphemia Tracy; Marriage of Hermione; The Holiday; Chedsy Place; The Old Man's Birthday, 1934; Quartet, 1935; Caroline; The First Morning, 1936; There Are Four Seasons, 1937; Journeying Wave, 1938; Merlin Bay, 1939; Steffan Green, 1940; Narcissa, 1941; Mrs. Frensham Describes a Circle, 1942; Weatherley Parade, 1943; Westover, 1946; The Ridleys, 1947; Family Roundabout, 1948; Jimmy, 1949; Jimmy Again, 1950; Frost at Morning, 1950; Linden Rise, 1952; The Gypsy's Baby, 1954; Four in Exile, 1955; Matty and the Dearingroydes, 1956; Blind Man's Buff, 1957; Wiseman's Folly, 1959; The Inheritor, 1960. Just William; More William; William Again; William the Fourth; Still William; William the Conqueror; William in Trouble; William the Outlaw; William the Good; William; William the Bad; William's Happy Days; William's Crowded Hours; William the Pirate; William the Rebel; William the Gangster; William the Detective; Sweet William; William the Showman; William the Dictator; William and A. R.P.; William and the Evacuees; William Does his Bit; William Carries On; William and the Brains Trust; Just William's Luck; William the Bold; William and the Tramp; William and the Moon Rocket; William and the Space Animal; William's Television Show; William the Explorer; William's Treasure Trove; William and the Witch; William and the Pop Singers; William and the Masked Ranger; William and the New Civilization. *Address:* Beechworth, Orpington Road, Chislehurst, Kent. *T.:* Orpington 26310.
[*Died* 11 *Jan.* 1969.

LAMBURY, 1st Baron *cr.* **1962. of Northfield; Leonard Percy Lord,** K.B.E., 1954; M.I.Mech.E.; Hon. President and Consultant to The British Motor Corporation Ltd. (President, Director and Consultant, 1963-66; formerly Executive Chairman); *b.* 15 Nov. 1896; *s.* of W. Lord; *m.* 1921, Ethel Lily Horton; three *d.* *Educ.:* Bablake Sch., Coventry. *Address:* Warren's Gorse, Nr. Cirencester, Glos.
[*Died* 13 *Sept.* 1967 (*ext.*).

LAMERT, Sidney Streatfield; Barrister-at-law; *b.* Agra, 1875; *s.* of Rev. M. Lamert, late Senior Chaplain Bengal establishment; *m.* 1910, Elizabeth (*d.* 1949), 2nd *d.* of late Rt. Rev. John Sheepshanks, Bishop of Norwich; three *d.* *Educ.:* Loretto. Managing Editor Sun, 1898-99; War Correspondent Daily Express (war medal), 1900-1; Asst. Editor Financial News, 1903-8; 2nd Lt., R.A.S.C. 1918-19; Editor of Money Market Review, 1910-23; Thos. De La Rue & Co. Ltd.: Chm. and Man. Dir., 1923-31; Chm. and Jt. Man. Dir., 1931-34; Chm., 1934-44. *Address:* Horleigh Green, Five Ashes, Sussex. *Club:* Union.
[*Died* 8 *Nov.* 1963.

LAMPARD-VACHELL, Benjamin Garnet, C.B.E. 1955; *b.* 26 Oct. 1892; *s.* of late Frank Lampard, Bath, Somerset; assumed additional surname of Vachell by Deed Poll in 1913; *m.* 1932, Lily, *y. d.* of late Col. T. Gracey, R.E., C.S.I.; one *d.* *Educ.:* Pembroke College, Cambridge. B.A.(Hons.) Cantab., Mech. Sci. Tripos, 1914; M.A. 1919; LL.B. (Lond.), 1923; Barrister-at-law, Middle Temple, 1923; A.M.I.A.E., 1917; A.F.R.Ae.S., 1917; Technical Officer (R.A.F.) at Air Dept. Admiralty and Air Ministry, 1916-19; contested (C.) Wednesbury Div. of Staffs, 1924, Lincoln, 1929, Barnstaple Div. of Devon, 1935; Torrington R.D.C., 1935; Devon C.C., 1937, Alderman, 1947 (Chm. A.R.P. Committee, 1939, Education Committee, 1946, C.D. Committee, 1951, Standing Joint Committee, 1958; Vice-Chm. Town and Country Planning Committee, 1939); J.P. Great Torrington, 1937, County of Devon, 1944; Chairman S.W. Regional Council for Further Education, 1947; Mem. Central Advisory Council for Education (England), 1956-61; Mem. National Advisory Council on Education for Industry and Commerce; Chm. Advisory Cttee. on Further Education for Agriculture, Ministry of Education, 1959; Pres. Assoc. of Educ. Cttees., 1956-57. Mem. Council, Rural Dist. Councils Assoc., 1947-49; Chm. Devon Assoc. of Parish Councils, 1947-49; Mem. Torrington Borough Council, 1937-46 (Mayor, 1937-1944); High Sheriff of Devon, 1944-45; Chm. Torrington Co. Petty Sessional Division, 1951-55. Treasurer University College of the South West, 1946, Deputy President, 1948; Pro-Chancellor of the University of Exeter, 1955; Burnham Cttee. on Teachers' Salaries, 1953; Chm. Devon County Playing Fields Association, 1947; Mem. Board of Governors, Bristol College of Advanced Technology; Vice-Chm. Board of Governors, Plymouth Technical College. Hon. LL.D. (Exeter), 1960. *Publications:* Critical Investigation into the Performance of Aeroplanes, 1919; Heraldic Shields at Weare Giffard Hall, 1934; Wild Birds of Torrington and District, 1944. *Recreations:* Hockey International, 1920-28 (26 caps), Captain 15 times; Cambridge Half-Blue, cricket; ornithology. *Address:* Weare Giffard, nr. Bideford. *T.A.* and *T.:* Bideford 357. *Clubs:* 1900, Royal Automobile, M.C.C; Devon and Exeter (Exeter)
[*Died* 4 *April* 1965.

LANCASTER, Joseph Torry, B.A., M.Litt.; J.P.; Headmaster, Ashville College, Harrogate, 1926-57; Chairman Y.M.C.A. Yorkshire Division, 1951, Vice-President: National Council; North-West Division Y.M.C.A.; Vice-Chairman Friends of Harrogate; *b.* Market Rasen, Lincs, 8 May 1892; *e. s.* of G. W. Lancaster; *m.* 1916, Alice Dora, *y. d.* of Henry Payne, Market Rasen. *Educ.:* De Aston School, Market Rasen (Lindsey Senior Scholarship, 1909); University College, London (Inter B.A. 1st Class Hons. English and Latin); B.A. (2nd Class Hons. English and French), Christ's College, Cambridge, M.Litt. (Thesis on Mrs. Gaskell). Queen's Royal West Surrey Regiment (wounded Aug. 1918); Capt. attached G.S. for educational organisation at Royal Victoria Hospital, Netley, 1918-19; Senior English Master, Leys School; President Harrogate Rotary Club, 1936-38. *Recreation:* motoring. *Address:* 10 Vernon Road, Harrogate. *T.:* 81598.
[*Died* 31 *Jan.* 1966.

LANCASTER-RANKING, Maj.-Gen. Robert P.; *see* Ranking.

LANDALE, David Fortune; Director: (Chairman, 1955-65), The Royal Bank of Scotland; The Northern & Employers Assurance Co. Ltd.; The British Investment Trust Ltd.; *b.* 7 Nov. 1905; *e. s.* of late David Landale, Dalswinton, Dumfries, and Mildred Sophia Fortune; *m.* 1st, 1929, Louisa (*d.* 1956), *y. d.* of late Charles William Forbes, Callendar House, Falkirk; one *s.* three *d.*; 2nd, 1957, Beatrice, *widow* of K. Lund. *Educ.:* Eton Coll.; Balliol Coll., Oxf. Managing Director Jardine Matheson & Co. Ltd. (Hong Kong, China and Japan), 1945-51. Unofficial Member: Executive Council, Hong Kong, 1946-51; Legislative Council, Hong Kong, 1946-50. Served War of 1939-45, Lieut. R.N.V.R., 1940-43; Minister of War Transport Representative in the Middle East, 1944-45. Member, Review Body on Doctors' and Dentists' Remuneration, 1967-. Member The Queen's Body Guard for Scotland, The Royal Company of Archers. *Address:* Dalswinton, Dumfries, Scotland. *T.:* Auldgirth 208. *Clubs:* Boodle's, Pratt's; New (Edinburgh). [*Died* 15 *Dec.* 1970.

LANDAU, Lev Davidovich; Soviet physicist; Professor of Theoretical Physics, Vavilov Institute of Physical Problems, Moscow, since 1937; *b.* Baku, 22 January 1908; *s.* of David and Lubov Landau; *m.* 1939, Konkordia; one *s.* *Educ.:* Baku Univ.; Leningrad Univ.; Leningrad Physical and Technical Inst.; scientific centres in Denmark, Switzerland, Germany, the Netherlands, Great Britain. Whilst abroad, began investigations leading him to study of low-temperature physics, 1929-30, resulting in explanation of de Haas-van Alphen effect, 1937-38; Head of Theoretical Div., Physical and Technical Inst., Kharkov, 1932-37; began work on theory of superfluidity, 1937. Member: Acad. of Sciences, U.S.S.R.; Danish and Netherlands Acad. of Sciences; Hon. Fell., Physical Soc.; For. Mem., Royal Soc.; For. Assoc., Nat. Acad. of Sciences, U.S.A.; Hon. For. Mem., Amer. Acad. of Arts and Sciences. Nobel Prize for Physics, 1962; Lenin Prize, 1962; Fritz London Award, 1960; three Stalin Prizes. *Publications:* The Theory of Superfluidity of Helium-II, 1941; On the Theory of the Intermedial State of Super-Conductors, 1943; (with E. M. Lifshitz) Course of Theoretical Physics (9 vols.), 1938-; numerous scientific papers and technical books. *Address:* The Institute of Physical Problems, Vorobjevskoe Shosse 2, Moscow, U.S.S.R. [*Died* 1 *April* 1968.

LANDIS, James McCauley; Hon. LL.D., Fouad University, Egypt; Lawyer; *b.* 25 Sept. 1899; *s.* of Henry M. and Emma S. Landis; *m.* 1st, 1927, Stella G. McGehee; two *d.*; 2nd, 1948, Dorothy P. Brown. *Educ.:* Princeton (A.B.); Harvard (LL.B. and S.J.D.). Sec. to Mr. Justice Brandeis (U.S. Sup. Court), 1924-25; Asst. Prof. of Law at Harvard, 1925-27; Professor of Legislation at Harvard, 1927-33; Member, Federal Trade Commission, 1933-34; Member, Securities Exchange Commission, 1934-37 (Chairman, 1935-37); Member, President's Fact Finding Board, National Railway Strike, 1937; Special Examiner, Dept. Labor, 1939; Consultant War Dept., 1940; Director, U.S. Office of Civilian Defense, 1941-43; Minister, American Director of Economic Operations to the Middle East, 1943-45. Dean of Law, Harvard University, 1937-46; Chm., U.S. Civil Aeronautics Bd., 1946-47; Chm., President's Special Bd. on Air Safety, 1947. Supervisor, Town of Harrison (N.Y.), 1955-57; Special Asst. to President Kennedy, 1961; Chief, Amer. Delegn. to negotiate Commercial Air Treaty with U.S.S.R., 1961. Medal for Merit (U.S.), 1946; Order of Leopold (Belgium), 1959. *Publications:* The Business of the Supreme Court of the United States (with Felix Frankfurter), 1928; Cases on Labor Law, 1932, Rev. Ed. 1942; The Administrative Process, 1938; The Surrender of King Leopold (with Joseph P. Kennedy), 1950. *Recreation:* bridge. *Address:* Griswold Road, Rye, N.Y., U.S.A. *Clubs:* Harvard, Westchester Country (New York); Harvard (Boston). [*Died* 30 *July* 1964.

LANDON, Col. James William Bainbridge, C.B.E. 1944; D.S.O. 1918; F.L.A.S.; *b.* 29 April 1890; *s.* of late Major-General Sir F. W. B. Landon, K.C.M.G., C.B.; *m.* 1918, Lilian Augusta Taylor (*d.* 1956); one *s.* one *d.* *Educ.:* Rossall School. Yorks Mtd. Brigade T. & S. Column, 2nd Lt. 1908; served European War, 1914-18, France, Egypt and Syria, Lt.-Col. comdg. 4th Cav. Divl. Train, R.A.S.C. (D.S.O.). Lt.-Col. T.A.R.O. R.A.S.C. 1919; Sector Commander Rotherham W.R.H.G. (C.B.E.). *Recreations:* cricket, golf, tennis, shooting and fishing. *Address:* The Granary, Woods Hill, West Chiltington, Nr. Pulborough, Sussex. *T.:* W. Chiltington 2364. *Clubs:* Lansdowne, M.C.C. [*Died* 2 *March* 1966.

LANDON, Philip Aislabie, M.C.; M.A.; Emeritus Fell., Trin. Coll., Oxford; formerly Univ. Reader in Criminal Law and the Law of Evidence; Barrister-at-law; Hon. Bencher of the Inner Temple; *b.* Exeter, 5 Dec. 1888; 3rd *s.* of late Col. A. Landon and Jane Mary, *d.* of Edward Giffard. *Educ.:* Kelly College; Brasenose College, Oxford (1st Lit. Hum. 1910; Diploma in Education with distinction, 1911). Served European War, Essex Regt., Staff Capt., D.A.Q.M.G. (M.C., despatches); Assistant Principal in Board of Education, 1919; Chairman of Examiners in Final Honour School of Jurisprudence, Oxford University, 1927, 1928, 1939 and 1946; Examiner in Cambridge Tripos, 1930-31 and 1946-47 and in Cambridge LL.B., 1949 and 1950; Rhodes Travelling Fellow, 1934; Member Governing Bodies of Malvern Coll., King's School, Canterbury, St. Edward's School, Kelly College, Tavistock; a Director of the French Hospital. Formerly Lecturer to Law Society and Imperial Defence College; Member of the Hebdomadal Council, 1931-49; Bursar, Trinity College, 1921-51; Chairman of Domestic Bursars' Committee, 1933-51. President Soc. of Public Teachers of Law, 1951-52. *Publications:* Pease and Landon, Contracts; Stephen's Commentaries, 17th and 18th edns.; Pollock, Torts, 14th and 15th edns.; articles in legal periodicals. *Recreations:* conversation and conservation. *Address:* Trinity College, Oxford. *T.:* 48405. *Club:* Vincent's (Oxford) (formerly Hon. Treasurer). [*Died* 12 *Oct.* 1961.

LANDOWSKI, Paul; Croix de Guerre (1914-18); Commandeur de la Légion d'Honneur; sculptor; *b.* 1 June 1875; *s.* of Dr. Landowski; *g. s.* of the violinist and composer, Henry Vieuxtemps; *m.* 1913, Mdlle. Cruppi; one *s.* one *d.* Membre de l'Institut de France; Membre de l'Académie des Beaux-Arts. Hon. Director, École Supérieure des Beaux Arts, Paris; Hon. Director, French Academy, Rome. *Principal works:* David Combattant, Fils de Cain, Hymne à l'Aurore, Cantique des Cantiques, Sainte Geneviève (Paris); Tombeau du Maréchal Foch aux Invalides; Reformation Monument in Geneva; Statue of Lord Haig at Montreuil-sur-mer; Monument aux Morts de la Ville d'Alger; Tomb of Sun Yat Sen, Nanking, China; the Christ of Mount Corcovado, Rio de Janeiro; Porte de Bronze de la nouvelle Faculté de Médecine, Paris, etc. Premier Grand Prix de Rome, 1900. Comdr., Crown of Oak, Luxembourg; Comdr., Order of St. James of Portugal, etc. *Publication:* Peut-on enseigner les Beaux-Arts?; various articles. *Address:* 12 rue Max Blondat, Boulogne, Seine, France. *T.:* Molitor 33.21. [*Died* 2 *April* 1961.

LANE, Sir Allen (Lane Williams), Kt. 1952; Hon. M.A. (Bristol); Hon. LL.D. (Manchester and Birmingham); Hon. D.Litt. (Oxon and Reading); Hon. Fellow: Royal College of Art; Royal Institute of British Architects; Chairman, Penguin Publishing Co.; Chairman, Allen Lane The Penguin Press; Director: Penguin Books Inc. (America); Penguin Books Australia Ltd.; City of London Board, Royal Insurance Co. Ltd.; *b.* 21 Sept. 1902; *e. s.* of late Allen Williams Lane, Bristol; *m.* 1941, Lettice, *e. d.* of late Sir Charles Orr, K.C.M.G.; three *d. Educ.:* Bristol Grammar School. Apprenticed to John Lane at The Bodley Head in 1919; resigned 1936 and founded Penguin Books Ltd. the same year. *Recreations:* farming, travel. *Address:* Priory Farm, Beech Hill, Berks.; Penguin Books, Harmondsworth, Middx. *T.:* Skyport 1984. *Club:* Garrick. [*Died* 7 *July* 1970.

LANE, Major-General Sir Charles (Reginald Cambridge), K.C.I.E., *cr.* 1946; C.B 1943; C.B.E 1943; M.C. 1917; *b.* 4 December 1890; *s.* of late F. G. A. Lane, J.P., of Bloxworth House and Poxwell, Dorset; *m.* 1st, 1915, Margaret (marriage dissolved 1948; she *d.* 1955), *d.* of late Col. H. James, C.B.; two *d.*; 2nd, 1948, Alison, *widow* of Squadron Leader H. A. MacBean, R.A.F. *Educ.:* Bradfield College, Berks; Royal Military College, Sandhurst. 2nd Lt., 1910; joined 19th Lancers. Indian Army, 1911; Ind. Ex. Force, France. 1914-18, Egypt, Palestine, Syria, 1918-19 (M.C., despatches twice, Bt. Major); p.s.c. Camberley, 1923; held various staff appts., India, 1924-34; Bt. Lt.-Col., 1932; commanded 20th Lancers, 1936-38; Col. 1939; Brig. 1940; Acting Maj.-Gen., 1941; Maj.-Gen., 1942; overseas in M.E.F. and Paiforce, 1942-43, as Deputy Adjt. and Q.M.G., 10th Army, and D.Q.M.G. Bases and L. of C. Paiforce; Commander 303 L. of C. Area in India Command, 1943; Deputy Principal Administrative Officer, H.Q. S.A.C.S.E.A., 1943-44; Representative in India of Supreme Allied Commander, S.E. Asia, 1944-46; retired from Army, 1947. Principal Regional Officer, Ministry of Health, 1947-57, retd. Knight, Polonia Restituta, 1945; Commander, Legion of Merit, U.S., 1946. *Address:* 3 Neville Terrace, S.W.7. *Club:* United Service. [*Died* 15 *Sept.* 1964.

LANE, Sir Charlton (Adelbert Gustavus), Kt., *cr.* 1945; *b.* 10 Feb. 1890; *s.* of Rev. C. G. and Adela Lane, Little Gaddesden, Herts; *m.* 1920, Millicent, *d.* of Lt.-Gen. Sir Henry Newdigate, K.C.B.; one *s.* one *d. Educ.:* Winchester; University College, Oxford. Administration, East Africa Protectorate, 1913; Zanzibar, 1923; Magistrate, Tanganyika, 1925; Kenya, 1928; Puisne Judge, Sierra Leone, 1939; Gold Coast, 1942; Chief Justice, Mauritius, 1943-49; retd., 1949. Called to Bar, Gray's Inn, 1928. *Address:* Broad Close, Church Enstone, Oxon. *Club:* East India and Sports. [*Died* 14 *Sept.* 1962.

LANE, Edward Arthur, M.A.; Keeper of the Department of Ceramics, Victoria and Albert Museum since 1950; *b.* 15 Dec. 1909; *s.* of late Rev. E. A. Lane, M.A., and Mary Elizabeth Luby; *m.* 1936, Angela Elizabeth, *d.* of late C. C. Lowis; one *d. Educ.:* St. John's School, Leatherhead; St. John's College, Cambridge (scholar). 1st Class in Classical Tripos; Scholar, British School at Athens, excavations in Greece, 1932-34. Assistant-Keeper, Victoria and Albert Museum, 1934; archæological excavations with Sir Leonard Woolley in Syria, 1937; R.A.F. Intelligence, Air Ministry, 1939-45; Visiting Professor, Farouk I University, Alexandria, 1949. *Publications:* Guide to the collection of tiles, V. & A. Museum, 1939 and 1960; Early Islamic Pottery, 1947; French Faïence, 1948; Greek Pottery, 1948, new edn. 1971 (posthumous); Style in Pottery, 1948; Italian Porcelain, 1954; Later Islamic Pottery, 1957, 2nd edn. 1971 (posthumous); English Porcelain Figures of the 18th Century, 1961. Periodical articles on art and archæology. *Address:* 19 Selwood Terrace, S.W.7. *T.:* Kensington 0768. [*Died* 7 *March* 1963.

LANE, Brigadier Frank, C.B.E. 1946; *b.* 1888; *m.* 1918; one *s.* one *d.* Joined R.E., 1915; served European War, 1914-18, overseas, 1915-19 (despatches twice). Director Army Postal Services, 1944-50; Regional Director, N.W. Region G.P.O., 1946-50. Order of Aviz, Portugal, 1918; Médaille de la Reconnaissance (France), 1947. *Address:* 64 School Road, Moseley, Birmingham 13. *T.:* Birmingham South 3358. [*Died* 4 *March* 1963.

LANE POOLE, Charles Edward; *see* Addenda: II.

LANG, Patrick Keith, C.B.E. 1920; *b.* 20 June 1863; *e. s.* of late Very Rev. J. Marshall Lang, C.V.O., D.D., LL.D., Principal of Aberdeen Univ.; *m.* Elizabeth Gentle Stevenson (*d.* 1950), Ingliston, Midlothian; one *s.* two *d. Educ.:* Glasgow Univ. Banker in India, Transvaal, Constantinople, and Egypt, 1881-1904; contested (U.) Bridgeton Division of Glasgow, 1909-10; Commissioner (unpaid) for C. Army Recreation Huts, Second Army, Western Front, 1916-17; served Ministries of Reconstruction and Munitions (Controller, unpaid), 1917-19. *Address:* Little Court, Merrow, near Guildford. *Club:* Oriental. [*Died* 30 *Sept.* 1961.

LANG, Robert Buntin, O.B.E. 1947; retired as Under Secretary, Ministry of Transport (1957-66); *b.* 15 Aug. 1906; *s.* of late Joseph Lang, Inverkip, Renfrewshire; *m.* 1944, Clare Church; no *c. Educ.:* Greenock High School; Glasgow University. Chartered Accountant (C.A.), 1930. Officer of Order of Orange-Nassau (Netherlands), 1947. *Address:* 37 Higher Green, Ewell, Epsom, Surrey. [*Died* 12 *March* 1970.

LANG, William Dickson, F.R.S. 1929; M.A., Sc.D. (Camb.); F.G.S., F.Z.S.; *b.* 1878; 2nd *s.* of late Edward Tickell Lang and Hebe, *d.* of John Venn Prior; *m.* 1908, Georgiana Catherine, *d.* of late Capt. Manley Charles Matthew Dixon, 8th The King's (Liverpool Regt); one *s.* one *d. Educ.:* Christ's Hospital; Harrow; Pembroke College, Cambridge (Exhibitioner and Scholar); 1st Class Nat. Sc. Tripos, 1901, Part I, 2nd Class, Part II, 1902; B.A. 1901; M.A. 1903; Sc.D. 1919; entered Geological Department of the British Museum, 1902; Assistant-Keeper, 1921; Deputy-Keeper, 1927; Keeper, 1928-38; Council of Geological Society, 1923-26; a Lyell Medal, Geological Society, 1928. *Publications:* British Museum Catalogue of Cretaceous Bryozoa, vols. iii. and iv. (1921-22); Handbook of British Mosquitoes, published by the Trustees of the British Museum, 1920; various papers in scientific journals on fossil Polyzoa and Corals, Recent Insects, philosophical biology, and the geology of the neighbourhood of Charmouth, Dorset. *Recreations:* Field Natural History, especially that of S.W. Dorset; gardening, etc. *Address:* Lias Lea, Charmouth, Bridport, Dorset. [*Died* 7 *March* 1966.

LANGBRIDGE, Rosamond Grant; *b.* Glen Alla, Co. Donegal; 2nd *d.* of late Rev. F. Langbridge, M.A., Canon of Limerick; *m.* J. S. Fletcher (*d.* 1935); one *s. Publica-*

tions: The Flame and the Flood; The Ambush of Young Days; The Third Experiment; The Stars Beyond; Imperial Richenda; The Single Eye; The Land of the Ever Young; The Golden Egg; The Psychology of Charlotte Brontë; The Green Banks of Shannon; The White Moth and Other Poems, 1932; contributor to the Manchester Guardian, Saturday Westminster, etc. Author of The Spell, produced by Sir John Martin Harvey at the Adelphi Theatre. *Recreations:* flowers, places, people. *Address:* Minerva, High St., W. Mersea, Essex. *T.:* Mersea 2123. [*Died* 2 *July* 1964.

LANGFORD, Caroline; *see* Hatchard, Caroline.

LANGFORD-JAMES, Reginald Hugh Lloyd; Director of Marine Insurance Company Ltd.; *b.* 1876; 2nd *s.* of Captain Francis Lloyd Langford-James, Tullaha, Co. Cork and Plas yn Penllech, Caernarvonshire; *m.* 1905, Amy Blanche (*d.* 1938), *d.* of Rev. John Clough, Rector of Wilford, Notts.; no *c.* *Educ.:* Oswestry School. Banking firm of I. and I. C. Wright and Co. Nottingham, 1893-98; Tea planting in Assam, 1898-1902; on Calcutta staff of James Finlay and Co. Ltd., 1902-23 (Manager 1920-23); Director Bank of Bengal (subsequently Imperial Bank of India); Member Bengal Legislative Council; Member of Committee, Bengal Chamber of Commerce; Chairman, Calcutta Hospital Nurses Institution; London Manager of James Finlay and Co. Ltd., 1923 (Chairman 1936-45); Chairman of National Bank of India Ltd., 1937-46. *Recreations:* shooting, fishing, etc. *Address:* Brynallt, Ellesmere, Shropshire. *T.:* Ellesmere 20. *Clubs:* Oriental, Bengal, Royal Calcutta Turf (Calcutta). [*Died* 15 *June* 1961.

LANGLEY, Commander Arthur Sydney, C.M.G. 1919; formerly Second Master and Senior Science Master, King Edward's School, Birmingham; retired, Aug. 1945; *b.* 1881. *Educ.:* Downing College, Cambridge (Scholar); M.A. In charge of Royal Naval Experimental Station, Stratford, during European War (C.M.G.). *Address:* 17 Devonshire Road, Hastings, Sussex. [*Died* 30 *March* 1964.

LANGLEY, Sir Carleton George, Kt., *cr.* 1946; Q.C., Leeward Islands, 1935 (retd.); A Commissioner of the Admiralty, Probate and Divorce Division, Royal Courts of Justice, since 1953; *b.* 21 May 1885; *er. s.* of late George Langley, Shepton Mallet, Som.; *m. d.* of late W. H. Lockett; one *d.* *Educ.:* City of London School. Called to Bar, Middle Temple, 1913; Military service Malta, France and Ireland, 1914-21, Captain 2nd Bn. The London Regt.; private practice Lincolns Inn and Bahama Islands, 1921-31; Attorney-General Leeward Islands, 1931-37; dual Appt. Acting Colonial Secretary and Attorney-General, 1934-5-6; Administrator Antigua, 1935-36; 2nd Puisne Judge, British Guiana, 1937-40; Chief Justice British Honduras, 1940-48. *Address:* 1 Plowden Buildings, Middle Temple Lane, Temple, E.C.4. *T.:* City 3537. *Clubs:* National, Royal Commonwealth Society. [*Died* 11 *Nov.* 1963.

LANGLEY, Very Rev. Henry Thomas, M.A.; *b.* The Rectory, Windsor, N.S.W., 30 Mar. 1877; 6th *c.* of late Rt. Rev. Henry A. Langley, First Bishop of Bendigo; *m.* 1901, Ethel Maud, *d.* of late C. I. Du Ve of Rosedale, Gippsland; four *s.* one *d.* *Educ.:* Caulfield Grammar School; graduated at Melbourne Univ. from Trinity College with honours in Logic and Philosophy. Curate of St. Paul's, Sale; Minister of Morwell, 1900; of Yarram, 1902; Curate of St. Clement's, Marrickville, Sydney, 1905; St. Phillip's, Sydney, 1906; Rector of Traralgon, Gippsland, 1907; Vicar of St. Mary's, Caulfield, 1911-42; Dean of St. Paul's Cathedral, Melbourne, 1942-47; retired, 1947. Canon of St. Paul's Cathedral, 1918; Examining Chaplain to the Bishops of Gippsland and Bendigo, 1911-17; Chap. to Bishop of Bendigo, 1917; Founder of Gen. Board of Religious Educ. for Ch. Eng. in Australia; Chm. Council for Christian Educ. in Schools (Vic.). *Recreations:* excursions into the country, visiting clergy and church organisations. *Address:* 19 Oulton St., Caulfield, Victoria, Australia. [*Died* 28 *Nov.* 1968.

LANGLEY, William Kenneth Macaulay, C.B.E. 1941 (O.B.E. 1937); *b.* 12 Jan. 1883; *s.* of Rev. William Langley, Narborough, Leicestershire, and Mary Heyrick Macaulay; *m.* 1937, May Penstone; one *s.* by former marriage. *Educ.:* Bromsgrove. Member, Madras Legislative Assembly (formerly Council), 1932-41, representing the Planting constituency; Chairman, Calicut Chamber of Commerce, 1926-44; Deputy President, Associated Chambers of Commerce of India, 1937; Chairman, Madras Branch European Association, 1936 and 1937; Vice-President, European Association, 1938-39; Deputy President, Employers' Federation of India, 1939. *Recreations:* reading, watching cricket. *Address:* c/o Lloyds Bank, Leamington Spa. *Clubs:* East India and Sports, M.C.C.; Madras (Madras). [*Died* 9 *April* 1965.

LANGLEY-TAYLOR, Sir George, Kt. 1964; F.R.I.B.A. (Dis. T.P.), F.R.I.C.S. (Forestry Dip.), F.L.A.S., M.T.P.I., F.R.S.H., F.R.S.A., F.R.G.S.; *b.* 26 July 1888; *y. s.* of Samuel and Mathilda Taylor, Bristol; *m.* Phyllis, *o. d.* of Mary Viner Allen. *Educ.:* Bristol Grammar School, College of Estate Management and privately. Served in Royal Horse Artillery, 1915-18; Captain in Home Guard, 1940-45; Member of St. Paul's Watch, 1943-45. Council for the Preservation of Rural England: Member, National Executive Committee, 1933- (Vice-Chm., 1944-57; Chm., 1957-68, Vice-Pres., 1968); Hon. Secretary, Bucks. Branch, 1933-46; Founder, Penn Country Branch. Founded Disraelian Soc. to enable Hughenden Manor and contents to be handed to Nat. Trust. Chm., Greater London Green Belt Coun.; One-time Chairman: Berks., Bucks. and Oxon. Architectural Soc.; Berks., Bucks. and Oxon. Branches, Royal Instn. of Chartered Surveyors and Land Agents Soc.; Hon. Sec., Nat. Playing Fields Assoc., Bucks. Branch, 1933-46; Vice-Pres., Nat. House Builders Registration Coun., 1957- (Chm., 1955-57). Member: Min. of Transport Adv. Cttee. on the Landscape Treatment of Trunk Roads; Exec. Cttee. and Hon. Architect to Alexandra Day; Exec. Cttee., London Soc., 1952-; Exec. Cttee. Soc. for Protection of Ancient Buildings, 1966-; New Forest Cttee., 1946-47; Forest of Dean Cttee., 1955-58. A Verderer of the New Forest, 1949-. Gov. and Chm., Harts Leap Children's Convalescent Home, Camberley. *Recreations:* the preservation of rural England; the ballet; travel. *Address:* 126 Gloucester Ct., Kew, Sy. *T.:* Richmond 1945. *Clubs:* Travellers', Farmers'; Kildare Street (Dublin). [*Died* 6 *Nov.* 1968.

LANGLOIS, Most Rev. Mgr. J. Alfred, D.D.; Bishop of Valleyfield since 1926; *b.* St. Claire, Dorchester, P.Q., 4 Sep. 1876. *Educ.:* St. Therese's Seminary; Quebec Laval University. Ordained, 1902; studied in Gregorian University in Rome, 1906-7; Doctor and Member of the Academy of St. Thomas Aquinas, Rome; Louvain University, 1907-8; Professor at the Laval University, theological course; Parish priest, 1917; founded the Parish of the Sacred Heart, Quebec, 1917-21; Rector of the Grand Seminary, Quebec, 1921-24; former Titular Bishop of Titopolis, 1924; Auxiliary to Cardinal Begin, 1924-25; and Administrator under

Archbishop P. E. Roy, 1925-26. *Address* Valleyfield, P.Q., Canada.
[*Died* 22 *Sept.* 1966.

LANGMAID, Brigadier Thomas John Robert, C.V.O. 1937; M.C. *b.* 7 Nov. 1887. *Educ.:* R.M.C. Sandhurst. Entered R.A.S.C. 1908; Capt., 1914; Major, 1926; Lt.-Col., 1934; Col., 1938; served European War, 1914-19 (despatches twice, M.C.); Assistant Director of Military Transport, 1938; retired pay, 1944. *Club:* United Service. [*Died* 20 *Dec.* 1965.

LANGMEAD, Frederick, M.D., F.R.C.P.; Professor of Medicine, University of London, retd.; Consulting Physician, St. Mary's Hospital, Paddington; *b.* Bovey Tracey, 1879; *y. s.* of late William Langmead of Climping, Sx.; *m.* 1913, Olive (*d.* 1956), *y. d.* of late Rev. T. T. Gray, Vice-Provost, Trinity College, Dublin; no *c.* *Educ.:* Cranleigh School; St. Mary's Hospital; M.D. London, 1904; F.R.C.P., 1913. Physician St. Mary's Hospital and Director of the Medical Unit, 1922-39, Physician in charge of Children's Department, St. Mary's Hospital, 1923-39; Physician to out-patients, The Hospital for Sick Children, Great Ormond Street, 1912-22; Assistant Physician Paddington Green Children's Hospital, 1906 - 11; Seamen's Hospital, Greenwich, 1908 - 13; Assistant Physician Pathologist and Demonstrator on Pathology, Royal Free Hospital and London School of Medicine for Women, 1911 - 13; Medical Tutor and Lecturer on Pharmacology and Therapeutics, St. Mary's Hospital Medical School, 1919-20; Examiner in Medicine, Conjoint Board Royal Colleges of Physicians and Surgeons, 1926-30; Examiner in Medicine, Univ. of Lond., 1930-34: Examiner in Medicine, Univ. of Manchester, 1936-40; Censor, R.C. of P., 1940-41, Senior Censor, 1943-44; Rep., of R.C.P. on Central Midwives' Bd., 1946-50. Recognised teacher in the University of London in Medicine, Pathology and Diseases of Children; Major R.A.M.C., European War, serving in Macedonia, retiring with that rank. *Publications:* Part Editor—Savill's System of Clinical Medicine, 2nd edition, and of The Dictionary of Practical Medicine; Editor of the Section on Medical Diseases of Children, Medical Annual, 1913 - 25; Chapters (with Dr. Thomas Hunt) on Alcohol in the Practice of Medicine and on the Body's Resistance to Disease in A Review of the Effects of Alcohol on Man, 1931, and various other contributions to medical literature. *Recreations:* mountaineering, gardening. *Address:* Beggars Bush, Ashurst, Steyning, Sussex. *T.:* Steyning 3045. [*Died* 29 *Oct.* 1969

LANGTON, Joseph L., M.Sc., M.I.E.E.; Senior Lecturer in High Voltage Electrical Engineering, College of Technology, Manchester University, 1903-43; *b.* 5 Nov. 1877; *m.* 1932, Lillian Carr; one *s.* *Educ.:* Grammar School and Univ., Manchester. Honours School of Physics, B.Sc. 1898, M.Sc. 1901; Assistant Lecturer in Physics and Lecturer in Electrical Engineering, Hartley University College, Southampton, 1898 - 1901; Lecturer in Electrical Engineering Technical College, Hull, 1901-03; The Services Education Tutor, 1940-1957; Elec. Research Assoc. Cttees. on Porcelain Research; Consultant on High Voltage Porcelain Insulators; Improved design and operation of many line insulators, designer of Sea-fog types. *Publications:* Papers in the Journal of Institution of Electrical Engineers on Porcelain Line Insulators; Radio Interference from Line Insulators; Overhead Conductor Vibration; Joint Author, Electric Arc Lamps, Overhead Transmission of Power, Electricity in the Textile Industries, German Technological Readers, I and II. *Recreations:* travel, bridge. *Address:* 4 Longton Ave., Withington, Manchester 20. *T.:* Didsbury 2133. [*Died* 4 *Feb.* 1961.

LANGTON-JONES, Commander Ronald, D.S.O. 1916; F.R.A.S.; F.R.G.S.; Royal Navy (retired); Inspector, Imperial Light-House Service in the Bahamas, 1929-49, retired; *b.* 22 Oct. 1884; *m.* 1949, Hon. Annie Forrestdale Weir, *e. d.* of 1st Baron Inverforth, P.C. *Educ.:* Stonyhurst College. Served in H.M.S. Triumph off Tsingtau, China, 1914; Beachmaster Lancs. Landing, Dardanelles, 1915-16 (despatches five times, D.S.O., Legion of Honour, Croix de Guerre, War medal and ten clasps); retired list, 1928; a Younger Brother of Trinity House; Liveryman Hon. Company of Master Mariners; Freeman of the City of London, 1933; Hon. Member Institut Historique et Héraldique de France; Life Governor Royal Society of St. George; Member R.U.S.I. Soc. of Nautical Research, Royal Over-Seas League, West India Cttee., British Commonwealth Union; Hon. Mem. Bahamas Chamber of Commerce. Shared the first prize, open competition awarded by Honourable Company Master Mariners, London, with essay, The Evolution of the Ship, 1946. K.C.S.G.; Vice-President, Navy League, 1951. *Publications:* The Modern Lighthouse (Lecture), 1931; Silent Sentinels, 1944 (2nd edn. 1950). *Recreations:* walking and motoring. *Address:* Dun-na-mara, Ledaig, Connel, Argyll. *T.:* Ledaig 233. *Clubs:* Army and Navy, Royal Automobile. [*Died* 9 *Jan.* 1967.

LANYON, (George) Peter; Professional Artist since 1933; *b.* St. Ives, Cornwall, 8 Feb. 1918; *s.* of W. Herbert Lanyon and L. P. Vivian; *m.* 1946, S. M. St. John Browne; four *s.* two *d.* *Educ.:* St. Erbyn's, Penzance; Clifton College; Penzance and Euston Road Art Schools. R.A.F. service, 1940-46. Italian Govt. Schol., 1953; Critics' Prize, 1954; Marzotto Prize, 1963. Commissions: ceramic mural for Liverpool Univ. Civil Engineering Building and a stained glass construction for the Arts Council, 1960; mural for Stanley J. Seeger Jr. Collection, New Jersey; mural for Birmingham Univ., Eng. First one-man show, Lefevre Gallery, London, 1949. One-man shows at the Gimpel Fils Gallery, London, 1952, 1954, 1958, 1960, 1962. One-man shows: Catherine Viviano Gall., New York, 1957, 1959, 1961, 1964. Visiting Lectr., West of England College of Art, Bristol. Visiting Teacher, San Antonio Art Inst., Texas, U.S.A., 1963. Bard of Cornish Gorsedd (Marghak an Gwyns). His paintings have been shown in numerous group exhibitions, in Europe, U.S.A. and S. America. Work represented in: Tate Gall., London; Arts Council of Gt. Brit.; Melbourne Museum; and in many American and European public and private collections. Member, Newlyn Soc. of Artists. *Recreation:* glider pilot. *Address:* Little Park Owles, Carbis Bay, St. Ives, Cornwall. *T.:* St. Ives 480. *Club:* Cornish Gliding and Flying. [*Died* 31 *Aug.* 1964.

LARCOM, Sir Philip, 4th Bt., *cr.* 1868; *b.* 13 Sept. 1887; 2nd *s.* of 2nd Bt. and Jeanie, *e. d.* of Alex. Perceval, Temple House, Co. Sligo; *S.* brother, 1950; *m.* 1920, Aileen Monica Royde, *d.* of late Rev. A. G. Colbeck, Rector of Easton, Wickham Market; one *s.* one *d.* *Educ.:* Cheltenham College. Formerly Lieutenant R.N.V.R. *Heir:* *s.* Charles Christopher Royde, *b.* 11 Sept. 1926. *Address:* Bridge View Cottage, Blandford St. Mary, Dorset. [*Died* 19 *July* 1967.

LARGE, Stanley Dermott, D.S.O. 1918; M.C.; Colonel (late R.A.M.C.), retired; *b.* Larne, Ireland, 22 Oct. 1889; *s.* of W. H. Large; *m.* 1st, 1918, Violet Muriel Elise (*d.* 1929), *d.* of D. Cowan of Coulport House, Dunbartonshire; four *s.*; 2nd, 1933, Mollie (*d.* 1937), *er. d.* of late Col. P. S. Lelean, C.B., C.M.G.; one *s.*; 3rd, 1943, Constance Murison

Barnsley Shaw, M.B., B.S. London. *Educ.:* Royal High School, Edinburgh; College of Surgeons, Edin. L.D.S. 1911; L.R.C.P. and S., Edin., 1912; entered R.A.M.C., 1913; Captain, 1915; Acting Major, 1918; Acting Lieut.-Colonel, 1918; served in France throughout War, commanded 76th F.A., 2 Sept. 1918 to end of war (M.C., D.S.O., despatches twice); retired Jan. 1923, with rank of Lieut.-Col.; was specialist in dermatology, Poona. Served throughout War of 1939-45; France, 1939-40; Col. 1944; Commanded Rehabilitation Centre. *Publications:* Rehabilitation, 1943; Repatriation, 1944. *Recreation:* photography. *Address:* Crag, Lochgoilhead, Argyll.
[*Died* 2 *April* 1965.

LARKEN, Rear-Admiral Edmund Thomas, C.B. 1960; O.B.E. 1946; *b.* Bushey, Herts, 24 September 1907; *s.* of late Edmund John Monson Larken and Violet Marian Larken (*née* Senior); *m.* 1936, Eileen Margaret, *d.* of Dr. William Webb Shackleton; one *s.* *Educ.:* Oakley Hall, Cirencester; R.N. Coll., Dartmouth. Joined R.N. as Cadet, 1921; Midshipman, H.M.S Emperor of India, 1925; Lieut. 1930; specialised in Gunnery, 1933; Lieut.-Comdr. 1937; Commander 1943; Captain 1949; Rear-Admiral 1959. Served War of 1939-45; H.M.S. Ark Royal, 1940-41; Admiralty, Naval Ordnance Dept., 1942-43; Staff of C.-in-C. British Pacific Fleet, 1944-45. Imp. Defence College, 1954; Captain (D) 8th Destroyer Squadron, 1955-56; Director, Trade Division, Admiralty, 1957-58; Flag Officer, Admiralty Interview Boards, 1958-61; retired, 1961. *Address:* S/B Five Sisters, Saltern Wood Quay, Yarmouth, Isle of Wight. *Club:* Army and Navy.
[*Died* 22 *July* 1965.

LARKEN, Rev. Prebendary Hubert; *e. s.* of late Francis Roper Larken, The Cantilupe Chantry, Lincoln, solicitor; unmarried. *Educ.:* Aysgarth Preparatory and Charterhouse Schools; Magdalen Coll., Oxford (M.A.). Held various country livings in his native county, and more especially as Rector of Brocklesby, 1912-18, and Rector of Croyland Abbey, 1922-1925; Vicar of Honington, Grantham, 1929-31; Rector of Wilsford, 1931-33; Archdeacon of Lincoln, 1933-37; Sub-Dean of Lincoln, 1937-46. *Recreation:* model railway engineering. *Address:* The Small House, South Collingham, Newark-on-Trent, Notts.
[*Died* 6 *April* 1964.

LARKING, Captain Dennis Augustus Hugo, C.M.G. 1916; R.N. retd.; Member of Lloyd's; *b.* Jan. 1876; *s.* of late Col. Cuthbert Larking and late Lady Adela Hare, *d.* of 2nd Earl of Listowel; *m.* 2nd, Nina Bianca, *d.* of late Charles Allatini, of Italy. *Educ.:* Stubbington House, Fareham; H.M.S. Britannia. Entered Royal Navy, 1889; served in Mediterannean, West Indian, and China Stations; retired, 1907; Naval attaché, Rome, 1915-19; Naval Attaché, Balkans, 1939-41; Admiralty, 1941-45. Legion of Honour (France); Order of Olaf (Norway); Order of White Eagle (Yugo-Slavia); Orders of S.S. Maurice and Lazarus and Crown of Italy (Italy). *Address:* Chalet Rosemary, Chemin des Sables, Juan les Pins, France. *Club:* Royal Yacht Squadron (Cowes).
[*Died* 20 *April* 1970.

LARMINIE, Margaret Rivers (Mrs. M. R. Tragett); *b.* 6 Sept. 1885; *y. d.* of late Col. Edward Merry Larminie, R.E., and Laura Frances, *d* of Sir Frederick Pollock, Bt., Lord Chief Baron of the Exchequer Court; *m.* 1911, Robert Clayton Tragett (marr. diss. 1934; he *d.* 1961). Received into R.C. Church, 1949. Won All England Ladies' Badminton Singles Championship, 1911, '12, '28, etc.; represented England 15 times. *Publications:* *novels:* Search, 1922; Echo, 1923; Deep Meadows, 1924; Soames Green, 1925; Galatea, 1928; The Visiting Moon, 1932; Doctor Sam, 1933; Gory Knight (with Jane Langslow), 1937; also under name of Mrs. R. C. Tragett, Badminton for Beginners, 1926; contributed articles on Badminton, short stories and verses to the Press. *Address:* c/o Westminster Bank Ltd., 195 Earl's Court Rd., S.W.5.
[*Died* 31 *March* 1964.

LARMOR, Sir (John) Graham, Kt., *cr.* 1948; *b.* 1897; *s.* of John S. Larmor, Lisburn, N.I.; *m.* 1st, 1924, Gladys (*d.* 1960), *d.* of George Maughan, Newcastle upon Tyne; two *s.* one *d.*; 2nd, 1964, Barbara, *d.* of Major H. Dixon, Keighley, Yorks. *Educ.:* Campbell Coll., Belfast. Agent for Min. of Supply and Govt. Purchasing Depts. in N.I., 1939-46, in providing textile equipment for the Services; Member Northern Ireland Housing Trust, 1945-58. Vice-Chairman Central Council of Irish Linen Industry; Member: Northern Ireland Advisory Cttee. for Civil Aviation; Robson Departmental Cttee. on Coal Distribution Costs, 1956; Adv. Cttee. for Textile Educn. (N.I.); Pres., Belfast Chamber of Commerce, 1957-58; Mem. Export Council for Europe, 1961; Pres. N.I. Bd. of Inst. of Directors, 1961; Member Industrial Coal Consumers' Council, 1962; Chm., Central Council of Irish Linen Industry, 1966-. Chairman: The Ulster Weaving Co. Ltd., Belfast; James Murland Ltd.; Hursts Ltd.; Killyleagh Flax Spinning Co. Ltd., Co. Down, N.I.; The Old Bleach Linen Co. Ltd., Co. Antrim, N.I. *Address:* (Home) 723a Antrim Road, Belfast, N.I.; 47 Linfield Road, Belfast, 12, N.I. *Club:* Brooks's.
[*Died* 13 *Oct.* 1968.

LASCELLES, Sir Daniel William, K.C.M.G., *cr.* 1954 (C.M.G. 1946); *b.* 19 March 1902. *Educ.:* Royal Naval Colleges, Osborne and Dartmouth; Balliol College, Oxford. 3rd Secretary, Diplomatic Service, 1926; 2nd Secretary, 1931; 1st Secretary, 1937; acting Counsellor, 1943; Counsellor, British Embassy, Athens, 1945-47; Chargé d'affaires, Athens, 1946 and 1947; Foreign Office, May 1947-48; Ambassador to Ethiopia, 1949-51 (Minister, 1948-49); to Afghanistan, 1953-57; to Japan, 1957-59. *Address:* Valley House, Cley, Holt, Norfolk.
[*Died* 17 *Oct.* 1967.

LASKI, Neville Jonas, Q.C. 1930; retired as Judge of the Crown Court and Recorder of Liverpool (1956-63); Vice-President Anglo-Jewish Association; *b.* 18 December 1890; *e. s.* of late N. Laski, J.P.; *m.* 1914, Phina Emily, *e. d.* of late Dr. M. Gaster; two *s.* two *d.* *Educ.:* Manchester Grammar School; Clifton College; Corpus Christi College, Oxford, M.A. Beit Prize, 1912; Bencher, Inner Temple, 1938. Served with 6th Lancashire Fusiliers, Gallipoli, Sinai and France, retiring with rank of Captain. Formerly Chairman Manchester Victoria Memorial Jewish Hospital; President London Committee of Deputies of British Jews, 1933-40. Judge of Appeal of the Isle of Man, 1953-56; Recorder of Burnley, 1935-56; Mem. General Council of the Bar, 1950-56, Chm. Professional Conduct Cttee., 1952-56, Hon. Treasurer, 1955-56. Pres. Elders of the Spanish and Portuguese Jews Congregation, 1961-67. Hon. LL.D. Liverpool, 1957. *Publications:* Jewish Rights and Jewish Wrongs, 1939, etc. *Recreation:* walking. *Address:* 20 Vale Court, W.9. *T.:* Cunningham 6663.
[*Died* 24 *March* 1969.

LATHAM, 1st Baron, *cr.* 1942, of Hendon; **Charles Latham,** J.P., F.A.C.C.A., F.C.I.S.; Certified Accountant; Founder and Senior Partner Latham & Co., Certified Accountants; Lord Lieutenant of Middlesex, 1945-56; *b.* 26 December 1888; *s.* of George Latham and Sarah Mason; *m.* 1st, 1913, Maya Helen Allman (marriage dissolved); three *d.* (one *s.* decd.); 2nd, 1957, Mrs. Sylvia May Kennard. *Educ.:* Elementary school, Norwich. Member of Public Works Loan Board, 1930-46; Member of Economy ("May") Committee appointed by Chancellor of Exchequer in 1931; Member of London and Home Counties Joint Electricity Authority, 1928-1934; Former member of Hendon Urban District Council, and later Alderman of Borough of Hendon, 1926-34; three times Parliamentary Candidate (Labour), 1922-23-1924; Alderman of L.C.C., 1928-34; L.C.C. representative for South Hackney, 1934-46, Alderman, 1946-47; Chm. of Finance Cttee. of L.C.C., 1934-40; Leader of London County Council, 1940-47. Member, London and Home Counties Traffic Advisory Cttee., 1933-46; Mem., Board London Passenger Transport Board, 1935-47; Chairman of London Transport Executive, 1947-53; Founder Mem. Admin. Staff Coll., Henley, 1946-59. Mem. Standing Advisory Cttee. on Pay of Higher Civil Service, 1956-67. Chm. Finance Cttee., Metropolitan Water Board, 1957-. Member: Council of Europe, 1960-1962; Western European Union, 1960-1962. K.St.J. Officer, Legion of Honour. *Recreations:* riding, walking, golf. *Heir: g.s.* Dominic Charles Latham [*b.* 20 September 1954; *er. twin s.* of Hon. Francis Charles Allman Latham (*d.* 1959) and of Gabrielle, *d.* of Dr. S. M. O'Riordan]. *Address:* Walter House, 418 Strand, W.C.2. *T.:* 01-836 3613; 58 Montagu Square, W.1. *T.:* 01-723 9003. [*Died* 31 *March* 1970.

LATHAM, Hon. Sir Charles George, Kt. 1948; retired from Parliament, Western Australia, May 1960; Hon. Deputy Director of Recruiting from 1950; *b.* 26 January 1882; 4th *s.* of Thomas and Isabella Latham; *m.* 1902, Marie Louise Allworden (*decd.*); two *s.* *Educ.:* Frogham, England; Hay, New South Wales. M.L.A. for York, W. Australia, 1921-42; Member of Commonwealth Senate, 1942-43; elected to the Legislative Council of Western Australia as Member for East Province, December 1946; Leader, Country Party of W.A., 1930-42; Deputy Premier and Minister for Lands, Migration and Health, 1930-33; Leader of the Opposition, 1933-42; Deputy Director of Commonwealth Loans 1943-46; Minister for Agriculture, Western Australia, 1952; retired Feb. 1953. Represented Western Australian Branch of Empire Parliamentary Assoc. at Silver Jubilee of King George V. in London, 1935; rep. W.A. Second Austr. Area, Commonwealth Parliamentary Conference, 1953. President: Children's Protection Soc. Inc., 1939-; Save the Children Fund (W. A. Branch), 1948-; Legislative Council, 1958. J.P. for State of Western Australia. *Recreations:* reading and fishing. *Address:* 8 Braydon Rd., Attadale, Western Australia. *T.:* 30-2482.
[*Died* 26 *Aug.* 1968.

LATHAM, Rt. Hon. Sir John Greig, P.C. 1933; G.C.M.G., *cr.* 1935 (C.M.G. 1920); Q.C. 1922; *b.* Victoria, 25 Aug. 1877; *s.* of late Thomas Latham, of Ivanhoe; *m.* 1907, Eleanor Mary, C.B.E. 1954 (*d.* 1964), *d.* of Richard Tobin, of Northcote; one *s.* (and one *d.* decd.). *Educ.:* State Sch.; Scotch Coll.; Univ. of Melbourne (exhibitions and final schols. in Logic, Philosophy, and Law, Supreme Court prizeman, M.A., LL.M.). Formerly Lecturer in Logic and Philosophy and subsequently Law of Contracts and Personal Property at University of Melbourne; Member of Commonwealth Parliament (House of Representatives) for Kooyong, 1922-34; Attorney-General, Australia, 1925-29, and Minister of Industry, 1928-29; leader of Opposition, 1929-31; deputy leader, 1931-32; Deputy Prime Minister, Attorney-General, Minister for External Affairs, and Minister for Industry, 1932-34; retired 1934 and resumed practice at the bar; Hon. Bencher, Inner Temple, 1935; Chief Justice of Australia, 1935-52; Lieut.-Comm. R.A.N.R. during war; member of staff Australian Delegation to Peace Conference, Paris, 1919; Assistant Secretary to British Delegation; British Secretary to Allied Commission on Czecho-Slovak affairs, etc.; first President League of Nations Union; Representative of Australia at League of Nations and Imperial Conference, 1926; Representative of Australia at Disarmament and Reparations Conferences, 1932; Leader of Australian Eastern Mission to Dutch East Indies, China and Japan, 1934; Deputy Chancellor, University of Melbourne, 1935-39, Chancellor, 1939-41; President Australian Law Council, 1935; President First Australian Legal Convention, 1935; President Free Library Movement, Victoria, 1937-48; Minister for Australia to Japan; 1940-41; Pres.: Australian-Netherlands Soc, 1943-47; Amateur Athletic Assoc. (Victoria), 1944-57; Library Assoc. of Australia, 1949-53; Australian-American Assoc., Vic., 1951-, Old Scotch Collegians Assoc., 1911, 1953; Aust. Elizabethan Theatre Trust, 1954-61; Austr. Cttee. for Cultural Freedom, 1954-61; Vice-Pres. Australian Red Cross Soc., 1944-61; Dir. Humes, Ltd.; Dir., Fulbright Bd., 1952-61; Chm. Gowrie Scholarship Trust. Hon. LL.D. Melb. *Publications:* The Significance of the Peace Treaty to Australia, 1919; Australia and the British Commonwealth, 1929; articles on legal subjects and international affairs. *Address:* 261 Domain Rd., South Yarra, Vic., Australia. *Club;* Melbourne (Melbourne). [*Died* 25 *July* 1964.

LATHAM, Russell, C.B.E. 1948; M.C. and Bar, 1917; J.P.; Deputy Chairman James Latham Ltd.; Director: Nigerian Hardwood Co. Ltd.; Trebartha Estates Ltd.; *b.* 1896; *s.* of Edward Locks Latham, Theydon Towers, Theydon Bois, Essex; *m.* 1925, Elsa Mary Andrews, *o. d.* of Arthur William Andrews, M.B.E., 112 Mount St., W.1; two *s.* one *d.* *Educ.:* Felsted. Enlisted Army at age of 17; served European War, in France, 1914-19, with London Rifle Brigade and R.A.S.C. Mons Star, General Service and Victory Medals. Regular Army Reserve Officers, 1919-25; retired with rank of Captain. First Chairman Timber Development Association, 1934-36; Assistant Timber Controller, Ministry of Supply, 1939-43; Deputy Timber Controller Board of Trade, 1943-49; Hardwood Timber Adviser to Board of Trade, 1950-. A Representative of the United Kingdom to: Economic Commission for Europe (Timber Committee), 1947-49; Organisation for European Economic Co-operation (Timber), 1949. J.P. Hertfordshire and Middlesex. *Recreations:* fishing, shooting; aquatints and mezzotints. *Address:* North Gate House, Hadley Common, Herts. *Club:* Bath. [*Died* 7 *April* 1964.

LATOURETTE, Kenneth Scott; Sterling Professor of Missions and Oriental History, Yale University, 1949-53, Professor Emeritus since 1953; *b.* Oregon City, Oregon, 9 August 1884; *s.* of De Witt Clinton and Rhoda Ellen Scott Latourette; unmarried. *Educ.:* Linfield (B.S.); Yale (B.A., M.A., Ph.D.). Hon. D.D. Glasgow, Oxford, Wales; other hon. degrees in the U.S.A., Japan, Canada, Europe. Travelling Secretary, Student Volunteer Movement, 1909-10; Staff of Yale-in-China, 1910-17 (on health leave after 1912); Lecturer in History, 1914-15; Assistant Professor, 1915-16, Reed College; Acting Assoc. Professor, 1916-17, Professor, 1917-18, Chaplain, 1918-21, Denison Univ.; Prof. of Missions, Yale Univ., 1921-27; Prof. of Missions and Oriental History, Yale Univ. 1927-53, Emeritus 1953. Chairman Executive Committee, Student Volunteer Movement, 1924-26; President: American Baptist Foreign Mission Soc., 1946-47; Amer. Soc. of Church History,

1945; Amer. Historical Assoc., 1948; Far Eastern Assoc., 1954-55; Chairman: Japan International Christian Univ. Foundation, 1951-; Research Committee Internat. Missionary Council, 1932-52; Exec. Cttee. World's Student Christian Federation, 1922-1924; Trustee and Member China Med. Board, 1934-49, etc. Pres. Am. Baptist Convention, 1951, 1952. Order of the Jade, China. *Publications:* The Development of China, 1917, 6th ed., 1946; History of the Early Relations between the U.S. and China, 1917; The Development of Japan, 1918, 4th ed., 1938; The Christian Basis of World Democracy, 1919; A History of Christian Missions in China, 1929; The Chinese, their History and Culture, 2 vols., 1934, 4th ed. 1964; Missions Tomorrow, 1936; A History of the Expansion of Christianity, 7 vols., 1937-45; Toward a World Christian Fellowship, 1938; Anno Domini, 1940; The Unquenchable Light, 1941; The U.S. Moves Across the Pacific, 1946; A Short History of the Far East, 1946, 4th edn., 1964; The History of Japan, 1947, 2nd ed., 1957; editor, The Gospel the Church and the World, 1947; (with W. R. Hogg) Tomorrow is Here, 1948; The Future of Christianity, 1948 (published in U.S.A. under the title The Christian Outlook, 1948); The Emergence of a World Christian Community, 1949; The China that is to be, 1949; These Sought a Country, 1950; The American Record in the Far East, 1952; A History of Christianity 1953; The Christian World Mission in Our Day, 1954; A History of Modern China, 1954; (with others) History of the Ecumenical Movement, 1954; Challenge and Conformity, 1955; Introducing Buddhism, 1955; World Service, 1957; Desafio a los Protestantes, 1957; A History of Christianity in the 19th and 20th Centuries, 5 volumes, 1958-62; China, 1964; Christianity through the Ages, 1965; Beyond the Ranges, 1967. *Recreations:* gardening, walking, mountain climbing, and geology. *Address:* 409 Prospect Street, New Haven 11, Conn., U.S.A. *T.:* 73131-667. *Clubs:* Elihu Graduates, Elizabethan (New Haven); Yale (New York). [*Died* 26 *Dec.* 1968.

LATTER, Arthur Malcolm, Q.C. 1922; *b.* 27 June 1875; *s.* of late Rev. A. S. Latter, North Mymms Hertfordshire; *m.* 1922, Amelia Mary (Mollie), (*d.* 1957), *o. d.* of late Alexander Curtis Cope, Bd. of Agriculture. *Educ.:* Marlborough College; Balliol College, Oxford (Brackenbury Scholar). Called to Bar, 1900; Lecturer for the Law Society, 1904-12; a Bencher of Hon. Society of Lincoln's Inn, 1926, Treasurer, 1946; Deputy Chairman West Sussex Quarter Sessions, 1931; Chairman, 1952; retired 1953. *Address:* Nutbourne Place, Pulborough, Sussex. *T.:* West Chiltington 3112. [*Died* 22 *Aug.* 1961.

LAUDERDALE, 16th Earl of, *cr.* 1624; **Rev. Alfred Sydney Frederick Maitland;** Baron Maitland, 1590; Viscount Lauderdale, 1616; Viscount Maitland, Baron Thirlestane and Boltoun, 1624; Bt. of Nova Scotia, 1672; *b.* 17 April 1904; *s.* of Rev. Hon. Sydney George William Maitland (2nd *s.* of 13th Earl), and Ella Frances, *d.* of Rev. James Richards; *S.* cousin 1953; *m.* 1st, 1938, Norah Mary (*d.* 1938), *d.* of William Henry La Touche; 2nd, 1940, Irene Alice May, *d.* of Rev. C. P. Shipton; no *c.* *Educ.:* Sidney Sussex College, Cambridge; 3rd Class Theological Tripos Part I, Sect. A, 1924, B.A.; 2nd Class Theological Tripos Part I, Sect. B, 1925, M.A. 1938. Cuddesdon College 1926. Deacon 1927, Priest 1928. Curate of Fenton, 1927-31; St. James, Wednesbury, 1931-32; All Saints, Sidley, 1932-37; Stoke-on-Trent, 1937-38; Curate-in-Charge, St. John, Heene, Diocese of Chichester, 1939-51; Curate in Charge of Conventional Dist. of St. John, West Worthing, 1951-53; Curate of All Saints, Woodham, Woking, Diocese of Guildford, 1953-1956; Rector of Catsfield, Sussex, 1957-60. *Heir:* b. Hon. Patrick F. Maitland (Master of Lauderdale). *Address:* St. John's, Lansdowne Road., Angmering, Sussex. *T.:* Rustington 2720. [*Died* 27 *Nov.* 1968.

LAUGHTON, Charles; actor; *b.* Scarborough, 1 July 1899; *s.* of Robert Laughton and Elizabeth Conlon; *m.* Elsa Lanchester; became an American citizen, 1950. *Educ.:* Stonyhurst; Royal Academy of Dramatic Art (gold medal). First appearance on stage, 1926; Mr. Prohack in Mr. Prohack, Court Theatre, 1927; Mr. Crispin in A Man with Red Hair, 1928; Poirot in Alibi, 1928; Harry Keegan and First Soldier in The Silver Tassie, 1929; Tony Perelli in On the Spot, 1930; William Marble in Payment Deferred, 1931; in the same part, Lyceum, New York, 1931; Old Vic Company, 1933. Produced and played in: Shaw's Don Juan in Hell and Major Barbara; Stephen Vincent Benet's John Brown's Body, and made many reading tours of the United States; produced and acted in, The Party, 1958; entered films 1932 and has appeared in, among others, Down River, The Sign of the Cross, The Private Life of Henry VIII., The Barretts of Wimpole Street, Ruggles of Red Gap, Les Miserables, Mutiny on the Bounty, Rembrandt, Vessel of Wrath, St. Martin's Lane, Jamaica Inn, Hunchback of Notre Dame, The Tuttles of Tahiti, The Man from Down Under, The Canterville Ghost, This Land is Mine, Captain Kidd, The Suspect, Because of Him, A Miracle can happen, The Big Clock, The Man on the Eiffel Tower, The Blue Veil, Full House, Young Bess, Salome, Hobson's Choice, Witness for the Prosecution, Under Ten Flags, Spartacus, Advise and Consent. Formed own film co., The Mayflower Pictures Corp., in partnership with Erich Pommer, 1937. *Publications:* (ed.) Tell Me A Story, 1957; (ed.) The Fabulous Country, 1962. *Address:* c/o M.C.A., 9370, Santa Monica Boulevard, Beverly Hills, California, U.S.A. [*Died* 15 *Dec.* 1962.

LAUGHTON, Very Rev. John George, C.M.G. 1948; Superintendent of Presbyterian Maori Missions; *b.* 2 Dec. 1891; *s.* of John Laughton and Mary Ann (*née* Shearer); *m.* 1921, Horiana Tekauru; two *s.* three *d.* *Educ.:* Otago University. Home Mission Service, 1913-18; joined Staff of Maori Mission, 1918; appointed Superintendent of Maori Missions, 1933; J.P. 1921; Moderator of General Assembly Presbyterian Church of N.Z., 1942; Chairman of Maori Bible Revision Committee, 1946. *Publications:* Maori Service Book of Presbyterian Church; translations of various works. *Address:* P.O. Box 72, Whakatane, N.Z. *T.A.* and *T.:* 318 Whakatane. [*Died* 3 *July* 1965.

LAURENCE, Admiral Sir Noel Frank, K.C.B., *cr.* 1938 (C.B. 1934); D.S.O. 1916; R.N.; *s.* of F. Laurence of Maidstone; *m.* 1917, Esme J. Coghlan White; two *s.* one *d.* Entered Navy, 1899; was in command of submarine E1; torpedoed two German battleships near Jutland, 1915 (despatches, D.S.O., bar); Commodore of the R.N. Barracks, Devonport, 1930-32; Naval A.D.C. to the King, 1932; Rear-Adm. (Submarines), H.M.S. Dolphin, 1932-34; Vice-Admiral Aircraft Carriers, 1936-37; Admiral Commanding Reserves, 1938-41; Chief Naval Representative at Ministry of Aircraft Production, 1941-43; retired from R.N., 1943. Russian Order of St. George, 4th cl.; Chevalier Legion of Honour; Russian Order of St. Vladimir, 4th cl.; Spanish Order of Naval Merit, 3rd cl. *Address:* Courtlands, Kingswood Firs, Hindhead, Surrey. [*Died* 26 *Jan.* 1970.

LAURIE, Brigadier Sir Percy Robert, K.C.V.O., *cr.* 1933; C.B.E. 1922; D.S.O.

1916; J.P.; one of H.M. Lieutenants for the City of London; *b.* 1880; *s.* of late Alfred Laurie, J.P., of Rockdale, Sevenoaks, Kent, and Devonshire Place, Eastbourne; *m.* Ethel Francis Lawson-Johnston, Addington Manor, Winslow, Bucks; one *s.* one *d.* *Educ.:* Harrow. Gazetted to Royal Scots Greys, 1902; Adjutant, 1909; Captain, 1911; Bt. Major, 1915; Lt.-Col. 1917; Brigadier, 1940; Local Major-General, 1942; A.D.C. to G.O.C. Southern Command, 1911; A.D.C. to Inspector-General the home forces, 1912; Military Secretary, 1913; Personal Assistant to Chief of Imperial General Staff, 1914; served European War, 1914-19 (despatches six times, D.S.O., Bt. Major); Deputy Assistant Commissioner Metropolitan Police, and Chief of the Mounted Branch, Scotland Yard, 1919-33; Assistant Comr. Metropolitan Police, 1933-36; retired, 1936; Assistant Chief Constable to War Dept. Constabulary in London, 1939 (civil appointment); re-employed and appointed Provost-Marshal, United Kingdom, 1940; retired Local Maj.-Gen. 1943. J.P. Home Counties, 1933; J.P. Wilts, 1939; Officer of the Order of St. John of Jerusalem; Order of Leopold; Commander of the Crown of Belgium; Commander of the Crown of Italy; Croix de Guerre, Français; Croix de Guerre, Belge; Mons Star; Lt. 3rd London Volunteer Rifle Corps, 1900; Master Merchant Taylors' Company, 1925-26; Master Saddlers' Coy., 1943-44; Member Grand Cttee., St. Thomas's Hosp., 1933; High Bailiff of Cricklade, 1937-47; Chairman, The North-West Wilts (Chippenham Div.) Conservative and Unionist Assoc., 1937-39; Land Tax and Income Tax Commissioner for County of Wilts, 1939-46; Wiltshire T.A. Assoc., 1939-46; Wiltshire County Welfare Officer, Army Cadet Force, 1944-46; Member St. Albans Diocesan Advisory Cttee., 1947. *Recreations:* hunting, polo, and shooting. *Address:* Wavendon Lodge, near Bletchley, Bucks. *T.:* Woburn Sands 3179. *Clubs:* Pilgrims, British Sportsman's, Royal Automobile. [*Died* 16 *Feb.* 1962.

LAURIE, Major-Gen. Rufus Henry, C.B. 1943; C.B.E. 1940; p.s.c. Camberley; *b.* 16 Sept. 1892; *m.* 1916, Dorothy, *d.* of Rev. T. H. Foulkes, M.A., Baldersby St James', Thirsk; one *d.* *Educ.:* Dover. Joined Royal Irish Rifles, 1912; Captain, 1916; served European War, 1914-18, Gallipoli, France, and Belgium; Staff of Mil. Gov., Cologne, 1918-19; Instructor R. Military College, Sandhurst, 1919-22; Staff College, Camberley, 1924-25; Staff Capt., 2nd Div., 1926; Staff Capt. N. China Spec. Force, 1927; G.S.O. 2 Southern Command, 1928-29; Bt. Maj. 1929; Maj., 1st Bn. R. Ulster Rifles, 1930; Bt. Lt.-Col. 1932; D.A.Q.M.G. War Office, 1932-33; G.S.O. 2 War Office, 1934-35; Lt.-Col. Commanding 2nd Bn. R. Ulster Rifles (Palestine), 1936-37; Col. A.A. and Q.M.G. 3rd Div., S. Comd., 1938 and War of 1939-45, France and Belgium, 1939-40; Brig. A.A. and Q.M.G. 3rd Corps, 1940-41; Major-Gen. 1941; M.G.A., S. Eastern Command, 1941-42; M.G.A., G.H.Q., Home Forces, 1942-43; M.G.A., 21 Army Group, 1943-44; G.O.C. Salisbury Plain District, 1944-47; retired, 1947. *Address:* Colston, 25 North Parade, Southwold, Suffolk. [*Died* 4 *Aug.* 1961.

LAVELLE, Rev. Canon Alexander Bannerman; Canon Residentiary and Precentor of Lichfield Cathedral since 1959; Examining Chaplain to the Bishop of Lichfield since 1960; *b.* 9 March 1899; *s.* of Alexander Lavelle and F. I. Lavelle, Belfast, North Ireland; *m.* 1933, Dr. Phyllis Anna Moore, Sheffield; two *s.* *Educ.:* Royal Belfast Academical Institution; Queen's University, Belfast (B.A.); Trinity College, Dublin (M.A., B.D.); Sheffield University (Ph.D.). Deacon 1924, Priest 1925, Liverpool; Assistant Curate, St. Paul, Prince's Park, Liverpool, 1924-26, Blundellsands, 1926-28; District Sec., British and Foreign Bible Society, S.E. Lancs. and E. Cheshire; Licensed to Preach, Diocese of Manchester, 1928-29; Vicar of Kimberworth, 1929-36; Rector of Darlaston, 1936-44; Vicar of Wednesbury, 1944-59; Rural Dean of Wednesbury, 1944-59. Prebendary of Gaia Major, 1956, of Bishop's Itchington, 1959. *Recreations:* reading and walking. *Address:* 9 The Close, Lichfield, Staffs. *T.:* Lichfield 2505. [*Died* 25 *Dec.* 1964.

LAVERY, Cecil; Hon. Mr. Justice Lavery; Judge of the Supreme Court of Ireland, 1950-66; *b.* 6 October 1894; *s.* of Patrick Lavery, Solicitor, Armagh, and Annie Rose Valleiy; *m.* 1927, Louisa Ormsby; two *s.* one *d.* *Educ.:* St. Vincent's College, Castleknock; University College, Dublin; National University of Ireland. LL.B. National University, 1916; called to Irish Bar, 1915; admitted member Senior Bar, 1927; Bencher King's Inns, 1932; Deputy Dail Eireann, Dublin County, 1935-38; Attorney-General for Ireland, 1948-1950; Senator, 1948-50. *Address:* Carrickbrennan, Monkstown, Co. Dublin. *Club:* Turf. [*Died* 16 *Dec.* 1967.

LAVIS, Rt. Rev. Sidney Warren, D.D.; Co-adjutor-Bishop of Capetown, 1931-Dec. 1957. *Educ.:* S. Boniface College, Warminster; S. Augustine's College, Canterbury. Deacon, 1898; Priest, 1899; Rector of S. Paul's, Capetown, 1905-28; Canon of S. George's Cathedral, Capetown, 1915; Archdeacon of the Cape, 1924; Dean of Capetown, 1928-32; Vicar-Gen. Dio. Capetown, 1930, 1934-35, 1938, 1948, 1955, 1957. B.D. Lambeth, 1926; Hon. Fellow S. Augustine's College, Canterbury, 1926; Hon. LL.D. Capetown Univ., 1951; D.D. Lambeth, 1958. *Publications:* pamphlets on housing, social conditions and the mixed race in South Africa. *Address:* 18 Burnside Road, Cape Town, S.A. [*Died July* 1965.

LAW, Henry Duncan Graves, C.I.E.; J.P. County of Kent; *b.* 13 Aug. 1883; *m.* 1st, 1910, Jean (*d.* 1956), *d.* of Peter Graham, R.A.; three *s.*; *m.* 2nd, 1958, Nancy, *yr. d.* of late Sir Henry Norbury and of Lady Norbury. *Educ.:* Westminster; Edinburgh University; Cambridge. Entered Indian Civil Service, 1906; Foreign and Political Department, 1912; H.M. Consul-General, Meshed, Persia, 1929-30; retired, 1932. *Address:* c/o Lloyds Bank, Tonbridge, Kent. [*Died* 28 *Jan.* 1964.

LAW, Ralph Hamilton; Under-Secretary, Department of Agriculture and Fisheries for Scotland since 1966; *b.* 18 Jan. 1915; 4th *s.* of John Law and Isabella Crombie Law; *m.* 1943, Nancy Murphie; one *s.* one *d.* *Educ.:* Perth Academy; Edinburgh University (M.A.); Christ Church, Oxford. Scottish Office, 1938. R.A.O.C., 1942-45. Principal, Scottish Home Department, 1946; Assistant Secretary, 1954; Under-Secretary, 1963. *Recreation:* walking. *Address:* 8 Dalrymple Crescent, Edinburgh 9. *T.:* Newington 6563. *Club:* Scottish Arts. [*Died* 11 *Nov.* 1967.

LAWRANCE, Major Sir Arthur Salisbury, K.C.M.G., *cr.* 1937 (C.M.G. 1931); K.B.E., *cr.* 1934; D.S.O. 1920; late Reserve of Officers; *b.* 1880; unmarried. *Educ.:* Reading; privately. Served South African War, 1900-2 (despatches, Queen's medal and three clasps, King's medal and two clasps); Somaliland, 1908-10 (despatches, medal and clasp); European War, 1914-15 (wounded, despatches, clasp); 1920 (despatches, D.S.O.); Secy. to the Government, British Somaliland, 1926-32; Commissioner and Commander-in-Chief British Somaliland Protectorate, 1932-35; Governor and Commander-in-Chief, 1935-39; British Red Cross representative, Lisbon, 1941-42; H.G.

(Intelligence Officer), 1943-45. *Club:* Victoria (Jersey, C.I.). [*Died* 12 *Jan.* 1965.

LAWRENCE; *see* Pethick-Lawrence.

LAWRENCE, 4th Baron, *cr.* 1869; **John Anthony Edward Lawrence,** Bt. 1858; *b.* 16 Oct. 1908; *s.* of 3rd Baron and Dorothy Helen, C.B.E. (*d* 1935), *d.* of 1st A. Pemberton-Hobson; *S.* father, 1947; *m.* 1st, 1936, Margaret Jean (marriage dissolved, 1947), *d.* of Arthur Downer, Rotherfield, Kent; one *s.*; 2nd, 1948, Joan Alice Mildred, *d.* of Major Arthur John Lewer, O.B.E., Norwood Green, Southall Middlesex. *Educ.:* Haileybury. *Heir: s.* David John Downer Lawrence; *b.* 4 Sept. 1937. [*Died* 8 *Oct.* 1968.

LAWRENCE, Albert; retired as Director: Pacific Steam Navigation Company; Royal Mail Agencies (Brazil) Ltd.; Royal Mail Lines Funds Trustees Ltd.; United Kingdom Mutual Steamship Assurance Association; United Kingdom Mutual War Risks Association; Member of Council, Chamber of Shipping; Chairman of United Kingdom/Brazil and River Plate Freight Conferences; Member of Institute of Transport; *b.* 3 Jan. 1893; *s.* of William Thomas Lawrence; *m.* 1921, Nora Charlotte Jolly (*d.* 1961). *Educ.:* St. Mary's School, Ware. Joined Royal Mail Steam Packet Co. (later named Royal Mail Lines, Ltd.) as junior clerk, 1909. Served European War, 1914-18, in Army, France and Balkans. Asst. Manager, Royal Mail Lines, Ltd., 1945; General Manager, 1946; Director, 1950; Managing Director, 1953-58, retired. *Recreations:* motoring, bowls and various sports. *Address:* 4 Little Crescent, Rottingdean, Sussex. *T.:* Rottingdean 4211. [*Died* 22 *Nov.* 1961.

LAWRENCE, Sir (Frederick) Geoffrey, Kt. 1963; Q.C.; Judge of the High Court, Queen's Bench Div., since 1965; *b.* 5 April 1902; *s.* of Frederick James Lawrence, Wrington, Nr. Bristol, Som.; *m.* 1941, Marjorie Avice, *d.* of late Charles Angelo Jones, Bodney Hall, Norfolk. *Educ.:* City of London Sch.; New Coll., Oxford. Barrister, Middle Temple, 1930; K.C. 1950; Bencher, Middle Temple, 1958. Mem. of Royal Commn. on Marriage and Divorce, 1951. Recorder of Tenterden, Kent, 1948-51; Recorder of Canterbury, 1952-62; Chairman, National Incomes Commission, 1962-65. Chm. of Gen. Council of the Bar, 1960-62. Chm., Q.S., W. Sussex, 1953. D.L. Sussex, 1964. *Address:* Royal Courts of Justice, Strand, W.C.2; Kents Farm, Hurstpierpoint, Sussex. *Clubs:* Athenæum, Brooks's. [*Died* 3 *Feb.* 1967.

LAWRENCE, Sir Henry Eustace Waldemar, 5th Bt., *cr.* 1858; *b.* 10 July 1905; *s.* of Sir Alexander Waldemar Lawrence, 4th Bt., and Anne Elizabeth Le Poer (*d.* 1950), *o. c.* of H. Le Poer Wynne; *S.* father, 1939. *Heir: b.* John Waldemar Lawrence [*b.* 27 May 1907; *m.* 1948, Jacynth Donaldson-Hudson, *d.* of late Rev. Francis George Ellerton]. *Address:* Brockham End, Bath. [*Died* 29 *Dec.* 1967.

LAWRENCE, Margery (Mrs. Arthur Towle); novelist, journalist and short-story writer; *b.* Shropshire; *d.* of Richard John Lawrence, barrister of the Inner Temple, and Grace, *d.* of Henry Banks, Tettenhall; *m.* Arthur E. Towle, C.B.E. (*d.* 1948); no *c.* *Educ.:* privately, at home and abroad. Published book of poems at 16; Art Schools in Birmingham, London, and Paris. *Publications:* Miss Brandt, Adventuress; Red Heels; Nights of the Round Table (short stories); Bohemian Glass (banned at first, subsequently great hit); Drums of Youth; Snapdragon (short stories); The Madonna of Seven Moons; The Terraces of Night (short stories); Silken Sarah; Madam Holle; The Crooked Smile; Overture to Life; The Bridge of Wonder; Step Light Lady; Ferry over Jordan; The Gilded Jar; Fourteen to Forty-Eight (poems); The Rent in the Veil (novel); Emma of Alkistan; Evil Harvest; Daughter of the Nile; Spanish Interlude; Master of Shadows (short stories); The Gate of Yesterday (novel); contributing to English and American papers. *Recreations:* travel, music, books, theatre; sailing, motoring, fine embroidery, singing and piano-playing. *Address:* 25 Riven Court, Inverness Terrace, Bayswater, W.2. *T.:* 01-229 0920. *Clubs:* P.E.N., Arts Theatre. [*Died* 13 *Nov.* 1969.

LAWRENCE, Robert Daniel, M.A., M.D., F.R.C.P; Consulting Physician, Diabetic Clinic, King's College Hospital, London; *b.* 18 Nov. 1892; 2nd *s.* of Thomas and Margaret Lawrence; *m.* 1928, Anne (*d.* 1964), *o. d.* of T. Batson, M.A., Oxon; three *s.* *Educ.:* Aberdeen Gram. School and University. Gold medallist in anatomy, surgery, and medicine; bio-chemist, King's Coll. Hosp., 1924-31; Specialist in Diabetes; First Pres. Internat. Diabetes Federation; F.R.Soc. Med. (formerly Pres Endocrine and Experimental Medicine Sections); Mem. Harveian, Physiological and Bio-chemical Societies; Banting Medallist, 1946; Fothergillian Gold Medal, 1956. Capt., R.A.M.C. (S.R.) 1914-19. Hon. LL.D. (Toronto), 1964. *Publications:* The Diabetic Life, 17th edition, 1965, trans. several langs.; Happiness and Our Instincts, 1947; Clinical Medicine, 1954; numerous articles on insulin and diabetes in medical journals. *Recreations:* tennis, golf, fishing, music. *Address:* 7 Sheffield Terrace, W.8. [*Died* 27 *Aug.* 1968.

LAWS, Samuel Charles, O.B.E. 1945; Principal, Northampton Polytechnic, London E.C.1, 1924-47; *b.* 1879; *s.* of James John Laws, Dereham, Norfolk; *m.* 1st, Ellen (*d.* 1936), *d.* of John and Margaret Phillipson, Brindle, Lancs; one *s* one *d.*; 2nd, Lucy Yvonne, *d.* of John Kendal Sadler and *widow* of Henry John Moon. *Educ.:* Norfolk County School; University College, Nottingham; St. John's College, Cambridge. Lecturer, King's College, London, 1904-05; Head of Physics and Engineering Department, Technical School, Blackburn, 1905-1909; Principal, Loughborough Technical College, 1909-1915; Principal, Wigan and District Mining and Technical College, 1915-24. *Publications:* Magnetic and Electrical Researches in Philosophical Magazine. *Address:* Whitehouse Farm, Bedmond, Herts. *T.:* King's Langley 2565. [*Died* 22 *March* 1963.

LAWSON, 1st Baron, *cr.* 1950, of Beamish, Co. Durham; **John James Lawson,** P.C. 1945; D.C.L. (Durham); Lord Lieutenant of County of Durham, 1949-58, retd.; Vice-Chairman National Parks Commission, 1949-57; *b.* Whitehaven, 16 Oct. 1881; *m.* 1906, Isabella Scott, Co. Durham; three *d.* *Educ.:* various Board Schools. Commenced work in the mine (Boldon Colliery, C. Durham) at 12 years of age; M.P. (Lab.) Chester-le-Street Division, Co. Durham, 1919-49, applied for Chiltern Hundreds, 1949; Financial Sec. to War Office, 1924; Parliamentary Sec., Ministry of Labour, 1929-31; Member Imperial War Graves Commission, 1930-47; Deputy Regional Commissioner, Civil Defence Northern Region, 1939-44; Vice-Chairman of British Council, 1944; Secretary of State for War, 1945-46. K.St.J. Brilliant Star, China. *Publications:* A Man's Life; Peter Lee; Man in the Cap—Herbert Smith. *Heir:* none. *Address:* 7 Woodside, Beamish, Co. Durham. [*Died* 3 *Aug.* 1965.

LAWTON, Frank; Actor; *b.* London, 30 Sept. 1904; *e. s.* of Frank Mokeley Lawton and Daisy Collier; *m.* 1934, Evelyn Laye,

First appearance 1923, Vaudeville Theatre, in Yes!; parts include George in The Last of Mrs. Cheyney, St. James's, 1925; Woodley in Young Woodley, Savoy, 1928; David in Michael and Mary, St. James's, 1930; Hec Hammond in London Wall, Duke of York's, 1931; first New York appearance, 1934, as Charles Tritten in The Wind and the Rain, Ritz; subsequently in following plays in New York: French Without Tears (as Hon. Alan Howard); Promise; I am my Youth (as Shelley); toured with Evelyn Laye in Three Waltzes and Elusive Lady, 1945-46; Tom Collier in Animal Kingdom, Playhouse, 1947; played in Summer in December, Comedy, 1949; Evan Davies in September Tide (provincial tour with Evelyn Laye), 1950; toured Australia and New Zealand in September Tide and Bell Book and Candle, 1951-52; Doctor Forrest in Four Winds, Phoenix, 1953; the Hon. William Stephen Fitzharding Bule in Waiting for Gillian, St. James's, 1954; Sir Robert Marlowe in The Silver Wedding, Cambridge, 1957; Suddenly its Spring, Duke of York's, 1959; The Big Killing, Prince's, 1962; Clive Champion Cheney in The Circle, Savoy, 1965. Since 1930 has played in several films, including: Cavalcade; David Copperfield; The Winslow Boy, 1948; A Night to Remember, 1958; etc. Served War of 1939-45, in Army; awarded American Legion of Merit. *Recreations:* golf, tennis, cricket. *Club:* Garrick.

[*Died* 10 *June* 1969.

LAWTON, Frank Warburton, C.B. 1945; O.B.E. 1918; *b.* 26 Oct. 1881; 4th *s.* of John and Hannah Lawton; *m.* 1903, Elizabeth Mary (*d.* 1964), *d.* of George Dickinson Savage; one *s.* *Educ.:* Christ Church, Crewe and Macclesfield Gram. Schs.; King's College, London. Served in South African War with 1st City of London (Rough Riders) Imp. Yeomanry; a solicitor, 1907; entered Dept. of H.M. Procurator-General and Treasury Solicitor, 1914; Assistant Solicitor, 1936; Principal Assistant Treasury Solicitor, 1944; a Master of the Supreme Court (Taxing Office), 1946-54. *Recreations:* all outdoor. *Address:* 22 Shirley Ave., Cheam, Surrey. *Club:* Athenæum.

[*Died* 14 *Sept.* 1966.

LAYBOURNE-SMITH, Louis, C.M.G. 1948; B.E., F.R.I.B.A., L.F.R.A.I.A.; Partner, Woods, Bagot, Laybourne-Smith and Irwin, Architects; *b.* Adelaide, 1 April 1880; *s.* of late Joseph Laybourne-Smith, Adelaide; *m.* 1903, Frances Maude, *d.* of late Edward Davies, Adelaide; one *s.* three *d.* *Educ.:* Way College, Adelaide; Adelaide University (B.E.); South Australian School of Mines (Fellow). Past President, South Australian Institute of Architects; Past Pres., R.A.I.A., 1938, 1940, now Life Fellow; F.R.I.B.A., 1928. *Address:* 87 Northgate Street, Unley Park, South Australia. *Club:* Adelaide.

[*Died* 13 *Sept.* 1965.

LAYCOCK, Major-General Sir Robert (Edward), K.C.M.G., 1954; C.B. 1945; D.S.O. 1943; J.P.; Hon. LL.D. (Malta); Colonel Commandant, Special Air Service Regt. and Sherwood Rangers Yeomanry, since 1960; Lord Lieut. of Nottinghamshire since 1962; *b.* London, 18 April 1907; *s.* of late Brig.-Gen. Sir Joseph Laycock, K.C.M.G., D.S.O.; *m.* 1935, Angela Clare Louise, D.St.J., *d.* of late Rt. Hon. William Dudley Ward, P.C.; two *s.* three *d.* *Educ.:* Eton; R.M.C. Sandhurst. Joined Royal Horse Guards, 1927. Served War of 1939-45 (D.S.O., C.B.). Chief of Combined Operations, 1943-47; retd. pay, 1947; Chm. Windsor Group Hosp. Management Cttee., 1953-54; High Sheriff, Notts., 1954; Governor and C.-in-C., Malta, 1954-59. Mem. Sheffield Regional Hospital Board, 1960-63; a Governor, Welbeck College; Younger Brother, Trinity House. K.St.J. Commander Legion of Merit (U.S.A.); Comdr. Légion d'Honneur (France); Grand Officer Order of Orange Nassau with Swords (Netherlands); Comdr., with Star, Order of St. Olav (Norway). *Address:* Wiseton, Doncaster, Yorks. *T.:* Wiseton 224. *Clubs:* White's; Royal Yacht Squadron (Cowes).

[*Died* 10 *March* 1968.

LAYH, Lieut.-Col. Herbert Thomas Christoph, C.M.G. 1919; D.S.O. 1917; V.D.; late Australian Military Forces; *b.* 3 Apr. 1885; *s.* of C. Layh, Hamilton, Victoria. Served European War, 1914-18 (wounded, despatches, D.S.O. and bar); joined staff of Commonwealth Bank, 1912. Retired, 1950. *Address:* 2 Nan St., Box Hill, E.11, Victoria, Australia.

[*Died* 10 *April* 1964.

LAYLAND-BARRATT, Captain Sir Francis Henry Godolphin, 2nd Bt., *cr.* 1908; M.C.; late Grenadier Guards; *b.* 11 December 1896; *o. s.* of Sir Francis Layland-Barratt, 1st Bt., and Frances (*d.* 1953), C.B.E., *e. d.* of Thomas Layland, Stonehouse, Wallasey, Cheshire; *S.* father 1933. *Educ.:* Eton; Royal Military College, Sandhurst. Served European War of 1914-18 (wounded, M.C., invalided 1917). County Councillor, Devon, 1928. *Heir:* none. *Address:* c/o Westminster Bank Ltd., 64 Knightsbridge, S.W.1.

[*Died* 16 *May* 1968 (*ext.*).

LAYTON, 1st Baron, *cr.* 1947, of Danehill; **Walter Thomas Layton,** C.H. 1919; Kt., *cr.* 1930; C.B.E. 1917; M.A.; Hon. LL.D. Columbia and Melbourne; Deputy-Chairman (late Chairman) of the Economist, Ltd.; Director, Reuters Ltd., 1945-53; Member, Reuters' Trust, 1953-63; Director, National Mutual Assurance, 1921-64; Director and Vice-Chairman, Daily News Ltd., 1930-63; *b.* London, 15 March 1884; *s.* of late Alfred John Layton and Mary Layton, F.R.C.O.; *m.* 1910, Eleanor Dorothea (*d.* 1959), *d.* of F. B. P. Osmaston, of Stonehill, Limpsfield, Surrey; three *s.* three *d.* (and *e. d.* decd.). *Educ.:* King's College School; Westminster City School; University College, London; Trinity College, Cambridge. B.A. (Lond.) 1904; B.A. (Camb.) 1907, M.A. 1911; Fell. Gonville and Caius Coll., Camb., 1909; Hon. Fell. 1931; Univ. Lectr. in Economics, 1912; Newmarch Lecturer Univ. Coll., London, 1909-12; Fellow of Univ. Coll. London. Mem. Munitions Council; Mem. Consultative Economic Committee, League of Nations; represented Ministry of Munitions in the Milner Mission to Russia, 1917, and the Balfour Mission to the U.S.A., 1917; Director of Economic and Financial Section of the League of Nations, and Director National Federation of Iron and Steel Manufacturers; Financial Adviser to Indian Statutory Commission, 1929-30; British Delegate to World Economic Conference, 1927; British Member of Organisation Committee of Bank of International Settlements (1929) of Committee appointed as result of London Conference to inquire into credit position of Germany, and of Advisory Committee under the Young Plan, 1931. Editor of the Economist, 1922-38; Dir.-Gen. of Programmes, Ministry of Supply, 1940-42; Chairman of Executive Cttee., Ministry of Supply, 1941-42; Chief Adviser on Programmes and Planning, Ministry of Production, 1942-43; Head of Joint War Production Staff, 1942-43; Chairman News Chronicle Ltd., 1930-50; Chm. Star Newspaper Co. Ltd., 1936-50. Dep. Leader of Liberal Party in House of Lords, 1952-55. Member Independent Television Authority, 1954-56. Vice-Pres. of Consultative Assembly of the Council of Europe, 1949-57; Director, Tyne Tees Television Ltd., 1958-61. Contested (L.) Burnley, Nov. 1922; South Cardiff, Dec. 1923; London University, 1929. *Publications:* An Introduction to the Study of Prices; Relations of Capital and Labour; Dorothy, 1961 (a biography of his wife); various articles in reviews and journals. *Recreations:* music and golf. *Heir:* s. Hon. Michael John Layton [*b.* 28 Sept. 1912; *m.* 1938, Dorothy Cross, Rugby; one *s.* one *d.*] *Address:* 57 Exeter House, Putney, S.W.15. *T.:* Putney 0234. *Clubs:* National Liberal, Royal Automobile. [*Died* 14 *Feb.* 1966.

LAYTON, Admiral Sir Geoffrey, G.B.E., *cr.* 1947; K.C.B., *cr.* 1940 (C.B. 1936); K.C.M.G., *cr.* 1945; D.S.O. 1918; R.N.; *b.* 20 April 1884; *s.* of George Layton, solicitor, Liverpool; *m.* 1908, Eleanor G. Langley; three *d.* *Educ.:* Eastman's, Winchester; H.M.S. Britannia. Sub-Lieut., 1903; Lieut., 1905; Commander, 1916; Capt., 1922; Rear-Adm., 1935; Adm., 1942; H.M.S. Renown, 1933-34; Commodore of Royal Naval Barracks, Portsmouth, 1934-36; Director of Personal Services, 1936-38; commanded Battle Cruiser Squadron, 1938; Vice-Adm. Commanding 1st Battle Squadron and Second-in-Command, Home Fleet, 1939-40; C.-in-C., China, 1940-42; Ceylon, 1942-45; Commander-in-Chief, Portsmouth, 1945-47; retired, 1947. Grand Cross of Orange Nassau with Swords; Chevalier of the Legion of Honour. *Recreation:* gardening. *Address:* Tower Cottage, Rowlands Castle, Hampshire. *Club:* United Service. [*Died* 4 *Sept.* 1964.

LAYTON, Thomas Bramley, D.S.O. 1918; M.S. Lond., F.R.C.S. Eng.; Consulting Surgeon to the Throat and Ear Dept. of Guy's Hosp.; Member of Royal Society of Medicine (Past Pres. Laryngological Section), and of Anatomical Society of Great Britain and Ireland; *b.* 8 June 1882; *s.* of late Thomas Layton, solicitor; *m.* 1909, Edney Eleanor Sampson; one *s.* one *d.* *Educ.:* Bradfield College; Guy's Hospital. Lt.-Col. R.A.M.C. (T.); retired. Late Otologist to the Fever Service of the L.C.C. and District Medical Officer to Sicily and Med. Supt. of the Hospital at Belsen under U.N.R.R.A.; Past Master Society Apothecaries; late Member of Insurance Committee (ex-Chairman) of County of London. *Publication:* An Industry of Health; Sir William Arbuthnot Lane, Bt., 1956. *Recreations:* reading, gardening. *Address:* The Shaws, Newchapel Road, Lingfield, Surrey. *T.:* Lingfield 338. *Club:* Athenæum. [*Died* 17 *Jan.* 1964.

LEA, Measham, C.I.E. 1929; O.B.E.; M.Inst.C.E; Chief Engineer Karachi Municipality, 1908-31; *s.* of Measham Lea; *b.* Crewe, 3 July 1869; *m.* 1897, Annie (*d.* 1957), *d.* of Alfred Kingston, F.R.Hist.S.; two *s.* two *d.* *Educ.:* Christ Church School and Mechanics Institute, Crewe. Assistant Engineer L. and N.W. Railways, 1891-96; Deputy Borough Engineer and Surveyor, Crewe, 1896-99; City Engineer and Surveyor, Truro, 1899-1908; engaged in the design and execution of Schemes of Water Supply, Main Drainage, Town Planning, Road Works, etc. Chairman of the Indian District of the Institution of Municipal and County Engineers for 10 years; Member of the Council of the Institution of Municipal and County Engineers, England for 10 years; and member of the Examination Board; Member of the Institution of Civil Engineers; President, Bombay Engineering Congress, 1927-28; Fellow Royal Society of Health. *Publications:* Papers on Bituminous Roads, Bombay Engineering Congress; Presidential Address Bombay Engineering Congress. *Recreation:* golf. *Address:* Roycroft, Culverden Park, Tunbridge Wells, Kent. *T.:* Tunbridge Wells 21683. *Club:* Sind (Karachi). [*Died* 9 *May* 1963.

LEACH, Frank Burton, C.I.E. 1932; *b.* 31 August 1881; *s.* of Rev. Robert Burton Leach, Sutton Montis, Somerset; *m.* 1928, Mrs. Ivy May Harcourt Field. *Educ.:* Eton; Magdalen College, Oxford. I.C.S. Burma, 1905; Deputy Commissioner, 1913; Commissioner, 1925; Chief Sec. to Govt. of Burma, 1930-32; retired, 1934; Political Secretary to the Burma Chamber of Commerce, 1934-38; Ministry of Information, India-Burma Section, 1939-45. *Publication:* The Future of Burma, 1936. *Address:* Wood Rising, Mont de la Rocque, St. Aubin, Jersey. *T.:* South 482. *Club:* East India and Sports. [*Died* 29 *Sept.* 1961.

LEAKE, Henry Dashwood Stucley, C.B. 1943; *b.* 17 Feb. 1876; *s.* of Lieut.-Col. Henry Leake, late 44th and 70th Regiments, and Jane Dashwood; *m.* 1910, Lucy Marie (*d.* 1959), *o. d.* of C. L. N. Ingram; one *d.* *Educ.:* Wellington College; University College, Oxford. Barrister-at-law, Inner Temple; Assistant Chief (Postal) Censor, War Office, 1918; Palmes d'Officier de l'Académie Française, 1920; Sec., Charity Commission, 1925-32; Charity Commissioner, 1932-39; Chief Charity Commissioner, 1939-44. *Recreation:* gardening. *Address:* Maypole Farm, Hawkinge, Kent. *T.:* Hawkinge 254. [*Died* 2 *June* 1970.

LEALE, Rev. Sir John, Kt., *cr.* 1945; Methodist Minister; President of the Controlling Committee, States of Guernsey, from 1940; Jurat of the Royal Court of Guernsey since 1934; *b.* 1892; *m.* 1918, Leonie, *d.* of John W. Dorey; one *d.* *Educ.:* Elizabeth College, Guernsey; Jesus College, Cambridge. *Address:* The Royal Hotel, Guernsey. [*Died* 22 *July* 1969.

LEAN, Captain John Trevor, D.S.O. 1940; R.N. retired; Secretary Royal Albert Yacht Club since 1954; *b.* 16 July 1903; *yr. s.* of John Edward and Ethel Lean, Truro, Cornwall; *m.* 1932, Ruth, *y. d.* of late T. M. Reed, Bridgwater, Somerset; two *d.* *Educ.:* Probus School, Cornwall; Royal Naval College, Osborne and Dartmouth. Cadet in H.M.S. Carnarvon, 1920; Lieutenant, 1926; Lt.-Comdr. in H.M.S. Philomel, 1934-37, New Zealand; H.M. Yacht, Victoria and Albert, 1937-39; Commander, 1938; in Command of H.M.S. Punjabi at Second Battle of Narvik, 13 April 1940 (D.S.O.); H.M.S. Roebuck, 1943-45; Capt. 1945; H.M.S. Ready, 1947; Assistant Director Naval Equipment, Admiralty, 1948; Commanding Officer, H.M.S. Manxman, 1951-53; retired, 1954. *Recreations:* golf and sailing. *Address:* Royal Albert Yacht Club, Clarence Parade, Southsea, Hants. [*Died* 31 *Dec.* 1961.

LEANE, Brig.-General Sir Raymond Lionel, Kt., *cr.* 1945; C.B. 1919; C.M.G. 1918; D.S.O. 1916; M.C., V.D.; J.P. State of S. Australia; *b.* Prospect, S. Australia, 12 July 1878; *s.* of T. J. Leane; *m.* Edith Louise, *d.* of J. Laybourne-Smith; five *s.* one *d.* *Educ.:* Public School, Adelaide. Forty-one years' service in Australian Volunteer and Citizen Forces; Garrison Artillery, West Australia, 1899; Infantry, 1900; 2nd Lieut. 1905; Lieut. 1906; Capt. 1910; at outbreak of European War joined 11th Bn. A.I.F. as Captain; served Gallipoli 25 April 1915 to 16 Nov. 1915; Temp. Major, 1915; Temp. Lt.-Col. Oct. 1915; temp. command of 11th Batt. Sept. 1915; Lt.-Col. March 1916; Brig.-Gen. 1918; commanded 48th Batt. Australian Imperial Forces in France, 1916-18; in command of 12th Bde., 1918-19 (despatches eight times, severely wounded, M.C., D.S.O. and bar, C.B., C.M.G., Croix de Guerre); commanded 4th Division, Salisbury Plain, 1919; returned to Australia, Oct. 1919; Chief Commissioner of Police, S. Australia, 1920-44; Chairman Bush Fires Advisory Committee, 1937-44; commanded 19th Australian Infantry Brigade, 1920; commanded 3rd Infantry Brigade, 1921-26; A.D.C. Gov.-General, 1920-23; unattached list, 1926; Hon. Col. 48th Bn. until 1953; Councillor, North Perth Municipality, 1903-1906; Chairman of Council, Regional Group

Institute Public Administration, 1927-32; Commander Home Guard, 1940-44; Deputy Chairman S.A. National Council Defence, 1940-44; Trustee Distressed Soldiers' Fund (Chm.); Seal Holder, Totally and Permanently Disabled Soldiers' Assoc.; Order of St. John of Jerusalem; Jubilee Medal, 1935; Coronation Medal, 1937. *Recreations:* military. *Address:* Greystone, 2/6 Dingera Ave., N. Plympton, S. Australia. *T.:* LF 2731. *Clubs:* Commonwealth, Commercial Travellers' (Adelaide).
[*Died* 25 *June* 1962.

LEARMONTH, Sir James (Rögnvald), K.C.V.O., *cr.* 1949; C.B.E. 1945; *b.* 23 March 1895; *s.* of William Learmonth; *m.* 1925, Charlotte Newell, *d.* of F. G. and Nellie Bundy, St. Johnsbury, Vermont, U.S.A.; one *s.* one *d.* *Educ.:* Girthon School; Kilmarnock Academy; Glasgow University; Mayo Clinic. M.B., Ch.B. (Honours), 1921; Ch.M. (High Com.) 1927; F.R.C.S. (Edin.), 1928; M.D. (h.c.) University Oslo, 1946; Doctor (*h.c.*) Univ. of Paris, 1953; Hon. F.R.F.P.S.(G.), 1954; Hon. F.R.A.C.S., 1954; Hon. D.Sc. (Sydney), 1954; Hon. F.R.C.S. 1949; LL.D. (Glas.) 1949, (St. And.) 1956; (Edin.) 1965; Doctor (*h.c.*) Univ. of Strasbourg, 1956; Extra Surgeon to the Queen in Scotland, 1960. Hon. F.A.C.S. 1950; Lister Medallist, 1951; Sir Arthur Sims Commonwealth Travelling Prof., R.C.S., 1954. Outstanding Achievement Award, University of Minnesota, 1964. Chevalier, Légion d'Honneur, 1950. *Publications:* papers on surgical subjects. *Address:* Ardbucho, Broughton, Biggar, Lanarkshire. [*Died* 27 *Sept.* 1967.

LEATHEM, Walter Henry; *b.* 4 Dec. 1894; *s.* of Andrew and Eliza Leathem; *m.* 1930, Eileen Holroyd (*d.* 1950); one *s.* one *d.* *Educ.:* Bradford Grammar School; Leeds University; London University. Assistant Solicitor, Bradford Corporation, 1917; Dep. Town Clerk, 1929; Town Clerk, 1946-60; Clerk to Aireborough U.D.C., 1960-64. *Address:* Bank House, Apperley Lane, Bradford. *T.:* Rawdon 2201. [*Died* 20 *March* 1967.

LEATHER, Lieut.-Col. Kenneth John Walters, C.B.E., late commanding 4th Militia Batt. Durham Light Infantry; *b.* 6 July 1878; *s.* of late Frederick John Leather of Middleton Hall, Belford, Northumberland; *m.* 1st, Beatrice Evelyn (*d.* 1905), 2nd *d.* of late Calverley Bewicke; 2nd, 1908, Sybil Margaret (*d.* 1942), 3rd *d.* of late Arthur Laing; one *s.*; 3rd, 1943, Gladys, *d.* of late H. A. Crinkley. *Educ.:* Wellington College, Trinity College, Cambridge. 2nd Lieutenant 3rd (now 4th) Battalion Durham L.I., 1898; 1st Battalion D.L.I., 1899; served South African War, 1899-1902 (Queen's medal 5 clasps, King's medal 2 clasps); second part of the War with Gough's Mt. Infantry; Major, 4th Batt. Durham L.I., 1912; to command, 1918; Lt.-Col. to command 20th Batt. (Wearside) Durham L.I., 1915, raised by the Sunderland Recruiting Committee; went to France with the 41st Division eight months later, and was severely wounded, 22nd July 1916; at Eastern Command Headquarters, 1917-1918. *Recreations:* shooting, golf. *Address:* Whalton, Northumberland. *T.:* Whalton 206.
[*Died* 2 *May* 1963.

LEATHERS, 1st Viscount, *cr.* 1954; Baron, *cr.* 1941, of Purfleet; **Frederick James Leathers,** P.C. 1941; C.H. 1943; LL.D.; *b.* 21 November 1883; *s.* of Robert and Emily Leathers, Stowmarket, Suffolk; *m.* 1907, Emily Ethel Baxter; two *s.* one *d.* Was associated with Ministry of Shipping in European War, 1914-18, subsequently serving on Government Committees dealing with labour at the Ports. In May 1940 joined Ministry of Shipping as adviser on all matters relating to Coal; Minister of War Transport, 1941-45. Secretary of State for the Co-ordination of Transport, Fuel and Power, 1951-53. Underwriting Member of Lloyd's; Warden of Company of Shipwrights. Hon. LL.D.: Leeds, 1946; Birmingham, 1951. *Heir:* *s.* Hon. Frederick Alan Leathers. *Address:* 48 Grosvenor Square, W.1. *T.:* Grosvenor 4711. [*Died* 19 *March* 1965.

LE BAS, Edward, C.B.E. 1957; R.A. 1954 (A.R.A. 1943); artist; *b.* 27 October 1904; *s.* of late Edward Le Bas, 28 Bryanston Square, W., of Channel Island descent. *Educ.:* Harrow; Cambridge. B.A. Cambridge Univ. Architectural School, 1925; A.R.C.A. (Lond.), 1928; London Group, 1942. *Recreations:* swimming and collecting contemporary paintings. *Address:* 49 Glebe Place, Chelsea, S.W.3. *T.:* Flaxman 9473; 3 Vine Place, Brighton 1, Sussex. *Club:* Travellers'. [*Died* 18 *Nov.* 1966.

LE BRETON, Col. Sir Edward Philip, Kt., *cr.* 1941; M.V.O. 1953; R.E; D.L.; J.P. and C.C. Dorset; *b.* 1883; *e. s.* of late Lieut.-Col. Edward Hemery Le Breton, Royal Irish Regiment, and Gemma Le Breton, Loders Court, Dorset (she *m.* 2nd, late T. Wentworth Falconer), *d.* of Col. J. J. Glossop, J.P., Inwood; *m.* 1920, Mary, 2nd *d.* of late Capt. E. H. B. Sawbridge, J.P., 24th Regt., East Haddon; one *d.* *Educ.:* Radley; R.M.A. Woolwich. 2nd Lieut. R.E., 1901; 1st K.G.O. Sappers and Miners, 1906; served N.W. Frontier of India, 1908 (medal and clasp); N.E. Frontier of India, 1911-12 (clasp); European War, 1914-19, in South Arabia and Mesopotamia as O.C. 5th Field Coy., 1st K.G.O. Sappers and Miners (despatches); a Gen. Staff Officer and C.R.E. 17th Division; retired 1920; Hon. Colonel Dorset Fortress R.E., 1936-1947; Freeman of City of London; member Co. of Stationers; High Sheriff of Dorset, 1933-34; Chairman Dorset Education Committee, 1933-46; one of H.M.'s Honourable Corps of Gentlemen at Arms, 1931-53. *Address:* Loders Court, near Bridport, Dorset. *T.:* Bridport 83. *Clubs:* Army and Navy; Dorset County (Dorchester). [*Died* 16 *Dec.* 1961.

LEBURN, (William) Gilmour, T.D.; M.P. (U.) Kinross and West Perthshire Division since 1955; Joint Parliamentary Under-Secretary, Scottish Office, since Oct. 1959; Parl. Priv. Sec. to Sec. of State for Scotland (1957-59); *b.* 30 July 1913; *er. s.* of late George Cheape Leburn and Mina Leburn (*née* Watt); *m.* 1944, Agnes Barbara May, M.B.E., J.P., *yr. d.* of Arthur J. May, Reading; two *s.* one *d.* *Educ.:* Strathallas School. Served War, 1939-44, Royal Signall (T.A.): 51st (H.) Div. 1939-42; wounded El Alamein, 1942; on staff, Staff College, Camberley, 1944 (despatches twice). Member Fife County Council, 1948-55; Vice-Convener, Fife, 1951-52. *Recreations:* golf, fishing, shooting. *Address:* Edenshead, Gateside, Fife. *T.:* Gateside 207. *Clubs:* Carlton; Conservative (Edinburgh); Royal and Ancient (St. Andrews).
[*Died* 15 *Aug.* 1963.

LECHMERE, Captain Sir Ronald Berwick Hungerford, 5th Bt., *cr.* 1818; late 5th Dragoon Guards; *b.* 16 May 1886; *s.* of Sir Edmund Arthur Lechmere, 4th Bart. and Alice (*d.* 1896), *d.* of E. Samuels, Canterbury, N.Z.; *S.* father 1937; *m.* 1915, Constance Marguerite, *d.* of late Lt.-Col. Wigram Long, R.A., M.P.; one *s.* one *d.* *Educ.:* Charterhouse. Served European War, 1914-15 (wounded). *Heir:* *s.* Berwick Hungerford [*b.* 21 Sept. 1917; *m.* 1952, Susan Adele Mary (marriage dissolved 1954), *o. c.* of late Comdr. G. H. Maunsell-Smyth, R.N., and of Mrs. Maunsell-Smyth, 49 Drayton Gardens, S.W.10; *m.* 1954, Norah G., *e. d.* of Bt. Col. Elkington, The Moat House, Cutnall Green, Worcs.]. *Address:* Whittemere, Hanley Castle, Worcestershire.
[*Died* 22 *Feb.* 1965.

LECONFIELD, 4th Baron (*cr.* 1895); **Hugh Archibald Wyndham;** F.S.A.; F.R.Hist.S.; *b.* 4 Oct. 1877; 4th *s.* of 2nd Baron Leconfield and Lady Constance Evelyn Primrose (*d.* 1939), sister of 5th Earl of Rosebery; *S.* brother 1952; *m.* 1908, Hon. Maud Mary Lyttelton (*d.* 1953), *e. d.* of 8th Viscount Cobham. *Educ.:* Eton; New College, Oxford. *Publications:* The Early History of the Thoroughbred Horse in South Africa, 1924; Problems of Imperial Trusteeship; Native Education, 1933; The Atlantic and Slavery, 1935; The Atlantic and Emancipation, 1937; A Family History, 1410-1688, 1939; Britain and the World, 1944; A Family History, 1688-1837, 1950; Petworth Manor in the Seventeenth Century, 1954; Sutton and Duncton Manors, 1956. *Heir:* *b.* Col. Hon. Edward Scawen Wyndham, D.S.O. *Address:* 3 Wyndham House, Sloane Square, S.W.1. *T.:* Sloane 1395. [*Died* 6 *July* 1963.

LECONFIELD, 5th Baron, *cr.* 1859; **Edward Scawen Wyndham,** D.S.O. 1914; late 1st Life Guards; *b.* 30 April 1883; *s.* of 2nd Baron and *b.* of 4th Baron; *S.* brother, 1963; *m.* 1907, Gladys Mary, *o. d.* of F. J. W. Farquhar and Ada Mary, *d.* of Sir J. W. Cradock-Hartopp, 4th Bt.; two *s.* one *d.* *Educ.:* Eton; Oxford. Entered Army, 1904; Capt. 1911; Maj. 1915; Lt.-Col. 1919; Col. 1924; served European War, 1914-15 (wounded, despatches, D.S.O.); retired pay, 1926. *Heir:* *s.* Baron Egremont, M.B.E. *Address:* 34 Hereford House, North Row, Park Lane, W.1. *T.:* Mayfair 1900. *Club:* Turf. [*Died* 17 *Oct.* 1967.

LE CORBUSIER, (Charles-Edouard Jeanneret); Grand Officier de la Légion d'Honneur; architect; *b.* La Chaux-de-Fonds, 6 Oct. 1887; *s.* of Georges-Édouard Jeanneret and Marie-Charlotte Amélie Perret; *m.* 1930, Yvonne Jeanne Victorine Gallis (*d.* 1957). Constructed first building at age of 17; built numerous private houses in France, etc.; planned cities of Buenos Aires, Stockholm, Antwerp, Algiers, Nemours (Africa), Bogotá, Chandigarh capital of Punjab, etc.; invited by govts. and professional centres to lecture on architecture and town planning; consultant for town and country planning to numerous govts. in Europe, Africa, America and Asia. Constructed pavilion l'Esprit Nouveau, Internat. Exhib. of Decorative Arts, Paris, 1925; Camp of Salvation Army, Paris; Swiss Pavilion, Univ. City, Paris, 1929-32; invited by Russian Govt. to make report for urbanization of City of Moscow, 1931; plan for constr. of Soviet Palace (rejected), 1932; planned Univ. City of Brazil, Rio de Janeiro, 1936; Palace of Min. of Educ. and Public Health, Rio de Janeiro (cons.); Pavilion des Temps Nouveaux, Internat. Exhibition, Paris, 1937; constructed Unité d'Habitation, Marseilles, 1945-50; constructed second Unité d'Habitation, Nantes-Rezé, 1953-55; 1st prize in contest for League of Nations Palace, Geneva, 1927 and in international contest for Palais du Centrosoyus, Moscow, 1928 (constr., 1928-32). Chief of Architectural Mission to U.S.A., 1945; Member: Council Ministry of Reconstruction, 1945; Commission of Urbanism, Min. of Colonies, 1945; French Delegate to U.N.O., New York (headquarters construction); Pres. and Founder of Ascoral Assoc. of Constructors for Architectural Renovation, Paris, 1943; Founder and Dir. l'Esprit Nouveau (review), 1919-25. Membre du Conseil National Économique au titre de la Pensée Française, 1947-51. Dr. h.c. University of Zürich; Hon. LL.D. (Cambridge), 1959; Hon. Corr. Mem. R.I.B.A.; Hon. Memb. Nat. Inst. of Arts and Letters, of New York; Member: Swedish Roy. Acad. of Fine Arts, Acad. of Architecture, U.S.S.R., Acad. of Fine Arts, Buenos Ayres, Acad. of Arts, Belgium; Member American Designers. Royal Gold Medal for 1953 (R.I.B.A.). Freedom of the City of La Chaux-de-Fonds, 1957. *Publications:* Vers une architecture, 1922 (Eng. edn. Towards a New Architecture); Urbanisme, 1924 (Eng. edn. The City of To-morrow); Quand les cathédrales étaient blanches, 1937; Destin de Paris, 1941; Sur les quatre routes, 1941; La Maison des hommes, 1942; Entretien avec les étudiants des écoles d'architecture, 1943; Les 3 Établissements humains, 1945; Manière de penser l'urbanisme, 1947; Propos d'urbanisme, 1946; United Nations Headquarters, 1947; L'Espace indicible, 1947; Le Modulor, 1948; The Marseilles Block, 1953; My Work, 1961 (trans. J. Palmes); le Corbusier, 1910-60, 1961. *Address:* 35 rue de Sèvres, Paris. [*Died* 27 *Aug.* 1965.

LEDGER, Air Vice-Marshal Arthur Percy, C.B. 1950; C.B.E. 1946 (M.B.E. 1921); Extra Gentleman Usher to the Queen since 1966 (Gentleman Usher, 1959-1966); *b.* 29 Aug. 1897; 2nd *s.* of late Arthur William Ledger, Canterbury; *m.* 1932, Elisabeth, *d.* of James Richard Forbes Elsmie, Kincardine, Scotland; one *s.* one *d.* *Educ.:* Canterbury. Served European War, 1914-18 with Royal West Kent Regiment, 1916-17 (wounded); R.F.C. and R.A.F. (58 Squadron), 1918; served in Egypt, Turkey, Iraq, 1919-23, with 70 and 55 Sqdns.; Staff Air Defence of Gt. Britain, 1925-28; R.A.F. Staff College, 1929; Iraq and Kurdistan (30 Squadron), 1930-31 (despatches); Comd. 40 Squadron R.A.F., 1935-1936; Staff Coll., Camberley, 1937-38; India, 1939-41. Instructor, Staff College, Quetta, 1939-40; H.Q. R.A.F., India, 1940-41. Director, Ground Defence Plans, Air Min., 1942-45; Air Officer Commanding 54 Group R.A.F. 1946; 28 Group, 1946-47; 23 Group, 1947-50; Air Officer Administration, H.Q. Flying Training Command. R.A.F., 1950-1952 retired 1952. President, Alpine Ski Club, 1959. Vice-President R.A.F. Mountaineering Assoc. J.P. (Kent) 1954. *Recreations:* mountaineering and ski-ing. *Address:* Lynton House, Bridge, nr. Canterbury, Kent. *Clubs:* Bath, Royal Air Force. [*Died* 6 *May* 1970.

LEDINGHAM, Mrs. Una Christina, F.R.C.P.; retired as: Senior Consultant Physician, Royal Free Hosp., and Physician in charge, Diabetic Dept.; Physician in charge, Diabetic Clinic, Hampstead Gen. Hosp.; Consultant Physician, Marie Curie Hospital; Recognized Teacher in Medicine, University of London; Examiner for membership of the R.C.P., and Staff Examiner in Medicine, University of London; *b.* 2 January 1900; *d.* of late James Louis Garvin, C.H., and Christina Wilson; *m.* 1925, John Ledingham, M.B., B.Ch., D.P.H.; one *s.* one *d.* *Educ.:* South Hampstead High School; Royal Free Hospital School of Medicine. M.B., B.S. Lond., M.R.C.S., L.R.C.P. 1923; M.D. and M.R.C.P. Lond. 1927; F.R.C.P. 1947. House Physician: Brompton Hospital for diseases of the chest, 1923; Royal Free Hosp., 1924; M.O. Out Patients, Royal Northern Hosp., 1924-25. Royal Free Hospital: Med. Registrar, 1925-1928; First Asst. Children's Dept., 1929-31; Asst. Physician, 1931. Physician Marie Curie Hosp., 1936-. First Fellow Asthma Research Council, 1928-29. Freewoman's Lectr., Clin. Med., 1936-46; Examiner Univ. of London: Diploma in Nursing, 1948-52, Medicine 1953-55, 1959-; Conjoint Bd., 1954-58; Reviewer in Gen. Med., Medical Annual, 1948-1956. *Recreation:* reading. *Address:* 47 Ladbroke Square, W.11. *T.:* Park 4767. [*Died* 19 *Nov.* 1965.

LEDLIE, Reginald Cyril Bell, F.R.C.S.; Consulting Surgeon: Miller General Hospital, East Ham Memorial Hospital; Consulting Surgeon Royal Marsden Hospital; Consulting Surgeon: Manor House Hospital; *b.*

1898; *s.* of Dr. Wm. Ledlie, M.A., M.D.; *m.* 1940, Elspeth Mary, *o. d.* of Dr. H. W. Kaye; two *s.* *Educ.:* Whitgift Sch.; London Univ. (Guy's Hospital). Treasurer's Gold Medal for Surgery at Guy's Hospital, 1919; Degree of M.B., B.S. (Hons.) London, 1921; F.R.C.S. (Eng.) 1924. *Publications:* Handbook of Surgery, 1951; Aids to Surgery, 8th edn., 1952. *Recreation:* ornithology. *Address:* 38 Rawlings Street, S.W.3. *T.:* Knightsbridge 2259. [*Died* 18 *Jan.* 1966.

LEDWARD, Richard Thomas Davenport, C.M.G. 1962; Counsellor, H.M. Foreign Service, since 1955; *b.* 29 June 1915; *s.* of late Harold and Lilian Ledward, Bowdon, Cheshire; *m.* 1941, Sylvia Josephine Watson; one *s.* one *d.* *Educ.:* Rugby; Trinity College, Cambridge. Entered Consular Service, 1937; served at Tokyo, 1937-40; Harbin, 1940-41; Foreign Office, 1942-44; Special Lecturer, School of Oriental and African Studies, London University, and Secretary of Scarbrough Commn. on Oriental, Slavonic, East European and African Studies, 1944-46; Grade 7, 1946; served at Helsinki, 1946-48; U.K. Deleg. to U.N., 1948-51; Foreign Office, 1952-54; Tokyo, 1954-56; Counsellor, 1955; Political Adviser to Hong Kong Govt., 1956-59; Washington, 1960. *Address:* c/o Foreign Office, Downing St., S.W.1. *Club:* Hong Kong (Hong Kong). [*Died* 7 *April* 1963.

LEE, Lieutenant-Colonel Sir (Albert) George, Kt., *cr.* 1937; O.B.E.; M.C.; B.Sc.; M.I.E.E.; *b.* 24 May 1879; *s.* of George Henry Payne Lee, Conway, and Maria Agnes Lee; *m.* 1st, 1903, Susie Lydia (*d.* 1944), *d.* of William Tanner; one *d.*; 2nd 1950, Ivy Laura Powell. Served during European War with R.E. and post-war with Royal Corps of Signals (Supplementary Reserve); represented British Government on numerous International Telecommunications Conferences; Chairman of Radio Research Board, 1928-47; Chairman Wireless Section, Institution of Electrical Engineers, 1927; Vice-President Institute of Radio Engineers, U.S.A., 1929; President Institution of Electrical Engineers, 1937; Member General Board National Physical Laboratory, 1935; Engineer-in-Chief, Gen. Post Office, 1932-39; Director of Communications Research and Development, Air Ministry, 1940; Senior Telecommunications Officer, Ministry of Supply, 1944-45; Member of Scientific Advisory Council, Ministry of Supply, 1946-49; Member of Royal Commission on Awards to Inventors, 1946-55. Medal of Honour, Institute of Radio Engineers, U.S.A., 1939. *Publications:* in Engineering and Scientific Journals. *Address:* Chedworth, Chalfont St. Giles, Bucks. [*Died* 26 *Aug.* 1967.

LEE, Sir Kenneth, 1st Bt., *cr.* 1941; Kt. 1934; Hon. LL.D. Manchester; Member, Commonwealth Shipping Committee; *e. s.* of late Harold Lee, Broughton Park, Manchester; *m.* 1910, Giulia (*d.* 1961), *e. d.* of Max Strakosch, New York; no *c.* Mem. Cttee. apptd. to examine the question of Govt. Machinery for dealing with Trade and Commerce, 1919, and of Industrial Fatigue Research Board, 1918-1921; Member Advisory Cttee. to Dept. of Overseas Trade (Development and Intelligence), 1918-25; Chairman Inter-Departmental Cttee. on Patents, 1921; Member: Royal Commission on the Coal Industry, 1925; Home Office Cttee. on the Factory Inspectorate, 1929; Cttee. on Registration of Accountants, 1930; Cttee. on Education for Salesmanship, 1930; U.K. Trade Mission to Egypt, 1931; U.K. Sugar Industry Inquiry Cttee., 1934; (ex-mem.) Advisory Council and Chairman Industrial Grants Cttee. of Dept. of Scientific and Industrial Research; Fuel Research Board, 1931-35; Royal Commission of Inquiry into Private Manufacture of and Trade in Arms, 1935-36. Director-General and Sec. to Ministry of Information, 1939-40; Member Willingdon Economic Mission to S. America, 1940-41; late representative in United States of the Industrial and Export Council of British Board of Trade; Director-General Raw Materials Controls, Ministry of Supply, 1942-1945. *Address:* Lukyns, Ewhurst, Surrey. *Club:* Athenæum. [*Died* 18 *Oct.* 1967 (*ext.*).

LEE, Hon. Sir Walter Henry, K.C.M.G., *cr.* 1922; Kt., *cr.* 1920; *b.* 27 April 1874; *s.* of Robert and Margaret Lee; *m.* 1897, Margaret, *d.* of late William Barnes; three *s.* four *d.* *Educ.:* Longford, Tasmania. Member House of Assembly for the District of Wilmot, 1909-46 (re-elected on nine occasions); Premier, Chief Secretary, and Minister for Education, 1916-22; Treasurer and Minister for Education, 1922-23; Treas. and Minister for Railways, 1923; Premier and Treasurer of Tasmania, 1923; Minister for Lands, Works, Agriculture, and Forestry, 1928-30; Minister for Lands, Works, and Agriculture, 1931; Minister of Lands and Works, 1932-34; Premier, Treasurer and Minister controlling Agricultural Bank and Hydro-Electric Dept., Tasmania, 1934. *Address:* Westbury, Tasmania. [*Died* 1 *June* 1963.

LEE, William Stevens, M.A.; J.P.; *b.* 5 Oct. 1871; 3rd *s.* of late John B. Lee, of Ravensbourne Park, Catford; *m.* 1906, Marion (*d.* 1923), 3rd *d.* of late T. C. Hounsfield, of Sèvres, France; one *s.* four *d.* *Educ.:* Dover College; Wadham College, Oxford (Open Classical Exhibitioner). Running Blue, 1894. Assistant Master at Dover College, 1894-1908; Headmaster Queen Elizabeth's School, Cranbrook, 1908-15, Dover College, 1915-34; retired 1934; Hon. Freedom of Dover, 1932. *Address:* 20 Waterloo Mansions, Dover, Kent. *T.:* Dover 947. [*Died* 31 *Oct.* 1965.

LEECH, George William, R.I. 1935; Painter; *b.* 1894; *e. s.* of late Joseph Haywood Leech; *m.* 1st, 1921, Helen Priestley (*d.* 1941); two *s.*; 2nd, 1941, Stella Elizma Boys. *Educ.:* Emanuel School. Studied Putney and Lambeth Schools of Art; three years L.C.C. Art Scholarship, 1912; Bronze Medal South Kensington (drawing from nude) 1915; commissioned A.P.W.O. Yorkshire Regt. (Green Howards), 1915; served European War, France (Machine Gun Corps), 1916-19. Exhibited Royal Academy since 1925; Art Editor Strand Magazine, 1930-39. *Address:* 1 Beaufort Street, Chelsea, S.W.3. [*Died* 14 *Oct.* 1966.

LEECH, William John, R.H.A. 1910; Painter; *b.* 10 April 1881; 3rd *s.* of late Prof. H. B. Leech, LL.D.; *m.* 1953, May Botterell. *Educ.:* St. Columba's College, Co. Dublin. Sch. of R.H.A.; Metropolitan School of Art, Dublin; Académie Julian, Paris. *Address:* Candy Cottage, Felix Drive, West Clandon, Surrey. [*Died* 16 *July* 1968.

LEEDS, 11th Duke of (*cr.* 1694); **John Francis Godolphin Osborne**; Bt., 1620; Viscount Latimer, Baron Osborne, 1673; Earl of Danby, 1674; Viscount Osborne of Dunblane, 1675; Marquis of Carmarthen, 1689; Baron Godolphin, 1832; *b.* 12 March 1901; *o. s.* of 10th Duke and Lady Katherine Frances Lambton (*d.* 1952), *d.* of 2nd Earl of Durham; *S.* father, 1927; *m.* 1933, Marianne (marriage dissolved, 1948), *d.* of late Iskender de Malkhazouny; *m.* 1948, Audrey (marriage dissolved, 1954), *yr. d.* of Brigadier Desmond Young; one *d.*; *m.* 1955, Caroline Fleur, *yr. d.* of late Col. Henry M. Vatcher, M.C., Valeran, St. Brelade's, Jersey. *Educ.:* Eton; Jesus Coll., Cambridge. *Heir:* *cousin,* Sir Francis D'Arcy Godolphin Osborne, K.C.M.G. *Address:* Melbourne House, Jersey, C.I.; La Falaise, Roquebrune, Cap Martin, A-M, France. [*Died* 26 *July* 1963.

LEEDS, 12th Duke of, *cr.* 1694; **(Francis) D'Arcy Godolphin Osborne;** Bt. 1620; Viscount Latimer, Baron Osborne, 1673; Earl of Danby 1674; Viscount Osborne of Dunblane, 1675; Marquis of Carmarthen, 1689; Baron Godolphin, 1832; K.C.M.G. 1943 (C.M.G. 1930); *b.* 16 Sept. 1884; *s.* of late Sidney F. Godolphin Osborne and Margaret Dulcibella (*d.* 1922), *d.* of late Hugh Hammersley; *S.* cousin, 1963; unmarried. *Educ.:* Haileybury. British Minister at Washington, 1931-35; Minister to the Holy See, 1936-47. K.St.J.; K.C.S.G. *Heir:* none. *Address:* 66 Via Giulia, Rome, Italy. [*Died* 20 *March* 1964 (*ext.*).

LEEDS, Commander Sir Reginald (Arthur St. John), 6th Bt., *cr.* 1812; R.N. (Ret.); D.L.; *b.* 13 May 1899; *s.* of late William Henry Arthur St. John Leeds and late Edith Mabel (she *m.* 2nd, 1920, John Hugh McNeale), *d.* of late Maj.-Gen. Jackson Muspratt Muspratt-Williams; *S.* cousin, 1924; *m.* 1926, Winnaretta, *o. d.* of late Paris Singer; one *s.* one *d.* *Educ.:* Osborne; Dartmouth. Retd., 1922. Lt. R.N.; F.O., R.A.F., 1922-23; Member, London Stock Exchange, 1928-69. Re-employed as Comdr. R.N. (Naval Liaison Officer, Fighter Command), 1939-45. High Sheriff of Devon, 1952-1953; D.L., County of Devon, 1964. *Heir: s.* George Graham Mortimer Leeds [*b.* 21 Aug. 1927; *m.* 1954, Nicola (marr. diss. 1965), *d.* of Douglas Robertson McBean, M.C.; three *d.*]. *Address:* Little Oldway, Paignton. *Clubs:* White's; Travellers' (Paris); Royal Torbay Yacht (Hon. Admiral); Royal Yacht Squadron (Cowes). [*Died* 18 *Jan.* 1970.

LEEPER, Sir Reginald Wildig Allen, G.B.E. 1948 (C.B.E. 1919); K.C.M.G. 1945 (C.M.G. 1936); Director De Beers Consolidated Mines Ltd., 1950-65, and other companies; Vice-President of the British Council since 1949; *b.* Sydney, N.S.W., 25 Mar. 1888; *s.* of late Alexander Leeper; *m.* 1916, Margaret Primrose Dundas, *d.* of G. Boyce Allen; two *d.* *Educ.*. Melbourne Grammar School; Trinity College, Melbourne; New College, Oxford. Intelligence Bureau, Department of Information, 1917; entered Foreign Office, 1918 (temp. clerk); 2nd Secretary, Foreign Office and Diplomatic Service, 1920; 1st Secretary, H.B.M. Legation, Warsaw, 1923-24; Riga, 1924; Constantinople, 1925; Warsaw, 1927-29; transferred to Foreign Office, 1929; Counsellor, 1933; Assistant Under-Secretary, 1940; Ambassador at the Court of the King of the Hellenes, 1943-46; Ambassador to Argentine Republic, 1946-48; retired 1948. *Publication:* When Greek meets Greek, 1950. *Address:* 9 Cornwall Gardens, S.W.7. [*Died* 2 *Feb.* 1968.

LEES, Sir Charles Archibald Edward Ivor, 7th Bt. *cr.* 1804; *b.* 6 March 1902; *s.* of Sir Jean Marie Ivor Lees, 6th Bt., and Beatrice Nora Mary (*d.* 1927), *d.* of late E. E. Davis, Kingston-on-Thames, Surrey; *S* father 1957; *m.* 1924, Lily, *d.* of Arthur Williams, Manchester; one *s.* (one *d.* decd.). *Educ.:* in Canada. Served War of 1939-45 as Captain, Royal Army Service Corps. *Heir:* . Thomas Harcourt Ivor Lees, *b.* 6 November 1941. *Address:* 30 Deauville Court, Elms Crescent, Clapham Common, S.W.4. [*Died* 4 *Jan.* 1963.

LEES, Rev. Harold M. H.; *see* Hyde-Lees.

LEES-JONES, John, O.B.E. 1953; Member, Advisory Council on Treatment of Offenders; *b.* 1887; *m.* 1921, Alice May, *d.* of late John Ryder, Manchester; three *s.* *Educ.:* Lymm Grammar School; Wrekin College, Shropshire. Served European War, 1914-19; called to Bar, Middle Temple, 1916; M.P. (U.) Blackley Division of Manchester, 1931-1945; J.P. 1926. *Address:* Foel, Llansannan, Denbigh, N. Wales. *T.:* Llansannan 205. *Club:* Farmers'. [*Died* 13 *Jan.* 1966.

LEESE, Charles William, C.M.G. 1932; *b.* 1876; *s.* of Charles Stuart Leese and Elizabeth Whitechurch; unmarried. Entered Colonial Civil Service as Asst. Dist. Comr., S. Nigeria, 1906; Treasurer, Gold Coast, 1924; Treasurer, Nigeria, 1928-35; retired 1935. *Address:* Centuries, Doddington, Sittingbourne, Kent. *Clubs:* Bath, Royal Commonwealth Society. [*Died* 26 *Feb.* 1969.

LE FANU, George Ernest Hugh, C.M.G. 1945; M.B.; retired; *b.* 18 Sept. 1874; *s.* of Joseph William Henry Le Fanu, Indian Civil Service; *m.* 1915, Mary Beatrice Fisher (*d.* 1961); two *d.* *Educ.:* School in Germany; Aberdeen Univ. W. African Med. Staff, 1907-26; Togoland Campaign, 1914-1916 (temp. Capt.); Consulting Physician in Liverpool to Colonial Office, 1928-45. *Recreations:* music and gardening. *Address:* Greenfield, South Brent, Devon. *T.A.:* Le Fanu, South Brent. *T.:* South Brent 3140. *Club:* University (Liverpool). [*Died* 25 *July* 1965.

LE FANU, Admiral Sir Michael, G.C.B. 1968 (K.C.B. 1963; C.B. 1960); D.S.C. 1941; Chief of Naval Staff and First Sea Lord, since 1968; *b.* 2 August 1913; *s.* of Captain H. B. Le Fanu, Royal Navy; *m.* 1943, Prudence, *d.* of Admiral Sir Vaughan Morgan, *q.v.*: two *s.* one *d.* Served in H.M. Ships Aurora, Howe and U.S. 3rd/5th Fleets, 1939-45. Commanded H.M.S. Eagle, 1957-58; Third Sea Lord and Controller of the Navy, 1961-65; C.-in-C. Middle East, 1965-68. U.S. Bronze Star, 1945. *Address:* 17 Stonehill Rd., S.W.14. *T.:* 01-876 1477. [*Died* 28 *Nov.* 1970.

LEFEAUX, Leslie; Governor Reserve Bank of New Zealand, 1934-40; *b.* 28 April 1886; *s.* of Harry I. Lefeaux; *m.* 1911, Ada Ethel, *d.* of the late W. E. Jones of Cheam, Surrey; one *d.* *Educ.:* Privately. Entered service of Bank of England, 1904; appointed Assistant to the Governors, 1932; resigned to take up above position. *Recreations:* golf, bowls. *Address:* 79 Manor Road, Worthing, Sussex. [*Died* 11 *Nov.* 1962.

LE FLEMING, Major-General Roger Eustace, C.B. 1947; O.B.E. 1943; M.C. 1918; retd.; *b.* 20 Apr. 1895; *s.* of John Le Fleming, Tonbridge; *m.* 1928, Jean, *d.* of Major A. Mirrlees; one *d.* *Educ.:* Tonbridge School; R.M.C., Sandhurst. Joined E. Surrey Regt., 1914; joined I.A., 1915; commanded 2nd Bombay Grenadiers, 1937; Bde. Comdr. 1941; Maj.-Gen. Commanding Waziristan Area, 1944 (wounded twice, despatches thrice), retired June 1948. *Address:* Windylow, Colemans Hatch, Hartfield, Sussex. *T.:* Colemans Hatch 11. [*Died* 9 *May* 1962.

LEFROY, Sir Edward Henry Bruce, Kt., 1955; J.P.; Pastoralist, Western Australia; *b.* Perth, Western Australia, 22 May 1887; *s.* of Sir Henry B. Lefroy, K.C.M.G., and Rose A. (*née* Wittenoom); *m.* 1915, Beatrice E. Vincent; three *s.* *Educ.:* Hale School, Perth, W.A. (formerly Perth High School); Haileybury College, England. Commenced pastoral career at Boolardy Station, Western Australia 1905; appointed to develop and manage large freehold area of virgin land at Cranmore Park, W.A., 1909; developed there a leading merino sheep stud and took a prominent lead in land development along scientific lines. Member of W.A. Cttee. of C.S.I.R., 1930; Chm. Cttee., and mem. Australian Council, 1934-43; mem. Advisory Council of C.S.I.R.O., 1943-55; Mem. W.A. Univ. Senate, 1945-61; formerly mem. and Chm. Moora Road Board; Director of a number of Pastoral Cos. Jubilee Medal,

1935; Coronation Medal, 1953. F.R.S.A. J.P., W.A., 1918-. *Publications:* agric. and pastoral articles for journals. *Recreations:* gardening and reading. *Address:* Colvin House, Round Hill, Western Australia; 63 Mount St., Perth. *Club:* Perth-Weld (Perth, Western Australia).
[*Died* 10 *Sept.* 1966.

LEGARD, Sir Digby Algernon Hall, 13th Bart., *cr.* 1660; B.A.; late Capt. R.A.F.; *b.* 7 Dec. 1876; *o. s.* of Rev. Cecil Henry Legard and Emily, *d.* of James Hall; *S.* uncle, 1923; *m.* 1904, Elaine (*d.* 1952), *d.* of W. J. S. Barber-Starkey; three *s.* one *d.* *Educ.:* Eton; Magdalene Coll., Cambridge. *Heir: s.* Thomas Digby Legard, Lt. R.A. [*b.* 16 Oct. 1905; *m.* 1935, Mary Helen, *er. d.* of Lt.-Col. L'Estrange Malone; three *s.*]. *Address:* Barton Cottage, Malton, Yorks. *Club:* M.C.C.
[*Died* 5 *Jan.* 1961.

LEGAT, Charles Edward, C.B.E. 1939; B.Sc.; retired; *b.* 16 Jan. 1876; 4th *s.* of late Robert Legat, W.S., Eskpark, Musselburgh; *m.* 1920, Frances Marion, *o. d.* of late Frederic Bennett, M.R.C.S., Okehampton; two *s.* *Educ.:* George Watson's College, Edinburgh; Edinburgh University (B.Sc.). Entered Forest Service, Cape Colony, 1898; transferred to Transvaal Forest Service. 1902 and absorbed into Union Forest Service. 1910; Conservator of Forests Transvaal, 1910-13; Chief Conservator of Forests, Union of South Africa, 1913-31; Editor Secretary of Empire Forestry Association, London, 1933-38; Hon. Member, Canadian Society Forest Engineers, New Zealand Forestry Society, South African Forestry Association. *Recreation:* gardening. *Address:* Beechdene, Lower Bourne, Farnham, Surrey. *T.A.* and *T.*: Farnham 5914. *Club:* Pretoria (Pretoria).
[*Died* 14 *Oct.* 1966.

LEGG, Leopold George Wickham; Fellow of New College, Oxford; *b.* 1877; *s.* of late John Wickham Legg, M.D., Hon. D.Litt. Oxon, F.R.C.P.; *m.* 1915, Olive Maud, *e.d.* of late William Percival Lindsay, W.S., Edinburgh; three *d.* (one *s.* decd.). *Educ.:* Winchester; New College, Oxford. *Publications:* English Coronation Records, 1902; A Short Survey of 26 Counties of England in 1634 by a Captain, a Lieutenant, and an Ancient, 1904; Select Documents of the Constituent Assembly, 1905; Matthew Prior, 1921; British Diplomatic Instructions, France, 1689-1721, 1925; Vol. II. 1927; Vol. III. 1930; Vol. IV. 1934; A relation of a short survey of the Western Counties by a Lieut. in 1635, 1936; and other works; Editor Dictionary of National Biography, Supplement 1931-40, Joint Editor, 1941-50. *Address:* c/o National Provincial Bank, Ltd., High Street Branch, Oxford. *Club:* United University.
[*Died* 19 *Dec.* 1962.

LEGGATT, Colonel Hon. Sir William Watt, Kt. 1957; D.S.O. 1945; M.C. 1918; E.D. 1946; Australian lawyer and politician, retd.; *b.* 23 Dec. 1894; *s.* of late Rev. T. W. Leggatt, ex-Moderator of Presbyterian Church of Victoria, Australia; *m.* 1926, Dorothy Meares Andrews; two *s.* one *d.* *Educ.:* Geelong College, Geelong, Victoria; Ormond College, University of Melbourne. B.A. (Melbourne) 1915, LL.B. 1920. Served European War in A.I.F., Egypt and France, 1915-18. Solicitor in Rushworth, 1921-1924, Murrayville, 1925, Mornington 1926-1940. War of 1939-45, comd. 2/40 Bn. A.I.F., 1941, on Timor; P.O.W., Changi Camp, 1942-45. Barrister in Melbourne from 1946. Member, State Legislative Assembly, 1947-56; Chief Sec. and Min. of Immigration, 1948-50; Minister of Education, State of Victoria, Australia, 1955-56; Agent-General for Victoria in London, 1956-64. *Recreation:* golf. *Address:* Aulua, 36 Herbert St., Mornington, Victoria, Australia. *Clubs:* Royal Automobile Club of Victoria, Naval and Military (Melbourne); Peninsula Country Golf (Frankston, Victoria).
[*Died* 27 *Nov.* 1968.

LEHMAN, Hon. Herbert H.; U.S. Senator, 1949-57; Director-General of United Nations Relief and Rehabilitation Administration, 1943-46; permanent and hon. Chairman since 1946; *b.* New York City, 28 March 1878; *s.* of Mayer Lehman and Babette Newgass; *m.* 1910, Edith Altschul; one *s.* one *d.* (and one *s.* decd.). Partner in Lehman Bros., bankers, New York City, 1908-28; Lt.-Governor, New York State, 1928, 1930; elected Governor New York State, 1932, re-elected 1934, 1936, 1938; Director U.S. Office of Foreign Relief, 1942-1943. Has received many decorations from his own and foreign countries, also honorary degrees from colleges and universities. *Address:* 820 Park Avenue, New York, U.S.A.; (office) 155 East 76th Street, New York 21, N.Y., U.S.A.
[*Died* 5 *Dec.* 1963.

LEICESTER, Sir Charles Byrne Warren, 9th Bt., *cr.* 1671; Lt.-Col., King's Dragoon Guards (retired); *b.* 30 March 1896; *s.* of late Major William Frederic and late Mary Lilian Leicester; *S.* kinsman, 1945 (family name changed from Byrne to Leicester by Special Act of Parliament, 1744, claim tail male descent from Maelmorda, King of Leinster). *Educ.:* Radley. Served with King's Dragoon Guards in European War, 1914-18, Persia and Iraq (medal); also War of 1939-45 (1939-45 Star, Africa Star (with 8th Army clasp), Defence Medal, War Medal, 1939-45). *Publication:* Bloodstock Breeding, 1957. *Recreations:* bloodstock, racing, hunting, polo. *Heir:* none. *Address:* at Kilcroney, Bray, Co. Wicklow, Ireland. *Club:* Cavalry.
[*Died* 18 *May* 1968 (*ext.*).

LEIGH, Alan de Verd, C.B.E. 1958 (M.B.E. 1920); Secretary, The London Chamber of Commerce, 1923-58, retd.; *b.* 7 June 1891; *s.* of late Canon John de Verd Leigh; unmarried. *Educ.:* Marlborough; Merton Coll., Oxford; B.A. 1914, 2nd Class Hons. Mod. Hist.; M.A. 1923. Admiralty, 1915-20; joined staff London Chamber of Commerce, 1920; asst. sec., 1921; awarded London Commercial Research Fellowship British Empire Exhibition, 1922 and visited Malaya, Borneo and New Guinea and reported on their economic position with suggestions for their future development; director Federation of Commonwealth and British Empire, Chambers of Commerce, 1923-58, and organised 10th - 19th triennial congresses of Chambers of Commerce of the British Empire; sent to Ottawa Conference in 1932 by London Chamber to press its views on monetary reform. *Publications:* articles on the reform of the monetary system. *Recreation:* golf. *Address:* 25 Woodland Court, Dyke Rd. Av., Hove 4, Sussex. *T.:* Brighton 55123. *Club:* Oxford and Cambridge.
[*Died* 7 *Nov.* 1961.

LEIGH, Arthur George, M.D., F.R.C.S.; Ophthalmic Surgeon; Surgeon, Moorfields Eye Hospital, since 1947; Consultant Ophthalmic Surgeon; St. Mary's Hospital, since 1947; Paddington Green Children's Hospital; Princess Louise Hospital for Children, Kensington; Lecturer in Ophthalmology, The Institute of Ophthalmology, Univ. of London; Mem. Bd. of Governors: St. Mary's Hosp., since 1962; Moorfields Eye Hospital, since 1966; *b.* 22 March 1909; *s.* of John McWhan Leigh and Catherine Abigail Hargrave, Liverpool; *m.* 1942, Margaret Eileen, M.B., Ch.B., *e. d.* of Edward Llewelyn Parry-Edwards, M.D., D.P.H., Caernarvon; two *d.* *Educ.:* Liverpool Collegiate School; University of Liverpool (Robert Gee Fell. in Human Anat., 1933; John Rankin Fell. in Anat., 1934; Thelwall Thomas Fell. in Surg. Path., 1936).

M.R.C.S., L.R.C.P. 1933; M.B., Ch.B. Liverpool, 1933; M.D. Liverpool, 1937; F.R.C.S. Eng. 1938. House Surg. and House Physician, Liverpool Roy. Infirmary, 1935-1936; House Surg. and Sen. Resident Officer, Roy. London Ophthalmic (Moorfields) Hosp., 1938-41; Ophthalmic Surgeon, National Temperance Hosp. 1946-52, King Edward VII Hosp., Windsor, 1947-54. Visiting Prof. of Ophthalmology, Roy. Medical Coll., Baghdad, 1957; January Lectr., North of England Ophthalmological Soc., 1966. Member: Editorial Bd. Ophthalmic Literature; Ophthalmological Soc. of U.K. (Hon. Sec., 1952-54, Mem. of Council, 1954-57); Oxford Ophthalmological Congress; Faculty of Ophthalmologists; Société Française d'Ophthalmologie; Liverpool Med. Instn.; Hon. Fellow, Louisiana-Mississippi Ophthalmological and Otolaryngological Soc. F.R.Soc. Med. (Vice-President Section of Ophthalmology). Served War of 1939-45, Sqdn. Leader (Ophthalmic Specialist), R.A.F.V.R., 1941-46. *Publications:* Corneal Transplantation, 1966; articles in various medical publications. *Recreations:* golf, ski-ing, painting. *Address:* 100 Harley Street, W.1. *T.:* Welbeck 8885; (home) 2 Park View Road, Ealing, W.5. *T.:* Perivale 7617. *Club:* Garrick. [*Died* 11 *Aug.* 1968.

LEIGH, Lt.-Col. John Cecil Gerard, J.P., D.L.; High Sheriff, Leicestershire, 1948-49; *b.* 21 Dec. 1889; *s.* of Capt. H. Gerard Leigh, Luton Hoo, Beds.; *m.* 1913, Helen, *d.* of late William J. Goudy, Chicago, U.S.A.; one *s.* two *d.* *Educ.:* Eton College; Royal Military College, Sandhurst. Joined 1st Life Guards, 1909; served European War, 1914-18, in France; member L.C.C., 1922-25; D.L., 1946; J.P., 1937; Leicestershire County Army Welfare Officer for Leicestershire and Rutland, 1939-45. *Address:* 4 Orchard Court, Portman Square, W.1. *T.:* Welbeck 1985. *Clubs:* Turf, Buck's. [*Died* 27 *Dec.* 1965.

LEIGH, Reginald Gerard, C.M.G. 1930; C.V.O. 1933; C.B.E. 1923 (O.B.E. 1920); *b.* 2 June 1880; *s.* of late Rev. Canon James Gerard Leigh. *Educ.:* Eton; Christ Church, Oxford, B.A. Called to Bar, Inner Temple, 1909. Appointed King's Messenger, Oct. 1919; assistant private secretary to Secretary of State for Foreign Affairs, 1919-32; retired, 1940. *Address:* Ferndale, Shankill, Co. Dublin, Eire. [*Died* 18 *March* 1962.

LEIGH, Richard Arthur A; *see* Austen-Leigh.

LEIGH, Vivien; Actress; *b.* 5 Nov. 1913; *d.* of Ernest and Gertrude Hartley; *m.* 1st, 1932, Leigh Holman (divorced, 1940); one *d.*; 2nd, 1940, Sir Laurence Olivier (later Lord Olivier) (marr. diss., 1960). *Educ.:* Roehampton; France. Six months' theatrical training in Paris; one year Academy of Dramatic Art, London. First stage appearance The Green Sash, Q Theatre; thereafter Henriette Duquesnoy in The Mask of Virtue, Ambassadors Theatre; Jenny Mere in Happy Hypocrite, His Majesty's Theatre; Ann Boleyn, Shakespeare's Henry the Eighth, Queen Anne in Richard the Second, Oxford; Because We Must, Wyndham's Theatre; Ophelia, Hamlet, Old Vic Company in Elsinore; Titania, Midsummer Night's Dream, Old Vic; title role, Serena Blandish, Gate Theatre; Romeo and Juliet, New York City, 51st St. Theatre; Jennifer Dubedat in Shaw's The Doctor's Dilemma, Haymarket Theatre; Sabina in Thornton Wilder's Skin of our Teeth, Phoenix Theatre, London; 6 months' tour of Australia and N.Z. with Old Vic Company, in Richard III, School for Scandal and Skin of Our Teeth, 1948. Season with Old Vic, New Theatre, 1949, in School for Scandal, Richard III, Antigone; A Streetcar Named Desire, Aldwych, 1949; Cleopatra in Anthony and Cleopatra, Cleopatra in Shaw's Caesar and Cleopatra, St. James's, 1951, New York, Dec. 1951; The Sleeping Prince, 1953; Stratford-on-Avon, 1955, as Lady Macbeth, Viola in Twelfth Night, Lavinia in Titus Andronicus; South Sea Bubble, Lyric, 1956; tour of Europe in Titus Andronicus, 1957; Paola in Duel of Angels, Apollo, 1958; Lulu in Look after Lulu!, Royal Court and New, 1959; Duel of Angels in New York and tour of U.S.A., 1960; Tour of Australia, New Zealand, 1961-1962, in Duel of Angels, Twelfth Night, The Lady of the Camellias; Tour of South America, 1962, in Twelfth Night, The Lady of the Camellias; Tovarich, U.S.A. 1963 (Tony Award); Ivanov, U.S.A., 1966. *Films include:* Sidewalks of London, A Yank at Oxford, Gone with the Wind (Academy award), Waterloo Bridge, Lady Hamilton, Caesar and Cleopatra, Anna Karenina, A Streetcar Named Desire (Academy award), The Deep Blue Sea, The Roman Spring of Mrs. Stone, Ship of Fools. Knight's Cross of the Légion d'Honneur, 1957. *Relevant Publications:* Light of a Star by Gwen Robins, 1968; Vivien Leigh: a Bouquet, by Alan Dent, 1969. [*Died* 8 *July* 1967.

LEIGH-BENNETT, Percy Raymond, C.I.E. 1945; V.D.; *b.* 1887; *s.* of late Herbert James Leigh-Bennett; *m.* 1920, Heather Mary, *d.* of J. J. Higgins. Formerly Transportation Manager, Bengal Nagpur Railway, Kidderpore, India. *Address:* Birkdown, 43 Greenwood Avenue, N. Bersted, Sussex. *Club:* Oriental. [*Died* 22 *Dec.* 1964

LEIGHTON OF ST. MELLONS, 1st Baron *cr.* 1962; **George Leighton Seager;** Bt. 1952; Kt. 1938; C.B.E. 1932; J.P.; H.M. Vice-Lieutenant, Monmouthshire, since 1957; *b.* 1896; *y. s.* of late Sir William Seager; *m.* 1921, Marjorie, *d.* of W. H. Gimson, Breconshire; two *s.* two *d.* *Educ.:* Queen's Coll., Taunton. Travelled on the Continent and in South America prior to becoming partner in firm of W. H. Seager & Co., Ltd., and Seagers Shipping Supplies, Ltd.; a Director of many Public Companies, including Tempus Shipping Co., Ltd., Victory Insurance Co., Ltd., Mountstuart Dry Dock, Ltd. (Chm.), Cardiff Channel Dry Dock Co., Barry Graving Dock Co., Atlantic Shipping and Trading Co., Victory Insurance Co., Ltd. (Chm.), and London Steam-ship Owners' Mutual Insurance Assoc. Ltd.; Member (Part-time) South Wales Area Electricity Board; Dir. British Sailors' Soc.; late President Chamber of Shipping of the U.K.; Member General Committee of Lloyd's Register; an Underwriter of Lloyd's; has been Chairman of Cardiff and Bristol Channel Shipowners' Association; Member Quarter Sessions and Chm. Standing Joint Cttee., Co., Monmouth; President of Cardiff Chamber of Commerce; a Governor of Cardiff Royal Infirmary; has made endowments to the University of Wales and other Welsh institutions; Dir. and Treas. of the Royal Merchant Navy School; and a Gov. of University College, Cardiff; during European War served with the Artist Rifles and on being invalided out served in an honorary capacity upon Secretariat of late Lord Rhondda at Ministry of Food; hon. adviser to Lord Privy Seal in 1929 on his Trade Mission to Canada; Member British Delegation to International Maritime Conferences at Geneva, 1935 and 1936; Chairman Cardiff Post Office Advisory Committee, Port of Cardiff Employment Committee and of S. Wales Advisory Committee to Unemployment Assistance Board; member of Tramp Shipping Advisory Committee under British Shipping Assistance Act, 1934; representative of Shipping Industry on Board of Trade Advisory

Council; Member: Advisory Council Ministry of War Transport; Milford Haven Conservancy Bd.; King George's Fund for Sailors; Chairman Hamadryad Seamen's Hospital; Chairman Committee of Visiting Justices Cardiff Prison; Member Monmouthshire Agricultural Wages Committee; a Welfare Officer County of Monmouthshire (Hon. rank of Captain); Chairman, National Liberal Organisation, 1956-62, resigned, continuing as Hon. Treasurer. Prime Warden of Worshipful Company Shipwrights; Freeman of City of London. High Sheriff of Monmouthshire, 1938. Jubilee Medal, 1935; Coronation Medal, 1953. *Recreations:* golf and motoring. *Heir: s.* Hon. John Leighton Seager [*b.* 11 January 1922; *m.* 1953, Elizabeth Rosita, *o. d.* of late Henry Hopgood; two *s.* one *d.* (one *d.* decd.)]. *Address:* Marleigh Lodge, St. Mellons, Monmouthshire. *Clubs:* Reform, Bath, National Liberal; Exchange (Cardiff); Monmouthshire County.
[*Died* 17 *Oct.* 1963.

LEIGHTON, Arthur Edgar, C.M.G. 1937; F.R.I.C.; F.R.A.C.I.; M.I.Chem.E.; formerly Consultative Member, Board of Factories Administration, Dept. of Munitions, Australia; *b.* London, 17 June 1873; *s.* of James Leighton; *m.* 1914, Norma, *d.* of George Stogdale, Melbourne; one *s.* one *d.* *Address:* c/o Australia and New Zealand Bank, Collins Street, Melbourne, Australia.
[*Died* 6 *Nov.* 1961.

LEIPER, Robert Thomson, C.M.G., 1941; D.Sc., M.D., LL.D. (Glas.); F.R.S.; F.R.C.P.; J.P.; Cons. helminthologist, since 1961, Commonwealth Bureau of Helminthology, St. Albans (Dir., 1928-58); Prof. Emer. of Helminthology in Univ. of London; *b.* Kilmarnock, 17 Apr. 1881; *o. s.* of John Leiper, Ayrshire; *m.* 1908, Ceinwen Saron (*d.* 1966), *y. d.* of William Jones, Bootle; one *s.* two *d.* *Educ.:* Warwick Sch.; Birmingham and Glasgow Universities, Helminthologist to London Sch. of Trop. Med., 1905-24; Director of the Prosectorium, Zoological Gardens, London, 1919-21; Director Dept. of Parasitology, London Sch. Hygiene and Trop. Med., 1924-46. Carnegie Research Scholar (Biol.), 1904; Wandsworth Research Scholar, 1912-14; M.D. 1917 with Hons.; Bellahouston, Straits Settlements, and West London Triennial, Gold Medals; Mary Kingsley Medalist, 1919; Bernhard Nocht Medaille, Tropeninstitut, Hamburg, 1961; Member of the Egyptian Government Survey in Uganda, 1907; Helminthologist to the Grouse Diseases Inquiry Committee, 1909; Research Expeditions to Gold Coast (1905), Nigeria (1912), China (1914), British Guiana (1921), Consultant Parasitologist and Temp. Lieut.-Col. R.A.M.C. Bilharzia Missions in Egypt, 1915-16, and 1928; Member of Colonial Advisory Medical Committee, 1942-45; Past Pres. of Tropical Diseases and Parasitology and of Comparative Medicine Sections, R.S.M., 1933-34. Mem. Council: Royal Society, 1939-41: Roy. Soc. of Trop. Med., 1916-22; Hon. Fellow: Nat. Inst. Sciences of India, 1955-; Roy. Soc. of Tropical Medicine and Hygiene, 1968-. Hon. Pres., Eighth Internat. Congress on Tropical Medicine and Malaria, 1968. Hon. Member: Amer. Soc. of Parasitologists; Italian Soc. Trop. Med. Order of Ismail (2nd class), 1946. Sometime external examiner for higher degrees in Science at London, Cambridge and other British Commonwealth and foreign Universities. *Publications:* Founder of Journal of Helminthology and Helminthological Abstracts; numerous papers on Medical Agricultural and general Helminthology. *Recreation:* reminiscences. *Address:* c/o J. W. G. Leiper, F.R.C.V.S., Nomansland Farm, Wheathampstead, Herts. *T.:* Wheathampstead 2083.
[*Died* 21 *May* 1969.

LEISHMAN, James Blair, F.B.A. 1963; Senior Lecturer in English Literature, University of Oxford, since 1947; Senior Research Fellow and Lecturer in English, St. John's College; *b.* 8 May 1902; *s.* of Matthew Shaw Leishman and Sarah Crossfield; unmarried. *Educ.:* Rydal School; St. John's College, Oxford. Asst. Lecturer, Lecturer and Senior Lecturer in English Literature at Univ. College, Southampton, 1928-46; Univ. Lecturer in English Literature, Oxford, 1946. *Publications:* The Metaphysical Poets: Donne, Herbert, Vaughan, Traherne, 1934; The Three Parnassus Plays, 1598-1602, 1949; The Monarch of Wit: a study of the Poetry of John Donne, 1951, 1962; Themes and Variations in Shakespeare's Sonnets, 1961; many vols. of trans. from Rainer Maria Rilke, 1934-1963; trans. from Hölderlin, 1944, 1954; Translating Horace, 1956. *Recreations:* walking, cycling, travel. *Address:* 10B Bardwell Road, Oxford. *T.:* 59463.
[*Died* 14 *Aug.* 1963.

LEITCH, Sir William, K.B.E., *cr.* 1943; C.B. 1926; *b.* 18 July 1880; *e. s.* of W. G. Leitch, Forres, Morayshire; *m.* 1906, Norah Gwendoline (*d.* 1951), *y. d.* of G. S. Kirkman, St. Austell; one *s.* *Educ.:* Forres Academy; King's College, London. Clerkship L.C.C., 1900; Local Government and Statistical Dept., 1900-5; Education Dept., 1905-12; National Health Insurance Commission (Scotland) District Inspector, 1912-14; Assistant Secretary, 1914; Seconded Ministry of Shipping, 1917-19; H.M. Treasury, 1919; Assistant Secretary H.M. Office of Works, 1920; Principal Assistant Secretary, 1935; Deputy Secretary, Ministry of Works, 1941-1943; Central Authority, under Treasury, for scrutiny of Explanatory Notes to subordinate Statutory Instruments, 1946-50; Secretary (part-time) War Works Commission, 1946-51; Dep. Chm. N. Surrey Valuation Panel and Court, 1948-51. *Address:* Kirkholm, Forres, Morayshire. *T.:* 143. [*Died* 30 *May* 1965.

LEITH-ROSS, Sir Frederick (William), G.C.M.G., *cr.* 1937 (K.C.M.G., *cr.* 1930); K.C.B., *cr.* 1933 (C.B. 1925); Deputy Chm., Nat. Provincial Bank, 1951-66; lately Director: Standard Bank Ltd.; National Discount Company; retired, 1966; *b.* 1887; *m.* 1912, Prudence, *d.* of late R. J. Staples; one *s.* three *d.* *Educ.:* Merchant Taylors' School; Balliol College, Oxford (Warner and Jenkyns Exhibitions and Hon. Scholar); 1st Class Mods. (1907) and Lit. Hum. (1909). Entered the Treasury, 1909; Private Secretary to the Prime Minister (Rt. Hon. H. H. Asquith), 1911-13; British representative on Finance Board of the Reparation Commission, 1920-25; Deputy Controller of Finance, H.M. Treasury, 1925-32; Chief Economic Adviser to H.M. Government, 1932-46; principal British financial expert at Hague Conferences, 1929 and 1930; Chairman of the International Committee on Inter-Governmental Debts, 1931; British representative on the Preparatory Committee and Member of British Delegation at World Economic Conference, 1933; War Debts Mission to Washington, 1933; Chairman of Industrial Property Conference, May 1934; negotiated Financial Agreements with Germany, Oct. 1934, and Italy, April 1935; Financial Mission to China, 1935-36; Delegate at International Sugar Conference, London, 1937; Member of Economic Committee of the League of Nations, 1932-39 (Chairman, 1936 and 1937); Director-General, Ministry of Economic Warfare, 1939-42; Chairman of Inter-Allied Post-War Requirements Committee, 1941-43; Dep. Director-General, U.N.R.R.A., 1944-45; Chairman of European Committee of Council, U.N.R.R.A., 1945-46; Governor, National Bank of Egypt, 1946-51. *Publication:* Money Talks (Memoirs), 1968. *Address:* St. Olaves, Bowring Road, Ramsey, Isle of Man.
[*Died* 22 *Aug.* 1968.

LE MARINEL, Very Rev. Matthew, M.A.; Retired as Rector of S. Helier (1938-

1959) and Dean of Jersey (1937-59); *b.* 18 July 1883; *s.* of Philip Le Marinel and Eva Louisa Pirouet. *Educ.:* Victoria Coll., Jersey; Elizabeth Coll., Guernsey; Jesus Coll., Oxford; St. Stephen's House, Oxford. Curate of S. Anne's Brookfield, N.6., 1906-9; S. Mary's, Brookfield, N.W.5, 1909-27; Vicar of S. Matthew's, Oakley Square, N.W.1., 1927-38; Hon. Canon of Winchester, 1944. *Recreations:* travel, cycling. *Address:* 13 Aquila Road, St. Helier, Jersey. *T.:* Central 23296. [*Died* 22 *Jan.* 1963.

LEMASS, His Hon. Judge Edwin Stephen; lately British Judge of the International Court, Tangier, Morocco (1949-57); *b.* 26 Dec. 1890; *s.* of late Peter Edmond Lemass, I.S.O., L.R.C.S.I., Monkstown, Co. Dublin, and Maria Patricia Scallan; *m.* 1949, Dora Anna Maria, *y. d.* of late Rocco Capozzi, Naples, and *widow* of Col. W. H. Thornton, C.B.E., M.C. (R.A.), Cairo. *Educ.:* University School; Trinity College, Dublin. B.A. Moderator Hons.; 1st prizeman Internat. Law. Auditor, Coll. Historical Soc. Called to Irish Bar, 1913, N.W. Circuit. Served European War, 1915-19, France and N. Russia (Archangel Force). Apptd. to Min. of Justice, Egypt, 1920; Private Sec. to the Judicial Adviser, 1921; Asst. and Legal Sec. to successive Judicial Advisers, 1922-31; Judge of Mixed (Internat.) Courts of Egypt, Nov. 1932; Counsellor, Mixed Court of Appeal, Alexandria, Nov. 1939-Oct. 1949. Chairman, United Forces Welfare Clubs Organisation, Alexandria, for British and Allied Troops in Egypt, 1940-47. Grand Officier, Order of the Nile, Egypt. *Recreations:* painting, all mediums, press drawings and cartoons, book illustration, travelling, motoring. *Address:* 1 Rue Scovasso, Tangier, Morocco. *Clubs:* Country Diplomatic (Tangier); Union (Alexandria).
[*Died* 12 *April* 1970.

LEMON, Brig. Arthur L. K.; *see* Kent-Lemon.

LEMONNIER, Admiral André Georges, Hon. K.C.B.; Grand Officier de la Légion d'Honneur; Commandeur du Mérite Maritime; Croix de Guerre; *b.* 1896. Served European War, 1914-18, and War of 1939-1945; Chief of Naval Staff, France, 1945-1947; formerly First Commandant N.A.T.O. Defence College; Naval Deputy to the Supreme Commander, S.H.A.P.E., 1951-56, retired. *Publications:* Paisible Normandie, 1954; Cap sur la Provence, 1956; Croiseurs en Action, 1959; Les Cent Jours de Normandie, 1961. *Address:* 2 rue Royale, Paris 8e. [*Died* 30 *May* 1963.

LENNARD, Sir Fiennes B.; *see* Barrett-Lennard.

LENNARD, Reginald Vivian, M.A.; *b.* Lightcliffe, Yorks, 3 Sept. 1885; *s.* of late Rev. V. R. Lennard, M.A. *Educ.:* Privately; New Coll., Oxford (exhibitioner), 1st Class Modern History, 1907; Cobden Prize, 1908, Social Research Prize (London School of Economics), 1914. Lecturer in Modern History, Wadham College, 1909; Lecturer to Workers' Educational Association, 1908-15; Labour Section, Ministry of Munitions, 1915; Paymaster Sub-Lieutenant R.N.V.R., 1917; Fellow of Wadham Coll., 1919; Member of Royal Commission on Agriculture, 1919; Lecturer in Agricultural History at Oxford School of Agriculture, 1919-1932; University Lecturer in Modern History, 1930-32; Sub-Warden of Wadham College, 1937-38, 1939-45; Reader in Economic History in the University of Oxford, 1932-51. *Publications:* Economic Notes on English Agricultural Wages, 1914; Rural Northamptonshire under the Commonwealth (in Vinogradoff's Oxford Studies in Social and Legal History), 1916; chapters on English Agriculture during and since the War in Some Aspects of Recent British Economics (Chicago), 1923; (as editor and part author) Englishmen at Rest and Play (1558-1714), 1931; Democracy: The Threatened Foundations, 1941 (German transl., 1946); Rural England 1086-1135, 1959; contributor to Hoops' Reallexikon der Germanischen Altertumskunde, 1912; Alfons Dopsch Festschrift, 1938; and various journals. *Address:* Paine's Close, Lower Heyford, Oxford. *T.:* Steeple Aston 461. [*Died* 6 *March* 1967.

LENNIE, Robert Aim, T.D.; M.D.; LL.D. (Glas.) 1955; F.R.F.P.S.G., F.R.C.O.G.; late Clinical Examiner in Gynæcology, University of Edinburgh; late Chairman of Central Midwives Board for Scotland; late Corps Comdt. St. Andrew's Ambulance Corps; *b.* 5 April 1889; 5th *s.* of late Ritchie Lennie, Cambuslang, Lanarkshire; *m.* 1926, Mary Kirk, M.B., Ch.B., *er. d.* of David Jeffrey, Glasgow. *Educ.:* Glasgow High School; University of Glasgow. Served European War, 1914-19, 1st Lowland Field Ambulance and attached 4th and 7th Royal Scots, 52nd (Lowland) Div., T.A. (despatches); O.C. 4th Scottish Gen. Hosp., 1939-41; Hon. Col. 4th Scottish Gen. Hosp. T.A., 1948-54; late Prof. Midwifery and Gynæcology, St. Mungo College, Glasgow; Regius Professor of Midwifery, University of Glasgow, 1946-54; formerly Obstetric Surgeon, Glasgow Royal Maternity Hosp.; Gynæcologist, the Western Infirmary, Glasgow; Col. late R.A.M.C., T.A.; Examiner for Fellowship, R.F.P. and S.G.; Examiner, Obstetrics and Gynæcology, Queen's University, Belfast, 1953. Hon. Fell. Edinburgh Obstetrical Soc., 1956. Hon. Fell. Glasgow Obstetrical Soc., 1960. *Publications:* (Part author) A Glasgow Manual of Obstetrics; various papers on Obstetrical and Gynæcological subjects. *Address:* Radernie, West Abercromby Street, Helensburgh, Dunbartonshire. *T.:* Helensburgh 616. *Clubs:* Conservative, Royal Scottish Automobile (Glasgow).
[*Died* 26 *March* 1961.

LEON, Paul; French Art Historian; Membre de l'Institut; Hon. Directeur-Général des Beaux-Arts, since 1933; Hon. Professor, Collège de France, since 1944; *b.* Rueil (Seine-et-Oise), 2 Oct. 1874; *s.* of Jules Léon and Louise Isay; *m.* 1906, Madeleine Alexandre; one *s.* one *d.* *Educ.:* Lycée Condorcet; École Normale Supérieure (agrégé ès lettres). Chef du Cabinet to Under-Sec. of State for Fine Arts, 1905-07; Director, Architecture Office, 1907-19 (in this capacity saved many monuments and works of art during European War); Directeur des Beaux-Arts, 1919; Mem. Acad. des Beaux-Arts, 1922; Directeur-Général des Beaux-Arts, 1928-33 (Hon. Dir.-Gen. 1933); Professor of History of Monuments, Collège de France, 1933-44 (Hon. Prof. 1944). Asst-Comr.-Gen., Internat. Exhibition of Decorative Arts (Grand Officer, Legion of Honour), 1925; Assistant Commissioner-General, International Exhibition of Art and Technology, 1937. Grand Croix, Legion of Honour, 1938; Conservateur du Musée Condé au château de Chantilly, 1955; numerous foreign decorations. *Publications:* La Renaissance des Ruines, 1918; Les Monuments Historiques (couronné en 1917 par l'Académie Française, en 1921 par l'Académie des Beaux-Arts); Art et Artistes d'aujourd'hui (tome I), 1925, (tome II), 1932; Rapport sur l'Exposition des Arts Décoratifs, 13 vol.; Eaux et Fontaines de Paris, 1946; Paris: Histoire de la Rue, 1947; Du Palais-Royal au Palais-Bourbon, Souvenirs, 1948; La Guerre pour la paix, 1950; La vie des monuments français, 1951; Les mémoires du Prince de Talleyrand (7 vols.), 1953-55; Mérimée et son Temps, 1962. *Address:* 15 Rue de la Pompe, Paris 16e, France. *T.:* Trocadéro 23. 42. [*Died* 1 *Aug.* 1962.

LEON, Sir Ronald George, 3rd Bart., *cr.* 1911; *b.* 22 Oct. 1902; *o. s.* of Sir George

Leon, 2nd Bt., and Mildred Ethel (*d.* 1951), *d.* of L. J. Jennings, M.P.; *S.* father 1947; *m.* 1st, 1924, Rosemary Armstrong; one *d.*; 2nd, 1932, Dorothy Katharine (marriage dissolved), *d.* of late Sir Guy Standing, K.B.E.; two *s.*; 3rd, 1947, Alice Mary, *o. d.* of late Dr. Thomas Holt, M.D. *Educ.:* Eton. Served War of 1939-45, Capt. K.R.RC. *Heir:* *s.* John Ronald *b.* 16 Aug. 1934. *Address:* 17 Chapel Street, S.W.1. *T.:* Sloane 5087. [*Died* 29 *Aug.* 1964.

LEONARD, Rt. Rev. Martin Patrick Grainge, D.S.O. 1916; M.A.; Suffragan Bishop of Thetford since 1953; Commissary to South African Church Railway Mission; Boy Scout Commissioner; Deputy Camp Chief; Hon. Chaplain to Forces (T.A.); *b.* Torpenhow, Cumberland, 5 July 1889; *s.* of Rev. John Grainge Leonard; *m.* 1933, Kathleen Mary (Head of St. Mildred's House, Isle of Dogs), *d.* of Rev. Leslie Knights-Smith, Brewood, Staffs; two *s.* two *d.* *Educ.:* Rossall School; Oriel College, Oxford; Egerton Hall, Manchester. While at Oxford obtained a commission in 4th Batt. the King's Own (R.L. Regt.) and served in Territorials for four years; at Rossall School Mission, Scoutmaster of the 15th Manchester Troop Boy Scouts; Deacon, 1913; Priest, 1914; Chaplain to the Forces, 1914; served European War, 1914-19 (despatches, D.S.O.); Resident Chaplain to Cheltenham Coll. 1919-1922; before and after the war, Asst. Missioner at Rossall School Mission, Manchester; Staff Padre Toc H Manchester, 1922-28; Administrative Padre at Toc H Headquarters, 1928-33; Chief Overseas Commissioner Toc H, 1933-36; Rector of Hatfield, 1936; Rural Dean of Hertford, 1940; Provost of St. Mary's Cathedral, Glasgow, 1944-53. *Publication:* Scouts' Owns, 1933. *Recreations:* gardening, philately. *Address:* 18 Albemarle Road, Norwich. *T.:* 53219. [*Died* 21 *July* 1963.

LEONARD, William, J.P.; Member, Board of North of Scotland Hydro Electric Scheme, 1950-55; *b.* 14 February 1887; *s.* of James Leonard, Glasgow and Vancouver; *m.* 1915, Mary Dunlop, *d.* of John Boyd, Glasgow. *Educ.:* Board Schools, Glasgow and Manchester. Journeyman Cabinetmaker; Canada, 1907-13 inclusive; Sergeant, 79th Cameron Highrs., Winnipeg; farming, Miami, Manitoba; carpenter, Vancouver, B.C.; National Secretary Scottish Labour College, 1918-20; Scottish Organiser Nat. Amal. Furnishing Trades Assoc., 1921-31; M.P. (Lab.) St. Rollox Div. of Glasgow, 1931-50; Parliamentary Private Secretary to Sir Andrew Duncan, M.P. at Board of Trade and also Ministry of Supply; Parliamentary Secretary, Ministry of Supply and Aircraft Production, 1945; Joint Parl. Sec. Min. of Supply, 1946-47; Member of I.L.P. 15 years; Member of Scottish Advisory Committee of Labour Party; Member of General Council Scottish Trade Union Congress; President Scottish Trade Union Congress, 1925 and 1931-32; Chairman of Housing Progress Panel for Scotland, 1951; Member of National Assistance Board, 1955-60. *Recreation:* gardening. *Address:* 2 Lochview Road, Bearsden, Glasgow. *T.:* 041-942 0047. [*Died* 14 *Oct.* 1969.

LESCAZE, William; Head of own firm, William Lescaze, Architect, since 1923; *b.* 27 March 1896; *s.* of Alexandre Lescaze and Marthe Caux; *m.* 1933, Mary Connick Hughes; one *s.* *Educ.:* Collège de Genève; École Polytechnique Fédérale, Zürich (M.Arch.). Naturalised American citizen, 1929. Principal works: Oak Lane Country Day School, 1929; Philadelphia Saving Fund Soc. Building (with George Howe), 1932; first modern residence to use glass brick in New York, 1933; summer camp for Internat. Ladies Garment Workers Union, Bushkill, Pa.; Public High School, Ansonia, Conn.; Kimble Glass Co. Admin. Bldg., Vineland, N.J.; Aviation Building and Pavilion of Switzerland, N.Y. World's Fair, 1939; Longfellow Bldg. (offices and stores bldg.), Washington, D.C.; Theatre, studios and offices for Columbia Broadcasting System, Hollywood, Calif.; Woods End War Workers Apartments, Roselle, N.J.; Chestnut Gardens War Workers Apartments, Bridgeport, Conn.; Elliott Houses (first post-war low-cost housing in N.Y.C.); Crossett Health Center, Arkansas; Theatre, Hempstead, L.I.; Harbor Homes, Port Washington, L.I., Spinney Hill Homes, Manhasset, L.I. (low cost housing); 711 Third Avenue (offices and stores building), New York City; City Civil Courts Buildings 111 Centre Street, New York City; Church Center at the United Nations Plaza, New York City; Brotherhood In Action, West 40th Street and 7th Ave. New York City; 777 Third Avenue, 38-storey office building with plaza and arcade, New York City; Chatham Center, Pittsburgh, Pa.; Junior High Sch. 24 Richmond, Staten Is.; No. 1 Oliver Plaza, Pittsburgh, Pa.; No. 1 New York Plaza, N.Y.C.; 110 East 59th Street, N.Y.C.; Prefabricated Steel House for Reliance Steel Products Co.; Metal clad Insulated Wall Research. Awards: Silver Medal, Intl. Exp Paris, 1937; Medal, Phila. Chapter of Am. Inst. Architects, 1940; Silver Medal, Pan Am. Congress Architects, Montevideo, Uruguay—all for Phila. Saving Fund Soc. Bldg.; Hon. Award, So. Calif. Chapter Am. Inst. Architects for Columbia Broadcasting Bldg.; Silver Medal for Pavilion of Switzerland, N.Y. World's Fair; Citation of Honor and Merit, The Stella Elkins Tyler School of Fine Arts, Temple Univ., Philadelphia, Pa. F.A.I.A., F.R.S.A.; Member N.Y. State Building Code Commn. *Publications:* Architecture for the New Theatre, 1935; The Intent of the Artist, 1941; On Being An Architect, 1942; articles in magazines. *Recreation:* painting. *Address:* 211 East 48 St., New York, N.Y. 10017. *T.:* Eldorado 5-3660. [*Died* 9 *Feb.* 1969.

LESLIE, Edward Henry John, C.M.G. 1918; M.V.O.; J.P., D.L.; *e. surv. s.* of late Robert Charles Leslie of Ballybay, Co. Monaghan, and Kilclief, Co. Down, J.P., D.L., and Charlotte Philippa Mary Kelso; *b.* 11 Aug. 1880; unmarried. *Educ.:* Eton. *Address:* 3 Piazza Campitelli, Rome, Italy. [*Died* 18 *Aug.* 1966.

LESLIE, Sir (Henry John) Lindores, 9th Bt., *cr.* 1625; *b.* 26 Aug. 1920; *s.* of Wing-Commander Sir Norman R. A. D. Leslie, 8th Bt., C.M.G., C.B.E., and Betty Elise, *d.* of late J. T. B. Sewell, C.B.E.; *S.* father, 1937; *m.* 1950, Colette Kathleen, *d.* of Dr. G. T. Cregan, M.C., Commonside House, Rogate, Petersfield, Hants.; one *d.* *Educ.:* Stowe. Commissioned 1939 XII Royal Lancers (Supplementary Reserve). Prisoner of War, 1940-45. A.C.I.S. 1947. *Recreations:* looking forward to affording them. *Address:* 9 Sloane Gate Mansions, S.W.1. *T.:* Sloane 1958. [*Died* 21 *June* 1967.

LESLIE, Lieut.-Col. John, D.S.O. 1919; M.C.; *s.* of late C. F. H. Leslie, 8 Carlos Place, W.; *b.* 1888; *m.* 1916, Margaret Nannette Helen, *d.* of late Howard Gilliat; two *s.* one *d.* Served European War, 1914-19 (despatches, D.S.O., M.C.); Director: Sheepbridge Engineering Ltd.; North British & Mercantile Insce. Co. Ltd.; Ocean Insce. Co. Ltd.; formerly Government Director British Sugar Corporation. D.L. for Norfolk, 1948, High Sheriff, 1950. *Address:* Brancaster, Norfolk. *Club:* White's. [*Died* 1 *Oct.* 1965.

LESLIE, Sir Lindores; *see* Leslie, Sir H. J. L.

LESLIE MELVILLE, Lt.-Col. Hon. Ian, T.D.; *b.* 14 Aug. 1894; *s.* of 11th Earl of Leven and 10th of Melville (*d.* 1906), and Hon. Emma Selina Portman (*d.* 1941), *e. d.* of 2nd Viscount Portman; *m.* 1915, Charlotte Isobel, *d.* of late Major W. Stirling of Fairburn, Ross-shire; one *s.* two *d.* (and one *d.* decd.). *Educ.:* Eton; Balliol College, Oxford, M.A. Lieut.-Col. commanding Lovat Scouts, 1936-40; served European War, 1914-18. Managing Director of Glyn, Mills & Co.; and Deputy Chairman Dalgety & Co. Ltd. until 1955. Member of Scottish Board, Legal and General Assce. Soc. Ltd. Mem. Royal Company of Archers, Queen's Body Guard for Scotland. *Address:* Bridgelands, Selkirk. *T.:* Selkirk 2370. *Clubs:* Brooks's, Lansdowne; New (Edinburgh).
[*Died* 10 *Feb.* 1967.

LESSER, Henry, C.B.E. 1950 (O.B.E. 1941); LL.B.; Barrister-at-Law; *e. s.* of Simon and Sarah Lesser; *m.* Jane, *d.* of Ralph and Ethel Lustig; two *d.* *Educ.:* City of London Cowper Street School; University College, London. Called to Bar, Gray's Inn; LL.B. (Hons.) London. Standing Member of National Health Service Tribunal; Member: Medical Practices Committee (National Health Service Act, 1946); N.W. Metrop. Reg. Hospital Board; Board of Governors Middlesex Hosp.; Chairman, Gen. Whitley Council, Min. of Health. Co-opted Mem. Health Cttee. of L.C.C., 1948-65; Mem. London Exec. Coun. (National Health Service Act, 1946), (Chm. 1947-53); President British Hospitals Contributory Schemes Assoc.; Trustee, Liverpool Victoria Friendly Soc.; Chairman: Hospital Saving Assoc.; Inst. Industrial Administration, 1951-53; Central Council for Health Education. 1946-1948; Founder-mem. and Mem. of Council and Exec. Cttee British Institute of Management, 1951-53; formerly Advisor on Industrial Relations to the South Eastern Gas Board; President National Associations of Pension Funds; Vice-President Insurance Inst. of London. Contested Peckham (Parl.) Division of Camberwell (Nat. L.), 1922; formerly President National Federation of Employees' Approved Societies; Chm., London Insurance Cttee., 1927; Pres., Nat. Assoc. of Insurance Cttees., 1927-28; Pres., Faculty of Insurance, 1931; Chm. Consultative Council to Minister of Health on Nat. Health Insurance. 1937-38; First Pres., Assoc. of Exec. Councils (Eng.) and Chm. Fed. of Exec. Councils, Eng., Scot., and Wales, 1948-49. Fellow, Royal Society of Health; Fellow, Chartered Insurance Institute; Fellow, British Institute of Management. Freeman and Liveryman of City of London; Member of Court of Assistants of Worshipful Company of Turners (formerly Master). *Publications:* standard work on The Law of National Health Insurance, 1939; numerous papers and articles on social insurance and public health services. *Address:* 47 Clifton Hill, N.W.8. *T.:* Maida Vale 1708; Goldsmith Building, Temple, E.C.4. *T.:* Central 8450. *Club:* Reform.
[*Died* 22 *Dec.* 1966.

LESSING, Edward Albert, O.B.E. 1918; Chairman of Alexandria Trading Corp. Ltd.; a Director, Contemporary Review, since 1960; *b.* 1890; *s.* of Albert Lessing, London. *Educ.:* Marlborough; University College, Oxford. Called to Bar, Inner Temple; served European War as Captain Grenadier Guards; a Member of Military Mission to Russia; M.P.(L.) Abingdon, 1923-24; Lieutenant and Paymaster Royal Army Pay Corps, 1939-42; Captain, Pioneer Corps, 1942-45, Interpreter I.O.; Civil Servant, 1945-47; formerly a director Baltic and Mercantile Exchange, Vice-Chm. Nat. Fed. Corn Trade Assocs. *Address:* 38 St. Mary Abbots Court, W.14. *Clubs:* Reform, National Liberal. [*Died* 25 *Aug.* 1964.

LESSING, Rudolf, C.B.E. 1958; Ph.D. (Munich), F.R.I.C., F.Inst.F., M.I.Chem.E.; Consulting Chemist and Chemical Engineer since 1907; *b.* 3 Apr. 1878; *s.* of Simon and Clara Lessing; *m.* 1912, Milly Fuld; one *d.* *Educ.:* Gymnasium Bamberg; Univs. of Munich, Geneva, Berlin, Manchester. Asst. to Prof. Willstaetter, Munich, 1900-02; Research Studentship, Owen's Coll., 1903; Research Chemist, Gas Light & Coke Co., Beckton, 1903-06; Chemist and Engineer, Mond Nickel Co., 1907. Specialises in Coal and its products, coal cleaning, air pollution, flue gas washing, packed towers for chemical processes. Founder and Man. Dir. Hydronyl Ltd., 1914, Deputy Chairman, 1961; Jt. Founder, Hon. Sec., Coal Research Club, 1921; Jt. Founder, Ed., Fuel in Science and Practice, 1922; Mem. Ed. Cttee. of Fuel; Mem. Ed. Bd. Internat. Jl. of Air and Water Pollution; evidence to Roy. Commn. on the Coal Industry, 1925; devised flue gas treatment plant, Fulham Power Station, 1931; Consultant to: Nuffield Trust, 1937; Nat. Trust, 1940; Admiralty, 1940; Dean and Chapter St. Paul's Cathedral, 1952. Chadwick Trustee, 1953, Vice-Chm. 1959; Mem. Cttee. on Air Pollution, 1953; Pres. Nat. Soc. for Clean Air, 1956-58. Past Vice-Pres. Faraday Soc.; Past Vice-Pres. Soc. Chem. Industry, Chm. London Section; Visitor and Manager Royal Institution; Vice-Chm. Brit. Chem. Plant Mfrs. Assoc., 1958. Hon. Member: Faraday Soc., 1957; Instn. of Gas Engineers, 1958; Coke Oven Managers Assoc., 1927; Mem. Parly. and Scientific Committee. *Publications:* William Young Memorial Lecture (Glasgow), Catalysis in the Gas Industry, 1914; Cantor Lectures, Coal Ash and Clean Coal, 1925; Keith Lecture (Edinburgh), Chemical Engineering, 1935. English edn. of Conversion of Coal into Oil, by Franz Fischer, 1925. Numerous original papers in scientific jls., 1900-62. *Recreations:* work and crossword puzzles; formerly mountaineering. *Address:* 3 Thorney Court, Palace Gate, W.8. *Clubs:* Reform, Savage.
[*Died* 2 *Sept.* 1964.

LESTRADE, Prof. Gérard Paul, M.A. (Cape Town); A.M. (Harvard); F.R.S.S.Af.; Professor Emeritus of Bantu Languages, University of Cape Town since 1935; *b.* Amsterdam, 22 August 1897; *s.* of Gerrit B. Lestrade and Pauline L. Goudman; *m.* 1925, Cornelia M. J. Aarts-de Vries. *Educ.:* Normal and S.A. College High School, S.A. College and University of Cape Town, Cape Town; Harvard University; University of London. B.A. University of Cape Town, 1918, M.A. 1919, A.M. Harvard University, 1922, University of London, 1923; Ethnologist, Native Affairs Department, Union of South Africa, 1925-29; Professor of Bantu Studies, University of Pretoria, 1930-34; Member: Council of University College of the North; Union Government Committee on S. African Place Names; Jt. Matric. Bd. of S.A. Univs.; Exams. Bd., Dept. of Bantu Educn. *Publications:* Contribs. scientific periodicals and other publications on languages, customs and history of S.A. Bantu. *Address:* c/o University of Cape Town, Rondebosch, South Africa. *Clubs:* Civil Service, Here Sewentien (Cape Town).
[*Died* 6 *Nov.* 1962.

LETCH, Sir Robert, Kt., *cr.* 1945; General Manager, British Transport Docks Division; Chairman, Docks Management Board, British Transport Commission; *b.* 10 Jan. 1899; *er. s.* of late R. J. Letch. Regional Port Director for Scotland, 1941-42; Regional Port Director North-Western Area, 1942-45; Chairman National Association of Port Employers and Joint Chairman, National Joint Council for Port Transport Industry 1945-47; in service of Port of London Authority, 1915-47. *Address:* Philips Hill, Old Shire Lane, Chorley Wood, Herts.
[*Died* 9 *July* 1962.

LETHBRIDGE, Colonel Alfred, C.B.E. 1932; I.A., retired; *b.* 29 Sep. 1884; *s.* of Robert Frederick Lethbridge and Mary Kathlene Hudson; *m.* 1922, Margery May Cockerton. *Educ.:* Tonbridge; Sandhurst. Late 4th/12th Frontier Force Regt. and Deputy-Inspector General Burma Military Police; retired, 1935. Home Guard, Group and Zone Commander, 1940-45. D.L. Devon, 1942-1947. *Recreation:* fishing. *Address:* Blair Hill, Gamberlake, Axminster, Devon. [*Died* 8 *Feb.* 1968.

LETHBRIDGE Major-General John Sydney, C.B. 1946; C.B.E. 1942; M.C. 1919; Director of Civil Defence, S.W. Region (Bristol), Sept. 1955 - Oct. 1960; *b.* 11 Dec. 1897; *s.* of Lt.-Col. Sydney Lethbridge, O.B.E., R.A.; *m.* 1925, Katharine Greville, *d.* of late Sir John Maynard, K.C.I.E., C.S.I.; one *s.* two *d.* *Educ.:* Gresham's School; Uppingham; R.M.A., Woolwich; Jesus Coll., Cambridge. 2nd Lt. R.E. 1915; served European War, France and Belgium, 1916-17; Aden F Force, 1917-1918; Afghanistan and N.W. Frontier, India, 1919-21; passed Staff College, Quetta, 1932; Lt.-Col. R.E. 1940; Acting Brig. 1940; Temp. Brig. 1941; Acting Maj.-Gen. 1942; Col. and Temp. Maj.-Gen. 1943; War Office, 1942-43; Commander 220 Military Mission, 1943-44; Chief of Staff XIV Army, 1944-45; Chief of Intelligence, Control Commission for Germany and B.A.O.R., 1945-48; retired Hon. Major-General, 1948; Commandant, Civil Defence Staff College, 1949-52. Commander, American Legion of Merit, 1946. *Recreations:* shooting, fishing, cricket. *Address:* Clapper Cottage, Bondleigh, nr. North Tawton, Devon. [*Died* 11 *Aug.* 1961.

LETHEM, Sir Gordon James, K.C.M.G., *cr.* 1936 (C.M.G. 1934); *b.* 16 Sept. 1886; *s.* of late James Lethem, Leith, Scotland, and late Marian Macintosh, Cambridge; *m.* 1923, Kate, *d.* of late R. W. Allen, Rowley Regis; one *d.* *Educ.:* Daniel Stewart's, Edinburgh; Mill Hill School; Edinburgh Univ.; Grenoble University; Spain. Called to Bar, Lincoln's Inn; Assistant Resident, Northern Nigeria, 1911; Served European War, 1914-1915, in Cameroons; Resident, Bornu Province, Nigeria, 1924; travelled on official mission in Sudan, Egypt, Hejaz, 1925; Staff Grade, 1928, Secretary for Native Affairs, and Secretary, Northern Provinces; acting as Lieutenant-Governor, 1931-2-3; Governor and Commander-in-Chief, Seychelles, 1933-1935; Leeward Islands, 1936-41; Governor Designate, Sierra Leone, 1941; Governor and C.-in-C., British Guiana, 1941-46; Hon. Col. British Guiana Regt., 1944; K.St.J. 1945; Hospitaller of Scottish Priory, Order of St. John, 1949. Contested (L.) Banffshire, 1950; Vice-Pres. Scottish Liberal Party, 1950; Pres. Scottish Nat. Council, United Nations Assoc. *Publications:* Colloquial Arabic, Nigeria and Lake Chad; articles on colonial administration. *Recreations:* various; black-face sheep farming on own land in Dumfriesshire. *Address:* Johnstone House, Johnstone-Craighaugh, Eskdalemuir, Dumfriesshire. *T.:* Eskdalemuir 210. *Clubs:* Athenæum, Royal Automobile; New (Edinburgh). [*Died* 14 *Aug.* 1962.

LETT, Sir Hugh, 1st Bt., *cr.* 1941; K.C.V.O. 1947; C.B.E. 1920; M.B., Ch.B. Vict., F.R.C.S. Eng., D.C.L. (hon.) Durham; Sc.D. (hon.) Cambridge; Retd. Cons. Surgeon and late Senior Surgeon to the London Hosp.; late Surgeon in charge of Genito-Urinary Department, London Hospital; Hunterian Trustee, R.C.S. (Chairman, 1955-59), Member of Council, 1927-43; President, 1938-41; Member, Court of Patrons, President B.M.A., 1946-48; Hon. F.R.S.M.; Hon. Member Section of Urology; Hon. Member British Association Urological Surgeons; Hon. Member International Society of Urology; Hon. Fellow Hunterian Society; Vice-President St. Peter's Hospital for Stone; late Member Court of Assistants (late Master) Society of Apothecaries; late Hon. Sec., King Edward's Hospital Fund for London; late Chm. Medical Advisory Cttee. Royal Masonic Hosp.; late Pres. Marlburian Club; late Pres. Section of Surgery and Section of Urology, R.S.M.; late Bradshaw Lecturer and Thomas Vicary Lecturer, R.C.S.; Moynihan Lecturer, Univ. of Leeds, 1942; late External Examiner in Surgery, University of Leeds; late Member of Court of Examiners, R.C.S.; Consulting Surgeon, Bushey Heath Cottage Hospital and King George Hospital, Ilford; Pres. and Orator, Hunterian Society; Vice-President Medical Society of London; late Assistant Surgeon, Belgrave Hospital for Children; *b.* April 1876; *s.* of R. A. Lett, B.A., M.D.; *m.* 1906, Nellie (*d.* 1963), *o. d.* of Sir Buckston Browne; three *d.* *Educ.:* Marlborough College; Leeds; London Hospital. Late Surgeon, Anglo-American Hospital, Wimereux, 1914-15, Belgian Field Hospital, Furnes, 1915, and Major R.A.M.C., 1915-16. *Publications:* papers on surgical subjects in the medical journals. *Address:* Waters Edge, Walmer, Kent. *T.:* Deal 758. [*Died* 19 *July* 1964 (*ext.*).

LETT, Phyllis, (Mrs Phyllis de Burgh Ker), A.R.C.M.; *b.* Redbourne, Lincolnshire; *d.* of R. A. Lett, B.A., M.D.; *m.* 1924, C. Rupert de Burgh Ker, M.C.; one *d.* *Educ.:* Royal College of Music (open Scholarship); Paris. Made début at Royal Albert Hall; Principal Contralto at all chief musical festivals in U.K., including Handel Festival and Eisteddfod; holder of the Musicians' Company's Medal; Associate Royal Philharmonic Society. *Recreation:* gardening. *Address:* Henderside, Yea, Victoria, Australia. *Club:* Victoria League (Melbourne). [*Died* 1 *June* 1962.

LEVER, Sir Ernest (Harry), Kt., *cr.* 1954; Hon. LL.D.; F.I.A.; Captain R.A. (S.R.) retired 1920; *b.* 22 November 1890; *s.* of late Thomas Bains Lever; *m.* 1913, Florence (whom he divorced), *d.* of Alfred Benjamin Millington; two *s.*; *m.* 1940, Mrs. Phyllis Blok, *d.* of late Frederic Ancill. *Educ.:* William Ellis Endowed School. Entered Prudential Assurance Company, 1907; served in European War, 1914-18 (British War Medal, Allied Victory Medal, despatches, Chevalier de la Légion d'Honneur, Croix de Guerre (with palm), Croix de Guerre (with gold star), Knight of Order of Dannebrog, Commander of Order of Polonia Restituta); Member of Board of Trade Departmental Committee on Fixed Trusts, 1936; Chairman Investment Protection Committee of British Insurance Association, 1938-40; Chairman, Richard Thomas & Baldwins Ltd., 1940-59; Chairman Steel Co. of Wales, Ltd., 1947-55; Chairman The Tinplate Conference (1925) and Welsh Plate and Sheet Manufacturers' Association, 1941-59; Director, Lloyds Bank Ltd., 1953-61; President British Iron and Steel Federation, 1956; active part in various international financial negotiations, 1919-40; Joint Secretary, Prudential Assurance Co., 1931-40; Former Member of Council of Foreign Bondholders; former Chairman of Cttee., British Long Term and Medium Term Creditors of Germany; former Chairman Czecho-Slovak (Financial Claims) Committee; Chairman or member of various war-time cttees., 1940-45. *Publications:* Foreign Exchange from the Investor's Point of View, 1925; several contributions to scientific journals on financial and actuarial subjects. *Recreation:* golf. *Address:* Blackbrook Farm, Blackbrook, Dorking, Surrey. *T.:* Dorking 6422. [*Died* 4 *Sept.* 1970.

LEVIEN, Jerome William John; Director, Atlas Assurance Company Ltd., since 1957; *b.* 28 Feb. 1893; *s.* of Martin David Willson Levien and Minnie Margaret Levien (*nee* Willson); *m.* 1918, Sybil May Scott; one *s.* one *d.* *Educ.:* Mill Hill School. Began career with Atlas Assur. Co. Ltd., 1910; joined Jardine Skinner & Co. (now Jardine Henderson Ltd.), Calcutta, 1912, by whom jointly employed with Atlas Assur. Co. Ltd. until 1935; appointed Eastern Sec., Atlas Assurance Co. Ltd., 1926; returned to London and apptd. Asst. Sec., 1935; Sec. 1938, Asst. Gen. Manager and Sec. 1944; Gen. Manager, 1946-58, retd. Director: Essex and Suffolk Insurance Co. Ltd.; Chm. London Salvage Corps, 1949-50; Chm. Fire Offices' Cttee., Fire Protection Assoc., 1949-1953. President: Insurance Inst. of London, 1950-51; Insurance Rifle Club, 1952-53; Insurance Boxing Club, 1952-; Insurance Offices' Rugby Football Union, 1953-54; Insurance Golfing Soc., 1954-55; Chairman British Insurance Assoc., 1953-55. *Publication:* Atlas at War, 1946. *Recreation:* golf. *Address:* Scaldsgrove, Cottered, Hertfordshire. *T.:* Cottered 250. *Club:* Oriental.
[*Died* 10 *April* 1961.

LEVIN, Dr. Nyman; Member for Weapons, Atomic Energy Authority, since 1965; *b.* 17 Feb. 1906; *s.* of Lewis Levin; *m.* 1933, Dora Hirsch; two *s.* one *d.* *Educ.:* Central Foundation School, London; Royal College of Science Imperial College of Science and Technology. Marconi's Wireless Telegraph Company, 1930-40; various posts in Admiralty, Royal Naval Scientific Service, 1940-55; Superintendent, Admiralty Gunnery Establishment, 1951-55; Chief of Research and Development, Rank Precision Industries, Ltd., 1955-1958; Deputy Director, Atomic Weapons Research Establishment, 1958-59, Director, 1959-65. *Address:* The Dyke House, Aldermaston, Berks. *T.:* Silchester 345.
[*Died* 25 *Jan.* 1965.

LEVY, Reuben, M.A., Litt.D.; Emeritus Professor of Persian, Cambridge University; Fellow of Christ's College; *b.* 28 April 1891; *s.* of Harris and Gertrude Levy, Manchester; *m.* 1st, 1921, Flora (*d.* 1962), *d.* of late M. Herz; 2nd, 1965, Margaret Sylvia, *d.* of late H. W. Sanderson. *Educ.:* Friars School, Bangor; Univ. of North Wales; Jesus College, Oxford; General Staff Intelligence, Mesopotamia (Captain), 1916-18; Iraq Political Service, 1918-20; Lectr. in Persian, Oxford, 1920-23; Resident in U.S.A., 1923-26; Lecturer in Persian, Cambridge, 1926-39. Chatham House, 1939-40; Served War of 1939-45, R.A.F. Intelligence, 1941-45 (Squadron Leader). *Publications:* Persian Literature, 1923; A Baghdad Chronicle, 1929; Sociology of Islam, 2 vols. 1931-33, 2nd edn. (Social Structure of Islam), 1957; Ma'alim al-Qurbah (Arabic text, etc.), 1938; Mirror for Princes (Qabus-nama), 1951; Qabus-nama (Persian text), 1951; The Persian Language, 1951; The Tales of Marzuban, 1959; The Shah-nama, 1966; articles in Journal of Royal Asiatic Soc., etc. *Recreations:* travel, keeping alive. *Address:* Christ's College, Cambridge. [*Died* 6 *Sept.* 1966.

LEVY, Richard Francis, Q.C. 1937; LL.B.; retired as Chairman Monopolies Commission, 1956-65; Chairman Workman's Compensation Supplementation Board, 1956-1962; Chairman Pneumoconiosis and Byssinosis Benefit Board, 1956-62; Chairman Committee of Inquiry into Precautions against Anthrax, 1957; lately Recorder of Margate; *b.* 13 July 1892; *s.* of late David and Catherine Levy; *m.* 1923, Jeanne Kasriel, Paris; two *d.* *Educ.:* Hackney Downs Secondary School; London University. Called to Bar, Middle Temple, 1918. Master of the Bench, Middle Temple. *Address:* 83 Oakwood Court, W.14. *T.:* Western 1708.
[*Died* 16 *Dec.* 1968.

LEVY, Stanley Isaac, Q.C. 1957; *b.* 24 Dec. 1890; *s.* of David and Catherine Levy; *m.* 1919, Mary Victoria, *d.* of Alfred and Bessie Emanuel. *Educ.:* City of London School; St. John's College, Cambridge. B.Sc. (Lond.) 1911; B.A. (Cantab.) 1912; Research, Cambridge, 1912-14. Chemical Asst. to Lord Moulton, Min. of Munitions, 1914-18; Consulting Chemist, 1919-35; F.R.I.C. 1919; Ph.D. (Lond.) 1920. Barrister, 1927; practised at the Bar, 1935-64, 1966-. Master of the Bench, Middle Temple, 1963. Asst. Dir., Min. of Supply, 1939-44. Fellow, Roy. Soc. of Bohemia, 1937. *Publications:* The Rare Earths, 1914, 2nd Edn. 1924; Modern Explosives, 1920; Introduction to Industrial Chemistry, 1926; Incandescent Lighting, 1922. *Recreations:* music, bridge, travel, swimming. *Address:* Carpmael Building, Temple, E.C.4. *T.:* Central 8791. *Club:* Savage. [*Died* 12 *Nov.* 1968.

LEWANIKA III, Sir Mwanawind; *see* Barotseland, Litunga of.

LEWES, Earl of; Henry John Montacute Nevill; *b.* 2 Feb. 1948; *s.* and *heir* of 5th Marquess of Abergavenny. *Educ.:* Eton. Page of Honour to the Queen, 1962-1964. [*Died* 2 *April* 1965.

LEWIS, Ven. Charles Gerwyn Rice; Archdeacon Emeritus, diocese of Monmouth; Archdeacon of Newport, 1953-64; Vicar of St. Mark's, Newport, 1954-64; Rural Dean of Newport since 1949; Hon. Canon of Monmouth since 1949. *Educ.:* St. David's College, Lampeter (B.A. 1923). Deacon 1923, priest 1924, Llandaff; Curate of St. John, Canton, Cardiff, 1923-25; Llanddewi-Rhondda, 1925-28; St. Woolos, Newport, 1928-31; Vicar of Treherbert, 1931-39. Served as Chaplain to the Forces 1940-41. Vicar of All Saints', Newport, 1939-1954. *Address:* 34 Fields Rd., Newport, Mon. [*Died* 17 *July* 1964.

LEWIS, Ven. Christopher Gwynne, M.C. 1918; Archdeacon of St. Davids since 1949; Rector of Prendergast since 1941; *b.* 13 March 1895; *s.* of late B. A. Lewis, Undercliff, Ferryside, Carmarthen; *m.* 1923 Mary, *d.* of late John Williams, Llandilo, Carmarthenshire; one *d.* *Educ.:* Queen Elizabeth's Grammar School, Carmarthen; Jesus College, Oxford. Served European War, 1914-18, Captain, Welsh Regt., 1915-19. Hon. Freeman of Borough of Carmarthen, 1923; B.A. 1921, M.A. 1932, Oxford. Curate of Llanelly (St. Paul), 1921, of Brecon, 1924; Curate-in-charge Llandefalle, 1930; Rector of Llanbadarnfawr (Radnorshire), 1934. *Address:* Prendergast Rectory, Haverfordwest, Pembrokeshire. *T.:* Haverfordwest 2625. [*Died* 31 *Jan.* 1963.

LEWIS, Clive Staples; Professor of Medieval and Renaissance English, Cambridge, 1954-66 (resigned Oct.); also Fellow of Magdalene College, Cambridge (Hon. Fell., Oct. 1963); *b.* 29 Nov. 1898; *s.* of late A. J. Lewis, Solicitor, Belfast, and Flora Augusta Hamilton; *m.* 1956, Mrs. Joy Gresham (*née* Davidman). *Educ.:* For one year at Malvern Coll.; afterwards privately by late W. T. Kirkpatrick, former Headmaster of Lurgan Coll. Scholar, Univ. Coll., Oxford, 1918; 2nd Lt. Somerset Light Infantry, 1918-19; Chancellor's Prize for English Essay; 1st in Hon. Mods., 1st in Greats., 1st in English; Lecturer at Univ. Coll., Oxford, 1924; Gollancz Memorial Prizeman, 1937; Library Assoc. Carnegie Medal, 1957. Fell. and Tutor of Magdalen Coll., Oxf., 1925-1954, Hon. Fell., 1955. Hon. D.D. St. And., 1946; F.R.S.L. 1948; Hon. D. ès Lettres,

Laval Univ., 1952; F.B.A. 1955; Hon. Fell., University Coll., Oxford, 1958; Hon. D.Litt., Manchester, 1959; Hon. Dr. Dijon, 1962; Hon. Dr. Lyon, 1963. *Publications:* Dymer, 1926 (under the name of Clive Hamilton); The Pilgrim's Regress, 1933; The Allegory of Love, 1936; Rehabilitations, 1938; Out of the Silent Planet, 1938; The Personal Heresy (with E. M. W. Tillyard), 1939; The Problem of Pain, 1940; The Screwtape Letters, 1942 (revised edn. The Screwtape Letters and Screwtape Proposes a Toast, 1961); A Preface to Paradise Lost (The Ballard Metthew Lecture for 1941), 1942; Perelandra, 1943; Christian Behaviour, 1943; Abolition of Man (Riddell Lectures, 1943), 1944; Beyond Personality, 1944; That Hideous Strength, 1945; The Great Divorce, 1945; George MacDonald: an Anthology, 1945; Miracles, 1947; Transposition, 1949; Mere Christianity, 1952; English Literature in the Sixteenth Century, 1954; Surprised by Joy (autobiography), 1955; Till We Have Faces, 1956; Reflections on the Psalms, 1958; The Four Loves, 1960; Studies in Words, 1960; Experiment in Criticism, 1961; They Asked for a Paper, 1962; (*Posthumous Publications*) Letters to Malcolm: Chiefly on Prayer, 1964; The Discarded Image, 1964; A Grief Observed, 1964; Letters of C. S. Lewis, 1966; Letters to an American Lady, 1969; Narrative Poems, 1969. *For children:* The Lion, the Witch, and the Wardrobe, 1950; Prince Caspian, 1951; The Voyage of the Dawn-Treader, 1952; The Silver Chair, 1953; The Horse and his Boy, 1954; The Magician's Nephew, 1955; The Last Battle, 1956. *Recreation:* walking. *Address:* Magdalene College, Cambridge. *Club:* Athenæum. [*Died* 22 *Nov.* 1963.

LEWIS, Dominic Bevan Wyndham, F.R.S.L. 1947. *Publications:* A London Farrago, 1922; At the Green Goose, 1923; At the Sign of the Blue Moon, 1924; At the Blue Moon Again, 1925; On Straw and Other Conceits, 1927; François Villon, 1928; The Anatomy of Dandyism (translated from Barbey d'Aurevilly), 1928; A Christmas Book (with G. C. Heseltine), 1928; King Spider: Louis XI. of France, 1930; The Stuffed Owl, an Anthology of Bad Verse (with Charles Lee), 1930; Emperor of the West (Charles V.), 1932; Take it to Bed, 1944; Ronsard, 1944; The Hooded Hawk, 1946 (republished as James Boswell, 1952); Four Favourites, 1948; The Soul of Marshal Gilles de Raiz, 1952; The Terror of St. Trinians (with Ronald Searle), 1954; Doctor Rabelais, 1957; A Florentine Portrait, 1959; Molière: The Comic Mask, 1959; The Shadow of Cervantes, 1962; The World of Goya, 1968. *Address:* c/o A. D. Peters, 10 Buckingham St., Adelphi, W.C.2. *Club:* Garrick. [*Died* 21 *Nov.* 1969.

LEWIS, Emily Catherine, M.S., F.R.C.S.; retd.; Surgeon to St. Saviour's and Marie Curie Hospitals; Cons. Surgeon to Royal Free and South London Hospitals; Past Member, Medical Tribunal, Min. of National Insurance; *d.* of James Lewis, Lieut. R.N., and Emily Catherine Wooldridge. *Publications:* Urology in Women; articles in Lancet, Medical Press, Medical World, etc. *Address:* 41 Cambridge Rd., Ely, Cambs. *Club:* University Women's. [*Died* 25 *Oct.* 1965.

LEWIS, Essington, C.H. 1943; Deputy Chairman The Broken Hill Pty. Co. Ltd., Melbourne, Aust., since 1952 (Chairman, 1950-52); *b.* Burra, S.A., 13 Jan. 1881; *s.* of late Hon. John Lewis, C.M.G., M.L.C. and Martha Brook; *m.* 1910, Gladys Rosalind Cowan (*d.* 1954); two *s.* three *d.* *Educ.:* St. Peter's Coll., Adelaide; S. Australian School of Mines (Diploma, 1903). General mining experience Broken Hill and Mt. Lyell; Foreman Sulphuric Acid and Zinc Plant, Broken Hill, 1904; Metallurgist and Asst. Manager Broken Hill Pty. Co's Smelting Works, Port Pirie; Manager Iron Knob Tramway and Ironstone Quarries; Manager Broken Hill Munitions Co. Pty. Ltd., 1915-1918; Asst. General Manager, B.H.P. Co., 1918; General Manager, 1921; Managing Director, 1926; Chief Gen. Manager, 1938; Chm., 1950. Director: Australian Iron & Steel Ltd. (Dep.-Chm.); Rylands Bros. (Australia) Pty. Ltd. (Dep.-Chm.); B.H.P. By Products Pty. Ltd.; B.H.P. Collieries Pty. Ltd.; Tube-makers of Australia Ltd. (Chm.); Stewarts & Lloyds (Australia) Pty. Ltd. (Chm.); British Tube Mills (Aust.) Pty. Ltd. (Chm.); Commonwealth Aircraft Corp. Pty. Ltd.; Hon. Member, Australasian Inst. M.M. (Bronze Medal 1940), M.Inst.Met., M.I.S.I. Hon. Amer. I.M. & Met. Eng., F.A.C.I., etc. Member Aust. Inst. of Metals (Florence M. Taylor Medal 1948); Hon. Mem. Institution of Engineers, Aust., 1948; Fellow Australian Academy of Science, 1954. Govt. Service: Chm. Advisory Panel on Industrial Organisation, 1938; Chairman of Defense Board of Business Administration, Nov. 1939; Director General of Munitions, 1940-1945 and of Aircraft Production, and Chm. Aircraft Advisory Cttee., 1942-45; Consultant to Commonwealth Immigration Planning Council, Oct. 1949; Chm. Australian Administrative Staff Coll., 1954-59; Chm. Industrial Design Council of Aust., 1957. Kernot Medal for 1943, Melbourne Univ.; Bessemer Gold Medal, 1944, Iron and Steel Institute, London. Hon. D.Sc. (Sydney), 1952; Gold Medal Inst. of Mining and Metallurgy, London, 1954. *Publications:* The Iron and Steel Industry of Australia, 1929; The Economics of the Australian Iron and Steel Industry, 1938; The Importance of the Iron and Steel Industry to Australia, 1948. *Recreations:* tennis, riding and billiards. *Address:* 500 Bourke Street, Melbourne, Australia. *T.A.:* Hematite. *T.:* MU8001; 283 Williams Rd., South Yarra, Vic.: Landscape. Tallarook, Vic. *Clubs:* Melbourne, Australian, West Brighton (Melbourne); Adelaide (Adelaide), Union (Sydney); Newcastle (Newcastle). [*Died* 2 *Oct.* 1961.

LEWIS, Brigadier-General Frederick Gustav, C.B. 1917; C.M.G. 1915; D.L., T.D.; Hon. Brig.-Gen.; Colonel T.F., late 13th Princess Louise's Kensington Battalion London Regiment; *b.* 1873; *s.* of late Leopold Lewis, Bradford; *m.* 1904, Annie Caton (*d.* 1963), *d.* of late Hugh Rose, Edinburgh. *Educ.:* Haileybury College; Trinity Hall, Cambridge B.A. 1895. Partner Dod Longstaffe & Co. Solicitors, 1906-16. Served European War, 1914-18 (despatches seven times, C.B., C.M.G., Belgian Croix de Guerre); commanded 142nd Infantry Brigade, 166th Infantry Brigade, section Tees garrison; Dep. Director Demobilisation at War Office; 4th Lond. Inf. Brig., T.F. Res. *Address:* c/o Midland Bank, 255 Kensington High St., W.8. [*Died* 6 *July* 1967.

LEWIS, Lt.-Col. George Alfred, C.M.G. 1916; C.B.E. 1948; Lt.-Col. late Commanding 5th Sherwood Foresters (Nottinghamshire and Derbyshire Regt.); *b.* Coleorton, Leicestershire, 1869; *e. s.* of late George Lewis of Derby; *m.* 1897, Mabel Frances, *d.* of late Alderman W. H. Marsden of Derby; one *d.* *Educ.:* Derby School (Scholar); Gonville and Caius College, Cambridge (Scholar) (B.A. 14th Wrangler, 1891; M.A. 1893); J.P. Derbyshire. Joined Territorial Forces as private, 1888; 2nd Lieut. 1892; Capt. 1895; Major, 1908; Lieut.-Col. 1915; served European War, 1914-16 (despatches, C.M.G.); Liquidator of the following Colliery Companies: Whitwick Colliery Co., Limited; The Wollaton Collieries, Limited; Hon. Fellow of Surveyors Institute; Past President, Midland Counties Institution of Engineers; Past Vice-President of the Institution of Mining

Engineers; Past-President of National Association of Colliery Managers. *Address:* Highfield House, Derby. *T.A.:* Lewis, Derby 43396. *T.:* Derby 43396. *Club:* Royal Automobile. [*Died* 9 *Feb.* 1961.

LEWIS, Sir Hawthorne; *see* Lewis, Sir W. H.

LEWIS, Henry, C.B.E. 1954; Professor Emeritus, University of Wales; Professor of Welsh Language and Literature, University College of Swansea, 1921–54; *b.* 21 Aug. 1889; *y. s.* of William Lewis, Heol y Coed, Ynystawe, Clydach, Glam.; *m.* 1921, Gwladys, *y. d.* of William Thomas Treorchy; two *d. Educ:* Ystalyfera County School; Univ. Coll., Cardiff, M.A., D.Litt. (Wales). President, Students Representative Council, Cardiff, 1911–12; represented Students of University of Wales at Imperial Universities Congress, 1912; Assistant Master at Ystalyfera and Llanelly Intermediate Schools; served in France with Welsh Guards (N.C.O.) and 13th R.W.F. (2nd Lieut.); Assistant Lecturer in Welsh. University College, Cardiff 1918–21; President Association of Past Students, U.C. Cardiff, 1919; Clerk of Guild of Graduates of Univ. of Wales, 1926–32, Warden, 1933–36: President Welsh Bibliographical Soc.; Chairman Council Coleg Harlech, Welsh Books Council; Member of Court of University of Wales, of Court and Council of National Library of Wales (Vice-Pres.), 1949–67, of Court of National Museum of Wales, of Welsh Joint Education Committee of Council of Univ. Coll. of Swansea. Formerly sec. of Cylch Dewi, Cardiff, ex-Chm. Swansea Cymmrodorion Soc. Hon. Life Gov., and Vice-Pres., C.&E.B.S.; Vice-Pres. Hon. Soc. of Cymmrodorion; Hon. Mem. R.I.A. 1957. Hon. D.Litt Celt. (N.U.I.), Hon. LL.D. (Wales). *Publications:* Life and Works of Iolo Goch in Iolo Goch ac Eraill, 1925, 1937; Llawlyfr Llydaweg Canol, 1922, 1935 (with J. Piette), 1966; Llawlyfr Cernyweg Canol, 1923, 1946; Chwedleu Seith Doethon Rufein, 1925, 1958; Delw y Byd, 1928; Hen Gerddi Crefyddol, 1931; Datblygiad yr Iaith Gymraeg, 1931, 1947; Darn o'r Ffestival, 1925; Brenin yr Ellyllon, 1921; Saith Stori (o'r Ffrangeg), 1930; Concise Comparative Celtic Grammar (with Holger Pedersen), 1937, 1962; Brut Dingestow, 1942; The Sentence in Welsh (Sir John Rhys Memorial Lecture, British Academy, 1942); Yr Elfen Ladin yn yr Iaith Gymraeg, 1943; ed. Hen Gyflwyniadau, 1948; Cydymaith i'r Hwsmon (Hugh Jones), Llanwynno (Glanffrwd), 1949; Morgannwg Matthews Ewenni, 1953; joint author of Mynegai i Farddoniaeth y Llawysgrifau, 1928; ed. Peniarth 53, 1927; ed. Welsh New Testament (in revised orthography for B. and F.B.S.), 1936, also Welsh Old Testament, 1955; ed. Welsh Apocrypha (in revised orthography for S.P.C.K.), 1958; joint-ed. Beibl y Plant, 1929; and of Cyfres y Werin, 1920–27; and of Welsh Congregational Hymn-book, 1959; consultant ed. (Celtic) 3rd ed. Webster's International Dictionary; ed. Collins-Spurrell Welsh Dictionary, 1960; contrib. Encyclopædia Britannica and to Welsh jls. *Recreation:* motoring. *Address:* y Gilfach Glyd, Plas Cadwgan Rd., Ynystawe, Swansea. [*Died* 14 *Jan.* 1968.

LEWIS, Maj.-Gen. Henry Augustus, C.B. 1937; C.B.E. 1920; Col. Comdt. R.A., 1942–47; *b.* 1879; *s.* of Major E. J. G. Lewis, B.S.C.; *m.* 1911, Mary Margaret (*d.* 1951), *d.* of Philip Arthur Newton; five *d.* Instructor at School of Gunnery, 1910–13; Superintendent of Experiments there, 1918–20; Secretary Ord. Committee, 1921–23; appointed a Member thereof, 1927; served China, 1900 (medal with clasp); European War, 1914–19 (Bt. Lt.-Col., Order of St. Stanislas of Russia, C.B.E.); Major-Gen. 1934; Director of Artillery, War Office, 1934–38; retired pay, 1938; Ordnance Board, 1939–43. *Address:* Oatlands Corner, Weybridge, Surrey. *Club:* United Service. [*Died* 14 *Oct.* 1966.

LEWIS, Brig. James C. W.; *see* Windsor Lewis.

LEWIS, John; *b.* 14 December 1912; *s.* of Leon Lewis and Bessie Felber; *m.* 1948, Joy Jocille (from whom he obtained a divorce 1955), *d.* of Horace N. Fletcher; one *d.* *Educ.:* Grocers' School; City of London College. Joint inventor high temperature thermal reclaiming process, adopted and sponsored by Ministry of Supply, 1941. Joint inventor of rubber substitute for cable and general rubber production. Developed Fire-resistant multiply belting for National Coal Board. Labour candidate in local Government elections for Golders Green Ward of Hendon, 1937 and 1938. Prepared Report on the Rubber Control Board for Minister of Supply, 1942. M.P. (Lab.) Bolton, Lancs, 1945–50, West Bolton, 1950–51; Parliamentary Private Sec. to P.M.G., April-July 1950, when appointed by P.M.G. to Sports Television Advisory Committee. Formerly Member: Select Cttee. on Estimates; Inter-Parliamentary Union; Empire Parliamentary Assoc.; British - American Parliamentary Union; Parliamentary and Scientific Cttee.; Member: Association of Supervisory Staffs, Execs. and Technicians; Exec. Committee of Central Council of Physical Recreation, 1948–51; Govt. Advisory Cttee. on Welfare of Colonial Peoples. Sponsored Nat. Coal Bd. Boxing Championships for Miners, 1947. Ex-Chm. House of Commons Motor Club; Chm. Empire Games Appeals Cttee., 1949–50; Steward British Boxing Board of Control, 1949–51. Freeman and Liveryman of the Carmen Company (Sen. Warden-Elect), also Liveryman Horners' Company. *Publications:* technical papers and miscellaneous journalism. *Recreations:* sport and art. *Address:* 4 Abbey Lodge, Hanover Gate, N.W.8. *T.:* 01-262 3717, 9965. *Clubs:* Savage, City Livery. [*Died* 14 *June* 1969.

LEWIS, John F.; Commissioner (retired) of the Salvation Army; late Manager and Chairman of Directors, Salvationist Publishing and Supplies Ltd. and Director Salvation Army Trustee Co. and Salvation Army Assurance Co.; *b.* Canterbury, New Zealand, 1876; *m.* 1904, Captain Edith Osborne (*d.* 1929); two *s.* two *d.* Associate Australian Society of Accountants, and Licensed Government Auditor (under Companies Act (Victoria)); J.P., N.S.W., Australia; entered Salvation Army as an Officer, 1896; greater part of Salvation Army Service spent in Colonies; has filled important executive positions in Australia, South Africa and British Isles, including Chief Secretaryship of Great Britain and Ireland; Territorial Commander for North of England, 1936; Governor, Men's Social Work for Great Britain and Ireland, 1939. *Recreation:* gardening. *Address:* Glebelands, Bidborough, Nr. Tonbridge Wells, Kent. *T.:* Southborough 765. [*Died* 8 *March* 1963.

LEWIS, John Llewellyn; American labour executive: President of United Mine Workers of America, 1920–60, resigned; President Emeritus since 1960; former President of Congress of Industrial Organizations; *b.* Lucas, Iowa, 12 Feb. 1880; *s.* of Thomas H. Lewis and Ann Louisa Watkins; *m.* 1907, Myrta Edith Bell; one *s.* (two *d.* decd.). *Educ.:* public schools. Mem., Fairless Commn., President's Citizen Advisers on the Mutual Security Program, 1956–57. Chm. Nat. Coal Pol. Conf., Inc., Wash. D.C., 1962. Has served as member various Governmental Agencies and Commissions. Former Chairman Board Labor's Non-Partisan League; former Vice-President of

American Federation of Labor. Presidential Medal of Freedom, 1964. *Address:* United Mine Workers Building, Washington, D.C., U.S.A. [*Died* 11 *June* 1969.

LEWIS, John Spedan; Founder of the John Lewis Partnership; *b.* 22 Sept. 1885; *er. s.* of late John Lewis and of late Eliza (*née* Baker); *m.* 1923, Sarah Beatrice Mary Hunter (*d.* 1953); one *s.* one *d.* *Educ.:* Westminster (Queen's Scholar). Partner, John Lewis and Co., Oxford Street, 1906; inherited control, 1928; formed John Lewis Partnership by settlement in trust, giving all profits to workers, 1929 (by 1962 about £11,000,000); completed foundation of Partnership, by second settlement, making consent of workers necessary to voluntary liquidation, 1950 (partners now number about 16,000; capital £28,500,000); retired as Chairman of Partnership's principal companies, Sept. 1955. President of the Classical Association, 1956-57. *Publications:* Partnership For All, 1948; Fairer Shares, 1954; Inflation's Cause and Cure, 1958. *Recreations:* gardening, natural history. *Address:* The Burrow, Longstock Park, Stockbridge, Hants. *T.:* Stockbridge 131. *Clubs:* Athenæum, Reform, Flyfishers'. [*Died* 21 *Feb.* 1963.

LEWIS, Michael Arthur, C.B.E. 1954; M.A.; Litt.D.; F.S.A.; F.R.Hist.S.; *b.* 3 Jan. 1890; 2nd *s.* of late Rev. Victor A. N. Lewis; *m.* 1933, Muriel Doris, *d.* of C. E. Cruikshank; one *s.* one *d.* *Educ.:* Uppingham; Trinity College, Cambridge. Assistant Master, R.N. College, Osborne, 1913; served European War of 1914-18, Royal Marine Artillery; Asst. Head of History and English Dept., R.N. Coll., Dartmouth, 1922; Professor of History and English, 1934-55, and Director of Sub-Lieutenants' General Education Course, 1946-55, Royal Naval College, Greenwich. On Councils and Publications Committees of Navy Records Society (Vice-Pres. since 1949), and Society for Nautical Research (Chm. of Council, 1951-60, Pres. since 1960); Member H.M.S. Victory Advisory Technical Committee, 1955-; Lectr. in English to R.N. Staff College, 1943-57, in Naval History, 1945-53, and R.N. Senior Officers' War Course, 1947-53. Introducer of TV film series "Victory at Sea", 1952-53. *Publications:* two volumes of Light Verse, 1921-24; *novels*, 1923-35; Beg o' the Upland; The Brand of the Beast; The Island of Disaster; Roman Gold; The Three Amateurs; The Crime of Herbert Wratislaus; When First We Practise; *history:* Naval Personnel; England's Sea Officers; British Ships and British Seamen; Armada Guns; The Ships and Seamen of Britain; The Navy of Britain; The Narrative of Admiral Sir William Dillon; The History of the British Navy (Pelican); Armed Forces and the Art of War, 1830-1870; A Social History of the Navy, 1793-1815; The Spanish Armada; Napoleon and his British Captives; The Navy in Transition, 1814-1864, a social history; Ancestors; The Hawkins Dynasty. Contributor to: Punch, 1918-31; The Dictionary of National Biography; The New Cambridge Modern History; The Times; The Mariner's Mirror; The Seafarer; Overseas; New Statesman; The Listener; History; U.S. Naval Institute Proceedings, etc. *Recreations:* fishing, gardening. *Address:* 36 Dartmouth Row, Greenwich, S.E.10. *T.:* 01-692 3517. [*Died* 27 *Feb.* 1970.

LEWIS, Oswald, M.A. (Oxon); *b.* Hampstead, 5 Apr. 1887; *yr. s.* of late John Lewis, founder of the firm of John Lewis & Co., silk mercers and drapers, Oxford Street; *m.* 1928, Frances Merriman, *e. d.* of late Dr. Harold Merriman Cooper, Hampton-on-Thames; one *s.* one *d.* *Educ.:* Westminster School; Christ Church, Oxford; Boulter Law Exhibition, Honours Degree in Jurisprudence. Called to Bar, Middle Temple, 1912; joined 2nd Co. of London Yeomanry (Westminster Dragoons), 1911; served European War, 1914-16; Member of the St. Marylebone Borough Council, 1908-12; Member of the London County Council, 1913-19; M.P. (C.) Colchester Division of Essex, 1929-45; formerly for many years a partner in John Lewis & Company; Past Master of Worshipful Company of Farriers; F.Z.S.; F.R.G.S. *Publications:* Because I've Not Been There Before; I'd Like to Go Again; After Dinner. *Recreations:* reading, bridge. *Address:* Beechwood, Hampstead Lane, N.6. *T.:* Mountview 3017. *Club:* Carlton. [*Died* 12 *Feb.* 1966.

LEWIS, Major-General Sir Richard (George), K.C.M.G. 1952; C.B. 1945; C.B.E. 1943; A.D.C.; late R.A.C., retired; *b.* 15 Apr. 1895; *o. s.* of Robert Travers Lewis, Ballinagar, County Galway; *m.* 1918, Eleanora Mary Clarkson McEwen; two *d.* *Educ.:* S. Columba Coll.; Trinity Coll., Dublin. Leinster Regt., European War, 1914-18 (despatches); Staff Coll.; Imperial Defence College; Staff and Allied Staff, War of 1939-45 (despatches); D.Q.M.G. War Office; Deputy Director-General for Finance and Administration European Regional Office of U.N.R.R.A., 1945; Personal Representative of Director-General of U.N.R.R.A. in Europe, 1947-48; A.D.C. to the King, 1948; Director General Foreign Office Administration of African Territories, 1949-52. Commander Legion of Merit (U.S.); Legion of Honour, Croix de Guerre (France). *Recreations:* motoring and horticulture. *Address:* Duns Tew Manor, Oxford. *T.:* Steeple Aston 332. *Clubs:* White's, Naval and Military. [*Died* 21 *July* 1965.

LEWIS, Stanley Radcliffe, C.M.G. 1958; Q.C. 1949; Barrister, Victoria, Australia, since 1900; *b.* Malvern, Victoria, 24 January 1878; *s.* of Robert Edward Lewis, London; *m.* 1907, Alice F. (deceased), *d.* of Robert Hicks; two *s.* *Educ.:* Toorak College, Melbourne; University of Melbourne. Called to the Bar, New South Wales, 1921; called to the Bar, Tasmania. Trustee of Melbourne Cricket Ground. *Address:* Athenæum Club, 87 Collins Street, Melbourne, Victoria, Australia. *Clubs:* Athenæum, Savage, Victoria Racing, Victoria Amateur Turf, etc., Royal Automobile of Victoria (all in Melbourne). [*Died* 30 *April* 1964.

LEWIS, Alderman Thomas, C.B.E. 1950; J.P.; Friendly Society official; *b.* 12 Dec. 1873. *Educ.:* Eastern District Board School, Southampton. Actively engaged in Trade Union and Labour Movement for over 50 years; Member, Southampton Borough Council for 40 years; M.P. (Lab.) Southampton, 1929-31 and 1945-1950; Past Chairman, Southampton, Board of Guardians; Past President, Hearts of Oak Benefit Society, and Trustee and Parliamentary Agent of that body; Past President, National Conference of Friendly Societies; for many years a member of the Management Committee, Seamen's National Insurance Society. Hon. Freeman of Borough of Southampton. Hon. LL.D., Southampton, 1955. *Address:* 66 Alma Road, Southampton. [*Died* 28 *Feb.* 1962.

LEWIS, Walter Samuel, C.B.E. 1947; J.P. 1937; Comp. I.E.E. 1949; Chairman Midlands Electricity Board, 1947-61, retd.; *b.* 6 Nov. 1894; *m.* Elizabeth Nellie Smith; two *d.* *Educ.:* Hadley, Salop; Highfield Road, Saltley, Birmingham. From 1908 served apprenticeship Electrical Engineering; four years R.F.C., European War, 1914-18. District Sec. Electrical Trades Union, 1923-35; Area Sec. of E.T.U., 1935-1947. City of Birmingham: Councillor,

1926; Lord Mayor, 1942-43; Alderman, 1943-54. Sec. to Trade Union Side of Dist. Jt. Industrial Council for Electricity Supply Industry, 1924-47; Member W. Midlands Jt. Electricity Authority for 18 years (Vice-Chm. until 1948). Member British Electricity Central Authority, 1948-50 and 1954-1955. *Recreations:* **fishing, bowls.** *Address:* **130 Stanmore Road, Edgbaston, Birmingham 16.** *T.:* **Bearwood 1180.**

[*Died* 4 *May* 1962.

LEWIS, Sir (William) Hawthorne, K.C.S.I., *cr.* 1940 (C.S.I. 1934); K.C.I.E., *cr.* 1938 (C.I.E. 1931); *b.* Kasauli, India, 29 June 1888; *s.* of late Thomas Crompton Lewis, Fellow of Trinity College, Cambridge, Director of Public Instruction, U.P., India, and Mary Olivia Hawthorne; *m.* 1st, 1929, Alice Margaret Rose Hewitt (*d.* 1953) (Kaisar-i-Hind Gold Medal; Comdr. Sister, Order of St. John of Jerusalem), *widow* of Lieut. Ronald Erskine Hewitt, R.N., and *d.* of late George Edward Woodhouse of Nordon, Blandford, Dorset; no *c.*; 2nd, 1957, Geraldine Susan Maud de Montmorency (F.L.A., UNESCO Travelling Fellowship, 1952), *d.* of late Professor J. E. G. de Montmorency. *Educ.:* Oundle School; Caius Coll., Camb. Appointed to the Indian Civil Service after the examination of 1911; arrived India, Dec. 1912; served in Bihar and Orissa as Assistant Magistrate and Collector; Censor Duty, Bombay, 1915-16; Under-Secretary to Government of Bihar and Orissa, 1918; Deputy Commissioner, 1923; Revenue Secretary, Government of Bihar and Orissa, 1925; on special reforms duty, Home Department, Government of India, 1927; Joint Secretary, Government of India, Reforms Office, 1930; on deputation to the Indian Round Table Conferences in London, 1930 and 1931; Reforms Commissioner to Government of India, 1932-35, and 1936-41; Governor of Orissa, 1941-46; Chairman St. John Council for Devon, 1951-52. K.St.J. *Address:* The Bridge House, Wilton, nr. Salisbury, Wilts. *T.:* Wilton 2233. *Club:* East India and Sports. [*Died* 19 *Oct.* 1970.

LEWIS, William Henry, M.A.; Hon. LL.D.; F.R.I.C.; Emeritus Professor of Chemistry, University of Exeter; *b.* 1869; *s.* of late William George and Susan Mary Lewis; *m.* 1898, Helen Mary Freeman; one *d.* (and one *d.* decd.). *Educ.:* University College, Aberystwyth; Jesus College, Oxford. Science Master, Exeter School, 1894-1901; Professor of Chemistry, University College, Exeter, 1901-35; Vice-Principal, 1925-35; Member of Council, Royal Institute of Chemistry, 1924-27; External Council, Univ. of London, 1930-35; retired 1935. *Publications:* papers on chemical research. *Address:* 2 Carlton Mansions, Esplanade, Sidmouth, Devon. [*Died* 25 *May* 1963.

LEWIS-CROSBY, Very Rev. Ernest Henry, M.A.; B.D.; Dean of Christ Church Cathedral, Dublin, since 1938; Precentor of Christ Church Cathedral, Dublin, 1927; *s.* of Robert Allen Cornwall and Harriett Elizabeth Crosby; *m.* Hilda Darley; two *s.* two *d.* (and *s.* decd.). *Educ.:* Trinity Coll., Dublin. Royal scholarship; 1st Honours in classics; 1st Prizeman, History; gold medallist, History and Political Science; Archbishop King's prizeman, Bishop Foster's prizeman, Biblical Greek Prizeman and Theological Exhibitioner Divinity School; Curate, Christ Church, Leeson Park; Head Church of Ireland Mission to the Jews; Rector of Drumcondra and N. Strand; Rector of Rathmines; Rector of Stillorgan, Co. Dublin; late Chaplain to Lord-Lieut. and Examining Chaplain to Bishop of Sodor and Man. Freeman of Dublin. Mem. of Order of Friendly Bros. *Publications:* Celtic Churches in the Diocese of Dublin 1932; The Ancient Books of Christ Church Cathedral, Dublin, 1947; A Short History of Christ Church Cathedral, 1949 (2nd. ed. 1956); The Annals of Christ Church Cathedral, 1950; Our Two Cathedrals, from foundation to Reformation, 1951. *Recreation:* gardening. *Address:* 10 Bushy Park Rd., Rathgar, Co. Dublin. *T.:* Dublin 909825. *Club:* Royal Irish Automobile (Dublin).

[*Died* 18 *May* 1961.

LEY, Henry George, M.A., Mus. Doc. Oxon, F.R.C.M., F.R.C.O.; Hon. R.A.M.; *b.* Chagford, Devon, 30 Dec. 1887; *s.* of Rev. G. L. H. Ley, Rector of Chagford, Devon; *m.* 1st, Evelyn Mary (*d.* 1946), *d.* of Rev. C. Heurtley; 2nd, Mary Elizabeth, *d.* of Rev. C. Walford. *Educ.:* St. George's School, Windsor (Chorister, St. George's Chapel); Uppingham (Musical Scholar); Royal College of Music (Council Exhibitioner); Keble College, Oxford (Organ Scholar). Conductor Keble College Musical Society; President Oxford University Musical Club, 1908; Precentor St. Peter's College, Radley, 1916-18; Teaching Staff (Organ) R.C.M., 1919-41; Organist and Choirmaster Christ Church Cathedral, Oxford, 1909-26; Organist of Sheldonian Theatre, Choragus Oxford University, 1923-26; Precentor and Director of Music, Eton College, 1926-45; President Royal College of Organists, 1933, 1934; Warden Music Masters' Association, 1936; Pres. Incorporated Assoc. of Organists, 1952, 1953. Hon. Fellow Keble Coll., Oxford; Fellow of Royal School of Church Music. *Publications:* Five albums of Songs; Church Music and Part Songs; two vols., Organ Solos and arrangements; Savernake, operetta for children; Joint Editor Oxford Psalter; Church Anthem Book; Oxford Chant Book (No. 2); articles on Walford Davies and Basil Harwood in Nat. Dict. Biog. *Recreations:* motoring, golf, chess. *Address:* Combewater Cottage, Metcombe, Ottery St. Mary, Devon.

[*Died* 24 *Aug.* 1962.

LIARDET, Major-General Sir Claude Francis, K.B.E., *cr.* 1944; C.B. 1937; D.S.O. 1917; D.L. County of London; Director of Bevington, Vaizey and Foster Ltd., Lloyd's; *b.* 26 Sept. 1881; *y. s.* of late Commander H. M. Liardet, H.M.I.N.; *m.* 1st, 1906, Dorothy, *y. d.* of A. R. Hopper, M.D.; one *s.* one *d.*; 2nd, 1928, Dorothy Clare, O.B.E. 1946, *o. d.* of late Adm. George Borrett, C.B.; one *s.* *Educ.:* Bedford Sch. 2nd Lt., Lancs. Artillery, 1899; Captain, 1905; transferred to Lancashire and Cheshire R.G.A. on formation of Territorial Force; Major, 1914; served European War (Brevet Lt.-Col., D.S.O., despatches five times); Commanded 125 Heavy Battery, R.G.A., France and Flanders, and 23rd Heavy Arty. Bde., also Bde. Major Heavy Arty. Australian Corps, G.S.O. 2, xiii Corps, 1914-18; Commanded: Lancs and Cheshire Coast Bde. R.A., 1919; 106 Lancs., Yeo. Bde. R.F.A., T.A., 1923; 64th (7th London) Field Bde. R.A., T.A., 1925. Lt.-Col., 1922; Bt. Col., 1926; Col. 1927; Major-General, 1938; C.R.A. 47th Div. and The London Div., 1934-38; Commander, The London Division, T.A., 1938; Director-General, Ground Defence, Air Ministry, and Commandant, Royal Air Force Regiment, 1942-45. Pres. Corp. of Insurance Brokers, 1947-51. *Address:* Greenacre, Chiddingfold, Surrey. *Club:* Junior Army and Navy. [*Died* 5 *March* 1966.

LICHTENBERGER, Rt. Rev. Arthur Carl; Prof. of Pastoral Theology, Episcopal Theological School, retd.; *b.* 8 Jan. 1900; *s.* of Adam and Theresa Lichtenberger; *m.* 1924, Florence Elizabeth Tate; one *s.* *Educ.:* Kenyon College; Episcopal Theological School. Professor N.T., St. Paul's Divinity School, Wuchang, China, 1925-1927; Rector, Grace Church, College Hill, Cincinnati, Ohio, 1928-33; Rector, St. Paul's Church, Brookline, Mass., 1933-41; Dean, Trinity Cathedral, Newark, N.J., 1941-48; Prof. Pastoral Theology, General

Seminary, N.Y., 1948-51; Bishop-Coadjutor, Dio. Missouri, 1951-52; Bishop of Missouri, 1952-58; Presiding Bishop, Episcopal Church, U.S.A., 1958-64. Hon. degrees: D.D.: Amherst, Bard and Kenyon Colleges, Virginia Theological Seminary, University of the South; Princeton; Huron College, London, Ont.; Wycliffe College, Toronto; Dr.Litt.: St. Augustine's Coll., Raleigh; S.T.D.: Berkeley Divinity Sch., Gen. Seminary, New York, Philadelphia Divinity Sch., Seabury-Western Seminary, Trinity Coll.; D.C.L.: Nashotah House; LL.D.: St. Paul's Univ., Tokyo; L.H.D.: Hobart Coll.; J.C.D.: Church Divinity Sch. of the Pacific. *Recreations:* fishing, gardening. *Address:* Suncoast Manor, 6909 9th St. South, St. Petersburg, Florida 33739, U.S.A. [*Died* 3 *Sept.* 1968.

LIDDALL, Sir Walter Sydney, Kt., *cr.* 1945; C.B.E. 1937; J.P.; *b.* Boston, 2 March 1884; *y. s.* of late Benjamin Liddall; *m.* 1910, Gertrude, *o. d.* of late G. R. Long, Scunthorpe; one *s.* two *d.* *Educ.:* De Aston Grammar School, Market Rasen. Played prominent part in bringing about the amalgamation in 1919 of the two urban districts of Scunthorpe and Frodingham and the two parishes of Crosby and Ashby; Chm., Scunthorpe and Frodingham U.D.C. 1920-21, 1923-24, 1924-25; Hon. Treas. Scunthorpe Conservative Club since 1927; Rotarian. Chm. Scunthorpe Savings Bank; Chairman, Rumex Oil Products, Ltd., Br. Traders & Shippers Ltd., Emery Cinema Circuit Ltd.; and director of other Ltd. Companies; M.P. (Nat. Con.) Lincoln City, 1931-45. Contested Don Valley division of W.R. Yorkshire, May 1929, Lincoln, 1945. *Recreations:* holds long-service medal Lincs Football Association. *Address:* Chequers, Scunthorpe, Lincs. *T.A.:* Liddall, Chequers, Scunthorpe. *T.:* 2150. [*Died* 24 *Feb.* 1963.

LIDDELL, Lieut.-Col. Arthur Robert, C.M.G. 1919; D.S.O. 1917; retired; formerly R.A.S.C.; *b.* 1872; *s.* of late Captain John Liddell, R.N.; *m.* Alice Maud (*d.* 1963), 3rd *d.* of late Thomas Mills, Sandhurst, Berks, and of Charters Towers, Queensland. Served in 3rd Batt. Dorset Regt., 1889-1894; gazetted to the 4th (R.I.) Dragoon Guards, 1894; transferred to the R.A.S.C., 1896; Adjutant, A.S.C. Training Establishment, 1907-09; served South African War, 1899-1900 (Queen's medal seven clasps); European War, 1914-19 (despatches 5 times, D.S.O., C.M.G.); served in R.O.C., 1939-1943. J.P. Bedfordshire. *Recreations:* shooting, fishing. *Club:* Army and Navy. [*Died* 20 *Dec.* 1966.

LIDDELL, Maximilian Friedrich, M.A. (Edinburgh, Dublin), Ph.D. (Birmingham); Professor of German and Lecturer in Anglo-Saxon, University of Dublin (Trinity College), 1933-58, retired; *b.* Barrow in Furness, 5 Feb. 1887; *s.* of late Arthur R. Liddell and Emilie J. Zimmermann; unmarried. *Educ.:* Germany; King Edward VI Grammar School, Morpeth; Universities of Edinburgh and Berlin. English Lektor, Kgl. Akademie, Posen, 1909-1911; Lecturer in German, Univ. of Birmingham, 1920-32; Member of Royal Irish Academy, 1934. *Publications:* Irland, 1931; Ferdinand Freiligrath: Poems (Selected and Edited), 1949; Der Stil der englischen Geschichtsschreibung im 18 Jahrhundert (in: Anglica, Palæstra 148, 1925); contributions to Modern Language Review, Year's Work in Modern Language Studies, Contemporary Review, Forum of Education, Hermathena, Dublin Magazine, etc. *Address:* 25 Butler Avenue, Harrow, Middlesex. *Club:* University (Dublin). [*Died* 28 *April* 1968.

LIDDELL HART, Sir Basil (Henry), Kt. 1966; Hon. D.Litt., Oxford, 1964; Hon. Fell., Corpus Christi College, Camb., 1965; *b.* Paris, 31 Oct. 1895; *yr. s.* of late Rev. H. Bramley Hart and Clara Liddell; *m.* 1st, 1918, Jessie, *d.* of J. J. Stone; one *s.*; 2nd, 1942, Kathleen, *d.* of Alan Sullivan, Toronto, Canada, and *widow* of H. P. Nelson, F.R.C.S. *Educ.:* St. Paul's; Corpus Christi College, Cambridge. K.O.Y.L.I.; served European War, 1914-18 (wounded); invalided, 1924; retired as captain, 1927. Evolved the Battle Drill system (in 1917), the "expanding torrent" method of attack, and other tactical developments adopted since. In 1920 wrote the post-war official manual Infantry Training; edited Small Arms Training. An early advocate of air-power and armoured forces; termed "the creator of the theory of the conduct of mechanised war" by the German encyclopædia, Der Grosse Brockhaus, and by Gen. Guderian, the creator and leader of the Panzer forces. In 1937 became personal adviser to the new War Minister, Mr. Hore-Belisha, when a belated effort was made to reorganise and mechanise the Army; drafted a programme; as official progress was slow compared with the imminent risk of war, gave up this advisory rôle in 1938 in order to press the needs publicly (many of the proposed reforms were achieved, but opposition had delayed the development of the tank and A.A. forces). Military Correspondent of the Daily Telegraph, 1925-35; of The Times, 1935-39, also its adviser on defence as a whole. Military Editor of the Encyclopædia Britannica, 14th edn. Lees-Knowles Lectr., Trinity College, Cambridge, 1932-33; Leverhulme Research Fellow, 1934; Editor of the section on The World Wars for the American Historical Association's Guide to Historical Literature, 1961; Editor-in-Chief, History of the Second World War, 1968-. Distinguished Visiting Professor of History, University of Calif., Davis, 1965-66; Visiting Professor of Strategy, Naval War Coll., U.S.A., 1970; lectured on strategy and tactics at the War and Staff Colleges of numerous countries. Chesney Gold Medal, Royal United Service Instn. *Publications:* some thirty books—among them Paris, or the Future of War, 1925; The Remaking of Modern Armies, 1927; The Strategy of Indirect Approach (1st edn., 1929; 6th enlarged edn., 1967); The British Way in Warfare; Thoughts on War; A History of the World War, 1914-18; The War in Outline; biographies of Scipio, Sherman, Foch, T. E. Lawrence; Why Don't We Learn from History; The Other Side of the Hill, 1948 (enlarged edn., 1951); Defence of the West, 1950; (edited) The Rommel Papers, 1953; The Soviet Army (ed.), 1956; The Tanks (the history of the Tank Corps, R.T.C. and R.T.R.), 1959; Deterrent or Defence, 1960; Memoirs, Vols. I and II, 1965; History of the Second World War, 1970 (posthumous). *Recreations:* discussion, croquet, chess, the history of fashion and habit. *Address:* States House, Medmenham, Marlow, Bucks. *Club:* Athenæum. [*Died* 29 *Jan.* 1970.

LIDDIARD, Mabel, C.B.E. 1952; *b.* 20 May 1882; *d.* of James Liddiard. *Educ.:* Bardon House School, High Wycombe. St. Thomas' Hospital: S.R.N. and S.C.M. Trained, 1911-1915; Charge Nurse, 1915-17; Night Sister (Acting), 1918. Mothercraft Training Society: Matron, 1918-36; Nursing Director, 1936-45. President Royal College of Midwives, 1949-52. F.R.S.H. *Publication:* Mothercraft Manual, 1923 (now in 12th edn.). *Address:* 9A Bisham Gardens, Highgate, N.6. *T.:* Mountview 9295. *Club:* Royal Over-Seas League. [*Died* 31 *March* 1962.

LIE, Trygve Halvdan, LL.D.; Norwegian Statesman; Minister of Commerce and Shipping, 1964-65; *b.* Oslo, Norway, 16 July 1896; *s.* of Martin and Hulda Arnesen Lie; *m.* 1921, Hjordis Joergensen (*d.* 1960);

three *d.* *Educ.:* Oslo Univ. Law degree, 1919; became mem. of Norwegian Social Dem. Youth Organisation, 1911; assistant to secretary of Norwegian labor party, 1919-22; legal adviser to Trade Union Fed., 1922-1935; national exec. sec. labor party, 1926; Minister of Justice labor party govt. (formed by Johan Nygaardsvold), 1935-39; mem. Norwegian Parl. 1935, re-elected 1945; Minister of Trade, Industry, Shipping and Fishing, 1939-40. Escaped to England with Norwegian govt., June 1940. Acting Foreign Minister, 1940, Foreign Minister, 1941; evolved provisional measures that saved Norwegian fleet for Allies; chm. Norwegian delegation to U.N. conf., San Francisco, Apr. 1945 (chm. Cttee. III for drafting charter of Security Council); resigned as Foreign Minister, 1945; appointed Foreign Minister interim coalition govt., 1945; Foreign Minister, Oct. 1945; chm. Norwegian delegation U.N. General Assembly in London, 1946; Secretary-General of United Nations, 1946-1953. Appointed Governor of Oslo and Akershus, 1955; Ambassador en mission speciale, 1959-66; Minister of Industry, 1963-64; Minister of Trade and Shipping, 1964-65. Active in Norwegian Sports Association. Has numerous Honorary degrees, principally from Universities in the U.S.A., Europe and South America. *Publications:* In the Cause of Peace, 1954; To Live or Die, 1955; With England in the Front Line, 1956; Homeward Bound, 1958. *Recreations:* ski-ing, shooting, tennis. *Address:* Hoffsveien 30.14, Oslo, Norway. *Club:* Det Norske Selskab (Oslo). [*Died* 30 *Dec.* 1968.

LIGERTWOOD, Hon. Sir George Coutts, Kt. 1956; Chancellor, University of Adelaide, 1961-66; Judge of the Supreme Court of South Australia, 1945-58; *b.* Maylands, South Australia, 15 October 1888; *s.* of William Leith Ligertwood, Aberdeen and Adelaide; *m.* 1915, Edith Emily, *d.* of Alexander Naismith, Jamestown, S.A.; one *s.* two *d.* (and one *s.* killed in action at Alamein). *Educ.:* Adelaide University (B.A., LL.B.). Q.C. 1930; Royal Commissioner for Commonwealth of Australia, 1945, 1949 and 1954, for W. Australian Government, 1959; Chairman, Commonwealth Committee on Taxation, 1959-61; Chairman, S.A. Committee on Tax Valuation, 1962-63. Member of Adelaide Univ. Council, 1942-66, Warden of Senate, 1945-59, Dep. Chancellor, 1959-61; Gov., Scotch Coll., Adelaide, 1930-. Former President Law Society of South Australia. Hon. LL.D.: W.A., 1963; Adel., 1964; Hon. D.Litt., Flinders Univ., S.A., 1967. *Address:* 1 Fife Avenue, Torrens Park, South Australia. *Club:* Adelaide (Adelaide, South Australia). [*Died* 13 *Oct.* 1967.

LIGHT, Sir Edgar (William), K.C.V.O., *cr.* 1953 (M.V.O. 1929); C.M.G. 1943; O.B.E. 1920 (M.B.E. 1918); *b.* 3 May 1885; *s.* of late Frederick Robert Light; *m.* 1925, Ethel Vera (*d.* 1968), *d.* of late Stanley Hicks, past master of Salters' Company. Entered Foreign Office, 1903; formerly Technical Adviser, Protocol Dept.; retired 1953. *Address:* Upover, Mayfield, Sussex. [*Died* 8 *Jan.* 1969.

LIGHTBODY, William Paterson Hay, C.B.E. 1943; L.R.C.P., L.R.C.S. (Ed.), L.R.F.P. & S. (Glas.); D.P.H. (Glas.); D.T.M. & H. (Camb.); *b.* 15 June 1893; *m.* 1st, 1920, Dorothy Mildred Cooke (*d.* 1959); one *s.*; 2nd, 1961, Hilda Mary. *Educ.:* Glasgow Acad.; Glasgow High School; Glasgow University and Extra-Mural Medical Schools; Glasgow Royal Infirmary, etc. Capt. R.A.M.C., 1916-20; Senior Medical Officer, Dept. of Health, Palestine, 1920-37; A.D.M.S. Sierra Leone, 1937-38; D.M.S., Sierra Leone, 1938-49. Senior Lecturer in Tropical Hygiene, Liverpool School of Trop. Med., 1949-59. *Publication:* (with T. H. Davey) The Control of Disease in the Tropics, 1956. *Address:* A1 Mount Court, The Mount, Heswall, Cheshire. *T.:* Heswall 1986. [*Died* 1 *June* 1962.

LIGHTFOOT, Ben, O.B.E. 1946; M.C.; M.A., F.G.S., M.I.M.M.; *b.* 30 Jan. 1888; *s.* of J. Lightfoot, Boston Spa; *m.* 1921, E. Longbottom, Allerton, Bradford; two *d.* *Educ.:* Bradford Gram. Sch.; Peterhouse, Cambridge. Harkness University Prize for Geology, Geological Survey of Scotland, 1909-10; Geological Survey of S. Rhodesia, 1911-14, Sorby Research Fellowship by Royal Society, 1914; served Royal Engineers, 1915-18 (despatches twice, M.C.), temp. Major; Mining Geologist to Perrin and Marshall in Hyderabad, 1919-20; rejoined Geological Survey of S. Rhodesia, 1921; retd. 1946; Lyell Fund Geological Soc. of London, 1928; Draper Medal, Geological Society of S.A., 1942. *Publications:* contributions to official publications of Geological Survey of Scotland and to numerous short reports and bulletins of Geological Survey of S. Rhodesia. *Address:* Bingley, Farm Lane, Barton-on-Sea, Hants. [*Died* 18 *Nov.* 1966.

LIGHTFOOT, Nicholas Morpeth Hutchinson, M.A.; F.R.S.E.; Principal, Chelsea College of Science and Technology, since 1950; *b.* 14 Oct. 1902; *s.* of Thomas and Mary H. Lightfoot; *m.* 1929, Janet Moulton (*d.* 1961), *d.* of John and Ellen Lightfoot, Hathersage, Derbyshire; one *d.* *Educ.:* Jarrow Grammar School, Co. Durham; Jesus College, Cambridge (Scholar). B.A. 1923, M.A. 1927. Assistant, Research Dept. Royal Arsenal, Woolwich, 1923-24; Asst. Lecturer: in Applied Mathematics, Univ. of Manchester, 1924-25; in Mathematics, Univ. of Sheffield, 1925-29; Lecturer in Mathematics, Heriot-Watt Coll., Edinburgh, 1929-38; Head of Mathematics Dept., Heriot-Watt Coll., 1938-43; Principal, South-East Essex Technical Coll., 1943-49. Pres. Assoc. of Principals of Technical Institutions, 1955-56. *Publications:* papers on mathematical theory of cooling steel in Proc. London Mathematical Soc. and Jour. of Iron and Steel Inst. *Address:* Tayinloan, Byne Close, Storrington, Pulborough, Sussex; Chelsea College of Science and Technology, Manresa Road, S.W.3. *T.:* Flaxman 5747. [*Died* 20 *Nov.* 1962.

LIGHTFOOT BOSTON, Sir Henry (Josiah); *see* Boston, Sir Henry J. L.

LILLICO, Hon. Sir Alexander, Kt. 1962; *b.* 26 Dec 1872; *s.* of Hugh and Mary Lillico, Tas.; *m.* 1896, Frances Emma Vertigan; three *s.* *Educ.:* Don, Tasmania. Farmer; M.L.C., Tasmania, 1924-54, retired. *Recreations:* his time was taken up so much with farming and parliament that he had very little left for recreation. *Address:* 47 Steele St., Devonport, North Tasmania, Australia. *T.:* Devonport 2.2096. [*Died* 16 *Dec.* 1966.

LILLICRAP, Sir Charles Swift, K.C.B., *cr.* 1947 (C.B. 1944); M.B.E. 1918; D.Sc. (Eng.); *b.* 12 Nov. 1887; *s.* of late Charles Lillicrap; *m.* 1911, Harriet Minnie (*d.* 1961), *d.* of late Richard Shears, Plymouth; two *s.* one *d.* *Educ.:* Stoke Public School, Devonport; H.M. Dockyard School, Devonport; R.N. Coll., Greenwich. Royal Corps of Naval Constructors, 1910; Instructor in Naval Architecture R.N. College, Greenwich, 1921-1924; Asst. Director of Naval Construction, 1936; Deputy Director of Naval Construction, 1941; Director of Naval Construction, 1944-51. Member of Council R.I.N.A. since 1937, Vice-Pres. 1945; Hon. Vice-Pres. 1955; Pres. British Welding Research Assoc.; Pres. Inst. of Welding, 1956-58. Fell. Imperial Coll. of Science and Technology, 1964. Liveryman and Past Prime Warden, Worshipful Co. of Shipwrights; Pres. Johnson Soc., 1955-56; Director: J. Samuel White

& Co., I.O.W.; Island Transport Co., I.O.W.; Henry Bannister Ltd., I.O.W.; Marinite Ltd. Hon. D.Sc. (Eng.) Bristol, 1951; Hon. Fell. Soc. of Engineers; Hon. Mem. British Ship Research Assoc.; Officer Legion of Honour; Grand Officer Orange Nassau. *Recreation:* books. *Address:* 9 Newstead Rd., Lee, S.E.12. *T.:* Kipling 5151. *Club:* Athenæum. [*Died* 17 *June* 1966.

LILLIE, Rev. Handley William Russell, S.J., M.A.; *b.* 2 Feb. 1902; *o.s.* of Cecil Firmin Lillie, M.A.; M.D. (Cantab.). Newchurch, Kent, and Caroline Margaret Lucy, *y. d.* of Rev. George Booth Perry, Ayscough, M.A., Vicar of Brabourne, Kent, and Hon. Emma Sophia Parnell. *Educ.:* Westminster School; Campion Hall, Oxford (2nd Cl. Hist.); St. Mary's Hall, Stonyhurst; Heythrop College, Chipping Norton, Oxon. Ordained priest, 1934; Chorister of Westminster Abbey, 1911-16; Asst. Master, Wimbledon College, 1922-23; Beaumont College, Old Windsor, 1929-31; Senior History Master, Beaumont College, 1936; Director of Music, Beaumont College, 1929-31 and 1936-41; Rector of Beaumont College, 1937-41; Chaplain to the Forces (R.A.F.V.R.), 1941-46; Assistant Principal Chaplain R.C. (Acting) Northern Area, 1944; Chaplain R.C. to Headquarters Fighter Command and Headquarters Balloon Command, 1944; Member of Headmasters' Conference, 1937-41. President of R.C. Schools Conference, 1938-39. English Colleges Retreat Preacher, Rome, 1948 and 1952; English Lecturer at Internat. Music Congress, Rome, 1950; National Director and Moderator-General for Sodalities B.V.M. in England, Scotland and Wales, 1950-53; Lenten Preacher, Gibraltar, 1954, 1966. F.R.G.S., 1966. *Address:* c/o 114 Mount St., W.1. *T.:* Grosvenor 1608. [*Died* 7 *April* 1967.

LIMERICK, 5th Earl of (*cr.* 1803), Edmund Colquhoun Pery, G.B.E. 1953; C.H. 1961; K.C.B. 1945; D.S.O. 1918; T.D.; Baron Glentworth, 1790; Viscount Limerick, 1800; Baron Foxford (U.K.), 1815; a Lieutenant of the City of London; Director of The Industrial & Commercial Finance Corporation, Ltd., The London Life Assoc., Ltd.; *b.* 16 Oct. 1888; *s.* of 3rd Earl and Isabella, *d.* of James Colquhoun; *S.* half-brother, 1929; *m.* 1926, Angela Olivia, *yr. d.* of late Lt.-Col. Sir Henry Trotter, K.C.M.G., C.B.; two *s.* one *d.* *Educ.:* Eton; New Coll., Oxford. Commanded 11th Brigade R.H.A. (T.A.); Bt. Col. R.A. (T.A.); retired, 1931; Hon. Col. City of London Yeomanry R.A.C. (T.A.), 1932-52; served European War, 1914-19 (despatches D.S.O.). Chm. of Council of Territorial and Auxiliary Forces Association, 1949-54; Pres., 1954-56. Chairman of City of London Territorial and Auxiliary Forces Association, 1941-50; Chairman Medical Research Council, 1952-Nov. 1960; formerly President Ski Club of Great Britain and Kandahar Ski Club. Hon. LL.D. (Aberdeen). *Recreation:* gardening. *Heir:* *s.* Viscount Glentworth. *Address:* Chiddinglye, West Hoathly, East Grinstead, Sussex. *T.:* Sharpthorne 214. [*Died* 4 *Aug.* 1967.

LIND, Hon. Sir Albert Eli, Kt. *cr.* 1951; retired from politics, May 1961; M.L.A. for Gippsland East, Victoria, Australia, from 1920; *b.* Charlton, Victoria, 1878; *s.* of Oliver Nicholas and Mary Annie Lind; *m.* 1905, Flora Arthur; four *s.* four *d.* *Educ.:* State Schs. (Primary). Building contractor, farmer and grazier. Has held following portfolios at intervals, 1935-52: Forests; Public Instruction; Soldier Settlement. Formerly Pres., Bd. of Land and Works, and Comr. of Crown Lands and Survey. Dep. Leader, Parl. Country Party and Dep. Premier, 1937-45; Dep. Speaker, 1947-50. *Address:* Hazel Dell, Mt. Taylor, via Bairnsdale, Vic., Australia. [*Died* 26 *June* 1964.

LIND-AF-HAGEBY, Emelie Augusta Louise; Speaker and Writer; *b.* Sweden, 20 Sept. 1878; *d.* of Emil Lind-af-Hageby. *Educ.:* Stockholm; Cheltenham. Naturalised British subject, 1912; founded the Animal Defence and Anti-Vivisection Society in 1906 of which she is President, Progress To-day; the Humanitarian and Anti-Vivisection Review, in 1909, The Purple Cross Service (with three hosps. for sick and wounded war-horses), authorized by French War Office, 1914; Sanatorium Beausoleil, Carqueiranne, France, used for French and Serbian soldiers, 1916, and later during many years for child-victims of the war; Diplôme de Grand Prix and Diplôme d'Honneur, French Ministry of Health; War Medal and Allied Victory Medal; President of the International Humanitarian Bureau of Geneva, founded in 1928; organised, in 1932, Animal Protection Deputation to Disarmament Conference of League of Nations, supported by 1400 societies; Silver Medal of French Ministry of Agriculture for services rendered to animals; Medal of the French Ministry of Foreign Affairs for work of Geneva International Bureau; organised the building of Pavilion Zoophilia with exhibition relating to humane education at Paris Exhibition, 1937 (awarded Grand Prix); received Gold Medal of Merit of Swedish S.P.C.A. and literary Prize at Oslo Congress, 1938; established First Aid Veterinary Post with ambulances, and promoted Evacuation of Animals Service of Animal Defence Society at outbreak of war, 1939. Acquired Ferne Estate, Dorset, in 1954, as memorial to Nina, Duchess of Hamilton; maintains it with object of preserving Ferne Animal Sanctuary and initiating a College for teaching and demonstration of humane methods in use of animals, the central idea being prevention of cruelty, in place of punishment. *Publications:* August Strindberg, 1913; Mountain Meditations, 1917; The Great Fox-Trot, 1938; numerous pamphlets and articles dealing with humanitarian and psychic subjects and the freedom of women. *Recreations:* mountains, motoring. *Address:* 7 St. Edmund's Terrace, Regent's Park, N.W.8; 15 St. James's Place, S.W.1; Ferne Animal Sanctuary, Shaftesbury, Dorset; Beausoleil, Carqueiranne, France. *Club:* P.E.N. [*Died* 26 *Dec.* 1963.

LINDEMANN, Lieut.-Col. (Hon. Brig.) Charles Lionel, D.S.O. 1917; *b.* Sidmouth, 20 Feb. 1885; *e. s.* of late A. F. Lindemann and Olga Davidson (*née* Noble), Sidmouth and Marlow; *b.* of late Viscount Cherwell, P.C., C.H., F.R.S.; *m.* Marie Madeleine de Lagotellerie-Tenré (*d.* 1939). *Educ.:* Blairlodge; Brussels; Darmstadt; Berlin University, Paris. Research work on physical subjects; served European War, 1914-18, in France (despatches twice, D.S.O., Chevalier (now Officer) Legion of Honour, 19 4 Star); Vice-Pres. and technical adviser to Brit. Mil. Claims Commn., Paris and War Office, 1919-24; scientific adviser, Anglo-Iranian (Persian) Oil Co. 1927-34; served as Liaison Officer at British Embassy in Paris with hon. rank of Brigadier, 1939-40, and at British Embassy in Washington, 1940-47; with rank of Counsellor, 1941; retired, 1947. *Publications:* various physical publications. *Recreations:* travelling, fishing, shooting, tennis. *Address:* 2500 East Las Olas Boulevard, Marine Towers Apartment 1408, Fort Lauderdale, Fla. 33301, U.S.A. *Clubs:* Athenæum (London); Knickerbocker (New York). [*Died* 13 *Aug.* 1970.

LINDOP, Colonel (Retd.) Carl Arthur Boys, O.B.E. 1938; D.L., J.P.; Chairman: H. W. Lindop & Sons Ltd.; G. Dyke & Son Ltd.; H. & J. Hill (Willenhall) Ltd.; Malleable Ltd.; R. E. Barker & Co. Ltd.; H. Richards (Willenhall) Ltd.; T. C. Neville & Sons Ltd.; Crystal Ware Products (Hereford) Ltd.; H. W. Lindop (Foundries)

Ltd.: Vice-Chairman: C. & L. Hill Ltd.; C. & L. Hill (Die Casting) Ltd.; Dir., Central Pattern Making Co.; *b.* 19 July 1899; *s.* of late H. W. Lindop; *m.* 1926, Eleanor Louise, *d.* of late John Hemming; two *s.* *Educ.:* Rossall School. Commn. in Royal Engineers (Signals), 1917; active service on Somme and remained with occupation forces in Germany until Sept. 1919. Joined 5th Bn. South Staffordshire Regiment (T.A.), 1921, and commanded battalion for eight years; retd., 1938. D.L. for Staffordshire, 1938; J.P. Walsall, 1938. Liveryman, Worshipful Co. of Glaziers. *Recreations:* Rugby football, tennis, golf. *Address:* Four Oaks House, 10 Moor Hall Drive, Four Oaks, Sutton Coldfield, Warwickshire. *Clubs:* Royal Automobile; Golf, Tennis (Sutton Coldfield). [*Died* 24 *Sept.* 1968.

LINDSAY, Sir Harry Alexander Fanshawe, K.C.I.E., *cr.* 1934 (C.I.E. 1926); C.B.E. 1919; I.C.S., retired; *b.* 11 March 1881; *s.* of late A. M. Lindsay, C.I.E., and of late Catherine Fanshawe; *m.* 1909, Kathleen Louise Huntington; two *s.* *Educ.:* St. Paul's School; Worcester College, Oxford (Oxford University Swimming and Water-polo team, 1901). Under-Secretary, Bengal Government, 1910-12; Bihar and Orissa, 1912; Commerce and Industry Dept. Govt. of India, 1912-15; Director-Gen. of Commercial Intelligence, Calcutta, 1916-21; Secretary to the Government of India, Commerce Dept., 1922; Government of India Trade Commissioner, London, 1923-34; delegate for India to Economic Committee League of Nations, 1924-34; Adviser to the Indian Delegation, Imperial Economic Conference at Ottawa, 1932; Director, Imperial Institute, 1934-53. Mem. of Council, Festival of Britain, 1951; Past-Chairman of Council, Royal Society of Arts; Past-President Royal Geographical Soc., Geographical Assoc. and Assoc. of Special Libraries and Information Bureaux; Vice-Pres., Royal Commonwealth Society. Editor, British Commonwealth Objectives (Royal Society of Arts, 1946). *Address:* Orchard, Shiplake, Oxon. [*Died* 2 *March* 1963.

LINDSAY, Howard; playwright, producer, actor; *b.* Waterford, N.Y., 29 March 1889; *m.* 1927, Dorothy Stickney; no *c.* *Educ.:* Boston Latin School; Harvard University. Graduated Boston Latin School, 1907; student Harvard Univ. for one year. Began as actor in Polly of the Circus, 1909; later became Stage Director and Playwright. Staged Dulcy and To the Ladies (by George Kaufman and Marc Connelly); The Wren and Hoosiers Abroad (by Booth Tarkington); The Haunted House (by Owen Davis); The Poor Nut (by J. C. Nugent and Elliott Nugent), etc.; also plays written by himself or in collaboration. Produced (with Russe Crouse) Arsenic and Old Lace, 1941; The Hasty Heart, 1945; Detective Story, 1949; One Bright Day, 1952; The Great Sebastians, 1955. She Loves Me Not (dramatized from novel by Edward Hope, 1934); Co-author: (with Bertrand Robinson) Tommy, 1927; Your Uncle Dudley, 1929; Oh Promise Me, 1930; (with Damon Runyon) A Slight Case of Murder, 1935; (with Russel Crouse) Anything Goes, 1934; Red, Hot and Blue, 1936; Hooray for What?, 1937; Life with Father, 1939 (created part of Father); Strip for Action, 1942; State of the Union (Pulitzer Prize, 1946), 1945; Life With Mother, 1948 (created part of Father); Call Me Madam, 1950; Remains to be Seen, 1951; The Prescott Proposals, 1953; The Great Sebastians, 1955; Happy Hunting, 1956; Tall Story, 1959, also book of The Sound of Music (musical), 1959; book of Mr. President (musical), 1962. *Address:* 13 East 94th St., New York 28, N.Y., U.S.A. *T.:* Sacramento 2-4428; Stanton, New Jersey. *Club:* The Players (Pres. 1955-65). [*Died* 10 *Feb.* 1968.

LINDSAY, Major Sir Humphrey; *see* Broun Lindsay, Major Sir G. H. M.

LINDSAY, Ian Gordon, O.B.E. 1956; R.S.A., F.R.I.B.A., F.R.I.A.S., F.S.A. Scot.; Member of Royal Commission on Ancient and Historical Monuments of Scotland; Royal Fine Art Commission of Scotland, Ancient Monuments Board of Scotland, Historic Buildings Council of Scotland, Council of National Trust of Scotland, etc.; *b.* 29 July 1906; *s.* of George Herbert Lindsay, Edinburgh; *m.* 1932, Hon. Maysie Elizabeth, *e. d.* of Major-General 2nd Baron Loch, of Drylaw; three *s.* three *d.* *Educ.:* Marlborough; Trinity College, Cambridge (B.A.). Served apprenticeship with late Dr. R. Fairlie, R.S.A.; commenced practice in Edinburgh, 1931. Responsible for various ecclesiastical and domestic works, memorial to 51st Highland Division at St. Valéry etc., also for restorations at Iona Abbey, Pluscarden Priory, Canongate Kirk, Inveraray Castle-Town, Mertoun, Aldie Castle, Cramond Village, etc. Served R.E., 1940-45, Major 1944. Foreign Mem. Royal Swedish Acad. of Letters, History and Antiquities, 1961. *Publications:* The Cathedrals of Scotland, 1926; Old Edinburgh, 1939; Georgian Edinburgh, 1948; The Scottish Parish Kirk, 1961; various contributions to architectural and other journals. *Recreation:* shooting. *Address:* Houstoun House, Uphall, West Lothian. *T.:* Broxburn 2570. *Club:* New (Edinburgh). [*Died* 28 *Aug.* 1966.

LINDSAY, Sir Lionel (Arthur), Kt., *cr.* 1941; artist; *b.* Creswick, Victoria, 18 Oct. 1874; *s.* of Robert Charles Lindsay, surgeon, and Jane Elizabeth Williams; *m.* 1903, Jane Ann Dyson, Melbourne; one *s.* one *d.* *Educ.:* State School; Creswick Grammar School. Pupil assistant, Melbourne Observatory, 1889; studied art National Gallery School, Melbourne, 1893. Trustee Nat. Gall. of N.S.W., 1918-. Drew for weekly papers. Went to Spain, 1902, to illustrate Carmen, Returned to Sydney, 1903; cartoonist, Evening News, Sydney, 1903-26; painted and etched in Spain, France, Italy, North Africa, and India, 1926-35. Prints in British Museum, New York Library, Modern Gallery, Madrid, and all Australian Galleries. Silver Medal, Paris Exhibition, 1937. *Publications:* A Consideration of the Art of Ernest Moffitt, 1899; The Art of Conrad Martens, 1920; The Art of Arthur Streeton, 1919; The Art of Hans Heysen, 1920; A Book of Woodcuts, 1922; Twenty-One Woodcuts, 1924; A. J. Munnings, R.A., 1927; Charles Keene The Artist's Artist, 1934; Addled Art, 1942; Discobolus and other verse, 1959. *Recreations:* gardening, print-collecting. *Address:* 7 Burns Road, Wahroonga, Sydney, Australia. *T.A.:* Wahroonga, Sydney. *T.:* J.W. 3182. *Club:* Arts. [*Died* 22 *May* 1961.

LINDSAY, Norman (Alfred William): black and white artist; *b.* Creswick, Victoria, 23 Feb. 1879; *s.* of Dr. Lindsay. Appointed to the artistic staff of the Bulletin, Sydney, 1901; subsequently its chief cartoonist for many years; illustrated in line and wash drawings Theocritus, Boccaccio and Casanova, Petronius, Hugh McCrae's Satyrs and Sunlight, Colombine and Gellert's Songs of a Campaign; a selection from his best work in line, published as The Pen Drawings of Norman Lindsay; has painted in oil and water-colour. *Publications:* A Curate in Bohemia, 1913; The Magic Pudding, 1919; Creative Effort, essays on Life and Art, 1920; Norman Lindsay's Book, No. 1, 1912, No. 2, 1915; The Cautious Amorist; Pam in the Parlour, 1934; Age of Consent, 1958; My Mask, 1970(posthumous), numerous uncollected stories and essays. *Address:* Spring Wood, New South Wales, Australia. [*Died* 21 *Nov.* 1969.

LINDSAY-HOGG, Sir Anthony Henry, 2nd Bt., *cr.* 1905; *b.* 1 May 1908;

e. s. of late William Lindsay Lindsay-Hogg and late Nora Cicely, *d.* of late Capt. J. J. Barrow of Holmewood, nr. Tunbridge Wells, Dornoch, Scotland, and 35 Hyde Park Gardens, W.; *S.* grandfather, 1923; *m.* 1929, Frances Mary (granted a divorce, 1934), *er. d.* of Arthur Richard Doble of Montreal; one *s.* Prior to joining R.A.F. was 1st Officer in A.T.A. 1939-41; A.D.C. to Sir Bede Clifford, Governor of Trinidad, 1942-43; late Squadron Leader, R.A.F. Transport Command. *Heir: s.* William Lindsay Lindsay-Hogg [*b.* 12 Aug. 1930; *m.* 1961, Victoria (marr. diss. 1968), *d.* of John Pares, Priory House, Kingsclere; one *d.* *Educ.:* Stowe. Lieut. 17/21st Lancers]. *Recreations:* landscape gardening, photography. *Address:* Carrington House, Hertford St., W.1. *Clubs:* Guards, St. James'. [*Died* 31 *Oct.* 1968.

LINDSEY, 13th Earl of (*cr.* 1626), and **ABINGDON,** 8th Earl of (*cr.* 1682); **Montagu Henry Edmund Cecil Bertie;** Baron, 1572; late Captain, Grenadier Guards; *b.* 2 Nov. 1887; *g. s.* of 7th Earl of Abingdon, and *o. s.* of late Lord Norreys and Hon. Rose Riversdale Glyn, *sister* of 4th Lord Wolverton; *S.* grandfather, as Earl of Abingdon, 1928 and kinsman as Earl of Lindsey, 1938; *m.* 1928, Elizabeth Valetta, *d.* of late Major-General Hon. Edward Stuart-Wortley, C.B., C.M.G., and Hon. Mrs. Stuart-Wortley, C.B.E., J.P. Captain Grenadier Guards (S.R.); formerly Capt. Royal Anglesey R.E.; has been employed under the Egyptian Government; served European War, 1914-18, temp. Flight Sub.-Lt. R.N.A.S. (wounded); Family Trustee, British Museum; High Steward of Abingdon. *Heir: cousin* Richard Henry Rupert Bertie, Lieut. Royal Norfolk Regt. [*b.* 28 June 1931; *m.* 1957, Norah Elizabeth Farquhar-Oliver]. *Address:* 2 Curzon Place, W.1. *Clubs:* Carlton, St. James'. [*Died* 11 *Sept.* 1963.

LINES, Vincent, R.W.S. 1945, Vice-President, 1964 (A.R.W.S. 1939); Principal, Hastings School of Art, since 1945; *b.* 19 June 1909. Art training: L.C.C. Central School of Arts and Crafts, The Roy. Coll. of Art. A.R.C.A. 1931; travelling scholar, 1932. Mem. N.E.A.C., 1946-, Hon. Sec., 1963; R.W.A. 1957. Work represented in series of water-colours in Royal Library, Windsor, and in British Museum, Victoria and Albert Museum, Imperial War Museum, Min. of Works, British Council, Manchester, Hastings, Eastbourne, Plymouth and other public galleries. Water-colours for Pilgrim Trust Scheme: Recording Britain, Londoner's England. Exhibited R.A., and British Council Exhibitions abroad. *Publications:* In the Byways of West Somerset, 1931; Shaping and Making, 1945; Mark Fisher and Margaret Fisher Prout, 1966; articles in the Old Water-colour Society vols. Illustrations for The English Windmill (by Rex Wailes), 1954. *Address:* 3 Pelham Street, Hastings, Sussex. *T.:* Hastings 2548. [*Died* 22 *April* 1968.

LINGEMAN, Eric Ralph, C.B.E. 1947; *b.* 19 June 1898; *s.* of Floris Lingeman and Marthe Marie de Bayser; *m.* 1929, Lois (*d.* 1936), *d.* of Sidney Rogers, Weybridge; two *s.* two *d.*; *m.* 1946, Damaris (*d.* 1964), *d.* of Carl Brunow, Helsingfors; one *s.* *Educ.:* Shrewsbury, Paris, Balliol. Inns of Court, O.T.C., Quetta Cadet College, 1st Bengal Lancers, 1917-20; Afghan War, 1919 (medal with clasp); Balliol, 1921-22; Hon. Attaché Brussels, 1922-23; Tehran, 1924-33; Buenos Aires, 1933-37; Helsingfors, 1938-41; Latin America, 1942-44; Baghdad, 1944-45; Economic Adviser to British Embassy, Athens, 1945-46; Counsellor (Commercial), British Embassy, Ankara, 1946-47; Economic Adviser to U.K. Liaison Mission, Tokyo, 1947-50; Minister (Commercial), Rome, 1950-51; British Ambassador to Afghanistan, 1951-53; British Ambassador to Uruguay, 1953-55; ret. 1956. Director of Britain in Europe, April 1958; retd. July 1961. *Publications:* Surveys of Persian, Argentine, Finnish, Turkish and Italian economies. *Recreation:* photography. *Address:* 51 Eaton Place, S.W.1. *T.:* Belgravia 3214. *Club:* St. James'. [*Died* 4 *Jan.* 1966.

LINNELL, John Wycliffe, M.C., B.A. (Lond.); B.A. (Cantab.); M.D. (Cantab.); F.R.C.P. (Lond.); retd. as: Cons. Physician; Consulting Physician, Metropolitan Hosp.; Consulting Physician, Mildmay Mission Hosp.; late Hon. Consulting Physician, Thyroid Clinic, New End Hospital, Hampstead; *b.* 31 Oct. 1878; 2nd *s.* of Rev. John Edward Linnell, Vicar of Pavenham, Beds, and Emmeline Elizabeth Darby; unmarried. *Educ.:* Bedford Modern School; St. John's College, Cambridge; London Hosp. Medical Superintendent, Mount Vernon Hospital, Hampstead; Gibbons Research Student, St. George's Hospital; Medical Registrar, London Hospital; late Consultant L.C.C. Hospitals Service; Co-Founder of the Thyroid Club. Served European War, 1914-19, France, Egypt and Gallipoli; 7th Division, 42nd Division, 2nd Mounted Division, and 40th Division; Major, R.A.M.C. (M.C., despatches). *Publications:* various articles in medical magazines; Old Oak, the Story of a Forest Village. Frequent Contrib. to Truth for some years. *Recreation:* formerly tramping. *Address:* The Retreat, Pavenham, Beds. *T.:* Oakley 247. *Club:* Royal Commonwealth Society. [*Died* 2 *Dec.* 1967.

LINSTEAD, Sir (Reginald) Patrick, Kt. 1959; C.B.E. 1946; F.R.S. 1940; D.Sc.; F.R.I.C.: Rector of the Imperial College of Science and Technology since 1955; *b.* 28 Aug. 1902; 2nd *s.* of Edward Flatman Linstead and Florence Evelyn Hester; *m.* 1st, 1930, Aileen Edith Ellis Rowland (*née* Abbott) (*decd.*); one *d.*; 2nd, 1942, Marjorie, *d.* of W. D. Walters, Aberdare. *Educ.:* City of London School; Imperial College of Science, London (D.I.C.). B.Sc. London, 1923; Ph.D. 1926; D.Sc. 1930; M.A. (Hon.) Harvard, 1942. Research Assistant to Sir Jocelyn Thorpe, 1927. Research Chemist, Anglo-Persian Oil Co., Ltd. 1928; Demonstrator and later Lecturer in Organic Chemistry, Imperial College, 1929-38; Firth Professor of Chemistry, The University of Sheffield, 1938-39; Professor of Organic Chemistry, Harvard University, 1939-42; Dep. Dir. of Scientific Research, Ministry of Supply, 1942-45; Director of Chemical Research Laboratory, Department of Scientific and Industrial Research, 1945-49; Professor of Organic Chemistry and Director of the Organic Chemistry Laboratories, Imperial College of Science and Technology, 1949-54; Dean of the Royal College of Science, 1953-54; Vice-President, 1959-65 (Foreign Secretary, 1960-65), Royal Soc.; Member: Senate, University of London; Court of Governors, London School of Economics and Political Science; Governing Body, Charterhouse, 1958-65; Govt. Cttee. on Higher Education, 1961-63; Trustee of the National Gallery; Member, Science Museum Adv. Council; formerly Vice-Pres. Chemical Society; formerly Vice-Pres. Royal Inst. of Chemistry. Hon. D.Sc. (Exeter), 1965. Hon. F.C.G.I., Hon. M.I.M.M. *Publications:* (jt.) Last Edition of Cain and Thorpe's Synthetic Dyestuffs; A Course in Modern Techniques of Organic Chemistry, 1955 (with Dr. J. A. Elvidge and Dr. M. Whalley); A Guide to Qualitative Organic Chemical Analysis (with Dr. B. C. L. Weedon); numerous papers on chemical research since 1921, mainly in Journal of Chemical Society.

Address: Imperial College, South Kensington, S.W.7. *Club:* Athenæum.
[*Died* 22 *Sept.* 1966.

LINTERN, Reep, C.B. 1961; M.Sc.; Barrister-at-Law; *b.* 9 April 1902; *o. s.* of late W. H. Lintern and Alice Reep; unmarried. *Educ.:* Shepton Mallet Grammar School; University of Bristol. B.Sc. (1st Class Hons.) Bristol 1922. M.Sc. 1924; Resident Engineer for late Sir Brodie Henderson, on construction of Poole Harbour Bridge, 1924; Chartered Civil Engineer, 1927, awarded Miller Prize and Telford Premium by Inst.C.E. Entered National Physical Laboratory, 1927, and Min. of Transport, 1929; Asst. Sec., 1943, and Director of Sea Transport, 1950. Under Secretary 1954-62; Hon Sec. Instn. of Professional Civil Servants and Member of National Whitley Council, 1935-38 Called to Bar, Middle Temple, 1935. *Publications* various scientific papers, in proc. Instn. of Civil Engineers, Soc. of Engineers and Public Works, Roads and Transport Congress. *Recreations:* music, reading and bridge. *Address:* 14 Selwood Terrace, S.W.7. *T.:* Fremantle 4785. *Clubs:* Roehampton, English-Speaking Union.
[*Died* 12 *June* 1967.

LINTOTT, Henry John, R.S.A., A.R.C.A.; painter of figure subjects and portraits; *b.* 25 Dec. 1877; *m.* 1st, 1907, Edith, *d.* of late John Lunn; one *s.*; 2nd, 1929, Audrey Ruth Mansell Wallace, *d.* of Rev. Walter Mansell Merry, M.A., of Oxford. Studied at Brighton, S. Kensington, Paris, and Italy. Scottish Modern Arts Association purchased Portrait of Artist's Wife, 1914; Thorburn Ross Fund for Scottish National Gallery purchased Orange and Grey. 1919. *Recreation:* music. *Address:* 9 Lennox Street, Edinburgh.
[*Died* 21 *Oct.* 1965.

LIPSON, Daniel Leopold, M.A. Cantab.; Alderman of Gloucestershire County Council since 1925 and Cheltenham Town Council since 1929; *b.* Sheffield, 26 March 1886; *s.* of H. R. Lipson; *m.* 1914, Juliet Lyon Barnett; two *d.* *Educ.:* Sheffield Royal Grammar School; Corpus Christi College, Cambridge. Assistant Master, Portsmouth Grammar School, 1908-12; Bradford Grammar School, 1912-14; Housemaster, Cheltenham College, 1914-23; Headmaster, Corinth College, Gheltenham, 1923-35; Mayor of Cheltenham, 1935-36, and 1936-37. M.P. (Ind.) for Cheltenham, 1937-50. Hon. Freeman, Cheltenham Borough, 1953. *Recreations:* walking, golf, reading. *Address:* 103 Old Bath Road, Cheltenham. *T.:* Cheltenham 2326.
[*Died* 14 *April* 1963.

LISBURNE, 7th Earl of (*cr.* 1776), **Ernest Edmund Henry Malet Vaughan,** J.P.; Viscount Lisburne and Lord Vaughan, 1695; Major, late Welsh Guards and Scots Guards; formerly Lord Lieut. Cardiganshire; *b.* 8 Feb. 1892; *o. s.* of 6th Earl and Evelyn (*d.* 1931), 2nd *d.* of Edmund Probyn, Longhope, Gloucestershire; *S.* father, 1899; *m.* 1st, 1914, Regina (*d.* 1944), *d.* of Don Julio de Bittencourt, Attaché to the Chilean Legation; one *s.* three *d.*; 2nd, 1961, Audrey Maureen Leslie, D.St.J. 1963, *d.* of James Meakin and *widow* of Hon. Robert Devereux, Hampton Ct., Herts. *Educ.:* Eton. Served European War, 1914-18 (wounded, despatches); re-employed War of 1939-45. Contested (C.) Cardiganshire, 1923; Vice-President of University College of Wales (Aberystwyth). *Heir:* *s.* Viscount Vaughan. *Recreations:* shooting, fishing. *Address:* Flat 7, 1 St. James's Street, S.W.1. *T.:* Whitehall 4286. *Clubs:* Carlton, Beefsteak.
[*Died* 30 *June* 1965.

LISMER, Arthur, C.C. (Canada) 1967; R.C.A. 1947 (A.R.C.A. 1919); O.S.A. 1913; Member of "Group of 7" Canadian Painters; Principal of School of Art and Design of Montreal Museum of Fine Art, 1942-67, Principal Emeritus since 1967; Assistant Professor of Fine Arts, McGill University, 1948-55; *b.* Sheffield, 1885; *m.*; one *d.* *Educ.:* Sheffield School of Art (Scholar); Académie Royale des Beaux Arts, Antwerp. Went to Canada, 1911; taught at Ontario Coll. of Art, 1915-16; Principal, Nova Scotia Coll. of Art, 1916-19; Vice-Principal, Ontario Coll. of Art, 1919-27; Educational Director Art Gallery of Toronto, 1928; Lecturer on Art, Dept. of Extension, Univ. of Toronto; Principal Teacher Training Course of Ontario Dept. of Education, 1920-33; lectured in South Africa in Union of S.A. and in British protectorates in Australia, N.Z., and the South Seas at invitation of Governments, 1936; Professor Fine Arts, Teachers' College, Columbia University, N.Y., 1938-39; directing Educational Activities, National Gallery of Canada, Ottawa, 1939-40; Educational Supervisor, Museum of Fine Arts, Art Association of Montreal, and Lecturer in Fine Arts and Aesthetics, McGill Univ. (Dept. of Architecture), Montreal, 1940; Honour Diploma N.S. College of Art; Hon. LL.D., by Dalhousie Univ., Halifax, N.S., 1942; F.R.S.A. (Lond., Eng.), 1948; Gold Medal, Univ. of Alberta, for Services to Canadian Art and Educ., 1953; Canada Council Medal, 1962. Hon. LL.D., McGill Univ., Montreal, 1963. *Address:* 2055 Fort St., Montreal. *T.:* WE 5-8118. *Clubs:* Arts and Letters (Toronto); Faculty, McGill University (Montreal).
[*Died* 23 *March* 1969.

LISTER, Charles Ashton, C.B.E. 1918; J.P.; *e. surv. s.* of late Sir Ashton Lister, C.B.E.; *b.* 1871; *m.* 1892, Laura Emmeline, *d.* of late A. Browning, M.A., Bath; five *s.* Has travelled a great deal in the U.S.A., Colonies, and on the Continent; served on Advisory Committees of Ministry of Munitions and Ministry of Reconstruction during the War, and also was a member of the West of England Munition Committee. *Address:* 7 Queens Rd., Hayward's Heath, Sussex. *Club:* Royal Automobile.
[*Died* 27 *March* 1965.

LISTER, Sir Frederick; *see* Lister, Sir T. F.

LISTER, Thomas, C.A.; Partner in Thomson McLintock & Co., Chartered Accountants, London, Glasgow and other Towns; Extraordinary Director, Scottish Amicable Life Assur. Soc.; Dir., Temperance Permanent Building Soc.; *b.* 3 July 1892; *s.* of late John Lister, Papermaker, Kilbagie, near Alloa, and late Jane Hannah Lister; *m.* 1918, Anna Rebecca, *d.* of late James and Sarah Black, Edinburgh; two *s.* one *d.* *Educ.:* Royal High School of Edinburgh; Edinburgh University (M.A.). Served European War, 1915-1919, Lieutenant, R.G.A. Mem. Interdepartmental (Spens) Cttees. on Remuneration of Medical and Dental Practitioners, 1946-48; Mem. North Midland District Valuation Board for Coal Industry, 1948-55. Member of Council, Institute of Chartered Accountants of Scotland 1952-56; Convener of Special Cttee. on Examination and Training of Apprentices, 1953-56; Vice-President, 1958-59; President, 1959-60. *Publications:* Lectures to Chartered Accountants Students' Societies of Edinburgh and Glasgow. *Recreation:* golf. *Address:* 33 King William Street, E.C.4. *T.:* Mansion House 3232; 19 Hurst Avenue, N.6. *T.:* Mountview 1314. *Clubs:* City of London, Reform; New (Edinburgh).
[*Died* 26 *Feb.* 1967.

LISTER, Sir (Thomas) Frederick, Kt. 1961; C.B.E. 1927; Insurance Manager (retd.); *s.* of late Thomas Lister, Surveyor; *m.* 1911, Isobel Lewis; no *c.* *Educ.:* Tranmere H.G. Sch., Birkenhead. Contested Ashton-under-Lyne, 1918; served Royal Garrison

Artillery; President National Federation of Dis. and Demob. Sailors and Soldiers, 1918-1921; Chairman British Legion, 1921-27; elected Life Member National Executive Council, 1927, National Vice-Pres., 1949; Chm. British Legion Central Service Cttee., 1949-62; Patron Lister House, Sharow, Ripon; Pres. Cheshire County British Legion; Chairman of: United Service Fund, 1942-48; Trustees, Prince of Wales British Legion Pension Fund; Mem. Exec. Council, St. Dunstans, 1953-63; Chm., British Legion Planning Cttee., 1941-47; Chm. Birkenhead and District Disablement Advisory Cttee., 1946-63; Chairman Conferences of British Empire Service League, London, 1923; Ottawa, 1925. *Recreation:* golf. *Address:* Corian, Reservoir Rd. North, Prenton, Birkenhead. *T.:* Birkenhead, Mountwood 1419. [*Died* 13 *March* 1966.

LISTER-KAYE, Sir Lister, 6th Bt., *cr.* 1812; *b.* 19 Dec. 1873; *s.* of Capt. Arthur Lister-Kaye (*d.* 1893, *s.* of 2nd Bt.), late Royal Artillery; *S.* cousin, Sir Kenelm Arthur Lister-Kaye, 5th Bt., 1955; *m.* 1910, Emily Mary (*d.* 1944), *d.* of late John Frederick Starkey, of Bodicote, Banbury; one *s.* one *d.* *Educ.:* privately. *Heir:* *s.* John Christopher Lister Lister-Kaye [*b.* 13 July 1913; *m.* 1942, Audrey Helen, *d.* of E. J. Carter; one *s.* one *d.*]. *Address:* Manor House, Stretton on Dunsmore, Rugby. *T.:* Wolston 206. [*Died* 12 *Feb.* 1962.

LISTON-FOULIS, Sir Archibald Charles, Bt.; *see* Foulis.

LITHGOW, Michael John, O.B.E. 1954; Deputy Chief Test Pilot, Vickers-Armstrongs (Aircraft) Ltd.; *b.* 30 Aug. 1920; *m.* 1946; two *s.* one *d.* *Educ.:* Cheltenham College. Served War of 1939-45 in Royal Navy; released, Nov. 1945, to join Vickers-Armstrongs Ltd. Holder of the world air speed record, Sept.-Dec. 1953. *Publications:* Mach One, 1955; (Editor) Vapour Trails, 1956. *Address:* Birchwood Cottage, Abinger Hammer, Surrey. *T.:* Abinger 283. *Club:* Royal Aero. [*Died* 22 *Oct.* 1963.

LITTLE, George Jerningham Knightley, C.B.E. 1927; Capt. late Coldstream Guards; *b.* 1886; *s.* of late E. Knightley Little, C.B.E., J.P., of Newbold Pacy Hall, Warwickshire. *Educ.:* Charterhouse. Private Secretary to Governor-General of New Zealand, 1924-27; comptroller of household to Governor-General of Canada, 1940-41. *Address:* Newbold Pacy Hall, Warwickshire. *T.:* Moreton Morrell 270. *Club:* Guards. [*Died* 25 *April* 1966.

LITTLEBOY, Colonel Charles Norman, C.B. 1959; D.S.O. 1940; M.C. 1917 (and Bar 1918); T.D. 1934 (and 2 clasps 1958); D.L.; J.P.; *b.* 25 May 1894; *e. s.* of Charles William Littleboy and Agnes Eveline Laverton; *m.* 1924, Violet Eldon Pratt; two *s.* three *d.* *Educ.:* Rugby School; Trinity College, Cambridge. Served European War, 1914-19, France and Flanders, with Durham L.I., 1914-16; with Notts and Derbyshire Regt., 1916-18; gazetted to Green Howards, 1920; Lieut.-Col. Green Howards, 1931; transferred to T.A.R.O., 1937. War of 1939-45, commanded 4th Green Howards in France, N. African Desert, Cyprus, 1939-42; transferred to T.A.R.O. County Cadet Comdt., 1946-50; Hon. Col. 4 Bn. Green Howards, 1949-61; Chm. North Riding T. & A.F.A., 1953-58. Hon. Col., 4th Green Howards, 1949-60. D.L. 1946. J.P. 1949, N.R. Yorks. District Comr., Scouts' Assoc. *Recreations:* tennis, shooting. *Address:* Howe, Thirsk, Yorkshire. *T.:* Sinderby 231. *Club:* Farmers'. [*Died* 7 *April* 1966.

LITTLEWOOD, James, C.M.G. 1963; a Vice-President of the Empire Cotton Growing Corporation; *b.* 2 September 1885; *s.* of John Littlewood, Royton, Lancashire; *m.* 1911, Amy, *d.* of Evan Jones, Southport; two *s.* one *d.* *Educ.:* Royton School; Oldham Technical School. Subseq. Empire Cotton Growing Corporation: Vice-Chairman of Administrative Council, 1944-46; Chairman, 1946-62; Vice-President, 1962-. *Address:* Dean Cottage, Buersil, Rochdale, Lancashire. *T.:* Rochdale 45218. [*Died* 14 *March* 1968.

LITTLEWOOD, Samuel Robinson; *b.* Bath 1875; *y. s.* of late Rev. W. E. Littlewood, Vicar of St. James's, Bath, and Lætitia Thornton; *m.* Phœbe Stella (*d.* 1948), *d.* of late Edwin Cooper Hayes, Solicitor, Dublin; one *s.* three *d.* *Educ.:* Merchant Taylors'; Dover College; St. Paul's. Dramatic Critic of Morning Leader, 1897-1903; Dramatic and Cinema Critic, Morning Post, 1928-38; Referee, 1915-33; Pioneer, 1920-30; Pall Mall Gazette, 1915-23; Daily Chronicle, 1904-1915, and 1918-20; Lady's Pictorial, 1914-21; Cinema Critic, Sphere, 1924-27; Fellow of Institute of Journalists, and Chairman London District, 1920; President Musical, Dramatic and Critics Circle, 1923; Member of Journalism Cttee., London Univ., 1920; B.B.C. Drama Critic, 1934-35; Editor, Men and Women, 1938-39; editor of The Stage, 1943-52, retired. *Publications:* The Story of Pierrot; Perrault's Fairy Tales; The Story of Santa Claus; Our Nursery Rhyme Book; The Fairies—Here and Now; The Romance of Petty France; The Child of the Sea; Valentine and Orson; Elizabeth Inchbald; King Arthur's Country; Somerset and the Drama; Anthology of Modern Drama; Dramatic Criticism. *Recreations:* chess, gardening, play-going. *Address:* 220 Worple Road, Wimbledon, S.W.19. *T.:* Wimbledon 1957. *Clubs:* Savage, Green Room. [*Died* 10 *Aug.* 1963.

LITTLEWOOD, Sir Sydney (Charles Thomas), Kt., *cr.* 1951; Chairman, Legal Aid Committee, Law Society, 1946-1952; President, Law Society, 1959-60 (Vice-President, 1958); *b.* 15 December 1895; *s.* of Charles Sydney Littlewood, Southampton; *m.* 1934, Barbara Langdon-Down; one *s.* Admitted Solicitor, 1922; Council, Law Society, 1940-64; President Justices' Clerks' Society, 1944-45; Member of Committee on Legal Aid and Legal Advice (Rushcliffe Committee), 1944-45; Chairman, Westminster Fire Office; Director, other Cos.; Mem. South-West Metropolitan Regional Hosp. Bd., 1952-59; Legal Mem. Town Planning Inst., 1956-; Hon. Mem. Amer. Bar Assoc., 1959-; Chm. Council, Professions Supplementary to Medicine, 1961-1966; Chm., Deptl. Cttee. on Experiments on Animals, 1963-64. Pres., London Rent Assessment Panel, 1965-67. *Recreation:* rose-growing. *Address:* Langwood, Bramley, Surrey. *Club:* Garrick. [*Died* 9 *Sept.* 1967.

LIVEING, Edward George Downing, M.A.; Author and commercial historian; *b.* 24 March 1895; *s.* of late Rev. H. G. D. Liveing and Margaret Rands; *m.* 1923, Gladys Constance Baker (*d.* 1959); one *d.* *Educ.:* Bradfield Coll.; St. John's Coll. Oxford (Exhibitioner in English Literature). Served during 1914-18 War with London Regt. in France and Palestine (wounded in Battle of Somme); Asst. to Military Censor, Egypt, 1918-19. Editor of Discovery, 1921-23. Joined B.B.C. in 1924; entrusted with creation of B.B.C.'s N. of England Region in 1928 and was its North Regional Dir. till 1937. Mem. of Lancashire Industrial Development Council, 1935-37. Managing Director, Motoring Abroad Publications Ltd., 1938-39. During 1939-45 War returned to B.B.C. for special war-time activities including establishment of Staff Welfare Unit, 1941, appt. as West Regional Director, 1941-42, assignment in Middle East 1942 for liaison between

B.B.C., the Minister of State's office, the service authorities, and Arab governments during El Alamein period; as its first Middle East Director established B.B.C. Office in Cairo, 1943. Joint Secretary, Educational Interchange Council, 1946-47. *Publications:* Attack; The House of Harrild; Adventure in Publishing; Pioneers of Petrol; A Century of Insurance; Across the Congo; contributions to Blackwood's Magazine, Fortnightly Review, etc. *Recreation:* travel. *Address:* 28 John Street, W.C.1. *T.:* Holborn 0955. *Club:* Savile. [*Died* 31 *Jan.* 1963.

LIVERPOOL, Earl of, 6th holder of title and 3rd of revived title; **Lieut.-Colonel Gerald William Frederick Savile Foljambe,** D.S.O. 1918; *b.* 12 May 1878; *s.* of 4th Earl of Liverpool; *S.* half-brother, 1941; *m.* 1909, Constance Isabelle, *o. c.* of late John Holden of Nuttall Temple, Nottingham. *Educ.:* Eton; R.M.C., Sandhurst. Served South Africa, 1900-2 (Queen's medal 3 clasps, King's medal 2 clasps); retired; European War of 1914-18 (D.S.O.). *Heir: b.* Hon. Robert Anthony Edward St. Andrew Savile Foljambe, *b.* 1887. *Address:* Merkland, Auldgirth, Dumfries. *T.:* Auldgirth 205. [*Died* 27 *July* 1962.

LIVERPOOL, 4th Earl of, *cr.* 1905 (but 7th holder of title); **Robert Anthony Edward St. Andrew Savile Foljambe**; *b.* 3 Apr. 1887; 4th *s.* of 1st Earl; *S.* brother, 1962. *Educ.:* Malvern. Inspector, Driffield Div., E. Riding Special Constabulary, 1926-45; Mem. Norton R.D.C., 1927-47. *Heir: great nephew* Edward Peter Bertram Savile Foljambe, *b.* (posthumously) 14 Nov. 1944. *Address:* Inverey, West Park Road, Cupar, Fife. [*Died* 13 *March* 1969.

LIVESEY, Rev. Herbert; *b.* 6 June 892; *e. s.* of late Walter Livesey, and Alice, *d.* of Christopher Wigglesworth, Lancashire. *Educ.:* Accrington Grammar School; S. Edmund Hall, Oxford, M.A., Dip Anthropology, L.Th. Durham, F.R.A.I. Lieut. South Lancashire Regt. (now the Lancashire Regt.) (wounded); Asst. Priest, Wigton, Cumberland; Chaplain and Tutor Lincoln Theological College; Chaplain to Bishop of Newcastle upon Tyne; Sub-warden, S. Saviour's College, Carshalton: Sub-warden, Diocesan House, Carshalton; Assistant Priest St. Martin in the Fields; Head of Cambridge University Settlement, 1936-39; Warden of Connaught Hall, University of Southampton and Director of Theological Studies, 1939-57. *Address:* Lower Farm, Madehurst, Arundel, Sussex; c/o F. Parkinson, Esq., J.P., Higher Antley Hall, Accrington, Lancs.; Barclays Bank, Accrington, Lancs. [*Died* 14 *Oct.* 1970.

LIVINGSTON, Henry Brockholst, C.B.E. 1953; retired; *b.* 26 August 1895; *s.* of late Edwin Brockholst Livingston and late Alice Mary (*née* de la Poer Power); *m.* 1919, Barbara (*née* Bancroft); one *s.* one *d.*; *m.* 1934, Elizabeth Rosemary (*née* Fitz-Gibbon Dillon); one *s.* *Educ.:* Stonyhurst College. Vice-Consul at San Francisco, Oct. 1919; subsequent appointments at Brussels, Ghent, Caracas, Los Angeles and Genoa; Consul at Leipzig, 1933; transferred to Geneva, 1938; Consul-Gen. at Los Angeles, 1945, Baden-Baden, 1946, Marseilles, 1950; Minister at San José, Costa Rica, 1951-52; retired, 1952. *Address:* Château de Bonmont, Chéserex, Vaud, Switzerland. *Club:* Royal Automobile. [*Died* 4 *June* 1968.

LIVINGSTONE, Dame Adelaide Lord, D.B.E. 1918; Vice-President, United Nations Association; Vice-President of Westminster Branch, U.N.A. (Chm. 1948-58); Associate mem. of American Outpost in Gt. Britain and of American Eagle Club; *d.* of late C. D. Stickney, Fall River, Mass., U.S.A., and of late Mrs. Sutherland Orr; *m.* 1915, W. H. D. Livingstone (*decd.*). Belclare, Co. Mayo. *Educ.:* Italy, Germany, Switzerland, France and America. Worked for Friends' Emergency Committee and International Women's Relief Committee in England, Germany, Austria, and the occupied districts of Belgium, November 1914-May 1915. Hon. Sec. of Govt. Cttee. on the Treatment of British Prisoners of War, 1915-18; in 1917 and 1918 was a member of the British Govt. Delegation sent to Holland to confer with German representatives regarding treatment of prisoners of war; Head of the War Office mission to search for missing in France and Flanders, 1919-20; Asst. Director of Graves Registration and Enquiries in Central Europe, 1920-22. Was a Member of three committees of the International Law Assoc. in 1920; Foundation member Information Service of Royal Institute of International Affairs until 1949; Head of Public Meetings Dept., League of Nations Union, 1923; Dir. of Special Activities to the League of Nations Union, 1928-34; Secretary National Declaration Committee, 1934-35 (Organiser of the Peace Ballot); Sec. and later Vice-Chm. Internat. Peace campaign, 1936-40; member Exec. Cttee., League of Nations Union, 1937-1944; Foundation Mem. of International Assembly, and member of two of its Committees, 1943-45. Member Exec. Cttee., U.N. Assoc., 1945-55. *Recreations:* gardening and telephoning. *Address:* 80 Carlisle Mansions, Carlisle Place, S.W.1. *T.A.:* Adingstone, London, S.W.1. *T.:* 01-834 0044. [*Died* 14 *Sept.* 1970.

LLEWELLYN, Captain Llewellyn Evan Hugh, C.B. 1928; O.B.E.: D.L.; R.N.; *b.* 1879; *e. s.* of late Walter J. Llewellyn, Southwood, Tiverton, Devon: *m.* 1907, Aileen (*d* 1969), *y. d.* of late Admiral Sir Digby Morant, K.C.B.; one *s.* one *d.* *Educ.:* Privately. Entered R.N. 1893; served E. Africa, 1896; W. Africa, 1895, 1897; Benin Expedition, 1897 (medal and clasp); China, 1900 (medal); specially promoted to Lieutenant, 1900, for meritorious examinations; Chief Inspector of Naval Ordnance, 1919-27; retired Captain, 1927; Director Bomb Disposal Dept., Admiralty, 1940-44. D.L. Cumberland, 1959. *Address:* Glenwood, Ravenglass, Cumberland. *Club:* United Service. [*Died* 4 *Feb.* 1970.

LLEWELYN, W. Craven; Colliery Owner and Companies' Director; Agriculturalist; *s.* of T. David Llewelyn, Clydach, Glamorganshire; *m.* 1932, Doris Mary Bell; no *c.* *Educ.:* Arnold College, Swansea; Technical College, Swansea; University College, Bangor. Studied mining privately under J. Henry Davies, M.E., F.G.S.; Forest Statistical Officer, Home-Grown Timber Dept., Board of Trade, 1918-19. Investigated timber regions of Central America, Central Europe and Russia. Travelled widely. Engaged in Colliery and Timber interests, Brick Manufacturer, and also engaged in Agricultural pursuits. Parliamentary Liberal Candidate for Chester in 1923 and Crewe 1929. President Swansea Chamber of Commerce, 1944-45. High Sheriff for Brecknockshire, 1944-45. Member Exec. Council Empire and Internat. Chambers of Commerce, 1948-63. Pres. Swansea Town Football Club Association. Member: N.F.U.; Farmers' Union for Wales. *Publications:* Afforestation of Wales, 1915; Forest Soils of Wales, 1917. *Recreations:* travelling, fishing, shooting, naturalist. *Address:* Forest, Clydach, Glamorganshire. *T.:* Clydach 2172; Woodlands, Penmaen, Gower, Glamorganshire. *Club:* Farmers'. [*Died* 4 *Jan.* 1966.

LLOYD, Capt. Arthur Wynell, M.C.; *b.* 4 April 1883; 2nd *s.* of late E. W. M. Lloyd. *Educ.:* Rugby; Queen's College, Oxford. Served with 25th R. Fusiliers in E. Africa, 1916 and 1917. *Address:* 1 The Grange, Hartley

Wintney, Basingstoke, Hants. *Club:* Athenæum. [*Died* 14 *May* 1967.

LLOYD, Cyril Edward, M.Inst.C.E.; *b.* 1876; *m.* 1909, Phyllis Gretchen, *d.* of Sir Ernest Waterlow, R.A.; one *d.* *Educ.:* Uppingham. Director N. Hingley & Sons Ltd., and other companies; M.P. (U.) Dudley, 1922-29, and 1941-45; contested Dudley, 1929; President, National Federation of Iron and Steel Manufacturers, 1925; High Sheriff of Worcestershire, 1935. Member United Kingdom Sugar Industry Inquiry Committee, 1934, 1935. *Address:* Church House, Broome, nr. Stourbridge, Worcs. *Clubs:* Carlton, Arts. [*Died* 19 *Feb.* 1963.

LLOYD, Edward Mayow Hastings, C.B. 1952; C.M.G. 1945; *b.* 30 Nov. 1889; 4th *s.* of late E. W. M. Lloyd and E. E. Lloyd, Hartford House, Hartley Wintney, Hants; *m.* 1918, Margaret Frances, *d.* of late Hon. Rollo Russell; two *s.* one *d.* *Educ.:* Rugby School; Corpus Christi Coll., Oxford. Inland Revenue, 1913; War Office, Contracts Dept., 1914-17; Ministry of Food, 1917-19; Economic and Financial Section of League of Nations Secretariat, 1919-21; Assistant Secretary, Empire Marketing Board, 1926-33; Secretary, Market Supply Committee, 1933-36; Assistant Director, Food (Defence Plans) Dept., 1936-39; Principal Asst. Secretary, Ministry of Food, 1939-42; Economic Adviser to Minister of State, Middle East, 1942-44; U.N.R.R.A., Economic and Financial Adviser for the Balkans, 1945; F.A.O., United Nations, 1946-47; Under Sec., Min. of Food, 1947-53. Pres. Agricultural Economics Soc., 1956; Consultant, P.E.P., 1958-64. *Publications:* Stabilisation, 1923; Experiments in State Control, 1924; Food and Inflation in the Middle East, 1940-45. *Address:* Tillingbourne Hey, Gravel Hill Terrace, Hemel Hempstead, Herts. *T.:* Hemel Hempstead 56514. *Club:* Reform. [*Died* 27 *Jan.* 1968.

LLOYD, Colonel Edward Prince, C.B.E. 1944; D.S.O.; Regular Army Officer (retired); *b.* 22 July 1887; *yr. s.* of late Lt.-Col. T. P. Lloyd, Longford House, Templemore, Ireland; unmarried. *Educ.:* Dover College; R.M.C., Sandhurst. Gazetted Lincolnshire Regt. 1906; commanded 2nd Bn. Lincolnshire Regt. 1933-37; Col. 1937-44; served European War, 1914-18 (despatches 5 times, Bt. Major, D.S.O. and Bar); Palestine, 1936-37 (despatches). *Club:* United Service. [*Died* 14 *May* 1970.

LLOYD, Captain Sir Humphrey (Clifford), K.C.V.O. 1962 (C.V.O. 1953; M.V.O. 1935); M.C. 1915; *b.* 24 April 1893; *s.* of late Colonel Wilford Neville LLoyd, C.B., C.V.O.; *m.* 1st, 1918, Constance, *d.* of late J. H. Loudon, O.B.E., of Olantigh, Wye, Kent; one *s.*; 2nd, 1932, Gladys Margery, *d.* of late Colonel H. W. A. F. Crichton-Browne, of Buildwas Park, Cressage, Shropshire; one *d.* *Educ.:* Eton; R.M.C. Sandhurst. Joined King's Royal Rifle Corps, 1913; served European War, 1914-1918 (wounded, despatches, M.C.); A.D.C. to Viceroy of Ireland, 1915; to General Lord Rawlinson, Comdg. 4th Army, 1916; seconded to R.A.F., 1917-19; retired, 1923; a Gentleman Usher to King George VI, 1925-1952; to Queen Elizabeth II, 1952-66, Extra Gentleman Usher, 1966-. An Assistant Chief Constable of the War Department Constabulary, 1932-36; Chief Constable of Montgomeryshire, 1936-48, and also of Radnorshire, 1946-48; Chief Constable of the Mid-Wales Constabulary, 1948-1959. O.St.J. *Recreations:* shooting, yachting, cricket. *Address:* Farthingworth House, 12 Montpelier Row, Twickenham, Middlesex. *T.:* Popesgrove 8233. *Clubs:* M.C.C., International Sportsmen's. [*Died* 11 *June* 1966.

LLOYD, Air Commodore Ivor Thomas, C.B. 1945; C.B.E. 1939; R.A.F. (retired); *b.* 2 March 1896; *s.* of late Major T. W. Lloyd; *m.* 1929, Phyllis Eleanor, *d.* of late Frank Pegler, J.P.; two *d.* *Educ.:* St. Bees; Royal Military College, Sandhurst. South Wales Borderers, seconded Royal Flying Corps, 1914-18; Royal Air Force, 1918-39; retired 1939 with rank of Group Capt.; recalled to active list on outbreak of war 1939; Coastal Command Headquarters for operational planning, 1939-41; Deputy Senior Air Staff Officer, 1941; Air Officer Commanding No. 16 Group, 1942; Deputy Air Officer-in-Charge Administration, Coastal Command, 1943-45 (despatches). *Address:* 44 Porchester Terrace, W.2. *T.:* Ambassador 5750. *Club:* R.A.F. [*Died* 28 *Oct.* 1966.

LLOYD, Colonel (Hon. Brig.) John Edward, C.B.E. 1943; D.S.O.; M.C.; E.D.; *b.* 13 April 1894; *s.* of late W. E. R. Lloyd, Melbourne, Victoria, Australia; *m.* 1920, M. M. Robinson, *d.* of late R. T. Robinson, K.C., Perth, W.A.; two *s.* one *d.* *Educ.:* The Grange and Brighton Grammar Schools, Victoria. Commission as Lieut. land forces and served European War, 1915-1918, Gallipoli and France, 1st A.I.F. (M.C. and bar); rose to rank of Major; in regular Indian Army, 1918-22; served in Afghan War, 1919-20; on land in West Australia, grazing and wheat property freehold, 1923-1928; in business Real Estate, 1928-39, Perth; 2nd in Command and later commanded 16 Bn. the Cameron Highlanders of W.A. 1936-39; with 2nd A.I.F., 1940-45; formed and commanded 2/28 Aust. Inf. Bn., from W.A.; early 1942 commanded 16 Aust. Inf. Bde. Group, A.I.F.; served Tobruk (D.S.O.), Syria, Ceylon, and New Guinea (C.B.E.); also Special Duties, India, Burma, New Guinea, Singapore, S.E. Asia (Repatriation of Aust. ex-P.O.W. and Internees), commanding Group. Resumed Farming and Grazing actively, 1948; Magistrate State Licensing Court, 1949-61. Hon. Col. Cameron Highlanders of W.A., 1955-60. Mem. W.A. Blinded ex-Servicemen's Assoc. *Address:* Dootamarra, Mayanup, W. Australia. *Clubs:* Navy, Army and Air Force, Perth (W.A.). [*Died Dec.* 1965.

LLOYD, Sir Robert Owen, Kt. 1959; O.B.E. 1946 (M.B.E. 1941); Chairman and Managing Director, Sir Robert Lloyd and Company Ltd.; *b.* 1894; *s.* of Charles and Mary Anne Lloyd; *m.* 1st, 1922, Ellen Lord (*d.* 1955); two *d.*; 2nd, 1960, Doris Martha, *d.* of late Mr. and Mrs. W. Davey. *Educ.:* Goosnargh (Oliversons') C.E. School. Apprentice carpenter-joiner, 1907. Served in France with R.E. Tunnelling company, 1914-1919. Director, Selwood Lloyd and Co., 1926-29; Director, Lloyd and Cross Ltd., 1929. President, Liverpool Regional Federation of Building Trades Employers, 1941-42 and 1957-58; President, National Federation of Building Trades Employers, 1950; Leader, Productivity Team on Building, 1949. President, Birkenhead Conservative Association. *Recreations:* golf, gardening. *Address:* Rock Mount, Thorsway, Caldy, Cheshire. *T.:* 051-625 8210. [*Died* 10 *March* 1970.

LLOYD, Rev. Canon Roger Bradshaigh; Residentiary Canon of Winchester since 1937; *e. s.* of Colonel W. E. Lloyd; *m.* 1927, Mildred Vera Frodsham Ward; one *d.* *Educ.:* Shrewsbury School; St. John's College, Cambridge. Curate of S. Wilfrid, Newton Heath, Manchester, 1924-26; S. Mary, Crumpsall, Manchester, 1926-28; Rector of S. Stephen, Harpurhey, Manchester, 1928-31; Vicar of Great Harwood, Lancashire, 1932-37. *Publications:* The Stricken Lute: a Biography of Abelard; The Religious Crisis; Christianity History and Civilisation; Crown Him Lord of

All; The Beloved Community; Revolutionary Religion; The Golden Middle Age; The Mastery of Evil; The Inspiration of God; The Glorious Liberty; The Church of England in the Twentieth Century; The Fascination of Railways; The Church and the Artisan Today; Railwaymen's Gallery; Adventure in Discipleship; Farewell to Steam; Letters of Luke the Physician; Letters from the Early Church; The Borderland; The Troubling of the City; The Ferment in the Church. *Address:* Cheyney Court, The Close, Winchester. *Club:* Athenæum. [*Died* 15 *Sept.* 1966.

LLOYD, Sir Thomas Ingram Kynaston, G.C.M.G., *cr.* 1951 (K.C.M.G., *cr.* 1947; C.M.G. 1943); K.C.B., *cr.* 1949; *b.* 19 June 1896; *e. s.* of late John Charles and Henrietta Elizabeth Lloyd, The Uplands, Shifnal, Shropshire; *m.* 1922, Bessie Nora, *er. d.* of late G. J. Mason, The Woodlands, Penn, Staffordshire; two *s. Educ.:* Rossall; R.M.A., Woolwich; Caius College, Cambridge. Commissioned R.E. 1916; served M.E.F., 1917-19 (despatches); retired and placed on Reserve, 1919; Assistant Principal Ministry of Health, 1920; transferred to Colonial Office, 1921; Principal, 1929; Secretary, Palestine Commission, 1929-30; Secretary, West India Royal Commission, 1938-39; Assistant Secretary, Colonial Office, 1939; Asst. Under-Secretary of State, Colonial Office, 1943; Permanent Under-Secretary for the Colonies, 1947-56; retired, 1956. Member of Council of Rossall School. *Address:* Faggots End, Radlett, Herts. *T.:* Radlett 6590. *Club:* Oxford and Cambridge. [*Died* 9 *Dec.* 1968.

LLOYD GEORGE of Dwyfor, 2nd Earl, *cr.* 1945; **Richard Lloyd George;** A.M.Inst.C.E.; Viscount Gwynedd, of Dwyfor, 1945; Major R.E.; *b.* 15 Feb. 1889. *s.* of 1st Earl and Margaret (*d.* 1941), G.B.E., *cr.* 1920, *d.* of Richard Owen, Mynydd Ednyfed, Criccieth; *S.* father, 1945; *m.* 1st, 1917, Roberta Ida Freeman (marr. diss., 1933), 5th *d.* of Sir Robert McAlpine, 1st Bt.; one *s.* one *d.*; 2nd, 1935, Mrs. Winifred Calvé. *Educ.:* Portmadoc; Christ's College, Camb. (B.A. Hons. 1910). Served in R.E., European War, 1914-18, and War of 1939-45. *Publications:* Dame Margaret, 1947; Lloyd George, 1960. *Heir: s.* Viscount Gwynedd. *Address:* House of Lords, S.W.1. [*Died* 1 *May* 1968.

LLOYD GEORGE, Lady Megan, C.H. 1966; J.P.; M.P. (Lab.) Carmarthen since 1957; *b.* Criccieth, Wales; *yr. d.* of 1st Earl Lloyd George of Dwyfor, P.C., O.M. (*d.* 1945) and Dame Margaret Lloyd George, G.B.E., J.P. *Educ.:* Garratt's Hall, Banstead; Paris. M.P. (L.), Anglesey, 1929-31, (Ind. L.) 1931-1943, (L.) 1945-51. Hon. LL.D. (Wales), 1949. *Address:* Brynawelon, Criccieth, North Wales. [*Died* 14 *May* 1966.

LLOYD-JACOB, Hon. Sir George (Harold), Kt., *cr.* 1950; **Hon. Mr. Justice Lloyd-Jacob;** Judge of the High Court of Justice, Chancery Division, since 1950; *b.* 1 October 1897; 7th *c.* of John Lloyd Jacob; *m.* 1928, Kay Winifred Surman; one *s.* two *d. Educ.:* Southgate; Christ Church, Oxford; King's College, London. Lieut. Royal Flying Corps, 1916-18; Flight Lieut. R.A.F., 1918-21; Called to Bar, Middle Temple, 1923. King Edward VII Scholar, 1924, Master of the Bench, 1950; Junior Counsel to Board of Trade in Patent Matters, 1937-45; Q.C. 1945. Lay Reader Diocese of Guildford. *Address:* 1 Garden Court, Temple, E.C.4. *T.:* 01-353 9187; Fredley Manor, Mickleham, Surrey. *T.:* Dorking 2054. *Club:* Knights of the Round Table. [*Died* 3 *Dec.* 1969.

LLOYD-WILLIAMS, Hugh, C.B.E. 1957; D.S.O. 1918; M.C. 1916; *b.* 1889; *m.* 1918, Dorothy Marian (*d.* 1967), *d.* of late Maj. the Hon. Frederick Le Poer Trench. *Educ.:* Univ. College of North Wales, Bangor (M.A.). Called to Bar, Middle Temple, 1921. Served War, 1914-18, Royal Welch Fusiliers (despatches, M.C., D.S.O.); Member, Industrial Court, and Industrial Disputes Tribunal, 1953-59. *Address:* 4 Paper Buildings, Temple, E.C.4. *T.:* Central 9568. *Club:* Army and Navy. [*Died* 2 *Dec.* 1968.

LLOYD-WILLIAMS, Captain James Evan, C.B.E. 1950; M.C. 1918; D.L.; *b.* 7 April 1888; *s.* of John Jordan Lloyd-Williams, M.A. (Oxon); *m.* 1923, Lilian Roche Brett; one *d.* (and one *d.* decd.). *Educ.:* Temple Grove; Westminster. Indian Police, 1907-27. Served European War, 1914-18, with Indian Cavalry, North West Frontier of India and Mesopotamia, 1915-19. Chief Constable: Montgomeryshire, 1927-31; Worcestershire, 1931-58, retd. D.L. Worcestershire, 1952. *Recreations:* shooting, gardening. *Address:* Elmley Castle, near Pershore, Worcs. *T.:* Elmley Castle 286. [*Died* 7 *May* 1969.

LLUBERA, Ignacio G.; *see* Gonzalez-Llubera.

LOBBAN, Charles Henry, D.Sc.; M.Inst.C.E.; Emeritus Professor of Civil Engineering in King's College, University of London; Fellow of King's College; *b.* 19 Jan. 1881; *s.* of Alexander Lobban, H.M. Inspector of Schools, and Katherine Edwards; *m.* 1906; one *d. Educ.:* Inverness College; Glasgow University. Demonstrator, Glasgow University, 1904-6; Lecturer, Manchester Univ., 1906-8; Prof. of Civil Engineering, Madras, 1908-10; in practice as Civil Engineer, Kilmarnock, 1910-14; war work, construction of camps, 1914-16; in Roy. Engineers in France (has rank of Major, R.E.), 1916-19; Assistant Controller, Disposals Board, 1919-20; Senior Lecturer in 1920, then Reader and later Prof. of Civil Engineering, and Head of the Dept. of Civil and Mechanical Engineering, Univ. of London, King's College; also consulting engineer for several large buildings; retired. *Publications:* Technical papers. *Recreations:* golf, yachting and fishing. *Address:* Morar, Boat-of-Garten, Inverness-shire. *T.:* Boat of Garten 269. [*Died* 13 *July* 1963.

LOCH, Lt.-Gen. Sir Kenneth Morley, K.C.I.E., *cr.* 1946; C.B. 1942; M.C.; *b.* 19 Sept. 1890; *s.* of late Lt.-Col. William Loch, C.I.E., and late Edith Mary, *d.* of James Gibbs, C.S.I., C.I.E.; *m.* 1929, Monica Joan Estelle Ruffer; two *s. Educ.:* Wellington College, R.M.A., Woolwich. Entered R.A. 1910; served European War, 1914-19 (despatches twice, M.C.); present at retreat from Mons, and battles of Marne and Aisne; p.s.c. Camberley; G.S.O. 2, T.A. Air Defence Formations, 1926-29; Instructor, Staff College, Quetta, 1932-35; G.S.O. 2, War Office, 1935-37; G.S.O. 1, Fighter Command R.A.F., 1937-38; Director A.A. and C.D., 1939-41; Special Employment, 1941; Master-Gen. of Ordnance, India, 1944-47; retired pay, 1947; British Council, 1947-48; Control Commission Germany, 1948-49; British Council, 1950-58. A Governor of Wellington College. *Recreation:* shooting. *Address:* 27 Chiltern Court, N.W.1. *T.:* Welbeck 5544. *Club:* Army and Navy. [*Died* 9 *Jan.* 1961.

LOCKE, George T., M.A.; *b.* Belfast, 13 Feb. 1872; widower; two *s. Educ.:* Roy. Academical Institution, Belfast; Queen's College, Belfast; St. John's College, Cambridge (Scholar). M.A. (Cantab.); B.A. (R.U.I.). Scholar of Q.C. Belfast and of R.U.I., 1891-94, obtaining 1st class honours in Mathematics and Physics at all exams.; Wrangler, 1897; studied German in Hanover for two years; Professor of Mensuration, Physics, and Applied Mechanics, Royal Agricultural College, Cirencester, 1899-1905;

Senior Mathematical Master, Wallasey Grammar School, 1906-17; Headmaster, Stand Grammar School, Whitefield, 1917-37; retired, 1937. *Recreations:* rowed while at St. John's, and afterwards in Germany; also taken interest in Rugby football, lawn tennis and golf. *Address:* 2 Chesham Place, Bowdon, Cheshire. [*Died* 17 *Dec.* 1968.

LOCKETT, Air Commodore Charles Edward Stuart, C.B. 1959; R.A.F. retd.; Shipowner, 1959, Lloyd's Agent in Jersey, 1961; *b.* 15 Apr. 1910; *s.* of late Robert Ker Lockett, The Priory, Hooton, Cheshire, and late Hilda Lockett (*née* Fielden); *m* 1933, Evelyn (*née* Mason); no *c.* *Educ.:* The Leas, Hoylake; Aston Clinton School, nr. Aylesbury, Bucks. Joined R.A.F., 1931; served in Army Co-operation Squadrons in India, Bomber Squadrons in U.K. and then in France, 1939; P.O.W., 1940-45; Station Comdr., Transport Comd. (Gp. Capt.); Staff Appointment, H.Q. Transport Command, 1948-49; Air Attaché, British Embassy, Warsaw, 1949-53; passed Operational Flying Course, R.A.F. Flying College, Manby; in Comd. Central Gunnery School, Leconfield, 1954-55; Air Attaché, British Embassy, Paris, 1955-59; retired, 1959. Apptd. German Consul at St. Helier, Jersey (having jurisdiction also throughout the Bailwick of Guernsey), 1966. Officier de la Légion d'Honneur (French), 1957. *Recreations:* fox-hunting and golf. *Address:* La Marotte, St. Helier, Jersey, Channel Islands. *Clubs:* Royal Air Force, United Hunts. [*Died* 20 *Aug.* 1966.

LOCKHART, Sir John B. S.; *see* Sinclair-Lockhart.

LOCKHART, Major-General Leslie Keith, C.B. 1949; C.B.E. 1946 (M.B.E. 1922); M.C. 1916, Bar to M.C. 1917; *b.* 5 June 1897; *m.* 1928; two *d.* *Educ.:* Brighton College; Royal Military Academy, Woolwich. Commissioned R.A. 1915; served European War, 1914-19, in France and Belgium. Appointed R.H.A. 1919; seconded for service with Royal Irish Constabulary, 1920-21; Palestine Gendarmerie, 1922-24; Transjordan Frontier Force, 1926-28. Staff Coll., Camberley, 1933-1934, p.s.c. Served in general staff, Southern Comd. (U.K.) 1935-36, and at War Office, 1937-40; Mil. Mission to U.S.A., 1941-42; War Office, Dep. Dir. R.A., 1942-43. A.A. Bde. Comd., and Second in Comd., G.H.Q. A.A. Tps., 21 Army Group, N.W. European Campaign, 1944-45, France and Belgium; G.O.C. 5th A.A. Group, 1947-50; G.O.C., East Anglian District, 1951-52; retired 1952. Lieutenant-Colonel, 1940, Colonel, 1944, Brigadier, 1947, Major-General, 1948. Dominion Chief Commissioner, Boy Scouts of New Zealand, 1953-60 (Silver Wolf, 1959). Comdr. Legion of Merit (U.S.A.); Comdr. Order of Leopold II with Palm and Croix de Guerre with Palm (Belgium). *Address:* Lower Mangorei Road, New Plymouth, N.Z. *Club:* United Service. [*Died* 27 *March* 1966.

LOCKHART, Sidney Alexander; Sheriff Substitute of Dumfries and Galloway at Kirkcudbright, Wigtown and Stranraer since 1955; *b.* 2 Nov. 1914; *yr. s.* of late William Masson Lockhart, solicitor, Ayr, and late Elizabeth Alexander; *m.* 1st, 1946, Helen Sheila Fotheringham, M.A. (*d.* 1961), *d.* of late William Fotheringham, Glasgow; no *c.*; 2nd, 1964, Jean Frazer, *widow* of William Montgomery. *Educ.:* Fettes Coll. M.A. Hons. (St. Andrews), 1938; LL.B. (Glasgow), 1947. Served in War, Glasgow Yeomanry (R.A.), with 1st and 8th Armies, 1939-46; Adjutant, 1943-46. Member, Faculty of Advocates, 1947; Mem. Supreme Court Legal Aid Cttee., 1950-55, Chm., 1953-55. Hon. Sheriff Substitute of Lanarkshire at Glasgow, 1952. *Recreations:* fishing, curling; railways, motor cars. *Address:* Janefield House, Kirkcudbright. *T.:* Kirkcudbright 421. *Clubs:* United Services and Northern (Edinburgh); Royal Scottish Automobile (Glasgow). [*Died* 3 *Aug.* 1969.

LOCKITT, Charles Henry, M.A., B.Sc. (Lond.); *b.* 30 May 1877; *s.* of late C. Clayton Lockitt and late M. A. Lockitt; *m.* 1st, 1905, Amy (*d.* 1921). 2nd, 1924, Helen (*d.* 1963), *daughters* of late Mrs. Stanton, Harley Road, N.W.; one *s.* (and one *s.* decd. 1931). *Educ.:* Whitgift School; University College, London. F. R. Hist. S.; Teaching posts at Rivington, Horsham, and Solihull Grammar Schools, 1897-1911; Headmaster of Bungay Grammar School, 1911-37; Member of Council of the Incorporated Association of Headmasters, 1927-30; Vice-President, Sussex County Playing Fields Assoc.; Vice-President, Sussex Rural Community Council; Member, East Sussex County Education Committee 1940-46; Governor, Brighton Coll. of Arts and Crafts, 1942-62; Army Welfare Officer (Lewes, Seaford Area), 1940-45. *Publications:* The Relations of French and English Society, 1763-93, 1920; Editor: Hamlet, 1925; The Adventure of Travel, 1936; The Imaginary Eye-Witness, 1937; Biography of To-day, Plays for Youth, 1938; Daviot's Richard of Bordeaux, 1938; Sheridan's The School for Scandal, and the Critic; Travel Pictures, 1939; More One-Act Plays, 1947; Editor: Luce's The Kingmaker, Berkeley's The Lady with a Lamp (school edns.), 1948, The Art of the Essayist, Short Stories of the Past, 1949. *Address:* c/o C. R. Lockitt, 91 Poulters Lane, Worthing. [*Died* 14 *Sept.* 1964.

LOCKWOOD, Sir John (Francis), Kt. 1962; Master of Birkbeck College, University of London, since 1951; *b.* 6 July 1903; *s.* of John and Elizabeth Lockwood; *m.* 1929, Marjorie, *d.* of W. Basil and Katherine Clitheroe; one *s.* one *d.* *Educ.:* The Grammar School, Preston; Corpus Christi College, Oxford. Assistant Lecturer in Latin, Victoria University, Manchester, 1927; Assistant Lecturer in Classics, University College, London, 1927-30; Lecturer in Greek, University College, London, 1930-40; Reader in Classics and Tutor to Arts Students, University College London, 1940-45, Professor of Latin, 1945-51; Dean of Faculty of Arts, Univ. of London, 1950-51; Public Orator, Univ. of London, 1952-55; Chairman of Collegiate Council, 1953-55; Deputy Vice-Chancellor, Univ. of London, 1954-55; Vice-Chancellor, 1955-58; Mem. of Court of Univ. of London, 1955-. Chairman: Secondary School Exams. Council, 1958-64; Working Party on Higher Education in East Africa, 1958; Grants Cttee. on Higher Education in Ghana, 1959; West African Examinations Council, 1960-64; Voluntary Societies' Cttee. for Service Overseas; Cttee. on Development of a Univ. in N. Rhodesia, 1963; Cttee. on Univ. and Higher Technical Educn. in N. Ireland, 1963-64. Member: U.S. Educn. Commn. in U.K., 1956-61; Commn. on Post-Secondary and Higher Education in Nigeria, 1959-60; Council of Royal College of Art, 1960; Council of Overseas Development Institute, 1960-; Univ. of Wales Commission, 1960-63; Council of Royal College, Nairobi, 1961-; U.N.E.S.C.O.-International Assoc. of Universities Study of Higher Education in Development of Countries of S.E. Asia, 1961-65; Provisional Council, University of Zambia, 1964-. Hon. LL.D., Leicester and Western Ontario. *Address:* 2 Gower St., W.C.1. *T.:* Museum 6930; 145 Green Dragon Lane, Winchmore Hill, N.21. *T.:* Laburnum 4066. *Club:* Athenæum. [*Died* 11 *July* 1965.

LOCKYER, Air Vice-Marshal Clarence Edward Williams, C.B. 1945; D.L.; M.A.; former Bursar and Fellow of Peterhouse, Cambridge (1945-57); *b.* 22 Aug. 1892; *s.* of James Edward Lockyer,

A.M.I.C.E.; *m.* Dorothy Rebecca Measures; one *s.* *Educ.:* University College, London; Peterhouse, Cambridge (Mechanical Sciences Tripos, John Bernard Seely Prize). Served European War with R.F.A. and R.F.C., 1914-1918; transferred to R.A.F.; Group Capt., 1939; Air Commodore, 1941; acting Air Vice-Marshal, 1944; Chief Instructor Cambridge University Air Squadron, 1936-39; Deputy Director, Directorate of Flying Training, Air Ministry, 1939; Deputy Director of Research and Development, Ministry of Aircraft Production, 1941-43. *Address:* 54 Storey's Way, Cambridge. *T.:* 56830.
[*Died* 7 *Aug.* 1963.

LOCOCK, Sir Charles (Bird), 3rd Bt., *cr.* 1857; *b.* 22 Nov. 1878; *e. s.* of 2nd Bt. and Fanny Bird, *d.* of Prebendary Pitman of Chichester; *S.* father, 1890; *m.* 1901, Christine, *y. d.* of Frederick Bennett, Ipswich; two *d.* (one *s.* decd.). *Educ.:* Harrow; Trinity College, Cambridge. *Heir:* none. *Address:* Blythswood, West Byfleet, Surrey. *T.:* Byfleet 45119.
[*Died* 18 *Sept.* 1965 (*ext.*).

LODER, Lieut.-Col. Giles Harold, M.C.; late Scots Guards; *b.* 2 Jan. 1884; *e. s.* of Wilfrid Hans Loder, 2nd *s.* of Sir Robert Loder, Bart.; unmarried *Educ.:* Eton College; Royal Military College, Sandhurst. Joined the Scots Guards, 1903; retired pay, 1931; served with 2nd Battalion during European War, 1914-18, going out with the 7th Division, Oct. 1914 (despatches, M.C.); wounded at Neuve Chapelle, March 1915; won the Derby with Spionkop, 1920; Sheriff of Sussex, 1942. *Recreations:* hunting, shooting, golf, tennis, etc. *Address:* Dencombe, Handcross, Sussex; Eyrefield Lodge, The Curragh Camp, Co. Kildare. *Clubs:* Guards, Turf, Boodle's, Bath: Kildare Street (Dublin). [*Died* 1 *Feb.* 1966.

LODGE, Rupert Clendon, M.A.; F.R.S.C.; Emeritus Professor of Philosophy, University of Manitoba; *b.* 8 Dec. 1886; *e. s.* of Charles S. Lodge and Amelia Smith Lodge, Manchester; *m.* Edith Warren Melcher, Lynn, Mass., U.S.A.; one *d.* *Educ.:* Manchester Grammar School; Brasenose Coll., Oxford; Universities of Manchester, Marburg, and Berlin. Junior Lecturer in Philosophy, Manchester University, 1910-11; Interim Professor of Philosophy, Dalhousie University, N.S., 1913; Instructor in Philosophy, Univ. of Minnesota, 1914-15; Lecturer in Philosophy, Univ. of Alberta, 1915-16; Asst. Prof. of Philosophy, Univ. of Minnesota, 1916-20; Prof. of Philosophy, Univ. of Manitoba, 1920-47; Queen's University, Kingston, Canada, 1948-49; Long Island University, 1949-54; Visiting Lecturer on Philosophy, Harvard Univ., 1928, 2nd semester; Visiting Prof. of Philosophy, New York Univ., Summer, 1938; Univ. of North Carolina, 1948, 2nd Term; Univ. of Alberta, Summer, 1948; Pres., American Philosophical Association, Western Division, 1926-27. *Publications:* Translation of Varisco's The Great Problems, 1914; The Meaning and Function of Simple Modes in the Philosophy of John Locke, 1918; Introduction to Modern Logic, 1920; Plato's Theory of Ethics; The Moral Criterion and the Highest Good, 1928; The Questioning Mind, 1937, 2nd ed. 1947; Philosophy of Education, 1937, 2nd ed., 1947; Manitoba Essays (Editor and contributor), 1937; Philosophy of Business, 1945; Plato's Theory of Education, 1947; The Great Thinkers, 1949; Applied Philosophy, 1951; Plato's Theory of Art, 1953; The Philosophy of Plato, 1956; contributions to the philosophical journals, and Canadian Reviews. *Recreation:* piano. *Address:* Bishop Hotel, 256, 1st Ave. N., St. Petersburg, Florida, U.S.A.
[*Died* 1 *March* 1961.

LODGE, Thomas Arthur, O.B.E. 1919; Litt.D. (Hon.); F.R.I.B.A. (Retd.); F.R.I.C.S. (Hon.); retired as Partner Lanchester & Lodge, architects, 1957; *b.* 2 April 1888; *s.* of Tom Arthur Lodge, Crookham, Hants.; *m.* 1925, Lydia June (*née* Martin). *Educ.:* Epsom College; Architectural Assoc., London. Served European War, 1914-19 (despatches, 1914-15 Star, O.B.E.); trained in Inns of Court; Capt. 24th London Regt., T.F.; Adjutant 2nd Field Survey Bn., R.E. *Buildings:* Town Halls: Beckenham, Hackney; The University of Leeds, St. Bartholomew's Hosp. and Medical School; Queen Elizabeth Hosp. and Med. Sch., Birmingham, and other hospitals; Science buildings at Universities of Oxford, Cambridge, Sheffield, Belfast; Palace for Rajah of Jodhpur; Council House and Post Office, Lucknow; technical schools at Reading, Bolton, Watford; Rayon Research Buildings, Manchester; buildings at Esso Oil Refinery, Fawley; Housing, L.C.C., Wandsworth; other private houses. Hon. Litt.D. Leeds, 1951. *Recreations:* fishing, riding, motoring. *Address:* 21 Priory Court, Granville Road, Eastbourne, Sussex. *T.:* Eastbourne 28628.
[*Died* 8 *Feb.* 1967.

LOEWI, Otto, M.D.; Sc.D. (Hon.) New York, 1944, Yale, 1951; Ph.D. (Hon.) Graz, 1950; M.D. (Hon.) Frankfurt, Graz, 1953; Research Professor of Pharmacology, New York University, College of Medicine, since 1940; *b.* Frankfurt a.M., 3 June 1873; *s.* of Jacob Loewi and Anna Willstatter; *m.* 1908, Guida Goldschmiedt (*d.* 1958); four *c.* *Educ.:* Frankfurt a.M.; Strassburg (M.D. 1896); Munich. Asst. Prof. of Pharmacology, Marburg, 1900; Assoc. Professor, Vienna, 1905; Prof., Graz, Austria, 1909-38; Franqui Professor, Brussels, 1938-1939; Walker-Ames visiting Professor, Seattle, 1942; Dunham Lecturer, Harvard, 1933; Harvey Lecturer, New York, 1933; Ferrier Lecturer to the Royal Society, London, 1935; Dohme Lecturer, Johns Hopkins, 1941; National Sigma Xi Lecturer, 1944; Hughlings Jackson lecturer, Montreal, 1946; visiting scholar Richmond area Univ. Center, 1948, etc.; shared Nobel Prize, 1936; Cameron Prize, Edinburgh, 1944; Foreign Member: Roy. Soc. (London); Roy. Soc. (Edin.); Accad. dei Lincei (Rome); Bavar. and Austrian Acad. of Sciences; Hon. Member: New York and Belgian Academies of Medicine; Amer. Soc. Pharmacol.; British and German Socs. Pharmacol. and Physiol., etc. *Publications:* numerous articles in medical journals. *Address:* 155 East 93rd Street, New York, U.S.A. *T.:* Atwater 9-6727. [*Died* 25 *Dec.* 1961.

LOFTHOUSE, Rt. Rev. Joseph, D.D.; *b.* 17 March 1880; *s.* of Thomas Lofthouse and Elizabeth Lint; *m.* 1914, Louisa Kelleway; one *s.* two *d.* *Educ.:* Wadsley Church School; Wycliffe College, University of Toronto. Deacon, 1907; priest, 1908; Incumbent of St. James, Rainy River, 1908-15; Canon of St. Alban's Pro-Cathedral, Diocese of Keewatin, 1914; General Missionary and Secretary-Treasurer of the Diocese, 1915-28; Domestic and Examining Chaplain to Bishop of Keewatin, 1921-38; Archdeacon of Kenora, 1928; Rector of St. Alban's Pro-Cathedral, 1929-38; Bishop of Keewatin, Rupertsland, 1938-53, retired. Hon. Brigade Chaplain (Major) 40th (R) Medium Regt. R.C.A., 1935-48, retd. (C.D.). *Recreations:* boating, gardening. *Address:* 120 St. Clair Ave., Hamilton, Ontario, Canada. *Club:* United Services Institute (Kenora, Ontario).
[*Died* 13 *July* 1962.

LOFTHOUSE, Rev. William Frederick, M.A. (Oxon); Hon. D.D. (Aberdeen); *b.* South Norwood, Surrey, 6 Sept. 1871; *s.* of William Beet and Alice Lofthouse; *m.* 1901, Kate Lyth (*d.* 1921), *d.* of Rev. H. J. Foster; no *c.* *Educ.:* City of London School; Trinity College, Oxford (open scholar); Gaisford University Prize (Greek verse), 1891; 1st class Classical Moderations, 1892; 1st class Lit. Hum., 1894; Hall Houghton Greek Testament Prize, 1896; Denyer and Johnson Scholarship, 1897; Asst. Tutor, Wesleyan Coll., Richmond, 1896; Asst. Tutor, Handsworth College, 1899; Minister in Bradford, Yorks, 1901-4; Tutor, Old Testament Languages and Literature and in Philosophy, Handsworth College, 1904; Principal and Tutor in Systematic Theology and Philosophy, 1925-1940; Secretary of Wesleyan Methodist Union for Social Service, 1905-15, President, 1915-16; Temp. C.F., 1916-19 (on Salonica front, 1917); President, Birmingham Free Church Council, 1924; Examiner in Theology, London University, 1924-26; Pres. Wesleyan Methodist Conference, 1929-30; President of Society for O.T. Study, 1931-1932; Co-President of Temperance Council of the Christian Churches, 1932; Delegate to Oxford and Edinburgh World Conferences, 1937; President Oxford Society of Historical Theology, 1945. *Publications:* Ethics and Atonement, 1906; Ezekiel (Century Bible), 1907; The Bible: its Origin and Authority, 1909; Ethics and the Family, 1912; The Making of the Old Testament, 1915; The Prophet of Reconstruction, 1920; Purity and Racial Health (with Mrs. Lofthouse), 1920; Altar, Cross and Community, 1921; Jeremiah, 1925; Christianity in Action, 1928; Israel after the Exile (Clarendon Bible), 1928; A Hebrew View of Evil (in Affirmations series), 1928; The Father and the Son, 1934; The Disciple whom Jesus Loved, 1936; Christianity in the Social State, 1936; The Family and the State, 1944; F. H. Bradley, 1949. Ed. two vols. essays: The Christian Use of Money, Christ and the Soldier, 1920; contributions to various magazines, volumes of essays, encyclopædias, and to Dummelow's, Peake's, and the Abingdon one-volume Bible Commentaries. *Address:* Hall Grange, Shirley Church Rd., Croydon, Surrey. [*Died* 5 *July* 1965.

LOGAN, David Gilbert, C.B.E. 1949; J.P.; M.P. (Lab.) Scotland Division of Liverpool since 1929; *b.* Liverpool, 22 Nov. 1871; *s.* of Thomas Logan; *m.* 1896, Susan Georgina, *d.* of G. H. S. Gains, Paignton; three *s.* three *d.* *Educ.:* St. Anthony's and St. Sylvester's Schools; privately. J.P., 1924, and City Alderman, 1929-35, Liverpool. Knight of the Order of St. Gregory the Great. A Founder Mem. of Knights of St. Columba in England. *Address:* 362 Scotland Road, Liverpool. [*Died* 25 *Feb.* 1964.

LOGAN, Sir William Marston, K.B.E., *cr* 1944 (O.B.E. 1933); C.M.G. 1939; *b.* 10 March 1889; *s.* of Rev. James Moffat Logan; *m.* 1920, Janet Colville McIntyre; one *s.* one *d.* *Educ.:* Bristol; Brasenose College, Oxford. Entered Colonial Administrative Service as a District Officer, Kenya, 1913; Lieutenant R.A. unattached list, 1915-17; held various Secretariat appointments, 1920-31, when appointed Commissioner for Local Government, Lands and Settlement; acted as Colonial Secretary in 1937; Chief Secretary, Northern Rhodesia, 1937-42; Acting Governor Northern Rhodesia, March-Sept. 1938 and April-Oct. 1941; Governor and C.-in-C., Seychelles Colony, 1942-47. *Recreation:* reading. *Address:* Ann Street, Gatehouse-of-Fleet, Kirkcudbrightshire. [*Died* 30 *Sept.* 1968.

LOMAS, Herbert; actor, stage and films; *b.* Burnley, Lancs, 1887. *Educ.:* Academy of Dramatic Art. First Stage appearance in The Winter's Tale, His Majesty's 1906. Repertory, Gaiety, Manchester, 1909; the original Nathaniel Jeffcote in Hindle Wakes; Season, Theatre Royal, Leeds, 1913 (Rev. James Morrell, in Candida, etc.); toured in the name-part in Abraham Lincoln, 1919-20; visited U.S., 1920- (Hornblower, in The Skin Game, etc.); repertory, Playhouse, Liverpool, 1924-27; Thomas Greenleaf, in Bird in Hand, Royalty, 1928; same part in New York, 1929; Werle in The Wild Duck, Everyman, 1930; subsequently played varied parts in the West End, repeating some early ones; Malvern Festival, 1939; played the Rev. Martin Gregory in long run of The Holly and the Ivy, Duchess, 1950. Has appeared in numerous films and on Television. *Address:* 85 Elm Avenue, Eastcote, Ruislip, Middlesex. [*Died* 11 *April* 1961.

LOMAX, Brig. Thomas B. T.; *see* Trappes-Lomax.

LONDESBOROUGH, 6th Baron, *cr.* 1850; **Ernest William Denison,** M.B.E. 1946; Capt. R.N., retd.; *b.* 9 Aug. 1876; *s.* of Rear-Admiral Hon. Albert Denison Sommerville Denison, 2nd *s.* of 1st Baron; *S.* to Barony of *cousin*, 4th Earl of Londesborough, 1937; *m.* 1905, Sybil May (*d.* 1963), *d.* of late Capt. H. T. Anley, The Firs, Binstead. *Heir: cousin*, Commander Conyngham Charles Denison, D.S.O., R.N. retd. *Address:* The Old Vicarage, Shalfleet, Newport, Isle of Wight. [*Died* 31 *Dec.* 1963.

LONDESBOROUGH, 7th Baron, *cr.* 1850; **Conyngham Charles Denison,** D.S.O. 1919; Comdr. R.N. retd.; *b.* 6 April 1885; *s.* of late Comdr. Hon. Conyngham A. Denison, R.N., and late Evelyn Maud Webster; *S. cousin*, 1964; *m.* 1912, Vera Baxendale; *m.* 1926, Mabel Megaw (*d.* 1951); *m.* 1952, Jocelyn Collins. *Educ.:* H.M.S. Britannia. Retired from Navy, 1908; Commander, 1918; served European War, 1914-19 (despatches, D.S.O.), and War of 1939-45. *Recreation:* yachting. *Heir: cousin*, John Albert Lister Denison, T.D., A.M.I.C.E. [*b.* 30 May 1901; *m.* 1st, 1949, Lesley Maxwell Gordon, M.B.E. (marriage dissolved, 1953), *widow* of Lt.-Col. J. H. Wooldridge, I.A., and *d.* of late Lt.-Col. H. F. Churchill, O.B.E.; 2nd, 1957, Mrs. Elizabeth Ann Roe, *d.* of late E. L. Sale, I.C.S.; one *s.*]. *Address:* Anchor Cottage, Bembridge, I. of Wight. *T.:* Bembridge 216. *Club:* Sailing (Bembridge). [*Died* 31 *Oct.* 1967.

LONDESBOROUGH, 8th Baron *cr.* 1850; **John Albert Lister Denison,** T.D. 1950; Joint Managing Director, W. Gerwin Ltd., since 1948; *b.* 30 May 1901; *s.* of Hon. Harold Albert Denison (*d.* 1948) (5th *s.* of 1st Baron) and Katherine (*d.* 1961) (*née* Lister); *S. cousin*, 1967; *m.* 1st, 1949, Lesley Maxwell Gordon, M.B.E. (marr. diss. 1953), *widow* of Lt.-Col. J. H. Wooldridge, I.A., and *d.* of late Lt.-Col. H. F. Churchill, O.B.E.; 2nd, 1957, Elizabeth Ann Roe, *d.* of late E. L. Sale; one *s.* *Educ.:* Wellington College; Trinity College, Cambridge. Employed as Engineer by Agricultural & General Engineers Ltd., 1927-30; Ransomes & Rapier, 1930-32; Austin Motor Co. Ltd., 1933-37; Henry Milward & Sons, 1937-39. Capt., Royal Artillery and then R.E.M.E., 1939-45, B.L.A. W. Gerwin Ltd., 1945-. A.M.I.C.E. 1927. *Recreations:* fishing, sailing, gardening. *Heir: s.* Hon. Richard John Denison, *b.* 2 July 1959. *Address:* Dragon House, Edgioak, Redditch, Worcs. *T.:* Astwood Bank 2459. *Clubs:* Royal Thames Yacht; Leander (Henley-on-Thames). [*Died* 5 *April* 1968.

LONDON, Heinz, Dr.phil.; F.R.S. 1961; Deputy Chief Scientist, Atomic Energy Research Establishment, Harwell, since 1958; *b.* 7 Nov. 1907; *s.* of late Prof. Franz London, Bonn University; *m.* 1946, Lucie, *née* Meissner; two *s.* two *d.* *Educ.:* Universities of Bonn, Berlin Munich, Breslau (Dr.phil.). Postgraduate Research at Clarendon Laboratory, Oxford, 1934-36; Research Grant at H. H. Wills Physical Lab., Bristol, 1936-41; worked on Atomic Energy Project at I.C.I. Alkali, Northwich, on Directorate of Tube Alloys, London, and at Birmingham University, 1942-46; Principal Scientific Officer, A.E.R.E. Harwell, 1946; Senior Principal Scientific Officer, 1949. Simon Memorial Prize, 1959. *Publications:* (ed.) Separation of Isotopes, 1961; papers on superconductivity, liquid helium, separation of isotopes. *Address:* 44 Cumnor Hill, Oxford. *T.:* Cumnor 2606. [*Died* 3 *Aug.* 1970.

LONG, 3rd Viscount (*cr.* 1921) of Wraxall, **Richard Eric Onslow Long,** T.D.; D.L.; J.P.; Major late Royal Wilts Yeomanry; *b.* 22 Aug. 1892; *s.* of 1st Viscount Long of Wraxall, and Lady Doreen Long; *S.* nephew, 1944; *m.* 1916, Gwendolyn (*d.* 1959), *d.* of Thomas Reginald Hague Cook; two *s.* one *d.* *Educ.:* Harrow. City, 1911-14; served with Regiment and 11th Indian Division and 13th Division and 3rd Army, European War, France, Suez Canal, Dardanelles (despatches); served War of 1939-45, R.A., 1939-43; M.P. (C.), Westbury Division of Wiltshire, 1927-31; President West Wilts Constitutional Association, 1925-33, re-elected Pres. 1948; D.L. Wilts, 1946. Past Mem. Nat. Exec. Council, British Legion, 1955; President British Legion for County of Wiltshire; Hon. Colonel 04 S/L Regt. R.A. (R.F.) T.A.; Knight Commander Order of King George I of Greece; Freeman City of Athens. *Recreations:* hunting, shooting, and cricket. *Heir:* *s.* Hon. Richard Gerard Long [*b.* 1929; *m.* 1957, Margaret Frances, *d.* of Ninian B. Frazer; one *s.* two *d.*]. *Address:* Steeple Ashton Manor, Trowbridge, Wilts. *Club:* Carlton. [*Died* 12 *Jan.* 1967.

LONG, Gavin Merrick, O.B.E. 1953; journalist and historian; *b.* Foster, Victoria, 31 May 1901; *s.* of George Merrick, Bishop of Newcastle, N.S.W.; *m.* 1926, Mary Jocelyn Britten; one *s.* one *d.* *Educ.:* All Saints College, Bathurst; St. Paul's College, Univ. of Sydney (B.A.). Assistant Master, The King's School, Parramatta, 1922-24; on staff The Argus, Melbourne, 1926-31; Sydney Morning Herald, 1931-43; Defence Correspondent, 1937-38; War Correspondent with B.E.F., France, 1939-40; with A.I.F. England, Libya, Greece, Australia, New Guinea, 1940-42; General Editor, Australian Official War History, 1943-63; Research Fellow, Australian National Univ., 1963-65. *Publications:* To Benghazi, 1952; Greece, Crete and Syria, 1953, The Final Campaigns, 1963 (volumes of Australian Official War History); MacArthur as Military Commander, 1969 (posthumous). *Address:* 10 Rawson St., Deakin, A.C.T. [*Died* 10 *Oct.* 1968.

LONG, Kathleen Ida, C.B.E. 1957; Pianist; *b.* 7 July 1896. *Educ.:* privately. Gained open scholarship to Royal College of Music at age of 14; first London Recital, at Aeolian Hall, at age of 19. Has played in many countries, including tours of Africa and America and has broadcast very frequently both from Gt. Britain and from many Continental stations. Hon. Fellow of Royal College of Music, 1953; Officier d'Académie (France) 1950. *Recreations:* needlework, reading, travelling. *Address:* 76 Whiting St., Bury St. Edmunds, Suffolk. [*Died* 20 *March* 1968.

LONG, William Henry, C.B. 1961; Permanent Secretary, Ministry of Agriculture, Northern Ireland, 1957-63, retd.; *b.* 10 May 1900; *s.* of Richardson Alexander Long and Elizabeth Crawford Long, Kilrea, Co. Londonderry; *m.* 1926, Winifred Simpson Cummings. *Educ.:* Rainey Endowed School, Magherafelt, Co. Londonderry. Entered Imperial Civil Service, in Dublin, 1916; served in the Congested Districts Bd. for Ireland; later apptd. to Irish Land Commission. During later stages of European War of 1914-18, joined Artists Rifles, and was later commissioned in Royal Irish (now Ulster) Rifles; transferred to Northern Ireland Civil Service, 1922, on estabt. of Northern Ireland Govt., and was posted to Min. of Finance in that year; transf. to Min. of Agric., Aug. 1934. Appointed: Principal Officer, 1940; Asst. Sec., 1946. Vice-President and Member of Council, Royal Ulster Agricultural Society. *Recreation:* fishing. *Address:* 9 Piney Hills, Malone Road, Belfast BT9 5NR, Northern Ireland. *T.:* Belfast 666172. [*Died* 5 *Jan.* 1969.

LONGBOURNE, Brig.-Gen. F. C. M. M.; *see* More-Molyneux-Longbourne.

LONGFORD, 6th Earl of (*cr.* 1785), **Edward Arthur Henry Pakenham;** Baron Longford, 1759; Baron Silchester (U.K.), 1821; Member of Senate, Eire, 1946-48; *b.* 29 Dec. 1902; *s.* of 5th Earl and Lady Mary Child-Villiers (*d.* 1933), 2nd *d.* of 7th Earl of Jersey; *S.* father, 1915; *m.* 1925, Christine, M.A. (Oxon), (author of many plays and novels), *d.* of late Richard Trew of Cheddar, Somerset. *Educ.:* Eton (Wilder Divinity Prize); Oxford, M.A.; Litt.D. (*h.c.*), Dublin, 1954. Author of plays produced in Dublin and London. Director Dublin Gate Theatre; Director Bovril (Eire) Ltd. D.Litt. (*h.c.*) Nat. Univ. of Ireland, 1958. *Heir:* *b.* Baron Pakenham. *Address:* Pakenham Hall, Castlepollard, Co. Westmeath; 123 Leinster Road, Dublin. *T.:* Dublin 92118. [*Died* 4 *Feb.* 1961.

LONGFORD, Rev. William Wingfield, D.D., F.S.A., F.R.S.L.; Rector of Sefton, Lancs, 1932-61; *b.* 1882; *e. s.* of William W. Longford, Northfield, Birmingham, and Clara Wade Powell; *m.* 1st, 1912, Lizzie Mansfield Templeton (*d.* 1916); one *d.*; 2nd, 1918, Georgina McIntosh (*d.* 1958); one *s.* two *d.*; 3rd, 1961, Bessie Hale. *Educ.:* King Edward's School, Birmingham; Christ Church, Oxford (Schol.). 1st Cl. Mod. Hist. 1904, 1st Cl. Theology 1906; Liddon Student, 1905; B.A. 1904; M.A. 1908; B.D. 1911; D.D. 1915. Deacon, 1906; Priest, 1907; Chaplain Queen's College, Birmingham, and Curate of St. Agatha, 1906; Lecturer in History, St. David's College, Lampeter, 1908-9; Vice-Principal Lichfield Theological College, 1909-12; Senior Curate of Huddersfield, 1912-13; Rector of Cononley-in-Craven, 1913-14; Vicar of Almondbury, Huddersfield, 1914-23; Assistant Rural Dean of Huddersfield, 1921-1923; Proctor in Convocation, Dio. Wakefield, 1922-23; Rector of Caversham, Oxon, 1923-32; Proctor in Convocation, Dio. Oxford, 1930-32. T.C.F. 1917; S.C.F. XXI Corps, Palestine; S.C.F. 1918, Force in Egypt (despatches); O.C.F. Western Command, 1939-45. Examiner, London Univ., 1920-24, 1926-29; Governor of Merchant Taylors' School, Gt. Crosby, 1935-63; Pres., Literary and Philosophic Soc. of Liverpool, 1937-39. *Publications:* Music and Religion, 1916; Contrib. Economic Review, Nineteenth Century, Editor Transactions Lancs and Cheshire Hist. Society, 1933-37. *Recreation:* fly-fishing. *Address:* Sephton Close, Wychbold, Droitwich. *Club:* Athenæum (Liverpool) (Pres. 1947). [*Died* 19 *Dec.* 1964.

LONGLEY, Stanislaus Soutten, R.I. 1932; R.B.A. 1924; Artist; *b.* 17 Aug. 1894; *s.* of Alfred John Longley and Blanche Soutten Bennett. *Educ.:* Aylesbury Grammar School. 3rd King's Own Hussars, 1914-18; commenced studying art at the Regent Street Polytechnic; first exhibited at Royal Academy 1924, and exhibited each year since. Camouflage Officer, 1941-44. *Recreations:* riding, tennis, swimming. *Address:* 94 Harewood Avenue, Bournemouth, Hants. [*Died Aug.* 1966.

LONGMAN, William; *b.* 14 November 1882; *s.* of late Charles James Longman; *m.* 1930, Katherine Elizabeth, adopted *d.* of Mrs. Stuart, Southwick, Sussex. *Educ.:* Harrow; University College, Oxford. Chairman, Book Trade Employers Federation, 1923-1924; President Booksellers Provident Institution, 1925-42; President Publishers Association, 1929-30; Chairman of Council of Croquet Association, 1924-26. *Publications:* Tokens of the Eighteenth Century connected with Booksellers, etc., 1917. *Recreations:* croquet, numismatics. *Address:* 42 Chelsea Square, S.W.3. *T.:* Flaxman 8977. *Clubs:* United University, Roehampton, Hurlingham.

[*Died* 1 *March* 1967.

LONGMORE, Air Chief Marshal Sir Arthur Murray, G.C.B., *cr.* 1941 (K.C.B., *cr.* 1935; C.B. 1925); D.S.O. 1919; *b.* 1885; *m.* 1st, 1913, Marjorie (*d.* 1959), *o. c.* of late W. J. Maitland, C.I.E.; two *s.* (and one killed in action, 1943) one *d.*; 2nd, 1960, Enid, *widow* of Lt.-Col. Geoffrey Bolster, and *d.* of late Col. M. R. de B. James. Late Lieut.-Commander Royal Navy; served European War, France, Battle of Jutland and Italy, 1914-19 (despatches, D.S.O.; officer Order of Crown of Belgium, Chevalier Legion of Honour, French Croix de Guerre, Italian Order of St. Maurice and St. Lazarus, Italian Croix de Guerre); Grand Cross of Royal Order of George I of Greece with swords; Greek War Cross. Commandant R.A.F. College, Cranwell, 1929-33; Air Officer Commanding Inland Area, 1933-34; Coastal Area, renamed Coastal Command, R.A.F., 1934-36; Commandant Imperial Defence College, 1936-38; A.O.C.-in-C., Training Command, 1939; Member of British Air Mission to Australia and New Zealand, 1939; Member of U.K. delegation to Pacific Defence Conference, New Zealand, 1939; A.O.C.-in-C. R.A.F., Middle East, 1940-41; Inspector-General of the Royal Air Force, 1941; retired list, 1942; Vice-Chm., Imperial War Graves Commission, 1954-57. *Publication:* From Sea to Sky, 1947. *Address:* Little Trees, Broomfield Park, Sunningdale, Berks. *Clubs:* Royal Over-Seas League; Royal Yacht Squadron (Cowes). [*Died* 10 *Dec.* 1970.

LONGSTAFF, Gilbert Conrad; Lieut.-Comdr. R.N.V.R. (Ret.); M.A., F.R.G.S.; *b.* 2 Aug. 1884; *s.* of late Llewellyn Wood Longstaff and late Mary Lydia Sawyer; *m.* Elizabeth, *d.* of late T. A. Falcon. *Educ.:* Eton; Cambridge. After leaving Cambridge studied Law but preferring to travel took up land development and farming in British Columbia and elsewhere in Canada and the Western States, also making two voyages before the mast in sail, rounding Cape Horn and the Cape of Good Hope; joined R.N.V.R. in 1914 as Lieut. and served throughout European War; formerly Chief Managing Director of Blundell, Spence and Co. Ltd., Hull, and of their overseas subsidiaries and associated companies; Past President of Hull Chamber of Commerce which he represented on Council of Assoc. of British Chambers of Commerce and on Humber Conservancy Board; joined Hampstead A.R.P. Wardens Service, Sept. 1939; enlisted as Able Seaman R.N.A.P. 1940, becoming Leading Seaman and Acting Petty Officer; granted Commission as Sub-Lieut. R.N.V.R., 1942; served in N. Africa, Sicily, Italy and Far East; invalided, Oct. 1947. *Publications:* Poems, by Gilbert Thorne; and in various periodicals. *Recreations:* field ornithology and gardening. *Address:* Chestnut Cottage, Burwash, Sussex.

[*Died* 15 *Dec.* 1964.

LONGSTAFF, Tom George, M.A., D.M. Oxon; F.Z.S.; *b.* 15 Jan. 1875; *e. s.* of late L. W. Longstaff, O.B.E., Wimbledon; *m.* 1st, 1911, Dora Mary Hamilton, 3rd *d.* of Bernard Scott, of Bournemouth; 2nd, 1938, Charmian Dorothy Isabel, *y. d.* of Duncan James Reid, M.B., C.M. *Educ.:* Eton; Christ Church, Oxford; St. Thomas's Hospital. Lt. 1/7th Battalion Hants Regiment, 1914; General Staff, Army Hdqrs., Simla, 1915-16; Assist. Commandant Gilgit Corps of Scouts, Frontier Militia, and Special Assistant at Fort Gupis to the Political Agent in Gilgit, 1916; Capt. 1917; retired with rank, 1918; Lt., 7th and 13th Battn. K.R.R.C., 1939-41, restored to rank on retirement. Has climbed in the Alps, Caucasus, Himalaya, Selkirk, Rocky Mountains, Greenland, and Spitsbergen; travelled in South Western Tibet, 1905; ascended Trisul in Garhwal Himalaya, 1907; awarded the "Gill Memorial" by R.G.S. for journeys in Himalaya and Tibet, 1908; explored the Siachen Glacier, and discovered the peaks of Teram Kangri, 1909; Oxford University Expedition to Spitsbergen, 1921; Mount Everest Expedition, 1922; Spitsbergen, 1923; Garhwal Himalaya, 1927; Leader of Oxford University Expedition to Greenland, 1928; awarded the Founder's Medal by R.G.S. for discovery of the Siachen Glacier and long continued geographical work in the Himalaya, 1928; West Greenland, 1931; Greenland and Baffinland, 1934; President, Alpine Club, 1947-1949; Vice-President, R.G.S., 1934-37, Hon. Sec. 1930-34; President Climbers, 1933-36 and Arctic Clubs, 1933; Cttee. British Ornithologists Union, 1931-33; travels in Transjordan and Lebanon, 1951-52. *Publications:* This my Voyage, 1950; papers in the Geographical, Alpine, Animal Ecology Journals, Ibis. *Recreations:* fishing, ornithology. *Address:* Badentarbat Lodge, Achiltibuie, Ross-shire. *Clubs:* Athenæum (Hon.), Alpine.

[*Died* 26 *June* 1964.

LOOMIS, Professor Roger Sherman; retired; *b.* 31 Oct. 1887; *s.* of Rev. Dr. Henry Loomis and Jane Herring Loomis; *m.* 1st, 1919, Gertrude Schoepperle (*d.* 1921); 2nd, 1925, Laura Hibbard (*d.* 1960); 3rd, 1963, Dorothy Bethurum; no *c.* *Educ.:* Williams College; Univs. of Harvard and Oxford. Instructor, Univ. of Illinois, 1913-1918; Instructor, Asst. Prof., Assoc. Prof., Prof., Columbia Univ., 1920-56. Eastman Visiting Prof., Oxford, 1955-56. Hon. D.Litt., Univ. of Wales, 1952; Docteur *h.c.*, Rennes, 1952; Hon. D.Litt., Columbia Univ., Williams Coll., 1957. *Publications:* Thomas of Britain, Romance of Tristram and Ysolt, 1923, 1951; (with Laura H. Loomis) Arthurian Legends in Medieval Art, 1938; (with Laura H. Loomis) Medieval Romances, 1957; Arthurian Tradition and Chrétien de Troyes, 1949; Wales and the Arthurian Legend, 1956; (ed.) Arthurian Literature in the Middle Ages, 1959; The Grail: from Celtic Myth to Christian Symbol, 1963; A Mirror of Chaucer's World, 1965; contribs. to literary and art jls., etc. *Recreation:* riding. *Address:* 76 Great Neck Rd., Waterford, Conn., U.S.A. *T.:* 443-4490.

[*Died* 11 *Oct.* 1966.

LORAINE, Rt. Hon. Sir Percy (Lyham), of Kirkharle, 12th Bt., *cr.* 1664; P.C. 1933; G.C.M.G., *cr.* 1937 (K.C.M.G., *cr.* 1925; C.M.G. 1921); F.R.G.S.; F.A.G.S.; Chairman Home Office Advisory Committee (Italian) since 1940; a Royal Commissioner for the Exhibition of 1851, 1945; Chm. departmental Cttee. appointed by Minister of Agriculture to report on policy and operation of National Stud, 1954-55; *b.* 5 Nov. 1880; *o. s.* of 11th Bt. and Frederica M. H., *d.* of Chas. Acton Broke, *co-heiress* of the Brokes of Nacton; *S.* father, 1917; *m.* 1924, Louise, *er. d.* of late Maj.-Gen. Hon. Edward Stuart-Wortley, C.B., C.M.G. and late Hon. Mrs. Stuart-Wortley, C.B.E., J.P. *Educ.:* Eton; New Coll., Oxford. Attaché at Constantinople, 1904; 3rd Secretary, Tehran, 1907; 2nd Secretary, Rome, 1909; Pekin, 1911; Paris, 1912-16; 1st Secretary, Madrid, 1916; Secretariat of the Peace Conference, Paris, 1919; 1st Secretary, Warsaw, Oct. 1919; British Minister to Persia, 1921-26; British Minister at Athens, 1926-29; High Commissioner for Egypt and the Sudan, 1929-33; British Ambassador

in Turkey, 1933-39; British Ambassador in Rome, 1939-40; retired from Diplomatic Service, 1941; Assistant to Sir George Clerk on the Special Mission to Budapest as Special Delegate of Supreme Council, Oct.-Dec. 1919; served South African War, 1901-2 (medal with five clasps); Hon. Lieut. in Army. *Heir:* none. *Address:* 19 Wilton Crescent, S.W.1. *T.:* Belgravia 7828; Styford Hall, Stocksfield-on-Tyne. *Clubs:* Turf, Beefsteak, Royal Automobile; Jockey (Newmarket); Irish Turf (Dublin); Jockey (Italy).
[*Died* 23 *May* 1961 (*ext.*).

LORD, Rev. Fred Townley, B.A., D.D., D.Litt.; Editor of The Baptist Times, 1941-56; Minister of Bloomsbury Central Church, 1930-58; Vice-President Baptist World Alliance, 1947- (President, 1950-55); *b.* Burnley, 1893; 2nd *s.* of Jonathan Lord; *m.* 1917, Sarah Alice Entwisle; one *s.* one *d.* *Educ.:* Accrington Grammar School; Rawdon Baptist College; Manchester and London Universities. Minister of Turret Green Baptist Church, Ipswich, 1916-20; Staff-Lecturer in Social History and Citizenship with the Army Service Schools, B.E.F.; Minister of Acton Baptist Church, 1920-26; Queen's Road Baptist Church, Coventry, 1926-30. B.A. Manchester, 1913; B.D. London, 1916. B.D. Hons., 1922; D.D. by thesis on Christian conception of soul and body in relation to modern Psychology, London, 1925; President of the Baptist Union, 1947-48. Visiting Prof. Furman Univ., U.S.A., 1958-59. *Publications:* Man and his Character (Christian Education Manuals); The Master and His Men; The Man in the Dark Room; The Unity of Soul and Body; The Acts of the Apostles; Christ on the Road; Light your Beacons; Christ in the Modern Scene; Great Women of the Bible; Great Women in Christian History; Conquest of Death—a Christian Interpretation of Immortality; Achievement: A History of the Baptist Missionary Society; Baptist World Fellowship: a History of the Baptist World Alliance; The Faith that Sings; The Treasure of the Gospel; You can master Life. *Recreation:* golf. *Address:* 14 Welbeck Mansions, N.W.6. [*Died* 10 *Feb.* 1962.

LORD, Sir Percy, Kt. 1968; Chief Education Officer, Lancashire County Council, since 1957; *b.* 20 Jan. 1903; *s.* of Joseph and Ann Lord, Springhead, Nr. Oldham; *m.* 1928, Doris (*née* Jones); two *d.* *Educ.:* Oldham High Sch.; Manchester University. B.Sc. 1st cl. hons. 1925; M.Ed. 1936. Teacher at Clitheroe Royal Gram. Sch., Oldham High Sch. and High Storrs Gram. Sch., Sheffield, 1926-42; Organiser, Bradford Educn. Cttee., 1942-44; Asst. Educn. Officer: Nottingham, 1944-47; Lancs, 1947-50; Dep. Educn. Officer, Lancs, 1950-57. *Recreations:* reading, bowling, walking; watching cricket (Vice-Pres., Lancs Co. Cricket Club). *Address:* 10 Yewlands Drive, Fulwood, Preston, Lancs. *T.:* Preston 79042.
[*Died* 31 *Dec.* 1968.

LORIMER, Lt.-Col. David Lockhart Robertson, C.I.E. 1917; Indian Army, retd. 1927; *b.* 24 Dec. 1876; *s.* of Rev. Robert Lorimer, of Mains and Strathmartine, near Dundee; *m.* Emily (*d.* 1949), *d.* of late T. G. Overend, K.C.; one *d.* (adopted). Entered Army, 1896; Q.V.O. Corps of Guides, 1898-1903; seconded with Khaibar Rifles, 1901-3; entered Political Dept. Govt. of India, 1903; H.B.M.'s Vice-Consul for Arabistan, 1903-9; Political Agent, Bahrein, 1911-12; H.M. Consul, Kerman and Persian Baluchistan, and ex-officio Assistant to Political Resident, Persian Gulf, 1912-14; Assist. Political Agent, Chitral, 1915; on Field Service with I.E.F.D. Mesopotamia, Civil Governor Amāra, 1915-16; H.B.M. Consul, Kerman, etc., 1916-17; Political Agent, Loralai, Baluchistan, 1920; Political Agent, Gilgit, 1920-24. Awarded Leverhulme Research Fellowship, 1933-35; Member of Norwegian Academy of Science and Letters; Triennial Burton Memorial Medal from Royal Asiatic Society, 1948; Hon. Fellowship School of Oriental and African Studies, University of London, 1953. M.R.A.S.; F.R.G.S. *Publications:* Syntax of Colloquial Pashtu, 1915; Persian Tales, 1919; Phonology of the Bakhtiari, Badakhshani and Madaglashti Dialects of Modern Persian, 1922; The Burushaski Language, Vols. I. and II., 1935, Vol. III., 1938; The Dumāki Language, 1939; The Wakhi Language, 2 Vols., 1958. *Address:* 32 Parkway, Welwyn Garden City, Herts. *T.:* Welwyn Garden 22696.
[*Died* 26 *Feb.* 1962.

LORIMER, Professor William Laughton, M.A. Oxon., LL.D. (St. Andrews); Professor of Greek in the University of St. Andrews from 1953 until Sept. 1955; *b.* 27 June 1885; *s.* of Rev. Robert Lorimer, Mains and Strathmartine, Angus, and Isabella Lockhart, *d.* of David Robertson, H.E.I.C.S.; *m.* 1915, Marion Rose (*d.* 1922), *d.* of late J. H. Gordon, Glasgow; one *s.* *Educ.:* High School of Dundee; Fettes College, Edinburgh; Trinity College, Oxford (scholar). Assistant and Lecturer in Greek, 1910-29, Reader in Latin (Univ. Coll., Dundee), 1929-53, in the University of St. Andrews. Chairman Council, Classical Association of Scotland, 1951-53; Chairman Executive Council and Member Editorial Committee of Scottish National Dictionary. F.B.A. 1953. *Publications:* Aristotelis qui fertur Libellus de Mundo (Paris), 1933; Aristoteles Latinus xii. 2 De Mundo (Rome), 1951, in Corpus Philosophorum Medii Aevi (Union Académique Internationale), etc.; articles and reviews in Classical Review, etc. *Address:* 19 Murray Park, St. Andrews, Fife, Scotland.
[*Died* 26 *May* 1967.

LORNE, Marion; Actress; *b.* Pennsylvania, 12 Aug. 1888; *d.* of Dr. William Lorne MacDougall; *m.* Walter Hackett (*d.* 1944). *Educ.:* Wyoming Seminary, Kingston, Pa.; American Academy of Dramatic Art. First appearance, Madison Square Theatre, New York, 1905; member of Hunter-Bradford Stock Company, Hartford, Conn., 1909-14; first London appearance, Prince of Wales's Theatre, 1915; has since played lead in the following productions among others: The Freedom of the Seas, Ambrose Applejohn's Adventure, Other Men's Wives, 77 Park Lane, The Way to Treat a Woman, The Gay Adventure, Afterwards, Hyde Park Corner, Espionage, London After Dark. *Address:* CBS-TV, 485 Madison Ave., N.Y.C. 22, U.S.A. [*Died* 9 *May* 1968.

LORT-WILLIAMS, Sir John (Rolleston), Kt., *cr.* 1936; Q.C. 1922; *b.* 14 Sept. 1881; *o. s.* of late Charles William Williams, solicitor, Walsall, Staffs., and Catharine, *d.* of late Joseph Morris, Hill House, Chilwell, Notts; *m.* 1st, 1923, Dorothy Margery Mary Russell (marriage dissolved, 1949); 2nd, 1950, Minnie Dorothy Margaret Lyal. *Educ.:* Merchant Taylors'; London Univ. Tancred Student, 1902; Barrister, Lincoln's Inn, 1904; Member Inner and Middle Temple; Pres., Hardwicke Society, 1911; contested (C.) Pembrokeshire, 1906 and 1908; Stockport, Dec. 1910; M.P. (C.) Rotherhithe, 1918-23; Recorder of West Bromwich, 1923-24; Recorder of Walsall, 1924-28; Puisne Judge of the High Court of Judicature at Fort William in Bengal, 1927-41; Officiating Chief Justice of Bengal in 1939 and 1940; Pres. R. Asiatic Soc. of Bengal, 1940-42; member of the Oxford Circuit. Served six years in Middlesex Imperial Yeomanry; member of the L.C.C. (Limehouse), 1907-10; Vice-Chairman of Housing Committee. *Recreations:* motoring, riding, walking. *Clubs:* Union; Royal Calcutta Turf.
[*Died* 9 *June* 1966.

LOTHIAN, Sir Arthur Cunningham, K.C.I.E., *cr.* 1941 (C.I.E. 1934); C.S.I. 1937; *b.* 1887; *s.* of D. B. Lothian, Strathgirnock, Aberdeenshire; *m.* 1920, Mary Helen *d.* of late W. O. Macgregor; one *s.* one *d.* *Educ.:* Aberdeen; Christ Church, Oxford; M.A., B.Sc., University of London; Hon. LL.D. (Aber.). I.C.S.: Bengal, 1911-15; thereafter in Political Department of Government of India; Pres., Council of State, Jaipur, 1930; Prime Minister, Alwar, 1933; Secretary (Federation) and Special Representative of the Viceroy in federal discussions with Indian States, 1935-37; Resident for Rajputana and Chief Commissioner, Ajmer-Merwara, 1937-42; Resident at Hyderabad, 1942-46. *Publications:* Kingdoms of Yesterday, 1951; articles in Quarterly and other Reviews; Ed. Murray's Handbook for India, Pakistan, Burma and Ceylon. *Recreations:* travelling, shooting, golf. *Address:* 23 Kensington Court Gardens, W.8. *T.:* Western 6571. *Club:* Athenæum. [*Died* 16 *Nov.* 1962.

LOUDON, Professor John, M.A., C.A.; partner in the firm of David Strathie & Co., Chartered Accountants, Glasgow, 1914-64, retd.; *s.* of late John Loudon, Glasgow; *m.* 1928, Vera Kathleen, *y. d.* of late F. J. Waring, C.M.G., Ealing. *Educ.:* Glasgow Academy; Fettes College, Edinburgh; Glasgow University. C.A. 1913; served with Cameronians (Scottish Rifles), 1914-1917; Director of Factory Accounts, Ministry of Munitions, 1917-19; Lecturer to Institute of Accountants and Actuaries in Glasgow; Prof. of Accountancy at Glasgow Univ., 1926-38. *Publications:* contribs. to professl. jls. *Address:* Dawn, Helensburgh, Dunbartonshire. *Club:* Western (Glasgow). [*Died* 3 *March* 1966.

LOUGH, Brig. John Robertson Stewart, C.B.E. 1945; D.S.O. 1918; M.C.; V.D.; Cdn. Army, retired; *b.* 13 Oct. 1887; *s.* of Robert F. Lough and Johan Hay Stewart; *m.* 1910, Lily McIlveen; one *s.* one *d.* *Educ.:* Edinburgh public schools. Served K.R.R.C. 1907-8; emigrated to Canada, 1908; European War, 1916-19, in France and Belgium (despatches, M.C. and bar, D.S.O., two medals); Staff Officer Cdn. Coronation Contg. 1937; commanded Seaforth Highlanders of Canada, 1936-38, Cdn. Reinf. Units, England, 1940-44; retired 1944. Coronation medal, 1937. *Recreations:* boating, amateur carpentry. *Address:* Lochmara, R.R.I., Wellington, V.I., B.C., Canada. [*Died* 26 *Jan.* 1970.

LOUGHBOROUGH, Major-General Arthur Harold, C.B. 1942; O.B.E. 1919; *b.* 20 Feb. 1883; 3rd *s.* of late Arthur Loughborough, Barrister-at-Law, of Lincoln's Inn; *m.* 1st, 1906, Norah Mary (*d.* 1909), *s. d.* of late Montague Alexis Pollard-Urquhart, Castle Pollard, Co. Meath; 2nd, 1921, Madeline Alice Frances, *o. d.* of late James Taylor and Mrs. E. L. Holbrooke; no *c.* *Educ.:* Doon House, Westgate-on-Sea, Kent; Bradfield College, Berks (Exhibitioner). 2nd Lt. Sussex R.G.A. Militia, 1900; 2nd Lt. R.G.A., 1902; Capt. and Adj. Clyde R.G.A. (T.), 1912; served European War, France (despatches, 1914-15 Star, British and Victory war medals, O.B.E.); Major, 1916; Secretary Royal Artillery Committee, 1923; Lt.-Col. 1932; Col. and Supt. of Experiments, 1932; Member, Ordnance Committee and Royal Artillery Committee, 1934; Brigadier and Commandant Military College of Science, 1936; Major-Gen. and Vice-Pres. Ordnance Committee and Pres. Royal Artillery Committee, 1938; Pres. Ordnance Board, 1940; retired, 1942. *Address:* c/o Lloyds Bank Ltd., Pier Street, Lee-on-Solent, Hants. [*Died* 26 *Dec.* 1967.

LOUW, Hon. Eric Hendrik, B.A., LL.B., D.Comm.; M.P. (Beaufort West, S. Afr.), 1924 and again since 1938; Minister of Foreign Affairs, South Africa, 1956-63, retd. (of Economic Affairs, 1948-54, of Finance, 1955-56); *b.* Jacobsdal, O.F.S., 21 Nov. 1890; *s.* of late J. A. Louw, Merchant, Beaufort West, C.P.; *m.* 1918, Anna Snyman, East London; one *s.* (and one *s.* decd.). *Educ.:* Victoria Coll., Stellenbosch; Rhodes Univ. Coll., Grahamstown. Admitted as a Barrister, 1917. First Trade Comr. of S. Africa in U.S. and Canada, 1925; High Comr. for S. Africa in London, 1929; first Minister of S. Africa to U.S., 1929; Minister to Italy, 1933; first S. African Minister to France and Portugal, 1934. Represented S. Africa: at Internat. Immigration Conf., Havana, 1928; at Internat. Red Cross and Prisoners of War Conf., Geneva, 1929; at League of Nations Assembly, 1929, 1934 and 1935; at U.N. Assembly, 1948, 1949, 1956, 1958, 1959, 1960, 1961, 1962. Represented S. African Prime Minister at Commonwealth Prime Ministers' Meeting, 1948, 1957 and 1960; also rep. S. Africa at Commonwealth Materials Conf., 1951, and at Commonwealth Economic Conf., 1952; Leader S. African delegn. at G.A.T.T. Conf., Geneva, Nov. 1954, and at meetings of Internat. Monetary Fund and Internat. Bank at Istanbul, Sept. 1955; Member, Electricity Supply Commn. *Address:* 38 Riverton Rd., Rondebosch, C.P., South Africa. [*Died* 24 *June* 1968.

LOVEDAY, Alexander, M.A.; Hon. D.Litt., McGill; Hon. Fellow, Peterhouse, Cambridge; Hon. Fellow, Nuffield College, Oxford; *b.* 1888; 5th *s.* of late J. E. T. Loveday, J.P., of Williamscote; *m.* 1916, Nathalie Irena (*d.* 1957), *e. d.* of late Field-Marshal Tarnoschi; two *s.* *Educ.:* Shrewsbury School; Peterhouse, Cambridge Univ. Fellow International Statistical Society; Hon. Member Swedish Royal Acad. of Science; Hungarian Statistical Society; Società Italiana di Demografia e Statistica; Asociatia Româna de Drept Financiar şi Fiscal; lectr. (political philosophy), Leipzig Univ., 1911-12; lectr. in economics, Cambridge Univ., 1913-15; War Office, 1915-19; League of Nations Secretariat, 1919, Director 1931-39 of the Financial Section and Economic Intelligence Service; of the Economic, Financial and Transit Dept., 1939-Feb. 1946; Member of the Inst. for Advanced Study, Princeton, N.J., 1946; Fellow of Nuffield College, 1946-49; Member of the U.N. Nuclear Economic and Employment Commission, 1946; Warden, Nuffield College, Oxford, 1950-54. *Publications:* History and Economics of Indian Famines, 1914; Britain and World Trade, Quo Vadimus and other essays, 1931; The Only Way; A Study of Democracy in Danger, 1950; Reflections on International Administration, 1957. Contributor to Economic Essays in honour of Gustav Cassel, 1933; The Lessons of Monetary Experience, 1937; The World's Future, 1938. *Address:* 18 Norham Gardens, Oxford. *Club:* Reform. [*Died* 19 *Jan.* 1962.

LOVEDAY, Arthur Frederic, O.B.E. 1920; *b.* 20 April 1878; 2nd *s.* of George Loveday, J.P., Manor House, Wardington, Banbury, Oxon; *m.* 1908, Mary Cornelia (*d.* 1963), *d.* of Jacob Backus, Lima, Peru, and Williamsburg, N.Y.; two *s.* two *d.* *Educ.:* Haileybury College. Business in Chile, 1900-1920; voluntary work in H.B.M. Consulate-General, Valparaiso and Intelligence Service in Chile, 1915-19 (O.B.E.); *Times* correspondent in Chile, 1914-20; business in Spain, 1921-33; Chairman British Chamber of Commerce in Spain, 1932-33; correspondent of Morning Post in Spain, 1927-33 Intelligence Service in Spain, 1924-33. Lay member of Church Assembly for Peterborough, 1935-39; Hon. Sec. Spanish Children's Repatriation Committee; Vice-Pres. Anglo-Chilean Society; British representative on Mission to S. American Republics on behalf of Intergovernmental Committee on Refugees, 1946-47. Commander Chilean Order of Merit, 1945; Knight Commander Spanish Civil Order of Merit, 1946. *Publications:* World War in Spain, 1939; Spain 1923-48, Through Civil War and World War, 1949; Three Stages of History in Rhodesia, 1961; Sir Hilgrove Turner, Soldier and Courtier under the Georges, 1965; articles and pamphlets on S. American, Spanish and Rhodesian subjects. *Address:* c/o Williams Deacon's Bank, 9 Pall Mall, S.W.1. *Clubs:* Travellers'; Salisbury (Rhodesia). [*Died* 22 *Dec.* 1968.

LOVEDAY, Thomas, M.A. Oxon.; Hon. LL.D. (Bristol, Capetown); Hon. Fellow, Bristol and King's College, London; *b.* 1875; *e. s.* of late J. E. T. Loveday, J.P.; *m.* Mildred (*d.* 1958), *d.* of late Rev. T. W. Fowle, Rector of Islip; two *d.* *Educ.:* Fettes College; Oxford (Magdalen College), John Locke Scholar, 1900; Leipzig. Principal of Univ. Coll., Southampton, 1920-22; Vice-Chancellor of University of Bristol, 1922-44; Chairman of the Committee of Vice-Chancellors and Principals, 1935-38; of the Executive Council of the Universities Bureau, 1943-45; of Committees on Veterinary and on Agricultural Education, 1936-38 and 1943-53; of the Bristol Evening Post Co., 1950-60. *Address:* Williamscote, Banbury, Oxon. *T.:* Cropredy 204. *Club:* Athenæum. [*Died* 4 *March* 1966.

LOVEJOY, Arthur Oncken, M.A. (Harvard); LL.D.: California, Missouri, Johns Hopkins; Litt.D.: Princeton, Columbia, Harvard, Maryland; L.H.D., Kenyon; Prof. of Philosophy Emeritus, Johns Hopkins University; *b.* Berlin, Germany, 10 Oct. 1873; *s.* of Rev. W. W. Lovejoy, Boston, Mass., and Sara Agnes Oncken, Hamburg; unmarried. *Educ.:* University of California; Harvard University; University of Paris. Assistant Professor, Stanford University, 1899-1901; Professor of Philosophy, Washington University, St. Louis, 1901-08; Lecturer in Philosophy, Columbia University, New York, 1907-08; Professor of Philosophy, University of Missouri, 1908-10; Johns Hopkins, 1910-38; F.A.A.; President American Association of University Professors, 1919; President American Philosophical Association, 1916; Member American Mission in England, 1918; Carus Lecturer American Philosophical Association, 1927; Lecturer, University of London, 1931; William James Lecturer, Harvard, 1933; Editor, Journal of the History of Ideas. *Publications:* The Revolt against Dualism, 1929; Primitivism and Related Ideas in Antiquity (with G. Boas), 1935; The Great Chain of Being, 1936; Essays in the History of Ideas, 1948; Philosophical Papers in American Journal of Theology; Hibbert Journal; Journal of Philosophy; Mind; Philosophical Review, and other periodicals; also in Essays in Critical Realism, 1920; Contemporary American Philosophy, 1929. *Address:* Johns Hopkins University, Baltimore, Maryland, U.S.A. *Club:* University (Baltimore). [*Died* 30 *Dec.* 1962.

LOVEL, Professor Raymond William; Professor of Operative Dental Surgery, University of Newcastle upon Tyne (formerly King's Coll., University of Durham), since 1946; Clinical Sub-Dean of the Dental School; Director of Newcastle upon Tyne Dental Hospital and Head of Department of Conservative Dental Surgery, Newcastle upon Tyne Dental Hospital; *b.* 15 May 1912; *o. s.* of William Henry Lovel, M.A., Wimbledon Park, S.W.19; *m.* 1946, Charmian Marrian Brown, Sutton Coldfield; one *s.* one *d.* *Educ.:* King's College Sch., Wimbledon; King's Coll. Hosp.; London Univ.; North-western Univ., Chicago. Wallace Memorial Prize, 1934, and other dental surgery prizes. L.D.S., R.C.S.Eng. 1934; D.D.S. Northwestern, 1935; H.D.D., R.C.S. Edin., 1937; F.D.S., R.C.S.Eng., 1948; M.D.S. Durham, 1958; F.D.S., R.C.S. Edin., 1959. Resident Dental House Surgeon, King's Coll. Hosp., 1935; Sen. Demonstr. in Clinical and Operative Dental Surgery, Univ. of Liverpool, 1935-1939. Commnd. in Army Dental Corps, 1939-1945, serving with B.E.F. France, 1940, and 8th Army, Middle East Land Forces, 1942-45. External Examr. in Dental Subjects: Univ. of Glasgow, 1951-54, 1966 and 1967; Univ. of Edinburgh, 1960-62; Univ. of Liverpool, 1962-64; Chairman of Board of Governors, Collierley Secondary Modern School, Dipton, 1955-62: President Newcastle Div., Assoc. of Univ. Teachers, 1956-58; Pres., N. of England Odontological Soc., 1958-59; Mem. Board of Governors, United Newcastle upon Tyne Hospitals, 1960-; Chm., N.E. Div. Hospital Group, B.D.A., 1961-63; Chm., Assoc. of Dental Hospitals of Great Britain and N. Ireland, 1964-65. *Publications:* Contributions to British Dental Jl., Dental Record, Dental Practitioner. *Recreations:* gardening, stamp collecting, mountaineering. *Address:* 6 Northumberland Avenue, Gosforth, Newcastle upon Tyne 3. *T.:* Gosforth 56024. *Club:* Wayfarers (Liverpool). [*Died* 8 *April* 1969.

LOVELACE, 4th Earl of (*cr.* 1838); **Peter Malcolm King;** Baron King and Ockham, 1725; Viscount Ockham, 1838; *b.* 30 Mar. 1905; *e. s.* of 3rd Earl and Lady Edith Anson (*d.* 1932), *d.* of 2nd Earl of Lichfield; *S.* father, 1929; *m.* 1st, 1939, Doris Evison (*d.* 1940); 2nd, 1951, Manon Lis, Baroness Blixen Finecke, *d.* of Axel Transo, Copenhagen; one *s.* *Educ.:* Eton. *Heir:* *s.* Viscount Ockham. *Address:* Ben Damph Forest, Torridon, Ross-shire. *Clubs:* Bath, Pratt's. [*Died* 4 *Dec.* 1964.

LOVETT, Rev. Canon John Percival Willoughby, M.A.; *b.* Bishop's Caundle Rectory, Dorset, 1 June 1880; *s.* of Rev. Robert Lovett and Elizabeth, *d.* of Hugh Lumsden of Pitcaple Castle, Aberdeenshire; *m.* 1925, Evelyn Cressie (*d.* 1965), *d.* of late Col. R. Maxwell-Hyslop, R.E.; two *d.* *Educ.:* Clifton Coll.; Trinity Coll., Oxford. Deacon, 1904; Priest, 1905; Curate of St. Mark, St. Helens, 1904-08; Domestic Chaplain to Bishop of Liverpool, 1908-10; Vicar of St. Mark, Newtown, Wigan, 1910-11; St. Mark, St. Helens, 1911-19; Vicar of Prescot, 1919-39; Rural Dean of Prescot, 1934-39; Canon of Liverpool Cathedral, 1928-39; Vicar of, Sherborne with Castleton and Lillington, 1939-47, Canon of Salisbury Cathedral, 1941-62, now emeritus; Rector of Gussage St. Michael and Gussage All Saints, 1947-52; Vicar of Melplash and Rector of Mapperton, Dorset, 1952-59. *Address:* Myrtle Cottage, Sherborne, Dorset. [*Died* 29 *Feb.* 1968.

LOVEYS, Walter Harris; M.P. (C.) Chichester, since Nov. 1958; *b.* 2 Nov. 1920; *s.* of late Walter Loveys and late Mrs. Loveys, Bilsham, Sx.; *m.* 1944, Muriel Helen, *d.* of Commander and Mrs. Redvers Prior; two *s.* one *d.* *Educ.:* Lancing College. Engaged in farming. Chairman, Chichester Conservative Association, 1953-58; Mem. Chichester Group Hospital Management Cttee. Mem., W. Sussex C.C., 1954-67. Member: Cons. Parly. Horticultural Cttee. (Hon. Sec. 1964-1965, Vice-Chm. 1966-); Estimates Cttee., House of Commons, 1968; The Speaker's Conf. on Electoral Law, 1968; various parly. delegns. to Continent, and to Tunisia, 1961; House of Commons Motor Club (Hon. Sec. 1964-). *Address:* Bonhams, Flansham, Bognor Regis, Sussex. *T.:* Middleton-on-Sea 3075. *Clubs:* Carlton, Lansdowne, Royal Automobile. [*Died* 7 *March* 1969.

LOW, Sir David (Alexander Cecil), Kt. 1962; Cartoonist and Caricaturist; *b.* Dunedin, New Zealand, 7 April 1891; 3rd *s.* of David Brown Low and Jane Caroline Flanagan; *m.* 1920, Madeline Grieve Kenning; two *d.* *Educ.:* Boys' High School, Christchurch. Political Cartoonist, The Spectator, Christchurch, 1902; The Bulletin, Sydney, 1911; the Star, London, 1919; the Evening Standard, 1927; The Daily Herald, 1950; The Manchester Guardian, 1953. Hon. LL.D. New Brunswick, 1958; Hon. LL.D. Leicester, 1961. Hon. Diploma of Associateship of Regional College of Art, Manchester, 1959. *Publications:* Low's Annual, 1908; Caricatures, 1915; The Billy Book, 1918; Man. 1921; Lloyd George and Co., 1922; Low and I, 1923; Low and I Holiday Book, 1925; Lions and Lambs, 1928; The Best of Low, 1930; Low's Russian Sketchbook, 1932; Portfolio of Caricatures, 1933; Low and Terry, 1934; The New Rake's Progress, 1934; Ye Madde Designer, 1935; Political Parade, 1936; Low Again, 1938; A Cartoon History of our Times, 1939; Europe since Versailles, 1939; Europe at War, 1940; Low's War Cartoons, 1941; Low on the War, 1941; British Cartoonists, 1942; The World at War, 1942; C'est la Guerre, 1943; Válka Začala Mnichovem, 1945; Dreizehn Jahre Weltgeschehen, 1945; Kleine Weltgeschichte, 1949; Years of Wrath, 1949; Low's Company, 1952; Low Visibility, 1953; Low's Autobiography, 1956; The Fearful Fifties, 1960. *Recreations:* walking, the cinema, and golf. *Address:* 33 Melbury Court, W.8. *Clubs:* National Liberal, Savile. [*Died* 19 *Sept.* 1963.

LOW, Sir Henry Telfer, Kt., *cr.* 1952; C.B.E. 1946; *b.* 13 Dec. 1880; *s.* of James Barrie Low; *m.* 1909, Kate Lily (decd.), *d.* of Donald McKay; one *s.* *Educ.:* Kelvinside Academy, Glasgow; South African College, Cape Town. Past Vice-Chm. Nat. Native Labour Bd., retd. 1954; Past Chm. Nat. War Fund; Vice-Chm.: Rhodesia Railways Bd.; Rhodesian Bd. of Standard Bank of S.A. Ltd., 1953, retired; director of Rhodesian cos. Has served various Internat. Rotary Cttees. and still actively interested as Rotarian. *Address:* 13 Clark Rd., Bulawayo, S. Rhodesia. *T.:* Byo 61115. *Clubs:* Bulawayo, Bulawayo Country (S.R.). [*Died* 15 *Oct.* 1964.

O W, William Alexander; M.C.; F.F.A.R.C.S.; retired; Consulting Anaesthetist to St. Thomas's Hospital. *Educ.:* Fettes Coll.; St. Thomas's Hospital. M.R.C.S. Eng., L.R.C.P. Lond. 1920; M.B., B.S. Lond. 1922; D.A. Eng. 1939; F.F.A.R.C.S. Eng. 1948. Formerly: Sen. Anaesth., St. Thomas's Hosp. and London Chest Hosp.; Anaesth., St. Mark's Hosp.; Fellow Fac. Anaesth., R.C.S. Eng.; Sen. Fellow Assoc. of Anaesths. of Gt. Brit.; Hon. Maj. R.F.A. *Publications:* contrib. to med. jls. *Address:* Woodside, Maple Avenue, Cooden, Bexhill-on-Sea, Sussex. [*Died* 26 *May* 1970.

LOWDON, Professor Andrew Gilchrist Ross, O.B.E. 1944; Professor of Surgery, since 1954, Dean of Medicine, since 1960, and Pro-Vice-Chancellor since 1965, University of Newcastle upon Tyne (lately King's College); Surgeon, Royal Victoria Infirmary, Newcastle upon Tyne; Member of General Medical Council; *b.* 12 April 1911; *s.* of Reverend C. Ross Lowdon and Alison Gilchrist; *m.* 1948, Glenys, *d.* of Professor Robert Donaldson; two *s.* two *d.* *Educ.:* Greenock Academy and Royal High School, Edinburgh; University of Edinburgh. M.A. 1932; M.B., Ch.B. (Hons. and Ettles Schol.) 1936; F.R.C.S.E. 1939; F.R.C.S. *a.e.g.*, 1959. Formerly House Phys. and House Surgeon, Royal Infirmary and Royal Hospital for Sick Children, Edinburgh, 1936-38; Senior President Royal Medical Society, 1936-37; Vans Dunlop Research Schol., Univ. of Edinburgh, 1938-39; R.A.M.C. 1939-45, Lieut.-Col. in charge of Surgical Div. Asst. Surg., Edin. Roy. Infirmary, 1946; Visiting Surg., Roy. Edinburgh Hosps. for Mental Disorders, 1946; Director of Post-graduate Surgical Studies, Edinburgh Post-graduate Board for Medicine, 1946-47; Lectr. in Surgery, 1947, and Sen. Lectr. in Surgery, 1950, Univ. of Edinburgh. *Publications:* various papers to medical journals. *Recreation:* golf. *Address:* Department of Surgery, Medical School, Newcastle upon Tyne, 1; 26 Brandling Park, Newcastle upon Tyne, 2. [*Died* 2 *Sept.* 1965.

LOWDON, John, C.M.G. 1931; *b.* Cardiff, 28 Dec. 1881; 2nd *s.* of late John Lowdon, J.P.; *m.* 1917, Edith, *yr. d.* of late Henry Jones; one *d.* *Educ.:* Privately. Vice-Consul at Havana, 1908; transferred to Sebastopol, 1910; to Rostov on Don, 1913; to Odessa, 1913; Acting Vice-Consul at Torneo, Finland, 1916 and 1917; Acting Consul-General at Moscow, 1917 and 1918; Acting Consul-General at Odessa, 1918, 1919 and 1920; Consul at Riga, 1920; employed at the Foreign Office, 1925; Consul at Lyons, 1926; Consul-General at Cologne, 1927-1934; Consul-General at Rio de Janeiro, 1934-1937; Consul-General at Algiers, 1937-40; employed at Foreign Office, 1940-41; retired, 1942. *Address:* 14 Highland Court, Church Road, Haywards Heath, Sussex. *T.:* Haywards Heath 947. [*Died* 28 *Feb.* 1963.

LOWE, Sir (Albert) George, Kt. 1961; Member, Foreign Compensation Commission, 1961-66; retired; Chief Justice, Fiji, Chief Judicial Commissioner Western Pacific, President Fiji Court of Appeal, 1958-61; *b.* Auckland, New Zealand, 5 June 1901; *s.* of William George and Sarah Lowe; *m.* 1930, Bertha Sharpe; two *d.* *Educ.:* Auckland (New Zealand) Grammar School; Auckland University Coll. Barrister and solicitor, N.Z. Legal practice on own account, 1928-38; Legal Secretary, Tonga, 1938-40 (Acting Chief Justice for period); Royal N.Z. Air Force (Sqdn. Ldr.), 1940-45; Crown Counsel, Kenya, 1945-49 (acted Solicitor-Gen. and Legal Draftsman for periods); Legal Secretary, Malta, 1949-53 (acted Lieut.-Governor for periods, 1949-53 incl.); Governor's Deputy, 1952, for period; Puisne Judge, Tanganyika, 1953-58. *Recreations:* silverwork, woodwork. *Address:* Charlwood, 31 Hillcrest Road, Purley, Surrey CR2 2JF. [*Died* 25 *Dec.* 1967.

LOWE, Hon. Sir Charles (John), K.C.M.G. 1956; Kt. 1948; M.A., LL.D.; Judge of Supreme Court, Victoria, 1927-64, retd.; *b.* Panmure, Vic., 4 Oct. 1880; *s.* of Thomas and Mary Ann Lowe, both of England; *m.* 1908, Clara Rhoda Dickason, Melbourne; one *s.* one *d.* *Educ.:* Panmure School; Surrey College, Melbourne; Trinity College, Melbourne University. Master at Choir School, St. Paul's Cathedral, Melbourne, 1897-1904; B.A. 1900; M.A. 1902; LL.B. 1904 (final honours in Arts and Law); a Barrister of Supreme Court, Victoria, 1906; Chancellor of Melbourne University, 1941-54; President Emeritus, Victorian Branch English-Speaking Union. Acting Chief Justice Supreme Court, Victoria, Sept. 1950-Sept. 1951, 1953 and 1961. Administrator, State of Victoria, July-Nov. 1953 and Feb.-Aug. 1961. *Recreation:* golf. *Address:* Myoora, Irving Road, Toorak, Victoria 3142, Australia. *Clubs:* Royal Automobile (Victoria), Australian, Melbourne Cricket, Royal Melbourne Golf (Melbourne). [*Died* 20 *March* 1969.

LOWE, Elias Avery, M.A.; Hon. D.Litt. Oxon.; Hon. LL.D. Univ. of North Carolina; D.Litt. National University of Ireland; Ph.D. Munich; Professor in Palaeography,

Institute for Advanced Study, Princeton, New Jersey, from 1936; *b.* 15 Oct. 1879; *s.* of Charles H. and Sarah Ragoler Lowe; *m.* 1911, Helen Tracy Porter; three *d.* *Educ.:* New York Grammar School; College of City of New York; Cornell University, A.B. 1902; Munich Univ., Ph.D. 1907. Associate of Carnegie Institution, Washington since 1911; Sandars Reader in Bibliography, Univ. of Cambridge, 1914; Lecturer and Reader in Palaeography, Univ. of Oxford, 1913-48. Corr. F.B.A.; Fell., Medieval Acad. of America (Haskins Medal, 1957); Hon. M.R.I.A.; Assoc. Mem., Institut de France; Corresponding Member, Linzei Acad. Consultant in Palaeography in Library of Congress, Washington, D.C.; Chichele Lecturer, Oxford, 1961. Gold Medal, Bibliographical Soc., 1959. *Publications:* Die aeltesten Kalendarien aus Monte Cassino, 1908; Studia Palaeographica, 1910; The Beneventan Script, 1914; The Bobbio Missal, 1920; A sixth-century fragment of the Letters of Pliny the Younger, 1922; Codices Lugdunenses antiquissimi, 1924; The Palæography of the Bobbio Missal, 1924; a Hand-list of Half-Uncial MSS., 1924; article, Handwriting, in Legacy of the Middle Ages, 1926; Palæographical Account of English Handwriting in S.P.E. Tract. xxiii., 1926; Regula S. Benedicti, 1929; Scriptura Beneventana, 1929; The Unique MS. of Tacitus' Histories (Laur. 68. 2) in Casinensia, 1929; English Uncial, 1960; Editor of *Codices Latini Antiquiores:* Part I, The Vatican City, 1934; Part II, Great Britain and Ireland, 1935; Part III, Italy (Ancona-Novara), 1938; Part IV, Italy (Perugia-Verona), 1947; Part V, France (Paris, 1950); Part VI, France (Abbeville-Valenciennes), 1953; Part VII, Switzerland, 1956; Part VIII, Germany (Altenburg-Leipzig, 1959); Part IX, Germany (Maria Laach - Würzburg), 1959; Part X, Austria, Belgium, Czechoslovakia, Egypt, Holland, 1963; Part XI, Hungary, Luxembourg, Poland, Russia, Spain, Sweden, The United States, and Yugoslavia, 1966; Part XII, Supplement, 1969; Handwriting (2nd rev. and enl. ed.), 1969. Contributions and reviews in historical, classical, and theological periodicals. *Recreations:* trout-fishing and golf. *Address:* Institute for Advanced Study, Princeton, N.J., U.S.A.; Corpus Christi Coll., Oxford. *Club:* Authors'. [*Died* 8 *Aug.* 1969.

LOWE, Sir George; *see* Lowe, Sir A. G.

LOWE, Ven. Sidney Edward; Archdeacon of Bradford and Rector of Guiseley, 1934 - Oct. 1953, Archdeacon Emeritus since 1953; *b.* 22 March 1882; *s.* of late Edward Lowe, Edgbaston, Birmingham; *m.* 1919, Olive Nelson, *d.* of late J. Dania Tomlinson; one *d.* (one *s.* killed in action). *Educ.:* King Edward's School, Birmingham; Queen's College and Univ. of Birmingham. Ordained, 1905; Curate of S. James', Gorton, Manchester, 1905-9; Vicar of Holy Trinity, Colne, Lancs, 1909-15; Vicar of S. Peter's, Rochdale, 1915-20; Vicar of All Saints', Bradford, 1920-25; Hon. Sec. Diocesan Board of Finance, 1923-28; Vicar of Otley, 1925-34; Rural Dean of Otley, 1925-34; Hon. Canon of Bradford Cathedral; Hon. O.C.F. 1940; F.R.S.A. *Recreations:* golf and swimming. *Address:* Brackens, Penmaen, Gower, S. Wales. *T.:* Penmaen 248. *Club:* Union (Bradford).

[*Died* 10 *Jan.* 1968.

LOWE, Lt.-Col. Thomas Alfred, D.S.O. 1918; M.C.; late Highland Light Infantry; Journalist; Military Correspondent, Daily Mail, 1939-45; Military Correspondent, Reuters, 1940; B.B.C.'s first Military Observer, 1938; *b.* 1888; *s.* of Alfred Lowe, Belfast; *m.* 1915, *d.* of J. B. McCutcheon, Belfast. Served France and Belgium, 1914-1918 (wounded twice, M.C., D.S.O., Brevet Major, Belgian Croix de Guerre, despatches twice). *Publications:* The Western Battlefields, 1919; A Guide to the Duties of an Adjutant, 1919; Physical Jerks, 1920; Wine, Women, and—Soldiers, 1932; Be Fit as a Fiddle, 1936; Fruit Farm in England; All the Know-How about Horse Racing, 1954; The Craft of the Cottage Garden, 1957; The Gardener's Year Complete, 1966; many short stories and articles. *Recreation:* golf. *Address:* Port Charlotte, Isle-of-Islay, Argyll. *Club:* Savage.

[*Died* 5 *Sept.* 1967.

LOWERY, Harry, M.Ed., B.A., Ph.D., D.Sc., F.Inst.P., F.T.C.L., F.B.O.A., F.C.P.; Music Lecturer and Adjudicator; *b.* Hensingham, Cumberland, 1896; *o. s.* of Henry and Annie Lowery; *m.* 1922, Everilda Mary (*d.* 1955), *d.* of John and Emily Butterill, Wolsingham, Co. Durham. *Educ.:* County Gram. Sch., Whitehaven; Univs. of London, Leeds, and Manchester. Mem. Bd., Trinity Coll. of Music; Vice-Pres., Coll. of Preceptors; Hon. Mem. Incorporated Soc. of Musicians; Mem. Worshipful Co. of Musicians. *Publications:* The Background of Music, 1952; Guide to Musical Acoustics, 1956; research papers in physics and music journals. *Address:* 32 Hainault Court, Forest Rise, E.17.

[*Died* 27 *Sept.* 1967.

LOWETH, Walter Ernest, C.B.E. 1935; D.L. Co. of London; J.P.; F.R.S.A.; *b.* 23 Oct. 1892; *s.* of William George and Helen Loweth; *m.* 1926, Irene Alice Marony; two *s.* Past Executive London Conservative Union; Mem. Hackney London Boro' Council, 1913-45; Mayor, 1926-27; Freeman of Boro' of Hackney, 1935; Pres. of Hackney and Stoke Newington Chamber of Commerce, 1934-35; represented Hackney on Association of Municipal Corps. for 7 years, on Metropolitan Water Bd. for 6 years; Lea Conservatory for 3 years; Past Mem. Exec. London Municipal Society; Past Chm. (now patron), Hackney Central Conservative Assocs. and Patron Stoke Newington and North Hackney Assoc.; Governing Dir. W. Loweth & Sons, Ltd., Hackney; Past Patron North Hackney British Legion; Vice-Pres. Council Disabled Soldiers and Sailors Foundation, Hackney; Past Pres. Hackney Div., Lifeboat Institution, Pres. R.S.P.C.C. Hackney Division; Trustee, Hackney Parochial Charities; President, Royal Society of St. George (City Branch); Chm. Royal Berks Association (Hackney and Stoke Newington); Hon. Col. 7th Royal Berks Regt. T.A., and Chairman and Trustee of its Old Comrades' Assoc.; European War, 1916-18; Patron Hackney Old Contemptibles' Assoc.; Liveryman: Basket Makers' Company (member of Court of the Company; Prime Warden, 1957-1958); Inn Holders' Company; Needlemakers', Farriers', Painters', Stainers', Companies; Freeman City of London and Member Guild of Freeman (on Court of Guild); Past Member City Corporation for Bishopsgate Ward; Common Councillor, City of London, 1946-64; Past Chm. Tower Hamlets Bench and Income Tax Commissioners, Tower Hamlets; Past Pres. Bishopsgate Ward Club; Past Chairman of Governors, Bishopsgate Institute. *Address:* 5 East Bank, N.16. *T.:* 01-800 1784. *Club:* City Livery. [*Died* 3 *March* 1968.

LOWIS, Frank Currie, C.I.E. 1914; *b.* 15 Nov. 1872; *s.* of Edmund Elliot Lowis, late B.C.S.; *m.* 1925, Marjorie Isabella Bucknall, of 7 Kensington Mansions, S.W. ; one *s.* one *d.* *Educ.:* Sherborne; Royal Indian Engineering College. Entered Public Works Department, India, 1896; Executive Engineer, 1907; special duty on the Semhu Lauhhaung Road, 1911; accompanied Hpimaw Expedition and constructed the road for it, 1913; in charge of construction Putaw Frontier Road, 1914; Commission Indian Army Reserve, 1915; Major; engaged in road-making in Southern Persia, 1917-18; Lt.-Col. 1919; retired from Burma

Public Works Dept., 1921. *Recreations:* polo, played in champion team three times; trains and rides own racing ponies; big-game shooting, first man in Burma to secure a tarkin. *Address:* Ford, Stockland, Honiton, Devon. [*Died* 11 *Oct.* 1963.

LOWLES, Sir (John) Geoffrey (Nelson), Kt., *cr.* 1952; *b.* 23 May 1898; *s.* of John and Lucy Lowles; *m.* 1921, Anna, *d.* of Felix Langley; one *d.* *Educ.:* Quaker School, Ackworth; Christ's College, Cambridge (M.A.). Chairman Woking and Chertsey Group H.M.C., 1948-54. Member: Surrey County Council, 1946-55; Council of Royal Yachting Association; Inland Waterways Re-development Advisory Cttee., 1959-. *Recreation:* yachting. *Address:* Binfield Manor, Binfield, Nr. Bracknell, Berks. *T.:* Bracknell 827. *Clubs:* Royal Thames Yacht; Royal London Yacht, Island Sailing (Cowes); Itchenor Sailing (Commodore, 1937-57, Admiral, 1957-); Bembridge Sailing; The Redwing. [*Died* 20 *June* 1962.

LUBBOCK, Percy, C.B.E. 1952; Author; *b.* 4 June 1879; *s.* of Frederic Lubbock and Catherine Gurney; *m.* 1926, Lady Sybil (*d.* 1943), *yr. d.* of 5th Earl of Desart, K.P., P.C., K.C.B.; no *c.* *Educ.:* Eton; King's College, Cambridge. *Publications:* The Craft of Fiction, 1921; Earlham, 1922; Roman Pictures, 1923; The Region Cloud, 1925; Shades of Eton, 1929; Portrait of Edith Wharton, 1947, etc. *Address:* Gli Scafari, Lerici, Italy. *Club:* Oxford and Cambridge. [*Died* 2 *Aug.* 1965.

LUCAN, 6th Earl of (*cr.* 1795), **George Charles Patrick Bingham;** Bt. 1632; Baron Lucan 1776; Baron Bingham, U.K., 1934; M.C. 1918; Col. (ret.); Chief Opposition Whip, House of Lords, since 1954; *b.* 24 Nov. 1898; *e. s.* of 5th Earl of Lucan, P.C., G.C.V.O., K.B.E., C.B., and Violet, O.B.E. 1920, *d.* of J. Spender Clay, Ford Manor, Lingfield; *S.* father, 1949; *m.* 1929, Kaitilin, *o. c.* of late Capt. Hon. Edward Dawson, Royal Navy, and late Lady Elizabeth Dawson; two *s.* two *d.* *Educ.:* Eton; R.M.C. Sandhurst. 2nd Lieut. Coldstream Guards, 1917; Lieut. 1918; served European War, 1917-18; A.D.C. to Governor-General of South Africa, 1924-25; Bde. Maj. British Troops in Sudan, 1932-34 and 11th Inf. Bde., 1934-36; D.A.A. and Q.M.G. London District, 1937-40; Commanded 1st Bn. Coldstream Gds., 1940-42; Dep. Dir. Ground Defence Air Ministry, 1942-45. Capt., 1926; Maj., 1934; Lt.-Col., 1941; Col., 1942; retired 1947. Captain of H.M. Bodyguard of the Yeomen of the Guard, 1950-51. Parl. Under-Sec. of State, Commonwealth Relations, June-Oct. 1951. *Heir:* *s.* Lord Bingham. *Address* 11 Hanover House, N.W.8. *T.:* Primrose 0092. *Club:* Guards. [*Died* 21 *Jan.* 1964.

LUCAS OF CHILWORTH, 1st Baron, *cr.* 1946, of Chilworth; **George William Lucas;** *b.* 1896; *s.* of Percy William Lucas, Oxford; *m.* 1917, Sonia, *d.* of Marcus Finklestein, Libau, Latvia; two *s.* two *d.* *Educ.:* London Tech. Schools. Pres. Motor Agents Assoc., 1927-29, 1941-46; Chairman National Joint Industrial Council of Motor Vehicle Retail and Repairing Trade, 1943-46; Chm Cttee. of Inquiry into Agricultural Marketing Acts, 1947; Member Motor Vehicle Maintenance Advisory Committee, 1940; Member of English National Committee Forestry Commission, 1945; New Forest Departmental Committee, 1945-46. A Lord in Waiting to the King, 1948-49; Captain of the Yeoman of the Guard, 1949-50. Parliamentary Secretary, Ministry of Transport, 1950-51. Mem. B.B.C. Gen. Advisory Council, 1952-56; Liveryman of Coachmakers Company. *Heir:* *s.* Michael Lucas (later 2nd Baron) [*b.* 26 April 1926; *m.* 1955, Ann-Marie, *o. d.* of Ronald Buck, Southampton; two *s.* (*er. s.* and *heir*, Hon. Simon William Lucas, *b.* 1957) one *d.*]. *Address:* Grey Walls, Cothill, nr. Abingdon, Berkshire. [*Died* 11 *Oct.* 1967.

LUCAS, Frank Laurence, O.B.E. 1946; F.R.S.L.; Fellow of King's Coll., Cambridge; formerly University Reader in English; *b.* 28 Dec. 1894; *er. s.* of Frank William Lucas and Ada Ruth Blackmur; *m.* 1st, Emily Beatrix Coursolles Jones; 2nd, Prudence Dalzell Wilkinson; 3rd, Elna Julie Dagmar Constance Kallenberg; one *s.* one *d.* *Educ.:* Rugby School; Trinity College, Cambridge. Pitt University Scholar, Porson Prize, 1914; served in 7th R. West Kent Regiment and Intelligence Corps (wounded 1916, gassed 1917, despatches); Browne medal, Chancellor's medal, 1920; Fellow of King's College, Cambridge, 1920; Student of British School at Athens, 1921; Foreign Office, 1939-45. *Publications:* Seneca and Elizabethan Tragedy; Euripides and his Influence; Euripides' Medea (translation); Authors Dead and Living; Tragedy; The Complete Works of J. Webster; Ten Victorian Poets; Studies French and English; The River Flows, Cécile, The Wild Tulip, Doctor Dido (novels); Time and Memory, Marionettes, Ariadne, Gilgamesh (poems); Poems, 1935; From Olympus to the Styx (with Prudence Lucas); The Art of Dying (with Francis Birrell); Tennyson, Beddoes, Crabbe, Rossetti (anthologies); Mount Peacock (from French of Marie Mauron); The Bear Dances (produced at the Garrick Theatre, Nov. 1932); Land's End (produced at Westminster Theatre, Feb. 1938); Four plays; The Decline and Fall of the Romantic Ideal; The Golden Cockerel Greek Anthology; The Woman Clothed with the Sun and other stories; The Delights of Dictatorship; A Journal Under the Terror, 1938; A Greek Garland; Messene Redeemed; Critical Thoughts in Critical Days; The Vigil of Venus; Homer's Hymn to Aphrodite; The Iliad; The Odyssey; Hero and Leander; Tennyson; Greek Poetry for Everyman; Greek Drama for Everyman; Literature and Psychology; From Many Times and Lands (poems); Style; The Search for Good Sense (Four 18th-century Minds); The Art of Living (Four 18th-Century Characters); The Greatest Problem, and other essays; Ibsen and Strindberg; Chekhov, Synge, Yeats and Pirandello. *Recreations:* walking and travel. *Address:* King's College, and 20 West Road, Cambridge. *T.:* Cambridge 52780. [*Died* 1 *June* 1967.

LUCE, Henry Robinson; Publisher and Editor; *b.* 3 April 1898; *s.* of Henry Winters and Elizabeth Middleton Luce; *m.* 1st, 1923, Lila Ross Hotz; two *s.*; 2nd, 1935, Clare Boothe Brokaw. *Educ.:* Hotchkiss Sch., Lakeville, Conn.; Yale Univ.; Oxford Univ. Founder and editor and publisher of Time, 1923, Editorial Chairman, 1964; began publishing Fortune in 1930, Architectural Forum, 1932, Life in 1936, House and Home, 1952, Sports Illustrated, 1954. *Address:* Time and Life Building, Rockefeller Center, New York, U.S.A. *T.:* Judson 6-1212 (Office). *Clubs:* Yale, Union, Racquet and Tennis, Century Association, University, The Links, Cloud, River, Hemisphere (New York); Chicago (Chicago). [*Died* 28 *Feb.* 1967.

LUCEY, Col. Walter Francis, C.M.G. 1919; D.S.O. 1916; Chairman and Managing Director of Hardings (Leeds) Ltd., textile machinery makers, Leeds, and Cocker Bros. Ltd., Sheffield; *b.* 1880; 2nd *s.* of late W. C. Lucey, M.D., Haslemere; *Educ.:* Merchant Taylors' School. Served European War, 1914-19 (C.M.G., D.S.O., Croix de Guerre, despatches 5 times). *Recreation:* golf. *Address:* Fulwith Brow, nr. Harrogate. *Clubs:* Royal Automobile; Leeds (Leeds). [*Died* 26 *Aug.* 1962.

LUCIE-SMITH, Sir John A(lfred), Kt. 1949; O.B.E. 1919; V.D.; retired as Chief Justice, Sierra Leone, W. Africa (1946-50); *b.* 27 January, 1888; *e. s.* of late Sir Alfred Lucie-Smith, sometime Chief Justice, Trinidad; *m.* 1914, Katie, *e.d.* of T. C. Pile; one *d.* *Educ.:* Stonyhurst College. Barrister-at-law, Middle Temple, 1910; Advocate and Solicitor, Straits Settlements, 1910-14; on active service (Royal Dublin Fusiliers), 1914-19 (despatches twice); Asst. Magistrate, Trinidad, 1920-23; President District Court, Cyprus, 1923-27; Puisne Judge, Cyprus, 1927-1929; Puisne Judge, Trinidad, 1929-31; Chairman Oil and Water Board, Trinidad; Puisne Judge, Kenya, Member of H.M.'s Court of Appeal for Eastern Africa, 1931-46; Acting Chief Justice 1934, 1937, 1945; Acting Chief Justice, Zanzibar, 1942; President Trade Disputes Tribunal, Kenya; Chairman Compensation Board, Kenya; Member West Africa Court of Appeal; retired, 1950. *Recreation:* fishing. *Address:* 20 Clifton Gardens, Folkestone, Kent.
[*Died* 17 *April* 1969.

LUCKNER, Felix, Count; Good-will Missioner and sailor; *b.* Dresden, 9 June 1881; *s.* of Heinrich, Count Luckner, and Maria, Countess Luckner; *m.* Ingeborg, Countess Luckner. *Educ.:* Sea. Went to sea at 13 years of age on a sailing ship; joined the Salvation Army in Australia; became a lieutenant; then lighthousekeeper's assistant in Australia; travelled through Australia with Hindoo-magicians as Billposter· sailed to America to meet Buffalo Bill; tramped, walked the ties of the railroad, and worked way from San Francisco to New York; then joined the Imperial Navy in Germany and gained lieutenant's commission from the Emperor on account of record for lifesaving; fought in the battle of Jutland on board the Crown Prince; later comdr. raider Seeadler; after a stay of seven years in the U.S.A. (hon. citizen several cities) returned to Germany, 1934, in his yacht Mopelia, which was destroyed by fire, 1935; 1937 he had built a new yacht called the Sea-Devil in which he started a new world tour through the South-Sea, New Zealand, Australia, Java, Borneo, Sumatra, Ceylon; returned, 1939. War of 1939-1945, was considered a state enemy for refusing to return hon. citizenships; never a member of Nazi Party; lecture-trip to U.S.A., 1949-50, for furthering understanding between peoples. *Publications:* in German: See-Teufel; Seeteufels, Weltfahrt; Aus 70 Lebensjahren; Der See-Teufel erobert Amerika; Vom Schiffsjungen zum Kapitän. In English: The Sea-Devil by Lowell Thomas; The Sea Devil's Fore-Castles by Lowell Thomas; A Boy Scout with the Sea-Devil, by David Martin; Out of an Old Sea Chest, by Edward Fitzgerald. *Recreations:* yachting and fishing on board his four-mast schooner Mopelia. *Address:* (Private) Jungfrauental 26, Hamburg; (Office; Manager) Frau Lindemann Kulturarchiv, Radekoppel 33, Hamburg Lemashl. *Clubs:* Hon. member of over 100 clubs, fraternities, and social organisations. [*Died* 13 *April* 1966.

LUCY, Capt. Sir Montgomerie R. F.; *see* Fairfax-Lucy, Capt. Sir H. M. R.

LUFF, Richard Edmund Relfe, C.B.E. 1946; formerly Joint Managing Director and Treasurer Cable & Wireless (Holding) Ltd., and associated companies; retired; *b.* 1887; *s.* of late Richard J. Luff, Croydon; *m.* 1930, Marjorie, *d.* of late Rev. H. H. Gibbon, vicar of Glasbury-on-Wye; one *d.* *Educ.:* Cranbrook School; Univ. Coll., London. LL.B.; chartered accountant on staff of Deloitte, Plender, Griffiths & Co., 1918; Eastern Telegraph Co. 1926; Cable and Wireless Ltd., 1929. *Address:* Lockets, Shamley Green, near Guildford, Surrey. [*Died* 25 *Aug.* 1969.

LUKE, Sir Harry (Charles), K.C.M.G., *cr.* 1939 (C.M.G. 1926); Kt. *cr.* 1933; M.A.; D.Litt. Oxon; Hon. LL.D. Malta; Bailiff of Egle and Bailiff Grand Cross, Order of St. John of Jerusalem; Grand Officer of Merit, Sovereign Military Order of Malta; *b.* London, December 1884; *o. s.* of late J. H. Luke, London; *m.* 1918, Joyce (from whom he obtained a divorce, 1949), *d.* of late Capt. J. L. Fremlin; two *s.* *Educ.:* Eton; Trinity College, Oxford (Hon. Fellow, 1952). Private Sec. and A.D.C. to the Governor of Sierra Leone, 1908-11 and to the Governor of Barbados, 1911; attached to Colonial Office, 1911 (Coronation Medals, 1911, 1937, 1953); Private Sec. to High Commissioner of Cyprus, 1911-12; Asst. Sec. to Govt. of Cyprus, 1912; Comr. of Famagusta, Cyprus, 1918; 2nd Lt. 2nd Co. of London Yeo. 1909-1911; served European War (Commander, R.N.V.R.), on Syrian Coast, 1914-15, on Staff of Admiral Sir Rosslyn Wemyss, Dardanelles, and as Government Sec., Mudros, February 1915-June 1916; Italian medal for military valour; Political Officer to Admiral of the Fleet Sir J. de Robeck, Constantinople and Black Sea, 1919-20; British Chief Commissioner in Georgia, Armenia and Azerbaijan, April-Sept. 1920; Assistant Governor of Jerusalem, 1920-24; a Commissioner to inquire into the Jaffa Riots of 1921 and into the affairs of the Orthodox Patriarchate of Jerusalem, 1921; Colonial Secretary of Sierra Leone, 1924-28; Chief Secretary of Palestine, 1928-30; Lieut.-Governor of Malta, 1930-38; Governor and Commander-in-Chief of Fiji and High Commissioner for the Western Pacific, 1938-42; Chief Rep. of the British Council in the Caribbean, 1943-46; Mem. of Foreign Relations Council of Ch. of England (and Chm. of its Oriental Churches Cttee.); Chm. Nikaean Club; President Malta League, 1955-1965; Member Council: British Commonwealth Ex-Services League; Hakluyt Soc.; occasional broadcaster and lecturer. *Publications:* The Fringe of the East, 1913; The City of Dancing Dervishes, 1914; Cyprus under the Turks, 1921 (2nd edn. 1969); Anatolica, 1924; Mosul and its Minorities, 1925; Prophets, Priests and Patriarchs, 1927; In the Margin of History, 1933; An Eastern Chequerboard, 1934; More Moves on an Eastern Chequerboard, 1935; The Making of Modern Turkey, 1936 (revised as The Old Turkey and the New, 1955); From a South Seas Diary, 1945; Malta 1949 (rev. enlarged edn. 1960); Caribbean Circuit, 1950; Cities and Men (an Autobiography), Vols. I and II, 1953, Vol. III 1956; Queen Salote and Her Kingdom, 1954; The Tenth Muse: an unconventional Book of Cookery, 1954 (rev. enlarged edition 1962); Cyprus: A Portrait and an Appreciation, 1957 (revised enlarged edition 1965); Islands of the South Pacific, 1962; ed. Sir George Hill's History of Cyprus, vol. iv, 1952. *Recreations:* formerly squash racquets; swimming; listening to music; has travelled widely in all continents (visited Easter Island and Juan Fernandez, 1952, Nepal and Sikkim, 1965). *Address:* 8 Bedford Gardens House, Bedford Gardens, W.8. *Clubs:* Athenæum, St. James'. [*Died* 11 *May* 1969.

LUKIS, Maj.-Gen. Wilfrid Boyd Fellowes, C.B.E. 1943; Maj.-Gen., Royal Marines, retd.; *b.* 24 Feb. 1896; *s.* of W. R. F. Lukis; *m.* 1922, Grace Holmes Simpson; one *s.* one *d.* *Educ.:* Switzerland. Prob. 2nd Lieut., 1913; Bt. Lt.-Col., 1937; Act. Maj.-Gen., 1943; G.O.C. Royal Marines M.N.B.D.O.I.; Maj.-Gen., 1945; G.O.C. Royal Marine Engineers.; retired 1946. *Address:* Scott's Paddock, Meonstoke, Hants. *Club:* Royal Naval (Portsmouth).
[*Died* 11 *Jan.* 1969.

LULING, Mrs. Peter; *see* Thompson, Sylvia.

LUMLEY, Sir Dudley (Owen), K.B.E. *cr.* 1953 (O.B.E. 1919; M.B.E. 1918); C.B. 1948; *b.* 6 March 1895; *s.* of late Edward Warner and late Theodora Algehr Lumley, Surbiton; unmarried. *Educ.:* Sherborne School; Selwyn College, Cambridge. Served European War, August 1914, 5th Wiltshire Regiment. Entered General Post Office, 1919. Private Sec. to Permanent Sec., G.P.O., 1922-27; Principal, 1927; i.d.c., 1932; Asst. Sec. G.P.O., 1937; Dep. Regional Director. Midland Region, 1939; Regional Director, Midland Region, 1944; Regional Director, London Postal Region, 1947; Director of Establishments and Organisation, G.P.O., 1949-52. Dep. Dir. Gen., G.P.O., 1952-55, retired. *Address:* 12 Littlemoor Road, Preston, Weymouth. *T.:* Preston (Dorset) 3166. *Club:* Junior Army and Navy.
[*Died* 23 *March* 1964.

LUMLEY-SMITH, Major Sir Thomas (Gabriel Lumley), Kt., *cr.* 1937; D.S.O. 1918; F.S.A.; Knight of Justice of the Order of St. John of Jerusalem; one of H.M.'s Lieuts. for City of London; *b.* 27 Oct. 1879; *o. s.* of late Sir Lumley Smith, K.C., Judge of City of London and Central Criminal Courts, 1901-13, and Jessie, *d.* of late Sir Thomas Gabriel, Bt.; *m.* 1st, 1911, Gwendolen (*d.* 1944), *y. d.* of late Charles Edward Coles, C.M.G., Pasha; two *s.* (one *d.* decd.); 2nd, 1946, Helen, O.St.J., *o. d.* of Hubert Blenkinsopp Coulson. *Educ.:* Eton; Trinity Coll., Cambridge. Received commission in 21st Lancers, 1900; served in Egypt and Gallipoli, 1915; in France and Belgium, 1916-19, with 3rd Division and Cavalry Corps (despatches twice, D.S.O.); Member of Council and Hon. Registrar, Imperial Society of Knights Bachelor; Grand Sec. of Mark Master Masons, 1923-55. *Address:* Kintbury Lodge, Kintbury, Berks. *T.:* 279. *Clubs:* Boodle's, Cavalry.
[*Died* 16 *Feb.* 1961.

LUMSDEN, Colonel Bruce (John David), C.B.E. 1958 (O.B.E. 1944); Royal Marines; Comdt. United Service Corps of Commissionaires, since 1958; Director: Pimms Ltd.; H. D. Davies and Co. Ltd.; Express Travel and Transport Co.; *b.* 23 July 1907; *s.* of late Colonel Henry Richmond William Lumsden and Ethel Gordon Davies; *m.* 1935, Betty Leida Lillian, *d.* of J. Holman Andrew, Plympton, S. Devon; one *s.* *Educ.:* Cheltenham College. Cadet, R.N., H.M.S. Thunderer, 1925; 2nd Lt. R.M., 1926; various courses to 1929; H.M.S. Valiant, 1930; H.M.S. Cornwall, China Stn., 1931; Phys. Trg. Officer, Plymouth Div. R.M., 1932-35; Capt. 1937; H.M.S. Sussex, Medit. Stn., 1937-39. Served War of 1939-45: Adjt. Chatham Div. R.M., 1939-40, R.M. Div. 1940-42 (Bt. Maj. 1941); A/Lt.-Col. 1942; C.O. 41st Commando R.M., Sicily and Salerno, 1943; Maj. 1943; A/Col. 1944; Brit. Combined Ops. Rep. with U.S. Amphibious Forces, Pacific, 1944-45. Staff of Combined Chiefs of Staff, Washington, D.C., as Chief of Combined Ops. Rep., 1945-47; War Office Observer, Bikini Atomic Bomb Tests, 1946; Lt.-Col. 1948. Raised R.M. Forces Vol. Reserve, 1948; C.O. 40th Commando, Hong Kong and Malaya, 1949-52; Fleet R.M. Officer, Home Fleet; H.M.S. Vanguard, 1953-55; Col. 1955; C.O. Depot R.M. and Comdt. R.M. School of Music, Deal, 1955-57; retd. pay, 1958. Common Cryer and Serjeant-At-Arms City of London, 1958; Swordbearer to the Lord Mayor of London, 1959-61. Hon. Col. R.M.F.V.R. (City of London) 1961-. *Recreations:* fishing, motoring, travel. *Address:* 1 Pelham Place, S.W.7. *T.:* Kensington 5080. *Club:* White's.
[*Died* 30 *April* 1965.

LUMSDEN, Sir James Robert, Kt. 1962; C.B.E. 1947; D.L.: *b.* 29 Sept. 1884; *s.* of James Lumsden, Arden, and Susan Campbell Mackenzie, *d.* of R. D. Mackenzie, of Caldarvan; *m.* 1914, Henrietta Macfarlane Reid, *d.* of George Macfarlane Reid, Prestwick; two *s.* *Educ.:* Fettes Coll., Edinburgh. Qualified C.A., 1903; practised in Glasgow firm Harvey & Lumsden, C.A.; retd., 1960. D.L. Dunbartonshire, 1930. *Recreations:* shooting, fishing. *Address:* Arden House, Arden, Alexandria, Dunbartonshire. *T.:* Arden 213. *Club:* New (Edinburgh).
[*Died* 30 *Oct.* 1970.

LUSHINGTON, Maj.-Gen. Godfrey E. W.; *see* Wildman-Lushington.

LUSHINGTON, Sir Herbert Castleman, 6th Bt., *cr.* 1791; *b.* 15 Sept. 1879; *s.* of late Algernon Hay Lushington and Emma Jane, *d.* of late Charles Castleman; *S.* cousin, 1937; *m.* 1st, 1908, Barbara Henrietta (*d.* 1927), *d.* of late Rev. William Greville Hazlerigg; three *s.*; 2nd, 1928, Roselia May, *d.* of Dr. Ernest Edward Elliot; one *s.* one *d.* *Heir:* *s.* Henry Edmund Castleman Lushington, Flt. Lt., R.A.F.V.R. [*b.* 2 May 1909; *m.* 1937, Pamela Elizabeth Daphne, *er. d.* of Major Archer R. Hunter, Hare Hatch Grange, Twyford, Berks; one *s.* two *d.*]. *Address:* Harrocks, Salt Hill, near Chichester.
[*Died* 5 *Oct.* 1968.

LUTHULI, Albert John; African liberation leader; former Zulu chieftain; teacher; elected Lord Rector of Glasgow University, 1962 (but has not yet been able to come to Scotland); *b.* 1899; *m.* 1927, Nokukanya; two *s.* five *d.* *Educ.:* Adams Mission Station College, Durban. Instructor, Adams College, 1921-36. Chieftain of Abasemakholweni tribe, Groutville, 1936, deposed by South African Government, 1952. President-General, African National Congress, 1952- (Mem., 1946-). Has been detained in South Africa and has had many political bans imposed against him by the Government; restricted to an area in Natal, 1961 and for a further 5 years, 1964. Nobel Prize for Peace, 1960 (accepted, 1961). United Nations Human Rights Prize, 1968. *Publication:* Let My People Go—an Autobiography, 1962. *Address:* Groutville, Umvoti Mission Reserve, Natal, South Africa.
[*Died* 21 *July* 1967.

LUTYENS, Lady Emily; author; *b.* 26 December 1874; 3rd *d.* of 1st Earl of Lytton, P.C., G.C.B., G.C.S.I., C.I.E.; *m.* 1897, Sir Edwin Lutyens, O.M., K.C.I.E., P.R.A., F.S.A., LL.D., D.C.L. (*d.* 1944); one *s.* four *d.* *Educ.:* at home. *Publications:* A Blessed Girl, 1953; The Birth of Rowland, 1956; Candles in the Sun, 1957. *Address:* 2 Hyde Park Street, W.2. [*Died* 3 *Jan.* 1964.

LUXTON, Rt. Rev. George Nasmith, D.D.; Bishop of Huron since 1948; *b.* 13 Aug. 1901; *s.* of Arthur G. H. Luxton and Margaret (*née* Gruer); *m.* 1929, Dorothy Catherine, *o. d.* of D'Arcy Martin, K.C., Hamilton, Ontario; three *s.* *Educ.:* University of Toronto; Trinity College, Toronto. D.D. (Trinity, Toronto), 1943; LL.D. (Western, London, Ont.), 1950. Deacon, 1924; priest, 1925; St. Patrick's Church, Guelph, Ont., 1923-25; Curate, Christ Church Cathedral, Hamilton, Ont., 1925-29; Rector: Christ Church, Calgary, Alta., 1929-33; St. George's, St. Catherine's, Ontario, 1933-39; Grace Church on the Hill, Toronto, Ont., 1939-43; Dean of Huron, 1943-48. *Address:* Bishopstowe, London, Ontario, Canada. [*Died* 2 *Oct.* 1970.

LYAL, David Hume, C.B. 1954; C.M.G. 1942; M.B.E.; *b.* 20 June 1892; *s.* of late George Lyal; *m.* 1918, Margaret, *d.* of Dr. John Cross. *Educ.:* King Edward's, Birmingham. Department of Overseas Trade; formerly Under Secretary, Board of Trade; Commissioned, 1916; Lieut. (acting Captain and Adjutant) 12th London Regiment,

1918. *Recreations:* tennis, golf. *Address:* Cluny, Baldslow Down, St. Leonards-on-Sea, Sussex. *T.:* Hastings 51274. [*Died* 6 *May* 1965.

LYALL, Archibald Laurence; *b.* 1904; *s.* of late G. H. H. Lyall and of late Dame Beatrix Lyall, D.B.E., J.P.; *m.* 1948, Diodata Hawkins (marriage dissolved, 1956), *d.* of late Count Caboga, Dubrovnik. *Educ.:* Winchester College; New College, Oxford (B.A.). Called to Bar, Lincoln's Inn, 1930. Attaché H.M. Legation, Belgrade, 1940-41; served in Intelligence Corps, Middle East, Italy and Austria, 1941-1947; demobilised with rank of Lt.-Col.; Chairman of Extradition Tribunal, British Zone of Germany, 1948; Head of British Element, Allied Information Services, Free Territory of Trieste, 1948-50; Director of Public Information Office, Allied Military Government, British/U.S. Zone, Free Territory of Trieste, 1950-51. Has acted in a number of American and Continental films. *Publications:* It Isn't Done; The Balkan Road, 1930; A Guide to the Languages of Europe; Envoy Extraordinary, a novel, 1932; Russian Roundabout, 1933; The Future of Taboo among the British Islanders, 1936; Black and White Make Brown, 1938; Soldier's Speakeasy, 1940; Rome, Sweet Rome, 1956; Well Met in Madrid, 1960; A Companion Guide to the South of France, 1963. *Clubs:* Oxford and Cambridge, St. James'. [*Died* 25 *Feb.* 1964.

LYDDON, Vice-Adm. Sir Horace (Collier), K.B.E. 1967 (O.B.E. 1953); C.B. 1964; Admiral President, Royal Naval College, Greenwich, since 1967; Chief Naval Supply and Secretariat Officer since 1964; *b.* 28 Sept. 1912; *s.* of late William James Lyddon, Plymouth, Devon; *m.* 1939, Dorothy Ida Oates; two *s.* *Educ.:* Plymouth Coll. Entered R.N., 1930. Dep. Sec. to C.-in-C. Eastern Fleet, 1942-44; Sec. to Adm. Sir Harold Walker, 5th Cruiser Sqdn., 1944-45, 3rd Battle Sqdn. 1945; Naval Forces, Germany, 1946-48; Sec. to Adm. Hon. Sir Cyril Douglas Pennant, 2nd i/c Mediterranean, 1949-50; B.N.S., Washington, 1950-52; C.-in-C., Nore, 1952-53; Exec. Asst. to Dep. S.A.C.L.A.N.T., 1954-56; Comdg. Officer, H.M.S. Phœnicia, 1958-60; Director of Service Conditions, Admty., 1960-62; Rear-Adm. (Personnel), Naval Air Comd., 1962-64; Director-General of Naval Manpower, 1964-1967. *Recreations:* Rugby football, athletics. *Address:* President's House, Royal Naval College, Greenwich. *Club:* Army and Navy. [*Died* 9 *June* 1968.

LYLE, Sir Oliver, Kt., *cr.* 1954; O.B.E. 1919; Managing Director, Tate & Lyle Ltd., since 1919; a Vice-Chairman Tate & Lyle Ltd., Tate & Lyle Investment, and Silvertown Services, since 1958; *b.* 22 Dec. 1890; 2nd *s.* of John Lyle, Finnart House, Weybridge; *m.* 1914, Lilian Isabel, *o. d.* of Charles Spicer, Weybridge; one *s.* three *d.* (and one *d.* decd.). *Educ.:* Uppingham; University of London. Served European War, 1914-18, Capt. H.L.I. (despatches twice, wounded); Inventions Dept., Ministry of Munitions, 1916-18. Sugar Refiner, 1911-. F.Inst.F. *Publications:* The Efficient Use of Steam, 1947 (Govt. publication); Technology for Sugar Refinery Workers, 1941, 3rd edn. 1957. *Address:* Shorehill, Kemsing, Kent. *T.:* Sevenoaks 61030. [*Died* 21 *Feb.* 1961.

LYLE, Robert, B.L. (Glas.); Town Clerk of Dundee since 1949; *b.* 19 Sept. 1905; *s.* of Robert Lyle and Mary Morrison; *m.* 1936, Helen M., M.A. (Hons.), *e. d.* of Daniel Fisher, Bathgate; three *s.* one *d.* *Educ.:* The Academy, Hamilton. Principal Assistant to Co. Clerk, West Lothian, 1930-32; Depute Town Clerk of Ayr, 1933-40; Town Clerk of Falkirk, 1940-49. *Recreations:* fishing and golf. *Address:* Selbie Lodge, Fairfield Rd., Broughty Ferry; City Chambers, Dundee. *T.:* 23141. *Club:* Golfers' (London). [*Died* 21 *Jan.* 1966.

LYLE, Thomas McElderry, C.S.I. 1941; C.I.E. 1928; B.E.; A.R.C.Sc.I.; I.S.E.; retired Chief Engineer, Irrigation Works, and late Secretary to Government United Provinces, India; *b.* 24 May 1886; 2nd *surv. s.* of late Rev. Thomas Lyle, M.A., Dublin; *m.* 1922, Mary Stewart, *e. d.* of Alexander Forsyth, of St. Catherine's Park, Leixlip, County Kildare. *Educ.:* St. Andrew's College, Dublin; Royal College of Science, Ireland; Queen's College, Belfast; Royal Univ. of Ireland. Graduated in Royal College of Science, 1906, with first place and also in the Royal University of Ireland, 1908, with first place and first class Hons. Served in the Engineering Department of L.C.C., 1908-09; appointed to the Indian Service of Engineers, 1909; employed on design and construction of various large hydraulic works, including The Sarda Canal Barrage and head reaches of the canal, 1921-29; also in charge of hydro-electric surveys U.P.; on military service in Waziristan, N.W.F., and in Persia with the Bushire Field Force, and in the Khyber Pass in the third Afghan War, 1918-19 (despatches, Bushire Field Force, 1919); Superintending Engineer, Irrigation Works, 1931-36; Chief Engineer to Govt. U.P., 1936-1941; Chairman Ganges River Inter-Provincial Flood Committee, 1939-41; Vice-President Central Board of Irrigation, India, 1940; Wheat Commr. and Sec. to Govt., U.P., in Price Control Dept., 1941-42; Adviser to Govt. of Ceylon on Reorganisation of Irrigation Dept., 1951-52. F.R.S.A., 1953. *Address:* Marshfield, Leixlip, Co. Kildare, Ireland. [*Died* 2 *Sept.* 1962.

LYNCH, Finian; Circuit Judge of North-West Circuit; Barrister-at-law; *s.* of late Finian Lynch of Kilmakerim, Caherciveen, Co. Kerry; *b.* 17 March 1889; *m.* 1919, Brighid, *d.* of Thomas Slattery, Tralee; six *s.* one *d.* *Educ.:* Rockwell and Blackrock Colls.; Nat. Univ., Dublin (B.A., Higher Diploma in Education). M.P. (S.F.) South Kerry, Dec. 1918-22; Member of Dáil Eireann, Cos. Kerry and West Limerick, 1921-23; Co. Kerry, 1923-1937; South Kerry, 1937-44; Minister of Education, Provisional Government, 1921-22; Minister of Fisheries, 1922-28; Minister for Lands and Fisheries, 1928-32; Deputy-Speaker, Dáil Eireann, 1938-39. *Address:* 44 South Hill, Dartry, Dublin 6. [*Died* 3 *June* 1966.

LYNCH, Capt. Vincent James, C.M.G. 1946; M.C. (and Bar); Barrister-at-Law, King's Inns, Dublin; Munster Circuit; *b.* 18 April 1892; *m.* 1926, Dorothy Smye. *Educ.:* Christian Coll., Cork; Univ. Coll., Cork. Royal Irish Fusiliers, 1914-20; Colonial Administrative Service, 1920-46; Under-Secretary, Gold Coast Government, 1942-46; acted as Colonial Secretary, Gold Coast Colony, 1943 and 1945. *Address:* Knockrobin, Kinsale, Co. Cork, Ireland. *Club:* Cork and County. *T.:* Cork 20836 and Kinsale 81. [*Died* 28 *March* 1961.

LYNCH-BLOSSE, Sir Henry, 15th Bt., *cr.* 1622; Retired Mining Engineer; *b.* 29 Oct. 1884; *s.* of Captain Edward Falconer Lynch-Blosse (*d.* 1926) and Edith Caroline (*d.* 1953), *d.* of Rev. George Alfred Walker; *S.* cousin, 1963; *m.* 1914, Cicely Edith, *d.* of late Francis Thomas Bircham, Gwentland, Chepstow, Monmouthshire; two *d.* *Educ.:* Repton. Former Lt. 7th Bn., Welch Regiment. Served European War, 1915-19, Royal Engineers (Captain). *Recreations:* golf, fishing. *Heir:* *nephew* David Edward Lynch-Blosse [*b.* 24 November 1925; *m.* 1950, Elizabeth, *er. d.* of Thomas Harold Payne, Welwyn Garden City; one *s.* two *d.*].

Address: Little Rainham, Southgate, Swansea, South Wales. *T.:* Southgate 350. [*Died* 17 *May* 1969.

LYNCH-BLOSSE, Sir Robert G.; *see* Blosse.

LYNE, Maj.-Gen. Lewis Owen, C.B. 1945; D.S.O. 1943; Chairman Executive Committee, U.N.A., 1951-57, Joint President, U.N.A., 1957; Chairman: The Manchester Oil Refinery (Holdings) Ltd., 1961-66; Petrocarbon Developments Ltd., 1960-68; Director, Lobitos Oilfields Ltd., 1963-66; Chm. Board of Governors, Moor Park College, 1954-60; President, The Knights' Association of Youth Clubs, 1946-69; *b.* 19 Aug. 1899; 2nd *s.* of Charles Lyne, Newport, Monmouthshire; unmarried. *Educ.*: Haileybury; R.M.C. Sandhurst. 2nd Lieutenant Lancs Fusiliers, 1921; Brevet Major, 1938; Brevet Lieut.-Colonel, 1939; Subst. Colonel, 1942; Acting Major-General, 1944; Maj.-Gen. 1946; served with 1st Bn. Lancs Fusiliers, 1921-38, in Ireland, England, Gibraltar, Egypt and N. China; p.s.c. 1936; staff appts. War Office, 1938-40; commanded 9th Bn. Lancs Fusiliers, 1940; Chief Instructor, Senior Officers' School, 1941; commanded 169 Inf. Bde. in England, Iraq, N. Africa and Italy, 1942-44; commanded 59 (Staffordshire) Division, 50th (Northumbrian) Division and 7th Armoured Div. in N.W. Europe (despatches, immediate D.S.O., C.B., French Legion of Honour, Officer, French Croix de Guerre). Military Governor, British Zone, Berlin, 1945; late Director of Staff Duties, War Office; retired, 1949. Pres. Haileybury Society, 1957-58. Pres., The British Diabetic Assoc., 1963. Russian Order of Kutuzov, 1st class, 1945. Liveryman Glaziers' Company, 1949. *Recreation:* travelling. *Address:* The Corner House, Kersey, Suffolk. *T.:* Hadleigh 3247. *Club:* Army and Navy. [*Died* 4 *Nov.* 1970.

LYNE, Robert Nunez, F.L.S., F.R.G.S.; retired; Brilliant Star of Zanzibar; *b.* 8 Aug. 1864; *s.* of De Castro F. Lyne, J.P., Barrister-at-law, late of Steartfield, Paignton; *m.* Hilda (*d.* 1935), *d.* of late David Bailey, Gymnastic Staff, 1st Life Guards. *Educ.:* Bloxham; Canterbury Agricultural College, University of New Zealand. Director of Agriculture, Zanzibar, 1896; reported on the Agricultural Prospects of the Plateaux of the Uganda Railway for the Commissioner of British East Africa, 1902; appointed to the British Committee of Tropical Agriculture and Colonial Development, 1909; Services lent to the Portuguese Government, to reorganise Department of Agriculture, Mozambique, and appointed Director of Agriculture of that Province, 1910; Director of Agriculture, Ceylon, 1912; founder and first Principal of School of Agriculture, Ceylon; nominated Ceylon Commissioner to the Fourth International Rubber and Allied Industries Exhibition, London, 1914. *Publications:* various reports on the Agriculture of Zanzibar, British East Africa, Portuguese East Africa, and Ceylon; Zanzibar in Contemporary Times, 1905; Mozambique: its Agricultural Development, 1913; Church of St. Peter in the East, Oxford, 1933 4th ed. 1936; An Apostle of Empire: The Life of Sir Lloyd William Mathews, 1936; Four Bishops, 1945; The Chathams in the Eighteen Eighties, 1958; East African Waters, 1959. Editor of The Tropical Agriculturist, 1912-16. *Recreations:* writing, astronomy. *Address:* 5 Beaufort East, Bath. *T.:* Bath 2100. [*Died* 21 *June* 1961.

LYNN, Col. Graham Rigby, C.B.E. 1941; D.S.O. 1917; Indian Medical Service, retired; *s.* of Graham Rigby and Jessie Lynn; *m.* 1925, Anna Marjorie Norman Ballantyne; two *s.* (and one *s.* decd.). *Educ.:* Tonbridge School; St. Bartholomew's Hospital. Entered Indian Medical Service, 1909; Captain, 1912; Major, 1921; Lt.-Col., 1929; Col. 1937; served European War, 1914-18 (despatches, D.S.O.); retired, 1938; served India, Middle East, Eritrea, 1939-45 (C.B.E.). *Recreation:* accepting geriatrism. *Address:* c/o Lloyds Bank Ltd., 6 Pall Mall, S.W.1. [*Died* 8 *Jan.* 1966.

LYNN, Ralph; actor; *b.* Manchester, 18 March 1882; *m.* Gladys Miles; one *s.* one *d.* First appearance on stage, Wigan, 1900; played in provinces and in America; first London appearance at the Empire in By Jingo, If We Do, 1914; in Hanky-Panky (the Empire), 1917; in various comedies in West End, 1918-22; Allington in Tons of Money (Shaftesbury), 1922-24; in a series of successes at the Aldwych, It Pays to Advertise, 1924; A Cuckoo in the Nest, 1925; Rookery Nook, 1926; Thark, 1927; Plunder, 1928; A Cup of Kindness, 1929; A Night Like This, 1930; Turkey Time, 1931; Wild Horses, 1952; The Party Spirit, Piccadilly, 1954; entered films, 1929; and has appeared in, among others, Rookery Nook, Tons of Money, Plunder, Summer Lightning, A Cuckoo in the Nest, A Cup of Kindness, Foreign Affaires, For Valour, Thark. Started on scheme to build theatre at Brighton, 1938. *Clubs:* Green Room, Stage Golfing Society. [*Died* 8 *Aug.* 1962.

LYON, Hon. Sir David B.; *see* Bowes-Lyon.

LYON, Malcolm Douglas; *b.* 22 April 1898; *s.* of Jeremiah Malcolm Lyon and Maria Soper; *m.* 1st. 1927, Helen Alice Elliot; 2nd, 1941, Doreen Healey; four *s.* three *d.* *Educ.:* Rugby School; Trinity College, Cambridge. 2nd Lt. R.F.A.; served European War, France, 1917-18. M.A., LL.B.; Cricket Blue; Pres. Footlights Dramatic Club, 1919-22; Cricket for Somerset, Cambridge, Gentlemen, and in Test Trials, 1920-31. Read for Bar and under contract to Charlot to write music for *revues intimes* at Vaudeville and Prince of Wales theatres, 1922-25; called to Bar, 1925; practised London, S.E. Circuit, and Essex and Herts Sessions, 1925-32. Magistrate, Gambia, 1932-35; Resident Magistrate, Tanganyika, 1935-38. D.A.A.G., A.G.6 War Office, 1939-41; commanded L.A.A. Regt., R.A., 1941-45. Resident Magistrate, Kenya, 1945-1948; Chief Justice, Seychelles, 1948-57; Puisne Judge, Uganda, 1957-61; retd. on pension, Oct. 1961. Contested (L.) West Suffolk, 1929. *Publications:* A Village Match and After; Cricket. Songs: Girls of the Old Brigade (B. Lillie); Lazy Melody (Blaney and Farrar), etc. *Recreations:* fishing, music, lawn tennis. *Clubs:* Reform, M.C.C., Royal Commonwealth Society. [*Died* 17 *Feb.* 1964.

LYON, Ursula Mary; *d.* of late Captain Pender, R.N.; *m.* 1908, Massey David E. G. Lyon, *s.* of late Edmund David Lyon, Captain, 68th Durham Light Infantry. *Educ.:* Wimbledon High School; privately. Journalist contributing to The Queen, Ladies Field, etc., since 1905; personal assistant to Editress (not editor) of The Queen, 1908; Editress (not Editor), 1916; resigned, 1924; regular contributor Daily Telegraph, 1924-29; Eve, 1925; Woman's Magazine, Times, Evening News, etc.; served on various committees, 1914-18; mentioned in despatches for service under D.G.V.O. (War Office), 1917; Chairman of various committees of Representative Women convened for special purposes; member of Executive Committee British Women's Patriotic League since 1915; Chairman, 1931-36; Vice-Chairman, Society of Women Journalists, 1927, Chairman, 1929-37, Vice-President, 1937; Hon. Governor of Middlesex Hospital in recognition of services, 1917; Member Royal Institute of Public Health, 1926; Council of Royal Society of St. George, 1937; and of Royal Society for the Prevention of Accidents, 1938; received Order of Mercy, 1916. *Publica-*

tions: Etiquette: A Guide to Public and Social Life, 1927; Mother and Child, 1928. *Recreations:* reading, fine needlework. *Address:* c/o Glyn, Mills & Co., Kirkland House, Whitehall, S.W.1. [*Died* 29 *Nov.* 1961.

LYON, Ven. William John; Archdeacon of Loughborough, 1940-53; Archdeacon Emeritus, since 1953; Hon. Canon of Leicester, 1935-40, Canon Theologian, 1940-58; *b.* 16 Jan. 1883; *s.* of George Hodgson and Susan Lyon; *m.* 1915, Mary Matilda Rodd (*d.* 1953); one *s.* one *d.* *Educ.:* Norwich Cathedral School; Emmanuel College, Cambridge; Ridley Hall, Cambridge. Carus Greek Testament Prize, 1909; Curate of S. George, E. Stonehouse, 1911-13; S. Andrew, Plymouth, 1913-15; Curate in Charge of S. Andrew, Bournemouth, 1915-19; Vicar of S. Andrew, Bournemouth, 1919-26; Rector of Sutton Coldfield, 1926-31; Rector of Handsworth, Birmingham, 1931-35; Hon. Chaplain to Bishop of Birmingham, 1927-28; Hon. Canon of Birmingham, 1928-35; Rector of Loughborough, 1935-58. *Address:* Brent Pelham Vicarage, Buntingford, Herts. *T.:* Brent Pelham 392. [*Died* 18 *March* 1961.

LYONS, Abraham Montagu, Q.C. 1933; Recorder of Great Grimsby since 1936; Leader of the Midland Circuit; Member, General Council of the Bar; *b.* Lincoln, 1894; *o. s.* of late R. and Mrs. R. Lyons, West Bridgford, Notts; unmarried. *Educ.:* Old Clee Grammar School, Lincs. Served in Army, 1914-16; Capt. and Staff Capt. 1940; Major and D.A.D. War Office, 1941; Col. 1944. Called to Bar, Middle Temple, 1922; M.P. (C.) East Leicester, 1931-45; contested (C.) Clay Cross Division of Derbyshire, 1929, East Leicester, 1945; travelled extensively Africa, Canada, and U.S.A. Member Court of Worshipful Company of Pattenmakers (Master, 1959, 1960). *Publications:* Canadian press series and miscellaneous articles. *Recreation:* golf. *Address:* 1 Pump Court, Temple, E.C.4. *T.:* Central 4122, City 5110. *Clubs:* Royal Automobile, Press, Unionist, 1900. [*Died* 29 *Nov.* 1961.

LYONS, Mrs. Miriam Isabel, CB.E 1919; *b.* Belfast, 1880; *d.* of W. R Nelson, linen manufacturer, Belfast; *m.* 1900, Major-General R. W. S. Lyons, Indian Medical Service, retired one *s.* three *d.* (and one *d.* decd.). President Poona Women's Branch of War and Relief Fund, Bombay, during European War. *Address:* Shierglas, Fleet, Hants. [*Died* 14 *March* 1968.

LYONS, Most Rev. Patrick Francis, D.D. (University of Propaganda Fide, Rome), 1927; Bishop of Sale since 1957; *b.* North Melbourne (Australia), 6 January 1903; *s.* of Patrick Joseph Lyons and Catherine Cecilia McMahon. *Educ.:* Sisters of Mercy School, North Melbourne (Australia); Christian Brothers' School, West Melbourne; Christian Brothers' College, North Melbourne. Matriculated (University, Melbourne) Dec. 1917; Public Service (Navy Dept., Melbourne), 1918-22; Ecclesiastical studies: St. Columba's College, Springwood, N.S.W.; St. Patrick's College, Manly, N.S.W.; Pontifical Urban College of Propaganda Fide, Rome, 1923-27. Ordained Priest, Rome, 1927; Curate in Archdiocese of Melbourne, 1927-34 (Collingwood, Geelong, and Brunswick); appointed to St. Patrick's Cathedral, 1934; Administrator at Cathedral, Chancellor of Archdiocese, Secretary to Archbishop Mannix, and Diocesan Consultor, 1938-44; also Vicar-Gen., 1939-44; Bishop of Christchurch, New Zealand, 1944-50; Auxiliary Bishop to Cardinal Gilroy, Sydney, Australia, 1950-56; in 1956 translated to Sale, Victoria, Australia, as Coadjutor Bishop with right of succession as Bishop of Sale; succeeded to See, 16 June 1957. *Address:* Bishop's House, Sale, Victoria, Australia. [*Died* 13 *Aug.* 1967.

LYSAGHT, Desmond Royse; *b.* 22 April 1903; *s.* of late W. R. Lysaght, C.B.E.; *m.* 1955, Jacqueline Mary, *d.* of late Major J. H. Whitehead, O.B.E., Minehead, Somerset. *Educ.:* Eton; Christ Church, Oxford. High Sheriff of Monmouthshire, 1942. Chairman, Chepstow Racecourse Co., 1945-64. *Recreations:* racing, travel, ornithology. *Address:* Dennel Hill, Chepstow, Mon. *T.:* 2056. [*Died* 1 *Jan.* 1970.

LYTTELTON, Hon. George William; late Assistant Master, Eton College; *b.* of 9th Viscount Cobham, K.C.B.; *b.* 6 Jan. 1883; *m.* 1919, Pamela Marie, *d.* of late Charles Adeane, C.B.; one *s.* four *d.* *Educ.:* Eton; Trinity College, Cambridge. *Address:* Finndale House, Grundisburgh, Suffolk. [*Died* 1 *May* 1962.

LYVEDEN, 4th Baron (*cr.* 1859), **Robert Fitzpatrick Courtenay Vernon;** *b.* 1 Feb. 1892; *e. s.* of 3rd Baron and Fanny Zelie (*d.* 1924), *d.* of Major Hill of Wollaston Hall, Wellingboro; *S.* father, 1926; *m.* 1949, Doris Violet, *widow* of Capt. Eric Paterson. *Educ.:* Harrow. *Heir:* kinsman, Sydney Munro Vernon [*b.* 21 Nov. 1888; *m.* (wife decd.); one *s.* four *d.*]. *Address:* Hunnersley, Burley, Ringwood, Hants. [*Died* 9 *Jan.* 1969.

M

MAAS, Paul, Dr. phil. (Munich); M.A. (Oxon); Hon. D.Litt. (Oxon.), 1959; Emeritus University Professor, Federal Republic of Germany; *b.* 18 November 1880; *s.* of Dr.iur. Maximilian Maas and Henriette Oppenheimer-Prins; *m.* 1909, Karen Raeder (*d.* 1960); three *d.* (one *s.* decd.). *Educ.:* Frankfort on Main; Freiburg, Baden; Universities of Berlin and Munich. Privatdozent, Univ. of Berlin, 1910; Professor Extraordinarius, Berlin, 1920; Professor Ordinarius, Königsberg, Prussia, 1930-1934. Life member of Balliol College, 1948; corresp. Fellow of The British Academy, 1941; Corresp. Mem. Deutsche Akademie der Wissenschaften, Berlin, 1955. Kt. Comdr., Royal Order of King George I, 1962; Knight's Cross of Order of Merit, West German Federal Republic, 1963. *Publications:* Griechische Metrik (Teubner), 1923 (English Trans. by Hugh Lloyd Jones, 1962); Textkritik, 3rd edn. (Teubner), 1957 (Italian Trans. by N. Martinelli, 1952), (English Trans. by Barbara Flower, Oxford, 1958); Romanos; treatises and articles on Greek, Roman, Byzantine and English Literature; Select list of writings (Clarendon Press, Oxford), 1951. *Address:* 217 Woodstock Road, Oxford. *T.:* 54578. [*Died* 15 *July* 1964.

MAASS, Prof. O(tto), C.B.E. 1946; F.R.S. 1940; F.R.C.S. 1932; F.R.S.A. 1953; LL.D., Hon. D.Sc., M.Sc., Ph.D.; Research Associate, McGill Univ., since 1958; Macdonald Professor of Physical Chemistry, 1923-55, and Chairman, Dept. of Chemistry, 1937-55, McGill Univ.; Gen. Dir., Pulp and Paper Research Institute of Canada, 1940-55; Scientific Adviser (Special Weapons) Chiefs of Staff, 1951-57; *b.* New York, 8 July 1890; *s.* of Max Maass and Sophie vom Kolke; *m.* 1926, Carol Edna Robertson; one *s.* *Educ.:* Montreal High School; McGill Univ.; Berlin Univ.; Harvard Univ. B.A. (McGill), 1911; M.Sc. 1912; 1851 Exhibition Scholar, 1912; Ph.D. (Harvard), 1919; LL.D. (Manitoba), 1941; Hon. D.Sc. (Laval), 1946, (Rochester), 1947, (Toronto), 1949. Professor in charge of Physical Chemistry, McGill Univ., 1917-55, Member, Montreal Section, Society of Chemical Industry (Chairman, 1932-33), London Soc. of Chemical Industry, Chemical Society,

Canadian Institute of Chemistry (President 1938-39); Dir. Chemical Warfare and Smoke, Dept. of Nat. Defence, 1940-46; member of National Research Council of Canada, 1939-1951, Asst. Pres. 1940-46; Scientific Adviser to Chief of General Staff, Dept. of National Defence, Ottawa, 1945-51; Member of Defence Research Bd., 1946-54; Sen. Research Officer, Nat. Res. Coun., 1955-58. Pres. Sect. III Royal Society of Canada, 1940-41. Medal Soc. Chem. Industry, 1943; Tory Medal, Roy. Can. Soc., 1944; Gold Medal, Civil Service Commn., 1947; U.S. Medal of Freedom with bough, 1947; Canadian Inst. of Chemistry Medal, 1952; Coronation Medal, 1953. *Publications:* Introduction to Physical Chemistry, 1931, rev. 1939; Papers dealing with physical chemistry and pulp and paper processing. *Address:* 32 Thornhill Avenue, Westmount, P.Q., Canada. *T.:* WE 26920. *Clubs:* Savage; University, McGill University Faculty (Montreal); (Hon. Mem.) Chemists (N.Y.). [*Died* 3 *July* 1196.

MABANE, 1st Baron, *cr.* 1962; **William Mabane,** P.C. 1944; K.B.E. 1954; M.A.; President, British Travel Association, 1964-1966 (Chm., 1960-63); *b.* 12 Jan. 1895; *s.* of Joseph Greenwood and Margaret Mabane, Leeds; *m.* 1944, Stella J., *d.* of late Julian Duggan, Buenos Aires. *Educ.:* Woodhouse Grove School; Gonville and Caius College, Cambridge. Served European War in Near East and France, E. Yorkshire Regt., 1914-1919; Warden, University Settlement, Liverpool, 1920-23; Chairman, Mabanes Properties Ltd.; Vice-President Building Socs. Association; formerly Dir. Kemsley Newspapers, Ltd.; M.P. (National Liberal) Huddersfield, 1931-45; Assistant Postmaster-General, 1939; Parliamentary Sec., Ministry of Home Security, 1930-42; Parliamentary Secretary, Ministry of Food, 1942-1945; Minister of State, 1945. *Publications:* various contributions to newspapers and periodicals. *Address:* 11 Stanhope Gardens, S.W.7. *T.:* Frobisher 2878. *Club:* Hurlingham. [*Died* 16 *Nov.* 1969 (*ext.*).

MABY, Sir Charles (George), Kt., *cr.* 1950; C.B.E. 1942 (O.B.E. 1933); Chief Constable, Bristol City Police, 1930-54, retired 1954; *b.* 4 Sept. 1888; *s.* of William Thomas and Sarah Maby; *m.* 1916, Rose Eileen (*née* Reynolds); no *c.* *Educ.:* St. George Secondary School, Bristol. Joined Bristol Constabulary, 1908. King's Police Medal, 1947. *Address:* 21 The Crescent, Henleaze, Bristol. *T.:* 626523. [*Died* 14 *May* 1967.

McADAM, William Alexander; C.M.G. 1946; Hon. LL.D. University of British Columbia, 1956; *b.* Manchester, 19 Dec. 1889; *s.* of John and Margaret F. McAdam; *m.* 1914, Inez, *d.* of late William Chalmers Duncan, founder of Duncan, B.C.; one *s.* one *d.* *Educ.:* Hulme Grammar School, Manchester. British Linen Bank, Edinburgh, 1905-10; Associate Member Institute of Scottish Bankers; Canadian Bank of Commerce, Vancouver, British Columbia, 1910-1913; Publicity and Industrial Commissioner for City of Victoria, B.C., 1919; entered service of British Columbia Govt., 1920; appointed Asst. Deputy Minister of Finance, 1922; transferred to London as Sec. to Office of Agent-General, 1923; Acting Agent-Gen., 1934-41; Agent-General, 1941-58, retired. Pres. Regional Council of Canadian Clubs of B.C.; Hon. Life Mem. Canadian Red Cross Society; Vancouver Bd. of Trade; The Canadian Legion; mem. Advisory Bd., The Royal Trust Co., Victoria, B.C.; Hon. Vice-Pres. Canadian Soccer Football Assoc. *Recreations:* Association football, cricket, and golf. *Address:* P.O. Box 755, Duncan, B.C., Canada. *Clubs:* Royal Automobile; (Hon. Life Mem.) Union Club of British Columbia (Victoria, B.C.). [*Died* 4 *July* 1961.

MacALEVEY, Major-General Gerald Esmond, C.B.E. 1946; D.S.O. 1942; M.C. 1918; *b.* 9 June 1894; *s.* of late William Charles MacAlevey, and late Mary Jane (*née* Bruin), Leicester; *m.* 1946, Hilda Mary Allport; three *s.* one *d.* *Educ.:* Mount St. Mary's College, Chesterfield; St. Mary's Hospital, Paddington. M.R.C.S., L.R.C.P. 1918. Commissioned into R.A.M.C. 1918; France, Germany, Irak, Egypt, 1918-24; Sudan (Egyptian Army and Sudan Defence Force), 1924-1932; United Kingdom, 1932-36; Major, 1930; India, 1936-41; Burma, 1941-45 (A.D.M.S. 17 Ind. Div.; D.D.M.S. 4 Corps; D.D.M.S. 220 Mil. Mission; D.D.M.S. 14th Army); D.D.M.S. Malaya Comd., 1946; United Kingdom, 1946-49; A.D.M.S., British Mil. Mission, Greece, 1949; D.D.M.S., B.T.E., 1950; Dep. Director of Med. Services, Western Command, 1951-52. *Address:* 15 The Drive, Roundhay, Leeds 8. *T.:* Leeds 663541. [*Died* 21 *Dec.* 1969.

MACALISTER, Sir Robert (Lachlan), Kt. 1956; *b.* Blenheim, New Zealand, 2 December 1890; *s.* of Sutherland John Macalister and Jane Harriet Gordon Macalister (*née* Sinclair); *m.* 1920, Katherine Featherston FitzGerald; two *s.* *Educ.:* Marlborough College, Blenheim, N.Z.; Victoria University, Wellington, N.Z. Qualified in Law, Wellington, 1911. Asst. Solicitor, Public Trust Office, 1911-19; private legal practice with Mazengarb, Hay & Macalister, barristers and solicitors (now Macalister, Mazengarb, Parkin and Rose), 1919. Public positions in Wellington: Member, City Council, 1938-56; Dep. Mayor, 1943-50; Mayor, 1950-56; Member, Harbour Bd., 1943-56; Past Chairman Regional Planning Council, Provincial Patriotic Fund Bd., and Queen Elizabeth Park Bd.; one-time member, Tongariro Nat. Park Bd., Dep. Chm. Nat. Art Gallery and Dominion Museum; Associate of Honour of Roy. N.Z. Inst. of Horticulture (A.H.R.I.H. (New Zealand)), Dominion President, 1947-50. *Recreations:* yachting and gardening. *Address:* 22 Anne Street, Wellington, N., New Zealand. *T.:* (home) 41904; (office) 43150. *Clubs:* No. 10 (London); Wellington, Wellington Racing; (Pres.) Royal Port Nicholson Yacht (Wellington). [*Died* 23 *May* 1967.

McALLISTER, Gilbert; Director, Gilbert McAllister and Partners, Ltd., since 1948; *b.* 26 March 1906; *y. s.* of late Archibald McAllister, J.P., Wishaw; *m.* 1937, Elizabeth May, *d.* of William Glen, Saltcoats; three *s.* *Educ.:* Wishaw High School; Glasgow University. President, Glasgow University Labour Club. Served on staff of Motherwell Times, Bulletin, Daily Record, and as special correspondent for United Press of America. Assignments covered included Plenary Sessions of League of Nations at Geneva, Moscow, and Lusitania Salvage Expedition in 1935. Secretary, Town and Country Planning Assoc., 1936-38; Editor, Town and Country Planning, 1936-42; Hon. Treasurer, Town and Country Planning Assoc. 1944; Manager, New Zealand Public Relations Council, 1938-40; served on Public Relations staff of Ministry of Food, and later as Public Relations Officer to Lord Reith's Reconstruction Group, 1940-42; Group Labour Manager, Parnall Aircraft, 1942-43. Former Hon. Secretary, Glasgow Press Club; Editor, Merchant Navy Journal, 1943-46. M.P. (Lab.) for Rutherglen Division of Lanarkshire, 1945-51. Member Public Accounts Committee, 1945-46; Chairman Executive, Margaret McMillan Memorial Fund; member Speaker's Committee on South Africa Gift Fund; member Commonwealth Parl. Assoc. deleg. to East Africa, 1948; visited Nigeria, the Gold Coast, and Liberia, 1949; toured U.S. of America for British - American Parliamentary Group, 1950; sec., Scottish Parliamentary Lab.

Party, 1948-50; Chairman, Parliamentary Group for World Government, 1950-51; Mem. U.K. delegation, Commonwealth Parliamentary Conference, N.Z., and joint conference with U.S. Senate, Canberra, Aust., 1950; Toured Middle East, 1952-53. Chairman of Council, World Parliament Association; General Administrator, National Music Council of Great Britain, 1959-; Mem. of Board, Trinity Coll. of Music; Mem. Central Music Advisory Committee, B.B.C. Managing Editor of Future, 1953-55. Margaret McMillan Memorial Medal, 1956. Editor of Sea; Editor of World. *Publications:* James Maxton: The Portrait of a Rebel, 1935; The Book Crisis (with J. B. Priestley and others), 1940: Town and Country Planning—The Prelude to Post-War Reconstruction (with Elizabeth McAllister), 1941; Homes, Towns and Countryside—A Practical Plan for Britain (edited, with Elizabeth McAllister), 1945; Houses as Homes, 1945; (with Elizabeth McAllister) The Pub and the Garden City, 1948; (ed.) The Bomb, Challenge and Answer, 1955; (ed.) Music in Britain Today and Tomorrow, 1960. *Recreations:* gardening and shopping. *Address:* 21 Hampstead Lane, Highgate Village, N.6. *T.:* Fitzroy 0088; 2 Manchester Square, W.1. *T.:* Hunter 1151. *Clubs:* Travellers', Royal Automobile.
[*Died* 27 *May* 1964.

McALPINE, Sir (Alfred) Robert, 3rd Bt., *cr.* 1918; *b.* 11 May 1907; *s.* of Sir Robert McAlpine, 2nd Bt. and Lillias Cooper (*d.* 1948), *d.* of Thomas Bishop; *S.* father, 1934. *Heir: kinsman,* Thomas George Bishop McAlpine [*b.* 23 Oct. 1901; *m.* 1st, 1934, Doris Frew (*d.* 1964), *d.* of D. C. Campbell and *widow* of W. E. Woodeson; 2nd, 1965, Mrs. Kathleen Mary Blackshaw]. *Address:* Farindons, Dormansland, Lingfield, Surrey.
[*Died* 25 *Aug.* 1968.

McALPINE, Sir Malcolm; *see* McAlpine, Sir T. M.

McALPINE, Sir Robert; *see* McAlpine, Sir A. R.

McALPINE, Sir (Thomas) Malcolm, K.B.E., *cr.* 1921; Public Works Contractor; Chairman, Sir Robert McAlpine & Sons Ltd.; Chairman, Dorchester Hotel, Ltd.; *b.* 19 June 1877; *s.* of Sir Robert McAlpine, 1st Bart., and Agnes Hepburn; *m.* 1903, Maud Dees; three *s.* *Educ.:* Kelvinside Academy. *Recreations:* racing, fishing. *Address:* Fairmile Court, Cobham, Surrey. *T.:* Cobham (Surrey) 90; North Foreland Hall, Broadstairs. *Clubs:* Bath, Carlton, Royal Automobile, St. Stephen's. [*Died* 12 *April* 1967.

MACANDIE, George Lionel, C.B.E. 1920; *b.* Brisbane, 26 June 1877; *s.* of William Macandie, Forres, Scotland; *m.* 1904, Alice, *d.* of William Hood, Brisbane; one *s.* two *d.* *Educ.:* Brisbane Grammar School. Queensland Public Service, 1896; Associate Federal Institute of Accountants; transferred to Commonwealth Defence Department, 1901; Secretary, Navy Office, Australia, 1914; retired list, 1946. *Publication:* The Genesis of the Royal Australian Navy, 1949. *Address:* 58 Rowland St., Kew, Melbourne, Australia. [*Died* 30 *April* 1968.

McARTHUR, Donald Neil, C.B.E. 1953; D.Sc., Ph.D., F.R.I.C., F.R.S.E.; retired as Director of the Macaulay Institute for Soil Research, Aberdeen, and as Research Lecturer in Soil Science, University of Aberdeen (1945-58); Professor of Agricultural Chemistry, and Interim Director of Research West of Scotland Agricultural College, Glasgow; *b.* Glasgow, 2 Aug. 1892; *o. c.* of Donald McArthur and Anne Dewar; *m.* Anne Videon Brough; one *s.* *Educ.:* Allan Glen's School, Glasgow; Univ. of Glasgow (Research Student). Demonstrator in Chemistry, West of Scotland Agricultural College; Physical Chemist to Glasgow and West of Scotland Radium Committee, University, Glasgow; Lecturer in Chemistry, West of Scotland Agricultural College. *Publications:* Agricultural progress; Papers in Transactions of Chemical Society, Transactions of Society of Chemical Industry, Journal West of Scotland Iron and Steel Institute. *Address:* 7 Orchard Drive, Edinburgh 4. *T.:* Edinburgh Dean 5915.
[*Died* 23 *Aug.* 1965.

MacARTHUR, General of the Army Douglas, Hon. G.C.B., *cr.* 1943; Congressional Medal of Honor; D.S.C.; D.S.M. (three oak leaf clusters); Navy D.S.M.; Chairman of Board of Remington Rand Incorporated, since 1952; *b.* Arkansas, 26 Jan. 1880; *s.* of Lieut.-General Arthur MacArthur and Mary P. Hardy; *m.* Jean Faircloth; one *s.* *Educ.:* U.S. Mil. Acad. (grad. 1903). 2nd Lt. Engineers, 1903; Capt. 1911; Major, 1915; Col. 1917; Temp. Brig.-Gen. 1918; Brig.-Gen. 1920; Maj.-Gen. 1925; General, 1930; General of the Army, 1944. Served European War (twice wounded); Superintendent United States Military Academy, 1919; in Philippines, 1922-25; commanding Philippine Dept., 1928-30; Chief of Staff, U.S. Army, 1930-35; Director Organisation of National Defense, Commonwealth Govt. of the Philippines, 1935; retired, 1937; Field Marshal of the Philippine Army, 1936; returned to active duty, 1941; C.-in-C. of Allied Forces, South-West Pacific Area, 1942; C.-in-C., U.S. Forces, Far East Command until 1951; Supreme Comdr. Allied Powers in Japan until 1951; C.-in-C. U.N. Forces in Korea until 1951. *Posthumous Publications:* Reminiscences, 1965; A Soldier Speaks, ed. V. E. Whan, 1966. *Address:* Waldorf-Astoria Hotel, New York, N.Y., U.S.A. [*Died* 5 *April* 1964.

McARTHUR, Hon. Sir Gordon Stewart, Kt. 1959; President, Legislative Council, Victoria, Australia, since 1958; *b.* Melbourne, 7 Apr. 1896; *s.* of late Hon. Sir W. G. Stewart McArthur, K.C.; *m.* 1936, Theodosia, *d.* of late Sir George and Lady Syme; three *s.* one *d.* *Educ.:* Geelong College; Jesus College, Cambridge (M.A.). Honours, Mechanical Science Tripos, 1921. Served European War, 1916-18, R.F.A. Called to the Bar, Inner Temple, 1929; Victoria, 1929. M.L.C., South-Western Province, Victoria, 1931-; Hon. Minister, 1955-; Minister for Forests and State Development, 1956-58. *Recreations:* golf, racing. *Address:* Meningoort, Camperdown, Victoria, Australia. *Clubs:* Leander (Henley, Eng.), University Pitt, Hawks (Cambridge, Eng.); Melbourne, Royal Melbourne Golf, Naval and Military, Victoria Racing (Melbourne).
[*Died* 10 *Aug.* 1965.

MacARTHUR, Lieut.-General Sir William Porter, K.C.B. 1939 (C.B. 1938); D.S.O. 1916; O.B.E. 1919; R.A.M.C. retd.; University Lecturer in Tropical Medicine, and additional member, Faculty of Medicine, University of Oxford; Consultant Roy. Masonic Hosp., London; Pres., Roy. Soc. of Tropical Medicine, 1959-61; Editor, Transactions of Royal Society of Tropical Medicine; Examiner (past or present), Univs. of Cambridge, Liverpool, London, Oxford, and R.C. of S., England; *b.* 11 March 1884; *o. s.* of J. P. MacArthur, Belfast, and Margaret, *d.* of William Baird, M.D., Donemara; *m.* Thérèse, *d.* of late Dr. L. F. Antelme, Paris and Mauritius; two *s.* *Educ.:* Queen's University, Belfast (M.D., B.Ch.), D.Sc. (Hon.), Belfast, 1935, Oxon, 1949; F.R.C.P., Lond., F.R.C.P. Ireland, D.P.H. (Oxford), D.T.M. and H. (Camb.). Vicary Lecturer, Royal College of Surgeons, 1931; Honeyman Gillespie Lecturer,

Edin. Univ., 1955; Arnott Medal, 1929; Chadwick Medal, 1935; Robert Campbell Orator and Medallist, 1951; Scott-Heron Medal, 1957. Professor of Tropical Medicine, R.A.M. College, 1922-29 and 1932-1934; Consulting Physician to the British Army, 1929-34; Deputy Director-General Army Medical Services, War Office, 1934-35; Commandant and Director of Studies, R.A.M. College, 1935-38; Director-General of Army Medical Services, 1938-41; K.H.P. 1930-41; retired pay, 1941; Col. Comdt. R.A.M.C., 1964-51. *Publications:* The Appin Murder, 1960; contrib. to The Great Famine, 1956; articles in Dict. of Nat. Biog., Brit. Encyc. of Med. Practice, and med. and hist. journs. *Address:* 48 Priory Avenue, W.4. *Club:* Army and Navy. [*Died* 30 *July* 1964.

MACARTNEY-FILGATE, John Victor Opynschae, C.B.E. 1964; M.C. 1917; T.D. 1945; Managing Director, Lazard Brothers & Co. Ltd., 1949-64; *b.* 1897; *s.* of Colonel E. J. P. F. Macartney-Filgate and Bertha Eugenie Lomax; *m.* 1920, Angela, *yr. d.* of Sir Reginald Neville, 1st Bt., Sloley Hall, Norfolk; two *s.* one *d.* *Educ.:* Rugby School. Served European War, 1914-1918: France and Flanders, 1915-18; Major, Royal Field Artillery (M.C., wounded twice); War of 1939-45: Lt.-Col., Royal Artillery; served in Far East; captured and became prisoner of war of Japanese. Asst. Parly. Sec., British Commonwealth Union, 1919-21. With Lazard Brothers and Co., Ltd., 1921-64, retired. F.I.B. and Mem. Council, 1954-64; Pastmaster, Worshipful Company of Bowyers. *Publication:* History of the 33rd Divisional Artillery in the War 1914-1918, 1921. *Recreations:* music, gardening. *Address:* Slough House, Danbury, Essex. *T.:* Danbury (Essex) 3128. [*Died* 23 *July* 1964.

MACASKIE, Charles Frederick Cunningham, C.M.G. 1946; *b.* 26 March 1888; *s.* of late C. F. C. Macaskie, Ilkley, Yorkshire; *m.* 1946, D. Cole-Adams, *d.* of W. H. Legg. *Educ.:* Uppingham. Barrister Gray's Inn; entered N. Borneo C.S., 1910; served War of 1914-18, Royal W. Kent Regt. (despatches); Chief Justice and Deputy Governor, North Borneo, 1934-45; Brig., Chief Civil Affairs Officer, British Borneo, 1945-46; Commissioner for War Damage Claims, Borneo Territories, 1947-51; acting British Judge, New Hebrides, Western Pacific, 1955, 1958, 1959. *Recreation:* golf. *Address:* Tuck Hill, Broadwater, Stanthorpe, Queensland, Australia. [*Died* 28 *Nov.* 1969.

MACASKIE, Nicholas Lechmere Cunningham, Q.C. 1930; Judge of Court of Admiralty of the Cinque Ports from 1954; *b.* 19 Aug. 1881; *e. s.* of Stuart Cunningham Macaskie, K.C., and Emily Lechmere Pugh; *m.* 1913, Jane Mary (*d.* 1965), *er. d.* of James Mark Tuohy; one *s.* four *d.* *Educ.:* Uppingham; Belgium; France. Bachelier ès lettres Paris Univ., 1901; called to Bar, Gray's Inn, 1905, Bencher, 1930, Treasurer, 1943; Revising Barrister on North Eastern Circuit, 1912-14; Recorder of York, 1930-1941; Recorder of Sheffield, 1941-57; served Army, 1917-19; Member of Council of Legal Education; Member of Board of Legal Studies, 1935-45; Chief of Legal Division of Control Commission of Germany, British Element, 1945-49; Chairman of Road and Rail Appeal Tribunal, 1949-51; Member of Special Panel of Transport Tribunal, 1951-61; Standing Arbitrator under the Railways Act 1921, 1952. A Comr. of Assize on three occasions, 1954. Elected an Appeal Steward of British Boxing Board of Control, 1950. *Address:* 27 Kensington Square, W.8. *T.:* Western 6763; 2 Temple Gdns., E.C.4. *T.:* Central 1807. *Club:* Pegasus. [*Died* 1 *Jan.* 1967.

MACASSEY, Sir Lynden (Livingston), K.B.E., *cr.* 1917; Q.C.; LL.D., Sc.D.; Chairman of the London Board, Scottish Amicable Life Assurance Society (President of the Society until 1962); Chairman Investment Registry Ltd.; Director: Settle Speakman & Co. Ltd.; Kinnaird Textiles Ltd., and of other Companies; *b.* 14 June 1876; *e. s.* of late L. L. Macassey, Holywood, Co. Down; *m.* 1903, Jeanne, *o. c.* of late Robert M'Farland, Melbourne and Barooga, N.S.W.; two *s.* one *d.* Trained and worked as an engineer; called to Bar, Middle Temple, 1899, Bencher and Past Treas.; K.C. 1912; Q.C. 1952 Hon. Mem. of American and Canadian Bar Associations; a Vice-Pres. International Law Association; Hon. Fell. Queen Mary Coll. (Univ. of London); Past-Master Drapers' Company; Past-Pres. and Hon. Mem. Institute of Transport; Past-Pres. Institute of Arbitrators; Sec. to Roy. Commission on London Traffic, 1903-06; Chm. of various Govt. Cttees. and Tribunals on questions of labour and wages, 1914-16; Dir. of Shipyard Labour, Admiralty, 1917-18; Mem. of War Cabinet Cttees.: on Labour, 1917-18; on Women in Industry, 1918-19; Chairman of Road Transport Fares Tribunal of Northern Ireland, 1928-35; Independent Chairman of the British Internal Combustion Engine Manufacturers' Assoc., 1940-53, and of Reuter Trust, 1941-51; Vice-President of the British Internal Combustion Engine Research Association, 1945-53. Member of Chatham House. A member of Board of Editors of American Arbitration Journal. *Address:* 6 Grafton Street, W.1. *T.:* Hyde Park 6455; 37 Alexandra Court, Queen's Gate, S.W.7. *T.:* Knightsbridge 1884. *Clubs:* Carlton; Ulster (Belfast); Royal Ulster Yacht (Bangor, Co. Down). [*Died* 23 *Feb.* 1963.

MACAULAY, William J. B.; *b.* 15 Dec. 1892; *s.* of Captain Patrick Macaulay of Waterside, Co. Antrim, and Elizabeth Murphy; *m.* 1937, Duchess Genevieve Brady (*d.* 1938). *Educ.:* privately. Served in R.N.R. 1915-20; Sec., Irish Legation, Washington. 1925-29; Counsellor, 1929-30; Consul-General in the U.S.A., 1930-34; Envoy Extraordinary and Minister Plenipotentiary to the Holy See, 1934-41, retired. *Address:* 34 East 50 St., New York 22, U.S.A. *Club:* New York Yacht (New York). [*Died* 7 *Jan.* 1964.

MACAULAY-OWEN, Peter, M.A., D.Phil. (Oxon.); Headmaster, Grammar School, St. Asaph, since 1934; *b.* 5 July 1906; *s.* of Thomas and Ellen Jane Macaulay-Owen; *m.* 1934, Glenys Ogwen Griffith; one *d.* *Educ.*; Ffestiniog County School; Jesus College, Oxford; Lecturer in Mathematics, University College, Hull, 1931-34. *Publications:* Articles in Journal and Proceedings, London Mathematical Society. *Address:* Grammar School, St. Asaph. *T.:* St. Asaph 3104. *Club:* Oxford Union Society (Oxford). [*Died* 8 *May* 1962.

MACBEATH, Alexander, C.B.E. 1953; Professor of Logic and Metaphysics, The Queen's University, Belfast, 1925-54; Chairman Belfast Council of Social Welfare, 1929-56; *b.* Applecross, Ross-shire, 1888; *m.* 1921, Grace, *d.* of Alexander Stewart, Woodend, Glenlyon, Perthshire; three *s.* one *d.* *Educ.:* Hutchesons' Boys' Grammar School and University, Glasgow (M.A. 1916). Served European War, 1915-19; Secretary to the Council of the Glasgow Charity Organisation Society, 1919; Lecturer in Moral Philosophy, Glasgow University, 1920; Senior Lecturer in Logic and Metaphysics, Glasgow Univ., 1923; Dean of Fac. of Arts, Q.U.B., 1929-32, 1938-41; Dean of Fac. of Law, 1941-45; Dean of Fac. of Commerce, 1945-1946; Chm. Jt. Cttee. on Adult Education, 1939-54; Director of Social Studies, 1945-53; Frazer Lecturer, Glasgow Univ., 1948;

Gifford Lecturer, St. Andrews Univ., 1948-49; Hobhouse Memorial Lecturer, 1957; Head of Dept. of Moral Philosophy, Edinburgh Univ., 1958-59; Visiting Prof., Univ. of Tasmania, 1959-61; Visiting Prof., Univ. of Auckland, N.Z., 1963. Hon. LL.D. Glasgow, 1952; Hon. Litt.D., Dublin, 1954; Hon. D.Lit. Belfast, 1957; Hon. D.Litt., Tasmania, 1961, and Auckland, 1963. *Publications:* The Relationship between Primitive Morality and Religion; Experiments in Living. *Address:* Lorne Cottage, Aberfeldy, Perthshire. [*Died* 15 *Dec.* 1964.

MACBEATH, Rev. John, M.A. (Glasgow); D.D. Glasgow; Hon. C.F.; Minister of Haven Green Church, Ealing, 1942-50; Minister Emeritus since 1950; *b.* Edinburgh; *m.* Margaret Mackenzie (*d.* 1947), Caberfeidh, Tain, Ross-shire; *m.* 1954, Eleanor Constance Millard, Streatham, London. *Educ.:* Warrender Park School; Heriot-Watt College, Edinburgh; Glasgow University; St. Mary's College, St. Andrews. Served in France with Y.M.C.A., 1915-16. Formerly Minister at St. Andrews, 1907-09; Cambuslang, 1909-21, and Fillebrook, London, 1923-29; Hillhead, Glasgow, 1929-42; Secretary for Scottish Churches Missionary Campaign, 1921-1923; Chaplain in France, Egypt, and Palestine; Lecturer in Comparative Study of Religion, Homiletics and Pastoral Theology in Baptist Theological College of Scotland, Glasgow, 1932-42; President, Baptist Union of Scotland, 1934-35. *Publications:* Gone West, The Face of Christ, The Great Unities, The Second Watch, The Round of the Year; The Hills of God; What is His Name?; The Voices of Revelation; The Life of a Christian; The Circle of Time; Taken Unawares; A Wayfarer's Psalter; In Time of Trouble; The Gift of Wings; also, for young people, Roadmakers and Road-menders, Lamps and Lamplighters, A Number of Things, Lilies Among the Wheat, Voices of the Woods, The Carpenter of Nazareth. *Recreations:* travel and literature. *Address:* 44 Croham Manor Road, South Croydon, Surrey. *T.:* Croydon 4588. [*Died* 3 *May* 1967.

McCAHEARTY, Ven. Reginald George Henry, M.A.; Archdeacon of Bromley since 1955; Rector of Chislehurst since 1955; Rural Dean of Orpington since 1954 (of Bromley, 1953-54); Hon. Canon of Rochester since 1950. *Educ.:* University of Leeds. B.A. 2nd class History and Boddington Prize, 1924; M.A. 1927. College of the Resurrection, Mirfield, 1920; ordained deacon, 1926; priest, 1927; curate, Gravesend, 1926-31; curate, Dartford, 1931-32; Vicar of Christ Church, Dartford, 1932-38; Vicar of Christ Church, Milton-next-Gravesend, 1938-47; Vicar of Orpington, 1947-55. *Address:* The Rectory, Chislehurst, Kent. [*Died* 24 *June* 1966.

McCALL, Robert Clark, C.M.G. 1955; Controller, Northern Ireland, British Broadcasting Corporation, 1956-66; *b.* 16 August 1906; *s.* of Robert McCall, Glasgow; *m.* 1930, Thelma K., *d.* of A. Brown, Ryde, New South Wales, Australia; one *s.* one *d.* *Educ.:* Fort Street High School, Sydney, Australia. Editorial staff, Sydney Daily Telegraph, 1922; Sales Manager, Parlophone Record Co., 1927; Sales Manager Assoc. Gramophone Cos., 1932; Australian Broadcasting Commission as Federal Programme Editor, 1936; Fed. Controller of Concerts 1937; Victorian Manager, 1938; seconded to B.B.C. as Pacific Service Director, 1940-1942; Federal Superintendent, Australian Broadcasting Commission, 1942; seconded to personal staff of Governor General, H.R.H. the Duke of Gloucester, as Press and Broadcasting Officer, 1945; Asst. Gen. Manager, Australian Broadcasting Commission, 1945; Asst. Controller, Overseas Services, B.B.C., 1946; Controller, Overseas Services, B.B.C., 1948; Asst. Director, External Broadcasting, 1952; Assistant Director, Television Broadcasting, B.B.C., 1952-56. *Recreations:* music, gardening. *Address:* 1 Portulla Drive, Lisburn, Northern Ireland. [*Died* 16 *Oct.* 1970.

McCALL, Rt. Rev. Theodore Bruce, B.A., Th.D.; Bishop of Wangaratta since 1963; *b.* London, 29 Dec. 1911; *s.* of late Sir John McCall, K.C.M.G., M.D., LL.D., Agent-General for Tasmania, and Claire McCall (*née* Reynolds); *m.* 1939, Helen Christie Wilmot, Corowa, N.S.W.; one *s.* three *d.* *Educ.:* Langley Place, St. Leonards-on-Sea; Launceston Church Grammar School, Tasmania; St. Peter's College, Adelaide, S. Australia. Mercantile Marine (A.U.S.N.Co.) as apprentice, 1927-30; St. Columb's Hall, Wangaratta, Victoria (theological college), 1931-35; Th.L., Aust. Coll. of Theology, 1934; Th. Schol. 1942; B.A. Univ. of Queensland, 1952. Deacon, 1935, priest, 1936; Curate of Milawa, 1935-36; St. Augustine's, Hamilton, Qld., 1936-37; Shepparton, Vic., 1937-39; Rector of Yea, 1939-43. Chaplain A.I.F., 1940-46. Rector of Macquarie Plains, 1946-49; Curate of Christ Church, St. Laurence, Sydney, 1949-1951; Rector of Holy Trinity, Launceston, 1951-53; Home Secretary, Australian Board of Missions, 1953-59; Editor of A.B.M. Review, 1953-59; Bishop of Rockhampton, 1959-63; Editor of Australian Church Quarterly, 1965-. *Publications:* Is the Church of England Changing?, 1957; Challenge in New Guinea, 1956; Blood and Race, 1958. *Recreations:* gardening, painting. *Address:* Bishop's Lodge, Wangaratta, Victoria, Australia. *T.:* 3643. [*Died* 16 *Jan.* 1969.

McCALLUM, Major John Dunwoodie Martin, C.B.E. 1921; D.S.O. 1916; late The Royal Ulster Rifles; *s.* of late John McCallum, Financial Sec., National Education Board, Ireland, and *e. d.* of Rev. J. D. Martin of Tullyallen, Co. Armagh; *b.* 2 Sept. 1883; *m.* 1915, Eveleen Lindsay, *e. d.* of Lindsay Hill Lloyd, Belfast; no *c.* *Educ.:* Royal Academical Institution, Belfast; Queen's College, Belfast. Graduated, 1906; admitted Solicitor, 1910; practised in Belfast; granted commission in T.F. (Unattached List), 1908, and posted to Belfast University, O.T.C.; Capt. 1911; Capt. and Adjutant of 8th Royal Irish Rifles, 1914; Resident Magistrate for Co. Clare, 1920; Commandant, R.I.C. Camp, Newtownards, 1920-22; Resident Magistrate, Newry, 1922-1943, and Belfast 1943-53; retired Sept., 1953; played for Ireland at Badminton in 1913-1914, 1920-27; French Croix de Guerre, 1918. *Recreations:* all games, principally cricket and Badminton (Pres. Internat. Badminton Fed., 1961; Pres. Badminton Union of Ireland); photography. *Address:* 41 Ormiston Crescent, Belfast. *T.:* Belfast 56536. [*Died* 14 *Jan.* 1967.

McCANNELL, Otway, R.W.A., R.B.A.; Hon. Member Paris Salon; figure and neo-abstract painter; Ex-Principal, Farnham Art School; *b.* 26 Dec. 1883; *s.* of William Cannell, Wallasey; *m.* Winifred Cooper; one *d.* *Educ.:* Nelson College, New Zealand. Studied at Kensington and in Italy; awarded the Royal Exhibition of Art in 1905; Royal College of Art Scholarship 1907, and Associateship, 1908; frequent exhibitor at Roy. Acad., and other leading London and Continental exhibitions; several one-man exhibitions; works purchased for municipal and private collections; in 1924 exhibited at the Academy The Devil's Chess-Board, which caused much controversy. *Publications:* (Author and Illustrator): Legends; Life and Destiny; Omar; Faith, etc. *Address:* High Moor, Moor Park, Farnham, Surrey. *T.:* Farnham 6192. [*Died* 29 *Sept.* 1969.

McCARRON, Edward Patrick; Barrister-at-Law; Peace Commissioner. *Educ.:* O'Connell Schools, Dublin; Univ. Coll., Dublin. Called to Irish Bar, King's Inns, 1914. Late Senior Auditor Local Government Board for Ireland; Permanent Secretary, Department of Local Government and Public Health, I.F. State, 1922-36; Registrar-General, 1926-36; retired, 1936; Director: Hibernian Fire and General Insurance Co. Ltd.; Waterford Ironfounders Ltd.; Masser-Waterford Ironfounders Ltd.; Dublin Savings Bank; Irish Pensions Trustees Ltd. *Address:* Anerley, Cowper Road, Rathmines, Dublin. *T.:* Dublin 971742. *Club:* St. Stephen's Green (Dublin).

[*Died* 4 *Oct.* 1970.

McCARTAN, Dr. Patrick, F.R.C.S.I.; L.R.C.P.I.; *b.* Co. Tyrone, 1878. Was resident Medical Officer in General Hospital, New York; M.P. Tullamore Division, King's Co., 1916; M.P. (Sinn Fein) King's County, Dec. 1918-22; Member Dail Eireann for King and Queen's Cos., 1921-23; was Republican Envoy of 1st Dail in the U.S.A.; Member 2nd Dail, Member of the Senate, Apr. 1948-Aug 1951. *Address:* Karnak, Greystones, Co. Wicklow, Ireland. [*Died* 28 *March* 1963.

McCARTHY, Admiral Sir (Edward) Desmond (Bewley), K.C.B. *cr.* 1950 (C.B. 1945); D.S.O. 1941; *b.* 1893; *s.* of Edward Adye McCarthy; *m.* 1925, Agatha, *d.* of late Brig.-Gen. H. J. J. Kentish; two *s.* *Educ.:* R.N. Colleges, Osborne and Dartmouth. Capt. 1935; Rear-Adm. 1944; Asst. Chief of Naval Staff, Admiralty, 1944-46; Rear-Admiral Destroyers, Mediterranean, 1946-47; Vice-Adm. 1948; C.-in-C. South Atlantic, 1948-50; retired, 1950; Admiral, retired list, 1952. *Address:* Cottman's Corner, Sturminster Marshall, Nr. Wimborne, Dorset. *T.:* Sturminster Marshall 200. *Club:* United Service.

[*Died* 8 *June* 1966.

McCARTHY, Sir Leslie (Ernest Vivian), Kt. 1949; Company Director since 1949; *b.* 22 December 1885; *o. s.* of J. A. McCarthy, formerly Queen's Advocate, Sierra Leone, and Solicitor-General, Gold Coast, and Lily McCarthy, Hull, and Freetown, Sierra Leone; *m.* 1947, Julia Bruce, Accra. *Educ.:* Keble College, Oxford. Called to bar, Gray's Inn, 1912; Law Officer, Gold Coast, 1921-39; Puisne Judge, Gold Coast, 1939-48. *Publication:* Edited 1936 Revised Edition, Gold Coast Laws. *Address:* P.O. Box 735, Accra, Ghana. [*Died* 20 *June* 1970.

McCARTHY, Sir Mortimer (Eugene), Kt. 1962; C.B.E. 1953; A.A.S.A.; Chairman, LM Ericsson Pty. Ltd.; *b.* 7 July 1890; *s.* of William and Elizabeth McCarthy, Fern Hill, Vic., Australia; *m.* 1919, Linda Gladys, *d.* of William and Evelyn Stuart, Subiaco, W.A.; two *s.* one *d.* *Educ.:* St Patrick's Coll., Ballarat, Vic.; Univ. of W.A. Joined Trade and Customs Dept., 1912. A.A.M.C., 1915-19 (despatches); transf. to Tariff Bd., 1929 (Sec. 1935-39); Sec. and Chief Exec. Officer, Prices Br., 1939-1941; Asst. Prices Comr., 1941-45; Commonwealth Prices Comr., 1945-49; Chairman: Tariff Bd., 1949-57; Consultative Cttee. on Import Policy, 1952-60; Advisory Authority, Japanese Trade Agreement, 1958-1960; Dairy Industry Cttee. of Enquiry, 1959; Sugar Enquiry Cttee., 1960. *Recreations:* motoring, gardening, bowls. *Address:* 18 Florence Avenue, Kew E.4, Victoria, Australia. *T.:* Melbourne 80-1553.

[*Died* 16 *May* 1967.

McCARTHY, Lt.-Col. W. H. Leslie, D.S.O. 1919; M.V.O. 1955; M.C.; *b.* 21 June 1885; *e. s.* of late Richard Hilgrove M'Carthy, J.P., Woodford House, Co. Kerry; *m.* 1921, Evelyn Marshall Porter; *m.* 1960, Evelyn Olivia Ward. *Educ.:* Trinity College, Dublin; St. Thomas's Hospital; Paris; Vienna. J.P.; Barrister-at-law of the Inner Temple; M.A., M.D. (Dub.), D.P.H. (Oxford); M.R.C.P. (Lond.); Arnott gold medal 1920; Senior Moderator and Gold Medallist in Natural Science; Stewart Medical Scholar; Reid Exhibitioner, Experimental Science; University Medallist in Political Economy and Aesthetics. Served European War (Belgium and France), 1914-1919 (thrice wounded, despatches thrice, D.S.O., M.C., and bar); Medical Officer, Guards Brigade, 1914-16; Commanded Infantry Field Ambulances, 1916-19. Formerly: Medical Officer of Health for the Inner and Middle Temples and for Chelsea. Coroner to the Queen's Household, 1934-55. *Publications:* Heredity and Environment in Relation to Crime; The Political Economy of War, and various contributions to contemporary medical literature. *Recreations:* fly-fishing, motoring, foreign travel. *Address:* Palais Ambassadeur, Rue du Congrès, Nice, A.-M., France. [*Died* 16 *Sept.* 1962.

McCARTNEY, James Elvins, M.D., Ch.B., D.Sc.; late Cons. Bacteriologist, Institute of Medical and Veterinary Science, Adelaide; formerly Director of Research and Pathological Services, London County Council, London; late Major, R.A.M.C.; *b.* 1891; *e. s.* of late James B. McCartney of Whithorn, Wigtownshire, and Warwick; *m.* 1st, 1916, Marjory (marriage dissolved, 1962), *e. d.* of late Joseph Macnaughton of Airdrie; one *s.* one *d.*; 2nd, 1962, Frances, *o. d.* of E. Taylor, Lewisham, S.E.13. *Educ.:* Warwick School; Edinburgh University. Served European War, 1914-19; Lecturer in Bacteriology, Edinburgh University, 1919-22, 1923-25; Fellow Rockefeller Institute, N.Y., 1922-23. *Publications:* (with T. J. Mackie) A Handbook of Practical Bacteriology; numerous publications on bacteriological and pathological subjects. *Address:* 16 Sherbourne Road, Medindie Gardens, S. Australia 5081, Australia.

[*Died* 24 *Sept.* 1969.

McCAY, Lieut.-Gen. (Hon.) Sir Ross (Cairns), K.B.E., *cr.* 1952 (C.B.E. 1943); C.B. 1946; D.S.O. 1917; retd.; *b.* 18 Sept. 1895; *s.* of Hugh D. McCay, Melb., Aust.; *m.* 1928, Ethel Dora Knight. *Educ.:* Scotch Coll., Melbourne; R.M.C.A. Duntroon. European War, 1914-18, A.I.F., Egypt, Gallipoli, France (Major, D.S.O., despatches, 1914-15 star, British War and Victory medals); Lieut. Indian Army 17 Cav. 1918; Capt. 1919; 6th Rajputana Rifles, 1924; Bt. Major, 1931; Lt.-Col. 1938; Col. 1941; Brig. 1942; Maj.-Gen. (acting), 1944; Temp. Maj.-Gen. 1945; Maj.-Gen. 1947; Lieut.-Gen. (actg.), 1948. N.W. Frontier, 1920-21, 1921-24, 1930-31, 1937, 1938-39 (two medals with 5 clasps, despatches); Deputy Military Secretary, India, 1940-41; Brig. General Staff, India Office, 1941-43; Brigade Comdr., I.A., 1943; Military Secretary, India, 1944; Area Commander, India, 1946; Comdr. Peshawar Area, 1947; Chief of Staff, Pakistan Army, 1948, Chief Mil. Adviser, 1951-53. *Recreations:* riding, shooting, golf. *Address:* Brownings Down Cottage, Warren Road, Guildford, Surrey. *Club:* United Service.

[*Died* 4 *April* 1969.

McCLEARY, George Frederick, M.D. (Cantab); D.P.H.; A.R.C.O.; *b.* 17 Aug. 1867; *m.* 1897, Hilda, *d.* of late Homersham Cox, Judge of County Courts; one *s.* two *d.* *Educ.:* Royal College of Music; Trinity Hall, Cambridge; Middlesex Hospital. Late Assistant Medical Officer of Health, Manchester; Medical Officer of Health, Battersea, Hampstead, Bedfordshire; Principal Medical Officer National Health Insurance Commission (England); Deputy Senior Medical Officer, Ministry of Health; Examiner in Public Health, Liverpool University; Lecturer on Public Health Administration, London School of Economics; De Lemar Lecturer, Johns Hopkins Univ., Baltimore, 1930-31; Ed., Public Health, 1908-12; Chairman, Nat. Assoc. for Maternity and Child Welfare; Ex-Pres. Metropolitan Branch, Society of Medical Officers of Health. *Publications:* Infantile Mortality, 1905; National Health Insurance, 1932; The Early History of the Infant Welfare Movement, 1933; The Maternity and Child Welfare Movement, 1935; The Menace of British Depopulation, 1937; Population: To-day's Question, 1938; Race Suicide?, 1945; Cricket with the Kangaroo, 1950; The Malthusian Population Theory, 1953; Peopling the British Commonwealth, 1955; On Detective Fiction and Other Things, 1960; numerous official reports and contributions to medical and lay journals. *Recreations:* mountaineering, music, golf. *Address:* 80 Corringham Road, N.W.11. [*Died* 2 *Jan.* 1962.

McCLELLAND, Rev. Henry Simpson, B.A., B.D.; Minister of Trinity Church, Claremont St., Glasgow, 1915-56; Writer, Broadcaster; *b.* Belfast, 1882; *m.* 1922, Ruby S. Frew-Gaff. *Educ.:* Nottingham College; New College, London Univ. First Charge: East Finchley, 1910-15. Lived disguised as tramp in London slums, 1912, Glasgow, 1925, to learn needs of destitute. Active Service, France, 1917-19; captured by Bedouin in Transjordania, 1920. Travelled through 13 European States, 1922; India, to meet Gandhi, 1930; Germany, Poland, Russia, 1933, for Ass. Sc. Newspapers. Interviewed Emperor Haile Sellassie in Addis Ababa, 1935; Spain, 1937; Tunisia, 1939. *Publications:* contrib. to British and American Press. *Recreation:* travel in search of trouble. *Address:* c/o Bank of Scotland, 711 Great Western Rd., Glasgow, W.2. [*Died* 20 *Oct.* 1961.

McCLELLAND, Hugh Charles, C.B.E. 1947; *b.* 15 Aug. 1893; *s.* of late William Dawson McClelland, Barberton, Eastern Transvaal and Belfast; *m.* 1929, Jean Ainslie, *d.* of late Alexander Hutchinson, Edinburgh; two *s.* *Educ.:* St. Andrew's Coll., Grahamstown, South Africa. Served R.F.C. and R.A.F., 1917-19. Consular Service, 1919; Vice-Consul, Lourenço Marques and Beira, Portuguese East Africa, 1919-24; Budapest, 1924-29; Rio de Janeiro, 1930-31; Consul at Guayaquil, 1932; Chargé d'Affaires, Quito, 1933-34; Consul at Tripoli, Libya, 1935-38; Delegate British Commercial Mission to Colombia, Aug.-Dec. 1938; Consul at St. Louis, 1939-43; Baltimore, 1943-45; Consul-Gen., Philadelphia, 1945-50; Consul-General Barcelona, 1951-53; retd. 1953. *Address:* c/o Barclays Bank, D.C.O., 1 Cockspur Street, London, S.W.1. *Club:* Royal Commonwealth Society. [*Died* 31 *Oct.* 1966.

McCLELLAND, William, C.B. 1923; O.B.E.; M.I.E.E.; Retired; *b.* 1873; *m.* 1898, Isabella Shepherd (*d.* 1933), Manchester; two *s.* one *d.* *Educ.:* Manchester. Assistant to C. H. Wordingham, M.I.C.E., Consulting Engineer, 1901-3; Electrical Engineer, Admiralty, on design and inspection of Warship Construction, 1903-6; Electrical Engineering Asst. to Director of Dockyards, Admiralty, 1906-18; Director of Electrical Engineering, Admiralty, S.W.1; Principal Electrical Adviser to Board of Admiralty, 1919-34; responsible for designs and equipment of Electrical Installations in all H.M. ships; served on Defence Committees; Ex-Hon. Treasurer and Member of Council of the Institution of Electrical Engineers; General Board of National Physical Laboratory, 1930-36; responsible for repair of electrical installations in all H.M. ships during the war in 1914-18; also for Electrical Equipment for many Naval Bases and Emergency Dockyards. *Publication:* The Applications of Electricity in Warships. *Address:* 76 Marine Court, St. Leonards-on-Sea. *T.:* Hastings 639. [*Died* 2 *Feb.* 1968.

MacCLURE, Victor; Author; *b.* 20 March 1887; *s.* of Thomas McClure, Kilchattan Bay, and Jean Reid Hutchison; *m.* Mrs. June Clarke. *Educ.:* Elgin; Glasgow; Dundee. Qualified as an architect; but took to the stage, acting and painting; Glasgow Repertory Company, Mr. (late Sir) Frank Benson's Company, 1912-14; painted for Mr. Granville Barker at the Savoy and St. James's Theatres, The Winter's Tale, Twelfth Night, Midsummer Night's Dream, Androcles and the Lion, Harlequinade; amongst others, Great Katherine; 1914-18, Med. Ex. Force, Gallipoli (wounded Sept. 1915); discharged the Army, unfit, Jan. 1916; Commissioned, Mar. 1916, Instructor of Signals, Anti-Aircraft Art., then with Dept. of Military Intelligence until June 1918, when invalided; painted for late J. B. Fagan at Court Theatre, Twelfth Night, The School for Scandal; after period of journalism, sub-editorship, commenced author 1921. *Publications:* Nicolette of the Quarter, 1923; Ultimatum, 1924; Boost of the Golden Snail, 1925; Esau, 1926; The Secret Fool; How to be Happy in London, 1927; The Crying Pig Murder; The practical Elocution Book, 1929; Galanty Gold, 1930; Gambletown, 1931; The Counterfeit Murders, 1932; Death Behind the Door; The Clue of the Dead Goldfish, 1933; Death on the Set, 1934; She Stands Accused; Scotland's Inner Man; If They Fall . . . ., 1935; Hi-Spy-Kick-the-Can; Frontéra, 1936; The Diva's Emeralds; The House of Dearth, 1937; I am Saxon Ashe, 1940; Saxon Ashe, Secret Agent, 1941; Gladiators over Norway, 1942; A Certain Woman, 1950; Good Appetite My Companion, 1955; Party Fare, 1957; Mainly Fish, 1959; *plays:* Latitude 15 South (Grand Guignol); with V. Woodhouse, The Limpet; *films:* The Great Mr. Handel; They knew Mr. Knight; Abide With Me. *Recreations:* fishing, painting, cookery, travel. *Address:* 1A Morpeth Terrace, S.W.1. *T.:* Victoria 2556. *Clubs:* Savage; Scottish Arts (Edinburgh). [*Died* 7 *April* 1963.

McCLURE-SMITH, Hugh Alexander, C.V.O. 1958; H.M. Australian Ambassador to Italy since 1959 (to the Netherlands 1955-58); *b.* 14 April 1902; *s.* of late W. A. McClure-Smith, Melbourne; *m.* 1936, Margaret Vincent, *o. d.* of late Lewis Buddy, N.Y.; one *d.* *Educ.:* Melbourne Grammar School; Balliol College, Oxford. Called to Bar, Inner Temple, 1928. Member staff of Price, Waterhouse and Co., 1929-31; contributed widely to British and Dominion press, 1931-32, visiting Australia, U.S.A. and Canada; rep. for Sydney Morning Herald at Imperial Economic Conf., Ottawa, 1932; correspondent for The Times, New York and Washington, 1933-35, and at London Naval Conf., 1936; member editorial staff, The Times, 1936; Associate Editor, Sydney Morning Herald, 1937; Editor-in-Chief, 1938-52; visited Netherlands E. Indies and British Malaya at Invitation of respective govts., 1941; mem. Aust. Press Deleg. visiting U.K. at invitation of British Govt., 1943; rep. Sydney Morning Herald at San Francisco Conf., 1945; Pres. N.S.W. Inst. of Journalists, 1938-44; Member Sydney University Extension Board, 1946-1952; Vice-President, Empire Art Council, 1951; H.M. Australian Minister to Egypt, 1953-55; Member Australian Delegation to Tenth General Assembly, U.N., 1955. *Publications:* sundry contributions to monthlies. *Address:* Australian Embassy, Rome. *Clubs:* Athenæum, Junior Carlton; Union (Sydney). [*Died* 8 *Oct.* 1961.

McCOLL, Sir Alexander Lowe, Kt., *cr.* 1946; formerly Director of Companies; *b.* 10 June 1878; *s.* of Hugh and Jean Boyd

McColl; *m.* 1909, Elizabeth Brown Lightfoot; one *s.* two *d.* *Educ.:* Kilmarnock Academy. Glasgow and South Western Railway, Locomotive Department, 1892-1905; Vacuum Oil Company Limited, 1905-1959 (Sales Manager, Director, Deputy Chairman, Chairman, retired); Chairman and Director Lubricating Oil Committee, Petroleum Board, 1939-49; formerly Chairman Alley & Maclellan Ltd.; formerly Chairman Superheater-Company Ltd.; formerly Director Glenfield & Kennedy (Holdings) Ltd., Indestructible Paint Co. Ltd., Pilchers Ltd., Alley & Maclellan (Polmadie) Ltd., Glasgow. Chairman Committee of Aberdeen Fishing Industry 1950; President MacColl Society; Past President London Ayrshire Society; F.I.P. *Recreations:* reading and sport. *Address:* Aikton, 109 Greenway, Totteridge, N.20. *Club:* American.
[*Died* 15 *Aug.* 1962.

McCOLLUM, Elmer Verner; Professor Emeritus of Biochemistry, Johns Hopkins Univ., Baltimore, U.S.A.; *b.* Kansas, 3 March 1879; *s.* of Cornelius A. McCollum and Martha Kidwell; *m.* 1st, 1907, Constance Carruth; one *s.* four *d.*; 2nd, 1945, Ernestine Becker. *Educ.:* Univ. of Kansas (B.A., M.S.); Yale Univ. (Ph.D.). Instructor, Asst. Prof., Assoc. Prof., Univ. of Wisconsin, 1907-13; Prof. Agric. Chem., 1913-17; Prof. of Biochem., Sch. of Hyg. and Public Health, Johns Hopkins Univ., Baltimore, 1917-46, Emeritus, 1946. Mem. Nat. Acad. of Sciences, 1920; Roy. Acad. Med., Belgium, 1920; Leopoldina, 1925; Mem. Swedish Roy. Acad. Sci., 1943; Mem. Amer. Philos. Soc., 1945; Roy. Soc. Arts (London), 1951; For. Mem. Roy. Soc., 1961, etc. Hon. degrees: Sc.D. Univ. of Cincinnati, 1920; LL.D. Univ. of Manitoba, 1937; LL.D. Johns Hopkins Univ., 1951; Dr. Humane Letters, Brandeis Univ., 1959. *Publications:* The Newer Knowledge of Nutrition, 1st edn. 1918, 5th edn., 1939; A History of Nutrition, 1957; very numerous papers on investigations relating to foods and nutrition; contrib. Jl. Biolog. Chem.; Amer. Journal of Nutrition. *Recreations:* history, autobiography, and walking in parks. *Address:* Johns Hopkins University, Baltimore 18, Maryland, U.S.A. (Home) 2402 Talbot Road, Baltimore 16, Maryland. *T.:* Wilkins 7-3274. *Club:* Johns Hopkins.
[*Died* 15 *Nov.* 1967.

McCOMBE, Francis William Walker, C.B. 1955; C.B.E. 1949; Chief Commissioner of Charities for England and Wales, 1953-60, retd.; *b.* 12 Dec. 1894; *o. s.* of late Rowan McCombe, F.R.C.S., D.P.H.; *m.* 1932, Blanche (*d.* 1953), *o. d.* of late F. F. Pitts; one *s.*; *m.* 1956, Alice Isabel Philip. *Educ.:* St. Lawrence College, Ramsgate; T.C.D. (M.A., LL.B.); Emmanuel College, Cambridge (M.A., LL.M.). European War, 1914-19, Capt. R.G.A. Called to Bar, Middle Temple, 1921; Dept. of H.M. Procurator General and Treasury Solicitor, 1923; personal assistant to Treasury Solicitor, 1927-34; transferred to Treasury, 1937; Controller of trading with the enemy and enemy property, 1939; Head of mission to U.S.A. on economic warfare, Oct. 1941; Counsellor, H.M. Embassy, Washington, and special adviser on enemy property and related financial blockade, 1942-45; Engaged in Washington, Paris, Lisbon, Madrid, Brussels and Ankara in discussions on German external assets, 1946-48; negotiated agreements with Switzerland, Sweden, Portugal, Spain, on enemy assets and looted gold. Vice-Pres., Governing Body, St. Lawrence Coll., Ramsgate; Legal Bd. of Church Assembly, 1952-65. *Publications:* Revenue and the Constitution, Halsbury, 1933; contribs. to Encyclopædia Britannica and law journals in U.K. and U.S.A. *Address:* 82 Morton Way, Southgate, N.14.
[*Died* 19 *April* 1969.

McCOMBIE, Major Hamilton, D.S.O. 1918; M.C.; M.A., D.Sc., Ph.D.; University Reader Emeritus in Chemistry; Fellow of King's Coll., Cambridge; *b.* 7 May 1880; *y. s.* of late Alex. McCombie; *m.* Jean, *e. d.* of late Sir John Craggs; three *d.* *Educ.:* Universities of Aberdeen, London and Strasbourg; formerly Lecturer in Chemistry, University of Birmingham; served European War (D.S.O., M.C.). *Publications:* several memoirs in Journal of Chemical Society. *Address:* Wendela, White Rose Lane, Woking, Surrey.
[*Died* 31 *May* 1962.

McCOMBIE, Col. William McC. D.; *see* Duguid-McCombie.

McCONACHIE, George William Grant; President, Canadian Pacific Air Lines Ltd., since 1947; *b.* 24 April 1909; *s.* of William Grant McConachie and Elizabeth (*née* Schnabel); *m.* 1935, Margaret MacLean; two *s.* *Educ.:* Edmonton, Alberta. Chief Pilot, Independent Airways Ltd., 1930, Pres. and Gen. Man., 1931-34; Pres. and Gen. Man., United Air Transport Ltd., 1934-37; Yukon Southern Air Transport Ltd., 1937-1941; Gen. Man., Canadian Pacific Air Lines, Ltd. (Western Lines), 1942-46; Asst. to President, 1946. Past President: Vancouver Board of Trade; Air Industries and Transport Assoc. (Ottawa). McKee Trophy award, 1945, for long and outstanding service in field of aviation. *Recreations:* tennis, golf, swimming. *Address:* 3875 Osler Street, Vancouver, B.C., Canada. *T.:* RE 8-2515.
[*Died* 29 *June* 1965.

McCONNEL, Maj.-Gen. Douglas Fitzgerald, C.B.1944; C.B.E. 1941; D.S.O. 1917; late R.A.; D.L. Ayrshire; *b.* 1893; *s.* of William Holdsworth McConnel, Heath End, Basingstoke; *m.* 1920, Ruth, *d.* of Major Walter Dutton Garnett-Botfield, of Beamish, Albrighton, Wolverhampton; one *d.* Served European War, 1914-18 (despatches, D.S.O.); G.O.C. Palestine and Transjordan, 1941-44; Comd. Lowland District, 1945-46; A.D.C. to the King, 1946-1947; retired pay, 1947. *Address:* Knockdolian, Colmonell, Ayrshire. *T.:* Colmonell 211.
[*Died* 7 *Feb.* 1961.

McCORMICK, Gerald Bernard, C.B. 1949; O.B.E. 1943; *m.* 1936, Reine Louise, *d.* of F. de Fontenay, Mauritius; one *d.* Late Director of Armament Supply, Admiralty; retired, May 1950. *Address:* L'Aragon, Pau, Basses-Pyrenées, France. *T.:* Pau 3957; Villa Magali, Capbreton, Landes, France. *Club:* English (Pau).
[*Died* 15 *April* 1966.

MacCORMICK, John MacDonald, LL.D. (Hon.); Chairman, Scottish Covenant Association, since 1949; *b.* 20 Nov. 1904; *yr. s.* of Captain Donald MacCormick and Marion (*née* MacDonald); *m.* 1938, Margaret Isobel Miller; two *s.* two *d.* *Educ.:* Woodside School, Glasgow; Glasgow University (M.A., LL.B.). Active in Scottish Home Rule movement since 1928: 1st Chm., Scottish National Party, 1928; Hon. Nat. Sec., 1928-42, when founded and became Chm. of Scottish Convention; Chm. of its National Assembly, 1947-; Rector of the University of Glasgow, 1950-53. Contested Inverness-shire, 1931, 1935, 1945, Paisley, 1948 and Border Counties, 1959. LL.D. (*hon. causa*) Glasgow, 1951. *Publications:* Experiment in Democracy, 1943; The Flag in the Wind, 1955. *Address:* 2 Park Quadrant, Glasgow. *T.:* Douglas 6138. *Club:* Glasgow Art (Glasgow).
[*Died* 13 *Oct.* 1961.

MacCORMICK, Brig. Kenneth, C.B. 1943; C.B.E. 1941; D.S.O. 1917; E.D.; M.B., Ch.B. N.Z.; F.R.C.S. Eng.; F.R.A.C.S.; Consulting Surgeon Auckland Hospital; President, New Zealand Branch, B.M.A., 1953; *b.* 13 Jan. 1891; *s.* of Charles

Edward MacCormick; *m.* Kathleen Reilly; *m.* 1943, Joan Stewart Fenwick; four *s.* one *d.* *Educ.:* Auckland Grammar School; University of Otago. Served European War, 1914-18, in Egypt, Gallipoli, and France; A.D.M.S. Northern Command, 1930-35; Director of Medical Services, Second N.Z. Expeditionary Force, 1939-43. Pres. N.Z. Red Cross Soc., 1961; K.H.S. *Address:* 98 Symonds Street, Auckland, N.Z. *T.:* 42059. *Clubs:* Northern, Officers (Auckland).

[*Died* 23 *Jan.* 1963.

McCORMICK-GOODHART, Leander, O.B.E. 1919; V.R.D.; K.St.J.; F.R.G.S.; Commercial Secretary (Hon.) British Embassy, Washington, D.C., U.S.A., 1925-1939, Counsellor (Hon.), 1942; *b.* 10 Aug. 1884; *e. s.* of F. E. McCormick-Goodhart; *g. s.* of Leander J. McCormick, Chicago; *m.* 1st, 1928, Janet, *e. d.* of Hon. T. W. Phillips, Butler, Pa., U.S.A.; one *s.* one *d.*; 2nd, 1952, Nita Kloeden, O.St.J. (Juanita Klo-Eden, A.L.C.M.), *y. d.* of Rev. O. Paul Kloeden, Adelaide, S.A.; one *s.* one *d.* *Educ.:* Cheam; Eton Coll.; New Coll., Oxf. Sub-Lt. R.N.V.R., 1907; passed as Naval Interpreter in three languages; research assistant to Lord Robert Cecil, M.P., 1907; R.N.V.R. officer selected to special sqdn. attending Tercentenary of Quebec, 1908; with Exhibns. Br. Bd. of Trade as Sec. (unpaid) to H.M. Comr.-Gen. for Argentine Centennial Exhibns., 1909-10; Asst. Leader, Brit. Univ. Students' Peace mission to Germany, 1913; accepted as Hon. Attaché, Washington, July 1914, but did not proceed owing to war; with Ops. Div., Admty. War Staff, 1914-19, dealing with blockade of Germany (despatches), and with Naval Section of British Peace Delegn., Paris, 1919; Mem. Supreme Economics Council (Communications Section); apptd. to Brit. Embassy, Washington, 1921, and served as Commercial Sec. (unpaid) to 1939; P.A. to H.M. Ambassador, the Marquess of Lothian, 1939-40, and supervisor of American Relief to Gt. Brit., 1939-42; retd., 1942 as Counsellor (Hon.) and received thanks of H.M. Govt. Comdr., ret. R.N.V.R.; Life Gov., Haileybury and Imperial Service Coll.; Mem., Maryland State Tercentennial, 1934; Mem., Adv. Cttee., Virginia 350th Anniversary Commn., 1957; Hon. Citizen of St. Augustine, Florida, 1950; Fell., Hon. Mem., or Mem., various hist. and numismatic socs. on both sides of Atlantic; Liveryman, Grocers' Company. Hon. Vice-Pres., Shakespeare and Audubon Naturalist Socs. of Washington, D.C. and of Washington Br., E.S.U. Mem. Gen. Council, Friends of the National Libraries; Middle Atlantic Regional Chm., Nat. Council, Metrop. Opera, 1958-59; Trustee (U.S.) Naval Historical Foundn.; Pres., Soc. for Preservation of Amer. Musical Heritage; informal "Adopter" of present H.M.S. Leander and her predecessor; personal McCormick family liaison with Univ of Va. Observatory founded by grandfather, 1922. *Publications:* Gentle Shafts (poems), 1942; Admiral Vernon Medals, 1944; Family Genealogical studies. *Recreations:* classical art, natural history and outdoor sports (Donor Mens' Doubles National Badminton Challenge Trophy (U.S.) 1937); Pres., Brit. Commonwealth Cricket Club (Washington, D.C.), 1953-. *Address:* Bellapais, 8303 Mount Vernon Memorial Highway, Alexandria, Virginia, U.S.A.; De le Brooke Manor, St. Mary's County, Maryland; 65 Hans Mansions, S.W.3. *Clubs:* Athenæum, St. James', R.N.V.R., Royal Automobile; Metropolitan (Washington); Casino (Chicago); Pilgrims, Ends of the Earth (N.Y.).

[*Died* 15 *Dec.* 1965.

McCOSH, Andrew Kirkwood, J.P., D.L.; mining engineer; *b.* 31 Aug. 1880; *e. s.* of Andrew Kirkwood McCosh, D.L., Cairnhill, Airdrie; *m.* 1920, Elizabeth, *d.* of H. B. Marshall, D.L., of Rachan, Broughton, Peeblesshire; three *s.* three *d.* *Educ.:* Fettes; Trinity College, Cambridge (B.A. Mechanical Science Tripos, 1902). Pres. British Iron and Steel Federation, 1936; Deputy Controller of Iron and Steel, Ministry of Supply, 1939-42; Pres. Mining Assoc. of Great Britain, 1944; President British Employers Confederation, 1945-46. *Address:* Culter Allers, Biggar, Lanarkshire. *Clubs:* Caledonian; Western (Glas.); New (Edin.).

[*Died* 27 *Sept.* 1967.

McCOWAN, Sir David James Cargill, 2nd Bt., *cr.* 1934; *b.* 15 Jan. 1897; *s.* of Sir David McCowan, 1st Bt. and Gertrude Margaret, C.B.E. 1923 (*d.* 1935), *d.* of David S. Cargill, Glasgow; *S.* father 1937; *m.* 1928, Muriel Emma Annie, *d.* of W. C. Willmott; two *s.* *Heir:* *s.* Hew Cargill, *b.* 1930. *Address:* Auchenheglish, Alexandria, Dunbartonshire.

[*Died* 29 *Aug.* 1965.

MacCRACKEN, Henry Noble; President, Vassar College, Poughkeepsie, N.Y., 1915-46, Emeritus; *b.* Toledo, Ohio, U.S.A., 19 Nov. 1880; *s.* of Henry Mitchell MacCracken and Catherine Hubbard; *m.* 1907, Marjorie Dodd; two *s.* two *d.* *Educ.:* New York University B.A., M.A.; Harvard University, Ph.D. Instructor, Syrian Protestant College, Beirut, 1900-03; John Harvard Fellow at Oxford, 1907-1908; Instructor in English at Sheffield Scientific School, Yale University, 1909-10; Asst. Professor, 1910-13, Professor of English, Smith College, 1913-15; during European War, was organizer and national director of Junior American Red Cross and in 1920 assisted in developing Red Cross organizations in several European countries; Hon. Chm. Kosciuszko Foundation; Member of Board of Polish Institute of Arts and Sciences in America; Trustee, Mackinac Coll., Mich., 1965-; Mem., Governors Adv. Cttee. on Hudson Valley 1964-. Chm. International Confs. of Christians, and Jews, Oxford, 1946, Fribourg, 1948. *Publications:* First Year English, 1903; English Composition in Theory and Practice, 1909; Introduction to Shakespeare, 1910; Manual of Good English, 1917; Minor Poems of Lydgate, 1912 and 1935; The College Chaucer, 1913; Shakespeare's Principal Plays, 1914 and 1935; The Family on Gramercy Park, 1949; The Hickory Limb, 1950; Old Dutchess Forever, 1956; Blithe Dutchess, 1958; Prologue to Independence, 1964. *Address:* 87 New Hackensack Rd., Poughkeepsie, N.Y., U.S.A.

[*Died* 7 *May* 1970.

McCREA, Rev. Alexander, M.A., D.D.; *b.* 5 Nov. 1879; *s.* of Edward McCrea and Elizabeth Moore; *m.* 1914, Kate Wolfe, Cork; two *s.* one *d.* *Educ.:* P.E.S. Methodist College, Belfast; Queen's Univ., Belfast. After four years in business, entered the ministry of the Methodist Church in Ireland; ministered in Londonderry, Dublin, Cork, and Belfast for 16 years; Theological Tutor, 1920; Principal of College, 1931-43. Methodist Dean of Residences in Queen's University, Belfast, 1931; a member of the Theological Faculty, 1932; President Methodist Church in Ireland, 1939-40. Chaplain: Parliament, Northern Ireland; Stranmillis Training College, Belfast. *Publications:* Why This Waste? A Defence of Christian Missions; The Mind of Christ; Irish Methodism in the Twentieth Century, a Symposium; The Work of Jesus in Christian Thought; Things concerning the Kingdom. *Address:* 21 Denorrton Park, Belfast, N.I.

[*Died* 26 *Jan.* 1963.

McCREERY, General Sir Richard Loudon, G.C.B., *cr.* 1949 (K.C.B., *cr.* 1943; C.B. 1943); K.B.E., *cr.* 1945 (M.B.E. 1926); D.S.O. 1940; M.C. 1918; *b.* 1 Feb. 1898; *s.* of Walter A. McCreery, Bilton Park, Rugby, and Emilia McAdam; *m.* 1928, Lettice, *d.* of late Lord Percy St. Maur; three *s.* one *d.* (and one *s.* decd.). *Educ.:* Eton; Royal

Military College, Sandhurst. 12th Lancers, 1915; served France, 1915-17, and August-November 1918 (M.C.); Staff College, 1928-1929; Brigade Major, 2nd Cavalry Brigade, 1930-33; commanded 12th Lancers (Armoured Car Regiment), 1935-38; G.S.O. 1 1st Division, 1938-39; served France, 1940 (D.S.O.); Maj.-Gen. 1943; Middle East, 1942, Tunisia, 1943, Italy, 1943-45 (C.B., K.C.B., K.B.E.); Chief of General Staff, Middle East, 1942; Lt.-Gen. 1944; commanded Eighth Army in Italy, 1944-45; G.O.C.-in-C. British Forces of Occupation in Austria and British representative on the Allied Commission for Austria, 1945-46; G.O.C.-in-C., B.A.O.R., 1946-48; General, 1948; British Army Representative, Military Staff Committee, U.N., 1948-49; retired, 1949; Colonel Commandant R.A.C., 1947-56; Colonel, 12th Lancers, 1951; Col., 9th/12th Royal Lancers, 1960. *Recreations:* hunting, steeplechasing (won Grand Military Gold Cup, Sandown Park, 1923, and rode winner again, 1928), and polo. *Address:* Stowell Hill, Templecombe, Somerset. *Club:* Cavalry. [*Died* 18 *Oct.* 1967.

McCROSTIE, Hugh Cecil, D.S.O. 1919; Director and Chief Secretary, Scottish Omnibuses Group of Companies, 1934-62; *b.* 1897; *y. s.* of Hugh McCrostie, Strath Tummel and Edinburgh, and Agnes Watson Hutchison; *m.* 1934, Doris Harcourt, Bebington, Cheshire; four *d.* *Educ.:* George Watson's Coll.; Edinburgh University (B.Com.). Member of Institute of Chartered Accountants of Scotland and of Institute of Transport. Served Royal Scots and Tank Corps, 1915-20, 2nd Lieut.-Capt., France, Belgium and North (Baltic) Russia (seriously wounded, despatches, D.S.O., Orders of St. Anne 2nd Class and St. Stanislas 2nd Class of Russia). Lieut.-Major 7/9th (Highlanders) Bn. The Royal Scots, T.A., 1920-31; Major, T.A.R.O., 1931-39; served War, 1939-42, Major, D.A.A.G., 4th Corps, N.W.E.F., and 5th Corps, T.D., (bar); Lt.-Col. Comdg. 1st Edinburgh Home Guard Bn., 1954-57. *Recreations:* country pursuits. *Address:* 27b Greenhill Gardens, Edinburgh 10. *T.:* Morningside 3848. *Club:* Caledonian United Service (Edinburgh). [*Died* 26 *Dec.* 1970.

McCULLAGH, (William) McKim (Herbert), D.S.O. 1918; M.C. 1914; T.D. 1949; F.R.C.S.; F.R.C.O.G.; Honorary Obstetric Surgeon, City of London Maternity Hospital; Honorary Gynæcological Surgeon, Samaritan Hospital, St. Mary's Hospital Group; Gynæcologist to St. Andrews Hospital, Dollis Hill, N.W.2; *b.* 1889; *e.* and *o. surv. s.* of S. W. McCullagh, B.A., Roselands, Rosetta Park, Belfast; *m.* 1932, Alison, *o. d.* of Henry Carrothers, Duneane, Ballynafeigh, Belfast; one *s.* two *d.* *Educ.:* Methodist Coll. and Queen's Univ., Belfast. Served European War, 1914-19, as an R.A.M.C. (S.R.) Officer; attached to No. 4 Field Ambulance Guards Division, 1914-18; Acting Lieut.-Colonel 137 Field Ambulance, 40th Division, 1918-19 (D.S.O., M.C., despatches five times). Served War of 1939-1945 as A.D.M.S. 47th London Division, 1939-42; A.D.M.S. Sierra Leone, 1942-44; O.C. Campbell College Military Hospital, Belfast, 1944-45. Arnott Medal, 1956. *Address:* 82 Harley Street, W.1. *T.:* Langham 3281; 7 Holly Lodge Gardens, Highgate, N.6. *T.:* Mountview 1911. [*Died* 17 *Aug.* 1964.

McCULLERS, Carson, (Mrs. Carson Smith McCullers); Author; *b.* 19 Feb. 1917; *d.* of Lamar Smith and Marguerite (*née* Waters); *m.* 1937, Reeves McCullers; no *c.* *Educ.:* Columbus High Sch.; Columbia and New York Universities. Guggenheim Fellow, 1942-43, 1946; award of American Academy of Arts and Letters, 1943; N.Y. Critics' Award, 1950. *Publications:* The Heart is a Lonely Hunter, 1940; Reflections in a Golden Eye, 1941; The Member of the Wedding, 1946; The Ballad of the Sad Café, 1951; Square Root of Wonderful, 1958; Clock Without Hands, 1961; Sweet as a Pickle and Clean as a Pig, 1964. *Address:* 131 South Broadway, Nyack, New York, U.S.A.; c/o Robert Lantz Ltd., 111 West 57th St., New York 19, N.Y. [*Died* 29 *Sept.* 1967.

McCULLOCH, Derek Ivor Breashur, O.B.E. 1939; *b.* Plymouth, Devon, 18 Nov. 1897; *y. s.* of Lionel and Bertha McCulloch; *m.* 1931, Eileen Hilda Barry; two *d.* *Educ.:* Croydon High School; Plymouth. Served European War, enlisting as private soldier when 17 years old, Public Schools Battalion; gazetted Green Howards (A.P.W.O.R.), 1917; transferred Royal Flying Corps, 1917; Adjt., served until 1921; First Asst. Secretary R.A.F. Memorial Fund: Central Argentine Railway, Buenos Aires, 1923; returned Europe for extraction of bullet from lung; Colonial Service appointment, 1925, withdrew for reasons of health; joined staff of B.B.C., 1926, as London Announcer; Children's Hour Organiser, 1933; Children's Hour Director, April 1938, appointment coincided with loss of leg in road accident; Head of Children's Hour, British Broadcasting Corporation, 1938-50; Children's Editor, News Chronicle, 1950-53. Author of many broadcast programmes and features; children's author; freelance lecturer and broadcaster. *Publications:* Cornish Adventure, 1937 (5 edns.); Cornish Mystery, 1950; The Son of the Ruler, 1954; Every Child's Birthday Book, 1956; Every Child's Pilgrim's Progress, 1956 (2 edns.); Editor of B.B.C. and various Annuals as Uncle Mac; contributor to Radio Times, Listener, Daily Telegraph, etc.; book reviews. *Recreations:* fishing, travel, cinematography. *Address:* The Crescent Corner, Keymer, Hassocks, Sussex. *T.:* Hassocks 2667. *Clubs:* M.C.C., Savage, B.B.C. [*Died* 1 *June* 1967.

McCULLOCH, Joseph, A.R.W.S. 1944; A.R.C.A.; *b.* 16 Feb. 1893; *s.* of William McCulloch and Frances Steward; *m.* 1934, Ethel Stone: one *d.* *Educ.:* Brudenell School, Leeds; Royal College of Art. Scholarship at Leeds School of Art when 16; a Royal Exhibitor in Painting to the Royal College of Art at 18; served Ireland and France, 1915-19; returned to the R.C.A., 1919; Painting Master at Ipswich School of Art, 1922-25; Instructor, Goldsmiths' College, 1941-50; Exhibitor at the Royal Academy, New English, etc. and Provincial galleries since 1928. *Publications:* 70 Illustrations in Highways and Byways in the Welsh Marches by S. P. B. Mais, 1939. *Recreations:* golf and billiards. *Club:* Chelsea Arts. [*Died* 11 *Nov.* 1961.

McCULLOCH, Sir Malcolm (McLeod), Kt. 1960; C.B.E. 1947; D.L.; King's Police Medal, 1941; Chief Constable, City of Glasgow Police, 1943-59; *b.* 26 October 1894; *er. s.* of late Archibald McCulloch, Corpach, Inverness-shire; unmarried. *Educ.:* Fort William High School, Inverness-shire. Joined City of Glasgow Police, 1912. Mem. of Standing Advisory Committee, Scottish Police Training School and College, 1947-59, Member of Board of Governors, Scottish Police College, 1956-59. Vice-Lieutenant, County of City of Glasgow, 1959-62; D.L. 1949-. President, Chief Constables' (Scotland) Association, 1957. King Christian the 10th Liberty Medal (Denmark), 1946; Medal of Freedom with Bronze Palm, U.S.A., 1946. *Recreation:* golf. *Address:* Staffa, 6 Arnwood Drive, Glasgow, W.2. *T.:* Western 4402. [*Died* 4 *June* 1969.

McCULLOCH, Norman George, C.B.E. 1952; resigned as Chairman Shirley Institute, Didsbury, Manchester, 1960; *b.* 30 June 1882; *s.* of late D. C. McCulloch and Mary McCulloch; *m.* 1933, Suzanne Gill. *Educ.:* Manchester College of Technology. *Recrea-*

tions: gardening, yachting. *Address:* 10 Madeira Court, Clifton Crescent, Folkestone, Kent. *T.:* Folkestone 55633. *Clubs:* National Liberal; Clarendon, Reform (Manchester). [*Died* 8 *March* 1965.

McCULLOCH, William Edward, M.D., M.B., Ch.B., F.R.S.T.M. & H.; F.Z.S.; F.R.I.P.H.H.; Fellow American Soc. of Tropical Medicine; Fellow British Medical Association, 1962; Chairman: Board of Governors, Jamaica Institute for Science and Literature; Advisory Board for the Printing Trade of Jamaica; Board of Visitors, Leper Hospital, Jamaica; Trustee, Jamaica Labour Party; *b.* 4 May 1896; *s.* of William McCulloch and Emma Esther Lindo; *m.* 1st, 1928, Eleanor Joan Wright (from whom he obtained a divorce, 1950); no *c.*; 2nd, 1950, Joyce Stewart, *Educ.:* Jamaica College (Captain, Musgrave Medallist, Prizeman in Chemistry and Mathematics, Jamaica Scholar, 1914); Aberdeen University. Private (University and Public Schools' Brigade) 20th Royal Fusiliers, 1915; wounded at Beaumont Hamel, 1916; Second Lt. Royal Flying Corps, 1917; Founder and first Pres. Aberdeen Univ. Labour Club; Pres. Aberdeen Univ. Sociological Society; Maunday Prizeman in Pathology, 1921; Certificate of London School of Tropical Medicine, 1923; West African Medical Staff, 1924; Pathologist, 1928; M.D. (Commendation for Thesis) Aberdeen, 1929; Dietetics Research Officer, West African Medical Staff, 1931; Secretary of Dietetics Committee of Nigeria; resigned from West African Medical Staff, 1934. Chairman: Caribbean Council of B.M.A., 1951-62; Nutrition Cttee. of Jamaica, 1952-1961. *Publications:* Viri Illustres Universitatum Abredonensium, 1923; Nutrition in Jamaica, 1945; Your Health in the Caribbean, 1954; and many papers in the West African Medical Journal, Nature, British Medical Journal, etc. *Recreations:* golf, motoring, gardening. *Address:* Norwich House, Port Antonio, Jamaica, W.I. *Clubs:* Athenæum, Royal Commonwealth Society. [*Died* 3 *July* 1963.

McCUNN, Major James, R.A.V.C., T.A. retired; Professor Emer. of Veterinary Anatomy, London University, at Royal Veterinary College; Acting Principal, Royal Veterinary College, 1954, Vice-Principal, 1955; *b.* 29 Dec. 1894; *s.* of Donald McCunn and Agnes McLellan; *m.* 1930, Eileen Carter; one *s.* one *d.* *Educ.:* private; Brunts School, Mansfield. M.R.C.V.S., Royal Veterinary College; served R.A.V.C., Mesopotamia and Kurdistan and in T.A. Army; retired 1932; M.R.C.S., L.R.C.P., London Hospital; F.R.C.S. 1955. Pathological Asst., Bacteriological Asst., London Hospital; Research Asst. Foot-and-Mouth Disease, Lister Institute; Royal Veterinary College, 1926-62; F.R.S.M. and Hon. Fellow, Hunterian Society; Examiner to R.C.V.S., Universities of: London, Cambridge, Liverpool, Edinburgh, Bristol, National University of Ireland and Wye Agricultural Coll.; Vice-Pres., Univ. of London Animal Welfare Soc.; Joint Editor Veterinary Journal, 1938-61; Treasurer, Past. Pres. and Victory Medallist, Central Veterinary Soc.; Member of Council, B.V.A.; Official Referee, Suffolk Horse Society; Pres. Section of Comparative Medicine, R.S.M. 1955-56; Treas. Victoria Veterinary Benevolent Fund. *Publications:* Editor Hobday's Surgical Diseases of the Dog and Cat and of Stubb's Anatomy of the Horse, 1938; papers on Surgical Subjects in Veterinary Record, Vety. Journal. *Recreations:* farming, horse and greyhound racing. *Address:* Larks Hall Farm, Chingford, Essex. *T.:* Silverthorn 1069. [*Died* 2 *April* 1967.

McCUTCHEON, Hon. (Malcolm) Wallace, P.C. (Can.); C.B.E. 1946; Q.C. (Can.); Senator, Government of Canada, since 1962; Chairman of Board, National Life Assurance Co. of Canada; Director: Canadian Enterprise Development Corp. Ltd.; Longmans Canada Ltd.; Montreal Trust Co.; Glens Falls Insurance Co.; Counsel, Shibley, Righton, Scane & McCutcheon, Toronto; *b.* London, Ont., 18 May 1906; *s.* of late Frederic W. C. McCutcheon and Mary (*née* Vining); *m.* 1934, Eva Trow Borland, *d.* of late York Borland, Toronto; three *s.* two *d.* *Educ.:* Oakwood Collegiate Inst., Toronto; Victoria Coll., Toronto Univ. (B.A.). Associate, Soc. of Actuaries, 1927; Osgoode Hall, Toronto; called to Bar of Ont., 1930. Practised law with Osler, Hoskin & Harcourt, Toronto, 1930-34. Asst. to Pres., Nat. Life Assce. Co. of Canada, 1934; Sec., 1937; Asst. Gen. Man., 1938. Served with Wartime Prices and Trade Bd., 1941-46 (latterly Dep. Chm.). Vice-Pres. and Man. Dir., Argus Corp. Ltd. and Dir. and/or Officer of a large number of industrial and financial cos., 1945-62. Minister-without-Portfolio, Govt. of Canada, 1962-63; Minister of Trade and Commerce, Feb.-Apr. 1963. K.C. (Ont.), 1947. Chm., Ont. Cancer Inst.; Chm., Princess Margaret Hosp.; Mem., Canadian Assoc. of Actuaries; Gov., Canadian Coun.; Gov., Internat. Chamber of Commerce; Trustee, United Community Fund of Metropolitan Toronto; Mem. academic and other Boards, etc. Holds hon. doctorates. Mem., United Church of Canada. Progressive Conservative. *Address:* (home) Ellanvannin Farms, R.R.1, Gormley, Ont., Canada; (office) 522 University Ave., Toronto, Ont., Canada. *Clubs:* Albany, Granite, National, Rosedale Golf, Tadenac, Toronto, University, York (Toronto); London (London, Ont.); Montreal, Mount Royal (Montreal); Rideau, Country (Ottawa); Vancouver (Vancouver). [*Died* 23 *Jan.* 1969.

McDAVID, Sir Herbert (Gladstone), Kt. 1957; C.B.E. 1944; Director: Glen Line Ltd., 1938-65 (late Managing Director and Chairman); McGregor, Gow & Holland Ltd., 1939-65 (late Managing Director and Chairman); McGregor, Gow & Robinson Ltd., Liverpool, 1945-63 (late Chairman); *b.* 19 May 1898; *e. s.* of Denis and Octavia McDavid; unmarried. *Educ.:* Liverpool Institute High School. Served Alfred Holt & Co., Liverpool (Blue Funnel Line), 1915-1965 (late Partner). Served European War, 1914-18, Liverpool Scottish, awarded M.S.M. Mem., Baltic Exchange; Liveryman, Worshipful Company of Shipwrights. Dep. Dir. of Sea Transport, Min. of War Transport, 1941-45; Dir. of Sea Transport, 1945; Ministry of Transport Representative for Middle East, 1956. Member, Port of London Authority, 1958-64. American Medal of Freedom with Silver Palm, 1947; Officer of Order of Orange Nassau (Netherlands), 1947. *Recreation:* fishing. *Address:* 35 Dorset House, Gloucester Place, N.W.1. *Clubs:* City of London, East India and Sports, Royal Automobile, City Livery. [*Died* 14 *Oct.* 1966.

McDAVID, James Wallace, C.B.E. 1945; D.Sc.; F.R.I.C.; M.I.Chem.E.; formerly Division Chairman, Imperial Chemical Industries Ltd., Nobel Division; *b.* 16 April 1887; *s.* of late John McKeand McDavid and of Jessie Ann Whyte; *m.* 1914, Jessie Elizabeth Wyllie Stewart; two *s.* one *d.* *Educ.:* Edinburgh University (B.Sc. 1908, Carnegie Research Scholar); Manchester University (1851 Exhibition Scholar, M.Sc. 1912). Joined Nobel's Explosives Co. Ltd., 1912. Served in France Sept. 1914-Feb. 1915 as 2nd Lieut. R.F.A. D.Sc. Edinburgh, 1916. Successively Dept. Manager, Works Manager, Production Director and Jt. Managing Delegate Director of I.C.I. (Explosives) Ltd. *Publications:* various papers in scientific journals. *Recreation:* golf. *Address:* Rosearden, West Kilbride,

Ayrshire. *T.:* West Kilbride 3107. *Clubs:* Royal Scottish Automobile, Conservative (Glasgow); Royal and Ancient (St. Andrews). [*Died* 22 *April* 1964.

MacDERMOT, Terence W. L., M.A. (Oxon.); LL.D. (McGill); Head of Department of Political Science, Bishop's University, Lennoxville, Canada, since 1961; *b.* 13 Sept. 1896; *s.* of Henry Miles Fleetwood MacDermot and Mary Emily Langdon; *m.* 1924; one *s.* two *d.* *Educ.:* Montreal High Sch; McGill Univ.; Oxford Univ. Served overseas with 7th Canadian Siege Battery, 1917-18; recommended on field for commission, Oct. 1918; Quebec Rhodes Scholar, 1919-22; Master Hotchkiss School, Conn., U.S.A.; Master Lower Canada Coll., Montreal; Asst. Professor of History, McGill University, 1929; on leave from University to be National Secretary, League of Nations Society in Canada, 1934-35; Principal, Upper Canada College, Toronto, 1935; on leave from Upper Canada College, Jan.-May 1942, with Bureau of Public Information, Ottawa; on Active Service Can. Army, 1942-45, Lieut.-Colonel. Dept. of External Affairs, Ottawa, 1945; High Comr. for Canada in S. Africa, 1950-1954; Ambassador to Greece and Ambassador to Israel, 1954-57; High Comr. for Canada in Australia, 1957-61. *Publications:* (with Francis Hankin) Recovery By Control, 1933; (Joint) Canada in World Affairs, 1940; pamphlet, Can We Make Good, 1940; historical articles, reviews, etc. and contributor to The Liberal Way, 1933; The Educational Year Book, 1937; The Seventh, 1953. *Address:* Bishop's University, Lennoxville, P. Que., Canada. *Clubs:* University (Montreal); St. George's (Sherbrooke). [*Died* 6 *May* 1966.

McDONAGH, James Eustace Radclyffe, F.R.C.S.; *b.* London, 17 Oct. 1881. *Educ.:* Bedford; St. Bartholomew's; Vienna. Surgeon, London Lock Hospitals; Hunterian Professor Royal College of Surgeons, 1916; Founder and Director Nature of Disease Institute since 1929; research work has led to reaching of conclusions on cause of syphilis, the common cold, influenza, the corresponding infections in animals, grass sickness, and other manifestations of disease in horses, etc., which are at variance with those generally held. *Publications:* Textbook on Venereal Diseases, 1915 and 1920; The Nature of Disease (three vols.), 1924-27-31; The Nature of Disease Journal (three vols.), 1932-1934; The Common Cold and Influenza, 1936; The Universe Through Medicine, 1940; The Nature of Disease To Date, 1946; The Nature of Disease Institute's First, Second and Third Annual Reports, 1948, 1949 and 1951; The Universe In The Making, 1948; A Further Study in the Nature of Disease, 1954; A Final Study in the Nature of Disease, 1959; The Nature of the Universe, Health and Disease, 1963. *Address:* Park Gate, Onehouse, Stowmarket, Suffolk. *T.:* Stowmarket 2848. *Club:* Pratt's. [*Died* 14 *Feb.* 1965.

MACDONALD, 7th Baron, *cr.* 1776; **Alexander Godfrey Macdonald of Macdonald,** M.B.E. 1944; T.D.; Lord Lieutenant since 1952, and Convener since 1968 (Vice-Convener, 1952), of the County of Inverness; *e. s.* of Hon. Godfrey Evan Hugh Macdonald and Helen, *e. d.* of Meyrick Bankes, and *g. d.* of late Meyrick Bankes, Winstanly Hall, Lancashire; *S.* grandfather, 1947; *m.* 1945, Anne, *o. d.* of late Alfred Whitaker and of Mrs. Maclachlan; two *s.* one *d.* *Educ.:* Eton; Magdalene College, Cambridge, M.A. J.P. and a C.C. for Inverness-shire; late Major Q.O. Cameron Highlanders. Member of: Agricultural Advisory Cttee. for Skye (Chm.), 1950-52; Skye Hosp. Board of Management (Chm.); North of Scotland Hydro-electric Board (part-time), 1961-, and Consultative Council (Chm.); Chairman Inverness-shire Unionist Association, 1945-50; Pres., Association of County Councils in Scotland, 1958-60. Grand Master Mason of Scotland, 1953-57. *Heir:* *s.* Hon. Godfrey James Macdonald, *b.* 28 Nov. 1947. *Address:* Armadale Castle, Isle of Skye. *Clubs:* Boodle's; New (Edinburgh); Highland (Inverness). [*Died* 29 *Nov.* 1970.

MACDONALD OF GWAENYSGOR, 1st Baron, *cr.* 1949, of Gwaenysgor, Flint; **Gordon Macdonald,** P.C. 1951; K.C.M.G., *cr.* 1946; Member of Colonial Development Corporation, 1952-59; National Governor, B.B.C. for Wales, 1952-60; Chairman National Broadcasting Council for Wales since 1953; *b.* Gwaenysgor, Prestatyn, N. Wales, 27 May 1888; *y. s.* of late Thomas and Ellen Macdonald, Ashton-in-Makerfield, nr. Wigan; *m.* 1913, Mary, *y. d.* of William and Margaret Lewis, Blaenau Festiniog, N. Wales; two *s.* two *d.* *Educ.:* St. Luke's Elementary School, Stubshaw Cross, Ashton-in-Makerfield, nr. Wigan; Ruskin College, Oxford. Commenced working underground in the Coal Industry at thirteen years, 1901; elected Wigan Board of Guardians, 1920 (Chm., 1929-30); Pres. Bryn Gates Co-operative Soc., 1922-24; elected Miners Agent, 1924-29, Mineworkers Fed. of Gt. Brit.; M.P. (Lab.) Ince Div., 1929-42; resigned from Parliament, July 1942; Regional Controller, Ministry of Fuel and Power, Lancashire, Cheshire, and North Wales region, 1942-46; Governor of Newfoundland and C.-in-C. of Newfoundland and its Dependencies, 1946-49; Chm. Commission of Govt. of Newfoundland until confederation with Canada, 1949; Paymaster-General, 1949-51. J.P. County of Lancashire; Labour Party Whip, 1931-34; Chairman of Committees, House of Commons, 1934-41; Nat. Pres. Band of Hope Union of Gt. Brit., 1951; Pres. N.W. Gt. Brit. Nat. Soc. for the Blind, 1951; Leader Deleg. to Commonwealth Conf. on Economic Aid to countries of S.E. Asia at Sydney, Aust., 1950; Deleg. to 5th Annual Conf. of U.N.O. Gen. Assembly, Lake Success, 1950. Hon. Doctor of Laws, Mount Allison Univ., Sackville, N.B., Canada; Hon. LL.D. University of Wales. *Publications:* Parliamentary Impressions (in Welsh), 1948; Newfoundland at the Crossroads (speeches and radio addresses made in Newfoundland), 1949. *Heir:* *s.* Hon. Gordon Ramsay Macdonald, M.A. [*b.* 16 Oct. 1915; *m.* 1941, Leslie Margaret, *d.* of John Edward Taylor, Rainford, Lancs; two *d.*]. *Address:* Prestatyn, North Wales. [*Died* 20 *Jan.* 1966.

McDONALD, Alexander, C.B.E. 1965; M.I.C.E.; late Secretary of the Institution of Civil Engineers; *b.* 18 May 1903; *m.* 1955. *Educ.:* Edinburgh University (B.Sc.). Public Works Department, Nigeria, 1925-54; Director of Public Works, Sierra Leone, 1942-43; Inspector-General of Public Works, Nigeria, 1951-54. *Publications:* various papers. *Recreation:* golf. *Address:* Institution of Civil Engineers, Great George Street, S.W.1. *T.:* 01-839 3611. *Clubs:* East India and Sports, Roehampton. [*Died* 27 *March* 1968.

MACDONALD, Angus Alexander, C.I.E. 1946; O.B.E. 1942; late I.C.S.; retired; *b.* 12 Nov. 1904; *s.* of Dr. Coll A. and M. I. Macdonald; *m.* 1932, Beatrice Mary Wolferstan-Tordiffe; no *c.* *Educ.:* Edinburgh Academy; Edinburgh University. Indian Civil Service; Assistant Commissioner, 1928-33; Deputy Commissioner, Lyallpur, 1933-36; Deputy Commissioner, Amritsar, 1936-41; Deputy Home Secretary, 1941-43; Home Secretary, Punjab, 1943-1947. *Recreations:* shooting, fishing. *Address:* Sealasdair, Ardentallen, Oban, Argyll. [*Died* 25 *Sept.* 1965.

McDONALD, Sir Charles (George), K.B.E. 1970 (C.B.E. 1950); Kt. 1962; M.B., Ch.M.; F.R.C.P. (London), 1956; F.R.A.C.P. 1938; Consulting Physician, Sydney, Australia, since 1927; *b.* Newcastle, N.S.W., 25 March 1892; *s.* of late William McDonald and Mary (*née* Slattery), Sydney; *m.* 1919, Elsie Isabel, *d.* of late William H. Hosie, Sydney; four *s.* one *d.* *Educ.:* Sydney High School; Univ. of Sydney. Hon. Asst. Phys. 1920-33, Hon. Phys. 1933-52, Consultant Phys. 1952-, Royal Prince Alfred Hosp., Sydney; Consultant Physician: Royal North Shore Hosp., Sydney; Lewisham Hosp. and St. Joseph's Hosp., Auburn, Aust. Lectr. in Clin. Med., Univ. of Sydney, 1938-52. Dep. Chancellor, 1954-1955, and Fellow of Senate, 1941-, Chancellor, 1964-, of University of Sydney. Hon. Secretary, 1944-48, Vice-President, 1948-50, Censor-in-Chief, 1950-54, President, 1954-56, R.A.C.P. Chm. Council, Sancta Sophia Coll., Univ. of Sydney, 1953-; Mem. Medical Bd. of N.S.W., 1946-62; Director: Royal North Shore Hosp., Sydney, 1959-62; Mutual Life and Citizens' Assurance Co. Ltd., 1951-66; Chm. Australian Rheumatism Council, 1959-; Pres. first Australian Rheumatism Congress, Sydney, 1963. Delegate of Univ. of Sydney at Congress of Empire Universities, Oxford, 1948 and at Congress of Univs. of the British Commonwealth, London, 1963. Trustee, Public Library of N.S.W., 1964-. Served European War, 1914-18, Capt. A.I.F; served War of 1939-45 (despatches): Lt.-Col. A.I.F.; Greece, Crete, Palestine, Egypt, 1941-43. K.C.S.G. 1960. *Publications:* The Physician and his Workshop, 1951; The Professions in Our National Life, 1955; medical and medico-historical articles. *Address:* 2/1 Winslow Gardens, 66 Darling Point Road, Darling Point, N.S.W., Australia. *T.:* FB 3927; 143 Macquarie St., Sydney, N.S.W. *T.:* BU 2071. *Clubs:* Royal Sydney Golf, Australian, Sydney University Staff (Sydney). [*Died* 23 *April* 1970.

MACDONALD, Col. Clarence Reginald, C.M.G. 1918; p.s.c.; late Royal Warwickshire Regt; *b.* 1876; *y. s.* of late Lieut.-Gen R. M. Macdonald, Madras Staff Corps; *m.* 1902, Violet Irene, *d.* of late T. Phelan, Clonmel; two *s.* *Educ.:* Rugby School. Served S. Africa, 1900-2 (Queen's medal with three clasps, King's medal with two clasps); N.W. Frontier of India, 1908 (medal with clasp); European War, 1914-19, G.S.O.2, N.Z. Military Forces in New Zealand (despatches, Bt. Lt.-Col., C.M.G.); Bde. Major, 8 Infantry Bde., Plymouth, 1920-22; commanded 1 Bn., The Royal Warwickshire Regt., 1923-27; A.A.G. British Army of the Rhine, 1928-29; Officer i/c Infantry Record and Pay Office, Perth, 1930-33; retired pay, 1933. *Address:* Grassmead, Beanacre, Nr. Melksham, Wiltshire. [*Died* 28 *Nov.* 1962.

MacDONALD, David Keith Chalmers, M.A., Ph.D., D.Phil.; F.R.S. 1960; F.R.S. (Can.) 1958; Principal Research Officer, Head, Low Temperature and Solid State Physics Group, National Research Council Ottawa, Canada, since 1951; *b.* Glasgow, Scotland, 24 July 1920; *s.* of George MacDonald, O.B.E., B.Sc. (Edin.) and Winifred Mary (*née* Halley); *m.* 1943, Moira Edwards (*née* Lawrie); two *d.* *Educ.:* Edinburgh University; Oxford University. M.A. (Edin.), 1941. Served War of 1939-45, with British Army (latterly Capt., R.E.M.E.), 1941-46; on staff of radar and telecommunications branch, Military Coll. of Science, 1943-46. Ph.D. (Edin.), 1946; Nuffield Research Fellow, I.C.I. Research Fellow, Clarendon Lab., Oxford, 1946-51; M.A. (by decree, Oxon.), 1948; D.Phil. (Oxon.), 1949; F.R.S.E., 1954; Hon. Chairman, Dept. of Physics, 1955-60, Hon. Professor, Dept. of Physics, 1960, Univ. of Ottawa. Gold Medal, Canadian Assoc. of Physicists, 1960. Gold Medal for Science, Professional Institute of Public Service of Canada, 1963. *Publications:* Near Zero (An Introd. to Low Temperature Physics), 1961 (New York); Thermoelectricity (An Introduction to the Principles), 1962 (New York); Noise and Fluctuations (An Introduction), 1962 (New York); Introductory Statistical Mechanics for Physicists, 1963 (New York); Faraday, Maxwell and Kelvin, 1964 (New York); papers on Brownian Movement and spontaneous fluctuations; topics in low temperature physics (particularly electronic conduction and related phenomena); thermodynamic properties of lattices; information theory, etc., in learned journals (*e.g.* in Proc. Roy. Soc., Philos. Mag., Phys. Rev., etc.). *Recreations:* thinking, television, arguing. *Address:* Division of Pure Physics, National Research Council, Sussex Drive, Ottawa 2, Ontario, Canada. *T.:* 992-0183. [*Died* 28 *July* 1963.

MACDONALD, Rev. Donald Bruce M.A., LL.D.; retd.; Chm. Bd. of Governors, University of Toronto, 1932-45, Member of Board, 1906-46; *b.* Toronto, 24 Feb. 1872; *s.* of John Kay Macdonald and Charlotte Emily Perley; *m.* 1st, Theresa K. Parfitt; no *c.*; 2nd, 1938, Frances M. Brigstocke; one *d.* *Educ.:* Toronto Collegiate Institute; Ridley College; University of Toronto; Knox College, New College, Edinburgh. Headmaster, St. Andrew's College, Aurora, 1900-35; University Royal Commission, 1905-6; Board of Trustees Toronto General Hospital; Chairman, Trustees Royal Ontario Museum; Chairman, Board of Governors, St. Andrew's College; President, Amateur Athletic Union of Canada, 1919-21; President, Canadian Club, Toronto, 1903-04. *Publications:* Sunday Evenings at St. Andrew's College; various addresses on educational subjects. *Address:* 86 Woodlawn Avenue East, Toronto, Canada. *Clubs:* Canadian, Faculty Union (Toronto). [*Died* 27 *Nov.* 1962.

MACDONALD, George, C.M.G. 1953; M.D.; Ch.B.; F.R.C.P.; D.P.H.; D.T.M.; Professor of Tropical Hygiene in Univ. of London since 1946 and Director Ross Institute of Tropical Hygiene, London School of Hygiene and Tropical Medicine, since 1945; *b.* 1903; *s.* of late Professor J. S. Macdonald, F.R.S.; *m.* 1932, Mary, *d.* of late Sir Roger Hetherington, C.B.; one *s.* two *d.* *Educ.:* Liverpool Institute; Liverpool University. Research Asst. Sir Alfred Lewis Jones Laboratory, W. Africa, 1924-29; Malaria Research Officer, Malaria Survey of India, 1929-31; Officer Mariani Medical Assoc., Assam, India, 1932-37; Assistant Director, Ross Institute, 1937; joined R.A.M.C. 1939; went with Malaria Field Laboratory to Middle East, 1940; Malaria Consultant M.E.F. 1943; Malaria Consultant C.M.F., 1944; Hon. Consultant in Malariology to the Army, 1949; member World Health Organization Expert Panel on Malaria, 1948- (Chm., 1958, 1963 and 1966), and on Environmental Sanitation, 1950-61 (Chm., 1953); Leader World Health Organization Mission to Korea, 1952; Member: Colonial Medical Research Cttee., 1953-1961; Tropical Medicine Research Board, 1961-64; Medical Advisory Cttee. on Technical Assistance Overseas, 1963-. Darling Foundation Award, 1954; Bernhard Nocht Medal, 1963; Fell. Royal Soc. of Tropical Medicine and Hygiene (President, 1965-67); Hon. Fellow, American Public Health Association. Hon. Corresp. Member: Deutsche Tropenmedizinische Gesellschaft; Société Belge de Médecine Tropicale. *Publications:* Epidemiology and Control of Malaria, 1957; (with Russell, West and Manwell) Practical Malariology, 1963; various papers on Tropical Medicine and Hygiene in Annals of Tropical Medicine and Parasitology, Indian Journal Medical Research, etc. *Address:* Byron House, North Road, Highgate, N.6. *T.:* Mountview 2166. *Club:* Athenæum. [*Died* 10 *Dec.* 1967.

MACDONALD, James, C.B.E. 1953; Director of Research and Education, Forestry

Commission, since 1948; Acting Deputy Director-General, 1960-63; *b.* 3 Aug. 1898; *s.* of Roderick and Christina Macdonald; *m.* 1933, Zoe Linton, *d.* of Ronald Sinclair, Edinburgh; two *s.* one *d.* *Educ.:* Blairgowrie High School; University of Edinburgh. Joined Forestry Commission, 1924; Research Officer, 1924-32; Research Officer and Lecturer at Imperial Forestry Institute, Oxford, 1932-36; Divisional Officer, Eastern England, 1936-39; Timber Production Department, in charge of divisions at Cambridge, Nottingham and Aberdeen, 1939-45; Conservator of Forests, 1946-48. President, International Union of Forest Research Organizations, 1957-61, Membre d'Honneur, 1962. F.R.S.E. 1957. *Publications:* papers in scientific and technical journals. *Address:* Woodcombe, Madeira Road, West Byfleet, Surrey. *T.:* Byfleet 43527. *Club:* Union. [*Died* 28 *April* 1963.

McDONALD, Sir John, Kt., *cr.* 1937; J.P. City of Glasgow; *b.* 24 May 1874; *m.* 1900, Janet Campbell Harrison; one *s.* one *d*; *m.* Christina McLachlan. *Educ.:* Glasgow. *Address:* Kilmardinny House, Kilmardinny, Bearsden, Dunbartonshire. *T.A.:* Litsun Glasgow. *T.:* Bearsden 1150. [*Died* 31 *Jan.* 1964.

MACDONALD, Most Rev. John Hugh; Archbishop of Edmonton (R.C.), since 1938; *b.* 3 April 1881; *s.* of Ronald MacDonald and Elizabeth Grant. *Educ.:* St. Francis Xavier University, Antigonish, Nova Scotia; Urban College, Rome. Teacher at St. F. X. Univ., 1906-11; Asst. Pastor, Glace Bay, N.S., 1911-14; Pastor, New Waterford, N.S., 1914-1924, Sydney, N.S., 1924-34; Bishop of Victoria, B.C., 1934-36; Coadjutor, Edmonton, 1936-38. Asst. Pontifical Throne, 1948. Hon. Dr. of Laws, Univ. of Alberta, 1960; St. Francis Xavier Univ., 1953. *Address:* 10044 113 St., Edmonton, Alberta, Canada. *T.:* 83242. [*Died* 17 *Jan.* 1965.

MACDONALD, John Robert, O.B.E.; Stipendiary Magistrate for Kingston-upon-Hull, 1925-52; *b.* 29 June 1879; 3rd *s.* of John Robert Macdonald of Craigengower and Jane Hamilton; *m.* 1916, Marrion Elizabeth Evetts (*d.* 1962), *d.* of John Galloway Watson and Janet Edward, *o. c.* of Capt. Edward Evetts, H.E.I.C. service. *Educ.:* Henley House, London; Streete Court, Westgate-on-Sea. Discount broker with his father (J. R. Macdonald & Co., London), 1900-06; Civil Engineer, 1906-08; called to Bar, Inner Temple, 1911; Member of the North-Eastern Circuit; Member of Bar Council, 1920-22; Pres. Soc. of Stipendiary Magistrates of England and Wales, 1952-. B.E.F. in ranks of London Scottish, 1914-15; later France, Salonica, Egypt, Palestine, commissioned in 17th London Regiment (Tower Hamlets Rifles, the Rifle Brigade), on the Staffs of 180th and 181st Infantry Brigades, 1916-17; Major on Staff of XXth Army Corps and H.Q., Egypt, 1917-19 (1914 Star, O.B.E., Order of the Nile, despatches). Home Guard, 1940-41. *Publications:* Traction Engine Law Codified, 1913 and 1921; Craigengower (privately), 1950; many contributions to the Press. *Recreations:* reading, tapestry. *Address:* Ventnor House, 25 Westgate, Hornsea, Yorks. [*Died* 5 *Sept.* 1965.

McDONALD, Niel, O.B.E. 1919; F.F.A., R.C.S.; Consulting Anaesthetist: Royal Northern Hospital; Hosp. for Sick Children, Gt. Ormond St.; Queen Mary's Hosp., Stratford; St. Peter's Hosp. for Stone; specialized in Anaesthetics since 1921; *b.* Preston, Lancs., 29 July 1886; *s.* of John McDonald, J.P., Preston, Lancs., and Barr, Ayrshire; *m.* 1927, Hilda Gladys May Bright (*d.* 1962); no *c.* *Educ.:* privately; Preston Gram. Sch.; University of Manchester. M.B., Ch.B. (Manch.) 1909; M.R.C.S. (Eng.), L.R.C.P. (Lond.) 1909; D.A. (Eng.) 1935; F.F.A., R.C.S. 1949. Res. surgical posts, Preston Roy. Infirmary and Ancoats Hosp., Manchester, 1909-12; general practice, Wellington, N.Z., 1912-13; M.O. in charge of Roy. Free Hosp. for Officers, London, 1915-19. Late Hon. Anaesthetist, Roy. Free Hosp. and Metropolitan Ear, Nose and Throat Hosp.; Specialist Anaesthetist, E.M.S., 1939-45. F.R.Soc.Med. (late Mem. Council Anaesthetic Section); F.Assoc. Anaesthetists of Gt. Britain and Ire.; Mem. B.M.A. *Publications:* various articles on anaesthetic subjects. *Recreations:* reading, walking, motoring. *Address:* 146 Wood St., Barnet, Herts. *T.:* Barnet, Herts, 6180. [*Died* 20 *Jan.* 1968.

MACDONALD, Captain Sir Peter Drummond, K.B.E., *cr.* 1945; M.P. (U.) Isle of Wight since 1924; *b.* Nova Scotia, 1895; *s.* of late Ronald A. Macdonald, of Nova Scotia; *m.* 1933, Lady Jean Alice Elaine Cochrane (*d.* 1955), 2nd *d.* of Lt.-Gen. the 12th Earl of Dundonald, K.C.B., K.C.V.O.; *m.* 1956, Dr. Phoebe Napier Harvey, M.B., F.F.A.R.C.S., D.A., Shanklin. *Educ.:* Dalhousie College; Trinity Hall, Cambridge. Bar, Inner Temple; served European War; contested Isle of Wight, 1923; Parliamentary Private Secretary to President Board of Trade, 1928-30; serving R.A.F.V.R., 1939. Squadron Leader. F.R.S.A. 1949. *Address:* 26 Whitelands House, S.W.3; Ningwood Manor, Yarmouth, I. of W. *T.:* Yarmouth 202. *Clubs:* Carlton; Royal Victoria Yacht. [*Died* 2 *Dec.* 1961.

McDONALD, Sir (Robert) Ross, Kt., *cr.* 1950; Q.C. (Australia) 1936; Barrister; *b.* Albany, W.A., 25 Jan. 1888; *s.* of Angus McDonald and Mary McDonald (*née* Elder); unmarried. *Educ.:* Scotch College, W.A.; Adelaide University, S. Australia. Admitted to Bar, 1910; LL.B. Adelaide Univ., 1914. Served European War, A.I.F., France and Belgium, 1916-18; Commonwealth Militia, Captain, 1920-30. Member for West Perth, W.A. Parliament, 1933-50; Leader Liberal Party, 1938-46; Member State Government, 1947-49, Attorney General, Minister for Native Affairs and for Housing; Member Senate, University of W.A., 1950-60. Hon. LL.D. Univ. of W.A., 1961. *Publications:* Digest of W.A. Law Reports. *Recreation:* bowls. *Address:* 6 Esplanade, Perth, Western Australia. *T.:* 23.4874. *Club:* Weld (Perth, W.A.). [*Died* 24 *March* 1964.

McDONALD, Thomas Pringle, Q.C. (Scot.) 1948; Sheriff of Aberdeen, Kincardine and Banff, since 1954; *b.* 18 August 1901; *s.* of late James McDonald, M.D., Belford, Northumberland; *m.* 1930, Harriet Selby McDowall; one *s.* two *d.* *Educ.:* George Watson's College, Edinburgh; Edinburgh University. M.A. 1922; LL.B. 1924. Admitted to Faculty of Advocates, 1927; served in The Royal Scots and Judge Advocate General's Department, 1940-45; Standing Counsel to War Dept. and Air Min., 1945-48; Chairman, Medical Appeal Tribunal, 1948-54; Keeper of Advocates Library, 1949-56; Vice-Dean, Faculty of Advocates, 1956-67; Procurator for the Church of Scotland, 1957-68. Chairman, Appeal Tribunal for Conscientious Objectors in Scotland, 1957. *Address:* 68 Northumberland Street, Edinburgh 3. *T.:* 031-556 5763. *Clubs:* Scottish Liberal; Royal Northern (Aberdeen). [*Died* 23 *July* 1969.

McDONALD, Sir Warren (D'Arcy), K.B.E. 1964 (C.B.E. 1957); Chairman, Commonwealth Banking Corporation, since 1959; Chairman, McDonald Industries Pty. Ltd., since 1947; Chairman, Reinsurance Co. of Australasia Ltd., since 1962; Director: I.C.I.A.N.Z., since 1961; Email, since 1964; *b.* 23 September 1901; *s.* of William and Christine McDonald; *m.* 1927, Christine O'Sullivan; three *d.* *Educ.:* Launceston Grammar School, Tasmania. Hydro Electric Department, Tasmania, 1919-24; Engrg. Contractor, 1926-38 (Chm. McDonald Constructions, 1938-). Served with A.I.F., 1939-45 (Middle East, India, S.W. Pacific). Mem. Aust. Nat. Airlines Commn., 1951-60; Mem. Council, Aust. Nat. Univ., 1951-64; Chm. Aust. Nat. Airways Commn., 1957-60; Vice-Chm., Perpetual Trustee Co. (Canberra), 1955-. *Recreations:* golf and fishing. *Address:* 8 Mugga Way, Red Hill, Canberra, A.C.T. *T.:* U1387. *Clubs:* Australian (Sydney); Commonwealth (Canberra); Royal Yacht Squadron, Royal Melbourne Golf, Royal Sydney Golf, Royal Canberra Golf. [*Died* 12 *Nov.* 1965.

MACDONALD-TYLER, Sir Henry Hewey Francis, Kt., *cr.* 1930; C.I.E. 1919; *b.* 13 Feb. 1877; *s.* of Canon Macdonald (who assumed name of Tyler); *m.* 1920, Winifred Judith, *d.* of T. D. Grimke-Drayton of Clifford Manor, Gloucestershire; two *d.* *Educ.:* St. Columba's College, Co. Dublin; Rossall School; Selwyn College, Cambridge (Exhibition). Passed into Indian Civil Service, 1900; served Madras Presidency, 1901-31; retired 1931; Secretary to Board of Revenue, Madras, 1912-15; Commission in Indian Army Reserve of Officers. Oct. 1915; served with 9th Gurkha Rifles, India and Mesopotamia, 1915-17; Political Officer Civil Administration, Mesopotamia, 1917-20 (despatches, C.I.E.); Board of Revenue, Madras, 1926; Commissioner of Labour, 1926-27; Sec. of Indian Central Committee, Indian Statutory Commission, 1928-29; High Sheriff for County Londonderry, 1940; Deputy Lieutenant Co. Londonderry, 1949; Volunteer Long Service Medal, 1912. *Recreations:* big-game shooting, fishing, gardening, shot for Cambridge against Oxford, 1898-99. Member of Irish XX., Bisley, 1898. *Address:* The Umbra, Magilligan, Londonderry, N. Ireland. *T.:* Castlerock 223; c/o National and Grindlays Bank, 54 Parliament Street, S.W.1; The Hermitage, Limavady, County Londonderry. *T.:* Limavady 2439. [*Died* 26 *Oct.* 1962.

McDONNELL, Colonel Hon. Angus, C.B. 1919; C.M.G. 1918; Canadian General Reserve; *b.* 1881; *s.* of 7th Earl of Antrim; *m.* 1913, Ethelwyn Sylvia (*d.* 1948), *d.* of late Henry Arthur Jones. Served European War, 1916-18 (C.B., C.M.G.); M.P. (C.) Dartford, 1924-29. Attaché to British Embassy, Washington, D.C., 1941-45. *Address:* Sypsies, Five Ashes, Mayfield, Sussex. *Club:* Brooks's. [*Died* 22 *April* 1966.

McDOUGALL, John Bowes, C.B.E. 1943; M.D., F.R.C.P.E., F.R.S.E., F.R.C.P.Glas.; retired; formerly Chief, Tuberculosis Section, W.H.O., Geneva, and Consultant in Tuberculosis to Egyptian Govt.; *b.* 5 Dec. 1890; *s.* of Allan and Margaret McDougall, Greenock, Scotland; *m.* 1920, Sarah Purdy Shepherd; two *s.*; *m.* 1954, Marietta Tsitseclis. *Educ.:* Greenock Acad.; Glasgow University (M.B., Ch.B. 1914, M.D. 1916). Medical Officer, Manchester Hospital for Consumption and Diseases of the Chest: Assistant Tuberculosis Officer, Stoke-on-Trent; Temporary Major, R.A.M.C., during European War as Officer-in-Charge, Medical Division No. 30 General Hospital, Calais; Chief Tuberculosis Officer, West Riding County Council; Medical Supt. Wooley Sanatorium, Northumberland; Medical Director, Preston Hall, near Maidstone, Douglas House, Bournemouth, and Nayland Sanatorium, Colchester. Has studied tuberculosis in Canada, U.S., France, and Germany, and specialised in problems concerning Occupational Therapy and Rehabilitation of the tuberculous. *Publications:* contrib. med. jls. *Recreations:* Rugby football (rep. Scotland against France 1914 and 1921, Ireland, 1914 and 1921, England 1922); music (A.R.C.M., L.R.A.M., L.T.C.L.); small livestock (books on rabbit culture). *Address:* 8 Karamanlaki St., Athens, Greece. [*Died* 30 *Sept.* 1967.

McDOUGALL, John Henry Gordon; *b.* 29 May 1889; *s.* of late Rev. T. H. McDougall, Vicar of Ledsham, Yorks; *m.* 1925, Nancy Elizabeth, *d.* of late H. T. Lewis; two *d.* *Educ.:* Marlborough College; St. John's College, Oxford. Asst. District Commissioner Uganda Protectorate, 1911; called to Bar, Inner Temple, 1921; Asst. Political Officer, Tanganyika Territory, 1921; Resident Magistrate, Tanganyika Territory, 1921; Puisne Judge, Tanganyika Territory, 1931; acted as Chief Justice on various occasions; retired, 1935; Chief Justice, Gibraltar, 1942-1946; Chief Legal Adviser to Civil Affairs Branch G.H.Q., M.E.L.F., 1946-47. *Recreations:* golf, gardening. *Address:* Marywood, Constantia, C.P., S. Africa. [*Died* 8 *June* 1969.

McDOUGALL, Sir Malcolm, Kt. 1962; Chairman, Thomas White & Sons Ltd.; Director: Coats Patons Ltd., 1961-69; Scottish Mutual Assurance Soc., Ltd.; Bruce Peebles Industries Ltd.; *b.* 22 Nov. 1899; *m.* 1927, Mary Regina Waddell; three *s.* *Address:* 155 St. Vincent Street, Glasgow, C.2. *T.:* 041-221 8711; Moorburn, Auchengreoch Road, Milliken Park, Kilbarchan, Renfrewshire. *T.:* Johnstone 20233. *Club:* Conservative (Glasgow). [*Died* 25 *June* 1970.

MacDUFF, John Levy, M.C. 1942; **Hon. Mr. Justice MacDuff;** Chief Justice, Fiji, since 1962; *b.* 11 December 1905; *s.* of Abraham Levy MacDuff; *m.* 1947, Kathleen Betty Garner; two *s.* one *d.* *Educ.:* Wellington College, New Zealand; Victoria University College, New Zealand (B.A., LL.M.). Served War of 1939-45 (M.C., despatches); Senior Magistrate, Fiji, 1945-1953; Puisne Judge, Kenya, 1953-62. *Recreations:* golf, tennis. *Address:* Supreme Court, Suva, Fiji. [*Died* 11 *July* 1963.

McELWAINE, Sir Percy Alexander, Kt., *cr.* 1939; LL.D.; *b.* 21 Sept. 1884; *s.* of A. J. McElwaine and Edith Leach; *m.* 1st, 1916, Evelyn MacNaught (*d.* 1918); 2nd, 1923, M. J. Belmar; two *s.* one *d.* *Educ.:* Campbell College, Belfast; Trinity College, Dublin. Member of Irish and Alberta Bars (Q.C. Northern Ireland); served European War, Lieut. Royal Irish Rifles; Magistrate, St. Lucia, 1920; Crown Counsel, Kenya, 1923; Attorney General, Fiji, 1927; Deputy Public Prosecutor, Singapore, 1930; Attorney General, Straits Settlements, 1933; Chief Justice of Straits Settlements, 1936-46; retired, 1946; interned, Feb. 1942-Aug. 1945; Commissioner, on administration of Income Tax Dept., Sierra Leone, 1948. *Publications:* Revised Edition of the Laws of the Straits Settlements, 1936; Revised Edition of the Laws of the Gold Coast, 1954. *Address:* Moorlands, Shaldon, Teignmouth, Devon. *T.:* Shaldon 2248. [*Died* 24 *Oct.* 1969.

McEWEN, Sir John (Helias Finnie), 1st Bt. *cr.* 1953; *b.* 21 June 1894; *e. s.* of late R. F. McEwen, F.S.A. (Scot.), D.L., J.P. of Marchmont and Bardrochat, and Mary Frances, *d.* of late R. H. D. Dundas; *m.* 1923, Bridget Mary, *e. d.* of late Rt. Hon. Sir Francis Lindley, P.C., G.C.M.G.; six *s.* one *d.* *Educ.:* Eton; Trinity Coll., Cambridge (M.A.). Served European War, 1914-18 in 5th Q.O. Cameron Highlanders (Capt. 1915) and R.A.F. (prisoner); 3rd Secretary, H.M. Diplomatic Service, 1920; 2nd Secretary, 1925; served Athens, Foreign Office, Rome; contested (U.) Berwick and Haddington, 1929 and 1945; M.P. (C.) Berwick and Haddington, 1931-45; Assistant Govt. Whip (unpaid), 1938-39; Parl. Under Sec. of State for Scotland, 1939-40; a Lord Comr. of the Treasury, 1942-44; Chairman of Cons.

Members' Cttee. in H. of C., Dec. 1944-June 1945. Mem. Council of Aliens (Foreign Office), 1939-40; Chm. of Scottish Cttee., Arts Council of Gt. Britain, 1957-; Trustee of National Galleries of Scotland, 1952-; Chairman Scottish Advisory Panel to British Council, 1953-57; Trustee, National Library of Scotland, 1958-. D.L., J.P. Co. Berwick; Pres. Scottish Unionist Assoc., 1949-50; Pres. Saltire Society, 1957-61; Mem. Queen's Body Guard for Scotland. Chevalier Légion d'Honneur. Hon. LL.D. (Glasgow). *Publications:* Poems, 1920; The Fifth Camerons, 1938; The Last of the Villavides, The Tapestry Bed (Vilmorin), If I were You (Julien Green), That which was lost (Mauriac), (and other translations from the French); Gallantry (with Sir Arnold Wilson); Three Scottish Ballads, 1941; There is a Valley, 1950; The Lyon of Scotland (play broadcast by B.B.C. Aug. 1951); (ed.) Fénelon Letters (posthumous), 1964. *Heir: s.* James Napier [*b.* 14 Dec. 1924; *m.* 1958, Clare, *d.* of Col. J. E. W. G. Sandars; one *d. Educ.:* Eton. Served War of 1939-45, Gren. Guards (wounded)]. *Address:* Marchmont, Berwickshire. *T.:* Greenlaw 221. *Clubs:* White's, Beefsteak; New, Conservative (Edinburgh). [*Died* 19 *April* 1962.

McFADDEN, Gertrude Violet; author. *Educ.:* privately. Native of Southampton, but of West Country stock; always lived in Hampshire. *Publications:* The Honest Lawyer, 1916; His Grace of Grub Street, 1918; The Preventive Man, 1920; The Trusty Servant, 1920; Maumbury Rings, 1921; Narcissus in the Way, 1922; The Turning Sword, 1923; Sheriff's Deputy, 1924; The Roman Way, 1925; So Speed We, 1926; The Bride's Groom, 1928; A Bridport Dagger (John Milbrook), 1930; contributor to The Dorset Year Book. *Recreations:* reading, gardening, rambles about the unfrequented country-side. *Address:* Durlston, Paisley Road, Bournemouth. [*Died* 15 *March* 1963.

MACFADYEN, Air Marshal Sir Douglas, K.C.B. 1956 (C.B.) 1951); C.B.E. 1943; i.d.c.; p.s.a.; Air Officer Commanding-in-Chief, Home Command, March 1956-March 1959 (retd.); *b.* 8 Aug. 1902; *s.* of late Frank Edward Macfadyen; *m.* 1939, Priscilla Alfrida Dafforn; two *s. Educ.:* Royal Grammar Sch., Newcastle upon Tyne Flight Cadet R.A.F. College, Cranwell, 1920-1922; Pilot Officer, 1922; Squadron Leader, 1936; Wing Commander, 1939; Group Capt. 1941; Air Commodore, 1947; Air Vice-Marshal, 1949; Air Marshal, 1956. Service Abroad: Iraq 1922-25, Palestine 1925-27, Aden, 1933-35, France 1939-40, N. Africa 1942-44; A.-O.-C. British Forces, Aden, 1952-53; Commandant, R.A.F. Staff College, Nov. 1953-Mar. 1956. *Recreation:* golf. *Address:* Eastmere, Shurlock Row, Berkshire. *T.:* Shurlock Row 318. *Club:* R.A.F. [*Died* 26 *July* 1968.

MACFADYEN, Sir Eric, Kt., *cr.* 1943; M.A.; J.P.; *b.* 1879; *y. s.* of late Rev. J. A. Macfadyen, D.D., Manchester; *m.* 1920, Violet, *d.* of late E. H. S. Champneys, Otterpool Manor, Sellindge; three *s.* three *d. Educ.:* Clifton College; Wadham College, Oxford. Trooper 59th Co. I.Y., S. Africa, 1900-1 (Queen's medal with 3 clasps); Pres. of Oxford Union, 1902; Cadet Malay Civil Service, 1902-5; contracting and planting, 1906-16; Chairman, Planters Association of Malaya; Member of Federal Council, F.M.S., 1911-16 and 1919-20; Lieut. R.G.A., 1917-1918; served in France, 1918; Captain 21st Bn. Home Guard, 1940-42; a Director of Plantation Companies; Pres., Imperial Coll. of Tropical Agriculture, Trinidad; Chairman Rubber Growers Assoc., 1927; Pres. Institution of Rubber Industry, 1930; Pres. Assoc. of British Malaya, 1931 and 1940; M.P. (L.) Wilts (Devizes), 1923-24. *Address:* Meopham Bank, nr. Tonbridge. *Clubs:* East India and Sports, City Universities. [*Died* 13 *July* 1966.

McFARLAND, Arthur; Stipendiary Magistrate for the City of Liverpool, 1947-1965; *b.* 25 Jan. 1893; 3rd *s.* of late Joseph William McFarland, Olive Mount, Birkenhead; *m.* 1921, Dorothy, *d.* of late J. George Evans, New Brighton; one *s.* one *d. Educ.:* St. Luke's, Tranmere, C. of E. School; University of Liverpool. Served European War, 1914-18, with Cheshire Regt. (Capt.). Called to Bar, Gray's Inn, 1930. Served War of 1939-45; 1940-41, with R.A.P.C. (Lieut. Paymaster). Chairman Appeals Tribunal, Liverpool, 1941-46; Asst. Recorder of Liverpool, 1942-47; Member Legal Commission Internat. Hospitals Assoc., 1939; Chairman: Liverpool City Justices, 1951; Merseyside Branch of the Magistrates Assoc., 1951; Standing Cttee. of Convocation, Univ. of Liverpool, 1950-53; Military Service (Hardship) Tribunal, Birkenhead, 1947. Royal Society of Arts Medal, 1926; Emmott Memorial Scholar in Law, Univ. of Liverpool, 1927; Vice-Chancellor of Duchy of Lancaster Prize, 1929; Board of Legal Studies Prize, 1929. Member: Liverpool Disablement Advisory Committee, 1946; Council of Liverpool Association of Boys' Clubs, 1948. *Publications:* Hawks Abroad (Play, broadcast), 1935; articles in "The Hospital". *Recreations:* walking, golf, hockey. *Address:* Iona, Groveland Avenue, Wallasey, Cheshire. *T.:* Wallasey 4172. *Clubs:* University (Liverpool); Wallasey Hockey. [*Died* 9 *May* 1966.

McFARLAND, Professor Bryan Leslie; Professor of Orthopædic Surgery, University of Liverpool, since 1951; *b.* 18 July 1900; *s.* of William John McFarland, N. Ireland, and Eileen McFarland; *m.* 1928, Ethel Ashton; two *s.* (and one *s.* decd.). *Educ.:* Wallasey Grammar School; Univ. of Liverpool. M.B., Ch.B. Liverpool, 1922; M.D. Liverpool, 1924 (thesis of special merit); M.Ch.Orth., Liverpool, 1926; F.R.C.S. Edin., 1928; F.R.C.S. Eng., 1949. Resident and demonstrator posts, 1922-25; Asst. Hon. Orth. Surg., David Lewis Northern Hosp., Liverpool, 1928; Asst. Hon. Orth. Surg., Roy. Southern Hosp., 1933, Hon. Orth. Surg., 1935; Lecturer, Orth. Surg., Univ. of Liverpool, 1944; Sen. Hon. Orth. Surg., Roy. Liverpool Children's Hosp., 1948; Director Orth. Studies, Univ. of Liverpool, 1948. President, British Orthopædic Association, 1953-55; Pres. International Orthopædic Society, 1960-; Consultant, Robert Jones & Agnes Hunt Hospital, Shropshire. Vice-Pres. R.C.S. (Edinburgh), 1961. Hon. mem. of many continental and overseas Orthopædic Assocs. *Publications:* Section, Congenital deformities of the spine and limbs, Modern Trends in Orthopædics, 1950; contributions to Brit. Jl. of Surgery, Jl. of Bone and Joint Surgery, etc. *Recreations:* gardening, fishing and shooting. *Address:* 41 Rodney Street, Liverpool. *T.:* Royal 1532; (residence) 10 Fulwood Park, Liverpool 17. *T.:* Lark Lane 2412; Bryn Ioan, Holyhead. *Clubs:* Constitutional; University (Liverpool); Holyhead Golf. [*Died* 23 *Jan.* 1963.

MACFARLANE, Robert Campbell, M.C. 1917; Q.C. (Scot.); *b.* 4 Aug. 1892; *e. s.* of late George Lewis Macfarlane, Senator of College of Justice in Scotland with judicial title of Lord Ormidale, and Mary Crichton, *d.* of James Hunter; unmarried. *Educ.:* Edinburgh Academy; Winchester College; B.N.C., Oxford (B.A.). Served European War, 1914-18, with Argyll and Sutherland Highlanders (France and Salonika), Major, 1917; War of 1939-45, with Royal Artillery (A.A.), 1939-42, Major, 1940. Called to Scottish Bar, 1921; K.C. (Scot.), 1951. Editor, Session Cases, 1952-59. *Recreations:*

fishing, shooting. *Address:* 57 Fountainhall Road, Edinburgh. *T.:* Newington 3687. *Club:* New (Edinburgh).
[*Died* 15 *March* 1963.

McFARLANE, Stuart Gordon, C.M.G. 1933; *b.* 4 May 1885; *s.* of late J. J. McFarlane, Malden, Vic.; *m.* Grace (decd.), *d.* of late Alfred McDermott, Orange, N.S.W.; one *s.*; *m.* 1958, Evelyn, *widow* of Hon. J. A. Perkins, M.P. Asst. Secretary (Finance), Commonwealth Treasury, 1926-32; Assistant Secretary (Administrative) Treasury, 1932-35; also Secretary to Australian Loan Council and Secretary to National Debt Commission, 1932-36; Official Secretary, Australia House, 1936-37; Secretary to Commonwealth Treasury, 1938-48; Member of Commonwealth Bank Board, 1938-45; Member of Commonwealth Bank Advisory Council, 1945-48. Member of Overseas Telecommunications Commission (Australia), 1946-1948; Exec. Dir. of Internat. Monetary Fund; also Internat. Bank for Development, Washington, 1948-50. *Address:* 22 Dampier Crescent, Canberra, A.C.T. *Club:* Australian (Sydney).
[*Died* 1 *Nov.* 1970.

MACFARLANE - GRIEVE, Lieut. - Col. Angus Alexander, M.C.; T.D.; M.A.; *b.* 11 May 1891; 3rd *s.* of late W. A. Macfarlane-Grieve, M.A., Impington Park, Cambridge and Edenhall, Roxburghshire; *m.* 1929, Sarah St Osyth, 2nd *d.* of late Rev. George Margoliouth; two adopted *s.* *Educ.:* Perse School, Cambridge; University College, Durham. B.A. 1913; Commissioned to Highland L.I. (S.R.) 1914 and later obtained a Regular Commission in Seaforth Highlanders; served with 2nd Highland L.I. and 2nd Seaforth Highlanders in France reaching rank of Acting Lieut.-Col. in 1918 (M.C.); Adjutant of Durham University and Leeds University Group of O.T.C.s. 1919-23; retired with rank of Major 1923; Bursar and Censor of University College, 1923; also Bursar of Hatfield College, 1926; Acting Master of Hatfield College, 1940-49; Master of University College, Durham, 1939-1953 and Sub-Warden of the Durham Colleges in the University of Durham, 1948-53. Sheep-Farming in Eskdale, Dumfriesshire, 1953-61. Commanded Durham University O.T.C., 1926-1934 and 1940-46, and 11th Bn. Durham H.G., 1941-42. Brevet Lieut.-Col. 1934; succeeded brother in Edenhall and Penchrise, Roxburghshire, 1934. *Publication:* A History of Durham Rowing, 1923. *Recreations:* farming, forestry, rowing, boys' clubs. *Address:* The Leap, Langholm, Dumfriesshire. *T.:* Langholm 358. *Club:* Royal Over-Seas League.
[*Died* 2 *Aug.* 1970.

McFEE, William; Novelist; Associate Member of Institution of Mechanical Engineers; Hon. M.A. Yale; Mem. Am. Historical Society; Natl. Inst. of Arts and Letters; *b.* London, 15 June 1881; *s.* of John Henry McFee and Hilda Wallace; *m.* 1st, 1920, Pauline Khondoff; no *c.*; divorced 1932; 2nd, 1932, Beatrice Allender (*decd.* 1952), West Virginia; 3rd, 1965, Dorothy North. *Educ.:* Culford, Suffolk. Apprentice at Richard Moreland & Sons, Engineers, City, as mechanical engineer; served in offices of W. Summerscales & Sons, Ltd., as assistant to the London Manager; went to sea as marine engineer, 1906; rose to chief engineer in ships of Woodfield S.S. Co.; went to United States and wrote books, afterwards going to sea in ships of United Fruit Company; served in War as engineer in transports and afterwards Eng.-Lieut. R.N.R. on various ships; returned to United States and was with United Fruit Co., as chief until 1922, when turned definitely to writing. *Publications:* An Ocean Tramp; Aliens; Casuals of the Sea; Captain Macedoine's Daughter; Harbours of Memory; A Six Hour Shift; Command; Race; Sunlight in New Granada; Swallowing the Anchor; Pilgrims of Adversity; Sailors of Fortune; North of Suez; Life of Sir Martin Frobisher; The Harbourmaster; No Castle in Spain; Sailor's Wisdom; The Beachcomber; Derelicts; Watch Below; Spenlove in Arcady; Ship to Shore; Family Trouble; The Law of the Sea; The Adopted. *Recreations:* motoring and travel. *Address:* P.O. Box 443, New Milford, Conn., U.S.A.
[*Died* 2 *July* 1966.

McFERRAN, Lieut.-Colonel Edwin Millar Gilliland, C.B.E. 1919; *s.* of John McFerran, Barnageeha, Belfast, and Millbrook, Larne, Co. Antrim; *b.* 1873; *m.* 1905, Pansey Mary, *e. d.* of James Jump, Horringer Court, Bury St. Edmunds. *Educ.:* Rossall School. Served S. Africa, 1901-2 (Queen's medal with five clasps); Uganda, 1904-6; European War, 1914-19 (despatches twice, C.B.E., two medals). *Club:* United Service. [*Died* 15 *June* 1962.

MacGEAGH, Colonel Sir Henry Davies Foster, G.C.V.O., *cr.* 1950; K.C.B., *cr.* 1946; K.B.E. *cr.* 1930 (C.B.E. 1919); Q.C. 1924; T.D.; Chairman of Council of Legal Education, since 1953; Judge Advocate General (Army and R.A.F.), 1934-54; *b.* 21 Oct. 1883; *o. s.* of late Foster MacGeagh, of Hadlow Castle, Kent; *m.* 1917, Rita (*d.* 1959), *o. d.* of late William Kiddle of Walbundrie, New South Wales. *Educ.:* St. Paul's; Magdalen Coll. Oxford; rowed in Magdalen Coll. Eight, Head of the River; Hons. Deg. History, B.A. 1905. Called to Bar, Middle Temple, 1906; South Eastern Circuit; Bencher of Middle Temple, 1931; Reader, 1943; Deputy Treasurer, 1949, during Treasurership of H.M. The Queen; Treasurer, 1950. Member Council of Soc. of Comparative Legislation; Vice-Pres. Ulster Association (London); held commission in Territorial Army (London Rifle Brigade), 1909-23; regular commission in the rank of Col., 1923-34, when retired from Army on appointment as Judge Advocate General of the Forces; served European War, France and Flanders, 1914-15 (Bt. Major, C.B.E., 1914 star and clasp); Military Assist. to the Judge Advocate General, 1916-23; D.A.A.G., 1917; Assistant Adjutant-General, War Office, 1918-23; Deputy Judge Advocate General British Forces in China (Shanghai Defence Force), 1927; Military Deputy of the Judge Advocate General (War Office and Air Ministry) and in charge of the Military and Air Force Department of his office, 1923-34; Silver Jubilee Medal, 1935; Coronation Medal, 1937 and 1953; Medal of Freedom, with gold palm (U.S.), 1947. *Publication:* Contributor of title Royal Forces in Halsbury's Laws of England (Hailsham Edition). *Address:* New Court, Temple, E.C.4. *T:* Central 8870. *Clubs:* Carlton, Leander, Pilgrims'.
[*Died* 29 *Dec.* 1962.

McGEOUGH, Most Rev. Joseph F.; *b.* 29 August 1903. Ordained 1930; Minutante, Sacred Congregation for the Oriental Church, Rome, 1938; attached to the Secretariat of State, 1945-57; appointed Apostolic Internuncio to Ethiopia, 1957; transferred to South Africa and consecrated Titular Archbishop of Emesa, 1960; Nuncio Apostolic to Ireland, 1967-69. [*Died* 12 *Oct.* 1970.

MacGILLIVRAY, Sir Donald Charles, G.C.M.G. 1957 (K.C.M.G. 1953; C.M.G. 1949); M.B.E. 1936; *b.* 22 September 1906; *s.* of late Evan James MacGillivray, Q.C.; *m.* 1936, Louisa Mai Knox-Browne; one *s.* *Educ.:* Sherborne School; Trinity Coll., Oxford. Administrative Officer, Tanganyika Territory, 1929-38, and Palestine, 1938-42; Deputy District Commissioner, Galilee, Palestine, 1942-44; District Commissioner, Samaria, Palestine, 1944-46; Under-Secretary, Palestine, 1946-47; Liaison Officer with U.N. Special Cttee. on Palestine, 1947; Colonial Secretary, Jamaica, 1947-52; Deputy High Commissioner, Federation of Malaya, 1952-54; High Commissioner, Federation of Malaya, 1954-58; Chairman, Kenya Council of State, 1958-63. Chairman,

Makerere Coll. Council, 1958-61; Deputy Chairman, Advisory Commission on Federation of the Rhodesias and Nyasaland, 1960; Chairman: Coun., Univ. E. Africa, 1961-64; Kenya Meat Commn., 1962-64. Dir., U.N. Special Fund for E. African Livestock Devolt. Survey, 1964-66; Chm. East African Bd., Standard Bank Ltd., 1966-. *Recreation:* farming. *Address:* Talanga, Gilgil, Kenya. *Clubs:* Oxford and Cambridge University; Muthaiga Country (Nairobi); Rift Valley (Nakuru). [*Died* 24 *Dec.* 1966.

MACGILLIVRAY, John Walker, C.M.G. 1943; O.B.E. 1934; retired; *b.* 15 Jan. 1884; *s.* of Duncan Macgillivray and Eliza Walker; *m.* 1907, Dorothy Smart; one *s.* one *d.* *Educ.:* private tuition. Survey of Trinidad, 1901-10; Trinidad Public Wks. Dept., 1912-17; Survey Dept., 1917-30; Director of Surveys and Sub-Intendant (i/c Lands and Surveys Dept.), 1930-42. Silver Jubilee Medal, 1935; Coronation Medal, 1937. *Address:* c/o Banco International del Peru, Plaza de la Merced, Lima, Peru, South America. [*Died* 31 *Oct.* 1961.

McGIVERN, Cecil, C.B.E. 1954; Executive, Granada Television Network, since 1961; *b.* 22 May 1907; *s.* of Stephen and Catherine McGivern; *m.* 1934, Elsie Collinson; one *s.* two *d.* *Educ.:* St. Cuthbert's Gram. Sch., Newcastle on Tyne; Armstrong Coll., Durham University. Schoolmaster, Actor, Producer, 1930-36. Joined B.B.C. in Manchester as Drama producer, 1936; transferred: to Newcastle in charge of programmes, 1937; to London Features Dept., 1940. Responsible for war-time programmes such as: Junction X, Radar, The First Thousand, Fighter Pilot, Bombers over Berlin, A Harbour called Mulberry. Joined Independent Producers Ltd. as screen-writer, 1945, working on films Blanche Fury, Great Expectations, etc. Rejoined B.B.C. as Television Programme Director, 1947; Controller of Television Programmes, 1950-56; Deputy Director of Television Broadcasting, 1956-61. *Publications:* Bombers over Berlin, 1942; *booklets:* Junction X, 1944; Harbour called Mulberry, 1945. *Recreation:* television. *Address:* Holly Lodge, Amersham Road, Chalfont St. Peter, Bucks. *T.:* Chalfont St. Giles 2121. [*Died* 30 *Jan.* 1963.

McGLASHAN, Sir George Tait, Kt. 1954; C.B.E. 1951; Convener of Co. of Perth, 1945-64; *b.* 1885; *s.* of Peter McGlashan, Stanley, and Jane Tait, Tarves, Aberdeenshire; *m.* 1914, Anne, *d.* of John Marshall, Perth; two *d.* *Educ.:* Perth Academy. Trained as engineer, Caledonian Rly. Co., and British Electric Plant Co. Ltd.; Chairman and Managing Director, 1919-45, Edmiston Brown and Co. Ltd., Engineers, Glasgow and Clarmac Engineering Co. Ltd., Glasgow. Member of North of Scotland Hydro-Electric Board, 1948-61; Chairman of Electricity Consultative Council for North of Scotland Dist., 1948-61. President Association of County Councils in Scotland, 1952-54. Chairman, Scottish Committee of Arts Council, 1951-57. *Recreations:* fishing, gardening, chess. *Address:* Summerbank, Auchterarder, Perthshire. *T.:* Auchterarder 2105. *Clubs:* Scottish Conservative (Edinburgh); Royal (Perth). [*Died* 17 *April* 1968.

McGOVERN, John; *b.* 13 Dec. 1887; *s.* of Thomas McGovern; *m.* 1909; two *s.* one *d.* Served seven years as apprentice plumber; master plumber, 1909-23; Australia, 1923-1925; master plumber at Shettleston, 1926-1929; insurance agent, 1930; Member of Glasgow Parish Council, 1928-30; Member of Glasgow Town Council, 1929-31. M.P. (Lab.; I.L.P. until 1947) Shettleston Div. of Glasgow, 1930-Sept. 1959. Led Hunger March, Glasgow to Edinburgh, and due to refusal of accommodation by Edinburgh Corporation, slept in Princes Street with 1000 men and women; protested against imprisonment of Tramp Preachers for speaking without permits on Glasgow Green and finally carried out of the House of Commons by eight attendants, July 1931. Arrested 1931 on two occasions and imprisoned in connection with Free Speech Campaign and Unemployed Riots, also arrested 1933; protested in House of Lords during King's Speech (Nov. 1933) against the failure to restore Unemployed Cuts and end the Means Test; led Hunger March from Glasgow to London, 22 Jan. 1934. Left Britain, to settle in Australia, 1962. *Recreations:* golf and pictures. [*Died* 14 *Feb.* 1968.

McGOVERN, William Montgomery, D.Phil.(Oxon); Professor of Political Science, Northwestern University; Commander U.S. Naval Reserve; *b.* Brooklyn, 28 Sept. 1897; *o. c.* of Felix Daniel McGovern, journalist, and Janet Blair Montgomery; *m.* 1927, Margaret, *d.* of Dr. C. J. Montgomery; one *s.* three *d.* *Educ.:* Abroad, including the Sorbonne, Paris, and Berlin University; Christ Church, Oxford. Has travelled all over the world, chiefly for purposes of scientific research; resided in principal monasteries of China and Japan in order to collect material and MSS.; granted honorary priesthood in the Nishi Honganji, Kyoto, Japan; lecturer in Chinese, Luchuan, and Japanese at the School of Oriental Studies, 1918-24; member of the Board of Oriental Studies, and Examiner, in the Univ. of London, 1920-27; Member of the Research Staff, Field Museum, 1927-28; lectured for L.C.C., 1919, and the Coll. of North Wales Univ. of Wales 1921-22; scientific adviser to research expedition to Tibet, 1922; explored a large portion of the North-West Amazon basin, and later carried out extensive excavations of the Inca and Pre-inca ruins in Peru, 1925-26; undertook extensive research work in the Balkans and in the Near and Middle East, 1931; Lecturer on Government, Harvard Univ. 1936 and 1940-41; Far Eastern Correspondent, Chicago Times, 1937; Visiting Prof., Univ. of Southern California, 1939. Lieut. U.S.N.R. 1940; on active duty, Dec. 1941-Feb. 1946; Lt.-Comdr. 1942; Comdr. 1945. Legion of Merit, 1946. *Publications:* The Child and the Flute, and other poems, 1919; Modern Japan, its Political, Military, and Industrial Organisation, 1920; Colloquial Japanese, 1921; Introduction to Mahayana Buddhism, 1922; Manual of Buddhist Philosophy, 1923; To Lhasa in Disguise, 1924; Jungle Paths and Inca Ruins, 1927; Growth of Institutions, 1929; Early Empires of Central Asia, 1937; From Luther to Hitler, the History of Fascist-Nazi Political Philosophy, 1941; Radicals and Conservatives, 1959; Stragetic Intelligence and the Shape of Tomorrow, 1961. *Recreations:* bridge, golf. *Address:* 1412 Judson Ave., Evanston, Illinois, U.S.A. *Clubs:* Adventurers Tavern (Chicago); University (Evanston); Cosmos, Army and Navy, Metropolitan (Washington). [*Died* 1964.

McGOWAN, 1st Baron, *cr.* 1937, of Ardeer; **Harry Duncan McGowan,** K.B.E., *cr.* 1918; Hon. LL.D. Glasgow University, 1934; Birmingham University, 1934; University of St. Andrews, 1950; Hon. D.C.L. (Oxon), 1935; Univ. of Durham, 1949; Hon. President of Imperial Chemical Industries, Ltd. (Chairman, 1930-50); President, Society of Chemical Industry, 1931; Hon. Colonel 52nd (Lowland) Divisional Signals, Royal Corps of Signals, 1934-39; *b.* Glasgow, 3 June 1874; *m.* 1903, Jean Boyle Young (*d.* 1952), Paisley; two *s.* two *d.* *Heir:* *s.* Hon. Harry Wilson McGowan [*m.* 1937, Carmen, *y. d.* of Sir Herbert Cory, 1st Bt., and Elizabeth, Lady Cory (*d.* 1956); three *s.* two *d.*]. *Address:* 1 Hyde Park Street, W.2. *T.:* Ambassador 1737. *Club:* White's. [*Died* 13 *July* 1961.

McGOWAN, 2nd Baron, *cr.* 1937; **Harry Wilson McGowan;** late Major, Middlesex Yeomanry; *b.* 18 May 1906; *er. s.* of 1st Baron McGowan, K.B.E.; *S.* father, 1961; *m.* 1937, Carmen, *d.* of Sir (James) Herbert Cory, 1st Bt.; three *s.* two *d.* *Educ.:* Uppingham; Clare College, Cambridge (B.A.). Served War of 1939-45, in Middlesex Yeomanry. *Heir: s.* Hon. (Harry) Duncan (Cory) McGowan [*b.* 20 July 1938; *m.* 1962, Lady Gillian Pepys, *y. d.* of 7th Earl of Cottenham; two *d.* *Educ.:* Eton]. *Address:* Bragborough Hall, Rugby, Warwickshire. *T.:* Braunston 210; 7 Princes Gate, S.W.7. *Club:* St. James'.
[*Died* 5 *July* 1966.

McGOWAN, Ven. Frank, M.B.E. 1945; Archdeacon of Sarum since 1951; Canon and Prebendary of Salisbury since 1944; *b.* 7 October 1895; *s.* of late Henry McGowan, Bristol; *m.* 1925, Ena Mary Craven (decd.); *m.* 1956, Lucy, *d.* of R. W. Shawcross, Leeds, and of late Mrs. Shawcross. *Educ.:* University of Bristol; St. Edmund Hall, Oxford. Served European War, 1914-1918; 2nd Lieut., Duke of Wellington's Regt., 1915-17; Lieut., Machine Gun Corps, 1917-18. B.A. (Oxon), 1920; Diploma in Theol., 1922; M.A. (Oxon), 1924. Deacon, 1922; priest, 1923; Curate, St. Michael and All Angels, Bournemouth, 1922; Vicar, St. Mark's, Birmingham, 1925; Rector of Cholderton, 1929. *Address:* Church House, Salisbury, Wilts. *T.:* Salisbury 5958. *Clubs:* Royal Commonwealth Society; Union Society (Oxford).
[*Died* 21 *Feb.* 1968.

MACGOWAN, Gault; Journalist; F.J.I.; Editor and Publisher, European Life, since 1955; *b.* England, Feb. 1894; *m.* 1923, Wendy (*d.* 1961), *y. d.* of late J. H. Corley Smith, Simla and Transvaal; one *s.* Late Capt. Indian Cavalry, R. of O.; served France, Italy, Mesopotamia; Associated Press Correspondent N. W. Frontier, India, 1922-23; Editor Times of Mesopotamia, 1924; Sub-Editor, The Times, 1925; Staff Correspondent Daily Express, Paris, 1926-27; Assistant Editor and Leader Writer Evening Express, Cardiff, 1927-28; Editor Londoner's Diary, Newspaper Features Ltd., 1928-29; Managing Editor, Trinidad Guardian, 1929-34; joined New York Sun, 1934, European Manager from 1946 until its amalgamation with New York World-Telegram, 1950. Delegate West Indies 4th Imperial Press Conference, 1930; Hon. Secretary on Council Institute of Journalists representing West Indies, 1930-35; Selfridge Prizeman; Company of Newspaper Makers, 1932; Officier de l'Instruction Publique, 1930; Officer of Military Order of Christ, Portugal, 1933; Chevalier de la Légion d'Honneur, 1934; Officer of the Order of Ouissam Alaouite Cherifien, Morocco, 1938; Croix de Guerre, 1943; Médaille de la France Libérée, 1949; Liveryman of the Stationers' Company and Freeman of the City of London since 1937. *Travels:* Notably, Himalayas, discovered new pass into Little Thibet (Received thanks survey of India); first flight over Orinoco delta and across Venezuelan Llanos Trinidad-Maracay; first flight, Trinidad, British Guiana; Special Correspondent, New York Times, with Beebe Bathysphere Expedition to Bermuda, 1934; Special Correspondent The Sun, at the Coronation of King George VI, Spanish Civil War, and with the French Foreign Legion in Algeria and Morocco, 1937; accredited War Correspondent with the British and U.S. Armies, War of 1939-45; Battle of Britain; Battle of the Atlantic and with the Commandos; African and European Campaigns, 1942-45 (wounded, Purple Heart). Captured by Germans in Allied drive to Paris; escaped and joined French Maquis until liberated, 1944. Potsdam Conference, 1945; U.N.O., London, 1946, and subsequently with N.A.T.O. forces. *Publications:* To the End of the World and Beyond; My Desert Dash to Damascus; Heidelberg Confidential!; Switzerland Confidential!; Bavaria Confidential!, 1956; Elizabeth Stuart: Her Story, 1963. *Address:* 15 Schlierbacher Aue, Heidelberg, Germany. *Clubs:* Authors', Press. [*Died* 30 *Nov.* 1970.

McGRATH, Mrs. Arthur T.; *see* Forbes, J. Rosita.

McGRATH, Most Rev. Michael Joseph, D.D., M.A., LL.D.; Archbishop of Cardiff (R.C.), since 1940; *b.* Kilkenny, 24 March 1882. *Educ.:* Rockwell College, Co. Tipperary; University College, Dublin. Ordained 1908; assistant priest, Diocese of Clifton, Bristol, 1908-19; Rector of Flint, 1920-27; Rector of Diocesan College, Aberystwyth, 1927-35; Bishop of Menevia, 1935-40. *Address:* Archbishop's House, 24 Newport Road, Cardiff. *T.:* Cardiff 30493.
[*Died* 28 *Feb.* 1961.

MacGREGOR, Alasdair Alpin; author; *b.* 1899; *e. s.* of late Col. John MacGregor, M.D., I.M.S.; *m.* 1958, Constance Patricia; *d.* of late Augustus Walker, and *widow* of Comdr. M. B. F. Colville, D.S.O., R.N. *Educ.:* Tain Academy; Inverness; George Watson's College, Edinburgh; graduate of Edinburgh University. Served European War, 1916-18, with 15th (Scottish) Division; contested (Soc.) County of Banff, 1929; West Hartlepool, 1931; Cathcart Div. of Glasgow, 1935; Private Sec. to the Chancellor of the Duchy of Lancaster and to Postmaster-General, 1929-31. Actively interested in all matters relating to animal welfare; one time Pres. of the League for the Prohibition of Cruel Sports; Vice-Pres. of London Robert Louis Stevenson Club. Is a vegetarian, teetotaller, and uncompromising antivivisectionist; returned graduation diplomas to Principal of Edinburgh Univ. as protest against its professional experiments upon living, unconsenting animals. Travelled in U.S.S.R., India, Ceylon, Malaya, Canada, United States, North-west Atlantic, Australia. Explored MacDonnell Ranges in Central Australia, 1952-53. Mem. British Humanist Assoc. *Publications:* (usually illustrated with his own photographs). Behold the Hebrides, or Wayfarings in the Western Isles, 1925; Over the Sea to Skye, 1926; Wild Drumalbain; The Road to Meggernie and Glen Coe, 1927; Summer Days among the Western Isles, 1929; A Last Voyage to St. Kilda, 1931 (upon which film, The Edge of the World, was based); Searching the Hebrides with a Camera, 1933; The Haunted Isles, 1933; Somewhere in Scotland, 1935 (enlarged edn., 1948); The Peat-Fire Flame, 1937; The Goat-Wife: Portrait of a Village, 1939 (enlarged edn., 1951); Vanished Waters: Portrait of a Highland Childhood, 1942; Auld Reekie: Portrait of a Lowland Boyhood, 1943; The Turbulent Years: A Portrait of Youth in Auld Reekie, 1945; The Western Isles, 1949; The Buried Barony, 1950; Skye and the Inner Hebrides, 1953; The Ghost Book: Strange Hauntings in Britain, 1955; (Ed.) Prof. Griffith Taylor's Journeyman Taylor: The Education of a Scientist, 1958; Phantom Footsteps, 1959; Percyval Tudor-Hart: Portrait of an Artist, 1961; The Golden Lamp: Portrait of a Landlady, 1964; Land of the Mountain and the Flood, 1965; The Enchanted Isles: Hebridean Portraits and Memories, 1967; The Farthest Hebrides, 1969; poems and essays in various anthologies; contributor to several leading Brit. and Amer. newspapers and magazines. *Recreations:* music (has given recitals of lyrics and ballads under auspices Australian Broadcasting Commission, and in the United States), swimming, mountaineering, field geology, photography, topography. *Address:* 48 Upper Cheyne Row, Chelsea, S.W.3. *T.:* 01-352 2023; King's Barn, Odiham, Hampshire. *T.:* Odiham 2123.
[*Died* 15 *April* 1970.

MacGREGOR, Professor Alexander Brittan, M.A., M.D., B.Chir. (Cantab.), M.R.C.S., L.R.C.P., F.D.S., R.C.S. (Eng.); Professor of Dental Surgery, and Director of Dental Studies, University of Birmingham, since 1953; *b.* 25 Jan. 1909; *o. s.* of Alexander Pendarves MacGregor and Mabel Brittan; *m.* 1934, Sybil (*née* Hawkey); one *s.* one *d.* *Educ.:* Marlborough College; Cambridge University. Sen. entrance Schol., St. Mary's Hosp., W.2, 1930; Dental Consultant St. Bartholomew's Hosp., 1938; Sqdn. Ldr. R.A.F.V.R., Maxillo-facial specialist, 1939-45; Dental Consultant to Royal Dental, Plastic Centre, Hill End and Amersham Hospitals, 1946; Civilian Dental Consultant to the Royal Navy, 1952. Dean of Faculty of Dental Surgery, R.C.S., 1962 (Mem. Bd., 1952; Vice-Dean, 1961); Mem. Gen. Dental Council. Colyer Res. Prize of Roy. Soc. of Med. and Mummery res. prize of B.D.A., etc. *Publications:* Section on Dentistry, Chambers's Encyclopædia. Contributions to Medical and Dental scientific jls., both English and foreign. *Recreations:* Alpine gardening, painting, fishing. *Address:* The Old Rectory, Maxstoke, Near Coleshill, Warwicks. *T.:* Coleshill 2248.
[*Died* 9 *Jan.* 1965.

MACGREGOR, Sir Alexander S. M., K.B.E., *cr.* 1955 (O.B.E. 1919; Kt., *cr.* 1941; M.D., D.P.H., F.R.C.P.Glas., LL.D. (Glasgow); J.P.; *b.* Arbroath, 1881; *m.* 1910, Margaret Whyte, Argyllshire; two *s.* two *d.* *Educ.:* Collegiate School; Hutchesons' Grammar School; Glasgow University, M.B., Ch.B., M.D., Honours and Gold Medallist (Glasgow), D.P.H. (Cambridge). Served European War, 1914-19; Gallipoli, Egypt, Palestine and Syria, Major R.A.M.C., (T.F.) (Brevet-Major, O.B.E., despatches four times); Medical Officer of Health, Glasgow, 1925-46; Ex-President, Royal Sanitary Association of Scotland; President Society of Medical Officers of Health, 1941-42; late Chm., Western Regional Hosp. Board (Scotland). *Publications:* various in medical journals. *Recreation:* golf. *Address:* 25 Corrour Road, Glasgow, S.3. *T.:* Langside 2585. *Club:* Western (Glasgow).
[*Died* 29 *June* 1967.

MACGREGOR, Rev. George Hogarth Carnaby; Professor of Divinity and Biblical Criticism in the University of Glasgow, 1933-1963; *b.* Aberdeen, 26 Nov. 1892; *s.* of Rev. George H. C. Macgregor, Minister in Aberdeen and London, and Agnes Amelia Rose; *m.* 1918, Christine E., *d.* of Rev. James G. Goold, Edinburgh; two *s.* two *d.* *Educ.:* Eastbourne College; Gonville and Caius College, Cambridge (Scholar); New College, Edinburgh; University of Glasgow; B.A. Cambridge (1st Class Honours, Classical Tripos), 1914; M.A. 1922; B.D. 1929; D.D. 1951; D.Litt. Glasgow 1929; Hon. D.D. Edinburgh, 1936; Minister, Chalmers Church, Bridge of Allan, 1918-23; St. John's-Renfield Church, Glasgow, 1924-28; Bruce Lecturer, Glasgow, 1928; Hosmer Professor of New Testament Exegesis in Hartford Theological Seminary, Connecticut, U.S.A., 1929-1933. President, Studiorum Novi Testamenti Societas, 1960. *Publications:* The Gospel of John, 1928; Eucharistic Origins, 1929; Jew and Greek; Tutors unto Christ (with A. C. Purdy), 1936; The New Testament basis of Pacifism, 1937; The Relevance of the Impossible, 1941; The Acts of the Apostles, 1954; The Structure of the Fourth Gospel (with A. Q. Morton), 1961; articles in Theological Periodicals. *Address:* Muskoka, Milngavie, Glasgow. *T.:* Milngavie 1344.
[*Died* 3 *July* 1963.

MACGREGOR, John, Q.C. (Scot.) 1931; M.A., LL.B.; Sheriff Substitute of Stirling, Dumbarton and Clackmannan at Falkirk, 1944-56, retd.; *s.* of late Donald Macgregor, Solicitor, Oban, and Jane McCallum Macgregor; *m.* Flora Emily Mary, *d.* of late John McGregor of Dunstaffnage, New South Wales, Australia; two *s.* *Educ.:* Royal High School, Edinburgh; Edinburgh University. Called to Scots Bar, 1907; joined Royal Scots Fusiliers as Subaltern, September, 1914; served in Palestine and France and retired in 1919 with rank of Major; Junior Counsel to the Post Office in Scotland, 1921. *Address:* Glengonnar, 14 Symington St., Leadhills, Lanarkshire.
[*Died* 31 *Jan.* 1967.

MACGREGOR, Sir Robert James McConnell, 6th Bt. *cr.* 1828; M.M.; late Canadian Infty.; late Lieut., Royal Air Force; *b.* 1890; *yr. s.* of late Patrick Eugene Macgregor and late Gertrude, *d.* of J. F. McConnell; nephew of Sir William Gordon Macgregor, 4th Bt.; *S.* brother, Sir Cyril Patrick McConnell Macgregor, 5th Bt., 1958; *m.* 1930, Annie Mary, *d.* of late Joseph Lane, Nanaimo, British Columbia; two *s.* three *d.* Served European War, 1914-18, with 10th Canadian Infty. Bn. *Heir:* *s.* Edwin Robert Macgregor [*b.* 1931; *m.* 1952, Margaret Alice Jean, *d.* of A. Peake, Haney, British Columbia; one *s.* one *d.* *Educ.:* University of British Columbia (M.A.Sc.)]. *Address:* 3316 W. 14th Avenue, Vancouver, British Columbia.
[*Died* 21 *Jan.* 1963.

MACHRAY, Robert, C.V.O. 1952; Anæsthetist to the Westminster Hospital since 1931; to the Brompton Hospital for Diseases of the Chest since 1932; and to King Edward VII Sanatorium, Midhurst, since 1944; *b.* 21 May 1906; *s.* of George and Laura Machray; *m.* 1936, Freda Mary (*née* Eveley) (*d.* 1967); one *s.* two *d.* *Educ.:* Beckenham County School; Westminster Hospital. M.R.C.S., L.R.C.P. 1929; M.B., B.S. Lond. 1931; F.F.A.R.C.S. 1948. Formerly Anæsthetist: Thoracic Unit, Horton Hospital, E.M.S.; Milford Sanatorium; and Sully Hospital (Welsh National Memorial Assoc.). *Publications:* contrib. to medical journals. *Address:* 2 Ellerdale Close, N.W.3. *T.:* Hampstead 2101.
[*Died* 21 *Jan.* 1968.

McILROY, Dame (Anne) Louise, D.B.E., *cr.* 1929; LL.D., M.D., D.Sc. Glas.; D.Sc. Lond.; D.Sc. Hon. Belfast; F.R.C.O.G.; F.R.C.P., L.M. Rotunda; Hon. Fellow Liverpool Medical Inst.; Retired; formerly: Consulting Obstetrician and Gynæcological Surgeon, Royal Free Hosp.; Pres., Medico Legal Soc.; Gynæcological Surgeon, Bermondsey Medical Mission Hosp.; Surgeon, Marie Curie Hosp. for Women; Consultant Obstetrician to Walthamstow Council; *b.* Lavin House, Co. Antrim; *d.* of late James McIlroy, M.D., J.P., Ballycastle, Co. Antrim. *Educ.:* Universities of Glasgow, London, Vienna, Berlin. Late Senior Assist. to Muirhead Prof. of Obstetrics and Gynæcology, Glasgow University; Médécin Chef, Scottish Women's Hospital, Troyes; later with l'Armée d'Orient in Serbia and Salonika (Croix de Guerre); R.A.M.C., Constantinople; late President Obstetrical Section of Royal Society of Medicine; late Member Central Council of B.M.A.; late President Metropolitan Branch of B.M.A.; late Gynæcological Surgeon E.M.S. Hospital, Slough; late Senior Obstetrician Fulmer Chase Maternity Hospital for Officers' Wives; late Obstetrical War Consultant, County Bucks; late Professor of Obstetrics and Gynæcology, Royal Free Hospital School of Medicine, University of London. C.St.J. *Publications:* From a Balcony on the Bosphorus; The Toxaemias of Pregnancy, 1936; Analgesia-Anæsthesia in Childbirth, Canadian Medical Association Journal, 1931; The Problem of the Damaged Heart in Obstetrical Practice (with Dr. O. Rendel), Journal of Obstetrics and Gynæcology, 1931; The Prevention and Treatment of Asphyxia in the New-born, Medical Journal and Record, New York, Vol. cxxxviii, 10, 11, 12, 1934. *Recreation:* fishing. *Address:* Little Turnberry, Girvan, Ayrshire.
[*Died* 8 *Feb.* 1968.

McILROY, William Ewart Clarke, C.B.E. 1943; J.P.; *b.* Reading, 4 Dec. 1893; *s.* of William and Henrietta McIlroy; *m.* 1920, Jeanne Smith; one *s.* two *d.* *Educ.:* Reading School and abroad. Served European War, 6th Oxford and Bucks Light Infantry, 1914-18; contested (Nat. Govt.) Reading, 1945; J.P. Reading, 1934; elected Reading Council, 1934; Mayor of Reading, 1938-42; Freeman Borough of Reading, 1943. *Recreations:* gardening, travel. *Address:* Hill Green, Leckhampstead, Berks. [*Died* 30 *June* 1963.

McILWRAITH, William, Q.C. (Scot.), 1960; Advocate; *b.* 8 May 1924; *s.* of James Campbell McIlwraith and Alicia Tait. *m.* 1952, Karin-Björg Johausen; two *d.* *Educ.:* Hamilton Academy, Glasgow University. Graduated M.A. (Glas.), 1943. Served in R.A.F., 1943-45. Graduated LL.B. (Glas.), 1947. Called to Scottish Bar, 1947. Sheriff Substitute of the Lothians and Peebles at Edinburgh, 1966-. *Address:* 20 Mansionhouse Rd., Edinburgh 9. *Club:* Scottish Liberal (Edin.). [*Died* 12 *May* 1968.

MacINNES, Rt. Rev. Duncan, M.B.E. 1946; M.C. 1944; Bishop of Moray, Ross and Caithness, since 1953; Rector of St. Mary, Glencoe (with St. Paul, Kinlochleven, 1938-45), North Argyllshire, since 1933. *Educ.:* Edinburgh Theological College. Deacon, 1926; Priest, 1927. Curate of St. Columba, Clydebank, 1926-28; Curate-in-Charge of Holy Cross, Knightswood, Glasgow, 1928-33; Chaplain to the Forces, 1939-45; Canon of Argyll and the Isles, 1941-; Dean of Argyll and the Isles, 1946-53. *Address:* Bishop's House, 43 Fairfield Road, Inverness. [*Died* 9 *Aug.* 1970.

MacINTOSH, Duncan William, C.M.G. 1949; O.B.E. 1946; K.St.J. 1952; retd.; *b.* 5 May 1904; *s.* of D. H. MacIntosh and Annabelle MacIntosh (*née* Fraser); *m.* 1937, Kathleen Helen Jones; no *c.* *Educ.:* Inverness High School. Royal Irish Constabulary, 1920-22; Airdrie Borough Police, 1924-29; Straits Settlements Police, 1929-1942; interned in Singapore, 1942-45; Singapore Police, 1945-46; Commissioner of Police, Hong-Kong, 1946-54; retired 1954. Police Adviser: to Government of Iraq, 1954-58; to Government of Jordan, 1962. King's Police Medal, 1931; Colonial Police Medal, 1941. *Recreations:* golf and motoring. *Address:* Summerlea, Hurst Green, East Sussex. [*Died* 14 *Sept.* 1966.

MACINTOSH, Edward Hyde, C.B.E. 1964; *b.* 21 May 1895; *s.* of A. C. Macintosh, sometime Pres. of Law Soc. of S. Wales; *m.* 1929, Doreen O'Hara Cross, *d.* of J. C. Cross, London; two *s.* two *d.* *Educ.:* Tonbridge. Joined R.F.A., Aug. 1914; France, 1915; Palestine Campaign, 1916-18; Staff Officer (D.A.A.G.), 1919-21. Sudan Political Service, 1921-45, ending as Governor Khartoum Province. Retd. as Chm. Northern Regional Hosp. Bd., 1965. Order of the Nile, 1931. *Recreations:* shooting, fishing. *Address:* Rebeg, Kirkhill, Inverness-shire. *T.:* Drumchardine 205. *Clubs:* Caledonian; Conservative (Edinburgh); Highland (Inverness). [*Died* 15 *Sept.* 1970.

MACINTYRE, David Lowe, V.C.; C.B. 1949; Under-Secretary Ministry of Works, Edinburgh, 1943-59 (retired); *b.* Portnahaven, Islay, Argyllshire, 18 June 1895; *s.* of Rev. A. S. Macintyre, B.A., B.D., and Elizabeth Lowe; *m.* 1929, Elspeth Moir, *d.* of W. M. Forsyth, Edinburgh; one *s.* one *d.* *Educ.:* George Watson's College, Edinburgh; Edinburgh University. Military Service, Argyll and Sutherland Highlanders and Highland Light Infantry, 1915-19. *Address:* 39 Buckingham Terrace, Edinburgh 4. *T.:* Edinburgh Dean 3344. *Club:* Scottish Arts (Edinburgh). [*Died* 31 *July* 1967.

MACINTYRE, Captain Ian Agnew Patteson, C.B. 1945; C.B.E. 1942; D.S.O. 1942; R.N. retired; *b.* 24 August 1893; *s.* of late Maj.-Gen. Donald Macintyre, V.C., and Alison Patteson; *m.* 1918, Gwendolen Beatrice Paine; three *s.* *Educ.:* Littlejohns, Greenwich. Navy, as Cadet, 1907; Midshipman in H.M.S. Bellerophon, 1911-13; served in destroyers and submarines in European War and in the Fleet and submarines until 1939; War of 1939-45, Chief Staff Officer to Adm. Sir Max Horton; commanded Scylla and Indefatigable; retd. list, 1947; C.C.G., 1947-48; Admiralty Regional Officer, North West, 1948-62. Legion of Honour, 1946. *Recreations:* fishing and golf. *Address:* 78 High Street, Old Portsmouth, Hants. [*Died* 17 *Aug.* 1967.

McINTYRE, William Keverall, C.M.G. 1950; M.C. 1918; M.D., F.R.C.O.G.; Consulting Gynecologist, Launceston General Hospital and Specialist in Obstetrics and Gynecology, Launceston, Tasmania, retired 1960; *b.* 12 Jan. 1882; *s.* of Mr. Justice McIntyre, Supreme Court, Tasmania, and Ada McIntyre; *m.* 1909, Margaret Edgeworth, *d.* of late Prof. Sir Edgeworth David, Sydney University; two *s.* two *d.* *Educ.:* Hutchins' School, Hobart; Sydney University (B.E.); Edinburgh University (M.D., Ch.B.). Trooper first Australian Bushman Contingent, S. African War, 1900-01; Member Australian Contingent King Edward VIIth Coronation, 1902; Mining Engineer, 1906-10. Served R.A.M.C. 28th Div., 1915-1919; France and the Balkans, Major Second in Command 80th Field Ambulance (despatches, M.C.). Greek Order of the Redeemer 2nd Class. *Publications:* professional articles in medical journals. *Recreation:* music. *Address:* Greycliff, Franklin Village, Launceston, Tasmania. *Club:* Launceston (Launceston). [*Died* *Feb.* 1969.

MacIVER, Robert Morrison; President, The New School for Social Research, 1963-1965, Chancellor, 1965-66; Lieber Professor of Political Philosophy and Sociology, Columbia University, 1929-50; now emeritus; Director, City of New York Juvenile Delinquency Evaluation Project, 1956-61; *b.* 17 April 1882; *s.* of Donald MacIver and Christine Morrison, Island of Lewis; *m.* 1911, Ethel Marion Peterkin; two *s.* one *d.* *Educ.:* Nicolson Institute, Stornoway; Edinburgh University (M.A. 1903, D.Phil. 1915); Oriel College, Oxford (B.A. 1907). Lecturer, Political Science, Aberdeen Univ., 1907; Professor, Political Science, Univ. of Toronto, 1915; Vice-Chm., Dominion of Canada War Labor Board, 1917; Prof., Barnard College, 1927. F.R.S.C., F.A.A.S., Fell. Amer. Philosophical Soc., etc.; Corresp. Mem., British Acad.; Mem., World Acad. of Arts and Science. Litt.D. Columbia, 1929, Harvard, 1936, Princeton, 1947; L.H.D. Yale 1951; LL.D., Edin. 1952, Toronto, 1957; Trustee, Russell Sage Foundation, New York. Comdr., Royal Order of Phœnix (Greece). *Publications:* Community, 1917; Labor in the Changing World, 1919; Elements of Social Science, 1921; The Modern State, 1926; Society, 1931, revised, 1937, (with C. Page) enlarged edition, 1950; Economic Reconstruction, 1934; Leviathan and the People, 1939; Social Causation, 1942; Towards an Abiding Peace, 1943; The Web of Government, 1946; The More Perfect Union, 1948; The Ramparts We Guard, 1950; Democracy and the Economic Challenge, 1952; The Pursuit of Happiness, 1955; Academic Freedom in Our Time, 1955; The Nations and the United Nations, 1959; Life: its Dimensions and its Bounds, 1959; Encounter with Time, 1962; Power Transformed, 1964; The Strategy of Delinquency Control, 1967; As a Tale that is Told (autobiography), 1968. *Recreations:* music, bridge, chess, golf, mycology, country life.

Address: Palisades, Rockland County, New York, U.S.A. *T.:* Elmwood 9-0864. [*Died* 15 *June* 1970.

MACK, Hon. Sir Ronald (William), Kt. 1967; President, Legislative Council of Victoria, since Sept. 1965; *b.* 20 May 1904; *s.* of late Frederick David Mack and late Elizabeth Edith Mack (*née* Hatton); *m.* 1st, 1935, Helen Isobel Janet (*née* Nicol); one *s.*; 2nd, 1958, Winifred Helen Crutchfield (*widow*) (*née* Trevelyan Campion). *Educ.:* Warrnambool, Victoria. Chartered Accountant. Served 2nd A.I.F., 1940-43 (Middle East; despatches twice; lost right eye El Alamein). Member: Victorian Legislative Assembly, 1950-52; Victorian Legislative Council, 1955-; Chairman of Committees, 1958-61; Minister of Health, 1961-1965. Fellow of the Institute of Chartered Accountants in Australia. *Recreations:* fishing, shooting. *Address:* 162 Power Street, Hawthorn, Victoria, Australia. *T.:* 81-6676. *Clubs:* Warrnambool, Warrnambool Racing (Warrnambool, Victoria). [*Died* 12 *Feb.* 1968.

McKAIG, Colonel Sir John Bickerton, K.C.B., *cr.* 1945 (C.B. 1932); D.S.O. 1917; D.L., T.D., M.A., late T.A.; Solicitor, formerly a partner in the firm of Alsop Stevens and Co., Liverpool; retired; *b.* 28 July 1883; *s.* of late William Rae McKaig and Agnes Fleming McKaig; *m.* 1921, Annie Wright, *er. d.* of Samuel Wright Lee, Liverpool; one *s.* one *d.* *Educ.:* Sedbergh School; Hertford College, Oxford. Received commission 6th Rifle Battalion King's Regiment (then 2nd V. B. The King's), 1906; admitted as solicitor, 1910; Captain, 1913; mobilised with 6th Rifle Bn. King's Regt., Aug. 1914; commanded Bn., Sept. 1916-Feb. 1929 (D.S.O. and bar, despatches 4 times); A.D.C. to the King, 1931-41; 17th Bn. Cheshire Regt. Home Guard from 1940, Capt.; Chairman West Lancashire Territorial Association, 1939-48; County Army Welfare Officer West Lancashire, 1939-48; Hon. Col. 573 H.A.A. Regt., 1949-; President Liverpool Law Society, 1940; Chm. Liverpool Savings Bank, 1951. *Recreation:* angling. *Address:* The Gate House, Broadwas-on-Teme, Worcs. [*Died* 7 *Sept.* 1962.

MACKARNESS, Cuthbert George Milford, C.I.E. 1941; *b.* 15 April 1890; 2nd *s.* of late Archdeacon Charles Coleridge Mackarness, D.D.; *m.* 1915, Eileen Lilias Godfrey, K.I.H., 1943; two *s.* *Educ.:* Radley College; St. John's College, Oxford. Joined Indian Forest Service, 1912; Deputy Conservator of Forests, 1919; Conservator of Forests, Assam, 1937-45. *Address:* Tas Combe, 104 Church St., Willingdon, Sussex. *T.:* Hampden Park 234. [*Died* 13 *June* 1962.

MACKAY, Hon. George Hugh; retired; *b.* Clermont, Queensland, 20 March 1872; *s.* of Hugh and Jane Mackay; *m.* Edith Ann Heard; one *s.* (and one *s.* one *d.* decd.). *Educ.:* Copperfield, Clermont and Bundaberg, Queensland, Legislative Assembly, Queensland, for Gympie, 1912-1915; House of Representatives for Lilley, Queensland, 1917-34; Temporary Chairman of Committees, 1929-31; Speaker, House of Representatives, Commonwealth of Australia, 1932-1934; Member of Parliamentary Standing Committee on Public Works, 1920-28, (Chairman, 1926-28); Member of Select Committee on case of ex-Gunner Yates, 1923; Member of Commonwealth delegation, Empire Parliamentary Assoc., which visited Canada in 1928; Jubilee Medal, 1935; Coronation Medals, 1937, 1953. *Recreation:* bowls. *Address:* 40 Red Hill Road, Gympie, Queensland, Australia. *T.:* 428. *Clubs:* Gympie Bowling (Gympie, Queensland) (Hon. Life Mem., Patron); Nundah Bowling (Patron). [*Died* 5 *Nov.* 1961.

MACKAY, Helen M. M., M.D., B.S.Lond., F.R.C.P. (Lond.); Hon. Consultant Physician Queen Elizabeth Hospital for Children; ex-Chairman of the Advisory Cttee. of Paediatricians, N.E. Metropolitan Regional Hospital Board; ex-President Section of Disease in Children, of Royal Society of Medicine; *b.* Inverness, 1891; *d.* of late Duncan L. M. Mackay, I.C.S., and Marion G. C. Wimberley. *Educ.:* Cheltenham Ladies' College; London (Royal Free Hospital) School of Medicine for Women. M.R.C.S., L.R.C.P., 1914; M.R.C.P. Lond., 1917; F.R.C.P. Lond. 1934; M.B., B.S. Lond. 1914; M.D. Lond. 1917; late Beit Memorial Research Fellow, Vienna, and Lister Institute of Preventive Medicine, 1929-1922; Ernest Hart Memorial Research Scholar of the British Medical Association; Dawson Williams Memorial Prize (paediatrics); Paediatrician to the Mothers' Hospital, Clapton and to Hackney Hospital; Member of staff of Medical Research Council; Paediatrician to General Lying-in Hospital, Asst. Physician to the Infants Hospital, Westminster; House Physician and Assistant Pathologist, Royal Free Hospital, etc.; Editor of the Magazine of the London School of Medicine for Women. *Publications:* (jointly) Studies of Rickets in Vienna, 1919-1922, M.R.C., Special Rep. Series, No. 77; (jointly) Nutritional Anæmia in Infancy, M.R.C., Special Report Series, No. 157, 1931; (jointly) Weight Gains, Serum Protein Levels, and Health of Breast Fed and Artificially Fed Infants, M.R.C. Special Report Series, No. 296; Diatetic deficiency diseases, Encyclopædia of Medical Practice, 1937; articles in med. journals, etc. *Address:* c/o National Provincial Bank, Holborn Hall, W.C.1. [*Died* 15 *July* 1965.

MACKAY, Lt.-Gen. Sir Iven Giffard, K.B.E., *cr.* 1941; C.M.G. 1919; D.S.O. 1917; V.D.; Hon.LL.D. (Sydney), 1952; High Commissioner for Australia, in India, 1944-48; retired, 1948; Esquire Bedell, University of Sydney, 1950; *b.* Grafton, New South Wales, Australia, 7 April 1882; *s.* of Rev. Isaac Mackay, of Armadale, Scotland, Free Presbyterian Church Minister, Grafton, and Emily Frances King, of Lake Erie, Canada; *m.* 1914, Marjorie Eveline, *e. d.* of Brig.-Gen. John Baldwin Meredith, Hunter River, N.S. Wales; one *s.* two *d.* *Educ.:* Newington College, Sydney; St. Andrew's College, University of Sydney. B.A.; Junior Demonstrator in Physics, University of Sydney, 1904; Resident Master in charge Science, Football, and Rowing, Sydney Church of England Grammar School, 1905-10; Assistant Lecturer and Demonstrator in Physics, University of Sydney, 1910; Pres., University Science Soc., 1913; Honorary Coach, University Football Club; admitted Emmanuel Coll., Cambridge, whilst working in Cavendish Laboratory, 1919; Student Adviser, University of Sydney, 1922; Headmaster, Cranbrook School, Sydney, 1933-40; Commonwealth Film Appeal Censor, 1932-40. Lt., Commonwealth Mil. Forces, 1911; Adjutant, 26th Infantry Regt., C.M. Forces; Captain and Adjt. 4th Battalion A.I.F., 1914; served Gallipoli; wounded Lone Pine, 1915; Major, 1915 (despatches); served France; Lt.-Col. 1916 (D.S.O. and bar, despatches); appointed command 1st Australian Machine Gun Battalion, March 1918; Col., 6 June 1918, temp. Brig.-Gen. commanding 1st Australian Infantry Bde., Oct. 1918 (French Croix de Guerre, C.M.G.); G.O.C. 2nd Div., Commonwealth Mil. Forces, 1937-40; Cdg. 6th Div. A.I.F., 1940-41; served Western Desert, Libya, Greece, Crete (Greek Military Cross); Lt.-Gen. 1941; G.O.C.-in-C. Home Forces, Australia, 1941-42; G.O.C. New Guinea Forces, 1943. *Recreations:* shooting, riding, ocean surfing; obtained University " blues " for football and rowing;

University 1st XI. *Address:* Pacific Highway, Turramurra, N.S.W., Australia. *Clubs:* Australian, Imperial Service, Pioneers, Royal Sydney Golf (Sydney). [*Died* 30 *Sept.* 1966.

McKAY, John; a miners' official. Ruskin College Student with Oxford Diploma for Economics and Political Science (Distinction). M.P. (Lab.) Wallsend, 1945-64. *Address:* 351 West Road, Newcastle upon Tyne 5. [*Died* 4 *Oct.* 1964.

MACKAY, Hon. John Keiller, S.M. 1967; D.S.O. 1916; V.D.; Q.C. (Can.); LL.D.; D.C.L.; Lt.-Governor of Province of Ontario, 1957-63; Director of cos.; *b.* Plainfield, Pictou County, N.S., 11 July 1888; *m.* 1943, Katherine Jean MacLeod, N.S.; three *s.* *Educ.:* Pictou Academy; St. Francis Xavier University; Dalhousie University Law School (LL.B.). Served European War 1914-18: commanded 6th Bde., Canadian Field Artillery, Lt.-Col. (wounded, despatches three times, D.S.O.). Member of law firm of Mackay, Matheson & Martin, Toronto. H.M. Counsel, 1933; Justice of Supreme Court of Ontario, 1935-50; Chairman of Board to review findings of all Courts Martial of War of 1939-45, 1945; Judge of Court of Appeal of Ontario, 1950-57. Pres., Canadian Civil Liberties Assoc.; Hon. Life Member: Royal Canadian Legion for Canada (Grand Pres. for Ont.); Canadian Bar Assoc., etc.; Past President St. Andrews Society of Toronto; Hon. Chieftain of Clan MacKay Soc. in Canada; Chancellor, Univ. of Windsor, Ont.; Mem. Bd. of Governors, Univ. of Toronto. Recognised Shakespearian Scholar and Orator; Hon. LL.D.: St. Francis Xavier Univ., 1951; Dalhousie Univ. 1958; Univ. of Ottawa, 1958; Univ. of Western Ontario, 1959; Univ. of Toronto, 1961; Law Soc. of Upper Canada, 1961; R.M.C. of Canada, 1967; Hon. D.C.L., Univ. of New Brunswick, 1959. Hon. Bencher, Law Society of Upper Canada, 1961. Hon. Pres., Oxfam of Canada. K.St.J. 1958. *Address:* 39 Kingsway Crescent, Toronto 18, Ontario, Canada. *Clubs:* Royal Canadian Military Institute, National, Empire, Arts and Letters (Toronto); Royal Canadian Yacht; Ashburn Golf and Country. [*Died* 13 *June* 1970.

MACKAY, John Martin; Sheriff Substitute of Stirling, Dumbarton and Clackmannan at Dumbarton, 1950-65; *b.* 9 June 1899; *s.* of John Martin Mackay, Solicitor in Glasgow; *m.* 1939, Muriel, *d.* of George Hill Scobbie, Dunglass, Bearsden, Glasgow; two *s.* *Educ.:* Glasgow Academy; Glasgow University. Served European War, 2nd Lieut. 5th Royal Scots, 1918-19. M.A. (Glasgow) 1921, LL.B (Glasgow) 1923. Partner in firm of Martin Mackay & Macquaker, Solicitors in Glasgow, 1924-47. Rector's Assessor on Glasgow University Court, 1945-47; Sheriff-Substitute of Dumfries and Galloway at Dumfries, 1947-50. *Publications:* articles in Modern Law Review, Juridical Review, etc. *Recreations:* shooting, fishing, lawn tennis, walking and gardening. *Address:* Hollingside, Helensburgh, Dunbartonshire. *T.:* Helensburgh 430. [*Died* 29 *Jan.* 1970.

McKEAN, Air Vice-Marshal Sir Lionel Douglas Dalzell, K.B.E., *cr.* 1945 (O.B.E. 1923); C.B. 1942; *b.* 1886; *m.* 1920, Phyllis Maude, *d.* of late A. J. Warren; (*s.* P.O., R.A.F., killed on active service, 1940). Joined R.N., 1904; served European War, 1914-18, with R.N.A.S. (despatches); transferred R.A.F. 1918. Head of R.A.F. Mission, Canada, 1940-45; retired from R.A.F. May 1945. Croix Militaire 1st Cl. (Belgium) 1943; Commander's Cross and Star of the Order of Polonia Restituta, 1945; Commander Legion of Merit, U.S.A., 1946; Grand Officer Order of Orange Nassau (Holland), 1947. *Address:* No. 2 The Field House, Market Drayton, Salop. [*Died* 28 *Dec.* 1963.

McKECHNIE, Hector, Q.C. (Scot.) 1945; B.A., LL.B., LL.D.; Sheriff of Perth and Angus, 1958-63, retd.; *b.* 19 May 1899; *o. s.* of late William Sharp McKechnie, M.A., LL.B., D.Phil., LL.D., writer in Glasgow and Prof. of Conveyancing, University of Glasgow; *m.* 1927, Dorothy May, *d.* of late Morris Carswell, of Glasgow and Murcia, Spain. *Educ.:* Cargilfield School; Winchester College; New College, Oxford; University of Glasgow. Lt. 5th/37th Northumberland Fusiliers, 1918-19; apprenticed solicitor, Glasgow, 1922-25; called Scots Bar, 1925; Faulds Fellow in Law of Glasgow University, 1926-28; Literary Director Stair Society, 1934-53, Chairman of Council, 1953-; Trustee Nat. Library of Scotland since 1936: standing Junior Counsel to Board of Trade in Scotland, 1937-45; Assistant Divisional Food Officer, S.E. Scotland, 1939-40; Member Scottish Records Advisory Council, 1941-; Chm. Departmental Cttee. on Diligence, 1956-58; David Murray Lecturer, Glasgow Univ., 1956; Sheriff of Inverness, Moray, Nairn, and Ross and Cromarty, 1953-58; Dep. Chm. for Scotland, Bd. of Referees, 1955-. *Publications:* Pursuit of Pedigree, 1928; articles in Encyclopædia of the Laws of Scotland and Juridical Review, 1926-33; The Lamont Clan, 1938. *Recreations:* natural history, antiquarian research. *Address:* 64 Great King St., Edinburgh 3. *T.:* Edinburgh Waverley 3171. *Club:* Royal Scottish Automobile (Glasgow). [*Died* 24 *April* 1966.

McKECHNIE, James; Actor; *b.* Glasgow, Scotland, 8 April 1911; *s.* of late William McKechnie, Glasgow and Buenos Aires, drysalter and exporter; *m.* 1940, Mary Hill Ross, Glasgow; one *s.* one *d.* *Educ.:* Glasgow High School and Hillhead High School, Glasgow. Started in oil concern (Anglo-Persian, Glasgow), 1928; then H. J. Heinz Ltd. till 1930. Repertory (2 companies), Glasgow and Edinburgh, till 1934 as amateur; became professional, 1934; B.B.C. Repertory Co., 1940; rejoined B.B.C. Drama Repertory Co., 1963. Has specialised in Radio from 1941, playing large range of parts in plays, features, etc. Won Daily Mail National Radio Award Trophy, 1949, 1950, 1953. Member Actor's Equity. Studies mental and nervous diseases in amateur capacity. *Recreations:* swimming; writing short stories. *Address:* 4 Cleveland Square, W.2. *T.:* Paddington 6567. *Club:* B.B.C. [*Died* 8 *May* 1964.

McKEE, J(ohn) Ritchie; President, Arts Council of Northern Ireland, since 1960 (Vice-President 1959-60); *b.* 25 October 1900; *s.* of William Barry McKee and Margaret Grey Burns Bulloch; *m.* 1941, Ada Maxwell Kirkpatrick; three *d.* *Educ.:* Bangor Gram. Sch., Co. Down. Partner in firm of W. B. McKee & Sons, Belfast. Hon. Treas., Belfast Philharmonic Soc., 1940; Mem. of Board, Council for the Encouragement of Music and the Arts (Northern Ireland), 1948; Hon. Administrator, Belfast Arts Theatre, 1950; Member Northern Ireland Advisory Council of British Broadcasting Corporation, 1957 (Chairman, 1958-62); Hon. Chairman Board of Directors, Ulster Group Theatre Ltd. (reconstituted as a non-profit distributing company), 1958; National Governor for Northern Ireland on Board of Governors of the British Broadcasting Corporation, 1958-62. *Recreations:* bridge and golf. *Address:* 124 Malone Road, Belfast. *T.:* 667857. *Club:* Ulster Reform (Belfast). [*Died* 26 *Feb.* 1964.

McKENNA, Stephen; novelist; *b.* 27 Feb. 1888; *y. s.* of late Leopold and Ellen McKenna; unmarried. *Educ.:* Westminster (Scholar);

Christ Church, Oxford (Exhibitioner); B.A. 1909 M.A. 1914. Has travelled in Europe, Asia, Africa, and America; Intelligence Section, War Trade Intelligence Department, 1915-19; a member of the Rt. Hon. A. J. Balfour's Mission to the U.S.A., 1917; Ministry of Economic Warfare, 1939-40. *Publications:* The Reluctant Lover, 1912; Sheila Intervenes, 1913; The Sixth Sense, 1915; Sonia, 1917; Ninety-Six Hours' Leave, 1917; Midas and Son, 1919; Sonia Married, 1919; Lady Lilith, 1920; The Education of Eric Lane, 1921; The Secret Victory, 1921; While I Remember, 1921; The Confessions of a Well-meaning Woman, 1922; Tex: A Chapter in the Life of Alexander Teixeira de Mattos, 1922; Soliloquy, 1922; The Commandment of Moses, 1923; Vindication, 1923; By Intervention of Providence, 1923; To-morrow and To-morrow, 1924; Tales of Intrigue and Revenge, 1924; An Affair of Honour, 1925; The Oldest God, 1926; Saviours of Society, 1926; The Secretary of State, 1927; Due Reckoning, 1927; The Unburied Dead, 1928; The Shadow of Guy Denver, 1928; The Datchley Inheritance, 1929; Happy Ending, 1929; The Redemption of Morley Darville, 1930; The Cast-iron Duke, 1930; Dermotts Rampant, 1931; Beyond Hell, 1931; Pandora's Box, 1932; The Way of the Phoenix, 1932; Superstition, 1932; Magic Quest, 1933; Namesakes, 1933; The Undiscovered Country, 1934; Portrait of His Excellency, 1934; Sole Death, 1935; While of Sound Mind, 1936; Lady Cynthia Clandon's Husband, 1936; Last Confession, 1937; The Home that Jill Broke, 1937; Breasted Amazon, 1938; A Life for a Life, 1939; Mean, Sensual Man, 1943; Reginald McKenna, 1863-1943: A Memoir, 1948; Not Necessarily for Publication, 1949; Pearl Wedding, 1951; Life's Eventime, 1954; That Dumb Loving, 1957; A Place in the Sun, 1962; and numerous contributions to the Press. *Recreation:* gardening. *Address:* 11 Stone Buildings, Lincoln's Inn, W.C.2. *T.:* Holborn 0558; Honeys, Waltham St. Lawrence, Berkshire. *T.A.:* McKenna, Shurlock-Row. [*Died* 26 *Sept.* 1967.

MACKENZIE, Alasdair Roderick; M.P. (L) Ross and Cromarty since 1964; *b.* 9 Aug. 1903; *m.* 1948, Annie Mackay; one *s.* one *d.* *Educ.:* Broadford Junior Secondary School, Skye. C.C. Ross and Cromarty, 1935-55; Convener, Council Educn. Cttee., 5 years; Mem. Crofters' Commn., 5 yrs.; Mem., Bd. of Govs. of N. of Scotland Coll. of Agriculture, 7 yrs. Farmer. Liberal Spokesman, House of Commons, for Agriculture and Fisheries. Gaelic Scholar. *Address:* Heathmount Tain, Ross-shire. *T.:* Tain 55. *Club:* National Liberal. [*Died* 8 *Nov.* 1970.

MACKENZIE, Surg. Vice-Adm. Sir Alexander; *see* Ingleby Mackenzie, Surg. Vice-Adm. Sir K. A.

MACKENZIE, Alexander George Robertson, A.R.S.A. 1948; F.R.I.B.A.; *b.* 1879; *s.* of late A. Marshall Mackenzie, R.S.A.; *m.* Jeannetta Cameron. Was articled to his father, afterwards with Sir Robert Edis, F.S.A., and René Sergent, Paris. Served European War with London Scottish, 1914. Pres.: Architectural Assoc., 1916; Royal Incorporation of Architects in Scotland, 1947. In partnership with A. Marshall Mackenzie, in London, until 1933, thereafter in Aberdeen. *Principal works:* Waldorf Hotel, Aldwych, and Australia House, Strand. Restorations: Medmenham Church, Bucks; Monymusk Church, and similar work in a number of Aberdeenshire Castles and Provost Ross's House, Aberdeen; additions to: Hursley Park, Hants; Swinfen Hall; Leicester University Buildings, etc. *Address:* Bourtie House, Inverurie, Aberdeenshire. *T.:* 2166. *Club:* Royal Northern (Aberdeen). [*Died* 20 *March* 1963.

MACKENZIE, Sir Clutha (Nantes), Kt. *cr.* 1935; *b.* 11 Feb. 1895; *s.* of late Hon. Sir Thomas Mackenzie, G.C.M.G., and Ida Henrietta Nantes; *m.* 1919, Doris Agnes Sawyer; two *s.* three *d.* *Educ.:* Waitaki. Served with Wellington Mounted Rifles N.Z.E.F., Egypt and Gallipoli, 1914-18 (blinded in action, 1915); M.P. for Auckland East, 1921-22; Director of N.Z. Institute for the Blind, 1923-38; Representative in N.Z. of St. Dunstan's Hostel for Blinded Soldiers; St. Dunstan's rep. in India, 1939-40, 1942-48; in U.S.A., 1940-42; temp. Maj., Gen. List, 1942; temp. Lt.-Col. 1943-48; special officer with Govt. of India to report on blindness in India, 1943-47; reported on blindness in China for Govt. of China, 1947, and in Malaya for Govt. of Malayan Union, 1947; appointed to U.N.E.S.C.O. to aid in solution of World Braille problems, 1949-51; on U.N. missions to report on blindness in Turkey, 1950, Ceylon, 1952, Singapore, 1952, Indonesia, 1952, India, 1953, Pakistan, 1953-55; preparatory Mission to East Africa for Royal Commonwealth Soc. for the Blind, 1953; Chm., World Braille Council, 1952-64; Member, Executive Council, World Council for the Welfare of the Blind, 1952-64, Hon. Vice-Pres., 1964; missions to: Egypt, Uganda and Aden Protectorate, 1954, and appointed Director Uganda Foundn. for the Blind, 1955-56, Ethiopia, 1956; U.N. appt. as Dir. Uganda Rural Project, 1956-58; commissioned by U.N. to write on Rural Training of the Blind of Emergent Countries, 1960. Kaisar-i-Hind Gold Medal, 1947. *Publications:* Edited and published Chronicles of the N.Z.E.F. 1916-19; The Tale of a Trooper, 1920; World Braille Usage (U.N.E.S.C.O.), 1954. *Recreation:* farming. *Address:* Wharematoro, Manurewa, N.Z.; c/o Westminster Bank, 34 Sloane Square, S.W.1. [*Died* 30 *March* 1966.

MACKENZIE, Rear-Admiral Colin, C.I.E. 1919; D.S.O. 1900; R.N., retired; *b.* 1872; *e. s.* of late Donald Mackenzie, Gairloch, Ross-shire; *m.* 1899, Clare (*d.* 1939), *e. d.* of Franklin Homan and *widow* of Henry Stanford Harris; one *d.*; *m.* 1946, Mary, *e. d.* of Thomas Milligan, Cowes, I. of Wight. Entered Navy, 1885; Lieut. 1894; Commander, 1906; served China, 1900 (D.S.O.); on Tigris River during operations north of Qurnah and occupation of Amara, 1915 (despatches, prom. Captain); retired list, 1923; Rear-Admiral, retired, 1926. *Address:* c/o Lloyds Bank, 115 Commercial Road, Portsmouth. [*Died* 22 *June* 1968.

MACKENZIE, Sir Duncan George, K.C.I.E., *cr.* 1937 (C.I.E. 1930); *b.* 1 July 1883; 4th *s.* of late T. D. Mackenzie, I.C.S.; *m.* 1st, 1919, Kathleen Millicent, *d.* of late S. Chandos-Pole; (one *s.* died of wounds received on active service, 1942); 2nd, 1947, Margaret Patricia, *er. d.* of late Brig.-Gen. H. W. Cobham, C.M.G., D.S.O. *Educ.:* Winchester; Brasenose Coll., Oxford. B.A. 1907, M.A. 1911. Joined I.C.S. 1907; Political Department, Govt. of India, 1912; served on N.W. Frontier of India during the War; Assistant Private Secretary to the Viceroy, 1918-19; Administrator, Bharatpur State, 1928-30; Resident, Jaipur, 1931-33, Hyderabad, 1933-38; Principal Officer, Northern Region, 1940-41; Commissioner, Red Cross and St. John War Org., Middle East, 1941-43. *Recreations:* shooting, golf, cricket. *Address:* The Manor, Wyke Champflower, nr. Bruton, Somerset. *T.:* Bruton 3203. *Club:* East India and Sports. [*Died* 9 *Aug.* 1965.

MACKENZIE, Rev. Francis Scott, M.A., B.D., Th.D., D.D., D.C.L.; Principal Emeritus Presbyterian Coll. Montreal; *b.* Lucknow, Ont., 9 Jan. 1884; *s.* of John Neil Mackenzie and Helen Scott; *m.* 1913, Alexandra Maclean (*d.* 1953), Lucknow, Ont.; one *s.* one *d.* *Educ.:* McGill University, Montreal; The Presbyterian College, Montreal Harvard University. Graduated in Arts B.A., McGill,

1914; 1st rank standing M.A. McGill, 1916; B.D. Presbyterian College, Montreal, 1916; Travelling Fellowship in Theology and Gold Medal, 1916; S.T.M., Harvard, 1917; Th.D. Harvard, 1918; Assistant Minister, Church of St. Andrew and St. Paul, Montreal, 1918-20; Minister, St. Andrew's Church, Sydney Mines, N.S., 1920-25; Minister, Presbyterian Church, Paris, Ont., 1925-26; Lecturer, Knox College, Toronto, 1925-26; Professor of New Testament and Systematic Theology, Presbyterian College, Montreal, 1926-58; Principal, 1929-45; retired 1958. President Western Section World Presbyterian Alliance, 1949-50. Moderator of General Assembly, Presbyterian Church in Canada, 1950. D.D. Knox College, Toronto, 1931; D.C.L. Acadia, 1938; D.D. Presbyterian College, Montreal, 1960. *Recreations:* curling, golf, fishing. *Address:* Ripley, Ontario, Canada. *Clubs:* Thistle Curling (Montreal), McGill University Faculty (Montreal).
[*Died* 26 *April* 1970.

MACKENZIE, Helen Margaret, H.R.O.I., A.R.C.A.; *e. d.* of Hugh J. Mackenzie, C.E., Ladyhill, Elgin, and Mrs. Mackenzie (*née* Lawson); *m.* 1915, Herbert Ashwin Budd, R.O.I. *Educ.:* Elgin Academy; Royal College of Art. Painter of figure subjects, portraits and designer; exhibitor in R.A. and principal provincial galleries; also in Pittsburg, Toronto, and New Zealand; principal works: Sleeping Shepherd, Hyde Park in Summer, Midsummer Mid-day, Victorian Family. *Recreations:* gardening and reading. *Address:* 10 Avenue Studios, 76 Fulham Road, S.W.3. *T.:* 01-589 2314. [*Died* 4 *May* 1966.

MACKENZIE, Sir (James) Moir, K.B.E., *cr.* 1951 (O.B.E. 1935); C.M.G. 1937; formerly Dep. Dir.-Gen., Federation of British Industries; *b.* Sunderland, 17 Oct. 1886; *s.* of James Mackenzie, Tweedmount, Melrose, and Barbara Mackenzie; *m.* 1914, Marguerite Stevenson, *o. c.* of Stevenson Haggie, Newcastle on Tyne; one *s.* two *d.* *Educ.:* Fettes College, Edinburgh; Edinburgh University. W.S. Edinburgh, 1911; Lieutenant R.N.V.R., 1914; served Royal Naval Division and Harwich Destroyer Force. Member Queen's Body Guard for Scotland, Royal Company of Archers. Member of British Industrial Mission to Eastern Canada, 1931; Represented Federation of British Industries at the Ottawa Conference, 1932; Member British Government Purchasing Mission to Canada, 1939. Pres. Scottish Rugby Football Union, 1948-49. *Recreations:* formerly Rugby football, golf, and motoring. *Address:* St. Ronans, Selsey, Sussex. *T.:* Selsey 2787. *Club:* Boodle's. [*Died* 22 *Jan.* 1963.

McKENZIE, John Grant, M.A., B.D., D.D. (Aberdeen); Jesse Boot Professor of Sociology and Psychology in Paton Congregational Coll., Nottingham, 1921-51, ret.; *b.* Aberdeen, 5 Feb. 1882; *m.* 1912, Margaret Ann, *d.* of William and Eleanor McDonald; one *s.* one *d.* *Educ.:* Robert Gordon's College and University of Aberdeen; United College, Bradford. Held pastorates in Holywell Green Congregational Church, Halifax, 1912-17; Snow Hill, Wolverhampton, 1917-21; Delegate to International Congregational Council, Boston, U.S.A., 1920; won the Williams Divinity Scholarship, open to all Nonconformist graduates of United Kingdom, 1910. Tate Lecturer, Manchester Coll., Oxford, 1944 and 1947. *Publications:* Modern Psychology and the Achievement of Christian Personality; A Study in the Psychology of Religious Education, etc.; Souls in the Making: an Introduction to Pastoral Psychology: Personal Problems of Conduct and Religion; Psychology, Psychotherapy and Evangelicalism, 1940; Re-Vitalising the Gospel; Pastoral Psychology and Psychotherapy; Nervous Disorders and Character; Religion and Nervous Disorders; Guilt: Its Meaning and Significance, 1962. *Recreation:* golf. *Address:* 37 Lauderdale Street, Edinburgh 9.
[*Died* 17 *May* 1963.

MACKENZIE, Colonel John Hugh, C.M.G. 1919; D.S.O. 1917; *b.* Kirkwall, Orkney, 2 July 1876; *s.* of late Maj. H. L. Mackenzie, R.A.; *m.* 1st, 1906, Lorna Gladys (*d.* 1937), *d.* of E. Bourne Lucas; one *d.*; 2nd, 1943, Helena Constance Strathearn, *d.* of late Rev. Hon. Arthur Gordon, D.D. *Educ.:* Merchiston Castle School, Edinburgh; Royal Military College, Sandhurst. 2nd Lt. The Royal Scots, 1896; Lt. 1899; Capt. 1903; Maj. 1914; Bt. Lt.-Col. 1917; Lt.-Col. commanding The Royal Scots, 1922-26; Col. 1921; Adjt. 2nd The Royal Scots, 1903-6; S.S.O. (1st Class), Pachmarhi, 1906-8; P.S.C. Quetta, 1909; Bde. Major, Jubblepore, 1911-14; G.S.O.3, 19th Div. 1915; 2, xvii. Corps, 1915-17; 1 (T.) First Army, 1917-18; 24th Div. 1918; 63rd (R.N.) Div. 1918-19; Lowland Div. 1919; O.C. 11th The Royal Scots, 1919 (despatches five times, Bt. Lt.-Col. 1917; C.M.G., D.S.O., Commander Order of Avis, Portugal); G.S.O.1 Poona District, 1920-22; A.A.G. War Office, 1927-31; Commander, 156th (West Scottish) Infantry Brigade, T.A., 1931-32; retired pay, 1932; Secretary Ex-Service Association, India, 1932-1935; Col. The Royal Scots, 1940-46. *Address:* Heather Brae, Seale, Surrey. *T.:* Runfold 2165. [*Died* 23 *Feb.* 1963.

MacKENZIE, Major-General John Percival, C.B. 1944; D.S.O. 1917; E.D.; M.E.I.C.; Railway Engineer; formerly Maj.-General in Canadian Militia; *b.* 1884. Professional Engineer; Assoc. Member, Inst. of Mining and Metallurgy; Associate Member, Inst. of Royal Engineers. Served European War, 1914-18 (D.S.O. and two bars); War of 1939-45 (C.B.). French Croix de Guerre with Star. *Address:* c/o Vancouver Club, Vancouver, B.C.
[*Died* 25 *Aug.* 1961.

MACKENZIE, Rt. Rev. Kenneth Donald; *b.* 16 Sept. 1876; *s.* of Major-General Hugh Mackenzie and Julia Vere Cameron of Lochiel; *m.* 1914, Elizabeth Janet Forbes (*d.* 1961). *Educ.:* Radley; Hertford Coll., Oxford (Scholar) (1st in Lit. Hum.); Wells Theological College. Deacon, 1901; Priest, 1902; Assistant Curate, All Hallows', E. India Docks, 1901-03; St. John's, Upper Norwood, 1903-05; Fellow, Dean and Chaplain, Pembroke College, Oxford 1905-10; Examining Chaplain to Bishop F. Paget of Oxford, 1909-11; Assistant Curate St. Mary Magdalene's, Paddington, 1910-15; Vicar, Selly Oak, Birmingham, 1915-20; St. John's, Richmond, Surrey, 1920-22; work for Anglo-Catholic Congress, 1923-34; Canon Residentiary of Salisbury, 1934-35; Bishop of Brechin, 1935-43; Select Preacher, Univ. of Camb., 1938; Pres., Church Union, 1951-56. *Publications:* The Way of the Church; The Confusion of the Churches; The Faith of the Church; An Echo of the World Call; The Case for Episcopacy; Anglo-Catholic Ideals; The Catholic Rule of Life; Christ the King; Women and the Liturgical Ministry; The Fruit of the Spirit, 1937; The Meaning of Churchmanship, 1940; Everyman's Religion, 1945; The Background of the Church of England, 1952; The Divine Prayer, 1956; The Prayer Book Epistles, 1957. Translator: Avancini, The Life and Teaching of Our Lord Jesus Christ, 1937. Contrib. to: Murray's Dictionary of the Bible; Confirmation, or The Laying on of Hands; Liturgy and Worship; The Apostolic Ministry, 1946; Joint Editor, Episcopacy, Ancient and Modern; Editor, Reunion of Christendom, 1938; Truth, Unity and Concord, 1948. *Address:* 12 Palmeira Court, Palmeira Square, Hove, Sussex. [*Died* 1 *Oct.* 1966.

MACKENZIE, Rear-Admiral Kenneth Harry Litton, C.B.E. 1942; *b.* 18 April 1888; *s. c.* of late Edward L. T. Mackenzie; *m.* 1933, Elizabeth Olwen, *yr. d.* of late Colonel W. Lyster-Smythe, D.L., J.P., Barbavilla, Co. Westmeath; two *d.* *Educ.:* Stubbington House. Joined H.M.S. Britannia as Naval Cadet,

1904; Lieutenant, 1910; specialised in Navigation, 1911; Lieut.-Comdr., 1918; Commander, 1923; Master of the Fleet, 1928-30; Captain, 1930; Rear-Admiral, 1941; A.D.C. to the King, 1940; Admiral Superintendent, H.M. Dockyard, Malta, January 1941-November 1943. *Address:* Farthings, Dundrum, County Dublin. [*Died* 30 *Oct.* 1970.

MACKENZIE, Sir Moir; *see* Mackenzie, Sir James M.

MACKENZIE-KENNEDY, Sir (Henry Charles) Donald (Cleveland), K.C.M.G., *cr.* 1939 (C.M.G., 1932); *b.* 1889; *e. s.* of late Maj.-Gen. Sir E. C. W. Mackenzie-Kennedy, K.B.E., C.B.; *m.* 1919, Mildred, 3rd *d.* of late Rev. J. G. Munday; three *s.* one *d.* *Educ.:* Marlborough; Clare College, Cambridge. Entered N. Rhodesia Administration, 1912; Assistant Native Commissioner, 1915; Native Commissioner, 1918; Temp. Lieut. Norforce, 1918; Assistant Magistrate, 1926; Principal Assistant Chief Secretary, 1927; Chief Secretary to the Government of Northern Rhodesia, 1930-34; Chief Secretary, Tanganyika Territory, 1935-39; Governor and Commander-in-Chief of Nyasaland Protectorate, 1939-42; Chief Political Liaison Officer, East Africa Force, Sept. 1939-April 1940; Governor and C.-in-C., Mauritius, 1942-49; retd. 1949. *Address:* c/o Standard Bank, 10 Clements Lane, E.C.4. [*Died* 2 *Aug.* 1965.

MacKERETH, Sir Gilbert, K.C.M.G., *cr.* 1952 (C.M.G. 1939); M.C.; *b.* 19 Oct. 1893; *s.* of Thomas MacKereth, F.R.S.; *m.* 1921, Muriel, *d.* of David J. Watson, Barrister-at-Law. *Educ.:* Keswick Grammar School; Rugby; Pembroke College, Cambridge, Served European War, 1914-18 (wounded despatches, M.C. Commander Order of Leopold of Belgium, Commander Order of Star of Ethiopia, French Croix de Guerre avec palmes, and Belgian Croix de Guerre); entered Consular service, 1919; Consul at Addis Ababa, 1930; Damascus, 1933; Consul-General, Addis Ababa, 1940; Ankara, Foreign Office, 1941; Counsellor, Legation, Beirut, 1944; Political adviser to C.-in-C. and Consul-General at Batavia, Java, 1946-47; H.M. Ambassador to Republic of Colombia, 1947-53; retired from Foreign Service, Nov. 1953. *Address:* BM/PB46, London, W.2. *Club:* Royal Automobile. [*Died* 11 *Jan.* 1962.

McKERIHAN, Sir (Clarence) Roy, Kt. 1967; C.B.E. 1958; M.S.M. 1917; financial consultant and adviser; retired; *b.* 6 May 1896; *s.* of Edward McKerihan, Brisbane; *m.* 17 Aug. 1921, Dorothy Juanita, *d.* of John McCallum; two *d.* *Educ.:* Tamworth, Tenterfield and Casino, Aust. Pres., Rural Bank of N.S.W., 1933-61. Pres., Board of Women's Hosp., Sydney, 1944-62. Hon. Federal Administrator, Aust. Comforts Fund, 1939-47. Hon. Federal Dir., Arts Council of Australia, 1949-62; U.N. Hon. Federal and State Treasurer: Unicef; Appeal for Refugees; Freedom from Hunger Campaign. Chm., R.A.A.F. Welfare Fund, 1948-62. Foundation President: Internat. Migration Movement; National Gallery Soc. of N.S.W.; Pres., National Trust of Australia. Life Mem., Royal Agricultural Soc. of N.S.W. *Recreations:* cricket, tennis and bowls (formerly Mem. A.I.F. Rugby Union Team.) *Address:* 895 New South Head Road, Rose Bay, N.S.W., Australia. *T.:* 37.6859 [*Died* 28 *Dec.* 1969.

McKERRAL, Andrew, C.I.E. 1931; M.A. (Glasgow), B.Sc. (Edinburgh); *b.* Southend, Kintyre, Argyllshire, 23 Sept. 1876; *s.* of late John McKerral, Midcalder. Entered Indian Agricultural Service, 1907; Director of Agriculture, Burma, 1923-35; retired, 1935. *Publications:* Kintyre in the Seventeenth Century; various papers on historical and technical subjects. *Address:* c/o National Bank of India, Bishopsgate, E.C.2. [*Died* 16 *Sept.* 1967.

McKERRON, Sir Patrick (Alexander Bruce), K.B.E., *cr.* 1950; C.M.G. 1945; *b.* 6 May 1896; *e. s.* of late Professor R. G. McKerron, Aberdeen University, and *g.s.* of late Dr. William Bruce, M.D., LL.D., The Castle, Dingwall; *m.* 1933, Marjorie Kennedy, *y. d.* of late Alexander Rettie of Ceylon; one *s.* one *d.* *Educ.:* Aberdeen Grammar School; Fettes College, Edinburgh. 4th Gordons, 1914-17, France, 1916, Capt.; Capt. 20th Punjabis, 1917-18; entered Malayan Civil Service, 1920; British Resident, Brunei, 1928-31; Asst. British Adviser, Kedah, 1934-36; Chief Censor, Malaya, 1939-41; Chief Civil Liaison Officer, 3rd Indian Corps, Malaya, 1942; Political Secretary, C.-in-C. Ceylon, 1942-43; Deputy Chief Civil Affairs Officer, Singapore (Brig.), Sept. 1945 (despatches); Colonial Secretary, Singapore, 1946-50; Officer Administering Govt., Singapore, May-Oct. 1947 and Nov. 1949-Apr. 1950; Pres. Assoc. of British Malaya, 1952-54. *Recreations:* golf, gardening. *Address:* Avington Park, Nr. Winchester, Hants. [*Died* 20 *March* 1964.

MACKESON, Brigadier Sir Harry Ripley, 1st Bart., *cr.* 1954; p.s.c.; *b.* 25 May 1905; *s.* of late Harry Mackeson, J.P., Littlebourne House, Littlebourne, Kent, and late Ella Cecil Ripley; *m.* 1940, Alethea Cecil, *d.* of late Commander R. Talbot, Royal Navy, Maxpoffle, St. Boswells; one *s.* one *d.* *Educ.:* Lockers Park, Hemel Hempstead; Rugby; R.M.C., Sandhurst. Joined Royal Scots Greys in India, 1925; Adjt. of Greys, 1933-35; Staff College, 1936; Bde. Maj. Egypt, 1938-40; G.S.O. 1, 1940-42; B.G.S., H.Q. Royal Armd. Corps, 1942; comd. Armd. Bde. U.K., France and Belgium, 1942-44. M.P. (C.) Hythe, 1945-1950, Folkestone and Hythe, 1950-Sept. 1959. Conservative Whip, 1947, Dep. Chief Conservative Whip, 1950; a Lord Commr. of the Treasury and a Dep. Govt. Chief Whip, 1951; Secretary for Overseas Trade, 1952-53. Chm. Dosco Overseas Engineering Co.; Pres. Kent Football Assoc., 1949-; Pres. Kent Cricket Club, 1951. *Heir:* *s.* Rupert Henry, *b.* 16 Nov. 1941. *Address:* Orchard Court, Portman Square, W.1; Eton House, Docking, Norfolk; The Old Rectory, Great Mongeham, Deal, Kent. *T.:* Deal 562. *Clubs:* Cavalry, Turf, International Sportsmen's. [*Died* 25 *Jan.* 1964.

MACKIE, Brig. Andrew Hugh, C.I.E. 1944; J.P.; late I.A.; *b.* 20 May 1897; *s.* of late J. H. Mackie, J.P., Castle Cary, Somerset; *m.* 1928, Enid M. Feaver; two *s.* *Educ.:* Sexey's School, Bruton; Military College, Wellington, India. Joined 2/4th Somerset L.I., Dec. 1914; 19th K.G.O. Lancers, 1917; special duty with Remount Commission, U.S.A., 1929; South Africa, 1944; Dep. Director Remounts, G.H.Q. India, 1935-41; late Director of Remounts, General Headquarters, India. Bursar, Millfield Sch., 1949-1962. *Address:* Cary Lodge, Burnham-on-Sea, Somerset. *T.:* Burnham-on-Sea 2183. [*Died* 20 *Feb.* 1968.

McKIE, Professor Douglas; Professor of the History and Philosophy of Science, University of London, Univ. Coll., 1957-64, Emeritus, 1964; *b.* 15 July 1896; *er. s.* of James McKie, Port William, Wigtownshire, and Janet Moseley, Mountain Ash, Glam.; *m* 1922, Mary, 2nd *d.* of T. Smith, Kirkby-la-Thorpe, Lincs.; one *s.* *Educ.:* The Grammar School, Tredegar; R.M.C. Sandhurst; University College, London. Formerly Lieut., 24th Regt. (South Wales Borderers); retired list, 1920, on account of wounds received in action. University College, London, 1920-23: B.Sc. 1st Cl. Hons.

Chem. 1923: Ramsay Medal, 1925; Ph.D. 1927; D.Sc. 1936. Asst., later Lectr. in History and Philosophy of Science, Univ. Coll., 1925-45, Sen. Lectr., 1945, Reader, 1946. Fell. of Univ. Coll., London, 1954. F.R.I.C. 1956; F.R.S.E. 1958; F.R.S.A. 1958 (Coun., 1962-64); F.S.A. 1962; Founder Mem. Faculty of Hist. of Med. and Pharmacy, Soc. of Apothecaries, and Pres. 2nd Brit. Congress, 1961. Mem. Soc. Apothecaries, 1963. Member of Commission Lavoisier, Académie des Sciences, Paris; Vice-Prés., Acad. Internat. d'Histoire des Sciences, 1956-1959; Chm. Soc. for the Study of Alchemy and Early Chemistry, 1959-. Chevalier de la Légion d'Honneur, 1957. Dexter Award, American Chemical Society, 1963. *Publications:* (with N. H. de V. Heathcote) The Discovery of Specific and Latent Heats, 1935; Antoine Lavoisier, The Father of Modern Chemistry, 1935; The Essays of Jean Rey, 1952; Antoine Lavoisier, Scientist, Economist, Social Reformer, 1952; ed. revised edns. of A. Wolf's History of Science, Technology and Philosophy in the 16th and 17th Centuries, and History of Science etc. in the 18th Century, 1950, 1952; (with N. H. de V. Heathcote) William Cleghorn's De Igne (1779) with translation and annotations, 1960; The Origins and Foundation of the Royal Society of London (in the Royal Society: its Origins and Founders, 1960); Science and Technology (Chaps. V in the New Cambridge Modern History, Vols. VIII, 1965, and XII, 1960); facsimile reprint of Lavoisier's Elements of Chemistry (1790) with introd., 1965; facsimile reprint of Boyle's Works (1772) with introd., 1965; Cochrane's Notes of Black's Lectures on Chemistry (1767-68), ed. with introd., 1966; founder and editor of Annals of Science, 1936-; numerous papers on the history of science. *Address:* 18 Brookland Hill, N.W.11. *T.:* Speedwell 8749. *Club:* Athenæum. [*Died* 28 *Aug.* 1967.

MACKINNON of MACKINNON, Commander Arthur Avalon; 36th Chief of the Clan Mackinnon; O.B.E.; R.N. (retired); *b.* 8 Nov. 1893; *s.* of late F. A. Mackinnon of Mackinnon and Emily Isabel Hood; *m.* 1921, Gunhild Kroyer (*d.* 1946); two *s.* one *d.*; *m.* 1948, Kathleen Mary, *widow* of Comdr. R. A. Nicholson, O.B.E., R.N. *Educ.:* Stone House, Broadstairs; R.N.C., Osborne and Dartmouth. Joined Naval College, 1906; went to sea, 1910; served European War, 1914-18, in Pacific, 1914-15; in destroyers in North Sea, 1916-18; retired, 1935; Naval Welfare Officer at Chatham, 1935-52. *Recreations:* cricket, hockey, shooting. *Address:* Charity Acre, Pilgrims Way, Hollingbourne, Maidstone, Kent. *T.:* Hollingbourne 320. [*Died* 8 *April* 1964.

MACKINNON, Kenneth Wulsten, M.B.E. 1945; T.D. 1953; Q.C. 1958; *b.* 20 January 1906; *s.* of Donald and Hilda Eleanor Marie Mackinnon; *m.* 1939, Dorothy Sparke, *d.* of Lewis James and Linda Sparke Davies; two *s.* *Educ.:* Geelong Grammar School, Australia; New College, Oxford. Barrister, Middle Temple, 1929. Served War of 1939-1945 with R.A. (T.A.). Staff College, Camberley, 1942-43. Lieutenant-Col. 1944. Bencher, Middle Temple, 1953. Mem. Gen. Council of the Bar (Exec. Cttee.), 1951-55; Mem. Bd. of Trade Departl. Cttee. on Company Law, under Lord Jenkins; Chm. Panel of Judges for the Accountants Award, 1960-. *Address:* 56 Kingston House North, S.W.7. *T.:* Kensington 1972. *Club:* Brooks's. [*Died* 30 *April* 1964.

MACKINTOSH OF HALIFAX, 1st Viscount, *cr.* 1957, of Hethersett, Norfolk; **1st Baron, *cr.* 1948; Harold Vincent Mackintosh, Bt., *cr.* 1935; Kt. 1922; D.L. W. Riding, Yorks; J.P.; LL.D. (hon.) Leeds University; Chairman of National Savings Committee since 1943, and President and Chairman since 1958; Chairman of John Mackintosh & Sons, Ltd., Halifax; *b.* 8 June 1891;** *s.* of John and Violet Mackintosh; ***m.* 1916, Constance Emily, *d.* of Edgar Cooper** Stoneham, O.B.E.; one *s.* one *d.* *Educ.:* New School, Halifax; Germany. President, The Advertising Association, 1942-46; Pres. Nat. Advertising Benevolent Soc., 1946-48; Pres. and Chm. Internat. Advertising Convention, 1951; Director of Martins Bank, Ltd. (London Bd.); a Dir. of Ranks Hovis McDougall Ltd.; a Trustee of East Anglia Savings Bank and of York County Savings Bank; Vice-Pres. Trustee Savings Banks Assoc.; Pres. World Council of Christian Education and Sunday Sch. Assoc. 1928-58 (Chairman, 1958-) (Hon. Treas. British Cttee.) President National Sunday School Union, 1924; Joint Hon. Treasurer, Home Missionary Committee of Methodist Church; Member Grand Council of British Empire Cancer Campaign, Chairman its Yorkshire Council; a Vice-President, Nat. Council of Y.M.C.A.; Jt. Hon. Treas. of Ashville Coll., Harrogate; Pres., Yorks. Agricultural Soc., 1928 and 1929; Pres., Royal Norfolk Agricultural Assoc., 1960. Chancellor, University of East Anglia, Norwich. Hon. Freeman of County Borough of Halifax. *Publication:* Early English Figure Pottery. *Heir:* *s.* Hon. John Mackintosh [*b.* 7 Oct. 1921; *m.* 1946 (marr. diss., 1956); two *d.*; *m.* 1956, Gwynneth Charlesworth, 2nd *d.* of Charles H. Gledhill, Halifax; two *s.*]. *Address:* Thickthorn Hall, Hethersett, Norfolk. *T.:* Norwich 52870; 55 Park Lane, W.1. *T.:* Grosvenor 1744. *Clubs:* Brooks's, Royal Automobile. [*Died* 27 *Dec.* 1964.

MACKINTOSH, James M., M.A., M.D., **LL.D., F.R.C.P.; Barrister-at-Law;** retired; ***b.* 17 February 1891;** *yr.* *s.* of **J. D. Mackintosh, Solicitor, Kilmarnock, Scotland; *m.* 1919, Marjorie, *d.* of David Strathie, C.A., Kilmacolm; one *s.* two *d.* *Educ.:* Glasgow High School and University. 2nd Lieut. 6th Cameron Highlanders, 1915-1916; Capt. R.A.M.C. 1917-20; Asst. Health Officer, Dorset, 1920-24; Burton-on-Trent, 1924-26; Leicestershire, 1926-30; County M.O.H.,** Northamptonshire, 1930-37; Chief M.O., Dept. of Health for Scotland, 1937-41; **Professor of Public Health: Glasgow, 1941-1944; Univ. of London, 1944-56. *Publications:*** Topics in Public Health, 1965; on housing, and social problems. *Address:* 3 Winford Court, Downs Park West, Bristol 6. [*Died* 20 *April* 1966.

MACKINTOSH, Stanley Hugh, D.S.O. 1917; O.B.E. 1930; *b.* 26 Jan. 1883; *m.* 1911, Isabella Jane Macleod (*d.* 1954); one *s.* one *d.* (and one *s.* died on active service). *Educ.:* Roy. Acad., Inverness. Maj. Northumberland Fusiliers; served in South Africa with Lovat Scouts, 1901-2; European War, 1914-19 (despatches, D.S.O.). Retired from Civil Service, 1944. Late Regional Controller for Scotland, Ministry of Labour and National Service, and National Service Hostels Corporation, Ltd. *Address:* 18 Braidburn Terrace, Edinburgh. [*Died* 24 *March* 1967.

MACKINTOSH, William Archibald; *see* Addenda: II.

McKISACK, Sir Audley, Kt. 1958; President, High Court of the Federation of South Arabia, since 1964 and Judge, Courts of Appeal, Bahamas, 1965, and Bermuda, 1965; *b.* 2 April 1903; *s.* of late Audley John McKisack and Elizabeth (*née* McCullough), Belfast; *m.* 1st, K. R. F. Gregorowski (marr. diss., 1947); one *s.* (and one *s.* decd.); 2nd, 1947, Elena Rose Jeannette Berger, M.B.E. *Educ.:* Bedford Sch.; Univ. College, Oxford (B.A.). Called to Bar, Inner Temple, 1935. Entered Colonial Service, 1924; Administrative Officer, N. Rhodesia, 1924-36; Magistrate 1936-38, Crown Counsel

1938-44, Uganda; Attorney-General, Gibraltar, 1944; Zanzibar, 1947; Secretary, Ministry of Justice, Gold Coast, 1950. Q.C. (Nigeria) 1951; Attorney-General, Federation of Nigeria, 1954-56 (Nigeria, 1951-1954). Chief Justice, Uganda, 1956-62. *Address:* Red Hedges, Northview Road, Budleigh Salterton, Devon. *T.:* Budleigh Salterton 758. *Club:* East India and Sports. [*Died* 16 *Aug.* 1966.

McKITTRICK, Thomas Harrington; retired banker; *b.* St. Louis, Mo., 14 March 1889; *s.* of Thomas Harrington and Hildegarde (*née* Sterling) McKittrick; *m.* 1921, Marjorie Benson; four *d.* *Educ.:* St Louis (Mo.) Manual Training School; Hackley School, Tarrytown, N.Y.; Harvard Univ. (A.B.).; St. Louis Univ. Law School. With Hargadine, McKittrick (Wholesale) Dry Goods Co., 1911-14; St. Louis (Mo.) Union Trust Co., 1914-15; Nat. City Bank of N.Y. in N.Y. City, 1916, in Genoa, Italy, 1916-18; with Lee Higginson & Co., in N.Y. City, 1919-1921; with Higginson & Co., London, 1922-1939; partner, 1924-39; Pres., Bank for Internat. Settlements, Basle, 1940-46; Chm. Northern Paper & Pulp Works, Tallinn, Estonia, 1935-61; Sen. Vice-Pres., Chase National Bank of N Y., 1949-54 (Vice-Pres., 1946); Dir. Chase Bank, 1946-54; Chief, Trade and Payments Div., Office of Special Representative, E.C.A., Paris, June-Dec. 1948; Actg. Chief, Mission to U.K., E.C.A., London, Aug.-Sept. 1949. Dir. Am. Chamber of Commerce, London, Eng., 1930-39; mem., Executive Cttee., U.S. Council, Internat. C. of C.; First Vice-Chm., Cttee. on Commercial and Monetary Policy, Internat. C. of C. Chairman Foreign Securities Cttee., Investment Bankers Assoc. of America, 1948; Chm. of the American-British Foundation for European Education, 1949-58; Chm. German Credits Arbitration Cttee. 1953-58 (Mem. 1931-39, Vice-Chm., 1933-1939); exec. cttee. and hon. treasurer American Relief Soc., London, England, 1930-39. Chief, Mission to India, Internat. Bank for Reconstruction and Development, Washington, Apr.-July, 1956; Pres. and Chm., Continental Amer. Fund, Inc., New York, 1956-59. Director: Canadian Internat. Growth Fund, Ltd., Montreal, 1956-; Institutional Shares, Ltd., N.Y., 1958-; Managed Funds, Inc., St. Louis, Mo., 1960-. Served as 2nd Lt., A.E.F., 1918, 1st Lt. 1919; cited for meritorious service. M.B.O.U.; Member American Ornithologists' Union; Member Am. Geog. Soc.; Corr. Mem. Statistisch-Volkwirtschaftliche Gesellschaft, Basel. Knight Grand Cross, Order of Crown of Roumania, 1947; Comdr. Order of Crown (Belgium), 1948; Comdr., Order of Merit (Italy), 1956. *Address:* (home) Slate Falls Blairstown, N.J., U.S.A. *Clubs:* American; University, Century (New York); Pilgrims (U.S.A.). [*Died* 21 *Jan.* 1970.

MACKNESS, Lieutenant-Commander George John, C.B.E. 1959 (O.B.E. 1944); D.S.C. 1917; D.L., J.P.. Royal Navy, retired; *b.* Broughty Ferry, Angus, 10 May 1892; *s.* of George Owen Carr Mackness, M.A., M.D. and Bertha, *d.* of John Raimes, Acaster Malbis, York; *m.* 1917, Helena Kathleen, *d.* of Sir Thomas Shipstone, Nottingham; three *s.* one *d.* *Educ.:* R.N. Colleges, Osborne and Dartmouth. R.N. till 1919; formerly director, Carter Gate Motor Co. Ltd., Motor Engineers, of Nottingham: director of J. Shipstone & Sons Ltd., Brewers, Nottingham. A.R.P. Controller of City of Nottingham during War of 1939-45; High Sheriff of Nottinghamshire, 1948-49. *Recreation:* fly-fishing. *Address:* Conery House, Whatton-in-the-Vale, Notts. *T.:* Whatton 266. *Club:* Royal Automobile. [*Died* 27 *Oct.* 1970.

MACKNESS, William Robert; H.M. Consular Service (retired); *b.* 15 June 1879; *o. s.* of late William Mackness; *m.* 1905, Ethel Jane Lawrence. *Educ:* University College School, London; privately. Temporary Vice-Consul, Santos, 1917; Bilbao, 1918; H.M. Consul, St. Louis, 1919; Trieste, 1921; Pernambuco, 1929; Malaga, 1934; Turin, 1937; H.M. Minister-Resident, Port-au-Prince, 1938-39. Coronation Medal, 1937. *Recreations:* golf and walking. *Address:* Glencree, Berkeley Rd., Frome, Somerset. *T.:* Frome 2144. [*Died* 2 *Aug.* 1963.

MACKNIGHT, Lieut.-Col. John James Thow, C.I.E. 1930; V.D. Lt.-Col. Surma Valley Light Horse, 1927-30; retired, 1930. Formerly Hon. A.D.C. to the Governor of Assam. *Address:* Kurkoorie, Bonaly Road, Colinton, Edinburgh 13. [*Died* 11 *April* 1965.

MACKWORTH-YOUNG, Gerard; *see* Young, G. M-.

McLAGGAN, Sir (John) Douglas, K.C.V.O. 1958 (C.V.O. 1950); M.A. (Aberdeen) 1914; M.B., Ch.B. (distinction Final Professional) 1920; F.R.C.S. (Ed.) 1924; F.R.C.S. (Eng.) 1926; Physiology Medal, Aberdeen, 1918; Formerly Lectr. in Diseases of the Ear, Nose and Throat and Surgeon in charge Ear, Nose and Throat Department of the Royal Free Hospital; *b.* 18 June, 1893; *s.* of James McLaggan and Sarah Ann Murray; *m.* 1928, Elsa V. Adams; two *s.* Formerly Aurist to King George VI, to Queen Mary, and to Queen Elizabeth. Served European War, 1914-18, with Gordon Highlanders. *Publication:* Diseases of the Ear, Nose and Throat, 1937, 2nd Edn. (with Miss J. Collier), 1952. *Recreation:* ornithology. *Address:* Daws Wood, Frensham, Surrey. *T.:* Frensham 2063. [*Died* 1 *Jan.* 1967

MacLAREN, Brig.-Gen. Charles Henry, C.M.G. 1918; D.S.O. 1916; President, McLaren Power & Paper Co., Quebec; *b.* 22 Nov. 1878; *s.* of late David MacLaren and late Katharine A. McGillivray; *m.* 1910, Dorothy Olivia, *d.* of late Lt.-Col. Fred White, C.M.G.; three *s.* *Educ.:* public schools, Canada; Queen's University (B.A.); Toronto University (LL.B.). Served European War, 1914-18, England, France (despatches twice, D.S.O., C.M.G.). [*Died* 15 *Aug.* 1962.

MacLAREN of MacLaren, Donald (The MacLaren of MacLaren); Chief of Clan Labhran; *b.* 22 July 1910; *s.* of late Rev. Duncan MacLaren, B.D., of Balquhidder, and Minister of Turriff; *m.* 1953, Margaret Sinclair, *d.* of Douglas Miller, M.D., F.R.C.S., F.R.C.P., F.R.C.O.G., of Edinburgh; *S.* uncle, 1957. *Educ.:* Turriff Academy; Edinburgh Univ.; Queen's Univ., Canada. Served 1939-48, with dept. of Foreign Office (Berlin, etc.) and with Cameron Highlanders, Major, 1944. Chartered Accountant (Can.); Director: United Baltic Corporation Ltd., London; Royal Caledonian Schools. *Heir:* *s.* Donald MacLaren, younger of MacLaren, *b.* 1954. *Address:* 3 Ennismore Gardens, S.W.7. *T.:* Kensington 8622; Creag an Tuirc, Balquhidder, Perthshire. *Clubs:* Reform; Puffin's (Edinburgh). [*Died* 8 *June* 1966.

McLARTY, Hon. Sir (Duncan) Ross, K.B.E. 1953; M.M. 1917; Farmer and Pastoralist, Western Australia; *b.* Pinjarra, W.A., 17 Nov. 1891; *d.* of late Hon. E. McLarty, M.L.C., of Pinjarra, W.A.; *m.* 1923, Violet, *d.* of Robert Herron, farmer, Coolup, W.A.; three *s.* *Educ.:* Pinjarra State Sch. and High (now Hale) Sch., Perth, W.A. M.L.A., for Murray-Wellington, W.A., 1930-50, and for Murray, 1950-; unopposed general elections, 1933, 1936, 1939, 1943,

1947, 1956, 1959; Leader of Liberal Party, Dec. 1946-March 1957; Premier and Treasurer of Western Australia, 1947-53, during which period also held portfolios of North-West, Housing and Forests; Leader of Opposition, W.A., 1953-57. Served European War, 1914-18, 44th Bn. A.I.F. (M.M.); War of 1939-45, Major commanding 4th Bn. V.D.C. Retired from politics, 1962. *Recreations:* cricket, football, golf. *Address:* Pinjarra, Western Australia. *T.:* Pinjarra 8. *Club:* West Australian (Perth, W.A.). [*Died* 21 *Dec.* 1962.

McLAUGHLIN, Rear-Adm. (retd.) Patrick Vivian, C.B. 1951; D.S.O. 1946; *b.* 7 April 1901; 3rd *s.* of late Vivian Guy Ouseley McLaughlin, J.P., Glos.; *m.* 1st, 1935, Anne Marguerite (marr. diss., 1949), *d.* of R. A. L. Broadley, Wincanton; *m.* 2nd, 1956, Elizabeth Viscountess Mountgarret (who *m.* 1931, 16th Viscount Mountgarret, marr. diss. 1941; one *s.* one *d.*), *er. d.* of Wm. Lorenzo Christie, J.P., Jervaulx Abbey, Yorkshire. *Educ.:* Brightlands Preparatory School, Gloucestershire; Royal Naval Colleges, Osborne and Dartmouth. Midshipman, 1917; Lieut. 1922; Lt.-Comdr. 1930; Comdr. 1935; Captain 1939; Rear-Admiral 1949; served War of 1939-45, in command H.M.S. Mashona, 1939 (North Sea Operations); H.M.S. Cairo, 1940 (despatches, Norwegian Campaign); Dep. Dir. of Naval Ordnance, Admiralty, 1941-43; comd. H.M.S. Spartan, 1943-1944; Capt. Comdg. Coastal Forces in Channel, 1944; H.M.S. Swiftsure (in command, 1945; British Pacific Fleet, Okinawa Campaign, Hong-Kong) (D.S.O.); Captain H.M.S. Excellent, 1947-49; Vice-Pres. Ordnance Bd., 1950-52; Sen. Naval Mem. and President Ordnance Board, 1952-53; retired list, 1953. Coronation Medal, 1937. *Recreations:* yachting, field sports, golf. *Address:* The Dolphins, Sandwich, Kent. *T.:* Sandwich 3343. *Clubs:* White's, United Service, M.C.C.; Royal Yacht Squadron (Cowes). [*Died* 8 *June* 1969.

MACLAY, 2nd Baron, *cr.* 1922, of Glasgow; **Joseph Paton Maclay,** Bt., *cr.* 1914; K.B.E., *cr.* 1946; *b.* 31 May 1899; *e. surv. s.* of 1st Baron Maclay, P.C.; *S.* father 1951; *m.* 1936, Nancy Margaret, *d.* of R. C. Greig, Hall of Caldwell, Uplawmoor, Renfrewshire; three *s.* two *d.* *Educ.:* Fettes College, Edinburgh; Trinity College, Cambridge. M.P. (L.) Borough of Paisley, 1931-1945; Head of Convoy and Admiralty Liaison Section, Ministry of War Transport, 1943-45. Pres. Chamber of Shipping of United Kingdom, 1946-47; Chm. Gen. Council of British Shipping, 1946-47; Lord Dean of Guild, Glasgow, 1952-54; Chm. Clydesdale & N. of Scotland Bank (Dir. 1947); Dir. Midland Bank. *Heir:* *s.* Hon. Joseph Paton Maclay, *b.* 11 April 1942. *Address:* Duchal, Kilmacolm, Scotland. *T.:* Kilmacolm 2255. *Clubs:* Western (Glasgow); Royal Yacht Squadron (Cowes). [*Died* 7 *Nov.* 1969.

MACLAY, Hon. Walter Symington, C.B. 1955; O.B.E. 1943; M.A. (Camb.), M.D. (Camb.), M.R.C.S. (Eng.), L.R.C.P. (London), F.R.C.P. (Eng.), D.T.M. and H. (Liverpool), D.P.M. (Eng.); Q.H.P. 1959; Emeritus Physician to Royal Bethlem-Maudsley Hospital; Regional Psychiatrist to Wessex Regional Hospital Board; Fellow of Royal Society of Medicine; Distinguished Fellow, Amer. Psychiatric Assoc.; Fellow of British Psychological Society; Hon. D.Sc., McGill, 1961; *b.* 29 October 1901; 2nd *s.* of 1st Baron Maclay, P.C.; *m.* 1928, Dorothy Russell Lennox; three *s.* one *d.* (and one *d.* decd.). *Educ.:* Fettes Coll., Edinburgh; St. John's Coll., Camb.; St. Bartholomew's Hosp., London. Worked as Medical Officer in native hospitals in Kenya, Nyasaland, and S. Africa, 1928-31; Clinical Assistant at Hospital for sick children, Great Ormond Street, and at City Road Chest Hospital, London, 1931-33; Medical Officer at Maudsley Hospital, 1932-38; Medical Supt. Mill Hill Emergency Hospital, 1939-1945; Medical Senior Commissioner, Board of Control and Principal M.O. of Ministry of Health, 1945-61. *Publications:* contrib. to Journal of Neurology and Psychopathology, and to Proc. Roy. Soc. Med. *Address:* Millwaters, London Road, Newbury, Berks. *T.:* Newbury 440; 40 Kensington Square, W.8. *T.:* Western 0364. [*Died* 27 *April* 1964.

MacLEAN, Col. Archibald Campbell Holms, C.B.E. 1918; retired list, The Royal Scots; *b.* Glasgow, 23 Oct. 1883; *s.* of late Charles James MacLean of Plantation; *m.* 1915; two *d.*; *m.* 1932; *m.* 1961. *Educ.:* Kelvinside; Royal Military College, Sandhurst. First commission in the Royal Scots, 1903; seconded R.F.C., 1912; Capt., 1913; Major, 1914; Lt.-Col., 1916; Colonel, 1918; attached Royal Air Force, 1918; promoted Brig. General, 1918; served European War, 1914-19 (despatches, C.B.E.); War of 1939-1945, Group Captain R.A.F.V.R., Regional Liaison Officer. Order Rising Sun, Japan. *Recreations:* golf, shooting, yachting. *Address:* Hillcroft Cottage, Bicknoller, Taunton, Somerset. *Club:* Naval and Military. [*Died* 30 *April* 1970.

McLEAN, Calvin Stowe; retired as Chairman of General Mining, and as a Director of all Mining and Finance Boards, 1965; *b.* 21 July 1888; *s.* of Hugh McLean; *m.* Olive Aileen, *d.* of late William Sealswood; one *s.* two *d.* *Educ.:* Rothesay Collegiate School, New Brunswick; McGill University, Montreal (B.Sc. (Mining)). Came to S. Africa, 1910. Joined Gen. Mining and Finance Corp. Ltd., 1920; Cons. Engr., 1936-50; Dep. Chm. and Tech. Dir., 1950-63; Chm., 1963-65. Mem., Assoc. of Mine Managers of the Transvaal, 1920- (Vice-Pres. 1935); Mem. Exec. Cttee., Transvaal and O.F.S. Chamber of Mines, 1941-65 (Pres., 1945-46, 1948-49, 1952-53); Mem., S.A. Atomic Energy Bd., 1955-64; Mem., S.A. Electricity Supply Commission, 1948-54. Pres., 7th Commonwealth Mining and Metallurgical Congress, S.A., 1961. Chm., St. Andrew's School for Girls, Johannesburg, S.A., 1939-68. Hon. LL.D. Witwatersrand, 1961. *Publications:* technical papers. *Recreations:* bowls, motoring. *Address:* 29 Bompas Rd., Dunkeld, Johannesburg, S.A. *T.:* 42-2418 and 836-1121. *Clubs:* Rand, Johannesburg Country, Wanderers' (Pres.), Royal Johannesburg Golf (all in Johannesburg); Durban Country (Durban). [*Died* 24 *Jan.* 1970.

McLEAN, Colonel Charles Wesley Weldon, C.M.G. 1919; D.S.O. 1915; *b* St. John, New Brunswick, Aug. 1882; *s.* of late Maj.-Gen. Hon. H. H. McLean, K.C.; unmarried. *Educ.:* R.M.C., Kingston. Served S. African War, 1899-1900; entered R.H.A. 1900; Capt. 1908; Major, 1914; Lt.-Col. 1923; Col. 1927; European War, May 1915-19, commanding 52nd Brigade Royal Artillery, 9th Division (wounded twice, 1914-15 Star, D.S.O. 2 bars, C.M.G., despatches thrice); M.P. (U.) Brigg Division of Lindsey, Lincolnshire, Dec. 1918-22; commanding 2nd Brigade Royal Horse Artillery, 1923-27; Comdr. Royal Artillery, 56th London Division, T.A., 1928-32; retired pay, 1932; War of 1939-45, H.Q., H.G. London District. *Clubs:* Carlton, Cavalry. [*Died* 5 *Sept.* 1962.

MacLEAN, Air Vice-Marshal Cuthbert Trelawder, C.B. 1933; D.S.O. 1919; M.C.; *b.* 18 Oct. 1886; *s.* of late Rev. T. B. MacLean, Wanganui, N.Z.; *m.* 1917, Maria Dorothy (*d.* 1965), *d.* of late Mrs. Lewin, Kirklivington Hall, Yarm; no *c.* *Educ.:* Wanganui Collegiate School; Auckland

University, N.Z. Served European War, 1914-19; seconded to R.F.C., 1915; R.A.F., 1918; Air Commodore, 1931; Air Vice-Marshal, 1935; Officer Commanding British Forces in Aden, 1929-31; Director of Postings, Air Ministry, 1931-34; Air Officer Commanding, R.A.F., Middle East, 1934-38; Air Officer commanding No. 2 (Bomber) Group, R.A.F., 1938; retired list, 1940; Chevalier Legion of Honour. *Address:* Whiteway Copse, Cirencester, Glos. *T.:* Cirencester 629. *Club:* Junior Army and Navy. [*Died* 25 *Feb.* 1969.

McLEAN, Sir Robert, Kt., 1926; B.Sc., F.R.Ae.S.; M.I.P.E.; late Director Vickers-Armstrong; late Managing Director and Chairman Vickers (Aviation) Limited and Chairman Super-marine Aviation Works Limited, 1927-38; late Managing Director Electrical and Musical Industries and the Gramophone Co.; *b.* 1884; *s.* of late Rev. D. McLean, B.D., Alloa; *m.* 1908, Evelyn Noel, *d.* of H. E. Girard, Calcutta; two *d.* *Educ.:* Edinburgh Academy and University. Indian State Railways: Assistant Secretary Railway Board, 1916; Secretary, 1919; Deputy Agent, G.I.P. Railway, India, 1920; General Manager, Great Indian Peninsular Railway, 1922-29; President, Indian Railway Conference Association, 1925; Trustee, Port of Bombay, 1922-27; served European War, Aden Field Force, Mesopotamia E.F. and B.E.F. France; Chairman, Society of British Aircraft Constructors, 1935-37; Past Pres., Instn. Production Engineers. *Address:* Laidlawstiel Farm, by Galashiels, Selkirkshire. *T.:* Clovenfords 8. *Club:* New (Edinburgh). [*Died* 9 *April* 1964.

McLEAN, Sir William Hannah, K.B.E., *cr.* 1938; J.P; Ph.D. (Glasgow), M.I.C.E.; honorary liaison officer with Members of both Houses of Parliament and economic and social development work in the Colonial Office since 1931; *b.* 25 Jan. 1877; *s.* of late William McLean, Dunoon, Argyll; *m.* 1922, Frances Gwendolin (*d.* 1960), *d.* of late Col. W. E. Donohue, C.B.E.; three *d.* *Educ.:* privately; University of Glasgow. Appointed to Sudan Civil Service, 1906; planned City of Khartoum under the personal direction of late Lord Kitchener, transferred, 1913, to the Egyptian Civil Service as Engineer-in-Chief, Ministry of Interior; planned the City of Alexandria, and initiated the national and regional development planning scheme for Egypt; prepared, in 1918, the protective town planning scheme for the old city of Jerusalem and the Holy Places; retired from Egyptian Civil Service in 1926, and engaged in technical and economic research in regional planning at the University of Glasgow; M.P. (C.) Tradeston Division of Glasgow, 1931-35; Chairman, Town Planning Institute (Scot. Branch), 1932-33; Member of the Advisory Committee on Education in the Colonies, 1932-38; Member of the Secretary of State's Educational Commissions to East Africa, 1937, and to Malaya (Chairman), 1938; Colonial Office Representative, New York World's Fair, 1939 and at Internat. Colonial Conf., Brussels, 1949; Member Royal Tunbridge Wells Corporation, 1936-46; Vice-Chairman of Kent Education (Tunbridge Wells District) Cttee., 1936-45; a Governor Imperial Coll., 1943-49; Member of Council, Royal Empire Society, 1949-52; Coronation Medal, 1953; C.St.J.; Commander of the Order of Ismail (1926), Commander of the Order of the Nile. *Publications:* Memoranda on colonial affairs for Colonial Office, 1931-63; The Social and Economic Development of the British Colonial Empire (Royal Society of Arts Cantor Lectures), 1940; Higher Education in East Africa, 1937, Malaya 1939 (part author); Survey of Technical Educn. in the Colonies, 1939; Economic and Social Development in the Colonies, 1936; An Economic Survey of the Colonial Empire, 1934 (part author); Regional and Town Planning, 1930; Principles of the Regional Development Planning of Colonies and Imperial Development Planning, 1929; National and Regional Development Planning Scheme for Egypt, 1925; City of Alexandria Town Planning Scheme, 1921; various contributions to publications of Learned Societies. *Recreations:* golf and fishing. *Address:* Cambridge Lodge, Camden Hill, Tunbridge Wells, Kent. *Club:* Athenæum. [*Died* 23 *Sept.* 1967.

McLEAN, Sir William Ross, Kt. 1965; V.R.D. 1942; Q.C. (Scot.); Sheriff of the Lothians and Peebles and Sheriff of Chancery in Scotland since 1960; *b.* 2 May 1901; *s.* of late Peter G. McLean, Clyde Shipping Co. Ltd., Glasgow; *m.* 1931, Marjorie Harvey, *d.* of late Robert Harvey Pirie, Solicitor, Glasgow; one *s.* one *d.* *Educ.:* Glasgow High School; Glasgow Univ. M.A., LL.B. 1924; admitted advocate, Scots Bar, 1927; K.C. (Scot.) 1948. Commissioned R.N.V.R., 1923; served War of 1939-1945, R.N.V.R., as Commander; retired list, rank of Commander, 1946. Contested (U.) Maryhill Div. of Glasgow, 1945; (U.) Greenock, 1951. Sheriff Principal of Roxburgh, Berwick and Selkirk, 1952-55; Sheriff of Renfrew and Argyll, 1955-60. *Recreations:* yacht racing and yacht cruising, ski-ing. *Address:* 39 Moray Place, Edinburgh. *T.:* Edinburgh Caledonian 8107. *Clubs:* Naval and Military; New (Edinburgh); Royal Scottish Automobile (Glasgow); Royal Forth Yacht (Edinburgh); Royal Northern Yacht (Rhu); Royal Highland Yacht (Oban); Mudhook Yacht; Ski Club of Great Britain; Scottish Ski; Scottish Mountaineering; Kandahar Ski. [*Died* 14 *Nov.* 1965.

MacLELLAN, Alexander Stephen; Managing Director, Alexander Stephen & Sons, Ltd., Linthouse, Glasgow, 1913-54, retired 1954; former Director: Glenfield & Kennedy Holdings Ltd., Kilmarnock; Alley & MacLellan (Polmadie) Ltd., Glasgow; *b.* 1 June 1886; 2nd *s.* of George Scott MacLellan and Maud Stephen; *m.* 1918, Anne Gellatly Mackinlay; two *s.* two *d.* *Educ.:* Merchiston Castle School, Edinburgh; Glasgow Univ. (B.Sc.Eng.). Mem. Management Bd. and Trustee for Funds of Engineering & Allied Employers Nat. Federation; Pres. Scottish Engineering Employers' Assoc., 1934-35; Pres. Anderson Coll. of Medicine, Glasgow, 1940-49; Director Glasgow Chamber of Commerce, 1942-49; Director Royal Hosp. for Sick Children, Glasgow, 1936-48; Dir.-Gen. of Ammunition Production, Ministry of Supply, 1940-41. M.I.Mech.E., M.I.N.A. Hon. LL.D. Glasgow, 1950. *Recreations:* shooting, fishing, golf (Capt. Prestwick Golf Club, 1953-54). *Address:* 10 Sydenham Road, Glasgow, W.2. *T.:* Glasgow Western 3301. *Clubs:* Caledonian; Western (Glasgow). [*Died* 15 *July* 1966.

MacLEOD, Douglas Hamilton, M.S. (Lond.), F.R.C.P. (Lond.), F.R.C.S. (Eng.), F.R.C.O.G.; Consulting Gynæcologist, St. Mary's Hospital and Putney Hospital; Consulting Surgeon, Queen Charlotte's Hospital and Royal Marsden Hospital; *b.* 9 May 1901; *s.* of late C. E. Alexander MacLeod, F.R.C.S. (Eng.); *m.* 1933, Lesley Frances, *e. d.* of late T. Martine Ronaldson, Portrait Painter; two *s.* one *d.* *Educ.:* Haileybury Coll. Entered Middlesex Hosp., 1920; qualified, 1925. Hunterian Professor, R.C.S. of Eng., 1946; President Obstetric and Gynæcological Section, Royal Society of Medicine, 1958-59. Examiner in Obstetrics and Gynæcology: to The Roy. Coll. of Obstetricians and Gynæcologists, to Univs. of Oxford, Cambridge and London and to Conjoint Board. *Publications:* (with J. H.

Howkins) Bonney's Gynæcological Surgery; (with late Sir Charles Read) Gynæcology; The Abnormal in Obstetrics; Endometriosis: a Surgical Problem, 1946; (jt.) Ten Teachers' Midwifery; Ten Teachers' The Diseases of Women; Queen Charlotte's Textbook of Obstetrics. Contribs. to Med. journals on Gynæcology and Obstetrics. *Recreations:* fishing and music. *Address:* 94 Harley Street, W.1. *T.:* Welbeck 4944.

[*Died* 27 *Jan.* 1970.

MACLEOD, Rt. Hon. Iain Norman, P.C. 1952; M.P. (C.) Enfield West since 1950; Chancellor of the Exchequer since June 1970; *b.* 11 Nov. 1913; *e. s.* of late Dr. Norman Macleod; *m.* 1941, Evelyn, *e. d.* of Rev. Gervase and Hon. Mrs. Blois, Fretherne, Glos.; one *s.* one *d. Educ.:* Fettes Coll.; Gonville and Caius Coll., Cambridge. B.A. 1935; with De La Rue's, 1935-38; Student, Inner Temple, 1938-39. Served War of 1939-1945: wounded in France, 1940; Staff College, 1943; D.A.Q.M.G., Major 50th (Northumbrian) Div., 1944; "D" Day Landing, 1944; served Norway, 1945-46. Contested Western Isles, 1945. Joined Conservative Parliamentary Secretariat, 1946; Head of Home Affairs Research Dept. of Conservative Party, 1948-50; Minister of Health, 1952-55; Minister of Labour and National Service, Dec. 1955-Oct. 1959; Sec. of State for the Colonies, 1959-61; Chancellor of the Duchy of Lancaster and Leader of the House of Commons, 1961-63; Joint Chairman, Conservative Party Organisation, 1963 (Chairman, 1961-63); Director: Lombard Banking, 1963-70; Provident Life Assoc. of London, 1969-70; Chairman, Television Advisers, 1968-70. Editor of The Spectator, Dec. 1963-Dec. 1965. *Publications:* Bridge is an Easy Game, 1952; Neville Chamberlain, 1961. *Address:* The White Cottage, Potters Bar, Herts. *T.:* Potters Bar 52381. *Clubs:* White's, M.C.C., Constitutional.

[*Died* 20 *July* 1970.

MacLEOD, Maj.-Gen. Malcolm Neynoe, C.B. 1942; D.S.O. 1918; M.C. 1917; *b.* 1882; *e. s.* of late Malcolm Neynoe MacLeod, Rajpur, Chumparun, India; *m.* 1924, Elsie May, *d.* of late W. E. Gould, of Wootton, New Milton. *Educ.:* Rugby School; R.M. Academy, Woolwich. Commissioned, 1900; served India, 1902-14; with Military Works Services, 1902-4, afterwards in the Survey of India; served in France, Belgium, and Germany during World War in command first of the 145th A.T. Company R.E., and afterwards of the 4th Field Survey Battalion; Chief Instructor, School of Artillery, Salisbury Plain, 1919-23; Ordnance Survey, Southampton, 1923-29; General Staff, War Office, 1929-1934; Director-General Ordnance Survey, 1935-43; A.D.C. to the King, 1936-39; retired pay, 1943; Col. Comdt. R.E. 1941-50. *Publications:* Articles in various journals on Military Survey and Aeroplane Photographic Survey. *Recreations:* Rugby football for Blackheath F.C. and Kent, 1901 and 1902; lawn tennis for Sussex, 1920, and Hampshire, 1927, 1928. *Address:* Little Haven, Dibden Purlieu, Southampton. *Club:* United Service.

[*Died* 1 *Aug.* 1969.

McLETCHIE, James Leslie, C.M.G. 1956; O.B.E. 1951; M.B., Ch.B. (Glas.); Senior Medical Officer, Ministry of Health, since 1960, Medical Officer, 1957-60; *b.* 17 March 1909; *s.* of late David B. McLetchie, Alexandria, Dunbartonshire, and Jane E. Leslie; *m.* 1936, W. S. Gunn; one *s.* one *d. Educ.:* Vale of Leven Acad.; Glasgow Univ.; London Sch. of Hygiene and Trop. Med.; Edinburgh University. D.T.M & H. Eng. 1936; D.P.H. 1957. Medical Officer, Nigeria, 1936; Senior Medical Officer, 1948; Epidemiologist, 1951; Adviser on rural health, 1952; Member Public Service Commission, 1954-56; Dir. Med. Services. E. Region, Nigeria, 1954-57. *Publications:* (part-author) Handbook for Dispensary Attendants and Field Unit Assistants, 1956; articles on control of trop. diseases in med. jls. *Address:* Ministry of Health, Elephant and Castle, S.E.1; 17 Foxgrove Road, Beckenham, Kent.

[*Died* 22 *Sept.* 1965.

MacMICHAEL, Sir Harold (Alfred), G.C.M.G., *cr.* 1941 (K.C.M.G., *cr.* 1932; C.M.G. 1927); D.S.O. 1917; *b.* 15 Oct. 1882; *s.* of late Rev. C. MacMichael and late Hon. Mrs. MacMichael; *m.* 1919, Nesta, *d.* of late Canon J. Otter Stephens; one *d.* (and one *d.* decd.). *Educ.:* King's Lynn and Bedford Schools; Magdalene College, Cambridge (Scholar, Hon. Fellow, M.A. 1939); 1st class Honours in Classics, 1904. Joined Sudan Political Service, 1905; successively Inspector in Provinces of Kordofan, Blue Nile, and Khartoum, Political and Intelligence Officer with Expeditionary Force which reoccupied Darfur, 1916 (despatches three times, D.S.O.); Sub-Gov. of Darfur Province; Asst. Civil Sec.; Civil Secretary, 1926-33, and, periodically, Acting Governor-General; Governor and Commander-in-Chief Tanganyika Territory, 1933-37; High Commissioner and Commander-in-Chief for Palestine and High Commissioner for Trans-Jordan, 1938-44; Special Representative of H.M. Govt. in Malaya, 1945; Constitutional Commissioner, Malta, 1946: Order of the Nile (2nd class), 1930; Burton Memorial Medal of the Royal Asiatic Society, 1928; Star of Ethiopia, 2nd class, 1930: Knight of the Order of St. John of Jerusalem, 1938. *Publications:* The Tribes of Northern and Central Kordofan, 1912; A History of the Arabs in the Sudan, 1922; The Anglo-Egyptian Sudan, 1934; The Sudan, 1954. *Recreations:* reading, won Public Schs. fencing championship, 1901. *Address:* Princes Hotel, Folkestone. *T.:* 53415. *Club:* Athenæum.

[*Died* 19 *Sept.* 1969.

McMICKING, Maj.-Gen. Neil, C.B. 1947; C.B.E. 1946 (O.B.E. 1941); D.S.O. 1919; M.C. 1916; D.L.; Brigadier, The Queen's Body Guard for Scotland, Royal Company of Archers; *b.* 3 June 1894; *o. s.* of late T. McMicking of Broomrigg, Dumfries, and late Margaret Rowand, *d.* of George Bulloch of Kinloch, Dunkeld; *m.* 1927, Margaret Winifred, *s. d.* of late David Landale of Dalswinton, Dumfries; two *s.* one *d.* *Educ.:* Eton; Sandhurst. Served European War, 1914-19. Adjutant T.F., 1915; General Staff Officer, 3rd Grade, 1917; Brigade Major, 1918; General Staff Officer, 2nd Grade, 1918 (wounded three times, despatches five times, M.C., D.S.O., 1914 Star); Commanded Tanks sent to General Denniken's Army, S. Russia, 1919 (Order of St. Anne, 2nd Class, with swords); served in Waziristan, 1920; Adjutant 2nd Bn. Black Watch, 1921-24; D.A.A. and Q.M.G. 1927-1928; Staff College, 1929-30; Brigade Major, 1933-34; D.A.A.G. Scottish Command, 1934-37; Brevet Lieut.-Col., 1937; Lieut.-Col. 1938. Commanded 2nd Bn. The Black Watch 1938-39 in Palestine Rebellion (despatches); War of 1939-45 A.A. and Q.M.G. 1939; A.Q.M.G., Western Desert Force, 1940; Brigadier in Command of Cairo Area, 1940; D.A. and Q.M.G., British Troops in Egypt, 1941, and D.A. and Q.M.G. XIII Corps, 1942; Commander Base for B.L.A. at Antwerp, 1944 (despatches four times, O.B.E., C.B.E., C.B., 1939-45 Star, Africa Star, N.W. Europe Star); Maj.-Gen. 1944; Maj.-Gen. i/c Administration, Scottish Command, 1945; Chief of Staff, Scottish Command, 1947; retired 1948. Colonel of The Black Watch (Royal Highland Regiment) 1952-60. D.L., Perthshire, 1961. *Address:* Eastferry, Dunkeld; Miltonise, Glenwhilly, Wigtownshire.

[*Died* 25 *April* 1963.

MACMILLAN, Daniel; Chairman of Macmillan Holdings, Ltd., since 1964; *b.* 1 Feb. 1886; *e. s.* of Maurice Crawford Macmillan; *m.* 1918, Margaret (*d.* 1957), *d.* of L. Matthews. *Educ.:* Eton (Newcastle Scholar); Balliol Coll., Oxford (Scholar); 1st Class Mods.; 2nd Class Lit. Hum.; Prox. Acc. Craven Scholarship. Joined Army, 1914; invalided, 1915; Admiralty, 1916-19. Director, Macmillan & Co. Ltd., 1911 (Chairman and Man. Dir., 1936-63). *Address:* 3 Grosvenor Square, W.1. *Clubs:* Athenæum, Garrick.
[*Died* 6 *Dec.* 1965.

MacMILLAN, Donald Baxter; explorer, lecturer, author; Technical Adviser to U.S. Army Engineers; Adviser to Research and Development Branch, office of The Quartermaster-General; *b.* Provincetown, Massachusetts, 10 Nov. 1874; *s.* of Neil MacMillan and Sarah Rebecca Gardner; *m.* 1935, Miriam Look. *Educ.:* Bowdoin (A.B. 1898; A.M. 1910; Sc.D. 1918), Harvard. Principal, Levi Hall School, N. Gorman, Me., 1898-1900; Head of Classical Department, Swarthmore Preparatory School, 1900-3; Instructor, Worcester (Mass.) Academy, 1903-1908; Assistant in Peary Arctic Club, North Polar Expedition, 1908-9; Member, Cabot Labrador Party, 1910; ethnological work among Esquimaux of Labrador, 1911 and 1912; Leader of Crocker Land Expedition, 1913-17; Ensign, U.S.N.R., Aviation, 1918-1919; Commander, expeditions to Baffin Land, Greenland, and Labrador, 1921-35 and 1938-48; various Arctic Expeditions, 1908-1954; Lieut.-Commander U.S.N.R., 1925; Tallman Foundation Professorship Bowdoin College, 1931-32; Frobisher Bay Expedition, 1937; recalled into U.S. Navy, 1941; Greenland Patrol May-Nov. 1941; Dept. of Secret Defense Work at Mass. Institute of Technology, 1942; Commander, 1942; attached to Hydrographic Office, Washington, 1942-1945; Greenland, Baffin Island, Labrador Aerial Survey, 1944; Rear-Admiral, 1955. Vice-President of James Otis Foundation; Member of National Advisory Board of National Gallery of the American Indian; Trustee of Emerson College, Boston, and of Worcester Academy. Congressional Medal, 1944; Elisha Kent Kane Gold Medal for daring exploration and scientific work; Medal of Explorers' Club, New York City; Gold Medal of Chicago Geographical Soc.; Hubbard Gold Medal of National Geographic Soc.; Bowdoin College Award. Hon. Sc.D. Boston Univ. 1937. *Publications:* Four Years in the White North, 1926; Etah and Beyond, 1927; Kah-da, an Eskimo Boy, 1929; How Peary Reached the Pole, 1934; Eskimo Place Names and Aid to Conversation, 1943. *Address:* Provincetown, Mass., U.S.A. *T.:* 323.
[*Died* 7 *Sept.* 1970.

McMORRAN, Donald Hanks, R.A. 1962; F.S.A. 1956; F.R.I.B.A. 1943; Architect; Treasurer, Royal Academy, 1965; *b.* 3 May 1904; *s.* of late William Edwin McMorran and Edith Hanks; *m.* 1937, Margaret, *d.* of late George Cox, Warnham, Sussex; two *s.* two *d.* *Educ.:* Harrow County Grammar School. Pugin Student, 1925; London Architecture Medals, 1946 and 1952. Hon. Sec., Board of Architectural Educn., 1952-54; Chm., R.I.B.A. Practice Cttee., 1955-58; Master of Art Workers Guild, 1956; Mem. Faculty of Architecture, British School at Rome. Work includes: Hammersmith Police Station and Section Houses at Greenwich and Hackney; housing estates in Hampstead, Poplar, Sydenham, Islington, Richmond and Dorking; Phoenix School, Poplar; Crigglestone Sec. Mod. School; Harlow Purford Green Primary Schools; Queen Elizabeth's School (extensions) and St. John's C. of E. Primary School, Wakefield; The King's School, Chester; Cranbrook School Memorial Gymnasium; Social Science and Education Departments and Cripps Hall, Nottingham University; 100 Pall Mall, S.W. (exterior); St. Stephen's Club, S.W.; United Free Church, Amersham; Devon County Hall, Exeter; County Library and Police H.Q., Bury St. Edmunds; Crosby Merchant Taylors' School Assembly Hall. Appointments include: new City Police Station and Central Criminal Court extensions for Corporation of London; Folkestone Civic Centre; West Suffolk Shire Hall extensions; Lenton Hall, Nottingham University; New Wye Bridge, Hereford. *Address:* 14 North Audley Street, W.1. *T.:* Mayfair 6036, 0250; Grinstead's, Dorking, Surrey. *T.:* Dorking 3401. *Clubs:* Athenæum, Savile.
[*Died* 6 *Aug.* 1965.

McMULLEN, Alexander Percy, C.B. 1931; M.A.; *b.* 9 Oct. 1875; *y. s.* of late A. P. McMullen, Hertford; *m.* 1902, Catherine Maude (*d.* 1959), *d.* of late L. T. Ashwell, Warlingham; two *s.* *Educ.:* Rugby School (Science Exhibitioner); Merton College, Oxon (Postmaster); 1st Class Nat. Sci. (Chem.) 1898. Assistant Master, Bradfield College, 1899; R.N. Coll., Osborne, 1904; R.N. Coll., Dartmouth, 1905; Head of Science Department, 1906; served in H.M.S. Agincourt as Tempy. Lieut., R.N.V.R., Aug. 1914-Dec. 1918; Jutland (despatches); Lieut.-Com., 1917; Adviser on Naval Education, 1919-36; Wartime Master R.N.C. Dartmouth, 1939-41. *Address:* Old Times Cottage, Tolleshunt Major, Nr. Maldon, Essex.
[*Died* 4 *Sept.* 1961.

McMULLEN, Maj.-Gen. Sir Donald Jay, K.B.E., *cr.* 1946 (C.B.E. 1940; O.B.E. 1937); C.B. 1944; D.S.O. 1918; M.I.Mech.E.; R.E.; retired; *b.* 1891; *m.* 1922, Evelyn Frances Packer; one *s.* two *d.* Served European War, 1914-18 (despatches, D.S.O., Brevet Major); Major, 1927; Lt.-Col. 1935; Brig. 1940; Maj.-Gen. 1943; Director of Transportation, War Office, 1940-1945; Dep. Chief Transport Division, Control Commission for Germany, British Element, 1945-48; retired, 1948. Commander Legion of Merit (U.S.A.), 1946; Commandeur de la Légion d'Honneur, 1947. *Address:* Rithe Cottage, Chidham, Nr. Chichester, Sussex. *T.:* Bosham 3301. *Club:* United Service.
[*Died* 12 *Nov.* 1967.

McMURRAY, Hon. Edward James, P.C., Q.C.; B.A., LL.B.; retired 1956; *b.* Thorndale, Middlesex County, Ont., Canada, 4 June 1878; *m.* 1st, 1906, Margaret M. (*d.* 1907), *d.* of Henry Wilton, Winnipeg, Man.; one *s.*; 2nd, 1922, Cecilia Makarski (*d.* 1962). *Educ.:* Country sch.; St. Mary's Collegiate Inst.; Manitoba Univ.; Manitoba Law School. Farmer's son; school teacher; law student; admitted to Manitoba Bar, 1906; specialised in defence of criminal cases; defended many capital cases in the Provinces of Manitoba and Ontario; defended strike leaders during the strike trials in Winnipeg; Member for Winnipeg North, House of Commons, 1921-25; Solicitor-General and Member of the Privy Council, 1923-25. Retired from practising law in the City of Winnipeg, 1956. *Recreations:* curling, golfing, and shooting. *Address:* (office) 7th floor Childs Building, Portage Avenue, Winnipeg 2, Man., Canada; 604 South Drive, Fort Garry, Winnipeg.
[*Died* 20 *April* 1969.

MACNAB of Macnab, Archibald Corrie, C.I.E. 1943; *b.* 1 Dec. 1886; 4th *s.* of James William Macnabb (*de jure* 19th of Macnab), H.E.I.C.S., J.P., Arthurstone, Binfield, Berks, and Alice Corrie; assumed in addition the name of MacLeod, 1943 (relinquished it and reverted to surname of Macnabb, 1949; recognised as 22nd chief of clan, as A. C. Macnab of Macnab, 1954); his wife assumed the name of Alice Macnabb MacLeod of MacLeod, 1943 (changed to Alice MacLeod Macnabb, 1949, to Alice MacLeod Macnab of Macnab, 1954); *m.* 1931, Alice (Kaisar-i-Hind silver and gold medals), *er. d.* of Hubert Walter and Dame Flora MacLeod of MacLeod; no *c.* *Educ.:* Eton Coll.; Balliol Coll., Oxford. Entered I.C.S. 1911. Dep. Comr.: Karnal, 1921, Shahpur, 1923, Attock, 1933; Commissioner Rawalpindi, 1934; Administrator, Lahore Municipality, 1937; Commissioner Jullundur, 1940; Financial Commissioner, Punjab, 1945; retired, 1948. *Publications:* Delhi Municipal Manual and History, 1917; Shahpur District Gazetteer, 1929; Brief Story of the Clan Macnab, 1951; various reports. *Recreation:* travel. *Heir:* *gt. nephew* James Charles Macnab, yr. of Macnab [*b.* 14 April 1926; *m.* 1959, Diana Mary, *er. d.* of Baron Kilmany; two *s.* two *d.*]. *Address:* Kinnell House, Killin, Perthshire. *T.:* Killin 212. *Clubs:* Leander, United University. [*Died* 13 *Nov.* 1970.

MACNAB, George Henderson, M.B., Ch.B., Edin.; F.R.C.S. Eng.; Surgeon Westminster Hospital; Surgeon The Hospital for Sick Children, Great Ormond Street; *b.* 12 March 1904; *s.* of late Andrew Macnab, Strathearn Lodge, Edinburgh, and Agnes Lyall Henderson, Edinburgh; *m.* 1946, Crystal Guina Lucy, *d.* of late Hon. St. Leger Jervis, D.S.O. *Educ.:* Edinburgh Acad.; Edinburgh Univ. M.B., Ch.B., Edin. Univ., 1926. House Surgeon Cameron Hosp. (West Hartlepool), Roy. Infirmary (Edin.), Royal Nat. Orthopædic Hosp. (London), West London Hosp.; House Surgeon Casualty Officer, Surgical Registrar, Res. Medical Supt., The Hosp. for Sick Children, Great Ormond St.; Dean, Westminster Hosp. Med. Sch., 1942-50. Honyman Gillespie Lecturer, 1944 and 1955; Mem. Bd. of Advanced Medical Studies, Univ. of London; F.R.S.M.; Fell. Assoc. of Surgeons of Gt. Br. and N. Ireland; Member: Internat. Soc. of Surgeons; James IV Assoc. of Surgeons; Soc. of Neurological Surgeons of Gt. Br.; Hunterian Prof., R.C.S. of Eng. 1962. *Publications:* Section on Diseases of the Alimentary Tract in Diseases of Children (Garrod, Batten and Thursfield), 1953; Maldescent of the Testicle (contrib. to Journal of Roy. Coll. of Surgeons of Edin.), 1955; Section on Spina Bifida Cystica and Hydrocephalus. Recent Advances in Pædiatrics (Gairdner), 1964; Section on Hydrocephalus and Spinal Anomalies. Surgery of Childhood (Mason Brown), 1962. *Recreations:* music, fishing, golf, squash rackets. *Address:* 15 The Boltons, S.W.10. *T.:* Fremantle 0792; Prince's Riding, Ringshall, Nr. Berkhamsted, Herts. *T.:* Little Gaddesden 3149; 149 Harley St., W.1. *T.:* Welbeck 4444. *Clubs:* Athenæum, Garrick; New (Edinburgh). [*Died* 1 *March* 1967.

MACNAB of Barachastlain, Iain, P.R.O.I.; R.E.; Painter and Engraver; Hereditary Armourer and Standard Bearer to The Macnab of Macnab; President Royal Institute of Painters in Oils; Chairman, Imperial Arts League; *b.* Iloilo, Philippine Islands, 21 Oct. 1890; *s.* of late John Macnab, Hongkong and Shanghai Bank; *m.* Helen Mary Tench (dancer, professional name Helen Wingrave); no *c.* *Educ.:* Merchiston Castle School, Edinburgh. Served in France 1914-16; Capt. 2nd Argyll and Sutherland Highlanders; wounded and invalided from the Army, 1916, and from R.A.F., 1942 and in 1945. Joint-Principal, The Heatherley School of Art, 1919-25; Prin. Grosvenor School of Art, 1925-40; Dir. of Art Studies, Heatherley School of Art, 1946-53. Honorary Auditor Royal Society of Painter-Etchers and Engravers. Fellow: National Society of Painters, Sculptors and Engravers; Society of Wood Engravers, etc. *Publications:* Figure Drawing; The Student's Book of Wood Engraving. *Address:* 33 Warwick Square, S.W.1. *T.:* Victoria 5933, 5492. *Club:* Arts. [*Died* 24 *Dec.* 1967.

McNAIR, Arthur James, M.A., M.B. Cantab.; F.R.C.S. Eng.; F.R.C.O.G.; Consulting Obstetric Surgeon Emeritus, Guy's Hospital; Hon. Consulting Gynæcologist, St. Thomas's Hospital, etc.; *b.* 27 April 1887; 2nd *s.* of late John McNair, of Lloyds, and Jeannie Ballantyne, both of Paisley; *m.* 1930, Grace Mary, *d.* of Major R. N. Buist, R.A.M.C. three *d.* *Educ.:* Aldenham; Emmanuel Coll., Cambridge. Nat. Science Tripos, Cambridge, 1908; M.B., B.C. Cambridge, 1911; F.R.C.S. England, 1921; Temp. Surgeon Royal Navy, 1914; Temp. Capt. R.A.M.C. (Surgical Specialist) Indian Expeditionary Force D., 1916; Afghan War, 1918; F.R.S.M.; Ex-Pres. of Gynæcological Section; late Vice-Pres. Roy. C.O.G.; late Examiner in Midwifery, Cambridge, Oxford, Liverpool, Sheffield, Birmingham Universities and Conjoint Board. *Publications:* Contributions to medical journals. *Address:* 9 Devonshire Mews West, W.1. *T.:* Welbeck 6241. [*Died* 30 *May* 1964.

McNAIR, Arthur Wyndham, C.S.I. 1924; O.B.E. 1919; *b.* 23 Aug. 1872; *s.* of Major John Frederick Adolphus McNair, C.M.G., R.A.; *m.* 1903, Elizabeth Eva Dawn, *d.* of David Charles Ballinger Griffith, Huntworth, Bedford; three *s.* two *d.* *Educ.:* St. Paul's School; Balliol College, Oxford. Entered I.C.S., 1891; Deputy Commissioner of Garwhal, 1898; Joint Magistrate, 1902; Assistant Commissioner, 1904; Commissioner, 1921; Member Board of Revenue, 1927-28; retired, 1928. *Address:* Lewdown, Devon. *T.:* Lewdown 213. *Club:* East India and Sports. [*Died* 31 *March* 1965.

McNAIR, Sir (George) Douglas, Kt., *cr.* 1943; *b.* 30 April 1887; *e. s.* of late George Burgh McNair and Isabel Frederica, *d.* of late Wm. Gowsmith; *m.* 1914, Primrose, *yr. d.* of late Douglas Garth; two *s.* one *d.* *Educ.:* Charterhouse; New College, Oxford. B.A. 1909; called to Bar, Middle Temple, 1911; Advocate Calcutta High Court 1912; 2nd Lt. Indian Army Reserve of Officers 1916: served Mesopotamia, 1916-19 (M.B.E., despatches); Judge, High Court of Judicature, Calcutta, 1933-45; President Dacca Riots Enquiry Committee, 1941; Legal Chairman Pensions Appeal Tribunal, 1946. Dep. Chm. Devon Quarter Sessions, 1954-56, Chm., 1956-58; Chm. Devon Standing Joint Cttee., 1956-58. J.P. Devon, 1950. *Recreation:* fishing. *Address:* Morden, Cockington Lane, Torquay. *T.:* Torquay 67651. *Clubs:* Oriental; Bengal (Calcutta). [*Died* 31 *Dec.* 1967.

McNAIR, John; Ex-General and Political Secretary Independent Labour Party, 1938-1955; obtained his B.A. degree, King's Coll. Durham University, 1959, and M.A., 1962; *b.* Boston, Lincs, Oct. 1887; unmarried. *Educ.:* Elementary school. Brought up on the Tyneside. Became member of I.L.P., 1908. Took an active part in industrial and political work in the locality. As a result could not find continuous employment. Went to Coventry, 1911. Same difficulties here and therefore went to France at end of 1911. Lived in Paris until 1923. Came to London, worked as Organising Secretary of I.L.P., 1923-24. Assisted in first Labour Govt.'s return to power. Through illness returned to France in 1924. Lived there, working in business and acting as international secretary to I.L.P. until July 1936. Decided that the Spanish Civil War was of tremendous importance. Joined I L.P. staff as Organising Sec. and was first British worker to enter Spain, early August 1936. Remained there one year. Sec. British Centre of Socialist Movement for United States of Europe, affiliated to European Unity Movement, 1945-. *Publications:* series of politica pamphlets for the I.L.P. dealing with: Spain, Socialist Britain, Conscription, Socialist Life or Atomic Death, 1939-48; James Maxton—The Beloved Rebel, 1955. *Recreations:* chess, continental travel. *Address:*

7 Easten Terrace, East Howdon, Wallsend-on-Tyne. [*Died* 19 *Feb*. 1968.

MacNALTY, Sir Arthur Salusbury, K.C.B., *cr.* 1936; M.A., M.D. Oxon., 1911; F.R.C.P., Lond., 1930; F.R.C.S. Eng., 1939; D.P.H., 1927; B.A. (2nd Class Hons. in Nat. Sc.), 1904; Hon. F.R.S.(Ed.); Hon. F.R.S.M. (late President Epidem. and Hist. Med. Sections); F.S.A.; Hon. F.R.S.H.; Hon. F.R.I.P.H.H.; Fellow, Univ. Coll. Lond.; Hon. Freeman Soc. Apothecaries; Hon. Freeman Barbers' Company; Freeman City of London; Hon. Fellow, Faculty of Hist. Med. and Pharmacy, Soc. of Apothecaries; Editor-in-Chief for Official Medical History of Last War since 1941; Life Governor of Council of Imperial Cancer Research Fund; Hon. Pres., British Society for the History of Medicine; *b.* 1880; *s.* of F. C. MacNalty, M.D., and Hester Emma Frances, *d.* of Rev. A. D. Gardner, M.A., Fellow of Jesus College, Oxford; *m.* 1913, Dorothea (*d.* 1968), *d.* of Rev. C. H. Simpkinson de Wesselow, M.A.; one *d.* (and one *d.* decd.). *Educ.:* privately, St. Catherine's Coll. and Corpus Christi Coll., Oxford; Univ. Coll. Hospital. R.M.O., Brompton Hosp. for Consumption; Medical Registrar, London Hosp.; Medical Inspector, H.M. Local Govt. Board, 1913-19; M.O. and Senior M.O., Ministry of Health, 1919-35; Chief Medical Officer Ministry of Health and Board of Education, 1935-41; K.H.P., 1937-41; Crown Nominee General Medical Council; Milroy Lecturer, R.C.P., London, 1925; Vicary Lecturer, R.C.S., 1945; Councillor, 1937-39 and FitzPatrick Lecturer, R.C.P. Lond., 1946, 1947; Secretary, Tuberculosis Committee of M.R.C., 1920-32; late Examiner in Public Health and Hygiene, Univs. of Oxford, Birmingham, and London; Examiner for M.D. Univ. of London. *Publications:* Epidemic Diseases of Central Nervous System, 2nd ed., 1932; History of State Medicine in England, 1948; The Three Churchills, 1949 (trans. into German); Henry VIII, 1952; Elizabeth Tudor, 1954; The Princes in the Tower, 1955; Mary Queen of Scots, 1960; (ed.) Civilian Health and Medical Services, Vol. I, 1953, Vol. II, 1954; The British Medical Dictionary (ed.), 1961; Official Reports on Tuberculosis, Nervous Diseases, Lymphadenoma, etc., to Ministry of Health and Medical Research Council. *Address:* Ministry of Health, Queen Anne's Mansions, S.W.1; Bocketts, Downs Road, Epsom, Surrey. *Club:* Athenæum. [*Died* 17 *April* 1969.

MacNAMARA, Arthur James, C.M.G. 1946; LL.D.; Deputy Minister of Labour for Canada, 1943-53; *b.* 4 March 1885; *s.* of John MacNamara; *m.* 1917, Myrtle Card. *Educ.:* Toronto and Montreal. Hon. LL.D. University of Manitoba. Deputy Minister of Public Works and Labour, Province of Manitoba, 1929-39, also acted as Chairman Manitoba Minimum Wage Board and Fair Wage Board; at outbreak of War, 1939, services loaned to Federal Government as Chm. Dependents Allowance Bd.; Associate Deputy Minister of Labour, 1940, and Acting Chief Commissioner, Unemployment Insurance Commission; Director, National Selective Service for Canada, Nov. 1942. Subseq. Chm. Advisory Cttee., Labour Dept., Canada, and Manager Canadian Assoc. of Equipment Distributors Office. *Address:* 72 Bronson Ave., Ottawa, Canada; Ottawa Journal Building, 237 Queen Street, Ottawa. *Clubs:* Manitoba, Rotary, Canadian (Winnipeg). [*Died* 4 *Oct*. 1962.

McNAMARA, Air Vice-Marshal (Retd.) Frank Hubert, V.C. 1917; C.B. 1945; C.B.E. 1938; B.A.; R.A.A.F., retd.; *b.* 4 April 1894; *m.* 1924, Hélène Marcelle Bluntschli; one *s.* one *d.* *Educ.:* Shepparton High School; Teachers' Training College, Melbourne; University of Melbourne (1913-14, B.A., 1933). 2nd Lt. Brighton Rifles (46th Infantry Bn.), 1913; called up, 1914; Lieut. No. 1 Squadron, A.F.C., A.I.F., 1916; attached to 42 Squadron, R.F.C., Bristol, England; Flying Instructor at 22 Reserve Squadron, R.F.C., Aboukir, Egypt; rejoined No. 1 Squadron, A.F.C., A.I.F., at Kantara; served in Egypt, Sinai, and Palestine, 1916-1917 (wounded); Captain and Flight Commander, 1917 (V.C.); invalided to Australia, 1917; Lieut. (Hon. Capt.) Aviation Instructional Staff (Permanent Forces), 1918; Staff Officer (Operations and Intelligence), R.A.A.F. Headquarters, Melbourne, 1921-22; O.C. No. 1 Flying Training School, Point Cook, 1922-25; Squadron Leader, 1924; to England on exchange duty, 1925-27; Second in Command No. 5 F.T.S. R.A.F. Sealand, and for 6 months Training Directorate Air Ministry; Second in Command No. 1 Flying Training School, Point Cook, 1927-30; C.O., 1930-33; Wing Comdr., 1931; C.O. No. 1 Aircraft Depot, and R.A.A.F. Station, Laverton, 1933-36; Acting Group Captain, 1936; Group Captain, 1937; graduated Imperial Defence College, 1937; Australian Air Liaison Officer, Air Ministry and Australia House, London, 1938-41; Air Commodore, 1939; Air Vice-Marshal, 1942; Air Officer commanding Overseas Headquarters R.A.A.F. London, 1942; on loan to R.A.F., as A.O.C. British Forces, Aden, 1942-45; R.A.A.F. Representative of Resident Minister's Staff in Offices of Cabinet and Minister of Defence, Whitehall, Oct. 1945 to July 1946; Education Branch (Control Commission for Germany), 1946-47; National Coal Board, London, 1947-59. *Recreation:* golf. *Address:* Brackendale, North Park, Gerrards Cross, Bucks. *Clubs:* United Service; Athenæum, Naval and Military (Melbourne) [*Died* 2 *Nov*. 1961.

MACNAMARA, Neil Cameron, C.B.E. 1955; M.I.Mech.E. 1919; M.I.C.E. 1956; President, Trollope & Colls Ltd., London, since 1963 (Chairman, 1923-62, Chairman and Managing Director, 1923-60); Chairman: Nuclear Civil Constructors Ltd.; Paternoster Development Ltd.; Director: Builders' Accident Insce. Ltd. and other Cos.; *b.* 26 May 1891; *s.* of Rt. Hon. T. J. Macnamara, M.A., LL.D., and Rachael Burr Cameron; *m.* 1915, Noeline Lufkin Skeet, *d.* of Robert Challen Skeet, Dunedin, N.Z.; one *d.* *Educ.:* Dulwich College; City and Guilds Technical College, London. Apprenticed to David Rowan Ltd., Engineers and Boilermakers, Glasgow; Man. Dir. Caversham Motor Co. Ltd., Reading, 1910-14. Served European War, 1914-19; B.E.F. France, Belgium and Army of Occupation, Germany (Major; despatches thrice, French Croix de Guerre). Director and Gen. Manager: Dunlop Rubber Co. (Far East Ltd.), Kobe, Japan; China Investment Trust Ltd.; Anglo-Japanese Cycle & Motor Manufacturing Co. Ltd., etc., 1919-23. *Address:* 18 Lowndes Lodge, Cadogan Place, S.W.1; Kings Wood, Penn, nr. High Wycombe, Bucks. *T.:* Penn 3220. *Club:* City of London. [*Died* 5 *March* 1968.

MAC-NAMEE, Rt. Rev. James Joseph; Assistant at Papal Throne, 1960; *b.* 1876. *Educ.:* St. Macarten's, Monaghan; St. Patrick's, Maynooth. Ordained, 1900; Professor in St. Macarten's, 1900-6; C. C. Clones, 1906-8; Monaghan, 1908-20; Administrator of Cathedral, Monaghan, 1920-1925; Parish Priest of Clones, 1925-27; Bishop of Ardagh and Clonmacnoise (R.C.), 1927-66. *Publication:* History of Diocese of Ardagh. *Address:* Bishop's House, St. Michael's, Longford, Ireland. [*Died* 24 *April* 1966.

McNAUGHTON, Gen. Hon. Andrew George Latta, P.C. (Can.) 1944; C.H.

1946; C.B. 1935; C.M.G. 1919; D.S.O. 1917; C.D. 1955; M.Sc.; Hon. LL.D. McGill Univ., 1920, Queen's Univ., 1941, Univ. of Birmingham, 1942, Ottawa, 1943, Saskatchewan, 1944; Michigan State Coll., 1955; Univ. of Toronto, 1961; Hon. D.C.L. Bishops Univ., 1937; Hon. D.Sc., Univ. of British Columbia, 1960; Dr. of Mil. Science, R.M.C. of Canada, 1963; soldier and engineer; *b.* Moosomin, Canada, 25 Feb. 1887; *s.* of late Robert Duncan McNaughton, Moosomin, Saskatchewan; *m.* 1914, Mabel Clara Stuart, *d.* of late Godfrey Weir, Montreal; two *s.* two *d.* (and *y. s.*, Sqdn. Ldr. R.C.A.F., killed in action over Germany, 1942). *Educ.:* Moosomin Public School; Bishop's College School, Lennoxville; McGill University, Montreal (B.Sc. 1910, M.Sc. 1912); Staff College, Camberley (p.s.c. 1921); Imperial Defence College, London (i.d.c. 1928). Served European War, 1914-19, in France and Belgium (wounded twice, despatches thrice); Maj.-Gen. 1929; Chief of Canadian General Staff, 1929-35; President National Research Council of Canada, 1935-44; Commanded 1st Division Canadian Overseas Force, 1939-40; Lt.-Gen. 1940; G.O.C. 7 Corps, 1940; Canadian Corps, 1940-1942; G.O.C.-in-C. First Canadian Army, 1942-43; General 1944; retd. 1944. Minister of National Defence Canada, 1944-45; Chairman Canadian Section, Canada U.S. Perm. Jt. Board on Defence, 1945-59; Canadian Rep.: in U.N. Atomic Energy Commission, 1946-49 (Pres. Canadian Atomic Energy Control Bd., 1946-48); on Security Council, 1948-49; Chm., Canadian Sect., Internat. Jt. Commn., 1950-62. Adviser Canadian Delegation to Imperial Conference, London, England, 1930; Adviser, Canadian Delegation to Conference for Limitation of Armaments, Geneva, 1932; Member Cttee. on Trans-Atlantic Air Service, Imperial Economic Conference, Ottawa, 1932; Chairman, Interdepartmental Committee on Trans-Canada Airway, 1933-35; Hon. Fellow, R.C.P. and S., 1939; Hon. Mem. Engineering Inst. of Canada (Sir John Kennedy Medal, 1940) 1957; Silver Medal of R.S.A., 1941; Hon. Member: Royal Society of Canada, 1942; Canadian Inst. of Forestry; Instn. of Electrical Engineers, 1942; R. Can. Institute, Toronto, 1942; American Institute of Electrical and Electronic Engineers, 1942 (Founders Award, 1964) Amer. Society of Mech Engineers, 1943; Mem. Assoc. of Professional Engineers of Ontario, 1950; Hon. Mem. Professional Engineers, Alberta, 1961; Hon. Fellow, Canadian Aeronautics and Space Inst., 1963. Hon. Colonel Commandant Corps of R. Can. Electrical and Mech. Engineers, 1949-64; Hon. Col. McGill Univ. C.O.T.C. 1951-; Mem. Kappa Alpha; Grand Officer of Order of Leopold (Belgium), 1946. Anglican. *Recreations:* shooting and fishing. *Address:* (home) 393 Fernbank Road, Rockcliffe Park, Ottawa, Canada. *Clubs:* (Hon.) East India and Sports; University, Royal St. Lawrence Yacht (Montreal); Rideau (Ottawa); Seigniory (Montebello, P.Q.).

[*Died* 11 *July* 1966.

McNAUGHTON, Sir George (Matthew). Kt. 1956; C.B. 1948; B.Sc. (Eng.); M.I.C.E.; M.I.Mech.E.; Chairman, East Surrey Water Company, since 1962; Dir., S.W. Suburban Water Company since 1961; Consultant to Wm. Zinn & Associates and to Haigh, Zinn & Associates, Consulting Engineers, since 1961. Chief Engineer: Department of Health for Scotland, 1938; Ministry of Health, 1944; Ministry of Housing and Local Government, 1951. Retired, 1960. *Address:* 25 Hambledon Vale, Woodcote, Epsom, Sy.

[*Died* 31 *Aug.* 1966.

MACNEAL, Sir Hector (Murray), K.B.E., *cr.* 1920; shipowner, Glasgow, London, etc.; *b.* 8 Feb. 1879; *s.* of late Frederick H. Macneal and *g.s.* of late George Macneal of Ugadale and Lossit, Argyllshire; *m.* 1st, 1912, Marjory (*d.* 1926), *d.* of late John Henderson and Mrs. Macfarlane Wilson; one *s.* two *d.*; 2nd, 1932, Edith (*d.* 1937), 3rd *d.* of late George J. Gould, New York. *Address:* 98 Piccadilly, W.1. *T.:* Grosvenor 1808.

[*Died* 12 *Nov.* 1966.

McNEELY, Most Rev. William, D.D.; Bishop of Raphoe (R.C.), since 1923; *b.* Donegal, 1888. Ordained Rome, 1912; Professor High School, Letterkenny; Chaplain, Western Front, 1917-19; Curate, St. Eunan's Cathedral; Command Chaplain Free State Army. *Address:* Ard Eunan, Letterkenny, Ireland.

[*Died* 11 *Dec.* 1963.

MACNEICE, Louis, C.B.E. 1958; writer; *b.* Belfast, 12 Sept. 1907; *s.* of late Rt. Rev. John Frederick MacNeice and Elizabeth Margaret Clesham; *m.* 1930, Giovanna Marie Thérèse Babette Ezra (marr. diss.); one *s.*; *m.* 1942, Hedli (*née* Anderson); one *d.* *Educ.:* Marlborough; Merton Coll., Oxford. Lectr. in Classics at Univ. of Birmingham, 1930-36; Lecturer in Greek at Bedford College for Women, 1936-40; Feature-writer and Producer for the B.B.C., 1941-1949; Director, British Institute, Athens, 1950. Hon. D.Litt. (Belfast), 1957. *Publications:* Blind Fireworks, 1929; Poems, 1935; The Agamemnon of Aeschylus, 1936; Out of the Picture, 1937; Letters from Iceland (with W. H. Auden), 1937; I Crossed the Minch, 1938; The Earth Compels, 1938; Modern Poetry, 1938; Zoo, 1938; Autumn Journal, 1939; The Poetry of W. B. Yeats, 1941; Plant and Phantom, 1941; Christopher Columbus, 1944; Springboard, 1944; The Dark Tower, 1946; Holes in the Sky, 1948; Collected Poems, 1949; Goethe's Faust, Parts I & II (verse trans.), 1951; Ten Burnt Offerings, 1952; Autumn Sequel, 1954; Visitations, 1957; Eighty-Five Poems, 1959; Solstices, 1961; The Burning Perch, 1963; The Administrator (radio play), 1961. *Posthumous publications:* Astrology, 1964; The Mad Islands; The Administrator (plays), 1964; The Strings are False; Varieties of Parable, 1965; One for the Grave (posthumous play), 1968. *Recreation:* tennis. *Address:* 10 Regent's Park Terrace, N.W.1.

[*Died* 3 *Sept.* 1963.

McNEIL, Charles, M.A., M.D. Edin. Univ.; F.R.C.P. Edin. and Lond.; retired, 1946; *b.* 21 Sept. 1881; *s.* of Dr. William McNeil, M.D.Edin., Stranraer, Wigtownshire; *m.* 1919, Alice Hill Workman, O.B.E., 4th *d.* of Thomas Workman, J.P., Belfast; no *c.* *Educ.:* John Watson's Institution, Edinburgh; George Watson's College, Edinburgh; Edinburgh University. Asst. Lecturer and Lecturer in children's diseases, Univ. of Edin., 1908-32; Mem. Staff Edin. Hosp. for Sick Children, 1908-46; Prof. of Child Life and Health, Edin. Univ., 1932-46. Pres. Roy. Coll. Physicians Edin., 1940-43. R.A.M.C., 1914-19 (despatches); Officer in Charge, Scottish Red Cross Hosp., Rouen, 1915-19. Hon. Mem.: Liverpool Med. Instn.; Irish Pædiatric Assoc. LL.D. Edin. 1953. *Publications:* various articles on Child Health in B.M.J., Lancet, Edin. Med, Jl., Archives of Disease in Childnood, etc. *Recreations:* fishing; classical and historica reading. *Address:* Nunraw Barns, Garvald by Haddington, Scotland. *T.:* Garvald 249.

[*Died* 27 *April* 1964.

McNEIL, Kenneth Gordon, C.B.E. 1962; J.P.; Deputy Chairman of Lloyd's, 1954, 1955, and 1965; *b.* 30 Sept. 1902; *s.* of late David and Evelyn Louise McNeil; *m.* 1931, Eleanor Mary Macgregor; two *s.* two *d.* *Educ.:* King's College School; Merton College, Oxford. Joined Lloyd's, 1924; Underwriting Member, 1926; Underwriter for Lion Motor Policies, 1931-56; Committee of Lloyd's, 1947-50, 1952-55; Dep. Chm., 1954-55. Chairman, Lloyd's

Motor Underwriters' Assoc., 1940-46; Member, War Office Claims Commn., 1950-; Managing Director of The K.G.M. Motor Policies, 1957-; Member of Committee of Lloyd's, 1957-60, 1962-65. Dir., Fenchurch Insurance Holdings Ltd., 1963-; Vice-Pres., Chartered Insurance Inst., 1963-66. A Gov., King's Coll. Sch., 1948-; Mem. of Governing Bodies Assoc.; Mem. Council, Benenden Sch., Kent, 1956-. Lay-Sheriff, City of London, 1968-69. J.P. Surrey, 1961-. *Recreations:* golf, ski-ing, lawn tennis, painting. *Address:* Hobbs Farm, Tandridge Lane, Lingfield, Surrey. *T.:* South Godstone 3137. *Clubs:* City Livery, Royal Automobile.
[*Died* 7 *Feb.* 1970.

MACNEIL of Barra, The; (Robert Lister), F.S.A. Scot.; 45th Chief of Clan Macneil and of that ilk; Baron of Barra; Member, Standing Council of Scottish Chiefs; *b.* 10 Dec. 1889; *s.* of Roderick Ambrose Macneil of Barra, 44th Chief, and Elizabeth, *d.* of Thomas Binns, of Michigan, U.S.A.; *m.* 1st, 1923, Kathleen (*d.* 1933), *e. d.* of Orlando Paul Metcalf, New York; one *s.* two *d.*; 2nd, 1936, Marie (from whom he obtained a divorce, 1946; she *d.* 1952), *o. d.* of late Major Pierre Christie Stevens, U.S. Army, *widow* of Frederick C. Hicks, Member of Congress; 3rd, 1953, Elizabeth, *o. d.* of late George A. Strow, and *widow* of Harold John Forster. Served in European War, 1914-18, with Canadian Engineers and as Trade Adviser, U.S. Government, and in War of 1939-45 as Chairman of Inventions Board, British Purchasing Commission, U.S.A. and Founder of Amer. Cttee. for Defense of British Homes; Boston Univ. Resident Architect, 1949-51. *Publications:* The Clan Macneil; Castle in the Sea, 1964. *Heir: s.* Ian Roderick Macneil, Yr. of Barra [*b.* 1929; *m.* 1952, Nancy, *d.* of James Wilson Ottawa; one *s.*]. *Address:* Barra House, Marlboro', Vermont, U.S.A. *T.:* 464-8837; Kisimul Castle, Isle of Barra, Scotland. *T.:* Castlebay 300. *Clubs:* British Officers' (Boston); New, Puffin's (Edinburgh).
[*Died* 24 *June* 1970.

McNEILL, Sir James (McFadyen), K.C.V.O. *cr.* 1954; C.B.E. 1950; M.C.; F.R.S. 1949; R.D.I.; B.Sc., LL.D. (Glas.); Deputy Chairman of John Brown & Co. (Clydebank) Ltd., until 1962; Director: John Brown & Co. Ltd., until 1962; British Linen Bank; *b.* 19 August 1892; *y. s.* of late Archibald McNeill, Clydebank; *m.* 1924, Jean Ross, *d.* of late Alexander McLaughlan, Glasgow; one *s. Educ.:* Allan Glen's School; Glasgow Univ. Served European War, 1914-19, Major R.F.A. (despatches, M.C.); President Shipbuilding Conference, 1955-57; Mem. Shipbuilding Advisory Cttee., 1956-59; Pres. Instn. Engineers and Shipbuilders in Scotland, 1947-49; Hon. Vice-Pres. Royal Instn. of Naval Architects; Governor, The Royal College of Science and Technology, Glasgow. Shipbuilding Rep. at Internat. Conf. on Safety of Life at Sea, 1948. Liveryman of Worshipful Company of Shipwrights. Chairman of British Shipbuilding Research Assoc., 1957-59. *Address:* Campsie Dene, Blanefield, Stirlingshire. *T.:* Blanefield 360. *Club:* Caledonian.
[*Died* 24 *July* 1964.

MACONACHIE, Sir Richard (Roy), K.B.E., *cr.* 1931; C.I.E. 1926; *b.* 1885; *s.* of late James Robert Maconachie, I.C.S.; *m.* 1921, Joan, *d.* of late Captain Edward Lethbridge and Mrs. Brooke, Ufford Place, Woodbridge; one *s. Educ.:* Tonbridge School; University College, Oxford, B.A. 1907; entered I.C.S. 1909; Foreign and Political Department, 1914; on military service, 1917-19; Counsellor, Kabul, 1922-24; British Minister to Afghanistan, 1930-35; Controller (Home Division) B.B.C., 1941-45. *Address:* 3 Kingston House, Odiham, Hants.
[*Died* 18 *Jan.* 1962.

MACONOCHIE, Sir Robert (Henry), Kt., *cr.* 1955; O.B.E.; Q.C. (Scot.) 1934; B.A. Oxon; Sheriff of Stirling, Dunbarton, and Clackmannan, 1942-61, retired; *b.* 11 May 1883; *s.* of Charles Cornelius Maconochie, C.B.E., K.C., Sheriff of The Lothians and Peebles, and Alice Mary Robertson; *m.* 1910, Laura Patricia Cowan; one *s.* three *d. Educ.:* Edinburgh Academy; Winchester College; University Coll., Oxford; Edinburgh University. B.A. 1906; called Scottish Bar, 1908; Lieutenant, General List, 1916; Ministry of National Service, 1917-18; Junior Counsel to Admiralty and Board of Trade; Sheriff Court Depute, 1926; Advocate Depute, 1927-29; Home Advocate Depute, 1932-34; Sheriff of Inverness, Elgin and Nairn, 1934-42; *interim* Sheriff of Ross and Cromarty, 1940; Covener of the Sheriffs, 1953 61; Mem. of Appeal Tribunal for Conscientious Objectors in Scotland, 1943, and Chairman 1953-57; Chairman of Hospital Board of Management for Stirling and Clackmannan, 1948-53; Chm., Nat. Jt. Council to deal with salaries of Teachers in Scotland, 1954-60. D.L. West Lothian, 1953-57. *Recreations:* music, shooting, fishing, golf. *Address:* 15 Moray Place, Edinburgh. *Clubs:* New (Edinburgh); Honourable Company of Edinburgh Golfers.
[*Died* 1 *July* 1962.

MacORLAN, Pierre (pseudonym of Pierre Dumarchey); Commandeur de la Légion d'Honneur; Croix de Guerre, 1914; Homme de Lettres; de l'Académie Goncourt; *b.* Péronne (Somme), 26 Feb. 1882; *m.* 1911, Marguerite Luc. *Educ.:* Lycée d'Orléans. *Publications:* La Maison du retour écœurant, 1912; Le Rire jaune, 1914; Le Chant de l'équipage, 1918; Le Bataillonnaire, 1920; A bord de l'étoile matutine, 1921; La Cavalière Elsa, 1922; La Vénus internationale, 1923; Sous la lumière froide, 1926; Le Quai des brumes, 1927; Villes, 1929; La Bandera, 1931; Malice, Les Jeux de demi-jour, Quartier réservé, 1932; Verdun, 1935; Le Camp Domineau, 1937; Masques sur mesure, 1937; Chronique de la fin d'un monde, 1940; L'Ancre de miséricorde, 1942; Picardie, 1943; Les Bandes, 1947; La Couronne de Paris, 1948; L'Écharpe de suie, 1948; Parades abolies, 1948; Filles, ports d'Europe et père Barbançon, 1950; Le Bal du Pont du Nord, 1950. *Recreation:* accordion. *Address:* St.-Cyr-sur-Morin, Seine et Marne, France. *T.:* 16.
[*Died* 27 *June* 1970.

MACPHERSON OF DRUMOCHTER, 1st Baron, *cr.* 1951, of Great Warley, Essex; **Thomas Macpherson;** *b.* 9 July 1888; *s.* of late James Macpherson, Muirhead, Chryston, Lanarkshire; *m.* Lucy, *e. d.* of late Arthur Butcher, Heybridge Basin, Maldon, Essex; one *s.* two *d. Educ.:* St. George's Road School, Glasgow. President (formerly Chairman) of Macpherson, Train & Co. Ltd., Foreign and Colonial Produce Importers and Exporters; Chairman London Provision Exchange, 1941. Three years member Romford U.D.C.; M.P. (Lab.) for Romford Borough, 1945-50. Regional Port Dir. for Scotland for the Ministry of War Transport, 1942-45; 1946, awarded American Medal of Freedom with Silver Palm for services to U.S. Army during War of 1939-45; Officer of Order of Orange Nassau for services with Netherlands shipping, War of 1939-45; Member of Re-organisation Commission for Hops, 1947; Chairman: Clan Macpherson Assoc., 1946-52; Chm. Council of Scottish Clan Societies, 1952-56. Member of Brown Committee on Domestic Food Production, 1949; Member Port of London Authority, 1949-; Member Essex River Board, 1956-; Chairman Thames Passenger Services Cttee. Ministry of Transport, 1949-; President, Domestic Poultry Keepers' Council of England and Wales, 1953-. For many years identified with Public work and Amateur sport in County of Essex, also interested in Agriculture. *Heir: s.*

Hon. (James) Gordon Macpherson, J.P. [*b.* 22 January 1924; *m.* 1947, Dorothy Ruth, *d.* of late Reverend Henry Coulter, B.A., B.D., Bellahouston, Glasgow; one *s.* two *d.*]. *Address:* Drumochter, Wickham Bishops, Witham, Essex; Adelaide House, London Bridge, E.C.4. *T.:* Mansion House 8621. [*Died* 11 *June* 1965.

MACPHERSON, Brig. Alan David, of Cluny and Blairgowrie, D.S.O. 1918; M.C.; R.A., retired; *b.* 1887; *er. s.* of late W. C. Macpherson, C.S.I.; *m.* 1922, Catharine Richardson (*d.* 1967), 2nd *d.* of late Robert H. Hill, 10 Kensington Park Gardens, W.; one *s.* one *d.* (and one *d.* decd.). *Educ.:* Winchester College; R.M. Academy, Woolwich. Served European War, 1914-18 (despatches thrice, D.S.O., M.C.); and 1939-44. Chief of Clan Macpherson. *Address:* The Newton of Blairgowrie, Perthshire. [*Died* 18 *June* 1969.

MACPHERSON, Lieutenant-Colonel Cluny, C.M.G. 1918; C.D. 1964; M.D., C.M.; F.R.C.S.; D.Sc.; J.P.; F.R.S.A.; *b.* St. John's, Newfoundland, 18 March 1879; *e. c.* of Campbell and Emma Duder Macpherson, St. John's; *m.* 1902, Eleonora Barbara, O.B.E., D.St.J. (*d.* 1964), *d.* of William MacLeod Thompson, Northumberland County, Ontario; one *s.* one *d.* *Educ.:* St. John's; McGill University, Montreal; Edinburgh, Paris. Surg. to R.N. Mission to Deep Sea Fishermen, Labrador, 1902-4; General Practitioner, St. John's, since 1904; Newfoundland Med. Bd. Registrar; Chm. Bd. of Commissioners in Lunacy; Mem. Med. Council of Canada, 1950 (Pres., 1954-55); Dir. Grenfell Assoc. of Newfoundland and Internat. Grenfell Assoc. Hon. Vice-Pres., Clan Macpherson Assoc. (Hon. Pres. Canadian Branch); Chm., 1953-57; Hon. Pres., St. John Ambulance Council for Newfoundland, 1953; Hon. Vice-President Newfoundland Divn., Canadian Red Cross Society, 1952; Captain and Principal Medical Officer 1st (afterwards Royal) Newfoundland Regt. on its inception, August 1914; Major, 1915; Lt.-Col., 1918; demobilised June 1919; in April 1915, while in France devised anti-gas helmet which was adopted for protection of the Army; Member first War Office Committee against Poisonous Gases. Service in France, Belgium, Gallipoli, Egypt, Salonica; invalided to Newfoundland, Oct. 1916; D.M.S., Newfoundland, 1916 (despatches twice, thanks of War Office for services in anti-gas work). Hon. Col. of 1 Medical Coy. R.C.A.M.C. (M), 1957. K.St.J. 1913; K.J.St.J. 1955. *Recreations:* sailing, fishing. *Address:* Calvert House, St. John's, Newfoundland. *T.A.:* Cluny Macpherson, St. John's (Newfoundland). *Club:* National (London). [*Died* 16 *Nov.* 1966.

MACPHERSON, Colin Francis, C.I.E. 1919; *b.* 1884; *s.* of late Sir William Macpherson, Judge of the High Court, Calcutta; *m.* 1924, Lily Isabel (*d.* 1954), *y. d.* of late Harry M. Oliver and Mrs. Oliver, of Williton, Somerset. *Educ.:* Cheltenham College. Served European War, 1914-19, in Mesopotamia (despatches, C.I.E.). *Address:* Shanna Cottage, Blairs, Kincardineshire. [*Died* 8 *Jan.* 1970.

MACPHERSON, Ewen; *b.* 1 Sept. 1872; *y. s.* of Sir A. G. Macpherson, K.C.I.E.; *m.* 1902, Dorothy, *d.* of Rev. Augustus De Morgan Hensley; two *s.* two *d.* *Educ.:* Haileybury; Trinity College, Oxford. Barrister-at-law, Inner Temple; Chief Charity Commissioner, 1932-39. *Address:* Goldhanger, Portland Road, East Grinstead, Sussex. [*Died* 14 *Feb.* 1962.

M'PHERSON, Sir Hugh, K.C.I.E., *cr.* 1924; C.S.I. 1919; *b.* 3 May 1870; *s.* of late Duncan M'Pherson, Paisley; *m.* 1897, Gertrude, *d.* of Dr. James Kelly; one *s.* two *d.* *Educ.:* Paisley Grammar School; Glasgow University; Balliol College, Oxford (Snell Exhibitioner). Passed open competition I.C.S., 1889; Assistant Magistrate, Bengal, 1891; Settlement Officer, Santal Parganas, 1898-1905; Director Land Records, Bengal, 1907-12; Revenue Secretary, Bihar and Orissa, 1912-15; Chief Secretary, Bihar and Orissa, 1915-19; Member, Board of Revenue, Bihar and Orissa, 1919; Secretary to Government of India, Home Department, 1919-20; Member Executive Council, Bihar and Orissa, 1921-25; Acting Governor, Bihar and Orissa, 1925; retired, 1926. *Address:* 171 Mayfield Road, Edinburgh 9. *T.:* 42478. [*Died* 17 *Dec.* 1960.

McPHERSON, Bt. Col. James, C.I.E 1933; M.A., M.B. Ch.B. (Glas.); F.R.C.S. (Edin.); M.R.C.P. London; I.M.S., retired; *b.* 16 Oct. 1876; *m.* 1908, Isabella Adamson; two *s.* one *d.* *Educ.:* Glasgow High School and University; London; Edinburgh; Vienna (1911 and 1934). Served Aden, 1903-4 (despatches); In Military Service 1902-08; Political Medical Dept. 1908-33; Residency Surgeon Bushire and War Service, 1914-19; I.E.F.D. Persian Gulf; Chief Medical Officer, Baroda State, 1920-23; Civil Surgeon Peshawar, 1923-25; Residency Surgeon, Mysore, 1925, K.H.S. (1931-33); retired, 1933. *Address:* c/o National and Grindlay's Bank Ltd., 54 Parliament Street, S.W.1. *Club:* Caledonian United Service (Edinburgh). [*Died* 13 *Jan.* 1963.

MACPHERSON, Rear-Admiral Kenneth Douglas Worsley; retired; *b.* 3 Nov. 1883; 2nd *s.* of W. D. L. Macpherson of Clifton College; *m.* 1915, Beryl Milne Willis; two *s.* *Educ.:* Clifton College; H.M.S. Britannia. Served European War, Dardanelles and Grand Fleet; Captain in charge Fishery Protection and Mine-Sweeping, 1932; Captain of the Dockyard and King's Harbour Master, Devonport, 1934; Naval A.D.C. to the King, 1936; retired, 1936. Served as Commodore R.N.R., 1939. Nautical Assessor to Court of Appeal, 1937; Nautical Assessor to House of Lords, 1946. *Address:* Adley, Chagford, Devon. [*Died* 26 *Aug.* 1962.

MacPHERSON, Major Hon. Murdoch Alexander, Q.C. 1927; *b.* Grande Anse, Nova Scotia, 16 April 1891; *s.* of Alexander MacPherson, Scotch-Canadian, farmer, and Margaret Campbell, Scotch-Canadian; *m.* 1915, Iowa Briggs; three *s.* two *d.* *Educ.:* St Peter's Academy, St. Peters, N.S.; Pictou Academy, Pictou, N.S.; Dalhousie University, Halifax, N.S., LL.B. Admitted to Nova Scotia Bar, 1913; Saskatchewan Bar, 1913; practised law in Saskatchewan at Swift Current and Regina; served European War with 10th Canadian Infantry Battalion, wounded at Arleux, 28 April 1917; discharged from Army and Hospital 22 May 1918; Candidate of Conservative Party for House of Commons, 1921; Member Legislative Assembly, Saskatchewan, 1925-34; Attorney-General, 1929-34, and Provincial Treasurer, 1931-34, Saskatchewan; Administrator for Canada, Farmers' Creditors' Arrangement Act since 1934. *Recreations:* gardening, fishing. *Address:* (Home) 202 Balfour Apts., Regina, Sask., Canada. *T.:* (Home) 6954 (Office) 7648. *Club:* Assiniboia (Regina). [*Died* 13 *June* 1966.

MACRAE, Herbert Alexander, C.M.G. 1942; M.B.E. 1918; M.A. Aberdeen Univ.; F.R.G.S.; *b.* 12 June 1886; *m.* 1933, Agnes Elsie Davidson Bruce, *d.* of Alexander Bruce, Fraserburgh. Served in H.M. Foreign Service in Japan, Norway, Hawaii, Philippine Islands, London, 1910-46; retd. 1946; served as Special Economic Adviser with rank of Minister to U.K. Liaison Mission in Japan, 1947. *Recreations:* mountaineering, yachting, fishing. *Address:* 123 Blenheim Place, Aberdeen. *T.:* Aberdeen 28803. *Clubs:* Alpine; University (Aberdeen). [*Died* 12 *Dec.* 1967.

MACRAE, Hugh, M.V.O. 1937; Chairman Isle of Wight Theatres Ltd.; *b.* 1880; *s.* of John Kenneth Macrae, deputy commissioner, Burmah; *m.* 1909, Elizabeth Pinkerton, *d.* of late Alexander Latta, solicitor, Edinburgh; one *s.* four *d.* *Educ.:* Elizabeth College, Guernsey; The College, Inverness. Treasurer Carnegie Dunfermline Trust and Carnegie Hero Fund Trust, 1909-14; served European War, Lieut. R.F.A. France, 1914-16 wounded); Assistant Accountant National Service Dept.; Dir. Statistics Admiralty; Sec. War Priorities Information Cttee. under Chairmanship of Field Marshal Smuts; Comptroller Statistics Department of Demobilisation and Resettlement; Principal Officer Statistical Department, Ministry of Labour; Departmental Secretary, King Edward's Hospital Fund for London, 1921-39; Finance Director Combined Appeal for Hospitals of London, 1922; Secretary British Charities Association, 1923-43; Secretary Thank-Offering Fund for recovery of King George V, 1929; Hon. Secretary National Wedding Gift Fund for late Duke of Kent, 1934; Vice-Chairman London Hospitals Street Collections Central Cttee., 1936-47; Deputy Chairman Red Cross Penny-a-Week Fund, 1939-43; Hon. Treas., British United Aid to China Fund, 1943-47. Partner, Hugh Macrae & Co., Chartered Accountants, 1921-58; Partner, Bird Potter & Macrae, Chartered Accountants, 1958-64. *Recreations:* fishing, gardening. *Address:* Ice Wood Cottage, Oxted, Surrey. *T.:* Oxted 2127. [*Died* 5 *July* 1965.

MacROBERT, Thomas Murray, M.A., D.Sc., LL.D.; Professor of Mathematics in Glasgow University, 1927-54; *b.* 4 April 1884; *e.s.* of Rev. Thomas MacRobert, M.A., Congregational Minister, Dreghorn, Ayrshire, and Isabella Edgely Fisher; *m.* Janet McGillivray Violet, *y. d.* of late James McIlreaith; two *s.* one *d.* *Educ.:* Irvine Royal Academy; Glasgow University; Trinity College, Cambridge. Euing Fellow, Glasgow University; Ferguson Scholar in Mathematics; Major Scholar of Trinity College, Cambridge; William Jack Prizeman, Glasgow University; Assistant and Lecturer in Mathematics, Glasgow University, 1910-1927; Lieutenant, R.G.A. (S.R.). *Publications:* Treatises on Functions of a Complex Variable, Spherical Harmonics, Bessel Functions (with Profs. Andrew Gray and G. B. Mathews); Trigonometry (with William Arthur); Editor of Bromwich's Infinite Series (second edition); numerous papers in the Proceedings of the Edinburgh Mathematical Society, the Proceedings of the Royal Society of Edinburgh; the Philosophical Magazine, the Proceedings of the Glasgow Mathematical Assoc., etc. *Address:* 20 Lilybank Gardens, Glasgow, W.2. [*Died* 1 *Nov.* 1962.

McSPARRAN, James, Q.C. (N.I.) 1945; Chairman, Anti-Partition League; *b.* Glasgow, 1 May 1892; *s.* of late James McSparran, C.C., Knocknacarry, Co. Antrim; *m.* 1927, Claire, *d.* of late Hugh McGuckin; one *s.* three *d.* *Educ.:* St. Mungo's Academy, Glasgow; St. Malachy's College, Belfast; Queen's University, Belfast; National University, Dublin; King's Inns, Dublin. Graduate B.A. Q.U.B. 1913; LL.B. 1st Place, 1st Class Hons. and Exhibition National Univ., Dublin, 1916; Victoria Prizeman, Bar Finals, King's Inns, Dublin, 1916; 2nd Place and Exhibition in John Brooke Scholarship, King's Inns, 1916; Barton Prizeman, King's Inns University students; Gold Medallist, King's Inns Debating Society. Called to Irish Bar, 1916. Elected to Northern Ireland Parliament, Anti-Partition Member for Mourne (Co. Down), 1945; re-elected 1949, now retd. Bencher of Inn of Court of Northern Ireland. *Recreations:* golf and gardening. *Address:* Knocknacarry, Cushendun, Co. Antrim, N. Ireland. *T.:* Cushendun 205; 4 Alexandra Gardens, Belfast. *T.:* 78823. [*Died* 15 *April* 1970.

McSWINEY, Col. (Hon. Brig.) Herbert Frederick Cyril, C.B.E. 1941; D.S.O. 1918; M.C. 1915; Indian Army, retired; *b.* 8 Nov. 1886; *s.* of Col. E. F. H. McSwiney, C.B., D.S.O.; *m.* 1st, 1913, Gladys De Brath (*decd.*); one *s.* one *d.*; 2nd, 1937, Eileen Mary Selwyn. *Educ.:* Cheltenham College; R.M.C., Sandhurst; Staff College. Commanded 1st Bn. 2nd K.E.O. Gurkha Rifles. *Address:* c/o National and Grindlay's Bank, Ltd., 54 Parliament Street, S.W.1. [*Died* 5 *July* 1963.

McVEY, Arthur Michael, F.C.I.S.; General Secretary, Timber Trade Federation of the U.K., Federated Merchant Freighters' Association Ltd., Timber Development Association Ltd. and other trade organisations, 1923-42, Secretary of Trade Delegations to Sweden, Finland, Canada and British Columbia, retired 1943; *b.* 17 May 1879; *s.* of Michael McVey, Glasgow; *m.* 1909; no *c.* Served European War, Lt. Suffolk Regiment, transferred to Northampton Regiment, served in Palestine (Lecturer and Instructor on Gas Warfare) and Salonika, 1917-19; Lt. Col. 1st Southwark Cadet Battalion, 1920-35; Vice-President County of London Cadet Committee, 1936; Parochial Reader Southwark, 1905-40; Diocesan Reader Guildford, 1928, Chichester, 1944-62; Member of Guildford R.D.C. 1943-44; Officer, First Class, Order of the White Rose of Finland. *Publications:* Contributions to Commercial and Trade Journals on trade organisation. *Address:* Avonstone, 28 Nutley Drive, Goring by Sea, Sussex. *T.:* Goring 41804. [*Died* 29 *April* 1964.

McVIE, John, O.B.E. 1954; M.S.M. 1917; Keeper of the Registers of Scotland, 1949-1957; *b.* 1 Mar. 1888; *s.* of John McVie and Thomasina McCracken Crocker; *m.* 1918, Jessie Gordon Hunter; two *s.* one *d.* *Educ.:* Stair Public School; Ayr Academy; Edinburgh University. Military Service 9th Royal Scots, 1909-19. Solicitor, 1911; entered Register House, 1911; Depute Keeper, 1946; Past President, Burns Federation; President, Scottish National Dictionary Association. *Publications:* Burns and Stair, 1927; Robert Burns, some Poems, Songs and Epistles, 1951; Burns Federation Song Book, 1956; The Burns Federation: a Bi-centenary Review, 1959; The Burns Country, 1962. Various articles and reviews in The Burns Chronicle. *Recreations:* music, fishing. *Address:* 13 Hillside Crescent, Edinburgh. *T.:* Waverley 4174. *Clubs:* Royal Scots, University Staff (Edinburgh). [*Died* 5 *Feb.* 1967.

McWATTERS, Sir Arthur Cecil, Kt., *cr.* 1929; C.I.E. 1918; I.C.S., retired; *b.* 1880; 3rd *s.* of late George McWatters, I.C.S.; *m.* 1920, Mary (*d.* 1938), *o. d.* of late Sir Stephen Finney, C.I.E.; two *s.* *Educ.:* Clifton; Trinity Coll., Oxford (scholar); M.A.; 1st Class Classical Moderations; 1st Class Literæ Humaniores; Hon. Mention Hertford Scholarship. Entered I.C.S. 1903 (1st place in Examination for Home and Indian Civil Service); Under-Secretary to Govt. of United Provinces, 1907-10; to Govt. of India, Commerce and Industry Dept., 1910-13; Wheat Commissioner for India, 1915; Controller Hides and Wool, Indian Munitions Board, 1917; Chairman Board of Special Referees, Excess Profits Duty Act, 1919; Secretary, Government of India Secretariat Procedure Committee; Indian representative on deputation to Persia, Jan. 1920; Controller of the Currency, Dec. 1920; Secretary to the Government of India in Depts. of Finance and Industries and Labour, 1923-31; acted as Member of the Governor-General's Council, Nov.-Dec., 1927, April-Oct. 1928, Oct. Dec. 1929, Sept.-Oct. 1930; on special duty as

Adviser to Indian Round Table Conference; Member of the Council of State and Indian Legislative Assembly; Secretary to the University Chest, Oxford, 1932-46; Fellow of Trinity Coll., Oxford, 1933-46. *Address:* 16 St. Giles, Oxford. *Club:* Athenæum.
[*Died* 25 *Sept.* 1965.

McWHAE, Brig. Douglas Murray, C.M.G. 1918; C.B.E. 1919; V.D.; M.D. (Melbourne), 1908; F.R.A.C.P. 1938; F.R.C.P. (London), 1940; late Australian A.M.C.; *b.* 28 May 1884; *m.* 1919, Gwynnyth Muriel Hope: two *s.* Consulting Physician, retd.; Hon. Physician to Governor-General of Australia, 1935-39; Hon. Physician to the King, 1941-45. Served European War (C.M.G. C.B.E., Legion of Honour). D.D.M.S. Western Command, 1925-41; D.D.M.S. 3rd Australian Corps, 1942-43. Retd. List, 1943. *Address:* 262 St. George's Terrace, Perth, West Australia.
[*Died* 22 *Sept.* 1969.

MADDAN, James Gracie, C.B.E. 1933; Postmaster-Surveyor of Manchester, 1920-35; *b.* 1873; *s.* of William Maddan and Anna Rosina Stevenson; *m.* Dorothy (*d.* 1962), *e. d.* of Commander Melville Tuke; three *s.* *Address:* Greathed Manor, Lingfield, Surrey.
[*Died* 31 *Jan.* 1966.

MADDEN, Admiral Sir Alexander Cumming Gordon, K.C.B., *cr.* 1951 (C.B. 1948); C.B.E. 1946; *b.* 21 Jan. 1895; *s.* of late Rev. Andrew Madden, M.A.; *m.* 1923, Evelyn Olive (*d.* 1958), *d.* of John Holroyde, F.R.C.S.; no *c.* *Educ.:* Royal Naval College, Dartmouth. During War of 1939-45 commanded Anti-Submarine School, H.M. Ships Birmingham and Anson, and served at Admiralty as Naval Assistant to Second Sea Lord; Deputy Controller of the Navy and Dir. of Naval Equipment, 1946-48; Flag Officer Commanding, 5th Cruiser Squadron and Flag Officer Second-in-Command, Far East Station, 1948-50; Lord Commissioner of the Admiralty, Second Sea Lord and Chief of Naval Personnel, 1950-53; Commander-in-Chief, Plymouth, November 1953-55; retired list, 1956. *Address:* c/o Lloyds Bank, Henley-on-Thames. *Clubs:* United Service, Royal Yacht Squadron. [*Died* 21 *Sept.* 1964.

MADDEN, William Thomas, C.B.E. 1923 (O.B.E. 1918); Secretary and Managing Director of the Surrey Public House Trust Co., Ltd., 1905-48; *b.* 1877; *s.* of John Thomas Madden. Hon. Technical Adviser, Central Control Board (Liquor Traffic), 1915; Organiser and Hon. General Manager of first State Liquor undertaking, Enfield, 1916-22. Hon. Ranger Surrey C.C. Green Belt, Wisley and Ockham, 1942-. *Recreations:* shooting and fishing *Address:* Lawn Cottage, Epsom Road, Guildford.
[*Died* 16 *Jan.* 1967.

MADDEN, Wyndham D'Arcy, C.B.E. 1953; J.P.; M.I.Mech.E.; F.I.E.E.; *b.* 2 August 1885; *s.* of late Wyndham Monson Madden, Haywards Heath, Sussex; *m.* 1912, Freda, *d.* of late Frederick Nassau Molesworth, Littleborough, Lancs.; two *d.* *Educ.:* Haileybury; Faraday House Engineering Coll. Director: Hick, Hargreaves & Co. Ltd. (Man. Dir., 1922-63; Chm. 1945-65), Law Land Co. Ltd. 1941-65, Martins Bank (Manchester Board) 1950-67; Manchester Ship Canal; Phoenix Assurance Co. Ltd. (Chm. Manchester Board); Chm. North Western Reg. Bd. for Industry and Mem. Nat. Production Adv. Coun. on Industry, 1949-58; Independent Mem. Cotton Board, 1948-59; Chm., County Borough of Bolton Cons. Assoc., 1945-52, Pres. 1955-58; Pres., Bolton and District Engineering Employers Assoc., 1932-57; Mem. Management Bd., Engineering and Allied Employers Nat. Fed., 1936-65 (Chm. Lancashire and Cheshire Regional Cttee., 1943-53); Mem. Council Brit. Electrical and Allied Manufacturers' Assoc., 1932-57; Pres. Bolton and District Chamber of Commerce, 1939-42; Chm. Bolton and District Employment Cttee., Min. of Labour and Nat. Service, 1948-65; Member: Cttee. of Investigation apptd. by Min. of Supply into Cotton Textile Machinery Industry, 1946; Army Manpower Sub-Cttee. on Manpower and Organisation in R.E.M.E. Workshops, 1947; Cttee. apptd. by Chancellor of Exchequer to review constitution, scope and functions of Reg. Bds. for Industry, 1953. Gen. Comr. of Income Tax, Bolton Div., 1955-66. Governor of Bolton School. M.A. (Hon.) Manchester, 1959. *Address:* White House, Parbold, Lancashire. *Club:* St. James's (Manchester).
[*Died* 3 *June* 1968.

MADDOCKS, Henry Hollingdrake; Barrister-at-Law; Metropolitan Stipendiary Magistrate, 1947-67; *b.* 7 Aug. 1898; *s.* of late Sir Henry Maddocks, K.C.; *m.* 1923, Hilda May Warren; one *s.* *Educ.:* Berkhamsted School. Joined R.F.C. 1916 (M.C. 1917); Demobilised, 1919; called to Bar, Inner Temple, 1921; practised in London and on Oxford Circuit; Recorder of Burton-upon-Trent, 1938-47. Member Royal Commission on Marriage and Divorce. *Address:* 68 Whitmore Road, Harrow. *T.:* 01-422 1150. *Club:* Reform. [*Died* 11 *July* 1969.

MADGE, Capt. Sir Frank William, 2nd Bt., *cr.* 1919; *b.* 24 Mar. 1897; *s.* of late Percy Frank Madge, 2nd *s.* of 1st Bt. and Fanny Julia, *d.* of late J. B. Lightburn; *S.* grandfather, 1927; *m.* 1922, Doris Annie, *d.* of John Beal (Master Mariner); four *d.* *Educ.:* Tonbridge. Served European War, 1915-17, H.A.C. (wounded); re-employed, 1941-43, with Royal Corps of Signals. *Recreation:* sailing. *Heir:* none. *Address:* Brambletye Gate, East Grinstead, Sussex. *T.:* E. Grinstead 554.
[*Died* 26 *May* 1962 (*ext.*).

MADGE, Sidney Joseph, D.Sc.; Hon. Assistant Keeper of British Museum, Dept. of Printed Books, 1943; *b.* West Hartlepool, Durham, 13 March 1874; 3rd *s.* of Benjamin John Madge, R.N., Tavistock, Devon, and Mary, *d.* of Henry Wilmer, Denton and Moulton, Northants; *m.* 1898, Flora Frances (*d.* 1945), *d.* of Dr. Nelson Hilder, Canterbury and Herne Bay, Kent; two *s.* two *d.*; *m.* 1947, Marjorie C. V., *widow* of Rev. A. Harrè. *Educ.:* Northampton School of Science; Oxford Central School; St. Paul's College, Cheltenham; London Univ. (London School of Economics and Political Science), B.Sc. 1921, M.Sc. (Thesis) 1922, D.Sc. (Thesis 1929, enlarged 1938). Inns of Court O.T.C. 1918, 2nd Lt. The Buffs, 1919; Member of Educational Staff, Hornsey, 1896-1934; also Lecturer in History, Economics, and Social Subjects, City of London Day Training College, 1897-1900, L.C.C. Literary and Commercial Institutes, 1900-32, Adult Education Movement, 1923-30; Member of Mosely Education Commission in U.S.A. and Canada, 1906. One of the Founders of the Oxford City Branch of University Extension, 1893-1894, Parish Register Society, 1896, and Phillimore's Marriage Registers Series, 1896; Editor of the British Record Society, 1900-1902, and London and Middlesex Archæological Society, 1921-23; Member of Council London Topographical Society, 1936-39, and Society of Antiquaries, 1938-40 (Library Committee 1938-45); Donor of Carey Centenary Bell, Moulton, 1934, and St. Alban Memorial Bell, St. Albans Cathedral, 1935; F.S.A., 1923-52. *Publications:* History of Moulton Parish Church, and Transcript of Parish Registers, 1895-1902; Gloucestershire Notes and Queries, 1895-1902; England under Stuart Rule, 1898; Inquisitions post mortem, Gloucestershire and London, 1901-1903; Rural

Middlesex under the Commonwealth, 1922-1923; Borzoi County Histories, 1928-1930; The Origin of the name of Hornsey, Early Records and Mediæval Records of Hornsey, 1936-39; The Domesday of Crown Lands, 1938; (with Sir Allen Mawer) Middlesex Place-Names (English Place Name Society), 1942; Worcester House in the Strand (Archæologia, 1945); The Parish Church of SS. Protus and Hyacinth, Blisland, Cornwall, 1947-50; The Chapel, Kieve and Gorge of St. Nectan, Tintagel, 1950, etc. Madge Collections are preserved in British Museum, Public Record Office, etc. *Recreations:* historical research and travel. *Address:* Harbledown, 23 Russell Hill Road, Purley, Surrey. [*Died* 3 *Feb.* 1961.

MADILL, Surgeon Rear-Admiral Thomas, C.B. 1952; O.B.E. 1941; Q.H.P. 1952; retd.; *b.* 14 Jan. 1895; *s.* of Rev. T. Madill, LL.D., Garvagh, Co. Londonderry, N.I.; *m.* 1930, Mary, *d.* of Dr. W. P. Panckridge, Petersfield, Hants; one *s.* *Educ.:* Coleraine Academy; Trinity College, Dublin. Surgeon Probationer, R.N.V.R., 1916; M.B., B.A., 1919; Surgeon Lt., R.N., 1921; Surgeon Lt.-Comdr. 1927; Surgeon Comdr., 1933; Surgeon Capt., 1943; Surgeon Rear-Admiral, 1950. Served in H.M. Ships, R.N. Hospitals and Marine Establishments. Surgeon Rear-Adm., R.N. Hosp. Malta, 1950-53; K.H.P. 1950-52, Q.H.P. 1952-53. *Address:* 7 Netley Mansions, South Parade, Southsea, Hants. *T.:* Portsmouth 33082. [*Died* 10 *Feb.* 1962.

MADSEN, Sir John (Percival Vissing), Kt. 1941; Professor of Electrical Engineering, Sydney University, 1920-1949, now Emeritus; Dean of the Faculty of Engineering and Fellow of the Senate, Sydney University, 1942-; Member of Council for Scientific and Industrial Research, Australia; Chairman of following Boards and Committees of Council for Scientific and Industrial Research: Radio Research Board, 1927-; Electrical Research Board, 1945-; Chairman of Australian National Research Council, 1945-; Chairman of Institute of Physics (Australian Branch), 1945-; *b.* 24 March 1879; *s.* of late H. F. Madsen; *m.* 1904, Maud Foster Molesworth; two *s.* one *d.* *Educ.:* Sydney High School; University of Sydney, B.Sc., B.E.; University of Adelaide, D.Sc., F.Inst.P.; M.I.E. (Aust.); Assistant Lecturer in Physics and Mathematics, Adelaide, 1901; Lecturer in Electrical Engineering, Adelaide, 1903-9; Lecturer in Electrical Engineering, Sydney, 1909; Major, Officer in Charge and Chief Instructor, Engineer Officers' Training School (Australia), 1915-18. *Publications:* various in scientific journals. *Address:* Talawa, Wandella Avenue, Roseville, Sydney, New South Wales, Australia. [*Died* 4 *Oct.* 1969.

MAGAN, Lt.-Col. Arthur Tilson Shaen, C.M.G. 1919; *b.* 21 May 1880; 2nd *s.* of late Percy Magan, J.P., of Correal, Roscommon, Ireland; *m.* 1906, Kathleen Jane, *e. d.* of late Assheton Biddulph, M.F.H.; two *s.* three *d.* *Educ.:* privately. Served European War in R.A.S.C., France and Belgium, 5 Aug. 1914-1 Mar. 1919 (despatches, C.M.G.). *Address:* Killyon Manor, Hill of Down, Co. Meath. *Club:* Friendly Brothers (Dublin). [*Died* 11 *Nov.* 1965.

MAGAURAN, Wilfrid Henry Bertram, M.D., M.Ch., F.R.C.S.; Ear, Nose and Throat Specialist; Consulting E.N.T. Surgeon to Hospital of St. John and St. Elizabeth, London, and Consulting Surgeon to St. Anthony's Hospital, Cheam, Surrey; formerly E.N.T. Surgeon to Wilson Hospital, Mitcham, Surrey; *b.* 13 July 1898; *s.* of late Dr. James Magauran, J.P., and Sarah, *d.* of Dr. James Mathews; *m.* 1938, Dr. Iris Mary Lamey, M.B., B.S. (Lond.) 1937; M.R.C.S. (Eng.); L.R.C.P. (Lond.) 1937; D.O.M.S. (Eng.) 1942, Ophthalmologist; one *s.* two *d.* *Educ.:* St. Patrick's Coll., Cavan, Co. Cavan; Univ. Coll., Galway; Univ. Coll., Dublin, National University of Ireland; St. Vincent's Hospital, Dublin; Guy's Hospital, London Hospital, Charing Cross Hosp. M.B., B.Ch., B.A.O. (N.U.I.), 1921; M.D. (N.U.I.), 1928; M.Ch. (Oto-rhino-laryngology (N.U.I.)), 1931; F.R.C.S. (Eng.), 1934; 1st Class Honours and Exhibnr.; Gold Medallist in Medicine, St. Vincent's Hospital. H.S. Roy. Sy. Co. Hosp.; A.M.O. St. Mary Islington Hosp.; A.M.O. London Metrop. Infectious Hosps. Sen. A.M.O. Downs Hosp., Sutton; i/c E.N.T. Clinic; Clin. Asst. Central London and Golden Square Throat, Nose & Ear Hosps. Clin. Asst. E.N.T., Guy's Hosp.; Reg. E.N.T. Charing Cross Hosp.; Asst. Aurist L.C.C.; E.N.T. Consultant Queen Mary's Hosp., Carshalton; E.N.T. Surg., Roy. Isle of Wight Hosp.; Actg. E.N.T. Surg. King Edward Memorial Hosp., Ealing; E.N.T. Surgeon: Queen Mary's Hospital in East End; Farnborough Co. Hosp., and Guy's Base Hosp.; Woking Victoria Hosp.; Roy. Mil. Hosp., Woolwich. Maj. R.A.M.C. (Otologist); Aural Surgeon E.M.S.; F.R.S. Med. Mem. Brit. Assoc. Otolaryngologists; Mem. B.M.A. K.C.S.G. 1955. *Publications:* various E.N.T. articles and publications on original work in Med. Jls. *Recreations:* golf, motoring. *Address:* Bayham Lodge, 25 Alexandra Road, Epsom, Surrey. *T.:* Epsom 2466. *Club:* Royal Automobile (including Country Club, Woodcote Park, Epsom). [*Died* 27 *May* 1964.

MAGEE, Allan Angus, C.B.E. 1943; D.S.O. 1919; Q.C.; *b.* 1881; *s.* of late Hon. Mr. Justice James Magee; *m.* 1910, M. Leslie Smith; one *s.* two *d.* *Educ.:* University of Toronto, Osgoode Hall. K.C. 1923. *Address:* Aldred Building, Place d'Armes, Montreal, Canada. *T.A.:* Magee. *Clubs:* University, Mount Royal (Montreal). [*Died* 3 *June* 1961.

MAGEE, Sir Cuthbert (Gaulter), Kt. 1961; C.B.E. 1952; F.R.C.P.E.; retired as Chief Medical Officer of the Ministry of Pensions and National Insurance (formerly Min. of Pensions), 1959-63; L.R.C.P., L.R.C.S.Ed., L.R.F.P.S.Glas, 1917; D.P.H. Manch. 1920; M.R.C.P.Ed. 1933; F.R.C.P. Ed. 1940. Formerly: House Physician, Royal Infirmary, Glasgow; Out-patients Medical Officer, Salford Royal Hospital, Manchester; Hon. Clinical Assistant, West End Hospital for Nervous Diseases. Fellow of the Royal Society of Medicine; Member British Medical Association. *Publications:* contributions to medical journals. *Address:* Stoke Grange, Clandon Road, Guildford, Surrey. [*Died* 29 *Aug.* 1963.

MAGEEAN, Most Rev. Daniel; Bishop of Down and Connor (R.C.), since 1929; *b.* 1882. *Educ.:* St. Malachy's College, Belfast; Maynooth. Ordained, 1906; Professor, St. Malachy's College, 1907-19; Dean of Maynooth, 1919-29. *Address:* Lisbreen, Somerton Road, Belfast. *T.:* 76185. [*Died* 18 *Jan.* 1962.

MAGGS, Joseph Herbert; formerly Director of United Dairies Ltd.; *b.* 23 July 1875; *s.* of Charles Maggs, Melksham; *m.* 1902, Ada Mary Fry; (*d.* 1963); no *c.* *Educ.:* Wycliffe Coll., Stonehouse, Glos. *Recreation:* fishing. *Address:* The Lodge, Rushall, Pewsey, Wilts. *T.A.:* Upavon. [*Died* 1 *Feb.* 1964.

MAGINNESS, Sir Greville (Simpson), K.B.E., *cr.* 1953; Kt., *cr.* 1947; Company Director; *b.* 14 June 1888; *s.* of late Edmund John Maginness, C.B.E., M.V.O., Southsea, Hants; *m.* 1928, Kathleen May, *d.* of Alfred Neale; one *d.* *Educ.:* Plymouth

and Mannamead College; also in France and Germany. Pres. Machine Tool Trades Assoc., 1940-43; Pres. Russo-British Chamber of Commerce from 1938; Pres. Engineering and Allied Employers' Nat. Federation, 1944-46; Pres. Brit. Employers' Confed., 1946-50; Member Engineering Advisory Council, Ministry of Supply, from 1946; Member Machine Tool Advisory Council, Ministry of Supply, from 1945; Member British Delegation at First Conference of I.L.O., Washington, 1919. *Recreations:* Rugby football, cricket, fishing. *Address:* The Court, Kent's Green, Callow End, Worcester. *Club:* Royal Automobile.
[*Died* 23 *Nov.* 1961.

MAGINESS, Rt. Hon. William Brian, P.C. (N. Ire.) 1945; Q.C. (N. Ire.) 1946; LL.D. (T.C.D.) 1922; County Court Judge of Down since 1964; *b.* 10 July 1901; *s.* of W. G. Maginess, Lisburn, County Antrim; *m.* 1954, Margaret Seeton, *d.* of W. Crawford, Ballyholme Road, Bangor, Co. Down; one *s.* *Educ.:* Lisburn; Trinity College, Dublin. Barrister, King's Inns, 1922. M.P. (U.) Northern Ireland, for Iveagh Div. of Co. Down, 1938-64; Under-Secretary to Ministry of Agriculture, Northern Ireland Government, 1941-43; Parliamentary Secretary to Ministry of Commerce, 1943-45; Minister: of Labour and Nat. Insurance, 1945-49; of Commerce, 1949; of Home Affairs, 1949-53; of Finance, 1953-56; Attorney-General, 1956-64. *Address:* Avonmore, Hillsborough Road, Lisburn, Co. Antrim, N.I.
[*Died* 18 *April* 1967.

MAGNAY, Brig. Arthur Douglas, C.I.E. 1944; I.A., retired; *b.* 14 May 1893; *s.* of F. W. Magnay, Drayton, Norfolk; *m.* 1944, Sophie Maud, *d.* of late Robert Charles and Hon. Mrs. Donner, and *widow* of Rear-Adm. Ion B. B. Tower, D.S.C., Royal Navy. *Educ.:* Harrow; R.M.C., Sandhurst. Joined Indian Army, 1912; posted to Skinners Horse; served European War, 1914-19; Indian Frontier, 1919, 1933-34, 1937, and 1938; Brig. 1940; retired, 1943. *Recreations:* riding, golf, bridge. *Address:* 38 Catherine Place, Buckingham Gate, S.W.1. *Club:* Army and Navy.
[*Died* 20 *Nov.* 1964.

MAGNUS, Henry Adolph, M.D. (Lond.); F.R.C.P.; F.C. Path.; Professor of Morbid Anatomy, King's Coll. Hospital Medical Sch., University of London, since 1948; Director of Pathology Department, King's College Hospital, since 1947; *b.* 11 Nov. 1909; *o. s.* of late D. G. H. Magnus and Lucy Swift; *m.* 1935, Kathleen, *d.* of late T. J. Aiken, J.P.; two *s.* *Educ.:* Mill Hill School; St. Bartholomew's Hosp. Casualty House Physician and House Physician, St. Bart's., 1932; Junior Demonstrator, Senior Demonstrator of Pathology, Lecturer in Morbid Anatomy, St. Bart's., up to 1939. M.D. London in Pathology, 1937 (University Gold Medal). Served in R.A.M.C., 1939-45, overseas 5½ years, Lt.-Col., A.D.P. Palestine and 9th Army and Eastern Command. Senior Lecturer, Morbid Anatomy, St. Bart's., 1945-46. Member Path. Soc. Gt. Brit. and Ireland; Assoc. of Clinical Path. Late Vice-Pres. and late Hon. Sec. Sect. of Path. Roy. Soc. Med.; Pres., Inst. of Medical Laboratory Tech., 1960-64; Mem. Bd. of Govs., King's Coll. Hosp. Examiner, Primary F.R.C.S. of England; late exmr., Primary F.F.A.R.C.S., Conjoint Board and University of London. *Publications:* various papers in scientific and medical journals. *Recreations:* sea fishing, gardening. *Address:* 28 Dulwich Village, S.E.21. *Club:* Athenæum.
[*Died* 12 *Sept.* 1967.

MAGRANE, Col. John Plunkett, C.B.E. 1944; E.D. 1940; *b.* 14 March 1896; *yr. s.* of late Lieutenant-Colonel V. J. Magrane, V.D., L.R.C.P.I., Darlaston, Staffs; *m.* 1928, Vera, *d.* of late Dr. J. Wingfield, Moseley, Birmingham; one *s.* *Educ.:* Mount St. Marys' College; Birmingham University. 2nd Lt. 6th South Staffordshire Regt. 1914; Lt. 1915; Capt. 1916: served European War, France and Flanders (wounded thrice, despatches) Major T.A.R.O 1922; Fiji Military Forces, Lt.-Col. 1940; Col. 1943; Colonial Police Service, 1922; Nigeria, 1922-1929; Mauritius, 1931-38; Fiji, 1939-46; Asst. Commissioner and British Resident, Germany, 1947-57. O.St.J. 1949. Cross of Merit First Class, Sovereign Military Order of Malta, 1958. *Address:* 100 Osborne Road, Southsea, Hants.
[*Died* 14 *June* 1963.

MAGRATH, Harry William, C.B.E. 1945; M.C. 1917; F.C.A.; *s.* of late William Magrath, Park House, Sparkbrook, Warwicks., and Roslin, Llandudno; *m.* 1916, Mabel Violette, *o. d.* of late Percy James Thomas Symes, Yeovil, Som., and Crouch End, Mddx.; no *c.* *Educ.:* Bedford School; Private Tutor; Continent. Asst. Director of Finance, 1918-19, Dir. of Finance, 1919-21, Min. of Food; District Auditor, 1921-38 (Chm. Dist. Auditors' Assoc., 1930-38); Dep. Chief Inspector of Audit, Min. of Health, 1938-40; Chief Auditor and Sec. of Nat. Insurance Audit Dept., 1940-55, retired 1955. Served European War, 1914-18 Inns of Court Regiment, 1914 (Aug.-Nov.), 60th Rifles, 1914-18 (gassed and invalided with Hon. rank of Capt.). *Recreations:* riding, walking, motoring. *Address:* 9 Riversleigh Avenue, Lytham St. Annes, Lancs. *T.:* Lytham 7887. *Clubs:* United Service, Royal Over-Seas League.
[*Died* 26 *March* 1969.

MAHADEVA, Sir Arunachalam, K.C.M.G. 1955; Kt. 1949; *b.* 4 Oct. 1885; *s.* of late Sir Ponnambalam Arunachalam; *m.* one *s.* one *d.* *Educ.:* Royal Coll., Colombo; Christ's College, Cambridge. Called to Bar, Lincoln's Inn, 1909; Advocate of the Supreme Court of Ceylon. Member of Ceylon Legislative Council, 1924-31; Manager, Ceylon State Mortgage Bank, 1932-33; Member of State Council of Ceylon, 1934-1947; Minister of Home Affairs, Ceylon, 1942-47. Ceylon Government Delegate to the International Trade Conference at Havana, 1947-48; High Commissioner for Ceylon in India, 1949. Member Public Service Commission, Ceylon. *Address:* Ponklar, Horton Place, Colombo 7, Ceylon.
[*Deceased.*

MAHAFFY, Alexander Francis, C.M.G. 1942; M.D., D.P.H. (Toronto); D.T.M. (Liverpool); *b.* 1891; *s.* of late Thomas Mahaffy; *m.* 1930, Elsie Evelyn, *d.* of late Engineer Captain W. H. James, C.B.E., R.N. Lieut. 4th Can. Machine Gun Coy. and 2nd Can. Machine Gun Bn., European War, 1914-18; Staff member International Health Div. of Rockefeller Foundation, 1923-1946; member West African Yellow Fever Commission, 1925-34; Director Yellow Fever Research Institute, Entebbe, Uganda, 1936-1946, and Joint Sec. Colonial Medical Research Committee, 1946-49; Director Colonial Medical Research, 1946-49; retd. 1949. *Publications:* papers on Yellow Fever. *Club:* Union (Victoria, B.C.).
[*Died* 4 *Dec.* 1962.

MAHER, Charles Ernest, C.B. 1954; Under-Secretary and Accountant-General in the Ministry of Labour since 1951; *b.* 13 August 1896; *er. s.* of late Charles Edward Maher, Plymouth, and of Amelia Virginia Hodge Maher (*née* Rogers), Modbury, Devon; *m.* 1922, Adelaide Ruth Wood (*d.* 1954), Gravesend; one *d.* *Educ.:* Midleton Coll., Co. Cork. Apptd. to staff of War Office, 1915; served European War, 1915-19; transferred to Min. of Labour, 1920.

Assistant Accountant-General, 1943; Deputy Accountant-General, 1945; Assistant Secretary for Finance, 1946. *Address:* 25 Sion Court, Twickenham, Mddx. *T.:* Popesgrove 9766. [*Died* 22 *June* 1961.

MAHESHWARI, Prof. Panchanan, F.R.S. 1965; Professor and Head of the Department of Botany, University of Delhi, India, since 1949; *b.* 9 Nov. 1904; *s.* of Bijay Lal and Laxmi Maheshwari; *m.* 1923, Shanti Maheshwari; three *s.* three *d.* *Educ.:* Jaipur and Allahabad, India. M.Sc. 1927, D.Sc. 1931, Univ. of Allahabad. Lectr. and later Assoc. Prof. of Botany, Agra Coll., 1930-37; Lectr., Univ. of Allahabad, 1937-1939; Lectr. and later Prof. and Head of Dept. of Biology, Univ. of Dacca, 1939-49. Corresp. mem., Amer. Botanical Soc., 1959; Deutsche botanische Gesellschaft, 1961; Hon. For. Fell., Amer. Acad. of Arts and Sciences, 1959; Fell. Nat. Inst. of Sciences, India, 1935; Pres. Nat. Acad. of Sciences, India, 1963-65. Hon. D.Sc. McGill Univ. 1959. *Publications:* An Introduction to the Embryology of Angiosperms, 1950; Recent Advances in the Embryology of Angiosperms, 1963; Dictionary of Economic Plants in India, 1965; Editor, Phytomorphology, 1950-. *Recreations:* music and stamp collection. *Address:* Department of Botany, University of Delhi, Delhi 7, India. *T.:* 228996. [*Died* 18 *May* 1966.

MAHIR, Thomas Edward, C.B.E. 1965; G.M. 1941; Assistant Commissioner (D. Department) New Scotland Yard, 1959-67; retired; *b.* 1 March 1915; *s.* of late Reverend Edward Alexander Mahir, M.A., B.Sc., and Dorothy Mahir (*née* Wardle); *m.* 1938, Dione Finnis, *o. d.* of George Finnis Moon, Warwick; no *c.* *Educ.:* Crewkerne School, Somerset. Schoolmaster, St. Aubyn's Prep. School, Tiverton, Devon, 1932-35; Direct Entrant Metropolitan Police College, Hendon, 1935-36; Junior Station Inspector, 1937; Station Inspector, 1939; Sub-Divisional Inspector, 1944; Chief Inspector, 1949; Superintendent, 1950; Chief Superintendent, 1954; Deputy Commandant, Police College, Ryton-on-Dunsmore, Warwickshire, 1955-57; Deputy Commander, 1956; Commander, 1958. F.R.S.A. 1964. K.St.J. 1966. *Recreations:* cricket, bowls, boxing, gardening. *Address:* Wayford, 21 Hill Brow, Hove 4, Sussex. *T.:* Brighton 52440. *Club:* Kennel. [*Died* 29 *Jan.* 1970.

MAHONEY, Charles, R.A. Elect, 1968 (A.R.A. 1961); A.R.C.A. 1924; painter; *b.* London, 18 Nov. 1903; *m.* 1941, Dorothy Bishop; one *d.* *Educ.:* Beckenham School of Art; Royal College of Art. Teacher, Painting School of Royal College of Art, 1928-53. Instructor of Painting and Drawing at the Royal Academy Schools. Has exhibited at New English Art Club, R.B.A. Galleries, etc. Work represented in Tate Gallery, galleries in Leeds, Newcastle, Sheffield, etc. Reproductions in periodicals. *Recreations:* gardening, studying modern art. *Address:* Oak Cottage, Wrotham, nr. Sevenoaks, Kent. *T.:* Borough Green 2406. [*Died* 11 *May* 1968.

MAHONEY, Sir John (Andrew), Kt. 1959; O.B.E. 1956; J.P. (Gambia); *b.* 6 March 1883; African (Gambian); *m.* 1910, Hannah Augusta Small; two *s.* three *d.* (and three *s.* decd.). *Educ.:* Methodist Elementary School, Bathurst, Gambia; C.M.S. Grammar School, Freetown, Sierra Leone. Shopkeeper and Clerk, 1900-11; Civil Servant, 1912-16; Mercantile Clerk, 1917-53; M.L.C. 1942-47; J.P. 1931-; Vice-Pres. Legislative Council, 1951-54; subsequently Speaker. Speaker, House of Representatives, Gambia, 1960-62, retired. *Recreations:* reading, walking, gardening. *Address:* 40 Buckle Street, Bathurst, Gambia, West Africa. *T.:* Bathurst 446. [*Died* 23 *Jan.* 1966.

MAINE, Henry Cecil Sumner, C.M.G. 1948; M.V.O.; Foreign Office, 1922-52, retd.; *b.* 1 July 1886; *s.* of late Charles Sumner Maine; *m.* 1912, Maude Barbara, *d.* of Frederick Kerr; two *d.* *Educ.:* Eton; Trinity Hall, Cambridge. Private Secretary's office, Buckingham Palace, 1912-16. Served European War, Grenadier Guards, 1916-19. War Office, General Staff, 1917-19. *Recreations:* cricket, tennis, golf. *Address:* 22 Shouldham St., W.1. *T.:* Ambassador 6461; Mill End Farm, Clavering, Essex. *Clubs:* Bath, Guards. [*Died* 24 *Sept.* 1968.

MAISTRE, Le Roy de, (Roy de Maistre); C.B.E. 1962; painter; *b.* N.S.W., Australia, 1894. Represented in a number of public galleries in England including the Tate Gallery; also in public galleries in Australia and Canada, and in many important private collections in Europe; in Westminster Cathedral and other churches. *Recreations:* various, numerous and private. *Address:* 13 Eccleston St., S.W.1. [*Died* 1 *March* 1968.

MAITLAND, Sir Alexander, Kt. 1962; Q.C. (Scot.), 1928; D.L.; Deputy Governor, Royal Bank of Scotland, 1953-62; *b.* 1877; *s.* of Thomas Maitland, Broughty Ferry; *m.* 1906, Rosalind Gertrude Craig (*d.* 1959), *d.* of Alexander Craig Sellar M.P.; no *c.* *Educ.:* Harrow; New College, Oxford, B.A., LL.B. Called to Scottish Bar, 1903; Advocate Depute, 1922-29; Sheriff of Caithness, Orkney and Zetland, 1929-31; served European War in R.A. in France and Salonica, 1914-18; D.L. City and County of Edinburgh, 1943; retired. *Address:* 6 Heriot Row, Edinburgh. *Club:* New (Edin.). [*Died* 25 *Sept.* 1965.

MAITLAND, Sir Alexander (Keith), 8th Bt. *cr.* 1818; *b.* 26 Oct. 1920; *s.* of Lieut.-Col. Sir (George) Ramsay Maitland, 7th Bt., D.S.O., and of Jean Hamilton Findlay; *S.* father, 1960; *m.* 1951, Lavender Mary Jex Jackson; two *s.* one *d.* (and one *d.* decd.). *Educ.:* Rugby; Peterhouse, Cambridge. Officer, Queen's Own Cameron Highlanders, 1940-51; retd. as Maj. *Recreations:* shooting, fishing. *Heir:* *s.* Richard John Maitland, *b.* 24 Nov. 1952. *Address:* Burnside, Forfar, Angus. *T.:* Forfar 39. [*Died* 18 *July* 1963.

MAITLAND, Sir Keith R. F. R.; *see* Steel-Maitland.

MAJDALANY, Fred, M.C. 1944; Author, Military Historian and Journalist since 1933; *b.* 22 May 1913; *s.* of Joachim and Victoria Majdalany; *m.* 1949, Sheila Howarth; one *d.* *Educ.:* King William's, I.O.M. (Schol.). Served War of 1939-45: enlisted, 1939; commnd. into Lancashire Fusiliers, 1940; First Army, N. Africa (wounded); Eighth Army, Sicily, Italy; Maj. 1943; Chief Instructor 164th Inf. O.C.T.U. (Eaton Hall), 1945. Theatrical publicist with Sir Charles Cochran, 1934-37; Dramatic Critic, Sunday Referee, 1937-39; Film Critic and Feature Writer, Daily Mail, 1946-61; Film Critic, Time and Tide, 1952-57. Pres. Critics' Circle, 1960. Author of revue sketches and lyrics for theatre and radio; documentary scripts for B.B.C. and Independent TV. F.R.S.L. *Publications:* The Monastery, 1945; Patrol, 1953; Cassino: Portrait of a Battle, 1957; The Red Rocks of Eddystone, 1959; State of Emergency, 1962; The Battle of El Alamein, 1965; The Crumbling of Fortress Europe, 1968; contribs. to Punch, Sunday Times, Evening Standard. *Recreations:* music, travel, spontaneous sociability. *Address:* Long Green Farmhouse, Little Saling, Braintree, Essex. *T.:* Shalford Green 339. *Club:* Royal Automobile. [*Died* 15 *Nov.* 1967.

MAJOR, Rev. Henry Dewsbury Alves, D.D. (Exeter College, Oxford); F.S.A.; Hon. Canon of Birmingham since 1941; Vicar of Merton, Bicester, 1929-60; Select Preacher, Oxford University, 1922; Cambridge, 1925, 1932; Examiner, University of London D.D.; Noble Lecturer, Harvard University, 1925-26; Hibbert Lecturer, 1946; Founded the Modern Churchman 1911 and has edited it from that date; *b.* 1871; *s.* of H. D. Major, Kati-Kati, New Zealand, and Mary Ursula, *d.* of W. Alves, Admiralty Commissioner at Haulbowline, Ireland; *m.* Mary Eliza, *d.* of C. C. McMillan, J.P., of Remuera and Waingaro, New Zealand; one *s.* one *d.* (and one *s.* killed in action, 1941). *Educ.:* St. John's Coll. and University Coll., New Zealand; Senior Scholar of University of New Zealand, M.A., 1st Class Honours (Nat.-Sc.); Exeter College, Oxford; M.A., D.D., 1st Class Honours (Theology), Canon Hall Greek Test. Prize, (Junior). Late Rector of Copgrove, and Vice-Principal of Ripon Clergy College; Principal of Ripon Hall, Oxford, 1919-48. *Publications:* The Gospel of Freedom; A Resurrection of Relics; Memorials of Copgrove; Jesus, by an Eye-Witness; Life and Letters of Bishop Boyd-Carpenter; English Modernism; Thirty Years After; The Church's Creeds and the Modern Man; Rome and the Modern Man, 1934; Towards Prayer Book Revision (essay in The Church and the Twentieth Century); The Mission and Message of Jesus, 1937; Revised Services, 1937; Basic Christianity, 1944; Civilization and Religious Values (Hibbert Lectures, 1948); Contrib. Encyclopædia Britannica (Modernism), etc. *Address:* Merton Vicarage, Bicester, Oxon. [*Died* 26 *Jan.* 1961.

MAKINS, Lt.-Col. Sir William Vivian, 3rd Bt., *cr.* 1902; D.L.; J.P.; one of H.M. Body Guard, Honourable Corps Gentlemen-at-Arms since 1951; Lt.-Col., Welsh Guards 1924-48, retd.; *b.* 19 Jan. 1903; *s.* of Sir Paul Makins, 2nd Bt., and Gladys Marie (*d.* 1919), *d.* of W. Vivian, 185 Queen's Gate, S.W.; *S.* father, 1939; *m.* 1932, Jean, *d.* of late Lord Arthur Hay and of Mrs. Robert Leatham; two *d.* *Educ.:* Eton. Served Sudan defence force, 1928-30, (Camel Corps; Kordofan operations, 1929-30 (despatches), Assistant Military Secretary, Gibraltar, 1937; Served War of 1939-45, with B.E.F., France) 1939-40; 1st Army, N. Africa, 1943-44 (despatches); Italy, 1944; Comd. R.M.C. O.C.T.U., Aldershot and Sandhurst, 1944-1946; A.M.S. Northern Command, 1947-48; Chm. Hampshire County Probation Cttee., 1953-; Chm. Winchester Diocesan Board of Finance, 1954-; Mem. House of Laity, Church Assembly, 1955-; J.P. Hants, 1948; High Sheriff, 1953-54; Member Hants C.C., 1956-; D.L. Hants, 1960; C.A., 1968. *Heir: b.* Paul Vivian Makins, Major, Welsh Guards, (retd.) [*b.* 12 Nov. 1913; *m.* 1945, Maisie, *d.* of Maj. O. H. Pedley and *widow* of Maj. C. L. J. Bowen]. *Address:* Littlehayes, Itchen Abbas, Hants. *T.:* Itchen Abbas 208. *Clubs:* Guards, Pratt's. [*Died* 22 *April* 1969.

MALAN, Group Captain Adolph Gysbert, D.S.O. 1940, and Bar, 1941; D.F.C. and Bar, 1940; *b.* Wellington, South Africa, 3 Oct. 1910; *s.* of William Adolph and Evelyn Forde Malan; *m.* 1938, Lynda Irene Fraser; one *s.* one *d.* *Educ.:* Wellington Public School, South Africa; South African Training Ship, General Botha. Joined Union Castle Mail S.S. Co. as Cadet, 1927; became officer, 1930; served as officer in same firm and as officer in Royal Naval Reserve until 1936 when accepted for Short Service Commission in R.A.F., terminated 1942; D.F.C. 1940 for operations at Dunkirk, Bar to D.F.C. 1940 for night operations; took over command of same Squadron in Aug. 1940 (D.S.O.); Fighter operations over England and Channel; Bar to D.S.O. 1941 for Fighter operations over France; commanded a Fighter Station, 1943; commanded a wing of R.A.F. Second T.A.F., Western Front, 1944; completed War course at R.A.F. Staff College, June 1945; a member of the Directing Staff at R.A.F. Staff College, 1945-46; retired, 1946. *Recreations:* riding, shooting, squash racquets. *Address:* Benfontein Farm, c/o De Beers Consolidated Mines Ltd., Kimberley, South Africa. [*Died* 17 *Sept.* 1963.

MALDEN, Edmund Claud, C.V.O. 1941; Surgeon Apothecary to H.M. Household, Windsor, 1938-52. Extra Surgeon Apothecary, 1952-58, retired; *b.* Pembury, Kent, 20 Aug. 1890; *s.* of late Walter Malden, M.D., Cambridge; *m.* 1st, 1921, Margaret Dorothy Durant (*d.* 1951); one *s.* one *d.*; 2nd, 1952, Bridget Landy. *Educ.:* Tonbridge Sch.; Gonville and Caius Coll., Cambridge; King's Coll. Hospital, London. Served European War in R.A.M.C. in France, 1915-19 (despatches). Consulting Physician and Pathologist King Edward VII Hospital, Windsor. *Recreations:* riding, golf, billiards. *Address:* 2 Hamilton Lodge, King's Road, Windsor. *T.:* Windsor 1347. *Club:* Berkshire Golf. [*Died* 11 *July* 1962.

MALIM, Frederic Blagden, M.A. Camb.; *b.* 1872; *s.* of late F. J. Malim, Chichester; *m.* 1907, Amy Gertrude (*d.* 1960), *d.* of G. R. Hemmerde: four *s.* (and one killed in the War) three *d.* *Educ.:* Blackheath School; Trinity College, Cambridge. Assistant Master in Marlborough College, 1895-1907; Headmaster of Sedbergh School, 1907-11; Haileybury, 1911-1921; Wellington College, 1921-37; visited Dominion Schools on behalf of H.M.C., 1938-1939. *Publication:* Almae Matres, 1948. *Address:* Myddylton House, Saffron Walden, Essex. *T.:* Saffron Walden 3263. [*Died* 5 *June* 1966.

MALINOVSKY, Marshal Rodion Yakovlevich; Minister of Defence, U.S.S.R., since 1957; *b.* Odessa, 1898. *Educ.:* Frunze Military Academy, Moscow. Enlisted in Tsarist Army, 1914; served in Ukraine (wounded) and France (Sergeant). Joined Red Army in Civil War. War of 1939-45: comd. army, Stalingrad, 1942; C.-in-C., S.W. Front, 1943; 2nd and 3rd Ukrainian Front, 1944; Marshal of the Soviet Union, 1944; Transbaikal Front, 1945. Far East, 1945-56; C.-in-C., Ground Forces, Moscow, 1956-57. Deputy to Supreme Soviet, 1946-. Hero of the Soviet Union; five Orders of Lenin; Order of Victory. *Address:* Ministry of Defence, Moscow, U.S.S.R. [*Died* 31 *March* 1967

MALKO, Nicolai; Musical Director, Sydney Symphony Orchestra, Australia, since 1957; *b.* 4 May 1888; *s.* of Andrew Malko, physician, and Olga Malko; *m.* 1924, Berthe Unik; two *s.* *Educ.:* Gymnasia, Odessa; Univ. of St. Petersburg, Russia. Studied music at Music Sch. Lagler, Odessa; Conservatory of Music, Petersburg; studied with Felix Mottl, Munich. Conductor of Ballet, later of Opera, Mariin Theatre, St. Petersburg, 1908-18; Conductor and Prof., Vitebsk, Kiev, Kharkov, 1918-25; Prof., Leningrad Conservatory of Music (conducting), 1925; Artistic Dir. and Conductor, Leningrad Philharmony Orch., 1926-29. First appearance W. Europe, Vienna and London, 1928; has appeared with all leading orchs. in Gt. Brit. Made S. Amer. and European Tour, 1929. Permanent Guest Conductor, Danish State Radio Symphony Orch. (Danish Nat. Orch.), 1930-. Settled in Chicago, 1940, conducting important orchestras; also Res. Conductor, Grant Park Symphony Orch., Chicago, 1946-1956; made tours abroad in Europe and S. America; toured U.S.S.R. and Japan, 1959. Hon. Dr. of Music. Kt. of Dannebrog (Denmark), 1950. *Publications:* Conductor and His Baton (Denmark), 1949;

articles in periodicals; arrangements for orchestra. *Address:* c/o A.B.C., 264 Pitt St., Sydney, N.S.W. *T.:* BO657.
[*Died* 22 *June* 1961.

MALLABY - DEELEY, Sir Anthony Meyrick, 3rd Bt., *cr.* 1922; *b.* 30 May 1923; *s.* of Sir Guy Meyrick Mallaby Mallaby-Deeley, 2nd Bt., and Marjorie Constance Lucy, *o. d.* of late James Ernest Peat, of Cranmer, Mitcham, Surrey; *S.* father 1946. *Heir:* none. *Address:* Fairfield Wadhurst, Sussex. *T.:* Wadhurst 85. [*Died* 1 *Dec.* 1962 (*ext.*).

MALLESON, (William) Miles; *b.* Croydon, Surrey, 25 May 1888; *s.* of Edmund Taylor Malleson and Myrrha Bithynia Malleson; *m.* 1st, Lady Constance Annesely (Colette O'Neil) (marr. diss.); 2nd, Joan Graeme Billson (marr. diss.); 3rd, Tatiana Lieven. *Educ.:* Brighton College (Head of School, Captain of Cricket); Emmanuel College, Cambridge, B.A. Historical Tripos., Part I. of Mus. Bac. First appearance as actor, Liverpool Repertory Theatre, 1912; first appearance in London, Royalty Theatre, 1913; dramatist. *Publications:* Youth, a Comedy in three acts; Paddly Pools, The Little White Thought, Maurice's Own Idea, three plays for children; Young Heaven, and three other plays; D Co. and Black 'Ell, two plays of the war; Conflict, a Comedy in three acts; Merrileon Wise, a play in three acts; The Fanatics, a Comedy in three acts: Four People, a play in three acts; Yours Unfaithfully: a comedy in three acts; Six Men of Dorset (with H. Brooks), a play in three acts; The Miser, an English version of Molière's L'Avare; Tartuffe, an adaptation from Molière; The Bachelor, The Provincial Lady, adaptations from Turgenev; The Prodigious Snob: an adaptation from Molière's Le Bourgeois Gentilhomme; The School for Wives, The Misanthrope, Sganarelle, The Imaginary Invalid, adaptations from Molière. *Address:* 14 Rugby St., W.C.1. *T.:* Chancery 3915. *Club:* Savage.
[*Died* 15 *March* 1969.

MALLET, Lady; (Matilde de Obarrio de Mallet); C.B.E. 1920; *b.* Guayaquil, Ecuador, 13 March 1872; *d.* of Don Gabriel de Obarrio Perez de Ochoa, Ponce de Leon, and Doña Rita de Vallarino; *m.* 1892, Sir Claude Coventry Mallet, C.M.G. (*d.* 1941), Diplomatic Service; one *s.* one *d.* *Educ.:* Academy, Manhattanville, New York, U.S.A.; Convent du Sacré-Cœur, Rue de Varennes, Paris. Founded Panama Red Cross, 1917 (which instituted Matilde Obarrio Medal, in schools of Panama, for literary merit, 1964); Baby Welfare, Antituberculosis Campaign (in recognition for services Panama Govt. authorised issue of stamps with Lady Mallet's portrait, for benefit of antituberculosis campaign); built and endowed Lady Mallet Panama Room at Star and Garter Hosp., Richmond, Surrey; also Costa Rica Memorial Reading Room, Star and Garter Hosp., Richmond, Surrey, chiefly with funds contributed by West Indian labourers of Panama Canal and banana plantations of Costa Rica. Established during 1914-18 war, 30 centres of British Red Cross and Queen Mary's Needlework Guild in Panama, Costa Rica, Colombia and Ecuador. Organised distribution of gifts to British West Indian Panama Contingent at the front, European War, 1914-18. Introduced and organised Girl Guide movement in Uruguay, 1922. Perm. Deleg. for Panama to Ligue des Sociétés de la Croix Rouge, Geneva, 1946. Appointed Hon. Attaché Panama Legation, London, 1947. Médaille de la reine Élisabeth of Belgium, 1918; Comdr. (Cross and Star) Order of Vasco Nuñez de Balboa of Panama, 1930; Reconnaissance Française, 1918; British Red Cross for War Work, 1922; Panama Red Cross, 1917; Coronation Medals Edward VII and George V; Panama Red Cross Medal of Merit (Honor al Merito), 1953; Gold Medal (commem. Panama Centenary celebrations of the Red Cross), 1964. *Publications:* Sketches of Spanish Colonial Life in Panama, 1915 (trans. into Spanish by the Academia Nacional de Historia, 1930). Articles in the Times, London, and in publications in Uruguay and Panama on Colonial subjects. Somerset and Dorset Notes and Queries (papers about the Mallet family), 1932, 1933; Letters from the Trenches, 1930. *Recreations:* music, riding, travelling. *Address:* The Manor House, Curry Mallet, Taunton, Somerset.
[*Died* 17 *Oct.* 1964.

MALLET, Sir Victor Alexander Louis, G.C.M.G., *cr.* 1952 (K.C.M.G., *cr.* 1944; C.M.G. 1934); C.V.O. 1939; *b.* 9 April 1893; *e. s.* of late Sir Bernard Mallet, K.C.B., and late Marie, *d.* of Henry John Adeane, M.P.; *m.* 1925, Christiana Jean, *e. d.* of Herman A. Andreae; three *s.* one *d.* *Educ.:* Winchester College; Balliol College, Oxford. Joined Cambridgeshire Regiment (T.F.) as 2nd Lieut. 1914; Captain, 1916; served for a time on personal staff of G.O.C. 37th Division B.E.F., and subsequently as Staff Captain, Midland District of Ireland; 3rd Secretary in the Diplomatic Service, 1919, and appointed to Teheran; 2nd Secretary in Foreign Office, 1922; First Secretary, 1925-26; appointed to Buenos Aires, 1926, and acted as Chargé d'Affaires there Dec. 1926-June 1927 and July-Sept. 1928; Brussels, 1929-32; transferred to Foreign Office, 1932; transferred to Teheran as acting Counsellor, 1933, where he acted as Chargé d'Affaires, June-Nov., 1933 and Oct.-Dec., 1935; Counsellor at Washington, 1936-39, where he acted as Chargé d'Affaires; Minister at Stockholm, 1940-45; Ambassador at Madrid, 1945-46; Ambassador at Rome, 1947-53; retired 1954. Chairman: Skefko Ball Bearing Co. Ltd., 1956-63; Northern Pulp Shippers Ltd., 1954-68. *Publication:* Life with Queen Victoria, 1968. *Recreations:* shooting, fishing, lawn tennis, golf. *Address:* Wittersham House, Wittersham, Nr. Tenterden, Kent. *T.:* Wittersham 238. *Club:* Brooks's. [*Died* 18 *May* 1969.

MALLEY, William Bernard, C.M.G. 1961; C.B.E. 1952 (M.B.E. 1942); Counsellor, H.M. Embassy, Madrid, since 1950; *b.* 24 Sept. 1889; *s.* of James Malley, late of Abingdon Lodge, Solihull, Warwickshire. *Educ.:* Cotton College, North Staffs.; University of Madrid, Lecturer, University College, El Excorial, Madrid, 1920-33. Entered H.M. Foreign Service, 1939; Assistant Press Attaché, 1939; Second Secretary, 1940; First Secretary, 1942. Coronation Medal, 1953. *Publications:* El Simbolismo Cristiano, 1935; Cartillas Escurialenses, 1936; Solihull and the Catholic Faith, 1939. *Address:* British Embassy, Madrid 4.
[*Died* 14 *Feb.* 1966.

MALLON, James Joseph, C.H. 1939; LL.D. (Liverpool); M.A. (Man.); J.P.; Warden of Toynbee Hall, 1919-54; Hon. Adviser to the Minister of Food on Feeding in Air Raid Shelters; Member National Trust, 1941; Advisory Cttee. on Internment and Repatriation of Enemy Aliens, 1939; Ministry of Labour Committee on Employment of Artists in War-time, 1939; Chairman of the People's Palace; Hon. Sec. of Wages Councils Advisory Council, Hon. Treasurer Workers' Educational Assoc., Workers' Travel Assoc.; Member Economic Advisory Council, Industrial Court, Central National Service Committee for Great Britain, and Aliens Deportation Advisory Committee (Home Office); Chairman of London Council for Voluntary Occupation during Unemployment; *b.* Manchester, 1875; *s.* of Felix Mallon, Co. Tyrone, and Mary O'Hare, Co.

Down; *m.* 1921, Stella Katherine, *e. d.* of late A. G. Gardiner. *Educ.:* Manchester University (Owens College). Secretary National League to establish a Minimum Wage, 1906; Member of first 13 Trade Boards established under Trade Boards Act, 1909, of Whitley Committee and of numerous other reconstruction Committees, 1917-20; of Committees appointed under Profiteering Act; Executive Committee, League of Nations Union; Executive Committee, British Empire Exhibition; Royal Commission on Licensing; Departmental Committee on Cinematograph Films Act; Departmental Committee on Adoption Societies and Agencies; Board of Governors of B.B.C., 1937-39 and 1941-46; Nat. Assistance Board, 1940-48; London Museum and Whitechapel Art Gallery; Post Office Advisory Committee. Margaret McMillan Medal, 1955. *Publications:* various booklets on women's work, minimum wage, etc.; contributor to Observer, Daily News, Guardian, etc. *Recreation:* golf. *Address:* Whiteleaf, Aylesbury, Bucks. *T.:* Princes Risborough 421. *Club:* Reform.
[*Died* 12 *April* 1961.

MALONE, Surgeon Rear-Admiral Albert Edward, C.B. 1946; B.A. Dublin, 1908; M.B., B.Ch., B.A.O. 1911; D.P.H. Belfast, 1923. *Educ.:* Trinity College, Dublin. Served European War, 1914-18 and War of 1939-45; Surgeon Capt. 1934; Surgeon Rear-Admiral 1943; retired list, 1947. *Address:* 16 Queens Keep, Palmerston Road, Southsea, Hants.
[*Died* 19 *May* 1970.

MALONE, Lt.-Col. Cecil L'Estrange, M.I.N.; *s.* of late Rev. Savile L'Estrange Malone; *m.* 1st, 1921, Leah (*d.* 1951), *yr. d.* of Arthur and Regina Kay; one *d.*; 2nd, 1956, Dorothy Nina Cheetham, *d.* of late Ernest H. and Nina Neal. *Educ.:* Cordwalles, Maidenhead; Royal Naval College, Dartmouth. Entered Royal Navy, 1905; selected to undergo flying course at Eastchurch (the 2nd course approved by the Admiralty), 1911; took part in Army Manœuvres, flying a twin-engined triple-screwed Short biplane, 1912; flew off foc'sle of H.M.S. London steaming 12 knots; commanded R.N.A.S. units in raid on Cuxhaven, 25 Dec. 1914 (despatches); in command H.M.S. Ben-my-Chree, March 1915; served in Dardanelles campaign till final evacuation (despatches); aeroplanes carrying torpedoes were used for the first time on record, and three seaplanes from H.M.S. Ben-My-Chree successfully torpedoed three enemy vessels, 1916; commanded E. Indies and Egypt Seaplane Squadron (Order of the Nile); appointed to Plans Division Admiralty, 1918; First British Air Attaché, Brit. Embassy, Paris, and Air Representative Supreme War Council, Versailles, 1918; M.P. (Co. L.) East Leyton, 1918-22; M.P. (Lab.) Northampton, 1928-31; Parliamentary Private Secretary to the Minister of Pensions, 1931; Staff Officer to Chief Warden, City of Westminster Civil Defence, 1942; Admiralty Small Vessels Pool, 1943-45. Chm., London Nautical School; Governor, School of Navigation, Southampton; Chm. and Hon. Organiser, " How Do I Go To Sea " Courses; Fellow Royal Aeronautical Society. *Publications:* The Russian Republic; New China; Manchoukuo, Jewel of Asia. *Recreation:* squash. *Address:* 1 Grove Court, Drayton Gardens, S.W.10. *T.:* Fremantle 5765. *Club:* Royal Aero. [*Died* 25 *Feb.* 1965.

MALONE, Sir Clement, Kt., *cr.* 1945; O.B.E. 1939; Q.C. (Windward Islands and Leeward Islands); 2nd *s.* of late Walter Whittingham Malone and Florence Henrietta Malone (*née* Hart), St. Johns, Antigua, B.W.I.; *m.* 1917, Ethel Louise, *e. d.* of late S. D. Malone and Mrs. Malone, Nevis, B.W.I.; three *s.* *Educ.:* Antigua Gram. Sch. Called to Bar, Middle Temple, 1916; practised as a Barrister-at-Law in the Leeward Is.; Mem. of Executive and Legislative Councils of St. Christopher and Nevis, and of Leeward Islands, 1923-40; Chief Justice of Supreme Court of Windward Islands and Leeward Islands and a Judge of the West Indian Court of Appeal, 1943-50; Puisne Judge, 1940-43; retired, 1950. *Recreations:* croquet and gardening. *Address:* 7 Parima Road. Valsayn Park, St. Joseph, Trinidad, W.I, *Club:* St. George's (Grenada).
[*Died* 9 *April* 1967.

MALONE, Herbert, Q.C. 1947; M.A., LL.B. (Belfast); *s.* of John Malone, Solicitor and Coroner for County Tyrone; *m.* 1925, Dorothy, *d.* of Major Clark, Barnt Green, Worcs.; one *s.* two *d.* *Educ.:* Castleknock Coll., Dublin; Queen's Coll., Belfast; Queen's College, Galway; Queen's University, Belfast (Law Scholar and Exhibitioner); Law School, Trinity College, Dublin. Joined Dublin Univ. Graduates O.T.C., 1915; commissioned R.F.A. (S.R.) and served overseas, 1915-16 (wounded); Home Service until 1919. Called to English Bar, Lincoln's Inn, 1919-21. Judicial Referee, one-third of England, under Insurance Acts. Practised in Newcastle upon Tyne and North-Eastern Circuit; moved to Temple, 1923; Contested (C.) S.W. Bethnal Green, 1929; Metropolitan Magistrate, 1948, resigned 1950; retired from Bar, 1952. *Publication:* ed. Law relating to Clubs. *Recreations:* tennis and swimming. *Address:* 14 Holman Court, Church Street, Ewell, Surrey.
[*Died* 9 *Sept.* 1962.

MALTBY, Henry Francis; Dramatist and Actor; *b.* Ceres, S. Africa, 25 Nov. 1880; *s.* of Henry Edward Maltby, C.E., and Johanna Henrietta Beck; *m.* 1924, Norah May Pickering. *Educ.:* Bedford School. First appeared on Stage with Sir Philip Ben Greet; one of the leading members of Miss Horniman's Manchester Company; appeared in many West End productions; since 1933 Dialogue and Scenario work on over 100 films including The Love Nest; Over the Garden Wall; Queen of Hearts; The Strange Adventures of Mr. Smith, and has acted in over seventy films; served during 1914-18 War in France and Flanders with Royal Garrison Artillery. *Publications:* Plays:—The Laughter of Fools, 1914; The Rotters, 1915; Petticoats, 1916; A Temporary Gentleman, 1919; Such a Nice Young Man, 1920; Maggie (with Fred Thompson), 1920; six Grand Guignol Plays, 1921-22; Mr. Budd of Kennington, 1922; Three Birds, 1923; The Right Age to Marry, 1925; What Might Happen, 1926; Our Countess, 1928; Something More Important, 1928; Bees and Honey, 1929; The Shingled Honeymoon, 1930; For the Love of Mike, 1931; The Age of Youth; Fifty-Fifty; Rings on Her Fingers; When Churchyards Yawn, 1932; Jack O'Diamonds (with Clifford Grey), 1935; The Shadow, 1936; Off the Gold Coast (with Clifford Grey), 1937; The Master Key, 1937; Susie; Nightingale House, 1942; Dusk to Dawn; The Complete Wangler, 1943; Meet Me Victoria, 1944; Have a Heart, 1945; Love Hunger, 1946; Ring Up the Curtain (Memoirs), 1950; Curtain Up (Further Memoirs), 1952; Wet Week at Westbourne; May I borrow your Wife?, 1953. *Recreations:* reading, swimming. *Address:* 60A Langdale Gardens, Hove, Sussex. *T.:* Hove 33485. *Clubs:* Savage, Dramatists.
[*Died* 25 *Oct.* 1963.

MALTWOOD, Mrs. Katharine, F.R.S.A.; sculptor and author. *Educ.:* The Slade. *Publications:* A Guide to Glastonbury's Temple of the Stars, 1935 (rev. edn. 1949); Air View Supplement to Temple of the Stars, 1937; The Enchantments of

Britain, King Arthur's Round Table of the Zodiac, 1946. *Recreation:* travel. *Address:* The Thatch, Royal Oak, Vancouver I., B.C. [*Died* 29 *July* 1961.

MANCE, Brigadier-General Sir H. Osborne, K.B.E., *cr.* 1929; C.B. 1918; C.M.G. 1917; D.S.O. 1902; late R.E.; Technical Adviser to Ottoman Bank, 1924-1962; President, Institute of Transport, 1949; *b.* 2 Oct. 1875; *e. s.* of Sir Henry C. Mance, C.I.E.; *m.* 1911, Elsie, *y. d.* of Major-General W. Stenhouse, Indian Army; two *s.* one *d.* *Educ.:* Bedford School. Served S. African War as Dep. Asst. Director of Railways and Armoured Trains, Kimberley line (despatches, Queen's medal with clasp, King's medal 2 clasps, D.S.O.); employed on construction of Baro-Kano Railway, 1908-11; European War, 1914-18; Director of Railways, Light Railways and Roads, War Office, 1916-20 (Bt. Lt.-Col. C.M.G., C.B.); Transportation Adviser to British Delegation, Paris, 1919-20; Pres. Communications Section of Supreme Economic Council, 1919-20; retired from the Army with rank of Colonel and hon. rank of Brig.-Gen., 1924; British Director on Board of German Railway Co., 1925-30; Financial Report Austrian Railways, 1933; Reported Co-ordination of Transport East Africa, 1936; Director of Canals, Ministry of War Transport, 1941-44; Brit. Mem. Transport and Communications Commn. of U.N., 1946-54; Brit. Delegate, Central Rhine Commn., 1946-1957; Hon. Member Roy. Inst. of Internat. Affairs; Triennial Gold Medal Institute of Transport, 1926. *Publications:* The Road and Rail Transport Problem, 1940; International Telecommunications, 1943; International Air Transport, 1943; International River and Canal Transport, 1944; Internat. Sea Transport, 1945; International Road Transport and Miscellaneous, 1946; Frontiers, Peace Treaties and International Organisation for Transport, 1946. *Address:* 38 Evelyn Mansions, Carlisle Place, S.W.1. *Club:* Army and Navy. [*Died* 30 *Aug.* 1966.

MANDER, Sir Frederick, Kt., *cr.* 1938; Hon. M.A. Oxford, 1935; Hon. F.E.I.S.; Chairman, Bedford C.C., 1952-62; General Secretary, N.U.T., 1931-Easter 1947; *b.* 12 July 1883; *s.* of Arthur and Caroline Mander, Luton; *m.* 1911, Hilda Irene, *d.* of Thomas William Sargent, Wakefield, Yorks; two *s.* one *d.* *Educ.:* Higher Grade School, Luton; Westminster Training College; Bachelor of Science (London University). Headmaster at Luton, 1915-31; Chairman, Newnes Educational Publishing Co. Ltd.; Member: Executive of Assoc. of Education Cttees., Cttee. on Education of Spastics (Vice-Chm.); Vice-Pres. of Nat. Foundation for Educational Research in England and Wales; Hon. Member, General Council of the Save the Children Fund. *Publications:* contribr. to educational press. *Address:* The White Lodge, Wainholm Gardens, Toddington, Beds. *T.:* Toddington 232. *Club:* National Liberal. [*Died* 27 *Feb.* 1964.

MANDER, Sir Geoffrey Le Mesurier, Kt., *cr.* 1945; *b.* 6 March 1882; *s.* of late S. Theodore Mander, Wightwick Manor, Wolverhampton, and Flora St. C., *d.* of H. N. Paint, M.P., Canada; *m.* 1st, 1906, R. Florence (from whom he obtained a divorce, 1930), *d.* of Col. Caverhill, Montreal; one *s.* two *d.*; 2nd, 1930, Rosalie Glynn, *o. c.* of A. C. Grylls, M.A.; one *s.* one *d.* *Educ.:* Harrow; Trinity Coll., Camb., M.A. Dir. (late Chm.), Mander Brothers, Ltd., Wolverhampton; M.P. (L.) East Wolverhampton, 1929-45; Parliamentary Private Secretary to Sir Archibald Sinclair, Secretary of State for Air, 1942-45; High Sheriff of Staffordshire, 1921; Barrister-at-law, Inner Temple; J.P. Staffs and Wolverhampton. *Recreations:* walking, tennis. *Address:* Wightwick Manor, Wolverhampton. *Clubs:* Reform, Royal Air Force. [*Died* 9 *Sept.* 1962.

MANDERS, Horace Craigie, C.I.E. 1931; V.D.; late A.D.C. to the Viceroy; late Colonel commanding Assam Valley Light Horse (Auxiliary Force, India); tea planter, Assam Frontier Tea Coy., Ltd.; *b.* 5 Dec. 1882; *s.* of late Horace Manders, M.D., F.R.C.S., V.D. and late Elizabeth Louisa, *d.* of G. P. Goode, Haverfordwest, Wales; *m.* Muriel Brenda (*d.* 1934), *d.* of late Vernon Hawkins, Southsea; no *c.* *Educ.:* Epsom College. Went out to South African War with Rough Riders 20th Batt. I.Y., April 1900; received a commission in 59th I.Y., Oxford Hussars, Dec. 1900; invalided home, May 1901; returned again in August 1901 and remained until end of War; came out to Assam as a tea planter with the Assam Frontier Tea Coy., Ltd., 1903; returned home and joined the Royal Berks Regt., 1914; served with the 2nd Hants Regt., 29th Division at Gallipoli (despatches); joined 11th K.E.O. Lancers, I.A., 1918. *Recreations:* polo, tennis, music. *Address:* c/o National and Grindlay's Bank Ltd., 13 St. James's Square, S.W.1. *Club:* Oriental. [*Died* 11 *Nov.* 1963.

MANDEVILLE, Rt. Rev. Gay Lisle Griffith, M.A.; retd.; *b.* 20 May 1894; *s.* of William Fitzherbert Mandeville and Helen (*née* Cook); *m.* 1921, Mary Ifil Buhot Glegg; three *d.* *Educ.:* Harrison College and Codrington College, Barbados. B.A. 1915; M.A. (Hons. Theol.) Dunelm, 1921. Deacon, 1917; priest, 1918; Curate of St. George, St. Kitts, 1917-21; Rector of Saba, Dutch West Indies, 1921-26; Vicar of St. Bartholomew, Barbados, 1926-28; Vicar of St. Stephen, Barbados, and Chaplain of the Leper Asylum, 1928-43; Secretary of the Barbados Synod, 1929-33; Chaplain of the Sisterhood of St. John the Baptist, 1929-43; Rector of St. Philip, Barbados, 1943-50; Vicar General, Barbados, 1948-51; Canon (St. Cyprian), 1950; Dean, 1950-51; Bishop of Barbados, 1951-60. *Address:* Pleshey, Paynes Bay, St. James, Barbados. [*Died* 19 *July* 1969.

MANGHAM, Sydney, M.A. (Cantab.); Emeritus Professor of Botany, University of Southampton, since 1951; *b.* 15 May 1886; *s.* of Harry and Louisa Mangham; *m.* 1912, Effie Alice Moorhouse (*d.* 1957); one *s.* one *d.* (and one *s.* killed in action, 1944). *Educ.:* Bancroft's School, Woodford, Essex; Emmanuel College, Cambridge (Exhibitioner). Nat. Sci. Trip., Pt. II, Botany, Cl. I, 1908; Univ. Frank Smart Student (Botany), 1908-1910; research in plant physiology, 1908-11. Lecturer in Botany, Armstrong (now King's) College, Newcastle on Tyne, 1911-20; Bacteriologist, R.N. Coll., Greenwich, 1915-18; Prof. of Botany, Southampton, 1920-51. Australian tour, Sept. 1951 - Jan. 1953; Curator of University Grounds, 1953-57. *Publications:* Introduction to Botany, 1926; A First Biology, A Second Biology (with W. R. Sherriffs), 1928, 1930; Textbook of Biology (with A. R. Hockley), 1938, 1951; Earth's Green Mantle, 1939, 1945, 1947. Papers in New Phytologist, Annals of Botany, Nature, etc. *Recreations:* gardening, photography, painting. *Address:* c/o Barclays Bank, 30 High St., Southampton. [*Died* 30 *July* 1962.

MANLEY, Norman Washington, M.M. 1917; Q.C. (Jam.); *b.* 4 July 1893; *m.* 1921, Edna Swithenbank; two *s.* *Educ.:* Jamaica College; Jesus College, Oxford. Rhodes Scholar, 1914. Called to Bar, 1921; apptd. K.C., 1931. Founder-Pres., People's National Party, Jamaica, 1938; Chief Minister, Jamaica, 1955-59; Premier, 1959-1962; Leader of the Opposition, 1962; retd. 1969. Hon. LL.D. Howard Univ., U.S.A., 1947. Hon. Fellow Jesus College, Oxford, 1960. *Recreations:* reading and music. *Address:* Kingston, Jamaica. [*Died* 2 *Sept.* 1969.

MANN, Harold Hart, D.Sc., F.R.I.C., F.L.S., F.R.G.S.; Assistant Director, Woburn Experimental Station (Lawes Agricultural Trust) 1928-56; *b.* 16 Oct. 1872; *s.* of late W. E. Mann of York; *m.* 1913, Katharine, *d.* of Rev. J. H. Collie, M.A., of Claughton, Birkenhead. *Educ.:* Elmfield School, York; Yorkshire Coll., Leeds; Pasteur Institute, Paris. Chemical Assistant for Research to the Royal Agricultural Society, 1895-98; Resident Chemist Woburn Experimental Farm of the Royal Agricultural Society, 1898-1900; Scientific Officer to the Indian Tea Association, Calcutta, 1900-7; Principal, Agricultural College, Poona, and Agricultural Chemist to the Govt. of Bombay, 1907-18; Director of Agriculture Bombay Presidency, 1918-20 and 1921-27; Agricultural Adviser to the Nizam's Government, 1928 and 1929; Adviser on tea cultivation to the Soviet Government, 1930, 1931 and 1933; to the Tanganyika and Nyasaland Governments, 1932; to the Iran Government, 1935; to the Turkish Government, 1940; Member Bombay Legislative Council, 1925; Kaiser-i-Hind Medal of the First Class, 1917. *Publications:* numerous on questions relating to tea culture and manufacture, and many other Indian agricultural questions; (with Sir G. Watt) The Pests and Blights of the Tea Plant; Statistical Atlas of the Bombay Presidency, 1925; also on sociological and economic subjects, specially Land and Labour in a Deccan Village, Parts I. and II., 1918 and 1921. *Recreation:* social study. *Address:* Bivia, Woodside, Aspley Guise, Bletchley, Bucks. *T.:* Woburn Sands 2316. *Club:* Royal Commonwealth Society. [*Died* 2 *Dec.* 1961.

MANN, Sir James Gow, K.C.V.O. 1957; Kt. 1948; M.A., B.Litt., F.B.A.; Surveyor of the Queen's Works of Art since 1952 (of King George VI's Works of Art, 1946-52); Master of the Armouries, The Tower of London, since 1939; Director of the Wallace Collection since 1936; Hon. Vice-President of the Society of Antiquaries (Director 1944-49, President 1949-54); Chairman, National Buildings Record; Member: Advisory Cttee., Royal Mint; Archbishop's Historic Churches Preservation Trust; Royal Commission on Historical Monuments (England); Historic Buildings Council for England; a Trustee, College of Arms; a Governor of the National Army Museum; *b.* 23 Sept. 1897; *s.* of Alexander Mann; *m.* 1st, 1926 Mary (*d.* 1956), *d.* of Rev. Dr. G. A. Cooke; one *d.*; 2nd, 1958, Evelyn Aimée, *e. d.* of late Charles Richard Hughes, Wilmslow, Cheshire. *Educ.:* Winchester; New Coll., Oxford. Served European War, 1916-19, Flanders and Italian fronts; late Major Royal Artillery, T.A. (Oxfordshire Yeomanry); Assistant-Keeper, Department of Fine Art, Ashmolean Museum, Oxford, 1921-24; Assistant to the Keeper of the Wallace Collection, 1924-32; Deputy-Director of the Courtauld Institute of Art, and Reader in the History of Art, University of London, 1932-36; mem. of committee of Exhibition of British Art, R.A., 1934, Portuguese Art, 1955-56, British Portraits, 1956-1957; visited Spain with Sir Frederic Kenyon at the request of the Spanish Government to inspect measures taken to protect works of art during the Civil War, 1937; Member and Hon. Secretary of British Committee for the Restitution of Works of Art in enemy hands, 1943-46. *Publications:* The Armoury of the Castle of Churburg (with Count Trapp), 1929; Armour of the Maximilian Period and of the Italian Wars, 1929; The Armour in The Sanctuary of the Madonna delle Grazie, near Mantua, 1930 and 1939; Catalogue of the Sculpture in the Wallace Collection, 1931; English Church Monuments, 1536-1625; Spanish Armour of the Xth-XVth Centuries, 1933; Plate Armour in Germany in the XIVth and XVth Centuries, 1935; The Lost Armoury of the Gonzagas, 1939-45; The etched Decoration of Armour (Harriet Hertz Annual Lecture, British Academy); Wallace Collection Catalogue of European Arms and Armour, 1962; articles in various journals and works of reference. *Recreations:* studying and collecting arms and armour, and European travel. *Address:* 23 Chapel Street, S.W.1. *Clubs:* Athenæum, Beefsteak. [*Died* 5 *Dec.* 1962.

MANN, Mrs. Jean, *d.* of Wm. Stewart, Glasgow; *widow* of Wm. Lawrence Mann (*d.* 1958); three *s.* two *d.* *Educ.:* Glasgow. Accountant. Ex-Convener of Housing and Ex-Senr. Magistrate City of Glasgow. M.P. (Lab.) Coatbridge Division of Lanark, 1945-50, Coatbridge and Airdrie, 1950-59. President Town and Country Planning Association (Scotland); Hon. Life Member of Royal Society for Prevention of Accidents; Vice-President, Hæmophilia Society; Member National Executive Labour Party, 1953-58. Ex-Editor, Scottish Town and County Councillor. Police Judge (Scotland). *Publications:* Replanning Scotland, 1942; Woman in Parliament, 1962. *Address:* Redcliff, 18 Albert Rd., Gourock, Renfrewshire. *T.:* Gourock 32385. [*Died* 21 *March* 1964.

MANN, Rt. Rev. John Charles; Hon D.D. Univ. of Glasgow, 1944; Assistant Bishop of Rochester since 1950; *b.* 6 Feb. 1880; *er. s.* of Charles and Eleanor Elizabeth Mann; *m.* 1908, Alice Ethel (*d.* 1950), *yr. d.* of Andrew and Jane Christina Maclure; two *s.* (one *d.* decd.). *Educ.:* Univ. of Glasgow; Ridley Hall, Camb. M.A. (Glas.) 1900. Curate St. Luke's, Maidstone, 1903; Church Missionary Society missionary, Nagasaki, 1905; Bishop in Kyushu, 1935-40; Asst. Bishop and Hon. Canon in Diocese of Rochester, 1941-47 and 1950-; Sec. of C.M.S., 1941-47; Proctor in Convocation, 1945-47 and 1953-59; formerly Secretary of the Church Missionary Society's Japan Mission and Examining Chaplain to Bishop in Kobe and Bishop of Osaka; Counsellor to Nippon Sei Ko Kwai (Japan Holy Catholic Church), 1947-50. *Address:* Mabledon, Tonbridge, Kent. [*Died* 28 *April* 1967.

MANN, Major William Edgar, D.S.O. 1917; late R.F.A.; *b.* 1885; 2nd *s.* of Sir Edward Mann, 1st Bt., and *b.* and *heir-pres.* to Sir John Mann, 2nd Bt.; *m.* 1913, Sarah Douglas, *d.* of late Col. Sir Alexander Sprot, 1st Bt.; two *d.* (one *s.* decd.). *Educ.:* Marlborough; R.M.A., Woolwich. Served European War, 1914-18 (twice wounded, despatches, D.S.O.); retired pay, 1926. *Address:* Earl Soham Lodge, Woodbridge, Suffolk. *Club:* Naval and Military. [*Died* 14 *Feb.* 1969.

MANN, Air Cdre. William Edward George, C.B. 1956; C.B.E. 1942; D.F.C. 1918; M.I.E.E.; p.s.a.; Air Commodore retired, Royal Air Force; *b.* 1899; *s.* of William Henry Mann; *m.*; one *s.* one *d.* *Educ.:* St. Paul's School. Joined Royal Naval Air Service, 1917 and served with No. 8 Royal Naval Squadron in France; transferred to R.A.F., 1918. Central Flying School, 1920-24, U.K., Iraq, Palestine, Egypt, 1925-38. Served War of 1939-1945; in Middle East as Chief Signal Officer; in N. Africa as Air Signals Officer-in-Chief (despatches, C.B.E., Officer of American Legion of Merit), 1939-42. Group Captain, 1939; Air Commodore, 1941; retired, 1945. Civil Aviation Signals representative, Cairo, 1945; Director of Telecommunications, Ministry of Civil Aviation, 1948-50; Dir.-General of Civil Aviation Navigational Services, Ministry of Transport and Civil Aviation, 1950-59; retired from Civil Service, Dec. 1959. Middle East Rep. of Decca Navigator Co., 1960-61; returned to U.K., 1961. *Address:* Yn Fea, Awbridge, Romsey, Hampshire. *T.:* Lockerley 366. *Club:* Royal Air Force. [*Died* 4 *May* 1966.

MANNING, Brian O'Donoghue, C.B.E. 1960; D.L., J.P.; *b.* 30 June 1891; *s.* of late Dr. T. Manning, Co. Kerry, and of late Dowager Viscountess Simon, D.B.E.; *m.* 1922, Gertrude Louise (*d.* 1962), *d.* of late John Joseph Bithell, Seville, Spain; two *d.* *Educ.:* St. Stephen's Green Sch., Dublin; Dover Coll. Chartered Acct.; Member of firm of Gundry, Cole & Co.; served European War, 1914-18, Lieut. Irish Guards (spec. res.); Member Departmental Committee on adoption societies and agencies; Member Home Secretary's Advisory Committee for House-to-House Collections Act, 1939; Member General Claims Tribunal, Compensation (Defence) Act, 1939; Director: Woolwich Equitable Building Society (Vice-Chairman); Shipman and King Cinemas, Ltd. (Chairman); Selayang Tin Dredging (Chairman), 1964-. D.L. 1936, J.P. 1934, County of London. Governor of Dover College and of Woolwich Polytechnic. Past Pres. London Irish Rugby Football Club. *Publications:* (with late Andrew Binnie) Receiver and Manager in Possession, 1935; The Technique and Principles of Auditing, 1951; Joint Editor, Simon's Income Tax. *Address:* 3 Selwyn House, Manor Fields, Putney Hill, S.W.15; Brewers' Hall, Aldermanbury Sq., E.C.2. *Clubs:* Guards, Royal Air Force. [*Died* 22 *Sept.* 1964.

MANNING, Sir Henry Edward, K.B.E. *cr.* 1939; Q.C. 1928; M.L.C. 1932-58; *b.* 1877; *s.* of late Sir William Patrick Manning; *m.* Nora (*d.* 1962), *d.* of late Sir James Martin two *d.* *Educ.:* St. Ignatius College, Sydney; University of Sydney. Admitted to Bar of N.S.W. 1902; Attorney General and Vice-President of Executive Council, New South Wales, 1932-41. *Address:* 11 Wentworth Street, Point Piper, Sydney. *Club:* Australian (Sydney). [*Died* 2 *May* 1963.

MANNIX, Most Rev. Daniel, D.D., LL.D.; Archbishop of Melbourne (R.C.), since 1917; late member of Senate, National Univ. of Ireland; *b.* Charleville, Co. Cork, Ireland, 4 March 1864. *Educ.:* Christian Schools, Charleville; St. Colman's College, Fermoy; St. Patrick's College, Maynooth. Professor of Mental and Moral Philosophy at St. Patrick's College, Maynooth, 1891; Professor of Theology, 1894; Vice-President, 1903; President, 1903-12; Coadjutor Archbishop of Melbourne, 1912-17. *Address:* Raheen, 94 Studley Park Road, Kew, Melbourne, E.4, Australia. [*Died* 5 *Nov.* 1963.

MANSEL, Major Rhys Clavell; *b.* 8 Feb. 1891; *s.* of Col. John Delalynde Mansel and Mildred, *d.* of late Arthur Guest; *m.* 1916, Sylvia (*d.* 1944), *d.* of Sir Guy Campbell, 3rd Bt.; one *s.* three *d.*; *m.* 1947, Archie Anne, *er. d.* of late H. M. Cairnes, Fox Hall, Raheny, Co Dublin, Ireland; one *s.* *Educ.:* Eton; Sandhurst. Rifle Bde., 1911; Capt. 1915; Major, 1917; served European War (wounded, despatches); War of 1939-45. J.P. 1930-52, D.L. 1933-52, Dorset; High Sheriff for Dorset, 1938-39 *Address:* Ropley Manor, Hampshire. *T.:* Ropley 3337. [*Died* 9 *Sept.* 1969.

MANSERGH, Gen. Sir (E. C.) Robert, G.C.B. 1956 (K.C.B. 1953; C.B. 1946); K.B.E. 1947 (C.B.E. 1946; O.B.E. 1942); M.C. 1932; Commander-in-Chief of the United Kingdom Land Forces, 1956-59, retd.; A.D.C. General to the Queen, 1956-59; Master Gunner, St. James's Park, since 1960; *b.* 12 May 1900; *s.* of C. L. W. Mansergh, C.B.E., I.S.O. *Educ.:* Rondebosch, South Africa; R.M.A., Woolwich. Commissioned in 1920 in R.F.A.; served U.K. and abroad, Regimental and Staff, appointed R.H.A.; Military Mission to Iraq, 1931-35; Adjt. R.M.A., Woolwich; served War of 1939-45. Eritrea, Abyssinia, W. Desert, Libya, Middle East, Persia and Iraq Force, Arakan, Assam, Burma, Liberation Singapore; Lt.-Col. 1941; Col. 1945; Actg. Maj.-Gen. 1944; Comdg. 11 (E.A.) Div 1945; 5th Indian Div. 1945; Maj.-Gen. 1946; Actg. Lieut.-Gen. 1946; Commander 15th Indian Corps; C.-in-C. Allied Forces, Netherlands East Indies, 1946; Director Territorial Army and Cadets, 1947; Lieut.-Gen. 1948; Military Sec. to Secretary of State for War, 1948-49; Commander, British Forces, Hong Kong, 1949-51; Deputy C.-in-C., Allied Forces, Northern Europe, 1951-53, Commander-in-Chief, 1953-56. Gen. 1953. Order of Rafidain, 1935. Col. Comdt. R.A. 1950-; Col. Comdt. R.H.A. 1957-. President, Westminster Chamber of Commerce, 1962-63. *Recreation:* gardening. *Address:* 66 Abbotsbury Close, W.14. *Club:* Travellers'. [*Died* 8 *Nov.* 1970.

MANSERGH, Admiral Sir Maurice (James), K.C.B., *cr.* 1952 (C.B. 1945); C.B.E. 1941; retired; *b.* 14 Oct. 1896; 2nd *s.* of Ernest Lawson Mansergh, M.Inst.C.E., and Emma Cecilia Fischer Hogg; *m.* 1921, Violet Elsie, *yr. d.* of Bernard Hillman, Hove; two *s.* two *d.* *Educ.:* Lindley Lodge, nr. Nuneaton; R.N. Colleges, Osborne and Dartmouth. Midshipman, H.M.S. Zealandia, 1914; Lieut., 1918; specialised in Navigation, 1921; Lieut.-Comdr. 1925; Commander, 1930; R.N. Staff College, 1933; Staff of C.-in-C., Med. 1934-36; H.M.S. Rodney (as Exec. Officer), 1936-37; Captain, 1937; Imperial Defence College, 1938; Director of Trade Division, Admiralty, 1939-41; Deputy Assistant Chief of Naval Staff (Trade) (as Commodore 2nd Class), 1941; Commanded H.M.S. Gambia, 1941-43; Deputy Chief of Staff and later Chief of Staff (as Commodore 1st class) to Allied Naval C.-in-C., Expeditionary Force for invasion of Normandy, 1943-45; Commodore 1st class commanding 15th Cruiser Squadron, 1945-46; Rear-Adm., 1946; Naval Sec. to First Lord of Admiralty, 1946-1948; Commanding 3rd Aircraft Carrier Squadron, 1948-49; Vice-Adm. 1949; Lord Commissioner of the Admiralty, Fifth Sea Lord, and Deputy Chief of the Naval Staff (Air), 1949-51; Admiral, 1953; Commander-in-Chief, Plymouth, 1951-53; retired 1954. Legion of Honour and Croix de Guerre (with palm), 1945; Legion of Merit (U.S.), 1946. *Address:* 48 Bilton Towers, Great Cumberland Place, W.1. [*Died* 29 *Sept.* 1966.

MANSERGH, Gen. Sir Robert; *see* Mansergh, Sir E. C. R.

MANSFIELD, Purcell James, Hon. R.C.M., F.R.C.O., A.R.C.M., L.Mus. T.C.L., L.L.C.M., Gold and Bronze Medallist, Bristol Eisteddfod 1905; Organist and Choirmaster of Hyndland Parish Church, Glasgow, since 1949; *b.* Torquay, 24 May 1889; *s.* of late Dr. Orlando A. Mansfield; *m.*; one *s.* one *d.* *Educ.:* Privately. Organist of Paignton Wesleyan Church, 1905-08; Bideford Wesleyan Church, 1908-10; Park Parish Church, Glasgow, 1910-19; Paisley Abbey, 1919-22; Organist to Corp. of Paisley (Clark Town Hall), 1919-24; Pollokshields-Titwood Parish Church, Glasgow, 1922-49. Organ Recitals: for Corp. of Glasgow (Art Galls., City Hall, St. Andrews Hall); at Westminster Cath. (R.C.), Newcastle Cath., St. Giles Cath., Edin., Glasgow Cath., etc.; also Organ Recitals for B.B.C. Conductor: Anchor Mills Ladies' Choir, Paisley, 1932-39; S.C.W.S. Welfare Choir, 1932-39; Peripatetic Singing teacher under Renfrewshire Educn. Authority, 1920-67. Pres. Glasgow Soc. of Organists, 1921-22; Pres. Glasgow Congress of Inc. Assoc. of Organists, 1956; Hon. Vice-Pres., Inc. Assoc. of Organists; Hon. Vice-Pres., Edin. Soc. of Organists; Chm. Alfred Hollins Memorial Cttee. *Publications:* Six Concert Overtures and over 60 miscellaneous pieces for Organ; Piano pieces and songs; Arrangements for Chorus of Negro Spirituals, Scots Songs, Christmas Carols (in 2, 3, and 4 parts); Operettas (4), etc. Musical Ed., British Students' Song Book, 1927. *Recreations:* photography, stamps, motoring. *Address:* 26 Mosspark Avenue, Glasgow, S.W.2. *T.:* Ibrox 0616.

[*Died* 24 *Sept.* 1968.

MANSFIELD, Wilfrid Stephen, C.B.E. 1946; M.A.; Fellow of Emmanuel Coll., Cambridge, since 1936; Vice-Master, 1958-61; Univ. Lecturer in Agriculture, 1926-59; Director Univ. Farm, Cambridge, 1929-59; *b.* 28 Feb. 1894; *s.* of Alfred Charles Mansfield and Alice Eliza, *d.* of S. L. Young; *m.* 1918, Sybil Madeline Southwell; three *d.* *Educ.:* Perse School; Emmanuel College, Cambridge. 2nd King Edwards Horse and 8th Hussars, 1914-18; Agricultural Officer Food Production Dept., 1918-19; Advisory Agriculturalist Cambridge University Dept. of Agriculture, 1919-26; Minister of Agriculture's Liaison Officer for the Eastern Counties, 1940-45. *Recreation:* shooting. *Address:* 12 Barton Road, Cambridge. *T.:* Cambridge 53396. [*Died* 27 *Nov.* 1968.

MANSHIP, Paul; Sculptor; *b.* St. Paul, Minnesota, 25 Dec. 1885; *s.* of Charles H. Manship and Marietta Friend; *m.* 1913, Isabel G. McIlwaine; one *s.* three *d.* *Educ.:* Public Schools, St. Paul; Pennsylvania Academy of Fine Arts, Philadelphia; winner of Prize Scholarship to American Academy in Rome, 1909-12; Barnett Prize for Sculpture, National Academy of Design, 1913 and 1917; Widener Gold Medal for Sculpture, Pennsylvania Academy of Fine Arts, 1913; gold medal Panama Pacific International Exposition, 1914; gold medal American Institute of Architects, 1921; medal for Numismatics, Am. Numismatic Soc., 1924; gold medal Phila. Art Assoc., 1925; Gold Medal Sesquicentennial Exposition, Philadelphia, 1926; Diplome d'Honneur, Paris Exposition, 1937; Medal of Honor National Sculpture Society, 1942; Gold Medal, National Institute of Arts and Letters, 1945; St. Luca Internat. Award for sculpture, Florence, 1960. Pres. Nat. Sculpture Soc., 1939-42; Pres., Alumni Assoc. Amer. Acad. Rome, 1939-42; Vice-Pres. Nat. Acad. of Design, 1942-48; Pres. Amer. Acad. of Arts and Letters, 1948-54; Chairman Smithsonian Commission of Fine Arts, Washington, D.C., 1946-64; Member Nat. Sculpture Soc., Amer. Acad. of Arts and Letters, Nat. Inst. of Arts and Letters, Commission of Fine Arts, Washington, D.C., 1937-41; F.A.A.S.; Fellow Amer. Acad. Rome; Corresponding Member Academia Nacional de Bellas Artes, Buenos Aires, 1944, Institut de France, 1946; Chevalier Légion d'Honneur, France, 1929; National Academy, St. Luca, Italy, 1952. Works, including a number of portrait busts, in many museums and art institutes. Designer of many medals. *Publications:* Contributor to Encyclopædia Britannica of articles on Decorative Sculpture and The History of Sculpture. *Address:* 15 Gramercy Park, New York 3, N.Y., U.S.A. *Clubs:* (Pres. 1950-54) Century, National Arts (New York); Art (Washington, D.C.).

[*Died* 31 *Jan.* 1966.

MANSON, Robert George, C.I.E. 1944; E.D.; M.Inst.T.; *b.* 16 April 1893; *s.* of late Robert Kirkland Manson; *m.* 1926, Mary E., *d.* of John Grant, Downpatrick; one *s.* one *d.* *Educ.:* Ayr Grammar School. Trained on Glasgow & South-Western Rly. Joined Assam Bengal Railway, 1914, as Asst. Traffic Supt.; Agent and General Manager, 1940; also Chairman, Chittagong Port Commissioners; Officiating General Manager, Bengal and Assam Railway, India, 1945-46; also Port Commissioner, Calcutta Port, 1945-46. *Recreation:* golf. *Address:* Shillong, Nutley Road, Donnybrook, Dublin, Eire. *T.:* Dublin 691028.

[*Died* 28 *April* 1969.

MANSON-BAHR, Sir Philip, Kt. 1941; C.M.G. 1938; D.S.O. 1917; Fellow Washington Acad. Med.; M.A., M.D., F.R.C.P. Lond., M.R.C.S. Eng., D.T.M. and H. Camb., F.Z.S.; Consulting Physician in Tropical Diseases; late Cons. Physician to the Colonial Office and Crown Agents for the Colonies, retd. 1961; late Dir., Clinical Division, London School of Hygiene and Tropical Medicine; President: Medical Art Society; Chairman British Ornithologists' Club; Consulting Physician Hosp. for Tropical Diseases; *b.* 1881; *m.* 1909, Edith Margaret (*d.* 1948), *d.* of late Sir Patrick Manson, G.C.M.G.; one *s.* three *d.*; *m.* 1950, Edith Mary Grossmith. *Educ.:* Rugby; Cambridge; London Hospital. Formerly Pres. Royal Soc. of Tropical Medicine and Hygiene; and Pres. Med. Society of London; in charge of Stanley Research Expedition to Fiji, 1909 and Ceylon, 1912-13; War Service (Egypt, Palestine), 1914-19. Hon. Member: French, Belgian, Dutch, American, German Socs. of Tropical Medicine. Brumpt prizeman, Paris, 1957. *Publications:* 7th to 16th editions of Manson's Tropical Diseases; The Life and Work of Sir Patrick Manson; The Dysenteric Disorders, 1939; Synopsis of Tropical Medicine, 1943; History of the School of Tropical Medicine in London, 1956; Patrick Manson, British Men of Science Series, 1962; also papers on ornithology and zoology and on tropical medicine. *Recreations:* painting, hunting, ornithology. *Address:* The Old Cottage, Pootings, Edenbridge, Kent. *T.:* Crockham Hill 242. *Club:* Athenæum.

[*Died* 19 *Nov.* 1966.

MANTON, 2nd Baron, *cr.* 1922, of Compton Verney, **George Miles Watson;** Captain The Life Guards; Director Newmarket Bloodstock Ltd.; *b.* 21 June 1899; *s.* of 1st Baron Manton and Frances Claire (*d.* 1944), *d.* of late Harold Nickols, of Sandford House, nr. Leeds; *S.* father, 1922; *m.* 1st, 1923, Alethea (who obtained a divorce, 1936), 2nd *d.* of late Col. Philip Langdale, O.B.E.; one *s.*; 2nd, 1938, Mrs. Leila Player, *o. d.* of late Major Philip Guy Reynolds, D.S.O. *Educ.:* Harrow School. Joined army Aug. 1917; 2nd Life Guards, 1918; resigned commission, 1923. *Heir:* *s.* Hon. Joseph Rupert Eric Robert Watson [*b.* 22 Jan. 1924; *m.* 1951, Mary Elizabeth, twin *d.* of Major T. D. Hallinan, Ashbourne, Glounthaune, Co. Cork; two *s.* three *d.*]. *Address:* Plumpton Place, near Lewes, Sussex. *Club:* White's.

[*Died* 10 *June* 1968.

MANTON, Brig. Lionel, D.S.O. 1917; O.B.E. 1923; late Royal Engineers; *b.* 1887; *m.* 1st, Beatrice Louise (*d.* 1920), *d.* of late R. L. Ross; one *s.* (and one son killed in action, Oct. 1943) one *d.*; 2nd, 1923, Joan, *d.* of G. H. Gifford, Lynch Cottage, Winchester; two *s.* Served European War, 1914-18 (despatches, D.S.O.); Inter-Allied Railway Commission, Cologne, 1922-26; Assistant Director of Transportation, British Troops in Egypt (temp.), 1935-36; Chief Engineer Malta, 1936; retired pay, 1936; Principal L.M. & S. Rly. School of Transport until Sept. 1939; Commandant No. 2 Railway Training Centre, 1939-41; Director of Transportation, India, Oct. 1941-June 1942; Principal, School of Transport (Railway Executive), 1937-51. *Address:* c/o Lloyds Bank Ltd., 6 Pall Mall, S.W.1.

[*Died* 23 *July* 1961.

MAPLESTONE, Philip Alan, D.S.O. 1917; D.Sc., M.B., B.S., D.T.M.; retd.; *m.* 1924, Isobel Alice, *d.* of C. V. Collins, Gisborne, Victoria; one *s.* Served European War, 1915-18 (despatches, D.S.O.). *Publications:* Nematode Parasites of Vertebrates (with

W. Yorke), 1926; numerous papers on Helminthology and Dermatology, etc., in Indian Journal Medical Research, Indian Medical Gazette and Records of the Indian Museum since 1927. *Recreation:* golf. *Address:* 25 Serpells Road, Templestowe, Victoria 3106, Australia. *Club:* Tasmanian (Hobart). [*Died* 13 *July* 1969.

MAPSON, Dr. Leslie William, F.R.S. 1969; Deputy Chief Scientific Officer, Agricultural Research Council, since 1967; *b.* 17 Nov. 1907; *s.* of William John and Elizabeth Mapson; *m.* 1949, Dorothy Lillian (*née* Pell); one *d. Educ.:* Univ. of Cambridge (B.A., Ph.D.). Scientific Officer, D.S.I.R., 1938; Principal Scientific Officer, 1950; Sen. Principal Scientific Officer, 1956. *Publications:* contribs. to The Vitamins; many scientific papers in Biochemical Jl. of New York Acad. of Sciences, and other scientific jls. *Recreations:* tennis, swimming, gardening. *Address:* Food Research Institute, Colney Lane, Norwich. *T.:* Norwich 56122 (ext. 57). [*Died* 3 *Dec.* 1970.

MAR, 29th Earl of, *cr. ante* 1404; **Lionel Walter Young Erskine,** Premier Earl of Scotland; 24th Baron Garioch, *cr. ante* 1404; *b.* 13 June 1891; *s.* of late Major Charles Walter Young (*d.* 1898) and Constance Barnes (*d.* 1936), *d.* of late Rev. John Lovick Johnson, Long Stratton, Norfolk; *S.* cousin, 1932; assumed surname of Erskine (registered in Court of Lord Lyon), 1933; unmarried. *Educ.:* privately. *Heir: cousin,* James Clifton of Mar, Master of Mar. *Address:* 12 Churchfield Road, Ealing, W.13. [*Died* 27 *Nov.* 1965.

MAR, Master of; *see* Garioch, Lord; David Charles of Mar.

MARATIB ALI, Sir Syed, Kt., *cr.* 1941; C.B.E. 1935; *b.* 1883; *m.* 1904, Syeda Mubarik Begam, *d.* of late Fakir Syed Iftikhar-ud-Din, C.I.E., Lahore. Director: industrial and commercial concerns. Ex-Pres. Pakistan Federation of Industries, etc.; Managing Proprietor, Syed A. & M. Wazir Ali, Importers/Exporters. *Address:* Nasheman, Davis Rd., Lahore, Pakistan. [*Died* 22 *May* 1961.

MARCHAND, Geoffrey Isidore Charles, C.B.E. 1949; J.P. (Herts and Middx.) 1951; *s.* of Isidore Henri Alphonse Marchand, M.B.E., C.A. Herts, J.P. Herts and Middx., and Anne Jane Marchand; *m.* 1st, 1913, Elsie Mary Russell-Smith (*d.* 1945); 2nd, 1948, Mary Ursula Atkins; no *c. Educ.:* Aldenham; St. John's College, Cambridge (M.A. 1912). Sec., Children's Country Holiday Fund, 1912-14; served European War, 1914-19, R.A.; France, Salonika, Palestine rank of Major; Deputy Mil. Sec. to F.M. Viscount Allenby, actg. Lt.-Col. (despatches); actg. Principal, Min. of Labour, Industrial Councils Div., 1919-20; Personal Asst. to Man. Dir. British Glass Industries Ltd., 1920-25; founded Glass Manufacturers' Fed., Director, 1925-49; Member: Bd. of Governors, Pottery and Glass Trades Benevolent Instn., 1923-49; Glass Delegacy, Sheffield Univ., 1928-49; Fellow Soc. of Glass Technology, Pres. 1946-49. Dep.-Chm. Nat. Youth Employment Council, 1946-; Vice-Chairman, National Dock Labour Board, 1951-53; Adviser on Professional Studies, British Institute of Management, 1951-53 and Deputy Chief Executive Officer, Institute of Industrial Administration, 1952-53. Ex-Vice-Chairman, Roy. Coll. of Art. Chm. Reg. Advisory Council for Higher Technological Education for London and Home Counties: Member: Employers' Panel, Nat. Arbitration Tribunal and Industrial Disputes Tribunal; Sen. Employers' Assessor, Nat. Service Hardship Appeal Court; Reinstatement in Civil Employment Appeal Court; various Govt. committees. F.I.A.A., Chm., 1943-46, Vice-President 1946; associated with British Employers' Confed. and F.B.I., 1922-49; frequently Employers' rep. at Internat. Labour Confs., Geneva, etc., 1924-45; Member, E. Barnet Urban D.C., 1927-38 and 1943-46, Chm. 1935. *Address:* Burles, Dippenhall, nr. Farnham, Surrey. [*Died* 5 *Feb.* 1965.

MARCHANT, Edgar Walford, D.Sc.; F.C.G.I.; Hon. M.I.E.E.; Emeritus Professor of Electrical Engineering in the Univ. of Liverpool; *b.* 1876; *o. s.* of John Harry and Fanny Ann Barnard Marchant; *m.* 1902, Mary Ethel Brooker (*d.* 1948); three *s.* (and one *s.* decd.). *Educ.:* University School, Hastings; Central Technical Coll., S. Kensington. Granville Scholar of the Univ. of London; Salomons Scholar of the Inst. of Electrical Engineers. After spending some time in a manufacturing firm, acted as director for three years of the private laboratory and works of Lord Blythswood near Glasgow; Demonstrator under Prof. Silvanus Thompson, 1900; Lecturer in Electrotechnics at University Coll., Liverpool, 1901; David Jardine Prof. of Electrical Engineering, University of Liverpool, 1903-41; Past-President of Institution of Electrical Engineers. *Publications:* Radio Telegraphy and Telephony, 1933; Introduction to Electrical Engineering, 1939; Scientific Papers to the Royal Society, Philosophical Magazine, Institution of Electrical Engineers, on Magnetic Properties of Iron at High Frequencies, Loss of Energy in Metal Plates due to Eddy Currents, Absorption of X-rays, Kelvin Lecture on High Frequency Currents, (with W. Duddell) on Oscillographs, Method of Testing Flaws in Metal Plates, a Portable Electrocardiograph, Measurement of Strength of Wireless Signals, the Heaviside Layer, Transmission of Electrical Energy at High Voltage, Transient Effects in Electricity Supply Systems, Heating of Buried Cables, Economic Limits of Electrical Transmission of Energy Electrical Canal Haulage, Electric Illumination, etc. *Recreations:* golf, fishing, gardening. *Address:* Brook Farm, Grendon, Atherstone, Warwickshire. *T.:* Polesworth 212. *Clubs:* Royal Commonwealth Society; University (Liverpool). [*Died* 14 *Nov.* 1962.

MARCKS, Violet O. C.; *see* Cressy-Marcks.

MARCOSSON, Isaac Frederick; journalist; *b.* Louisville, 13 Sept. 1876; *s.* of Major Louis Marcosson, Confederate Army; *m.* 1942, Ellen Petts. *Educ.:* Public Schools. Began life as journalist in Louisville; Member of Staff Louisville Times, 1894-1903; Associate Editor World's Work, New York, 1903-7; Financial Editor Saturday Evening Post, Philadelphia, 1907-10; Associate Editor Munsey's Magazine, 1910-13; special representative of the Saturday Evening Post mainly in Europe, 1913-37. Among his achievements have been his discovery and publication, The Jungle; he was the first interviewer to make the great American money captains talk for publications; secured first war interviews with Lloyd George, Kerensky, and Sir Douglas Haig. *Publications:* How to Invest your Savings, 1908; The Autobiography of a Clown, 1910; The War after the War, 1917; The Re-birth of Russia; Leonard Wood, Prophet of Preparedness; The Business of War, 1918; S.O.S.—America's Miracle in France; Peace and Business; Adventures in Interviewing, 1919; An African Adventure, 1921; The Black Golconda, 1924; Caravans of Commerce, 1926; David Graham Phillips and His Times, 1932; Turbulent Years, 1938; Wherever Men Trade, 1945; Colonel Deeds, Industrial Builder, 1947; Metal Magic, The Story of the American Smelting and Refining Co., 1949; Marse Henry, the biography of Henry Watterson, 1951; Industrial Main Street—the Story of Rome, New

York, 1952; Copper Heritage, The Story of The Revere Copper & Brass Company, 1955; Anaconda, 1957; Before I Forget—A Pilgrimage to the Past, 1959; co-author, Charles Frohman, Manager and Man. *Recreations:* golf, walking and motoring. *Address:* 16 Gramercy Park, New York. *Clubs:* Savage, American; Players (New York); Union Interalliée (Paris). [*Died* 14 *March* 1961.

MARCOTTE, Rev. F. X., O.M.I., Ph.D., D.D.; Professor in the Faculty of Arts at University of Ottawa, 1928-58, Professor Emeritus, Faculty of Arts, 1958; *b.* St. Paul, Minnesota, U.S.A., 18 Oct. 1883. *Educ.:* Ottawa; Rome. Priest; Professor of Philosophy, Church History and Holy Scripture at St. Joseph's Scholasticate, 1911; Rector of the College of Gravelbourg, Saskatchewan, 1920; Rector of the University of Ottawa, 1921-27; Provincial Treasurer of the Oblate Order at Montreal, 1927-28; Secretary of the University of Ottawa, 1928-33; Chevalier de la Légion d'Honneur, 1926. [*Died* 1 *March* 1967.

MARDY JONES, Thomas Isaac; *s.* of Thomas Jones Brynamman, Carmarthen; *m.* Margaret Moredecai, Cowbridge; two *d.* *Educ.:* Ruskin College, Oxford. M.P. (Lab.), Pontypridd Division of Glamorgan, 1922-31. Author several books, local Government work and rating reforms; made many study tours in India, the Middle East, and in South Africa, 1928-46; Staff Officer, Ministry of Supply, 1942-44; Education and Welfare Officer with the British Forces in Middle East, 1945-46; Public Lecturer on World Affairs; Specialist on India and the Middle East; F.R.Econ.S.; Official Lecturer to the National Coal Board on the Economics of the Coal Industry. *Publications:* Character, Coal and Corn—The Roots of British Power, 1949; India as a Future World Power, 1952. *Recreations:* tennis, bowls and book collecting. *Address:* 85 Canterbury Road, Herne Bay, Kent. *Club:* Royal Over-Seas League. [*Died* 26 *Aug.* 1970.

MARGAI, Rt. Hon. Sir Milton Augustus Strieby, P.C. 1962; Kt. 1950; M.B.E., 1943; M.L.C. 1951; Prime Minister of Sierra Leone, since 1960; Minister of Internal Affairs since 1954, and Minister of Defence since 1961; *b.* 1895; *s.* of M. E. S. Margai, Bonthe; *m.* 1924, Gladys, *d.* of Edward Gosman. *Educ.:* Albert Acad., Freetown; Fourah Bay Coll., the Univ. Coll. of Sierra Leone, Freetown; Durham Univ. Coll. of Medicine; Liverpool School of Tropical Medicine (M.A., M.B., B.S.). In private medical practice, 1927-28; Government Medical Officer, 1928-50; Minister of Health, Agriculture and Forestry, 1953-54; Premier and Minister of Internal Affairs and Development, 1954-60. Hon. D.C.L.: Univ. of Liberia, 1959; Durham Univ., 1961. *Recreations:* music and tennis. *Address:* The Lodge, Hill Station, Freetown, Sierra Leone, West Africa. [*Died* 28 *April* 1964.

MARGESSON, 1st Viscount, *cr.* 1942, of Rugby; **Captain Henry David Reginald Margesson,** P.C. 1933; M.C.; Director, International Nickel Company,; Martins Bank (London Board); *b.* 1890; *s.* of late Sir Mortimer Margesson, and Lady Isabel Margesson (*d.* 1946); *m.* 1916, Frances (from whom he obt. a div., 1940), *d.* of late F. H. Leggett; one *s.* two *d.* *Educ.:* Harrow; Magdalene Coll. Camb. Served World War, 1914-18 (M.C.); was Adjutant 11th Hussars; M.P. (U.) Upton Division of West Ham, Nov. 1922-23; Rugby, 1924-42; Parliamentary Private Secretary to Rt. Hon. Sir C. A. Montague Barlow, Minister of Labour, 1922-23; Assistant Government Whip, Nov. 1924; Junior Lord of the Treasury, 1926-29 and Aug.-Oct. 1931; Parliamentary Secretary to the Treasury, and Government Chief Whip, 1931-40; Secretary of State for War, 1940-42. *Heir:* *s.* Hon. Francis Vere Hampden Margesson [*b.* 17 April 1922; *m.* 1958, Helena, *d.* of Haki Backstrom Oulu, Finland; one *s.* three *d.*]. *Address:* 70 Eaton Square, S.W.1. *Clubs:* Turf, Buck's. [*Died* 24 *Dec.* 1965.

MARIX, Air Vice-Marshal Reginald Lennox George, C.B. 1940; D.S.O. 1914; late R.A.F.; *b.* 17 Aug. 1889; *s.* of James Marix; *m.* 1st, Vera, *d.* of Clifford Trevor-Wadmore (marriage dissolved); one *s.*; 2nd, 1955, Helen, *widow* of Duncan Holmes. *Educ.:* Radley; France. Served Belgium, France and Dardanelles, European War, 1914-17 (despatches twice, D.S.O., wounded, Order of Crown of Belgium, Belgian Croix de Guerre); War of 1939-45, Coastal Command (despatches) and Transport Command (Polonia Restituta 2nd class); retired 1945. *Address:* Sa Serra, Paguera, Majorca. *Clubs:* Royal Air Force; United Services (Montreal). [*Died* 7 *Jan.* 1966.

MARKAR, Hadji Sir Mohamed M.; *see* Macan-Markar.

MARKS OF BROUGHTON, 1st Baron *cr.* 1961, of Sunningdale; **Simon Marks,** Kt. 1944; Chairman and Joint Managing Director, Marks & Spencer Ltd.; *b.* 9 July 1888; *s.* of Michael and Hannah Marks; *m.* 1915, Miriam, *d.* of Ephraim Sieff; one *s.* one *d.* *Educ.:* Manchester Grammar School. Hon. D.Sc. (Econ.) London, 1939; Hon. LL.D. Manchester University, 1962; Leeds University, 1964; Hon. Ph.D. Hebrew University of Jerusalem, 1962; Hon. F.R.C.S.: Hon. Fellow of Weizmann Institute of Science, Rehovoth, Israel; Hon. Fellow of University Coll., London. *Heir:* *s.* Hon. Michael Marks [*b.* 27 Aug. 1920; *m.* 1st, 1949, Ann Catherine, (marriage dissolved 1958), *d.* of Major Richard Pinto, M.C.; one *s.* two *d.*; 2nd, 1960, Hélène, *d.* of Gustav Fischer]. *Address:* 47 Grosvenor Square, W.1; Titlarks Farm, Sunningdale, Berks. *T.:* Ascot 552. [*Died* 8 *Dec.* 1964.

MARKS, Eric A. D.; *see* Marshall, Eric.

MARKS, Captain Percy D'Evelyn, C.M.G. 1919; C.B.E. 1944; R.N. retired; *b.* Cork, 1883; 7th *s.* of late J. Christopher Marks, Mus.Doc.; *m.* 1917, Dorothy, 2nd *d.* of W. J. Walpole, J.P., Castlenode, Strokestown, Co. Roscommon; one *s.* one *d.* *Educ.:* Magdalen College School, Oxford. Entered Navy, 1901; Paymaster Lieut.-Comdr. 1914; Paymaster-Comdr. 1922; Paymaster-Captain, 1932; served European War, 1914-1919, China, Egypt, Mesopotamia, and Grand Fleet; Secretary to Paymaster Director-General, 1918; Secretary to Commander in Chief, Africa, 1922-25; Secretary to C.-in-C., Plymouth, 1926-29; Fleet Accountant Officer, Home Fleet, H.M.S. Nelson, 1935-36; Port Accountant Officer, the Nore, 1936-38; retired list, 1938; Base Accountant Officer, Dover, 1939-41; Base Supply Officer, Liverpool, 1942-45. Chevalier of Legion of Honour, 1919. *Address:* Whistley House, Potterne, Devizes, Wilts. [*Died* 11 *Jan.* 1968.

MARLOW, Arthur Herbert, C.M.G. 1954; C.B.E. 1945; *b.* 29 Sept. 1893; *s.* of late John Marlow, Northampton; *m.* 1919, Hilda Dexter; one *d.* *Educ.:* Northampton School. Entered Home Civil Service, 1913, and Foreign Office, 1914, being released for military service in Feb. 1917. Joined Inns of Court O.T.C., commissioned in R.G.A. and served overseas. After the war entered Consular Service, serving at Boston, Mass., Santos and Sao Paulo, Brazil, and Barcelona; Consul at Bahia, Brazil, 1932; transferred to Lima, Peru, with additional ranks of Commercial Secretary and 1st Secretary in

Diplomatic Service; Chargé d'Affaires at Lima on various occasions; H.M. Consul-General at Buenos Aires, Argentina, 1942-47; Chicago, 1947-50; Paris, 1950-53; retired December 1953. *Address:* 46 Sheen Court, Richmond, Surrey. *T.:* Prospect 6620. *Recreations:* golf, music, bridge. *Club:* Royal Mid-Surrey Golf (Richmond). [*Died* 12 *April* 1964.

MARLOW, Ewart, C.B.E. 1960; M.C. 1918; J.P.; a Chief Executive Officer since 1932; *b.* 11 Aug. 1895; *s.* of Jesse and Ann Marlow; *m.* 1919, Ethel Kathleen Curtis; one *s.* *Educ.:* Wellingborough School. Served European War, Northamptonshire Regiment, 1915-18, A/Captain. Northamptonshire County Council: County Councillor, 1938; County Alderman, 1946; Vice-Chm., 1952; Chairman, 1954. J.P. for Northamptonshire, 1941-. Chm. Kettering Petty Sessions, 1956-; Chm. Mid-Northamptonshire Water Board, 1948-; Mem. Central Advisory Water Cttee., Ministry of Local Government, 1959-. *Recreations:* ornithology, gardening. *Address:* Copelands House, Desborough, Northamptonshire. *Club:* County (Northampton). [*Died* 4 *July* 1965.

MARLOW, Louis; *see* Wilkinson, L. U.

MARLOWE, Anthony Alfred Harmsworth, Q.C. 1945; M.P. (C.) Brighton, 1941-50, Hove, 1950-65; *b.* 25 October 1904; *s.* of late Thomas Marlowe, Osborne Cottage, Isle of Wight, formerly Chairman of Associated Newspapers Ltd., and Alice Davidson; *m.* 1st, 1929, Patricia Mary (marriage dissolved, 1955), 2nd *d.* of late Sir Patrick Hastings, Q.C.; one *s.* three *d.*; 2nd, 1956, Mrs. Marion Slater, *d.* of late Comdr. Robert Tennant-Park, O.B.E., R.N.R. *Educ.:* Marlborough; Trinity Coll., Cambridge. B.A. (Hons. Cantab.); called to Bar, Inner Temple, 1928; Master of the Bench, 1953. Served in Army, 1939-45 (Lt.-Col., on staff of Judge-Advocate-Gen.). *Address:* (Professional) 3 Hare Court, Temple, E.C.4. *T.:* Central 7742; Mill House, Wimborne-St.-Giles, Dorset. *Club:* Brooks's. [*Died* 8 *Sept.* 1965.

MARR, James William Slesser, M.A., D.Sc.; Principal Scientific Officer in the Royal Naval Scientific Service (National Institute of Oceanography) since 1949; Lieut.-Comdr. R.N.V.R., 1943; *b.* 9 Dec. 1902; 2nd *s.* of late John George Marr, farmer, formerly of Coynachie, Aberdeenshire; *m.* 1937, Dorothea Helene, 4th *d.* of late G. F. Plutte, Sydenham; two *s.* three *d.* *Educ.:* Aberdeen Grammar School and University. At 18 years of age, when a Boy Scout, served with Shackleton-Rowett Antarctic Exp. in the "Quest" under late Sir Ernest Shackleton, 1921-22; zoologist to British Arctic Exp., 1925; appointed zoologist in the Colonial Service ("Discovery" Investigations), 1926, and in this service subs. took part in three expeditions to Antarctic in Royal Research Ships "William Scoresby", 1927-29, "Discovery II", 1931-33 and 1935-37; seconded in charge of oceanography to British Australian New Zealand Antarctic Research Exp. under Sir Douglas Mawson. 1929-30. Scouts' Silver Cross and Bronze Medal of Royal Humane Soc. 1919; Polar Medal in bronze, 1934; W. S. Bruce Memorial Prize of Royal Scottish Geog. Society, 1936; Bar to Polar Medal, 1942; Polar Medal in Silver, 1954. Back Grant of Royal Geog. Society, 1946; at outbreak of war of 1939-45 carried out research in Antarctic into canning, drying and freezing of whale meat for human consumption, 1939-40; Lieut. R.N.V.R. 1940; served Iceland, Scapa and Eastern Fleet; seconded to S. African Naval Forces, 1942-43; Lt.-Comdr. 1943; organised and commanded advance parties of Falkland Is. Dependencies Survey in Graham Land region of Antarctica, 1943-45. *Publications:* various papers in the "Discovery" Reports and other scientific journals. *Recreation:* gardening. *Address:* Chase Lodge, Haslemere, Surrey. *T.:* Hindhead 273. [*Died* 29 *April* 1965.

MARRIOTT, Rev. Stephen Jack, M.A. Cantab.; Archdeacon of Westminster, 1946-1951 and 1959-63, Canon 1937-63, Sub-Dean, 1951-59 of Westminster; *b.* 8 Nov. 1886; *s.* of Stephen and Louise Marriott, Redhill, Sy.; *m.* Emilie Luzia (*d.* 1954), *d.* of Edouardo Alvarez da Nobrega, Lisbon; three *s.* two *d.* *Educ.:* Christ Coll., Brecon; Christ's College, Cambridge. Deacon, 1911; Priest, 1913; Curate Emmanuel Church, Southport, 1913-14; Curate in Charge Rye Park, Herts, 1914-15; Holy Trinity, Folkestone, 1915-17; Temp. Naval Chaplain and R.A.F., 1917-18; Incumbent Priory Church, South Queensferry, 1918-20; Rector of St. Baldreds, North Berwick, 1920-37; National President of Brotherhood Movement, 1941-42; Archbishop's Visitor to R.A.F., 1944-45. Retired July 1963. *Address:* Flat 3x, Artillery Mansions, 75 Victoria Street, S.W.1. [*Died* 25 *Dec.* 1964.

MARSDEN, Col. Sir Ernest, Kt. 1958; C.M.G. 1946; C.B.E. 1935; M.C.; D.Sc.; F.R.S. 1946; J.P.; Hon. LL.D.; M.I.E.E.; F.R.S.N.Z.; *b.* 19 February 1889; *s.* of Thomas and P. Marsden; *m.* 1913, Margaret Sutcliffe; one *s.* one *d.*; *m.* 1958, Joyce W. Chote. *Educ.:* Queen Elizabeth Grammar School, Blackburn; Victoria Univ. John Harling Fellow. Univ. of Manchester; Lecturer in Physics, Univ. of London; Prof. of Physics, Victoria University College, Wellington, N.Z., 1914-22; Assistant Director of Education, N.Z., 1922-27; Secretary, Department of Scientific and Industrial Research, N.Z., 1927-47; N.Z. Scientific Liaison Officer, London, 1947-57. Chm. N.Z. Defence Science Advisory Council, 1956; Past President R.S.N.Z. Hon. D.Sc.: (Oxon.; Wellington, N.Z.); Hon. LL.D (Manch.). U.S. Medal of Freedom (with palms). Commander, Royal Swedish Order of the North Star, 1966. *Publications:* Proc. Royal Society; Phil. Mag.; Proc. Phys. Soc.; papers on Atomic Physics and Bio-physics. *Address:* Cheviot Rd., Lowry Bay, Wellington, New Zealand. [*Died* 15 *Dec.* 1970.

MARSH, Sir Percy William, Kt., *cr.* 1946; C.S.I. 1939; C.I.E. 1929; I.C.S. (retired); *b.* 14 Oct. 1881; 2nd *s.* of late Henry Marsh, C.I.E.; *m.* 1931, Joan Mary, 2nd *d.* of P. W. Beecroft, Kingsthorpe, Northampton; one *s.* one *d.* *Educ.:* Wellington College (Scholar); Wadham College, Oxford (Scholar). 1st Class Lit. Hum., B.A. 1904; I.C.S. 1905; served in U.P. as Asst. City and District Magistrate, Commissioner, Board of Revenue, and Adviser to the Governor, 1905-1942; services lent to War Office, 1915-19; Chairman Joint Public Service Commission, Punjab and N.W.F.P., Lahore, 1942-47. *Recreations:* formerly pigsticking, golf. *Address:* Orchard Cottage, Dorchester-on-Thames, Oxon. *T.:* Warborough 466. *Club:* East India and Sports. [*Died* 16 *Jan.* 1969.

MARSHALL, Sir Archie (Pellow), Kt. 1959; **Hon. Mr. Justice Marshall;** Judge of High Court of Justice, Queen's Bench Div., since 1961; Commissioner of Assize, Oxford Circuit, 1959; Chm. of Cornwall Q.S. since 1957; *b.* 20 November 1899; *yr. s.* of Alfred Ernest Stanley Marshall, Roche, Cornwall; *m.* 1926, Meta, *yr. d.* of William Hawke, Bugle, Cornwall; one *s.* one *d.* *Educ.:* Truro School, Cornwall; Gonville and Caius College, Cambridge. Served European War, 1914-18, R.N. in North Sea, Mediterranean and South Russia, 1917-20; M.A., LL.B. (Camb.), 1921-25; Pres., Cambridge Union, Michaelmas Term, 1924; called to Bar and joined Midland Circuit, 1925; practised in Birmingham, 1925-47; Q.C. 1947; Recorder of Warwick, 1949-51; Recorder of City of Coventry, 1952-59; Dep. Chm., Quarter Sessions: Northants, 1947-54, Warwickshire, 1950-54, Cornwall, 1954-57. Master of the Bench, Gray's Inn, 1950; elected to Gen. Council of Bar, 1958. Mem. Standing Cttee. on Criminal Law Revision, 1959-; Judge of High Court of Justice, Probate, Divorce and Admiralty Division, 1959-61. Liberal Candidate, King's Norton, 1929 and 1931, South Hereford, 1945. Pres. London Cornish Assoc. *Recreations:* walking, fishing. *Address:* (home) North Acre, Brighton Road, Banstead, Surrey. *T.:* Burgh Heath 54648. *Club:* Reform. [*Died* 20 *June* 1966.

MARSHALL, Arthur, A.C.G.I., F.R.I.C., F.C.S.; *b.* 1873; *e. s.* of Henry Marshall; *m.* 1901, Ada Milly (*d.* 1962), *e. d.* of George Watts. *Educ.:* Univ. Coll. School; Central Technical College, S. Kensington. Chemist to Cogswell & Harrison, Ltd., gun-makers; Chemist, Royal Gunpowder Factory, Waltham Abbey; Manager, Curtis & Harvey's Explosives and Gas Mantle Factories, Dartford; Chemical Inspector, Indian Ordnance Department; organised chemical sections of Faraday Centenary Exhibition, 1931. Experimental Officer, Armament Research Dept., 1939-45. *Publications:* Explosives; A Short Account of Explosives; Dictionary of Explosives; various scientific and technical papers, mostly in Journals of Chemical Society and Society of Chemical Industry. *Address:* 10 Aubrey Walk, W.8. *T.:* Park 7957. *Club:* Athenæum. [*Died* 9 *May* 1968.

MARSHALL, Eric; (Eric Astor David Marks); Concert Singer; *b.* London, 26 Feb. 1891; *s.* of late Major Claude Marks, D.S.O., 4th Battalion Highland Light Infantry, and late Caroline, Marchioness of Winchester; *nephew* of late Harry Marks, M.P. Was an Officer in 19th County of London Regt. (T.F.); retired through ill-health and went round the world; has been through every phase of the stage; toured with Mme. Tettrazzini, 1921. *Recreations:* hunting, steeplechasing, sculling, boxing and fencing. *Address:* 21 Grafton St., Bond St., W.1. [*Died* 8 *July* 1961.

MARSHALL, Eric Stewart, C.B.E. 1919; M.C.; M.R.C.S., L.R.C.P.; *b.* 1879; *m.* 1922, Enid Dorothy May (Mrs. Hibbert), (*d.* 1935), *d.* of late Sir William Hood Treacher, K.C.M.G. Served European War, 1914-19 (despatches, M.C., C.B.E.); British Antarctic Expedition, 1907-09; British Expedition to Dutch New Guinea, 1909-11; 2nd class Order of St. Stanislas. *Address:* Eastmora, Yarmouth, I.O.W. [*Died* 26 *Feb.* 1963.

MARSHALL, Fred, J.P.; *b.* 1883; *s.* of John Marshall, S. Anston, Yorks.; *m.* 1912; one *s.* one *d.* *Educ.:* Elementary School; South Anston, Yorks. Member Sheffield City Council, 1919, Alderman, 1926; Lord Mayor, City of Sheffield, 1933-34. M.P. (Lab.), Brightside Division of Sheffield, 1930-31 and 1935-50; Parliamentary Secretary, Ministry of Town and Country Planning, 1945-47. J.P. Sheffield, 1928. *Address:* Millthorpe, Monks Hill, Westbourne, Nr. Emsworth, Hants. [*Died Nov.* 1962.

MARSHALL, George Leslie, O.B.E. 1938; F.R.S.A.; M.A.; Life-member Royal Scottish Pipers Soc.; Northern Ireland Director, British Broadcasting Corporation, 1932-48 (retd.); *s.* of late Andrew Marshall, Edinburgh and Jocotepec, Mexico, and Margaret Elizabeth, *e. d.* of late W. K. Coubrough, Liverpool; *m.* Dorothy Norman, *d.* of late Charles W. Cropper, M.D., New York. *Educ.:* Victoria College, Jersey; Merchiston Castle School, Edinburgh; Edinburgh and Oxford Universities. Formerly Secretary to late Sir Edmund Walker, Chancellor of Univ. of Toronto, Canada; served European War, 1914-19, with Canadian Expeditionary Force; Lieut. 48th Highlanders (Toronto); in France with 4th Bn. (1st Div.) Canadian Infantry; joined British Broadcasting Corporation, 1924; Station Director at Edinburgh, Glasgow, and Newcastle upon Tyne; Member the Society of Antiquaries of Newcastle upon Tyne. *Recreations:* music, fishing, antiquities. *Address:* 40 Mount Charles, Belfast, Northern Ireland. *T.:* Belfast 21969. *Clubs:* Ulster (Belfast); Bruntsfield Links Golfing Society (Edinburgh). [*Died* 12 *Dec.* 1964.

MARSHALL, Herbert Brough Falcon (Herbert Marshall); actor, stage and screen; *b.* 23 May 1890; *s.* of Percy Falcon Marshall and Ethel May Turner; *m.* 1st, 1915, Mollie Maitland; 2nd, 1928, Edna Best; one *d.*; 3rd, 1940, Elizabeth Russell; one *d.*; 4th, Patricia Mallory (*d.* 1958); 5th, Mrs. Dee Anne Kahmann. *Educ.:* privately; St. Mary's College, Harlow. Articled clerk to a firm of chartered accountants in the City; made first appearance on stage Buxton, 1911, and London, 1913; served European War, 1916-1918; joined company of Lyric Opera House, Hammersmith, 1918; associated with Mr. Gilbert Miller from 1929, during which appeared with his wife, Edna Best, in Michael and Mary, The Swan, There's Always Juliet (London and New York), and together in British pictures of Michael and Mary, The Calendar, Faithful Heart, Hollywood (Paramount) during summer and autumn of 1932, doing Blonde Venus with Dietrich, Trouble in Paradise under Lubitsch, and Evenings for Sale; returned to London and appeared with Edna Best in Another Language; returned to Hollywood in July 1933, and temporarily left stage; remained in Hollywood doing Rip Tide with Norma Shearer, Iris March with Constance Bennett, and Painted Veil with Greta Garbo; The Good Fairy; The Dark Angel; Accent on Youth; If You could only Cook; Till we meet again; Girls Dormitory; A Woman Rebels; Angel (another Lubitsch production) and a succession of motion pictures in Hollywood and radio broadcasts from Hollywood and New York; several television appearances; in London, 1955-56, for pictures The Weapon and Wicked As They Come; returned to Hollywood for television series. *Recreations:* games of almost every description, and poker as only card game. *Address:* Beverly Hills, California, U.S.A. *Clubs:* Garrick, Green Room. [*Died* 22 *Jan.* 1966.

MARSHALL, John, M.C. 1917; T.D. 1930, F.R.C.P.S.G., D.O.M.S.(Eng.); Hon. Surgeon Glasgow Eye Infirmary; Member, Advisory Committee, W. H. Ross Foundation (Scotland) for Prevention of Blindness; *b.* 18 January 1895; *s.* of Wm. Marshall, schoolmaster, and Christina Burns; *m.* 1928, Florence Christian Macrae, M.B., Ch.B.; one *s.* two *d.* *Educ.:* Allan Glen's School; Glasgow University M.B., Ch.B. Glas. (hons.) 1917; F.R.C.P.G. 1923; D.O.M.S. Eng. 1926. Surgeon Oculist, Glasgow, 1921-. Formerly: Surgeon Oculist to the Queen in Scotland, also to King George VI; Civilian Cons. Ophthalmologist, Admiralty in Scotland; Cons. Oculist, Glas. Corp. Fever Hosps.; Ophth. Surg., Dumfries and Galloway Roy. Infirmary; Sch. Oculist, Stewartry of Kirkcudbright and Wigtownshire C.C.; Surgeon, Glasgow Eye Infirmary; Hon. Clin. Lectr. to Glasg. Univ. in Ophthalmology; Surgeon, Glasg. Blind Certifying Clinic. Served War, 1917-20, Lt.-Col. R.A.M.C. (T.A.). Vice-Pres. Ophth. Soc. of U.K.; Ophth. Sect., B.M.A. President Faculty of Ophthalmologists; Mackenzie Memorial Medal, 1953, F.R.Soc.Med. *Publications:* ophthalmic subjects in Trans.

Ophthal. Soc. U.K., and British Journal of Ophthalmology. *Address:* Ashestiel, Bridge of Weir Road, Kilmacolm, Renfrewshire. *T.:* Kilmacolm 2620. [*Died* 9 *Aug.* 1970.

MARSHALL, Robert Ian, B.Com.; C.A.; *b.* 2 July 1899; *s.* of David Marshall and Marion Mitchell Irons; *m.* 1st, 1928, Elizabeth Mary Hannah (*d.* 1934); three *s.*: 2nd, 1935, Lilian May Hannah; one *d.* *Educ.:* Viewpark, Edinburgh; Edinburgh Academy; Edinburgh University. Served European War, Royal Field Artillery, 1917-1919; 2nd Lt., France, 1918, Germany, 1919. B.Com. Edin. Univ., 1923. Qualified as Chartered Accountant, 1924. War of 1939-45: Major, Royal Field Artillery, then Staff, 1940-45. President, The Institute of Chartered Accountants of Scotland, 1958-59. *Recreations:* golf, gardening. *Address:* Southgate, 20 Pentland Avenue, Colinton, Edinburgh 13. *Club:* Caledonian United Service (Edinburgh). [*Died* 5 *April* 1970.

MARSHALL, Septimus; *b.* 1876; *m.* 1949, Irene (Ingrid) Emanuelson, *widow* of Gösta Emanuelson, formerly of Sherborne, Somerset West, Cape, S. Africa; Liveryman, Dyers Co. Alderman for Dowgate Ward of City of London, 1941-47, Sheriff, 1944-45. *Address:* 50 Upper Thames St., E.C.4; Sherborne, Oathall Avenue, Oathall Road, Haywards Heath, Sx. [*Died* 15 *Sept.* 1962.

MARSHALL, Sir William Marchbank, Kt., *cr.* 1937; J.P. County of Lanark; Solicitor; *b.* Greenock, 24 Jan. 1875; *s.* of Rev. George A. Marshall, Mount Park Free Church, Greenock; *m.* 1905, Helen Dron Stewart; two *d.* *Educ.:* George Watson's College, Edinburgh; Edinburgh University. Partner, W. M. Marshall, Ross and Munro, Solicitors, Motherwell; Member of Lanark County Council, 1906-12; Chairman Executive Council for Lanarkshire (National Health Service); Hon. Sheriff; Mem. of Government Cttee. on Scottish Health Services, 1933; Chm. of the Unemployment Assistance Board for Lanarkshire, 1935; Dean of the Society of Solicitors at Hamilton, 1934-36; Deacon of the Incorporation of Skinners and Glovers of Glasgow, 1935; President, Uddingston Cricket Club, 1936 and Bothwell and Blantyre Angling Club, 1937. *Publications:* Pamphlets: Medical Benefit in Scotland, Medical Treatment of the Sick Poor, etc. *Recreations:* angling, motoring. *Address:* Knowehead, Uddingston, by Glasgow. *T.:* Uddingston 36. *Clubs:* National Liberal; Western (Glasgow). [*Died* 5 *April* 1967.

MARSILLAC, Jacques J. B. de Hon. C.B.E. 1919; Officier de la Légion d'Honneur, Croix de Guerre 1940, etc.; Ed. in Chief of Paris-Reportages; *b.* 1 August 1879; *m.* 1913, Myrtle Thomas: one *d.* *Educ.:* Lycée Louis le Grand and Sorbonne, Paris. Special Correspondent for Le Journal and other newspapers in Great Britain, Northern Africa, Spain, the Balkans, Germany, the United States, Soviet Russia, China, Japan, etc.; for some time attached to the Allied Press Mission with the British Armies. Captain in the French Army, 1944-45. *Publications:* A book of verse, Lilas et Roses; various technical papers on engineering, etc. *Address:* 102 rue de Richelieu, Paris. [*Died* 8 *April* 1962.

MARSTON, Archibald Daniel, C.B.E. 1953; F.R.C.S. (Eng.), L.R.C.P. (Lond.), L.D.S.R.C.S. (Eng.); D.A.R.C.P. and S. (Eng.); F.F.A.R.C.S. (Eng.); formerly Consultant Adviser in Anæsthetics to Ministry of Health; Hon. Anaesthetist to Guy's Hospital: Anaesthetist and Lecturer in Anaesthetics, Guy's Hospital Dental School; Anaesthetist to the Royal Masonic Hospital; *b.* 28 Mar. 1891; *s.* of late Daniel Marston and late Annie Bell; *m.* 1923, Emily Phyllis Irene (*d.* 1961), *d.* of Henry Norris-Cox; no *c.* *Educ.:* Privately; Guy's Hosp. First qualified as a Dental Surgeon but proceeded to medicine and specialised in Anaesthesia; Temp. Surgeon-Lieut. R.N.; Fellow Royal Soc. of Medicine (Past Pres. Anaesthetic Section); Fellow Hunterian Soc.; Held Resident House Appointments at Guy's Hospital; late Obstetric Registrar and Tutor Guy's Hosp.; Member of the British Medical Association; formerly Anaesthetist to the West End Hospital for Nervous Diseases; Anaesthetist in Emergency Medical Service of Ministry of Health; Past Pres. Association of Anaesthetists of Great Britain and Ireland; Examiner in Anaesthetics for Royal College of Surgeons of England, and Dean of Faculty of Anæsthetists, 1948-52. Hickman Medal, Faculty of Anæsthetists, R.C.S., 1957; John Snow Memorial Medal, Assoc. of Anæsthetists of Gt. Brit. and Ireland, 1958. *Publications:* Notes on the Use and Technique of General Anaesthesia in Dental Surgery, with special reference to Evipaw Sodium, 1934, contributions on Anaesthesia in Medical Journals. *Recreations:* gardening, billiards. *Address:* Flat 2, 26 Brunswick Terrace, Hove 1, Sussex. *T.:* Hove 36871. *Clubs:* Bath, Surrey County Cricket, National Sporting. [*Died* 14 *Jan.* 1962.

MARSTON, Hedley Ralph, F.R.S. 1949; D.Sc. (Aust. Nat. Univ.); (a.e.g.) D.Sc. (Adelaide Univ.); F.R.A.C.I., F.Aust. Academy of Science, etc.; retired as Chief of Division of Biochemistry and General Nutrition, Commonwealth Scientific and Industrial Research Organisation, Univ. of Adelaide (1945-1965); *b.* Bordertown, South Australia, 26 August 1900; *s.* of S. H. Marston; *m.* 1933, Kathleen Nellie Spooner. *Educ.:* University of Adelaide, South Australia; Cambridge. Principal Research Officer, Division of Animal Nutrition, C.S.I.R., 1930-32; Officer in charge of Nutrition Laboratory, C.S.I.R., 1932-44. Fellow of Nat. Research Council; Petitioner, Foundation Fell. and first Treas. Aust. Acad. of Science, 1954-. Annie Cunning Lecturer to Royal Australian College of Physicians, 1959. Mueller Medal, 1959. *Publications:* many publications of original research in General Physiology and Biochemistry. *Recreation:* Experiments! *Address:* 23 Harrow Road, St. Peter's, South Australia. [*Died* 25 *Aug.* 1965.

MARTEN, Sir Amberson Barrington, Kt., *cr.* 1924; LL.D., M.A.; *b.* 8 Dec. 1870; *e.s.* of late Sir Alfred Marten, K.C., M.P.; *m.* 1898, Lois (*d.* 1947), *d.* of late W. Tarn, Lancaster Gate, W.; 2nd, 1957, Kathleen, *widow* of Maj. C. Rodney Wimshurst, B.Sc., Glenmead, Matfield. *Educ.:* Eton; Trinity College, Cambridge (1st Class Law Tripos); Cambridge University Association Football XI., 1892-93. Studentship of Council of Legal Education. Called to Bar, Inner Temple, 1895; Member of Bar Council 1909-10; practised in Chancery Division until 1916; Puisne Judge, High Court, Bombay, 1916-26; Chief Justice, 1926-30. *Address:* Glenmead, Matfield, Kent. *Club:* Oxford and Cambridge. [*Died* 1 *July* 1962.

MARTEN, Ven. George Henry, M.A.; Archdeacon of Kingston-on-Thames, 1931-1946, Emeritus since 1946; *b.* 20 Jan. 1876; *y. s.* of Charles Henry Marten, Blackheath; *m.* 1922, Gertrude Isabel Kathleen (*d.* 1964), 2nd *d.* of T. S. Medill, Wimbledon; no *c.* *Educ.:* Clifton Coll.; King's Coll., Cambridge; Wells Theological College. Ordained, 1900; Assistant, Curate, Holy Trinity, Southwark, 1900-4; Limpsfield, Surrey, 1904-8; Rector of Tatsfield Surrey, 1908-13; Vicar of St. Marks, Woodcote, Purley, 1913-22; Rural Dean of Caterham, 1918-22; Vicar of St. Marks with St. Andrews, Surbiton, 1922-33; Rural Dean of Kingston, 1926-31; Hon. Canon of Southwark Cathedral, 1929-37; Rector of Godstone, 1936-45; Warden of the Homes of St. Barnabas, Dormans, Surrey, 1945-55. Fishmongers' Company, 1914, Livery and Freedom of City of London. Served as Chaplain under Missions to Seamen at Naval Base of Oban in 1918. *Publications:* Book of Sermons, 1917; Under Six Bishops, 1961. *Address:* St. Paul's House, Upper Maze Hill, St. Leonard's-on-Sea, Sussex. [*Died* 13 *Jan.* 1966.

MARTIN, Sir Albert Victor, Kt. 1966; C.B.E. 1961; Chairman of Albert Martin & Co. Ltd. and its associate companies; *b.* 12 May 1897; *s.* of Arthur and Sarah Martin, Smalley, Nr. Derby; *m.* 1920, Edith Anne Hartshorne (decd.); one *s.*; *m.* 1961, Councillor Thelma Idina Street, M.B.E. *Educ.:* Heanor Grammar Sch.; Nottingham Univ. College. Served in R.F.A., 1915-16; Capt. 102 "Z" A.A. Battery, War of 1939-45. Part-time lecturer in textiles, Nottingham Univ. Coll., for some years. Chm. Sheffield Regional Hosp. Bd., 1956-; Past Mem. Council, Nottingham Chamber of Commerce (now Vice-Pres.); Chm. Council Sub-Cttee. which reported Nottingham's road traffic problems (suggesting Traffic Wardens); Mem. Notts. War Pensions Cttee., 1940 (Past Chm.); Chm., Nat. Hospitals Staff Cttee. Mem. E. Midlands Reg. Industrial Adv. Savings Cttee.; Mem. General Nursing Council; Chm. Nottingham Gen. Dispensary (Mem. Cttee., 1940-); Past Chm. or Mem. various hosp. cttees. Mem. Council of Nottingham University and Sheffield University. *Recreations:* Reserve to Coxswainless Four represented England Olympic Games, Amsterdam, 1928; rowed in final of Wyfolds, Henley, 1931; Capt. Wollaton Park Golf Club, 1943. *Address:* Little Dalby Hall, Little Dalby, Leics. *T.:* Somerby 320. [*Died* 25 *Nov.* 1968.

MARTIN, Arthur Campbell, C.V.O. 1951; F.R.I.B.A.; *b.* 20 Aug. 1875; 3rd *s.* of Rev. Charles Martin, Dartington, Devon; *m.* 1911, Hope, *d.* of Alex. Johnston, Singapore; one *s.* one *d.* *Educ.:* Winchester College. Architect, articled in London, 1894. Country Houses and Churches, 1900-52; Architect for Memorial Chapel, R.M.C., Sandhurst; Consulting Architect to Duchy of Cornwall, 1930. *Publication:* The Small House, 1906. *Address:* The Coach House, Englefield Green, Surrey. *T.:* Egham 2365. [*Died* 2 *July* 1963.

MARTIN, (Basil) Kingsley; Editor, New Statesman and Nation, 1930-60 (Editorial Director, 1961-62; retired 1962; Editorial Consultant, 1962-); *b.* 28 July 1897; *s.* of Rev. Basil Martin, Unitarian Minister. *Educ.:* Mill Hill School; Magdalene Coll., Camb. Bye-Fellow, Magdalene Coll., 1921-23; M.A. Princeton, N.J. Asst. Lectr., Dept. of Political Sci. at London School of Economics, 1923-27; Editorial Staff, Manchester Guardian, 1927-31. *Publications:* The Triumph of Palmerston, 1924 (republished with new chapter, 1963); The British Public and the General Strike, 1927; French Liberal Thought in the Eighteenth Century, 1929 (re-published 1955); Low's Russian Sketch Book, in collaboration with David Low, 1932; The Magic of Monarchy, 1937; Propaganda's Harvest, 1942; The Press the Public Wants, 1947; Harold Laski, A Memoir, 1953; Critic's London Diary, 1960; The Crown and the Establishment, 1962; Father Figures, 1966; Editor, 1968. *Recreations:* chess and painting. *Address:* Hilltop, Rodmell, Lewes, Sussex. [*Died* 16 *Feb.* 1969.

MARTIN, Sir Charles Carnegie, Kt. 1957; C.B.E. 1951; one of H.M.'s Inspectors of Constabulary since 1958; *b.* 24 May 1901; *s.* of George Thornton Martin and Jane Warren; *m.* 1930, Margaret Roberts; one *s.* two *d.* Metropolitan Police, 1921-41; Chief Constable: Leamington Spa, 1941-42; Southport, Lancs., 1942-46; Asst. Chief Constable, Liverpool, 1946-48; Chief Constable, Liverpool City Police, 1948-58; Director, Securicor North-West, 1967-. *Publication:* Police and Children, 1956. *Recreations:* fishing, ornithology. *Address:* c/o The Home Office, Whitehall, S.W.1; Dry Grange, Allerton, Liverpool 18. *T.:* Garston 7873. *Club:* Royal Commonwealth Society. [*Died* 22 *Feb.* 1969.

MARTIN, Daisy Maud, C.B.E. 1938; R.R.C. 1935; *d.* of late William Thomas Martin; The Pines, Ilfracombe. Trained King's College Hospital, 1910-13. Joined Queen Alexandra's Imperial Military Nursing Service, 1913, served European War in France, (Despatches); A.R.R.C. 1919; Matron-in-Chief, Queen Alexandra's Imperial Military Nursing Service, 1934-38; retired pay, 1938. *Address:* 18 Chambercombe Terrace, Ilfracombe, Devon. [*Died* 23 *Aug.* 1964.

MARTIN, Frederick John, C.B.E. 1942; M.A., Ph.D.; F.R.I.C.; Director (Deputy Chairman) of Allied Retail Trades (London) Ltd. since 1947, Second General Operative Investment Trust Ltd. since 1945; P. G. Hicks & Sons Ltd. since 1950 and Gosdens Ltd. since 1959; *b.* 5 September 1891; 3rd *s.* of late B. W. Martin; *m.* 1st, 1919, Gladys Eve (*d.* 1919), *d.* of R. Heffer; 2nd, 1925, Dorothy Evelyn (*d.* 1956), *d.* of late Colonel Evelyn Cloete, C.B.E.; one *s.* *Educ.:* Selwyn Coll., Camb. Served European War, 1914-19, with Leicester Regt., R.F.C. and R.A.F., demobilised with rank of Captain (Flight Commander); Sudan Govt. Service, 1919-24; transferred to Sierra Leone Govt. Service in 1924; Director of Agriculture, 1934-44, and Food Controller, 1939-42, Sierra Leone; also Controller of Merchandise, 1940-42; Member of Legislative Council, 1934-44; assisted in raising Sierra Leone Defence Corps, 1939-40; retired from Colonial Service, November 1944. *Publications:* various in scientific journals on agricultural, chemical, and allied subjects. *Recreations:* tennis and shooting. *Address:* 66 Hamilton Terrace, N.W.8. *Clubs:* Junior Carlton, M.C.C., Hurlingham, Royal Commonwealth Society, Arts Theatre. [*Died* 4 *May* 1964.

MARTIN, Henry, Editor-in-Chief, Press Assoc., 1928-54, retired; *b.* London, 19 April 1889; *s.* of Henry Martin, Brighton, and Annie Elizabeth Holland, Ninfield, Sussex; *m.* 1st; one *s.* one *d.*; 2nd, one *s.*; 3rd, 1948, Ivy Coleman. *Educ.:* privately. Trained at Worcester, 1905-8; London News Agency, 1908-19; Daily Sketch News Editor, 1919-1925; Evening Standard News Editor, 1925-1928. *Publication:* The Place of Religion in the Post-War Press. *Recreations:* music (ancient and modern), archæology, literature, poetry, philosophy, theology. *Address:* 11 Cornwall Court, Wilbury Avenue, Hove, Sussex. [*Died* 24 *Sept.* 1964.

MARTIN, Rev. Hugh, C.H. 1955; M.A., Hon. D.D. (Glasgow); Retired; *b.* 7 April 1890; *s.* of Rev. Thomas Henry Martin, D.D., and Clara Thorpe; *m.* 1918, Dorothy Priestley Greenwood; two *s.* *Educ.:* Glasgow Academy; Royal Technical College, Glasgow; Glasgow Univ.; Baptist Theological Coll., Glasgow; Trinity Coll., Glasgow. Entered Baptist Ministry, 1914; Assistant Secretary, Student Christian Movement, 1914-29; Chairman, C.O.P.E.C. National Executive, 1920-24; Hon. Treasurer, World's Student Christian Federation, 1928-35; Ministry of Information, 1939-43 (Director, Religions Division); Joint Hon. Secretary, Friends of Reunion, 1933-1943; Managing Director and Editor, Student Christian Movement Press Ltd., 1929-50; Vice-President, British Council of Churches, 1950-52; Moderator, National Free Church

Federal Council, 1952-53; Chm., Exec. Cttee. Brit. Council of Churches, 1956-62; has travelled widely in interests of Student Christian Movement. *Publications:* The Calling of the Church; According to St. Luke; The Meaning of the Old Testament; The Kingdom Without Frontiers; Christ and Money; Morality on Trial; The Parables of the Gospels; Edinburgh, 1937; The Christian as Soldier; Christian Reunion; Great Christian Books; Luke's Portrait of Jesus; The Lord's Prayer; Puritanism and Richard Baxter; The Seven Letters; The Claims of Christ. Editor, The Teacher's Commentary; Towards Reunion Christian Social Reformers of the Nineteenth Century; A Book of Prayers for Schools; Prayers in Time of War; A Christian Year Book; Christian Counter-Attack; A Treasury of Christian Verse, etc. *Recreation:* gardening. *Address:* Lynton, College Lane, East Grinstead, Sussex. *T.:* East Grinstead 1070. *Club:* Athenæum. [*Died* 1 *July* 1964.

MARTIN, Lieut.-Gen Hugh Gray, C.B. 1941; D.S.O. 1918; O.B.E. 1920; Colonel Comdt. R.A., 1942-52; *b.* 28 Feb. 1887; *y. s.* of late J. M. Martin, J.P., formerly of Auchendennan, Dunbartonshire; *m.* 1st, 1915, Violet, *d.* of Colonel Forteath of Newton, Morayshire; one *d.*; 2nd, 1930, Lorna, *widow* of Major N. C. Healing, D.S.O., M.C., R.A. *Educ.:* Marlborough College; Royal Military Academy, Woolwich. Joined Royal Artillery, 1906; appointed Royal Horse Artillery, 1912; served European War (D.S.O., despatches); Afghan War, 1919 (O.B.E., despatches), passed Staff Coll., 1921; Brevet-Lt.-Col., 1926; Instructor, Staff College, Quetta, 1928-31; Imperial Defence College, 1936. Col., 1937; G.S.O. 1st grade, 3rd Division, 1937-38; Commander R.A. 4th Division, 1938; Maj.-Gen. 1938; M.G.A.A. at G.H.Q., B.E.F., 1940; Temp. Lt.-Gen., 1941; retired, 1942; Military Correspondent, Daily Telegraph, 1943-59. *Publications:* papers in Blackwood's, Cornhill, etc.; History of the 15th (Scottish) Div.; Sunset From The Main, 1951. *Address:* 136 Chester Road, Hazel Grove, Cheshire. *T.* Stepping Hill 7896. [*Died* 2 *Oct.* 1969.

MARTIN, Brig. John Crawford, C.B.E. 1942; D.S.O. 1943; M.C. 1915; retired, 1947; *b.* 5 June 1896; *s.* of F. W. Martin, Woodlands, Davidson's Mains, Midlothian; *m.* 1920, Elma, *d.* of A. Gray Muir, W.S.; one *s.* one *d.* *Educ.:* Edinburgh Academy. Indian Army; served in France and India, 1914-18 (despatches); third Afghan War; p.s.c. 1929; Burma Campaign, 1942-45 (despatches). *Recreations:* fishing, gardening, sailing. *Address:* Port-na-Mairt, Ganavan, by Oban, Argyll. *T.:* Oban 2626. [*Died* 24 *June* 1963.

MARTIN, Kingsley; *see* Martin, Basil K.

MARTIN, Olive F., M.A. (Cantab.); *b.* 4 Jan. 1887; *d.* of A. B. Martin, Muxton, Salop. *Educ.:* City of London School; Newnham Coll., Cambridge. Vice-Principal of The Ladies' College, Cheltenham, 1924-31; Headmistress, SS. Mary and Anne, Abbots Bromley, 1931-47. *Address:* 31 Brampton Rd., St. Albans, Herts. *T.:* 51882. [*Died* 12 *April* 1967.

MARTIN, Reginald James; Retired Bank Manager; writer on coinage and cognate subjects; with National Provincial Bank Ltd., 1911-52; Manager Muswell Hill Branch, 1935-43; Long Acre Branch, 1943-1952; Member L.C.C. Banking Consultative Committee (on Educ.), 1938-52 (Chm., 1947-1948); *b.* Runcorn, 27 Sept. 1892; *yr. s.* of Rev. James Martin, Methodist minister, and of Eliza Jane, *d.* of John Mills, Ipswich; unmarried. *Educ.:* Ashville College, Harrogate. President Ashvillian Society, 1938-1939. Served European War, 1914-18, with Artists' Rifles and Queen's Westminsters; Capt. and Adjutant 2nd/10th London Regt. (wounded twice); private, Home Guard, 1940-44. Since 1937 has broadcast frequently on popular side of coinage and banking. *Publications:* chatty articles on modern coinage matters in The Times and other papers; articles on Royal Mint and Coinage in new Chambers's Encyclopædia. *Recreations:* golf; meeting interesting people. *Address:* c/o National Westminster Bank Ltd., 1 Long Acre, W.C.2. *Club:* National Liberal. [*Died* 2 *Nov.* 1970.

MARTIN, Lt.-Col. Sir Robert Edmund, Kt. 1939; C.M.G. 1916; T.D.; V.L. 1949 J.P., late 4th Bn. Leicestershire Regt. (T.F.), County Alderman, Leicestershire C.C.; Member of the Church Assembly; Chm. since 1916 of the Midland Dist. Miners' Fatal Accident Relief Soc.; Chm. of Directors Ecclesiastical Insurance Office *s.* of late Robert Frewen Martin, of Anstey Pastures, Leicestershire; *b.* 1 Dec. 1874; *m.* 1925, Hon. Ethel Laura, *e. d.* of 2nd Baron Crawshaw, *widow* of Captain Laurence Peel, Green Howards. *Educ.:* Eton; King's Coll. Camb. Served European War, 1914-16 (wounded, despatches, C.M.G.). Chm., Leicestershire C.C., 1924-60. *Recreations:* shooting and sailing. *Address:* The Brand, near Loughborough, Leics. *T.:* Woodhouse Eaves 269. *Club:* Oxford and Cambridge. [*Died* 13 *June* 1961.

MARTINDALE, Rev. Cyril Charlie, S.J., M.A., writer; *b.* 25 May 1879; *s.* of late Sir Arthur Henry Temple Martindale, K.C.S.I., and Marion Isabella Mackenzie. *Educ.:* Harrow; Stonyhurst; Campion Hall, Oxford. 1st class classical Mods. and Gts.; Hertford, Craven and Derby sch., Chancellor's Gr. verse and Gaisford Latin verse prize; Ellerton Theological Essay prize; taught at Stonyhurst, Manresa House, Roehampton, and Oxford (sub. fac. Litt. Hum.); Ordained 1911; on staff of Farm St. Church, since 1927. *Publications:* Lives of R. H. Benson; Fr. B. Vaughan; Fr. C. D. Plater; The Risen Sun (after visits to Australia and New Zealand); African Angelus (after visiting S. Africa Union and the Rhodesias); Athens, Argentine, Australia (after visits); Faith of the Roman Church; Vocation of Aloysius Gonzaga; What are Saints?; Broadcast Sermons; The Message of Fatima; Notes for Schools on Gospel and Acts (5 vols.); The Castle and the Ring, etc. *Address:* Burton Hill, Petworth, Sussex. *T.:* Petworth 3206. [*Died* 18 *March* 1963.

MARTINDALE, Louisa, C.B.E. 1931; J.P.; M.D., B.S. (Lond.), F.R.C.O.G.; Hon. Consulting Surgeon, Marie Curie Hospital, London; Hon. Consulting Surgeon, New Sussex Hospital, Brighton; Past President Medical Women's International Association; Past President of the Medical Women's Federation; *d.* of late William Martindale and late Louisa Spicer of Horsted Keynes, Sussex. *Educ.:* Royal Holloway College, Egham; London (Royal Free Hospital) School of Medicine for Women; Vienna, Berlin, Freiburg. F.R.S.M.; late President London Association of the Medical Women's Federation; late M.O. Roedean School, Brighton; late M.O. Brighton and Hove High School. *Publications:* The Woman Doctor and her Future; a Woman Surgeon (autobiography); papers to medical journals. *Address:* 14 Avenue Lodge, Avenue Road, N.W.8. *T.:* Primrose 0418. [*Died* 5 *Feb.* 1966.

MARTINEAU, Reverend Canon George Edward, M.A.; Hon. Canon St. Mary's Cathedral, Edinburgh, since 1959; Canon Missioner of Diocese and Rector of St. Columba, Edinburgh, since 1959; *b.* 18 Jan. 1905; *s.* of Alfred Martineau, Advocate, Aberdeen, and Maud Martineau; *m.* 1st, 1933, Christian Burnett (*d.* 1957), Powis, Aberdeen; three *s.* one *d.*; 2nd, 1959, Hester Dickson; one *s.* *Educ.:* Uppingham; St. John's College,

Cambridge. B.A. 1926; M.A. 1931. Asst. Master, Ardvreck Preparatory School, Crieff, 1926-28; Cuddesdon Theological Coll., 1928-1930; Deacon, 1930; Priest, 1931. Curate at Chesterfield Parish Church, 1930-33; Curate at Old St. Paul's, Edinburgh, 1933-1935; Vicar of New Mills, Diocese of Derby, 1935-39; Rector of St. Thomas, Aboyne, Dio. of Aberdeen, 1939-44; Rector of Christ Church, Falkirk, Dio. of Edinburgh, 1944-48; Rector of St. John's, Jedburgh, Dio. of Edinburgh, 1948-58; Dean of Edinburgh, Scottish Episcopal Church, 1962-67. *Address:* 9 Ramsay Garden, Edinburgh 1. *T.:* Caledonian 1634. *Club:* New (Edinburgh).
[*Died* 3 *Jan.* 1969.

MARTINEAU, Sir Wilfrid, Kt., *cr.* 1946; M.C., T.D., M.A.; Solicitor and Notary Public; Clerk to the Birmingham Assay Office, 1923-60; Member, General Board (Past Chm.), Midland District Board of Martins Bank Ltd.; Member Midland Local Board Sea Insurance Co. Ltd., since 1952; *b.* 11 Dec. 1889; *e. c.* of late Col. Ernest Martineau, C.M.G., V.D., T.D.; *m.* 1916, Elvira Mary Seton Lee, *yr. d.* of Dr. F. R. Lee Strathy; two *s.* one *d.* *Educ.:* Rugby School; Trinity Hall, Cambridge. Commissioned 6th Bn. R. Warwickshire Regt. T.A. 1908. Service European War, 1914-19 (despatches, M.C.); transferred to Royal Corps of Signals, commanded 48 Divisional Signals, 1929-1933; Colonel 1937. Member Birmingham City Council, 1932-52; Lord Mayor of Birmingham, 1940-41; Alderman, 1941; Chm. Education Cttee., 1943-52; Pres. Assoc. Educ. Cttees., 1955-56; Mem. Burnham Cttee., 1949-; Leader of Authorities' Panel, Burnham Cttee., 1959-63; Member Nat. Advisory Council on the training and supply of Teachers, 1956- (Vice-Chairman, 1959-); Member Executive Committee of Nat. Foundation for Educational Research, 1958- (Chm. 1958-63). West Midland Group on Post-War Reconstruction and Planning since 1942; Chm. Edgbaston Div. Unionist Assoc., 1936-40 and 1945-52; Life Governor and Mem. Council, Univ. of Birmingham; Dep. Pro-Chancellor, 1957; Gov., numerous schools; Bailiff, King Edward's Schools, 1954-55; Mem. Management Cttee., City of Birmingham Symphony Orchestra; Liveryman of Goldsmiths' Company, 1952; Dir. Birmingham Repertory Theatre Ltd., 1952; Chairman B.B.C. Midland Regional Advisory Council, 1952-57. Member of numerous Birmingham Cttees. *Address:* 30 Rotton Park Road, Edgbaston, Birmingham. *T.:* (Birmingham) Edgbaston 1591; Upper Coscombe, Temple Guiting, nr. Cheltenham. *T.:* Stanton 227. *Clubs:* United University; Union (Birmingham). [*Died* 8 *July* 1964.

MARTINSON, Rt. Rev. Ezra Douglas, C.B.E. 1956 (M.B.E. 1943); retired; *b.* 16 March 1885; *s.* of Jonas and Salome Martinson; *m.* 1912, Bernice Ohene; two *s.* eight *d.* (and two *s.* decd.). *Educ.:* Basel Mission Schools and Theological College, Akropong; King's College, London (short study). Teacher Catechist, 1905-15; Diocese of Accra: Deacon, 1915; Priest, 1916; Archdeacon, 1937; Archdeacon of the whole Diocese, 1937; Assistant Bishop, 1951-63. Canon of Collegiate Church of St. George the Martyr, Jerusalem, 1955-63. Coronation Medal, 1953. *Publications:* (first translator) Anglican Prayer Book, with Ancient and Modern, into Twi language, Akan, in Ghana, 1957; Anglican Church Doctrine in Twi, 1963; Twi Catechism for Baptism and Confirmation Candidates, 1963. *Address:* c/o P.O. Box 8, Bishop's House, Accra, Ghana.
[*Died* 28 *March* 1968.

MARTYN, David Forbes, F.R.S. 1950; Chief Officer, Upper Atmosphere Section, Commonwealth Scientific and Industrial Research Organization, since 1958; *b.* 27 June 1906; *s.* of Dr. H. Somerville Martyn and Elizabeth Craigallan Martyn, Cambuslang, Scotland; *m.* 1944, Margot Adams, Sydney, Australia. *Educ.:* Plymouth College; Allan Glen's School; Royal College of Science, London. B.Sc., A.R.C.Sc. 1926, Ph.D. 1929, D.Sc. 1936, London. Lyle Medal, Aust. Nat. Research Council, 1947; Sidey Medal, Royal Soc. N.Z. 1947; Burfitt Medal, Roy. Soc., N.S.W., 1950; Charles Chree Medal of Physical Soc., London, 1954. Houldsworth Fellow, Univ. of Glasgow, 1927-1929; Radio Research Board, Australia, 1930-; mission on behalf of Commonwealth Govt. to U.K., 1939 initiating radar development in Australia; first Chief Radiophysics Laboratory, Sydney, 1939-41; Director Operational Research, Aust. fighting services, 1942-44. Chairman, U.N. Sci. and Tech. Cttee. on Peaceful Uses of Outer Space, 1962-; Pres., Australian Acad. of Science, 1969-. *Publications:* papers in learned journals, 1926-. *Recreations:* golf, tennis, trout-fishing. *Address:* Upper Atmosphere Section, C.S.I.R.O., Camden, N.S.W. Australia. [*Died* 5 *March* 1970.

MARTYR, (Joseph) Weston; author; *b.* Southampton, 1885; *m.* 1918, Norah Christine Bainbridge (*d.* 1942); no *c.* *Educ.:* Sea. Went to sea at 15, served in square-rigged ships and then steamers; became a gold-miner in South Africa; recruited labour in China for Rand Mines; merchant and steamship business in Japan; S. Sea trader; banker in Formosa; Consul for Netherlands, Denmark and Sweden in Shimonoseki; 1st Sherwood Foresters and Tunnelling Co. R.E. in France, Captain R.E.; trading in Far East; steamship business in New York, etc.; gave it all up and began to write in 1922; introduced ocean yacht racing into England, 1923. *Publications:* The Southseaman, 1923; Paradise Enow, 1936; Not without Dust and Heat, 1930; The £200 Millionaire, 1931; A General Cargo, 1935; The Pipe Pushers, 1938; The Wandering Years, 1939; many short stories and Radio Talks. *Recreations:* ocean yacht racing, croquet, archery. *Address:* Lawnside, Westfield Road, Budleigh Salterton, Devon. *Clubs:* Royal Ocean Racing; Budleigh Salterton Croquet. [*Died* 27 *March* 1966.

MARWICK, Hugh, O.B.E. 1938; M.A., D.Litt., Edinburgh; Chevalier of Royal Norwegian Order of St. Olaf, 1946; Hon. Sheriff-Substitute of Orkney, 1936; Executive Officer and Director of Education, Orkney Education Authority, 1929-46; retd., 1946; *b.* 30 Nov. 1881; *s.* of late Hugh Marwick, Rousay, Orkney, and late Lydia Gibson; *m.* 1914, Jane Barritt, Burnley, Lancs; no *c.* *Educ.:* Edinburgh Univ. Chief English Master, Burnley Grammar School, 1910-14; Headmaster, Kirkwall Secondary School, 1914-29. Foreign Corresp. Mem. Kungel. Vitterhets Historie och Antikvitets Akademi, Stockholm, 1952; Hon. Mem. Gustav Adolfs Akademi, 1953; Mem. Det. Norske Videnskaps Akademi Oslo, 1954. Freedom of Kirkwall, 1954. Hon. LL.D. (Aberdeen), 1956; Hon. D.Phil., Bergen University, 1964. Hon. Fellow, Soc. of Antiquaries of Scotland, 1960. *Publications:* The Orkney Norn, 1929; Merchant Lairds of Long Ago, Pt. I. 1936, Pt. II. 1939; The Place-Names of Rousay, 1947; Orkney (Hale's County Series), 1951; Official Guide to Orkney Ancient Monuments, 1952; Orkney Farm-Names, 1952, various antiquarian articles in Proceedings of Society of Antiq. Scot., and Orkney Antiquarian Society. *Recreations:* archæology, place-names. *Address:* Alton House, Kirkwall, Orkney. *T.:* Kirkwall 61.
[*Died* 21 *May* 1965.

MARYON, Herbert, O.B.E. 1956; F.S.A.; Fellow of the International Institute for the Conservation of Museum Objects; *b.* 9

March 1874; *s.* of John S. Maryon; *m.* 1st, Annie Elizabeth Stones; one *d.*; 2nd, Muriel Dore Wood; one *s.* one *d.* *Educ.:* John Lyon School, Harrow. Director School of Industrial Arts, Keswick, 1900-05; Teacher of Sculpture, Reading University, 1908-27; Master of Sculpture, King's College (University of Durham), Newcastle upon Tyne, 1927-39; Technical Attaché, British Museum Laboratory, 1945-62; Exhibitor at the Salon, Roy. Acad., Walker Art Gall., etc. *Publications:* Metalwork and Enamelling, 4th edn. 1959; Modern Sculpture its Aims and Ideals, 1933; 40 archæological papers. *Recreations:* travel, archæology. *Address:* 54 Craigleith View, Edinburgh 4.
[*Died* 14 *July* 1965.

MARYON-WILSON, Rev. Canon Sir (George) Percy (Maryon), 12th Bt. of East Borne, *cr.* 1661; M.A.; Lord of the Manor of Hampstead; Rector of Christ Church, St. Leonards-on-Sea, 1941-64; Canon and Prebendary of Chichester Cathedral since 1953; Member of Executive Committee of Standing Council of the Baronetage since 1951; Custos, St. Mary's Hospital, Chichester, since 1964; *b.* 22 February 1898; *o. s.* of late George Maryon-Wilson and late Hon. Stephanie Allanson-Winn, sister of 5th Baron Headley; *S.* uncle, 1944. *Educ.:* Eton; Magdalen College, Oxford, 2nd class Honours in Modern History and Diploma in Theology with distinction. Lieutenant (temporary Captain) Grenadier Guards, 1916-20; aide-de-camp to Governor-General of South Africa (Earl Buxton), 1919-20; Pilkington Prize, 1923; ordained priest, 1924; Assistant Magdalen College Missioner till 1927; Head of Magdalen College Mission, 1927-41; Vicar of St. Mary the Virgin, Somers Town, 1929-1941; Vice-Chairman St. Pancras House Improvement Society, 1924-41, now Vice-Pres.; Chairman Christ Church St. Leonards-on-Sea Housing Society, 1941-63. Preached before University of Oxford, 1940 and 1946. Proctor in Convoc., Dio. Chichester, 1957-1964. *Publications:* In whose heart are thy ways, 1937; Whom the Lord hath redeemed, 1938; Caritas Christi, 1940; The Vocation of the Laity, 1940; Is He sure to bless ?, 1943; Transition to Peace, 1945; Some common obstacles to Faith, 1945· The Paradoxical Society, 1946; Advent to Easter, 1946; The Way of Love, 1948; The Sound of that Spiritual Trumpet, 1951; Plain Talks on the Religion of the Church, 1953; contributor to A Lantern for Lent, 1931. Harvest Home, 1930. Catholic Sermons, 1932; articles in Dict. of National Biography on Basil Jellicoe and Dr. Maude Royden. *Recreations:* squash racquets, riding, chess. *Heir: kinsman,* Hubert Guy Maryon Wilson, *b.* 27 July 1888. *Address:* 21 West Street, Chichester, Sussex. *T.:* Chichester 85958. *Clubs:* Reform, National Liberal.
[*Died* 10 *July* 1965.

MASANI, Sir Rustom Pestonji, Kt., *cr.* 1943; M.A., J.P.; *b.* 23 Sept. 1876; *m.* 1902; three *s.* one *d.* *Educ.:* Elphinstone College, Bombay. Fellow: Institute of Bankers; Univ. Bombay; Medallist, Asiatic Soc., Bombay; President K.R. Cama Oriental Inst.; Vice-Pres. P.E.N. All-India Centre; Member of Indian Nat. Commission for Co-operation with U.N.E.S.C.O.; Member, Indian Council for Cultural Relations; Editor: Gup-Sup; English Columns, Kaisar-i-Hind; Indian Spectator. Vice-Chancellor, Univ. of Bombay, Provincial Leader, National War Front, Bombay; Trustee: Prince of Wales Museum; N.M. Wadia and other Charities; People's Free Reading Room and Library; President: Anthropolog. Soc., Adult Educ. Assoc.; Indian Inst. for Educ. and Cultural Co-operation; Society for Protection of Children in Western India; Parsi Girls' School Association; Vice-President Bhandarkar Oriental Research Inst.; Municipal Secretary, Deputy Municipal Commissioner and Municipal Commissioner, Bombay; Manager, Central Bank of India; Sec. Indian Central Banking Enquiry Cttee.; Director, Reserve Bank of India. *Publications:* (English) Child Protection; Folklore of Wells; Law and Procedure of Municipal Corporation, Bombay; The Conference of the Birds, a Sufi Allegory; Evolution of Local Self-Government in Bombay; Court Poets of Iran and India; The Religion of the Good Life: Zoroastrianism; Dadabhai Naoroji: the Grand Old Man of India; Education for World Understanding: The Role of Wealth in Society; The Five Gifts; Britain in India; N.M. Wadia and His Foundation, also (in Gujarati) Gharni tatha Nishalni Kelavni, "Tansukh Mala"; *novels:* Bodhlu, Chandra Chal, Abysiniano Habsi. *Address:* Mody Mansion, Merewether Road, Bombay, India.
[*Died* 14 *Nov.* 1966.

MASCHWITZ, Eric, O.B.E. 1936; Producer (Special Projects) Rediffusion Television, since 1963; *b.* Birmingham, 10 June 1901; *o.s.* of late Albert Arthur Maschwitz and Leontine Hilda, *d.* of Augustus Boekemann, Sydney, N.S.W.; *m.* 1st, 1926, Hermione Ferdinanda, *e. d.* of James Gingold (marr. diss.); 2nd, 1945, Phyllis (*d.* 1969), *d.* of T. C. Gordon. *Educ.:* Arden House, Henley-in-Arden; Repton (Classical Scholar); Gonville and Caius Coll., Cambridge (Mod. Language Scholar). Edited group of Hutchinson's magazines, 1922-23; joined B.B.C. in 1926; Variety Dir. of the B.B.C., 1933-37, Editor of the Radio Times, 1927-33; under contract to Metro-Goldwyn-Mayer, Hollywood, 1937-38; enlisted Intelligence Corps, 1940; sent on mission to U.S.A., 1941-42; inaugurated Army Broadcasting Section, War Office, 1942; devised Overseas Recorded Broadcasting Service for troops; Lt.-Col. i/c Broadcasting, 21 Army Group, 1945. Head of Light Entertainment (Television), B.B.C., 1958-61; Assistant and Adviser to Controller of Television Programmes, B.B.C., 1961-63. Director of the Performing Right Society; Ivor Novello Award for services to music, 1961; *Plays:* The Double Man (Blackpool, 1930); Evidence for the Defence (Swanage, 1930); Gay Hussar (provinces, 1933-34); Spread it Abroad (with Herbert Farjeon) (Saville Theatre, 1935); Balalaika (Adelphi and His Majesty's Theatres, London, 1936-38); Magyar Melody (His Majesty's, 1939); New Faces (Comedy, 1940); Waltz without End (Lyric, 1942-43); Flying Colours (with Ronald Jeans), 1943; Between Ourselves, 1946; Good Night, Vienna, 1946; Starlight Roof (Hippodrome), 1947-48; Carissima (Palace), 1948-49; Belinda Fair (Saville), 1949; Zip Goes A Million (Palace), 1951-53; Love from Judy (Saville), 1952-54; Pink Champagne, 1953, Happy Holiday (Palace), 1954; Romance in Candlelight (Piccadilly), 1955; Three Waltzes (new version), 1955; Summer Song (Princes), 1956; White Horse Inn (new version), 1957; Passion Flower, 1957. *Autobiography:* No Chip on my Shoulder, 1957. *Film Scenarios:* Good Night, Vienna, 1932; Invitation to the Waltz, 1935; Goodbye Mr. Chips, 1939. *Songs:* These Foolish Things, Nightingale Sang in Berkeley Square, Room 504 and many other ballads. *Recreations:* tennis and travelling. *Address:* 8 Queen Anne St., W.1. *Club:* Savile.
[*Died* 27 *Oct.* 1969.

MASEFIELD, John, O.M. 1935; C.Lit. 1961; Litt.D.; LL.D.; writer; Poet Laureate since 1930; *m.* 1903, Constance (*d.* 1960), *d.* of Nicholas de la Cherois-Crommelin, late of Cushendun, Co. Antrim, Northern Ireland; one *d.* (and one *s.* killed in action). *Publications:* The Tragedy of Nan; The Tragedy of Pompey the Great; Multitude and Solitude;

Poems and Ballads; William Shakespeare; The Everlasting Mercy; The Widow in the Bye-Street; Dauber; The Daffodil Fields, etc.; Philip the King; The Faithful; Sonnets and Poems; Good Friday; Gallipoli; Lollingdon Downs; Reynard the Fox, etc.; Right Royal; King Cole; Melloney Holtspur, 1922; Sard Harker, 1924, etc.; Odtaa, 1926; Recent Prose, 1924; The Midnight Folk, 1927; The Hawbucks, 1929; The Wanderer of Liverpool, 1930; Minnie Maylow's Story and other tales and scenes, 1931; A Tale of Troy, 1932; The Conway, 1933; The Bird of Dawning, 1933; The Taking of the Gry, 1934; The Box of Delights, 1935; A Letter from Pontus, 1936; The Country Scene, 1937; Dead Ned, 1938; Tribute to Ballet, 1938; Live and Kicking Ned, 1939; Basilissa, 1940; The Nine Days Wonder, 1941; In the Mill, 1941; New Chum, 1944; a Macbeth Production, 1945; Thanks Before Going, 1946; Badon Parchments, 1947; On the Hill, 1949; So Long to Learn, 1952; The Bluebells, 1961; Grace Before Ploughing, 1966. *Address:* Burcote Brook, Abingdon, Berks. [*Died* 12 *May* 1967.

MASON, Arnold Henry, R.A. 1951 (A.R.A. 1940); R.P.; Portrait and Landscape Painter; *b.* Birkenhead, 20 March 1885; *s.* of Rev. W. H. Mason. *Educ.:* Royal College of Art; Slade; studied in Paris and Rome. Cheshire County Council Scholar, 1903-6; Assistant to Sir W. B. Richmond, R.A., 1906-8; British Institution Scholar, Painting, 1908-11; Joined Artists Rifles, July 1915; Commissioned Shropshire Light Infantry, 1917. Exhibitor in principal London exhibitions; Pictures in Tate, Manchester, Hanley Art Galleries and Private Collections. *Recreations:* reading, billiards, gardening. *Club:* Chelsea Arts. [*Died* 17 *Nov.* 1963.

MASON, Professor Eudo Colecestra, M.A., Dr.Phil.; D.Litt. (Oxford); Professor of German, University of Edinburgh, since 1951; *b.* Colchester, 26 September 1901; 3rd *s.* of Ernest N. Mason and Bertha B. (*née* Kitton); *m.* 1939, Esther K. Giesecke (*d.* 1966). *Educ.:* Perse Sch., Cambridge; St. Catherine's Soc., Oxford; Jesus College, Cambridge. B.A. Oxford, English Hons., 1926; Lector, Münster, Westphalia, 1926-31; B.A. Cambridge, Mod. Lang. Trip. II, 1932; Lector, Leipzig, 1932-39; D.Phil. Leipzig, 1938; Lector, Basel, Switzerland, 1939-46; Lecturer in German Literature, Edinburgh, 1946-51. Vis. Prof., Univ. of California, Berkeley, 1963. Gold Medal, Goethe-Institut, 1967; Prize of the Deutsche Akademie für Sprache und Dichtung for Germanistik im Ausland, 1967. Dr. (*h.c.*) Berne. *Publications:* Rilke's Apotheosis, 1938; Lebenshaltung und Symbolik be, R. M. Rilke, 1939, 1964; H. Füssli, Aphorismen über die Kunst, 1944; Der Zopf des Münchhausen, 1949; Unveröffentlichte Gedichte H. Füsslis, 1951; The Mind of Henry Fuseli, 1951; Rilke und Goethe, 1958; Deutsche und englische Romantik, 1959 (rev. edn., 1966); Rilke, Europe and the English-Speaking World, 1961; Exzentrische Bahnen, 1962; R.M. Rilke (Writers and Critics), 1963; Füsslis Bemerkungen über Rousseau, 1962; Miscellany of German and French Poetry, 1963; Goethe's Faust: Its Genesis and Purport, 1967; contrib. British and continental jls. on German and English literature. *Recreations:* walking; wild flowers; country-dancing. *Address:* 20 Warriston Gardens, Edinburgh 3. [*Died* 10 *June* 1969.

MASON, Frank H., R.I.; marine painter; *b.* Seaton Carew, County Durham, 1876; *s.* of Felix Gibson and Catherine Everet Mason; *m.* 1st, 1899, Edith Ann (decd.), *y. d.* of late Capt. Townley Fullam, Hull; one *d*; 2nd, 1954, Charlotte, *d.* of Charles Groves, Eastbourne. *Educ.:* private schools; H.M.S. Conway. Followed the sea for a while; later engaged in engineering and shipbuilding at Leeds and Hartlepool; has travelled abroad extensively and made several voyages for purposes of sketching. Lieutenant R.N.V.R. Dec. 1914; served European War, North Sea and Egypt, 1914-19. Min. of Home Security and Admiralty for Special duties, 1941; Mem. Society of Marine Artists, 1961. *Publications:* The Book of British Ships, various articles and pamphlets; illustrations and posters for railway companies. *Recreations:* yachting and mechanical work. *Address:* 3 Primrose Hill Studios, Fitzroy Road, N.W.1. *T.:* Primrose 3105. *Clubs:* Royal Thames Yacht (Hon. Life Mem.); Royal Yorkshire Yacht (Bridlington); Anchorites. [*Died* 24 *Feb.* 1965.

MASON, Sir Laurence, Kt. 1942; C.I.E. 1930; O.B.E. 1919; M.C.; *b.* 27 Aug. 1886; *s.* of late Herbert W. Mason, J.P., The Manor House, Sproughton, nr. Ipswich; *m.* Margaret Menella (*d.* 1959), *d.* of late Rev. H. C. Jollye, Walton Rectory, Warwick; one *s.* *Educ.:* Charterhouse; Christ Church, Oxford (B.A.). I.F.S., 1907; joined in India, 1910, as Assistant Conservator of Forests; Deputy Conservator, 1915; Inspector-General of Forests, India; retired from Indian Forest Service, 1941; Deputy Director-General Supply, India, 1941-44; served on Staff of Cabinet Mission to India, 1946. Served European War in France with Royal Artillery, 1914-1918 (M.C., O.B.E., Croix de Guerre des Belges, temp. rank of Major). *Address:* 19 Hollycombe Close, Liphook, Hants. *T.:* 2129. [*Died* 4 *June* 1970.

MASON, Robert Heath, C.M.G. 1963; O.B.E. 1944; H.M. Diplomatic Service; Assistant Under Secretary of State, Foreign and Commonwealth Office, since 1968; *b.* 10 Sept. 1918; *e. s.* of Hugh Campbell Mason and Grace Ann Mason, N.Z.; *m.* 1951, Angelica Vernon Mann, New York; one *s.* two *d.* *Educ.:* Waipukurau and Waipawa District High Schools, Hawke's Bay, N.Z., Commissioned R.A.F. (Equipment Br.), 1938; served War of 1939-45 (O.B.E.): in Coastal and Bomber Commands, 1941; Soviet Union, 1943; India and Burma, 1945; studied Arabic, 1947; joined H.M. Foreign Service, 1949; Foreign Office, 1951; Warsaw as First Secretary, 1953; Foreign Office, 1955; Amman, as First Secretary and Consul, later Counsellor, 1960; Head of Northern Dept., F.O., 1960-63; Counsellor, Washington, 1963-64; Counsellor and Head of Chancery, British Embassy, Leopoldville, 1964-66; Ambassador to the Mongolian People's Republic, 1966-67; Commonwealth Office, 1968. *Address:* The Terrace, Boston Spa, Yorkshire. *T.:* Boston Spa 3200. *Club:* Travellers'. [*Died* 4 *Aug.* 1969.

MASON, William, D.Sc., M.Inst.C.E., M.I. Mech.E.; Emeritus Professor, University of Liverpool, 1938; *b.* 1872; *e. s.* of Joseph Mason, of Heywood, Lancs; *m.* Jean, *d.* of George Flett of Wick, Caithness; one *s.* *Educ.:* private school; Owens College, Manchester. Pupilage with James Diggle, A.M.Inst.C.E., late of Heywood and Westminster; 1st Class Hons. Engineering and Physics, Victoria University (Manchester) and University Scholar; railway contractor's engineer; Assistant Engineer P.W.D., India; Senior Demonstrator King's College, London; Lecturer in Engineering, University of Liverpool; Professor of Engineering (Applied Mechanics), University of Liverpool, 1920-37; D.Sc. University of Manchester, 1914; Emeritus Professor, University of Liverpool, 1938; President Liverpool Engineering Society, 1936-37. *Publications:* papers published by scientific and technical societies. *Recreation:* garden. *Address:* 140 Mount Gold Road, Plymouth. *T.:* Plymouth 62310. [*Died* 1 *Nov.* 1961.

MASSEY, Rt. Hon. Vincent, C.C. (Canada), 1967; P.C. 1941; C.H. 1946; Royal Victorian Chain, 1960; *b.* Toronto, 20 Feb. 1887; *e. s.* of Chester D. Massey and Anna Vincent; *m.* 1915, Alice Stuart (*d.* 1950), *d.* of late Sir George Parkin, K.C.M.G.; one *s.* (and one *s.* decd.). *Educ.:* St. Andrews Coll., Toronto; Univ. of Toronto, B.A.; Balliol Coll., Oxford, M.A. Lecturer in Modern History, University of Toronto, and Dean of Residence, Victoria College, 1913-15; directed building of Hart House, Toronto; on staff Military District No. 2 (Canada), 1915-18; Assoc. Secretary, War Committee of the Cabinet (Ottawa), Jan.-Dec. 1918; with Government Repatriation Committee as Secretary, and later Director, 1918-19; President, Massey-Harris Co., Toronto, 1921-25; appointed Minister without portfolio in Dominion Cabinet and contested Durham (Liberal), 1925; attended Imperial Conference, London, 1926, with Canadian Delegation; H.M. Canadian Minister to the U.S.A., 1926-30; President, National Liberal Federation of Canada, 1932-35; High Commissioner for Canada in United Kingdom, 1935-46; Canadian delegate, League of Nations Assembly, 1936; a Trustee of National Gallery (London), 1941-46 (Chairman, 1943-46); a Trustee of Tate Gallery, 1942-1946; Chairman, Royal Commission on National Development in the Arts, Letters and Sciences, 1949-51; Chancellor, Univ. of Toronto, 1947-53; Governor-General and Commander-in-Chief of Canada, 1952-59. Chairman, Massey Foundation; Chairman, H.R.H. The Duke of Edinburgh's Second Commonwealth Study Conf., 1959-62; Pres. Third Commonwealth Educn. Conf. (Ottawa), 1964. Romanes Lecturer (Oxford), 1961. Hon. Fell.: Balliol Coll., Oxford; R.I.B.A.; Royal Society of Canada; Royal Architectural Institute of Canada; Royal College of Physicians and Surgeons (Canada); Hon. F.R.C.O.G.; Hon. Life Member, Can. Hist. Assoc.; Hon. Member, Cdn. Bar Assoc.; Hon. Mem. Canadian Medical Assoc.; Hon. Life Mem. Parly. Press Gall., Ottawa; For. Hon. Mem., Acad. of Arts and Sciences (U.S.A.); Visitor, Massey Coll., Toronto; Hon. D.C.L. Oxford, Bishop's and Acadia Univs.; Hon. LL.D., Aberdeen, Birmingham, B.C., California, Carleton, Columbia, Dalhousie, Kentucky, Liverpool, Manitoba, McGill, McMaster, Michigan, New Brunswick, N.Y., Ottawa, Princeton, Queen's (Canada), St. Francis Xavier, Saskatchewan, Sherbrooke, Toronto, Yale Universities and Dartmouth and Hobart Colleges; Royal Military College, Kingston; D. de l'Univ. Laval; Litt.D., Univ. Western Ontario; Hon. Fellow, Trinity College, Toronto; Bailiff Grand Cross, St. John of Jerusalem; Albert Medal, R.S.A., 1959; Canada Council Medal, 1962. *Publications:* Good Neighbourhood and other Addresses, 1931; The Sword of Lionheart and other Wartime Speeches, 1943; On Being Canadian, 1948; Speaking of Canada, 1959; What's Past Is Prologue, 1963; Confederation on the March, 1965. *Address:* Batterwood House, nr. Port Hope, Canada. *Clubs:* Athenæum, Brooks's, Beefsteak; Toronto, York, University (Toronto); Century (N.Y.).

[*Died* 30 *Dec.* 1967.

MASSIE, Grant, C.B.E. 1944; M.S., F.R.C.S.; Surgeon Guy's Hospital; Surgeon Putney Hospital; *b.* 31 Dec. 1896; *s.* of Thomas and Katherine Massie. *Educ.:* Guy's Hospital, London University. M.B., B.S. (Hons. Surgery) 1922, M.S. 1924; M.R.C.S. Eng., L.R.C.P. Lond., 1920, F.R.C.S. Eng. 1922; Treas. Gold Medal in Clin. Surg., Arthur Durham Trav. Student, 1921. Poulton Student and Ashley Cooper Student, 1924. Fell. Roy. Soc. Med. and Assoc. Surgs.; Assoc. Mem. Brit. Orthop. Assoc.; Brigadier, Cons. Surg. India Command and 11th Army Group; formerly Exam. Anat. for F.R.C.S. Eng.; Asst. Orthop. Surg. Sen. Demonst. Anat. and Surg. Regist. Guy's Hosp. *Publications:* Surgical Anatomy, 4th ed., 1940; contrib. to medical jls. *Address:* 55 Wimpole St., W.1. *T.:* Welbeck 8607. *Club:* Athenæum.

[*Died* 12 *Aug.* 1964.

MASSIE, Lt.-Col. Robert John Allwright, D.S.O. 1918; retd.; *b.* 1890; *s.* of Hugh Hamon Massie, Sydney; *m.* 1st, Phyllis Wood, *d.* of H. H. Lang, Newcastle, N.S.W.; one *s.* (killed in action) two *d.*; *m.* 2nd, 1947, Elizabeth, *widow* of E. C. Squire, Washington, D.C. *Educ.:* Sydney Univ. (B.E.). Served European War, 1914-18 (despatches, D.S.O., French Croix de Guerre with Palm). *Recreations:* sailing, motoring, Life member N.S.W. Cricket Assoc. *Address:* 17 Upper Spit Road, Mosman, N.S.W., Australia. *Clubs:* Union, Royal Sydney Yacht Squadron, Cricketers' (Sydney); Elanora Country.

[*Died* 14 *Feb.* 1966.

MASSON, Sir (James) Irvine (Orme), Kt., *cr.* 1950; M.B.E. 1918; F.R.S. 1939; D.Sc. (Melbourne); Hon. LL.D. (Edinburgh and Sheffield); Fellow of Univ. Coll., London; F.R.I.C.; *b.* Melbourne, 3 Sept. 1887; *o. s.* of late Prof. Sir David Orme Masson, K.B.E., F.R.S., and Mary, *d.* of Sir John Struthers, M.D.; *m.* 1913, Flora Lovell (*d.* 1960), *o. d.* of late Prof. G. Lovell Gulland, C.M.G., M.D.; one *s.* *Educ.:* Melbourne Grammar School; University of Melbourne (Ormond College). 1851 Exhibition Research Scholar, 1910-12 (Edinburgh, London); Lecturer and Reader in Chemistry, Univ. Coll., London, 1912-15, 1919-24; R.N.V.R. 1914-15; at Research Department Royal Arsenal, Woolwich, 1915-1919; Secretary of the Chemical Society, 1921-24; Professor of Chemistry and Head of Department of Pure Science, University, Durham, 1924-38; Member of Senate, University of Durham, 1930-36, 1938; Vice-Chancellor of the University of Sheffield, 1938-52; retired. Court, 1939-48, and Board of Governors, 1948-52, of United Sheffield Hospitals, and Chairman of Liaison Cttee. between University, Regional Hospitals, and United Sheffield Hospitals. Trustee and Member Exec. of Carnegie Trust for Univs. of Scotland, 1953-; Statutory Comr., Univ. of St. Andrews, 1953-58. *Publications:* chiefly investigations in physical, inorganic, and organic chemistry published by Royal Society, Chemical Society, etc., 1909-38; Three Centuries of Chemistry, 1925; contributor on chemistry to various co-operative volumes; Problems in the National Teaching of Science, 1931; occasional typographical studies in Trans. Bibliographical Society; monograph on Mainz printing, 1457-59 (Bibl. Soc., 1954), etc. *Address:* c/o Pringle & Clay, W.S., 21 Ainslie Place, Edinburgh 3. *Club:* Athenæum. [*Died* 22 *Oct.* 1962.

MASSON, Sir John Robertson, Kt., *cr.* 1946; Director, John Swire & Sons Ltd., 1939-63; *b.* 30 Nov. 1898; *e. s.* of late George Masson, Kingussie; *m.* 1945, Jean Gordon, *d.* of Charles Gordon Mackie, Montrose; one *d.* *Educ.:* Fettes; Merton College, Oxford (Exhibition). Chief Representative for India, Burma and Ceylon, Ministry of War Transport, 1942-45. *Club:* Junior Carlton.

[*Died* 10 *March* 1965.

MASSY, Lt.-Gen. Hugh Royds Stokes, C.B. 1940; D.S.O. 1917; M.C.; *b.* Jan. 1884; *e. s.* of late Arthur Wellington Massy of Cottesmore, Pembroke, and Emma Stokes of Cuffern, Pembroke; *m.* 1912, Maud Ina Nest (*d.* 1960), *o. d.* of late Col. Roch, Llether, Pembroke; one *s.* one *d.* *Educ.:* Bradfield College; R.M.A., Woolwich. Received Commission in R.F.A. 1902; served in W. Africa, 1907-11; Adjutant to 4th East Lancs. Brigade R.F.A., 1913-14; served European War in Gallipoli, Egypt, and France (D.S.O.

M.C.); India, 1922-28, including Instructor, Staff College, Quetta, 1925-28; Imperial Defence College, 1930; Col., 1932; Instructor Senior Officers' School, Belgaum, 1932-34; Brigadier, Royal Artillery, Southern Command, 1934-38; Maj.-Gen., 1938; Director of Military Training, War Office, 1938-39; Deputy Chief of Imperial General Staff, 1939-40; Corps Commander, 1940-41; retired pay, 1943; Col. Comdt. R.A., 1945-51. High Sheriff of Pembrokeshire, 1946. *Address:* Mashumbas, Marandellas, S. Rhodesia. [*Died* 21 *May* 1965.

MASTER, Col. W. A. C.; *see* Chester-Master.

MASTERS, Albert Edward Hefford, C.B. 1956; C.B.E. 1952; M.I.Mech.E.; Managing Director: Petters Ltd. since 1960; Director: Hawker Siddeley Diesels Ltd.; Air Pumps Ltd.; *b.* 9 August 1902; *s.* of late A. E. H. Masters; *m.* 1928, Elsie, *d.* of late F. J. Littlewood; two *s.* Chief Designer, Lagonda cars, 1930-35; Tank Designer, Vickers-Armstrong, 1935-40; Dep. Director, Fighting Vehicles Research and Development Establishment, Ministry of Supply, 1941-45, Director, 1945-59. *Recreation:* farmer. *Address:* Iris Copse, Nowhurst Lane, Broadbridge Heath, Horsham, Sussex. *T.:* Horsham 5142. *Club:* Farmers'. [*Died* 7 *June* 1968.

MASTERS, David. *Publications:* The Romance of Excavation, 1923; The Wonders of Salvage, 1924; The Conquest of Disease, 1925; New Cancer Facts, 1925; How to Conquer Consumption, 1926; Perilous Days, 1927; The Glory of Britain, 1930; When Ships go Down, 1932; S.O.S., 1933; On the Wing, 1934; Deep-Sea Diving; I.D.—New Tales of the Submarine War, 1935; Crimes of the High Seas, 1936; What Men Will Do For Money, 1937; Divers in Deep Seas, 1938; So Few—Immortal Record of the Royal Air Force, fully authenticated, 1941; Up Periscope, the Immortal Record of His Majesty's Submarines, 1942; With Pennants Flying, the Immortal Record of the Royal Armoured Corps, 1943; A Combined Wonders of Salvage and S.O.S., 1944; Miracle Drug, the Inner History of Penicillin, also 8th edition So Few, and revised editions of Wonders of Salvage and When Ships Go Down, 1946; Epics of Salvage—Wartime Feats of the Marine Salvage Men, 1952 (Amer. edn. 1954, French translation, Arraches à la Mer, 1955), The Plimsoll Mark, 1955; Epics of Salvage, 1956; So few, 1957; Up Periscope, 1957; In Peril On The Sea, War Exploits of Allied Seamen, 1960. *Recreations:* gardening, photography, the study of Nature, economics and the interplay of natural forces. *Address:* c/o David Higham Associates, 76 Dean Street, Soho, W.1. [*Died* 24 *May* 1965.

MASTERS, Hon. Robert, C.M.G. 1953; *b.* 15 June 1879; *s.* of Jonas and Barbara Masters; *m.* 1906, Alice G. Hopkins; one *s.* three *d.* *Educ.:* Brunnerton Public School, N.Z. Entered business at Stratford in firm which is now Masters, Ltd., Taranaki, of which he is Managing Director; Managing Director Taranaki Publishing Coy. and other Companies; Taranaki Provincial representative at Rugby and Hockey; 12 years Member and 4 years Chairman Taranaki Education Board; President Stratford Agricultural and Pastoral Association; Chairman N.Z. Transport Board, 1929; Chairman N.Z. Railways Royal Commission, 1930; Member Legislative Council, 1930-37; Minister without portfolio and Deputy-Leader Legislative Council, 1930-31; Minister of Industries and Commerce, 1931-1935; Minister of Education, 1931-34; Member of Cabinet Economy Committee, 1931; Leader of the Legislative Council of New Zealand, 1933-35; Represented the Government in the Hawkes Bay Earthquake area in connection with earthquake in Feb. 1931; with the Prime Minister attended the World Monetary and Economic Conference, London, 1935, as New Zealand delegation; Member New Zealand Electricity Council. *Recreations:* was an active Rugby and hockey player, and now takes keen interest in administrative side of these sports. *Address:* 17 Hamlet Street, Stratford, New Zealand. [*Died* 29 *June* 1967.

MATANIA, Chevalier Fortunino, R.I. 1917; portrait painter; specialist in historical paintings; *b.* Naples, 1881; *s.* of Professor Cav. (Chevalier) Eduardo Matania and Clelia Della Valle, Naples; *m.* 1905, Elvira Di Gennaro (*d.* 1952); one *s.* one *d.*; *m.* 1960, Ellen Jane Goldsack. *Educ.:* Naples, in his father's studio. Showed since then a strong inclination to follow his father's steps; made the illustration of the first historical book with his father at fourteen; went to Milan as a special artist for the Illustrazione Italiana; at twenty in Paris with Illustration Française and London with The Graphic; at twenty-two in Italy for military service in the Bersaglieri; at twenty-four in London again engaged by The Sphere; Guest of H.M. at the Durbar (Coronation Medal); in 1914 became a war artist and went to the front several times to draw from life; nearly every year exhibited at R.A. and R.I. mostly pictures of Roman life. *Publications:* pictures published in newspapers, every week in Illustrazione Italiana from 1895-1902, in The Graphic, 1901-4, in The Sphere since 1904; principal magazines Europe and America, regularly in Britannia and Eve since 1929; became a writer of historical stories in 1931. *Recreations:* fencing, painting, reconstruction of historical furniture and dresses, music, modelling. *Address:* Studio, 104 Priory Road, N.W.6; 121 Hendon Way, N.W.2. *T.:* Maida Vale 6314. [*Died* 8 *Feb.* 1963.

MATHER, John Chadwick, J.P.; Deputy-Chairman, Cammell, Laird & Co. Ltd., since 1960 (Chairman 1951-59); Vice-Chairman, John Holt & Co. (Liverpool) Ltd. since 1949; *b.* 28 May 1904; *e. s.* of Ernest Mather and Constance, *d.* of John Holt; *m.* 1931, Dorothy, *d.* of J. H. Rodier; two *s.* two *d.* *Educ.:* Uppingham School; Balliol College, Oxford. Entered John Holt & Co. (Liverpool) Ltd., 1927; Director, 1946. Served War with R.A., 1939-45. Director: Cammell, Laird & Co. (Shipbuilders and Engineers) Ltd., 1954; Metropolitan-Cammell Carriage and Wagon Co. Ltd., 1951; Patent Shaft Steel Works Ltd., 1956; Reliance Marine Insurance Co. Ltd.; Guinea Gulf Line Ltd., 1949; Holt Sons & Co. Ltd., 1958. J.P. Flintshire; High Sheriff, Flintshire, 1959. *Recreation:* shooting. *Address:* Plas-yn-Llan, Nanmerch, Flints. *Club:* Palatine (Liverpool). [*Died* 6 *Sept.* 1961.

MATHER, Richard; Chairman Skinningrove Iron Co. Ltd., 1942-62; Ex-Member, Iron and Steel Board, Ministry of Supply; *b.* 19 September 1886; 2nd *s.* of Richard and Ellen Mather; *m.* 1914, Marie C. L. G. A. Schultze; one *s.* one *d.* *Educ.:* Royal Grammar School, Sheffield; Univ. of Sheffield. Metallurgist, Cochrane & Co., Middlesbrough, 1907-11; Metallurgist, Research Dept., Woolwich (W.O.), 1911-19; Metallurgical Inspector, Govt. of India, 1919-1925; Technical Adviser, Indian Tariff Board, 1923-24 and 1926-27; Dep. Gen. Manager, Tata Iron & Steel Co., Jamshedpur, 1927-29; Technical Director, Tata Iron & Steel Co., Bombay, 1930-40; Past Pres. and Bessemer Medallist, Iron & Steel Inst. *Address:* 124 Knightsbridge, S.W.1. *T.:* Kensington 7376. *Club:* East India and Sports. [*Died* 8 *Nov.* 1964.

MATHER, Colonel William, C.B. 1952; T.D. 1927; D.L.; Member: Council Scottish Branch, British Red Cross Society (Chm.

Glasgow Branch, 1945, Pres. 1959); Committee Erskine Hospital for Disabled Servicemen; Earl Haig Fund (Scotland); *b.* 22 Aug. 1888; *s.* of James Mather, Pollokshields, Glasgow, and Janet Morrison French; *m.* 1918, Catherine Grant Duff; two *d.* *Educ.:* Glasgow High School; Collegiate School, Glasgow. Served European War, 1914-18, with 7th Cameronians (Scottish Rifles) which he commanded, 1923-27; Hon. Col. 7th and 6/7th Cameronians, 1948-53. Member Glasgow T. & A.F.A., 1923-53, Chm. 1947-50. Commanded 4th Lanark Bn., H.G., 1940-45. Board of Management, Glasgow Western Hospitals, and Convenor Finance Committee, until 1962. D.L. City of Glasgow, 1945. *Address:* Sarona, Busby, Lanarkshire. *T.:* Busby 1322. *Clubs:* Western, Royal Scottish Automobile (Glasgow)

[*Died* 2 *Oct.* 1966.

MATHER, William Allan; B.Sc. (C.E.), LL.D., D.C.L.; Chairman, Member of Executive Committee and Director: Canadian Pacific Railway Company; Canadian Pacific Steamships, Ltd.; Chairman and Director Canadian Pacific Air Lines, Ltd.; Member of Executive Cttee., and Director Consolidated Mining and Smelting Co. of Canada, Ltd.; Director: Scottish Trust Company; West Kootenay Power and Light Co. Ltd.; Canadian Marconi Co.; Canadian Pacific Express Co.; Toronto, Hamilton and Buffalo Rly. Co.; Royal Trust Co.; *b.* Oshawa, Ontario, 12 Sept. 1885; *s.* of late David Low Mather and late Katherine Allan; *m.* 1925, Maynard Cruickshank, Moose Jaw, Sask.; one *s.* one *d.* *Educ.:* public and high schools, Kenora Ont.; McGill University. Degree in civil engineering, 1908. Began working for C.P.R. in 1903, as axeman on construction gang; gen. supt., Moose Jaw, Sask., 1918; gen. supt., Calgary, 1932; asst. to vice-pres., Montreal, 1933; general manager, Western Lines, Winnipeg, 1934; vice-pres. Western Lines, Winnipeg, 1942; vice-pres. Prairie Region, Winnipeg, 1947; pres., Montreal, 1948. Member various associations and committees in Canada. Hon. D.C.L. (Bishop's Univ., Lennoxville, Que.), 1951; Hon. LL.D. (Univ. of Western Ontario), 1952. K.St.J., 1952. *Address:* Windsor Station, Montreal, 3. *T.A.:* Prescanpac. *T.:* UN 1-6811; 1227 Sherbrooke St. W., Montreal, Quebec, Canada. *Clubs:* University, Mount Royal (Montreal); Manitoba (Winnipeg); Assiniboia (Regina); Vancouver (Vancouver). [*Died* 2 *Jan.* 1961.

MATHERS, 1st Baron, *cr.* 1951, of Newtown St. Boswells; **George Mathers,** K.T. 1956; P.C. 1947; D.L. Edinburgh, 1946; President Edinburgh Y.M.C.A. since 1947; *b.* Newtown, St. Boswells, Roxburghshire, 28 Feb. 1886; *s.* of late George Mathers, J.P.; *m.* 1st, 1916, Edith Mary Robinson (*d.* 1938), Carlisle; no *c.*; 2nd, 1940, Jessie Newton, 3rd *d.* of late George Graham, J.P., of Peebles and Edinburgh. *Educ.:* Newtown St. Boswells Village School. From 1899 served as clerk with N. British Railway (now British Rlys.); active in Trade Union and Labour Movement from 1908; President of Carlisle Trades Council and Labour Party, 1917-20, and its first Hon. Life member; Carlisle City Council, 1919; transferred to Edinburgh, 1921; was Chairman of Edinburgh Central I.L.P. and Pres. Edinburgh Branch of Scottish Home Rule Assoc.; elected to London and North Eastern Railway No. 1 Sectional Council and Railway Council; contested West Edinburgh, 1923 and 1924; M.P. (Lab.) West Edinburgh, 1929-31, Linlithgowshire, 1935-50, W. Lothian, 1950-51. Parliamentary Private Secretary to Parliamentary Under-Secretary of State for India, July 1929, and transferred to same position with Under-Secretary of State for the Colonies, Nov. 1929; Comptroller of H.M. Household, Oct. 1944-May 1945; Scottish Labour Whip, 1935-45, Treasurer of H.M. Household and Deputy Chief Whip, 1945-April 1946; Lord High Commissioner to General Assembly of Church of Scotland, 1946, 1947, 1948, 1951. Pres. Edinburgh and District Trades and Labour Council, and Chairman of Edinburgh and Lothians Labour Parties Federation, 1933; Member of Scottish Rating and Valuation Committee, 1943-44. Chairman: Brit. Gp. Inter-Parl. Union, 1950-51; Cttee. of Selection, House of Commons, 1946-51; Member Speakers' Panel of Chairmen and of Standing Orders Cttee., House of Commons, 1947-51; Chairman, South-Eastern Regional Hospital Board, Scotland, 1951-54; Pres. Nat. Temperance Fedn., 1950-; Mem. Council, U.N. Assoc., and Pres. Edin. Branch, 1954-; Fellow Roy. Commonwealth Soc. and Chm. Edin. Branch. *Recreations:* travelling, bowls. *Heir:* none. *Address:* 50 Craiglea Drive, Edinburgh 10. [*Died* 26 *Sept.* 1965 (*ext.*).

MATHESON, Professor Angus; Professor of Celtic Languages and Literatures, University of Glasgow, since 1956; *b.* Harris, Inverness-shire, 1 July 1912; *yr. s.* of Malcolm Matheson and Mary Murray; *m.* 1st, 1941, Sylvia A. Terry-Smith (marriage dissolved, 1950); 2nd, 1951, Flora C. Macraild; one *s.* one *d.* *Educ.:* Dunskellar Public School, North Uist; Inverness Royal Academy; University of Edinburgh; University College, Dublin (N.U.I.); University of Bonn. M.A. 1st Cl. Hons. in Celtic (Edinburgh) 1934; McCaig Schol. in Celtic, 1934; Macpherson Schol. in Celtic, 1936; Asst. Lecturer, Univ. of Edinburgh, 1936; McCallum-Fleming Lecturer in Celtic, Univ. of Glasgow, 1938, Sen. Lecturer, 1953; attached to Monitoring Unit of B.B.C., 1940-1942. Served War of 1939-45, with Royal Corps of Signals and Intelligence Corps at home and overseas (France, Belgium, India), 1942-46. Governor: Highlands and Islands Education Trust, 1957; Jordanhill Coll. of Education, 1959; Chief of Gaelic Soc. of Inverness, 1960; President, Scottish Gaelic Texts Soc., 1960. *Publications:* Ed Carmina Gadelica, Vol. V, 1954; More West Highland Tales, Vol. II, 1960; contrib. to Everyman's Encyclopaedia, Cassell's Encyclopaedia of Literature, and to journals of Celtic studies. *Recreations:* tennis, shooting, billiards. *Address:* 52 Kersland Street, Glasgow, W.2. *T.:* Western 4430. *Club:* The College (Glasgow). [*Died* 2 *Nov.* 1962.

MATHESON, General Sir Torquhil George, 5th Bt., of Lochalsh, *cr.* 1882; K.C.B., *cr.* 1921 (C.B. 1918); C.M.G., 1919; *b.* 4 Feb. 1871; 5th and *y. s.* of late Sir Alexander Matheson, 1st Baronet of Lochalsh, and 3rd wife, Eleanor Irving Perceval, *g.d.* of late Spencer Perceval (Prime Minister); S. brother 1944; *m.* 1st, 1900, Ella Louisa, *d.* of late Captain James Wingfield Linton and Countess of Aylesford; no *c.*; 2nd, 1923, Lady Elizabeth Keppel (despatches, as V.A.D. Nurse also 1915 Star, General Service and Victory Medals; A.R.R.C.), *o. d.* of 8th Earl of Albemarle; two *s.* *Educ.:* Eton. Served in 4th Battalion Bedfordshire Regiment (Herts Militia), 1890-94; Commission in Coldstream Guards, 1894; Adjutant 1st Batt 1897-1902; Regimental Adjutant, 1903-5; attached General Staff, London District, 1907-11; appointed to the command of 3rd Batt. Coldstream Guards, 1915; served S. African War as Adj. 1st Batt. (King's and Queen's medal, despatches); European War, Aug. 1914-18, where he commanded in succession 3rd Bn. Coldstream Guards; 46th (Scottish) Infantry Brigade; 20th (Light) Div, gassed and invalided; 4th Div. and Guards Div. (despatches ten times, Brevet Lieut.-Col., Bt. Col., C.B., C.M.G., Major-General); appointed to command an Infantry Brigade, 1915; a Division, 1917; operations in Waziristan, 1920-24 (despatches four times, K.C.B.); G.O.C. Waziristan Force, 1920-24, and Waziristan District from April-October 1924; Commanded 54th East Anglian Division T.A., 1927-30; General Officer Commanding-in-Chief, Western Command, India, 1931-35; General, 1934; retired pay, 1935; Member Ross and Cromarty C.C. 1938-45; raised and commanded D Coy. 2nd Ross-shire Battalion Home Guard, 1940-42. Croix de Guerre (France) with Palms; Order of St. Stanislas, 3rd cl. with swords. *Heir:* *s.* Torquhil Alexander, Major Coldstream Guards, [*b.* 15 Aug. 1925; *m.* 1954, Serena Mary Francesca, *o.d.* of Lieut.-Col. Sir Michael Peto; two *d.*]. *Address:* White Lodge, Springfield Road, Camberley, Surrey. *Club:* Guards. [*Died* 13 *Nov.* 1963.

MATHEW, Sir Charles, Kt. 1953; C.M.G. 1950; *b.* 24 March 1903; 3rd *s.* of late Theobald Mathew and Ruth Mathew; unmarried. *Educ.:* Wimbledon College; Downside School; Trinity College, Oxford (M.A.). Called to Bar, 1927; entered Colonial Service, 1929; Nigeria Cadet, 1929; Assistant District Officer, 1932; Uganda Magistrate, 1933; Crown Counsel, 1936; Judicial Adviser, 1939; Judicial Adviser to Emperor of Ethiopia, 1941, with rank of Lt.-Col.; Officer of Order of the Star of Ethiopia, 1944; Attorney-General, Nyasaland, 1944; Attorney-General and Member for Law and Order, Tanganyika, 1947; Chief Justice, Federation of Malaya, 1951-56; Judicial Adviser to Ethiopian Govt., 1956-62. Q.C. (Nyasaland) 1946, (Tanganyika) 1951. *Address:* Manor Farm House, Brede, Sussex. *Clubs:* Travellers', East India and Sports. [*Died* 14 *Feb.* 1968.

MATHEW, Francis; Manager of The Times since 1949; Director, Times Book Co. Ltd., since 1949; *b.* 8 Nov. 1907; 5th *s.* of late Theobald Mathew and Ruth Mathew; *m.* 1938, Emma Margaret, *o. d.* of late Thomas Lloyd Bowen-Davies; five *s.* six *d.* *Educ.:* Downside School; Grenoble University. Managing Director of St. Clements Press Ltd., 1947-48; Works Director of W. Speaight & Sons Ltd., 1946-48. *Address:* 15 Albert Hall Mansions, Kensington, S.W.7; Hatchlands, East Clandon, Surrey. *Club:* Athenæum. [*Died* 29 *March* 1965.

MATHEW, Robert, T.D. 1950; M.P. (C.) Honiton Division of Devon since 1955; *b.* 9 May 1911; *yr. s.* of late Major-General Sir Charles Massy Mathew, K.C.M.G., C.B., D.S.O., and Janet Muir, *yr. d.* of Sir James Knox, of Place, Kilbirnie, Ayrshire; *m.* 1944, Joan Leslie, *o. c.* of late John Synnot Bruce, Barrister-at-Law, Glamorgan; three *s.* *Educ.:* Eton Coll.; Trinity College, Cambridge (M.A.). Barrister-at-Law, Lincoln's Inn, 1937; served war, 1939-45: K.R.R.C. (T.A.); Staff College, Camberley, 1942; G.S.O. 2 (I), War Office, 1943; Special Operations (Italy, Greece), 1944-45. Lieut.-Col., (T.A.R.O.) 1944-; contested (C.) S. Ayrshire, 1945 and 1946; contested (C.) Chatham and Rochester, 1950 and 1951; Chelsea Borough Councillor, 1945-1949. Parliamentary Private Secretary to Minister of Health (lately Min. of State, Bd. of Trade), 1957-59; Parly. Under-Sec. of State, Foreign Office, Jan.-Oct. 1964. Liveryman, Salters' Company. *Recreations:* riding, travel. *Address:* Stedcombe, Manor, Axmouth, Nr. Seaton, Devon. *T.:* Seaton 2. *Clubs:* Brooks's, Pratt's, M.C.C. [*Died* 8 *Dec.* 1966.

MATHEW, Sir Theobald, K.B.E., *cr.* 1946; M.C. 1918; Director of Public Prosecutions since 1944; *b.* 4 Nov. 1898; *s.* of late Charles J. Mathew, K.C., and Anna Mathew, J.P.; *m.* Phyllis Helen, *d.* of Hon. Cyril Russell; one *s.* two *d.* *Educ.:* Oratory School; R.M.C. Sandhurst. Served European War, 1917-20, with Irish Guards (M.C.); A.D.C. to General Sir Alexander Godley, 1919; called to the Bar, 1921; joined Charles Russell & Co., Solicitors, 1925; Board of Middlesex Hospital, 1930; Departmental Committee on Imprisonment for Debt, 1934; Home Office, 1941; Head of Criminal Division, 1942-44; Mem. Magistrates Courts Rules Cttee., 1952-; Mem. Standing Cttee. on Criminal Law Revision, 1959-. *Address:* 12 Buckingham Gate, S.W.1. *T.A.:* Public Prosecutions, Sowest, London. *T.:* Victoria 6912. *Club:* Travellers'. [*Died* 29 *Feb.* 1964.

MATHEWSON, Sir Alexander (Robert), Kt. 1964; C.B.E. 1959; *b.* 21 January 1907; *s.* of late Robert W. Mathewson and Jessie C. (*née* Lockhart); *m.* 1935, Iris Christie; two *d.* *Educ.:* George Watson's Coll., Edinburgh; Edinburgh University. Mem. Inst. of Chartered Accountants of Scotland, 1931. Served with Royal Air Force, 1940-46. Member of the High Constables and Guard of Honour of Holyroodhouse, 1949-66; Liveryman, Worshipful Company of Distillers, 1960. *Address:* c/o Lloyds Bank Ltd., 39 Piccadilly, W.1. [*Died* 25 *Sept.* 1968.

MATHIAS, Alfred Ernest, C.I.E. 1932; Indian Civil Service (retd.); *b.* 24 Jan. 1880; *m.* 1st, 1915, Enid Janet Davies; one *s.* one *d.*; 2nd, 1945, Winifred Margaret Legh. *Educ.:* Clifton College; Oriel College, Oxford, B.A. Member and President, Indian Tariff Board, 1926-30; Commissioner Central Provinces, 1930. *Address:* c/o Lloyds Bank Ltd., Langport, Somerset. [*Died* 20 *March* 1963.

MATHIAS, Most Rev. Louis, S.D.B., D.D.; Archbishop of Madras-Mylapore (R.C.), since 1952; *b.* Paris, 1887. Prefect Apostolic of Assam, 1922; Bishop of Shillong, 1934; Archbishop of Madras, 1935. Croix de Guerre; Silver Jubilee Medal; grand officer Order Holy Sepulchre; Commander of the Crown of Italy; Legion of Honour (France). *Address:* Archbishop's House, San Thome-Mylapore, Madras 4, India. [*Died* 3 *Aug.* 1965.

MATHIAS, Ronald Cavill, O.B.E. 1967; Full-time Member, National Board for Prices and Incomes, since 1967; *b.* 21 Sept. 1912; Welsh parentage; *m.* 1938, Annie Ceridwen Hall; one *d.* *Educ.:* Gowerton Grammar School, S. Wales. On staff of Rd. Thomas & Co. (now Rd. Thomas & Baldwins Ltd.), Iron and Steel Mfrs., South Wales, 1924-45; Transport and General Workers' Union: Merthyr District Organiser, 1945-49; Cardiff District Secretary, 1949-53; South Wales Regional Secretary, 1953-67. *Publications:* Articles for journals and newspapers. *Recreations:* walking, pianoforte playing, reading, lecturing on industrial relations, and related subjects. *Address:* 2 Lon-y-Mynydd, Rhiwbina, Cardiff. *T.:* Cardiff 65560. [*Died* 15 *April* 1968

MATHIEU-PEREZ, Sir Joseph Leon; *see* Perez.

MATTHEW, Thomas Urquhart, Ph.D. (Cantab.), M.Sc. (Birmingham); Company Director since 1955; *b.* Edinburgh, 4 November 1909; *s.* of late Thomas Matthew and late Jane Williamson, Edinburgh; *m.* 1938, Elizabeth F. Murdoch, *d.* of late J. C. Murdoch, Burnside, Rutherglen; three *s.* *Educ.:* George Heriot's Sch., Edinburgh; Roy. Tech. Coll., Glasgow; King's College, Cambridge. Engineering Apprentice Babcock & Wilcox, Renfrew; Senior Whitworth Scholar and Sir James Caird Senior Scholar at King's College, Cambridge; Engaged on Consulting Production Engineering Practice in South African Mining and other industries; War of 1939-45, Technical Adviser South African War Supplies Directorate and Chemical Defence Factories of U.D.F.; engaged on Industrial and Municipal Investigations since 1945; Lucas Prof.

in the Principles of Engineering Production, the University, Edgbaston, Birmingham, 1948-55. Leader of I.L.O. Technical Assistance Productivity Mission to Indian Engineering and Textile Industries, 1952-53. *Publications:* various technical papers. *Recreation:* reading. *Address:* 42 Westfield Road, Edgbaston, Birmingham 15. *T.:* Edgbaston 2885. [*Died* 11 *May* 1962.

MATTHEWS, Ven. Cecil Lloyd, M.A.; Archdeacon Emeritus, 1956; *b.* 8 Feb. 1881; *s.* of Rev. William and Amelia Mary Matthews; *m.* 1911, Ennis Beddoe; two *s.* *Educ.:* Monmouth Grammar School; Keble College, Oxford. Ordained 1904; Curate of S. Laurence and S. Gregory, Norwich, 1904-06; Priest in Charge, S. Marks, Bourne End, 1907-11; Rector of Clophill, Beds., 1911; Temp. C.F. (France), 1915-19; H.C.F., 1919; Vicar of Hungarton, Twyford and Thorpe Satcheville, Leic., 1919; Vicar of Hinckley, 1923; Vicar of Knighton, Leicester, 1929-48; Rural Dean of Christianity (Leicester), 1933-38; Hon. Canon in Leicester Cathedral, 1933-37, Canon Residentiary, 1937-38; Archdeacon of Leicester, 1938-56; Vicar of All Saints, Leicester, 1954-1956 (priest-in-charge, 1948); Examining Chaplain to the Bishop of Leicester, 1953-56. *Recreation:* golf. *Address:* Green Shutters, Well End, Bourne End, Bucks. *T.:* Bourne End 796. [*Died* 26 *Feb.* 1962.

MATTHEWS, Gilbert, C.V.O. 1949; C.B.E. 1947; Operating Superintendent, British Railways, Western Region, 1948-55, retd.; *s.* of late Sir Thomas Matthews, London; *m.* 1st, 1916, Emily Louise Gough (*d.* 1929); one *s.*: 2nd, 1933, Doris Esmae A'Court (*d.* 1949), Christchurch, N.Z.; one *d.*; 3rd, 1951, June Beverly Robinson, Christchurch, New Zealand; one *d.* *Educ.:* Westminster School, Joined Great Western Railway, 1908, General Manager's Office. Toured U.S.A. to study operating matters. Traffic Department, 1911. Operating Assistant Supt. of Line, 1934; Divisional Supt., Swansea, 1937; Principal Asst. Supt. of Line, 1939; Supt. of Line, 1941. Chairman R.E.C. Operating Cttee., 1945. Lt.-Col. Railway Engineer and Staff Corps, 1944. *Address:* Villa Gardenia, Upper Gardens, St. Julian's, Malta, G.C. *T.:* 36599. *Club:* Union (Sliema, Malta). [*Died* 22 *Oct.* 1969.

MATTHEWS, Rev. Chancellor Norman Gregory; Chancellor of Llandaff Cathedral since 1952; Rector of St. Fagan's with Llanilterne since 1953; *b.* 12 Feb. 1904; *o. s.* of William John and Agnes Amelia Matthews; *m.* 1953, Mary Laurella Thomas, M.A. (Oxon.), *er. d.* of Walter Rees and Kathleen Olga Thomas. *Educ.:* Swansea Grammar Sch.; Jesus Coll., Oxford; St. Stephen's House, Oxford. Meyricke Exhibr., Jesus Coll., Oxf., 1922; B.A. (2nd Cl. Honour Sch. of Theol.) 1926; M.A. 1930. Deacon, 1927; priest, 1928; Asst. Curate, St. Dyfrig's, Cardiff, 1927-35; First Warden of St. Teilo's Hall of Residence, Univ. Coll. of S.W. and Mon., 1935-40. Llandaff Diocesan Missioner, 1936-40; Member: Governing Body of the Church in Wales, 1937-; Central Cttee. for the Training of Ordination Candidates, 1937-; Examining Chaplain to Bishop of Llandaff from 1938; Chaplain to H.M. Prison, Cardiff, 1940-45; Vicar of Roath St. Saviour, 1940-53; Canon of Llandaff, 1946-1952. Lecturer in English Literature under Local Educ. Authority from 1942; also courses of lectures at British Council; religious and literary broadcasts; literary reviewing. Member of the Standing Liturgical Commn. of Church in Wales; Ct. of Govs.: Univ. Coll. of S.W. and Mon.; Corp. of Sons of Clergy. *Recreations:* reading, piano, conversation. *Address:* The Rectory, St. Fagan's, Cardiff. *T.:* Cardiff 73132. [*Died* 6 *Aug.* 1964.

MATTHEWS, Percy John, M.C., Croix de Guerre; Newspaper Proprietor; *b.* 25 May 1895; *y. s.* of late Aaron Matthews and Sarah Fox; *m.* 1919, Florence Lauraine, *y. d.* of late William Nethway and Catherine Gallavan; one *s.* Served European War, 1914-18, France (with 4th Hussars), Salonika, Egypt, Palestine, Irish Rebellion (despatches twice, wounded, M.C., Croix de Guerre); upon retiring from Army (Captain), 1920, entered journalism, Times and Mirror, Bristol; Director, Weston Gazette Ltd., 1922; founded Clevedon News, Ltd., 1926, and was first chairman of company; joined The Times of Ceylon Company, Ltd., 1929; Chairman and Managing Director, The Times of Ceylon Co., Ltd., 1934-42 (relinquished to return to Britain for special war service); Ministry of Production, 1942; Ministry of Information Speaker on British Commonwealth of Nations and Far East, 1943-45; chief proprietor, Burton Chronicle, 1936-55; director of other newspaper and allied companies. *Recreations:* horse-riding, motoring, shooting, fishing. *Address:* Stormont, The Crescent, Westbury-on-Trym, Bristol. *T.:* Bristol 62 5333. [*Died* 5 *Aug.* 1964.

MATTHEWS, Sir William (Thomas), K.C.M.G. 1944; C.B. 1941; O.B.E. 1931 (M.B.E. 1918); *b.* 28 May 1888; *s.* of John Edward and Isabella Matthews; *m.* 1914, Violet Boreham (*d.* 1965); one *s.* one *d.* Assistant Principal H.M. Treasury; Private Secretary to Controller of Supplies, H.M. Treasury; Principal, H.M. Treasury, 1920; Asst. Sec., Assistance Board, 1934; Prin. Asst. Sec., Assistance Board, 1937; Civil Adviser to Intendent Gen., Cairo, 1941; Dir.-Gen. Middle East Relief and Refugee Administration, 1942; Dir.-Gen. U.N.R.R.A. in Balkans, 1944; Under Sec., Ministry of Nat. Insurance, 1945; Under-Sec. H.M. Treasury, 1948. Former Member Admin. and Budgetary Cttee., U.N.O. *Recreations:* golf, fishing. *Address:* c/o Lloyds Bank, 6 Waterloo Place, Pall Mall, S.W.1. [*Died* 26 *July* 1968.

MATTINGLY, Professor Garrett; Professor of European History, Columbia University, since 1948; *b.* 6 May 1900; *s.* of Leonard H. and Ida Garrett Mattingly; *m.* 1928, Gertrude McCollum; one *c.* (decd.). *Educ.:* Harvard, A.B. 1923; Ph.D. 1935. Instructor, Northwestern Univ., 1926-28; Instructor to Assoc. Prof., Long Island Univ., 1928-42. Served in U.S.N.R., active duty, 1942-46. Head of Division of Social Philosophy, Cooper Union, N.Y., 1946-48. George Eastman Visiting Professor, Oxford Univ., 1962-63. F.R.S.L. 1960; Litt.D., Wesleyan Univ., 1962. *Publications:* Catherine of Aragon, 1942; Renaissance Diplomacy, 1955; The Defeat of the Spanish Armada, 1959; contrib. to English Historical Review, Amer. Hist. Rev., Canadian Hist. Rev., etc. *Recreation:* reading. *Address:* Columbia University, New York 27, N.Y., U.S.A. [*Died* 18 *Dec.* 1962.

MATTINGLY, Harold, C.B.E. 1960; F.B.A. 1946; F.S.A. 1947; M.A.; late Assistant Keeper, Dept. of Coins and Medals, British Museum (1910-48); *b.* Sudbury, Suffolk, 24 Dec. 1884; *s.* of Robert and Gertrude E. Mattingly; *m.* 1915, Marion Grahame Meikleham; three *s.* one *d.* *Educ.:* Leys, Cambridge; Gonville and Caius College, Cambridge. 1st class 1st Division Pt. I. Classical Tripos, 1st class Pt. II. Classical Tripos (distinction in History), Craven University Scholarship, Chancellor's Medal for Classics; entered British Museum, 1910; Pres. Royal Numismatic Society, 1942-48 (Hon. Vice-Pres. 1953); Visiting Prof. in Classics, Dunedin, N.Z., 1954; Vice-Pres. Society for Promotion of Roman Studies; Hon. Fellow, Gonville and Caius College, Cambridge; Hon. Litt.D., N.Z., 1955. *Publications:* The Imperial Civil Service of

Rome, 1909; Outlines of Ancient History, 1914; Handbook of Roman Coins, 1928; Five volumes (1923, 1930, 1936, 1940, 1950) of the British Museum Catalogue of Roman Imperial Coins; Roman Imperial Coinage (with Rev. E. A. Sydenham), 1922-51; The Man in the Roman Street, 1947; Imperial Roman Civilization, 1957. *Address:* 9 Missonden Rd., Chesham, Bucks. *T.:* 8224.
[*Died* 26 *Jan.* 1964.

MAUDE, Sir (Evelyn) John, K.C.B., *cr.* 1941 (C.B. 1929); K.B.E., *cr.* 1937; *b.* 1883; *s.* of late John Maude, Oberhofen, Switzerland; *m.* 1914, Evelyn, *d.* of Frederick Baker Gabb; one *s.* four *d.* *Educ.:* Rugby; Exeter College, Oxford. Called to Bar, Lincoln's Inn, 1908. Deputy Secretary to Ministry of Health, 1934-1940; Secretary, 1940-45; Deputy Chairman, Local Government Boundary Commission, 1945. *Address:* Hall Hill, Oxted, Surrey. *T.:* Oxted 2422. *Club:* Oxford and Cambridge.
[*Died* 5 *Feb.* 1963.

MAUDSLAY, Cecil Winton, C.B. 1937; M.A. (Oxon.); *b.* 26 Sept. 1880; *s.* of late Athol Maudslay, Littlebourne, Twyford, Hants; *m.* 1944, Charity Magdalen, *e. d.* of late Rev. C. Mallam Johnston, formerly Vicar of Cookham Dean; one *s.* one *d.* *Educ.:* Clifton College (Scholar); Exeter Coll., Oxford (Exhibitioner). First Class Hons. in Modern History, 1902; entered Board of Education as Junior Examiner, 1904; Private Secretary to Parliamentary Secretary, 1915-19; Assistant Secretary, 1924-35; Principal Assistant Secretary, 1935-40; part-time employment in connection with provision of School Canteens, 1940-42; returned to full-time service in charge of Child Care Division, 1942-44; Chairman of Association of First Division Civil Servants, 1928-31; Chairman of Higher Grades Conference of Civil Service Organisations, 1929-34; Member of Interdepartmental Committee on the Nursing Services, 1937-39; Freeman of City of London. Master of the Musicians' Company, 1955-56, and Liveryman of the Shipwrights' Company. *Recreations:* travel, music, photography. *Address:* The Beacon, Duddleswell, Uckfield, Sussex. *T.:* Nutley 2661. [*Died* 8 *Dec.* 1969.

MAUGHAM, (William) Somerset, C.H. 1954; F.R.S.L., M.R.C.S., L.R.C.P.; Commander of the Legion of Honour; Hon. D.Litt.: Oxford, Toulouse; C.Lit. 1961; Fellow Library of Congress, Washington; Hon. Mem. National Society of Arts and Letters, U.S.A.; Hon. Senator of Heidelberg University, 1961; *b.* 25 Jan. 1874; *y. s.* of late Robert Ormond Maugham; *m.* 1916, Syrie (*d.* 1955), *d.* of Dr. Barnardo; one *d.* *Educ.:* King's Sch., Canterbury; Heidelberg Univ.; St. Thomas's Hosp. *Publications:* (among others) Liza of Lambeth, 1897; Mrs. Craddock, 1902; The Land of the Blessed Virgin, 1905; The Magician, 1908; Of Human Bondage, 1915; The Moon and Sixpence, 1919 (prod. as Opera, 1957); The Trembling of a Leaf, 1921; On a Chinese Screen, 1922; The Painted Veil, 1925; The Casuarina Tree, 1926; Ashenden, 1928; The Gentleman in the Parlour, 1930; Cakes and Ale, 1930; First Person Singular, 1931; The Narrow Corner, 1932; Ah King, 1933; Altogether, 1934; Don Fernando, 1935; Cosmopolitans, 1936; Theatre, 1937; The Summing Up, 1938; Christmas Holiday, 1939; The Mixture as Before, 1940; Up at the Villa, 1941; The Razor's Edge, 1944; Then and Now, 1946; Creatures of Circumstance, 1947; Catalina, 1948; A Writer's Notebook, 1949; The Complete Short Stories, III Volumes, 1951; The Vagrant Mood, 1952; A Choice of Kipling's Prose, 1952; Ten Novels and their Authors, 1954; The Partial View, 1954; Points of View, 1958; *plays:* (among others) A Man of Honour, 1903; Lady Frederick, 1907; Jack Straw; Mrs. Dot; Penelope, 1908; Smith, 1909; The Land of Promise, 1914; Caroline, 1916; Cæsar's Wife; Home and Beauty, 1919; The Unknown, 1920; The Circle, 1921; East of Suez, 1922; Our Betters, 1923; The Letter, 1927; The Constant Wife, 1927; The Sacred Flame, 1929; The Breadwinner, 1930; For Services Rendered, 1932; Sheppey, 1933; *films:* short stories adapted as Quartet, Trio, Encore. *Relevant Publication:* Somerset Maugham, by Richard Cordell, 1961. *Address:* St. Jean-Cap Ferrat, A.M., France. *Club:* Garrick.
[*Died* 16 *Dec.* 1965.

MAURAULT, Rt. Rev. Mgr. Olivier, C.M.G. 1943; Rector (or President) of Université de Montréal from 1934; retired as Rector, 1955; *b.* 1 January 1886; *s.* of Élie Maurault and Lucie Boucher. *Educ.:* Montreal; Paris. Professor Collège de Montréal, 1913-15; Assistant St. James Church, 1915-26; Parish Priest Notre-Dame Church, 1926-29; President André Grasset College, 1929-34. Member, Royal Society of Canada, 1931-; Pres. Société Historique de Montréal, 1941-. Jubilee Medal of George V; Coronation Medal of George VI; Médaille Kornman de l'Académie française; Commandeur de l'Ordre Equestre du St.-Sépulcre, 1950; Commandeur de l'Ordre de Léopold II, 1950; Chapelain de l'Ordre de Malte, 1953; Médaille de Polonia Restituta, 1953. *Publications:* Le Petit Séminaire de Montréal, 1918; Brièvetés, 1928; La Paroisse, 1929; Marges d'histoire, 3 vols., 1929-30; "Nos Messieurs", 1936; Propos et portraits, 1941; Moisson de Ville-Marie, 1943; Aux Louisianais, 1943; Le Mexique de mes Souvenirs, 1945; Par voies et par chemins de l'air, 1947; L'École Polytechnique de Montréal, 1948; L'Oeuvre et Fabrique de Notre-Dame, 1959. *Address:* 3461 Jeanne Mauce, Montreal, Canada. *Club:* Cercle Universitaire (Montreal).
[*Died* 14 *Aug.* 1968.

MAURIAC, François, de l'Académie Française; *b.* 1885. *Educ.:* Collège des Marianites, Grand-Lebrun. Former President Société des Gens de Lettres; Winner Grand Prix of Académie Française, 1926; Nobel Prize for Literature, 1952. *Publications:* La Chair et Le Sang, 1920 (trans. 1954); Le Baiser au lépreux (trans.), 1922; Génitrix (trans.), 1924; Le Désert de l'amour (trans.), 1925; Le Nœud de vipères (trans.), 1932; Asmodée (play); Les Chemins de la mer (trans.); Le Sagouin, 1951 (Eng. trans.: The Little Misery, 1952), Memoires Intérieurs (trans. by Gerard Hopkins, 1960); Ce que je crois, 1962; other trans.: Woman of the Pharisees; The Enemy; Thérèse; That Which Was Lost; The Dark Angels; Questions of Precedence; The Son of Man; Young Man in Chains; Second Thoughts; De Gaulle (trans.), 1966; Mémoires politiques, 1968; Un Adolescent d'autrefois, 1969; Le nouveau bloc-notes, 1965-1967, 1970 (posthumous). *Address:* 38 Av. Théophile Gautier, Paris (XVI).
[*Died* 1 *Sept.* 1970.

MAUROIS, André, Hon. K.B.E. *cr.* 1938 (C.B.E.); Mem. of French Acad., since 1938; *b.* 1885, Elbeuf, France; *m.* 1st, 1912, Janine de Szymkiewicz (*d.* 1924); two *s.* one *d.*; 2nd, 1926, Simone de Caillavet; one *d.* *Educ.:* Lycée de Rouen. D.C.M.; Grand Croix of the Legion of Honour; Hon. D.Litt. Oxon., Hon. D.C.L. Edinburgh, St. Andrews; Hon. Doctor of Letters, Princeton; attached to British G.H.Q. as French eye-witness, 1939-1940. *Publications:* Silences du Colonel Bramble, 1918; Discours du Docteur O'Grady, 1920; Ariel, or the Life of Shelley, 1923; Dialogues sur le Commandement, 1925; Mape, 1926; Bernard Quesnay, 1926; The Life of Disraëli, 1927; Climats, 1928; Aspects of Biography, 1929; Whatever Gods

May Be, 1929; Byron, 1930; Lyantey, 1931; Tourgueniev, 1931; The Weigher of Souls, 1932; Voltaire, 1932; The Family Circle, 1932; Mes songes que voici, 1933; King Edward and his Times, 1933; Dickens, 1934; Poets and Prophets, 1936; A History of England, 1937; The Thought-Reading Machine, 1938; Chateaubriand, 1938; The Art of Living, 1940; Battle of France, 1940; Tragedy in France, 1940; A Time for Silence, 1941; Fattypuffs and Thinifers, 1942; Call No Man Happy, 1943; History of the United States, 1944; Woman without Love, 1945; J.-L. David, 1949; A History of France, 1949; The Quest for Proust, 1950; Lelia, or the life of George Sand, 1952; Olympio or the Life of Victor Hugo, 1954; Les roses de Septembre, 1956 (trans. September Roses, 1958); To the Fair Unknown, 1957; The Three Musketeers (Les Trois Dumas), 1957; The Life of Sir Alexander Fleming, 1959; The Art of Writing, 1960; Adrienne, ou la Vie de Madame de La Fayette, 1960; De Proust à Camus, 1962; Choses Nues, 1963; An Illustrated History of England, 1963; Napoleon, 1964; A History of the United States from Wilson to Kennedy, 1964 ; Prométhée ou la Vie de Balzac, 1965; Victor Hugo and his World, 1966; Lettre ouverte à un Jeune Homme, 1966; An Illustrated History of Germany, 1966; The Chelsea Way, or, Marcel in England, 1966. *Posthumous publications:* An Illustrated History of the United States, 1969; Memoirs, 1970; Points of View, 1970. *Address:* 86 Blvd. Maurice-Barrès, Neuilly-sur-Seine, France; (summer) Essendiéras, Excideuil, Dordogne. [*Died* 9 *Oct.* 1967.

MAVROGORDATO, John Nicolas, M.A.; *b.* London, 19 July 1882; *m.* 1914, Christine Humphreys; two *s.* *Educ.:* Eton (King's Sch.); Exeter Coll., Oxford (Scholar). Work for J. M. Dent and other publishers, 1908-12; Mem. Internat. Commn. for care of Turkish Refugees, Salonica, 1913; lecturer on Koraes Foundation, King's Coll., Univ. of London, 1919; Bywater and Sotheby Professor of Byzantine and Modern Greek Language and Literature, and Fellow of Exeter Coll., Oxford, 1939; retired, 1947 (Professor Emeritus); Hon. Fell. Exeter Coll., 1956. *Publications:* Tragedy of Cassandra in Troy, 1914; The World in Chains (socialism and war), 1917; The Erotokritos, 1929; Introduction to F. H. Marshall's Three Cretan Plays, 1929; Modern Greece (1800-1931), 1931; Elegies and Songs, 1934; Poems of C. P. Cavafy, 1951; Digenes Akrites, 1956; contrib. Chambers's Encyc. D.N.B., etc. *Recreations:* anything except theology or mathematics. *Address:* 3 Montpelier Walk, S.W.7. *Club:* Athenæum. [*Died* 24 *July* 1970.

MAWHOOD, Mrs. L.; *see* Clare, Mary.

MAXWELL, Sir Alexander, G.C.B., *cr.* 1945 (K.C.B., *cr.* 1939; C.B. 1924); K.B.E., *cr.* 1936; *b.* 9 March 1880; *e. s.* of late Rev. J. T. Maxwell, Plymouth; *m.* Jessie Macnaughton, *d.* of late Rev. John Campbell, D.D., Kirkcaldy; two *s.* *Educ.:* Plymouth College; Christ Church, Oxford. Entered Home Office, 1904; Assistant Secretary, 1924; Chairman of Prison Commission England and Wales, 1928-32; Deputy Under-Secretary of State, Home Office, 1932-38; Permanent Under-Secretary of State, Home Office, 1938-48; retired, 1948. *Address:* Chasemores, Coldharbour, Nr. Dorking, Surrey. *T.:* Dorking 73116. *Club:* United University. [*Died* 1 *July* 1963.

MAXWELL, Arthur Crawford, C.M.G, 1956; Commissioner of Police, Hong Kong, 1953-59, retd.; Organiser, The Royal Society for the Prevention of Accidents, Northern Ireland, 1960-63; *b.* 25 May 1909; *s.* of Rev. Robert Maxwell; *m.* 1933, Phrena Ramplen Jones; one *s.* one *d.* *Educ.:* Methodist College, Belfast. Joined Colonial Police (Malaya), 1928. Interned, Singapore, 1942-1945. Supt. of Police, Malaya, 1946; Comr. of Police, Sarawak 1947-49; Dep. Comr. of Police, Hong Kong, 1949-53. King's Police Medal, 1952. *Address:* 45 Maryville Park, Belfast 9. [*Died* 11 *May* 1964.

MAXWELL, Constantia Elizabeth, M.A., Litt.D.; Member of the Irish Academy of Letters; Lecturer in History, 1909-39, Professor of Economic History, 1939-45, Lecky Professor of Modern History, 1945-51, Trinity Coll., Univ. of Dublin. *Educ.:* St. Leonards School, St. Andrews; Trinity College, Dublin. *Publications:* A Short History of Ireland, 1914; Irish History from Contemporary Sources, 1923; The English Traveller in France, 1932; Dublin under the Georges, 1936, new edn. 1956; Country and Town in Ireland under the Georges, 1940; A History of Trinity College, Dublin, 1946; editor of Arthur Young's Tour in Ireland, 1925, and Young's Travels in France, 1929; The Wisdom of Dr. Johnson (anthology), 1948; The Stranger in Ireland, from the reign of Elizabeth to the Great Famine, 1954. *Address:* 5 Waterloo Terrace, Cranbrook, Kent. [*Died* 6 *Feb.* 1962.

MAXWELL, Vice-Adm. Hon. Sir Denis (Crichton), K.C.B. 1952 (C.B. 1948); C.B.E. 1945; M.I.Mech.E.; F.R.S.A.; *b.* 26 Sept. 1892; *s.* of Somerset Henry Maxwell, 10th Baron Farnham and Lady Florence Jane Taylour, 5th *d.* of 3rd Marquess of Headfort; *m.* 1923, Theodora Mary, *d.* of A. W. Hickling, J.P.; one *d.* *Educ.:* R.N. Colleges, Osborne and Dartmouth; R.N. Engineering College, Keyham; R.N. Coll., Greenwich. Midshipman, 1910; Sub-Lieut., 1913. Specialised in Engineering and became Lieut. (E), 1915; qualified in Advanced Course in Engineering, 1923; Comdr. (E), 1927; Capt. (E), 1939; Rear-Adm. (E), 1946; Vice-Adm. (E), 1950. Dep. Engineer-in-Chief of the Fleet, 1946-48; Rear-Adm. (E) on staff of C.-in-C., Plymouth, 1949-50. Engineer-in-Chief of the Fleet, 1950-53. *Recreations:* golf and shooting. *Address:* Flagstaff House, P.O. Box 609, Umtali, Rhodesia. *Club:* Rhodes (Umtali). [*Died* 16 *Jan.* 1970.

MAXWELL, Douglas Rider, C.B.E. 1934; M.A.; *b.* 22 July 1885; *s.* of John Maxwell and Alice Marcella Wyndham; *m.* 1922, Gladys Maude (*d.* 1962), *d.* of Rev. Canon William Gardiner, B.D. *Educ.:* Marlborough; Keble Coll., Oxon. Entered British North Borneo C.S., 1906; held various senior appointments including those of acting Resident of the Interior, Superintendent of Census, Protector of Labour and Inspector of Schools, Assistant Government Secretary, Resident of the East Coast, Resident of Kudat, and acting Resident of Sandakan; became a Magistrate of the first class, 1911, a Sessions Judge, 1930, and a Judge of the High Court, 1930; held appointment of Government Secretary and Official Member of the Legislative Council, 1927-34; was Officer Administering the Government on ten different occasions between March, 1927, and March, 1934; retired, 1934. *Publication:* Census of North Borneo, 1921. *Address:* c/o National Provincial Bank Ltd., Chancery Lane Branch, W.C.2. [*Died* 1 *Oct.* 1967.

MAXWELL, Gavin, M.A.; F.R.S.L.; F.Z.S.(Sc.); F.R.G.S.; F.A.G.S.; F.I.A.L.; Sponsor of the Dolci Cttee.; Hon. Life Member: Wildfowl Trust; Cttee., Wildlife Youth Service; Fauna Preservation Soc.; Internat. Cttee., Centro Studi e Scambi Internazionali; Cttee. of Honour Nat. Campaign for the Abolition of Capital Punishment; Pres., British Junior Exploration Soc.; writer since 1952; portrait painter, 1949-52; *b.* 1914; *y. s.* of late Lt.-Col. Aymer Edward Maxwell and of Lady Mary Percy, 5th *d.* of 7th Duke of Northumberland; *g.s.* of Rt. Hon. Sir Herbert Eustace Maxwell, 7th Bart. of

Monreith, K.T., P.C.; *m.* 1962, Lavinia (marriage dissolved, 1964), *e. d.* of Rt. Hon. Sir Alan and Hon. Lady Lascelles. *Educ.:* Stowe; Hertford Coll., Oxford (M.A.). Scots Guards, 1939-41, seconded to S.O.E., 1941, invalided with rank of Major 1944; bought Island of Soay and started Island of Soay Shark Fisheries, 1944. *Publications.* Harpoon at a Venture, 1952; God Protect Me from My Friends, 1956; A Reed Shaken by the Wind, 1957 (Heinemann Award of Royal Society of Literature); The Ten Pains of Death, 1959; Ring of Bright Water, 1960 (Book Society non Fiction Choice); The Otters' Tale, 1962; The Rocks Remain, 1963; The House of Elrig, 1965 (Book Society non-fiction choice); Lords of the Atlas, 1966; Seals of the World, 1967; Raven Seek thy Brother, 1968 (Book Society choice). *Address:* 9 Paultons Square, S.W.3; Sandaig, by Kyle of Lochalsh, Ross-shire. *T.:* Glenelg 206; Kyleakin Lighthouse, Isle of Skye. *T.:* Kyleakin 222. *Clubs:* Guards, Special Forces. [*Died* 7 *Sept.* 1969.

MAXWELL, Gerald Verner, C.M.G. 1931; *b.* 23 June 1877; 5th *s.* of late Sir William Edward Maxwell, K.C.M.G.; *m.* 1900, Jane Crawford (*d.* 1959), *d.* of late David Blyth, M.B., C.M.; two *s.* two *d.*; *m.* 1960, Dorothy Vivienne May, *d.* of late Oswald Ira Lewis. *Educ.:* Bedford Sch. (Exhib.); Peterhouse, Camb. (Schol.). Cadet, Fiji, 1898; held Magisterial and Admin. appts. in Fiji till 1912; Chairman of Native Lands Commission, Fiji, 1912-21; Chief Native Commissioner, Kenya, 1921-31; ex-officio member of Executive and Legislative Councils; retired, 1931. *Address:* Delana, Campbelltown, N.S.W. *T.:* 21143. *Clubs:* East India and Sports; Nairobi. [*Died* 4 *June* 1965.

MAXWELL, James Robert, C.M.G. 1952; owner of Lapuet Estate, Kitale; engaged in general mixed farming; *b.* 5 Aug. 1902; *s.* of James Maxwell, Kisumu, Kenya; *m.* 1927, Margaret, *d.* of late James Gardner Davidson; Nairobi; two *s.* three *d.* *Educ.:* Nairobi Kenya Colony. Farming, 1920; Director, Kisumu Hotel, 1930-46; Nairobi City Council; Elected, 1946; Alderman, 1948; Mayor, 1951-52; resigned from Aldermanic Bench, 1952. President East Africa Hotelkeepers' Association, 1945. M.L.C. for Trans Nzoia Dist., 1956-60. *Address:* 3 Kingsway, Pinelands, C.P., South Africa. *Club:* Nairobi (Kenya). [*Died* 30 *March* 1970.

MAXWELL, Sir John, Kt., *cr.* 1941; C.B.E.; *b.* 24 Dec. 1882; *s.* of James and Margaret Maxwell; *m.* 1905, Mary Warburton; two *s.* *Educ.:* Public School, Muirkirk, Ayrshire. Served in Manchester City Police Force, 1901-43; Chief Constable of Manchester, 1927-43. *Publication:* Manchester City Police Instruction Book, 1924. *Recreation:* golf. *Address:* 39 Whitegate Park, Flixton, Urmston, Lancs. [*Died* 14 *Feb.* 1968.

MAXWELL, John, R.S.A. 1949 (A.R.S.A. 1945); Teacher, Edinburgh College of Art, 1955-61; *b.* 12 July 1905. *Educ.:* Dalbeattie High School; Dumfries Acad.; Edinburgh College of Art; France, Spain and Italy. Teacher in Edinburgh College of Art, 1935-46. Member Society of Scottish Artists. *Recreations:* gardening, music. *Address:* Millbrooke, Dalbeattie, Kirkcudbrightshire. *Club:* Scottish Arts (Edinburgh). [*Died* 3 *June* 1962.

MAXWELL, Joseph, V.C., M.C. and Bar, D.C.M.; journalist; *b.* Sydney, N.S.W.; *s.* of John Maxwell, 8 Fairlight St., Manly, N.S.W. *Educ.:* Gilberton Public School. Served European War in Gallipoli and France (V.C., M.C. and Bar, D.C.M.). *Publication:* Hell's Bells and Mamselles, 1932. *Address:* 25 Ocean Street, Bondi, New South Wales, Australia. [*Died* 6 *July* 1967.

MAXWELL, Sir Reginald Maitland, G.C.I.E., *cr.* 1944 (C.I.E. 1923); K.C.S.I., *cr.* 1939 (C.S.I. 1933); *b.* 1882; *s.* of John Maxwell of Richmond; *m.* 1913, Mary Lyle, *d.* of Rev. Henry Haigh, D.D.; one *s.* one *d.* (and one *s.* decd.). *Educ.:* Marlborough; Corpus Christi College, Oxford. Indian Civil Service, Bombay Presidency, since 1906; Private Secretary to H.E. Sir George Lloyd, G.C.S.I., D.S.O., Governor of Bombay, 1920-21; Secretary to Bombay Retrenchment Committee, 1921-23; Collector and Magistrate and Political Agent, 1924-28; Secretary to Govt. of Bombay, General Department, 1928; Private Secretary to H.E. Sir Frederick Sykes, P.C., G.C.I.E., Governor of Bombay, 1929; Secretary to Government of Bombay, Home Department, 1931; Commissioner of Excise, Bombay, 1935-36; Secretary to Govt. of India, Home Dept., 1936; Home Member of Governor-General's Executive Council, 1938-44; Adviser to the Secretary of State for India, 1944-47. *Address:* Barford House, St. Mary Bourne, Andover, Hants. *T.:* St. Mary Bourne 218. [*Died* 29 *July* 1967.

MAXWELL, Brigadier Richard Hobson, C.B. 1948; *b.* 24 August 1899; *s.* of D. A. Maxwell. *Educ.:* Marlborough; Royal Military College, Sandhurst. Suffolk Regiment: 2nd Lieut., 1918; temp., Lieut.-Colonel, 1940; temp. Brig. 1943; Colonel, 1946; Brig., 1950. Instructor R.M.C., Sandhurst, 1934-37; Brigade Major Eastern Command, 1937-38. Served War of 1939-45 (despatches). A.D.C. to the Queen, 1952-55; Provost Marshal, 1952-54; retd. from Army, 1955. Hon. Col. 23rd London Regt., 1955-60; Colonel, The Suffolk Regiment, 1957-59 and 1st East Anglian Regt., 1959-62. Vice-Chairman, The Royal Tournament, 1955-63. *Address:* c/o Lloyds Bank Ltd., 6 Pall Mall, S.W.1. *Club:* Army and Navy. [*Died* 28 *Aug.* 1965.

MAXWELL, Rear-Adm. Sir Wellwood George Courtenay, K.B.E., *cr.* 1943; C.M.G. 1919; D.L.; Hon. D.C.L. (Dunelm); *b.* 11 Aug. 1882; *s.* of George Maxwell, late of Glenlee, New Galloway, Scotland; *m.* 1917, Elizabeth Compton, *o. d.* of late Brig.-Gen. Hon. W. E. Cavendish, M.V.O.; one *s.* one *d.* *Educ.:* Moorland House, Heswall; H.M.S. Britannia. Lt., 1904; Comdr., 1915; Capt., 1922; Rear-Admiral, 1934; served European War, 1914-1918; present at Capture of Tsingtau (Sacred Treasure of Japan, 2nd Cl.); Dardanelles, 1915-1917 (Legion of Honour, Italian Silver Medal for Valour, despatches twice); Grand Fleet, 1917-18 (C.M.G.); commanded Gunnery School, Chatham, 1923-25; H.M.S. Ceres, 1925-27; H.M.S. St. Vincent, 1928-30; H.M.S. Valiant, 1932-33; retired list, 1934; recalled as Flag Officer Tyne Area, 1939-46; (King Haakon VII Norwegian Liberty Cross); Pres. of Northamptonshire Royal Naval Assoc., 1936-; County Commissioner Boy Scouts, Northamptonshire, 1946-51; D.L. County Northampton, 1949; Pres. Northamptonshire British Legion, 1950-; Midland Area Pres. British Legion, 1953-54; Vice-Chm. Kettering and Wellingborough Pensions Appeal Board, 1953. *Recreations:* racing, shooting. *Address:* Sudborough Manor, near Kettering, Northants. *T.:* Lowick 208. [*Died* 9 *July* 1965.

MAY, James Lewis; Author and Critic; *b.* 10 Aug. 1873; *er. s.* of late Dr. L. J. May; *m.* 1896, Elizabeth Hyde; one *s.* one *d.* *Educ.:* University College School; privately in France. For some time reader and literary adviser to John Lane, The Bodley Head; Editor of the English edition of The Works of Anatole France; Editor, with late Henry D. Davray, of Anglo-French Review; Member of Committee of Help for Devastated Areas in France, 1914-18. Translator of numerous works from Latin, French and Italian, contributor to Edinburgh Review,

Dublin Review, English Review, Clergy Review, The Tablet, Dictionary of National Biography, etc. Vice-Pres. Charles Lamb Society; Member of Council Virgil Society. Chevalier de la Légion d'Honneur. *Publications:* Anatole France, 1924; Cardinal Newman, 1929; (trans. Dutch and German) The Path Through the Wood, 1930; George Eliot, 1930; Father Tyrrell and the Modernist Movement, 1932; An English Treasury of Religious Prose, 1932; The Oxford Movement, 1933; Charles Lamb, 1934; The Unchanging Witness, 1935; Thorn and Flower, 1935; John Lane and the Nineties, 1936; Fénelon, 1938. *Recreations:* reading, listening to music. *Address:* 2 Winterstoke Gardens, Mill Hill, N.W.7. *T.:* Mill Hill 2077. [*Died* 28 *May* 1961.

MAY, Richard William Legerton, C.V.O. 1959; M.A., M.B., B.Ch. (Cantab.); retd. as Surgeon Apothecary to H.M. Household, Windsor, (1952-65) and to H.M. The Queen Mother's Household at the Royal Lodge, Windsor (1956-65); Hon. Cons. Physician to Eton Coll., Royal Holloway Coll. and King Edward VII Hospital; Consultant Physician to King Edward VII Hosp., Windsor; *b.* 30 Dec. 1902; *s.* of late William May, L.D.S., and late Minnie F. May, Thurlestone, Devon; *m.* 1931, Winifred Amy Kaye; one *s.* decd. *Educ.:* Rugby Sch.; Trin. Coll., Cambridge; St. Thomas's Hospital, London. M.R.C.S.Eng., L.R.C.P.Lond. 1927; M.A. Cantab. 1930; M.B., B.Ch. Cantab. 1930. Late House Surgeon St. Thomas's Hospital; House Physician Evelina Hospital for Sick Children and West London Hospital. Divisional Surgeon St. John's Ambulance Association. Hon. Mem. Old Etonian Soc. O.St.J. *Publication:* contrib. to Med. Jl., 1950. *Recreations:* golf, travel. *Address:* Woodcote, Windsor Road, Ascot, Berks. *T.:* Ascot 20308. *Clubs:* Buck's (Hon. Mem.); Berkshire Golf, Thurlestone Golf. [*Died* 23 *April* 1967.

MAY, Rt. Hon. William Morrison, P.C. (N. Ire.) 1957; Minister of Education, Government of Northern Ireland, since 1957; M.P. Ards Division (N. Ireland Parliament) since 1949; *b.* 8 Apr. 1909; *e. s.* of William May, J.P., Marlborough Park, Belfast; *m.* 1934, Olive Muriel (*née* Dickinson); one *s.* two *d.* *Educ.:* Methodist College, Belfast. Chartered Accountant, 1931; admitted partner Quin, Knox & Co., C.A., 1935; F.C.A. 1940. Served Aux. Air Force, 1936-39; served R.A.F. 1939-45, Wing Comdr. Member of Lloyd's, 1954. *Recreations:* golf, photography. *Address:* Mertoun Hall, Holywood, Co. Down, N. Ireland. *T.:* Belfast 63177. *Clubs:* R.A.F.; Ulster Reform (Belfast). [*Died* 2 *March* 1962.

MAYALL, Robert Cecil, C.M.G. 1941; D.S.O. 1919; M.C.; *b.* 1 June 1893; *s.* of late Rev. S. B. Mayall, Vicar of St. Paul's Church, Finchley, N.3; *m.* 1929, Rhoda Anne (*d.* 1957), *d.* of late C. Stote, Swindon, Wilts.; one *s.* one *d.* *Educ.:* St. Lawrence College, Ramsgate; Sidney Sussex College, Cambridge (History Scholar). B.A. (Hist. Hons. 2nd Class), 1914; M.A., 1920. Served European War, the 11th Northumberland Fusiliers, 1914-20, in England, Belgium, France and Italy; in Egypt with the 11th Brigade (D.S.O., M.C. and bar, Italian Medal for Valour, 1919, despatches); Assistant District Commissioner, Sudan Government, 1920; District Commissioner, Headquarters Kordofan Province, El Obeid, Sudan, 1931-1933; Assistant Civil Secretary (Personnel Section) Sudan Government, Khartoum, 1933-34; Deputy Civil Secretary, Sudan Government, 1934-1936; Governor Gezira Province, Sudan, 1936-40; retired, 1940; Sudan Agent in London, 1941-1951; Public Relations Consultant to Sudan Government in London, 1951-56, retired. 3rd Class of Order of the Nile; King's Jubilee Medal, 1935; Coronation Medal, 1937. *Address:* Flat 2, Westering, Bishops Down Road, Tunbridge Wells, Kent. [*Died* 19 *Sept.* 1962.

MAYCOCK, Alan Lawson, M.C. and Bar, 1918; Keeper of the Old Library, Magdalene College, Cambridge, since 1965; *b.* 8 June 1898; *s. s.* of late Canon Herbert William Maycock and Mildred Mary Maycock; *m.* 1929, Enid, *d.* of late Lawrence and Constance Nathan; one *d.* *Educ.:* Marlborough College; Clare College, Cambridge. Served European War: commissioned service in Royal Garrison Artillery, B.E.F., France, 1917-19. Mathematical schol., Clare Coll., Camb.; B.A. 1921; M.A. 1925. Employed as geodetic surveyor by Royal Dutch-Shell Oil Companies in Egypt and U.S.A., 1921-25. Studied for Univ. of London Diploma in Librarianship, 1925-26; Administrative Staff, London Sch. of Economics, 1926-28; Education Officer, Royal Air Force, 1928-31. Asst. Secretary (Educn.), Univ. of Cambridge Appts. Board, 1931-62; Acting Sec., 1940-45; Principal Asst. Sec., 1962-65. *Publications:* The Inquisition, 1927; An Oxford Note-Book, 1929; Things Seen in Cambridge, 1934; Nicholas Ferrar of Little Gidding, 1938; The Apocalypse, 1941; Chronicles of Little Gidding, 1954; The Man Who was Orthodox, 1963. *Recreation:* water-colour painting. *Address:* 10 Latham Road, Cambridge. [*Died* 24 *Sept.* 1968.

MAYER, John, C.B.E. 1962; Chairman International Combustion Ltd. since 1955; Jt. Managing Director, International Combustion (Holdings) Ltd.; *b.* 6 March 1904; *s.* of John Mayer, M.B.E., and Alice Howe; *m.* 1st, 1931, Mary Fynn (*d.* 1942); one *d.*; 2nd, 1948, Dorothy Maude Fynn. *Educ.:* Christ's Hospital, Horsham, Sussex; Owens College, Manchester. Engineer, Mather & Platt Ltd., Manchester, 1924-26; International Combustion Ltd.; Engineer, 1926; Chief Engineer and Director, 1952; Chairman and Jt. Managing Director, 1955. *Publications:* Contribution to jls. of Inst. of Fuel and Inst. of Mechanical Engineers. *Recreation:* mountain walking. *Address:* 6 West Bank Avenue, Derby. *T.:* Derby 42881. [*Died* 12 *Dec.* 1967.

MAYERS, Thomas Henry, Q.C. (Jamaica) 1943; Puisne Judge, Kenya, 1952-64, retd.; *b.* 5 Nov. 1907; *s.* of late Henry Donald and late Bertha Greenidge Mayers; *m.* 1946, Mary Beatrice, *e. d.* of late G. H. Barrington. *Educ.:* Harrison College, Barbados; Downing College, Cambridge (M.A., LL.B.); Middle Temple. Barrister at Law, Middle Temple, 1929; Oxford Circuit, 1931-36; Resident Magistrate, Jamaica, 1936; Solicitor-General Jamaica, 1940; Attorney-Gen. for Jamaica, 1943-52. Member Privy Council, Executive Council and Legislative Council, Jamaica; Legal Adviser to Jamaica representatives Caribbean Closer Assoc. Conf., 1947; Chm. Jamaica Govt. (sugar) Delegation to U.K., 1949. *Recreations:* golf, walking. *Address:* 345 Lonsdale Road, S.W.13. [*Died* 20 *Sept.* 1970.

MAYHEW, Sir Basil (Edgar), K.B.E., *cr.* 1920; F.C.A.; Knight of Grace of the Order of St. John of Jerusalem, 1919; Joint Founder of the firm of Barton, Mayhew & Co., Chartered Accountants (retd. 1936); Director Reckitt & Colman Holdings, Ltd. (retd. 1962); *b.* 9 November 1883; *e. s.* of late T. Edgar Mayhew, Ipswich; *m.* 1st, 1911, Dorothea Mary (*d.* 1931), *d.* of late Stephen Paget, F.R.C.S.; two *s.* (and one killed in action, 1942), three *d.*; 2nd, 1932, Beryl Caroline Rees, *d.* of late Russell J. Colman; High Sheriff of Norfolk, 1940-41; Secretary to the Joint War Finance Committee, 1915-36, and to the Central Demobilisation Board, 1918-20, of the

British Red Cross Society and the Order of St. John of Jerusalem; Trustee (Chm., 1952-62) Rural Industries Bureau, 1921; Member of Departmental Committee (Lord Linlithgow's) on Disparity in Prices of Agricultural, etc., Produce, 1923; Member Standing Committee to advise on grants to assist Agricultural Co-operation or Credit, 1924; Member Committee of Enquiry into Co-operative Bacon Factory Industry, 1925; Member Standing Committee (Agricultural Section) Merchandise Marks Act 1926; Member Economic Advisory Council Committee on Centralised Slaughtering, 1931; Chairman British Industries Fair Site and Buildings Committee, 1933; Member of Joint Committee set up by the British and Argentine Governments to enquire into the conditions of the Anglo-Argentine Meat Trade, 1935; Silver Jubilee Medal, 1935. Member Agric. Marketing Cttee. (Lucas), 1947. *Address:* 35 Abbey Lodge, Park Road, N.W.8. *T.:* Paddington 1573. *Clubs:* St Stephen's; Norfolk County (Norwich); Royal Norfolk and Suffolk Yacht. [*Died* 2 *Nov.* 1966.

MAYNARD, Charles Gordon, C.B.E. 1959; C.A.; J.P.; Chairman, Welwyn Garden City and Hatfield Development Corporations, 1958-66 (ex-Vice-Chairman); *b.* 1889; *s.* of late Charles Riley Maynard; *m.* 1920, Irene Constance, *d.* of I. Stevenson, Londonderry; one *s.* two *d.* *Educ.*: Elmfield College, Yorkshire. Formerly Governing Director: C. Gordon Ltd.; Arnold Perfections Ltd.; Black Boy Chocolate Co. Ltd., etc. Chairman, Digswell Arts Trust; Chairman, Digswell Lake Society. J.P. 1938, C.A. 1948 (C.C. 1937), High Sheriff (1952-53), Hertfordshire. *Recreation:* fishing. *Address:* Springfield, Northaw, Potters Bar, Middlesex. *T.:* Potters Bar 52007. [*Died* 1 *April* 1970.

MAYNARD, Richard de Kirklevington, C.I.E. 1946; *b.* 26 Feb. 1892; *s.* of late A. C. H. Maynard; *m.* 1915, Susan Boag Miller, O.B.E. (*d.* 1967); one *d.* (one *s.* missing, presumed killed, on active service, Malta, 1942). *Educ.:* Aysgarth Sch., Yorks.; Malvern College. Traffic Apprentice N.E. Rly., 1908-13; Asst. Traffic Supt. Madras and Southern Mahratta Rly., India, 1913; Chief Operating Supt., 1935; Gen. Manager, 1944. In 1931 acted as Adviser for Company Railways with Govt. of India Rly. Retrenchment Cttee.; appointed by Govt. of India Railway Board as their rep. on Permanent Commission of Internat. Railway Congress Assoc., 1947; retired; joined C.C.G. as Dep. Director, Rail Branch, Dec. 1947; retired Feb. 1949. Director West of India Portuguese Guaranteed Rly. Co. Ltd. *Address:* The Quarry, Allerston, Pickering, Yorkshire. *T.A.* and *T.:* Snainton (Yorks) 315. *Clubs:* East India and Sports; Madras (Madras). [*Died* 27 *Feb.* 1969.

MAYNE, Very Rev. William Cyril, M.A.; Dean of Carlisle, 1943-59, Dean Emeritus, 1959; *b.* 1877; *yr. s.* of late Canon J. Mayne, Christian Malford, Chippenham; *m.* 1930, Mary Onslow, *e. d.* of Major G. A. Onslow, Dorrington, Salop. *Educ.:* Westminster; Trinity Coll., Cambridge (Scholar and Stewart of Rannoch Scholar). 1st Class Classical Tripos, 1899; Deacon, 1906; Priest, 1907; Asst. Master, Rugby Sch., 1907-12; Assist. Curate, All Saints, Poplar, 1912-14; Vice-Principal, Bishops' College, Cheshunt, 1914-20; Chaplain to Forces, 1914-19; Principal, Bishops' College, Cheshunt, 1920-25; Rector and Rural Dean of Poplar, 1925-30; Vicar of Chiswick, 1930-34; Professor of Greek and Classical Literature in University of Durham and Canon Residentiary of Durham Cathedral, 1934-43; Examining Chaplain to Bishop of St. Albans, 1924-34; to Bishop of London, 1925-34; to Bishop of Durham, 1934-43; to Bishop of Carlisle, 1943-59. Boyle Lecturer, 1929-1931; Warden of the Order of St. Elizabeth of Hungary, 1934-59; Rural Dean of Durham, 1940-43; Chaplain to High Sheriff of Durham, 1942; Chaplain to High Sheriff of Cumberland, 1947. *Publications:* verse translation of Pindar's Olympian Odes, 1906. *Address:* Applegarth, Hayton, Carlisle. *T.:* Hayton 232. [*Died* 20 *July* 1962.

MAYO, 9th Earl of (*cr.* 1785), **Ulick Henry Bourke,** Baron Naas, 1766; Viscount Mayo, 1781; *b.* 13 Mar. 1890; *e. surv. s.* of 8th Earl and Ethel Kathleen Jane (*d.* 1913), *d.* of late Capt. John W. Freeman, of Rockfield, Herefordshire; *S.* father 1939; *m.* 1937, Noel Jessie Haliburton Wilson, F.R.G.S., late Pte. in W.R.A.F., also nurse (Red Cross) 1914, *d.* of late William James Wilson, High Park, near Kendal. *Educ.:* Uppingham. Late 2nd Lieutenant Special Reserve of Officers attached 1st Bn. K.R.R.C. and Lieutenant King's African Rifles, European War, 1914. Member Society for Individual Freedom. *Heir:* *n.* Lieutenant Terence Patrick Bourke, R.N. [*b.* 26 Aug. 1929; *m.* 1952, Margaret Jane Robinson, *o. d.* of Gerald Harrison; three *s.*]. [*Died* 17 *Dec.* 1962.

MAYO, Dr. Charles William; Emeritus Surgeon, Mayo Clinic (Surgeon, 1931-64); Prof. of Surgery Mayo Foundation (Univ. of Minnesota), Rochester, Minnesota, from 1947; Member Board of Regents, Univ. of Minnesota, 1951; Chm., Bd. Regents, Univ. of Minn., 1961- ; Mem. Bd. of Trustees, Carleton Coll., Northfield, Minn., 1940- ; Mem. Bd. Trustees, Univ. of Pa., 1955-61; Medical adviser to Northwest Airlines since 1953, President Amer. Assoc. for the U.N. 1954-57 (was Alternate Delegate, Eighth Gen. Assembly, U.N., 1953); Editor-in-Chief of Postgraduate Medicine; Chairman, Mayo Assoc., 1953; Member: Board of Governors, Mayo Clinic, 1933-64; Rehabilitation Medical Advisory Bd., American Legion, 1946-Dec. 1957; Chairman, Special Medical Advisory Group, Veterans Administration, 1946-53; Editorial Bd. of Surgery; Bd. of Directors of Mutual of Omaha (Chief Medical Consultant, 1964-); College of Electors, Hall of Fame, New York Univ., 1955- ; *b.* Rochester, Minnesota, 28 July 1898; *s.* of Charles Horace Mayo and Edith Graham; *m.* 1927, Alice V. Plank; four *s.* two *d.* *Educ.:* Princeton University; University of Pennsylvania; University of Minnesota. A.B. (Princeton), 1921; M.D. (Pennsylvania), 1926; M.S. (Surgery) (Minnesota), 1931; LL.D. (Hon.): St. Lawrence Univ., Canton, N.Y.; Drake Univ.; Des Moines, Ia.; Gonzaga Univ., Spokane; D.Sc. (Hon.) Franklin and Marshall Coll., Lancaster, Pa.; L.H.D. (Hon.); Nasson Coll., Springvale, Maine; Nebraska-Wesleyan University, Lincoln; intern. Robert Packer Hospital, Sayre, Pa., 1926-27; Fell. in Surgery, Mayo Foundation, 1927-31; Consulting Surgeon and head of a section in surgery, Mayo Clinic, 1931-1964; Instructor in Surgery, Mayo Foundation, 1932; Asst. Prof. of Surgery, 1935; Assoc. Prof. of Surgery, 1940. Served 1942-1945; head of one of Mayo Clinic military units, with rank of Colonel at time of discharge from military service. Delegate to World Health Assemblies: Mexico City, 1955; Geneva, Switzerland, 1956; Minneapolis, U.S.A., 1958. Member various surgical and other Assocs. in U.S.A.; Hon. Member: Med. Instn., Liverpool, Eng., and other foreign Assocs., etc. F.A.C.S., 1933; Associate Fellow International Society of Surgery, 1946; Hon. F.R.C.S. Eng. 1958; Hon. F.R.A.C.S. 1962. Is a Freemason. Holds various awards and medals, for his work. Order of Crown of Italy; Order al Merito of Chile (Comdr.). *Publications:* Surgery of the Small and Large Intestine, 1955; many articles on medical and surgical subjects. *Recreations:* farming, fishing, riding, boating. *Address:* Mayo Clinic, Rochester, Minnesota; Mayowood, Rochester, Minnesota. *T.:* 282-2-2511; 282-1712. *Clubs:* Minneapolis (Minn.); Rotary University (Rochester, Minn.); University (St. Paul, Minn.); University (Chicago, Ill.); Princeton (New York).

[*Died* 28 *July* 1968.

MAYRS, Edward Brice Cooper; Emeritus Prof. of Pharmacology, Queen's University of Belfast; Hon. Consultant, Northern Ireland Hospitals Authority; *b.* 1891; *s.* of late J. C. Mayrs, J.P., Belfast. *Educ.:* Methodist College, Belfast; Queen's University Belfast (Scholar), M.B., B.Ch. (Honours), 1914; D.P.H. 1919; M.D. (gold medal), 1920. Lieutenant and Captain, R.A.M.C., 1915-17; former Demonstrator in Physiology, Q.U.B.; Lecturer in Materia Medica, Edinburgh University; Lecturer in Pharmacology, Q.U.B. *Publications:* various scientific papers in Journal of Physiology, Quarterly Journal of Medicine, British Medical Journal, etc. *Address:* Collin Grove, Dunmurry, Co. Antrim. *T.:* Dunmurry 2280.

[*Died* 15 *April* 1964.

MAYSTON, Very Rev. Richard John Forrester, C.B.E. 1956 (M.B.E. 1944); Provost of Leicester and Vicar of St. Martin's Cathedral Church since Nov. 1958; *b.* Dublin, 23 Jan. 1907; 3rd *s.* of late Albert E. Mayston and M. Maud Mayston (*née* Forrester), professional musicians; *m.* 1937, Margaret Annetta Fisher, B.A. (T.C.D.), *y. d.* of late John Fisher, solicitor, and Ellen (*née* Livingston), Newry, Co. Down; no *c.* *Educ.:* High School, Dublin; Dublin Univ. (T.C.D.). Organ Exhibnr. and Scholar, R.I.A.M., 1923, 1924, 1925: Organist, All Saints, Raheny, 1922-25; Holy Trinity, Killiney, 1925-31; B.A. (T.C.D.). Divinity Testimonium, and Composition Prize, 1931; M.A. 1936; ordained, 1931; Curate of Holywood, Co. Down, 1931-36. Commissioned Royal Army Chaplains' Dept., 1936; served Palestine, 1938-40; Staff Chaplain to Chaplain-General, War Office, 1940-44; D.A.C.G., N.I.D., Burma (despatches, 1946), India, H.Q. Brit. Commonwealth Occupation Force (Japan) S.P.D., and B.A.O.R.; A.C.G., British Troops, Egypt, 1951-52; A.C.G., B.A.O.R., Germany, 1953-55; Asst. Chaplain-Gen., W.O., 1955-58; retired from Army, 1958. Hon. Chaplain to the Queen, 1954-58, to the Bishop of Leicester, 1956-1958. *Recreations:* music, fishing. *Address:* Provost's House, 7 St. Martin's East, Leicester. *T.:* Leicester 25294/5. *Clubs:* National, English-Speaking Union (London); University (Dublin); Leicestershire.

[*Died* 13 *May* 1963.

MAYURBHANJ, Maharaja of, Flight Lt. Maharaja Sir Pratap Chandra Bhanj Deo, G.C.I.E., *cr.* 1946 (K.C.I.E., *cr.* 1935); Hon. Flight Lieut. R.A.F.; is a Director of several companies; *b.* Feb. 1901; *s.* of Maharaja Sri Ram Chandra Bhanj Deo and Maharani Lakshmi Kumari Devi; *m.* 1925, Maharani Prem Kumari Devi, *d.* of Maharaj Sirdar Singhji of Shahpura, Rajputana; two *s.* one *d.* *Educ.:* Mayo College, Ajmer; Muir Central College, Allahabad. After merger of Indian States, joined firm of Messrs. Gladstone Lyall & Co. Ltd., as Managing Director; retired, 1958. *Address:* Baripada, Mayurbhanj, India.

[*Deceased.*

MBOYA, Tom, (Thomas Joseph); Minister of Economic Planning and Development, Kenya, since 1964; *b.* 15 Aug. 1930; *m.* 1962; Pamela Odede; one *s.* three *d.* (and one *s.* decd.). *Educ.:* Holy Ghost Coll., Mangu; Roy. Sanitary Institute's Med. Trng. Sch.; Jeanes Sch.; Ruskin Coll., Oxford (British Workers' Travel Assoc. Scholar). Sanitary Inspector, Nairobi City Council, 1951-52. Mem. African Staff Assoc., 1951 (Pres., 1952); Mem. Kenya African Union, 1952; Nat. Gen. Sec., Kenya Local Government Workers' Union, 1952; Gen. Sec., Kenya Fedn. of Labour, 1953-62; M.L.C. Kenya, 1957-; Sec.-Gen., Kenya African Nat. Union, 1960-; Minister of Labour, Kenya, 1962-63; Minister of Justice and Constitutional Affairs, 1963-64. Chairman: 1st All African People's Conf., Accra, 1958; I.C.F.T.U. East and Central African Cttee., 1959-62; P.A.F.M.E.C.A., 1959; U.N. Econ. Commn., for Africa, 1965-67; Mem. United Nations Development Planning Committee 1968. Hon. LL.D. Howard Univ., Washington, 1959. *Publication:* Freedom and After, 1963; Challenge of Nationhood, 1970 (posthumous). *Recreations:* swimming, reading. *Address:* Box 10818, Nairobi, Kenya. *T.:* Nairobi 28360.

[*Died* 5 *July* 1969.

MEABY, Kenneth Tweedale, C.B.E. 1942; D.L. Notts; J.P.; Clerk of the Lieutenancy since 1920; Clerk of the Peace and of the County Council for Nottinghamshire, 1920-54; Clerk of the Court Magistrates Courts Committee; County Controller for Civil Defence, Secretary of Nottinghamshire War Agricultural Executive Committee, legal adviser to Midland Agricultural College, and Clerk of War Zone Court for North Midland Region; *b.* 11 Feb. 1883; *e. s.* of late Rev. G. K. Meaby, M.A., and *g.s.* of Dr. George Meaby, LL.D., Cartmel; unmarried. *Educ.:* St. Bees School, Cumberland. Formerly Deputy Town Clerk for Plymouth and Wolverhampton and Deputy Clerk of the Peace and of the County Council for Devon and Durham Counties; late Pres. Law Society for Nottingham and Nottinghamshire. Late Flag Officer R.N.V.R., retd. J.P. 1954. *Publications:* Conservation of Water Supplies, 1934; Survey of County Govt. in Nottinghamshire during 50 years 1939; Nottinghamshire County Records during the 18th Century, 1943; Relations between Parish Councils, Rural District Councils and County Councils, 1948. *Recreations:* yachting and golf. *Address:* Burgage Court, Southwell, Notts. *T.:* Southwell 2261. *Clubs:* Royal Cruising; Royal Southern Yacht (Southampton); Royal Western Yacht (Plymouth); Royal Fowey Yacht (Fowey); Hamble Sailing; Nottinghamshire County (Nottingham).

[*Died* 6 *April* 1965.

MEADE-FETHERSTONHAUGH, Adm. Hon. Sir Herbert, G.C.V.O., *cr.* 1934 (K.C.V.O., *cr.* 1929), C.B. 1925; D.S.O. 1915; Royal Navy, retired; Extra Equerry to the Queen since 1952 (formerly to King George VI and to King George V); *b.* 3 Nov. 1875; *b.* of 5th and *heir-pres.* to 6th Earl of Clanwilliam; assumed additional name of Fetherstonhaugh by Royal licence, 1932; *m.* 1911, Margaret, *e. d.* of late Rt. Rev. Hon. E. C. Glyn; one *s.* two *d.* (and one *s.* decd.). Employed Naval Mobilisation; Captain, 1915; Rear-Admiral, 1925; Vice-Admiral, 1930; Admiral, 1934; served European War, 1914-18 (despatches, prom.), including Heligoland Bight, 1914, off Dogger Bank, 1915, and Battle of Jutland, 1916 (despatches); Naval Assist. to the Second Sea Lord, 1918-19; Chief of Staff to the Comdr.-in-Chief at Rosyth; commanded H.M.S. Renown, 1921-23; commanded R.N. College, Dartmouth, 1923-25; Rear-Adm. commanding Destroyer Flotillas of the Mediterranean Fleet, 1926-28; commanded H.M. Yacht, 1931-34; Naval A.D.C. to the King, 1924; retired list, 1936. Served in war of 1939-45 as Commodore of Convoys, R.N.R.; Lt.-Col. H.G., and Lieut. R.N.V.R. Admiralty Small Vessels Pool. Sergeant-at-Arms, House of Lords, 1939-46. *Address:* Uppark, Petersfield, Hants. *Club:* Turf.

[*Died* 27 *Oct.* 1964.

MEADON, Ernest John, C.B. 1960; Deputy Secretary, Ministry of Power, 1965-68; *b.* 11 November 1911; *s.* of late John Henry Meadon and Annie Meadon (*née* Hodgkiss); *m.* 1st, 1937, Elizabeth Mildred (*d.* 1957), *d.* of late Councillor Harold Harrison, Greenmount, Bury, Lancs.; two *s.*; 2nd, 1959, Mary Lilian, *d.* of late A. F. Parsons, Boscombe, Bournemouth. *Educ.:* Manchester Grammar School; Gonville and Caius College, Cambridge (B.A.). Assistant Principal, Mines Department, 1934; Private Secretary to Sec. for Mines, 1937-38; Principal, 1939; Assistant Secretary, Min. of Fuel and Power, 1942. Under-Secretary, Safety and Health Division, 1954; Accountant-General and Under-Secretary for Finance, Ministry of Power, 1955-62, Director of Establishments, 1962-65. *Recreations:* music, sailing, chess, gardening. *Address:* 8 Red House Lane, Walton-on-Thames, Surrey. *T.:* 28221. *Club:* Devonshire. [*Died* 6 *May* 1970.

MEALING, Sir Kenneth William, Kt., *cr.* 1945; Director: Yule Catto & Co. Ltd.; Ultramar Co. Ltd.; *b.* 17 Mar. 1895; *o. s.* of William Robert and Edith Lucy Mealing; *m.* 1929, Molly Eileen Sandifer; two *d.* *Educ.:* Privately. Served with Sussex Yeomanry, Royal Sussex Regiment and (in France) with R.F.A., 1914-19; joined Andrew Yule & Co. Ltd. in Calcutta, 1920; Director, 1934; Deputy Chairman, 1936; Chairman, 1941; retired 1945. President, Bengal Chamber of Commerce and Associated Chambers of Commerce, India, 1944-45; Member, Council of State, India, 1944-45. *Recreations:* astronomy, reading. *Address:* Aston Valentine, South Ascot, Berks. *Clubs:* Oriental; Bengal (Calcutta). [*Died* 4 *Oct.* 1968.

MEARS, Sir Grimwood, K.C.I.E., *cr.* 1928; Kt., *cr.* 1917; Knight of the Order of the Crown of Belgium, 1919; *b.* 21 Jan. 1869; *o.s.* of William Mears, B.A. Winchester; *m.* 1896, Annie (*d.* 1943), *d.* of late G. P. Jacob of Bryngoleu, Shawford; one *s.* one *d.*; *m.* 1951, Margaret Mary Tempest. *Educ.:* Exeter College, Oxford. Called to Bar, Inner Temple, 1895; requested in September 1914 by the Government to investigate cases of alleged German atrocities, and for this purpose gave up a considerable practice at the Bar; and with the assistance of some twenty members of the Bar, voluntarily collected the greater part of the evidence laid before the Bryce Committee on Alleged German Outrages; acted as joint Honorary Secretary to that Committee; later, wrote a reply to the German White Book; after the outbreak of the Irish Rebellion in April 1916 gave his services as Secretary to the Royal Commission appointed to inquire into the causes of the rising; Secretary to the Dardanelles Commission, 1916-17; accompanied Lord Reading to America, and was with him during his Ambassadorship, 1918-19; British Representative on the Inter-Allied Cereal Committee at Washington; Chief Justice of High Court, Allahabad, 1919-1932; retired, 1932; Chairman Bombay Back Bay Enquiry Committee, 1926-27; formerly J.P., Hants and Dep. Chm. Quarter Sessions. *Recreations:* fly-fishing, shooting and occasional broadcasting. *Address:* 3 St. Edmund's Road, Ipswich, Suffolk. [*Died* 20 *May* 1963.

MEASURES, Wing Comdr. Arthur Harold, C.B.E. 1945 (O.B.E. 1918); M.I.M.E.; R.A.F. (R.); Member of Board, British European Airways Corporation, 1946-1956; *b.* 20 February 1882; *m.* 1906, Grace Dorey; one *s.* one *d.* *Educ.:* Southwell Collegiate Grammar School, Nottinghamshire. Served apprenticeship Simpson & Co., London; joined Air Bn. R.E. 1912; France, Aug. 1914-18; transferred R.A.F. as Squadron Leader, 1919; retired as Wing Commander, 1930; joined Imperial Airways, Divisional Engineer, E. Africa, 1932; Operations Manager, India, 1933; Railway Air Services, 1934; Manager, Scottish Airways, 1937; Superintendent, Associated Airways Joint Cttee., 1940; Dir. of Isle of Man Air Services, Great Western & Southern Airways. Médaille Militaire (France), 1914. *Address:* Creech Cottage, 36 Longdown Lane, Ewell, Surrey. *T.:* Ewell 7465. [*Died* 12 *June* 1969.

MEASURES, Sir Philip Herbert, Kt., *cr.* 1946; C.B.E. 1931; *b.* 2 Jan. 1893; *s.* of late Herbert James Measures; *m.* 1935, Muriel, 3rd *d.* of W. S. Steventon. *Educ.:* Stonyhurst College. Commission in the Special Reserve of Officers (3rd Battalion The East Surrey Regiment), 1911-13; passed the examination for appointment to Indian Police; arrived in India, 1913; served in different districts of the United Provinces until 1916, when services were lent to the Govt. of the N.W.F.P. in the Police and Frontier Constabulary until 1920; returned to the U.P. in 1921; was in charge of police arrangements at Hardwar Kumbh Mela, 1927; Superintendent of Police, Allahabad, 1928-32; Assistant to Inspector-General of Police, 1933-1934; Superintendent of Police, Agra, 1935-38; Deputy Inspector-General of Police, Southern Range, U.P., 1939-44; Deputy Inspector-General of Police Headquarters, 1944-45; Inspector-General of Police, U.P., 1945-47, retired, Apr. 1947. *Recreation:* golf. *Address:* Bradda Brae, Port Erin, I.O.M. *T.:* Port Erin 2351. [*Died* 25 *Oct.* 1961.

MEDFORTH, Marguerite Elizabeth, C.B.E. 1931; R.R.C.; *b.* Sept. 1879; 2nd *d.* of late Robert Medforth, J.P., West End House, Bridlington. *Educ.:* Privately; Oxford High School. Trained Metropolitan Hospital, 1903-6; joined Q.A.I.M.N.S., 1906; served European War in France, Mudros, Egypt, Salonika (R.R.C. 1st Class, despatches twice); Matron-in-Chief, Queen Alexandra's Imperial Military Nursing Service, 1930-34; retired, 1934; Regional Nursing Officer, London, Ministry of Health, 1940-45. *Recreations:* outdoor sports, gardening. *Address:* Flat 5, Wilton House, Grosvenor Gardens, St. Leonards-on-Sea. *T.:* Hastings 6778. *Club:* United Nursing Services (Hon. Vice-President). [*Died* 29 *May* 1966.

MEDILL, Brig. Percy Montgomery, D.S.O. 1918; *b.* 1882; *y. s.* of late T. S. Medill, Wimbledon; *m.* 1930, Muriel Edith, J.P. *d.* of late Clive Davies, Hawkley Hurst, Hants and Honolulu; one *d.* *Educ.:* Haileybury. Served European War, 1914-18 (despatches, D.S.O.); Chief Instructor in Gunnery, School of Artillery, Larkhill, 1934-36; Brigadier R.A. Western Command, India, 1936-38; retired pay, 1939. *Address:* The Grange, Shiplake Cross, Henley-on-Thames. [*Died* 4 *March* 1963.

MEDLAND, Hubert Moses; retired Civil Servant: Part-time Member, S.W. Electricity Board; *b.* 1 July 1881; *s.* of Alderman Charles Medland and Elizabeth Medland, Okehampton, Devon; *m.* 1906, Mary Ellen Smith, Newark-on-Trent; two *s.* two *d.* *Educ.:* Elementary School, Okehampton; Tavistock Grammar School. Served an apprenticeship to Mechanical Engineers; Member of Amalgamated Society of Engineers five years as full-time District Secretary, Plymouth; Vice-Chairman of H.M. Dockyard, Devonport, Whitley Committee, nine years; Member Devonport Board of Guardians, 1920; Member of Plymouth City Council, 1923; Lord Mayor of Plymouth, 1935-36; J.P. 1937; M.P. (Lab.) Drake Division of Plymouth, 1945-50; Pres. of British Waterworks Assoc. 1938; Shipyard Labour Supply Offices, Ministry of Labour, 1940; Deputy Regional Commissioner, South West Region, 1941. King

George VIth Coronation Medal, 1937; Imperial Service Medal, 1940. *Recreations:* cricket, bowling, reading. *Address:* 44 Quarry Park Road, Peverell, Plymouth. *T.:* Plymouth 60621. *Club:* Golfers'. [*Died* 11 *Dec.* 1964.

MEDLEY, Charles Douglas; Hon. LL.D. (Birmingham); Solicitor, retired; *b.* 6 June 1870; *e.s.* of Rev. Edward Medley and Emily, *d.* of Rev. C. M. Birrell, and *sister* of Rt. Hon. A. Birrell; *m.* 1901, Anne Gwendoline Owen (*d.* 1961); four *s.* two *d.* *Educ.:* Leys School, Cambridge; London University, B.A. Formerly Senior Partner in firm of Field Roscoe & Co.; Chairman of Trustees of Barber Institute of Fine Arts, Univ. of Birmingham; formerly Dir. and Chm., Guardian Assurance Co. Ltd. *Recreations:* literature, fishing. *Address:* 24 York House, York House Place, Kensington Church St., W.8. *T.:* Western 0490. *Clubs:* Reform, Arts. [*Died* 12 *Aug.* 1963.

MEDLEY, Sir John (Dudley Gibbs), Kt., *cr.* 1948; Hon. D.C.L. Oxon; M.A. (Oxon and Melbourne); Hon. LL.D. (Melbourne); *b.* 19 April 1891; *s.* of late Professor Dudley Julius Medley; *m.* 1916, Emmeline Mary, 2nd *d.* of late Sir Francis Newbolt, K.C.; one *s.* one *d.* *Educ.:* Winchester; New Coll., Oxford (Scholar). 1st Class Honours Honour Moderations, 1912; 1st Class Honours Litteræ Humaniores, 1914; Fellow of Corpus Christi College, Cambridge, 1914; 2nd Lieutenant 6th Battalion Welsh Regiment (T.F.), 1914; served in France throughout European war; demobilised with rank of Major, 1919; entered service of Anthony Gibbs & Sons, London; went to Australia to Gibbs, Bright & Co., 1920; Manager of their Adelaide Office, 1922-24; Manager in Sydney, 1924-30; resigned 1930 and became Headmaster of Tudor House School, Moss Vale, N.S.W.; Vice-Chancellor Univ. of Melbourne, 1938-51; F.R.S.A. 1948; Mem. A.B.C., 1942-61; Pres. Australian Council of Educational Research, 1950-58; Chm. Trustees, Nat. Gall., 1950-57. *Publications:* Addresses, 1938-40, 1940; What Next (4 Broadcasts), 1941; The Future of Australian Universities, 1944; An Australian Alphabet, 1953. *Recreations:* gardening, fishing. *Address:* Wickham, Harkaway, Victoria, Australia. *Club:* Melbourne (Melbourne). [*Died* 26 *Sept.* 1962.

MEDLYCOTT, Sir Hubert Mervyn, 7th Bt., *cr.* 1808; J.P. Somerset and Dorset; Major, Dorset Yeomanry; retired, 1918; *b.* 29 Sept. 1874; *s.* of late Rev. Sir Hubert James Medlycott, 6th Bt., and Julia Ann, *d.* of Rev. Charles Glyn; *S.* father, 1920; *m.* 1906, Nellie Adah, *d.* of Hector E. Monro, Edmondsham, Dorset; two *s.* (and one *s.* decd.). *Educ.:* Harrow; Trinity College, Cambridge (B.A.). Served in Dorset Yeomanry, 1902-10; rejoined, 1914-18. *Heir:* *s.* James Christopher, *b.* 17 April 1907. *Address:* Manor House, Sandford Orcas, Sherborne, Dorset. *T.:* Corton Denham 206. [*Died* 2 *Sept.* 1964.

MEECHAM, Bert, C.M.G. 1961; O.B.E. 1957; Chairman: Hadfields (W.A.) 1934 Ltd.; A. T. Brine & Sons Ltd.; Ajax Plaster Co. Pty. Ltd.; Ceiloyd Pty. Ltd.; Director: Griffin Coal Mining Co. Ltd.; Mineral Mining & Exports (W.A.) Proprietary Ltd.; Palatine Insurance Co. of Australia Ltd.; *b.* 22 Sept. 1886; *s.* of A. J. Meecham; *m.* 1907, Muriel A. Custard, Yeovil, Som.; three *s.* *Educ.:* Royal Grammar School, High Wycombe, Bucks. Past Pres. Chamber of Manufactures, W.A.; Past Vice-Pres. Associated Chambers of Manufactures, Australia; Leader, Australian Industrial Delegn. to India, 1946; Mem. Export Development Council, 1958-61. Member: State Cttee., Commonwealth Sci. & Indust. Research Organisation; Co-op. Mem., Adv. Council, C.S.I.R.O. Is interested in gold, coal and base metal mining, plaster of Paris manuf., steel making, building. *Recreation:* interest in sport (Life Mem. W.A. Cricket Assoc.), etc. *Address:* Hendford, 146 Forrest St., Peppermint Grove, Western Australia. *T.:* 32004. *Clubs:* West Australian (Perth); (Past Pres. and Life Mem.) Lake Karrinyup Golf; W.A. Turf; Royal Freshwater Bay Yacht. [*Died* 27 *Nov.* 1964.

MEEK, Charles Kingsley, M.A., D.Sc. (Oxon.); *b.* 24 June 1885; *s.* of Rev. J. B. Meek, Rothesay; *m.* 1919, Helen Marjorie, (*d.* 1960), *e. d.* of Lt.-Col. C. H. Innes Hopkins; two *s.* *Educ.:* Rothesay Acad.; Bedford School; Brasenose College, Oxford. Joined Administrative Service, Nigeria, 1912; Asst. Resident, N. Nigeria, 1912; District Officer, 1921; Commissioner for decennial Census, 1921; Anthropological Officer for Northern Provinces, 1924; Resident, 1929; retired 1933; Wellcome gold medal, Royal Anthropological Institute, 1936; Heath Clark lectr., London Univ., 1939; Senior Research Fellow, Brasenose Coll., Oxford, 1943; Univ. Lectr. in Anthropology, Oxford, 1947; retired, 1950. *Publications:* The Northern Tribes of Nigeria, 1925; A Sudanese Kingdom, 1931; Tribal Studies in Northern Nigeria, 1931; Ibo Law in Essays Presented to C. G. Seligman, 1934; Law and Authority in a Nigerian Tribe, 1937; (with W. M. Macmillan and E. R. J. Hussey) Europe and W. Africa, 1940; Land Law and Custom in the Colonies, 1946; Colonial Law—A Bibliography, 1948; Land Tenure and Land Administration in Nigeria and the Cameroons, 1957. *Address:* c/o The Scott Hospital, Beacon Park Road, Plymouth, Devon. [*Died* 28 *March* 1965.

MEEK, Sir David Burnett, Kt., *cr.* 1937; C.I.E. 1933; O.B.E. 1924; M.A. and D.Sc. Glasgow Univ.; Indian Trade Commissioner, London, from 1935; *b.* 10 March 1885; *s.* of late Robert Meek; *m.* Retta Young, 2nd *d.* of late David Gemmell; (one *s.* killed in action 1942). Director of Industries, Govt. of Bengal, 1920-26; Chairman, Conciliation Board on Calcutta Tramway Strike, 1922; Director-General of Commercial Intelligence and Statistics, Govt. of India, 1926-35; Chairman, Hides Cess Committee, 1928; Govt. of India Delegate to International Conference on Economic Statistics, Geneva, 1928; Leader Govt. of India Trade Mission to Persia, Iraq, Palestine, Syria, Soudan, Egypt, Zanzibar, Kenya, Tanganyika, Portuguese East Africa and the Union of South Africa, 1929; Deputation to Federal Reserve Bank, U.S.A., 1930; Dep. High Comr. for India in London, 1944. Attended Internat. Food Conf. Hot Springs, U.S.A., and Monetary Conf., Bretton Woods, U.S.A. Govt. of India delegate, International Sugar Conference, London, 1937; Govt. of India Delegate on International Rubber Regulation Committee, International Tea Committee, International Sugar Council, Wheat Advisory Cttee. Comdr., Orange Nassau, 1948. *Clubs:* Oriental, Athenæum. [*Died* 23 *June* 1964.

MEGAW, Arthur Stanley, (Arthur Stanley), M.A. (h.c.), Queen's University, Belfast; Solicitor (retd.) and Writer; *y. s.* of late Robert Megaw, Holywood, Co. Down and Eliza Morison, *e.d.* of William Pirrie, Rockferry, Cheshire; *m.* Bertha, *y. d.* of late John Augustus Smith, Clonmult, Co. Cork, and Annie, *e. d.* of Jonathan Richardson, M.P., Kirkassock, Co. Down; two *s.* (and two *s.* decd.). *Educ.:* Sullivan Upper School, Holywood; Queen's University, Belfast (B.A. Hons., Prizeman). Silver Medallist of Incorporated Law Society of Ireland; Member of Board of Social Science Studies, Queen's University, 1917-21; Chairman Belfast War Pensions Appeals Committee, 1919-1922; Hon. Sec. Belfast Lit. Soc., 1927-54. *Publications:* Patriotic Song—a British Empire Anthology; The Book of the Garden; The

Bedside Book; The Out-of-Doors Book; The Fireside Book; The Testament of Man—an Anthology of the Spirit; The Golden Road—an Anthology of Travel; The Seven Stars of Peace—an anthology for the times; Good Company; The House of Tranquility; The Bedside Bible; Britain at War; Madame de Sévigné—her Letters and her World; The Bedside Bunyan; The Monkhurst Case; The Bedside Shakespeare; The Bedside Book for Children; Under Italian Skies; The New Bedside Book; Peace at the Close; A Backroom Boy; Contributor to Blackwood's Magazine, The Times, The Times Literary Supplement, etc. *Address:* Arden, Fortwilliam Drive, Belfast. [*Died* 23 *Sept.* 1961.

MÉGROZ, Rodolphe Louis; Journalist and lecturer; *b.* Pimlico, 2 Aug. 1891; *e. s.* of R. F. Mégroz and Alice Jane Bull; Pyrenean brigands and East Anglian farmers as ancestors; *m.*; three *d.* In B.B.C. European News Service, 1942-45. Editor of Overseas Food Corp. publications, 1949-51. First book (verse) published during last year of Military service; contributor of poems, essays, articles and book reviews to numerous journals. Drama: Rossetti, a play with Herbert de Hamel; Mr. Absalom, a play with Alan Sullivan; Mosquito Day and other plays for B.B.C.; St. Genevieve, a Masque, with Leighton Lucas. *Publications:* Personal Poems, 1919; Walter de la Mare, a Biographical and Critical Study, 1924; A Talk with Joseph Conrad, 1926; Joseph Conrad's Mind and Method, 1931; (re-issued for libraries, by N.Y. publisher, 1964); The Three Sitwells, a Biographical and Critical Study, 1926; Francis Thompson, The Poet of Earth in Heaven: a Study in Poetic Mysticism and the Evolution of Love Poetry, 1927; The Story of Ruth: an Idyll (verse), 1927; From the Scrip of Eros, Poems, 1934; Dante Gabriel Rossetti, the Poet of Heaven in Earth, 1928; Sir Ronald Ross, Discoverer and Creator, 1931; Modern English Poetry, 1882-1932, 1933; Guide to Poetry for Reciters and Teachers, 1934; English Poetry for Children, 1934; Modern Poems for Children (Anthology), 1936; A Treasury of Modern Poetry (Anthology), 1936; The Lear Omnibus (anthology of Edward Lear's Nonsense), 1938 (reprint, 1945); The Dream World, 1939; The Real Robinson Crusoe, Life of Alexander Selkirk, 1939; The Book of Lear (Penguins, 2 vols.), 1940; The Cook's Paradise, being Verral's Complete System of Cookery (1759) with Thomas Gray's unpublished Cookery Notes, 1948; Profile Art Through the Ages, 1948; Pedagogues are Human (an anthology of Teachers and Pupils), 1950; 31 Bedside Essays, 1951. The following (all signed C. D. Dimsdale): Come Out of Doors (illustr. Tunnicliffe), 1951; The Story of Grass, 1960; Countryside and Coast, 1964. *Recreations:* billiards; explaining the peace. *Address:* Cheverells, Pickford Road, Markyate, Herts. [*Died* 30 *Sept.* 1968.

MEIKLEJOHN, Col. John Forbes, C.I.E. 1942; *b.* 10 Oct. 1889; *s.* of G. Forbes Meiklejohn, Chief Justice, Mysore; *m.* 1917, Julia Chester Woodhouse (*d.* 1948); *m.* 1949, Barbara Mary Hyde. *Educ.:* Cheltenham; R.M.C., Sandhurst. Served European War, 1914-18 (despatches 4 times); N.W. Frontier, 1929-30; Burma, 1931-32; War of 1939-1945, South-East Asia Command. Cabinet Office, Military Histories Branch, 1946-55. *Address:* c/o Lloyds Bank Ltd., 6 Pall Mall, S.W.1. *Club:* United Service. [*Died* 6 *March* 1966.

MEIKLEJOHN, Surgeon Rear-Adm. Norman Sinclair, D.S.O. 1919; *b.* 15 June 1879; *s.* of J. W. S. Meiklejohn, M.D., Dep. Inspector-General, R.N. *Educ.:* St. Paul's School; St. George's Hospital. Served European War, 1914-19 (D.S.O.); retired list, 1934. *Address:* Royal Naval Club, Portsmouth. *Club:* Reform. [*Died* 27 *June* 1961.

MEIKLEJOHN, Sir Roderick Sinclair, K.B.E., *cr.* 1931; C.B. 1911; Commandeur de l'ordre de la Couronne (Belgium); *b.* 30 May 1876; *e. s.* of late John William Sinclair Meiklejohn, M.D., Deputy Inspector-General of Hospitals and Fleets, R.N. *Educ.:* St. Paul's School; Hertford College, Oxford (Scholar). Entered War Office, 1899; transferred to Treasury, 1902; Private Secretary to Sir E. Hamilton, 1903-4; to the Duke of Devonshire, 1904-5; to the Right Hon. H. H. Asquith as Chancellor of the Exchequer and Prime Minister, 1905-11; Deputy Controller of Supply Services in H.M. Treasury; First Civil Service Commissioner, 1928-39. *Address:* 9 Wythburn Court, Seymour Place, W.1. *T.:* Ambassador 4305. *Clubs:* Brooks's, Beefsteak. [*Died* 18 *Jan.* 1962.

MEIKLEREID, Sir (Ernest) William, K.B.E., *cr.* 1955; C.M.G. 1947; *b.* 12 October 1899; *s.* of late W. Meiklereid; *m.* 1939, Katherine Perouse de Montclos (*d.* 1958). *Educ.:* Monkton Combe School; Emmanuel College, Cambridge. Served in H.M. Forces, 1918-19, Student interpreter in Siam, 1923; served in various consular capacities in Siam, Netherlands East Indies, and French Indo-China; Consul-General, Dakar, 1943-45; Saigon, 1945-47; San Francisco, 1947-49; Minister (Commercial) British Embassy, Paris, 1950-55; Head of U.K. Delegation to High Authority of the European Coal and Steel Community, 1955-1958; Government's Representative with Commission of European Atomic Energy Community, 1958; retd. from H.M. Foreign Service, 1958. *Address:* Bec Melar, Lanmodez, Pleubian, C. du N., France. *Club:* Royal Automobile. [*Died* 12 *Jan.* 1965.

MEINERTZHAGEN, Col. Richard, C.B.E. 1957; D.S.O. 1916; late Duke of Cornwall's Light Inf.; ornithologist; *b.* 3 March 1878; *s.* of late Daniel and Georgina Meinertzhagen, Mottisfont Abbey, Romsey; *m.* 1921, Annie Constance Jackson (*d.* 1928); two *s.* one *d.* *Educ.:* Harrow. Joined Army (Royal Fusiliers), 1899; served in India till 1902, when joined King's African Rifles till 1905; served on various expeditions in E. Africa (medal, three clasps, wounded, despatches); graduated at Staff College; retired pay, 1925; served in E. Africa, Palestine, and French fronts during the European War, and was afterwards Member of Paris Peace Delegation; Chief Political Officer in Palestine and Syria, 1919-1920; Military Adviser, Middle East Dept., Colonial Office, 1921-24; Council of the Royal Geog. Soc., 1927-30; extensive travel Asia, Africa and U.S.A.; War Office, 1939-40; Home Guard, 1940-45. *Publications:* Birds of Egypt, 1930; Life of a Boy, 1947; Review of the Alaudidae, 1951; Birds of Arabia, 1954; Kenya Diary, 1902-1906, 1957; Pirates and Predators, 1959; Middle East Diary, 1959; Army Diary, 1960; Diary of a Black Sheep, 1964; various on ornithology in scientific magazines. *Recreations:* biology, geography, silence, solitude and space. *Address:* 17 Kensington Park Gardens, W.11. *T.A.:* Montezuma, London. *T.:* Park 4928. [*Died* 17 *June* 1967.

MELAS, Michael Constantine; Grand Cross of Order of George I (Greece); Greek Ambassador in London, 1962-64; *b.* 1902; *m.* 1930, Christine Carapano (*d.* 1942); one *s.* one *d.*; *m.* 1946, Frosso Eugenidi. *Educ.:* École des Sciences Politiques, Paris. Attaché, Greek Ministry of Foreign Affairs, 1924; Ambassador, Cairo, 1952; Greek Member of N.A.T.O. Council, 1956. G.C.V.O. (Hon.) 1963. *Recreation:* golf. *Address:* 15 rue de Franqueville, Paris XVI, France. [*Died* 4 *March* 1967.

MELCHER, Frederic Gershom; Chairman R. R. Bowker Co., Publishers' Weekly Library Journal; *b.* Malden, Mass., 12 April 1879; *s.* of Edwin Forrest Melcher and Alice Bartlett; *m.* 1910, Marguerite Fellows; one *s.* two *d.* *Educ.:* Public schools of Newton, Mass. Bookselling, Boston and Indianapolis, 1895-1918; R. R. Bowker Co. Publishers, N.Y., Vice-Pres. 1918-33, Pres., 1933-59, Chm. 1959-; Co-ed. Publishers' Weekly, 1918-59; Sec. Amer. Booksellers Assoc., 1918-20; Exec.-Sec. Nat. Assoc. of Book Publishers, 1920-24. Hon. Life Member American Library Association. Lecturer and writer on publishing and book-trade matters. Founder of Children's Book Week. Established, 1924, John Newbery Medal for most distinguished children's book and, 1937, Caldecott Medal for best picture book. Hon. Member Society of Bookmen (London). Director P.E.N. (American). Hon. Litt.D. Rutgers Univ., 1958; Syracuse Univ. 1959. *Address:* 228 Grove Street, Montclair, New Jersey, U.S.A. *T.A.:* Pubweekly New York. *T.:* Murray Hill (N.Y.) 2-0150. *Club:* Grolier (New York). [*Died* 9 *March* 1963.

MELDRUM, Sir Peter (Lowrie), Kt. 1965; Lord Provost of Glasgow and Lord Lieutenant of County of City of Glasgow since 1963; *b.* 6 March 1910; *m.* Jessie Cockburn Downie; one *d.* *Educ.:* Glasgow. Mem. Glasgow Corp., 1939- (Chm. various Cttees.); Magistrate, 1944-47. Member: S. of Scotland Elec. Bd.; Scottish Tourist Bd.; Scottish Coun. (Develt. & Industry); Clyde Navigation Trust; B.T.C., Scottish Area Bd.; Scottish Omnibus Gp.; Chm. Clyde Valley Planning Adv. Cttee.; served on various Govt. Cttees. of Enquiry. Hon. LL.D. Strathclyde, 1965. *Address:* 28 Muirhill Ave., Glasgow, S.4. [*Died* 31 *Oct.* 1965.

MELDRUM, Brig.-Gen. William, C.B. 1919; C.M.G. 1916; D.S.O. 1917; *s.* of late A. L. Meldrum, St. Andrews, Scotland; *b.* Kamo, North Auckland, 28 July 1865; *m.* 1st, 1893, Nora Elizabeth, *d.* of late Capt. Howard Carthew, New Plymouth, N.Z.; one *s.* one *d.*; 2nd, 1927, Clare Beatrice Cicin, *d.* of late Leonard Reid Dodsun, Greymouth, N.Z.; one *s.* two *d.* *Educ.*: Auckland Grammar School. Barrister and solicitor, 1889; farming, 1906-21; Stipendiary Magistrate, New Zealand, 1921-1933; Mayor of Greymouth, 1935-38; Com. Wellington Mounted Rifles Regiment, 1914-17; New Zealand Mounted Rifles Brigade, 1917-19; served European War, 1914-18 (C.B., C.M.G., D.S.O., despatches six times), Serbian Order of the White Eagle; retired list, 1921. *Recreation:* chess (won N.Z. Chess championship 1896) *Address:* 187 Tainui Street, Greymouth, N.Z. [*Died* 13 *Feb.* 1964.

MELLANBY, Molly, C.B.E. 1957; formerly Commissioner of Prisons; Member Council of Dr. Barnardo's Homes; *b.* 2 Nov. 1893; *d.* of late Henry and Frances Mellanby, Yarm-on-Tees, Yorks. *Educ.:* Princess Helena Coll., Ealing; Newnham College, Cambridge. Assistant Mistress and House Mistress, Tunbridge Wells High School, 1917-21; Assistant Mistress and House Mistress, Roedean School, 1921-35; Governor H.M. Borstal Institution, Aylesbury, 1935-43. *Club:* Oxford and Cambridge. [*Died* 16 *Sept.* 1962.

MELLER, Grahame Temple, C.B.E. 1947; F.C.A.; Permanent Member, Transport Tribunal, since 1964; *b.* 27 April 1905; 2nd *s.* of late Sir Richard Meller, sometime M.P. for Mitcham, and late Jeanie Frances (*née* Sibley); *m.* 1934, Mary Eleanor, *d.* of late Charles Nixon; three *s.* *Educ.:* Lancing. Chartered Accountant, 1928; in Malaya, 1930-33; Sec., Imperial Airways, 1934-39; Chief Accountant, B.O.A.C., 1940-45; Asst. Dir.-Gen. and Administration Dir., B.O.A.C., 1945-48; Royal Dutch/Shell Group, 1949-1963; first Chairman Financial Cttee., Internat. Air Transport Assoc., 1944-45; Mem. Nat. Jt. Coun. for Civil Aviation, 1945-48; nominated Mem. Oil Consumers Coun., 1948; Hon. Treas., British Soc. for Internat. Health Educn., 1 63. Lieut., East Surrey Regt. (T.A.), 1925-30. Chevalier, Order of Oranje Nassau (Netherlands), 1948. *Recreations:* golf, racing, reading, modern art, travel. *Address:* Whiteoaks, Horley, Surrey. *T.:* Horley 2215. *Club:* Junior Carlton. [*Died* 22 *June* 1965.

MELLISH, Rev. Edward Noel, V.C. 1916; M.C.; *b.* 1880; *s.* of Edward Mellish; *m.* 1918, Elizabeth Wallace Molesworth; three *s.* one *d.* *Educ.:* King Edward VI. School, Saffron Walden; King's College, London. Served South African War, 1900-02; ordained, 1912; Curate of St. Paul's, Deptford, 1912; Acting Army Chaplain, 1915-19; served European War, 1915-18 (V.C.); Vicar of St. Mark's, Lewisham, 1919; of Wangford-cum-Henham and Reydon, 1925-28; of Great Dunmow, 1928-48; Perpetual Curate, Baltonsborough, 1948-53; retired 1953. *Address:* The Court House, South Petherton, Somerset. [*Died* 8 *July* 1962.

MELLOR, Lieut.-Col. Abel, C.M.G. 1919; D.S.O. 1916; late R.H.A.; *b.* 18 Jan. 1880; *s.* of late C. W. Mellor, J.P., late I.C.S.; *m.* 1918, Barbara Janet, *d.* of late E. A. Smithers; one *d.* Served S. African War 1899-1902 (Queen's medal two clasps, King's medal two clasps), ; European War, 1914-18 (despatches, D.S.O. and bar). *Address:* Parsonage Farm, Hungerford, Berks. *T.:* Hungerford 153. [*Died* 7 *Feb.* 1967.

MELLOR, Brigadier John Seymour, C.B.E. 1946 (O.B.E. 1919); M.C. 1917; Chief Constable, War Department Constabulary, 1928-52; Hon. Commandant of the Force, since 1952; *b.* 1883; 2nd *s.* of late James Mellor, Onslow Square, S.W.7; *m.* 1909, Elizabeth Love, 2nd *d.* of late Frederick Marquand, New York; two *s.* one *d.* *Educ.:* Eton. Served in S. African War, 1899-1901, with Sussex Militia; given free commission, by Lord Roberts in K.R.R.C., 1902; Adjutant, Eton College O.T.C., 1911-14; European War, 1914-19 (despatches four times); retired 1921. King's Foreign Service Messenger, 1921-28. Provost Marshal of the United Kingdom, 1943-45. Croix de Guerre with Golden Star (France), 1918. *Recreation:* golf. *Address:* The White House, Watton at Stone, Hertford. *Club:* M.C.C. [*Died* 26 *Sept.* 1962.

MELVILLE, Frances Helen, O.B.E. 1935; M.A., B.D., LL.D.; *b.* 1873; *d.* of late Francis Suther Melville, D.C.S., Edinburgh. *Educ.:* Edinburgh; Germany; University of Edinburgh, M.A., Hon. Phil.I., 1897; University of St. Andrews, B.D., 1910-9; University of Glasgow, LL.D., 1927; Lecturer in Mental and Moral Science, Ladies' College, Cheltenham, 1899; Warden of University Hall, Univ. of St. Andrews, 1900-09; Mistress of Queen Margaret College, Univ. of Glasgow, 1909-35. *Address:* 16 Merchiston Place, Edinburgh 10. *T.:* Fountainbridge 7189. *Clubs:* Lady Artists' (Glasgow); Overseas (Edinburgh). [*Died* 7 *March* 1962.

MELVILLE, Lt.-Col. Hon. Ian L.; *see* Leslie Melville.

MENNINGER, William C., M.D.; President of The Menninger Foundation, Topeka, Kansas; *b.* 15 Oct. 1899; *s.* of Charles Fredrick and Flo Knisely Menninger; *m.* 1925, Catharine Wright; three *s.* *Educ.:* Washburn Municipal University, Topeka; Columbia University and Cornell Medical School, New York City. A.B. 1919 (Washburn), M.A. 1922 (Columbia), M.D.

1924 (Cornell). Has taken active part in educational phase of psychiatry for many years; now Prof. of Psychiatry in Menninger Foundation School of Psychiatry (associated with Veterans Administration Hospital). Medical Director Menninger Sanitarium, 1930-45; interested in application of dynamic principles of psycho-analysis to psychiatric hospital therapy. President: Am. Psychiatric Assoc., 1948-49, Councillor, 1949-52; Am. Psychoanalytic Assoc., 1947-1949, Councillor, 1949-51; Central Neuro-psychiatric Assoc., 1947-48; Chairman, Group for Advancement of Psychiatry, 1946-50, President, 1950-51; Fellow, American College of Physicians, First Vice-President, 1964-65. Advisor to several governmental committees. Director, Neuro-psychiatry Consultants Division, Office of Surgeon-General, U.S. Army, 1943-46. Brigadier-General Medical Corps (D.S.M., Army Commendation Ribbon). U.S. Chamber of Commerce Award for Great Living Americans, 1957; Gold Medal of Nat. Inst. of Social Sciences (with brother, Dr. Karl Menninger) 1961. Holds several Hon. Degrees, from 1949. Chevalier Légion d'Honneur (France), 1948. *Publications:* Juvenile Paresis, 1936; Psychiatry in a Troubled World, 1948; (with Munro Leaf) You and Psychiatry, 1948; Psychiatry: Its Evolution and Present Status, 1948; over 200 papers, mostly on psychiatric subjects, in various scientific journals. *Recreations:* philately, ornithology; Boy Scout work (member, National Executive Board since 1935). *Address:* (office) The Menninger Foundation, 3617 W. Sixth Avenue, Topeka, Kansas, U.S.A.; (home) 1724 Collins Avenue, Topeka, Kansas, U.S.A. *Clubs:* American Philatelic Society; University (Chicago). [*Died* 6 *Sept.* 1966.

MENON, Rao Bahadur Vapal Pangunni, C.S.I. 1946; C.I.E. 1941; *b.* 30 Sept. 1894; *s.* of C. Sankunni Menon and Srimathi Vapal Kunhikutty Amma; *m.* 1st, 1925; 2nd, 1941, Srimathi Kanakamma; two *s.* one *d.* *Educ.:* Ottapalam High School. Joined service, 1914; Asst. Sec., Govt. of India, Reforms Office, 1933; Under-Sec., 1934; Dept. Sec., 1936-40; Joint Sec., June-Oct. 1937 and June-Oct. 1938; Deputy Secretary to Governor-General (Reforms), 1940-42; Joint Sec. to Governor-General (Reforms), Feb.-June 1941; Reforms Commissioner, 1942-47; Secretary to the Governor-General (Public), June 1945-Aug. 1946; Cabinet Secretary, 1945; Sec. to Govt. of India in States Ministry, July 1947-Oct. 1948; Adviser to Govt. of India in the Ministry of States, 1948-49; Secretary to the Govt. of India, Ministry of States, 1949-51; Governor of Orissa, May 1951-July 1951; Member, Finance Commission 1951-52; retired from service, March 1952. *Publications:* The Integration of the Indian States, 1956; The Transfer of Power in India, 1957. *Address:* Shelter Cooke Town, Bangalore 5, India. [*Died* 1 *Jan.* 1966.

MENSON, Sir Charles W. T.; *see* Tachie-Menson.

MENZIES, Sir Robert, Kt., *cr.* 1943; O.B.E. 1918; V.D.; C.A.; *b.* Edinburgh, 12 July 1891; *y. s.* of late Archibald Menzies, S.S.C., Edinburgh; *m.* 1932, Jenny Hamilton, *e. d.* of late Thomas Young, Edinburgh; no *c.* *Educ.:* George Watson's College, Edinburgh; Morrison's Academy, Crieff; Edinburgh Univ. Served European War, 1914-1918, with 9th Royal Scots (wounded, O.B.E., despatches thrice). Member Inst. of Chartered Accountants of Scotland, 1914. Commandant, Cawnpore Contingent, A.F.I., 1921-1933 and 1940-47; Hon. A.D.C. to Viceroy, 1941-47; President Upper India Chamber of Commerce, 1939-41 and 1944-45. Chairman (1938-56) and Managing Director (1930-56), Brit. India Corp., Ltd., Kanpur, U.P., India. Chm. Federation of Woollen Manufacturers in India, 1941-47; Vice-Pres. Federation of Employers in India, 1942-56. *Address:* Heather Wells, Lightwater, Surrey. *T.:* Bagshot 2341. *Clubs:* Caledonian, Oriental, Royal Automobile; Cawnpore (Kanpur); Bengal (Calcutta). [*Died* 6 *Aug.* 1967.

MENZIES of Menzies, Ronald Steuart, D.L., J.P.; Hereditary Chief of Clan Menzies; *b.* 1884; *o. s.* of late William George Steuart-Menzies, Arndilly, Craigellachie, Banffshire; *m.* 1912, Olive (marriage dissolved, 1931), 2nd *d.* of late T. Turner-Farley, Wartnaby Hall, Melton Mowbray; one *d.*; *m.* 1931, Sybil Mary Willoughby, *d.* of Gerald Bowman Boulton, Beverley, Yorkshire; one *s.* two *d.* *Educ.:* Eton. Served European War, 1914-19, Scots Guards; Capt., 1915; Major, 1919; comd. 6 Bn. Gordon Highlanders, 1927-31; Lt.-Col., 1927. Surname Menzies of Menzies recognised by Lord Lyon, 1957. D.L. 1948, J.P. 1946, Banffshire; Vice-Lieutenant of Banffshire, 1952. *Address:* Arndilly, Craigellachie, Banffshire. [*Died* 2 *Oct.* 1961.

MENZIES, Maj.-Gen. Sir Stewart Graham, K.C.B., *cr.* 1951 (C.B. 1942); K.C.M.G., *cr.* 1943; D.S.O. 1914; M.C.; *b.* 30 Jan. 1890; *s.* of Lady Holford; *m.* 1st, 1918, Lady Avice Sackville (from whom he obtained a divorce, 1931) *d.* of 8th Earl De la Warr; 2nd, 1932, Pamela (*d.* 1951), *d.* of late Hon. Rupert Beckett; one *d.*: 3rd, 1952, Audrey Clara Lilian (formerly wife of Hon. Niall Greville Chaplin, and previously widow of Lord Edward Hay), *yr. d.* of Sir Thomas Paul Latham, 1st Bt. *Educ.:* Eton. Grenadier Guards, 1909-10; Life Guards, 1910-39. Served European War, 1914-18 (despatches, D.S.O., M.C., Bt. Major). Subsequently Bt. Col. Grand Officer Legion of Honour; Grand Officer Order of Leopold, Crown of Belgium; Legion of Merit (U.S.A.); Polonia Restituta (Poland); Grand Officer Orange Nassau (Holland); Commander St. Olaf (Norway). *Address:* Bridges Court, Luckington, Chippenham, Wilts. *Clubs:* White's, St. James', Turf. [*Died* 29 *May* 1968.

MENZIES, Major-General Thomas, C.B. 1950; O.B.E. 1943; late R.A.M.C.; retired from Active List, 1953; *b.* 5 March 1893; *s.* of late T. Menzies, M.A., J.P., Farragon, Cults, Aberdeenshire; *m.* 1919, Euphemia, *e. d.* of Gilbert Anderson, Findlins, Hillswick, Shetland; two *s.* one *d.* *Educ.:* Aberdeen Grammar School; University of Aberdeen. M.B., Ch.B. (Aberd.), 1915; D.T.M. & H. (Edin.), 1932. Commissioned Lieut., R.A.M.C. (S.R.), 1914; served European War, 1914-18; mobilised, 1915; India and Mesopotamia, 1915-18; British War and Victory Medals. Commissioned Capt. R.A.M.C. (Regular), 1919; Major, 1927; Lieut.-Col., 1941; Col., 1946; Brig., 1947; Maj.-Gen., 1949. Specialist in Medicine, Aldershot Comd., 1924, Eastern Comd., India, 1928, Scottish Comd., 1931, Southern Comd., India, 1936; Queen Alexandra Mil. Hosp., Millbank, 1938. Served War of 1939-45, France, 1939-40; N. Africa and Italy, 1942-46 (despatches, 1939-45 Star, Africa Star (1st Army), Italy Star, Defence Medal, Victory Medal); Professor of Tropical Medicine, Royal Army Medical Coll., 1940; O.C. 31 Gen. Hosp., 1942; O.C. 94 Gen. Hosp. 1943; A.D.M.S. (Admin.), A.F.H.Q., 1944; D.D.M.S., 3 Dist., Italy, 1946; O.C. Royal Victoria Hosp., Netley, 1946; A.D.M.S., Aldershot and Hants Dist., 1947; D.M.S., G.H.Q., M.E.L.F., 1948-50; D.D.M.S., Southern Command, 1951-53; K.H.P. 1949-1952; Q.H.P. 1952-53; retd. 1953; Provost, Burgh of Kirriemuir, 1958-64; J.P. Angus, 1958-64. *Recreations:* fishing, philately. *Address:* 72 Roods, Kirriemuir Angus. *T.:* 2870. [*Died* 17 *Oct.* 1969.

MENZLER, Frederick August Andrew, C.B.E. 1949; Consulting Actuary; Director, Throgmorton Management Ltd.; *b.* 18 Oct. 1888; *m.* 1st, Edith Carpenter; one *s.*; 2nd, Marguerite Bowie. *Educ.:* St. Marylebone Grammar School; Strand School, King's College, London; B.Sc. Lond. (private study). Ecclesiastical Commission, 1907-19; served European War, 1915-19; Government Actuary's Department, 1919-1929; Secretary, Permanent Consultative Committee on Official Statistics, 1922-1928; Underground Group of Companies 1929-33; London Passenger Transport Board, 1933-47, London Transport Executive, 1948-54: Actuary, 1930-39; Chief Financial Officer, 1939-45; Chief Development and Research Officer, 1945-54. Member, staff side, National Whitley Council for the Civil Service, 1926-29; Chm. Instn. of Professional Civil Servants, 1928-29; Pres., 1950-52, Inst. of Actuaries. Vice-Pres., Roy. Statistical Soc., 1957-58. Member: Phillips Cttee. on Economic and Financial Problems of the Provision for Old Age, 1953-1954; Royal Commission on the Civil Service, 1953-55; London and Home Counties Traffic Advisory Cttee., 1946-54. Guy Medallist in Silver, Roy. Statistical Soc. Croix de Guerre Belge, 1917. *Publications:* Institute of Actuaries Students' Society: The First Fifty Years 1910-1960, 1960; The Stock Exchange, 1961; contributions to: Jls. of Inst. of Actuaries; Roy. Statistical Soc.; Inst. of Transport. *Recreations:* walking and reading. *Address:* 36 Grandcourt, King Edward's Parade, Eastbourne, Sussex. *T.:* Eastbourne 30931. *Club:* Reform. [*Died* 1 *Nov.* 1968.

MERCER, George Gibson, C.B.E. 1941; J.P.; Farmer; *b.* 1873; *s.* of James Mercer, J.P., Southfield, Dalkeith, Midlothian; *m.* 1911, Marjorie, *d.* of late Alexander Campbell, S.S.C., Edinburgh; one *s.* *Educ.:* Dollar Academy; Royal High School, Edinburgh. Chairman of Midlothian Agricultural Executive Committee, 1939-47; Ex-President of Scottish Chamber of Agriculture; Ex-President of Animal Diseases Research Association, Moredun, Edinburgh; Ex-Pres. Scottish Agricultural Organisation Soc. *Address:* Wellwood, Ladybank, Fife. *T.:* Ladybank 400. *Clubs:* Farmers'; Scottish Liberal (Edinburgh). [*Died* 14 *Nov.* 1964.

MERCER, Rev. Dr. Samuel Alfred Browne; Prof. Emer. of Semitic Languages and Egyptology, Trinity College, Univ. of Toronto (Dean of Divinity, 1923-24, Professor 1924-26); *b.* Bay Roberts, Newfld., 10 May 1879; *s.* of Samuel Mercer and Elizabeth Browne Mercer; *m.* 1910, Genevieve Magee (*d.* 1959), Duxbury Mass., U.S.A.; one *d.* *Educ.:* Bishop Field Coll., St. John's, Newfld.; Harvard University (B.A.); Univ. of Wisconsin (M.A.); Univ. of Heidelberg; Sorbonne; Univ. of Munich (Ph.D.). Professor of Hebrew and Old Testament, Western Theological Seminary, Chicago, 1910-22; Dean of Bexley Hall, Gambier, Ohio, U.S.A., 1922-23; Dean of Divinity, Trinity College, Toronto, 1923-24; Pres., Society of Oriental Research. Founder, Anglican Theological Review; Editor: Biblical and Oriental Series; Egyptian Religion, 1933-; Jl. of Soc. of Oriental Research, 1917-. Lauréat de l'Académie Française, 1930. Holds several hon. degrees. F.R.G.S. *Publications:* 39 books including The Oath in Babylonian and Assyrian Literature; Sumero-Babylonian Sign-List; Ethiopic Liturgy; Ethiopic Grammar; Assyrian Grammar; Egyptian Grammar; The Book of Genesis; Religious and Moral Ideas in Babylonia and Assyria; Tutankhamen and Egyptology; The Recovery of Forgotten Empires; Etudes sur les Origines de la Religion de l'Egypte; Extra-Biblical Sources for Hebrew History; The Ethiopic Text of Ecclesiastes; The Tell el-Amarna Tablets; Horus, Royal God of Egypt; The Supremacy of Israel; Sumero-Babylonian Year-Formulae; Religion of Ancient Egypt; The Pyramid Texts, Translation and Commentary; Earliest Intellectual Man's Idea of the Cosmos; Origin of Writing and Our Alphabet; numerous articles on Old Testament Assyriology and Egyptology, etc. *Recreation:* walking. *Address:* c/o Mrs. R. Spaulding, 110 Roosevelt Road, Toronto 6, Canada. [*Died* 10 *Jan.* 1969.

MERCHANT, Professor Wilfred, M.A., S.M., D.Sc., M.I.Struct.E., M.Inst.C.E., A.M.I.Mech.E., A.M.Am.Soc.C.E.; Professor of Structural Engineering, College of Science and Technology, Manchester, since 1957; *b.* 12 Aug. 1912; *yr. s.* of Fred Merchant, Salford; *m.* 1946, Beatrice Mary Aitken; one *s.* one *d.* *Educ.:* Manchester Grammar School; Corpus Christi College, Oxford; Massachusetts Institute of Technology. Various structural engineering work in London, 1933-1937; Development work on jet engines, Metropolitan-Vickers Electrical Co. Ltd., Manchester, 1939-46; College of Science and Technology, Manchester: Lecturer in Structural Engineering, 1946-51; Reader in Applied Mechanics 1951-57. *Publications:* (with A. Bolton) Introduction to the Theory of Structures, 1956; (with M. R. Horne) Stability of Frames, 1965; articles in Jour. Mathematics and Physics, and in reports and memoranda of: Aeronautical Research Council, Proc. Instn. of Mech. Engineers, Proc. Instn. of Struct. Engineers, IX Internat. Congress of Applied Mechanics Brussels, VI Internat. Congress of I.A.B.S.E., Stockholm, VII, Rio de Janeiro. *Address:* College of Science and Technology, Manchester 1. [*Died* 12 *Oct.* 1965.

MERCIECA, Hon. Sir Arturo, Kt., *cr.* 1926; M.A., LL.D.; *b.* Victoria, Gozo, 14 June 1878; *s.* of Dr. Bartolomeo Mercieca and Julia Garroni; *m.* 1908, Josephine Tabone; six *s.* two *d.* *Educ.:* Jesuits' College, Gozo; University, Malta (Govt. Scholarship). Member of the Council of Government representing Gozo, 1907-10; Assistant Crown Advocate and Professor of Commercial Law at Malta University, 1915-1919; Crown Advocate and *ex officio* M.E.C. and M.L.C.; Legal Adviser to Naval, Military and Air Force Authorities, and Crown Officer in connection with Prize matters; President of Control Board, Controller of Clearing Office, 1919-21; Puisne Judge of Malta, 1921-23; Chief Justice and President of the Court of Appeal, Malta, 1924-40. *Address:* Cloe, Ta Xbiex, Malta. *Club:* Casino Maltese. [*Died* 31 *July* 1969.

MEREDITH, Hubert Angelo, O.B.E. 1944 (M.B.E. 1918); Wing Commander, R.A.F.V.R.; *b.* 7 November 1884; *o. s.* of late John Meredith. *Educ.:* St. Paul's. Mem. of London Stock Exchange, 1913-24; Anglo-Austrian Bank (afterwards Anglo-International Bank), 1924-29; City Editor, Saturday Review, 1924-31; City Editor, Daily Mail, Evening News, Daily Mirror, and Sunday Pictorial, 1931-35; Captain and Adjutant R.D.C., London District, 1915-18; Staff-Captain, War Office, 1918-1919. Pilot Officer R.A.F.V.R. 1941; retired Aug. 1944, Wing Comdr. *Publications:* various manuals and brochures on Tin and Mining subjects; The Drama of Money Making, 1931. *Address:* 120 North Gate, Regent's Park, N.W.8. *T.:* Primrose 9846. *Club:* Union. [*Died* 31 *March* 1965.

MEREDITH, Prof. Hugh Owen, O.B.E.; M.A. Cantab.; M.Com. Manchester, Hon. Lecturer, Magee University College; Londonderry, 1951-58; Prof. of Economics, Queen's Univ., Belfast, 1911, now emeritus; *b.* 1878; *s.* of Thomas and Isabella Meredith;

m. 1906, O. C. M. Iles (*d.* 1945); three *s.* two *d.*; *m.* 1946, A. M. Blyth, M.B.E. (*d.* 1951); *m.* 1957, M. A. Spring-Rice, M.R.C.S., L.R.C.P. *Educ.:* Shrewsbury; King's Coll., Cambridge, Fellow, 1903-08. Lecturer in Economic History and Commerce, Manchester University, 1905-08; Girdler's Lecturer in Economics, Cambridge University, 1908-11; attached Ministry of Munitions, 1916-18; Ministry of Labour, 1918-19. *Publications:* Protection in France, 1904; Outlines of English Economic History, 1908; Week-day Poems, 1911; Four Dramas of Euripides, 1937. *Address:* Larkbeare, 85 Cumnor Hill, Oxford. [*Died* 31 *July* 1964.

MEREDITH, Rt. Rev. Lewis Evan; an Asst. Bishop, Diocese of Gloucester, 1965-1966; *b.* 21 Feb. 1900; *s.* of Arthur Evan and Frances Charlotte Meredith; *m.* 1929, Evelyn Mary Juckes; one *s.* one *d.* *Educ.:* Lancing College; Trinity College, Cambridge; Westcott House, Cambridge. Asst. Curate, Oswestry, Diocese of Lichfield, 1923-27; Minor Canon, Precentor and Sacrist, Canterbury Cathedral, 1927-31; Vicar of Wath-on-Dearne, with Adwick upon Dearne, Diocese of Sheffield, 1931-36; Vicar of Bognor Regis, 1936-47; Vicar and Rural Dean of Eastbourne, 1947-57; Hon. Canon in Chichester Cathedral, 1951-57; Proctor in Convocation 1955-57; Suffragan Bishop of Dover, 1957-1964. *Recreations:* walking, music. *Address:* St. Martins, Butts View, Bakewell, Derbyshire. [*Died* 4 *Jan.* 1968.

MEREDITH, Rev. Canon Ralph Creed; Vicar of Windsor, 1940-58, retired; Chaplain to The Queen 1952-69 (to King George VI, 1946-52), Rural Dean of Poole since 1962; *b.* 10 July 1887; *y. s.* of late Sir James Creed Meredith, Dublin; *m.* 1915, Sylvia, *e. d.* of Joseph Aynsley, Bournemouth; two *s.* one *d.* *Educ.:* Trinity College, Dublin. B.A. Jun. Mod. Ethics and Logics, 1909, M.A. 1912. Pres. Univ. Philosophical Soc., 1909; auditor and oratory medallist, Coll. Theological Soc., 1910; Curate of Armley, Leeds, 1914-17; Vicar of Bournville, 1920-24; Wanganui, N.Z., 1924-31; Archdeacon of Waitotara N.Z., and member of General Synod, 1924-1931; Pres. N.Z. Croquet Council, 1928-31; Pres. N.Z. Badminton Assoc., 1929-31. Vicar of Cheshunt, 1932-40; Rural Dean of Ware, 1932-39; Proctor in Convocation, 1936-40 and 1950-59; Hon. Canon of Oxford 1953-59; Rural Dean of Maidenhead, 1950-1958; Chairman Windsor Divisional Executive Education Committee, 1949. *Publication:* Editor, Sermons for Lay Readers in New Zealand, 1928-30. *Recreations:* chess, croquet, badminton. *Address:* 9 Kingsbridge Road, Parkstone, Dorset. *T.:* Parkstone 2561. [*Died* 10 *Jan.* 1970.

MEREDITH, Sir Vincent Robert Sissons, Kt. 1952; Q.C. (N.Z.), 1957; *b.* Whangarei, N.Z., 31 March 1877; *s.* of Henry Mark Meredith and Emily Meredith (*née* Sissons); *m.* Hilda Ray Staples; one *s.* two *d.* *Educ.:* Auckland Grammar School, N.Z. Admitted Barrister and Solicitor, N.Z., 1910; Crown Solicitor, Wellington, 1916; Crown Solicitor, Auckland, 1921-52. *Recreations:* golf, fishing; formerly football (managed two All Black sides overseas, Australia, 1910, Gt. Britain, 1935). *Address:* Mission Bay, Auckland, N.Z. *T.:* 50144. *Club:* Northern (Auckland). [*Died* 14 *Jan.* 1965.

MEREDITH, Colonel William Rice, C.B.E. 1935; D.S.O. 1918; *b.* 24 Aug. 1882; *s.* of late Right Hon. Richard Edmund Meredith, P.C., K.C., and Anne Pollock; *m.*, 1910, Yolande Perceval, *y. d.* of late Lt.-Colonel Francis Corbet-Singleton, C.B.; one *s.* *Educ.:* Clifton College; R.M.C., Sandhurst. 2nd Lt. The Royal Inniskilling Fusiliers, 1902; Lieut., 1905; Capt., 1914; Major, 1917; Lt.-Colonel (Brevet) 1928; Colonel, 1932; Staff College graduate, 1919; served in Egypt, Cyprus, Somaliland, East Africa, Uganda, India, Iraq, Malaya, Nigeria; employed with King's African Rifles, 1908-13; specially employed, War Office, 1915; Brigade Major, Home Forces; G.S.O. 2 Mersey Garrison, G.S.O. 2 France; D.A.Q.M.G., India; Commandant F.M.S. Volunteer Forces; Commandant Nigeria Regiment, and Mem. Nigerian Executive and Legislative Councils, 1932-36; served East Africa (Somaliland), 1908-10 (medal and clasp); Waziristan, 1921 (medal and clasp); European War, France, Belgium, Gallipoli (wounded, despatches, 1914-15 star, B.W.M. and Victory Medal); retired pay, 1936; 1940 restored to active list and served in France; reverted to retired pay, 1943. Gold Staff Officer Coronation of King George VI. *Address:* Englishcombe, Camberley, Surrey. *T.:* 1263. [*Died* 14 *March* 1964.

MERER, Air Vice-Marshal John William Frederick, C.B. 1949; R.A.F.; retired; Director, U.K. Committee for U.N.I.C.E.F., since 1959; *b.* 28 July 1899; *m.* 1933; one *s.* one *d.* Commissioned R.F.C., France, 1918; Indian Frontier, 1919-23; Experimental Pilot, R.A.E., 1924-27; qualified as specialist navigator, 1927; adjutant, R.A.F. College, Cranwell, 1929-31; p.s.a., 1934; served in Middle East, 1939-42; British Joint Staff Mission, Washington, 1942-44; No. 5 Group Bomber Command, 1944-45; Director of Allied Co-operation and Foreign Liaison, Air Ministry, 1945-47; A.O.C. No. 46 Group, 1947-49; commanded British element of Berlin Airlift, 1948-49; Director of Navigation and Control, Air Ministry, 1950-52; Head of British Military Delegation with European Defence Community Interim Commission, Paris, April 1952; retired from R.A.F. 1955. Deputy Co-ordinator for the International Geophysical Year, Brussels, 1957-58. F.I.N. Commander, U.S. Legion of Merit, 1949. *Address:* Glentworth, Ledborough Lane, Beaconsfield, Bucks. *T.:* Beaconsfield 1114. *Club:* R.A.F. [*Died* 31 *Oct.* 1964.

MEREWETHER, Edward Rowland Alworth, C.B. 1956; C.B.E. 1948; M.D.; F.R.C.P.; F.R.S. Edin. 1940; Consultant in Industrial Health, Admiralty; H.M. Senior Medical Inspector of Factories, Ministry of Labour and National Service, 1942-1957, retired; Chief Medical Adviser to Ministry of Agriculture and Fisheries; Member: Industrial Health Research Board; I.L.O. Corresp. Commission on Industrial Hygiene; *b.* 2 March 1892; *s.* of Alworth Edward Merewether; *m.* 1918, Ruth Annie Hayton, *d.* of Robert Waddell. *Educ.:* Christ's Hospital; Durham Univ. M.B., B.S., Durham, 1914; M.D. (Gold Medal), 1916; M.R.C.P. Lond. 1938; F.R.C.P. 1946. Served War of 1914-18 (despatches): Surg.-Lieut. R.N. in Balkans, R.N.A.S., Grand Fleet, and France. Barrister-at-law, Gray's Inn, 1926. Sometime Lectr. in Industrial Hygiene, Univs. of Aberdeen and Glasgow; Hon. Physician to the King, 1944-47. Hon. Fell. Amer. Public Health Assoc. C.St.J. 1957. Order of St. Sava, Serbia. *Publications:* articles on Industrial Hygiene and Medicine, etc. *Address:* Falaise, The Ridgway, Pyrford, Surrey. *T.:* Byfleet 42936. *Clubs:* Savage, National Liberal, Civil Service. [*Died* 13 *Feb.* 1970.

MERRIAM, Sir Laurence (Pierce Brooke), Kt. 1949; M.C. 1916; D.L., J.P.; *b.* 28 Jan. 1894; *s.* of Charles Pierce Merriam, Bluebridge House, Halstead, Essex; *m.* 1921, Lady Marjory Kennedy, *d.* of 3rd Marquis of Ailsa; two *s.* *Educ.:* St. Paul's School; University College, Oxford. Represented Oxford University at Rugby Football, Swimming and Water Polo; Rep. England at Rugby Football *v.* Wales and France, 1920; Capt. Blackheath Football Club, 1922. Commissioned in Rifle Brigade, served throuthout European War, 1914-18 (wounded twice, M.C.); attached Tank Corps, Temp. Capt., acting Major, 1918-19. British Xylonite Co., 1919 (Chm., 1957-63); Chairman: B.X. Plastics Ltd., 1957-63. Director: Ilford Ltd., 1950-63; Municipal Mutual Insurance Ltd.; Distillers Co., 1961-1963; Chairman: Furniture Development Council, 1957-63; Furniture Industry Research Assoc.; Vice-Pres. Assoc. of Chemical & Allied Employers, 1959-63. Mem. N.E. Metropolitan Regional Hospital Board, 1961-64; Chairman, Royal Eastern Counties Hospital Management Committee. Seconded to Ministry of Supply, 1940-45; lent to Board of Trade, 1948-50. Examiner of Controls. J.P. Essex; Essex C.C., 1955-65 (Chm. Finance Cttee.); D.L. Essex, 1962. *Address:* Loom House, Dedham, nr. Colchester, Essex. *T.:* Dedham 2257. *Clubs:* Bath, Buck's. [*Died* 27 *July* 1966.

MERRICK, Sir John Edward-Siegfried, Kt., *cr.* 1945; C.M.G. 1937; O.B.E. 1931; *b.* 29 Feb. 1888; *s.* of late Karl Richter; assumed name of Merrick by deed-poll, 1916; *m.* 1916, Elinor, *d.* of late T. A. Gray; one *s.* one *d.* *Educ.:* Winchester; University College, Oxford. Assistant District Commissioner, Uganda, 1912; Senior Assistant Secretary, East Africa Protectorate, 1919; Assistant Colonial Secretary, Kenya, 1926; Principal Assistant Colonial Secretary, Kenya, 1927; Deputy Chief Secretary, Uganda, 1932; Chief Secretary, Uganda Protectorate, 1935-45; officer administering Govt., 1937, 1940, and 1942; retired, 1946. *Address:* Twelve Trees Cottage, Dover Road, Branksome Park, Poole, Dorset. *T.:* Westbourne 61093. [*Died* 2 *March* 1968.

MERRIMAN, 1st Baron, *cr.* 1941, of Knutsford; **Frank Boyd Merriman,** P.C. 1933; G.C.V.O., *cr.* 1950; Kt., *cr.* 1928; O.B.E. 1918; Hon. LL.D. McGill Univ., 1930; President Probate, Divorce and Admiralty Division of the High Court of Justice since 1933; Hon. Member American and Canadian Bar Associations; *b.* 1880; *e. s.* of late Frank Merriman, J.P., of Hollingford House, Knutsford; *m.* 1st, 1907, Eva Mary (*d.* 1919), 2nd *d.* of late Rev. Henry Leftwich Freer; two *d.*; 2nd, 1920, Olive McLaren (*d.* 1952), M.B.E., 3rd *d.* of late Frederick W. Carver, J.P., of Oakhurst, Knutsford; 3rd, 1953, Jane, *yr. d.* of late James Stormonth, Belfast. *Educ.:* Winchester. Barrister, Inner Temple, 1904; K.C., 1919; Bencher, 1927; Deputy Treasurer, 1949. Served European War, 1914-19; D.A.A.G. from 1917 (O.B.E., despatches thrice); Recorder of Wigan, 1920-28; Solicitor-General, 1928-29 and 1932-33; M.P. (C.) Rusholme Division of Manchester, 1924-33. Chairman, Bishop of London's Commission on the City Churches, 1941-46. Conservative, Church of England. *Recreations:* golf, fishing. *Address:* 2 Crown Office Row, Temple, E.C.4. *T.:* Central 6446. *Clubs:* Carlton, Savile. [*Died* 18 *Jan.* 1962 (*ext.*).

MERTON, Sir Thomas (Ralph), K.B.E. 1956; Kt. 1944; M.A., D.Sc. (Oxon); F.R.S. 1920; *b.* 12 Jan. 1888; *m.* 1912, Marjory, *d.* of Lt.-Col. W. H. Sawyer; five *s.* *Educ.:* Eton; Balliol College, Oxford. Formerly Professor of Spectroscopy, Oxford University, and Fellow of Balliol College. Treasurer Royal Society, 1939-56; Fellow of Eton College, 1945-63; Trustee, National Gallery, 1955-62; Trustee, National Portrait Gallery; Member Royal Fine Art Commission. Bakerian Lecturer, Royal Society, 1922. Holweck Prize, 1951; Rumford Medal of Roy. Soc., 1958. Hon. LL.D. (Aberdeen); Hon. D.Sc. (London). *Publications:* papers in the Proceedings and Transactions of the Royal Soc. and other scientific journals. *Recreation:* fishing. *Address:* Stubbings House, Maidenhead Thicket, Berks. *T.:* Littlewick Green 2022. *Clubs:* Athenæum, Brooks's, Savile. [*Died* 10 *Oct.* 1969.

MESTROVIC, Ivan; professor and sculptor in residence, Notre Dame University, South Bend, Indiana, since 1955; *b.* 1883. Apprenticed to a master-mason at Split; went to Vienna; exhibited at the Austrian Exhibition in London, 1906; Internat. Art Exhibition at Rome, 1911, Victoria and Albert Museum, 1915; Grafton Galleries, 1917; Paris, 1907, 1908, 1918, 1933; International Art Exhibition at Venice, 1914; Metropolitan Museum, New York City, 1947. *Principal Works:* a memorial chapel to the Račić family at Cavtat, Dubrovnik; a seated memorial figure of Bishop Strosmajer, the Croat patriot; a portrait of President Masaryk of Czechoslovakia; two equestrian statues in bronze of American Indians, sculptured for the City of Chicago; a large bronze statue of Gregory of Nin, the Bishop Chancellor of the Old Croatian Kingdom, at Split, Dalmatia (Croatia); portraits: of President Hoover; of Pope Pius XI; of Pius XII; memorial chapel to Mestrovic family at Otavice near Drniš, Dalmatia (Croatia); a monument of thankfulness to France at Belgrade; memorial Chapel to the Unknown Soldier on Avala Mount, Belgrade; monument to G. Bratianu at Bucharest; memorial Church to the Croatian King, Zvonimir, at Biskupija, Dalmatia (Croatia); Project and 46 fragments to the Temple of Kossovo; several portraits in England and America; several woodcarvings on biblical subjects. Works during last years preceding war of 1939-45: Two equestrian statues in bronze of King Ferdinand I and Carol I of Rumania (Bucharest); an exhibition pavilion in Zagreb; his own house in Split (which is now the Mestrovic Gallery); a reconstruction of an ancient Convent. Works during the war in immigration: a pieta in marble; four stone reliefs representing: St. Girolamo, Pope Sixto V, Pope Leon X, Pope Pius XII. (The latter two were destroyed by the Germans) for the Colegio di St. Girolamo, Rome. 22 feet figure, Man and Freedom, for Mayo Clinic, Rochester, Minn., 1953. Figure of Prince-Bishop Petar Petrovic Njegos, Cetinje Crna-Gora, Yugoslavia, 1953; 20-feet relief, stone, Christ on the Cross lamented by women, Trinity Lutheran Church, Rochester, Minn., 1955; heroic figure, Father Grajales, St. Augustine, Fla., 1955; Pietà, twice life-size, bronze, Miami, Fla., 1956; heroic size bronze figure of inventor Nikola Tesla. Zagreb, Yugoslavia, 1956; 18-foot relief Madonna in stone on façade of R.C. Shrine in Washington, D.C.; above door of same church over-life size Madonna with two angels, 1957; bronze, over-life size, sitting figure of Pope Pius XII for St. Louis, Mo., 1958. Six Wood carvings (to complete earlier-begun biblical series); 8 paintings on wood, and other smaller works. Hon. Doctorates: Syracuse, Marquette, Notre Dame, Ohio Wesleyan, Colgate, Columbia Univs.; Mem. of academies of arts and sciences: Edinburgh, Prague, Munich, Vienna, Bucharest, Zagreb, Belgrade, Brussels. Mem. Nat. Inst. of Arts and Letters, U.S.A.; American Acad. of Arts and Letters, U.S.A. Grand Officier, Légion d'Honneur, 1940. *Publications:* a Monography, by M. Curčin; (London), 1919; 1933, Engl. Ed., 1935; Our Lady of the Angels, 1937; Religious Art, 1944 (all published in Zagreb); a Monography, Ivan Mestrovic, 1948, a Monography, Ivan Mestrovic, sculptor and patriot, 1959 (both publ. Syracuse). *Recreations:* reading and writing. *Address:* 214 East Pokagon Street, South Bend, Ind., U.S.A. *T.:* CE 33215; Mletačka ul. 8, Zagreb, Yugoslavia. *Clubs:* Rotary, P.E.N. [*Died* 16 *Jan.* 1962.

METALIOUS, Grace (Mrs. G. Metalious); author; *b.* Manchester, New Hampshire, U.S.A., 8 Sept. 1924; *m.* 1st, 1942, George Metalious (marriage dissolved 1958); one *s.* two *d.*; 2nd, 1958, T. J. Martin (marr. diss., she re-married 1st husband, 1960). *Educ.:*

New Hampshire public schools. *Publications:* (in U.S. and Eng.): Peyton Place, 1957; Return to Peyton Place, 1960; Tight White Collar, 1960; No Adam in Eden, 1964. *Address:* c/o Jacques Chambrun, 7 45 5th Avenue, New York 22. [*Died* 25 *Feb.* 1964.

METCALFE, Sir Frederic William, K.C.B., *cr.* 1949 (C.B. 1939); *b.* 4 December 1886; *s.* of late W. P. Metcalfe, of Ceylon and Stone Hall, Oxted; *m.* 1919, Helen, *d.* of late C. J. Goodman, Oxted. *Educ.:* Wellington College; Sidney Sussex College, Cambridge (Hon. Fell. 1953). 6th S.R. Bn. The Rifle Brigade, 1914-18, served European War, France and Belgium. Asst. Clerk, House of Commons, 1919; 2nd Clerk Asst., 1930; Clerk Asst., 1937; Clerk of the House of Commons, 1948-54; retired 1954. Speaker, House of Representatives, Nigeria, 1955-60. Formerly a Governor of Wellington College. *Address:* 27 North End House, W.14. *T.:* Empress 3025. *Clubs:* Public Schools, M.C.C.; Royal Mid-Surrey Golf. [*Died* 3 *June* 1965.

METCALFE, Percy, C.V.O. 1937; R.D.I. 1938; Sculptor and Medallist; *b.* 14 Jan. 1895; 2nd *s.* of John and Hannah Metcalfe; *m.* 1920, Eveline Mabel Smith; two *d.* *Educ.:* Royal College of Art (associate). *Address:* 70 Madrid Road, S.W.13. *T.:* 01-748 3786. [*Died* 9 *Oct* 1970.

METHVEN, Sir Harry (Finlayson), K.B.E. 1952; Kt. 1944; Director Dorchester Hotel Ltd.; *b.* 2 Jan. 1886; *s.* of late James Methven, Barcaldine, Ledaig, Argyll; *m.* 1913, Gladys Hulbert (*d.* 1966), *d.* of late Frederick Foreshew, Streatham; one *s.* one *d.* *Educ.:* privately. *Recreations:* yachting, fishing, and golfing. [*Died* 26 *Aug.* 1968.

METHVEN, John Cecil Wilson, C.B. 1950; M.R.C.S. (Eng.), L.R.C.P. (Lond.); *b.* 27 June 1885; *yr. s.* of late James Methven, Southampton; *m.* 1913, Gladys Kate (*d.* 1939), *o. d.* of late J. S. W. Edmunds, Twyford, Berks; one *s.* one *d.* *Educ.:* Woolston College, Southampton; London Hospital. Medical Officer, H.M. Prison Service; served European War, 1915-19; Captain, Acting Major, R.A.M.C. (T.F.); Governor, H.M. Borstal Institution, Rochester, Kent; Governor, H.M. Prison, Maidstone; Asst. Commissioner of Prisons i/c of Borstal Institutions, 1930-38; H.M. Commissioner of Prisons, England and Wales, 1938-50; Dep. Chm. Prison Commn., 1948-50; Medical Adviser Home Office, 1946-50; Inspector under Inebriates Acts, 1938-50. *Recreations:* gardening, golf, walking. *Address:* 76 Baker Street, Weybridge, Surrey. [*Died* 6 *Aug.* 1968.

MEYENDORFF, Alexander, Hon. D.C.L. Durham; retired; (holder of Swedish barony recognised by Imperial Russia); *b.* 10 April 1869; *s.* of late Felix Meyendorff, Russian Diplomat, and late Olga, Princess Gorchakov; *m.* 1st, Princess Nina Tsulukidze (*d.* 1906); 2nd, 1907, Princess Barbara Shervashidze (*d.* 1946). *Educ.:* Weimar and Stuttgart Gymnasium; St. Petersburg University, Faculty of Law. Military service, 1892-93, 1st Dragoons at Tver; Civil Service, 1893-1906 in local and Central Government Offices; Inspector of S.P.B. Law School, 1906-1907; Member of the Duma for Livonia, 1907-17; Vice-President, 1907-9; Senator, 1917; left Petersburg, Aug. 1918; taken with his wife by British Mine-layer, Princess Margaret, from Riga to London, 1919; 1919 domiciled in England; Reader (London University) in Russian Institutions and Economics at School of Economics, 1922-34. *Publications:* Translations into Russian of German Text-books in Roman and Constitutional Law; Case Law Collections in Land Law; Monograph on the Peasants joint family in Russian Customary Law and Statute Law, 1907; Correspondence Diplomatique du Baron de Staal, 1929; Background of the Russian Revolution, 1929; The Cost of the War to Russia, 1932; Tragedy of Modern Jurisprudence, in Interpretations of Modern Legal Philosophies (N.Y.), 1947. *Address:* 115 Cromwell Road, S.W.7. *T.:* Frobisher 3230. [*Died* 20 *Feb.* 1964.

MEYRIC HUGHES, Reginald Richard, T.D. 1950; Secretary of the Royal Agricultural Society of England since 1962; *b.* 28 Jan. 1915; *s.* of late Hugh Meyric Hughes and Elsie Margaret (*née* Middleton); *m.* 1941, Jean Mary Carne, *d.* of Edward Bickerton Pratt; two *s.* *Educ.:* Shrewsbury School. Admitted solicitor, 1938; Asst. Solicitor, Cheshire County Council, 1938-39; Dorset C.C., 1939-50 (Senior Asst. Solicitor, 1947-50); Dep. Secretary, County Councils Assoc., 1950-61. Vice-Chm. London Police Court Mission, 1957-. Served War of 1939-45, in K.S.L.I., 1939-46; p.s.c. 1939; Hon. Lt.-Col. *Recreations:* foreign affairs and travel; gardening and fishing. *Address:* High Crouch, Crouch, Near Borough Green, Kent. *Club:* Farmers'. [*Died* 1 *Feb.* 1962.

MEYSEY-THOMPSON, Capt. Sir Algar de Clifford Charles, 3rd Bt., *cr.* 1874; *b.* 9 Nov. 1885; *s.* of late Col. R. F. Meysey-Thompson, 2nd *s.* of 1st Bt., and Charlotte, *d.* of Sir James Walker, 1st Bt.; *S.* baronetcy of uncle, 1st Baron Knaresborough, 1929. *Educ.:* Eton; Trinity College, Cambridge (M.A.). Late P.A.S.I.; served European War, 84th and 93rd Batteries R.F.A., 1914-22 (three medals, 1914-15 Star); late Capt. Army Educational Corps. *Heir: kinsman,* Humphrey Simon Meysey-Thompson, *b.* 31 March 1935. *Address:* The Retreat, York. [*Died* 11 *Jan.* 1967.

MICHELL, Humfrey, M.A.; F.R.S.C.; *b.* London, 21 Feb. 1883; *y. s.* of G. D. Michell, Capt. 19th Foot, and Mary, *e. d.* of Lt.-Gen. David Babington, Madras Army; *m.* 1910, Dorothea (*d.* 1955), *d.* of Albert Edwards, solicitor, Ottery St. Mary, Devon; one *s.* one *d.* *Educ.:* Dulwich; Queen's College, Oxford. B.A. 1905. M.A. University of Manitoba, 1911; University of Heidelberg. Lecturer, St. John's Coll., Winnipeg, Manitoba, 1911; Instructor Queen's University, Kingston, Ontario, 1913; Professor of Political Economy, McMaster University, Hamilton, Ontario, 1919-48; retired. Pres. Canadian Political Science Assocn., 1941. *Publications:* an Index of General Business Conditions, and an Index of Physical Volume of Production in Canada, 1924; Prices in Canada from 1848, 1931; Elementary Economics, 1932; Outlines of Economic History, 1937, 4th edn. 1958; The Economics of Ancient Greece, 1940, 2nd edn., 1957; Sparta, 1951, 2nd edn., 1964; French edn., Sparte et les Spartiates; many articles in reviews and journals on economic subjects. *Address:* Lowell Lodge, North Hatley, Quebec, Canada. [*Died* 5 *May* 1970.

MICHELL, Commander Kenneth, D.S.O. 1941; M.V.O. 1925; D.S.C. 1917, and Bar 1941; *b.* 1887; 3rd *s.* of late G. B. Michell, Sussex; *m.* 1917, Helen (*d.* 1963), 2nd *d.* of late Prof. W. Frecheville; two *s.* one *d.* *Educ.:* H.M.S. Britannia. Joined R.N. 1902; served European War; commanded H.M. Submarines A9, C28, B10, B7, and E50; Senior Submarines Officer, Venice, 1916 (Order of St. Maurice and Lazarus, Silver Medal for Valour); D.S.C. in action with German Submarine, North Sea, 1917; Senior Officer, Norwegian Convoy Destroyer Escort Flotilla, 1918; in command H.M. Monitor 33, N. Russia, Dwina River Expedition, 1919; Senior Officer, Danube M.L. Flotilla, 1920; 1st Lt.-Comdr, H.M.S. Revenge, 1921-23; in command H.M.S. Truro; escorted H.M. Yacht Britannia, 1924-25; Officer Instructor to London Division, R.N.V.R.,

H.M.S. President, Victoria Embankment, 1926-1928; in command H.M.A.S. Marguerite, 1928-1929; Executive Officer, Royal Australian Naval College, 1929-30; awarded Royal Humane Society's Medal, 1926; retired with rank of Commander, 1931; Chief Officer, Training Ship, Exmouth, 1933; Liaison Officer, R.N. and R.M. Officers Civil Employment Committee, 1935-39; Sea Transport Officer, Dieppe, 1939; Technical Delegate to Danube International Commission, Belgrade, 1940; Staff of Naval Attaché, Athens; Sea Transport Officer, Piræus (D.S.O.); Sea Transport Officer, Suda Bay, Crete (Bar to D.S.O.); in command H.M.S. Northney II. and III., 1942; Staff of Operations Division Admiralty, N. Africa and Adriatic, 1943-44; Admiralty Liaison Officer to Ministry of Labour and National Service, 1945-46. Master of M.V. Sir Edward P. Wills II. R.N. Mission to Deep Sea Fishermen, 1947-1948; Superintendent, Training Ship Foudroyant, Portsmouth, 1950-51; Hon. Local Sec. Sussex Archæological Soc. Amberley; Mem. Soc. Sussex Downsmen. *Address:* Dower Cottage, Amberley, Arundel, Sussex. *T.:* Bury (Sx.) 402. [*Died* 25 *Dec.* 1967.

MICHIE, James Kilgour; Director of National & Grindlay's Bank Limited, 1940-66 (Chm., 1946-63); *b.* 18 September 1887; *m.* 1st, 1916, Barbara Allen Springett Sanders (*d.* 1919); one *d.*; 2nd, 1922, Marjorie Crain Pfeiffer; three *s.* *Educ.:* Falkland, Fife. Joined Steel Bros. & Co. Ltd., London, 1905; Burma, 1907 (Chairman, 1940-60). Served European War, 1914-1918, India Defence Force; Consular Agent for France in Burma, 1922-26. Chairman, Rice Advisory Committee, Ministry of Food, 1939-43; Member: India Cttee., Min. of Information 1940-42; Far East Relief Cttee., 1942-46; East India Cttee., London Chamber of Commerce, 1945-49; Joint Cttee. on India, 1945-50. Officier d'Académie (France), 1921. *Recreation:* golf. *Address:* 42 Great Cumberland Place, W.1; Gunsite, Thorpe Road, Aldeburgh, Suffolk. *Clubs:* Oriental, City of London [*Died* 5 *March* 1967.

MICKLEM, Colonel Henry Andrew, C.B. 1919; C.M.G. 1918; D.S.O. 1898; *b.* Farnborough, 29 June 1872; *e. s.* of late Maj.-Gen. Edward Micklem. *Educ.:* Winchester College. Joined Royal Engineers, 1891; Egyptian Army, 1897; Sudan Expedition, 1897-98 (wounded, despatches; D.S.O., 4th class Medjidie, medal and Egyptian Government medal with 2 clasps); served South African War, 1899-1902 (severely wounded, despatches, brevet of Major, Queen's medal with three clasps, King's medal with two clasps); retired, 1909; served European War, 1914-18 (Bt. Lieut.-Col., C.B., C.M.G.). *Address:* 9 Green Street, Mayfair, W.1. *T.:* Mayfair 3802; Rosehill, Henley-on-Thames. *Clubs:* Army and Navy, Carlton. [*Died* 9 *March* 1963.

MICKLEM, Very Rev. Philip Arthur, D.D.; *b.* 5 April 1876; *s.* of Leonard Micklem; *m.* 1932, Evelyn, *d.* of P. Edmonde Auriac. *Educ.:* Harrow School; Hertford College, and Cuddesdon Theological College, Oxford. First-Class Mods. and Greats; Liddon Student; B.A. 1899; M.A. 1902; Assistant Master, Harrow School, 1902-3; Deacon, 1902; Priest, 1903; Assistant Curate, Shere, Surrey, 1903-09; Lecturer, St. Augustine's College, Canterbury, 1909-10; Canon Residentiary, Brisbane Cathedral, and Principal, Theological College, Brisbane, 1910-17; Rector of St. James's, Sydney, 1917-37; Provost of Derby and Vicar of All Saints, Derby, 1937-47; Bampton Lecturer, 1946. *Publications:* Westminster Commentary on St. Matthew; Principles of Church Organisation; Values of the Incarnation; The Secular and the Sacred. *Address:* Marigolds, Staplecross, nr. Robertsbridge, Sussex. *Club:* Oxford and Cambridge. [*Died* 5 *Dec.* 1965.

MICKLETHWAIT, The Hon. Mrs.; Ivy Mary; *b.* 4 Oct. 1895; 2nd *d.* of Miles, 10th Baron Beaumont; *m.* Richard Gerald Micklethwait, of Ardsley House, Barnsley; one *s.* one *d.* *Address:* Harston Hall, Grantham. *T.:* Knipton 239. [*Died* 31 *Jan.* 1967.

MICKS, Robert Henry; formerly Physician, Sir Patrick Dun's Hospital, Dublin (1927-1962); Cons. Physician, Royal Victoria Eye and Ear Hospital, Dublin; Consulting Physician Teac Ultain; King's Professor of Materia Medica, University of Dublin, since 1945; *b.* 30 Dec. 1895; *s.* of W. L. Micks and E. I. Meyrick; *m.* 1940, Fanny Geraldine Townsend MacFetridge; two (adopted) *s.* *Educ.:* St. Stephen's Green School; Trinity College, Dublin. Professor of Pharmacology, R.C.S.I., 1935-45. *Publications:* The Essentials of Materia Medica, Pharmacology and Therapeutics, 9th edn., 1965; Approach to Clinical Medicine, 1955. Articles in medical journals. *Recreation:* sailing. *Address:* 2 Merlyn Park, Dublin 4. *T.:* Dublin 694157. [*Died* 9 *Feb.* 1970.

MIDDLEMAS, Noel Allan, C.M.G. 1946; Retired (Colonial Civil Service); *b.* 7 June 1892; *s.* of Joseph Middlemas; *m.* 1929, E. I. Jeffreys; one *d.* *Educ.:* Auckland Grammar School, N.Z.; Victoria University College, N.Z. Served with New Zealand Forces in Egypt, Gallipoli and France, 1914-1918; Survey Dept., Malaya, 1921-25; Superintendent of Surveys, Sarawak, 1925-1933; Superintendent of Lands and Surveys, Sarawak, 1933-39; Director of Surveys, Land Officer and Commissioner of Mines, Uganda, 1940-46. *Recreation:* bowls. *Address:* c/o Standard Bank of South Africa, Umkomaas, Natal, S. Africa. *Club:* Royal Commonwealth Society. [*Died* 2 *May* 1967.

MIDDLETON, 11th Baron (*cr.* 1711), **Michael Guy Percival Willoughby,** Bt., *cr.* 1677; K.G. 1957; M.C.; T.D.; LL.D.; Major late 10th Lancers, I.A.; late Colonel commanding 5th Battalion The Green Howards (T.); also commanded 5th and 30th Battalions, East Yorks Regt.; Lord-Lieut. for East Riding, Yorkshire, 1936-68; Chancellor, The University of Hull; *b.* 21 October 1887; *er. surv. s.* of 10th Baron and Ida Eleanora Constance (*d.* 1924), *d.* of G. W. H. Ross; *S.* father, 1924; *m.* 1920, Angela Florence Alfreda, *er. d.* of Charles Hall, Eddlethorpe Hall, Malton, Yorkshire; two *s.* two *d.* J.P., East Riding; K.St.J.; Director, Thirsk Race Co. Ltd., Birdsall Estates Ltd. Owns about 13,000 acres. Hon. Freeman, City of Hull, 1968. Hon. LL.D.: Leeds University, 1955; Hull University. Silver Wolf, Boy Scouts, 1968. *Heir:* *s.* Hon. (Digby) Michael (Godfrey John) Willoughby, M.C. *Address:* Birdsall House, Malton, Yorks. *Clubs:* Cavalry; Yorkshire (York). [*Died* 16 *Nov.* 1970.

MIDDLETON, Admiral Gervase Boswell, C.B. 1947; C.B.E. 1943; *b.* 22 December 1893; *s.* of late Reginald E. Middleton, M.Inst.C.E.; *m.* 1938, Dora Thacher Clarke; no *c.* *Educ.:* Osborne and Dartmouth. European War in Zealandia, Queen Elizabeth, Resolution; qualified in Torpedo, 1917-18 (Ogilvy Medal); Capt. 1935; Capt. H.M.S. Aurora, 1938-40; Dir. of Torpedoes and Mining, 1942; Capt. H.M.S. Revenge; Captain H.M.S. Ramillies (despatches twice, U.S.A. Legion of Merit, Officer, Legion of Honour, Croix de Guerre avec Palme); A.D.C. 1944-45; Rear-Adm. 1945; Admiral Superintendent H.M. Dockyard, Chatham, 1946-50; Vice-Admiral, 1948; retired list, 1950; Admiral, retired list, 1952. *Address:* 38 Farm Avenue, N.W.2. *T.:* Gladstone 4547. *Club:* United Service. [*Died* 12 *June* 1961.

MIES van der ROHE, Ludwig, F.A.I.A.; architect; Professor Emeritus of the Illinois Institute of Technology, Chicago, Illinois, U.S.A.; *b.* Germany, 27 March 1886. Director Bauhaus school of modern design, Dessau, 1930; Member Prussian Academy of Arts, 1931; Professor and Director of Department of Architecture, 1938-58, Illinois Inst. of Technology. American citizen, 1944. Works include: German Pavilion for International Exposition, Barcelona, 1929; Tugendhat house, Brno, Czechoslovakia, 1930; new buildings for Illinois Inst. of Technology; Promontary Apartments, Chicago, 1949; 860 Lake Shore Drive Apartments, 1951; 900 Esplanade Apartments, Chicago, 1956; Pavilion Apartments, Detroit, Michigan, 1958; Seagram Building, New York, 1958; Colonnade Apartments, Newark, N.J., 1960; Bacardi Building, Mexico City, 1961; Lafayette Towers, Detroit, 1963; One Charles Center, Baltimore, 1963; Chicago Federal Center, 1964; New National Gallery, Berlin, Germany, 1968; District of Columbia Public Library, Washington, D.C., 1969. Also designs furniture, etc. Fellow Amer. Inst. of Architects; Hon. Corresp. Mem. R.I.B.A., 1949, and Mem. or Hon. Mem. of other architectural assocs. and acads. Holds many Hon. Degrees, 1950-. Mem. German Order Pour le Merite, 1957 (Cross of Comdr., 1959); Medal of Honor, New York Chapter of The Amer. Inst. of Architects, 1958; R.I.B.A. Gold Medal, 1959; A.I.A. Gold Medal, 1960; holds many major architectural medals, prizes and awards. U.S. Presidential Medal of Freedom, 1963. *Address:* 230 East Ohio Street, Chicago, Ill. 60611, U.S.A.
[*Died* 17 *Aug.* 1969.

MIFSUD, Edward Robert, C.M.G. 1932; O.B.E. 1927 (M.B.E. 1925); *b.* 1875; *s.* of late Prof. Anthony Mifsud, Malta. *Educ.:* Privately Malta University. Joined Malta Civil Service, 1892; Chief Clerk, Lieutenant Governor's Office, 1913; Deputy Assist. Secretary to Government and Clerk of Council, 1920; Private Secretary to the Governor and Clerk of the Executive, Nominated, and Privy Councils, 1921; Secretary to Maltese Imperial Govt., 1927; Secretary to Government, 1934; retired, 1938. *Address*: 148 Tower Road, Sliema, Malta.
[*Died* 6 *May* 1970.

MILBANK, Major Sir Frederick Richard Powlett, 3rd Bt., *cr.* 1882; late Yorks Regiment; *b.* 7 Sept. 1881; *s.* of Sir Powlett Milbank, 2nd Bt., and Edith Mary, *d.* of Sir Richard Green-Price, 1st Bt.; *S.* father, 1918; *m.* 1904, Dorothy, *e. d.* of late Col. John Gerald Wilson, C.B., Cliffe Hall, Yorks; three *s.* *Educ.:* Eton. 2nd Lt. Yorkshire Hussars I.Y., 1901-03; M.F.H. 1901-16; Captain 5th Bn. Yorkshire Regiment, 1914-20 (despatches twice, granted rank of Major, Belgian Croix de Guerre); J.P. North Riding of Yorkshire. *Heir:* *s.* Major Sir Mark Vane Milbank, K.C.V.O. *Address:* Barningham Park, Richmond, Yorkshire. *T.A.:* Barningham. *T.:* Barningham 202.
[*Died* 29 *April* 1964.

MILES, Sir Charles Watt, Kt. 1947; O.B.E. 1945; Chairman since 1962, and Managing Director since 1954, R. G. Shaw & Co. Ltd., London; *b.* 15 March 1901; *m.* 1926, Lilian Hope Sykes; one *s.* one *d.* *Educ.:* Coopers' Company's School, London. Joined R. G. Shaw & Co., London, 1917; proceeded to India, 1921, to Shaw Wallace & Co.; Partner, 1938; firm became limited company, 1947; Managing Director 1947-49. Vice-Chm. Indian Tea Assoc., 1939-40-41. Representative in India for U.K. Commercial Corp., 1941-45. Member Bengal Legislative Assembly, 1941-47. President Bengal Club, 1948-49. Director, R. G. Shaw & Co. Ltd., London, 1949; Chm. Indian Tea Assoc. (London), 1953-55; Dep. Chm., Chartered Bank, 1966; Chairman: Capital & National Trust Ltd., 1963; Orient and General Investment Trust Ltd. *Address:* Whyteladies, Wildernesse Ave., Seal, Sevenoaks, Kent. *T.:* 61165. *Clubs:* Oriental, Royal Automobile; Bengal (Calcutta).
[*Died* 20 *Oct.* 1970.

MILES, Sir Charles William, 5th Bt. *cr.* 1859; O.B.E.; *b.* 7 July 1883; *s.* of 4th Bt. and Mary (*d.* 1938), *d.* of Frederick Neame of Luton, Selling, Kent; *S.* father, 1915; *m.* 1912, Favell Mary, *d.* of Charles Gathorne Hill, Claverton Manor, Bath; two *s.* *Educ.:* Uppingham. Served European War (Mesopotamia), 1914-16 (wounded, O.B.E., despatches); Lieut. Col. Reserve of Officers; late Captain Somerset L.I.; D.L. Somerset. Owns about 1000 acres. *Heir:* *s.* William Napier Maurice, *b.* 19 Oct. 1913. *Address:* Old Rectory House, Walton-in-Gordano, Clevedon, Somerset.
[*Died* 28 *Dec.* 1966.

MILES, Rev. Frederic James, D.S.O. 1917; O.B.E. 1919; V.D. 1927; D.D.; Litt.D., Th.D.; F.Ph.S.; Retd. as Internat. Sec. The Russian Missionary Society, Inc., 1949; Instructor, Miami Bible Institute, Miami, Florida, U.S.A., from 1953; Past P. Grand Chaplain, A.O. Freemasons; Pres. National C.E. Union of Wales, 1929-1930; Pres., C.E. Union of Great Britain and Ireland, 1930-31; Ex-President Newport and District C.E. Union and of Victorian and other Australian C.E. Unions; *b.* London, 18 Nov. 1869; *m.* 1894, Isabella Killick (*d.* 1937), of N.S.W.; *m.* 1950, Gwendolyn Adelle Yungblut. *Educ.:* London; West Australian Baptist College. Royal Warwickshire Regt.; Industrial Missionary in Ceylon, 1892-1900; various pastorates in Australia, 1900-14; Senior Baptist Chaplain for five years in Victoria; appointed to Australian Imperial Force when first formed; with the First Division in Egypt, Gallipoli, Sinai Peninsula, and France (D.S.O.), Australian Headquarters Staff; Senior Chaplain, O.P.D. and U.B.; A.I.F. till 1920; prominent worker in Y.M.C.A., Council of Churches, etc.; probation officer under Crown Law Department to deal with Juvenile Offenders. Editor, The Friend of Russians (retired, 1949). *Publications:* Why was Jesus our Fileleader?, 1930; The Miracle of Miracles, 1934; Even at the Doors, 1936; The Christ, the Coming and the Comforter, 1937; The Spirit of Jesus, 1937; The World's Best Seller and Why?, 1938; Triumph for the Troops, 1938; Through the Holy Spirit, 1939; The Parable of the Eagles' Nest, 1939; His Life on Earth and Ours, 1940; A Cluster of Camphire, 1941; Understandest Thou?, 1946; The Horsemen are Riding, 1947; The Debt we owe to the Jew, 1946; The Inspiration of the Wonderful Book, 1947; Russia and Palestine in Prophecy, 6th Ed. enlarged, 1949; Editor of religious periodicals, Australia, and constant contributor to such journals. *Recreations:* tennis, golf, bowls. *Address:* 1643 N.W. 1st St., Miami, Florida, U.S.A. *Club:* Authors'.
[*Died* 18 *March* 1962.

MILES, Sir John Charles, Kt., *cr.* 1919; M.A., B.C.L. Oxon; Hon. D.Litt. (Trinity College, Dublin); Hon. Fellow of Exeter Collgee, Oxford, 1937; Hon. Fellow of Merton Coll., Oxford, 1947; Mem. Court of Weavers' Company, London; *b.* 29 Aug. 1870; *s.* of John Miles, 32 Kensington Park Gardens, London; *m.* 1904, Marion Frances Charlotte (*d.* 1949), *y. d.* of Henry Langley, 2nd Life Guards; no *c.* *Educ.:* Shrewsbury Sch.; Exeter Coll., Oxford. Barrister-at-law; a Gov. of Shrewsbury Sch., 1917-44; Tutor of Merton Coll., Oxf., 1899-1930; Senior Research Fell., 1930-36; Domestic Bursar, 1904-23; Warden, 1936-47; Legal Assist. Min. of Munitions, 1915-18; Solicitor Min. of Labour, 1918-19; Emeritus Member of Society of Public Teachers of Law, 1946.

Publications: on English Law and Laws of the Ancient Near East. *Address:* 2 Northmoor Road, Oxford. *T.:* Oxford 59181. *Club:* Union (Hon. Life Member)
[*Died* 12 *Jan.* 1963.

MILES, Capt. Wilfrid; employed in Historical Section, Cabinet Office, 1923-54; *b.* 20 July 1885; 3rd *s.* of J. J. Miles, of Ash, Surrey; *m.* 1918, Kate Crichton. *Educ.:* Farnham Grammar School. Asst. Manager, Times of India, Bombay, 1909-14; Bombay Volunteer Rifles, 1910-14; Royal Fusiliers, Aug. 1914; 2nd Lt. Durham Light Infantry 1914; Captain 1915; European War, France and Belgium, War Office (Intelligence) 1918. *Publications:* Official: Military Operations, Western Front: 2nd July 1916 to end of the Battle of the Somme, 1938; The Battle of Cambrai, 1917, 1949; Unofficial: The Service Battalions of the Durham L.I., 1920; The Gordon Highlanders, 1919-45, 1961. Reviews of Military books; articles in military magazines. *Address:* Woodcote Grove House, Woodcote Park, Coulsdon, Surrey. [*Died* 13 *Sept.* 1962.

MILFORD, 1st Baron, *cr.* 1939, of Llanstephan; **Laurence Richard Philipps,** 1st Bt., *cr.* 1919; Hon. LL.D. Aberystwyth; J.P. Hampshire and Radnorshire; 6th *s.* of late Sir James E. Philipps, 12th Baronet, and Hon. Lady Philipps; *b.* 1874; *m.* 1901, Ethel Speke of Jordans, Ilminster, Somerset; four *s.* one *d.* *Educ.:* Felsted School; Royal School of Mines. Founder of Hosp. for Paralysed ex-Service Men at Rookwood, Llandaff; Member of Council of University College of Wales, Aberystwyth; Founder of National Welsh Plant Breeding Institute, Aberystwyth and The Milford Chair of Animal Health, Aberystwyth. Member of the Jockey Club: late Member of the Air Registration Board under the Air Ministry; Hon. Vice-President of Wales and Monmouthshire Conservative Association and of Suffolk Conservative and Unionist Association. High Sheriff, Hampshire, 1915. *Recreations:* racing, shooting, and fishing. *Heir:* *s.* Hon. Wogan Philipps. *Address:* Llanstephan House, Llyswen, Radnorshire. *T.:* Erwood 229. *Clubs:* Boodle's, Turf, Royal Automobile: Jockey (Newmarket). [*Died* 7 *Dec.* 1962.

MILFORD HAVEN, 3rd Marquess of, *cr.* 1917; **David Michael Mountbatten,** O.B.E. 1942; D.S.C. 1942; Earl of Medina, *cr.* 1917; Visc. Alderney, *cr.* 1917; R.N. (retd.); Chairman, Atlas Copco (Great Britain) and Atlas Copco (Manufacturing) since 1966; Director, George Brodie & Co. Ltd.; *b.* 12 May 1919; *s.* of 2nd Marquess and Nadejda (*d.* 1963), 2nd *d.* of Grand Duke Michael of Russia and Countess Torby; *S.* father, 1938; *m.* 1st, 1950, Mrs. Romaine Dahlgren Pierce Simpson (marr. diss., 1960); 2nd, 1960, Janet Mercedes Bryce; two *s.* *Educ.:* Roy. Naval Coll., Dartmouth. Entered R.N. 1933; Midshipman R.N., H.M.S. London, 1937; Sub. Lt. H.M.S. Kandahar, 1939-41; Lt. H.M.S. Bramham, 1942; Signal Course, H.M.S. Victory, 1943; Flotilla Signal Officer, H.M.S. Quilliam, 1944; Staff Signal Officer, Adm. Comdg. Carriers, British Pacific Fleet, 1945; Naval Air Station, St. Merryn, 1946-47; retired list, 1948. Worshipful Co. of Shipwrights. M.I.E.R.E. 1967. *Recreations:* yacht racing, golf, ski-ing. *Heir:* *s.* Earl of Medina. *Address:* Tindon Manor, Saffron Walden, Essex. *Clubs:* White's, Royal Corinthian Yacht, Royal London Yacht, Royal Thames Yacht.
[*Died* 14 *April* 1970.

MILL, William Allin, M.S.Lond., F.R.C.S. Eng.; *b.* 26 April 1902; *s.* of Robert Mill, Dunedin, New Zealand, and London; *m.* Nancy McKenzie: one *s.* two *d.* *Educ.:* Whitgift; Guy's Hospital (Treasurer's Gold Medals in Clinical Medicine and Surgery). Distinction in Anatomy and Surgery M.B., B.S. (Lond.) Honours. War of 1939-45 served in R.A.M.C., Temp. Lt.-Col. E.N.T. Adviser, A.F.H.Q., C.M.F. (despatches). Late Pres. Section of Laryngology, R.S.M.; Late Treas. Brit. Assoc. of Otolaryngologists. W. J. Harrison Prize in Laryngology, R.S.M., 1956/57. Formerly: Surgeon, Ear, Nose, and Throat Dept., St. Thomas's Hospital; Surgeon, Ear Nose and Throat Dept., Roy. Marsden Hosp.; Consultant E.N.T. Surgeon, Royal Masonic Hosp.; Aural Surgeon to Florence Nightingale Hosp.; Registrar of Ear, Nose, and Throat Department, Guy's Hosp.; Surgeon, Central London Throat, Nose, and Ear Hospital. Member of the Court of Examiners, R.C.S. *Publications:* various papers in Medical Journals. *Address:* 22 Melcombe Court, Dorset Square, N.W.1. *T.:* Paddington 3372. *Club:* Bath.
[*Died* 9 *March* 1968.

MILLAR, Edric William Hoyer, C.B.E. 1942; formerly Assistant Secretary, Treasury; *b.* 5 Sept. 1880; *s.* of late Henry Edward Millar; unmarried. *Educ.:* Rugby School; Corpus Christi College, Oxford. 1st class Classical Mods. 1901; 1st class Lit. Hum. 1903; entered Treasury, 1903; retired, 1945. *Address:* Wykeham, Bushey Heath, Herts. *T.:* Bushey Heath 1748.
[*Died* 4 *March* 1963.

MILLAR, Eric George, M.A., D.Litt. (Oxon), F.S.A. (Vice-President, 1952-56); Keeper of Manuscripts and Egerton Librarian, British Museum, 1944-47; *b.* 24 Oct. 1887; *o. s.* of late George T. J. Millar and late Edith Mary, *d.* of T. A. Guthrie; unmarried. *Educ.:* Charterhouse; Corpus Christi College, Oxford. Assistant in Department of MSS., British Museum, 1912; Deputy Keeper, 1932; served with 4th Batt. The Buffs, 1915-19; Rhind Lecturer, Edinburgh, 1933; Sandars Reader in Bibliography, University of Cambridge, 1935; seconded to Ministry of Home Security, 1940-44. *Publications:* The Lindisfarne Gospels, 1923; English Illuminated Manuscripts from the 10th to the 13th Century, 1926; English Illuminated Manuscripts of the 14th and 15th Centuries, 1928; The Library of A. Chester Beatty, A Descriptive Catalogue of the Western MSS. Vol. I., 1927, Vol. II., 1930; The Luttrell Psalter, 1932; The Rutland Psalter, 1937; The St. Trond Lectionary, 1949; A Thirteenth Century York Psalter, 1952; An Illuminated MS. of La Somme le Roy, 1953; A Thirteenth Century Bestiary, 1958; The Parisian Miniaturist Honoré, 1959; articles, etc. on Illuminated MSS. for the Société Française de Reproductions de MSS. à Peintures. *Recreations:* collecting MSS. and drawings, trout fishing, gardening. *Address:* The Summer House, Dinton, Salisbury. *Club:* Athenæum.
[*Died* 13 *Jan.* 1966.

MILLARD, Ven. Ernest Norman; *b.* 20 September 1899; *e. s.* of Sidney Ernest and Eleanor Lucy Millard, Streatham Park, S.W.; unmarried. *Educ.:* City of London School; Worcester College, Oxford (Scholar); Cuddesdon. B.A. 1920; 3rd class Lit. Hum., 2nd class Hons. Theology, 1923; M.A. 1927; Liddon Student, 1922: Ellerton Essay Prize, 1924; Deacon, 1924; Priest, 1925; Curate of Rugby, 1924-1929; Vicar of S. James, Northampton, 1929-37; Vicar of S. Mark, Portsea, 1937-46; Rural Dean of Portsmouth, 1943-46; Archdeacon of Oakham and Canon Residentiary of Peterborough Cathedral, 1946-66; Emeritus, 1967. Vice-Chairman Central Council of the Board of Social Responsibility for Moral Welfare, 1952-60. Examining Chaplain to Bishop of Peterborough since 1927. *Recreations:* motoring, walking, sailing. *Address:* 4 Thorpe Ave., Peterborough. *T.:* Peterborough 4045. *Clubs:* United

University; City and Counties (Peterborough). [*Died* 7 *March* 1969.

MILLER, Sir Alastair George Lionel Joseph, 6th Bt., *cr.* 1788; *b.* 5 Mar. 1893; *s.* of Sir William Miller, 5th Bt., and Mary Augusta, *d.* of Charles John Manning, *niece* of Cardinal Manning; *S.* father 1948; *m.* 1st, 1919, Kathleen (marriage dissolved, 1926), *y. d.* of Major Stephen Howard, C.B.E.; one *s.*; 2nd, 1927, Margaret May (marriage dissolved, 1933), *d.* of Frederick Shotter; two *d.*; 3rd, 1938, Cynthia Rosemary, *d.* of F. E. Huish; two *s.* one *d.* *Educ.:* Beaumont. Served European War, 1914-18; formerly Captain Irish Guards and Flight Comdr. R.A.F. *Heir: s.* Frederic William MacDonald [*b.* 21 March 1920; *m.* 1947, Marian Jane Audrey, *d.* of R. S. Pettit. [*Died* 1 *April* 1964.

MILLER, Professor A(rthur) Austin; Emeritus Professor of Geography in the University of Reading (Professor of Geography, 1943-65); Council, British Association for the Advancement of Science, 1961-1965; *b.* 6 July 1900; *s.* of Dr. W. F. Miller, Wrangle, Lincolnshire, and Charlotte Ions; *m.* 1925, Faith Madeline Woolgar; one *s.* one *d.* *Educ.:* Magdalen College School, Oxford; University College, London. B.Sc. 1st Class Hons. in Geology, 1922; M.Sc., 1925; D.Sc., 1940. Demonstrator in Geology, U.C., London, 1922-25; Lecturer in Geography, Univ. of Reading, 1926. Council Royal Geographical Society; President Institute of British Geographers, 1946-48; Advisory Editor for Geography, Chambers's Encyclopædia, 1945-49; Member of Commission on Terraces, International Geographical Union, 1948-52; President Section E (Geography) British Association, Sheffield Meeting, 1956. Chairman, International Geographical Congress: Washington 1952 (Climatology Section); Rio de Janeiro, 1956; Stockholm, 1960 (Climatology and Hydrology section). Fellow of University College, London, 1958. Visiting Prof., Univ. of Indiana, U.S.A., Jan. 1958-Jan. 1959; Visiting Professor: Univ. of British Columbia (Vancouver), summer session, 1958, 1965; Univ. of Western Ontario, London, 1965. Pres., Geographical Assoc., 1960. Murchison Award, 1963. *Publications:* Climatology, 1930; The Skin of the Earth, 1953; Everyday Meteorology (with M. Parry), 1958. Papers on geology, geomorphology and climatology. *Recreations:* sailing, camping, touring, rivers. *Address:* Woodlands, 67 Eastern Avenue, Reading. *T.:* Reading 62112. [*Died* 31 *March* 1968.

MILLER, Edmund Morris, C.B.E. 1963; Litt.D. Professor of Psychology and Philosophy (Emeritus, since 1952), University of Tasmania (previously Lectr., 1913-24) State Psychological Clinic (Director, 1922 - 46, 1951-52, Consultant 1946-52); Vice-Chancellor, University of Tasmania, 1933-45; *b.* Natal, 1881; *s.* of David and Georgina Miller, of Dundee and Melbourne; *m.* Catherine MacKinnon, *d.* of Rev. John Carson; one *d.* *Educ.:* Wesley College, Melbourne; M.A., Litt.D., University of Melbourne; Edinburgh University; Research Scholar in Philosophy, 1911 - 12. Visited for Tasmanian Government universities, psychological clinics, institutions for feeble-minded in U.S. and Canada, 1921; Sec. Imperial Federation League of Australia, 1908-13; Chairman Library Association of Victoria, 1912-13; President Tasmanian Institution for Blind, Deaf and Dumb, 1923-40; Chairman Board of Trustees, Tasmanian Public Library, 1922-43; Chairman Mental Deficiency Board, 1925-46, 1951-52; Member of Indeterminate Sentences Board, 1923-52; President, Australian Association of Psychology and Philosophy, 1928-29; Chairman Australian Army Psychology Advisory Committee, 1941 - 42; Fellow: British Psychological Society, 1939; Internat. Inst. of Arts and Letters, 1958. *Publications:* Some Phases of Preference in Imperial Policy, 1911; Libraries and Education, 1912; Kant's Doctrine of Freedom, 1913; Basis of Freedom, Study of Kant's Theory, 1924; Brain Capacity and Intelligence, 1926; Moral Law and the Highest Good (Kant's Theory), 1928; Australian Literature, 2 vols., 1940, rev. edn., 1956; Pressmen and Governors, 1952; contributor to journals on literature, psychology and philosophy. *Recreations:* bowling and reading. *Address:* The University, Hobart, Tasmania. [*Died* 21 *Oct.* 1964.

MILLER, Emanuel, M.A. (Cantab.); F.R.C.P.; D.P.M. (Cantab.); Hon. Physician, Child Psychiatry, St. George's Hospital; Emeritus Physician, Maudsley Hospital; Hon. Director, East London Child Guidance Clinic; Member of Child Guidance Council; Hon. Physician, London Jewish Hospital; Hon. Psychiatrist, Tavistock Clinic; Co-Editor, British Journal of Criminology; *b.* London, 1894; *y. s.* of Abram Miller, London; *m.* 1933, Betty (*d.* 1965), 2nd *d.* of S. Spiro, J.P.; one *s.* one *d.* *Educ.:* City of London School (Times Scholar); St. John's College, Cambridge (Exhibitioner and Prizeman). Natural Science Tripos, Pt. I; Moral Science Tripos, Pt. II; Prizeman, London Hospital Medical School; Lt.-Col., R.A.M.C., Psychiatric Specialist since 1940; Army Psychiatrist to Directorate of Medical Research and Statistics, 1943-45; Lecturer to Medical Post Graduates in Psychology, Cambridge University, 1924-25; Sometime Member, Council for Treatment of Offenders, Home Office; F.R.Soc.Med.; Fellow Eugenic Soc.; Membre de la Société de Morphologie, Paris; Fellow and late Chairman, Medical Section, British Psychological Society. Chm. Association of Child Psychiatry. Joint Editor: Jl. Child Psychology and Psychiatry, 1959-; Brit. Jl. of Criminology, 1948-; Library of Criminology, 1960-. *Publications:* Types of Mind and Body; Modern Psychotherapy; Insomnia and Disorders of Sleep; Editor and part author, Neurosis in War, 1940; Editor, Foundations of Child Psychiatry, 1967; papers on Psychopathology and Disorders of Childhood. *Recreations:* painting and modelling. *Address:* Tenby Mansions, Nottingham St., W.1. *T.:* Welbeck 7055. *Club:* Athenæum. [*Died* 29 *July* 1970.

MILLER, Frederick Robert, F.R.S. 1932; M.A.; M.B. (Toronto); M.D. (Munich); F.R.S.C.; F.R.C.P. (Canada); lately Professor of Physiology, Faculty of Medicine, University of Western Ontario; *b.* Toronto; *s.* of Allan F. Miller and Elizabeth Crean. *Educ.:* Universities of Toronto, Munich, Strasburg, Liverpool, and Oxford. Assistant in Physiology, Cornell University, 1903 - 5; Demonstrator of Physiology, University of Toronto, 1907-10; student in Universities of Munich, Strasburg, and Liverpool, 1910-12; Lecturer on Physiology, McGill University, Montreal, 1912-14. *Publications:* papers in British and American physiological journals: subjects—galvanotropism, the stomach, salivary reflexes, deglutition, centres in medulla oblongata, mastication, cerebellum, reflexes, electrophysiology. *Recreation:* gardening. *Address:* c/o The Public Trustee, 145 Queen Street West, Toronto 1, Canada. [*Died* 11 *Nov.* 1967.

MILLER, Col. Sir Geoffry C.; *see* Christie-Miller.

MILLER, Gilbert Heron; Theatrical Producer; *b.* N.Y.C., 3 July 1884; *s.* of Henry and Helène Stoepel (Bijou Heron) Miller; *m.* 1927, Kathryn King Bache. *Educ.:* de la Salle Inst., N.Y.; Frères des Écoles Chrétiennes-Passy, Paris; Muller-Gelenick Realschule, Dresden; Bedford

County Sch., Bedford, England. Theatre Mgr., 1927-; Producer, 1916-; Vice-Pres., Charles Frohman Inc., 1921-32; Lessee: Hy. Miller's Theatre, 1921-, Lyric Theatre, London, 1919-. Producer numerous successful plays; most recent among the American Productions: Edward my Son, 1949; The Cocktail Party, 1950; Ring round the Moon, 1951; Gigi, 1954; The Living Room, 1954; Witness for the Prosecution, 1954; The Reluctant Debutante, 1956; The Sleeping Prince, 1956; Under Milkwood, 1957; The Rope Dancers, 1957; Patate, 1958; The Golden Fleecing, 1959; The Caretaker, 1961; The White House, 1964; The Diamond Orchid, 1965; and among the London productions: Dear Ruth, 1946; The Happy Time (with Sir Laurence Olivier), 1952; The Caine Mutiny Court Martial (with Henry Sherek), 1956, Change of Tune, 1959; Write me a Murder (with H. M. Tennent Ltd.), 1962. Served as 1st Lt. in A.E.F. Intelligence Dept., 1918-19; served as Aviation Technician, U.S.S. Shangri-la, Sept. 1944-Feb. 1945. Officier d'Académie; Officier, Légion d'Honneur (French); Order of Isabel la Catolica (Spanish). *Address:* (Home) 550 Park Avenue, N.Y.C., U.S.A.; Drungewick Manor, Loxwood, Sussex, England; 40B Hill St., London, England; (Office) 124 W. 43rd St., N.Y.C., U.S.A.; 6B Hertford St., London, England. *Clubs:* Players' (N.Y.C.); Buck's (London); Travellers' (Paris).

[*Died* 2 *Jan.* 1969.

MILLER, René; *see* Fülop-Miller.

MILLER, Robert Brown, M.A., LL.B.; Sheriff-Substitute of Renfrew and Argyll at Campbeltown, since 1955; *b.* 2 Dec. 1905; *o. s.* of David Miller, Clerk, Dundee, and Marjory Isabella Brown; *m.* 1948, Janet Officer, *o. d.* of Thomas Yule, Glasgow. *Educ.:* Morgan Academy, Dundee; Universities of St. Andrews and Glasgow. First place (equal) St. Andrews Univ. Open Bursary Competition in 1924; awarded Russell Bursary for four years; also Spence (Classics) Bursary in 1925, at St. Andrews Univ. Medallist in General Greek (equal) and in Special Greek; First Place for Latin Prose; M.A. (St. Andrews): 2nd Cl. Hons. in Classics, 1928. Trained as teacher, Dundee Training Coll., 1928-29. Began legal studies at Glasgow Univ., 1931; LL.B. (Glasgow), 1935. Admitted as solicitor, 1936; admitted to Faculty of Advocates, 1938. Editor of Sheriff Court Reports for Scots Law Times, 1940-41. Served War of 1939-45, R.A.F., 1941-45. Sheriff-Substitute of Inverness, Moray, Nairn and Ross and Cromarty at Stornoway, 1947-55. *Address:* Dunara, Campbeltown, Argyll. [*Died* 11 *Oct.* 1963.

MILLER, Samuel V. C.; *see* Christie-Miller.

MILLER, Sinclair, D.S.O. 1918, M.C., M.A., B.Sc., M.D., M.R.C.P. (Lond.); Senior Physician, Duchy House Clinic, Harrogate; Consulting Physician, Ilkley Coronation Hospital; Physician in charge of Blood Transfusion Service, Harrogate General Hospital; Consulting Pathologist, Ripon and District Hospital; Consulting Pathologist, Harrogate General Hospital and Royal Bath Hospital, Harrogate; *b.* 19 March 1885; *s.* of James and Sarah M. Miller; *m.* 1st, 1916, Norah Isabel, *d.* of late Rt. Hon. R. G. Glendinning, D.L., P.C., Belfast; three *s.* one *d.*; 2nd, 1958, Isabel Wales (Iddie) Dick. *Educ.:* The Rainey Endowed School, Magherafelt; Queen's University, Belfast (Scholar and Dunville Research Student); The London Hospital. Served European War France, 1914-1918, Lt.-Col. commanding Divisional Field Ambulance (D.S.O., M.C., despatches); Officer in charge Malarial Research Department 4th London General Hospital, under Sir Ronald Ross, 1919. *Publications:* Diabetes; Chronic Arthritis; Nutrition and Diet in Rheumatism; Gastric Function in Chronic Arthritis and Fibrositis; Thrombo-phlebitis Migrans; Sub-arachnoid Hæmorrhage. *Recreations:* walking and gardening. *Address:* 9 Queen's Road, Harrogate. *T.:* Harrogate 2323.

[*Died* 24 *Aug.* 1961.

MILLER, William Thomas, O.B.E. 1941; Secretary of Federation of Colliery Deputies Associations of Great Britain since 1939; President, General Federation of Colliery Firemen's Examiners and Deputies since 1926; *b.* 21 July 1880; *s.* of Simon Miller and Juliet Lever. *Educ.:* St. Peter's C. E. Schools, Hindley, Wigan. Commenced work underground at 12 years; Assistant Fireman 1903; Emigrated to Nova Scotia 1906, worked in Local Mine; returned 1908; resumed position as Mine Deputy at Cross Tetleys Ltd.; President of Lancashire and Cheshire Colliery Deputies Association 1913; Secretary Lancashire, Cheshire and North Wales Colliery Deputies and Shot-firers Association 1922; Represented General Federation on several Mine Disasters, Haig Pit, Bentley, Lyme Pit, Garswood Hall, Gresford Explosions; Member of Royal Commission on Safety in Mines, 1936; employed as a pony driver when underground fire took place at Bamfurlong Colliery No. 2 Pit where 16 men lost their lives, 1892; Investigation Officer (chief), Ministry of Fuel and Power (North-Western Region), 1943-47; retired, 1947. 54½ years in connection with coal mining. *Address:* 71 Scot Lane, Newtown, Wigan.

[*Died* 23 *Oct.* 1963.

MILLERS, Harold Cuthbert Townley, T.D.; Registrar, Probate, Divorce and Admiralty Div. of Supreme Court, since 1949; *b.* 11 Sept. 1903; *s.* of John Townley and Ellen Elizabeth Millers. *Educ.:* Wrekin; London University (B.A. Hons.). Preparatory Schoolmaster, 1925-31; called to Bar, Gray's Inn, 1931; practised on Northern Circuit to Sept. 1939. Lancashire Fusiliers, T.A., 1936-39; R.A. 1939-42; General Staff in Middle East, 1942-45; Legal Adviser to B.M.A., Dodecanese, 1945; District Registrar, Manchester, 1946-48. *Recreations:* walking, and watching village cricket. *Clubs:* Garrick, Farmers'.

[*Died* 28 *Feb.* 1968.

MILLIGAN, John Williamson, D.S.O. 1917; *b.* 7 Sept. 1875; *s.* of Wyndham Carmichael Anstruther Milligan, Shipowner, Liverpool, and Margaret Whitson Gibson, Dundee. *Educ.:* St. John's Coll., Oxford (B.A.); Caen, Sorbonne (Paris), Heidelberg and Berlin Universities. Settled in British E. Africa, 1911; founded J. W. Milligan & Co. Ltd., Land, Estate & Insurance Agents, Importers & Exporters, 1912, and Anglo-Baltic Timber Co. Ltd., 1913, including The East African Hides, Wool and Skins Mart, and Ruiru Timber Co. Ltd.; Rep. Messrs. John K. Gilliat & Co. Ltd., London. Joined E. African Mounted Rifles, Aug. 1914, serving throughout campaign against German East Africa in that unit and at G.H.Q. (despatches, D.S.O.). Founder and late Pres. Land and Estate Agents and Valuers Assoc. of Kenya; Past Mem. Exec. and Treas. Assoc. of Chambers of Commerce and Industry of E. Africa. Past Pres. Coffee Trade Assoc. of E. Africa and of Nairobi Coffee Exchange. Pres. Royal Agricultural Soc. of Kenya, 1948-49, and of Show Jumping Assoc. of Kenya, 1950-54; and Past Pres. etc. of various sporting activities in Kenya, including Sec. and Hon. Treas. Jockey Club of Kenya, 1912; Past Steward and Clerk of Course, 1913-48. *Publication:* Handbook of British East Africa, 1912. *Recreations:* golf, squash rackets, shooting, fishing. *Address:* Muthaiga, P.O. Box 148, Nairobi, Kenya. *T.:* Nairobi 65269. *Clubs:* Bath; Muthaiga Country, Nairobi (Nairobi). [*Died* 1 *July* 1965.

MILLIGAN, Lt.-Col. Stanley Lyndall, C.M.G. 1918; D.S.O. 1916; *b.* Aberdeen, 27 Apr. 1887; *s.* of Robert Angus Milligan, solicitor, Aberdeen; *m.* 1934, Sylvia Nora Evelyn, *d.* of Col. C. F. A. Turnbull, late D.C.L.I.; one *s.* one *d.* *Educ.:* South African College, Cape Town. Australian Military Citizen Forces, 1908-1914; served European War with 1st Australian Forces; 1914-15: Egypt and Gallipoli; 1916-19: Staff and Regimental Service France and Flanders; commanded 2nd Australian Battalion, 1917 (rank Lieut. Col., C.M.G. D.S.O., five times despatches); attached Egyptian Army 1919-24; Sudan Defence Force, 1924-27; operations in Southern and Western Darfur 1921 (Sudan General Service medal and clasp); served on Anglo-French Sudan Boundary Commission, 1922-23; gazetted Captain, 1917; Highland Light Infantry, resigned 1927; Lt.-Col. Reserve of Officers: Director of Surveys, Anglo-Egyptian Sudan, 1927-37; War of 1939-1945, recalled to Army and commanded Training Bn. and Training Centre, 1940-44; Order of the Nile, 3rd class, 1936. *Recreation:* sailing. *Address:* Flat 2, Minterne House, Minterne Magna, Dorset. *T.:* Cerne Abbas 226. *Club:* United Service. [*Died* 15 *April* 1968.

MILLIN, Albert, C.M.G. 1961; C.B.E. 1953 (O.B.E. 1935); J.P.; Solicitor and Notary Public; *b.* Montagu, Cape Province, South Africa, 1 June 1893; *s.* of late Barnett Millin; *m.* 1924, Frances Sybil Emmett-Deal; one *s.* *Educ.:* South African College School, Cape Town; South African College, Cape Town. Served War, German South-West Africa, 1914-15; 2nd Lieut., Sherwood Foresters Regt. Overseas, 1917-18. Mem., European Adv. Coun., Swaziland, 1921-, and Member, Executive Committee. *Recreation:* bowls. *Address:* P.O. Box 24 Mbabane, Swaziland. *Clubs:* English (Lourenço Marques); Wanderers (Johannesburg); Mbabane (Swaziland). [*Died* 26 *Oct.* 1964.

MILLIN, Sarah Gertrude; *d.* of Isaiah and Olga Liebson, Barkly West District, C.P., S. Africa; *m.* Hon. Philip Millin (*d.* 1952), Judge of Supreme Court of S. Africa. Hon. D.Litt., Univ. of the Witwatersrand, 1952. *Publications:* An Explanation of South Africa called The South Africans 1926; new and enlarged ed., 1934; 3rd ed., 1951, The People of South Africa; Men on a Voyage (short pieces), 1930; British Commonwealth Series: South Africa, 1941; B.B.C. Play, General Smuts, 1943; W.O.R. (U.S.A.) Series of 13 plays, The Life of General Smuts, 1944; War Diaries, World Blackout, (1) 1944, (2) 1945, (3) The Reeling Earth, 1945, (4) The Sound of the Trumpet, 1947, (5) Fire Out of Heaven, 1948, (6) The Seven Thunders, 1948; Social Study, the People of South Africa, 1950; *biography:* Rhodes: A Life, 1933 (new edn. with Eng. preface and appendix, 1952, new edn. 1968; filmed as Rhodes of Africa); General Smuts, 1936; *autobiography:* The Night is Long, 1941; The Measure of my Days, 1955; *novels:* The Dark River, 1920; Middle-class, 1921; Adam's Rest, 1922; The Jordans, 1923; God's Stepchildren, 1924 (new edition with preface, 1952); Mary Glenn, 1925 (a play, No Longer Mourn, based on Mary Glenn, produced in London, 1935); An Artist in the Family, 1927; The Coming of the Lord, 1928; The Fiddler, 1929; The Sons of Mrs. Aab, 1931; Three Men Die, 1934; What Hath a Man?, 1938; The Herr Witch Doctor, 1941; King of the Bastards, 1950; The Burning Man, 1952; Two Bucks Without Hair, 1957; The Wizard Bird, 1962; Goodbye, Dear England, 1965; *compilation:* White Africans Are Also People, 1966. *Address:* 34 Pallinghurst Road, Westcliff, Johannesburg, S.A. [*Died* 6 *July* 1968.

MILLS, 1st Viscount *cr.* 1962; **Percy Herbert Mills;** 1st Baron, *cr.* 1957; 1st Bt., *cr.* 1953; P.C. 1957; K.B.E. 1946; Kt. 1942; Director, Electrical & Musical Industries Ltd.; Chairman, E.M.I. Electronics Ltd.; Chairman, Stocklund Property Ltd.; *b.* 4 January 1890; *m.* 1915, Winifred Mary Conaty, Birmingham; one *s.* one *d.* *Educ.:* North Eastern County School, Barnard Castle. Controller-General of Machine Tools, 1940-44; Head of Production Division, Ministry of Production, 1943-44; President of the Economic Sub-Commission of British Element of Control Commission for Germany, 1944-46; Pres. Birmingham Chamber of Commerce, 1947-48. Hon. Adviser on Housing to Minister of Housing and Local Govt., 1951-52; Chairman, National Research Development Corporation, 1950-55; Chm. W. & T. Avery Ltd., Soho Foundry, Birmingham, 1955-56. Minister of Power, 1957-59; Paymaster-General, 1959-61; Min. without Portfolio, 1961-62; Deputy Leader of House of Lords, 1960-62. Master, Gunmakers' Co., 1965-66. *Heir:* *s.* Hon. Roger Clinton Mills [*b.* 14 June 1919; *m.* 1945, Joan Sheriff; one *s.* two *d.* *Educ.:* Canford School; Cambridge]. *Address:* 38 Campden Hill Gate, W.8. *Clubs:* Carlton, Constitutional, Beefsteak. [*Died* 10 *Sept.* 1968.

MILLS, Maj.-Gen. Sir Arthur Mordaunt, Kt. 1938; C.B. 1932; D.S.O. 1917 and two bars, 1917-18; Indian Army retired; *b.* 13 August 1879; *s.* of late Col. A. McL. Mills, I.A.; *m.* 1st, 1908, Winifred Alice (*d.* 1931), *d.* of late Col. R. H. Carew, D.S.O., R.A.M.C.; three *s.* one *d.*; 2nd, 1940, Hilda Grace Shirley, *yr. d.* of late Harry Gavin Young, Madras Police. *Educ.:* Wellington College. Served with 3rd R. Sussex Regt. 1st Devons, 18th K.G.O. Lancers I.A. and 4th P.W.O. Gurkhas; S. African War (five clasps); European War (wounded, despatches three times, D.S.O. and 2 bars, Bt. of Lt.-Col.); Instructor, Senior Officers' School, Woking, 1921-24; N.-W. Frontier, India, 1930 (despatches); commanded Razmak Brigade, Waziristan, India, 1930-34; Military Adviser-in-Chief, Indian States Forces, 1935-39; A.D.C. to the King, 1933-35; retired, 1939. Colonel 4th P.W.O., Gurkha Rifles, 1935-50. *Address:* The Little House, Enton Green, Godalming; c/o National and Grindlay's Bank, 26 Bishopsgate, E.C. *Club:* English-Speaking Union. [*Died* 8 *Oct.* 1964.

MILLS, Arthur Stewart Hunt, R.E. 1948 (A.R.E. 1934); Artist; *b.* Portsmouth, 1897; *s.* of Henry Hunt Mills and Maud Clay Carter; *m.* 1934, Dora Marian, *d.* of Whitfield Taylor, Blackheath; one *s.* one *d.* *Educ.:* Portsmouth Grammar School; Magdalene College, Cambridge; Goldsmiths' College School of Art. Served European War, 1914-18; R.F.C., 1916-19 (despatches); War of 1939-45; Territorial A.A., R.A., 1939-40; R.A.F., 1940-45 (despatches). *Exhibited:* Royal Academy, Painter Etchers, Society of Wood Engravers, principal provincial exhibitions, also in Europe and N. America. *Recreations:* field natural history. *Address:* Stonerdale, Church Road, Steep, Petersfield, Hants. [*Died* 24 *Dec.* 1968.

MILLS, Eric, C.B.E. 1934 (O.B.E. 1919); B.A. (Cantab.); retired; *b.* 22 January 1892. War Service, 1914-20. Public appointments in Palestine, 1917-48; retired, 1948. Special duty: Jamaica, 1949; Fiji, 1950; Anglo-Egyptian Sudan, 1950-51; British Guiana, 1952-54; University College, Ibadan, Nigeria, 1956. Officer, Knights of St. John. *Publication:* Report of the Census of Palestine, 1931. *Address:* Red Cottage, Mill Lane, Chiddingfold, Godalming, Surrey. [*Died* 16 *Oct.* 1961.

MILLS, Air Vice-Marshal Reginald Percy, C.B. 1930; M.C., A.F.C.; *b.* 1885; *y. s.* of William Henry Mills, J.P., Parkstone, Dorset; *m.* 1919, Helen (marriage dissolved, 1936), *d.* of Major W. H. Bulpett, Alresford, Hants; one *d.* *Educ.:* Felsted. Royal Fusiliers, 1909; seconded Royal Flying Corps, 1913; served European War, 1914-19 (despatches twice, M.C., A.F.C.); Deputy Director Air Ministry, 1922-26; Chief Staff Officer, Royal Air Force in India, 1926-31; Director of Organisation and Staff Duties, Air Ministry, 1931-33; Air Officer Commanding, Oxford Bombing Area 1933-34; Director of Postings, Air Ministry, 1934-35; retired list, 1936; re-employed R.A.F. with rank of Group Captain, 1939, and Air Vice-Marshal, 1941-42. *Address:* 50 Proctors Road, Hobart, Tasmania. [*Died* 4 *July* 1968.

MILMAN, Brig.-Gen. Sir Lionel Charles Patrick, 7th Bt. *cr.* 1800; C.M.G. 1917; late R.A.; 3rd *s.* of Sir F. J. Milman, 4th Bt.; *b.* 23 Feb. 1877; *S.* brother, Sir William Ernest Milman, 6th Bt., 1962; *m.* 1911, Marjorie Aletta, *d.* of Col. A.H. Clark-Kennedy, late I.S.C.; three *s.* one *d.* *Educ.:* Sidney Sussex College, Cambridge (Classical Exhibitioner; B.A. Classical Tripos, 1899). Entered R.A. 1900; Capt. 1912; Major, 1915; Instructor in Artillery, R.M.A., Woolwich, 1910-14; joined Ministry of Munitions, Jan. 1916; Controller of Gun Ammunition Filling Division since July 1916 (C.M.G.); served European War, 1914-1918; retired, 1919. General Manager for I.C.I. Ltd. in S. Africa and later in Birmingham, 1919-28; Director, Small Arms Ammunition Dept. of Ministry of Supply, 1940-46. *Recreations:* cricket, golf. *Heir:* *s.* Major Dermot Lionel Kennedy Milman, R.A.S.C. [*b.* 24 Oct. 1912; *m.* 1941, Muriel, *o. d.* of J. F. S. Taylor; one *d.*]. *Address:* c/o Lloyds Bank, 6 Pall Mall, S.W.1. [*Died* 2 *Nov.* 1962.

MILMAN, Sir William Ernest, 6th Bt, *cr.* 1800; *b.* 11 Aug. 1875; *s.* of 4th Bt. and Katharine, *d.* of Stephen C. Moore, D.L., J.P., Barne, Clonmel; *S.* brother 1946; *m.* 1934, Elder Wilse Samson (*d.* 1959). Served Boer War and European War, 1914-19 (M.M.). *Heir:* *b.* Brig.-Gen. L. C. P. Milman. *q.v.* *Address:* Wilses Vei 13, Jar-i-Baerum, Norway. [*Died* 30 *Aug.* 1962.

MILNER-WHITE, Very Rev. Eric, C.B.E. 1952; D.S.O. 1918; Dean of York since 1941; Fellow of King's College, Cambridge, since 1918; *b.* 23 April 1884; *s.* of Sir Henry Milner-White; unmarried. *Educ.:* Harrow; King's College, Cambridge (Scholar); Cuddesdon Theological College. 1st Class Historical Tripos, Pt. I. 1905; University Lightfoot Scholar, 1906; 1st Class Historical Tripos, Pt. II. 1907; B.A. 1907; M.A. 1911; D.D. (Lambeth) 1952; Deacon, 1908; Priest, 1909; Curate of St. Paul's, Newington, 1908-09; St. Mary Magdalene, Woolwich, 1909-12; Chaplain of King's, 1912; Lecturer in History, Corpus Christi, Cambridge, 1912-14; Dean of Kings, 1918-41; Canon of Lincoln Cathedral, 1937-1941; Examining Chaplain to the Bishop of London, 1913-36; to Bishop of Lincoln, 1936-41, to Archbishop of York, 1942; Chaplain to the Forces, B.E.F. 1914; served with the Seventh Division, S.C.F. 7th Division, 1917 (D.S.O.). Pres. of Henry Bradshaw Soc., 1943-59; Provost, Woodard Corporation, Northern Division, since 1945; Mem. Advisory Council of V.A. Museum, 1944-1959; Hon. Mem. of Worshipful Company of Glaziers with Freedom of City of London, 1948. Hon. Litt.D. (University of Leeds), 1962. *Publications:* Cambridge Offices and Orisons, 1921; One God and Father of All, 1929; Memorials upon Several Occasions, 1933; A Cambridge Bede-Book, 1935; The Book of Hugh and Nancy, 1937; The Daily Prayer, 1941; A Procession of Passion Prayers, 1950; My God my Glory, 1954. 16th Century Glass in York Minster, 1960. *Recreations:* modern pottery, stained glass, rose growing. *Address:* The Deanery, York. *T.:* York 23608. *Clubs:* M.C.C., Oxford and Cambridge. [*Died* 15 *June* 1963.

MILNE, Sir James (Allan), Kt. 1959; C.B.E. 1949; *b.* 11 November 1896; *s.* of late James Murray Milne and Martha Burney; *m.* 1923, Sarah Emma Ridge (*d.* 1962); two *d.* *Educ.:* Barrow Grammar School. Commenced training as shipbuilder at Barrow Yard of Messrs Vickers Ltd.; went to France, 1922, to join Société des Ateliers et Chantiers de France of Dunkerque where finally became General Manager; returned to England, 1940. Pres. of the Shipbuilding Conference, 1957-59; Past Chm. British Shipbuilding Research Assoc., 1959; Past Prime Warden Worshipful Company of Shipwrights. Vice-Pres. Royal Instn. of Naval Architects; M.I.Mar.E.; Mem. N.E. Coast Instn. of Engineers and Shipbuilders; Hon. Vice-Pres. Southern Br. Royal Instn. of Naval Architects and Inst. of Marine Engineers. Chm. of Govs., Isle of Wight Technical Coll.,1951-; Dir., Shipwrights Hall Ltd.; Vice-Pres., Hampshire County Cricket Club. Chevalier du Mérite Maritime, France, 1937. *Recreations:* golf, shooting, cricket. *Address:* Avalon, Cowes, Isle of Wight. *T.:* Cowes 2796. *Clubs:* Royal Automobile; Royal London Yacht, Royal Corinthian Yacht, Island Sailing. [*Died* 22 *May* 1966.

MILNE, Sir John S. W.; *see* Wardlaw-Milne.

MILNE, Oswald Partridge, F.R.I.B.A.; J.P.; *b.* 1881; *s.* of William Oswald Milne, F.R.I.B.A. and Louisa Katherine, *d.* of F. R. Partridge, Kings Lynn; *m.* 1920, Irene (Jessie Powys) (*d.* 1965), *d.* of C. H. Murray. *Educ.:* Bedford School. Articled to Sir Arthur Blomfield, A.R.A. Started practice in London, 1905. Past Chairman Council of Royal Soc. of Arts. Works include many country houses amongst which: Huntercombe Place, Oxfordshire; Rhowniar, Towyn, N. Wales; Coleton Fishacre, Kingswear, Devon; Tirinie, Blair Atholl, Perthshire. School Buildings: Bedford School; Dame Alice School, Bedford; Christ's Hospital; Cheltenham College; St. John's, Leatherhead; Blundell's School; Highgate School; Dartington School and other buildings, Dartington, Devon; schools for County Councils of Beds., Berks., Herts. and Surrey; Bishop Bell School, Eastbourne. Work includes also new building Claridge's Hotel, etc. Served European War 1914-18, Major R.A.S.C. (despatches); War of 1939-1945, Captain Home Guard. Served Hampstead Borough Council as Councillor and Alderman, 1937-53; Mayor, 1947-49; J.P. County of London (Hampstead), 1941. *Recreations:* painting and gardening. *Address:* Lower Heath House, 101 South End Road, Hampstead, N.W.3. *T.:* Hampstead 5926. *Club:* Arts. [*Died* 15 *Jan.* 1968.

MILNE, William Proctor, LL.D., M.A., D.Sc. (Aberdeen), M.A. (Cambridge); Professor of Mathematics, University of Leeds, 1919-46; Emeritus Professor since 1946; *b.* Wester Rora, Longside, Aberdeenshire, 22 May 1881; *e. s.* of Andrew Milne and Jessie Proctor; *m.* Mary Deas, *d.* of Robert Carr Burnett, M.A. (St. Andrews), Echt, Aberdeenshire; one *s.* one *d.* *Educ.:* Peterhead Academy; Aberdeen Grammar School; Aberdeen University. Graduated with First Class Honours in Mathematics and Natural Philosophy, gaining Simpson Mathematical Prize, Greig Prize in Natural Philosophy, David Rennet Gold Medal, bracketed for Lyon Prize with Professor W. M. Calder of Edinburgh University, Fullerton Scholarship, Ferguson Scholarship; Cambridge University, Fourth Wrangler, First Class Part II., Mathematical Tripos; Mathematical Master at Clifton College, Bristol, 1907-19; Examiner, Universities of St. Andrews, Durham, Bristol, Birmingham, Liverpool, London, Manchester, Cambridge; Pro-Vice-Chancellor, University of Leeds, 1943-45; President of Buchan Field Club, 1940-48; Hon. Mem.

Malayan Mathematical Soc., 1953-. Hon. LL.D. (Aberdeen), 1946; Hon. LL.D. (Leeds), 1955. *Publications:* Eppie Elrick, an Aberdeenshire Tale of the '15; Researches on Synthetic Geometry, published in a series of papers in the Proceedings of the London Mathematical Society; text-books on Homogeneous Co-ordinates, Projective Geometry, Higher Algebra, First Course in Calculus (with G. J. B. Westcott of Bristol Grammar School). *Address:* 16 Monkbridge Road, Headingley, Leeds. [*Died* 3 *Sept.* 1967.

MILNE HENDERSON, Captain Thomas Maxwell Stuart, C.I.E. 1941; O.B.E. 1919; R.I.N. (retd.); Captain, R.N. Emergency List; *b.* 18 May 1888; *e. s.* of late John Milne Henderson, J.P., C.A., late Manager North of Scotland Bank Ltd., Edinburgh; *m.* 1917, Evelyn Henderson, *d.* of late Dr. John Haldane Bain, Edinburgh; no *c.* *Educ.:* George Watson's Coll. and Roy. High School, Edinburgh; H.M.S. Conway, Birkenhead. Midshipman R.N.R., 1906; Cadet; 3rd and 2nd Officer Barque Inverclyde of Aberdeen, 1907-10; Sub-Lt., R.I.M., 1910; Lt. R.I.M., 1914; served European War with Royal Navy, 1914-16; Marine Transport Officer, Mesopotamia, 1916-17; lent to Royal Engineers as Capt. R.E. for service with Inland Water Transport, 1917; Major R.E. and D.A.D.I.W. and D., France and Italy, 1917-18; D.A.D.I.W.T., Mesopotamia, 1918; Lt.-Col. R.E. and A.D.I.W.T. Mesopotamia, 1919-20 (O.B.E.); Commander R.I.N., 1930; Surveyor in Charge, Marine Survey of India, 1930-35; Divisional Sea Transport Officer, India, 1935-37; Capt. R.I.N., 1937; Capt. Supt. H.M. Indian Naval Dockyard, Bombay, and Officiating Chief of Staff, R.I.N., 1937; Chief of Staff, R.I.N., 1938-42; Officiating Flag Officer Comdg. R.I.N., June-Sept., 1939; Hon. A.D.C. to Viceroy of India, 1938-42; Commodore, R.I.N., 1940-42 (C.I.E.); Officer on special duty with Govt. of India, 1941-42; retired, 1942. *Recreations:* playing bad golf, destructive gardening, plain cooking. *Address:* 25 Braidburn Crescent, Edinburgh 10. *T.:* 031-447 5802. [*Died* 10 *Dec.* 1968.

MILNER OF LEEDS, 1st Baron *cr.* 1951, of Roundhay, in the City of Leeds, **James Milner,** P.C. 1945; M.C. and Bar; T.D., D.L. (West Riding of Yorkshire); Hon. LL.D. (Leeds) 1953; Solicitor and Comr. for Oaths; late senior partner of J. H. Milner & Son, Leeds and London; Chairman, Cleaver-Hume Ltd.; late Member, Court and Council, Leeds University; *b.* 12 Aug. 1889; *s.* of late J. H. Milner, City Coroner for Leeds; *m.* 1917, Lois Tinsdale, *d.* of Thomas Brown, Roundhay, Leeds; one *s.* two *d.* *Educ.:* Easingwold Grammar School; Leeds University; LL.B., Leeds, 1911. Late Member W.R. Territorial Assoc.; late Trustee Haig Memorial Homes; Trustee Liverpool Victoria Friendly Soc.; Vice-Pres. Assoc. of Municipal Corporations and Building Soc. Assoc.; Patron, Leeds Trustee Savings Bank; Past Pres. N.E. Leeds United Nations Assoc.; President: Leeds Civic Trust; Seamen and Boatmen's Friend, Society; Leeds Flower Show; Vice-President, Leeds Thoresby Society; Vice-Pres., Leeds Nat. Savings Cttee; Hon. Member Leeds Chamber of Commerce; President Leeds Law Soc., 1936; late Mem. Council, London Law Soc.; Mem. Adv. Coun., E.S.U.; Pres. Society of Yorkshiremen in London and of Yorkshire Society, 1957. Past High Chief Ranger Independent Order of Foresters; late President Sanitary Inspectors' Association (now Public Health Inspectors' Association); served European War, Major, R.A.S.C. and Devon Regiment (wounded, despatches, M.C. and bar); Chairman Leeds City Labour Party, 1926; Dep. Lord Mayor, Leeds, 1928-29; Mem. Leeds City Council, 1923-29; M.P. (Lab.) Sth. East Leeds, 1929-51; Parl. Private Sec. to Lord Addison, 1929-31; late Chm., subsq. Mem. History of Parliament Trust; late Chm. British Gp. Inter-Parl. Union, and attended Confs. at: The Hague, 1938, Oslo, 1939, Copenhagen, 1946, Cairo, 1947, Rome, 1948, Dublin, 1950, Vienna 1954, Bangkok, 1956; Leader Parl. Deleg. presenting Speaker's Chair and Mace to Ceylon Parl., 1949, and of Parl. Deleg. to Austria, 1948, Turkey, 1953; late Chm. British-American Parliamentary Group; Lecture Tour in U.S.A., 1953; Hon. Citizen, Texas State, U.S.A.; Hon. Member British Empire Club, Rhode Island, U.S.A.; Founder and First chm., Labour Party Services Cttee. and of Solicitors' Group, House of Commons; Mem. of Indian Franchise Cttee. 1932, of Cttee. Commonwealth Parl. Association, of Roy. Inst. of Internat. Affairs; and of many House of Commons Cttees.; Chairman: Select Cttee. Revising Standing Orders relating to Private Bills, 1945; Cttees. on Standing Orders on Public Bills, 1948; on Chairmen's Panel, House of Commons, 1935-43; Deputy Chairman of Ways and Means, Jan. 1943; Chairman of Ways and Means and Deputy Speaker of the House of Commons, 1943-45 and Aug. 1945-Oct. 1951; Chairman of the Fire Cttee. in charge of Civil Defence of the Houses of Parliament, etc., 1943-45. Mem. Cttee. on Standing Orders of House of Lords, 1953; former Peers' Rep., Nat. Counc. Labour. Former Dep. Speaker, House of Lords. *Recreations:* gardening, travel. *Heir:* *s.* Hon. Arthur James Michael Milner [*b.* 12 Sept. 1923; *m.* 1951, Sheila Margaret, *d.* of Gerald Hartley, of Weetwood, Leeds; one *s.* two *d.*]. *Address:* 34 and 35 Norfolk St., W.C.2. *T.:* Temple Bar 7608; Whitehall Court, S.W.1; Sanderson House, Leeds. *T.:* Leeds 20852; The Grove, Roundhay, Leeds, 8. *Clubs:* United Sports, Royal Automobile. [*Died* 16 *July* 1967.

MILNER, Thomas Stuart, R.W.S. 1953 (A.R.W.S. 1947); Artist and Designer; *b.* 27 April 1909; *yr. s.* of late Francis Henry Milner and late Lillian Jane Chandler; *m.* 1966, Joyce Mary Wellings, Bungay, Suffolk. *Educ.:* Sir George Monoux Gram. Sch., E.17; Central School of Arts and Crafts, Southampton Row. Practising as designer of Interior Decoration; Painter in oils and water colours, specialising in landscapes, still life and portraits. First exhibited in R.A., 1933; thereafter regularly; also at Paris Salon, and many other Galleries. Sometime R.B.A. Illustrated Articles in: The Studio, The Artist, etc. Works in London Museum and other public and private collections. *Publications:* Relevant publications; Biograph. details and illustr. in: The History of British Water-colour Painting by Adrian Bury, R.W.S.; Water-colour by Percy Bradshaw. *Recreations:* study of architectural antiquities; collecting and restoring antiques. *Address:* Home Farm, Thrandeston, Diss, Norfolk. [*Died* 10 *April* 1969.

MILNES GASKELL, Lady Constance, D.C.V.O. 1960 (C.V.O. 1953); Extra Lady-in-Waiting to Princess Marina, Duchess of Kent, since 1961; *b.* 21 April 1885; *d.* of 5th Earl of Ranfurly, P.C., G.C.M.G.; *m.* 1905, Evelyn Milnes Gaskell (*d.* 1931), *s.* of Rt. Hon. Charles Milnes Gaskell; one *d.* (one *s.* killed on active service, Coldstream Guards, 1943). *Educ.:* privately. Lady-in-Waiting to Queen Mary from Sept. 1937 until Her Majesty's death, 1953; Lady-in-Waiting to the Duchess of Kent, 1953-60. D.J.St.J. 1919. *Address:* St. Milburga, Much Wenlock, Shropshire. *T.:* Much Wenlock 289. *Clubs:* Lansdowne, Royal Over-Seas League. [*Died* 29 *April* 1964.

MINOR, Clark H(aynes), Hon. G.B.E. 1946; Chairman, Board of Trustees, Hamilton College, U.S.A.; *b.* 11 Dec. 1878; *s.* of

James Smith Minor and Mary Elizabeth Burrows; *m.* 1933, Allice C. Archibald. *Educ.:* Hamilton College, Clinton, N.Y. (Ph.B.). With Western Electric Co., 1902-1924: in N.Y. City office, 1902-04; Chicago office, 1904-05; Kansas City (Mo.) office, 1905-06; mgr. Omaha (Neb.) office, 1907-08, Kansas City office, 1908-09; mgr. dir. Bell Tel. Mfg. Co., Antwerp, Belgium, 1909-15, also dist. mgr. Internat. Western Elec. Co., 1912-15, acting for Sales mgr. N.Y. City, Central dist. mgr., Chicago, contract sales mgr., N.Y. City, 1915-16; organizer China Elec. Co. Ltd., Pekin, China, 1918; European comm'l mgr. Internat. Western Elec. Co., London, 1921-24; vice-pres., Internat. Gen. Elec. Co. Inc., 1924-25, pres., 1925-45. Chm. Courier Associates, Investments. Member: Newcomen Society of England; St. George's Society of New York; Society of the Cincinnati (Connecticut Chapter). Dr Eng., Rensselaer Poly. Inst., 1940; LL.D. Hamilton Coll., 1945. Holds several foreign orders. *Recreations:* sculpturing, fishing. *Address:* (business) 570 Lexington Ave., New York 22, N.Y., U.S.A.; (home) 730 Park Avenue, New York 21, N.Y., U.S.A. *Clubs:* American (London); Union Interalliée, Travellers' (Paris); Metropolitan (Washington); University (New York); Pilgrims of U.S., Ends of the Earth, India House, Canadian (N.Y.).
[*Died* 4 *Feb.* 1967.

MINORSKY, Vladimir, Corr. F.B.A. 1943; M.R.A.S., Doct. *h.c.* (Univ. Brussels), 1948; Litt.D. *h.c.* (Cantab.), 1963. Professor Emeritus, 1944, in Univ. of London; Hon. Fell. School of Oriental Studies, 1944; Hon. Member: Société Asiatique (Paris), 1946; Deutsche Morgenländische Gesellschaft, 1957; *b.* Korcheva, 6 February 1877; *s.* of Fedor M. Minorsky and Olga M. Golou-bitsky; *m.* 1913, Tatiana Schébounine. *Educ.:* University of Moscow (Faculty of Law); Institute of Oriental Languages, Moscow. Entered Russian Ministry of Foreign Affairs, 1903; served in Persia (Tabriz, Tehran) and travelled extensively in N.W. Persia, 1904-8; served in St. Petersburg and visited Russian Turkestan and Western Persia, 1908-12; 2nd Secretary Embassy in Constantinople, 1912; Imperial Russian Commissioner on Mixed Commission for delimitation of Turco-Persian frontier, 1913-1914; 1st Secretary and Councillor of Legation in Tehran, 1916-19; attached to Russian Embassy in Paris, 1919; Lecturer of Persian literature, Turkish and Oriental history at the École Nationale des Langues Orientales, Paris, 1923-34; Oriental Secretary to Persian Art Exhibition, London, 1930-31; Lecturer in Persian at London School of Oriental Studies, 1932; Reader in Persian in the University of London, 1933; Prof. of Persian in Univ. of London, 1938; Visiting Prof. Fuad I Univ., Cairo, 1948-49. Triennial Gold Medal, R.A.S., 1962. Hon. Member Inst. Peruano de Altos Estudios Islamicos, 1961; Member Assoc. de l'Académie des Inscriptions et Belles Lettres, France, 1963. *Publications:* A Visit to the Russian Cossacks in Asia Minor (in Russian), 1902; Matériaux sur la secte persane des Ahlé-Haqq (in Russian), 1911 (gold medal of the Sect. of Ethnography of Moscow); Notes sur les Ahlé-Haqq (in French), 1920-21; 110 articles in the Enc. of Islam (Leiden), 1925-36; Hudud al-Alam, a Persian geography of A.D. 982 (Gibb Memorial series), 1937; Marvazi on China, the Turks and India (Royal Asiatic Society), 1942; A Manual of Safavid Administration (Gibb M.S.), 1942; Studies in Caucasian History, 1953; Persia in 1478-1490 (R. Asiatic Society), 1957; History of Sharvan and Darband, 1958; Complete Bibliography in presentation volume of the Bulletin School of Oriental Studies, 1952; Iranica, 1964. *Recreation:* music. *Address:* 27 Bateman Street, Cambridge.
[*Died* 25 *March* 1966.

MIRRLEES, Maj.-Gen. William Henry Buchanan, C.B. 1945; D.S.O. 1941; M.C.; Colonel Commandant, Royal Regiment of Indian Artillery, 1945; *b.* 4 Oct. 1892; *s.* of W. J. Mirrlees, J.P., and Emily Lena Moncrieff, Mount Blow, Shelford, Cambs.; *m.* 1st, 1922, Iris Irma (marriage dissolved, 1927), *d.* of Sir George G. Leveson-Gower, K.B.E., M.P.; 2nd, 1931, Frances de La Lanne, Philadelphia, U.S.A. (*d.* 1962); no *c.* *Educ.:* Marlborough Coll.; R.M.A., Woolwich. Commissioned in R.F.A. 1912. Served European War, 1914-19 (M.C., Chevalier of the Legion of Honour); War of 1939-45 (D.S.O. and bar, C.B.); retired, 1946. Commander, Legion of Honour, 1954. *Recreation:* golf. *Address:* 115 Rue de la Pompe, Paris; 43 Avenue de Budé, Geneva. *Clubs:* Cavalry, Buck's; Travellers' (Paris).
[*Died* 22 *Oct.* 1964.

MIRZA, Maj.-Gen. Iskander, C.I.E. 1945; O.B.E. 1938; retired; *b.* 13 November 1899; *m.* 1934. *Educ.:* Elphinstone College, Bombay; Roy. Milit. Coll., Sandhurst. First cadet from continent of India to be gazetted into Army from R.M.C.; Cameronians (2nd Scottish Rifles), Kohat, 1921; 17th Poona Horse, Jhansi, 1924; selected for Indian Political Service, 1926, and served as Asst. Comr., Abbottabad, Bannu, Nowshera and Tank; Dep. Comr., Hazara and Mardan, 1931-36; Political Agent, Khyber 1938; Dep. Comr., Peshawar, 1940; Political Agent, Orissa States, 1945; Jt. Sec. to Govt. of India, Min. of Defence, 1946; Defence Secretary, Pakistan Govt., 1947; Governor, East Pakistan, 1954; Minister for Interior, States and Frontier Regions, Pakistan, 1954; Actg. Gov.-Gen. of Pakistan, Aug. 1955; Gov.-Gen., 1955; (first) Pres. of the Islamic Republic of Pakistan, 1956-58; left Pakistan after military coup d'état, 1958; now living in retirement in London. *Recreations:* riding, shooting and horse-racing; formerly cricket (blue, R.M.C.). *Address:* 49 Prince's Gate, S.W.7.
[*Died* 12 *Nov.* 1969.

MISA, Brigadier Lawrence Edward, D.S.O. 1940; O.B.E. 1945; *b.* 21 Feb. 1896; *s.* of V. P. Misa; unmarried. *Educ.:* Eton; R.M.C., Sandhurst. Joined 2nd Dragoon Guards, The Queen's Bays, 4 Aug. 1914 (Special Reserve); Regular Commission 4th Royal Irish Dragoon Guards, 1915; commanded 4/7 Royal Dragoon Guards, 1939-42; served European War, 1914-18 (wounded); war of 1939-45 (D.S.O., O.B.E.); retired pay, 1946. *Address:* Thuja, Bath Road, Marlborough, Wilts. *Clubs:* Cavalry, Royal Automobile.
[*Died* 9 *Feb.* 1968.

MISRA, Sir Lakshmipati, Kt., *cr.* 1944; General Manager, Hindustan Motors Ltd., Calcutta, since 1946; *b.* 4 July 1888; *s.* of Benarsi Das Misra, Mainpuri, United Provinces; *m.* 1905, Shyama, *d.* of Girwar Lal Chaturvedi; three *s.* one *d.* *Educ.:* Agra College; Thomason College of Engineering, Roorkee (B.Sc.). Joined Indian State Railways, 1911; lent to Baroda State as Engineer-in-Chief, Baroda State Railways, 1924; proceeded to Europe, 1927, to study Railways; Executive Engineer, East India Railway, 1928; on special duty with Rly. Bd., 1929, Controller of Stores, N.W. Rly., 1930; Dep. Gen. Man., E.I.R., 1932-35; Divl. Supt., E.I.R., Howrah, 1935-38; Mem. Fed. Public Service Commn., Govt. of India, 1938-39; Gen. Man., E. Bengal and Bengal & Assam Rly., 1939-43; Comr. for Port of Calcutta, 1939-43; Pres., Instn. of Engrs. (India), 1942-43. Burma Campaign, 1942-43 (despatches); Mem. (Eng.) Rly. Bd. (Govt. of India), 1943-44; Chief Comr. of Rlys., Rly. Bd., New Delhi, 1945; retired from railway service, 1945. Chairman, Machine Tool Panel, Govt. of India, 1948-49; Chm. Road Transport Development Cttee., U.P., 1948-1949; Pres. Indian Branch Inst. of Welding (London), 1949-53; Chairman, Road Transport Development Cttee., U.P., 1948-1949; Chm. Workshops Co-ordination & Development Cttee., U.P., 1950-51; Mem., Automobile Expert Cttee., India, 1950-51. Commandant, Calcutta Special Constabulary, 1950-; Mem. Nat. Railway Users' Consultative Council, 1953; Mem. Development Council for Internal Combustion Engines and Power Driven Pumps, Govt. of India, 1953-; Mem. Reviewing Cttee. on report of Railway Accidents Enquiry Cttee., 1954; Mem. Calcutta Advisory Panel, Central Board of Film Censors, 1951-56; Mem. Indian Railway Equipment Cttee., 1955-56; Mem. Fact Finding Cttee. to make recommendations for development of new Industries in U.P., 1956; Chm. Advisory Cttee. of Calcutta branch, Indian Standard Instn., 1956-; Pres., Calcutta Branch, Indian Roads and Transport Development Assoc. Ltd., 1960-62; Chm. Assoc. of Indian Automobile Manufacturers, 1961-62. Mem. Central Posts and Telegraphs Advisory Council, Min. of Transport and Communications, 1962-. Dr. of Engineering, Univ. of Roorkee, 1959. *Address:* c/o Birla Brothers Private Ltd., 15 India Exchange Place, Calcutta 1, India. *Clubs:* Delhi Gymkhana (Delhi); Chelmsford (New Delhi); Calcutta, Calcutta South (Calcutta); Boathouse (Naini Tal). [*Died* 8 *Feb.* 1964.

MITCHELL, Sir Angus (Sinclair), Kt. 1956; Director: Australian Cement Ltd.; Australian Portland Cement Pty. Ltd.; Noske Industries Ltd.; Noske Flour Mills Pty. Ltd.; Queen's Bridge Motor and Engineering Co. Pty. Ltd.; Queen's Bridge Investments Pty. Ltd.; *b.* Shanghai, 1 Apr. 1884; *s.* of James Alexander Mitchell, Aberdeen, Scotland, and Elizabeth Anderson, Melbourne; *m.* 1910, Teenie Robertson McKenzie; three *d.* *Educ.:* Scotch Coll., Melbourne. Pres. Vic. Soc. for Crippled Children; Pres. Rotary Internat., 1948-49. Hon. Treas. Boy Scouts Assoc. (Vic. Branch); Hon. Treas. Australian Boy Scouts Assoc.; Dir. Y.M.C.A. of Melbourne; Trustee Victorian Overseas Foundation. Hon. Dr. of Laws, Baylor Univ., Waco, Texas, U.S.A. *Address:* Hotel Windsor, Spring St., Melbourne, Vic., Australia. [*Died* 16 *Aug.* 1961.

MITCHELL, Arthur James, O.B.E. 1948; Resident Engineer for Water Supply Scheme in East Kesteven, Lincolnshire, since 1955; *b.* 18 November 1893; *s.* of John Robert Mitchell, M.A., and Agnes Mackie (*née* Thomson); *m.* 1926, Doreen Milnes Harris; two *s.* *Educ.:* Montrose Academy, Scotland. Pupil with G Somervel Carfrae, Civil Engineer, Edinburgh, 1912-17 (served European War, 1914-16, with Royal Scots, in France); Assistant Engineer, Westminster City Council, and H.M. Office of Works, Dover Naval Dockyard, 1917-19; Engineer and Partner, John P. Mitchell, Public Works Contractor, Egypt, Sudan and Palestine, 1919-27; various posts including Water Engineer, Dep. and Actg. Director of Public Works, Government of Tanganyika, 1930-49; Director, Colonial Development Corporation, 1949-51; Regional Controller, Colonial Development Corporation, for Central Africa and the High Commission Territories, 1951-53. Member of the Institution of Civil Engineers; Mem. Inst. of Water Engineers. *Publications:* various contributions to Technical Societies and Journals on engineering subjects. *Recreations:* golf, bridge, etc. *Address:* Seeley's End, Baring Crescent, Beaconsfield, Bucks *T.* Beaconsfield 1108. *Clubs:* Royal Commonwealth Society; Beaconsfield Golf. [*Died* 12 *Nov.* 1967.

MITCHELL, Sir David George, K.C.I.E., 1936 (C.I.E. 1923); C.S.I. 1932; I.C.S. retd.; *b.* 1879; *s.* of Alexander Mitchell; *m.* 1906, Elizabeth Duncan Wharton; one *d.* *Educ.:* George Heriot's School, Edinburgh; Edinburgh University (B.Sc); Oxford University, Entered I.C.S. 1903; District Judge, 1916; Legal Secretary to Government Central Provinces, and Secretary, Legislative Council, 1919; Joint Secretary to the Government of India, Legislative Department, 1927; Secretary to Government of India, Industries and Labour Department, 1933; officiated as Member of the Viceroy's Executive Council, 1935; retired, 1937. *Address:* The Hope, Moffat, Dumfriesshire. [*Died* 10 *March* 1963.

MITCHELL, Edward Rosslyn, M.A., LL.B.; J.P.; solicitor senior partner, Rosslyn Mitchell & Son, Glasgow; *b.* 16 May 1879; *m.* 1st, 1907, Constance Regina (*d.* 1936), *d.* of late James T. Bell, tobacco manufacturer, Glasgow; one *s.* one *d.*: 2nd, Marguerite Antoinette Marie, *d.* of Donald Ferguson; one *d.* *Educ.:* Hillhead High School and University, Glasgow. President Students' Representative Council, 1901, entered Town Council of Glasgow, 1909; resigned, 1925, re-elected, 1932; Magistrate, 1913; contested (L.) Buteshire, 1910; (Soc.) Glasgow Central, 1922; Glasgow Central, 1923; M.P. (Soc.) Paisley, 1924-29; Governor Royal Scottish Academy of Music. *Publications:* Impressions, 1932; Ladies and Gentlemen: The Craft of Public Speaking, 1933; Passing By, 1935; Many Phases, 1937. *Recreations:* golf, bicycling, gardening. *Address:* 18 Woodside Place, Glasgow; 25 Queensborough Gardens, Glasgow, W.2. [*Died* 31 *Oct.* 1965.

MITCHELL, Sir James, Kt. 1959; C.B.E. 1953; *b.* 30 May 1905; *s.* of late William Mitchell and Agnes Scott Mitchell; *m.* 1935, Edith Theresa Bona; one *s.* *Educ.:* Rothesay Academy. Clydesdale Bank Ltd., 1920; Harrisons and Crosfield (Borneo) Ltd., 1927-1959. *Address:* Mill Lane, South Harting, Nr. Petersfield, Hants. [*Died* 25 *April* 1968.

MITCHELL, Sir Kenneth Grant, K.C.I.E., *cr.* 1946 (C.I.E. 1934); Kt., *cr.* 1941; F.C.G.I.; M.I.C.E.; M.Inst.T.; lately Chief Controller Road Transport and Development, Government of India, Dept. of War Transport; County Chief Warden, Civil Defence Corps, W. Suffolk, 1953-59; *b.* 28 Aug. 1885; *s.* of late Capt. Hugh Mitchell, R.E.; *m.* 1911, Lilian (*d.* 1938), *d.* of late Edward Westlake, Southampton; (one *s.* killed in Italy, 1942) one *d.* Assistant Engineer, Indian Service of Engineers, 1909; Executive Engineer, 1917; Temp. Capt. R.E., India, 1917-19; Under-Secretary, Punjab Govt., 1919; Road Engineer with Govt. of India, 1930; Consulting Engineer to Govt. of India, Roads, 1934-42. Retired, 1946. *Address:* St. Michael's House, Peckham Bush, Tonbridge, Kent. *Club:* East India and Sports. [*Died* 23 *Sept.* 1966.

MITCHELL, Oliver Worden; *b.* 7 March 1898; 4th *s.* of Charles Mitchell, London; *m.* 1929, Jean, *yr. d.* of John S. Wingate, J.P., Greenock; two *s.* one *d.* *Educ.:* Owen's Sch.; Magdalen Coll., Oxford. Observer and Pilot, R.N.A.S. and R.A.F., 1916-19; Exhibitioner and honorary Academic Clerk at Magdalen College, Oxford, 1919-21; Senior English and History Master, and House Master, King William's College, Isle of Man, 1921-1932; Headmaster, The King's School, Peterborough, 1932-39; Headmaster, Owen's School, 1939-48; Headmaster, Royal Grammar School, Newcastle upon Tyne, 1948-60. F.R.S.A. 1949. Member: Educational Advisory Council of R.A.F.; Professional Classes Aid Council; and of Girls' Public Day School Trust. Governor, Hamilton House School, Tunbridge Wells. *Recreation:* golf. *Address:* The Cedar House, Butlers Cross, Aylesbury, Bucks. *Club:* Savage. [*Died* 25 *Oct.* 1963.

MITCHELL, Maj.-Gen. Sir Philip Euen, G.C.M.G., *cr.* 1947 (K.C.M.G., *cr.* 1937, C.M.G. 1933); M.C.; *b.* 1 May 1890; 5th *s.* of late Captain Hugh Mitchell (late R.E.); *m.* 1925, Margery, *d.* of late John D'Urban Tyrwhitt Drake; no *c.* *Educ.:* privately; St. Paul's School; Trinity College, Oxford. Assistant Resident, Nyasaland, 1912; Lieut. K.A.R., 1915; Captain, 1917; Adjutant, 1917-18 (M.C., despatches); A.D.C. and private secretary to acting Governor, Nyasaland, 1918-19; Assistant Political Officer, Tanganyika Territory, 1919; Assistant Secretary, Native Affairs, 1926; Provincial Commissioner, 1928; Secretary for Native Affairs, Tanganyika Territory, 1928; Chief Sec. 1934-35; Governor and Commander-in-Chief, Uganda, 1935-40; Deputy Chairman of Conference of East African Governors, 1940; Political Adviser to General Sir Archibald Wavell, 1941; British Plenipotentiary in Ethiopia and Chief Political Officer on Staff of G.O.C.-in-C. East Africa, 1942; Governor of Fiji and High Commissioner for Western, Pacific, 1942-44; Governor and C.-in-C. Kenya 1944-52. *Publication:* African Afterthoughts; 1954. *Recreations:* golf, shooting, fishing. *Clubs:* Savile, Little Ship.
[*Died* 11 *Oct.* 1964.

MITCHELL, Col. Thomas John, D.S.O. 1918; late Member Board of Management Perthshire General Hospitals; late Medical Member Pensions Appeal Tribunals for Scotland; late Hon. Lecturer, Anatomy Department, and Regent University of St. Andrews; late R.A.M.C.; *b.* 2 Oct. 1882; *s.* of Robert Mitchell, J.P., Perth, and Mary Rollo; *m.* 1914, Blanche Katherine, *d.* of Robert Bruce, M.D., F.R.C.S., Edinburgh. *Educ.:* Perth Academy; George Watson's College, Edinburgh; St. Andrews University. M.B., Ch.B. with distinction 1904, M.D. 1908, Ch.M. 1925, St. Andrews University. Entered R.A.M.C. 1908; served India, 1910-14; European War, 1914-19, France, Egypt, Mesopotamia, O.C. No. 7. B.F.A.; D.A.D.M.S. 15th Indian Division; Brevet Major 1916 (D.S.O., despatches five times); Bt. Lt.-Col., 1930; Assistant Editor Official Medical History of War, 1920-24; Editor, 1928-31; (with Miss G. M. Smith, M.A., M.B.E.) final vol. of War Casualties and Medical Statistics; D.A.D.G. War Office, 1924-28; D.A.D.M.S. Egypt, 1931; retired 1931; re-employed A.D.M.S., Sept. 1939-42. *Publications:* Memoirs of a Motorist; Joint Editor General History Official Medical History of the Great War, Vol. IV, and Casualties and Medical Statistics final volume; articles in Diseases of the War, Volumes 1 and 2. *Recreations:* shooting, fishing, golf (Captain, Royal Perth Golfing Soc., 1953-54; Mem. Rules of Golf Cttee. Royal and Ancient, 1938-54; late Mem. General Cttee., Championship Cttee., Royal and Ancient), motoring. *Address:* c/o Lloyds Bank Ltd., 16 St. James's St., S.W.1. *Clubs:* Caledonian; New, Caledonian United Service (Edinburgh); Royal and Ancient (St. Andrews); Hon. Company of Edinburgh Golfers (Muirfield); Prestwick Golf (Prestwick, Ayrshire); Royal County (Perth).
[*Died* 17 *Jan.* 1966.

MITCHELL, Sir William, K.C.M.G., *cr.* 1927; M.A., D.Sc., Litt.D.; Emeritus Professor of Philosophy, University of Adelaide, South Australia, since 1942; formerly Vice-Chancellor and Chancellor; *b.* Inveravon, Banffshire, Scotland, 27 March 1861; *s.* of P. Mitchell; *m.* Margery Erlistoun (*decd.*), *d.* of R. Barr Smith, Adelaide; one *s.* one *d.* *Educ.:* Edinburgh University. Was Lecturer on Ethics, Edinburgh University, and on Education, University College, London; Gifford Lecturer in Aberdeen University for 1924-27. *Publications:* Structure and Growth of the Mind, 1907; The Place of Minds in the World, 1933. *Address:* Fitzroy Terrace, Prospect, S. Australia. [*Died* 25 *June* 1962.

MITCHELL-COTTS, Sir Campbell; *see* Cotts, Sir W. C. M.

MITCHESON, John Moncaster Ley, C.M.G. 1942; O.B.E. 1939; *b.* 28 May 1893; *er. s.* of late Richard Edmond Mitcheson, Asst. Sec., Bd. of Education; *m.* 1925, Mrs. Valerie Violet Marley, *yr. d.* of late E. Howard Stafford. *Educ.:* Winchester; St. John's College, Oxford. Acting Vice-Consul, 1914; 2nd Lieut. Royal Marines, 1917; Vice-Consul, 1919; Consul, 1924; transferred to Commercial Diplomatic Service, 1935; Commercial Counsellor Warsaw, 1938 and Stockholm, 1940; Dir.-Gen., Commercial Br., C.C.G. (British Element), 1945; Consul-Gen., Batavia, 1947; Dep. High Comr. for U.K. in India, 1947-49; Consul-General, San Francisco, 1949-52; retired, 1952. *Recreations:* gardening, walking, swimming. *Address:* Grove Hill House, Nr. Hailsham, Sussex.
[*Died* 2 *Sept.* 1966.

MITCHISON, Baron *cr.* 1964 (Life Peer); **Gilbert Richard Mitchison,** C.B.E. 1953; Q.C. 1946; *b.* 23 March 1890; *s.* of late Arthur Maw Mitchison and late Mary Emmeline Russell; *m.* 1916, Naomi M. Haldane (Naomi M. Mitchison); three *s.* two *d.* *Educ.:* Eton; New College, Oxford. Service in Queen's Bays and Staff appointments, 1914-18, finally as Major, G.S.O. 2, British Mission to French Forces in Italy (French Croix de Guerre). Barrister, Inner Temple, 1917. Contested (Lab.) King's Norton (Birm.), 1931 and 1935; M.P. (Lab.) Kettering Div., Northants, 1945-64. Joint Parliamentary Secretary, Ministry of Land and Natural Resources, 1964-66. Mem., Harlow Development Corp., 1966-. *Publications:* First Workers' Government, 1934; various chapters and articles, etc. on economic, social and legal subjects. *Recreation:* fishing. *Address:* Carradale House, Carradale, Argyll. *T.:* Carradale 234; 2 Harcourt Buildings, Temple, E.C.4. *T.:* 01-353 2193. *Club:* Athenæum.
[*Died* 14 *Feb.* 1970.

MITRA, Sir Dhirendra Nath, Kt., *cr.* 1944; C.B.E. 1939; Assoc. K.St.J., 1949; Chairman: Durgapur Projects Ltd.; United Industrial Bank Ltd.; Richardson & Cruddas Ltd.; Durgapur Chemicals Ltd.; Director or Chairman of 20 other Cos. and Corps.; Secretary to the President of India, 1952; Legal Adviser and Solicitor to the High Commissioner for India in the U.K.; Solicitor for Government of India, New Delhi; *b.* 18 April 1891; *s.* of Upendranath Mitra; *m.* 1916, Suchandra, *d.* of S. C. Mallik; two *d.* *Educ.:* St. Xavier's Coll.; Presidency Coll.; Univ. Coll., Calcutta. Solicitor of Supreme Court, England; rep. at World Health Assembly, U.N. Conf. on Freedom of Information and Adviser U.N. Conf. on Human Rights; Governor League of Red Cross Socs.; Leader of Indian Deleg. to the Diplomatic Conf. for Establishment of Internat. Conventions for protection of war victims. Sheriff of Calcutta, 1954; Chief Adviser, Hindusthan Co-operative Insurance Society, Ltd., 1952-54; formerly: Minister on the High Commission for India; Chairman Banks' Liquidation Proceedings Committee, 1952. Hon. Doctorate, Visva-Bharati University. Member Executive Council, Rabindra Bharati University. *Recreation:* walking. *Address:* 7 Ballygunge Circular Rd., Calcutta. *T.:* 44.5278. *Clubs:* Calcutta, Royal Calcutta Turf (Calcutta).
[*Died* 31 *Dec.* 1966.

MITRA, Professor Sisir Kumar, M.B.E. 1936; F.R.S. 1958; Emeritus Professor of Physics, University of Calcutta, since 1956; National Research Professor, 1962; *b.* 24 October 1890; *s.* of late Joykrishna and Saratkumari Mitra; *m.* 1914, Lilavati (*d.* 1939), *d.* of Rai Bahadur Harakisore Biswas,

Barisal (Bengal); one *s.* (and two *s.* decd.). *Educ.:* Calcutta University; Sorbonne, Paris. Joined University of Calcutta as Lecturer in Physics, 1916; Khaira Professor of Physics, Calcutta University, 1923; Sir Rashbehary Ghose Professor of Physics, Calcutta University, 1938-55, retired. *Publications:* Active Nitrogen (Monograph), 1945; The Upper Atmosphere, 2nd revised edn., 1952 (transl. into Russian by Russian Acad. of Sciences); numerous other scientific papers. *Recreations:* walking; chess. *Address:* 9 Hindusthan Road, Calcutta 29, India. *T.:* 46-1041; Institute of Radio Physics and Electronics, 92 Upper Circular Road, Calcutta, India. *T.:* 35-1319. *Club:* Chakra Baithak (Calcutta, India).
[*Died* 13 *Aug.* 1963.

MITTELHOLZER, Edgar Austin; professional writer since 1952; *b.* 16 Dec. 1909; *s.* of William Austin and Rosamond Mabel Mittelholzer (*née* Leblanc); *m.* 1st, 1942, Roma Erica Halfhide (marriage dissolved, 1958); two *s.* two *d.*; 2nd, 1960, Jacqueline Rose Pointer; one *s.* *Educ.:* various private schools; Berbice High School, New Amsterdam, British Guiana. Casual Customs officer, agricultural asst. and meteorological observer, cinema inspector, free lance journalist, hotel receptionist until 1941. Enlisted Trinidad Royal Naval Volunteer Reserve, 1941. Came to London, 1948. Employed Books Dept., British Council, 1948-52. Guggenheim Fellow, 1952. *Publications: novels:* Corentyne Thunder, 1941; A Morning at the Office, 1950; Shadows Move Among Them, 1951; Children of Kaywana, 1952; The Weather in Middenshot, 1952; The Life and Death of Sylvia, 1953; The Harrowing of Hubertus, 1954; My Bones and My Flute, 1955; Of Trees and the Sea, 1956; A Tale of Three Places, 1957; Kaywana Blood, 1958; The Weather Family, 1958; A Tinkling in the Twilight, 1959; Latticed Echoes, 1960; Eltonsbrody, 1960; Thunder Returning, 1961; The Mad Macmullochs, 1961; The Piling of Clouds, 1961; The Wounded and the Worried, 1962; Uncle Paul, 1963; *non-fiction:* With a Carib Eye, 1958; A Swarthy Boy, 1963. *Recreations:* walking, observing the weather (amateur meteorologist), reading, and listening to the music of Wagner. *Address:* Loushall House Cottage, Dippenhall, Farnham, Surrey. *T.:* Farnham 4750.
[*Died* 6 *May* 1965.

MOBERLY, Lieut.-General Sir Bertrand Richard, K.C.I.E., *cr.* 1937; C.B. 1929; D.S.O. 1915; p.s.c.; Indian Army, retired; *b.* 15 Oct. 1877; 2nd *s.* of late John Cornelius Moberly, Bassett, Southampton; *m.* 1910, Hylda (*d.* 1955), *e. d.* of late Arthur Clevedon Willis, Union Bank of Australia, Ltd.; two *d.* *Educ.:* Winchester; Royal Military College, Sandhurst; Staff College, Camberley. 2nd Lieutenant, Indian Army, Unattached List, 1897; Indian Army, 1899; joined 2nd Punjab Infantry, Punjab Frontier Force, 1900; served in North-West Frontier of India, 1901-2 and 1930; Somaliland, 1903-4 (despatches); European War, 1914-18 (despatches five times); Brevet Lieutenant-Colonel, 1918; Brevet Col., 1921; Major-General, 1930; Lieut.-Gen., 1938; retired, 1940; Red Cross Commissioner, India, 1940-43. *Recreation:* sketching. *Address:* Stoneham, Lymington, Hants. *T.:* Lymington 2731.
[*Died* 17 *Feb.* 1963.

MOBERLY, Charles Noel, C.I.E. 1919; V.D.; late Gen. Man., The Bombay Electric Supply and Tramways Co., Ltd., Bombay; *b.* 24 Dec. 1880; *s.* of George Ernest Moberly, Ipswich; *m.* 1908, Kate Charlotte (*d.* 1961), 2nd *d.* of John Edward Fottrell, Dublin; two *d.* (and one *s.* one *d.* decd.). *Educ.:* Rugby. Served engineering pupilage with the Brush Electrical Engineering Co. Ltd., Loughborough, by whom sent to Bombay after 2 years technical training at the Yorkshire College, Leeds; Member of the Institution of Civil Engineers; awarded C.I.E. for services during the Great War; Lieut.-Colonel, Indian Defence Force (retired); awarded V.D. *Recreation:* gardening. *Address:* Teddars Leas House, Etchinghill, Folkestone. *T.:* Lyminge 87515. *Clubs:* Radnor (Folkestone); Yacht (Bombay).
[*Died* 1 *Jan.* 1969.

MODY, Sir Homi, K.B.E. 1935; M.A., LL.B.; Chairman: Central Bank of India Ltd.; Indian Hotels Co. Ltd.; Patron-in-Chief, Cricket Club of India Ltd.; Sir Dorab Tata Trust; Life President: Indo-American Society; Indian Council of World Affairs, Bombay Branch; *b.* 23 September 1881. *Educ.:* St. Xavier's College, Bombay. Member Indian Legislative Assembly, 1929-1943 and Constituent Assembly, 1948-49; First Round Table Conf., 1929, and Reserve Bank Cttee. of the Conf., 1934; Employers' delegate, Internat. Labour Conf., Geneva, 1937; Mem. for Supply, Viceroy's Exec. Council, 1941-43; Governor of Bombay, September 1947; Governor of U.P., 1949-1952. Ex-Director, Tata Sons Ltd. Past President or Chairman of: Millowners' Association, Bombay; Bombay Municipal Corp.; Indian Merchants' Chamber; Associated Cement Cos. Ltd.; Tata Group of Hydro-Electric Companies; Indian Banks Assoc. (Founder and first President); Indian Inst. of Art-in-Industry; Employers' Fedn. of India. F.R.S.A. Hon. LL.D.: Banaras, Aligarh and Poona Univs.; D.Litt., Agra Univ.; Grand Commander, Order of George I of Greece. *Publications:* The Political Future of India, 1908; Biography of Sir Pherozeshah Mehta, 1921 (2nd edn. 1964); Reflections, Wise and otherwise, 1961. *Address:* Spirospero, Carmichael Rd., Bombay, India. *Clubs:* Royal Automobile, Royal Over-Seas League, International Sportsmen's (London); Willingdon Sports, Royal Western India Turf (Past Pres.); Cricket Club of India (Bombay). [*Died* 9 *March* 1969.

MOFFATT, Paul McGregor, F.R.C.S.; Surgeon, Moorfields, Eye Hospital; Ophth. Surgeon: Hammersmith and West London Hosps.; Ophthalmic Consultant, L.C.C. Central Medical Staff, etc. *Educ.:* Guy's Hosp. M.R.C.S. Eng., L.R.C.P. Lond. 1923; M.B., B.S. 1924; D.P.H. 1930; D.O.M.S. 1932; M.R.C.P. Lond. 1933; M.D. Lond. 1933; F.R.C.S. Eng. 1937. F.R.Soc.Med. (late Vice-Pres. Ophth. Section); Mem. Ophthalmological Soc. of the U.K.; Mem. Société Française d'Ophthalmologie. *Publications:* Aids to Ophthalmology, 11th edn., 1957; contributions to medical journals. *Address:* 73 Harley Street, W.1. [*Died* 27 *Aug.* 1963.

MOHAN SINGH, Sardar Bahadur Sardar, C.I.E. 1941; Landlord and House Proprietor; Director Punjab National Bank Ltd. and several other Companies; *b.* 6 June 1897; *s.* of Sardar Hardit Singh; *m.* Laj Mohan Singh, Sardarni; three *s.* *Educ.*. Government College and Aitchison Chiefs' College, Lahore, India. Member Secretary of State for India's Council, London, 1935-37 and then Adviser to the Secretary of State for India, 1937-40; Member Punjab and N.W.F.P. Joint Public Service Commission, 1943-47; Chairman Patiala and East Punjab States Union Public Service Commission, 1948-56. Life Member Royal Over-Seas League, London; Red Cross Society; Life Patron of Provincial Boy Scouts' Association; was President Sikh Educational Conference. Takes special interest in Educational, Temperance, Social, Religious and other public activities; Vice-President World Fellowship of Faiths, London. *Address:* 23/39 Kautilya Marg, New Delhi. *Clubs:* Royal Over-Seas League; Delhi Gymkhana (New Delhi); National Sports Club of India. [*Died* 27 *Dec.* 1961

MOISEIWITSCH, Benno, C.B.E. 1946; Pianist; *b.* Odessa, 22 February 1890; *s.* of David Leon and Esther Miropolsky; granted certificate of British naturalisation, 1937; *m.* 1st, 1914; two *d.*; 2nd, 1929; one *s.* *Educ.:* Imperial School of Music, Odessa (Rubinstein Prize at age of 9); Vienna, under Leschetitzky, 1905-8; in England since 1908; début at Queen's Hall, London, 1909, achieving instantaneous success; now one of the world's great pianists. Has travelled extensively; 7 visits to Australia, New Zealand, and Tasmania; 3 to the Far East and Dutch East Indies; 4 to South America; over 20 to U.S.A. and Canada; 3 to South Africa; visited most countries on the Continent, 1936. He gave 100 concerts for Mrs. Churchill's Aid to Russia Fund, and played for many other charities during the War of 1939-45. World Tour, 1948. *Relevant Publication:* Moiseiwitsch by Maurice Moiseiwitsch, 1965. *Recreation:* golf. *Clubs:* Savage, Devonshire.
[*Died* 9 *April* 1963.

MOLD, Brigadier Gilbert Leslie, C.I.E. 1946; Indian Army (retd.); *b.* 3 Sept. 1893; *s.* of Charles Mold, Oxfordshire; *m.* 1928, Barbara Honor, *d.* of late Sir Hugh Crosthwaite, C.I.E. *Educ.:* Merton College, Oxford. Commissioned Oct. 1914, in T.A.; regular commission Indian Army, 1916; served European War, 1914-18, N.W.F.P., India, Mesopotamia, Palestine; War of 1939-45, Comdt. Trng. Bn., 15 Punjab Regt., 1939-41; G.H.Q. India, 1941-46; Director of Personal Services, G.H.Q., India, 1943-46; retired, 1946. *Address:* Kyrenia, Cyprus.
[*Died* 26 *July* 1963.

MOLE, Sir Charles Johns, K.B.E., *cr.* 1953 (O.B.E. 1942; M.B.E. 1920); Kt., *cr.* 1947; M.V.O. 1937; F.R.I.B.A.; Director-Gen. of Works, Ministry of Works, 1946-58, retired; *b.* 1886; *s.* of late Charles and Mary Mole, Broadhempston, Devon; *m.* 1913, Annie (*d.* 1962), *d.* of Richard Hugh Martin, Plymouth; one *s.* two *d.*; *m.* 1962, Marjorie, *d.* of late Capt. F. W. Butt-Thompson. *Educ.:* Lipson Gram. Sch. H.M. Office of Works, 1911. Architect to Coronation of King George VI. *Address:* Broadston, Ashley Drive, Walton-on-Thames. *T.:* 20710.
[*Died* 4 *Dec.* 1962.

MOLESWORTH, 10th Viscount (*cr.* 1716); **Charles Richard Molesworth;** Baron Philipstown, 1716; *b.* 3 Jan. 1869; 2nd *s.* of 8th Viscount Molesworth and Georgina, *d.* of George Bagot Gosset, 4th Dragoon Guards; *S.* brother 1947; *m.* 1906, Elizabeth Gladys, *d.* of late Edwin Martin Langworthy; one *s.* (and one died on active service) one *d.* *Heir:* *s.* Hon. Richard Gosset Molesworth [*b.* 31 Oct. 1907; *m.* 1958, Mrs. Florence Womersley (*née* Cohen); one *s.*]. *Address:* 29 Clarendon Road, St. Heliers, Jersey, C.I.
[*Died* 24 *Feb.* 1961.

MOLESWORTH, Lt.-Gen. George Noble, C.S.I. 1941; C.B.E. 1958 (O.B.E. 1950) p.s.c.; i.d.c.; Col. 4/15th Punjab Regt. 1941-60; Hon. Col. 12/Punjab Regt. 1961; *b.* 14 July 1890; *e. s.* of late Henry B. Molesworth, and *g. s.* of late Sir Guilford Molesworth; *m.* 1927, Marjorie Frances, *d.* of late B. F. Simpson; no *c.* *Educ.:* Bradfield College; R.M.C., Sandhurst. 2nd Lieut Somerset Light Infantry, 1910; Adjt. 2nd Somerset L.I., 1916-19; served in Malta, North China, and India (Great War Medal); 3rd Afghan War, 1919 (medal and clasp, despatches); D.A.A.G., A.H.Q., 1919-21 and 1924; Brigade Major, 1925; D.A.Q.M.G., A.H.Q., 1926-27; transferred to Indian Army, 15th Punjab Regiment, 1928; Instructor, Staff College, Quetta, 1929-33; Bt. Lieutenant-Colonel, 1932; commanded 4/15th Punjab Regiment 1934-36; Imperial Defence College, 1935; Deputy Director of Military Operations and Intelligence, India, 1936-38, Director, 1938-41; Deputy Chief of General Staff, Army Headquarters, India, 1941-42; Sec. Military Dept., India Office, 1943-44; retired, 1945. Member, Nat. Savings Cttee. for Southern Region, 1949-60; Vice-President H nts. Scout Council, 1966. *Publications:* Notes on Infantry Machine Guns, 1915; History of the Somerset Light Infantry (1919-45), 1951; edited, annotated and produced the maps for the Diary of Arthur Cook and published it privately as A Soldier's War, 1958; Three Centuries of Parish Life, 1960; Sancta Cruce de Durie, 1961; Afghanistan 1919, 1963; Curfew on Olympus, 1966. *Address:* c/o Lloyds Bank Ltd., 6 Pall Mall, S.W.1.
[*Died* 7 *Jan.* 1968.

MOLLISON, William Mayhew, C.B.E. 1920; M.A., M.Ch. Cantab., F.R.C.S. Eng. 1905; retired; *b.* 20 Dec. 1878; *o. s.* of late W. L. Mollison; *m.* 1908, Beatrice Marjory Walker; (d. 1966) three *s.* two *d.* *Educ.:* Haileybury Coll.; King's College, Cambridge (Exhibitioner and Prizeman); Guy's Hospital; Vienna; Berlin. Arthur Durham Travelling Student, Guy's Hospital. Formerly Consulting Aurist and Laryngologist to Guy's Hospital. *Publications:* various papers in medical journals. *Recreation:* golf. *Address:* Picket Hill, Ringwood, Hants. *T.:* Ringwood 3845.
[*Died* 18 *Jan.* 1967.

MOLONEY, Henry J., S.C.; member of the Munster Circuit; *b.* Oldcourt, Skibbereen, 19 Aug. 1887; *e. s.* of late John Moloney, solicitor, Midleton; *m.* 1915, Josephine, *d.* of late Denis O'Mahony, Midleton; one *s.* three *d.* *Educ.:* University School, Skibbereen; Presentation College, Cork; Queen's College, Cork; King's Inns, Dublin. John Brooke Scholar, 1909; called to Irish Bar, 1909; Professor of Real Property and Equity, University College, Cork (N.U.I.), 1912-24; called to the Inner Bar, 1927; Bencher of Kings Inns, 1939; Member Committee dealing with reform of the law relating to Medical Practitioners medical education and research, 1947; Mem. Cttee. to deal with reform of Company Law, 1950; Mem. Council, Civics Institute of Ireland (Pres. 1947-52); Mem. Photographic Soc. of Ireland. *Publications:* The Law relating to Criminal Injury. *Address:* Cranna, Cowper Road, Rathmines, Dublin. *T.:* Dublin 971681. *Clubs:* National Liberal; United Service, Milltown Golf (Dublin).
[*Died* 18 *July* 1965.

MOLONY, Rev. Brian Charles, O.B.E., T.D., M.A.; Rector of Easton, 1953-59; Headmaster, Worksop College, 1936-52; Hon. Canon of Dunham in Southwell Cathedral from 1939; Rural Dean of Winchester from 1958; *b.* 25 Oct. 1892; *s.* of Henry William Elliot Molony and Edith Gertrude Marian Tatham; *m.* 1917; one *s.* three *d.* *Educ.:* Rugby (Scholar); Trinity College, Cambridge (Scholar). 1st Class Maths. Tripos Part I., 1912; Part II, 1914; Bell University Scholar. Served with 1st Herts Regt. in France, 1914-18; Staff Captain, 5th Army, later at G.H.Q., 1918; Assistant Master Rugby School, 1919-35; House Master Rugby School, 1927-35; deacon, 1920; priest, 1921. *Publications:* Analytical Geometry; Numerical Trigonometry. *Recreation:* climbing. *Club:* Authors'. [*Died* 17 *Oct.* 1963.

MOLYNEUX, Sir John (Harry), Kt. 1966; O.B.E. 1956; *b.* 29 March 1882; *m.* 1906, Mary Annie, *d.* of John Burton, Stafford; two *d.* (and one *s.* decd. on active service). *Educ.:* Owen Street Council Sch., Dudley. Engineers' Wood Patternmaker, retd. 1955. Mem., Dudley Borough Coun., 1919-66. J.P. 1926-57; now on supplemental list. *Address:* 28 Bunns Lane, Dudley, Worcs.
[*Died* 6 *Feb.* 1968.

MONCK, Sir John Berkeley, G.C.V.O., *cr.* 1950 (K.C.V.O., *cr.* 1938; C.V.O. 1926); C.M.G. 1934; an Extra Gentleman Usher to the Queen since 1952 (to King George VI, 1950-52); *b.* 18 Dec. 1883; *yr. s.* of late W. B. Monck of Coley Park, Reading, and Althea, *e. d.* of Captain Charles Fanshawe. *Educ.:* Eton. Hon. Attaché in H.M. Diplomatic Service, 1907-17; served in St. Petersburg, Berlin, The Hague; Second Secretary at Paris, 1917-19; Assistant Marshal of the Diplomatic Corps, 1920-36; Vice-Marshal, 1936-45, acting as Marshal, 1939-45; resigned from Foreign Office, 1945, on appt. as H.M. Marshal of the Diplomatic Corps, 1945-50; Grand Officer of the Legion of Honour; Commander of Orders of Leopold and of the Nile; Grand Officer of Order of the Star of Roumania. *Address:* c/o Messrs. Child & Co., 1 Fleet Street, E.C.4. *Clubs:* Travellers', St. James', Brooks's. [*Died* 31 *March* 1964.

MONCKTON OF BRENCHLEY, 1st Visc. *cr.* 1957; **Walter Turner Monckton,** P.C. 1951; G.C.V.O. 1964 (K.C.V.O. 1937); K.C.M.G. 1945; M.C. 1919; Q.C. 1930; Hon. D.C.L. (Oxon.) 1952; Hon. LL.D. (Bristol) 1954; Hon. LL.D. (Sussex), 1963; Director, Midland Bank Ltd. and Midland Bank Executor and Trustee Co. Ltd. (Chairman, 1957-64); Chairman: Iraq Petroleum Company; Committee of London Clearing Bankers; Chancellor, University of Sussex, since 1961; *b.* Plaxtol, Kent, 17 Jan. 1891; *e. s.* of late F. W. Monckton, Ightham Warren, Kent; *m.* 1914, Mary Adelaide Somes (marr. diss., 1947; she *d.* 1964), *d.* of Sir Thomas Colyer-Fergusson, 3rd Bt.; one *s.* one *d.*; *m.* 1947, Hon. Bridget Helen (later Baroness Ruthven of Freeland, 10th in line), *e. d.* of 9th Baron Ruthven, C.B., C.M.G., D.S.O.; one step *s.* (12th Earl of Carlisle) one step *d.* *Educ.* Harrow; Balliol Coll., Oxford (M.A.). Pres. Oxford Union Society, 1913; called to Bar, Inner Temple, 1919; Bencher, 1937. South-Eastern Circuit; Recorder of Hythe, 1930-1937; Chancellor of the Diocese of Southwell, 1930-36; Attorney-Gen. to Prince of Wales, 1932-36; Attorney-Gen. to the Duchy of Cornwall, 1936-47 and again 1948-1951; Standing Counsel to Oxford Univ., 1938-51; Dir. General of the Press and Censorship Bureau, 1939-40; subsequently Deputy Director-General of Ministry of Information, an additional Deputy Under-Secretary of State for Foreign Affairs, 1940, Director-General, 1940-41; Director-General of British Propaganda and Information Services at Cairo, 1941-42; Solicitor-General, 1945; United Kingdom Delegate Allied Reparation Commission, Moscow, 1945; Chairman, Governors St. George's Hospital, 1945-51; M.P. (C.) Bristol West, Feb. 1951-Jan. 1957; Minister of Labour and National Service, 1951-55; Minister of Defence, Dec. 1955-Oct. 1956; Paymaster-General, Oct. 1956-January 1957. Chairman, Advisory Commn. on Central Africa, 1960. President Surrey County Cricket Club, 1950-52 and 1959-; President of the M.C.C. for 1956-57. Hon. Fellow Balliol College, Oxford, 1957; Visitor Balliol College, Oxford, 1957. President, Institute of Bankers, 1958-60; President, Overseas Bankers Club, 1961-62; President, British Bankers' Association, 1962-. *Heir:* *s.* Maj.-Gen. Hon. Gilbert Walter Riversdale Monckton, O.B.E., M.C. *Address:* 6 King's Bench Walk, Temple, E.C.4. *Clubs:* Brooks's, Buck's. [*Died* 9 *Jan.* 1965.

MONDOR, Henri Jean; French Surgeon; Professor, Faculté de Médecine de Clinique chirurgicale; Member of the French Academy; *b.* Saint-Cernin, Auvergne, 20 May 1885; *s.* of M. Mondor and Jeanne (*née* Vidal). *Educ.:* Lycée d'Aurillac; Faculté de Médecine de Paris. President, Cercle Carpeaux; Pres. des Amis de Proust. *Publications:* Diagnostics urgents; Vie de Mallarmé; Histoire d'un faune; Alain, etc.; Précocité de Valéry; Propos familiers de Paul Valéry. *Address:* 92 rue Jouffroy, Paris 17e, France. [*Died* 6 *April* 1962.

MONEY, Rev. Canon Frank Reginald, M.A.; Rector of Folkingham with Threekingham, Osbournby, Swarby, Pickworth, Walcot, since 1961, and of Aswarby, since 1965; Canon and Preb. of Leighton Beaudesert in Lincoln Cathedral; *b.* 10 June 1905; *o. s.* of A. S. Money; *m.* 1948, Gwendoline Mary Bradock; no *c.* *Educ.:* High Pavement School, Nottingham; St. Chad's College Durham University. Curate of St. Werburgh, Derby, 1928-30; Priest in charge of St. George, Derby, 1930-34; Vicar of Holy Trinity, Ilkeston, 1934-49; Vicar of Wootton St. Lawrence, Hants., 1949-54. Chaplain of Park Prewett Mental Hospital, 1950-54; Rooksdown Plastic Surgery Hosp., 1950-54. Rural Dean of Basingstoke, 1953-1954; Canon Residentiary of Winchester, and Cath. Treas., 1954-61. *Recreations:* local history and walking. *Address:* Folkingham Rectory, Folkingham, Lincs. *T.:* 241. [*Died* 4 *Aug.* 1968.

MONEY, Brigadier Harold Douglas Kyrle, C.B.E. 1945; D.S.O. 1940; J.P.; *b.* 3 Sept. 1896; *s.* of late Brig.-Gen. E. D. Money, C.I.E., C.V.O., D.S.O.; *m.* 1920, Margery Ruth, *d.* of late Sir John Oakley, G.B.E.; one *s.*; *m.* 1947, Nancy Proes, *widow* of Major Geoffrey Proes, R.A. *Educ.:* Wellington College; R.M.C., Sandhurst. Joined Q.V.O. Corps of Guides F.F. in Aug. 1914; served European War in France, 1915, Persia, Mesopotamia, 1916-17, Palestine, 1918; transferred to Royal Scots, 1923; commanded 1st Bn. Royal Scots in France and Flanders 1940 (wounded, despatches, D.S.O.); commanded 44th Lowland Bde., 1941-44, including operations in Normandy (despatches, C.B.E.); Commander Airborne Establishments, 1944-46; retired 1946. J.P. Co. Tyrone. *Recreations:* shooting and fishing. *Address:* Rossclare, Killadeas, Co. Fermanagh, Northern Ireland. *Clubs:* Naval and Military, M.C.C. [*Died* 7 *Sept.* 1965.

MONK (Mary) Beatrice Marsh, C.B.E. 1929; R.R.C.; Cmdr. of Order of St. John of Jerusalem; *d.* of late John Monk, of Woodchurch, Cheshire. House Steward of the London Hospital, 1918-19; Matron's Assistant, 1908-18; Matron, London Hospital, 1919-31; Pres. of Royal College of Nursing, 1938-40; Regional Matron for Joint War Organization of British Red Cross and Order of St. John of Jerusalem, Eastern Region, 1940-46. *Recreations:* gardening, occupational therapy. *Address:* The Glebe House, Bramford, E. Suffolk. *Club:* Cowdray. [*Died* 2 *June* 1962.

MONKHOUSE, John Parry, F.R.C.S.; Hon. Civil Consultant in Otology to R.A.F.; *b.* 1899; *e. s.* of John and Leah Monkhouse; *m.* 1927, Mary Godfrey Mackwood Ling; one *d.* *Educ.:* Worksop Coll., Notts.; St. Mary's Hosp., London. M.R.C.S., Eng. L.R.C.P. Lond., 1925; M.B., B.S. Lond., 1926; F.R.C.S. Eng., 1928. Formerly: Hon. Asst. Surg., Golden Square Throat Hosp.; Aural Surg., King Edward Memorial Hosp., Ealing; Cons Aural Surg., L.C.C.; Senior Aural Surgeon, Ear, Nose and Throat Department, Middlesex Hospital; Consulting Aural Surgeon: Queen Charlotte's Maternity Hospital; National Heart Hospital; Royal National Orthopædic Hospital; Pres., Otological Section, Roy. Soc. Med.; F.R.Soc.Med. *Publications:* Fenestration for Otosclerosis in Grey Turner's Modern Operative Surgery, 1956; contrib. to Archives of Middlesex Hosp.; Proc. Roy Soc. Med., etc. *Address:* 10 Claredale Rd., Exmouth, Devon. *T.:* Exmouth 3738. [*Died* 28 *Dec.* 1968.

MONKSWELL, 3rd Baron (*cr.* 1885), **Robert Alfred Hardcastle Collier;** *b.* London, 13 Dec. 1875; *e. s.* of 2nd Baron and Mary, 3rd *d.* of J. A. Hardcastle, M.P.; *S.* father 1909; *m.* 1st, 1908, Ursula Mary (*d.* 1915), *d.* of late Hugh Gurney Barclay, M.V.O., Colney Hall, Norwich; one *d.*; 2nd, 1925, Katharine Edith, *er. d.* of late William S. H. Gastrell (one *s.* decd.). *Educ.:* Eton; Trinity College, Cambridge. Entered Foreign Office, 1900; Attaché, Berlin, 1900; 3rd Secretary, 1902; transferred to Madrid, 1903; to Washington, 1904; to Pekin, 1904; 2nd Secretary, 1905; Junior Clerk Foreign Office, 1905; resigned, 1910; served in European War as Interpreter, and 2nd Lieut. R.F.A. *Publications:* French Railways, 1911; The Railways of Great Britain, 1913. *Heir: n.* William Adrian Collier [*b.* 1913; *m.* 1939, Erika, *d.* of Dr. E. Kellner]. *Address:* 95 Beachlands, Pevensey Bay, Sussex. *T.:* Pevensey Bay 342. *Clubs:* Athenæum, M.C.C. [*Died* 14 *Jan.* 1964.

MONRO, Major-General David Carmichael, C.B. 1946; C.B.E. 1943; F.R.C.S. (Edinburgh); *b.* 19 May 1886; *s.* of late Charles John Monro, Craiglockhart, Palmerston North, N.Z.; *m.* 1942, Kathleen Noone; one adopted *d.* *Educ.:* Wellington College, N.Z.; Edinburgh Univ. (M.B., Ch.B. 1911, F.R.C.S.Ed. 1934). Temp. Commission R.A.M.C. 1914, Regular 1917; went to India 1918; Specialist in Surgery in India, U.K. and Malta; Personal Surgeon to C.-in-C. in India (F.M. Sir P. Chetwode), 1931; Asst. Professor Military Surgery, R.A.M. College, London, 1938; Consulting Surgeon to British Army and Prof. Mil. Surgery, R.A.M. College, 1940-45; Consultant Surgeon M.E.F., Cairo, 1941-42; Army Representative on Allied Surgical Mission to Moscow, June-July 1943; K.H.S.; retired pay, 1945, but re-employed as Consultant Surgeon M.E.L.F. until final retirement, Nov. 1948. External Examiner in Surgery, Fouad I Univ., Cairo, and Kitchener Medical School, Khartoum. Legion of Merit, degree of Commander (U.S.A.), 1947; King Haakon VII Liberty Cross (Norway), 1947. *Publications:* contributions to Medical Journals; The Medical Services in Burma (Surgery), Army Quarterly, 1946. *Recreations:* golf, swimming, yachting, fishing. *Address:* Fiftyone, Roehampton Lane, S.W.15. *T.:* Prospect 6087. *Club:* Roehampton. [*Died* 6 *Dec.* 1960.

MONROE, Vice-Adm. Hubert Seeds, D.S.O. 1917; *b.* Dublin, 4 Nov. 1877; *s.* of late Rt. Hon. John Monroe, P.C., Judge of the High Court of Justice, Ireland, and Elizabeth Moule; *m.* 1925, Helen (*d.* 1955), *widow* of Adm. Sir Charles Dundas of Dundas, K.C.M.G. *Educ.:* Stubbington House, Fareham; H.M.S. Britannia, Dartmouth. Went to sea, 1894; Lieut. in H.M.S. Forte, 1902-5; S. Africa (war medal); Senior Officer of the Nore Defence Flotilla during European War, 1914-18 (3 war medals, Croix de Guerre with palm); Captain, 1918; A.D.C. to the King, 1929; Rear-Admiral, 1929; retired list, 1931; Vice-Adm., retired, 1934. *Address:* Flat 7, Englefield Court, Woodlands Road, Bickley, Kent. *T.:* Imperial 5105; c/o National Provincial Bank Ltd., 208 Piccadilly, W.1. *Club:* United Service. [*Died* 13 *July* 1966.

MONSARRAT, Keith Waldegrave, M.B., C.M., F.R.C.S.; Consulting Surgeon (retd.); Major R.A.M.C.(T.); T.D.; Group Officer, E.M.S. Liverpool, 1939-45; *b.* Kendal, 11 Jan. 1872; *s.* of Rev. Henry Monsarrat; *m.*; one *s.* one *d.*; *m.* 1947, Marie, *widow* of Dr. J. George Adami, C.B.E., F.R.S., M.D. *Educ.:* King William's College, Isle of Man; Edinburgh Univ. Degree in Medicine, 1894; House Surgeon, Nottingham and Great Yarmouth Hospitals, 1894-97; Assistant Surgeon, Liverpool Children's Infirmary, 1899; Hon. Surgeon, Northern Hospital, Liverpool, 1902; Dean of the Faculty of Medicine, Univ. of Liverpool, 1908-14; Lecturer on Clinical Surgery, University of Liverpool, 1907; Lecturer on Operative Surgery, 1911; Surgeon 1st Western Base Hospital and 37th General Hospital, Salonika (despatches twice, Order of St. Sava, 1st class); Member of General Medical Council, 1927; Pres. Liverpool Medical Institution, 1930; External examiner in Surgery, Edinburgh and Manchester Universities. *Publications:* Poems, 1920-21; Health and the Human Spirit, 1923; Praise, A Tale of Knowledge, 1933; Human Understanding and its World, 1937; Human Powers and their Relations, 1938; Thoughts, Deeds and Human Happiness, 1945; Human Desires and their Fulfilment, 1950; On Human Thinking, 1955. *Address:* 29 Aigburth Drive, Liverpool. 17. [*Died* 28 *April* 1968.

MONSELL, 1st Viscount, *cr.* 1935, of Evesham, **Bolton Meredith Eyres-Monsell,** P.C. 1923; G.B.E., *cr.* 1929; R.N.; Government Director on Board of British Airways, 1937; *s.* of late Lt.-Col. Bolton Monsell and Mary Beverley, 2nd *d.* of late Sir E. Ogle, 6th Bart.; *m.* 1st, 1904, Caroline Mary Sybil, C.B.E. (marriage dissolved, 1950; she died 1959), *d.* of late H. W. Eyres, of Dumbleton Hall, Evesham; one *s.* three *d.*; 2nd, 1950, Mrs. Essex Leila Hilary Drury, *g. d.* of late Field Marshal the Earl of Ypres. *Educ.:* Stubbington House, Fareham. Entered Britannia, 1894; went to sea as midshipman, 1896; obtained first-class certificates in all examinations; specialised as a Torpedo Lieutenant, 1903; placed on Emergency List, 1906; M.P. (C.) South Worcestershire, now Evesham Division, 1910-35. High Steward of the Borough of Evesham. A Unionist Whip, 1911; returned to Navy, Aug. 1914; received Order of the Nile for services in Egypt, 1915 (despatches); Commander, 1917; Treas. of the Royal Household, 1919; Civil Lord of the Admiralty, 1921; Financial Secretary to the Admiralty, 1922-23; Parliamentary Secretary to the Treasury, 1923-24, 1924-29, and 1931; First Lord of the Admiralty, 1931-36. Elder Brother of Trinity House. Chief Conservative Whip, 1923-31; Regional Commissioner for Civil Defence, South Eastern Region, 1941-45. *Heir: s.* Hon. Henry Bolton Graham Eyres-Monsell, *b.* 21 Nov. 1905. *Address:* 78 Whitehall Court, S.W.1. *Clubs:* Carlton, Royal Yacht Squadron (Cowes). [*Died* 21 *March* 1969.

MONSLOW, Baron *cr.* 1966 (Life Peer), of Barrow-in-Furness; **Walter Monslow;** M.P. (Lab.) Borough of Barrow-in-Furness, 1945-66; Parliamentary Private Secretary: Min. of Civil Aviation, 1949-50; Min. of Food, 1950-51. Retired as Organising Secretary of Associated Society of Locomotive Engineers and Firemen. *Address:* Ashleigh, 100 Crouch Hill, Hornsey, N.8. [*Died* 12 *Oct.* 1966.

MONSON, Sir Edmund St. John Debonnaire John, 3rd Bt., *cr.* 1905; K.C.M.G., *cr.* 1938; *b.* 9 Sept. 1883; *s.* of late Sir Edmund Monson, 1st Bt., Ambassador in Vienna and Paris, and Eleanor Catherine Mary, *d.* of Major Munro, Consul-General at Monte Video; *S.* brother 1936. Entered Diplomatic Service, 1906; served in Constantinople, Tokyo, Paris, and Teheran; Minister to Colombia, 1926-29; to Mexico, 1929-34; to Baltic States, 1935-37; to Sweden, 1938-39. *Heir: b.* George Louis Esme John Monson, *q.v.*, *b.* 1888. *Club:* St James'. [*Died* 16 *April* 1969.

MONSON, Sir George Louis Esmé John, 4th Bt. *cr.* 1905; *b.* 28 Oct. 1888; *s.* of Sir Edmund John Monson, 1st Bt., P.C., G.C.B., G.C.M.G., G.C.V.O., and Eleanor Catherine Mary (*d.* 1919), *d.* of James St. John Munro; *S.* brother, 1969. *Educ.:* Eton; Balliol College, Oxford. [*Died* 21 *Nov.* 1969 (*ext.*)

MONTAGU, Hon. Lilian Helen, C.B.E. 1955 (O.B.E. 1937); J.P.; D.H.L.; President of the West Central Jewish Club, and of the West Central Jewish Day Settlement; Pres. and Founder of the Union of Liberal and Progressive Synagogues; Hon. Life Pres. of the World Union for Progressive Judaism; Chairman and Lay Minister of the West Central Liberal Jewish Synagogue; *b.* London, 1873; *d.* of 1st Lord Swaythling. *Educ.:* Doreck College; private tuition. Most of life been spent in social work; connected with the Women's Industrial Council and the National Council of Women for many years; lay preacher for the Jewish Religious Union; Chairman of the Chelsea Juvenile Court, 1942-45. *Publications:* Naomi's Exodus; Broken Stalks; What Can a Mother Do? and other Stories; Thoughts on Judaism; The Faith of a Jewish Woman, 1943; My Club and I, 1943; Letters to Anne and Peter, 1944; God Revealed: An Anthology of Jewish Thought; numerous essays. *Address:* The Red Lodge, 51 Palace Court, W.2. *T.:* Bayswater 1124. [*Died* 22 *Jan.* 1963.

MONTAGUE, Lt.-Gen. Hon. Percival John, C.B. 1943; C.M.G. 1919; D.S.O. 1918; M.C.; V.D.; C.D.; late Chief of Staff, Canadian Military H.Q. in London; Judge of Appeal for Manitoba since 1951 (Puisne Judge, King's Bench, 1932); was member of legal firm of Pitblado, Hoskin, Montague & Drummond-Hay, Barristers, Winnipeg; *b.* 1882; *e. s.* of late Hon. W. H. Montague, P.C., L.R.C.P. Edin.; *m.* 1907, Anne Isabel (*decd.*), *d.* of late Rev. Hugh Fletcher, D.D.; two *d.* *Educ.:* Upper Canada Coll., Toronto Univ. and Osgoode Hall. Called to Bar in Ontario and Manitoba, 1907; K.C., 1928; Pres. Manitoba Bar Assoc., 1931; served France, 1915-19 (despatches, C.M.G., D.S.O., M.C.); commanded Fort Garry Horse, 1920-23, and 6th (Can.) Mounted Bde., 1928-36; Hon. A.D.C. to Gov.-Gen., 1932-1940; served 1939-46; Maj.-Gen. i/c Admin. etc.; also Judge-Advocate Gen. Canadian Army overseas. Hon. LL.D. Manitoba Univ., 1942; Toronto, 1946; D.C.L. Mt. Allison, 1946. *Address:* 103 Wilmot Place, Winnipeg, Canada. *Clubs:* Army and Navy; Manitoba (Winnipeg). [*Died* 11 *June* 1966.

MONTEATH, Sir David Taylor, K.C.B., *cr.* 1944 (C.B. 1938); K.C.S.I., *cr.* 1947; K.C.M.G., *cr.* 1942; C.V.O. 1931; O.B.E. 1918; *b.* 1887; *y. s.* of late Sir James Monteath, K.C.S.I.; *m.* 1933, Mary Lindsay, *o. d.* of late Kenneth Eady; one *d.* *Educ.:* Clifton College; Trinity College, Oxford. Admiralty, 1910; Junior Clerk, India Office, 1911; Services lent to Admiralty, Feb. 1915; Deputy Director, Naval Sea Transport, 1917; Lieut. R.N.V.R., N. Russia, 1918-19; Private Secretary to Parliamentary Under-Secretary of State for India, 1919; to successive Secretaries of State for India, 1927-31; Assist. Secretary, India Office, 1931-37; Secretary, Burma Round Table Conference, 1931; Assistant Under-Secretary of State for Burma, 1937-1941; Under-Secretary of State for India and for Burma, 1941-47, for Burma, 1947; retired, 1948; Imperial Russian Order of St. Stanislas. *Recreations:* golf, gardening. *Address:* Brushwood, Frilford Heath, nr. Abingdon, Berks. [*Died* 27 *Sept.* 1961.

MONTEATH, Harry Henderson; Professor of Conveyancing in the University of Edinburgh, 1935-55; President of the Law Society of Scotland, 1953-55; Member of Law Reform Committee (Scotland), 1954-; Hon. LL.D. Glasgow, 1954; *b.* 26 June 1885; *s.* of Henry Monteath and Helen Guthrie; *m.* 1st, 1917, Margaret Frances Alice Warrand (*d.* 1920); (one *d.* decd.); 2nd, 1925, Margaret Frew McNeill; one *s.* three *d.* *Educ.:* Edinburgh Academy (Dux of School); Merton College, Oxford (Classical Exhibn.). B.A. 1907, 2nd Cl. Classical Mods., 2nd Cl. Lit. Hum.; LL.B. Edin. (distinction) 1911; W.S. 1912. Served European War, 1914-18, Capt. R.A.S.C., Mesopotamia (despatches). *Recreation:* golf. *Address:* 62 Palmerston Place, Edinburgh 12. *T.:* Caledonian 5324. *Club:* New (Edinburgh). [*Died* 5 *March* 1962.

MONTEUX, Pierre; conductor; *b.* Paris, 4 August 1875; *s.* of Gustave Monteux and Clémence (*née* Brisac); *m.* 1928, Doris Hodgkins, Brussels. *Educ.:* Paris Conservatoire. Served European War, French Army, 1914-16. Started career as vio a player; Conductor: Metropolitan Opera Company, New York, 1917-19; Boston Symphony Orchestra, 1919-24; (with Mengelberg) Concertgebouw Orchestra, Amsterdam, 1924-34; Paris Symphony Orchestra, 1930-38; San Francisco Symphony Orchestra, 1935-52, also Musical Director. Principal Conductor, London Symphony Orchestra, 1961-. Has conducted leading orchestras in many European cities. His (Aug.) school for conductors, at Hancock, is international. Mem. Santa Cecilia, Rome; Mem. Royal Academy of Music, London. Gold Medal, Royal Philharmonic Soc., 1963. Holds several hon. degrees. Comdr. Legion of Honour; Officer of Crown of Roumania; Comdr. of Order of Orange-Nassau. *Recreations:* reading, walking on estate, clocks. *Address:* Domain of the Great Pine, Hancock, Maine, U.S.A. [*Died* 1 *July* 1964.

MONTGOMERY, Sir Basil Purvis-Russell Hamilton-, 8th Bt., *cr.* 1801, of Stanhope; *b.* 25 Sept. 1884; *e. s.* of Sir Henry James Purvis-Russell-Montgomery, 7th Bt., and Mary Maud, M.B.E. (*d.* 1947), *o. c.* of Thomas Purvis Russell of Warroch Kinross-shire; *S.* father, 1947; *m.* 1915 Amelia A. Richards; two *d.* *Educ.:* Uppingham School; Trinity Hall, Cambridge. *Heir:* *n.* Basil Henry David Purvis Russell-Montgomery [*b.* 20 March 1931; *m.* 1956, Delia, *o. d.* of Admiral Sir Peter Reid, G.C.B., C.V.O.]. *Address:* 1 Gwynfa Avenue, Cashmere Hills, Christchurch, New Zealand. *Club:* Automobile Association (Canterbury, N.Z.). [*Died* 28 *Jan.* 1964.

MONTGOMERY, Bo Gabriel de, Count; F.K., D.Phil. (Oxon.); *b.* 21 April 1894; *m.* (1933-57) Brita Dahl; two *s.* five *d.* *Educ.:* Stockholm; Trinity College, Oxford. *Publications:* Politique Financière d'Aujourd'hui, 1918; British and Continental Labour Policy, 1923; Issues of European Statesmanship, 1925 and 1926; Pax Britannica, 1928; Versailles, a Breach of Agreement, 1932; Gustavus Adolphus, 1944; Origin and History of the Montgomerys, 1948; Ancient Migrations and Royal Houses, 1968. *Address:* Jarnvagsgatan 6 Nyköping, Sweden. [*Died* 16 *Oct.* 1969.

MONTGOMERY, George Allison, Q.C. (Scot.) 1945: Professor of Scots Law at Edinburgh University, 1947-68; *b.* 17 Feb. 1898; 2nd *s.* of late Sir Matthew Montgomery, who was Lord Provost of Glasgow, 1923-26; *m.* 1929, Nancy, *o. d.* of late Rt. Hon. Lord Morison, P.C., a Senator of the College of Justice in Scotland; two *s.* *Educ.:* Glasgow Academy; Kelvingrove School, Bridge-of-Allan; Glasgow University. Served European War with 2/5th Highland Light Infantry and with 11th Bedfordshire Regt.; M.A. 1920; LL.B. (with distinction) 1923; admitted to Faculty of Advocates, 1923; Junior Counsel to Board of Trade in Scotland, 1933-37; Extra Advocate-Depute, 1937-45; Advocate-Depute, May-Sept. 1945; Member Royal Commission on Capital Punishment, 1949; Chairman of Scottish Local Tribunal for Conscientious Objectors; Chairman of Council, Queen's Institute of District Nursing

(Scottish Branch), 1960-69. Hon. Sheriff-Substitute of Perth and Angus at Dunblane; and of Roxburgh and Selkirk at Selkirk. *Publications:* various contributions to legal journals. *Recreation:* golf. *Address:* Heathmount, Dunblane, Perthshire. *T.:* Dunblane 3108. *Clubs:* New (Edinburgh); Honourable Company of Edinburgh Golfers (Muirfield). [*Died* 9 *Aug.* 1969.

MONTGOMERY, Colonel John Willoughby Verner, C.M.G. 1918; D.S.O. 1917; V.D.; Retired list; *b.* Brantford, Canada, W., 1867; *s.* of late Captain Alexander Nixon Montgomery, J.P., The Royal Fusiliers, and late Istere Alicia Atrutel; *m.* Flora McDonald Seton, *d.* of late Henry Gordon Reid and late Agnes Kelt Reid; two *s.* *Educ.:* Hilton College, Natal; Repton; St. Mary's Hospital. West Indies sugar-planting, 1886-7; Natal farming, 1887; joined Natal Carbineers, 1888; served S. African War, 1899-1902 (despatches, Queen's and King's medals with 6 clasps); Native Rebellion, 1906 (medal and clasp); European War, commanded 1st Natal Carbineers in South-West Africa (despatches, C.M.G.); long service medal; formed and commanded 10th South African Infantry for service in East Africa (despatches, D.S.O. for conspicuous gallantry on the field, 1914 Star, British medal, Victory medal, regiment presented with King's Colour). Hon. Col. Royal Natal Carbineers, 1952. *Address:* 32 Fairholm Avenue, Durham North, Natal, S. Africa. [*Died* 2 *April* 1968.

MONTGOMERY, Leslie Alexander; *see* Doyle, Lynn.

MONTGOMERY, Robert Ernest, C.I.E. 1938; retired from the Civil Service; *b.* 9 July 1878; 2nd *s.* of late William Jamison and Eleanor Harper Montgomery, formerly of Bangor, Co. Down; *m.* 1910, Marion Blackwood Jarvie, Edinburgh; one *s.* three *d.* *Educ.:* King's College, London. Joined Civil Service, India Office, 1898, as Second Class Clerk; Staff Clerk, 1915; Junior Clerk (Administrative Grade) 1919; Principal, 1921; transferred to Office of High Commissioner for India, as Asst. Sec. 1922, and Sec. General Dept.; retired, 1938; served with a Home Guard Bn., Devonshire Regt., 1940; Commissioned 1942-43; Deputy Sub-Controller, Torbay Area A.R.P., 1944-45; a School Manager, Brixham County Primary Schools, 1946-56; School Governor, Brixham Secondary Boys' School, 1954-56. Hon. Sec., Brixham Sea Cadet Corps, 1946, Chm. 1949, retired 1954. *Address:* Rock Hill House, Heath Road, Brixham, S. Devon. *T.:* Brixham 3330. [*Died* 25 *Oct.* 1962.

MONTGOMERY CAMPBELL, Rt. Rev. and Rt. Hon. Henry Colville, P.C. 1956; K.C.V.O. 1961; M.C.; D.D.; *b.* 11 Oct. 1887; *s.* of Rev. Sidney Montgomery Campbell; *m.* 1915, Joyce Mary (*d.* 1928), *er. d.* of late Archdeacon F. N. Thicknesse; one *s.* four *d.* *Educ.:* Malvern Coll.; Brasenose Coll., Oxford (M.A.). Curate of Alverstoke; Vicar of St. Saviours, Poplar, 1917-19; Rector, W. Hackney, 1919-26; Rector of Hornsey, 1926-33; Rural Dean of Hornsey, 1929-33; Rector of St. George, Hanover Sq., 1933-40; Suffragan Bishop of Willesden, 1940-42; Suffragan Bishop of Kensington, 1942-49; Rector of St. Andrew Undershaft with St. Mary Axe, London, E.C., 1940-49; Bishop of Guildford, 1949-56; Bishop of London, 1956-61. C.F., 1915-17 (M.C.); Chaplain T.A., 1926-38; Sub-Prelate Order of St. John of Jerusalem, 1940; Dean of the Chapels Royal, 1956-61; Prelate of Order of British Empire, 1956-61. D.D. (Lambeth), 1950. F.K.C. 1962. *Address:* 8 Vincent Sq., S.W.1. [*Died* 26 *Dec.* 1970.

MONTGOMERY-SMITH, Col. Edwin Charles, C.M.G. 1919; D.S.O. 1917; T.D.; M.R.C.S., L.R.C.P.; formerly K.H.S.; Dep. Asst. Dir-Gen., A.M.S., War Office, 1919-25; *b.* 1869; *s.* of James Montgomery Smith, Atherton, Lancs; *m.* 1st, 1895, Margaret (*d.* 1956), *d.* of T. H. Hope, solicitor, Atherton; one *s.* (one *s.* decd.); 2nd, 1959, Sybil Constance, *o. d.* of Dr. C. J. Wyatt, Penygraig, Glam. *Educ.:* private; City of London Coll.; London Hospital. Health Officer, Bermudas, 1895; Poor Law Officer and Public Vaccinator, Bermudas; Hon. Fellow Royal Hunterian Soc.; late Member of Council British Medical Association; Surgeon St. John's Wood Dispensary; Hon. Life Member St. John's Ambulance Association; Examiner in First Aid and Hygiene, L.C.C.; served European War, 1914-18 (despatches five times, D.S.O., C.M.G.); France and 28th Division and 56th London Division; later A.D.M.S. of the City of London Division, B.E.F. *Publications:* Beri-beri Stricken Cases, 1897, B.M.J.; Clothing for Sub-tropical Climates, 1899, P.J.; Colitis and its Toxic Effects in the Human System. *Address:* Gosfield Hall, Halstead, Essex. *T.:* Halstead 2542. [*Died* 14 *Jan.* 1963.

MONTGOMERIE, Harvey Hugh, C.B. 1945; O.B.E. 1938; *b.* 19 April 1888; *y. s.* of late Archibald Montgomerie; *m.* 1918, Elisabeth Parlane, *d.* of late James Kinloch, J.P., Tullichewan, Dunbartonshire; two *s.* one *d.* *Educ.:* Dumbarton Academy; Glasgow University. M.A.(Hons.), B.Sc. 1909; Carnegie Research Scholar, 1910-11; entered Civil Service, 1912; Barrister, Middle Temple (Certificate of Honour), 1928; Asst. Sec. Ministry of Labour, 1939; Principal Asst. Sec., Ministry of Works, 1941; Under-Secretary, Ministry of Works, 1946-52. *Address:* 88 Etheldene Avenue, N.10. *T.:* Tudor 2883. [*Died* 22 *April* 1965.

MONTGOMERIE, James, C.B.E. 1943; D.Sc. (Eng. Lond.); *b.* 3 Aug. 1873; *m.* Margaret Gray Buchanan (*d.* 1960); one *s.* *Educ.:* Roy. Technical Coll., Glasgow; Univ. of London. Ship Surveyor to Lloyd's Register of Shipping, 1901; Principal Surveyor for Scotland, 1917; Asst. to Chief Ship Surveyor, 1919; Chief Ship Surveyor, 1928; retired, 1944. *Address:* Pen-Y-Bryn, Howell Hill, Ewell, Surrey. [*Died* 8 *Oct.* 1962.

MOODIE, Alexander Reid, M.A., M.D., F.R.C.S.E.; late Hon. Surgeon to the King; late Lecturer in Ophthalmology, University of St. Andrews; Cons. Ophthalmic Surgeon to Royal Infirmary, Dundee, and Royal Infirmary, Perth; Col., A.M.S. retired (late T.A.); *b.* 30 Sept. 1886; *er. s.* of David and Christina Reid Moodie; *m.* 1917, Emily Susan Herald Cochrane; two *s.* *Educ.:* Dundee; St. Andrews; Vienna. Served with Serbian Army in Macedonia (Order of St. Sava); T.D.; late A.D.M.S. 51st (Highland) Division. *Publications:* Articles to professional journals. *Recreations:* Rugby football, golf. *Address:* The Wynd, St. Andrews, Fife. *T.:* 1251. *Club:* Royal and Ancient (St. Andrews). [*Died* 21 *May* 1968.

MOODIE, Donald, R.S.A. 1952 (A.R.S.A. 1943); Secretary, Royal Scottish Academy, since 1959; *b.* 24 March 1892; *s.* of William Moodie and Margaret Mowat; *m.* 1925, Susan A. Binnie, M.B., Ch.B.; two *d.* *Educ.:* George Heriot's School; Edinburgh College of Art. Served 5th Royal Scots M.G.C. (despatches), 1910-18. On staff of Edinburgh College of Art, 1919-55. Guthrie Award, 1924. President Society of Scottish Artists, 1937-41. *Address:* Newstead, East Suffolk Road, Edinburgh. *T.:* Newington 4573. *Club:* Scottish Arts. [*Died* 19 *June* 1963.

MOODY, Charles Harry, C.B.E. 1920; Mus.D. Cantuar, 1923; F.S.A. 1927; Hon. R.C.M. 1933; F.R.C.O. (Hon.) 1920; F.R.S.A. 1945; Liveryman of Company of Musicians,

1918; Organist and Master of the Choristers of Ripon Cathedral, 1902-54, retired 1954; *b.* 22 Mar. 1874; *y. s.* of late Charles Moody of Stourbridge, Worcester; *m.* Mary Grindal (*d.* 1958), 2nd *d.* of late Dr. John Grindal Brayton, Medical Officer of Health for Hindley, Lancs; one *s.* two *d.* Pupil of T. Westlake Morgan, at Bangor Cathedral; Acting Organist of St. Michael's College, Tenbury, 1893; Deputy Organist and Master of the Choristers of Wells Cathedral, and private organist to the Bishop of Bath and Wells, 1894; Organist and Choirmaster of the Parish Church, Wigan (on the nomination of Sir John Stainer), 1895; Conductor of the Wigan and District Choral Society, of the Church Choral Association, and of the Wigan Amateur Operatic Society, 1896; Organist and Choirmaster of Holy Trinity, Coventry, and Conductor of the Trinity Festival Choir, 1899; Lecturer in Music at the Ripon and Wakefield Diocesan Training Coll., 1902-52; Conductor of the Festival Chorus, and of the Ripon Choral Society; Music Master to the Duchess of Leeds at Hornby Castle, Yorkshire, 1903; Conductor of the Huddersfield Glee and Madrigal Society, 1912, and of the Halifax Choral Society, 1917-21; Conductor Leeds New Choral Society, 1923-26; Chairman of the Ripon Diocesan Music Committee, 1928; Hon. Member of the Ripon Rotary Club, 1929; Member of the Ripon Diocesan Advisory Committee, 1928; Senior Adjudicator at chain of Musical Festivals in Canada, and Lecturer on English Cathedrals and Abbeys, under auspices of National Council of Education of Canada, 1940; Hon. Organising Secretary of The Friends of Ripon Cathedral, 1941-52; Hon. Treasurer, Ripon Hospital, 1942; received Freedom of City of Ripon, 1952; Lady Maud Warrender Award of Merit, 1954. *Publications:* A Choral Elegy, The Choir Boy in the Making; A Festival Magnificat, performed at the Festival of North-Eastern Cathedral Choirs in York Minster, 1902; Lectures on Church Music; Music and Emotion; The Evolution of Ecclesiastical Music; Selby Abbey, from 1069 to 1908; A Handbook to Ripon Cathedral, 1920; Fountains Abbey: a Pictorial History (Pride of Britain Series), 1959. Songs (under the pen name Coulthart Brayton); Anthems, etc.; a Magnificat for the 800th Anniversary of Fountains Abbey, 1932. Articles in The Times, Cambridge Review, Manchester Guardian, etc. *Recreation:* archæology. *Address:* Woodbridge, Ripon. *T.:* Ripon 342.

[*Died* 10 *May* 1965.

MOODY, John C., R.I. 1931; R.E. 1946; President Society Graphic Art, 1948; President, Society of Sussex Artists, 1954; *b.* 21 June 1884; *m.* 1914. *Educ.:* privately. Studied London, Paris, Italy, etc., painting and allied arts; firstly about 1910 until today exhibited R.A.; International Soc. Roy Inst. Oils, Paris, and all Provincial Galleries. Late Principal Hornsey College of Arts and Crafts, Mddx. C.C. *Publications:* etchings. *Address:* Hillside Cottage, Burpham, nr. Arundel, Sussex. *Club:* Chelsea Arts.

[*Died* 7 *Jan.* 1962.

MOODY, Robert Ley, M.B., B.S. Lond. 1935; D.P.M. 1938; Physician-in-charge, Department of Child Psychiatry, St. George's Hosp., S.W.1; *b.* 7 Jan. 1909; *s.* of Percivale Sadleir and Louisa Marian Moody; *m.*; one *d.* *Educ.:* Bromsgrove Sch.; St. Thomas's Hosp. Sir Alfred Fripp Memorial Fellowship in Child Psychiatry (Guy's Hosp.) 1939; Cons. Psychiatrist, E.M.S., 1940-45; Clin. Dir. Child Guidance Trg. Centre, 1946; Psychiatrist to St. George's Hosp. and Victoria Hosp. for Children, 1948. Chm. Soc. Analytical Psychol., 1952; Pres. Internat. Assoc. for Analytical Psychol., 1957. *Publications:* contrib. Lancet, Jl. Med. Psychol., Jl. Analytical Psychol., etc. *Recreations:* music (piano), painting. *Address:* 50 Palace Mansions, W.14. *T.:* 01-603 5863.

[*Died* 26 *Aug.* 1970.

MOOKERJI, Radha Kumud, M.A. Ph.D., Hon. D.Litt.; F.A.S.B.; Emeritus Professor of History, Lucknow Univ. Padmabhushana; *b.* 20 Jan. 1884; *s.* of Gopalchandra Mookerji, M.A., B.L., Vakil, Berhampore (Bengal); *m.* 1910, Anasuya Devi; one *s.* *Educ.:* Krisnanath Coll., Berhampore; Presidency Coll., Calcutta; Cobden Medallist, Mouat Medallist, and Premchand Roychand Scholar (Calcutta Univ.); H.H. the Gaekwad Prizeman and Lecturer (1925-30); Mysore University Extension Lecturer, 1918-20; Calcutta University Readership Lecturer, 1925; Manindra Nandy Lecturer at the Benares Hindu University, 1928; Punjab University Extension Lecturer, 1930-34 and 1939; Sir William Meyer Lecturer, Madras University, 1940; Professor and Head of the Department of History, Lucknow University, 1921-45; sometime Mallik Professor of Indian History, National Council of Education, Bengal, Manindra Professor, Benares Hindu University, and Professor of History, Mysore Univ.; President of History Section of All-India Oriental Conference, Mysore Session; President, All-Bengal Teachers' Conference, Khulua Session; General President of Indian History Congress, Gwalior, 1952; Member of the Bengal Legislative Council (Upper House), 1937-43; Member of Bengal Land Revenue Commission, 1938-40; Government of India Delegate to F.A.O. Preparatory Commission at Washington, D.C., U.S.A., 1946-47; Member of Council of States of Central Indian Legislature; M.P. (India), 1952-58. *Publications:* A History of Indian Shipping and Maritime Activity from the Earliest Times; The Fundamental Unity of India (from Hindu sources, with Introduction by J. Ramsay MacDonald); Local Government in Ancient India (Foreword by Lord Crewe); Men and Thought in Ancient India, 1924; An Introduction to Indian Economics; Nationalism in Hindu Culture; Harsha (Rulers of India Series); Asoka (Gaekwad Lectures), 1928; Hindu Civilisation, 1936; Early Indian Art; India's Land-System; Akhand Bharat; A New Approach to the Indian Communal Problem; Chandragupta Maurya and His Times; Gupta Empire; Ancient Indian Education, 1948; Ancient India, 1956. *Address:* 6 Goode Road, Darjeeling; 39 Ekdalia Road, Calcutta; Kumud-Kutir Puri (Orissa).

[*Died* 9 *Sept.* 1963.

MOON, Arthur, Q.C. 1928; Chairman, General Claims Tribunal, 1945-59; *b.* 1882; *s.* of late Sir Ernest Moon, K.C.B., K.C.; *m.* Marjorie *e. d.* of Major Charles and Lady Kathleen Skinner; one *s* two *d.* *Educ:* Eton; New College, Oxford. Called to Bar, 1907; Bencher, Inner Temple, 1936; Mem. Gen. Claims Tribunal, 1939, Chm. 1945; contested (C.) N. St. Pancras, Dec. 1910; served in 8th Batt. The London Regt. (T.F.), 1914-19 (Capt., M.C.). *Recreations:* rackets for Eton, tennis for Oxford. *Address:* Balholmie, Cargill, Perth. *Club:* Oxford and Cambridge, M.C.C., Brooks's.

[*Died* 4 *April* 1961.

MOON, Sir Richard, 3rd Bt., *cr.* 1887; *b.* 12 April 1901; *s.* of Reginald Blakeney Moon (*d.* 1927; *g. s.* of 1st Bt.) and Lucy Annie (*d.* 1935), *d.* of J. Crowther; *S.* cousin 1951; *m.* 1st, 1929, Bertha (from whom he obt. a divorce, 1954), *d.* of J. H. Edwards; two *d.*; 2nd, 1954, Mary Gertrude Hinton Burlington, Iowa, U.S.A. *Heir:* *b.* Joh Arthur Moon, *b.* 27 Oct. 1905. *Address:* Maitland St., Toronto, Ont.

[*Died* 23 *Feb.* 1961.

MOONEY, Herbert Francis, C.I.E. 1946; C.B.E. 1960 (O.B.E. 1939); E.D. 1945; M.A. (Oxon.), Sc.D. (Dub.), F.L.S.; Indian Forest Service, retd.; *b.* 6 Nov. 1897; *s.* of late H. C. Mooney, M.B., F.R.C.S.I., and of Mrs. Mooney (*née* Dolan); *m.* 1st, 1927,

Ruby Lyons (*d.* 1931); one *s.* one *d.*; 2nd, 1933, Muriel Maher; one *d.* *Educ.:* Clongowes Wood Coll., Eire; Trinity Coll., Dublin; Oxford University. Served European War, in the Indian Cavalry, 1916-19. Joined I.F.S., 1921, ret. 1947, Conservator of Forests, Orissa. Forestry Adviser, Brit. Middle East Development Div., Beirut, 1951-62. *Publications:* A Supplement to the Botany of Bihar and Orissa (India), 1950; A Glossary of Ethiopian Plant Names, 1963; various botanical papers in Indian Forest Records, Journ. Ind. Bot. Soc., Journ. Asiatic Soc., etc. *Address:* Broumana, Ballinclea Rd., Killiney, Co. Dublin. *Clubs:* Royal Irish and Royal St. George Yacht.
[*Died* 20 *Aug.* 1964.

MOORE, Hon. Arthur Edward, C.M.G. 1958; J.P.; Director, A.M.P. Society and Queensland Trustees; *b.* Napier, New Zealand, 9 Feb. 1876; *s.* of Edward Moore, Manager Union Bank of Australia, and Emma, *d.* of Captain Newman, Royal Navy; *m.* 1899, Mary Eva Warner, Toowoomba; three *s.* *Educ.:* Church of England Grammar School, Melbourne. Vineyard in N. Victoria 4 years; farming on Darling Downs, Queensland, since 1898; Cheese Manufacturer; Chm. Shire Council 18 years; Member of Queensland Parliament, 1915-41; Premier of Queensland, 1929-32. *Recreations:* fishing and shooting. *Address:* Bulimba House, Bulimba Brisbane, Queensland, Australia. *T.:* Brisbane JY 1111. *Club:* Queensland (Brisb.). [*Died* 7 *Jan.* 1963.

MOORE, Charles Joseph Henry O'Hara, C.V.O. 1945; M.C.; Manager of H.M.'s thoroughbred stud, 1937-63; *b.* 1880; *s.* of late Arthur John Moore, M.P., D.L., J.P., Mooresfort, County Tipperary; *m.* 1917, Lady Dorothie Mary Evelyn Feilding (*d.* 1935), 2nd *d.* of 9th Earl of Denbigh; one *s.* four *d.* Served European War, 1914-1918 (despatches, M.C.). Extra Equerry to King George VI, 1937-52. *Address:* Mooresfort, Tipperary. [*Died* 25 *April* 1965.

MOORE, Brig. Harold Edward, D.S.O. 1919; M.C.; A.R.I.B.A.; late Royal Engineers; late Chief Engineer; *b.* 11 Feb. 1888; *s.* of John Whitehead Moore Eye, Peterborough; *m.* 1927, May (*d.* 1932), *d.* of Walter Howard King, Peterborough; one *s.* one *d.* *Educ.:* Berkhamsted School. Served European War, 1914-19 (despatches, M.C., D.S.O.); Deputy Assistant Director of Works, War Office, 1929-33; Chief Instructor (Construction), School of Military Engineering, 1937-39; Home Office, 1939; B.E.F., France, 1940 (despatches); retired pay, 1944; Dep. Comr. British Red Cross, N.W. Europe, 1944-1945. *Address:* Scio House, Putney, S.W. 15. *Club:* United Service. [*Died* 28 *July* 1968.

MOORE, Sir Henry Monck-Mason, G.C.M.G., *cr.* 1943 (K.C.M.G., *cr.* 1935; C.M.G. 1930); K.St.J. 1941; LL.D. Ceylon (Hon.); *b.* 1887; *y. s.* of late Rev. E. W. Moore, M.A., and Laetitia M. Monck-Mason; *m.* Daphne, *o. d.* of late W. J. Benson, C.B.E.; one *d.* (and one *d.* decd.). *Educ.:* King's College School; Jesus College, Cambridge B.A. 1909; Cadet Ceylon Civil Service, 1910; 4th Assistant Colonial Secretary, 1914; temporary commission R.G.A., Salonika, and B.E.F. 1916-19; Additional Assistant Colonial Secretary, Ceylon, 1919; Colonial Secretary, Bermuda, 1922; Principal Assistant Secretary, Nigeria, 1924; Deputy Chief Secretary, Nigeria, 1927; Colonial Secretary, Kenya, 1929-34; Governor of Sierra Leone, 1934-37; Assistant Under-Secretary of State, Colonial Office, 1937-39; Deputy Under-Secretary of State for the Colonies, 1939; Governor and C.-in-C. of Kenya, 1939-44; Governor and C.-in-C. Ceylon, 1944-48; Governor-General and C.-in-C., 1948-49; retired. *Address:* 409 Grosvenor Sq., Rondebosch, Cape Town, S. Africa. *Clubs:* Athenæum, Oxford and Cambridge; Civil Service (Cape Town).
[*Died* 26 *March* 1964.

MOORE, John Cecil; F.R.S.L.; Author; *b.* 10 November 1907; *m.* 1944, Lucile Douglas Stephens. *Educ.:* Malvern College. Organised Tewkesbury Play Festival, 1934-39; Hon. Director, Cheltenham Festival of Contemporary Literature, 1949-1956 and 1963; Chairman, Society of Authors, 1956-57. Served in Royal Navy, pilot, Fleet Air Arm, 1939-43, in Admiralty, 1944-45. Lieut.-Commander R.N.V.R. *Publications:* Dixons Cubs, 1930; Dear Lovers; Tramping Through Wales, 1931; King Carnival; English Comedy, 1932; The Walls are Down; The Welsh Marches, 1933; Country Men, 1934; The New Forest, 1935; Overture, Beginners, 1936; The Cotswolds, 1937; Clouds of Glory, 1938; The Countryman's England, 1939; A Walk Through Surrey; Life and Letters of Edward Thomas, 1939; Wits End, 1942; Fleet Air Arm, 1943; Escort Carrier, 1944; Portrait of Elmbury, 1945; Brensham Village, 1946; The Blue Field, 1948; Dance and Skylark, 1951; Midsummer Meadow; Tiger, Tiger, 1953; The White Sparrow; The Season of the Year, 1954; The Boys' Country Book, 1955; Come Rain, Come Shine, 1956; September Moon, 1957; Jungle Girl, 1958; Man and Bird and Beast, 1959; You English Words, 1961; The Year of the Pigeons: The Elizabethans (play), 1963; The White Sparrow (play), 1964; The Waters under the Earth, 1965; Among the Quiet Folks, 1966; (with H. T. Sheringham) The Book of the Fly-Rod, 1931; (with Eric Taverner) The Anglers' Week-end Book, 1935; also many plays and programmes for broadcasting and TV. *Recreations:* country sports, cats, cricket, natural history. *Address:* Lower Mill Farm, Kemerton, nr. Tewkesbury, Glos. *T.:* Overbury 308. *Club:* Savile.
[*Died* 27 *July* 1967.

MOORE, Rev. John Walter Barnwell, C.B.E. 1939; M.A.; R.N., retired; *b.* 19 Dec. 1886; *s.* of Skinner Moore, Clifton Terrace, Brighton; *m.* 1913, Millicent, *d.* of A. W. Smythe; one *s.* one *d.* (and *er. s.*, Lieut. R.N., killed, 1941). *Educ.:* Tonbridge; Selwyn College, Cambridge. Deacon, 1909; Priest, 1910; Curate, St. Simon, Southsea, 1909; Chaplain R.N., 1911-46; K.H.C. 1938-41; retired list, 1941. Hon. Chaplain, R.N.V.R., 1947. *Address:* Gaybrook, Brockenhurst, Hants. *T.:* Brockenhurst 2075.
[*Died* 22 *Nov.* 1969.

MOORE, Kathleen Ella, B.A. Hons.; *b.* 11 Dec. 1874; *e. d.* of Rev. E. W. Moore, M.A., Rector of Stoke Doyle, Northants; *Educ.:* Wimbledon High School (G.P.D.S.T.); La Printanière, Vevey; Westfield College; University of London. Assistant Mistress, High School, Cork, Jan.-July 1899; Second Mistress, Sherborne Girls' School, Dorset, 1899-1917; Headmistress, Queen Anne's School, Caversham, 1918-38; retired, 1938. *Address:* St. Joseph's Nursing Home, Boar's Hill, Oxford. [*Died* 29 *April* 1969.

MOORE, Maj. Montagu Seymour, V.C. 1917; *b.* 1896; *m.* 1933, Audrey, *o. d.* of late Dr. J. Penn Milton; one *s.* Served European War (V.C.): Hants Regt., Flanders, N. Russia, 1919; Ireland, Constantinople, 1920-21. K.A.R., 1921-26, ret. as Major. Game Ranger, 1926-44, Game Warden, 1944-51, Tanganyika. *Address:* P.O. Kiganjo, Kenya. [*Died* 9 *Sept.* 1966.

MOORE, Percival, A.R.C.A. (Lond.), Painter in watercolour; Illustrator; *b.* 1886; *s.* of John Moore, Coal Merchant and Farmer; *m.* Margaret Wright (*d.* 1956); one *d.*; *m.* 1963, Freda M. Durkin. *Educ.:* Keighley Boys Grammar School; Royal College of

Art, London (Royal Exhibitioner) Full Diploma of College 1910. Served European War 1916-19 (France one year) Lieutenant, N. Staffordshire Regiment; Principal, Wakefield School of Art, 1920-27; Principal, Southampton School of Art (Southern College of Art, Southampton Centre), 1927-44. *Principal Works:* The Quest, Royal Academy Exhibition, 1914; Watercolours: Sand Dunes; Receding Tide, Ryde, both purchased by Southampton Art Gallery. *Recreation:* cricket. *Address:* 22 Lordswood Court, Coxford Rd., Southampton. [*Died* 22 *Dec.* 1964.

MOORE, Ramsey Bignall, O.B.E. 1955; *b.* 23 January 1880; *s.* of James Moore, Douglas, J.P. and Sarah Jane Clucas; *m.* 1905, Agnes Cannell Clague; two *s.* *Educ.:* Grammar School and Secondary School, Douglas. Articled to G. A. Ring, H.M. Attorney-General; on expiration of articles joined Mr. Ring in partnership; practised as Ring & Moore until 1921; H.M. Attorney-General, Isle of Man, 1921-1945; Member of Education Authority, 1907-19; Member of House of Keys, 1919-21; Acting Deemster, 1921, 1923, 1956 and 1957; Chairman, Health Insurance and Pensions Board, 1920-45; Chairman, Council of Education, 1936-45; Trustee, Manx Museum. *Recreation:* gardening. *Address:* Brookdale, Cronkbourne Road, Douglas, I.O.M. *T.:* Douglas 5746. [*Died* 2 *July* 1969.

MOORE, Reginald, B.Mus. (Dunelm), F.R.C.O.; Lecturer in Music, The University of Exeter, 1955-65; Lecturer in Music, 1965; Hon. Local Representative, Roy. Acad. of Music, since 1956; Examr. for Associated Bd. of Royal Schools of Music, 1958; *b.* 19 May 1910; *s.* of Leonard and Sarah Moore; *m.* 1939, Grace Estelle, *d.* of Albert and Kathleen Muriel Houghton; one *d.* *Educ.:* Central High Sch., Leeds. Organist, St. Saviour's, Leeds, 1926; Organist and Choirmaster, Bramley Parish Church, Leeds, 1929; Asst. Organist, Salisbury Cathedral, 1933; Music Master, Salisbury Cath. Sch., 1933. Conductor Salisbury Musical Soc., 1934. Served R.A.F., 1941-45. Asst. Music Master, Winchester Coll., 1947-52; Organist and Master of the Choristers, Exeter Cathedral, 1953-57; Conductor Exeter Musical Society, 1953-57; Diocesan Choirmaster, Exeter Diocesan Choral Association, 1953-57. *Recreations:* squash, walking. *Address:* Department of Music, The University, Exeter. [*Died* 25 *May* 1968.

MOORE, Robert Foster, O.B.E. 1919; J.P.; M.A. Cantab., F.R.C.S. Consulting Surgeon Moorfields Eye Hospital; Consulting Ophthalmic Surgeon, St. Bartholomew's Hospital, Member of Committee, Ministry of Health on possible Cocaine substitutes; Officer in Charge, Ophthalmic Centre, Etaples, B.E.F.; Past President Ophthalmological Society of the United Kingdom; Ophthalmic Surgeon, Ministry of Pensions; Examiner in Ophthalmology, Conjoint Board and University of London; Ophthalmological Consultant, Min. of Supply, 1946; *b.* 1877; *m.* 1919. *Educ.:* Christ's Coll., Cambridge (Scholar); Class I, Natural Science Tripos; St. Bart.'s Hosp., Scholar, Middlemore Prize, 1914; Lang Research Scholar 1913; Montgomery Lecturer, Trinity Coll., Dublin, 1927; Demonstrator of Anatomy, St. Bart.'s, 1907-13; Middlemore Lecture, 1949. O.St.J. *Publications:* Medical Ophthalmology; 2nd edition, 1925; Notes on the Dissection of the Head of an Australian Native; Studies from the Anthropological Laboratory University of Cambridge; Melanomata of the Choroid, Moorfields Reports, vol. xix.; Lipæmia Retinalis, Lancet, 20 Feb. 1915; Renal Retinites in Trench Nephrites, Lancet, Dec. 1915; Retinal Circulation in Arterio Sclerosis, Transac. Ophthal. Soc. vol. xxxvi.; Retinites of Arterio-Sclerosis, Quarterly Journal of Medicine, 1919, etc. *Recreations:* sketching, climbing, fishing. *Address:* The Red House, Bemerton, Salisbury, Wilts. *T.:* Salisbury 3722. [*Died* 1 *March* 1963.

MOORE, Sir Richard (Greenslade), Kt. 1960; O.B.E. 1951; Mayor of Kalgoorlie, State of W. Australia, since 1937; *b.* Neereman, Victoria, 21 June 1878; *s.* of John and Annie Moore, Devonshire, England; *m.* 1st, 1902, Margaret McIntyre (*d.* 1952); two *s.* two *d.* (and two *s.* decd.); 2nd, 1953, Rose Sarah Fennell. *Educ.:* Eddington, Victoria. Blacksmith and wheelwright; worked for two years as a journeyman blacksmith; started own business in Broad Arrow, W.A., 1902; ran own coachbuilding business, Kalgoorlie, 1905-37; building and repairing house property, 1937-. Pres., Royal Flying Doctor Service; Pres., Silver Chain Bush Nursery Assoc., etc. Life Member: Kalgoorlie Goldfields Methodist Mission; Kalgoorlie Mechanics Inst.; Pres., Repatriation Committee, Goldfields; Patron: Goldfields Nat. Football Club; Police and Citizens Month Club; Amateur Swimming Club. S.B.St.J. 1956. *Recreations:* gardening, fishing. *Address:* 169 Egan Street, Kalgoorlie, W.A. *T:* 489. [*Died* 15 *Sept.* 1966.

MOORE, Very Rev. Robert Henry, M.A.; Dean Emeritus of Perth, Western Australia (St. George's Cathedral); *b.* Mullingar, Co. Westmeath, Ireland, 1872; *s.* of late Joseph H. Moore, A.I.M.; past President and M.I.C.E.I., and late County Surveyor of Meath; *m.* 1st, 1901, Jane Josephine (*d.* 1916), *e. d.* of Joseph Watterson of Ardglass, Co. Down; one *s.* one *d.* (and one *s.* died on active service, lost at sea, P.O.W. of Japanese, 1942); 2nd, 1921, Margaret, 2nd *d.* of late Most Rev. C. O. L. Riley, Archbishop of Perth; two *s.* one *d.* *Educ.:* Drogheda Grammar School; Trinity College, Dublin. Graduated 1894; medal in Logics and Ethics; took keen interest in College Theological Society and was one of founders of present College paper "T.C.D."; ordained in 1896 to curacy in St. Luke's, Belfast; volunteered for service in diocese of Perth, West Australia, 1898; there pioneered in back country of goldfields, building churches at Kanowna and Mt. Morgans; Rector of Boulder City, 1901; of Northam, 1905; Canon of St. George's Cathedral, 1910; Rector of Fremantle, 1911-21; served as Chaplain with the A.I.F. in Egypt and Palestine, 1917-19; Archdeacon of Northam, 1921-29; Dean of Perth (St. George's Cathedral), 1929-47; retired, 1947. Pioneered new parish of Scarborough, W.A., 1947-55, as Hon. Rector. Hon. Org. S.P.C.K. for Province of W.A., 1956-62. Is a Freemason. *Address:* c/o 72 Barker Rd., Subiaco, Western Australia. [*Died* 20 *Feb.* 1964.

MOORE, Tom Sidney, M.A. (Oxon), B.Sc (Lond.); Professor of Chemistry, Royal Holloway College, University of London, 1914-1946, Professor Emeritus since 1948; Secretary of the Chemical Society, 1928-1934, Vice-Pres. 1934-37; *b.* 19 Feb. 1881; *m.* 1907, Mabel (*d.* 1954), 3rd *d.* of C. C. Moore, Liverpool; one *s.* one *d.* *Educ.:* East London College; Merton College, Oxford; University of Würzburg. Lecturer in Chemistry at University of Birmingham, 1903-5; Fellow of Magdalen College, 1905; Tutor of Magdalen College and Lecturer at St. John's College, 1907-14; Fellow of Queen Mary College, 1938. *Publications:* various papers in the Journal of the Chemical Society; the Philosophical Magazine; Berichte der deutschen chemischen Gesellschaft, and the Zeitschrift für physikalische Chemie; The Chemical Society, 1841-1941, 1947. *Recreation:* golf. *Address:* Lodge Hotel, Englefield Green, Surrey. [*Died* 26 *Nov.* 1966.

MOORE, W(illiam) Arthur, M.B.E. 1919; *b.* 1880; *s.* of Rev. W. Moore, B.D., Rector of St. Patrick's, Newry, and Mary Frizelle;

m. Maud (*d.* 1957), *d.* of George Maillet; one *s.* *Educ.:* Campbell College, Belfast; St. John's College, Oxford. President, Oxford Union Society, 1904; Secretary Balkan Committee, 1904-8; Special Correspondent of The Times in Young Turk Revolution, 1908; Persia, 1909-12; Balkan War, Russia, Spain, Portugal, Albania, 1913-1914; Retreat from Mons, Marne, 1914; Lieut. Rifle Brigade, Jan. 1915; Dardanelles (attached Scottish Rifles), 1915; Salonika, G.S.O. 1916-17; R.F.C. and R.A.F. Squadron Leader, 1918; British Military Mission, Balkans, G.S.O.2, 1918-19 (despatches twice); Times Correspondent in Middle East, Afghanistan, India, 1919-22; Assistant Editor of the Statesman (Calcutta), 1924; Managing Ed., 1933-42; Public Relations Adviser to Adm. Mountbatten, S.A.C.S.E.A., 1944-46; syndicated correspondent, Korean War, 1950; Peking, Siam, Indo-China, Nepal, Persia, etc., 1951. Question-master, All-India Radio Brains Trust. Editor of Thought, 1949; M.L.A., India, 1926-33; Chm. Indian Branch Empire Press Union, 1933-43; Pres. Indian and Eastern Newspaper Society, 1939-43; Founder Member Himalayan Club; founded Bengal Flying Club and has been Chairman of Aero Club of India and Burma. Serbian White Eagle; Greek Order of the Redeemer. *Publications: novel:* The Miracle (by Antrim Oriel), 1908; The Orient Express, 1914; This Our War, 1942; articles on problem of keyboard scale with solution in The Times, Musical Times, etc. *Address:* 84 Cadogan Place, S.W.1. *Club:* Savile.

[*Died* 23 *July* 1962.

MOORE, William Harvey, Q.C. 1948; Vice-President, International Law Association, 1959 (Hon. Secretary General, 1951, Deputy Hon. Secretary, 1944); *b.* Ilfracombe, North Devon, 5 November 1891; formerly of Highbullen, Chittlehamholt, North Devon; *e. s.* of late William Robert Moore, Barrister-at-law; *m.* 1920, Maud Kirkdale, *d.* of late Sir George Baden-Powell, M.P., and of Lady Baden-Powell; four *d.* *Educ.:* Clifton College; New College, Oxford (M.A.). Called to Bar, Inner Temple, 1919; Barrister-at-law, Western Circuit. Stood as Labour candidate for Chatham Division, 1924, and for West Derby Div. of Liverpool, 1929. *Recreations:* camping, fishing; travelling in the interests of international understanding and goodwill, particularly among lawyers. *Address:* 3 Paper Buildings, Temple, E.C.4. *T.:* Central 2904; Court Lodge, Westwell, Ashford, Kent. *T.:* Charing 555.

[*Died* 4 *July* 1961.

MOORE DARLING, Canon Edward; Canon Emeritus of Coventry since 1958; *b.* 29 Feb. 1884; *s.* of Edward Henry and Adeline Darling; *m.* 1912, Louisa Elizabeth Longden; one *s.* one *d.* *Educ.:* privately; Univ. of London; Lichfield Theol. College. 1st Cl. Univ. Prelim. Theol. Exam. 1910. Deacon 1910; Priest 1911; Curate: Bloxwich, 1910-13; Walsall, 1913-16; Great Barr, 1916-19; Vicar: Streetly, 1919-22; St. Giles, Shrewsbury, 1922-27; Great Barr, 1927-30; St. Chads, Shrewsbury, 1930-36. Prebendary of Lichfield Cath., 1936; Chaplain, Shrewsbury Sch., 1936-37; Vicar and Rural Dean of Oswestry, 1937-44; Rural Dean of Whitchurch, 1944-46; Vicar and Rural Dean of Eccleshall, 1946-51; Residentiary Canon of Coventry and Diocesan Missioner, 1951-58. *Publications:* Highways, Hedges and Factories, 1957; Making the Most of Life, 1959; frequent articles in Expository Times. *Recreations:* (in chronological order) football, cricket, fly-fishing. *Address:* 2 St. James Close, Alveston, Stratford-on-Avon, Warwicks.

[*Died* 23 *Oct.* 1968.

MOORE-GUGGISBERG, Lady, Decima, C.B.E. 1918; Médaille de Reconnaissance Française, Première Classe; Hon. Organiser and Director General, British Navy, Army and Air Force Leave Club, Paris, European War, 1914-18 and War of 1939-1945 (Overseas Medals, 1939-45 Star, France and Germany Star, War Medal 1939-45); *d.* of Edmund Henry Moore and Emily Strachan; *m.* 1905, Brig.-Gen. Sir Gordon Guggisberg, K.C.M.G., D.S.O. (*d.* 1930). *Educ.:* Boswell House Coll.; Blackheath Conservatoire of Music (Scholarship). Originated Casilda in The Gondoliers at the Savoy Theatre, followed by Miss Decima and many operas and comedies; sang at concerts in the Albert Hall, St. James's Hall and Queen's Hall, etc.; travelled round the world; war work; Originator and Founder of the Women's Emergency Corps, the first organisation of women to replace men, 9 Aug. 1914; from this corps sprang the Women's Volunteer Reserve, the Women's Legion; the National Food Fund, etc., and the Women's Emergency Canteen, working in France; attached to the French Army, 1915; Directrice de la Cantine at Depôt des Eclops-Conty, Compiègne, Corneuve, Rambervilles, Vosges, and nursed at the Hôpital Militaire 103, Amiens; founder of several Leave Clubs in France, 1915-18, 1939-40, and 1944, and British Empire Leave Club, Cologne, 1919; voluntary work in Paris, 1946, for British Army Welfare Service; Hon. Organiser of a section of Remembrance Day, 11 Nov., of the British Legion from its inception, and Founder of the sales of Poppies on 11 Nov. in the West Coast of Africa; Exhibition Commissioner and Chm. of the Gold Coast Building at Wembley, British Empire Exhibition, 1923-24-25; Chairman Overseas Section and Director Forum Club. *Publications:* We Two in West Africa; adaptation of a playlet, A Black Mark, and many articles on various subjects. *Recreations:* shooting, golf, riding, tennis. *Club:* Royal Over-Seas League.

[*Died* 18 *Feb.* 1964.

MOORHEAD, Major-General Charles Dawson, C.B. 1943; D.S.O. 1940; M.C.; p.s.c.; retired. 1947; *b.* 17 Sept. 1894; *s.* of Thomas Dawson Moorhead; *m.* 1923, Margaret Hamilton, *d.* of Brig.-Gen. Sir Arthur Long, K.B.E., C.B., C.M.G., D.S.O.; no *c.* *Educ.:* Cheltenham College; R.M.C., Sandhurst. Served European War, 1914-19; War of 1939-45, Middle East 1942-43 (despatches). C.C. Kent, 1958-. *Address:* Mountfield Farm, Warehorne, Ashford, Kent.

[*Died* 30 *Dec.* 1965.

MOORING, Sir (Arthur) George (Rixson), K.C.M.G. 1961 (C.M.G. 1955); Kt. 1958; British Resident, Zanzibar, 1959-64, retired, 1964; *b.* 23 Nov. 1908; *s.* of late Arthur Mooring and of Martha Mooring, Biddenham, Bedford; *m.* 1947, Patricia Josephine, *d.* of late Algernon and Irma Hare Duke, Craigavad, County Down; one *s.* one *d.* *Educ.:* Bedford Modern School; Queen's College, Cambridge. B.A. (Hons.) 1930. Entered Colonial Service, Nigeria, 1931; Financial Secretary to Western Region of Nigeria, 1949; Permanent Sec., Ministry of Finance, 1954; Dep. Governor, Western Region, Nigeria, 1957-1959. Served War of 1939-45 with Royal West African Frontier Force in West Africa, India and Burma (despatches), 1940-45; Lt.-Col. 1945. Mem. Constituency Delimitation Commn., St. Vincent, West Indies, 1967; Chm., Gilbert and Ellice Is. Colony Socio-Economic Survey, 1967. K.St.J. 1960. *Recreations:* golf, sailing. *Address:* Moat House, Earl Soham, Woodbridge, Suffolk. *T.:* Earl Soham 277. *Clubs:* Royal Commonwealth Society, East India and Sports; Hawks (Cambridge). [*Died* 13 *Jan.* 1969.

MORCOM, Lieut.-Col. Reginald Keble, C.B.E. 1919; M.I.C.E. M.I.E.E., M.I.M.E., M.R.I.N.A.; M.A. (Camb.); Chairman Belliss & Morcom, Ltd., etc.; *m.* Frances Isobel (*d.*

1941), *d.* of late Sir Joseph Swan, F.R.S. *Educ.:* Marlborough; Trinity College, Cambridge. Served European War, 1914-19 (despatches, C.B.E.); Member of British Economic Mission to the Far East, 1930; Vice-President British Electrical and Allied Manufacturers' Assoc. and F.B.I. *Address:* The Clockhouse, Bromsgrove, Worcs. *Club:* United University. [*Died* 5 *May* 1961.

MORE-MOLYNEUX-LONGBOURNE, Brig.-Gen. Francis Cecil, C.M.G. 1919; D.S.O. 1915; The Queen's Royal Regt.; *b.* 20 June 1883; *s.* of Charles Ranken Vickerman Longbourne, of Ripsley, Sussex; *m.* 1919, Gwendoline Carew (*d.* 1946), *d.* of Admiral Sir Robert More-Molyneux, G.C.B., Loseley Park, Guildford; one *s.* *Educ.:* Marlborough. With Mounted Infantry West African Frontier Force, 1911; served S. African War, 1900-2 (Queen's medal 3 clasps); European War, 1914-1918; commanded Bn. The Queen's; Bt. Major, 1915; Bt. Lt.-Col., 1918; Brig.-Comdr., 1917-19 (Chevalier Légion d'Honneur, despatches 13 times); retired, 1921; Col. R. of O., 1922; hon. rank of Brig.-General, 1921; took the name of More-Molyneux, 1928, Longbourne added, 1943. *Address:* Loseley Park, Guildford. *Club:* United Service. [*Died* 5 *Nov.* 1963.

MORETON, Rev. Canon H. A. V., B.A.; M.Litt., D. ès L., Hon. C.F., F.R.Hist.S.; Hon. corresponding member of Institut Historique et Héraldique de France; Canon Residentiary, Librarian and Chancellor of Hereford Cathedral, 1935-64; C.F. Reserve of Officers since 1939; Chaplain to Forces, 1941-45; *b.* 21 July 1889; *s.* of Albert Frampton Moreton, Brockweir, Glos.; *m.* 1921, Anne Dorothy, *d.* of Major Farrington; two *s.* two *d.* *Educ.:* University of Wales; St. Michael's Theological College, Llandaff; University of Besançon. Curate of Windhill, Yorks, 1914-17; Chaplain to Forces, 1917-20; Curate of Castleford, Yorks, 1920 22; Vicar of Flamborough, Yorks, 1922-32; Rector of Pencombe, Herefordshire, 1932-35; Editor of Oecumenica, 1934-40. *Publications:* La Réforme anglicane au XVIe siècle; Rome et l'Église primitive; l'Anglicanisme (Editor). *Address:* The Cloisters, Hereford. *T.:* Hereford 2817. [*Died* 11 *Dec.* 1966.

MORFORD, Howard Frederick; Director, Inchcape & Co. Ltd.; *b.* 21 February 1894; *s.* of Frederick Morford; *m.* 1922, Marguerite Lilian Deniau; one *s.* two *d.* *Educ.:* Dover County School. Entered service of Chartered Bank, 1913; served in Indo-China, 1919-37; and later in Borneo, Sumatra and Hong Kong; Head Office, London, 1940-58 (Chief General Manager, 1955-58). *Recreations:* fishing and gardening. *Address:* Orchard Rise, Buxted, Sussex. *T.:* Buxted 3224. *Clubs:* Oriental, Overseas Bankers. [*Died* 25 *Dec.* 1963.

MORGAN, Cecil Lloyd; *b.* 22 Aug. 1882; *s.* of Rev. Canon John and Anne Morgan; *m.* 1913, Margaret Eleanor Monk; three *s.* (and one son killed on active service) one *d.* *Educ.:* Rossall; Corpus Christi Coll., Oxford (M.A.). Asst. Master at County School, Bethesda, N. Wales, 1905-6; King Edward VII School, Sheffield, 1906-8; High School, Nottingham, 1908-14; Head Master of Grammar School, Haverfordwest, 1919-21; Ardwyn County School, Aberystwyth, 1921-28; The Judd School, Tonbridge, 1928-46; served European War, 1914-18, Major, 11th Suffolk Regiment. *Address:* Tan y Graig, Pentrefelin, Criccieth, Cærnarvonshire. *T.:* Criccieth 275. [*Died* 12 *Aug.* 1965.

MORGAN, Lieut.-Gen. Sir Frederick Edgworth, K.C.B., *cr.* 1944 (C.B. 1943); Colonel Commandant Royal Artillery, 1948-1958; *b.* 5 Feb. 1894; *s. s.* of Frederick Beverley Morgan, Paddock Wood, Kent; *m.* 1917, Marjorie, *d.* of Col. T. du B. Whaite, C.B., C.M.G., Westport, Co. Mayo; one *s.* two *d.* *Educ.:* Clifton College; Royal Military Academy, Woolwich. 2nd Lt. Royal Artillery, 1913; served European War, France and Belgium, 1914-18 (despatches twice); Capt. 1916; Staff College, Quetta, 1927-28; Major 1932; G.S.O. 2 (Royal Artillery), India, 1931-34; Bt. Lt.-Col. 1934; G.S.O. 2, War Office, 1936-38; Col. 1938; G.S.O. 1, 3rd Division, 1938-39; Temp. Brig. 1939; Commanded 1st Support Group, 1 Armoured Division, 1939-40 (France, 1940); B.G.S. 2nd Corps, 1940-41; Commanded Devon and Cornwall Division, 1941; Acting Maj.-Gen. 1941; Commanded 55th (West Lancashire) Division, 1941-42; Acting Lt.-Gen. 1942; Commanded 1st Corps, 1942-43; Chief of Staff to Supreme Allied Commander (Designate), 1943-44; Deputy Chief of Staff to Supreme Commander, Allied Expeditionary Force, 1944-45; Chief of U.N.R.R.A. Operations in Germany, 1945-1946; retired, 1946. Controller of Atomic Energy, 1951-54; Controller of Atomic Weapons, 1954-56. Commander, Legion of Honour, France, 1945; Croix de Guerre, France, 1945; Distinguished Service Medal, U.S.A., 1945; Comdr. Legion of Merit, U.S.A., 1945. *Publications:* Overture to Overlord (an account of planning of invasion of N.W. Europe), 1950; Peace and War, a soldier's life (Autobiography), 1961. *Address:* 30 Kewferry Road, Northwood, Middlesex. *T.:* Northwood 21828. *Clubs:* Army and Navy, Special Forces. [*Died* 19 *March* 1967.

MORGAN, Major-General Harold de Riemer, D.S.O. 1918; D.L. Brecknock; *b.* 12 March 1888; *m.* 1st, 1915, Frances C. Anderson (*d.* 1958); two *s.* one *d.*; 2nd, 1960, Ann, *widow* of Lt.-Col. T. C. L. Redwood. *Educ.:* Harrow Sch.; Worcester Coll., Oxf. Commissioned: The Buffs, 1910; 7th Duke of Wellington, 1918; Comd. Oxford Univ. O.T.C., 1919-22. M.A. (by decree). Comd. 2nd Bn. 5th Fusiliers, 1936-39; 148 Bde., Norway, 1940; 45th Div., 1941-43. Retired pay, 1946. Colonel, The Royal Northumberland Fusiliers, 1947-53. *Address:* Llandefaelog House, Brecon. *Club:* United Service. [*Died* 1 *June* 1964.

MORGAN, Heaton Andrew Kenneth, M.C. 1916; *b.* 26 May 1889; *s.* of Rev. John Morgan; *m.* 1927, Constance Isobel Currie; no *c.* *Educ.:* Clifton College; London University. B.Sc. (Engineering); called to Bar Middle Temple, 1912; entered Director Public Prosecutions Dept., 1920; Assistant Director of Public Prosecutions, 1 Jan. 1949-Jan. 1952; retired. *Recreations:* golf, bridge. *Address:* 20 Roehampton Close, S.W.15. *T.:* Prospect 2722. *Club:* Roehampton. [*Died* 2 *July* 1962.

MORGAN, Hywel Glyn, Q.C. (Nyasaland and N. Rhodesia); Legal Officer, Foreign Compensation Commission, 1959; Barrister-at-Law, Lincoln's Inn, 1924; Wales and Chester Circuit; *b.* 1899; *s.* of late Thomas Morgan and Ann Dare Morgan; *m.* Edna Janet Armstrong; one *d.* *Educ.:* Univ. of Wales (LL.B.). Crown Counsel, Gold Coast, 1926; Asst. Attorney-Gen., Nyasaland, 1932; Attorney-Gen., Nyasaland, 1936; Attorney-Gen., Northern Rhodesia, 1944; Judge of Supreme Court, Gold Coast, 1951-53; retired Dec. 1953. Chairman, Tribunals, Kenya, 1955-56; Special Court, Cyprus, 1956-58. *Recreations:* golf, riding. *Address:* 11 Old Square, Lincoln's Inn, W.C.2. *T.:* Holborn 8206; Wongona, The Roman Way, Cowbridge, Glam. *T.:* Cowbridge 366. *Clubs:* East India and Sports; Royal Porthcawl Golf (Porthcawl). [*Died* 2 *May* 1966.

MORGAN, James, C.M.G. 1934; *b.* 18 Nov. 1882; *m.* 1937, Countess Marie-Louise Salm, Salzburg. Student Interpreter, 1905;

Consul at Aleppo, 1920; Consul-General at Smyrna, 1928; Consul-General at Stamboul, 1930; Counsellor at H.M. Embassy in Turkey, 1930-40, Minister 1940; retired 1943. *Address:* Ravenscliff, Moville, Co. Donegal. *Club:* Royal Societies.

[*Died* 29 *March* 1968.

MORGAN, Sir John V. H., Bt.; *see* Hughes-Morgan.

MORGAN, Rev. Richard J. B. P.; *see* Paterson-Morgan.

MORGAN, Sydney Cope, M.B.E. 1918; Q.C. 1946; *b.* 25 Oct. 1887; *e. s.* of late George Ernest Morgan, Cookham Dean, Berks. *Educ.:* Taunton; Trinity Coll., Cambridge. European War, 1914-18, Major S.W. Borderers. Called to Bar 1921. Capt., General List, 1940-44. Contested (L.) Cambridge Borough, 1922, 1923, and Northampton, 1929; Leader of the Parliamentary Bar, 1952-62. Bencher, Middle Temple, 1954. *Address:* 5 Ashley Gdns., S.W.1. *Club:* United University. [*Died* 14 *Oct.* 1967.

MORGAN, Admiral Sir Vaughan, K.B.E., 1949 (C.B.E. 1937); C.B. 1945, M.V.O. 1918; D.S.C. 1917; D.L.; retd.; *b.* 20 Mar. 1891; *y. s.* of late Joseph John Morgan; *m.* 1st, 1916, Mary Julia (*d.* 1961), *o. d.* of late Dillon Ross Lewin Lowe; one *s.* two *d.*; 2nd, 1962, Eirene Marjorie, *widow* of Capt. C. A. Allen, R.N. *Educ.:* Horris Hill; R.N.C., Osborne; R.N.C., Dartmouth. Operations against Zeebrugge and Ostend; Flag-Lieut. to Adm. of the Fleet Sir Roger Keyes, 1918, Adm. of the Fleet Earl Jellicoe, 1919; Second Naval Mem., Navy Bd., New Zealand, 1934-36; Commanding Fifth Destroyer Flotilla, 1937-39; Chief Staff Officer, Dover, 1939-41; Captain of H.M.S. Revenge, 1941; Flag Liaison Officer, New Delhi, 1943; Director of Signal Div., Admiralty, 1943-45; Admiral-Supt. H.M. Dockyard, Portsmouth, 1945-49. Retired list, 1949; Admiral, 1949. D.L. Hants., 1955. *Recreation:* fishing. *Address:* Webb's Green Cottage, Soberton, Hants. *T.:* Droxford 477. *Club:* United Service.

[*Died* 9 *Oct.* 1969.

MORGAN, Air Cdre. Wilfred W.; *see* Wynter-Morgan.

MORGAN, Rev. Prebendary William Edgar, M.A.; Master of Sexey's Hospital, Bruton, 1954-67 and Chaplain, 1956-67; Prebendary of Combe XIII, Wells Cathedral, 1954-67; *b.* 17 March 1888; *s.* of late Rev. William C. Morgan, North Shoebury, Essex, *m.* 1914, Lily Amery Waite, *d.* of late Rev. J. H. Hinchcliffe; one *s.* *Educ.:* St. John's School, Leatherhead; Emmanuel College, Cambridge. Assistant Master at Forest School, Walthamstow, 1910-13; Deacon, 1911; Priest, 1912; acted as temporary chaplain to the Forces, December 1914-December 1916; Minor Canon, Sacrist, and Headmaster of the Cathedral Choir School, Rochester, 1913-18; Headmaster, The Abbey School, 1918-21; Curate St. Margaret's, Westminster; C.F. 1925-26; Rector of Fairsted with Terling, 1926-28; Rector of Warsop, Notts., 1928-46; Rector of Huntspill, 1946-54. Rural Dean of Mansfield, 1938-46; of Pawlett, 1948-54; O.C.F. 1941-46. *Address:* Bruton, Seaton Down Road, Seaton, Devon. *T.:* Seaton 1011.

[*Died* 3 *Aug.* 1968.

MORGAN, Major William Henry, C.B.E. 1942; D.S.O. 1917; M.I.C.E.; *b.* 1883; *e. s.* of E. F. Morgan of Coombe Dell, Croydon; *m.* 1919, Evelyn Mary (*d.* 1939), *e. d.* of W. H. Wright, Addiscombe; one *s.* (*er. s.* killed in June 1942); *m.* 1942, Eileen Gertrude, *o. d.* of Mrs. G. M. W. Webb, late of Purley. Served European War, 1915-19 (despatches, D.S.O.). County Engineer of Middlesex, 1932-49; retired 1949. Former Vice-Pres., Institution of Civil Engineers. *Address:* 15 Woodcote Village, Purley, Surrey. *Club:* Royal Automobile.

[*Died* 29 *Jan.* 1966.

MORGAN-GRENVILLE, Lieut.-Col. Hon. Thomas George Breadalbane, D.S.O. 1918; O.B.E. 1946; M.C.; p.s.c.; V.L., J.P.; late the Rifle Brigade; *b.* 26 Feb. 1891; *e. surv. s.* of 11th Baroness Kinloss, C.I.; *m.* 1916, Georgina May St. John, 3rd *d.* of Albert St. John Murphy of Little Island House, Eire; three *d.* *Educ.:* Eton; Royal Military College, Sandhurst. Served European War, 1914-18 (D.S.O., M.C., despatches four times, Légion d'honneur); North Russia, 1918-19; War of 1939-45 (O.B.E., despatches). V.L., J.P. Bedfordshire; High Sheriff of Bedfordshire, 1950-51. *Address:* Wootton House, Wootton, near Bedford. *T.:* Lower Shelton 231. *Club:* Naval and Military.

[*Died* 10 *Jan.* 1965.

MORGAN-POWELL, Samuel; *b.* London, 4th June 1878; *s.* of Charles Powell, Wetherby, Yorks, and Emma Morgan, Blaenavon, Monmouth; *m.* Velma Alberta, *d.* of John Dawson, Coaticook, P.Q. *Educ.:* Ellesmere. Began newspaper work in Bradford Office of the Yorkshire Post; took up music studies, drama, and fiction; engaged in various capacities on numerous papers in North-west and Midlands; Freelance for few years, touring Europe, West Coast of Africa, etc.; Sub-editor, Demerara Daily Chronicle; toured West Indies and South America; Editor, Demerara Argosy; went to Canada, 1905, joining staff of Witness; later went to Montreal Herald, then to Montreal Star; retired from chief editorship, 1946; retired from dramatic and literary editorships in December 1953. *Publications:* Night Thoughts, 1896; Memories that Live, 1929 (David Literary Prize, Quebec); Down the Years (poems), 1938; Lilac Time in Arcady (verse); short stories: Love in the Hands of Fate; A Muted Melody; The Devil in Heaven; From Palm to Pine. Articles and short stories to Canadian Magazine, Vanity Fair, etc. *Recreations:* motoring, writing plays. *Address:* Haddon Hall, 2150 Sherbrooke Street, W., Montreal, Canada. *T.A.:* Morgan-Powell, Montreal. *T.:* Wilbank 6812 Montreal. *Club:* P.E.N.

[*Died* 4 *June* 1962.

MORGENTHAU, Henry, Jr.; *b.* N.Y. City, 11 May 1891; *s.* of late Henry Morgenthau, G.B.E. (Hon.), and Josephine Sykes; *m.* 1916, Elinor Fatman (*d.* 1949); two *s.* one *d.*; *m.* 1951, Mrs. Marcelle Hirsch. *Educ.:* Cornell University. LL.D. Temple Univ. 1938; Amherst College, 1942; D.H.L. Hebrew Union College, Cincinnati, O., 1945 Dr. Humane Letters, Yeshiva Univ., 1948. Publisher American Agriculturist, 1922-33; Chairman Governor Roosevelt's Agricultural Advisory Commission, State of New York, 1929-33; Conservation Commissioner State of New York, 1931-33; Member of Taconic State Park Commission; Chairman, Federal Farm Board, Washington, D.C., 1933; Governor, Farm Credit Administration, 1933; Acting and Under-Sec. of the Treasury, 1933-1934; Sec. of the Treasury, U.S.A., 1934-45. General Chairman, United Jewish Appeal, since 1947. Lieut. (J.G.) U.S. Navy, 1918-19. Medal for Merit, 1945; Grand Officer, Legion of Honor, 1946; Chinese Order of the Auspicious Star, Grand Cordon, 1948. Hebrew Member of the Obed and Jordan Lodges; Jewish Religion. *Publications:* Germany is Our Problem, 1945; The Morgenthau Diaries, vol. 1, Years of Crises, 1928-1938; vol. 2, Years of Urgency, 1938-1941. *Address:* Hopewell Junction, New York, U.S.A. *Clubs:* Century Country (New York), Dutchess Golf and Country (N.Y.); Metropolitan, National Press (Washington, D.C.).

[*Died* 6 *Feb.* 1967.

MORISON, Cecil Graham Traquair, M.A.; Student Emeritus of Christ Church, Oxford, since 1948; *b.* 12 July 1881; *s.* of J. Morison, M.D., Thirlestane, St. Albans, Hertfordshire; *m.* 1910, Nora Georgina, *d.* of late Capt. John Wardell, R.M.L.I., and Mrs. Wardell, The Abbey, Shangolden, Co. Limerick; two *s.* *Educ.:* Rugby School; Balliol College, Oxford; Rothamsted Experimental Station. European War, Assistant Chemical Adviser, III. Army in France, 1916, and Co. Officer R.M.C., Camberley, 1917, Captain. Official student, Christ Church, Oxford, 1928-46, ordinary student, 1946-48. Lecturer and Reader in Agricultural Chemistry, Univ. of Oxford, 1909-28; Reader in Soil Science, Oxford, 1928-48; sometime Lecturer Univ. and Lincoln Colleges; Rhodes Travelling Fellow, 1929-31; sometime member Hebdomadal Council and general Board of Faculties; Curator of Univ. Chest and the Bodleian Library. Ecological Expeditions to Sudan, Tanganyika and Central Africa, 1933, 1935, 1938, 1947, 1949, 1951, 1954, 1956. *Publications:* various scientific papers. *Address:* Christ Church, Oxford; The Orchard, Drewsteignton, Exeter, Devon. *T.:* Drewsteignton 252. [*Died* 6 *April* 1965.

MORISON, Stanley; F.B.A. 1954; R.D.I., 1960; on the staff of The Times, 1930-60; Typographical Adviser to University Press, Cambridge, 1923-44, 1947-59, and to The Monotype Corporation since 1923; Member, Editorial Board, Encyclopædia Britannica, 1961; *b.* 6 May 1889. Editor, The Fleuron, 1926-1930; Sandars Reader in Bibliography in the University of Cambridge, 1931; Editor, The Times Literary Supplement, 1945-47; Lyell Reader in Bibliography, Oxford, 1957. Gold medal Amer. Institute of Graphic Arts, New York, 1946; Gold medal Bibliographical Soc., London, 1948; Hon. Litt.D., Cambridge, 1950; Hon. D.Litt., Birmingham, 1950; Hon. Ph.D., Chatham, N.B. 1959; Hon. LL.D. Marquette, Wis., 1960; Senior Fellow of Royal College of Art, 1950; Hon. Mem. Society of Industrial Artists; Hon. Mem. Art Workers Guild; Hon. Assoc. Manchester Coll. of Art, 1958; Hon. For. Corresp. Mem. Grolier Club, N.Y.; Fell. Newberry Library, Chicago; Hon. Fell. Pierpont Morgan Library, New York. *Publications:* Four Centuries of Fine Printing; Type Faces and Type Design; The Calligraphy of Ludovico degli Arrighi; The Alphabet of Damianus Moyllus; Eustachio Cellebrino; German Incunabula in the British Museum; (with Henry Thomas) Andres Brun, Calligrapher of Saragossa, 1929; The Writing Book of Gerard Mercator; Memoir of John Bell 1745-1832; Ichabod Dawks and His News-Letters; The English Newspaper, 1622-1932; Fra Luca de Pacioli (for the Grolier Club of New York), 1933; First Principles of Typography, 1936; The Art of Printing, (British Academy Annual Lecture on Aspects of Art), 1938; Black Letter, 1941; English Liturgical Books, 3rd ed. 1949; Editor history of The Times four volumes, 1935, 1939, 1947, 1952; Printing The Times, 1953; The Portraiture of Thomas More, 1957; Talbot Baines Reed, 1960; The Likeness of Thomas More, 1963; The Typographic Book, 1450-1935, 1963; John Fell: The University Press and the Fell Types (with Harry Carter), 1967. Many articles on medieval and humanistic manuscripts. Contributor Encyclopædia Britannica 14th Edition (Calligraphy, Printing Type, and Typography). *Address:* 2 Whitehall Court, S.W.1. [*Died* 11 *Oct.* 1967.

MORLAND, William Vane, M.I.Mech.E., M.Inst.T., F.R.S.A.; Road Transport Consultant; *b.* 26 Apr. 1884; *m.* 1949, A. M. Hinton. *Educ.:* Southport and privately. General Manager and Engineer: Notts. & Derbyshire Tramways Co., Ilkeston Tramways, Midland General Omnibus Co., 1919-24; General Manager and Engineer: St. Helen's Corp. Transport, 1924-26, Walsall Corp. Transport, 1926-32; General Manager and Chief Engineer: Leeds City Transport Dept., 1932-49. Served European War, 1914-19; Mechanical Transport in France with First Exped. Force; transferred to Railway Operating Div. of Royal Engineers; on War Office Staff subs. until demobilisation in 1919. Vice-Pres. International Union of Public Transport; President Municipal Passenger Transport Association, 1949-; Road Passenger Transport Executive, 1949-52. *Publications:* has written numerous technical papers for various Chartered Institutions. *Recreations:* literature and music. *Address:* 162 Chiltern Court, Baker Street, N.W.1. *T.:* Welbeck 5544, Ext. 162. [*Died* 10 *Dec.* 1962.

MORLEY, 5th Earl of, *cr.* 1815; **Montagu Brownlow Parker;** Viscount Boringdon, 1815; Baron Boringdon, 1784; late Captain, Grenadier Guards; President of Port of Plymouth Trade and Commerce; *b.* 13 Oct. 1878; 2nd *s.* of 3rd Earl of Morley and Margaret, *d.* of late R. S. Holford, Weston Birt; *S.* brother 1951. *Educ.:* Eton Coll. 2nd Lt. 3rd Bn. Gloucester Regt., 1898; 2nd Lt. Grenadier Guards, 1899 (Queen's medal 3 clasps, King's medal 2 clasps); S. African War, 1900-02 (wounded); A.D.C. Maj.-Gen. R. Campbell, 1901-02; to Maj.-Gen. L. Oliphant, commanding Johannesburg, 1902; to Maj.-Gen. L. Oliphant, commanding London District, 1903-06; Captain, 1907; resigned, 1909; served European War, 1914-18 (despatches five times, Croix de Guerre). *Heir:* *n.* John St. Aubyn Parker, *b.* 29 May 1923. *Address:* Saltram, Plympton, Plymouth, Devon. *T.:* Plympton 3254. *Clubs:* Turf, Royal Thames Yacht; Royal Western Yacht (Vice Cdre.) (Plymouth). [*Died* 28 *April* 1962.

MORLEY, Arthur, O.B.E. 1937; D.Sc., Hon. M.I.Mech.E.; *b.* Cheadle Hulme, Cheshire, 1876; *s.* of James Bolton and Letitia Agnes Morley; *m.* 1903, Catherine Brown of Liverpool; two *s.* one *d.* *Educ.:* Univ. of Manchester. Apprenticed to L. Gardner & Sons, engineers, Patricroft; Demonstrator in Engineering, Yorkshire College, Leeds, 1900-01; Senior Lecturer in Mechanical Engineering, University College, Nottingham, 1901-05; Professor of Mechanical Engineering at University College, Nottingham, 1905-12; H.M. Inspector of Schools, 1912; Staff Insp. (Engineering) Board of Educ., 1919-37. *Publications:* Mechanics for Engineers, 1905; Strength of Materials, 1908; Elementary Applied Mechanics, 1911; Theory of Structures, 1912; Applied Mechanics, 1943; (with Dr. E. Hughes) Elementary Engineering Science, 1937, and Mechanical Engineering Science, 1938; various scientific and technical papers. *Address:* Applegarth, Sham Castle Lane, Bath. *T.:* Bath 5943. [*Died* 5 *Jan.* 1962.

MORLEY, Austin; Director, Averys Ltd.; *b.* 14 November 1898; *s.* of J. W. A. Morley; *m.*; two *s.* *Educ.:* Dudley Grammar School; Birmingham Univ. General Manager, W. & T. Avery Ltd., 1936; Managing Director, Averys Ltd., 1955-64. President, West Midland Engineering Employers' Assoc., 1966-68. *Recreations:* golf and gardening. *Address:* Hunters Moon, Endwood Drive, Little Aston Park, Sutton Coldfield, Warwickshire. *Club:* Conservative (Birmingham). [*Died* 22 *Jan.* 1970.

MORLEY, Edith Julia, O.B.E.; J.P.; Hon. Secretary Reading and District International Advice Bureau; Emeritus Professor, University of Reading; *b.* London, 1875; *d.* of Alexander Morley, M.R.C.S., surgeon-dentist. *Educ.:* privately in London; Hanover; University of London King's College for Women, and University College. Oxford Final Honours School of

English Language and Literature, 1899; Associate of King's College, 1899; Fellow of King's College for Women, 1913; Lecturer King's College for Women, 1899-1914; Lecturer, University College, Reading, 1901; Prof. of English Language, University of Reading, 1908-40; F.R.S.L.; Hon. M.A. (Oxford). *Publications:* Hurd's Letters on Chivalry and Romance, 1911; Women Workers in Seven Professions, 1913; Young's Conjectures on Original Composition, 1917; Blake, Coleridge and Wordsworth, being Selections from Crabb Robinson's Remains, 1922; Correspondence of Crabb Robinson with the Wordsworth Circle, 1927; Crabb Robinson in Germany, 1929; The Life and Times of Henry Crabb Robinson, 1935; Henry Crabb Robinson on Books and their Writers, 1938, etc. *Address:* 96 Kendrick Rd., Reading. *T.:* 82191. *Club:* Crosby Hall. [*Died* 18 *Jan.* 1964.

MORONY, Thomas Henry, C.S.I. 1931; C.I.E. 1925; *s.* of William Casey Morony, Bellmullet, Co. Mayo; *m.* Evelyn Myra, *e. d.* of late Rt. Rev. E. N. Lovett, C.B.E.; one *s.* one *d.* *Educ.:* Fettes Coll., Edinburgh. Entered India Police, 1899; District Superintendent of Police, 1907; seconded as Inspector-General, Indore State Police, 1912-17; Inspector-General of Police, Central Provinces, India, 1922; retired 1933; King's Police Medal, 1918. *Address:* Avon Close, Crane St., Salisbury, Wilts. *T.:* Salisbury 3704. [*Died* 23 *Nov.* 1961.

MORPHETT, Lieut.-Colonel George Charles, C.M.G. 1918; D.S.O. 1916; late Royal Sussex Regiment; *b.* 23 December 1878; *m.* (wife decd. 1960); one *s.* Served South Africa, 1899-1902 (Queen's medal with four clasps, King's medal with two clasps); European War, 1915-18 (despatches, D.S.O., Brevet Lt.-Col., Legion of Honour, C.M.G.); retired pay, 1921. *Address:* 9 Wilbury Avenue, Hove, Sussex. *Club:* East India and Sports. [*Died* 29 *Feb.* 1968.

MORRELL, Capt. Sir Arthur Routley Hutson, K.B.E., 1941; *b.* Oct. 1878; *s.* of Robert and Charlotte Elizabeth Morrell; *m* 1924, Audrey Louise Alston; two *s.* *Educ.:* Bedford. Went to sea as apprentice in 1895 in the sailing ship Crusader of Shaw Savill & Albion Line; joined West India and Panama Telegraph Co., 1903, in command 1906-22, retiring on election Active Elder Brother of Trinity House; Deputy Master of Trinity House, 1935-48; retd. from active service, 1948; one of members of Foundation Council of Hon. Company of Master Mariners; Past Director, Royal Exchange Assurance. J.P. retd., 1948. D.L. Co. Lond., resigned, 1961. *Recreations:* golf and bridge. *Address:* Flat 12, Saffron Court, Eastbourne, Sussex. [*Died* 2 *Feb.* 1968.

MORRILL, Thomas James, C.B. 1946; T.D., D.L.; County Representative, Emergency Help Scheme, St. John and British Red Cross Society; *b.* 1 Dec. 1886; *s.* of Henry Morrill, Withernsea, E. Yorks; *m.* 1936, Zilla P. Rosenthal; no *c.* *Educ.:* Hull Technical College; in Sweden. Joined E. York. Regt., 1904; served throughout European War, 1914-18; commanded 4th E. York. Regt., 1921-26; commanded 1st E.R. (E. Hull) Home Guard during war of 1939-45; Hon. Colonel 4th E. York. Regt., 1926-51, *Recreation:* yachting. *Address:* The Firs, Newland Park, Hull. *T.:* Hull 42897. *Club:* Royal Yorkshire Yacht (Bridlington). [*Died* 4 *April* 1969.

MORRIS, Air Cdre. Alfred D. W.; *see* Warrington-Morris.

MORRIS, Air Vice-Marshal Sir (Alfred) Samuel, K.B.E., *cr.* 1946 (O.B.E. 1919); C.B. 1943; *b.* 4 Jan. 1889; *s.* of late George Morris, Tunbridge Wells; *m.* 1942, Henrietta, *d.* of late Graves Stoker, F.R.C.S., Hertford St., W.1. Served European War, 1914-18; Royal West Kent Regt., 1914; R.F.C., 1915; R.A.F., 1919; retired, 1946. *Address:* c/o Glyn, Mills & Co., Whitehall, S.W.1. *Club:* Royal Air Force. [*Died* 9 *Nov.* 1964.

MORRIS, General Sir Edwin Logie, K.C.B., *cr.* 1944 (C.B. 1941); O.B.E. 1919; M.C.; *b.* 10 March 1889; *s.* of late Clarke Morris, M.R.C.S., L.R.C.P., J.P.; *m.* 1st, 1921, Celia (marriage dissolved, 1953), *d.* of Arthur Meade, St. Ives, Cornwall: no *c.*; 2nd, 1953, Mary Sinclair, *widow* of John Sinclair, Farnham, Surrey. *Educ.:* Wellington; R.M.A., Woolwich. R.E. 1909; served European War, 1914-18, France and Italy; Brigade Major 10 and 144 Inf. Bdes.; G.S.O. 2 14 Corps; Brevet-Maj. (despatches five times, O.B.E., M.C.); Brigade Major; Turkey, 1919-20; Student Staff College, 1921-22; Instructor Staff College, 1927-1929; Imperial Defence College, 1933; C.R.E. India, 1934; Deputy Director Operations and Intelligence A.H.Q. India, 1934-36; Deputy Director Operations, War Office, 1936-38; Brigadier General Staff Northern Command, 1938-39; Major-Gen. 1939; Director of Staff Duties, War Office, 1939-40; Divisional Comdr. 1940; Corps Comdr. 1941; Lieut.-Gen. 1943; Chief of the General Staff, India, 1942-44; G.O.C.-in-C Northern Comd., 1944-46; Gen., 1946; British Army Representative Military Staff Committee, United Nations, 1946-48; A.D.C. General to the King, 1947-48; retd. pay, 1948. Chief Royal Engineer, 1951-58; Col. Comdt., R.E., 1944-58. Master of the Skinners' Company, 1954-55. *Address:* Westwood Place, Normandy, Nr. Guildford, Surrey. *T.:* Normandy 2358. *Club:* Army and Navy. [*Died* 29 *June* 1970.

MORRIS, Geoffrey O'C.; *see* O'Connor-Morris.

MORRIS, Gwilym Ivor, C.B. 1953; Under-Sec., Min. of Aviation, since 1959; *b.* 15 May 1911; *s.* of Rev. John Morris, Chepstow; *m.* 1941, Audrey Brown; one *s.* one *d.* *Educ.:* Pontypridd County Sch.; Jesus Coll., Oxf. Asst. Principal: Min. of Agriculture (N.I.), 1934, Min. of Shipping, 1940; Private Sec.: to Rt. Hon. Lord Leathers, P.C. (now Viscount Leathers) in 1945 and to Rt. Hon. Alfred Barnes, P.C. in 1946; Under-Sec., Min. of Transport, 1948-59. *Address:* 23 Reynolds Close, N.W.11. *T.:* Speedwell 0376. *Club:* Royal Automobile. [*Died* 3 *Aug* 1965.

MORRIS, Sir Harold, Kt., *cr.* 1927; M.B.E. 1919; Q.C. 1921; President of the Industrial Court, 1926-45; Chairman National Wages Board for Railways since 1925; *b.* Dec. 1876; *s.* of late Sir Malcolm Morris, K.C.V.O; *m.* Olga, *d.* of late Emil Teichman, Sitka, Chislehurst; one *s.* four *d.* *Educ.:* Clifton; Magdalen College, Oxford M.P. (N.L.) East Bristol, 1922-23; Recorder of Folkestone, 1921-1926; called to Bar, Inner Temple, 1899; Bencher 1934; South-East Circuit; served European War, 1914-19 (despatches, M.B.E.). *Publications:* The Barrister, 1932; Back View, 1960. *Address:* 21 Lichfield Road, Kew, Surrey. *T.:* Richmond 4728. *Club:* Athenæum. [*Died* 11 *Nov.* 1967.

MORRIS, Brig. Herbert Edwin Abrahall, C.I.E. 1942; O.B.E. 1934; *b.* 7 May 1894; *s.* of Edwin Henry Morris, Ross-on-Wye, Herefs.; *m.* 1920, Rhoda, *er. d.* of Rev. William Ellison, Rector and Lord of the Manor of Harlton; one *s.* one *d.* (and one *s.* died on active service). *Educ.:* Cambridge High School; Cambridge University (M.A.). 2nd Lieut. T.A. 1915; with Cambs. Regiment to end of 1917; transferred to Indian Army with Regular Commission and served with 2/30th Punjab Regt.

and 2/154th Infantry; Indian Army Ordnance Corps, 1921. Served European War, 1914-19 (Egyptian Expeditionary Force); Waziristan N.W.F. of India, 1919-20; Mohmand Operations, 1933 (despatches, O.B.E.); operations N.W.F. 1935 (despatches, Bt. Lt.-Col.); Chief Ordnance Officer, 1936-37; Asst. Director, 1937-40; Deputy Director, 1940-43; Director, 1943; Director of Ordnance Services of an Army Group; A.D.C. to the King, 1944; retd. 1945. Director Entries and Exits Branch, C.C.G. (British Element), 1946-49. Director-General, Tripartite Travel Board for Western Germany, 1949-53; Chief Military Observer to U.N. Peace Mission to the Balkans, H.Q. Salonica, Greece, 1953-54; Financial Secretary to the Society for the Propagation of the Gospel, 1955-60. Order of Merit in Silver of Swedish Red Cross, 1949. *Address:* 4 Hillview Court, Woking, Surrey. *T.:* Woking 2865; Lloyds Bank, Cox's & Kings Branch, 6 Pall Mall, S.W.1.
[*Died* 20 *Sept.* 1969.

MORRIS, Major John Patrick; *b.* 21 March 1894; *s.* of Joseph Thomas and Ellen Morris. *Educ.:* SS Peter and Pauls, Bolton; Municipal Secondary School, Bolton. Civil Service; served European War, 1914-19, Lieut. R.E. (despatches); served War of 1939-45, Burma Campaign, 1939-45. M.P., (U.) Salford North, 1931-45. Member London Stock Exchange. *Recreation:* golf. *Address:* 21 Blenheim Rd., N.W.8.
[*Died* 31 *July* 1962.

MORRIS, Brig. John Sidney, C.B.E. 1935; *b.* 24 April 1890; *s* of David Morris and Annie Kent; *m.* 1917, Kathleen Lynch; two *s.* one *d.* *Educ.:* Manchester Grammar School Commissioned B.S.A. Police, 1914; Assistant Commissioner, 1929; Commissioner, 1933; Commandant, Southern Rhodesia Forces, 1936; Inspector-General, British South Africa Police, S. Rhodesia, from 1940, now retired; served European War, Rhodesia, 1914-18; Colonial Police Medal, 1942; King's Police Medal, 1945. War of 1939-45, East Africa and Middle East. K.St.J. *Recreations:* lacrosse, football, tennis *Club:* Salisbury (S. Rhodesia).
[*Died* 18 *Nov.* 1961.

MORRIS, Lawrence Henry, F.F.A.R.C.S.; Hon. Consulting Anæsthetist, St. Mary's Hospital, Westminster Hospital (Gordon Hospital and Prince of Wales Hospital (Bearsted Memorial Hospital), since 1967; *b.* Ceres, South Africa, 10 April 1902; *s.* of late Dr. Frank Mayo Morris, Cape Town; *m.* 1935, Mary MacDonnell; one *s.* *Educ.:* South African College School; Diocesan College, Rondebosch; Emmanuel College, Camb.; London Hosp. Med. College. B.A. Camb.; M.R.C.S. Eng., L.R.C.P. Lond. 1928; F.F.A.R.C.S. Eng. 1948. Formerly: Senior Resident Anæsthetist, Receiving Room Officer and House Surgeon, Ear, Nose and Throat Dept., London Hospital; House Surgeon, Dudley Road Hosp., Birmingham; Hon. Anæsthetist, Croydon General Hospital; Hosp. for Epilepsy and Paralysis, Maida Vale; Consulting Anæsthetist, L.C.C. Surgical Mission to Radium Inst., Bogota, Colombia, South America, 1949 (British Council). Fell. Association of Anæsthetists. *Publications:* on Anæsthesia in medical journals; articles in Modern Practice in Anæsthesia (Evans), 1949. *Recreations:* fishing, cinematography, gardening. *Address:* 9 Rede Place, W.2. *T.:* Bayswater 3355.
[*Died* 7 *Nov.* 1969.

MORRIS, Alderman Percy, C.B.E. 1963; J.P.; *b.* 6 October 1893; *s.* of Thomas and Emma Morris; *m.*1920, Elizabeth Davies; *m.* 1956, Catherine Evans. *Educ.:* Manselton Elementary and Dynevor Secondary School, Swansea. Joined G.W. Railway Service, 1908 (Administrative Staff); Member of Swansea County Borough Council since 1927: Deputy Mayor, 1944-45; Mayor, 1955-56. Deputy Regional Commissioner for Civil Defence, Wales Region, 1941-45; President Railway Clerk's Assoc. of Great Britain and Ireland, 1943-53. M.P. (Lab.) Swansea West, 1945-Sept. 1959. Member Western Area Board, British Transport Commission, 1960-62. Member of Parliamentary Far East Delegation, 1955. Member Council, University College, Swansea. Member, National Assistance Bd., 1961-66 (Dep. Chm., 1965-66); the National Assistance Bd. was replaced by the Supplementary Benefits Commn. (Dep. Chm., 1966-). Freeman, Co. Borough of Swansea, 1958. J.P., Swansea, 1939. *Recreation:* motoring. *Address:* 30 Lon Cedwyn, Cwmgwyn, Swansea. *T.:* Swansea 24030. *Club:* Reform.
Died 7 *March* 1967.

MORRIS, R(obert) Schofield, B.Arch.; R.C.A. 1959; F.R.A.I.C. 1944; F.R.I.B.A. 1952; F.R.S.A. 1954; Partner, Marani, Morris & Allan, Architects, Toronto; *b.* 14 Nov. 1898; *s.* of Robert Simpson Morris and Jessie Corinne Parker; *m.* 1948, Elsie Strachan Johnston. *Educ.:* Ashbury Coll., Ottawa; Royal Military Coll., Kingston; McGill Univ., Montreal, Canada. Lt., Royal Artillery (Field), 1917-18. Pres. Ontario Association of Architects, 1942-43; Pres., Royal Architectural Institute of Canada, 1952-53; Hon. F.A.I.A., 1953. Royal Gold Medal for Architecture, 1958. *Recreations:* golf, gardening. *Address:* 37 Dunloe Road, Toronto, Canada. *T.:* Hudson 3-7072. *Clubs:* York, University (Toronto); University (Montreal).
[*Died* 5 *June* 1964.

MORRIS, Air Vice-Marshal Sir Samuel; *see* Morris, Air Vice-Marshal Sir A. S.

MORRIS, Rev. Canon Walter Edmund Harston, M.A.; Vicar of All Saints, Southport, 1918-56; Rural Dean of North Meols, 1934-1956; Hon. Canon Liverpool Cathedral, 1928-38, Residentiary Canon, 1938-56, Canon Emeritus, 1956; Proctor in Convocation and Member Nat. Church Assembly, 1938; *b.* Everton, Liverpool, 1872; *s.* of Rev. David Morris, Chaplain of H.M. Prison, Liverpool; *m.* 1906, Edith Nield; two *s.* one *d.* *Educ.:* Royal Institution, Liverpool; Trinity College, Cambridge (Bp. Jacobson Mem. Scho.). Deacon, 1899; Priest, 1900; Curate of St. George, Stockport, 1899-1902; St. Augustine, Highbury, 1902-5; Chaplain Blind and Deaf Asylum, Manchester, 1905-10; Vicar of Emmanuel, Preston, 1910-17; Balderston, Blackburn, 1917-18; Chairman, Bishop Liverpool's Building Campaign, 1927. *Address:* Chard Vicarage, Somerset.
[*Died* 29 *May* 1968.

MORRIS-EYTON, Lieut.-Col. and Brevet Colonel Charles Reginald, M.C.; R.A.; Deputy Lieut. Co. of Stafford, 1927; landowner; *b.* 21 July 1890; *e. s.* of late Charles Edward Morris-Eyton, Wood Eaton Manor, Stafford and Oxon, Shrewsbury; *m.* 1932, Marie Violetta Robertson-Grant; three *s.* one *d.* *Educ.:* Eton; Brasenose College, Oxford. First Commission, 1910; Capt., 1916; Lt.-Col. Commanding 61st Bde. R.F.A.(T.), 1920-1924; retired with rank of Brevet Col., 1924; Salop County Council since 1938; High Sheriff of Salop, 1938-39; succeeded to Wood Eaton and Bicton Estates on death of father, 1930, and Walford Estate was in part made over to him in 1921; greatly interested in Agriculture, and manages all estates himself; Chairman Salop Chamber of Agriculture, 1929, 1930. *Recreations:* shooting, and has done a lot of big game shooting in Africa and Canada in his young days. *Address:* Belgownie, P.B. 241A, Salisbury, S. Rhodesia; P.B.S. Ranch, Lancaster, S. Rhodesia.
[*Died* 22 *June* 1961.

MORRISON OF LAMBETH, Baron, *cr.* 1959 (Life Peer); **Herbert Stanley Morrison,**

P.C. 1931; C.H. 1951; High Steward of the City of Kingston upon Hull, 1956; *b.* 3 January 1888; *s.* of Henry and Priscella Morrison; *m.* 1st, 1919, Margaret Kent (*d.* 1953); one *d.*; 2nd, 1955, Edith, *d.* of late John Meadowcroft and of Mrs. William Davies. *Educ.:* Elementary Schools. Errand boy; shop assistant; telephone operator; deputy newspaper circulation manager; M.P. (Lab.) South Hackney, 1923-24, 1929-1931 and 1935-45, East Lewisham, 1945-1951; S. Lewisham, 1951-59; Minister of Transport, 1929-31; Minister of Supply, 1940; Home Secretary and Minister of Home Security, 1940-45; Member of War Cabinet, 1942-45; Deputy Prime Minister, 1945-51; Lord President of the Council and Leader of House of Commons, 1945-51; Sec. of State for Foreign Affairs, Mar.-Oct. 1951; Deputy Leader of Opposition, 1951-1955. Mayor of Hackney, 1920-21 (Alderman, 1921-25); Member L.C.C., 1922-45 (Leader of the Council, 1934-40); J.P. County of London. Member of Metropolitan Water Bd., 1925-28; London and Home Counties Jt. Elec. Authority, 1925-29; Jt. Town Planning Advisory Cttee. for London Traffic Area, 1927-28; Standing Joint Cttee. of Quarter Sessions and the L.C.C., 1922; Greater London Regional Planning Cttee., 1936; Nat. Service Cttee. for London, 1939-1940; London Regional Council for Civil Defence, 1939-40. Sec. to London Labour Party, 1915-47, Treas., 1948-62; Chm. Nat. Labour Party, 1928-29. Pres. Workers' Travel Assoc., 1951; Pres. Assoc. of Municipal Corporations, 1958-61. Pres. Brit. Bd. of Film Censors, 1960. Hon. Fellow of Nuffield College. Hon. LL.D. London, 1952; Hon. LL.D. Cambridge, 1956; Hon. LL.D., Maine, U.S.A., 1956, Leicester 1960; Hon. D.C.L. Oxford, 1953. *Publications:* Socialisation and Transport, 1933; How Greater London is Governed, 1925; Looking Ahead, 1943; How London is Governed, 1949; The Peaceful Revolution, 1949; Government and Parliament: A Survey from the Inside, 1954; Herbert Morrison: An Autobiography, 1960. *Address:* 14 Colepits Wood Rd., S.E.9.
[*Died* 6 *March* 1965.

MORRISON, Colonel Frank Stanley, C.M.G. 1918; D.S.O. 1917; Royal Canadian Dragoons, retd.; p.s.c.; *b.* 1881; *s.* of Francis Robert Morrison and Isobel McKay; *m.* 1st, 1910, Alice Coffin Dillingham (*d.* 1965); 2nd, 1965, Dorothy S. Roehrs. Served South African War (medal four clasps); European War, 1914-1918 (despatches, C.M.G., D.S.O., Russian Order of St. Anne, Montenegran Order of St. Danilo, 1914-15 Star, British War Medal, Allied War Medal); D.A.A.G. 2nd Canadian Division, 1915; D.A.A.G. Canadian Corps H.Q., 1916; A.A. and Q.M.G. 2nd Canadian Division, 1917; Director of Organisation, Canadian Overseas Forces, 1918; D.A.G. Can. Overseas Forces, 1918-19. *Address:* c/o Bank of Montreal, King and Bay Sts., Toronto. Ontario. Canada.
[*Died* 9 *Sept.* 1969.

MORRISON, Herbert Needham, C.B. 1947; *b.* 4 Sept. 1891; *s.* of late John Morrison, Magherafelt, Londonderry; *m.* 1917, Kathleen, *d.* of late Rev. H. M. Knox; one *s.* one *d.* *Educ.:* Queen's College, Galway; Trinity College, Cambridge. Secretary's Dept. Admiralty, 1921; Private Secretary to the Civil Lord, 1925; Principal in Secretary's Dept., 1930; Director of Greenwich Hospital, 1934-38 and 1948-51; Asst. Sec., Admiralty, 1939; Prin. Asst. Sec., 1942; Under Sec., 1946; retired, 1951. *Address:* 2 Glencree Park, Jordanstown, Co. Antrim, N. Ireland.
[*Died* 5 *March* 1963.

MORRISON, Joseph Albert Colquhoun; *b.* 17 May 1882; *y. s.* of late William Epps Morrison, Mondello Lodge, Eastbourne; unmarried. *Educ.:* Forest School; Trinity Hall, Cambridge, B.A. (Classical Tripos), 1904. Has exhibited pictures at Royal Academy, New English Art Club, etc. *Address:* Rockleigh, Chalford, Gloucestershire. *Club:* Chelsea Arts.
[*Died* 28 *July* 1964.

MORRISON-BELL, Sir Charles Reginald Francis, 3rd Bt., *cr.* 1905; Capt. XII (Royal) Lancers (R.A.C.); *b.* 26 June 1915; *s.* of Sir Claude W. H. Morrison-Bell, 2nd Bt., and Frances Isabel (*d.* 1966), *d.* of Lt.-Col. Charles Atkinson Logan, Royal Scots; *S.* father, 1943; *m.* 1955, Prudence Caroline, *o. d.* of Lt.-Col. W. D. Davies (60th Rifles, Retd.), Redesdale Cottage, Otterburn, Northumberland; two *s.* *Educ.:* Eton; Trinity Coll., Camb. High Sheriff of Northumberland, 1955-56. *Heir:* *s.* William Hollin Dayrell Morrison-Bell, *b.* 21 June 1956. *Address:* Highgreen, Tarset, Northumberland. *T.:* Greenhaugh 223. *Club:* Northern Counties (Newcastle upon Tyne).
[*Died* 22 *Dec.* 1967.

MORROW, Cdre. James Cairns, C.B.E. 1956; D.S.O. 1940; D.S.C. 1944; R.A.N. retd., Naval Officer-i/c and Sea Transport Officer, W.A. Area; *b.* 6 Feb. 1905; *m.* 1935, Elizabeth Sinton; *m.* 1946, Dulce McWhannell; two *s.* *Educ.:* Melbourne Grammar School; R.A.N. College. Cdre. 1st class 1956. Retd., 1960, rank Cdre. *Recreations:* golf, tennis. *Club:* Imperial Service (Sydney).
[*Died* 8 *Jan.* 1963.

MORSE, Sir Arthur, K.B.E. 1961 (C.B.E. 1944); Kt. 1949; Director: Bowmakers Ltd. since 1954 (Chairman, 1954-62); Mercantile Bank Ltd. 1959-65; British Bank of the Middle East 1960-65; *b.* 25 April 1892. Member of the London Committee of The Hongkong and Shanghai Banking Corporation. Chairman British Travel and Holidays Association, 1954-60. Hon. LL.D. (Hong Kong). Order of Benemerencia, Portugal, 1951. *Recreations:* racing and golf. *Address:* 84 Arlington House, Arlington Street, S.W.1. *Clubs:* Junior Carlton, Oriental.
[*Died* 13 *May* 1967.

MORT, David Llewellyn; M.P. (Lab.) East Swansea since 1940; Secretary South Wales Branch of Iron and Steel Trades Confederation since 1915; *b.* Briton Ferry, 1888; M.P. (Lab.) Eccles, 1929-31. *Address:* Plas Gwyn, Caereithin, Swansea. *T.:* 32743 Swansea.
[*Died* 1 *Jan.* 1963.

MORTIMER, Brig. Philip, C.I.E. 1939; Indian Army, retd.; *b.* 22 April 1882; *s.* of Col. Francis James Mortimer, R.A.; *m.* 1906, Ruth, *d.* of Maj. R. Johnston, H.L.I.; one *s.* *Educ.:* Cheltenham College; R.M.C., Sandhurst. 2nd Lt., East Surrey Regt., 1901; Indian Army, 1903; France and Flanders in European War, 1914-18; 3rd Afghan War, 1919; Waziristan Campaign, 1920-22 (despatches); Lt.-Col., 1929; Col., 1932; Brigadier, 1935. *Address:* Kiln Cottage, Saltwood, Kent. *T.:* Hythe 67518.
[*Died* 3 *July* 1963.

MORTLOCK, Rev. Canon Charles Bernard, M.A.; F.S.A.; Hon. A.R.I.B.A.; Hon. C.F.; Rector of St. Vedast, Foster-lane, E.C., since 1947; Canon and Treasurer of Chichester Cathedral since 1950; Proctor in Convocation of Canterbury, 1931-60; Chairman: of Council, Actors' Church Union; Palestine Exploration Fund (Hon. Sec., 1936-55); a Gov. of Royal Ballet School, and of Heathfield School, Ascot; F.J.I.; Mem. editorial staff of Daily Telegraph; Member: C. of E. Council on Inter-Church Relations (inception—1961); Bd. of Studies in Architecture, Univ. of London (Chm., 1946-60); Grand Council of Roy. Acad. of Dancing; Grand Council of Imperial Soc. of Teachers of Dancing; Cttee. of Management, Nat. Bldgs. Record, 1952-61; Cttee. of the Victorian Soc.; *b.* 27 Feb. 1888;

o. s. of late James Charles Mortlock; unmarried. *Educ.:* Jesus Coll., Cambridge. Ordained, 1913; Asst. curate successively Batcombe, Somerset, St. Mary-le-Bow, St. Silas, Kentish Town, St. John, Gt. Marlborough Street and St. Mary-le-Strand, London; Vicar of Epping, Essex, 1936-47; Ed. of The Challenge, 1914-16; temp. C.F., 1916-17 (relinq. commn. on account of illness contracted in France); Assistant Editor of Country Life, 1918-19; Editor Treasury Magazine, 1918; Lecturer on Ecclesiastical Art, King's Coll., London, 1936-40; Chairman Press Committee of Church Assembly, 1936-57; Member Financial Commn. and Publicity Commn. of Church Assembly; Member, Central Council for the Care of Churches, from inception till 1960; Archbishop's Commission on Evangelism; Council of Society of Antiquaries, 1952-1953; Ecclesiastical Corresp. to Daily Telegraph, 1921-; Archæological Corresp., 1929-; special Corresp. in Europe, India and Middle East; Urbanus, of the Church Times, 1919-; dramatic and ballet criticism in Daily Telegraph, Weekly Dispatch, Punch, City Press, and Church Times; President Critics Circle, 1946-47; magazine and review articles in England and America; contributor, D.N.B.; Poor Law Guardian for the city of Westminster, 1928-30. *Publications:* People's Book of the Oxford Movement, 1933; Famous London Churches, 1934; Inky Blossoms: a collection of essays, 1949. *Address:* St. Vedast's Rectory, Foster Lane, E.C.2; 2 Vicar's Close, Chichester. *Clubs:* Athenæum, Garrick; Royal Fowey Yacht (Fowey); Royal Western Yacht (Plymouth). [*Died* 31 *Oct.* 1967.

MORTON, Guy Mainwaring; author; (nom-de-plume, Peter Traill); *b.* 9 Sep. 1896; *s.* of late Captain Harry Mainwaring Dunstan, *stepson* of late Michael Morton; *m.* 1924, Clare, *o. d.* of late M. H. Horsley, J.P., West Hartlepool, Co. Durham; one *s.* *Educ.:* Rugby; Univ. Coll., Oxford. Joined R.G.A., 1915; promoted Actg.-Capt., 1917; Actg.-Major, 1918; despatches, 1918; B.A. 1920; Barrister, Inner Temple, 1921; Ministry of Information, 1939-45. *Publications:* Woman to Woman, 1924; Memory's Geese, 1924; The Divine Spark, 1926; Under the Cherry Tree, 1926; The White Hen, 1927; Some Take a Lover, 1928; The Life Fashionable, 1929; Great Dust, 1932; Here Lies Love, 1932; The Angel, 1934; Carry Me Home, 1934; Red, Green and Amber, 1935; Half Mast, 1936; The Sleeve of Night, 1937; Not Proven, 1938; Six of One, 1938; Golden Oriole, 1940 The Wedding of the Jackal, 1943; No Farthing Richer, 1944; The Deceiving Mirror, 1946; Under the Plane Trees, 1947; Midnight Oil, 1947; So Sits the Turtle, 1948; The Portly Peregrine, 1948; Caravanserai, 1949; The Singing Apple, 1949; Wings of Tomorrow, 1950; Mutation Mink, 1950; The Rope of Sand, 1951; French Dressing, 1952. Plays produced: Fallen Angels (with Michael Morton), 1924; After the Theatre (with Michael Morton), 1924; By Right of Conquest (with Michael Morton), 1925; Salvage (with Michael Morton), 1926; The Stranger in the House (with Michael Morton), 1928; Because of Irene (with Michael Morton), 1929; Tread Softly, 1936. *Address:* 24 Cliveden Place, S.W.1. *T.:* Sloane 7388 *Club:* Bath. [*Died* 11 *Nov.* 1968.

MORTON, Air Vice-Marshal (retd.) Terence Charles St. Clessie, C.B. 1950; O.B.E. 1935; M.D. (Ed.) 1921; F.R.C.P. (Lond.) 1944; retired as Area Pathologist, West Cornwall Clinical Area (1951-60); *b.* 25 Sept. 1893; *o. s.* of R. A. Morton, Mussoorie, U.P., India; *m.* 1921, Emily Frances, *d.* of late Dr. Robertson Dobie, Crieff, Scotland. *Educ.:* Stewart's College, Edinburgh; Edinburgh University. Surgeon Probationer. R.N.V.R., 1914-15; Surgeon, R.N., 1915-19; Ft. Lt. R.A.F., 1919; Z expedition Somaliland, 1919-20; P.M.O., British Forces, Iraq, 1940 (despatches); Consultant in Pathology and Tropical Medicine, R.A.F., 1943; Senior Consultant, R.A.F., 1948; retd. 1951. Member of Council: Royal Soc. of Tropical Medicine, 1948-51; Assoc. of Clinical Pathologists, 1950-53. K.H.P., 1944-1951. *Publications:* (novel) All Square with Fate, 1933; Malaria, Brit. Encyc. of Med. Practice, 1952; contributions to Lancet, B.M.J., etc. *Recreations:* fly-fishing, golf. *Address:* Saffron Meadow, Penryn, Cornwall. *T.:* Penryn 2576. *Clubs:* United Hunts, Royal Cornwall Yacht. [*Died* 16 *Oct.* 1968.

MOSELEY, Sydney Alexander; author and journalist; Radio Columnist, U.S.A.; Director, The Outspoken Press; Chairman and Managing Editor, Television Press, Ltd.; Vice-President Newspaper Press Fund; Founder and Life Member Overseas Press Club of America; Founder and First President Broadcast Critics Circle; *b.* London, Mar. 1888; married. Began journalism in London; joined staff, Daily Express, 1910; edited first English daily published in Cairo, where he conducted a world-wide campaign against the Capitulations, 1913; also edited other English weeklies in Egypt, and was Cairo correspondent of the New York Times, Paris Daily Mail, Central News, London; Univ. of London, O.T.C., Aug. 1914; official corresp. with the Mediterranean Expeditionary Forces, 1914; commission in the R.N.V.R., attached to the C.-in-C. Coast of Scotland; founded and edited Southend Times; contested (I.L.P.) Southend-on-Sea, 1924; instrumental in obtaining broadcast of television in this country; was first to broadcast speech and vision simultaneously; first radio critic; has been special correspondent of Daily Express, Evening News, Sunday Express, Daily Herald, People, etc.; has contrib. to Encyclopædia Britannica, Cassell's History of the Great War, Harmsworth's Universal Encyclopædia. Prospective Indep. Parl. candidate for Bournemouth, 1959. *Publications:* With Kitchener in Cairo, 1917; Truth about the Dardanelles, 1916; The Fleet from Within, 1919; An Amazing Seance and an Exposure, 1919; Night Haunts of London; Haunts of the Gay East, 1920; A Singular People, 1921; The Much Chosen Race, 1921; Love's Ordeal, 1923; Brightest Spots in Brighter London; The Mysterious Medium, 1925; New Light Side of London, 1926; Truth About Borstal, 1926; The Convict of To-Day, 1927; Money Making in Stocks and Shares, 1927; The Small Investor's Guide, 1929; Television To-Day and To-Morrow, 1930; Short Story Writing and Free-Lance Journalism, 1928; The Truth about Journalism, 1931; Who's Who in Broadcasting, 1932; Broadcasting In My Time, 1935; Founded Liberty Press Ltd., 1934; The Truth about a Journalist, 1935; Television for the Intelligent Amateur, 1936; Russia Without Prejudice, 1937; Simple Guide to Television, 1938; From Fleet Street to Times Square (New York), 1945; God Help America!, 1951; John Baird, The Romance and Tragedy of the Pioneer of Television, 1952; Private Diaries of Sydney Moseley (1903-60), 1960. Began For Editors Only, a new monthly publication, 1950; publisher and editor of The Critic, a monthly. *Recreations:* singing, study of opera, swimming, tennis, golf, and losing money made by writing by speculating on the Stock Exchange, travelling. *Address:* 36 Christchurch Rd., Bournemouth. *Clubs:* Press, Royal Automobile; Overseas Press Club of America (New York). [*Died* 5 *Dec.* 1961.

MOSS, Abraham; M.A., J.P.; *b.* 1899; *m.* 1935, Doris Lewis. *Educ.:* Salford Grammar School. Elected Manchester City Council, 1929; J.P., 1943; Alderman, 1946; Lord Mayor of Manchester, 1953-54; Chairman: Town Hall Cttee., 1950-53; Libraries, 1938-1942; Blind Welfare, 1935-38; Chairman:

Manchester Education Committee, 1959; Nathan Laski Memorial Trust; Manchester King David Schools; [Chairman: Manchester Victoria Memorial Jewish Hospital; Manchester Wireless for the Blind; North Manchester Hospital Management Cttee.; Mem. Manchester Regional Hosp. Bd.; Vice-Chairman: Manchester Corporation Airport Cttee.; Manchester Northern Hosp.; President: Manchester Luncheon Club; Manchester and Regional Cttee. for Poliomyelitis Research; Manchester Jewish Blind Society; Vice-President: Assoc. of Education Cttees.; Manchester and Salford Blind Aid Society; Board of Deputies of British Jews; Henshaw's Institute for the Blind; Manchester Jewish Homes for the Aged; President: Youth Hostels Association (England and Wales); Manchester and Dist. Regional Group; Exec. Mem. Duke of Edinburgh's Award; Governor: De La Salle Training Coll.; Manchester Gram. Sch.; William Hulme's Gram. Sch.; Bury Gram. Sch.; Manchester High School for Girls; Manchester College of Science and Technol.; Manchester Coll. of Music; Northern School of Music: Past Pres. Council of Manchester and Salford Jews. Member: Departmental Cttee. on Central Criminal Court, in S. Lancs.; Court of Governors of University of Manchester; Council, Univ. of Manchester. Manchester Emergency Cttee., 1940-46. Executive: National Institute for the Blind; Hallé Concerts Soc.; Friends of the Hebrew University of Jerusalem. M.A. (Honoris Causa), Manchester, 1952. *Recreations:* swimming, walking. *Address:* 85 Park Road, Prestwich, Lancs. *T.:* Deansgate 3011/2/3 and Cheetham Hill 1938. [*Died* 20 *June* 1964.

MOSSE, Robert Lee; *b.* 6 Jan. 1877; *s.* of late James Robert Mosse, of the Admiralty; *m.* 1st, 1910, Dorothy (*d.* 1957), *d.* of late Thomas Bowater Vernon; four *s.*; 2nd, Eileen, *widow* of Robert Elphinstone Bradley, Indian Police. *Educ.:* Highgate Sch. Admitted a solicitor, 1899; formerly a partner in firm of Gibson and Weldon, 27 Chancery Lane, W.C.2; Master of the Supreme Court, Chancery Division, 1930-50. *Address:* Loriners, The Green, Pembury, Tunbridge Wells. *T.:* Pembury 97. [*Died* 10 *Feb.* 1963.

MOSSOP, Sir Allan (George), Kt., *cr.* 1937; *b.* 30 July 1887; *s.* of late Joseph Mossop, Cape Town; *m.* 1st, 1920, Linda Maud (*d.* 1949), *o. d.* of late Alexander William Elliot, Rangoon; 2nd, 1950, Jean Maud Bennett, M.B.E., *widow* of Lieut.-Commander William Alexander Elliot, R.N.; no *c.* *Educ.:* Kingswood College, Grahamstown; South African College, Cape Town; Pembroke College, Cambridge (MA.., LL.B.). Called to Bar, Inner Temple, 1908; Acting Crown Advocate of Weihaiwei, 1915-16; Crown Advocate, 1916-30; Acting Crown Advocate in China frequent periods, 1916-23; Crown Advocate, 1925-33; British Custodian in China of Enemy Property, 1918-20; Commissioner on the Sino-British Joint Commission on Nanking Claims, 1928-29; Judge of H.B.M. Supreme Court for China, 1933-43; Counsellor (Legal) at British Embassy in China, 1945-46; retired, 1946. *Address:* c/o Barclays Bank (D.C. & O.), Adderley Street, Cape Town, S. Africa. *Clubs:* Junior Carlton; Civil Service (Cape Town). [*Died* 14 *June* 1965.

MOSTON, Henry E., C.B.E. 1937; J.P.; Secretary of Labour and Chief Inspector of Factories, New Zealand, 1932-47, retd.; *b.* Runcorn, Cheshire, 3 June 1881; *s.* of William and Martha Moston; *m.* 1908, Margaret Hill, Runcorn; three *d.* *Educ.:* Runcorn Parish Church School; United Kingdom College. Before coming out to New Zealand employed for 11 years by Manchester Ship Canal Co.; studied with a view to entering the Civil Service; attracted by the progressive industrial legislation which had been introduced under the Seddon regime decided to come out to New Zealand; joined Labour Department in 1908; charge of Westland District with headquarters at Greymouth, then transferred to Wanganui and subsequently became first Officer in Charge of the Wellington District; later, Officer in Charge, Auckland; Deputy Chief Inspector of Factories for the Dominion, 1918. Chairman, Industrial Advisory Council, N.Z., 1952-. *Recreations:* music (Chairman of Royal Wellington Choral Union, 1934-48; President British Music Society). *Address:* Hamilton Road, Hataitai, Wellington, N.Z. *T.:* 81385. [*Died* 30 *Oct.* 1962.

MOSTYN, 4th Baron (*cr.* 1831); **Edward Llewelyn Roger Lloyd-Mostyn,** Bt. 1778; *b.* 16 March 1885; *s.* of 3rd Baron and Lady Mary Florence Edith Clements, O.B.E. (*d.* 1933), *sister* of 4th Earl of Leitrim: *S.* father, 1929; *m.* 1918, Constance Mary, *o. c.* of W. H. Reynolds, Aldeburgh; one *s.* one *d.* (and two *s.* decd.). *Educ.:* Eton. Joined Irish Guards, 1905; 3rd Bn. Roy. Welch Fus., 1908; temp. Capt. Denbighshire Yeomanry, 1916-18; temp. Lt. R. Horse Guards, 1918-19; J.P., D.L. Flint. *Heir:* *s.* Capt. Hon. Roger Edward Lloyd-Mostyn, M.C. *Address:* Mostyn Hall, Mostyn, Flint. [*Died* 2 *May* 1965.

MOTT, Sir Adrian Spear, 2nd Bt., *cr.* 1930; *b.* 5 Oct. 1889; *s.* of Sir Basil Mott, 1st Bt., C.B., F.R.S. and Florence Harmar Parker; *S.* father, 1938; *m.* 1914, Mary Katharine, *d.* of Rev. Alfred Herbert Stanton, formerly Vicar of St. Peter's, Oxford; one *s.* two *d.* *Educ.:* Radley; Merton College, Oxford, M.A. Barrister, Inner Temple, 1915; served European War, 1915-18; Capt., R.F.A.; a publisher. *Heir:* *s.* John Harmar [*b.* 21 July 1922; *m.* 1950, Elizabeth, *o. d.* of Hugh Carson, Weoley Hill, Birmingham; one *s.* two *d.* *Educ.:* Radley; New Coll., Oxford. Served R.A.F., 1943-46]. *Address:* Appletree Cottage, 115 Victoria Rd., Oxford. *T.:* Oxford 58926. [*Died* 23 *May* 1964.

MOTTISTONE, 2nd Baron, *cr.* 1933, of Mottistone; **Henry John Alexander Seely,** O.B.E. 1961; F.S.A.; F.R.I.B.A.; D.L. Co. Southampton; Surveyor of the Fabric of St. Paul's Cathedral; Chairman of the London Society; Lay Canon of Portsmouth Cathedral; *b.* 1 May 1899; *e. s.* of 1st Baron Mottistone, P.C., C.B., C.M.G., D.S.O., and Emily Florence Crichton; *S.* father 1947. *Educ.:* Harrow; Trinity College, Cambridge. Served European War, 1914-18, with R.F.A. in Italy and War of 1939-45 as Flight-Lieut. Auxiliary Air Force (A.E.A.) and Emergency Works Officer, Ministry of Works. Principal Architectural works, with his partner Paul Paget, include: Restoration, Eltham Palace; Reconstruction, after war damage, of Lambeth Palace; the Deanery and Canons' Houses, Westminster Abbey; Fulham Palace; the Charterhouse, London; Eton College; All Hallows by the Tower; S. Mary's, Islington; St. George's, Stevenage New Town; St. Mary's, West Kensington; Chapel for the Order of The British Empire in St. Paul's Cathedral; New Chapel, St. John's School, Leatherhead; Orpington Public Library. New buildings for Educational Training Colleges at Oxford, Bishop's Stortford, Bristol, Cambridge, Culham, Norwich and Carmarthen. Architect to St. George's Chapel, Windsor, and Portsmouth Cathedral. Pres. Royal Isle of Wight Agricultural Soc., 1961 and 1962. C.St.J. *Heir:* *b.* Hon. (Arthur) Patrick William Seely, T.D. *Address:* 41 Cloth Fair, E.C.1. *T.:* Central 0321; Mottistone Magna, Isle of Wight. *T.:* Brighstone 322. *Clubs:* Athenæum; Royal Solent Yacht. [*Died* 18 *Jan.* 1963.

MOTTISTONE, 3rd Baron, *cr.* 1933, of Mottistone; **Arthur Patrick William Seely,** T.D.; Land Agent; *b.* 18 Aug. 1905; 2nd *surv. s.* of 1st Baron Mottistone, P.C., C.B., C.M.G., D.S.O., and Emily Florence Crichton; *S.* brother, 2nd Baron Mottistone, O.B.E., 1963; *m.* 1939, Wilhelmina Josephine Philippa (from whom he obtained a divorce, 1949), *o. d.* of Baron Van Haeften, The Hague, Holland, and of Lady Ley, Pitt Manor, Winchester. *Educ.:* Harrow; Trinity College, Cambridge. Lieut. R.A. 1939; Captain, 1940; Major, 1942; Lt.-Col. (T.A.) 1947 (Comdg. 313 H.A.A. Regt. R.A. (T.A.)). Contested E. Division of Nottingham (L.) July 1945. County Councillor, Isle of Wight, 1934-38. *Heir: half b.* Capt. Hon. David Peter Seely, R.N. [*b.* 16 Dec. 1920; *m.* 1944, Anthea Christine, *d.* of Victor McMullan; two *s.* two *d.*]. *Address:* Mottistone Magna, Isle of Wight. *Club:* National Liberal. [*Died* 4 *Dec.* 1966.

MOULD, John, O.B.E. 1954; retired as Chairman, The East Midlands Electricity Board (1957-59); *b.* 7 April 1890; *e. s.* of John Thomas Mould and Minnie (*née* Bird); *m.* 1918, Mabel Hawkins (*d.* 1962); no *c.* *Educ.:* Essex County High School; City and Guilds Technical College, Assistant to Professor Sylvanus Thompson, F.R.S., 1910-13; Generator Designer, Siemens Bros. Dynamo Works, Stafford, 1913-19; Deputy Chief Engineer, Leicester Corporation Electricity Dept., 1919-27; General Manager and Chief Engineer, Leicester Corporation Electricity Dept., 1927-48; Deputy Chairman, East Midlands Electricity Board, 1948-1957. *Recreations:* walking, sailing. *Address:* Fair Acre, Chapel Lane, Minchinhampton, Glos. [*Died* 13 *Dec.* 1964.

MOULD, Sam Carter, C.I.E. 1932; *b.* Edgbaston, 27 Sep. 1880; *m.* 1908; one *s.* one *d.* *Educ.:* Penrhyn House School, Edgbaston; King Edwards, Birmingham (Junior and Senior Scholar, Leaving Exhibitioner), Jesus Coll., Cambridge (Scholar and Prizeman); 13th Wrangler in 1902; Mechanical Sciences Tripos, 1903. Joined Indian Service of Engineers, 1904. Posted to Bombay Presidency and served on the Jamrao Canal, Sind, 1905-08; Assistant Engineer in charge Lake Beale Dam Construction in Nasik District, 1909-11; Executive Engineer, Dam Construction and Irrigation Management Nasik and Ahmednagar Districts and also had Executive Charge of Roads and Buildings Construction and Maintenance in Ahmednagar and Poona Districts for short periods, 1912-22; returned to Sind Aug. 1923 as Superintending Engineer of the Rohri Canal Circle in the Lloyd Barrage and Canals Construction; in charge. Joint Chief Engineer in Sind, 1932. Chief Engineer, 1933; retired, 1935; special duty in Bombay in connection with amalgamation of Public Works and Civil Accounts, Feb. 1916. *Address:* Russet House, Hindhead, Surrey. [*Died* 30 *March* 1963.

MOULLIN, Eric Balliol, M.A., Sc.D. M.I.E.E.; Chartered Electrical Engineer; Fellow of King's College, Cambridge; Professor of Electrical Engineering, Cambridge University, 1945-60; *b.* 10 Aug. 1893; *s.* of Arthur D. Moullin, A.M.I.C.E., and *g.s.* of W. Bailleul Moullin, St. Peter Port, Guernsey; *m.* 1st, Christobel, *yr. d.* of late Prof. E. S. Prior, A.R.A.; two *d.*; 2nd, 1934, Joan Evelyn, *er. d.* of L. F. Salzman, F.S.A. *Educ.:* privately; Downing College, Cambridge (Mathematical Scholar); 1st class honours, Mechanical Sciences Tripos; John Winbolt Prizeman; M.A. 1919, Sc.D. 1939; M.A., Oxon, 1930; LL.D. (*honoris causa*) Glasgow University, 1958. Univ. Lecturer in Engineering at Cambridge and Assistant Lecturer, King's College, Cambridge, till 1929; Donald Pollock Reader in Engineering Science, Oxford, 1930-45; Fellow of Magdalen College, Oxford, 1932-45; served as temporary Senior Experimental Officer at Admiralty Signals Establishment, Portsmouth, 1940-42; Member of Senior Research Staff of Metropolitan Vickers Electrical Co. Ltd., Manchester, 1942-44; President Inst. Electrical Engineers, 1949-50; Chairman of Radio Section, 1939; a Governor of the College of Aeronautics until 1949; Member of the Radio Research Board of the Ministry of Scientific and Industrial Research, 1934-1942; Vice-Pres. and Past Chm. of Council Guernsey Society; Seigneur du Fief des Éperons, and Vavasseur du Fief de la Chapelle and du Fief de Bruniaux de Noirement, Guernsey. Associated with work on the vibration of ships; inventor of Moullin Torsionmeter, Voltmeter, and various electrical measuring instruments. *Publications:* Radio Frequency Measurements, 1926 and 1930; Principles of Electro-magnetism, 1932, 1950, and 1955; Spontaneous Fluctuations of Voltage and Shot Effect, 1938; Radio Aerials, 1949; Electromagnetic Principles of the Dynamo, 1955; scientific papers before the Royal Society, Cambridge Philosophical Society, Institution of Electrical Engineers, etc.; Antiquarian papers, Guernsey. *Address:* 21 Sedley Taylor Rd., Cambridge. [*Died* 18 *Sept.* 1963.

MOULTON, Hon. Hugh Fletcher; Barrister-at-law; *s.* of Lord Moulton of Bank and Clara, *widow* of R. W. Thomson, Edinburgh; *m.* 1st, 1902, Ida (*d.* 1933), *y. d.* of Boydell Houghton; no *c.*; 2nd, 1937, Marie Josephine, *d.* of late Sebastien Bergaentzle. *Educ.:* Eton; King's College, Cambridge (Scholar); 5th Wrangler, 1898. Called to Bar, 1899; L.C.C. Education Committee, 1913-15, 1919-1922; M.P. (L.) Salisbury, Dec. 1923-Oct. 1924; served in R.G.A., chiefly in France and Belgium, Major R.G.A., 1915-19 (M.C.). Fellow, Imperial Coll. of Science and Technology. *Publications:* Life of Lord Moulton; Fletcher Moulton on Patents; Articles on Patents, Designs and Trademarks, Hailsham Edition Laws of England; Articles on Patents in Encyclopædia Britannica; Merchandise Marks Act; Companion to the Company Act, 1929; The Importers Guide to Customs and Tariffs; Powers and Duties of Education Authorities; The National Tariff Policy; Trial of Steinie Morrison; Trial of Mason; Without the Law; Urgent Private Affairs; The Unofficial Executor; The Man in the Turkish Bath etc. *Address:* 16 Argyll Road, W.8. *T.:* Western 2687; 2 Paper Buildings, Temple, E.C.4. *T.:* Central 2487. *Clubs:* Garrick, Savage. [*Died* 4 *Jan.* 1962.

MOUNSEY, Sir George Augustus, K.C.M.G., *cr.* 1933 (C.M.G. 1924); C.B. 1931; O.B.E. 1915; *b.* 21 Dec. 1879. *Educ.:* Harrow; New College, Oxford. Entered Diplomatic Service, 1902; served at The Hague, Berlin, Constantinople, Rome, and then F.O.; Third Secretary, 1904; Second Secretary, 1908; First Secretary, 1915; Counsellor, 1924; Assistant Under Secretary of State, Foreign Office, 1929; Secretary, Ministry of Economic Warfare, 1939-40. *Address:* 96A Mount Street, W.1. *Clubs:* Royal Automobile, Lansdowne. [*Died* 3 *April* 1966.

MOUNTAIN, John Francis, C.B. 1958; retired as Under-Secretary, Admiralty (1951-1958); *b.* 24 June 1895; *m.* 1st, 1927, Doris Gordon (*née* Burrell) (*d.* 1951); one *s.* one *d.*; 2nd, 1953, Greta Gordon (*née* Burrell). Entered Civil Service (Admiralty) June 1914. Various posts, from 1914, in H.M. Dockyards and in Admiralty. Sub-Lt., R.N.V.R. (63rd R.N. Div.), 1918-19. Called to Bar (Middle Temple), 1921. *Address:* Merok, Oakwood Avenue, Purley, Surrey. [*Died* 12 *Sept.* 1965.

MOUNT EDGCUMBE, 6th Earl of *cr.* 1789; **Kenelm William Edward**

Edgcumbe, T.D.; D.L.; Visc. Mount Edgcumbe and Valletort, 1781; Baron Edgcumbe of Mount Edgcumbe, Co. Cornwall (U.K.), 1742; Fellow of University College, London; late Lt.-Col. R.E. (T.A.); J.P. Herts; *s.* of late Richard Edgcumbe; *S. cousin*, 1944; *m.* 1906, Lillian Agnes (*d.* 1964), *d.* of Col. A. C. Arkwright, of Hatfield Place, Essex; three *d.* (one *s.* killed in action, 1940). *Educ.:* Harrow. Studied Electrical Engineering in Germany and at University College, London. Served throughout European War, 1914-18. Hon. Member and Past President of the Institution of Electrical Engineers; late Hon. Secretary of the International Electrotechnical Commission; Fellow (Past President) of the Illuminating Engineering Society of Great Britain; Member of the American Institute of Electrical Engineers; M.I.C.E., F.Inst.P., etc.; a keen Territorial for twenty-five years. D.L., County of Cornwall, 1961-. O.St.J. 1964. *Heir: cousin*, Edward Piers Edgcumbe [*b.* 1903; *e. s.* of late George Valletort Edgcumbe; *m.* 1944, Victoria Effie Warbrick, *y. d.* of late Robert Campbell]. *Address:* Mount Edgcumbe, Plymouth. *T.:* Millbrook 311. *Club:* Athenæum.
[*Died* 10 *Feb.* 1965.

MOUNTGARRET, 16th Viscount (Ireland), *cr.* 1550; **Piers Henry Augustine Butler;** Baron, *cr.* 1911; *b.* 28 Aug. 1903; *s.* of 14th Viscount Mountgarret and Robinia Marion (*d.* 1944), *d.* of Col. E. Hanning Lee, Bighton Manor, Alresford; *S.* brother, 1918; *m.* 1st, 1931, Eglantine Marie Elizabeth (from whom he obtained a divorce, 1941; she *m.* 1956, Rear-Admiral P.V. McLaughlin, C.B., D.S.O.); *e. d.* of late W. L. Christie; one *s.* one *d.*, 2nd, 1941, Margarita, *d.* of Sir John Barran, 2nd Bt. *Educ.:* R.N. College, Dartmouth; Trinity College, Cambridge. Owns about 14,700 acres. *Heir: s.* Hon. Richard Henry Piers Butler [*b.* 8 Nov. 1936; *m.* 1960, Gillian Margaret, *o. d.* of Francis Buckley; two *s.* one *d.*]. *Address:* Nidd Hall, Harrogate; Eaglehall, Pateley Bridge, Yorks; Ballyconra, Kilkenny.
[*Died* 2 *Aug.* 1966.

MOUSLEY, Edward Opotiki, M.A., LL.B. (Cantab.), LL.B. (N.Z.) and Lincoln's Inn; Barrister-at-Law and Writer; *b.* 27 March 1886; *s.* of William Thorp Mousley and Sophia Allday; *m.* Mona (*d.* 1952), *e. d.* of late Colonel F. C. King-Hunter; three *s.* one *d.* *Educ.:* Victoria College (N.Z.); Emmanuel College, Cambridge. Active service, 1914-18; wounded and prisoner of war with General Townshend's army in siege of Kut-el-Amara; Capt., Royal Field Artillery, mentioned in special post-war despatch for gallantry in attempting escape over Marmora Sea; Chief Legislative Draftsman, Judicial Dept. Mesopotamia, 1919-20; member, British Empire delegation to Washington Conference, 1921-22, Hague Conference, 1922, Third Assembly League of Nations, etc.; Legal Advisor Reparation Claims Dept. (Sumner Commission). *Publications:* The Place of International Law in Jurisprudence (awarded Camb. Univ. Diploma as original contribution to world's knowledge); An Empire View of the Empire Tangle; The Secrets of a Kuttite; Blow Bugles Blow: An English Odyssey (a novel); A British Brief: England's Reparation Victims and War Debt: Mr. Salt Finds Happiness (novel); Le Siège de Kut-el-Amara; Man or Leviathan?; Federal Union (with others); The Democratic Advance. *Recreations:* travel, fishing. *Address:* Far Curlews, Hayling Island. *Club:* Oxford and Cambridge.
[*Died* 17 *Jan.* 1965.

MOWAT, Colonel Sir Alfred Law, 2nd Bt., *cr.* 1932; D.S.O. 1919; O.B.E. 1944; M.C.; D.L.; Vice-Lieutenant, West Riding, Yorks, since 1951; J.P.; *b.* 1890; *o. s.* of Sir J. G. Mowat, 1st Bt.; *S.* father 1935; *m.* 1920, Dorothy Louise, *d.* of H. Hirst Waller, J.P., Westvale, Halifax; one *d.* Served European War, 1914-19 (despatches, D.S.O., M.C. and bar); War of 1939-45 to Sept. 1941. A.A. Royal Artillery. J.P. 1921, D.L. 1943, West Riding, Yorks. *Heir:* none. *Address:* Oldfield Nook, Scholes, Cleckheaton, Yorks.
[*Died* 20 *Oct.* 1968 (*ext.*).

MOWBRAY (25th Baron, *cr.* 1283), **SEGRAVE** (26th Baron, *cr.* 1283), **and STOURTON,** of Stourton, co. Wilts (22nd Baron, *cr.* 1448), **Capt. William Marmaduke Stourton,** M.C.; late Grenadier Guards; late Lieut. 8th (King's Royal Irish) Hussars; *b.* 31 Aug. 1895; *e. s.* of 24th Baron Mowbray, 25th Baron Segrave and 21st Baron Stourton and Mary (*d.* 1961), *o. c.* of late Thomas Angus Constable, Manor House, Otley, Yorks.; *S.* father, 1936; *m.* 1921, Sheila, *er. d.* of late Hon. Edward Gully, C.B.; one *s.* one *d.* *Educ.:* Downside School; R.M.C., Sandhurst. Served European War, 1915-18 (M.C.); retired, 1928. *Heir: s.* Hon. Charles Edward Stourton, 2nd Lt. Grenadier Guards [*b.* 11 March 1923; *m.* 1952, Hon. Jane Faith de Yarburgh-Bateson, *o. d.* of Baron Deramore; two *s.*]. *Address:* Allerton Park, near Knaresborough, Yorkshire.
[*Died* 7 *May* 1965.

MOWBRAY, Sir George Robert, 5th Bt., *cr.* 1880; K.B.E. 1957; D.L.; *b.* 15 July 1899; *s.* of 4th Bt. and Caroline Elwes (*d.* 1941), *d.* of late Gen. G. T. Field, R.A.; *S.* father, 1919; *m.* 1927, Diana Margaret, *d.* of Sir Robert Heywood Hughes, 12th Bt.; one *s.* two *d.* *Educ.:* Charterhouse; New Coll., Oxford, M.A. Served European War in France with R.F.A.; High Sheriff of Berkshire, 1930; Alderman of Berkshire, 1938; Vice-Chm. of Berks. County Council, 1957-60 (Chm., 1944-1946 and 1960-65). A.R.P. Controller for Berkshire, 1939-45. Vice-Chm. of County Councils Assoc., 1946 and 1949-50, Chm., 1950-56; Mem. Royal Commission on Civil Service, 1953-55; President of the University Council, University of Reading, 1933-66 (Treasurer, 1931-33). Warden of Bradfield College Council, 1945-46. D.L., Berks., 1967. *Heir: s.* John Robert Mowbray [*b.* 1 March 1932; *m.* 1957, Lavinia Mary, *d.* of late Lt.-Col. Francis Hugonin, Stainton House, Stainton in Cleveland, Yorkshire; three *d.*]. *Address:* Warennes Wood, Mortimer, Berks. *Club:* Oxford and Cambridge.
[*Died* 9 *Nov.* 1969.

MOWLL, Rt. Rev. Edward Worsfold, M.A.; Canon Emeritus of Manchester Cathedral since 1952; Assistant Bishop, Diocese of Bath and Wells, 1952-58; *b.* 1881; *s.* of late Worsfold and Mary Mowll; *m.* 1st, 1909, Josephine Denham Gildea (*d.* 1912); one *s.*; 2nd, 1915, Margaret Cicely (*d.* 1958), *d.* of late Colonel and Lady Mary Skrine; 3rd, 1959, Alice Hone, *d.* of late Bishop and Mrs. Kempson. *Educ.:* The King's School, Canterbury; Jesus College and Ridley Hall, Cambridge. Curate, Leyton Parish Church, 1905-11; Assistant Secretary, Church Pastoral-Aid Society, 1911-15; Vicar of Benwell, Newcastle upon Tyne, 1915-19; Vicar of Christ Church, Southport, 1919-28; Rector of St. Aldate's, Oxford, 1928-33; Provost of Bradford Cathedral, Vicar of Bradford and Surrogate, 1933-43; Rural Dean of Bradford, 1935-43; Suffragan Bishop of Middleton, 1943-51; Hon. Canon of Liverpool Cathedral and Surrogate, 1926-28. *Recreation:* at Cambridge gained Trial Cap for University Boat Race, 1901. *Address:* Ram Alley, Burbage, Marlborough, Wilts. *T.:* Burbage 373.
[*Died* 12 *June* 1964.

MOXHAM, Sir Harry Cuthbertson, Kt. 1935; D.D.S., F.A.C.D.; Chairman of a group of Industrial and Mining Companies. *Educ.:* Sydney High School; University of Pennsylvania, U.S.A. President Australian Dental Association, 1934-37; ex-President

Australian Dental Assoc., N.S.W. Branch; ex-Chairman Dental Research Department, University of Sydney, etc. *Address:* 175 Macquarie Street, Sydney, N.S.W.; 687 New South Head Road, Rose Bay, Sydney, N.S.W. *Clubs:* Royal Sydney Golf; Elanora Country Golf; American National.
[*Died* 3 *Jan.* 1965.

MOYLAN, Sir John FitzGerald, Kt., *cr.* 1932; C.B. 1923; C.B.E. 1918; *b.* Grenada, 16 June 1882; *s.* of late Edward Kyran Moylan, Barrister-at-law; *m.* 1914, Ysolda Mary Nesta, (*d.* 1966), *d.* of late Hon. John Donohoe FitzGerald, K.C.; two *s.* four *d.* *Educ.:* Bedford School; Queens' College, Cambridge. 1st Class, Classical Tripos, 1904; M.A. 1947; Receiver for Metropolitan Police District and Courts, 1919-45; also Assistant Under-Secretary of State, Home Office, 1940-45; O.St.J.; Commander Order of Crown, Belgium. *Publications:* Scotland Yard, 1929, 2nd edition, 1934; The Police of Britain, 1947. *Address:* Church Lane Cottage, Bury, Pulborough, Sx. *Club:* Oxford and Cambridge.
[*Died* 15 *June* 1967.

MOYNIHAN, 2nd Baron, *cr.* 1929, of Leeds; **Patrick Berkeley Moynihan,** Bt., *cr.* 1922; O.B.E. 1945; T.D.; Partner in firm of Stokes, Priest & Co.; *b.* 29 July 1906; *o. s.* of 1st Baron Moynihan, K.C.M.G., C.B., and Isabella Wellesley (*d.* 1936), *d.* of T. R. Jessop, F.R.C.S., J.P.; *S.* father 1936; *m.* 1st, 1931, Ierne Helen (who obtained a divorce, 1952), *er. d.* of late Cairnes Candy, Mount Barker, W.A., and *o. d.* of Mrs. Cairnes Candy, 72 Kensington Court, W.8; one *s.* two *d.*; 2nd, 1952, June Elizabeth, *yr. d.* of Arthur Stanley Hopkins; one *s.* one *d.* *Educ.:* Winchester; University College, Oxford, B.A. Called to Bar, Lincoln's Inn, 1929. Served in Royal Artillery, 1939-45, commanded 453 Heavy A.A. Regiment, R.A. (T.), 1947-52. Chm. of Edith Cavell Homes of Rest for Nurses, 1948-52; Chm. Liberal Party Exec., 1949-50; Chm. Management Cttee. Epsom Group of Hospitals, 1956-60. Master of the Haberdashers' Company, 1963-64. Director Simms Motor and Electronics; Director Tileyard Press Ltd.; Hon. Treas., Queen's Institute of District Nursing; Chm., North-West Metropolitan Regional Hospital Board; Member Bd. of Hospital for Sick Children. *Heir:* *s.* Hon. Antony Patrick Andrew Cairnes Berkeley Moynihan, *b.* 2 Feb. 1936. *Address:* High Warren, Ashtead, Surrey. *T.:* Ashtead 2094; Rock Cottage, Dymchurch, Kent. *T.:* Dymchurch 2148. *Clubs:* Royal Automobile, Garrick.
[*Died* 30 *April* 1965.

MOYSEY, Edward Luttrell, C.I.E. 1922; Indian Civil Service, retired; 2nd *s.* of late Henry Luttrell Moysey, I.S.O., Ceylon Civil Service; *m.* 1913, Ethel Sidney (*d.* 1961), *d.* of late Sidney Wilson, Rusthall, Bexhill. *Educ.:* Cheltenham College; Merton College, Oxford. Entered Indian Civil Service, 1901; served in Bombay Presidency; retired, 1923. *Address:* 1 Eversley Road, Bexhill-on-Sea, Sussex. [*Died* 17 *Sept.* 1970.

MUCHMORE, Alfred, C.B.E. 1948 (O.B.E. 1942); retired; *b.* 27 Dec. 1893; *s.* of Alfred John and Harriet Williams Muchmore; *m.* 1920, Amy Mildred Mayers; two *d.* *Educ.:* St. Germans, Cornwall; and privately. U.K. Civil Service, 1912; served European War, 1914-19; U.K. Civil Service, 1919-20; Tanganyika Government, 1920-37; Financial Secretary, Aden Colony, 1937-48; Colonial Office, 1948-49; Gold Coast Govt., 1949-50; Treasurer, St. Helena Government, 1950-52. *Recreation:* gardening. *Address:* Venoon, East Taphouse, Liskeard, Cornwall. *T.:* Dobwalls 397. [*Died* 12 *Nov.* 1962.

MUIR, Lt.-Col. Wingate Wemyss, C.B.E. 1926 (O.B.E. 1918); M.V.O. 1922; *b.* 12 June 1879; *s.* of late Col. W. J. W. Muir, 27 De Vere Gardens, Kensington; unmarried. *Educ.:* Haileybury College; Sandhurst. Entered Army 1898; joined Indian Army, 15th Sikhs, 1900; A.D.C. to Earl of Minto, Viceroy of India, 1908-10; A.D.C. to Lord Hardinge, Viceroy of India, 1910-14; served European War (wounded); returned to India, 1916; A.D.C. to General Sir Charles Monro, C.-in-C. in India, 1917-20; Comptroller of the Household to the Marquis of Reading, 1921-26, and Lord Irwin, 1926-30; Lt.-Col. 1924; retired, 1931; Officer of the Star of Roumania, 1918; Commander of the Crown of Belgium, 1926. *Recreations:* golf, fishing, shooting. *Address:* c/o Coutts & Co., bankers, 440 Strand, W.C.2. *Clubs:* United Service, M.C.C.
[*Died* 25 *May* 1966.

MUIR MACKENZIE, Sir Robert (Henry), 6th Bt., *cr.* 1805; *s.* of Sir Robert Cecil Muir Mackenzie, M.C., 5th Bt. and Kate Brenda Blodwen (she *m.* 2nd 1929, Major John Campbell-Holberton, who *d.* 1962; she *d.* 1958), *d.* of late Henry Jones, Cardiff; *b.* 6 Jan. 1917; *S.* father, 1918; *m.* 1st, 1947, Charmian Cecil de Vere (*d.* 1962), *widow* of Brig. W. G. Glencairn-Campbell, O.B.E., and *o. d.* of Col. and Mrs. Cecil Brinton, Yew Tree House, Belbroughton, Worcestershire; one *s.* one *d.*; 2nd, 1963, Mrs. J. G. Turner, 98 Mount Street, W.1. *Educ.:* Marlborough; New College, Oxford. Served War of 1939-45, R.A., reaching rank of G.S.O. 3 (wounded, despatches). *Heir:* *s.* Alexander Alwyne Brinton Muir Mackenzie, *b.* 8 Dec. 1955. *Address:* Kingsdene, Hampstead Lane, N.W.3. *T.:* Speedwell 9121.
[*Died* 4 *Dec.* 1970.

MUIRHEAD, Charles Alexander, C.I.E. 1941; *b.* 3 September 1888; *s.* of late A. Muirhead, C.I.E.; *m.* 1917, *d.* of J. Parsloe, Pretoria, S. Africa; one *s.* *Educ.:* Cheltenham College. Agent and General Manager, South Indian Rly., 1935-40; General Manager, Pondicherry Rly., 1935-40; Trustee of Port of Madras, 1935-40; Member of Advisory Board, Cochin Harbour, 1937-1940; President, Indian Rly. Confce. Assn., 1940. *Recreations:* philately, and thinking over the good old days. *Address:* Kia-Ora, Palmeria Av., Westcliff-on-Sea, Essex. *Club:* Royal Commonwealth Society.
[*Died* 2 *June* 1967.

MUIRHEAD, Lt.-Col. (Hon. Brig.) James Ingram, C.I.E. 1944; M.C. 1916; *b.* 6 June 1893; *s.* of late James Muirhead, J.P., Heath, near Wakefield, Yorkshire; *m.* 1921, Dorothy Alayne Denholm (K.-I.-H. Silver Medal 1935, bar 1944), *d.* of late Colonel H. A. D. Fraser, C.B.; two *s.* one *d.* *Educ.:* Haileybury Coll. Land Agency, 1911-14; Officer in 4th K.O.Y.L.I. (T.F.), 1911-17; in France, 1915-18; Brigade Major, 100th Infantry Brigade in France, 1917-18; joined 28th (now 7th) Light Cavalry, Indian Army, Oct. 1918, and served in this Regiment and in various staff appts. until July 1940; Assistant Commandant (G.S.O.1) O.T.S. Bangalore, July 1940-May 1941; Commander Delhi Area, June 1941-1944; Commandant Jaipur State Forces, July-Nov. 1944, on retirement from Indian Army; Assistant Chief Constable, War Dept. Constabulary, 1947-58. French Croix de Guerre, 1918. *Recreations:* fishing, golf, gardening. *Address:* Craigieburn House, Moffat, Dumfriesshire. [*Died* 29 *Oct.* 1964.

MUKERJEE, Most Rev. Arabinda Nath; *see* Addenda: II.

MUKERJEE, Radhakamal, M.A., Ph.D.; Padmabhusan, 1966; Indian Academic and writer on Sociology; *b.* 7 Dec. 1889; *s.* of late Gopalchandra Mukerjee; *m.* 1914, Nalini Devi; two *d.* *Educ.:* Krishnath College, Berhampore; Presidency College, Calcutta. Mouat Medallist and Premchand Roychand Scholar (Calcutta Univ.), 1915; Editor of the Upasana; Special Lecturer in

India Economics, University of the Punjab, 1917; Lecturer in Economics, Post-Graduate Department, Calcutta University, 1917-21; Banaili Reader, Patna University, 1925; Extension Lecturer, Nagpur University, 1925; Reader, Calcutta University, 1928; Pres. Indian Economic Assoc., 1932; Sir William Meyer Lecturer, Madras Univ., 1935; Convener, First Indian Population Conference and Secretary, Indian Institute of Population Research, Lucknow, 1936; visited and lectured at European and American Universities, 1937; Economic Adviser, Gwalior State, 1945-47; Chm., Economics and Statistics Commn., F.A.O., Copenhagen, 1946; Member: Govt. of India deleg. to consider proposals regarding World Food Council, Washington, 1947; Technical Cttee., I.L.O., 1947-48; Advisory Bd. of Industries, Govt. of India, 1948-49; Working Party on Textile Industry, Govt. of India, 1950-51; Research Professor and Director of J.K. Inst. of Sociology, Ecology and Human Relations; Prof. and Head Dept. Economics and Sociology, Univ. of Lucknow, Vice-Chancellor, 1955-57. Vice-Pres. Internat. Inst. of Sociology; Hon. Mem. Amer. Sociological Soc.; Mem. Internat. Inst. of Population Research; President of Academies, etc., in U.P. *Publications:* The Foundations of Indian Economics, 1916; Principles of Comparative Economics, vol. i., 1921; vol. ii., 1922; Democracies of the East, 1923; Borderland of Economics, 1925; Civics, 1926; Groundwork of Economics; Regional Sociology, in The Century Social Science Series; The Rural Economy of India, 1926; Introduction to Social Psychology: Mind in Society (with Dr. N. N. Sen-Gupta), 1930; Land Problems of India, 1933, being the Calcutta University Readership Lectures; Migrant Asia: a problem in World Population, 1934; Limits and Potentialities of Agriculture in India Analysed; Theory and Art of Mysticism, 1937; The Regional Balance of Man: an Ecological Theory of Population, 1938; The Changing Face of Bengal: a Study in Riverine Economy, 1938; Food Planning for Four Hundred Millions, 1938; Man and His Habitation, 1939; Economic History of India, 1600-1800, 1944; The Indian Working Class, 1945; Planning the Countryside, 1945; Social Ecology, 1945; The Political Economy of Population, 1946; The Social Structure of Values, 1946; Races, Land and Food, 1946; The Social Function of Art, 1946; The Dynamics of Morals, 1951; Intercaste Tensions, 1952; The Social Transition in an Indian City, 1952; The Horizon of Marriage, 1957; The Frontiers of Social Science (essays), 1957; The Lord of the Autumn Moons, 1957; The Culture and Art of India, 1958; The History of Indian Civilization, Vol. I, 1958; The Symbolic Life of Man, 1958; The Philosophy of Social Science, 1960; Cosmic Art of India, 1961; The Dimensions of Human Evolution, 1963; The Philosophy of Personality, 1964; The Flowering of Indian Art, 1964; The Destiny of Civilization, 1964; The Dimensions of Values, 1964; The Sickness of Civilization, 1964; The Oneness of Mankind, 1964; Social Sciences and Planning, 1965; The Institutional Theories of Economics, 1965; Indian Scheme of Life, 1966; The Community of Communities, 1966; The Way of Humanism, East and West, 1967; Bhagarad Gita, the Dialogue with the Self Divine, 1968; The Multi Dimensional Man, 1968; Society beyond Societies, 1968; The Song of the Self Supreme Astravakra Gita, 1968; The Multi Dimensional System of Sociology, 1968. Economic Problems of Modern India (Editor), 1938; Population Problems in India (Editor), 1939. Associate Editor, Journal of Applied Sociology, University of California; Ed. Uttara Bharati, Jl. of Research of U.P. Univs., 1954-57. Ed. Indian Jl. of Social Defence, Indian Jl. of Social Research, 1958; many Bengali works. *Address:* The University, Lucknow, India. [*Died* 24 *Aug.* 1968.

MUKERJI, Rai Bahadur P. N., C.B.E. 1933; *b.* 22 Dec 1882; *s.* of H. C. Mukerji and Haridasi Banerjee; *m.* 1902, Samir Bala Chatterjee; one *s.* two *d.* *Educ.:* Presidency Coll., Calcutta, M.A. Joined the Postal Dept. of India as Superintendent of Post Offices, 1904; Secretary of the Postal Enquiry Committee, 1920; Member of the Committee of Reorganisation, 1921; studied Postal Systems in Europe, 1922; Secretary of the Indian Delegation to the Universal Postal Congress at Stockholm, 1924; Rai Bahadur, 1926; Assistant Diretor General, Posts and Telegraphs, 1927; Delegate to the Universal Postal Congress at London, 1929; Deputy Director General, Posts and Telegraphs, 1931; on deputation to Afghanistan to settle postal relations, 1932; Postmaster General Madras, 1933; led the Indian Delegation to the Universal Postal Congress at Cairo, 1934; Postmaster General, Bengal and Assam Circle, 1934; Senior Deputy Director General, Posts and Telegraphs, India, 1938-39; retired, 1939; rejoined as Welfare Officer, Posts and Telegraphs, Bengal and Assam Circle, 1942; Deputy Controller General of Civil Supplies, Eastern Region, 1944-45. *Publications:* Samkhya O Yoga — Parichaya O Sadhana. Also, an English rendering of Yoga Philosophy of Pantanjali. *Recreations:* tennis, bridge. *Address:* Raceview, Hastings, Calcutta. *Club:* Calcutta. [*Died* 20 *Dec.* 1965.

MUKLE, May, F.R.A.M.; *b.* 14 May 1880; *d.* of Leopold Mukle and Anne Ford; unmarried. *Educ.:* Royal Academy of Music. Played in public from age of 9; toured extensively as soloist in all the 5 Continents. *Publication:* Two Fancies, for 'cello and piano. *Recreations:* bridge and walking. *Address:* 11 Bulstrode Street, W.1. *T.A.:* BM/Mukle, London. *T.:* Welbeck 8938. *Died* 20 *Feb.* 1963.

MULLALLY, Gerald Thomas, M.C.; M.S. (Lond.); F.R.C.S. (Eng.); Consulting Surgeon, Westminster Hospital, Emeritus Surgeon, Hospital of St. John and St. Elizabeth, N.W.8; *b.* 1887; 2nd *s.* of late W. T. Mullally, M.D.; *m.* Adelaide, *d.* of late J. C. Redpath; one *s.* two *d.* *Educ.:* St. Vincent's, Castleknock; Guy's Hospital. Gold Medal in Surgery, Guy's Hospital; Captain (acting Major) R.A.M.C. (SR) 1914-1919; Surgeon Specialist 8 Casualty Clearing Station, France (M.C., despatches); Surgeon: Ministry of Pensions, 1920-28; Westminster Hosp., 1920-50; Hosp. of St. John and St. Elizabeth, 1921-50. *Publications:* Various, in medical journals. *Address:* 3 Batsford, The Park, Cheltenham, Glos. [*Died* 16 *April* 1969.

MULLAN, Charles Seymour, C.I.E. 1942; M.A.; late I.C.S.; *b.* 17 June 1893; *o. s.* of late Francis Curran Mullan; *m.* 1924, Kathleen, *d.* of late Sir Charles Griffin, Q.C.; two *s.* two *d.* *Educ.:* St. Vincent's College, Castleknock; Trinity College, Dublin (Scholar, Double Senior Moderator, University Student). Served European War, Royal Artillery, 1915-19; entered I.C.S., 1919, and posted to Assam; Under-Secretary to Govt. of Assam, 1924-27; Deputy Commissioner, 1929; Superintendent census operations, 1930-32; Excise Commissioner, 1933-35; Reforms Officer and Additional Secretary to Govt., 1935-36; Secretary to Govt. of Assam, 1937-38; Commissioner of Income Tax, Bengal, 1939-45; acting Member, Central Board of Revenue, Govt. of India, 1945; retired, 1946. *Publications:* Census of India, 1931, Vol. III, Assam; A Scholar in Clive Street (1946), under pseudonym of Rhadamanthus. *Address:* Deepdene, Aldeburgh, Suffolk. *Club:* Aldeburgh Yacht. [*Died* 19 *Oct.* 1969.

MULLER, Hermann Joseph; Prof. of Zoology, Indiana Univ., from 1945; Distinguished Service Prof. since 1953, Emeritus, since 1964; *b.* 21 Dec. 1890; *s.* of Hermann J. Muller and Frances Louise Lyons; *m.* 1st, 1923, Jessie M. Jacobs; one *s.*; 2nd, 1939, Dorothea Kantorowicz; one *d.* *Educ.:* Columbia University. Ph.D. (Columbia), 1915; D.Sc. (Edin.), 1940; Hon. D.Sc.: (Columbia), 1949, (Chicago), 1959, (Swarthmore), 1964; Hon. M.D. (Jefferson Med. Coll.), 1963. Instructor in Biology, Rice Institute, Houston, 1915-18 (head of dept. 1916-18); Instructor in Zoology, Columbia Univ., 1918-20; Assoc. Prof. of Zoology, Univ. of Tex., 1920-25, Prof. 1925-36 (on leave 1932-36); Guggenheim Fellow, 1932-33; Senior Geneticist, Inst. of Genetics of Academy of Sciences of U.S.S.R., Leningrad, 1933-34, Moscow, 1934-1937; guest investigator, Inst. of Animal Genetics of Univ. of Edinburgh, 1937-38; Macaulay Fellow and Lecturer, 1938-40; Research Associate in Biology, Amherst Coll., 1940-42; Visiting Prof., 1942-45; Member, Inst. for Advanced Learning in the Medical Sciences, City of Hope Medical Center, Duarte, California, 1964-65. Vis. Prof., Depts. of Zoology and Genetics, Univ. of Wisconsin, 1965-66. Mem. Nat. Acad. of Sciences, 1931; Vice-pres., Amer. Com. for Cultural Freedom, 1950; Pilgrim Trust Lectr., Royal Society, 1945; Messenger Lecturer, Cornell Univ., 1945; Swarthmore Centennial Lectr., 1963; for. mem. Roy. Swedish Acad. of Sciences, 1946, Acad. Naz. dei Lincei, 1947, Roy. Danish Acad. Science, 1948, Nat. Inst. of Sciences of India, 1951. Annual Award of American Association for Advancement of Science, 1927; Nobel Laureate in Physiology and Medicine, 1946; Kimber Genetics Award, 1955; Darwin-Wallace Commemorative Medal, Linnean Society, 1958; hon. mem. Mendelian Soc. of Lund, 1946, Genetical Soc. of Great Britain, 1947 Genetics Soc. of Japan, 1950; Indian Genetics Society, 1960; Zoological Society of India, 1963; President Eighth International Congress of Genetics, 1948; President American Humanist Assoc. 1956-59 (designated Humanist of the Year, 1963); Vice-Pres., World Acad. of Art and Science, 1961-. Foreign Member: Royal Society, London, 1953; Royal Society, Edinburgh, 1959; Ital. Soc. Agric. Genetics, 1959; Acad. Sc. et Lit. Moguntina (Mainz), 1958; Akad. Naturforsch. Leopoldina (Halle), 1960; Japan Acad., 1960. *Publications:* The Mechanism of Mendelian Heredity (co-author), 1915, 1923; Out of the Night, a Biologist's View of the Future, 1935, 1936. 1938; Genetics, Medicine and Man (co-author), 1947; Studies in Genetics, 1963; over 350 articles on biological subjects, including The Gene, Proc. Roy. Soc., Ser. B, 134:1-37, 1947. *Address:* Dept. of Zoology, Indiana University, Bloomington, U.S.A.

[*Died* 5 *April* 1967.

MULLER, Walter Angus, C.M.G. 1946; *b.* 30 July 1898; 2nd *s.* of late Arthur A. Muller, Dorking and Lymington; *m.* 1st, 1924, Vera Maude Campbell (*d.* 1942); two *d.*; 2nd, 1943, Irene Selina O'Reilly. *Educ.:* Univ. College School; Royal College of Science. Served European War, 1915-19, The Queens (Royal West Surrey Regt.) and R.G.A.; Lieut., Acting Major. Entered Colonial Police Service, 1920; Ceylon Police, 1920-38; Commissioner of Police, Trinidad and Tobago, 1938-1948. Held additional offices in Trinidad; Commandant Local Forces, 1938-40, and O.C. Troops, Trinidad, 1939-40 (Colonel); ex-officio M.L.C., 1938-41; Director of Civil Aviation, 1940-42; Commissioner Trinidad District, St. John Ambulance Brigade Overseas, 1945-48; Commissioner of Police, Tanganyika, 1948-51; Commissioner, Tanganyika District, St. John Ambulance Brigade Overseas, 1948-51; Inspector-General of Colonial Police, 1951-57; Member Kenya Police Commn., 1953. Assistant Secretary of the National Association of Youth Clubs, 1957-58. King's Police Medal, 1944; Colonial Police Medal, 1950. C.St.J. *Address:* The Old Grange, Hampton-on-Thames. *T.:* 01-979 2304

[*Died* 18 *Jan.* 1970.

MULLINGS, Sir Clement Tudway, Kt., *cr.* 1934; C.S.I. 1929; *b.* April 1874; *s.* of late John Mullings, Cirencester, Glos; *m.* 1914, Letitia Livingstone, Adelaide, S. Australia; one *s.* one *d.* (one *d.* decd.). *Educ.:* Bath College; R.I.E. College, Coopers Hill. P.W.D., Madras, 1896-1931; Chief Engineer, 1925; retired, 1931.

[*Died* 24 *Nov.* 1962.

MULLINS, Arthur, C.M.G. 1935; C.B.E. 1920; Under-Secretary Tourist Catering and Holiday Services Division of the Board of Trade since 1946; late Comptroller-General of the Department of Overseas Trade; *b.* 1895; 2nd *s.* of late Josiah Edgar Mullins and of Emily Mullins; *m.* 1918; one *d.* *Educ.:* Boxford Hall; privately. Served European War, 1914-16; Personal Assistant to Controller of Mechanical Warfare, 1916-17; Private Secretary to Deputy Minister of Munitions, 1917-20; Private Secy. to successive Secretaries of the Department of Overseas Trade, 1920-26; Secretary and Assistant Manager of the Export Credits Guarantee Department, 1926-1930; Secretary Overseas Trade Development Council, 1930; Commissioner to the Council, 1932; Director of the Department of Overseas Trade, 1934; Deputy Comptroller-General, 1936-39; Official Member of the Scottish Woollen Trade Delegation to the U.S.A. and Canada, 1931; member of a number of official delegations to European Countries, 1932-35. *Club:* Boodle's.

[*Died* 23 *March* 1963.

MULLINS, Claud; Writer, mainly on Law Reform; Vice-Pres. of London Marriage Guidance Council; Vice-Pres., Family Planning Association; Member of Council of Magistrates Association, 1933-44, and 1947-1962; Member Midhurst Rural District Council, 1950-63; has broadcast occasionally; *b.* 6 Sept. 1887; *e. s.* of late E. Roscoe Mullins and late Alice Mullins; *m.* 1925, Gwendolen, *yr. d.* of late A. P. Brandt, Castle Hill, Bletchingley; one *s.* two *d.* *Educ.:* University College School, London; Mill Hill School; abroad. On administrative staff of London County Council, 1907-12; called to Bar, Gray's Inn, 1913 (Bacon Scholarship, 1911; Certificate of Honour, 1912); in Army, 1915-19; served Mesopotamia and India, 1917-19; Member of British Commission to War Criminal Trials at Leipzig, 1921; Chairman of Courts of Referees (Unemployment Insurance), 1930; Metropolitan Magistrate, 1931-47; South-Western Magistrates' Court; formerly North London; Mem. Departmental Cttee. on employees of Animal Welfare Societies, 1951-52; Fellow Royal Commonwealth Society since 1912. Gave Maudsley Lecture, 1948. *Publications:* London's Story, 1920; The Leipzig Trials, 1921; In Quest of Justice, 1931; Marriage, Children, and God, 1933; Wife *v.* Husband in the Courts, 1935; Crime and Psychology, 1943; Why Crime?, 1945; Fifteen Years' Hard Labour, 1948; Are Findings Keepings?, and other Stories from the Law for Young People, 1953; Marriage Failures and the Children (Beckly Social Service Lecture), 1954; The Sentence on the Guilty, 1957; One Man's Furrow, 1963. *Recreations:* reading, hearing good music, walking. *Address:* Glasses, Graffham, Petworth, Sussex. *T.:* Graffham 260.

[*Died* 23 *Oct.* 1968.

MULOCK, Air Commodore Redford Henry, C.B.E. 1919; D.S.O. 1916 *b.* 11 Aug.

1886; *s.* of late W. R. Mulock, K.C. *Educ.:* Graduate in Electrical Engineering (B.Sc.), McGill University, Montreal, Canada. Served European War, 1914-19 (despatches, D.S.O. and bar, Chevalier of Legion of Honour, C.B.E.); First Canadian Contingent, B.E.F.; Hon. A.D.C. to Governor-General of Canada, 1931. *Address:* 3484 Marlowe Avenue, Montreal. [*Died* 23 *Jan.* 1961.

MUNBY, Lt.-Col. Joseph Ernest, C.M.G. 1919; D.S.O. 1917; late King's Own Yorkshire L.I.; *b.* Myton-on-Swale, Yorkshire, 26 March 1881; *y. s.* of late Edward Charles Munby, Oswaldkirk, Yorkshire; *m.* 1915, Helena Maud, *y. d.* of late J. G. Lyon of Carleton Close, Pontefract. *Educ.:* Malvern; R.M.C., Sandhurst. Joined 1st Yorkshire L.I., 1900; Passed Staff College, 1912-13; raised the 6th (Service) Batt. K.O.Y.L.I. at beginning of European War, and served with it till the end of 1914; Brigade-Major, 83rd Brigade, at and near Ypres till May 1915; with 2nd Batt. K.O.Y.L.I. till July 1915; with 14th Light Division as G.S.O., 3rd and 2nd grade, July 1915 till Feb. 1917; G.S.O. 1st Grade, 38th (Welch) Division, till end of war at Ypres. Arras, and on the Somme (despatches, D.S.O., C.M.G., Bt. Lt.-Col.); retired pay, 1927; raised and commanded a company of 8th (H.D.) Bn. Green Howards, 1939-42; M.F.H. Derwent Hunt, 1930-34. *Address:* The Lodge, Ebberston, Scarborough. *T.:* Snainton 200. [*Died* 11 *Feb.* 1962.

MUNCH, Charles; Grand Officier, Légion d'Honneur; Music Director, Boston Symphony Orchestra, 1949-62; Director, Orchestre de Paris, since 1967; *b.* 26 Sept. 1891; *s.* of Ernest Munch and Celestine Munch (*née* Simon); *m.* 1933, Genevieve Maury. *Educ.:* Gymnase Protestant and Conservatorium, Strasbourg. Prof. of Violin, Strasbourg Conserv. and Concertmaster Strasbourg Orch., 1919-25; Prof. of Violin, Conserv. and Concertmaster, Gewandhaus Orch., Leipzig, 1925-32; Conducting debut, Paris, Straram Orch., 1932; Founder and Cond. Paris Philharmonic Soc. Orch., 1935-1938; Prof. of Violin, École Normale, Paris, 1936; Prof. of Conducting, Paris Conserv. and Cond. Paris Conserv. Concerts Soc., 1938-1946; Cond. French Nat. Orch. tour of U.S. and Canada, 1948; Director, Berkshire Music Center, U.S.A., 1951-62; European tours Boston Symph. Orch., 1952, 1956, Australasian tour, 1960. Grand Prix du Disque, 1949, 1951, 1952, 1954, 1955, 1956, 1959, 1961. Hon. degrees: Dr. of Music, Boston Univ., 1955, Boston Coll., 1956, Harvard Univ., 1956; Dr. of Humane Letters, Tufts Univ., 1956. Légion d'Honneur (France), 1940, Commander, 1952, Grand Officier, 1967; Commander, Order of Arts and Letters (France), 1957; Commander, Order of the Cedar (Lebanon), 1957; Nat. Acad. of Recording Arts and Sciences Award, 1959, 1962 (2). *Publication:* Je suis chef d'orchestre (Paris, 1954; New York, 1955; London, 1956, etc.). *Recreation:* golf. *Address:* 15 Place Dreux, Louveciennes, Seine et Oise, France. [*Died* 6 *Nov.* 1968.

MUNI, Paul; Stage and motion picture actor; *b.* Lemberg, Austria, 22 Sept. 1895; *s.* of Phillip and Sally Weisenfreund; *m.* 1921, Bella Finkle; no *c.* *Educ.:* Public schools. First appeared Yiddish Theatre, New York, 1908; Jewish Art Theatre Company, New York; first English-speaking part, 1926; returned to London stage in Death of a Salesman, Phœnix, 1949. Entered films, 1929, and has appeared in The Valiant, Scarface, Fugitive from a Chain Gang, Dr. Socrates, The Story of Louis Pasteur, The Life of Emile Zola, The Good Earth, etc. Returned to films after 12 years, 1960, appeared in; The Last Angry Man, 1960. *Recreations:* swimming, reading, music. [*Died* 26 *Aug.* 1967.

MUNN, Rt. Rev. Eric George; Bishop of Caledonia since 1959; *b.* 8 March 1903; *s.* of George Stace and Alice Lucy Munn; *m.* Thyra Mary Hutchins. *Educ.:* Leeds University; College of Resurrection, Mirfield. Deacon, 1929; Priest, 1930; Curate, Wigan, 1929-32; Missionary, Quesnel, 1932-34; Indian Missionary, Lytton, 1934-36; Curate, St. James, Vancouver, 1936-42; Vicar of Fernie with Michel, 1942-45; Rector of St. Barnabas, Victoria, B.C., 1945-55; Hon. Canon, British Columbia, 1951-56; Examining Chaplain to Archbishop of British Columbia, 1952-55; Missionary at Lytton, Diocese of Cariboo, 1955-59; Archdeacon of Lytton, 1958. Hon. D.D., Anglican Theological College of British Columbia, 1961. *Address:* Bishop's Lodge, 208 Fourth Avenue West, Prince Rupert, British Columbia. [*Died* 26 *Dec.* 1968.

MUNN, Mrs.; *see* Bryant, Marguerite.

MUNRO, Sir Alan (Whiteside), K.B.E. 1965; Company Director and Consultant to firm of A. W. Munro & Co. since 1965; *b.* 12 May 1898; *s.* of George Whiteside Munro, Brisbane, Qld.; *m.* 1921, Beryl, *d.* of James Nicholson, Esk, Qld.; one *s.* (and one *s.* killed in action, R.A.A.F. 1942). *Educ.:* Brisbane Gram Sch. In practice as C.A., 1929-57 (F.C.A.); Chm. Qld. State Coun. of Inst. of C.A.s (Aust.), 1938-40; Pres., Brisbane Chamber of Commerce, 1940-42; M.P. (M.L.A.), Qld., Apr. 1950-65; Minister for Justice and Attorney-General of Qld., 1957-1962; Dep. Premier and Minister for Industrial Devel., 1962-65. *Recreations:* four grandchildren (much more important to him than reading and bowls). *Address:* 33 Volga Street, Indooroopilly, Brisbane, Australia. *T.:* 7.3284. *Clubs:* Queensland, Brisbane (Brisbane). [*Died* 8 *July* 1968.

MUNRO, Major-General Archibald Campbell, C.B. 1942; M.D.; *b.* 16 Jan. 1886; *s.* of A. C. Munro, M.B., D.Sc., Medical Officer of Health, Renfrewshire; *m.* 1925; one *d.*; *m.* 1945, Aldyth, *o. d.* of Denbigh Jones, Llanelly, Carmarthenshire. *Educ.:* Glasgow High School; Glasgow University (M.B., Ch.B. (Hons.), 1908; M.D. 1911). D.T.M. and H. (London), 1914; D.P.H. (Cantab.) 1923; Lt. Indian Medical Service, 1908; Capt. 1911; Major, 1920; Lt.-Col. 1928; Col. 1937; Maj.-Gen. 1940. Served European War, 1914-18, France and Irak (despatches); N.W. Frontier, 1937; served War of 1939-45 (despatches); Hon. Physician to the King, 1939-43; Director of Medical Services, India, 1941; retired, 1943. *Publications:* articles in medical journals. United Services Journal of India and Scottish Geographical Society's Journal. *Address:* Prospect Cottage, Coach Hill, Titchfield, Hants. *Club:* United Service. [*Died* 6 *July* 1961.

MUNRO, Sir (Richard) Gordon, K.C.M.G. 1947 (C.M.G. 1946); M.C. 1918; Member of Council and Exec. Committee, British Red Cross Society; *b.* 1895; *s.* of late Richard Gordon Munro, London; *m.* 1st, 1919, Diana (marr. diss., 1933), *e. d.* of 1st Earl Baldwin of Bewdley, K.G.; one *s.*; 2nd, 1934, Muriel, *yr. d.* of late Sir Otto Beit, Bt.; two *s.* *Educ.:* Wellington; R.M.C., Sandhurst. Commissioned 4th Dragoon Guards, 1914. Served European War, 1914-18, France and Flanders (severely wounded); Capt. 1917; Adjutant, 1918; Staff Capt. 2nd Cav. Bde., 1918; Staff Capt. and D.A.D. War Office, 1919-22; invalided on account of wounds, 1923 (Captain retired pay). Entered Helbert, Wagg & Co., Ltd., Bankers, 41 Threadneedle Street, 1923; a Man. Dir., 1934-46, resigned, 1946; Dep. Director, Prisoners of War Dept., British Red Cross and St. John War Organisation, 1939; Admiralty Liaison Officer War Office, 1940; Financial Adviser to U.K. High Commissioner in Canada, 1941-46; H.M. Treasury Rep. in U.S., 1946-49, Minister British Embassy, Washington, 1946-49; U.K. Exec. Dir. and Alternate Gov. of Internat. Bank for Reconstruction and Development, 1947-49; Financial Adviser to Govt. of S. Rhodesia, and Chm. S. Rhodesia Currency Bd. (serving S. and N. Rhodesia, Nyasaland), 1950-52; High Commissioner for Southern Rhodesia, in the U.K., 1953; H.M. Government Representative on Board of British Petroleum Co. Ltd., 1954-56. A Governor of Wellington College. *Recreations:* riding, walking, racing. *Address:* 81 Onslow Square, S.W.7. *Clubs:* Cavalry, Traveller's, Turf. [*Died* 4 *Oct.* 1967.

MUNRO, Thomas Arthur (Howard), M.D. Edin., D.Psych., F.R.C.P. Edin.; F.R.S.E.; Physician Superintendent of Royal Edinburgh Hospital; Hon. Senior Lecturer in Psychiatry, University of Edinburgh, since 1955; *b.* Calcutta, 1 October 1905; *s.* of T. M. Munro, Hooghly River Survey; *m.* 1935, Kathleen Carlton; one *d.* *Educ.:* Edinburgh Academy and University; Harvard and Johns Hopkins Univs. Ho. Phys. to Prof. of Clin. Med., Edin. Roy. Infirmary, 1929; Interne, Boston Psychopathic Hosp., U.S.A., 1931; Asst. Phys., Phipps Psychiatric Clinic, Johns Hopkins Hosp., 1932; Asst. Phys., Roy. Edin. Mental Hosp., 1930, 1933-35; Grantee of Med. Research Council, 1935-36; Beit Memorial Research Fellow, 1937-41; Psychiatrist i/c Neurosis Centre, Emergency Service, 1942-43. Service in R.A.M.C., 1943-46; Brig., A.M.S.; Cons. psychiatrist, Allied Land Forces, S.E. Asia and later to Army in India. Physician in Psychological Medicine, Guy's Hospital, 1947; Physician, Bethlem Royal and Maudsley Hosps., 1953. *Publications:* various articles in med. text-books and jls. *Recreations:* travel, music. *Address:* 5 Morningside Place, Edinburgh 10. *Club:* New (Edinburgh). [*Died* 18 *Dec.* 1966.

MURCHIE, Lt.-Gen. John Carl, C.B. 1945; C.B.E. 1943; *b.* 7 June 1895; *m.* 1920, Sybil Kirkpatrick; no *c.* *Educ.:* Edmundston Private School; Royal Military College, Canada. Lieut. Royal Canadian Horse Artillery, 1915; served European War regimental duty; Gunnery Staff Course, 1924; Chief Instructor Artillery, Kingston, Canada, 1928; Staff College, Camberley, 1929-30; G.S.O. 2, War Office, London, 1935-37; D.M.O., N.D.H.Q. Ottawa, 1940; B.G.S., C.M.H.Q. London, 1941-42; Vice-Chief of General Staff, Ottawa, 1942-43; Chief of General Staff, Canada, 1943-45; Chief of Staff Canadian Military H.Q. in London, 1945-46; retired, 1946. *Recreations:* fishing and golf. *Address:* 421 Laurier Avenue East, Ottawa, Canada. [*Died* 5 *March* 1966.

MURDOCH, Sir Walter, K.C.M.G. 1964; C.B.E. 1939; Chancellor of University of Western Australia, 1943-47, Prof. Emeritus; *b.* Aberdeenshire, 1874; *s.* of Rev. James Murdoch; *m.* 1st, 1897, Violet Catherine Hughston; one *s.* two *d.*; 2nd 1962, Barbara Cameron. *Educ.:* Scotch College, Melbourne, Aust. For some years a schoolmaster in Victoria, Aust.; became lecturer at the University of Melbourne, and, later, leader-writer on the Melbourne Argus; Professor of English Literature, Univ. of Western Australia, 1912-39. *Publications:* The Struggle for Freedom; The Australian Citizen; Loose Leaves (a book of essays); A New Primer of English Literature; The Making of Australia (an introductory history); The Oxford Book of Australian Verse; A Memoir of Alfred Deakin, 1923; Speaking Personally (essays); Saturday Mornings (essays); Moreover (essays); The Wild Planet (essays); Lucid Intervals (essays); The Spur of the Moment (essays); Steadfast (on the war). *Address:* Blithedale, South Perth, Western Australia. [*Died* 30 *July* 1970.

MURISON, Alfred Ross, C.B.E. 1953 M.A., Ph.D., LL.D.; J.P.; F.E.I.S.; Rector Emeritus, Marr College, Troon, Ayrshire; *b.* Fraserburgh, 1891; *s.* of late George Murison, Jeweller; *m.* 1920, Christian Ewen, *e. d.* of late Rev. William Cowie, M.A., Parish Minister of Maud; one *s.* one *d.* *Educ.:* Fraserburgh Academy; Aberdeen University; M.A. 1st class Honours in Classics, Mathematics and Natural Philosophy, Economic Science; Ph.D. Glasgow; LL.D. Aberdeen. Home Civil Service, 1915; War Service, Inns of Court O.T.C. and Royal Air Force; Principal Mathematical Master and 2nd Master, Vale of Leven Academy, 1919; Rector, Miller Academy, Thurso, 1920; Rector, Hamilton Academy, 1924; Rector of Marr College, 1930-57; President Educational Institute of Scotland, 1952; President, Scottish Schoolmasters' Association, 1938-41. *Recreations:* golf, bridge. *Address:* 20 Rowan Road, Dumbreck, Glasgow. *T.:* Ibrox 3433. [*Died* 21 *Feb.* 1968.

MURPHY, Brigadier-General Cyril Francis de Sales, D.S.O. 1917; M.C.; *b.* 1882; *s.* of Jerome Murphy, Ashton, Cork; *m.* 1926, Marguerite, *d.* of Garrett Nagle, Byblox, Doneraile, Co. Cork. *Educ.:* Beaumont. 2nd Royal Berks Regt., 1902-10; Army Gymnastic Staff, 1910-13; Royal Flying Corps, 1914-19; retired, 1919; European War Western Front, 1914-18, Ypres, Messines, and Somme (D.S.O., M.C., Officer de Croix de Couronne); R.A.F., Air Ministry, 1939-44; National Institute of Agricultural Botany, Cambridge, 1922-27 and 1944-47. *Address:* 3 Chesham Street, S.W.1; The Bridge, Banagher, S. Ireland. [*Died* 7 *Jan.* 1961.

MURPHY, Air Vice-Marshal (Retd.) Frederick John, C.B. 1949; C.B.E. 1946; Medical Officer, Ministry of Health, since 1951; *b.* 1892; *s.* of Prof. J. E. H. Murphy, M.A., Trinity College, Dublin; *m.* 1924, Margaret Vera (*decd.*), *d.* of R. C. Oliver, J.P., Morpeth; *m.* 1950, Félice Grant Mulholland, *widow* of Group Capt. D. O. Mulholland, C.B.E., A.F.C. *Educ.:* The Abbey and Trinity Coll., Dublin, B.A., M.B., B.Ch., B.A.O. (Dub.) 1916, D.P.H. (Eng.) 1935. Joined Royal Air Force, 1918; served War of 1939-45. Egypt, Western Desert, Normandy, Germany; Wing Commander, 1935. Principal Medical Officer: 2nd T.A.F., 1943-45; Bomber Command, 1945-47; Technical Training Command, 1947-48; Air Vice-Marshal, 1947; Principal Medical Officer, Royal Air Force Mediterranean and Middle East Command, 1948-51; K.H.S., 1947-51; retired, 1951. *Address:* The Lodge, California Lane, Bushey Heath, Herts. *T.:* Bushey Heath 1231. [*Died* 22 *May* 1969.

MURPHY, Sir George (Francis), 2nd Bt., *cr.* 1912; *b.* 31 March 1881; *s.* of 1st Bt. and Mary (*d.* 1882), *d.* of James and Mary Freeman of Rathmines, Co. Dublin; *S.* father, 1925; *m.* 1913, Frances, *d.* of late Richard Davoren. *Heir:* none. *Address:* Hawthorn, Shrewsbury Road, Dublin. *T.:* Dublin 683336. *Clubs:* St. Stephen's Green (Dublin); Royal Irish Yacht (Kingstown, Co. Dublin). [*Died* 4 *July* 1963 (*ext.*).

MURPHY, Colonel George Francis, C.M.G. 1918; D.S.O. 1917; E.D. 1946; A.M.F.; Director Volunteer Defence Corps since 1940; Provost Marshal Allied Land Forces, Australia; Director of Military Prisons and Detention Barracks, Australia; Comptroller-General of Prisons, N.S.W., 1939-53; Director Home Guard, Army H.Q. *b.* Sydney, N.S.W., 24 Sept. 1883; *m.* 1908 and again

1936; three *s.* five *d.* *Educ.:* Public Schools, Sydney; Sydney University. Teacher, Education Department, 1900-20; Service 20th and 18th Batts., A.I.F., Capt., Maj., Anzac (wounded); Egypt, France and Belgium (wounded); Lieut.-Colonel, 1916; commanding 18th Battalion, A.I.F. (C.M.G., D.S.O. and bar, despatches seven times); transferred Justice Department, 1920; Sheriff of the State of New South Wales, 1925-1939; Deputy Marshal of the High Court of Australia, 1925-39. President, Returned Sailors', Soldiers' and Airmen's Imperial League of Australia, N.S.W. Branch, 1939-40; Hon. Mem. Soldiers' Children Educ. Bd., N.S.W. *Recreations:* tennis, shooting, bowls (Mem. Exec. Roy. N.S.W. Bowling Assoc., Advisory Cttee. Aust. Bowling Council). *Address:* 14 McLean Ave., Chatswood, N.S.W. *Clubs:* C.T.A., Chatswood Bowling (N.S.W.). [*Died* 13 *Sept.* 1962.

MURPHY, Sir William (Lindsay), K.C.M.G., *cr.* 1946 (C.M.G. 1944); Director, Rhodesian Selection Trust Ltd., Mufulira Copper Mines Ltd. and other companies in the same group, since 1953; *b.* 4 May 1887; *s.* of Canon R. W. Murphy, M.A., Clifden, Co. Galway, Eire; *m.* 1922, Betty Mary, M.B.E., *d.* of Col. the Rev. T. Ormsby, D.S.O., Milford, Tuam, Co. Galway; three *s.* two *d.* *Educ.:* The Abbey, Tipperary; Trinity College, Dublin (Classical Scholar; Senior Moderator and Gold Medallist, B.A., 1909; LL.D. *jure dig.* 1945; Vice-Pres. College Historical Society). Entered Ceylon Civil Service, 1910; Principal Assistant Colonial Secretary, Ceylon, 1928; Chairman, Municipal Council and Mayor of Colombo, 1932-37; Colonial Sec., Bermuda, 1942-45; Governor and Commander-in Chief of the Bahamas, 1945-49, retired. 1949. Acting Governor of Southern Rhodesia, 1954; Actg. Gov. of S. Rhodesia and Actg. Governor-General and Comdr.-in-Chief, Rhodesia and Nyasaland, 1957. K.St.J. *Address:* Kiltullagh, P.O. Bromley, S. Rhodesia. *Clubs:* Junior Carlton, Royal Commonwealth Society, Royal Over-Seas League; University (Dublin); Salisbury (Salisbury, S.R.). [*Died* 15 *April* 1965.

MURRAY, Prof. Emeritus Adam George, M.A. (Edin.), C.A.; Professor of Accounting and Business Method, University of Edinburgh, 1945-57; Editor of The Accountants' Magazine (Scottish C.A. official publication), 1923-52; Senior Partner of A. G. Murray & Co., C.A., 4 Rothesay Place, Edinburgh 3; *b.* 3 Oct. 1893; *s.* of Robert Murray, Bonnyrigg, Midlothian; *m.* 1921, Maud Wilkinson, Leicester; one *s.* one *d.* (and one *s.* decd.). *Educ.:* George Watson's College, Edinburgh. Served European War, 1914-18, London Scottish and Royal Scots. Commenced practice as professional accountant, 1919. Past Member of Council of Society of Accountants in Edinburgh and of Institute of Taxation; Member of Institute of Chartered Accountants of Scotland; Mem. Inst. of Taxation. *Address:* 4 Rothesay Pl., Edinburgh 3. *T.:* Caledonian 3071; Elanora, N. Berwick, East Lothian. *T.:* 2424. [*Died* 10 *Dec.* 1966.

MURRAY, Albert Victor; Emeritus Professor of Education, University of Hull, since 1945; *b.* 1 September 1890; *e. s.* of John Ridley Murray and Elizabeth Lawther, Scotland Gate, Choppington, Northumberland; *m.* 1923, Winifred, *y. d.* of Henry and Mary Seares, Prestwich, Manchester; two *s.* one *d.* *Educ.:* Choppington National School; Morpeth Grammar School; Magdalen College, Oxford. B.A. 1913; M.A. 1920; B.Litt. 1931; M.A. Cantab. 1943 (St. John's College); B.D. 1945; S.T.D. Dickinson Coll., Carlisle, Pa., 1950; Mansfield Coll., Oxford, 1913-14; a Sec. of Student Christian Movement, 1913-22; Lecturer in Education, Selly Oak Colleges, Birmingham, 1922-33; Prof. of Education, Univ. Coll., Hull, 1933-45; Travelling Research Fellowship in Africa, 1927-28; Vice-Pres. of the Conf. of the Primitive Methodist Church, 1932; Educational Adviser to the Christian Council of Nigeria, 1932; President of the Birmingham Free Church Council, 1932-33; Lectured in S. Africa, 1934; Gov. of Roy. Holloway Coll.; Fernley-Hartley Lecturer, Methodist Conf., 1939; Pres. Training Coll. Assoc., 1940-42; President of Cheshunt Coll., Cambridge, 1945-59. Vice-Pres. Conf. of the Methodist Church, 1947-48; Hyde Lecturer, Andover-Newton Theological Coll., Boston, U.S.A., 1947; Chm. World Inst. of Christian Education, Toronto, 1950; Vice-President Methodist Ecumenical Council, 1947-51; Essex Hall Lectr., 1954; Cole Lecturer, Vanderbilt Univ., Nashville, U.S.A. 1955; Hibbert Lecturer, 1957; Fellow of Woodbrooke College, Selly Oak, Birmingham, 1959-60. *Publications:* The School in the Bush: a critical study of the Theory and Practice of Native Education in Africa, 1929 (2nd edit. enlarged, 1939); Education under Indirect Rule, 1935; Personal Experience and the Historic Faith, 1939 (3rd ed., 1962); The School and the Church, 1945; How to Know your Bible, 1952; Education into Religion, 1953; Truth and Certainty, 1954; Teaching the Bible, 1955; Natural Religion and Christian Theology, 1956; The State and the Church in a Free Society, 1958; contrib. to New Cambridge Mod. Hist. Vol. XI. 1962; Abelard and St. Bernard, 1966. *Recreation:* sketching. *Address:* 6 Brooklyn, Grassington, Skipton, Yorks. *T.:* Grassington 242. [*Died* 10 *June* 1967.

MURRAY, Sir Angus Johnston, Kt. 1966; O.B.E. 1945; M.B., Ch.M.; President, Australian Medical Association, 1964-1967; Hon. Consulting Obstetrician and Gynæcologist, Royal North Shore Hospital, Sydney. *Educ.:* University of Sydney. Served European War of 1914-18, 18th Battery, 6th Army Field Artillery Brigade; served World War of 1939-45, Australian Army Medical Corps, 2/5 Aust. Gen. Hosp., 1940-45 (O.C. Surgical Division, 1942-44; C.O., 1944-45); Colonel A.A.M.C., retired. President: B.M.A. (N.S.W. Branch), 1953; Confederation of Medical Associations of Asia and Oceania, 1964; Fellow of Senate, University of Sydney, 1964; Member of Council, St. Andrew's College, Univ. of Sydney (Chairman, 1957-60). F.R.C.S.Edin.; F.R.A.C.S.; F.R.C.O.G. *Address:* 149 Macquarie Street, Sydney, New South Wales, Australia. [*Died* 24 *Sept.* 1968.

MURRAY, Group Captain Charles Geoffrey, C.B.E. 1937 (O.B.E. 1919); *b.* 1880; *y. s.* of Charles Oliver Murray, R.E., Painter Etcher; *m.* 1914, Ramah Barbara, *d.* of Thomas Murray, Haswell, Co. Durham; one *s.* three *d.* *Educ.:* Godolphin School. Joined R.N.V.R. 1903; transferred Royal Marines, 1914; served Flanders, Middle East Expeditionary Force and France; transferred to Royal Air Force, 1918, apptd. to Air Ministry; permanent commission R.A.F. 1918; transferred to Accountant Branch, R.A.F.; served Command Accountant, Halton, 1921-23; Command Accountant Coastal Area, 1923-26; Command Accountant Iraq, 1926-28; Command Accountant Halton, 1929-35; Command Accountant, Coastal Command, 1935-39; Command Accountant, Far East Command, 1939; retired, 1942. *Recreations:* golf, sailing. *Address:* Bermuda, Sandy Point, Hayling Island, Hants. *Club:* Royal Air Force Yacht (Calshot). [*Died* 21 *Dec.* 1962.

MURRAY, David Leslie, F.R.S.L.; *b.* 1888; *s.* of Charles Murray; *m.* 1928, Margaret Leonora Eyles (*d.* 1960). *Educ.:* Harrow (Entrance Scholarship, Classics and History); Balliol College, Oxford (Brackenbury History

Scholar; First Class Lit. Hum., 1910; John Locke Scholar, 1912. Intelligence Dept War Office, 1916-19; Dramatic Critic (Nation and Athenæum), 1920-23; joined staff of The Times, 1920; Editor Times Literary Supplement, 1938-44. *Publications:* Pragmatism, 1912; Scenes and Silhouettes, 1926; Disraeli, 1927; (with W. Macqueen-Pope) Fortune's Favourite, the Life and Times of Franz Léhar, 1953; *novels:* The Bride Adorned, 1929; Stardust, 1931; The English Family Robinson, Trumpeter, Sound ! 1933; Regency, 1936; Commander of the Mists, 1938; Tale of Three Cities, 1940; Enter Three Witches, 1942; Folly Bridge, 1945; Leading Lady, 1947; Royal Academy, 1950; Outrageous Fortune, 1952; Come Like Shadows !, 1955; Roman Cavalier, 1958; Hands of Healing, 1961. *Address:* 32 Eton Avenue, N.W.3. *T.:* Swiss Cottage 4691.
[*Died* 30 *Aug.* 1962.

MURRAY, Reverend Canon Edmund Theodore; *b.* 16 Aug. 1877; *s.* of W. Murray, M.D., Scaur Bank, Longtown, Cumberland; *m.* 1911, Catherine (*d.* 1956), *widow* of A. H. Sharp, Aston Somerville Hall, Broadway and *d.* of T. Dymond, Burntwood Hall, Barnsley; no *c.* *Educ.:* Uppingham; Christ's Coll., Cambridge; Leeds Clergy School. B.A. 1898; M.A. 1922; Deacon, 1900; Priest, 1902; Curate of Bedale, Yorks, 1900-04; of Wymondham, Norfolk, 1904-05; of Wem, Salop, 1905-06; Rector of Bourton on the Hill, 1906-46; Archdeacon of Cheltenham, 1943-51. C.F., 1917-19; Hon. Canon, Gloucester, 1939-55, Canon Emeritus, 1955. *Address:* Daglingworth House, Cirencester, Glos.
[*Died* 16 *Feb.* 1969.

MURRAY, Everitt George Dunne, O.B.E., 1918; M.A., L.M.S.S.A., M.D (Hon.), D.Sc. (Hon.), F.R.S.C.; Medal of Freedom (U.S.); Visiting Professor, Univ. of Western Ontario, London, Ontario, since 1955; *b.* Johannesburg, 21 July 1890; *e. s.* of G. A. E. Murray, M.B., F.R.C.S., and Kathleen, *y. d.* of Capt. J. J Dunne; *m.* 1917, Winifred, *e. d.* of T. Hardwick Woods, J.P., Blundeston Hall, Blundeston, Suffolk; one *s.* one *d.* *Educ.:* St John's College and Johannesburg College; Christ's College, Cambridge; St. Bartholomew's Hospital, London. Captain R.A.M.C.; Staff Central Cerebrospinal Fever Laboratory, 1915-16; Member of War Office Committee on Dysentery, 1918; Staff Vaccine Department, R.A.M. College, 1917-19; Senior Demonstrator in Pathology, St. Bartholomew's Hospital, 1919-20; Research Bacteriologist, Medical Research Council, 1920-26; Fellow Christ's College, Cambridge, 1923-31; Lecturer in Pathology, University of Cambridge, 1926-30; Professor of Bacteriology and Immunology, McGill Univ., Montreal, 1930-55; Hon. Consultant: Royal Victoria Hosp., Montreal General Hosp.; Children's Memorial Hosp. and Alexandra Hosp., Montreal, 1930-55; Councillor, Municipal Council, City of Montreal, representing McGill University, 1947-55; Vice-Pres.: Section VII of Third Congress, Section I of Fifth Congress, Section VI of Fourth Congress, and mem. Cttee. on Bacteriological Nomenclature (Chm. 1953), Cttee. of Honour, VII Congress, 1958, Pres. VIII Congress, 1962; Pres. Sect. V, Roy. Soc. Canada, 1954-55; Mem. Nat. Res. Council of Canada, 1953-56. Member of Judicial Commission of Internat. Association of Microbiologists; Member Perm. Commission, Internat. Federation of Culture Collections of Micro-organisms; Pres. of Montreal Medico-Chirurgical Soc., 1942-1943. During War of 1939-45, Member of various Committees of National Research Council of Canada and of Dept. of National Defence, Ottawa; Canadian Chm. of Joint U.S.-Canadian Commission and Chairman of Biological Warfare Committee of Directorate of Chemical Warfare and Smoke, N.D. H.Q. Ottawa, Superintendent of Research in Directorate of Chemical Warfare and Smoke. A member of the Wartime Prices and Trade Board Pharmaceutical Advisory Committee. Flavelle Medal, Royal Society of Canada, 1953. Coronation Medal Queen Elizabeth II. *Publications:* number of papers in Scientific Periodicals; one of 3 Editor-Trustees of Bergey's Manual of Determinative Bacteriology. Chapters in several textbooks; The Meningococcus (Med. Research Council Special Report Series). *Address:* Dept. Medical Research, Univ. Western Ontario, London, Ont., Canada
[*Died* 6 *July* 1964.

MURRAY, Brig. Sir (George David) Keith, Kt. 1959; O.B.E. 1938; M.C. 1918; T.D.; D.L., J.P.; Lord Lieutenant of Caithness, since 1964 (Vice-Lieutenant, 1952-64, and Convener, 1938-64, Caithness); Chm., Northern Agricultural Executive Council, 1947; Pres., Caithness T.A. Association; Hon. Sheriff Substitute; Past-Pres. Aberdeen-Angus Society of G.B.; *b.* 24 May 1898; *o. s.* of late Donald Murray, Garth House, Castletown; *m.* 1939, Christine Truscott Auld; one *s.* *Educ.:* George Watson's Coll.; Edinburgh University. Joined Special Service Bn., 1915; commissioned Seaforth Highlanders, Nov. 1915; Capt. and Adjt., 8th Bn. Seaforth Highlanders, 1918; served 5th and 4/5th Seaforths until 1937; comd. Bn., 1932-37; raised and comd. 226 Hy. A-A Battery, R.A., comd. 101 Regt. R.A., and two A-A brigades, 1939-43; Mil. Governor Osnabruck, R.B., 1945. A.D.C. (Extra) King George VI and to the Queen, Farmer: pedigree A.-A. cattle, North Country Cheviot sheep and Shetland Ponies. President Caithness Boy Scouts Association; Chairman Caithness Savings Committee; Member: Consultative Council, N. of Scotland Hydro-electric Bd.; Council, North Country Cheviot Sheep Society (Past-Pres.); Director, Royal Highland and Agricultural Society of Scotland (Past-Chm.). Croix de Guerre avec palme, 1918. *Address:* Borgie House, Castletown, Caithness. *Clubs:* New (Edinburgh); Royal Scottish Automobile (Glasgow).
[*Died* 12 *Oct.* 1965.

MURRAY, George McIntosh, C.B.E. 1958; Chief Leader Writer, Daily Mail, since 1939; *b.* 16 Dec. 1900; 2nd *s.* of Samuel and Amy Murray; *m.* 1st, 1927, Irene Bill (*d.* 1963); one *s.* one *d.*; 2nd, 1967, Loris Taylor, Auckland, N.Z. *Educ.:* Archbishop Tenison's Sch. On staff of: Farnham Herald, 1923; Dudley Herald, 1925; Hampshire Herald, 1925; Southern Daily Echo, 1930; Sunday Dispatch, 1931; Daily Mail, 1933. Mem. Press Council, 1953, Vice-Chm., 1957, Chm., 1959-1963; Dir. Associated Newspapers Ltd., 1955. F.J.I., 1957; Mem. Council Commonwealth Press Union. *Publications:* The Life of King George V, 1935; His Majesty King Edward VIII, 1936; King George VI and the Coronation, 1937; *for children:* The Impatient Horse, 1952. *Recreation:* gardening. *Address:* 45 Grove Way, Esher, Surrey. *T.:* 01-398 4766; 28 Mowlem Court, Swanage, Dorset. *T.:* Swanage 3128. *Clubs:* Garrick, Press.
[*Died* 2 *Nov.* 1970.

MURRAY, George William Welsh, M.C., F.R.G.S.; F.R.A.I.; *b.* 9 Sept. 1885; *s.* of late G. R. M. Murray, F.R.S.; *m.* 1926, Edith Agnes, *d.* of late W. D. Cairney, Glasgow; no *c.* *Educ.:* Westminster School. Joined Survey of Egypt, 1907; conducted many survey expeditions in the deserts of Egypt; Political Officer, Northern Red Sea Patrol, 1915; served with 7th Field Survey Coy. R.E. in Sinai and Palestine, 1916-19; Captain, 1918; Director, Desert Surveys, 1932-37; Director, Topographical Survey, 1937-47; Technical Expert, Survey of Egypt, 1948-51; Mem. Council Fuad I Desert Inst., 1950; Founder's Medal Royal Geog. Society, 1936; President, Cairo Scientific Society, 1936-38; Membre de

l'Institut d'Egypte, 1938 (Vice-Pres., 1946-47). *Publications:* Sons of Ishmæl, 1935; Contributions to Journal of Egyptian Archæology and Journal of Royal Anthropological Institute. *Recreation:* mountaineering. *Address:* Rimhan, Milltimber, Aberdeen. *T.:* Culter 2164. *Club:* Alpine.
[*Died* 31 *Jan.* 1966.

MURRAY, Gladstone; *see* Murray, W. E. G.

MURRAY, Lt.-Col. Henry William, V.C. 1917; C.M.G. 1919; D.S.O. 1916, Bar to D.S.O. 1917; *b.* near Launceston, Tas., 30 Dec. 1883; *s.* of late E. K. Murray of St. Leonards, Tasmania; *m.* 1926, Ellen P., *d.* of D. Cameron; one *s.* one *d.* Served European War, 1914-18 (wounded four times, C.M.G., D.S.O. and bar, V.C., Croix de Guerre); War of 1939-45, organised defence force of Queensland bushmen. Coronation Medal, 1937. *Address:* Glenlyon Station, Richmond, Queensland.
[*Died* 7 *Jan.* 1966.

MURRAY, Hubert Leonard, C.B.E. 1936; Administrator of Papua, Dec. 1940 till 1942, now retired; Official Secretary, Territory of Papua, 1916-40; late Member of Executive and Legislative Councils; Master of Official Vessel, Laurabada; *b.* 13 Dec. 1886; *s.* of James Aubrey Murray and Marion Edith Lewis: *m.* 1915, Pauline Anna Herbert (decd.); (one *s.* decd.). *Educ.:* Fort Street Model Public School, Sydney. Dept. of Trade and Customs, Commonwealth of Australia, 1905-9; Government Service of Papua from 1909; Private Secretary to the Lieutenant-Governor 8 years; Member of Commonwealth Committee to advise *re* combined administration for New Guinea and Papua. Attached to a section of U.S.A. Gen. Headquarters in Australia, 1942-45; Mem. Cttee., War Damage Commn., 1942-45. *Publications:* Sailing Directions of the Territory of Papua. *Recreations:* yachting, swimming, billiards. *Address:* c/o Ministry for Territories (Papua), Canberra, A.C.T.
[*Died* 10 *Dec.* 1963.

MURRAY, James Dixon; Independent Methodist Minister; *b.* 17 Sept. 1887; *m.* 1908; three *d.* *Educ.:* East Howie Elementary School and then to Evening Classes, W.E.A. Classes, University Classes, and Summer School College (2). Miners Asst. Sec., 1914 and 1927. County Councillor, 1925; County Alderman, 1937. Representative on Miners' Federation of Great Britain Executive Committee, 1936, and Delegation to U.S.S.R. President Spennymoor Divisional Party, 1925-42. M.P. (Lab.) Spennymoor (County Durham), 1942-50, North-West Division of Co. Durham, 1950-55. *Recreations:* work, music, religious services. *Address:* 11 Frederickson, Meadowfield, Co. Durham. *T.:* Brandon Colliery 125.
[*Died* 24 *Jan.* 1965.

MURRAY, Sir John, K.C.V.O., *cr.* 1932; D.S.O. 1918; F.S.A.; D.L. County of London; senior director of publishing house of John Murray, 50 Albemarle Street, W.1; editor of the Quarterly Review; *b.* 12 June 1884; *s.* of Sir John Murray, K.C.V.O. (*d.* 1928); *m.* 1916, Lady Helen de Vere, *y. d.* of 1st Earl Brassey, G.C.B. *Educ.:* Eton; Magdalen Coll., Oxford (M.A., 2nd Class Mod. Hist.). Lt.-Col. formerly Scottish Horse, T.A.; commanded 12th Bn. the Royal Scots, 1918-19; served First World War, 1914-18, in Gallipoli, Egypt and France (despatches, D.S.O. and bar, Croix de Guerre, Belgium); T.D.; Home Guard, 1940-42; Comdr. Order of St. John of Jerusalem; High Sheriff, County of London, 1914; editor of the Magdalen College Record, 1922. Member of Board, Hospital for Sick Children, Great Ormond St., 1907-48; formerly Hon. Treasurer Royal Literary Fund and Deafened Ex-Servicemen's Fund. *Address:* Flat 5, 49 Lowndes Square, S.W.1; 50 Albemarle St., W.1. *Club:* Athenæum.
[*Died* 6 *Oct.* 1967.

MURRAY, John, M.A. Oxford and Aberdeen, Hon. LL.D. Aberdeen; Hon. Litt.D. Columbia University, New York; Hon. D.Litt. Exeter University; Principal of the University College of the South West of England, Exeter, 1926-51; Chm., Consultative Cttee. for Independent Education; *b.* Fraserburgh, Aberdeenshire, 28 Feb. 1879; *e. s.* of late Francis Robert Murray, Fraserburgh; *m.* 1921, Mrs. Harwood, *widow* of George Harwood, formerly M.P. for Bolton, *d.* of late Sir Alfred Hopkinson, K.C. *Educ.:* Robert Gordon's Coll., Aberdeen; Aberdeen Univ.; Christ Church, Oxford; Prize-Fellow of Merton Coll., Oxford, 1905; Student and Tutor of Christ Church, 1908; Censor of Christ Church, 1910-15; Ministry of Munitions (Labour), 1915-18; M.P. (Co. L.) for West Leeds, 1918-23; Chm. of Central Profiteering Cttee., 1920-21. Governor: Bryanston School; St. Martin-in-the-Fields High School for Girls; Gordonstoun School. *Address:* 62 Porchester Gate, W.2. *T.:* Bayswater 6810. *Clubs:* Athenæum, Reform, English-Speaking Union.
[*Died* 28 *Dec.* 1964.

MURRAY, Brig. Sir Keith; *see* Murray, Sir G. D. K.

MURRAY, Margaret Alice, D.Lit.; F.S.A. (Scot.); F.R.A.I; Fellow of University Coll., London; *b.* 1863; *y. d.* of J. C. Murray of Calcutta. Entered University College, London, as a student, 1894; Junior Lecturer on Egyptology, 1899; University Extension Lecturer for Oxford University, 1910; for London University, 1911; retired from Assistant Professorship in Egyptology at University College, 1935; excavated in Egypt, 1902-4; excavated a Neolithic Temple in Malta, 1921-1923; excavated an early mediæval site in Hertfordshire, 1925; excavated megalithic remains in Minorca, 1930-31; excavated Nabatean remains at Petra, 1937; excavated Bronze-age site at Tell Ajjul, South Palestine, 1938; President, Folklore Society, 1953-55. *Publications:* Osireion at Abydos; Saqqara Mastabas, vols. i. and ii; Elementary Egyptian Grammar; Elementary Coptic Grammar; Tomb of Two Brothers; Ancient Egyptian Legends; Witch Cult in Western Europe; Egyptian Elements in the Grail Romance; Notes on Egyptian Standard; Descent of Property in the Old Kingdom; Royal Marriages and Matrilineal Descent; Index of Names and Titles in the Old Kingdom; Excavations in Malta; Egyptian Objects found in Malta; Handbook of Egyptian Sculpture; Egyptian Temples; Excavations in Minorca, Trapucó I and II and Sa Torreta; Maltese Folk-tales; (with D. Pilcher) Coptic Reading-Book; The God of the Witches; Petra, The Rock of Edom; A Street in Petra; Connexions between Ancient Egypt and Russia; The Splendour that was Egypt; Egyptian Religious Poetry; The Divine King in England; The Genesis of Religion; My First Hundred Years, 1963. *Recreation:* travelling. *Address:* c/o University College, Gower Street, W.C.1. *Club:* Society of Visiting Scientists.
[*Died* 13 *Nov.* 1963.

MURRAY, Sir Patrick (Ian Keith), 10th Bt. *cr.* 1673; Technical Adviser to Mutron Ltd. (Electronic Instruments), since 1947; *b.* 28 Aug. 1904; *s.* of Patrick Keith Murray (*d.* 1937) (3rd *s.* of 8th Bt.) and Dorothea Sprot; *S.* uncle, Sir William Keith Murray, 9th Bt., 1956; *m.* 1929, Liska Creet; one *s.* *Educ.:* Harrow; Faraday House. Represented Goodman Mining Machinery, Chicago, in India, 1926-29; Agent for Sathgram Colliery, India, 1929-31; Technical Writer, The Statesman, Calcutta, 1931-33; B.B.C., 1934-42; Foreign Office, Political Intelligence Dept., 1942-44; Electrician, Plean

Colliery, 1944-46; private research on electronic apparatus, 1946-47. *Publications:* Radio Communication Applied to Mines, 1933, etc. *Recreations:* science and invention. *Heir:* *s.* William (Patrick Keith) Murray, *b.* 7 Sept. 1939. *Address:* Aberturret, Crieff, Perthshire.
[*Died* 18 *June* 1962.

MURRAY, Brigadier Terence Desmond, C.B.E. 1945; D.S.O. 1918; M.C. 1917; *b.* Parramatta, N.S.W., 19 Jan. 1891; *s.* of late Sir J. H. P. Murray, K.C.M.G.; *m.* 1917, Philippa Chevallier, *d.* of late Lt.-Gen. Sir F. W. Kitchener, K.C.B.; three *d.* *Educ.:* Beaumont; Stonyhurst; R.M.A., Woolwich. Commissioned 1910; 1st Suffolk Regt., 1922; Royal Tank Regt., 1925; Brig., 1939; served European War, 1914-18, with 1st Leinster Regiment, France, Salonika, Palestine (despatches four times, D.S.O., M.C.); served War 1942-45, N. Africa, Italy, N.W. Europe; retired pay, 1945. Military Cross and Order of White Lion of Czechoslovakia, 1945. *Address:* c/o Lloyds Bank, 6 Pall Mall, S.W.1.
[*Died* 17 *July* 1961.

MURRAY, Violet Cecil, M.A. (Oxon.); *b.* 29 March 1885; *er. d.* of James Murray, M.A., M.D., and Cecilia Scott. *Educ.:* Privately in Inverness and London; St. Hugh's College, Oxford. 2nd Mistress Grassendale School for Girls, Southbourne, Hants., 1915-18; French Mistress, St. Leonards School, St. Andrews, 1918-19; Joint Headmistress Heatherley School for Girls, Inverness, 1919-28; Warden of University Hall for Women, University of Sheffield, 1928-36; Warden, University Hall, St. Andrews, Fife, 1936-50, retired. *Recreations:* music, reading, walking, travel. *Address:* 6 Gibson Place, St. Andrews, Fife. *T.:* St. Andrews 199. *Club:* St. Rule (St. Andrews). [*Died* 21 *Feb.* 1961.

MURRAY, (William Ewart) Gladstone, D.F.C., M.C.; late Royal Flying Corps; Policy Counsel (Canada, British Commonwealth and U.S.A.) since 1943; *b.* 8 April 1893; *s.* of Paul Murray and Hannah Mackay; *m.* 1923, Eleanor, *d.* of John Powell, J.P., Wrexham; one *s.* one *d.* *Educ.:* King Edward's High School, Vancouver, B.C.; McGill College of British Columbia; McGill University, Montreal; New College, Oxford. Journalism, Canada, U.S.A., and South America, 1912; Rhodes Scholar from Province of Quebec to Oxford University, 1913, 1914; Active Service, 1914-18 (2000 hrs. combatant flying); Aeronautical Correspondent, Daily Express, 1919, 1921; Publicity Director, League of Nations Union, 1921, 1922; Publicity Manager, Radio Communication Co., Ltd., 1922, 1924; Director of Public Relations, Information, and Publications, B.B.C., 1924-35; Acting Controller of Programmes and Assistant Controller, B.B.C., 1935; General Manager, Canadian Broadcasting Corp. 1936-42; Director-General of Broadcasting, Canada, 1942-43; Founder of the Responsible Enterprise Movement, Canada, 1943-44. Was on Special Mission to advise Government of Canada on development of broadcasting, 1933. Life Associate, The Royal Society of St George LL.D. (Hon.) Florida Southern College, 1948. Croix de Guerre; Italian Medal. *Publications:* contributor to reviews and magazines on Empire subjects, Economics, Politics, Business, Canada, Travel, Foreign Affairs, Broadcasting, Journalism, and Publicity. *Recreations:* running, squash, tennis, golf. *Address:* 125 Lowther Ave., Toronto 5, Canada. *Clubs:* Oxf. and Camb.; Univ., Badminton and Racquet, Toronto Hunt (Toronto). [*Died* 28 *Feb.* 1970.

MURRAY, William Staite; painter and potter; inventor first crude oil high temperature pottery kiln; Trustee to the National Arts Council of Southern Rhodesia; Visiting Inspector and Adviser to Government Schools of Southern Rhodesia for Art in Education; *b.* London, 1881; *s.* of James Murray, Edinburgh, and Arabella Caroline Staite, Greenwich; *m.* Kathleen Harriet Medhurst. *Educ.:* Colfe's Grammar School. Late Head of School of Pottery, Royal College of Art, South Kensington. One man Show, London, New York, Tokio, The Hague, etc.; official purchases, Victoria and Albert Museum, Metropolitan Museum, New York; Manchester Art Gallery, Fitzwilliam Museum, Cambridge, etc. Served Machine Gun Corps during European War, 1914-18. *Publications:* contributed Art Work, etc. *Recreation:* gardening. *Address:* Murray House, Odzi, Southern Rhodesia.
[*Died* 7 *Feb.* 1962.

MURRAY-AYNSLEY, Sir Charles Murray, Kt., *cr.* 1950; *b.* 28 Nov. 1893; *s.* of Rev. A. E. Murray-Aynsley; *m.* 1st, 1920, Elsa Marianova (*d.* 1951); no *c.*; 2nd, 1952, Annamaria Eleanor, *o. d.* of late Emil Curth, Trebnitz, Silesia. *Educ.:* Marlborough; St. Paul's; St. John's Coll., Camb. (Schol.). First Class Law Tripos, Part II, 1920; Barrister-at-Law, Inner Temple, 1920; North Eastern Circuit; in practice in England till 1927; District Commissioner, Belize, British Honduras, 1927-30; acted as Attorney-General on various occasions; Chief Justice of Tonga, 1930-35; Chief Justice of Grenada, 1935-38; Puisne Judge Supreme Court of Straits Settlements, 1938; was interned Singapore. Chief Justice, Singapore, 1946-55, retired 1955. Served King's Royal Rifle Corps, 1914-1919; in France 1915-16 (severely wounded). *Address:* c/o Union de Banques Suisses, Lugano, Switzerland. *Club:* Oxford and Cambridge University. [*Died* 31 *Aug.* 1967.

MURRAY-HARVEY, Captain Edward, O.B.E. 1920; M.C.; F.R.G.S.; *b.* Norwich, 1886; *o. s.* of late Edward Palmer Harvey and Margaret Harvey, of Bacton and Hunstanton, Norfolk; *m.* 1st; two *d.*; 2nd, Ruby, *d.* of J. H. Lee, Hunstanton; two *s.* *Educ.:* King Edward VI. School, Norwich; privately. Served in the Irish Guards, Special Reserve, during European War (twice wounded, M.C. and Bar); was head of a mission at Danzig, under Sir William Goode's organisation, 1919-20; Commercial Secretary to H.M. Legation at Belgrade, 1920-28; H.M. Legation (now H.M. Embassy) at Santiago, Chile, 1928-31; Commercial Counsellor to H.M. Embassy, Rio de Janeiro, 1931-1942; Brit. Govt. Commercial Agent in Palestine and Transjordan, 1944-46; retd., 1946. Alderman, Norfolk C.C. and mem. of New Hunstanton U.D.C. *Publications:* Economic reports on Jugoslavia; Economic reports on Chile, published by H.M. Stationery Office; article (economic) on Jugoslavia for the Encyclopædia Britannica, and Economic Reports on Brazil, etc. *Recreations:* shooting, fishing, motoring. *Address:* Green Tiles, Old Hunstanton, Norfolk. *T.* Hunstanton 2235. *Club:* Norfolk (Norwich).
[*Died* 20 *June* 1967.

MURROW, Edward R., K.B.E. (Hon.); reporter and news analyst since 1939 (Columbia Broadcasting System, Inc., Dec. 1935); *b.* Greensboro, North Carolina, 25 April 1908; *s.* of R. C. Murrow; *m.* 1934, Janet Huntington Brewster; one *s.* *Educ.:* Washington State Coll. (B.A.). Pres. National Student Federation of America, 1929-32; Assistant Director, Institute of International Education 1932-35; Director of Talks and Education, Columbia Broadcasting System, Inc., 1935-37; European Director, Columbia Broadcasting System, Inc., 1937-45; War Correspondent, 1939-45; President of American Correspondents, London, 1944-45; Vice-Pres. and Director of Public Affairs, Columbia Broadcasting System, Dec. 1945-

July 1947; Mem. C.B.S. Bd. of Directors, 1947-56; Director of the United States Information Agency, 1961-64. Holds numerous hon. degrees, and also awards for Radio, TV, etc. Hon. O.B.E. 1947; Chevalier Légion d'Honneur (France), 1954; Officer, Order of Leopold (Belgium), 1959. *Publications:* This is London, 1941; various magazine articles, book reviews, etc. *Recreations:* golf, fishing. *Address:* 1776 Pennsylvania Ave., Washington, D.C. *Clubs:* Savile; Century, Lambs (New York). [*Died* 27 *April* 1965.

MUSELIER, Vice-Am. d'Escadre Emile Henry; Grand Officier de la Légion d'Honneur; Compagnon de La Libération (France); *b.* Marseilles, 17 Apr. 1882; *m.* 1908, Marie-Anne Jacquemont du Donjon (*d.* 1961); two *s.* two *d.*; *m.* 1962, Monique Gibeau. *Educ.:* Brest French Naval School on board Le Borda. Aspirant de 1ere classe, 1902; Enseigne de Vaisseau, 1904; Lieutenant de Vaisseau, 1912; Capitaine de Corvette, 1918; Capitaine de Frégate, 1922; Capitaine de Vaisseau, 1926; Contre-Amiral, 1933; Vice-Amiral, 1939; Vice-Amiral d'Escadre, 1940; among his many commands, Admiral Muselier was in charge of the Defences of Cherbourg, was Major-General at Ferryville (Bizerta), was in command of the Second Division of cruisers in the Mediterranean, and in 1938 was appointed Admiral Commanding the Navy and Defences of the port of Marseilles where the War of 1939-45 found him; joined General de Gaulle in July 1940; C.-in-C. of Free French Naval Forces, 1940-42, and of Free French Air Forces, 1940-41; National Commissioner of Navy and Merchant Navy in the French National Committee, resigned March 1942; Assistant to General Giraud in Algiers, 1943; Chief of the French Naval Delegation of the Military Mission for German Affairs till February 1945; active service, 1940-46. Founded a group, Union for the Defence of the Republic, 1946. Membre du Comité National des Combattants de la Paix; Président de l'Association Nationale d'Entr'aide à la Vieillesse. Hon. K.C.B. *Publications:* Marine et Résistance, 1945; De Gaulle contre le gaullisme, 1947. *Address:* Château de Seymiers, Fayet-Le-Château (Puy-de-Dôme), France; Toulon (Var), Villa Taravao, Cap Brun. [*Died* 2 *Sept.* 1965.

MUSGRAVE, Sir Charles, 14th Bt., *cr.* 1611; *b.* 9 November 1913; *s.* of Thomas Charles Musgrave (3rd *s.* of 11th Bt.), and Ethel, *d.* of C. A. Frost, Melbourne, Australia; *S.* cousin, Sir Nigel Courtenay Musgrave, 13th Bt., 1957; *m.* 1948, Olive Louise Avril (marriage dissolved, 1960), *d.* of Patrick Cringle, Norfolk; two *s.* *Educ.:* West Buckland School, Devon; Thurlestone College. Employed Metropolitan Railway, 1930-34. H. A. C. (Territorial Army), 1932-33; Regular Army, 1934-46: Rifle Brigade, India, Palestine, Egypt, 1934-43; R.E., Sicily, Italy, France, Belgium, Holland, Germany, 1943-46. On demobilization, engaged in farming in South Creake, Norfolk; subseq. lived Suffolk. *Recreation:* tennis. *Heir:* *s.* Christopher Patrick Charles Musgrave, *b.* 14 April 1949. *Address:* Sunnymead, Rushlake Green, Heathfield, Sussex. [*Died* 26 *July* 1970.

MUSKERRY, 7th Baron (Ire.), *cr.* 1781; **Mathew Fitzmaurice Tilson Deane;** Bt. (Ire.), *cr.* 1710; *b.* 30 July 1874; *s.* of Hon. Mathew James Hastings Fitzmaurice Deane (3rd *s.* of 3rd Baron); *S* kinsman 1954; *m.* 1st, 1897, Mabel Kathleen Vivienne (*d.* 1954) *d.* of C. H. Robinson, M.D.; one *s.* one *d.* (and two *s.* decd.); 2nd, 1964, Muriel Sellers, *d.* of Arthur Simpson. *Heir:* *s.* Hon. Hastings Fitzmaurice Tilson Deane, M.A., M.B. (Dublin); D.M.R. (Lond.) [*b.* 12 March 1907; *m.* 1944, Betty Palmer, Glenstone, Grahamstown, S. Africa; one *s.* one *d.* *Educ.:* Dublin University. Served War of 1939-45: Capt. S. African Med. Corps, 4th Armoured Car Regt., M.E.F., and with Allied Armies in Italy]. *Address:* c/o Frederick Bowman Publications, Humanimal House, Sandown Lane, Liverpool 15. *T.:* Sefton Park 5772. [*Died* 2 *Nov.* 1966.

MUSSON, Major-General Arthur Ingram, C.B. 1936; late Chief Paymaster, War Office and Inspector of Army Pay Offices; *b.* 1877; *s.* of W. Musson, Clitheroe, Lancs.; *m.* Teresa M. I. (*d.* 1961), *d.* of I. McDonnell, Water Park, Co. Cork; two *d.* *Educ.:* Tonbridge; R.M.C. Sandhurst. Joined East Yorks. Regt., 1897; transferred. to R.A.P.C., 1908; served South African War, 1899; European War, 1914-1919; Iraq Operations and N.W. Persia, 1919-20; retired pay, 1937; re-employed on Staff, 1940-41. *Address:* c/o Lloyds Bank Ltd., Cox's & King's Branch, 6 Pall Mall S.W.1. [*Died* 30 *Dec.* 1961.

MUSSON, Francis William, C.B. 1958; C.M.G. 1945; A.F.C. 1918; A.F.R.Ae.S. 1929; *b.* Clitheroe, Lancs., 31 May 1894; *e. s.* of Alfred William Musson, M.B., and Alice Maude Slater; *m.* 1926, Margaret Edith Withecomb, *d.* of Solomon John Brice; one *s.* *Educ.:* Tonbridge; Emmanuel Coll., Camb. (Scholar). European War, 1914-19, served with Loyal North Lancs Regt. and R.F.C. (wounded France 1915, 1914-15 Star, A.F.C.); on transfer to R.F.C. was engaged on scientific work connected with aerial gunnery and ballistics; B.A. Cambridge, 1916; M.A. 1950; Asst. Principal, Air Min., 1919; Principal, 1930; Dep. Director of Aircraft Production, 1937; Director of Labour and Priority, 1939; British Air Commission, Washington, D.C., 1940; Controller of Programmes and Administration at British Air Commission, Washington, 1942-45; Principal Asst. Sec., Min. of Aircraft Production, 1945; attached Foreign Office, 1946; retired as Under-Secretary, 1958. *Recreations:* cricket and golf—also music. Played cricket for Lancashire. *Address:* Wayside, Priestfields, Rochester, Kent. *T.:* Chatham 43002. *Clubs:* United University, M.C.C. [*Died* 2 *Jan.* 1962.

MUSTERS, Col. John N. C.; *see* Chaworth-Musters.

MYBURGH, Brig. Philip Stafford, C.B.E. 1945; D.S.O. 1919; M.C.; R.A., *b.* 12 May 1893; *m.* 1st, 1919, Marie Louise (who obtained a divorce, 1929; she *m.* 2nd, 1929, Hon. Patrick Johnstone), *d.* of Albert Picard, Paris; one *d.*; 2nd, 1930, Elizabeth Marjorie Reed (divorced for desertion); two *s.* (and one *s.* decd.); 3rd, 1947, Margaret Constance Dibb, *d.* of late A. D. Barr. Entered R.A., 1912; served European War, 1914-18 (despatches twice, D.S.O., M.C., Croix de Guerre); War of 1939-1945, Middle East, Burma Campaign and S.E.A.C. (despatches, Bar to D.S.O., C.B.E.); retired pay, 1946. *Address:* Rogues Roost, Moiben, Kenya, E. Africa. [*Died* 21 *May* 1963.

MYERS, Leonard William, M.A., Headmaster, Simon Langton School, Canterbury, 1926-Dec. 1954; *s.* of Thomas Myers, Bishop's Stortford; *m.* 1945, Mrs. M. A. Sheppard. *Educ.:* Bishop's Stortford College; Magdalen College, Oxford. Assistant master, St. Olave's School, S.E., 1913-26: War service H.A.C. (France). Member Council Nat. Assoc. of Head Teachers, 1946-54. *Recreation:* travel. *Address:* The Red House, London Road, Canterbury, Kent. *T.:* Canterbury 3578. [*Died* 26 *July* 1962.

MYRDDIN-EVANS, Sir Guildhaume, K.C.M.G. 1947; C.B. 1945; retired as Chief International Labour Adviser to H.M. Government (1955-59) and Deputy Secre-

tary, Ministry of Labour and National Service (1945-59); Chairman, Local Government Commission for Wales, 1959; *b.* 17 December 1894; 2nd *s.* of Reverend Thomas Towy Evans, Blaenau Gwent, Abertillery, Mon., and of Mary James; *m.* 1919, Elizabeth, *d.* of Owen Watkin, Sarn, Caernarvonshire; two *s.* *Educ.:* Llandovery; Christ Church, Oxford. 1st Cl. Hons. Mathematical Mods. 1913; hon. mention, Junior Mathematical Schol., 1915; M.A.; served European War, 1914-18 as Lt. South Wales Borderers, France and Flanders; invalided; attached to Prime Minister's Secretariat, 1917; Asst. Sec. War Cabinet, 1919; Assistant Principal, Treasury, 1920; Private Secretary to Controller of Supply Services, 1920-27, to Controller of Finance and Supply Services, 1927, and to Financial Secretary to Treasury, 1927-29; attended Middle East Conference, Cairo and Jerusalem, 1921; Asst. Sec. to British Delegation to Hague Conferences on Reparations, 1929 and 1930; Principal, Ministry of Labour, 1929; Deputy Chief Insurance Officer under Unemployment Acts, 1935; Principal Private Sec. to Minister of Labour, 1938; Asst. Sec. Ministry of Labour, 1938; Principal Asst. Sec. Ministry of Labour and National Service, 1940; loaned to War Cabinet Offices as Head of Production Executive Secretariat, 1941; loaned to U.S.A. Govt. as adviser to War Manpower Commission, 1942; advised Govt. of Canada on manpower, 1942; Under-Secretary, Ministry of Labour and National Service, 1942. British Govt. Delegate to International Labour Conference, 1939 and 1944-59; President of the Conference, 1949. British Govt. rep. on Governing Body of Internatonal Labour Office, 1945-59, Chm., Nov. 1945-Dec. 1947, and 1956-57; member of British Govt. Delegation to U.N. Conf., San Francisco, 1945, and to Gen. Ass. U.N., 1946-53; mem. Council Baptist Union of Gt. B. and Ire. 1943-. U.S.A. Medal of Freedom with palms. *Publication:* The Employment Exchange Service of Great Britain (with Sir Thomas Chegwidden, C.B., C.V.O.), 1934. *Recreation:* foreign travel. *Address:* 6 Chester Place, Regent's Park, N.W.1. *T.:* Welbeck 5696. *Club:* Bath.
[*Died* 15 *Feb.* 1964.

MYTTON, Alderman Sir Thomas Henry, Kt. 1966; *b.* Brynmawr, 1878. *Educ.:* Garnfach Sch., Nantyglo. Formerly: colliery worker; Mem., S. Wales Miners' Fedn. (now N.U.M.). Member: Bedwellty Bd. of Guardians, 1909; Abertillery Urban Coun., 1919 (Chm., 1923, 1937); Monmouthshire C.C., 1938 (Alderman, 1953; Chm., 1961-62). *Address:* 9 Granville St., Abertillery, Mon. [*Died* 13 *Nov.* 1966.

N

NAESMITH, Sir Andrew, Kt., *cr.* 1953; C.B.E. 1948 (O.B.E. 1942); J.P.; M.A. (h.c.); retired as a Director of the Bank of England (1949-57); part-time mem. Iron and Steel Board, 1953-60; Empire Cotton Growing Corporation; Vice-Pres., British Cotton Growing Association; *b.* 24 July 1888; *s.* of Thomas Naesmith; *m.* 1917, Emily Woods. J.P. for Lancashire. *Address:* 202 Haywood Rd., Accrington, Lancs. [*Died* 23 *Oct.* 1961.

NAIRN, Sir Douglas (Leslie) Spencer-, 2nd Bt. *cr.* 1933; T.D.; *b.* 24 December 1906; *e. s.* of Sir Robert Spencer-Nairn, 1st Bt., T.D.; *S.* father, 1960; *m.* 1st, 1931, Elizabeth Livingston (marr. diss., 1946), *d.* of late Arnold J. Henderson; two *s.* one *d.*; 2nd, 1947, E. Louise, *d.* of late Frederick Vester; one *s.* one *d.* *Educ.:* Trinity Hall, Cambridge (M.A.). Member of firm of Nairn-Williamson Ltd., Director, October 1960-68. Served War of 1939-45, Black Watch, ending with rank of Lt.-Col. Farmed in Southern Rhodesia, 1947-54. M.P. (C.) Central Ayrshire, 1955-Sept. 1959. *Heir:* *s.* Robert Arnold Spencer-Nairn [*b.* 11 Oct. 1933; *m.* 1963, Joanna Elizabeth, *d.* of late Lt.-Comdr. G. S. Salt, R.N., and Mrs. W. J. Lamb; one *s.* one *d.* *Educ.:* Eton; Trinity Hall, Cambridge. Late Lieutenant, Scots Guards]. *Address:* Rankeilour, Cupar, Fife; Culligran, Struy, Inverness-shire; 4 Stanhope Mews East, S.W.7; Villa Franca, Glendale, Rhodesia. *Clubs:* Carlton, Caledonian; New (Salisbury, Rhodesia). [*Died* 8 *Nov.* 1970.

NAISH, Albert Ernest, M.A., M.D. (Cantab.); F.R.C.P. (Lond.); Consulting Physician, Sheffield Royal Hospital and Sheffield Children's Hospital; Consulting Physician, Jessop Hospital for Women, and to the Royal Albert Institution; *b.* 15 Oct. 1871; *s.* of Henry Naish, of Holdenhurst, nr. Bristol, and Elizabeth Pinsent Keddle; *m.* Lucy Wellburn, M.B.; five *s.* three *d.* *Educ.:* Monkton Combe School; Trinity College, Cambridge; St. Bartholomew's Hospital. Served as Major R.A.M.C. (T.) in Wharncliffe War Hospital, 1915-19, and as Consulting Physician to Ministry of Pensions Hospital, 1919-21; Professor of Medicine in the University of Sheffield, 1931-36; Examiner in Medicine for Univ. of Cambridge, 1933-41, and for Royal College of Physicians, 1932-36. *Publications:* various contributions to medical journals. *Recreation:* walking. *Address:* Derwen, Valley, Holyhead. *T.:* Valley 265.
[*Died* 2 *Aug.* 1964.

NAISH, John Paull; Chief Oriental Reader, University Press, Oxford; *s.* of Charles E. Naish, Charlbury; *m.* 1913, Jessie Evelyn, *d.* of Arthur Hall, Woburn Sands, one *s.* *Educ.:* King Edward's High School, Birmingham; read Theology and Philosophy in Birmingham and Nottingham, 1905; 1906, studied Hebrew and Syriac in Birmingham under Professor J. Rendel Harris, and Arabic in London under Sir Thomas W. Arnold; further study in Beirut and Cairo in 1906; in Central Provinces and Punjab, India, 1907-10; studied Urdū, Persian and Arabic in St. Stephen's College, Delhi, under Professor Abdurrahman; took B.A. and B.D. degrees in London University, 1914; after the War, studied at Mansfield Coll., Oxford, and read with Prof. D. S. Margoliouth; travel and study in Holland, France, Germany, Italy, Sicily, Spain, 1921-32 and S. Africa, 1949-50; B.D. Hons. in Church History, 1st Class (Lond.), 1919; studied Theology and Oriental Languages in Strasbourg, 1921, under Profs. G. Baldensperger and Ch. Jaeger; B. Litt. (Oxon), and University Syriac Prize, 1921-22; D.D. (Lond.), 1923; Oriental Languages Reader at University Press, Oxford, 1921-23; Lecturer in Hebrew and Old Testament Exegesis in Mansfield College, Oxford, 1923-32; External Tutor in Hebrew and Old Testament, Keble College, Oxford, 1927-31; M.A. (Oxon), 1930; studied Egyptian Hieroglyphic and Hieratic under Dr. A. M. Blackman, 1925-29. Member of the Oxford Society of Historical Theology since 1923; of the Royal Asiatic Society, 1928-41; of the Deutsche Morgenländische Gesellschaft, 1931-40; Assistant Editor of the Palestine Exploration Fund Quarterly Statement during 1932; Examiner for Elmslie Hebrew Scholarship, 1928; External Examiner for M.A. Degree, Univ. of Manchester, 1934; studied Sanskrit, Pali, Russian and Japanese. Hon. Fellow, Mansfield College, since 1947. *Publications:* The Fourth Gospel and the Sacraments, 1922; translation from the German of Dr. A. Schweitzer's Civilization and Ethics, 1923; The Semitic Background of the Gospels, 1923; The Book of Job and the Early Persian Period, 1925; Egyptian Influence on Israelite History (in Amicitiæ Corolla), 1933; The Book of Micah (in Ad. Sch. Trans. Series), 1934; Indexes to Dr.

J. H. Hertz's ed. Pentateuch and Haftorahs, 1936; translation from the French of Mahmūd Muhtār Pasha's Wisdom of the Qur'ān, 1937; Indexes to Dr. P. P. Argenti's Istoria di Scio, 1943, and Libro di Oro, 1944; Index to Dr. G. Yazdānī's Bidar, 1947; wrote the Foreign Impressions pages in the Congregational Quarterly, 1925-32; articles in Enquiry, 1948-1949; assisted with: Lady Drower's Mandaic Dictionary, 1959; Madame Foat-Tuğay's Autobiography, Three Centuries, 1960. *Recreation:* ornithology. *Address:* Stone Walls, Kiln Lane, Shotover, Oxford. *T.:* Oxford 61184.
[*Died* 13 *April* 1964.

NALL, J(ohn) Spencer, C.M.G. 1954; Chairman and Managing Director of Bright and Hitchcocks Pty. Ltd., 1927-65; Chairman of Commissioners, Geelong Harbor Trust, 1933-58; *b.* 2 Sept. 1887; *s.* of late Rev. John Nall, Geelong, Vic.; *m.* 1920, Marjorie St. Aubyn, *d.* of late Rev. Joseph Snell, Geelong, Vic.; one *s.* two *d.* *Educ.:* Grenville Coll., Ballarat, Vic. Served European War, 1914-18, France, 114th Howitzer Battery 5th Div. A.I.F. Mem. Council Geelong Chamber of Commerce and Manufacturers, 1927- (Pres. 1936, 1937). Chairman, Geelong & District War Funds Board, War of 1939-45; President, Geelong Rotary Club, 1932. Trustee various Charitable and Philanthropic Organizations. F.R.G.S. 1950. *Recreation:* golf. *Address:* St. Aubyn, 10 Layton Crescent, Geelong, Vic., Australia. *T.:* X7676. *Clubs:* Rotary (Geelong); Athenæum (Melbourne); Golf (Barwon Heads); Golf (Point Lonsdale).
[*Died* 13 *Sept.* 1970.

NALLY, Will; *b.* Astley, nr. Manchester 13 Dec. 1914; *s.* of Tom Nally, coalminer and Tess Nally; *m.* 1937, Hilda, *d.* of Joseph and Martha Clarkson, Manchester; two *s.* *Educ.:* Elementary Schools. Solicitor's clerk; later journalist. President Manchester and District Federation Labour Leagues of Youth, 1930-35; National Committee Labour League of Youth, 1931-1935. Co-operative Press, reporter and feature writer; Gunner, Royal Artillery; Daily Herald reporter; War Correspondent in Europe; youngest delegate to inaugural meetings of Consultative Assembly, Council of Europe; Vice-pres., Council of Europe Commn. on Social Affairs, 1949-50; M.P. (Labour Co-operative) Bilston Division of Wolverhampton, 1945-50, Bilston, 1950-55; Parl. Private Sec. to Min. of Town and Country Planning, 1949-51. *Recreations:* gambling reform; film fan; Manchester historical research. *Address:* The Meads, Croft Hill Rd., Moston, Manchester 10. *T.:* Failsworth 2592. *Clubs:* National Trade Union, London Press; Manchester Press.
[*Died* 4 *Aug.* 1965.

NANAVATI, Dr. Sir Manilal B., Kt., *cr.* 1941; B.A., LL.B. (Bombay); M.A. (Penn., U.S.A.); President, Indian Society of Agricultural Economics, 1942-53; *b.* 11 Jan. 1877. *Educ.:* Baroda; St. Xavier's College and Government Law College, Bombay; Wharton School of Finance, Pennsylvania. Joined Baroda State Service, 1904; Director of Commerce and Industries, 1912; between 1912 and 1931 held at various times posts of Registrar, Co-operative Societies, Director of Commerce and Industries, Development Commissioner, Collector and Accountant-General; Secretary and then President of Okha Harbour Board; Revenue Commissioner, 1932-33; Naib Dewan (Member of Executive Council), 1934-35; Deputy Gov., Reserve Bank of India, 1936-41; Member, Famine Inquiry Commission. Pres. Indian Soc. of Agricultural Economics, 1941-59. Title of Arunaditya conferred by Baroda Govt. in 1936. Hon. D.Sc., Sardar Vallabhbhai Vidyapith Univ., 1962. *Publications:* Report on the Agricultural Indebtedness in the Baroda State, 1913; Report on the Sociological survey of the Servants of the Khangi Department, 1917; The Indian Rural Problem (with J. J. Anjaria), 1944. *Address:* Leela, Juhu, Bombay. *T.:* 88315.
[*Died* 29 *July* 1967.

NANDRIS, Grigore, M.A., Ph.D.; Professor Emeritus of Comparative Philology of the Slavonic Languages in the University of London (apptd. Prof., 1948, retired 1962); *b.* 30 Jan. 1895; *m.* 1937, Mabel W. Farley, B.A. (T.C.D.), *d.* of Prof. W. J. Farley, Magee Coll., Londonderry; one *s.* *Educ.:* University of Bucharest; University of Vienna; University of Cracow; Paris. Professor of Slavonic Philology, University of Cernăuti, Bucovina, 1926; Prof. of Slavonic Philology, Univ. of Bucharest, 1940; Chm. of Soc. for Culture and Literature in Bucovina, 1929-42; Mem. Roumanian Parl.; Commander of Polonia Restituta. *Publications:* Slavo-Rumanian Charters in the Monasteries of Mount Athos, 1937; Slavonic influence in the Rumanian language (2nd Internat. Congress of Slav Philologists, Warsaw), 1934; Colloquial Rumanian, 1966; The development and structure of Rumanian, 1951; Old Church Slavonic Grammar, 1966; The historical Dracula, 1966; Phonemic and phonetic principles, 1966; Neo-Byzantine Wall-painting in Eastern Europe; Contrib. to Slavonic and East European Review, Encyclopædia Britannica, Chambers's Encyclopædia. *Address:* 13 Chelwood Gardens, Kew, Surrey. *T.:* Prospect 8926.
[*Died* 29 *March* 1968.

NAPIER, Albert Napier Williamson; *b.* 5 Oct. 1894; 2nd *s.* of late James Williamson Napier; *m.* 1945, Marion, *d.* of late Brig.-Gen. F. A. Curteis, R.A. *Educ.:* Oundle; Germany, France, Switzerland, Italy; Pembroke College, Cambridge. 2nd Lt. Intelligence Corps, B.E.F., France, 1914; transferred to D.C.L.I., Aug. 1916, and continued to serve with B.E.F. till March 1918. Levant Consular Service, 1922; served at various posts abroad; Asst. Oriental Secretary (Press and Publicity) British Embassy, Cairo, 1936-1942; H.M. Consul, Casablanca, 1942-45; Foreign Office, 1945-47; Consul-General Zürich, 1947-49; Istanbul, 1949-52; retired 1952. *Recreations:* golf, travel, bridge. *Address:* Old Cottage, Burchetts Green, Berks. *T.:* Littlewick Green 3053.
[*Died* 3 *Jan.* 1969.

NAPIER, Brig. John Lenox Clavering, C.B.E. 1944; *b.* 9 Dec. 1898; *s.* of late Capt. A. L. Napier, O.B.E., late Green Howards; *m.* 1925, Grace Edythe Muriel, *d.* of late Col. C. A. Young, C.B., C.M.G.; two *s.* one *d.* *Educ.:* Wellington College; R.M.A., Woolwich. Joined R.A. 1916; R.H.A. 1918; transferred to Royal Tank Corps, 1923; Adjt. 1926-27; officer of a Company of Gentleman Cadets, R.M.A., Woolwich, 1928-31; India with Armoured Car Company, 1932; Staff College, Quetta, 1934-35; Armoured Car Company, 1936, and later G.S.O. 3, Madras District; G.S.O. 2 War Office, 1938; M.E.F. 1940. Served European War, 1914-18 (B.W.M., V.M.); Mohmand Ops., N.W. Frontier, India, 1933 (Indian G.S. medal); War of 1939-45 (despatches, Africa Star, Italy Star, 1939-45 Star, B.W.M., Defence Medal, C.B.E., Legion of Merit, U.S.); retired pay, 1952. *Recreations:* shooting and fishing. *Address:* Puddicombe House, Drewsteignton, Nr. Exeter. [*Died* 27 *May* 1966.

NAPIER, Sir Robert (Archibald), 12th Bt., of Merchiston, *cr.* 1627; *b.* 19 July 1889; *s.* of Sir Archibald Napier, 10th Bt. and Mary, *d.* of Sir Thomas Fairbairn, 2nd Bt.; *S.* brother 1954; *m.* 1st, 1914, Violet (marriage dissolved, 1929), *d.* of E. Payn; one *s.*; 2nd, 1929, Margaret Anne Searle Hinton, M.B.E. (*d.*1962), *d.* of Thomas James Hinton, Horwell Lodge, Copplestone, Devon, and late Mrs. Mary Hinton. *Educ.:* Eton. Trooper in the City of London Yeomanry (Roughriders); held commission in 1st Royal East Kent Mounted Rifles, European War, 1914-18; served War of 1939-45 as Flight Lieut., R.A.F. *Heir:* *s.* William Archibald, *b.* 19 July 1915 [*m.* 1942, Kathleen Mabel, *d.* of late Reginald Greaves, Tafleberg, C.P.; one *s.*]. *Address:* Merchiston Croft, P.O. Sandown, Johannesburg, S. Africa. *T.:* 426353. [*Died* 25 *June* 1965.

NAPIER-CLAVERING, Maj.-Gen. Noel Warren, C.B. 1944; C.B.E. 1941; D.S.O. 1917; late R.E.; *s. s.* of Francis Napier-Clavering and Elizabeth, *d.* of Thomas Cowan; *b.* 24 Dec. 1888; *m.* 1921, Margaret, *d.* of T. W. Vigers of Montville, St. Peter Port, Guernsey; one *d.* *Educ.:* Clifton Coll.; R.M.A., Woolwich. Served European War (despatches, D.S.O., Bt. Major, Chevalier du Mérite Agricole); Palestine, 1936-37; War of 1939-45 (despatches, C.B.E., C.B.); Major, 1925; Bt. Lt.-Col., 1931; Lt.-Col., 1932; Col., 1936; Maj.-Gen., 1940; A.A. and Q.M.G. 4th Division, 1937-39; Brigadier in charge of Administration, British Troops in Egypt, 1939-40; D.A.G., G.H.Q., M.E.F. 1940-42; Chief of British Military Mission to Egyptian Army, 1942-45; retired pay, 1945; p.s.c. *Address:* Tundry House, Dogmersfield, Hants. *Club:* Army and Navy. [*Died* 30 *Sept.* 1964

NARANG, Sir Gokul Chand, Kt., *cr.* 1935; *b.* Baddoki Gosain, District Gujranwala, Punjab, 15 Nov. 1878; *o. s.* of L. Mul Raj Narang; *m.* 1904, Sumitra Devi, 2nd *d.* of Ra Sahib Seth Chuhar Lal, Banker, Abbottabad, N.W.F. Province; one *s.* (and two *s.* decd., one of whom killed in action on Burma Front, 1944, the other *d.* 1965) four *d.* *Educ.:* Gujranwala, Lahore, M.A. (Punjab). 1901, M.A. (Cal.), 1902; PhD. (Bern.), 1910, Served as a Professor in D.A.V. College, Lahore, 1901-7; called to Bar, Lincoln's Inn, 1910; practised as Advocate at the High Court of Judicature at Lahore for twenty years; is Chairman of the Punjab Sugar Mills Co., Ltd., the Basti Sugar Mills Co., Ltd., the Nawabganj Sugar Mills Co., Ltd., the Narang Bank of India Ltd., etc.; Director Punjab National Bank Ltd. for 18 years; Member Punjab Legislature for 22 years; Ex-Fellow of the Punjab University; President Punjab Provincial Hindu Sabha, 1923-30; President High Court Bar Association, 1930; Minister for Local Self-Government, Punjab, 1930-37. *Publications:* Message of the Vedas; Transformation of Sikhism; Real Hinduism, etc. *Address:* 5 Cavalry Lines, Delhi 8, India. [*Died* 24 *Feb.* 1970.

NARBOROUGH, Rt. Rev. (Frederick) Dudley Vaughan, M.A.; *b.* 13 June 1895; 2nd *s.* of Frederick William and Edith Narborough. *Educ.:* King's Sch., Norwich; Worcester Coll., Oxf. (Exhibitioner and Squire Schol.). First class hons. in Theology, Junior Denyer and Johnson scholarship; Fellow and Chaplain of Worcester College, 1921-26; Examining Chaplain to the Bishop of Southwark, 1922-30; Resident Chaplain to the Archbishop of Canterbury, 1926-28; Canon Residentiary of Bristol, 1928-39; Provost of Southwark Cathedral and Rector of St. Saviour with St. Peter, Southwark, 1939-41; Lecturer, St. Martin-in-the-Fields, 1941; Examining Chaplain to the Bishop of Newcastle, 1927-36; and to the Bishop of Bristol, 1933; Treasurer of Bristol Cathedral, 1929-1933; B.D. Oxford, 1931; Select Preacher, Oxford, 1931-32; Cambridge, 1933 and 1940. Boyle Lecturer, 1944-46; Archdeacon of Colchester, 1946-59; Bishop of Colchester, 1946-65; retired, 1965. Hon. Canon of Chelmsford, 1959-. *Publication:* Commentary on the Epistle to the Hebrews (Clarendon Bible); contributor to Essays on the Trinity and the Incarnation. *Address:* 279 Queen Edith Way, Cambridge. [*Died* 21 *Jan.* 1966.

NARRACOTT, Arthur Henson; Air Correspondent, The Times, since 1940; *b.* Torquay, 10 April 1905; *er. s.* of late P. T. Narracott, Keelby, Torquay; *m.* 1st, Catherine Aeron, *er. d.* of T. H. Franklin, Torquay; one *d.*; 2nd, Daphne Lilian, *y. d.* of late H. S. and Mrs. Hook, Guildford. *Educ.:* Homelands School, Torquay; Torquay Grammar School. Entered journalism, 1921, as member editorial staff of Torbay Express; four years staff of Torbay Herald and Express; joined reporting staff of Press Association, 1928; Parliamentary staff of The Times, 1938; deputy Lobby Correspondent of The Times, 1939. Served with R.A.F. in France, 1939-40, and subsequently acted as The Times war correspondent with Allied Air Forces in France, North Africa, Italy and on the Continent (despatches). *Publications:* War News Had Wings (A Record of the R.A.F. in France), 1940; How the R.A.F. Works, 1941; Unsung Heroes of the Air, 1943; Air Power in War, 1945; In Praise of the Few (Editor), 1946. *Recreations:* golf, flying, angling. *Address:* 807 Endsleigh Court, W.C.1. *T.:* Euston 4025. *Club:* Royal Aero. [*Died* 16 *May* 1967.

NASH, Norman E. Keown, C.M.G. 1946; *b.* Geelong, Victoria, Australia, 14 March 1885; *m.* 1915, Alice May Clarke (*d.* 1959), Whalley Range, Manchester; one *d.* Called to Bar, Gray's Inn; journalism in Manchester and London; News Department, Foreign Office, 1920; retired 1950. United Kingdom Correspondent of the Council of Europe, 1950-55. *Address:* 1 The Pound, Westcott, Dorking, Surrey. [*Died* 16 *Sept.* 1966.

NASH, Rt. Hon. Sir Walter, P.C. 1946; G.C.M.G. 1965; C.H. 1959; Member, New Zealand Parliament since 1929; Prime Minister, New Zealand, 1957-60, also Minister for External Affairs and Minister for Maori Affairs, 1957-60; Leader of H.M. Opposition, New Zealand, 1950-57 and 1960-63; *b.* 1882; *s.* of Alfred Arthur Nash; *m.* 1906, Lotty May (*d.* 1961), *d.* of Thomas Eaton, Selly Oak; three *s.* *Educ.:* St. John's Church School, Kidderminster; N.Z. Delegate to the Second International Labour Conference at Geneva in 1920; Leader N.Z. Deleg. to Conf. of Inst. of Pacific Relations at Honolulu, 1927, at Banff, Canada, 1933; and at Mont Tremblant, Canada, 1942; and to Conf. Brit. Commonwealth Relations at Toronto, 1933. Member Nat. Exec. Labour Party, 1919-60, Secretary N.Z. Labour Party, 1922-32, National Pres., 1935-36; Vice-Pres. N.Z. Institute of International Affairs, 1936-41; Member Wellington Harbour Board, 1933-38; Minister of Social Security, 1938; Minister of Marketing, New Zealand, 1936-41; Minister of New Zealand in the United States 1942-44; Minister of Finance, Customs, etc., New Zealand, 1935-49; Member, New Zealand War Cabinet, 1939-45; Dep. Prime Minister of New Zealand, 1940-49. Mem. of Pacific War Council, Washington, 1942-44; Pres., I.L.O. Conference, Philadelphia, U.S.A., 1944; New Zealand Representative, Imperial Conference, 1937; Leader, New Zealand Delegation, International Monetary Conference, Bretton Woods, U.S.A., 1944; N.Z. Deleg. British Commonwealth Prime Ministers' Conf., London, 1946; Leader, N.Z. Deleg. to Confs. on Trade and Employment, Geneva, 1947, Havana, 1947-48; Leader N.Z. Deleg. to Conf. of Commonwealth Finance Ministers, 1949; Leader, New Zealand Delegations: 14th Session E.C.A.F.E., Kuala Lumpur, 1958; 4th Session S.E.A.T.O. Council of Ministers, Manila, 1958; 13th Sess. U.N.

Gen. Assembly, N.Y., 1958; 10th Meeting Colombo Plan Consultative Cttee., Seattle, 1958; Antarctic Conf., Washington, 1959; ANZUS Counc. Meeting, Washington, 1959; 14th Sess. U.N. Gen. Assembly, N.Y., 1959; 11th Meeting, Colombo Plan Consult. Cttee., Jogjakarta, 1959; 6th Sess. S.E.A.T.O. Counc. of Ministers, Washington, 1960. Chm. 5th Session. S.E.A.T.O. Council of Ministers, Wellington, 1959. Attended: Commonwealth Prime Ministers' Conf., London, 1960; 15th Session, United Nations General Assembly, New York, 1960. Visited Antarctica and South Pole, 1964. Hon. LL.D. (Cambridge Univ., Eng.; Tufts Coll., Mass., and Temple University, Phil., U.S.A.); Hon. D.C.L. (Victoria College of Wellington, N.Z.). *Publication:* New Zealand, a Working Democracy, 1943. *Address:* Parliament Buildings, Wellington, New Zealand; 14 St. Albans Grove, Lower Hutt, New Zealand. *T.:* 63-401. [*Died* 4 *June* 1968.

NASMITH, Admiral Sir Martin (Eric) Dunbar-, V.C. 1915; K.C.B., *cr.* 1934 (C.B. 1920); K.C.M.G., *cr.* 1955; Vice-Admiral of the United Kingdom and Lieutenant of the Admiralty, 1945-62; *s.* of late Martin A. Nasmith, of Clevehurst, Weybridge; *m.* 1920, Beatrix Justina (*d.* 1962) (Dep. Superintendent-in-Chief, St. John Ambulance Bde., 1942-53; C.B.E. 1949; D.St.J. 1951), *o. d.* of late Commander Harry Dunbar-Dunbar-Rivers, Glen Rothes; two *s.* one *d.* Served European War, 1914-19; destroyed 96 Turkish vessels of various types in the Sea of Marmora while in command of Submarine E11 (V.C., promoted Comdr.); Commanded R.N.C., Dartmouth, 1926-1928; Naval A.D.C. to the King, 1927-28; Rear-Adm., 1928; Rear-Adm., Submarines, 1929-31; Vice-Admiral, 1932; Commander-in-Chief East Indies Station, 1932-34; a Lord Commissioner of the Admiralty and Chief of Naval Personnel, 1935-38; Admiral, 1936; Commander-in-Chief, Plymouth, and Western Approaches, 1938-41; Flag Officer in Charge, London, 1942-46; Vice-Chairman Imperial War Graves Commission, 1948-1954. D.L. Morayshire, 1942, Vice-Lieutenant, 1957. Grand Officier Legion of Honour and Croix de Guerre avec Palmes, 1946, Knight Grand Cross Orange Nassau and St. Olaf of Norway, Order of Polonia Restituta, 1st Class. *Address:* Glen Rothes, Morayshire. *Clubs:* United Service, Royal Ocean Racing. [*Died* 29 *June* 1965.

NASSER, President Gamal Abdel; President of the United Arab Republic since 1958 (of the Republic of Egypt, 1956-58); Prime Minister since 1967; Chairman Supreme Arab Socialist Union Committee, 1962; *b.* Ben Mor, Assiut Province, Egypt, 15 January 1918; *e. s.* of late Abdel Nasser Hussein, postal clerk, Cairo and Alexandria; *m.* 1944; three *s.* two *d.* *Educ.:* El-Masria Secondary Sch., Cairo; Military Acad., Cairo. Served as infantry officer, Egypt and Sudan. Lecturer, Military Academy, 1942; graduated Staff College. Served Palestine War of 1948-1949 (wounded). Led Revolution of 23 July 1952 which led to abdication of King Farouk and the establishment of Republic of Egypt. Deputy Premier of Egypt, 1953, and Minister of the Interior, June-Oct. 1953; Sec.-Gen. of the Liberation Rally, 1953; Temporary Premier of Egypt, Feb.-March 1954; Prime Minister and Mil. Gov. of Egypt, 1954-56. Nationalized Suez Canal Company, 1956; proclaimed Socialist laws, 1961 and 1963; diverted Course of the Nile, 1964. *Recreations:* reading and sports. *Address:* Presidency, Cairo, U.A.R. [*Died* 28 *Sept.* 1970.

NATHAN, 1st Baron, *cr.* 1940, of Churt; **Col. Harry Louis Nathan,** P.C. 1946; T.D.; F.B.A. 1960; F.S.A. 1955; D.L., J.P. County of London; a Lieutenant of City of London; Solicitor; Hon. Col. L.A.A./S.L Regt. R.A., T.A., 1937-55, of 512 L.A.A. Regt. R.A., T.A., 1955-61, of 300 Regt. R.A., T.A., 1961-63; Honorary Air Commodore No. 906 (County of Middlesex) Balloon Squadron Auxiliary Air Force, 1939-49; *b.* 1889; *s.* of late Michael Henry Nathan, J.P.; *m.* 1919, Eleanor Joan Clara Stettauer (known as Eleanor Lady Nathan, when widowed); one *s.* one *d.* *Educ.:* St. Paul's School. Volunteer Officer prior to 1908, and one of original officers of Territorial Force; served with London Regiment in Gallipoli, Egypt and France (1914-15 Star); Major (temp. Lt.-Col.), late 1st London Regt.; mem. Co. of London T. & A.F.A., 1942-45, 1948-59. Col. (actg.), Comd. Welfare Officer, Eastern Comd., 1939-41, London Dist., 1941-43; on retirement granted hon. rank of Colonel; M.P. North-East Bethnal Green, 1929-35 (Liberal till 1934 when joined Labour Party); M.P. (Lab.) Central Wandsworth, 1937-40; Parliamentary Under-Secretary of State for War and Vice-President of the Army Council, 1945-46; Minister of Civil Aviation, 1946-48. Contested (L.) Whitechapel and St. George's, 1924; (Lab.) Cardiff (South), 1935. F.R.S.A. (Chm. R.S.A., 1961-63); F.R.S.S.; F.R.Econ.S.; F.R.G.S. (Pres. 1958-61); Pres. Geographical Assoc., 1956; Chm. Mount Everest Foundation, 1959-60; Pres. Assoc. of Technical Institutes, 1958-60; Pres. London and Middlesex Archæological Soc., 1946-49; Chm. Westminster Hosp., 1948-63; Chm. Isaac Wolfson Foundation since its creation, 1955; Chairman Committee on Charitable Trusts, appt. by Prime Minister, 1950; Dep. Chm. Cttee. on Consolidation and Amendment of Law of Customs and Excise, appt. by Chancellor of Exchequer, 1951; Chairman Queen Elizabeth Coronation Forest in Israel; Mem. Gen. Medical Council as Crown appointee, 1949-1959; Chm., Exec. Cttee., British Empire Cancer Campaign since 1954; Pres. Old Pauline Club, 1957-60; Governor of St. Paul's School and of St. Paul's Girls' School, 1960-. Master Worshipful Co. of Pattenmakers, 1951-52 and 1952-53; Master Worshipful Co. of Gardeners, 1955-56; Hon. Pres. Hillel Foundation to 1961; Trustee Jewish Bd. of Deputies. Ex-Mem. Min. of Pensions Cent. Adv. Cttee. Coronation Medal, 1937, 1953. Hon. Citizen, City of Washington, D.C., 1958. K.St.J. *Publications:* Free Trade To-day, 1929; Medical Negligence, 1957. Contrib. to new (3rd) edn. of Halsbury's Laws of England. *Heir:* *s.* Captain Hon. Roger Carol Michael Nathan, late 17/21 Lancers [*b.* 5 December 1922; *m.* 1950, Philippa, *er. d.* of Major J. B. Solomon, M.C.; one *s.* two *d.*]. *Address:* 20 Copthall Avenue, E.C.2; 71 Park Street, W.1. *T.A.:* Client, London. *T.:* National 9611, Grosvenor 2071. *Clubs:* Athenæum, Travellers', Reform, City Livery. [*Died* 23 *Oct.* 1963.

NAWANAGAR, Maharaja Jam Saheb of, Lt.-Gen. H.H. Maharaja Jam Shri Digvijaysinhji Ranjitsinhji Jadeja, G.C.S.I., *cr.* 1947 (K.C.S.I., *cr.* 1935); G.C.I.E., *cr.* 1939; Hon. A.D.C. to H.M., 1936-46; Extra Hon. A.D.C., 1946-50; *b.* 1 Sept. 1895; *S.* 1933; elected Raj Pramukh or Constitutional Head of United State of Saurashtra, 15 Feb. 1948, and Permanent Raj Pramukh, 1949; *m.* 1935, Princess Gulabkunverba, *d.* of late Maharao Shri Swaroopramsinghji of Sirohi; one *s.* three *d.* *Educ.:* Rajkumar Coll., Rajkot; Malvern Coll.; Univ. College, London. Captain late 5th/6th Rajputana (Napier's) Rifles; active service with Egyptian Exp. Force, 1920, Wazir Force, 1922-24. Rep. India at War Cabinet and Pacific War Council, London, 1942. Chancellor, Chamber of Princes, 1937-44. Indian Deleg. to sessions of U.N., 1948, 1949, 1950 (Chm. of several cttees., and of U.N.O. Admin. Tribunal, 1950, 1951; Chm. U.N. Negotiating Cttee. for Korean Rehabilitations. *Recreations:* all games such

as rackets, cricket, squash, tennis, and shooting. *Address:* The Palace, Jamnagar, India. *Clubs:* Willingdon Sports, National Sports Club of India (Bombay); (Patron-in-Chief) Rifle, (Patron) Rotary (Jamnagar).
[*Died* 3 *Feb.* 1966.

NAYLOR, Very Rev. Alfred Thomas Arthur, D.S.O. 1940; O.B.E. 1918; M.A.; Dean of Battle, 1946-59, retired; *b.* 27 Dec. 1889; *s.* of Rev. Alfred James Naylor; *m.* 1930, Muriel Emma Acheson (*née* Mosse), *widow* of Major C. D. Acheson; one *s.* one *d.* *Educ.:* King Edward's High School, Birmingham; Emmanuel Coll. and Ridley Hall, Cambridge. Deacon, 1912; Priest, 1913; Curate Pudsey, Leeds; C.F., 1914-18, Belgium and France (despatches twice); Chaplain Wemyss Castle and Wemyss Coal Coy., 1919-20; C.F. Guards' Chapel, Chelsea, 1921-23; R.M.A., Woolwich, 1923-26; Tientsin, 1926-29; Guards' Depot, Caterham, 1929-32; London District, 1932-34; Aldershot, 1934-36; Palestine, 1936; Assistant Chaplain General, Aldershot, 1939; Deputy Chaplain-General B.E.F. France, 1939-40 (despatches); Assist. Chaplain-General South-Eastern Army, 1940-45; Hon. Chaplain to the King, 1945; retired pay, 1945; Rural Dean of Battle and Bexhill, 1953. *Recreation:* Captain of College Boats, 1912. *Address:* Home Place, Whatlington, Battle, Sussex. *T.:* Battle 85. *Club:* Army and Navy.
[*Died* 1 *March* 1966.

NAYLOR, Thomas Humphrey; Director (past Chairman): Royal Insurance Co. Ltd.; Liverpool & London & Globe Insurance Co. Ltd.; Liverpool & Lancashire Insurance Co. Ltd.; Director: Martins Bank Ltd.; *b.* 1 July 1890; 2nd *s.* of John Naylor, Leighton Hall, Montgomeryshire; *m.* 1st, 1922, Quenelda Anne, *d.* of Charles J. Williamson, Liverpool; one *s.*; 2nd, 1935, Dorothy Isabel Durning, *d.* of Sir Richard D. Holt, 1st Bt., Liverpool; two *s.* two *d.* *Educ.:* Eton; Trinity Coll., Cambridge (B.A.Mech.Sci.). Served European War, 1914-18, as commissioned officer in Montgomeryshire Yeomanry, Palestine and Flanders (despatches). Partner in Sandbach Tinne & Co., Merchants of Liverpool and British West Indies, 1921-38; Chm. Demarara Co. Ltd. and allied companies, 1936-58. High Sheriff of Cheshire, 1950-51. *Recreations:* shooting; formerly flying. *Address:* The Grange, Ashton, Nr. Chester; 49 Lowndes Square, S.W.1. *Clubs:* Bath, Leander. [*Died* 5 *Sept.* 1966.

NAZIMUDDIN, (Sir) Al-Haj Khwaja, (K.C.I.E., *cr.* 1934; C.I.E. 1926); President of All Pakistan Muslim League; *b.* 19 July 1894; *s.* of late Khwaja Nazimuddin, Ahsan Munzil, Dacca; *m.* 1924, Shah Bano, *d.* of K. M. Ashraf, Zamindar; two *s.* one *d.* *Educ.:* M.A.O. Collegiate Sch., Aligarh; Dunstable Gram. Sch., England; Trinity Hall, Cambridge (M.A.); Hon. Fellow, Trinity Hall, Cambridge, 1952. Barrister-at-Law. Member Executive Council, Dacca University, 1923-1929; Chm. Dacca Municipality, 1922-29; Minister of Education, 1929-34 (piloted Compulsory Primary Education Bill in Bengal Legislative Assembly, 1930); Member of Bengal Executive Council, 1934-36 (piloted Bengal Agricultural Debtors' Bill and Bengal Rural Development Bill in Bengal Leg. Assembly); Home Minister, Government of Bengal, 1937; resigned from Cabinet, Dec. 1941. Leader of the Muslim League Parl. Party, Bengal, and Leader of Opposition in Bengal Legislative Assembly, 1942-1943; Chief Minister of Bengal Government, 1943-45. Food delegate, on behalf of Govt. of India, to U.S.A., 1945-46; rep. India at last meeting of League of Nations, Geneva, 1946. Dep. Leader of Muslim League Parl. Party and Central Legislative Assembly, India, 1946; Member of Working Cttee. of All India Muslim League, 1937-47. On establishment of Pakistan, elected Chief Minister of East Pakistan, 1947; Governor-General of Pakistan, 1948-51; Prime Minister of Pakistan, 1951-53. Nishan-i-Pakistan, 1958. *Recreations:* President of All India Hockey Federation for two successive terms, and Pres. of Mohammedan Sporting Club, Calcutta (premier Club of Muslims), for 10 years; hobbies: tennis, billiards, shooting, fishing, and interested in gardening and poultry. *Address:* 27 Eskaton Rd., P.O. Ramna, Dacca, East Pakistan.
[*Died* 22 *Oct.* 1964.

NEAL, His Honour John, M.C.; retired as County Court Judge (1942-61); *b.* 17 August 1889; *s.* of late Arthur Neal, M.P., Parliamentary Secretary to Ministry of Transport, and Annie Elizabeth Neal; *m.* 1940, Rosemary, *d.* of late Canon John Young; three *s.* *Educ.:* Leys School; King's Coll., Cambridge. Served European War, 1914-19, R.N.V.R., then in France in Royal Artillery, Major (M.C., 1914-15 Star). Called to Bar, Inner Temple, 1920. Contested Wansbeck Div. of Northumberland, 1922, and Barnsley Borough, 1923 and 1924; Officers' Emergency Reserve, 1938-40; Ministry of Economic Warfare and Ministry of Food, 1940-42; Deputy Chairman of Quarter Sessions of West Riding of Yorkshire, 1942-1945. *Publications:* contrib. Law Quarterly Review. *Recreations:* trying to find one; formerly lacrosse (half blue, 1909, 1910, 1911). *Address:* Stone Hall, Great Mongeham, nr. Deal. *Club:* Reform. [*Died* 8 *Sept.* 1962.

NEALE, Lt.-Col. Sir (Walter) Gordon, K.C.V.O., *cr.* 1941 (C.V.O. 1937); C.I.E. 1929; Political Department, Government of India, retired; *b.* 2 Oct. 1880; *s.* of W. E. Neale, I.C.S.; *m.* Grace Margaret (*d.* 1945), *d.* of late Adolph Fass; two *s.* (and one killed on active service). *Educ.:* Wellington College; Corpus Christi College, Oxford. Political A.D.C. to Secretary of State for India, 1933-1945. *Club:* United Service.
[*Died* 26 *April* 1966.

NEAME, Humphrey; Retired as: Cons. Ophthalmic Surgeon, University College Hospital; Cons. Surgeon, Royal London Ophthalmic Hosp.; Hon. Cons. Ophthalmic Surgeon, Dr. Barnardo's Homes; *s.* of late Frederick Neame of Luton, Selling, Faversham; *m.* 1st, 1924, Minnie Goodwin (*d.* 1932), *d.* of late J. B. Skirving, S. Africa; two *s.*; 2nd, 1938, Elizabeth Monroe. *Educ.:* Cheltenham College. Examiner for Diploma of Ophthalmology, Oxford Univ. etc. Fellow, Royal Society of Medicine (Past Pres. Section of Ophthalmology, Roy. Soc. Med.); late Ophthalmic Surgeon, Ministry of Pensions; President Cheltonian Society, 1951-52. European War, 1914-18, Capt. R.A.M.C. (French Croix de Guerre). *Publications:* Handbook of Ophthalmology, 8th Ed. (jointly); contrib. to Beren's The Eye and its Diseases; Atlas of External Diseases of the Eye; Articles on Ophthalmology in Encyclopædia Medica (1924); contrib. to various medical jls. *Recreation:* gardening. *Address:* 4 Fairlawn End, Upper Wolvercote, Oxford. *T.:* Oxford 57723.
[*Died* 25 *July* 1968.

NEAME, Lawrence Elwin; Editor, The Cape Argus, S. Africa, 1938-46; *b.* Wolverhampton; *e. s.* of Louis Marsh Neame of Brighton; *m.* Mary Gwendoline, *g.d.* of late Baron da Costa Ricci, Financial Adviser to Portuguese Embassy, London. Journalism in England and India and S. Africa; special correspondent Curzon's great Durbar at Delhi, 1903; joined Rand Daily Mail, 1904; editor, 1920-24. *Publications:* The Asiatic Danger in the Colonies; Some South African Politicians; General Hertzog, White Man's Africa, A City Built on Gold, The History of Apartheid, etc. *Address:* 103 Triborough, Illovo, Johannesburg, S. Africa. [*Died* 30 *June* 1964.

NEATE, Horace Richard, C.B.E. 1957; J.P., D.L., C.A., F.R.G.S.; *b.* 17 Mar. 1891; *s.* of Henry and Clara Neate, late of Cheltenham; *m.* 1916, Dorothy Claire, *d.* of John and Evie Wall, late of Cheltenham. *Educ.:* Cheltenham, privately. Bedford Town Council, 1928- (Alderman, 1934-46); Mayor of Bedford, 1933-36. Bedfordshire C.C. 1931- (Alderman, 1942- ; Vice-Chairman, 1952-56); Vice-Chairman, Bedfordshire Standing Joint Committee, 1942- ; Member: Police Council of England and Wales; Mem. Police Cttee. of County Councils Association for England and Wales (Chm. 1960-63, Vice-Chm. 1950-1960); Board of Governors, Police College; North-West Metropolitan Regional Hosp. Board, 1947 (Vice-Chm. 1949-). Sec. Bedford County Hosp., 1938-48; a Governor of Middlesex Hosp., London, 1948-63. J.P.1936. D.L. 1951, Bedfordshire. High Sheriff of Bedfordshire, 1955. *Recreations:* cricket (Hon. Treas., Minor Counties Cricket Assoc., 1945-57; Chm., 1957- ; Pres. Beds. County C.C.), Rugby football (Vice-Pres. Bedford R.F.C.), walking. *Address:* 4 Rothsay Gardens, Bedford. *T.:* Bedford 66858.
[*Died* 12 *Nov.* 1966.

NEAVE, James Stephen, LL.B. (Lond.); a Master of the Supreme Court of Judicature, Chancery Division, since 1953; *b.* 23 Dec. 1898; *o. s.* of late Stephen Gooch Neave and of Alice Maude Neave (*née* Langford); *m.*; one *d.* *Educ.:* Tiffin School, Kingston-on-Thames. Served European War in P.O.W. Civil Service Rifles, 15th London Regt., 1917-19. Articled to late Harry Knox of Linklaters & Paines; admitted a Solicitor, 1922; member firm of Dalston, Sons, Elliman & Neave, 1927-53; sometime Legal Adviser to Brit. Road Federation, Internat. Road Federation and Inst. of Road Transport Engineers. *Address:* Greenhays, Fleet, Hants. *T.:* Fleet 7573. *Club:* Royal Automobile.
[*Died* 3 *Sept.* 1970.

NEAVE, Sheffield Airey, C.M.G. 1941; O.B.E. 1933; *b.* 20 April 1879; *s.* of Sheffield H. M. Neave and *g.s.* of Sheffield Neave, Governor of the Bank of England; *m.* 1915, Dorothy (*d.* 1943), *d.* of Col. A. T. Middleton, 13th Hussars; two *s.* three *d.* 1946, Mary Irene, *d.* of Henry Hodges, Broadway Hall, Churchstoke. *Educ.:* Eton; Magdalen College, Oxford, M.A. and B.Sc. 1906; D.Sc. 1918; Naturalist, Geodetic Survey of Northern Rhodesia, 1904-05; Entomologist, Katanga Sleeping Sickness Commission, 1906-08; Entomologist, Entomological Research Committee (Tropical Africa), 1909-13; Assistant Director, Imperial Institute of Entomology, 1913-41; Director, 1942-46; Hon. Secretary, Association of Economic Biologists, 1916-21; Hon. Secretary, 1918-33, President, 1934-35, Special Life Fellow, 1945, Royal Entomological Society of London; Hon. Sec., Zoological Soc., 1942-52 (Vice-Pres. 1953); Chairman, World List of Scientific Periodicals, 1935-52. Membre d'Honneur, Circle Zoologique Congolais; Hon. Member Nederlandsche Entomologische Vereeniging; Hon. Fellow Société Fouad Ier d'Entomologie. *Publications:* Many memoirs on the fauna of Africa in Proceedings and Transactions of Zoological and Royal Entomological Societies, and other Scientific Journals; a Summary of data relating to Economic Entomology in the British Empire, 1930; the Centenary History of the Entomological Society of London, 1933; Editor of Nomenclator Zoologicus, 1939-49. *Recreations:* horticulture, agriculture, big-game shooting, philately. *Address:* Mill Green Park, Ingatestone, Essex. *T.:* Ingatestone 36. *Club:* Athenæum.
[*Died* 31 *Dec.* 1961.

NEEDHAM, Maj.-Gen. Henry, C.B. 1931; C.M.G. 1918; D.S.O. 1916; *b.* 1876; *e. s.* of late Lt.-Col. Hon. H. C. Needham, Grenadier Guards; *m.* 1902, Violet (*d.* 1962). *d.* of late Capt. H. Andrew, 8th Hussars, and Mrs. Yates Browne; one *d.* *Educ.:* privately. Lieut. 5 Regiment, Canadian Artillery; joined Gloucester Regiment, 1900; p.s.c. 1908-9; Staff, England, 1910-1914; France, Egypt, Salonika, Russia, 1914-18 (Legion of Honour, St. Vladimir, U.S. Distinguished Service Medal, C.M.G., D.S.O., 1914 Star, Queen's S.A. Medal, St. Stanislas, Comdr. Belgian Order of the Crown, Belgian Croix de Guerre); commanded 4th Worcestershire, 1922-23; Col., 1919; Military Attaché, Brussels, Berne, Luxembourg, 1922; Military Attaché, Paris, 1927-31; Major-General, 1931; Commander Bombay District, 1931-35; retired pay, 1935; Comptroller, Hospital for Sick Children, Great Ormond Street, 1938-1939; special appointments Near East and Belgium, 1939-40 (wounded, 1939-43 Star); Montgomeryshire War Agricultural Executive, 1940-45. *Recreation:* golf. *Address:* 1 Orchardwood, Ascot, Berks.
[*Died* 29 *Aug.* 1965.

NEEDHAM, Sir Raymond (Walter), Kt. 1957; Q.C.; J.P.; F.S.A.; Master Treasurer, Middle Temple, 1953; Reader (1945) General Commissioner of Taxes, Middle Temple; a Trustee of the Ciba Foundation for Medical and Chemical Research; Hon. Treas. Outward Bound Trust; *s.* of Herbert Needham, schoolmaster; *m.* 1st, Sarah Gertrude (*née* Hull) (*d.* 1945); 2nd, Helen Mary, *o. d.* of late Alexander Speak, Culgaith, Cumberland. *Educ.:* Dronfield Grammar School; Sheffield Technical School and Private Tutors. Inland Revenue Department, 1897; called to Bar, Middle Temple, 1908; seconded to War Office and Lord-Lieutenant of Ireland, 1915-16; Private Secretary to Minister of Information, Secretary to Ministry, Accounting Officer to H.M. Treasury, 1917-19, and Liquidator of Ministry. Controller of Aerodromes and Aerial Licensing, Air Ministry, 1919; practised at Bar, 1920-40; K.C. 1928; Q.C. 1952; Dir., Min. of Information, 1939; Hon. Counsel to Finnish Legation in London, 1940; Member of Air Supply Board, 1940-46; Director of Priorities, Ministry of Aircraft Production, and Adviser to Minister, 1940-1942; Advisory Staff, Ministry of Production and Deputy Chairman Materials Committee, 1942-44. Resumed practice at Bar, 1943. J.P. (1931) Herts, (1938) Dorset, (1941) Hants, (1950) Kent. Member of Quarter Sessions Appeal Cttees. for Herts, Dorset, Hants and Kent, successively; Dep. Chm. Kent, 1946-52. *Publications:* Somerset House, Past and Present (with Alexander Webster); The Income Tax Acts; The Death Duties; Income Tax Principles. *Recreation:* idling. *Address:* Nevill Court, Tunbridge Wells. *T.:* Tunbridge Wells 27027: Old Hunstanton, Norfolk. *Club:* White's.
[*Died* 16 *March* 1965.

NEERUNJUN, Sir Rampersad, Kt. 1962; O.B.E. 1947; Q.C. (Mauritius) 1957; Chief Justice of Mauritius since 1960; *b.* 15 Aug. 1906; *s.* of S. J. Neerunjun and L. Biltoo; *m.* 1932, Nancie Muriel Waite, Stamford, Lincolnshire; one *s.* *Educ.:* St. Enfant Jesus School (Schol.); Royal College, Mauritius (Laureate and Gold Medallist); London Sch. of Economics, Univ. Coll. and King's Coll., London. Called to Bar, Middle Temple, 1930. Practised at Mauritius Bar, 1931-38; Dist. Magistrate, 1938; Judge, Profiteering Court, 1942; Magistrate, Industrial Court, 1944; Substitute Procureur and Advocate-Gen., 1949; Puisne Judge, 1954; Procureur and Advocate-Gen., 1956 (title changed to Attorney-Gen., 1958). Hon. Legal Adviser to Military during War of 1939-45; Member or Pres. various Commns. of Enquiry including: Arbitration Courts (Wages) in Industry and Agriculture, 1947-49; Pres. Commn. of

Enquiry, Supplies Control Dept., 1949; Mem. Commn. of Enquiry, Local Govt., 1956; also served as Chm. or Mem. on a number of educational and administrative Boards, Cttees. and Trusteeship Foundations. *Recreations:* tennis, table tennis, Badminton, fishing. *Address:* The Grange, Belle Rose, Mauritius. *T.:* R.H. 371; Supreme Court, Port Louis, Mauritius. *T.:* P.L. 1905. *Club:* Royal Commonwealth Society. [*Died* 6 *Jan.* 1967.

NEHRU, Shri Jawaharlal, M.A. (Cantab.); Prime Minister and Minister for External Affairs, India, since 1947, also Minister of Atomic Energy (Minister of Defence, Nov. 1st-Nov. 20th 1962); Barrister-at-Law; Indian Congress, Uttar Pradesh-Phulpur, since 1957; *b.* Allahabad, 14 Nov. 1889; *s.* of Pandit Motilal Nehru and Swarup Rani Nehru; *m.* 1916, Shrimati Kamala (*d.* 1936); one *d.* *Educ.:* Harrow School; Trinity College, Cambridge. Barrister-at-Law, Inner Temple, 1912; Advocate, Allahabad High Court; Secretary, Home Rule League, Allahabad, 1918; Member, All India Congress Committee, since 1918; joined non-violent non-cooperation movement under Gandhiji, 1920; associated with labour and nationalist movements; imprisoned on several occasions for political activities; General Secretary, All India Congress Committee, 1929; succeeded father as President of Indian National Congress, 1929; President also in 1936, 1937, 1946, 1951-54; President, All India States Peoples Conference and Chairman, National Planning Committee, 1939; Vice-President, Interim Government, and Minister for External Affairs and Commonwealth Relations, 1946. Member, Constituent Assembly, Provisional Parliament, and first Lok Sabha. *Publications:* India and the World; The Unity of India; Soviet Russia; Eighteen Months in India, 1936; Autobiography, 1936; Glimpses of World History, 1939; Discovery of India, 1946; Independence and After; Jawaharlal Nehru's Speeches, 1949-1953; A Bunch of Old Letters, 1958; Nehru's Letters to his sister (ed. Krishna Nehru), 1963; *Relevant publication:* Profile of Jawaharlal Nehru, by K. T. Narasimha Char, 1966. *Address:* Anand Bhawan, Allahabad, India. [*Died* 27 *May* 1964.

NEILL, Col. Sir Frederick (Austin), Kt. 1958; C.B.E. 1942; D.S.O. 1917; T.D.; D.L.; J.P.; late Royal Engineers (T.A.); President, James Neill and Co. (Sheffield) Ltd.; *b.* 11 Nov. 1891; *s.* of late James Neill, J.P.; *m.* 1918, Winifred Margaret, *y. d.* of late Robt. Colver, J.P., Rockmount, Ranmoor; one *s.* three *d.* *Educ.:* Wrekin Coll. Served European War, 1914-18 (despatches four times, D.S.O., Croix de Guerre, 1914 Star); Lt.-Col. 1920; Bt. Col. 1927; Col. 1930. Hon. Col. 49th Divisional Engineers (T.A.). Master Cutler, The Company of Cutlers in Hallamshire, 1937-38. D.L. West Riding; High Sheriff of Yorkshire, 1955; High Sheriff of Hallamshire, 1962. *Address:* Whinfell, Whirlow, Sheffield 11. [*Died* 11 *Aug.* 1967.

NEILSON, Francis, D.Litt.; author; *b.* Birkenhead, 26 Jan. 1867; *s.* of Francis Butters, Liverpool, and Isabel, *d.* of William Neilson, Dundee; name changed to Neilson by deed poll, 1902; *m.* 1st, 1893, Catherine Eva (decd.), *d.* of James O'Gorman; two *d.*; 2nd, 1917, Helen Swift Morris (*d.* 1945), *d.* of Gustavus Swift and *widow* of Edward Morris, Chicago. *Educ.:* Liverpool High School; privately. Went to America, 1885; critic, Theatre Mag., N.Y., 1889; later with reportorial depts., Sun and Recorder; actor with Gillette and Frohman Cos., N.Y.; returned to England, 1897; stage director for Charles Frohman and Royal Opera, London; contested Newport Division of Salop, 1906 and 1908; M.P. (L.) Hyde Division, Cheshire, 1910-16, resigned. Founder of the Brotherhood Movement, 1904; President of the English League for the Taxation of Land Values, 1912-15; returned to U.S., 1915; became U.S. citizen, 1921; Editor, Democratic Monthly (Eng.), 1906-08, The Freeman (New York), 1920-24, and Unity (Chicago), 1919-26; Pres., Nat. Drama League of America, 1920-26; Member of Governing Body of Shakespeare Memorial Theatre; Hon. Governor, The John Rylands Library; Fellow in Perpetuity, Metropolitan Museum of Art; Assoc. Member, Poetry Soc. of America; Life Member: Nat. Art Collections Fund; Gorgas Memorial Inst. of Tropical and Preventive Medicine; R. Soc. of St. George; Member Dean's Chapter Council Liverpool Cathedral; Founder Neilson Exped. to Near East (Univ. of Liverpool). Donor of Fund for Publication of Collected Vocal Works of William Byrd. *Publications:* Libretti: Prince Ananias; Manabozo (also in German); Plays produced and published: The Bath Road; The Crucifixion of Philip Strong; The Crucible; A Butterfly on the Wheel; The Sin-Eater's Hallowe'en; The Desire for Change; The Impossible Philanthropist (Tourbillon, prod. Paris, 1925); A Mixed Foursome; The Day before Commencement; The Queen of Nectaria; Le Baiser de Sang (with Jean Aragny), Grand Guignol, Paris, 1929, etc.; The March of Christendom; Novels; Madame Bohemia; A Strong Man's House; The Garden of Doctor Persuasion; Other works: How Diplomats Make War, editions in French, Swedish and German; The Old Freedom; A Journal to Rosalind; Blue and Purple (verse) Duty to Civilization (also in German); Control from the Top; The Eleventh Commandment; Sociocratic Escapades; The Professor's Hotchpotch (Adam Savage); Man at the Crossroads; A Professor's Balderdash (Adam Savage); The Tragedy of Europe, 5 vols.; In Quest of Justice; Hate, the Enemy of Peace—a reply to Lord Vansittart; The Devil and All (Rhadamanthus); The Roots of Our Learning; The Story of The Freeman; A Task for Diogenes (Rhadamanthus); Modern Man and the Liberal Arts (essays); A Key to Culture; Hamlet and Shakespeare; The Makers of War; A Study of Macbeth; My Life in Two Worlds (2 vols.); The Churchill Legend; Shakespeare and The Tempest; Poems; The Freudians and the Oedipus Complex; The Cultural Tradition; From Ur to Nazareth; regular contrib. Amer. Jl. of Economics and Sociology. *Address:* Harbor Acres, Port Washington, New York, U.S.A. *Clubs:* Authors'; Players (New York). [*Died* 13 *April* 1961.

NEILSON, Lt.-Col. John Fraser, C.B.E. 1919; D.S.O. 1917; late 10th Royal Hussars; *b.* 1884; 3rd *s.* of William Neilson of Arnewood, Kelvinside, Glasgow; *m.* 1st, 1916, Helen Vera (*d.* 1930), *d.* of William Cazalet, Moscow; 2nd, 1959, Oonagh Marguerite Burton Scrimgeour. *Educ.:* Uppingham; Sandhurst. Joined 10th Hussars in India, 1904; went to S. Africa with the regiment; went to Russia, Dec. 1913; on the outbreak of European War was attached to the Russian armies (C.B.E., D.S.O.); holds Russian Orders of St. Vladimir, St. Stanislas, St. Anne. *Address:* The Small House, Weedon, Aylesbury, Bucks. [*Died* 30 *Dec.* 1962.

NELSON OF STAFFORD, 1st Baron *cr.* 1960; **George Horatio Nelson;** Bt. 1955; Kt. 1943; LL.D., F.C.G.I., Hon. D.I.C., M.I.Mech.E., M.I.E.E.; Chairman: The English Electric Co. Ltd., London, since 1956; English Electric Export and Trading Co. Ltd.; D. Napier & Son, Ltd.; The Vulcan Foundry Ltd.; Robert Stephenson & Hawthorns Ltd.; Director: Lloyds Bank Ltd.; John Inglis Co. Ltd., Toronto; Marconi's Wireless Telegraph Co. Ltd.; English Electric

Co. of Canada, Ltd.; *b.* London, 1887; *e. s.* of George and Emily Walsh Nelson; *m.* 1913, Florence Mabel, *o. d.* of late Henry Howe, J.P., Leicestershire; one *s.* one *d.* *Educ.:* City and Guilds Technical Coll., London (awarded Diploma, Mitchell Exhibition and Brush Studentship). Pres. F.B.I., 1943-44, 1944-45; Vice-Pres. 1936-49. Pres. (Chm. of Council, 1947), British Electrical and Allied Manufrs. Assoc., 1950-53, Vice-Pres. (re-elected), 1954, Counsellor, 1961; Member of Advisory Council, Board of Trade, 1938; of Heavy Bomber Group Cttee., Air Ministry, 1939-45; of Executive Cttee., 1942 and of Grand Council, 1944, of F.B.I.; Chairman of U.K. Tank Mission to America and Canada, 1942; Member: Council of Instn. of Mechanical Engineers, 1943 (Vice-Pres., 1951-57, Pres., 1957-58), Council of Instn. of Electrical Engineers, 1949 (Vice-Pres. 1950-55, Pres. 1955), Reconstruction Joint Advisory Council, 1943-44; Higher Technological Education Cttee., 1944-45; Cttee. on future scientific policy, 1945; General Board and Executive Committee National Physical Laboratory, 1945-51; Governing Body of Queen Mary Coll. University of London (Hon. Fellow, 1947); Chm. Census of Production Cttee., 1945; Co-opted Member of University of Cambridge Appointments Board, 1946-51; Assistant of the Court of the Worshipful Company of Goldsmiths, 1950; President: Union of Educational Institutions, 1946-47; Brit. Electrical & Allied Research Assoc., 1952; Member: Bd. of Professional Engineers Appts. Bd., 1952; Heavy Electrical Plant Consultative Council, 1952-. Vice-Pres. Hispanic and Luso-Brazilian Councils, 1954; Member Governing Body of Imperial Coll. of Science and Technology, 1955 (Hon. Fellow, 1955); Hon. D.I.C. 1955; Member Ct. of Governors, Manchester Coll. of Sci. and Tech., 1956; President, Locomotive and Allied Manufacturers Assoc., 1958-60; Vice-Pres., The British Electrical Power Convention, 1956-57, Pres., 1957-58. Hon. Freeman, Borough of Stafford, 1956; Hon. LL.D. (Victoria University of Manchester), 1957. Third Warden, Court of Worshipful Co. of Goldsmiths, 1957, Second Warden, 1958, Prime Warden, 1960. Rep. of Goldsmiths' Company on Council of City & Guilds of London Inst., 1958, and Vice-Pres. of the Institute; Mem. Exec. Cttee. of the Pilgrims, 1957; First Class Mem. Smeatonian Soc. of Civil Engineers, 1959. Responsible for the manufacture and installation of steam and hydro-electric power equipments, electric traction equipments, etc., in various parts of the world: Chief Outside Engineer, British Westinghouse Co., Trafford Park, 1911; Chief Electrical Supt. there, 1914; Manager, Sheffield Works of Metropolitan Vickers Electrical Co., 1920; Managing Dir., The English Electric Co. Ltd., 1930; Chairman and Managing Director, 1933-56. *Publications:* include some Papers; Train lighting; Works Organisation; Trade after the War; Increased production—decreased unemployment; Post-war prospects and the place of private enterprise, 1943. *Heir:* *s.* Hon. Henry George Nelson. *Address:* Hilcote Hall, Eccleshall, Stafford; Flat 61A, Grosvenor House, Park Lane, W.1. *Clubs:* Athenæum, Carlton. [*Died* 16 *July* 1962.

NELSON, Charles Gilbert; *b.* 19 Sept. 1880; *m.* 1909, Agnes Whyte; two *s.* one *d.* *Educ.:* Girvan Burgh School (pupil-teacher); Training College for Teachers, Glasgow; Glasgow University (1st Cl. Hons. Classics); Balliol College, Oxford (Snell Exhibitioner; 1st Cl. Hon. Mods. and Lit. Hum.). Junior Examiner, Civil Service Commission, 1907; Senior Assistant Director of Examinations, 1933-39; Assistant Commissioner and Director of Examinations, 1939-44. *Address:* 4 Palma Court, 31 Manor Rd., Worthing. [*Died* 2 *Nov.* 1962.

NELSON, Sir Frank, K.C.M.G., *cr.* 1942; Kt., *cr.* 1924; *b.* 1883; *m.* 1st, 1911, Jean (*d.* 1952), *o. d.* of late Col. Patrick Montgomerie, R.E.; one *s.*; 2nd, Dorothy Moira Carling, Ripon, Yorks. *Educ.:* Bedford Gram. Sch.; Neuenheim Coll., Heidelberg. Chairman, Bombay Chamber of Commerce, 1922 and 1923; President, Associated Chambers of Commerce of India and Ceylon, 1923; Member, Bombay Legislative Council, 1922, 1923; Bombay Light Horse, 1914-18; Member of Council of Royal Colonial Institute; M.P. (C.) Stroud Division of Gloucestershire, 1924-31; led a party of four Unionist M.P.s to tour Russia in April 1926; Member of Empire Parliamentary Delegation to Australia, 1927; Consul at Basle, 1939. Pilot Officer, R.A.F.V.R., 1940; Actg. Air Cdre. whilst in comd. of Special Ops. Exec., 1941-43: Wing Comdr. Air Intelligence, Washington, 1944; in Comd. Air Force Intelligence, C.C.G., rank Air Cdre., at Detmold, until Demobilisation, 1946. *Address:* 20 Norham Gardens, Oxford. [*Died* 11 *Aug.* 1966.

NELSON, Colonel John Joseph Harper, C.I.E. 1936; O.B.E. 1919; M.C.; M.D., M.R.C.P.E., F.R.C.S.E.; I.M.S., retired Medical Member, Pensions Appeal Tribunal, since 1946, and Council B.M.A.; *b.* 12 Jan. 1882; *s.* of Rev. J. Nelson; *m.* 1909, Annabel, *d.* of N. MacCormick, Achaban House, Fionnphort, Isle of Mull; one *s.* two *d.* *Educ.:* Edinburgh University. Entered Indian Medical Service, 1908; Principal and Professor of Medicine, King Edward Medical College, Lahore, 1930-36; retired 1937. Director of Medical Services Kashmir and Jammu States, India, 1938; rejoined I.M.S. 1940, retd. 1944. Director of Medical Services, 1st Corps Area, U.N.R.R.A., 1944. *Recreations:* fishing, shooting, lawn tennis. *Address:* Achaban House, Fionnphort, Isle of Mull. *T.:* 205. *Clubs:* Dumfries and Galloway County (Dumfries); Punjab (Lahore). [*Died* 10 *March* 1961.

NELTHORPE, Col. Oliver S.; *see* Sutton-Nelthorpe.

NEPAL, Maharaja, H.H. Mohan Shamsher Jang Bahadur Rana; Ojaswi Rajanya; Projjwala Nepal Tara; Om Ram Patta; Atula Jyotirmaya Tri-Shakti Patta; Ati Pravala Gorkha Dakshina Bahu; Sainik Deergha Seva Patta; G.C.B. (Hon.), *cr.* 1950; G.C.I.E. (Hon.), *cr.* 1945; G.B.E. (Hon.) *cr.* 1937; Hon. Lieut.-Gen. in British Army; Hon. Col.-in-Chief of Bde. of Gurkhas, British Army; Hon. Lieut.-Gen., I.A.; Hon. Col. of all Gurkha Rifle Regts. of I.A.; *b.* 23 Dec. 1885; *s.* of H.H. Maharaja Chandra Shamsher Jang Bahadur Rana; *m.* H.H. Bada Maharani Dikshya Kumari Devi, 2nd *d.* of Kunwar Indra Bir Singh Rathor of Marma, Doti, Nepal; two *s.* six *d.* *Educ.:* privately. Entered service, at age of 15, 1900; Chief of Staff of H.H. Maharaja Chandra Shamsher Jang Bahadur Rana, 1902-29; visited U.K., France, Italy, and Switzerland with his father, 1908; Comdg.-Gen., in charge of Council, 1929; Southern Comdg.-Gen., in charge of H.H.'s Personal Office, 1932; Sen. Comdg.-Gen. in charge of War Office and Tarai Dept., 1933; in charge of War Office during War of 1939-45; C.-in-C. Nepalese Army and Head of Home and other Civil Depts., 1945-48; Prime Minister and Supreme C.-in-C. of Nepal, 1948-50, and also Minister of Foreign Affairs, Feb.-May 1951; Prime Minister and Minister of Foreign Affairs and Defence, May-Nov. 1951; resigned, Nov. 1951. Grand Croix, Légion d'Honneur, France, 1949; Legion of Merit, Degree of Chief Commander, U.S., 1948; Grand Cross Order of Netherlands Lion, 1950; Grand Order of Cloud and Banner, China, 1946. *Recreations:* riding, billiards and chess. *Address:* Laxmi Nivas, Maharajganj, Kathmandu, Nepal. [*Died* 6 *Jan.* 1967.

NESBITT-HAWES, Sir Ronald, Kt., *cr.* 1948; C.B.E. 1941; E.D; M.I.E.E., M.I.R.E.; English Electric M.I.R.E.; English Electric Co. since 1949; *b.* 11 November 1895; *s.* of A. J. Hawes, London; *m.* 1920, Kathleen Anne, *d.* of R. B. Dawson, A.R.C.A.; two *s.* *Educ.:* Taunton School. Royal Engineers (Signals), 1914-19; Wireless Branch Indian Posts and Telegraphs, 1920-36; Chief Engineer Posts and Telegraphs, Burma, 1936-39; Director General Posts and Telegraphs, Burma, 1939-Apr. 1950. Held mil. rank Brig., 1942-45 (despatches). *Recreation:* sailing. *Address:* 2 Newcastle Lane, Springfield, Gosford, N.S.W., Australia. *Club:* Royal Over-Seas League. [*Died* 3 *Jan.* 1969.

NESS, Mrs. Patrick; (E. Wilhelmina); Member Council Royal Geographical Society, 1930-34, 1935-38, 1946-50, and 1956; Vice-President Lambeth Housing Ltd.; Member of Council R. African Soc., 1938-45, 1955, 1956, Vice-Pres. 1946-49; Diploma and Hon. Member, Royal Antwerp Society; Hon. Member Soc. of Women Geographers of America; National Council of Women of Great Britain: President, 1940-41 and 1943-1945 (Vice-Pres. 1938-39); Mem. Royal Institute of International Affairs; lectured to R. Geog. Soc. (London), R. Central Asian Soc., R. Antwerp Geog. Soc., L.C.C., etc., on expeditions; made gift to R. Geog. Soc., 1953, for annual presentation to young geographers (Mrs. Patrick Ness award). *Publications:* Ten Thousand Miles in Two Continents. Also articles in The Geographical Journal, Royal Central Asian Journal, Royal African Society Journal, Fortnightly, Story of Exploration and Adventure, etc. *Address:* 15 Rutland Court, Knightsbridge, S.W.7. *T.:* Kensington 3810. [*Died* 22 *April* 1962.

NETHERSOLE, Sir Michael (Henry Braddon), K.B.E., *cr.* 1948; C.S.I. 1946; C.I.E. 1942; D.S.O. 1919; late I.C.S.; *b.* 15 Sept. 1891; *yr. s.* of late Sir Michael Nethersole, K.C.S.I.; *m.* 1925, Hermione (*d.* 1944), *yr. d.* of late General K. J. Buchanan, C.B.; one *d.* Served European War, 1914-1919 (despatches, D.S.O.). *Address:* c/o National and Grindlay's Bank Ltd., 54 Parliament Street, S.W.1. [*Died* 14 *Feb.* 1965.

NETTLETON, Martin Barnes, M.A. Oxon., F.R.G.S.; Headmaster, Northampton Grammar School, since 1945; *b.* 24 Feb. 1911; *s.* of late W. H. Nettleton, Headmaster, Cardiff; *m.* 1945, Joan Constance, *d.* of Capt. (S) H. C. Pinsent, R.N.; one *s.* one *d.* *Educ.:* Clifton; Lincoln College, Oxford. 1st Class Classical Hon. Mods., 1931; 2nd Class Lit. Hum., 1933; President Oxford University Mountaineering Club, 1933. Classical Master: Rossall, 1935; Repton, 1938. Royal Air Force Officer, 1941. Hon. Lieutenant-Colonel, 1958. *Publications:* Scottish and Icelandic Mountain literature and history. *Recreations:* mountain climbing and Faeroese/Icelandic research. *Address:* The School House, Northampton. *T.:* Northampton 33510. [*Died* 6 *April* 1964.

NEVILE, Christopher; retired; *b.* 12 April 1891; *s.* of Edward Horatio and Alice Edith Nevile, Skellingthorpe Manor, Lincoln; *m.* 1918, Vera Brantingham Burtt; two *s.* (and *e. s.* decd.). *Educ.:* Winchester. Past Pres. National Farmers' Union 1942-43; Part-time Member Railway Executive, 1947-50. *Recreation:* fishing. *Address:* Whisby Hall, Lincoln. *T.:* Doddington 332. [*Died* 27 *Jan.* 1962.

NEVILE, Sir Sydney Oswald, Kt., 1942; a Director of Whitbread & Co., Ltd., 1919-68; Vice-President, Brewers Society; Senior Past Master Brewers Co.; Past Chm. National Trade Defence Assoc.; Past Pres. of the Institute of Brewing; Member of Council, State Management Districts, 1921-1955; *b.* 12 July 1873; *s.* of Rev. Christopher Nevile, Thorney, Notts.; *m.* 1946, Madeleine (Madge) de Lacy, *d.* of late Dr. C. A. Wickham, Willesborough, Kent. Was a Mem. Central Control Bd. (Liquor Traffic), Hop Control Committee, Home Office Committee on Damaged Licensed Premises and Reconstruction, etc. Entered brewing industry, 1888; interested in policy of Improved Public Houses since 1909; formerly Vice-Pres., Federation of British Industries. *Publications:* Seventy Rolling Years, 1958; various technical papers connected with the brewing and allied industries. *Address:* 9 Mill Road, Worthing, Sussex. *T.:* Worthing 2580. [*Died* 3 *Sept.* 1969.

NEVILLE, Eric Harold; Professor of Mathematics, University of Reading, 1919-54; Mem. National Cttee. for Mathematics; Mem. Council, British Assoc., 1946-52, Pres. Section A, 1950, Chm. Mathematical Tables Cttee., 1931-47. Pres. Mathematical Assoc., 1934, Librarian, 1923-53; *b.* 1 Jan. 1889; 2nd *s.* of Mynott and Edith Neville; *m.* 1913, Alice Maud Emily (*d.* 1956), *e. d.* of Samuel and Sarah Farnfield; no *c.* *Educ.:* William Ellis School, London; Trinity College, Cambridge. Fellow of Trinity College, Cambridge, 1911-17. *Publications:* The Fourth Dimension; Prolegomena to Analytical Geometry; Jacobian Elliptic Functions, Farey Series of Order 1025; Rectangular-Polar Conversion Tables, etc. *Address:* The Copse, Sonning, Berks. *T.:* Sonning 3202. *Club:* Athenæum. [*Died* 21 *Aug.* 1961.

NEWALL, 1st Baron, *cr.* 1946, of Clifton-upon-Dunsmoor; **Marshal of the Royal Air Force Cyril Louis Norton Newall,** G.C.B., *cr.* 1938 (K.C.B., *cr.* 1935; C.B. 1929); O.M. 1940; G.C.M.G., *cr.* 1940 (C.M.G. 1919); C.B.E. 1919; *b.* 15 Feb. 1886; *s.* of late Lt.-Col. William Potter Newall, I.A.; *m.* 1925, Olive Tennyson Foster, D.St.J., *o. d.* of Mrs. Francis Storer Eaton, Boston, U.S.A.; one *s.* two *d.* *Educ.:* Bedford School; R.M.C., Sandhurst. Entered Royal Warwickshire Regt. 1905; transferred to 2nd K.E.O. Gurkhas, Indian Army, 1909, to R.F.C. 1914 and to R.A.F. 1919; served Zakkha Khel Expedition, 1908 (medal and clasp); European War, 1914-19 (despatches thrice, C.M.G., C.B.E., Albert Medal 1st Class, Bt. Major, officer Legion of Honour, Crown of Italy and Leopold of Belgium, Belgian Croix de Guerre); Deputy Director of Personnel Air Ministry, 1919-22; A.D.C. to H.M. the King, 1923-24; Director of Operations and Intelligence and Deputy Chief of the Air Staff, 1926-31; additional Member of the Air Council, 1930-31; Air Officer Commanding Wessex Bombing Area, 1931; Air Officer Commanding Royal Air Force, Middle East, 1931-34; Member of Air Council for Supply and Organization 1935-37; Air Chief Marshal, 1937; Chief of Air Staff, 1937-40; Marshal of the Royal Air Force, 1940; Governor-General and Commander-in-Chief of New Zealand, 1941-46. K.St.J; Vice-President R.A.F. Benevolent Fund. *Heir: s.* Hon. Francis Storer Eaton Newall [*b.* 23 June 1930; *m.* 1956, Pamela Elizabeth Rowcliffe; two *s.* one *d.*] *Address:* c/o Lloyds Bank Ltd., 6 Pall Mall, S.W.1. *Clubs:* Buck's, Beefsteak, Oriental. [*Died* 30 *Nov.* 1963.

NEWBOLT, Captain (Arthur) Francis, C.M.G. 1949; *b.* 1893; *o. s.* of late Sir Henry Newbolt, C.H., D.Litt., poet and historian; *m.* 1st, 1921, Nancy Kathleen (*d.* 1948), *d.* of John Triffitt, York; one *s.* two *d.*; 2nd, 1953, Sheila Vivien, *d.* of late Eric Mills, C.B.E., Chiddingfold; one *step-d.* *Educ.:* Winchester; New College, Oxford (B.A.). First commission (Army), March 1914; served European War; on active service Oxfordshire Light Infantry and D.C.L.I., 1914-19; Capt. 1915; Adjutant, 1918-19. Asst. Private Secretary at Colonial Office; to Viscount Milner, 1919, Mr.

Churchill, 1921, Duke of Devonshire, 1922, Mr. J. H. Thomas, 1924, Mr. Amery, 1924, Lord Passfield, 1929. Visited, on official business, Malta, Cairo and East, South and West Africa, 1946; Director of Recruitment, Colonial Service, 1948-54. *Publications:* The King's Highway (Song); Shakespeare Plays for Community Players. *Recreations:* writing music and plays, trout fishing. *Address:* Brook House, Chiddingfold, Nr. Godalming, Surrey. *Club:* Vincent's (Oxford).
[*Died* 6 *Sept.* 1966.

NEWBOROUGH, 6th Baron *cr.* 1776; **Robert Vaughan Wynn;** Bt. 1742; O.B.E. 1944; J.P., D.L.; late 9th (Q.R.) Lancers; *b.* 17 July 1877; *e. s.* of Hon. Charles Henry Wynn (*d.* 1911) (3rd *s.* of 3rd Baron), Rhug, Corwen, Merioneth, and Frances Georgiana (*d.* 1919), *d.* of Lt.-Col. Romer, Bryncemlyn, Co. Merioneth; *S.* cousin 1957; *m.* 1913, Ruby Irene (*d.* 1960), 3rd *d.* of Edmund Wigley Severene of Thenfor, Banbury and Wallop Hall, Salop; two *s.* *Educ.:* Stubbington House, Fareham. Sligo Artillery, 1896-99; 9th (Q.R. Lancers, 1899-1907; Montgomeryshire Yeomanry, 1907-1913; rejoined 9th Lancers, 1914-18; Royal Air Force, 1918; Reserve of Officers, 9th Lancers; served in South African War, 1899-1902 (despatches twice, one of which for exceptional gallantry); European War, 1914-19 (despatches 4 times); Major, 1918; Brevet Lt.-Col., 1919. Sector Comdr. Home Guard, 1940-44. *Heir:* *s.* Hon. Robert Charles Michael Vaughan, D.S.C. *Address:* Bodfean Hall, Pwllheli, N. Wales; Fort Belan, Llandwrog, Caernarvonshire. *Clubs:* Junior Carlton; Royal Yacht Squadron (Cowes); Bembridge Sailing (Bembridge); Royal Welsh Yacht (Carnarvon).
[*Died* 27 *Oct.* 1965.

NEWBOULT, Sir Alexander Theodore, K.B.E., *cr.* 1948; C.M.G. 1946; M.C. 1918; E.D. 1946; *b.* 3 Jan. 1896; *er. s.* of late Rev. A. W. Newboult; *m.* 1923, Nancy, *d.* of late Rev. W. R. Gilbert, M.A., J.P., R.N.; two *d.* *Educ.:* Oakham and Kingswood Schools; Exeter College, Oxford. Served European War, 1914-1919, with R.N.D. and D.C.L.I.; entered Colonial Administrative Service, Malaya, 1920; Under-Secretary F.M.S., 1940; Colonial Secretary, Fiji, 1942; administered the Government, 1943; Deputy Chief Civil Affairs Officer, Malaya, 1945, with rank of Brig.; Chief Secretary, 1946-50; administered the Govt. July-Oct. 1948; retired, 1950. *Recreations:* music, gardening. *Address:* Glynn Gdns., Bodmin, Cornwall. *T.:* Cardynham 271. *Club:* East India and Sports.
[*Died* 5 *Jan.* 1964.

NEWCOMB, Lt.-Col. Clive, C.I.E. 1937; I.M.S., retired; *b.* 1882; *s.* of William Newcomb; *m.* 1919, Doris Emmie Holdsworth; one *s.* one *d.* *Educ.:* Merchant Taylors' School; St. John's College, Oxford; St. Thomas' Hospital. B.A. Oxford, 1905; M.B., B.Ch. 1910; D.M. 1919; F.R.I.C. 1925; entered I.M.S. 1910; served European war in Mesopotamia, 1914-18 (Prisoner of War with Turks, 1916-18); Chemical Examiner, Madras, 1920; Prin., Medical Coll., Madras, 1932; Officiating Surgeon General, Madras, 1935; retired, 1937. Examiner of Medical Stores, India Store Department, 1937-45. *Publications:* various scientific papers. *Recreation:* book-binding. *Address:* Dudley Cottage, Walberswick, Southwold, Suffolk. *T.:* Southwold 2315.
[*Died* 7 *Nov.* 1968.

NEWCOME, Major-General Henry William, C.B. 1923; C.M.G. 1919; D.S.O. 1915; *b.* 14 July 1875; *e. s.* of Major Henry George Newcome, R.A., Aldershot Manor, Hants; *m.* 1st, 1925, Lady Helen Alice Whitaker (*d.* 1929), *e. d.* of 2nd Earl of Lathom; one *s.*; 2nd, 1935, Sybil, *d.* of J. Ll. Brinkley and *widow* of Major Sydney Boddam-Whetham, D.S.O., M.C., R.A. Entered army, 1895; Captain, 1901; Adj., 1902-05; Major, 1911; A.D.C. to Major-General commanding R.A., Natal, 1900; Instructor, Ordnance College, 1909-12; Major Instructor, School of Gunnery, 1914; General Staff Officer, 3rd Grade, 1912-14; 2nd Grade, 1914; served South Africa, 1899-1900 (despatches, Queen's medal 6 clasps); European War (D.S.O. for distinguished work in reports, and especially at Givenchy (wounded twice, despatches six times); General Staff Officer, 1st Grade, temp. Lieut.-Colonel, Headquarters, France, 1916; Lt.-Col. Instructor Gunnery School, Salisbury Plain, 1916 (despatches); C.R.A. 21st Division Artillery (C.M.G.); temp. Brig.-Gen. May 1917; Col. 1918; Commandant, School of Artillery, Larkhill, 1918-22; C.R.A. Northern Command, India, 1922-26; Major-General, 1927; G.O.C. 50th Northumbrian Division T.A., 1928-31; Comm. Baluchistan District, 1931-32; Major-General R.A., Army Headquarters, India, 1933-1935; retired pay, 1935; Col. Commandant R.A. 1938-45. Lt.-Colonel, Home Guard, 1940-42. *Address:* Hale Place, Farnham, Surrey. *Club:* Army and Navy.
[*Died* 25 *Feb.* 1963.

NEWELL, Prof. Gordon Ewart, T.D. 1946; B.Sc., Ph.D., D.Sc. (London); Emeritus Professor of Zoology, University of London, 1968; *b.* 14 April 1908; *s.* of Joseph Newell and Gertrude Rowden; *m.* 1937, Winifred Violet Young; five *s.* one *d.* *Educ.:* Simon Langton's School, Canterbury; Taunton School, Taunton; King's College, London. Lecturer, subsequently Reader and Professor, in Zoology, at Queen Mary Coll., 1933-68. University Colours for Boxing, 1931-32. Served War of 1939-45, with Cambridge S.T.C. and Army Operational Research Group; Italy, 1944 (wounded); retired with rank of Major, 1945. A Governor Wye College. *Publications:* Animal Biology, 1942; Marine Plankton, 1963; papers on marine and experimental zoology in scientific jls. *Recreations:* golf, painting, old cars. *Address:* 3 Kemsdale House, Hernehill, Nr. Faversham, Kent.
[*Died* 4 *Aug.* 1968.

NEWLAND, Sir Henry Simpson, Kt., *cr.*, 1928; C.B.E.; D.S.O.; M.B., M.S. (Adelaide); D.Sc.(Hon.) (Univ. of W. Australia) 1948; Dr. of Laws, h.c., Melb., 1952; F.R.C.S. Eng., F.R.C.S. Edin. (Hon.), F.R.A.C.S., F.A.C.S.; Vice-Pres. B.M.A. (Past President of Federal Council) in Australia; Consulting Surgeon, Adelaide Hospital and Adelaide Children's Hospital; *b.* Adelaide, 24 Nov. 1873; *s.* of late Simpson Newland, C.M.G., and Jane Isabella Newland; *m.* Ellen Mary Lindon; one *s.* two *d.* *Educ.:* St. Peter's College; University of Adelaide; London Hospital. Everard Scholar, 1896; studied medicine and surgery, London, Paris, Prague, Vienna, and U.S.A.; Surgical Registrar, London Hospital, 1901; served European War, 1914-18 (despatches), Australian Army Medical Corps, Egypt, Lemnos, Gallipoli, France; Major, promoted Lt.-Col. 1916; commanded 1st Australian Casualty Clearing Station, 1916-17; Surgical Specialist, 3rd Australian Casualty Clearing Station, 1917-18; C.O. Australian Section, Queen's Hospital, Sidcup, 1918; represented Australian Army Medical Corps on Council of Consultants, War Office, 1918-19, and at Interallied Surgical Conferences, Paris, 1918; President: Section of Surgery, Australasian Medical Congress, 1920; R.A.C.S., 1929-34; Vice-Pres., B.M.A., Eng., 1932-1965. Gold Medal, B.M.A., Australia, 1949; Gold Medal, B.M.A., Eng., 1955. *Publications:* Papers in Medical Journal of Australia, B.M.J., etc. *Recreations:* tennis, golf. *Address:* Luilyl, 12 Burlington St., Walkerville, S. Australia. *Clubs:* Leander, Public Schools; Adelaide (Adelaide), Australasian Pioneer. [*Died* 13 *Nov.* 1969.

NEWMAN, Bernard; F.R.S.A.; Author and Lecturer; *b.* 8 May 1897; *s.* of William and Annie Newman, Ibstock, Leicestershire; *m.* 1st, 1923, Marjorie Edith Donald; three *d.*; 2nd, 1966, Helen Freda Johnston. *Educ.:* Bosworth. Served European War with B.E.F., France, 1915-19; entered Civil Service, 1920. Lecturer on Espionage, Travel, and European Affairs since 1924; with B.E.F. as lecturer, 1940; later, with French Army; Staff Lecturer, Ministry of Information, 1940-45; toured North America for M.O.I., 1942; toured Europe and Middle East for Army Education, 1945-46; India, South East Asia and Japan, 1947; Mediterranean and North Africa, 1948; since then travelled in more than 60 countries. Chevalier, Legion of Honour, 1954. *Publications:* Round About Andorra, 1928; The Cavalry Went Through, 1930; Armoured Doves, 1931; Hosanna, 1933; Death in the Valley, 1934; In the Trail of the Three Musketeers, 1934; Death of a Harlot, 1934; Pedalling Poland, 1935; Spy, 1935; Secret Servant, 1935; The Blue Danube, 1935; Anthology of Armageddon, 1935; German Spy, 1936; Tunnellers, 1936; The Mussolini Murder Plot, 1936; Albanian Back-door, 1936; Cycling in France, 1936; Lady Doctor—Woman Spy, 1937; I Saw Spain, 1937; Death under Gibraltar, 1938; Danger Spots of Europe, 1938; Ride to Russia, 1938; Maginot Line Murder, 1939; Death to the Spy, 1939; Baltic Roundabout, 1939; Secrets of German Espionage, 1939; The Story of Poland, 1940; Siegfried Spy, 1940; Savoy! Corsica! Tunis!, 1940; Death to the Fifth Column, 1941; One Man's Year, 1941; Secret Weapon, 1942; The New Europe, 1942; Black Market, 1942; American Journey, 1943; Second Front—First Spy, 1944; Balkan Background, 1944; Spy Catchers, 1945; British Journey, 1945; The Spy in the Brown Derby, 1946; Russia's Neighbour—the New Poland, 1946; Baltic Background, 1947; Dead Man Murder, 1946; Middle Eastern Journey, 1947; The Red Spider Web, 1947; Moscow Murder, 1948; News from the East, 1948; The Captured Archives, 1948; The Flying Saucer, 1948; Mediterranean Background, 1949; Lazy Meuse, 1949; Shoot!, 1949; Come Adventuring with Me, 1949; Cup Final Murder, 1950; The Sisters Alsace-Lorraine, 1950; Epics of Espionage, 1950; Turkish Cross-Roads, 1951; Centre Court Murder, 1951; Oberammergau Journey, 1951; They Saved London, 1952; Death at Lord's, 1952; Soviet Atomic Spies, 1952; Both Sides of the Pyrenees, 1952; Tito's Yugoslavia, 1952; Morocco Today, 1953; Ride to Rome, 1953; Yours for Action, 1953; Report on Indo-China, 1953; The Wishful Think, 1954; Berlin and Back, 1954; The Sosnowski Affair, 1954; Double Menace, 1955; North African Journey, 1955; Still Flows the Danube, 1955; Operation Barbarossa, 1956; Inquest on Mata Hari, 1956; Real Life Spies, 1956; The Three Germanies, 1957; Spain on a Shoestring, 1957; A Hundred Years of Good Company, 1957; The Otan Plot, 1957; Unknown Germany, 1958; Flowers for the Living (with Guy Bolton), 1958; Taken at the Flood, 1958; Portrait of Poland, 1959; Danger Spots of the World, 1959; Visa to Russia, 1959; Speaking from Memory (autobiography), 1960; Unknown Jugoslavia, 1960; Silver Greyhound, 1960; Bulgarian Background, 1961; Far Eastern Journey, 1961; Let's Look at Germany, 1961; The Blue Ants, 1962; The World of Espionage, 1962; Mr Kennedy's America, 1962; This is Your Life, 1963; Unknown France, 1963; The Travelling Executioners, 1964; Round the World in Seventy Days, 1964; Behind the Berlin Wall, 1964; Spies in Britain, 1964 Background to Vietnam, 1965; South African Journey, 1965; The Spy at No. 10, 1965; Spain Re-visited, 1966; Evil Phœnix, 1966; To Russia and Back, 1967; The Bosworth Story, 1967; The Dangerous Age, 1967; Draw the Dragon's Teeth, 1967; Portrait of the Shires, 1968; Turkey and the Turks, 1968; The Jail Breakers, 1968. Also, under *pseudonym* Don Betteridge Scotland Yard Alibi, 1938; Cast Iron Alibi, 1939; Balkan Spy, 1942; The Escape of General Gerard, 1944; Dictator's Destiny 1945; The Potsdam Murder Plot, 1947; Spies Left!, 1950; Not Single Spies, 1951; Spy-Counter-Spy, 1953; The Case of the Berlin Spy, 1954; The Gibraltar Conspiracy, 1955; The Spies of Peenemünde, 1957; Contact Man, 1960; The Package Holiday Spy Case, 1962. *Recreation:* cycling. *Address:* 3 Gerard Road, Harrow on the Hill. *T.A.* and *T.:* 01-907 2468. [*Died* 19 *Feb.* 1968.

NEWMAN, Bertram; late Lecturer at Southampton University; formerly Staff Inspector, Ministry of Education; *b.* 1886; *s.* of late Dr. A. J. Newman, Godalming; *m.* 1921, Josephine, *d.* of late J. Eteson Robinson, Sheffield. *Educ.:* Charterhouse; University College, Oxford. 1st class Honour Moderations and Lit. Hum., Gaisford Prize (Verse), 1905; Hertford Scholar, 1906, Derby Scholar, 1908; served in France, 1916-18 (Capt. and Adjutant R.G.A.). *Publications:* Cardinal Newman, 1925; Edmund Burke, 1927; Lord Melbourne, 1930; Jonathan Swift, 1937; English Historians (Selections), 1957. *Address:* 203 Bassett Avenue, Southampton. *T.:* 68274. [*Died* 25 *Aug.* 1962.

NEWMAN, Major Edward William Polson, B.A.; O.St.J.; Officer (1st class) Order of the White Rose of Finland; Editor, Oxford University Press, 1945-52; *b.* 1887; *o. s.* of late David Newman, M.D. Craig Ailey, Cove, Dunbartonshire, and Jean McFadyean, *d.* of late William Polson, J.P., Edgehill, Paisley, Renfrewshire; *m.* 1923, Eileen Merlyn, *o. d.* of late John Edward Hussey, J.P., Edenburn, Co. Kerry; two *s.* *Educ.:* Marlborough; Christ Church, Oxford. Entered The Cameronians (Scottish Rifles), 1910; served European War (1914 Star and war medals); attached General Staff, 1915-16; Staff Captain, 195th Infantry Brigade, 1917-18; Royal Air Force, 1918-19; retired as Major, 1920; private secretary to the Anglican Bishop in Jerusalem, 1923-25; Received into the Church of Rome, 1945; Internal Oblate, O.S.B., Farnborough Abbey, Hants., 1953-61; press correspondent in Palestine and Syria, 1924-1926; war correspondent with the French Army in Syria, 1925-26; assignments in Europe, the Middle East and N.E. Africa, 1926-38; lectured before the Imperial Defence Coll., 1928; R.N. Staff Coll., 1935; British member Africa Conference, Royal Acad. of Italy, 1938; Press Adviser to Finnish Legation, London, 1927-32; to Egyptian Legation, 1930-32; to Italian Embassy, 1936-39; industrial missions in Scotland, 1933-34; Foreign Public Relations Officer, Imperial Airways, 1939; Min. of Food, 1940; Internal Relations, de Havilland Aircraft Co., 1942-44. *Publications:* The Middle East, 1926; The Mediterranean and its Problems, 1927; Great Britain in Egypt, 1928; Britain and the Baltic, 1930; Ethiopian Realities, 1936; Italy's Conquest of Abyssinia, 1937; The New Abyssinia, 1938; Britain and North-East Africa, 1940; Masaryk, 1960; contributor to the Encyclopædia Britannica, Nineteenth Century, Quarterly Review, The Times, etc. *Address:* Huntly, Bishopsteignton, Devon. *T.:* Bishopsteignton 201. [*Died* 17 *Dec.* 1967.

NEWMAN, Major-General Hubert Thomas, C.B. 1948; C.B.E. 1945; Royal

Marines (retd.); *b.* 26 Aug. 1895; *s.* of Thomas Newman, Ore, Sussex, and Harriet Matilda Newman; *m.* 1924, Kathleen Mary, *d.* of H. R. Corbett, M.D., Plymouth, Devon; no *c.* *Educ.:* Eastbourne College. Commissioned Aug. 1914; Captain 1917; Major, 1933; Bt. Lt.-Col. 1938; Lt-Col. 1940; Col. 1943; Major-Gen. 1946; p.s.c. 1930. Seconded South African Defence Force, 1939-42. Maj.-Gen., General Staff, Royal Marine Office, 1944; Maj.-Gen. R.M., East Indies, 1945; A.D.C. to the King, 1946; commanding Royal Marines, Portsmouth, 1946-48. Hon. Col. Comdt., 1954-58; retd. list, 1948. *Address:* Hill House, Cranbrook, Kent. *T.:* Cranbrook 2359.
[*Died* 2 *May* 1965.

NEWMAN, Sir Ralph Alured, 5th Bt., *cr.* 1836; *b.* 28 April 1902; *e. s.* of Robert Lydston and Alfreda Newman, both late of 11 Cadogan Sq., S.W.1, and Blackpool House, near Dartmouth, S. Devon; *S.* to Baronetcy of his cousin, Baron Mamhead, 1945; *m.* 1946, Ann Rosemary Hope, *d.* of late Hon. Claude Hope-Morley, *q.v.*; two *s.* two *d.* *Educ.:* Eton; Corpus Christi Coll., Cambridge. B.A. 1923; M.A. 1927; Merchant of City of London; Liveryman of Fishmongers; Freeman of City of London; Member Society of Merchants trading to the Continent. Served War of 1939-45, R.A.S.C. Motor Transport, England, 1939-42, and in Middle East in M.T. R.A.S.C. and Horse Transport, R.A.S.C., Sept. 1942-Sept. 1945. *Recreations:* all sports and gardening. *Heir:* *s.* Geoffrey Robert Newman, *b.* 2 June 1947. *Address:* Blackpool House, nr. Dartmouth, Devon. *Clubs:* Carlton, M.C.C.; Pitt.
[*Died* 20 *July* 1968.

NEWMAN, Rev. Canon Richard, M.A. Oxon; Hon. Canon of Blackburn, 1946, Canon Emeritus since 1947; *b.* 1871; *s.* of Rev. Frederick William Newman; *m.* 1900, Alice Dorothea, *d.* of Arthur Page, F.R.C.O.; one *s.* two *d.* *Educ.:* Hereford Cathedral School; Brasenose College, Oxford; University of Bonn; Leeds Clergy School. 2nd class Lit. Hum. Oxon; Curate S. Mary's, Nottingham; New Mills; Vicar of Goodshaw; Whalley; Rural Dean of Whalley, 1912-17; Rector of Church Kirk, 1917-32; Vicar of Holy Trinity, Preston, 1932-42; on staff of Blackburn Cathedral, 1942-46; Rural Dean of Accrington, 1922-32; Proctor in Convocation, 1922 and 1929-36; Hon. Canon of Blackburn, 1927-36; Archdeacon of Blackburn, 1936-46; Examining Chaplain to Bishop of Blackburn, 1927-46. *Address:* 5A Hillside St., Hythe, Kent.
[*Died* 3 *June* 1961.

NEWNHAM, Hubert Ernest, C.M.G. 1937; V.D.; M.A. (Oxon.); Major Ceylon Light Infantry retired; *b.* 1 Oct. 1886; *s.* of H. S. Newnham, Guildford, Surrey; *m.* 1930, Mary Garneys Latter; two *d.* *Educ.:* Dean Close School; St. John's College, Oxford. Entered Ceylon Civil Service, 1909; Mayor of Colombo, 1924-31; Comr. of Local Government, 1931-35; Commissioner for Relief of Distress during Famine and Malaria Epidemic, 1935-36; Principal Collector of Customs, Ceylon, and Chairman, Colombo Port Commission, 1936-38; retired from Ceylon Civil Service, 1939; Nominated Member Ceylon State Council, 1939-43; Dep. Chm. Ceylon Chamber of Commerce, 1943-45. Godalming Borough Councillor, 1947-50. *Address:* The Cross House, Childswickham, Broadway, Worcs.
[*Died* 1 *Oct.* 1970.

NEWSAM, Sir Frank (Aubrey), G.C.B. 1957 (K.C.B. 1950); K.B.E. 1943; C.V.O. 1933; M.C.; Permanent Under-Secretary of State, Home Office, 1948-57; *b.* 1893; *s.* of late William Elias Newsam, Barbados: *m.* 1927, Jean, *d.* of late James McAuslin. *Educ.:* Harrison Coll., Barbados; St. John's Coll., Oxford. Served European War, 1914-1919 (despatches, M.C.); Private Sec. to successive Secretaries of State for Home Dept., 1927-33; Deputy Under-Secretary of State for Home Dept., 1941-48. Chairman: Board of Governors, Police College, 1947-; State Management Districts Council; Nat. Fire Brigades Advisory Council, 1947-. K.St.J. 1955. Commander of the Order of St. Olav (Norway). *Publication;* The Home Office, 1954. *Club:* United University.
[*Died* 25 *April* 1964.

NEWTON, Algernon, R.A. 1943 (A.R.A. 1936); landscape painter; *b.* Hampstead, 23 February 1880; *y. s.* of Arthur Henry Newton and Georgina Tregonning Newton of Potterspury Lodge, Northamptonshire; *m.* 1st, 1903, Marjorie Emelia Balfour Rider; one *s.* two *d.* (and one *s.* decd.); 2nd, 1921, Elsie Mary Willmott, *er. d.* of Rev. Arthur Willmott Richards. *Educ.:* Farnborough School; Clare College, Cambridge. Studied at Frank Calderon's School of Animal Painting; Slade School, and London School of Art. Works purchased by Tate Gallery (Chantrey Bequest), City of Birmingham Art Gallery, Brighton Corporation Art Gallery, Walker Art Gallery, Liverpool, Ferens Art Gallery, Hull, Nottingham Art Gallery, Buxton Art Gallery, Lady Lever Art Gallery, Art Gallery, Preston, Nat. Gall. of Victoria, Nat. Gall. of N.S.W., Pietermaritzburg Art Gall., Minneapolis Art Gall., U.S.A. *Address:* 16 Vicarage Gate, W.8.
[*Died* 21 *May* 1968.

NEWTON, Sir Basil Cochrane, K.C.M.G., *cr.* 1939 (C.M.G. 1929); *s.* of George Onslow and Lady Alice Newton of Croxton Park, Cambridgeshire; *b.* 1889; unmarried. *Educ.:* Wellington; King's College, Cambridge. Served in Foreign Office, 1912-25; attached to British Delegation to Special Tariff Conference, Peking, 1925-26; Acting Counsellor, Peking, 1927-29; Counsellor, Berlin, 1930-35, Minister, 1935-37; Minister to Czechoslovakia, 1937-39; Ambassador to Iraq, 1939-41; served in F.O., 1942-46; retired, 1946. *Recreations:* shooting, ski-ing. *Address:* 17 Kensington Mansions, Trebovir Road, Earl's Court, S.W.5. *T.:* Frobisher 1071. *Clubs:* St. James', Boodle's. [*Died* 15 *May* 1965.

NEWTON, Eric, C.B.E. 1964; Art Critic to The Guardian; Lectr. on Art History to the Central School of Arts and Crafts since 1963; *b.* 28 Apr. 1893; *m.* 1st, 1915, Isabel Aileen Vinicombe; two *s.*; 2nd, 1934, Stella Mary Pearce. B.A. Manchester University, 1913 (M.A. 1951). M.A. Oxon., 1959. Mosaic designer, craftsman, with L. Oppenheimer Ltd., Manchester, 1913-14 and 1918-33. Served European War, 1914-18, as Captain, 2/9 Manchester Regiment. Art Critic: Manchester Guardian, 1930-47; Sunday Times, 1937-51; Pres. Brit. sect. of Assoc. Internat. des Critiques d'Art, 1949-61; Lecture tour, Canada, U.S. 1936, 1953 and 1956; U.S. 1952; Mem. of Carnegie jury, Pittsburgh 1952. Slade Professor of Fine Art, Oxford University, 1959-60; Art Adviser, Commonwealth Inst., 1960-63. *Publications:* The Artist and His Public, 1935; Masterpieces of Figure Painting, 1936; Christopher Wood, 1938; European Painting and Sculpture (Penguin), 1941, enlarged edn. Introduction to European Painting (Longmans), 1949 (republished by Cassell, 1962); British Painting (British Council), 1945; Stanley Spencer (Penguin), 1947; British Sculpture, 1944-46, 1947; The Meaning of Beauty, 1950; In My View (Collected Essays), 1950; Wyndham Lewis (part author), 1951; Tintoretto, 1952; The Arts of Man (New York), 1960; The Romantic Rebellion, 1962. *Recreations:* painting, foreign travel. *Address:* 3 Cumberland Gardens, W.C.1. *T.:* Terminus 4443. *Club:* Savile. [*Died* 10 *March* 1965.

NEWTON, Lieut.-Col. Frank Graham, C.B.E. 1918; D.S.O 1918; V.D.; grazier; *b.* 5 Oct. 1877; *s.* of late Richard Newton, Brisbane, Queensland; *m.* 1912, Kathleen, *d.* of late Frederick Verney, Botolph House, Winslow, Bucks; one *s.* three *d.* *Educ.:* Brisbane Grammar School. Enlisted in Queensland Mounted Infantry as private, 1899; commission granted on active service, South Africa, 1900; wounded, Aug. 1900; A.D.C. to Sir Herbert Chermside, Private Secretary to Lord Chelmsford, successive Governors of Queensland; joined 5th Australian Light Horse Regiment as Lieut., 1914; Captain in Gallipoli, 1915; Major, 1916; A.A.G., A.I.F. in Egypt with Desert Mounted Corps, H.Q.; Lieut.-Col. 1917 (C.B.E., D.S.O.); returned to Australia, 1919; Colonial Auxiliary Forces Officers' Decoration, 1924. *Address:* 129 Windermere Road, Ascot, Brisbane, Australia. *Club:* Queensland (Brisbane).
[*Died* 1 *Nov.* 1962.

NICHOLAS, His Honour Judge Montagu Richmond; County Court Judge, Wandsworth, since June 1960; *b.* 17 June 1905; *yr. s.* of late W. S. Nicholas; *m.* 1927, Morna Mary Stuart, *yr. d.* of late Sir Louis Stuart, C.I.E.; one *s.* *Educ.:* Royal Naval Colleges, Osborne and Dartmouth; Trinity Hall, Cambridge. Called to Bar, Inner Temple, Nov. 1927. County Court Judge, Bow, 1957-60. *Address:* 11 Esmond Court, Thackeray Street, W.8. *T.:* Western 9834. *Club:* Oxford and Cambridge University.
[*Died* 27 *May* 1964.

NICHOLLS, John Ralph, C.B.E. 1949; D.Sc.; F.R.I.C.; *b.* 1889; 4th *s.* of late John Fry and Amelia Nicholls; *m.* 1915, Alice (*d.* 1968), *o. d.* of late Henry Gibbons; one *s.* *Educ.:* Dr. Morgan's School, Bridgwater; Merchant Venturers, Bristol; City and Guilds Technical College, Finsbury. Government Chemist's Dept., 1911 - 57; Superintending Chemist, 1936; investigations on food and drugs; Deputy Govt. Chemist, 1946-54; Member Council Soc. for Analytical Chemistry, 1932-33, 1936-37, 1947-1948; Vice-Pres. 1938-39, 1944-45, 1949-50, 1954-; President 1951-53; Mem. Council Roy. Inst. of Chemistry, 1936-39, 1940-43; Examiner, 1943-; Streatfeild Memorial Lectr., 1938; Tatlock Memorial Lectr., 1948. League of Nations Commission for Opium and Coca Leaves, 1933; W.H.O. Expert Committee on Drug Dependence, 1947-. Mem. of Food Additives and Contaminants Cttee. *Publications:* Opium, 1938; The Determination of Alcohol, 1948; Aids to Analysis of Food and Drugs, 1952; papers on chemical subjects in scientific and technical journals. *Recreations:* hockey (Middlesex), tennis, swimming bowls. *Address:* 23 Willow Way, Finchley, N.3. [*Died* 17 *Feb.* 1970.

NICHOLLS, Sir John (Walter), G.C.M.G. 1970 (K.C.M.G. 1956; C.M.G. 1948); O.B.E. 1941; formerly Member of H.M. Diplomatic Service; *b.* 4 Oct. 1909; *er. s.* of late W. H. Nicholls, Radlett; *m.* 1935, Dominie, *d.* of Peter Vlasto, Liverpool; one *s.* two *d.* *Educ.:* Malvern; Pembroke College, Cambridge. Entered Foreign Office, 1932; Second Sec., 1937; First Sec., 1942; Counsellor, 1946; Asst. Under-Sec. of State, 1951; British Ambassador to Israel, 1954-57; Ambassador to Yugoslavia, 1957-60; Ambassador to Belgium, 1960-63; Dep. Under-Sec., Foreign Office, 1963-66; Ambassador to S. Africa, 1966-69; also served at Athens, Lisbon, Vienna, Moscow. Grand Cross, Order of the Crown (Belgium). *Recreations:* gardening, manual labour. *Address:* Thorpes, Frenches Green, Felsted, Essex. *T.:* Felsted 277. *Club:* Travellers'.
[*Died* 25 *Oct.* 1970.

NICHOLLS, Lucius, C.M.G. 1945; M.D., B.C., B.A. (Cantab.); formerly Director of Medical Laboratories, Ceylon; Nutrition Adviser to Special Commission, South-East Asia; Acting Director Far East Epidemiological Bureau of World Health Organisation; retired 1949; *b.* 22 Jan. 1885; *s.* of late Dr. F. L. Nicholls; *m.* 1926, Gladys Evelyn Johnson (*d.* 1946); one *s.* two *d.* *Educ.:* Downing College, Cambridge. Pathologist, Seamen's Hospital, Greenwich, 1907; Surgeon, Victoria Hospital, St. Lucia, B.W.I., 1909-13; Capt. R.A.M.S., O.C. Kadjiado Hospital, Brit. East Africa, 1914-1915. *Publications:* Tropical Nutrition and Dietetics, 1938 and 1945; Tropical Hygiene, 1945; numerous papers. *Recreations:* shooting, golf. *Address:* Raylands Nursing Home, Marine Parade, Brighton, Sussex. *T.:* Brighton 62705. *Club:* Royal Commonwealth Society.
[*Died* 3 *Sept.* 1969.

NICHOLLS, Sir Marriott Fawckner, Kt. 1969; C.B.E. 1946; M.A., M.Chir. (Cantab.); F.R.C.S. Eng., L.R.C.P. (Lond.); Professor of Surgery, Univ. of Khartoum, Sudan; late: Director of Surgical Unit, Surgeon in Charge, Genito-Urinary Department, St. George's Hosp., London; Consulting Surgeon to Belgrave Hosp. for Children; Surgeon Royal National Orthopædic Hospital; F.R.S.M. (Hon. Sec., 1939. Vice-President, Surgical Section, 1937); Fellow Medical Society, London, Harveian Society (Council 1936), Association of Surgeons Great Britain and Ireland (Council 1938); Fell. Brit. Assoc. of Urological Surgeons (Council 1945-49); *b.* London, 12 May 1898; *o. s.* of Marriott Edwin Nicholls. *Educ.:* City of London School; Clare College, Cambridge; St. George's Hospital, London (Allingham Scholarship in Surgery, Sir Francis Laking Research Scholarship). Served in European War, 1915-19, Captain Royal Fusiliers; Usual House Appointments, also Assistant Pathologist, Assistant Curator, Surgical Registrar, Resident Assistant Surgeon, St. George's Hospital, London; Clinical Assistant, St. Peter's Hospital; Assistant Surgeon St. George's Hosp., 1932; Surg. 1939; Dean of Medical School; late Brig., R.A.M.C.; Consulting Surg., S.E.A.C. Member Court of examiners, R.C.S., 1940-41, 1946-51, Chm., 1950-51; Pres. Section of Urology, Roy. Soc. Med., 1960-61. *Publications:* publications on surgical subjects to medical journals. *Recreation:* fishing. *Address:* P.O. Box 102, Khartoum, Sudan; Radways Close, Hampnett, Glos. *Club:* United University.
[*Died* 25 *Aug.* 1969.

NICHOLLS, Hon. Sir Robert Dove, Kt. 1941; J.P.; Director: South Australian Farmers' Union Ltd. and Farmers' Executors Ltd. (retired as Chairman of both July 1962); Director: Cresco Fertilisers Ltd. (retired as Chairman); Deputy Chairman, South Australian Housing Trust; *b.* Nantawarra, South Australia, 27 June 1889; *s.* of James Nicholls; *m.* 1915, Rose Evelyn Marshall Cowan; two *s.* two *d.* M.P., 1915-56; Speaker House of Assembly, State of S. Australia, 1933-56; Chairman of Committees and Dep. Speaker, 1927-30; Pres. Australian American Movement (S.A. Branch), 1941-46. Member: Council, School of Mines and Industries, 1936-54; Bd. of Governors, Botanic Garden, 1933-56; Council, Institutes Assoc., 1927-48; Chairman Advisory Committee Roy. Adelaide Hospital and University, 1933-62; President Royal Society of St. George, 1949-54. *Address:* 34A, South Esplanade, Glenelg, S. Australia.
[*Died* 18 *Jan.* 1970.

NICHOLLS, William, M.A.; Sudan Political Service, retired; *b.* Lifford, Co. Donegal, 18 Nov. 1882; *s.* of late Wm. Nicholls

Rathmines, Dublin; *m.* 1935, Ena. *e. d.* of late Charles Somerville and Mrs. Somerville, Wellington Court, Knightsbridge, S.W.1; one *d.* *Educ.:* Arlington House, Portarlington; Trinity College, Dublin. Entered the Sudan Political Service, 1907; served as Commissioner in Dongola, Khartum, Kordofan Halfa and Darfur Provinces; Darfur Expedition, 1916 (medal and clasp); Deputy Governor Sennar Province, 1917; special service in Egypt (Western Frontier); mentioned in despatches for War Services, 1917; Deputy Governor, Darfur, 1919; Officer of the Order of the Nile, 1919; Commander, 1929; Political Officer Anglo-French Equatorial African Boundary Commission, 1922; Governor of the White Nile Province, 1922-26; Governor of Berber Province, 1926-32. *Publication:* The Shaikiya, a history of Dongola, 1913. *Address:* Rostellan, Pyrford, Surrey. *T.:* Byfleet 45582. *Club:* Junior Carlton.
[*Died* 8 *March* 1970.

NICHOLS, Sir Philip Bouverie Bowyer, K.C.M.G., *cr.* 1946 (C.M.G. 1941); M.C.; *b.* 7 Sept. 1894; *yr. e.* of late John Bowyer Buchanan Nichols and Katherine Pusey, Lawford Hall, Manningtree, Essex; *m.* 1932, Phyllis, *e. d.* of late Lieut.-Col. Right Hon. H. H. Spender Clay, C.M.G., M.C., M.P., and Pauline Astor; two *s.* two *d.* *Educ.:* Winchester; Balliol College, Oxford. Served European War, 1914-19, Suffolk Regt., on Western Front (M.C., wounded, despatches) Entered Foreign Service, 1920; Vienna, 1920-23; seconded for service New Zealand, 1928-30; First Secretary, Rome, 1933-37; Foreign Office, 1937-41; Minister to Czechoslovak Govt. in London, 1941; Ambassador to the Czechoslovak Republic, 1942-47; Ambassador to the Netherlands, 1948-51; retired at own request, Dec. 1951. J.P. Essex, 1952; D.L. Essex, 1953; Mem. General Purposes, Exec. and Finance Cttees., Nat. Trust, 1953; Chairman Dedham Vale Society, 1957; Chairman Batte-Lay Trust, Colchester, 1958. *Address:* Lawford Hall, Manningtree, Essex; 9 Morpeth Mansions, S.W.1. *Clubs:* Brooks's, Bath, Beefsteak.
[*Died* 6 *Dec.* 1962.

NICHOLSON, Rear-Admiral Charles Hepworth, C.B. 1947; C.B.E. 1944; R.N.; *b.* 29 Sept. 1891; *s.* of Capt. C. S. Nicholson, R.N., and Mary Nicholson; *m.* 1922, Dora Barwis (*d.* 1954), Plymouth; two *s.* one *d.*; *m.* 1956, Mary Hill Straus, *widow* of P. J. W. Straus. *Educ.:* R.N. Colleges, Osborne and Dartmouth. Retired. *Address:* The Old Manor House, Ropley, Hants.
[*Died* 10 *Sept.* 1966.

NICHOLSON, Frank Carr, M.A.; Hon. LL.D. (Edinburgh); Librarian to the University of Edinburgh, 1910-39; *s.* of late Henry Alleyne Nicholson, M.D., F.R.S., Professor of Natural History at the University of Aberdeen; *m.* 1939, Mary, *d.* of late A. M. M'Leod, Dunosdale, Barnton, Edinburgh. *Educ.:* University of Aberdeen; Christ's College, Cambridge. Classical Tripos, 1896; 1st Class Medieval and Modern Languages Tripos, 1898; Assistant Librarian, University Library, Aberdeen, 1901-3; Acting Librarian, Royal College of Physicians of Edinburgh, 1903-09. *Publication:* Old German Love Songs, translated from the Minnesingers of the 12th to 14th centuries, 1906. (With Georgina Sime), Brave Spirits, 1952, A Tale of Two Worlds, 1953, Inez and her Angel, 1954. *Address:* Idlethorpe, Keswick. [*Died* 11 *March* 1962.

NICHOLSON, Joseph Sinclair, C.B. 1939; C.B.E. 1932; Commander of Order of Leopold II, 1920; M A.; *b.* 23 Oct. 1882; *s.* of Daniel Nicholson, St. Lawrence, I. of W., and Eleanor Elizabeth Sinclair; *m.* 1910, Gertrude Sylvia, *d.* of Rev. R. W. Sealy, Abbotsham, Devon; three *s.* two *d.* *Educ.:* Malvern College; Oriel College, Oxford Resident, Toynbee Hall, 1907-10; Poor Law Guardian; assisted in enquiries for Royal Commission on the Poor Laws, 1908-9; Temporary appointment Board of Trade, 1909-11; Insurance Officer under Unemployment Insurance Act, 1912; Ministry of Labour, 1916-45. *Address:* Russettings, 18 Tupwood Lane, Caterham Valley, Surrey. *T.:* Caterham 43135. *Club:* Oxford and Cambridge. [*Died* 9 *April* 1968.

NICHOLSON, Colonel Walter Norris, C.M.G. 1918; D.S.O. 1916; late 1st Batt. Suffolk Regt.; *b.* 10 June 1877; 8th *s.* of William Norris Nicholson, Master in Lunacy; *m.* 1924, Una Phyllis Higgs; two *d.* *Educ.:* Charterhouse; Trinity College, Cambridge. Served South African War, 1899-1902 (Queen's medal and three clasps, King's medal and two clasps); European War, 1914-18 (despatches, C.M.G., D.S.O., Bt. Lt.-Col.); retired pay, 1933; Colonel The Suffolk Regt., 1939-47. *Publications:* Behind the Lines, 1939; History of the Suffolk Regt., 1948. *Address:* Norney Rough, Eashing, nr. Godalming, Surrey. *T.:* Godalming 94. [*Died* 5 *April* 1964.

NICKOLLS, Lewis Charles, C.B.E. 1964; M.Sc. (Lond.), A.R.C.S., D.I.C., F.R.I.C.; retd.; *b.* 26 July 1899; *s.* of Charles Albert and Clara Rose Nickolls; *m.* 1939, Dorothy Diana Crawley; one *s.* one *d.* *Educ.:* Brighton Grammar School; London Univ. (Royal Scholar, 1917). Government Laboratory, 1922-35; Metropolitan Police Laboratory, 1935-40; Director, Forensic Science Laboratory, Wakefield, 1940-51; Director Metropolitan Police Laboratory, 1951-64. *Publications:* The Scientific Investigation of Crime, 1956; assisted in 12th edn. Taylor's Principles and Practice of Medical Jurisprudence, Vol. 2, 1957; contribs. to various scientific journals. *Recreations:* golf, gardening (roses). *Address:* 226 Chislehurst Road, Petts Wood, Kent. *T.:* Orpington 21287.
[*Died* 2 *March* 1970.

NICKSON, Colonel John Edgar, M.C. and Bar, 1918; T.D.; D.L.; *b.* 21 April 1899; *e. s.* of late Richard Nickson, Cefn, Tyn-y-Groes, Caernarvonshire. *Educ.:* Shrewsbury. 2nd Lt., Roy. Welch Fusiliers, 1914-18 served European War, 1918; (wounded), and War of 1939-45; Lt.-Col. 1942; Bt.-Col. 1951. D.L. 1951, Vice-Lieut. 1960, Caernarvonshire; C.C. Caernarvonshire, 1958. *Recreations:* shooting, fishing, gardening. *Address:* Cefn, Tyn-y-Groes, Conway, Caernarvonshire. *T.:* Tyn-y-Groes 233. *Clubs:* Boodle's; Racquet (Liverpool)
[*Died* 23 *March* 1969.

NICOL, Brigadier Cameron Macdonald, C.I.E. 1941; M.D. Aberdeen, 1919; *b.* 20 July 1891. *Educ.:* Aberdeen University, M.B., Ch.B., 1915. Indian Medical Service; Deputy Assistant Director of Hygiene, India, 1929-34; Assistant Director of Public Health, Rawalpindi, 1934; Director of Public Health, Punjab, 1936-41. *Address:* Three Gates, Oaklands, Welwyn, Herts. *T.:* Welwyn 368. *Club:* East India and Sports.
[*Died* 19 *Feb.* 1965.

NICOL, Sir Thomas Drysdale, K.B.E. 1920; *b.* 16 Feb. 1878; *m.* 1902, Jane Henderson (*d.* 1943), *d* of Robert Simpson; one *d.* decd. *Educ.:* High School, Glasgow; Universities of Glasgow and Sheffield. Director of Contracts, Ministry of Munitions, 1917; Controller of Aircraft and Mechanical Transport Contracts, 1918; Chairman of Liquidation Committee, 1919. *Club:* Royal Automobile.
[*Died* 1 *March* 1961.

NICOLAY, Colonel Bernard Underwood, C.B. 1924; *b.* 23 Dec. 1873; *s.* of late Lieut.-Col. F. W. Nicolay, 2nd P.W.O. Gurkha Rifles, of Rose Hill, Bideford, N. Devon; *m.* Alice Gertrude, *d.* of late Rt. Hon. Sir E. N. C. Braddon, P.C., K.C.M.G.; (one *s.* lost on active service, H.M.S. Submarine Perseus, 1941) one *d.* *Educ.:* United

Services College, Westward Ho!; R.M.C., Sandhurst. Gazetted 1st Batt. Hampshire Regt., 1894; transferred to Indian Army, 17th Bombay Infantry, 1898; to the 1/4 Gurkha Rifles, 1898; served N.-W. Frontier, India, 1897-98; China, 1900; European War, 1914-19, in Egypt and France (despatches, severely wounded); Afghanistan, 1919 (despatches); Waziristan, 1920-21 (despatches twice, Bt.-Col.); formed in 1916 the 4th Batt., 3rd Q.A.O. Gurkha Rifles, and disbanded the same, 1922; Deputy Military Secretary, A.H.Q., India, 1922-27; retired, 1928. *Address:* Birchcroft, Chobham Road, Camberley, Surrey. *Club:* United Service. [*Died* 8 *Dec.* 1960.

NICOLLE, John Macarthur, O.B.E.; retired; *b.* 9 Sept. 1885; *s.* of late Joshua Mauger and Mary Catherine Nicolle; *m.* 1918, Katherine Myra Faith, *d.* of Rev. George Battiscombe; no *c.* *Educ.:* Godolphin School; Mercers' School. Joined Trinity House Service as an Upper Grade Clerk, 1905; Secretary of Corporation of Trinity House, London, 1935-46; served European War, 1914-18, 3rd Bn. S. Staffordshire Regt. and Royal Air Force (O.B.E.). *Address:* Gaines, Gerrards Cross, Bucks. *T.:* Gerrards Cross 3544. [*Died* 20 *Aug.* 1964.

NICOLLS, Arthur Edward Jefferys, C.B.E 1938; M.C.; late Director of Mangles Bros. Coorg Coffee Estates Ltd.; late Manager of a Coffee Estate, Coorg, S. India; *b.* Knipton Rectory, Grantham; *s.* of late Rev. E. R. J. Nicolls, M.A., lately Rector of Saxelbye, Melton Mowbray; *m.* 1918, Catherine Fraser Duff; no *c.* *Educ.:* Summerfields; Winchester. Began Coffee Planting in Coorg, 1906; Chairman United Planters Association of S. India, 1936; Vice-Chairman, Indian Coffee Cess Committee, 1936; Represented European Constituency on Coorg Legislative Council, 1924-36; served in ranks of 2nd Battn. Loyal North Lancashire Regiment, 1914-15; and held commission in 4th Battn. King's African Rifles, 1915-19; attained rank of Captain and Adjutant of 4/4th King's African Rifles (wounded, M.C.). *Address:* 39 Chancellor House, Tunbridge Wells. *Clubs:* United Service (Bangalore); Ootacamund. [*Died* 8 *March* 1963.

NICOLLS, Sir Basil (Edward), Kt., *cr.* 1953; C.V.O. 1950; C.B.E. 1945; retired from B.B.C. as Acting-Director-General, 1952; *b.* 29 Aug. 1893; *s.* of Ven. G. E. Nicolls; *m.* 1922, Norah, *d.* of late General F. C. Godley, M.V.O. *Educ.:* Wellington College (Scholar); Christ Church, Oxford (Slade Prize Exhibition, distinction in war course of Lit. Hum., 1921). Farming in Ontario, 1912-14; N. Staffordshire Regiment and Staff in Gallipoli, Mesopotamia, India, Afghanistan, 1914-19; at Oxford, 1920-21; with Bird and Co., Calcutta (steel project), 1921-22; Assistant Secretary Carnegie U.K. Trust Dunfermline, 1923; 1924 onwards in service of the B.B.C., as, successively, Manchester Station Director, London Station Director, General Editor of Publications, Controller of Administration, Controller of Programmes; Senior Controller, 1944; Director of Home Broadcasting, 1947. *Address:* Reed House, Northam, N. Devon. *Club:* Athenæum. [*Died* 3 *Aug.* 1965.

NICOLLS, Edward Hugh Dyneley, C.M.G. 1927; O.B.E. 1918; A.M.I.C.E. (Retd.); *b.* 1871; 6th *s.* of late Captain Francis Hastings Gustavus Nicolls, 4th Dragoon Guards, of Ashorne, Warwick; *m.* 1898, Florence Mary (*d.* 1942), *d.* of late Ebenhard Granberg, Abo, Finland. *Educ.:* All Saints School, Bloxham. Superintendent of Public Works, Cyprus, 1898; Director Public Works, 1904-18; served European War, 1914-18 (despatches); Director Public Works, Gold Coast, 1918-28; retired. *Recreations:* fishing, shooting. *Address:* Uplands, Crapstone, Yelverton, S. Devon. *T.:* Yelverton 566. [*Died* 7 *Jan.* 1963.

NICOLSON, Hon. Sir Harold (George), K.C.V.O., *cr.* 1953; C.M.G. 1920; author and critic; formerly in Diplomatic Service; lately Chm. Committee of London Library (1952-57); Vice-Chairman of Executive of National Trust; Hon. Fell. of Balliol; *b.* Tehran, Persia, 1886; *s.* of 1st Baron Carnock; *m.* 1913, Hon. Victoria Mary Sackville-West, C.H. (*d.* 1962), *o. c.* of 3rd Baron Sackville; two *s.* *Educ.:* Wellington; Balliol College, Oxford. Entered Foreign Office, 1909; appointed to H.M. Embassy, Madrid, 1910; Constantinople, 1911; transferred to Foreign Office, 1914; served on British Delegation to Peace Conference, 1919; 2nd Secretary Diplomatic Service, 1919; First Secretary, 1920; joined League of Nations, Oct. 1919; returned to Foreign Office, June 1920; Counsellor, 1925; appointed to H.M. Legation, Tehran, Oct. 1925; to H.M. Embassy, Berlin, 1927; resigned, 1929; employed on editorial staff of Evening Standard, 1930; contested combined Universities as New Party Candidate, 1931; accompanied De La Warr educational Commission to East Africa, 1937; M.P. (Nat. Lab.) W. Leicester, 1935-45; Parl. Sec. to Ministry of Information, 1940-41; a Governor of the B.B.C., 1941-46. Joined Labour Party, 1947. Hon. Doctor Univs. of Athens, Grenoble, Glasgow, Dublin, Durham; a Trustee of Nat. Portrait Gall., 1948-64; President Classical Association, 1950-51. F.R.S.L. Commander of the Legion of Honour. Hon. Member, New York Academy. *Publications:* Paul Verlaine, 1921; Sweet Waters, 1921; Tennyson, 1923; Byron, The Last Journey, 1924; Swinburne (in English Men of Letters Series), 1926; Some People, 1927; Development of English Biography, 1928; Lord Carnock, 1930; People and Things, 1931; Public Faces, 1932; Peacemaking, 1919, 1933; Curzon: The Last Phase, 1934; Dwight Morrow, 1935; Small Talk, 1937; The Meaning of Prestige (Rede Lecture, 1937); Helen's Tower, 1937; Diplomacy, 1939; Marginal Comment, 1939; Why Britain is at War, 1939; The Desire to Please, 1943; Friday Mornings, 1944; Some People, 1944 (new edition, 1959); Another World Than This (Anthology, with V. Sackville West), 1945; The Congress of Vienna, 1946; The English Sense of Humour, 1947; Comments, 1948; Benjamin Constant, 1949; King George V: His Life and Reign, 1952; Evolution of Diplomatic Method (Chichele Lectures), 1954; Good Behaviour, 1955; Sainte-Beuve, 1957; Journey to Java, 1957; The Age of Reason, 1960; Monarchy, 1962; Diaries and Letters, 1930-39, ed. by Nigel Nicolson, 1966, 1945-62, 1968. *Address:* Sissinghurst Castle, Kent. *Clubs:* Travellers', Beefsteak. [*Died* 1 *May* 1968.

NICOLSON, Sir (Harold) Stanley, 12th Bart. of that Ilk and Lasswade, *cr.* 1629; *b.* 22 Oct. 1883; *s.* of 10th Bt. and Annie (*d.* 1936), *d.* of late John Rutherford, Bruntsfield Place, Edinburgh; *S.* brother 1952; *m.* 1927, Jean, *d.* of late Alexander Landles; no *c.* *Educ.:* Merchiston Castle; Edinburgh University. Late Lieut. R.N.V.R.; Lt.-Colonel i/c H.G. Bn. *Recreations:* shooting, fishing, golf. *Heir:* none. *Address:* Brough Lodge, Fetlar, Shetland. *T.:* Fetlar 2. [*Died* 5 *June* 1961 (*dormant*).

NICOLSON, Sir John (William), Kt. 1962; M.M. 1917; Senior Resident Surgeon, Manor House Hospital, N.W.11, since 1958; *b.* 26 June 1895; *s.* of Samuel Nicolson; *m.* 1931, Dorothie, *d.* of Henry Cowell; one *s.* one *d.* *Educ.:* Portree High School; Glasgow Univ. Served War with Cameron Highlanders, 1914-19. Glasgow University, 1919-24; M.B., Ch.B. 1924. Manor House Hospital, 1926. *Publications:* contributions to B.M.J., etc. *Recreations:* shinty and fishing. *Address:* Hillside, North End Road, N.W.11.

T.: Speedwell 6601. *Clubs:* Royal Commonwealth Society, Glasgow University (London). [*Died* 1 *June* 1965.

NICOLSON, Sir Kenneth, Kt., *cr.* 1944; M.C.; Partner, Gladstone, Wyllie & Co., London, East India Merchants, since 1922. Senior Partner since 1936; *b.* 2 Oct. 1891; *s.* of William Paterson Nicolson, Bridge-of-Weir, Renfrewshire; *m.* 1920, Mignon, 5th *d.* of Allen Thornton Shuttleworth, Indian Forest Service; two *s.* one *d.* *Educ.:* Glasgow Academy. East India Merchant; arrived India, 1911. Served in France and Belgium, European War, 1914-18, with R.H. and R.F.A. (M.C., despatches); returned to India, 1919. A commissioner for the Port of Calcutta, 1930-41; Chief Controller of Purchase (Munitions), Dept. of Supply, Govt. of India, 1941-45. *Recreations:* hunting, golf. *Address:* Norton Bavant Manor, Warminster, Wilts. *Clubs:* Caledonian, Oriental; Royal Bombay Yacht (Bombay); Bengal, Royal Calcutta Turf (Calcutta); Sind (Karachi). [*Died* 3 *April* 1964.

NICOLSON, Sir Stanley; *see* Nicolson, Sir H. S.

NILAND, D'Arcy Francis; author; *m.* 1942, Ruth Park; two *s.* three *d.* *Educ.:* St. Joseph's, N.S.W., Australia. Novelist, short-story writer, radio dramatist, television playwright, journalist. *Publications:* The Shiralee, 1955; Make Your Stories Sell, 1955; The Drums Go Bang (autobiography with Ruth Park), 1956; Call Me When the Cross Turns Over, 1957; Gold in the Streets, 1959; The Big Smoke, 1959; The Ballad of the Fat Bushranger, 1961; Logan's Girl, 1961; Dadda Jumped Over Two Elephants, 1963; The Apprentices, 1965; Pairs and Loners, 1966; Travelling Songs of Old Australia (with Leslie Raphael), 1966. *Recreation:* travel. *Address:* 61 Woodland St., Balgowlah Heights, N.S.W. *T.:* 94-2147. [*Died* 29 *March* 1967.

NIMITZ, Fleet Adm. Chester W., G.C.B. (Hon.) 1945; D.S.M. (U.S.) (4 times awarded); *b.* Fredericksburg Texas, U.S.A., 24 February 1885; *s.* of Chester Bernhard Nimitz and Anna Henke; *m.* 1913, Catherine Vance Freeman; one *s.* three *d.* *Educ.:* U.S. Naval Academy; U.S. Naval War College (1922-23). Ensign, U.S. Navy, 1907; Commanding Officer, U.S.S. Plunger, 1909; Lieut. 1910; Commander Third Submarine Division, Atlantic Torpedo Fleet, 1911-12; Commander Atlantic Submarine Flotilla, 1912-13; Lt.-Comdr. 1916; Executive and Engineering Officer, U.S.S. Maumee, 1916-17; Chief of Staff, Commander Submarine Force, Atlantic Fleet, 1918; Executive Officer, U.S.S. South Carolina, 1919; attached to University of California Naval Reserve Unit, 1926-29; Commanding Officer, U.S.S. Augusta, 1933-35; Assistant Chief of Bureau of Navigation, Navy Dept., 1935-38; Commander Battleship Division 1, Battle Force, 1938-39; Chief of the Bureau of Navigation, Navy Dept., 1939-41; Fleet Admiral, 1944; Commander-in-Chief, U.S. Pacific Fleet and Pacific Ocean Areas, 1941-1945; Signatory of Japanese Surrender as U.S. Representative; Chief of Naval Operations, U.S., 1945-47; Special Assistant to Secretary of U.S. Navy, 1947-49. Holds many other decorations both American and foreign; hon. degrees from American Univs. and Colleges. *Address:* 728 Santa Barbara Road, Berkeley 7, Calif., U.S.A. [*Died* 13 *Feb.* 1966.

NIND, William Walker, C.I.E. 1936; *b.* 26 Sept. 1882; *s.* of Lieut.-Colonel Frederick William Nind and Isabelle Agnes Walker; *m.* 1917, Feodore Scott; one *s.* one *d.* *Educ.:* Blundell's School, Tiverton; Balliol College, Oxford. Joined Indian Imperial Customs Service, 1906; served in Rangoon, Chittagong, Calcutta and Bombay as Asst. Collector of Customs and as Collector of Customs; Collector of Salt Revenue, Bombay; Member, Central Board of Revenue, Government of India; retired, 1937; British Delegate to Anglo-Afghan Trade Conference, 1922-23; Leader of Indian Trade Delegation to Afghanistan, 1934; working temporarily at India Office, Whitehall, 1940-48; Representative of India on League of Nations Advisory Committee in regard to opium and other dangerous drugs. *Address:* 3B Norham Gardens, Oxford. *T.:* Oxford 55995. *Club:* East India and Sports. [*Died* 11 *Nov.* 1964.

NISBET, Hugh Bryan, C.B.E. 1963; Ph.D., D.Sc. (Edin.); F.H.W.C.; F.R.I.C.; F.Inst. Pet.; F.Inst. Fuel; F.R.S.E.; Principal and Vice-Chancellor, Heriot-Watt University, 1966-67; Principal, Heriot-Watt College, Edinburgh, 1950-66; *b.* 31 March 1902; *yr. s.* of Hugh B. Nisbet and Robina Currie Cockburn; *m.* 1st, 1929, Emily Murray Donmall (*d.* 1967); 2nd, 1969, Flora Pellow, *née* Bigsby. *Educ.:* George Heriot's Sch., Edinburgh; Edinburgh Univ.; Heriot-Watt College, Edinburgh; also studied at University of Graz and University of Vienna. Heriot-Watt College: Demonstrator in Chemistry, 1921; Lecturer in Applied Chemistry, 1924-46; Professor of Chemistry, 1946-50. Vice-Chairman, Scottish Technical Education Consultative Council, 1964-1966. Hon. D.Litt. Heriot-Watt, 1968. Commander, Royal Norwegian Order of St. Olav, 1964. *Publications:* numerous papers on organic chemistry, mainly dealing with pyrazoline local anaesthetics, pyridine bases in shale oil and coal tar and analytical problems in Jl. of Chem. Soc., Jl. Inst. of Petroleum, Jl. Inst. of Fuel; Analyst, Jl. of Pharmacy and Pharmacology, Jl. of Pharmacology and Experimental Therapeutics. *Recreation:* fishing. *Address:* 30 Lockharton Ave., Edinburgh EH14 1AZ. *Club:* University (Edinburgh). [*Died* 21 *Nov.* 1969.

NITCH, Cyril Alfred Rankin, M.B., M.S. Lond.; F.R.C.S. Eng.; Consulting Surgeon, St. Thomas's Hospital, Evelina Hospital, etc.; *s.* of George H. Nitch; *m.* 1907, Amy A. (*d.* 1957), *d.* of late Surgeon Major J. L. Bryden, I.M.S.; two *d.* *Educ.:* Westminster School; St. Thomas's Hospital. B.S.Lond.; Gold Medal and University Scholarship; M.S.Lond., Gold Medal; served European War in England and France, 1914-17; Member of International Urological Association; Hon. Member British Assoc. of Urological Surgeons, Assoc. d'Urologie Français and Soc Italiana di Urologia; late President, Section of Surgery, and Section of Urology, Royal Society of Medicine; Fellow of Association of Surgeons of Great Britain and Ireland; late Examiner in Surgery, Universities of London and Wales Hon. Mem. Section of Surgery, Royal Soc. Med., 1962. *Publications:* articles on Surgery and Urology in various journals and text-books *Recreation:* golf. *Address:* Croyde, E. Coker Rd., Yeovil, Somerset. *T.:* 3283. [*Died* 17 *Sept.* 1969.

NIVEN, William Dickie, M.A., D.D., LL.D.; *b.* 26 Apr. 1879; *s.* of Charles Niven and Jane M. Mackay; *m.* 1908, Isabella M. Cumming; two *d.* *Educ.:* Fyvie Public Sch.; Gordon's Coll., Aberdeen; Universities of Aberdeen, Berlin, Halle. M.A. Aberdeen as most distinguished graduate in Arts of Year 1900; Lumsden and Sachs Fellowship, Aberdeen United Free Church Coll. 1906; Asst. to Professor of Logic in Aberdeen, 1903-1906; Croom Robertson Fellowship, 1901; Minister at Macduff, 1907-10; Blairgowrie, 1910-18; Causewayend, Aberdeen, 1919-27; External Examiner in Philosophy, Aberdeen, 1910-13; Professor of Church History in

Trinity College, Glasgow, 1927; External Examiner for B.D. Degree, Aberdeen, 1932-1935; Professor of New Testament Language and Literature in Glasgow University, 1935-1946; Professor of Ecclesiastical History in Glasgow University, 1946-49, retired, 1949. *Publications:* The Conflicts of the Early Church, 1930; John Knox and the Scottish Reformation, 1938; Reformation Principles after Four Centuries, 1953; Articles in Encyclopædia of Religion and Ethics and Dictionary of Apostolic Church. *Address:* 93 Hyndland Road, Glasgow, W.2. *T.:* Western 5817. [*Died* 26 *Feb.* 1965.

NIXON, Sir Frank Horsfall, K.C.M.G. *cr.* 1941; C.B. 1932; *b.* Leeds, 26 Jan. 1890; *s.* of William Nixon; *m.* Yvonne, *d.* of Joseph Vilbois; one *s.* *Educ.:* Leeds Grammar School; Pembroke Coll., Cambridge. Wrangler, Mathematical Tripos, 1st Class Historical Tripos. Appointed to Treasury, 1912; Director Economic and Financial Section League of Nations, 1920-1923; Commissioner of Austrian Government for floating Austrian Reconstruction Loans, 1923; Financial Mission to Poland, 1923-24; President of the International Union of Credit Insurers, 1935 and 1939; Comptroller General Export Credits Guarantee Department, 1926-44; Joint Managing Director of United Kingdom Commercial Corporation, 1940-46; Director John Brown & Co. Ltd., 1946-50; President London Chamber of Commerce, 1949-52; Member of China Government Purchasing Commission, 1949-51; Member of Council of Foreign Bondholders since 1950; Chairman: Greek House, 1946-51; City General Insurance Co. Ltd., 1951-65; Emerson Associates Ltd., 1961-63. Hon. Treasurer National Inst. for the Deaf, 1952-; Trustee and Chm., College for Deaf Welfare, 1964-. Master, Worshipful Company of Glass Sellers, 1956. Officier of the Ordre de la Couronne de Belgique, 1919; Officier of the Order Corona Italia, 1919; Officier of the Order Polonia Restituta, 1924; Silver Jubilee Medal, 1935; Coronation Medal, 1937. *Recreation:* travel. *Address:* 8 Dunstable Mews, W.1. *T.:* Welbeck 2008. *Clubs:* Athenæum, Royal Automobile. [*Died* 6 *July* 1966.

NIXON, Ven. George Robinson; *s.* of John and Elizabeth Nixon, Enniskillen, Co. Fermanagh; *m.* 1912, Kathleen Maud Morgan. *Educ.:* Portora Royal School, Enniskillen; Trinity College, Dublin (Exhibitioner and Classical Honorman); B.A. (Respondent), 1905; B.D., 1914; Senior Classical Master at the Educational Institution, Dundalk, 1900-5, and at the Grammar School, Drogheda, 1905-8; Curate of Tuam Cathedral, 1908; Curate of St. George, Dublin, 1910-11; Curate of Kilnamanagh Union, 1911-14; Rector of Killasnett (Kilmore), 1914-15; Rector of Turlough (Tuam), 1915-18; Rector of Kilcommon Union, Diocese of Tuam, 1918-50; Secretary to Tuam Diocesan Council, 1942-50; Examining Chaplain to the Bishop of Tuam, 1923-; Canon of Tuam Cathedral, 1925; Provost of Tuam, 1928-39; Archdeacon of Tuam, 1939-1950. *Recreations:* local history and archæology. *Address:* 11 Herbert Rd., Sandymount, Dublin. *T.:* Dublin 683944. [*Died* 13 *April* 1963.

NIXON, Wilfrid Ernest, F.C.I.S.; retired as Chairman and Managing Director, de Havilland Holdings Ltd. and Director of individual de Havilland Companies, 1959; *b.* 1892; *m.*; one *s.* (and one *s.* killed serving in R.A.F., War of 1939-45, and two *d.* decd., 1958). Sec., de Havilland Aircraft Co. Ltd., when it was formed at Edgware, 1920; Director, 1931, Man. Dir., 1944, Chm., 1954. Hon. Companion, Roy. Aeronautical Soc., 1958; Liveryman, Guild of Air Pilots and Air Navigators, 1959. Formerly Mem. Mid Herts Group Hospital Management Cttee., and various Sub-Committees; Part-time Member Eastern Electricity Board. Supporter of institutions such as National Trust, Zoological Society, London, etc. *Recreations:* formerly all forms of sport and is still interested. *Address:* The Grange, Harpenden, Herts. *T.:* Harpenden 3040. [*Died* 26 *Sept.* 1970.

NIXON, William Charles Wallace, C.B.E. 1965; M.D.; F.R.C.S.; F.R.C.O.G.; Professor of Obstetrics and Gynæcology, Univ. of London, and Dir., Obstetric Unit, University College Hosp., since 1946; *b.* 22 Nov. 1903; *s.* of Professor William Nixon, Malta University. *Educ.:* Epsom College; St. Mary's Hospital. Epsom Scholar, St. Mary's Hospital, 1922; Obstetric Surgeon, St. Mary's Hospital, 1934, and Queen Charlotte's Hospital, 1935; Professor of Obstetrics, Hong Kong University, 1935; Surgeon, Soho Hospital for Women, 1938; Professor of Obstetrics, Istanbul University, 1943. Foundation Mem. Chinese Obstetrics Soc., 1936; Hon. Member: Athens Obstetrics Soc.; French Gynæcological Soc.; Gynæcological Soc., Uruguay; Roy. Belgian Soc. of Obstetrics and Gynæcology; Turkish Obstetric Soc.; Società Italiana di Ostetricia e Ginecologia. Petrus Pazmany Commemorative Medal, Budapest Univ. 1947; Commemorative Medal, Université Libre de Bruxelles, 1954; Hon. M.D. Univ. of Bristol, 1961. Examr. in Obstetrics and Gynæcology, Univs. of London Cambridge, Durham. *Publications:* A guide to Obstetrics in General Practice. 1954; Childbirth, 1962; contrib. to medical journals. *Recreations:* swimming, shooting. *Address:* University College Hospital, Gower Street, W.C.1. *T.:* Euston 5050. *Club:* Savage. [*Died* 9 *Feb.* 1966.

NOBBS, Percy Erskine, M.A., D.Litt., F.R.I.B.A., R.C.A.; architect; *b.* Haddington, Scotland, 11 Aug. 1875; 3rd *s.* of John L. Nobbs, of Petersburg, and Agnes Fletcher Brown, of Haddington; *m.* Mary Cecilia, *e. d.* of Francis J. Shepherd, M.D., of Montreal; one *s.* one *d.* *Educ.:* Edinburgh Collegiate School; Edinburgh University; pupil Sir Robert Lorimer, R.S.A. M.A. Edin. Univ., D.Litt. McGill Univ., Montreal. Served throughout War of 1914-18; rank Major; Professor in Architecture, McGill Univ., 1903-1940; Past Pres., Province of Quebec Assoc. of Architects, Town Planning Institute of Canada, Royal Architectural Institute of Canada, Royal Canadian Academy and Province of Quebec Assoc. for the Protection of Fish and Game; founded Atlantic Salmon Assoc., Montreal, 1948. *Works:* The Union and Macdonald Engineering Building at McGill; Univ. Club, and Protestant Board Schools, Montreal; Arts Building, Univ. of Alberta, Edmonton; Naval Monuments, Halifax. *Publications:* Salmon Tactics; Fencing Tactics; Design. *Recreations:* fencing, angling. *Address:* 38 Belvedere Rd., Westmount, Montreal. *Club:* University Montreal). [*Died* 5 *Nov.* 1966.

NOBLE, Dennis; Baritone, Grand Opera; *b.* 25 Sept. 1898; *m.* 1960, Mrs. Sylvia McCormack; previously widower; no *c.* *Educ.:* Choir School of Bristol Cathedral. Served European War, 1914-18. Has sung at Covent Garden, on the Continent and in America. Sang lead in Waltzes from Vienna, both in London and New York. Took part of Earl of Essex in a production of Merrie England, Prince's Theatre. Was for four years Lay Vicar at Westminster Abbey. Professor of Singing, Guildhall School of Music and Drama, until December 1959, now at Royal Irish Academy of Music. Is one of the artists who started broadcasting in Marconi House. *Recreations:* cricket and gardening. *Address:* Royal Irish Academy of Music, Dublin. *Clubs:* Savage, M.C.C. [*Died* 14 *March* 1966.

NOBLE, Frederick A. W.-; *see* Williamson-Noble.

NOBLE, Sir Humphrey Brunel, 4th Bt., *cr.* 1902; M.B.E. 1946; M.C.; Major, late Northumberland Hussars; *b.* 9 May 1892; *s.* of Sir Saxton Noble, 3rd Bt. and Celia Brunel (*d.* 1962) (author of The Brunels, Father and Son, 1938), *d.* of Arthur James of Eton Coll.; *S.* father, 1942; *m.* 1926, Celia, *d.* of late Capt. Stewart Weigall, R.N.; two *s.* one *d.* *Educ.:* Eton; King's Coll., Cambridge (M.A.). Served European War, Northumberland Hussars, 7th Division, 1914-19 (despatches twice, M.C., Order of Leopold of Belgium, Belgian Croix de Guerre); served War, 1940-45. High Sheriff of Northumberland, 1956. *Recreations:* Tennis, hunting, music. *Heir: s.* Major Marc Brunel Noble, late Royal Dragoons [*b.* 8 Jan. 1927; *m.* 1956, Jennifer Lorna, *yr. d.* of late John Mein Austin, Flinthill, West Haddon, Northants., and late Mrs. R. B. Butler, Castle Carrock, Cumberland; two *s.* one *d.*]. *Address:* Walwick Hall, Humshaugh, Northumberland. *Clubs:* Athenæum Beefsteak, Northern Counties. [*Died* 14 *Aug.* 1968.

NOBLE, Rev. Walter James, D.D.; *b.* Darlington, 2 Feb. 1879; *s.* of James and Ellen Noble; *m.* 1904, Elizabeth Annie Bewick; three *s.* one *d.* *Educ.:* Grammar School, Darlington; Didsbury College, Manchester. Entered the Ministry of the Wesleyan Methodist Church, 1900, and went to Ceylon as a missionary same year, working in Vernacular and English for 22 years; from 1922 to 1947 a Gen. Sec. of the Wesleyan Methodist (now Methodist) Missionary Society, with charge of Home Organisation till 1927, subsequently with charge of the Society's work in India, Ceylon, Burma, South and West Africa and Europe; has visited the Middle East, South Africa, and the U.S.A., in the interests of the work; Vice-President of British and Foreign Bible Society; Chairman Standing Committee of Conference of British Missionary Soc., 1937-42; Pres. Conference of Methodist Church, 1942-43. *Publications:* Christ and the Changing World, 1926; World Service, 1927; Ploughing the Rock, 1928; Yarns of Ceylon, 1929; The Black Trek, 1930; Christian Union in South India, 1936; Guidance, 1936; Flood Tide in India, 1937; Pollard of Stone-Gateway, 1937; Something to Remember (autobiography), 1957. *Recreations:* walking, reading, especially history and poetry. *Address:* 59 Central Avenue, Herne Bay, Kent. *T.:* Herne Bay 1277. [*Died* 21 *Feb.* 1962.

NOCK, Arthur Darby, M.A.; Hon. LL.D. Birmingham; Dr. (*h.c.*) Paris; Litt. D., Jewish Theological Seminary of America; Corr. F.B.A.; Editor Harvard Theological Review; Frothingham Professor of History of Religion in Harvard University since 1930; a Senior Fellow, Society of Fellows, since 1937; *b.* 21 Feb. 1902; *s.* of late Cornelius Nock and Alice Page; unmarried. *Educ.:* Portsmouth Grammar School; Trinity College, Cambridge. Waddington University Scholar and Members' Prizeman for Latin Essay, 1920; Chancellor's Medal for Classics, 1923; Fellow of Clare College, Cambridge, 1923-30; University Lecturer in Classics, 1926-30; visiting Lecturer at Harvard University, 1929; Donnellan Lecturer at Trinity College, Dublin, 1931; Lowell Lecturer at King's Chapel, Boston, 1933; Swander Lecturer at Seminary of Reformed Church, Lancaster, Pennsylvania, for 1938; Gifford Lecturer at Aberdeen, 1939, 1946; Haskell Lect., Oberlin, 1942; Corr. Member Berlin, Göteborg, Lund, Munich, Oslo, Stockholm (History and Antiquities) Academies; Hon. Mem. Soc. Roman Studies, Sodalicium Neotestamenticum Upsaliense, Soc. des Bollandistes; Member American Philosophical Society. *Publications:* Sallustius Concerning the Gods and the Universe, 1926; Early Gentile Christianity and its Hellenistic Background (in Essays on the Trinity and the Incarnation, ed. A. E. J. Rawlinson), 1928; Magical Texts from a bilingual papyrus in the British Museum (with H. I. Bell and Sir Herbert Thompson), 1932; Conversion, 1933; St. Paul, 1938; (with A. J. Festugière) Hermès Trismégiste, 1946-54 (vols. I-II had Prix du Budget of Académie des Inscriptions); contribs. Pauly-Wissowa, Cambridge Ancient History, learned jls., etc.; joint-editor, Oxford Classical Dictionary, 1949; associate editor, Vigiliae Christianae. *Recreation:* travel. *Address:* Eliot House, Harvard University, Cambridge, Mass., U.S.A. *Clubs:* Century (New York); Odd Volumes (Boston). [*Died* 11 *Jan.* 1963.

NOON, Firoz Khan, (K.C.S.I. 1941; K.C.I.E. 1937; Kt. 1933); M.A. (Oxon.); Leader, Republican Party, Pakistan, from 1958; M.P., Pakistan, from 1955; *b.* 7 May 1893; *s.* of late Hon. Nawab Sir Malik Mohammed Hayat Khan Noon, Kt., C.S.I.; *m.* Alam Khatoon; three *s.* two *d.*; *m.* 1945, Elizabeth Rikh. *Educ.:* Aitchison Chiefs' Coll., Lahore; Wadham Coll., Oxford. Called to the Bar, Inner Temple, London. Advocate Lahore High Court, 1917-26; Member of the Punjab Legislature, 1920-36; Minister for Local Self-Government, Punjab Government, 1927-30; Minister for Education and Medical and Public Health, Punjab, 1931-36; High Commissioner for India in United Kingdom, 1936-41; Labour Member of Viceroy's Executive Council, India, 1941-42, Defence Member, 1942-45; Indian rep., British War Cabinet, 1944-45; Member Punjab Provincial Legislature and All Pakistan Constituent Assembly and Legislature, 1947-50; Governor of East Pakistan, 1950-53; Leader (elected) Punjab Moslem League, 1953; Chief Minister of West Punjab, 1953-55; Foreign Minister, Pakistan, 1956-57; Prime Minister, Minister for Foreign Affairs and Commonwealth Relations, and Minister of Interior, Pakistan, 1957-Oct. 1958; former Member: Governing Body of I.L.O., Geneva; Perm. Cttee. Int. Inst. of Agriculture, Rome; Int. Rubber Regulation Cttee.; Int. Tea Cttee; Imperial Economic Cttee.; Int. Sugar Council, London; Imperial Communication Advisory Council; Imperial Shipping Cttee.; Hon. Fellow of Wadham College, Oxford; Hon. LL.D. Toronto, Can., 1938. *Publications:* Canada and India, 1939; Wisdom from Fools, 1940; Illustrated "India," 1940; Scented Dust, 1941. *Address:* Al Viqar, Lahore, Pakistan. [*Died* 9 *Dec.* 1970.

NORBURY, Captain Herbert Reginald, C.B. 1919; R.N.; *b.* 21 May 1876; *s.* of late Sir Henry Norbury, K.C.B.; *m.* 1924, Violet Catherine (*d.* 1967), *d.* of late Adrian Hope and *widow* of Lt.-Commander Herbert F. Guinness, R.N. *Educ.:* H.M.S. Britannia. Captain, 1913; served European War. Order of Rising Sun, Japan); retired list, 1923. *Address:* 88 Albion Gate, W.2. *T.:* Paddington 9313. *Club:* United Service. [*Died* 15 *March* 1967.

NORBURY, Lionel Edward Close, O.B.E., M.B., B.S., F.R.C.S. (Eng.); Consulting Surgeon, Royal Free Hospital, St. Mark's Hospital, West Middlesex Hospital, and Belgrave Hospital for Children; late Member Council Royal College of Surgeons (late Vice-President); *b.* Cape of Good Hope, Jan. 1882; *s.* of late Sir Henry Norbury, K.C.B.; *m.* 1915, Grace, *d.* of A. W. Rogerson, Lewes; four *d.* *Educ.:* Merchant Taylors' School; St. Thomas's Hospital (Tite and Peacock Scholar); Cheselden Medal for Surgery, Beaney Scholarship in Surgery and Surgical Pathology and Treasurer's Gold Medal; Lecturer on Surgery, Royal Free

Hospital; late Resident Assistant Surgeon and Surgical Registrar, St. Thomas's Hospital; late Assistant Surgeon, Mildmay Hospital; Surgeon, British Red Cross Hospital, Netley; Capt., R.A.M.C., 1914-19; Fellow, Royal Society of Medicine; President, Sub-Section Proctology, 1930-31; Fellow Assoc. of Surgeons, Great Britain; Fellow, Medical Soc. of London (President), Hunterian Soc. (Life Fellow) and Harveian Soc. (President) and Medico-Legal Soc.; Hunterian Prof., 1941, late Member Court of Examiners, and Bradshaw Lecturer, 1948, Royal College of Surgeons; Late Arris and Gale Lecturer, Roy. College of Surgeons; Hunterian Orator Royal College of Surgeons, 1953; Orator Hunterian Society, 1955; Gordon-Watson Memorial Lecturer, R.C.S., 1959; Orator Med. Soc. of London, 1960. Medical Inspector in Nullity, 1913-63. Late Examiner in Surgery, Univs. of Liverpool and Belfast. Vice-Pres. Medico-Legal Society. Liveryman, Society of Apothecaries; Freeman of City of London. *Publications:* Cardiac Massage as a Means of Resuscitation; The Sigmoidoscope and some of its uses; Treatment of certain Atonic and Atrophic conditions of the Cæcum; Surgical treatment of Goitre; Multiple Primary Malignant Tumours; Cancer of the Colon, Cancer of the Rectum; Proctology throughout the Ages, 1948; The Hunterian Era: Its Influence on the Art and Science of Surgery, 1953; The Times of John Hunter, 1955. *Recreations:* motoring, tennis. *Address:* The Priors, Cowden, Nr. Edenbridge, Kent. *Club:* Internat. Sportsmen's. [*Died* 31 *Oct.* 1967.

NORDHOFF, Heinrich; Grand Cross of German Federal Order of Merit, with Sash and Star, 1964; Grand Cross, Distinguished Service Order, with Star, 1955; Chairman, Administrative Council, Deutsche Automobil Gesellschaft; President of the Volkswagen enterprise; *b.* Hildesheim, Germany, 6 January 1899; *s.* of Johannes Nordhoff and Ottilie Lauenstein; *m.* 1930, Charlotte Fassunge; two *d.* *Educ.:* Hildesheim and Berlin. Diplom-Ingenieur, Technische Hochschule, Berlin-Charlottenburg, 1927. Served as Private in European War, 1914-18 (wounded). Bayerische Motoren-Werke, Munich, 1927-29; Opel Automobile Co., 1929-45; joined Volkswagen, 1948. Board of Directors of: Dresdner Bank, A.G. Hamburg; Deutsche Continental Gas-Gesellschaft, Düsseldorf; Frankfurter Versicherungs A.G., Frankfurt; Berlinische Feuerversicherungsanstalt, Munich; August Thyssen-Hutte A.G. Duisberg; Erste Allgemeine Unfall und Schadens-Versicherungs-Gesellschaft, Wien. Adv. Bd.: Braunschweigische Staatsbank, Brunswick; Allianz-Versicherüngs-AG, Munich. Vice-Pres., Verband der Automobilindustrie Frankfurt; B.D.I., Düsseldorf. Member, World Brotherhood, New York; Hon. Member Senate of Technische Universität, Berlin-Charlottenburg, 1951. Has hon. degrees and freemanships, also several awards and foreign decorations. *Address:* Volkswagenwerk A.G., Wolfsburg, Niedersachsen, Germany; (private) Kiefernweg 7, Wolfsburg, Han., Germany. [*Died* 12 *April* 1968.

NORFOLK, Rear-Admiral George Anthony Francis, C.B. 1959; D.S.O. 1952; *b.* Saltash, 4 April 1907; *s.* of late Comdr. Stanley Bernard Norfolk, R.N. and late Mary Carmen Norfolk (*née* Galliano); *m.* 1941, Mary Joan, *d.* of late Adolphus Matthews, Chignal Smealey, Essex; no *c.* *Educ.:* St. George's College, Weybridge; R.N. Colleges, Osborne and Dartmouth. Joined R.N. as Naval Cadet, Osborne, 1921; specialised in Torpedo duties, H.M.S. Vernon, 1932; promoted Commander, 1939, whilst mine-laying at Dover; commanded: H.M.S. Agamemnon, mine-layer, 1941; H.M.S. Whelp (British Pacific Fleet for final phase War with Japan), 1944-46; Captain, 1947; Supt. Torpedo Experiment and Design, 1948-50; Comd. H.M.S. Black Swan (and Capt. (F) 3rd Frigate Squadron) on Far East station (Korean War), 1950-52; Director, Trade Div. Naval Staff, Admiralty, 1952-54; Chief of Staff to C.-in-C. Far East Station (as Commodore 1st Cl.), 1954-56; Rear-Adm. 1957; Deputy Chief of Naval Personnel (Personal Services), Admiralty, 1957-May 1959; Director-General Personal Services and Officer appts., May-July 1959; retired, 1959. Joined Staff of McKinsey & Co. Inc., Management Consultants, 1960. Younger Brother of Trinity House. *Recreations:* swimming, shooting, talking, amateur dramatics, dancing and skylarking. *Address:* (business) McKinsey & Co. Inc., 25 St. James's Street, S.W.1. *T.:* Trafalgar 8040; (home) Park Cottage, Burhill Park, Walton-on-Thames, Sy. *T.:* Walton-on-Thames 20206. *Clubs:* United Service; R.N.R. (Officers); Royal Naval (Portsmouth); Burhill Golf; Seven Seas. [*Died* 11 *Feb.* 1966.

NORMAN, Brigadier-General Claude Lumsden, D.S.O. 1917; M.V.O. 1908; D.L. Somerset, 1931; *b.* 19 Feb. 1876; *y. s.* of late Field-Marshal Sir H. W. Norman, G.C.B., G.C.M.G., C.I.E.; *m.* 1905, Emlyn Margaret (*d.* 1961), *o. d.* of late Sir Alfred Reynolds, of Ayot Bury, Welwyn, Herts; one *s.* one *d.* *Educ.:* Marlborough. Gazetted 2nd Lieut. 1896; Bt. Lt.-Col. 1915; Bt. Col. 1918; in charge Indian Orderly Officers to the King, 1908; served N.W. Frontier of India, 1897-98, operations of the Samana, and in the Kurram Valley (medal with 2 clasps); Tirah, 1897-8 (clasp); East Africa, 1903-4, operations in Somaliland (medal with clasp, despatches); European War, 1914-1918 (despatches, D.S.O.); A.D.C. 1918; retired, 1922. *Address:* Orchard Hill, Kingston St. Mary, Taunton, Somerset. *T.:* Kingston St. Mary 28427. [*Died* 3 *April* 1967.

NORMAN, Frederick, O.B.E. 1947; M.A.; F.S.A.; Academic Vice-President (formerly European Academic Director), Institute of European Studies (Chicago) since Oct. 1965; Mellon Professor, Univ. of Pittsburgh, 1966; Emeritus Prof., Univ. of London; Prof. and Head of Dept. of German at King's College, 1937-65; Director, Institute of Germanic Studies, Univ. of London, 1956-1965; Deputy Vice-Chancellor, Univ. of London, 1962-64; *b.* London, 23 November 1897; *s.* of late A. E. Norman and Jenny Norman; *m.* 1st, 1923, Elizabeth, M.A., F.B.Ps.S., Department of Psychological Medicine, Guy's Hospital (*d.* 1955), *d.* of Arthur A. and Cecil Elsie Dixon; one *d.*; 2nd, 1957, Martha Catherine, M.A., *d.* of late Robert Stewart McNicol, Helensburgh; one *d.* *Educ.:* Private School in London; abroad (Prisoner of War in Germany, 1914-18); Univ. Coll., London, 1919-22. Fellow of King's Coll. and of Univ. Coll., London; Corr. Mem. Deutsche Akademie für Sprache und Dichtung. Assist., later Lecturer in German, University College, London, 1922-30; Head of Department of German, Reading University, 1926-1930; Reader in Mediæval German, King's College and Univ. College, London, 1930-1937; served War of 1939-45, attached to Foreign Office, Sept. 1939-July 1945, latterly as liaison officer to Air Ministry, with hon. rank of Wing-Comdr.; Member of Senate, Univ. of London, 1938-66; Dean, Fac. of Arts, Univ. of London, 1946-50; Dean, Fac. of Arts, King's Coll., 1946-48. Member of Council, School of Slavonic and East European Studies, 1946- (Chm. 1949-65); former member of Governing Body of: School of Oriental and African Studies; Institute of Child Health; Inst. of Archæology (Dep. Chm.): Courtauld Inst.; Warburg Inst.; Mem. for Gt. Britain on Comité International Permanent des Linguistes since 1950; Acad. Planning Board, Univ. of Kent, 1960-65;

Court, Univ. of Kent; Anglo-Austrian Mixed Commn., 1962-; Governor, Sadler's Wells Foundation, 1964-66. Gold Medallist, Goethe Institut, Munich, 1964; prize as "Leading Foreign Germanist" from Deutsche Akademie für Sprache und Dichtung, 1965. *Publications:* (Special field of work: Germanic Antiquities and Mediæval Germanic Languages and Literatures); Henry Crabb Robinson and Goethe (2 vols.), 1929 and 1931; (with H. Röhl) Wörterbuch zur deutschen Literatur, 1931; Waldere, 1933; A Sketch of Old High German Grammar, 1949; articles and reviews in English, American and foreign learned journals; general editor (with Prof. A. H. Smith) Methuen's Old English Library, 1932-; ed. (with Prof. A. H. Smith) London Mediæval Studies and London Mediæval Studies Monograph Series, 1937-; ed.: Trans. Philological Society, 1937-40; Proc. 7th Internat. Congress of Linguists, London, 1952; Schiller Bicentenary Lectures, 1960; Hofmannsthal Studies in Commemoration, 1963; Hauptmann Centenary Lectures, 1964; Essays in German Literature I, 1965; editorial bd.: Euphorion, Anglia, Germanistik, Slavonic and East European Review. *Recreations:* music, travel. *Address:* 63 Yarnell's Hill, Oxford. *T.:* Oxford 42551. *Club:* Athenæum.
[*Died* 8 *Dec.* 1968.

NORMAN, Henry Gordon, C.M.G. 1944; retired; *b.* 4 March 1890; *s.* of Harry and Elizabeth Mary Norman, London, Eng.; *m.* Marie Murielle Hill (*d.* 1967), London, Eng.; two *s.* one *d.* Formerly Pres. Montreal Stock Exchange, Canada. *Address:* Hudson Heights, Quebec, Canada. *Club:* Whitlock Golf. [*Died* 27 *Nov.* 1967.

NORMAN, Ronald Collet; *b.* 1873; 2nd *s.* of late F. H. Norman of Moor Place, Much Hadham, Herts; *m.* 1904, Lady Florence Sibell Bridgeman (*d.* 1936), *d.* of 4th Earl of Bradford; three *s.* two *d.* *Educ.:* Eton; Trinity Coll., Cambridge. Assistant Private Secretary to Rt. Hon. G. Wyndham, 1899; Private Secretary to Lord Chancellor (Earl of Halsbury), 1900-5; Member of the L.C.C., 1907-22; Alderman, 1922-34; Chairman, 1918-19; Vice-Chairman of British Broadcasting Corp., 1933-35, Chairman, 1935-39; Member of Royal Fine Art Commission, 1934-49; Vice-Chairman of National Trust, 1924-48, Vice-President 1948; Vice-President of National Council of Social Service. *Address:* Moor Place, Much Hadham, Herts. *Club:* Athenæum. [*Died* 5 *Dec.* 1963.

NORMANBROOK, 1st Baron, *cr.* 1963, of Chelsea; **Norman Craven Brook,** P.C. 1953; G.C.B. 1951 (K.C.B. 1946; C.B. 1942); Chairman of Governors of the B.B.C. since 1964; Director: B.O.A.C. since 1964; Barclays Bank since 1963; Tube Investments since 1963; *b.* 29 April 1902; *s.* of late Frederick Charles Brook; *m.* 1929, Ida Mary Goshawk. *Educ.:* Wolverhampton School; Wadham Coll., Oxford. Hon. Fell. Wadham Coll., 1949. Entered Home Office, 1925; Principal, 1933; Asst. Sec., 1938; Principal Private Secretary to Sir John Anderson when Lord Privy Seal, 1938-39, and when Home Secretary, 1939-40; Principal Assistant Secretary, 1940; Personal Asst. to Sir John Anderson when Lord President of the Council, 1940-42; Deputy Secretary (Civil) to the War Cabinet, 1942; Permanent Secretary, Office of Minister of Reconstruction, 1943-45; Additional Secretary to the Cabinet, 1945-46; Secretary of the Cabinet, 1947-62; Joint Secretary of the Treasury and Head of the Home Civil Service, 1956-62. Trustee, British Museum, 1963; Member Advisory Council on Public Records, 1964. Hon. LL.D. Bristol Univ., 1954; Birmingham Univ., 1958; Cambridge Univ., 1960; Hon. D.C.L., Oxford Univ., 1961. *Recreation:* golf. *Heir:* none. *Address:* 11 The Vale, S.W.3. *T.:* Flaxman 9553. *Clubs:* Oxford and Cambridge; Royal and Ancient (St. Andrews); Woking.
[*Died* 15 *June* 1967 (*ext.*).

NORMAND, Baron (Life Peer), *cr.* 1947, of Aberdour; **Wilfrid Guild Normand,** P.C. 1933; K.C. 1925; a Lord of Appeal in Ordinary, 1947-53; Lord Justice General of Scotland and Lord Pres. of Court of Session, 1935-1947; *b.* 1884; *s.* of late Patrick Hill Normand of Whitehill, Aberdour, Fife; *m.* 1st, 1913, Gertrude Lawson (*d.* 1923); one *s.* one *d.*; 2nd, 1927, Marion Cunningham. *Educ.:* Fettes College, Edinburgh; Oriel College, Oxford; Paris; Edinburgh University. Admitted to the Faculty of Advocates, 1910; served in the Royal Engineers, 1915-18; Editor of the Juridical Review, 1920; contested (U.) West Edinburgh, 1929; M.P. (U.) West Edinburgh, 1931-35; Solicitor-General for Scotland, 1929, and 1931-33; Lord-Advocate for Scotland, 1933-35; Hon. Bencher of Middle Temple since 1934; Hon. Fellow Oriel College, 1935; Hon. Fellow University College, London, 1952; Hon. LL.D. Edin., 1936; President Classical Association of Scotland, 1938; Trustee of National Library of Scotland, 1925-46, 1953-; Trustee of British Museum, 1950-53; Chairman Trustees, Scot. Nat. Museum of Antiquities, 1954-60; Mem. Advisory Cttee., Scot. Nat. Museum, 1954-59; Pres. Internat. Law Assoc., 1954-55. *Address:* 6 Succoth Pl., Edinburgh. *Club:* New (Edinburgh).
[*Died* 5 *Oct.* 1962.

NORMAND, Robert Casley, C.M.G. 1962; Director of Statutory Consolidation for Victoria, Australia, since 1955; *b.* 16 March 1897; *s.* of Robert Normand, Kew, Vic.; *m.* 1928, Estelle May, *d.* of Edgar Fullwood, Canterbury, Vic.; two *s.* *Educ.:* Melbourne High School; Univ. of Melbourne. Served European War, 1914-18, with A.I.F. in Middle East, France and Flanders (M.M.); commnd. 1918. LL.B. Melb. 1921; admitted to Victorian Bar, 1922; Parliamentary Draftsman for Victoria, 1935-55. *Publications:* various articles in Australian Law Journal. *Recreation:* horticulture. *Address:* 33 Trafalgar St., Mont Albert E.10, Vic., Australia. *T.:* 89-2264.
[*Died* 11 *Oct.* 1962.

NORMANTON, 5th Earl of (*cr.* 1806), **Edward John Sidney Christian Welbore Ellis Agar;** Baron Somerton, 1795; Viscount Somerton, 1800; Baron Somerton (U.K.), 1873; Capt. late Royal Horse Guards; *b.* 29 March 1910; *o. s.* of 4th Earl and Lady Amy Frederica Alice Byng (*d.* 1961), *d.* of 4th Earl of Strafford, K.C.V.O.; S. father, 1933; *m.* 1st, 1937, Hon. Mrs. Prior-Palmer (from whom he obtained a divorce, 1943), *o. d.* of Sir Frederick Frankland, 10th Bt., and Baroness Zouche; 2nd, 1944, Lady Fiona Fuller, 2nd *d.* of 4th Marquis Camden; two *s.* *Educ.:* Eton; Cambridge (B.A.). *Heir:* *s.* Viscount Somerton. *Address:* Somerley, Ringwood, Hants. *T.A.:* Ringwood. *T.:* Ringwood 3253. *Clubs:* Turf, White's, Royal Ocean Racing; Royal Yacht Squadron. [*Died* 28 *Jan.* 1967.

NORRIS, Arthur Gilbert, C.B.E. 1952 (O.B.E. 1946); *b.* 16 Oct. 1889; *y. s.* of William Arthur Norris and Mary Hannah Beck; *m.* 1919, Grace Mary Sullivan; one *s.* one *d.* *Educ.:* Gresham's School, Holt. Admitted Solicitor, 1913; entered Public Trustee Office, 1914; Chief Administrative Officer, 1944; Assistant Public Trustee, 1949-52; retired, 1952. Served European War, 1914-18; Temporary Lieut. Royal Marines; served in R.M. Bn. which landed from H.M.S. Vindictive at Zeebrugge, 1918 (despatches), and also in N. Russia (Murmansk). *Recreation:* country life. *Address:*

Meyrick Park Mansions, Bodorgan Road, Bournemouth. [*Died* 7 *Dec.* 1962.

NORRIS, Donald Craig, M.D., B.S., L.R.C.P. (London); F.R.C.S. (England); Barrister-at-Law (Inner Temple); Chief Medical Officer, Metropolitan Water Board and Lee Conservancy Board, Royal Exchange Assurance, Royal London Mutual Insurance Society and Employers' Liability Assurance Corporation; late Medical Officer, Bank of England; Medical Referee to various Insurance Cos.; Past Chairman Advisory Medical Council, Industrial Welfare Soc.; Member Editorial Bd., Brit. Jl. of Industrial Medicine; Assoc. Ed., Medico-Legal Jl.; Founder Member (Exec. Cttee.) British Council for Rehabilitation of the Disabled; *s.* of Charles Alfred Norris and Elizabeth Craig; *m.* Hélène Righthouse (*d.* 1958), M.D. Geneva, L.M.S.S.A. London; one *s.* *Educ.:* Aske's, Hatcham, School; Univ. College, London; London Hospital; Univ. of Paris. Served in French Army as Stretcher-Bearer, 1914-15, and in Serbian Red Cross during Typhus Epidemic, 1915; Order of St. Sava (Serbia), 1915. Captain R.A.M.C. 1916-20 (India, Mesopotamia, East Africa, France); late House Surgeon, London Hospital, Senior Resident Medical Officer, Poplar Hospital for Accidents (2 years) and Tutor and Lecturer, Insurance Institute of London (15 years); Pres. Hunterian Society, 1937-38; Pres., Assurance Medical Society, 1959-60. Major, 39th County of London (M.W.B.) Bn. Home Guard; Incident M.O. Corp. of London (A.R.P. Dept.). *Publications:* A Red Cross Unit in Serbia, 1916; The Nervous Element in Accident Claims (Transactions of Assurance Medical Society, 1932); Industrial Accidents, Medical Examinations and Reports, and Malingering, British Encyclopædia of Medical Practice, 1937, 2nd Edn., 1951; Physically Handicapped Persons and Employment (British Journal of Physical Medicine and Industrial Hygiene, Oct. 1942). *Recreations:* making and mending all sorts of things. *Address:* 53 Portland Place, W.1. *T.:* Langham 6906. *Club:* Athenæum. [*Died* 17 *Jan.* 1968.

NORRIS, Francis Edward Boshear, C.B.E. 1920; F.R.S.A.; F.G.S., F.R.G.S., F.Z.S.; *o. s.* of late Francis Boshear Norris, Charmouth, Dorset, and Rosalind Hodge, Sidmouth, Devon; *m.* 1916, Nancy (*d.* 1960), *er. d.* of Frank William Jenkins, Aylesbury; one *s.* *Educ.:* Park House, Southborough; Rugby School; Corpus Christi Coll., Oxford. After some years of geological research at Oxford established an Observatory at Guildford for the recording and study of earthquakes; this was brought to an end by European War, during which undertook administrative Red Cross work; Red Cross County Director for Surrey, 1918-19 (C.B.E.); took up social welfare work. During and after Nazi War, made systematic photograph records of Church Buildings. *Recreations:* music, photography, stamps, coins. *Address:* Sunnylands House, Pinhoe, nr. Exeter, Devon. *T.:* Exeter 67388. [*Died* 21 *Dec.* 1966.

NORRIS, Rt. Rev. Ivor Arthur, D.D. (St. John's College, Manitoba); Bishop of Brandon since 1950; *b.* 9 July 1901; *m.* 1930, Madeline Grace Thomas, *d.* of first Bishop of Brandon; two *s.* *Educ.:* St. John's College, Winnipeg; King's College, London, Eng. Curate, All Saints, Winnipeg, 1926; Rector of Christ Church, Russell, 1930; Neepawa, 1935; St. George's, Brandon, 1938; Hon. Canon, 1938. Served War of 1939-45, Chaplain, R.C.A.F., 1940. Archdeacon of Brandon, 1947. Prolocutor Provincial Synod of Rupert's Land, 1949. *Address:* Bishop's Lodge, Brandon, Manitoba, Canada. *T.:* 2632. [*Died* 24 *Jan.* 1969.

NORRIS, John Alexander, C.M.G. 1936; *b.* 28 March 1872; *m.* 1901, Ellen Heffernan, Sunbury; one *s.* one *d.* (and one *s.* killed in action, 1944). Entered State Service of Victoria, 1885; Auditor General of Victoria, 1919-37; retired, 1937. *Recreation:* golf. *Address:* 60 Queens Road, Melbourne, Australia. *Club:* Roy. Melb. Golf. [*Died* 23 *July* 1962.

NORRIS, Kathleen; *b.* San Francisco, California, 16 July 1880; *d.* of James Alden Thompson and Josephine Moroney; *m.* 1909, Charles Gilman Norris (*d.* 1945); one *s.* *Educ.:* Home. Early years in Mill Valley, a small mountain village in California; orphaned in 1900; Librarian, Social Worker, and Newspaper Writer. *Publications:* Novels: Mother, 1911; The Rich Mrs. Burgoyne, 1912; Poor Dear Margaret Kirby, 1913; Saturday's Child, 1914; The Treasure, 1914; The Story of Julia Page, 1915; The Heart of Rachel, 1916; Martie the Unconquered, 1917; Undertow, 1917; Josselyn's Wife, 1918; Sisters, 1919; Harriet and the Piper, 1920; The Beloved Woman, 1921; Lucretia Lombard, 1922; Certain People of Importance, 1922; Butterfly, 1923; The Callahans and the Murphys, 1924, Rose of the World 1924; Noon, 1925; Little Ships, 1925; The Black Flemings 1926; Hildegarde, 1926; The Sea Gull, 1927; Barberry Bush, 1927; My Best Girl, 1927; The Fun of Being a Mother, 1928; Outlaw Love, 1928; What Price Peace? 1928; Home, 1928; The Foolish Virgin, 1928; Mother and Son, 1929; Storm House, 1929; Red Silence, 1929; Passion Flower, 1930; Lucky Lawrences, 1930; Beauty in Letters, 1930; The Love of Julie Borel, 1931; Hands Full of Living, 1931; Belle-Mère, 1931; Second Hand Wife, 1932; Younger Sister, 1932; Treehaven, 1932; Walls of Gold, 1933; My California, 1933; Wife for Sale, 1933; Angel in The House, 1933; Tangled Love, 1933; My California, 1934; Victoria: a play, 1934; Manhattan Love Song, 1934; Three Men and Diana, 1934; Shining Windows, 1935; Tamara, 1935; Beauty's Daughter, 1935; Secret Marriage, 1936; The American Flaggs, 1936; Bread into Roses, 1937; You Can't Have Everything, 1937; Heartbroken Melody, 1938; Baker's Dozen, 1938; The Sea-Gull, 1938; The Runaway, 1939; Lost Sunrise, 1939; The World is Like That, 1940; The Mystery of The Marshbanks, 1940; These I Like Best, 1941; The Venables, 1941; An Apple for Eve, 1943; Corner of Heaven, 1944; Burned Fingers, 1945; Mink Coat, 1946; Over at the Crowleys, 1946; The Secret of Hillyard House, 1947; Christmas Eve, 1949; Mary-Joe, 1950; Shadow Marriage, 1952; Miss Harriett Townsend 1955; The Best of Kathleen Norris, 1955; Through A Glass Darkly, 1957; Family Gathering, 1959. *Address:* 1623 Palou Avenue, San Francisco 24, Calif., U.S.A. [*Died* 18 *Jan.* 1966.

NORRIS, His Honour Richard Hill; County Court Judge, Circuit no. 25, 1947-December 1958, retired; Deputy Chairman of Warwickshire Quarter Sessions, Supplementary List, June 1961: *b.* 1 June 1886; *o. s.* of Richard Hill Norris, M.D., and Emma Susan Norris; *m.* 1918, Maude Mary Parker; no *c.* *Educ.:* King Edward VI High School, Birmingham. Called to Bar, Middle Temple, 1911; Member of Midland Circuit until 1947. *Recreations:* fishing and gardening. *Address:* 62 Sir Harry's Rd., Edgbaston, Birmingham. *T.:* 021-440 2872. [*Died* 25 *March* 1970.

NORRITT, Sir James (Henry), Kt., *cr.* 1953; J.P.; D.L.; Director Cantrell & Cochrane Ltd., Mineral Water Manufacturers, since 1942, and of other associated companies; *b.* 27 Nov. 1889; unmarried. *Educ.:* Belfast. High Sheriff of Belfast, 1948-49; Deputy Lord Mayor of Belfast, 1949-50; Lord Mayor of Belfast, 1951-53. Pres. Ulster Industries Assoc., 1944-. Past Pres. Belfast Wholesale Merchants' and Manufacturers'

Assoc., 1948-54; Past Pres. Belfast Rotary Club; Past Dist. Chm. Irish Rotary; Past Chm. and Vice-Pres., Chartered Inst. of Secretaries, N.I. Branch; Mem. many Trade, Industrial and Business Assocs. in Belfast; Pres. Belfast Chamber of Commerce, 1958; Councillor for Shankill Ward, Belfast Corp., 1942-60. D.L. for City of Belfast, 1953, J.P. 1943; Freeman, City of Belfast, 1953. LL.D. (*h.c.*), Queen's University, Belfast, 1953. *Recreations:* interested in sports and youth activities; former Commissioner, Boy Scout Movement. *Address:* Glen-Wilten, 732 Antrim Road, Whitewell, Belfast, Northern Ireland. *T.:* Belfast 76963. *Clubs:* Constitutional; Ulster (Belfast). [*Died* 21 *July* 1963.

NORTH, Admiral Sir Dudley Burton Napier, G.C.V.O., *cr.* 1947 (K.C.V.O., *cr.* 1937; C.V.O. 1920); C.B. 1935; C.S.I. 1922; C.M.G. 1919; D.L.; Royal Navy, retd.; Extra Equerry to the Queen; *b.* 25 Nov. 1881; *s.* of late Col. Roger North, Royal Artillery; *m.* 1st, 1909, Eglantine (*d.* 1917), *d.* of Hon. William Campbell of Sydney, N.S.W., Australia; no *c.*; 2nd, 1923, Eilean, *d.* of late Edward Graham, J.P., Forston House, Dorchester; one *s.* three *d.* *Educ.:* H.M.S. Britannia; Mid., 1897; Lieutenant, 1903; Commander, 1914; Captain, 1919; Rear-Admiral, 1932; Vice-Admiral, 1936; Admiral, 1940; was 1st Lieut. of Battle Cruiser New Zealand at Battle of Heligoland, 1914; Commander of that ship during Battle of Dogger Bank, 1915, and Jutland, 1916. Commander of Russian Order of St. Stanislas with swords; French Croix de Guerre with Palme; Order of Rising Sun of Japan, 3rd Class; Order of the Nile, Egypt, 2nd Class; Order of Merit, Chile; Legion of Merit, U.S.A., Degree of Commander. Commanded H.M.S. Caledon, Revenge and Tiger; Director of the Operations Division, Admiralty Naval Staff, 1930-32; Chief of Staff, Home Fleet, 1932-33; Commanded H.M. Yachts, 1934-39; Vice-Admiral Comdg. Royal Squadron for T.M. Visit to Canada and U.S.A., 1939; Admiral Commanding North Atlantic Station, 1939-40; retd. 1942; Flag Officer-in-Charge Great Yarmouth, 1942-45; Major 1st Bn. Dorset Home Guard, 1942; a Younger Brother of Trinity House; Naval A.D.C. to Prince of Wales during Canadian Tour, 1919 (M.V.O.); Extra Equerry to Prince of Wales during tours to Australia, India, Japan, Africa and South America (C.V.O.); Extra Equerry-in-Waiting to Duke of Connaught during Indian Tour, 1920-1921; A.D.C. to the King, 1932; Extra Equerry to King George VI. D.L. Dorset 1952. *Address:* The Lodge, Parnham, Beaminster, Dorset. *Clubs:* Army and Navy; (Hon.) Royal Yacht Squadron (Cowes). [*Died* 15 *May* 1961.

NORTH, John Dudley, C.B.E. 1962; Chairman and Managing Dir. Boulton Paul Aircraft Ltd.; *b.* 2 Jan. 1893; *o. s.* of Dudley North and Marion Felgate; *m.* 1922, Phyllis Margaret Huggins; two *d.* *Educ.:* Bedford School. Began career in marine engineering: attracted to aviation in its earlier days, he joined Horatio Barber at Hendon and, later, the Grahame White Aviation Co., of which he became Chief Engineer. Designed G-W charabanc (for so long holder of world's passenger-carrying record) and a small single-seater, which was first British aircraft to loop. Joined Austin Motor Co. as Supt. Aircraft Dept., but in 1917 returned to design-work as Chief Engineer, Boulton & Paul Ltd., Norwich. There he worked on development of high-performance twin-engine bombers and on metal construction and armament. Boulton Paul Aircraft Ltd. was incorporated in 1934 to acquire aircraft dept. of Boulton & Paul Ltd., Coachmakers Livery. Hon. Fellow, Royal Aeronautical Society. Hon. D.Sc., Birmingham, 1967. *Recreation:* collection and cultivation of Alpine plants. *Address:* Eversley, Bridgnorth, Salop. *T.A.* and *T.:* Bridgnorth 3296. *Clubs:* Athenæum, Royal Aero. [*Died* 11 *Jan.* 1968.

NORTH, Roland Arthur Charles, C.M.G. 1946; *b.* 28 Jan. 1889; *s.* of late John William North, A.R.A., R.W.S.; *m.* 1928, Leo Catherine Greening; one *s.* one *d.* *Educ.:* Blundell's School; Balliol College, Oxford. Administrative Officer, Hong Kong Government Service, 1912-46; Secretary for Chinese Affairs, Hong Kong, 1936-46; retired, 1946. *Address:* La Vista, Blaxland Road, Wentworth Falls, N.S.W. *Club:* Royal Commonwealth Society. [*Died* 18 *June* 1961.

NORTHAM, Sir Reginald, Kt. 1961; C.B.E. 1954; Principal of Swinton Conservative College, Masham, since its foundation in 1948; *o. s.* of Samuel Northam, Hatherleigh and Exeter, Devon. *Educ.:* Queens' Coll., Cambridge. (M.A., LL.B.; Pres. Union, 1923). A Director of Studies, Cambridge. Called to Bar, Inner Temple, 1928. Formerly in Board of Trade; Parly. Cand. (C.) Batley and Morley, 1951, Hull West, 1955. *Publication:* Conservatism, the only way. *Address:* Radleigh House, Masham, Nr. Ripon, Yorks. *T.:* Masham 277; Swinton Conservative College, Masham. *T.:* Masham 230. *Club:* United University. [*Died* 19 *March* 1967.

NORTHCOTT, General Sir John, K.C.M.G. 1950; K.C.V.O. 1954 (M.V.O. 1927); C.B. 1941; p.s.c.; i.d.c.; Governor of New South Wales, 1946-57; Administrator, Commonwealth of Australia, 1951 and 1956; *b.* 24 March 1890; *s.* of John Northcott, Dean, Vict.; *m.* 1915, Winifred M. (*d.* 1960), *d.* of Archibald Paton, Kew, Victoria; two *d.* *Educ.:* Grenville College; Melbourne Univ. Lieut. 9th A.L.H., 1908; Adj. 12 Bn. A.I.F., 1914; severely wounded, Gallipoli; G.S.O. 5th Mil. Dist., 1918; Staff College, Camberley, 1923-25; Director of Supplies & Transport, A.H.Q., 1926; G.S.O. 3 Div., 1931; G.S.O. War Office, 1933; G.S.O. 44th (Home Counties) Div. 1934; Imperial Defence College, 1935; Committee Imperial Defence, 1936; Special duty in U.S.A. and Canada, 1936-37; Director of Military Intelligence and Operations, 1938; Military Adviser, Dominions War Conference, Lond., 1939; Deputy Chief of General Staff, Australia, 1939-41; Commander 1st Australian Armoured Div., 1941-42; Commander, 2nd Aust. Corps, Australia, 1942; Chief of the General Staff, Australia, 1942-45; commanded Empire Occupation Force in Japan, 1945-46; General, 1951. Chairman, Commonwealth Transport Committee, 1926-28; Commonwealth Staff Officer attached to Duke and Duchess of York's Staff, Royal visit, 1927. Honorary Air Commodore, R.A.A.F. Mem. Council, New England University. Hon. D.Litt.: Sydney Univ.; New England Univ.; Hon. D.Sc., Univ. N.S.W. K.St.J. 1946. *Recreations:* bowls, garden. *Address:* Water St., Wahroonga, New South Wales, Australia. *Clubs:* Union, Australian, Imperial Service, Sydney, (all in Sydney). [*Died* 4 *Aug.* 1966.

NORTHEN, Lieut.-Colonel Arthur, C.B.E. 1919; D.S.O. 1916; late South Lancashire Regt. and R.A.S.C.; *b.* 24 Oct. 1873; *m.* 1896, Ada Constance (marriage dissolved, 1925, she died 1946), *d.* of F. C. Winby, Portland Place, W.1.; one *s.* one *d.*; *m.* 1926, Germaine Marie Adèle, *d.* of Armand Belison, Paris. *Educ.:* Oundle. Served S. African War, 1899-1902 (Queen's medal with three clasps, King's medal with two clasps); attached I.A., 1904-08; European War, 1914-19 (despatches six times, Mons Star, D.S.O., Brevet Lieut.-Col., C.B.E.); Commandant, R.A.S.C. Training Estabt., 1918-20; retd. 1922; re-employed, 1940-41 (Medal); Capt. Home Guard,

Engineer, S.O.S., U.S.A. Army, 1942-45. *Address:* Villa Robert, Biarritz, France. [*Died* 29 *Aug.* 1964.

NORTHESK, 11th Earl of (*cr.* 1647), **David Ludovic George Hopetoun Carnegie;** Baron Rosehill, 1639; Hon. Major, Intelligence Corps; late 2nd Lt. Coldstream Guards; Representative Peer for Scotland, 1959-63; *b.* 24 Sept. 1901; *s.* of 10th Earl and Elizabeth (*d.* 1950), *d.* of Maj.-Gen. George Skene-Hallowes; *S.* father, 1921; *m.* 1st, 1923, Jessica Ruth (marriage dissolved, 1928), *d.* of late F. A. Brown, U.S.A.; 2nd, 1929, Elizabeth Vlasto; one adopted *d.* *Educ.:* Gresham's School, Holt. *Heir: cousin,* John Douglas Carnegie, *b.* 1895. *Address:* Bear Farm, Binfield, Bracknell, Berks. *T.:* Shurlock Row 286. *Club:* Kennel. [*Died* 7 *Nov.* 1963.

NORTHEY, Sir Armand (Hunter Kennedy Wilbraham), Kt. 1958; J.P.; Deputy Chairman, Wiltshire Quarter Sessions, since 1945; *b.* 16 Jan. 1897; *s.* of George Wilbraham Northey, D.L., J.P.; *m.* 1929, Mollie, *d.* of late Comdr. Percy Helyar, D.S.O.; one *s.* one *d.* *Educ.:* privately; Balliol College, Oxford. Barrister, Inner Temple, 1923. Employed Foreign Office, 1918-19; Admiralty, 1941-45. J.P. Wilts., 1936. *Address:* Cheney Cottage, Box, Wilts. *T.:* Box 592. *Clubs:* Carlton, M.C.C. [*Died* 30 *Dec.* 1964.

NORTHUMBERLAND, Helen, Dowager Duchess of, G.C.V.O., *cr.* 1938; C.B.E. 1920; Order of Mercy, 1942; *d.* of 7th Duke of Richmond and Gordon, K.G.; *m.* 1911, Earl Percy, afterwards Duke of Northumberland (*d.* 1930); three *s.* (and *e. s.* killed in action in Belgium, May 1940) two *d.* Mistress of the Robes to Queen Elizabeth the Queen Mother, 1937 - 64. *Address:* 114 Eaton Square, S.W.1. *T.:* Belgravia 3332; Lesbury House, Alnwick, Northumberland. *T.:* Alnmouth 330; Albury Park, Guildford. *T.:* Shere 16. [*Died* 13 *June* 1965.

NORTON, 6th Baron (*cr.* 1878), **Hubert Bowyer Arden Adderley;** *b.* 21 Feb. 1886; *s.* of 5th Baron and Grace Stopford Sackville of Drayton, Northants; *S.* father, 1945; *m.* 1912, Elizabeth (*d.* 1952), *d.* of W. J. Birkbeck; two *s.* three *d.* *Educ.:* Eton; R.M.C., Sandhurst. Lieut. Scots Guards, 1906-10; served European War, 1914-18, on staff and in M.G.C.; retired as Major, 1918. Lt.-Colonel Suffolk Home Guard, 1943-44. J.P. Co. Warwick. President Church Union, 1947-51; Member of House of Laity, Church Assembly; a lay guardian of the Sanctuary of Our Lady of Walsingham. *Heir: s.* Hon. John Arden Adderley [*b.* 24 Nov. 1915; *m.* 1946, Betty Margaret, *o. d.* of late James McKee Hannah; two *s.*]. *Address:* Fillongley Hall, Coventry, Warwickshire. *T.:* Fillongley 303. [*Died* 17 *Feb.* 1961.

NORTON, Sir Evan (Augustus), Kt. 1964; C.B.E. 1958; Senior Partner in firm of Wragge & Co., solicitors, Birmingham since 1928; *b.* 9 October 1901; *o. s.* of late William Joseph Norton and of Rose Norton; *m.* 1928, Mildred Anness Bryan Smith; one *s.* two *d.* *Educ.:* Balliol College, Oxford. B.A. 1922, M.A. 1933. Treas., 1925-48, and Dep. Chm., 1948-1953, Birmingham Civic Society; Director, Birmingham Repertory Theatre, 1935-53; Trustee, Sir Barry Jackson Trust, 1935-; Life Governor (Mem. Council and Treasurer, 1962-64), Birmingham University; Guardian of Assay Office, Birmingham, 1946-; Chm. General Hospital, Birmingham, 1951-53; Chm. Board of Governors, United Birmingham Hospitals, 1953-63, Deputy Chairman, 1963-; Trustee, Nuffield Provincial Hospitals Trust, 1957-; Chairman: Teaching Hospitals Assoc., 1961-65; The British Rollmakers Corporation Ltd., Charles Clifford Industries Ltd., Kalamazoo Ltd., Mercian Builders Merchants Ltd.; Director of Birmingham Industrial Trust Ltd. (Chm., 1959-1967), The Expanded Metal Co. Ltd., The Midland Assurance Ltd., Midland Caledonian Investment Trust Ltd., Richard Lloyd Ltd., and other Cos.; Mem. of Birmingham Committee of Lloyds Bank Ltd. *Recreations:* farming, gardening and foreign travel. *Address:* Carpenters Hill, Beoley, Nr. Redditch. *T.:* Redditch 2247; Windsor House, 3 Temple Row, Birmingham 2. *T.:* Central 0031. *Club:* Union (Birmingham). [*Died* 8 *Aug.* 1967.

NORTON, Colonel Gilbert Paul, C.B.E. 1950; D.S.O. 1916 and Bar 1918; T.D., M.A., F.C.A.; late Senior Partner of Armitage & Norton, Chartered Accountants; retd. as Chairman (late Man. Dir.) Yorkshire Copper Works, Leeds; *b.* 17 Aug. 1882; *s.* of George Pepler Norton, Highroyd, Honley, nr. Huddersfield; *m.* 1908, Daisy, *d.* of late Thompson Naylor, Huddersfield; one *s.* two *d.* *Educ.:* Shrewsbury School; Caius College, Cambridge. Joined firm of Armitage & Norton, Chartered Accountants, Huddersfield, London, Leeds, Bradford, etc., partner, 1906. On outbreak of European War volunteered for active service with territorial unit (5th Duke of Wellington's Regt.); served, 1915-18 (despatches thrice, D.S.O. and Bar); comd. 2/10th Manchester Regt. and 15th West Yorkshire Regt., Hon. Col. 5th Duke of Wellington's Regt. 1940-49. Formerly J.P., D.L., West Riding of Yorks. Joint Director of Finance, Wool Control, 1939-49. *Recreations:* hunting, fishing. *Address:* Edenbank, Wetheral, near Carlisle. [*Died* 6 *Jan.* 1962.

NORTON, Ven. Hugh Ross, O.B.E.; M.A.; *b.* 3 Apr. 1890; *y. s.* of George Everitt Norton, M.R.C.S., and Jane Helen, 2nd *d.* of Hugh Ross, Tobermory, Isle of Mull; *m.* 1922, Jessie Muriel (*d.* 1965), *y. d.* of G. H. Glover, Barbourne, Worcester; three *s.* one *d.* *Educ.:* Monkton Combe School; Wadham College, Oxford. Deacon, 1913; Priest, 1914; Asst. Curate St. Mary, Whitechapel, 1913-15; St. Dunstan, Stepney, 1915-19 (T.C.F. 1916-19, Egypt, Palestine, Mesopotamia); St. Benetfink, Tottenham, 1919-21; Precentor of Wakefield Cathedral, 1921-24; Chaplain to the Forces, Tidworth, 1924; Larkhill, 1926; Tientsin, 1929-33; York, 1933; Catterick, 1935; Palestine, 1936; Chaplain to the Brigade of Guards, 1938-44; S.C.F. London District, 1938; D.A.C.G., London District, 1940-44; A.C.G., Eastern Command, 1944; D.A.C.G., Aldershot and Hants Dist., 1944-1945. Hon. Chap. Bp. of Ripon, 1937; Rector of Horringer with Ickworth, Bury St. Edmunds, 1945-58; Canon Residentiary of St. Edmundsbury Cathedral, 1958-64. Archdeacon of Sudbury, 1945-62. Archdeacon Emeritus, 1962. *Recreation:* music. *Address:* 17B Northgate Street, Bury St. Edmunds, Suffolk. *T.:* 3006. [*Died* 10 *Jan.* 1969.

NORTON, Rt. Rev. John F.; *b.* Lucan, Co. Dublin, 30 Jan. 1891. Bishop of Bathurst (N.S.W.) (R.C.), from 1928. *Educ.:* Mungret Coll.; National Univ. of Ireland; All Hallows Coll., Dublin. Priest, 1915; went to Bathurst, 1915; Diocesan Inspector of Schools, Bathurst, 1921; Bishop's Secretary and Administrator of Cathedral, 1922-26; Bishop of Lunda and Coadjutor Bishop of Bathurst, 1926-28. LL.D. (*h.c.*) N.U.I. 1958; Freeman of Dublin, 1958. *Address:* Bishop's House, Bathurst, N.S.W., Australia. [*Died* 20 *June* 1963.

NORTON, William, T.D. for Kildare Irish Parliament since 1948, Member Council of State since 1938; *m.* Helena McNamee; five *c.* T.D. for Co. Dublin, 1926-27, for Kildare,

1932-37; for Carlow-Kildare, 1937-48, for Kildare, 1948-. First place in Ireland in P.O. Learners' Exam., 1916; P.O. Clerk, 1918; elected to Nat. Exec. of Post Office Workers' Union, 1920 (Hon. Organising Sec., 1922-23; Hon. Gen. Sec., 1923-24; full-time Sec. 1924-57). Pres. Exec. Council Postal and Telegraph and Telephone International. 1926-60 (President, 1959-60). Leader of Labour Party in Dàil, 1932-60. Tánaiste and Minister for Social Welfare, 1948-51; Tánaiste and Minister for Industry and Commerce, 1954-57. *Address:* 6 Merlyn Park, Ballsbridge, Dublin.

[*Died* 4 *Dec.* 1963.

NORWOOD, Sir Charles John Boyd, Kt., 1937; Chairman: Wellington Gas Company Ltd.; The Dominion Motors Ltd.; Governing-Director, C. B. Norwood Ltd.; Chm. Dirs., E. W. Mills Ltd.; *b.* Gympie, Queensland, 1871; *s.* of John Boyd and Marion Norwood, both of Belfast, Ireland; *m.* 1904, Rosina Ann (*d.* 1957), *d.* of George Tattle, Wellington, N.Z.; one *s.* two *d.* *Educ.:* Normal Schools, Gympie and Maryborough. Served his apprenticeship as Mechanical Engineer, and after a varied career, in which he became interested in mining and sugar plantations, came to Wellington, New Zealand, 1897, joining the Wellington Gas Company; subsequently appointed to Executive Staff; resigned 1912, and founded Dominion Motors Ltd. Member Wellington City Council, 1917-23; Mayor of Wellington, 1925-27; founder of Wellington City Milk Dept.; as Mayor was Founder and Chairman Wellington Fire Board; Founder and Pres. of Wellington Free Ambulance Service; Pres. The Australian Assoc.; Pres. Wellington Show Assoc.; Past-Pres. Wellington Manufacturers' Assoc., Wellington Chamber of Commerce, Navy League, and Rotary; Past Mem. Town Planning Board and Board of Health; for 35 years a Mem. Wellington Harbour Bd. (Chm., 1921-38); Pres. N.Z. Crippled Children Soc.; Chm. and Trustee, Nuffield Trust for Benefit of Crippled Children in N.Z.; Mem. Council, Internat. Soc. for Rehabilitation of the Disabled, New York. Mem. Inst. Directors, London. Patron various Wellington Sporting Assocs. *Address:* 9 Upland Road, Wellington, W.1, New Zealand. *Clubs:* Wellesley, Rotary (Wellington, N.Z.).

[*Died* 26 *Nov.* 1966.

NOSWORTHY, Sir Richard Lysle, K.C.M.G., *cr.* 1945 (C.M.G. 1936); Director Mercantile and General Reinsurance Co. Ltd.; *b.* 20 November 1885; *e. s.* of late Richard Nosworthy; unmarried. *Educ.:* Christ Church, Oxford. Vice-Consul, New York, 1911; Private Sec. to Sir A. Steel-Maitland, Additional Parliamentary Under-Secretary of State for Foreign Affairs, 1917-18; Acting Commercial Secretary, Washington, 1920; Consul, Turin, 1922; seconded for service on the Reparations Commission, 1927-30; Consul, Los Angeles, 1930-31; Envoy Extraordinary and Minister Plenipotentiary to Bolivia, 1931-34; Commercial Counsellor at Rome, 1934-40; seconded to the Treasury, 1940-42; Commercial Counsellor at Rio de Janeiro, 1942-44; Minister (Commercial) at Rome, 1944-46; retired, 1946; called to the Bar, Inner Temple, 1921. *Recreations:* mountaineering, gardening. *Address:* 35 Brompton Square, S.W.3. *Clubs:* Travellers', Beefsteak. [*Died* 25 *July* 1966.

NOTESTEIN, Wallace, M.A., Ph.D., Hon. Litt.D. (Harvard, 1939, Birmingham 1950, Yale, 1951); Hon. LL.D. (Glasgow) 1950; Hon. D.Litt (Oxford) 1958; Sterling Prof. of English History, Yale University, 1928-1947, Professor Emeritus since 1947; *b.* 16 Dec. 1878; *s.* of Professor J. O. Notestein, College of Wooster, and Margaret Wallace; *m.* 1943, Ada Comstock, Cambridge, Mass. *Educ.:* College of Wooster; Yale University. Assistant Professor History, Kansas University, 1905-8; Instructor History, 1908, Assistant Professor, 1910, Associate Professor, 1914, Professor, 1917-20, University of Minnesota; Research Assistant to Committee on Public Information, Washington, 1917; attached to U.S. State Dept., Washington, 1918, and American Commission to Negotiate Peace, Paris, 1919; Professor of English History, Cornell University, 1920-28; Member Treasury Committee on House of Commons Records, 1931-33; Eastman Professor Oxford University, 1949-50; Mem. American Philos. Soc.; Corres. F.B.A.; Corres. F.R.Hist.S.; Hon. Mem., Hist. Assoc. (London). *Publications:* History of English Witchcraft, 1913; Source Problems in Engl. Hist. (with A. B. White), 1915; Commons Debates, 1629 (with F. H. Relf), 1921; Sir Simonds D'Ewes's Journal of the Long Parliament, 1923; Winning of the Initiative by the House of Commons (Raleigh Lecture, British Academy), 1924; Commons Debates, 1621, 7 vols. (with F. H. Relf and H. Simpson), 1935; English Folk, A Book of Characters, 1938; The Scot in History, 1946; The English People on the Eve of Colonization, 1603-1630, 1954; Four Worthies, 1956. *Recreation:* chess. *Address:* 236 Edwards Street, New Haven, Conn., 06511, U.S.A. *Clubs:* Athenæum; Yale, Century (New York). [*Died* 1 *Feb.* 1969.

NOTTIDGE, Sir William Rolfe, Kt., *cr.* 1948; *b.* 22 Aug. 1889; *s.* of late Albert James Nottidge and late Keziah King; *m.* 1916, Gertrude Rachel Barcham Green (*d.* 1950); two *s.* two *d.* *Educ.:* Tonbridge School; St. John's Coll., Oxon (M.A.). Served European War, 1914-18, with Bedfordshire Regt. (despatches twice). Called to Bar, Lincoln's Inn, 1919. Mem. Kent C.C., 1928-58; Chairman 1952-58; J.P., D.L., Kent; Chairman Tonbridge Magistrates. Inter-Departmental Cttee. on Road Safety for School Children, 1935; Chairman Kent Education Committee, 1932-49; Rochester Bridge Warden since 1940. *Recreations* golf and gardening. *Address:* Fairmile, Tonbridge, Kent. *T.:* Tonbridge 2941. *Club:* County (Maidstone).

[*Died* 8 *June* 1966.

NOWELL, Air Cdre. Henry Edward, C.B. 1946; O.B.E. 1942; D.L.; Executive Officer to the Chm., The Hunting Group of Cos., since 1955; *b.* 15 Nov. 1903; *s.* of J. G. Nowell, Swindon, Wilts; *m.* 1st, 1931, Freda (marriage dissolved, 1962), *d.* of Alfred Mason, Swindon; two *s.*; 2nd, 1963, Pauline, *d.* of late Albert Biage, Montreal. *Educ.:* The College, Swindon; R.A.F. Apprentices School, Cranwell; R.A.F. Coll., Cranwell. Pilot Officer, 1924; R.A.F. Egypt, 1925-28; R.A.F. engineering course, 1929-31; R.A.F. India, 1934-37; Personnel Staff 22 Group, 1937-38; Army Staff College, Quetta, India, 1939; Senior Air Staff Officer, Peshawar, 1940-41; Joint Planning Staff, Delhi, 1942; Air Ministry, Air Staff Policy, 1943-44; R.A.F. Delegation, Washington, 1944-45; Commanded R.A.F., Moreton in Marsh, 1946-47; Deputy Head, British Joint Service Mission, (R.A.F.), Washington, 1948-1950; Assistant Commandant, R.A.F. Staff College, Bracknell, 1950-52; Director of N.A.T.O. Affairs, Air Ministry, 1953-54; Director of Organization (F.P.), Air Ministry, 1954-55; retired from R.A.F., 1955. A.F.R.Ae.S., 1959. D.L., Co. Berkshire, 1966. Commander of Legion of Merit (U.S.A.), 1946. *Recreations:* gardening, woodwork, golf. *Address:* c/o Lloyds Bank, West Drayton, Mddx. *Clubs:* R.A.F., United Hunts, R.A.F. Reserves.

[*Died* 1 *Feb.* 1967.

NOWELL, William, C.M.G. 1936; C.B.E. 1929; D.I.C.; *b.* Heptonstall, Yorkshire, 9 May 1880; *s.* of John and Elizabeth F. Nowell; *m.* 1st, Jennie (*d* 1933), *d.* of William Rushworth, Halifax; no *c.*; 2nd,

Dorothy Mary, *d.* of H. Willett Huxham, J.P., Bideford; one *s.* one *d.* *Educ.:* Halifax Municipal Technical School; Royal College of Science, S. Kensington. Assistant Superintendent, Dept. of Agriculture, Barbados; Mycologist and Agricultural Lecturer, Imperial Department of Agriculture for the West Indies; Assistant Director, Dept. of Agriculture, Trinidad and Tobago; Director of Science and Agriculture, British Guiana; Director of the East African Agricultural Research Station, Amani; retired 1936; Chairman W. African Cocoa Commission, 1938. Ed. of Empire Cotton Growing Review, 1940-57. Fellow, Imperial Coll. of Science and Technology. *Publications:* Diseases of Crop Plants in the Lesser Antilles, 1923; papers on Tropical Plant Pathology in West Indian Bulletin, Annals of Applied Biology and Annals of Botany. *Address:* 15 Thornden, Cowfold, Horsham, Sussex. [*Died* 1 *Oct.* 1968.

NUFFIELD, 1st Viscount, *cr.* 1938, of Nuffield; 1st Baron, *cr.* 1934; **William Richard Morris,** 1st Bt., *cr.* 1929; G.B.E. 1941 (O.B.E. 1917); C.H. 1958; F.R.S. 1939; F.R.C.S. 1948; M.A.; Hon. D.C.L. Oxon, 1931; Hon. LL.D. Sydney and Birmingham, 1938, London, 1947, Melbourne, 1949, Belfast, 1950; Hon. D.Sc. New South Wales Univ. of Technology, 1952; Hon. M.D. Pretoria University, 1958; D.L. Oxfordshire; K.St.J.; motor manufacturer; Chairman of Morris Motors Ltd., and its associated Cos., 1919-52; Hon. Pres. British Motor Corp., Ltd.; *b.* 10 Oct. 1877; *s.* of Frederick Morris, Oxford; *m.* 1904, Elizabeth Maud (*d.* 1959), *d.* of William Jones Anstey, Oxford; no *c.* *Educ.:* Cowley, Oxford. Hon. Freeman of Cities of Coventry, Worcester, Cardiff, Oxford, Droitwich and Whitehaven; of Borough of Rhondda; of Worshipful Society of Apothecaries of London; Freeman, Incorporation of Coopers of Glasgow, 1935; Hon. Member: British Medical Assoc.; British Orthopædic Assoc.; British Dental Assoc.; Hon. Company of Master Mariners; Worshipful Company of Grocers, 1955; Hon. Mem. City of Coventry Freemen's Guild, 1955; New Zealand Soc.; Roy. Naval Club, Portsmouth; Roy. Scottish Soc. of Arts; Oxford Union; Hon. Fellow of Pembroke College, Oxford, and of Worcester College, Oxford; Hon. F.F.A.R.C.S., 1953; Hon. F.R.C.O.G. 1956; Hon. Fell. R.A.C.S., 1959; Hon. President of Guy's Hospital; Vice-President Oxford Society; Life Governor or Vice-President of many hospitals and charitable institutions in Great Britain and Dominions; awarded Albert Gold Medal by Royal Society of Arts and Commerce, 1937; Hon. Medal, Roy. Coll. of Surg. of Eng., 1942; Colyer Gold Medal, Roy. Coll. of Surg. of Eng., 1957; Albert Lasker Award by Internat. Soc. for the Welfare of Cripples, 1957; Golden Heart Award by the Variety Club of Gt. Britain, 1958. *Relevant Publication:* The Nuffield Story, by Robert Jackson, 1964. *Recreation:* golf. *Heir:* none. *Address:* Nuffield Place, nr. Henley-on-Thames. *Clubs:* Leander (Hon. Mem.), Royal Aero, Royal Automobile; Royal Scottish Automobile (Glasgow). [*Died* 22 *Aug.* 1963 (*ext.*).

NUGEE, Francis John, M.C., M.A.; Headmaster of Eastbourne College, 1938-56; *b.* 30 May 1891; *e. s.* of late Canon F. E. Nugee; *m.* 1930, Lucy Maud, 3rd *d.* of late Charles Smith Morris, Llandaff House, Llandaff; two *d.* *Educ.:* Radley; Magdalen College, Oxford. Asst. Master at Radley 1919-38 (Sub-Warden from 1924); served with 4th Bn. Leicestershire Regt. 1914-19 (wounded, M.C.); Commanded Radley O.T.C. 1923-28; Brev. Lt. Col. T.A. Gen. List; E.D.; retired 1933. *Address:* The Bungalow, Marle Hill, Evesham Road, Cheltenham. *T.:* Cheltenham 25815. [*Died* 29 *Jan.* 1966.

NUGENT, Sir (George) Guy (Bulwer), 4th Bt., *cr.* 1806; formerly Captain Grenadier Guards; *b.* 5 Nov. 1892; *s.* of late Brig.-Gen. G. C. Nugent, M.V.O., and Isabel Mary, *d.* of late General Sir Edward Gascoigne Bulwer, G.C.B.; *S.* grandfather, 1928; *m.* 1921, Maisie Esther, *d.* of J. A. Bigsby; two *s.* one *d.* *Educ.:* Eton; R.M.C., Sandhurst. Served European War, 1914-18. *Heir:* *s.* Robin George Colborne Nugent [*b.* 1925; *m.* 1947, Ursula Mary, *er. d.* of late Lt.-Gen. Sir Herbert Cooke, K.C.B., K.B.E., C.S.I., D.S.O.; two *s.* one *d.*]. *Address:* Bannerdown House, Batheaston, Bath. *T.:* Bath 88377. [*Died* 17 *Aug.* 1970.

NUGENT, Rt. Hon. Sir Roland Thomas, 1st. Bt. *cr.* 1961; P.C. (N. Ire.) 1944; Kt. 1929; J.P.; H.M. Lieutenant, Co. Down; Speaker of the Senate, N. Ireland, 1950-61; Minister in the Senate, 1949; Leader of the Senate, 1944-50; *b.* 19 June 1886; *o. s.* of E. H. S. Nugent, J.P., D.L., of Portaferry, Co. Down; *m.* 1917, Cynthia Maud, *d.* of Captain F. and Lady Maud Ramsden; one *d.* (two *s.* killed in action, 1943, 1944). *Educ.:* Eton; Trinity College, Cambridge, B.A. (Minor Scholar History), University of Bonn. Entered Diplomatic Service, 1910; exchanged to Foreign Office, 1913; retired, 1918; Grenadier Guards, 1918 and again 1940-43; Director, Federation of British Industries, 1916-17, and 1919-32; Minister without Portfolio, Northern Ireland, 1944-45; Minister of Commerce, 1945-1949; H.M. Lieutenant, Co. Down. LL.D. *h.c.* Queen's University, Belfast, 1958. *Heir:* none. *Address:* Portaferry House, Co. Down, Northern Ireland. *Club:* Ulster (Belfast). [*Died* 18 *Aug.* 1962 (*ext.*).

NUGENT, Colonel Walter Vyvian, C.B.E. 1919; D.S.O. 1916; late R.A.; *b.* Sowerby, Yorkshire, 3 Dec. 1880; *s.* of Nicholas Nugent and Caroline Adelaide Perry; *g.s.* of Sir Oliver Nugent, of Antigua, West Indies; *m.* 1911, Dorothy Florence, *y. d.* of J. Selwyn Rawson, J.P.; two *s.* two *d.* (and one *s.* killed in War of 1939-45). *Educ.:* Pocklington School; Royal Military Academy, Woolwich. 1st Commission in Royal Artillery, 1900; served in Malta, Ceylon, and China, 1900-1906; special service in China, 1906; Assistant Commissioner, Yola-Cross River Boundary Commission, 1907-9 (Anglo-German Nigeria Cameroons Boundary); General Staff Officer 3rd Grade, Military operations, War Office, 1909-1912; Chief Commissioner, Nigeria Cameroons Boundary Delimitation Commission, 1912-13; General Staff, War Office, 1913-14; served through the Dardanelles and Palestine Campaigns (despatches five times, D.S.O.); G.S.O. 3rd Grade, General Headquarters, June–Nov. 1915; G.S.O. 2nd Grade, General Headquarters Nov. 1915; G.S.O. 1st Grade, H.Q., Egypt, March 1917; Intelligence Branch General Staff, H.Q. Egypt; G.S.O. 1st Grade, Military Operations Directorate, War Office, 1919; Instructor Staff College, Camberley, 1921-25; Commander 7th Medium Brigade R.A., 1926-28; G.S.O. 1st Grade Directorate of Military Operations and Intelligence, War Office, 1929-32; G.S.O. 1st Grade, Western Command, 1932-34; retired pay, 1934; Gen. Staff Intelligence War Office, Sept. 1939; Deputy Regional Transport Commissioner, N.W. Region, 1942-46; Knight of Order of Crown of Italy, 1917; Knight, Legion of Honour, 1918. *Address:* Bullace Trees, Triangle, Halifax, Yorks. [*Died* 14 *Sept.* 1963.

NUTTALL, Sir James, Kt. 1944; Vice-Chairman, Binny & Co. Ltd., London; *b.* 1891; *s.* of late J. J. Nuttall, Paxford, Glos.; *m.* 1919, Ella Margaret, *d.* of late F. W. Gooch of Westcott, Surrey; one *d.* Served in South India, 1913-45. Director: Binny & Co. (Madras) Ltd., Buckingham & Carnatic Co. Ltd., Bangalore Woollen Mills, 1926-45. Member, Madras Legislative Assembly, 1937-39. Member National Service Advisory Committee, 1941; Member Provincial Advisory Committee on War supplies, 1941-45; Member Board, Imperial Bank of India, 1941-45; Chairman, Madras Chamber of Commerce, 1942-44; Member, Madras Town Planning Committee, 1944; Chairman, European Association (S. India), 1945; Member Requisitioning Committee, 1945. *Address:* Thanington, Chichester Rd., Dorking, Surrey. [*Died* 16 *Nov.* 1962.

NUTTING, Arthur Ronald Stansmore, O.B.E.; M.C.; *b.* 3 Mar. 1888; *s.* of Sir John Nutting; *m.* 1st, 1912, Edith, *d.* of Walter Brooks, New York; 2nd, 1932, Patricia, *e. d.* of H. R. Jameson, Drumleck, Howth, County Dublin; two *s. Educ.:* Eton; Trinity Hall, Cambridge, B.A. Governor, Bank of Ireland, 1926-30; Director of: A. Guinness Son & Co.; E. & J. Burke, Ltd., Dublin, Liverpool and N.Y.; Cantrell & Cochrane, Ltd., Dublin and N.Y.; Coast Lines Ltd.; Guardian Eastern Insurance Co. Ltd.; Trust Houses Ltd.; British and Irish Steam Packet Co., Ltd., (Chm.), London Electrical and Gen. Trust, Ltd., Tyne & Tees Shipping Co., Ardrossan Harbour Board, Belfast Steamship Co. Ltd., Guardian Assurance Co., Standard Trust Co. (Chm.). Chairman, Westinghouse Brake and Signal Co. Ltd., 1944-62, resigned. Captain, Irish Guards. *Recreation:* fishing. *Address:* North Breache Manor, Ewhurst, Surrey. *Clubs:* Guards, White's, Royal Automobile; Kildare Street (Dublin). [*Died* 23 *March* 1964.

NUTTING, Air Vice-Marshal Charles William, C.B.E. 1940; D.S.C.; Telecommunications adviser to the Minister Resident in Middle East; *b.* 1889; *m.* Amy Georgina (*d.* 1951). Served European War with R.N.A.S. and R.A.F., 1914-19; Air Staff Signals Officer, R.A.F., 1931; commanded No. 3 Flying Training School, 1932-1937; Air Commodore, 1937; Director of Signals, Air Ministry, 1937; served War of 1939-45, 1939-40 (C.B.E.); Air Vice-Marshal, 1941; retired, 1942. *Address:* Elm Cottage, Galmpton, Nr. Kingsbridge, S. Devon. *T.:* Galmpton 269. *Club:* Royal Air Force. [*Died* 25 *Feb.* 1964.

NYE, Lieut.-General Sir Archibald (Edward), G.C.S.I., *cr.* 1947; G.C.M.G., *cr.* 1951; G.C.I.E., *cr.* 1946; K.C.B., *cr.* 1946 (C.B. 1942); K.B.E., *cr.* 1944; M.C.; Hon. D.C.L. Bishop's University; Hon. LL.D. McGill, Toronto and McMaster Univs.; a Director of the Royal Bank of Canada; *b.* 23 April 1895; *s.* of Charles E. and Mary Nye; *m.* 1939, Colleen (Kaisar-i-Hind Gold Medal, 1947), *d.* of General Sir Harry Knox, K.C.B., D.S.O.; one *d. Educ.:* Duke of York's School, Dover. Enlisted in ranks, 1914; 2nd Lt. Leinster Regt. 1915; Lieut. Leinster Regt., 1916; Capt. R. Warwickshire Regt. 1923; Bt. Major, 1930; Bt. Lt.-Col. 1934; Major South Lancashire Regt. 1935; Lt.-Col. R. Warwickshire Regt. 1937; Col. (temp. Brig.), 1939; Maj.-Gen. (acting), 1940; Maj.-Gen. (subst.), 1941; Lieut.-Gen. (acting), 1941; Lt.-Gen. (subst.), 1944; Adjutant Leinster Regt., 1919-22; Student Staff College, Camberley, 1924-25; G.S.O. for Air Co-operation, 1926-28; Brigade Major, 1928-30; G.S.O. (War Office), 1931-1932; G.S.O. (Staff College), 1932-35; G.S.O. (War Office), 1936-37; Commander, Nowshera Brigade, 1939; Deputy Director of Staff Duties, 1940; Director of Staff Duties, 1940; Vice-Chief of Imperial Gen. Staff, 1941-46; Governor of Madras, 1946-1948; High Commissioner for the U.K. in India, 1948-52; High Commissioner for the U.K. in Canada, 1952-56. Barrister-at-law, Inner Temple, 1932. A Rhodes Trustee; Freeman of City of Ottawa. *Recreation:* gardening. *Address:* Alderstone House, Whiteparish, Wiltshire. *Club:* United Service. [*Died* 13 *Nov.* 1967.

O

OAK-RHIND, Edwin Scoby, C.B.E. 1942; Chairman, Civil Defence Committee, Kent C.C., 1939-55, and Chairman, Kent Federation of Civil Defence Associations, 1946; *b.* 17 July 1883; *s.* of William Oak-Rhind; *m.* 1st, 1907, Katharine Sevecke (*d.* 1951), *d.* of William Hughes; one *s.*; 2nd, 1952, Nancy Layfield Hewitt. *Educ.:* privately. Served in R.N.A.S., 1914-18 (despatches). Managing Director and Sec. North Foreland Golf Club, 1920-39; Member Broadstairs and St. Peter's U.D.C., 1920-36, Chairman, 1924-25; Member Kent C.C. 1922-60; County Alderman, 1939; Chairman Isle of Thanet Conservative Assoc., 1936-52 (Pres. 1952-); Member Local Govt. Advisory Cttee. to Conservative Party, 1948-54. Chairman Fire Brigade Cttee., 1952. *Recreations:* golf, fishing, and model yacht racing. *Address:* Whitegates, Northumberland Avenue, Cliftonville, Margate. *T.A.:* and *T.:* Thanet 20752. *Club:* North Foreland Golf. [*Died* 8 *May* 1963.

OAKE, George Robert, C.B. 1954; Chief Officer, Pig Industry Development Authority, 1957-67; *b.* 13 July 1903; *m.* 1928, Mary Elizabeth Benson; one *s. Educ.:* Jesus College, Oxford. Colonial Service, Nigeria, 1926-30; Asst. Registrar, Univ. of London, 1930-35; Sec., London School of Hygiene and Tropical Medicine, 1935-39; Ministry of Food, 1939-55; Dir. of Establishments, Min. of Agriculture, Fisheries and Food, 1955-57. *Recreation:* painting. *Address:* Sherborne, Ingleden Park Rd., Tenterden, Kent. *Club:* Savile. [*Died* 4 *Aug.* 1969.

OAKES, Sir Sydney, 2nd Bt., *cr.* 1939; *b.* 9 June 1927; *s.* of Sir Harry Oakes, 1st Bt., and Eunice Myrtle McIntyre, Sydney, Australia; *S.* father, 1943; *m.* 1948, Greta, *y. d.* of Gunnar Hartmann, Copenhagen; one *s.* two *d.* President, Sydeta Securities Ltd., and associated companies. *Heir:* *s.* Christopher, *b.* 10 July 1949. *Address:* Nassau, Bahamas. [*Died* 8 *Aug.* 1966.

OAKEY, John Martin, C.B.E. 1958; M.C. 1917; D.L.; J.P.; Chairman, National Heart Hospital and Tooting Bec Hospital since 1951; *b.* 13 June 1888; 2nd *s.* of late Herbert Oakey, Streatham, and Wellington Mills, S.E.1, and of Fanny Eliza Oakey. *Educ.:* Cheltenham; Trinity Coll., Cambridge. Called to the Bar, Lincoln's Inn, 1912. Served European War, Artists Rifles, Rifle Brigade, Royal Engineers (Special Brigade), 1914-19, Major; Artists Rifles, 1920-1940; Royal Engineers, 1940; War of 1939-1945, Ships Adjutant, Troop Ships, 1942-45. Alderman, London County Council, 1931-49; Member L.C.C. for North Lewisham, 1949-1958; Dep. Chm. L.C.C., 1947-48; sometime Mem. Public Assistance Cttee., Health Cttee., Welfare Cttee., Parks Cttee., General Purposes Cttee., Mental Hospitals Cttee., 1931-1958; of several Mental Hosp. Cttees.; also Vice-Chm. Mental After Care Assoc.; Mem. Licensing Planning Cttee.; Quarter Sessions of Co. of London. Chairman John Oakey & Sons Ltd., abrasive manufacturers, Wellington Mills, London, S.E.1. J.P., Westminster Petty Sessional Bench and Licensing Cttee. Past Master of the Worshipful Company of Plumbers. J.P. 1941, D.L. 1950, Co. London. *Recreations:* touring, philately. *Address:* 7 Broadbent St., W.1. *Clubs:* Union, Oriental. [*Died* 30 *Jan.* 1963.

OBEYESEKERE, Sir James Peter, Kt., *cr.* 1936; Maha Mudahyar; *b.* 17 Jan. 1879; *e. s.* of late Hon. J. P. Obeyesèkere and Cornelia Henrietta, *e. d.* of D. C. H. D. Bandaranayake, Gate Mudaliyar; *m.* 1914; one *s. Educ.:* St. Thomas' College, Colombo;

Trinity College, Cambridge, M A. Barrister-at-Law, Inner Temple, 1903; J.P., 1912; Mudaliyar of Siyane Korale East, 1914; Maha Mudaliyar, 1927. *Address:* Batadola, Veyangoda, Ceylon. [*Died* 3 *Sept.* 1968.

O'BRIEN, Brigadier Brian Palliser Tiegue, C.S.I. 1947; O.B.E. 1943; M.C. 1917, Bar 1920; I.A. retd.; *b.* 16 July 1898; *s.* of Pierce O'Brien, Durra, Ennis, Co. Clare, Ireland; *m.* 1928, Elinor Laura, *d.* of late S. N. Mackenzie, I.C.S.; two *s.* *Educ.:* Masonic School, Dublin. Commissioned 8th Gurkha Rifles, 1916; served European War, Mesopotamia (wounded); Afghan War, 1919; Waziristan Campaign, 1919-20; Malabar Rebellion, 1921; Waziristan, 1924; Staff College, Quetta, 1934, 1935; General Staff, 1937-40; Comd. 1/4th Gurkha Rifles, 1941; G.S.O. 1, G.H.Q. India, 1942; Deputy Director Military Intelligence, 1943; Director of Intelligence, India Command, 1945; retired 1947. *Recreation:* golf. *Address:* Birchwood Farm, Biddenden, Kent. [*Died* 9 *Nov.* 1966.

O'BRIEN, Lt.-Colonel Edward, C.B.E. 1927; Indian Army, retired; *b.* 20 Sept. 1872; *s.* of Edward O'Brien, Indian Civil Service; *m.* 1898, Mary Elma Travers (*d.* 1952), *d.* of R. W. Hunter, I.C.S.; no *c.* *Educ.:* Dover College; R.M.C., Sandhurst. 2nd Lieutenant Royal Irish Regiment, 1891; Indian Army, 1894; Bombay Political Dept., 1897; Kaisar-i-Hind medal 2nd class, 1901; Winner of Bombay Gymkhana Athletic Challenge Cup, 1899-1902 and 1908-9; Winner of 120 yards hurdles, Irish Championship, Ireland *v.* Scotland, and Army Championship, 1911; Administrator of the Porbandar State in Kathiawar, 1916-20; Resident at Kolhapur, 1925-28; retired, 1928; Adviser to Raja of Ramdurg, 1939-40, after Ramdurg riots; Adviser to the Rani of Mudhol, 1940-41; Adviser to the Jahagirdar of Ichalkaranji, 1941-42. *Recreation:* natural history. *Club:* Bangalore (Bangalore). [*Died* 20 *March* 1965.

O'BRIEN, Lt.-Col. Hon. Henry Barnaby, M.C.; D.L.; late Irish Guards; *b.* 9 Jan. 1887; *y. surv. s.* of 14th Baron Inchiquin, K.P.; *m.* 1st, 1925, Lady Helen Baillie-Hamilton (*d.* 1959), *o. d.* of late Brig.-Gen. Lord Binning, C.B., M.V.O.; two *s.*; 2nd, 1964, Edith, *widow* of Thomas M. Steele, Evelick. Served European War, 1914-18 (wounded, despatches, M.C.). D.L. for East Lothian. *Address:* 3 Ibris Place, North Berwick. [*Died* 7 *Jan.* 1969.

O'BRIEN, Sir John (Edmond Noel), 5th Bt., *cr.* 1849; M.C. 1940; *b.* 23 Dec. 1899; *s.* of late Edmond Lyons O'Brien (*y. b.* of 3rd Bt.) and of Audrey Townshend, *d.* of late David Crawford, New York; *S.* cousin 1952; *m.* 1st, 1928, Moira Violet (marriage dissolved, 1940), *d.* of Capt. R. B. Brassey; 2nd, 1940, Rosemary Brent Staniland, *d.* of Edgar Grotrian, Knapton Hall, Malton; one *d.* Served War of 1939-1945 as Captain, H.Q. Staff, 46 Division. *Heir:* *b.* David Edmond O'Brien [*b.* 19 Feb. 1902; *m.* 1927, Mary Alice, *y. d.* of Sir Henry Foley Grey, 7th Bt.; two *s.* one *d.*]. *Address:* Knockeen, Fethard, Co. Tipperary. [*Died* 28 *Sept.* 1969.

O'BRIEN, Richard Alfred, C.B.E. 1920; M.D. (Melb.), B.S., D.P.H.; *b.* 1878; *m.* Nora McKay; two *s.* one *d.* *Educ.:* Trinity College, Melbourne University. Director Wellcome Physiological Research Laboratories, 1914-39. *Publications:* Papers on bacteriological subjects in Journal of Pathology, etc. [*Died* 19 *Oct.* 1970.

O'BRIEN, Sir Tom, Kt. 1956; General Secretary of National Association of Theatrical and Kine Employees since 1932; *b.* 17 Aug. 1900; *m.* 1922; two *s.* two *d.* *Educ.:* St. Mary's School, Llanelly. Started work as an errand-boy at age of 12 years; overstated age and joined Army, 1915, and served in the Dardanelles. Member Nat. Assoc. of Theatrical and Kine Employees, 1919; District Organiser for South Wales and West of England, 1921; National Organiser, 1924. M.P. (Lab.) Nottingham West, 1945-50, 1955-Sept. 1959 (Nottingham North-West, 1950-55). Member T.U.C. Gen. Council, 1940- (Chm., 1952-53); Mem. Cinematograph Films Council; Pres. Federation of Theatre Unions; Pres. Federation of Film Unions; Went to Italy, 1944, to advise Italian workers and appointed to visit U.S.A. 1945, 1946 and 1947, and World Trade Union Congress at Paris 1945, Czechoslovakia 1946, Austria 1947, Germany and Sweden, 1952 and 1953, as a fraternal delegate; Special T.U. missions, U.S.A. and Canada, 1954, 1958, 1960, 1966, South and North Africa, 1957 and U.S.S.R., 1959. Member National Council of Labour and General Council of I.C.F.T.U., 1950; rep. T.U.C. as adviser to I.L.O., Geneva, 1950-54. Pres. T.U.C., 1952, 1953, Vice-Pres. 1954. Subsequently Director, Daily Herald. Chief Barker, Variety Club of Gt. Britain, 1958; Delegate to Internat. Conventions of Variety Clubs at New York, San Francisco, Miami, New Orleans, Toronto, Buffalo, Dublin, Houston. Member of Board, British Travel Association; Mem. Council, Imp. Soc. of Knights Bachelor. *Recreations:* walking, reading, nature study, music, plays. *Address:* 57 Parliament Hill, Hampstead, N.W.3. *T.A.:* Stageland, London W.C.2. *T.:* 01-836 8526. *Club:* Eccentric. [*Died* 5 *May* 1970.

O'BRYAN, Hon. Sir Norman, Kt. 1958; Q.C. Austr. 1937; Judge of the Supreme Court, State of Victoria, 1939-66; *b.* 16 Oct. 1894; *s.* of Michael J. O'Bryan, South Melbourne; *m.* 1st, 1921 Elsa Mary, *d.* of G. M. Duncan, Kew; 2nd, 1929, Violet Leila also *d.* of G. M. Duncan; four *s.* two *d.* *Educ.:* Christian Brothers' College, Melbourne; University of Melbourne. Exhibitioner in Law, Melbourne Univ., 1915. Began practice as Barrister-at-law, 1916; served War, 1916-19, Artillery, A.I.F.; practised at Bar, Victoria, 1920-38; Mem. Victoria Bar Council, 1934-1938. Formerly Lecturer in Law and Member of Faculty of Law, Univ. of Melbourne. Chm. St. Vincent's Hospital Advisory Council, 1943-63; Mem. Electoral Coll., St. Vincent's Hospital. Mem. Committee, M.C.C. *Recreations:* golf, bowls and gardening. *Address:* 2 Huntingfield Road, Toorak, Victoria, Australia. *T.:* BY 3882 (Melb.). *Clubs:* Australian, Victoria Racing, Moonee Valley Racing, Melb. Cricket, Royal Automobile of Victoria (Melbourne); Peninsula Country (Frankston). [*Died* 5 *June* 1968.

O'CALLAGHAN, Timothy Patrick Moriarty, C.I.E. 1933; *b.* 25 Nov. 1886. Joined Indian Police, 1906; Inspector-General of Police, Assam, 1929-37; retired, 1937. *Address:* c/o Lloyds Bank, Ltd., Guernsey, C.I. [*Died* 17 *March* 1961.

O'CASEY, Sean; Irish dramatic author; *b.* Dublin, 30 March 1880; *s.* of Michael and Susanna O'Cathasaigh; *m.* 1927, Eileen Reynolds (stage name Eileen Carey); two *s.* one *d.* *Educ.:* in the streets of Dublin. Worked as a builder's labourer, railway labourer, and general labourer. Won Hawthornden Prize, 1926. *Publications: plays:* The Shadow of a Gunman, 1925; Juno and the Paycock, 1925; The Plough and the Stars, 1926; The Silver Tassie, 1929; Within the Gates, 1933; Windfalls, 1934; The Star Turns Red, 1940; Purple Dust, 1940; Red Roses for Me, 1942; Oak Leaves and Lavender, 1946; Cockadoodle Dandy, 1949; The Bishop's Bonfire, 1955; The Drums of Father Ned, 1960; Behind the Green Curtains (Three plays), 1961; *Collected* *plays:* (2 vols.) 1949; (2 vols.) 1951; *essays:* The Flying Wasp, 1936, The Green Crow (essays and stories), 1956; *autobiography:* 6 vols.: I Knock at the Door, 1939; Pictures in the Hallway, 1942; Drums under the Windows, 1945; Inishfallen, Fare Thee Well, 1949; Rose and Crown, 1952; Sunset and Evening Star, 1954; Under a Colored Cap, 1963; Blasts and Benedictions, 1967 (posthumous). *Relevant Publications:* (Ed. Robert Hogan) Feathers from the Green Crow: Sean O'Casey 1905-1925, 1963 Sean; O'Casey, The Man I knew, by Gabriel Fallon, 1965. *Recreations:* everything except work. *Address:* 40 Trumlands Rd., St. Marychurch, Torquay, Devon. *T.:* Torquay 87766. [*Died* 18 *Sept.* 1964.

OCHTERLONY, Sir Charles Francis, 5th Bt., *cr.* 1823; F.S.A. (Scot.); *b.* 27 June 1891; *y. s.* of Sir David F. Ochterlony, 3rd Bt., and Somerville (*d.* 1930), *d.* of B. Grahame of Morphie, Kincardineshire; *S.* brother 1946. *Educ.:* George Watson's College; Edinburgh University. *Recreations:* genealogical res., water-colour painting. *Heir:* none. *Address:* Overburn, Currie, Midlothian. [*Died* 2 *Nov.* 1964 (*ext.*).

O'CONNELL, Thomas J., LL.D.; F.E.I.S. (Hon.); Gen. Sec., Irish Nat. Teachers' Organization, 1916-48; *b.* Bekan, Co. Mayo, Nov. 1882; 2nd *s.* of Thomas and Maria O'Connell, Bekan, Co. Mayo; *m.* 1905, Kathleen O'Connor (*d.* 1956); two *s.* three *d.* (and one *s.* decd.). *Educ.:* Bekan Nat. School; St. Patrick's Coll., Drumcondra. National Teacher, 1902-16; elected mem. of Dail Eireann for Co. Galway, 1922 and 1923; S. Mayo in June and Sept. 1927; Vice-Chm. of Labour Party, 1923; Leader of Labour Party in Dail Eireann, 1927-32; Member of Executive of Irish Labour Party and Trade Union Congress, 1921-31; President of that body, 1929-30; Member of Seanad Eireann, 1941-44, 1948-51 and 1954-57. Member of Youth Unemployment Commission, 1943-51. Director World Federation of Education Associations, 1927-40; Member of Central Council, Irish Red Cross Society, 1939-49. *Publications:* various pamphlets, essays, etc., on questions of educational administration; History of the Irish National Teachers' Organisation, 1868-1968, 1968. *Recreations:* gardening and reading. *Address:* Killasheeda, Elton Park, Sandycove, Dublin. *T.:* 805616. *Club:* Teachers' (Dublin). [*Died* 22 *June* 1969.

O'CONNOR, Frank; *pseud.* of Michael O'Donovan; Writer and Journalist; *b.* 1903; *s.* of Michael and Mary O'Donovan; *m.* 1st, 1939, Evelyn Bowen; two *s.* one *d.*; 2nd, 1953, Harriet Randolph Rich; one *d.* *Educ.:* Christian Brothers, Cork. By profession Librarian. Hon. Litt.D. (University of Dublin), 1962. *Publications:* Guests of the Nation, 1931; The Saint and Mary Kate, 1932; The Wild Bird's Nest, 1932; Bones of Contention, 1936; Three Old Brothers, 1937; The Big Fellow, 1937; Lords and Commons, 1938; Fountain of Magic, 1939; Dutch Interior, 1940; Three Tales, 1942; A Picturebook, 1942; Crab Apple Jelly, 1944; The Midnight Court, 1945; Towards an Appreciation of Literature, 1945; Selected Stories, 1946; Irish Miles, 1947; Art of the Theatre, 1947; The Common Chord, 1947; The Road to Stratford, 1948; Leinster, Munster and Connacht, 1950; Travellers' Samples, 1950; The Stories of Frank O'Connor, 1953; More Stories by Frank O'Connor, 1954; Selected Stories of Frank O'Connor, 1956; The Mirror in the Roadway, 1956; Domestic Relations, 1957; The Book of Ireland, 1958; Kings, Lords and Commons, 1960; An Only Child, 1961; The Little Monasteries, 1962; The Lonely Voice, 1963; Collection Two, 1964; The Backward Look, 1966; *plays* (in collaboration): In the Train, 1937; The Invincibles, 1937; Moses' Rock, 1938; *other plays:* Time's Pocket, 1939; The Statue's Daughter, 1940. *Recreation:* cycling. *Address:* c/o A. D. Peters, 10 Buckingham St., Adelphi, W.C.2. [*Died* 10 *March* 1966.

O'CONNOR-MORRIS, Geoffrey; Hon. A.R.C.M.; Organist at 7th C.S. Church, London, 1930-60; *b.* Thun, 1886; parents Irish; *m.* 1912, Christian Helena, *y. d.* of Col. Sir James Gildea, G.B.E., K.C.V.O., C.B. *Educ.:* Dublin; Royal College of Music, London. Organist to St. Cuthbert's, Carlisle, and Assistant Organist to the Cathedral; St. John's Church, Wilton Road, London; Organist and Choirmaster to St. Paul's, Onslow Square; Conductor to the Carl Rosa Opera Co., 1919; on the Staff of B.B.C., 1926-27; Professor of Conducting and Orchestration at Guildhall School of Music, 1944-47. *Publications:* various songs, piano, and violin music. *Recreations:* billiards and tennis. *Address:* 16b Trebovir Road, Earl's Court, S.W.5. [*Died* 19 *Feb.* 1964.

ODDIN-TAYLOR, Harry Willoughby, C.I.E. 1946; C.B.E. 1937 (O.B.E. 1933); A.C.G.I. B.Sc.; A.M.I.C.E.; Consulting Engineer; *b.* 12 July 1886; *s.* of Francis Oddin-Taylor, Thuxton House, Norfolk, and Elizabeth Mary, *d.* of Rev. Thomas Paddon, M.A., Norfolk; *m.* 1910, Margaret Elizabeth Dickens Bradley; no *c.* *Educ.:* Royal Grammar School, Lancaster. Assistant Engineer Chiswick Urban District Council, 1907-9, joined Imperial Service of Engineers, India, 1909; in charge of design and construction of road and railway bridge over River Krishna near Satara, Deccan, 1910-14; Executive Engineer in charge design, building, and organisation of Bombay Govt. Central Workshops, Poona, 1915-18; Executive Engr. Fuleli Canals, Hyderabad, Sind, 1918-19; retired from Govt. Service and practised as Consulting Engr., Karachi, 1920-26; rejoined Imperial Service of Engineers as Executive Engineer in charge construction northern half of Lloyd Barrage at Sukkur, and of right bank regulators, 1926-32; in charge running and organisation of Lloyd Barrage, Sukkur, 1932-35; Supt. Eng. and Joint Secretary to A.G.G. in charge of clearance and reconstruction of Quetta City and Civil Station after the earthquake of 31 May 1935; Joint Secretary, in the Public Works Dept., to the Agent to the Governor-General in Baluchistan and Superintending Engineer Baluchistan Irrigation; retired 1945; Engineer Adviser to the Supply Directorate, Baluchistan, 1945-46; Inventor of the "Satara Director" for indirect fire by machine guns and of the "Quetta Bond" method of construction used for earthquake-proof buildings in Quetta and by the Ministry of Home Defence for blast-proof buildings in England. *Publications:* Mechanical Transport in India, 1913; Felling of a Masonry Chimney at Dapuri, 1916; Difficulties met with during the Construction of the Lloyd Barrage at Sukkur, 1933 (All papers before Engineering Congresses or Govt. publications). *Recreations:* tennis; photography, both still and cine. *Address:* The Maltings, Garboldisham, Diss, Norfolk. [*Died* 12 *Jan.* 1967.

O'DELL, Andrew Charles, M.Sc.; F.R.S.E.; Professor of Geography, University of Aberdeen, since 1951; *b.* 4 June 1909; *o. s.* of late Charles and Jemima O'Dell, formerly of Lluipaardsvlei, Transvaal; *m.* 1938, Queenie Louise Smith; one *s.* one *d.* (and one *d.* decd.). *Educ.:* Westminster City School; King's College, London. B.Sc. (Lond.) 1st Cl. Hons. Geography; M.Sc. Demonstrator in Dept. of Geography, London School of Economics, 1930-33; Lectr. Birkbeck College, 1931-45; seconded to Naval Intelligence Div., 1941-43; seconded to Dept. of Health for Scotland, 1943-45; Lectr. and Head of Dept. of Geography, Univ. of Aberdeen, 1945; Reader in Geography, 1949. Mem. Building Materials Cttee. Scottish Council; Mem. Highland and Islands Advisory Panel, 1963-65. Leader of Aberdeen Univ. Archæological Excavations. Shetland Islands, 1955-59 (St. Ninian's Isle Treasure, 1958). Jelf Medallist, Faculty of Science, K.C.L., 1930; Newbigin Memorial Medallist, Royal Scottish Geographical Society, 1938. *Publications:* The Historical Geography of the Shetland Islands, 1939; Railways and Geography, 1956; The Scandinavian World, 1957; (with K. Walton) Highlands and Islands of Scotland, 1962; papers on historical geography and transport. *Recreations:* travel, collecting railway literature. *Address:* The Barn, 80 St. Machar Drive, Aberdeen. *T.:* 43710; 86 Goldhurst Terrace, N.W.6. [*Died* 17 *June* 1966.

ODETS, Clifford; Playwright; *b.* Philadelphia, Pa., 18 July 1906; *s.* of Louis J. Odets and Pearl Geisinger; *m.* 1936, Luise Rainer (marriage dissolved 1939); *m.* 1943, Bette Grayson (*d.* 1953); one *s.* one *d.* *Educ.:* Public Sch. and High Sch., N.Y.C. Acted character parts in stock productions and small parts in Broadway plays, 1923-28; played juvenile rôles in Theatre Guild Productions, 1928-30; Member and Actor with Group Theatre, 1930-35; adapted for screen, and directed, None but the Lonely Heart, 1944; adapted for Screen: Sweet Smell of Success, 1957; Wild in the Country, 1961. Original story for screen, and directed Story on Page One, 1959. Member of: Actors' Equity Association, Dramatists' Guild, Screen Writers' Guild. *Publications:* Waiting for Lefty, Awake and Sing, Till the Day I Die, 1935; Paradise Lost, 1936; Golden Boy, 1937; Rocket to the Moon, 1939; Night Music, 1940; Clash by Night, 1942; The Big Knife, 1949; The Country Girl (entitled Winter Journey, in England), 1950; The Flowering Peach, 1953; Sweet Smell of Success (scenario), 1956; The Story on Page One (original story, scenario, directed), 1959. *Recreations:* music, philately, painting. *Address:* Actors' Equity Association, New York City, U.S.A. [*Died* 15 *Aug.* 1963.

ODGERS, Sir Charles Edwin, Kt., *cr.* 1930; M.A., B.C.L.; *b.* Bridgwater, Somerset, 17 Jan. 1870; *e. s.* of late Rev. J Edwin Odgers, M.A., D.D., Manchester College, Oxford; *m.* 1909, Elsa Lily, O.B.E., *e. d.* of late Charles Fellows Pearson: two *s.* *Educ.:* Bath College; Lincoln College, Oxford (Open Classical Scholar). Bar, Middle Temple, 1896; Professor of Law and Vice Principal, Madras Law College, 1902-11; acted on several occasions as Principal; Administrator-General and Official Trustee of Madras, 1912-20; acted as Chief Judge, Madras Court of Small Causes, 1916-20; Chief Judge, 1920; acted as Judge of High Court, Madras, 1919 and '20; Puisne Judge, High Court, Madras, 1921-30; retired 1930; Lecturer in Laws, King's College, London, 1931-37; Vice-Dean of Laws, 1934-37. *Publications:* (Joint) Chitty on Contracts, 20th ed.; (Joint) Clark and Lindsell on Torts, 10th ed.; The Construction of Deeds and Statutes, 4th ed. 1956; An Introduction to the Law of Contracts, 1948; Craies, Statute Law, 5th ed. 1952; numerous articles in Encyclopaedia of the Laws of England. *Address:* Brockwell Gate, Walton-on-the-Hill, Tadworth, Surrey. *T.:* Tadworth 2196. [*Died* 4 *Aug.* 1964.

ODGERS, Walter Blake, Q.C. 1933; M.A.; Metropolitan Magistrate, 1941-54; *b.* 14 Dec. 1880; 2nd *s.* of late William Blake Odgers, K.C., LL.D., Recorder of Bristol, and Director of Legal Studies under Council of Legal Education and of late Frances Odgers, J.P.; *m.* 1914, Janet Fortune Cleghorn (*d.* 1967). *Educ.:* Sedbergh Sch.; Balliol Coll., Oxford. Called to Bar at Middle Temple, 1906; joined Western Circuit and Hants Sessions; in the Army, 1915-19, 2½ years in France; Recorder of Southampton, 1937-41; Member of General Council of the Bar, 1925-41. *Publications:* (with his father) Odgers on the Common Law; Senior Editor of Odgers on Libel and Slander (6th ed.). *Recreations:* O.U.R.U.F.C., 1901-3; Middlesex R.F.C. 1906-10 (Capt. 1907-9); Richmond R.F.C. 1903-10. *Address:* Calverly Hotel, Tunbridge Wells, Kent. [*Died* 25 *April* 1969.

O'DONNELL, Elliott; Author, Lecturer; *s* of Rev. Henry O Donnell, M.A. (T.C.D.); and of E. S. Harrison, Oxendon, Northants. *m.* 1905, Ada *d.* of Henry W. Williams, M.D. no *c.* *Educ.:* Clifton College; Dublin. Henry Neville Dramatic Academy, London, 1898-1899. Experience of Stage and Films. Ranched in Far West, and has lectured, broadcast and televised. *Publications:* Escaped from Justice; For Satan's Sake; Dinevah the Beautiful; Jennie Barlowe; The Unknown Depths; Some Haunted Houses of England and Wales; Haunted Houses of London; Ghostly Phenomena; Scottish Ghosts; Dreams and their Meanings; Werwolves; The Sorcery Club; Animal Ghosts; Haunted Highways; The Irish Abroad; Twenty Years' Experience as a Ghost Hunter; Byways of Ghostland; The Haunted Man; Haunted Places in England; Banshees; More Haunted Houses of London; Spiritualism Explained; Strange Sea Mysteries; Kate Webster (Notable Trial Series); Ghosts Helpful and Harmful; Ghostland; Strange Disappearances; Confessions of a Ghost Hunter, Fatal Kisses; Famous Curses; Great Thames Mysteries Women Bluebeards; Rooms of Mystery; Ghosts of London; The Devil in the Pulpit; Family Ghosts; Strange Cults and Secret Societies of London; Haunted Churches; Murder at Hide and Seek; Caravan of Crime; Hell Ships; The Dead of Night; Cornered at Last; Haunted and Hunted; Haunted Britain; Adventures with Ghosts; Ghosts with a Purpose; The Dead Riders; Dangerous Ghosts; Haunted People; Phantoms of the Night; Haunted Waters; Trees of Ghostly Dread; Screaming Skulls; edited Ghosts; contributed to Nineteenth Century Magazine, Harmsworth's Encyclopædia (Sir J. Hammerton), etc. *Recreations:* investigating queer cases and frightening crooks within the Law; walking, talking. *Address:* c/o Westminster Bank, Queen's Rd., Clifton, Bristol. *Club:* Royal Commonwealth Society. [*Died* 6 *May* 1965.

O'DONOGHUE, Charles Henry, D.Sc.; F.Z.S., F.R.S.E.; F.R.S.C.; Professor of Zoology, University of Reading, 1939-52; Professor Emeritus since 1952; *b.* 23 Sept. 1885; *y. s.* of Charles Henry and Mary A. E. O'Donoghue, Lidlington, Bedfordshire; *m.* 1913, Elsie Joste, *e. d.* of Henry Broadbent Smith; one *s.* *Educ.:* King's College, University College, London. D.Sc. London, 1912; Assistant Univ. Coll. Lond. 1908-12; Senior Assistant, 1913-18; Prof. of Zoology, Univ. of Manitoba, 1918-27; Lecturer Zoology, Univ. of Edinburgh, 1927-28; Reader and Director of Studies, Edinburgh, 1929-39; Beit Memorial Fellow Medical Research, 1912-13; Director Biological Station, Nanaimo, B.C., Summer, 1923; Prof. Stanford University, California, by invitation, 1926; Neil Gold Medal, Royal Society, Edinburgh, 1932; President Royal Physical Society, 1933-36; Secretary to Ordinary Meetings, Royal Society, Edinburgh, 1937-39. *Publications:* Introduction to Zoology for Medical Students; numerous papers in scientific journals and proceedings on Bryozoa, Opisthobranchs and Anatomy of the Vertebrata particularly the Blood-vascular system. *Recreation:* the outdoors. *Address:* University, Reading. [*Died* 28 *Nov.* 1961.

O'DONOVAN, Michael; *see* O'Connor, Frank.

O'DONOVAN, Brigadier Morgan John Winthrop (The O'Donovan), M.C.; *b.* 2 May 1893; *s.* of late Colonel The O'Donovan, C.B., late of Liss Ard, Skibbereen, Co. Cork; *m.* 1926, Cornelia, *d.* of late Dr. William Henry Bagnell, Pau; one *s.* one *d.* *Educ.:* Marlborough College; R.M.C., Sandhurst. Gazetted Royal Irish Fusiliers and joined 1st Bn., 1913; served France and Flanders, 1914-1918 (M.C., wounded); served N.W. Persia and Iraq, 1919 and 1920 (despatches); G.S.O. 3 Eastern Command, 1923-27; Commanded Royal Irish Fusiliers and after expansion 1st Bn., 1937-40; Colonel, 1940; Temp. Brigadier, 1940; retired pay, 1944. Hon. rank of Brig. *Recreations:* fishing and shooting. *Address:* Hollybrook House, Skibbereen, County Cork. *T.:* Skibbereen 59. *Clubs:* United Service; Kildare Street (Dublin); Cork and County (Cork).
[*Died* 28 *April* 1969.

O'DOWDA, Lieut.-General Sir James Wilton, K.C.B., *cr.* 1934 (C.B. 1918); C.S.I. 1919; C.M.G. 1916; late Royal Dublin Fusiliers; Col. Queen's Own Royal West Kent Regiment, 1928-36; *b.* 14 Dec. 1871; *m.* 1910, Gaynor, *d.* of late Maj.-Gen. C. R. Simpson, C.B.; one *d.* (one *s.* decd.). Entered Royal West Kent Regt., 1891; Capt. 1900; Adjutant, 1903-5; Major, 1909; Lt.-Col. Royal Dublin Fusiliers, 1915; Brigadier-General, 1915; Maj.-Gen. 1923; Lt.-Gen. 1931; served N.W. Frontier, India, 1897-98 (medal with clasp); European War, Gallipoli, Egypt, and Mesopotamia, 1914-18 (Bt. Col., C.M.G., C.B., C.S.I.); Afghan Campaign, 1919; commanded Nowshera and Jubbulpore Brigades, 1919-23; in charge of Administration Eastern Command, Horse Guards, 1923-27; commanded Baluchistan District, India, 1927-31; retired pay, 1934. Zone Comdr. East Lancs Area, 1940-44; H.G. Adviser Preston Sub. Dist., 1944. *Address:* The Old Coach House, Rye, Sussex. *Club:* Army and Navy.
[*Died* 2 *Jan.* 1961.

O'DWYER, William; lawyer, U.S.A.; *b.* 11 July 1890; *s.* of Patrick O'Dwyer and Bridget McNicholas; *m.* 1st, 1916, Catherine Lenihan (*d.* 1946); no *c.*; 2nd, 1949, Elizabeth Sloan Simpson. *Educ.:* National School, Bohola, Eire; St. Nathys College, Roscommon, Eire; University of Salamanca, Spain; Fordham University, New York, N.Y., U.S.A. D.C.L. (Fordham), 1946. New York City Policeman, 1917-24; New York City Magistrate, 1932; King's County Judge, 1937-39; King's County District Attorney, 1940-45; Mayor, City of New York, U.S.A., 1946-50; U.S. Ambassador to Mexico, 1950-1952. In 1942, while District Attorney, obtained leave of absence; Major, U.S. Army Air Corps, 1942; Brig.-Gen., 1944. Grand Officer of Crown of Italy, 1945; Officer of French Legion of Honour, 1948. *Recreations:* golf, music, theatre, historical novels, and biographies. *Clubs:* Brooklyn Bar Association, Knights of Columbus, Ancient Order of Hibernians (N.Y.); North Hills Golf (Douglaston, N.Y.)
[*Died* 24 *Nov.* 1964.

OEHLERS, Sir George Edward Noel, Kt. 1958; O.B.E. 1953; President, Industrial Court of Malaysia, since August 1967; *b.* 1 April 1908; *s.* of late George Rae Oehlers and late Frances Maude Oehlers; *m.* 1940, Daphne Eleanor (*d.* 1960), *o. d.* of late John Hayward Pye, Penang and London, and late Eleanor Margaret Pye, Penang and Singapore; two *s.* three *d.*; *m.* 1965, Annie Wilson Kirkwood Tessensohn (*widow*), *d.* of late John Patrick Flynn, Edinburgh and late Jessie Knox Watt, Edinburgh. *Educ.:* St. Andrew's School, Singapore; Raffles Institution, Singapore. Barrister-at-Law, Gray's Inn, London, 1928-31. Municipal Comr. and City Councillor Singapore, 1933-41 and 1947-54; Speaker of the Legislative Assembly: Singapore, 1955-63; Sabah, 1963-64. Chairman: Public Utilities Bd., Singapore, 1963-65; Industrial Arbitration Tribunal, 1965-67. Formerly Mem. in Singapore of: Raffles Museum and Library Cttee.; Silver Jubilee Fund Cttee.; Advisory Cttee., T.B. Treatment Allowance; Singapore Education Bd.; Allocation Cttee., National Service; Queen's Scholarship Bd. *Address:* 296 D Jalan Ampang, Kuala Lumpur, Selangor, Malaysia. *T.:* (office) Kuala Lumpur 21070; 109 H Emerald Mansions, Emerald Hill Road, Singapore. *T.:* Singapore 21261. *Clubs:* Singapore Recreation, Singapore Hockey Assoc., Singapore Eurasian Assoc., Singapore Cricket; Selangor, Lake, Selangor Eurasian Assoc., Arthur's Cave (Kuala Lumpur).
[*Died* 26 *Oct.* 1968.

OFFICER, Sir (Frank) Keith, Kt., *cr.* 1950, O.B.E., M.C.; *b.* Melbourne, Australia, 2 Oct. 1889. *Educ.:* Melbourne Grammar School; Ormond College, University of Melbourne (LL.B.). Served with A.I.F., 1914-19. Egypt, Gallipoli, France, Belgium (to Res. with rank of Major); Political Officer, Nigeria, 1919-24; Australian Dept. of External Affairs, Canberra, 1927-33; Australian External Affairs Officer, London, 1933-37; Australian Counsellor, British Embassy, Washington, 1937-40; Counsellor, Australian Legation, Washington, 1940; Counsellor, Australian Legation, Tokio, 1940; Chargé d'Affaires, 1941; Counsellor Australian Legation, Moscow, 1943, Chargé d'Affaires, 1943; Australian Chargé d'Affaires, Chungking, 1944-45; Australian Minister in S.E. Asia, 1946; Australian Minister to the Netherlands, 1946-1948; Australian Ambassador to China, 1948-49; Australian Ambassador to France, 1950-55, retired. *Address:* Darkwater, Blackfield, Hants. *Clubs:* Boodle's; Royal Yacht Squadron; Melbourne, Royal Cruising, Royal Yacht Club of Victoria (Melbourne).
[*Died* 21 *June* 1969.

OFFNER, Professor Richard, Ph.D.; Professor of History of Fine Arts, New York University, from 1923, now Professor Emeritus; *b.* Vienna, 30 June 1889; *s.* of Bernard Offner and Antonia Schmeidler; *m.* 1940, Philippa Gerry Whiting; one *s.* one *d.* *Educ.:* Harvard, 1912, University of Vienna, Ph.D., 1914. Fellow, American Acad., Rome, 1912-14; Sachs Fellow, Harvard, 1920-22. Served European War, 1914-18, as 2nd Lt., Camp Gordon, Georgia. Doctor (*h.c.*), University of Vienna, 1964. *Publications:* Studies in Florentine Painting, 1927; Italian Primitives at Yale University, 1927; The Works of Bernardo Daddi, 1930; A Corpus of Florentine Painting, Sec. III, vols. I-VIII, 1930-58; Sec. IV, vols. I, II, 1960-62; articles in Dial, Art in America, Burlington Magazine, Dedalo, L'Arte, Bollettino d'Arte, Gazette des Beaux-Arts, etc. *Address:* 1 East 78th Street, New York City, N.Y., U.S.A.; Via Michele Di Lando 7A, Florence, Italy.
[*Died* 26 *Aug.* 1965.

OFFOR, Richard, O.B.E. 1961; B.A., first class honours in History, Ph.D.; Fellow of University College, London; *b.* 12 May 1882; *s.* of Henry Offor; *m.* 1917, Eveline, *d.* of Walter Butters, J.P. *Educ.:* Grocers' Company's School and Univ. College, London. Assistant Librarian, University College, London, 1907-19; Librarian of Brotherton Library and Keeper of Brotherton Collection, University of Leeds, 1919-47; Emeritus Librarian, 1947-. Library Adviser to Inter-University Council for Higher Education Overseas, 1947-60. *Publications:* A MS. in the University Library at Leeds containing the Report of the Jesuit Province of Paraguay for 1626-27; The Papers of Benjamin Gott in the publication of the Thoresby Society v. 32; A series of articles on the Influence of Great Britain over France up to 1800 as illustrated by a collection being formed at Leeds; A Survey of American Library Buildings; Guide to the Library of the University of Leeds; contributions to the Library Association Record, Universities Quarterly, etc. *Recreation:* collecting editions of Bunyan. *Address:* Homestead, 24 Tangier Road, Guildford. *T.:* Guildford 5072. [*Died* 7 *Jan.* 1964.

OGDEN, George Washington; author; *b.* Kansas, U.S.A., 9 Dec. 1871; *s.* of Ambrose Ogden and Charlotte Gibbs; *m.* 1st, 1895, Eleanor Nolan (*decd.*), Montreal, Canada; two *s.* one *d.*; 2nd, 1940, Kathleen (Nolan) Heimaster (*d.* 1965), Montreal, Canada. *Educ.:* public schools, Kansas. Newspaper Reporter, Correspondent and Editor; contributor of articles and short stories to leading Amer. magazines. *Publications:* Home Place; Land of Last Chance; Duke of Chimney Butte; The Long Fight; Rustler of Wind River; Trail's End; Claim Number One; The Road to Monterey; The Trail Rider; The Man from Brazos; The Valley of Adventure; Sheep Limit; Cherokee Trails; Sooner Land; Wasted Salt; Steamboat Gold; Fenced Water; White Roads; A Man from the Bad Lands; The Ghost Road; Deputy at Bernal; Ranger of Blackwater; West of Dodge; Whisky Trail; Stockyards Cowboy; Windy Range; There Were no Heroes; West of the Rainbow; Custodian of Ghosts, etc. *Address:* 538 Ninth Street, Santa Monica, California, U.S.A. [*Died* 31 *March* 1966.

OGG, David; Hon. Fellow of New College, Oxford, since 1959; formerly Fellow, Tutor and Librarian, New College; Visiting Professor: University of South Carolina, 1956-57; College of Charleston, 1957-58; University of Texas, 1958-59; William Marsh Rice University, Houston, Texas, 1959-60; *b.* Glasgow, 19 June 1887; *s.* of late Archibald Ogg; *m.* 1917, Emily Louise, *y. d.* of late Alfred J. White, Witley, Worcestershire; one *s.* *Educ.:* Glasgow University; Lincoln College, Oxford. *Publications:* Europe in the Seventeenth Century, 1925; John Selden's Dissertatio ad Fletam, 1925; Louis XIV, 1933; England in the Reign of Charles II 1934; Herbert Fisher, a short biography, 1947; England in the Reigns of James II and William III, 1955. *Address:* New College, and Radbrook House, Lonsdale Road, Oxford. *T.:* Oxford 58438. [*Died* 28 *March* 1965.

OGILBY, Col. Robert James Leslie, D.S.O. 1917; late Colonel of the London Scottish; J.P., D.L.; *b.* 27 Nov. 1880; *o. s.* of Capt. R. A. Ogilby, D.L., and Helen Sarah, 2nd *d.* of Rev. G. B. Wheeler, Rector, Ballysax, Co. Kildare; *m.* 1936, Isabel Katherine (*d.* 1940), *widow* of Rev. C. H. Brocklebank, Westwood Park, Colchester. *Educ.:* Eton. D.L. and J.P., Co. Londonderry; High Sheriff, 1911. Late Lieutenant 2nd Life Guards and 4th Dragoon Guards. Served European War (D.S.O. and bar, Belgian Croix de Guerre, 1914 Star). *Address:* Coldham, Sandwich, Kent; Ardnargle, Limavady, Co. Londonderry; 22 Down St., W.1. *Clubs:* Cavalry, Caledonian. [*Died* 27 *Jan.* 1964.

OGILVIE, Alex., C.B.E. 1919 (O.B.E. 1918); *b.* 8 June 1882; 2nd *s.* of late Arthur Graeme Ogilvie, mining engineer; *m.* 1934, Angela N. Le Cren (*d.* 1958), 2nd *d* of Mrs. E. I. Newbold, Imberley Lodge, East Grinstead. *Educ.:* Rugby; Trinity College, Cambridge. In charge of Repair Depot, Dunkirk, 1916-17; in charge of New Design Branch, Technical Department Air Ministry, 1917-19. *Address:* Clonmore, Linwood, Ringwood, Hants. [*Died* 18 *June* 1962.

OGILVIE, Sir Charles (MacIvor Grant), Kt., *cr.* 1944; C.S.I. 1941; C.B.E. 1928; Lecturer in Modern History, University of St. Andrews, 1945-56, retired; *b.* 6 May 1891; *s.* of late Alexander Grant Ogilvie and late Charlotte Ogilvie; *m.* 1916, Gwladys Evelyn Mary Thomson (*d.* 1956); one *s.* three *d.* *Educ.:* Bedford School; Exeter College, Oxford. Passed I.C.S. Examination, 1914; Deputy Commissioner, Gurdaspur, 1919; Administrator Nabha State, 1923; Deputy Commissioner Lahore, 1925-28; Senior Secretary to the Financial Commissioners, 1928; Home Secretary to Government, Punjab, 1929; Fellow Commoner of Corpus Christi College, Cambridge, 1931; elected Exhibitioner, 1932; First Class Historical Tripos, 1933; reappointed Home Secretary, Punjab, 1933; Finance Secretary, Punjab, 1933; Joint Secretary, Army Dept. Government of India for the reorganisation of the Military Medical Services, 1934; re-appointed Finance Secretary, Punjab, 1934; on deputation to Imperial Defence College, 1936; Secretary, Defence Dept., Govt. of India, 1937-45; retd., 1947. *Publication:* The King's Government and the Common Law, 1471-1641, 1958. *Address:* Owlswood, Tekels Avenue, Camberley, Surrey. *Club:* Royal Naval (Portsmouth). [*Died* 17 *Feb.* 1967.

OGILVIE, Lieutenant-Colonel Sir George Drummond, K.C.I.E., *cr.* 1936 (C.I.E. 1925); C.S.I. 1932; *b.* 18 Feb. 1882; *e. s.* of late George Macartney Ogilvie, Bengal Civil Service; *m.* 1907, Lorna (*d.* 1961), *d.* of Thomas Rome, J.P., Glos; one *s.* one *d.* *Educ.:* Cheltenham College; R.M.C., Sandhurst. Entered Indian Army, 1900; appointed Indian Political Dept., 1905; Captain, 1909; Assistant Secretary, Govt. of India, Army Dept., 1915; Major, 1915; Lt.-Col., 1926; Deputy Secretary, Govt. of India, Foreign and Political Dept., 1919; Officiating Political Secretary, Govt. of India, 1923; President of the Council of State, Jaipur, 1925; Resident in Mewar, Rajputana, 1925-27; Secretary Indian States Committee, 1927-29; Resident in Kashmir, 1929-31; Agent to the Governor-General in Central India, 1931-32; Agent to the Governor-General in Rajputana, 1932-37; retired, 1937. *Address:* 191 Bickenhall Mansions, W.1. [*Died* 12 *Oct.* 1966.

OGILVIE, Lieut.-Col. Sholto Stuart, C.B.E. 1947; D.S.O. 1916; late Wilts Regt.; *b.* 1884; *s.* of late Glencairn Stuart Ogilvie; *m.* 1910, Gladys Mina Henrietta, *e. d.* of Mortimer Rooke; one *s.* four *d.* (and one *s.* killed in war, 1940). *Educ.:* Rugby; University College, Oxford. Served European War, 1914-18 (despatches, D.S.O. and two Bars). *Address:* Ness House, Sizewell, Leiston, Suffolk. *T.:* Leiston 203. *Club:* Junior Carlton. [*Died* 27 *March* 1961.

OGILVIE, William Henry; author, journalist; *b.* Holefield, Kelso, Scotland, 21 Aug. 1869; *e. s.* of late George Oglivie; *m.* 1908, K. M., *o. d.* of late T. Scott Anderson of Ettrick Shaws; one *s.* one *d.* *Educ.:* Fettes College, Edinburgh. Went out to Australia 1889; spent eleven years in the bush, sampling sheep-station life in all its phases; wrote verse for Sydney Bulletin; returned to Scotland, 1901; Professor of Agricultural Journalism in the Iowa State College, U.S.A., 1905-07; J.P. Co. Roxburgh and Co. Selkirk. *Publications:* Fair Girls and Grey Horses (verse), 1899; Hearts of Gold (verse), 1901; Rainbows and Witches (verse), 1907; My Life in the Open, 1908; Whaup o' the Rede, 1909; The Land we Love (verse), 1910; The Overlander and other Verses, 1913; The Honour of the Station, 1914; The Australian and other Verses 1916; Galloping Shoes (Hunting Verses), 1922; Scattered Scarlet (Hunting Verses), 1923; Over the Grass (Hunting Verses), 1925; A Handful of Leather (Hunting verses), 1928; A Clean Wind Blowing (verse), 1930; Collected Sporting Verse, 1932; Saddles Again, 1937; From Sunset to Dawn (War verses), 1947; Saddle for a

Throne, 1953; Border Poems (selection), 1959. *Songs:* Lavender of Life; The Silent Squadron; The New Moon; Seagulls in Town; Gipsies, set by Graham Peel (record); Timber Lore; A Scotch Night; The Witch of Bowden (record); Lovelight; The Barefoot Maid; The Challenge; A Woodland Bouquet; Little Grey Water; A Bunch of Snowdrops; Wind of the Autumn; Heart if You've a Sorrow; Apple Winds; Daffodils in London Town; The Hoofs of the Horses; A Border Home; Wake Little Bees; Hills in Heaven; Ettrick; Coo-ee; The White Swan; Berries (part-song); Apple Blossom (part-song); A Clean Wind Blowing (part-song). Verses recorded in Australia, 1955 (spoken by Harry Borradale). *Address:* Kirklea, Selkirk. *T.:* Ashkirk 226. [*Died* 30 *Jan.* 1963.

OGILVY-DALGLEISH, Wing Comdr. James William, O.B.E. 1917; *b.* 20 March 1888; *s.* of late Capt. James Ogilvy Dalgleish and Mary, *d.* of Andrew Carden, J.P., D.L., Barnane, Co. Tipperary; *m.* 1916, Guinevere, *d.* of Myles Kennedy, J.P., D.L., Stone Cross, Ulverston; two *d.* *Educ.:* Winton House, Winchester; Harrow; H.M.S. Britannia. Cadet Royal Navy 1903; Lieutenant 1910; Lieut.-Cmdr. and Squadron Cmdr. 1917; Wing Comdr. 1918; served throughout European War in R.N.A.S. and R.A.F. (despatches); retired, 1920. High Sheriff of Rutland, 1943. Zone Commander and Col. Rutland Home Guard, 1940-43. *Club:* United Service. [*Died* 9 *April* 1969.

O'HAGAN, 3rd Baron (*cr.* 1870), **Maurice Herbert Towneley Towneley-O'Hagan;** *b.* 20 Feb. 1882; *s.* of 1st Baron and Alice, *d.* and *co-heiress* of Col. Charles Towneley, Towneley, Lancashire and Lady Caroline Molyneux; *S.* brother, 1900; *m.* 1st, 1911, Frances (*d.* 1931) *o. d.* of 1st Baron Strachie; one *d.* (one *s.* decd.), 2nd, 1937, Evelyn, *widow* of Lt.-Col. H. O. S. Cadogan, The Royal Welch Fusiliers. *Educ.:* Marlborough; Trin. Coll., Camb., M.A. 2nd Lt. Middlesex (D. of Cambridge's Own); Major Essex R.H.A.; raised a battery of R.H.A. (T.) 1914; invalided out of Army, 1918; late Hon. Col. 6th Batt. Essex Regt. (T.); J.P. Hants; a Deputy Speaker and Deputy Chairman House of Lords. Former Member of National Council of King's Roll, Chm. Central Chamber of Agriculture, 1929; Member of Council of Central Landowners Assoc.; former Member of National Executive of British Red Cross Society and of V.A.D. Council; Pres. British Dairy Farmers' Assoc., 1914-15; Vice-Pres. English-Speaking Union; Mem. of Ecclesiastical Committee of Parliament, 1920-1932 and 1943-55; Assistant Private Secretary to First Lord of Admiralty, 1906-7; Lord-in-Waiting to H.M. King Edward VII., 1907-10. Grand Cross Queen Isabella (Spain) and North Star (Sweden); Jubilee Medal, 1935. *Heir:* *g. s.* Charles Towneley Strachey (father assumed, 1938, surname of Strachey), *b.* 6 Sept. 1945. *Recreations:* travelling, riding, fencing, shooting. *Address:* Little Salterns, Beaulieu, Hants. *T.:* Bucklers Hard 231. *Club:* Carlton. [*Died* 18 *Dec.* 1961.

O'HALLORAN, Hon. Cornelius Hawkins; Justice of Court of Appeal of Province of British Columbia, since 1938; *b.* Pavilion, British Columbia, 10 Jan. 1890; *s.* of Cornelius O'Halloran and Bridget Hawkins, pioneer residents of Irish birth (County Clare); *m.* 1917, Ada, *d.* of Ernest Schaper and Ada Crabb; two *s.* two *d.* *Educ.:* University of Ottawa; University of New Brunswick, B.A. 1912; M.A. 1914. Called to British Columbia Bar, 1915; served as private in France and Belgium with C.E.F. in European War; unsuccessful candidate (Nanaimo-Riding) for House of Commons in 1926 and 1930; Board Member St. Joseph Hospital and Children's Aid Society until 1938; Captain (Militia reserve of officers); Militia Staff course certificate; Hon. Consul for Belgium at Victoria, 1933-38; Chief Counsel to Coal and Petroleum Products Royal Commission, 1935-37; Counsel for British Columbia before Dominion Tariff Board, Ottawa, on Petroleum reference, 1935, and on Automotive references, 1935-36; K.C. 1936. *Publications:* contributor to Law Periodicals. *Address:* Law Courts, Victoria B.C. Canada. *Club:* Union (Victoria). [*Died* 9 *Sept.* 1963.

O'HARA, Most Rev. Gerald Patrick, S.T.D., J.U.D.; Apostolic Delegate in Great Britain since 1954; also to Malta, Gibraltar and Bermuda; *b.* Scranton, Pennsylvania, U.S.A., 4 May 1895; *s.* of Patrick J. O'Hara, D.D.S., and Margaret M. Carney. *Educ.:* St. Joseph's Coll. High School, Philadelphia; St. Charles Seminary, Overbrook, Pennsylvania; Pontifical Roman Seminary, Rome (S.T.D., J.U.D.). Priest, 1920; Auxiliary Bishop of Philadelphia and Vicar General, Archdiocese of Philadelphia, 1929; Bishop of Savannah-Atlanta, 1935; Regent of Apostolic Nunciature, Rumania, 1946; received title of Archbishop, 1950; Nuncio to Ireland, 1951; Bishop of Savannah, 1956; promoted titular Archbishop of Pessinus, Nov. 1959. *Address:* 54 Parkside, S.W.19. *T.:* Wimbledon 1410. [*Died* 16 *July* 1963.

O'HARA, John (Henry); author and journalist; *b.* 31 Jan. 1905; *e. s.* of Patrick Henry O'Hara, M.D., and Katharine E. Delaney O'Hara, Pottsville, Pa.; *m.* 1st, 1931, Helen Petit (marr. diss. 1933); 2nd, 1937, Belle Wylie (*d.* 1954); one *d.*; 3rd, 1955, Mrs. Katharine Barnes Bryan. *Educ.:* Niagara Preparatory School, U.S.A. Entered journalism, 1924; worked on newspapers and magazines in Pennsylvania and New York as reporter, re-write man, copy reader, columnist, drama and motion picture critic, war correspondent. Member: Nat. Institute of Arts and Letters; Authors Guild; Dramatists Guild; Screen Writers Guild; The Silurians; Sigma Delta Chi. Donaldson Award, 1952; Critics Circle Award, 1952; Nat. Book Award, 1956; Amer. Acad. of Arts and Letters Award (in the Novel), 1964. *Publications:* Appointment in Samarra, 1934; The Doctor's Son, 1935; Butterfield 8, 1935; Hope of Heaven, 1938; Files on Parade, 1939; Pal Joey, 1940; Pipe Night, 1945; Hellbox, 1947; A Rage to Live, 1949; The Farmers Hotel, 1951; Ten North Frederick, 1955; A Family Party, 1956; Sweet and Sour, 1956; From the Terrace, 1958; Ourselves To Know, 1960; Sermons and Soda-Water (three novellas), 1960; Five Plays by John O'Hara, 1961; Assembly, 1961; The Big Laugh, 1962; The Cape Cod Lighter, 1962; Elizabeth Appleton, 1963; The Hat on the Bed, 1963; The Horse Knows the Way, 1964; The Lockwood Concern, 1965; My Turn, 1966; Waiting for Winter, 1966; The Instrument, 1967; And Other Stories, 1968; The O'Hara Generation, 1969; Lovey Child's, A Philadelphia Story, 1969. Author of libretto of Pal Joey (music and lyrics by Rodgers and Hart), 1940. *Recreations:* music, golf. *Address:* c/o Random House, 457 Madison Avenue, New York, U.S.A. *Clubs:* Savile; Century, Coffee House, The Leash (New York); Bedens Brook Golf, Nassau (Princeton); Racquet (Philadelphia); Field (Quogue, L.I.); National Golf Links of America (Southampton, L.I.). [*Died* 11 *April* 1970.

O'HARE, Patrick Joseph, M.D., Ch.B., J.P., *b.* 9 June 1883, *s.* of Bailie Patrick O'Hare, M.P.; *m.* Helen, 3rd *d.* of Joseph Lynas J.P.; two *s.* four *d.* *Educ.:* St. Mungo's Academy and Glasgow University. *Recreations:* golf, swimming. *Address:* 360 Wedderlea Drive, Glasgow, S.W. [*Died* 31 *Aug.* 1961.

OJUKWU, Sir Odumegwu, Kt. 1960; O.B.E. 1951; Chairman: Nigerian Produce Marketing Co. Ltd.; Eastern Nigeria Marketing Board; Eastern Nigeria Development Corp.; African Continental Bank, Ltd.; Nigerian National Line Ltd.; Eastern Nigeria Construction and Furniture Co. Ltd.; and Director of many companies, Nigeria; *b.* 1909; *s.* of Ezeokigbo and Ukonwa Ojukwu; *m.* 1956, Virginia Nbanu Obimma; three *s.* *Educ.:* Hope Waddell Trg. Inst., Calabar. 1st Mem. Onitsha Div., Nigeria House of Parliament, 1954-58. Coronation Medal, 1953. Hon. LL.D. 1963. *Recreations:* shooting, tennis. *Address:* Eastern House, Alexander Avenue, Ikoyi, Lagos, Nigeria. *Clubs:* Metropolitan, Island (Lagos).
[*Died* 13 *Sept.* 1966.

O'KELLY, Sean Thomas; D.Litt., D.C.L.; President of Ireland, 1945-59; Minister of Finance, 1939-45; Vice-President of the Executive Council and Minister for Local Government and Public Health, Irish Free State, 1932-45; Minister of Education, 1939; Member Dáil Éireann, Dublin North, 1918-45; Proprietor and Editor The Nation, Dublin; Vice-President Fianna Fáil, Republican Party; one of the founders Sinn Féin with A. Griffith; Honorary Secretary Sinn Féin, 1908-10; Manager Daily, Sinn Féin; General Secretary Gaelic League, 1915-20; Alderman Dublin Corporation, 1906-24; Contributor to Irish and American Press on Irish politics; Speaker First Dáil Éireann, 1919-21; *b.* 25 Aug. 1882; *e. s.* of Samuel O'Kelly, Berkley Road, Dublin; *m.* 1st, 1918, Mary Kate (*d.* 1934), 2nd *d.* of John Ryan, Tomcoole, Wexford; 2nd, 1936, Phyllis, *y. d.* of John Ryan. *Educ.:* O'Connell Schools, Dublin. M.P. (Republican), North Dublin, Dec. 1918-24. Was Irish Envoy to Paris and Rome, 1919-22, and U.S.A., 1924-26; Grand Cross, Order of St. Gregory the Great, 1933; Grand Cordon, Legion of Honour, 1950; Grand Cross Charles III, Spain; Grand Cross, Order of Merit, Germany, 1955; Grand Cordon, Order of Merit, Italy, 1957; Grand Cross, Order of Pius, 1957; Collar of Gold, Order of Pius, 1958; Hon. LL.D.: T.C.D., 1956; University of Ottawa, 1956; De Paul Univ., Chicago, 1959; Boston College, U.S.A., 1959; Fordham Univ., 1959. *Address:* Roundwood Park, Co. Wicklow.
[*Died* 23 *Nov.* 1966.

O'KELLY de GALLAGH et TYCOOLY, Count Gerald Edward (creation Holy Roman Empire, Marie-Theresa, 1767); Knight of the Sovereign Order of Malta; Grand Officer Legion of Honour; Grand Officer of the Order of Christ; *b.* Gurtray, Portumna, Ireland, 1890; 3rd *s.* of Count John O'Kelly and Mary, *d.* of late Count O'Byrne of Corville and *g. d.* of Baron von Hübner, Austrian Ambassador in Paris, 1849-1858; *m.* 1920, Amy Marjorie (*d.* 1957), *d.* of late John Stuart, Liverpool; no *c.* *Educ.:* Clongowes Wood College; Royal University, Ireland. Travelled extensively in Far East and America; served European War, 1914-1918; Irish Agent, Switzerland, 1919; transferred to Brussels, 1921; Irish Representative in Brussels, 1921-29; Envoy Extraordinary and Minister Plenipotentiary of Irish Free State to Paris, 1929-35 (and to Belgium, 1932-35); retired from diplomatic service, 1935, returning to it in 1948 as Minister Plenipotentiary, Chargé d'Affaires, Lisbon; retired, Aug. 1955 and named Hon. Counsellor to the Legation; recalled to duty, Apr. 1962 as Minister Chargé d'Affaires. *Recreations:* reading, surviving. *Address:* Irish Embassy, 17A, rue Sacramento à Lapa, Lisbon, Portugal. *T.:* 662225. *Clubs:* Stephen's Green (Dublin); St. Cloud (Paris); Gaulois (Brussels); Eça de Queiroz (Lisbon).
[*Died* 3 *Jan.* 1968.

OLDFIELD, Claude Houghton; author; *b.* Sevenoaks, Kent; *y. s.* of George Sargent Oldfield and Elizabeth Harriet Thomas; *m.* Dulcie Benson. *Educ.:* Dulwich College. Visited Czechoslovakia as guest of the Government, 1936. *Publications: verse:* The Phantom Host, 1917; The Tavern of Dreams, 1919; *plays:* Judas, 1922; In the House of the High Priest, 1923; *essays:* The Kingdoms of the Spirit, 1924; *novels:* Neighbours, 1926; The Riddle of Helena, 1927; Crisis, 1929; I am Jonathan Scrivener, 1930; A Hair Divides, 1930; Chaos is Come Again, 1932; Julian Grant Loses His Way, 1933; This Was Ivor Trent, 1935; The Passing of the Third Floor Back (based on Jerome K. Jerome's play), 1935; Christina, 1936; Strangers, 1938; Hudson Rejoins the Herd, 1939; All Change, Humanity!, 1942; Six Lives and a Book, 1943; Passport to Paradise, 1944; Transformation Scene, 1946; The Quarrel, 1948; Birthmark, 1950; The Enigma of Conrad Stone, 1952; At the End of a Road, 1953; The Clock Ticks, 1954; Some Rise by Sin, 1956; More Lives than One, 1957; *short stories:* Three Fantastic Tales, 1934; The Beast, 1936; The Man Who Could Still Laugh, 1943. *Recreation:* Devonshire. *Club:* Savage.
[*Died* 10 *Feb.* 1961.

OLDFIELD, William Henry, J.P.; M.P. (Lab.) Gorton Division of Manchester, 1942-1955; Parliamentary Private Secretary to Minister of Education, 1945-51; Alderman Manchester City Council. J.P. Manchester. *Address:* 266 Dickenson Road, Longsight, Manchester 13. [*Died* 16 *Nov.* 1961.

OLDHAM, Joseph Houldsworth, C.B.E. 1951; M.A., D.D.; *b.* 20 Oct. 1874; *e. s* of Lt.-Col. G. W. Oldham, R.E.; *m.* 1898, Mary (*d.* 1965), *d.* of Sir Andrew H. L. Fraser, K.C.S.I. *Educ.:* Edinburgh Acad.; Trinity Coll., Oxford. Sec. of the Student Christian Movement, 1896-97; Secretary of the Young Men's Christian Association at Lahore, India, 1897-1900; Secretary of the World Missionary Conference, 1908-10, and of its Continuation Committee, 1910-21 and of the International Missionary Council, 1921-38; Editor of the International Review of Missions, 1912-27; Administrative Director of the International Institute of African Languages and Cultures, 1931-38; Chairman of the Research Commission of the Universal Christian Council for Life and Work, 1934-1938; Member of the Advisory Committee on Education in the Colonies, 1925-36; of the East Africa Commission on Closer Union, 1927-28; Editor of the Christian News-Letter, 1939-45. Senior Officer of the Christian Frontier Council, 1942-47. *Publications:* Christianity and the Race Problem; Real Life is Meeting; Florence Allshorn; Life is Commitment. *Address:* The Briers, Old Roar Road, St. Leonards-on-Sea, Sussex. *T.:* Hastings 51146. *Club:* Athenæum.
[*Died* 16 *May* 1969.

OLDMAN, Cecil Bernard, C.B. 1952; C.V.O. 1958; M.A., F.S.A.; Principal Keeper of Printed Books, British Museum, 1948-59; *b.* 2 April 1894; *er. s.* of Frederick James Oldman and Agnes Barnes Nightingale; *m.* 1933, Sigrid, *yr. d.* of Vice-Admiral Adolf Sobieczky and Adele, Baroness Potier des Echelles, Baden bei Wien, Austria. *Educ.:* City of London School; Exeter College, Oxford. Assistant, afterwards Assistant-Keeper, Printed Books Dept., British Museum, 1920-43; Deputy-Keeper, 1943-46; Keeper, 1946-47. Vice-Pres. of Royal Musical Assoc., 1948; Vice-Pres. of Library Association, 1949; President 1954. Hon. Fellow Exeter College Oxford, 1956. Hon. D.Mus. (Edin.), 1956; Hon. Litt.D. (Sheffield) 1959. *Publications:* Thomas Attwood's Studies with Mozart, 1925; Mozart-Drucke (with O. E. Deutsch), 1931-32; Mozart and Modern Research, 1932; Musical First Editions, 1934, new edition, 1938; Thomson's Collections of National Song (with Cecil Hopkinson), 1940; contributor to third, fourth and fifth editions of Grove's Dictionary of Music and Musician's and to various musical and bibliographical periodicals. *Recreations*: music, gardening, reading. *Address*: Flat 3, 37-41 Gower St., W.C.1. *T.*: 01-580 8135. *Club*: Athenaeum. [*Died* 7 *Oct.* 1969.

OLDS, Irving Sands, Hon. C.B.E.; partner, White & Case, N.Y., since 1917; Hon. Degrees: D.Sc. Bus. Admin. (Bryant) 1946; M.A. (Yale) 1948; D.Sc. Comm. (Drexel Inst. of Tech.), 1952; D.Pub.Serv. (Univ. of Denver) 1952; LL.D. (Roanoke Coll.) 1952, (Trinity Coll.) 1953, (Long Island Univ.) 1954. (Brigham Young Univ.) 1955, (Syracuse Univ.) 1955, (Swathmore College) 1956, (Yale Univ.) 1956; (Wabash College) 1957; (Williams Coll.) 1959; (Franklin and Marshall Coll.) 1959; (Univ. of Akron) 1959; D.C.L. (Union College) 1954; D.H.L. (Oberlin) 1958; Hon. Chancellor, Union College, 1954-55; *b.* Erie, Pa., 22 Jan. 1887; *s.* of Clark Olds and Livia Elizabeth Keator: *m.* 1917, Evelyn Foster (*d.* 1957), New York, N.Y.; no *c. Educ.:* Erie High School; Yale Coll.; Harvard Law School. B.A. Yale, 1907; LL.B. Harvard 1910; Secretary to Justice Oliver Wendell Holmes, U.S. Supreme Court, 1910-11; admitted to Bar, Pennsylvania, 1910, and N.Y. 1912; entered N.Y. law firm, White & Case, 1911. Counsel for Export Dept., J. P. Morgan & Co., *re* war purchases in U.S. by British and French Governments, 1915-17; Counsel for Purchasing Department of British War Mission to U.S.A., 1917-19; Special Asst. to Asst. Sec. of War, Stettinius, in U.S. War Dept., 1918; member Board of Directors and Finance Cttee. (now Exec. Cttee.), U.S. Steel Corp., 1936-60 (retd.); Chm., Board of Directors, 1940-52 (retired); Trustee: Metropolitan Museum of Art (member Executive Committee); Metropolitan Opera Association; N.Y. Public Library; Pierpont Morgan Library; American Shakespeare Festival Theatre and Academy; N.Y. Hist. Soc. (President); Cooper Union for Advancement of Science and Art (Chm.); Fell., Yale Corp., 1947-55; Mem. Yale Univ. Council, 1956-61; (Pres., 1959-61); Dir., Teachers Insurance & Annuity Association of America Stock; Council for Financial Aid to Education (Chm.) Member: Bd. of Directors Lincoln Center for the Performing Arts; Member of Board of Governors, Amer. Nat. Red Cross, 1953-54; Member of Bd. of Managers, N.Y. Inst. for Education of the Blind; National Sponsor, Hadley Sch. for the Blind; Member-at-large Yale Alumni Bd.; former Vice-Pres.: N.Y. State Chamber of Commerce; Counsellor, Nat. Industrial Conf. Bd.; Mem., Council on Foreign Relations; Trustee, American Heritage Foundation; National Trust for Historic Preservation; Heritage Foundation (Deerfield, Mass.); Shelburne (Vt.) Museum; Mem. Assoc. of Bar of City of N.Y., American Bar Assoc., N.Y. State Bar Assoc., Am. Iron and Steel Inst., Iron and Steel Inst. (Eng.), Am. Antiquarian Soc.; Roy. Soc. of Arts; Am. Acad. of Arts and Sciences; Acad. of Polit. Science, Am. Acad. of Polit. and Social Science, Bibliographical Soc. of America, Newcomen Soc. of England, The Pilgrims of the U.S., etc. Served with Squadron A, N.Y. Nat. Guard, 1911-16. *Publications:* The United States Navy, 1776-1815, 1942; Bits and Pieces of American History, 1952; numerous business, economic and historical addresses. *Recreations:* hunting, fishing, riding. *Address:* 14 Wall St., New York 5, New York; 141 East 72nd Street, New York 21, New York. *Clubs:* Knickerbocker, Century, University, Yale, Grolier, Down Town, The Recess, Pinnacle (N.Y. City); Graduates (New Haven); New Haven Lawn (New Haven); Walpole Society (Chm.), Club of Odd Volumes (Boston); Rowfant (Cleveland); Blooming Grove Hunting and Fishing (Hawley, Pa.). [*Died* 4 *March* 1963.

O'LEARY, Major Michael J., V.C. 1915; Building Contractor; *b.* Kilbarry Lodge, Macroom, County Cork, 1888; Private, Irish Guards, 1909-13; Royal North-West Mounted Police, 1913-14; promoted from Sergeant, 1915; to 1st Bn. Connaught Rangers, 1915, on commission; served European War, 1914-18 (despatches, Cross of St. George (Russia), V.C.).; War of 1939-45; rejoined Army from R.A.R.O., 1939; Capt. 1939; Capt., Pioneer Corps, 1944; Middlesex Regt., 1940-44; discharged on medical grounds, 1945. *Address:* 3 Oakleigh Ave., Edgware, Middx. *T.:* Edgware 5028. [*Died July* 1961.

OLIPHANT, Sir Lancelot, K.C.M.G., *cr.* 1931 (C.M.G. 1917(; C.B. 1929; retd.; *b.* 1881; 3rd and *o. surv. s.* of Arthur C. Oliphant; *m.* 1939, Christine (Officier de l'Ordre de Léopold, 1946), *widow* of Victor, 1st Viscount Churchill, G.C.V.O. Entered Foreign Office, 1903; Acting 3rd Secretary in H.M. Diplomatic Service, 1905; at British Embassy, Constantinople, 1905-6, and again at British Legation, Teheran, 1909-11; visited the Khanates of Central Asia, 1911; Assistant Secretary, Foreign Office, 1920; Counsellor, 1923; Assistant Under-Secretary of State, 1927-36; Deputy Under-Secretary of State for Foreign Affairs, 1936-39; Ambassador to Belgium and Minister to Luxembourg, 1939; was captured by enemy forces in France while proceeding from Bruges to Le Havre to join the Belgian Govt. and was interned in Germany from 2 June 1940 till 27 Sept. 1941. Resumed his duties with Belgian and Luxembourg Govts. in London, 1 Oct. 1941-Sept. 1944; retired, Nov. 1944. Vice-Pres. (Hon.) Anglo-Belgian Union. Silver Jubilee Medal, 1935; Coronation Medal, 1937. *Publication:* An Ambassador in Bonds, 1946. *Address:* 6 Cumberland Mansions, George Street, W.1. *Club:* Turf. [*Died* 2 *Oct.* 1965.

OLIVE, George William, C.B.E. 1952; M.A. (Cantab.); *s.* of late George Olive, Hemel Hempsted; *m.* Charlotte Cook; one *s.* one *d. Educ.:* Berkhamsted School; Clare College, Cambridge. VIth form Master, Housemaster, Oundle School; late Headmaster, Dauntsey's School, Wilts. *Publications:* Monographs on Modern Education and the Teaching of Science: A Schools Adventure; The Most Precious Gift of All. *Address:* Fearnoch, 15 Latham Road, Cambridge. [*Died* 10 *Nov.* 1963.

OLIVER, Major Alfred Alexander, C.B.E. 1929; T.D.; *b.* 23 Oct. 1874; *yr. s.* of Alfred Oliver, Highbury; *m.* Edith Mary (*d.* 1949), *d.* of J. E. Hayes, St. Albans; one *d. Educ.:* Owens School, Islington. H.M. Customs, 1893; Inland Revenue, Somerset House, 1894; Controller of Repayments, 1920; Clerk to the Special Commissioners of Income Tax, 1921, Special Commissioner, 1925; retired, 1936; late Major 15th Battn. London Regt. (P.W.O. Civil Service Rifles); served S. Africa with the C.I.V. 1900 (Queen's medal and 4 clasps); European War 1914-19 in France, Macedonia, Egypt, and Palestine (despatches twice). *Address:* Briarfields, Warminster, Wilts. *T.:* Warminster 2225. [*Died* 19 *Jan.* 1965.

OLIVER, Hon. Dame Florence G. C.; *see* Cardell-Oliver, Hon. Dame A. F. G. C.

OLIVER, Admiral of the Fleet Sir Henry Francis, G.C.B., *cr.* 1928 (K.C.B., *cr.* 1916; C.B. 1913); K.C.M.G., *cr.* 1918; M.V.O. 1905; Hon. LL.D. (Edin.), 1920; *b.* 22 Jan. 1865; *s.* of late Robert Oliver, Lochside, Kelso; *m.* 1914, Beryl (later Dame Beryl Oliver), *d.* of Francis Edward Carnegy and of Mrs. Carnegy of Lour. Entered Navy, 1878; Lieutenant, 1888; Commander, 1899; Captain, 1903; Rear-Admiral, 1913; Director of Intelligence, Admiralty War Staff, 1913-14; Acting Vice-Admiral and Chief of Admiralty War Staff, 1914-17; on Admiralty reorganisation in 1917 became a member of the Board and Deputy Chief of Naval Staff; Rear-Admiral Commanding First Battle Cruiser Squadron, 1918; Vice-Admiral, 1919; Vice-Adm. commanding the Home Fleet, 1919; Vice-Admiral commanding Reserve Fleet, 1919-1920; Second Sea Lord, 1920-24; Commander-in-Chief, Atlantic Fleet, 1924-27; Vice-Admiral; 1919; Admiral, 1923; Admiral of the Fleet, 1928; retired list, 1933; restored to active list, 1940. Jubilee Medal, 1935; Coronation Medals, 1937 and 1953. American Dist. Service Medal; Commander Legion of Honour; Orders of St. Anne of Russia, Swords of Sweden. *Address:* 20 South Eaton Place, S.W.1. *T.:* Sloane 7370. *Club:* United Service. [*Died* 15 *Oct.* 1965.

OLIVER, Laurence Herbert, C.B.E. 1946; J.P.; *b.* 15 Oct. 1881; *s.* of late Walter E. Oliver, Hampstead, N.W.; *m.* 1915, Amelia, *d.* of late G. Oettle, Lee, S.E.; one *d.* *Educ.:* Bancroft's School. Entered service of L.C.C., 1900; Asst. Clerk, 1930, Dep. Clerk, 1939, Actg. Clerk, 1946, and Clerk, 1947: retired, 1947. J.P. County of London since 1945, on Hampstead bench until 1956. Member London Licensing Planning Cttee. and of Visiting Cttee. H.M. Prison Wormwood Scrubs, until 1956. Member of Public Works Loan Board, 1948-59. Served European War, 1914-18, with R.A.S.C. in East Africa (commissioned officer); rendered services to Civil Defence during War of 1939-1945. *Address:* 8 The Rise, Edgware, Middlesex. *T.:* Stonegrove 7969. *Club:* Reform. [*Died* 19 *June* 1962.

OLIVER, Sir Roland Giffard, Kt., 1938; M.C.; Judge of High Court of Justice, King's Bench Division, 1938-57, retd.; *b.* 1882; 3rd *s.* of Edmund Ward Oliver of Orlestone, Kent; *m.* 1st, Winifred (*d.* 1959), 3rd *d.* of Lt.-Colonel Burnaby; 2nd, 1961, Mrs. Madelaine Mary Kean. *Educ.:* Marlborough; Corpus Christi College, Oxford. Recorder of Folkestone, 1926-38. Member of Budget enquiry tribunal, 1936; Chairman of Committee on Court Martial Procedure, 1938; Chairman Prison and Detention Barracks enquiry, 1943. *Address:* Capel, Orlestone, Ashford, Kent. [*Died* 14 *March* 1967.

OLIVER, Victor; Film and Stage Star; Conductor of the British Concert Orchestra; *b.* 8 July 1898; *s.* of Baron Victor von Samek and Josephine Rauch; relinquished father's title in 1922; *m.* 1936, Sarah (from whom he obtained a divorce, 1945, and who *m.* 1949, Antony Beauchamp), *d.* of Rt. Hon. Sir Winston S. Churchill, K.G., M.P.; *m.* 1946, Natalie Frances Conder; one *d.* *Educ.:* University of Vienna. Started as concert-pianist in America; later turned to the legitimate stage and in 1935 entered the revue field; has appeared in many British and American films. B.B.C. Radio and Television Opera Department. *Publications:* writes for newspapers and magazines. *Recreations:* tennis, golf, riding. *Address:* 66 Westminster Gardens, S.W.1. *T.:* Victoria 2640. *Clubs:* Wentworth Golf (Surrey); Royal Birkdale Golf. [*Died* 15 *Aug.* 1964.

OLIVER, Professor William, B.Sc., A.M.I.C.E., F.R.S.E.; Professor of Organisation of Industry and Commerce, University of Edinburgh, 1925-52, retired 1952; *m.*; one *s.* one *d.* *Educ.:* George Watson's College, Edinburgh; University of Edinburgh. *Recreation:* golf. *Address:* 76 Inverleith Row, Edinburgh 3. *T.:* Waverley 4631. *Club:* University Union (Edin.). [*Died* 19 *Nov.* 1962.

OLIVER-BELLASIS, Captain Richard, C.B. 1951; C.V.O. 1946; C.St.J.; A.M.I.E.E.; Royal Navy (retired); *b.* 15 September 1900; *s.* of late Capt. R. J. E. Oliver-Bellasis, Shilton, nr. Coventry; *m.* 1928, Lorna, *d.* of H. L. Richardson, Shiremark, Capel, Surrey; two *d.* *Educ.:* The Golden Parsonage, Hemel Hempstead; R.N. Colleges, Osborne and Dartmouth. Specialized in Torpedo (Ogilvie Medal). Commander, 1933; H.M.S. Vernon in charge of experimental mine-sweeping, 1939; Capt. 1941; Naval Staff, Admiralty, 1941; H.M.S. Euryalus, 1943; Director of Underwater Weapons, Admiralty, 1947-50; ret., 1950. Sec. Cooper Technical Bureau, 1952. *Address:* Old Oak Farm, Ashley Green, Chesham, Bucks. *T.:* Berkhamsted 707. *Club:* United Service. [*Died* 24 *Oct.* 1964.

OLLARD, Lt.-Col. John William Arthur, O.B.E. 1960; *b.* 4 July 1893; *s.* of Arthur Ridgway Ollard and Agnes C. C. de Havilland. *Educ.:* St. Edmund's Coll., Ware; Downing Coll., Camb. Gazetted 1st Bn. Cambridgeshire Regt. 1912; served in France, 1915; retired, 1919, Captain; re-employed 1941, Lt.-Col. Isle of Ely County Council, 1922, Alderman, 1934, Chairman, 1957; Wisbech Town Council, 1926, Alderman, 1931; Mayor of Wisbech, 1927. High Sheriff Cambs and Hunts, 1943; D.L. Cambridgeshire 1935; Knight Commander Order of St. Gregory, 1948; O.St.J. 1943. Hon. Freeman Borough of Wisbech, 1944. *Address:* Petercroft, Wisbech. *T.A.:* Wisbech. *T.:* Wisbech 230. [*Died* 28 *Jan.* 1961.

OLVER, Col. Sir Arthur, Kt., *cr.* 1937; C.B. 1919; C.M.G. 1916; F.R.C.V.S.; F.R.S.E.; late R.A.V.C.; *s.* of R. S. Olver, of Trescowe, Par Station, Cornwall; *b.* 1875; *m.* 1914, Marjorie Beart; one *s.* Served South African War, 1901-2 (Queen's medal, 5 clasps); P.V.O. Egyptian Army and Sudan C.V.D., 1907; Assistant Director General, A.V.S., 1908; European War, 1914-18 (despatches twice, C.M.G., Brevet Lt.-Col.); D.D.V.S. British Remount Commission, Canada and America, 1917 (C.B.); Deputy Director of Veterinary Services, India, 1928-30; retired pay, 1930; Expert Adviser in Animal Husbandry, Government of India, 1930-38; Principal Royal (Dick) Veterinary College, Edinburgh, 1938-45. *Address:* 7 The Avenue, Summersdale, Chichester, Sussex. [*Died* 15 *Aug.* 1961.

O'MEARA, Maj.-Gen. (Retd.) Francis Joseph, C.B. 1956; Deputy Director of Medical Services, Western Command, 1956-1959; *b.* 4 July 1900; *s.* of Dr. T. J. O'Meara, Skibbereen, County Cork, Eire; *m.* 1935, Janet Glendower, *d.* of H. W. Croft, Ledbury, Herefordshire; two *s.* one *d.* *Educ.:* Clongowes; Trinity College, Dublin. M.A., M.D. Dub. 1926; F.R.C.P.I. 1928; D.T.M. & H. Eng. 1932. Lt., R.A.M.C. 1923; Major, 1934; served War of 1939-45 in France and Germany (P.O.W., 1940-44; despatches, 1946). Cons. Physician, B.A.O.R., 1946-50; Cons. Physician, F.A.R. E.L.F., 1950; Director of Medical Services, G.H.Q., M.E.L.F. 17, 1954-56. Q.H.P. 1955-59; Lt.-Col., 1944; Col. 1948; Brig. 1953; Maj.-Gen. 1955. Fellow Roy. Soc. Med. and Roy. Soc. Tropical Med. C.St.J. 1948. *Publications:* numerous papers on medical subjects; Jl. R.A.M.C. *Recreations:* fishing, shooting, golf, bridge, history. *Address:* c/o Glyn, Mills & Co., Whitehall, S.W.1. *Club:* Army and Navy. [*Died* 15 *Oct.* 1967.

OMOLOLU, Olumide Olusanya; Judge of the High Court of Lagos, Nigeria, since Sept. 1964; *b.* 27 July 1925; *s.* of late Adebayo Omololu, M.B.E., and of Adebisi Omololu; *m.* 1954, Abimbola Aina Da

Rocha Afodu, M.A., LL.B., Barrister-at-Law. *Educ.:* The Grammar School, Lagos; Trinity College, Dublin; Middle Temple, London. Legal Practitioner, Nigeria, 1950-52; Crown Counsel, 1952-54; Legal Adviser to Inland Revenue, 1954-57; joined External Affairs Service, 1957; Nigerian Attaché: at British Embassy, Rio de Janeiro, 1958; at British Embassy, Paris, 1958-59; Chancellor of the Lagos Diocese, 1955-57; Asst. Registrar, Church of Province of W. Africa, 1954-57; Actg. Permanent Sec., Min. of Foreign Affairs and Commonwealth Relations, Lagos, Oct. 1960; Member, first Nigerian Delegation to U.N., 1960. Deputy High Commissioner for Nigeria in the United Kingdom, 1961-62; Solicitor-General of the Federation of Nigeria, 1962-1964; Queen's Counsel, 1963. Chief Bajiki of Owu, 1961. *Recreations:* cricket, reading. *Address:* Judges' Chambers, High Court, Lagos, Nigeria. *Clubs:* Royal Commonwealth Society; Island, Metropolitan (Lagos). [*Died* 18 *March* 1967.

O'MORCHOE, The, Captain Arthur Donel MacMurrogh, Chief of O'Morchoe of Oulartleigh and Monamolin; *b.* 3 June 1892; *e. s.* of late Rev. Thomas Arthur O'Morchoe, M.A., The O'Morchoe, and late Anne, *d.* of late John George Gibbon, LL.D., B.L., of Kiltennell, Co. Wexford; *m.* 1st, 1926, Isabel Hester Louise (*d.* 1947), *o. d.* of late Richard George Carden, J.P., D.L., of Fishmoyne, Co. Tipperary; two *d.*; 2nd, 1948, Eva Augusta Elizabeth, *widow* of Lt.-Col. George Meredyth Grogan, D.S.O., 18th Royal Irish Regt., and *o. d.* of late Ernest F.L. Ellis, St. Austins, Inch. *Educ.:* Trinity Coll., Dublin. Joined the Leinster Regiment (Royal Meaths) Aug. 1914; served European War, A.D.C. to Maj.-Gen. Hon. E. J. Montague-Stuart-Wortley and Camp Commandant 65th Division, 1917-18; served in the Provost Marshal's Department, 1918-22; entered the Colonial Service, 1924; A.D.C. to British Resident, Zanzibar, 1930-31; Private Secretary to Acting British Resident, 1931; Commissioner of Police, Gold Coast, 1934; attached General Staff War Office, 1940. Colonial Police Medal, 1941. *Address:* St. Austins, Coolgreany, Gorey, Co. Wexford. *Club:* Kildare St. (Dublin). [*Died* 29 *Aug.* 1966.

O'NEILL, Colonel Eugene Joseph, C.M.G. 1919; D.S.O. 1915; V.D.; M.B. (N.Z.); F.R.C.S., Ed.; M.R.C.S. Eng.; F.R.A.C.S.; N.Z. Medical Corps, retired; Cons. Surgeon, Dunedin Hospital, N.Z.; late Hon. Physician to Governor-General, New Zealand; *b.* Dunedin, N.Z., 1875; *s.* of Patrick O'Neill, Dunedin, N.Z.; *m.* Josephine, *d.* of Dr T. Monaghan, London; three *d.* (one *s.* killed in action War of 1939-1945). *Educ.:* Christian Brothers' School, Dunedin; Otago Univ.; London. Senior House Surgeon Dunedin Hospital, N.Z., 1899-1900; Served South Africa, 1901-2 (despatches, Queen's medal 5 clasps); in Dardanelles, Egypt, France, European War, 1914-19 (despatches, C.M.G., D.S.O.). Formerly Resident Surgeon Lock Hosp., London; Hon. Surgeon, Dunedin Hosp., 1903-27. Served War of 1939-45, Merchant Navy, Pacific, 1939-41. *Address:* 3 Embassy Court, Boulcott St., Wellington, N.Z. [*Died* 24 *April* 1962.

O'NEILL, Col. Patrick Laurence, C.I.E. 1919; Indian Medical Service, retired; *b.* 28 Feb. 1876; *s.* of Dr. P. L. O'Neill of Geraldine, Athy, Co. Kildare; *m.* 1906, Doretta, *d.* of Stephen Telford, Barrowford, Athy; two *s.* two *d.* Served E. Africa, 1914-18 (C.I.E., despatches); Inspector-General Civil Hospitals, Burma, 1929-32; retired, 1933. *Address:* Lodge Cottage, Upper Warren Avenue, Caversham, Reading, Berks. *T.:* Reading 71838. [*Died* 4 *Dec.* 1962.

ONIONS, Charles Talbut, C.B.E. 1934; F.B.A. 1938; Fellow of Magdalen College since 1923 (Librarian, 1940-55); *b.* 10 Sept. 1873; *e. s.* of late Ralph John Onions and Harriet Onions (*née* Talbut), Birmingham; *m.* Angela (*d.* 1941), *y. d.* of late Rev. Arthur Blythman, Rector of Shenington; seven *s.* three *d.* *Educ.:* King Edward VI. School, Camp Hill, and Mason College, Birmingham. Engaged in teaching, 1892-95; on the staff of the Oxford English Dictionary from 1895 (co-editor, 1914-33); B.A. Lond. 1892; M.A. Lond. 1895 (classics); Hon. M.A. Oxon, 1914; Naval Intelligence Division, Admiralty, 1918 (Hon. Capt. R.M.); Lecturer in English, Oxford, 1920-27; Reader in English Philology, Oxford, 1927-49; Deputy for Prof. of Anglo-Saxon, Oxford, 1921-22; Hon. D.Litt. Oxon; Hon. Litt.D. Leeds; Hon. Fellow of the Royal Society of Literature, 1928; President of the Philological Society, 1929-33; Hon. LL.D. Birmingham, 1930; Sir Israel Gollancz Memorial Prizeman (British Academy), 1933; Leverhulme Research Fellow, 1938-40; Hon. Director Early English Text Society, 1945-1957; Corresponding Fell. of the Mediæval Acad. of Amer., 1953. Has examined in English in Univs. of Oxford, London, Wales, Belfast, Leeds, and Reading. *Publications:* Advanced English Syntax, 1904, etc.; (with H. E. Berthon) Advanced French Composition, 1904, 1924; A Shakespeare Glossary, 1911, etc.; completed editing of Shakespeare's England, in succession to Sir Sidney Lee, 1916; revised Sweet's Anglo-Saxon Reader, 1922, 1946, etc.; editor of Shorter Oxford English Dictionary, 1933, etc.; editor of Medium Ævum, 1932-56. *Address:* 7 Staverton Road, Oxford. [*Died* 8 *Jan.* 1965.

ONIONS, Oliver; *b.* Bradford, 1873; *m.* Berta Ruck,; two *s.* Studied Art. Worked as draughtsman for Harmworth Press. *Publications:* The Compleat Bachelor; Tales of a Far Riding; The Odd Job Man, The Drakestone; Back of the Moon; Admiral Eddy; Pedlar's Pack; Little Devil Doubt; Draw in your Stool; The Exception; Good Boy Seldom; Widdershins; In Accordance with the Evidence; The Debit Account; The Story of Louie; The Two Kisses; A Crooked Mile; Mushroom Town; The New Moon, 1918; A Case in Camera, 1920; The Tower of Oblivion, 1921; Peace in Our Time, 1923; Ghosts in Daylight, 1924; The Spite of Heaven, 1925; Whom God hath Sundered, 1926; Cut Flowers, 1927; The Painted Face, 1929; The Open Secret, 1930; A Certain Man, 1931; Catalan Circus, 1934; The Collected Ghost Stories of Oliver Onions, 1935; The Hand of Kornelius Voyt, 1939; The Italian Chest, 1939; Cockcrow, or Anybody's England, 1940; The Story of Ragged Robin, 1945; Poor Man's Tapestry, 1946 (awarded James Tait Black Memorial Prize, 1947); Arras of Youth, 1949; A Penny for the Harp, 1951; Bells Rung Backward, 1953. *Address:* c/o A. P. Watt and Son, Hastings House, Norfolk Street, W.C.2. [*Died* 9 *April* 1961.

ONSLOW, Sir Richard Wilmot, 7th Bt., *cr.* 1797; T.D. 1943; Major Duke of Cornwall's L.I. (T.A.); *b.* 30 July 1906; *er. s.* of Sir Roger Onslow, 6th Bt., and Mildred (who *m.* 2nd, 1932, Capt. Ughtred A. F. Knox), *e. d.* of late Sir R. R. Wilmot, 6th Bt.; *S.* father, 1931; *m.* 1st, 1929, Constance (*d.* 1960), *d.* of Albert Parker; one *s.* three *d.*; 2nd, 1961, Mary (Molly) Russell, Belfast. *Educ.:* Cheltenham College. *Heir:* *s.* John Roger Wilmot [*b.* 21 July 1932; *m.* 1955, Catherine Zoia Greenway; one *s.* one *d.*]. *Address:* Casa Onslow, Marsaxlokk, Malta, G.C. *Club:* Royal Fowey Yacht. [*Died* 14 *July* 1963.

OPPENHEIMER, Charles, R.S.A. 1934 (A.R.S.A. 1927); R.S.W. 1912; *b.* Manchester, 10 Oct. 1875; 4th *s.* of Ludwig and Susan McCulloch Oppenheimer, Manchester; *m.* 1903, Constance Emily, *e. d.* of R. L. Taylor, F.I.C., F.C.S., Manchester. *Educ.:* Manchester.

Studied at Manchester School of Art under R. H. A. Willis and Walter Crane and in Italy. Kirkcudbright, and Evening, Lake of Lucerne, purchased by Manchester City Art Gallery; The Artist's Garden, Oldham Art Gallery; Low Tide, Kirkcudbright, Southport Art Gallery; Granite Quarry, Whitworth Art Gallery; Harnessing the Dee, Galloway, Kelvingrove Art Gallery, Glasgow; Lily Pool, University Art Gallery, Michigan, U.S.A.; February Sunshine, Newport (Mon.) Art Gallery; A Late Snowfall, The Scottish Modern Arts Assoc.; Early Morning, A Solway Port, Worthing Art Gallery; The Old Tolbooth, Manchester City Art Gallery; Barlochan Pool, National Gallery of South Africa, Capetown; White Gables, Pilgrim Trust; Winter Landscape, Blackpool Art Gallery; My Garden at Twilight, Broughton House Collection, Kirkcudbright. Served in France, Royal Artillery. *Recreations:* golf, fishing. *Address:* Woodlea, Kirkcudbright, Scotland. *T.:* 586. *Club:* Scottish Arts (Edinburgh) [*Died* 16 *April* 1961.

OPPENHEIMER, Sir Francis (Charles), K.C.M.G., *cr.* 1919; Kt., *cr.* 1907; *b.* London, 17 Dec. 1870; *s.* of Sir Charles Oppenheimer, Kt., H.B.M.'s Consul-General at Frankfort; *m.* 1931, Jane, Lady Horlick. *Educ.:* Lycée, Frankfort; M.A. Balliol College, Oxon. Barr.-at-Law Middle Temple; H.B.M.'s Consul-General at Frankfort-on-Main, 1900-1911; Commercial Attaché for Northern Central Europe, with the rank of an acting Counsellor, of Embassy in the Diplomatic Service, to reside in Frankfort, 1912-14; retired from Diplomatic Service, 1920. At outbreak of war sent to The Hague, where he devised and negotiated establishment (Christmas Day, 1914) of the Netherland Oversea Trust (the N.O.T.)—the first of the private bodies constituted in neutral countries in connection with the blockade; entrusted with similar mission to Switzerland, 1915, where he negotiated the S.S.S. (Société Swiss de Surveillance Economique). Acted as British Delegate on several occasions when inter-allied matters were discussed in Paris; left The Hague, Oct. 1918; proceeded on a Special Mission to Vienna as British Financial Commissioner, May 1919. *Publications:* Frankish Themes and Problems, 1952; The Legend of the Ste. Ampoule, 1953; Stranger Within (autobiography), 1960. *Address:* Point House, Point Hill, Rye, Sussex. *T.:* Rye 3273; 20 Lowndes Square, S.W.1. *T.:* Sloane 3161. *Club:* St. James'. [*Died* 25 *June* 1961.

OPPENHEIMER, Joseph, R.P.; Painter; *b.* 13 July 1876; *m.* 1908, Fanny (*née* Sternfeld); one *s.* one *d.* Studied at Munich Academy; stayed in Italy; visited U.S.A., France, Canada, etc. Since 1904 has been exhibiting at Royal Academy and later at Royal Society of Portrait Painters; also at Continental Exhibitions (Europe) until 1933; in recent years active also in Canada and U.S.A.; Munich International Exhibition Gold Medal, 1910; Hon. Mention Carnegie Inst., Pittsburgh, 1916. *Publications:* Occasional until 1908; Studio ABT, 1908; Continental European art magazines until 1933; covers of Woman's Journal. *Address:* 42 Wolfington Road, West Norwood, S.E.27. [*Deceased.*

OPPENHEIMER, J. Robert; physicist; Director and Professor of Physics, Institute for Advanced Study, Princeton, N.J., 1947-1966; *b.* New York, N.Y., 22 April 1904; *s.* of Julius Oppenheimer and Ella (*née* Freedman); *m.* 1940, Katherine Harrison; one *s.* one *d.* *Educ.:* Harvard University (B.A.); Cambridge University; Göttingen University, Germany (Ph.D.). National Research Fellow, 1927-28; Internat. Educ. Board Fellow, Univs. of Leyden and Zürich, 1928-1929; Asst. Prof. of Physics, Univ. of California and Calif. Inst. of Technology, 1929-31; Assoc. Prof., 1931-36; Professor, 1936-47; Director, Los Alamos Scientific Laboratory, Los Alamos, N.M. 1943-45. Chairman General Advisory Cttee. to U.S. Atomic Energy Commn., 1946-52; Mem. Board of Overseers, Harvard Coll., 1949-55; Fell. or Mem. of numerous acads. and socs. in America, also For. Mem. Royal Society, and Foreign or Hon. Mem. of many in other countries, and holds fellowships and hon. degrees, including some in Great Britain. Enrico Fermi Award, 1963. *Address:* (Home) Olden Farm, Princeton, N.J., U.S.A. [*Died* 18 *Feb.* 1967.

ORAM, Hon. Sir Matthew Henry, Kt. 1952; M.B.E. 1919; Speaker, House of Representatives, New Zealand, 1950-57; M.P. (Nat.) Manawatu, New Zealand, 1943-57; retired 1957; *b.* 2 June 1885; *s.* of Matthew Henry Oram and May Oram (*née* Eltham); *m.* 1913, Margarette Anne Florence (*née* Johnson); two *s.* two *d.* *Educ.:* Wellington College; Victoria University College, N.Z. M.A. (Hons. in Mathematics) 1909; LL.B. 1912; Barrister and Solicitor, 1913. Senior Partner firm Oram & Yortt, Palmerston North, N.Z. Held many positions on educational bodies (Victoria Coll. Council; Massey Agricultural Coll. Bd. of Governors, School of Agriculture; High School Board of Governors, etc.). Chm. Bd. Directors of N.Z. Players; President: N.Z. Air League; The Constitutional Society of N.Z. *Recreations:* golf, tennis, flying, acting, racing. *Address:* Norton, Featherston St., Palmerston North, N.Z. *T.:* 85344. *Clubs:* Wellesley (Wellington, N.Z.); Manawatu (Palmerston North, N.Z.); Feilding (Feilding, N.Z.). [*Died* 22 *Jan.* 1969.

ORCHARD, W(illiam) Arundel, O.B.E. 1936; D.Mus. Durham University; F.R.C.M.; *b.* London; *s.* of William Edward and Anne Elizabeth Orchard. *Educ.:* private tuition. Formerly music master Forest School, Essex, and Conductor of Colet Orchestral Society, London; also formerly Conductor Royal Sydney Liedertafel, Sydney Symphony Orchestra, Sydney Madrigal Society; Director of State Conservatorium of Music, New South Wales, and Conductor of Conservatorium Orchestra, 1923-34; Lecturer-in-charge of the Degree Course in Music in the University of Tasmania, 1935-38; since then visiting examiner in Australasia for Trinity College of Music, London; composer of various choral and orchestral works, chamber music, songs, etc. *Publications:* The Distant View, 1943; Music in Australia, 1953. *Address:* University Club, Sydney, N.S.W., Australia. [*Died* 7 *April* 1961.

ORD, Bernhard (Boris), C.B.E. 1958; M.A., Mus.B. (Hon. Mus.D. Durham 1955, Cambridge 1960); F.R.C.O. 1916; A.R.C.M. (piano playing, 1st pl.) 1920; Fellow, King's College, Cambridge, 1923; *s.* of late Clement Ord, M.A., Lecturer in the University of Bristol. *Educ.:* Clifton College (Scholar), 1907-14; Organ Scholar, Corpus Christi Coll., Cambridge, 1919; John Stewart of Rannoch Schol. in Sacred Music, 1920. Organist of King's College and Organist to the University, 1929-58; University Lecturer in Music, 1936-58; Conductor, Cambridge University Musical Society, 1938-54, and of Univ. Madrigal Society from its inception in 1920 to 1958. Conductor: Royal Albert Hall; Royal Festival Hall; B.B.C., etc.; Harpsichordist, specializing in continuo; Adjudicator, most Music Festivals; retired 1958. Served European War, 1914-1918, R.F.C. (Pilot), 1916-19 (twice wounded); Flight-Lieut. R.A.F., 1941-45; served in Normandy invasion. *Address:* King's College, Cambridge. [*Died* 30 *Dec.* 1961.

ORDE, Major Sir Simon Arthur Campbell-, 5th Bt., *cr.* 1790, of Morpeth; T.D.; Lovat Scouts; *b.* 15 July 1907; *s.* of Sir Arthur

John Campbell-Orde, 4th Bt., and Maie (*d.* 1955), *e. d.* of J. C. Stewart of Fasnacloich, Argyll; *S.* father, 1933; *m.* 1938, Eleanor Hyde, *e. d.* of Col. Humphrey Watts, O.B.E., T.D., Haslington Hall, Cheshire; two *s.* one *d.* *Educ.:* Charterhouse. *Heir:* *s.* John Alexander Campbell-Orde, *b.* 11 May 1943. *Address:* 31 The Little Boltons, S.W.10 *Club:* Caledonian. [*Died* 23 *Aug.* 1969.

ORIEL, John Augustus, C.B.E. 1947; M.C. 1917; F.R.I.C., M.I.Chem.E.; F.Inst.Pet.; Fellow Extraordinary, Churchill College, Cambridge, 1960, Fellow Emeritus, 1963; *b.* 17 June 1896; *s.* of late David Morgan Oriel, Dowlais, South Wales; *m.* 1923, Margaret Hester Evans; two *d.* *Educ.:* University of Wales (B.Sc.); Jesus College, Cambridge (M.A.). Natural Science Tripos, Part II. Served European War, 1915-19: Royal Engineers and Royal Garrison Artillery (wounded thrice, M.C.); temporarily blinded by mustard gas. Joined The Shell Petroleum Co. Ltd., 1921; Refinery Manager, Suez, 1933-35; Chief Chemist, The Shell Petroleum Co. Ltd., and Gen. Manager, "Shell" Refining and Marketing Co. Ltd., until 1950; Leader, Combined Intelligence Objectives Sub-Cttee. (Fuel and Oils), 1944-1945. Became blind from effects of mustard gas, 1950. Vice-Pres. Soc. of Chem. Industry, 1954-57; Mem. Exec. Council, Roy. Nat. Institute for the Blind; Mem. Board of Governors, Worcester College for the Blind; President Institution Chemical Engineers, 1955-57. Osborne Reynolds Medallist, Institution of Chemical Engineers, 1953 (Hon. Member 1958); Eastlake Medallist, Inst. of Petroleum, 1955 (Hon. Fell. 1959). *Address:* Springfield House, Brailes, Banbury, Oxon. *T.:* Brailes 225. *Club*: Oxford and Cambridge University. [*Died* 16 *June* 1968.

ORME, Lieut.-Col. Frank Leslie, O.B.E. 1946; T.D., J.P.; D.L.; Director: Royal Insurance Co. Ltd.; Liverpool & London & Globe Insurance Co. Ltd.; London & Lancashire Insurance Co. Ltd.; Midland Bank Ltd.; British & Foreign Marine Insurance Co. Ltd.; Thames & Mersey Marine Insurance Co. Ltd.; *b.* 10 May 1898; *s.* of late Edward Banks Orme; *m.* 1927, Margaret Ann (decd.), *o. c.* of Mrs. McKinnon Clark; four *s.*; *m.* 1948, Joan Cunliffe, *d.* of late W. R. Nielson. *Educ.:* Charterhouse; St. John's College, Cambridge; R.M.A., Woolwich. Served European War (despatches); R.F.A. in Salonika, 1916-1919; War of 1939-45 (despatches, O.B.E.): served in R.A.; comd. 25 L.A.A. Regt., 1941-43, 150 L.A.A. Regt., 1943-45. President of Liverpool Cotton Association, 1947. D.L. County of Chester, 1962. High Sheriff of Cheshire, 1962. *Recreations:* golf (Capt. of Royal Liverpool G.C., 1946-47), shooting. *Address:* Friars Park, Backford, nr. Chester. *T.:* Great Mollington 258. *Club:* Bath. [*Died* 25 *Dec.* 1968.

ORME, William Bryce; Principal Medical Officer, Johore, Malay States (retired); *b.* 16 Jan. 1871; *s.* of William Orme, Royal Sussex Militia; unmarried. *Educ.:* Lancing College; University College, London. M.R.C.S. England, L.R.C.P. London, 1894; Member of the Straits Settlements and Federated Malay States Medical Council; Diploma Tropical Medicine and Hygiene, Cantab. 1907; Diploma (with distinction), London School of Tropical Medicine, 1907; Egyptian Medical Service, 1897-1906; Medical Service of the Federated Malay States, 1907-19; seconded for a period of 3 years to reorganise the British North Borneo Medical Service, 1913-16; Order of the Medjidieh. *Publications:* in various Medical Journals. *Address:* 14 Cromwell Road, Hove, Sussex. *T.:* Hove 34160. [*Died* 29 *April* 1962.

ORMEROD, Frank Cunliffe, M.D. (Manch.) 1920; F.R.C.S.(Edin.) 1921; F.R.C.S. (Eng.) 1926; Professor Emeritus in the University of London, since 1959; Director of Research, Institute of Laryngology and Otology, 1959-62; Professor of Laryngology and Otology (University of London) at the Institute of Laryngology and Otology, Gray's Inn Rd., W.C.1, 1949-59; Hon. Cons. Surgeon, Roy. Nat. Throat, Nose and Ear Hospital, Throat and Ear Department, Brompton Chest Hospital; Consulting Laryngologist, King Edward VII Sanatorium, Midhurst; Hon. Consultant, Ear, Nose and Throat Department, Westminster Hospital, Royal National Hospital for Consumption, Ventnor; late Hon. Surgeon, Ear and Throat Dept. Marylebone Dispensary, and Golden Square Throat, Nose and Ear Hospital; *b.* 23 August 1894; *s.* of George Henry Ormerod and Clara, *d.* of Joseph Cunliffe, J.P., Chorley, Lancs; *m.* 1921, Mary, *o. d.* of William Burton, M.A., F.C.S.; two *s.* *Educ.:* Manchester Grammar School; Manchester University (Dreschfeld and Dauntesey Scholarships, M.B., Ch.B. 1916). H.S. and H.P. Manchester Royal Infirmary; House Surgeon, Birmingham and Midland Ear, Nose and Throat Hospital; Surgical Registrar, Golden Square Throat and Ear Hospital; Aural Specialist, Ministry of Pensions; Temp. Captain R.A.M.C., Mesopotamia, 1916-19 (Surgical and X-Ray Specialist); Afghanistan, 1919 (Med. Off. 1/4 Ghurkha Rifles); late member Court of Examiners, R.C.S.; Semon Lectr., Univ. of Lond., 1953; James Yearsley Lectr., 1965. Hon. Life Fell., Med. Society of Lond.; F.R.Soc.Med. (Ex. Hon. Sec. and Vice-Pres., Sect. Laryngology; Past Pres. and Ex. Hon. Sec., Section of Otology); late Hon. Sec. Brit. Assoc. of Otolaryngologists; Mem. Brit. Med. Assoc.; Hon. Sec. Sect. Oto-Rhino Laryngology, Eastbourne, 1931; Hon. Member: Société Française d'Otorhinolaryngologie; Deutsche Gesellschaft der Hals-Nasen-Ohrenärzte; Society of Head and Neck Surgeons of America; American Broncho-œsophagological Assoc.; Assoc. of Otorhinolaryngologists of Yugoslavia; American Laryngological, Rhinological and Otological (Triological) Society. *Publications:* Tuberculosis of the Upper Respiratory Tract, 1939; Articles on Disease of Throat, Nose and Ear in Proceedings of Royal Society of Medicine, Journal of Laryngology and Otology and other Medical Periodicals. *Address:* 37 Portland Place, W.1. *T.:* Langham 5621; 89 Belsize Park Gardens N.W.3. *T.:* Primrose 1480. [*Died* 25 *Jan.* 1967.

ORMEROD, Henry Arderne, M.A., M.C.; Rathbone Professor of Ancient History, Liverpool University, 1928-51; *b.* 16 March 1886; 3rd *s.* of late J. A. Ormerod, M.D., F.R.C.P.; *m.* Mildred Robina, 2nd *d.* of late Richard Caton, M.D., F.R.C.P.; two *s.* *Educ.:* Rugby School; Queen's College, Oxford (Scholar). Student at the British School at Athens, 1909-11; travelled in Greece and Asia Minor; Lecturer in Greek, University of Liverpool, 1911-23; Professor of Greek, University of Leeds, 1923-28; served in R.F.A., 1915-19 (M.C., despatches, Chevalier of Order of King George I. of Greece). *Publications:* Piracy in the Ancient World, 1924; The Liverpool Free School, 1951; The Early History of the Liverpool Medical School, 1953; The Liverpool Royal Institution, 1953; sections in Cambridge Ancient History, Vol. IX.; papers on Classical subjects in Journal of Hellenic Studies, Journal of Roman Studies, Annual of British School at Athens, Classical Review, Liverpool Annals of Archæology and Anthropology, Proceedings of the Leeds Philosophical and Literary Society. *Recreation:* fishing. *Address:* Cootes, Crookham Common, Newbury, Berks. [*Died* 21 *Nov.* 1964.

ORMOND, Arthur William, C.B.E. 1920; F.R.C.S.; Emeritus Consulting Ophthalmic Surgeon, Guy's Hospital; Bt. Major late R.A.M.C.T.; Ophthalmic Surgeon, No. 2 General Hospital, Chelsea; late Surgeon, Royal Eye Hospital; Ophthalmic Surgeon, St. Dunstan's Hostel; Hon. Consulting Oculist, London Orphan School, Watford, and Royal Asylum for the Deaf, Margate; Fellow Royal Society of Medicine; Member of Ophthalmological Society, Great Britain; Examiner in Ophthalmology, Oxford University; Examiner in Ophthalmology, Universities of Ireland; *b.* 1871; *m.* Mary C., *o. d.* of E. H. P. Eason. *Publications:* Some Notes on the Etiology of Strabismus, Guy's Hospital Reports, 1902; Notes on 100 Cases of Cerebral Tumour, Transactions of Medico-Chirurgical Society, 1906; editor, 2nd edition Higgens' Ophthalmic Practice; Notes on Two Cases of Leprosy affecting the Eyes, The Practitioner. *Address:* The Summit, Mt. Ephraim, Tunbridge Wells, Kent. *T.:* Tunbridge Wells 20611.
[*Died* 14 *Feb.* 1964.

ORMOND, Ernest Charles (Mr. Justice Ormond), retired High Court Judge, Pakistan; *b.* 24 Oct. 1896; *e. s.* of late Mr. Justice Ernest William Ormond, Barrister-at-law and Judge Chief Court, Lower Burma, and of Ellinor, *d.* of late Lewis Pugh Pugh, Barrister-at-law, of Calcutta, D.L., M.P.; *m.* 1930, Nancy, *d.* of R. K. Magor, D.L.; one *s.* two *d.* *Educ.:* Winchester Coll.; King's Coll., Camb. Barrister-at-law; Commissioned R.A., 1915; active service in France (severely wounded) and in Afghanistan; demobilised with rank of Capt. Called to Bar (Gray's Inn), 1925; Barrister-at-law practising in the High Court, Calcutta, 1926-40; Member Bengal Legislative Council; rejoined R.A.: G.S.O.1, 1940; released from military service with rank of Lt.-Col. 1944; Acting Judge Calcutta High Court, 1944; Addl. Judge, 1945; Judge, High Court, Calcutta, 1945-47; Judge of High Court, Dacca, Pakistan, 1947-50. *Publications:* The Law of Patents in India; The Rules of the Calcutta High Court. *Recreation:* gardening. *Address:* 21 Upper Phillimore Gardens, W.8. *T.:* Western 9771.
[*Died* 2 *June* 1962.

ORPHOOT, Burnett Napier Henderson, R.S.A. 1942; F.R.I.B.A. (Ret.); *b.* 13 Apr. 1880; *s.* of Thomas Henderson Orphoot and Edith Carmichael Smythe Burnett; *m.* 1915, late Marjory Harriet White; no *c.* *Educ.:* Rugby; Edinburgh Univ.; school of Applied Art, Edinburgh, Studio of J. Umbdenstock, Paris. In practice from 1910, now retired. Served European War in R.E. (T.) *Publications:* Etchings, Italy, etc. *Address:* Wellhouse, Murrayfield, Edinburgh. *T.:* Donaldson 3131. *Clubs:* New Scottish Arts (Edinburgh); Taw and Torridge Sailing (N. Devon).
[*Died* 8 *April* 1964.

ORR, Christine Grant Millar; Writer of fiction, journalism, radio features, and plays; *d.* of late Sheriff R. L. Orr, K.C.; *m.* 1944, Robin Hynde Forsyth Stark. *Educ.:* St. George's High School, Edinburgh; Somerville College, Oxford. *Publications: novels:* The Glorious Thing, 1919; Kate Curlew, 1922; The Player King, 1931; Immortal Memory; Gentle Eagle: A Stewart Portrait, 1937; The Happy Women, 1947; You Can't Give Them Presents, 1949; Other People's Houses, 1951; *plays:* Pearl for James, 1950; Miss Scott of Castle Street, 1952; East Wind House, 1954; The Crystal Rose, 1955. *Address:* 5 Grosvenor Crescent, Edinburgh 12. *T.:* Caledonian 8179.
[*Died* 18 *May* 1963.

ORR, John, M.A., B.Litt. (Oxon); Lic. ès Lettres (Paris); Hon. D.Litt. (Manchester); Docteur, h.c., Univ. Caen and Sorbonne; Hon. LL.D. (St. Andrews); F.B.A. 1952; Prof. of French, University of Edinburgh, 1933-1951, Professor of French Language and Romance Linguistics, 1951-55; Dean of the Faculty of Arts, 1950-54; *b.* 4 June 1885; *s.* of Peter Orr, Launceston, Tasmania, and Lilias Duncan Allan; *m.* 1910, Augusta Berthe, *d.* of Victor Brisac, St. Petersburg. *Educ.:* The High School, Launceston, Tasmania; Univ. of Tasmania (Classical Schol.); Balliol College, Oxford (Rhodes Scholar); The Sorbonne, École des Hautes-Études, Collège de France, and École des Langues Orientales, Paris. Lecturer in French, Manchester University, 1913-15; Lecturer in French, East London Coll., 1915-18; Professor of French Language, Manchester University, 1918-33; Dean of the Faculty of Arts, 1924-26; Pro-Vice-Chancellor, 1931-33; University representative on the Committees of the Whitworth Institute and the Manchester City Art Gallery till 1933; Chairman, Edinburgh-Caen Fellowship, Hon. Vice-Pres., Soc. of Scottish Artists; Romance Editor for Modern Language Review, 1948-57; Joint Editor of French Studies; Président, Soc. de Linguistique romane; Pres. Modern Humanities Research Assoc., 1954. Pres. Assoc. Internationale des Études françaises, 1955-57; Corresp. Member, Real Academia de Buenas Letras, Barcelona, 1957. Commandeur de la Légion d'Honneur; Knight Commander, Orden Civil of Alfonso X, el Sabio; Vigneron d'Honneur and Bourgeois de St. Emilion, 1961. Pres., Internat. Fedn. Modern Languages and Literatures, 1963-66. *Publications:* Les Œuvres de Guiot de Provins, 1915; French the Third Classic, 1933; An Introduction to Romance Linguistics (translated and revised from the Rumanian version by I. Iordan), 1937; On Homonymics (in Pope Presentation Volume), 1939; Le Boucher d'Abbeville, 1947; Le Lai de l'Ombre, 1948; Contes et poèmes by J. Supervielle, 1950; Words and Sounds in English and French, 1953; Old French and Modern English Idiom, 1962; Three Studies in Homonymics, 1962; Essais d'Etymologie et de Philologie françaises, 1963; papers on French Language, Romance Philology and English Linguistics, in British and foreign journals. *Address:* 20 Dundonald St., Edinburgh, 3.
[*Died* 10 *Aug.* 1966.

ORR, William James, C.B.E. 1920; cotton spinner and manufacturer; James Orr & Sons, Ltd., and A. S. Orr & Co. Ltd.; *b.* 1873; *s.* of James Orr; *m.* 1902, Kathleen Marguerite (*d.* 1939), *d.* of late Sir Joseph Leigh, Stockport; one *s.* one *d.* Has Order of Crown of Belgium. *Address:* Plovers Moss, Sandiway, Cheshire; Empire House, Manchester. *T.:* Central 2294.
[*Died* 24 *Jan.* 1963.

ORRIN, Herbert Charles, O.B.E. 1919; F.R.C.S.; Lecturer in Operative Surgery and Surgical Pathology, New School of Medicine Edinburgh; Examiner in Anatomy and Pathology, Royal College of Surgeons (Edin.) late Surgeon, Craigleith Hospital, Edinburgh; *b.* 22 May 1878; *y. s.* of late Henry Orrin, Colchester, Essex; *m.* Margery, *d.* o. late T. Burnett Ramsay of Banchory; one *s.* *Educ.:* Royal Albert School of Art and Science; Royal College of Surgeons, Edinburgh; Edinburgh Royal Infirmary. Held various London Hospital appointments, including (1914-18) Civil Surgeon attached to 3rd London General Hospital; R.A.M.C. (T.) and Weir Auxiliary Hospital. Former House Surgeon and Clinical Assistant, Royal Infirmary, Edinburgh. *Publications:* Aids to Operative Surgery; the X-Ray Atlas of the Systemic Arteries of the Body; The "First Aid" X-Ray Atlas of the Arteries, 1921; First Aid X-Ray Atlas of Fractures and Dislocations; Emergency Operations for General Practitioners on Land and Sea, 1924;

Fascial Grafting in Principle and Practice, 1928; contributions to medical and surgical literature. *Recreations:* motoring, writing. *Address:* 19 Cumlodden Avenue, Edinburgh 12. *T.:* Donaldson 2700.
[*Died* 5 *July* 1963.

ORSBORN, Albert William Thomas, C.B.E. 1943; *b.* 4 Sept. 1886; *e. s.* of Rev. Albert Orsborn, Toronto; *m.* 1947, Phillis Taylor, Leader, Salvation Army Women's Social Work in G.B.; four *s.* two *d.* (and one *s.* decd.) (by former marriage). *Educ.:* Board Schools. Salvation Army Officer, 1906. Served in New Zealand as Chief Sec. S.A. work; held positions in Salvation Army International Training College; Territorial Commander for S.A. work in Scotland and Ireland; British Commissioner, 1940-46. General of the Salvation Army, 1946-54; retired July 1954. *Publications:* The House of My Pilgrimage, 1958; mostly poetry and songs in Salvation Army periodicals. *Address:* c/o 101 Queen Victoria Street, E.C.4.
[*Died* 4 *Feb.* 1967.

OSBORNE, Sir Cyril, Kt. 1961; M.P. (C.) for Louth, Lincolnshire, since 1945; Stockbroker and Company Director; *b.* 19 June 1898; *s.* of Thomas Osborne, Nottingham; *m.* 1935, Joyce Lawrence Feibusch, Wolverhampton; two *s.* two *d.* *Educ.:* University College, Nottingham. Served with R.F.A., 1914-18. Past Master, Framework Knitters; Member, Court of Assistants, Bakers' Company. Chairman, Anglo-Soviet Parliamentary Gp.; Hon. Treasurer, Inter-Parliamentary Union, British Group, 1964-67. Mem. Pilgrims' Soc. J.P. County of Leicester. *Recreation:* golf. *Address:* Kinchley House, Rothley, Leicestershire. *T.:* Rothley 2636. *Clubs:* English-Speaking Union; Leicestershire (Leicester).
[*Died* 31 *Aug.* 1969.

OSBORNE, Lieut.-General Edmund Archibald, C.B. 1939; D.S.O. 1914; *b.* 26 July 1885; *m.* 1922, Vera (*d.* 1962), *d.* of late James Fitzgerald Bannatyne, of Haldon, Devon, and Fanningstoun, County Limerick, and late Mrs. Bannatyne; one *s.* (one *s.* decd.). Entered army, 1904; Captain, 1914; Bt. Major, 1916; Major, 1921; Bt. Lieut.-Colonel, 1921; Lieut.-Colonel, 1926; Col., 1930; Maj.-Gen., 1937; Lt.-Gen., 1940; served European War, 1914-18 (despatches eight times, D.S.O.); Officer Commanding School of Signals, 1926-30; G.S.O. 1 3rd Div. 1930-33; Commander 157th (Highland Light Infantry) Brigade T.A., 1933-34; Commander, Cairo Brigade, Egypt, 1934-38; Commander 44th (Home Counties) Division T.A., 1938-40; specially employed, 1940; retired, 1941. Col. Comdt. Royal Corps of Signals, 1938-46. *Address:* Ley Grait, Milton Lilbourne, Pewsey, Wilts. *T.:* Pewsey 3293. *Club:* United Service. [*Died* 1 *June* 1969.

OSBORNE, Malcolm, C.B.E. 1948; R.A. 1926; P.P.R.E., A.R.C.A.; President Royal Society of Painter-Etchers and Engravers, 1938-62; *b.* Frome, Somerset, 1 Aug. 1880; 4th *s.* of Alfred Osborne, Schoolmaster; *m.* 1927, Amy Margaret Stableford. *Educ.:* Merchant Venturers' Technical Coll., Bristol. Royal Coll. of Art, S. Kensington, 1901-6; studied Etching and Engraving under Sir Frank Short, R.A., P.R.E.; served in Artists' Rifles and 60th Division in France, Salonika and Palestine; late Professor of Engraving, Royal College of Art. A.R.A. 1918. *Publication:* Etched Plates. *Recreation:* sports. *Address:* 44 Redcliffe Gardens, South Kensington, S.W.10. *Club:* Chelsea Arts. [*Died* 22 *Sept.* 1963.

OSBORNE, William Alexander, M.B., D.Sc. (Tübingen, Melbourne (Hon.) and Belfast (Hon.)); F.A.C.S. (Hon.); F.R.A.C.P. (Foundation); M.D. Melbourne (Hon.); Prof. of Physiology 1903-38 and Dean of the Faculty of Medicine, 1929-38, now Prof. Emeritus, Univ. of Melbourne; *b.* Holywood, Co. Down, 26 Aug. 1873; *y. s.* of Rev. Henry Osborne, M.A.; *m.* 1903, Ethel Elizabeth, *d.* of James Goodson, Armley, Leeds; one *s.* three *d.* *Educ.:* Upper Sullivan School, Holywood; Queen's College, Belfast; University College, London; University of Tübingen. 1851 Exhibitioner, 1897; Sharpey Scholar, University College, London, 1901; Assistant Professor of Physiology, University College, London; Scientific Assistant, London University, 1902. *Publications:* German Grammar for Science Students, 3rd ed.; The Laboratory and other Poems, 1907; William Sutherland, a Biography, 1920; Practical Biochemistry, 6th edition, 1946; A Primer of Dietetics, 6th edition, 1943; The Visitor to Australia, 1934; Essays and Literary Sketches, 1943; Essays and Studies, 1946; various papers in Journal of Physiology, British Medical Journal, Biochemical Journal, etc. *Recreations:* mediæval and American history; history of science. *Address:* Horseshoe Bay, Magnetic Island, N. Queensland Australia. *Clubs:* Melbourne (Melbourne); North Queensland (Townsville). [*Died* 28 *Aug.* 1967.

OSBOURNE, Air Cdre, Sir Henry P. S.-; *see* Smyth-Osbourne.

OSMASTON, Bertram Beresford, C.I.E. 1919; F.C.H., M.B.O.U.; Chief Conservator of Forests, India, retired; *s.* of John Osmaston, late of Osmaston Manor, Derby; *b.* 1868; *m.* 1892, Catherine Mary (*d.* 1960), *d.* of Gen. C. H. Hutchinson, R.A.; two *s.* three *d.* *Educ.:* Trent College; Cheltenham College; Coopers Hill. Joined the Indian Forest Service, 1888; served in United Provinces, Bengal, Andamans, Burma and Central Provinces; President of Forest Research Institute and College, Dehra Dun, 1916-19. *Recreations:* ornithology, botany. *Address:* 116 Banbury Road, Oxford. [*Died* 6 *Sept.* 1961.

OSSIANNILSSON, Karl Gustav; *see* Addenda: II.

OSTENSO, Martha; author; *b.* Bergen, Norway, 17 Sept. 1900; *d.* of Sigurd Brigt Ostenso and Lena Tungeland; brought to U.S. in infancy; *m.* 1944, Douglas Durkin. *Educ.:* public schools, Minn.; Brandon (Can.) Collegiate School; Univ. of Manitoba. Began writing at Winnipeg, 1920. *Publications:* A Far Land (verse), 1924; Wild Geese (novel), 1925; The Dark Dawn, 1926; The Mad Carews, 1927; The Young May Moon (novel), 1929; The Waters under the Earth (novel), 1930; Prologue to Love (novel), 1932; There's Always Another Year (novel), 1933; The White Reef (novel), 1934; The Stone Field (novel), 1937; The Mandrake Root (Novel), 1938; Love Passed this Way (novel), 1941; (with Sister Elizabeth Kenny) And They Shall Walk (biography), 1943; O River, Remember! (novel), 1943; Milk Route (novel), 1948; The Sunset Tree (novel), 1949; A Man Had Tall Sons (novel), 1958; also numerous short stories and serials. *Address:* Route 6, Brainerd, Minn., U.S.A.
[*Died* 29 *Nov.* 1963.

O'SULLIVAN, Hon. Sir Neil, K.B.E. 1959; Solicitor; Senator for Queensland, Australia, 1946-62, retired; *b.* Brisbane, 2 Aug. 1900; *s.* of late P. A. O'Sullivan, Brisbane; *m.* 1929, Margaret, *d.* of late Dr. J. M. McEncroe; two *s.* *Educ.:* St. Joseph's College, Nudgee, Queensland. Served in the R.A.A.F., 1942-1945. Minister for Trade and Customs, 1949-56, and Leader of the Government in the Senate, 1949-58; Attorney-General and Vice-President of Executive Council, Commonwealth of Australia, 1956-58. *Recreations:* golf, tennis, turf. *Address:* Conon Street, Windsor, Queensland, Australia. *Clubs:* American National (Sydney); Brisbane, Johnsonian, Tattersall's, Royal Qld. Golf, Royal Automobile of Qld. (Brisbane).
[*Died* 4 *July* 196

O'SULLIVAN, Richard, Q.C. 1934; Bencher of Middle Temple, 1940; Reader,

1952; *b.* 1888; *s.* of Richard O'Sullivan, Cork; *m.* 1942, Dorothea Close, *o. d.* of late Lt.-Col. A. C. Borton, D.L., J.P., Cheveney, Kent. Called to Bar, Middle Temple, 1914; served in the R.A., 1915-19; Recorder of Derby, 1938-62; Member of General Council of the Bar, 1939-53; member of Lord Chancellor's Cttee. on Law of Defamation, 1939-47. Hon. Lecturer in Common Law, Univ. Coll., London, 1946-60; Reader in Common Law at Inns of Court; Senior Master Tutor, Post Final Course, 1959-60. Hon. Sec. of the Thomas More Soc. of London since 1928; Hon. Sec. Grotius Society, 1955 1958. *Publications:* On Military Law and the Supremacy of the Civil Courts, 1921; Freedom in the Modern World (trans. from the French of Jacques Maritain), 1935; Gatley on Libel and Slander (4th edition), 1953; Christian Philosophy in the Common Law, 1947; The Inheritance of the Common Law, 1950; (ed.) The King's Good Servant, 1948; Under God and The Law, 1949; Edmund Plowden (A Reading), 1953; (ed.) Man and the State, by Jacques Maritain, 1954. *Address:* 72 Northways, Swiss Cottage, N.W.3. *Clubs:* Athenæum, Reform. [*Died* 18 *Feb.* 1963.

OSWALD, Colonel Christopher Percy, C M.G. 1935; O.B.E. 1919; Controller, Imperial War Graves Commission, 1928-43 (retired); *b.* 5 Mar. 1875; *s.* of Charles Christopher Oswald; *m.* 1909, Evelyn Ida (*d.* 1953), *d.* of late George Hardie, J.P., Sydney, N.S.W., and Barnet, Herts; one *s.* Chartered Accountant; served European War in France, 1915-19; Lieut.-Colonel, Aug. 1918 (General List) (despatches, O.B.E.); re-employed. Col. 1939. *Address:* The Grange, Goring-on-Thames, Nr. Reading, Berks. [*Died* 7 *Oct.* 1966.

OTTAWAY, Eric Carlton, R.D.I., M.I.Mech.E., M.Inst.T.; Full-time Member of the London Transport Board since 1963; *b.* 28 June 1904; *s.* of late Joe Caleb and Edith Ottaway; *m.* 1929, Marion Emily, *d.* of late Arthur Venner, St. Austell, Cornwall; one *s.* *Educ.:* Westminster City School; Battersea Polytechnic. Rolling Stock Engr., Midland Red Omnibus Co., 1925; Asst. Experimental Engr., London General Omnibus Co., 1929; Tech. Officer (Buses and Coaches), London Passenger Transport Bd., 1933. Seconded for work in connection with manufacture of Halifax bombers by London Aircraft Production Gp., 1940; Jt. Gen. Man., 1943. Works Man. (Buses and Coaches), L.P.T.B., 1945, being largely responsible for design of the post-war fleet of buses and coaches; Chief Supplies Officer, 1951, redesignated Chief Supplies and Services Officer, 1958-63; Chm., British Transport Advertising Ltd., June-Dec. 1962. *Publications:* papers to Instn. of Mechanical Engineers. *Recreations:* sailing, painting. *Address:* 19 Westfield Court, Portsmouth Road, Surbiton, Surrey. *T.:* Kingston 9628. *Club:* Royal Thames Yacht. [*Died* 27 *Jan.* 1967.

OVERSTREET, Harry Allen, Professor Emeritus of Philosophy, College of the City of New York, since 1939; *b.* San Francisco, Oct. 25, 1875; *s.* of William Franklin and Julia Detje Overstreet; *m.* 1st, 1907, Elsie Burr; three *s.*; 2nd, 1932, Bonaro Wilkinson. *Educ.:* University of California; Balliol College, Oxford. Instructor to Associate Professor of Philosophy in the Univ. of California, 1901-11; Head of Department of Philosophy and Psychology, College of the City of New York, 1911-39; Lecturer in New School for Social Research, 1924. *Publications:* Influencing Human Behaviour, 1925; About Ourselves, 1927; The Enduring Quest, 1931; We Move In New Directions, 1933; A Guide to Civilized Loafing, 1934; A Declaration of Interdependence 1937; Town Meeting comes to Town (with Bonaro W. Overstreet), 1938; Let Me Think, 1939; Our Free Minds, 1941; The Mature Mind, 1949. Leaders for Adult Education (with Bonaro W. Overstreet), 1941; Where Children Come First (with Bonaro W. Overstreet), 1949; The Great Enterprise; Relating Ourselves to our World, 1952; The Mind Alive, 1954, The Mind Goes Forth, 1957, What We Must Know about Communism, 1958; The War Called Peace: Khrushchev's Communism, 1961; The Iron Curtain: Where Freedom's Offensive Begins, 1963 (all with Bonaro W. Overstreet); The Strange Tactics of Extremism, 1964.; The F.B.I. in Our Open Society, 1969. *Address:* 3409 Fiddler's Green, Falls Church, Virginia, U.S.A. [*Died* 17 *Aug.* 1970.

OVEY, Sir Esmond, G.C.M.G., *cr.* 1941 (K.C.M.G., *cr.* 1929; C.M.G. 1917); M.V.O. 1907; *b.* 23 July 1879; *s.* of late Richard Ovey of Badgemore House, Oxon; *m.* 1st, 1909, Blanche Willis, *d.* of late Rear-Adm. W. H. Emory, United States Navy; 2nd, 1930, Mme. Barrios (*d.* 1954), *d.* of Réné Vignat. *Educ.:* Eton; abroad. Attaché, 1902; passed competitive examination, 1903; appointed to Tangier, 1904 (did not proceed); Stockholm, 1904; Tangier, 1904; 3rd Secretary, 1905; passed an examination in Public Law, 1905; granted an allowance for knowledge of Arabic, 1905; transferred to Paris, 1906; visited Moscow, Caucasus Mountains, and Crimea, 1900; Morocco, accompanying Diplomatic Mission to Fez, 1905; 2nd Secretary H.M. Diplomatic Service, Washington, 1908-15; also Florida, Cuba, and Jamaica; Councillor of Embassy, British Legation, Tehran, 1924, and Rome 1925; H.B.M. Minister to Mexico, 1925-29; Ambassador at Moscow, 1929-33; Brussels, 1934-37; Ambassador to Argentine Republic and Minister to Paraguay, 1937; retired, 1942; restricted permission to wear Grand Cross of Order of Leopold. *Recreations:* gardening, motoring, travelling. *Address:* Culham Manor, Oxon, nr. Abingdon, Berks. *Club:* St. James'. [*Died* 30 *May* 1963.

OWEN, Sir (Arthur) David Kemp, K.C.M.G. 1970; M.Com. (Leeds) 1929; Hon. LL.D. (Leeds) 1954; Secretary-General, International Planned Parenthood Federation, since 1969; *b.* Pontypool, Monmouthshire, 26 Nov. 1904; *s.* of Rev. Edward Owen and Gertrude Louisa Kemp; *m.* 1st, 1933, Elizabeth Joyce Morgan (marr. diss.); one *s.* one *d*; 2nd, 1950, Elisabeth Elsa Miller; two *s.* *Educ.:* Leeds Grammar School; University of Leeds. Asst. Lectr. in Economics, Huddersfield Technical Coll., 1926-29; Director, Sheffield Social Survey Committee, 1929-33; Secretary, Civic Division, Political and Economic Planning, 1933-1936; Co-Director, Pilgrim Trust Unemployment Enquiry, 1936-37; Stevenson Lecturer in Citizenship, University of Glasgow, 1937-1940; General Secretary, Political and Economic Planning, 1940-41; Personal Assistant to Sir Stafford Cripps, Office of the Lord Privy Seal, 1942, Ministry of Aircraft Production, 1942-43; Member of the Cripps Mission to India, 1942; Member Reconstruction Department of Foreign Office, in charge League of Nations Affairs, 1944-45; Member, United Kingdom Delegation, International Labour Conference, Philadelphia, 1944, San Francisco Conference, 1945; Deputy Executive Secretary, Preparatory Commn. of U.N., London, 1945-46; Exec. Asst. to Sec-Gen. of U.N. Feb.-April 1946; Asst. Sec.-Gen. in charge of Economic Affairs, 1946-51. Exec. Chm. U.N. Technical Assistance Board, 1951-65; Mem. Edtl. Adv. Bd., Encyclopædia Britannica, 1959-68; Co-Administrator, U.N. Develt. Programme, 1966-69. Hon. LL.D. Wales, 1969. *Publications:* Social Survey of Sheffield-Reports on Unemployment, Standard of Living, Housing,

1931-33; British Social Services, 1940; many contributions to periodical journals. *Recreations:* mountain walking, reading. *Address:* International Planned Parenthood Federation, 18-20 Lower Regent Street, S.W.1. *T.:* 01-839 2911. *Club:* Athenæum. [*Died* 29 *June* 1970.

OWEN, George Douglas, C.M.G. 1935; *b.* 1 April 1887; *s.* of late Alfred Owen and Sarah Bushe; *m.* 1923, Ruth, *e. d.* of late Sir Wm. Knaggs, K.C.M.G.; one *s.* one *d.* *Educ.:* Highgate School. Entered Trinidad Civil Service, 1907; served with H.M.'s Forces 1916-19; Private Secretary to successive Governors of Trinidad, 1910-24; Assistant Colonial Secretary, British Guiana, 1925-31; Colonial Secretary, Barbados, 1931-38; British Guiana, 1938-43. *Recreation:* tennis. *Address:* 16 Palliser Court, Palliser Road, West Kensington, W.14. *T.:* Fulham 1709. [*Died* 21 *Dec.* 1965.

OWEN, George Elmslie, R.B.A. 1933; Artist; *b.* 13 Dec. 1899; *s.* of late George Owen and Catherine Banks; *m.* 1935, Margaret Fell, B.Sc. *Educ.:* George Watson's College and College of Art, Edinburgh. *Publications:* Stirling, Twenty Drawings. *Address:* Saint Ronan, The Crescent, Steyning, Sussex. [*Died* 13 *June* 1964.

OWEN, Lt.-Col. Sir Goronwy, Kt., *cr.* 1944; D.S.O.; *b.* Penllwyn, Aberystwyth, 22 June 1881; *m.* 1925, M. Gladwyn, *widow* of Owen Jones, J.P., of Caernarvon, High Sheriff of Caernarvonshire, 1950-51. *Educ.:* Univ. College, Aberystwyth; M.A. Called to Bar, Gray's Inn, 1919; served European War, 1914-19 (despatches twice, D.S.O.); M.P. (L.) Caernarvonshire, 1923-31 (Ind. L.), 1931-45; Comptroller of the Household, 1931; Liberal Chief Whip, 1931; D.L. County of Caernarvon, 1936; Alderman of Caernarvonshire C.C. 1945; ex-Chm. Agricultural Wages Committee for Counties of Anglesey and Caernarvon, Montgomery and Merioneth; ex-Chm. of Caernarvonshire and Anglesey Territorial and Auxiliary Forces Assoc.; County Army Welfare Officer; Chm., Gwynedd Police Authority, 1955-56 (Vice-Chm., 1954-55); President S. Caernarvon Creameries, 1940- (Hon. Pres. 1962). Has served on numerous Select and Inter-Departmental Cttees. Freedom of Borough of Conway, 1943. *Address:* Plas Ty Coch, Caernarvon. *Club:* Royal Welsh Yacht (Caernarvon). [*Died* 26 *Sept.* 1963.

OWEN, Grace, O.B.E. 1931; B.Sc. (Columbia); M.Ed. (Hon. Manchester); formerly President Nursery School Association of Great Britain; *b.* 1873; *d.* of Samuel and Sarah Elizabeth Owen; unmarried. *Educ.:* Blackheath High School; Blackheath Kindergarten Training College; Royal Academy of Music; Teachers' College, Columbia University, New York. Lecturer at the Blackheath Kindergarten Training College and at the Summer Schools of Educational Handwork Association; Lecturer in connection with the beginnings of the Nursery School Movement in the U.S.; Columbia University, N.Y.; Lecturer for the West Riding, Bradford and Leeds L.E.A.s.; Lecturer in Education, Manchester University, 1906-10, Reading University College, 1910-12, Leeds Training College, 1913-16; Organised Course for Nursery School Teachers and became Principal of the Mather Training College for Nursery and Junior School Teachers, 1917-24; Principal of City of Manchester and Mather Training College, 1924-26; Hon. Sec. of the Nursery School Association of Great Britain, 1923-33; Hon. Adviser to the Nursery School Association of Great Britain, 1933-41. *Publications:* Nursery School Education; various pamphlets and articles on the education of young children and especially in relation to Nursery Schools. *Address:* Appleton-le-Moors, York. [*Died* 20 *Nov.* 1965.

OWEN, Harrison; *see* Addenda: II.

OWEN, Leonard, C.I.E. 1938; M.A; I.C.S. (retired); *b.* 1890; *s.* of late David Owen, Solicitor, Bangor; *m.* 1923, Dilys, *d.* of Joseph Davies Bryan, LL.D., Alexandria; one *s.* one *d.* *Educ.:* Friars School; Univ. Coll. of North Wales. Passed into I.C.S., 1914; R.F.A. 1914-19; Asst. Magistrate, Meerut, 1919; District Magistrate, Benares, 1924; Settlement Officer, Bara Banki, 1927; Deputy Commissioner in charge Kumaon division, 1934; Chief Govt. Whip Indian Legislative Assembly, 1935; District Magistrate, Cawnpore, 1936; Ministry of Home Security, 1939-44; Ministry of Supply, 1945; Board of Trade, 1946-52. A Vice-Pres. Honourable Soc. of Cymmrodorion; Mem., Court of Governors and Council of National Library of Wales; a Governor of Chalfont County Secondary Sch. *Recreation:* translating Welsh classical verse into English. *Address:* 15 Ethorpe Close, Gerrards Cross, Bucks. *Club:* East India and Sports. [*Died* 4 *Nov.* 1965.

OWEN, Lloyd, C.B.E. 1964 (M.B.E. 1952); Chairman, Rowntree & Co. Ltd., since 1957; *b.* 30 May 1903; *s.* of late Thomas Owen, Cardiff; *m.* 1932, Gladys Brown; one *d.* *Educ.:* Howard Gardens School, Cardiff; London University (B.Com.). Joined Rowntree & Co. Ltd., 1928: Director, 1952; Deputy Chairman, 1957. Member, University of Wales Appointments Board, 1950. Trustee, Joseph Rowntree Memorial Trust, 1951. President, Cocoa, Chocolate and Confectionery Alliance, 1962-64. Hon. Treasurer, Univ. of York, 1963. Hon. LL.D., Univ. of Wales, 1963. *Recreation:* reading. *Address:* Clifton Lodge, York. *T.:* York 23253. [*Died* 9 *March* 1966.

OWEN, Peter M.; *see* Macaulay-Owen.

OWEN, Most Rev. Reginald Herbert, D.D. Lambeth, 1952; Bishop of Wellington N.Z., 1947-60; Primate and Archbishop of New Zealand, 1952-60; *b.* 25 May 1887; *s.* of Herbert C. Owen, Sydenham Hill, S.E.; *m.* 1913, Jane, *d.* of late Arthur William Hunt, Longlands, Lancaster. *Educ.:* Dulwich Coll.; Wadham Coll., Oxford (Open Scholarship). 1st Cl. Classical Moderations, 1908; 3rd Cl. Literae Humaniores, 1910; Assistant Master Clifton College, 1910-12; Fellow and Classical Lecturer Worcester College, Oxford, 1912-1915; School of Instruction for Officers, 1914-15; Hon. Fellow of Worcester College, Oxford, 1932; Joint Secretary Oxford and Cambridge Schools Examination Board, 1913-1915; Headmaster of Uppingham School, 1916-34; Fellow, Chaplain and Classical Lectr., Brasenose College, Oxford, 1934-46, Tutor, 1937-46, Hon. Fellow, 1954; Select Preacher at Oxford Univ., 1926-27, at Cambridge Univ., 1935; Chaplain R.N.V.R., 1939-45; Examining Chaplain to the Bishop of Ripon, 1939-46. Episcopal Canon of Collegiate Church of St. George, Jerusalem, 1958-60. *Publications:* Prayers in Use at Uppingham School, 1928. *Recreation:* formerly rowing (Oxford v. Cambridge, 1910). *Address:* White Cottage, Paraparaumu Beach, New Zealand. *Club:* Leander. [*Died* 24 *Feb.* 1961.

OWENS, Capt. Sir Arthur Lewis, Kt., *cr.* 1943; R.D.; R.N.R., retired; Master, Merchant Navy. *Address:* c/o Ministry of Defence, S.W.1. [*Died* 6 *July* 1967.

OWENS, Tom Paterson, C.B.E. 1951; *b.* 30 December 1888; *s.* of Richard and Elizabeth Owens, Maryport, Cumberland; *m.* 1921, Emily Pearse (*d.* 1961), Pietermaritzburg, Natal; (son lost on active service as midshipman Jervis Bay), two *d.* *Educ.:* Liverpool; Borough Road Coll., Isleworth. Governor, Portland Borstal Institution and Feltham, 1912-31; Governor Wandsworth Prison, 1931-35; Director Borstal Association for after care of Borstal lads; Director Central Association for after care Convicts, 1935-38; Asst. Comr. and Inspector of Prisons, 1938-40; Chief Inspector, Children's Department, Home Office, 1940-50, retd., 1950. War service, King's African Rifles in East Africa, seconded from The Buffs, 1915-19 (despatches); Home Guard Bn., County of London Regt., 1940-1944. *Address:* c/o I. F. Garland, Esq., Twin Streams. P. B. Gingindhlovu, Zululand, S. Africa. [*Died* 20 *April* 1968.

OWLES, Thomas Arthur, C.B.E. 1948 (O.B.E. 1939), *b.* Sale, Cheshire, 2 July 1890; *s.* of late Arthur Hatsell Owles, M.Inst.C.E., and of Irene Prudence Griffin; *m.* 1922, Alice Mackay Brown; two *d.* *Educ.:* Dover College. Harbour Engineer, Colombo Port Commission, Ceylon, 1924-47. Served R.E., 1916-20, Captain. *Recreations:* gardening, fishing. *Address:* Sandside Cottage, Kirkcudbright, Scotland *T.:* Kirkcudbright 675. [*Died* 9 *Oct.* 1966.

OWST, Gerald Robert, M.A., Litt.D. Cantab.; D.Lit., Ph.D. (Theol.) London; F.S.A.; Life Fellow of Emmanuel College and Professor Emeritus, University of Cambridge, since 1959; Fellow of King's College, London, since 1939; *b.* April 1894; *o. s.* of late Robert Clement Owst (*g.g.s.* of Robert Owst of Wilberfoss, E. Yorks), and Agnes H. Ledger; *m.* 1928, May, *o. d.* of Albert and Mary Duckett; two *d.* *Educ.:* Cheltenham College; Emmanuel College, Cambridge (Litt.D., 19 3); King's College Theological Departm t (postgraduate), London. Assistant Editorial Secretary to the Medieval-Latin Dictionary Committee of the British Academy, 1924-27; tutor to Prince Chichibu of Japan, for his English visit, 1925-26; H.M. Inspector of Schools, Board of Education, Elementary Branch, 1928-29, Secondary Branch, 1929-38, Staff Inspector for History, 1937-38; Temp. Principal, Board of Education, 1941-44; first Professor of Education, Cambridge University and Fellow of Emmanuel College, 1938-59. Fellow Royal Historical Society 1926-57; Hon. Member and Vice-President, Herts Archæological Society, since 1929; Syndic of Cambridge Univ. Press, 1938-40. *Publications:* Preaching in Medieval England (Cambridge Studies in Medieval Life and Thought), 1926; Literature and Pulpit in Medieval England, 1933 (rev. ed., 1961); The Destructorium Viciorum of Alexander Carpenter, 1952; contribution to Dictionary of English Church History (3rd ed.) and encyclopædias, Studies presented to Sir H. Jenkinson, 1957, Prince Chichibu Memorial Vol., and B.B.C. talks in An Outline of Church History; articles and reviews in various jls. *Recreation:* examining antiques. *Address:* Cudworth Cottage, High Street, Great Wilbraham, Cambs.; Emmanuel College, Cambridge. *T.:* Fulbourn 329. [*Died* 19 *Feb.* 1962.

OZANNE, Major-General William Maingay, C.B. 1947; C.B.E. 1941; M.C.; *b.* 15 Sept. 1891; British; *s.* of E. C. Ozanne, C.S.I., Guernsey; *m.* 1st, 1920, Dorothy (*d.* 1927), *d.* of Douglas Osborne, Rosnaree, Ire.; two *d.*; 2nd, 1942, Susie (*d.* 1950), *widow* of Capt. R. G. Kerrison and *d.* of Mr. van Citters, Wroxham, Norfolk; one *d.* *Educ.:* Elizabeth College, Guernsey; R.M.C., Sandhurst. 2nd Lt. The Duke of Wellington's Regt., 1911; served European War of 1914-18, France and Belgium (wounded twice, despatches, 1914 Star and clasp, British War and Victory Medals, M.C. and bar). Bt. Lt.-Col., 1932; Lt.-Col., 1936; Col., 1939; Brig., 1939; Maj.-Gen., 1941; G.S.O.3; France, 1917-18; Brigade Major, France, 1918-19; Brigade Major, U.K., 1919-22; Instructor, Small Arms School, 1924-28; Chief Instructor, Small Arms School, 1933-1936; commanded The Duke of Wellington's Regiment, 1936-39; served War of 1939-45; retired pay, 1946. *Recreations:* golf, shooting, fishing, and sailing. *Address:* Appletrees, Barton Mills, Bury St. Edmunds, Suffolk. *T.:* Mildenhall 3123. *Clubs:* Army and Navy; Royal and Ancient (St. Andrews); Royal St. George's Golf (Sandwich); Royal Worlington and Newmarket Golf (Worlington). [*Died* 24 *March* 1966.

P

PACKER, Admiral Sir Herbert Annesley, K.C.B. *cr.* 1950 (C.B. 1945); C.B.E. 1945; *b.* 9 Oct. 1894; *o. s.* of W. H. Packer, M.D., Cressage, Shropshire; *m.* 1925, Joy, *d.* of late Dr. Julius Petersen, Cape Town, South Africa; one *s.* *Educ.:* Royal Naval Colleges, Osborne and Dartmouth. Entered Navy, 1907; Lt. 1916; Comdr. 1929; Capt. 1935; Rear-Admiral, 1944; Vice-Admiral, 1948; Admiral, 1952. Served European War, 1914-18, Pacific (H.M.A.S. Australia) and Grand Fleet (H.M.S. Warspite) (despatches); Naval Attaché Athens, Ankara and Belgrade, 1937-39; commanded H.M.S. Calcutta, 1939-40; H.M.S Manchester, 1940-41; Captain of Gunnery School, Whale Island, 1941-43; Captain of H.M.S. Warspite, 1943 (despatches); Commodore Administration to C.-in-C. Mediterranean, 1944 (C.B.E.); Chief of Staff to C.-in-C. Mediterranean, 1944 (C.B.); Rear-Admiral Comdg. 2nd Cruiser Squadron, 1946-48; a Lord Commissioner of the Admiralty and Chief of Supplies and Transport, 1948-50; C.-in-C., South Atlantic Station, 1950-52; retired, 1953. Officer U.S. Legion of Merit, 1945; Commandeur, and Croix de Guerre avec Palme, Légion d'Honneur (France), 1947. *Address:* Cressage, Hillwood Avenue, Claremont, Cape Province, S. Africa. *Clubs:* United Service, All-England Lawn Tennis; Civil Service (Cape Town); Royal Cape Golf (Cape Peninsula). [*Died* 23 *Sept.* 1962.

PACKMAN, Lt.-Colonel Kenneth Chalmers, C.I.E. 1946; *b.* 14 May 1899; *s.* of late T. C. Packman; *m.* Dorothy Stevenson; two *d.* *Educ.:* Gresham's School. South African Heavy Artillery, 1917; 25th Cavalry (F.F.), 1919; Afghan War, 1919; Commandant Mekran Levy Corps, 1920; Political Department, 1924; Waziristan Operations, 1930; H.M. Consul-General in Chinese Turkistan, 1938; Waziristan Operations, 1941 (despatches): Resident in Waziristan, 1944-47. *Address:* c/o National and Grindlay's Bank, 13 St. James's Square, S.W.1. [*Died* 5 *Oct.* 1969.

PADDON, Lieut.-Colonel Sir Stanley Somerset Wreford, Kt., *cr.* 1932; C.I.E. 1919; *s.* of late S. W. Paddon of Parkfield, Esher, Surrey; *b.* 1881; *m.* 1911, Nora Howell, (*d.* 1943), 2nd *d.* of late S. Earnshaw Howell; no *c.*; *m.* 1944, Lilian Emily (*nee* Holden). *Educ.:* Wellington College. Served with 3rd Dragoon Guards in the South African War (Queen's medal with five clasps); transferred to Indian Cavalry (36th Jacob Horse), 1904; European War, 1914-19, on the Imperial General Staff (two Brevets, Russian Order of St Anne, despatches, C.I.E.); Dir.-Gen., India Store Dept., 1923-40; late Gov., Sch. Oriental Langs. Now in California. Comp., I.Mech.E. Freeman of the City of London. *Address:* c/o Bank of America, Redlands, California, U.S.A. [*Died* 5 *Dec.* 1963.

PADLEY, Wilfred, C.M.G. 1956; O.B.E. 1943; H.M. Colonial Service, retired; Director, Brush Aggregates, since 1968; *b.* 22 Feb. 1910; *s.* of Fred and Edith Padley; *m.* 1st,

1934, Nora Cecilia McDonnell (*d.* 1941); 2nd, 1944, Dorothy Helen Perkins; two *s.* three *d.* *Educ.:* Keighley Grammar School; Royal College of Science (A.R.C.S., B.Sc.). Royal Navy, 1932-40; Officer for Co-ordination of Supplies, Malta, 1941-42; Governor of Malta's Rep. in Middle East, 1942-45. Kenya: Asst. Sec., 1946, Asst. Financial Sec., 1948, Sec. to Treasury, 1951; Financial Secretary, Uganda, 1953; Minister of Finance, Uganda, 1955-Sept. 1956; retired 1956. Dir., Metal Industries, 1956-67. *Recreation:* music. *Address:* The Red Lodge, Oakway, Chesham Bois, Bucks. *Clubs:* Devonshire, Royal Commonwealth Society. [*Died* 23 *Nov.* 1968.

PAGE, Sir (Charles) Max, K.B.E., *cr.* 1946; C.B. 1944; D.S.O. 1919; M.A. Oxon; M.S., F.R.C.S.; Officer of the Legion of Honour (France); Consulting Surgeon to Metropolitan Police; Consulting Surgeon to St. Thomas's Hospital; Adviser in Surgery to S.E. Metropolitan Regional Hospital Board; Hunterian Orator, 1951; Robert Jones Lecturer, 1952; Hunterian Professor, Member of Council, late Vice-Pres. of Royal College of Surgeons of England; *b.* Sept. 1882; *m.* 1913, Helen, *d.* of late Sir T. W. Holderness, 1st Bt., G.C.B.; one *s.* one *d.* *Educ.:* Westminster School; St. Thomas's Hospital. Gold Medal, London University M.S., 1908; Musgrove and Beaney Scholarships and Cheselden and Bristowe Medals at St. Thomas's Hospital; Senior Medical Officer, British Red Cross Societies Detachment in Turkey, 1912-13; served with B.E.F. in France, Aug. 1914 to Jan. 1919, Surgical Specialist, 1915-16; with 29th Div. 1917; O.C. a Field Ambulance of 32nd Div. 1918; promoted Act. Lt.-Col. March 1918 (despatches 3 times; D.S.O.); Consulting Surgeon, B.E.F. France, 1939-40. Late Consulting Surgeon to Army; Major-General; President of Assoc. of Surgeons, 1945-46; Director of Accident Service, Radcliffe Infirmary, Oxford, 1943-46. *Publications:* The Treatment of Fractures in General Practice; many contributions to the Medical Societies and Press. *Address:* Luton House, Selling, Faversham, Kent. *T.:* 234. *Club:* Union. [*Died* 1 *Aug.* 1963.

PAGE, Rt. Hon. Sir Earle (Christmas Grafton), P.C. 1929; G.C.M.G. *cr.* 1938; C.H. 1942; D.Sc. (Sydney 1952, Univ. of New England 1955); F.R.C.S., F.R.A.C.S., M.B., Ch.M.; M.H.R. Cowper Division since 1919; *b.* 8 Aug. 1880; 4th *s.* of late Charles Page, Grafton, N.S.W.; *m.* 1906, Ethel Blunt (*d.* 1958), Stanmore, Sydney; three *s.* one *d.*; *m.* 1959, Jean Thomas, Sydney. *Educ.:* Sydney High School and University. Mayor of South Grafton, 1918; Acting Prime Minister Aug. 1923 to March 1924, Sep. 1926 to Jan. 1927, Feb. to Aug. 1935 and April to July 1937; Commonwealth Treasurer, 1923-1929; Minister of Commerce and Deputy Prime Minister, Australia, 1934-39; Minister for Health, 1937-38; Prime Minister, April 1939; Minister of Commerce, 1940-41; Special Australian Envoy to British War Cabinet, 1941-42; Minister for Health, 1949-1956. Leader Australian Country Party, 1920-39; First Chairman Australian Loan Council, 1924-29; First Chairman Australian Agricultural Council, 1934-39; Member Australian War Cabinet, 1942-43; Australian Advisory War Council, 1942-45. First Chairman New England University Council, Armidale, N.S.W., 1938-55; First Chancellor, University of New England, 1955-60. Served European War in France and Egypt, 1914-1918. *Publications:* Pamphlets on Creation of New States and Constitutional Reconstruction in Australia, and Development of Mechanical Power; Clarence River Gorge Hydro-Electric Scheme. *Recreation:* tennis. *Address:* Commonwealth Parliament, Canberra, A.C.T.; Boolneringbar, via Grafton, N.S.W. *Club:* Australian. [*Died* 20 *Dec.* 1961.

PAGE, Sir Frederick Handley, Kt., *cr.* 1942; C.B.E. 1918; Hon. F.R.Ae.S.; Hon. M.Inst.T.; F.C.G.I., Hon. F.I.Ae.S. (America), Hon. A.R.I.B.A.; Founder and Man. Director Handley Page Ltd., Chairman since 1948; Chairman and Managing Director Handley Page (Reading) Ltd.; Member of Council, Hon. Treasurer since 1943, Chairman 1929-31 and 1937-38, Pres. 1938-1939, of Society of British Aircraft Constructors, Ltd.; Chairman of Council and Exec. Cttee. of City and Guilds of London Inst.; Governor and Fellow of Imperial College of Science and Technology; Chairman of Board of Governors, College of Aeronautics, Cranfield; Assoc., Manchester College of Technology; Hon. Assoc., Birmingham College of Technology; *b.* 1885; *m.* Una Helen Thynne (*d.* 1957); three *d.* Vice-Chm., Air Registration Board, 1937-58; Pres. Royal Aeronautical Soc., 1945-47; Pres. Inst. of Transport, 1945-46; Master, Worshipful Company of Coachmakers and Coach Harness Makers, 1943-44; Pres., Harrow East Conservative Association; D.L. Middlesex, 1954-1956; Lord Lieutenant of Middlesex, 1956-60. Officer de la Légion d'Honneur; Officer de l'Ordre de la Couronne, Belgium. W.G.L. (German Scientific Soc. for Aviation) Ludwig Prandtl Ring, 1960; R.S.A. Albert Gold Medal, 1960; Gold Medal, R.Ae.S., 1960. *Address:* Limes House, Stanmore, Middlesex. *T.:* Grimsdyke 295; 18 Grosvenor Square, W.1. *T.:* Mayfair 2370. *Clubs:* Carlton, (Vice-Pres.) Royal Aero. [*Died* 21 *April* 1962.

PAGE, Sir Max; *see* Page, Sir C. M.

PAGE, Lieut.-Colonel Stanley Hatch, C.M.G. 1918; T.D. 1919; F.R.I.C.S., F.R.S.H., L.R.I.B.A.; Architect and Surveyor; *b.* 21 June 1874; 2nd *s.* of late William Gray Page, Ramsgate; *m.* 1st, 1899, Mary Caroline (*d.* 1940), *o. d.* of late Alvis Stapley, Maidstone; three *s.* three *d.*; 2nd, 1940, Lottie Wootton (Dot), *o. d.* of late William Mascall, Newington, St. Laurence, Thanet. *Educ.:* King's School, Canterbury. Served in European War, 1914-19, R.F.A. (T.F.) (despatches, C.M.G.); King George V. Coronation Medal; Freeman of City of London; Liveryman of Worshipful Company of Haberdashers; Special Diploma of Royal Institution of Chartered Surveyors in Sanitary Science; Past Chairman Kent Branch; Past Pres. Ramsgate Chamber of Commerce; Vice-Pres. Kent Automobile Club. *Recreations:* motoring, photography, architectural archæology. *Address:* Tancrey House, 47 Vale Square, Ramsgate. *T.:* Thanet 53070. [*Died* 7 *May* 1962.

PAGE, William Walter Keightley, Q.C. 1946; M.C. 1917; *b.* 1878; 3rd *s.* of late David Page, M.D., and Mary, *d.* of John Rauthmell; *m.* 1923, *o. d.* of late Herbert Weston Sparkes, Dawlish, formerly of Calcutta; one *d.* *Educ.:* Christ Church Cath. Choir School; Magdalen College School, Oxford. Admitted solicitor, 1902; practised at Calcutta, 1905-14 and 1919-20; served 1914-19: in France and Palestine (1915-19) with 38th K.G.O. Central India Horse (wounded, M.C., despatches). Barr., Inner Temple, 1921; practised at Calcutta, 1922-38, and before the Judicial Cttee. of the Privy Council, 1938-50; Pres. European Association (India), 1934-35, 1937-38. *Recreation:* shooting. *Address:* Greenways, Forder Lane, Bishopsteignton, S. Devon. *Club:* Oriental. [*Died* 30 *Aug.* 1962.

PAGET, Gen. Sir Bernard (Charles Tolver), G.C.B., *cr.* 1946 (K.C.B., *cr.* 1942; C.B. 1940); D.S.O. 1918; M.C. 1915; D.L.; I.d.c.; p.s.c.; Hon. M.A. Christ Church, Oxford; *b.* 15 Sept. 1887; 3rd *s.* of late Francis Paget, Bishop of Oxford, and Helen Beatrice, *d.* of late Very Rev. R.

W. Church, Dean of St. Paul's; *m.* 1918, Winifred Nora, *d.* of Sir John Paget, 2nd Bt.; one *s.* (and *yr. s.* died of wounds, 1945). *Educ.:* Shrewsbury School; Royal Military College, Sandhurst. Served European War, 1914-18 (Bt. Major, wounded twice, despatches, D.S.O., M.C., Italian Silver Medal for Military Valour); Bt. Lieut.-Col., 1925; Col. 1929; G.S.O. (1 grade) Staff College, Quetta, 1932-34; War Office, 1934-36; Maj.-Gen., 1937; Lt.-Gen. 1941; General, 1943; Commander Quetta Bde. and Baluchistan District, 1936-37; Comdt. Staff College, Camberley, 1938-39; Commander, 18th Division, and in Norway, 1939-40; Chief of General Staff, Home Forces, 1940; C.-in-C. South Eastern Command, 1941; C.-in-C. Home Forces, Dec. 1941-43; C.-in-C. 21st Army Group, June-Dec. 1943; C.-in-C. Middle East Force, 1944-46; A.D.C. General (Extra) to the King, 1944-46; retired pay, 1946. Governor of Royal Hospital, Chelsea, October 1949-1957. Colonel Commandant Reconnaissance Corps and Intelligence Corps, 1943-1952; Col., Oxford and Bucks Light Infantry, 1946-55 D.L. Hampshire; National Chm.: Forces Help Society; Lord Roberts' Workshops; Vice-Pres. Royal Commonwealth Society for the Blind; Vice-Pres. Eastbourne College; Governor Corps of Commissionaires. Hereditary Freeman of Cork. Grand Cross Order of Polonia Restituta; Grand Officer Order of Leopold with Palm; Belgian Croix de Guerre; Chief Commander United States Legion of Merit; Grand Cross Order of St. Olav, Norway; Grand Officer Order of George I of Greece; Greek Gold Medal for Valour; Grand Comdr. Czechoslovak Order of the White Lion. *Address:* The Old Orchard, Heath Road, Petersfield, Hants. *Clubs:* United Service, Royal Commonwealth Society. [*Died* 16 *Feb.* 1961.

PAIN, Sir Charles John, Kt., *cr.* 1936; Chartered Accountant; *b.* 29 Aug. 1873; *e. s.* of John Pain, River, Dover; *m.* 1st, 1902, Lucy Adelaide (*d.* 1943), 2nd *d.* of Reuben Morley, Nottingham; one *d*; 2nd, Constance Eveline Smith. *Educ.:* Blue Schools, Isleworth. J.P. for City of Nottingham; past Pres. of Nottingham Society of Chartered Accountants. Chevalier of the Order of St. Olaf (Norway), 1949. *Recreation:* golf. *Address:* Elmcroft, Harlaxton Drive, Nottingham. *Club:* Borough (Nottingham). [*Died* 12 *Oct.* 1961.

PAKENHAM-WALSH, Ernst, B.A. (T.C.D. Dublin); *b.* 19 June 1875; *s.* of late Rt. Rev. W. Pakenham-Walsh, Bishop of Ossory and late Clara Jane Ridley; *m.* 1st, L. E. F. Ashe; 2nd, M. L. M. Strachan; one *d.* *Educ.:* Birkenhead School; Trinity College, Dublin (Junior Exhibitioner, Scholar, Littledale Prizeman, Sen. Mod., Classics). Passed I.C.S. 1898; joined Service 1899; served in various districts as Assistant Collector, Assistant Supt. Police, Sub. Collector, acting Collector and acting District and Sessions Judge; District and Sessions Judge, 1919; Acting Judge High Court, Madras for periods in 1928, 1929, 1930, 1931; Puisne Judge High Court Madras, 1932-1935; retired 1935. *Recreation:* music. *Address:* Kyngeshene, Warren Road, Guildford. *T.:* Guildford 2559. [*Died* 11 *Aug.* 1964.

PAKENHAM-WALSH, Major-Gen. Ridley P., C.B. 1940; M.C.; retired; *b.* 29 April 1888; *s.* of late Rt. Rev. W. Pakenham-Walsh, Bishop of Ossory, Ferns and Leighlin; *m.* 1915, Mabel, *d.* of E. A. Smith, Sydney, N.S.W.; two *s.* one *d.* *Educ.:* Cheltenham College; R.M.A. Woolwich. Commissioned R. Engineers, 1908; Instructor R.M. College, Duntroon, Australia, 1914-15; served European War, Dardanelles and France, 1915-18 (M.C., Bt. Major, despatches); British Representative International Commission, Teschen, 1919-20; Bt. Major, 1919; Instructor in Tactics and Brigade Major, S.M.E., 1923-26; G.S.O.II, War Office, 1927-30; Bt. Lieut.-Col., 1928; Imperial Defence College; A.A.G. War Office, 1934-35; Brig., Gen. Staff, Eastern Command, 1935-39; Major-General, Commandant S.M.E. and Inspector R. Engineers, 1939; Engineer in Chief, B.E.F. 1939-40 (wounded, despatches, C.B.); G.O.C. Northern Ireland District, 1940-41; Corps Commander (acting Lt.-Gen.), 1941; Commander Salisbury Plain Dist., 1942; Controller General Army Provision (E.G.), 1943-46. Vice-Chairman Development Corporation Harlow New Town, 1947-50. Pres. Cheltonian Soc., 1948-49. *Publications:* Outline History of Russo-Japanese War, 1924; Elementary Tactics, 1925; History of the Roy. Engineers, Vols. VIII and IX, 1938-48, 1959; several articles in military publications. *Recreation:* gardening. *Address:* Redcot, Three Gates Lane, Haslemere, Surrey. [*Died* 3 *Nov.* 1966.

PALIN, Ven. William; Archdeacon of Cleveland, 1947-65; Archdeacon Emeritus since 1965; Rector of Skelton-in-Cleveland and Vicar of Upleatham, 1947-65; *b.* 1893. *Educ.:* Hertford College, Oxford Deacon, 1923, priest, 1924, Diocese of York. Curate of North Ormesby, 1923-28; Vicar of Thornaby-on-Tees, 1928-38; Offg. Chaplain R.A.F., 1936-38; Vicar of S. John, Middlesbrough, 1938-47. Rural Dean of Middlesbrough, 1938-47; Prebend of Husthwaite in York Minster, 1943; Proctor in Convocation, 1932-50, and 1957-. Hon. Chap. to Bp. of Kimberley and Kuruman, 1963-65. *Address:* Bidston, Britannia Terrace, Saltburn-by-the-Sea, Yorkshire. *T.:* Saltburn 2164. [*Died* 1 *May* 1967.

PALING, Gerald Richard, C.B. 1957; C.B.E. 1948; *b.* 29 September 1895; *s.* of Walter John Paling; *m.* 1924, Ann Kathleen Richards; one *d.* *Educ.:* Brighton. Admitted Solicitor, 1918. Served European War; H.M. Army, 1914-16, France (wounded). Legal Asst. Dir. of Public Prosecutions Dept., 1918; Asst. Dir. of Public Prosecutions, 1944; Deputy Director of Public Prosecutions, 1948-58; Member, Amateur Swimming Assoc. Council. *Publication:* contrib. to Encyclopædia of the Laws of England, 1939. *Recreations:* swimming, association football. *Address:* 62 Braemore Road, Hove 3, Sussex. *T.:* Hove 36461. [*Died* 25 *Jan.* 1966.

PALLISER, Herbert William, F.R.B.S.; Sculptor; Member, Society of Portrait Sculptors; *b.* Northallerton, 1883; *s.* of late Robert Shotton Palliser, Hadley Wood, nr. Barnet; *m.* Jane, *d.* of J. Moncur, Stafford; one *d.* *Educ.:* London Central School of Arts and Crafts; Slade School of Sculpture. *Principal Works:* Calcutta War Memorial Statues; Figures on Pediments of the London Life Assoc. Building, King William Street; Statue of St. George, Old Bedfordians Memorial, Bedford School; Victoria House—Figures on Pediments facing Bloomsbury Square and Southampton Row; Group, Vintry House, Queen Street; Kenton Church, Harrow—Madonna; St. Edmund's, Muswell Hill—Pieta; St. Anne's Well, Buxton—Statue of St. Anne; Memorial to President Roosevelt, Westminster Abbey, in collaboration with C. Terry Pledge, A.R.I.B.A. M.B. Laboratories, Porton, nr. Salisbury; Labours of Hercules stone panels; Bronze Medallion Portrait of Lord Ashfield, Broadway House, Westminster; Bronze Portrait Relief of Canon F. J. Shirley, D.D., Headmaster, The King's School, Canterbury. *Publications:* contributions to Architectural Review, Builder, Studio. *Address:* 96 Kingsley Way, N.2. [*Died* 9 *Oct.* 1963.

PALMELLA, 5th Duke of; Dom Domingos de Sousa Holstein Beck; Portuguese

Ambassador to the Court of St. James, 1943-1949; *b.* 6 June 1897; *s.* of Luiz and Helena, 4th Duke and Duchess of Palmella; *m.* 1918, Maria do Carmo Pinheiro de Mello, 2nd *d.* of Count de Arnoso; five *s.* six *d.* *Educ.:* Beaumont; King's College, Cambridge (B.A. 1918, M.A. 1947, Hon. LL.D. 1947). Director of Bank of Portugal, 1926-50; Director of Banco Esperito Santo e Comercial de Lisboa, 1950-; Director, Calouste Gulbenkian Foundation, 1956-. Hon. G.C.V.O., 1957. *Recreations:* golf, shooting, and fishing. *Heir:* *s.* Dom Luiz de Sousa e Holstein Beck, Marquis de Faial. *Address:* 140 Rua da Escola Politecnica, Lisbon, Portugal. *Club:* Turf (Lisbon). [*Died* 16 *Nov.* 1969.

PALMER, Alexander Croydon, O.B.E., M.B., F.R.C.S., F.R.C.O.G.; Cons. Gynæcological and Obstetric Surgeon, King's College Hospital; Surgeon, Samaritan Free Hospital; Hon. Consulting Gynæcologist to Epsom and Ewell Cottage Hospital, Sutton and Cheam General Hospital, and to Jewish Maternity Home, Underwood Street, E.; Examiner in Midwifery and Diseases of Women, University of London; late senior Examiner in Midwifery and Diseases of Women, Conjoint Board London, Oxford University; External Examiner in Midwifery and Diseases of Women, Birmingham Univ.; *b.* 2 July 1887; *s.* of A. Palmer, St. Clair, Dunedin, N.Z.; *m.* Geraldine Louise, *d.* of late Percy Savill, Carr End, Reigate, Surrey; one *s.* (and one *s.* decd.). *Educ.:* Waitaki, New Zealand; Otago University; London Hospital; London University. English International (Rugby) 1908-09; late Consulting Gynæcologist, The Hospital for Epilepsy and Diseases of the Nervous System, Maida Vale; late Assistant Obstetric Surgeon, Royal Northern Hospital; late Examiner in Midwifery and Diseases of Women to the Society of Apothecaries, etc.; late Obstetric Tutor and Registrar London Hospital; late Receiving-Room Officer, House Surgeon, Senior Resident, etc., London Hospital East; late Examiner to the Central Midwives Board; Pres. of Section of Obst. and Gynæ., Royal Soc. of Medicine, 1952-53; Pres. Med. Soc. London, 1951-52. Late Major in charge Surgical Div., 32 Stationary Hospital, B.E.F.; late Surgeon, Horton Emergency Hospital. *Publications:* Two Cases of Rupture of the Vagina in Labour and other papers, Proceedings of the Royal Society of Medicine; Report on the Cause of Stillbirth for the Medical Research Council, 1922; Prolapse; The Prolapse Syndrome and its Treatment, Med. Press, Dec. 1934; Sterility in Women, Clin. Journal, Feb. 1935. *Recreation:* golf. *Address:* 130 Harley Street, W.1. *T.:* Welbeck 3349; Heath Lodge, Walton Heath, Tadworth, Surrey. *T.:* Tadworth 3228. [*Died* 16 *Oct.* 1963.

PALMER, Francis Noel; *s.* of Henry Nathaniel Palmer, of Yarmouth; *m.* 1916, Hannah (*d.* 1954), *d.* of Joseph Cree, Chesterfield; one *s.* one *d.* *Educ.:* Dulwich Hamlet. Labour candidate, Farnham Div., Surrey, 1919; joined Labour Party, 1906; joined Trade Union, 1911; worker for Women's Suffrage; ejected from Labour Party, Oct. 1931; M.P. (Nat. Lab.) S. Tottenham, 1931-35; discharged army, suffering tuberculosis, 1917. *Recreations:* politics, reading. *Address:* Briarpatch, Normandy, Surrey. *T.A.:* Palmer, Normandy, Guildford. *T.:* Normandy 112. [*Died* 18 *Jan.* 1961.

PALMER, Henry Alleyn, T.D. 1944; *b.* 13 Nov. 1893; *s.* of Alfred Henry Palmer; *m.* 1925, Maud, *e. d.* of Lt.-Col. O. J. Obbard; one *s.* one *d.* *Educ.:* Charterhouse; University Coll., Oxford. Commissioned in Middlesex Regt. (T.A.), 1914; demobilised, 1919. Called to the Bar, 1921; in practice, 1921-40. Recalled from Reserve, for Army Service, 1940; demobilised and placed on retired list, 1945. Asst. Registrar, Court of Criminal Appeal, 1948; Registrar, Courts-Martial Appeal Court and Assistant Master of the Crown Office, 1952; Master of the Crown Office, Queen's Coroner and Attorney, and Registrar of the Court of Criminal Appeal, 1962-65. *Publications:* Managing editor, New Zealand Statutes (reprint), 1931; Part editor, Harris and Wilshere's Criminal Law, 1954 and 1960 editions. *Recreation:* gardening. *Address:* Alderman's Cottage, Knowl Hill, Nr. Twyford, Berks. [*Died* 15 *Aug.* 1965.

PALMER, Herbert Edward; Poet and Literary Critic, and occasional Lecturer; *b.* Market Rasen, Lincs, 1880; *s.* of Rev. A. Palmer, Wesleyan Methodist Minister, and Eliza J. Coleman; *m.* Harriet Emily, *d.* of Rev. Chas. J. Preston, Wesleyan Methodist Minister; one *s.* *Educ.:* Woodhouse Grove School; Birmingham University; Bonn University. Commenced career in 1899 as a Schoolmaster; taught in various types of English schools and three French (State) schools; also private tutor in Germany during seven years before the war; and after 1919 English Literature Lecturer during several Winter-evening sessions to Workers' Educational Association. Last school post, English Master at St. Albans School, relinquished in 1921 for a literary career. *Publications:* Two Fishers (verse), 1918; Two Foemen (verse), 1920; Two Minstrels (verse), 1921; The Unknown Warrior (verse), 1924; Songs of Salvation, Sin, and Satire (verse), 1925; The Judgment of François Villon (a play), 1927; The Lady of Laws (a translation with Colonel L. W. Charley, of Susanne Trautwein's Die Schöne Richterin), 1929; The Teaching of English, 1930; The Armed Muse (verse), 1930; Jonah comes to Nineveh (verse), 1930; Selections in Augustan booklet (verse), 1931; Cinder Thursday (verse), 1931; What the Public Wants, 1932; Collected Poems, 1933; The Roving Angler, 1933; Summit and Chasm (verse), 1934; The Mistletoe Child: autobiography of Childhood, 1935; The Vampire (verse), 1939; Post Victorian Poetry (criticism), 1938; The Gallows-Cross (verse), 1940; Season and Festival (selected verse in Sesame Book), 1943; The Dragon of Tingalam (fairy play) 1945; A Sword in the Desert (verse), 1946; The Greenwood Anthology of New Verse, 1948; The Old Knight (verse), 1949; The Ride from Hell (verse), 1958. *Recreations:* fly-fishing for trout and grayling; long-distance hill-walking. *Address:* 22 Batchwood View, St. Albans, Herts. [*Died* 17 *May* 1961.

PALMER, Horace Stanley, T.D. 1950; **Hon. Mr. Justice Palmer;** retired as a Judge of the High Court, Eastern Nigeria (1956-63); Director, Glebe Rentals Ltd. since 1965; *b.* 9 March 1904; *s.* of Stanley Palmer and Mabel Matilda (*née* Stone); *m.* 1934, Edith Marjorie (*née* Lockwood); one *s.* two *d.* *Educ.:* Westminster School; St. John's College, Oxford (M.A.). Called to Bar, Inner Temple, 1927; Legal Staff, Ministry of Health, 1936; Resident Magistrate, Northern Rhodesia, 1937. Commission in 54th (E.A.) Divisional Signals, T.A., 1926; served in Northern Rhodesia Regiment, 1939-40 (Staff Captain). Chairman Minimum Wages Advisory Board, Northern Rhodesia, 1946. Puisne Judge, Nigeria, 1951. Master of Plaisterers Company, 1950-51. Mem. Judicial Service Commn., Eastern Nigeria, 1959 (Acting Chm. 1959). Acting Chief Justice, Eastern Nigeria, Aug. 1959-Nov. 1959, March 1960-Oct. 1960, June 1961-Sept. 1961. Divl. Pres., B.R.C.S., 1963-64; Mem. and Reserve Chm., N.W. London Rent Tribunal, 1965-67; Staff Officer, Civil Defence, 1965-. War Medal and Coronation Medal. *Publications:* Leases, 1934; Law of Arbitration and Awards, 1935. Contributor to Halsbury's Laws of England (1st edn.). Editor of Northern Rhodesia Law Reports, 1939-50. *Recreations:* archery, billiards. *Address:* 162 Upper Woodcote Road, Caversham, Reading, Berks. *Clubs:* Bath, Royal Toxophilite Soc. [*Died* 11 *Aug.* 1968.

PALMER, James L., O.B.E. 1941; Member of the Press Council; President, Guild of British Newspaper Editors, 1949; Chairman: Joint Editorial Committee of Guild and Newspaper Society; presided four-party conferences, 1951, on national training scheme for journalists; native and freeman of Chester; *m.* Ellen Marsland, Hoole; three *s.* *Educ.:* Chester. Journalist. Courant and Observer, Chester; Chief Reporter, The Western Morning News; first News Editor of amalgamated The Western Morning News and Mercury; Editor from 1920's until retirement, 1948; Director, 1949, Westcountry Publications Ltd., and The Cornishman; Chief Regional Officer for South-west England of Ministry of Information, with headquarters at Bristol, 1939-42; studied newspaper conditions in European countries, U.S.A., and Canada; revisited Canada, 1927, as Member of British Newspaper Society's Party, participating in the Confederation Jubilee celebrations; journeyed up River Amazon, 1931; visited Iceland, Spitzbergen and Arctic, 1932; Holy Land and Near East, 1933; Deleg. to Imperial Press Conf., South Africa, 1935; toured devastated Germany as war correspondent, 1946; leader of party of nine English and Welsh editors who toured France, 1946; President, 1939-40, 1942-45, and 1945-46, of Plymouth Athenæum and Devon and Cornwall Natural History Soc.; President, Penzance Library, Morrab Gardens; Hon. Mem., Devon and Cornwall Bird Watching Societies; President, Penzance Natural History and Antiquarian Soc.; initiated Cornish Bard, Palmor Tyr Sans, at Roche, 1933; Mason: P.P.J.W., Devon, 1940; Pres. Western District Masonic Assoc., 1941; first Master, Plymouth and Dist. Masters' Lodge, No. 5898. *Publication:* The Cornish Chough through the Ages. *Recreations:* natural history, gardening. *Address:* Trethias, Lidden, Penzance, Cornwall. *T.:* Penzance 3124. *Club:* Press. [*Died* 17 *Sept.* 1961.

PALMER, Sir John Archdale, 7th Bt. *cr.* 1791; *b.* 10 Nov. 1894; *s.* of 6th Bt. and Lilian, *d.* of General E. A. Somerset, C.B.; *S.* father, 1933; *m.* 1922, Kathleen, *yr. d.* of late Mr. Herbert Smith; two *s.* Served War of 1939-45, with R.A., 1939-48. D.L. Gloucestershire, 1956. C.St.J., 1959. *Heir:* *s.* John Edward Somerset [*b.* 27 Oct. 1926; *m.* 1956, Dione Catharine, *d.* of Duncan Skinner, Usk, Monmouthshire; one *s.* one *d.*]. *Address:* Newland, near Coleford, Glos. *T.:* Coleford 2158. [*Died* 24 *June* 1963.

PALMER, Reginald Howard Reed, M.C.; D.L.; Past President National Association of Biscuit Manufacturers; past Chairman: Huntley & Palmers, Ltd.; Assoc. Biscuit Manufacturers Ltd.; *b.* 1898; *s.* of late W. Howard Palmer of Heathlands, Wokingham, Berks; *m.* 1924, Lena F., *d.* of A. B. Cobham; two *s.* *Educ.:* Eton. Served in Grenadier Guards, 1916-19; Joint Master, The Garth Hunt, 1931-36; High Sheriff of Berkshire, 1935; D.L. 1953. *Address:* Hurst Grove, Twyford, Berks. *T.:* Hurst 12. *Clubs:* Guards, Bath. [*Died* 15 *Feb.* 1970.

PALMER, Lt.-Col. Roderick G. F.; *see* Fenwick-Palmer.

PALMER, Sir William, G.B.E. 1959 (K.B.E. 1941); C.B. 1938; Chairman, British Rayon Federation since 1946; *b.* 1883; *s.* of late Henry Palmer, Buckingham; *m.* 1914, Dorothy, *d.* of William Catmur; two *s.* two *d.* (and one *s.* decd.). *Educ.:* Alleyn's School, Dulwich; London University. Second Secretary, Ministry of Supply, 1939-42; Second Secretary, Ministry of Production, 1942-44; Principal Industrial Adviser to Board of Trade, 1944-46. *Address:* 67 Grand Drive, S.W.20. *Club:* Union. [*Died* 26 *Sept.* 1964.

PALTRIDGE, Hon. Sir Shane Dunne, K.B.E. 1966; Minister for Defence, Australia, since 1964; Senator for Western Australia since 1951 and Leader of the Government in the Senate since 1964 (Dep. Govt. Leader in the Senate, 1958-64); *b.* 11 January 1910; *s.* of A. D. Paltridge, Moora; *m.* 1947, Mary E., *d.* of J. McEncroe; two *d.* *Educ.:* state schools; Fort Street High School. Served War of 1939-45; R.A.A.F., 1940-42; A.I.F., 1942-45; Gunner, 217 Australian Field Regiment. Joined National Bank of Australasia, 1926, Western Australia, 1929-36; in hotel business, Western Australia, from 1936. Minister for: Shipping and Transport, 1955-60; Civil Aviation, 1956-64; (Actg. Labour and National Service, May-July 1960; (Actg). Defence, May-June 1061; Defence and Civil Aviation, April-June. 1964. *Recreation;* reading. *Address:* 122 Forrest Street, South Perth Western Australia. *Clubs:* Perth (Perth W.A,); Celtic (Melbourne). [*Died* 21 *Jan.* 1966.

PANAPA, Rt. Rev. Wiremu Netana, C.B.E. 1954; L.Th.; *b.* 7 June 1898; *m.* 1925, Agnes Waikeria Anderson; four *s.* three *d.* *Educ.:* St. Stephen's Coll., Parnell; Te Rau Theological Coll., Gisborne; St. John's Coll., Auckland. New Zealand Board of Theological Studies Licentiate in Theology, 1921; Deacon, 1921, Priest, 1923, Auckland. Curate, Diocese of Auckland, 1921-40; Maori Diocesan Missioner, 1930-40; Chaplain to the Forces (N.Z.), 1940-44; Vicar of Ohmemutu Pastorate, 1944-47; Taupo Maori District, Diocese of Waiapu, 1947-51; Bishop of Aotearoa, Suffragan to the Bishop of Waiapu, 1951-68. Coronation Medal, 1953. *Address:* P.O. Box 399, Hastings, Hawkes Bay, New Zealand. [*Died* 10 *June* 1970.

PANIKKAR, Kavalam Madhava; Vice-Chancellor Jammu and Kashmir University, Srinagar, since 1961; Ex-Member of Parliament, Rajya Sabha; *b.* 1895. *Educ.:* Madras Christian Coll.; Ch.Ch., Oxford (Dixon Scholar, Hist. Research). 1st Class Mod. History, Oxford; Barrister-at-Law (Middle Temple); D.Litt. (Delhi); LL.D. (Aligarh), etc. Prof., Aligarh Univ.; Editor, The Hindustan Times; Sec. to Chancellor, Chamber of Princes; Foreign Minister, Patiala; Prime Minister, Bikaner State, 1944-47; Sec. Indian States Deleg. to Round Table Conf.; Indian States' Rep. to Pacific Relations Conf., 1942, and Commonwealth Relations Conf., 1945; Mem. Indian Deleg. to U.N. Gen. Assembly Session, 1947; Ambassador of India in China, 1948-52; Ambassador of India in Egypt and Minister for India accredited to the Lebanon, Syria and Libya, 1952-53; Member, States Reorganisation Commission, 1954-55; Indian Ambassador to France, 1956-59. Chm., U.N.E.S.C.O. Advisory Cttee., Major Project for Eastern and Western Cultural Values, 1957. *Publications:* Indian States and Government of India, 1927; Caste and Democracy, 1933; The New Empire, 1934; India and the Indian Ocean, 1945; A Survey of Indian History, 1947; The Indian Revolution, 1951; Asia and Western Dominance, 1953; In Two Chinas, 1954; The Geographical Factors in Indian History, 1954; In Two Chinas, 1955; Hindu Society at Crossroads, 1956; India and China, 1957; The Afro-Asian States and their Problems, 1959; Problems of Indian Defence, 1960 In Defence of Liberation, 1962; The Foundations of New India, 1963; novels, dramas, poems in Malayalam language. *Address:* c/o Jammu and Kashmir University, Srinagar, Kashmir, India. [*Died* 10 *Dec.* 1963.

PANNETT, Charles Aubrey, F.R.C.S., M.D., B.S., B.Sc.; Professor Emeritus, University of London, since 1950; *b.* 1884; *s.* of Charles Yeatman Pannett; *m.* 1914, Nora Kathleen (*d.* 1952), *d.* of John Moon, Dublin; *m.* 1954, Diana Margaret, *d.* of late Col. Hon. F. W. Stanley, D.S.O. and of Lady Alexandra Stanley. *Educ:* Westminster City Sch.; St. Mary's Medical Sch.; Exhibnr. in Anatomy and in Physiology, Univ. of London; Gold Medallist in M.B., B.S., and in M.D. examinations. Hunterian Professor Royal College of Surgeons; Prof. of Surgery, Univ. of London, and Dir. of the Surgical Unit, St. Mary's Hosp., London, 1922-1950. *Publications:* Surgery of Gastro-duodenal Ulceration; Text-book of Surgery, 1945; and various papers upon abdominal and renal diseases in medical journals. *Address:* 39 Cliddesden Road, Basingstoke, Hants. *T.:* 21136. [*Died* 28 *July* 1969.

PANOFSKY, Erwin, Ph.D.; Professor Emeritus of the History of Art, Institute for Advanced Study, Princeton, N.J., U.S.A.; Samuel F. B. Morse Professor, New York Univ. from 1962; *b.* 30 March 1892; *s.* of Arnold Panofsky and Caecilie (*née* Solling); *m.* 1916, Dorothea Mosse; two *s.* *Educ.:* Joachimsthalsches Gymnasium, Berlin; Universities of Munich, Berlin, Freiburg (Baden). Ph.D. Freiburg (Baden), 1914; Privatdozent, Univ. of Hamburg, 1921; full Prof. Univ. of Hamburg, 1926; dismissed by Nazi régime, 1933; Visiting Professor, New York Univ. and Princeton Univ., 1934-35; Prof. Institute for Advanced Study, 1935. Mem. Amer. Philosophical Soc.; American Acad. of Arts and Sciences; Corresp. Fellow: American Mediæval Acad.; Koninklijke Akademie van Wetenschapen; British Academy; Acad. Royale de Belgique; Royal Swedish Acad. of History and Antiquities; Accademia delle Arti del Disegno (Florence). Hon. degrees: Ph.D., Utrecht Univ., 1936; Litt.D., Princeton Univ., 1947; Dr. of Letters, Oberlin Coll., 1950, Rutgers Univ., 1954; Bard Coll., 1956; Ph.D., Uppsala Univ., 1953; Dr. of Arts, Harvard Univ., 1957; Dr. of Arts, New York Univ., 1962; Ph.D. Berlin Univ. 1962; Ph.D. Rome, 1963; Dr. of Fine Arts, Philadelphia Coll. of Art, 1965; Dr. of Letters, Columbia Univ., 1965. Ph.D. Bonn Univ., 1967. Hon. Senator, Freiburg Univ., 1967. Jungius Medal (Hamburg); Haskins Medal (Amer. Mediæval Acad.); National Gallery of Art Medal, 1966. Order Pour le Mérite for Arts and Sciences, 1967. *Publications:* Dürers Kunsttheorie, 1915; Dürers Stellung zur Antike, 1922; Dürers Kupferstich "Melencolia I" (with F. Saxl); Die deutsche Plastik des 11. bis 13. Jahrhunderts, 1924; Idea, 1924 (Italian trans., 1952); Hercules am Scheidewege, 1931; Studies in Iconology, 1939; The Codex Huyghens, 1940; Albrecht Dürer, 1943; Abbot Suger on the Abbey of St. Denis and its Art Treasures, 1946; Gothic Architecture and Scholasticism, 1951; Early Netherlandish Painting, 1953; Meaning in the Visual Arts, 1955; Galileo as a Critic of the Arts, 1955; Pandora's Box (with D. Panofsky), 1956; Renaissance and Renascences, 1960; A Mythological Painting by Poussin in the National Museum at Stockholm, 1960; The Iconography of Correggio's Camera di San Paolo, 1961; Tomb Sculpture: Its Changing Aspects from Ancient Egypt to Bernini, 1964 (New York). Contrib. to periodicals, "Festschriften" and Symposia, in England, various other European countries and the U.S.A. *Recreations:* detective stories, music, moving pictures. *Address:* 97 Battle Road, Princeton, N.J., U.S.A. *T.:* Princeton 924-1679. [*Died* 14 *March* 1968.

PANTER, Air Vice-Marshal Arthur Edward, C.B. 1946; B.A., M.R.C.S., L.R.C.P.; late R.A.F.; *b.* 17 June 1889; *s.* of late Rev. C. E. Panter, M.A., Royal Navy; *m.* 1st, 1917, Isobel (*d.* 1925), *d.* of late W. Mill Saunders; 2nd, 1927, Marie Howard, *d.* of late Lieutenant-Colonel J. H. Kemple, O.B.E., 9th Lancers; one *s.* *Educ.:* St. Helen's College, Southsea; Clare College, Cambridge; King's College Hospital London. R.N. Medical Service, 1913-19; R.A.F. Medical Service, 1919-46; Principal Medical Officer, Middle East Command, R.A.F., 1939-44 (despatches twice); Coastal Command, April-October 1944; Technical Training Command, October 1944-October 1946; K.H.S. 1942-47. Retired from National Health Service as Medical Supt. Rooksdown House, 1959. *Recreations:* rowing, tennis, ski-ing. *Address:* The Coach House, 31 Withdean Road, Brighton, BN1 5BL. *T.:* Brighton 54233. *Club:* Royal Air Force. [*Died* 12 *March* 1969.

PANTIN, Prof. Carl Frederick Abel, F.R.S. 1937; M.A., Sc.D. (Cantab.); Hon. Dr. (Univ. São Paulo); Hon. D.Sc. (Durham); Fell, Trinity Coll., Camb.; Hon. Fell., Christ Coll., Camb.; Prof. of Zoology in the Univ., 1959-66; *b.* 30 Mar. 1899; *er. s.* of Herbert and Emilie Pantin, Blackheath, London; *m.* 1923, Amy, 2nd *d.* of Dr. J. C. Smith, Edinburgh; two *s.* *Educ.:* Tonbridge; Christ's College, Cambridge. 2nd Lt. R.E. 1918; Physiologist to Marine Biological Laboratory, Plymouth, 1922-29; Trail award of Linnean Society, 1937; Royal Medal of Royal Society, 1950; Pres. Sect. D (Zoology), Brit. Assoc. (Edinburgh), 1951; Croonian Lecture, Royal Society, 1952; For. Mem. Academia Brasileira de Ciência, 1953; Hon. Member Royal Society of New Zealand, 1955; President, Linnean Society of London, 1958, 1959, 1960; President, Marine Biological Assoc., 1960-66; Trustee, British Museum, 1960; Chm. Bd. of Trustees, Brit. Museum (Natural Hist.), 1963-. Gold Medal, Linnean Soc., 1964. *Publications:* papers in Jl. of Experimental Biology, Proceedings of Royal Soc., Journal of Marine Biological Association, etc. *Recreation:* fishing. *Address:* Trinity College, and 25 Bentley Road, Cambridge. *T.:* Cambridge 57435. [*Died* 14 *Jan.* 1967.

PAPWORTH, Rev. Sir Harold (Charles), K.B.E. *cr.* 1950 (O.B.E. 1941); Priest in charge of St. Michael and All Angels, Exeter, 1961-66; *b.* 16 December 1888; *s.* of late A. C. Papworth, Cambridge, and Stamford, Lincs; *m.* 1932, Florence Mary, *d.* of late Captain John Moore, Coonoor, India. *Educ.:* Ipswich School; March Grammar School; University of Leeds. M.A. Leeds; D.Litt. Travancore. Entered Indian Educational Service, 1916; Professor of English, Presidency College, Madras, 1916-28; Principal, Victoria College, Palghat, 1928-32; Principal, Government Mohamadan College, Madras, 1932-1934; Principal, Presidency College, Madras, 1934-43. Director of Public Instruction, Government of Madras, 1938 and 1940. Chairman, Travancore Education Reforms Commission, 1943-44; Pro-Vice-Chancellor, University of Travancore, 1944-47; Vice-Chancellor, University of Travancore, Trivandrum, India, 1947-50; Curate, Holy Trinity, Stroud Green, N.4, 1950-52; Vicar of St. Luke, Jersey, 1952-57; Curate, St. John, Torquay, 1958-60. Travancore Gold Medal of Merit, 1946. *Publications:* Report of Travancore Education Reforms Commission; articles on educational subjects. *Recreations:* amateur theatricals, singing. *Address:* c/o National and Grindlay's Bank, 26 Bishopsgate, E.C.2. *Club:* Madras (Madras). [*Died* 22 *Feb.* 1967.

PARAMORE, Richard Horace, M.D. Lond., F.R.C.S. Eng.; *b.* 12 Aug. 1876; *s.* of Richard Paramore, M.D.; *m.* 1904, Lilian Mabel, *y. d.* of late Rev. E. Godson of Boroughbridge, Somerset; two *d.* *Educ.:* Merchant Taylors' School; St. Bartholomew's Hospital. House Surgeon at Windsor, 1900; House Surgeon and Resident Medical Officer, General Hospital, Birmingham, 1901-3; Registrar and Pathologist, Hospital for Women, Soho Square, 1910-13; Hunterian Professor Royal College of Surgeons of England, in 1910 and 1911; Surgeon Hospital St. Cross, Rugby, 1916, and later with charge of Gynæcological Department. Member Renal Assoc., 1952. Served European War, 1914-18, Major, R.A.M.C.; Officer-in-Charge, Surgical Division, Belton Park Military Hospital, 1918. *Publications:* The Statics of the Female Pelvic Viscera, vol. i., 1918, vol. ii., 1925; The Toxæmia of Acute Intestinal Obstruction or Vomiting as a Pathological Force, 1923; Eclampsia and its Treatment: An Experience with Spinal Anæsthesia in One Case, Proc. R.S.M., 1928: 21,1334; Eclampsia and its Renal Lesion, Journal Obst. and Gyn. British Empire, 1929, xxxvi. 341; Fondements d'une Théorie Mécaniste de l'Eclampsie, Gyné. et Obst., Paris, 1931, xxiii. 114; The Hepatic Lesions, Journ. Obstet. and Gyn., Brit. Emp., 1932, xxxix. 777; The intra-abdominal pressure in pregnancy newly considered: ibid., 1937, xliv. 1056; Vesalius: Anatomist (1514-64)-Tabulae Anatomicae Sex; An Historical Note: Brit. Med. Bulletin, 1949, vi. 1436; Cortical Necrosis, Proc. R.S.M. 1951, 44, 402; Treatment of Anuria: Discussion (ibid: 1952, 45, 855); and numerous publications in journals since 1908 *Address:* Rose Cottage, Thursley Rd., Elstead, Surrey. [*Died* 21 *Oct.* 1965.

PARANJPYE, Sir Raghunath Purushottam, Kt. 1942; M.A. (Cantab.). B.Sc. (Bombay); D.Sc. (Hon.) Calcutta; Litt.D. (Hon.) Poona; *b.* Murdi, Ratnagiri District of Maharashtra (India), 16 Feb. 1876; *s.* of Púrushottam Keshav Paranjpye, caste, Konkanastha Brahmin; *m.* 1905, Saibai Joshi (*d.* 1931); one *d.* *Educ.:* The Maratha High School, Bombay; Fergusson Coll., Poona; St. John's College, Cambridge (Fellow); Paris and Göttingen. First in all his University examinations in India; went to England as a Government of India scholar; bracketed Senior Wrangler at Cambridge, 1899; returned to India, 1901; Principal and Professor of Mathematics, Fergusson College, Poona, 1902-26; Minister of Education, Bombay Presidency, 1921-23, Member of the Reforms Inquiry Committee, 1924; Member of the Auxiliary and Territorial Forces Committee, 1924; Member Indian Taxation Inquiry Committee, 1924-25; Pres. Nat. Liberal Federation of India at Lucknow, 1924 and at Allahabad 1939; has taken a prominent part in all social, political, and educational movements in Bombay Presidency; Fellow Bombay University, 1905-27, and Poona University, 1949-; Vice-Chancellor of the new Indian Women's Univ., 1916-20; Bombay Legislative Council as nominee of Govt., 1913-16; representative of the University of Bombay on Council, 1916-23; re-elected, 1926; Minister of Excise and Forests, 1927; Member of the India Council, London, 1927-32; Vice-Chancellor, Lucknow University, 1932-38; High Commissioner for India in Australia, 1944-47; Vice-Chancellor Univ of Poona, 1956-59; Hon. Associate R.P.A. 1931; Hon. Fellow of St. John's College, Cambridge, 1945. Kaisar-i-Hind gold medal, Jan. 1916. *Publications:* besides some mathematical publications, has written short lives of Gopal Krishna Gokhale and Dhondo Keshav Karve, two recent political and social leaders of India; The Crux of the Indian Problem 1931; Rationalism in Practice, 1936; Eighty-Four Not Out, 1961. *Recreations:* reading, bridge. *Address:* Poona 4, India. *Clubs:* Deccan Liberal, Deccan Gymkhana (Poona). [*Died* 6 *May* 1966.

PARDOE, John George, C.M. F.R.C.S., M.B.; Consulting Surgeon, West London Hospital; *b.* 1871; 3rd *s.* of late Rev. George Pardoe, Vicar of Alkham, Kent; *m.* Mary, *e. d.* of late Arthur Woodman Dixon, Newcastle; one *d.* *Educ.:* University of Aberdeen; King's College Hospital, London. Fellow of the Royal Society of Medicine; Member of the Société Internationale de Chirurgie; Corresponding Member of the Association Française d'Urologie, and of the American Association of Genito-Urinary Surgeons; Member of the Association Internationale d'Urologie. *Publications:* Contributions to the Surgery of the Urinary Organs in an Index of Treatment; Proceedings of the Royal Medical and Chirurgical Society, the Royal Society of Medicine, etc. *Address:* St. George's Nursing Home, Milford-on-Sea, Hampshire. *T.:* Milford-on-Sea 258. [*Died* 23 *April* 1965.

PARHAM, Rt. Rev. Arthur Groom, M.C., M.A.; Hon. Canon of Christ Church, Oxford, since 1934; Hon. Assistant Bishop in Diocese of Oxford since 1954; *b.* 25 June 1883; *s.* of Edmund and Ann Parham; *m.* 1946, Margaret Elizabeth Montagu, J.P. Berkshire, 1959, *widow* of Major T. G. H. Kirkwood, Royal Engineers; two *d.* *Educ.:* Magdalen College School, Oxford; Exeter College, Oxford; Leeds Clergy School. Deacon 1909; Priest, 1910; Curate of Bromley, Kent, 1909-12; Chaplain and Precentor of Christ Church Cathedral and Chaplain of Magdalen College, Oxford, 1912-1921; Temporary Chaplain to the Forces with the 2nd Mounted Division, the 47th and 17th Divisions, and D.A.C.G., 17th Corps, 1914-19 (M.C., despatches twice); Rector of Easthampstead, 1921-26; Vicar of S. Mary the Virgin, Reading, 1926-46; Rural Dean of Reading, 1934-42; Archdeacon of Berkshire, 1942-54; Suffragan Bishop of Reading, 1942-54; Proctor in Canterbury Convocation, 1935-54. Member of Government Committee of Enquiry into Detention Barracks, 1943; Member Home Office Advisory Council on Treatment of Offenders, 1947-57. *Address:* Wittenham House, Little Wittenham, nr. Abingdon, Berks. *T.:* Clifton Hampden 278. *Club:* Oxford and Cambridge University. [*Died* 8 *Jan.* 1961.

PARISER, Sir Maurice (Philip), Kt. 1965; Alderman, Manchester City Council; *b.* 4 Dec. 1906; *s.* of Lewis Alexander Pariser, Manchester; *m.* 1934, Irene Marks; two *s.* *Educ.:* privately; Manchester Univ. War Service, 1940-46; Maj. E. Lancs. Regt. Member: Manch. City Council, 1946- (Leader, 1962-66); Court and Council, Manch. Univ. 1954-. Chairman: Manch. Educ. Cttee., 1950-54; Univ. of Manch. Inst. of Science & Tech., 1956-; Manch. Coll. of Art & Design, 1959-65; Manch. Libraries Cttee., 1959-62. M.A. (h.c.) Manchester University, 1958. Member: N.W. Economic Planning Council, 1965-; National Theatre Board, 1965-; a Local Director, Henry Ansbacher and Co., 1965-. *Recreations:* bibliography and book collecting. *Address:* 84 Upper Park Rd., Salford 7, Lancs. *T.:* Cheetham Hill 2819. [*Died* 3 *Feb.* 1968

PARK, Rev. William Robert, C.I.E. 1917, O.B.E. 1919; M.A.; *b* 12 Jan 1880; *m.* 1910, Rosamond Ella (*d.* 1932), 3rd *d.* of Rev. C. Eveleigh Woodruff, M.A., Six-Preacher of Canterbury Cathedral three *d.* *Educ.:* Christ's Hosp., London; Exeter Coll., Oxford. Curate, South Hill, Cornwall, 1905-06, Holy Trinity, Oxford, 1906-10, Holy Trinity, Margate, 1910; Organising Sec. (Gloucester and Hereford Dioceses), C.M.S. 1910-12; Chaplain on Bengal Establishment (Rangoon Diocese), 1912; Rangoon Cantonments, 1912; Meiktila (Burma), 1912-14; Port Blair, Andaman Islands, 1914-16; Mesopotamian Expeditionary Force, Assistant Principal Chaplain, 1916; Senior Chaplain to the Forces, 1st Indian Army Corps, 1917; Principal

Chaplain, 1919; Maymyo Cantonments (Burma), 1920; Dagshai, 1923; Rangoon Cathedral, 1924; Mandalay, 1927; Moulmein, 1929; Maymyo, 1930; Archdeacon of Rangoon, 1934-37; Rector of Campsea Ashe, 1937-49; Rural Dean of Wilford, 1942-49; Vicar of Stalisfield with Otterden, Faversham, Kent, 1949-58; Chap. to the Earl of Stradbroke, 1959. *Address:* The Vicarage, Wangford, Beccles, Suffolk. [*Died* 25 *Dec.* 1961.

PARKER, Dom Anselm (Edward Stanislaus); Titular Abbot of Westminster, 1961; Titular Cathedral Prior of Rochester, 1949; priest and monk of the Order of St. Benedict; Assistant Priest at St. Mary's, Leyland, since 1947; *b.* Birmingham, 7 May 1880. *Educ.:* Ampleforth Coll., Yorkshire; Oxford Univ.; graduated, 1900; M.A., 1904. Entered the English Congregation of the Benedictine Order, 1900; priest, 1907; assistant master at Ampleforth, 1903-08; Master of St. Benet's Hall (formerly Parker's Hall), Oxford, 1908-20; Headmaster of Abbey School, Fort Augustus, 1920-24; Assistant-Priest, St. Mary's, Warrington, 1924-28; Assistant-Priest, St. Mary's, Merthyr Tydfil, 1928-30; Rector of St. Mary's, Leyland, Lancs, 1930-47. *Publications:* writer of articles in Catholic periodicals in England and America; co-translator (with Rt. Rev. T. L. Parker, M.A.) of A Manual of Modern Scholastic Philosophy by Cardinal Mercier and others. *Address:* St. Mary's, Leyland, Lancs. *T.:* 21183. *Club:* Oxford Union (Oxford). [*Died* 19 *Dec.* 1962.

PARKER, Rt. Hon. Dame Dehra, P.C. (N. Ire.) 1949; G.B.E. 1957 (D.B.E. 1949; O.B.E. 1918); J.P.; Minister of Health and Local Government, Northern Ireland, 1949-1957; M.P. (U.) N. Ireland Parliament, Londonderry County and City, 1921-29, S. Londonderry, 1933-60, resigned; *o. c.* and *heiress* of late James Kerr-Fisher, The Manor House, Kilrea, Co. Londonderry, and of Chicago, U.S.A.; *m.* 1st, 1901, Lt.-Col. Robert P. D. Spencer Chichester, D.L., M.P. of Moyola Park, Castledawson, Co. Londonderry (*d.* 1921); one *d.*; (one *s.* decd.); 2nd, 1928, Adm. H. W. Parker, C.B., C.M.G. (*d.* 1940). Parliamentary Secretary to Ministry of Education, Northern Ireland, 1937-44. President of C.E.M.A. (N. Ireland), 1949-60. *Recreation:* fishing. *Address:* Shanemullagh House, Castledawson, Co. Derry, N. Ireland. *Clubs:* Guards; Alpha (Belfast). [*Died* 28 *Nov.* 1963.

PARKER, Dorothy (Mrs. Alan Campbell); Writer; book reviewer for Esquire since 1958; *b.* 22 August 1893; *d.* of Jacob Henry Rothschild and Eliza Ann Marston; *m.* 1917, Edwin Pond Parker II; divorced, 1928; *m.* 1934, Alan Campbell. *Educ.:* Miss Dana's School, Morristown, New Jersey; Blessed Sacrament Convent, New York. Editorial staff of Vogue, 1916-1917; editorial staff of Vanity Fair, 1917-1920; book-reviewer for The New Yorker for several years; later screen-writer in Hollywood; at present free-lance writer. Winner of Marjorie Waite Peabody Award, 1958. F.I.A.L. 1959. *Publications:* Close Harmony (play: with Elmer Rice), 1925; Enough Rope (verse), 1926; Sunset Gun (verse), 1928; Laments for the Living (short stories), 1930; Death and Taxes (verse), 1931; After such Pleasures (short stories), 1933; Not so Deep as a Well (verse), 1936; Here Lies (short stories), 1939; The Ladies of the Corridor (play: with Arnaud d'Usseau), 1953. The Portable Dorothy Parker (collected verse and short stories), 1944; contributor of short stories to numerous magazines. *Address:* 8983 Norma Place, Los Angeles 69, California, U.S.A. [*Died* 7 *June* 1967.

PARKER, Hampton Wildman, C.B.E. 1957; M.A., D.Sc.; lately Keeper, Dept. of Zoology, British Museum (Natural History) (1947-57); *b.* 5 July 1897; *e. s.* of late Stephen and Bertha Leonora Parker, Giggleswick; *m.* 1924, Nora Whatling, Cambridge. *Educ.:* Giggleswick; Christ's Hosp.; Selwyn College, Cambridge. Served European War, 6th Duke of Wellington's (West Riding) Regt., 1915-19. Asst. Keeper in charge of Amphibians and Reptiles, Brit. Mus. (Nat. Hist.), 1923. Temp. Naval Store Officer, Admiralty, 1940-45. Deputy Keeper, Dept. of Zoology, Brit. Mus. (Nat. Hist.), 1944. *Publications:* Frogs of the family Microhylidae, 1934; Snakes, 1963; Natural History of Snakes, 1965; numerous zoological papers in scientific periodicals of the U.K., U.S.A., Belgium and Holland. *Recreation:* yachting. *Address:* c/o Midland Bank, Gloucester Road, S. Kensington, S.W.7. [*Died* 2 *Sept.* 1968.

PARKER, Harold; Sculptor and Painter; *b.* 1873; *s.* of late D. Parker and Jane Parker, Brisbane, Queensland; *m.* 1911, Janet (*d.* 1951), *d.* of late Lieut.-Col. Sir T. B. Robinson, G.B.E., K.C.M.G.; no *c.* *Educ.:* West End State School, South Brisbane; privately. Student of Art School, Brisbane, under late Mr. Clark and late R. Godfrey Rivers; came to London, 1896; student of City and Guilds of London Institute under late W. S. Frith; whilst there won £100 Scholarship, County Council Scholarship, First for Sculpture, Gilbert-Garret Sketch Club, etc.; R.B.S. 1906-26; Foundation Member Australian Academy of Arts. *Principal Works:* Ariadne, statue, marble (Chantrey purchase, Tate Gallery); Esther, bust, marble; The First Breath of Spring, marble figure (Queensland National Art Gallery) and marble figure, National Art Gallery, Melbourne; The Long, Long Dreams of Youth; Narcissus; Prometheus; Mention Honorable, Salon, 1910; Marble Bronze Memorial to Mrs. M'Connel of Queensland; Memorial Busts of Mr. John Forrest; Marble Bust of Lady M'Ilwraith; two colossal groups main entrance doorway Australia House, Strand; The Pioneer, marble (medal, Paris Salon, 1928); marble bust, Iris, purchased for National Gallery, Melbourne (Felton Bequest). *Principal oil paintings include*—The Resurrection, The Marriage in Cana, Orpheus and Eurydice, Horses hauling Timber (Hon. Mention, Paris Salon, 1928), etc.; has exhibited Painting and Water Colour Drawings in Paris Salon, 1928-29; held exhibitions of seventy works in Sydney, 1930, and fifty-four works in Melbourne, 1933, etc. *Address:* Ningwood, 34 Dornoch Terrace, West End, S. Brisbane, Australia. *T.:* Brisbane J2096. [*Died* 23 *April* 1962.

PARKER, Lt.-Col. Hon. Hubert Stanley Wyborn, D.S.O. 1919; V.D.; Barrister; *b.* 16 October 1883; *s.* of the late Hon. Sir Stephen Henry Parker, K.C.M.G., K.C., and Amey Katherine Leake; *m.* 1923; one *s.* one *d.* *Educ.:* Hale School, Perth; Malvern College. M.L.A., N.E. Fremantle, 1930-33; M.L.C., W. Australia, 1934-54; Attorney-General, 1933; Minister for Health, 1947; Minister for Mines, 1947-50; Chief Sec., Minister for Police, 1948, and Native Affairs, 1949. Served Australian Field Artillery A.I.F., 1914-19 (D.S.O.); Home Service, 1940; A.I.F. 1941 and R.A.N.V.R. 1942. *Address:* 26 Wright Avenue, Swanbourne, W. Australia. *T.:* F 1205. *Clubs:* Royal Automobile of W.A., Royal Freshwater Bay Yacht, Cottesloe Golf (W.A.). [*Died* 26 *July* 1966.

PARKER, John Williams, C.B. 1945; *b.* 1885; *y. s.* of F. W. Parker, Rolvenden, Kent; *m.* 1926, Maude Vivien, *y. d.* of F. W. Barnes; one *d.* Entered Scottish Education Department, 1904; Assistant Secretary, 1936; Second Secretary, 1940; Deputy

Secretary, 1946-48. *Address :* 27 Woodberry Crescent, N.10. *T. :* Tudor 4873. [*Died* 4 *Dec.* 1961.

PARKER, Brig.-Gen. Walter Mansel, C.B. 1928; C.M.G. 1916; D.S.O. 1918; late R.A.S.C.; 2nd *s.* of late Col. Walter Parker, Exeter; *b.* 1875; *m.* 1931, Audrey Stanley, *d.* of S. Weigall. *Educ.:* Elizabeth College, Guernsey. Joined Northamptonshire Regt. 1895; served Tirah Expedition, N.W. Frontier, India, 1897-98 (medal and 3 clasps); joined Army Service Corps, 1902; London School of Economics, 1912; went to Argentina, Supervising War Office Contracts, 1913; Staff Capt., War Office, 1914. Served European War—War Office, Gallipoli, Salonika, Egypt, Mesopotamia, France (C.M.G., Brevet-Colonel, D.S.O., despatches five times). Assistant Director of Supplies, War Office, 1919-1922; Deputy Director Mechanical Transport, A.H.Q., India, 1923-28; retired pay, 1928. *Address:* Dundridge House, Harberton, Totnes, Devon. *T.:* Totnes 2366. [*Died* 18 *April* 1962.

PARKER, Rt. Rev. Wilfrid, M.A.; Honorary C.F.; *b.* 23 Jan. 1883; *s.* of late Hon. Cecil Parker; *m.* 1933, Charlotte (*d.* 1965), *e. d.* of Sir George Albu, 1st Bart. *Educ.:* Radley Coll.; St. Andrew's College, Grahamstown; Christ Church, Oxford. Assistant Priest, Christ Church Mission, Poplar, 1908; Domestic Chaplain to the Archbishop of York, 1909-13; Asst. Priest, St. Mary's, Johannesburg, 1913-15; Asst. Priest, St. Martins-in-the-Fields, 1915-19; Chaplain to the Forces, France and Italy, 1916-19 (Croce di Guerra, 1918). Vicar, St. George's Parktown, Johannesburg, 1919-23; Priest in Charge, St. Cyprian's Native Mission, Johannesburg, 1923-31; Canon of Johannesburg Cathedral, 1926; Archdeacon and Director of Native Missions, Diocese of Pretoria, 1931-33; Bishop of Pretoria, 1933-50, resigned. Sub-prelate of Order of St. John of Jerusalem, 1946. *Address:* Papenboom, Newlands, Cape of Good Hope. [*Died* 23 *June* 1966.

PARKES, Sir Fred, Kt. 1958; Chairman and Managing Director, Boston Deep Sea Fisheries Ltd., and associated companies, since 1924; *b.* 14 Jan. 1881; *s.* of Frank Parkes, Sleaford, and Elizabeth, *d.* of J. Young; *m.* 1902, Gertrude Mary Bailey; one *s.* two *d.* *Educ.:* Elementary School. Underwriting Member of Lloyd's, 1948. President, North Fylde Conservative Assoc.; President, Blackpool and Dist. Branch of S.S. & A.F.A.; Director, Fleetwood Fishing Vessel Owners Assoc., President, 1938-47; Member of Blackpool and Fylde War Pensioners' Welfare Cttee. Director, British Trawlers' Federation. Liveryman Worshipful Company of Poulters; Liveryman Worshipful Company of Shipwrights. Hon. Freeman of Borough of Fleetwood, 1956. Chevalier de l'Ordre du Mérite Maritime, 1948. Lord of the Manor of Winmarleigh. *Recreation:* golf, *Address:* Wellvale, 60 Warbreck Hill Road. Blackpool. Lancs. *T.:* Blackpool 52667. *Clubs:* City Livery; North Shore Golf (President) (Blackpool). [*Died* 22 *June* 1962.

PARKES, Sir Sydney, Kt. 1946; C.B.E. 1943; Chief General Manager, Lloyds Bank Ltd. 1938-45, Director 1941-56; Chairman Crosse & Blackwell (Holdings) Ltd., 1946-1956; Vice-President City of London Savings Committee (Chairman, 1941-53); Mem. National Savings Committee, 1942-55; *b.* 23 Feb. 1879; *s.* of late Tom Burchall Parkes, Altrincham, Cheshire; *m.* 1904, Hilda Mary, *d.* of Rev. John H. Corson; two *s.* *Educ.:* Truro School; Manchester University (Cobden Prizeman). Master of Glovers Company, 1941-43; Member, Court of Common Council, 1934-58; Dep. Chm. Bank of British West Africa Ltd., 1948-54; Dir. National Bank of New Zealand, Ltd. 1936-58 (Chm. 1945-55). *Address:* Oatlands Park Hotel, Weybridge, Surrey. *T.:* Weybridge 4242. [*Died* 21 *Jan.* 1961.

PARKIN, Benjamin Theaker; M.P. (Lab.) for North Paddington since Dec. 1953; *b.* 1906; *s.* of Capt. B. D. Parkin; *m.* 1st, 1929, Phyllis Lunt (marriage dissolved, 1957); two *s.*; 2nd, 1957, Pamela Tuffnell (*née* Coates); one *s.* *Educ.:* Wycliffe Coll.; Lincoln College, Oxford; Strasbourg University, Schoolmaster and R.A.F. (Flt. Lt.). M.P. (Lab.) for Stroud, Mid-Gloucester Div., 1945-50. *Recreations:* foreign travel and junk shops. *Address:* House of Commons, S.W.1; 75 Winchester Street, S W.1. [*Died* 3 *June* 1969.

PARKINSON, Sir (Arthur Charles) Cosmo, G.C.M.G. 1942 (K.C.M.G. 1935; C.M.G. 1931); K.C.B. 1938; O.B.E. 1919; M.A. (Oxford); hon. LL.D. (St. Andrews); Chairman, Court of Governors, London Sch. of Hygiene and Tropical Medicine, 1951-64; a Crown Trustee, City Parochial Foundation, 1946-66; *b.* 18 Nov. 1884; *s.* of late Dr. S. G. Parkinson, Wimborne, Dorset; unmarried. *Educ.:* Epsom Coll.; Magdalen Coll., Oxford. Appointed to Admiralty, 1908; transferred to Colonial Office, 1909; Assistant Secretary, 1925-31; Assistant Under-Secretary of State, 1931-37; Permanent Under-Secretary of State for the Colonies, 1937-40; Permanent Under-Sec. of State for Dominion Affairs, Feb. 1940; appointed to act as Permanent Under-Sec. of State for Colonies, May 1940; seconded for special duty in the Colonies, April 1942; retired 31 Dec. 1944; re-employed 1 Jan. to 30 Sept. 1945 on special duty for the Secretary of State for the Colonies; absent on military service, 1915-19; Inns of Court O.T.C. and King's African Rifles, held appointment of D.A.A.G. with rank of Major in King's African Rifles, 1917-18; Order of the Brilliant Star of Zanzibar (3rd class), 1929. *Publication:* The Colonial Office from Within, 1909-1945, 1947. *Address:* c/o Messrs. Coutts & Co., 440 Strand, W.C.2. *Club:* Athenæum. [*Died* 16 *Aug.* 1967.

PARKINSON, Joseph Ernest, C.I.E. 1938; M.A.; late Indian Educational Service, *b.* 13 Apr. 1883; *s.* of Joseph Edward Parkinson, Burnley; *m.* 1915, Kathleen (*d.* 1954), *d.* of J. McDonnell, Leeds; one *s.* one *d.* *Educ.:* Burnley Gram. Sch.; King's College, Cambridge. Joined Indian Educational Service, 1913; Educational Commissioner with Govt. of India, 1936; retired, 1938; re-employed as Educational Commissioner with Govt. of India, Apr.-Nov. 1938. *Address:* Bryn Estyn, Trefriw, Caerns. [*Died* 1 *Jan.* 1962.

PARKINSON, Wilfrid, M.C., M.A.; *b.* Norland, nr. Halifax, Yorks, 1887; *m.* 1916, Grace Booth Bidwell, Cambridge; one *s.* one *d.* *Educ.:* Leicester; Peterhouse, Cambridge (Open Mathematical Scholar). 18th Wrangler, 1909; Natural Science Tripos, Part II, 1910; held teaching posts at Wolverhampton School, Edinburgh Academy; chief mathematical master, Merchant Taylors' School, 1919-25; Headmaster of the City of Oxford School, 1925-32; Headmaster of Bridlington School, Yorkshire, 1932-47; served in R.E. (Signals) European War (despatches, M.C.). *Publication:* A Primer of Geometry. *Address:* Beechurst, Duxford, Cambs *T.:* Sawston 3167. [*Died* 15 *Aug.* 1965.

PARMAR, Rt. Rev. Philip; Bishop of Delhi, since 1966; *b.* 28 Nov. 1909; *m.* 1938, Eleanor, *d.* of Rev. J. Isudas; two *s.* one *d.* *Educ.:* Univ. of Bombay (M.A., B.T., LL.B.); Bishop's Coll., Calcutta. Deacon, 1943; Priest, 1944. Bishop of Bhagalpur, Bihar, 1955-66. *Recreation:* reading. *Address:* Bishop's House, 1 Church Lane, New Delhi 1, India. *T.:* 34748 and 33080. [*Died* 9 *May* 1970.

PARMINTER, Brigadier Reginald Horace Roger, C.B.E. 1940; D.S.O. 1917; M.C.; *b.* 28 March 1893; *s.* of Major William George Parminter and Leila M. E. Heyn; *m.* 1919, Muriel Davis; one *s.* *Educ.:* Dover College; Royal Military College, Sandhurst. Entered Army, 1913; posted Manchester Regiment; Captain, 1915; Bt. Major, 1919; Major, 1926; Lt.-Col., 1933; Bt. Col. 1935; Col. 1937; served European War (D.S.O., M.C.); commanded 2nd Bn. The Manchester Regt., 1933-35; Commandant Royal Military School of Music and Inspector of Army Bands, 1935-1939; Assistant Adjutant and Quarter-Master-General, i/c Administration, 1939-1944; Comd. Area in France and Belgium, 1944-45. Chief of U.N.R.R.A. Mission to Austria, 1946-47. A.D.C. to the King, 1943-1948; retired. Member U.N. Secretariat, New York, 1948-54. *Recreations:* flying, cricket. *Address:* Witherhurst Farm, Burwash, Sussex. *Clubs:* Royal Air Force, M.C.C. [*Died* 7 *May* 1967.

PARR, George Herbert Edmeston, C.B. 1953; C.B.E. 1948; *b.* 28 April 1890; *s.* of late S. G. Parr, S. Norwood; *m.* 1918, Amy Grace, *d.* of late H. J. Martin, Cheam; three *s.* three *d.* *Educ.:* Marlborough Coll.; Berlin; Paris. H.M. Consular Service, 1914; transf. to Govt. of N. Ire., 1921; Asst. Sec., Ministry of Commerce, 1922; seconded to Ministry of Food, 1939; Divisional Food Officer, N. Ireland, 1939-44; Permanent Secretary, Ministry of Commerce, 1944-49; Comptroller and Auditor-General, Northern Ireland, 1949-55; retired 1955. Mem., Restrictive Practices Ct., 1957-61; Chm., Adv. Cttee. on Inland Fisheries in N. Ireland, 1961-63. *Recreation:* gardening. *Address:* Cranley, Groomsport, Bangor, Co. Down. *T.:* Groomsport 303. [*Died* 31 *Dec.* 1969.

PARR, Raymond Cecil; *b.* 8 Oct. 1884; *s.* of Cecil F. Parr of Kimpton Grange, Welwyn, Herts, and Amy Dimsdale, *d.* of 6th Baron Dimsdale; *m.* 1913, Audrey Bapst; two *s.* *Educ.:* Eton; New College, Oxford. Entered Diplomatic Service as Attaché, 1908; appointed to Cairo, 1909; transferred to Paris, 1910; 3rd Secretary, 1911; transferred to Rome, 1913; Rio de Janeiro, 1916; 2nd Secretary, 1919; transferred to Brussels 1919; 1st Secretary, 1920; transferred to Copenhagen, 1920; First Secretary British Legation, Budapest, 1924-27; Counsellor of Embassy, 1927; Counsellor at British Legation, Tehran, Persia, 1927-31; acted at various times as Chargé d'Affaires in last four posts; retired, 1935. *Address:* Old Dove House, near Harpenden, Herts. [*Died* 10 *Jan.* 1965.

PARRISH, Maxfield; Artist; *b.* 1870; *s.* of Stephen Parrish and Elizabeth Bancroft; *m.* Lydia Austin; three *s.* one *d.* Doctor of Laws, Haverford College, 1914; Phi Beta Kappa; Hon. Member Philadelphia Water Color Society; Gold Medal Architectural League of New York, 1917; Honorable Mention Paris World's Fair; Silver Medal Pan-American Exposition, Buffalo, 1918; Member National Academy of Design, New York; Mural paintings in The Curtis Building, Philadelphia; Mask and Wig Club, Philadelphia; Meeting House Club, New York; Palace Hotel, San Francisco; Sherman Hotel, Chicago; Raquet Club, New York; Eastman Theatre, Rochester, New York; Mr. Irénée du Pont, Wilmington, Delaware; Mrs. James Storrow, Lincoln, Mass. Dr. of Fine Arts, Univ. of New Hampshire, 1954. *Address:* The Oaks, Cornish, New Hampshire, U.S.A. *Club:* Coffee House (New York). [*Died* 30 *March* 1966.

PARRY, Hon. Sir Henry W.; *see* Wynn Parry.

PARRY, Engineer Rear-Admiral Herbert Lyell, C.B. 1931; O.B.E. 1919; *b.* 1875; *s.* of S. Parry, Chester; *m.* 1904, Charlotte Ethel (*d.* 1956), *d* of R. Parnall, Glan-Mor, Newport, Mon.; one *d.* *Educ.:* King's Sch., Chester; R.N. Engineering College, Keyham. Engineer Admiral for Personnel, 1928-31; retired list, 1931. *Address:* c/o Mrs. M. Willis, Springfield, Nottington, nr. Weymouth. *T.:* Upwey 251. *Club:* Royal Dorset Yacht (Weymouth). [*Died* 12 *Feb.* 1963.

PARRY, Rev. Kenneth Loyd, B.Sc. (Liverpool); Moderator of the Free Church Federal Council, 1956-57; *b.* 11 Nov. 1884; *s.* of late Joseph Parry, M.I.C.E., City Water Engineer, Liverpool; *m.* 1st, 1911, Hope Gladys Blakeley (*d.* 1921); one *s.* one *d.* (and one *s.* decd.); 2nd, 1923, Margaret Yvonne Addyman (*d.* 1949); one *s.* one *d.* *Educ.:* Merchant Taylors' Grammar School (Crosby); Liverpool University; Mansfield College, Oxford. Congregational Minister: Oxted, Surrey, 1909-13; Lion Walk, Colchester, 1913-21; Chorlton Road, Manchester, 1921-33; Highbury Chapel, Bristol, 1933-54. Actg. Principal, Western Coll., Bristol, 1939-41; Chairman: Board of Dirs., London Missionary Soc., 1941-42; Congregational Union of England and Wales, 1942-43; Governors of Redland High School, Bristol; on Board of Bristol United Hosps. *Publications:* The Mystery of Godliness, 1934; Companion to Congregational Praise, 1953; Christian Hymns, 1956. Frank Crossley (chapter in Great Christians), 1933; Prayer and Praise (chapter in Christian Worship), 1936. *Recreations:* music, golf. *Address:* 24 Clarendon Road, Bristol 6. *T.:* 44928. [*Died* 20 *Jan.* 1962.

PARRY, Air Vice-Marshal Rey Griffith, C.B. 1941; D.S.O. 1915; D.I.C., A.F.R.Ae.S.; R.A.F., retd. formerly R.N.; *b.* 7 Sept. 1889; *s.* of late W. Griffith-Parry; *m.* 1920, Joan Brunner, M.B.E., *y. d.* of late Major T. W. Buckley, of Clopton Manor, Kettering; two *d.* Entered H.M. Navy, 1905; Eng.-Lieut. 1911; served Dardanelles, 1914-15 (despatches, D.S.O. for services in H.M.S. Inflexible when she was struck by a mine); Croix de Guerre with Palm (French), 1917; Eng.-Lieut. Commander, 1919; granted permanent commission as Squadron Leader R.A.F., 1919; Wing Commander, 1929; Group Captain, 1935; Air Commodore, 1938; Air Vice-Marshal (acting), 1939; served War of 1939-45 (despatches, C.B.); retired with Hon. rank of Air Vice-Marshal, 1943. *Address:* Pasea Hall, Tortola, Virgin Is. *Clubs:* Royal Automobile; R.A.F. Yacht. [*Died* 8 *Aug.* 1969.

PARRY, Brigadier Sir Richard G.; *see* Gambier-Parry.

PARSONS, Sir (Alfred) Alan Lethbridge, K.C.I.E., *cr.* 1935 (C.I.E. 1925); Kt., *cr.* 1932; *b.* 22 Oct. 1882; *s.* of late J. F. Parsons, M.R.C.S., of Garston House, Frome, Somerset, and late Alice Marion Down; *m.* 1920, Katharine, *d.* of S. G. Parsons of Pelham House, Lindfield, Sussex; three *d.* *Educ.:* Bradfield College; University College, Oxford (Scholar). B.A. 1905; Indian Civil Service, 1907; Under-Secretary to the Punjab Government, Finance Department, 1912; Under-Secretary to the Government of India, Finance Department, 1916; Deputy Controller of the Currency, 1922; Secretary to Government of India, Department of Industries and Labour, 1925; Financial Commissioner, Railways, 1926; Temp. Member of the Executive Council of the Governor-General of India, June 1932; Secretary to the Government of India, Finance Department, 1932-34; Member of Council of India, 1934; Adviser to Secretary of State for India, 1937-40. *Recreations:* fishing, shooting, bridge. *Address:* 19 Cotman Close, Westleigh Avenue, S.W.15. *Club:* East India and Sports. [*Died* 11 *Oct.* 1964.

PARSONS, Major-General Sir Arthur Edward Broadbent, K.C.I.E., *cr.* 1938; C.B.E. 1927; D.S.O.; late Indian Political Department; *b.* 1884; *s.* of Frederick Parsons, Frome, Somerset; unmarried. *Educ.:* Bradfield College; Exeter College, Oxford. 2nd Lt. The Sherwood Foresters, 1906; 52nd Sikhs F.F., 1908; served European War, 1914-19 (despatches) Political Dept., 1919; Afghan War, 1919 (despatches, O.B.E.); Waziristan Operations, 1921-22 (despatches, D.S.O.); Agent to Governor General, Baluchistan, 1936-39; Acting Governor, N.W. Frontier Prov., 1939; Representative of War Organisation of the British Red Cross Society and Order of St. John of Jerusalem in Russia, 1942; G.H.Q. Middle East, 1943-44. *Address:* c/o National & Grindlay's Bank, 13 St. James's Sq., S.W.1. *Club:* United Service. [*Died* 8 *Aug.* 1966.

PARSONS, George Richard, C.B. 1955; C.B.E. 1951; Director of Establishments and Organisation, General Post Office, 1952-58; *b.* 11 July 1898; *s.* of George Parsons; *m.* 1926, Florence Mary, *d.* of James Amis; one *d.* Served European War, 1917-18, with Royal Flying Corps. *Address:* 3 South Bank Terrace, Surbiton. [*Died* 20 *Feb.* 1961.

PARSONS, John Randal; Chairman, Gillett Brothers Discount Co., 1926-46; *b.* 1884; 4th *s.* of late Hon. Richard Clere Parsons and *g.s.* of 3rd Earl of Rosse; *m.* 1909, Hon Alice Esmeralda, 3rd *d.* of 2nd Baron O'Neill. *Educ.:* Wellington (King's Gold Medal); Trinity College, Cambridge, B.A. In business in Canada, 1910-14; served Russia 1915-18, Flag Lieut. to Admiral Phillimore attached to Russian Imperial Headquarters 1915-16; Assistant Naval Attaché, Petrograd 1917; Naval Attaché 1917-18; 3rd Class Order of St. Anne; 2nd Class Order of St. Stanislas. *Recreations:* fishing, yachting, shooting. *Address:* Little Gillions, Croxley Green, Herts. *T.:* Rickmansworth 2021. *Clubs:* Travellers', Royal Yacht Squadron (Cowes). [*Died* 15 *March* 1967.

PART, Lt.-Col. Sir Dealtry Charles, Kt. 1957; O.B.E.; J.P.; 2nd *s.* of late Charles Thomas Part, D.L., J.P., of Aldenham Lodge, Herts, and Isabella A., 3rd *d.* of late Alex. Mackintosh of Mackintosh (The Mackintosh), Moy Hall, Inverness-shire; *m.* Edith M. (*d.* 1957), *d.* of late W. Christie-Miller, D.L., J.P., Britwell Court, Burnham, Buckinghamshire; *m.* 1958, Mrs. Avice Long. *Educ.:* Harrow. Formerly Capt. 21st Lancers; Lieut.-Col. retired; Sheriff of Bedfordshire, 1926; H.M. Lieutenant for Bedfordshire, 1943-57. *Recreation:* Joint Master Hertfordshire Hounds, 1931-48. *Address:* Houghton Hall, Houghton Regis, Bedfordshire; Morvich, Rogart, Sutherland, Scotland. *Club:* Cavalry. [*Died* 9 *Feb.* 1961.

PARTINGTON, James Riddick, M.B.E., D.Sc.; Emeritus Professor of Chemistry in the University of London; *b.* Bolton, Lancs., 20 June 1886; *s.* of Alfred and Mary Agnes Partington; *m.* 1919, Marian (*d.* 1940), *d.* of Thomas Jones, Buckley, Chester; one *s.* two *d.* *Educ.:* Manchester University; University of Berlin. University Scholar and Beyer Fellow of Manchester University, 1910-11; 1851 Exhibition Scholar; Research at the Universities of Manchester and Berlin, 1909-13; Lecturer and Demonstrator in Chemistry, Univ. of Manchester; served in Army, and conducted special researches in Applied Chemistry for Inventions Dept. of Min. of Munitions; Prof. of Chemistry, Univ. of London, 1919-51; President, British Soc. for the History of Science, 1949-51. Dexter Award, 1961; Sarton Medal 1965. *Publications:* General and Inorganic Chemistry, 1965; A Text-Book of Inorganic Chemistry, 1961; Origins and Development of Applied Chemistry, 1935; A Short History of Chemistry, 1965; Thermodynamics, 1950; An Advanced Treatise on Physical Chemistry 1949-54; A History of Greek Fire and Gunpowder, 1960; A History of Chemistry, 1961-64; and other books; papers in Journal of Chemical Society, Isis, and other journals. *Address:* 80 Carlton Road, Witton Park, Northwich, Cheshire. *Club:* Athenaeum. [*Died* 9 *Oct.* 1965.

PARTRIDGE, Edward Hincks, M.A.; J.P.; Headmaster, Giggleswick School, 1931-1956, retired; *b.* 24 Oct. 1901; *s.* of late Edwin Partridge, Derby; *m.* 1927, Brenda de Mestre, *d.* of late Admiral J. de M. Hutchison, C.M.G., C.V.O.. *Educ.* Rossall (scholar); Corpus Christi Coll., Oxford (scholar); 2nd Class Hons. Mods.; 2nd Class Lit. Hum. Classical VI Form Master, Wellington Coll., 1924-31. *Publications:* Freedom in Education, 1943; Journey Home, 1946. *Address:* Shaws Farm, Storth, Milnthorpe, Westmorland. [*Died* 9 *March* 1962.

PASCOE, Sir (Frederick) John, Kt. 1957; Chairman, British Timken Division of The Timken Roller Bearing Company, since 1959 (Chairman 1950-59, Dep.-Chairman, 1940-50, Director, 1930-, Managing Director, 1940-59, British Timken Ltd.; Chm. and Man. Dir., 1950-59, Fischer Bearings Co. Ltd.); *b.* 19 March 1893; *s.* of late Frederick Richard Pascoe, Truro, Cornwall; *m.* 1936, Margaret Esson, *er. d.* of late Col. F. J. Scott; one *s.* one *d.* *Educ.:* Exeter School; St. John's Coll., Cambridge (B.A. Mech. Sciences). Apprenticeship, Leeds Forge. Served European War, 1914-18: commnd. in D.C.L.I., afterwards Indian Signal Service. Sec. Electric and Railway Finance Corp., 1926-30. Chairman: Aberdare Holdings Ltd.; Aberdare Cables Ltd.: Aberdare Engineering Ltd.; South Wales Switchgear Ltd. Chm. Kettering Conservative and Unionist Assoc., 1948-1953. Mem. Nat. Council of Aims of Industry; Mem. Regional Advisory Council for the Organization of Further Education in the East Midlands. Freeman of City of London; Liveryman: Worshipful Co. of Tin Plate Workers alias Wire Workers; Fishmongers' Company. *Recreations:* fishing; encouragement all forms of sporting activity (Vice-Pres. English Schools Cricket Assoc., etc.). *Address:* 8 Eaton Place, S.W.1. *T.:* Belgravia 4899 (Lady Pascoe: Belgravia 6718). *Clubs:* Carlton, Boodle's; Travellers' (Paris). [*Died* 5 *Feb.* 1963.

PASK, Edgar Alexander, O.B.E. 1944; M.A.; M.R.C.S., M.D.; Professor of Anæsthetics, Univ. of Newcastle upon Tyne (formerly King's Coll., Univ. of Durham), since 1949; Vice-Dean, Fac. of Anæsthetists, Royal College of Surgeons of England, 1958; *b.* 4 September 1912. *Educ.:* Rydal School; Downing College, Cambridge; London Hospital. M.A. Camb. 1933, M.D. 1947, F.F.A.R.C.S. 1949. Mem. Cttee. of Management, Royal Nat. Life-Boat Instn. *Address:* Department of Anæsthetics, The Medical School, Newcastle upon Tyne 1. [*Died* 30 *May* 1966.

PASS, (Alfred) Douglas, O.B.E. 1946; D.L., J.P.; *b.* 1885; *o. s.* of Alfred Capper Pass, Wootton Fitzpaine Manor, Charmouth, Dorset; *m.* 1912, Katharine Olive, *d.* of late C. T. Heycock, F.R.S.; five *d.* *Educ.:* Harrow; King's College, Cambridge. First class Nat. Sci. Tripos. J.P. 1911; D.L. 1943; High Sheriff of Dorset, 1922; Elected to Dorset C.C., 1913; Alderman, 1925-; for many years Chm. County Finance Cttee.; Vice-Chm. Council, 1939-46; Chm., 1946-55. Served European War, 1914-18, Dorset Yeomanry; Capt. 1915. From 1920, active interest in Boy Scout Movement; Dist. Comr. W. Dorset and subseq. County Pres. until 1962. War of 1939-45: County Army Welfare Officer for Dorset, with acting rank Lieut.-Colonel. President, Capper Pass & Son Ltd., Smelters, Bristol and Hull (part of

R.T.Z. Group, 1968), Chm. 1934-60. *Recreations:* fishing, hunting, shooting, stalking. *Address:* Wootton Fitzpaine Manor, Charmouth, Dorset. *T.:* 302.
[*Died* 9 *March* 1970.

PASSMORE, John Reginald Jutsum, C.B.E. 1937; retired; late Asst. Secretary Ministry of Aircraft Production; *b.* 4 Dec. 1878; 4th *s.* of late Edmund Passmore, Mornacott, Bishop's Nympton, Devon; *m.* 1906, Blanche Powell Jutsum; one *d.* *Educ.:* South Molton Collegiate School. Entered Permanent Civil Service, 1898; India Office, 1899-1912; Divisional Accountant, Board of Trade Labour Exchange and Unemployment Insurance Department, 1912-14; Assistant Divisional Officer, 1914-17; Divisional Controller, Ministry of Labour, 1917-23; Deputy Controller of Training, 1923-29; Director of Training, 1929-35; Chief Inspector of Training, 1935-39. *Recreation:* walking. *Address:* St. Leonards Park, Horsham, Sussex.
[*Died* 20 *Feb.* 1965.

PASTURE, 5th Marquis *cr.* 1768, France; **Major Gerard Hubert de la;** M.C. (and bar); late King's African Rifles; *b.* 3 May 1886; 2nd *s.* of 4th Marquis and Georgiana Mary (*d.* 1934), *d.* of Robert J. Loughnan, an Indian Judge; *S.* father, 1916; *m.* 1918, Ida, 3rd *d.* of late Sir Alexander Mosley, C.M.G.; two *s.* one *d.* *Heir:* *s.*, *b.* 30 Jan. 1921. *Address:* Stable Yard Cottage, Street End, nr. Canterbury, Kent. *T.:* Petham 288. [*Died* 12 *Nov.* 1962.

PATENAUDE, Hon. Esioff Léon, P.C., Q.C. (Can.); LL.D. (Hon. Montreal, McGill and Laval), D.C.L. (Bishop's); lawyer; Honorary President, Alliance Mutual Life Insurance Co.; Vice-President, Crédit Foncier Franco-Canadien; Chairman, Administration & Trust Co.; Director, Texaco Canada Limited; *b.* St. Isidore, Laprairie Co., P.Q., Canada, 12 February 1875; *s.* of Hilaire Patenaude and Angèle Trudeau, both French-Canadians; *m.* 1900, Georgianna, *d.* of Antoine Deniger, Laprairie; one *s.* one *d.* Admitted to the Bar of the Province of Quebec, 1899; Member Legislature of the Province of Quebec, for the County of Laprairie, 1908-15; and for Jacques-Cartier, 1923-25; Member House of Commons and Minister of Inland Revenue, 1915-17; Secretary of State, 1917; Minister of Justice, 1926; Lieut.-Governor of the Province of Quebec, 1934-40. *Address:* (home) 1321 Sherbrooke St. W., Montreal, P.Q.; (office) 680 Sherbrooke St. W., Montreal, P.Q.
[*Died* 11 *Feb.* 1963.

PATERSON, Donald Hugh, B.A. (Manitoba); M.D. (Edin.); F.R.C.P. (Lond.), F.R.C.P. (Can.); formerly Clinical Professor, Department of Pædiatrics in the Faculty of Medicine, University of British Columbia, 1952; Consultant in Pædiatrics, Vancouver General Hosp.; Consulting Pædiatrician Westminster Hosp.; Cons. Physician to Hospital for Sick Children, Great Ormond Street; *b.* 11 May 1890; *s.* of H. S. Paterson, Winnipeg; *m.* 1923, Dorothy Reed, *d.* of G. W. Blaikie, Toronto; three *s.* (and one *s.* decd.). *Educ.:* Edinburgh Univ.; Manitoba Univ. Late Capt., R.A.M.C., Special Reserve; F.R.S.M. (Pres. Children's Section, 1942-43); Mem. Brit. Pædiatric Assoc. (Pres. 1947-48); late Lecturer in Diseases of Children, London Univ.; late Member the General Nursing Council Board of Examiners for Sick Children's Nurses; Hon. Member Canadian Pædiatric Society; Member of American Pædiatric Society; Member of the Assoc. of Physicians of Gt. Britain and Ireland; Assoc. Member of Pædiatric Soc. of Paris; Hon. Fellow of American Acad. of Pædiatrics. *Publications:* Modern Methods of Feeding in Infancy and Childhood (with G. Newns), 10th edn., 1955; Sick Children: Diagnosis and Treatment (with R. Lightwood), 8th edn., 1962; editor of Garrod, Batten, Thursfield and Paterson's Diseases of Children, 4th edn. (with Alan Moncrieff), 1947; Jt. Editor (with J. F. McCreary) Pediatrics (Lippincott), 1956. *Recreations:* golf, fishing and shooting. *Address:* 1707 Angus Drive, Vancouver, B.C. *T.:* Regent 3-2401. *Clubs:* Vancouver; Capilano Golf
[*Died* 12 *Dec.* 1968.

PATERSON, John Sidney, C.B.E. 1943; retired as Assistant Secretary, Home Office (1945-59); *b.* 4 August 1899; *s.* of late Colonel Sidney Paterson, Ministry of Interior, Egypt; *m.* Brada Elizabeth, *o. d.* of late Judge A. Spencer Hogg; two *d.* *Educ.:* Eton; R.M.C., Sandhurst (winner, Sword of Honour and Saddle). Grenadier Guards, 1918-20; Egyptian Police, 1931-37; Foreign Office, Communications Department, 1937-1938; Ministry of Home Security, 1938-1944; attached S.H.A.E.F. Mission to Belgium for Civil Defence duties, Nov. 1944-Jan. 1945; U.N.R.R.A., 1944-45. Officer, Order of Leopold II, 1946. *Address:* c/o Post Office, Puerto de Andraitx, Majorca. *Club:* Guards. [*Died* 17 *March* 1965.

PATERSON, John Wilson, C.V.O. 1936 (M.V.O. 1926); M.B.E. 1920; F.R.I.A.S., A.R.I.B.A.; *b.* 1887; *s.* of William Paterson; *m.* 1920, Elizabeth Robertson (decd.), *d.* of H. Doig, Edinburgh. *Educ.:* George Watson's College, Edinburgh. Formerly Senior Architect, Ministry of Works, Scotland. *Address:* 6 Melville Crescent, and (home) 1 Murrayfield Drive, Edinburgh. *T.:* 031-337 7586. [*Died* 31 *May* 1970.

PATERSON-MORGAN, Rev. Richard James Basil, C.B.E. 1929; M.A.(Oxon); *b.* 1879; *m.* 1910, Agnes Wilhelmina, *o. d.* of William Dronsfield, J.P.; one *d.* Curate of Runcorn, 1903-08; Weaverham, 1908-09; Rector of Bangor Is-y-Coed, 1909-19; Member of S. Asaph Diocesan Association of Schools, 1915-19; Standing Committee Diocesan Conference, 1915-19; Commissioner under Pluralities Act (Amendment Act), 1915-19; Parish Councillor (Bangor-Is-y-Coed), 1912-19; Member of Ellesmere Board of Guardians, 1914-19; of Overton Rural District Council, 1914-19; of Denbighshire County Council, 1914-1919; of Denbighshire Local Education Authority, 1914-20; Divisional Chief Warden for Eddisbury Wardens Div., 1938-46; Pres. Northwich Divisional Conservative Assoc., 1950 (Chairman 1919-36 and 1944-50); Vice-Chairman Lancashire, Cheshire, and Westmorland Conservative Provincial Division, 1933-1936; Recorder of Mid-Cheshire Pitt Club, 1933-. Hon. Chaplain, Chester Sea Cadet Corps, 1944-61. Life Mem. Northwich Conservative Assoc., 1959. *Address:* Sandiway Lodge, Sandiway, Cheshire. *T.A.:* Sandiway, Cheshire. *T.:* Sandiway 3009.
[*Died* 25 *May* 1966.

PATON, Herbert James, M.A., D.Litt. (Oxon); Hon. D.Litt. (Edinburgh); LL.D. (Glasgow, St. Andrews, and Toronto); F.S.A. Scot., F.B.A. 1946; Author and editor; Emeritus Professor, Univ. of Oxford; Hon. Fell. of The Queen's College, Oxford; Hon. Fellow of Corpus Christi College, Oxford; *b.* 30 March 1887; *s.* of late Rev. William Macalister Paton, B.D., Abernethy, Perthshire, and Jean Robertson Millar; *m.* 1st, 1936, Mary Sheila (*d.* 1959), *d.* of late Henry Paul Todd-Naylor, I.C.S.; 2nd, 1962, Sarah Irene (*d.* 1964), *d.* of late Professor W. Macneile Dixon. *Educ.:* High School of Glasgow; Univ. of Glasgow; Balliol College, Oxford. Fellow and Praelector in Classics and Philosophy, Queen's College, Oxford, 1911-27; Dean, 1917-22; Intelligence Division of the Admiralty, 1914-19; British representative on the sub-Commission for Polish Affairs, Paris, 1919; Junior Proctor,

1920; Laura Spelman Rockefeller Research Fellow, University of California, 1925-26; Professor of Logic and Rhetoric, University of Glasgow, 1927-37; Dean of the Faculty of Arts, 1935-37; White's Professor of Moral Philosophy, Univ. of Oxford, and Fellow of Corpus Christi College, 1937-52; Foreign Research and Press Service (after 1943 Foreign Office Research Dept.), 1939-44; Mem. Exec. Cttee. of League of Nations Union, 1939-48; Curator of Bodleian Library, Oxford, 1938-52; Member of General Board of the Faculties, 1943-48; Chm. Board of Faculty of Social Studies, 1944-46; Chm. of Board of Studies for Psychology, 1950-52; Forwood Lecturer, Univ. of Liverpool, 1948-1949; Gifford Lecturer, Univ. of St. Andrews, 1949-51; Visiting Professor, University of Toronto, 1955. Crown Assessor on Court of St. Andrews Univ., 1953-60. *Publications:* The Good Will; Kant's Metaphysic of Experience; The Categorical Imperative; The Moral Law; In Defence of Reason; The Modern Predicament; The Claim of Scotland. *Recreation:* golf. *Address:* Nether Pitcaithly, Bridge of Earn, Perthshire. *T.:* 248. *Club:* Oxford and Cambridge University. [*Died* 2 *Aug.* 1969.

PATRICK, Rt. Hon. Lord; William Donald Patrick; P.C. 1949; Q.C. 1933; LL.D.; one of the Senators of H.M. College of Justice in Scotland, 1939-63; *b.* 1889; *s.* of William Smith Neill Patrick, Sheriff Clerk of Ayrshire. *Educ.:* Glasgow High School; Glasgow University. Admitted a member of Faculty of Advocates in 1913; Dean of the Faculty of Advocates, 1937-1939; served European war with Royal Flying Corps and Royal Air Force. *Club:* New (Edinburgh). [*Died* 17 *Feb.* 1967.

PATRICK, Adam, M.A. (Glas.), M.D. (Glas.), LL.D. (Glas. and St. Andrews), F.R.C.P. (London, Edin. and Glas.); late Lecturer on History of Medicine, Emeritus Prof. of Medicine, Univ. of St. Andrews; *b.* Greenock, 29 June 1883; *s.* of William Patrick; *m.* Esther Margarete Roe; one *s.* one *d. Educ.:* Greenock Academy; Glasgow University. *Publications:* various papers on medical subjects. *Address:* 5 Whitehall Road, Rugby, Warwicks. *T.:* Rugby 2950. [*Died* 19 *Sept.* 1970.

PATTERSON, Professor Jocelyn; Professor of Chemical Pathology, Charing Cross Hospital Medical School, University of London, since 1948; *b.* 15 Sept. 1900; *s.* of John Patterson and Isabella G. Patterson (*née* Howe); *m.* 1926, Kathleen (*née* Thompson); one *s. Educ.:* Universities of Durham and St. Andrews. King's Coll., Univ. of Durham, 1916, B.Sc. 1919; B.Sc. 1st Class Hons., 1920; Research Student, Univ., of St. Andrews, 1920; Research Asst. to Sir James Irvine, 1922-23; M.Sc. Durham, 1921; Ph.D. St. Andrews, 1922. Appointed Biochemist, Charing Cross Hospital, and Lecturer in Pathological Chemistry, Charing Cross Hosp. Med. Sch., 1924. Mem. Bd. of Governors, Charing Cross Hosp., 1957-63; F.R.S. (Edin.) 1942. *Publications:* (jointly) The Adrenal Cortex and Intersexuality, 1938; Recent Advances in Clinical Pathology, 1952. Contributions to Journal of Chem. Soc., Biochem. Jl., Jl. Experimental Pathology, Lancet and Brit. Med. Jl. *Recreations:* walking and gardening. *Address:* Hill Top, Chestnut Avenue, Rickmansworth, Herts. *T.:* Rickmansworth 5008. [*Died* 6 *Sept.* 1965.

PATTINSON, George Norman; J.P. Westmorland; Alderman, Westmorland County Council; *b.* 14 June 1887; *s.* of George Henry and S. A. Pattinson, Gossel Ridding, Windermere; *m.* 1st, 1917, Ethel Muriel, *er. d.* of J. R. Smith, The Priory, Windermere; three *s.* three *d.*; 2nd, 1964, Mary, *er. d.* of Graham Bridge, Chester. *Educ.:* Sedbergh; Emmanuel Coll., Cambridge (M.A.). Solicitor and Company Director. High Sheriff of Westmorland, 1941. *Recreation:* golf. *Address:* Gossel Ridding, Windermere. *T.A.* and *T.:* Windermere 238. *Club:* Royal Windermere Yacht. [*Died* 17 *Aug.* 1966.

PATTISON, Harold Arthur Langston, C.B.E. 1947; *b.* London, England, 30 June 1897; *s.* of late A. L. Pattison, Horley, Sy., and London; *m.* 1921, Suzan Mackenzie Baird; one *s.* one *d. Educ.:* Bedford Sch.; Downing College, Cambridge. M.A. Cambridge; served European War, 1914-18, in Army and R.A.F. (wounded); permanent commission R.A.F., 1919, served in India, Transjordan, and in R.C.A.F. as Exchange Officer; Air Ministry rep., Newfoundland, to organise experimental Atlantic flights, 1936; retired from R.A.F., 1937; J.P. 1938; Director of Civil Aviation, Newfoundland, 1937-49; Mem. Air Navigation Commission, I.C.A.O., 1951-57; Civil Aviation and Communications Attaché, Office of High Comr. for Canada, London, 1957-63; Canadian Member, Commonwealth Communications Bd., 1957-63. *Address:* 5 Warburton Close, Park Lane, Eastbourne, Sussex. [*Died* 21 *May* 1966.

PAUL, Sir Aubrey Edward Henry Dean, 5th Bt., *re-cr.* 1821; *b.* 19 Oct. 1869; *e. s.* of 4th Bt. and 2nd wife, Eliza Monckton, 2nd *d.* of Maj.-Gen. James Ramsay; *S.* father, 1895; *m.* 1901, Irene Regine (*d.* 1932), *d.* of late Henry Wieniawska of Warsaw; one *s.* (and one *d.* decd.). Late Lieut. 3rd Batt. Northumberland Fusiliers; Captain in 9th (Service Batt.) 5th Northumberland Fusiliers, 1915. *Heir: s.* Brian Kenneth, *b.* 18 May 1904. [*Died* 16 *Jan.* 1961.

PAUL, Professor Eric Barlow; Professor of Physics, Rice University, Houston, Texas, since 1964; *b.* 8 March 1919; Canadian; *m.* 1948, Vivien Margaret (*née* Bedford); one *s.* one *d. Educ.:* Queen's (Canada); Cambridge. B.A., M.A. Queen's Univ., Canada, 1941; Scientific Officer, Nat. Research Council of Canada, 1942-46; Ph.D. (Cambridge), 1948; Scientific Officer, Atomic Energy of Canada, Chalk River, 1948-56; Principal Scientific Officer, U.K.A.E.A., Harwell, 1956-58; Dep. Chief Scientist, Harwell, 1958-61; Professor of Physics, Manchester Univ., 1961-64. *Publications:* papers on nuclear physics in learned journals. *Address:* Department of Physics, Rice University, Houston, Texas, U.S.A. [*Died* 9 *July* 1968.

PAUL, Francis Kinnier, T.D. 1950; Headmaster Exeter School, Devon, since 1950; *b.* 6 May 1911; *y. s.* of late Rev. Principal F. J. Paul, D.D., of Belfast, and Edina Hately Paul (*née* Wilson); *m.* 1944, Daphne Mary Frearson; one *s.* two *d. Educ.:* Campbell Coll., Belfast; Pembroke College, Cambridge (M.A.); also studied at Univs. of Bonn, Leipzig, Marburg, Berlin, Dijon, Rennes, and Paris. Assistant Master (Mod. Langs.), Merchant Taylors' School, Northwood, Middlesex, 1933-40 and 1946-49. Served War of 1939-45, Intelligence Corps; Middle East and E. Africa, 1941-44; U.K. and Germany, 1944-46; Lieut.-Colonel. Chm. Combined Cadet Force Cttee., Devon T. & A.F.A. *Recreations:* walking, fishing. *Address:* High Meadow, Barrack Road, Exeter, Devon. [*Died* 11 *May* 1965.

PAUL, Rev. Sir Jeffrey; *see* Paul, Rev. Sir W. E. J.

PAUL, Leslie Douglas, M.A., B.Mus. (Oxon), Mus.Doc (Edinburgh), F.R.A.M., F.R.C.O.; Organist and Master of the Choristers, Bangor Cathedral, 1927-69; Organ and Piano Tutor, University College of North Wales, and North Wales Training

College; Examiner for Associated Board of Royal Schools of Music since 1945, including examination tours: India, 1946; New Zealand, 1948; West Indies, 1957; Adjudicator at Festivals; *b.* Bangor, 8 March 1903; *s.* of William Paul, Parkstone, Dorset; *m.* 1940, Elizabeth, *o. d.* of R. Lloyd-Jones, Caernarvon; one *s.* one *d.* *Educ.:* Clifton Coll.; Royal Academy of Music (Organ Schol.); Keble Coll., Oxford. Assistant Music Master, Winchester Coll. War Service in R.A.F.V.R., 1941-45, with rank of Flt.-Lieut. Has adjudicated at leading Musical Festivals and broadcast extensively as Organist and as Pianist. Member of Council, Incorporated Society of Musicians; Member Musical Advisory Board, 1961-62, and special Comr., Royal School of Church Music, 1961-. Represented Wales in Coronation Choir, Westminster Abbey, 1937 (Coronation Medal). *Publications:* Songs, Pianoforte, Church Music. *Address:* Gwern, 64 Penrhos Road, Bangor, N. Wales. *T.:* Bangor 2685.
[*Died* 12 *Oct.* 1970.

PAUL, Stuart, J.P. East Suffolk; President of R. and W. Paul Ltd.; Mem. East Suffolk C.C., 1944-52; breeder of Pedigree Stock; President, of the Suffolk Agricultural Association, 1945; *b.* 30 June 1879; *s.* of late William Francis Paul, J.P., O.B.E.; *m.* 1909, Gladys, *d.* of late William Henry Hamilton; two *s.* one *d.* *Educ.:* Bath College. High Sheriff of Suffolk, 1938; Chm. E. Suffolk War Agricultural Exec. Cttee., 1939-46. Owns 6500 acres in E. Suffolk, 4000 of which are farmed by Stuart Paul & Sons. *Address:* Freston Lodge, near Ipswich. *T.A.:* Freston, Near Ipswich. *T.*; Ipswich 52508. *Club:* County (Ipswich).
[*Died* 18 *Nov.* 1961.

PAUL, Rev. Sir (William Edmund) Jeffrey, 6th Bart., *cr.* 1794; *b.* 23 Sept. 1885; *s.* of Sir William Joshua Paul, 4th Bt., and Richenda Juliet Paul (*née* Gurney) (*d.* 1933); *S.* brother 1955; *m.* 1927, Alice May Ellen Henly (*d.* 1957); no *c.* *Educ.:* Repton; Trinity Coll., Cambridge (B.A., LL.B.). Ordained Deacon, 1908 (Church of Ireland), Priest 1909; Curate at Lismore, Waterford, Ireland, 1908-11; Diocese of Saskatchewan: Superintending Clergyman, Lloydminster Mission Belt, 1911-1912; North Battleford Mission Belt, 1912-1921; Missionary to Indians at Sturgeon Lake and Stanley Missions, 1921-27; Archdeacon of Indian Missions, 1927-55, retired. Hon. D.D. St. John's College, Winnipeg, 1940. *Heir:* none. *Address:* Gaultier, Woodstown, Waterford, Ireland.
[*Died* 9 *Oct.* 1961 (*ext.*).

PAULIN, George Henry, R.B.S. A.R.S.A.; H.R.I. sculptor; *b.* Muckart, 14 Aug. 1888; *s.* of George Paulin, minister; *m.* 1921, Muriel Margaret, *e. d.* of Rev. J. E. Cairns, M.A., Muckart; one *s.* two *d.* *Educ.:* Dollar Academy; Edinburgh College of Art. Studied in Rome, Florence, and Paris, 1911-14; served during the War with the Lothians and Border Horse, later with the R.A.F. in Italy. *Principal Works:* War Memorials at Kirkcudbright, Dollar, Denny, Milngavie, Muckhart, Coalsnaughton, the 8th Argylls at Beaumont Hamel, France; also Memorials to Sir William Ramsay, Glasgow University; Dr. Hunter, Trinity Church, Glasgow; Dr. McEwen, Claremont Church, Glasgow; Dr. Barrett, Mitchell Library, Glasgow; Dr. Corbett, Camphill Church, Glasgow; Statue to Lord Lister, Kelvingrove, Glasgow; War Memorial to 51st (Highland) Division, Beaumont Hamel, France; Memorial to Sir William McEwen, Erskine Hospital; Statue to Anna Pavlova, Ivy House, Hampstead, 1952; Special Coronation Year Hallmark on precious metals. *Recreation:* golf. *Address:* Watchfield House, Watchfield, Swindon, Wilts. [*Died* 10 *July* 1962.

PAULINE, Sister; *see* Young, Hilda B.

PAUS, Christopher L., C.B.E. 1920 (O.B.E. 1918); *b.* 6 Nov. 1881; *m.* 1909, D. Resch Knudsen. *Educ.:* Bradford Grammar School; Jesus College, Oxford. Commercial Attaché at H.M. Legation, Oslo, 1914; Commercial Diplomatic Secretary at Oslo, 1919-39; Commercial Counsellor at Oslo, 1939-40; retired, 1941. Coronation Medal 1937. *Address:* c/o Umaria, Grantown-on-Spey, Morayshire. [*Died* 28 *May* 1963.

PAVY, Emily Dorothea, C.B.E. 1917; B.A. (Adel.), D.Sc. (Econ.) (Lond.); Solicitor, retd.; *d.* of Cornelius Proud; *m.* Gordon A. Pavy, Barrister; one *s.* one *d.* *Educ.:* Universities of Adelaide and London. South Australian Spence Scholar, 1913; Welfare Department, Ministry of Munitions, 1915-19; Lecturer University of Adelaide. *Publication:* Welfare Work, 1916. *Address:* 7 Rutland Avenue, Unley Park, South Australia.
[*Died* 8 *Sept.* 1967.

PAWSEY, Joseph Lade, F.R.S. 1954; M.Sc., Ph.D.; D.Sc.; Assistant Chief, Div. of Radiophysics, Commonwealth Scientific and Industrial Research Organization, Sydney, Australia, since 1951; *b.* 14 May 1908; *s.* of Joseph Andrews and Margaret Pawsey; *m.* 1935, Greta Lenore Nicoll, B.A., of Battleford, Saskatchewan, Canada; two *s.* one *d.* *Educ.:* Wesley Coll., Melbourne; Queen's Coll., Melbourne Univ. (M.Sc.); Sidney Sussex Coll., Camb. (Ph.D.) 1851 Exhibition Overseas Scholarship, 1931. Research on ionosphere, Cavendish Laboratory, Camb., 1931-34; Television development with Electric and Musical Industries Ltd., Hayes, Middlesex, 1934-39; Radar development, 1939-45; Radio Research, particularly on radio astronomy and the ionosphere, Radiophysics Division C.S.I.R.O., 1945-. Fell. Austr. Acad. of Science, 1954; Lyle Medal, 1954; Mathew Flinders Lecture, 1957; Hughes Medal, Royal Society, 1960; President radio astronomy commission of Internat. Astronomical Union, 1952-58. *Publications:* (with R. N. Bracewell) Radio Astronomy, 1955; various scientific papers. *Address:* Radiophysics Laboratory, C.S.I.R.O., University Grounds, Sydney, Australia. [*Died* 30 *Nov.* 1962.

PAYNE, Charles Frederick, C.S.I. 1920; *b.* 1875; *s.* of F. Payne of The Priory, Rotherfield, Sussex; *m.* 1907, Doris Jeannie Macpherson; no *c.* *Educ.:* St. John's, Leatherhead; Brasenose College, Oxford (Classical Scholar). Passed Indian Civil Service, 1897; first appointment in Bengal, 1898; Chairman of the Calcutta Corporation, 1913-22; Fellow of the Chartered Surveyors' Institution 1923. *Recreation:* golf. *Club:* East India and Sports.
[*Died* 29 *Sept.* 1966.

PAYNE, Rev. Francis Reginald Chassereau, O.B.E. 1920 (M.B.E. 1919); Rector of Market Bosworth, 1931-54; Canon Chancellor, Leicester Cathedral, 1927-54, Canon Emeritus, 1954; Proctor in Convocation, 1925; *b.* St. James's, South Elmham, 17 June 1876; *s.* of Rev. William John Payne and Eliza Hannah Boughey; *m.* Ethel Annie, *d.* of John Ambrose and Annie Cope; one *s.* one *d.* *Educ.:* Saffron Walden; Keble College, Oxford; St. Stephen's House. Deacon, 1899; Priest, 1900; Curate of St. Andrew's, Leicester, 1899–1905; Assistant Chaplain, H.M. Prison, 1900-4; Curate of Knighton, 1905-11; Vicar of St. Margaret's, Leicester, 1911-23; Surrogate, 1917-54; Priest Canon, St. Martin's Collegiate Church, 1922-24; Canon Chancellor; 1924-54; Vicar of Knighton, Leicester, 1923-29; Canon Missioner, Diocese of Leicester, 1929-31; Secretary to the Bishop's Fund, 1929-31; Rector of Stockerston, 1931; Chaplain H.M. Prison, Leicester, 1904-31; Rural Dean of Christianity,

1924-31; Rural Dean Sparkenhoe I, 1931-54; Hon. Clerical Sec. Leicester Diocesan Conference, 1921-46. *Recreation:* gardening. *Address:* The Monastery, Happisburgh, Norwich. [*Died* 2 *May* 1961.

PAYNE, Sir William (Labatt), Kt. 1960; C.M.G. 1959; O.B.E. 1941; President of the Land Court of Queensland, 1938-61; *b.* 5 Sept. 1890; *s.* of late Christopher J. Payne, Brisbane. *Educ.:* Brisbane Gram. Sch., Barrister-at-law, 1917. Chm., Land Administration Board of Queensland, 1928-38; Chairman of a number of Royal Commissions on matters associated with rural development; Chairman of Commission of Inquiry to improve land administration in Malaya, 1957. *Publications:* numerous Reports and Publications on land settlement matters. *Address:* 6 Villiers Street, New Farm, Brisbane, Qld.; Coolangatta, Gold Coast, Queensland. *Clubs:* Royal Automobile of Queensland (Brisbane); Pioneers (Sydney). [*Died* 14 *Feb.* 1962.

PAYNE-GALLWEY, Sir Reginald F., Bt.; *see* Gallwey.

PAYTON, Wilfrid Hugh, C.M.G. 1945; I.C.S.; *b.* 7 Apr. 1892; *s.* of Hugh Payton, Birmingham; *m.* 1919, Kathleen Adelaide Lewis; no *c.* *Educ.:* King Edward's School, Birmingham; Trinity College, Cambridge (Scholar). Entered Indian Civil Service, 1915; I.A.R.O. 1916-19; Deputy Commissioner, 1923; Chairman, Rangoon Development Trust, 1935-37; Commissioner, 1938; Chief Secretary to Govt. of Burma, 1937-38, 1942-43, 1944-45; Financial Commissioner, 1945; retired, 1949. *Address:* Forest Edge, Lyndhurst, Hants. *T.:* Lyndhurst 2515. [*Died* 2 *May* 1965.

PEACEY, Rt. Rev. Basil William, M.A. (Leeds); General Licence, Dio. Cape Town; *b.* 1889; *s.* of R. D. Peacey, Winchcombe Glos.; *m.* 1931, Anna, *d.* of Senator Hofmeyr; two *s* one *d.* *Educ.:* Christ's Hosp.; Leeds Univ.; Coll. of the Resurrection, Mirfield; Curate at Dairycoates, Hull, 1913-17; Priest-Vicar, Grahamstown Cathedral, S. Africa, 1917-23; Priest in charge Pessene and Maputoland Districts of the Diocese of Lebombo, Portuguese East Africa and Principal of St. Christopher's Coll., Hlamankulu, Lourenço Marques, 1923-29; Bishop of Lebombo, 1929-1935; Rector of Krugersdorp, 1935-41; Rector of Constantia, 1941-54. *Publications:* papers in Journal of South African Bureau of Racial Affairs, 1953. *Recreation:* carpentry. *Address:* 43 Second Crescent Fish Hoek, Cape, South Africa. *T.:* 8.790[illegible]. *Club:* Christ's Hospital. [*Died* 23 *July* 1969.

PEACHEY, Captain Allan Thomas George Cumberland, C.B.E.; D.S.O.; R.N.; *b.* 1896; *o. s.* of late Doctor Allan Thomas Peachey and late Alice Katherine Peachey (*née* le Fleming); *m.* 1929, Nina Muriel Paterson (*née* Sutherland); no *c.* *Educ.:* Haileybury; Trinity College, Cambridge. Entered R.N., 1914; served European War, 1914-18: Grand Fleet, 2nd Battle Squadron (Jutland), 1st Battle Cruiser Squadron, also "Q" Ships. Subsequently, in that order: Atlantic Fleet, China Squadron, Admiralty Yacht, Mediterranean Fleet, Home Fleet Flotillas, Yangtse Flotilla, Home Fleet Carriers. Commander, 1933; served, Signal Division, Admiralty; Executive Officer, H.M.S. Royal Oak; Operations Officer, Coast of Scotland; Captain, 1940. War of 1939-45: Commanded H.M.S. Queen of Bermuda, H.M.S. Delhi, H.M.S. Enterprise, H.M.S. Royal Sovereign, Build-Up Group Far Eastern Assault Force. Commodore, 1947-48, as last Commodore, Palestine and Levant. Retired List, 1950. Attached H.M. Foreign Service, 1951-54. U.S.A. Legion of Merit; Order of George I of Hellenes. *Address:* 43 Lowndes Square, S.W.1. *Club:* White's. [*Died* 15 *March* 1967.

PEACOCK, Sir Edward Robert, G.C.V.O., *cr.* 1934; Hon. D.C.L. Oxford, 1932; Hon. LL.D. Edinburgh, 1938; a Director of the Canadian Pacific Railway Company and Harris and Partners, Toronto; formerly a Director of Baring Brothers & Co.; retired from Bank of England, 1946, after serving for 20 years as a Director; a Lieutenant of the City of London; a Rhodes Trustee; Chairman of Trustees, Imperial War Graves Commission; Chairman, Board of Management, Royal Commission for the Exhibition of 1851; a Trustee, King George's Jubilee Trust; *b.* Glengarry, Canada, 2 Aug. 1871; *e. s.* of Rev. W. M. Peacock, Canada; *m.* 1912, Katherine (*d.* 1948), *d.* of John Coates; two *d.* *Educ.:* Queen University, Kingston, Canada (M.A., LL.D.). English master and senior house master at Upper Canada College, Toronto, 1895-1902; with Dominion Securities Corporation of Canada and London, 1902-15; concerned with the direction of Light, Power and Traction Companies in Spain, Brazil and Mexico, 1915-24. *Recreation:* golf. *Address:* The Thatched House, Swinley Forest, Ascot, Berks. *T.:* Ascot 18. *Clubs:* Athenæum, Brooks's; York (Toronto). [*Died* 19 *Nov.* 1962.

PEACOCK, Frederick Hood, C.M.G. 1961; Chairman, Gibsons Ltd., Flourmillers, Hobart, since 1927; *b.* Franklin, Tasmania, 13 Nov. 1886; *s.* of C. M. Peacock; *m.* 1920, Lydia, *d.* of W. Cripps; four *s.* one *d.* *Educ.:* Hutchins School, Hobart. Director, W. D. Peacock and Co. Ltd., Hobart (for 25 years). President, Hobart Savings Bank, 1950-. *Recreations:* tennis, yachting. *Address:* Beach Road, Sandy Bay, Tasmania; H. Jones and Co. Pty., Hobart, Tasmania. *Clubs:* Tasmanian, Royal Yacht Club of Tasmania, Rotary, Derwent Sailing Squadron (Tasmania). [*Died* 29 *Dec.* 1969.

PEACOCK, Sir Kenneth (Swift), Kt. 1963; President and Consultant, Guest, Keen & Nettlefolds Limited since 1965; Past Director: Steel Company of Wales, Ltd.; United Steel Cos. Ltd.; Lloyds Bank Ltd.; *b.* 19 February 1902; *o. s.* of Tom Swift Peacock and Elizabeth Amy Richards; *m.* 1st, 1925, Hilaria (*d.* 1926), *d.* of late Sir Geoffrey Syme, K.B.E. and late Lady Syme, Melbourne, Australia; one *d.*; 2nd, 1934, Norah, *d.* of Norman Rigby, Birmingham; two *s.* *Educ.:* Oundle School. Served with Guest, Keen & Nettlefolds Ltd. in varying capacities; Managing Director, 1936-53; Chairman and Managing Director, 1953-63; Exec. Chairman, 1964-65. *Recreations:* riding, hunting, sailing. *Address:* Lower Coscombe, Temple Guiting, Gloucestershire. *T.:* Stanton 221. *Clubs:* Junior Carlton, Royal Automobile; Union (Birmingham). *Died* 6 *Sept.* 1968.

PEACOCK, Rev. W. Arthur; Press Officer, Unitarian Church Headquarters; Editor Modern Free Churchman; Minister, Putney Unitarian Church; *b.* 23 August 1905. Edited Clarion, 1927-30, New Nation, 1932-34. Secretary-Manager, National Trade Union Club, 1931-46. Ordained Minister, 1937. Hon. Sec. World Congress of Faiths, 1951-59; Member: Churches Council on Gambling; Central Churches Group, National Council of Social Service; National Peace Council. *Publications:* Tom Mann: Militant Trade Unionist; (with George Jeger) Medical Mission in Spain; Who are the Universalists; Spiritual Leadership of Jesus; Yours Fraternally; Christian Modernism and other faiths; Fellowship Through Religion; I'm not religious But—; Religion Can Make Sense; (ed.) The Family and Society; (with Alan Ruston) Prisons, Punishment and People; Christian Encounter. Contributor to various literary and religious newspapers. *Address:* Gt. Frenches Park, Crawley Down, Sussex. [*Died* 16 *Sept.* 1968.

PEACOCK, Rev. Canon Wilfrid Morgan, M.A.; *b.* 24 January 1890; 2nd *s.* of late Reverend R. Peacock, M.A., Vicar of Woodlands St. Mary, Lambourn, Berkshire; *m.* 1913, Adela Marian, *y. d.* of Arthur Rutter, Mon Abri, Cambridge; two *d. Educ.:* Marlborough; Jesus College, Cambridge. Deacon, 1913; Priest, 1914; Assistant Curate, St. Michael and All Angels, Belgrave, Leicester, 1913-14; served with Leicestershire Regt., 1914-19, Captain (wounded); Assistant Master, Uppingham School, 1919; Aldenham School, 1919; Cheltenham College, 1919-22; Headmaster, Collyer's School, Horsham, 1922-26; Principal of King's College, Lagos, West Africa, 1926-31; Canon, Christchurch Cathedral, Lagos, 1929; Hon. Canon, 1931; Canon Emeritus, 1941; Headmaster of King Alfred's School, Wantage, 1932-49; Warden of S. Augustine's House, Reading, 1949-59. Served with R. Sussex Regt. and Royal West African Frontier Force (Nigeria), 1940-41. *Address:* 37 The Drive, Shoreham-by-Sea, Sussex. *T.:* Shoreham-by-Sea 3692. [*Died* 25 *Jan.* 1970.

PEACOCKE, Emilie Hawkes; *b.* 1883; *er. d.* of late John Marshall, Editor and co-proprietor, Northern Echo, Darlington; *m.* 1909, late Herbert Peacocke, journalist; one *d. Educ.:* privately. Trained at Northern Echo, 1899; Reporter: Daily Express, 1904; Tribune, 1906; Daily Mail, 1908; Ministry of Information, 1918; Daily Express Feature and Woman's Page, 1918-28; Journalist, Daily Telegraph and Morning Post, 1928-46; Member of Livery of Stationers and Newspaper Makers Co.; F.J.I.; Hon. Home Sec. Inst. of Journalists, 1962; Life member Nat. Union of Journalists. *Publications:* Writing For Women, 1936; several cookery books. *Address:* 12 Hillsleigh Rd., W.8. *T.:* Park 9456; St. John's Studio, Grayshott, nr. Hindhead, Hants. [*Died* 25 *Jan.* 1964.

PEACOCKE, Rt. Rev. Joseph Irvine, D.D.; *b.* Monkstown, Co. Dublin, 28 Nov 1866; *e. s.* of late Most Rev. J. F. Peacocke, D.D., Archbishop of Dublin; *m.* 1902, Ada Victoria Stanley, *d.* of Lindsey Bucknall Barker; two *s.* one *d. Educ.:* Corrig School, Kingstown; Trinity College, Dublin. Classical Scholar, 1888; Senior Moderator, History and Political Science, 1889; 1st prize Political Economy, and 1st prize Eccles. History, 1890; 1st Theological Exhibitioner, 1891; Ordained, 1891; Rector of Christ Church, Lisburn, 1894-1901; Rector of St. Mary's, Dublin, 1902-3; Rector of Bangor, Co. Down, 1903-16; Prebendary of St. Andrew's, Down Cathedral, 1911; Bishop of Derry and Raphoe, 1916-45. *Address:* Dunderry, Ballycastle, Co. Antrim. [*Died* 31 *Jan.* 1962.

PEAKE, Brigadier Edward Robert Luxmoore, C.B.E. 1947; M.C.; *b.* 9 Oct. 1894; *s.* of late Thomas Pendril Peake; *m.* 1928, Audrey Danvers Rutherfoord Hyde Turner; one *s.* one *d. Educ.:* Cheltenham College. R.M.A., Woolwich, 1913-14; commissioned R.E., Aug. 1914; served European War, 1914-18; Survey in Gold Coast, 1920-1925; Geographical Section, Gen. Staff, War Office, 1925-30; Senior British Comr., Northern Rhodesia-Belgian Congo Boundary Commission, 1930-33; Ordnance Survey Office, 1934-46; retired as Dep. Director Gen., Oct. 1946; with Internat. Civil Aviation Organization, 1946-52, as Chief of Aeronautical Charts and Information Branch. *Address:* 10 Avonmore Avenue, Guildford, Surrey. [*Died* 27 *April* 1964.

PEAKE, Frederick Gerard, C.M.G. 1939; C.B.E. 1926 (O.B.E. 1923); *b.* 1886; *o. s.* of late Lieut.-Colonel Walter Ancell Peake, D.S.O., of Burrough, Melton Mowbray; *m.* 1937, Elspeth Maclean (*d.* 1967), *yr. d.* of late Norman Ritchie, St. Boswells; one *d. Educ.:* Stubbington House, Fareham; R.M.C., Sandhurst. Received first Commission in the Duke of Wellington's Regt., 1906; served in India till 1913, when seconded to the Egyptian Army and posted to the Camel Corps in the Sudan; served in Darfur expedition, 1916 (Sudan medal, two clasps, and 4th Class Order of Nile); served in Royal Flying Corps in Salonika, 1916, and in the Hedjaz Sector of the Egyptian Expeditionary Force; Inspector-General of Gendarmerie, Transjordan, 1921, and Director of Public Security, 1923; raised the Arab Legion, 1922 (King's medal, Victory medal, 1st Class Order of Nahda, 2nd Class Order of Istiqlal, Zikra Istiqlal; Syrian Order pour la Mérite); Min. of Civil Defence, 1939; Home Office, Acting Inspector Constabulary, 1942. Commander of the Order of St. John of Jerusalem, 1934; Laurence Memorial Gold Medal, 1940; patron of one living. *Publications:* History and Tribes of Jordan; Change at St. Boswells. *Address:* Hawkslee, St. Boswells, Roxburghshire. *T.:* St. Boswells 2209. *Clubs:* Royal Air Force; New (Edinburgh). [*Died* 30 *March* 1970.

PEAKE, Mervyn; F.R.S.L.; poet, novelist painter, playwright and illustrator; *b.* China, 9 July 1911; *s.* of E. C. Peake, M.D.; *m.* 1937, Maeve Gilmore (artist); two *s.* one *d. Educ.:* Tientsin Grammar School; Eltham College, Kent. *Publications:* Rhymes Without Reason, 1944; Captain Slaughterboard Drops Anchor, 1945 (rep. 1966); The Craft of the Lead Pencil, 1946; Titus Groan (novel), 1946; Letters from a Lost Uncle, 1948; The Glassblowers (poem) and Gormenghast (novel) were awarded W. H. Heinemann Foundation Prize (Royal Society of Literature) 1950; Mr. Pye, 1953; The Wit to Woo (play), 1957; Titus Alone (novel), 1959; The Rime of the Flying Bomb, 1962; Titus Groan novels (as trilogy; in U.K. and U.S.), rep. 1967; A Reverie of Bone (poems), 1967. *Address:* 1 Drayton Gardens, S.W.10. *T.:* Fremantle 7448. [*Died* 17 *Nov.* 1968.

PEAL, Lt.-Col. Edward Raymond, C.B.E. 1919 (O.B.E. 1919); D.S.C.; *b.* 1884; *s.* of Henry Walter Peal, J.P.; *m.* 1923, Kathleen, *d.* of late Lt.-Gen. Sir Bertram Richard Kirwan, K.C.B., C.M.G.; two *s.* one *d. Educ.:* Tonbridge. Served European War, 1914-19 (despatches, D.S.C., O.B.E., C.B.E.). Master, Worshipful Company of Cordwainers, 1955. *Address:* 34 The Close, Salisbury, Wilts. *Club:* R.A.F. [*Died* 24 *April* 1967.

PEARCE, Sir (Charles) Frederick (Byrde), Kt., *cr.* 1948; C.B.E. 1941; *b.* 13 June 1892; *s.* of C. W. Pearce, Mus. Doc. Trinity College of Music, London; *m.* 1949, Olwen, *widow* of Lieut.-Colonel John Lawson, Skinner's Horse. *Educ.:* Marlborough College; Balliol College, Oxford (Exhibitioner). Served European War, 1914-19; entered I.C.S., 1920; Deputy Commissioner, 1931; Finance Secretary to Govt. of Burma, 1934; Secretary to Governor of Burma, 1939; Commissioner, 1941; Administrator Refugee Areas, North Assam, 1942; Major-General; Chief Civil Affairs Officer (Burma), 1943; Director, Frontier Areas, Burma, 1945; Counsellor to Governor, 1946; Member of the Application Committee on the Indo-Burma Debt, 1936; Auditor-General, Burma, 1947; retired, 1948; Chief Secretary, Eritrea, 1949-1952. *Publication:* Report on the Settlement of the Pakokku District, Burma, 1932. *Recreations:* golf, music. *Address:* Wynne House, Boxford, Colchester. *Club:* Oxford and Cambridge. [*Died* 26 *Aug.* 1964.

PEARCE, C. Maresco; painter; *b.* 1874; *o. s.* of Maresco Pearce, painter and solicitor, and Sarah A. Tyerman; *m.* 1914, Anna (*d.* 1959), *d.* of Halsey Ricardo; two *s.* three *d.* *Educ.:* Private school; Christ Church, Oxford. Apprenticed to Sir Ernest George, architect; studied painting under Augustus John and William Orpen, Jacques Emile Blanche, Walter Sickert; F.R.G.S.; Member of the London Group; Works in British Museum, Victoria and Albert Museum and various galleries in England and abroad. Represented in Exhibn.: Some Contemporary British Painters, Wildenstein Gall., 1962. *Recreations:* forestry and painting. *Address:* 117 Church Street, Chelsea, S.W.3. *T.:* Flaxman 4392; Carpenter's Town, Graffham, Sussex. *Club:* Chelsea Arts. [*Died* 9 *Dec.* 1964.

PEARCE, Alderman E(dward) Ewart, M.B.E. 1945; J.P.; in practice as Chartered Accountant; *b.* 19 April 1898; *o. c.* of Simon and Minnie Pearce, Stoke-sub-Hamdon, Somerset; *m.* 1922, Winifred Constance Blackmore; two *s.* twin *d.* *Educ.:* Howard Gardens High School, Cardiff. Served in Army, 1916-19, England and Egypt. Served in Army, 1916-19, England and Egypt. Served in Home Guard, 1940-45, Troop Commander. Entered Chartered Accountant's Office in Cardiff, 1915; qualified as Incorporated Accountant, 1925; commenced to practise, June 1931. Member Cardiff City Council, 1941-45 and 1947-62; Alderman, 1955-58 and 1960-62; Chairman of Finance Committee. Lord Mayor of Cardiff, 1961-62; J.P. Cardiff, 1950. Hon. Life Mem. British Legion, 1945. *Recreations:* cricket and gardening. *Address:* 119 Heath Park Avenue, Cardiff. *T.:* Cardiff 52281. [*Died* 3 *Jan.* 1963.

PEARCE, Sir Frederick; *see* Pearce, Sir C. F. B.

PEARCE, Harold Seward, C.B.E. 1941; *b.* 1 February 1880; *s.* of late James Seward Pearce, formerly of Southampton; *m.* 1st, 1904, Bessie Snow Findlow (*d.* 1914); one *s.*; 2nd, 1920, Gertrude Mary Elizabeth Barry (*d.* 1952). *Educ.:* King Edward VI. School, Southampton. Admitted a Solicitor of Supreme Court; Treasury Solicitor's Dept., 1901; transferred to Dept. of the Director of Public Prosecutions, 1908; Assistant Solicitor to the Post Office, 1921-44; a Taxing Master of the Supreme Court, 1944-1952. *Recreations:* golf and motoring. *Address:* Whitesands, Reigate. *T.:* Reigate 3462. *Club:* Reigate Heath Golf (Reigate). [*Died* 7 *March* 1961.

PEARL, Amy Lea, (Mrs. F. Warren Pearl), C.B.E. (Hon.) 1952; *b.* 12 Nov. 1880; *d.* of John P. and Susan Duncan, New York City; *m.* 1909, Frederic Warren Pearl (*d.* 1952); two *s.* two *d.* (and one *s.* two *d.* decd.). *Educ.:* Miss Brown's, New York City. Served with Canadian and American Red Cross in England and France, 1916-18; served with British Red Cross (Prisoners of War Section), War of 1939-45; also associated American Eagle Club, American Trailer Ambulance and many other American charities. Actively connected with N.S.P.C.C., R.N.L.I., Queen's Nurses, and numerous other British charities; one-time Governor St. George's Hospital; Chairman American Relief Society. *Recreations:* hospitality, charity and friendships. *Address:* c/o Stuart Pearl, 2 Plowden Buildings, Middle Temple, E.C.4. *Club:* American Women's (London). [*Died* 1 *Feb.* 1964.

PEARSALL, William Harold, F.R.S. 1940; F.L.S.; F.I.Biol.; D.Sc.; Hon. D.Sc. (Dun.); Hon. D.Sc. (Birmingham); Professor Emeritus, lately Quain Professor of Botany, University of London, University College, 1944-57; Hon. Research Associate U.C.L.; Member Nature Conservancy since 1949 (Chairman Scientific Policy Cttee., 1955-63); Chairman of Council, Freshwater Biological Association; Trustee, Society for Experimental Biology; Hon. Trustee, Tanganyika Nat. Parks; *b.* 23 July 1891; *o. s.* of William Harrison Pearsall; *m.* 1917, Marjory Stewart Williamson; two *s.* *Educ.:* Ulverston Grammar School; Manchester University (Graduate Schol.). War Service, R.G.A. and R.E.; Reader in Botany, Univ. of Leeds, 1922; Prof. of Botany, Univ. of Sheffield, 1938-44; President, Institute of Biology, 1957-58; Hon. Mem. Soc. Phytogeographica Suecica; Hon. Mem. Indian Bot. Soc.; Hon. Mem. British Ecological Soc. Linnean Gold Medal, 1963. *Publications:* Mountains and Moorlands, 1949; Report on an Ecological Survey of Serengeti National Park, Tanganyika, 1957; numerous scientific papers on freshwater biology, ecology and plant physiology; Editor of Annals of Botany. *Recreations:* fishing, walking and golf. *Address:* University College, W.C.1; 6 Pemberton Drive, Morecambe, Lancs. [*Died* 14 *Oct.* 1964.

PEARSE, James, C.B.E. 1920; M.D.; late Medical Officer, Ministry of Health; *b.* 1871; 2nd *s.* of Rev. J. Pearse, Madagascar; *m.* 1902, Amy (*d.* 1944), *e. d.* of Joseph Nodal; one *s.* two *d.* *Educ.:* Edinburgh University. In medical practice, Trowbridge, 1895-1914; Medical Officer, National Health Insurance Commission, 1914-18. *Publications:* various articles in Medical Press. *Recreations:* horticulture. *Address:* Eltermere, Elterwater, near Ambleside. [*Died* 2 *Nov.* 1962.

PEARSON, Hon. (Bernard) Clive; Chairman, S. Pearson & Son Ltd., 1927-54; Director of Southern Railway, 1936-47; *b.* 1887; 2nd *s.* of 1st Viscount Cowdray; *m.* 1915, Hon. Alicia Mary Dorothea Knatchbull-Hugessen, *d.* of 1st Baron Brabourne; three *d.* *Educ.:* Rugby; Trinity College, Cambridge. B.A. Formerly Captain Sussex Yeomanry; Sheriff of Sussex, 1940; Chairman British Overseas Airways Corporation, 1940-43; Joint Master Cowdray Hounds, 1922-33, Master, 1933-35. *Address:* Parham Park, Pulborough, Sussex. *Clubs:* Bath; Royal Yacht Squadron (Cowes). [*Died* 22 *July* 1965.

PEARSON, Drew, (Andrew Russell); Columnist; Radio and Television Commentator; *b.* Evanston, Illinois, U.S.A., 13 December 1897; *s.* of Paul Martin Pearson and Edna Wolfe; *m.* 1st, 1925, Countess Felicia Gizycka; one *d.*; 2nd, 1936, Luvie Moore. *Educ.:* Phillips Exeter Academy, Exeter, N.H.; Swarthmore College, Swarthmore, Pa. A.B. 1919. U.S. Army, 1918; Dir., Amer. Friends Service Commission in Serbia, Montenegro, and Albania, 1919-21; instr. in industrial geography, Univ. of Pa., 1921-22; lectured on Am., Australian, and New Zealand chautauquas, 1921-23; visited Japan, China, and Siberia, reporting results of Washington Arms Conf. for newspaper syndicate, 1922; interviewed Europe's Twelve Greatest Men for newspaper syndicate, 1923; Lecturer in Commercial Geography, Columbia Univ., 1924; reported: Communist infiltration of China, 1925; Geneva Naval Conf. for Japan Advertiser, 1927; staff U.S. Daily, 1926-33, Baltimore Sun, 1929-32; reported 6th Pan-Am. Conf., Havana, 1928; accompanied Sec. of State Kellogg to Paris to sign Anti-War Treaty, 1928; reported London Naval Conf., 1930, Cuban Revolution, 1931, Rio de Janeiro Conf., 1942, San Francisco United Nations Conf., 1945; Paris Peace Conf., 1946; "Summit" Conf., 1955; Paris "Summit" Conf., 1960; organised Friendship Trains to Western Europe, 1947-48; U.S. delegate to Atlantic Conference, London, 1959; Mem., President's Food for Peace Cttee., 1961. *Publications:* Washington Merry-Go-Round, 1931; More Merry-Go-Round, 1932; The American Diplomatic Game, 1935; The Nine Old Men, 1936; U.S.A. 2nd Class Power?, 1958; The Case Against Congress, 1968; The Senator (novel), 1968; daily newspaper column The Washington Merry-Go-Round since 1932. *Recreation:* farming. *Address:* 2820 Dumbarton Ave., N.W., Washington, D.C.; Rockville, Md.; 1313 29th St., N.W., Wash. *T.:* Adams 2-4321. *Clubs:* Overseas Writers, National Press, Cosmos (Washington). [*Died* 1 *Sept.* 1969.

PEARSON, Hesketh, F.R.S.L.; *b.* Hawford, Worcs., 20 Feb. 1887; *s.* of T. H. G. Pearson and Constance Biggs; *m.* 1st, 1912, Gladys Rosalind Bardili (*d.* 1951); (one *s.* decd.); 2nd, 1951, Dorothy Joyce Ryder. *Educ.:* Bedford Grammar School. Wasted two years in a City shipping office. Went on the stage in 1911, appearing in the London productions of Sir Herbert Tree, H. Granville-Barker, and Sir George Alexander. Joined the army as a private in the 1914-18 war, spent three years on active service in Mesopotamia and Persia (despatches, Capt.). Returned to the stage and acted in the productions of Dennis Eadie, Ethel Irving, Sir Nigel Playfair, Phyllis Neilson-Terry, Basil Dean, Godfrey Tearle, Anmer Hall, etc.; left the stage to write biographies in 1931. Pres. Edinburgh Sir Walter Scott Club, 1959-60. Edited Oscar Wilde's Works for Everyman Library, 1930; Essays by Oscar Wilde, 1950. Introduction to: Selected Essays and Poems by Oscar Wilde (Penguin Books) 1954; Five Plays of Oscar Wilde (Bantam Books) U.S.A., 1961; Articles on Bernard Shaw for Chambers's, Colliers and New Universal Encyclopaedias; Introduction to: Portrait of G.B.S., by Feliks Topolski. *Publications:* Modern Men and Mummers, 1921; A Persian Critic, 1923; Iron Rations, 1928; Ventilations, 1930; Doctor Darwin, 1930; The Smith of Smiths, 1934; The Fool of Love, 1934; Gilbert and Sullivan, 1935; Labby, 1936; The Swan of Lichfield, 1936; Tom Paine, 1937; Common Misquotations, 1937; Thinking It Over, 1938; The Hero of Delhi, 1939; Bernard Shaw, 1942; A Life of Shakespeare, 1942; Conan Doyle, 1943; The Life of Oscar Wilde, 1946; Dickens, 1949. The Last Actor-Managers, 1950; G.B.S. A Postscript, 1951; Dizzy, 1951; The Man Whistler, 1952; Walter Scott, 1954; Beerbohm Tree, 1956; Gilbert, 1957; Johnson and Boswell, 1958; Charles II, 1960; Bernard Shaw (complete edition), 1961; The Pilgrim Daughters, 1961; Lives of the Wits, 1962; Henry of Navarre, 1963. With Hugh Kingsmill: Skye High, 1937; This Blessed Plot, 1942; Talking of Dick Whittington, 1947; With Colin Hurry: (play) Writ for Libel, 1950. With Malcolm Muggeridge: About Kingsmill 1951; (Posthumous) Hesketh Pearson, by Himself, 1965; articles, broadcasts, etc. *Recreations:* walking, talking, idling. *Address:* 14 Priory Rd., N.W.6. *T.:* Maida Vale 5686. *Club:* Savage. [*Died* 9 *April* 1964.

PEARSON, Vice-Adm. John Lewis, C.M.G. 1919; R.N., retired; *b.* 1879; *s.* of late Admiral Sir Hugo Lewis Pearson, K.C.B.; *m.* 1912, Phoebe Charlotte, *d.* of Col. Cecil Beadon, Indian Army; three *s.* Commodore in charge of Naval Establishments at Hong-Kong, 1926-28; a Naval A.D.C. to the King, 1929; Rear-Adm. 1929; retd. list, 1931; Vice-Adm., retd., 1934; D.L., J.P., Herefordshire; Chevalier Legion of Honour. *Address:* The Old Rectory, Brampton Abbots, Ross-on-Wye. *T.:* Ross 2279 *Club:* United Service. [*Died* 31 *May* 1965.

PEARSON, William George, C.B.E. 1938. *Educ.:* Jarrow-on-Tyne; privately. Member of Jarrow Town Council since 1920; Deputy Mayor of Jarrow, 1926 and 1927; Mayor of Jarrow, 1928, 1929, 1930; contested (C.) Houghton-le-Spring (Durham) Division, 1929; M.P. (Nat. C.) Jarrow Division of Durham, 1931-35; J.P. 1932. *Address:* Elmwood, 48 Morpeth Avenue, South Shields. [*Died* 4 *Oct.* 1963.

PEASE, Sir Edward, 3rd Bt., *cr.* 1882, of Hutton Low Cross and Pinchinthorpe; *b.* 15 December 1880; *e. s.* of Sir Alfred E. Pease, 2nd Bt., and Helen (*d.* 1910), *d.* of late Sir Robert Fowler, 1st Bt., of Gastard, Wiltshire; *S.* father, 1939; *m.* 1919, Ida Mary, *d.* of late J. Lawrance, Cambridge. *Educ.:* Winchester; Trinity College, Cambridge. Sudan Civil Service, 1903-11; travelled in Algeria, Abyssinia, Somaliland, Kenya, Rhodesia, etc.; served European War, 1915-19. *Heir: half-b.* Alfred Vincent, *b.* 2 April 1926. *Address:* Lowcross Gate, Hutton, Guisborough, North Yorkshire. *T.:* Guisborough 191. [*Died* 14 *Jan.* 1963.

PEASE, Sir Richard Arthur, 2nd Bt., *cr.* 1920; J.P. D.L.; *b.* 18th Nov. 1890; *s.* of late Sir Arthur Francis Pease, 1st Bt., and Laura Matilda Ethelwyn (*d.* 1936), *d.* of late Charles Peter Allix, Swaffham Prior House, Cambridge; *S.* father, 1927; *m.* 1st, 1917, Jeannette Thorn (*d.* 1957), *d.* of late Gustav Edward Kissel, New York; two *s.* one *d.* (and one *s.* decd.); 2nd, 1961, Launa Keppel, *widow* of Lt.-Col. Arnold Keppel. *Educ.:* Eton; Trinity College Cambridge M.A. Capt. (retd.) Northumberland Yeomanry; served European War, 1914-18. *Heir: s.* Richard Thorn Pease [*b.* 20 May 1922; *m.* 1956, Anne, *d.* of late Lt.-Col. Reginald Francis Heyworth; one *s.* two *d.*]. *Address:* Prior House, Richmond, Yorks. *T.:* Richmond Yorks 3340 *Club:* Brooks's. [*Died* 13 *Nov.* 1969.

PEASGOOD, Osborne Harold, C.V.O. 1953; D.Mus.; Sub-Organist, Westminster Abbey, since 1924; Professor, Royal College of Music; member of teaching staff, Reading University; *b.* 5 March 1902; *s.* of Robert Harold and Laura Ellen Peasgood; *m.* 1936, Dora H. Livesey; one *d.* *Educ.:* Kilburn Grammar School; Royal College of Music. A.R.C.M. 1920, Graduate of Royal College of Music, 1922; F.R.C.O. 1926; B.Mus. 1933, D.Mus. 1936, Dublin University (T.C.D.); Organ Schol. R.C.M., 1918-24. Acting Organist and Master of the Choristers, Westminster Abbey, 1941-46. Played organ at Coronations, 1937, 1953, and at wedding of the Queen, 1947. *Publications:* compositions: church music and arrangements for organ. *Recreations:* trout fishing, tennis, motoring. *Address:* Greystones, 123 Woodcock Hill, Harrow, Middx. *T.:* Wordsworth 2509. *Club:* Constitutional. [*Died* 25 *Jan.* 1962.

PEAT, Stanley, F.R.S. 1948; D.Sc. (Birm.), B.Sc. (Dunelm); Professor of Chemistry, University College of North Wales, Bangor, since 1948; Head of Department of Chemistry; *b.* 23 August 1902; *er. s.* of John H. Peat, Bolden, Co. Durham; *m.* 1939, Elsie Florence, *d.* of Henry H. V. Barnes, Birmingham; two *d.* *Educ.:* Rutherford College Boys' School, Newcastle on Tyne; Universities of Durham (King's College) and Birmingham. Lecturer in Physiology, 1928-34, then Lecturer and later Reader in Organic Chemistry, 1934-48, University of Birmingham. *Publications:* scientific papers on Carbohydrates, published mainly in Jour. Chem. Soc. *Address:* Dept. of Chemistry, University College, Bangor, N. Wales. [*Died* 22 *Feb.* 1969.

PECHEY, Archibald Thomas, *noms de plume* Valentine, and Mark Cross; author, lyrist, and playwright; *b.* 26 Sept. 1876; *s.* of late John Thomas Primrose Pechey and late Alice Emily Vallentin; *m.* Bijou Sortain, *y. d.* of late Surgeon-

Major C. J. Sortain Hancock, M.D.; one *s.* one *d.* *Educ.:* Repton. Imperial Insurance Company, 1892-93; Corn Exchange, Mark Lane, 1894-1912; journalist, 1912-14; Wylie Tate Productions, 1915-21; lyrist in Maid of the Mountains, The Beauty Spot, Some; part author of Cinderella, London Hippodrome, and numerous pantomimes; part author of Lads of the Village and Tons of Money (Shaftesbury and Aldwych Theatres); winner of D. C. Thomson £1000 Serial Prize—with story entitled Her Mother's Honour, 1924. *Publications:* Novels—Cud-dl'ums; The Adjusters; The Unseen Hand; One Good Turn; A Flight to a Finish; The Blue Pool; The Things that Count; Young Desire; God's Clearing House; Round the Corner; At Your Beginnings; The Longest Way Round; That Certain Thing; One Hour Before Dawn; Rising Mists; Shadows on the Grass; Strange Experiment; The Silver Cord; Anne Adventures; Nor equal nor unequal; Cobwebs to Cables; Youth in Revolt; Leaves of Memory; Much Abides; Garden by the Water; Twilight Hour; Reckless Youth; Brave Endeavour; Gay Adventure; The Moving Finger; Yvonne runs Away; Green Ridges; The Cartland Heritage; Youth takes a Hand; Life's Meaning; The Enchanted Glade; Passing By; Let's Pretend; Marilyn; Once the Young Heart; Minx; Pamela's Progress; Dream Cottage; The Way of a Man with a Maid; Would She Were Mine; Love Gives Itself; The Little God of Love, Yet Love breaks through; Let the Maiden Understand; Love Will Venture In; Woman has her Way; Love Conquers All; Stepping Stones; Hid in the Heart; When Love Calls. Leave it to Love; Joy be Mine; The Truly Lov'd And When Love Speaks. 47 detective novels as Mark Cross. Serials in Daily Mirror, Sunday Pictorial, Daily Chronicle; Play, Compromising Daphne; Talking Films Dialogue, Compromising Daphne, etc. (British International Pictures). *Recreations:* billiards, entomology, old horse brasses. *Address:* Ivey House, West Shepton, Shepton Mallet, Somerset *T.:* Shepton Mallet 2101. *Club:* Savage.

[*Died* 29 *Nov.* 1961.

PECK, Vice-Admiral Ambrose Maynard, D.S.O. 1917; *s.* of Jasper Kenrick Peck, Barrister-at-law; *m.* 1908, Dorothy Agnes Henn-Gennys (*d.* 1957), *d.* of Adm. Sir Robert Hastings Harris, K.C.B., K.C.M.G. *Educ.:* H.M.S. Britannia. Served Boer War, 1899-1901; European War, commanded H.M.S. Swift, 1916-17, when that ship with H.M.S. Broke engaged six German destroyers off Dover (Croix de Guerre); Chief Staff Officer to Rear-Admiral, Gibraltar, 1921-23; Operations Division, Naval Staff, Admiralty, 1923-26; Commanded H.M.S. Benbow, Atlantic Fleet, 1926-27; Rear-Admiral and retired list, 1928; Vice-Adm. retired, 1932. *Address:* Coltfoot, Yelverton, S. Devon. [*Died* 2 *March* 1963.

PECK, Major-Gen. Henry Richardson, C.B. 1926, C.M.G. 1915; D.S.O 1917; Col Commandant, R.A., 1938-44; *b.* 1874; *e. s.* of late P. W. Peck, of Temple Combe House, Somerset; *m.* Kathleen Dulcibella (*d* 1954). *d.* of late Col. Charles Hore, C.M.G. Served S. African War, 1899-1902 (severely wounded, despatches twice, Bt. Major, Queen's medal 4 clasps, King's medal 2 clasps); European War, 1915-18 (despatches five times, C.M.G., D.S.O. Bt. Col); Colonel Commandant R.A. 2nd Division, Aldershot, 1923-27; Maj.-Gen. 1926 G.O.C 44th Home Counties Division T.A. 1929 1933; retired pay, 1933. *Address:* 133 Cranmer Court, S.W.3. [*Died* 3 *June* 1965.

PECK, Sir James Wallace, Kt., *cr.* 1938; C.B. 1920; M.A.; F.R.S.E.; *b.* Glasgow, 1875; 2nd *s.* of W. Edwin Peck, Glasgow; *m.* 1911, Winifred Frances (*d.* 1962) (author of books, as Winifred Peck); two *s.* *Educ.:* Royal Technical College, Glasgow; Glasgow University; Christ Church, Oxford. Lecturer Mathematical Physics at Glasgow University, 1899-1903; Inspector Scottish Education Department, 1903-1905; Principal Assistant L.C.C. Education Department, 1905-1910, Clerk Edinburgh School Board, 1910-12; Chief Inspector in National Health Insurance Commission (Scotland), 1912-14, and in Scottish Board of Health, 1921-24; Captain Royal Field Artillery, 1914-18; Assistant Secretary Ministry of Food, 1918-21; Assistant Secretary, Royal Commission on Nat. Health Insurance, 1924-26; Second Secretary Scottish Education Department, 1930-36; Permanent Secretary, Scottish Education Department, 1936-40; Chief Divisional Food Officer for Scotland, 1940-46. *Address:* 6 Abbotsford Crescent, Church Hill, Edinburgh. *Club:* Caledonian United Service (Edinburgh). [*Died* 3 *Feb.* 1964.

PECK, Very Rev. Michael David Saville; Dean of Lincoln and Prebendary of Aylesbury since 1965; *b.* 7 January 1914; *s.* of Major E. Saville Peck, Cambridge; *m.* 1949, Virginia Forman. *Educ.:* King's College Choir School, Cambridge; Sedbergh; King's College, Cambridge. Curate, Holy Cross, Greenford, 1937-1946; Vice-Principal, St. Chad's College, Durham, 1946-49; Vicar of St Mark's, Mansfield, 1949-56; Archdeacon of Portsmouth. 1956-64. *Recreation:* sailing. *Address:* The Deanery, Lincoln. *T.:* Lincoln 23608. *Club:* Royal Naval (Portsmouth).

[*Died* 22 *April* 1968.

PECK, Lady; (Winifred Frances); 2nd *d.* of late Rt. Rev. Dr. E. A. Knox; *m.* 1911, Sir James Wallace Peck, C.B., M.A.; two *s.* *Educ.:* Wycombe Abbey School; Lady Margaret Hall, Oxford. *Publications:* The Court of a Saint; Twelve Birthdays; The Closing Gates; The Patchwork Quilt; A Change of Master; The King of Melido; The Warrielaw Jewel; The Skirts of Time; The Skies are Falling, 1936; They Come, They Go, 1937; Coming Out, 1938; Let Me Go Back, 1940; Bewildering Cares, 1940; A Garden Enclosed, 1941; Housebound, 1942; Tranquillity 1943, There is a Fortress, 1945; Through Eastern Windows 1947; Veiled Destinies, 1948; Arrest the Bishop, 1949; A Clear Dawn, 1949; Facing South, 1950; Unseen Array, 1951; Winding Ways 1952; A Little Learning, 1952; Home for the Holidays, 1955. *Address:* 54a George Square, Edinburgh. *T.:* New 44178. *Club:* University Women's.

[*Died* 20 *Nov.* 1962.

PEEBLES, James Ross; Head Master, The Cathedral School, Hereford, since 1957; *b.* 12 June 1909; *yr. s.* of late Rev. Guy Steel Peebles and Anne Eleanor (*née* Ross); *m.* 1942, Betty Anna Anderson; two *s.* one *d.* *Educ.:* Glasgow Academy; Glasgow University; University College, Oxford. 2nd Class Honours in Modern History, Oxford, 1931. Asst. Master, Westminster School, 1931; Housemaster, 1945-57, also Head of English and History Departments. Served in Intelligence Corps, 1941-45, attached to War Office, with rank of Major. *Recreations:* music, cricket, golf. *Address:* Cathedral School, Hereford. *T.:* Hereford 3757. *Clubs:* M.C.C., Public Schools.

[*Died* 15 *Dec.* 1967.

PEEL, 2nd Earl, *cr.* 1929; **Arthur William Ashton Peel;** Viscount Peel, *cr.* 1895; 7th Bt., *cr.* 1800; *b.* 29 May 1901; *o. s.* of 1st Earl and Hon. Ella Williamson (*d.* 1949), *e. d.* of 1st Baron Ashton; *S.* father, 1937 and *S.* to Baronetcy of cousin, 1942; *m.* 1946, Kathleen McGrath; two *s.* *Educ.:* Eton; Balliol College, Oxford, B.A. Lord Lieutenant and custos rotulorum of Lancaster, 1948-50; hon freeman of Lancaster; President Lancashire Association of Boys' Clubs, 1934-68; Vice-Chairman, Nairn & Williamson (Holdings) Ltd.; Director, District Bank Ltd. Assistant Secretary, Royal Commission on Land

Drainage, 1927, attached to Indian Statutory Commission, 1928. Deputy Chairman L.M. & S. Rly. Co., 1946-48. Upper Bailiff, Worshipful Company of Weavers, 1958-59. Hon. LL.D. Lancaster University, 1967. K.St.J. *Heir:* *s.* Viscount Clanfield. *Address:* Hyning Hall, Carnforth, Lancashire. *T.:* Carnforth 2684; 4 Mayfair House, 14 Carlos Place, Grosvenor Square, W.1. *T.:* 01-629 8367; Gunnerside Lodge, Richmond, Yorks. *T.:* Gunnerside 230. *Clubs:* St. James', Carlton. [*Died* 22 *Sept.* 1969.

PEEL, Sir Edward Townley, K.B.E., *cr.* 1944; D.S.O. 1918; M.C.; Order of the Nile 2nd Class (Egypt); Grand Officer Order of King George 1st (Greece); Chairman Peel & Co. Ltd., Alexandria, since 1908; Director of several commercial companies, Egypt; *b.* Knutsford, Cheshire, 31 May 1884; *s.* of late William Felton Peel, Wargrave Hall, Wargrave, Berks, and Sarah Edith Peel; *m.* 1923, Françoise Nora, (*d.* 1953), 2nd *d.* of Francis de Revière, Calvados, France. *Educ.:* Arnold House, Llandulas, N. Wales; Cheltenham College; Lycée Français, Tours. Joined Peel & Co., Ltd., Alexandria, Egypt, 1902. Served European War, 1914-18, France, Dardanelles and M.E.F., Egypt, Palestine and Syria (despatches five times, M.C., D.S.O.). *Recreations:* shooting, fishing, world record Rod-caught Tunny, 812 lbs. (1935), yachting (winner 3 times Cumberland Cup 8-metre International contest *v.* France), marine biological research (Vice-Pres. Roy. Marine Biological Assoc. of Gt. Brit.); F.R.G.S., F.R.Z.S., and Challenger Soc. *Address:* Fleming, Alexandria, Egypt; Peel & Company Limited, Alexandria. *T.A.:* Perpetual. *Clubs:* Royal Thames Yacht, International Sportsmen's, Royal Automobile; Union (Alexandria); Turf (Cairo); Royal Danish Yacht; Royal Yacht Club of Egypt; British Tunny, etc. [*Died* 6 *Sept.* 1961.

PEEL, His Honour Robert, O.B.E. 1917, Q.C. 1930; County Court Judge, Circuit No. 4, 1933-53; Deputy of the Chancellor of the Duchy of Lancaster, 1933-59; *b.* 3 Feb. 1881; *e. s.* of late William Peel of Knowlmere Manor, Clitheroe; *m.* 1907, Mary Beatrice (*d.* 1959), *er. d.* of late Sir Henry Worsley-Taylor, Bart., K.C.; four *d.* *Educ.:* Winchester; New Coll. Oxford. 2nd class Hon. Mods. and Litt. Hum.; Called to Bar, Lincoln's Inn, 1906; served European War, 1914-19, 16th London Regiment (Queen's Westminster Rifles); Deputy Judge-Advocate-General, British Salonika Force, and subsequently Army of the Black Sea, 1915-1919 (despatches, O.B.E., Brevet Major, Serbian Order of White Eagle). *Recreations:* shooting, forestry. *Address:* Knowlmere Manor, Clitheroe, Lancs. *T.:* Dunsop Bridge 226. *Club:* United University. [*Died* 28 *April* 1969.

PEERS, Roger Ernest, C.B.E. 1966; Secretary, King Edward's Hospital Fund for London, since 1960; *b.* 22 May 1906; *s.* of Sir Charles Peers, C.B.E., F.B.A., Chiselhampton, Oxon., and Gertrude Katharine (*née* Shepherd); *m.* 1st, 1931, Rosalind Harvey (*d.* 1964); one *s.* two *d.*; 2nd, 1966, Valerie Wagner (*née* Kemp). *Educ.:* King's College School, Wimbledon. Joined staff of King's Fund, 1936, Asst. Secretary, 1947; organised Emergency Bed Service, 1938, Sec., 1938, Director, 1953; Member, Fact-finding investigation for Designated Grades of Hosp. Service, 1958-59. Served War of 1939-45. R.N.V.R. Mine Disposal Unit, 1941-45 (commendation). *Address:* Flat 1, 5 Kensington Park Gardens, W.11. *T.:* 01-727 9731. *Club:* Athenæum. [*Died* 27 *May* 1968.

PEIRSE, Air Chief Marshal Sir Richard Edmund Charles, K.C.B., *cr.* 1940 (C.B. 1936); D.S.O. 1915; A.F.C.: Order of Polonia Restituta, 1942; Knight Grand Cross of Orange Nassau, 1943; Commander Legion of Merit, United States; Special Necklet, Cloud and Banner, China; late R.A.F.; *b.* 1892; *o. s.* of late Admiral Sir Richard Peirse, K.C.B., K.B.E.; *m.* 1st, 1915; one *s.* one *d.*; marriage dissolved; 2nd, Jessie Auchinleck, *d.* of late Alexander Stewart of Innerhadden, Perthshire. *Educ.:* Monkton Combe School; H.M.S. Conway; King's College, London. Served European War, 1914-18 (D.S.O., A.F.C.); Deputy Director of Operations and Intelligence, Air Ministry, 1930-33; Air Officer Commanding British Forces, Palestine and Transjordan, 1933-36; Deputy Chief of Air Staff, 1937-1940; Member of Air Council, 1939; Vice-Chief of Air Staff, 1940; Air Officer Commanding-in-Chief Bomber Command, 1940-1942; A.O.C.-in-C., India, 1942-43; Allied Air C.-in-C., S.E. Asia Command, 1943-44; retired list, 1945. *Address:* The Cottage, Shillingford Court, Shillingford, Oxon. *Club:* Royal Automobile. [*Died* 5 *Aug.* 1970.

PEIRSON, Garnet Frank; Chairman, Midlands Electricity Board, since 1962; *b.* 26 April 1911; *s.* of Frank Ernest Peirson and Alice M. Morton, Coventry; *m.* 1937, Barbara Heathcock; one *s.* one *d.* *Educ.:* King Henry VIII School, Coventry; Birmingham University. Entered Elec. Supply Industry, 1934. Chief Engineer, Midland Electric Corp. for Power Distribution Ltd., 1944; Chief Engineer, Midlands Elec. Board, 1948, Dep. Chairman, 1957. Pres. Birmingham Electric Club, 1951-52 and 1952-53; Chairman, S. Midland Centre of I.E.E., 1959-60. *Publications:* papers on Automatic Circuit Reclosers and Use of Radio in Elec. Supply Industry in Jl. of I.E.E. *Recreations:* Rugby football; cinematography and sound recording; boats. *Address:* Highfields, Wollescote Road, Stourbridge, Worcs. *T.:* 5422. [*Died* 7 *Nov.* 1963.

PELLEW, Lancelot Vivian, C.M.G. 1964; President of the Industrial Court of South Australia, Oct. 1952-Dec. 1964, retd.; *b.* 15 Dec. 1899; *s.* of Joseph Henry Pellew and Laura Lee; *m.* 1924, Ray Lilian Smith; one *d.* *Educ.:* Queen's School, North Adelaide; St. Peters College, St. Peters. Admitted to Bar, S.A. Supreme Court, 1923. In practice Adelaide, 1926-42; Actg. Dep. Master, Supreme Court, Adelaide, 1942-45; Special Magistrate, Dec. 1945-48. Dep. Pres., Industrial Ct., 1948-52. *Recreations:* golf, bowls. *Address:* 3 Bedford St., Kensington Park, Adelaide, South Australia. *T.:* Adelaide 3-5079. *Clubs:* Adelaide, Royal Adelaide Golf, S.A. Lawn Tennis Assoc., Adelaide Oval Bowls, S.A. Cricket Assoc. (Adelaide); Mt. Lofty Golf. [*Died* 8 *Dec.* 1970.

PEMBERTON, Horatio Nelson; Chief Engineer Surveyor, Lloyd's Register of Shipping, 1957-67; Chairman, Council of Engineering Institutions, since 1966; *b.* 10 Jan. 1902; *e. s.* of late H. Nelson Pemberton, London; *m.* 1st, 1936, Margaret (*d.* 1938), *o. d.* of David Gemmell; one *s.*; 2nd, 1938, Vera, *d.* of George Judd, Sheringham, Norfolk; one *d.* *Educ.:* Middlesbrough High Sch. Engineering apprenticeship at Scott's Shipbuilding & Engineering Co., Greenock; Merchant Navy, 1922-30; Engineer and Ship Surveyor, Lloyd's Register of Shipping, 1930; Deputy Chief Engineer Surveyor, 1953. M.I.Mech.E. (Member of Council, 1957); M.I.Mar.E. (Vice-Pres., 1964; Chm. of Council, 1965); M.R.I.N.A. Chm. B.S.I. Council for Codes of Practice; Mem. General Council B.S.I.; Member American Society of Marine Engineers and Naval Architects; Member Research Committees, British Ship Research Assoc.; Member Min. of Power Nuclear Safety Advisory Cttee.; Member: U.K. Atomic Energy Authority Cttees. on

safety of nuclear plant, and Admiralty and Min. of Transport Cttees. on nuclear propulsion of ships; Min. of Transport Cttee. on prevention of pollution of the sea by oil; U.K. Delegation at the 1960 Safety of Life at Sea Conference. Thomas Lowe Gray Memorial Lecturer, 1953. City and Guilds Insignia Award (*h.c.*), 1963. *Publications:* papers to learned societies. *Recreation:* country life. *Address:* St. Faiths, High St., Blakeney, Norfolk. *T.:* Cley 372.
[*Died* 6 *April* 1967.

PEMBERTON-PIGOTT, Maj.-Gen. Alan J.. K.; *see* Pigott.

PEMBLETON, Edgar Stanley, C.M.G. 1941; B.A. (Oxon.); *b.* 14 Apr. 1888; *s.* of late George Pembleton, Grantham; *m.* 1916, Elizabeth Colhoun (*d.* 1959), *y. d.* of late James Colhoun, Philadelphia, Pa.; two *s.* *Educ.:* King's School, Grantham; Corpus Christi Coll., Oxford. Assistant Resident, Northern Nigeria, 1911; Resident, 1928; Senior Resident, 1934; retired from Colonial Administrative Service, 1944; Executive Secretary, British Section, Anglo-American Carribean Commission, 1944-46; Deputy Chairman, Caribbean Research Council, 1946-1948. *Address:* 2 Worcester Road, Clifton, Bristol 8. *T.:* Bristol 37853.
[*Died* 10 *Feb.* 1968.

PEMBROKE, 16th Earl of, *cr.* 1551, and 12th Earl of **Montgomery,** cr. 1605; **Sidney Charles Herbert,** C.V.O. 1945; J.P.; Baron Herbert of Caerdiff, 1551; Baron Herbert of Shurland, 1604; Baron Herbert of Lea (U.K.), 1861; Hereditary Grand Visitor of Jesus College, Oxford; present Earl is a direct descendant of 1st Earl; Alderman Wilts. C.C., 1954-67; Lord Lieutenant for Wiltshire, since 1954; *b.* 9 Jan. 1906; *e. s.* of 15th Earl of Pembroke and Montgomery, M.V.O.; *S.* father 1960; *m.* 1936, Lady Mary Dorothea Hope (later Countess of Pembroke and Montgomery), *o. d.* of Hersey, Marchioness of Linlithgow; one *s.* one *d.* *Educ.:* Eton; Pembroke Coll., Oxford. Served War of 1939-45, R.A. and Staff. Comptroller and Private Secretary to the Duchess of Kent, 1942-48; Equerry to the late Duke of Kent. Trustee of National Gallery, 1942-49 and 1953-60; Trustee of Nat. Portrait Gall., 1944-58; Mem. Historical Manuscripts Commission, 1941-58. President: Wilts T. & A.F.A.; St. John Council; Boy Scouts Assoc.; Historic Churches Trust. J.P. 1954. *Publications:* (edited) Henry, Elizabeth and George (Pembroke Papers), 2 vols., 1939, 1950; Letters and Diaries of Henry, Tenth Earl of Pembroke, and his Circle; A Catalogue of the Paintings and Drawings at Wilton House, Salisbury, 1968. *Recreations:* shooting, fishing, racing. *Heir:* *s.* Lord Herbert. *Address:* Wilton House, Salisbury, Wilts. *T.:* Wilton 3211. *Club:* Turf.
[*Died* 16 *March* 1969.

PENDER, 2nd Baron, *cr.* 1937, of Porthcurnow; **John Jocelyn Denison-Pender,** C.B.E. 1946; Governor, Cable and Wireless (Holding) Ltd.; Chairman: Cables Investment Trust Ltd.; Globe Telegraph and Trust Co. Ltd.; African Direct Telegraph and Trust Co. Ltd.; Eastern and South African Investment Trust Co. Ltd.; Electra Finance Co. Ltd.; Second Electra Finance Co. Ltd.; Third Electra Finance Co. Ltd.; Electra House Ltd.; Director: Direct Spanish Telegraph Co. Ltd.; Commercial Union Assurance Co. Ltd.; Pres., Royal Albert Hall, since 1952; Vice-Chm. Board of Governors of Charing Cross Hosp., since 1960; *b.* 26 Jan. 1907; *e. s.* of 1st Baron and Irene (*d.* 1943), *o. c.* of Sir Ernest de la Rue, K.C.V.O.; *S.* father 1949; *m.* 1930, Camilla Lethbridge, *o. d.* of late Willoughby Arthur Pemberton; two *s.* one *d.* *Educ.:* Eton; Magdalen College, Oxford. After a cable-laying expedition in 1926, entered service of The Eastern Telegraph Co. Ltd. in 1928 and passed through its numerous branches; appointed Asst. Sec. of Cable and Wireless Ltd. (the Operating Company), 1930; Dep. Chief Gen. Manager, 1933; Gen. Manager, 1935; Joint Managing Director, 1945-46, which office he vacated on nationalisation of Company. *Recreations:* shooting, fishing, racing, bridge. *Heir:* *s.* Hon. John Willoughby Denison-Pender [*b.* 6 May 1933; *m.* 1962, Julia, *yr. d.* of Richard Cannon; one *d.*]. *Address:* 105 Cadogan Gardens, S.W.3. *T.:* Sloane 3144. *Clubs:* White's, St. James'.
[*Died* 31 *March* 1965.

PENDER, Major Henry Denison Denison, D.S.O. 1918; O.B.E. 1942; M.C.; late Royal Scots Greys; *b.* 2 April 1884; 2nd *s.* of late Sir John Denison-Pender, G.B.E., K.C.M.G.; *m.* 1913, Doris Louise Sydney (*d.* 1952), *e. d.* of Sydney Fisher of Amington Hall, Tamworth, Staffs; three *d.* *Educ.:* Eton. Second Lieut. Royal Scots Greys, 1907; served European War, France and Belgium, Aug.-Nov. 1914 and May 1915-March 1918: temp. Capt. Nov. 1914; Capt. May 1915 (despatches four times, Bt. Major, D.S.O., M.C.), High Sheriff of Dorsetshire, 1935; J.P. Dorset, 1926; Deputy Chief Telegraph Censor, Central Telegraph Office, 1939-42; Director of the Telegraph Construction and Maintenance Co. Ltd., 1921-59. Chm. Sturminster R.D.C., 1949-53. Mem. Council Bath and West Agric. Soc., 1929-50 (Vice-Pres. 1950); Mem. Council Roy. Agric. Soc., 1943-53; Pres. Yeovil Agric. Soc., 1936 and 1937; Life Hon. Mem. Hunters Improvement and Light Horse Breeding Soc., 1953. *Address:* Hartletts, Hook, Hants. *T.:* Hook 2451. *Club:* Boodle's.
[*Died* 16 *Feb.* 1967.

PENFOLD, Capt. Marchant Hubert, C.B.E. 1919; R.N. (retired); *b.* Exeter, 16 Nov. 1873; *s.* of Captain H. M. Penfold, R.N.R.; *m.* 1896, Ella Marion, *y. d.* of E. J. Harvey, Admiralty Solicitor, Portsmouth; one *s.* *Educ.:* Gill's School, Muizenberg, Cape Colony. Entered Royal Navy, 1886; Lieutenant, 1894; Commander, 1906; retired with rank of Captain, 1922; granted C.B.E. for services at Sheerness Dockyard during the War. *Recreations:* golf, badminton, stamp collecting, Fellow of the Royal Philatelic Society. *Address:* 47 Hove Park Villas, Hove, Sussex. *T.:* Hove 3423. *Club:* Sussex Sports (Hove).
[*Died* 28 *Jan.* 1961.

PENGELLY, Herbert Staddon, C.B. 1954; *b.* 1 Oct. 1892; *s.* of James Edward Pengelly, and Mary Jane Pengelly (*née* Staddon); *m.* 1924, Kate Lilian, *d.* of late Arthur J. Beecroft. *Educ.:* Stoke Public Higher School, Devonport; H.M. Dockyard School, Devonport; R.N.C., Greenwich. Assistant Constructor, Roy. Corps of Naval Constructors, 1916-29; Constructor Lieut., H.M.S. Renown, 1917-18; Professor of Naval Architecture, R.N. College, Greenwich, 1929-34; Constructor and Chief Constructor, Battleship Design, 1934-42; Fleet Constructor Officer, Eastern Fleet, 1942-44 (rank of Constructor Captain); Asst. Director of Naval Construction, 1944-51; Principal Deputy Dir., Oct. 1951-Nov. 1954; retd. from Admiralty Service, 1954. Vice-Pres. Royal Inst. of Naval Architects. Liveryman, Worshipful Company of Shipwrights. *Publication:* (with E. L. Attwood) Theoretical Naval Architecture, 1931. *Recreations:* golf, walking, reading. *Address:* 28 Monkridge, Crouch End Hill, N.8. *T.:* Mountview 6040. *Clubs:* Athenæum; Bath and County (Bath); South Herts Golf.
[*Died* 18 *Dec.* 1963.

PENGILLY, Sir Alexander, Kt., *cr.* 1929; *b.* 8 June 1868; three *d.* Chairman of South Dorset Conservative Assoc., 1918-40; Chairman, Wessex Area of National Union of Conservative

and Unionist Associations, 1926-29. *Recreation:* golf. *Address:* Lostwithiel, Grosvenor Road, Weymouth. *T*: 2344
[*Died* 21 *June* 1965.

PENMAN, David, C.I.E. 1937; D.Sc., late Asst. Chief Engineer (Scot.) Home Office (Civil Defence Dept.). *Educ.:* Heriot-Watt College, Edinburgh. D.Sc., Engineering, Edinburgh University; B.Sc. 1st class honours in Mining, London University; B.Sc. Distinction in Electrical Engineering, Edinburgh University; Research Assistant, Mine Rescue Apparatus Research Committee, 1916-1918; Organiser of Mining Education (Eastern District) Fife Education Committee, 1919-20; Inspector of Mines, Govt. of India, 1921-26; Principal, Indian School of Mines (Government of India), Dhanbad, India, 1926-32; Chief Inspector of Mines in India, 1932-38. Retired, 1949. *Publications:* The Electrical Equipment of Collieries; Compressed Air Practice in Mining; Treatise on Mine Ventilation; All about Coal, etc. *Recreations:* tennis, golf, motoring. *Address:* 6 Dalhousie Terrace, Edinburgh 10. [*Died* 24 *Aug.* 1961.

PENN, Will C., M.C., R.O.I., R.P., R.C.A.; portrait and figure painter. *Educ.:* London. Studied at Royal Academy Schools and on the Continent; frequent exhibitor at the Royal Academy since 1902; was gazetted to the 5th King's Liverpool Regt., and served with the 57th Division in France. *Address:* Kirkdale Vicarage, Nawton, Yorks.
[*Died* 27 *May* 1968.

PENNANT, Adm. Hon. Sir Cyril E. D.; *see* Douglas-Pennant.

PENNEFATHER, Harold W. A. F.; *see* Freese-Pennefather.

PENNEFATHER - EVANS, Lt. - Colonel Granville, C.B.E. 1920; *s.* of late Matthew Pennefather-Evans; *m.* 1st, 1893, Grace Woodburn (*d.* 1908), *d.* of late Major Douglas Hennessy, Indian Army; one *s.* (and two *s.* decd. of whom one was killed on active service in France, 1916); 2nd, 1923, Ethel Margaret, *d.* of late Charles Banastre Lloyd, of Janearo, Naivasha, B.E.A. *Educ.:* Rugby. Entered South Wales Borderers, 1890; transferred to Indian Army, 1893; Lt.-Col. commanding 22nd Punjabis, 1916-20; retired, 1920. Served European War, 1914-18 (despatches thrice, Brevet Lieut.-Col.); Afghan War, 1919 (despatches). *Publications:* Big-game shooting in Upper Burma, 1912; Small-game shooting, 1951. *Address:* c/o Westminster Bank Ltd., Exmouth, Devon.
[*Died* 12 *Jan.* 1963.

PENNELL, Lt.-Col. Richard, D.S.O. 1917; (retired) K.R.R.C; *b* 4 Feb. 1885; *s.* of late Richard and Maria Pennell; *m.* Catherine Hunt; three *s.* Served European War, 1914-1918 (wounded, despatches, D.S.O. with bar). Military Knight of Windsor. *Address:* 17 Lower Ward, Windsor Castle. [*Died* 13 *July* 1963.

PENNEY, Air Commodore Howard Wright, C.B. 1957; C.B.E. 1951; retd.; *b.* 14 August 1903; *s.* of late Charles Gregory Penney, Raynes Park, S.W.20; *m.* 1943, Beryl Enid, *d.* of late William Tucker, Slough, Bucks; one *s.* one *d.* *Educ.:* Friars Sch., Bangor, N. Wales. Joined R.A.F., 1927; served Iraq, 1930-32; Graduate R.A.F. Staff College, 1935; served Far East, 1936; Air Ministry and Ministry of Aircraft Production, 1937-47; promoted Group Capt. 1947; Air Cdre. 1958; served Far East, 1948-50; Maintenance Command, 1950-55; Air Ministry, 1956-58; S.A.S.O., H.Q. No. 41 Group 1958-61; Air Commodore (Operations), H.Q. Maintenance Command, 1961-62; retired, 1962. *Address:* The Cottage, North End, Newbury, Berks. [*Died* 19 *June* 1970.

PENNEY, Maj.-Gen. Sir (William) Ronald Campbell, K.B.E. 1958 (C.B.E. 1943; O.B.E. 1933); C.B. 1944; D.S.O. 1937; M.C.; late R. Signals; retd. pay, 1949; *b.* 1896; 2nd *s.* of J. Campbell Penney, Accountant of Court for Scotland; *m.* 1st, 1925, Shirley Mary (*d.* 1960), *d.* of Vice-Admiral V. G. Gurner; two *d.*; 2nd, 1963, Stella, *widow* of Lt.-Cdr. R. M. Marshall, R.N.V.R., and *d.* of late Rev. P. M. Daubeny and of Mrs. Daubeny, Old House Farm, Cublington, Bucks. *Educ.:* Wellington; Royal Military Academy, Woolwich. Commissioned Royal Engineers, 1914; Captain, 1917; transferred R. Signals, 1921; Major, 1927; Bt. Lieut.-Colonel, 1934; Lieut.-Col. 1935; Col. 1939; Maj.-Gen. 1941; served European War, France and Belgium (despatches, M.C., French Croix de Guerre, Belgian Croix de Guerre); India, 1921-26; p.s.c. 1928; War Office, 1929-30; Brigade Major, Shanghai, 1931-33; India, 1935-1939; N.W. Frontier, 1937 (despatches, D.S.O.); War of 1939-45 (wounded, C.B.E., C.B., American Legion of Merit, Czecho-Slovak Order of the White Lion). Colonel Comdt. R. Signals, 1947-57. Ministry of Supply, 1946-49; employed Foreign Office, 1953-57. *Address:* West Pavilion, Paxton House, Berwick-on-Tweed. *T.:* Paxton 263. *Club:* United Service. [*Died* 3 *Dec.* 1964.

PENNOYER, Richard Edmands, B.Sc.; Assoc. Inst. Loco. Eng.; *b* 25 Dec. 1885; *e. s.* of late Albert Adams Pennoyer, Oakland, California, and Virginia, *e. d.* of Henry Geddes; *m.* 1917, Winifred Constance Hester (*d.* 1965), *e. d.* of Lord Alexander Paget, and *widow* of Viscount Ingestre, M.V.O.; one *s.* *Educ.:* private schools; University of California, B.Sc. Member of Newcomen Society. *Publications:* occasional contributor to railway press. *Club:* Beefsteak. [*Died* 17 *Nov.* 1968.

PENNYCUICK, Brig. (Retired) James Alexander Charles, D.S.O. 1914; late R.E.; *b.* 9 June 1890; *s.* of late C. E. D. Pennycuick, C.M.G., Ceylon Civil Service; *m.* 1923, Marjorie, *d.* of Sir G. R. L. Hare, 3rd Bt.; one *s.* two *d.* Entered Army, 1910, Royal Engineers; served European War, 1914-18 (twice wounded, despatches thrice, D.S.O. and bar, Order of St. Anne); went back with another to blow up bridge at Pontoise during Mons retreat; p.s.c. War of 1939-45 served with Allied Commission Italy (despatches). *Address:* Cunliffes, Horam, E. Sussex. *Club:* Royal Automobile. [*Died* 21 *Feb.* 1966

PENRHYN, 5th Baron, *cr.* 1866; **Frank Douglas - Pennant;** Lieut.-Col.; J.P. Northants; *b.* 21 Nov. 1865; *s.* of late Lieut.-Col. Hon. Archibald Charles Douglas-Pennant (2nd *s.* of 1st Baron Penrhyn) and late Hon. Harriet Ella Gifford, *d.* of 2nd Baron Gifford; *S.* kinsman 1949; *m.* 1st, 1892, Maud (from whom he obtained a divorce, 1903), *d.* of late Col. John Hardy, 9th Lancers; two *d.*; 2nd, 1905, Alice Nellie (*d.* 1965), *o. d.* of Sir William Charles Cooper, 3rd Bt.; two *s.* one *d.* *Educ.:* Eton; R.M.C., Sandhurst. Lt.-Col. 60th King's Royal Rifle Corps; served S. Africa, 1900-2; European War, 1914-16. *Heir:* *s.* Colonel Hon. Malcolm Frank Douglas-Pennant, D.S.O., M.B.E. *Address:* Sholebroke Lodge, Towcester, Northants. *T.A.:* Pennant-Whittlebury. *T.:* Silverstone 240.
[*Died* 3 *Feb.* 1967.

PENRHYN - HORNBY, Charles Windham Leycester, J.P.; *b.* 5 Nov. 1873. *Educ.:* Rossall; Royal Agricultural College, Cirencester. Handicapper under Jockey Club Rules, 1911-35; High Sheriff of Westmorland, 1940. *Recreations:* watching cricket; billiards and shooting. *Address:* Brook House, Lymm, Cheshire.
[*Died* 21 *Sept.* 1966.

PENROSE-WELSTED, Col. Reginald Hugh, C.I.E. 1943; Indian Army, retired; *b.* 23 April 1891; *s.* of late S. Q. Penrose-Welsted, Ballywalter, Co. Cork; *m.* 1918, Gertrude Eugenie, *d.* of G. Perfect; two *d.* *Educ.:* Rossall School; R.M.A., Woolwich. 2nd Lt. Indian Army, 1910; Capt. 1915; Major, 1927; Lt.-Col. 1936; Bt. Col. 1935; Col. 1938. Director of Farms, General Headquarters India, 1936-42; retired, 1942. *Address:* 73 Cantelupe Road, Bexhill-on-Sea Sussex. *T.:* 2795. [*Died* 1 *Feb.* 1966.

PENSON, Dame Lillian Margery, D.B.E., *cr.* 1951; Ph.D. (Lond.); Hon. LL.D., Cantab., Leeds, McGill, St. Andrews, Southampton; Hon. D.C.L., Oxford; Hon. D.Litt., Sheffield, Western Ontario; Hon. D.Lit. Belfast; Hon. Fellow R.C.S., 1959; Professor of Modern History in the University of London (Bedford College), 1930-1962; Emeritus Professor, 1962; Member Council of University College of Rhodesia and Nyasaland since 1955; *b.* 18 July 1896; *e. d.* of Arthur Austin Penson. *Educ.:* privately; Birkbeck Coll. and Univ. College, London. Junior Administrative Asst., Min. of National Service, 1917-18; War Trade Intelligence Department, 1918-19; Lecturer in History, Birkbeck College, University of London, 1921-1930, and at Queen Mary College, 1923-25; Dean of the Faculty of Arts in University of London, 1938-44; Member of Senate since 1940; Chairman of the Academic Council, 1945-48; Member of Commission on Higher Education in the Colonies, 1943-45; Mem. U.S. Educ. Commission in U.K., 1949-56; Vice-Chancellor of Univ. of London, 1948-51. *Publications:* The Colonial Agents of the British West Indies, 1924; Contributions to: the Cambridge History of the British Empire, Vol. I, 1929, Cambridge History of India, Vol. VI, 1932, English Historical Review, Transactions of the Royal Historical Society, Cambridge Historical Journal, etc.; (as assistant to G. P. Gooch and H. Temperley, editors) British Documents on the Origins of the War, 1898-1914, Vols. I-X, 1925-38; (with H. Temperley) A Century of Diplomatic Blue Books, 1938, and Foundations of British Foreign Policy, 1938; (editor), 6th Ed. Grant and Temperley, Europe in the Nineteenth and Twentieth Centuries, 1952. *Address:* 5 Wood Vale, Forest Hill, S.E.23. [*Died* 17 *April* 1963.

PENTIN, Rev. Herbert, M.A.; Founder and Warden of International Society for promoting study of Apocrypha, 1905; Editor of the International Journal of Apocrypha, 1907-17; Canon of Gibraltar Cathedral, 1935; *b.* 1873; *s.* of late Capt. P. M. Pentin, Rodwell, Weymouth; *m.* 1st, Margaret Gwynevor, *d.* of late E. Vaughan Williams of The Manor House, Weymouth; 2nd, Margit, *d.* of late Judge A. F. Akerman, LL.M., Knight of the North Star, Sweden; one *s.* *Educ.:* Weymouth College. Theological Exhibitioner, Univ. of Durham; L.Th. 1896; B.A. 1898; M.A. 1901; F.R.Hist.S. 1895; F.S.A.Scot. 1904; M.R.A.S. 1907; Curate, Coton, Nuneaton, 1896-99; Stratford-on-Avon, 1899-1901; Vicar of Milton Abbey, 1901-14; Vicar of St. Peter's, Portland, and Acting C.F. 1914-26; Chaplain, R.N. Division, 1914-15; Chaplain, Australian Imperial Forces, 1917-19; Acting Chaplain, H.M. Anti-Submarine School, 1924-1926; Chaplain in Diocese of Gibraltar, 1926-37; Chaplain to H.M. Embassy, Madrid, 1933-36; Chaplain to H.M. Embassy, Lisbon, 1936-37. *Publications:* Deutero-Canonica, 1905-6; The Apocrypha in Greek and English, 1906; The Book of Judith, 1908; Memorials of Old Dorset, 1908. *Recreation:* archæology. *Address:* Largo of the Count of Ericeira, Ericeira, Portugal. *Club:* Royal British (Lisbon). [*Died* 4 *Oct.* 1965.

PENTON, Brigadier Bertie Cyril, C.B. 1935; D.S.O. 1919; Indian Army, retired; *b.* 1 July 1880; *s.* of Major General H. E. Penton; *m.* 1912, Grace Caroline, *d.* of A. E. Ashley; one *d.* decd. *Educ.:* Marlborough. Served N.W.F. of India, 1908 (medal with clasp); European War 1914-19 (despatches twice, D.S.O.); Waziristan, 1921-24 (despatches); retired, 1936. *Address.* Atherton, 104 Park Road, Camberley, Surrey. [*Died* 24 *July* 1962.

PENTON, Sir Edward, K.B.E., *cr.* 1918; *b.* 18 June 1875; *e. s.* of late Edward Penton, Cavendish Sq., W.; *m.* 1902, Eleanor (*d.* 1951), 2nd *d.* of W. A. Sharpe, Broadlands Road, Highgate; four *s.* three *d.* *Educ.:* Rugby; New College, Oxford. Honours History School, B.A., 1897; travelled in S. Africa, India, Burma, Persia; Mayor of Metropolitan Borough of St. Marylebone, 1912-1913; Alderman, 1913; Superintendent Royal Army Clothing Department (Boot Section), 1914-19; contested Tiverton Division of Devonshire, 1918; East Lewisham Division, 1923 and 1929; Chief Inspector of Clothing, Central Ordnance Depot, Branston, Burton-on-Trent, until 30 June 1946; then acted as Secretary to the Commonwealth Conference on design, devel. and inspection of Stores and clothing. *Address:* Brooks's, St. James's, S.W.1. *T.:* Hyde Park 3745. *Clubs:* Garrick, Brooks's, Beefsteak. [*Died* 21 *Dec.* 1967.

PEPPER, George Wharton; Attorney-at-law, Senator from Pennsylvania, 1922-27; *b.* 16 March 1867; *s.* of George Pepper, M.D., and Hitty Markoe Wharton; *m.* 1890, Charlotte R. (decd.), New Haven Conn., *o. d.* of Professor George P. Fisher of Yale University; one *s.* two *d.* *Educ.:* Univ. of Pennsylvania. Became a member of the teaching staff of the Law School of the University of Pennsylvania, 1889; Algernon Sydney Biddle Professor of Law, 1894-1910; identified with movements for the reform of legal education in the United States; has been engaged since 1889 in the active practice of law in the State and Federal Courts in Philadelphia and throughout the United States; Hon. LL.D. University of Pennsylvania, 1907; Yale University, 1914; University of Pittsburg, 1921; Lafayette University of Rochester and Pennsylvania Military College, 1922; Kenyon Coll., 1924; Bucknell Univ., 1926; Williams Coll., 1936; Univ. of Toronto, 1944; Hon. D.C.L. Univ. of the South, 1908; Trinity College, 1918; Hahnemann Medical College and Hospital of Philadelphia, 1941; Rutgers College, 1940; Jefferson, 1952; has taken an active part in philanthropic and educational work; Trustee of Univ. of Pennsylvania; Past Pres. American Law Institute; Mem. of Amer. Philosophical Soc. and of Chapter of Washington Cathedral; former Chancellor of Philadelphia Bar Association; Mem. of Republican Nat. Cttee., 1922-28; Philadelphia Award, 1953; Grand Officer Order Leopold II, Belgium; Award of Merit, Order of the Sangreal. *Publications:* A Digest of Pennsylvania Decisions (with William Draper Lewis); The Way, a devotional book for boys; A Voice from the Crowd, being the Lyman Beecher Lectures for 1915 before Yale University; Men and Issues; In the Senate; Family Quarrels: the President; the Senate; the House, being the White Lectures before the Univ. of Virginia; Philadelphia Lawyer; an Analytical Index to the Book of Common Prayer, 1948; essays on legal topics. *Recreations:* tramping and camping, tennis, etc. *Address:* 123 S. Broad Street, Philadelphia, Pa., U.S.A. *Clubs:* University, Racquet, Penn Athletic, Rittenhouse, Union League (Philadelphia); Metropolitan (Washington); Century Association (N.Y). [*Died* 24 *May* 1961.

PEPPIATT, Sir Leslie (Ernest), Kt. 1959; M.C. and Bar, 1918; formerly Senior Partner of Legal Firm of Freshfields; *b.* 7 Nov. 1891; *s.* of William Robert Peppiatt; *m.* 1927, Cicely Mallyn Howse; two *s.* *Educ.:* Bancroft's School: London Univ. Member of

Departmental (Spens) Cttees. on remuneration of Medical Specialists and remuneration of Dental Practitioners, 1947. Director of Equity & Law Life Assurance Society Ltd., 1948. Chairman of 1930 Fund for Benefit of Trained District Nurses, 1954; Pres. Law Society, 1958-59; Chairman Departmental Committee on Betting on Horse-racing, 1960. Governor, Dominion Students' Hall Trust (London House) and the Sister Trust (William Goodenough House). *Recreation:* fishing. *Address:* Cleve Cottage, Wisborough Green, Sussex. *T.:* Wisborough Green 465. *Club:* Athenæum. [*Died* 15 *Nov.* 1968.

PEPYS, Walter Evelyn, C.M.G. 1938; *b.* 12 April 1885; *s.* of Hon. Walter Courtenay Pepys, 60th Rifles and Barrister-at-law; *m.* 1932, Violet Maude (*d.* 1960), *d.* of T. Carr-Ramsey, Dunvegan House, Swatow, South China. *Educ.:* Malvern; Brasenose College, Oxford (M.A.). Held various appointments in Malayan Civil Service from 1908, including District Officer, Pasir Puteh, Kelantan; Superintendent of Lands, Kelantan; Commissioner of Lands, Trengganu; Commissioner of Lands and Mines, Johore; Under Secretary to Government, F.M.S.; Commissioner of Customs and Excise, S.S. and F.M.S.; General Adviser, Johore, 1935; retired 1940; General Adviser, Sarawak, 1940; Liaison Officer Sarawak and North Borneo, 1940; Interned in Singapore, 1942-45. *Recreations:* games, reading, music. *Address:* c/o Chartered Bank, 38 Bishopsgate, E.C.2. *Clubs:* M.C.C., Royal Commonwealth Society. [*Died* 15 *Nov.* 1966.

PERCEVAL, Col., Hon. Maj.-Gen., Christopher Peter Westby, C.B.E. 1940; D.S.O. 1917; *b.* Christchurch, New Zealand, 11 June 1890; *y. s.* of late Sir Westby Brook Perceval, K.C.M.G. *Educ.:* Wimbledon College; R.M.A., Woolwich. Entered Royal Artillery, 1910; served European War, 1914-18; War of 1939-45, France and Middle East; Chief Instructor in Gunnery, School of Artillery, Larkhill, 1938-39; Commander R.A., 1939; Maj.-Gen. R.A., 1944; Area Comd., 1945; retired pay, 1946. *Address:* Aynho Park, Banbury, Oxon. *Club:* Army and Navy. [*Died* 21 *Nov.* 1967.

PERCIVAL, Lieutenant-General Arthur Ernest, C.B. 1941; D.S.O. 1918, and Bar 1919; O.B.E. 1921; M.C.; *b.* Aspenden, Herts, 26 Dec. 1887; *s.* of Alfred Reginald and Edith Percival; *m.* 1927, Margaret Elizabeth MacGregor (*d.* 1953), *d.* of Thomas MacGregor Greer of Sea Park, Carrickfergus and Tullylagan Manor, Co. Tyrone; one *s.* one *d.* *Educ.:* Rugby School. In business in London with Naylor, Benzon & Co. Ltd. 1907-14; serving U.K. 1914-15; B.E.F. France, 1915-19 (D.S.O., M.C., French Croix de Guerre, wounded September 1916); North Russia, 1919 (bar to D.S.O.); Ireland, 1920-22 (O.B.E., despatches twice); Staff College, Camberley, 1923-24; General Staff Officer 2, Nigeria Regt., 1925-27; Staff Officer, Nigeria Regiment, Nigeria, 1927-29; commanding 7th (S.) Bn. and 2nd Bn. Bedfordshire Regt., 1918-19; Capt. Essex Regt., 1916-18; Brevet Major, Essex Regt., 1919-24; Major, Cheshire Regt., 1924-28; Bt. Lt.-Col. Cheshire Regt., 1929; Lt.-Col. 1932; Col. 1936; Maj.-Gen. 1940, antedated to 1938; Royal Naval Staff College, Greenwich, 1930; General Staff Officer, 2nd Grade, Staff College, Camberley, 1931-32; commanded 2nd Bn. The 22nd (Cheshire) Regt. 1932-36; Imperial Defence College course, 1935; General Staff Officer, First Grade, Malaya, 1936-38: Brigadier, General Staff, Aldershot Command, 1938-39; Brigadier General Staff, 1st Corps, B.E.F., 1939-40; G.O.C. 43rd (Wessex) Div., 1940; Asst. Chief of Imp. General Staff, War Office, 1940; G.O.C. 44th (Home Counties) Div., 1940-41; G.O.C., Malaya, 1941-42; released from captivity in Manchuria, 1945; retired pay, 1946. Hon. Col. the 479 (Herts. Yeomanry) H.A.A. Regt. T.A., 1949-54; Col. The 22nd (Cheshire) Regt. 1950-55. D.L. Hertfordshire, 1951. *Publication:* The War in Malaya, 1949. *Recreations:* polo, tennis, cricket (Gentlemen of Essex), hockey, squash, etc. *Address:* Bullards, Widford, Ware, Herts. *T.:* Much Hadham, 169. *Club:* United Service. [*Died* 31 *Jan.* 1966.

PERCY, Col. Lord William (Richard), C.B.E. 1919; D.S.O. 1917; late Grenadier Gds.; *b.* 17 May 1882; 2nd *s.* of 7th Duke of Northumberland; *m.* 1922, Mary, *d.* of late Capt. George S. C. Swinton; two *s.* *Educ.:* Oxford (B.A.). Called to Bar, Inner Temple, 1906; served European War, 1914-18 (wounded, despatches twice, Bt. Major, Serbian Order of the White Eagle with Swords; Commander Order King George of Greece); retired with rank of Colonel, 1919. *Address:* Horstead House, Norwich. *T.:* Coltishall 357. *Club:* Travellers'. [*Died* 8 *Feb.* 1963.

PEREIRA, Adeodato Anthony; Metropolitan Magistrate, 1949-61; *b.* 19 Feb. 1889; *s.* of Adrian Aloysius Pereira and Angelina Mary Anne, *d.* of Adeodato da Silva Lima; *m.* 1921, Enid Winifred, *d.* of Frank Cartwright Rimington; two *s.* two *d.* *Educ.:* Wimbledon College, Wimbledon; University College, Oxford. Wimbledon Coll., 1901-7; Univ. Coll. Oxf., 1908-11, 2nd Cl. Hon., M.A.; Inner Temple, 1913. Served European War, 1914-18, Army Pay Dept.; demobilised, 1919, with rank of Capt. Called to bar, Inner Temple, 1920; practised on Common Law side, S.E. Circuit. Chm. of an Appeal Tribunal Assistance Board (part-time), 1935; Inspector, Ministry of Transport (part-time), 1936; Referee, Ministry of Health (part-time), 1939; Stipendiary Magistrate, East and West Ham, 1946-49. *Publications:* Law of Hire and Hire-Purchase. 1932, 2nd Ed., 1939; Hire-Purchase in Halsbury's Laws of England (Hailsham Ed.); Hire and Hire-Purchase in last Ed. of Encyclopaedia of Forms and Precedents. *Recreation:* painting. *Address:* 18 Lancaster Rd., Wimbledon, S.W.19. *T.:* Wimbledon 3185. *Club:* Oxford and Cambridge. [*Died* 28 *Dec.* 1965.

PEREIRA, Sir Horace (Alvarez de Courcy), Kt., *cr.* 1950; *b.* 21 July 1879; *o. s.* of late Rt. Reverend H. H. Pereira, Bishop of Croydon; *m.* 1905, Christian Mary Isabel Gordon (*d.* 1953); one *s.* *Educ.:* Marlborough; Trinity College, Oxford. Called to Bar, Inner Temple, 1903; temporary Captain in Army, 1915-19. Senior Registrar of Principal Probate Registry, 1948-53 (Registrar 1924); retired Jan. 1953. *Address:* 48 Cheniston Gdns., W.8. *Club:* Athenæum. [*Died* 29 *Sept.* 1963.

PEREZ, Sir Joseph Leon Mathieu-, Kt., *cr.* 1955; *b.* 19 March 1896; *o. c.* of John Adhemar Perez and Leonie, *d.* of Leon Mathieu; *m.* 1920, Marie Andreide Peschier; one *d.* *Educ.:* St. George's Coll., Weybridge; London University (Middle Temple). Barrister-at-Law, 1917; Q.C. (Trinidad and Tobago); Chief Magistrate, 1936; Puisne Judge, 1941; Attorney-General, 1950. Chief Justice, Trinidad and Tobago, and President, West Indian Court of Appeal, 1952-58, retd. *Publication:* Digest of Law Reports of Trinidad and Tobago. *Recreations:* racing and fishing. *Address:* Port-of-Spain, Trinidad, W.I. *Clubs:* West Indian; Union (Trinidad); Trinidad Turf, Trinidad Yacht, Queen's Park Cricket. [*Died* 24 *Aug.* 1967.

PERIES, Sir (Pattiya Pathirannahalgae) Albert (Frederick), K.B.E. 1954; Speaker, House of Representatives, Ceylon, since 1965; *b.* 12 May 1900; *m.* 1926, Mary Cilesta Susan Silva; one *s.* three *d.* *Educ.:* St. Joseph's Coll., Colombo; Ceylon Law Coll., Colombo. Passed out as Lawyer,

1924; practised in Colombo and Chilaw Courts; Chm., Medapalata Village Cttee., Nattandiya, 1934-51. Speaker, 1951-56; elected to Nattandiya Seat, House of Representatives, 1947, 1952, 1960; Chairman of Committees and Deputy Speaker, 1948; Speaker, House of Representatives, Ceylon, 1951-56. *Recreations:* cricket, reading. *Address:* Mavila, Nattandiya, Ceylon.
[*Died* 21 *Sept.* 1967.

PERKINS, Frances, Hon. LL.D., University of Wisconsin and Amherst College; retired Government Official, U.S.A.; *d.* of Frederick Winslow and Susan W. Perkins; *m.* 1913, Paul Caldwell Wilson; one *d.* *Educ.:* Mt. Holyoke College; Columbia Univ. Executive Director of Voluntary Association for Social Work, 1908-19; Consumers' League; Committee on Safety; Maternity Center Assoc.; Council on Immigrant Education, etc. Member N.Y. State Industrial Commission (Chairman), 1919-29; Labor Commissioner, State of New York, 1929-33; Sec. of Labor, U.S.A., 1933-45; Commissioner, U.S. Civil Service Commission, 1946-53. Visiting Professor: Univ of Illinois, 1953; Salzburg Seminars (Amer. Subjects), 1956; Cornell Univ., 1957, 1958, 1959, 1960, 1961, 1962, 1963; Princeton Univ., 1961-62, *Publications:* People at Work, 1934; The Roosevelt I Knew, 1946. *Recreations:* usual: theatre, concerts, country life. *Address:* Ithaca, N.Y., U.S.A. *Clubs:* Cosmopolitan, Colony (New York); F Street (Washington).
[*Died* 14 *May* 1965.

PERKINS, Rev. Jocelyn Henry Temple, C.V.O. 1948 (M.V.O. (4th Cl.) 1938); F.S.A.; D.C.L. (Hon.) Bishops' Univ., Lennoxville, Canada, 1925; Minor Canon Emeritus of Westminster Abbey since 1958 (Sacrist and Minor Canon, 1899-1958, resigned); Pro-Precentor, 1940-46; Gen. Sec. British Columbia and Yukon Church Aid Society since 1910; *b.* Hendon, Mx. 5 Aug. 1870; *e. s.* of late John Robert Perkins, M.R.C.S., and Emma Kate, *d.* of late Jasper Holmes; *m.* 1896, Emma Zillah, *e. d.* of late Alfred Claude Taylor, M.D., of Colston House, Nottingham; two *s.* *Educ.:* Bedford School (Exhibitioner); Magdalen College, Oxford (History Exhibitioner). Leathersellers Company Exhibitioner, B.A.; 2nd Class Modern History, 1892; M.A. 1896; St. Stephen's House, Oxford; Cuddesdon College, 1894; Deacon, 1894; Priest, 1895; Organist and Assistant Master at St. Edward's School, Oxford, 1894-95; Minor Canon of Ely Cathedral, 1895-1900; Assistant Curate of St. Mary's, Ely, 1896-1900; Central Secretary of Melanesian Mission, 1900-01; Chaplain to Hospital for Ladies of Limited Means, 1900-1903; Organizing Secretary of the New Westminster and Kootenay Missionary Association, 1902-10; Secretary to the Archbishop of Canterbury's South African Education Fund, 1905-11; Chaplain at Highfield, Hendon, 1907-12; Secretary to the Central Council of Diocesan Conferences, 1901-07; Assistant Member of the College of St. Saviour, Southwark, 1903-19; Conductor of St. Margaret's Musical Society, 1902-15; Chairman of the Festival of English Church Art, 1930. Councillor, Westminster City Council, 1919-45. *Publications:* The Coronation Book, 1902, 2nd edition, 1911; The Honourable Order of the Bath, 1913, 2nd ed. 1920; Westminster Abbey, 1913, 2nd ed. 1920; Walks in Rouen, 1919, 2nd ed. 1920; Some French Cathedrals, 1925; The Ornaments of Westminster Abbey, 1933; Historic Occasions in Westminster Abbey (with Archdeacon Storr), 1933; The Cathedrals of Normandy, 1935; The Chapel of King Henry VII in Westminster Abbey and its High Altar, 1935; The Crowning of the Sovereign, 1937, 2nd ed. 1953; The Organs and Bells of Westminster Abbey, 1937; Westminster Abbey: The Empire's Crown, 1937; Westminster Abbey: Its Worship and Ornaments, Vol. I., 1938; Vol. II., 1939; Vol. III., 1952; A Wealth of Treasure, 1942; Westminster Abbey Benedictine Monastery and Collegiate Church, 1945; The Chapel of the Royal Air Force and the Battle of Britain Window, 1948; The Nurses' Chapel, 1954; 60 Years at Westminster Abbey, 1960; editor of Across the Rockies; frequent contributor to various London journals. *Recreations:* music, foreign travel, architecture. *Address:* 5 Little Cloister, Westminster Abbey, S.W. *T.:* Abbey 5121.
[*Died* 21 *April* 1962.

PERRIS, Ernest A.; former Editor of The Daily Chronicle, The Sunday Times; founder of the London News Agency; *s.* of late Rev. Henry Woods Perris; *m.*; one *d.* *Recreations:* travel, fishing.
[*Died* 6 *Oct.* 1961.

PERROTT, Arthur Finch, C.I.E. 1943; *b.* 13 Nov. 1892; *s.* of Finch Perrott and Jeanette Elisabeth Phillips; *m.* 1930, Marjorie Maude Croome; one *s.* one *d.* *Educ.:* Dulwich College. Joined Indian Police, 1912; Commandant, Frontier Constabulary, 1926; Political Agent, North Waziristan, 1928; Deputy Inspector-General of Police, Punjab, 1934; Inspector-General of Police, N.W.F.P., 1940; Chairman, Provincial Transport Authority and Provincial Rationing Authority, N.W.F.P., 1943; Provincial Motor Transport Controller, N.W.F.P., 1943. King's Police Medal, 1919. Bar to King's Police Medal, 1925; despatches, 1940; Indian Police Medal, 1945; retired, 1947; Ministry of Food, London, 1947-49. Field Organiser, Christchurch (N.Z.) Presbyterian Social Service Assoc., 1952-59. *Recreations:* tennis, hockey, golf. *Address:* 7 Cavendish Court, Bexhill-on-Sea, Sussex.
[*Died* 23 *Nov.* 1969.

PERROTT, Samuel Wright, B.A., M.A.I.; *b.* 1870; *s.* of Charles Leslie Perrott, Lawyer, Dublin; *m.* Charlotte Elizabeth (*d.* 1956), *d.* of Col. W. R. Mayo; one *s.* three *d.* *Educ.:* Trinity College, Dublin. Joined Eng. Dept., Lancashire and Yorkshire Railway, 1898. Contractor's Engineer on Meon Valley Railway in Hampshire, 1899-1901; Extension of Victoria Station, Manchester, Contractor's Engineer, 1901-05; Professor of Civil Engineering and Dean of the Faculty, University of New Brunswick, 1905-08; Professor of Civil Engineering, University of Liverpool, 1908-36. M.I.C.E. 1907, and M.E.I.C. *Publications:* Railway Surveying and Permanent Way; Surveying for Schools; Surveying for Young Engineers. *Address:* Highfriars, 6 Eastbury Ave., Northwood, Mx. *T.:* Northwood 25428.
[*Died* 6 *Feb.* 1964.

PERRY, Lieut.-Col. Ernest Middleton, C.B.E. 1919; T.D.; F.R.C.V.S.; Officier du Mérite Agricole (France); *b.* 1878; *s.* of S. Perry; *m.* 1904, Gladys L. Weston; two *s.* two *d.* *Educ.:* Whitgift. Major, R.F.A. (T.A.); Lt.-Colonel, R.A.V.C. (T.A.); served European War, 4 Aug. 1914-Nov. 1919 (despatches four times, C.B.E.). *Address:* Mannerhead, 20 Parkside, Wimbledon, S.W.19. *T.:* Wimbledon 0613.
[*Died* 3 *Feb.* 1963.

PERRY, Hon. Sir Frank (Tennyson), Kt. 1955; M.B.E. 1951; Chairman, Perry Engineering Co. Ltd., since 1938; Mem. for Central District No. 2, Legislative Council, South Australian Parliament, since 1947; *b.* 4 Feb. 1887; *s.* of late Rev. Isaiah Perry; *m.* 1911, Hildagarde Theresa, *d.* of Rev. F. W. Matschoss; one *d.* (and one *s.* one *d.* decd.). *Educ.:* State Schs.; Prince Alfred Coll. Mem., St. Peter's Coun., 1923-33 (Mayor, 1933); Mem., House of Assembly, S. Australian Parliament, for Dist. of East Torrens, 1933-38; Mem., State Cttee. C.S.I.R.O. 1930-61; Chm. Bd. of Area Management, S. Aust. Min. of Munitions, 1940-45; Mem. Adelaide Univ. Council, 1950-62; Chm., Ammunition Industry Advisory Cttee. Dept. of Defence Production (Commonwealth Govt.), 1952-55; Dep. Pres., Liberal and

Country League of S. Australia, 1952-55. Past President: Australian Metal Industries Assoc., 1943-48; Metal Industries Assoc. of S. Australia, 1940-48; Associated Chambers of Manufactures of Australia, 1942; S. Australian Chamber of Manufactures, 1940-41. *Address:* 415 Glynburn Road, Leabrook, South Australia. *T.:* 31 2007. *Club:* Adelaide (Adelaide).
[*Died* 20 *Oct.* 1965.

PERRY, Hon. Sir William, Kt., *cr.* 1946; LL.B.; New Zealand; Barrister and Solicitor; *b.* 23 Aug. 1885; *s.* of William Perry and Bridget Crowe; *m.* 1st, 1909, Eva Teresa Hurley (*d.* 1910); 2nd, 1917, Eva Sarah Bird; one *d.* *Educ.:* Wellington College; Victoria Univ. Coll., Wellington, N.Z. Executive N.Z. Rugby Football Union, Councillor Eastbourne Borough Council, 1914-15; served European War, 1915-18, Lieut. Wellington Infantry Regt. (wounded, lost right arm); Pres. Wellington Returned Services' Assn., 1921-22; Dominion Vice-Pres. N.Z. Returned Services' Assn., 1925-1935; Pres. 1935-43; Member N.Z. War Council, 1940-42; Minister of Armed Forces and War Co-ordination in N.Z. War Cabinet, 1943-45; Pres. N.Z. Defence League since 1936. *Recreation:* bowls. *Address:* 96 Bolton St., Wellington, N.Z. *T.A.:* Perypope, Wellington, N.Z. *T.:* 44-888 Wellington. *Club:* Wellesley (Wellington).
[*Died* 20 *March* 1968.

PERTWEE, Roland; dramatic author, novelist and short story writer; formerly an actor. *Plays:* Out to Win (with D. C. Calthrop), 1921; I Serve, 1922; revised The Creaking Chair, 1924; wrote Interference (with Harold Dearden), 1927; Hell's Loose, 1929; Heat Wave, 1929; Pursuit, 1930; A Prince of Romance, 1932; This Inconstancy (with J. Hastings Turner), 1933; To Kill a Cat (with Harold Dearden), 1939; Pink String and Sealing Wax, 1943; School for Spinsters, 1947; The Paragon (with Michael Pertwee); House on the Sand, 1948; Master of None (autobiography), 1938; The Camelion's Dish, 1940; The Islanders, 1950; Rough Water, 1951; Young Harry Tremayne, 1952; The Story of Willie Syme, 1957. Also wrote numerous film scripts including: Madonna of the Seven Moons, They were Sisters, Carnival. Television series (with Michael Pertwee) The Grove Family. *Address:* Appletrees, Spondon, Sandhurst, Kent. [*Died* 26 *April* 1963.

PETER, Bernard Hartley, C.B.E. 1943; M.I.E.E.; Royal Engineers (retired); *b.* 6 June 1885; 2nd *s.* of Claude Hurst Peter, Town Clerk, Launceston, Cornwall; *m.* Eileen Mary, *d.* of Francis Plunkett, Dublin. *Educ.:* Blundell's School, Tiverton; City and Guilds College, London. Central London Railway, 1902-3; District Railway & London Underground Railways, 1903-11; McKenzie Holland & Westinghouse Power Signal Co. Ltd. and Westinghouse Brake Co., 1911-47. [*Died* 28 *Dec.* 1970.

PETERKIN, Lieut.-Col. (Brevet Col.) Charles Duncan, C.B.E. 1919; T.D.; Advocate in Aberdeen from 1914, now retired; Treasurer Society of Avocates in Aberdeen, 1949-51; President 1952-54; *b.* 14 June 1887; *yr. s.* of late Henry Peterkin, Solicitor, Aberdeen; *m.* 1918, Netta Macgregor, adopted *d.* of late Sir Thomas Jaffrey, Bt.; no *c.* *Educ.:* Aberdeen Grammar School; Aberdeen University, M.A., LL.B. Served European War with 4th Bn. The Gordon Highlanders in France and Flanders as Capt. and Maj. 1915-17; Administrative Commandant of Railheads (Lieutenant-Colonel) 2nd Army, 1918; British Army of the Rhine, 1919 (despatches twice, C.B.E.); Commanded 4th Bn. The Gordon Highlanders (T.A.) 1924-28; Brevet Colonel, Feb. 1928. *Recreation:* golf. *Address:* 64 Rubislaw Den South, Aberdeen. *T.A.:* Peterkin, Aberdeen. *T.:* Aberdeen 34259. *Club:* Royal Northern (Aberdeen).
[*Died* 8 *May* 1962.

PETERS, Professor Bernard George, M.Sc. (Bristol), Ph.D. (London); Professor of Parasitology in the University of London since 1955; *b.* Isleworth, 21 Aug. 1903; *s.* of G. Peters, Bristol, and Mary (*née* Furber), Massachusetts; *m.* 1928, Vera May Beese; one *d.* *Educ.:* Bristol Grammar School; Bristol University. Min. of Agric. Research Scholar, Grocers' Company Research Scholar. Dep. Dir., Imperial Bureau of Agricultural Parasitology, 1929-32; Demonstrator, then Lectr., in Helminthology, London School of Hygiene and Tropical Medicine, 1932-36; Research Officer, Inst. of Agricultural Parasitology, St. Albans, 1936-43; Operational Research, Bomber Command H.Q., 1943-45; Principal Scientific Officer, Inst. of Agric. Parasitology and Rothamsted Experimental Station, 1942-52; Head of Nematology Dept., Rothamsted, 1952-55. Hon. A.R.C.S. *Publications:* numerous articles in learned jls., mainly Journal of Helminthology. *Recreation:* photography. *Address:* Rafters, Larch Avenue, Sunninghill, Berks.
[*Died* 9 *Sept.* 1967.

PETERS, Sir William, Kt., *cr.* 1947; C.M.G. 1928; formerly Senior U.K. Trade Commissioner in South Africa and Economic Adviser to U.K. High Commissioner; *b.* 1889; *s.* of James Seaton Peters, Beltonford, Dunbar; *m.* Margaret, *d.* of James Strachan, Newmachar, Aberdeenshire; two *s.* one *d.* *Educ.:* Aberdeen Grammar School; Aberdeen University. Commercial Secretary, 1919; Assistant Agent, British Commercial Mission to Russia, 1921-24; Commercial Secretary to British Mission, Moscow, 1924-27; Commercial Secretary, H.B.M. Legation, Stockholm, 1928-1929; United Kingdom Trade Commissioner in the Irish Free State, 1929-35. *Address:* 21 The Abbey, Romsey, Hants. *T.:* Romsey 2017.
[*Died* 5 *March* 1964.

PETHICK-LAWRENCE, 1st Baron, *cr.* 1945, of Peaslake; **Frederick William Pethick-Lawrence,** P.C. 1937; M.A.; Barrister-at-Law; *b.* 28 Dec. 1871; *s.* of Alfred Lawrence; *m.* 1st, 1901, Emmeline (*d.* 1954) (author of My Part in a Changing World, 1938), *d.* of late Henry Pethick, Weston-super-Mare; 2nd, 1957, Mrs Duncan McCombie, *d.* of late Sir John Craggs. *Educ.:* Eton (Captain of the Oppidans, 1891) Trinity College, Cambridge. 4th Wrangler, 1894; 1st Class Nat. Science Tripos, 1895; 2nd Smith's Prizeman, 1896; President of the Union, 1896; Adam Smith Prizeman for Economics, 1897; Fellow of Trinity, 1897; opposed S. African War; obtained a controlling interest in The Echo newspaper, 1901; edited the paper, 1902-5, and when it ceased paid the staff and the creditors out of his own pocket; editor of Labour Record and Review, 1905-7; joint-editor of Votes for Women, 1907-14; sentenced to nine months' imprisonment in 1912 for conspiracy in connection with one of the militant demonstrations of women suffragists; became Hon. Treasurer of U.D.C., 1916; contested South Aberdeen as peace-by-negotiation candidate, April 1917, and South Islington for Labour, 1922; M.P. (Lab.) West Leicester 1923-31; M.P. (Lab.) E. Edinburgh, 1935-45; Financial Secretary to the Treasury, 1929-1931; Member of Indian Round Table Conference, 1931; Secretary of State for India and for Burma, 1945-47; Trustee of the Nat. Library of Scotland, 1942-; Dep. chm. of Commonwealth Parl. Assoc., U.K. branch, 1945-52; Member Political Honours Scrutiny Committee, 1949-; Governor: Shakespeare Memorial Theatre; King Edward's School, Witley. *Publications:* Local Variations in Wages; Women's

Fight for the Vote; The Man's Share; A Levy on Capital; Why Prices Rise and Fall; Unemployment: The National Debt; (joint) The Heart of the Empire; Reformers' Year Book, 1904-8; This Gold Crisis, 1931; The Finance Chapter in Twelve Studies in U.S.S.R., 1932; The Money Muddle and the Way Out, 1933; Fate Has Been Kind (autobiography), 1943; (joint) Mahatma Gandhi, 1949; (joint) If I had my Time again, 1950; various pamphlets and articles on mathematics, economics, free trade, woman suffrage, etc. *Recreations:* lawn tennis, billiards. *Heir:* none. *Address:* 11 Old Square, Lincoln's Inn, W.C.2. *T.A.:* Pethlawro-Holb, London. *T.:* Holborn 7087. *Clubs:* Royal Aero, P.E.N. [*Died* 10 *Sept.* 1961.

PETRE, Major Henry Aloysius, D.S.O. 1916; M.C.; late Squadron Commander R.A.F.; *b.* 12 June 1884; *e. s.* of Sebastian Henry Petre and Elise, *d.* of W. Edmund Sibeth, *o.s.* of Hon. H. W. Petre of the Manor House, Writtle; *m.* 1929, Kathleen Coad, *d.* of Robert L. Defries, 173 Roxborough Street East, Toronto. *Educ.:* Mount St. Mary's College, Chesterfield. Admitted a solicitor, 1905; took up aviation, 1910; went to Australia to found Australian Flying Corps, Dec. 1912; served in Mesopotamia, 1915-16 (despatches 5 times, M.C., D.S.O.); transferred from Australian Flying Corps to R.A.F. 1918; retd. from R.A.F., 1919; joined firm of Blount Petre & Co., Solicitors; retd., 1958. Obtained British Glider Duration Record with flight of 3 hrs. 28 mins. 5 secs., 24 May 1931; Gliding Instructor to Air Training Corps during War of 1939-45. *Recreations:* aviation, ski-ing, skating. *Address:* 38 South Lodge, Grove End Road, N.W.8. *Clubs:* Royal Aero; Elstree Flying; London Gliding; Ski Club of Great Britain; Scottish Ski Club. [*Died* 24 *April* 1962.

PETRI, Egon, Hon. Mus. D., Manchester, 1938; Concert-Pianist and Piano Teacher; Professor at the Conservatory of Music, San Francisco, California, since 1958; *b.* 23 March 1881; *s.* of Henri Petri and Katharina Tornauer; *m.* 1905, Maria Schoen; two *s.* one *d.* *Educ.:* Leipzig; Dresden. At the age of 5, received violin instruction from mother, then from father; started piano when 7; when 11, pupil of Teresa Carreno; when 18, played 2nd violin in father's quartette and in Dresden Opera under Schuch; composition with Hermann Kretzchmar and Felix Draeseke, Organ with Uso Seifert, also French Horn, 1901 Master-class at Weimar, given by Ferruccio Busoni, friend of parents since 1886; first piano recitals in 1902; first appearance in London 1903 (under Sir Henry Wood); Professor at the Royal Manchester College of Music, 1905; Berlin, 1911; Zakopane (Poland), 1917; Professor Conservatorium at Basle, 1920; Prof Hochschule für Musik, Berlin, 1921; Tours in Russia, 1923-37; left Hochschule in 1925, settled in Zakopane; first tour in America, 1932. Pianist in Residence: Cornell Univ., Ithaca, N.Y., 1940-46; Mills College, Oakland, Calif., 1947-57; *Publications:* Bach's Piano Works (with Busoni and Mugellini); Kadenzas for Mozart-Concertos. *Address:* 391 Fairmount Ave., Oakland 11, California, U.S.A. [*Died* 27 *May* 1962.

PETRIE, Alfred Alexander Webster, C.B.E. 1945; M.D., F.R.C.P. (Lond.); F.R.C.S.E.; Consulting Physician in Psychological Medicine, Charing Cross Hosp.; late Medical Adviser, Mental Health, L.C.C.; *b.* 9 Oct. 1884; *s.* of Lt.-Colonel A. E. Petrie; *m.* 1926, Joyce Victoria Sarah Williams; two *s.* one *d.* *Educ.:* Portsmouth Grammar School; University of Edinburgh. Qualified Medicine, 1908; usual Hospital appointments; Temp. Captain R.A.M.C., 1915-19; late Deputy Medical Superintendent and Lecturer, Maudsley Hospital; formerly Physician Superintendent, Banstead Hospital for Nervous and Mental Disorders; formerly (W.E.) actg. Lt.-Col. R.A.M.C.; Ex-Pres. Royal Medico-Psychological Assoc.; Fellow and Ex-President Psychiatric Section Royal Society Medicine. *Publications:* Chapters on Pathology and Bacteriology of War Wounds in Mull's Surgery in War; Chapters Character and Conduct, Lancet Book on Mental Disorders, 1926, etc.; (jointly) Psychiatric Section Medical Progress, 1947. *Address:* Green Court, 1 Banstead Rd., Ewell, Surrey; Glenton, Summerley, Bognor Regis. [*Died* 5 *Oct.* 1962.

PETRIE, Sir David, K.C.M.G., *cr.* 1945; Kt., *cr.* 1929; C.I.E. 1915; C.V.O. 1922; C.B.E. 1919 (O.B.E. 1918); Indian Police, retired 1936; Member Public Service Commission, India, 1931-32, Chairman 1932-36; 2nd *surv. s.* of late Thomas Petrie; *b.* Inveraven, 1879; *m.* 1920, Edris Naida (*d.* 1945), *y. d.* of late W. H. Elliston Warrall. *Educ.:* Aberdeen University; M.A. 1900. Entered Indian Police, 1900; Punjab Police, 1900-3; seconded for service with Samana Rifles (Kohat Border Military Police), being successively Quartermaster and Adjutant, 1904-8; Assistant to Deputy Inspect.-Gen. of Police, C.I.D., Punjab, 1909-10; Assistant Director of Criminal Intelligence, Govt. of India, 1911-12; United Service Institution of India Gold Medal Essay, 1911; King's Police Medal, 1914; Additional Supt. of Police, Delhi, 1912-14; on special duty in Far East with Home Department, Govt. of India, 1915-19; on Staff of Duke of Connaught, India, 1921; on Staff of Prince of Wales, India, 1921-22; Senior Supt. of Police, Lahore, 1923; Member of the Royal (Lee) Commission on the Public Services in India, 1923-24; Director, Intelligence Bureau, Home Department, Government of India, 1924-31; Chairman, Indian Red Cross Society and St. John Ambulance Association, and Chief Commissioner for the Empire of India of St. John Ambulance Brigade Overseas, 1932-36; served under Colonial Office in Palestine, Dec. 1937-Jan. 1938; served Intelligence Corps, 1940-45, as 2nd Lt., Act. Col. and local Brig.; Knight of Grace of St. John of Jerusalem, 1933; American Legion of Merit (Commander); Czechoslovak Order of the White Lion, Cl. III.; Commander Order of Orange Nassau with Swords. *Recreations:* shooting, fishing. *Address:* c/o Lloyds Bank, Ltd., 6 Pall Mall, S.W.1. *Club:* Oriental. [*Died* 7 *Aug.* 1961.

PEYTON, Sir Algernon, 7th Bt., *cr.* 1776; late Lt.-Col. XI (P.A.O.) Hussars; *b.* 4 Jan. 1889; *s.* of 6th Bt. and Ida (*d.* 1938), *d.* of James Mason, Eynsham Hall, Oxfordshire; *S.* father 1916; *m.* 1916, Joan Stratford, *d.* of late John Stratford Dugdale, K.C.; two *d.* (and one *s.* killed in action 1945). *Educ.:* Eton; R.M.C., Sandhurst. Owns about 2000 acres. Served European War, 1914-18 (wounded). D.L. 1936, J.P. 1921, High Sheriff of Oxon, 1928. *Heir:* none. *Address:* Swift's House, Bicester, Oxfordshire. *Club:* Cavalry. [*Died* 14 *March* 1962 (*ext.*).

PFEIL, Leonard Bessemer, O.B.E. 1947; F.R.S. 1951; D.Sc.; F.I.M.; A.R.S.M.; Vice-Chairman, The International Nickel Co. (Mond) Ltd.; formerly Man., Development and Research Dept.; Dir. Henry Wiggin & Co. Ltd.; *b.* 13 Mar. 1898; *m.* 1924, Brenda Beatrice Butler; two *s.* *Educ.:* St. Dunstan's College, Catford; The Royal School of Mines, London. Lecturer, University College of Swansea, 1921-30; Assistant Manager, Development and Research Department The Mond Nickel Co. Ltd., 1930-45. *Publications:* numerous papers published by learned societies. *Address:* Hillcroft, Rose Walk, Purley, Surrey. *T.:* Uplands 4417 [*Died* 16 *Feb.* 1969.

PHAIR, Rt. Rev. John Percy; *b.* 1 Nov. 1876; *s.* of Peter Phair, Ram Park, Castlerea; *m.* 1st, Alice Maud (*d.* 1945), *d.* of

Edward Nevill Banks, C.E., Belfast; one *s.* three *d.*; 2nd, 1958, Pauline Beryl, *d.* of Benjamin Fawcett Eustace, J.P., Dublin. *Educ.:* Ranelagh Sch., Athlone; Trinity Coll., Dublin. Ordained 1900; Curate of Conwall, 1900-1902; St. Matthias, Dublin, 1902-06; Monkstown, 1906-09; Incumbent of St. Catherine's, Dublin, 1909-12; Christ Church, Leeson Park, 1912-23; Chaplain to Lord Lieut., 1913-21; Chaplain to Archbishop of Dublin and Canon of Christ Church Cathedral, Dublin, 1920-23; Rural Dean of Rathdowney, 1926-40; Dean of Ossory and Rector of Kilkenny, 1923-40; Canon of Aghold in Leighlin Cathedral, 1925-40; Examining Chaplain to Bishop of Ossory 1938-40; Bishop of Ossory, Ferns and Leighlin, 1940-61. *Address:* The Old Rectory, Kilbride, Carlow, Eire. *Club:* University (Dublin). [*Died* 28 *Dec.* 1967.

PHELAN, Edward Joseph; retired Civil Servant; *b.* Tramore, Co. Waterford, Ireland, 25 July 1888; *s.* of Thomas Edward Phelan, Master Mariner; *m.* 1940, Fernande Crousaz. *Educ.:* St. Francis Xavier's Coll. and Univ. of Liverpool. B.A., B.Sc. (Hons. Physics), M.Sc. Entered British Civil Service, 1911. Served in B. of Trade, Min. of Labour, Foreign Office. Mem., Mission to Russia, 1918; Mem., Brit. Delegn. to the Peace Conference, 1918. Sec., Organising Cttee. of Washington Labour Conf.; successively Chief of Div., Asst. Dir., Dep. Dir., and Director-Gen. of I.L.O.; kept I.L.O. in active operation during War, 1941-44; secured adoption of Declaration of Philadelphia and its insertion in revised Constitution of I.L.O. and obtained recognition of I.L.O. as a Specialised Agency of United Nations. Retired, 1948. Hon. LL.D., N.U.I.; Hon. D.Sc.: Laval Univ., Univ. of Montreal. Mem., Mexican Acad. of Labour Law and Social Legislation. Commandeur de la Légion d'Honneur (France); Commander, Order of Southern Cross (Brazil); Grand Officer, Order of Aztec Eagle, Mexico; Hon. Citizen of Mexico City. *Publications:* Yes and Albert Thomas (biog. study of first Dir. of I.L.O.), 1936; numerous reports and articles on international questions. *Address:* La Pernette, Chemin de la Voile, Genthod, Geneva, Switzerland. [*Died* 15 *Sept.* 1967.

PHELAN, Maj.-Gen. Frederick Ross; *see* Addenda: II.

PHIBBS, Sir Charles, Kt., *cr.* 1936; *b.* 27 May 1878; *s.* of Charles Phibbs, Doobeg, Bunnanadden, Co. Sligo; *m.* 1908, Beatrice Gwendoline, *d.* of Walter Lanyon Nickels, Chenotrie Noctorum, Birkenhead; two *s.* *Educ.:* Rossall. Farming and Land Agency work in Ireland, 1894-1922; Farming and public work in Merioneth since 1922; Conservative and National Government Candidate in Merioneth, 1926-35; Sheriff of Merionethshire, 1938. Alderman, Merioneth C.C., 1949, Chairman, 1950-51. J.P. County of Merioneth, now retired. O.St.J. *Address:* Plas Gwynfryn, Llanbedr, Merioneth. *T.A.:* Llanbedr, Merioneth. *T.:* Llanbedr 205. *Club:* Farmers'. [*Died* 2 *July* 1964.

PHILBY, Captain Ralph Montague, C.I.E. 1939; R.I.N. (retired); *b.* 1 April 1884; *e. s.* of H. M. Philby; *m.* 1910, Katharine Mary, (*d.* 1957), *er. d.* of Dr. W. Kebbell, Brisbane, Australia; one *d.* (one *s.* decd.). *Educ.:* St. Paul's Sch., London; H.M.S. Worcester. Served in sailing ships (Barque, Inverclyde of Aberdeen); Sub. Lieut. R.I.N. late Royal Indian Marine, 1906; Cmdr. 1922; Capt. 1929; Nautical Adviser to the Government of India from 1935; retd. from R.I.N. 1939; served throughout European War afloat and ashore (Persian Gulf Medal with Clasp, 1914-15 Star, Allied and Victory Medals); Inspector of Lighthouses and Light vessels etc. in the Persian Gulf, 1921-22, while in command of R.I.M.S. Nearchus; held administrative posts in Mercantile Marine dept. etc. in ports of Madras, Mandalay, Rangoon, Aden and Bombay. War of 1939-45: re-employed from retired list for service in the R.I.N. and Indian Observer Corps. *Recreations:* bridge, walking, gardening. *Address:* 42 Gordon Road, Camberley, Surrey. [*Died* 24 *Feb.* 1969.

PHILIPPS, Lt.-Col. Sir Grismond (Picton), Kt., *cr.* 1953; C.V.O. 1945; Lord Lieutenant of Carmarthenshire since 1954; Capt. Grenadier Guards, retd.; *b.* 20 May 1898; *o. s.* of late Major Grismond Philipps, Cwmgwili, Carmarthen; *m* 1925, Lady Marjorie Joan Mary Wentworth-Fitzwilliam (from whom he obtained a divorce, 1949), 2nd *d.* of 7th Earl Fitzwilliam; one *s.* 2nd Lt. Grenadier Guards, 1917; Capt 1925; retired pay, 1933; Bt. Major, 1941; Lt.-Col. comdg. 4th Bn. The Welch Regt. (T.A.), 1939 (Hon. Col., 1960-64). Member: Court of Governors and Council National Library of Wales; The National Museum of Wales County Council, 1945-52; Chm. Historic Buildings Council for Wales, 1955-. D.L. 1935, J.P. 1938, C.C. 1946, Vice-Lieut. 1936-54, Carmarthenshire. *Address:* Cwingwili, Bronwydd Arms, S. Wales. *T.:* Carmarthen 6229. *Club:* Guards. [*Died* 8 *May* 1967.

PHILIPPS, Sir Richard F.; *see* Foley-Philipps.

PHILLIMORE, Colonel Reginald Henry, C.I.E. 1944; D.S.O. 1918; *b.* 19 June 1879; *s.* of Admiral Henry Bouchier Phillimore, C.B., and Anne Ellen Bourdillon; *m.* 1910, Eileen Elizabeth Crosthwait; no *c.* *Educ.:* Westminster School; R.M.A., Woolwich. 2nd Lieut. Royal Engineers, 1898; served in India. 1900; posted Survey of India, 1903; served British Expeditionary Force, France, Aug. 1915; Mediterranean Expeditionary Force, Salonica, March 1916-1919 (despatches four times, D.S.O., Brevet Lt.-Colonel); rejoined Survey of India, 1919; Officiated Surveyor-General of India, 1931; Colonel, 1923; retired, 1934; re-employed, Dec. 1940, as Captain Royal Engineers, General Staff, G.H.Q., Simla, India; resigned Feb. 1942 and re-employed Survey of India, Delhi, India, till May 1946. *Publication:* Historical Records Survey of India, Vol. I. 18th Century, 1946, Vol. II. 1800-15, 1950, Vol. III. 1815-30, 1954, Vol. IV. 1830-43, 1958; Vol. V. 1844-61, 1964. *Recreation:* historical research. *Address:* c/o Survey of India, Dehra Dun, U.P. India. *Club:* United Service. [*Died* 30 *Oct.* 1964.

PHILLIPS, Major-Gen. Sir Farndale, K.B.E. 1957 (C.B.E. 1953); C.B. 1955; D.S.O. 1944; President, British Trawlers' Federation, since 1957; *b.* 11 Sept. 1905; *s.* of Major E. S. Phillips; *m.* 1938, Lovering Catherine Russell, *widow* of John Edward Russell, Auckland, New Zealand; one *s.* *Educ.:* Colchester Royal Grammar School. Entered R.M., 1923; Lieutenant 1926; served in various ships, 1926-29; Adjt., Plymouth Div. R.M. 1931-34; H.M.S. Sussex, 1934-37; Capt. 1935; H.M.S. Rodney, 1937; H.M.S. Achilles (N.Z.) 1937-39; H.M.S. Courageous (torpedoed), 1939; Staff College, Camberley, 1940; G.S.O.2, 1st Div. 1941, G.S.O. 1, R.M. Div. 1942; 47 Commando, 1943-44; Comdr. 116 Inf. Bde. R.M. 1945; Fleet Royal Marine Officer, British Pacific Fleet, 1945-46; Major 1945; Lieut.-Col. 1948; Col. 1950; Maj.-Gen. 1952; Jt. Services Staff Coll., 1947-48; Sch. of Amphibious Warfare, 1949-50; Comdr. 3 Commando Bde. R.M., 1951-52. Malaya; Commander, Portsmouth Group, Royal Marines, 1952-54; Chief of Amphibious Warfare, 1954-57. Knight Comdr. Order of Orange

Nassau, 1947. *Address:* The Old Vicarage, Northorpe, Gainsborough, Lincs. *T.:* Scotter 218. *Club:* United Service.
[*Died* 25 *Feb.* 1961.

PHILLIPS, Colonel Geoffrey Francis, C.B.E. 1919; D.S.O. 1915; late Duke of Cornwall's Light Infantry; *b.* 3 May 1880; *o. surv. s.* of late Mrs. Hawtin Phillips; *m.* 1920, Pamela, *y. d.* of late Arthur Ridley; two *d.* Entered Army, 1900; Capt., 1910; Major, 1915; employed with King's African Rifles, 1906-12; Staff Capt., 1914; Brigade Major, 1915; served East Africa, 1906-10 (medal with clasp); European War, 1914-18 (despatches seven times, wounded, D.S.O., Bt. Lt.-Col.); General Staff Officer 2nd Grade, General Headquarters, East Africa, 1916; General Staff Officer, 1st Grade, 1916; Bt. Lt.-Col., 1917; Commandant King's African Rifles, 1919-23; retired pay, 1924. *Address:* 35 Cranmer Court, Sloane Avenue, S.W.3. [*Died* 18 *Jan.* 1968.

PHILLIPS, George Godfrey, C.B.E. 1943; *b.* 7 June 1900; *s.* of late George Charles Phillips, M.D., Grantley, Wotton-under-Edge, Gloucestershire, and late Ethel Nancy Phillips (*née* Mosley); *m.* 1932, Betty Mary, *d.* of late Trevor Bright, Friar's Gate, Freshford, and of Mary Lindsay Bright; two *s.* one *d.* *Educ.:* Harrow School; Trinity College, Cambridge (M.A., LL.M.). Called to the Bar, Gray's Inn, 1925; practised at the Bar, 1925-31; Prosecuting Counsel to G.P.O., Midland Circuit, 1931; Agent and Counsel for H.M. Govt. before Anglo-Mexican Special Claims Commn., Mexico City, 1931; joined Secretariat, Shanghai Municipal Council, 1934, Sec., 1936, Comr. Gen., 1940; returned to England, 1942. Solicitor, 1945, Partner in Linklaters and Paines, 1945-53; re-admitted to the Bar, 1955. Dep. Chm. Quarter Sessions, Lindsey (Lincs.), 1946-63; Man. Dir., Lazard Brothers & Co. Ltd., 1953-1964. Director: Equity and Law Life Assurance Society Ltd. (late Chm.); English Electric Co. Ltd.; Winterbottom Trust Ltd.; Chloride Electric Storage Co. Ltd.; Birmingham Small Arms Co. Ltd.; Longmans, Green & Co. Ltd. *Publications:* (joint) Wade and Phillips Constitutional Law, 1931; Ed. 14th and 15th edns. of Kenny's Outlines of Criminal Law, 1933 and 1936. *Address:* 135A Ashley Gardens, S.W.1. *Club:* White's. [*Died* 24 *Oct.* 1965.

PHILLIPS, Rev. Godfrey Edward, B.A. (London), M.A. (Oxon.), D.D. (Glasgow); *b.* 4 March 1878; *s.* of Edward and Clara Phillips, Birmingham; *m.* 1902, Clarissa May Stevens (*d.* 1961), two *s.* *Educ.:* King Edward's School, Birmingham; Mansfield College, Oxford. Missionary in India, chiefly Madras and Bangalore, 1901-26; Foreign Secretary London Missionary Soc., 1926-36; Professor of Missions, Selly Oak Colleges, Birmingham, 1936-45; ordained C. of E. 1945. Hon. D.D. Glasgow Univ., 1948. *Publications:* The Outcaste's Hope, 1911; The Ancient Church and Modern India, 1919; Doings and Dreams, 1926; The Missionary's Job, 1928; Our Sixth Form in India, 1930; (with C. M. Phillips) Back to India, 1934; The Untouchables' Quest, 1936; The Gospel in the World, 1939; The Old Testament in the World Church, 1942; The Transmission of Christian Faith and Life, 1947; The Religions of the World, 1948; The Imagery of the Pilgrim Psalms, 1957. *Address:* Jersey House, The Bishops Avenue, N.2. *T.:* Speedwell 6443. [*Died* 29 *Nov.* 1963.

PHILLIPS, Vice-Admiral Sir Henry Clarmont, K.B.E., *cr.* 1946; C.B. 1944. Served European War, 1914-18; Capt. 1932; Rear-Admiral, 1942; Vice-Adm. 1945 (retd.). *Address:* Littlefield, Rowledge, Farnham, Surrey. [*Died* 26 *Aug.* 1968.

PHILLIPS, Hubert; Author, Journalist and Broadcaster; *b.* 13 Dec. 1891; *s.* of Arthur Phillips and Alice Ellen Heritage; *m.* 1st, 1919, Margery Mary Davies (*d.* 1960); one *s.* decd.; 2nd, 1962, Madeleine Bartlett. *Educ.:* Sexey's Sch., Bruton; Merton College, Oxford. Postmaster in Modern History; Cl. 1 Mod. Hist. 1913; Dip. Ec. and Pol. Sc. (Distinction), 1914; served in Army, 1914-19 (despatches twice; Actg. Lt.-Col. 1918, Essex Regt.) Tutor in History, Ordination Test School, Knutsford, 1919; Head of Dept. of Economics, Bristol University, 1919, also Dir. Extra-Mural Studies, 1923; rep. Univ. on Bd. of Educn.'s Adult Educ. Cttee., etc.; Dir. Liberal Research Dept., 1924; Economic Adviser and Sec. Liberal Industrial Enquiry, 1926; contested Wallasey, 1929; Sec. and Adviser to Liberal Parliamentary Party, 1929; Research Officer Telephone Development Assoc., 1929; guest lecturer, Univ. of Minnesota, 1930; Chairman, Radical Policy Committee, 1931. Editorial staff, News Chronicle, 1930-54; contributed Dogberry's Column, 1931-52; Bridge Editor, 1932; created Inspector Playfair (problems in detection), 1936; principal leader-writer, 1942-46; Caliban of the New Statesman, 1930-38, and subsequently, of the Law Journal. Contributor, at various times, to: Evening News; Evening Standard; Star; Daily Telegraph; Lilliput; Picture Post; Lady, etc. Bridge: founded Duplicate Bridge Control Bd.; English Bridge Union; London and Home Counties Contract Bridge Assoc.; Pres., Nat. Bridge Assoc.; rep. England in Internat. Matches, (Capt. 1937-38). Numerous Broadcasts (Round Britain Quiz, etc.) and Television Programmes. Theme Convenor, Lion and Unicorn Pavilion, Festival of Britain. Gilchrist Lecturer, 1949. *Publications:* under various pseudonyms, about 200 Crime-Detection Stories; about ninety books now out of print, including: The Week-End Problems Book; The Elements of Contract; How to Play Bridge; Ask Me Another; Try This One; Question Time. Books not out of print: Bridge is only a Game; Making Bridge Pay; Bridge with Mr. Goren; Profitable Poker. Hubert Phillips Asks You (2 Vols.); Compendium of Indoor Games (Vol. I: Card Games; Vol. II: Party Games; Vol. III: Chess (Joint); Vol. IV: Games of Skill for Two); The Penguin Hoyle; Pools and the Public (based on evidence given to Royal Commission on Gaming, Betting and Lotteries). Selected Verse. *Autobiography:* Journey to Nowhere, 1960 (further vols. planned but never written). Editor, Ptarmigan Books. *Recreations: semper aliquid novi.* *Address:* Staffordway, 25 Vincent Road, Selsey, Sussex. [*Died* 9 *Jan.* 1964.

PHILLIPS, Major-General Sir Leslie Gordon, K.B.E., *cr.* 1946 (C.B.E. 1938); C.B. 1943; M.C.; *b.* 11 Feb. 1892; *s.* of late Benjamin Phillips; *m.* 1914, Maud Constantia, *d.* of late J. Wells Thatcher; two *d.* *Educ.:* Bedford; Sandhurst. 2nd Lt. Worcs. Regt., 1911; R. Signals, 1920; Col. 1934; Maj.-Gen. 1940; served European War, France and Belgium, 1914-18 (M.C., despatches thrice); Waziristan Operations, 1936-37 (despatches twice); Director of Signals, 1943-46; retd. 1946. Col.-Comdt. Royal Signals, 1946-53. *Address:* Rosemary, Hartley Wintney, Hants. *T.:* Hartley Wintney 2220.
[*Died* 19 *March* 1966.

PHILLIPS, Mrs. McGrigor; (Dorothy Una Ratcliffe), F.R.A.S., F.R.G.S., F.R.H.S.; Hon. LL.D. Leeds University, 1955; Una O'r Dyffrynoedd (National Eisteddfod of Wales, August 1933); Vice-Pres. of Yorkshire Dialect Society; Freeman of Arachova, North Greece, 1946; Chevalier of the Order of King George I, 1949; *e. d.* of Mr. and Mrs. Benson Clough, The Inner Temple, London, and of Oxshott, Surrey; *m.* 1932,

Noel McGrigor Phillips (*d.* 1943); *m.* 1947, Alfred Phillips (*d.* 1965). Temple Sowerby Manor given to Nat. Trust, 1950. *Publications:* Singing Rivers (verse), 1922; Dale Dramas (plays), 1923; Nathaniel Baddeley, Bookman (play), 1924; The Shoeing of Jerry-go-Nimble (verse), 1926; Dale Lyrics (verse), 1926; Dale Folk (prose), 1927; Fairings (prose), 1928; Nightlights (verse), 1929; The Gone Away (three-act play), 1930; Lillilows (character sketches), 1931; Gypsy Dorelia (three-act play), 1932; Dale-Courtin' (dialect lyrics); South African Summer (travel essays), 1933; Lapwings and Laverocks (dale sketches), 1934; Equatorial Dawn (Travel), 1936; Swallow of the Sea (a 40-ton Yawl in Northern Waters: prose), 1937; The Smuggling Hob and other One-Act Plays, 1938; News of Persephone (travel), 1939; From all the Airts (Verse), 1940; What Do They Know of Yorkshire (character sketches), 1940; Grecian Glory (travel), 1941; Mrs. Buffey in Wartime, 1942; Rosemary Isle (verse for children), 1944; Delightsome Land, 1945; Island - of - the - Little Years, 1947; The Daystar, 1947; Little Gypsy in the Wood, 1948; Until that Dawn, 1949; Icelandic Spring (travel), 1950; The Queen Rides (play), 1951; Up Dale (selected verse), 1952; Jingling Lane (3-act play), 1954; Over hill over dale (verse), 1956; Lady of a Million Daffodils (Recollections), 1958; Yorkshire Lyrics (collected verse), 1960; The Cranesbill Caravan, 1961; The Letter (one-act play), 1964; Hazelthwaite Hall (9 one-act plays), 1966. Editor, Northern Broadsheet. *Recreations:* yachting, caravaning. *Address:* Angus House, West Bay, North Berwick, East Lothian. [*Died* 20 *Nov.* 1967.

PHILLIPS, Montague Fawcett, F.R.A.M., F.R.C.O., Composer; *b.* 13 Nov. 1885; *s.* of Richard L. Phillips; *m.* Clara Butterworth, singer; one *s.* one *d.* *Educ.:* R. Acad. of Music. Henry Smart and Macfarren Scholarships for Composition, also Battison Haynes Prize for Prelude and Fugue for Organ, R.A.M. Club Prize for Organ Playing and Improvisation, and the Chas. Lucas Memorial Medal for the composition of Symphonic Scherzo for Orchestra. *Compositions:* Symphony in C Minor, 1911; Heroic Overture, 1914; Phantasy for Violin and Orchestra, 1912; Overture Boadicea, 1907. The Death of Admiral Blake, for Baritone solo, chorus, and orchestra. String Quartet. A Romantic Light Opera, The Rebel Maid; Two Pianoforte Concertos, 1907 and 1919; The Song of Rosamond, Scena for Soprano and Orchestra, 1922; Suite for Orchestra, In Maytime, 1923; Light Opera, The Golden Triangle; A Hillside Melody for Orchestra, 1924; Two Light Orchestral Pieces: Violetta (Air de Ballet) and Arabesque, 1926; Suite for Orchestra, Dance Revels, 1927; Balletto (No. 1) for Orchestra, 1928; A Forest Melody for Orchestra, 1929; Miniature Suite, Village Sketches, 1932; Suite for Orchestra, The World in the Open Air, 1933; Harlequin Dance for Orchestra, 1933; Three Country Pictures for Orchestra, 1936; A Surrey Suite for Orchestra, 1936; Overture, Charles II, 1936; A Moorland Idyll, for Orchestra, 1936; Overture, Revelry, 1937; Empire March for Orchestra, 1941; Sinfonietta for Orchestra 1943; Festival Overture, 1944; Overture, Hampton Court, 1954; over 150 songs; numerous part songs and piano pieces. *Recreation:* golf. *Address:* Clare Cottage, Clare Hill, Esher, Surrey. *T.:* Esher 62419. *Club:* R.A.M. [*Died* 4 *Jan.* 1969.

PHILLIPS, Morgan Walter; General Secretary, British Labour Party, 1944-62, retd.; *b.* 18 June 1902; *e. s.* of William Phillips; *m.* 1930, Norah, *o. d.* of William and Catherine Lusher; one *s.* one *d.* *Educ.:* elementary school, Bargoed, S. Wales; London Labour College. Sec. Bargoed Local Labour Party, 1923-25; Chm. Bargoed Steam Coal Lodge of S. Wales Miners Fedn., 1924-26; Sec./Agent: W. Fulham Constituency, Labour Party, 1928-30, Whitechapel, 1934-37; Mem. Fulham Borough Council and Chm. of its Finance Cttee., 1934-37; Examr. for Nat. Council of Labour Colls., 1930-32. Joined Labour Party Head Office Staff, 1937; Propaganda Officer, 1937-40; Eastern Counties Organiser, 1940-41; Sec., Research Dept., 1941-44; Chm. Socialist Internat., 1948-57. *Publications:* East meets West; various political and economic pamphlets. *Recreations:* bowls, football, snooker and reading. *Address:* 115 Rannoch Road, W.6. [*Died* 15 *Jan.* 1963.

PHILLIPS, Lieut.-Colonel Noel Clive, D.S.O. 1917; M.C. 1916; Chairman of the Wolseley Engineering Ltd.; *b.* 30 July 1883; *e. surv. s.* of late P. S. Phillips, J.P., Crumlin Hall, Mon., and Tyn-y-Graig, Builth, Breconshire; *m.* 1922, Irene Mary, *d.* of late Dr. Arthur Pallant; no *c.* *Educ.:* Marlborough. Commission, 1901, 3rd Bn. Loyal North Lancashire Regt.; served S. Africa, 1901-03 (Queen's Medal, 5 clasps); resigned Commission, 1904; joined Bombay Burmah Trading Corporation at Rangoon, 1904; Recommissioned 3rd L.N. Lancs., 1915; served 1st Bn. L.N. Lancs. Regt., 1st Div. B.E.F., France, 1915-18, Officer Commanding, 1916-18 (D.S.O., M.C., despatches); O.C. 49th R.D. Battalion, 1918-19; resigned Commission, 1920, with rank Lieut.-Colonel; returned to Burma; Manager, Bombay Burmah Trading Corporation; left Burma, 1931; High Sheriff Radnorshire, 1938; Member Radnor County Agricultural Executive Committee, 1942-49. D.L., 1943-55, J.P. 1942, C.C. 1940-46, Radnorshire. *Recreations:* fishing, shooting. *Address:* Perrycroft, Colwall, nr. Malvern, Worcs. *Clubs:* M.C.C., Farmers'. [*Died* 15 *Aug.* 1961.

PHILLIPS, Major-Gen. Owen Forbes, C.M.G. 1919; D.S.O. 1917; *b.* 9 June 1882; *s.* of late A. O. H. Phillips. Served European War, 1914-19 (despatches, D.S.O., C.M.G.); commanded Field Troops 4th Military District S.A. and District Base Commandant, 1926-29; Director of Ordnance Services, 1929-1932; Commander 1st Division and Base Commandant 2nd District Base, 1933-34; Quarter-Master General, G.H.Q., Melbourne, 1934-39; Inspector of Coastal Anti-Aircraft Defences, Australia, 1939-40. *Address:* Beaumaris, Melbourne, Australia. [*Died* 15 *May* 1966.

PHILLIPS, Sir Philip David, Kt. 1967; C.M.G. 1964; M.M. 1918; Q.C. (Vict.) 1946; retired as Chairman, Commonwealth Grants Commission, Australia (1960-1966); *b.* 22 March 1897; *s.* of Morris Mondle Phillips, Melbourne; *m.* 1st; two *d.*; 2nd, 1949, Olive Catherine, *d.* of Henry Rosenthal, Melbourne. *Educ.:* Melbourne C. of E. Gram. Sch.; Melbourne University. M.A., LL.M., 1922. Admitted to Vict. Bar, 1923; ret. 1957. Chm., Vict. Transport Regulation Board, 1934-37; Dep. Chm., Commonwealth Liquid Fuel Control Board, 1940-45. S. Korman Special Lecturer, Melb. Univ., 1957-. Chm. of Directors, Automotive & General Engineers Ltd., 1964. *Recreations:* lawn-bowls, woodwork. *Address:* Velden, Cromwell St., Eltham, Victoria, Australia. *T.:* 4399015. *Clubs:* University (Sydney); Royal Automobile (Melbourne); Heidelberg Golf. [*Died* 19 *Sept.* 1970.

PHILLIPS, Robert Randal, Hon. A.R.I.B.A.; journalist; editor of Homes and Gardens from founding in 1919 till 1941; formerly for many years editor of The Architects' and Builders' Journal and The Architectural Review and general editor of publications issued by Technical Journals, Ltd.; English correspondent of The Architectural Forum, Boston; established Details, 1908; *b.* Monmouthshire, 1878; *m.* 1911; one *d.* *Educ.:* Clytha College,

Newport; École Industrielle, Lausanne. Joined Royal Engineers as a Sapper, April 1917; served in France, March 1918-Feb. 1919; joined Ministry of Works and Buildings (Directorate of Post-War Building), 1941; retd. from Min. of Works (Library), Feb. 1955. *Publications:* The Servantless House, 1920 (2nd ed. 1923); The Book of Bungalows, 1920 (3rd ed. 1926); Furnishing the House, 1921; The House Doctor, 1923; The House you Want, 1923; Small Family Houses, 1924; Small Country Houses of To-day, 1925; The Modern English House, 1927; The Modern English Interior, 1928; The £1000 House, 1929; The House Improved, 1931; Houses for Moderate Means, 1936 (3rd ed. 1949). *Recreations:* punting and sculling. *Address:* 6 Homefield Road, Chiswick, London, W.4. *T.:* Chiswick 7113.
[*Died* 17 *Jan.* 1967.

PHILLIPS, Sidney Hill, C.B. 1941; *b.* 8 April 1882; *s.* of late Godfrey Phillips, J.P., Risca, Mon.; *m.* 1917, Isobel Gladys Custance; one *s.* one *d.* *Educ.:* Cheltenham College; St. John's College, Cambridge. Bracketed third Wrangler, 1903; 1st class Natural Science Tripos, 1904; entered Admiralty as Clerk Class 1, 1904; Principal Assistant Secretary, Admiralty, 1936-42. *Address:* 9 Park Place, Wadebridge, Cornwall.
[*Died* 28 *Feb.* 1962.

PHILLIPS, Lieut.-Colonel Thomas Richmond, C.M.G. 1917; late R.A.; D.L. Surrey, 1929; *b.* 24 Dec. 1866; *m.* Hilda, *d.* of late Fred Mellersh, banker, Godalming; one *s.* one *d.* *Educ.:* Clifton College. Entered R.A. 1886; Capt. 1896; Major, 1904; Lt.-Col. 1914; retired, 1920; Adjutant Militia, 1898-1903; served European War, 1914-18 (C.M.G., despatches four times). *Address:* Downderry, Godalming, Surrey. *Club:* M.C.C.
[*Died* 5 *June* 1963.

PHILLIPS, Sir Thomas Williams, G.B.E., *cr.* 1946 (K.B.E., *cr.* 1934; C.B.E. 1918); K.C.B., *cr.* 1936 (C.B 1922); Commander Order of the Crown (Belgium); Hon. LL.D. (Wales) 1946; Hon. Fellow, Jesus College, Oxford, 1948; *b.* 20 April 1883; 2nd *s.* of Thomas Phillips, of Cemmaes, Mont.; *m.* 1913, Alice Hair (*d.* 1965), *d.* of late Falconer Martin Potter, Highbury; two *s.* one *d.* *Educ.:* Machynlleth County School; Jesus Coll., Oxford. 1st Class, Class. and Math. Mods., 1st Class, Lit. Hum.; Gaisford Prize (Greek Prose), 1905; B.A. (London); M.A. (Oxon); entered Civil Service (1st Div.), 1906; Jt. Sec., British Delegation to Berlin Internat. Copyright Conference, 1908; Secretary, Copyright Committee, 1909; Joint Secretary, Imperial Copyright Conference, 1910; Barrister, Gray's Inn, 1913; Assistant Secretary (Ministry of Labour), 1919; Principal Assistant Secretary, 1919; Deputy Secretary, 1924-34; Permanent Secretary, Ministry of Labour, 1935-44, Ministry of National Insurance, 1944-48; Chairman of Central Land Board, and of War Damage Commission, 1949-59; Chairman Building Industry Working Party, 1948-49; Chairman Committee on Economic and Financial Problems of Provision for Old Age, 1953-54; Independent Chairman, National Joint Council for Local Authorities, Administrative, Professional, Technical and Clerical Services, 1951-63; Chairman of War Works Commission, 1949-64. *Address:* Cliff Top, North Foreland Avenue, Broadstairs, Kent.
[*Died* 21 *Sept.* 1966.

PHILLIPS, William; *b.* 30 May 1878, American parentage; *m.* 1910, Caroline Astor Drayton; three *s.* two *d.* *Educ.:* private schools; Harvard College. Private Secretary to Hon. J. H. Choate, 1903-5; 2nd Secretary American Legation, Peking, 1905-7; Assistant to 3rd Asst. Secretary of State, 1907-8; Chief of Division of Far Eastern Affairs, March-Dec. 1908; 3rd Assistant Secretary of State, 1908-1909; 1st Secretary American Embassy, London, 1909-12; on leave of absence as Regent of the College, and Secretary of Corporation of Harvard University, 1912-14; 3rd Assistant Secretary of State, 1914-17; Assistant Secretary of State, 1917-20; Minister to the Netherlands, 1920-22; Under-Secretary of State, 1922-24; Ambassador to Belgium, 1924-27; Minister to Canada, 1927-29; Under-Secretary of State, 1933; Ambassador to Italy, 1936; Personal Representative of the President of the United States to India, 1942; Political Officer (U.S.) on General Eisenhower's Staff, London, 1943-44. Member British-American Committee of Inquiry on Palestine. *Publication:* Ventures in Diplomacy. *Recreation:* golf. *Address:* Beverley, Mass., U.S.A.
[*Died* 23 *Feb.* 1968.

PHILLIPS, Lieut.-Col. William Eric, C.B.E. 1943; D.S.O. 1917; M.C.; LL.D.; Chairman of Board, Duplate Canada Ltd.; Chm. Bd. and Chief Executive Officer, Massey-Ferguson Ltd.; Chairman of Board: Canadian Pittsburgh Industries Ltd.; Argus Corporation Ltd.; Director: Royal Bank of Canada; Pittsburgh Plate Glass Co., Brazilian Traction Light and Power Co. Ltd., Dominion Tar and Chemical Co. Ltd.; Hollinger Consolidated Gold Mines Ltd.; F.C.I.C., M.E.I.C., F.S.G.T.; Hon. Chm. Bd. of Governors of Toronto Univ.; *b.* Toronto, 1893; *m.* Doris Delano Eustace Smith; three *s.* two *d.* *Educ.:* Upper Canada Coll., University of Toronto (B.A.Sc. 1914). Travelled Europe after leaving school until outbreak of war in 1914. Joined Leinster Regt. 1914; served with Royal Warwickshire Regt. (wounded, despatches twice, D.S.O., M.C.); loaned to the French for work in Poland, 1919; retd. from Army, 1920. Church of England. Hon. LL.D. Univ. Toronto, 1946. *Address:* 174 Teddington Park, Toronto 12, Canada. *Clubs:* York, Toronto Hunt, Toronto (Toronto); Mount Royal (Montreal; Royal Yacht Squadron.
[*Died* 26 *Dec.* 1964.

PHILLIPS, William James, M.V.O. 1955; Mus. Doc. (Queen's Coll., Oxford); F.R.C.O., A.R.C.M.; Hon. F.G.S.M.; Organist and Choirmaster at the Chapel Royal, Hampton Court Palace, 1930-56; Member of Council and Examiner, R.C.O., 1930; Professor Lectr. and Examiner in Harmony, Composition, History, etc., at the Guildhall Sch. of Music, 1921; Lectr. in Practical Harmony at London Day Training College, 1917; Conductor Bermondsey Univ. Settlement, 1917; Hon. Fellow Guildhall School of Music, 1926; Vice-President, Union of Graduates in Music, 1926; Chairman, London Musical Competitions Festival, 1930; *m.* 1920, Jessie Edith (*d.* 1940), *d.* of Walter Hanbury, Worcester Park, Surrey; *m.* 1941, Constance Edith, *d.* of A. W. Bradley, Surbiton. Organist SS. Mary and John, Oxford, 1894-96; S. John's, Hammersmith, 1896-1902; S. Barnabas, Pimlico, 1902-17; S. Cuthbert's, Kensington, 1917-1924; Hon. Secretary of the Union of Graduates in Music, 1921-26; Liveryman of Worshipful Company of Musicians, 1926; Master of Worshipful Company of Musicians, 1947; Grand Organist, Grand Lodge of Freemasons, 1920. *Publication:* Carols, their Origin, Music, and Connection with Mystery Plays, and Church Music. *Address:* Kenward, 28 Corkran Road, Surbiton, Surrey. *Club:* City Livery.
[*Died* 2 *Feb.* 1963.

PHILLIPSON, Sir Sydney, K.B.E. 1958; Kt. 1949; C.M.G. 1946; M.A. (Manchester); retired as Chairman, Council, University College, Ibadan, Board of Management, University College Hospital, Ibadan, Council, Nigerian College of Technology, 1958; *b.* 1892; *m.* 1919, Gladys (*d.* 1953), *d.* of C. H. Paley; *m.* 1965, Mrs. Margaret Sayers, *widow* of Rev. Denton Sayers, Hertfordshire. Cadet, Ceylon Civil Service, 1919; Financial Sec., Uganda, 1941-45; Financial Sec., Nigeria, 1945-48; Adviser to Southern Cameroons Government on financial and constitutional problems, 1959, 1960 and 1961. Author of various reports on financial and administrative problems in Nigeria and the Gold Coast. Hon. LL.D. (Ibadan). *Address:* 49 Hallam Street, Portland Place, W.1. *T.:* Langham 2717. *Club:* Athenæum. [*Died* 16 *Jan.* 1966.

PHILP, Hon. Sir Roslyn (Foster Bowie), K.B.E. 1958; Judge of Supreme Court of Queensland since 1939; Senior Puisne Judge since 1956; *b.* 27 July 1895; *s.* of J. A. Philp, Brisbane, Austr.; *m.* 1917, Marjorie Alice Hewson, *d.* of Walter Ferrier; one *s.* (and two *s.* decd.). *Educ.:* Brisbane Grammar School. Served European War, 1914-18, A.I.F. in France. Called to the Bar, 1923; Judge, 1939. Chairman: Aliens Internment Cttee., 1939-45; Air Court of Inquiry, 1943; Roy. Commn. on Espionage in Australia following Petrov's defection, 1954-55. Pres., Qld. Art Gall. Trustees; Mem. Law Faculty Bd., Qld. Univ.; Mem. Qld. Rhodes Scholarship Selection Cttee. Chm. Commonwealth Wool Inquiry Cttee., 1961. *Recreation:* golf. *Address:* Supreme Court, Brisbane, Qld. Australia. *Club:* Queensland (Brisbane). [*Died* 18 *March* 1965.

PHIPPS, Captain William Duncan, C.V.O. 1954; (M.V.O. 1909); late R.N.; a Gentleman Usher in Ordinary to the Queen, 1952-64 (to King George VI, 1937-52); *b.* 1882; *m.* 1917, Pamela May, *d.* of late Brig.-Gen. Sir Walter Ross, K.B.E., C.B., and *widow* of Lieut.-Com. Hon. P. R. Heathcote-Drummond Willoughby; two *s.* Entered Navy, 1898; retired, 1920. *Club:* United Service. [*Died* 2 *June* 1967.

PHYTHIAN-ADAMS, Canon (sometime Lieut.-Colonel) William John Telia Phythian, D.S.O. 1918; M.C.; D.D.; Canon of Carlisle, 1932-58; a Chaplain to the Queen since 1952 (to King George V, 1933-36; Edward VIII, 1936; George VI, 1937-51); Examining Chaplain to Bishop of Carlisle since 1947; *b.* 27 May 1888; *s.* of Rev. E. C. Phythian-Adams, sometime Fellow of Worcester College, Oxford, and Rector of Dyndor, Herefordshire; *m.* 1935, Adela Noël Evelyn, 2nd *d.* of Thomas Houghton and Josephine Constance Robinson; three *s.* *Educ.:* Marlborough and Corpus Christi College, Oxford. Late Assist. Director of the British School of Archæology at Jerusalem, and Keeper of the Museums to the Palestine (Govt.) Administration; collaborated with Prof. Garstang, M.A., in archæological excavations in Northern Syria, the Sudan, and Palestine; ordained deacon, 1925; priest, 1926; Vicar of Millom, 1927-31; Bishop's Messenger, Diocese of Carlisle, 1931-32; Warburtonian Lecturer, 1935-37; Editor of Church Quarterly Review, 1940-45. *Publications:* With Unveiled Face; The Way of At-onement; The People and the Presence; The Fulness of Israel; The Call of Israel; Mithraism; contributions to Journal of Roman Studies, Palestine Exploration Fund Quarterly Statement, Bulletin of British School of Archæology in Jerusalem, New Commentary on Holy Scripture, Journal of Palestine Oriental Society, Church Quarterly Review, The Juridical Review, A Companion to the Bible. *Address:* 16 Manor Way, Onslow Village, Guildford. *T.:* Guildford 67451. [*Died* 20 *Feb.* 1967.

PIAGGIO, Henry Thomas Herbert, M.A. (Cambridge); D.Sc. (London); Emeritus Professor of Mathematics, University of Nottingham (formerly Univ. Coll., Nottingham), 1951; *b.* London, 2 June 1884; *s.* of late Francis Piaggio; unmarried. *Educ.:* Lyulph Stanley School, St. Pancras; City of London School; St. John's College, Cambridge. Lecturer at Univ. Coll., Nottingham, 1908-19. Professor 1919-50. *Publications:* Differential Equations, 1920; contributions to mathematical and psychological journals. *Address:* 5 Lenton Avenue, The Park, Nottingham. [*Died* 25 *June* 1967.

PICCARD, Auguste; Commandeur Légion d'Honneur; Commandeur Ordre de Léopold; Grand Officier de l'Ordre de la Couronne; Professor *honoraire*, Univ. of Brussels; *b.* 28 Jan. 1884; *s.* of Jules Piccard, professor, Univ. of Basle, and Hélène Haltenhoff; *m.* 1920, Marianne Denis; one *s.* four *d.* *Educ.:* Basle; Zürich. Prof. ord. Ecole Polytecn., Zürich, 1920; Prof. ord. University of Brussels, 1922-54. He invented the stratospheric balloon with air-tight cabin, and the bathyscaphe; ascent in the stratosphere at 15,500 m., May, 1931; ascent at 16,900 m., Aug. 1932; dive at 1080 m. in the bathyscaphe, "Trieste," Aug. 1953; dive at 3150 m., Sept. 1953. Dr. (*h.c.*) Strasbourg, Lausanne. *Publications:* Au dessus des nuages; entre terre et ciel; En bathyscaphe au fond des mers, 1954; Ueber den Wolken, unter den Wellen, 1954; In Balloon and Bathyscaphe. *Address:* 3 Chemin du Grand-Praz, Lausanne, Switzerland. [*Died* 25 *March* 1962.

PICKARD, Lieut.-Col. Jocelyn Arthur Adair, C.B.E. 1948; D.S.O. 1918; late R.E.; *b.* 1885; *o. s.* of late Rev. H. Adair Pickard; *m.* 1920, Angela Mary, *y. d.* of A. Conyers Baker; one *s.* one *d.* *Educ.:* Rugby; R.M. Acad., Woolwich. Commissioned Royal Engineers, 1904; transferred to Special Reserve, 1911; served in France, Aug. 1914-April 1919; Captain, 1914; Major, 1918; Lt.-Col. 1920 (D.S.O., despatches four times); London Traffic Branch, Board of Trade, 1912-14; Ministry of Transport, Director, Tramways and Road Services Branch; Assistant Inspecting Officer of Railways, 1919-23; Chief Exec. Officer, Roy. Soc. for the Prevention of Accidents, 1923-50. *Address:* 23 Hill Court, Surbiton. *T.:* Elmbridge 3376. [*Died* 18 *April* 1962.

PICKERING, Brigadier Ralph Emerson, C.B.E. 1947; *b.* 13 Sept. 1898; *s.* of Thomas Pickering, Tyneholm, Newcastle upon Tyne, and the Hill House, Gilsland, Cumberland; *m.* 1927, May Frances, *d.* of Sir Edward A. H. Blunt, K.C.I.E., O.B.E., I.C.S., and *widow* of M. H. Bates, R.F.A., Gyrn Castle, Llanasa; one *d.* *Educ.:* Uppingham; R.M.C., Sandhurst, 1916; 2nd Lieut. The Queen's R.W. Surrey Regt., 1917; served European War, 1914-18 (wounded); Waziristan Ops., N.W. Frontier of India, 1920-1921 (despatches twice, medal and two clasps). A.D.C. to His Excellency the Governor of United Provinces, India, 1922; Sudan, 1926-27; T.A. Adjutant, 1928-32; Adjutant 2nd The Queen's Royal Regiment, 1934-1937; Brigade Major, 1937-39; comd. Depot, Queen's Royal Regt. and Inf. Trg. Centre, 1939-40; served War of 1939-45, and until 1946; Lieut.-Col. Comdg. 1/6 The Queen's, 1940-41; Sub-Dist. and Bde. Comdr., 1942-1945; Comdr. British Troops, N. Africa, 1945-46; R.A.R.O. 1946; (temp.) King's Messenger, 1947. Mem. Exec. Cttee. Conservative and Unionist Films Assoc., 1947-1959. *Recreation:* sailing. *Address:* The Walled Garden, Netley Hill, Bitterne, nr. Southampton. *T.:* Bursledon 409. *Clubs:* Naval and Military; Royal Thames Yacht. [*Died* 27 *March* 1962.

PICKFORD, Sir Anthony Frederick Ingham, Kt., *cr.* 1949; Commander of the Legion of Honour; Commander of Order of Orange-Nassau; Commander of Order of the Dannebrog; *b.* 27 June 1885; *o. s.* of Rev. Joseph Ingham and Mary Pickford;

m. 1913, Lillian, *e. d.* of late Ernest Thomas George Crowdy: one *s.* one *d.* *Educ.:* Merchant Taylors' School, London; Trinity Coll., Dublin. Admitted. 1907; Honours Final Law Examination; Comptroller and City Solicitor, London, 1924-46; Freemason; Glazier; Past-Master of the City of London Solicitors' Company; Vice-Pres. British Red Cross Society, City of London Branch; Town Clerk of City of London, 1946-53. Capt. 62nd (W.R.) Division, 1915-19; France, 1916-18. *Recreation:* golf. *Address:* Ormont, 3 Richmond Grove, Bexhill-on-Sea, Sussex. *T.:* Bexhill 173.
[*Died* 16 *Sept.* 1970.

PICKLES, William Norman, C.B.E. 1957; M.D., F.R.C.P. (Lond.); General Practitioner, Aysgarth, Wensleydale, 1912-64; lecturer; *b.* 6 March 1885; *s.* of Dr. John J. Pickles and Lucy Pickles; *m.* 1917, Gertrude Adelaide Tunstill; one *d.* *Educ.:* Leeds Grammar School; Leeds School of Medicine. M.D. London 1918; F.R.C.P. London 1963. Served European War, as Surgeon Lt. R.N.V.R., 1914-19. Interest in Epidemiology and Infectious diseases and writings on these subjects, led to invitations to give lectures in most medical schools, and to many medical societies in Britain, including Milroy Lectures, R.C.P., 1942, and in U.S. (Cutter Lecture, Harvard) and Canada, 1948; Post-graduate Lecturer, Australia and N.Z., 1951; lectured in S. Africa, 1953, and again in U.S.A., 1955. First Pres. Coll. of General Practitioners, 1953-56. Hon. D.Sc. Leeds 1950; Hon. F.R.C.P.E. 1955; Bisset Hawkins Medal, R.C.P., 1953; 1st James Mackenzie Medal, R.C.P.E., 1955. *Publications:* Epidemiology in Country Practice, 1939; papers in Lancet, B.M.J., Practitioner on Epidemiology and Infectious Disease, etc. *Relevant publication:* Will Pickles of Wensleydale, by John Pemberton, 1970. *Recreations:* epidemiology and a commonplace book. *Address:* Aysgarth, Yorkshire. *T.:* Aysgarth 285. [*Died* 2 *March* 1969.

PICTON, Ven. Arnold Stanley, M.A.; Archdeacon of Blackburn since 1959; Vicar of the united parish of St. George, Preston, since 1951; *b.* 28 June 1899; *s.* of Thomas and Maggie Maud Picton; *m.* 1935, Mary Margaret Marr; two *s.* one *d.* *Educ.:* S.W. Polytechnic Institute, Chelsea; King's College, London; Christ Church, Oxford; Cuddesdon College. B.A.; A.K.C. (Lond.) 1920; M.A. (Oxon.) 1929. Curate: Warrington, 1925-27; Millom, 1927-31; Vicar: St. Luke's, Barrow-in-Furness, 1931-42; Holy Trinity, Preston, 1942-51. Rural Dean of Dalton, 1942-45; Proctor in Convocation, 1945-59; Examining Chaplain to Bishop of Blackburn, 1945-. *Address:* St. George's Vicarage, Preston, Lancs. *T.:* Preston 4416.
[*Died* 8 *June* 1962.

PIDSLEY, Brigadier Wilfrid Gould, C.B.E. 1951 (O.B.E. 1945); D.S.O. 1918; M.C. 1917; *b.* 19 August 1892; *s.* of late Tom G. Pidsley, Exeter; *m.* 1919, Bertha May Wreford; one *s.* *Educ.:* Exeter. 2nd Lieut. First Surrey Rifles, 1913; served France, Belgium and Italy, 1915-18 (despatches thrice); Lieut., Army Educational Corps, 1919; Germany, 1919-20; Instructor, R.M.C., Sandhurst, 1921-26; served India, Staff Capt., 1927-31; Gen. Staff (1st Grade), Gibraltar, 1939-40; Dep. Adjt.-Gen., 1st Army 1942, 18 Army Group 1943; Col. on Staff Italian Army Mission, 1944-47 (despatches thrice); Army Education Directorate, War Office, 1948; Director of Army Education (War Office), 1950-52; retired 1952. Alderman Lymington Borough Council, 1964-. Italian Croce di Guerra, 1918; U.S. Legion of Merit, 1946. *Publication:* History of First Surrey Rifles, 1920. *Recreations:* sailing, painting. *Address:* Bays, Captains' Row, Lymington, Hants. *T.:* Lymington 2577. [*Died* 4 *March* 1967.

PIERCE, Robert, F.R.I.B.A.; private practice; *b.* 3 April 1884; *s.* of Captain O. Pierce, Llanfair P. G., Anglesey; *m.* Olwen, *d.* of late Rev. W. Jones-Williams, Cemaes, Anglesey; one *s.* two *d.* *Educ.:* Friars School and University College, Bangor; Architectural Association Architectural Schools, London. *Recreations:* sketching and golf. *Address:* Craig-y-Don, St. David's Road, Caernarvon. *T.:* 2910. *T.A.:* Pierce, Architect, Carnarvon.
[*Died* 13 *March* 1968.

PIERCE, Stephen Rowland, F.R.I.B.A. 1938; Dist. T.P. 1947; F.S.A. 1961; Architect and Town Planning Consultant; *b.* 6 Apr. 1896; *s.* of Stephen Pierce, Hastings, and Louisa (*née* Pigram); *m.* 1930, Betty Scott, A.R.I.B.A., *d.* of Roderick Mackenzie Scott and Helen (*née* Llewelyn); no *c.* *Educ.:* St. Leonards-on-Sea. Articled to Arthur Wells, F.R.I.B.A., of Hastings; Rome Scholar in Architecture, 1921. Master at Architectural Assoc. Schools, 1919-32; Dir. of Architecture, Hastings School of Art, 1936-42; Lecturer School of Architecture, Manchester University, 1941-42. In Partnership with late C. H. James, R.A., 1933-47. Works include: Haig Memorial, Whitehall, 1929; Slough Town Hall, 1936; Norwich City Hall, 1938; Hertfordshire County Hall, 1940; Assembly House, Norwich, 1950, etc. War Memorials: British Medical Association; Corner Brook, Newfoundland; etc. Town Planning Consultant: Malta, Norwich, Leamington Spa, Southampton, etc. Past Hon. Librarian, Architectural Association, 1934; Past Member Council and Vice-President R.I.B.A. 1951-55; Chairman Faculty of Architecture, British School at Rome; Chairman Codes Cttee. (Building), Brit. Standards Instn. *Publications:* (jointly) Planning, 1935, 8th edn. 1959; Norwich Cathedral at the end of the 18th century, 1965; articles in Town Planning Review, Jl. of Roman Studies Walpole Society Vols., Jl. Soc. of Antiquaries, R.I.B.A. Journal and other technical and professional journals, etc. *Recreations:* travelling, snooker, study of English drawings and water-colours. *Address:* (home) 44 Aubrey Walk, W.8. *T.:* Park 1688; (private office) 21 Bedford Square, W.C.1. *T.:* Museum 8985. *Clubs:* Arts (Chm.); Strangers (Norwich). [*Died* 15 *Feb.* 1966.

PIERCY, 1st Baron, *cr.* 1945, of Burford; **William Piercy,** C.B.E. 1919; Member of Board (formerly Chairman), Industrial and Commercial Finance Corporation Ltd.; Chairman, Ship Mortgage Finance Co. Ltd.; Chairman, Estate Duties Investment Trust; Member of Court and Senate of University of London; a Governor of University of Birmingham and of London School of Economics; *b.* 1886; *s.* of late Augustus Edward Piercy; *m.* 1st, 1915, Mary Louisa, O.B.E. (*d.* 1953), *d.* of late Hon. Thomas Henry William Pelham, C.B.; one *s.* three *d.*; 2nd, 1964, Veronica, *yr. d.* of Mrs. Ann Warham. A Director of the Bank of England, 1946-56. Pres., Nat. Inst. of Industrial Psychology, 1946-63; Chairman, Wellcome Trust, 1960-1965. *Heir:* *s.* Hon. Nicholas Pelham Piercy [*b.* 1918; *m.* 1945, Oonagh Lavinia, *d.* of Major Edward Baylay, D.S.O., Muden, Natal; two *s* three *d.*]. *Address:* Swan Lane House, Burford, Oxon. *Club:* Athenæum. [*Died* 7 *July* 1966.

PIERSSENÉ, Sir Stephen (Herbert), Kt., 1953; T.D. 1950; *b.* 9 August 1899; *s.* of Rev. R. Pierssené, Chandlers Ford, Hants.; *m.* 1st, 1927, Avice (marr. diss. 1936), *d.* of Rev. Ll. C. W. Bullock; two *s.*; 2nd, 1942, Maureen Ava, *d.* of Capt. D. Suttie, R.A.M.C.; one *d.* *Educ.:* St. John's Sch., Leatherhead; R.M.C., Sandhurst. 2 Lt. Queen's Roy. Regt.; served France, 1918 (wounded) and Asia Minor (Intell. Corps), 1920. Joined Leeds Rifles (T.A.),

1936. Served War of 1939-45 in Regtl. and Staff Appts. in R.A. (A.A.), Lt.-Col., 1941; retd. 1945. Conservative Agent, Rugby Div., 1924; Central Office Agent Yorks. Area, 1930. Brotherton & Co. Ltd., Chemical Manufacturers, as Secretary, 1935, Director, 1937. General Director, Conservative Central Office, 1945-57. C.C. East Sussex, 1961-. *Address:* Corryard, Crawley Down, Sussex. *Clubs:* Carlton, Junior Carlton, Constitutional, St. Stephen's. [*Died* 29 *Jan.* 1966.

PIGGOTT, Major-General Francis Stewart Gilderoy, C.B. 1937; D.S.O. 1917; *b.* London, 18 Mar. 1883; *e. s.* of late Sir Francis Taylor Piggott, Chief Justice of Hong-Kong, and late Mabel Waldron, *e. d.* of late J. W. Johns, J.P., D.L.; *m.* 1909, Jane (*d.* 1955), *d.* of late W. James Smith, J.P., of Gibraltar, and Villa Vieja, Algeciras; one *s.* (*y. s.* died on active service, 1941) one *d.* *Educ.:* Cheltenham Coll.; Roy. Military Acad., Woolwich. 2nd Lieut. R.E. 1901; Lieut. 1904; Capt., 1911; Maj., 1916; Bt. Lieut.-Col. 1919; Col. 1923; Major-Gen. 1935; specially employed in Tokyo during Russo-Japanese War, 1904-6; Adjutant, R.E., Gibraltar, 1906-8; attached to H.M. Embassy, Tokyo, 1910-13; qualified 1st Class Interpreter in Japanese, 1906 and 1912; General Staff, War Office, 1914; served in Egypt and France during European War (D.S.O., Bt. Lieut.-Col., despatches 5 times; 3rd Class Order of the Rising Sun; Officer of the Legion of Honour; Officer of the Order of Leopold; 3rd Class Order of the Sacred Treasure; French Croix de Guerre; Belgian Croix de Guerre); graduated, Staff College, Camberley, 1919; attached to Crown Prince of Japan during visit to England, 1921; General Staff, War Office, 1920-21; Military Section of British Empire Delegation to Washington Conference on Limitation of Armament, 1921; Military Attaché to H.M. Embassy, Tokyo, 1921-26 and 1936-39; General Staff Officer, 1st grade, War Office, 1927-30; Deputy Military Secretary, War Office, 1931-35; retired pay, 1939; a Senior Lecturer in Japanese at School of Oriental Studies, London, 1942-46; Member of Cheltenham College Council, 1931-35; President of the Cheltonian Society, 1944-47; Col.-Comdt. R.E., 1941-51; Chairman, Japan Soc. of London, 1958-61; accompanied Crown Prince of Japan during 6 week's visit to Britain, 1953; visited Japan as Foreign Minister's guest, 1955. Grand Cordon, Orders of Sacred Treasure, 1955, and Rising Sun, 1961, Japan. *Publications:* The Elements of Sōsho, 1913; Broken Thread, 1950; ed. Japan and her Destiny by Mamoru Shigemitsu, 1958. *Address:* Oak Cottage, Cranleigh, Surrey. *T.:* Cranleigh 107. *Clubs:* Army and Navy, M.C.C., Surrey C.C., I Zingari, Free Foresters. [*Died* 26 *April* 1966.

PIGGOTT, Julian Ito, C.B.E. 1933 (O.B.E. 1925); M.C. 1962; Chairman, Anglo-German Association; *b.* Tokyo, Japan, 25 March 1888; *y. s.* of late Sir Francis Taylor Piggott; *m.* 1930, Helen Maud, 2nd *d.* of late William Mackenzie, and *niece* of late Hon. Robert Randolph Bruce; two *d.* *Educ.:* Cheltenham College; Pembroke College, Cambridge. Hon Attaché, H.B.M. Legation, Tangier, 1912-14; served European War, 1914-18 (M.C., despatches); Commissioner at Cologne, Inter-Allied Rhineland High Commission, 1920; resigned, 1925, to join David Colville & Sons, Glasgow; Manager British Steel Export Assoc., 1929-36; Regional Controller Ministry of Aircraft Production, 1940-42; Ministry of Production, 1943-44; Regional Controller, North Midland Region, Board of Trade, 1944-49; Chairman, Jewellery and Silverware Council, 1949-53; Member Steel Trades Advisory Delegation, Ottawa Conference, 1932; Member Federation of British Industries Mission to Japan and Manchukuo, 1934. Grand Cross of Merit, Order of Merit of the Federal Republic of Germany, 1958. *Recreations:* cricket (captained Cheltenham College XI, 1907), golf, shooting. *Address:* Chasemore End, Coldharbour, Dorking. *Clubs:* M.C.C. Royal Automobile, Free Foresters, I Zingari [*Died* 23 *Jan.* 1965.

PIGOTT, Maj.-Gen. Alan John Keefe, C.B. 1946; C.B.E. 1941; *b.* 4 July 1892; *s.* of late Col. F. K. Pigott and Amy, *d.* of late Rev. J. K. Robinson; *m.* 1915, Viola Constance *d.* of S. M. Fox, Fawe Park, Keswick; one *s.* (and two *s.* decd.). *Educ.:* Shrewsbury School; Queen's College, Oxford. R. Irish Regt. 1914-22; R. Northumberland Fusiliers, 1922-24; R. Berkshire Regt. 1924-39; Col. 1939; Brig. 1940; Maj.-Gen. 1943; retired, 1947. *Address:* 123 Winchmore Hill Road, Southgate, N.14. *T.:* 01-886 2274. [*Died* 2 *Dec.* 1969.

PIKE, Cecil Frederick; *b.* 1898; *m.* 1922, Elinor, *d.* of James Dunn, Darlington; two *d.* *Educ.:* Aylesbury Road Council School, Bromley; Manchester University. Served European War, 1915-19; M.P. (U.) Attercliffe Division of Sheffield, 1931-35. *Address:* 50 Cartledge Lane, Holmesfield, Nr. Sheffield. *T.:* Holmesfield 308. [*Died* 12 *May* 1968.

PIKE, Colonel Ebenezer John Lecky, C.B.E. 1942; M.C.; D.L.; *b.* 29 Feb. 1884; *s. s.* of Robert Lecky Pike, D.L., Kilnock, Co. Carlow, Ireland; *m.* 1913, Olive (*d.* 1962), *d.* of Edward Snell, Monkokehampton, Devon; (one *s.* killed on active service), two *d.* (and one *d.* decd.). *Educ.:* Harrow. Entered Grenadier Guards, 1903. Served European War (M.C., despatches four times); Staff College, Camberley, 1921; commanded 1st Bn. Grenadiers, 1927-29; A.A.G., War Office, 1929; retired, 1933; Assistant Military Secretary at G.H.Q. Expeditionary Force and went to France, 1939; Zone Commander of Sussex Home Guard, 1940-44. Comdr. Order of Sacred Treasure (Japan). *Recreations:* fishing, shooting, walking, fencing. *Address:* Little Glebe, Fontwell, Arundel, Sussex. *Club:* Turf. [*Died* 13 *Oct.* 1965.

PIKE, Leonard Henry; *b.* 8 Aug. 1885; *s.* of late Thomas Pike, Brisbane, Queensland; *m.* 1923, Margaret, *d.* of late Robert Hutton, Whitby, Yorks.; one *s.* one *d.* *Educ.:* Emanuel School, Streatham; Birkbeck College. Served South African War, City of London Rough Riders, 1901-2; served European War, A.I.F., 1915-18. 9th A.F.A. Brigade; 14th A.L.H. and 3rd Div. Ammunition Col.; was Official Secretary to Premier of Queensland; Official Secretary, Queensland Govt. Office, London, 1927-32; Acting Agent-Gen. in London for Queensland Government, 1932-36; Agent-General, 1936-1951; Director for Queensland visit of Empire Parliamentary Association, 1926; Director for Queensland visit of Duke and Duchess of York, 1927; represented Australian Sugar Industry as adviser to Australian Delegation, Ottawa Conference, 1932; adviser to Rt. Hon. Lord Bruce of Melbourne at Monetary and Economic Conference, London, 1933; adviser to Australian Delegation at International Sugar Conference, London, 1937; Australian Govt. representative on Internat. Sugar Council, 1938-52; late Chairman, Statistical Committee, and Vice-Chairman International Sugar Council; Representative of Australian Football Assoc. on Football Assoc. Council. Silver Medallist, R.S.A. *Recreation:* golf. *Address:* 16 Withyham Road, Cooden, Bexhill-on-Sea, Sussex. [*Died* 24 *March* 1961.

PILCHER, Rt. Rev. Charles Venn, D.D., S.T.D.; Bishop Coadjutor of Sydney, Australia, 1936-56, retd.; *b.* 4 June 1879; *s.* of Francis Pilcher and Mary Alma Eleanor Wood Elliott; *m.* 1908, Eva Alberta Jones;

one *s.* one *d.* *Educ.:* Charterhouse; Hertford College, Oxford. Curate of St. Thomas', Birmingham, 1903-5; Domestic Chaplain to Bishop of Durham and Principal of Bishop's Hostel, 1905-6; Professor of the New Testament at Wycliffe College in University of Toronto, Canada, 1906-8; Secretary for Sunday Schools of Diocese of Toronto, 1909-10; Curate of St. James' Cathedral, Toronto, 1910-16; Tutor in Wycliffe College, Toronto, 1916-19; Professor of the Old Testament, Wycliffe College, 1919-33; Professor of the New Testament, 1933-36; Canon Precentor of Diocese of Toronto, 1931-36. Hon. Fellow Nat. Icelandic League of America, 1935; Lecturer Moore Theological Coll. 1936-; Recognised Lecturer: on Church History, 1938-44, on New Testament Lang. and Lit. 1944-56, University of Sydney. Knight Commander, Icelandic Order of the Falcon, 1954. *Publications:* The Passion Hymns of Iceland; Icelandic Meditations on the Passion; Hosea, Joel, Amos; Three Hebrew Prophets and the Passing of the Empires; The Prayer that Teaches to Live; Twelve Hymns and Tunes; The Hereafter in Jewish and Christian Thought (Moorhouse Lectures for 1938); To Bethlehem came Mary Mild, and other Hymns and Tunes; Life in Christ—The Teaching of the Prayer Book for Confirmed Members of the Church of England, 1945. Sec. Compilation Cttee. of Australian Hymn Supplement, 1945-48. That I may know Him—Thoughts on the Holy Communion, 1947; The Conduct of Public Worship, 1947; Icelandic Christian Classics, 1949; St. Paul's Epistle to the Romans, translated in Paraphrase, 1951. *Recreations:* music, astronomy. *Address:* St. Andrew's Cathedral, Sydney, Australia. [*Died* 4 *July* 1961.

PILCHER, George; Barrister-at-law (Inner Temple); *b.* 26 Feb. 1882; *s.* of W. G. Pilcher, Folkestone; *m.* Muriel Annie, *d.* of Dr. J. G. Blackman, Portsmouth. *Educ.:* Kent College, Canterbury; Wadham College, Oxford (Mod. Hist. Hons.). Joined staff of Morning Post, 1907; Private Secretary to Sir F. Ware; Foreign Editor of Morning Post, 1909-14; Special Correspondent with Turkish Army, Balkan War, 1912, and at various times in Finland, Albania, etc.; Morning Post Correspondent, Calcutta, and Assistant and Joint Editor, Calcutta Statesman, 1914-24; Special Correspondent, N.W. Frontier, 1920, Sikkim, Himalayas, etc.; Morning Post Correspondent during Duke of Connaught's and Prince of Wales's Indian Tours; M.P. (C.) Penryn and Falmouth Division, 1924-29; Secretary of the Royal Empire Society, 1929-35; lectured on India in Canada at invitation of National Council of Education, Canada, 1930; Member and Secretary of House of Commons All-Party Delegation to Empire Parliamentary Conference, Canada, 1928; Chairman Parliamentary Delegation to Brazil, 1927; Member Indian Imperial Assembly, 1924. *Publications:* Steel a Factor in India's Progress; has contributed to Edinburgh, Fortnightly, Nineteenth Century, and other Reviews. *Recreation:* travel. *Address:* Green Bank, Reed Vale, Teignmouth, Devon. *Club:* Royal Over-Seas League. [*Died* 8 *Dec.* 1962.

PILCHER, Sir Gonne (St. Clair), Kt. 1942; M.C.; retired as Judge of High Court of Justice, 1961 (Queen's Bench Div., 1951-1961; Probate, Divorce and Admiralty Div., 1942-51); *b.* 19 Sept. 1890; *e. s.* of late Maj.-Gen. Thomas David Pilcher, C.B., and Kathleen Mary, *yr. d.* of late Col. T. Gonne, 17th Lancers; *m.* 1918, Janet, *er. d.* of late Allan Hughes; one *d.* *Educ.:* Wellington College; Trinity College, Cambridge. Called to Bar, 1915; K.C. 1936; served European War in France and Belgium, 1914-18 (despatches, M.C.); Junior Counsel to Admiralty, Admiralty Court, 1935-36; Dep. Chm. Somerset Quarter Sessions 1938; Attached Officer, War-Office, Sept. 1939-Oct. 1942; Vice-Pres. Comité Maritime International, 1947-62; Pres. British Maritime Law Assoc., 1950-62; Chm. Cttee. appointed to enquire into administration of justice under Naval Discipline Act, 1950-51; headed U.K. deleg. to the Brussels Diplomatic Conf. on International Maritime Conventions, May 1952, Sept. 1958 and May 1961. *Recreation:* hunting. *Address:* Lynch, Allerford, Minehead, Somerset. *T.:* Porlock 509. *Club:* Boodle's. [*Died* 3 *April* 1966.

PILCHER, Robert Stuart, C.B.E. 1943; F.R.S.E.; M.Inst.T.; *b.* 28 Jan. 1882; *m.* 1909, Louise C. G. Niven; one *d.* *Educ.:* British School, Wallasey. Training as Electrical Engineer, Montreal Street Railway; Assistant Electrical Engineer, Birkenhead Corporation Tramways; Traffic Manager, Burton Corporation Tramways, 1905-7; General Manager, Aberdeen Corporation Tramways, 1907-19; General Manager, Edinburgh Corporation Tramways, 1919-29; Gen. Manager, Manchester Corporation Transport Dep., 1929-46; Chairman of Traffic Commissioners for the West Midland Area of England, 1946-51; Pres. Inst. of Transport, 1946-47; Leader of the Employers' side of the National Joint Industrial Council for the Road Passenger Transport Industry (Municipal) for nine years. *Publications:* Road Transport Operation Passenger, 1930; Road Passenger Transport, 1937. *Recreations:* sketching, painting. *Address:* Keith Marischal, Humbie, East Lothian. *T.:* Humbie 51. [*Died* 7 *Aug.* 1961.

PILLEAU, Major-Gen. Gerald Arthur, C.B.E. 1945; M.C.; p.s.c.; *b.* 1896; *s.* of late Maj. Arthur Langston Pilleau, I.A.; *m.* 1921, Eileen Georgina (*d.* 1945), *d.* of late Maj.-Gen. Sir Menus O'Keeffe, K.C.M.G., C.B.; one *s.*; *m.* 1947, Doris Kathleen (who *m.* 1929, Air Chief-Marshal Sir Harry Broadhurst), *d.* of William John French; one *d.* *Educ.:* Wellington College; R.M.C., Sandhurst. 2nd Lt. Queen's Royal Regiment, 1914; served European War, 1914-19; Capt. 1921; Maj. 1934; Lt.-Col. 1940; Col. 1943; Brig. 1941; Maj.-Gen. 1944. Chief of General Staff Middle East, 1944-45; Acting Commander Ninth British Army, 1945; G.O.C. British Troops North Levant, 1946; retd. pay, 1947. *Recreations:* shooting, fishing, motoring. *Address:* Bridge House, Mordiford, Herefordshire. *T.:* Holme Lacy 227. *Clubs:* Royal Automobile, United Hunts. [*Died* 6 *June* 1964.

PILLEY, Professor John Gustave; Professor Emeritus of Education in the Univ. of Edinburgh (Professor, 1951-66); *b.* 6 Jan. 1899; *s.* of John James Pilley and Annie Maria Young; *m.* 1943, Marjorie Dora Weston; two *s.* *Educ.:* Dulwich College; R.E. Signal Corps; Exeter College, Oxford. Lecturer in Education: Liverpool Univ., 1926-27, Bristol Univ., 1927-37; Visiting Prof. (Rockefeller Foundation) at Teachers' Coll., Columbia Univ., 1937-38; Visiting Prof., Wellesley Coll., Mass., 1938-39; Chm. Dept. of Educ., Wellesley Coll., 1939-46; Lectr. in Educ., Bristol Univ., 1946-47; Chm. Dept. of Educ., Wellesley Coll., 1947-1951. *Publications:* Electricity 1927; numerous articles *Address:* c/o The University, Edinburgh. [*Died* 11 *July* 1968.

PIM, Brigadier George Adrien, C.I.E. 1941; D.L.; *b.* 7 Feb. 1888; *s.* of late Canon John Pim, R.D., Easton Lodge, Monkstown, Co. Dublin, and Mrs. Jane Pim, Castle Kevin, Co. Wicklow; *m.* 1927, Audrey, *d.* of Robert Harries, J.P., M.F.H., of Carmarthenshire; two *s.* *Educ.:* Rossall School; Trinity College, Dublin (B.A. Hons., 1908). Indian Army, 1909; served European War, 1914-19 (despatches twice). Indian Frontier, 1921-24 and 1930, India, 1939-45; retired 1943. High Sheriff, Pembrokeshire, 1952; D.L. Pembrokeshire, 1957. *Address:* Wyncliffe,

St. David's, Pembrokeshire. *T.:* 233. [*Died* 26 *June* 1965.

PIMLOTT, John Alfred Ralph, C.B. 1953; Assistant Under-Secretary of State, Department of Education and Science, since 1960; *b.* 24 Oct. 1909; *e. s.* of late Frederick Ralph Pimlott and of Lillie Elizabeth Pimlott, Newbury; *m.* 1939, Ellen Dench Howes, Washington, D.C.; one *s.* two *d.* *Educ.:* Hele's School, Exeter; Worcester College, Oxford. Stanhope Univ. Historical Essay Prize, 1930. Entered Home Office, 1932; Private Secretary to Home Secretary, 1943-45; Private Secretary to Lord President of the Council, 1945 - 47. Home Civil Service Commonwealth Fellow, 1947-48; Office of the Lord President of the Council, 1949-51; Under-Secretary, Ministry of Materials, 1951-54; Under-Secretary, Board of Trade, 1954-55; Secretary, Monopolies and Restrictive Practices Commission, 1955-56; Under-Secretary, Board of Trade, 1956-60. Member, Council of Toynbee Hall. *Publications:* Toynbee Hall: Fifty Years of Social Progress, 1935; The Englishman's Holiday, 1947; Public Relations and American Democracy, 1951; Recreations, 1968. *Recreations:* gardening, writing. *Address:* 15 Belvedere Grove, Wimbledon, S.W.19. *T.:* 01-946 5545. *Club:* Reform. [*Died* 6 *Sept.* 1969.

PINCKNEY, John Robert Hugh, C.B.E. 1920; *b.* 11 May 1876; *yr. s.* of Erlysman Pinckney, J.P., of Wraxall Lodge, Bradford-on-Avon; *m.* 1903, Winifred, *d.* of J. Ledger Hill of Combe Down, Bath; three *d.* (two *s.* killed in action and one *d.* decd.). *Educ.:* Wellington Coll.; Trinity Coll., Cambridge. Served in War Trade Intelligence Department during the War (C.B.E.). Director of National Bank of India, 1934-53. *Address:* Hidden Cottage, Hungerford, Berks. *T.A.:* Hungerford. *T.:* Hungerford 27. [*Died* 20 *Feb.* 1964.

PINEY, Alfred, M.D., Ch.B., M.R.C.P., M.R.C.S.; retired as Consulting Physician, St. Mary's Hospital, E.13; *b.* 3 Feb. 1896; *m.* Dorothy L., *d.* of late A. French, Doncaster. *Educ.:* King Edward VI High Sch., Birmingham; Birmingham Univ. Capt. late R.A.M.C. (S.R.); Lectr. in Pathological Histology in Univ. of Birmingham; Asst. Pathologist Gen. Hosp., Birmingham; Director of the Institute of Pathology, Charing Cross Hospital, W.C.; Director, Pathological Dept., Cancer Hospital, London; Consulting Physician, Chelmsford and Essex Hospital; Consulting Physician, E.M.S.: Arris and Gale Lectr. of R.C.S., 1926 and 1927; Sec. Scientific Committees, British Empire Cancer Campaign; member B.M.A.; European Hæmatological Soc.; Swiss, German, French and Italian Hæmat. Society; Corr. Member Soc. de Méd. de Paris (Medallist 1949); Internat. Soc. Hæmat.; Internat. Soc. Internal Med.; Assoc. des Médecins de langue française. *Publications:* Text-book of Surgical Pathology (with C. J. Marshall), 1925; Recent Advances in Hæmatology, 4th ed., 1939; Editor 14th ed. of Green's Manual of Pathology, 1928; Diseases of the Blood, 2nd ed., 1932; Atlas of Blood Diseases, 7th ed. 1952. Recent Advances in Microscopy (ed.), 1931; Blood Diseases in General Practice, 1934; Sternal Puncture, 4th ed. 1949; Synopsis of Blood Diseases, 1946; Translation of Morawitz' Blood Diseases in Clinical Practice, 1933; Moeschlin's Spleen Puncture, 1951; papers in Medical and Scientific Journals. *Address:* 152 Harley Street, W.1. [*Died* 16 *Oct.* 1965.

PININFARINA, Battista; car body designer and coachbuilder; *b.* Turin, Italy, 2 November 1895; *s.* of Giuseppe Farina and Giacinta Vigna; *m.* 1921, Rosa Copasso. *Educ.:* elementary school. Italy. Founder and Administrator of Carrozzeria Pininfarina J.S. Co., 1930-. Hon. Royal Designer for Industry (R.D.I.), awarded by Roy. Soc. of Arts, London, 1954. Cav. del Lavoro (Italy); Commendatore, Corona d'Italia; Grand Cross of Military Order of Malta, etc. *Address:* 61 Corso Stati Uniti, Turin, Italy. *Clubs:* Circolo degli Artiati; Rotary (Turin); Circolo del Golf. [*Died* 3 *April* 1966.

PINK, Sir Ivor (Thomas Montague), K.C.M.G. 1963 (C.M.G. 1953); H.M. Diplomatic Service; *b.* 9 September 1910; *er. s.* of late Leonard M. and Ethel M. Pink; *m.* 1950, Dora Elizabeth Hall (*née* Tottenham), *widow* of Lieut. (E) B. E. Hall, R.N.; one *d.* *Educ.:* Uppingham; New College, Oxford. Entered Diplomatic Service, 1934; served in Foreign Office until 1938; Tehran, 1938-40; Foreign Office, 1940-45; Berlin, 1945-47; Counsellor, Tokyo, 1948-49; National Defence College, Kingston, Ontario, 1949-50; Minister, U.K. Delegation to O.E.E.C., Paris, 1950-53; Member of Directing Staff, Imperial Defence College, 1953-54; Assistant Under Secretary of State, Foreign Office, 1954-58; British Ambassador to Chile, 1958-61; Minister, 1961-63, Ambassador, 1963-65, to Hungary. *Recreation:* riding. *Address:* c/o D.S.A.O., King Charles St., S.W.1. *Clubs:* St. James', Hurlingham. [*Died* 28 *Jan.* 1966.

PINTO, Vivian de Sola, M.A., D.Phil. (Oxon), F.R.S.L.; Emeritus Professor, University of Nottingham; *b.* 9 December 1895; *o. s.* of J. de S. Pinto; *m.* 1922, Irène Adeline, *d.* of Charles Emile Pittet, Switzerland; two *s.* *Educ.:* University College School; Christ Church, Oxford. Served in Royal Welch Fusiliers, 1915-19, and in Intelligence Corps and Royal Engineers, 1940-42; Lecteur d'anglais, Université de Paris, 1922-23; Lecturer in English Literature, University College, Nottingham, 1923-26; Professor of English, University College, Southampton, 1926-38; Professor of English, Univ. of Nottingham, 1938-61; Visiting Professor, Univ. of California, 1965-1966. *Publications:* Sir Charles Sedley, A Study in the Life and Literature of the Restoration, 1927; the Poetical and Dramatic Works of Sir Charles Sedley, edited with Prefaces, Commentary, etc., 1928; Peter Sterry, Platonist and Puritan, 1934; The Invisible Sun (Poems), 1934; Rochester, Portrait of a Restoration Poet, 1935; Lord Berners, a Selection, 1937; The English Renaissance, 1938 (3rd rev. edn. 1966); This is my England (Poems), 1941; The Wild Geese (Russian Folk Tales), 1944; The Road to the West (Soviet War Poems, with Alan Moray Williams), 1945; John Skelton, a Selection from his Poems, 1950; Crisis in English Poetry, 1880-1940, 1951 (5th rev. edn. 1967); English Biography in the Seventeenth Century, 1951, Poems by John Wilmot, Earl of Rochester (edited), 1953; Restoration Carnival, 1954; R. M. Hewitt, A Selection, edited with a Memoir, 1955; (edited, with A. E. Rodway) The Common Muse, 1957; (edited) The Divine Vision, 1957; Enthusiast in Wit, A Portrait of John Wilmot, Earl of Rochester, 1962; (edited) Byron's Poems, 1963; (ed. with Warren Roberts) The Complete Poems of D. H. Lawrence, 1964; The Restoration Court Poets, 1965; William Blake, A Selection with Introduction, 1965; (ed.) Poetry of the Restoration, 1966; The City that Shone: an autobiography, 1895-1922, 1969; Essays and Studies by Members of the English Assoc., Essays by Divers Hands, The Review of English Studies, English, etc. *Recreations:* reading, walking, and sketching. *Address:* Ninety Nine, Hayling Rise, High Salvington, Worthing, Sussex. *T.:* Swandean 2399. *Club:* Savile. [*Died* 27 *July* 1969.

PIPER, Professor Stephen Harvey, D.S.O. 1919; T.D.; D.L., D.Sc., F.Inst.P.; Emeritus Professor of Physics, University of Bristol, since 1954; *b.* 1887; *s.* of Alfred Towry and Ada Ellen Piper; *m.* 1914, Mary Joyce Casswell; two *s.* (and one *s.* killed in action, 1941). *Educ.:* King's Coll. School; King's College, London. 1st Cl. Hons. Physics, London Univ., 1910; Research Scholar, 1910, Lecturer in Physics, 1911, University College, Nottingham. Served European War, Gallipoli, France, with Sherwood Foresters, 1914-18 (wounded, despatches three times, D.S.O.), rank of Major. Lt.-Col. Home Guard, 1940-1944. Lecturer, Bristol University, 1921; Reader in Physics, 1933; Assistant Director, Wills Physical Laboratory, 1948, Professor 1951-54; Scientific Adviser, Civil Defence, to Home Office, S.W. Region, 1951. D.Sc. London, 1931. D.L. 1953. *Publications:* contrib. to scientific journals, particularly Biochem. Jl., mainly on the structure of aliphatic compounds and the nature and metabolism of plant and insect waxes. *Address:* 65 Walliscote Road, Weston-super-Mare. *T.:* 335. *Club:* Bristol (Bristol).
[*Died* 5 *March* 1963.

PIPPARD, Alfred John Sutton, M.B.E., F.R.S. 1954; D.Sc.; F.I.C.E.; Hon. F.C.G.I.; Fellow of Imperial College of Science and Technology; Prof. of Civil Engineering, Univ. of London (Imperial College), 1933-56; Professor Emeritus, 1956; *b.* 6 April 1891; *s.* of late A. W. Pippard, Yeovil; *m.* Olive (*d.* 1964), *g.d.* of late Mrs. F. Tucker, Yeovil; two *s.* *Educ.:* Yeovil School; University of Bristol. D.Sc. (Bristol), 1920. Articled Assistant to A. P. I. Cotterell, Bristol and Westminster; Assistant Engineer, Pontypridd Water Board, 1913-14; Admiralty Air Department and Air Ministry, 1915-19; Director of Ogilvie and Partners, Consulting Engineers, London, 1919-22; Prof. of Engineering, Univ. of Wales, Cardiff, 1922-28; of Civil Engineering Univ. of Bristol, 1928-33. Mem. Council Inst.C.E., 1944-49, 1950-64, Vice-President 1954-58, President, 1958-59. James Alfred Ewing Medallist, 1963. Hon. Member, Inst. Royal Engineers, 1959; Hon. Fellow, Inst. Public Health Engineers, 1960; Hon. LL.D. (Bristol) 1966; Hon. D.Sc. (Birmingham), 1966; Hon. D.Tech. Brunel, 1968. *Publications:* Aeroplane Structures; Strain Energy Methods of Stress Analysis; Analysis of Engineering Structures; The Experimental Study of Structures; Studies in Elastic Structures; numerous papers in Philosophical Magazine Procs. of Institutions of Civil and Mechanical Engineers; reports of Aeronautical Research Committee, etc. *Address:* 1 Dorset House, St. John's Ave., S.W.15. *T.:* 01-788 2898.
[*Died* 2 *Nov.* 1969.

PIPPETT, Roger Samuel; literary critic and adviser; reader for the Book-of-the-Month Club; *b.* St. John's Wood, 13 Nov. 1895; *o. s.* of late Samuel and Frances Mary Pippett; *m.* Aileen Side. *Educ.:* Board School; Christ's Hospital, Horsham. Book Editor of "PM", New York, 1940-48. *Publications:* several hundred dramatic and literary reviews in the Daily Herald, "PM" and the New York Times. *Recreations:* anything but sport. *Address:* 15 West Eighth Street, New York City.
[*Died* 30 *Sept.* 1962.

PIRE, Rev. Père Dominique-Georges, Th.D., O.P.; Belgian ecclesiastic and social worker; *b.* Dinant, Belgium, 10 Feb. 1910. *Educ.:* Ancient Humanities, Coll., Bellevue, Dinant; Studium de la Sarte-Huy; Angelicum University, Rome; Louvain University (law and social sciences). Lecturer in Moral Philosophy, Studium de la Sarte-Huy, 1937-47. Founded various charitable organisations, including Les Stations de Plein-Air de Huy (for poor children), 1938, and Le Service d'Entr' Aide Familiale (for poor families), 1940; active in the Resistance, 1940-45; founded Aide aux Personnes Déplacées, 1949 (an internat. refugee relief organisation); four Homes for old refugees have been set up in Belgium, and seven European Villages for refugees have been founded, five in Germany and one each in Belgium and Austria; founded The Heart Open to the World Assoc., 1959; founded a Peace University where idealists, regardless of colour, creed and nationality are formed, to work for universal peace), 1960; founder of Fraternal Dialogue between Black, White and Yellow (to promote better understanding between the different races), 1959; founder of a pilot-village in Asia, 1962, called Island of Peace (centre at Gohira, E. Pakistan), and of a second Island of Peace, 1967, in India (State of Madras). Nobel Peace Prize, 1958, for the climate of respect of consciences and mutual understanding above all barriers (national, political, confessional, etc.) in which he has achieved all his humanitarian works; Sonning Prize (Denmark), 1964. Chevalier Légion d'Honneur; Croix de Guerre avec Palmes, Médaille de la Résistance, Médaille de la Guerre, 1940-45; Médaille de la Reconnaissance Nationale; Croix d'Honneur du Mérite Civique Français; Cross of Merit (1st class) of Order of Merit of the Federal Republic of Germany. *Publications:* Bâtir la Paix (English edn., London) Building Peace, 1967; numerous articles. *Address:* 35 rue du Marché, Huy, Belgium.
[*Died* 30 *Jan.* 1969.

PITT, Dame Edith (Maud), D.B.E. 1962 (O.B.E. 1952); M.P. (C.) Edgbaston Division of Birmingham since July 1953; *b.* 14 Oct. 1906; *e. d.* of Ernest George Pitt. *Educ.:* Bordesley Green Council Sch., Birmingham; Evening Institute, Birmingham. Industrial Welfare Officer; City Councillor, Small Heath Ward, Birmingham, 1941-45 and 1947-1954. Chm. Birmingham Women Conservatives, Vice-Chm. Birmingham Conservative Assoc., 1950-53. Dep. Chm. Birmingham Sanatoria Management Cttee., 1948-54. Contested (C.) Stechford Div., Birmingham, General Elections, 1950 and 1951, and Small Heath Div., Nov. 1952. Joint Parliamentary Secretary, Ministry of Pensions and National Insurance, Dec. 1955-Oct. 1959; Parliamentary Secretary, Ministry of Health, Oct. 1959-July 1962. *Recreations:* politics, social work, gardening. *Address:* 20 Blakesley Road, Yardley, Birmingham 25. *T.:* Stechford 3590; 44 Westminster Gardens, S.W.1. *T.:* Victoria 4660.
[*Died* 27 *Jan.* 1966.

PITT, Frances, J.P.; F.L.S., M.B.O.U.; student of Animal psychology and behaviour and writer on natural history; lectures, and shows own Nature colour cine films; *b.* 25 January 1888; *d.* of William James Pitt and Frances Jane, *d.* of Samuel Harvey. Joint Master, Wheatland Hounds, 1929-35, Sole Master, 1935-52; Member of Committee of Enquiry on Cruelty to Wild Animals, 1949-51. *Publications:* Wild Creatures of Garden and Hedgerow, 1920; Woodland Creatures, 1922; Shetland Pirates, 1923; Waterside Creatures, 1925; Wild Life Studies, 1926; Animal Mind, 1927; Moses, My Otter, 1927; Tom, My Peacock, 1928; Toby, My Fox-Cub, 1929; Diana, My Badger, 1929; Katie, My Roving Cat, 1930; The Intelligence of Animals, 1931; Tiny, My Terrier, 1931; Scotty, the Story of a Highland Fox, 1932; The Naturalist on the Prowl, 1934; Birds by the Sea, 1935; Wild Nature's Day, 1936; Editor, Romance of Nature, 1936-37; Editor, Animal Writings, 1937; Wild Animals in Britain, 1939; How to see Nature, 1940; Jane Squirrel, 1942; Betty, 1943; Friends in Fur and Feather, 1946; Meet me in the Garden, 1946; The Year in the Countryside, 1947; Birds in Britain, 1948; Hounds, Horses and Hunting, 1948; Follow

Me, 1949; Nature through the Year, 1950; My Squirrels, 1954; Country Years, 1962; regular contributor to many journals, including weekly articles in the London Evening News, since 1926. *Address :* Castle House, Harley, Shrewsbury. *T.:* Cressage 283. *Club:* English-Speaking Union. [*Died* 9 *March* 1964.

PITT-RIVERS, George Henry Lane Fox, B.Sc. (Oxon.); Captain late, The Royal Dragoons; F.R.A.I.; F.R.G.S.; Owner-Director of the Pitt-Rivers Museum, Farnham, Blandford, Dorset; Life Member and Fellow, and for 20 years Member of Council of Eugenics Society; *b.* 22 May 1890; *e. s.* of late A. E. Lane Fox Pitt-Rivers, F.S.A., of Rushmore, Wilts, and Ruth, *d.* of Lord Henry Thynne, and *g.s.* of Lieut.-General Pitt-Rivers, F.R.S.; *m.* 1st, 1915, Emily Rachel Forster; two *s.*; 2nd, 1931, Rosalind Venetia Henley, F.R.S.; one *s.*; 3rd, Stella Edith Howsen Clive. *Educ.:* Eton. Owns lands in Dorset and Wiltshire; Lieutenant, Royal Wilts Yeomanry, 1909; Royal Dragoons, 1910; served European War, 1914-18 (severely wounded); R. of O., 1919-36; Fellow Commoner of Worcester College, Oxford, 1920; Private Secretary (1920-21) and A.D.C. (1920-24) to Governor-General of Australia; did field work in anthropology in New Guinea and Bismarck Archipelago in 1921; Sec.-Gen. and Hon. Treas., Internat. Union for Scientific Investigation of Population Problems, 1928-37. Contested N. Dorset Constituency, 1935, as Independent Agriculturist. From 1939 responsible for reclaiming considerable area of waste land; 1940-42, held a political prisoner by order of Home Secretary. Inaugurated Wessex Musical Festival, 1945. Established the methodology of the science of ethnogenics, interaction of race, population, and culture. *Publications:* Conscience and Fanaticism, 1919; The World Significance of the Russian Revolution, 1920; Variations in Sex Ratios as Indices of Racial Decline, in Proceedings 2nd Pan-Pacific Science Congress, 1925; Aua Island, vol. iv, Journal of the Royal Anthropological Institute, 1925; The Clash of Culture and the Contact of Races, 1927; Weeds in the Garden of Marriage, 1931; (Ed.) Problems of Population (Proc. Internat. Union for the Scientific Investigation of Population), 1932; Revolt against Tithe, 19th Century, March 1934, and other exposures of the Tithe System; The Czech Conspiracy, 1938; various papers on anthropology and the science of population. *Recreations:* historical research; refuting politicians. *Address:* The Manor House, Hinton St. Mary, Dorset; 77 Cadogan Gardens, S.W.3. *Clubs:* Athenæum; Union Interalliée (Paris). [*Died* 17 *June* 1966.

PITT-WATSON, Very Rev. Prof. James, D.D.; Professor of Practical Theology, Trinity College, Glasgow, since 1946; Moderator of General Assembly of Church of Scotland for 1953; *b.* Edinburgh, 9 Nov. 1893; *s.* of John Watson and Margaret Robertson; *m.* 1918, Margaret Munro Ritchie; one *s.* two *d.* *Educ.:* George Heriot's Sch., Edinburgh; Univ. of Edinburgh. War Service, 1917-19. M.A. (Hons. in Philosophy), B.D. Ordained, 1920. Parochial Charges: Dalmuir, Clydebank, 1920-23; Sandyford, Glasg., 1923-29; St. Mungo's, Alloa, 1929-46; convener of various Cttees., General Assembly, including Church and Nation, 1944-49; Chaplain to the Queen since 1952 (to King George VI, 1951-52). Rep. Church of Scotland at 1st Gen. Assembly, World Council of Churches, 1948. Lectured in U.S.A., 1951. Led Church of Scotland delegation to Coronation, 1953, and presented the Holy Bible to the Queen. Appointed Baird Lecturer, 1954; Vice-Pres. Brit. Council of Churches, 1954-56; Mem. Conferring Panel on Christian Unity with C. of E. Hon. D.D. Edin., 1947. *Publication:* For Such a Time as This, 1953. *Address:* The Manse of New Kilpatrick, Bearsden, Dunbartonshire. *T.:* 0035. [*Died* 25 *Dec.* 1962.

PLATT, Benjamin Stanley, C.M.G. 1945; M.B., Ch.B., M.Sc., Ph.D.; Professor of Nutrition, University of London, and Head of Dept. of Human Nutrition, London Sch. of Hygiene and Tropical Medicine; *b.* 5 June 1903; *e. s.* of Benjamin Gelder Platt; *m.* 1932, Muriel Bessie Shuter; two *s.* three *d.* *Educ.:* Leeds University and Medical School. B.Sc. Leeds (1st Class Hons. Chemistry), 1923; M.B., Ch.B. (2nd Class Hons.), 1930; Research Scholar, D.S.I.R. 1923-25; Beit Medical Research Fellow, 1926-27 and 1931-1932; Associate in Medicine and Head of Department of Medicine, Henry Lester Institute of Medical Research, Shanghai, 1932-38; Senior Member of Central Organisation for Co-ordination of Nutritional Research in Colonial Empire, 1939-42. Director of Nutrition Survey Unit (Nyasaland), 1939-40; Joint Secretary Scientific Food Policy Committee of War Cabinet, 1940-45. Member, of Cttee. on Medical and Nutritional Aspects of Food Policy. Bishop Harman Prize of British Medical Association, 1939; Hon. Mem. American Institute of Nutrition, 1966. *Publications:* in various scientific journals. *Address:* Ebor Cottage, The Ridgeway, Mill Hill, N.W.7. *T.:* Mill Hill 2926; Nutrition Building, National Institute for Medical Research, The Ridgeway, Mill Hill, N.W.7. *T.:* 01-959 3378. [*Died* 18 *July* 1969.

PLATT, Sir Thomas Comyn-, Kt., *cr.* 1922; *s.* of Rev. T. D. Platt, Vicar of Holy Trinity, Portsea, Hants; *b.* 1875; *m.* 1917, Henriette (Etta) (*d.* 1932), *o. d.* of Capt. William Degacher, C.B., S.W. Borderers; no *c.* [assumed the name of Comyn, 1922]. *Educ.:* privately. Hon. Attaché to Embassy in Constantinople, 1904; served in Foreign Office, 1906-7; transferred to Athens, where he was employed at the British Legation; Secretary to the Commissioner in Uganda, 1908; again employed at the Foreign Office, 1909-11; appointed Assistant to the Representative of H.M. Government on the South African Deportation Commission; was a Gold Staff Officer at the Coronations of Edward VII., George V. and George VI., and received the Medal; Railway Officer and Interpreter in France during the War; invalided, 1916; appointed a Member of Game Committee under the Food Ministry; contested (C.) Louth Division Lincolnshire, 1891, Southport, 1923, Portsmouth, Central, 1929; travelled extensively in Central Asia and Asia Minor, also Africa. *Publications:* By Mail and Messenger, 1925; The Turk in the Balkans. The Abyssinian Storm, 1935; various articles on Eastern Questions. *Recreations:* none; *Clubs:* Turf, Naval and Military. [*Died* 18 *March* 1961.

PLATTS, Col. Matthew George, C.I.E. 1939; O.B.E., M.C.; late Chief Engineer for Electricity, Govt. of Madras; *b.* 17 Dec. 1886; 2nd *s.* of late Walter Platts, J.P. and Elizabeth Ann Platts, Bingley, and Scarborough; *m.* 1920, Helen Adah, *widow* of Capt. J. R. Cook, 21st Punjab Regt. I.A., and *o. d.* of late Ralph A. Sadler, Blandford, Dorset; one *s.* one *d.* *Educ.:* Leys School, Cambridge; Leeds University; School of Military Engineering, Chatham. Commissioned R.E. Spl. Res. of Officers, 1907; Indian Service of Engineers, 1910; Public Works Dept. Madras Presidency, 1910-14; served European War, Gallipoli and France, 1914-19 (despatches twice, O.B.E., M.C.); P.W.D., Coorg, 1919-24; P.W.D. Madras Presidency, 1924-25; Hydro-Electric Development, Madras, 1926-45; M.I.C.E.; Telford Premium and Indian Prize, 1935; Hon. A.D.C. to the Viceroy, 1935-40; A.I.R.O., Remount Dept., 1927-40. *Recreations:* hunting and riding. *Address:* The Down Wood, Blandford, Dorset. [*Died* 14 *March* 1969.

PLEDGE, Humphrey Thomas, C.B.E. 1960; Keeper, Science Museum Library, South Kensington, since 1945; *b.* 6 Nov. 1903; *s.* of Thomas Pledge and of Isabella Allen; *m.* 1934, Ruth, *d.* of Rev. H. M. Brown; one *d.* *Educ.:* Tonbridge Sch.; Trinity Coll., Camb. (Exhibitioner, 1st Cl. Nat. Sciences Tripos). Asst. Master, Wrekin Coll., 1925-26; Asst. Keeper, Science Museum Library, 1927. *Publications:* Science since 1500, 1939; articles. *Address:* 30 Woodlands Road, Redhill, Surrey.
[*Died* 28 *Dec.* 1960.

PLENDER, The Lady (Mabel Agnes); *d.* of Peter G. Laurie, Heron Court, Brentwood, Essex; *m.* 1st, 1910, George N. Stevens (*d.* 1930), 7 Hyde Park Gardens, W.2; 2nd, 1932, 1st Baron Plender of Sundridge, G.B.E., LL.D., J.P. (*d.* 1946). Dame of Grace, Order of St. John of Jerusalem; Order of Mercy; Member of Council of Metropolitan Hospital Sunday Fund; Council of Central Club Y.W.C.A.; Committee Member Friends of the Poor; Shaftesbury Homes; Vice-Chm. Roy. Soc. of St. George. *Address:* 12 Chancellor House, Tunbridge Wells, Kent. *T.:* 21558. *Clubs:* Naval and Military, Bath; Union Interalliée (Paris).
[*Died* 12 *June* 1970.

PLOWDEN, Brig. Bryan Edward Chicheley, D.S.O. 1937; Indian Army (retired); *b.* 16 June 1892; *e. s.* of late Richard Chicheley Plowden, Indian Police, and Ethel Sarah Plowden; *m.* 1921, Tempe Mary, *o. d.* of late Dr. Edward Bagot; two *s.* *Educ.:* Blundell's School; R.M.C., Sandhurst. 2nd Lt. 1912; joined 82nd Punjabis (I.A.), 1913; Brevet Major, 1929; Lt.-Col., 1935; commanded 2nd Bn. 4th Bombay Grenadiers (K.E. VII's Own), 1935-37; Brevet Col., 1937; Col., 1938; Commander Mhow (Independent) Area, 1941-1943; retired, 1943. Served N.W.F.P. 1915; Mesopotamia, 1916-17; N.W.F.P., 1919-20; Khaisora Operations, 1936 (despatches); Waziristan Operations, 1937 (D.S.O., despatches). *Address:* Newry, Mayhill, Ramsey, Isle of Man. *T.:* 3484. *Club:* United Service.
[*Died* 15 *March* 1965.

PLOWDEN-WARDLAW, Rev. James Tait; *b.* 23 Nov. 1873; *e. s.* of James Campbell Wardlaw and Augusta Ellen Chichele Plowden, assumed by deed poll registered in the High Court of Judicature the extra surname of Plowden, 1901; *m.* 1904, Edith (*d.* 1957), 2nd *d.* of late Campbell of Craigie, M.P. for the Ayr Burghs, Vice-Lieutenant of Ayrshire; two *s.* one *d.* *Educ.:* King's College, Cambridge; Lincoln's Inn, London. Barrister-at-law, 1901; Advocate of the Supreme Court of Cape Colony, 1901; the Transvaal, 1903; acting Crown Prosecutor of the Special Criminal Court, Pretoria, 1902; Public Prosecutor of Pretoria, 1902; ordained, 1910; Select Preacher, Cambridge, 1914 and 1941; Chaplain of St. Edward's, Cambridge, 1913; Chaplain to the Forces, B.E.F. 1916-18; Rector of Beckenham, 1919-25; Chaplain of St. Paul's, Cannes, 1928-29; Vicar of St. Clement's, Cambridge, 1931-41. *Publications:* Examination Papers in Constitutional and General History of England; The Test of War, 1916; Religious Reconstruction after the War, 1916; Vox Domini, 1929; Vox Dilecti, 1931; Oxford Centenary (Supplementary) Missal, 1933; Catholic Reunion, 1935; A Modern Imitation, 1960. *Recreations:* travelling, religious philosophy. *Address:* The Old House, Milverton, Taunton. *T.:* Milverton 369. *Club:* Anglo-American.
[*Died* 19 *Nov.* 1963.

PLUCKNETT, Theodore Frank Thomas, M.A. (Lond.); LL.B. (Camb.); F.B.A. 1946; Emeritus Professor of Legal History in the University of London since 1963, Professor, 1931-63; Dean of Faculty of Laws, 1954-58; *b.* Bristol, 2 Jan. 1897; *o. s.* of late Frank Plucknett; *m.* 1923, Marie, *e. d.* of Ferdinand Guibert, Clermont-Ferrand; one *s.* *Educ.:* Ald. Newton's Sch. Leicester; Univ. Coll., London (Gladstone Prize); Emmanuel College, Cambridge (research exhibitioner and student; Sudbury-Hardiman Prize); Harvard Law School (Choate Memorial Fellow). Tutor in History, Radcliffe College, 1923-24; Instructor in Legal History, Harvard Law School, 1923-26; Asst. Prof., 1926-31; Ford's Lecturer, University of Oxford, 1946-47; Creighton Lecturer, Univ. of London 1953; Wiles Lecturer, Univ. of Belfast, 1958; Chairman, Master of the Rolls' Archives Cttee., 1949; member of editorial bd. of the History of Parliament; Pres.: Royal Historical Soc., 1948-52; Society of Public Teachers of Law, 1953-54; Member of International Academy of Comparative Law, Vice-Pres., 1956-; Fellow of U.C., London; Hon. Fellow of Emmanuel College, Cambridge. Hon. LL.D. Glasgow, 1958; Hon. Litt.D. Cambridge, 1959. *Publications:* Statutes and their interpretation in the 14th century, 1922; Readings on the History and System of the Common Law (3rd edn. with Dean Roscoe Pound), 1927; Concise History of the Common Law, 1929, 6th edition, 1960; The Year Books of Richard II, 1929; 11th edn. of Taswell-Langmead's Constitutional History of England, 1960; Legislation of Edward I, 1949; The Mediæval Bailiff, 1954; Early English Legal Literature, 1958; Edward I and Criminal Law, 1960; General Editor of the Ames Foundation, 1928-42; Literary Director of the Selden Society. *Address:* 17 Crescent Road, S.W.20. *T.:* Wimbledon 6278; London School of Economics, Houghton Street, W.C.2.
[*Died* 14 *Feb.* 1965.

PLUME, William Thomas, Hon. A.R.I.B.A.; Editor of The Builder, 1918-37. Editor Emeritus since 1937; *b.* Jan. 1869; *m.* 1909, Alice Gertrude, *d.* of John Lloyd Edwards, Liverpool; two *s.* five *d.* *Educ.:* Richmond, Surrey. Joined The Builder, 1885. *Publications:* contributor to various publications. *Recreations:* cricket, swimming, etc. *Address:* Coombeland, Bickleigh, Tiverton, Devon.
[*Died* 12 *Feb.* 1962.

PLUMER, Hon. Eleanor Mary; *b.* 22 July 1885; *d.* of Field-Marshal Viscount Plumer. *Educ.:* King's College for Women. Oxford Final Honours English Language and Literature; Lecturer and Tutor to Women Students, King's College, 1915-17 and 1919-23; Warden, Mary Ward Settlement, 1923-27; Warden, St. Andrew's Hall, University of Reading, 1927-31; Principal of St. Anne's College, Oxford, 1940-53. *Recreation:* travel. *Address:* Flat 6, 69 Holland Park, W.11.
[*Died* 29 *June* 1967.

PLUMMER, Sir Leslie Arthur, Kt., *cr.* 1949; M.P. (Lab.) Deptford since 1951; farmer; *b.* Demerara, British Guiana, 2 June 1901; *s.* of George Henry and Sara Eliza Plummer; *m.* 1923, Beatrice Lapsker; no *c.* *Address:* Berwick Hall, Toppesfield, Essex. *T.:* Gt. Yeldham 264. *Club:* Savile.
[*Died* 15 *April* 1963.

PLUNKETT - ERNLE - ERLE - DRAX Admiral Hon. Sir Reginald Aylmer Ranfurly, K.C.B. *cr.* 1934 (C.B. 1928); D.S.O. 1918; J.P.; D.L.; *b.* 28 Aug. 1880; 2nd *s.* of 17th Baron Dunsany and Ernle Elizabeth Louisa Maria Grosvenor, *o. c.* of Col. Francis Augustus Plunkett Burton, Coldstream Guards [assumed by Royal Licence, 1916, additional names of Ernle-Erle-Drax]; *m.* 1916, Kathleen, *o. d.* of Quintin Chalmers, M.D.; one *s.* four *d.* *Educ.:* Cheam School; H.M.S. Britannia. Went to sea, 1896; Lieut. 1901; Commander, 1912; served afloat in the Grand Fleet from 1914 onwards; present, on board H.M.S. Lion, at the Heligoland Action, Dogger Bank, and Jutland (despatches, pro-

moted to Captain); awarded Russian Order of St. Stanislas (2nd cl.) with swords, 1916; D.S.O. 1918, when commanding H.M.S. Blanche; Director of Royal Naval Staff College, Greenwich, 1919-22; Pres. of Naval Allied Control Commission (Berlin), 1923 and 1924; Naval A.D.C. to the King, 1927-28; Rear-Adm. 1928; Rear-Adm., 1st Battle Squadron, 1929-30; Director of Manning Dept., Admiralty; 1930-32; Vice-Adm. 1932; Commander-in-Chief America and West Indies Station, 1932-34; Commander-in-Chief, Plymouth Station, 1935-38; Adm., 1936; Commander-in-Chief, The Nore, 1939-1941; First and Principal Naval A.D.C. to the King, 1939-41; Home Guard, 1941-43; Commodore of Ocean Convoys, 1943-45. *Publications:* England's Last Chance, 1938; Mission to Moscow, 1939; The Art of War, 20th Century Version, 1943; World War III, some pros and cons, 1954; History of Charborough, 1056-1956, 1956; Solar Heated Swimming Pools, 1962; A Few Notes on Health, Happiness and Wisdom, 1965; Quotes and Notes, 1966; The Uncertain Future, 1967. *Recreations:* writing, gardening, swimming, experiments with solar heating. *Address:* Charborough Park Wareham, Dorset. *Club:* United Service.
[*Died* 16 *Oct.* 1967.

POATE, Sir Hugh Raymond Guy, Kt., *cr.* 1952; M.V.O. 1947; E.D. 1951; Hon. Consulting Surgeon, Royal Prince Alfred Hospital, Sydney, since 1938; *b.* 16 Jan. 1884; *o. s.* of Fred Poate, Surveyor-General, N.S.W., and Julia Rooke; *m.* 1st, Beatrice Ellis (*d.* 1912), Sydney; one *d.*; 2nd, 1916, Aida Diacono (*d.* 1951), Cairo; three *s.* two *d.* *Educ.:* Sydney Grammar School; University of Sydney. M.B., Ch.M. (Syd.). 1907; F.R.C.S. Eng. 1909; F.R.A.C.S. (Foundation Fellow). Served European War, 1914-17, Capt. 1st Field Ambulance, Egypt, Gallipoli (Major), Egypt (Lt.-Col.), England, France, Belgium. Wing-Comdr., R.A.A.F., 1928; Group Capt. 1942. President Roy. Aust. Coll. Surg., 1945-47. Hon. Surg. Royal Prince Alfred Hospital, Sydney, 1911-38; Director Post Graduate Surgery, 1938-42. Chancellor, Order of St. John, The Priory in Australia, 1946; G.C.St.J. *Publications* many in Med. Jls. of Australia, Jl. of Roy. Austr. Coll. of Surgeons, etc. *Recreations:* gardening (past Pres. Roy. Hort. Soc. of N.S.W.; Member of Orchid Society of N.S.W.). *Address:* 38 Victoria Rd., Bellevue Hill, Sydney, N.S.W. *T.:* F.M. 3364; (professional) 225 Macquarie St., Sydney. *T.:* B.W. 9944. *Clubs:* Australian (Sydney); Royal Sydney Golf. [*Died* 26 *Jan.* 1961.

POCHIN, Horace Wilmer; *b.* 1903; *s.* of late H. Stanley Pochin, J.P., and Ethel, *d.* of late F. B. Wilmer; *m.* 1927, Sheila. *d.* of late Dr. A. L. Macleod; one *d.* *Educ.:* Uppingham. J.P. Leicestershire; High Sheriff for Leicestershire, 1944. *Address:* The Willowsic, Houghton on the Hill, Leicestershire. *T.:* Thurnby 2093.
[*Died* 10 *Dec.* 1961.

PODE, Sir (Edward) Julian, Kt. 1959; Chairman: Prince of Wales Dry Dock Co., Swansea, Ltd.; The Steel Company of Wales Ltd., 1962-67 (Managing Director 1947-62); Wm. France, Fenwick & Co., since 1966; Director: The Steetley Company Ltd.; Lloyds Bank Ltd. (Chairman, South Wales Cttee), and other public companies; also Chairman, National Industrial Fuel Efficiency Service, 1965-; Dep. Chm., The Hodge Group Ltd. since 1963; Pres. of British Iron and Steel Fedn.. 1962, 1963, 1964; *b.* 26 June 1902; *s.* of Edward Pode; *m.* 1930, Jean Finlay, *d.* of F. Finlayson, Gwynfa, Caswell, Swansea; one *s.* one *d.* *Educ.:* H.M.S. Conway. Joined Guest, Keen & Nettlefolds Ltd., as District Accountant, 1926; Director, 1945-68. Secretary, 1930, and later Assistant Managing Director, 1943, of Guest, Keen, Baldwins Iron & Steel Co. Ltd. High Sheriff of Glamorgan, 1948; F.C.I.A.; F.C.I.S.; J.Dip. M.A.; J.P. 1951-66; Hon. Freeman of Borough of Port Talbot, 1957; C.St.J. 1963. *Recreations:* farming and golf. *Address:* Great House, Bonvilston, Nr. Cardiff. *T.:* Bonvilston 200. *Clubs:* East India and Sports; Cardiff and County (Cardiff). [*Died* 11 *June* 1968.

POLAND, Vice-Adm. Sir Albert (Lawrence), K.B.E., *cr.* 1953; C.B. 1942; D.S.O. 1940 and Bar 1941; D.S.C. 1918; R.N. retd.; *b.* 18 June 1895; *m.* 1931, Leila Helen Beatrice Sly; two *s.* *Educ.:* Osborne and Dartmouth. Served European War, 1914-18 (D.S.C.); War of 1939-45 (D.S.O. and Bar, C.B.). Chief of Staff to C.-in-C., The Nore, 1946-48; Senior British Naval Officer and Flag Officer Liaison, Middle East, 1948-50; Admiral Superintendent H.M. Dockyard, Chatham, 1950-54; retired Jan. 1955. Order of George I of Greece, III Class, *Address:* Overcliff, St. Merryn, Nr. Padstow. Cornwall. *T.:* St. Merryn 359. *Club:* United Service. [*Died* 20 *March* 1967.

POLAND, Commander John Roberts; *b.* London, 20 Jan. 1893; *yr. s.* of late John Poland, F.R.C.S.; *m.* 1916, Karin, *y. d.* of late N. J. Bengtson, Stockholm; two *s.* two *d.* *Educ.:* Royal Naval Colls., Osborne and Dartmouth. Joined Royal Navy, 1905; Lt. 1915; Lieutenant-Commander, 1923; retd. Commander, 1936; City Marshal of London, 1936-38; Common Cryer and Serjeant-at-Arms, City of London, 1938-57; Asst. Naval Attaché, Stockholm and Oslo, 1939-40, Swordbearer, City of London, 1957-58, retd. Prime Warden, Guild of Mace-bearers, 1946-1952, Joint Master, 1952-59. *Address:* Home Cottage, Seal, Sevenoaks, Kent. *T.:* Sevenoaks 61046. [*Died* 23 *Feb.* 1961.

POLE-EVANS, Illtyd Buller, C.M.G. 1921; M.A. (Cantab.), D.Sc. (Wales); LL.D. (University of Witwatersrand); *b.* 1879; *s.* of Rev. Daniel and Caroline Jane Evans; *m.* 1922, Mary Ross Hall Thomson; one *s.* one *d.* *Educ.:* Cowbridge Grammar School; University Coll. of S. Wales and Monmouthshire; Selwyn College, Cambridge. Mycologist to Transvaal Govt. 1905; Chief of Division of Plant Pathology and Mycology to Union of S. Africa, Dept. of Agric. 1911; Pres. of the S. African Association for the Advancement of Science, 1919; Chief, Division of Botany, Plant Pathology, Horticulture and Entomology, 1927; Chief, Division of Plant Industry, Department of Agriculture, Union of S. Africa, 1929-39, retired; Director of Botanical Survey of S. Africa, 1918-39. President of the South African Biological Society; Scott Medal for Research, 1919; Medal of the S.A. Association for the Advancement of Science, 1922, Represented the Government of the Transvaal at the Fourth International Botanical Congress at Brussels, 1910, and at the opening of the Royal Botanic Gardens at Potsdam, 1910; also represented the Union Government at an International Phytopathological Conference in Philadelphia, 1922; sent on special mission to Portuguese East Africa to investigate Cocoanut Palm diseases, 1913. *Publications:* numerous scientific papers dealing with the vegetation of S. Africa and the diseases of plants in S. Africa. Formerly Editor of the Flowering Plants of South Africa and of Bothalia. *Recreation:* bird photography. *Address:* Clogheen, P.O. Box 291, Umtali, Rhodesia.
[*Died* 16 *Oct.* 1968.

POLING, Daniel Alfred, D.D., Litt.D., S.T.D., LL.D.; Hon. Life Pres., World's Christian Endeavor Union; Chaplain, Chapel of Four Chaplains, Phila., Pa.; Chairman of Bd., Christian Herald, Christian Endeavor World; *b.* Portland, Oregon, U.S.A.,

30 Nov. 1884; *s.* of Charles C. Poling and Savilla Kring; *m.* 1st, 1906, Susan J. Vandersall (*d.* 1918), Akron, O.; 2nd, 1919, Lillian Diebold Heingartner (*d.* 1967), Canton, O.; one *s.* six *d.* (and one *s.* killed in action). *Educ.:* A.B. and A.M. Dallas (Ore.) College; Lafayette (Ore.) Seminary; Ohio State University. LL.D. Albright College; Litt.D. Defiance College; D.D. Hope College; S.T.D. Syracuse; D.D. Univ. of Vermont; LL.D. Temple Univ.; D.D., Phillips Univ., 1939; Prohibition candidate for governor of Ohio, 1912; Temporary Chm. Prohibition Nat. Conv. 1916; Sec. Flying Squadron Foundation and leader in campaign covering 250 cities, 1914-15; Pastor, Marble Collegiate Ref. Ch., New York, 1923-29; Minister, Baptist Temple, Phila., 1936-48. Dir., J. C. Penney Foundation, New York, Presbyterian Ministers Life Insurance Fund, Phila; Trustee, Bucknell Univ.; engaged overseas in special war work in British Isles, France and Germany, 1918-19; Pres., Greater New York Fed. of Churches, 1926-27, General Synod of Reformed Church in Am., 1920-30; Member Gen. War Time Commission of the Churches; Major Chaplain Officers' Reserve; Member Pres. Truman's Civilian Advisory Commission on Universal Training; Mem. Newcomen Soc.; American Legion; etc. Holds War Dept. Citation for Work as accredited War Corresp.; Humanitarian award, Welcome Chapter, Penna.; Eastern Star, 1940; Medal of Merit, U.S. Govt., 1947; various other awards and hon. degrees received, including Benjamin Franklin Award, 1961. Is a Freemason. *Publications:* Mothers of Men, 1914; Huts in Hell, 1918; Learn to Live, 1923; What Men Need Most, 1923; An Adventure in Evangelism, 1925; The Furnace (novel), 1925; John of Oregon (novel), 1926; Radio Talks to Young People, 1926; Dr. Poling's Radio Talks, 1927; The Heretic (novel), 1928; Youth and Life, 1929; Between Two Worlds (novel), 1930; John Barleycorn, His Life and Letters, 1933; Youth Marches, 1937; Opportunity Is Yours, 1940; 52 Storey Sermons for Children, 1940; A Treasury of Best Loved Hymns, 1942; A Preacher Looks at War, 1943; Your Daddy Did Not Die, 1944; A Treasury of Great Sermons, 1944; Faith is Power for You; Prayers for the Armed Forces, 1950; Your Questions Answered with Comforting Counsel, 1956; Mine Eyes Have Seen, 1960; Jesus Says to You, 1961. Daily Column, Americans All, in N.Y. Syndicate papers. *Recreations:* riding, fishing, tennis. *Address:* 141 Pelham Rd., Philadelphia 22, Pa., U.S.A.; 305 East 40th St., N.Y.C., N.Y.; (office) Christian Herald, 27 E. 39th St., N.Y.C., N.Y. *T.:* Mur 6 0712. *Clubs:* Poor Richard (Phila.); Union League, Overseas Press, Explorers (N.Y.C.); National Press (Wash.). [*Died* 7 *Feb.* 1968.

POLLARD, Rt. Rev. Benjamin, T.D.; D.D. (Lambeth), 1953; M.Sc., B.D.; retired as Bishop of Sodor and Man, 1954-66; Bishop Suffragan of Lancaster, 1936-54; Archdeacon of Lancaster, 1950-54; *b.* 12 Sept. 1890; *s.* of Benjamin Pollard and Cecilia Beatrice, *d.* of Farnham Foxwell; *m.* 1st, 1916, Marjorie (*d.* 1961), *e. d.* of William Beckwith Bradbury, Endcliffe, Sheffield; one *s.*; 2nd, 1962, Mrs. Eileen Vellan, *widow* of Alexander Vellan. *Educ.:* Manchester Grammar School; Victoria University of Manchester. President of University Union, Manchester, 1916; Research Student in Chemistry, University of Manchester, 1913; ordained 1914; served Ministry of Munitions, 1914-16; Chaplain to Forces, 1916-19; Precentor, Sheffield Cathedral, 1919; Rector of Bradfield, 1920-24; Rector of St. Chrysostom's, Victoria Park, Manchester, and Chaplain Royal Infirmary, Manchester, 1924-28; Vicar of Lancaster, 1928-54; Canon of Blackburn Cathedral, 1932-54; Hon. Chaplain to the Forces, T.A.: Member of the Council: of Rossall School; King William's College, Isle of Man; formerly: Prolocutor of York Convocation; Chairman, House of Clergy of Church Assembly; Member Board of Governors of the Church Commissioners. *Address:* 3a Coburg Rd., Ramsey, Isle of Man. *Club:* Ellan Vannin (Douglas, Isle of Man). [*Died* 11 *April* 1967.

POLLARD, Major Hugh B. C., F.R.M.S.; late London Regiment; authority on modern and ancient firearms. Special correspondent and staff, Daily Express, 1912-1920; Director Publicity Department, Ministry of Labour Appointments Dept., 1918-19; Staff Intelligence Directorate W.O., 1916-18; Irish Office, 1920-22; Major, General Staff, War Office, 1940; Formerly Sporting Editor, Country Life; Order of St. Anne, 2nd Class; Chevalier Imperial Order Red Arrows of Spain. *Publications:* A Busy Time in Mexico; The Book of the Pistol; Story of Ypres; Automatic Pistols; Modern Shotguns; Secret Societies of Ireland; Sportsman's Cookery Book; sections of the official Text-Book of Small Arms; A History of Firearms; Wildfowl and Waders; Game Birds; The Biology of the Pheasant; Hard up on Pegasus; The Gun Room Guide; The Mystery of Scent; and numerous articles on scientific subjects. *Recreations:* hunting, criminology. *Address:* 2 West Lavington Hill, Midhurst, Sussex. *Clubs:* Savile, Authors'. [*Died* 17 *March* 1966.

POLLEN, Sir Walter Michael Hungerford, Kt. 1959; M.C. 1915; Captain (retired) Cameronians (Scottish Rifles); J.P.; C.C.; *b.* 10 Aug. 1894; *s.* of late Capt. Francis Gabriel Hungerford Pollen, C.B.E., R.N.; *m.* 1925, Rosalind Frances, *d.* of late Robert Benson; one *s.* one *d.* Served European War, 1914-17, with The Cameronians in France, Capt. Comdg. a Machine Gun Co. (wounded twice, despatches M.C.). In Egyptian Army with Sudan Political Service, 1918-26. Retired from Army, 1926; from Sudan, 1928. Formerly Chairman and Man. Dir. Fras. Hinde & Sons Ltd.; Chm. Sheffield Steel Products Ltd.; and other companies. C.C. 1946. J.P. 1949, Gloucestershire. *Recreations:* shooting, fishing, photomicrography; study of insects. *Address:* Norton Hall, Mickleton, Gloucestershire. *T.:* 218; 25 Bryanston Square, W.1. *T.:* Ambassador 5826; Balranald, North Uist, Outer Hebrides. *Clubs:* Brooks's, Naval and Military. [*Died* 21 *June* 1968.

POLLITT, George Paton, D.S.O. 1917; M.Sc., Ph.D.; *b.* Mellor, near Blackburn, Lancashire, 1878. *Educ.:* Bruges; Manchester University; Zürich Polytechnicum. Director Imperial Chemical Industries from its formation till 1945. 1914-1919, enlisted as Despatch Rider in 1914; commanded 11th Battn. Lancs. Fusiliers, 1918 (wounded 4 times, despatches four times, D.S.O. and 2 bars, 1914 Star); granted rank of Lt.-Col. on demobilisation. Zone Commander L.D.F. and Home Guard, 1939-41; granted Hon. rank of Col. Farmed 900 acres in Shropshire, 1932-47 and 2800 acres in Southern Rhodesia, 1947-52. High Sheriff of Shropshire, 1945-46. Awarded Gold Medal of Society of Chemical Industry, 1927; Silver Medal of Royal Society of Arts, 1937. *Publications:* Britain can Feed Herself, 1942; various contributions to technical and agricultural press. *Address:* Nansavallon, St. Mawes, Truro, Cornwall. *Clubs:* Royal Automobile, Farmers': Salisbury (Salisbury, S.R.). [*Died* 9 *March* 1964.

POLLOCK, Maj.-Gen. Arthur Jocelyn Coleman, C.B.E. 1941 (O.B.E. 1918); retd.; *b.* 1891; *s.* of H. F. Pollock, Hanworth, Mx.; *m.* 1936, Ann Maria Theresa Brigitte, *d.* of Patrick Kirwan, Co. Galway. *Educ.:* Wellington; R.M.A., Woolwich. Joined R.A., 1911; served European War, 1914-19, in

France, Belgium (despatches thrice, O.B.E.); Staff Captain Military Interallied Missions, Berlin, 1920-26; Chief Instr., School A.A., 1930-33; Bt. Lt.-Col. 1935; Lt.-Col. 1937; Col. 1938; commanded 41st Anti-Aircraft Bde., 1938; War of 1939-45 (despatches thrice); Staff G.H.Q., M.E.F., 1940-42; G.O.C. A.A. Group Eastern Mediterranean, 1942-44; retired pay, 1944; Director Ministry of Information, 1944-46; Head of Middle East Information Department, Foreign Office, 1946-49; retd. 1950. Member, W.R.D. Council, 1952; County Chief Warden C.D., 1954. *Address:* Timber Cottage, Warningcamp, Arundel, Sx. *Club:* United Service. [*Died* 19 *Feb.* 1968.

POLLOCK, Hon. Surg. Comdr. Sir Donald; *see* Pollock, Hon. Surg. Comdr. Sir J. D.

POLLOCK, Sir (Frederick) John, 4th Bt., *cr.* 1866; Author *b.* 26 Dec. 1878; *o. s.* of Rt. Hon. Sir Frederick Pollock, 3rd Bart. and Georgina Harriett (*d.* 1935), *d.* of John Deffell, Calcutta; *S.* father, 1937; *m.* 1st, 1920, Princess Lydia Bariatinsky (Mme. Lydia Yavorska) (*d.* 1921), *d.* of late General de Hubbenet; 2nd, 1925, Mme. Alix l'Estom Soubiran; one *s.* *Educ.:* Eton; Trinity College, Cambridge (Scholar, 1899; Fellow, 1902); B.A. (1st class Historical Tripos) 1900, M.A. 1903; Law School, Harvard University, 1903-4. Called to Bar, Lincoln's Inn, 190; Member of Olympic Games Committee, 1908; Chief Commissioner in Russia and Poland of the Great Britain to Poland and Galicia Fund under the Russian Red Cross, 1915-18; correspondent of The Times, Daily Mail, or Daily Express in Finland, Berlin, and Paris, 1919-25; Paris correspondent of the Morning Post, 1928 1932; Associate Editor of France, the London French daily, 1940; diplomatic Staff, Reuters, 1942. Officer, Legion of Honour; Russian Red Cross; St. Anne (with Swords). *Publications:* The Popish Plot, 1903; new ed. 1944; The Policy of Charles II. and James II. in the Cambridge Modern History, vol. v., 1908; Damaged Goods and Maternity (tr., in Three Plays by Brieux), 1911; Damaged Goods (tr., republished separately), 1914, revised ed. 1943; War and Revolution in Russia, 1918; The Bolshevik Adventure, 1919; Anatole France Himself, 1925; German Militarism at Work, 1925; Listening to Lacoste, 1926; Twelve One-Acters, 1926; Anatole France Abroad, 1927; Paris and the Parisians, 1929; The Everlasting Bonfire, 1940; The Pollock-Holmes Letters, 1942; Time's Chariot, 1950; Curtain Up!, 1958. *Plays produced:* The Invention of Dr. Metzler, 1905; Rosamond, 1910; The Love of Mrs. Pleasance, 1911; Mlle. Diana, 1913; Anna Karenina (from Tolstoy's novel), 1913 fresh production 1943; For Russia!, 1915; In the Forests of the Night, 1920; The Dream of a Winter Evening, 1921; The Luck King, 1921; The Vulture, 1931; The King's Arms, 1939. *Translations and adaptations produced:* The Parisienne (Henry Becque), 1911; The Great Young Man (Prince Bariatinsky), 1911; I Love You and Mlle. Fifi, 1913; The Man who was Dead (Tolstoy), 1912; Lolotte (Meilhac and Halévy), 1913; Damaged Goods (Brieux), 1914, revised, 1943; Maternité (Brieux), 1933. *Heir:* *s.* George Frederick [*b.* 13 Aug. 1928; *m.* 1951, Doreen Mumford, *o. d.* of N. E. Nash, *q.v.*]. *Address:* 9 Wilbraham Place, S.W.1. *Clubs:* Athenæum, Royal Automobile, Dramatists'. [*Died* 22 *July* 1963.

POLLOCK, Sir John; *see* Pollock, Sir F. J.

POLLOCK, Hon. Surgeon Commander Sir (John) Donald, 1st Bt., *cr.* 1939; O.B.E.; R.N.V.R.; LL.D.; D.L.; M.D. (distn.), C.M. Edin.; Hon. D.Sc. Oxon.; F.R.S. Edin.; late Rector of the University of Edinburgh (1939-45); Hon. Colonel Royal Army Ordnance Corps, 1939; Hon. Col. City of Edinburgh Cadet Corps, 1943; Hon. Wing Commander Royal Air Force, 1939; Hon. Fellow Royal Scottish Society of Arts; Chm.: Edinburgh Motor Engineering Co. Ltd., 1939; Hon. Director: Edinburgh and Dumfriesshire Dairy Co., Ltd., since 1929; Member of Advisory Committee of Three appointed by City of Edinburgh to report upon its future lines of Development, 1943; *b.* 1868; *s.* of late Rev. J. Barr Pollock, Galashiels; unmarried. *Educ.:* Private; Glasgow University (Science); Edinburgh University (Medicine). Medical Practice S. Kensington, 1895-1908; Personal Physician and General Adviser to late Duke of Leinster, 1907-26; Captain in Glasgow and Lanarkshire Yeomanry till 1911; in Navy Medical Service from 1914; Ex-Chairman and President of British Oxygen Co. Ltd. and Ex-Hon. Pres., late Chm., Metal Industries Ltd.; late Member of Scottish Milk Marketing Board; Member of Senior Common Room, Balliol Coll., Oxf.; late Mem. and Interim Chm., Carnegie Trust for Univs. of Scotland, also on Executive Committee; Ex-Chairman of Executive Committee of Newbattle College for Adult Education; Convener: Cockburn Society; Pres. Edinburgh School for Spastics; late Member of Economic Committee of Scottish National Development Council; President of the XIIth International Congress of Acetylene, Oxy-Acetylene Welding and Allied Industries, London, 1936; Ex-President of British Acetylene Association; Vice-President of Navy League, Edinburgh Branch; President Leith Boys' Brigade, 1937; Fellow of Scottish Zoological Society; Member of National Trust for Scotland for Places of Historical Interest or Natural Beauty; a Vice-Pres., British Assoc., 1951. *Recreations:* Nautical Training of young lads; gardening, engineering. *Address:* Manor House, Boswall Road, Edinburgh 5. *T.:* 83041 Edinburgh. *Clubs:* Athenæum, Union; New (Edinburgh). [*Died* 4 *June* 1962 (*ext.*).

POLTIMORE, 4th Baron, *cr.* 1831, **George Wentworth Warwick Bampfylde;** Major, T.F. Res. (Yeo.), retd.; *b.* 23 Sept. 1882; *e. s.* of 3rd Baron Poltimore and Hon. Margaret Harriet (*d.* 1931), *d.* of 1st Baron Allendale; *S.* father, 1918; *m.* 1st, 1910, Cynthia Rachel (*d.* 1961), *d.* of Hon. Gerald Lascelles, C.B.; one *d.*; 2nd, 1962, Barbara Pitcairn (Walker), *d.* of Peter Nicol, Kirkintilloch. *Educ.:* Eton. Late Grenadier Guards; Major Royal North Devon Yeomanry; served European War, 1914-18 (despatches twice). *Heir:* *b.* Hon. Arthur Blackett Warwick Bampfylde [*b.* 29 Nov. 1883; *m.* 1st, 1916, Catharine Frances Graham (*d.* 1938), *d.* of late Gen. Hon. Sir David Macdowall Fraser, G.C.B.; 2nd, 1939, Mrs. Mabel Meyrick (from whom he obtained a divorce), *d.* of late Col. Arthur Montgomery, Rifle Brigade, Grey Abbey, Co. Down]. *Address:* Benwell, P.O. Box 6, Bindura, Rhodesia. [*Died* 13 *July* 1965.

POLTIMORE, 5th Baron, *cr.* 1831; **Arthur Blackett Warwick Bampfylde;** Bt. 1641; *b.* 29 Nov. 1883; 2nd *s.* of 3rd Baron Poltimore; *S.* brother 1965; *m.* 1st, 1916, Catharine Frances Graham (*d.* 1938), *d.* of late Gen. Hon. Sir David Macdowall Fraser, G.C.B.; 2nd, 1939, Mrs. Mabel Meyrick (marr. diss. 1948; she *d.* 1957), *d.* of late Col. Arthur Montgomery, Rifle Brigade, of Grey Abbey, Co. Down. *Educ.:* Eton. *Heir:* *b.* Hon. Hugh de Burgh Warwick Bampfylde. *Address:* P.O. Tigoni, Nairobi, Kenya. [*Died* 10 *June* 1967.

PONSONBY, Hon. Bertie Brabazon; *b.* 1885; *s.* of 8th Earl of Bessborough; *m.* 1933, Constance Evelyn, *o. d.* of late Rev. Canon H. Rollo Meyer. *Educ.:* Harrow; Trinity College, Cambridge, B.A. Bar, Inner Temple, 1909; late Lieut. Grenadier Guards; served European

War, 1914-16 (wounded). *Address:* 44 Hallmores, St. Catharine's Road, Broxbourne, Herts. *T.:* Hoddesdon 65676.
[*Died* 24 *June* 1967.

PONSONBY, Sir George Arthur, K.C.V.O., *cr.* 1939 (C.V.O. 1929; M.V.O.); Extra Equerry to the Queen since 1952 (to King George VI, 1939-52); Comptroller of the Household and Private Secretary to Queen Maud of Norway, 1919-38; *b.* 1878; *s.* of Robert Charles Ponsonby; *m.* 1st, Sheila Oldfield (*d.* 1918); two *s.* one *d.*; 2nd, Elisa Broch; two *d.* *Educ.:* Harrow. With Child & Co., bankers, till the War; Lieut., Grenadier Guards, in European War (severely wounded Dec. 1915); Secretary (Officers Branch) Statutory Committee; Hon. Secretary, Lady Haig's Fund for Disabled Officers; Administrative Officer, Artificial Limbs, Ministry of Pensions; Grand Cross of St. Olav. *Address:* Chaffinches Farm, Birdham, Chichester, Sx. *T.:* Birdham 232.
[*Died* 12 *Nov.* 1969.

POOL, Professor Arthur George; Professor of Economics, University of Leicester, since 1948; *b.* 2 April 1905; *s.* of Thomas and Edith Marian Pool; *m.* 1930, Mary Elizabeth, *d.* of John Robert and Mary Ann Fenton; one *s.* one *d.* *Educ.:* High Pavement School, Nottingham; University College, Nottingham. Asst. Lecturer in Economics, 1927-30, Lecturer in Economics, 1930-47, Univ. of Sheffield. Principal, Min. of Shipping and Min. of War Transport, 1941-45. Senior Lecturer in Economics, Univ. of Sheffield, 1947-48; Dean of Faculty, Univ. of Leicester, 1948-60. *Publications:* A Survey of Transport in Sheffield, 1933; Wage Policy in Relation to Industrial Fluctuations, 1938; (with G. P. Jones) A Hundred Years of Economic Development in Great Britain, 1940; (with G. Llewellyn) Three Reports on the British Hosiery Industry, 1955, 1957, 1958; papers in learned journals. *Recreations:* walking, music, gardening. *Address:* 26 Stoughton Drive North, Leicester. *T.:* Leicester 37533.
[*Died* 6 *March* 1963.

POOL, William Arthur, M.R.C.V.S.; Editor, The Veterinary Annual; formerly Director of Commonwealth Bureau of Animal Health, Weybridge, retired 1955; *b.* 26 November 1889; *s.* of A. G. Pool, Penzance, Cornwall; *m.* Margery Annie, *d.* of H. J. Alsopp, Manchester; one *s.* (and one *s.* killed on service with R.A.F., 1944). *Educ.:* Exeter School. Graduated as Member of Royal College of Veterinary Surgeons, 1911; Indian Veterinary Service, 1912-24; served 1914-18 War, Captain, Indian Army Reserve of Officers (Vet. Branch); formerly Director Moredun Institute, Animal Diseases Research Assoc. of Scotland, 1926-29. *Publications:* scientific, relating to the diseases of animals. *Address:* 9 Effingham Road Surbiton, Surrey. [*Died* 4 *Feb.* 1969.

POOLE, Austin Lane, M.A.; D.Litt. (Oxon.); F.B.A. 1952; Hon. Fellow of St John's College and of Corpus Christi College Oxford; *b.* Oxford, 6 Dec. 1889; 2nd *s.* of late Reginald Lane Poole and Rachael Emily, *d.* of F. R. Malleson; *m.* 1916, Vera Ellen, *d.* of late Dr. Arthur Dendy, Professor of Zoology at King's College, London; one *d.* *Educ.:* Magdalen College School; Corpus Christi Coll., Oxford. 1st Class Mod. History, 1911; Lothian Prize, 1912; Lecturer in History at Selwyn Coll., Cambridge, 1912-13; Fellow and Lecturer, St. John's Coll., Oxford, 1913-47; Lieut. 8th Service Battn. Glouc. Regt. 1914-18 (France, wounded); Senior Tutor St. John's College, Oxford, 1931-45; President of St. John's College, Oxford, 1947-57. University Lecturer in Medieval History, 1927-35; Ford's Lecturer in English History, 1944-45; Senior Proctor, 1924-1925; Pro-Vice-Chancellor, 1948-57; Member of the Hebdomadal Council, 1924-31 and 1935-57; Delegate of University Press; Curator of the University Park since 1924. Chevalier de la Légion d'Honneur, 1953. *Publications:* Henry the Lion, 1912; (joint ed.) Poems of Gray and Collins in Oxford Standard Authors, 1917, 3rd edn., 1937; Chapters on German History in Vols. III., V., VI. of the Cambridge Medieval History; Obligations of Society in the XII. and XIII. centuries, 1946; Domesday Book to Magna Carta, 1951, 2nd edn. 1955; (ed.) Medieval England, 1957; articles in the English Historical Review and elsewhere. *Address:* 28 Belsyre Court, Woodstock Rd., Oxford. *T.:* Oxford 59453. [*Died* 22 *Feb.* 1963.

POOLE, Granville, B.Sc., M.I.M.E., F.G.S.; F.R.S.A.; Past-President, North of England Institute of Mining and Mechanical Engineers; Consulting Mining Engineer; Director Coldberry Lead Co., Seghill Lead Mining Co.; Chm. Blanchland Fluor Mines Ltd.; *b.* Stourbridge, 1885; *s.* of David Poole; *m.* Mary Hilda, *d.* of John Dick, Consett, Co. Durham; one *s.* one *d.* (of a previous marriage). *Educ.:* King Edward VI. Grammar School, Stourbridge; Birmingham University. Lecturer in Mining, Birmingham University; H.M. Inspector of Mines, 1909; acted as Private Secretary to H.M. Chief Inspector of Mines at Home Office, 1911-13; Secretary to Departmental Committee to inquire into spontaneous combustion in mines; held appointment as H.M. Inspector in Northern, Midland, and Southern Divisions; promoted to senior rank, 1917; Prof. of Mining, Univ. of Leeds, 1919-23; Prof. of Mining, King's Coll., Newcastle, 1923-1951, retd. 1951, Prof. Emeritus since 1952. Arbitrator under 1930 Coal Mines Act; Member Northern Division Valuation Board. *Publication:* Haulage and Winding. *Recreations:* music, fishing. *Address:* 62 The Rise, Ponteland, Newcastle upon Tyne. *T.:* Ponteland 2193. [*Died* 26 *May* 1962.

POOLE, Brig. Ivan Maxwell Conway, D.S.O. 1916; Indian Army, retired; *b.* 23 Feb. 1878; *s.* of late Lt.-Col. M. Conway Poole, Burmah Commission; *m.* Hazel, *d.* of late Major R. Johnston, A.P.D.; one *s.* one *d.* *Educ.:* Malvern College. Unattached List. Indian Staff Corps, 1898 (attached 2nd E. Lanc. Regt.); 13th Rajputs, 1899; Supply and Transport Corps, 1901; served France, I.E.F.(A.), 1914-15; Mesopotamia, 1915-16; A.D.T. Tigris Army Corps (despatches, D.S.O.); A.D.S.T. Aden F.F., 1918; Afghanistan, 1919; Waziristan F.F., 1923; D.D.S.T. Northern Command, India, 1928; D.D.S.T. A.H.Q., India, 1930; retired 1932. *Address:* 59 West Street, Faversham, Kent.
[*Died* 23 *Dec.* 1963.

POOLE, Maj.-Gen. Leopold Thomas, C.B. 1945; D.S.O. 1918; M.C. 1917; M.B., Ch.B., D.P.H.; late R.A.M.C.; *b.* 21 Apr. 1888; *m.* 1922, Elizabeth Taylor Bruce; one *s.* (and one *s.* decd.). *Educ.:* Edinburgh Instn.; Edinburgh Univ. Sen. H.S. and Res. Surg. and M.O. Roy. Inf. Preston, 1910-12; Lt. R.A.M.C. 1912; Capt. 1915; Actg. Lt.-Col. 1918-19; Maj. 1924; Lt.-Col. 1934; Bt. Col. 1938; Brig. 1940; Maj.-Gen. 1941. Asst. Prof. of Pathology, 1934-39; Director of Pathology, War Office, 1941-45; K.H.P., 1938-46; retired pay, 1946. Served European War, 1914-18, France and Belgium (despatches thrice, 1914 Star and Clasp, B.W.M., V.M., D.S.O., M.C.); Iraq. Ops. 1919-20 (Iraq Medal and Clasp); N.W. Frontier of India (Mohmand), 1933 (Medal and Clasp). *Publications:* Gassing and Poison Gases in War, 1937. The British Encyclopædia of Medical Practice; many articles in Medical Annual and medical journals. *Address:* Sunnyside, Jedburgh, Scotland. *T.:* Jedburgh 3266.
[*Died* 9 *April* 1965.

POOLE, Sir Lionel (Pinnock), Kt. 1966; J.P.; Member, Bd. of Trade Adv. Cttee., since 1960; Industrial Estates Management Corp. for England since 1960; *b.* 28 Oct. 1894; *m.* 1916, Beatrice Emma Goodson; one *d.* *Educ.:* Elementary; Workers Educational Association. Nat. Union of Boot and Shoe Operatives: Branch Pres., Wellingborough, 1919; Nat. Organiser, 1929; Asst. Sec., 1943; Gen. Sec., 1949. Chm. Nat. Council, Recruitment and Training, 1957-59; Fellow, British Boot and Shoe Instn. (Vice-Pres. 1956); Member: T.U.C. Gen. Council, 1957-59; Part-time Member Board of B.O.A.C. 1960-64; British Productivity Council; Industrial Training Council; Nat. Production Advisory Council on Industry; Bd. of Governors, Loughborough Coll. of Technology; Governor, Nat. Leathersellers' College. J.P. Northamptonshire, 1949. *Recreations:* gardening, reading, motoring. *Address:* Bergholt, Earls Barton Road, Great Doddington, Wellingborough, Northants. *T.:* Wellingborough 3768. [*Died* 13 *Jan.* 1967.

POOLE, Maj.-Gen. William Henry Evered, C.B. 1944; C.B.E. 1945; D.S.O. 1942; South African Ambassador to Greece, 1960-65; *b.* 8 October 1902; *s.* of late Major W. J. Evered Poole, 60th K.R.R., and Henrietta Constance Van Breda; *m.* 1927, Elsie Irene (marriage dissolved, 1951); 2nd *d.* of late Sir J. G. van Boeschoten; one *d.*; *m.* 1951, Maureen, 2nd *d.* of late M. Naish-Gray. *Educ.:* S. Andrews College, Grahamstown; Diocesan College, Cape Town. Private, Cape Peninsula Rifles, 1919; Pte. 1st S.A. Mtd. Rifles, 1922; attended S.A. Cadet Course, passed 1st place, 1922-23; Commissioned into 3rd Bty. S.A. Field Artillery, 1923; transferred to S.A. Garrison Artillery, 1925; Comd. Signals Wing, S.A. Military College, 1929; Bty. Capt. 2nd S.A. Field Bty., 1931; S.A. Staff Duties Course, 1931-32; Bt. Lt.-Col. 1935; Comd. Special Service Bn., 1932-36; Comd. Small Arms Wing, S.A. Military College, 1937; Comdt. S.A. Military College, Roberts Heights, 1938; G.S.O.1 1st S.A. Division, Aug. 1940; G.S.O.1 2nd S.A. Division, Oct. 1940; Brig. 2nd S.A. Inf. Bde. (1st S.A. Div.) M.E.F. 1941; G.O.C. 6th South African Armoured Division U.D.F., M.E.F., 1943; General Officer Admin U.D.F., M.E.F. and C.M.F., 1945; Dep. Chief G.S., U.D.F., 1946-48; Head of South African Military Mission in Berlin, 1948-51; Head of Mission of Union of South Africa, Cologne, 1949-51; South African Minister to Italy, Greece and Egypt, 1951-54, Argentine and Chile, 1954-57, Argentine, 1958-60. K.St.J. *Recreations:* formerly Rugby, tennis, polo; now golf and yachting. *Address:* c/o Box 34, Pretoria, S. Africa. *Club:* Civil Service (Cape Town). [*Died* 9 *March* 1969.

POOLEY, Sir Ernest (Henry), 1st Bt., *cr.* 1953; G.C.V.O. 1957 (K.C.V.O. 1944); Kt. 1932; M.A., LL.B., Hon. LL.D. (Lond.), 1948; Member of the Council of King Edward's Hospital Fund for London; Hon. Fell. Pembroke College, Cambridge, and Queen Mary College, London; War Service (1914-18) in R.N.V.R. and R.G.A., France and Gallipoli; *b.* 20 Nov. 1876; *e. s.* of late Henry Fletcher Pooley, Assistant Secretary to the Board of Education, and Susan, *d.* of late Edward Bond; *m.*, 1953, Christabel, *widow* of H. C. Marillier, and *d.* of late Arthur Hopkins, R.W.S. *Educ.:* Winchester College; Pembroke College, Cambridge. Called to Bar, 1901; Legal Assistant in the Board of Education, 1903-5; Secretary to the Departmental Committee on Physical Deterioration, 1903-4; Assistant Clerk to Drapers' Company, 1905-08; Clerk to Drapers' Company, 1908-44; Master of Drapers' Company, 1944-45; Warden of Drapers' Company, 1952-53, 1962-63; Mem. of the Senate and the Court of the University of London, 1929-48; Member of the Hambledon Committee on Industrial Design, 1936; of the Goodenough Committee on Medical Education, and the Fleming Committee on Public Schools, 1944. Chairman Arts Council of Great Britain, 1946-53. C.St.J. *Publication:* The Guilds of the City of London (Britain in Pictures). *Heir:* none. *Address:* Westbrook House, Upperton, Petworth, Sussex. *T.:* Petworth 2185. *Clubs:* Athenæum, Royal Automobile, Savile. [*Died* 13 *Feb.* 1966 (*ext.*).

POPE, Arthur Upham, A.B., M.A., Ph.D.; Director, American Institute for Iranian Art and Archæology (subsequently renamed Iranian, then Asia, Institute, expanded and transferred to Pahlavi University of Shiraz), since 1930; Emeritus since 1952; *b.* 7 Feb. 1881; *s.* of Louis Atherton Pope and Imogene Titus; *m.* 1920, Dr Phyllis Ackerman. *Educ.:* Brown University; Cornell University; Harvard University. Instructor, Brown University; Assistant Professor, University of California; Acting Associate Professor Amherst College; Personnel Division, General Staff U.S. Army (rank corresponding to Major), 1918-19. Director of San Francisco Museum, 1923; Research work in Persia, 1925-50. Initiated Survey of Persian architecture; organised 1st International Exhibition Persian Art, Philadelphia, 1926; various exhibitions Persian Art, U.S.A.; (with Sir Arnold Wilson) Internat. Exhibition Persian Art, London, 1931; (with Sir Dennison Ross) 2nd Congress Persian Art, London, 1931; Joint Director above Exhibition and Congress; Exhibition: Photographs Persian Architecture principal European and American cities, R.I.B.A., 1931-35; Chairman, American Committee for Chinese War Orphans, 1939; Director, Exhibition of Persian Art, New York, 1940; Chairman, Committee for National Morale, 1940-48; Executive Secretary International Association for Iranian Art and Archæology; Joint Director of the Third International Congress, Leningrad - Moscow, September 1935, and Associate Director of the Third International Exhibition of Persian Art, Hermitage, Leningrad, Sep.-Dec., 1935; Adviser in Persian Art, Pennsylvania Museum; Adviser in Art to the Gov. of Persia, 1925; State visit Persia, 1964; Hon. Ph.D., Univ. of Teheran; Harvard University Lecturer to French Universities for 1934-35; Lecturer at many European and American Societies and Institutions (Museums and Universities). Mem. various learned Societies, 1926-; Mem. Iranian Acad., 1944; President of the International Association Iranian Art and Archaeology, 1960- (Ex-Sec., 1931); Director, 4th Internat. Congress, Persian Art and Archaeology, N.Y. and Washington, 1960, editor, Proceedings; President, Vth Internat. Congress, Persian Art and Archaeology, Tehran, Isfahan, Shiraz, 1968. Order Elmi, 1925. Comdr. Order of the Crown, 1945, Order Danesh (Iran), 1960; Order Homayoun (Iran), 1964. *Publications:* Early Oriental Carpets, 1926; An Introduction to Persian Art, 1931; Lincoln and Urgent World Problem, 1943; Maxim Litvinoff 1943; Editor, Survey of Persian Art (7 vols.), 1938 (re-issue 12 vols., 1965; XIVth, XVth vols. (Proc. IVth Internat. Congress), 1967); Masterpieces of Persian Art, 1945 (in Persian, 1958-59); Persian Architecture, 1965; numerous articles both general and scientific on various phases of Persian Art. *Recreation:* music. *Address:* Asia Institute, Pahlavi University, Shiraz, Iran; Warren, Connecticut, U.S.A. [*Died* 3 *Sept.* 1969.

POPE, Frank Aubrey, C.I.E. 1945; M.Inst.T.; *b.* 3 Aug. 1893; *s.* of the Rev. Martin Pope and Phoebe Hunter; *m.* 1918; two *d.* *Educ.:* The Leys School. L.N.W. and L.M.S. Railways. European War 1914-18, France 1914-15, Salonika 1916-18 (despatches, White Eagle of Serbia, Greek Order of Merit). Colonial Railway Service, Nigeria, 1925-30; L.M.S. Railway, 1930; Supt. of Operation, 1937; loaned to Indian Govt. to report on State Railways 1932-33 and 1933-1934. B.E.F. France 1940, Col., Director of Railways (despatches); Manager L.M.S. Northern Ireland, 1941-43; Chief Commercial Manager L.M.S., 1943-46; Vice-Pres., 1946-1947. Loaned to Indian Govt. as Regional Port Director, Calcutta, 1944-45; first Chm. Ulster Transport Authority, 1948-51; Member British Transport Commission, 1951-58; Director: John Bull Rubber Co.; Metro-Cammell Carriage & Wagon Co.; Nyasaland and associated Railways. *Recreation:* golf. *Address:* 18 Hanover Square, W.1. *Clubs:* Oriental; Bengal (Calcutta). [*Died* 15 *Jan.* 1962.

POPHAM, Arthur Ewart, C.B. 1954; F.B.A. 1949; Hon. R.E. 1945; Keeper, Department of Prints and Drawings, British Museum, 1945-54; *b.* Plymouth, 22 March 1889; *m.* 1st, 1912, Brynhild Olivier; two *s.* one *d.*; 2nd, 1926, Rosalind Thornycroft. *Educ.:* Dulwich Coll.; Univ. Coll., London; King's College, Cambridge. Entered British Museum, 1912; served European War, 1914-1918, Flight Lieutenant, R.N.A.S., and Capt. R.A.F., Egypt and Palestine; Hon. Secretary Vasari Society, 1925-35. Hon. Fellow, King's College, Cambridge, 1955. *Publications:* Catalogue of Dutch and Flemish Drawings in the British Museum Vol. V. 1932; The Drawings of Leonardo da Vinci, 1946; Catalogue of Italian Drawings of XV cent. in British Museum (with Philip Pouncey), 1950; Correggio's Drawings, 1957; Catalogue of Drawing of School of Parma in the British Museum, 1967; Catalogue of the Drawings of Parmigiano, 1971 (posthumous). Contributions to Burlington Magazine and foreign periodicals. *Address:* 4 Canonbury Place, N.1. *T.:* Canonbury 4640. *Club:* Athenæum. [*Died* 8 *Dec.* 1970.

POPKESS, Captain Athelstan, C.B.E. 1956 (O.B.E. 1942); Chief Constable of Nottingham, 1930-59; *b.* Knysna, S. Africa, 23 Nov. 1893; *s.* of Edward Peter Popkess and Lilian Thorne; *m.* 1st, 1923, Gilberta Lilian, *d.* of Richard Popkess; two *s.* two *d.*; 2nd, 1938, Dorothy, *d.* of Patrick Walsh. *Educ.:* Queen's Coll., Queenstown, S.A.; St. George's Coll., Salisbury, S.R.; King's Coll., London Univ. (studying Russian language). Speaks also Afrikaans, Arabic and Swahili. Served with 1st Bn. Rhodesia Regt., in German S.W. Africa, under Gen. Louis Botha, 1914; commnd. Regular Army, in N. Staffs. Regt. (The Prince of Wales's), 1915 (1914-15 Star); seconded first to Legion of Frontiersmen and then to K.A.R., in German E.A., 1916; rejoined 1st Bn. N. Staffs. Regt. on the Curragh, Ire., 1919 (opns. against Sinn Fein); seconded to Palestine Gendarmerie (Native), 1921; rejoined 2nd Bn. N. Staffs. Regt., 1924; seconded to be Asst. Provost Marshal, Aldershot Command, 1928. Pioneered in Police wireless and Scientific Crime Investigation. Has done much broadcasting for B.B.C. British War and Victory Medals; Civil Defence Medal; Police Long Service Medal; King's Police Medal, 1935; Jubilee Medal, 1935; Coronation Medals, 1937 and 1953. Sword of Honour, Swedish Police. *Publications:* Mechanized Police Patrol; Traffic Control and Road Accident Prevention; Sweat in my Eyes. Articles, etc., in many periodicals. *Recreation:* boxing, Rugby football, and cricket, although now unable to participate in them actively. *Address:* 2 Willenhall, Guestland Road, Torquay, Devon. [*Died* 29 *April* 1967.

PORCELLI, Lt.-Col. The Baron Ernest George Macdonald di S. Andrea; late The Duke of Cornwall's Light Infantry; *b.* 27 May 1886; *o. s.* of Col. The Baron Alfred Porcelli di S. Andrea, a naturalized British subject who was commissioned in the Corps of Royal Engineers, and *g. s.* of Col. The Baron A. S. R. Porcelli di S. Andrea, Inspector of the Royal Palace of Caserta, Italy, a Garibaldian who married Anne Sarah Macdonald of Clanranald; *m.* 1927, Ethel Donaldson, *d.* of late R. S. Sloan of Long Island, New York, U.S.A., and *widow* of Lt.-Col. J. S. Liddell; one *s.* one *d.* *Educ.:* R.M.C. Sandhurst. 2nd Lieut. D.C.L.I. 1906; served with D.C.L.I. at Gibraltar, Bermuda, S. Africa, N. Ireland, India, Channel Islands, Gt. Britain; seconded to K.A.R. 1913-19; served in Marehan Somalis Jubaland Expedition, 1913-14; European War, British East Africa, German East Africa, Expedition against Aulihan Somalis, Jubaland, 1917-18 (wounded, despatches, Bt. Major); O.C. Troops, Jubaland; seconded to Egyptian Army, 1919-21; served in Darfur, Sudan; Retd. as Lieut.-Col. 1931; rejoined 1st Sept. 1939; proceeded to France, 10 Sept. 1939 as Group Commander, Labour Group, later Pioneer Corps; evacuated France, June 1940; served in M.E., 1940-43, Asst. Dir. of Pioneers and Labour, Sudan and Canal Zone, also as Gp. Comdr., Pioneer Corps, with 8th Army; Comdt. P.O.W. Camps, 1943-44; U.N.R.R.A. 1944-1946; proceeded to France and Germany, April 1945 (despatches, 1939-1945 Star, Africa Star). *Publications:* The White Cockade, 1949; The Mayflower Story, 1956; (Ed.) The Eve of Victorianism, 1940. *Recreations:* all outdoor sports, writing. *Heir:* *s.* Ronald Macdonald Vernon Porcelli, *b.* 17 Dec. 1927. *Address:* c/o Lloyd's Bank Ltd., Cox's & King's Branch, 6 Pall Mall, S.W.1. *Club:* United Service. [*Died* 3 *July* 1965.

PORTER, Annie (Mrs. H. B. Fantham), D.Sc.Lond.; Hon. Parasitologist to the Zoological Society of London; *e. d.* of late S. Porter, Brighton; *m.* 1915, H. B. Fantham (*d.* 1937). *Educ.:* University College, London; Quick Laboratory, Cambridge. Beit Memorial Research Fellow, Cambridge, 1914-16; formerly Assistant in Helminthology, Cambridge; Head of the Department of Parasitology, South African Institute for Medical Research, Johannesburg, 1917-33, and Senior Lecturer in Parasitology, University of the Witwatersrand; Examiner in Zoology and in Animal Parasitology in the Universities of the Witwatersrand and South Africa; Research Associate in Zoology, McGill University, Montreal, 1933-38; President, South African Geographical Society, 1924; Fellow of the Royal Society of South Africa and former Vice-Pres. and Member of Council; President, Section D (Zoology), South African Association for the Advancement of Science, 1922; South Africa Medallist, 1927; F.L.S., F.Z.S. *Publications:* numerous zoological papers, especially on Protozoa and Helminthes. *Address:* Zoological Society of London, Regent's Park, N.W.1. [*Died* 9 *May* 1963.

PORTER, Cole; Composer, Lyricist; *b.* Peru, Ind., 9 June 1893; *s.* of Samuel Fenwick Porter and Kate Cole; *m.* 1919, Linda Lee Thomas (*d.* 1954); no *c.* *Educ.:* Worcester (Mass.) Acad.; Yale; Harvard Law Sch.; Harvard Music Sch. A.B., Yale, 1913; enlisted in Foreign Legion, 1917; transferred to French Army and served until 1919. Mem. Delta Kappa Epsilon, Scroll and Key (Yale). Hon. Degrees: Doctor of Music, Williams College, U.S.A., 1955; Doctor of Humane Letters, Yale University, U.S.A., 1960. *Publications:* Composer and Lyricist for musical comedies: See America First, 1916; Hitchy Koo, 1919; Greenwich Follies, 1923; Paris, 1928; Wake Up and Dream, 1929; 50 Million Frenchmen, 1929; The New Yorkers, 1930; Gay Divorce, 1932; Nymph Errant, 1933; Anything Goes, 1934;

Jubilee, 1935; Born to Dance (motion picture), 1936; Red Hot and Blue, 1936; Rosalie (motion picture), 1937; You Never Know, 1938; Leave It to Me, 1938; Broadway Melody 1940 (motion picture), 1939; Dubarry Was a Lady, 1939; Panama Hattie, 1940; You'll Never Get Rich (motion picture), 1941; Let's Face It (Broadway musical show), 1941; Something to Shout About (motion picture), 1942; Something for the Boys (Broadway musical show), 1942; Mexican Hayride (Broadway musical show), 1943; 7 Lively Arts (Revue), 1944; Around the World in Eighty Days (Broadway musical show), 1946; Kiss Me, Kate (Broadway musical show), 1949, (Coliseum), 1951; Can-Can (musical), 1954; Silk Stockings (Broadway musical show), 1955; High Society (film), 1956; Les Girls (film), 1957; Aladdin (TV), 1958; Can-Can, 1960. *Address:* Waldorf-Astoria Towers, New York, N.Y., U.S.A. [*Died* 15 *Oct.* 1964.

PORTMAN, 8th Viscount (U.K.), *cr.* 1873; **Gerald William Berkeley Portman;** Director, Alliance Assurance Company; *b.* 20 Aug. 1903; *er. s.* of 7th Viscount and Dorothy Marie Isolde (*d.* 1964), *d.* of Sir Robert Sheffield, 5th Bt.; *S.* father, 1948; *m.* 1st, 1926, Marjorie Bentley, *d.* of George Bentley Gerrard, Montreal, Canada; 2nd, 1946, Nancy Maureen, 4th *d.* of Capt. (S) Percy Herbert Franklin, R.N. retd. *Educ.:* Eton; R.M.C., Sandhurst. Joined R.A.S.C., 1940, Capt. 1942; served War of 1939-45, in East African Command and Eastern Command, 1940-45. *Recreations:* fishing, shooting, golf. *Heir:* *n.* Edward Henry Berkeley Portman, now 9th Viscount Portman [*b.* 22 Apr. 1934; *m.* 1st, 1956, Rosemary Joy (marr. diss., 1966), *e. d.* of Charles Farris, Coombe Bissett, Wiltshire; one *s.* (Hon. Christopher Edward Berkeley Portman, *b.* 30th July, 1958; now *heir* to Viscountcy) one *d.*; 2nd, 1966, Penelope Anne Hassard, *yr. d.* of Trevor Allin, North Moreton, Berkshire; two *s.*]. *Address:* Burtley House, Beaconsfield, Bucks. *T.:* Beaconsfield 255. *Clubs:* Carlton, Turf, Royal Automobile. [*Died* 3 *Nov.* 1967.

PORTMAN, Eric; stage and film actor; *b.* Yorkshire, 13 July 1903; *s.* of Matthew Portman and Alice Harrison. *Educ.:* Rishworth School, Yorks. First appearance on London stage in The Comedy of Errors, Savoy, 1924; parts include: Horatio in Hamlet, Old Vic, 1927; Stephen Undershaft in Major Barbara, Wyndham's, 1929; Aimwell in The Beaux' Stratagem, Royalty, 1930; Eben in Desire Under the Elms, Gate, 1931; Ragnar Brovik in The Master Builder, Duchess, 1931; George D'Alroy in Caste, Embassy, 1932; Captain Absolute in The Rivals, 1933; Count Orloff in Diplomacy, Prince's, 1933; Lord Byron in Bitter Harvest, Arts, and St. Martin's, 1936; Brutus in Julius Caesar, Open-Air Theatre, 1937; Rodolph Boulanger in Madame Bovary, Broadhurst, New York, 1937; Oliver Farrant in I Have Been Here Before, Guild, New York, 1938; Mark Anthony in Julius Caesar (modern dress), Embassy, and His Majesty's, 1939; Stanley Smith in Jeannie, Torch, and Wyndham's, 1940; on tour, 1943; leading rôles in Playbill, Phoenix, 1948; The Governor in His Excellency, Princes, 1950; The Marshal in The Moment of Truth, Adelphi, 1951; The Priest in The Living Room, Wyndham's, 1953; Mr. Malcolm and Major Pollock in Separate Tables, St. James's, 1954-56, and went to New York with the production, 1956; A Touch of the Poet (New York), 1958; A Passage to India (New York), 1962; The Claimant, 1964; Justice, St. Martin's, 1968. *Films include:* 49th Parallel, One of Our Aircraft is Missing, We Dive at Dawn, Millions Like Us, A Canterbury Tale, Men of Two Worlds, Wanted for Murder, Dear Murderer, Cairo Road, His Excellency, The Colditz Story, The Good Companions, Freud, West Eleven, Deadfall. *Address:* Lower Penpol, St. Veep, Cornwall; 2 Bray House, Duke of York St., S.W.1. [*Died* 7 *Dec.* 1969.

PORTMAN, Guy Maurice Berkeley, C.B. 1952; T.D., D.L.; Chairman Allen Harvey and Ross Ltd., Discount Brokers; *b.* 4 Aug. 1890; *m.* 1922, Miriam Katharine, *d.* of Capt. G. W. and Lady Elizabeth Taylor; one *s.* one *d.* (and one *d.* decd.). *Educ.:* Winchester College; New College, Oxford. Barrister-at-Law, 1914. T.A. Commission, 1914. European War, 1914-18 (P.O.W., Germany). Commanded Rangers, 1929-34; Queen's Westminsters, 1938-39; War of 1939-45: Brigadier, 168 Inf. Bde. T.A. 1939-42; G.H.Q. India, 1942-45. A.D.C. to King George VI, 1941-52; Chairman County of London Territorial and Auxiliary Forces Association, 1948-54. Chairman London Discount Market Association, 1955-57. Chairman Hambledon R.D.C., 1955-59. *Address:* Hangerfield, Witley, Surrey. *Clubs:* Beefsteak, Garrick. [*Died* 16 *July* 1961.

POST, Rear-Adm. Simon Edward, C.B. 1962; O.B.E. 1944; retd.; *b.* 10 May 1910; *s.* of late Donnell Post and late Hon. Mrs. Post; *m.* 1944, Annette Mary, *d.* of William MacMurray, Surgeon; one *s.* one *d.* *Educ.:* R.N.C., Dartmouth. Naval Cadet, 1924-27; Midshipman in H.M.S. Nelson, First Commission, 1928-30; Submarines in China, 1932-35; Destroyers in period of Abyssinian War and Spanish Civil War, 1935-37; qualified as Torpedo Officer, 1938. Served War of 1939-45, in Cruisers; H.M.S. Norfolk at sinking of Scharnhorst, 1943; Commander, 1944; transferred to newly formed Electrical Branch, 1946; Captain, 1952; Commanded: H.M.S. Ariel, Air Electrical School, Winchester, 1955-57; H.M.S. Collingwood, Main Electrical School, Fareham, 1957-59; Chief Staff Officer (Technical) to Commander-in-Chief, Portsmouth, 1960-61; Director, Engineering and Electrical Training Division, Training Department, Admiralty, and Dep. Chief Engineering Officer, 1961-62; retired, Aug. 1962. *Address:* The Chestnuts, St. Cross, Winchester. *T.:* Winchester 4894. [*Died* 5 *Feb.* 1965.

POTIER, Gilbert George, D.F.C. 1942 and Bar, 1944; Deputy Chairman, Consolidated Gold Fields Ltd. since 1961 (Managing Director, 1958-61); *b.* 28 June 1915; *s.* of late Cecil William Louis Potier; *m.* 1945, Mary, *d.* of Thomas White Moore; two *d.* *Educ.:* Caterham Sch., Surrey. A.C.A. 1937. Served War of 1939-45 as Pilot, R.A.F., 210 and 53 Squadrons. Partner in Limebeer & Co., Chartered Accountants, 1947-57. Dir., Johnson Matthey & Co. Ltd. and various other companies. *Recreations:* tennis, golf, walking. *Address:* 8 Victoria Grove, W.8. *T.:* 01-584 8416; Sea Shells, Selborne Way, East Preston, Sx. *T.:* Rustington 4200. *Clubs:* Hurlingham; Royal and Ancient (St. Andrews). [*Died* 11 *Jan.* 1969.

POTT, Anthony Percivall, C.B. 1961; A.R.I.B.A.; A.A.dip.; Chief Architect, Ministry of Education, since 1956; *b.* 28 July 1904; *s.* of late Henry Percivall Pott and Magdalen Margaret Ord; *m.* 1934, Janet, *d.* of late Henry Martineau Fletcher; one *s.* one *d.* *Educ.:* Oundle School; Architectural Association School. Senior Architect, Building Research Station, Department of Scientific and Industrial Research, 1943-49; Principal Architect, Ministry of Education, 1949-56. *Publications:* papers on technical subjects. *Address:* 56 Addison Avenue, W.11. *T.:* Park 5301. [*Died* 23 *Feb.* 1963.

POTT, Gladys Sydney, C.B.E. 1937; *b.* 1867; *d.* of Ven. Alfred Pott, D.D., Archdeacon of Berkshire. *Educ.:* Privately. Woman

Inspector under Women's Branch of Board of Agriculture, 1916-19; Woman Delegate to Canada under Dominion Office to enquire into post-war conditions of Women's Work, 1939; Woman Officer of Oversea Settlement Dept of Dominions Office and Chairman of Society for Oversea Settlement of British Women, 1920-37; visited India and S. Africa and Rhodesia, 1921; Delegate on Migration to Australia and New Zealand, 1923; Attended International Conference on Migration in Rome on behalf of Dominion Office, 1921; International Labour Office Conference on Migration in Geneva on behalf of Dominion Office, 1926; has taken part in various Conferences on Migration. *Address:* Little Place, Clifton-Hampden, Oxon. *T.:* Clifton-Hampden 202. [*Died* 13 *Nov.* 1961.

POTT, H(enry) Percivall; M.P. (C.) Devizes Division of Wiltshire since 1955; director and farmer; *b.* 29 March 1908; *s.* of late Henry Percivall Pott, Upham House, Upham, Hants; *m.* 1946, Mary Vera, *d.* of Falconer Balston Larkworthy. *Educ.:* Oundle School. Member of County Executive Committee of National Farmers' Union, Northamptonshire, 1936, Hampshire, 1947-1952; Member of Estate Management Cttee. of Hampshire Agricultural Executive Cttee., 1948-53; Member of Hampshire County Council, 1949-; J.P. Hampshire, 1951. Chairman of Wey Valley Water Co.; Director of Mid-Wessex Water Co. Served War of 1939-45 with Royal Air Force Volunteer Reserve, 1941-46; retired with rank of Squadron Leader. *Address:* Coopers Bridge, Bramshott, Liphook, Hants; c/o House of Commons, S.W.1. [*Died* 17 *Jan.* 1964.

POTTER, Sir Alan (Graeme), Kt. 1960; *b.* England, 14 February 1891; *m.* 1926, Barbara Bowker; two *d.* *Educ.:* Winchester College, England. *Recreation:* golf. *Address:* 2 Castlereagh Street, Sydney, N.S.W., Australia. *Club:* Union (Sydney). [*Died* 20 *Nov.* 1969.

POTTER, Carlyle Thornton, M.D., C.M.; F.R.C.P.; retired; late Physician: Children's Department, West London Hospital, Evelina Hospital for Sick Children, Queen Elizabeth Hospital for Children; Pædiatrician, Kingsbury Maternity Hospital; Medical Consultant National Institute for the Blind; Associate Lecturer in Pædiatrics, Guy's Hospital Medical School. *Educ.:* McGill Univ. M.D., C.M. McGill 1923; L.C.P.S. Quebec 1923; M.R.C.P. Lond. 1934; F.R.C.P. Lond. 1944. Formerly: Med. Registrar, Maida Vale Hosp.; House Phys., Children's Hosp., Paddington Green and West End Hosp. for Nervous Diseases, Regent's Park. F.R.Soc.Med.; Past Pres. Section Pædiatrics, Roy. Soc. Med.; Mem. Brit. Pædiatric Assoc. *Address:* 27 Manor Road, Barnet, Herts. [*Died* 6 *Nov.* 1962.

POTTER, Lt.-Col. Claud Furniss, C.M.G. 1919; D.S.O. 1916; late R.A.; *b.* 26 May 1881; *s.* of W. Furniss Potter, M.Inst.C.E., Arundel Lodge, Ilkley; *m.* 1st, 1920, Ann Janet Baird (*d.* 1920), *widow* of Farquhar Gray Tinn of Kirkhill Castle, Colmonell, Ayrshire; 2nd, 1922, Annie Gwendolen Shelley, 2nd *d.* of H. Fell, Rostherne, Ilkley, Yorks; two *s.* one *d.* *Educ.:* Marlborough College; Royal Military Academy, Woolwich. Served S. African War, 1902 (Queen's medal and four clasps); European War, 1914-19 (wounded, despatches, C.M.G., D.S.O., Bt. Lt.-Col.); p.s.c. 1913; retired pay, 1926. *Address:* c/o Lloyds Bank, Ltd., 6 Pall Mall, S.W.1. *Club:* United Service. [*Died* 29 *Jan.* 1965.

POTTER, Colonel Colin Kynaston, D.S.O. 1917; O.B.E. 1944; M.C.; T.D.; D.L.; Territorial Army, retired; *b.* 27 Sep. 1877; *o. surv. s.* of late Edmund Peel Potter, J.P., Bowfell, Windermere; *m.* 1908, Hazel (*d.* 1960), *d.* of late Rev. P. Read, Bolton; four *s.* *Educ.:* Malvern Coll. Joined 2nd V.B. Loyal North Lancs Regt., 1900; served S. African War, 1901-02 (Queen's medal 4 clasps); transferred 5th Bn. L.N. Lancs Regt. T.F., 1908; served European War, 1914-18; commanded 1/7th Bn. The Kings (Liverpool) Regt., 1916-19; commanded 5th Bn. The Loyal Regt. T.A., 1920-26 (M.C., D.S.O. and bar, despatches 5 times, T.D.). Commanded 5th County of Lancaster Regt. Home Guard, 1940-44. *Address:* Knowle Hotel, Sidmouth, Devon. *T.:* Sidmouth 955. [*Died* 28 *Feb.* 1964.

POTTER, Brig.-Gen. Herbert Cecil, C.B. 1927; C.M.G. 1918; D.S.O. 1917; late The King's (Liverpool Regt.) and The Royal Warwickshire Regt.; late Colonel Commandant 3rd Indian Infantry Brigade, Peshawar; *b.* 1875; *s.* of late Frederick Anthony Potter, B.A., B.Sc.; *m.* Mary Kingston (*d.* 1935), *d.* of late Rev. Moule Griffith; one *s.* two *d.* *Educ.:* Bedford Modern School. Served South African War, 1901-2 (Queen's medal and three clasps); Sudan, 1908 (medal and clasp, 4th Class Osmanieh, 3rd Class Mejidieh), European War, 1914-18 (despatches, C.M.G., D.S.O., Legion of Honour, Bt. Lt.-Col., Bt. Col.); retired pay, 1927. *Address:* Exning Lawn, Christ Church Road, Cheltenham. *T.:* 54953. [*Died* 11 *June* 1964.

POTTER, Lt.-Col. James Archer, C.B.E. 1919; T.D.; *b.* 1875; *s.* of W. H. Potter; *m.* 1921, Helen May *d.* of late G. S. Beaumont, Bradford. Major and Brevet Lt.-Col., Leicestershire Regt. (T.A.) Served European War, 1914-19 (C.B.E.). *Address:* Barn Close, Oadby, Leicester. [*Died* 12 *Nov.* 1962.

POTTER, Rupert Barnadiston; President (late Chairman), Simon Engineering Ltd.; *b.* 23 Oct. 1899; *y. s.* of late John Wilson Potter and Jane Boyd Potter; *m.* 1946, Barbara (*d.* 1970), *widow* of Stanley Cooper; no *c.* *Educ.:* Winchester; Trinity Coll., Cambridge. Served European War, R.F.A., 1918-19; B.A. Hons. Engineering, Cambridge, 1921. *Recreations:* racing, reading; formerly golf. *Address:* 34 Parkside, Knightsbridge, S.W.1. *Clubs:* Bath; Royal St. George's Golf (Sandwich). [*Died* 19 *Aug.* 1970.

POTTER, Stephen; Author; *b.* 1 February 1900; *s.* of Frank Collard Potter and Elizabeth Reynolds; *m.* 1st, 1927, Mary Attenborough (marriage dissolved, 1955); two *s.*; *m.* 2nd, 1955, Heather, *o. d.* of late Brig. C. A. Lyon, D.S.O.; one *s.* *Educ.:* Westminster School; Merton College, Oxford. Hons. English Language and Literature, 1923; Sec. to Henry Arthur Jones, the dramatist, 1925; Lecturer in English Literature, London University, 1926; joined staff of B.B.C., 1938, as writer-producer. 1942 Editor of literary features and poetry. 1943 Chairman of Literary Committee. Principal programmes: How series, with Joyce Grenfell; Professional portraits; Originator and Editor of New Judgment series. Dramatic critic of the New Statesman, 1945-46; book critic of the News Chronicle, 1946-47; Editor of Leader Magazine, 1949-51. *Publications:* The Young Man, a novel, 1929; D. H. Lawrence, A First Study, 1930; The Nonesuch Coleridge, 1934; Minnow among Tritons, Letters of Mrs. S. T. Coleridge, 1934; Coleridge and S.T.C., 1935; The Muse in Chains, A Study in Education, 1937; Gamesmanship, 1947; Lifemanship, 1950; One-Upmanship, 1952; Humour Anthology, 1954; Potter on America, 1956; Supermanship, 1958; The Magic Number, 1959; Steps to Immaturity, 1959; Squawky: The Adventures of a Clasperchoice, 1964; Anti-Woo, 1965; The Complete Golf Gamesmanship, 1968; Pedigree: The Evolution of English nature words. *Address:* 23 Hamilton

Terrace, N.W.8. *T.:* 01-286 5567. *Clubs:* Savile, Garrick; Leander; Royal and Ancient; Edinburgh Croquet.
[*Died* 2 *Dec.* 1969.

POULENC, Francis; French composer; *b.* Paris, 7 Jan. 1899; pupil of Ricardo Viñes (piano) and of Charles Koechlin (composi, tion). *Works* include: Rapsodie nègre, 1916; Mouvement perpétuel, 1917; Le Bestiare d'Apollinaire, 1919; Sonata for Clarinet and Piano, 1921; Poems of Ronsard, 1925; Les Biches (ballet prod. by Diaghilev), 1925; Trio, 1926; Concert champêtre, 1927; Aubade (ballet), 1929; Les Animaux modèles (ballet), 1942; Figure humaine (cantata for double choir, first performed B.B.C., 25 March 1945), 1943; Les Mamelles de Tirésias (opéra-bouffe), 1944; Dialogues des Carmelites (opera), 1956 (prod. as The Carmelites, Covent Garden, 1958). Hon. D.Mus. Oxford Univ., 1958. *Address:* 5 rue de Médicis, Paris. *T.:* Danton 52.23.
[*Died* 30 *Jan.* 1963.

POUND, Roscoe; University Professor Emeritus, Harvard; *b.* Lincoln, Nebraska, U.S.A., 27 Oct. 1870; *s.* of Judge Stephen Bosworth Pound of Lincoln, Nebraska; *m.* 1st, 1899, Grace (*d.* 1928), *d.* of Leander Gerrard of Columbus, Nebraska; 2nd, 1931, Lucy Berry, *widow* of Lieut.-Colonel James E. Miller, U.S. Army. *Educ.:* University of Nebraska (A.B. 1888; A.M. 1889; Ph.D. 1897): Harvard Law School; Hon. LL.D., Universities of Michigan, 1913, of Nebraska, 1913, of Chicago, 1916, of Missouri, 1916; Brown Univ., 1919; Harvard Univ, 1920; Univ. of Cambridge, 1922; and others; Hon. L.H.D., Boston Univ., 1933; J.U.D., Univ. of Berlin, 1934. Admitted to Bar, 1890; Commissioner of Appeals, Supreme Court of Nebraska, 1901-3; Prof. of Law and Dean of the Law School, Univ. of Nebraska, 1903-7; Prof. of Law, North-western Univ., 1907-9; Prof. of Law, Univ. of Chicago, 1909-10; Story Professor of Law, 1910-13; Carter Professor of Jurisprudence, 1913-37; and Dean of the Faculty of Law of Harvard University, 1916-36; University Professor, 1937-47; Prof. of Law, Univ. of Calif., at Los Angeles, 1949-53. Tagore Prof. of Law, Univ. of Calcutta, 1948 (lectures delivered, 1953); member of several foreign academies; member of National Commission on Law Observance and Enforcement, 1929; Legal Adviser to Chinese Ministry of Justic, 1946-1949. President American Academy of Arts and Sciences, 1935-37; President Académie Internat. de Droit Comparé, 1950-56; Hon. Fellow Stanford University. *Publications:* The Spirit of the Common Law, 1921; An Introduction to the Philosophy of Law, 1922 (revised ed., 1954); Interpretations of Legal History, 1923; Law and Morals, 2nd edition, 1926; Criminal Justice in America, 1930; Lectures on the Philosophy of Freemasonry, 1915; Lectures on Masonic Jurisprudence, 1920; Readings on the History and System of the Common Law, 3rd ed., 1927; Readings in Roman Law, 2nd ed., 1915; Pound's Edition Ames and Smith's Cases on Torts, 1917; Outlines of Lectures on Jurisprudence, 5th ed., 1943; Outlines of a Course on Legislation, 1934; The Formative Era of American Law, 1936; The History and System of the Common Law, 1939; Contemporary Juristic Theory, 1940; Organization of Courts, 1940; Appellate Procedure in Civil Cases, 1941; Administrative Law, its Growth, Procedure, and Significance, 1942; Social Control through Law, 1942; New Paths of the Law, 1950; Justice According to Law, 1951; The Lawyer from Antiquity to Modern Times, 1953; Masonic Addresses and Writings of Roscoe Pound, 1953; Jurisprudence, 5 vols., 1959. *Recreation:* botany (Director of the Botanical Survey of Nebraska, 1891-1901). *Address:* Hotel Commander, Cambridge 38, Massachusetts, U.S.A. [*Died* 1 *July* 1964.

POUNSETT, Clement Aubrey, C.M.G. 1965; Member, South Australian Forestry Board; Public Service Commissioner and Chairman, Public Service Board, South Australia, 1961-65; *b.* 16 May 1900; *s.* of Henry Walter and Mary Blanche Pounsett; *m.* 1930, Mona Ruth, *d.* of Kenneth and Grace Campbell; no *c.* *Educ.:* Pulteney Grammar School, Adelaide. Entered Public Service, South. Australia, 1917; Secretary: Public Service Classification and Efficiency Board, 1926; South Australia Public Stores Dept., 1936; Public Service Comrs. Dept., 1941; Asst. Public Service Comr., 1949. Chm., S. Aust. Supply and Tender Board, 1958-65. F.C.I.S. (past Chm., S. Aust. branch), A.A.S.A. *Recreations:* football, cricket, tennis, bowls, reading. *Address:* 19 Kennaway St., Tusmore, S. Australia. *T.:* 3.5808. *Club:* Commonwealth (Adelaide).
[*Died* 28 *April* 1968.

POVAH, Reverend John Walter; Major, retired pay; *b.* 31 May 1883; *s.* of Rev. F. K. Povah and Mary Eleanor, *e. d.* of D. Haydon, Guildford; *m.* 1919, Winifred, *yr. d.* of H. Keith; one *d.* *Educ.:* Charterhouse. Royal Field Artillery, 1901-19; served France, 1914-18 (despatches); studied at King's College, London; B.D. 1922, 1st class Honours in Hebrew and Aramaic, including Syriac, 1923; General Secretary Church Tutorial Classes Association, 1923-26; Tutorial Secretary, 1926-1929; ordained in Diocese of Birmingham, 1931; Assistant Curate, St. Stephen's, Selly Hill, Birmingham, 1931-32; Vicar, St. Mark's, Londonderry, Smethwick, 1934-42; Rector of Ullingswick, 1942-45. *Publications:* A Study of the Old Testament; The New Psychology and the Hebrew Prophets; The Old Testament and Modern Problems in Psychology; Helps to the Study of the Historical Books of the Old Testament; Concerning the Editing of the Gospel Narratives, 1960. *Recreation:* walking. *Address:* 26 Broad Street, Bromyard, Herefordshire.
[*Died* 14 *Jan.* 1961.

POWELL, A. R. P. B., 2nd Baron; *see* Baden-Powell.

POWELL, Canon Arnold Cecil, M.A.; *b.* 18 Sept. 1882; *s.* of W. H. Powell, London; *m.* 1909, Mary Winnifred (*d.* 1954), *d.* of A. Walker, Haxby Hall, York; two *s.* one *d.*; *m.* 1955, Eva, *widow* of Canon Salwey, Chichester. *Educ.:* St. Olave's School, London; Trinity College, Cambridge (Open Exhibitioner). 2nd Classes in Parts I. and II. of The Natural Sciences Tripos; Assistant Master at Gresham's School, Holt; King's School, Grantham; Sedbergh School; Headmaster of Skipton Grammar School; Bedford Modern School; Headmaster of Epsom College, 1922-39; Rector of Graffham with Lavington, 1939-47; Rural Dean of Petworth, 1945-47; Prebendary of Highleigh, 1947; Custos of St. Mary's Hospital, Chichester, 1954-62. *Address:* 1 Mount Lane, Chichester, Sussex. *Club:* Public Schools. [*Died* 15 *Nov.* 1963.

POWELL, Cecil Frank, F.R.S. 1949; M.A., Ph.D. (Cantab.); Hon. Sc.D. (Dublin, Bordeaux, Warsaw, Berlin, Padua, Moscow); Melville Wills Professor of Physics in the University of Bristol, 1948-63; Director of the H. H. Wills Physics Laboratory, 1964-69; *b.* 5 December, 1903; *s.* of Frank and Elizabeth Powell, Tonbridge, Kent; *m.* 1932, Isobel Therese Artner; two *d.* *Educ.:* Judd School, Tonbridge; Sidney Sussex College, Cambridge (Scholar). 1st Class Hons. in Parts I and II of Natural Science Tripos, 1924-25; Research Assistant to Professor A. M. Tyndall, in Bristol, 1928; Member Expedition, organised jointly by Royal Society and Colonial Office, to investigate seismic and volcanic activity in Montserrat, British West Indies. 1935; Director of European expedition for making high altitude balloon flights, Sardinia, 1952,

Po Valley, 1954, 1955 and 1957; Chm. Scientific Policy Cttee. of European Organisation for Nuclear Research (C.E.R.N.), Geneva, 1961-63; Mem. Science Research Council of the U.K. and Chm. of its Nuclear Physics Bd., 1965-68. Foreign Member: Roy. Dublin Academy; Acad. Sciences of the U.S.S.R.; Vernon Boys Prizeman; Hon. Fellow: Physical Soc. of London, 1947; Sidney Sussex Coll., Cambridge, 1966; Hughes medallist of the Royal Soc., 1949; Nobel Prize for Physics, 1950; Royal Medal, Roy. Soc., 1961; Lomonosov Gold Medal (Sov. Acad. Sci.), 1967; Guthrie Medal of the Inst. of Physics and Physical Soc., 1969. *Publications:* (with G. P. S. Ochialini) Nuclear Physics in Photographs, 1947; (with P. H. Fowler and D. H. Perkins) Studies of Elementary Particles by the Photographic Method, 1959; numerous papers to learned societies on discharge of electricity in gases, and on development of photographic method in nuclear physics. *Recreations:* squash racquets and tennis. *Address:* 12 Golney Avenue, Clifton, Bristol 8. [*Died* 9 *Aug.* 1969.

POWELL, Lt.-Col. Evelyn George Harcourt; late Grenadier Guards; *b.* 21 Feb. 1883; *m.*; two *d.* Entered army, 1901; retired pay, 1927; M.P. (U.) S.E. Southwark, 1931-35. *Address:* 31 Hillgate Place, W.8. [*Died* 15 *July* 1961.

POWELL, Emeritus Professor Raphael, D.C.L.; Professor of Roman Law in the University of London, 1955-64; *b.* Bristol, 4 Aug. 1904; *e. s.* of Maurice and Esther Powell; *m.* 1927, Catherine, *e. d.* of Julius and Elizabeth Rosenthal; one *s.* one *d.* *Educ.:* Hereford Cathedral School; Brasenose College, Oxford. Somerset Thornhill Schol. in Classics, 1922; B.A., 1st cl. hons., 1925; B.C.L. 1926; Senior Hulme Schol., 1926; Harmsworth Law Schol., 1927; Barstow Law Schol., 1929; M.A. 1929; called to Bar, Middle Temple, 1929; D.C.L. 1953. Asst. in Law, Univ. Coll., London, 1931; Lectr. in Law, Univ. of Leeds, 1932-36; Head of Law Dept., Univ. Coll., Hull, 1937-1949; Reader in Law, Univ. Coll., London, 1949-55; Dean, Faculty of Laws: Univ. Coll., London, 1957-59; University of London, 1962-. War service, 1940-45; commissioned in R.A., 1940; Staff Capt., War Office (S.P.3), 1944-45. Chm., Central British Fund for German Jewry (Leeds cttee.), 1934-36; Pres. Leeds Zionist Soc., 1933-36; Mem. Provincial Exec. Cttee., Zionist Fedn., 1935-37; educational work in youth clubs, 1934-39; Chm. Central Hull Divl. Lab. Party, 1939; Chm. Hillel Foundation Education Cttee., 1954-60; Mem., U.K. Committee of Comparative Law, 1950-64. *Publications:* Law of Agency, 1933; Law of Agency, 1952, 2nd edn., 1961. Ed. and contrib. The Principles and Practice of Judaism (essays), 1959. Articles in Current Legal Problems and other periodicals. *Recreations:* cooking, crosswords, cricket. *Address:* 86b Marlborough Mansions, N.W.3. *T.:* Hampstead 0091. *Club:* M.C.C. [*Died* 30 *Nov.* 1965.

POWELL, Richard, C.I.E. 1947; Indian Police Service, retired; *b.* 4 Apr. 1889; *s.* of late Richard John Powell and late Alice Alethia Powell; *m.* 1955, Dorothy Coxon. *Educ.:* Bedford School (Head of School). Indian Police Service, 1908; Deputy Inspector-General of Police, United Provinces, 1935-40; Inspector-General of Police, Ajmer and Rajputana, 1940-43; War Transport Department, Govt. of India, 1944-45; Inspector-Gen. of Police, Jammu and Kashmir, 1946-47. Organised evacuation by air of British residents in Kashmir in 1947. With Indian Army in European War, 1915-16, and Third Afghan War, 1919. *Recreations:* Rugby football (School XV), hockey, pig-sticking and lawn tennis (played in Wimbledon championships). *Address:* The Dell, Seven Corners Lane, Beverley, Yorkshire. *T.:* Beverley 82308; c/o National and Grindlay's Bank Ltd., 54 Parliament Street, S.W.1. *Clubs:* East India and Sports, Queen's. [*Died* 14 *July* 1961.

POWELL, Ronald Arthur; *b.* 15 Sept. 1888; *s.* of late Arthur Powell, K.C.; *m.* 1925, Violet, 2nd *d.* of late Sir W. G. Alcock, M.V.O. *Educ.:* Winchester; New College, Oxford. Called to Bar, Middle Temple, 1914; Oxford Circuit and C.C.C.; served European War, 1914-19; Hampshire Regt., Macedonia. Metropolitan Magistrate, Tower Bridge, 1926; Greenwich and Woolwich, 1927; West London, 1928; Westminster, 1934, till closed, 1942; Lambeth, 1942-44; Marylebone, 1944-49; retired, 1949. *Address:* Heathercliff, Northview Road, Budleigh, Salterton, Devon. *Club:* United University. [*Died* 30 *Oct.* 1966.

POWELL, Samuel M.; *see* Morgan-Powell.

POWELL, Sidney, C.M.G. 1957; Chartered Accountant, in practise since 1919, Australia; *b.* 26 June 1894; *s.* of Alfred and Eliza Powell; *m.* 1921, Linda Dorothy Barns; one *s.* one *d.* *Educ.:* Sturt St. Public School; Muirden College, Australia. Pres. Associated Chambers of Commerce in Australia, 1953-55; Pres. Adelaide Chamber of Commerce, 1940-42; Chairman State Council, Chartered Institute of Accountants in Australia, 1942-44. Director: Bank of Adelaide; Adelaide Cement Co. Ltd. (Chm.); Guinea Airways Ltd. (Chm.); Quarry Industries Ltd. (Chm.); Salt Industries Ltd.; Australian Cotton Textile Industries Ltd.; Onkaparinga Woollen Co. Ltd.; Executor Trustee & Agency Co. of S.A. Ltd.; and various other companies. *Recreation:* golf. *Address:* Kumara, Hawthorn Crescent, Hawthorn, South Australia. *T.:* U 2152. *Clubs:* Adelaide, Royal Adelaide Golf (Adelaide). [*Died* 17 *Dec.* 1964.

POWELL, Colonel William Jackson, C.I.E. 1930; M.D. Dublin; *b.* 17 Dec. 1881; *s.* of Ven. Dacre H. Powell, D.D., Archdeacon of Cork, and E. L. Cummins; *m.* 1913, Moila Deane (Artist); four *d.* *Educ.:* Llandaff Cathedral School; Dover College; Trinity College, Dublin; The Purser Medal, the Fitzpatric Scholarship, and the Haughton Clinical Medals at Sir P. Dun's Hospital, Dublin. Entered I.M.S., 1905; House Surgeon, Sir P. Dun's Hospital, Dublin, 1906; served in Mesopotamia, India, Persia, and Russia, European War (despatches, severely wounded, Battle of Ctesiphon); Inspector-General of Prisons, C.P., 1923-35; Represented India Commission Internationale Pénal et Pénitentiaire, 1930-35; Officiating Inspector-General of Civil Hospitals and Director of Public Health, C.P., 1933-34; A.D.M.S. Kohat District, 1935-37; A.D.M.S. Peshawar District, India, 1937-38; Hon. Surgeon to the King, 1937-38; retired, 1938; R.A.F., 1938-39. Hon. M.O. Savernake Hospital, Marlborough, 1940-49. Mem. Marlborough and Ramsbury R.D.C., 1949-55; Wilts. C.C. 1952-58. *Publications:* Indian Prisons, 1927. *Recreations:* riding, fishing, sailing. *Address:* The Croft, Great Bedwyn, Marlborough, Wilts. [*Died* 8 *Feb.* 1961.

POWELL-PRICE, John Cadwgan, C.I.E. 1941; E.D.; M.A.; *b.* 11 June 1888; *s.* of late Chancellor C. Powell-Price, of Bangor Cathedral, and Marion Lewis; *m.* 1923, Evelyn, *d.* of late Rev. E. S. Oakley, Almora, India; one *s.* *Educ.:* St. John's School, Leatherhead; Selwyn College, Cambridge (Exhib. Classics). B.A. 1910, M.A. 1919; Asst. Master, Portsmouth Grammar School, 1912; Vice-Principal, Meerut Coll., India, 1913-14; Indian Army, R. of O., 8th Rajputs, 1914; Special Service Officer, Alwar Imperial

Service Infantry, 1915-19, Suez Canal, Sinai and Palestine (despatches); entered Indian Educational Service, 1920; Educational Commissioner with the Government of India, 1936; Director of Public Instruction, United Provinces, 1939-43; Lieut.-Col. commanding Allahabad Contingent A.F.(I), 1937-43. Councillor, Oxford City Council, 1945-46. *Publications:* The Teaching of History in Indian Schools, 1934; Indian Coins and Inscriptions (with Professor R. K. Mukherji and R. B. Prayag Dayal), 1937; A History of India, 1955; articles in historical and educational journals. *Address:* 119A Ladbroke Road, W.11. *T.:* Park 8287.
[*Died* 13 *Feb.* 1964.

POWER, Hon. Charles Gavan, P.C. Can., 1935; Q.C. Can.; M.C.; LL.L.; LL.D.; Senator, Canada, since 1955; appointed a Fellow under Skelton-Clark Memorial Foundation, Queen's University, 1960-61; *b.* Sillery, Quebec, 18 Jan. 1888; *s.* of William Power and Susan Rockett; *m.* 1912, Rosemary, *d.* of late William H. Pendleton, Montreal; two *s.* one *d.* *Educ.:* Loyola College, Montreal; Laval Univ., Quebec. M.P. House of Commons, Canada, 1917; Minister of Pensions and National Health in Mr. King's Cabinet, 1935; Postmaster-General of Canada, Sept. 1939; Minister of National Defence for Air, Canada, May 1940-1944, and Associate Minister of National Defence, July 1940-44. Enlisted Jan. 1915; served Overseas, Captain and Acting Major (twice wounded, M.C.); invalided from service, 1918. *Address:* 10 Du Fort St., Quebec, Can. *T.:* 3-9619. *Clubs:* Garrison, Lake Ste. Anne Fish and Game (Quebec); Rideau (Ottawa). [*Died* 30 *May* 1968.

POWER, Gerald, C.M.G. 1941; *b.* 7 Feb. 1891; *m.* 1943, Elizabeth Primrose, *d.* of late F. J. L. Shaw, Bournemouth and Tientsin, North China. *Educ.:* Denstone Coll.; Queen's College, Oxford. Superintendent Education Dept. Northern Nigeria, 1914; Assistant Director of Education, Gold Coast, 1929, Dir. of Educ., 1933-Jan. 1947. *Address:* c/o National Provincial Bank Ltd., 208-209 Piccadilly, W.1. [*Died* 25 *Sept.* 1967.

POWER, General Thomas Sarsfield, D.S.M. (U.S.) 1945; Silver Star, 1945; Legion of Merit with one Oak Leaf Cluster, 1945; D.F.C. 1944; Bronze Star 1945; Army Commendation Medal with one Oak Leaf Cluster, 1946, etc.; Vice-Chairman, Eversharp Inc.; Director: Bucyrus-Erie Co.; Hedge Fund of America Inc.; *b.* 18 June 1905; *s.* of late Thomas S. and Mary Rice Power; *m.* 1936, Mae Ayre of Newcastle upon Tyne, England; no *c.* *Educ.:* Graduate Barnard Preparatory School, New York City, 1922. Commissioned 2nd Lieut. U.S. Army Air Corps, 1929. Served War, 1941-45: Exec. and Dep. Comdr. 304th Bomb Wing, Italy, Jan.-Aug. 1944; Comdr., 314th Bomb Wing, Peterson Field, Colorado and Guam, 1944-45; Dep. Chief, Ops., U.S. Strategic A.F., Pacific, Aug.-Dec. 1945; H.Q. A.A.F., Washington, D.C., Dec. 1945-March 1946; Asst. Dep. Task Force Comdr. for Air (Op. Crossroads) Bikini Atoll, Pacific, March-Sept. 1946. Dep. Asst. Chief of Staff, Ops., H.Q.U.S.A.F., 1946-1947; Chief, Training Div. and later Chief, Requirements Div., Dep. Chief of Staff, Ops., H.Q.U.S.A.F., 1947-48; Air Attache, U.S. Embassy, London, June-Oct. 1948; Vice C.-in-C., Strategic Air Comd., Oct. 1948-April 1954; Comdr., Air Research and Development Comd., 1954-57; Commander-in-Chief, Strategic Air Command, United States Air Force, 1957-64, and, as additional duty, Director, Joint Strategic Target Planning Staff of Department of Defense, 1960-1964. Kt. of St. Sylvester, 1964; Kt. of St. Brigette, 1967. French Croix de Guerre with Palm, 1949. *Recreations:* golf, fishing and holds the black belt in judo. *Address:* (office) 5933 W. Slauson Ave., Culver City, Calif. 90232; (home) Thunderbird County Club, Palm Springs, Calif. 92262, U.S.A.
[*Died* 6 *Dec.* 1970.

POWICKE, Sir (Frederick) Maurice, Kt., *cr.* 194; M.A.; D.Litt.; Hon. D.Litt., (Cambridge and Durham); Hon. LL.D. (St. Andrews and Glasgow); Hon. Litt.D. (Manchester, Liverpool, Queen's Univ. Belfast, London, and Harvard); Hon. Doctor, University of Caen; F.B.A. 1927; Corresponding Fellow of the Mediaeval Academy of America, 1929; For. Associate Académie des Inscriptions et Belles-Lettres (Institut de France), 1951; Hon. Member Amer. Historical Assoc.; Hon. Member Massachusetts Historical Soc., 1947; Hon. Member Royal Irish Academy, 1949; Corr. Mem. Monumenta Germaniae Historica, 1955; Fell. of Merton Coll., Oxford, 1908-15, Hon. Fellow since 1932; Hon. Fellow of Balliol College since 1939; and of Oriel College since 1947; *b.* Alnwick, 16 June 1879; *s.* of Rev. F. J. Powicke, D.D.; *m.* 1909, Susan Irvine Martin, *d.* of late Rev. T. M. Lindsay, D.D.; two *d.* *Educ.:* Owens College, Manchester; Balliol College, Oxford. Professor of Modern History in the Queen's Univ., Belfast, 1909-19; Professor of Mediæval History in the University of Manchester, 1919-28; Ford's Lecturer in English History, Oxford, 1926-27; Regius Professor of Modern History, University of Oxford, 1928-47; President of Royal Historical Society, 1933-37. *Publications:* The Loss of Normandy, 1913, 2nd edn. 1961; Ailred of Rievaulx, 1922; Stephen Langton, 1928; Medieval England, 1931; The Medieval Books of Merton College, 1931; The Christian Life in the Middle Ages, 1935; 2nd edn. (with A. B. Emden) of Rashdall's Univs. of Europe in the Middle Ages, 1936; History, Freedom and Religion (The Riddell Lectures, University of Durham, 1937), 1938; editor of Handbook of British Chronology (Royal Historical Society), 1939; The Reformation in England, 1941; King Henry III and the Lord Edward, 1947; Ways of Medieval Life and Thought, 1950; Walter Daniel's Life of Ailred, 1950; The Thirteenth Century, (Oxford History of England), 1953, 2nd edn. 1962; Modern Historians and the study of history, 1955; articles in the English Historical Review and elsewhere. *Address:* 6 Oriel Square, Oxford. *T.:* Oxford 47384.
[*Died* 19 *May* 1963.

POWLETT, Vice-Adm. Frederick Armand, C.B.E. 1919; R.N., retired; *b.* 1873; *s.* of late Admiral Armand Temple Powlett, Manor House, Frankton, near Rugby; *m.* 1905, Nora (*d.* 1934), *d.* of Ernest Chaplin, Brooksby Hall, Leicester. Chief of Staff to Vice-Admiral Commanding E. Coast during European War (C.B.E.); Rising Sun (Japan) 3rd Class. *Address:* c/o Westminster Bank, Farnham, Surrey. [*Died* 3 *Dec.* 1963.

POWLEY, Edward B., D.Phil. (Oxon.); author; *b.* Narborough, Norfolk, 1887; *e. s.* of James Powley, farmer; *m.* 1st, 1914, Hilda Mary (*d.* 1960), *e. d.* of George Reeder, Narford; 2nd, 1962, Florence Mary Pomeroy (authoress); *Educ.:* King Edward VII Grammar School, King's Lynn; King's College, London (B.A. Hons. Philosophy), A.K.C. Master, Deacon's School, Peterborough; F.R.Hist.S. Served in Royal Navy during War of 1914-18 (Grand Fleet, Dover Patrol, Admiralty); at Royal Grammar School, Lancaster, 1919-20; followed research under Sir C. H. Firth, Balliol College, Oxford (B.Litt. Modern History); returned to teaching and, while at Caistor Grammar School, Lincs, 1922-25, simultaneously farmed in Norfolk; Merchant Taylors' School, Crosby, Lancs. (librarian), 1925-51; M.A. (Mediæval Hist.), Liverpool, 1941; Sometime Member Bootle Education Committee; Organiser of Education,

H.M. Borstal Institution, Gaynes Hall, Hunts. (part time appointment), 1953 - 57. C.C., Huntingdonshire, 1954-65; Mem. St. Neots Rural District Council, 1955-65; Dep. Traffic Comr., Eastern Traffic Area, 1955-67; Member Minister of Transport's Committee on Rural Bus Services, 1959-. Organised The Cromwell Museum, Huntingdon, opened 1962. Chairman, Grafham Parish Council; President, Hunts. and Peterborough Parish Councils' Assoc.; re-elected C.C. Huntingdon & Peterborough, 1967. D.Phil. (Oxon.) 1962. Began Literary career by contrib. to the Spectator under Strachey. *Publications:* The English Navy in the Revolution of 1688, with Foreword by Earl Jellicoe, 1928; Vicisti, Galilaee ? or Religion in England (To-day and To-morrow Series), 1929; A Hundred Years of English Poetry (the Cambridge continuation of Palgrave's Golden Treasury), 1931; republished in Canada, 1933; The Laurel Bough (English Epical Verse, 1380-1932), 1934. The House of de la Pomerai (Berry Pomeroy, Devon) 1066-1719, with Appendix, Post 1719, 1944; Poems 1914-1950, 1951; Cat., Cromwell Mus., Huntingdon, 1964; King William's War—Naval Affairs Nov. 1688 to June 1690, 1967. *Recreations:* gardening, travel. *Address:* The Old Rectory, Grafham, Huntingdon. *T.:* Buckden 261. *Clubs:* Authors', Pepys (Chm.). [*Died* 7 *Feb.* 1968.

POWNALL, Lt.-Gen. Sir Henry Royds, K.C.B., *cr.* 1945 (C.B. 1936); K.B.E. *cr.* 1940; D.S.O. 1918; M.C.; Col. Comdt. R.A., 1942-52; *b.* 1887; 2nd *s.* of late C. A. W. Pownall, Blackheath; *m.* 1918, Lucy Louttit Gray (*d.* 1950), *y. d.* of late William Henderson, Aberdeen. *Educ.:* Rugby School; Royal Military Academy, Woolwich; Staff College, Camberley; Imperial Defence College. Served in R.F.A. and R.H.A. in England and India, 1906-14; served in France, 1914-19 (D.S.O., M.C.); operations N.W.F. India, 1930-31 (Bar to D.S.O.); Brigade Major R.A., 17th Division, 1917-19; Brigade Major, School of Artillery, 1924-25; G.S.O. II. Staff College, Camberley, 1926-29; Military Assistant Secretary, Committee of Imperial Defence, 1933-35. Deputy Secretary, 1936; Commandant, School of Artillery, Larkhill, 1936-38; Director of Military Operations and Intelligence, War Office, 1938-39; Chief of General Staff, B.E.F., 1939-40; Inspector-General of Home Guard, 1940; commanded British Troops in Northern Ireland, 1940-41; Vice-Chief of Imperial General Staff, War Office, 1941; Commander-in-Chief, Far East, Dec. 1941-Jan. 1942; Lt.-Gen., 1942; Chief of Staff "A.B.D.A." Command, Far East, Jan.-Feb., 1942; G.O.C.Ceylon, March 1942-March 1943; C.-in-C. Persia-Iraq, 1943; Chief of Staff to Supreme Allied Comdr., S.-E. Asia Command, 1943-44; retd., 1945. Chm. Friary Meux Ltd.; Mem. Cttee., Lloyds Bank, 6 Pall Mall, Chief Commissioner St. John Ambulance Brigade, 1947-49; Vice-Chancellor Order of St. John, 1950, Chancellor 1951. G.C.St.J. *Recreation:* fishing. *Address:* 6 Launceston Place, W.8. *T.:* Western 4133. *Club:* Army and Navy. [*Died* 9 *June* 1961.

POWNALL, John Cecil Glossop, C.B. 1949; *b.* 11 March 1891; *e. s.* of Henry Harrison Pownall, J.P., Ades, Chailey, and of Blanche, *d.* of Col. J. J. Glossop, J.P.; *m.* 1925, Margaret Nina, *d.* of J. C. Jesson; two *s.* *Educ.:* Rugby School; Trinity College, Cambridge. Barrister-at-Law, Lincoln's Inn. Served European War, 1914-19, in France, Macedonia and Palestine; recalled for service 1940-42, Captain, R.A. Entered Charity Commission, 1921; Secretary, Charity Commission, 1942-44; Chief Charity Comr. 1944-53. *Address:* Byways, Steep, Petersfield, Hants. *Club:* Junior Carlton. [*Died* 19 *Dec.* 1967.

POWYS, John Cowper; author and poet; *b.* Shirley, Derbyshire, 8 October 1872; *s.* of Rev. C. F. Powys and Mary Cowper Johnson; *m.* Margaret Alice Lyon (*d.* 1947), Middlecot, S. Devon; one *s.* (decd.). *Educ.:* Sherborne Sch.; Corpus Christi Coll., Cambridge. Lectr. in Gt. Brit. and America. *Publications: novels:* Wood and Stone; Rodmoor; Ducdame; Wolf Solent (new edn., 1961); *poetry:* Wolfsbane; Mandragora; Samphire; Lucifer: a Narrative Poem, 1956; *philosophy:* The Complex Vision; The Religion of a Sceptic; *criticism:* Visions and Revisions; Suspended Judgments; The Meaning of Culture, 1930; In Defence of Sensuality, 1930; A Glastonbury Romance, 1933; A Philosophy of Solitude, 1933; John Cowper Powys: Autobiography, 1934; Jobber Skald, 1935; The Art of Happiness, 1935; Maiden Castle, 1936; Morwyn, 1937; The Pleasures of Literature, 1938; Owen Glendower, 1941; Mortal Strife, 1941; The Art of Growing Old, 1943; Dostoievsky, 1946; Rabelais, 1947; Porius, 1951; The Inmates, 1952; In Spite Of, 1953; Atlantis, 1954; The Brazen Head, 1956; Up and Out, 1957; Letters to L. U. Wilkinson, 1957; Homer and the Æther, 1959; All or Nothing, 1960. *Recreation:* walking. *Address:* 1 Waterloo, Blaenau-Ffestiniog, Merionethshire, North Wales. [*Died* 17 *June* 1963.

POWYS-JONES, Lionel, C.B.E. 1954; retired; served in Department of Native Affairs, Southern Rhodesia, 1915-54; Secretary for Native Affairs, Chief Native Commissioner and Director of Native Development, Southern Rhodesia, 1949-54; *b.* 14 July 1894; *s.* of Llewelyn Powys-Jones, J.P., resident Magistrate, Bulawayo; *m.* 1918' Dorothy Mary, *d.* of Lt.-Col. Charles Clayton; one *d.* *Educ.:* Blundell's School, Tiverton; Victoria College, Jersey; Oriel College, Oxford (Rhodes Scholar, Hons. Degree in Jurisprudence). Served European War, 1916-19: 2nd Rhodesia Regt. and 4th-60th Rifles (wounded 1918). *Recreations:* tennis and golf. *Club:* Salisbury (Salisbury, Rhodesia). [*Died* 27 *Nov.* 1966

POYNTER, Sir Hugh (Edward), 3rd Bt., *cr.* 1902; retired; Chairman, Richard Thomas & Baldwins (Aust.) Pty. Ltd., Sydney, N.S.W., from 1927; *b.* London, 28 Jan. 1882; *s.* of Sir Edward John Poynter, Bt., G.C.V.O., Pres. Royal Academy, and Agnes, *d.* of Rev. George Macdonald; *S.* brother, 1923; *m.* 1st, 1905, Mary Augusta Mason (*d.* 1930), *d.* of Charles M. Dickinson, U.S. Consul-General, Constantinople; no *c.*; 2nd, 1933, Linda Rule King (*d.* 1939), *d.* of late Ernest Rule Taylor, Pymble, N.S.W.; 3rd, 1939, Irene May (*d.* 1965), *d.* of late Cornelius E. Williams, Abertillery, Mon. *Educ.:* St. Michael's Sch., Westgate-on-Sea; St. Paul's Sch., London. Sec. to Sir Adam Block, K.C.M.G., President of the Council of Administration, Ottoman Public Debt, Constantinople, 1904; resigned on outbreak of war from the post of Assistant Comptroller of Technical Services; decorated with the Order of the Medjidieh; served four years in R.A.S. Corps in England and France; is honorary Captain in the Army; Agent in Paris for Baldwins, Ltd., 1919-21; President, Baldwins Canadian Steel Corporation, Ltd., Toronto, 1921-26; K.St.J.; Chevalier Legion of Honour. *Publications:* Contributions on finance to the Near East, and other financial papers. *Recreation:* motoring. *Heir:* none. *Address:* c/o Mrs. E. Drake, 6 Hume St., Wollstonecraft, Sydney, N.S.W., Australia. [*Died* 28 *June* 1968 (*ext.*).

PRANCE, Brig. Robert Courtenay, C.B.E. 1948; D.S.O. 1916; *b.* Evesham, 19 Feb. 1882; *s.* of Courtenay Garrard Prance; *m.* 1909, Estelle Veronica Cotter; no *c.* *Educ.:*

Haileybury; Woolwich. R.A., 2nd Lieutenant, 1900; Captain, 1910; Major, 1914; Lieut.-Colonel, 1925; Colonel, 1929; South Africa, 1902 (Queen's medal with four clasps); European War, 1914-18, France, Belgium, Balkans and Palestine (despatches four times, D.S.O., 1914 star, two medals); Commander R.A., 3rd Div., 1935-39; retired pay, 1939; War of 1939-45. B.R.A. Southern Command, 1939-42. *Address:* Eversfield, Broughton, nr. Stockbridge, Hants. [*Died* 4 *Feb.* 1966.

PRASAD, Dr. Rajendra, M.A., M.L., LL.D.; President of the Indian Republic, 1950-62; *b.* 3 Dec. 1884; *m.* Rajbansi Devi (*d.* 1962); two *s.* *Educ.:* Presidency Coll., Calcutta. Professor of English, G.B.B. College, Muzaffarpore, 1908; practised as lawyer, Calcutta High Court, 1911-16, Patna High Court, 1916-20; joined Mahatma Gandhi in Champaran Agrarian Movement; suspended practice as lawyer and joined non-co-operation movement, 1920; Gen. Sec., Indian National Congress; member, Congress Working Cttee.; President, Indian National Congress, 1934, 1939, 1947-48; imprisoned several times for taking part in Civil Disobedience Movement, for last time Aug. 1942; released, 1945; Minister for Food and Agriculture in Govt. of India, 1946-48; President Indian Constituent Assembly, Dec. 1946-50; other activities include propagation of Hindi, journalism, and social, humanitarian and relief work in general; one of founders of Patna English daily, Searchlight, and the Hindi Weekly, Desh. Bharat Ratna, 1962. *Publications:* India Divided; Atma Katha (autobiography); Mahatma Gandhi in Champaran; At the feet of Mahatma Gandhi. *Address:* Rashtrapati Bhavan, New Delhi, India. [*Died* 28 *Feb.* 1963.

PRATT, David Doig, C.B.E. 1955 (O.B.E. 1947); M.A., B.Sc., Ph.D., LL.D. St. Andrews; F.R.I.C.; retired as Director of the National Chemical Laboratory (Department of Scientific and Industrial Research), Teddington (1951-59); *b.* 8 March 1894; British; *m.* 1917, Minnie Elizabeth Hayman; two *s.* *Educ.:* Wald Academy, Anstruther, Fife; St. Andrews University; Manchester University. Served European War as Capt., H.L.I., 1914-19 (despatches). Chemical Research Laboratory, Teddington, 1925-59. *Publications:* (with late Sir G. T. Morgan) Rise and Development of British Chemical Industry, 1938; series of papers in Jl. of Chem. Soc. and Jl. of Soc. of Chem. Industry. *Recreation:* gardening. *Address:* Adastra, Ormond Crescent, Hampton, Middx. *T.:* Molesey 2588. *Club:* Savage. [*Died* 5 *May* 1962.

PRATT, Edwin John, C.M.G. 1946; M.A., Ph.D., F.R.S.C., Litt.D., D.C.L.; formerly Professor of English, Victoria College, University of Toronto, Canada, retired 1953; *b.* 4 Feb. 1883; *s.* of John and Fanny Pratt; *m.* 1918, Viola L. Whitney; one *d.* *Educ.:* University of Toronto, Canada. Awarded Canada Council Medal, 1962. *Publications:* Newfoundland Verse, 1923; The Witches' Brew, 1926; Titans, 1926; The Iron Door, 1927; The Roosevelt and the Antinoe, 1930; Verses of the Sea, 1930; Many Moods, 1933; The Titanic, 1935; The Fable of the Goats (Governor-General's Award), 1937; Brebeuf and His Brethren (Governor-General's Award), 1939; Dunkirk, 1941; Still Life, 1943; Collected Poems, 1944; They are Returning, 1945; Behind the Log, 1947; Towards the Last Spike (Governor-General's Award), 1952; Collected Poems, 1958; Here the Tides Flow, 1962. *Recreation:* golf. *Address:* 5 Elm Ave., Toronto 5, Canada. *T.:* Wa 5-6853. *Clubs:* P.E.N.; Arts and Letters (Toronto). [*Died* 26 *April* 1964.

PRATT, Sir John (Thomas), K.B.E., *cr.* 1929; C.M.G. 1919; *b.* 13 Jan. 1876; 6th *s.* of late Edward Pratt, of Indian Salt Revenue Service; *m.* 1st, 1914, Edith Violet (*d.* 1937), *d.* of late James Houson Parker, of Great Baddow, Essex, and of Slatwoods, East Cowes; one *d.*; 2nd, 1943, Dorothy, *d.* of A. H. Barker, Beckenham. *Educ.:* Dulwich College. Called to Bar, Middle Temple, 1905 (Certificate of Honour); Student Interpreter in China, 1898; British Assessor in Mixed Court at Shanghai, 1909; Vice-Consul in China, 1910; Consul at Tsinan, 1913; Consul-General, Tsinan, 1919; Nanking, 1922; Shanghai, 1924; transferred to Foreign Office, 1925; acting Counsellor in Diplomatic Service, 1929; retired, 1938; Head of Far East Section, Min. of Information, 1939-41; late F.O. Rep. on Universities China Cttee.; Chm. British and Chinese Corporation; Vice-Chm. Governing Body of School of Oriental and African Studies; Member of Scarborough Commission *Publications:* Great Britain and China; Japan and the Modern World, 1942; War and Politics in China, 1943; Before Pearl Harbour, 1943; China and Japan; China and Britain, 1944; Expansion of Europe into the Far East, 1947; several pamphlets. *Address:* Hollyoak, Nairdwood Lane, Prestwood, Nr. Great Missenden, Bucks. *T.:* Great Missenden 2521. [*Died* 23 *Jan.* 1970.

PRATT, Brigadier Reginald S.; *see* Sutton-Pratt.

PRATT, William Henry; *see* Karloff, Boris.

PRAUSNITZ GILES, Carl, M.D. Breslau; M.R.C.S., Eng. L.R.C.P. Lond.; Physician; late Hon. Research Fellow University of Manchester; *b.* 11 Oct. 1876; *s.* of Otto Prausnitz, M.D., Hamburg, and Edith Maria Giles, Bonchurch, Isle of Wight; changed name by deed poll to C. Prausnitz Giles; *m.* Margot Bruck; two *s.* one *d.* *Educ.:* Realgymnasium des Johanneums, Hamburg; Technical High School, Darmstadt; Universities of Leipzig, Kiel and Breslau. German medical qualification, 1901; M.D., 1903; Conjoint Board London qualification, 1908; Assistant, State Hygienic Institute, Hamburg, 1902-5; Demonstrator of Bacteriology, Royal Institute of Public Health, London, 1905-8; Assistant Bacteriologist, Metrop. Asylums Board, London, 1908-10; Assistant Hygienic Institute, University of Breslau, 1910-1923; Privatdozent of Hygiene, University of Breslau, 1912; Deputy Professor of Hygiene, University of Greifswald, Germany, 1923-26; Professor of Hygiene, University of Breslau, 1926-33; Hon. Research Fellow, University of Manchester, 1933-35; Medical Practitioner, 1935-. Hon. M.D. (Hamburg), 1960. *Publications:* Publications on cotton workers' asthma, cholera, typhoid, hay fever, allergy, Wassermann reaction, standardisation of sera, medical education, etc. *Address:* Kingseat, St. Boniface Road, Ventnor, I.W. [*Died* 21 *April* 1963.

PREBENSEN, Per Preben, Hon. G.C.V.O. 1951; Hon. C.B.E. 1930; Knight Grand Cross, Order of St. Olav, 1953, etc. Norwegian Ambassador to Italy since Dec. 1958; Norwegian Ambassador in London, 1946-58; Norwegian Minister to Irish Republic, 1950-1958; *b.* Risör, Norway, 6 Aug. 1896; *s.* of J. W. Prebensen, Shipowner; *m.* 1925, Ragnhild Fougner; two *s.* one *d.* *Educ.:* Norwegian Naval College. Served in Antwerp, Montreal, Moscow, and several periods in Min. of Foreign Affairs, Oslo; Head of Treaty Div., Min. of Foreign Affairs, 1935; Director, Foreign Trade Dept., Min. of Supply, later Min. of Commerce, 1939; Permanent Under-Sec. Min. of Foreign Affairs, 1945. Hon. D.C.L. Durham, 1958. *Address:* Norwegian Embassy, Largo dei Lombardi 21 Rome. [*Died* 21 *Oct.* 1961.

PREMPEH, II, Otumfuo Sir Osei Agyeman, K.B.E., *cr.* 1937; nephew to late Nana Agyeman Prempeh I; Kumasihene and direct descendant of late King Osei Tutu, the Founder of Ashanti Empire; Hon. Zone Organiser (with rank of Hon. Lt.-Col.) in Home Guard, 1942; *b.* 1892. *Educ.:* Wesleyan School, Kumasi. Became Kumasihene in 1931, in succession to his uncle Prempeh I; became Asantehene when Ashanti Confederacy was restored in 1935 by British Government. Silver Jubilee Medal, 1935; Coronation Medals, 1937, 1953. *Address:* Asantehene's Office, Manhyia, Kumasi, Ashanti, Ghana. *T.:* 2214. [*Died May* 1970.

PRENDIVILLE, Most Rev. Redmond; Archbishop of Perth (Australia) (R.C.), since 1935; *b.* 11 Sept. 1900. *Educ.:* National University of Ireland; All Hallows College, Dublin. Ordained 1925; Administrator of St. Mary's Roman Catholic Cathedral, 1928-1933; Coadjutor Archbishop of Perth, W.A., 1933-35. *Address:* St. Mary's Cathedral, Perth, W. Australia. [*Died* 28 *June* 1968.

PRENTICE, Frank Douglas; Secretary, Rugby Football Union, since 1947; *b.* 21 Sept. 1898; *s.* of Thomas and Catherine Prentice; *m.* 1921, Doris Hunter, *d.* of Robert and Agnes Goodacre; twin *s.* *Educ.:* Wyggeston School, Leicester. Served European War, 1914-18, in France, Royal Garrison Artillery; War of 1939-45 in R.A.O.C. International Rugby Union player, 1927-28; Captain, British Rugby team, New Zealand and Australia, 1930; Manager, British Rugby team, Argentina, 1936. *Recreations:* cricket, fishing. *Address:* Rugby Football Union, Twickenham, Middlesex. *T.:* Popesgrove 1697. *Clubs:* East India and Sports, Public Schools. [*Died* 3 *Oct.* 1962.

PRESCOTT, James C.; retired as Prof. of Electrical Engineering, King's Coll., Newcastle upon Tyne, 1959; now employed by English Electric Co.; *b.* 1894; *s.* of late James Mulleneux and Margaret Prescott; *m.* 1943; Doreen, *d.* of late H. Clark, Newcastle upon Tyne; one *s.* one *d.* *Educ.:* The Univ. of Liverpool. Research engineer, Metropolitan Vickers Ltd.; Lieut. R.N.V.R. attached to H.M. Mining School, Portsmouth; Lecturer in Electrical Engineering, University of Liverpool; Warden of the Halls of Residence for Men, University of Liverpool. *Publications:* contributions to technical journals. *Address:* c/o English Electric Company, Kidsgrove, Stoke-on-Trent. [*Died* 12 *June* 1964.

PRESCOTT, Richard Gordon, Bathgate, C.M.G. 1943; C.B.E. 1946 (O.B.E. 1941); retired; *b.* 30 May 1896. Joined Indian Police, 1915; Deputy Commissioner Police, Rangoon, 1937; Commissioner of Police, Rangoon, 1939; Inspector-General of Police, Burma, 1942. Deputy Director, Civil Affairs (Burma), 1944-1946. King's Police Medal, 1931. *Address:* Torphin, Harelaw Road, Colinton, Edinburgh 13. [*Died* 6 *Jan.* 1963.

PRESCOTT, Sir Richard Stanley, 2nd Bt., *cr.* 1938; *b.* 26 Jan. 1899; *s.* of Colonel Sir William Prescott, 1st Bt., C.B.E., and Bessie Smith (*d.* 1940), *d.* of late Mark Stanley, of Ambleside; *S.* father, 1945; *m.*; no *c.* *Educ.:* Caterham. Civil Engineer. Served, 1914-18, Beds. Regt., 1939-45, R.C.A.F. *Heir:* *n.* Mark Prescott, *b.* 3 March 1948. *Address:* 27 Maniton Rd., Centre Is., Toronto. [*Died* 21 *Jan.* 1965.

PRESCOTT, (William Robert) Stanley; *b.* 25 Apr. 1912; *yr. s.* of Col. Sir William Prescott, 1st Bt. and *heir-pres.* to 2nd Bt.; *m.* 1st, 1939, Gwendolen, *o. c.* of late Leonard Aldridge, C.B.E.; one *s.*; 2nd, 1951, Sheila Walker, *er. d.* of late Surgeon Rear-Adm. D. Walker Hewitt, C.B., C.M.G., F.R.C.S., and of Mrs. D. Walker Hewitt, Alverstoke, Hants. *Educ.:* St. John's College, Cambridge. Barrister, Gray's Inn, 1935. Freeman City of London. War of 1939-45, served in U.K. and overseas, 1939-43, when invalided. M.P. (C.) for Darwen Division of Lancashire, 1943-51. Member Court of Common Council, City of London, 1945-51; Member, Parl. Mission to Japan, 1947. *Address:* Flat 2, 66 Cadogan Square, S.W.1. *Club:* Devonshire. [*Died* 6 *June* 1962.

PRESTIGE, Major Sir John (Theodore), Kt., *cr.* 1919; *b.* 15 July 1884; *m.* 1917, Iris, *d.* of late Major C. R. E. Radclyffe; one *s.* two *d.* Contested (U.) Deptford, 1918; L.C.C., 1918-19; High Sheriff of Kent, 1931-32; much interested in Local Government work. Before retirement, for many years Dep. Chm. of J. Stone & Co. Ltd., Deptford, S.E. *Address:* Bourne Park, Canterbury, Kent. *Club:* Carlton. [*Died* 8 *Nov.* 1962.

PRESTON, Bryan Wentworth, M.B.E. 1945; *b.* 21 Feb. 1905; 2nd *s.* of late Sir Walter Preston; *m.* 1932, Jean, 2nd *d.* of William Reid; two *s.* *Educ.:* Rugby; New College, Oxford. Played Rugby football for Oxford, 1925-26; Lt.-Comdr. R.N.V.R., 1940-45. Dep. Chm., Stone-Platt Industries Ltd. *Recreation:* yachting. *Address:* Oldown, Tetbury, Glos. *Clubs:* Carlton, Brooks's: Royal Yacht Squadron (Cowes). [*Died* 12 *June* 1965.

PRESTON, Lt.-Col. Sir Edward Hulton, 5th Bt., *cr.* 1815; D.S.O. 1918; M.C.; late 2nd Batt. Royal Sussex Regt.; *b.* 17 Sept. 1888; *s.* of 3rd Bt. and Mary Hope, *d.* of late Edmund Lewis Clutterbuck, Hardenhuish Park, Wiltshire; *S.* brother, 1918; *m.* 1920, Margaret, *e. d.* of late Benjamin Bond-Cabbell and Mrs. Bond-Cabbell of Cromer Hall, Norfolk; two *d.* Served European War, 1914-18 (D.S.O., M.C.). Owns about 1500 acres. D.L. Norfolk, 1951; Sheriff of Norfolk, 1956. *Heir:* *cousin*, Thomas Hildebrand Preston, O.B.E. *Address:* Beeston Hall, Neatishead, Norwich. *Club:* Royal Automobile. [*Died* 7 *Dec.* 1963.

PRESTON, Frank Sansome, M.A. Camb.; *b.* 1875; *y. s.* of T. Sansome Preston of Hampstead; *m.* 1909, Frances Audley, *e. d.* of late Sir Godfrey Y. Lagden, K.C.M.G., K.B.E.; one *s.* two *d.* *Educ.:* Marlborough; Pembroke College, Cambridge (Scholar). 1st class Class. Trip., Pt. I., 1897; Assistant Master in Marlborough College, 1899-1914; Headmaster of Malvern College, 1914-1937. *Address:* Flat 1, Thirlestone Court, Hindhead, Surrey. *T.:* Hindhead, 860. [*Died* 8 *Feb.* 1970.

PRESTON, Lt.-Col. Hon. Richard (Martin Peter), D.S.O. 1917; late R.H.A.; *b.* 12 August 1884; *s.* of 14th Viscount Gormanston; *m.* 1st, 1908, Belle (*d.* 1936), *d.* of late F. H. Hamblin; two *s.* three *d.*; 2nd, 1943, Sheilah (*d.*). 1951), *widow* of Lieutenant-Commander J. H. Forbes, D.S.O., R.N., and *er. d.* of R. de Crecy Steel, Walton-on-Thames, one *s.* (decd.) *Educ.:* Oratory School; R.M. Academy Woolwich. Served European War, 1914-18 (D.S.O. and bar, despatches five times); M.Inst.Met. (Pres. 1940-42, platinum Medallist). *Publication:* The Desert Mounted Corps, 1921. *Recreations:* none. *Address:* Barford House, Wokingham, Berks. *Club:* Army and Navy. [*Died* 20 *May* 1965.

PRESTON, Colonel Thomas, C.B.E., 1937; M.C.; T.D.; D.L.; J.P. Yorks (East Riding); *b.* 6 Dec. 1886; *o. s.* of late H. E. Preston, Moreby Hall, York; *m.* 1st, 1917, Gladys May (*d.* 1955), 3rd *d.* of J. H. Love, Hawkhills, Easingwold, Yorks; one *s.* two *d.*; 2nd, 1956, Frances Betty, *widow* of H. B. Emley and *e. d.* of W. L. Illingworth, Vale Lodge, Ripley, Harrogate. *Educ.:* Eton.

Joined Yorkshire Hussars (Yeomanry), 1910; served European War, 1914-18 (despatches, M.C.); commanded Yorkshire Hussars, 1932-36 (Hon. Col. 1946-56); Commander 5th Cavalry Brigade T.A., 1938-39; Colonel (Movements), 1940-45; A.D.C. to the King, 1939-46. *Address:* The Grange, Tadcaster, Yorks. *T.:* Tadcaster 2206 *Club:* Yorkshire (York). [*Died* 2 *July* 1966.

PRETTY, Eric Ernest Falk, C.M.G. 1951; Agent in the United Kingdom for the Government of Brunei since 1957; *b.* 8 March 1891; *s.* of late Herbert Pretty, Reading, Berks; *m.* 1934, Merrall Josephine, *d.* of J. Bouch-Hissey and Mary Merrall; two *d.* *Educ.:* Temple Grove; Harrow School (Open Scholar); Magdalen College, Oxford (Demy). Cadet Malayan Civil Service, 1914; British Resident, Brunei, 1923-1928; Sec. to High Commissioner, 1931-37; Under Sec. to Govt., F.M.S., 1940-42; Resident Commissioner, Johore, 1946; British Adviser, Johore, 1948; British Resident, Brunei, 1948-51; Adviser to Lee Foundation, Singapore, 1952-54. Dato Setia Negara Brunei, 1962; Order of the Crown of Brunei, 1966. *Recreations:* golf, billiards, racing. *Address:* Kingswood Manor, Lower Kingswood, Surrey. *T.:* Reigate 43878. *Clubs:* Royal Commonwealth Society; Vincent's (Oxford); Singapore.
[*Died* 15 *July* 1967.

PREZIOSI, Professor Count Luigi, Kt., *cr.* 1948; M.D.; Ophthalmologist, Malta; *m.*; two *s.* *Educ.:* Royal University, Malta (B.Sc., M.D.). D.O. Oxon. Formerly President of the National Assembly, Malta; Professor, Royal University, Malta. *Address:* Villino Preziosi, St. Paul's Bay, Malta, G.C.
[*Died* 30 *July* 1965.

PRICE, Allen, C.M.G. 1954; H.M. Diplomatic Service, retired; *b.* 21 May 1905; *s.* of Rev. William Richard Price and Edith Mary (*née* Anscombe); *m.* 1937, Catherine Eleanor Harr; one *s.* one *d.* *Educ.:* Silcoates School, Wakefield; St. Catharine's College, Cambridge. H.M. Consular Service in China, 1929-42. Served at Detroit, 1944-45; St. Paul-Minneapolis, 1945; Consul-Gen.: Amoy, 1946-49; Valparaiso, 1950-52; Peking, 1953-54; Stuttgart, 1954-58; Houston, Texas, 1958-63; retired, 1963. *Address:* 4 The Glen, Farnborough Park, Kent. *Clubs:* Royal Automobile, M.C.C.
[*Died* 27 *Jan.* 1970.

PRICE, Lt.-Col. Sir Charles (James Napier) Rugge-, 8th Bt. *cr.* 1804; Royal Artillery; *b.* 4 Sept. 1902; *s.* of Sir Charles Frederick Rugge-Price, 7th Bt., and Isabella Napier Keith (*d.* 1947), *er. d.* of Maj.-Gen. Sir James Keith Trotter, K.C.B., C.M.G.; *S.* father 1953; *m.* 1935, Maeve Marguerite, *y. d.* of Edgar Stanley de la Pena, Hythe, Kent; one *s.* three *d.* *Educ.:* Harrow; Royal Military Academy, Woolwich. 2nd Lt. R.A., 1923. Served War of 1939-45: France, Germany; Lt.-Col. 1943. *Heir:* *s.* Charles Keith Napier Rugge-Price, *b.* 7 Aug. 1936. *Address:* 5 The Layne, Middleton-on-Sea, Sussex. *T.:* Middleton 3014.
[*Died* 7 *Nov.* 1966.

PRICE, Maj.-Gen. Denis Walter, C.B. 1961; C.B.E. 1945; retd.; Minister of Presbyterian Church, U.S., since 1963; *b.* 28 Oct. 1908; *s.* of Walter Cromwell Price and Elva Margaret Jowitt; *m.* 1951, Audrey de Beaufort; two *s.* two *d.* *Educ.:* Blundell's; Royal Military Academy; Gonville and Caius College, Cambridge. Commissioned in Royal Engineers, 1929; Iraq Desert Survey, 1936-38; Instructor, R.M.A., 1938-39; on staff of Royal Marine Div., 1941; combined ops. H.Q., 1942-43; H.Q., S.A.C.S.E.A., 1944-45; Commander, 41 Indian Beach Gp., 1945; Comdr. R.E. 5 Indian Div. and Force 110, 1946-47; i.d.c. 1952; Comdr. British Services Security Organisation, Germany, 1956-58; Major-General 1959; Chief of Staff, British Defence Staffs, Washington, 1959-62; retired, 1962. *Recreation:* sailing. *Address:* Natural Bridge, Virginia, U.S.A. *Clubs:* United Service; Achilles. [*Died* 19 *March* 1966.

PRICE, Ernest Griffith; *b.* 13 May 1870; *s.* of John T. Griffith Price, of Ilford, Essex, and Sarah, *d.* of Thomas Arkell Abraham, of Upminster; *m.* 1900, Maude Ethel (*d.* 1957), *yr. d.* of Maj. W. S. Marshall, J.P., of Johannesburg. *Educ.:* Ilford College. Is a contractor and wharfinger; a Director of Bridge Wharves Co. (Limited), of Shepwood Partition Brick Co. Ltd., and of various other companies; a past President of Trade Association; a member of Board of Management of Reedham Orphanage, and Past Master of the Paviors' City Company; a Conservative. M.P. (N.L.), Shoreditch, 1922-23. *Recreations:* golf and billiards. *Address:* Aston, Foxley Lane, Purley, Surrey. *T.:* Uplands 0397. *Clubs:* Constitutional, 1920, Golfers'. [*Died* 5 *Jan.* 1962.

PRICE, G. Ward; *s.* of late Rev. H. Ward Price *Educ.:* St. Catharine's College, Cambridge. Special Foreign Correspondent of the Daily Mail; War Correspondent with Turkish Army in First Balkan War; Official War Correspondent at Dardanelles and with Salonica Army; War Correspondent in France, 1939; with 1st Army in Tunisia; and with Allied Armies in France, 1944; Director, Associated Newspapers, Ltd. *Publications:* The Story of the Salonica Army, 1917; With the Prince to West Africa, 1925; Through South Africa with the Prince, 1926; In Morocco with the Legion, 1934; I Know These Dictators, 1937; Year of Reckoning, 1939; Giraud and the African Scene, 1944; Extra-Special Correspondent, 1957. *Address:* c/o National Provincial Bank, Lincoln's Inn, W.C.2. *Clubs:* Bath, R.A.C.
[*Died* 22 *Aug.* 1961.

PRICE, Sir Henry Philip, 1st Bt. *cr.* 1953, of Ardingly, Sussex; Kt., *cr.* 1937; *b.* 17 Feb. 1877; *s.* of late Joseph Price, Leeds; *m.* Anne Elizabeth (*d.* 1936), *d.* of late Robert Craggs, Boston, Lincs; one *d.* decd.; *m.* 1939, Eva Mary Dickson, Tudor Close, Old Hollow, Worth, Sx.; one *s.* (adopted) one *d.* (adopted). Chairman, Executive Committee of the National Liberal Council, 1952-53; A Founder of the Royal Institute of International Affairs. *Recreations:* golf, horticulture, and travel. *Address:* Wakehurst Place, Ardingly, Sussex. *T.:* Ardingly 207; Wilbraham House, Wilbraham Place, Sloane Square, S.W.1. *T.:* Sloane 4711.
[*Died* 12 *Dec.* 1963 (*ext.*).

PRICE, John C. P.; *see* Powell-Price.

PRICE, Sir John G., Bt.; *see* Green-Price.

PRICE, (Lilian) Nancy (Bache), C.B.E. 1950; apptd. Hon. Dir., People's National Theatre, 1933; *b.* 3 Feb. 1880; *d.* of Wm. Henry Price and Sarah Julia Mannix; *m.* 1907, Col. Charles Raymond Maude (*d.* 1943); two *d.* *Educ.:* Malvern Wells, Worcester. On the stage since 1899; played over 442 parts; played Gran in Whiteoaks (1327 performances); produced 87 plays; one of the original three founders of the Council of Justice to Animals. *Publications:* A Vagabond's Way; Shadows on the Hills; The Gull's Way; Nettles and Docks; Jack by the Hedge; Hurdy Gurdy; I had a Comrade Buddy; Tails and Tales; The Wonder of Wings; Where the Skies Unfold; Acquainted with the Night; Ta-Mera; Bright Pinions; In Praise of Trees; Feathered Outlaws; Into an Hour-Glass; Pagan's Progress; The Heart of a Vagabond; I Watch and Listen; Winged Builders; Each in his own Way, Editor of the Pedlar's Pack Magazine.

Recreations: walking, riding, climbing, sailing and tennis. *Address:* Arcana, High Salvington, nr. Worthing, Sussex. *T.:* Worthing 64473; 145 Rowlands, Worthing, Sussex. *T.:* Worthing 20 2287.
[*Died* 31 *March* 1970.

PRICE, Major Sir Robert H. G.; *see* Green-Price.

PRICE, Walter Harrington C.; *see* Crawfurd-Price.

PRICE, Wilfrid; Barrister-at-Law; Recorder of Tewkesbury, 1931-51; *b.* 22 April 1879; 2nd *s.* of Edward E. Price, Chartered Acct., London; *m.* 1912, Eleanor Margaret (*d.* 1960), 2nd *d.* of W. E. Hill, Blackheath, S.E., Solicitor; one *s.* one *d. Educ.:* St. Dunstan's College (Foundation Scholar). Qualified as Chartered Accountant, 1901; called to Bar, Middle Temple, 1904; Bencher, 1936; Oxford Circuit; Referee under Landlord and Tenant Act, 1927; Member of Court of Assistants of Salters Company, Master, 1938-39. *Address:* 16 Leonard Court, Edwardes Square, W.8. *Club:* Reform.
[*Died* 21 *June* 1961.

PRICE, Lieut.-Colonel Hon. William Herbert, Q.C. 1921, LL.B.; *b.* Owen Sound, County of Grey, Ontario, 24 May 1877; *e. s.* of late William Herbert Price and Jane Gardiner Price, Gore Bay, Ontario; *m.* 1910, Alice, *d.* of late John Gentles, Kincardine, Ontario; two *s.* (and one *s.* killed in action). *Educ.:* Law School, Osgoode Hall, University of Toronto. Practised law in Toronto until appointed Treasurer of the Province of Ontario in the Conservative Government of 1923-26; Attorney-General, Province of Ontario, 1926-34; represented Parkdale (Toronto) in the Ontario Legislature, as a Conservative, 1914-37, when he retired to resume practice of law; organised High Park Rifle Association, and in 1915 became Captain in the Canadian Expeditionary Force; commanded 204th Infantry (Beavers); served with British Army in France, June 1917-Dec. 1918; retired from Army, rank of Lt.-Col., 1938. *Recreations:* golf and curling. *Address:* 6 Ridout Street, Toronto, Ontario, Canada. *Clubs:* Albany, Canadian Military Institute, Empire (Toronto).
[*Died* 21 *Dec.* 1963.

PRICE-DAVIES, Maj.-Gen. Llewelyn Alberic Emilius, V.C. 1901; C.B. 1927; C.M.G. 1918; D.S.O. 1900; late King's Royal Rifle Corps; *b.* 30 June 1878; 3rd *s.* of late L. R. Price, Marrington Hall, Chirbury, Salop; *m.* 1906, Eileen Geraldine Edith, *d.* of late James Wilson, D.L., of Currygrane, Edgeworthstown, Ireland. *Educ.:* Marlborough; Sandhurst. Entered army, 1898; Capt. 1902; Major, 1915; p.s.c.; served South Africa, 1899-1902 (despatches twice, Queen's medal 5 clasps, King's medal 2 clasps); European War, 1914-18 (despatches, Bt. Lt.-Col. and Bt. Colonel, 1914 Star, Victory medal and Allied medal); Brigade Commander 1915-18; President Standing Committee of Enquiry regarding Prisoners of War, 1918-19; A.D.C. to the King, 1920-30; A.A.G. Aldershot Command, 1920-24; Commanding 145th Infantry Brigade, 1924-27; A.A. and Q.M.G. Gibraltar, 1927-30; retired pay, 1930 (Hon. Maj.-Gen.); one of H.M.'s Body Guard of the Hon. Corps of Gentlemen-at-Arms, 1933-1948; Battalion Commander Upper Thames Patrol (Home Guard), 1940-45. General Secretary Odney Club, Cookham, 1930-45; served on various Cttees. of Nat. Council, Y.M.C.A., since 1930. *Address:* Corndon, Sonning; Reading, Berks. *T.:* Sonning 2184 *Club:* Army and Navy.
[*Died* 26 *Dec.* 1965.

PRICHARD, Katharine Susannah; authoress; *m.* 1919, Hugo Vivian Hope Throssell, V.C. (*d.* 1933); one *s. Publications:* Hodder and Stoughton £1000 prize novel on Australia, The Pioneers, 1915; Windlestraws, 1916; The New Order Black Opal, 1921; Working Bullocks, 1926; The Wild Oats of Han, Coonardoo, 1929; Haxby's Circus, 1930 (Fay's Circus in American Ed.); The Earth Lover, poems; Kiss on the Lips, Short Stories, 1932; The Real Russia, 1934; Intimate Strangers, 1937; Brumby Innes, play, 1940; Moon of Desire, 1941; Potch and Colour, short stories, 1945; The Roaring Nineties, 1946; Golden Miles, 1948; Winged Seeds, 1950; N'goorla, 1959; Child of the Hurricane, 1963; On Strenuous Wings, selections from Works, 1965; Happiness, selected short stories, 1967; Subtle Flame, 1967; Moggie and Her Circus Pony, 1967; translations into numerous languages. *Address:* Greenmount, W. Australia.
[*Died* 20 *Oct.* 1969.

PRICHARD, Brig. Walter Clavel Herbert, C.B. 1945; C.B.E. 1941; D.S.O. 1918; *b.* 1883. Served European War, 1914-18 (despatches, D.S.O., Bt. Lt.-Col.); retired pay, 1929; re-employed until 1945. *Address:* White Cottage, Iver, Bucks.
[*Died* 3 *May* 1965.

PRIDEAUX, Rev. Canon Walter Archibald, M.A.; Vicar of Charlton All Saints, 1951-1958; Canon of Salisbury and Preb. of Stratford in Salisbury Cathedral, 1948-61; Canon Emeritus, Salisbury Cathedral, since 1961; *b.* 3 Dec. 1882; 3rd *s.* of Rev. Canon Walter Cross and Georgina Louisa Prideaux; *m.* 1931, Pamela, *o. d.* of late John and Evelyn Verity; two *s.* one *d. Educ.:* Newton College; Corpus Christi, Oxford; Wells Theological College. Deacon, 1909; Priest, 1910; Assistant Master, Ridley College, St. Catherine's, Ontario, 1904-07; Lecturer in Church History, Diocese of Saskatchewan, 1907-08; Curate St. Chad's, Gateshead, 1909-13; St. Ignatius', Sunderland, 1913-14; Vicar St. Mary Magdalene, Sunderland, 1914-24; St. James', West Hartlepool, 1924-27; temporary Chaplain of the Forces, 1917-19; attached 3rd British General Hospital, H.M.A T. Varela, and 35th Brigade, Indian Army, Mesopotamia Expeditionary Force; Hon. C.F.; Archdeacon of Damaraland, and Priest in Charge of the Northern Area (Walvis Bay to Grootfontein), 1927-31; Member of the Advisory Educational Council of S.W. Africa, 1929-31; Member of S. African Provincial Synod, 1929; Vicar General of the Diocese of Damaraland, 1930; Rector of St. Edmund, Salisbury, 1932-40; Member of Salisbury Education Committee, 1938-40; Rector of Pewsey, 1940-51; Rural Dean of Pewsey, 1945-50. *Address:* Newmans, Bodenham, Salisbury, Wilts.
[*Died* 26 *Aug.* 1965.

PRIEST, Maj.-Gen. Robert Cecil C.B. 1941; Army Medical Service, retired; 4th *s.* of late Thomas Priest, Harborne, Warwicks.; *m.* Emelie Pauline, 2nd *d.* of late R. Addison-Newman, Hove; one *s.* one *d. Educ.:* King Edward's School, Birmingham; Gonville and Caius Coll., Cambridge Univ.; St. Thomas's Hosp., Lond. First class honours, Natural Sciences Tripos, 1904; Prizeman for Natural Sciences and Foundation Scholarship, Gonville and Caius Coll., 1904; M.A., M.D., B.Ch., Cambridge; F.R.C.P. London, M.R.C.S. Eng. land, D.T.M. and H. England; entered R.A.M.C. 1909; served European War, India and Mesopotamia, 1914-18; Brevet Lieut.-Colonel, 1930; Leishman Memorial Medal and Prize, 1930; Brevet Colonel, 1934; Consulting Physician to the Forces in Egypt and Palestine, 1936-37; Examiner in Medicine and Pharmacology, Egyptian University, Cairo, 1933-37; Professor of Tropical Medicine, R.A.M. College, and Consulting Physician to the Brit. Army, 1937-39; Consulting Physician to the B.E.F. (France), 1939-40; Inspector of Medical Services, 1940-41; K.H.P., 1934-41; Maj.-Gen. 1937; retired pay, 1941. Consulting Physician, Western Command 1941-1946; House Governor, King Edward VII Convalescent Home for Officers, Osborne, I.W., 1946-52. Life Member, The British Red Cross Society, 1958 (Badge of Honour).

Publications: Multiple neuritis amongst British Troops in India, 1912; cysticercus cellulosae in man, 1926; Cerebrospinal Fever in the B.E.F., France, 1939-40; Meningococcal Infections in the Army, 1939-45; and many other articles in medical journals. *Address:* 627 Nell Gwynn House, Sloane Ave., S.W.3. *T.:* Kensington 4066. [*Died* 22 *Feb.* 1966.

PRIESTLEY, Henry, M.D., Ch.M., B.Sc.; Emeritus Prof. of Biochemistry, Univ. of Sydney; *b.* Bradford, 19 June 1884; *s.* of Herbert Priestley; *m.* Katie Geraldine Gray, *d.* of late Canon Gray Maitland; two *s.* *Educ.:* Newington College, Sydney; University of Sydney. Beit Memorial Research Fellow, 1911-12; Assistant Australian Institute of Tropical Medicine, 1913-17; Lecturer in Physiology, Univ. of Sydney, 1918-19; Associate Prof. of Physiology, 1920-37; Prof. of Biochemistry, 1938-48. *Publications:* papers on biological, physiological and pathological subjects. *Recreation:* gardening. *Address:* Bundeena, Fuller's Rd., Chatswood, Sydney, N.S.W. [*Died* 28 *Feb.* 1961.

PRIESTMAN, Major-General John Hedley Thornton, C.B. 1939; C.B.E. 1937, D.S.O. 1917; M.C.; *b.* 1885; *s.* of J. Priestman; East Mount, Holderness; *m.* 1915, Hilda Louise (*d.* 1958), *d.* of J. H. Corner of Esk Hall, Sleights, Yorks; (one *s.* killed in action, 1943) one *d.* Served European War, 1914-18 (despatches, D.S.O., M.C., Brevet Major, French Croix de Guerre); Palestine, 1936-; Commander 13th Infantry Brigade, 1934-38; A.D.C. to the King, 1937-38; retired pay, 1941; Colonel Royal Lincolnshire Regt., 1938-1948. *Address:* Highmead, Bengeo, Hertford. *Clubs:* United Service, M.C.C. [*Died* 22 *Feb.* 1964.

PRIMO DE RIVERA, Duke of, Miguel Primo de Rivera; Marqués de Estella; twice a Grandee of Spain; Knight of Order of Santiago; Gran Cruz de la Orden de Carlos III; Gran Cruz de la Orden del Mérito Agricola. Civil Governor of Madrid, 1940-41; Minister of Agriculture, Spain, 1941-45. Spanish Ambassador to the Court of St. James's, 1951-58. *Address:* Madrid, Spain. *Clubs:* St. James' (London); Nuevo (Madrid). [*Died* 8 *May* 1964.

PRINCE-SMITH, Sir William, 3rd Bt., *cr.* 1911; O.B.E. 1944; M.C.; *b.* 10 Aug. 1898; *s.* of Sir Prince Prince-Smith, 2nd Bt., and Maud Mary (*d.* 1939), *d.* of Henry Wright, of Mayfield, Keighley; *S.* father, 1940; *m.* 1923, Marian Marjorie, *d.* of Thomas Nickell-Lean of Waterloo, Liverpool; one *s.* one *d.* *Educ.:* Charterhouse. Served European War, 1918 (despatches, M.C.). *Heir:* *s.* William Richard [*b.* 27 Dec. 1928; *m.* 1955, Margaret Ann, *d.* of Dr. John Carter, Goldings, Loughton, Essex; one *s.* one *d.*]. *Address:* Southburn House, nr. Driffield, E. Yorks. [*Died* 10 *July* 1964.

PRINGLE, G. L. Kerr, M.C., M.D., C.M. (Edin.); retired; Consulting Physician, Harrogate Royal Bath Hospital; *b.* Edin.; *s.* of John Pringle, M.D., H.E.I.C.S. Deputy Inspector-General of Hospitals; *m.* 1st, Emily, *y. d.* of William Wilkie of Gartferry, Lanarkshire; 2nd, Dorothy Isabel, *o. d.* of Alfred Foster Gradon, Indian Woods and Forests, and *widow* of Seward Hunt of Alta Gracia, Argentine Republic; no *c.* *Educ.:* Edinburgh Academy; Edinburgh University. M.B.C.M. 1893; M.D. 1897; joined the 2/5th West Yorks Regt., Oct. 1914; went out to France Jan. 1917; transferred to 29 Cas. Clearing Station; Majority, Jan. 1918; M.C. June 1918; demobilised, July 1918; resumed practice as Consulting Spa Physic. at Harrogate; Ex-President Balneological Section Royal Society of Medicine; British Representative International Society of Medical Hydrology; Fellow (Ex. Pres.) Royal Medical Society, Edinburgh. *Publications:* Some Notes of the Classification of Arthritis, Edin. M.J., July 1911; Review of Recent Work on Morbid Anat. of Chronic Arthritis, Lancet, 1920; Pathways of Infection in the Rheumatic Group of Diseases, Pract. 1921; Glucose Tolerance in Chronic Arthritis (jointly), Lancet, 1923; The Treatment of Rheumatic Conditions by Waters, Baths, Archives of Med. Hydrology, Sept. 1924; Osteoarthritis, Prescriber Nov. 1926; Endocrine Imbalance and its relation to Chronic Arthritis, British Medical Journal, 1928; a Summary of Two Thousand Consecutive Cases of Rheumatic Disease, Proc. Roy. Soc. Med., Jan. 1930. *Recreations:* fishing, golf. *Address:* 16 Charles Cope Road, Orton Longueville, Nr. Peterborough, Northants. [*Died* 6 *Nov.* 1961.

PRINGLE, Sir Norman Hamilton, of Newhall, Selkirkshire, 9th Bt., *cr.* 1683; Sqdn. Ldr. R.A.F.V.R.; *b.* 13 May 1903; *o. s.* of 8th Bt. and Madge (*d.* 1960), *d.* of T. Vaughan; *S.* father, 1919; *m.* 1927, Winifred Olive, *d.* of J. Curran. *Heir:* *s.* Stuart Robert [*b.* 21 July 1928; *m.* 1953, Jacqueline Marie, *o. d.* of W. H. Gladwell, Ipoh, Malaya]. *Address:* Bunbury, Pound Lane, Burley, Ringwood, Hants. [*Died* 8 *Feb.* 1961.

PRINGLE, William Henderson, M.A., LL.B.; *b.* 1877; *s.* of Rev. John Pringle, B.A., Crossford, Lanarkshire; *m.* Annie Nelson Forrest (*d.* 1961); one *s.* one *d.*; *m.* 1965, Agnes Ross. *Educ.:* Hamilton Academy and privately; Universities of Edinburgh and Glasgow; London School of Economics. Called to Bar, Lincoln's Inn, 1905; recognised teacher of Economics and University Extension Lecturer, University of London, 1910-20; Lecturer on Economics, Birkbeck College, University of London, 1918-20; Professor of Economics, University of New Zealand, 1920-22; Ministry of Munitions, Labour Department, 1915-16; Ministry of Reconstruction, 1917-19; Lecturer London School of Economics, 1923-24; contested (L.) Berwickshire and East Lothian, 1922; Ayr Burghs, 1923; Berwickshire and East Lothian, 1924; Principal, City of Birmingham Commercial College, 1925-42. Scottish Representative of the New Commonwealth Society. *Publications:* Part Author of The Industrial Outlook, 1917; edited Economic Problems in Europe To-day, 1928; an Introduction to Economics, 1930; Editor of The Library of Advertising, 1931. *Recreations:* walking and cycling. *Address:* The Meadow, Balerno, Midlothian. *Club:* Royal Over-Seas (Edinburgh). [*Died* 23 *April* 1967.

PRIOR, Arthur Norman, F.B.A. 1963; M.A.; Fellow of Balliol College, Oxford, since 1966 and Reader in Philosophy, University of Oxford, since 1969; *b.* Masterton, N.Z., 4 December 1914; *s.* of Dr. N. H. Prior, Masterton, New Zealand; *m.* 1943, Mary Laura, *d.* of Reverend F. H. Wilkinson; one *s.* one *d.* *Educ.:* Wairarapa High Sch.; Otago University (M.A.). Asst. Lecturer in Philosophy, Otago Univ., 1937. Served Royal N.Z. Air Force, 1942-45. Lecturer, Canterbury University College, 1946-49, Senior Lecturer, 1949-52, Professor, 1953-58; Professor of Philosophy, Manchester University, 1959-66. John Locke Lecturer, Oxford Univ. 1955-56. Editor, Journal of Symbolic Logic, 1960. Vis. Lectr., Polish Acad. of Science, 1961; Vis. Prof. of Philosophy, Univ. of Chicago, 1962; British Council Univ. Visitor to New Zealand, 1965; Flint Vis. Prof., Univ. of California, Los Angeles, 1965; Vis. Prof. Univ. of Oslo, 1969. *Publications:* Logic and the Basis of Ethics, 1949; Formal Logic, 1955; Time and Modality, 1957; Past, Present and Future, 1967; Papers on Time and Tense, 1968;

articles and reviews in philosophical periodicals. *Recreations:* walking and canal cruising. *Address:* 21 The Paddox, Banbury Road, Oxford. [*Died* 7 *Oct.* 1969.

PRIOR, Sir Henry Carlos, K.C.I.E., *cr.* 1946; (C.I.E. 1936); C.S.I. 1943; *b.* 1890; *s.* of late Rev. C. H. Prior; *m.* 1926, Irene Beryl Mitchell; two *d.* *Educ.:* Eton; King's Coll., Cambridge. Indian Civil Service, 1914; Indian Army, Reserve of Officers, 1915-1919; served in Bihar, 1919-39; Govt. of India from 1939; Secretary Labour Dept., 1941; Sec. Dept. of Works, Mines and Power, India, 1946; Ironstone Adviser, Min. of Housing and Local Govt., 1951-64. *Recreations:* croquet, golf. *Address:* Lynchets, Bridport, Dorset. *Club:* East India and Sports. [*Died* 29 *March* 1967.

PRIOR, Comdr. Redvers Michael D.S.O.; D.S.C.; R.N., Emergency list Served War of 1914-18 and War of 1939-1945 (D.S.O., D.S.C. and Bar). M.P. (C.) Aston Division of Birmingham, 1943-45. Member Kent County Council, 1949. *Address:* Maison du Douet, St. Lawrence, Jersey, C.I. *T.:* Northern 599. [*Died* 4 *Nov.* 1964.

PRIOR, Ven. William Henry; Archdeacon Emeritus and Hon. Canon of Truro; *b.* 30 September 1883; *s.* of William Prior; *m.* 1910, Mary Hole (*d.* 1956); two *s.* two *d.*; *m.* 1961, Eleanor Rachel (*d.* 1969), 2nd *d.* of 4th Marquess of Ormonde and *widow* of Captain Edward Brassey Egerton, 17th Lancers. *Educ.:* King's College, London (A.K.C.). Deacon 1907, Priest 1908. Curate at Chipping Barnet, 1907-10; Rector, Beachburg, Ontario, 1910-15; St. Barnabas' Ottawa, 1915-25; Vicar, Saltash, 1925-56. Hon. Canon, Truro, 1947; Proctor in Convocation, 1950-61 (Surrogate, 1931); Prebendary and Rector of Collegiate Church of St. Endellion, 1956-65 (Archdeacon of Bodmin, 1956-61). *Address:* Apartment 1, Porthgwidden, Feock, Truro, Cornwall. [*Died* 17 *Nov.* 1969.

PRITCHARD, Eric Alfred Blake, M.D., F.R.C.P.; Physician to University College Hospital since 1936; Physician to National Hospital for Nervous Diseases, Maida Vale, since 1931; *b.* 25 March 1889; *s.* of Thomas and Minnie Pritchard; *m.* 1930, Clodagh *d.* of Major H. W. Lewin; one *s.* two *d.* *Educ.:* Whitgift School; King's College, Cambridge; University College Hospital, London. *Publications:* Aids to Neurology, 1959; various contributions to medical journals. *Address:* 15 Devonshire Place, W.1; Ousebourne, Godmanchester, Hunts. *Club:* Athenæum. [*Died* 9 *June* 1962.

PRITCHARD, Sir Harry Goring, Kt., *cr.* 1929; D.L.; member of the firm of Sharpe Pritchard & Co.. Solicitors and Parliamentary Agents; *b.* 1868; *s.* of late Andrew Goring Pritchard; *m.* 1899, Amy Louisa Harriet Bayly (*d.* 1956); two *s.* three *d.* *Educ.:* Epsom College; King's College, London. Sec., Assoc. of Municipal Corporations, 1910-44. Member of Royal Commission on Local Government; Past-President of the Law Society and of Society of Parliamentary Agents. *Address:* 29 Heath Drive, Hampstead, N.W.3. *T.A.:* Pritchard, London. *T.:* Hampstead 1786. [*Died* 9 *June* 1962.

PRITCHARD, Lt.-Col. Hugh Robert Norman, C.I.E. 1929; O.B.E. 1920; Indian Army (retd.); *b.* 11 April 1879; *s.* of late Thomas Pritchard, Madras, India; *m.* 1906, Letitia de la Cloche Gordon (*d.* 1945), *d.* of Lt.-Col. Francis William Snell, Bombay Political Dept.; one *s.* one *d.* *Educ.:* George Watson's Coll., Edinburgh; University of Bonn, Germany. Gazetted Cheshire Regt., 1899; 5th Bombay Light Infantry, 1900; 2nd Sikhs, Punjab Frontier Force, 1902; Foreign and Political Dept. Govt. of India, 1904; District Judge, Peshawar; Political Agent, Bhopawar; Secretary to Agent to Governor-General, Baluchistan; Secretary to Agent to Governor-General, Rajputana; Political Agent, Bhopal; Political Agent: Eastern Rajputana States; Southern Rajputana States; Resident in Mewar; Officiating Agent to Governor-General in Central India, 1929; Agent to Governor-General, Madras States, 1930-33; Served European War, France, 1915-16, and Afghan War, 1919 (despatches, O.B.E.); retired, 1933. *Address:* Otterden Place, Eastling, Nr. Faversham, Kent. [*Died* 19 *June* 1967.

PRITCHARD, Captain John Laurence, C.B.E. 1950; late R.A.F.; Secretary, Royal Aeronautical Society, 4 Hamilton Place, W.1, 1925-51; *o. s.* of John Hewitt Pritchard, Shrewsbury; *b.* 25 Feb. 1885; *m.* Winifred, *d.* of W. J. Ross. *Educ.:* Dulwich College; Christ's College, Cambridge. Entered Fleet Street, 1908; author and journalist; writer on scientific subjects and aeronautics; joined Royal Fusiliers as private, 1915; transferred to Admiralty R.N.A.S., 1916; transferred to Air Ministry, 1918; retired with rank of captain, 1919; editor Journal of Royal Aeronautical Society, 1920-45; technical editor of Wireless Encyclopædia, 1923-24; Mem. of Council, Roy. Aeronautical Soc., 1952-55; Sec. Anglo-American Conf., 1951; Member, Roy. Inst.; Hon. F.R.Ae.S.; Hon. F.A.I.A.A. *Publications:* Aeroplane Structures, with A.J.S. Pippard, 1920) new edition, 1935); The Story of the Aeroplane, 1927 (third edition, 1935); Sir George Cayley: The Inventor of the Aeroplane, 1961; Technical Editor Handbook of Aeronautics, 1931-54; contrib. technical entries, The Shorter Oxford Eng. Dictionary; over twenty novels. *Recreations:* criminology, writing novels and verse. *Address:* Garden House, Castle Keep, London Road, Reigate, Surrey. *T.:* Reigate 46842. [*Died* 23 *April* 1968.

PRITCHETT, Sir Theodore Beal, Kt., *cr.* 1953; M.C. 1916; D.L.; *b.* 1890; *s.* of Theodore Pritchett; *m.* 1931, Winifred; two *s.* one *d.* *Educ.:* Bromsgrove School. Solicitor. Served European War, 1914-19. Mem. Birmingham City Council, 1924, Alderman, 1939, Lord Mayor, 1939-40; Clerk to Justices Redditch and Wythall, 1923; D.L. Warwickshire, 1945. *Address:* 93 Cornwall Street, Birmingham; Woodnorton, Ullenhall, Henley-in-Arden, Warwickshire. *Clubs:* Constitutional; Conservative (Birmingham). [*Died* 29 *Aug.* 1969.

PROCTOR, Surgeon Rear-Admiral Richard Louis Gibbon, C.B. 1958; M.A., M.D., B.Ch., F.R.C.P.I., D.P.H.; *b.* 13 May 1900; *er. s.* of late Reverend R. Gibbon Proctor, B.D., Dublin; *m.* 1937, Dorothy Joan, *er. d.* of late Eng. Rear-Admiral J. H. Hocken, C.B.E., Plymouth; one *s.* one *d.* (and one *s.* (R.A.F. Officer) killed, 1968, nr. El Adem, Libya, as result of flying accident). *Educ.:* Campbell College, Belfast; Cadet College, Quetta; Trinity College, Dublin. I.A. Cadet, Quetta, 1918. Began to study Medicine, 1919; B.A. 1923; M.B., B.Ch., B.A.O., 1924. Entered R.N. Med. Service, 1924; M.R.C.P. (Ire.), 1931, Fellow, 1935; M.A., M.D., 1936, D.P.H., 1937 (T.C.D.); specialised in Clinical Pathology, Hygiene and Preventive Med. Clin. Pathologist: R.N. Hosp., Plymouth, 1935-37; R.N. Hosp. Haslar, Gosport, 1939-1941; Naval M.O.H.: Rosyth, 1941-44; Alexandria, 1944-45; Malta, 1945-46; Sen. M.O. Zymotic Sect. of R.N. Hosp., Chatham, Naval M.O.H. The Nore Comd., 1946-51; Asst. to Med. Dir.-Gen., 1951-55; Deputy Med. Dir.-Gen., 1955-58. Q.H.P. 1955-58. Surgeon Lieut., 1924; Surgeon Comdr., 1936; Surgeon Captain, 1946; Surgeon Rear-Admiral. 1955; retired, 1958. C.St.J.

1956 (O.St.J. 1952). *Publications:* contrib. on Clinical Pathology in Journals of Royal Naval Medical Service. *Recreations:* walking, reading, writing, chess. *Address:* 81 St. Margaret's Street, Rochester, Kent. *T.:* Medway 43393. *Club:* Royal Over-Seas League. [*Died* 10 *May* 1969.

PROCTOR, William Thomas; *b.* 1896; *s.* of late William Proctor, Longtown; *m.* 1930, Lucy Playsted, Pontypool; one *s.* *Educ.:* Longtown Council School. M.P. (Lab.) Eccles, 1945-64. P.P.S. to Sec. of State for Colonies, 1945-51. *Address:* Crown Cottage, Longtown, Abergavenny, Mon. [*Died* 13 *Jan.* 1967.

PROTHEROE-SMITH, Lieut.-Colonel Sir Hugh (Bateman), Kt., *cr.* 1928; O.B.E. 1919; D.L. Cornwall 1936; *b.* 1872; *y. s.* of late Sir Philip and Lady Protheroe-Smith, Tremorvah, Truro, Cornwall; unmarried. *Educ.:* Wellington College; Sandhurst. Joined Dorset Regiment, 1892; Lieutenant, 1895; exchanged 21st Lancers, 1897; Captain, 1900; Major, 1906; resigned commission 21st Lancers, 1909; served Nile Expedition, 1898, Battle of Khartoum (Egyptian medal with clasp, British medal); S. African War, 1899-1900, on Staff, relief of Kimberley, actions at Paardeberg, Poplar Grove, Dreifontein, Karee Siding, and Zand River; Johannesburg, Pretoria, Diamond Hill, operations in Cape Colony, south of Orange River, 1899-1900, including actions at Colesberg (Queen's medal with 5 clasps); East Africa, 1903-4, on Staff as Special Service Officer (Director of Signalling), operations in Somaliland (despatches, medal with clasp); European War, 1914-19, France and Egypt (despatches, Légion d'Honneur, Croix d'Officier; Order of the Nile; Officier George Premier); Chief Constable, Cornwall, 1909-35; retired, 1935. *Address:* Pentowan, Falmouth. [*Died* 28 *Nov.* 1961.

PROUT, Margaret F.; *see* Fisher Prout.

PROWER, Brigadier John Mervyn, D.S.O. 1916; Canadian Permanent Force (ret.); *b.* Quebec, 8 March 1885; *s.* of late Lieut.-Colonel J. Elton Prower; *m.* 1st, 1910, Una Catherine Corse-Scott (*d.* 1915); one *d.*; 2nd, 1920, Ella Sylvia Mundy; one *s.* one *d.* *Educ.:* Bedales School, Petersfield. Lt. 1st Batt. Hampshire Regiment, 1905-10; served with Cdn. Corps European War, 1914-18 (despatches five times, D.S.O. and bar), and in War of 1939-45; commanded Quebec Military District until retirement in 1945. *Address:* Knowlton, Quebec, Canada. *Clubs:* Naval and Military; United Service (Montreal). [*Died* 8 *Sept.* 1968.

PRYCE-JONES, Sir Pryce Victor, 2nd Bt., *cr.* 1918; *b.* 10 June 1887; *s.* of 1st Bt. and Beatrice, *d.* of Herbert Hardie, of Orford House, Cheshire; *S.* father, 1926; *m.* 1938, Syra, *d.* of Francis O'Shiel, Highfield, Omagh, Co. Tyrone. *Educ.:* Eton; Cambridge. Served European War from start to finish. *Heir:* none. *Recreations:* hunting, coursing. *Address:* The Manor House, Great Ryburgh, near Fakenham, Norfolk. *T.:* Great Ryburgh 238; Dolerw, Newtown, North Wales. [*Died* 27 *Feb.* 1963 (*ext.*).

PRYDE, Professor George Smith; Professor of Scottish History and Literature at Glasgow University since 1957; *b.* 1 Oct. 1899; 2nd *s.* of D. H. Pryde, school teacher, Dundee, and Georgina Smith, Kirriemuir; *m.* 1929, Florence Mills, Brookline, Mass., U.S.A. *Educ.:* Harris Academy, Dundee; St. Andrews University. First Class Hons. in History, 1922; Ph.D. 1926; Commonwealth Fund Fellow, Yale Univ., 1926-27. Asst. in Scottish History, Glasgow Univ., 1927; Lecturer, 1929; Senior Lecturer, 1947; Reader, 1953. Served with 4/5th Black Watch, 1918-19, and with Ministry of War Transport, 1941-46. President Glasgow Branch, Historical Association of Scotland, 1953-59; President Historical Assoc. of Scotland, 1959-. Chairman of Council, Scottish History Soc., 1959-. *Publications:* The Estate of the Burgesses in the Scots Parliament (with J. D. Mackie), 1923; Scotland (with Sir Robert Rait), 1934, 2nd edn., 1954; Ayr Burgh Accounts, 1937; The Treaty of Union, 1950; The Scottish Universities and the Colleges of Colonial America, 1957; reviews and articles in journals and newspapers. *Recreation:* swimming. *Address:* 72 Kelvin Court, Glasgow, W.2. *T.:* Western 7078; Trenant, Lamorna, Penzance, Cornwall. *T.:* Mousehole 372. *Club:* The College (Glasgow). [*Died* 6 *May* 1961.

PRYOR, Maurice Arthur; Chairman, Truman Hanbury Buxton & Co. Ltd., since 1964 (Director, 1934); *b.* 23 June 1911; *m.* 1935, Verona Beatrice Greenwell; one *s.* three *d.* *Educ.:* Stowe. Lt.-Comdr. R.N.V.R., 1940. Chairman: Daniell & Sons Breweries, Ltd.; Haven Inns Ltd.; Russell's Gravesend Brewery Ltd.; The Writtle Brewery Co. Ltd.; Director: Gilbert Reeves & Co. Ltd.; Fowler Ltd.; Vice-Pres., Inst. of Brewing (Pres. 1958-60); Past Master, Brewers' Co., 1962; Vice-Pres., Brewers' Soc. (Chm. 1964-65); Mem. Coun., Carlisle State Management Scheme. *Recreations:* shooting, gardening, sailing. *Address:* Gallops, Ditchling, Sussex. *T.:* Plumpton 280. *Clubs:* Bath, M.C.C. [*Died* 20 *Dec.* 1969.

PRYOR, Lt.-Col. Walter Marlborough, D.S.O. 1917 (and Bar 1918); D.L., J.P., M.A.; *b.* 1880; *s.* of M. R. Pryor, D.L., J.P., Weston Park, Hitchin, Herts; *m.* 1910, Ethne Philippa, *o. d.* of Sir Norman Moore, 1st Bt.; three *s.* *Educ.:* Eton; Trinity College, Cambridge. Served European War, 1914-18; commanded 1/6th Royal Warwickshire Regt., France and Italy, 1917-19. Italian Bronze Medal, 1918. *Address:* Lannock Manor, Hitchin. *T.:* Weston 338. *Club:* Oxford and Cambridge. [*Died* 28 *May* 1962.

PRYSE, Sir Pryse L. S., Bt.; *see* Saunders-Pryse.

PUCKLE, Sir Frederick Hale, K.C.I.E., *cr.* 1942 (C.I.E. 1930); C.S.I. 1938; *b.* 8 June 1889; *e. s.* of late Selwyn Hale Puckle, M.B., J.P., Ivy House, Churchstoke, Mont.; *m.* 1914, Violet Marion, O.St.J., *e. d.* of Salusbury Vaughan-Thomas; two *d.* *Educ.:* Uppingham; King's Coll., Camb. I.C.S. 1913; served European War, 1915-19; Deputy Commissioner (and various posts) in the Punjab, 1919-37; Govt. of India, 1937-1943; Counsellor, British Embassy, Washington, 1944-48. *Address:* 14 Brookside, Headington, Oxford. [*Died* 5 *Aug.* 1966.

PUGH, Rev. Canon John Richards; Canon Emeritus of Llandaff, and Commissary to the Bishop of Willochra; *b.* 18 May 1885; *m.* 1912, Anne, *d.* of John Evans, Cefn Banadl, Tregaron; one *s.* two *d.* *Educ.:* Tregaron County Sch.; St. John's Coll., Ystradmeurig; St. David's College, Lampeter. Ordained, 1908; Curate of Dinas and Penygraig, 1908-1912, of Llanwonno, 1912-15; Curate-in-charge, Nantymoel, 1915-19; Vicar of Llwynypia, 1919-21; Rector of Merthyr Tydfil, 1921-41; Vicar of Carmarthen, 1941-1955; Canon of Llandaff, 1928; Canon in Residence, St. David's, 1948. Archdeacon of Carmarthen, 1950-60, retired. *Address:* The Kieffe, St. Clears, Carmarthen. *T.:* St. Clears 261. [*Died* 4 *Dec.* 1961.

PULLAN, Ayrton John Seaton, C.B.E. 1961; *b.* 21 Aug. 1906; *s.* of Henry Alexander Seaton Pullan and Marie (*née* Robertson); *m.* 1st, 1933, Mary Hooke Platt (marr. diss.); two *s.* two *d.*; 2nd, 1954, Gladys (Dilys) Vandeminden; two *d.* *Educ.:* Edinburgh

Academy; Cheltenham College; St. John's College, Oxford. M.A. Modern Languages. Entered H.M. Consular Service, 1929; Student Interpreter and Vice-Consul, Bangkok, 1929-33; Acting Consul, Batavia, 1934-1936, and Medan, 1938; Acting Consul-General, Saigon, 1939-40; Acting Consul, Songkhla, 1940-41; Vice-Consul, New York, 1942-44; Consul, San Francisco, 1944-47 (Acting Consul-General, 1945 and 1946); Consul, Surabaya, 1948-50; Foreign Office, 1950-51; Consul, Innsbruck, 1951-53; Consul, Luanda, 1954-56; Consul-General, Shanghai, 1956-58; Oporto, 1958-62; retd. 1962. *Recreations:* music, golf, cricket, walking. *Address:* Kinrara, Carrington Terrace, Crieff, Perthshire. [*Died* 6 *Feb*. 1967.

PULLEIN-THOMPSON, Mrs. H. J.; *see* Cannan, Joanna.

PULLINGER, Henry Robert, M.A. (Oxon); *b*. 25 Oct. 1884; *s*. of late William Henry Russell Pullinger, Southgate, Middlesex and Sarah Ann Moir; *m*. 1912, Lilian (*d*. 1961), *e. d.* of late Dr. W. A. H. Lloyd, Llandilo, Carmarthenshire; one *s*. *Educ.:* Christ's Hospital, Queen's Coll., Oxford. 1st Class Mathematical Moderations, 1st Class Mathematical Finals; Senior Housemaster and Mathematical Master, St. Paul's School, till 1928; Headmaster of The Royal Grammar School, Worcester, 1928-50. *Recreation:* gardening. *Address:* Hallow Bank, Hallow Road, Worcester. [*Died* 10 *Aug*. 1970.

PUMPHREY, Professor Richard Julius, F.R.S. 1950; Sc.D. 1949; Derby Professor of Zoology, University of Liverpool, since 1949; *b*. 3 Sept. 1906; *s*. of Julius Pumphrey and Alice Lilian (*née* Towgood); *m*. 1933, Sylvia Margaret, 2nd *d*. of late Dr. W. H. Mills, F.R.S.; two *s*. one *d*. *Educ.:* Marlborough; Trinity Hall, Cambridge (Scholar). 1st Class Pt. II Nat. Sci. Tripos, 1929; Frank Smart Price, 1929; A. M. P. Read Scholar, 1931; Ph.D. 1932; Rockefeller Fellow, 1934; Beit Fellow, 1936-39, 1945-46. Admiralty Signal Establishment, 1939-45; Asst. Director of Research in Zoology, Cambridge, 1947-49. *Address:* 61 Caldy Road, West Kirby, Cheshire. [*Died* 25 *Aug*. 1967.

PUNCH, Arthur Lisle, M.B., B.S. (Lond.), M.R.C.P. (Lond.); Senior Physician, Royal Northern Hospital, Holloway; Physician to the Brompton Hospital for Consumption and Diseases of the Chest; Consulting Physician to the West Norfolk and King's Lynn Hospital, Norfolk; 2nd *s*. of John Joseph Punch; *m*. 1st, 1916, Dorothy Alice Shorrocks (marriage dissolved, 1929); no *c*.; 2nd, 1933, Sybil Olive Williams. *Educ.:* St. Paul's School; Guy's Hospital, Entrance Science Scholarship, Gold Medal Clinical Medicine. Served in Royal Naval Hospitals and in H.M.S. Cassandra and H.M. Hospital Ship Berbice, European War. *Publications:* Intra-thoracic Neoplasms, Journal of Clinical Research; Treatment by Ultra Violet Radiation, some illustrative cases, Lancet; The Value of the Complement fixation Test in the diagnosis of Pulmonary Tuberculosis, Lancet; The Treatment of the Diabetic in general practice (Journal of Clinical Research). *Recreations:* tennis, golf, and squash rackets. *Address:* 64 Harley St., W.1; 3 Egerton Terrace, S.W.3. *Club:* Junior Carlton. [*Died* 1 *Jan*. 1964.

PUNNETT, Reginald Crundall, F.R.S., 1912; M.A.; *b*. Tonbridge, 1875; *s*. of George Punnett and Emily Crundall; *m*. 1913, Eveline Maude Froude Nutcombe-Quicke (*d*. 1965), *d*. of John Froude Bellew, Stockleigh English, Devon. *Educ.:* Clifton College; Caius College, Cambridge; Natural Science Tripos, 1898; Walsingham Medal, 1900; Balfour Student, 1904-8. Lecturer in St. Andrews University, 1899-1902; Fellow of Caius College, 1901; Superintendent of Museum of Zoology, 1909; Professor of Biology, Cambridge University, 1910-12; Professor of Genetics, 1912-40; Darwin Medal, Roy. Soc., 1922; Pres., Genetical Soc., 1930-32, Hon. Mem. 1948; Corr. Acad. Nat. Sc. Philadelphia; Hon. Mem. Poultry Sc. Assoc. Amer.; Hon. Mem. Genet. Soc. Japan; Originator of the Sex-linked Method to Poultry Breeding. *Publications:* Mendelism, 1905 (7th edition, 1927); Mimicry in Butterflies, 1915; Heredity in Poultry, 1923; Editor of the Journal of Genetics, 1910-46; various papers dealing with biological subjects. *Address:* Bilbrook Lodge, Bilbrook, Minehead, Somerset. *Club:* Savile. [*Died* 3 *Jan*. 1967.

PURCELL, Hubert Kennett, C.B.E. 1944 (O.B.E. 1937); *b*. 10 Dec. 1884; *yr. s.* of late Sir John Purcell, K.C.B.; *m*. 1914, Mary L., *e. d.* of late William B. Pritchard. *Educ.:* privately. Entered office of the Crown Agents for the Colonies, 1901; Chief Clerk Crown Agents for the Colonies, 1933-1947; retired, 1947. *Address:* Loughmoe, 16 Burntwood Road, Sevenoaks, Kent. *T.:* Sevenoaks 2910. [*Died* 10 *Aug*. 1962.

PURCELL, Pierce Francis, M.A., M.A.I. (Dublin), M.Inst.C.E.; LL.D. (h.c.) N.U.I.; Professor of Civil Engineering, University College, Dublin, National University of Ireland, 1910-53; *b*. Kilkenny, 6 October 1881; *o. s.* of late Thomas P. Purcell, Albert House, Dalkey, Co. Dublin; *m*. 1910, Amy Austral (*d*. 1940), *o. d.* of G. H. Oatway, Highgate, London, late of Dunedin, New Zealand; four *s*. *Educ.:* St. Vincent's College, Castleknock, Co. Dublin. Engineering School, Dublin University, 1899-1902; first place with honours and B.A.I. degree, 1902; senior moderatorship and gold medal in Experimental Physics and Chemistry, 1903; M.A. and Master of Engineering (M.A.I.), 1908; an Assistant Engineer with London Co. Council, 1904-10; engaged on the construction of Kingsway and Aldwych, and some large drainage schemes in South London; acted as Secretary to the Irish Peat Enquiry Committee, 1917-18; Peat Investigation Officer to the Fuel Research Board, 1918-31; acting as consulting engineer for design and construction of various bridges, waterworks and drainage schemes in Ireland; various publications and contributions on engineering subjects; Past President of the Institution of Civil Engineers, Ireland; Member Governing Body U.C.D.; Member Senate N.U.I.; Chairman, Alliance and Dublin Consumers Gas Co. Captain Portmarnock G.C., 1925 and 1937. Pres., Golfing Union of Ireland, 1949-50. *Recreations:* golf, swimming. *Address:* Ashton, Killiney, Co. Dublin. *T.A.:* P.F.Purcell, Killiney. *Clubs:* St. Stephen's Green (Dublin); Royal Irish Yacht (Kingstown); Portmarnock; Royal and Ancient (St. Andrews). [*Died* 18 *Jan*. 1968.

PURCELL, Ronald Herbert, C.B. 1957; Ph.D., D.I.C., F.R.I.C.; Chief of the Royal Naval Scientific Service, 1962-68; retired, 1968; *b*. 14 July 1904; *m*. 1st, 1936; one *d*.; 2nd, 1953, Pierrette Marie-Marthe Rosenthal, Cannes, France. *Educ.:* Gravesend Co. Sch.; Imperial Coll. of Science and Technology; Univ. of Amsterdam, Univ. of London Travelling Fellowship, 1927; Ramsay Memorial Fellowship, 1928. Lectr. in Physical Chemistry, Imperial Coll. of Science and Technology, 1929-46; War of 1939-45, seconded to Admiralty for work as scientific adviser to Director of Miscellaneous Weapons Development; joined Royal Naval Scientific Service, 1946; Admiralty Materials Laboratory, 1947-50; Admiralty Research Laboratory, 1950-51; Deputy Director of Physical Research, Admiralty, 1951-54; Chief Scientific

Adviser, Home Office, 1954-62. *Publications:* contrib. to chemical journals, including Jl. Chem. Soc., Trans. Faraday Soc. *Recreations:* garden and theatre. *Address:* 55 Newton Wood Road, Ashtead, Surrey. *T.:* Ashtead 3503. *Club:* Athenæum.
[*Died* 8 *July* 1969.

PURCELL, Victor, C.M.G. 1946; Ph.D., Litt.D. (Cantab.); University Lecturer in Far Eastern History, Cambridge, since 1949; *b.* 26 Jan. 1896; *s.* of Victor and Eva Purcell, Normandy, Sy.; *m.*; one *s.* *Educ.:* Bancroft's Sch.; Trinity Coll., Cambridge (ed. The Granta; Mem., Union Ctte.); Commissioned Green Howards, 1914, B.E.F. 1915-18 (twice wounded, prisoner); Cadet, Malayan Civil Service, 1921; studied Chinese in Canton; held many appointments including Magistrate. Protector of Chinese, and Director-General of Information, Malaya. Lectured in U.S.A. for Ministry of Information, 1941. Lieut.-Col. Green Howards (S.O.I., War Office), 1944; Col., Principal Adviser on Chinese Affairs, British Military Administration, Malaya, 1945; Consultant, United Nations, Lake Success, Sec. to Working Group (Twelve Nations) on Asia and Far East, 1946; Consultant to Econ. Commission for Asia and Far East, 1947. Research Associate, Institute of Pacific Relations, 1946; Delegate to I.P.R. Conf., Lucknow, 1950; Visiting Lectr. Sch. of Advanced Internat. Studies of Johns Hopkins University, Washington, D.C., July-December 1955; Lecturer in Canada for I.P.R. September 1955; Revisited China and South-east Asia, 1956 and 1962, also Turkey 1959, and Iran, 1961. Delegate, XXV International Congress of Orientalists, Moscow, 1960, visited Soviet Central Asia; visited Persia, 1961; Lecturer European Forum, Alpbach, 1962; visited U.S.A., 1964. *Publications:* The Further Side of No-Man's Land, 1929; The Spirit of Chinese Poetry, 1929; An Index to the Chinese Written Language, 1929; Problems of Chinese Education, 1936; Chinese Evergreen, 1938; Cadmus, 1944; Malaya, 1946; The Chinese in Malaya, 1948; The Chinese in Southeast Asia, 1951 (rev. edn. 1965); The Colonial Period in Southeast Asia, 1953; Malaya: Communist or Free?, 1954; The Rise of Modern China (Hist. Assoc. Pamphlet), 1962; China (Nations of the Modern World), 1962; The Revolution in Southeast Asia, 1962; A Background to the Boxer Uprising, 1962; The Memoirs of a Malayan Official, 1965 (posthumous publication); contributor to New Cambridge Modern History. *Address:* 10 Lyndewode Road, Cambridge. *T.:* Cambridge 53894. *Clubs:* Athenæum, East India and Sports.
[*Died* 2 *Jan.* 1965.

PURCHASE, Sir (William) Bentley, Kt. 1958; C.B.E. 1949; M.C. 1917; Borough Coroner for Ipswich since 1959; Hon. Sec. Coroners' Society of England and Wales since 1938; *b.* 31 Dec. 1890; *s.* of late Sir William H. and late Lady J. N. Purchase; *m.* 1924, Beryl Edith Rickards Chapman; one *s.* one *d.* *Educ.:* Bradfield; Sidney Sussex Coll., Cambridge; London and University College Hospitals. M.B., B.Ch. Cantab. 1919; M.R.C.S., L.R.C.P., D.P.H.; Barrister-at-Law, Inner Temple, 1919; Bar, 1921-30, Treasury Counsel (Appeal Cases) at County of London Sessions, 1924-30; Coroner, 1930-59; Coroner to the Queen's Household, 1955-59; Chairman, St. Helier Hosp. Management Cttee., 1948-50; Lecturer: Criminal Law, Supply and Accountant Officer Courses, Royal Navy, 1925-; Forensic Medicine, Royal Free Hosp., St. Thomas's Hosp. and Univ. Coll. Hosp. Medical Schools, 1947-. M.O.H. Inner and Middle Temple, 1955-. White Eagle of Serbia, 1921. *Publications:* (with H. Wollaston) Jervis on Coroners, 9th Edn.; (with Dr. F. E. Camps) Practical Forensic Medicine; various legal compilations. *Relevant Publication:* Coroner: The Biography of Sir Bentley Purchase, by R. Jackson, 1963. *Address:* Purdis Hall, Nacton, Ipswich, Suffolk. *T.:* Kesgrave 106. *Club:* Bath.
[*Died* 27 *Sept.* 1961.

PURDIE, Edna, M.A., D.Lit. (London); Hon. F.T.C.L.; Fellow of King's College, London; Emeritus Professor of German, University of London, since 1962; *b.* 27 November 1894; *d.* of George R. Purdie. *Educ.:* Privately; Universities of London and Oxford. Lecturer in German, University of Liverpool, 1917-21; Independent Lecturer in German and Teutonic Philology, Univ. Coll. of North Wales, Bangor, 1921-33; Prof. of German Language and Literature, University of London (Bedford College), 1933-62; Member of Senate, University of London, 1950-62. Hon. Fellow, Warburg Institute. *Publications:* Von deutscher Art und Kunst: einige fliegende Blätter, 1773 (Ed.) 1924; The Story of Judith in German and English Literature, 1927; Friedrich Hebbel: a Study of his Life and Work, 1932; Ed. of Hebbel; Herodes und Mariamne, 1943; Poems, 1953; Studies in German Literature of the 18th Century, 1965; articles in Publications of English Goethe Soc., Germanic Review, Shakespeare Jahrbuch, German Life and Letters, Euphorion. *Address:* 5 Wood Vale, Forest Hill, S.E.23.
[*Died* 17 *June* 1968.

PURDOM, Charles Benjamin; Author and Editor; *b.* London, 15 October 1883; *e. s.* of Benjamin Purdom (*y. s.* of Henry Purdom, Southwark); *m.* 1912, Lilian, 2nd *d.* of late Peter Aloysius Cutlar, M.D., Waterford; one *s.* one *d.* Finance Director, Welwyn Garden City, Ltd., 1919-28; Editor of Everyman, 1928-32; Editor of New Britain, 1933-34; Editor of Theatregoer, 1935; Treasurer, International Housing and Town Planning Federation, 1931-35; Hon. Secretary, 1918-31; General Secretary, British Equity, 1939-40; Joint Secretary, London Theatre Council, 1939-40; appointments in Ministry of Food (1941-43), Ministry of Supply (1943), Ministry of Information (1944). Associated with Garden City movement since 1902; has devoted much attention to the finance of garden cities and financial questions connected with town planning. *Publications:* The Garden City, 1913; The Garden City After the War, 1918; Town Theory and Practice, 1921; The Building of Satellite Towns, 1925; (re-written, 1949); Producing Plays, 1929 (re-written, 1951); The Pleasures of the Theatre, 1932; A Plan of Life, 1932; The Perfect Master, 1937; The New Order, 1941; Britain's Cities To-morrow, 1942; How Should We Rebuild London?, 1945; Economic Wellbeing, 1947; Producing Shakespeare, 1950; Life Over Again, 1951; Drama Festivals and their Adjudication, 1951; Harley Granville Barker, 1955; Letters of Bernard Shaw to Granville Barker, 1956; A Guide to the Plays of Bernard Shaw, 1963; The Letchworth Achievement, 1963; What Happens in Shakespeare, 1963; The God-Man, 1964. Edited, Everyman at War, 1930; Edited, The Swan Shakespeare, 1930, etc. *Recreations:* books, theatre. *Address:* 39 Woodland Rise, Welwyn Garden City, Herts. *T.:* Welwyn Garden 22289.
[*Died* 8 *July* 1965.

PURVES, William Donald Campbell Laidlaw, C.B.E. 1938; Civil Servant; retired; *b.* 4 July 1888; *s.* of late William Laidlaw Purves, M.D., 20 Stratford Place, W., and Hardwicke Cottage, Wimbledon Common, S.W., and of late Elizabeth Adie; *m.* 1917, Mabel, *d.* of late Dr. Arthur Maude, Westerham and Forest Edge, Forest Row, Sussex; no *c.* *Educ.:* Fettes Coll., Edinburgh (Scholar); Trinity Coll., Cambridge (Exhibitioner), Vidil Prize, 1909; 1st class Hons. French and 2nd class Hons.

German in Mod. Language Tripos; B.A. 1910; Asst. Master Wellington College, 1910; Eton College, 1911-12; joined Sudan Political Service, 1913; Governor Dongola Prov. 1930-32, Halfa Prov. 1933-34, Berber Prov. 1934; Northern Prov. 1935-38; retired, 1938; Deputy Censor Kenya Govt., 1939-41; re-engaged by Sudan Govt., 1941 as Principal, School of Administration and Sudanese Relations Officer; retired for second time, 1944; 4th Cl. Order of Nile, 1924; 3rd Cl., 1935; Jubilee and Coronation Medals. *Recreations:* played Rugby football for Cambridge 1907-1909 (Capt.), and for Scotland 1911-13. *Address:* Aynhoe Park, Banbury, Oxon. *Club:* Royal Over-Seas League.
[*Died* 19 *Sept.* 1964.

PYKE, Rev. R.; *b.* 6 Dec. 1873; *s.* of Samuel and Elizabeth Pyke; *m.* 1900, Mary Dyer; two *s.* three *d.* *Educ.:* Shebbear College, N. Devon. Minister of St. James Church, Forest Hill, S.E., for ten years; Resident Governor of Shebbear College, 1915-1922; churches in Bristol, Bideford, Plymouth, and Southport; President United Methodist Conference, 1927, and Methodist Conference, 1939. *Publications:* John Wesley came this Way; The Protestant Faith and Challenge; The Dawn of American Methodism; Men and Memories; The Story of Shebbear College. *Address:* 10 King's Drive, Bishopston, Bristol 7.
[*Died* 20 *Sept.* 1965.

Q

QUARTERMAINE, Leon; Actor; *b.* Richmond, Surrey, 24 Sept. 1876; *s.* of Fred Quartermaine and Alice Ann Egg; *m.* 1st, Aimée de Burgh (marriage diss.); 2nd, 1922, Fay Compton (from whom he obtained a divorce, 1942); *m.* 1943, Barbara Wilcox. *Educ.:* Whitgift Grammar School. First stage appearance Alexandra Theatre, Sheffield, 1894; first London appearance, Pavilion Theatre, Mile End, 1894; toured with Ben Greet's, George Alexander's and Forbes-Robertson's companies; first West End appearance, under Forbes-Robertson, Comedy Theatre, 1901; first New York appearance, Knickerbocker Theatre, in The Light that Failed, 1903; parts in, among others, A Butterfly on the Wheel, The Winter's Tale, Twelfth Night, Typhoon, The Doctor's Dilemma, The Silver Box, Ghosts, 1911-14; in New York, 1915; army service, 1916-19; played in Mary Rose, Quality Street, The Man with a Load of Mischief, Trelawny of the Wells, Journey's End (London and New York, 1929-30), Hamlet, Heartbreak House, Escape Me Never, As You Like It, 1936; John Gielgud Season Queen's Theatre, 1937-1938 (Richard II, School for Scandal, Three Sisters, Merchant of Venice), Dear Octopus, 1938-39, etc.; Stratford Memorial Theatre: 1949, in Much Ado about Nothing; 1950, Buckingham in King Henry VIII (before the King and Queen); films: Escape Me Never, and Dark World, 1935. *Address:* Coombe Bissett, Salisbury, Wilts. *Club:* Green Room. [*Died* 25 *June* 1967.

QUASHIE-IDUN, Sir Samuel Okai, Kt. 1961; President, Court of Appeal for Eastern Africa, since 1964; *b.* Cape Coast, Ghana, 15 Jan. 1902; *s.* of late Joseph Albert Idun and Mercy (*née* Quashie); *m.* 1928, Charlotte Eunice Amoah, M.B.E.; two *s.* two *d.* *Educ.:* Mfantsipim School, Cape Coast, Ghana; Selwyn College, Cambridge. B.A. 1927, M.A. 1938, Cambridge. Called to the Bar, Inner Temple, London, 1927; practised at Bar, Gold Coast, 1927-36; apptd. Dist. Magistrate, Gold Coast, 1936; Puisne Judge, Gold Coast, 1948; Acting Chief Justice, Ghana, on various occasions, 1956-57; retired from the Bench, Ghana, 1958; apptd. Judge, High Court, Western Nigeria, Oct. 1958; Chief Justice, Western Nigeria, Oct. 1960-64. Chm. War Charities Org., Ashanti Reg. and E. Reg. Gold Coast, 1939-43; Mem. Govt. Selection and Schol. Bds., Gold Coast, 1942-50; Mem. Students Adv. Bd., Gold Coast, 1947-50; Mem. Commn. of Enquiry into Enugu (Nigeria) disturbances, 1949. First Pres. Ashanti Cultural Soc., Ghana, 1955-58; Pres. Ghana Soc. for the Prevention of Tuberculosis, 1956-58. Hon. Sec. Churches' Chaplaincy Council, Univ. Coll., Nairobi. Vice-President, Child Welfare Soc., Kenya. *Recreations:* golf; chiefly interested in church work and music; has been Choir Master of Methodist Churches in Ghana. *Address:* President's Chambers, Court of Appeal for Eastern Africa, P.O. Box 30187, Nairobi, Kenya. *Clubs:* Royal Commonwealth Society, Corona (London); (Hon. Mem.) Ibadan Recreation, (Past Pres.) Rotary (Ibadan); Rotary (Nairobi).
[*Died* 12 *March* 1966.

QUASIMODO, Salvatore; Italian poet and critic; Professor of Italian Literature, Giuseppe Verdi Conservatory, Milan, since 1941; *b.* Syracuse, Sicily, 20 Aug. 1901. *Educ.:* Polytechnic and private study, Rome. Assistant Editor, Il Tempo, 1938-40, and its Dramatic Critic. Corresp. Mem. Nat. Acad. Luigi Cherubini, Florence. Mem. Acad.: Amer. Arts and Sciences; Deut. Akad. der Künste zu Berlin; Acad. Internat. des Sciences Politiques de Genève (Suisse); Accad. Italiana di Scienze Biologiche e Morali. Etna-Taormina Internat. Prize (jointly with Dylan Thomas), 1953; Nobel Prize for Literature, 1959. Hon. D.Litt., Oxford, 1967. *Publications: verse:* Acque e terre, 1930; Oboe Sommerso, 1932; Odore di Eucalyptus ed altri versi, 1933; Erato e Apollion, 1936; Poesie, 1938; Ed è subito sera, 1942; Giorno dopo giorno, 1946; La vita non è sogno, 1949; Billy Budd (story of H. Melville, music of G. F. Ghedini), 1949; Il falso e vero verde, 1953; La terra impareggiabile, 1958; L'amore di Galatea (libretto for music of Michele Lizzi), etc.; *anthologies:* in 1957 and 1958; *translations include:* Romeo and Juliet, Macbeth, Othello, Richard III, The Tempest (Shakespeare); Il fiore dell' Antologia Palatina; Poesie di E. E. Cummings; Eracle (Euripides); Ecuba (Euripides); Antony and Cleopatra (Shakespeare); Mutevoli pensieri (Conrad Aiken); Edipo Re (Sophocles). Contributions to literary journals. *Address:* Corso Garibaldi 16, Milan, Italy. [*Died* 14 *June* 1968.

QUASS, Phineas, O.B.E. 1919; Q.C. 1952; *b.* London; *s.* of Michael Quass; *m.* 1933, Eleanor Ruth Grey; two *d.* (one *s.* decd.). *Educ.:* Univ. Coll. School; St. John's Coll., Cambridge (Foundation Schol.; MacMahon Law Student; Hons. in History, Law, Economics, Natural Sciences and Mathematical Triposes; Whewell Schol. in Internat. Law). Sometime Director of Requirements and Assistant Legal Adviser, Ministry of Food. F.R.S.M. Admitted to Gold Coast Roll of Legal Practitioners and Ceylon Roll of Advocates. *Recreations:* walking, music; studying medical statistics and foreign railway and air time tables. *Address:* 2 Paper Buildings Temple, E.C.4. *T.:* Central 9119, 7951; 2 Harcourt Buildings, Temple, E.C.4. *T.:* Central 9949. *Club:* Athenæum. [*Died* 28 *Sept.* 1961.

QUAYLE, Thomas, C.I.E. 1936; *b.* 13 Sept. 1884; 3rd *s.* of Thomas and Margaret Anne Quayle, Egremont, Cumberland; *m.* Phyllis Gwendolen, *yr. d.* of C. D. Johnson, formerly Comptroller to the London County Council; one *s.* one *d.* *Educ.:* University College of Wales, Aberystwyth; Balliol Coll., Oxford. B.A. (University of London) with Honours in English and French; M.A. (Lond.) with Mark of Distinction in English Language and Literature; D.Lit. (Lond.) in English; B.A.

(Wales) with First Class Honours in English; Eyton-Davies Research Student in the University of Wales; William Noble Fellow of the University of Liverpool. Secretary to the High Commissioner for India (Education Department), 1921-47; Rep. of India on Conf. of Allied Ministers of Education, 1942-1945; Adviser to Indian Delegation to first Gen. Conf. of U.N.E.S.C.O., Paris, 1946. *Publications:* Poetic Diction; A Study of Eighteenth Century Verse; (with Walter de la Mare) Readings; occasional contributions to various newspapers and periodicals. *Address:* 31 Parkside, Mill Hill, N.W.7. *Club:* Savage. [*Died* 7 *March* 1963.

QUERIPEL, Colonel Leslie Herbert, C.M.G. 1918; D.S.O. 1915; late R.A.; *b.* 14 July 1881; *s.* of Col. A. E. Queripel, C.B., Army Veterinary Service, and Mary Watson; *m.* 1st, 1914, Margaret Kidner (*d.* 1914); 2nd, 1918, Sybil, *d.* of John Kidner, Dodhill House, Taunton; two *d.* (one *s.* killed in action, 1944). *Educ.:* private; R.M.A., Woolwich. Second Lt. R.A. 1899; Capt. 1908; Major, 1914; Lt.-Col. 1921; Col. antedated 1920; served China, 1900 (medal with clasp); European War, 1914-1918 (C.M.G., D.S.O., Bt. Lt.-Col.); retired pay, 1930. *Address:* 52 Warwick Park, Tunbridge Wells, Kent. *T.:* Tunbridge Wells 308. *T.A.:* c/o Mensarius, London. [*Died* 31 *Dec.* 1962.

QUIBELL, 1st Baron, *cr.* 1945, of Scunthorpe; **David John Kinsley Quibell,** J.P. for Lindsey, Lincolnshire, and for Flintshire; builder and contractor; *b.* 21 Dec. 1879; *m.* 1st, Edith Jane (*d.* 1953), *d.* of J. Foster, Scunthorpe; one *d.*; 2nd, 1954, Catherine Cameron Rae. Contested Brigg Division of Lincs. six times; M.P. (Lab.) Brigg Division of Lincs, 1929-31 and 1935-1945; Member of the Scunthorpe Corporation; Chairman of the U.D. Council, 1914-15 and 1935-36; first Freeman of Borough of Scunthorpe, 1948; Coronation Mayor for Scunthorpe, 1953. A Forestry Commissioner, 1942-45. Chm. Stewart and Arnold, High Wycombe. *Address:* Manston, Cliff Gardens, Scunthorpe, Lincs. *T.A.:* Quibell, Scunthorpe. *T.:* 2996: Russell Hotel, W.C.1. [*Died* 16 *April* 1962 (*ext.*).

QUIG, Alexander Johnstone; Deputy-Chairman Imperial Chemical Industries Ltd., 1948-56, retired; Director, Birmingham Small Arms Co. Ltd. and Rawlplug Co. Ltd.; *b.* 5 January 1892; *m.* 1952, Mrs. Joan Leason, *widow.* *Educ.:* Glasgow High School. Joined Nobel Industries Ltd., 1908. Served European War, 1914-18 with Glasgow Highlanders and London Scottish, France, and Highland Light Infantry, India. Joined Nobel Chemical Finishes Ltd., 1925; successively General Manager, Managing Director, Chairman; Director Imperial Chemical Industries Ltd., 1940; Chairman Industrial Management Research Assoc., 1946-49; Chairman cttee. appointed by Air Ministry to review Air Ministry organisation, 1948-49; founder member British Institute of Management. *Recreations:* farming, golf, music. *Address:* Combe Farm, Bramley, Surrey. *Clubs:* Caledonian, Farmers'. [*Died* 13 *Dec.* 1962.

QUINN, Harley; *see* Thorley, Wilfred.

QUIRK, Roger Nathaniel, C.B. 1960; F.S.A.; Under-Secretary, Department of Education and Science, since 1964; *b.* Winchester, 1909; *s.* of Rev. Canon Robert Quirk; *m.* 1941, Paula, *d.* of Dr. A. Weber; three *d.* *Educ.:* Winchester Coll. (scholar); King's Coll., Camb. (scholar). First Class Natural Science Tripos; Wiltshire Prize for Geology; B.A. 1931; M.A. 1935. Entered civil service, 1931; Commonwealth Fund (Harkness) Fellowship in U.S.A., 1937-1938. Under-Sec., Ministry of Fuel and Power, 1948; Office of the Lord President of the Council, 1952; Office of the Minister for Science, 1959. Member Historical Manuscripts Commn., 1959-; Mem., Council, Society of Antiquaries, 1962-; Mem. Council, British Records Association, 1962-; Mem. Council, Royal Archæological Inst., 1964; Member, Institute of Historical Research Cttee., 1963; Mem., Winchester Excavations Cttee. *Publications:* articles on Anglo-Saxon and mediæval archæology and art-history. *Recreations:* archæology, geology. *Address:* 10 Landsowne Crescent, W.11. *T.:* Park 9677. *Club:* Athenæum. [*Died* 22 *Nov.* 1964.

QURAISHI, Khan Bahadur Nawab, Sir Makhdum Murid Hussain, Kt., *cr.* 1944; a Spiritual Head (Sajjada-Nashin, Hazrat Ghaus Bahaud-din Zakaryya), Pakistan; *b.* Multan City, Punjab, December 1878; *s.* of Khan Bahadur, Makhdum Hassan Bakhash, Sahib Quraishi, Multan; *m.* 1908; one *s.* four *d.* *Educ.:* Aitchison Chiefs College, Lahore. Has presided over many Muslim League Conferences; was Vice-Chairman of Multan Municipal Board for many years; Vice-Chairman of Multan Central Co-operative Bank Ltd., from 1929. Khan Bahadur, 1924; Nawab, 1936; M.L.A., India, 1936. *Recreation:* landlordship. *Address:* Multan City, Punjab, Pakistan. *T.:* 2752. [*Deceased.*

R

RABAGLIATI, Herman Victor, Q.C. 1937; *b.* 22 July 1883: 3rd *s.* of late A. C. F. Rabagliati, M.D., F.R.C.S.E., and Helen Priscilla, *d.* of late Duncan McLaren, M.P., Edinburgh: *m.* 1912, Marguerita Lilian Chamier Waring, J.P. Bucks, *d.* of late Bannatyne McLeod, I.C.S., and *widow* of H. A. Waring, Indian Police; two *s.* one *d.* *Educ.:* Bradford Grammar School; Edinburgh Univ. M.A. Edinburgh, 1906; Senior Pres. Students Representative Council, 1904-5; Lanfine Bursar in Economic Science, 1904; called to Bar, Lincoln's Inn, 1908; Bencher, 1942; North Eastern Circuit; served European War in R.F.C. and R.A.F.; Recording Officer 57 and 70 Squadrons, 1916-17; Captain and Adjutant, 13th Wing, 1918; Member of Linslade U.D.C., 1925-26. Served in R.A.F.V.R. Sept. 1939-June 1945; lecturer in Air Force Law at Initial Training Wing, Liaison Officer Fleet Air Arm, member of Standing Court Martial, and Permanent President of Courts of Inquiry for the investigation of flying accidents, etc. Retired with rank of Wing Commander. Deputy Chairman, Panel of Arbitrators, and Chairman, Midland District Valuation Board, 1948-55, Coal Industry Nationalisation Act, 1946. *Publications:* Historical Reviews, Westminster Gazette, 1908-15; articles on mining legislation, etc. *Recreations:* history, walking golf. *Address:* 19 Old Bldgs., Lincoln's Inn, W.C.2. *T.:* Chancery 5916; Southcourt House, Linslade, Leighton Buzzard. *T.:* Leighton Buzzard 3170. *Clubs:* Royal Automobile, Edinburgh University (London). [*Died* 16 *April* 1962.

RABETT, Brigadier Reginald Lee Rex, C.M.G. 1915; V.D. 1925; Royal Australian Artillery (retd.); Fellow: Real Estate Inst. (Aust.); Commonwealth Inst. of Valuers (Aust.); formerly Managing Director Raine and Horne, Ltd., Real Estate Agents and Valuers, Sydney; *b.* 23 May 1887; *s.* of late Percy Arundel Rabett, Sydney, N.S.W.; *m.* 1915, Marjory Enston, *d.* of late John Enston Squier, Westcott, Surrey; one *d.* (one *s.* died of wounds, Malaya, 1942). *Educ.:* All Saints

College, Bathurst; Sydney Grammar School. Served European War, 1914-18, with A.I.F.; comd. 2nd Batt. 1st Fd. Bde. Roy. Australian Artillery, 1st Aust. Div., 1914-16, Dardanelles (despatches, C.M.G.); attached 29th (British) Div., May-Oct. 1915; C.O. 12th (Army) Fd. Artillery Bde. R.A.A. (originally part of 4th Aust. Div.), 1916; Suez Canal, France and Belgium, 1916-17 (despatches); C.R.A. 2nd Aust. Div. Artillery, 1921-26; Bde. Comdr. 9th Inf. Bde. (2nd Aust. Div.), 1926-31; Brig. 1951 (ante-dated, 1944); retd. list, A.M.F. Founded Corinthian Hockey Club, Sydney, 1906 (first men's hockey club in Austr.) and 2 other clubs; first Hon. Sec. N.S.W. Hockey Assoc. (for some years); Member: Constitutional Assoc. of N.S.W.; United Service Instn. of N.S.W.; Life Member: Roy. Artillery Assoc. (City of London Branch); 29th (British, 1914-18 War) Divisional Assoc.; Vice-President: Roy. Aust. Artillery Assoc. (N.S.W.); Returned Sailors'. Soldiers' and Airmen's Imperial League of Australia. *Recreations:* golf, gardening, rowing (rowed for Sydney Rowing Club, 1904-14; Inter-state eight-oar crew (N.S.W.), 1913), riding, fencing, swimming. *Address:* Bognor, 17 Gladswood Gardens, Double Bay, N.S.W. *T.:* Sydney FM2218. *Clubs:* Imperial Service (for 14 yrs. Vice-President) Royal Sydney Golf, Life Member and Vice-Pres., Sydney Rowing, (Sydney); Gallipoli Legion of Anzacs.
[*Died* 15 *June* 1966.

RABY, Frederic James Edward, C.B. 1934; Litt.D., Cambridge; D.Litt. (Hon.). Oxford; F.B.A.; Hon. Fellow, Jesus College, Cambridge; *b.* 11 December 1888; *e. s.* of late E. J. Raby; *m.* 1917, Joyce (*d.* 1942), *d.* of late W. H. Mason; one *s.* one *d.* *Educ.:* King's School, Chester; Trinity College, Cambridge: Senior Scholar; 1st Class, Parts I. and II. Historical Tripos; H.M. Office of Works, 1911-48; Hon. Fellow, Jesus College, Cambridge, 1941-1948, Fellow and Lecturer, 1948-54; Fellow (Vice-President, 1940-46), Society of Antiquaries; Corresponding Fellow of Mediæval Acad. of America; formerly Mem. of Central Council for Care of Churches; (member Cathedrals' Advisory Committee); Member Ely Diocesan Advisory Committee; Trustee and Governor of Dr. Johnson's House, Gough Square. Chairman of Council of Additional Curates Society, 1949-54; Member Council of Westcott House, Cambridge, 1951-54. *Publications:* A History of Christian Latin Poetry from the Beginnings to the Close of the Middle Ages, 1927 (2nd ed., 1953); Bède le Vénérable, in Dictionnaire d'histoire et de géographie ecclésiastiques; The New Learning, a contribution to a general view of the world, 1933 (edited); Friedrich von Hügel, in Great Christians, 1933; A History of Secular Latin Poetry in the Middle Ages, 2 vols., 1934; 2nd ed. 1957; The Poetry of the Eucharist, 1957. Poems of John of Hoveden, Surtees Soc., 1939; ed. The Oxford Book of Medieval Latin Verse, 1959; contributions to Cambridge Bibliography of English Literature, to Cassell's Encyclopædia of Literature, to the Encyclopædia Britannica and to Chambers's Encyclopædia. *Address:* Jesus College, Cambridge; 2 Park Lodge, Park Tce., Cambridge. *Club:* Athenæum. [*Died* 30 *Oct.* 1966.

RACKHAM, Bernard, C.B. 1937; *b.* 26 July 1876; *s.* of Alfred Thomas Rackham, Admiralty Marshal; *m.* Ruth (*d.* 1963), *y. d.* of Francis Adams, London and Natal; one *s.* one *d.* *Educ.:* City of London School; Pembroke College, Cambridge (Scholar); B.A., 1st Class Classical Tripos, 1898; M.A. 1907. At Victoria and Albert Museum, 1898-1938, retired as Keeper of Department of Ceramics; F.S.A.; Vice-President: English Ceramic Circle (President 1939-46); British Society of Master Glass Painters; Art Section of Ceramic Society; Surrey Archæological Society; Hon. Member: Oriental Ceramic Society; Museenverband; Member of Cttee., International Museum of Ceramics, Faenza; Hon. Member of Maatschappij der Nederlandsche Letterkunde, Leiden. *Publications:* A Book of Porcelain; Victoria and Albert Museum, Catalogue of the Schreiber Collection; Catalogue of the Herbert Allen Collection of English Porcelain, Catalogue of the Le Blond Collection of Corean Pottery, Dutch Tiles, Guide to Italian Maiolica; English Pottery (with Herbert Read); Early Netherlands Maiolica; Catalogue of the Glaisher Collection, Fitzwilliam Museum; Guide to the Collections of Stained Glass, Victoria and Albert Museum; Catalogue of Italian Maiolica, Victoria and Albert Museum; A Key to Pottery and Glass; Medieval English Pottery; The Ancient Glass of Canterbury Cathedral; Early Staffordshire Pottery; Italian Maiolica; Animals in Staffordshire Pottery; The Stained Glass Windows of Canterbury Cathedral; Islamic Pottery and Italian Maiolica (in a Private Collection); edited and translated Old Dutch Pottery and Tiles, by E. Neurdenburg, Pottery and Porcelain, by E. Hannover, Egyptian Art, by W. Worringer, Raphael, by Oskar Fischel; articles in Burlington Magazine, and other art periodicals. *Address:* 26 Fort Road, Guildford, Surrey. *T.:* Guildford 3733.
[*Died* 13 *Feb.* 1964.

RACKHAM, Clara Dorothea, M.A., J.P.; *b.* London; *y. d.* of late Henry S. Tabor; *m.* 1901, H. Rackham (*d.* 1944). *Educ.:* Notting Hill High School; St. Leonard's School, St. Andrews; Newnham Coll., Cambridge. Classical Tripos, Cambridge, 1898; Poor Law Guardian, 1904-17; H.M. Inspector of Factories, 1915-19; Member Departmental Cttees. (Home Office) on Fitness of Young Persons for Factory Employment, 1924; Offences against Young Persons, 1925; Factory Inspectorate, 1929; Roy. Commn. on Unemployment Insur., 1930. *Publication:* Factory Law, 1938. *Address:* Meadowcroft, Trumpington Road, Cambridge.
[*Died* 11 *March* 1966.

RADCLIFFE, Sir Clifford (Walter), Kt., *cr.* 1953; C.B.E. 1942; D.L.; M.A.; Clerk of the Peace, Middlesex, Clerk and Solicitor of Middlesex C.C., retd. 1954; Group Controller, London Civil Defence, Group 6; Hon. Sec. Middlesex A.T.C.; *b.* 18 Dec. 1888; *s.* of late Professor Radcliffe, Manchester Univ.; *m.* 1915, Florence Eva Wright; one *d.* *Educ.:* Manchester Grammar School; St. John's College, Cambridge. Articled to Town Clerk, York; Assistant to Town Clerk, Sunderland; Managing Clerk to Sharpe, Pritchard & Co., London; Asst. Solicitor, County Borough of Tynemouth; Solicitor to Fulham Borough Council; Clerk of the Peace, Middlesex; Clerk of the Middlesex Lieutenancy. Hon. Secretary: London and Home Counties Advisory Cttee. on Town Planning; Soc. of Chairmen and Deputy Chairmen of Quarter Sessions for England and Wales; Consultative Cttee. London and Northolt Airports; Asst. Commissioner Local Govt. Boundary Commission; Part-time Mem., North Thames Gas Board. *Publication:* Middlesex, 1939, new edn., 1954. *Recreations:* golf, fishing, etc. *Address:* 53 Wildcroft Manor, Putney Heath, S.W.15. *Club:* East India and Sports.
[*Died* 4 *Feb.* 1965.

RADCLIFFE, Sir Everard Joseph, 5th Bt., *cr.* 1813; K.C.S.G.; J.P.; *b.* 27 Jan. 1884; *e. s.* of Sir Joseph Radcliffe, 4th Bt. and Mary Katherine (*d.* 1943), *d.* of J. R. F. G. Talbot of Rhode Hill, Lyme Regis; *S.* father 1949; *m.* 1909, Daisy (*d.* 1943), *d.* of Capt. H. Ashton Case of Beckford Hall,

Tewkesbury; four *s.* (and 3rd *s.* killed in action, 1940, 6th *s.* decd.). *Educ.:* Downside; Christ Church, Oxford. Captain Yorks. Hussars; G.S.O.3 Military Intelligence, 1916. J.P., N.R. Yorks, 1910. *Heir*; *s.* Capt. Joseph Benedict Everard Henry Radcliffe, M.C., late 60th Rifles [*b.* 10 March 1910; *m.* 1937, Elizabeth, *e. d.* of Gilbert Butler, Utica, New York; one *d.* (one *s.* decd.)]. *Address:* St. Trinians Hall, Richmond, Yorkshire. *T.:* Richmond, Yorks, 3300. [*Died* 23 *Nov.* 1969.

RADCLIFFE, Sir Ralph H. J. D.; *see* Delmé-Radcliffe.

RADDEN, Prof. Horace Gray, B.D.Sc. Melb., L.D.S. Vict., D.D.Sc. Melb., M.Sc. Manc., F.D.S.R.C.S. Eng., F.D.S.R.C.S. Edin.; Professor of Dental Surgery, University of Manchester, England, since 1953; Dean of Turner Dental School and Dir. of the Dental Hospital of Manchester; Member Bd. of Governors of United Manchester Hospitals; Consultant to Manchester Royal Infirmary; Member General Dental Council; Member Dental Sub-Committee, Medical Research Council; *b.* Claremont, W.A., 6 May 1903; *s.* of late W. H. Radden, Melbourne; *m.* 1929, Edna, *d.* of G. H. Stewart, Melbourne; two *s.* *Educ.:* Melbourne High Sch.; University of Melbourne. Private dental practice at Caulfield, Vic., 1926-46; Hon. Pathologist, Dental Hospital, Melbourne, 1943-46; Hon. Dental Surg., 1939-46; Hon. Dental Surg., Alfred Hospital, Melbourne, 1940-46. First Prof. of Dental Science, Univ. of Western Australia, 1946. Formerly Member Dental Bd. and Physiotherapy Bds. of W. Aust. and of Council of W. Aust. Branch of Aust. Dental Assoc. *Publications:* numerous contributions to dental journals on research and oral pathology. *Address:* Turner Dental School, University of Manchester, Bridgeford Street, Manchester 15. *T.:* Ardwick 5252. [*Died* 31 *May* 1966.

RADFORD, Professor Arthur; Emeritus Professor of Social Administration, Nottingham University; *b.* 22 Feb. 1888; *s.* of Alfred Radford and Hannah Scott; *m.* 1st, 1917, Norah Frances Elliott (*d.* 1930); 2nd, 1931, Lena Lawry; two *s.* *Educ.:* University College, Nottingham; London School of Economics. Schoolmaster, 1909-1915. Served European War, Royal Artillery, 1915-19. Lecturer in Economics, 1919-1931; Director of Social Studies, Nottingham Univ., 1931-48; Prof. of Social Administration, 1948-53, retired, 1953. Independent member of Hosiery Working Party, 1946; Chairman: Joint Univ. Council of Social Studies, 1948-51; Nottingham Social Service Council, 1945-53; and of many local cttees. *Publications:* Plain Ordinary Man, 1935; Patterns of Economic Activity, 1935; Goodwill in a Great Society, 1950. *Recreation:* photography. *Address:* Seafields, Rosudgeon, Penzance, Cornwall. [*Died* 10 *March* 1963.

RADLEY, Sir (William) Gordon, K.C.B. 1956; Kt. 1954; C.B.E. 1946; Ph.D., C.Eng., F.I.E.E.; Director-General, General Post Office, 1955-60; *b.* 18 Jan. 1898; *s.* of late William A. Radley, O.B.E., Blackheath; *m.* 1938, Dorothy Margaret Hines; one *s.* one *d.* *Educ.:* Leeds Modern School; Faraday House Electrical Engineering College, B.Sc. (Eng.) Lond., Ph.D. Lond. Served European War, 1914-18, in Royal Engineers. Apprentice Bruce Peebles Ltd., Edinburgh; entered G.P.O. Engineering Dept., 1920; Controller of Research, 1944-49; Deputy Engineer-in-Chief, 1949-51; Engineer-in-Chief, 1951-54; retired as Dir.-Gen. and entered industry, 1960. Chairman: Marconi Internat. Marine Co., 1961-68; English Electric Computers Ltd., 1963-68; Director: English Electric Co. and various subsids., 1960-68; Canadian Marconi Co., 1961-67. Chairman: Electro-Acoustics Cttee., Medical Research Council, 1944-49; Materials Cttee., Radio Research Board, 1948-52; Measurements Section, Institution of Electrical Engineers, 1944-45, Vice-Pres., 1951-56, Pres. 1956-57; Pres. British Electrical and Allied Industries Research Assoc., 1957-58; Christopher Columbus Internat. Prize for Communications, 1955. Hon. Mem. Société Royale Belge des Electriciens, 1957. Faraday Medal, Instn. of Electrical Engineers, 1958. Hon. F.I.E.R.E., 1964. Comdr., Order of Merit, Research and Invention, France, 1965. Member: Abbeyfield Soc.; British Churches Housing Trust. *Publications:* numerous scientific papers. *Recreation:* walking. *Address:* 13 Gills Hill, Radlett, Herts. *T.:* Radlett 5904. [*Died* 16 *Dec.* 1970.

RADNOR, 7th Earl of (*cr.* 1765), **William Pleydell-Bouverie,** K.G. 1960; K.C.V.O., 1946; Bt. 1713-14; Viscount Folkestone, Baron Longford, 1747; Baron Pleydell-Bouverie, 1765; late Captain 4th Bn. Wiltshire Regt.; Official Verderer of the New Forest, 1964-66; Lord Warden of the Stannaries, 1933-65; Chm. Rothamsted Experimental Station, 1938-64; Chairman, Forestry Commission, 1952-63; Chairman of Council of Royal Society of Arts, 1953; *b.* 18 Dec. 1895; *e. s.* of 6th Earl and Julian (*d.* 1946), *d.* of Charles Balfour, Newton Don; *S.* father, 1930; *m.* 1st, 1922, Helena Olivia (from whom he obtained a divorce, 1942; she *m.* 2nd, 1943 Brig. M. W. W. Selby-Lowndes, D.S.O.), *d.* of late Charles R. W. Adeane, C.B.; two *s.* four *d.*; 2nd, 1943, Isobel, O.B.E. 1961, *d.* of Lieut.-Col. Richard Oakley, D.S.O., and *widow* of R. T. R. Sowerby; one *s.* *Educ.:* Harrow; The Royal Agricultural College, Cirencester. Served European War, 1914-19 (wounded). Hon. LL.D. Aberdeen, 1959. *Heir:* *s.* Viscount Folkestone. *Address:* Longford Castle, Salisbury, Wilts. *T.:* Bodenham, Wilts 232. [*Died* 23 *Nov.* 1968.

RADOT PASTEUR, Louis; *see* Vallery-Radot Pasteur.

RAE, Brig. Cecil Alexander, C.B.E. 1945; E.D.; M.D.; F.R.C.S.E.; Surgical Staff Toronto General Hospital from 1925; *b.* 14 July 1889; *s.* of Rev. James W. Rae; *m.* 1926, Marion Wilson Richardson; two *s.* *Educ.:* Aylmer Collegiate Institute; University of Toronto (M.B. 1917, M.D. 1930). Served European War, 1915-16, 1917-19. F.R.C.S. Edinburgh, 1924; F.R.C.S. (C.), 1934; Senior Demonstrator, Univ. of Toronto. O.C. No. 15 Cdn. Genl. Hospital, Sept. 1939; D.D.M.S. Cdn. Military H.Q., London, 1941; D.D.M.S. H.Q. 2nd Cdn. Corps, 1943; Inspector of Hospitals, Cdn. Military H.Q., 1944. *Address:* 211 Richview Avenue, Toronto, Ontario. *Clubs:* Arts and Letters, York Downs Golf Granite (Toronto). [*Died* 14 *May* 1966.

RAE, Duncan McFadyen, C.M.G. 1963; Chargé d'Affaires for New Zealand in Indonesia since 1963; *b.* 2 June 1888; *s.* of William Rae and Susan Rae (*née* McFadyen); *m.* 1921, Marjorie Tucker; one *s.* one *d.* (and one *d.* decd.). *Educ.:* Otago University; Knox Coll., Dunedin. M.A. 1st Cl. Hons., Diploma in Education. Began teaching, 1906. Served 1914-18 War, Capt. 1st N.Z.E.F. (despatches). Headmaster, Riverton Dist. High Sch., 1921-23; Vice-Principal, 1924-28, Principal, 1928-46, Auckland Teachers' College. Member of Parliament, N.Z., 1946-60, when resigned. Consulate-General for N.Z., in Indonesia, 1961-63. F.R.Hist.S. *Recreations:* rowing, Rugby, athletics, golf. *Clubs:* Northern (Auckland, N.Z.); British Cricket (Indonesia). [*Died* 3 *Feb.* 1964.

RAE SMITH, Sir Alan, K.B.E., *cr.* 1948 (O.B.E. 1918); Kt., *cr.* 1935; Chartered Accountant, formerly senior partner of Deloitte Plender Griffiths and Co.; a director of Savoy Hotel Ltd.; was Financial Adviser to Ministry of Shipping, 1939-41, and to Ministry of War Transport (later Ministry of Transport), from 1941; *b.* 28 May 1885; *s.* of late Arthur Edward Smith, Pencarrow, Enfield, and Julia Tarling; *m.* 1912, Mabel Grace, *d.* of late W. J. Eales; three *s.* one *d.* (and *e. s.* killed on active service, 1945). Member of Colonial Development Advisory Committee, 1929-40 (Chairman, 1935-40); Member of Housing (Rural Authorities) Committee, 1931-34; Member of special committee on expenditure appointed by Imperial War Graves Commission, 1938; Member of Conference on War Damage to Fixed Property, 1939; Chairman Shipbuilding Loans Committee and Payment for War Losses of Ships Committee, Ministry of Shipping, 1939-40; and of Bunker Prices (Oil and Coal) Committees and Reinsurance Premium Committee, Ministry of War Transport, 1940-46; Chairman of Advisory Committee of Accountants to Minister of War Transport on Road Haulage Scheme, 1942-43; Financial Adviser in connection with formation of National Dock Labour Corporation, 1941; Member (nominated by Government) of Arbitration Tribunal to determine sum payable to Courtaulds Ltd. for shares in American Viscose Corporation acquired by H.M. Treasury in 1941; advised Home Secretary on revision of London taxi fares, 1950 and 1951; Mem. Taxicab Committee, 1952; Hon. Treas. and Chairman Finance Committee of R.I.I.A.; Chairman Gresham Club, 1951; served European War, Major, R.A.S.C. *Recreations:* golf, tennis, shooting, fishing. *Address:* Copynsfield, Westerham, Kent. *T.:* Westerham 3201. *Clubs:* Flyfishers', Gresham.
[*Died* 11 *July* 1961.

RAEBURN, Sir Colin, Kt. 1960; C.B.E. 1945 (O.B.E. 1934); D.Sc.; Water Engineer, Cyprus; *b.* 1894; *s.* of James Raeburn and Annie, *d.* of Hugh Lambie, Glasgow; *m.* Antoinette Blanche, *d.* of Edwin Evans, M.B.E. Served European War, 1914-18, Lieut. Cameron Highlanders, Salonica. Formerly Chm. Cyprus Airways. *Address:* P.O. Box 822, Nicosia, Cyprus.
[*Died* 27 *Oct.* 1970.

RAGG, Rt. Rev. Harry Richard; *b.* 6 Jan. 1889; *s.* of Frank Hugh Ragg and Priscilla Ann Butler; *m.* Winifred Mary, 2nd *d.* of Ernest Groves, Armstrong, B.C.; *g.d.* of Sir John Groves, Weymouth; three *s.* two *d.* *Educ.:* Hereford School; St. John's College, Cambridge; Bishop's Hostel, Liverpool. B.A. 1911; M.A. 1915; D.D. (Hon.) St. John's College, Winnipeg, 1939, Emmanuel College, Saskatoon, 1944. Member of the Cambridge University Athletic Club, 1909, 1910, 1911 (First string 100 yards); Secretary, 1910-11; Deacon, 1912; Priest, 1913; Assistant-Curate, St. Paul's, Southport, Lancashire, 1912-14; Vicar of Fruitvale, B.C., 1914-15; Rector of Trail, B.C., 1915-20; Rector of Chilliwack, B.C., 1920-25; Rural Dean of Yale, 1921-25; Rector of All Saints Church, Winnipeg, 1925-33; Rector of the Cathedral Church of the Redeemer, and Dean of Calgary, 1933-43; Bishop of Calgary, 1943-51; Hon. Asst. to Bp. of New Westminster, 1956-66. Association Padre, Toc H. 1926-51; Member: General Synod of Church of England in Canada, 1924-; Exec. Council General Synod, 1931-65; Provincial Synod of Rupert's Land, 1927-51; Prolocutor of Lower House, 1939-43. *Recreations:* motoring, carpentering, gardening. *Address:* 2635 Cranmore Road, Victoria, B.C., Canada. *T.:* 384-5032.
[*Died* 15 *Aug.* 1967.

RAGG, Sir Hugh Hall, Kt., *cr.* 1947; J.P.; Sen. Nominated M.L.C., Fiji, since 1947; M.E.C. and leader unofficial mems. Legislative Council since 1944; *b.* Suva, Fiji, 26 Jan. 1882; *s.* of Hugh Hall Ragg; *m.* 1st, Dora, *d.* of Capt. W. S. Petrie; eight *c.*; 2nd, Adrienne Josephine, *d.* of Capt. McMicham. *Educ.:* Marist Brothers School, Suva. Elected M.L.C., 1926-47. *Recreations:* bowls, golf and boating. *Address:* Tamavua, Suva, Fiji. *Clubs:* Fiji, Defence (Suva); Northern (Lautoka).
[*Died* 24 *May* 1963.

RAGGATT, Sir Harold George, Kt. 1963; C.B.E. 1954; F.A.A.; Geological and Mining Consultant to: Broken Hill Pty. Co. Ltd.; Australian Mutual Provident Soc.; Australian Atomic Energy Commn.; Director: Ampol Exploration Pty. Ltd.; Ampol Petroleum; *b.* 25 Jan. 1900; *s.* of P. Raggatt, Roseville, N.S.W.; *m.* 1927, Edith Thora, *d.* of F. C. Hellmers; one *d.* *Educ.:* Sydney Technical High Sch.; Sydney Univ. (D.Sc.). Geol. Survey, N.S.W., 1922-40; Chm., Mining Industry Advisory Panel, 1944; Commonwealth Geologist, 1940-51; Dir., Bureau of Mineral Resources, Geology and Geophysics, Dept. of Supply and Development, 1942-51; Secretary, Commonwealth Department of National Development, 1951-1965; Deputy Chairman, Australian Atomic Energy Commission, 1957-65; Chairman, Snowy Mountains Council, 1958-65. Member: Linnæan Society of New South Wales; Amer. Assoc. of Pet. Geologists; Soc. of Econ. Geologists; Life Member: Roy. Soc. of N.S.W.; Hon. Life Mem., Aust. Inst. of Mining and Metallurgy; Hon. Mem., Geological Soc. of Aust. *Publication:* Mountains of Ore, 1967. *Recreations:* swimming, gardening. *Address:* 17 Glasgow Place, Hughes, Canberra, A.C.T. *Clubs:* Commonwealth (Canberra); C.T.A. (Sydney).
[*Died* 2 *Nov.* 1968.

RAGLAN, 4th Baron (*cr.* 1852), **FitzRoy Richard Somerset;** F.S.A.; Order of the Nile; H.M.'s Lieutenant for Co. Monmouth; *b.* 10 June 1885; *e. s.* of 3rd Baron Raglan and Lady Ethel Jemima Ponsonby (*d.* 1940), *d.* of 7th Earl of Bessborough; *S.* father, 1921; *m.* 1923, Hon. Julia Hamilton, *d.* of 11th Baron Belhaven, C.I.E.; two *s.* two *d.* *Educ.:* Eton; R.M. College, Sandhurst. Entered Grenadier Guards, 1905; Captain, 1914; Major, 1919; A.D.C. to Governor, Hong-Kong, 1912-13; with Egyptian army, 1913-19; Political Officer, Palestine, 1919-1921; retired pay, 1922; President, Section H, British Association, 1933; President Folk-Lore Society, 1945-47; Chairman, Art and Archæology Cttee., National Museum of Wales, 1949-51, Treasurer, 1950-52, Vice-Pres., 1952-57, President, 1957-62, National Museum of Wales; Pres., Roy. Anthropological Institute, 1955-57; J.P. Co. Monmouth, 1909; Monmouth C.C., 1928-49; D.L. 1930. County Commissioner for Boy Scouts, 1927-54. Owns about 1100 acres, and Cefntilla Court; Tory. *Publications:* Jocasta's Crime, An Anthropological Study, 1933; The Science of Peace, 1933; If I were Dictator, 1934; The Hero; A Study in Tradition, Myth and Drama, 1936; How Came Civilisation? 1939; Death and Rebirth, 1945; The Origins of Religion, 1949; Monmouthshire Houses (with Sir Cyril Fox), Parts I-III, 1951-54; The Temple and the House, 1964. *Heir:* *s.* Hon. FitzRoy John Somerset, Captain Welsh Guards (Reserve), *b.* 8 Nov. 1927. *Address:* Cefntilla Court, Usk, Monmouthshire. *Club:* Beefsteak.
[*Died* 14 *Sept.* 1964.

RAHILLY, Captain Denis Edward, C.B.E. 1937; R.N. (retired); *b.* 1 Sept. 1887; *yr. s.* of Lt. Col. J. R. Rahilly, R.A.M.C.; *m.* 1916, Jean, *e. d.* of Geo. Dixon, Row, Doune, Perthshire; one *s.* *Educ.:* Epsom College, H.M.S. Britannia. Midshipman 1903, H.M.S.

Crescent, Cape Station; served as Gunnery Officer of H.M. Australian Ship Sydney, 1913-16, including the taking of German New Guinea and destruction of German cruiser Emden; invalided 1919 for War injuries and joined Royal Naval Ordnance Inspection Department; Inspector of Naval Ordnance, 1928-31: Member of Ordnance Committee, 1932-37. *Address:* 23 Clarence Road North, Weston-super-Mare. [*Died* 25 *Nov.* 1966.

RAIKES, Colonel David Taunton, D.S.O. 1919; M.C.; late South Wales Borderers and Royal Tank Regt.; *b.* 1897; *y. s.* of late Robert Taunton Raikes and 2nd wife, Rosa Margaret Cripps; *m.* 1930, Cynthia Birkett, *er. d.* of Ronald Stewart-Brown, Bryn-y-Grog, Wrexham; one *s.* one *d.* *Educ.:* Radley College; Merton College, Oxford. Served European War, 1915-18 (despatches, D.S.O., M.C. and bar). Served R.T.R. R.A.R.O. at War Office and Ministry of Supply, 1940-41; Chief Instructor D. and M. Schools; Colonel, Chief Inspector of Fighting Vehicles, 1943-45; Director, Ship Repairs, Ministry of Transport, 1945-46. Late chairman Roxburgh, Colin Scott and Co. Ltd., Glasgow. *Recreations:* rowed in Oxford VIII, 1920-22; President, O.U.B.C., 1922; English Rugby Union Trials, 1924-25. *Address:* Haycroft House, Sherborne, Glos. *Clubs:* United University, Leander [*Died* 8 *July* 1966.

RAILING, Sir Harry, Kt., *cr.* 1944; formerly Chairman and Joint Man. Director, General Electric Co. Ltd.; *b.* 10 Dec. 1878; *s.* of I. Railing and Hannah (*née* Bing); *m.* 1933, Clare (*d.* 1959), O.B.E. 1946, *d.* of Joseph Nauheim; no *c.* *Educ.:* Munich Univ. (Doctor of Engineering). After gaining experience in U.S.A. joined G.E.C. Engineering Works in Birmingham; held various positions on administrative and production side, Director 1911, General Manager, 1941, Vice-Chairman, 1942, and Chairman, 1943-57; President British Electrical and Allied Manufacturers Assoc., 1952, (Vice-President and Chairman, 1944-45); President I.E.E., 1944-45; Vice-President Engineering and Allied Employers' National Federation, 1944-54; Member: Tank Committee, 1916; Advisory Council to Department of Overseas Trade, 1944; Engineering Advisory Council, Ministry of Supply, then Board of Trade, 1946-58; Heavy Electrical Plant Cttee., 1944-56. Past Master Worshipful Company of Pattenmakers. *Address:* 12 Gloucester Square, W.2. *T.:* Paddington 8990; Long Furrow, Abbot's Drive, Virginia Water, Surrey. *Club:* Athenæum. [*Died* 16 *Oct.* 1963.

RAINEY, Lieutenant-Colonel John Wakefield, C.B.E. 1919; M.R.C.V.S.; Lieut.-Colonel R.A.V.C. (retired); Govt. Veterinary Officer Tasmanian Department of Agriculture, 1940-51; *b.* Totnes, 1881; 2nd *s.* of John Crofton Rainey; *m.* 1910, Elsie Clare, *o. d.* of Francis Dominic Bowles, J.P., C.C., London; two *s.* *Educ.:* Oxford High School; Royal Veterinary College, Edinburgh. Served (Corporal) 74th Irish Yeomanry, South Africa, 1901-2 (Queen's medal and five clasps); entered Army Veterinary Dept., 1905; Captain A.V.C. 1910; served European War, 1914-19 (despatches, Brevet Major, O.B.E., C.B.E.); Assistant Director General Army Veterinary Service, 1917-19; Govt. Veterinary Officer, Fiji Islands, 1920-21. *Publications:* editor and part author of Official History of the War, Veterinary Services, 1925. *Recreations:* none. *Address:* Barra, Deloraine, Tasmania. *Club:* Savile. [*Died* 13 *April* 1967.

RAINS, Claude; actor; *b.* London, 10 Nov. 1889; *m.* five times; one *d.* Made his first stage appearance, Haymarket, 1900, as small child, in Sweet Nell of Old Drury; then (during 7 years) from call-boy to asst. stage-man. at His Majesty's and at Haymarket, 1911; toured in Australia, 1911-12, as stage-manager, and played in You Never Can Tell; West End, 1912-13; toured U.S. as gen. man. for Granville Barker, also played, 1914-15. Served in H.M. Army until 1919. Subsequent years in the West End, playing notably Klestakoff in The Government Inspector; toured (with Henry Ainley) as Cassius in Julius Caesar, 1920. Further London successes included: Daniel Arnault in Daniel, St. James's, 1921; Giannetto in The Jest, St. James's, 1921; Faulkland in The Rivals, Queen's, 1925, and varied leads, 1922-1926, particularly at the Everyman in Shaw's plays. Went to America and appeared in leading theatres in New York and on tour, 1926; continued successes there, culminating in 1934, after which he was absent from the stage for 16 years (having entered films, in which he has played many leads, 1933). Re-appeared on regular stage, at Philadelphia, Dec. 1950, as Rubashov in Darkness at Noon, and played this part at the Alvin, New York, 1951 (won, for this, in a single season: Antoinette Perry Award; best actor of 1950-1951 season, of New York critics' annual poll; 1950-51 Donaldson award for best performance by an actor; gold medal (for good speech on the stage) from Amer. Acad. of Arts and Letters, 1951; also 2 other medals); continued playing in New York, notably as Sir Claude Mulhammer in The Confidential Clerk, 1954. Dramatic prof. at Roy. Academy of Dramatic Art, London, for a few years while in the London Theatre. *Films include:* The Invisible Man; Anthony Adverse; Juarez; The Sea Hawk; Here Comes Mr. Jordan; King's Row; Casablanca; Forever and a Day; Phantom of the Opera: Mr. Skeffington; Mr. Smith Goes to Washington; Deception; This Earth is Mine; Notorious; Passage to Marseilles; Caesar and Cleopatra; Lawrence of Arabia; The Greatest Story Ever Told. *Address:* Lower Corner, Sandwich, N.H., U.A.S. *Club:* Players' (New York). [*Died* 30 *May* 1967.

RAIT KERR, Colonel Rowan Scrope, C.B.E. 1946; D.S.O. 1918; M.C. 1917; late R.E.; *b.* 13 April 1891; *e. surv. s.* of late Sylvester Rait Kerr, of Rathmoyle, Edenderry, King's County; *m.* 1916, Helen Margaret, *y. d.* of late Francis Metcalfe, of Metcalfe Park, Enfield, Co. Kildare; one *d.* *Educ.:* Arnold House, Llandulas; Rugby; Royal Military Academy, Woolwich. Commission in Royal Engineers, 1910; retired pay, 1936; Secretary of M.C.C., 1936-52. *Publications:* The Laws of Cricket, 1950; Cricket Umpiring and Scoring, 1957. *Address:* c/o Lloyds Bank, Ltd., 6 Pall Mall S.W.1. [*Died* 2 *April* 1961.

RAJAGOPALACHARI, Sir Shrinivas Prasonna, Kt., *cr.* 1945; retired; *b.* 24 June 1883; one *s.* two *d.* *Educ.:* Presidency Coll., Madras; Law Coll., Madras. Advocate, High Court, Madras, 1906; joined Mysore Civil Service, 1906; Under-Sec. to Govt. 1914; Deputy Commissioner, 1918; Assistant Private Secretary to Maharaja of Mysore, 1919-27, Excise Commissioner in Mysore, 1927, and Revenue Commissioner, 1930; Second Member of Council, Mysore, 1932, and First Member, 1935; acted as Dewan of Mysore in 1936 and 1937; represented Mysore on Committee of Ministers and other All-India Conferences; retired from Mysore Service, 1939; late Home Minister and Vice-Pres., Executive Council, Gwalior State; Government Director, Central Board, Imperial Bank of India, 1949-53. *Publication:* Some Aspects of Indian Federation, 1938. *Recreations:* walking, golfing and bridge. *Address:* Basavangudi, Bangalore, India. *T.:* Bangalore 2019. *Clubs:* National Liberal (London); Century (Bangalore); Cosmopolitan (Madras). [*Died* 2 *Jan.* 1963.

RALLI, Sir Strati, 2nd Bt., *cr.* 1912; M.C.; Comdr. Order George I, Greece; Director Maritime Shipping & Trading Co.; *b.* New York, 14 July 1876; *o. surv. s.* of 1st Bt. and Eugénie, *d.* of late Leonidas P. Argenti of Marseilles; *S.* father, 1931; *m.* Jan. 1915, Louise W. Williams; two *s.* two *d.* *Educ.:* Eton; New Coll., Oxford. Served S. African War, 1900-01; European War, 1914-19. High Sheriff, County of Southampton, 1943. Retd. as Chm. and Dir. Orion Insurance Co. Ltd., 1958. *Heir: s.* Godfrey Victor Ralli [*b.* Sept. 1915; *m.* 1st, 1937, Nora Margaret Forman (from whom he obtained a divorce 1947); one *s.* two *d.*; 2nd, 1949, Jean, *er. d.* of late Keith Barlow, 3 Vicarage Gate, W.8]. *Address:* Kingston House, S.W.7. *Clubs:* City of London, White's
[*Died* 12 *Nov.* 1964.

RALPH, Annabella, C.B.E. 1942; R.R.C. 1940 (and Bar, 1946); late Matron-in-Chief Queen Alexandra's Royal Naval Nursing Service; *b.* 13 July 1884; *e. d.* of late Alexander Ralph, Rothes, Morayshire, and of late Jessie Ralph, Easter Elchies, Craigellachie, Banffshire. *Educ.:* Higher Grade School, Hopeman, Morayshire. Trained at Aberdeen Royal Infirmary; joined Queen Alexandra's Royal Naval Nursing Service, 4 Aug. 1914; served in H.M. Hospital Ship, St. Margaret of Scotland, 1916-17, in Near East; in Home Naval Hospitals, 1917-33; Superintending Sister, 1933; at R.N. Hospital, Hong Kong, 1933-36; Matron, 1936; at R.N. Hospitals, Haslar and Plymouth 1936-38; at R.N. Hospital, Malta, 1938-40; Matron-in-Chief, 1940; at R.N. Hospital, Haslar, 1940-41; Matron, Royal Naval Auxiliary Hospital, Kilmacolm, 1942-46; retired, 1946. *Recreations:* travel, walking. *Address:* The Gardens, Cullen House, Cullen, Banffshire, Scotland. [*Died* 28 *June* 1962.

RALPH, Helen Douglas Guest, B.A. (Lond.); *b.* Bristol, 31 July 1892; *y. d.* of late Benjamin Ralph, LL.D. *Educ.:* Nottingham High School for Girls; Westfield Coll., Univ. of London. B.A. (Honours in Classics), London University, 1915; Classical Mistress, The Mount School, York, 1916-19; Assistant Mistress, St. Paul's Girls' School, 1919-28; Head Mistress of Guildford High School, 1929-37. Leader-Organiser Y.W.C.A. Centre, Merthyr Tydfil, 1942-46; Secretary to Society for the Equal Ministry of Men and Women in the Church (Interdenominational), 1946-47. *Recreations:* (formerly) walking, golf. *Address:* Rodborough, Long Crendon, nr. Aylesbury, Bucks. [*Died* 9 *Sept.* 1961.

RAM, Sir Shri, Kt., *cr.* 1941; Landlord, Banker; Chairman: Kirloskar Oil Engines Ltd.; *b.* Delhi, India, 26 April 1884; *s.* of Lala Girdhar Lal; three *s.* *Educ.:* Delhi. Apprentice, engineering section, Delhi Cloth Mills, 1904-5; started ginning factory, 1907-1908; rejoined Delhi Cloth Mills, 1909; Manager, 1912, Managing Director until end of 1946, Chairman since 1951; Member, Executive Committee, Punjab Chamber of Commerce for 20 years; first Industrialist of Northern India to be elected President of Federation of the Indian Chamber of Commerce; Member, Delhi Municipality, 15 years, and Vice-Pres. 6 years. Created Shri Ram Research Institute for Scientific and Industrial Research. Created with two others, Commercial Educational Trust, which endowed Commercial College and Commercial Higher Secondary School, etc.; Managing Agent, Jay Engineering Works Ltd., Bengal Potteries Ltd.; Director, Central and Local Boards of the Reserve Bank of India, Suidri Fertilizers & Chemicals Ltd.; Mem., Trade Mission to Afghanistan, 1934. Former Pres., International Chamber of Commerce and All India Federation of Employers of Labour. Hon. Official Adviser to Government on Indo-Japanese Trade Negotiations 33, 34, 36 and 37. One of the signatories to the Bombay Plan. Member: Panel on Indian Textile Industry; Exec. Cttees. of Federation of Indian Chambers of Commerce and Industry; Dictionary of Economic Products and Industrial Resources of India; All India Organization of Industrial Employers; Indian Industrial Research Council; Bd. of Scientific and Industrial Research; Council, Lady Shri Ram College for Women, and A.S.V.J. Higher Secondary School. Formerly Chairman: Panel Post-War Planning on Sugar, Alcohol and Food Yeast and Heavy Chemicals; Governing Bodies and Trusts of the Indraprastha, Ramjas and Hindu Colleges; Reception Cttee., Inter-Asian Relations Conf., 1947. Donates entire income above necessary living appointed by Chamber of Princes to consider expenses to Shri Ram Charitable Trust. *Publication:* Municipal Problems in Delhi. *Address:* 22 Curzon Road, New Delhi. *T.:* 7605. *Club:* Roshanara (New Delhi).
[*Died* 11 *Jan.* 1963.

RAM, William Francis Willett; Chairman, The Charterhouse Group Ltd., since 1964 (Deputy Chairman, 1962-64); *b.* 10 Nov. 1907; *s.* of Willett Ram and Ethel (*née* Blackiston); *m.* 1934, Kate Margaret, *d.* of Henry Marshall; two *d.* *Educ.:* Brighton College. Served War of 1939-45: Royal Artillery, 1939-45 (Lt.-Col.). Solicitor, Slaughter & May, 1933-39 and 1945-46; Partner, Clifford Turner & Co., 1946-62. Chairman: Charterhouse Japhet & Thomasson Ltd.; Charterhouse Japhet Securities, Ltd., Charterhouse Group Properties Ltd., Charterhouse Group Canada Ltd., Charterhouse Canada Ltd., Film Industry Defence Organisation Ltd., The Delta Metal Company Ltd.; Director: Charterhouse Investment Trust Ltd., Clover Dairies Ltd., James Booth Aluminum Ltd., Film Industries Assignees Ltd. Legion of Merit, U.S.A.; Officer, Order of Orange-Nassau, Netherlands; Norwegian Freedom Medal. *Recreation:* gardening. *Address:* (private) 48 Grosvenor Square, W.1. *T.:* Mayfair 5468; (business) Charterhouse Group Ltd., 1 Paternoster Row, St. Pauls, E.C.4. *T.:* 01-248 3999. [*Died* 17 *Jan.* 1968.

RAMAN, Sir (Chandrasekhara) Venkata, Kt., *cr.* 1929; M.A.; Hon. D.Sc.; Hon. Ph.D., Hon. LL.D.; Nobel Laureate in Physics; Director, Raman Research Institute, Bangalore; *b.* 7 Nov. 1888. *Educ.:* Presidency College, Madras. B.A. 1st class, 1904, and University medal; M.A. 1st class, and joined Indian Finance Department, 1907; Curzon Research Prizeman, 1912; Sir Rashbehari Ghosh Travelling Fellow and British Association Lecturer, 1924; Research Associate, California Institute of Technology, Pasadena, 1924; Mateucci medallist, Rome, 1929; Hughes Medallist of Royal Society, 1930; Franklin Medallist, 1942. Foreign Associate: Paris Acad. of Sciences, 1949; Pontifical Acad. of Sciences, 1961; Academies of Science, U.S.S.R., 1962; Hungary, Czechoslovakia, 1963; Romania, 1966. F.R.S. 1924-68. Pres., Indian Acad. of Sciences, 1934. Hon. Member, Société Philomathique de Paris; Hon. Fellow, Optical Society of America, Franklin Institute, Royal Irish Academy, Zürich Physical Society, Royal Philosophical Society, Glasgow, and Royal Society of New Zealand. *Publications:* Molecular Diffraction of Light; Mechanical Theory of Bowed Strings and Violin-Tone; Diffraction of X-rays; Theory of Musical Instruments, and many scientific papers in the Philosophical Magazine and the Physical Review, Nature, The Astrophysical Journal, the Proceedings of the Royal Society, and of the Indian Academy of Sciences. *Address:* Raman Research Institute, Hebbal Post, Bangalore 6, India. [*Died* 21 *Nov.* 1970.

RAMASWAMI AIYAR, Sir C. P., K.C.S.I. 1941; K.C.I.E. 1925 (C.I.E. 1923); LL.D., D.Litt.; Vice-Chancellor, Annamalai Univ. (for the second time, 1962); Fellow Madras Univ.; *b.* 12 Nov. 1879; *o. s.* of late C. R. Pattabhi Ramayyar Vakil, High Court and afterwards a Judge, Madras City Court; *m.* Sitammal, *g. d.* of C. V. R. Sastri, the first Indian Judge in Madras; three *s.* *Educ.:* Wesleyan High School, Presidency College, and Law College, Madras. Joined the Madras Bar, 1903, and led the original side soon afterwards; enrolled specially as an Advocate, 1923; Fellow of Univ., 1912; Member of Madras Corporation, 1911; served on many committees; Member of the Indian National Congress and was its All-India Secretary, 1917-18; Madras Delegate to Delhi War Conference; Univ. M.L.C., Madras, 1919; Member of Committee to frame Rules under Reform Act, 1919; M.L.C. under Reformed Constitution for Madras, 1920; Advocate-General for the Presidency, 1920; engaged from 1910 in almost all heavy trials in Madras; one of the Indian representatives at the Assembly of the League of Nations at Geneva, 1926 and 1927; Rapporteur to League of Nations Cttee. on Public Health, 1927; Law Member of Madras Govt., 1923-1928; Vice-Pres. Exec. Council, 1924; resigned membership of Madras Govt., March 1928, and rejoined the Bar, April 1928; delivered the Sri Krishna Rajendra Univ. Lecture at Mysore, 1928; Convocation Address of Delhi Univ., 1931, Osmania Univ., 1942, Patna Univ., 1944. Rep. State of Cochin before Butler Enquiry Cttee., 1928; member of sub-cttee. to draft constitution for uniting British India and the Indian States in a Federation, 1930; Deleg. to Indian Round Table Conf. and member Federal Structure Cttee. R.T.C., 1931; acting Law Member, Govt. of India, 1931; Legal and Constitutional Adviser to Govt. of Travancore; Member Consultative Cttee. R.T.C.; Tagore Law Lecturer, Calcutta Univ., 1932; Acting Commerce Member Government of India, 1932; Chairman Cttee. the White Paper, 1933; Member of Joint Select Cttee. of Parl. on Indian Reforms, 1933; Deleg. to World Economic Conf., 1933; drafted a new constitution for Kashmere, 1934; Member Govt. of India Cttee. on Secretariat Procedure, 1935; title of Sachivothama conferred, 1936; Member for Information, Gov.-Gen.'s Exec. Council, India, 1942; Vice-Chancellor, Travancore Univ., 1937; presided over All-India Law Conf., Hyderabad, 1944; gave evidence before Commission on Indian Reforms and Cttee. on Finance, and, in London, before Joint Parl. Cttee. Chairman Shipping Policy Cttee. of Govt. of India, 1946. Rep. States before the British Cabinet Deleg., 1946; Member Negotiating Cttee. on behalf of States in respect of Const. reforms, 1947; as Dewan declared Indep. of State, 1947. Initiated various irrigation and hydro-electric schemes. Dewan of Travancore, 1936-47, resigned Aug. 1947; travelled extensively. Member Indian Press Commission, 1952; Vice-Chancellor, Annamalai Univ., 1953; Vice-Chancellor, Banaras Hindu University, 1954; Leader Indian Univs. Delegation to China, 1955; Mem., Public Service Recruitment Cttee., 1955; Mem. Univ. Grants Commn., 1955; delivered Convocation Address of Lucknow Univ., also of Banaras Hindu Univ. (Dr. of Laws), 1956; Maharaja Sayaji Rao Lectr., Baroda Univ., 1956; Delegate to Brit. Commonwealth Univs. Conf. and P.E.N. Internat. Conf., London, 1956. Delivered the Sivell-Visvesvarayya lectures, on Long Range Planning, 1959. Chm. Hindu Religious Endowments Commn. of Govt. of India, 1960. Mem., Nat. Integration Council, 1961; Mem. Punjab Commn. apptd. by Govt. of India, 1961; delivered Convocation Address of Vikram University, Ujjain, 1961; Chm. Nat. Integration Cttee. on Regionalism, 1962; Chitale Lectr., Madras Univ., 1962; Delegate, Commonwealth Univs. Conf., 1963; Pres. Inter-Univ. Bd. of India and Ceylon, 1965; delivered first Malaviya Memorial lectures, 1965. F.R.S.A. 1937; LL.D., Univ. of Travancore, 1939; D.Litt., Annamalai Univ., 1955; Dr. Laws: Madras Univ., 1957; Mysore Univ., 1960. *Publications:* Selection of Essays and Addresses, 1948; Biography of Dr. Annie Besant; contributions to various periodicals: on Hinduism and Jainism, political, financial, and literary topics. *Recreations:* lawn-tennis, riding, and walking. *Address:* The Grove, Mylapore, Madras; Delisle, Ootacamund, India. *Clubs:* Athenæum (Hon. Mem.), National Liberal, Royal Automobile; Cosmopolitan (Madras).
[*Died* 26 *Sept.* 1966.

RAMPUR, Major-Gen. H.H. the Nawab (Alijah, Nasir-ul-Mulk, Mukhlis-ud-Daulah, Amir-ul-Umara, Nawab Dr. Sir Syed Mohammed Raza Ali Khan Bahadur, Mustaid Jung), G.C.I.E., *cr.* 1944; K.C.S.I., *cr.* 1936; D.Litt. (Aligarh); LL.D. (Benares); *b.* 17 Nov. 1906; *m.* 1921, H.H. Nawab Rafaat Zamani Begum Sahiba, *e. d.* of late Sahibzada Sir Abdussamad Khan, C.I.E.; three *s.* six *d.* *Educ.:* Rajkumar College, Rajkot. Succeeded 1930; has a taste for music and fine arts; Hon. Col. of Hodson's Horse and 11/9th Jat. Regt. Grand Master, Grand Lodge of India. *Address:* Rampur, U.P., India. [*Died* 6 *March* 1966.

RAMSAY, Sir Alexander, Kt., *cr.* 1938; O.B.E.; ex-Director Engineering and Allied Employers' National Federation, retired; *b.* 1887; *m.* Mary (*d.* 1964) *d.* of Richard Callan, late of Motherwell; one *s.* two *d.* Formerly Director of Ruston & Hornsby, Ltd., and Chairman of Enfield Cycle Co. Ltd.; M.P. (C.) West Bromwich, 1931-35. *Address:* 81 The Drive, Hove, Sussex. *Club:* Athenæum.
[*Died* 17 *Oct.* 1969.

RAMSAY, Sir Alexander Burnett, 6th Bt., *cr.* 1806; attached to firm McLaghlan and Campbell, Orange, N.S.W.; *heir-pres.* to late Sir Alexander Edwin Burnett, 14th Bt., of Leys, until 1959 (did not claim as 15th Bt.); *b.* 26 March 1903; *S.* father, 1924; *s.* of 5th Bt. and Mabel, *d.* of late William Joseph Hutchinson, Queensland; *m.* 1935, Isabel Ellice, *e. d.* of late William Whitney; one *s.* two *d.* *Educ.:* The King's School, Parramatta. *Heir:* *s.* Alexander William Burnett, *b.* 4 Aug. 1938. *Address:* Haddon Rig, Warren, N.S.W. Australia.
[*Died* 25 *Sept.* 1965.

RAMSAY, Louis E. B. C.; *see* Cobden-Ramsay.

RAMSAY, Hon. Sir Patrick William Maule, K.C.M.G., *cr.* 1932 (C.M.G. 1929); *b.* 20 Sept. 1879; 2nd *s.* of 13th Earl of Dalhousie, and Ida, *d.* of 6th Earl of Tankerville; *m.* 1917, Dorothy Cynthia (*d.* 1957), *d.* of Brig.-Gen. Sir Conyers Surtees, C.B., C.M.G., D.S.O., *widow* of C. C. Tower, Essex Yeomanry; one *s.* *Educ.:* Winchester. Nominated an Attaché, 1904; Constantinople, 1905; 3rd Secretary, 1906; Peking, 1910; 2nd Secretary, 1911; Paris, 1911; St. Petersburg, 1914; Paris, 1915; Foreign Office, 1918; 1st Secretary, 1918; Stockholm, 1919; acted as Chargé d'Affaires, 1919, 1920, 1921, 1922, 1923, and 1924; Counsellor of Embassy, 1922; Rio de Janeiro, 1925; acted as Chargé d'Affaires, 1925 and 1926; Counsellor at Madrid, 1927-29; Minister in Athens, 1929-33; in Budapest 1933-1935; in Copenhagen, 1935-39. *Club:* Travellers'.
[*Died* 19 *June* 1962.

RAMSBOTTOM, John William, M.A., M.Com.; *b.* 27 Feb. 1883; *s.* of late John Ramsbottom; *m.* 1918, Grace, *d.* of W. Goudie, Marple,

Cheshire. *Educ.:* Central High School, Manchester; Univ. of Manchester. H.M. Inspector of Factories, 1906-12; Hunter Lecturer in Social and Industrial Economics, Armstrong Coll., Newcastle on Tyne, 1913-19; Served European War, 1914-19; temp. service Jt. Industrial Councils (Whitley) Div., Min. of Labour, 1919-22; Univ. of London Lecturer in Applied Economics, London School of Economics, 1922-23; H.M. Inspector of Schools (Technical), 1923-25; Director, 1925-45 and Governor, 1945-56, City of London Coll.; Chm. Assoc. of Principals of Technical Institutions, 1929; member of Educ. Panel, Committee on Educ. for Salesmanship, 1931; Chairman Assoc. of Technical Institutions, 1937; Member of Ministry of Labour Committee, 1945, to frame courses in Business Administration for ex-service men and women; Pres. Nat. Assoc. for Advancement of Educ. for Commerce, 1950; charter mem. of executive of Brit. Council; Hon. Member and former Vice-Pres. British Assoc. for Commercial and Industrial Educ.; Vice-Pres. Roy. Soc. of Arts, 1948-52. *Publications:* articles and papers on Commercial Education. *Address:* The Bushes, Durlston, Swanage, Dorset. *T.:* Swanage 2368. [*Died* 25 *Feb.* 1966.

RAMSDEN, Major-General William Havelock, C.B. 1943; C.B.E. 1940; D.S.O. 1939; M.C.; retired; *b.* 3 Oct. 1888; *s.* of Rev. Henry Plumptre Ramsden; *m.* 1st, 1918, Christine Baldwin; one *s. decd.*; 2nd, 1946, Gena Wathen, *d.* of J. Whale-Ure. *Educ.:* Bath College; R.M.C., Sandhurst. 2nd Lt. W. India Regt. 1910; Cameroons, 1915-16; Capt. E. York Regt., 1916; France, 1917-18 (M.C.; Major, G.S.O. (Weapon Training), 1926-30; Bt. Lt.-Col. 1933; E. York Regt. (India) Razmak, etc., 1934; Lt.-Col. 1st Bn. Hampshire Regt. 1936; Operations Waziristan, 1936-37, (despatches, medal); Operations Palestine, 1938-39 (despatches, medal, D.S.O.); Colonel (antedate to 1936) and Temp. Brigadier, 1939; Comdr. West Lancs Area, 1939; Comdr. 25th Inf. Bde., France 1939-40; Comdr. 50 Div., Mid. East, 1940-1942 (despatches); Maj.-Gen. 1941; Comdr. 30 Corps (acting Lt.-Gen.), Mid. East, July-Sept. 1942; Commander 3rd Division, Dec. 1942-43; Commander S.D.F. and British Troops, Sudan and Eritrea, Jan. 1944-June 1945; retired pay, Sept. 1945. *Recreations:* general. *Address:* Green Banks, West Chiltington, Sussex. *T.:* 3337. [*Died* 16 *Dec.* 1969.

RAMSEY, Admiral Sir Charles Gordon, K.C.B., *cr.* 1940 (C.B. 1935); *b.* 1882; *m.* 1st, 1912, Luleen Clare (*d.* 1939), *d.* of William Handcock; one *d.*; 2nd, 1945, Helen, *widow* of George M'Murtrie Godley of Long House, Greenwich, Connecticut, U.S.A. Joined R.N. 1897; Captain, 1922; Rear-Admiral, 1934; Vice-Admiral, 1938; Admiral, 1942; served European War, 1914-19 (despatches Jutland); A.D.C. to the King, 1933; Rear-Adm. 2nd Battle Squadron, 1935-37; Commander-in-Chief, Rosyth, 1939-42; retired, 1942; Commodore of Convoys. *Address:* Long House, Greenwich, Connecticut, U.S.A.; Capricorn, Hope Sound, Florida, U.S.A. *Clubs:* Army and Navy; Century (N.Y.). [*Died* 19 *Dec.* 1966.

RAMSEY, Stanley Churchill, F.R.I.B.A.; retired from architectural practice, 1957; Past Dir. (Dep. Chm.), Abbey National Building Society; *b.* 2 Dec. 1882; *e. s.* of late Herbert Edward Ramsey and late Eva Catherine Ramsey (*née* Churchill); *m.* 1920, Cecilia Violet Martin, *y. d.* of late Dr. Henry Plumridge and late Mrs. Plumridge; one *s.* one *d.* *Educ.:* Aske's Sch., Hatcham; King's College, London; Royal Academy Schools. Articled to, and afterwards in partnership with C. Stanley Peach, F.R.I.B.A.; in partnership with Professor Adshead, 1911-33; Senior Partner in firm of Ramsey, Murray, White and Ward, 1945-57. Served European War, 1914-18 as Lieut. R.N.V.R. and Captain R.A.F. Past Vice-President, R.I.B.A.; former Member of Council of the Architectural Association. *Publications:* Editor of Masters of Architecture and author of Inigo Jones in that series, 1925; Small Houses of the Late Georgian Period, 1st Vol. 1920, 2nd Vol. 1925; many contribs. to professional jls., etc. *Address:* 27 Claire Court, Woodside Ave., N.12. *T.:* Western 3569. *Club:* Athenæum. [*Died* 25 *Dec.* 1968.

RAND, Ivan Cleveland; D.C.L., LL.D.; retired as Justice, Supreme Court of Canada, (1943-59); retired as Dean of Law School, University of Western Ontario, London, Ontario; *b.* 27 April 1884; *s.* of Nelson Lawrence Rand and Minnie Turner Rand; *m.* 1913, Iredell Baxter; two *s.* *Educ.:* Mount Allison University; Harvard Law School. Private practice: Medicine Hat, Alta., 1913-20; Moncton, N.B., 1920-26; Counsel, Can. Nat. Rlys., 1926-43. Member U.N. Special Cttee. on Palestine, 1947. Hon. D.C.L. Mt. Allison Univ., 1945; Hon. LL.D. Univ. of New Brunswick, 1950. *Publications:* contrib. to law reviews. *Address:* Moncton, New Brunswick, Canada. *Clubs:* Rideau (Ottawa); University (Montreal). [*Died* 2 *Jan.* 1969.

RANDALL, Henry John, LL.B. (Lond.); F.S.A.; retired from practice as a Solicitor, 1962; *b.* Bridgend, 13 December 1877; *s.* of William Richard Randall, Solicitor, and Hannah Johnston; *m.* 1916, Olga Ruth Brewis; no *c.* *Educ.:* Bradfield. Admitted a Solicitor, 1900; Officer in Volunteers and Territorial Force, 1895-1918; Member of Council of Nat. Museum of Wales; Treas., 1952; Pres. of Cambrian Archæological Association, 1928-1929; Treasurer, 1936; President of Bridgend District Law Society, 1928 and 1960 (Secretary, 1911-21); President, Cardiff Naturalists Society, 1946-47; Member of Council of Society of Antiquaries, 1949; member Ancient Monuments Board for Wales. Hon. LL.D. University of Wales, 1963. *Publications:* Law and Geography, in Evolution of Law Series, Vol. III., 1918; Beginnings of English Constitutional Theory in Wigmore Celebration Legal Essays, 1919; History in the Open Air, 1936; The Creative Centuries, 1944; Bridgend: the story of a market town, 1955; The Vale of Glamorgan, 1961. Joint Editor of South Wales Record Society, 1929. *Recreations:* fishing, archæology. *Address:* Erw Graig, Bridgend, Glamorgan. *T.:* Bridgend 2226. *Club:* Athenæum. [*Died* 4 *Nov.* 1964.

RANDALL, Henry John, C.B.E. 1950; *b.* 30 Dec. 1894; *m.* 1923, Kathleen Elsie Wells; two *s.* one *d.* *Educ.:* Sibford School, Oxon. City of London Electric Lighting Co. Ltd.; Secretary, 1931; Manager, 1936; Managing Director, 1940. Chairman, Electrical Development Association, 1946-47; Chairman, London Electricity Supply Association, 1946-1947; Member, British Electricity Authority, 1947-50 and 1954-55; Chairman, London Electricity Board, 1947-56. *Recreations:* gardening (Vice-Pres. The Iris Society); photography, painting. *Address:* The Gower, Burkes Road, Beaconsfield, Bucks. *T.:* Beaconsfield 4245. *Club:* Athenæum. [*Died* 5 *May* 1967.

RANDELL, Major Charles Edmund; Journalist; Editor, The Brewers' Journal and Hop and Malt Trades Review, 1930-60, retd.; *b.* Aysgarth, Yorks, 17 Nov. 1893; *y. s.* of William Randell and Edith Macdonnell, *d.* of Rev. John White, Chevington, Suffolk; *m.* 1941, Barbara Constance, *e. d.* of Frederick Taylor, Leicester; (one *s.* decd.), one adopted *s.* one adopted *d.* *Educ.:* Pocklington Grammar School; Thames Nautical Training College, H.M.S. Worcester; University of London; Inns of Court (Middle Temple).

Enlisted Public School Corps, 1914; Lieut. 1916; Capt. 1918; served Eastern Theatre, Salonika, Constantinople, etc., demobilised 1919; Assistant Secretary, Institute of Brewing, 1921-30, inaugurated and organised annual trade tours to Continent, viz., 1930, Berlin; 1931, Munich; 1932, Copenhagen; 1933, Belgium; 1934, Alsace-Lorraine; 1935, Sweden; 1936, Switzerland; 1937, Holland; 1938, Czecho-Slovakia; 1939, Paris; rejoined Army, 1941, for duration, Captain Intelligence Corps; G.S.O. 3; War Office, 1943-45, G.S.O. 2. *Publications:* Compiled English-speaking section of Bibliographie des Brauwesens by Fritz Schoellhorn, 1928; Contributor to The Times and many other newspapers and trade journals. *Recreations:* golf, motoring, gardening. *Address:* Glenmore, Brighton Road, Crawley, Sussex. *T.:* Crawley 25674. [*Died* 29 *Dec.* 1961.

RANKEILLOUR, 3rd Baron, *cr.* 1932, of Buxted; **Henry John Hope**; *b.* 20 Jan. 1899; 2nd *s.* of 1st Baron Rankeillour, P.C. (*d.* 1949), and Mabel Ellen, O.B.E. (*d.* 1938), *d.* of Francis Riddell, Cheeseburn Grange, Northumberland; *S.* brother, 1958; *m.* 1933, Mary Sibyl, *y. d.* of late Colonel Wilfrid Ricardo, D.S.O., Hook Hall, Surrey; one *s.* one *d.* *Educ.:* Oratory School; Christ Church, Oxford. Hon. Attaché, H.M. Legation, Berne, 1917. Served European War, 1914-18 (despatches, severely wounded). Parliamentary Barrister, 1925. Served throughout War of 1939-45. Administrative Secretary to Preparatory Commission of U.N.O., 1945. Chairman St. John and St. Elizabeth's Hospital, 1949-57. Knight of Malta; Knight Commander of St. Gregory, 1952. *Publications:* Death on the Pack Road, 1933; Men Who March Away, 1934; Dennisdale Tragedy, 1936; Hope's Education Act, 1936. *Heir:* *s.* Hon. Peter Thomas More Hope, *b.* 29 May 1935. *Address:* Covar's Farm, Liphook, Hants. [*Died* 2 *Dec.* 1967.

RANKIN, Lt.-Col. (Arthur) Niall (Talbot); *b.* 6 Aug. 1904; *s.* of Lt.-Col. Sir Reginald Rankin, 2nd Bt., and Hon. Nest Rice (*d.* 1943), 2nd *d.* of 6th Baron Dynevor, and *heir-pres.* to brother, Sir Hugh Rankin, 3rd Bt.; *m.* 1931, Lady Jean Margaret Florence Dalrymple (C.V.O. 1957, Order of Mercy, 1930; appointed a Woman of the Bedchamber to Queen Elizabeth the Queen Mother, 1947), *er. d.* of 12th Earl of Stair, K.T., D.S.O.; two *s.* *Educ.:* Eton; Christ Church, Oxford (M.A.). Official photographer to Oxford Univ. Arctic Expedn., 1924, to Spitzbergen and North-East Land; Staff-photographer to the Field Newspaper, 1929-31; producer of various travel films, mainly in the Orient, including travels through Tibet, Indo-China, China, and the Dutch East Indies, 1936-38. Emergency Reserve of Officers, Scots Guards, 1939; Lt.-Col. 1943. Since War of 1939-45 has made extensive journeys to Antarctic, 1946-47, Canada, 1948, Arctic Alaska, 1950, Northern Hudson's Bay, 1951, Iceland, 1954, Nepal Himalayas, 1954, Assam, 1955, Central Africa, 1957, Central Africa, 1957-59, Australia, 1961, on various nature surveys. F.R.P.S., F.R.G.S. Member of the Royal Company of Archers (Queen's Body Guard for Scotland). *Publications:* Haunts of British Divers, 1947; Antarctic Isle, 1951. Many articles on ornithological subjects. *Recreations:* gardening, climbing, yachting. *Address:* House of Treshnish, Calgary, Isle of Mull, Argyll. *T.:* Dervaig 49; 35 Cambridge Square, W.2. *T.:* Ambassador 4500. *Clubs:* Buck's; Royal Highland Yacht. [*Died* 7 *April* 1965.

RANKIN, Major-Gen. Henry Charles Deans, C.I.E. 1943; O.B.E. 1919; *b.* 16 Sept. 1888; *o. s.* of late Henry C. D. Rankin, Briarfield, Skelmorlie, Ayrshire; *m.* 1918, Edith Watson, *y. d.* of late James Gardner, Skelmorlie; two *s.* *Educ.:* Glasgow Acad., Glasgow Univ. (M.B., Ch.B. 1911). Surgeon to Red Cross Unit with Serbian Army, Balkan War, 1912-13 (Order of St. Sava IV Cl.); Lieut. R.A.M.C. 1913; served European War, 1914-18 (despatches thrice, O.B.E., twice prisoner); Surgeon to C.-in-C. India, (Lord Rawlinson, Lord Birdwood, Lord Chetwode): 1923-25 and 1927-31; Physician and Surgeon Royal Hospital, Chelsea, 1931-1935; Surgeon to Governor of Bombay (Lord Brabourne), 1936-37; D.D.M.S. G.H.Q., India, 1941-43; D.D.M.S. Southern Army, India, 1943-45; D.D.M.S. Eastern Command, 1945-46; retired from Army, 1946; Member of Pensions Appeal Tribunals, 1947. V.H.S. 1941. *Recreations:* "Age still leaves us Friends and Wine." *Address:* Romarin, Rosemary Lane, Rowledge, Farnham, Surrey. *T.:* Frensham 2625. *Club:* United Service. [*Died* 4 *June* 1965.

RANKIN, Lt.-Col. Niall; *see* Rankin, Lt.-Col. A. N. T.

RANKINE, Sir Richard Sims Donkin, K.C.M.G., *cr.* 1932 (C.M.G. 1919); *b.* North Shields, Northumb.; *s.* of John Rankine; *m.* Hilda Gertrude Akerman (*d.* 1958), *e. d.* of Joseph Steele Dalzell of Hayton, Oamaru, N.Z.; one *s.* one *d.* *Educ.:* privately. Entered Colonial Service, Fiji, 1894; Private Secretary to Governors Sir G. T. M. O'Brien, Sir H. M. Jackson, Sir Everard im Thurn; Assistant Colonial Secretary, Fiji, 1909; Receiver-General, Commissioner of Stamps, 1910; acted Colonial Secretary on many occasions; proceeded to India as personal representative of Governor on Special Mission on question of emigration of Indians to Fiji, 1919; Chief Secretary, Nyasaland, 1920; acted as Governor, 1921, 1923, 1924 and 1926; represented Nyasaland at Colonial Office Conference; Chief Secretary to the Government of Uganda, 1927-29; Acting Governor, Uganda, June 1928; British Resident for the Zanzibar Protectorate, 1930-37; retired 1937; Brilliant Star of Zanzibar (1st Class). *Recreations:* tennis, golf, cricket. *Address:* Flat 8, Arundel House, 22 The Drive, Hove 3, Sussex. [*Died* 24 *June* 1961.

RANKING, Major-General Robert Philip Lancaster-, C.B. 1946; C.B.E 1943; M.C. 1918; p.s.c.; *b.* 26 Nov. 1896; *s.* of late Lt.-Col. G. S. A. Ranking, C.M.G.; *m.* 1929, Marjorie Christian, *d.* of late A. S. Elder, Leatherhead. *Educ.:* Bradfield College, Berks; Cadet College, Quetta. 2nd Lt. 1915; Capt. 1919; served European War, 1916-18, France, Palestine, and Syria (M.C.); Major, 1933; Bt. Lt.-Col. 1936; Col. 1939; Brig. 1940; Maj.-Gen. (temp.) 1942. Served from 1940 in War of 1939-45, Middle East, Greece, East Frontier of India, Bmaur (despatches thrice, C.B.E., Greek Military Cross Class A); retd. 1948. *Recreations:* riding, shooting, fishing, stamp-collecting. *Address:* Bucks Close, Teffont Magna, nr. Salisbury, Wilts. *T.:* Teffont 282; Lloyds Bank, 6 Pall Mall, S.W.1. *Clubs:* Cavalry; Phyllis Court (Henley); Bibury (Salisbury). [*Died* 29 *Dec.* 1961.

RANKL, Karl; Conductor (Free Lance); *b.* 1 October 1898; *m.* 1923, Adele Jahoda. *Educ.:* Vienna. Became Conductor of the Vienna Volksoper, 1922; Opera Director Reichenberg, 1925-27; Conductor of the Opera, Koenigsberg (Prussia), 1927; Conductor of State Opera, Berlin, 1928-31; Principal Conductor State Opera, Wiesbaden, 1931; Opera Director Graz (Austria), 1933-1937; Opera Director, Prague, 1937; after Hitler's occupation of Czechoslovakia emigrated to England; Musical Director Royal Opera House, Covent Garden, W.C.2, 1946-1951. Principal Conductor, Scottish National Orchestra, 1952-57; Director of Elizabethan

Opera Company of Sydney, 1958. From 1944 Guest Conductor of London Philharmonic Orchestra, Liverpool Philharmonic Orchestra, and B.B.C. *Compositions:* Deirdre of the Sorrows, Opera; 8 Symphonies; 1 String Suite; 1 Quartet; Music from Deirdre; Suite for Orchestra; Sinfonietta Nos. 1 and 2; Theme and Variations; Der Mensch, Secular Oratorio for Solo, Choir and Orch.; 60 Songs. *Address:* 25 Acacia Road, St. John's Wood, N.W.8.
[*Died* 6 *Sept.* 1968.

RANSFORD, Ella; *d.* of Thomas Davis Ransford, F.R.C.S., L.R.C.P. *Educ.:* St. Leonards School, St. Andrews; Girton College, Cambridge; Sorbonne, Paris. Assistant Mistress County School, Penarth, Glam., Belvedere School (G.P.D.S.T.) Liverpool; Headmistress Ipswich High School (G.P.D.S.T.) 1919-25; Headmistress of Croydon High School for Girls, G.P.D.S.T., 1925-39. *Address:* Nyewood, Walberton, Arundel, Sussex.
[*Died* 2 *May* 1968.

RANSOME, Maj.-Gen. Algernon Lee, C.B. 1937; D.S.O. 1918 and bar 1918; M.C. 1914; F.R.E.S.; *b*, 1883; *s.* of Lee Johnstone Ransome, San Francisco, Cal., U.S.A. and Winchester, Hants and of Mary Elizabeth Wodehouse; *m.* 1927; Catherine Violet Burton. *Educ.:* privately; R.M.C. Dorset Regt., 1903-31. Served European War, 1914-18 (despatches 6 times, Bt. Maj., Bt. Lt.-Col., D.S.O. and bar, M.C.); staff, 1915-16; Comd. 7 Bn. The Buffs, 1916-18; comd. 170 Inf. Bde., 1918-19; on staff, 1920-1925, 1927-28 (R.M.C. Duntroon, Australia) and 1931-33; Comd. 2 (Rawalpindi) Inf. Bde., 1933-35, Maj.-Gen. 1935; ret. 1938; re-called 1939; Comd. 46 div., 1939; Comd. 10 (Romsey) Bn. Hampshire Home Guard, 1942-45. p.s.c. 1919. *Address:* The Close, Braishfield, Romsey, Hampshire.
[*Died* 6 *May* 1969.

RANSOME, Arthur, C.B.E. 1953; Hon. Litt.D. (Leeds); Hon. M.A. (Durham); *b.* 18 Jan. 1884; *s.* of Prof. Cyril Ransome, M.A. (*d.* 1897); *m.* 1st, 1909; one *d.*; 2nd, 1924, Evgenia, *d.* of Peter Shelepin. *Educ.:* Rugby. *Publications:* A History of Storytelling, 1909; Edgar Allan Poe, 1910; The Hoofmarks of the Faun, 1911; Oscar Wilde, 1912; Portraits and Speculations, 1913; The Elixir of Life, 1915; Old Peter's Russian Tales, 1916; Six Weeks in Russia, 1919; Aladdin, 1919; The Soldier and Death, 1920; The Crisis in Russia, 1921; Racundra's First Cruise, 1923; The Chinese Puzzle, 1927; Rod and Line: with Aksakov on Fishing, 1929; Swallows and Amazons, 1930; Swallowdale, 1931; Peter Duck, 1932; Winter Holiday, 1933; Coot Club, 1934; Pigeon Post, 1936 (Library Association's Carnegie Medal); We Didn't Mean To Go To Sea, 1937; Secret Water, 1939; The Big Six, 1940; Missee Lee, 1941; The Picts and the Martyrs, 1943; Great Northern?, 1947; Mainly about Fishing, 1959. *Recreations:* fishing, sailing, fairy stories. *Address:* c/o Jonathan Cape Ltd., 30 Bedford Square, W.C.1. *Clubs:* Royal Cruising, Garrick.
[*Died* 3 *June* 1967.

RAPHAEL, Geoffrey G.; retired as Metropolitan Police Magistrate (1945-65); *b* 21 Dec. 1893; *s.* of late Joseph Henry Raphael; *m.* 1st, 1933, Nancy, *er. d.* of Lt.-Col. E. A. Rose; one *s.* two *d.*; 2nd, Patricia, *d.* of late Sir Patrick Hastings, Q.C., and of Lady Hastings. *Educ.:* Frinton College; University College School; privately in Germany. Served throughout European War, 1914-19; B.E.F., London Rifle Brigade, 1914 (wounded; Star and clasp). Called to Bar, Inner Temple, 1924; President Harwicke Society, 1930; Junior Counsel to the Treasury at County of London Sessions and Junior Counsel in the Court of Criminal Appeal, 1934; Officers' Emergency Reserve, 1938; Staff of Judge-Advocate-General, 1940; North Africa and Italy, 1942-45. Lt.-Col. A.D.J.A.G. at A.F.H.Q. C.M.F. (despatches). *Recreation:* painting. *Address:* Chilston House, Burwash, Sussex. *T.:* Burwash 568.
[*Died* 21 *Dec.* 1969.

RASCH, Sir (Frederic) Carne, 2nd Bt., *cr.* 1903; *b.* 27 Sept. 1880; *s.* of Sir Frederic Carne Rasch, 1st Bt.; *S.* father, 1914; *m.* 1921, Catherine Margaret (J.P. Essex), *o. d.* of late Hon. John Richard de Clare Boscawen, J.P., D.L., and Lady Margaret Boscawen, and *widow* of 16th Lord Petre. *Educ.:* Eton. Entered the Service, 1st Batt. Essex Regt., 1901; transferred to The Carabiniers, 1903; Captain, 1908; Major, 1915; served South Africa, 1901-2 (Queen's medal 5 clasps); European War, 1914-1919 (despatches); retired pay, 1920; Lt.-Col. retired pay, 1924; Lt.-Col. Commanding 5th Batt. Essex Regt. 1922-28. Hon. Col. since 1935; Brevet Col. 1926; Col., 1928; J.P., D.L., Essex; High Sheriff, 1924-25; commanded 161st (Essex) Infantry Brigade T.A 1928-32; H.M. Bodyguard, 1929-38; served River Emergency Services, 1939-40; comd. 2nd Bn. Essex Home Guard, 1940-43; served Admiralty Ferry crews, 1943-45; A.D.C. to the King, 1931-41. *Heir:* *n.* Major Richard Guy Carne Rasch [*b.* 10 Oct. 1918; *m.* 1st, 1947, Anne Mary Dent-Brocklehurst (marriage dissolved, 1959); one *s.* one *d.*; 2nd, 1961, Fiona Mary Salmon]. *Address:* Woodhill, Danbury, Essex. *Clubs:* Army and Navy; Royal Yacht Squadron (Cowes).
[*Died* 12 *June* 1963.

RASCHEN, George H., C.B.E. 1937; late Senior Managing Director Forbes Forbes Campbell and Co., Ltd., India; retired from India, 1938; *b.* 3 Feb. 1889; *s.* of John and Eleanor Raschen; *m.* 1918, Adelaide Majolier Brabazon Urmston, Fintonagh, Maidstone; one *d.*; *m.* 1922, Jane Katharine Irwin, Justicetown, Cumberland; one *s.* *Educ.:* Birkenhead School. Served in the Indian Army during European War (twice wounded); Chairman Karachi Chamber of Commerce 3 years; Trustee and Vice-Chairman Karachi Port Trust; Member of Governor of Sind's Advisory Council; Member of Sind Legislative Assembly. *Recreation:* fishing. *Address:* Innisfree, Dawlish, Devon.
[*Died* 12 *April* 1964.

RATCLIFF, Rev. Canon Edward Craddock; Regius Professor of Divinity, University of Cambridge, 1958-64; Emeritus Professor, since 1964; Fellow of St. John's College, Cambridge, 1950; Canon Emeritus of Ely Cathedral, 1959; *b.* 16 December 1896; *o. s.* of late John Ratcliff and Marie-Louise, *d.* of Vaughan Craddock; unmarried. *Educ.:* Merchant Taylors' School; St. John's Coll., Cambridge (Scholar). Army Y.M.C.A. of India, 1916-18 (unfit for military service); 2nd Class, Oriental Languages Tripos, Pt. I, and B.A. 1920; 1st Class, Theological Tripos, Pt. II, and George Williams Prize, 1922. Deacon, 1922; Priest, 1923; Curate, St. Mary's, Ely, Cambs., 1922-24; Vice-Principal, Westcott House, Cambridge, 1924-29; Fellow, and Praelector in Church History and Theology, Queen's College, Oxford, 1930-43; Chaplain, 1930-37; University Lecturer in Liturgiology, Oxford, 1933-39; Asst. Minister, St. George's, Hanover Square, London, 1944-45; Prof. of Liturgical Theology in Univ. of London, attd. King's College, London, 1945-1947; Preb. of Fittleworth in Chichester Cathedral, 1946-47; Ely Prof. of Divinity, University of Cambridge, and Canon of Ely, 1947-58; Commissary to the Archbishop of Capetown, 1950-57. Select Preacher, Cambridge Univ., 1931, 1934, 1948 and 1954; Oxford Univ., 1933-34, 1952-53; Catechist, Exeter Coll., Oxford, 1957-58; Examining Chaplain to Bp. of Chichester, 1934-50. President, Henry Bradshaw Society, 1960-. *Publications:* The English Coronation Service,

1936; The Booke of Common Prayer: its making and revisions, 1949; The Coronation Service of Queen Elizabeth II, 1953; contributor to: New Commentary on Holy Scripture, 1928; Encyclopædia Britannica, 1929, 1963; Chambers's Encyclopædia, 1963; Liturgy and Worship, 1932; The Study of Theology, 1939; From Uniformity to Unity, 1962; Biblical and Patristic Studies in memory of R. P. Casey, 1963; Studies in Church History, II, 1965. *Address:* St. John's College, Cambridge. *Clubs:* Athenæum, Royal Societies.
[*Died* 30 *June* 1967.

RATCLIFFE, Arthur; *b.* 17 Feb. 1882; *s.* of Joseph and Ann Ratcliffe; *m.* Ellen, *d.* of G. H. and M. Horrobin; one *s.* *Educ.:* British School, Leek. Plumber and Decorator; President of the National Federation of Master Painters and Decorators of England and Wales, 1932; Urban District Councillor for Leek, 1923-1934; connected with the Building Society movement; Director of the Leek United and Midlands Building Society since 1929; M.P. (U.) Leek Division, Staffordshire, 1931 - 35; Leek Rural District Council, 1937. *Address:* The Hillochs, Ecton, Wetton, Ashbourne, Derbyshire. *T.:* Hartington 203.
[*Died* 3 *May* 1963.

RATCLIFFE, Dorothy Una; *see* Phillips, Mrs. McGrigor.

RATHBONE, Basil, M.C. 1918; **stage and film actor; *b.* Johannesburg, Transvaal, 13 June 1892; *s.* of Edgar Philip Rathbone and Anne Barbara George; *m.* 1st, Ethel Marian Forman (marriage dissolved); one *s.*; 2nd, Ouida Bergere; one *d.* *Educ.:* Repton College. With Sir Frank Benson's No. 2 Company, 1911, and went with Company to America, 1912, playing various Shakespearean parts. First London appearance as Finch in The Sin of David, Savoy, 1914. Served European War, 1914-18, as private in the London Scottish; commissioned in Liverpool Scottish (M.C.). With New Shakespeare Company at Stratford-on-Avon, 1919. Played title-rôle in Peter Ibbetson, Savoy, 1920; since then leading parts in West End, New York and other American theatres. Commenced film career, 1925, and has appeared in many films. Has often taken the part of Conan Doyle's Sherlock Holmes in films and in radio productions. Lecture tour, with dramatic readings, 1951. *Publication:* (with Walter Ferris) Judas, 1925. *Address:* 135 Central Park West, New York 23, N.Y.,** U.S.A. [*Died* 21 *July* 1967.

RATTEN, Victor Richard, C.B.E. 1925; M.D.; Senior Cons. Surgeon of Royal Hobart Hospital and Major Australian Army Medical Corps; *b.* 12 Dec. 1878; *s.* of Rev. G. W. Ratten, Melbourne, Australia; one *s.* (and *e. s.* died on active service, England, 1945). Served European War, 1914-19. *Address:* 167 Macquarie Street, Hobart, Tasmania.
[*Died* 30 *Dec.* 1962.

RATTENBURY, John Ernest, D.D.; Methodist Minister; *b.* 10 Dec. 1870; *s.* of Rev. H. Owen Rattenbury, Wesleyan Minister; *m.* 1898, Edith Mary (*d.* 1934), *d.* of R. S. Mantle, of Wykes and Mantle, chartered accountant, Leicester; one *s.* one *d.* *Educ.:* Woodhouse Grove School; Didsbury College, Manchester. Entered Wesleyan ministry, 1893; Leicester, 1893-1902; founded Mission at Belgrave Hall, 1897, church at Clarendon Park, 1900, Leicester; Nottingham, 1902-7; the largest Public hall in Nottingham, the Albert Hall was purchased by a syndicate of Wesleyans; started a mission there with empty hall and £12,000 debt; the Mission is the centre of great social and religious activity; since transferred to West London Mission, founded 1887, headquarters Kingsway Hall, formerly Gt. Queen St. Chapel; Superintendent West London Mission, 1907-25; Quillian Lecturer, Emory University, U.S.A.; Fernley-Hartley Lecturer, 1941. Pres. National Free Church Council, 1936; Pres. Methodist Sacramental Fellowship, 1939-50. *Publications:* Sermons on Social Subjects, 1908; The Twelve, 1916; Roman Errors, 1920; Our Father and His Family; Wesley's Legacy to the World, 1928; The Testament of Paul, 1930; Vital Elements of Public Worship, 1936; The Conversion of the Wesleys, 1938; The Evangelical Doctrines of Charles Wesley's Hymns, 1940; The Eucharistic Hymns of John and Charles Wesley, 1948; Thoughts on Holy Communion, 1958. *Recreation:* chess. *Club:* National Liberal. [*Died* 19 *Jan.* 1963.

RATTENBURY, Robert Mantle, M.A.; Fellow of Trinity College since 1926; *b.* 9 Dec. 1901; *s.* of late John Ernest Rattenbury, D.D.; *m.* 1934, Monica Mary Miller Jones; three *d.* *Educ.:* Westminster School; Trinity College, Cambridge. First Class Honours in Classical Tripos Part I, 1921, Part II, 1923; George Charles Winter Warr Scholar, 1923-24; Asst. Lecturer in Classics, Univ. of Leeds, 1924-27; Classical Lecturer, 1930-52, Steward, 1937-45, Tutor, 1945-46, Senior Tutor, 1946-52, of Trinity Coll., Cambridge; Lecturer in Classics, Univ. of Camb., 1932-52; Registrary of Univ. of Cambridge, 1953-69; Hon. Secretary of Classical Association, 1931-35; Editor (with C. J. Fordyce) of the Classical Review, 1943-60; Member Governing Body of Westminster School, 1951-66. *Publications:* Romance: Traces of Lost Greek Novels (New Chapters in the History of Greek Literature, third series, ed. J. U. Powell), 1933; (with T. W. Lumb) Ed. of the Aethiopica of Heliodorus in the Budé Series, vol. i, 1935, vol. ii, 1938, vol. iii, 1943; articles and reviews in classical periodicals. *Address:* Trinity College, Cambridge; 10 Amhurst Court, Grange Road, Cambridge.
[*Died* 29 *July* 1970.

RATTRAY, Rear-Admiral Sir Arthur Rullion, K.B.E., *cr.* 1947; C.B. 1945; **C.I.E. 1943; *b.* 1891; *s.* of Arthur Rattray, late Indian Navy, Gatehouse-of-Fleet, Kirkcudbrightshire, Scotland; *m.* 1917, Doris Gertrude (*d.* 1942), *d.* of late James Muir, and of Mrs. James Muir, The Wyck, Hitchin, Herts; one *s.* *Educ.:* privately; H.M.S. Conway. Master Mariner. Served in George Milne & Co.'s Sailing Ships, of Aberdeen; joined R.I.M. (later R.I.N.), 1912. Served European War, 1914-18, at sea, also with R.F.C. Commander, 1934. Served War of 1939-45; held important staff appointments in India; Commodore, 2nd class, 1941, 1st class, 1943; Rear-Adm. 1944; Flag Officer, Bombay, 1944-47; retired, 1948; Captain Emergency, Royal Navy. *Address:* c/o Lloyds Bank Ltd., 6 Pall Mall, S.W.1; c/o The Bank of London and South America, Ltd., 40/8 Rua-Aurea, Lisbon, Portugal.**
[*Died* 10 *Aug.* 1966.

RATTRAY, Robert Fleming, M.A., Ph.D.; Extension Lecturer, University of Cambridge, since 1945; *s.* of late Wm. Rattray, Monifieth, Angus; *m.* 1915, Mary Currall Heygate Brooks, B.A. (*d.* 1963), *d.* of late H. R. F. Brooks, Banbury. *Educ.:* Glasgow University (1st Cl. hons. in English); Manchester College, Oxford; Kiel, Marburg and Harvard Universities. Assistant Minister, Ullet Road Church, Liverpool, 1913-15; Minister, Hindley, near Wigan, 1915-17; Great Meeting, Leicester, 1917-21; first Principal, University College, Leicester, 1921-31; Minister, Memorial Church (Unitarian), Cambridge, 1931-45; President, General Assembly of Unitarian and Free Christian Churches of Great Britain and Ireland, 1938-39; Upton Lecturer, Manchester Coll., Oxford, 1945; President, Manchester Coll., Oxford, 1951-54; Vice-Chairman Council, R.S.P.C.A. *Publications:* Fundamentals of Modern Religion, 1932; Bernard

Shaw: A Chronicle and an Introduction, 1934; Samuel Butler: A Chronicle and an Introduction, 1935; From Primitive to Modern Religion, 1937; Bernard Shaw: A Chronicle, 1951; Poets in the Flesh, 1961; articles in Mind, Philosophy, Hibbert Journal, Quarterly Review, Wetenschappelijke Bladen, etc. *Address:* 26 Queen Edith's Way, Cambridge. [*Died* 18 *Nov.* 1967.

RAU, Sir Benegal Rama, Kt., *cr.* 1939; C I.E. 1930; Governor Reserve Bank of India, 1949-57; *b.* 10 Jan. 1889; *s.* of Dr. B. R. Rau; *m.* 1919, Dhanvanthi, *d.* of Pandit R. K. Handoo; two *d.* *Educ.:* Presidency College, Madras; King's College, Cambridge. Joined Indian Civil Service, 1913; Under Secretary, Government Madras, 1920; Deputy-Secretary, Government of Madras, 1922; Secretary, Indian Taxation Committee, 1925-26; Deputy-Secretary Finance Department, Government of India, 1926; Financial Adviser, The Indian Statutory Commission, 1928-30; Joint Secretary, Industries Department, Government of India, New Delhi, 1930-31; Secretary, Indian Delegation Round Table Conferences and Joint Parliamentary Committee, 1931-34; Dep. High Commissioner for India in London, 1934-38; Agent-General for the Government of India in the Union of South Africa, 1938-40; High Commissioner for India in South Africa, 1941; Chairman, Bombay Port Trust, 1942; Ambassador for India, Tokyo, 1947-48; Leader Indian Deleg., Commonwealth Conf., Canberra, 1947; Indian Ambassador to the U.S.A., 1948-49. *Recreation:* tennis. *Address:* Mafatlal Park, Warden Road, Bombay, India. *Club:* Willingdon (Bombay). [*Died* 13 *Dec.* 1969.

RAVEN, Rev. Charles Earle, D.D.; Hon. D.D. (Glasgow), 1929, (Aberdeen), 1946, T.C.D.), 1950, (McGill), (Trin. Coll., Toronto), 1952; Hon. D.Sc. (Manchester), 1948; Hon. D.Litt. (Delhi) 1955; F.B.A.; F.L.S.; Chaplain to the Queen since 1952 (formerly to King George V and VI); *b.* 4 July 1885; *s.* of John E. Raven, barrister-at-law; *m.* 1st, 1910, Margaret E. Buchanan Wollaston (*d.* 1944); one *s.* three *d.*; 2nd, 1954, Ethel Paine (*d.* 1954), *widow* of J. F. Moors, Boston, U.S.A.; 3rd, 1956, Mme N. Hélène Jeanty, *widow* of M. Paul Jeanty, Brussels. *Educ.:* Uppingham; Caius College, Cambridge (Scholar). Fellow, Dean, and Lecturer in Theology, Emmanuel College, 1909-1920; ordained, 1909; Army Chaplain, 1917-18; Rector of Bletchingley, 1920-24; Canon of Liverpool, 1924-32; Chancellor, 1931-32; Chancellor Emeritus since 1932; Regius Professor of Divinity, Cambridge Univ., 1932-50; Master of Christ's College, Cambridge, 1939-50; Warden of Madingley Hall, Cambridge, 1950-54; Canon of Ely, 1932-40. Examining Chaplain to Bishop of Southwark, 1911-18; of Llandaff, 1920-24; of Liverpool, 1924; of Lichfield, 1942; Donnellan Lecturer, Trinity College, Dublin, 1919; Hulsean Lecturer, Cambridge, 1926-1927; Noble Lecturer, Harvard, 1926; Robertson Lecturer, Glasgow, 1931; Halley Stewart Lecturer, 1934; Herbert Spencer Lecturer, Oxford, 1945; Hobhouse Lecturer, London, 1946; Vice-Chancellor, Cambridge University, 1947-49; Gifford Lecturer, Edinburgh, 1950-52; Owen Memorial Lecturer, Canada, 1952; Forwood Lecturer, Liverpool University, 1954; Trustee British Museum, 1950-63; Hon. Chaplain to Bishop of Portsmouth, 1951-59; President, Botanical Society of British Isles, 1951-55; Hon. Fellow, Caius College. *Publications:* What think Ye of Christ?, 1916; Christian Socialism, 1920; Apollinarianism, 1923; In Praise of Birds, 1925; Our Salvation, 1925; The Creator Spirit, 1927; A Wanderer's Way, 1928; Christ and Modern Education, 1928; Bird Haunts and Bird Behaviour, 1929; Jesus and the Gospel of Love, 1931; Musings and Memories, 1931; Is War Obsolete?, 1935; War and the Christian, 1938; The Gospel and the Church, 1939; John Ray, Naturalist, 1942; Science, Religion and the Future, 1943; Good News of God, 1944; English Naturalists from Neckam to Ray, 1947 (James Tait Black prize); Natural Religion and Christian Theology (Gifford Lectures, 2 vols.); Science and Religion, Experience and Interpretation, 1953; Science, Medicine and Morals, 1959; Teilhard de Chardin, Scientist and Seer, 1962; (with Eleanor Raven) The Life and Teaching of Jesus Christ, 1933. *Address:* 10 Madingley Road, Cambridge. *T.:* Cambridge 3880; 32 Avenue Franklin Roosevelt, Brussels. [*Died* 8 *July* 1964.

RAVENSDALE, 2nd Baroness, *cr.* 1911; **Mary Irene Curzon;** Baroness in her own right; also *cr.* Life Peeress, 1958, with title of Baroness Ravensdale of Kedleston; *b.* 20 January 1896; *e. d.* of late Marquess Curzon of Kedleston and Mary Victoria, C.I., *d.* of late L. Z. Leiter, Washington, U.S.A.; *S.* father to Barony of Ravensdale, 1925. Vice-Pres. The Highway Clubs of East London Inc.: Vice-Pres. of Nat. Assoc. of Girls' Clubs and Mixed Clubs; Joint Pres. London Union of Youth Clubs; Treas. of Musicians' Benevolent Fund; President, World Congress of Faiths; Vice-Chm. of Royal India Soc. *Publication:* In Many Rhythms (autobiography), 1953. *Heir: n.* Nicholas Mosley, *b.* 25 June 1923. *Address:* 9 The Vale, Chelsea, S.W.3. [*Died* 9 *Feb.* 1966.

RAW, Brigadier Cecil Whitfield, C.B.E. 1942; T.D.; D.L.; *b.* 19 Oct. 1900; *s.* of late N. Whitfield Raw; *m.* 1929, Barbara Marion Alice Harker; two *s.* *Educ.:* Dover College. Fellow Institute of Chartered Accountants; Partner in Hyland Riches & Raw, Chartered Accountants, 7 Southampton Place, W.C.1., and in Ernest James & Co., Chartered Accountants, 11-13 Dowgate Hill, E.C.4; Governor of Dover College; Chm., Rochester Diocesan Board of Finance. D.L. Kent, 1952. Former Hon. Colonel 265 L.A.A. Regiment, R.A. T.A. A.D.C. (Additional) to the Queen, 1951-61. *Address:* 8 Tootswood Road, Bromley, Kent. [*Died* 15 *Feb.* 1969.

RAW, Vice-Adm. Sir Sydney (Moffatt), K.B.E., *cr.* 1954 (C.B.E. 1942); C.B. 1951; retd.; President, Submarine Old Comrades' Assoc.; *b.* 19 Aug. 1898; *e. s.* of late Dr. Nathan Raw, C.M.G., and late A. L. Raw; *m.* 1927, Grace Léonie, *d.* of F. Gibson Ward, Rosemont, Bermuda; two *d.* *Educ.:* Osborne and Dartmouth Naval Colleges; Trinity College, Cambridge. Entered Osborne as cadet, 1911; went to sea from Dartmouth, 1914; served European War, H.M.S. Nottingham, 1914 (Heligoland Bight), H.M.S. Tiger, 1914-17 (Dogger Bank, Jutland), H.M.S. Geranium, Mediterranean, 1917-18; joined Submarines, 1918, then almost continuously in Submarines in Baltic, China, Home Waters, and Mediterranean; Naval Staff College, 1929; Military Staff College, Camberley, 1934; 2½ years Naval Staff, Admiralty, 1935-37; War of 1939-45 entirely with Submarines: raising of Thetis, 1939, Captain (S/M) Colombo, 1939-40, (S/M) Malta, 1940, (S/M) Mediterranean, 1940-41; Chief of Staff to Admiral (Submarines), 1942-44; Commanded H.M.S. Phoebe, 1944-45 (despatches twice for operations on Burma coast); Imperial Defence College, 1946; Commodore, Royal Naval Barracks, Devonport, 1947-49; Flag Officer, (Submarines), 1950-51; a Lord Commissioner of the Admiralty, Fourth Sea Lord and Chief of Supplies and Transport, 1952-1954, retired 1954. *Address:* 7 Shortheath Crest, Farnham, Surrey. *Club:* United Service. [*Died* 4 *Feb.* 1967.

RAWLINGS, Admiral Sir (Henry) Bernard (Hughes), G.B.E., *cr.* 1946 (K.B.E., *cr.* 1945; O.B.E. 1920); K.C.B., *cr.* 1944 (C.B. 1942); D.L.; *b.* 21 May 1889; *s.* of W. J. Rawlings, Downes, Hayle, Cornwall; *m.* 1922, Eva Loveday, *d.* of William Hastings Beaumont, Esher; two *s.* one *d.* *Educ.:* Stanmore Park; H.M.S. Britannia. Entered R.N., 1904; Midshipman, 1905; served War of 1914-18; with Foreign Office and Military Missions in Poland, 1918-21; commanded H.M. ships Active, Curacoa. Delhi; Naval Attaché, Tokyo, 1936-39; H.M.S. Valiant, 1939 (despatches); A.D.C. to the King, 1940; Rear-Admiral commanding 1st Battle Squadron, 1940; commanded 7th Cruiser Squadron, 1941 (despatches, Hellenic War Cross). Assistant Chief of Naval Staff, Foreign, 1942-43. Vice-Adm. 1943; Flag Officer West Africa, 1943; Flag Officer Eastern Mediterranean, 1943-44; Second in Command British Pacific Fleet, and Commanding British Task Forces, 1944-45; retired list, 1946; Adm. (retd.), 1946. Commander U.S.A. Legion of Merit; Grand Officer Order of George I (Greece). High Sheriff of Cornwall, 1950; D.L. Cornwall; *Recreations:* gardening, fishing. *Address:* Clerkenwater House, Bodmin. *Club:* United Service. [*Died* 30 *Sept.* 1962.

RAWLINGS, Rear-Adm. Henry Clive, C.B. 1943; D.S.O. 1920; Royal Navy; *b.* Mar. 1883; *s.* of Edward Rawlings, Padstow, Cornwall; *m.* 1909, Georgina Helen Watson; one *s.* one *d.* *Educ.:* St. Andrew's School, Eastbourne; H.M.S. Britannia, Dartmouth. Served European War, 1914-19; Battle of Jutland and Baltic (D.S.O., despatches); commanded cruiser Devonshire, 1929-31; Director, Naval Air Division, Admiralty, 1932-34; commanded H.M.S. Glorious, 1935-1936; A.D.C. to the King, 1936; retired list, 1936; served War of 1939-45 (C.B.); Commodore of Convoys, Sept. 1939-May 1940; Rear-Admiral on Staff of C.-in-C. Nore, 1940-1942; Commodore of Convoys, 1942-43; Rear-Admiral Naval Air Stations, Indian Ocean, 1944-45; Head of Admiralty Technical Mission, Canada, 1945-46. *Address:* Gloyns House, Yealmpton, S. Devon. *Club:* United Service. [*Died* 29 *Dec.* 1965.

RAWLINS, Francis Ian Gregory, C.B.E. 1960; retired as Scientific Adviser to Trustees of National Gallery (1934-60) (Deputy Keeper, 1948); *b.* 8 July 1895; *y. s.* of late William Donaldson Rawlins, K.C., White Waltham Grove, Berkshire; unmarried. *Educ.:* Privately; Trinity College, Cambridge; University of Marburg. M.Sc. (Cambridge), 1926; A.Inst.P. 1927; F.Inst.P. 1929; Supervisor in Crystallography, Fitzwilliam House, 1929; Director of Natural Science Studies, Fitzwilliam House, 1932; University Research Assistant in Crystallography, 1933; Cantor Lecturer, Royal Society of Arts, 1937; Visiting Lecturer, Harvard University, and Robert Trowbridge Memorial Lectr., Yale, 1939; F.R.S.E. 1937; Fenton Foundation Lectr., Buffalo Univ., 1947; Sec. Gen. Internat. Institute for Conservation, 1949-58, Vice-Pres., 1958-64, Hon. Fell., 1964; Mem., I.C.O.M. Scientific Laboratories Committee, 1955-60; Editor of Studies in Conservation, 1951-58. A Governor of Liddon House, since 1934. (Chm. 1953-65); Tech. Dir. Central Council for the Care of Churches, 1956; Member Cathedrals Advisory Cttee., 1956; Consultative Member, New York Univ. Inst. of Fine Arts, 1959; Member, Advisory Cttee., National Army Museum, 1959; Member, Hon. Scientific Advisory Cttee., Nat. Gall., 1960; Mem. Council, Nat. Buildings Record, 1962-64. F.S.A. 1954. *Publications:* Infra-Red Analysis of Molecular Structure (with A. M. Taylor), 1929; From the National Gallery Laboratory, 1940; Editor. The First Fifty Years of the Faraday Society, 1953; Aesthetics and the Gestalt, 1953; numerous papers in Proc. Roy. Soc., Philosophical Magazine, Trans. Faraday Society, Technical Studies, dealing with molecular physics and the application of physical principles to paintings. *Recreations:* Ecclesiastical Architecture; country life. *Address:* Danny, Hurstpierpoint, Hassocks, Sussex. *T.:* Hurstpierpoint 2299; Ribblesdale House, Appleby, Westmorland. *T.:* Appleby 526. *Clubs:* Athenæum; County (Carlisle). [*Died* 2 *May* 1969.

RAWLINS, Morna Lloyd, M.B., B.S. Lond.; Cons. Surgeon to In-patients and Department for Venereal Diseases, Elizabeth Garrett Anderson Hospital (retired); late Asst. Director Female Venereal Diseases Department, Guy's Hospital; Surgeon Marie Curie Hospital; Consulting Surgeon, Bermondsey Medical Mission; *b.* Mussoorie, 4 August, 1882; *d.* of T. W. Rawlins, I.C.S., and Caroline Stanley, *d.* of Sir John Irvine Murray, K.C.B.; *m.* 1917, Commander F. C. Vaughan, R.N.; no *c.* *Educ.:* Cheltenham College; London School of Medicine for Women. Assistant Anæsthetist, 1911, House Surgeon, 1912, and Senior Obstetric Assistant, 1912-14, Royal Free Hospital; R.M.O. Female Lock Hospital, 1914; Assistant Surgeon Endell Street Military Hospital, 1915-16; Gynæcologist, Female Lock Hospital, 1917; M.O. in charge of V.D. Clinic, St. Helier, Carshalton, 1944-46; Vice-President V.D. Section B.M.A. (Cambridge), 1920; F.R.S.M. *Publications:* Treatment of Venereal Diseases in Women (jointly), 1917; Gonorrhœa in the Female; the Venereal Clinic; The Diagnosis, Treatment and Prevention of Syphilis and Gonorrhœa, 1921; papers in Proc. Roy. Soc., etc. *Recreations:* gardening, motoring. *Address:* Rockhurst, Budletts, Uckfield, Sussex. *T.:* Uckfield 2596. [*Died* 31 *July* 1969.

RAWLINSON, Sir (Alfred) Frederick, 4th Bt., *cr.* 1891; *b.* 23 Aug. 1900; *s.* of Lt.-Col. Sir Alfred Rawlinson, 3rd Bt. and Margarette Kennard (*d.* 1907), 5th *d.* of William Bunce Greenfield, J.P., D.L., of Haynes Park, Bedford; *S.* father, 1934; *m.* 1934, Bessie Ford Taylor, *d.* of Frank Raymond Emmatt, Harrogate; two *s.* one *d.* Served War of 1939-45, R.A.F.V.R., 1941-45. *Heir:* *s.* Anthony Henry John Rawlinson [*b.* 1 May 1936; *m.* 1960, Penelope Byng Noel, 2nd *d.* of Capt. G. J. B. Noel, R.N., of Haslemere, Sy.; one *s.* one *d.*]. *Address:* 22 Bryanston Road, Winton, Bournemouth, Hants. [*Died* 15 *June* 1969.

RAWSON, Brigadier Creswell Duffield, C.B.E. 1937; D.S.O. 1915; *b.* 22 Oct. 1883; *s.* of Edward Creswell Rawson, I.C.S., and Marion Emma Duffield; *m.* 1918, Gladys, *y. d.* of Arthur Niblett; one *s.* one *d.* *Educ.:* Malvern College; R.M. Academy, Woolwich. Commission in R.A. 1902; served in operations, Suez Canal, 1915 (despatches); operations, Gallipoli (Anzac), 1915 (wounded, despatches, D.S.O.); Mesopotamia, 1916-18 (despatches); Waziristan Operations, 1937 (despatches, C.B.E.); ret. 1939. *Address:* The Cottage, Orchard Close, Carroll Avenue, Ferndown, Dorset. [*Died* 9 *Feb.* 1964.

RAWSTORNE, Brigadier George Streynsham, C.B.E. 1944; M.C. 1915; retired Regular Army (The Seaforth Highlanders); Lord Lieutenant of County of Sutherland since 1950; *b.* 22 Jan. 1895; 2nd *s.* of Rt. Rev. Atherton Gwillym Rawstorne, D.D. (late Bishop of Whalley); *m.* 1933, Joyce, *e. d.* of Major W. Priestley, of Rovie, Rogart; two *d.* *Educ.:* Eton; Royal Military College, Sandhurst. Served in European War, 1914-19, Seaforth Highlanders (despatches twice); Major, 1936; served War of 1939-45 in China, Madagascar, India, Persia, Syria, Sicily, Italy, Egypt, and Palestine (despatches twice);

Brigadier, 1943; Comdr. Inverness sub-district, 1945-47; retired, 1947. A.D.C. and Mil. Sec. to Governor of Bombay (late Lord Lloyd), 1921-24. Order of Polonia Restituta (3rd class), 1945. *Recreations:* shooting, fishing. *Address:* Rovie, Rogart, Sutherland, Scotland. *T.:* Rogart 210; 4 Seymour Walk, S.W.10. [*Died* 15 *July* 1962.

RAYBURN, Hon. Sam; Speaker, House of Representatives, 1940-47, 1949-1953, and since 1955; *b.* Roane County, Tennessee, 6 January 1882; *s.* of William Marion Rayburn and Martha Waller; unmarried. *Educ.:* Flagg Springs Country School, East Texas State Teachers College and University of Texas. Member of Texas House of Reps., 1907, served six years, last two as Speaker; Member of Nat. House of Reps., 1913, and has served continuously since that time. Permanent Chm., Democratic National Convention, 1948-1952-1956. *Recreations:* fishing, helping to take care of cattle on his ranch at Bonham, Texas. *Address:* Bonham, Texas, U.S.A. *T.:* 379. *Clubs:* Alfalfa, National Press (Washington, D.C.). [*Died* 16 *Nov.* 1961.

RAYMOND, Air Vice-Marshal Adélard, C.B.E. 1945; E.D.; A.D.C.; Chevalier de la Légion d'Honneur; Croix de Guerre with Palm; President and Managing Director, Queen's Hotel, Montreal, Que.; Director: Canadair Ltd.; Crown Trust Co.; The Imperial Life Assurance Co.; Canadian Aviation Electronics; President: Raymond Distributing Co. Ltd.; Gleneagles Investment Co. Ltd.; Past Pres. Montreal Tourist and Convention Bureau; *b.* St. Stanislas de Kosta, Beauharnois County, Quebec, 10 July, 1889; *s.* of Adélard and Priscille (Quesnel) Raymond; *m.* 1932, Marguerite Burnside; two *s.* *Educ.:* Valleyfield Coll. Served with Royal Flying Corps, 1915-18, and Royal Canadian Air Force, 1939-45. President Canadian Hunter Saddle and Light Horse Improvement Soc.; Member Chambre de Commerce; Governor Queen Elizabeth Hospital; Member Newcomen Society, of England. Roman Catholic. *Recreations:* riding, hunting, golf. *Address:* 3940 Cote des Neiges, Montreal, Que., (office) 700 Windsor St., Montreal. *Clubs:* Mount Royal, Canadian, Montreal Hunt, Lake of Two Mountains Hunt (M.F.H.), Laval-sur-le-Lac (Past Pres.), Montreal Amateur Athletic Assoc. (Life Mem.), Forest and Stream (Dir.), Royal Automobile, St. James's, etc. (Montreal). [*Died* 23 *Feb.* 1962.

RAYNES, Harold Ernest; Director of Legal and General Assurance Society, 1951-61; *b.* 1 January 1882; *s.* of late Sidney H. Raynes, M.R.C.S., L.R.C.P.; *m.* 1918, Helen Ida Morrish; two *s.* (and one *s.* decd.). *Educ.:* William Ellis Endowed School, Hampstead. Entered City, 1898, starting with marine insurance with Lloyd's Brokers; actuarial work with Legal and General Assurance Soc., 1901, as Secretary and Actuary; Chairman of Life Offices Assoc., 1940-42; Fellow Inst. of Actuaries, 1909 (past Hon. Sec. and Vice-Pres.); Corresp. member Institut des Actuaires Français and Association des Actuaires Suisses; Fellow Chartered Insurance Inst., 1926 (Hon. Treas., 1938-49). A Governor: London School of Economics, 1937-63; Polytechnic, Regent Street, 1942-58. Member: Carr-Saunders Cttee. on Commercial Educ., 1949; Nat. Advisory Council on Educ. for Industry and Commerce, 1948-1958; Secondary School Certificate Council, 1949-52. *Publications:* Insurance Companies Investments, 1930; A History of British Insurance, 1948; Principles of British Insurance, 1953; Social Security in Britain, A History, 1957; Insurance, 1959; various actuarial and insurance articles. *Recreation:* gardening. *Address:* Glenroy, Seymour Road, Finchley, N.3. *T.:* Finchley 1203. *Club:* Reform. [*Died* 3 *April* 1964.

RAYNES, William Robert; Alderman, Derby, since 1923; *b.* Chasetown, Staffs, 26 Jan. 1871; *m.* 1893, Alice E. Foster, Heanor; no *c.* *Educ.:* Elementary Schools. Son of working blacksmith; started work at 13; apprenticed to decorating trade at 14; became active in Trade Union circles at 22; entered Derby Town Council, 1911; Mayor of Borough, 1921-1922; Parliamentary candidate, 1922; M.P. (Lab.) Derby, 1923-24 and 1929-31; Hon. Freedom of the Borough of Derby, 1935; J.P. *Address:* The Lois Ellis Home, Greenwich Drive North, Kingsway, Derby. [*Died* 30 *Jan.* 1966.

RAYNSFORD, Lt.-Col. Richard Montague, D.S.O. 1919; D.L. Northamptonshire; J.P.; *b.* 19 May 1877; *s.* of Lieut.-Col. F. M. Raynsford, Indian Army; *m.* Daphne Mildred, Alderman, Northants. C.C. 1954, *y. d.* of Major-Gen. W. W. Pemberton, Indian Staff Corps; one *s.* (and one killed war of 1939-45) one *d.* *Educ.:* Highgate School; R.M.C., Camberley. 2nd Lieutenant, Leinster Regiment, 1897; served South African War (Queen's medal 3 clasps, King's medal 2 clasps); European War, 1914-18, in Salonika and France; commanded 5th Connaught Rangers and 10th Devons, and served on the staff at G.H.Q., France, as Deputy Assistant Director-General of Transportation (despatches, D.S.O.); Lt.-Col. 1925; commanding 1st Northamptonshire Regiment, 1925-26; retired pay, 1926; Secretary of theNorthamptonshire and Huntingdonshire T.A. Assoc., 1926-42; High Sheriff Northamptonshire, 1945-46. Editor, The Fighting Forces, 1926-50. *Address:* Milton Malzor Manor, Northampton. *T.:* Bilsworth 251. *Club:* United Service. [*Died* 5 *March* 1965.

READ, Ernest, C.B.E. 1956; F.R.A.M. 1923 (A.R.A.M. 1906); F.R.C.O. 1907 (A.R.C.O. 1889); F.R.C.M., 1962; Professor and Examiner at the Royal Academy of Music since 1914; Founder and Conductor of London Junior and Senior Orchestras (1926 and 1931) and of Ernest Read Children's Concerts (1944); *b.* 22 Feb. 1879; *s.* of late Frederick Read; *m.* 1st, 1906, Dorothea Johanna, *d.* of Rev. Canon G. Jackson; one *s.* (one *d.* decd.); 2nd, 1923, Helen Frieda, *d.* of W. F. Webster, Barrister-at-Law; two *d.* *Educ.:* Royal Academy of Music (Robert Newman Prize); privately. Studied with the late Tobias Matthay, Sir Walter Alcock and Emile Jaques-Dalcroze. Formerly: Organist Shere Parish Church and St. Mary's Church, Guildford; Founder and Conductor of Guildford Orchestral and Choral Society; Organist and Choirmaster at St. Peter's, Cranley Gdns., S.W.7, 1905-23. Studentship at R.A.M. included Sub-Professorships; Mem. Cttee. of Management, R.A.M. for 20 years. Served during 1914-18 War. Apptd. Examr. to Associated Board of Royal Schools of Music (Mem. Bd. for 30 years). Appointed Conductor, Free Church Choral Union, 1928. Gave Music Broadcasts to Schools, 1935 and 1936; Orchestral Summer Course at Queenswood School, 1949-; Director of Music, Queenswood School, 1920-. Pres. Music Teachers' Assoc., 1944-; Pres. London Schools Symphony Orchestra, 1955-; Chm. Dalcroze Society Inc., 1942-. Examiner to: London University, National Froebel Foundation, Royal Military School of Music, etc. *Publications:* Aural Training Based on Musical Appreciation, 3 vols., 1912; Studies in Sight Singing, 1916; Melody Making, 1916; various school songs and piano pieces, etc.; arrangements for school choirs and Women's Institutes of Messiah (Handel), St. Matthew's Passion and Christmas Oratorio (Bach), Creation (Haydn), etc. *Address:* 151 King Henry's Road, Hampstead, N.W.3. [*Died* 9 *Oct.* 1965.

READ, Rt. Rev. Henry Cecil; Chaplain, St. Paul's, Poona, since 1961; *b.* 25 Dec. 1890; unmarried. *Educ.:* Wellington College; Caius College, Cambridge. 1st Cl. Classical Tripos; M.A. 1918; Deacon, 1914; Priest, 1915; C.M.S. Missionary at Poona, 1922-23; Nasik, 1924-27; Aurangabad, 1927-29; Missionary at Manmad, 1929; Principal St. Andrew Divinity School, 1930-1939; Archdeacon of Aurangabad, 1940-44. Bishop of Nasik, 1944-57; Res. Canon, Rochester, 1957-61. *Address:* 1A Staveley Rd., Poona, India. [*Died* 29 *May* 1963.

READ, Sir Herbert, Kt. *cr.* 1953; D.S.O. 1918; M.C.; Litt.D. (Hon. Leeds); M.A. (Edin.); a Trustee of the Tate Gallery since 1965; *b.* 4 December 1893; *e. s.* of late Herbert Read of Muscoates Grange, Kirbymoorside, Yorks; *m.* 1st, Evelyn Roff; 2nd, Margaret Ludwig; four *s.* one *d.* *Educ.:* Crossley's School, Halifax; University of Leeds. Commissioned Jan 1915 to the Yorkshire Regt. (The Green Howards); Captain, 1917; fought in France and Belgium, 1915-18 (M.C., D.S.O., despatches); Assistant Principal, H.M. Treasury, 1919-22; Assistant Keeper, Victoria and Albert Museum, 1922-31; Watson Gordon Professor of Fine Art in the University of Edinburgh, 1931-33; Sydney Jones Lecturer in Art, University of Liverpool, 1935-1936; Editor, the Burlington Magazine, 1933-39; Leon Fellow, University of London, 1940-42; Charles Eliot Norton Professor of Poetry, Harvard Univ., 1953-1954; A. W. Mellon Lecturer in Fine Arts, Washington, 1954; Senior Fellow, Royal College of Art, 1962; Prof. honorario, Univ. of Córdoba, Argentine, 1962; hon. Doctor of Fine Arts, University of Buffalo, New York, 1962; Hon. Litt.D. University of Boston, Mass., 1965; University of York, 1966; Hon. Fellow, Society of Industrial Artists; President: Soc. for Education through Art; Institute of Contemporary Arts; Yorkshire Philosophical Society; British Society of Aesthetics; Foreign Corr. Mem. Académie Flamande des Beaux Arts, 1953; Foreign Mem. Académie Royale des Beaux Arts, Stockholm, 1960; Fell., Center for Advanced Studies, Wesleyan Univ., Connecticut, 1964-65; Hon. Member: National Institute, 1966; American Acad. of Arts and Letters, 1966. Erasmus Prize, 1966 (with René Huyghe). *Publications:* Naked Warriors, 1919; Eclogues, 1919; Mutations of the Phœnix, 1923; In Retreat, 1925; Reason and Romanticism; English Prose Style, 1928; Phases of English Poetry, 1928; The Sense of Glory, 1929; Wordsworth (Clark Lectures), 1930; The Meaning of Art, 1931; Form in Modern Poetry, 1932; The Innocent Eye, 1933; Art Now, 1933; The End of a War, 1933; Art and Industry, 1934; Poems, 1914-34; The Green Child; In Defence of Shelley, 1935; Art and Society, 1936; Poetry and Anarchism; Collected Essays, 1938; The Knapsack, 1939; Annals of Innocence and Experience; Thirty-five Poems, 1940; The Politics of the Unpolitical, Education through Art, 1943; A World within a War (poems), 1944; A Coat of Many Colours (essays), 1945; Collected Poems, 1946; The Grass Roots of Art, 1947; Education for Peace, 1949; The Philosophy of Modern Art, 1952; The True Voice of Feeling, 1953; Icon and Idea, 1955; Moon's Farm (poems), 1955; The Art of Sculpture, 1956; The Tenth Muse, 1957; A Concise History of Modern Painting, 1959; The Forms of Things Unknown, 1960; A Letter to a Young Painter, 1962; To Hell with Culture, 1963; The Contrary Experience, 1963; Selected Writings, 1963; A Concise History of Modern Sculpture, 1964; The Origins of Form in Art; Henry Moore: A Study of his Life and Work, 1965; Collected Poems, 1966; Poetry and Experience, 1967; Art and Alienation, 1967. *Posthumous Publications:* Arp, 1968; The Cult of Sincerity, 1969; The Redemption of the Robot, 1970. *Address:* Stonegrave House, Stonegrave, York. *Club:* Reform. [*Died* 12 *June* 1968.

READ, Herbert Harold, F.R.S. 1939; F.R.S.E., F.G.S., D.Sc., A.R.C.S.; *b.* Whitstable, Kent, 17 Dec. 1889; 2nd *s.* of late Herbert Read; *m.* Edith, *d.* of late F. T. Browning; one *d.* *Educ.:* Simon Langton School, Canterbury; Royal College of Science, London. Joined H.M. Geological Survey, 1914; service with Royal Fusiliers in Egypt, Gallipoli, and France, 1914-17; Geological Survey in Scotland, 1917-31; George Herdman Professor of Geology, University of Liverpool, 1931-38; Professor of Geology in the University of London, Imperial College of Science and Technology, 1939-55; Senior Research Fellow, Imperial College, 1955-64; Professor Emeritus, 1955. Pres., Section C, Brit. Assoc., Dundee, 1939; President, Geologists Association, 1942-44; Pres. Geological Society of London, 1947-49 (Bigsby Medallist, 1935; Wollaston Medallist, 1952); Pres. International Geological Congress, 18th Session, London, 1948. Dean, Royal School of Mines, Imperial College, 1943-45. Pro-Rector, Imperial College, 1952-1955. Membre Correspondant, Société Géologique de Belgique, 1946; (André Dumont Medal, 1950); Foreign Mem., Geol. Soc. of Portugal, 1947; Corr. Geol. Soc. of America, 1948 (Penrose Medal, 1967); Correspondant étranger de la Société Géologique de France, 1948 (Associé étranger, 1963); Walker-Ames Prof., Univ. of Washington, Seattle, Fall Term, 1949; Member Norwegian Academy of Science and Letters, 1950. Nuffield Visiting Lectr. South Africa, 1951; Alexander du Toit Memorial Lecturer, Johannesburg, 1951; Correspondant de l'Académie des Sciences de l'Institut de France, 1954; Associate of Royal Academy, Belgium, 1954 (Prix Paul Fourmarier, 1960); Hon. M.R.I.A., 1958. Hon. D.Sc. (Columbia Univ.), 1954; Hon. Sc.D. (Dublin), 1956. Fellow of Imperial College of Science and Technology, 1957; Steinmann Medal, Geologische Vereinigung, 1960; Royal Medal, Royal Society, 1963. Hon. Member, Geological Society, India, 1962. *Publications:* The Granite Controversy, 1957; Memoirs and Papers dealing with the Geology and Petrology of the Scottish Highlands and Donegal. *Recreation:* none. *Address:* c/o Imperial College of Science and Technology, South Kensington, S.W.7. [*Died* 29 *March* 1970.

READ, Professor John, F.R.S. 1935; M.A., Sc.D. (Cantab.); B.Sc. (Lond.); Ph.D. (Zürich); Professor of Chemistry and Director of the Chemistry Research Laboratory in the United College of St. Salvator and St. Leonard, University of St. Andrews, since 1923; *b.* 17 Feb 1884; *s.* of late John Read, yeoman, formerly of Hinton St. George, Som.; *m.* 1916, Ida, *e. d.* of Arthur Suddards, Leeds; one *s.* (and one *s.* decd.). *Educ.:* Sexey's School, Bruton; Finsbury Technical College; University of Zürich; Technological School, Manchester; Emmanuel College, Cambridge. Chemist, Thames Conservancy Laboratory, 1904-05; lecturer and demonstrator in chemistry, Cambridge University, 1908-16; Professor of Organic Chemistry, Pure and Applied, Univ. of Sydney, 1916-23; Pres. of the Chemistry Section of the British Association, 1948; Associate Editor of Chymia, 1949; Member, Mixed Commission, Anglo-Italian Cultural Convention, 1953. Dexter Award, Amer. Chem. Soc., 1959. *Publications:* Numerous original memoirs dealing with essential oils, petroleum, marine fibre and other natural products, the terpene series, the preparation of halogenohydrins, methods of optical resolution, simple asymmetric substances, and generally with organic chemistry, stereochemistry, alchemy and historical chemistry, published in Transactions of the Chemical Society, and other scientific and historical journals; Text-book of Organic Chemistry, 1926, rewritten (with F. D. Gunstone), 1958; Introduction to Organic Chemistry, 1931; Prelude to Chemistry (historical), 1936, 1939, 1961; Explosives, 1942, Spanish edition, 1947; The Alchemist in Life, Literature and Art, 1947; Humour and Humanism in Chemistry (historical), 1947, Spanish edition, 1953; A Direct Entry to Organic Chemistry, 1948 (awarded Premio Europeo Cortina Prize, 1949), 1953, 1961. German edn. 1950, Italian edn. 1952, Amer. edn. 1960; What is Science? (Chemistry), 1955; Through Alchemy to Chemistry, 1957, 1961, French edn. 1959, Spanish and Italian edns. 1960, Amer. edn. 1963; articles on organic chemistry in Encyclopædia Britannica, 1929, and on organic chemistry and alchemy in Chambers's Encyclopædia, 1950. Various plays (West-country dialect), prose sketches, etc., including Farmer's Joy, 1949. *Recreations:* walking, folk-study, travel. *Address:* The University, St. Andrews, Scotland. *T.:* (Laboratory) St. Andrews 216. (Residence) St. Andrews, 379. [*Died* 21 *Jan.* 1963.

READ, Col. Richard Valentine, C.V.O. 1939; C.B.E. 1944; D.S.O. 1918; M.C. 1916; *b.* Brentwood, Essex, 14 Feb. 1892; 3rd *s.* of late John Jervis Read, High House, Brentwood, Essex and Roundwood, Virginia Water, Surrey; *m.* 1953, Joyce, *d.* of late James Ince, Toronto, Canada, and *widow* of Dr. Charles B. Crawford, M.D., Washington, D.C. *Educ.:* Malvern Coll.; R.M.C., Sandhurst. Joined 2nd Bn. The Essex Regiment, 1911; served with 2nd Bn., B.E.F., during 1914 and 1915; wounded Aisne, 1914, and Ypres, 1915; Adjutant, 12th (Service) Battalion The Essex Regiment, 1915; specially employed War Office, 1916; Brigade-Major, 10th Canadian Infantry Brigade, B.E.F., 1917; Brigade-Major, 92nd Infantry Brigade, and General Staff 1st Corps, B.E.F., Dec. 1917-March 1918; Brigade-Major 180th Infantry Brigade, E.E.F., March-Oct. 1918; G.S.O. 2 75th Division, E.E.F., Oct. 1918-April 1920 (D.S.O., M.C., despatches twice); Adjutant, 4th Battalion The Essex Regiment (Territorial Army), 1921-25; with 2nd Battalion Essex Regiment, Ambala, Cawnpore, and the Khyber, India, 1925-29; D.A.A.G. Northern Command, India, 1929-33; Commanded Depot, the Essex Regiment, 1933-35; Assistant Military Secretary (Personal) to Commander-in-Chief in India, 1936; commanded 1st Bn. The Essex Regiment, in Palestine and Egypt, 1936-38; Military Attaché, British Embassy, Washington, 1938-41; Asst. Military Sec. Northern Command, 1941-45; retired, 1945. Secretary, Essex Territorial and Auxiliary Forces Association, 1945-52. Lieutenant, 1913; Captain, 1915; temp. Major, 1918-20; Major, 1930; Lieut.-Col., 1936; Col., 1938. D.L. Essex, 1947-54. *Address:* 4 Lowell Place, Fredonia, New York State, U.S.A. *Clubs:* Army and Navy, Royal Automobile. [*Died* 15 *Jan.* 1964.

REAKES, George Leonard; Journalist, Director Wallasey News; *b.* 31 July 1889; 4th *s.* of Henry James Reakes, Bath, Somerset. *Educ.:* Bath City Secondary School. Served European War, Artists' Rifles, O.T.C., 1916-19. Member Wallasey County Borough Town Council, 1922-50; Mayor Coronation Year, 1936-37; J.P., 1939; Chm. of Juvenile Court of Wallasey; a Wallasey Rotarian and Past Pres. of the Club; served Postal Censorship, 1939-42; M.P. (Ind.) Wallasey, 1942-45. *Publications:* Booklets: Technical Education (Preface by Sir Henry Bellingham, Bt., Commissioner Nat. Educ., Ireland), 1913; Modern Education (foreword by Rt. Hon. Bonar Law, M.P.), 1919; The Juvenile Offender (foreword by the Hon. Justice Lynskey), 1953; Man of the Mersey (foreword by Lord Brabazon of Tara), 1956. *Address:* 43 St. Mary's St., Wallasey, Cheshire. *Clubs:* Farmers': Whitehall, Warren (Wallasey). [*Died* 15 *April* 1961.

REAY, 13th Baron (*cr.* 1628), of Reay, County Caithness, Scotland; **Aeneas Alexander Mackay,** Baronet of Nova Scotia, 1627; Chief of Clan Mackay; a Representative Peer of Scotland, 1955-59; *b.* 1905; *s.* of 12th Baron and Baroness Maria Johanna Bertha Christina Van Dedem; *S.* father, 1921; *m.* 1936, Charlotte Mary, *o. d.* of late William Younger; one *s.* two *d.* *Heir:* *s.* Hugh William Mackay, Master of Reay. *Address:* Ophemert, Holland. *T.:* 281; Langlee House, Galashiels, Scotland. *T.:* Galashiels 2333. [*Died* 10 *March* 1963.

REBBECK, Sir Frederick (Ernest), K.B.E., *cr.* 1953; Kt., *cr.* 1941; D.Sc.; D.L.; J.P.; Whitworth Exhibitioner; *m.* 1907, Amelia Letitia (*d.* 1955), *d.* of Robert Glover; two *s.* three *d.*; retired as Chairman and Managing Director of Harland and Wolff, Ltd., shipbuilders and marine engineers, of Belfast, Glasgow, London, Liverpool and Southampton (1930-62), also as Director of Colvilles Ltd., Ocean Transport Co. Ltd., and Watertight Door Co. Ltd., 1962, and as Mem. Gen. Cttee. of Lloyd's Register of Shipping and Mem. Shipbuilding Conf. Exec. Bd., 1962; Director: Heaton Tabb & Co. Ltd., of London and Liverpool; Short Brothers & Harland Ltd.; Past-Pres. Inst. of Marine Engineers; Past-Pres. Shipbuilding Employers' Federation. Formerly: Belfast Harbour Commissioner, and Vice-Pres. R.I.N.A. Member: Institution of Engineers and Shipbuilders in Scotland; Institution of Mechanical Engineers; North-East Coast Institution of Engineers and Shipbuilders; Institute of Metals; Iron and Steel Institute; Institute of Fuel; Liverpool Engineering Society; Society of Naval Architects and Marine Engineers, New York. Liveryman of the Worshipful Company of Shipwrights. *Address:* Sandown House, Knock, Belfast 5. *T.:* Belfast 654482. [*Died* 27 *June* 1964.

RÉBORA, Piero, M.A.; Emeritus Professor of English at University of Milan (Professor, 1957-59); *b.* Milan, 21 June 1889; *m.* 1917; three *s.* *Educ.:* Milan; Univ. of Turin. Lectr. in Italian at Liverpool University, 1914-23; Captain in European War; Professor of Italian Studies at the University of Manchester, 1923-32; Director of Studies, British Institute, Florence, 1932-40; Prof. of English at Univ. of Urbino, 1937-56. *Publications:* Jonathan Swift, 1922; La Scuola in Inghilterra, 1924; L'Italia nel dramma inglese, 1925; Francesco Ferrucci, 1926; Civiltà italiana e civiltà inglese, 1936; I Sonetti di Shakespeare, 1941; Tragici elisabettiani, 1946; Shakespeare, his message, 1946; G. B. Shaw, 1948; La letteratura inglese del novecento, 1950, etc. Translations from Shakespeare, Lamb, Meredith, etc. *Recreation:* reading. *Address:* c/o Dept. of English, University of Milan, Italy. [*Died* 1963.

REDDING, Rt. Rev. Donald Llewellyn, M.B.E. 1944; *b.* 11 July 1898; *s.* of Joseph James and Sarah Elizabeth Redding; unmarried. *Educ.:* City of London School; Friends' School, Saffron Walden; St. Barnabas Theological College, North Adelaide. Curate of Christ Church, Mt. Gambier, 1921; Priest in charge: St. Peter's, Robe, 1925, Waikerie and Loxton, 1926; Curate of St. Paul's, Point Adelaide, 1927; Priest in charge, Henley Beach, 1928; Rector of: St. John's, Maitland, 1929, St. Mary's, Burra, 1933, St. Barnabas, Clare, 1939; Chaplain A.I.F., 1939; Rector and Archdeacon, Mt. Gambier, 1946; Hon. Canon of Adelaide, 1949; Vicar of St. Andrew's, Brighton, Victoria, 1949; Bishop of Bunbury, 1951-57; Vicar of St. Mary's, South Camberwell, Diocese of Melbourne, 1957-60; Coadjutor Bishop of Melbourne, 1960-63, retired. *Address:* 109 Glengyle Terrace, Plympton, South Australia. [*Died* 15 *Oct.* 1969.

REDESDALE, 3rd Baron, *cr.* 1902; **Bertram Thomas Carlyle Ogilvy Freeman-Mitford,** D.S.O. 1919; J.P.; Capt., Royal Navy; 3rd *s.* of 1st Baron Redesdale and Lady Clementine Gertrude Helen Ogilvy (*d.* 1932), *d.* of 10th Earl of Airlie; *S.* brother, 1958; *m.* 1925, Mary Margaret Dorothy Cordes, *o. d.* of late Thomas Cordes, of Silwood Park, Sunninghill. Entered Navy, 1894; Commander, 1913; Captain, 1918; served European War (D.S.O., Croix de Guerre, Military Medal for Valour, Italy); retired, 1922; High Sheriff of Oxfordshire, 1935; D.L. Oxfordshire, 1940; Lt.-Col. Home Guard, 1941. Royal Humane Society Bronze Medal, 1916. *Heir: b.* Capt. Hon. John Power Bertram Ogilvy Freeman-Mitford. *Address:* Westwell, Burford, Oxfordshire. *T.:* Burford 2251. *Clubs:* Carlton; (Hon.) Royal Yacht Squadron. [*Died* 24 *Dec.* 1962.

REDESDALE, 4th Baron, *cr.* 1902; **John Power Bertram Ogilvy Freeman-Mitford;** *b.* 31 Jan. 1885; 4th *s.* of 1st Baron Redesdale, G.C.V.O., K.C.B. (*d.* 1916) and Lady Clementine Gertrude Helen Ogilvy (*d.* 1932), *d.* of 10th (*de facto* 7th) Earl of Airlie, K.T.; *S.* brother, 1962. Joined Warwickshire Yeomanry; 1st Life Guards (Special Reserve); served European War, France, 1914-19, also served 1941-45, Capt. Gen. List. *Heir: n.* Clement Napier Bertram Freeman-Mitford [*b.* 28 Oct. 1932; *m.* 1958, Sarah Georgina Todd; three *d.*]. *Address:* Mitford Cottage, Westwell, Burford, Oxfordshire. *T.:* Burford 3222. *Clubs:* Carlton, Pratt's, Buck's. [*Died* 31 *Dec.* 1963.

REDFORD, Professor Arthur; Professor of Economic History, University of Manchester, since 1945; *b.* 25 May 1896; *m.* 1925, Lucy Ashton; two *s.* *Educ.:* University of Manchester. Served European War: Army, 1915-19, Lieutenant 4th Manchester Regiment and Special List, attached General Staff (despatches). 1st cl. hons. in history, 1915 (Bradford Schol., Graduate Schol.), 1st cl. hons. in economics, 1920 (Shuttleworth Economic Schol., Langton Fell.); M.A. (*in absentia*), 1916; Ph.D., 1922. Lecturer in Economics, Univ. of Liverpool, 1922-25; Cassel Lecturer in Commerce, Univ. of London (London Sch. of Economics), 1925-26; Reader in Economic History, Univ. of Manchester, 1926-45. *Publications:* Labour Migration in England, 1926; Economic History of England, 1760-1860, 1931, rev. edn. 1960; Manchester Merchants and Foreign Trade, Vol. I, 1794-1858, 1934. Vol. II, 1850-1939, 1956; The History of Local Government in Manchester (3 vols.), 1939-40. Articles and reviews in various learned jls. *Address:* 57 Manor Drive, Manchester 21. *T.:* Didsbury 1623. [*Died* 25 *July* 1961.

REDHEAD, Edward Charles; M.P. (Lab.) Walthamstow West since March 1956; Minister of State: Dept. of Educn. and Science, 1965-67 (Board of Trade, 1964-1965); J.P.; *b.* 8 April 1902; *s.* of Robert Charles and Elizabeth Redhead; *m.* 1928, Gladys Mary Pannell; one *d.* *Educ.:* Walthamstow Higher Elementary School; privately. Entered Civil Service (Post Office) as Boy Clerk, 1917; Asst. Clerk (later Clerical Officer), Customs and Excise, 1919. Exec. Officer, 1932, and Higher Exec. Officer, 1940. Various hon. offices in Civil Service Clerical Assoc. and Soc. of Civil Servants until Gen. Secretary of latter, 1948-56. Opposition Whip (Eastern), Oct. 1959-64. Walthamstow Borough Council, 1929-65; Alderman 1945-1965; Mayor, 1949-50 and 1961-62. J.P. Essex, 1946. *Address:* 2 Mapperley Drive, Oak Hill, Woodford Green, Essex. *T.:* Larkswood 1671. [*Died* 15 *April* 1967.

REDLICH, Professor Hans Ferdinand; M.A. (Manchester), 1966; Professor of Music, University of Manchester, since Oct. 1962; *b.* 11 Feb. 1903; *s.* of late Professor Joseph Redlich and of Alix Leo (*née* Simon); *m.* 1st, 1930, Elise (*née* Gerlach) (*d.* 1959); 2nd, 1961, Erika (*née* Burger). *Educ.:* Schotten-gymnasium, Vienna; Universities of Vienna, Munich, Frankfurt-am-Main. Asst. Conductor, Opera House, Berlin-Charlottenburg, 1924-25; Conductor, Municipal Theatre, Mainz, 1925-29; Dr.Phil., Univ. Frankfurt-am-Main, 1931. Lectr. for Extra-Mural Depts. (Music), Univs. of Cambridge and Birmingham, 1942-55; Lectr. in Hist. of Music. Univ. of Edinburgh, 1955-62. Vice-Pres., Internat. Alban Berg Soc., N.Y., 1967. Hon. Mus.D. Edinburgh, 1967. *Publications:* Claudio Monteverdi Das Madrigalwerk, 1932 (Berlin); Claudio Monteverdi: Life and Works, 1952 (London); Bruckner and Mahler, 1955 (London), Revised Edn., 1963 (London); Alban Berg — The Man and His Music, 1957 (Vienna and London); critical editions of Handel's Concerti Grossi, op. 6, Water Music and Fireworks Music, 1962-66; New Oxford History of Music, Vol. IV (The Age of Humanism), 1968 (Ch. V/c and Ch. X). See article in Grove's Dictionary of Music and Musicians, 5th edn., 1954 and Supplement Vol., 1960 (original compositions, edns. of old music and musicological papers). *Address:* 1 Morville Road, Manchester 21. *T.:* 061-881 6496. [*Died* 27 *Nov.* 1968.

REDMAN, Brigadier Arthur Stanley, C.B. 1919; late R.E.; *b.* 25 Sept. 1879; *e. s.* of late T. E. Redman, J.P., The Knoll, Shawford, Hants; *m.* 1909, Vera Mary, (*d.* 1962), *y. d.* of late James Kay, of Larkhill, Timperley, Cheshire; one *s.* one *d.* *Educ.:* Repton; Royal Indian Engineering College, Coopers Hill. 2nd Lieut. R.E. 1901; Lieut. 1904; Capt. 1912; Maj. 191; Lt.-Col. (temp.), 1916; Col. (temp.), 1918-20; Subs. Col. 1922; Brig. 1941; employed on survey of Orange River Colony, 1905-8; Assistant Instructor S.M.E., 1909-12; G.S.O. 3, War Office, 1913-14; Movements Directorate, War Office, 1914-20; Deputy Director of Railways, War Office, 1918-20; Traffic Supt. Somerset and Dorset Railway, 1920-21; Asst. Director of Movements, War Office, 1921-24; Asst. Director of Transportation, War Office, 1924-25; Asst. Adj.-Gen., War Office, 1926-30; retired pay, 1931; Chairman of West Midland Traffic Commissioners, 1931-37, and Licensing Authority, West Midland Traffic Area, 1934-37; Deputy Director, Ministry of Supply, 1939-41; served European War, 1914-18 (Bt.-Major, despatches, Bt. Lieut.-Col., C.B.); re-employed as Colonel, R.A.R.O., Sept. 1939; retired, 1941, with hon. rank Brigadier. *Address:* c/o Lloyds Bank Ltd., Cox's & King's Branch, 6 Pall Mall, S.W.1. [*Died* 9 *March* 1963.

REDMAYNE-JONES, Sir Edward, Kt. 1948; *b.* 11 Oct. 1877; *e. c.* of William and Alexandrina Jones, Wavertree; *m.* 1909, Margaret (*d.* 1957), 2nd *d.* of William Pierpoint, J.P., Grappenhall, Cheshire; one *d.* *Educ.:* Liverpool Institute. Whole business life spent in International Grain Trade; Chm. British Federation of Commodity Assocs. Ltd., 1951-52; Member Exec. Cttee.

Internat. Chamber of Commerce and other similar organisations. Chairman National Federation of Corn Trade Associations, 1941-1947; Pres. Liverpool Corn Trade Association 1934-35; Chairman Liverpool Grain Contract Insurance Co., 1934-35. *Recreations:* golf, curling. *Address:* Sandringham Road, Birkdale, Lancs. *T.:* Southport 66472. *Clubs:* National Liberal; Exchange (Liverpool). [*Died* 8 *Sept.* 1963.

REDPATH, Anne, O.B.E. 1955; A.R.A. 1960; R.S.A. 1952; R.B.A. 1946; R.O.I. 1948; R.W.A. 1957; A.R.W.S. 1962; *b.* 29 March 1895; *d.* of Thomas Brown Redpath and Agnes Milne, Galashiels, Selkirkshire; *m.* 1920, James Beattie Michie (*d.* 1958); three *s.* *Educ.:* Hawick High Sch.; Edinburgh Coll. of Art. With diploma in drawing and painting in 1918 gained Post-Graduate Scholarship; Travelling Scholarship, 1919; studied in Paris, Brussels and Florence; lived in France for 15 years; returned to Scotland in 1934. Member Society of Scottish Artists and Glasgow Institute; Member Manchester Academy. Pictures in permanent collections: Tate Gallery; L.C.C.; Coventry; Wellington National Gallery (New Zealand); Sydney, Australia, Glasgow, Edinburgh, Aberdeen, Hull, Vancouver B.C., Manchester, Dundee, Queensland, Adelaide, R.W.A. Coll., Bristol, Perth; Laing collection, Newcastle, Preston Art Gallery, Edinburgh Gall. Contemporary Art. Exhibits regularly: Royal Academy; Royal Scottish Academy, Glasgow Institute, Society of Scottish Artists. Hon. LL.D. (Edin.), 1955. F.A.M.S., 1957. *Address:* 7 London St., Edinburgh. *T.:* Waverley 5150. [*Died* 7 *Jan.* 1965.

REDWOOD, Rev. Canon Frederick Arthur, M.A.; Canon Residentiary and Guestmaster of Liverpool Cathedral, 1960-64, retired; *b.* 18 April 1891; *s.* of late William and Mary Redwood; *m.* 1922, Constance Mary, *d.* of Alderman Arthur Wakerley, J.P., Leicester and Suffolk; two *s.* *Educ.:* Bishop Wordsworth School, Salisbury; Queens' Coll., Cambridge (Schol. and Stewart of Rannoch Hebrew Scholar). Deacon, 1914; priest, C.F., 1915; Curate of St. James the Less, 1914-15; Domestic Chaplain to Bishop of Chelmsford, 1919-23; Vicar: Holy Trinity, Bordesley, 1924-26; St. James Hill, 1926-32; Vicar and Rural Dean of Ormskirk, 1932-60. Exam. Chaplain to Bishop of Birmingham, 1925-32; Chaplain: Ormskirk Poor Law Instn., 1932-42; Ormskirk County Hosp., 1949-60. *Address:* Home Green, Wick's Lane, Formby, Lancs. *T.:* 2318. [*Died* 15 *July* 1964.

REDWOOD, (William Arthur) Hugh, O.B.E. 1955; Journalist, Author and Evangelist; *b.* Bristol, 15 Feb. 1883; *s.* of William Redwood and Mary Rawlins; *m.* 1st, 1908, Florence Edith Board (*d.* 1939); one *d.*; 2nd, Elsie Parslow. *Educ.:* Bristol Cathedral School. Reporter Western Daily Press, Bristol, 1898-1905; editorial staff Central News Agency, London, 1905-18; successively Foreign Editor, Night Editor, Deputy Editor. Religious Editor, Daily News and News Chronicle, 1919-53; F.J.I. Became actively associated in 1928 with the Slum Work of the Salvation Army and described it (1930) in God in the Slums, published in 15 languages and 32 English editions; engaged in evangelistic work since 1931. *Publications:* God in the Shadows, 1932; Kingdom Come, 1934; God in the Everyday, 1936; Practical Prayer, 1937; Brotherhood, 1939; Year's Journey, 1946; The Book of Lazarus, 1946; Bristol Fashion, 1948; The Forgiving Minute, 1950; Promise Box, 1952; Residue of Days, 1958; collected broadcast talks; and various others. *Recreations:* music, radio. *Address:* 5 Hillcrest Road, Orpington, Kent. *T.:* Orpington 23067. [*Died* 26 *Dec.* 1963.

REECE, B(razilla) Carroll; lawyer and banker; Chairman Republican National Committee for Tennessee; *b.* Butler, Tenn., 22 Dec. 1889; *s.* of John Isaac Reece and Sarah E. Maples; *m.* 1923, Louise Despard Goff; one *d.* *Educ.:* Carson and Newman Colleges; New York University; University of London. LL.D. Cumberland Univ., 1928. Asst. Sec., Instr. Economics, 1916-17, Dir. Sch. of Commerce, Accounts and Finance, and Instr. Economics, 1919-20, New York Univ. Enlisted in Army, 1917; served, 1917-19, with 26th Div. A.E.F.; Comd. 3rd Bn. 102nd Inf. (D.S.C., D.S.M., Purple Heart (U.S.); French Croix de Guerre with palm). Congressman, 1921-31 and 1933-47. Pres. Carter Co. Bank, First Nat. Bank of Jonesboro, Sullivan Co. Bank. Member various associations. Mason. Baptist. *Address:* Johnson City, Tenn., U.S.A. [*Died* 19 *March* 1961.

REECE, John H.; *see* Holroyd-Reece.

REED, Sir Arthur Conrad, Kt., *cr.* 1945; *s.* of William Henry Reed, J.P., Exeter; *m.* 1905, Emily Ward (*d.* 1947), *d.* of John Berry, Bondleigh, Devonshire. *Educ.:* Queen's Coll., Taunton. M.P. (U.) Exeter, 1931-45; Member Exeter City Council; Chm. of Dirs. of Reed Smith, Ltd., Wansborough Paper Co. Ltd., and F. Tremlett and Co. Ltd.; Pres. of Paper Makers Association of Great Britain and Northern Ireland, 1935-37; J.P. Exeter, 1937. Hon. LL.D. Exeter Univ., 1959. *Recreations:* golf and shooting. *Address:* Cumbre, Exeter. *T.A.:* Reed, Cumbre, Exeter. *T.:* Exeter 2329. *Clubs:* Carlton, Constitutional. [*Died* 15 *Jan.* 1961.

REED, Bellamy A. C.; *see* Cash-Reed.

REED, Rt. Rev. Ernest Samuel; Bishop of Ottawa since 1954. *Educ.:* Univ. of Manitoba. B.A. 1930; L.Th. St. John's Coll., Manitoba, 1931; M.A. McGill Univ., 1938; B.D. Bishop's Univ., Lennoxville, 1951. Deacon, Yukon for Rupertsland, 1931; Priest, Rupertsland, 1932; Curate of St. Luke, Winnipeg, 1931 (on leave, studying, 1932-34); Rector of Cowansville, 1934-37; Incumbent of Noranda, 1937-40; Curate of Trinity Memorial Church, Montreal, 1940-42; Rector of St. John Divine, Verdun, Montreal, 1942-46; Rector of Gaspé, 1946-52; Archdeacon of Gaspé, 1946-52; Rector of St. Matthew, City and Diocese of Quebec, 1952-1954; Archdeacon of Quebec, 1952-54. Chm. Exec. Cttee., Vanier Inst. of the Family; Vice-Pres., Canadian Council of Churches; Mem. Central and Exec. Cttees., World Council of Churches. Hon. degrees: D.D., St. John's Coll., Winnipeg, Manitoba, 1954; D.C.L., Bishop's Univ., Lennoxville, P.Q., 1955; D.D., Trinity Coll., Toronto, Ont., 1955. *Address:* Bishop's Court, Ottawa, Ontario, Canada. [*Died* 28 *Feb.* 1970.

REED, Hon. Sir Geoffrey Sandford; *see* Addenda: II.

REED, Sir (Herbert) Stanley, Kt., *cr.* 1916.; K.B.E., *cr.* 1919; LL.D. (Glasgow); *b.* Bristol, 28 Jan. 1872; *m.* 1901, Lilian (*d.* 1947), *d.* of John Humphrey; no *c.* Joined staff Times of India, 1897; Special Correspondent, Times of India and Daily Chronicle, through famine districts of India, 1900; tour of Prince and Princess of Wales in India, 1905-6; Amir's visit to India, 1907, and Persian Gulf, 1907; Editor, The Times of India, Bombay, 1907-23; Joint Honorary Secretary Bombay Presidency King Edward Memorial; represented Western India, Imperial Press Conferences, 1909 and 1930; Vice-President Central Publicity Board, 1918; Conservative candidate, Stourbridge Division of Worcestershire, 1929; M.P. (U.) Aylesbury division of Bucks, 1938-50. *Publications:* From Delhi to Bombay; The Royal Tour in India; The King and Queen in India; India:

The New Phase; The India I Knew, 1897-1947; Founder of the Indian Year-Book. *Address:* 24 Whitehall Court, S.W.1. *Clubs:* Athenæum; Willingdon Sports (Bombay). [*Died* 17 *Jan.* 1969.

REED, Sir John S. B.; *see* Blake-Reed.

REED, Sir Stanley; *see* Reed, Sir H. S.

REES, E(dgar) Philip, C.M.G. 1947; M.C. 1917; retd.; *b.* 28 June 1896; *s.* of late Dr. Alfred Rees, J.P., and late Margaret Rees; *m.* 1921, Natalie Goddard; one *d.* *Educ.:* Cardiff Grammar School. Formerly director of companies. *Address:* 1535 Marlowe Ave., Montreal 28, Canada. *T.:* Hv. 6-3635. [*Died* 28 *Nov.* 1964.

REES, Sir (James) Frederick, Kt. 1945; Hon. LL.D. (Birmingham, Wales and Edinburgh); Hon. Fellow of Lincoln College, Oxford; *b.* Milford Haven, Pembrokeshire, 13 Dec. 1883; *m.* 1913, Dora Lucile, *e. d.* of late Dr. Gethin Davies, Principal of the North Wales Baptist Coll.; one *s.* *Educ.:* Univ. College, Cardiff; Lincoln College, Oxford (Open History Scholar); B.A. (Wales), 1904, with First Class Honours in History; First Class in the Oxford School of Modern History, 1908; Assistant Lecturer in History in University College, Bangor, 1908-12; Lecturer in Economic History in the Queen's University of Belfast, 1912-13; Lecturer (later Reader) in Economic History in the University of Edinburgh, 1913-25; Prof. of Commerce, Univ. of Birmingham, 1925-29; Principal of Univ. College of South Wales and Monmouthshire, Cardiff, 1929-49; Vice-Chancellor of the Univ. of Wales, 1935-37 and 1944-46; Warden of Guild of Graduates of University of Wales, 1950-53; Chm. of Advisory Council Welsh Reconstruction Problems, 1942-46; Member of Ceylon Commission on Constitutional Reform, 1944-45; Visiting Professor in Economics, Univ. of Ceylon, 1953-54; Member Local Govt. Boundary Commission, 1946-49; Mem. Nat. Reference Tribunal, under Coalmining Industry Conciliation Scheme, 1943-56; Mem. Cttee. of Inquiry into Working of Dock Labour Scheme, 1955-56; Chm. Cttee. on Night Baking, 1950-51; President, Cambrian Archæological Association, 1956-57. High Sheriff of Pembrokeshire, 1955; Head of Department of Economic History, University of Edinburgh, 1956-58. *Publications:* Social and Industrial History of England, 1815-1918; A Short Fiscal and Financial History of England, 1815-1918; A Survey of Economic Development; Studies in Welsh History; The Story of Milford (Milford Haven); The Problem of Wales and other Essays; contributions to Encyclopædia Britannica (14th edition), Encyclopædia of the Social Sciences, Dictionary of National Biography (1922-1930); Cambridge History of the British Empire, The Dictionary Of Welsh Biography, etc. *Address:* 11 Celyn Grove, Cyncoed, Cardiff. *T.:* Cardiff 755649. [*Died* 7 *Jan.* 1967.

REES, Lt.-Col. John Gordon, D.S.O. 1918; late 13th Hussars; 2nd *s.* of late William Thomas Rees and late Alice Rachel, *d.* of late William Powell; *b.* 1884; *m.* 1942, A. M. D. T., *d.* of Major F. T. James, Pendarren House, Merthyr Tydfil. *Educ.:* Rugby; R.M.C., Sandhurst. Late Captain 13th Hussars; late Lt.-Col. Welsh Horse and Royal Welch Fusiliers; High Sheriff Radnors, 1915; served European War (D.S.O. and 2 bars); also 1939-40, Lt.-Col. South Wales Borderers. D.L., J.P., of Breconshire. *Address:* Glan-Nant, Crickhowell, Breconshire. *T.:* Crickhowell 234. [*Died* 15 *Nov.* 1963.

REES, John Rawlings, C.B.E. 1946; M.A., M.D. (Camb.); F.R.C.P. (Lond.); D.P.H.; President, 1948-49. Director, 1949-62, World Federation for Mental Health (Hon. President 1962-); *b.* 25 June 1890; *s.* of late Rev. R. Montgomery Rees; *m.* 1921, Mary Isabel (*d.* 1954), M.B., Ch.B., *d.* of late C. R. Hemingway, C.B.E.; one *d.* *Educ.:* Bradford Gram. Sch.; King's Coll., Cambridge. The London Hospital (House Physician and House Surgeon, etc.); Consulting Psychiatrist to the Army, 1939-45 (Brigadier); Hon. Cons. Psychiatrist to the Army, 1945-55. Served European War, 1914-19, Temp. Capt. R.A.M.C. (1914 Star, Order of the Belgian Crown); Belgium, France, Mesopotamia and North Persia; formerly Neurological Specialist, Ministry of Pensions, Medical Supt. Bowden House; late Physician and Medical Director, the Tavistock Clinic; Pres. Internat. Cttee. for Mental Hygiene; Member B.M.A.; Fellow of Royal Society of Medicine (late Pres. Sect. of Psychiatry); Royal Medico Psychological Association (late Council) and of Société Medico-Psychologique of Paris; Hon. Member Am. Psychiatric Assoc.; Psychiatric Assocs. of India, Vienna, Peru, Germany, New Jersey and Mexico; Corresp. Member Swiss Psychiatric Soc., etc. Thomas Salmon Memorial Lecturer at Academy of Medicine, New York, 1944; William Withering Lectr., Birmingham Univ., 1945; Maudsley Lectr., 1956; Barton Pope Lectr., Adelaide, 1960. Lasker, Rubin and Adolf Meyer Awards (U.S.). Grand Officer, Order Hipolito Unanue (Peru), 1960; Commander, Order of Public Health (France), 1961. *Publications:* An Introduction to Psychological Medicine (with Gordon and Harris); The Health of the Mind (3rd edn. 1951); The Shaping of Psychiatry by War; Contribution to Recent Advances in the Study of the Psychoneuroses; Three Years of Military Psychiatry; The Case of Rudolf Hess (Ed.), 1947; Modern Practice in Psychological Medicine (Ed.), 1949; Reflections, 1967; numerous contributions to medical and sociological journals. *Address:* 116 Bickenhall Mansions, Baker St., W.1. *T.:* 01-935 8872. *Club:* Royal Automobile. [*Died* 11 *April* 1969.

REES, Sir Richard (Lodowick Edward Montagu), 2nd Bt., *cr.* 1919; Author; *b.* 4 April 1900; *s.* of 1st Bt. and Hon. Mary, *sister* of 14th Lord Dormer; *S.* father, 1922. *Educ.:* Eton; Trinity College, Cambridge. Hon. Attaché, Berlin Embassy, 1922; in Cambridge University Press, 1923; Hon. Treasurer and Lecturer, London District, W.E.A., 1925-27; Editor of The Adelphi, 1930-36; served in R.N.V.R., 1940-45; (French Croix de Guerre, 1944); has exhibited paintings at R.A., R.S.A., London Group, R.S.B.A., etc. *Publications:* Brave Men, 1958; For Love or Money, 1960; (Ed.) J. Middleton Murry; Selected Criticism, 1960; George Orwell, 1961; (Ed.) Simone Weil: Selected Essays, 1962; A Theory of My Time, 1963; (Ed.) Simone Weil: Seventy Letters, 1965; Simone Weil: A Sketch for a Portrait, 1966; (Ed.) Simone Weil: On Science, Necessity, and the Love of God, 1968; (Ed.) Simone Weil: First and Last Notebooks, 1970; (Ed.) J. Middleton Murry: Poets, Critics, Mystics, 1970. *Address:* 16 Burnsall Street, S.W.3. [*Died* 24 *July* 1970 (*ext.*).

REEVE, Ada; Actress; *b.* London, 3 March 1874; *d.* of Charles Reeve; *m.* 1st, Bert Gilbert (Hazlewood) (marriage dissolved); 2nd, Wilfred Cotton (decd.). Appeared first in London as a child actress at the Pavilion, Whitechapel, and later at various Music Halls in London and the Provinces; first West End appearance in Musical Comedy, Gaiety, 1894, as Bessie Brent in The Shop Girl; subsequent successes in comedy, variety, pantomime, etc., London and provinces. Toured Australia, 1898, 1914, 1922, 1926, 1929-35; South Africa, 1906, 1909,

1911, 1913, 1918; U.S., 1893, 1911, 1912, 1925, 1927-8. First appearance in cabaret, Trocadero, 1935; toured in variety theatres, 1938-39: reappeared in London as Mrs. Batley in They Came to a City, Globe, 1943; played for over a year as Mrs. Catt in The Shop at Sly Corner, St. Martin's, 1945-46; Julie Bille-en-Bois, in Don't Listen, Ladies!, St. James's, 1948-49; has appeared in films and television and made recent broadcasts. *Publication:* Autobiography, Take it for a Fact, 1954. *Address:* 29 Stanley Gardens, W.11. [*Died* 25 *Sept.* 1966.

REEVE, Charles William, C.B.E. 1937; A.C.I.S.; *b.* Feb. 1879; *e. s.* of Charles Reeve, Gunthorpe, Notts; *m.* 1908, Annie A. (*d.* 1961); *e. d.* of R. Williamson, Pinchbeck, Lincs; one *d.* *Educ.:* De Aston School, Market Rasen; University College, Nottingham. Chief Accountant Associated Equipment Co. Ltd., now Associated Commercial Vehicles Ltd., 1929, Man. Dir., 1933-51, Chm. and Man. Dir., 1957, retired from the Board; Managing Director, D. Napier & Sons Ltd. 1938-42. Chief Stores Superintendent group of companies controlled by the Underground Electric Railway Company, London (now London Passenger Transport Board); President, Motor Trade Association, 1922-23; Member Advisory Council of the Board of Trade; Liveryman of Coachmakers' and Coach Harnessmakers' Company. *Publications:* articles on Motor Transport, Works Organisation, Cost Accounts. *Recreation:* gardening. *Address:* Hillside, Barnet Lane, Totteridge, N.20. *T.:* Hillside 2244. [*Died* 15 *May* 1965.

REEVE, Russell, R.E. 1955; R.B.A. 1932; Visiting Teacher of Drawing and Painting, Hornsey College of Art, since 1929; Painter, Etcher and Writer; *b.* Hethersett, Norwich, 3 June 1895; *s.* of Thomas Sidney Reeve, Norwich, and Alice Louisa Reeve (*née* Davies), Diss; *m.* 1922, Lucy Boag (*d.* 1964), Norwich; no *c.* *Educ.:* Crooks Place School and School of Art, Norwich. Junior Asst., City Engineers Dept., Norwich, 1908-14. Lt., R.E., 1917-18 (France). Slade School of Fine Art: Robert Ross Schol. and Orpen Bursary, 1919-22; Part-time student of Etching at Royal College of Art, 1921-22. Brother of Art Workers Guild, 1954-; Mem. Council Royal Society of Painter-Etchers, 1957-; Mem. Anglo-Portuguese Society. Works shown in many societies' exhibitions at home and abroad, and in one-man shows: Wilton Gallery, Luzo-Brazilian Council, Norwich, Ipswich, Cape Town, Lisbon. Works in Public Collections: Belfast; Bradford; Sheffield; Barnsley; Stoke; Camberwell; Hornsey, St. Marylebone, Guildhall Art Gallery, Royal College of Music; War Museum; V. & A. Museum; Ministry of Works; Nat. Students' Library; Duke of York's H.Q., Chelsea; Portuguese Embassy; Braganza Foundation, Lisbon; Deventer, Holland; Camara de Cascais; Institution Agricultural Engineers (Portrait of Founder); Recording Britain (Pilgrim Trust); *Publications:* drawings and articles: The Artist, Studio, Musical Times, Christian Science Monitor, Countrygoer Books; contrib. etchings to School Prints. *Recreations:* water-colour sketching; roaming in Portugal; looking through field glasses. *Address:* 24 St. Ann's Terrace, St. John's Wood, N.W.8. *T.:* 01-722 3429. [*Died* 1 *April* 1970.

REEVES, Joseph; *b.* 28 Jan. 1888; *s.* of Walter Cookson and Ruth Reeves; *m.* 1940, Florence Gladys Holdup; three *d.* *Educ.:* L.C.C. Past-Pres. International Cremation Fed., Vice-Chm. Cremation Soc.; Director: London Crematorium Ltd.; H. I. Thompson Press Ltd.; Pemberton Press; Educn. Secretary, Royal Arsenal Co-operative Society, 20 years. Secretary, Manager and Founder, Workers' Film Assoc. Member: B.B.C. Advisory Cttee. on adult educational broadcasts; Beveridge (1949) Committee on renewal of charter; Management Cttee. Workers' Travel Assoc. Ltd. Alderman and Councillor, Deptford, 1920-49. Took parties to Russia in 1927, 1929 and 1935. M.P. (Lab.) Greenwich, 1945-59; Member National Executive, Labour Party; Education Exec., Co-operative Union Ltd., National Cttee. Co-operative Party. Lecturer, Summer Schools, Conferences, etc. Member of Parliamentary Delegation to Finland, 1954, to West Indies, 1955; Mem. Exec. British Assoc. for World Government. *Publications:* A Century of Rochdale Co-operation, 1945; numerous pamphlets. *Recreations:* tennis, cricket, billiards. *Address:* 3 Weatherby Close, Park Lane, Eastbourne, Sussex. *T.:* Eastbourne 54465. [*Died* 8 *March* 1969.

REID, Sir Alexander (James), Kt. 1958; C.M.G. 1952; I.S.O. 1946; *b.* 12 October 1889; *s.* of late David Hay and late Jane Reid; *m.* 1915, Florence Sarah Jones; one *s.* one *d.* *Educ.:* Glasgow, Scotland; University of Western Australia (B.A.). Entered public service of Government of W.A., 1910; Asst. Under Treasurer, 1931; Under Treasurer, Government of Western Australia, 1938-54. Other positions held: Chairman: State Electricity Commission; Board of Management, Royal Perth Hosp.; Senate, Univ. of W.A. (now Chancellor). Director: A. T. Brine & Sons (Pty.) Ltd.; Australian Fixed Trusts (W.A.) Pty. Ltd. Hon. LL.D. Melb. and Qld. *Address:* 22 St. George's Terrace, Perth, W.A. *T.:* 21 9411; 92 Circe Circle, Dakeith, W.A. *T.:* 86.4197. *Clubs:* Weld, Rotary (Perth). [*Died* 30 *Aug.* 1968.

REID, Arthur Beatson, C.I.E. 1932; *b.* Kensington, 16 March 1888; *s.* of John Maitland Reid and Isabel Beatson; *m.* 1919, Eva Norah Stonehewer Bird; two *d.* *Educ.:* Cheltenham College; St. John's College, Oxford. Served in Indian Civil Service, 1912-1938. *Recreations:* tennis, golf. *Address:* 14 Ernle Road, S.W.20. *Club:* East India and Sports. [*Died* 2 *Dec.* 1965.

REID, Charles, M.A. (hons.); B.Sc. (spec. dist.); M.B., Ch.B. (hons.); M.D. (hons.); D.Sc. (Aberdeen); D.P.H. (Cantab); *b.* Cove, Kincardineshire, 1892; *s.* of Charles Reid, M.A. (ret.), Gillingham, Kent; *m.* Edith, *y. d.* of late Robert Laing, Aberdeen; one *d.* *Educ.:* Gordon's College, Aberdeen; Universities, Aberdeen and Cambridge. House Physician, Aberdeen Royal Infirmary, 1916-17; M.O., R.A.M.C. (S.R.) in France, 1917-20; Post-graduate work, Cambridge, 1920-21; Assistant, Physiology, Aberdeen University, 1920-21; Lecturer, Experimental Physiology, Aberdeen University, 1921-28; Examiner in Physiology, London Univ.; Professor of Physiology, Prince of Wales Medical College, Patna, India, 1929-32; Lecturer, Physiology Dept., University College, London, 1933-36; Reader in Physiology, London Univ., 1936-48; Professor of Physiology, Medical Faculty of Abbassia, Cairo University, 1948-52; W.H.O. Professor of Physiology Dow Medical College, Karachi, Pakistan, 1952-57, retired, 1957. *Publications:* Abnormal coronary artery in ox-heart, 1922; Diastatic activity in blood and urine, 1925; Effect on renal efficiency of lowering blood-pressure, 1926; Effects of electrolytes on the rhythmical contractions of the isolated mammalian intestine, 1927; The mechanism of voluntary muscular fatigue, 1927-28; Experimental ischæmia, Effects on blood-pressure, etc., 1929; Blood-pressure in its clinical application, 1930; Studies in blood-diastase, 1930; Glycolysis in blood, 1931; Fibrillary twitchings, 1931; Contrib. Proc. Phys. Soc. on Insulin and endocrines in relation to metabolism. *Address:* 81 Old Henley Village, Nr. Midhurst, Sussex. *Clubs:* Liphook Golf; Cowdray Park. [*Died* 24 *Oct.* 1961.

REID, Sir Charles Carlow, Kt., *cr.* 1945; *b.* 27 Jan. 1879; *s.* of William Reid and Isabella Carlow; *m.* 1st; one *s.* one *d.*; 2nd, 1920, Olive Lumsden. *Educ.:* Leven Public School (Fife). Mining Engineer; till 1942 General Manager and Director of Fife Coal Co. Ltd.; Production Director. Ministry of Fuel and Power, London, 1942-45; Past Pres. Mining Institute of Scotland; Chairman of Technical Advisory Cttee. on Coal Mining, 1945; Medallist of Institute of Mining Engineers, 1947; Member of National Coal Board, London, 1946-48. *Recreation:* golf. *Address:* Rosayres, 57 Blackwater Rd., Eastbourne. *T.:* Eastbourne 991. [*Died* 19 *Feb.* 1961.

REID, Major-General Denys Whitehorn, C.B. 1945; C.B.E. 1942; D.S.O. 1918; M.C. 1916; Indian Army, retired; *b.* 24 March 1897. Served European War, 1915-18, with Seaforth Highlanders (wounded, despatches twice, M.C. and bar, D.S.O.); War of 1939-45 in Middle East and commanded 10th Indian Division in Italy (wounded, Bar to D.S.O., C.B.E., C.B.); late 5th Mahratta Light Infantry; retd., 1947. *Address:* Lane End Cottage, Sampford Arundel, Nr. Wellington, Somerset. *T.:* Greenham 465. *Club:* Naval and Military. [*Died* 28 *Nov.* 1970.

REID, Ven. Ernest Gordon, M.A.; *s.* of Percy Thomas Reid, Mill Hall, Cuckfield, Sussex; *m.* Nancy Ida, *d.* of late Frederick Webb, Babraham; two *s.* one *d.* *Educ.:* Harrow; Pembroke College, Oxford; Wells Theological College. Deacon, 1909; priest, 1910. Curate of St. Anthony, Stepney, 1909; Chaplain of Oxford House, Bethnal Green, 1912; Vicar of St. Peters, Stepney, 1914; Rector of Sedlescombe with Watlington, Sussex, 1920; Vicar of Holy Trinity, Hastings, 1926-38; Chaplain Royal East Sussex Hospital, 1926-38; Archdeacon of Hastings, 1938-56; Surrogate, 1938. *Recreations:* shooting, golf, tennis. *Address:* Windmill Hill Place, nr. Hailsham, Sussex. *T.:* Hurstmonceux 3286. *Clubs:* M.C.C., Sussex. [*Died* 25 *Dec.* 1966.

REID, Brig. Sir Francis (Smith), Kt. 1964; C.B.E. 1945 (O.B.E. 1942); Secretary to the Speaker, House of Commons, since 1955; *b.* 2 Jan. 1900; *s.* of late George Whyte Reid, Inchanga, Bearsden, nr. Glasgow; *m.* 1928, Dorothy Muriel, *er. d.* of late Maj.-Gen. R. St. C. Lecky, C.B., C.M.G., Ballykealy, Co. Carlow, Eire; one *d.* (one *s.* decd.). *Educ.:* Fettes College, Edinburgh; R.M.A. Woolwich. 2nd Lieut. R.F.A. 1919; Capt. R.A. 1932; Major, 1938; Lt.-Col. 1945; Col. 1946; Brig. 1950; retd. 1955. War service: Kurdistan and Iraq (G.S. Medal and 2 clasps), 1919-20; French N. Africa and Italy, 1939-45; Brig. Gen. Staff, Allied Force Headquarters, 1943; C.R.A. (temp. Brig.) 78 Div., 1944-45; Comdr. Ceylon Garrison and U.K. Troops in Ceylon, 1949-50; Comdr. Cyprus District, 1950-51; Comdr. Cyrenaica District, 1951-52; Comdr. Ceylon Army, 1952-55. Officer Legion of Merit (U.S.A.), 1946. *Address:* Berden Hall, Nr. Bishop's Stortford, Herts. *T.:* Brent Pelham 258. *Club:* Army and Navy. [*Died* 18 *Jan.* 1970.

REID, Frank Aspinall, C.M.G. 1918; *b.* London, Ontario, 19 July 1875; *s.* of William John Reid; *m.* 1900, Laura, *d.* of Sidney A. King, M.D., Kingsville, Ontario; two *s.* one *d.* *Educ.:* Upper Canada College, Toronto. Formerly Colonel, D.A.A.G.; Dir. of Recruiting and Organization, Act. Adj. Gen. Canadian Overseas Mil. Forces, 1916. [*Died* 1 *Sept.* 1961.

REID, Very Rev. G. R. S., M.A., D.D., Minister Emeritus in Presbyterian Church, Roseville, Sydney; Moderator-General of Presbyterian Church of Australia, 1933-36; Member of Australian Historical Society; *b.* Fifeshire 1871; *s.* of late David Reid, farmer, Cruivie and Peacehills, and Annie Beattie, Cupar, Fife; *m.* Frances (*d.* 1948), *d.* of late Rev. John Robertson, Arbroath and Manchester; one *s.* three *d.* *Educ.:* High School, Dundee; St. Andrews University (prizeman in several classes); United College (theological), Edinburgh. Ordained by Edinburgh Presbytery and appointed minister of Scotch Church, Brussels, where he lectured to British-American colony on English Literature; proceeded to Australia in 1907 and became Minister of Pastoral Charge of Narandera, N.S.W.; afterwards Minister in Glebe, Sydney, and Roseville; acted as overseas Chaplain with Australian Imperial Forces during war; took interest in religious education and was for twelve years Chairman of Welfare of Youth Council; Steel Lecturer in Pastoral Theology to united classes under Theological Faculty in St. Andrews College within University of Sydney; Moderator of Presbyterian Church in New South Wales, 1929-30 and as official head visited throughout State in many congregations, city and country; also visited Presbyterian and other mission fields in India; lectured on his travels to schools and other audiences in Sydney. *Publications:* Editor of College Echoes while at St. Andrews University (Students' organ); Editor annual Book of Family Worship; brochure on Battle of Waterloo; "Royalty and Loyalty, the value of the British Monarchy" on occasion of visit of Duke of York to Australia; Presbyterian Pioneers in Australia, 1937; Anthony Trollope; Travels and Impressions in Australia, 1947; Ebenezer: Australia's Oldest Church, 1950; John Knox, Leader of the Scottish Reformation, 1959; frequent contributor to Church papers and press. *Recreations:* chess and walking. *Address:* Elston, Roseville Avenue, Roseville, Sydney, N.S.W. *Club:* Presbyterian (Sydney). [*Died* 29 *July* 1964.

REID, Sir George Thomas, K.B.E., *cr.* 1942; C.B. 1937; *b.* 19 April 1881; *s.* of Archibald Reid; *m.* Helen McL. Pennycook (*d.* 1944); two *d.*; *m.* 1947, Dorothy Rosamund Underwood. *Educ.:* London School of Economics. B.Sc. (Econ.) First Class Hons., Mitchell Studentship, 1906. Secretary, Assistance Bd., 1938-44, formerly Asst. Sec., Ministry of Labour; Secretary of Industrial Court, 1919-23; Secretary of Trade Boards, 1912-19; Director of Welfare Division, European Regional Office of U.N.R.R.A., 1944-45; Vice-Chm. C.S. Selection Board, 1946-49. *Address:* 21 Rugby Road, Worthing, Sx. *T.:* Worthing 47544. *Club:* Reform. [*Died* 14 *Nov.* 1966.

REID, Colonel Hector Gowans, C.M.G. 1919; C.B.E. 1920; D.S.O 1917; Barrister-at-law, Gray's Inn, 1930; F.R.P.S.L.; *b.* 6 June 1881; *s.* of George Patrick Reid, Toronto, Canada; *m.* 1905, Edythe Alsop (*d.* 1956), *d.* of T. A. Brock, Woodville, Adelaide, Australia; one *s.* one *d.* *Educ.:* Upper Canada College, Toronto; Royal Military Coll. Kingston, Canada. Served S. African War, 1899-1902 (Queen's medal and five clasps); European War, 1914-18, Egypt, Gallipoli, France and Belgium (despatches six times, Bt. Lt.-Col., C.M.G., D.S.O., Médaille du Roi Albert, 1914-15 Star, General Service and Victory medals); Armed Forces of South Russia, British Military Mission, 1919-20, (C.B.E., 2nd Class Order of St. Anne, crossed swords); Iraq, 1920-21 (Iraq General Service medal). Seconded for service under Canadian Government, 1906-07; Australian Government, 1908-1909; New Zealand Government, 1913-18; R.A.F. as Colonel i/c Administration Palestine, 1922-24; British Army of the Rhine, 1924-26; Colonel i/c R.A.S.C. Records, 1926-30; retired pay, 1930; Hudsons Bay Company; Winnipeg, 1930-38; R.C.A.F., 1939-44; Private Secretary to Gov. of Barbados, 1944-45; Canadian Vol. Service medal. *Address:* St. Lucia, West Indies. [*Died* 7 *March* 1966.

REID, Helen Rogers, (Mrs. Ogden Reid); *b.* 23 November 1882; *d.* of Benjamin Talbot Rogers and Sarah Louise Johnson Rogers; *m.* 1911, Ogden Reid; two *s.* (and one *d.* decd.). *Educ.:* Grafton Hall, Wisconsin; Barnard College, New York. A.B. 1903. Newspaper work with New York Herald Tribune, 1918-58; Vice-pres. and Advertising Director, 1922-47, President, 1947-53, Chairman of Board, 1953-55; Hon. degrees: Dr. of Letters: Miami Univ., 1931; Columbia Univ., 1949; Bates Coll., 1951; Manhattanville Coll. of the Sacred Heart, 1953; Dr. of Humanities, Rollins Coll., 1933; Dr. of Laws: Oglethorpe Univ., 1935; Univ. of Toronto, 1947; Smith Coll., 1948; Univ. of Wisconsin, 1953; Temple Univ., 1953; Mount Holyoke, 1954; Dr. of Humane Letters: Lafayette Coll., 1941; New York Univ., 1944; Yale Univ., 1950; C.W.Post Coll., Long Island Univ., 1964; Dr. of More Humane Letters, Syracuse Univ., 1941. *Address:* (home) 834 Fifth Avenue, New York City, N.Y. 10021, U.S.A. *Clubs:* Colony, Women's University, Women's City, New York Newspaper Women's (N.Y.C.). [*Died* 27 *July* 1970.

REID, Vice-Adm. Howard Emerson, C.B. 1944; Royal Canadian Navy (retd.); *b.* 5 June 1897; *s.* of George E. Reid and Louisa M. Amy; *m.* 1936, Edith A. Houston; two *s.* one *d.* *Educ.:* Ashbury College, Ottawa; Royal Naval College of Canada, Halifax. Joined H.M.S. Berwick as Midshipman, 1914; H.M.C.S. Rainbow, 1916; H.M.S. Attack, Channel and Western Approaches, 1917; H.M.S. Viscount, Grand Fleet, 1918-19; H.M.S. Titania, China Station, 1920-22; H.M.C.S. Patriot, in command, 1923-25; various R.C.N. appointments, 1923-28; H.M.S. Sepoy, China Station, in command, 1929-30; R.N. Staff College, Greenwich, 1931; H.M.S. Warspite, 1932; Commander, 1933; Appts. as: Comdr. in Charge, Halifax, Director of Operations and Training, Naval H.Q., Ottawa, and Comdr. "D" of West Coast Destroyers, 1936-38. Capt. 1939; Commanding Officer Atlantic Coast, 1939-40, with rank of Commodore 1st Class; Vice-Chief of Naval Staff, Naval Service H.Q., Ottawa, and Naval Member of U.S.-Canada Joint Defence Board, 1941-42; Flag Officer, Newfoundland Force, 1943; Rear-Admiral, 1943; Naval Member of Canadian Joint Staff, Washington, U.S.A., 1943-46; Vice-Admiral, 1946; Chief of Naval Staff, Royal Canadian Navy, 1946-47; retired, 1948. *Recreations:* fishing and shooting. *Address:* 1530 Despard Ave., Victoria, B.C., Canada. [*Died* 3 *May* 1962.

REID, Rev. James, M.A.; D.D. (Edin.); *b* 1877; *s.* of William Reid, Leven, Fife; *m.* Isabella (*d.* 1954), *d* of Robert Gerrett, J.P., Leven; three *s.* *Educ.:* Leven; Edinburgh Univ.; New Coll., Edin. Minister at Oban, 1905-10; Sherwood United Free Church, Paisley, 1910-1915; Minister of St. Andrew's Presbyterian Church, Eastbourne, 1915-45. President of National Free Church Council of England and Wales, 1932-33; Moderator of the General Assembly of the Presbyterian Church of England, 1935. Freeman of Eastbourne, 1945. *Publications:* Materials of Moral Instruction; The Victory of God; In Quest of Reality; The Bible for Youth; The Key to the Kingdom; In Touch with Christ; The Springs of Life; Why be Good; Making Friends with Life; The Temple in the Heart; Facing Life with Christ; Where the New World begins; Living in Depth. *Address:* 7 Grassington Road, Eastbourne, Sussex. *T.:* Eastbourne 3427 [*Died* 19 *July* 1963.

REID, His Honour John Alexander, M.C.; Judge of County Courts, 1950-67, retd.; *b.* 14 Sept. 1895; *er. s.* of late James Robert Reid, C.I.E., Indian Civil Service; *m.* 1940, Jean Ethel, *d.* of Sidney Herbert Ashworth, St. Albans; two *s.* two *d.* *Educ.:* Marlborough; R.M.C. Sandhurst. Second Lieut. York and Lancaster Regt., 1914. Served European War, 1914-16 (despatches, M.C.); invalided 1917. Called to the Bar, Lincoln's Inn, 1919; practised at Chancery Bar till 1950. *Address:* Eastfield Cottage, Mickleham, Dorking, Surrey. *T.:* Leatherhead 2066. [*Died* 1 *June* 1969.

REID, Mrs. Ogden; *see* Reid, Helen Rogers.

REID, Colonel Percy Lester, C.B.E., 1944; J.P., D.L.; late Irish Guards; *b.* 20 Nov. 1882; *e. s.* of late Percy T. Reid, Mill Hall, Cuckfield, Sussex; *m.* 1909, K. M. E., *e. d.* of Fergus Fergusson, London and Johannesburg; two *s.* *Educ.:* Eton; Sandhurst. Joined Irish Guards, 1902; commanding 2nd Bn. Irish Guards in France, 1916-17 (despatches four times, O.B.E.); Lt.-Col. retired 1919; Member of the Northamptonshire County Council, 1926-1937; Director of the Prudential Assurance Co., 1926-59; High Sheriff of Northants., 1931-1932; Zone Commander, Home Guard for Northamptonshire, 1941, rank Col. (C.B.E.); Master Merchant Taylors' Company, 1947-48. *Recreations:* shooting, fishing. *Address:* Manor Ho., Thorpe Mandeville, Northants. *T.:* Sulgrave 316. *Clubs:* Guards, M.C.C., Bath. [*Died* 12 *July* 1968.

REID, Sir Robert Niel, K.C.S.I., *cr.* 1937 (C.S.I. 1934); K.C.I.E., *cr.* 1936 (C.I.E. 1930); I.C.S. retired; *b* 15 July 1883; *y. s.* of David Reid, Sevenoaks, Kent; *m.* 1909, Amy Helen, *o. d.* of G. W. Disney, Muzaffarpur, India; three *s.* one *d.* *Educ.:* Malvern; Brasenose College, Oxford. Passed into I.C.S., 1906; joined in Bengal as Assistant Magistrate, 1907; Under Secretary, 1911-14; I.A.R.O., 1916-19; Secretary to Government of Bengal, 1927-28; Commissioner, Rajshahi Division, 1930; Chief Secretary (offg.), 1930; Commissioner, Chittagong Division, 1931; Chief Secretary to the Government of Bengal, 1932-34; Acting Member of Executive Council, Bengal, 1932; Member of Executive Council, Bengal, 1934-37; Governor of Assam, 1937-42; Acting Governor of Bengal, June-Oct. 1938 and Feb.-June 1939; China Relations Officer, Calcutta, 1942-43; Director-General, Post and Telegraph Censorship, 1945. Chairman, East Suffolk Executive Council under National Health Service Act, 1947-55; Chairman, Suffolk Local Valuation Panel, 1949-63. Kaisar-i Hind gold medal, 1924; Hon. Fellow of Brasenose, 1940. *Address:* Heath Lodge, Woodbridge, Suffolk. [*Died* 24 *Oct.* 1964.

REID, Thomas, C.M.G. 1931; Ceylon Civil Service, retired; *b.* 26 Dec. 1881; *s.* of John Reid, Mt. View, Co. Carlow; *m.* 1913, Brenda Broadway, L.R.A.M., A.L.C.M., A.R.C.M.; one *s.* two *d.* *Educ.:* Queen's College, Cork; Royal University, Dublin, B.A. (Senior Classical Scholar, Senior Scholar Jurisprudence, Economics and Modern History, Prizeman, Ancient History). Passed Home, Indian and Eastern Civil Service, 1905; entered Ceylon Civil Service; various judicial and administrative posts in Ceylon; Mayor and Chairman, Municipal Council, Colombo, 1919-1924; Labour Controller, Ceylon, 1925-29; Member Legislature, 1926-31; on special duty in connection with introduction of new Ceylon Constitution, 1930-31; retired Dec. 1931; Financial Commissioner to report on Seychelles Colony, 1933; Chairman League of Nations Commission on Sanjak of Alexandretta, 1937-38; member of Palestine Partition Commission, 1938. M.P. (Lab.) Swindon Division of Wilts, 1945-50, Borough of Swindon, 1950-55, retired 1955. *Publications:* Where White and Brown Meet, novel, 1934; articles in various political periodicals and broadcasts. *Recreation:* books. *Address:* 15A Tring Ave., Ealing Common, W.5. *T.:* Acorn 4320. [*Died* 28 *Jan.* 1963.

REID, William, J.P., Glasgow; *s.* of Hill Reid, merchant and manufacturer. *Educ.:* Whitehill Secondary School, Glasgow. Entered Glasgow Town Council, 1920; Magistrate, 1927-30; J.P. 1930-: Police Judge, 1930-50. Chairman: Glasgow Corporation Transport Cttee., 1936-39; Public Health Cttee., 1946-49. M.P. (Lab.) Camlachie Div. of Glasgow, 1950-55, Provan Div., 1955-1964. Member, Scottish Western Regional Hospital Board. *Address:* c/o W.R.H.B. (Scot.) 351 Sauchiehall St., Glasgow, C.2. [*Died* 16 *July* 1965.

REID, William David, O.B.E. 1944; J.P. 1938; D.L.; *b.* 20 April 1883; *s.* of James Reid, Shipmaster, and Elizabeth Dougall; *m.* 1902, Ann Wyllie; one *d.* (and one *d.* decd.). *Educ.:* Robert Gordon's Coll., Aberdeen; Univ. of Aberdeen. Solicitor in Aberdeen, 1907-. Served European War, 1917-18. Mem. of Aberdeen Town Council, 1934-; Senior Magistrate, 1937-38. Pres. Society of Advocates in Aberdeen, 1950; Lord Provost of the City of Aberdeen, 1951-52; Member Solicitors' Discipline Cttee. for Scotland; Vice-Pres. Law Society of Scotland. D.L. Aberdeen, 1952. *Recreations:* bridge, golf, bowls, chess, billiards. *Address:* Kingshill, King's Gate, Aberdeen. *T.:* Aberdeen 33018. [*Died* 26 *Sept.* 1964.

REID DICK, Sir W(illiam), K.C.V.O., *cr.* 1935; R.A. 1928 (A.R.A., 1921); Hon. R.S.A.; F.R.B.S.; Queen's Sculptor in Ordinary for Scotland since 1952 (Sculptor to King George VI, 1938-52); Member of Royal Fine Art Commission since 1928; Member of the Mint Advisory Committee; Trustee of Royal Academy; *b.* Glasgow, 13 Jan. 1879; *m.* 1914, Catherine, *d.* of William John Treadwell, Northampton; one *s.* two *d.* *Educ.:* Glasgow School of Art; London. Pres. Royal Society of British Sculptors, 1933-38; Trustee of Tate Gallery, 1934-41; Albert Medal of Royal Society of Arts (presented by Princess Elizabeth), 1948. Exhibited at Royal Academy since 1905, Paris Salon, and International Society; Femina Victrix, purchased by New South Wales Gallery, 1914; bronze mask, purchased by Chantry Trustees, 1919; other works: Silence, figure for a tomb, various works in public and private collections; Bust of Viscount Bryce, Washington, Earl of Chatham, Pittsburg, Lord Riddell; War Memorials Rickmansworth and Bushey; Kitchener Memorial Chapel for St. Paul's Cathedral; large Bronze Eagle, on Royal Air Force Memorial, Embankment, London; Lion, Menin Gate, Ypres; on active service in France and Palestine, 1914-19; Medal, Royal Society British Sculptors, 1928; Lord Leverhulme Memorial, Port Sunlight, Cheshire; Large Stone Equestrian Groups on Unilever House, Blackfriars; Statue Lord Irwin, Delhi; Statue of Sir John Soane, Bank of England; Bust Sir Edwin Lutyens; Bust of Lord Duveen, National Portrait Gallery; Bronze Figure, Welcome, Nottingham Town Hall; Bust of King George V. 1933; Statue of Livingstone, Victoria Falls; Statue of Lord Willingdon, Delhi; Bust Canon Alexander, St. Paul's Cathedral; Stone Figures, New Government Building, Edinburgh; Tombs of King George V., and Queen Mary, St. George's Chapel, Windsor; Memorial to King George V. and Queen Mary, Sandringham Church; Memorial Bust, Crathie Church, Balmoral; Bust of Queen Mary; Statue of King George V., for National Memorial, Westminster; Equestrian Statue of Lady Godiva, Coventry; Portrait of King George VI.; Portrait of Winston S. Churchill; Portrait of the Queen (now Queen Elizabeth, The Queen Mother); Portrait of Princess Elizabeth; Bronze Statue, President Roosevelt, Grosvenor Square; The Rani Kaiser Portrait (bronze); Bronze bust of Dr. Parkinson, Leeds Univ.; Bronze bust of Isaac Wolfson; Memorial to King George VI., Sandringham Church; Portrait bust of Sir Reginald Bloomfield, National Portrait Gallery. *Address:* 16 Maida Vale, W.9. *T.:* Cunningham 5313. *Club:* Arts. [*Died* 1 *Oct.* 1961.

REILLY, Lt.-Col. Sir Bernard Rawdon, K.C.M.G., *cr.* 1934; C.I.E. 1926; O.B.E. 1918; employed in Colonial Office, 1940-1961; *b.* 1882; *s.* of late Col. B. L. P. Reilly, Indian Army. *Educ.:* Bedford. Entered Indian Army, 1902; entered Political Department, 1908; served in India and Aden; H.M.'s Commissioner and Plenipotentiary to H.M. the King of the Yemen, Dec. 1933, and concluded a treaty with the Yemen, Feb. 1934; Resident and Commander-in-Chief at Aden, 1931-37; Chief Commissioner, Aden, 1932-37; Governor and Commander-in-Chief of Aden, 1937-40; accompanied British Delegation to Refugees Conference at Bermuda, April 1943. Member of British Delegation to Ethiopia which concluded Anglo-Ethiopian Agreement in Dec. 1944; Head of War Office Working Party sent to advise on British Military Admin. of former Italian Colonies in Africa, 1946-47; on special duty in East Africa, 1948. Chairman: Royal Commonwealth Society for the Blind (previously British Empire Society for the Blind), 1950-59; Commission of Inquiry into importation and possession of qat in Aden, 1958. *Publication:* Aden and the Yemen, 1960. *Club:* United Service. [*Died* 28 *Oct.* 1966.

REILLY, Joseph, M.A.; D.Sc. (N.U.I.); M.A. (Cantab. and Dub.); Sc.D. (Dub.); D.ès.Sc. (Geneva); F.R.C.Sc.I.; F.R.I.C.; F.Inst.P.; M.R.I.A.; Prof. of Chemistry; National Univ. of Ireland (University College; Cork), 1925-59, Emeritus Professor, 1960, *b.* Dublin, 3 September 1889; *s.* of J. Reilly of Granard, Longford; *m.* Chevaun, B.A., *d.* of late M. O'Brien, M.D., Galway; four *s.* two *d.* *Educ.:* Christian Brothers School, Dublin. St. Mary's College, Dublin; Royal College of Science for Ireland; University College, Dublin; University of Cambridge; University of Geneva; University of Berlin. Assistant State Chemist, Dublin, 1924; Head of Branch (Acting Deputy-Director) Research Dept. Royal Arsenal, Woolwich, 1921-24; Chemist-in-Charge, Royal Naval Cordite Factory, Dorset, 1915-21; formerly Member of Committee of Science, Royal Dublin Society; Member of Council of Chemical Soc. and of Society of Chemical Industry; Member Faraday Soc. and Biochemical Soc.; Boyle Medallist, Royal Dublin Society. *Publications:* Aims in School Science; Explosives; Distillation; (Joint) Physico-Chemical Methods, 5th ed. (3 vols.); Practical Physical Chemistry, Laboratory Chemistry, Inorganic Chemistry, Quantitative Analysis, etc.; The Growing of Oil-Producing Plants, Our Daily Bread, The Dietetics of Vegetables, etc.; Editor of the Blarney Magazine, 1948-; 250 research, scientific and general papers mainly in Organic and Physical Chemistry in the Trans. of the Chem. Soc., J. Soc. of Chem. Industry, Scientific Proc. of the Royal Dublin Soc., Proc. Royal Irish Academy, Helvetica Chemica Acta, Berichte (Chem.), Biochemical Journal, J. Amer. Chem. Soc., J. of Organic Chem., J. Chem. Educ., Nature, etc. *Recreations:* travel, editor of magazine, book reviews. *Address:* Glengorm, The Ridgeway, Bishopstown Ave., Cork, Ireland. [*Died* 18 *Sept.* 1965.

REINOLD, Vice-Admiral Harold Owen, C.B. 1930; C.V.O. 1924; Royal Navy; *b.* 1877; *s.* of Professor A. W. Reinold, C.B., F.R.S., and M. S. Owen; *m.* 1917, Frances Olwen Fisher-Rowe (*d.* 1958); three *s.* one *d.* *Educ.:* St. Christopher's, Blackheath; R.N. Colleges. Naval cadet, 1891; Lieut. 1899; Capt. 1917; Rear-Adm. 1928; Vice-Adm. 1933; retired list,

1933; Commanded H.M.S. Prince Rupert on Belgian Coast, 1915-16 (despatches twice); K.H.M. Plymouth, 1917-18; Commanded H.M.S. Ceres, Mediterranean and Black Sea, 1919-21; H.M. Navigation School, 1922-24; Commanded H.M.S. Hood, Atlantic Fleet, 1925-27; Director of Naval Equipment, Admiralty, 1930-31; Admiral Superintendent, Devonport Dockyard, 1931-35. *Address:* Paulsgrove, Hayling Is. *T.:* 77555. [*Died* 4 *Jan.* 1962.

RELF, Ernest Frederick, C.B.E. 1944; A.R.C.Sc.; F.R.Ae.S.; F.R.S. 1936; *b.* 2 Oct. 1888; *s.* of Thomas J. and Marion Relf, Maidstone, Kent; *m.* 1917, Elfreda Grace Day; no *c.* *Educ.:* Portsmouth Royal Dockyard School; Royal College of Science, London. Apprenticeship in Portsmouth Dockyard 1904-9; Royal Scholarship to R.C.S. 1909; Scientific Staff, N.P.L., 1912; Superintendent Aerodynamics Division National Physical Laboratory, 1925-45; Principal of College of Aeronautics, 1946-51. James Forrest Lecturer, 1936; Wilbur Wright Lecturer, 1946. *Publications:* numerous papers in Reports and Memoranda of Aeronautical Research Council, Philosophical Magazine, and Aeronautical Technical Journals. *Recreation:* music—piano, organ, composition. *Address:* Spinney Dene, 28 Spinney Hill, Addlestone, Surrey. *T.:* Weybridge 47833. [*Died* 25 *Feb.* 1970.

RELTON, Frederick Ernest, D.Sc., M.A.; *b.* 19 May 1883; *s.* of Thomas Relton; *m.* Janet Orr; three *s.* one *d.* *Educ.:* Queen Mary College, London; Worcester College, Oxford. Mathematical Scholar, Worcester College, 1901-4; Lieut. in R.G.A. 1915-1919; Principal, Bingley Technical School; Mathematics Staff of Imperial College, South Kensington; Prof. of Mathematics and Mechanics, Cairo University, 1931-47. Mathematical Lecturer at King's College, University of London, 1947-54, retired. *Publications:* Applied Bessel Functions, 1946; Applied Differential Equations, 1947; various papers in pure and applied mathematics. *Recreations:* journalism, gardening; *Address:* 34 Hengistbury Road, Bournemouth. [*Died* 14 *Jan.* 1963.

REMARQUE, Erich Maria; *b.* Osnabrück, 1898; *m.* 1957, Paulette Goddard. Served European War. *Publications:* All Quiet on the Western Front, 1929; The Road Back, 1931; Three Comrades, 1937; Flotsam, 1941; The Arch of Triumph, 1946; Spark of Life, 1952; A Time to Love, and a Time to Die, 1954; The Black Obelisk, 1957; Heaven has no Favorites, 1961; The Night in Lisbon, 1964. Script for film The Last Act, 1955. *Play:* The Last Station, 1956. *Address:* Porto-Ronco, Ticino, Switzerland. [*Died* 25 *Sept.* 1970.

REMINGTON, Geoffrey Cochrane, C.M.G. 1960; Solicitor, N.S.W.; Chairman, Standard Telephones and Cables Pty. Ltd.; Director: W. R. Carpenter Holdings Ltd.; Dalton Bros. Holdings Ltd.; Trustee, Public Library of New South Wales; *b.* Summer Hill, 27 November 1897; *s.* of J. C. Remington; *m.* 1930, Joan, *d.* of J. E. Daly; one *s.* one *d.* *Educ.:* Sydney Church of England Grammar School; Armidale School. Assistant Director, Dept. of War Organisation of Industry, 1941; Asst. Dir. of Personnel, Allied Works Council, 1942-43; Actg. Dir. of U.N.R.R.A., S.W. Pacific, 1945. Pres. Rotary Club, Sydney, 1948-49. Exec. Chm. Free Library Movement; Mem. Libraries' Advisory Cttee., N.S.W.; Mem. Mitchell Library Cttee.; Dep. Chm. N.S.W. Library Bd. Counsellor, Australian Administrative Staff College. *Address:* 263 George Street, Sydney, N.S.W., Australia. *Clubs:* Union (Sydney); Royal Sydney Yacht Squadron; Commonwealth (Canberra). [*Died* 23 *Jan.* 1968.

REMNANT, 2nd Baron, *cr.* 1928, of Wenhaston; **Robert John Farquharson Remnant,** M.B.E. 1945; Bt., *cr.* 1917; *b.* 29 Mar. 1895; *er. s.* of 1st Baron and Frances Emily (*d.* 1944), *d.* of late Robert Gosling of Hassobury, Bishop's Stortford; *S.* father, 1933; *m.* 1924, Norah Susan, *yr. d.* of Lt.-Col. A. J. Wogan-Browne; one *s.* one *d.* *Educ.:* Eton; Magdalen College, Oxford. Served European War, 1914-18 and War of 1939-45. *Heir:* *s.* Hon. James Wogan Remnant [*b.* 23 Oct. 1930; *m.* 1953, Serena Jane, *o.d.* of Commander Sir Clive Loehnis, K.C.M.G; three *s.* one *d.*]. *Address:* Bear Place, Twyford, Berks. *T.:* Wargrave 39. *Clubs:* Constitutional, City. [*Died* 4 *June* 1967.

REMNANT, Hon. Peter Farquharson; *b.* 21 September 1897; *yr. s.* of 1st Lord Remnant; *m.* 1923, Betty (*d.* 1965), *d.* of late W. G. Tanner of Frenchay, Gloucs.; (only son killed in action 26 Jan. 1945) two *d.* *Educ.:* Eton; Magdalen Coll., Oxford. Lt. R.G.A., 1916-19; Lt.-Col. R.A., A.A. and Staff, 1939-45. M.P. (C.) Wokingham Division of Berkshire, 1950-59. *Address:* Ipsden House, Ipsden, Oxford. *T.:* Checkendon 271. *Club:* Constitutional. [*Died* 31 *Jan.* 1968.

RENALS, Sir Herbert, 3rd Bt., *cr.* 1895; *b.* 29 Sept. 1919; *s.* of Sir James Herbert Renals, 2nd Bt., and Susan Emma Crafter, Bromley, Kent; *S.* father, 1927. *Heir:* *b.* Stanley Renals, *b.* 20 May 1923. [*Died* 19 *Aug.* 1961.

RENAUD, Maj.-Gen. Ernest James, C.B. 1945; C.B.E. 1943 (O.B.E. 1919); C.D. 1950; Major-General, Canadian Militia, retd. Served European War, with Canadian Overseas Forces, 1914-19 (O.B.E.); also War of 1939-45 (C.B.E., C.B.). G.O.C., Quebec Command, till 1948; retired, 1948. *Address:* 309 Clemow Avenue, Ottawa, Ont., Canada. [*Died* 28 *Jan.* 1967.

RENIER, Gustaaf Johannes, Ph.D., Phil.lit.cand.; Professor Emeritus of Dutch History and Institutions in the University of London since 1957; *b.* Flushing, Holland, 25 Sept. 1892; *s.* of Pieter Renier, Flushing; *m.* 1939, Olive Mary Corthorn; no *c.* *Educ.:* Flushing Sch.; Louvain Sch.; Univs. of Ghent and London (U.C.L.). London correspondent of Dutch newspapers, 1914-27; from 1927, author and translator; Lectr. English History, U.C.L., 1934; Reader in Dutch History, Univ. London, 1936; Professor, 1945-57; during War of 1939-45, Literary Adviser, Netherlands Govt. in London. Corresp. Royal Acad., Amsterdam; Fellow of Univ. Coll., London, 1948; Officer Order of Orange Nassau, 1947; Knight Order of Netherlands Lion, 1957. *Publications:* Great Britain and the Establishment of the Kingdom of the Netherlands, 1813-15, 1930; The English: are they human?, 1931; The Ill-fated Princess: Life of Charlotte, daughter of the Prince Regent, 1932; William of Orange, 1932; Oscar Wilde, 1933; He came to England, a self-portrait, 1933; A Tale of Two Robins, 1934; Robespierre, 1936; The Dutch Nation, an historical Study, 1944; The Criterion of Dutch Nationhood, 1946; De Noord-Nederlandse Natie, 1949; History, its Purpose and Method, 1950; numerous translations from the Dutch, the French and the German. *Recreations:* conversation, dogs. *Address:* 7 Montpelier Row, Twickenham, Mdx. *T.:* Popesgrove 6528. [*Died* 4 *Sept.* 1962.

RENISON, Sir Patrick (Muir), G.C.M.G. 1962 (K.C.M.G. 1955, C.M.G. 1950); J.P.; Joint Vice-Chairman, British Red Cross Society, since 1964; Member, Governing Body, Queen Elizabeth House, Oxford; *b.* 24 March 1911; *yr. s.* of late William John Henry Renison; *m.* 1936, Eleanor Hope

Gibb; one *d.* *Educ.:* Uppingham; Corpus Christi College, Cambridge. Colonial Administrative Service, 1932; seconded Colonial Office, 1932-35; Ceylon Civil Service, 1935-44; seconded Colonial Office, 1944-1946 and 1947-48; Colonial Secretary, Trinidad and Tobago, 1948-52; Governor and C.-in-C., Brit. Honduras, 1952-55; Governor and Commander-in-Chief of British Guiana, 1955-59; Governor and Commander-in-Chief of Kenya, 1959-62; Adviser to Lord Hailsham on Sport and Physical Recreation, 1963. K.St.J. 1955. Hon. Fellow of Corpus Christi College, Cambridge, 1959. J.P. Sussex, 1965. *Address:* Freeman's Farm House, Mayfield, Sussex. *Club:* Oxford and Cambridge.
[*Died* 11 *Nov.* 1965.

RENNIE, Charles Robert, C.B.E. 1933; retired Civil Servant; *b.* 7 Oct. 1880; *s.* of R. A. Rennie and Mary Jordan; *m.* 1st, 1921, Mary Hylda (*d.* 1922), *d.* of Rev. J. G. Munday; no *c.*; 2nd, 1937, Mary Ellen, (*d.* 1966), *d.* of Frederick McQuade, Sydney, N.S.W. Entered Northern Rhodesia Administration, 1903; Assistant Native Commissioner, 1906; Native Commissioner, 1910; Assistant Magistrate, 1914; District Commissioner and Magistrate, 1924; Provincial Commissioner, 1929; retd. 1932; served Nyasaland Govt. as Asst. Sec., 1940-42; Controller of Supplies and Prices, 1943-45. *Recreation:* fishing. *Address:* c/o Standard Bank of S.A. Ltd., Cape Town, South Africa.
[*Died* 10 *Feb.* 1969.

RENOLD, Sir Charles Garonne, Kt., *cr.* 1948; J.P.; Director, Renold Chains Ltd., since 1906; Hon. President since 1967 (Chairman, 1943-67); *b.* 29 October 1883; *s.* of Hans Renold of Aarau (Switzerland) and Manchester; *m.* 1st, 1909, Margaret Hilda (*d.* 1958), *d.* of Charles Hunter, Manchester; three *s.* one *d.*; 2nd 1960, Noël Garry (*d.* 1966), *e. d.* of late E. A. Dunne, Sale and Dublin. *Educ.:* Abbotsholme School; Cornell Univ., U.S.A. Hon. LL.D. (Manchester), 1960. *Publication:* Joint Consultation over Thirty Years, 1950. *Recreations:* fishing, gardening. *Address:* Little Lydgate, Eccles Road, Chapel-en-le-Frith, Derbyshire. *T.:* Chapel-en-le-Frith 2847. *Club:* Engineers (Manchester). [*Died* 7 *Sept.* 1967.

RENWICK, William Lindsay; Regius Professor of Rhetoric and English Literature, University of Edinburgh, 1945-1959; now Emeritus Professor; *b.* Glasgow, 6 January 1889; *s.* of W. K. Renwick, Glasgow; *m.* Margaret, *d.* of Robert Lang. *Educ.:* Glasgow University; Toulouse; the Sorbonne; Merton College, Oxford. M.A. Glasgow, 1910, and Clark Scholar, 1912; served with the Cameronians (Scottish Rifles), 1914-19; B.Litt. Oxon, 1920; Lecturer in Glasgow University; Joseph Cowen Professor of English Language and Literature, King's College, Newcastle upon Tyne, in the University of Durham, 1921-45; Visiting Professor, China, 1943-44; D.Litt. (Glas.), 1926; D. (*hon. caus.*), Bordeaux, 1934; F.B.A. 1946; LL.D. (Glasgow), 1953. *Publications:* Edmund Spenser, An Essay on Renaissance Poetry, 1925; Spenser's Works, 1928; John of Bordeaux, 1936; (with H. Orton) The Beginnings of English Literature, 1939; English Literature 1789-1815, 1963. *Address:* Arthur Lodge, 60 Dalkeith Road, Edinburgh 9. *T.:* Newington 5163.
[*Died* 25 *Nov.* 1970.

REUTHER, Walter Philip; President, United Automobile, Aerospace and Agricultural Implement Workers, since 1946; *b.* Wheeling, W. Va., 1 Sept. 1907; *s.* of Valentine and Anna Stoker Reuther; *m.* 1936, May Wolf; two *d.* *Educ.:* Wayne University. Tool and die maker: Wheeling Steel Co., 1922-27; Ford Motor Co., 1927-1933 (fired for union activity); travelled in Germany, U.S.S.R. (18 months, working at Ford plant in Gorki, U.S.S.R.), and other European and Asian countries. Helped found U.A.W., Detroit, 1935; Mem. Internat. Exec. Bd., 1936-; Vice-Pres., 1942-46; Dir., General Motors Dept., 1939-48. Pres., Congress of Industrial Organisations, 1952 to merger with American Federation of Labor, 1955; Vice-Pres., A.F.L.-C.I.O., 1955-1967, and Pres., Industrial Union Dept., 1956-68; Vice-Pres. and Mem. Exec. Bd.: I.C.F.T.U., 1951-68; Mem. Exec. Bd., 1949- (Pres. Automotive Div., 1949-); Internat. Metalworkers Fedn.; Member many govt. cttees. and commns., incl.: President's Adv. Cttee. on Labor-Management Policy; President's Cttee. on Equal Employment Opportunity; Officer, Director, or Trustee of: U.N.A of U.S.A.; N.A.A.C.P.; Nat. Housing Conf.; Citizens Crusade against Poverty (Nat. Chm.); Metropolitan Detroit Citizens Develt. Authority (Chm. Bd.); Dept. of Church and Economic Life, Nat. Coun. of Churches, and many other organisations. Holds honorary degrees. *Publications:* Selected Papers of Walter P. Reuther (ed. H. M. Christman). 1961; (with Edith Green) Education and the Public Good, 1963; contrib. New Horizons of Economic Progress (ed. L. A. Seltzer), 1964; numerous articles and pamphlets. *Address:* 8000 East Jefferson Avenue, Detroit, Michigan 48214, U.S.A. *T.:* 926-5000. [*Died* 9 *May* 1970.

REVEL, John Daniel, R.O.I., P.S., A.R.C.A.; Director Glasgow School of Art, 1925-32; Headmaster, Chelsea School of Art, 1912-24; *b.* Dundee, 2 Feb. 1884; *m.* Lucy Elizabeth Babington (*d* 1961), 2nd *d* of Hugh J. Mackenzie, C.E., Elgin. *Educ.:* Royal Coll. of Art. Mem. International Society of Painters, 1913, Royal Institute of Oil Painters, 1923, and Society of Portrait Painters, 1924; Associate of Royal College of Art in Painting and Architecture since 1912; served European War. *Address:* Lydds, White Shute, Blewbury, Berkshire. *Club:* Chelsea Arts.
[*Died* 25 *Nov.* 1967.

REVENTLOW, Count Eduard; Hon. G.C.V.O. 1951; retired; Danish Minister at the Court of St. James, 1938-47, Ambassador 1947 - 53; Hon. President, Assoc. of Free Danes in Great Britain and N. Ireland, 1942-45; *b.* 28 Nov. 1883; *s.* of late Count C. B. Reventlow and Sophie Schiaer; *m.* 1910, Else, *d.* of Admiral F. de Bardenfleth; two *s.* one *d.* *Educ.:* Copenhagen University. Studied law, passed examination, 1908; entered Danish Foreign Service, 1909; held posts in Copenhagen, Berlin and Paris, 1909-1913; 1st Secretary to Danish Legation in London, 1913-19; Permanent Under-Secretary of State for Foreign Affairs, 1922-32; Minister in Stockholm, 1932-37. *Publication:* I Dansk Tjeneste, 1956. *Address:* 21 Østbanegade, Copenhagen, Denmark.
[*Died* 26 *July* 1963.

REW, Lt.-Col. Horace Edward, D.S.O. 1940; Farmer; *b.* 5 June 1899; *s.* of Edward Charles Ashurst Rew, Sheepdrove, Lambourn, Berks; *m.* 1927, Kathleen, *d.* of L. R. Neate; two *s.* *Educ.:* Hurstpierpoint; R.M.C., Sandhurst. Commissioned 1918, Royal Berkshire Regt.; R.A.F., 1925-29; Major I.R. Berks Regt., 1938; commanded 1/8 Lancashire Fusiliers, 1940-42; retired, 1947. *Address:* Wolds Farm, Nottingham Road, Natal, South Africa.
[*Died* 5 *Feb.* 1967.

REWCASTLE, His Honour Cuthbert Snowball, B.A., LL.B.; Judge (jt.) of County Courts (West London and Shoreditch), 1955-61, retired; *b.* 21 Feb. 1888; *s.* of Cuthbert Rewcastle, J.P.; *m.* 1st, 1918, Annie Evelyn Goddard (*d.* 1923); 2nd, 1926, Dr. A. Genevieve Candon (*d.* 1951): two *s.* one *d.* *Educ.:* Rugby; Trinity Coll.,

Cambridge. Editor of The Granta; Called to Bar, Inner Temple, 1913; Senior Advocate, Federal Court of India; Secretary of the Royal Commission on the Sugar Supply; Referee under the Landlord and Tenant Act, 1927; called within the Bar, 1935; Judge (jt.) of County Courts (Kingston and Wandsworth), 1952. Chm., Commission on Silicosis Legislation, N. Rhodesia, 1949; Chm., Commission on Pulmonary Disability, 1954. Contested, as a Liberal, Hallam Division of Sheffield, 1922, and 1923 and Kettering Division of Northants, 1929; sometime Hon. Secretary of the Eighty Club. *Publications:* Joint Editor with late A. A. Hudson, K.C., of 4th Edition of Hudson on Building Contracts; Editor of 2nd Edition of Mahaffy and Dodson on the Law relating to Motor Cars. *Recreations:* fly-fishing, walking. *Address:* 2 Paper Buildings, Temple, E.C. *T.:* Central 9119. [*Died* 8 *June* 1962.

REY, Lt.-Col. Sir Charles Fernand, Kt., *cr.* 1938; C.M.G. 1932; *b.* London, Aug. 1877; *m.* Georgina (*d.* 1958), *y d* of late J. Hume Webster. *Educ.:* privately, for the Army; passed R M A Woolwich Examination; studied for Mining Engineering at Royal School of Mines and elsewhere; exploring and prospecting expedition through West Africa, 1899; joined Board of Trade, 1900; Secretary to China Tariff Commission, 1902; to Imperial Institute Advisory Cttee. and Imperial Institute Trustees, 1903; to All Red Route Cttee., 1904; proceeded to Roumania for Commercial Treaty Negotiations with that country, 1905; thence on Special Mission to Constantinople and Sofia; Secretary to Swiss Commercial Treaty Negotiations in London, 1906; despatched to Germany to study Labour Exchanges; General Manager of Labour Exchanges, 1909; General Manager of Unemployment Insurance, 1912; Director of Labour Supply, Dept. Ministry of Munitions, 1915; Assistant General Secretary Ministry of Munitions, 1916; Director of Employment Dept. Board of Trade, 1917; Director-General of National Labour Supply, Ministry of National Service, Aug 1918; Assistant Secretary, Ministry of Labour, 1918; Chairman British Commission, Rotterdam, and Chief British Representative Inter-Allied Commission, Rotterdam, for Food Supply to Germany, March 1919; granted leave, June 1919-Nov. 1920, for work in Abyssinia; second journey to Abyssinia, 1922-1923; third, 1925-26; fourth, 1926-27; Unemployment Grants Committee, 1927-29; Resident Commissioner, Bechuanaland Protectorate, 1930-37 and Commandant B.P. Police; retired, 1937; F.R.G.S., 1923; Commander of the Star of Ethiopia, 1924. Mem. Portuguese Acad. of Hist., 1945-. Hon. Life Vice-Pres., S.A. Assoc. of Arts, 1952. *Publications:* Unconquered Abyssinia as it is To-day, 1923; In the Country of the Blue Nile, 1927; The Romance of the Portuguese in Abyssinia, 1929; The Lady or the Leopard, 1929; The Real Abyssinia, 1935; Revision of Articles on Abyssinia, etc., in Encyclopædia Britannica, 1929, 1953; The Union of South Africa and some of its Problems, 1948. *Address:* Whitehall Court, Rondebosch, Capetown. *Clubs:* Civil Service, Royal Automobile Club of S.A. (Cape Town). [*Died* 30 *March* 1968.

REYNAUD, Paul, G.C.V.O. (Hon.); LL.D. Chevalier de la Légion d'Honneur; Croix de Guerre; Member, Assemblée Nationale, France; *b.* Barcelonnette (B.-A.), 15 Oct. 1878; *m.*; two *s.* two *d.* Barrister, Paris Court of Appeal. M.P. for: the Basses-Alpes, 1919; Paris, 1928, 1932, 1936; the Nord, 1946, 1951, 1955, 1958. Former Minister: for the Colonies; of Justice (twice); of Finance (thrice); also for National Defence; and for Foreign Affairs. Prime Minister of France, 1940; a Deputy Prime Minister (Laniel Government), France, 1953. Delegate to Council of Europe, 1949; Chm. Economic Committee of Council of Europe, 1952-. *Publications:* Waldeck-Rousseau, Les Trois glorieuses, Jeunesse, quelle France veux-tu?, Le Problème militaire français, Courage de la France, S'unir ou périr, Finances de guerre, La France a sauvé l'Europe, 1946; Au cœur de la mêlée (Eng. trans., 1955, in the Thick of the Fight, 1930-1945); Mémoires: Vol. 1, Venu de ma montagne, 1960; Vol. 2, Envers et contre tous; La Politique étrangère du gaullisme; Et après?, 1963. *Address:* 5 Place du Palais-Bourbon, Paris VIIe. *T.:* Invalides 69-86. [*Died* 21 *Sept.* 1966.

REYNOLDS, Alfred Charles; Composer and conductor; *b.* Liverpool, 15 Aug. 1884; *s.* of Charles Reynolds and Eva Gertrude (*née* Allinson); *m.* 1913, Barbara Florack; one *d.* *Educ.:* Merchant Taylors'; Institut Commercial de Vincennes, Paris; Hochschule and Meisterschule, Berlin. Studied music in Paris and Berlin; Pupil for composition of Engelbert Humperdinck. Organist at British Embassy Church, 1908-10; conducted operas and operettas in Germany and Russia; returned to England, conductor for P. M. Faraday and George Edwardes. Invalided out of the Army, 1917; toured in India and Far East. Conducted The Insect Play, The Immortal Hour and Bethlehem, Regent Theatre for Sir Barry Jackson, 1923; musical director for Sir Nigel Playfair, Lyric Theatre, Hammersmith, 1923-32, where he composed and arranged the music for The Duenna, Lionel and Clarissa, Riverside Nights, Love in a Village, The Fountain of Youth, Derby Day; also incidental music for plays. Conducted Cosi fan Tutte, Kingsway and Royal Court Theatre, 1927. Also wrote music for 1066 and All That, composed originally for Birmingham Repertory Theatre; The Bookie's Opera, composed for Television; operetta, The Limpet in the Castle, 1958. A.I.L. 1945. *Publications:* (vocal scores) The Duenna, 1924; Lionel and Clarissa, 1925; The Policeman's Serenade, 1926; Love in a Village, 1928; The Fountain of Youth, 1931; Derby Day, 1932; 1066 & All That, 1934; Five Centuries of Love, 1946; various songs, articles, lectures, etc. *Recreation:* motor-boating. *Address:* 16 Crescents Walk, Bognor Regis, Sussex. *T.:* Bognor Regis 3444. *Clubs:* Savage, Green Room, Linguists'. [*Died* 18 *Oct.* 1969.

REYNOLDS, Air Marshal Sir Bryan (Vernon), K.C.B., *cr.* 1955 (C.B. 1954); C.B.E. 1943; D.L.; retired; *b.* Highgate, 1902; *s.* of Austin Reynolds, M.R.C.S.; *m.* 1947, Geraldine, *d.* of John Redington, Galway, Ireland; one *d.* *Educ.:* St. Olave's, S.E.1. Served War of 1939-45 (despatches, C.B.E.); formerly A.O.C., R.A.F. N. Ire., and Sen. Air Force Officer, N. Ire.; Air Vice-Marshal, 1950; A.O.C. No. 22 Group, Technical Training Command, 1950-52; Actg. Air Marshal, 1953; A.O.C. Malta, 1952-55; Dep. C.-in-C. (Air), Allied Forces, Mediterranean, 1953-55; Air Marshal, 1956; C.-in-C. Coastal Command, C.-in-C. Air East Atlantic, C.-in-C. Air Channel Command, 1955-59; retired, 1959. Commander, Order of Orange Nassau (Netherlands), 1943. D.L., County of Sussex, 1962. *Address:* The Old Vicarage, Walberton, Arundel, Sussex. *T.:* Yapton 293. [*Died* 6 *Dec.* 1965.

REYNOLDS, Rt. Hon. Gerald William, P.C. 1968; M.P. (Lab.) for Islington N. since 1958; Minister of Defence for Administration, since 1967; *b.* 17 July 1927; *s.* of Arthur Reynolds and Florence (*née* Hambridge); *m.* 1949, Dorothy F. Budd; two *d.* *Educ.:* Acton Co. School; Ealing School of Art (Evening Classes). D.P.A. 1949. Mem. Acton Borough Coun., 1949-65 (Mayor, 1961-1962); parly. candidate, Worthing, 1951; Local Government Officer to National Executive of Labour Party, 1955-58 (Local Govt. Assistant, 1952-55). Parliamentary

Under-Secretary of State for Defence for the Army, Ministry of Defence, 1964-65. Minister of Defence for the Army, 1965-67. Chm., London Borough of Ealing, 1964-65. *Publication:* (with Anthony Judge) The Night the Police Went on Strike, 1968. *Recreations:* local government, cars. *Address:* 45 Mill Hill Rd., W.3. *T.:* Acorn 8334. [*Died* 7 *June* 1969.

REYNOLDS, Sir Jeffery (Fellowes Crofts), Kt., *cr.* 1947; C.I.E. 1944; M.C. 1917; M.I.Mech.E.; *b.* Oct. 1893; 2nd *s.* of William Benbow Reynolds; *m.* 1924, Hilda E. P. Duffes; one *s.* *Educ.:* Lancing. Served European War, 1914-18. South Indian Railway, 1919-48; General Manager, 1941-48; General Manager, Tata Locomotive and Engineering Co., Ltd., India, 1949. *Address:* The Island House, Bray, Berks. [*Died* 15 *March* 1966.

REYNOLDS, Major Sir Percival Reuben, K.B.E., *cr.* 1928 (O.B.E. 1921); Director B.C.R. Factories Ltd., Welwyn Garden City, 1937; *b.* 1876; *s.* of late R. Reynolds, J.P., Wakefield; *m.* Constance (*d.* 1962), *d.* of late J. S. Booth, J.P., Wakefield; two *s.* one *d.* *Educ.:* Wakefield Grammar School. Served European War, 1914-19 M.E.F. and E.E.F. (despatches); ex-President of National Association of British and Irish Millers, 1925-27; Member of Ships Replacement Committee, 1935-37. *Address:* c/o B.C.R. Factories Ltd., Welwyn Garden City. [*Died* 28 *Nov.* 1965.

REYNOLDS, Quentin James; Writer; *b.* 11 April 1902; *s.* of James Reynolds, New York City, and Katherine Mahoney, New York City; *m.* 1942, Virginia Peine, actress, New York. *Educ.:* Brown University, Rhode Island; Law School of St. Lawrence University, New York City. Journalist on New York Evening World, 1924-28; foreign correspondent for International News Service, 1928-32; Assoc. Ed., Collier's Weekly, 1933-45; Editor, The United Nations World, 1951. Hon. degrees: LL.D. St. Lawrence University; Brown University, Doctor of Letters. *Publications:* The Wounded Don't Cry, 1940; London Diary, 1940; Don't Think It Hasn't Been Fun, 1941; Only the Stars are Neutral, 1942; Dress Rehearsal (Story of Dieppe), 1943; The Curtain Rises, 1944; Officially Dead, 1946; Courtroom, 1950; I, Willie Sutton, 1953; The Amazing Mr. Doolittle, 1953; The Man Who Wouldn't Talk, 1953; Headquarters, 1955; They Fought for the Sky, 1958; (with Katz and Aldouby) Minister of Death, 1961; By Quentin Reynolds, 1964; *for children:* The Wright Brothers, 1950; Custer's Last Stand, 1951; The Battle of Britain, 1953; The F.B.I., 1954; The Life of St. Patrick, 1955. *Address:* Bedford Village, New York 22. *Clubs:* University (N.Y.); River. [*Died* 17 *March* 1965.

REYNOLDS, Russell John, C.B.E. 1932; M.B., B.S.(Lond.); M.R.C.S., F.R.C.P.(Lond.), D.M.R.E. Camb. F.F.R.; M.I.E.E.; Consulting Physician Departments of Radiology and Electrotherapeutics, Charing Cross Hospital; late Lecturer in Radiology, Charing Cross Hospital Medical School; Honorary Adviser in Radiology to Minister of Pensions and Minister of Supply; late Manager of the Royal Institution of Great Britain; Consulting Radiologist, National Hospital for Paralysed and Epileptic, Queen Square, British Home for Incurables, Streatham, King George Hosp., Ilford, Samaritan Free Hosp., Caernarvonshire and Anglesey Infirmary, Bethlem Royal Hospital and Lambeth Hospital; Examiner Royal Army Medical College; late Examiner in Radiology, University of Cambridge, Conjoint Board; Faculty of Radiologists; Hunterian Prof. R.C.S., 1936-37; Capt. (late R.A.M.C.); F.R.S.M. (Past Pres. Radiology Section); Past-President British Institute of Radiology; late Hon. Secretary and Librarian Röntgen Society; late Hon. Medical Editor British Journal of Radiology; *b.* 1880; *o. c.* of John Reynolds, M.D.; *m.* Annie (*d.* 1941), *o. c.* of A. Romer, London; two *s.* *Educ.:* Westminster; Guy's Hospital; Univ. of London. Introduced Improvements in Apparatus for producing X-rays since the discovery, 1895; in Induction Coils in 1898 and in X-ray Tubes in 1901; Radiologist to certain L.C.C. Ringworm Clinics, 1912-14; graduated, 1907; European War; Radiologist, Tooting Military Hospital, Holborn Military Hospital, 2nd London General Hospital; Hon. Radiologist to Federated Malay States Government Hospital, Wheathamstead, Herts; Electrical Specialist Karachi Brigade, India, 1917-1919. Hon. Member: American Röntgen Ray Society; Canadian Radiological Association; New York Röntgen Society; Mem. Comité d'Honneur and Béclère Medallist, 1957, Centre Antoine Béclère, Paris; Association of Physicians of Vienna; Society of Radio Biologists of Italy. Hon. Fell. Soc. Radiographers; Hon. Mem. British Institute of Radiology; Hon. F.A.C.R. Retired. International award of Antoine Béclère Medal for Radiology, Paris, 1957. *Publications:* The Early History of Radiology in Britain (Clinical Radiology), 1961; article on Radiography & Radiotherapy, British Encyclopædia of Medical Practice, 1940; papers in medical journals. *Recreation:* yachting. *Address:* Flat 41, 6 Hall Road, St. John's Wood, N.W.8. *Clubs:* Athenæum, Savage. [*Died* 5 *Nov.* 1964.

RHIND, Edwin S. O.; *see* Oak-Rhind.

RHODES, Sir Christopher (George), 3rd Bart., *cr.* 1919; *b.* 30 April 1914; *s.* of Lieutenant-Colonel Sir John (Phillips) Rhodes, 2nd Bt., D.S.O.; *S.* father 1955; *m.* 1st, 1936, Mary (from whom he obtained a divorce, 1942), *d.* of Horace Kesteven; 2nd, 1943, Mary Florence, *er. d.* of late Dr. Douglas Wardleworth; two *s.* one *d.* Served War of 1939-45, Essex Regiment. Hon. Lt.-Colonel. Officer Legion of Merit (U.S.A.); Croix de Guerre (France). *Heir: s.* John Christopher Douglas, *b.* 24 May 1946. *Address:* 86 High Street, Blakeney, Norfolk. *T.:* Cley 260. *Club:* Boodle's. [*Died* 22 *June* 1964.

RHODES, His Honour Harold; Judge of County Courts, Circuit No. 8 (Manchester), 1942-58, retired; J.P. Lancs and Cheshire; *b.* 1885; 2nd *s.* of late George Rhodes, K.C.; *m.* 1915, Ena (*d.* 1955), *y. d.* of late Thomas Wolverson, M.D.; two *s.* one *d.* *Educ.:* Bowdon Coll.; Corpus Christi Coll., Oxford, M.A. Called to Bar, Inner Temple, 1910; Mem. of Northern Circuit. Served European War, 29th Divisional Artillery, France, 1915-18, retiring with rank of Captain. Chairman Midland (Amalgamated) District Committee of Investigation under Coal Mines Act, 1936; appointed to sit as Tribunal to examine Enemy Aliens in Derbyshire, 1939. Commissioner of Assize, Northern Circuit, 1946. Dep. Chairman Lancashire Quarter Sessions, 1942-60; Chairman Altrincham Petty Sessional Div., 1942-60; Chairman, N.W. Conscientious Objectors' Tribunal, 1955-58. *Address:* 18 Belsize Court, Hampstead, N.W.3. *Clubs:* Oxford and Cambridge; St. James's (Manchester). [*Died* 17 *Oct.* 1964.

RHODES, Harold Vale, C.B. 1947; *m.* 1913, Jessie Helen, *d.* of John Lodge Sykes, Huddersfield; one *s.* one *d.* Called to the Bar, Gray's Inn, 1928. Under-Secretary and Director of Establishments and Organisation, Min. of Nat. Insurance, 1946-1951. *Publications:* The Politics of Naval Disarmament, by Giovanni Engely (trans. from Italian), 1932; Setting up a New Government Department, 1949. *Recreation:* music. *Address:* 11 Rowsley Rd., St.

Anne's-on-Sea, Lancs. *T.:* St. Annes 24914. *Club:* Lytham Yacht. [*Died* 23 *Feb.* 1970.

RHODES, Kathlyn ; *b.* Thirsk, Yorkshire. *Educ.:* London; France. *Publications: Novels:* Sweet Life; Desert Dreamers; Afterwards; Lure of the Desert; Sands of Gold; The City of Palms; The Golden Apple; The Mirage of the Dawn; East o' the Sun; The Golden Journey; Crime on a Cruise; The Lady Was Warned; The Glory of the Moon; It Happened in Cairo; The Bright Company; The Fifth Act; The Envious Gods; Roses in December (autobiography); Moon over Madeira, Libretto, Opera, Robin Hood (Open-Air Theatre, Scarborough, 1949). Book filmed: Afterwards. *Other Books:* Schoolgirl Honour; Dodo's Schooldays, etc. *Play:* (broadcast) Don Quixote Brown. *Recreations:* motoring, music, travel, golf. *Address:* The Elms, Cherry Orchard, Staines. *T.:* Staines 53572. [*Died* 15 *Jan.* 1962.

RHODES, Colonel Stephen, C.B. 1931; D.S.O. 1918; D.L.; T.D.; E D.; *m.* 1924, Wilfreda (*d.* 1929), *widow* of Major Crawfurd V. Monier-Williams, D.S.O., M.C., of Chequers, Esher, Surrey, and *o. d.* of Craster M. Usher, Wilford Lodge, Esher. Served European War, 1914-18 (despatches, D.S.O.); commanded 147th 2nd West Riding Infantry Brigade, 1929-33; Hon. Col. 467 (5th York and Lancaster) A.A. Regt. R.A., 1930-54. Served attached to R.A.F., 1940-41. *Address:* South Hill, Whixley, York. [*Died* 7 *Oct.* 1966.

RHODES, Walter Harpham, C.B.E. 1947; President of Allied Industrial Services Ltd., London, Bradford, Glasgow, Birmingham; *b.* 6 March 1888; *e. s.* of late Walter Rhodes, Bradford; *m.* 1912, Marguerite, *d.* of late Robert Mobbs; no *c. Educ.:* Bradford Grammar School; Worksop Coll. Served European War with R.F.A. and Labour Corps; Vice-Pres. Royal Over-Seas League; Founder, 1938, W. H. Rhodes' Canada Educational Trust, which provides for annual educational visits to Canada of Senior Secondary Schoolboys. *Recreations:* yachting, travel, walking. *Address:* Shenley, Burn Bridge, nr. Harrogate. *T.:* Harrogate 81639. *Club:* Union (Bradford). [*Died* 7 *May* 1962.

RHYDDERCH, Sir William Edmund Hodges, K.B.E., *cr.* 1951; C.B. 1946; *b.* 16 Aug. 1890; *s.* of late Richard Rhydderch, Rhyl. *Educ.:* Llandovery College; Hertford College, Oxford; Deputy Chairman of Board of H.M. Customs and Excise, 1949-52. *Address:* Brick Cottage, Hatfield Broad Oak, Bishop's Stortford, Herts. [*Died* 27 *Oct.* 1961.

RHYS WILLIAMS, Juliet, Lady (Juliet Evangeline), D.B.E. 1937; Vice-President, Economic Research Council; Chairman, United Europe Movement, since 1958; Founder Member National Birthday Trust, 1928, Chairman, since 1957; European League of Economic Co-operation since 1948; *b.* 17 December 1898; *yr. d.* of late Clayton Glyn and Mrs. Elinor Glyn (authoress); *m.* 1921, Lt.-Col. Sir Rhys Rhys Williams, 1st Bt., D.S.O., Q.C. (*d.* 1955); one *s.* (Sir Brandon Meredith Rhys Williams, 2nd Bt, M.P.) two *d.* (and one *s.* killed in action in Tunisia, 1943). *Educ.:* The Links, Eastbourne. Private Secretary to Director of Training and Staff Duties, Admiralty, 1918; Assistant Secretary War Cabinet Demobilisation Committee, 1919; Private Secretary to Parliamentary Secretary Minister of Transport, 1919-20. Hon. Treas., Queen Charlotte's Hosp. Anæsthetic Fund, 1928-39; Hon. Secretary Joint Council of Midwifery, 1934-39; Member of Inter-Departmental Committee on Abortion, 1937-1938. Contested (L.) Pontypridd by-election, 1938; Assistant Commercial Relations Officer, Ministry of Information, 1939-40; Asst. Section Officer, W.A.A.F., 1940; D.G.St.J. 1942; Hon. Sec. Women's Liberal Federation, 1943. Contested (L.) Ilford (North), 1945; Chm. Publications and Publicity Cttee. of the Liberal Party, 1944-46. Hon. Sec.: Economic Section Congress of Europe at the Hague, 1948; United Europe Movement, 1947-58. Hon. Editor, European Review, 1951-54; Director, Economic Digest, 1954-58; a Governor of the B.B.C., 1952-1956; Chm. Cwmbran Development Corporation, 1955-60. *Publications:* In Search of Reality, 1925; Something to Look Forward to, 1943; Aircraftswoman Grey, 1943; Family Allowances and Social Security, 1944; Stern Daughter, 1944; Dr. Carmichael, 1946; 49 Chances, 1947; Taxation and Incentive, 1952; An Economic Policy for Britain, 1963. *Address:* Miskin Manor, Pontyclun, Glamorgan; 47 Eaton Place, S.W.1. [*Died* 18 *Sept.* 1964.

RIBERI, Cardinal Antonio; Nuncio Apostolic to Spain since 1962; *b.* 15 June 1897. Ordained, 1922; Privy Chamberlain to His Holiness, 1925; Secretary of Apostolic Nunciature in Bolivia, 1925-29; Auditor of Apostolic Nunciature in Ireland, 1929-34; apptd. Apostolic Delegate to Africa for the Missions, 1934; consecrated Titular Archbishop of Dara, 1934; Director of Vatican Relief Service for non-Italian Refugees, 1942-1946; first Apostolic Internuncio to China, 1946-59; Nuncio Apostolic to Ireland, 1959-1962. *Address:* Nunciatura Apostolica, Avenida Pio XII 46, Madrid 16, Spain. [*Died* 16 *Dec.* 1967.

RICE, Elmer; Playwright, novelist, stage director; *b.* New York City, 28 September 1892; *m.* 1915; one *s.* one *d.*; *m.* 1942; two *s.* one *d*; *m.* 1966, Barbara Marshall. *Educ.:* New York Public Schools; New York Law School (LL.B. 1912). Regional Director, Federal Theatre Project, 1935-36; Officer and Director, Playwrights' Producing Co.; Member National Institute of Arts and Letters; President Dramatists' Guild, 1939-43; President Authors' League of America, 1945-46; Member, Board of Directors of American Civil Liberties Union; Member of Council of British Dramatists; Chairman National Council on Freedom from Censorship; Member of Panel of American Arbitration Assoc.; Vice-President P.E.N. Club, N.Y. Centre; Vice-President, International P.E.N., Lecturer in English, University of Michigan; 1954; Adjunct Professor, New York University, 1957-58. Hon. Litt.D., University of Michigan, 1961. *Plays produced:* On Trial, 1914; The Iron Cross, 1917; For the Defense, 1919; Wake up Jonathan (with Hatcher Hughes), 1921; It is the Law (with Hayden Talbot), 1922; The Adding Machine, 1923; Close Harmony (with Dorothy Parker), 1924; Cock Robin (with Philip Barry), 1928; Street Scene, 1929; (Pulitzer Prize); The Subway, 1929; See Naples and Die, 1929; The Left Bank, 1931; Counsellor-at-Law, 1931; Black Sheep, 1932; We, The People, 1933; Judgment Day, 1934; Between Two Worlds, 1934; Not for Children, 1936; American Landscape, 1938; Two on an Island, 1939; Flight to the West, 1940; A New Life, 1943; Dream Girl, 1945; Street Scene (musical version, with Kurt Weill and Langston Hughes), 1947; The Grand Tour, 1951; The Winner, 1954; Cue for Passion, 1958; Love Among the Ruins, 1963. *Published:* On Trial, Wake up Jonathan, The Adding Machine, Close Harmony, Cock Robin, Street Scene, The Subway, See Naples and Die; The Left Bank; Counsellor-at-Law; We, The People; Judgment Day; Between Two Worlds; Not for Children; American Landscape; Two on an Island; Flight to the West; A New Life; Dream Girl; Street Scene (musical version); The Grand Tour, 1951; The Winner, 1954; Cue for Passion,

1959; Love Among the Ruins, 1963. *Produced in England:* On Trial, The Adding Machine, Cock Robin, The Subway, Street Scene, See Naples and Die; The Left Bank; Counsellor-at-Law; Not for Children; Judgment Day; Dream Girl. Between Two Worlds, The Winner. *Novels published:* A Voyage to Purilia; Imperial City; The Show Must Go on 1949; *other publications:* The Living Theatre, 1960; Minority Report: An Autobiography, 1963. *Address:* 815 Long Ridge Road, Stamford, Conn., U.S.A.
[*Died* 8 *May* 1967.

RICE, Colonel Henry James, C.I.E. 1935; M.C.; M.D.; I.M.S., retired; *b.* 20 Oct. 1894; *s.* of Dr. T. W. Rice, Portarlington; *m.*; one *s.* one *d.* *Educ.:* Trinity College, Dublin. Served European War; Lieut. R.A.M.C. 1917; Capt. 1918; Lieut. I.M.S. 1922; Capt. 1923; Major, 1932; Lt.-Col. 1940; Col. 1943; served 1930, N.W.F. (despatches); retired, 1945. *Address:* Coosan Point, Athlone, Eire.
[*Died* 8 *May* 1964.

RICE, Percy Christopher, O.B.E. 1926 (M.B.E. 1918); I.S.O. 1930; *b.* 21 Feb. 1877; *e. s.* of John Norman Rice; *m.* 1910, Edith Beatrice Colman (*d.* 1947); two *s.* one *d.* *Educ.:* King's College, London. Entered the Foreign Office, 1895; Staff Officer, 1916; Finance Officer in the Dept. of Overseas Trade, 1918; Chief Establishment and Finance Officer, 1922-34; Assistant Director, 1922-38. Temporarily re-employed in Foreign Office, 1939-45. Pres. Civil Service Christian Union, 1950-62. Vice-Pres. National Young Life Campaign, 1957. *Publications:* Senior Editor of the Foreign Office List, 1915-38 and again, 1942-46. *Recreations:* social and religious work. *Address:* Meriton, Downsway, Merrow, Guildford. *T.:* Guildford 3648. *Club:* National.
[*Died* 6 *March* 1963.

RICH, Adena M. (Mrs. Kenneth F. Rich); Director Emeritus, Immigrants' Protective League (Director, 1926-54); *b.* Erie, Pennsylvania, U.S.A., New England parentage; *m.* 1917, Kenneth F. Rich. *Educ.:* Oberlin College, A.B. 1911; Certificate of Graduation, Chicago School of Civics and Philanthropy, 1912; Graduate study at New York School of Social Work and University of Chicago. Supervisor of Visitors, Immigrants' Protective League, 1912-14; Supervisor of Field Work, Chicago School of Civics and Philanthropy, 1914-16; Civic Director Women's City Club of Cincinnati, 1916-17; Director, Girls' Protective Bureau (a Wartime Agency), 1918-19; Lecturer, Courses in Civics to Women's Clubs, 1920-21; Director of Surveys, Chicago Community Trust, 1921-22; Executive Vice-President, Illinois League of Women Voters, 1923-1926; Trustee, Oberlin College, since 1935; State Chairman, Woman's Division, War Finance Committee of Illinois, 1941-44; Lecturer, University of Chicago, Courses in Immigration in the School of Social Service Administration, for a number of years; Resident in Chicago Social Settlements; Eli Bates House, Henry Booth House, Hull House; Head Resident, Hull House, 1935-1937; for many years on Board of Directors, Women's City Club of Chicago; State of Illinois, Committee on Citizenship and Naturalization; Chm., Div. X, The Immigrant, Nat. Conference of Social Work, Boston, 1930; represented Immigrants' Protective League, Second Internat. Conference of Emigration and Immigration at Havana, Cuba, 1928. Member Phi Beta Kappa. *Publications:* Short articles in Club Organs and Bulletins; pamphlet for Chicago Community Trust, Prenatal Care in Chicago; Various Reports regarding Care of Women Offenders; special articles on Immigration and Naturalization, particularly for the Social Service Review; annual Reports for Immigrants' Protective League. *Recreations:* music, theatre. *Address:* Westminster Place, 1 Calvin Circle, Evanston, Illinois, U.S.A. *Club:* Chicago Woman's.
[*Died* 10 *March* 1967.

RICH, Roy; Head of Light Entertainment, British Broadcasting Corporation, since 1964; *b.* 16 Sept. 1912; *s.* of Charles Rich and Elsie Rich (*née* Tookey); *m.* 1st, 1939, Pamela Titheradge (marriage dissolved, 1946); 2nd, 1946, Brenda Bruce; one *s.* twin *d.* *Educ.:* Dulwich College. Repertory at Dundee, 1930-31; Stage Manager, London Hippodrome, 1931-32; Producer of Rep., Bradford and Leeds, and of Pantomime, Princes, Bristol, 1932-36; Production Controller, Moss Empires and General Theatre Corp., 1936-38. Asst. Head of Presentation, B.B.C., 1938-40. R.A.F., 1940-46. Film Director, Gainsborough Films Ltd., 1946-50; Director of Productions, Arts Theatre, London, 1950-55; Executive Producer, British Lion Films Ltd., 1955-58. Controller of Programmes, Southern Television, 1958-64. *Recreations:* travel, looking and listening. *Address:* King's Head Hotel, Wellesbourne, Warwicks. *T.:* Wellesbourne 206. *Clubs:* Garrick, Lord's Taverners, M.C.C.
[*Died* 24 *March* 1970.

RICHARDS, Alfred Newton, Medal for Merit (U.S.) 1946; Emeritus Prof. of Pharmacology, University of Pennsylvania, 1946 (Professor of Pharmacology, 1910-46); *b* 22 March 1876; *s.* of Rev. Leonard E. Richards and Mary E. (*née* Burbank); *m.* 1908, Lillian L. Woody; one *s.* *Educ.:* Yale College; Columbia University, College of Physicians and Surgeons. Asst. in Physiological Chemistry, Coll. of Physicians and Surgeons, N.Y., 1898-1904; Instructor in Pharmacology, Coll. of Physicians and Surgeons, N.Y., 1904-1908; Professor of Pharmacology, Northwestern Univ. Med. Sch., Chicago, 1908-10. Asst. Editor, later managing editor, Jl. of Biological Chemistry, 1905-14. Vice-Pres. i/c Medical Affairs, Univ. of Pa., Philadelphia, 1939-48. Chm., Cttee. on Medical Research, Office of Scientific Research and Development, U.S. Govt., 1941-46. Mem. Bd. of Trustees, Rockefeller Foundation, 1937-41; Mem., Bd. of Dirs., Merck & Co., Inc., 1948-58. Croonian Lectr., Royal Society, 1938; Pres., Nat. Acad. of Sciences, 1947-50; Vice-Pres. Amer. Philosophical Soc., 1944-47. Mem. Scientific Staff, Medical Research Cttee., Great Britain, 1917-18; Major, Sanitary Corps, A.E.F., France, 1918. Hon. Sc.D.: Univ. of Pa., 1925; Western Reserve, 1931; Yale, 1933; Harvard, 1940; Columbia, 1942; Williams, 1943; Princeton, 1946; N.Y. Univ., 1955; Rockefeller Inst., 1960; Oxford, 1960; Hon. LL.D.: Edinburgh, 1935; Johns Hopkins, 1949; Hon. M.D.: Univ. of Pa., 1932; Louvain, 1949. Holds numerous awards and medals. Hon. C.B.E. (U.K.) 1948. *Publications:* Methods and Results of Direct Investigations of the Function of the Kidney (The Beaumont Foundation Lectures, Detroit, 1929). Contrib. Amer. Jl. of Physiology, Jl. of Physiology, Jl. Biological Chemistry, Proc. of Roy. Soc. *Address:* 737 Rugby Road, Bryn Mawr, Pennsylvania, U.S.A. *T.:* Lawrence 5-0917.
[*Died* 24 *March* 1966.

RICHARDS, Francis John, D.Sc., F.R.S. 1954; Director of Agricultural Research Council Unit of Plant Morphogenesis and Nutrition, Wye College, Ashford, Kent, 1960; *b.* 1 October 1901; *s.* of Robert Richards, Burton-upon-Trent; *m.* 1928, Lilian Kingsley Mason; two *d.* *Educ.:* Burton-upon-Trent Grammar School; Birmingham University. Research officer, Research Institute of Plant Physiology, Imperial College of Science and Technology (stationed at Rothamsted Experimental Station), 1926-39; Head of Imperial College Laboratory, Rothamsted, 1939-59. *Publications:* scientific contributions to botanical journals. *Recreations:* scientific dilettantism. *Address:* Orchard Bank, Oxenturn Rd., Wye, Ashford, Kent. *T.:* Wye 471. [*Died* 2 *Jan.* 1965.

RICHARDS, Frank (pen-name); real name was Charles (Harold St. John) Hamilton; Author of the "Billy Bunter" books and plays; *b.* 1875; unmarried. *Publications:* over 30 books so far published, and about 45 plays on television; two new books every year (spring and autumn) and the Bunter annual for Christmas; Autobiography, 1952. *Recreations:* chess; the classics, especially Horace and Lucretius; music. *Address:* Rose Lawn, Kingsgate, Broadstairs, Kent. *T.:* Thanet 62713. [*Died* 24 *Dec.* 1961.

RICHARDS, John Gower Meredith, C.M.G. 1959; Secretary-General, International Superphosphate Manufacturers' Association Ltd., since 1960; *b.* 23 May 1900; *e. s.* of Dr. H. M. Richards and Mrs. Richards (*née* Todd); *m.* 1st, 1927, Nina Wayzer (*d.* 1949); one *d.*; 2nd, 1953, Maud Connell (*née* Hargroves); two *step s.* one *step d.* *Educ.:* Hereford Cathedral School; Jesus College, Oxford (M.A.); Sorbonne (L.-ès-L.). Assistant Master, Sutton Valence School, 1926-27; Assistant Master, Dulwich College, 1927-34; H.M. Inspector of Schools, 1934-1939; Principal, Board of Trade, 1939-43; Assistant Secretary, Board of Trade and Ministry of Materials, 1943-55; Counsellor, U.K. Delegation to O.E.E.C., 1955-60. *Recreations:* travel, gardening, wine tasting. *Address:* The Vineyard, Sparepenny Lane, Farningham, Kent. *T.:* Farningham 2404. *Clubs:* United University, Civil Service. [*Died* 21 *June* 1968.

RICHARDS, Sir Joseph, Kt. 1966; retired Company Director; *b.* 2 May 1888; *m.* 1909 (wife decd.); two *s.* one *d.* *Educ.:* Barnsley. Has spent all his working life with collieries, and coke and bye-products. *Recreations:* Association football (Past Pres. Football League and Vice-Pres. Football Assoc.). *Address:* Highstones, Keresforth Hall Road, Barnsley, Yorkshire. *T.:* Barnsley 3487. [*Died* 24 *May* 1968.

RICHARDS, Maurice John, O.B.E. 1946; M.C.; *b.* 7 May 1894; 3rd *s.* of late W. Richards; *m.* 1917, Mary Anderson McMurtrie; one *s.* two *d.* *Educ.:* Clifton College. Gazetted to R.F.A., 1915; served European War, 1914-18, France and Belgium (wounded twice, M.C.). Solicitor, 1920; Public Trustee Office, 1921-25; Charity Commission, 1925; Assistant Commissioner, 1939-44; Secretary, 1944-58 (O.B.E.). *Recreations:* sea fishing, boats, country life. *Address:* 1033 Oxford Road, Tilehurst, Reading. *Club:* East India and Sports. [*Died* 16 *Sept.* 1969.

RICHARDS, Hon. Mrs. Noel Olivier; *see* Addenda: II.

RICHARDS, Air Commodore William Edward Victor, C.B. 1955; C.B.E. 1944; *b.* 12 Dec. 1897; *s.* of Edward V. Richards, Ruggin Court, West Buckland, Somerset, and Clara, *d.* of Sir Edward Matthew Hodgson, Dublin; *m.* (wife decd.); one *d.* (one *s.* killed in action, 1944); *m.* 1942, Florence Hilda Hinton (*d.* 1963). *Educ.:* Wellington Sch., Somerset. Entered Royal Flying Corps from school (via Somerset Light Infantry), 1916, and thereafter served with R.F.C. and R.A.F. War of 1939-45 (despatches 4 times, C.B.E.). A.O.C. R.A.F. Record Office Group, Gloucester, Sept. 1951-March 1956. *Address:* c/o Glyn, Mills & Co., Kirkland House, Whitehall, S.W.1. *Club:* Royal Air Force. [*Died* 6 *April* 1964.

RICHARDS, Maj.-Gen. William Watson, C.B. 1942; C.B.E. 1941; M.C. 1919; *b.* 14 December 1892; *s.* of Thomas William Watson Richards, St. Helier, Jersey; *m.* 1936, Alice Marie de los Angeles Cecile, *d.* of Eugene Neuville, late Consul-General of France at Gibraltar. *Educ.:* privately. Served European War, 1914-18 (M.C.); employed under Air Ministry, 1924 - 27; specially employed, 1937-39; served War 1939-40, B.E.F., France, 1940-43, M.E.F. (despatches thrice, C.B., C.B.E.); Director, Clothing and Stores, War Office, 1943-46; Maj.-Gen. 1945. Controller of Ordnance Services, War Office, 1946-48; retired, 1948. Colonel Commandant Royal Army Ordnance Corps, 1947-57 (Representative, 1951, 1953, 1955). Commander Legion of Merit, U.S.A.; Czech War Cross, 1939; Czech Medal of Merit, 1st Class. Order of Rising Sun of Japan, 4th Class. *Recreations:* fishing, shooting, golf. *Address:* Braeside, 31 Preston Drove, Brighton, Sussex. *T.:* Brighton 54827. *Club:* Royal Air Force. [*Died* 6 *March* 1961.

RICHARDSON, Sir Albert (Edward), K.C.V.O. 1956; P.P.R.A. (P.R.A. 1954; R.A. 1944; A.R.A. 1936); F.S.A., F.R.I.B.A.; Hon. M.A. (Cantab.); Hon. Litt.D. (Dublin); Hon. R.W.S.; Hon. R.E.; Professor of Architecture, London University (University College), 1919-46, emeritus since 1947; Hon. Fellow St. Catharine's College, Cambridge; Pres., Guild of Surveyors, since 1951; Architect in private practice; *b.* 1880; *m.* Elizabeth (*d.* 1958), *d.* of John Byers, Newry, Co. Down; one *d.* Member of Royal Commission on Historical Monuments; Member of Central Council for the Care of Churches; Member of Diocesan Advisory Cttees. of London, St. Albans, Ely and Southwark. Mem. of Royal Fine Art Commission, 1939 - 56. Royal Gold Medal of R.I.B.A. 1947. President of the Royal Academy, 1954-1956. Grande Oficial da Orden Militar de Sant Tagoda Espada, 1955. *Publications:* various on Architecture. *Recreations:* water colour drawing, travel, and research. *Address:* Avenue House, Ampthill, Beds. *T.:* Ampthill 2172; 29A Wimpole Street, W.1. *T.:* Langham 0502. *Clubs:* Athenæum, Brooks's. [*Died* 3 *Feb.* 1964.

RICHARDSON, Major-General Alexander Whitmore Colquhoun, C.B. 1943; D.S.O. 1917; late Royal Tank Corps; *b.* 11 May 1887; *s.* of James Colquhoun Richardson; *m.* 1914, Agnes Mackay, *d.* of Alexander Thackeray, J.P., of Glan Ely, St. Fagans, Glam.; one *s.* (and one killed in action, 1942) one *d.* *Educ.:* Denstone College, Staffs. Commission in the 4th Bn. West Yorks Regt. 1907; regular Commission, Bedfordshire Regt. 1909; Capt. 1913; served European War, 1915-1918 (D.S.O., Bt. Major); Bt. Lt.-Col. 1927; Lt.-Col. 1930; commanded 4th Bn. Royal Tank Corps, 1930-31; retired pay, 1931; Operating Manager London General Omnibus Company, 1931-36; Chief Welfare Officer, L.P.T.B., 1937; Lt.-Col. 84th A.A. Brigade, 1938; embodied, 1939; general staff, War Office, 1940; Brig., 1941; Major-General, 1942; retired, 1945. *Address:* Crathorne, Southhampton Road, Lymington, Hants. *T.:* Lymington 2052. *Clubs:* Royal Lymington Yacht; Poole Yacht. [*Died* 22 *July* 1964.

RICHARDSON, Cyril Albert, C.B. 1948; M.A.; *b.* 19 September 1891; *s.* of A. E. Richardson, Chatham; *m.* 1916, Alice Marguerite Sharp; one *s.* *Educ.:* Mill Hill School; Sidney Sussex College, Cambridge. Senior Science Master, St. Bees School, 1914; H.M. Inspector of Schools, 1920; Staff Inspector for Training of Teachers, 1936; visited Newfoundland as educational adviser, 1933; Chief Inspector, Ministry of Education, 1945-52; retired, 1952. Member Royal Institute of Philosophy. *Publications:* Spiritual Pluralism, 1919; The Supremacy of Spirit, 1922; Happiness, Freedom and God, 1944; Strategy of Living, 1944; Knowledge, Reality and Life, 1950; The Education of

Teachers in England (U.N.E.S.C.O.), 1953; Introduction to Mental Measurement, 1954; Methods and Experiments in Mental Tests, 1922; The Growth and Variability of Intelligence (Pt. II in Collaboration)—Special Monograph Supplement British Journal of Psychology, 1933; Pluralism (art. Ency. Brit. 1929 ed.); articles in Mind, Philosophical Review, Brit. Journal of Psychology, etc. Author of Simplex and Simplex Junior Group Intelligence Scales. *Recreations:* tennis, bridge, chess. *Address:* Herries, 9 Orchard Lane, West Wimbledon, S.W.20. *T.:* Wimbledon 5511. *Club:* English-Speaking Union [*Died* 9 *April* 1966.

RICHARDSON, E(dward) Ryder, Q.C. 1952; Barrister-at-law; Recorder of Stoke-on-Trent since 1954; *b.* 3 Oct. 1901; *s.* of J. C. Ryder Richardson, M.B., B.Ch., and Mary E. Ryder Richardson; *m.* 1928, Marjorie (Glyn) Hollings; two *s.* *Educ.:* Epsom Coll.; University Coll., London. Called to Bar, Middle Temple, 1926; Master of the Bench, Middle Temple, 1960. Recorder of Walsall, 1946-51. *Recreations:* cooking, gardening, yachting. *Address:* 1 Paper Buildings, Temple, E.C.4 *T.:* Central 0165; 53 Townshend Road, N.W.8. *T.:* Primrose 5324. [*Died* 30 *May* 1961.

RICHARDSON, Rev. Canon Frederick, M.A. Camb.; Prebendary and Canon of Stillington in York Minster, 1933-61, Canon Emeritus, 1961; *b.* Nottingham, 3 April 1885; *s.* of Frederick Grunwell and Rosa Richardson; unmarried. *Educ.:* Nottingham High Sch.; Fitzwilliam House, Cambridge; St. Stephen's House, Oxford. Deacon, 1908; Priest, 1909; Curate of Higham Ferrers, 1908-11; St. Clement's, York, 1911-16; Vicar of Cudworth, 1916-24; Rural Dean of Hemsworth, 1922-24; Assistant Chaplain of Montreux, 1924-26; Vicar 1926-36 and Rural Dean 1928-36 of Easingwold; Rector of Beeford, 1936-43; Vicar of Pocklington with Yapham and Kilnwick Percy, 1943-60; also Vicar of Millington with Great Givendale (in plurality) 1947-60. *Address:* Sharston House, Manor Park, Knutsford, Cheshire. *T.:* Knutsford 4113. [*Died* 4 *Oct.* 1967.

RICHARDSON, Major Guy F.; *see* Richardson, Major T. G. F.

RICHARDSON, Harry, C.B.E. 1956; Principal, Technical College, Bradford, 1920-56; *b.* 25 June 1891; unmarried. *Educ.:* Hulme Hall, Manchester; Manchester Univ.; M.Sc., F.Inst.P., F.C.I.S., Hatfield and Graduate, Scholar and Beyer Fellow, Research Student and Fellow with Prof. Sir E. Rutherford, 1912-15; Demonstrator in Physics, Manchester University, 1914; Registrar, College of Technology, Manchester, 1916; Director of University Studies, College of Technology, Manchester, 1919; Educational Adviser to Indian Students under H.M. India Office, 1915-20; Senior Resident Tutor, Hulme Hall, Manchester, 1919; former Member of the Council for External Students of the University of London; during the war of 1914-18 served as Lt. R.N.V.R. with special mine-sweeping service; former member of Council Bradford Chamber of Commerce; Chm. Assoc. of Principals of Technical Institutions, 1926; Officier d'Académie. *Publications:* (with Professor Sir Ernest Rutherford) several papers upon X-Rays and the radioactive radiations published in the Philosophical Magazine and the Proceedings of the Royal Society. *Recreations:* walking, tennis. *Address:* 65 St. Mary's Terrace, Heaton, Bradford 9. *T.:* Bradford 43309. [*Died* 20 *June* 1966.

RICHARDSON, Major Sir Ian R. H. S.-, Bt.; *see* Stewart-Richardson.

RICHARDSON, John Henry, C.M.G. 1965; M.A. Cambridge, Ph.D. London; President, Government of Aden Industrial Court, 1960-1966; Montague Burton Professor of Industrial Relations, Leeds University, 1930-55; Pro-Vice-Chancellor of the Univ., 1954-55; *b.* Runcorn, Cheshire, 1 July 1890; *o. c.* of late William Henry Richardson and Anne Richardson, Runcorn; *m.* 1925, Emily Moore Hamilton, M.B.E.; two *d.* Emmanuel Coll., Cambridge (Exhibitioner); Wrenbury Scholar, Cambridge University. European War, 1914-1918, Commission in Royal Tank Corps; Research Division, International Labour Office of the League of Nations, Geneva, 1921-30; Assistant Chief of Section, 1929-1930; Technical Adviser to Conferences and Committees of the International Labour Organisation; Visiting Professor of Social Legislation, Columbia University, New York, 1928; Assistant Director, Geneva School of International Studies, 1935-39. Investigations into industrial relations and labour conditions in U.S.A., the U.S.S.R., Australia and New Zealand, 1932-38; member of Trade Boards; Ministry of Labour Manpower Survey, Regional Investigator, 1940; Nuffield Coll. Social Reconstruction Survey, Investigator for West Yorkshire, 1941; Visiting Professor of Economics, Toronto Univ., 1941-42; Economic Adviser, Bermuda Govt., 1942-43, Bahamas, 1943-1944, Gold Coast, 1944-45; Delegate for Bahamas at Anglo-American Caribbean Conference, Barbados, 1944; Chairman Board of Enquiry into wage dispute in Antigua Sugar Industry, Leeward Islands, 1944; Impartial investigator into political, economic and social conditions for Joint Cttee. of Bermuda Legislature, 1947-48; adviser on Social Security to Govt. of Venezuela, 1948-49; Bermuda Govt., 1950; Govt. of British Guiana, 1954, Govt. of Barbados, 1954; adviser on wages to Govt. of Burma under U.N. Technical Assistance Prog., 1953 and 1956; Chm. Arbitration Tribunal, Nigerian tin mining industry wage dispute, 1954; I.L.O. Consultant on freedom of association, 1955; Mem. Colonial Labour Advisory Cttee., 1949-55; Visiting Prof. of Economics, Univ. of Calif., 1955-56; Cassidy Research Visiting Prof., Toronto Univ., 1956-1957; Visiting Prof., School of Industrial and Labor Relations, Cornell University, 1957-58; Economic Consultant, U.N., N.Y., 1958. Mem. Council, Royal Statistical Soc., 1949-53; U.N. Technical Assistance Adviser (I.L.O.) to Govts. of India, 1958, Pakistan, 1959-61; Director of I.L.O. Training Courses in Labour Administration for Ethiopia and other East African countries, 1962-64; Vis. Prof. of Labour Economics, M.E. Technical University in Ankara (O.E.C.D.), 1964-65. Hon. Member British Universities' Industrial Relations Association. *Publications:* A Study on the Minimum Wage, 1927; Economic Disarmament, 1931; Business Forecasting, 1931; Industrial Relations in Great Britain, 1933, revised edition, 1938; British Economic Foreign Policy, 1936; Industrial Employment and Unemployment in West Yorkshire, 1936; An Introduction to the Study of Industrial Relations, 1954; Economic and Financial Aspects of Social Security, 1960. *Address:* 2 Claremont Road, Mont Millais, Jersey, C.I. *Club:* Royal Commonwealth Society. [*Died* 8 *June* 1970.

RICHARDSON, Very Rev. John Macdonald; *b.* 10 April 1880; *s.* of James and Elizabeth Richardson; *m.* 1st, 1912, Florence L. Christie; 2nd, 1920, Muriel Jean Mapple; one *s.* three *d.* *Educ.:* Stirling High School; Glasgow University, M.A., B.D.; Marburg University. Minister Freuchie, Fifeshire; Dunfermline, Fifeshire; St. Andrew's, Waterloo, Liverpool; Trinity Church, Bath; War Chaplain to Scottish Horse, 2nd Bn. Scots Guards; Moderator of Presbyterian

Church of England, 1939; President Liverpool Free Church Centre 1939-40; President Free Church Council Bath, 1945-46, President Bath Council of Christian Churches, 1946-47; Moderator of Nat. Free Church Federal Council, 1947-48. *Recreations:* golf, curling. *Address:* Perrymead Lodge, Bath. [*Died* 7 *May* 1964.

RICHARDSON, Philip John Sampey, O.B.E. 1951; Knight of Royal Order of Dannebrog (R.D.), 1951; Editor of The Dancing Times, 1910-57; Vice-President and first Hon. Fellow (1962) of the Royal Academy of Dancing; Director, Royal General Theatrical Fund; President, Official Board of Ballroom Dancing (which he founded, 1929); President, International Council of Ballroom Dancing; *b.* Winthorpe, Notts, 1875; *m.* 1909, Edith Aldersey (*d.* 1953), *d.* of John Brough Hallam; no *c.* *Educ.:* Beaumont Coll.; University Coll. School. Founded Dancing Times, 1910; was largely instrumental in the founding in 1920 of Association of Operatic Dancing of Gt. Britain (now Royal Acad. of Dancing); instrumental with A. L. Haskell, 1929-30, in founding Camargo Society for the production of ballet before a subscription audience; organised ten Sunshine Matinees in aid of the Blind Babies; acted as Adjudicator at innumerable Dance Competitions—both stage and ballroom. *Publications:* The Art of the Ballroom (with Victor Silvester), 1936; History of English Ballroom Dancing, 1910-1945, 1946; Social Dances of the Nineteenth Century, 1960; many articles on dancing to general press. *Address:* 12 Henrietta Street, Covent Garden, W.C.2. *T.:* Temple Bar 7854. *Clubs:* Garrick, Aldwych.
[*Died* 17 *Feb.* 1963.

RICHARDSON, Rev. Raymond William, C.B. 1965; *b.* 16 Oct. 1909; *s.* of late Rev. Canon W. A. Richardson; *m.* 1939, Jocelyn Carroll; three *s.* *Educ.:* Dragon Sch. and Magdalen Coll. Sch., Oxf.; Trinity Coll., Dublin. B.A. 1934; M.A. 1943. Deacon 1935, Priest 1936, Dio. of Ossory; Curate of Ardamine 1935, Queenstown 1937. H.M.S.: Victory, 1939; Resolution, 1939; Osprey, 1941; Swiftsure, 1944; Heron, 1946; Gannet, 1949; Ocean, 1951; Condor, 1953; Peregrine, 1955; Victorious, 1958; Vernon, 1960. H.M. Dockyard, Portsmouth, 1961. Hon. Chaplain to the Queen, 1963-66; Chaplain of the Fleet and Archdeacon of the Royal Navy, 1963-66. Home Secretary, Jerusalem and the East Mission, 1966-. *Recreations:* yachting, fishing. *Address:* 76 Dora Road, Wimbledon, S.W.19. *Clubs:* United Service; Royal Naval (Portsmouth).
[*Died* 11 *Aug.* 1968.

RICHARDSON, Major (Thomas) Guy (Fenton), C.C.; *b.* 18 October 1885; *s.* of Thomas Fenton Richardson; *m.* 1947, Gladys Lewis (*née* Edisbury); no *c.* *Educ.:* Old Quintinian. Underwriting Member of Lloyd's, 1938; Life Governor Royal United Kingdom Beneficent Association; Sheriff City of London, 1948-49 (Under Sheriff, 1945-48); Life Governor of Sheriffs Fund Society; Deputy Alderman and H.M. Lieut., City of London. Freeman of City of London; Member Court of Assistants of Worshipful Co. of Wheelwrights, 1927 (Master, 1952-53); Member of Guild of Freemen. Private in The Artists' Regt.; gazetted Queen's Royal West Surrey 2/22nd Bn. London Regt.; served European War; France, 1915; Salonika, 1917; Palestine, 1917-19; General Staff G.H.Q. 3rd Echelon E.E.F., 1917-19; Major, retired, 1936. Home Guard, 1940-44. *Recreations:* golf, shooting. *Address:* Denewood, The Grove, Epsom, Surrey. *T.:* 23587. *Clubs:* United Service; Royal Automobile, United Wards.
[*Died* 11 *July* 1966.

RICHARDSON, Major-General Thomas William, O.B.E. 1919; *b.* 24 February 1895; *y.* and *o. surv. s.* of late T. W. Richardson, M.R.C.S., Norwich, and of Rose Louise, *d.* of Maj.-Gen. A. T. Etheridge, C.S.I.; *m.* 1st, 1921, Josephine Mary Wickham Herbert Clarke (whom he divorced, 1932); one *s.* one *d.*; 2nd, 1933, Elizabeth Evelyn Langworthy (*d.* 1958); one *s.*; 3rd, 1959, Doris Edith (Peggy) Cooper. *Educ.:* King Edward VI's School, Norwich. Royal Military College, Sandhurst, 1912-13; 2nd Lieut. A.S.C., 1914; Temp. Capt. 1915; Actg. Major, 1918, 1920, 1922; Bt. Major, 1931; Major, 1935; Bt. Lt.-Col. 1936; Lt.-Col. 1940; Col. 1940; Brig. 1941; Maj.-Gen. (temp.) 1943; Maj.-Gen. (retired) 1946. Adjutant, A.S.C., 3rd Division, France, 1915, and commanded 37th Division M.T. Company, France, 1916-1918 (O.B.E., despatches twice); Middle East, 1919-24; Instructor, R.A.S.C. Training Centre, 1925-28; Adjutant, R.A.S.C. Rhine Army, 1929; Adjutant, R.A.S.C., Catterick, 1930-33; D.A.D.S. & T. War Office, 1933-1937; A.D.S. & T. Hong-Kong, China Command, 1937-39; formed and commanded No. 2 Mobilisation Centre, 1940 (Col.); D.D.S.T. (Supplies), War Office, 1941-43 (Brig.). Inspector R.A.S.C., 1943-1946 (Maj.-Gen.); travelled widely, 1943-44, inspecting and reporting to Q.M.G. on Supplies and Transport Services. Assisted in planning N. Africa and Normandy landings. Hon. Col., 110 Transport Column R.A.S.C. (T.A.), 1948-53; Regional Food Officer, Midland Region, 1947-53. U.S. Legion of Merit, degree of Commander, 1945. *Address:* Eaton Cottage, 462 Unthank Rd., Norwich (NOR 32E). *T.:* Norwich 52503
[*Died* 6 *March* 1968.

RICHARDSON, Violet Roberta S.; *see* Stewart-Richardson.

RICHEY, James Ernest, M.C., F.R.S. 1938; F.S.E. 1952, A.I.C.E. 1965; B.A., B.A.I., Sc.D.; Lecturer in Geology, Univ. of Dundee (formerly St. Andrews), and Cons. Geologist, 1946; *b.* 1886; *s.* of Rev. John Richey, Rector, Desertcreat, County Tyrone; *m.* 1924, Henrietta Lily McNally; three *d.* *Educ.:* St. Columba's; Trinity College, Dublin (Senior Moderator and large gold medallist). Demonstrator, Oxford Univ., 1910; H.M. Geological Survey, Scotland, 1911-46; commission Royal Engineers, 1914, retired as Capt. 1919. *Publications:* Elements of Engineering Geology, 1964; part author of various memoirs of Geological Survey, Scotland, Communications to Scientific Societies. *Address:* The Coach House, Grange, Monifieth, Angus. *T.:* Monifieth 2611.
[*Died* 19 *June* 1968.

RICHMOND, Sir Arthur (Cyril), Kt. *cr.* 1955; C.B.E. 1946; *b.* 27 January 1879; 5th *s.* of Sir W. B. Richmond, K.C.B., R.A., and his wife Clara (*née* Richards); *m.* 1st, 1907, Theodora Anna van Riemsdyk; 2nd, 1941, Margaretta Josephine Hamilton Williams. *Educ.:* Repton; France, Germany and Italy. Transvaal Civil Service, 1902-1905; Board of Education, Private Secretary to Sir Robert Morant, K.C.B., 1905-1907; Deputy Director, Victoria and Albert Museum, 1907-10; after long illness, Assistant Director, Kent Education Cttee., 1919-1926; Dep. Secretary Nat. Council of Social Service, 1926-35; Vice-Chm. Land Settlement Assoc., 1935, Controller, 1940-50; Chm., 1948-58, retd.; Chm. of Agricultural Co-operatives of Gt. Brit. and Ire., 1951-57; member Royal Fine Art Commission, 1949-1961; Chairman of the Horace Plunkett Foundation, 1954-62. *Publications:* Twenty-Six Years (Autobiography) 1961; Another Sixty Years, 1965. Translations from Marcel Prévost and Louis Hémon and from Italian and Dutch publications; articles in Nineteenth Century and other Journals. *Recreations:* water-colour painting; the study of foreign languages and gardening. *Address:* 49 Paultons Square, Chelsea, S.W.3. *T.:* Flaxman 2467. *Clubs:* Athenæum, Chelsea Arts. [*Died* 6 *Nov.* 1968.

RICHMOND, Brigadier Arthur Eaton, C.B.E. 1945; M.R.C.S., L.R.C.P., D.P.H., D.T.M.; *b.* 28 February 1892; *s.* of late Richard Richmond, M.D., and Ellen Bush; *m.* 1916, Margaret Mary, *d.* of William Kelly, Tuam, Galway, Ireland; one *s. Educ.:* Oundle School; St. Thomas's Hospital, London. Commissioned R.A.M.C. 1915. Service in Egypt and Palestine, 1915-18; Khajuri Operations, N.W.F.P. India, 1931; Mohmand Operations, N.W.F.P. 1933; Service in U.K. and Middle East, War of 1939-45; Director of Army Health, War Office. 1945-49; K.H.S. 1946-49; retired pay, 1950. Temp. Medical Officer, Ministry of Health, 1950-59. *Recreation:* golf. *Address:* c/o Glyn, Mills, Kirkland Hse., Whitehall, S.W.1. [*Died* 9 *Jan.* 1961.

RICHMOND, Sir Bruce Lyttelton, Kt., *cr.* 1935; Hon. D. Litt. (Oxon) 1930; Hon. Litt.D. (Leeds) 1922; Journalist; *s.* of late Douglas Close Richmond; *m.* Elena, *d.* of late William G. Rathbone. *Educ.:* Winchester (scholar); New College, Oxford (scholar). Called to the Bar (Inner Temple) 1897; editorial staff of The Times, 1899-1938. *Address:* The Old Rectory, Islip, Oxford. *Club:* Oxf. and Camb. [*Died* 1 *Oct.* 1964.

RICHMOND, Sir Ian, Kt. 1964; C.B.E. 1958; F.B.A. 1947; F.S.A. (Scot.); M.A.; President, Society of Antiquaries; Professor of the Archæology of the Roman Empire, Oxford University, since October 1956; *b.* 1902; *twin s.* of late Daniel Richmond, O.B.E., J.P., M.D., F.R.C.S.E., and Helen Harper; *m.* 1938, Isabel, *e. d.* of late J. A. Little; one *s.* one *d. Educ.:* Ruthin School, N. Wales; Corpus Christi College, Oxford; held the Gilchrist Studentship of the British School at Rome and the Craven Fellowship and the Goldsmiths' Senior Studentship of the University of Oxford. Lecturer in Classical Archæology and Ancient History at the Queen's University of Belfast, 1926-30; Director of the British School at Rome, 1930-32; Lecturer 1935-43, Reader 1943-50, Univ. of Durham, at King's College, Newcastle upon Tyne; Professor in Roman-British History and Archæology, University of Durham, at King's College, Newcastle upon Tyne, 1950-Oct. 1956. Rhind Lecturer, 1933; Dalrymple Lecturer, Univ. of Glasgow, 1938 and 1956; Riddell Memorial Lecturer, Univ. of Durham, 1948; Ford's Lecturer in English History, Oxford, 1950-51; J. H. Gray Lecturer, Cambridge, 1951-52; Cadbury Lecturer, Univ. of Birmingham, 1952-53. Royal Comm. for Historical Monuments (England) since 1944 and (Scotland) since 1944. Member, Ancient Monuments Board for England, since 1959. Pres. Soc. for the Promotion of Roman Studies, 1958-61. Public Orator, Durham University, 1949-51. Corr. Fell. German Archæolog. Institute. Hon. Fellow, Corpus Christi Coll., Oxford, 1965. Hon. LL.D. Edin., 1946; Hon. Litt.D. Leeds, 1956; Hon. D.Lit. Belfast, 1956; Hon. D.Litt. Manchester, 1960; Hon. Litt.D.: Cantab., 1964; Newcastle upon Tyne, 1965. *Publications:* City Wall of Imperial Rome, 1930; Editor of T. Ashby's The Aqueducts of Ancient Rome; Roman Britain, 1948. *Address:* All Souls College, Oxford. [*Died* 5 *Oct.* 1965.

RICHMOND, Sir John Ritchie, K.B.E., *cr.* 1939 (C.B.E. 1918); LL.D. 1945; retired 1954; *b.* 1869; *m.* 1893; *m.* 1949. *Educ.:* Glasgow High School and University. President N.W. Engineering Employers Assoc., 1903, 1917-18; Hon. Pres. Glasgow School of Art; Chairman Scottish Architectural Advisory Cttee., 1935. Served on Advisory Cttee. of Board of Trade. *Address:* Blanefield, Kirkoswald, Ayrshire. *Clubs:* Automobile, Conservative, Art (Glasgow). [*Died* 25 *Feb.* 1963.

RICHMOND, Lawrence, C.B.E. 1942 (O.B.E. 1927); Ex-Chm. West Riding of Yorks. Exec. Council under Nat. Health Service Act (1946-62); *b.* Sheffield, 6 Nov. 1885; *s.* of Edwin Richmond, J.P., Incorporated Accountant; *m.* 1911, Alice Mary Beard; one *s.* one *d. Educ.:* Sheffield Royal Gram. Sch. Assistant Clerk to Guardians, Ecclesall Bierlow Union, 1902-10; Deputy Clerk to Guardians, (former) Sheffield Union, 1910-1925; Clerk to Guardians (amalgamated) Sheffield Union, 1925-30; Clerk to Sheffield Union Assessment Committee, 1925-27; Clerk to Sheffield County Borough Assessment Committee, 1927-30; Clerk to Norton R.D.C., 1926-30; County Welfare Officer and Blind Persons Officer, County of West Riding of Yorkshire, 1930-45; Clerk to Yorkshire Casual Poor Assistance Committee, 1934-48. Former Chairman of Wakefield "A" Hospital Management Committee. *Publication:* Local Authorities and the Welfare of the Blind, 1938. *Address:* Fieldside, 9 Gagewell Lane, Horbury, Nr. Wakefield. [*Died* 20 *April* 1968.

RICHMOND, Leonard, R.B.A. 1914; R.O.I. 1918; painter (landscape and figure). *Educ.:* Taunton. Student at the Taunton School of Art, and the Chelsea Polytechnic, London; commissioned by the Canadian Govt. to go to the Front in France, dating from March 1918, to make sketches and gather materials for the purpose of executing a large war picture, entitled Canadian Soldiers Constructing Railways at the Front; awarded a bronze medal in the International Section at the Panama-Pacific Exhibition held in San Francisco, 1915, for a pastel picture; awarded the William H. Tuthill purchase prize in the Chicago International Water-Colour Exhibition, 1928; awarded the Tattersall Cup for the best Railway Poster of the year 1937 in Great Britain; awarded Silver Medal at Paris Salon for oil painting of St. Ives Harbour, Cornwall, 1947. Gave series of lectures on Art at well-known Universities and Art Galleries from Montreal to Vancouver, B.C., 1925-26; similar series New York to Chicago, Ill., 1928-29. Apptd. Editor, The Artist (magazine), 1952. Annual visits to U.S.A., giving radio talks, television and pictorial demonstrations, 1950-. *Publications:* The Art of Landscape Painting; The Technique of Oil Painting; Studies in water colour; The Technique of the Poster; Essentials of Pictorial Design; The Technique of Still Life Painting in Oil Colours; Landscape Composition in Colour; also Co-Author of The Technique of Water-Colour Painting and The Art of Pastel Painting. *Recreation:* general literature. *Clubs:* Chelsea Arts; Salmagundi, National Arts (New York). [*Died May* 1965.

RICHMOND, Col. Wilfrid Stanley, C.M.G. 1918; M.Inst.C.E.; *b.* 1881; *s.* of late John Richmond, Harpenden, Herts; *m.* 1909, Viola, *d.* of late John Allen, Brondesbury, London; one *s. Educ.:* Bedford Modern School. Served European War, 1914-18 (despatches twice, C.M.G., Officer Legion of Honour). Divisional Road Engineer. Min. of Transport, 1921-45. *Address:* 77 Platts Lane, Hampstead, N.W.3. *T.:* Hampstead 7466. [*Died* 28 *Jan.* 1962.

RICKARD, Charles Ernest, O.B.E. 1919; Engineer; retired 1949; *b.* London, 31 May 1880. *Educ.:* Univ. Coll., London. Joined The Wireless Telegraph and Signal Company, Limited (now Marconi's Wireless Telegraph Company, Ltd.), as Electrical Assistant to Marchese Marconi, 1898; was successively Engineer-in-Charge, Inspector-General of Wireless Telegraphy, and Technical Adviser to the Chilian Navy, 1906-18; assistant to Chief Engineer of Marconi's Wireless Telegraph Co. Ltd., London, 1919; Assistant General Manager, 1923; Deputy Engineer-in-Chief, 1927; Engineer-in-Chief, 1932; Technical General Manager, 1935; Dep. Managing Director, 1937; General Manager, 1941-46; Hon. Consultant Marconi Instruments Ltd.; retd., 1949; has undertaken numerous missions abroad as consulting engineer and has served as a member of British Govt. Committees dealing with wireless telegraph regulations; represented the Marconi Companies at the International Radio Telegraph Conferences at Washington, 1927, and Madrid, 1932, the European Broadcasting Conference, Prague, 1929, the International Technical Consultative Committee for Radioelectric Communications at the Hague, 1929, Copenhagen, 1931, and Lisbon, 1934; delegate to the International Television Conference at Nice, 1935; M.I.E.E.; Chairman ot Wireless Section I.E.E., 1930-31; M.I.Mech.E.; Fellow of Physical Society. *Recreation:* gardening. *Address:* Windrush, Salisbury Rd., Seaford, Sussex.

[*Died* 11 *May* 1961.

RICKARD, Mrs. Victor (Jessie Louisa); novelist; *b.* Dublin; *d.* of late Canon Courtenay Moore, Rector of Mitchelstown, Co. Cork, and late Jessie Mona Duff; *m.* 1st, Robert Dudley Innes Ackland, of Boulston Manor, Pembrokeshire; one *d.*; 2nd, Lt.-Col. Victor G. H. Rickard, Royal Munster Fusiliers (killed in action, May 1915); one *s.* *Publications:* Young Mr. Gibbs, 1912; Dregs, 1914; The Story of the Munsters, 1915; The Light Above the Crossroads, 1916; The Frantic Boast; The Fire of Green Boughs, 1917; The House of Courage, 1918; Cathy Rossiter, 1919; A Reckless Puritan, 1920; A Fool's Errand, 1921; Blindfold, 1922; Without Justification, 1923; Old Sins have Long Shadows, 1924; Upstairs, 1925; Not Sufficient Evidence, 1926; The Light that Lies; A Bird of Strange Plumage, 1927; The Guests of Chance; The Perilous Elopement, 1928; The Scarlet Sin; The Mystery of Vincent Dane, 1929; The Empty Villa; The Dark Stranger, 1930; Yesterday's Love; Young Mrs. Henniker, 1931; Spring Hill, 1932; Sorel's Second Husband, 1932; The Young Man in Question, 1933; Sensation at Blue Harbour, 1934; House Party, 1935; Cuckoo Street, 1937; Murder by Night, 1938; The Mystery of Tara Heston, 1939; The Guilty Party, 1940; Ascendancy House, 1944; White Satin, 1945; Shandon Hall, 1950. *Address:* c/o A. P. Watt and Son, 10 Norfolk Street, W.C.2.

[*Died* 28 *Jan.* 1963.

RICKETSON, Staniforth, D.C.M.; Member of Stock Exchange of Melbourne since 1914; Senior Partner of J. B. Were & Son, Stock and Share Brokers, Underwriters and Distributors of Securities Melb., Sydney, Brisb., Adelaide, Perth; Chm. Austr. Foundn. Investment Co. Ltd., Nat. Reliance Investment Co. Ltd., Capel Court Investment Co. (Australia) Ltd., Jason Investment Co. (Australia) Ltd., Sherbourne Investments Ltd., Brenton Investments (Australia) Ltd., Clonmore Investments (Australia) Ltd., Haliburton Investments (Australia) Ltd., Jonathan Investments Ltd., Capel Court Underwriting and Development Ltd., Bonville Underwriting and Development Ltd.; Capel Court Securities Ltd.; *b.* Malvern, Melbourne, 1 Aug. 1891; 2nd *s.* of late Henry Joseph Ricketson and Sophia Henrietta Sheppard, Barratta, Deniliquin, N.S.W.; *m.* 1st, 1916; three *s.* two *d.* (and one *s.* decd.); 2nd, 1946, Edna, *d.* of late George S. Holmes, Melbourne; one *s.* one *d.* *Educ.:* Prahran State School; Wesley Coll. (Government Scholar, Corrigan Entrance Scholar). With Australian Mercantile Land and Finance Company Limited, 1908; Journalist in Tasmania, 1910-11; joined J. B. Were & Son, 1911, partner, 1914; served European War; enlisted A.I.F. 17 Aug. 1914 and served mainly with 5th Bn. till end of War; Gallipoli Landing, 1915 (D.C.M., promoted Second Lieutenant, wounded thrice, despatches); Captain, 1916; Adjutant 65th Battalion Sixth Division, 1917; rejoined 5th Battalion, 1917, as Adjutant and Company Commander on Western Front till end of War. *Recreation:* walking. *Address:* Mornington, Adeney Avenue, Kew E.4, Victoria, Australia Toolebewang Farm, Launching Place, Victoria; Australia. *Clubs:* Melbourne (Melbourne); Australian, Australasian Pioneers (Sydney).

[*Died* 6 *Dec.* 1967.

RICKETT, Harold Robert Norman, C.B.E. 1966; T.D.; President, Amateur Rowing Association, since 1968; Member of the London Stock Exchange and Partner in R. Nivison & Co. since 1935; *b.* 20 July 1909; *e. s.* of late A. N. Rickett, Reigate, Surrey; *m.* 1934, Dorothy, *o. c.* of late E. O. Barry, Lower Kingswood, Surrey; one *s.* one *d.* *Educ.:* Eton; Trinity College, Cambridge. Hons. Nat. Sciences Pt. I, Law Pt. II; B.A. 1931, M.A. 1936. At Cambridge: rowed Head of the River 1929, won Fours 1929 and 1930, Pairs 1930; rowed for Cambridge in Universities' Boat Race 1930, 1931, and 1932 (Pres.). Rowed in British Olympic Eight, Los Angeles, 1932. Served War of 1939-45 in Queen's Royal Regt.; France, 1940 (despatches); Adjt. 2/5th Bn., 1940-42; G2, War Office, 1943-44; G2 Instructor, Staff College, 1944-45 Steward of Henley Royal Regatta, 1935- and Chm., Cttee. of Management, 1951-65. Coached several Cambridge crews for Boat Race and Olympic eights of 1948 and 1952. President: Eton Mission Rowing Club, 1949-; Thames Punting Club, 1959-; Eton Vikings Club, 1961-66 and 1967-; Leander Club, 1967-. Chairman, Council for Youth Rowing, 1965-. Member, Technical Commission of Fédération Internationale des Sociétés d'Aviron, 1968-. *Publication:* (with R. D. Burnell) A Short History of Leander Club, 1968. *Recreations:* rowing, delphiniums. *Address:* Ford's Farm, Pirbright, Surrey. *T.:* Brookwood 3272. *Club:* Bath.

[*Died* 31 *Jan.* 1969.

RICKETTS, Major Arthur, C.M.G. 1901; M.D. (Lond.), M.R.C.S.; *b.* 7 Aug. 1874 *s.* of late W. T. Ricketts of Burchetts, Chailey, Sussex; *m.* 1917, Betty (*d.* 1953), *widow* of E. A. Salaman. *Educ.:* Dulwich Coll.; U.C. London. Ho. Phys., U.C.H.; then Civil Surg. (1900-01) and Surg. Captain Irish Horse, South African Field Force, 1902; Major, R.A.M.C. (T.), 1918. Fellow, B.M.A., 1961. *Address:* 122 Holden Road, North Finchley, N.12. *T.:* Hillside 5888. [*Died* 14 *May* 1968.

RICKETTS, Rt. Rev. Clement Mallory; *b.* 19 August 1885; *s.* of late Rev. R. E. Ricketts, previously Vicar of Crambe-with-Whitwell-on-the-Hill, Yorks, and Mabel Rose, *d.* of late Major Arthur Wellesley Williams; *m.* 1920, Dorothy Frances, 2nd *d.* of late Rt. Rev. G. R. Eden; two *s.* one *d.* *Educ.:* King's School, Canterbury; Keble College, Oxford; Cuddesdon College, Oxford. 2nd Class in Honour School of Theology at Oxford; Deacon, 1910; Priest, 1911; Curate of S. Martin's, Salisbury, 1910-12; Chaplain of Bishops' College, Cheshunt, 1912-14; Vicar of S. Michael and All Angels', Colombo, Ceylon, 1914-23; Commissary to Bishop of Colombo, 1923-36; Domestic and Diocesan Chaplain to the Bishop of Wakefield, 1923-1924; Vicar of Holy Trinity, Weymouth, 1924-37; Rural Dean of Weymouth, 1936-1937; Canon Residentiary and Missioner of Gloucester, 1937-45; Bishop Suffragan of Dunwich, 1945-Oct. 1954. Rector of Dennington and Badingham, 1945-Oct. 1954; Examining Chaplain to the Bishops of Gloucester and St. Edmundsbury and Ipswich; Commissary to Bishop of Kimberley and Kuruman, 1943-51. *Address:* Madehurst Vicarage, Arundel, Sussex. *T.:* Slindon 291. [*Died* 28 *Feb.* 1961.

RICKETTS, Gordon Randolph, M.A., Secretary, Royal Institute of British Architects, since 1959; *b.* 27 Oct. 1918; *s.* of Major F. J. Ricketts, late Director of Music, Royal Marines, and Mrs. A. L. Ricketts; *m.* 1947, Lesley, *d.* of Col. A. C. T. White, V.C., M.C.; two *s.* one *d.* *Educ.:* St. Lawrence Coll.; Keble Coll., Oxford. R.A.F. (pilot), 1941-46. Regional Secretary, Federation of British Industries, at Cambridge, 1948-1949; Personal Assistant to Sir Norman Kipping, Director-General, F.B.I., 1949-1951; Appointments Secretary, University of Nottingham, 1951-56; Secretary for Professional Relations, Royal Institute of British Architects, 1957-59. *Recreations:* music, gardening, tennis, squash. *Address:* Windrush, Bulstrode Way, Gerrards Cross, Bucks. *T.:* Gerrards Cross 3121. *Club:* Athenæum. [*Died* 5 *Jan.* 1968.

RICKMERS, W. Rickmer, Hon. Ph.D.; F.R.G.S.; Explorer and Writer; Leader of Expeditions; *b.* 1 May 1873; *s.* of W. Rickmers and Alice Hellbardt; *g.s.* of R. C. Rickmers, Heligoland, K.C.M.G.; *m.* 1897, Christian Mabel, *g.d.* of Dr. Alexander Duff. *Educ.:* Bremen; London; Vienna Univ. Since 1894 explored the glacier ranges of the Caucasus and the Pamirs (Russian Turkestan, Bukhara), mostly with his wife; led large expeditions in 1903, 1906, 1913 and notably 1928 (German-Russian Pamirs Expedition); Pioneer of Continental ski-ing; a Vice-Pres., Brit. Mountaineering Assoc.; served in the war as army interpreter and member of the German Caucasus Delegation; Gold medallist R.G.S.; works for friendly relations between Britain and Germany. *Publications:* The Duab of Turkestan, 1913; Ski-ing, 1910; Alai! Alai!, 1930; Scientific Results (Co-editor), 1932, 6 vols.; Die Wallfahrt zum Wahren Jakob, 1926; The Alai-Pamirs, Geogr. Journal, 1929; Lazistan and Ajaristan, G.J. Dec. 1934; Many contributions to geographical and climbing journals; Translated many English books on travel and mountaineering. *Recreations:* climbing, ski-ing, organisation, philosophy. *Address:* 5 Unertl Strasse, Munich, Bavaria, Germany. *Clubs:* Ski of Great Britain; (Hon.) Alpine; (Hon.) Appalachian Mountain; (Hon.) British Mountaineering Assoc. (Vice-Pres.). [*Died* 15 *June* 1965.

RIDDELL, Walter Alexander, M.A., B.D., Ph.D., LL.D.; late Prof. of International Relations, Univ. of Toronto; former Canadian High Commissioner in New Zealand; *b.* Stratford, Canada, 5 Aug. 1881; *s.* of George Bradshaw Riddell and Georgina Cawston; *m.* 1916, Mary Gordon, *d.* of late J. Murray Clark, K.C.; one *s.* three *d.* *Educ.:* Manitoba College; University of Manitoba, B.A., 1907; Columbia University, M.A., 1908; Ph.D., 1916; Union Theological Seminary, B.D., 1912; Post-graduate research in Archives at Ottawa, Paris and London. Director of Social Surveys for the Presbyterian and Methodist Churches, 1913; Superintendent of Trades and Labour, Ontario Government, 1916; Dep. Minister of Labour, 1919; Chief of Section, International Labour Office, League of Nations, 1920-25; Canadian Advisory Officer, League of Nations, 1925-37; Counsellor, Canadian Legation, Washington, 1937-40. Member of Canadian Delegations to Assembly of League of Nations and to International Labour Conference, 1925-37 and 1949; Member of Governing Body of International Labour Office and Chairman of Governing Body, 1935-36; Delegate Plenipotentiary, Conference for Limitation of Naval Armament, Second Opium Conference, Arms Control Conference; International Conference on Economic Statistics; Diplomatic Conference for the Revision of the Geneva Red Cross Convention, 1929, and the Preparation of a Code for Prisoners of War; Delegate Second Passports Conf., Third Conf. of Labour Statisticians, Economic Conf., Conf. for Abolition of Import and Export Prohibitions and Restrictions; Preparatory Conf. for Second Wheat Conf. (Rome), Conf. of wheat-exporting countries (London), Conf. on Limitation of Manufacture of Narcotic Drugs; 4th Communications and Transit Conf.; Member of Canadian Deleg. to Disarmament Conf.; Mem. Co-ordination Cttee. on the Italo-Ethiopian Dispute; substitute rep. of Governing Body of I.L.O. to Monetary and Economic Conf.; represented it at Regional Labour Conf., Santiago-de-Chile, 1936; Canadian Govt. at 2nd Regional Labour Conf., Havana, 1939. *Publications:* The Rise of Ecclesiastical Control in Quebec; World Security by Conference; Canadian Foreign Policy, 1917-40; The Making of the Commonwealth. *Recreations:* golf, motoring. *Address:* 76 Douglas Drive, Toronto, Canada. [*Died* 27 *July* 1963.

RIDDICK, Col. John Galloway, C.B.E. 1925; D.S.O. 1919; D.L., J.P. Cheshire; *b.* 1879; *s.* of R. F. Riddick, J.P. of Ashley, near Altrincham; *m.* Margery, *d.* of Theodore Bower, Farnborough, Kent; three *s.* *Educ.:* Rugby. Served European War, 1914-19 (despatches, D.S.O., Chevalier Legion of Honour); commanded R.E., 42nd (E. Lancashire) Div. (T.A.), 1918-25. *Address:* Hanson House, Mobberley, Cheshire. *T.:* Mobberley 2132. [*Died* 4 *Aug.* 1964.

RIDDOCH, John William, M.C.; M.B.Ch.B. (Ed.), F.R.C.S. (Ed.); Surgeon, Solihull Hospital, Warwicks., 1949-60, retd.; *b.* Edinburgh, 3 March 1893; *s.* of late John Riddoch, M.R.C.V.S., and late Elizabeth Hart; *m.* 1931, Norah Hutchin; one *s.* two *d.* *Educ.:* George Watson's College and University, Edinburgh. Graduated 1915; served R.A.M.C. 1915-1920, Egypt, Salonica, France; House Physician and House Surgeon, Cumberland Infirmary, Carlisle, 1920-21; Senior House Surgeon Rochdale Infirmary, 1921-22; Resident Surgical Officer, Ministry of Pensions Hospital, Craigleith, Edinburgh, 1923-25; Senior Resident Medical Officer, Highbury Hospital, Birmingham, 1925-1927. Surgeon: Midland Hospital, Birmingham, 1926-49; Corbett Hospital, Stourbridge, 1939-58. *Publications:* articles in medical jls. *Recreations:* golf, fishing. *Address:* 7 Chad Road, Edgbaston, Birmingham 15. *T.:* Edgbaston 3375. [*Died* 31 *Dec.* 1969.

RIDLEY, 3rd Viscount (*cr.* 1900), **Matthew White Ridley,** C.B.E. 1938; T.D.; 4th Baron Wensleydale, *cr.* 1900; Bt. *cr.* 1756; Hon. Col., Northumberland Hussars, T.A., since 1962; Chairman Northumberland County Council, 1940-46 and 1949-52; J.P.; Vice-Lieutenant since 1939; Regional Controller for the North, Ministry of Production, 1942-49; *b.* 16 Dec. 1902; *e. s.* of 2nd Viscount Ridley and Hon. Rosamond Guest, D.B.E. (*d.* 1947), *y. d.* of 1st Baron Wimborne; *S.* father, 1916; *m.* 1924, Ursula, O.B.E. 1953, 2nd *d.* of late Sir Edwin Lutyens, O.M., K.C.I.E., R.A.; two *s.* *Educ.:* Eton. Director of Producer-Gas Vehicles, Ministry of Transport, 1942. Owns about 10,200 acres. Hon. D.C.L. (Durham). *Heir:* *s.* Hon. Matthew White Ridley, 2nd Lt. Coldstream Guards [*b.* 29 July 1925; *m.* 1953, Lady Anne Lumley, 3rd *d.* of 11th Earl of Scarbrough, K.G., G.C.S.I., G.C.I.E., G.C.V.O.; one *s.* three *d.*]. *Address:* Blagdon, Seaton Burn, Northumberland. *T.:* Stannington 236; 11 Binney St., W.1. *T.:* Mayfair 4372. *Club:* Turf. [*Died* 25 *Feb.* 1964.

RIDLEY, Maurice Roy, M.A. Oxon; Hon. L.H.D. Bowdoin College, U.S.A.; *b.* 25 Jan. 1890; *s.* of Rev. W. D. Ridley; *m.* 1st, Katharine Bishop, *e. d.* of Col. F. A. Scott, Cleveland, Ohio, U.S.A.; two *d.*; 2nd, Jean Evelyn

Lawther, *d.* of Robert Carlisle, Helens Bay, Co. Down, N. Ireland; two *s.* *Educ.:* Clifton College; Balliol College, Oxford (Exhibitioner and Hon Scholar), Craven and Passmore Edwards Scholarships, Newdigate, Chancellor's English Essay, and Charles Oldham Prizes. Assistant Master, Clifton College, 1914-20; Fellow, and Tutor in English Literature, Balliol Coll., 1920-45 (Chaplain, 1920-31); relinquished the exercise of orders, 1945; Rhodes Travelling Fellow, 1928; Tallman Visiting Professor, Bowdoin College, U.S.A., 1931-32; Lecturer, Bedford College, London, 1948-67. *Publications:* Poetry and the Ordinary Reader, 1930; Keats' Craftsmanship, 1933; Oxford Crosswords, 1934; New Temple Shakespeare (editor), 1934-36; Shakespeare's Plays, a Commentary, 1937; Gertrude Bell, 1941; Sir Gawain and the Green Knight, 1944; Abraham Lincoln, 1944; Antony and Cleopatra (New Arden edn.), 1953; Othello (New Arden edn.), 1957; Studies in Three Literatures, 1961; Second Thoughts, 1965. *Address:* 18 Clifton Park, Bristol 8. *T.:* Bristol 3-4356. [*Died* 12 *June* 1969.

RIETCHEL, Julius; Fellow of Institute of Actuaries; late General Manager, Secretary and Actuary, Sun Life Assurance Soc., retd. 1941. *Address:* Saxonbury, Wadhurst, Sx. *T.:* 305. [*Died* 22 *Jan.* 1963.

RIEU, Sir (Jean) Louis, K.C.S.I., *cr.* 1929 (C.S.I. 1920); Indian Civil Service (retd.); *b.* 23 Nov. 1872; *e. s.* of late Dr. Charles Rieu, formerly Keeper of the Oriental MSS. at the British Museum, and Prof. of Arabic at Cambridge; *m.* 1st, 1899, Ida Augusta (*d.* 1921), *d.* of late John Edwards, J.P., Knockrobin, Co. Wicklow; one *d.*; 2nd, 1930, Eileen Dorothy, *d.* of late Cyril Kirkpatrick. *Educ.:* University College School, London; Balliol College, Oxford. Entered Indian Civil Service, 1893, and posted to Bombay Presidency served as Assistant Collector and Collector in Sind, and in other capacities till 1911, when appointed Secretary to the Government of Bombay in the General Department; Collector of Karachi, 1917; Secretary to the Government of Bombay in the Revenue and Financial Departments, 1918; Commissioner in Sind, 1919-25; Member of Executive Council of the Governor of Bombay, 1926-29. *Address:* Casa San Giorgio, Alassio, Italy; c/o Lloyds Bank, 6 Pall Mall, S.W.1. *Club:* Athenæum. [*Died* 4 *Nov.* 1964.

RIGBY, Brigadier Thomas, C.B. 1949; D.S.O. 1944; M.C. 1918; Retired Army Officer; Fruit Grower since 1949; *b.* 11 Nov. 1897; *s.* of late Geo. Henry Rigby, solicitor, and late Caroline Florence (*née* Male); *m.* 1925, Ruth Ramsay (*née* Brown); one *s.* one *d.* *Educ.:* Sandroyd; Winchester College; R.M.A. Woolwich. Commissioned 1915; served European War, 1914-18, Lieut. and Temp. Capt. R.A., France, Belgium and Germany, 1916-19 (M.C.) Lt. "L" Bty. R.H.A., 1919-28; Capt. 1928; Staff Coll., Camberley, 1932-33; staff appointments, India, 1935-39; War of 1939-1945, Instructor Senior Officers' School, 1939-40; A.Q.M.G. G.H.Q., B.E.F. and 10 Corps., G.S.O. 1 38 Div., 1940-41; Comdg. 30 Fd. Regt., 1941; Deputy Director Military Operations, War Office, 1941-42 (Temp. Brig.); C.R.A. 46 Div., N. Africa, Italy, 1942-44 (despatches, D.S.O.); D.D.R.A. War Office, 1944-46; B.R.A., M.E.L.F., 1946-49; retired as Hon. Brig., 1949. *Recreations:* golf, tennis, gardening. *Address:* Hill House, Long Melford, Sudbury, Suffolk. *T.:* Long Melford 217. [*Died* 27 *July* 1969.

RIGG, Ven. William Harrison, D.D.; Archdeacon of Bodmin, 1939-52, now Archdeacon Emeritus; Canon of Truro, 1936-56; Hon. Warden of Trelawne (Home for retired Clergy and their wives), 1953-56; *b.* 1 Nov. 1877; *e. s.* of Rev. W. H. Rigg; *m.* 1913, Margaret Elizabeth Scott Moncrieff; one *s.* two *d.* *Educ.:* Harrow; Hertford College, Oxford. 2nd Cl. Hons. Mod. Hist., 1900; 2nd Cl. Hons. Theology, 1901; M.A. 1903; B.D. and D.D. 1921; Curate of St. Mary's, Lewisham, 1901-5; St. Alfege, Greenwich, 1905-7; Vicar of Christ Church, Bermondsey, 1907-13; Christ Church, Greenwich, 1913-21; Vicar of Beverley Minster, 1921-36; Rural Dean of Beverley, 1932-36; Vicar of St. Mary Magdalene, Launceston, 1936-45; Examining Chaplain to Archbishop of York, 1927-39, and to Bishop of Truro, 1938-59; Canon of York, 1933-36. *Publications:* Devotional Commentary on the 1st and 2nd Book of Samuel, 2 Vols., 1926; Contributor to Essays on the Atonement in History and in Life, 1929; to Essays on Authority and the Christian Faith, 1935; The Fourth Gospel and its Message For To-day, 1952; to Churchman, Expository Times, and Church Quarterly Review. *Address:* Garth House, 38 Frant Road, Tunbridge Wells. *T.:* Tunbridge Wells 26664. [*Died* 2 *May* 1966.

RIGGALL, Robert Marmaduke, M.R.C.S. Eng., L.R.C.P. Lond., L.R.C.P. and S. Edin. and Glas.; Medical Supt. of Northumberland House Psychiatric Nursing Home, N.3; Surg. Lieut.-Comdr. (Retired) R.N.; late Cons. Physician (Psycho-Analysis); Hon. Psychologist to West End Hospital for Nervous Diseases; *b.* London, 23 May 1881; *s.* of late Rev. Marmaduke Riggall, Sutton-on-Sea, Lincs.; *m.* 1st, 1913, Mary Douglas (*d.* 1964), *d.* of late Lt.-Col. George Moore, Great Meadow, Castleton, Isle of Man; one *s.* two *d.*; 2nd, Paulette Nixon. *Educ.:* Kingswood; Universities of Manchester and Edinburgh; London Hospital. Qualified, 1907 and after hospital appointments entered the Royal Navy as Surgeon-Lieut. 1908; served in China Station for two years, and shipwrecked in H.M.S. Bedford, 1910; retired, 1914; studied tuberculosis at Davos Platz, Switzerland; rejoined R.N., Aug 1914; Surgeon Lt.-Comdr., 1917; served in North Sea, West Africa, and Haslar Hospital for Psycho-therapeutic research work; demobilised 1918 for Psycho-therapeutic work under Ministry of Pensions; late Hon. Sec. Medical Section of British Psychological Soc.; Mem., British Psycho-Analytical Society. *Publications:* papers to Lancet, etc. *Recreations:* punting, ski-ing, etc. *Address:* Dr. R. M. Riggall, Northumberland House, 237 Ballards Lane, N.3. *T.:* 01-346 5283. *Club:* Royal Over-Seas League. [*Died* 3 *Oct.* 1970.

RILEY, Maj.-Gen. Sir (Henry) Guy, K.B.E., *cr.* 1944; C.B. 1938; *b.* 5 Nov. 1884; *s.* of late Col. H. W. D. Riley, 55th Foot (The Border Regt.); *m.* 1920, Frances Dorothy (*d.* 1959), *er. d.* of late John Atkinson, J.P., of Newbiggin, Hexham. *Educ.:* Bedford School. Joined 1st Bn. The North Staffordshire Regt. from 3rd Militia Bn. The Border Regt., 1906; transferred to R.A.P.C., 1910; served European War (despatches twice); Paymaster-in-Chief, War Office, 1937-43; Col. Comdt. R.A.P.C., 1943-55. *Address:* Gatton, 26 Nightingale Road, Guildford, Surrey. *Club:* Army and Navy. [*Died* 24 *Oct.* 1964.

RILEY, William; author; *b.* 23 Apr. 1866; *s.* of Joseph and Hannah Riley; *m.* 1st, 1892, Clara Hirst (*d.* 1929), Morley, nr. Leeds; no *c.*; 2nd, 1932, Edith Mary Berry, Silverdale. *Educ.:* Bradford Grammar School. Was associated for some years with his father's business of stuff merchant; then helped to inaugurate the business of optical lantern slide makers which was carried on in England and America by Riley Brothers, Limited, of which company he was Managing Director; wrote Windyridge in 1911 to interest friends and without thought of publication; book was published in 1912 and became instantly popular; since then has devoted himself to writing and lecturing, chiefly on Yorkshire subjects. *Publications:* Windyridge; Netherleigh; The Way of the Winepress; No. 7 Brick Row; Olive of Sylcote; Jerry and Ben; The Lady of the Lawn; Men of Mawm; Rachel Bland's Inheritance; The Garden of Delight; Laycock of Lonedale; Peter Pettinger; Through a Yorkshire Window; A Yorkshire Suburb; A Village in Craven; Children of the Outcast; Windyridge Re-visited; Witch Hazel; Doctor Dick; Squire Goodall; Kit of Kit's Folly; The Silver Dale; Old Obbut; The North-West Yorkshire Pennines; Jack and John; Man of Anathoth; Old Ara; The Sixpenny Man; Gold Chains; The Valley of Baca; The Voice in the Garden; Common Clay; Grapes from Thorns; A Stick for God; Sunset Reflections. *Recreations:* walking, gardening. *Address:* Yew Tree House, Silverdale, nr. Carnforth, Lancs. *T.:* Silverdale, Carnforth 229. [*Died* 4 *June* 1961.

RIMMER, Edward Johnson, Q.C. 1952; A.M.Inst.C.E.; *b.* 28 Mar. 1883; *s.* of E. J. Rimmer and Helen R. Rimmer (*née* Milne); *m.* 1913, Muriel Oldroyd; one *s.* two *d.* *Educ.:* Bickerton House, Birkdale; Liverpool University (B.Sc.; M.Eng.). Pupil to J. T. Wood, M.Inst.C.E., 1900-04; Engineer with S. Pearson and Sons, 1905-09; reading for Bar with late A. R. Kennedy, 1909-12. Served Royal Engineers, 1914-18. Federation Civil Engineering Contractors (Director, 1919-24). *Publication:* The Law Relating to the Architect, 1952. *Recreations:* riding and gardening. *Address:* Peachfield Cottage, Hayes Bank Road, Malvern Common, Malvern, Worcs. *T.:* Malvern 5197. *Club:* St. Stephen's. [*Died* 15 *May* 1962.

RINFRET, Rt. Hon Thibaudeau; P.C. (Gt. Brit.), 1947 (Can.), 1953; LL.D., Hon. LL.D. (University of Montreal, McGill University, University of Ottawa, Laval University, Bishop's College, University of Caen, Univ. of Poitiers, New York Univ., Univ. of Toronto, Univ. of Adelaide); *b.* Montreal, 22 June 1879; *s.* of F. O. Rinfret, Barrister, and Albina Pominville; *m.* 1903, Georgine, *d.* of late S. J. B. Rolland, Montreal; three *s.* one *d.* *Educ.:* St. Mary's College; Laval and McGill Universities, Montreal. B.A. (St. Mary's College), 1897; B.C.L. (McGill University), 1900; called to Bar of P.Q., 1901; K.C. 1912; practised in partnership with Hon. Jean Prévost, 1901-10; with Hon. J. L. Perron, K.C., 1910-22; Judge of the Superior Court at Montreal, 1922-24; Judge of the Supreme Court of Canada, 1924-1944; Chief Justice of Canada, 1944-54, retd. A director of L'Alliance Française of Ottawa; Vice-Pres. of La Fédération de L'Alliance Française aux États-Unis et au Canada; Président, Comité d'Ottawa de France-Amérique; Chm. Bd. of Regents, Ottawa Univ. Grand Croix de l'Ordre de Saint-Grégoire-le-Grand; Grand Officer Legion of Honour of France; Knight Grand Cross of Order of Malta. Roman Catholic. *Clubs:* Canadian, Rideau Country (Ottawa); University, Cercle Universitaire, Montreal (Montreal); Union Interalliée de Paris. [*Died* 25 *July* 1962.

RIPPER, Walter Eugene; Chairman Ripper Robots Ltd., and of other cos.; *b.* 24 Jan. 1908; *s.* of Ministerialrat Max Ripper and Amelie Wokatsch; *m.* 1st, 1938, Bertha Siedek (marr. diss.); one *s.* two *d.*; 2nd, 1952, Nancy Deacon. *Educ.:* Gymnasium Hietzing, Vienna; Vienna University (Ph.D.). Scientist, inventor, company director, farmer, pioneer in crop protection in U.K. and Africa. Introduced to Britain first synthetic selective herbicide 1940 (DNC), systemic insecticides in 1947, crop spraying by helicopter, 1949, aerial robot sprayers, 1957. Entomologist, U.S. Dept. of Agriculture, 1931-36; Founder and Man. Director, Pest Control Ltd., 1938-53; Chairman, Pest Control (Sudan) Ltd., 1947-57; Vice-Chairman, Fisons Pest Control Ltd., 1954-58; Managing Director, Dow Agrochemicals Ltd. (which he founded in partnership with Dow Chemical Co.), 1958-62. Fellow Roy. Entomological Soc., Entomological Soc. of America, Entomological Soc. of South Africa; Fellow Royal Aeronautical Soc., American Association of Agricultural Engineers. Silver Medal, Internat. Congress of Entomology, Paris, 1953, for Systemic Insecticides; Premium Society of Engineers, 1955, for Spraying Crops by Helicopter. *Publications:* The Cotton Pests of the Sudan, 1964; numerous papers on insect physiology, the control of agricultural pests, particularly by systemic insecticides, biological control, selective toxicity, selective weed control in beet, equipment for application of agricultural chemicals, in particular aircraft spraying. *Recreations:* ski-ing on snow and water; shooting. *Address:* The Manor, Docking, Norfolk. *T.:* Docking 235. *Clubs:* Savage, Farmers'. [*Died* 21 *March* 1965.

RITCHIE, Arthur David, M.A.; Emeritus Professor of Logic and Metaphysics, Edinburgh University, Prof. 1945-59; *b.* Oxford, 22 June 1891; *s.* of late Prof. D. G. Ritchie and late Mrs. E. S. Ritchie; *m.* 1921, Katharine Victoria, *d.* of late Rev. Preb. S. G. Ponsonby; one *s.* one *d.* *Educ.:* Fettes College, Edinburgh; St. Andrews University; Trinity Coll., Cambridge. Chemist in Naval Airship Service, 1914-18; Fellow of Trinity College, Cambridge, 1920-26; Assistant-Lecturer, Manchester University, 1920; Lecturer in Chemical Physiology, Manchester University; Rockefeller Travelling Fellowship, 1925; Tarner Lecturer, Trinity College, Cambridge, 1935; Professor of Philosophy, Victoria University of Manchester, 1937-45. *Publications:* Scientific Method, 1923; Comparative Physiology of Muscular Tissue, 1928; Natural History of Mind, 1936; Civilization, Science and Religion, 1945; Science and Politics, 1947; Essays in Philosophy, 1948; Studies in the History and Methods of the Sciences, 1958; papers in scientific and philosophical journals. *Address:* 8 Hope Park Square, Edinburgh. [*Died* 12 *March* 1967.

RITCHIE, Douglas Ernest; *b.* London, 26 Mar. 1905; *e. s.* of Ernest G. Ritchie, Dorking, Surrey; *m.* 1933, Evelyn, *d.* of James Bissett, Glen Red, British Bechuanaland; one *s.* one *d.* *Educ.:* City of London School. Chorister at Temple Church, London. Farmed in Orange Free State, Transvaal and Cape Province, South Africa. Joined staff of Rand Daily Mail and Johannesburg Sunday Times as reporter; literary, musical and dramatic criticism; special correspondent for Rand Daily Mail, Cape Times, Natal Mercury and other South African morning newspapers with late Duke of Kent during his tour of South Africa and Southern Rhodesia, 1934; editorial staff of Daily Telegraph, 1935; joined B.B.C. European Service, March 1939; Assistant Director B.B.C. European Broadcasts, 1941-44; Director European News Department, B.B.C., 1944-46; seconded to British Information Services, New York, as Director of Press and Radio Division, 1946-49; Gen. Overseas Service Organiser, B.B.C., 1949-50; Head of Publicity, 1950-1956. Organiser of B.B.C.'s "V" campaign: first broadcast as "Colonel Britton", June 1941; official broadcaster of Supreme Allied Commander's messages and instructions to Europe from May 1944 until the close of the war in Europe. King Haakon VII Liberty Cross; King Christian X Liberty Medal. *Publication:* Stroke: A Diary of Recovery, 1960. *Address:* Mickleham Priory, Nr. Dorking, Surrey. *T.:* Leatherhead 2063. [*Died* 15 *Dec.* 1967.

RITCHIE, Capt. Sir Lewis Anselmo (*pseudonym* Bartimeus), K.C.V.O., *cr.* 1947 (C.V.O. 1939); C.B.E. 1944; R.N. retd.;

b. 29 April 1886; *m.* 1915, Harriet Marguerita Scott; one *s.* one *d.*; surname altered to Ritchie from Ricci by Deed Poll, 1941. Entered Britannia, 1901; reverted to retired list, 1944. Press Secretary to the King, 1944-1947. *Publications:* Naval Occasions, 1914; Tall Ship on Other Naval Occasions, 1915; The Long Trick, 1917; Navy Eternal, 1918; Awfully Big Adventure, 1919; Unreality, 1920; Seaways, 1923; Great Security, 1925; The Elephant's Head, 1930; Overlooked, 1932; A Make and Mend, 1934; An Off-Shore Wind, 1936; Under Sealed Orders, 1938; A Ditty Box, 1940; Steady As You Go, 1942; East of Malta, West of Suez, 1943; The Mediterranean Fleet, Part II, 1944; Malta Invicta, 1943; The Turn of the Road, 1946. *Recreations:* fishing, gardening. *Address:* Bagley Wood House, Nr. Kennington, Oxford. *Club:* Flyfishers' (Pres. 1944-45).
[*Died* 7 *Feb.* 1967.

RITCHIE-SCOTT, A., D.Sc. (Lond.), B.Sc. (Edin.); F.R.S.E.; *b.* Edinburgh, 1874; *m.* 1938, Alison Struan, *d.* of late David Robertson, London. *Educ.:* George Heriot's School and University, Edinburgh, University College, London. Assistant Sir John Murray Challenger Expedition Reports, 1894-96; Edinburgh University Research Fellowship, 1896; Teaching, 1896-1907; Assistant Registrar, University, Cape of Good Hope, 1907-9; Principal, L.C.C. Beaufoy Institute, 1909-39; Director of Returns and Deputy Director of Statistics, Ministry of Food, 1917-1919; Chief-Examiner, London County Council, 1920-22; Member London Math. Society. *Publications:* A Complete School Algebra; Scientific Papers, chiefly Mathematical, to: Edin. Math. Soc., Nat. Sci., Biometrika, etc. *Address:* 7 Muirton Bank, Perth, Scotland. *T.:* Perth 1682. [*Died* 23 *Nov.* 1962.

RITSON, Lady Kitty (nom de plume, Lady Kitty Vincent); *d.* of 11th (*de facto* 8th) Earl of Airlie and Lady Mabell Gore; *b.* 5 Feb. 1887; *m.* 1926, Lt.-Col. Ralph Gerald Ritson (*d.* 1966). *Educ.:* Home. *Recreations:* travelling, dog-breeding. *Address:* 44 Dennekamp, Main Road, Wynberg, C.P., South Africa.
[*Died* 17 *Oct.* 1969.

RITTER, His Eminence Cardinal Joseph Elmer; Archbishop of St. Louis, Missouri, since 1946; *b.* New Albany, Indiana, 20 July 1892; *s.* of Nicholas Ritter and Bertha Luette. *Educ.:* St. Meinrad Minor and Major Seminaries. Priest, 1917; named Rector of the Cathedral of SS. Peter and Paul, Indianapolis, in 1924. Titular Bishop of Hippus and Aux. Bishop to Bishop of Indianapolis, 1933; Vicar-General of Diocese of Indianapolis, 1933; Bishop of Indianapolis, 1934; Archbishop of Indianapolis, 1944-46. Named Assistant at the Pontifical Throne, 1956; created and proclaimed Cardinal under the title of St. Alphonsus, 1961. *Address:* 4396 Lindell Blvd., St. Louis 8, Mo., U.S.A. *T.:* Jefferson 3-1887.
[*Died* 10 *June* 1967.

RIVALLAND, Sir Michel (Jean Joseph Laval), Kt. 1968; M.B.E. 1952; Chief Justice of Mauritius since 1967; *b.* 23 Mar. 1910; *s.* of Maurice Rivalland and Marie Majastre; *m.* 1941, Josephe Marie Therese (*née* Rivalland); three *s.* two *d.* *Educ.:* Royal Coll., English Schol., 1929. Called to the Bar (Middle Temple), 1934. Private Practice, 1934-42; Legal Adviser, 1942; Crown Counsel, 1947; Controller of Supplies, 1949-57; Solicitor General, 1958; Puisne Judge, 1960; Senior Puisne Judge, 1961. *Recreations:* walking, fishing, gardening. *Address:* Quatre Bornes, Mauritius. *T.:* 4-3856. [*Died* 29 *Jan.* 1970.

RIVERS, George H. L. F.; *see* Pitt-Rivers.

RIVETT, Sir (Albert Cherbury) David, K.C.M.G. 1935; F.R.S. 1941; M.A., B.Sc., Hon. D.Sc. (Oxon), D.Sc. (Melb.), Hon. D.Sc. (Manch.); Hon. LL.D. (Aust. Nat. U.); Hon. Fellow of Lincoln College, Oxford; Hon. A.C.T. (Manch.); *b.* Port Esperance, Tasmania, 4 Dec. 1885; *e. s.* of late Rev. A. Rivett, Sydney; *m.* 1911, Stella, 2nd *d.* of late Hon. Alfred Deakin; two *s.* *Educ.:* Wesley College, Melbourne; Queen's College, University of Melbourne; Lincoln College, Oxford; Nobel Institute, Stockholm. Victorian Rhodes Scholar, 1907; Lecturer and Demonstrator in Chemistry, Univ. of Melbourne, 1911; Associate Professor, 1920; Professor, 1924-27; Deputy Chairman and Chief Executive Officer of Commonwealth C.S.I.R., 1927-45, Chairman, 1946-49; General Organising Secretary for visit to Australia of the British Association for the Advancement of Science, 1914; President of Australian and New Zealand Association for the Advancement of Science, 1937-39; Gen. Pres. Australian Chemical Institute, 1940 and 1948; Pres. of Soc. of Chemical Industry, 1948-49; Hon. Capt. A.A.M.C. Reserve, 1915-16; served under Department of Munitions, H.M. Factory, Swindon, 1917-1918. *Publications:* The Phase Rule and the Study of Heterogeneous Equilibria, 1923; Papers on Chemistry in various scientific journals. *Recreation:* gardening. *Address:* 11 Eton Square, 474 St. Kilda Road, Melbourne, S.C.2, Australia.
[*Died* 1 *April* 1961.

RIVETT-CARNAC, Vice-Admiral James William, C.B. 1945; C.B.E. 1944; D.S.C.; D.L.; *b.* 1891; 2nd *s.* of late Rev. Sir George Rivett-Carnac, 6th Bart.; *b.* and *heir-pres.* of Sir Henry George Crabbe Rivett-Carnac, 7th Bt.; *m.* 1922, Isla Nesta, 2nd *d.* of late Major Harry Blackwood, J.P., Kincurdy, Ross-shire; two *s.* one *d.* *Educ.:* Royal Naval College, Dartmouth. Served European War, 1914-19 (D.S.C.); Commodore New Zealand Div. 1938-39: Captain H.M.S. Rodney, 1941-1943; Rear-Admiral, 1943; Flag-Officer British Assault Area, 1944; Vice-Adm. (Q) British Pacific Fleet, 1945-47; retired list, 1947. Chm., Thingoe R.D.C., 1958-61. D.L. Suffolk, 1958. Legion of Honour, Croix de Guerre. *Address:* Fornham House, Bury St. Edmunds, Suffolk. *T.:* 4636.
[*Died* 9 *Oct.* 1970.

ROBB, Prof. Andrew McCance; Professor of Naval Architecture in the University of Glasgow, 1944-57, retired; *b.* 31 March 1887; 2nd *s.* of Andrew Robb and Margaret McCance; *m.* 1914, Evelyn Taylor, *y. d.* of Rev. Alexander Brown, Pollokshields, Glasgow; one *s.* *Educ.:* Pollokshields public school, Glasgow; Glasgow University. B.Sc. 1910, D.Sc. 1921. Assistant to professor Sir John H. Biles, 1912-16, and 1920-25; service in Mesopotamia, 1916; Assistant in Dept. of Deputy-Controller for Auxiliary Shipbuilding and Controller-General of Merchant Shipbuilding, 1917-19; Technical Assistant with Harland and Wolff, Belfast, 1919-20; in practice as consulting naval architect, 1925-44. LL.D. Glasgow, 1958. *Publications:* Studies in Naval Architecture, 1927; Theory of Naval Architecture, 1952. Sundry technical papers. *Address:* 9 Falkland Street, Glasgow, W.2. *T.:* Western 5008. *Club:* College (Glasgow).
[*Died* 30 *Dec.* 1968.

ROBB, Air Chief Marshal Sir James (Milne), G.C.B. 1951 (K.C.B. 1949; C.B. 1941); K.B.E. 1945; D.S.O. 1926; D.F.C.; A.F.C.; F.S.A.; *s.* of late James Thomas Robb, J.P., Hexham; *m.* 1927, Bessie Murray, *y. d.* of late Mrs. Elizabeth Johnston, Pulborough; one *s.* one *d.* *Educ.:* George Watson's; Durham Univ. Served European War, 1914-18, Northumberland Fusiliers and R.F.C. (D.F.C.); Germany 1919; Kurdistan, 1922-25 (D.S.O.); Chief Instructor, Central Flying School, 1927-30; Senior Air Force Officer, H.M.S. Eagle, China,

1933-34; Fleet Aviation Officer to Commander-in-Chief, Mediterranean, 1935-36; Commandant, Central Flying School, 1936-1940; A.O.C. No. 2 Bomber Group, 1940, No. 15 Coastal Group, 1941; Deputy Chief of Combined Operations, 1942; A.O.C., R.A.F., North-West Africa, 1943-44; Chief of Staff (Air) to General Eisenhower, 1944-45; A.O.C.-in-C. R.A.F. Fighter Command, 1945-47; Vice-Chief of the Air Staff, Air Ministry, 1947-48; C.-in-C. Air Forces, Western Europe, 1948-51; Inspector-General of the Royal Air Force, 1951; retd. from active list, 1951. King of Arms of Order of the Bath, 1952-65; Cabinet Office, Historical Section; Mem. Cttee., Lloyds Bank, 6 Pall Mall. Legion of Honour (France), Order of White Lion, 1st Class (Czecho-Slovakia), Legion of Merit and D.S.M. (U.S.A.). *Recreations:* ornithology, archæology. *Address:* Hollow Meadow, Chagford, Devon. *Club:* Royal Air Force.
[*Died* 18 *Dec.* 1968.

ROBBINS, Alan Pitt, C.B.E. 1954; retired as Secretary of General Council of the Press (1954-60); *b.* 21 Jan. 1888; *s.* of late Sir Alfred and Lady Ellen Robbins; *m.* 1912, Olive Pardon, *o. d.* of late Edgar Searles and Charlotte Louisa Pardon. *Educ.:* City of London School. Engaged in journalism since 1904; Reporter on the Yorkshire Observer 1904-8 and on Birmingham Post 1908-9. Editorial staff of The Times, 1909-1953; Parliamentary Correspondent, 1923-1938; News Editor, 1938-53. Fellow of the Institute of Journalists, 1920, Chairman of London District, 1926, President, 1935; Treasurer, 1939-51; Chairman of the Parliamentary Lobby Journalists, 1925; Master of the Gallery Lodge of Freemasons, 1932; Past Chm. and a Vice-President Newspaper Press Fund; a Governor of St. Dunstan's. Mem. Exec. Council Commonwealth Press Union. Toured Canada at invitation of Assoc. of Canadian Clubs to speak on The British Press in Wartime, 1945. Represented The Times Weekly Review at 7th Imperial Press Conf., Canada, 1950. Livery Representative in Court of Stationers' and Newspaper Makers' Company, 1962-63. *Publication:* Newspapers To-Day, 1956. *Recreations:* watching cricket and play-going. *Address:* Pembroke House Hotel, Hove 3, Sussex. [*Died* 4 *Feb.* 1967.

ROBERTS, Lt.-Col. Sir Alexander (Fowler), K.B.E., *cr.* 1926; Managing Director, Murray, Roberts & Co., Ltd., Wellington, New Zealand, since 1929; *b.* Dunedin, N.Z., 1882; *s.* of late Sir John Roberts, C.M.G., Dunedin; *m.* 1907, Hannah Ruby Farquhar; three *s.* *Educ.:* Merchiston Castle, Edinburgh; Clare College, Cambridge. Cambridge Rugby XV., 1901-3; entered Murray, Roberts & Co., Ltd., 1903; Staff Embarkation Officer, N.Z.E.F., 1914-18 and 1939-45; N.Z. Comr. to British Empire Exhibition, 1924-25; Mayor of Lower Hutt, 1929-31. N.Z. Rep. British Ministry of War Transport, 1941-45. *Recreations:* golf, tennis. *Address:* 99 Woburn Road, Lower Hutt, N.Z. *Clubs:* Wellington; Dunedin; Hawkes Bay. [*Died* 19 *March* 1961.

ROBERTS, Sir Alfred, Kt., *cr.* 1955; C.B.E. 1950; Member, Cotton Board, since 1948; Director, Bank of England, since 1956; Governor, Commonwealth Institute, since 1962; Mem., Commonwealth Scholarship Commission in Britain since 1961; *b.* 30 Nov. 1897; *m.* 1921, Gladys Bertha McEntyre; two *d.* *Educ.:* Chalfont St. Council School, Bolton. Chairman, T.U.C. General Council, 1950-51; Vice-Chairman, Governing Body, I.L.O., 1954-60; General Secretary, National Association of Card, Blowing and Ring Room Operatives, 1935-62; Chm., International Cttee. of T.U.C., 1958-63; Mem., Nationalised Industries Advisory Cttee., 1963. M.A. (*h.c.*) Manchester Univ., 1954. *Address:* Priory Close, Penwortham, Preston, Lancs. *T.:* Preston Priory 83542.
[*Died* 18 *Nov.* 1963.

ROBERTS, Allan Arbuthnot Lane, C.I.E. 1932; *b.* 11 Oct. 1884; *s.* of late Lt.-Col. A. S. Roberts; *m.* 1911, Gladys, *d.* of late Rev. Edward Steele, Vicar of St. Neot, Cornwall; two *s.* *Educ.:* Cheltenham College; St. John's College, Oxford. Ashburton Shield, 1902; Oxford University Trial Eights, 1905. Entered I.C.S. 1908; Assistant Commissioner Punjab, 1909; Under-Secretary Punjab Govt., 1915-17; Secretary Delhi Municipal Committee, 1918-21; Deputy Sec. Punjab Govt., 1921-24; Deputy Comr. Lahore, 1929-31; retired, 1934. *Address:* c/o National Provincial Bank, Cornmarket Street, Oxford. *Club:* Leander.
[*Died* 6 *Aug.* 1967.

ROBERTS, Rev. Arthur Betton; retired; *b.* 27 Dec. 1880; *s.* of Arthur Edmund Simmonds Roberts and Ella Francesca Bright. *Educ.:* Merchant Taylors' School; Stubbington House, nr. Fareham; London College of Divinity. Deacon, 1904; Priest, 1905; Assistant Curate Holy Trinity, Kingsway, W.C., 1904-06; Assistant Curate Goring on Thames, 1907-09; A.C.S. Chaplain, Ajmer, Rajputana, 1909-13; Chaplain Bengal (Nagpur) Ecclesiastical Establishment, 1913; Archdeacon of Nagpur, 1928-32; Bishops Commissary in Charge of Diocese of Nagpur, 1930; Rector of Stanton with Dale Abbey, 1933-39; Rector of Exton, 1939-48; Vicar of Wookey, 1948-54. *Address:* c/o Stockcross Vicarage, Newbury, Berks.
[*Died* 3 *Jan.* 1961.

ROBERTS, Bryn; General Secretary, National Union of Public Employees, 1934-1962; retired (ill health) July 1962; *b.* 7 April 1897; *s.* of William and Mary Roberts; *m.* 1922, Violet Sheenan; one *s.* two *d.* *Educ.:* Abertillery Elementary School; Central Labour College. Left school and started as a coal miner at age 13; won scholarship to Central Labour Coll., 1919, and on returning in 1921, was appointed Checkweighman for Rhymney Miners; Rhymney Valley Miners' Agent, and Exec. Member of South Wales Miners' Fed., 1926; prominent as a Councillor in Welsh local govt. life. T.U.C. Fraternal Deleg. to American Fed. of Labour Convention, 1942; Member of Parliamentary and trade union delegation to China, 1954. Mem. of Cttee. on Social Workers in Mental Health Service. *Publications:* The American Trade Union Split and Allied Unity, 1943; At the T.U.C., 1947; Topical comments, 1952; As I See It, 1957; The Price of T.U.C. Leadership, 1961; At the T.U.C., No. 2, 1962. *Address:* White Cottage, 10 Scotts Lane, Shortlands, Kent. *T.:* Beckenham 9038.
[*Died* 26 *Aug.* 1964.

ROBERTS, Very Rev. Edward Albert Trevillian, M.A. (Oxon); *b.* 10 Oct. 1877; *s.* of Griffith Roberts, formerly Dean of Bangor, and Jane Lloyd Roberts; unmarried. *Educ.:* Llandovery College; Jesus College, Oxford. Curate of Neath, 1901-06; Cwmbach-Llechryd, 1906-14; Rector of Llanelly, Breconshire, 1914-21; Canon and Subdean Brecon Cathedral, 1925-39; Dean of Brecon, 1939-49; Vicar of Brecon, 1921-1949; Rural Dean of Brecon, Part 1, 1941-1949; resigned, 1949. *Recreation:* fishing. *Address:* Spa Nursing Home, Temple Street, Llandrindod Wells, Radnorshire.
[*Died* 2 *May* 1968.

ROBERTS, Sir Ernest Handforth Goodman, Kt. 1936; Q.C. 1949; Dep. Chairman, Flint Quarter Sessions, 1949-61, variously, Commissioner Central Criminal Court and Acting Deputy Chairman London

Sessions; Commissioner of Assize various circuits 18 times from 1949-55 inclusive; *b.* Pen-y-Ffordd, Flintshire, 20 April 1890; *o. s.* of late Hugh Goodman Roberts and late Elizabeth, *d.* of Edward Lewis; unmarried. *Educ.:* Malvern Coll.; Trinity Coll., Oxford. M.A.; President of the Oxford Union, 1914; H.M. Forces, 1914-19; Captain (temp.) in Royal Welch Fusiliers; served in Palestine, Court-martial Officer (despatches); Member of Governing Body, Church in Wales, 1916-36. and 1947-59; Chancellor of diocese of Bangor, 1947-59, of Chelmsford since 1950. Barrister-at-law, Inner Temple, 1916; contested (C.) Flintshire, 1923; M.P. (C.) Flintshire, 1924-29; Chief Justice of High Court of Judicature at Rangoon, 1936-48; retired, 1948. *Publication:* Principles of the Law of Contract, 1923. *Recreation:* travel by sea. *Address:* 39 Ashley Gardens, S.W.1. *Clubs:* Junior Carlton, Naval and Military. [*Died* 14 *Feb.* 1969.

ROBERTS, Francis Noel, C.B. 1954; C.B.E. 1947; Retired as Secretary and Commissioner of H.M. Customs and Excise (1952-1957); *b.* 25 December 1893; *s.* of late Charles G. Roberts, Claremont, Jersey. *Educ.:* Victoria College, Jersey; Exeter College, Oxford. Served European War in Army, 1914-19; Act. Maj., R.G.A. Joined H.M. Customs and Excise, 1919. *Address:* 10 Nursery Avenue, Shirley, Surrey. [*Died* 20 *April* 1969.

ROBERTS, Geoffrey Dorling, O.B.E.; Q.C., 1937; retired; *b.* 27 August 1886; *s.* of Charles Tanner Kingdom Roberts; *m.* 1st, 1915, Margaret Gertrude Petrie (*d.* 1944); two *d.* (and one *d.* decd.); 2nd, 1947, Margot Sandys (*née* Von der Mühlen), (marriage dissolved, 1953), *widow* of Captain G. J. Sandys; 3rd, 1953, Louise Mary Orford (*née* Maxwell). *Educ.:* Exeter School; Rugby; Oxford. Blue for Rugby football and half blue for lawn tennis; played Rugby football for England in 1907 and 1908; M.A. Oxford Honour School of Law; called to Bar, Inner Temple, 1912; served in Army, Aug. 1914-April 1919, in Devonshire Regiment and on the Staff, four years in France; returned to Bar, 1919; practised at Criminal Bar under Sir Richard Muir and Sir Travers Humphreys; late Senior Treasury Counsel Central Criminal Court; Recorder of Exeter, 1932-46; Recorder of Bristol, 1946-61. *Publications:* Without My Wig, 1957; Law and Life, 1964. *Recreations:* golf, tennis, lawn tennis, billiards, bridge. *Address:* 11 King's Bench Walk, Temple, E.C.4. *Clubs:* Garrick, M.C.C., Nineteenth, A.E.L.T.; Hampshire (Winchester). [*Died* 7 *March* 1967.

ROBERTS, George Augustus, C.B.E. 1920; F.R.C.S.; Retd. Cons. Surgeon, Royal Hants County Hospital, Winchester; *b.* 1875; *s.* of Rev. A. Roberts; *m.* 1906, Florence Muriel, *d.* of Colonel A. McLeod Mills; three *s.* two *d.* *Educ.:* Marlborough College. Surgeon to Winchester Red Cross Hospital during European War. *Address:* Preston House, Winchester. [*Died* 25 *Sept.* 1962.

ROBERTS, George Lawrence, M.B., Ch.B., Liverpool; B.D.S., Liverpool; F.D.S.R.C.S.; F.F.D.R.C.S.I.; Director of Dental Studies and Prof. of Dental Surgery, Univ. of Sheffield; Hon. Dental Surgeon Sheffield Royal Hosp. since 1935, and Sheffield Royal Infirmary since 1937; Mem. of Bd. of Faculty of Dental Surgery, R.C.S., since 1954 (Vice Dean, 1963-64); Mem. Gen. Dental Council since 1956; Examiner for Final F.D.S. to R.C.S. since 1963; Ext. Examr. in Dental Subjects to N.U.I. and to Univ. of Newcastle upon Tyne since 1965; Member, Sheffield Regional Hosp. Bd. since 1962 (also 1947-59); Member of Board of Governors, United Sheffield Hospitals; Cons. Advisor in Dental Surgery to Ministry of Health since 1964; *b.* Liverpool, 14 Jan. 1904; *s.* of George Roberts, Hoylake; *m.* 1939, Joyce Spring-Rice, *er. d.* of C. E. Smith, Rothley, Leicestershire; two *s.* *Educ.:* Calday Grange Grammar School; University of Liverpool. M.B., Ch.B. Hons. 1927, B.D.S. Hons. 1928, Liverpool; F.D.S. Royal College of Surgeons, 1948; Tutor in Dental Surgery, University of Leeds, 1928; Demonstrator in Dental Surgery, University of Liverpool, 1930; Tutor in Clinical Dental Subjects, University of Birmingham, 1931; External Examiner in Dental Subjects to Univ. of Leeds, 1941-44; to Univ. of Durham, 1944-47; to Univ. of Manchester, 1945-1947; to Univ. of Birmingham, 1947-49; to Univ. of London, 1951-54; to Queen's Univ. Belfast, 1955-58; to Liverpool Univ., 1955-58; to Univ. of Birmingham, 1958-1961; to University of Edinburgh, 1960-1963; Examiner for Final F.D.S. to R.C.S. 1952-57 (for Primary F.D.S., 1948-52); F.R.S.M.; Past Pres. Yorkshire Branch of British Dental Assoc., 1946-47; Pres. Odontological Section of Roy. Soc. Med., 1962-63. *Publications:* A Technique of Apicectomy, British Dental Journal, 1933; Notes on Uses of Fused Porcelain in Dental Surgery; The All Porcelain Jacket Crown, Dental Journal of Australia, 1935 and 1936; Contributor to American Year Book of Dentistry, 1937; Dental Jl.; Dental Practitioner. *Address:* Brook Lodge, Fulwood, Sheffield 10. [*Died* 14 *Dec.* 1967.

ROBERTS, Sir George (William Kelly), Kt. 1958; C.B.E. 1953; J.P.; President Legislative Council, Bahamas, since Nov. 1954; *b.* 19 July 1907; *m.* 1929, Freda Genevieve (*née* Sawyer); three *s.* *Educ.:* Queen's College, Nassau, Bahamas. Member, House of Assembly, Bahamas, 1934-54; Member Executive Council, Bahamas, 1946-1954. J.P. Bahamas, 1953. *Address:* Lucky Hill, Nassau, Bahamas. *T.:* 6151. *Clubs:* East India and Sports; Royal Nassau Sailing (Nassau, Bahamas). [*Died* 24 *June* 1964.

ROBERTS, H(ugh) Gordon, C.I.E. 1928; M.D.; Hon. LL.D. University of Wales, 1946; *b.* 1885; *s.* of David Roberts, Liverpool; *m.* 1913, Katharine, *d.* of John Jones, Liverpool; one *s.* one *d.* *Educ.:* Liverpool College and University (M.B. and Ch.B., 1912, M.D. 1920); Civil Surgeon, Shillong, 1914-19 (services having been lent by the Mission to the Govt. of Assam); a member of Assam Legislative Council, 1921-1924; a member of Assam Medical Council, 1920-43; Pres. of Assam Branch (British Medical Association), 1932-33; President English Conference Presbyterian Church of Wales, 1937; late Senior Medical Missionary of Welsh Presbyterian Mission, Assam, India; General Secretary and Editor of Medical Missionary Association of London, 1946-48, retired 1948; short term appt. superintending building of Jowai new mission hosp., Shillong, Assam, 1949-53. King's Jubilee Medal, 1935; Kaisar-i-Hind Gold Medal. *Address:* 9 Sandlea Park, West Kirby, Cheshire. [*Died* 20 *Dec.* 1961.

ROBERTS, Hon. James, C.M.G. 1958; M.L.C. 1947; President New Zealand Labour Party from 1937; *b.* Cork, Ireland, 25 Feb. 1881; *m.* 1912, Lucy (*d.* 1944), *d.* of T. Wallace; one *s.* four *d.* *Educ.:* National Schools in Ireland. Went to sea at age of 16; settled in New Zealand, 1901; employed on railways, in gasworks and on waterfront. Joined N.Z. Labour Party; Secretary N.Z. Waterside Workers' Fedn., 1915-41; Sec. N.Z. Alliance of Labour, 1920-35; Vice-Pres. N.Z. Labour Party, 1934-37. Was first N.Z. Labour delegate to I.L.O. Conference, 1930; Dep. Mem. Governing Body, I.L.O., 1930-38. Chairman: N.Z. Worker Publishing Co.;

New Zealand Labour Newspapers. *Address:* 41 Durham St., Wellington C.2, New Zealand. [*Died* 4 *Feb*. 1967.

ROBERTS, Sir John, Kt., *cr*. 1953; J.P.; Woollen Manufacturer; *b*. 16 Jan. 1876; 2nd *s*. of Sir John Roberts, C.M.G., Dunedin, N.Z.; *m*. 1901, Agnes A. (decd.), *d*. of Dr. J. S. Muir, Selkirk; two *s*. two *d*. (and one *s*. decd.). *Educ.:* High School, Dunedin, N.Z.; Merchiston Castle, Edinburgh. Provost of Selkirk, 1908, 1915-20, 1935-41; J.P. Selkirk; C.C.; Freeman of Selkirk, 1952; Hon. Sheriff Substitute, Selkirkshire. *Recreations:* hunting, golf. *Address:* Craigallan, Selkirk. *T.:* Selkirk 3253. *Club:* Constitutional. [*Died* 23 *Jan*. 1966.

ROBERTS, Maj.-Gen. John Hamilton, C.B. 1945; D.S.O. 1942; M.C.; *b*. 21 Dec. 1891; *s*. of William Percy Roberts and Mary Mackinnon; *m*. 1st, 1917, Isabelle Mary Waldron (*decd.*); three *s*. one *d*.; 2nd, 1943, Anne Caroline Fullerton, *widow*. *Educ.:* Epsom College, Surrey; Upper Canada College, Toronto; Royal Military College, Kingston, Ont. Commissioned in Royal Canadian Artillery, 1914; served throughout European War, 1914-18, in Royal Canadian Horse Artillery (wounded); War of 1939-45, arrived England Dec. 1939 in command R.C.H.A.; C.R.A. 1st Canadian Div. 1940; Commander 1st Bde. 1st Canadian Div., Feb. to July 1941; C.C.R.A. 1st Canadian Corps, July to Nov. 1941; 2nd Canadian Division, 1941-43; Major-General, 1942; Commander Canadian Reinforcement Units, 1943; retired, 1945. Commandeur Légion d'Honneur, Croix de Guerre avec palmes, 1945. Chief Administrative Officer, Imperial War Graves Commission, North-West Europe, 1945-50. *Recreations:* shooting, fishing. *Address:* Les Mouettes, Fauvic, Jersey, C.I. [*Died* 17 *Dec*. 1962.

ROBERTS, Ven. Richard Henry, M.A.; Archdeacon of St. Asaph, 1942-59; Vicar of Rhyl, 1935-54. *Educ.:* Keble College, Oxford. B.A., 1906; M.A., 1912; deacon, 1908; priest, 1909; Vicar of Llangennech, 1914-20; Bettws with Ammanford, 1920-35; Cursal Canon of St. Asaph, 1939-42. *Address:* 2 Heatherslade Road, Pennard, Nr. Swansea, Glam. [*Died* 6 *July* 1970.

ROBERTS, Sir Sydney (Castle), Kt. 1958; M.A., Hon. LL.D. (St. And.), Hon. L.H.D. (Brown); F.R.S.L.; Hon. F.L.A.; Fellow, and formerly Master, of Pembroke College, Cambridge; *b*. Birkenhead, 3 April 1887; *s*. of late Frank Roberts, M.Inst.C.E., Worthing; *m*. 1st, Irene (*d*. 1932), 2nd *d*. of late A. J. Wallis, Fell. of Corpus Christi Coll., Camb.; one *d*. (one *s*. killed in action 1944 and one *d*. decd.); 2nd, 1938, Marjorie, *widow* of M. B. R. Swann, M.D. *Educ.:* Brighton Coll.; Pembroke Coll., Cambridge (Scholar). 1st Class Classical Tripos, Part I (1909) and Historical Tripos, Part II (1910); Asst. Secretary, Cambridge University Press, 1911; Sec., 1922-48; served in Suffolk Regt. (Lieut.), 1915-19; wounded, Ypres, 1917; Lecturer for English Tripos, 1919-45; Pres. Johnson Society, 1929; Fellow of Pembroke College, 1929; Bursar, 1935-36; Member of Council, Publishers' Assoc., 1933-1940; Bd. of Trade Representative, Eastern Region, 1940-44; Cambridge Borough Councillor, 1946-49; Master of Pembroke, 1948-58; Vice-Chancellor of Cambridge, Univ., 1949-51; Pres., Library Association, 1953; Sandars Reader in Bibliography, 1954. Vice-President International Association of Universities, 1950-55; Trustee, Shakespeare's Birthplace, Barber Institute, Dr. Johnson's House, and Cambridge Union; Associate Fellow, Calhoun College, Yale University; Hon. Liveryman Goldsmiths' Company; Member U.S. Educational Commission, Victoria and Albert Museum Advisory Council; Chm., British Film Institute, 1952-56 and Cinematograph Films Council, 1954-64; Chairman Cttee. of enquiry into Public Library Services, 1957-58; Chairman Gabbitas-Thring Educational Trust, 1960-; Pres. English Assoc., 1962-63. *Publications:* Picture Book of British History (3 vols.), 1914-32; Story of Doctor Johnson, 1919; History of Cambridge University Press, 1921; Doctor Johnson in Cambridge, 1922; Boswell's Tour to Corsica, 1923; Piozzi's Anecdotes of Johnson, 1925; Samuel Johnson, Writer; The Charm of Cambridge; Browne's Christian Morals, 1927; translator of Aspects of Biography (André Maurois), 1929; An XVIII Century Gentleman, and other Essays, 1930; Doctor Watson, 1931; translator of A Frenchman in England, 1933; Introduction to Cambridge, 1934; Doctor Johnson (Great Lives), 1935; editor of Essays and Studies, Vol. XXIII., 1938; Zuleika in Cambridge, 1941; British Universities, 1947; Sherlock Holmes (Selected Stories), 1951; Holmes and Watson, 1953; The Evolution of Cambridge Publishing, 1956; Dr. Johnson and others, 1958; Richard Farmer, 1961; Adventures with Authors, 1966 (*posthumous*). *Recreation:* books. *Address:* The Loke House, 21 West Rd., Cambridge. *T.:* 50040. *Club:* Athenæum. [*Died* 21 *July* 1966.

ROBERTS, Ven. Windsor; Archdeacon of Dorking since 1957; Rector of Bisley since 1957; *b*. 4 May 1898; *s*. of John Wesley and Mary Jane Roberts; unmarried. *Educ.:* West Monmouthshire School; Durham University. Ordained, 1922; Curate, St. Paul's, Bedminster, Bristol, 1922-26, The Temple Church, Bristol, 1926-27, St. Mary, Portsea, 1928-31; Vicar of St. James's, Milton, Portsmouth, 1931-47; Rector of Alverstoke, Hants, 1947-57. Proctor in Convocation, 1945-; Examining Chaplain to Bishop of Guildford, 1957-. *Recreation:* golf. *Address:* Bisley Rectory, Woking. *T.:* Brookwood 3377. *Clubs:* English-Speaking Union; County (Guildford). [*Died* 23 *Dec*. 1962.

ROBERTSON, Alexander, F.R.S. 1941; Director; Heath Harrison Professor of Organic Chemistry, University of Liverpool, until 1957 now Professor Emeritus; *s*. of Andrew Robertson and Jane Cantlay; *m*. Margaret Mitchell Chapman (*d*. 1960), M.B., Ch.B. (Aberdeen); one *s*. *Educ.:* Aberdeen and Glasgow Universities. Lord Kitchener National Memorial Scholar at Glasgow University, 1919-22; Carnegie Scholar at Glasgow University, 1922-24; Rockefeller International Science Fellow at Manchester University, 1924-26; Graz University, Austria, 1926; M.A. (Aberdeen) 1919; B.Sc. (Glasgow) 1922; Ph.D. (Glasgow) 1924; LL.D. (Aberdeen); Asst. Lectr. in Chemistry at Manchester Univ., 1926-28; Reader in Chemistry, East London College, University of London, 1928-30; Reader in Biochemistry, London, School of Hygiene and Tropical Medicine, University of London, 1930-33; Pro-Vice-Chancellor, University of Liverpool, 1949-54. Member, Univ. Grants Cttee., 1955-59; Mem. of Agricultural Research Council, 1960-65. Davy Medal of Royal Society, 1952. *Publications:* Papers on Organic Chemistry in Journal of Chemical Society. *Recreations:* golf, shooting, fishing. *Address:* Roxholme Estates, Sleaford, Lincolnshire. *T.:* Ruskington 469. *Club:* University (Liverpool). [*Died* 9 *Feb*. 1970.

ROBERTSON, Sir Alexander, Kt. 1961; D.C.M. 1916. Formerly Metropolitan Police: Assistant Commissioner, 1956-58, Deputy Commissioner, 1958-61; retired 31 October 1961. *Recreations:* golf, fishing. *Address:* Dunkeld, Wansunt Rd., Bexley, Kent. *T.:* Crayford 21878. [*Died* 27 *Aug*. 1970.

ROBERTSON, Archibald Wallace; retd.; *b*. 23 Jan. 1895; *s*. of late Charles

Henry Everton Robertson and Henriette Anna Philippine van Dolder; *m.* 1927, Irene Elizabeth McLeod (*d.* 1954); no *c.* *Educ.:* King's School, Warwick; King's School, Grantham; Château du Rosey, Rolle, Switzerland; Dulwich College; Trinity Hall, Cambridge. Pro-Consul at Batavia, Java, 1916; Vice-Consul, Batavia, 1920; Sourabaya, 1921-23; Rotterdam, 1924; San Francisco, 1925-26; La Paz, Bolivia, 1926-29, with local rank of 2nd Secretary; Vice-Consul, Tunis, 1931-34; Consul at Cluj, Roumania, 1934; Bucharest, 1935-38; Cairo, 1938-44; Assistant Judge of the Consular Court in Egypt in 1939; Consul at New York, 1944-45; H.M. Envoy Extraordinary and Minister Plenipotentiary to Nicaragua, and Consul-General for the Republic of Nicaragua, 1945; H.M. Consul-Gen. at Amsterdam, 1948-53; retd. June 1953. *Recreation:* golf. *Address:* c/o Hongkong & Shanghai Banking Corp., 9 Gracechurch St., E.C.3. [*Died* 26 *Sept.* 1966.

ROBERTSON, Commodore A(rthur) Ian, C.B. 1953; R.D. 1938 (and Clasp, 1954); R.N.R. retired; *b.* 22 November 1898; *s.* of J. W. Robertson, M.A., Dalbeattie, Scotland; unmarried. *Educ.:* Lincoln City School. Went to sea as apprentice, Prince Line, Dec. 1912; entered R.N.R. as midshipman, 1916; served 2nd Cruiser Sqdn., then in Hydrophone Trawlers; took part in N. Russian Relief Force; demobilized, Dec. 1918. N.Z.S. Co., 1918; Lieut. R.N.R. 1923; Lieut.-Comdr. 1931; Comdr. 1939. Was Chief Officer of liner Rangitata at outbreak of war of 1939-45; mobilised, 1940; Comdr. of Humber Escort Force; Naval Berthing Officer, Tilbury, during collapse of Low Countries. In comnd. various major war vessels: E. Coast Convoy Protection, special service to Persian Gulf, and U.S.A. Comd. H.M.S. Invicta in combined ops., Dieppe Raid, then H.M.S. Princess Josephine Charlotte, also combined ops. in Force " J ". Landed first American troops at Orange Beach, Sicily, 1943; Capt. R.N.R. 1943; went U.S.A. and took comd. H.M.S. Patroller, Escort Aircraft Carrier; worked in Pacific, ferrying aircraft to India, Pearl Harbour; comd. H.Q. Ship, Lothian; Merchant Navy Liaison Officer to Flag Officer Fleet Train in Pacific; demobilized, 1945; re-joined N.Z.S. Co. in comd. A.D.C. to King George VI, 1950, to the Queen, 1952. Cdre. R.N.R., 1952. Senior Officer on active list of R.N.R., retired, 1953; Master of R.M.V. Ruahine (18,000 ton liner), New Zealand Shipping Co. Ltd., retired, 1954. Younger Brother of Trinity House, 1942; Mem. Hon. Company of Master Mariners, 1950. Mem. Roy. Naval Sailing Assoc. *Recreations:* golf, sailing. *Address:* Wayside, Welcomes Road, Kenley, Surrey. *T.:* Uplands 0097. *Clubs:* Naval and Military, R.N.R. Officers' (Pres.). [*Died* 24 *March* 1961.

ROBERTSON, Sir Carrick Hey, Kt., *cr.* 1929; M.B., B.S.(Lond.); F.R.C.S., F.R.C.A.S., F.A.C.S. (Hon.); Hon. Consulting Surgeon Auckland Hospital; *s.* of late Blair Robertson; *m.* 1st, 1906, Constance (*d.* 1950), *yr. d.* of late C. Maxwell-Hibberd; three *s.* one *d.*; 2nd, 1957, Delta, *d.* of late B. F. Cranwell. *Educ.:* St. Dunstan's Coll.; Guy's Hosp. Past President of N.Z. Branch B.M.A.; Foundation Fellow of Royal Australasian College of Surgeons; Honorary Fellow of American College of Surgeons; Hon. Fellow Assoc. of Surgeons of Gt. Brit. and Ireland, 1947; Chevalier Legion of Honour, 1939. *Address:* 1 Alfred Street, Auckland, C.1, N.Z. *Club:* Northern (Auckland). [*Died* 7 *July* 1963.

ROBERTSON, Charles; *b.* 23 Feb. 1874; *s.* of John and Margaret Robertson; *m.* 1910, Lilian Rose FitzRoy (*d.* 1960), *er. d.* of 8th Duke of Grafton. *Educ.:* Minto School; Edinburgh University. Ministry of Education, Egypt, 1902-25; Member of L.C.C. for East Islington, 1931-34; Alderman L.C.C., 1934-52; Vice-Chairman, 1934-37, Chairman, 1937-45, of L.C.C. Education Comm.; Chairman London County Council, 1945-46. Formerly Trustee of City Parochial Foundn. *Address:* 205 Hampstead Way, N.W.11. *T.:* Speedwell 1837. *Club:* Athenæum. [*Died* 6 *Jan.* 1968.

ROBERTSON, Sir David, Kt., *cr.* 1945; *b.* 19 Jan. 1890; *s.* of John Robertson, Chief Inspector, G.P.O., Glasgow, and Susie Scott Merrylees; *m.* May, *d.* of Robert Weir Ritchie and Amelia McDonald, Prestwick, Ayrshire; two *d.* *Educ.:* Woodside; Allan Glen's Schools, Glasgow; Glasgow Univ. Apprenticed Mitchell & Smith, C.A., Glasgow, 1907; joined Staff Cole Dickin and Hills, 18 Essex St., W.C.2., 1912; joined army, 1915; from Glasgow University O.T.C. commissioned to Argyll and Sutherland Highlanders; served B.E.F., France (wounded); attached Ministry of Food, 1918, as Sectional Accountant Fish, Game, Poultry, Eggs Section, promoted to Assistant Director of Finance and at the Armistice, Chief Accountant to the Ministry at the Peace Conference in Paris; after the war entered Fishing and Cold Storage Industries; Managing Director of several important companies; resigned Fishing Industry appointments, 1940. M.P. (C.) Streatham Division of Wandsworth, 1939-50; M.P. (U.) Caithness and Sutherland, 1950-64. First Freeman of Thurso, 1963. *Recreations:* golf, fishing. *Address:* 39 Hyde Park Gate, S.W.7. [*Died* 3 *June* 1970.

ROBERTSON, Sir Dennis Holme, Kt., *cr.* 1953; C.M.G. 1944; M.C. 1916; M.A., F.B.A.; Hon. D.Comm. (Amsterdam); Hon. Litt.D. (Harvard, Durham, Manchester); Hon. D.Econ. (Louvain); Hon. D.Sc.Econ. (Lond.); Hon. D.H.L. (Columbia); Hon. D.L.E.S. (Sheff.); Professor of Political Economy in the University of Cambridge, 1944-57, retd.; *b.* 23 May 1890; *s.* of late Rev. James Robertson, Headmaster of Haileybury, and late Constance E. Wilson. *Educ.:* Eton Coll.; Trinity Coll., Cambridge; Craven scholar, Chancellor's Medallist for English Verse, Cobden Prizeman; President of Union Soc. and Amateur Dramatic Club. Served European War (Egypt and Palestine) with 11th Batt. London Regt.; Fellow of Trinity College, Cambridge, 1914-38, and since 1944; Reader in Economics, Cambridge University, 1930-38; Sir Ernest Cassel Professor of Economics in the University of London, 1939-44; an adviser at H.M. Treasury, 1939-44. Member of the Royal Commission on Equal Pay, 1944; President of Royal Economic Society, 1948-50; Fellow of Eton College, 1948-57. Member of Council on Prices, Productivity and Incomes, 1957-1958; Member Amer. Phil. Soc.; hon. Member Amer. Acad. Arts Sci.; For. Mem. Naz. Acc. dei Lincei; Hon. Fellow of London School of Economics. *Publications:* A Study of Industrial Fluctuation, 1915; Money, 1922, revised 1928 and 1947; The Control of Industry, 1923, revised (with S. R. Dennison) 1960; Banking Policy and the Price Level, 1926; Economic Fragments, 1931; Economic Essays and Addresses (with A. C. Pigou), 1931; Essays in Monetary Theory, 1940; Utility and All That and other essays, 1952; Britain in the World Economy, 1954; Economic Commentaries, 1956; Lectures on Economic Principles, three vols., 1957-59; Growth, Wages, Money, 1961; articles in Economic Journal, etc. *Address:* Trinity College, Cambridge. *Club:* United University. [*Died* 21 *April* 1963.

ROBERTSON, Professor Donald James, M.A. (Glasgow); Principal's Assessor and Professor of Industrial Relations, University of Glasgow, since 1969; Member, Commission on the Constitution, since 1969; *b.* 17 May

1926; *s.* of Adam Robertson and late Margaret Gibson; *m.* 1955, Amy Affleck Mitchell; two *d. Educ.:* Hutcheson's Boys' Gram. Sch., Glasgow; Univ. of Glasgow. Asst. in Political Economy, Univ. of Glasgow, 1949-50; Research Asst., Oxford Univ. Inst. of Statistics, 1950-51; Lecturer: in Social and Economic Research, 1951-52; in Political Economy, 1952-57, Senior Lecturer in Political Economy, 1957-61, Univ. of Glasgow; Prof. of Applied Economics and Head of Dept. of Social and Economic Research, Univ. of Glasgow, 1961-69; Visiting Prof. of Business Administration, Univ. of California, Berkeley, 1966. Sub-Lieut. R.N.V.R. 1945-47. Mem. and Chm., Wages Council, 1955-69. Member Court of Inquiry on Electricity Supply Industry, 1964; Chairman, Court of Inquiry: on Railway Guards, 1967; on Rootes (Scotland) Ltd., 1968; on Dispute at Girling Factory, Bromborough, 1968; on Labour Relations at Heathrow Airport, 1970. Economic consultant for Lothians Regional Survey and Plan and Falkirk/Grangemouth Survey and Plan. Mem., National Economic Development Council; Chm., Railway Staff National Tribunal. Economic Consultant to Sec. of State for Scotland; Director, Glasgow Chamber of Commerce, 1966-69. Member: Council Royal Economic Soc.; Academic Adv. Cttee., Univ. of Salford. Ed., Scottish Journal of Political Economy; Chm., Bd. of Management, Urban Studies. President: Sect. X of British Assoc., 1963; Univ. Industrial Relations Association, 1962-65. M.B.I.M., 1967. Hon. M.T.P.I. 1970. Sidney Ball Memorial Lectr., Univ. of Oxford, 1965. *Publications:* Factory Wage Structures and National Agreements, 1960; The Economics of Wages, 1961; Public Expenditure; Appraisal and Control (Ed. with A. T. Peacock), 1963; Fringe Benefits, Labour Costs and Social Security (Ed. with G. L. Reid), 1965; British Balance of Payments (Ed.), 1966; Economics of Wages and Labour (with L. C. Hunter), 1969; articles in Scottish Jl. Polit. Econ.; Bulletin of Oxford Univ. Inst. of Statistics; Political Quarterly; The Manager; and other jls. *Address:* Woodend, 19 Blackwood Road, Milngavie, Glasgow. *T.:* 041-956 3700.

[*Died* 22 *Aug.* 1970.

ROBERTSON, Donald Struan, F.B.A., F.S.A.; M.A.; Hon. D.Litt. (Durham); Hon. LL.D. (Glasgow): Hon. D.Phil. (Athens); Hon. A.R.I.B.A.; Emeritus Professor of Greek, University of Cambridge (Regius Professor, 1928-50); Fellow of Trinity College, Cambridge, since 1909; *b.* 28 June 1885; *o. s.* of late H. R. Robertson, R.E., R.M.S.; *m.* 1st, 1909, Petica Coursolles (*d.* 1941), 4th *d.* of late Major Charles Jones, R.A.; two *s*; 2nd, 1956, Margaret Ann, 2nd *d.* of late Rt. Hon. Sir Eric Phipps, G.C.B., G.C.M.G., G.C.V.O., and *widow* of George Anthony Cary. *Educ.:* Westminster; Trinity College, Cambridge. Classical Lecturer, Trinity College, 1913-28; Vice-Master of Trinity Coll., 1947-51; held temporary commission in R.A.S.C. 1914-19; Member of the German Archæological Institute. *Publications:* A Handbook of Greek and Roman Architecture, 1929, edn. 2, 1943; articles in classical periodicals; editor with A. S. F. Gow, of W. Ridgeway's, The Early Age of Greece, vol. ii., 1931; editor, with Prof. Paul Vallette of Paris, of the Metamorphoses of Apuleius in the Budé Series, vols. i. and ii., 1940, vol. iii., 1945. *Address:* Trinity College, Cambridge. *T.:* Cambridge 58201; 37 Madingley Road, Cambridge.

[*Died* 5 *Oct.* 1961.

ROBERTSON, Edward, M.A., B.D., D.Litt., D.D. (St. A.); M.A. (Man.); D.D. (Wales); LL.D. (Manchester); Emeritus Professor; *b.* Cameron, Fife; *s.* of John Robertson, schoolmaster, Cameron; *m.* 1915, Gertrude Mary Coventry; (one *s.* decd.) two *d.* *Educ.:* Cameron School; Madras College, St. Andrews (Dux and Gold Medallist in Mathematics); St. Andrews Univ. (First in open Bursary Competition); Universities of Leipzig, Berlin, Heidelberg; one year in Syria studying Arabic. Assistant to Professor of Hebrew, St. Andrews, 1905-06; Carnegie Research Scholar, 1907-08; Carnegie Research Fellow, 1909-10; Lecturer in Arabic, Edinburgh University, 1913-21; Professor of Semitic Languages and Literature. University College of North Wales, Bangor, 1921-34; Dean of Faculty of Theology, 1922-1934; Vice-Principal, 1926-28; D.Litt. (St. Andrews), 1913; External Examiner, Universities of St. Andrews, Edinburgh, Glasgow, Oxford, Liverpool, Wales, London; D.D. (St. Andrews) 1929; Gunning Lecturer in the University of Edinburgh, 1929-32; Professor of Semitic Languages and Literatures, University of Manchester, 1934-45 (retired); Ops. Officer, North Western Reg. (Civil Defence), 1939-41; Pro-Vice-Chancellor, University of Manchester, 1944. President of Old Testament Study Society, 1948. Royal Asiatic Society. Librarian of John Rylands Library, 1949-62; Hon. Gov. of John Rylands Library, 1962. *Publications:* Translation of Arabic MS. on Calligraphy; A Descriptive Catalogue of Arabic and Persian MSS. in Edinburgh University Library (in collaboration); articles on Syrian and Palestinian Place-Names in Encyclop. Britannica (14th ed.); Catalogue of Samaritan Manuscripts in the John Rylands Library, Vol. I, 1938, Vol. II. 1962; The Old Testament Problem; articles in journals. Editor The Bulletin of the John Rylands Library; Co-ed. Modern Hebrew periodical, Melilah. *Recreation:* chess. *Address:* Box 131. Hudson, P.Q., Canada. *T.:* 236-4233.

[*Died* 29 *April* 1964.

ROBERTSON, E. Arnot; (Lady Turner); writer, broadcaster and lecturer; *d.* of late Dr. G. A. Robertson; *m.* 1927, Sir Henry (Ernest) Turner, *q.v.*; one *s. Educ.:* Sherborne, Paris, and Switzerland. *Publications:* Cullum, 1928; Three Came Unarmed, 1929; Four Frightened People, 1931; Ordinary Families, 1933; Thames Portrait, 1937; Summer's Lease, 1940; The Signpost, 1943; Devices and Desires, 1954; Justice of the Heart, 1958; The Spanish Town Papers, 1959. *Address:* 98 Heath Street, Hampstead, N.W.3.

[*Died* 21 *Sept.* 1961.

ROBERTSON, Sir Frederick Wynne, Kt., *cr.* 1945; C.S.I. 1941; C.I.E. 1935; *b.* 3 Feb. 1885; *s.* of late Major J. A. Robertson, Struan Hill, Delgany, Wicklow, Ireland; *m.* 1924, Gladys, *d.* of Dr. E. J. Jerome, Camelford, Cornwall; no *c. Educ.:* Charterhouse; Trinity College, Dublin. Entered Indian Civil Service, 1909; Settlement Officer Bankura, 1917; Secretary, Board of Revenue, Bengal, 1923; Commissioner, Presidency Division, 1930; Commissioner, Rajshahi Division, 1933; retired from I.C.S., 1937; Chairman Bengal Public Service Commission, 1937; Chairman, Federal Public Service Commission, 1942-47. *Address:* Dromore, Portland Road, Greystones, Wicklow, Eire. *Club:* Royal Irish Automobile.

[*Died* 24 *Nov.* 1964.

ROBERTSON, Sir George Stuart, Kt., *cr.* 1928; Q.C. 1920; F.S.A.; *b.* London, 25 May 1872; *e. s.* of late John Abel Robertson of Sutton Court, Sutton, Surrey, and Barbara Price, *d.* of late Thomas Keay of Oakley, Staffordshire; *m.* 1912, Helen Lawson, (*d.* 1954), 2nd *d.* of Wm. Lawson Peacock, Reigate; one *s. Educ.:* Winchester College (Scholar); New College, Oxford (Scholar and Fellow). M.A.; 1st Class Moderations, Classics; 1st Class Lit. Hum.; Ireland Scholar; Craven Scholar; Denyer and Johnson Scholar; Derby Scholar; Eldon Law Scholar; Chancellor's Prize, Latin Prose;

Gaisford Prizes, Greek Verse and Greek Prose; Canon Hall Junior Greek Testament Prize; Barrister, Inner Temple, 1899; Oxford Circuit; Secretary to Lord Alverstone as President of the Alaska Boundary Tribunal, 1903; Chief Registrar of Friendly Societies, 1912-37; and Industrial Assurance Commissioner, 1923-37; Deputy Chairman, Devon Quarter Sessions, 1939-46; Director of the Prudential Assurance Co. Ltd., 1937-52; Member of the General Council of the Bar, 1907-11; Knight of the Order of the Saviour of Greece; threw the hammer for Oxford against Cambridge, 1892-1893-4-5 (winner, 1893-4-5), for Oxford against Yale, 1894, and for the London Athletic Club against the New York Athletic Club, 1895; threw the discus and composed and recited a Greek ode at the Olympic Games, Athens, 1896; Vice-Pres. London Athletic Club. *Publications:* The Law of Tramways and Light Railways; Civil Proceedings by and against the Crown; Oswald on Contempt of Court (3rd edition); The Law of Copyright. *Recreations:* applied arts, music, travelling. *Address:* 41 Queen's Gate Gardens, S.W.7. *T.:* Knightsbridge 5012. *Club:* Athenæum. [*Died* 29 *Jan.* 1967.

ROBERTSON, Sir Howard (Morley), Kt. 1954; M.C.; R.A. 1958 (A.R.A. 1949); P.P.R.I.B.A., S.A.D.G.; Hon. D.Litt. (Reading) 1957; A.R.C.A.; partner in firm of Easton & Robertson, Cusdin, Preston and Smith, retd.; *b.* Salt Lake City, 16 Aug. 1888; *y. s.* of Casper Ludovic Van Uytrecht Robertson, Liverpool, and Ellen Duncan, Ohio, U.S.A.; *m.* 1927, Doris Adeney Lewis, A.R.I.B.A., Melbourne; no *c.* *Educ.:* Eastfield House, Ditchling, Sussex; Malvern College. Received architectural education at Architectural Assoc. Schools, 1905-07, then at École des Beaux Arts, Paris, 1908-12; French Govt. Architectural Diploma, 1913; served in France, 1915-19 (M.C., Legion of Honour, U.S.A. Certificate of Merit, Officier de l'Étoile Noire); President Royal Institute of British Architects, 1952-1954. R.I.B.A. Godwin Bursar, 1933; Royal Gold Medal for Architecture, 1949. *Principal Works:* British Government Pavilion, Paris Exhibition of Decorative Arts, 1925; private houses in London, provinces, and abroad; works at Berkeley, Savoy, and Claridge's Hotels; New Hall for the Horticultural Society, London; British Pavilion, Brussels, 1935, Johannesburg, 1936, and New York World's Fair, 1939; offices, industrial buildings, flats and schools; Printing Works for Bank of England, Faculty of Letters, Reading Univ., 1956; Shell Centre, South Bank. U.K. Mem., Board of Design, U.N. Headquarters, New York. *Publications:* Principles of Architectural Composition, 1924; Architecture Explained, 1926; Modern French Details (with F. R. Yerbury), 1928; Modern Architectural Design, 1932; Architecture Arising, 1944; contributor to various architectural reviews. *Recreations:* music, motoring, travel. *Address:* 58 Bedford Square, W.C.1. *T.:* Museum 8121. *Club:* Royal Automobile. [*Died* 5 *May* 1963.

ROBERTSON, Sir James Jackson, Kt., *cr.* 1956; O.B.E. 1948; J.P.; retired as Rector of Aberdeen Grammar School, (1942-59); *b.* 14 May 1893; *s.* of late Alexander K. Robertson, Kilmarnock, Ayrshire; *m.* 1924, Aline Mathieson Woodrow, *d.* of late James R. Woodrow, Washington, D.C.; one *s.* one *d.* *Educ.:* Kilmarnock Academy; Hutchesons' Grammar School; Glasgow High School; Glasgow University. First Bursar, Glasgow Univ.; Mil. Service, 1916-19. M.A. Hons. Classics (Glasg.), 1919; B.D. (Lond.), 1930; F.R.S.E. 1941; F.E.I.S. 1949; Hon. LL.D. (Aberdeen), 1956. Classical Masterships, 1920-26; Headmaster, Fort William Secondary School, 1926; Rector of: Falkirk High School, 1931; Royal High School of Edinburgh, 1940. Secretary, Scottish Secondary Headmasters' Assoc., 1936-39, Pres. 1944-46; Member: Advisory Council on Educn. in Scotland, 1942-52 (Convener of its Secondary Committee), and Vice-Chm., 1957; Advisory Committee on Education in Colonies, 1946- (Chm. of its Africa Sub-Committee, 1956); reported on Achimota School to Govt. of Gold Coast, 1952; Member, U.K. Deleg. to 8th Gen. Conf. of U.N.E.S.C.O., Montevideo, 1954; Chairman, School Broadcasting Council for Scotland, 1965; Member: School Broadcasting Council for U.K., 1957; Council for Overseas Colleges of Arts, Science and Technology, 1957; Pres. Education Section of British Assoc., 1959; Mem. Tribunal of Inquiry into Waters Case, 1959; Chm. of Scottish Council for Training of Teachers, 1959-61; Mem. Scottish Council for Research in Education, 1959-; Mem. Royal Commission on the Police, 1960; Mem. National Council for Supply of Teachers Overseas, 1960; Mem. U.K. National Commn. for Unesco, 1960-66. J.P. 1950. *Publications:* contrib. to Year Book of Education and educl. jls. *Recreation:* walking. *Address:* 10 Hamilton Place, Aberdeen. *T.:* 23295. [*Died* 9 *June* 1970.

ROBERTSON, Jean F.; *see* Forbes-Robertson.

ROBERTSON, John Archibald Campbell, C.B. 1961; Under Secretary, H.M. Treasury, since 1951; *b.* 21 Nov. 1912; *m.* 1941, Diana Van Cortlandt, *d.* of Charles Read, Ottawa, Canada; three *s.* two *d.* *Educ.:* Univ. Coll. School; St. John's Coll., Cambridge. First Class, Historical Tripos, Parts I and II. Administrative Class, Home Civil Service, 1935; India Office, 1935-36; transferred to Treasury, 1936; Private Secretary to Financial Secretary, 1939-40, and to Permanent Secretary, 1943-45; Assistant Secretary, 1945. Home Civil Service Commonwealth Fund Fellow, 1949-50; Director of Personnel, United Nations, 1954-57. *Address:* Voel House, 18 South Grove, Highgate, N.6. *T.:* Mountview 0454. [*Died* 27 *May* 1962.

ROBERTSON, John Henry; *see* Connell, John.

ROBERTSON, John Williamson; journalist; *b.* 27 March 1900; *s.* of David Robertson, journalist, and Elizabeth Hume; *m.* 1928, Violet Isobel Duncan (decd.); two *d.* *Educ.:* Woodside Higher Grade School, Glasgow. Began as office-boy in Glasgow Evening News, 1915, subsequently absorbed by Kemsley Newspapers; Reporter, Asst. Ed., then Ed. of Evening News (1941); finally Editor-in-Chief in Glasgow (1946); Managing Editor of Kemsley Newspapers in Manchester, 1948-52, then editor Sunday Chronicle; returned to Glasgow as Managing Editor of (now defunct) Evening News; formerly Editor of the Sunday Mail. Served one year in European War, 1914-18, as Second-Lieutenant R.A.F., 1918; Pilot ever since; Hon. Flying Instructor, R.A.F., 1939-45. *Recreations:* flying, golf, swimming, motoring. *Address:* 8 North Campbell Avenue, Milngavie, Dunbartonshire. *T.:* Milngavie 1735. *Clubs:* Glasgow, Old Troon, Scottish Flying, Royal Scottish Automobile (Glasgow), etc. [*Died* 29 *May* 1969.

ROBERTSON, Norman Alexander, C.C. (Can.); Director, Graduate School of International Affairs at Carleton University, Ottawa, 1965; *b.* 4 Mar. 1904; *s.* of L. F. and F. Robertson; *m.* 1928, H. J. Welling; two *d.* *Educ.:* University of British Columbia; Balliol Coll., Oxford. Entered Department of External Affairs of Canada, 1929; Under-Sec. of State for External Affairs, 1941-46 and 1958-64; Clerk of Privy Council and Sec. to Cabinet 1949-52; High Commissioner for Canada in U.K., 1946-49 and 1952-57; Canadian Ambassador to Washington, 1957-58.

Hon. Fellow, Balliol College, Oxford, 1963. *Address:* Carleton University, Ottawa 1, Canada. [*Died* 16 *July* 1968.

ROBERTSON, Thomas Logan, C.M.G. 1969; Chairman of Council, Western Australian Institute of Technology, since 1967; President, Australian Council for Educational Research since 1967; *b.* 12 Nov. 1901; *s.* of Andrew H. F. Robertson; *m.* 1927, Marion Gibson; one *s.* one *d.* *Educ.:* Perth Modern Sch.; Univs. of Western Australia and London. W. Aust. Education Service, 1918-40; Inspector of Schools, W. Aust., 1941-46. Dep. Asst. Dir., Aust. Army Educn. Service, Major, 1942-45. Asst. Dir., Commonwealth Office of Educn., 1946-50; Dir. Gen. of Educn., W. Aust., 1951-66; Pro-Chancellor, Univ. of W. Aust., 1956-66; Chm. Council, Canberra Coll. of Advanced Educn., 1967-68. F.A.C.E. 1960; Hon. LL.D. (W.A.), 1968. Britannica Australia Award for services to Education, 1967. *Recreations:* swimming, gardening. *Address:* 59 Tyrell Street, Nedlands, W. Australia 6009, Australia. *T.:* 865698. [*Died* 29 *Aug.* 1969.

ROBERTSON, Wheatley Alexander, C.M.G. 1948; *b.* Brixham, 4 Aug. 1885; *s.* of Col. Wheatley Robertson, Madras Staff Corps, and Christina M. Grieve; unmarried. *Educ.:* Rugby; Royal Indian Engineering College, Cooper's Hill. Joined Indian Forest Service 1906 in Burma; research staff at Forest Research Institute Dehra Dun, 1921; Conservator of Forests Utilisation Circle in Burma, 1924; Retired from Indian Forest Service, 1933; Editor Empire Forestry Journal, 1932-33; Director Forest Products Research under Dept. of Scientific and Industrial Research at Forest Products Research Laboratory, Princes Risborough, Bucks, 1933-45; Forestry Adviser, Colonial Office, 1941-50. *Recreations:* walking, travel. *Club:* East India and Sports. [*Died* 7 *Nov.* 1964.

ROBERTSON - GLASGOW, Raymond Charles; *b.* 15 July 1901; *yr. s.* of late R. P. Robertson-Glasgow, formerly of Craigmyle, Aberdeenshire, and late Muriel Barbara (*née* Holt-Wilson), Redgrave, Suffolk; *m.* 1943, Elizabeth Edward (*née* Powrie), *widow* of P. Y. Hutton; one step *s.* *Educ.:* St. Edmund's School, Hindhead; Charterhouse (Scholar; Gordon Whitbread Prize for Greek and Latin Literature, Thackeray Prize for English Literature); C.C.C., Oxford (Open Scholar). B.A. (Hons.) Oxon. 1923, M.A. 1948. Master, St. Edmund's Sch., Hindhead, 1923-33; Golf, then Cricket, Correspondent, The Morning Post, 1933-37, Daily Telegraph, 1937-38, Observer, 1938-56, Sunday Times, 1956, contrib. to Punch and many other magazines. *Publications:* The Brighter Side of Cricket, 1933; I Was Himmler's Aunt, 1941; No Other Land, 1943; Cricket Prints, 1943; Men Only in Sport, 1943; More Cricket Prints, 1948; 46 Not Out (Autobiog.), 1948; Rain Stopped Play, 1948; The Brighter Side of Cricket, 1951; All in the Game, 1952; How to Become a Test Cricketer; Crusoe on Cricket, 1966 (*posthumous*). *Recreations:* cricket (played for Oxford v. Cambridge, 1920-23, Somerset, 1920-35, Gentlemen v. Players, Lords, 1924, for an England Eleven v. Australians at Folkestone, 1930); golf (Mem. Oxford and Cambridge Golfing Soc.). *Address:* Lime Tree Cottage, St. Andrew's School, nr. Pangbourne, Berkshire. *T.:* Bradfield (Berks) 265. *Clubs:* Savage, Press, M.C.C.; Vincent's (Oxford). [*Died* 4 *March* 1965.

ROBERTSON SCOTT, John William, C.H. 1947; M.A. (*h.c.*) Oxon., 1949; *b.* Wigton, 1866; *m.* 1906, Elspet Keith (*d.* 1956). *Educ.:* grammar and Quaker schools. Birmingham Daily Gazette, 1886-1887; Pall Mall Gazette, 1887-93; Westminster Gazette, 1893-99; Daily Chronicle 1899 till South African War; subsequently lived in Essex and wrote on rural subjects, above the signature Home Counties; contributed monthly country article to World's Work, 1903-16, and 1922-24, and weekly to County Gentleman, 1902-9; rural commissioner in Netherlands and Denmark for Daily Chronicle, 1910; contributor Quarterly Review, Nineteenth Century, Spectator, Nation, Times, etc., 1910-14. Member of rural housing advisory committees at Whitehall under four Ministers. Member of the Councils of Nat. Education Assoc., Nat. Soc. for the Abolition of Cruel Sports, Rationalist Press Assoc. Soc. for the Liberation of the Church from State Control, Agricultural Economics Soc., Japan Soc.; Member: Vegetarian, Cremation, and Voluntary Euthanasia Socs.; Rationalist Press Assoc. *Publications:* pamphlets against the South African War, 1900; People of China, 1900; In Search of £150 Cottage (with J. St. Loe Strachey), 1904; The Little Farm, 1905; Country Cottages, 1905; Poultry Farming: Some Facts and Some Conclusions, 1905; The Case for the Goat, 1908; The Townsman's Farm, 1908; Strange Story of the Dunmow Flitch, 1909; Sugar Beet: Some Facts and Some Illusions: A Study in Rural Therapeutics, 1911; A Free Farmer in a Free State (Holland), 1912; The Land Problem, 1913; Practical Hints from the Note-book of an Old Farmer (edited); A Plea for an Open-Air Museum; War and Peace in Holland; Despatches on the War in a Dutch Translation (edited), 1914; Japan, Great Britain, and the World (English and Japanese), 1916; The Ignoble Warrior (English and Japanese), 1917; Our Obligations to the Japanese; The Foundations of Japan: 6000 Miles in its Rural Districts, 1922; The Farmer's Problem, 1923; The Story of the Women's Institute Movement, 1925; England's Green and Pleasant Land, 1925; extended ed., 1947; The Dying Peasant and the Future of his Sons, 1926; The Country Citizen, 1938, etc.; founded (1915) and edited (until 1918) the New East (English and Japanese), Tokyo; founded the Village Press, 1926, and The Countryman, 1927; edited it until 1947; Faith and Works in Fleet Street, 1947; The Countryman Book, 1948; The Countryman's Breakfast Poser and Townsman's Rural Remembrancer, 1950; The Story of the Pall Mall Gazette, its first Editor, Frederick Greenwood, and its Publisher, George Smith, 1950; The Day Before Yesterday, 1951; The Life and Death of a Newspaper (Memories of the Pall Mall Gazette and its Editors), 1952; 'We' and Me, 1956. *Recreations:* J.P.; founder of the Quorum Club (educational soc. of sixty Oxfordshire magistrates). Most outdoor occupations except hunting, shooting, racing and fishing. *Address:* Idbury Manor, Kingham, Oxford. *T.:* Shipton-under-Wychwood 226. *Club:* Farmers'. [*Died* 21 *Dec.* 1962.

ROBIN, Rt. Rev. Bryan Percival, M.A., Th. Soc.; *b.* 12 Jan. 1887; *s.* of late Rev. P. C. Robin, Rector of Woodchurch, Cheshire; *m.* 1921, Frances Nathalie Mary, *d.* of late Canon H. J. Glennie; three *s.* two *d.* *Educ.:* Rossall Sch.; Univ. of Liverpool, B.A. 1909, M.A. 1941; Leeds Clergy School. Th. Soc. Aust. Coll. Theol. 1941; Deacon, 1910; Priest, 1911; Assistant Curate S. Margaret, Ilkley, 1910-14; Member Bush Brotherhood of S. Barnabas, N. Queensland, 1914-20; Canon and Sub-Dean of St. James's Cathedral, Townsville, 1922-25; Warden of St. John's College, Brisbane, and Canon of Brisbane, 1926-30; Rector of Woodchurch, Cheshire, 1931-41; Rural Dean of Wirral North, 1936-1941; Hon. Canon of Chester, 1940-41; Bishop of Adelaide, 1941-56; Hon. Canon of Portsmouth, 1958; Assistant Bishop of Portsmouth, 1959-67; retired. *Publication:* The Sundowner, 1921. *Recreations:* golf, tennis, etc. *Address:* 135 Sussex Road, Petersfield, Hants. [*Died* 17 *June* 1969.

ROBINS, 1st Baron *cr.* 1958, of Rhodesia and of Chelsea; **Thomas Ellis Robins,** K.B.E. 1954; Kt. 1946; D.S.O. 1919; E.D. 1933; President of the British South Africa Company; Director: Barclays Bank D.C.O., African Explosives and Chemical Industries, Anglo-American Corporation of South Africa, Wankie Colliery Co., Premier Portland Cement (Rhodesia), De Beers Consolidated Mines, Union Corporation, and other companies; Trustee Rhodes-Livingstone Museum; *b.* Philadelphia, U.S.A., 31 Oct. 1884; *s.* of late Major Robert P. Robins, U.S. Army, and Mary, *d.* of late Thomas de la Roche Ellis; *m.* 1912, Mary St. Quintin, *y. d.* of late Philip Wroughton, D.L., of Woolley Park, Berks; two *d.* *Educ.:* privately; University of Pennsylvania, B.A.; Christ Church, Oxford. Was the first Rhodes Scholar from State of Pennsylvania to Oxford University, 1904-07; Assistant Editor Everybody's Magazine, New York, 1907-1909; Private Secretary to Earl Winterton, M.P., 1909-14; a British subject by naturalisation, 1912; mobilised with City of London Yeo., 4 Aug. 1914 and served overseas in M.E.F., and E.E.F., April 1915-Jan. 1921; Provost Marshal, E.E.F. (Egypt and Palestine), Feb. 1919-Jan. 1921 (despatches twice, D.S.O.); Secretary of Conservative Club, 1921-28; commanded City of London Yeomanry Battery, R.H.A., T.A., 1925-28 (winners of the King's Prize, 1928). Served East Africa Command, 1939-40; O.C., 1st Bn. The Rhodesia Regt., 1940-43; Military Delegate from Southern Rhodesia to Eastern Group Conference, Delhi, 1940; General Staff, India, 1943; A.A. & Q.M.G. Southern Rhodesia Forces, 1943-45; Commissioner for Boy Scouts, Southern Rhodesia, 1930-45. K.St.J.; Grand Officier, Ordre Royal de l'Étoile d'Anjouan. *Address:* 76 Sloane St., S.W.1. *Clubs:* Carlton, Cavalry, Pratt's, Bath, Brooks's; various, in Rhodesia and South Africa.
[*Died* 21 *July* 1962 (*ext.*).

ROBINSON, Charles Stanley, C.B.E. 1943; M.A. Camb.; F.R.I.C.; C.Eng., M.I.Chem.E.; *b.* 25 Dec. 1887 *s.* of late Frederick Robinson, Nottingham; *m.* 1930, Barbara Lang Johnson (*d.* 1968), *d.* of late Sir Alexander Richardson, M.P. *Educ.:* Nottingham High Sch.; Emmanuel Coll., Cambridge (Scholar). B.A. 1910, M.A. 1922; served as a private, European War, 1914-16 (1914-15 Star); 1916-18 with Ministry of Munitions; Works Manager Cape Explosives Works, South Africa, 1918-24; Technical Adviser to Union Sulphur Co. of Louisiana in Marseilles, 1924-25; a Technical Manager to Nobel Industries Ltd., 1925-29; to I.C.I. Ltd., 1929-38; Chairman of I.C.I. (General Chemicals) Ltd., 1938-39; seconded to Ministry of Supply, Oct. 1939; Deputy Director-General of Ordnance Factories, 1940; Director-General of Filling Factories, Ministry of Supply, 1941-45; Deputy Chief, Economics Division, Allied Control Commission (British Element), 1945-46. Member, Peterlee Development Corp., 1949-54; Chairman, Aycliffe Development Corp., 1953-63. Mem. Royal Commission on Equal Pay; Liveryman, Gunmakers Company; Freeman, City of London. *Address:* 5 Trumpington Rd., Cambridge. *T.:* Cambridge 53037. *Clubs:* Savage, M.C.C.; Union Society (Cambridge).
[*Died* 27 *Nov.* 1969.

ROBINSON, Rear-Admiral Eric Gascoigne, V.C. 1916; O.B.E. 1919; R.N. retired; *b.* Greenwich, 16 May 1882; *s.* of Rev. J. L. Robinson, M.A., R.N.; *m.* 1913, Edith Gladys Cordeux (*d.* 1938); (two *s.* both killed in War of 1939-45) one *d.* *Educ.:* St. John's, Leatherhead; The Limes, Greenwich. Joined Britannia, 1897; Rear-Adm. and retired list, 1933. *Recreations:* golf, tennis. *Address:* The White House, Langrish, Nr. Petersfield, Hants. *T.:* Petersfield 579.
[*Died* 20 *Aug.* 1965.

ROBINSON, Sir Foster (Gotch), Kt. 1958; President: E. S. and A. Robinson (Holdings) Ltd., 1961 (Chm. 1929-61); Bristol Waterworks Co., 1964 (Chm., 1935-60); Teleflex Products Ltd., 1964 (Dir., 1934-64); *b.* 19 Sept. 1880; *s.* of Edward Robinson and Katherine Frances Robinson, Bristol; *m.* 1st, 1908, Marguerite Victoria Mary Clarke (*d.* 1963); one *s.*; 2nd, 1966, Mrs. Jeanie Monsell, *widow* of the Rt. Rev. J. N. Bateman-Champain. *Educ.:* Clifton Coll., Bristol; Exeter Coll., Oxford. After university took up business career. *Recreations:* cricket, golf, fishing, and racing. *Address:* Eastwood Manor, East Harptree, Bristol. *Clubs:* St. James', Portland; Clifton (Bristol); Jockey.
[*Died* 31 *Oct.* 1967.

ROBINSON, Godfrey, C.B.E. 1953; M.C. 1917; Chairman Royal National Institute for the Blind since 1952 (Member Council since 1933); Director Thomas Robinson Sons & Co. Ltd.; *b.* 27 Dec. 1897; 2nd *s.* of late T. A. Robinson, J.P., North Ferriby; *m.* 1924, Margaret Enid, *d.* of late Horace Vipan Wright, J.P., North Ferriby; three *s.* two *d.* *Educ.:* Uppingham. Lieut. R.F.A., 1915-18; blinded in action, France, 1917. Chairman, Hull and East Riding Institute for the Blind, 1938- (Committee 1920-); Sheriff of City and County of Kingston upon Hull, 1941-42; Member Advisory Cttee. to Minister of Health on Health and Welfare of Handicapped Persons, 1950-; Hull City Council, 1955. *Address:* Fouracres, North Ferriby, Yorks. *T.:* Ferriby 87311. *Club:* United Service.
[*Died* 19 *Dec.* 1961.

ROBINSON, Rt. Rev. Hector Gordon; Bishop of Riverina since 1951; *b.* 9 June 1899; *s.* of late John Graham Robinson and late Muriel Helen Robinson, Melbourne, Vict.; *m.* 1930, Elsie Hamilton, *d.* of late William Hamilton Brownless of Jerilderie, N.S.W. *Educ.:* Scotch College, Melbourne; Australian Coll. of Theology (Th.L. 1921); Trinity Coll., Melbourne (B.A. 1923). Deacon, 1922; priest, 1923; Curate of St. Peter Melbourne, 1922-24; Chaplain, Royal Australian Navy, 1924-27; Priest-in-charge, Boort, 1927-29; Rector of Home Hill, 1930-37; St. Matthew, Townsville, 1937-39; Mackay, Diocese of N. Queensland, 1939-51; Archdeacon of Mackay, 1943-51. *Address:* Bishop's Lodge, Narrandera, N.S.W., Australia.
[*Died* 9 *Dec.* 1965.

ROBINSON, Henry Morton; Author; *b.* Boston, Mass., 7 Sept. 1898; *s.* of Henry M., and Ellen Robinson (*née* Flynn); *m.* 1926, Gertrude Ludwig (marr. diss.); one *s.* two *d.*; *m.* 1954, Vivian Wyndham. *Educ.:* Columbia College; Columbia University. Served U.S. Navy, Gunner's Mate 3rd Class, 1917-19. Instructor in English, Columbia Coll., 1924-27. Editor, Contemporary Verse, 1925-27; Assoc. Editor, Reader's Digest, 1932-37, Senior Editor, 1937-45. Since then, has devoted full time to writing. Member: Poetry Society of America (Vice-Pres. 1953-1954); Authors' League, N.Y. City. *Publications:* Children of Morningside, 1924; Buck Fever, 1929; Stout Cortez, 1931; Science Versus Crime, 1935; Second Wisdom, 1936; Public Virtue, Private Good, 1937; D. W., 1940; Fantastic Interim, 1943; A Skeleton Key to Finnegans Wake (with J. Campbell), 1944; The Perfect Round, 1945; The Great Snow, 1947; The Cardinal, 1950; The Enchanted Grindstone, 1952; (with A. Zaidenburg) Out of Line, 1952; Tale of Two Lovers, 1955; The Willingdone Museyroom, 1956; Water of Life, 1959. *Recreations:* yachting, falconry, small arms. *Address:* 100 Creston Ave., Tenafly, N.J., U.S.A. *T.:* LO-9, 9574. *Clubs:* Century, Columbia University, New York Athletic, N.Y.A. Yacht Club (New York); P.E.N. (Internat.).
[*Died* 13 *Jan.* 1961.

ROBINSON, Col. John Poole Bowring, C.M.G. 1919; D.S.O. 1917; (p.s.c.); late Royal Dublin Fusiliers and Royal Berkshire Regt.; *b.* 1881; 2nd *s.* of late Rev. A. D. J. Robinson; *m.* 1912, Ethna Pauline (*d.* 1958), *d.* of late Very Rev. T. A. Hackett, Dean of Limerick; one *d.* (and one *s.* decd.). *Educ.:* Westminster; Sandhurst. Served South African War, 1899-1902 (Queen's medal five clasps); Aden Hinterland, 1903; European War, 1914-19 (despatches five times, C.M.G., D.S.O.); Co. Commander, R.M.C. Sandhurst, 1923-25; commanded 2nd Batt. Royal Berks Regiment, 1928-32; G.S.O. 1st Grade, 5th Division, Catterick, 1932-33; A.Q.M.G., Aldershot Command, 1933; retired pay, 1933; Senior Regional Officer, A.R.P. and C.D., Southern Region, 1938-42. War Organisation B.R.C.S. and Order of St. John, Dir. of Personnel, 1944-47. O.St.J. *Address:* Park Cottage, Letcombe Regis, Berkshire. *Club:* Army and Navy. [*Died* 8 *Aug.* 1966.

ROBINSON, John William Dudley, M.Sc., Ph.D., F.G.S.; Officier de l'Ordre de la Santé Publique; Secretary, Royal Sanitary Inst. 1928-52, Vice-President, 1953-1955; Vice-President Royal Society for the Promotion of Health, 1955-63 (Life Vice-Pres., 1963); *b.* 1886; *s.* of John and C. S. Robinson; *m.* 1913, Mildred Blanche Chapman, B.Sc., D.I.C., F.G.S.; no *c.* *Educ.:* Sir Joseph Williamson's Mathematical School, Rochester; South Western Polytechnic. On staff of Kent and Surrey Education Committees; Secretary in the University of London, 1912-14; Secretary of the Institution of Municipal and County Engineers, 1914-28; served European War in Honourable Artillery Company and as Lieutenant, Royal Engineers, 1916-19. *Publications:* editor, Journal of Institution of Municipal and County Engineers, 1914-28; papers on geological subjects. *Recreations:* walking, gardening *Address:* 23 Trescobeas Road Falmouth, Cornwall. *T.:* Falmouth 313. [*Died* 15 *July* 1967.

ROBINSON, Joseph, C.B.E. 1955; *b.* 7 Feb. 1905; *s.* of late Alfred Robinson, J.P., shipowner, North Shields, and Constance Alice (*née* Goodes); *m.* 1931, Katherine (*née* Garrison), New Jersey, U.S.A.; one *s.* two *d.* *Educ.:* Malvern Coll.; Corpus Christi Coll., Cambridge. Entered H.M. Consular Service, 1928; served at: New York, 1929-31; Antwerp, 1932-36; Santiago de Chile, 1937-1944 (Lima, 1940); Tegucigalpa, 1945-46; St. Paul-Minneapolis, 1946-47; H.M. Foreign Service: Head of Chancery, Caracas, 1947-50; Head of Information Services Dept., F.O., 1950-53; H.M. Ambassador to Paraguay, 1953-56; H.M. Consul-Gen., Zürich, 1957-60; retd. 1960. Served in Central Office of Information for planning towns in Britain by moulders of opinion from abroad, 1961-69, retd. *Recreations:* gardening, music, advancing a measure of law around the Earth. *Address:* 6 Hawkswell Gardens, Summertown, Oxford OX2 7EX. *T.:* Oxford 55497. [*Died* 4 *Jan.* 1970.

ROBINSON, Rev. Canon Reginald Henry, M.A., D.D.; *b.* 7 Aug. 1881; *s.* of late Rev. Francis Edward Robinson and Mary Caroline Butler; *m.* 1932, Miriam Jane Robertson; one *d.* *Educ.:* St. Oswald's College, Ellesmere; King Edward's School, Bromsgrove; Oxford University, B.A. 1903, M.A. 1906. Shute Exhibitioner, 2nd Cl. Classical Mods., 1901. Assistant Master, Bramcote, Scarborough, 1906-09; Classical Master, Heidelberg College, 1909-10; Cuddesdon Theological College, 1910; Deacon, 1911; Priest, 1912; Assistant Curate, All Saints', King's Heath, 1911-15; Priest-in-charge of St. Catherine's Edson, with St. Mary's Jasper, 1915-17; Head of Edmonton Mission and Examining Chaplain to Bishop of Edmonton, 1917-20; Associate Rector, Pro-Cathedral, Calgary, 1920-26; Canon Residentiary, 1921-26; Rector of Pro-Cathedral, Calgary, and Dean of Calgary, 1926-32; Examining Chaplain to Bishop of Calgary, 1921-32; B.D. (Honours), St. John's College, Winnipeg, 1925; D.D. (Hon.), 1930; Bishop's Commissary, 1930; resigned from Calgary and returned to England, 1932; Bishop's Messenger, 1935-50; Examr., Peterborough Diocesan Readers' Assoc., 1935-66; Rector of St. Mary's, Wilby, Wellingborough, 1933-37; Vicar of St. James', Northampton, 1937-49; Rural Dean of Northampton, 1946-1949; Vicar of Mears Ashby, Northamptonshire, 1949-54, Rector of Hardwycke, Northamptonshire, in plurality, 1952-54, Canon (non-residentiary) of Peterborough, 1946, Emeritus 1967. *Recreations:* photography, gardening. *Address:* 66 Brookland Road, Northampton. *T.:* 32026. [*Died* 19 *Aug.* 1970.

ROBINSON, Samuel, C.M.G. 1945; *b.* 1893; *m.* 1924, Ella Motley; one *s.* one *d.* Served with H.M. Forces, 1914-19; Civil Service, 1919-53; Secretary of the Iron and Steel Board, 1953-59. *Address:* 11A High St., St. John's Wood, N.W.8. [*Died* 19 *Oct.* 1967.

ROBINSON, Brig.-General Stratford Watson, C.B. 1919; D.S.O. 1917; late Royal Artillery; *b.* 1871; 4th *s.* of late J. H. Robinson, Examiner of Private Bills, House of Commons; *m.* 1909, Doris Ethel (*d.* 1956), 2nd *d.* of Vincent Mackinnon, Mussoorie, India; one *s.* *Educ.:* Elizabeth College, Guernsey; R.M. Academy, Woolwich. Commissioned R.A., 1890; served N.W.F. India and Tirah, 1897-98 (medal and 3 clasps); South Africa (on Staff), 1901-2, (Queen's medal and 3 clasps); N.W.F. India, 1908 (medal with clasp); European War, 1914-1919, on Staff (Indian Corps, 2nd Div. and 13th Corps), (Bt. Lt.-Col., D.S.O., Bt. Col., C.B.); A.A.G. Eastern Command, 1919-23; retired as Colonel with hon. rank of Brig.-Gen., 1923. *Address:* c/o Lloyds Bank, 6 Pall Mall, S.W.1. [*Died* 16 *April* 1962.

ROBINSON, Theodore Henry, Litt.D. (Cantab.), D.D. (Lond.), Hon. D.D. (Aberdeen and Wales); Hon. D.th. (Halle-Wittemberg); *b.* Edenbridge, Kent, 9 August 1881; *s.* of Rev. W. Venis Robinson, B.A., Baptist minister, and Emily Jane, *y. d.* of W. W. Page; *m.* 1906, Marie Helen (*d.* 1959), *e. d.* of Rev. C. Joseph; one *d.* *Educ.:* Mill Hill School; St. John's College, Cambridge; Regent's Park Coll., London; University of Göttingen. Lecturer, Woodbrooke Settlement, 1905-8; Professor of Hebrew and Syriac, Serampore College, Bengal, 1908-15; Lecturer in Semitic Languages, Univ. College, Cardiff, 1915-27; Prof. 1927-44; Schweich Lecturer, 1926; Murtle Lecturer, 1928; Visiting Prof., Univ. of Chicago, 1929, University of Halle-Wittenberg, 1931; Hon. Sec. Society for Old Testament Study, 1917-46, President, 1928 and 1946. Burkitt Bronze Medal for Biblical Studies (British Academy), 1946; Hon. Mem. (American) Soc. of Biblical Literature and Exegesis. *Publications:* Paradigms and Exercises in Syriac Grammar; Adult School translations; general editor of O.T. Series; volumes on Genesis and Amos; The Life of Jesus according to S. Mark; The Book of Amos, Hebrew Text, with Notes and Vocabulary; Prophecy and the Prophets in the Old Testament; The Clarendon Old Testament, vol. iii., Eighth and Seventh Centuries, The Decline and Fall of the Hebrew Kingdoms; An Introduction to the History of Religions; The Genius of Hebrew Grammar; Commentary on the Gospel according to St. Matthew; Commentary on the Epistle to the Hebrews; Handbuch zum Alten Testament, Pt. 6 (commentary on Hosea - Micah); Text of Ruth and Lamentations in Biblia Hebraica; (with W.O.E. Oesterley) Hebrew Religion; A

History of Israel (Vol. I.); Introduction to the Books of the Old Testament; (with E. Evans) The Bible: What it is and what is in it; The Poetry of the Old Testament; A School Introduction to the Old Testament; Job and his Friends; numerous articles in British and foreign periodicals; and in the Encyclopædia Britannica. *Recreation:* philately. *Address:* Flat 2, 1 Elmgrove Road, Ealing, W.5. *T.:* Ealing 8173. *Club:* Old Millhillians. [*Died* 26 *June* 1964.

ROBINSON, Sir Victor Lloyd, Kt. 1959; C.B.E. 1954 (O.B.E. 1953); Q.C. (S. Rhodesia) 1945; *b.* 19 Mar. 1899; *s.* of Leo G. Robinson and Mabel Lloyd, Natal, S. Africa; *m.* 1923, Marguerite Beck, Cape Province; one *s.* one *d.* *Educ.:* Hilton College, Natal; University of Cape Town; Oxford University. Native Department, S.R., 1922; Public Prosecutor, Bulawayo, 1926; Department of Justice, S.R., 1930. Attorney-General, S. Rhodesia, 1949-53; Federal Attorney-General of Rhodesia and Nyasaland, 1954-59, retired. Chairman, S. Rhodesia Constitutional Council, 1962-. *Recreations:* cricket and golf. *Address:* 42 Lofts Hall, 143 Baines Ave., Salisbury, S. Rhodesia. [*Died* 23 *March* 1966.

ROBINSON, Sir William, Kt., *cr.* 1946; D.L.; J.P.; Managing Director Robertson, Ledlie, Ferguson & Co. Ltd., and Bank Buildings Co. Ltd., 1928-61; Dir. J. N. Richardson Sons & Owden Ltd. and Bessbrook Spinning Co. Ltd.; *b.* 21 Oct. 1879; *s.* of William Robinson, Seagoe House, Portadown; *m.* 1907, Olive Humphreys Perrott, Cork and Dublin; four *s.* two *d.* *Educ.:* Portadown; Dublin. Mem. Newry U.D.C., 1923-29, Chm. 1926-29; President Municipal Authorities Assoc. Northern Ireland, 1926-27; Chairman Belfast City Administrators, 1942-45; Member Electricity Board, Northern Ireland, 1942-52, Chairman 1944-52. *Address:* Montana, Greenisland, Co. Antrim. *T.:* Belfast 833/3218. [*Died* 11 *Dec.* 1961.

ROBINSON, Sir William Henry, K.C.M.G., *cr.* 1937; C.B.E. 1920; *b.* 1874; *s.* of late William Thomas Robinson, Sunningdale; *m.* 1902, Emily Frances (*d.* 1956), *d.* of late John Tomblin; two *s.* one *d.* Foreign Office, 1893; Asst. to Principal Establishment Officer, 1916-1938. *Address:* Holmsted Manor, Cuckfield, Sussex. *T.:* Cuckfield 312. [*Died* 12 *Feb.* 1964.

ROBINSON, William Oscar James; M.P. (Lab.) East Walthamstow since 1966; J.P.; Solicitor; *b.* 20 March 1909; *y. s.* of Walter George Edwin and Eleanor Robinson; *m.* 1949, Florence Anne Minot; no *c.* *Educ.:* elem. and secondary schs., Leyton; London Univ. and Law Soc. Sch. of Law. Qualified as Solicitor, 1947. Local Govt. Service for 25 years. Legal and Administrative Officer, Harlow Development Corp., 1947-49; Sec., Overseas Food Corp., 1949-51; Sec. and Legal Adviser, Essex Local Medical Cttee., and in private practice, 1952-. J.P., Essex, 1953. *Recreations:* cricket and football (reluctantly now only as a spectator); bowls. *Address:* 120 Eastern Avenue, Wanstead, E.11. [*Died* 18 *Oct.* 1968.

ROBINSON, William Sugden; Journalist; *b.* Leeds; *m.* 1st, 1906, Winifred Skinner (*d.* 1942), Sheffield; one *s.*; 2nd, 1943, Ada Bentham, Hessle, East Yorks. *Educ.:* Leeds Grammar School. Joined E. Hulton & Co., Ltd., 1904; Editor Daily Dispatch, Manchester, 1910-14; Editor Daily Sketch, London and Manchester, 1914-19; Managing Editor Lloyd's Sunday News, 1919-23; Managing Director Reynolds's Illustrated News, 1924-25; Managing Editor, Sheffield Independent Press, Ltd., 1926; Managing Editor Bradford and District Newspaper Co. Ltd., 1927-30; Director and Editor-in-Chief, Hull and Grimsby Newspapers, Ltd., 1930-46. Was Vice-Chairman, Sailors' Children's Society for 14 years. *Address:* Hatfield House, West Ella Road, Kirkella, E. Yorks. *Club:* Pacific (Hull). [*Died* 30 *June* 1968.

ROBISON, Lionel MacDowall, C.B.E. 1942; late Director of Education, Ceylon; *b.* 4 July 1886; *s.* of William Robison, Elland, Yorks; *m.* 1916, Rose, *d.* of late R. B. Hellings, C.M.G.; two *d.* *Educ.:* Grace Ramsden's School; Manchester Univ. Dept. of Education, Ceylon, 1909-43. Lecturer and Vice-Principal, Govt. Training College, Colombo; Inspector of Schools; Deputy Director of Education; Visiting Lecturer in Geography, Ceylon University College, 1920-1930. Asst. Educational Adviser, Colonial Office, 1945-55. *Publications:* some school text-books in Geography. *Recreations:* football, cricket, boxing, the theatre. *Address:* Broadlands, Broad Avenue, Queen's Park, Bournemouth. *T.:* Bournemouth 35957. [*Died* 20 *Nov.* 1967.

ROBSON, Hon. Harold (Burge); Member Committee of Management, Royal National Life-Boat Institution, since 1936, Vice-President, 1955; *b.* 10 March 1888; *e. s.* of late Rt. Hon. Lord Robson, G.C.M.G., and Catherine, *d.* of late Charles Burge; *m.* 1st, 1912, Ysolt (from whom he obtained a divorce, 1920), *e. d.* of late Colonel H. Le Roy-Lewis, C.B., C.M.G., D.S.O.; one *s.*; 2nd, 1922, Iris Emmeline Abel, *yr. d.* of late Reginald Abel Smith and Hon. Mrs. R. Abel Smith; one *s.* one *d.* *Educ.:* Eton; New College, Oxford. Capt., Northumberland Hussars Yeomanry: Colonel commanding 7th Batt. Northumberland Fusiliers (T.A.) 1927-32; called to Bar, Inner Temple, 1910; served European War (France and Italy), 1914-18 (despatches, Croix de Guerre, Belgium); Secretary of Commissions, Lord Chancellor's Office, 1919-23; contested (L.) Berwick Division (Northumberland) by-election, 1923, General Election, Dec. 1923 and Oct. 1924; South Shields, General Election, 1929; D.L., J.P., Vice-Lieutenant, Northumberland; Vice-Chairman, Northumberland County Council, 1935-37. Home Guard, 1940-45. Governor Bridewell Royal Hospital. *Address:* Pinewood Hill, Witley, Surrey. *Clubs:* Brooks's, Union. [*Died* 13 *Oct.* 1964.

ROBSON, Leonard Charles, C.B.E. 1955; M.C., M.A. (Oxon.); B.Sc. (Sydney); Headmaster, Sydney Church of England Grammar School, North Sydney, 1923-58, retired; *b.* Sydney, New South Wales, 17 October 1894; *m.* 1920, Marjorie G. Grindrod. *Educ.:* Sydney Grammar School; Sydney University (Scholar); Oxford (Rhodes Scholar for N.S.W.); B.A. 1920, with First Class in Final Honours Schools. Rowed in Trials; served in War with Australian Imperial Forces, 1915-19, 18th Infantry Battalion (despatches, M.C.). Member: Board of Secondary School Studies, 1937-49; Soldiers' Children Education Board, 1932-; Commonwealth Scholarships Board, 1958-1964; Chm. Headmasters' Conf. of Australia, 1940-43; Mem. Senate of University of Sydney; Chm. Commonwealth Bank Appeals Board, 1959-64; Chm., Commonwealth Advisory Cttee. on Science Facilities in Schools, 1964-; F.A.C.E. *Address:* 34 Pentecost Highway, Pymble, N.S.W. *Clubs:* University, Schools (Syd.). [*Died* 5 *Dec.* 1964.

ROCH, Walter Francis; *b.* 20 Jan. 1880; *y. s.* of late Walter Francis Roch of Butter Hill, Pembroke, and *d.* of late Walter Powell; *m.* 1911, Hon. Fflorens Mary Ursula Herbert, *o. d.* of 1st and last Baron Treowen, C.B., C.M.G.; M.P. (L.) Pembrokeshire, 1908-18. *Address:* Ty'r Nant, Llanarth, Raglan, Monmouthshire. *Club:* Reform. [*Died* 3 *May* 1965.

ROCHE, Alexander Ernest, M.A., M.D., M.Ch. (Cantab.); F.R.C.S. (Eng.); late Consulting Surgeon; Speciality Diseases of the Urinary Organs; Surgeon-in-Charge of the Genito-Urinary Dept., West London, Royal Northern and Hounslow Hospitals; *b.* 1896; *s.* of Raphael Roche, London, and Grace Simon; *m.* 1932, Cicely Mary, *o. d.* of F. W. Briggs; three *s.* one *d.* *Educ.:* St. Paul's School; Magdalene College, Cambridge (classical scholar); St. Bartholomew's Hospital, London. Fell. of the Roy. Soc. of Medicine (ex-Pres. Sect. Urol.), and the Hunterian Soc. (ex-Pres.); West London Medico-Chirurgical Soc. (ex-Pres.); late Clinical Asst., House Surgeon, and Resident Surgical Officer, St. Peter's Hosp. for Stone and other Urinary Diseases; and Chief Assistant to a Surgical Unit, St. Bartholomew's Hospital (5 years). *Publications:* Pyelography, its History, Technique, Uses, and Dangers, 1927; Urology in General Practice, 1935; Medical and other Verses, 1935; An Anthology of Wit, 1935; Practical Urology, 1956; articles on surgical and genito-urinary subjects in various medical journals. *Recreations:* literature, music, walking. *Address:* 6 Parkside Gardens, Wimbledon Common, S.W.19. *T.:* Wimbledon 2913. *Club:* Savage. [*Died* 25 *July* 1963.

ROCKE, Colonel Cyril Edmund Alan, D.S.O. 1918; late Irish Guards; President British Legion, Menton Branch; *b.* 7 Sept. 1876; *s.* of late General Currie, I.M.S.; *m.* 1917, Betty, *o. c.* of late Hon. L. M. Iddings, U.S.A. Foreign Service; one *d.* *Educ.:* Sandhurst. Entered army (31st East Surrey Regt.), 1898; attached R.F.C., 1914-15; transferred Irish Guards, 1916 (commanded 2nd Batt. 15 Sept. 1916); Military Attaché, Rome, 1918-20; retired, 1920; served S. Africa, 1899-1902 (King's medal 2 clasps, Queen's medal 5 clasps); European War, 1914-18 (wounded, despatches thrice, D.S.O., Kaisar-i-Hind, Légion d'Honneur, St. Maurice and Lazarus, Croix de Guerre). *Recreation:* anti-communism. *Address:* Beauregard sous St. Antoine, 34 Blvd. de Garavan, Menton, A.M., France. *Clubs:* Royal Commonwealth Society, Royal Thames Yacht; Papal Court. [*Died* 16 *June* 1968.

RODDIE, Lieut.-Col. William Stewart, C.V.O. 1929; retired; *b.* 1878; *s.* of W. Stewart Roddie. *Educ.:* Royal Academy, Inverness; France and Germany. Served European War, 1914-18; H.M. Treasury for Ministry of Information, 1918-19; Intell. Dept., War Office, 1919; special missions to Germany for W.O.; Minister of Munitions and Dept. of Overseas Trade; appointed to Interallied Disarmament Commission (Berlin), 1920-27; financial missions to Far East and U.S.A., 1919-32; Lecture Tours in U.S.A., Middle European Conditions, 1933-1948; Admiralty, Special Service, 1944. *Publications:* Peace Patrol, 1932; History of Post-war Germany. *Address:* 2 Morpeth Mansions, Westminster, S.W.1. *T.:* Victoria 5589. *Club:* Royal Automobile. [*Died* 22 *Jan.* 1961.

RODGER, T(homas) Ritchie, O.B.E. 1941; J.P. 1933; M.D., F.R.C.S.Ed.; retired Aural Surgeon; *b.* 3 Oct. 1878; *s.* of Alexander Rodger; *m.* 1906, Daisy Bartram (*d.* 1964), Cambuslang, Glasgow; four *s.* *Educ.:* Lanark Gram. Sch.; Glasgow University; Edinburgh; Univ. of Pennsylvania. M.B., Ch.B. 1901; M.D. 1906; F.R.C.S.Ed. 1908; Sen. Surgeon Ear, Nose and Throat Dept.: Hull Royal Infirmary, 1919-38; Hull Children's Hosp., 1928-43. Group Officer, Min. of Health, 1939-46. Pres. Otology Section Roy. Soc. Med., 1939; Pres. North of Eng. Otolaryngological Soc., 1947. Sheriff of Hull, 1928-29. *Publications:* contributions to: Journal Laryngology, Brit. Med. Journal, Practitioner, Medical World. *Recreations:* golf, gardening, travel. *Address:* 3 South Road, Newton Abbot, Devon. [*Died* 23 *Sept.* 1968.

RODGERS, William Robert; author, poet; *b.* 1 Aug. 1909; *s.* of Robert S. Rodgers and Jane Ferris McCarey; *m.* 1st, 1935, Mary Harden Waddell; two *d.*; 2nd, 1953, Marianne Gilliam (*née* Helweg); one *d.* *Educ.:* Queen's Univ., Belfast. Minister of Loughgall Presbyterian Church, Co. Armagh, 1934-46; B.B.C. producer and script-writer, 1946-52. Elected to Irish Academy of Letters, 1951. *Publications:* Awake, and Other Poems, 1941; Europa and the Bull, 1952; Ireland in Colour, 1956. *Recreation:* talking. *Address:* Breffny, 6 Victoria Road, Colchester, Essex. *T.:* Colchester 4072. [*Died* 1 *Feb.* 1969.

RODWELL, Air Commodore Robert John, C.B. 1947; R.A.F.; retd.; *b.* 13 Jan. 1897; 3rd *s.* of late J. B. Rodwell, Exmouth, Devon; *m.* 1919, M. H. Livock; two *d.* *Educ.:* St. Edmund's Coll., Ware. Enlisted Hampshire Regiment, 1914; 2nd Lieut. Devonshire Regiment, 1916; transferred to R.F.C. as Pilot, 1917; served European War, 1914-18, India, Egypt, France (Croix de Guerre); regular commission, R.A.F., 1919; served in Ireland, Egypt, Iraq, Palestine, 1920-25; Adjt. Staff Coll., 1925-28; specialised and qualified as Engineer Officer, 1928-1930; served in Iraq, 1932-34; Iraq and Sudan, 1934-36; on transfer to Tech. Branch Staff Duties and Command of Tech. Training Schools in Tech. Training Command, 1936-1948; President R.A.F. Central Trade Test Board, 1947; Group Capt. 1940; Air Commodore, 1948; retired, 1952. *Address:* Kingsley, Chine Walk, Ferndown, Dorset. [*Died* 27 *Dec.* 1970.

RODZIANKO, Colonel Paul, C.M.G. 1917; *s.* of Gen. Paul Rodzianko and Princess Marie Galitzine, Petrograd; *m.* 1949, Joan, *widow* of Enrique De Udy and *d.* of late Major Denis and Hon. Mrs. Farrer; one *s.* one *d.* *Educ.:* Corps des Pages, Petrograd. Entered Regiment of Chevaliers Guard, Petrograd; A.D.C. to General Bezobrazoff, Commander of the Guards; during war became a Colonel; attached to Russian Embassy in Rome; after Russian Revolution joined British Army as a Tommy; was made Hon. Colonel in the British Army and Liaison Officer to the British Military Unit in Siberia; War of 1939-45, Hon. Col. British Army, Syria, Palestine, N. Africa, Sicily, Sardinia, Italy, Scotland, Germany. *Publications:* Modern Horsemanship, 1936; Tattered Banners, 1939; Life of Mannerheim, 1940. *Recreation:* riding. *Address:* Brayfield Lodge, Olney, Bucks. *T.:* Turvey 249. *Club:* International Sportsmen's. [*Died* 16 *April* 1965.

ROE, Harold Riley, C.I.E. 1933; *b.* 1883; *m.* 1913, Edith Louise, *d.* of late Rev. Edward Guilford, C.I.E., O.B.E.; one *s.* one *d.* *Educ.:* Sutton Valence. Joined Indian Police, 1903; posted to United Provinces; Deputy Inspector-General, 1930; Officiating Inspector-General, 1933; retired, 1935. *Address:* Abbotsford, Cedar Drive, Chichester. *T.:* 5570. [*Died* 17 *April* 1963.

ROE, Maj.-Gen. (Retd.) Sir William Gordon, K.B.E. 1960 (C.B.E. 1945; O.B.E. 1944; M.B.E. 1940); C.B. 1957; late R.A.S.C.; A.M.I.Mech.E. 1942; M.Inst.T. 1960; Assistant Master General of Ordnance, War Office, 1960-64; *b.* 16 September 1904; *s.* of late Captain F. H. Roe, R.A.S.C.; *m.* 1932, Annette, *d.* of F. A. Stiles, Welling, Kent; one *s.* *Educ.:* R.M.C., Sandhurst (King George V's Gold Medal and Sword). Commissioned R.A.S.C., 2nd Lt., 1929; served War of 1939-45 (despatches thrice); France and Belgium (M.B.E.), 1940; French N. Africa, Sicily (O.B.E.), 1942-43;

Italy, 1943-45; Brig. A./Q., 13th Corps, 1944-45 (C.B.E.); Greece, 1945; Brig. in charge of Admin., Palestine and Transjordan, 1945-46; W.O., 1948-51; D.S.T.: Far East, Malaya, 1951; B.A.O.R., 1953; Maj.-Gen. i/c Admin., H.Q., B.A.O.R., 1954-57; Director of Supplies and Transport at the War Office, 1957-60, retired. A.D.C. to the Queen, 1952-55. Col. Comdt., R.A.S.C., 1963-65 and of Royal Corps of Transport, 1965-67. Legion of Merit (U.S.A.), Degree of Officer, 1944; Chevalier, Legion of Honour (France), 1944; Croix de Guerre avec Palmes (France), 1944. *Address:* Lone Gable, Poverest Road, Petts Wood, Kent. *T.:* Orpington 20232.
[*Died* 27 *July* 1969.

ROE-THOMPSON, Edwin Reginald; *b.* 23 Oct. 1894; *s.* of Edwin Thompson, Bridlington. *Educ.:* Bridlington School; University of London; Keble College, Oxford. B.Sc. Lond. 1915; B.A. Oxon 1922. Invalided, 1917. Master, Mill Hill, 1917; St. Edward's School, 1918; Wellington College, 1923; Headmaster, Kendal School, 1925-46; Vice-Pres. Windsor Division Liberal Assoc., 1923, 1924. *Publications:* Text-books on Chemistry; That House Across the Way, 1947; What You Will, 1948; various papers, scientific, general, and social; contributor Nature, Science Review, and professional journals. *Address:* 16 Kingsgate, Bridlington, Yorks. *T.:* 3701. *Club:* National Liberal.
[*Died* 20 *June* 1970.

ROEBUCK, Alfred, Hon. M.I.Mech.E.; retd. from any full-time business appointment, *b.* 2 May 1889; *s.* of late Wade and Mary Elizabeth Roebuck; *m.* 1915, Blanche Elizabeth Roebuck (*née* Peters); two *d.* *Educ.:* Sheffield University. Hadfields Ltd., steel makers and engineers, Sheffield; apprentice, then engineering draughtsman; Asst. Chief Engineer, 1914; Chief Engineer, 1924; Director, 1929; Works Director, 1931-45; Director with special duties, 1945-50; Director: John Baker & Bessemer, Ltd., 1945-50; Millspaugh, Ltd., 1946-50; Engineering Director, M.A.P. Factory, Swinton, 1939-43. President, Junior Instn. Engineers, 1949-50; M.I.Mech.E. 1929; Mem. Council, 1937-42 and 1945-; Vice-Pres., 1949-53, Pres., 1953-54. Mem. Sheffield Univ. Engineering and Metallurgical Cttee. Has held various positions in local Sheffield socs. and associations. Serving Brother, Order of St. John of Jerusalem, 1951. *Publications:* articles in Proc. Inst. Mech. Engrs. *Recreations:* motoring, gardening and bowls. *Address:* 79 Huntley Road, Sheffield 11. *T.:* Sheffield 60794.
[*Died* 19 *Jan.* 1962.

ROGER, Sir Alexander, K.C.I.E., *cr.* 1941; Kt., *cr.* 1916; Hon. President: British Insulated Callender's Cables, Ltd.; Automatic Telephone & Electric Co. Ltd.; formerly Deputy Chairman of the Midland Bank Ltd. (retired, 1959); Chairman Telephone and General Trust Ltd., and several telephone operating companies in Portugal and the West Indies until 1960; Vice-President Federation of British Industries; Vice-President Anglo-Portuguese Society; *b.* 30 January 1878; *s.* of late James Paterson Roger, Rhynie, Aberdeenshire; *m.* 1908, Helen Stuart, *y. d.* of James Campbell Clark, Connel Ferry, Argyllshire; three *s.* *Educ.:* Robert Gordon's College, Aberdeen. Director, Motor Ambulance Dept., British Red Cross Society, 1914-15; Director-General, Trench Warfare Supply Department, Ministry of Munitions, 1915-17; Member of Council, Ministry of Reconstruction, 1917-18; Chairman, Transport of Wounded Dept., War Organisation of British Red Cross Society and Order of St. John of Jerusalem, 1939-40; Chairman of Tank Board, 1940; Chairman, Ministry of Supply Mission to India, South Africa, Australia, New Zealand, Hong Kong, Burma, and Malay States, 1940-41; Chairman Appeals Council Great Ormond Street Hospital for Sick Children, 1934-47; Commander of Military Order of Christ, Grand Cross of the Order of Industrial Merit (Portugal); Orders of Polonia Restituta of Poland and St. Anne of Russia. *Recreations:* golf, stalking. *Address:* Binfield Lodge, Binfield, Berks. *Clubs:* Carlton, Caledonian, Royal Automobile.
[*Died* 4 *April* 1961.

ROGERS, Rev. Guy; *see* Rogers, Rev. T. G.

ROGERS, Prof. Lambert Charles, C.B.E. 1958; V.R.D. 1946; M.Sc., M.D., M.Ch.; F.R.C.S., F.R.C.S.E. F.R.A.C.S., F.A.C.S.; Professor of Surgery, University of Wales; Director of Surgical Unit, Welsh National School of Medicine, Cardiff Royal Infirmary; Consultant in Neuro-surgery to Royal Navy; Surgeon to United Cardiff Hosps.; Hon. Consulting Surgeon, Prince of Wales Orthopædic Hospital, Cardiff; Adviser in Surgery, Welsh Regional Hospital Board; External Examiner in Surgery for Fellowship of R.C.S.(I.) and R.C.S.(Edin.); Mem. Council R.C.S. of Eng., 1943-59 (Examiner in Anatomy for Fellowship); Fellow of Anatomical Society of R. Soc. Med. and of Assoc. of Surgeons of Great Britain and Ireland (Pres. 1951-52); Hon. Mem. Soc. of Brit. Neurological Surgeons (Pres. 1948-50), Moynihan Chirurgical Club (Hon. Sec. 1940-50, Pres. 1950-52); B.M.A. Pres. Section of Surgery, 1953. Pres. S. Wales and Mon. Branch, 1960-61; Cardiff Medical Soc. (Pres. 1954-1955) and of Welsh Surgical Soc. (Pres. 1953-1958); Pres. local branch of Royal College of Nursing, 1955-56; Pres. Section of Surgery, Roy. Soc. Med., 1960-61; Hon. Mem. Society of Australasian Neurological Surgeons; Membre Honoraire Étranger de la Soc. Belge de Chirurgie; Member International Soc. of Surgery (British Delegate, 1947-); Hon. Life Mem., and Vice-Pres. Glamorgan Branch, British Red Cross Society; Vice-Pres. Cardiff Business Club; *b.* 8 April 1897; *s.* of Charles Robert Rogers and Janet Chant; *m.* 1952, Barbara Mary, *widow* of Lt. J. K. Ainsley, R.A.; one *d.* one *step-s.* *Educ.:* Melbourne; Univ. of London (Middlesex Hosp.); Edinburgh. Formerly Reader in Surgery, Univ. of London (British Postgraduate Medical School); Hunterian Prof. R.C.S. of England, 1935, Arris and Gale Lecturer, 1947; Arnott Demonstrator, 1952; Bradshaw Lecturer, 1954; Vice-President R.C.S., 1953-55. M.D. Melb. (*h.c.*), 1952; M.Ch. (*h.c.*), National Univ. of Ireland, 1961. Late Examiner in Anatomy to Conjoint Board, London, and in Surgery to Univs. of Cambridge, Dublin, London, Glasgow, Belfast, Bristol and to National Univ. of Ireland; Member Court of Examiners, R.C.S. of England; Prosector to Univ. of London and R.C.S. England (distinction); served in R.N. in European War and War of 1939-45; Surgeon Capt. R.N.V.R. (retd.). *Publications:* various papers on surgical and allied subjects; Editor: 10th, 11th, 12th, 13th and 14th edns. Treve's Surgical Applied Anatomy, 1939, 1947, 1952, 1957, 1962; Editor: 4th edn. Grey Turner's Modern Operative Surgery, 1955-56. *Recreations:* motoring and travelling. *Address:* Steynton, Lisvane, Cardiff; Surgical Unit, The Royal Infirmary, Cardiff. *T.:* Cardiff 24639, Cardiff 51607. *Clubs:* Athenæum, Junior Army and Navy, Royal Automobile, Seven Seas; Cardiff and County.
[*Died* 10 *Oct.* 1961.

ROGERS, Major-General Sir Leonard K.C.S.I., *cr* 1932; Kt., *cr.* 1914; C.I.E. 1911; F.R.S. 1916; LL.D. (Glasgow and St. Andrews); M.D., B.S. (London), F.R.C.P., F.R.C.S.; Indian Medical Service; retired; late Pres. of Medical Board, India Office; late Physician London Hospital for Tropical Medicine; late Prof. of Pathology, Medical College, Calcutta;

late President Royal Soc. of Tropical Medicine; Hon. Member of Cambridge Philosophical Society; Moxon Gold Medallist of the Royal College of Physicians of London; Fothergillian Gold Medallist, Medical Society of London; Laveran Gold Medal, Paris, 1956; *b.* 18 Jan. 1868; *s.* of Henry Rogers, R.N.; *m.* 1914, Una Elsie (*d.* 1951), *d.* of C. N. McIntyre North; three *s.* *Educ.:* Plymouth College; St. Mary's Hospital, London. Entered Indian Med. Service, 1893; Croonian Lecturer, Royal College of Physicians, 1924. *Publications:* Recent Advances in Tropical Medicine, 1928; Tropical Medicine, 4th Ed. (with Megaw); numerous scientific papers in medical journals and Royal Society publications on Fevers, Snake Poisons, Liver Abscess, Tuberculosis, and Leprosy; works on Kala-Azar, Tropical Fevers, Cholera, Dysenteries and Leprosy. *Address:* Melville Hotel, Falmouth, Cornwall. [*Died* 16 *Sept.* 1962.

ROGERS, Lindsay; *see* Addenda: II.

ROGERS, Thomas Arthur, C.B.E. 1956; H.M. Chief Inspector of Mines and Quarries, 1958-62; *b.* 5 June 1897; *s.* of Thomas Henry and Elizabeth Rogers; *m.* 1922, Gwendoline Wetmore Davies; two *d.* *Educ.:* South Wales and Monmouthshire School of Mines. Colliery Manager, 1922; Junior Inspector of Mines, Newcastle on Tyne, 1927; Senior Inspector of Mines, Swansea, 1939; Senior District Inspector of Mines, Edinburgh, 1946; Divisional Inspector of Mines, Cardiff, 1947; Deputy Chief Inspector of Mines, London 1951. Past Pres. S.W. Soc. of Mining Engineers; Past Pres. and Hon. Mem. S. Wales Inst. of Engineers; Mem. Council Southern Counties Institution of Mining Engineers; President Institution of Mining Engineers, 1959-60. *Publications:* papers and presidential addresses in Trans. of I.M.E. *Recreations:* gardening, fishing. *Address:* Flat 9, Southwood Court, Middle Warberry Road, Torquay, Devon. *T.:* Torquay 27641. [*Died* 20 *Dec.* 1965.

ROGERS, Rev. (Travers) Guy, M.C.; B.D.; Chaplain to the Queen since 1952 (formerly to King George V, to King Edward VIII, and to King George VI); Canon Emeritus of Birmingham; Proctor in Convocation, 1921-49; Rector of Birmingham, 1925 (now retired); *s.* of late David Gregory Rogers, of Oldcastle, Co. Sligo; *m.* 1924, Marguerite Inez, 2nd *d.* of James Bishop Hartley, Titlark's Cottage, Sunningdale; one *s.* one *d.* *Educ.:* Trinity College, Dublin. Curate of S. Matthias, Dublin, 1900-2; Monkstown, Dublin, 1902-3; S. Barnabas, Kensington, 1903-6; Holy Trinity, Marylebone, 1906-9; Vicar of S. John the Evangelist with S. Stephen's, Reading, 1909-15; temporary Chaplain to the Forces, 1915-16; Vicar and Rural Dean of West Ham, 1916-25; Hon. Canon of Chelmsford, 1920; Lecturer in Pastoral Theology, Cambridge, 1928, and Durham University, 1938; Select Preacher Cambridge University, 1920 and 1926, Oxford University, 1938-39. *Publications:* The Church and the People, 1930; Joint Editor and Contributor, Liberal Evangelicalism, 1923; The Inner Life: Second Series of Liberal Evangelical Essays, 1925; Return to God, 1933; contributor to The Church and the Twentieth Century, 1936, and The Chronicle U.S.A.; Autobiography: A Rebel at Heart, 1956. *Recreation:* lawn tennis. *Address:* 40 Wimbledon Close, The Downs, S.W.20. *T.:* Wimbledon 4082. [*Died* 18 *July* 1967.

ROGERS, Major Vivian Barry, C.B.E. 1950 (O.B.E. 1942); D.S.O. 1919; M.C.; D.L.; J.P.; formerly Senior Partner in firm of Rogers, Chapman & Thomas, chartered surveyors, chartered auctioneers and estate agents, incorporating Henry Chapman & Co., 36 Southampton Street, Strand, W.C.2, and elsewhere (retd. 1958); *b.* London, 1887; 6th *s.* of late William Bennett Rogers J.P., of Danehurst, Westgate-on-Sea; *m.* 1915, Helen Thérèse (*d.* 1965), *d.* of late Patrick Galway Costello Shaw; one *s.* *Educ.:* Marlborough College; Lausanne Univ. Mayor of Westminster, 1928-29; Alderman of Westminster City Council, 1941-49; Commandant-in-Chief, Metropolitan Special Constabulary, New Scotland Yard, S.W.1, 1943-49; General Commissioner for Income Tax, 1938-59. Fell. Royal Institution of Chartered Surveyors; Mem. of Council of Chartered Auctioneers and Estate Agents Institute, 1939-59. Served European War, 1914-19, Northumberland Fusiliers, Staff Captain, 108th Infantry Brigade and D.A.Q.M.G., 36th (Ulster) Division (D.S.O., M.C., French Croix de Guerre, despatches twice). O.St.J. 1945. *Address:* Sunwood, The Bramblings, Rustington, Sussex. *T.:* Rustington 3443. *Club:* Constitutional. [*Died* 3 *Oct.* 1965.

ROGERSON, Colonel Sidney; *b.* 22 Oct. 1894; *s.* of Reverend S. Rogerson; *m.* 1st, 1928, Ethel Dorothy, *y. d.* of Sir Henry Gibson; one *s.*; 2nd, 1935, Nancy Winifred, *d.* of R. L. Allport; one *s.* one *d.* *Educ.:* Worksop Coll.; Sidney Sussex Coll., Cambridge. Open Schol. S. Sussex Coll., Modern History, 1912; B.A. 1916. Served European War; commissioned West Yorks Regt., Aug. 1914; France, B.E.F., 2nd Bn. W. Yorks R., 1916-19; Staff 23rd Inf. Bde. and 8th Div., 1917-18; demobilised, 1919. Federation of British Industries, 1919; Publicity Manager F.B.I., 1923-30; joined Imperial Chemical Industries, 1930; Publicity Controller, I.C.I. Ltd., 1937-52. Publicity and Public Relations Adviser to Army Council, War Office, 1952-3-4. Hon. Col. 44th (Home Counties) Infantry Div. Signals Regt. T.A., 1955-58; Col. 1958, retd. Gov., Allied Schools. *Publications:* Twelve Days, 1933; Last of the Ebb, 1937; Propaganda in Next War, 1938; Old Enchantment, 1938; Our Bird Book, 1946; Both Sides of the Road, 1949; Wilfred Rhodes (biography), 1960. *Recreations:* cricket, agriculture, elkhounds. *Address:* Barningham, nr. Bury St. Edmunds, Suffolk. *T.:* Coney Weston 256. *Club:* Travellers'. [*Died* 26 *Nov.* 1968.

ROGOSINSKI, Professor Werner Wolfgang, F.R.S. 1954; Dr.Phil.; Professor of Mathematics, Aarhus University, Denmark, since 1959; Emeritus Professor, Universities of Durham and Newcastle upon Tyne; *b.* 24 September 1894; *s.* of Herman Rogosinski and Helma Brann; *m.* 1928, Erna Raphael; one *s.* *Educ.:* St. Maria Magdalena, Breslau; Univ. of Göttingen. Dr.phil., Göttingen, 1922; Privatdozent and Ausserordentlicher Prof., Univ. of Königsberg i.Pr., 1923-36; Asst. Lecturer, Univ. of Aberdeen, 1941-45; Lecturer, 1945, Reader, 1947, Prof. of Pure Mathematics, 1948-59, King's Coll., Newcastle upon Tyne, Durham University. For. Mem., Danish Acad. of Sciences and Letters, 1962. *Publications:* Fouriersche Reihen, 1930; Fourier Series: (with G. H. Hardy) Cambridge Tract, 1944; Volume and Integral, 1952. Contributions to: Mathem. Annalen, Math. Zeitschrift, Compositio Mathematica, Jl.L.M.S., Proc.L.M.S., Quarterly Jl. of Mathem., Proc. Roy. Soc., Proc. Cambridge Phil. Soc., Acta Mathematics. *Recreation:* music. *Address:* Nordborggade 13. st.th., Aarhus, Denmark. [*Died* 23 *July* 1964.

ROLFE, Douglass H. B.; *see* Boggis-Rolfe.

ROLLAND, Very Rev. Sir Francis (William), Kt. 1958; C.M.G. 1955; O.B.E. 1953; M.C., M.A.; *b.* Geelong, 1878; *s.* of late Very Rev. W. S. Rolland; *m.* 1919, Aline (*d.* 1964), *d.* of late Sir Charles Ballance, K.C.M.G. *Educ.:* Toorak Coll.; Melbourne, Edinburgh, and Oxford Universities. Served European War, 1915-19, as Chaplain with Australian Imperial Force (M.C.); Principal, Geelong Coll., Victoria, Australia, 1920-46;

Chm. Headmasters' Conference of Australia, 1936-39; Moderator Presbyterian Church, Victoria, 1937-38; Moderator General, Presbyterian Church of Australia, 1954-57. Hon. D.D. Edin., 1960. F.A.C.E. *Address:* 26 Nott St., East Malvern, Melbourne, Australia. *Clubs:* Roy. Automobile of Vic., (Hon.) Melbourne (Vic.).
[*Died* 22 *Jan.* 1965.

ROMANNE-JAMES, Mrs. Helena Constance (Mrs. H. C. Aylen); author and journalist; *d.* of Henry Higgins, Willsbridge House, Gloucestershire; *m.* Captain Lionel Aylen, A.F.C. and M.I.C.E.; one *d.* *Educ.:* Bath; Bonn am Rhein; Reading Univ. Spent four years in Far East—China, Japan, Siam, Java; commenced journalistic work in Hong-Kong for China Newspapers; on return to England became London correspondent for Siam; wrote London Letter for China Newspapers; edited Buddhist Review, and has since then worked in London as editor, author, regular contributor and free lance; has broadcast frequently from B.B.C.; Winner of the Smedley Memorial Prize (1931) for best piece of Journalism published in any reputable paper or journal; F.R.S.A.; Member Society of Authors; Chairman Society of Women Journalists, 1939. Hon. Sec. Prison Gardens Association, for Nat. Gardens Guild. *Publications:* Intercepted Letters; The Islanders of Hong-Kong; O Toyo Writes Home; Herb Lore for Housewives; Flowers For the House And How to Arrange Them; Joint Author of Choosing a Career. *Recreations:* gardening, herb growing and drying, pot-pourri making. *Address:* Fair Croft, Brecon, S. Wales. *T.:* 46. *Club:* Forum. [*Died* 8 *July* 1966.

ROMER, General Sir Cecil Francis, G.C.B., *cr.* 1935 (K.C.B., *cr.* 1929; C.B. 1915); K.B.E., *cr.* 1925; C.M.G. 1917; D.L. Kent; late Royal Dublin Fusiliers; *b.* 14 Nov. 1869; 4th *s.* of late Rt. Hon. Sir R. Romer; *m.* Frances Grace Wilkinson (*d.* 1944); one *d.* Entered Army, 1890; Capt., 1898; Major, 1910; Brev. Lt.-Col., 1913; Brev. Col. 1916; Lt.-Gen. 1927; Gen. 1932; General Staff Officer, 2nd Grade, 1904; A.D.C. to H.M. 1916; served S. African War, 1899-1902 (despatches; Bt. Major; Queen's medal 5 clasps, King's medal 2 clasps); European War, 1914-18 (despatches, C.B., C.M.G., promoted Maj.-Gen.); Commanded 1st Division, Aldershot, 1926-27; General Officer Commanding-in-Chief Western Command, 1928-31; General Officer Commanding-in-Chief, Southern Command, 1931-33; Adjutant-General to the Forces, 1933-35; retired pay, 1935; Officer Legion of Honour. *Address:* c/o Lloyds Bank, 6 Pall Mall, S.W.1.
[*Died* 1 *Oct.* 1962.

ROMER, Rt. Hon. Sir Charles Robert Ritchie, P.C. 1951; Kt. 1944; O.B.E.; Chairman of Committee of Inquiry into Breaches of Security, 1961; *b.* 19 Jan. 1897; *s.* of late Baron Romer, P.C.; *m.* 1st, Lorna Buchanan; one *d.*; 2nd, Frances Evelyn Lebeau Kemp; two *s.* *Educ.:* Rugby. Served in the Army, 1914-18; Called to Bar, Lincoln's Inn, 1921; K.C. 1937. Legal Adviser to Regional Commissioner, N. Midland Region, 1940-44; Judge of Chancery Division, High Court of Justice, 1944-1951; a Lord Justice of Appeal, 1951-60, retired. Hon. Fellow Trinity Hall, Cambridge, 1957. *Recreations:* golfing and fishing. *Address:* Orchard House, Littlestone-on-Sea, Kent. *T.:* New Romney 2324. *Club:* English-Speaking Union.
[*Died* 15 *Feb.* 1969.

ROMERIL, Herbert George; J.P. Middlesex; railway clerk; *b.* Walworth, 1881. *Educ.:* Castle Hill School, West Ealing. M.P. (Lab.) South-East St. Pancras, 1923-24 and 1929-31; President of Railway Clerks' Assoc., 1912-16; gave evidence before Departmental Committee on Railway Amalgamations and Working Agreements, 1909. *Address:* 57 Grenoble Gardens, Palmers Green, N.13.
[*Died* 2 *Oct.* 1963.

ROOME, Major-General Sir Horace Eckford, K.C.I.E., *cr.* 1946; C.B. 1944; C.B.E. 1941; M.C. 1916; D.L. 1951; *b.* 17 May 1887; *s.* of Dr. H. A. Roome; *m.* 1916, Helen Isabel, *d.* of Col. W. S. Walford, late R.A.; three *s.* (and one *d.* decd.). *Educ.:* R.M.A., Woolwich. India on 1st commission; served European War, France, Mesopotamia, Persia; service in India with Survey of India Dept., 1918-26; in England, 1926-30; in India in regimental and staff employ, 1931-46; Engineer-in-Chief, India; retired, 1947. *Address:* St. Lawrence, Totland Bay, Isle of Wight. *T.:* Freshwater 107. *Club:* United Service.
[*Died* 29 *June* 1964.

ROOSEVELT, (Anna) Eleanor (Mrs. F. D. Roosevelt); Member American Assoc. for U.N. in charge of organization; *b.* 11 Oct. 1884; *d.* of Elliott Roosevelt and Anna Hall; *m.* 1905, Franklin Delano Roosevelt (*d.* 1945), President of United States, 1933-45; four *s.* one *d.* *Educ.:* private. United States representative at U.N. General Assembly, 1945-52. Awarded United Nations Human Rights Prize, 1968. *Publications:* When you grow up to Vote, 1932; It's up to the Women, 1933; A Trip to Washington with Bobby and Betty, 1935; This is my Story, 1937; My Days, 1938; If you ask me, 1946; This I Remember, 1950; India and the Awakening East, 1953; On My Own, 1959; You Learn By Living, 1960; The Autobiography of Eleanor Roosevelt, 1962; Tomorrow is now, 1964 (*posthumous*). Editor, The Moral Basis of Democracy, 1940, etc. *Address:* Hyde Park, Dutchess County, N.Y., U.S.A.
[*Died* 7 *Nov.* 1962.

ROOTES, 1st Baron *cr.* 1959, **William Edward Rootes,** G.B.E., 1955 (K.B.E., 1942); British motor car manufacturer; Chancellor Designate, University of Warwick, since 1964; Chairman of Promotion Committee, University of Warwick; *b.* 17 Aug. 1894; *s.* of late William Rootes, Hawkhurst, Kent; *m.* 1st, 1916, Nora Press (marr. diss., 1951; she *d.* 1964); two *s.*; 2nd, 1951, (Ruby Joy) Ann, formerly wife of Sir Francis Henry Grenville Peek, 4th Bt., previously *widow* of Sir Charles Thomas Hewitt Mappin, 4th Bt., and *o. d.* of Capt. Gordon Duff, late R.G.A. *Educ.:* Cranbrook School. Served European War, 1915-18: Lieut. R.N.V.R., 1915-17; Aircraft Engineering, 1917-18. Member: Board of Trade Advisory Council, 1931-34, and 1939-40; Overseas Trade Development Council, 1933-40; Bd. of Trade Deptl. Cttee. on Gift Coupon Trading Stamps, 1933; Deleg. to British Week in Finland, 1933; Cttee. of Education and Training of Students from Overseas, 1933-34; U.K. Trade Mission to Poland, 1934; Jt. Aircraft Engine Cttee. (Shadow Industry), 1936-40, Chm. 1940-41; Chairman: Ministry of Transport Motor Vehicle Maintenance Advisory Cttee., 1941; Supply Council, Min. of Supply, 1941-42; Pres., Soc. of Motor Manufacturers and Traders, 1939-42. Mem. U.K. Trade Mission to Canada, 1958. Chairman of Dollar Exports Council (re-formed 15 Dec. 1960 and named Western Hemisphere Exports Council), 1951-1964. Member: Nat. Advisory Council for Motor Manufacturing Industry, Board of Trade, 1947-64; Engineering Advisory Council, Board of Trade, 1947-62; Council and Exec. Cttee., British Council; Council of Society of Motor Manufacturers and Traders. Formed Rootes, Ltd., 1917; Chairman: Rootes Motors, Ltd., and associate company, Rootes, Ltd.; Director: Humber Ltd., Hillman Motor Car Co., Ltd., Sunbeam-Talbot, Ltd., Singer

Motors Ltd., Rootes (Scotland) Ltd., Commer Cars Ltd., Karrier Motors Ltd., Thrupp and Maberly Ltd., Tilling-Stevens Ltd., Warwick Wright Ltd., George Heath Ltd., Tom Garner Ltd., British Light Steel Pressings Ltd. Vice-Pres. Roy Smithfield Club (Pres. 1962). Benjamin Franklin Award, Roy. Society of Arts, 1962. *Heir: s.* Hon. William Geoffrey Rootes. *Address:* Devonshire House, Piccadilly, London, W.1. *T.:* Grosvenor 3401; Ramsbury Manor, Ramsbury, Wiltshire. *T.:* Ramsbury 381/2; Glenalmond House, Perthshire, Scotland. *T.:* Glenalmond 220. *Clubs:* St. James', Buck's, Travellers', Royal Automobile. [*Died* 12 *Dec.* 1964.

ROPNER, Sir (Emil Hugo Oscar) Robert, 3rd Bt., *cr.* 1904; *b.* 8 Oct. 1893; *s.* of late Emil Hugo Oscar Robert Ropner, 2nd *s.* of 1st Bt.; *S.* uncle 1936; *m.* 1918, Lillian Rochfort, *d.* of Colonel Rochfort Snow, Christchurch, N.Z.; one *s.* two *d.* *Educ.:* Harrow. Joined Ropner & Sons, Ltd. Shipyard, 1912; with them till firm closed down, 1928; European War, 1914-18; Staff-Captain, Boulogne Base, 1916-18. *Recreations:* walking, motoring, gardening, riding on engine footplates. *Heir: s* Robert Douglas [*b.* 1 Dec. 1921; *m.* 1943, Patricia Kathleen, *d.* of W. E. Scofield, West Malling, Kent; one *s.*, one *d.*]. *Address:* 19 Parkside, Knightsbridge S.W.1. *Club:* Royal Thames Yacht. [*Died* 5 *May* 1962.

ROPS, Henry D.; *see* Daniel-Rops.

ROQUES, Frederick William, C.B.E. 1955; M.A., M.D., M.Chir. (Cantab.), F.R.C.S. (Eng.), F.R.C.O.G.; Hon. Air Commodore, Consultant in Gynæcology, R.A.F.; Obstetric and Gynæcological Surgeon, The Middlesex Hospital and the Royal Masonic Hospital; Consulting Gynæcological Surgeon, The Hospital of St. John, St Elizabeth, and The Chelsea Hospital for Women; The West Herts Hospital and The Gerrard's Cross Hospital; Examiner in Obstetric Medicine to the Univs. of Cambridge, London, Leeds and Bristol, to the Conjoint Board of R.C.P. and R.C.S., and to the Central Midwives' Board; *b.* London, 2 Aug. 1898; *o. s.* of late A. W. Roques, F.R.I.B.A.; *m.* Jean Wanklyn (*d.* 1956); two *s.* *Educ.:* Highgate; Clare Coll., Cambridge. Served European War, Lt., 2nd Bde. R.A.; Entered Middlesex Hosp., 1921; Qualified, 1924; Lyell Gold Medallist and Scholar; Freeman Scholar; filled offices of House Surgeon, Obstetric House Surgeon. Senior Demonstrator in Anatomy and Obstetric and Gynæcological Registrar; Fellow of the Royal Society of Medicine (President of the Section of Obstetrics). *Publications:* Epidemic Encephalitis in Association with Pregnancy, Labour and Puerperium; Director Diseases of Women by "Ten Teachers"; papers in Proc. Roy. Soc. Med., etc. *Address:* Tal-y-Llyn Farm, Wigginton, Herts. *Club:* Royal Air Force. [*Died* 14 *July* 1964.

ROQUES, Mario Louis Guillaume; Professeur honoraire au Collège de France; École des Hautes Etudes (Romance Philology); administrateur honoraire de l'École des Langues Orientales; member of Institut de France; Président du Conseil de perfectionnement de l'École des Chartes; *b.* 1 July 1875; *s.* of Anselme Roques and Marguerite Bordes; *m.* 1905, Julienne Blanc; one *s.* *Educ.:* Lycée Henri IV. École Normale Supérieure, École des Hautes Études, École des Langues Orientales, Paris. Agrégé de l'Université; diplomé de l'École des Langues Orientales et de l'École des Hautes Études; maître de conférences à l'École Normale Supérieure; lieutenant d'artillerie et chef de cabinet d'Albert Thomas, ministre de l'armement, 1915-18; Académie des Inscriptions et Belles Lettres, 1933, et président de l'Académie, 1940; Docteur honoris causa de l'Université d'Oxford, 1934, de l'Université de Sofia, 1939; de l'Université de Bucarest, 1945 et de l'Université de Liège, 1950; Académie de langue et littérature françaises de Belgique, 1947; Accademia dei Lincei, Roma, 1955; Académie de Stockholms 1957; missions en Roumanie; conférences en Belgique, Bulgarie, Danemark, Grande-Bretagne, Roumanie. *Publications:* Romania; Classiques français du moyen âge; editions of Old French, Provençal, Rumanian, and Albanian Texts; Linguistic Geography; Rumanian Literature; Lexiques français du moyen âge. *Recreation:* vie à la campagne. *Address:* Paris (5), rue de Poissy, 2. *T.:* Odéon 03.94; Cuissy sur Loire, par Saint-Gondon, Loiret, France. [*Died* 8 *March* 1961.

RORIMER, James J.; Bronze Star (U.S.); Director and Trustee, The Metropolitan Museum of Art, New York, since 1955; *b.* Cleveland, Ohio, 7 Sept. 1905; *s.* of late Louis Rorimer and Edith (*née* Joseph); *m.* 1942, Katherine Newton Serrell; one *s.* one *d.* *Educ.:* University School, Cleveland, Ohio; Harvard University (B.A. *cum laude*). Joined staff of Metropolitan Museum of Art, 1927; Asst., Dept. of Decorative Arts, 1927-1929; Asst. Curator, 1929-32; Assoc. Curator, 1932-34; Curator, Dept. of Medieval Art, 1934-55, of The Cloisters, 1938-1949; Director of The Cloisters, since 1949. Member: Amer. Acad. of Political and Social Sciences; Amer. Assoc. of Museums (Coun. Mem., 1956-62); Amer. Fed. of Arts; Archaeological Inst. of Amer.; France-America Soc.; Medieval Acad. of America (Councillor, 1955, Exec. Cttee. 1957-58), International Institute of Conservation; U.S. National Committee for ICOM, 1956 (Internat. Council of Museums, Pres., 1965); Assoc. of Art Museum Directors (Exec. Cttee., 1963); Asia Society (Trustee 1956); New York University (Inst. of Fine Arts Advisory Cttee.); Art Advisory Cttee., Dartmouth College; N.Y. State Museums Assoc. (Vice-Pres. 1961-65); International Council of Museums (re-elected Vice-Pres.); and various other American and foreign societies and academies; Hon. Member American Inst. Decorators; Fellow, American Acad. of Arts and Letters; F.A.G.S.; Adviser, Cleveland Inst. of Art; Trustee, Museum of the City of N.Y.; Fellow Pierpont Morgan Library. Hon. Doctor of: Humanities, Western Reserve University, Cleveland, Ohio, 1956; Humane Letters, Columbia University, 1957; Laws Union College, 1957; Fine Arts, Hamilton College, 1957; Fine Arts, Adelphi, 1963; Fine Arts, N.Y. Univ., 1964. On leave of absence from the Museum for War Service, 1943-46. Holds various medals and awards including Croix de Guerre (silver star); Officer, Legion of Honour; Officer, Order of Arts and Letters (France); Cross of Commander of Order of the Dannebrog. *Publications:* in U.S.A.; Ultra-Violet Rays and Their Use in the Examination of Works of Art, 1931; A Guide to the Collections (Medieval Sect.), 1934; The Cloisters—The Building and the Collection of Medieval Art, 1938 (rev. 1963); Medieval Monuments at The Cloisters—As They Were and As They Are, 1941; Survival: The Salvage and Protection of Art in War, 1950; Picture Books: Medieval Jewelry, 1940; The Unicorn Tapestries, 1938 (revised edn., 1962); Medieval Tapestries, 1947; The Nine Heroes Tapestries at The Cloisters, 1953; contrib. to journals. *Address:* The Metropolitan Museum of Art, New York 28, N.Y., U.S.A.; (home) 1000 Park Avenue, New York 28, N.Y., U.S.A.; Chagrin Falls, Ohio, U.S.A. *Clubs:* Harvard, Grolier, Century, Dutch Treat (New York). [*Died* 11 *May* 1966.

ROSCOE, Prof. Kenneth Harry, M.C. 1940; T.D. 1954; Professor of Engineering,

University of Cambridge, since 1968; Fellow of Emmanuel College, Cambridge, since 1948; Consultant in Soil Mechanics; *b.* 13 Dec. 1914; *s.* of late Col. H. Roscoe, O.B.E., T.D., Stoke-on-Trent, and Elizabeth A. (*née* Schofield); *m.* 1945, Janet Dinah, Consultant Pædiatrician, *d.* of late B. L. Gimson, M.A.; one *s.* one *d.* *Educ.:* Newcastle-under-Lyme High Sch.; Emmanuel Coll., Cambridge (Sen. Schol.). M.A. 1943; A.M.I.Mech.E. 1943; A.M.I.C.E. 1967. Techn. Trainee, Metropolitan-Cammell Ltd., 1938-39. Adjt. to C.R.E. Forward Sub Area, France, 1939-1940; P.O.W., Germany, 1940-45. Univ. Dept. of Engrg., Cambridge: Research Student, 1945; Demonstrator, 1946; Lectr., 1948; Reader, 1965; Head of Soil Mechanics Lab., 1946-; Head of Survey, 1950-60; Tutor, 1952-65 and Domestic Bursar, 1955-1965, Emmanuel Coll., Cambridge. Min. of Supply: Rate of Strain Panel, 1953-59; R.E. Adv. Cttee., 1957-68; Ministry of Defence: Adv. Council on Scientific Research and Techn. Develt., 1968-69; Vehicles Council (formerly Vehicles Bd.), 1969-. Ed. Panel, Géotechnique, 1964-68. Vis. lectr. to many N. Amer. and European univs., res, estabs. and engrg. institutes. T.A. Service. R.E., 1934-60: 2nd in Comd., C.U.O.T.C., 1952-60; Lt.-Col. 1946. Brit. Geotech. Soc. Prize, 1958. *Publications:* numerous papers in scientific and techn. jls. on stress-strain behaviour of soils and on interaction of soils and structures. *Recreations:* ball games, odd jobs. *Address:* 4 Millington Rd., Cambridge. *T.:* 50505; University Dept. of Engineering, Trumpington St., Cambridge. *T.:* 55691; Emmanuel Coll., Cambridge. *T.:* 58356. [*Died* 10 *April* 1970.

ROSE, (Charles) Archibald (Walker), C.I.E. 1911; F.R.G.S.; J.P.; *b.* 14 July 1879; *s.* of late Thomas Edward Rose; *m.* Elsie Mabel, *d.* of late James Rolland Morse. Was present at Siege of Peking and received China medal and clasp for defence of Legations; has acted as Consul at Chungking, Chefoo, and Ningpo, Hangchow, on Burma-China Frontier; travels in China, Mongolia, and Central Asia; represented Foreign Office at Tripartite Conference *re* Tibet at Simla, 1913-1914; Commercial Attaché, Shanghai, 1915; Peking, 1917; rank 1st Secretary Diplomatic Service; retired, 1921. *Address:* The Moat Farm, Framlingham, Suffolk. *Club:* Reform. [*Died* 3 *March* 1961.

ROSE, Sir Charles Henry, 3rd Bt., *cr.* 1909; late Royal Navy; *b.* 13 Oct. 1912; *s.* of 2nd Bt. and Daphne, *y. d.* of late Capt. H. Brooks Gaskell, of Kiddington Hall, Oxford; *S.* father, 1914; *m.* 1937, Hon. Phoebe Margaret Dorothy Phillimore, *o. d.* of 2nd Baron Phillimore; one *s.* two *d.* (and one *s.* decd.). *Educ.:* Dartmouth. *Heir:* *s.* Julian Day Rose, *b.* 3 March 1947. *Address:* Hardwick House, Whitchurch, Oxon. [*Died* 8 *April* 1966.

ROSE, Sir David James Gardiner, G.C.M.G. 1966 (C.M.G. 1966); C.V.O. 1966; M.B.E. 1954; Governor-General of Guyana, since Dec. 1966; *b.* 10 April 1923; *yr. s.* of late Dr. Frederick Gardiner Rose, O.B.E., M.D., M.R.C.P., of British Guiana, and Thyrza Rachel (*née* Mould), of London; *m.* 1948, Patricia Mary Catherine, M.R.C.S., L.R.C.P., *o. d.* of late G. W. Firkins, Worcester, and Mary Ellen (*née* Moore); two *s.* four *d.* *Educ.:* Mount St. Mary's Coll., Derbyshire, England. War Service, British Army, 1941-48 (Europe and Caribbean); Lieut. K.O.Y.L.I. Colonial Police Service, 1948: Asst. Supt., British Guiana, 1948; Supt. 1953; Senior Supt., 1955; Asst. Commissioner, 1958. Administrative Service, 1960. Federal Defence Officer, W. Indian Fedn., Trinidad, 1960-62; served on Interim Commission, W. Indies, May-Aug., 1962; Actg. Administrator, Antigua, Aug. 1962; Actg. Administrator, St. Lucia, 1963; Administrator of Antigua, 1964-66. Colonial Police Medal for Meritorious Service (and Bar for Gallantry), 1960. K.St.J., 1967. *Recreations:* Rugby football, riding, walking, music, reading. *Address:* Guyana House, Georgetown, Guyana; Old Sandalls, Mayfield, Sussex. *T.:* Mayfield 3357. *Clubs:* Royal Commonwealth Society, West Indian (both in London). [*Died* 10 *Nov.* 1969.

ROSE, Herbert Jennings, M.A. (Oxon.); Professor of Greek, United College of St. Salvator and St. Leonard, St. Andrews, 1927-53; retired Sept. 1953; *b.* Orillia, Ontario, 5 May 1883; *e. surv. s.* of Rev. S. P. Rose, D.D., and Jean Andrews; *m.* 1911, Elsie (*d.* 1939), *e. d.* of late Samuel Plimsoll, M.P. (the Sailors' Friend); four *s.* two *d.* *Educ.:* Private tuition; Collegiate Institute, Ottawa; McGill University, Montreal; Balliol College, Oxford. Fellow and Lecturer of Exeter College, Oxford, 1907-11; Associate Professor of Classics, McGill University, 1911-15; Army Service, 1915-19; Professor of Latin, Aberystwyth, 1919-27; President of Folk-lore Society, 1932-35; President of Scottish Anthropological Society, 1932-52; Pres., Classical Assoc. of Scotland, 1955; Socio Corrispondente R. Istituto lombardo di Scienze e Lettere, 1932; F.B.A., 1934; Fellow of the Scottish Anthropological Society, 1935; Foreign Member, Royal Society of Letters, Lund, 1935; Sather Professor Univ. of California, July-Dec. 1939; Hon. Fellow of Exeter College, 1944; For. Mem. Roy. Netherlands Acad. of Sciences, 1951; Hon. LL.D. St. Andrews, 1954. *Publications:* The Roman Questions of Plutarch, 1924; Primitive Culture in Greece, 1925; Primitive Culture in Italy, 1926; Blodau o Hen Ardd, 1927 (with T. Gwynn Jones); A Handbook of Greek Mythology, 1928; Modern Methods in Classical Mythology, 1930; The Origin and Growth of Religion (translated from the German of Father W. Schmidt), 1931; Hygini Fabulae, 1934; A Handbook of Greek Literature, 1934; A Handbook of Latin Literature, 1936; The Eclogues of Vergil, 1942; Greek Piety (translated from the Swedish of M. P. Nilsson), 1948; Ancient Greek Religion, 1948; Folklore of Chios (with P. P. Argenti), 1949; Ancient Roman Religion, 1949; Essays on the History of Religion (from the Italian of R. Pettazzoni), 1954; Two Thunderclouds (from the Dutch of B. A. van Proosdij), 1954; The Ancient Chronology of Western Asia and Egypt, 2nd edn. (from the Dutch of P. van der Meer), 1955; The All-knowing God (trans. from the Italian of R. Pettazzoni), 1956; Gods and Heroes of the Greeks, 1957; A Commentary on the surviving plays of Aeschylus, I, 1957, II, 1958; Some Problems of Classical Religion, 1958; Heroes of the Greeks (from the German of K. Kerényi), 1959; Classical Literature for Students of English, 1959; various articles and reviews, mostly in the journals of learned societies in Europe and America; several articles in Hastings' Encyclopædia of Religion and Ethics, the Encyclopædia Britannica, 14th and 15th edns., Oxford Classical Dictionary, Chambers's Encyclopædia, and other works of reference. *Recreations:* miscellaneous reading, chess. *Address:* 16 Queens Gardens, St. Andrews, Fife. *T.:* St. Andrews 986. [*Died* 31 *July* 1961.

ROSE, Colonel Richard Aubrey De Burgh, C.M.G. 1919; D.S.O. 1916; late Worcestershire Regiment; *b.* 9 May 1877; *s.* of late Surg.-Gen. H. J. Rose; *m.* Vera Lambert, (*d.* 1942), *o. d.* of late Dr. J. A. Turner, C.I.E.; one *d.* *Educ.:* Dover College. Joined Worcestershire Regt. from the 3rd E. Surrey Regt. in April 1900; served S. African War, 1900-2, with 2nd Batt. Worcestershire Regt.; seconded for service with Gold Coast Regt. W.A.F.F. 1906; 2nd in Command, 1911; Commanded The Gold Coast Regiment W.A.F.F.,

1914-22; served European War, 1914-17, in the Cameroons and East Africa (C.M.G., D.S.O. and bar, Bt. Lt.-Col., Croix d'Officier Légion d'honneur, Officer Military Order of Avis); retired pay, 1922. *Recreations:* cricket, lawn tennis. *Address:* 82 Redcliffe Gardens, S.W.10. [*Died* 23 *Jan.* 1962.

ROSE, Professor William, M.A., Ph.D.; Professor of German Language and Literature, University of London, since 1949; Head of Dept. of Modern Languages, London School of Economics, since 1935; Chm. Inst. of Germanic Languages and Literatures, Univ. of London; *b.* 13 July 1894; *s.* of Joseph and Anne Rose; *m.* 1926, Dorothy Wooldridge; one *s.* one *d.* *Educ.:* King Edward VI School, Five Ways, Birmingham; Universities of Birmingham and London. Served European War, 1914-18, in Royal Warwickshire Regt., Machine Gun Corps, and Royal Air Force, 1915-20; War of 1939-45, in Intelligence Corps, 1939-44. Lecturer in German, King's College, Univ. of London, 1920-27; Reader in German, Univ. of London (King's College), 1927-35; Sir Ernest Cassel Reader in German, Univ. of London and Head of Dept. of Modern Languages, London School of Economics, 1935-49. Member of Council, English Goethe Society. *Publications:* From Goethe to Byron, 1924; Men, Myths and Movements in German Literature, 1931; Heinrich Heine: Two Studies of his Thought and Feeling, 1956; (Ed.) The History of Dr. John Faustus, 1925; (Ed., with J. Isaacs) Contemporary Movements in European Literature, 1928; (Ed.) Modern German Poetry, An Anthology, 1932; (Ed., with G. Craig Houston) R. M. Rilke, Aspects of his Mind and Poetry, 1937; (Ed.) Essays on Goethe, 1949; A Book of Modern German Lyric Verse, 1960; (Trans.) Goethe: The Sorrows of Young Werther, 1929; Gen. Ed.: The Republic of Letters series; Benn's Sixpenny Library; (Ed.) An Outline of Modern Knowledge, 1931; contributor to learned journals and annuals. *Recreation:* travelling abroad. *Address:* Kine Croft, Sutton Courtenay, Berks. *T.:* Sutton Courtenay 273; 5 Chamberlain St., N.W.1. [*Died* 13 *July* 1961.

ROSE, Prof. William John, M.A. Oxon. Ph.D. Cracow; F.R.Hist.S.; F.R.S.C.; Hon. LL.D., University of British Columbia; D.D., Union College of British Columbia; Emeritus Professor, University of London and University of B.C.; *b.* Minnedosa, Canada, 7 August 1885; *s.* of Henry Rose and Prudence McKinney; *m.* 1912, Emily Mary Cuthbert; no *c.* *Educ.:* Univ. of Manitoba, Oxford, Leipzig, Cracow. Rhodes Scholar, Magdalen Coll., Oxford, 1905-8; Lecturer in History, Univ. of Manitoba, 1908-12; Prisoner of War (civilian) in Austrian Silesia, 1914-18; Student Relief and Y.M.C.A. Sec. Cracow and Warsaw, 1919-27; Asst. Prof. of Sociology, Dartmouth College, Hanover, N.H., U.S.A., 1927-35; Reader from 1935, Professor, 1938-50, of Polish Literature and History, University of London; Director of School of Slavonic and East European Studies, 1939-47; Editor of Slavonic and East European Review, 1945-1950. Foreign Research and Press Service of Foreign Office, 1939-43. *Publications:* The Desire of All Nations, 1919, and Danzig and Poland, 1922, both trans. from Polish; Stanislas Konarski, 1929; The Drama of Upper Silesia, 1936; Poland (as Penguin Special), 1939; Three Chapters in Cambridge History of Poland, Vol. II, 1941; The Rise of Polish Democracy, 1944; Poland Old and New, 1948; contributor to Chambers's Encyclopædia, new edn.; numerous review and newspaper articles. *Recreations:* tramping, golf, gardening. *Address:* Naramata, B.C., Canada. [*Died* 10 *March* 1968.

ROSEVEARE, Richard Victor Harley, M.C., M.A., F.I.M.A.; Sen. Mathematical Master, Winchester College, 1944-57, retd.; *b.* 1897; 2nd *s.* of late William Nicholas Roseveare, M.A.; *m.* 1931, Frances Alice, *d.* of late Allan C. Fraser, Ottawa, Canada; one *s.* one *d.* (and one *s.* decd.). *Educ.:* Winchester College; Trinity Coll., Cambridge, 1st Class Mathematical Tripos. Served in R.F.A., 1915-19; wounded 1916; attached Ordnance Committee, 1917 (M.C., French Croix de Guerre); Assistant Master, Winchester College, 1922-32; taught for a year at Upper Canada College, Toronto, 1927-28; Headmaster of Cheltenham College, 1932-37, Gordonstoun School, 1938-39; Director of Education, Sudan, 1939-44. *Recreations:* walking, music. *Address:* Corpus Christi Cottage, Chalford Glos. [*Died* 14 *May* 1968.

ROSEWAY, Sir (George) David, K.B.E. *cr.* 1947 (C.B.E. 1941); C.B. 1944; B.A.; *b.* 9 April 1890; *e. s.* of late David Roseway; *m.* 1920, Norma MacIntosh (*d.* 1950), *d.* of late William Hynd; one *s.* one *d.* *Educ.:* Merchant Taylors' School; Christ's College, Cambridge (Scholar). 1st Class Nat. Sci. Tripos, 1911; B.A. 1912; Higher Divn. Clerk, War Office, 1914; Private Sec. to successive Under-Secretaries of State (Mr. Ian Macpherson, Lord Peel and Sir Robert Sanders), 1916-22; Principal, 1922; Private Secretary to successive Secretaries of State (Mr. A. Duff Cooper, Mr. Leslie Hore-Belisha, Mr. Oliver Stanley, and Mr. Anthony Eden), 1936-40; Assistant Secretary, 1937; Director of Finance, War Office, 1940; Deputy Under-Secretary of State, War Office, 1945-55; retired. F.R.P.S.L. *Recreations:* gardening, philately. *Address:* Greenways, 59 West End Lane, Pinner, Middlesex. *T.:* 01-866 1342. [*Died* 25 *Nov.* 1969.

ROSING, Vladimir; Director of Rosing Productions, Inc.; *s.* of a Russian barrister and landowner, Serge Rosing; *m.* 1st, Marie Falle; one *s.*; 2nd, Margaret Williamson; 3rd, 1939, Winifred Campbell; 4th 1952, Jean Hillard; one *s.*; 5th, Ruth Scates. *Educ.:* Petrograd Univ. for Law. Singing with Jean de Reszke, Sbriglia, Sir George Power, Mrs. Rosing; originally intended by the family for the Bar, but the call of art and singing was stronger, and on receiving his first engagement to the opera of Petrograd left the Bar; sung in the opera as their chief tenor, 1912-13; first appearance in London Albert Hall, 1913: tour in Switzerland and South Russia, 1913-14; engaged in June 1914 as the leading tenor for the Imperial Opera, Vienna, fortunately did not get there; sang in England, 1914-20; created the rôle of Herman in opera Queen of Spades in London, 1915; began his series of Recitals in London as interpreter of songs, 1916; tour in England, 1919-20; first singer to give Vocal Recital, Albert Hall, 6 March 1921; 100th Recital in London; created Opera Intime, London, 25 June 1921; 1st American tour, Nov. 1921-April 1922; 1st Recitals, Paris, May-June 1922; Belgium, England, France, Autumn 1922; America, Canada, Dec. 1922-April 1923; tour, Paris, England, America, Canada, 1923-24; organised the Rochester American Opera Co., 1923-26; artistic director of the American Opera Company, 1927-30; produced plays New York, 1931-1935; producing director of Covent Garden English Opera Co., 1936-39; producing director of Southern California Opera Co. of Hollywood, 1939; Director of Entertainment, U.S. Army, Camp Roberts, 1943-45; Artistic Director, American Opera, Cal., 1946-50; Directing Operatic Films, R.O. Century and M.G.M., 1949-50; California Centennial Pageant, Hollywood Bowl; staging opera films, M.G.M. Air Force Pageant, Hollywood Bowl; music, theatre, television, Hollywood; Dennis Day TV Show; Hollywood Bowl Productions, 1950-1955: Faust, Fledermaus, Merry Widow, Song of Norway, etc.; film Interrupted

Melody. Director of: City Center Opera Co., N.Y.; Los Angeles Civic Light Opera; Phœnix Civic Light Opera; Lyric Opera of Chicago. Author and director of: Oregon Story for Centennial of State of Oregon, 1959; Kansas Story for Cent. of Kansas, 1961. *Recreations:* skating, tennis, chess, bridge; won championship for roller-skating in Petrograd, 1911. *Address:* 4540 N. 44th St., Phœnix, Arizona, U.S.A. [*Died* 24 *Nov.* 1963.

ROSMAN, Alice Grant; journalist and novelist; *b.* South Australia; *g.-g.d.* of one of the men who bought paper land in the new Colony in London in 1836 and sailed there with his house and family. *Educ.:* Dominican Convent, Cabra, South Australia. Began writing at school, and soon after leaving became Adelaide correspondent for Sydney Bulletin; after four years' journalism in Australia came to London for Coronation and has remained ever since; published two novels during the War, but as they made no money, turned to editorial work and short stories which did; left these excitements in 1927 to concentrate on fiction. *Publications:* Miss Bryde of England, 1916; The Tower Wall, 1917: The Back-Seat Driver, 1928; The Window, 1928; Visitors to Hugo, 1929; The Young and Secret, 1930; Jock the Scot, 1930; The Sixth Journey, 1931; Benefits Received, 1932; Protecting Margot, 1933; Somebody Must, 1934; The Sleeping Child, 1935; Mother of the Bride, 1936; Unfamiliar Faces, 1938; Truth to Tell, 1938; William's Room, 1939; Nine Lives (U.S.A.), 1941. *Recreations:* motoring, travelling and returning to London, especially the last. *Address:* 15 Wood Lane, Highgate, N.6. *T.:* Tudor 3170. [*Died* 20 *Aug.* 1961.

ROSS, Rev. Alexander, D.D.; B.D.; Senior Minister of Burghead Free Church, Morayshire; *b.* 9 Sept. 1888; *s.* of Robert and Jane Ross; *m.* 1922, Williamina Roberts; one *s.* *Educ.:* Kiltearn Public Sch.; Dingwall Academy; Aberdeen University; Free Church College, Edinburgh. Minister of Partick Free Church, Glasgow, 1913-22; Burghead Free Church, Morayshire, 1922-26; St. Columba Free Church, Aberdeen, 1926-1928; St. Andrew's Presbyterian Church, Swift Current, Sask., Canada, 1928-30; Free High Church, Dumbarton, 1930-37; Professor of New Testament Exegesis, Free Church College, Edinburgh, Scotland, 1937-1952; Minister, Burghead Free Church, 1952-1958; Moderator of Free Church of Scotland, 1935. Hon. D.D. (Montreal), 1950. *Publications:* Editor of The Instructor, Young People's Magazine of Free Church of Scotland, 1918-28; articles in The New Bible Handbook (Inter-Varsity Fellowship), 1947; Commentary on Epistles of James and John in New International Commentary, 1954; contributions in The New Bible Dictionary (I.V.F.), 1962. *Recreations:* golf and cricket. *Address:* Free Church Manse, Whiting Bay, Isle of Arran. [*Died* 26 *May* 1965.

ROSS, Alexander David, C.B.E. 1949; M.A., D.Sc., Diploma in Education (Glasgow); B.Sc. (Lond.); D.Sc. (Adelaide); Hon. LL.D. (W.A.) 1963; F.R.A.S.; F.R.S.E.; F.R.S.A.; F.Inst.P.; Hon. F.A.I.P. 1964; F.I.E.S. (Aust.); Hon. F.E.I.S. 1951; Executive Officer, Pan Indian Ocean Science Association; Consultant, East-West Centre, Univ. of Hawaii, Honolulu, 1961-64; Professor of Physics, University of Western Australia, 1912-52; *b.* Glasgow, 1883; *s.* of late Dr. David Ross; *m.* 1913, Euphemia W., B.Sc., *d.* of late Bailie Murchie, Irvine; one *d.* *Educ.:* Glasgow C. of S. Normal School and Training College; Glasgow High School: Royal Technical College, Glasgow; Universities of Glasgow and Göttingen. Thomson Research Scholar, 1905; Houldsworth Research Fellow, 1906; Assistant to the Professor of Natural Philosophy, 1907; Lecturer on Natural Philosophy, University of Glasgow, 1908; Examiner, Scotch Education Department and Civil Service Commission, 1908-13; President of the British Astronomical Association, Scottish Branch, 1911-13, and W.A. Branch, 1927-29; President, Royal Society of W.A., 1916-17; 1923-25 and 1940-41; President, W.A. Astronomical Soc., 1915-17, 1950-52; Pres., Illuminating Engineering Soc., W.A.; 1944-45, National President, Australia, 1948-49; held combined Chair of Mathematics and Physics in the University of Western Australia, 1912-29; Kelvin Medal and Prize for researches in Natural Philosophy, 1914; Member of the Crocker Solar Eclipse Expedition of the Lick Observatory, 1922; Hon. Secretary, Australian Branch Inst. of Physics, 1924-43, President, 1944-45; Member, Inventions Board, Aust. Military Forces, W. Comd., 1939-42; Chairman, Defence State Camouflage Committee (W.A.), and Dep. Director of Camouflage (Commonwealth Dept. of Home Security), 1941-43; Officer R.A.A.F., War of 1939-45. Consultant Physicist, Royal Australian Navy, 1940-43; Member, Aust. Scientific Instruments and Optical Panel, 1940-45; Member, W.A. State Committee C.S.I.R.O., 1926-; Member, 1916-55, Chairman, 1938-55, Soldiers' Children's Scholarship Trust; Foundation Member, Soldiers' Children Education Board, 1921-; Member, W.A. Optometrical Registration Bd., 1940-52. Chairman W.A. Division, Aust. Nat. Research Council, 1944-54; Local Hon. Sec. for W.A., Aust. and N.Z. Assoc. for Adv. of Science. 1945-58, and Hon. Life Member of the Association; took active part in establishing Aust. Inst. of Physics, 1964; Hon. F.A.I.P. 1964; W.A. Government representative Council of National Association of Testing Authorities (Aust.); Hon. Life Mem., Royal Soc. of Mauritius. *Publications:* numerous researches in magnetism, spectroscopy, astrophysics, and metallography in the Philosophical Magazine, Annalen der Physik, Physikalische Zeitschr., etc. *Recreations:* music, motoring, photography. *Address:* Balnagown, Golf Links Road, Albany, Western Australia. *Clubs:* Weld (Perth), Albany (W. Australia). [*Died* 14 *Dec.* 1966.

ROSS, Alexander Howard, C.B.E.; J.P.; retired Political Officer, Gold Coast and Sierra Leone Governments; *b.* Wiltshire, 31 Jan. 1880; *er. s.* of Doctor R. A. Ross, F.R.C.S.; *m.* Ianthe, *widow* of Lieut.-Commander R. Ussher, D.S.O., R.N.; no *c.* *Educ.:* Epsom College; H.M.S. Worcester. Entered service of Gold Coast Government, 1905; served as Assistant District Commissioner, District Commissioner, and acting Provincial Commissioner in Ashante, Northern Territories of Gold Coast; acting Secretary for Native Affairs, 1919; Provincial Commissioner, Sierra Leone, 1920; Commissioner of the Southern Province, Sierra Leone, 1920-28; County Councillor, Hertfordshire; Platoon Commander Herts Bn. Home Guard, 1940. *Publications:* a series of articles on the activities of pirates in West Africa in the publication West Africa. *Recreation:* shooting. *Address:* c/o Bank of West Africa, 37 Gracechurch Street, E.C.3. [*Died* 6 *April* 1965.

ROSS, Archibald Hugh Houstoun, C.B.E. 1957 (O.B.E. 1953); Director of Forestry for Scotland, 1953-March 1957, retired; *b.* 23 March 1896; *s.* of Hugh Houstoun Ross and Edith Margaret Macnider; *m.* 1929, Winifred Mary Frank; two *d.* *Educ.:* Shrewsbury School; Trinity College, Oxford (B.A.). Royal Engineers, 1915-18; Indian Forest Service, 1921-24; Forestry Commn., 1925-57. *Address:* The Dowery House, Ford, Midlothian. *T.:* Ford 368. *Clubs:* East India and Sports; New (Edinburgh). [*Died* 27 *April* 1969.

ROSS of that Ilk, yr., Charles Campbell, Q.C. (Grenada) 1938, (Gibraltar), 1947; Sheriff-Substitute of Elgin and Nairn 1961-1965 (at Stornoway and Lochmaddy, 1955-1961); Chief-Designate of the Clan Ross; *b.* 1901; *yr.* but *o. surv. s.* of late Sir Ronald Ross, K.C.B., K.C.M.G., F.R.S., F.R.S.E., F.R.C.S.; *m.* 1930, Beatrice, *er. d.* of late Major A. E. Saner; two *s.* one *d.* *Educ.:* Charterhouse; Magdalen College, Oxford (M.A.) Barrister-at-Law, Lincoln's Inn, 1927; Advocate (Scotland), 1947; Private practice, 1927-34 and 1953-55; Colonial Legal Service, 1934-53. *Publications:* The Law relating to Inn-keepers, 1928; The Law of Licensing, 1933; The Laws of Gibraltar, 1950; various official handbooks and contributions to legal encyclopædias and periodicals. *Address:* Spey Bay, Morayshire. *T.:* Spey Bay 209. *Club:* Scottish Arts (Edinburgh). [*Died* 29 *June* 1966.

ROSS, Sir Frederick W. L.; *see* Leith-Ross.

ROSS, Sir James Stirling, K.B.E., *cr.* 1937 (C.B.E. 1919); C.B. 1928; M.A.; *b.* 3 Aug. 1877; *s.* of late John Ross, V.D., F.E.I.S., Edinburgh; *m.* 1st, 1904, Christina MacDonald, M.A. (Scholar of Newnham College, Cambridge), *d.* of John Ross, M.A., Rector of Arbroath High School; two *s.* one *d.*; 2nd, 1928, Henrietta Wilson, *d.* of late J. P. Halket, 51 Woodside Park Road, N.12 *Educ.:* Royal High School, Edinburgh; Univ. of Edinburgh (1st Class honours in Classics and Baxter Scholar); Balliol College Oxford (Warner Exhibitioner and 1st Class in Classical Moderations). War Office, 1900; Private Secretary to Chief of General Staff, 1904-5; served in Aldershot, Scottish and Northern Commands, 1905-12; Finance Dept., War Office, 1912-18; Deputy to Assist. Financial Secretary, Air Ministry, 1918; Director of Accounts, 1921; Principal Asst. Secretary, 1930-34; Deputy Secretary and (later) First Deputy Under Secretary of State, 1934-38; retired May 1938; rejoined Air Ministry Sept. 1939 for war service; served as Air Ministry Representative in S. Africa and Southern Rhodesia, 1940-43; Air Ministry Secretariat and Planning Executive, Jan. 1944-Feb 1946; Chm., Selection Board, Allied Control Commission (Germany), Feb.-Aug. 1946; served with Ministry of Health as a Regional Officer for introduction of Nat. Health Service, 1946-49 Member of Board of Trustees of Imperial War Museum, 1930-38; Vice-Chairman Bacon Development Board, 1938-39; Chairman West Surrey and Aldershot Hospital League, 1938-48; President Civil Service Pensioners' Alliance, 1954- and First Div. Pensioners' Group, 1957-61. *Publication:* The National Health Service in Great Britain: an Historical and Descriptive Study, 1952. *Recreations:* golf, fishing. *Address:* Dunkeld, 10 Green Lane, Merrow, Guildford, Surrey. *Club:* National Liberal. [*Died* 2 *Oct.* 1961.

ROSS, John, C.B. 1951; formerly Assistant Under-Secretary of State, Home Office; *b.* 1 Sept. 1893. Head of Children's Department of Home Office, 1947-55; retired 31st December 1955. *Address:* Pall Mall Chambers, 104 Pall Mall, S.W.1. *Club:* Reform. [*Died* 5 *Dec.* 1967.

ROSS, Brigadier John Ellis, C.V.O. 1947; C.B.E. 1950; Comptroller to Governor of Southern Rhodesia, 1950-56; *b.* 7 June 1893; *y. s.* of John Arthur and Florence Ross; *m.* 1922, Jean Rousell, *d.* of E. W. Morey. *Educ.:* King's School, Worcester. Joined British South Africa Police, 1913, Asst. Commissioner, 1940, Commissioner of Police, 1945 Retired 1950; O.St.J. 1950. *Address:* Salisbury Cottage, Robinson Rd., Kenilworth, C.P., S. Africa. [*Died Oct.* 1965.

ROSS, Rev. Kenneth Needham; Canon and Chancellor of Wells Cathedral, since 1969; *b.* Worcester, 28 Nov. 1908; *s.* of William George and Elizabeth Ann Ross. *Educ.:* King's School, Worcester; Merton College, Oxford; Cuddesdon College, Oxford. Postmaster of Merton, 1926-31; 1st cl. Classical Hon. Mods. B.A. (2nd cl. Lit. Hum.) and Liddon Student, 1930; 1st cl. Theology 1931; M.A. 1933. Deacon, 1932; priest, 1933; Curate, St. Michael and All Angels, Radford, 1932-33; Chaplain, Salisbury Theological Coll., 1933-36, Vice-Principal, 1936-41; Vicar of Malden, Surrey, 1941-51; Vicar of All Saints', Margaret Street, W.1, 1951-69. Examining Chaplain to Bishop of London, 1951; a proctor in Convocation, 1954-. *Publications:* History of Malden, 1947; Why I am not a Roman Catholic, 1953; The Thirty-nine Articles, 1957; Is Religion a Racket?, 1961; The Christian Mysteries, 1964; What the Spirit Says to the Churches, 1965; regular contributor to Church Times. *Address:* 8 The Liberty, Wells, Somerset. *T.:* Wells 8763. [*Died* 8 *June* 1970.

ROSS, Robert, O.B.E. 1939; *b.* 25 Jan. 1893; *e. s.* of late John and Jessie Ross, Seaforth, Alness; *m.* 1919, Margaret M. Hood; two *s.* *Educ.:* Bridgend Public School, Alness: Dingwall Academy; Edinburgh University (M.A. 1914). Served European War, 1914-18 (severely wounded); War Office, 1917-18. Entered Consular Service, 1920; served at: Rio de Janeiro, Frankfort, Katowice, Chicago, Reykjavik, Teneriffe, Moscow (Commercial Counsellor), Hamburg (Consul-General); retired 1952. *Recreations:* microscopy, fishing, philology. *Address:* Seaforth, Alness, Ross-shire. *T.:* Alness 261. [*Died* 11 *July* 1969.

ROSS, Air Commodore Robert Peel, D.S.O. 1917; A.F.C.; late R.A.F.; *m.* 1916, Muriel Valerie, *d.* of late E H Kinnard; one *s.* H.M.S. Britannia, 1903; R.N.A.S., 1914. Served European War, 1914-18 (D.S.O., A.F.C.); Air Aide-de-Camp to the King, 1927-30: Deputy Director of Manning, Air Ministry, 1928-31; Chief Staff Officer, Middle East Command, 1931-33; retired, 1934; Commandant, Scottish Area, Royal Observer Corps, 1938-44. *Address:* Belmore, Gullane, East Lothian. *Clubs:* Shikar; Hon. Company of Edinburgh Golfers. [*Died* 30 *Dec.* 1963.

ROSS WILLIAMSON, Reginald Pole; Regional Director, British Information Services, Melbourne, Australia; *b.* 25 January 1907; *s.* of late Rev. Hugh Ross Williamson; *m.* 1932, Eileen Sybil, *d.* of late A. C. Buchanan, Sydney, N.S.W. *Educ.:* Emmanuel College, Cambridge. Worked for British Museum in Egypt and at Ur of the Chaldees; Editor of the original The Bookman, 1934; attached to Observer, 1934-39; Admiralty (Press Division), 1939-43; U.K. Press Attaché, Dublin, 1943-53; Office of U.K. High Commission, India, 1953-54; First Secretary, British Embassy, Dublin, 1955-57; Regional Director, British Information Services, Cape Town, South Africa, 1957-62. *Recreation:* painting. *Address:* c/o H.M. Diplomatic Service, Whitehall, S.W.1. *Club:* Oxford and Cambridge. [*Died* 22 *April* 1966.

ROSSITER, Dr. James Leonard, C.B.E. 1960; J.P. (in West Australia); M.A., D.Litt.; D.Ed.; Headmaster Wesley College, Perth, West Australia, 1930-52; Grand Master, Grand Lodge of W.A. of A.F. and A.M.; Past Provincial Prior of Knights Templar in Western Australia; *b.* 9 November 1887; *s.* of Samuel Rossiter and Emma Thyrza Mitchell; *m.* 1912, Mary Marguerite Sparkman Jacobs; two *s.* two *d.* *Educ.:* Prince Alfred College, Adelaide; Universities of Adelaide and Sydney. Formerly: Director of Education for the Northern Territory of Australia, 1913 and 1914; Tutor in Universities of Sydney and Queensland; Chm., Adult Education Board, Mem. of the Senate and Warden of Convocation, Univ. of Western Australia. Acting Principal, Methodist Ladies' College, Perth, W.A., for 1960. Defence Medal, 1939-1945; Jubilee Medal, 1935; King George VI Coronation Medal, 1937; Queen Elizabeth II Coronation Medal, 1953. *Publications:* Educational Pamphlets, Articles, etc. *Recreations:* golf, gardening. *Address:* Karrinyup, via Mt. Hawthorn W. Australia. *Clubs:* Royal Automobile of W.A., Freemasons'; Rotary; Lake Karrinyup Country. [*Died* 3 *Sept.* 1963.

ROTH, Cecil; Reader in Jewish Studies, Oxford, 1939-64; *b.* London, 5 March 1899; *y. s.* of Joseph and Etty Roth; *m.* 1928, Irene Rosalind Davis, London. *Educ.:* City of London School. Military Service, 1917-19; Merton College, Oxford, 1919-24; B.Litt. 1923; D.Phil., M.A. 1924; F.R.Hist.S. 1925; F.R.S.L. 1941; Leverhulme Research Fellow, 1935-36; contributor to the Encyclopædia Britannica, Encyclopædia Judaica, Cambridge Medieval History, etc.; has lectured extensively in Europe, Africa and America. President of Jewish Historical Soc. of England, 1936-1945 and 1955-56; Visiting Lectr. in History, Jews' Coll., London. 1939-48; Visiting Prof., Columbia Univ., New York, 1958; Visiting Prof. of History: Bar Ilan Univ., 1964-65; Queen's College, N.Y., 1966-69. Editor, Encyclopedia Judaica, since 1965. *Publications:* The Last Florentine Republic, 1925 (Italian translation, 1929); Iscariot, 1929; The Casale Pilgrim, 1929; L'Apôtre des Maranes, 1930; History of the Jews in Venice, 1930 (Italian translation, 1932); A Jewish Book of Days, 1931, 1966; Lettere inedite di Donato Giannotti a Piero Vettori, 1932 (with Marchese Roberto Ridolfi); History of the Marranos, 1932 (Spanish trans., 1941, Hebrew, 1951); The Nephew of the Almighty, 1933; Life of Menasseh ben Israel, 1934; A Short History of the Jewish People, 1936 (translated into Hungarian 1943, Hebrew 1946, French 1948, German, 1954, Italian and Portuguese, 1962, Japanese 1965); Spanish Inquisition, 1937; The Jewish Contribution to Civilisation, 1938 (Translations into Spanish, Arabic, Serbo-Croat, Hebrew); Anglo-Jewish Letters, 1939; The Magnificent Rothschilds, 1939 (also in Dutch); The Sassoon Dynasty, 1941; History of Jews in England, 1941; History of Jews in Italy, 1946, etc.; Life of Gracia Nasi, 1947; Life of Duke of Naxos, 1948 (also in Hebrew and Spanish); Intellectual Activities of Medieval English Jewry, 1949; The Great Synagogue, 1950; Rise of Provincial Jewry, 1950; Catalogue of MSS. in the Roth Collection, 1950; The Jews of Medieval Oxford, 1951; Life of Benjamin Disraeli, 1952; The Historical Background of the Dead Sea Scrolls, 1958 (also in Hebrew); The Jews in the Italian Renaissance, 1959 (also in Hebrew); Personalities and Events in Jewish History, 1953; Essays and Portraits, 1962; The Dead Sea Scrolls: a new historical approach, 1965; Gleanings, 1967, etc. Ed. Soncino Press Haggadah, 1930; Magna Bibliotheca Anglo-Judaica, 1937; Beaconsfield Press Haggadah (Illustr. Arthur Szyk), 1939; Standard Jewish Encyclopedia, 1959; History of Jewish Art, 1961; Sarajevo Haggadah, 1962; Ben Shahn Haggadah, 1965; Chinese Jews, 1966, etc. *Relevant publication:* Bibliography of Remember the Days (Honorific Volume issued by Jewish Hist. Soc., Eng.) 1966. *Recreation:* sleep. *Address:* 21 Rehov Balfour, Jerusalem, Israel; c/o Lloyds Bank, 263 Tottenham Court Road, W.1. *Club:* Arts. [*Died* 21 *June* 1970.

ROTH, Leon, M.A., D.Phil.; F.B.A. 1948; *b.* London, 31 March 1896; 3rd *s.* of late Joseph Roth and Etty Jacobs; *m.* 1925, Winifred Marguerite, *d.* of late Alderman Abraham Davis, J.P.; three *s.* one *d.* *Educ.:* City of London School; Exeter College, Oxford. Military service (England and France), 1916-18; John Locke Scholar in Mental Philosophy, 1920; James Mew Hebrew Scholar, 1921; Officier d'Académie, 1926; Lecturer in Philosophy at the University of Manchester, 1923-28; Ahad Haam Professor of Philosophy at the University of Jerusalem, 1928-53 (Rector, 1940-43, Dean of the Faculty of Humanities, 1949-51); visiting Prof. in Philosophy, Coll. of Jewish Studies, Chicago, 1957, Brown Univ., 1958. *Publications:* Spinoza, Descartes and Maimonides, 1924; Correspondence of Descartes and Constantyn Huygens, 1926; Jewish Thought in the Modern World (in the Oxford Legacy of Israel), 1927; Science of Morals, 1928; Spinoza, 1929; Maimonides, Introduction to Logic, 1935; In Memory of Ahad Haam, 1937; Descartes' Discourse on Method, 1937; Illustrations of Post-Biblical Jewish Ethical and Religious Thought, 1938; Guide to the Study of Greek Philosophy, 1939; Problems of Hebrew Secondary Education in Palestine (Editor), 1939; Guide to the Study of Modern Philosophy, 1941; Ex Ore Altissimi, an Anthology of the Hebrew Scriptures, 1944; England and English Democracy, 1945; Introduction to the study of Political Thought, 1946; The Guide for the Perplexed: Moses Maimonides, 1948; Education and Human Values, 1949; On the Education of the Citizen (Ed.), 1949; Jewish Thought as a Factor in Civilization (Unesco), 1954; God and Man in The Old Testament, 1955; Judaism, a Portrait, 1960; Translator and Editor of philosophical classics in Hebrew. *Address:* 3 Sudeley Street, Brighton 7. *T.:* Brighton 64215. *Club:* Reform. [*Died* 1 *April* 1963.

ROTH, Paul Bernard, M.B., Ch.B. (Aberd.), F.R.C.S. (Eng.); late Surgeon, M.V. City of Poona, Ellerman Line; Hon. Consulting Orthopædic and Fracture Surgeon to North Staffordshire Royal Infirmary, Stoke-on-Trent; late Medical Member, Pensions Appeal Tribunals; late Med. Referee for County Court Circuit No. 26; Member B.M.A.; late Fellow British Orthopædic Assoc.; late F.R.S.M.; *b.* Brighton, 1882; *s.* of late Bernard Roth, F.S.A., F.R.C.S., and *g.s.* of Rt. Hon. John Bright, P.C., M.P.; *m.* 1st, 1911, Emilie Harding Lauder; one *s.* one *d.* (and one *s.* killed on active service, R.A.F., 1942); 2nd, 1933, Iris Darbyshire. *Educ.:* Tonbridge School; Aberdeen University; London Hospital. *Publications:* Orthopædics for Practitioners, 1920; numerous papers on orthopædic subjects, especially fractures, deformities of the feet, injuries to joints. *Address:* Hotel Clare, 67 Springfield Road, Kings Heath, Birmingham. *T.:* Highbury 1381. *Club:* Reform. [*Died* 29 *Dec.* 1962.

ROTHERY, Professor William; *see* Hume-Rothery.

ROTHKO, Mark; artist; *b.* Dvinsk, Russia, 25 September 1903; *s.* of Jacob Rothkovich and Kate (*née* Goldin); taken as child to United States, 1913; *m.* 1945, Mary Alice Beistle. *Educ.:* Yale College. Taught children's classes at Center Academy, Brooklyn, 1929-52; on staff of Brooklyn College, 1951-54; Visiting Artist, University of Colorado at Boulder, 1955, and Tulane University, 1956. One-man exhibitions include: Contemporary Arts Gallery, New York, 1933; Portland (Oregon) Art Museum, 1933; Peggy Guggenheim Gallery, 1945; Santa Barbara, California, 1946: Providence, Rhode Island and Chicago, 1954; Houston, Texas, 1957; Phillips Collection, Washington, D.C., 1960; Whitechapel Art Gallery, London, 1961. Annual exhibitions, Betty Persons Gallery, 1947-51; has exhibited regularly at Sidney Janis Gallery, New York, 1954-, and frequently abroad. Member, Federation of Modern Painters and Sculptors. *Address:* 118 East 95th Street, New York City, N.Y., U.S.A. [*Died* 25 *Feb.* 1970.

ROTHSCHILD, Anthony (Gustav) de, D.L.; *b.* 26 June 1887; 3rd *s.* of late Leopold de Rothschild, C.V.O.; *m.* 1926, Yvonne, *e. d.* of Robert Cahen d'Anvers, Paris; one *s.* two *d.* *Educ.:* Harrow; Cambridge (M.A.), 1st class Historical Tripos, Parts 1 and 2. Represented the University at tennis. Late Major, Bucks Yeomanry; served European War, 1914-1918 (despatches), Gallipoli (wounded); General Staff, France. Chairman, The Industrial Dwellings Soc. (1885) Ltd.; Pres. Norwood Home for Jewish Children. *Address:* Ascott Wing, Leighton Buzzard, Beds. *T.:* Leighton Buzzard 2219. *Clubs:* Turf; Jockey (Newmarket). [*Died* 5 *Feb.* 1961.

ROTHWELL, Brig. Richard Sutton, D.S.O. 1917; late Royal Artillery; *b.* 1882; *e. s.* of late Col. J. S. Rothwell; *m.* 1922, Gwendoline Marion (*d.* 1941), *d.* of Mrs. Allardice, Tregenna Longcross, Port Isaac, Cornwall. Served European War, 1914-18 (despatches, D.S.O.); Commander 27th (London) Air Defence Brigade T.A., 1935, 26th (London) Anti-Aircraft Group, 1935-39; retired pay, 1939. *Address:* The Red Lodge, Crowthorne, Berks. *T.:* Crowthorne 2757. [*Died* 28 *June* 1962.

ROTTER, Godfrey, C.B. 1936; C.B.E. 1925 (O.B.E. 1918); G.M. 1945; D.Sc., F.R.I.C., F.Inst.P.; *b.* 1879; *s.* of Charles G. Rotter, Croydon; *m.* 1905, Gertrude Elizabeth Plank; four *s.* one *d.* *Educ.:* City of London School; University College, North Wales. Entered Experimental Establishment of the War Office Explosives Committee, 1903; Director of Explosives Research, Research Dept., Royal Arsenal, Woolwich, 1921-42; award in connection with design of No. 106 fuze of which 88,000,000 were manufactured during European War, 1914-18. Developed many explosives and processes employed by the Fighting Services. Late Consultant to the Ministry of Supply. *Address:* Tyhen, Llwyndafydd, Llandyssul, Cards. *T.:* Newquay (Cards.) 346. [*Died* 16 *Feb.* 1969.

ROUNTREE, His Honour Judge Gilbert Harry; Judge of Plymouth and Cornwall County Courts since 1962; Deputy Chairman, Cornwall Quarter Sessions, since 1962; *b.* 27 Aug. 1907; *s.* of late Harry Rountree, artist, and Stella Rountree; *m.* 1932, Catherine Mary, *o. d.* of Douglas Mackie, Darjeeling; one *d.* *Educ.:* Westminster. Admitted Solicitor, 1930. Served R.A.F.V.R., 1940-45 (despatches); rank of Sqdn. Ldr. Called to Bar, Inner Temple, 1946; Western Circuit. *Recreation:* fly fishing. *Address:* Trehalvin, Trewidland, Liskeard, Cornwall. [*Died* 20 *Sept.* 1962.

ROUS, (Francis) Peyton, A.B., M.D.; Member Emeritus of the Rockefeller Institute for Medical Research, U.S.A.; Editor, Journal of Experimental Medicine; Scientific Consultant, Sloan-Kettering Institute for Cancer Research; *b.* 5 October 1879; *s.* of Charles Rous and Frances Wood; *m.* 1915, Marion Eckford de Kay; three *d.* *Educ.:* Public schools, Baltimore, Maryland; Johns Hopkins University, A.B.; Johns Hopkins Medical School, M.D. Hon. Sc.D. Cambridge, Michigan, Yale, Birmingham, McGill, Chicago, Rockefeller Inst.; Hon. LL.D.: St. Lawrence, Jefferson, Hartford; Hon. M.D., Zürich; Hon. Fell. Trinity Hall, Cambridge; Member: National Academy of Sciences; American Philosophical Society; foreign correspondent Académie de Médecine, Paris; for. mem. Roy. Soc.; hon. F.R.S.M. London; For. Corres. Mem. B.M.A.; hon. member Physiological Soc., Pathological Soc. of Great Britain and Ireland, New York Pathological Soc., Amer. Soc. Microbiology; member Royal Academy of Sciences of Denmark, Norwegian Acad. of Science and Letters; Hon. Fell., Weizmann Inst. of Science, Israel, Coll. of Pathologists, London; resident house officer, Johns Hopkins Hosp., 1905-06; instructor in pathology, Univ. of Michigan, 1906-08; assistant, 1909-10, associate, 1910-12, associate member, 1912-1920, member in pathology and bacteriology, 1920-45, Rockefeller Institute for Medical Research; John Scott medal and award, 1927; Linacre Lecturer, Cambridge Univ., 1929; Walker Prize, Royal College of Surgeons, 1941; Anna Fuller Memorial Prize, 1952; Kober Medal, Assoc. of Amer. Physns., 1953; Bertner Medal and Award, Univ. of Texas, 1954; Kovalenko Medal, National Academy of Sciences, 1956; Distinguished Service Award, American Cancer Society, 1957; Lasker Award, Am. Publ. Health Assoc., 1958; Judd Award, Memorial Center for Cancer, 1959; W.H.O. United Nations prize for Cancer Research; Gold Medal, R.S.M. (London), 1962; Gold Headed Cane Award, Amer. Assoc. of Pathologists and Bacteriologists, 1964; Nat. Medal of Science, U.S.A.; Paul Ehrlich Award, Germany, 1966; Nobel Prize in Med. (jointly), 1966, etc. *Publications:* Papers on cancer, the viruses, and physiological subjects. *Recreation:* relishing life. *Address:* 122 E. 82nd St., New York N.Y. *T.:* Butterfield 8-4567. *Club:* Century (N.Y.). [*Died* 16 *Feb.* 1970.

ROUSE, Sir Alexander Macdonald, Kt., *cr.* 1930; C.I.E. 1913; F.C.H. 1900; M.I.C.E.; M.T.P.I.; *b.* 14 Sept. 1878; *s.* of George Woodford Rouse; *m.* 1910, Jean Lois (*d.* 1958), *d.* of Major C. J. Jameson, B.S. Corps; two *s.* *Educ.:* St. Paul's School R.I.E.C., Coopers Hill. P.W.D., India, 1900-33; Chief Engineer, Central P.W.D., 1925-33; Chief Engineer, Ministry of Home Security and Home Office, 1938-49; retired. *Address:* Riverside, Beccles, Suffolk. *Clubs:* East India and Sports; Royal Norfolk and Suffolk Yacht (Lowestoft) [*Died* 9 *Dec.* 1966.

ROUSE-BOUGHTON, Sir E. H., Bt.; *see* Boughton.

ROUTH, Colonel Guy Montgomery, C.B.E. 1922; D.S.O. 1916; *b.* 18 June 1882; *s.* of Alfred Curtis Routh, M.D., F.R.C.S. (Lond.), and A. J. A., *d.* of C. H. F. Routh, M.D.; *m.* 1911, Flora Aiton Bell (*d.* 1959); one *s.*; *m.* 1959, Coraline Maud Norris. *Educ.:* Tonbridge School; R.M.A., Woolwich. R.G.A. 1900; in charge Ordnance, East Africa, 1914-15; Ordnance appointments in peacetime (India), 1908-14 and 1922-36, in wartime, 1914-22 and (York), 1940-42. Bt. Colonel 1930; retired, 1936; A.R.P. Officer, Middlesex, 1937-40; A.D.O.S. York (Colonel), 1940-42; Min. of Supply, 1942-44. Vice-Pres. (Emeritus) Inst. of Civil Defence, 1958. Languages include: Persian, Arabic, Urdu (High Proficiency Standards). *Publications:* in monthly Journals. *Address:* 61 Philbeach Gardens, S.W.5. [*Died* 23 *Aug.* 1963.

ROUTH, Robert Gordon; *b.* 18 Jan. 1869; *s.* of Charles Richard Augustus Routh and Sarah Eleanor Gordon; unmarried. *Educ.:* Dulwich College; Trinity College, Oxford. B.A. 1892; M.A. 1895; Assistant Master in Bromsgrove School, 1894; Bromsgrove District Council, 1901-13; County Education Committee, selected member, 1908-11; Headmaster, Bromsgrove School, 1912-31. *Address:* Charlecote Park, Warwick. *T.:* Wellesbourne 277. *Club:* United University. [*Died* 14 *March* 1964.

ROUTLEY, Dr. Thomas Clarence, C.B.E. 1946; Consultant General, the World Medical Association; *b.* 11 March 1889; *s.* of Obadiah and Eliza Silverwood Routley; *m.* 1916, Florence Johnston; one *s.* three *d.* *Educ.:* University of Toronto. M.B. 1915; R.A.M.C. and R.C.A.M.C., 1915-19. General Secretary Canadian Medical Assoc., 1923; M.D. Toronto, 1930; F.R.C.P.(C.) 1931. Rep. Canada on Interim Commn. of W.H.O., 1946-48; Chm. Council, World Med. Assoc., 1946-50. Pres., British Medical Assoc., 1955-56, Vice-Pres. 1957; Pres., Canadian Medical Association, 1955-56. Hon. LL.D.: (Canadian Univs.) Queen's, 1931; Dalhousie, 1952; Toronto, 1955; Hon. D.Sc., Laval (Quebec), 1956. *Publications:* numerous papers on various subjects in medical journals for many years. *Recreations:* music, trees, reading *Address:* 17 Heathdale Road, Toronto, Canada. *T.:* RU 3-8222. *Clubs:* York, Granite, Rotary (Toronto); University (Montreal).
[*Died* 31 *March* 1963.

ROUX, François C.; *see* Charles-Roux.

ROWCROFT, Maj.-Gen. Sir (Eric) Bertram, K.B.E., *cr.* 1946 (C.B.E. 1941; M.B.E. 1926); C.B. 1944; *b.* 28 January 1891; *yr. s.* of late Colonel George Francis Rowcroft, D.S.O.; *m.* 1917, Mary Anderson (*d.* 1963), 2nd *d.* of late Cecil Grahame Traill, M.B., C.M., of Fallowfield, Bagshot, Surrey; one *s.* one *d.* *Educ.:* Haileybury College; R.M.C., Sandhurst. In ranks, R.E. (T.A.), 1908-9, R.M.C., 1910-11; gazetted 2nd Lieutenant A.S.C., 1911; Captain, 1917; Major, 1930; Lieut-Col., 1938; Bt.-Col., 1939; Col. 1939; Temp. Brig., 1940; Acting Maj.-Gen., 1942; Maj.-Gen., 1943. Served European War, France and Flanders, 1914-18 (despatches); Palestine, 1936 (despatches). Staff Capt., War Office, 1918-22; Inspector of Tanks, 1932-36; Deputy Director of Supplies and Transport, War Office, 1939-42; Director of Mechanical Engineering, War Office, 1942-46; retired 1947. Director, Civil Service Supply Association Ltd., 1947-1962. A.M.I.Mech.E. 1925; M.I.Mech.E. 1942; M.I.E.E. 1942; Member Worshipful Company of Turners and Freeman of City of London, 1943; Col. Comdt. R.E.M.E., 1947-1956. C.C. Sy., 1949-52. Mem., Surrey County T. and A.F.A., 1950-52; Dorset County President, British Legion, 1961; S.W. Area President, Old Contemptibles' Assoc., 1962. *Address:* Colway Rise, Lyme Regis, Dorset. *T.:* Lyme Regis 487. *Club:* United Service. [*Died* 27 *Dec.* 1963.

ROWE-DUTTON, Sir Ernest, K.C.M.G., *cr.* 1949 (C.M.G. 1932); C.B. 1946; *b.* 1891; *m.*; three *d.* Entered Civil Service, Inland Revenue, 1914; transferred Treasury, 1919. Financial Adviser to H.M. Embassy, Berlin, 1928-32; to H.M. Embassy, Paris, 1934-39. Third Secretary, Treasury, 1947; U.K. Exec. Director of Internat. Bank for Reconstruction and Development, 1949-51. Retired from Treasury, Dec. 1951. Member, Board of Governors and Guardians, National Gall. of Ireland, 1960-62. *Address:* Coolakay Lodge, Enniskerry, Co. Wicklow, Ireland.
[*Died* 8 *Aug.* 1965.

ROWELL, Sir Reginald Kaye, Kt., *cr.* 1947; *b.* 29 May 1888; *s.* of late John Rowell, Stroud, Glos.; *m.* 1914, Gertrude Mary, *d.* of late Freeman Aldridge, Eastbourne. *Educ.:* Marling School, Stroud. Called to Bar, Lincoln's Inn, 1915; Controller of Death Duties, Board of Inland Revenue, 1944-48. *Address:* The Imperial Hotel, Devonshire Place, Eastbourne, Sussex. *T.:* Eastbourne 5280. [*Died* 15 *Aug.* 1964.

ROWLAND, Christopher John Salter; M.P. (Lab.) Meriden since 1964; Parliamentary Private Secretary to Ministers of State, Foreign Office, since 1964; *b.* 26 September 1929; *er. s.* of Tom Rowland and late Joan Rowland; *m.* 1955, Leslie, *d.* of Claude and Ethel Branch; one *s.* one *d.* *Educ.:* elementary schools, Chesterfield Grammar School; London School of Economics, B.Sc. (Econ.); Corpus Christi College, Oxford (Scholar), Postgraduate B.Phil. Joined Labour Party, 1946. Nat. Service, Royal Artillery, 1948-49. Chm. Nat. Assoc. of Labour Student Organisations, 1953-54. Talks producer, B.B.C. Overseas Services (dismissed on selection as prospective Parly. cand.) 1954-59. Commonwealth Fund Fellowship to the U.S.A., 1957-58. Broadcasting Dept. of Labour Party, 1959. Contested (Lab.) Eastleigh Div. of Hampshire, 1959. Information Officer to Booker Group, 1960-. Hon. Treasurer, Africa Bureau. Member, Council, Institute of Race Relations. *Recreations:* soccer, music, looking at buildings, travelling by train. *Address:* 12 Blackheath Park, S.E.3.
[*Died* 5 *Nov.* 1967.

ROWLAND, Sir John Edward Maurice, Kt., *cr.* 1941; *b.* 30 April 1882. *Educ.:* Dulwich College. Served European War, R.E., 1914-19, Capt. 1917. Joined Indian State Railways, 1904; Agent, Burma Railways, 1935; Chief Railway Commissioner, Burma, 1937-41. *Address:* c/o The Standard Bank of South Africa, Adderley Street, Cape Town, South Africa.
[*Died* 19 *Jan.* 1969.

ROWLAND, Sir Wentworth (Lowe), 2nd Bt., *cr.* 1950; Senior Partner, Rowland & Co., Chartered Accountants, since 1949 (Partner, 1934); Director of Courtin & Warner Ltd. and several other cos.; *b.* 7 Nov. 1909; *s.* of Sir Frederick Rowland, 1st Bt., of Taunton, and of Alice Blanche (*née* Reynolds); *S.* father, 1959; *m.* 1947, Violet Mary Elizabeth Macbeth, *d.* of late A. C. Macbeth Robertson; one *d.* *Educ.:* Marlborough College. Articled to E. E. Smith, F.C.A., 1928; qualified as Chartered Accountant, 1934; F.C.A., 1943. Territorial Army, 2nd Bn. Queen Victoria Rifles, April 1939; Commissioned 1st Bn. K.R.R.C., Feb. 1940, transf. R.A.F.V.R., June 1940; served U.K. and India; demob. Nov. 1945, rank Sqdn. Ldr. Partner in: Sewell, Hutchinson & Co., Chartered Accts., 1958; Albert Goodman & Co.; Sheen & Co. Member: Inst. of Directors; Court of Common Council of Corporation of London, 1951-; Chairman: Bridge House Estates Cttee.; Gresham Cttee., 1965; Comr. of Taxes, City of London: Corporation Representative: on Dickens House Trust (Trustee, 1956-); on Council of British Travel and Holiday Assoc.; Mem. Lord Mayor and Sheriffs Cttee., 1938, 1949, 1969. Mem., B.T.A., 1963-. Chm., Special Reception Cttee. for visit of King Hussein of Jordan and Princess Muna, 1966. Governor: Christ's Hosp.; Bridewell Hosp. Mem. Worshipful Co. of Bowyers; Past Master, Worshipful Co. of Horners. *Recreations:* hockey, tennis, squash, cricket, golf. *Heir:* none. *Address:* The White Cottage, Leigh, Nr. Tonbridge, Kent. *T.:* Hildenboro 3035. *Clubs:* City Livery, Public Schools, Mining, Coleman Street Ward (Hon. Sec. 1946-, Chm. 1955), City Pickwick (Hon. Sec. and Vice-Pres., 1956-); Warlingham R.F.C. (Chm. 1956-65).
[*Died* 19 *Sept.* 1970 (*ext.*).

ROWLANDSON, Edmund James, C.I.E. 1932; *b.* 27 Oct. 1882; *s.* of Frederick Rowlandson, B.A., LL.B.; *m.* 1912, Kate Millicent Lister, *d.* of late Col. H. H. Crookenden, R.A.; one *s.* (and one *s.* killed in action, 1943). *Educ.:* King's School, Bruton; Selwyn College, Cambridge. Joined Indian Police Service, 1903; retired, 1935. *Address:* Swiss Cottage, Haddenham, Aylesbury. *T.:* Haddenham 232.
[*Died* 10 *Jan.* 1962.

ROWLEY, Baron *cr.* 1966 (Life Peer), of Rowley Regis; **Arthur Henderson,** P.C. 1947; Q.C. 1939; *b.* Newcastle on Tyne, 27 Aug. 1893; *s.* of late Rt. Hon. Arthur Henderson, M.P.; *m.* 1958, Mrs. Mary Elizabeth Gliksten, U.S.A. *Educ.:* Central School, Darlington; Queen's College, Taunton; Trinity Hall, Cambridge. Hons. in Law and Economics (M.A., LL.B.); Chairman, Cambridge University Labour Club, 1920-21; called to Bar, 1921; Secy. of Univ. Lab. Federation, 1921-24; contested North Portsmouth, 1922; M.P. (Lab.) South Cardiff, 1923-24 and 1929-31, Kingswinford division of Staffordshire, 1935-50, Rowley Regis and Tipton, 1950-66; late Standing Counsel to the Labour Party; Mem. Royal Economic Society, Hardwicke Society, and Cambridge Union Soc.; War Service, 1914-18; served on General Staff, Sept. 1939-March 1942; Joint Parliamentary Under-Sec. of State for War, 1942-43; Financial Secretary to War Office, 1943-45; Parliamentary Under-Sec. of State, India Office and Burma Office, 1945-47; Minister of State for Commonwealth Relations, 1947; Secretary of State for Air, 1947-51. D.L. County of London, 1948. Mem. of Plowden Committee, on the Representational Services Overseas; Vice-President British Parl. Group for World Government; Pres. United Nations Parl. Group; Senior Vice-Pres., Council of Europe Assembly, 1961-62. *Publications:* Trade Unions and the Law; (with Sir Henry Slesser) Treatise entitled Industrial Law; joint author of Treatise on Housing Law. *Address:* 710 Hood House, Dolphin Square, Westminster, S.W.1. *T.:* Victoria 3800.
[*Died* 28 *Aug.* 1968.

ROWLEY, Lieut.-Col. Sir Charles Samuel, 6th Bt. *cr.* 1786; T.D.; D.L.; 55th (Suffolk and Norfolk Yeo.) Anti-Tank Regt. R.A. (T.A.); *b.* 23 Dec. 1891; *s.* of 5th Bt. and Hon. Louisa Helen Brownlow (*d.* 1922), *d.* of 2nd Baron Lurgan, K.P.; *S.* father 1931; *m.* 1920, Margery Frances, *e. d.* of Sir N. H. Bacon, 12th and 13th Bt.; one *s.* two *d.* *Educ.:* Eton; Trinity College, Cambridge. Served European War, 1914-15 in Grenadier Guards (wounded); Hon. Col. 358th (Suffolk Yeo.) Medium Regt., R.A., T.A. *Heir:* *s.* Joshua Francis Rowley [*b.* 31 Dec. 1920; *m.* 1959, Hon. Celia Monckton, 2nd *d.* of 8th Viscount Galway, P.C., G.C.M.G., D.S.O., O.B.E.]. *Address:* Holbecks, Hadleigh, Suffolk. *T.:* Hadleigh, Suffolk, 3211 *Clubs:* Guards, Pratt's. [*Died* 19 *Jan.* 1962.

ROWLEY, Rev. Harold Henry; Professor of Hebrew Language and Literature, University of Manchester, 1949-59, now Professor Emeritus; M.A. (Brist. and Manc.), D.D. (Lond.), B.Litt. (Oxon.), Hon. D.D. (Durham, Wales, Oxon., Edin., Manc.), Hon. Theol.D. (Uppsala), Hon. D.Th. (Zürich and Marburg), Hon. LL.D. (McMaster), Hon. Docteur de Strasbourg; F.B.A., Mem. of Norwegian Acad. of Science and Letters; Foreign mem. Roy. Flemish Acad.; Mem., Roy. Soc. of Letters of Lund; Hon. Mem., Soc. of Biblical Literature (U.S.A.); Hon. Fell., Sch. of Oriental and Afr. Studies, London; *b.* 24 March 1890; *s.* of Richard and Emma Rowley; *m.* 1918, Gladys B. Shaw; one *s.* three *d.* *Educ.:* Wyggeston School, Leicester; Bristol Baptist College and Bristol University; Mansfield College and St. Catherine's Society, Oxford; Dr. Williams' Divinity Scholar, 1913; Baptist Union Scholar, 1914; Elmslie Memorial Scholar 1914; Houghton Syriac Prizeman, 1915; Minister of United Church (Baptist-Congregational), Wells, Somerset, 1917-22; Missionary of Baptist Missionary Society in China, 1922-1930; Associate-Professor of Old Testament Literature, Shantung Christian University, 1924-29; Assistant Lecturer in Semitic Languages, University College o South Wales and Monmouthshire, Cardiff, 1930-34; Prof. of Semitic Languages, Univ. Coll. of North Wales, Bangor, 1935-45, and Lectr. in the History of Religions, 1940-45; Vice-Principal, 1940-45; Dean of Bangor School of Theology, 1936-45; Prof. of Semitic Languages and Literatures, Univ. of Manchester, 1945-49; Schweich Lectr., 1948; Jordan Bequest Lectr., 1954; Edward Cadbury Lectr., 1965; Examiner in Theology, London University, 1936-38, 1943-45; Examiner in Hebrew, Birmingham, 1936-38; Durham, 1938-39; Bristol, 1938-40, 1950-52; Wales, 1957-61; Examiner in Semitic Languages, Manchester, 1943-45; Liverpool, 1950-54; London, 1957-63. Joint Secretary of Society for Old Testament Study, 1946-60, President, 1950; Dean of the Faculty of Theology, Manchester University, 1953-56; President, Baptist Union of Great Britain and Ireland, 1957-58. Burkitt Medal of British Academy, 1951. *Publications:* Aspects of Reunion, 1923; The Aramaic of the Old Testament, 1929; Darius the Mede and the Four World Empires in the Book of Daniel, 1935; Israel's Mission to the World, 1939; The Relevance of the Bible, 1942; The Relevance of Apocalyptic, 1944; The Missionary Message of the Old Testament, 1945; The Rediscovery of the Old Testament, 1946; The Growth of The Old Testament, 1950; The Biblical Doctrine of Election, 1950; From Joseph to Joshua, 1950; Submission in Suffering and Other Essays on Eastern Thought, 1951; The Servant of the Lord, 1952; The Zadokite Fragments and the Dead Sea Scrolls, 1952; The Unity of the Bible, 1953; Prophecy and Religion in Ancient China and Israel, 1956; The Faith of Israel, 1956; Teach Yourself Bible Atlas, 1961; Men of God, 1963; From Moses to Qumran, 1963; Worship in Ancient Israel, 1967; A Dictionary of Bible Themes, 1968; A Dictionary of Bible Personal Names, 1968; Editor: Studies in Old Testament Prophecy, 1950; The Old Testament and Modern Study, 1951; Journal of Semitic Studies, 1956-60; Peake's Commentary on the Bible (Jt. Ed.), 1962; Hastings' Dictionary of the Bible (Jt. Ed.), 1963; Companion to the Bible, 1963; The Century Bible. *Address:* The Field, Cowie Road, Stroud, Glos. *T.:* Stroud 3888.
[*Died* 4 *Oct.* 1969.

ROWORTH, Edward; Emeritus Professor of Fine Art, University of Cape Town, since 1954; *b.* 1880; *e. s.* of Arthur Hewitt Roworth, Hathersage, Derbys.; *m.* 1911, Henrica Molony (*d.* 1958), *e. d.* of Roderick Molony O'Connor, Cragenowen Castle, Co. Clare; one *d.* *Educ.:* studied under Prof. Herkomer and at The Slade. Painted portrait-group of National Convention of South Africa (now hanging in Parliament House, Cape Town), 1911. Portraits (also in Parliament House, Cape Town) include: Cecil Rhodes, Gen. Louis Botha, Gen. Hertzog, J. H. Hofmeyr. Has painted five portraits of General Smuts and portraits of the King and Queen of Greece. Michaelis Professor of Fine Art, University of Cape Town, 1937-50. Director and Trustee, National Gallery of S. Africa, 1937-50. *Recreations:* reading, music, more painting. *Address:* Soete Inval, Parel Vallei, Somerset West, Cape Province, South Africa. *Club:* Civil Service (Cape Town).
[*Died* 13 *Aug.* 1964.

ROWSE, Herbert James, F.R.I.B.A.; Architect, practising in Liverpool; *s.* of James William Rowse and Sarah Cammack; *m* 1918, Dorothy, 2nd *d.* of late Thomas Parry, Crosby, Lancashire; two *s.* one *d.* *Educ.:* privately; University of Liverpool. Holt Travelling Scholar in Architecture; Architectural Competitions: India Buildings, Liverpool (in partnership), 1st Premium, 1924; New Library and Chambers at King's College, Cambridge (in partnership), 1st Premium, 1924; New Headquarters Building for Martin's Bank, Limited, Liverpool, 1st Premium, 1927; commenced practice in Liverpool, 1918; Headquarters at Liverpool for Lloyds Bank, Limited, and other Branches, 1927-29; Assessor in Architectural Competition for New Police and Fire Station, Accrington, 1929; designed New Headquarters Building for Compania de Aplicaciones Electricas S.A., Barcelona, Spain, 1930; Architect to the Mersey Tunnel Joint Committee, 1931; Bronze Medal of the Royal Institute of British Architects for the Woodside Ventilation Station of the Mersey Tunnel; New Headquarters Building for Pharmaceutical Society of Great Britain in Brunswick Square, 1935; new University of London building; various Domestic works and Housing Schemes and Flats for Local Authorities since 1918, including Woodchurch Housing Estate 1944 for Birkenhead Corporation; New Concert Hall for Liverpool Philharmonic Society; United Kingdom Government Pavilion, Empire Exhibition, Scotland, 1938; various Industrial and Scholastic commissions; design of new Research Labs. for British Electrical and Allied Industries Research Assoc. at Leatherhead, 1945; Diplomatic Buildings, Delhi and Karachi, 1951. Ministry of Health Housing Medal, 1950. Mem. of Council, R.I.B.A., 1944-50; External Examiner at the Univ. of Liverpool, 1931-33; High Sheriff of Anglesey, 1942-43; Officier de l'ordre de Leopold II (Belgium), 1950. *Recreation:* travel. *Address:* Martins Bank Building, Liverpool, 2; Chapel House, Puddington Wirral, Cheshire. *T.A.:* Classic Liverpool. *T.:* Central 2428, Burton 223. *Clubs:* Architecture, Constitutional, Palatine (Liverpool). [*Died* 22 *March* 1963.

ROWSE, William Crapo, M.E.; M.A.S.M.E.; Consulting Engineer, Los Angeles, California; *b.* Davenport, Iowa, U.S.A., 24 Jan. 1883; *s.* of Edward T. Rowse and Elizabeth E. Lawton; *m.* 1909, Amy Collins; one *d.* *Educ.:* Oberlin College, Ohio; Purdue University, La Fayette, Indiana. Designer with Bettendorf Steel Car Co.; in charge design of 500,000 steel foundry, 1907-1910; instructor in steam engineering, University of Wisconsin, Madison, 1910-13; experimental engineer, the Cutler-Hammer Manufacturing Co., New York, 1913-14; Professor of Mechanical Engineering, University of Manitoba, 1914-16; in charge experimental work, Franklin Automobile Co., Syracuse, N.Y., 1916-17; Assistant Manager of Machinery Fabrication, Hog Island Shipyards, Philadelphia, Pa., 1917-19; Assistant to President, Franklin Automobile Co., Syracuse, N.Y., 1919-23; Asst. City Engineer, Pasadena, California, 1923-26; Principal Mechanical Engineer in charge of Steam Plant Design, Department of Water and Power of City of Los Angeles, 1926-48; retired, 1948. *Publications:* (Paper) Pitot Tubes for Gas Measurement, etc. *Recreations:* travel, camping, etc. *Address:* 1880 Hill Drive, Los Angeles 41, Calif. [*Died* 12 *June* 1961.

ROYDE SMITH, Naomi Gwladys; writer; *d.* of late Michael Holroyd Smith and Ann Daisy, *d.* of Rev. Ebenezer Williams; *m.* 1926, Ernest Milton. *Educ.:* Clapham High School; Geneva. Literary Editor Westminster Gazette, 1912-22. *Publications:* A Private Anthology, 1924; The Tortoiseshell Cat, 1925; The Housemaid, 1926; A Balcony (play), 1926; Skin-Deep, 1927; John Fanning's Legacy, 1927; Children in the Wood, 1928; The Lover, 1928; Summer Holiday, 1929; The Island, 1930; The Delicate Situation, 1931; The Mother, 1931; The Double Heart, 1931; Madame Julia's Tale, 1932; The Bridge, 1932; Incredible Tale, 1932; Portrait of Mrs. Siddons, 1933; Pilgrim from Paddington, 1933; The Queen's Wigs, 1934; David, 1934; Private Room (play), 1934; Jake, 1935; All Star Cast, 1936; For Us in the Dark, 1937; Miss Bendix, 1938; The Younger Venus, 1938; The Altar-Piece, 1939; Urchin Moor, 1939; Jane Fairfax, 1940; Outside Information, The Unfaithful Wife, 1941; Mildensee, 1943; Fire-Weed, 1945; The State of Mind of Mr. Sherwood, 1947; Love in Mildensee, 1948; The Iniquity of Us All, 1949; The Idol and the Shrine, 1949; Rosy Trodd, 1950; The New Rich, 1951; She Always Caught the Post, 1953; All Night Sitting (play), 1954; Melilot: a tale, 1954; Love at First Sight, 1956; The Whistling Chambermaid, 1957; How White is my Sepulchre, 1958, A Blue Rose, 1959; Love and a Birdcage, 1960. *Address:* c/o Barclays Bank, Winchester. [*Died* 28 *July* 1964.

ROYLANCE, Robert Walker, C.B.E. 1948; D.L., J.P. Middlesex; *b.* 8 Aug. 1882; *er. s.* of Robert William Roylance; *m.* 1908, Olive Kathleen, *d.* of Charles Gerald Drinan, M.A.; two *d.* *Educ.:* Godolphin School. Served 3rd Middlesex Artillery (Vols.) 1899-1902; Intelligence Corps, 1915-17; Royal Flying Corps and Royal Air Force, 1917-19; Lieut.-Col. 1918; Committee of Lloyd's 1925-28, 1930-33, 1935-38 and 1940-43, Dep. Chm., 1936. Chm., 1937; High Sheriff of Middlesex, 1942-43, *Address:* Wellesley House, Lower Sloane Street, S.W.1. *Club:* R.A.F. [*Died* 2 *Oct.* 1962.

ROYLE, Charles, J.P.; President National Federation of Meat Traders Associations, 1929 and 1942; *b.* 17 Jan. 1872; *s.* of Samuel and Mary E. Royle; *m.* Maria, *d.* of Oliver Wolfe; four *s.* two *d.* *Educ.:* Portwood Wesleyan Higher Grade School. A master butcher; Town Council 44 years; Mayor of Stockport four times; President of National Council of Brotherhoods, 1923; M.P. (L.) Stockport, 1923-24; President, Nat. Fed. Meat Traders, 1929, 1942. Freeman of Borough of Stockport, 1947. *Publication:* (autobiography) Opened Doors, 1949. *Recreation:* public service. *Address:* Abbeville, Stockport. *T.:* Stepping Hill 2798. [*Died* 3 *Nov.* 1963.

ROYLE, Thomas Wright, C.V.O. 1944; M.B.E. 1918; M.Inst.T.; *b.* 27 Sept. 1882; *e. s.* of Thomas Wright Royle, Manchester; *m.* 1915, Mary Ellen, *d.* of Charles Elliott, Manchester; one *s.* one *d.* Joined Lancashire & Yorkshire Railway, 1898; Confidential Assistant to Supt. of the Line in connection with Railway Executive Committee work, 1914; Asst. Supt. of the Line, Lancashire & Yorkshire Railway, 1919; Assistant Divl. General Supt., Northern Division, L.N.W.R., 1922; Asst. General Supt., Western Division, L.M.S.R., 1923; Asst. Chief Commercial Manager, L.M.S.R., 1932; Chief Asst. Commercial Manager, L.M.S.R., 1935; Chief Operating Manager, L.M.S.R.; 1938; Vice-Pres. L.M.S.R., 1944-47. Lt.-Col., Engineer and Railway Staff Corps, 1938; Pres. Institute of Transport, 1947-48. American Medal of Freedom with Silver Palm, 1947. *Address:* 147 Nether Street, North Finchley, N.12. [*Died* 17 *July* 1969.

RUBINSTEIN, Helena, (Princess Gourielli); Founder and President, Helena Rubinstein Inc., New York; President, Helena Rubinstein Ltd., London, Canada, France, etc; *b.* Cracow, 1871; *d.* of Horace Rubinstein and Augusta (*née* Silberfeld); *m.* 1st, Edward J. Titus; one *s.*; 2nd, Prince Artchie Gourielli-Tchkonia. *Educ.:* Universities of Cracow and Zürich. *Publication:* My Life for Beauty, 1965 (*posthumous autobiog.*). *Recreations:* bridge, theatre, art. *Address:* (office) 655 5th Avenue, New York, N.Y. U.S.A.; (home) 625 Park Avenue, New York. N.Y. [*Died* 1 *April* 1965.

RUGBY, 1st Baron, *cr.* 1947, of Rugby; **John Loader Maffey,** G.C.M.G., *cr.* 1935

(K.C.M.G., *cr.* 1931); K.C.B., *cr.* 1934; K.C.V.O., *cr.* 1921; C.S.I. 1920; C.I.E. 1916; late I.C.S.; *b.* 1 July 1877; *s.* of late Thomas Maffey; *m.* 1907, Dorothy, O.B.E., *d.* of late Charles L. Huggins, J.P., Hadlow Grange, Buxted: two *s.* one *d.* *Educ.:* Rugby; Christ Church, Oxford. Entered I.C.S. 1899; transferred to Political Department, 1905; served with Mohmand Field Force, 1908 (medal and clasp); Political Agent, Khyber, 1909-12; Deputy Commissioner, Peshawar, 1914-15; Deputy Secretary in the Foreign and Political Dept., Govt. of India, 1915-16; Chief Political Officer in Afghanistan with North-West Frontier Field Force, 1919; Private Secretary to the Viceroy, 1916-20; Chief Secretary to Duke of Connaught, 1921; Chief Commissioner North-West Frontier Province, India, 1921-24; Governor-General of the Sudan, 1926-33; Permanent Under Secretary of State for the Colonies, 1933-37; Director: Imperial Airways, Rio Tinto Co. Ltd., 1937-39; U.K. Representative to Eire, 1939-49, retd. 1949; Governor of Rugby School, resigned 1939; Hon. Student of Christ Church, Oxford; Order of the Rising Sun; Grand Cordon of the Crown of Italy, 1928: Grand Cordon. Egyptian Order of Ismail, 1929; Star of Ethiopia, 1930. *Heir:* *s.* Hon. Alan Loader Maffey [*b.* 16 April 1913; *m.* 1947, Margaret Bindley; four *s.* two *d.* *Educ.:* Stowel. *Address:* Quay House, Halesworth, Suffolk. *T.:* 3210.
[*Died* 20 *April* 1969.

RUGGE-PRICE, Lt.-Col. Sir Charles J. N.; *see* Price.

RUKIDI III, H.H. Sir George David Kamurasi, Kt. 1962; Omukama of Toro since 1929; *b.* 6 March 1906; *s.* of late Kyebambe IV; *m.* 1935, H.H. Byanjeru Keziah Bonabana; four *s.* three *d.* (and two *s.* one *d.* decd.). *Educ.:* Toro and Mengo High Schools; King's Coll., Budo; Private Tutor, London. Insp. of Police, Uganda, 1926. Served, 4th Bn. (Uganda) K.A.R., Lt., 1928-1930. Mem. Automobile Assoc. and Mem. British Legion, London. Uganda Independence Conf., London, 1962. *Recreations:* football, tennis, squash, billiards, table tennis, badminton. *Address:* Kabarole Palace, P.O. Box 80, Fort Portal, Toro, Uganda. *T.:* Fort Portal 42, Kampala 4657. *Club:* Royal Commonwealth. [*Died* 21 *Dec.* 1966.

RULE, Frank Gordon; *b.* 22 July 1882; *m.* 1st, 1919, Corinne Dorothea (*d.* 1945), *d.* of late Godfrey Clive, Preston; 2nd, 1946, Elizabeth Cairns Rule, M.A., B.Sc., *widow* of H. Gordon Rule, Ph.D., D.Sc., Lecturer in Organic Chemistry at Edinburgh University. Vice-Consul, Marseilles, 1908; Buenos Aires, 1910; Beira, 1912; Port Arthur, Texas, 1917; Consul, Seville, 1919; Bordeaux, 1922; Chargé d'Affaires, Monrovia, 1927; Consul-General, New Orleans, 1930-33; Rotterdam, 1933-39; retired, 1939; interned in Holland and Germany, 1940-45. *Address:* c/o Barclays Bank Ltd., 78 Victoria St., Westminster, S.W.1. [*Died* 31 *July* 1965.

RULE, Mrs. Mollie, M.B.E. 1948; Deputy Field Representative and Senior Resettlement Officer, World Council of Churches, Greece, since 1953; *b.* 9 Sept. 1899; *d.* of George Edward Albert Hamerton and Mary Cook Jones; *m.* 1928, George Edward Litchfield Rule (marriage dissolved, 1935); one *s.* (and one *s.* decd.). *Educ.:* Roedean, Brighton; Dartford Physical Training College, Kent. Physical training mistress in schools in London, Port Elisabeth and Johannesburg, S. Africa, and Umtali, S. Rhodesia, 1920-28, and in Salisbury, S. Rhodesia, 1935-39. Mobilised in Rhodesia Regiment for work in internment camps, transferred to Southern Rhodesia Women's Internment Camp Corps when formed, serving 1939-47; continued in charge of Dept. of Internment Camps and Refugee Settlements until 1949; I.R.O., S. Rhodesia, 1949, Uganda and Tanganyika, 1949-50, Philippine Islands, 1950-53. *Recreation:* motoring. *Address:* Odos Aphroditis 48, Phaleron, Athens, Greece. *T.:* Athens 990269. *Club:* German Automobile. [*Died* 5 *March* 1965.

RUMBOLD, Etheldred, Lady, C.B.E. 1920; *b.* 31 July 1879; *d.* of Sir Edmund Fane, K.C.M.G.; *m.* 1905, Rt. Hon. Sir Horace Rumbold, G.C.B., G.C.M.G., 9th Bt. (*d.* 1941); one *s.* one *d.* *Address:* 33 Kensington Court, W.8. [*Died* 23 *Oct.* 1964.

RUNCORN, Baron, *cr.* 1964 (Life Peer), of Heswall; **Dennis Forwood Vosper,** P.C. 1957; T.D. 1950; B.A.; *b.* 2 Jan. 1916; *yr. s.* of Gerald and Marjorie Vosper, *g.s.* of late Sir William Forwood, K.B.E., D.L., J.P.; *m.* 1st, 1940, Margaret Eva (marr. diss. 1966), *o. c.* of Sidney and Ada Ashford, Gayton, Cheshire; 2nd, 1966, Helen Norah, *yr. d.* of late Sir Crosland Graham and of Lady Graham, Ruthin, N. Wales. *Educ.:* The Leas, Hoylake; Marlborough Coll.; Pembroke Coll., Camb. Wilson, Vosper & Coltart, Ships Store & Export Merchants, in Liverpool. Joined Territorial Army, April 1939; served 1939-46, Cheshire Regt. Secretary, Knutsford Division Conservative Assoc., 1946. M.P. (C.) Runcorn Div. of Cheshire, 1950-64. Conservative Whip, 1950-54; a Lord Commissioner of the Treasury, 1951-54; Parliamentary Secretary Ministry of Education, Oct. 1954-Jan. 1957; Minister of Health, 1957, resigned owing to illness, Sept. 1957; Leader, Parliamentary Delegation to West Indies, 1958; Jt. Parl. Under-Sec. of State, 1959-60, Minister of State, Home Office, 1960-61; Secretary for Technical Cooperation, 1961-63; Chairman of Supplementary Benefits Commission, 1966 (of Nat. Assistance Bd., 1964-66). Hon. Sec. Anglo-Turkish Soc., 1953; Mem. Albemarle Cttee., 1959. *Recreations:* tennis, travelling, and gardening. *Address:* Plaish Hall, Nr. Church Stretton, Shropshire. *T.:* Longville 375; 24 Mulberry Close, Beaufort Street, S.W.3. [*Died* 20 *Jan.* 1968.

RUNGE, Rev. Charles Herman Schmettau, D.S.O. 1918; M.C.; M.A.; *b.* 4 June 1889; *s.* of Julius Joseph Runge and Bertha Schmettau. *Educ.:* Charterhouse; Trinity Coll., Oxford. Employed in British Bank of South America, Buenos Aires, 1908-1912; Runge, Wolters & Co., London, 1912-1914; Army, 1914-19, Commissioned in 12th Middlesex Regt., later General List as Staff Capt. 54th Infantry Brigade, 1916; Brigade Major, 55th Infantry Brigade, 1917; D.A.Q.M.G. 58th Division, 1918 (M.C. and bar, D.S.O.); Deacon, 1921; Priest, 1922; Warden of Buxton Hostel, Lecturer in Theology Transvaal University College, Pretoria, 1922-24; Curate of St. Saviour, Paddington, 1924-26; Member of Community of the Resurrection, 1928; Headmaster of St. John's College, Johannesburg, 1930-35; Provincial of Community of the Resurrection in South Africa, 1935-40; Principal Chaplain, Union Defence Forces (South Africa), M.E.F. and C.M.F., 1941-44; Chief Welfare Officer, 1944-46 (despatches); Rector of St. Paul's, Rondebosch, Cape Town 1947-50; received into the Catholic Church, 1952; Beda College, Rome, 1952-55; Ordained Priest, Rome, 1955; Pastor in Archdiocese of Pretoria, 1955-63; Lectr., Beda Coll., Rome, 1964-68; retd., 1968. *Address:* Cressy Collegio, Woodmancote, Cheltenham, Glos.; 399 Bosman Street, Pretoria, Transvaal, South Africa.
[*Died* 13 *Sept.* 1970.

RUNGE, Sir Peter (Francis), Kt. 1964; Chairman, British National Export Council, since 1968; Joint Vice-Chairman, Tate & Lyle Ltd., 1958; Director: Vickers Ltd.;

Lloyds Bank; *b.* 11 May 1909; 2nd *s.* of late J. J. Runge and Norah C. Hasluck; *m.* 1935, Fiona Margaret Stewart Macpherson, *er. d.* of 1st Baron Strathcarron of Banchor, P.C.; three *s.* one *d.* *Educ.:* Charterhouse; Trinity Coll., Oxford. B.A. (Chemistry) 1931. Joined Tate & Lyle Ltd., 1931; Director, 1935; Joint Vice-Chm., 1958. Chairman: London and S.E. Region, F.B.I., 1958-60; Roy. Commonwealth Soc. for the Blind, 1965-70; President: F.B.I., 1963-65 (Vice-Pres., C.B.I., 1965-68); British Industrial and Scientific Film Assoc., 1965-1970; London Internat. Youth Science Fortnight; Member: Exec. Cttee., Industrial Welfare Soc., 1950-56; Coun., Industrial Society (formerly Industrial Welfare Soc.), 1950- (Chairman 1966-69); N.E.D.C., 1964-1966; Council, Duke of Edinburgh's 1st Study Conf., 1956; Court of Governors, Administrative Staff Coll., 1966-. Comdr., Order of Duarté Sanchez y Mella (Dominican Republic), 1959. *Recreation:* fishing. *Address:* Finings, Lane End, Bucks. *T.:* Lane End 241. *Club:* United University.
[*Died* 19 *Aug.* 1970.

RUNNETT, Henry Brian; Organist and Master of the Choristers, Norwich Cathedral, since 1967; Conductor, Norwich Philharmonic Society, since 1970; *b.* 20 Jan. 1935; *s.* of Henry and Florence Runnett; unmarried. *Educ.:* Waterloo Grammar School, Liverpool; Matthay School of Music, Liverpool; St. John's Coll., Cambridge. M.A. (Cantab.), B.Mus. (Dunelm), F.R.C.O. (CHM), L.R.A.M., A.R.C.M. Asst. Organist, Chester Cathedral, 1955-60; Organ Scholar, St. John's Coll., Cambridge, 1960-63; Lectr. in Music and University Organist, Manchester Univ., 1963-66. *Recreation:* enjoying good food. *Address:* 19 The Close, Norwich, NOR 16P. *T.:* Norwich 26589.
[*Died* 20 *Aug.* 1970.

RUSHBURY, Sir Henry (George), K.C.V.O. 1964 (C.V.O. 1955); C.B.E. 1960; R.A. 1936 (A.R.A. 1927); R.W.S. 1926; R.E. 1922; Hon. A.R.I.B.A. 1948; Keeper of the Royal Academy, 1949-64; *b.* Harborne, nr. Birmingham, 28 October 1889; *m. e. d.* of H. Lazell; two *d.* Studied Art under R. M. Catterson-Smith, M.A., at Birmingham School of Art; executed drawings and paintings, London in War-time, for the Imperial War Museum; drawings and prints purchased by Brit. Museum, Tate Gall., Birmingham and Liverpool Art Galleries, and elsewhere. *Recreation:* walking. *Address:* 6 St. Martins Lane, Lewes, Sussex. *T.:* Lewes 3210. *Clubs:* Chelsea Arts, Arts.
[*Died* 5 *July* 1968.

RUSHTON, Major Harold P., T.D.; D.L.; J.P.; *s.* of W. T. Rushton, J.P.; *b.* Sept. 1895; *m.* 1921, Ruth, *d.* of G. E. H. Bearcroft, of Himbleton, Worcs.; two *d.* *Educ.:* Haileybury. Served European War, 1914-19, with R.F.A. (despatches): Major (Worcestershire and Oxfordshire Yeomanry) Brigade R.A. (T.A.), 1925; High Sheriff of Worcestershire, 1943; D.L. Worcestershire, 1958. M.F.H. Worcestershire, 1929-37. *Recreations:* hunting, shooting, racing. *Address:* Phepson Manor, Droitwich. *T.:* Himbleton 206. *Club:* Cavalry.
[*Died* 31 *Aug.* 1968.

RUSHTON, Martin Amsler, C.B.E. 1960; Professor Emeritus of Dental Medicine in the University of London; *b.* 29 March 1903; *s.* of W. Rushton; *m.* 1949, Dorothy (*née* Whiteside); one *d.* *Educ.:* Caius College, Cambridge; Guy's Hospital. Additional Dental Surgeon to Guy's Hospital; Hon. Consulting Dental Surgeon to St. Thomas's Hosp.; Dental Surgeon i/c Maxillo-facial Unit, Basingstoke, 1939-46. Dean, Faculty of Dental Surgery, R.C.S., 1959-62. Pres., B.D.A., 1964-65. Hon. degrees: Odont. D. Stockholm, 1958; LL.D.: Toronto, 1959; Belfast, 1965; D.Odont. Copenhagen, 1964. F.R.C.S. 1964. Colyer Gold Medal, R.C.S., 1968. *Address:* Alcala, Kippington Rd., Sevenoaks, Kent. *T.:* 55627.
[*Died* 16 *Nov.* 1970.

RUSHWORTH, Geoffrey Harrington, C.M.G. 1967; Deputy Chairman, Commonwealth Banking Corporation, Australia, since 1962; *b.* 5 Mar. 1899; *s.* of D. H. Rushworth; *m.* 1925, Vida Gowenlock; two *s.* *Educ.:* Melbourne Church of England Grammar School. Chairman: Unilever Aust. Pty. and Lever Bros. (N.Z.) Ltd., 1944-61; Levers Pacific Plantations Pty., 1944-64. Director: National Heart Foundation Aust. (N.S.W. Div.), 1958-; Aust. Finance an dInvestment Co., 1962-. Federal President, National Safety Council, Aust., 1963-64. Member, Council Aust. Admin. Staff College, 1956-. *Recreation:* golf. *Address:* 21 Killara Avenue, Killara, N.S.W., Australia.
[*Died* 8 *Nov.* 1969.

RUSS, Sidney, C.B.E. 1931; Professor of Physics, Medical School, Middlesex Hospital, 1920-46, Professor Emeritus, 1946; Physicist to the Middlesex Hosp., 1913-46; Scientific Sec. of the National Radium Commission, 1929-1935; Fellow of University College, London; *b.* 2 Dec. 1879; 4th *s.* of late Charles Russ, St. John's Wood; *m.* Mary Priestley, *e. d.* of late Major F. N. Priestley, Leeds; one *s.* one *d.* *Educ.:* Shebbear College, North Devon; University College, Gower Street; B.Sc. (1st Class Honours), London University, 1905, D.Sc. 1909; Demonstrator in Physics at the University, Manchester, 1906-10; Beit Memorial Fellow at the Cancer Research Laboratories, Middlesex Hospital, 1910-12. *Publications:* (with H. A. Colwell) Radium X-Rays and the Living Cell; Physics in Medical Radiology (with L. H. Clark and B. D. Watters); X-Ray and Radium Injuries (with H A. Colwell); Radon, its Use and Technique (with W. A. Jennings); Cancer, Where w Stand; Smoking and its Effects (with special reference to Lung Cancer). *Address:* The Hut, Fish Lane, Bognor Regis, Sussex.
[*Died* 27 *July* 1963

RUSSELL, 3rd Earl (*cr.* 1861), **Bertrand Arthur William Russell,** O.M. 1949; F.R.S. 1908; M.A.; Viscount Amberley 1861; Fellow of Trinity Coll., Camb.; *b.* Trelleck 18 May 1872; 2nd *s.* of late Viscount Amberley and Katherine, *d.* of 2nd Baron Stanley of Alderley; *S.* brother, 1931 *m.* 1st, 1894, Alys Whitall Pearsall Smith (marriage dissolved, 1921, she *d.* 1951); 2nd, 1921, Dora Winifred, M.B.E. (author of The Right to be Happy, 1927; marriage dissolved, 1935), *d.* of late Sir Frederick Black, K.C.B.; one *s.* one *d.*; 3rd, 1936, Patricia Helen, *d.* of H. E. Spence (marriage dissolved, 1952); one *s.*; 4th, 1952, Edith, *d.* o Edward Bronson Finch, New York. *Educ.:* Trinity Coll. Cambridge (scholar); 1st class in Mathematics and in Moral Sciences, Part II.; Sylvester Medal of Royal Society, 1934; de Morgan Medal of London Mathematical Society, 1934; Nobel Prize for Literature, 1950. Hon. Fell. L.S.E. 1961. *Publications:* German Social Democracy, 1896; Essay on the Foundations of Geometry, 1897; Philosophy of Leibniz, 1900; Principles of Mathematics, 1903; Philosophical Essays, 1910; Problems of Philosophy, 1911; (with Dr. A. N. Whitehead) Principia Mathematica, 1910; Our Knowledge of the External World as a Field for Scientific Method in Philosophy, 1914; Principles of Social Reconstruction, 1917; Mysticism and Logic, 1918; Roads to Freedom, 1918; Introduction to Mathematical Philosophy, 1919; The Practice and Theory of Bolshevism, 1920; The Analysis of Mind, 1921; The Problem of China, 1922; The A B C of Atoms, 1923; (with Dora Russell)

The Prospects of Industrial Civilization, 1923; Icarus, 1924; What I Believe, 1925; The A B C of Relativity, 1925; On Education, 1926; The Analysis of Matter, 1927; An Outline of Philosophy, 1927; Sceptical Essays, 1928; Marriage and Morals, 1929; The Conquest of Happiness, 1930; The Scientific Outlook, 1931; Education and the Social Order, 1932; Freedom and Organisation, 1814-1914, 1934; In Praise of Idleness, 1935; Which Way to Peace? 1936; (with Patricia Russell) The Amberley Papers, 1937; Power: A New Social Analysis, 1938; An Inquiry into Meaning and Truth, 1940; History of Western Philosophy, 1946; Human Knowledge, its Scope and Limits, 1948; Authority and the Individual, 1949; Unpopular Essays, 1950; New Hopes for a Changing World, 1951; The Impact of Science upon Society, 1952; Satan in the Suburbs (five short stories), 1953; Nightmares of Eminent Persons, 1954; Human Society in Ethics and Politics, 1954; Portraits from Memory, 1956; Why I am not a Christian, 1957; Common Sense and Nuclear Warfare, 1958; My Philosophical Development, 1959; Wisdom of the West, 1959: Fact and Fiction, 1961; Has Man a Future?, 1961; Unarmed Victory, 1963; Political Ideals, 1963; War Crimes in Vietnam, 1967; Autobiography, Vol. I 1967, Vol. II, 1968, Vol. III, 1969. *Relevant Publication:* Bertrand Russell: The Passionate Sceptic, by Alan Wood, 1957. *Heir: s.* Viscount Amberley. *Address:* Plas Penrhyn, Penrhyndeudraeth, Merionethshire; Trinity College, Cambridge. *Club:* Athenæum.
[*Died* 2 *Feb.* 1970.

RUSSELL, Brig.-Gen. Hon. Alexander Victor Frederick Villiers, C.M.G. 1918; M.V.O. 1908; late Grenadier Guards; Director, Sun Life Assurance Society, Sun Insurance Office, Ltd., 1929-56, Proved Securities Ltd., National Group of Fixed Trusts Ltd., Moorgate Unit Trust Managers Ltd.; Steward National Greyhound Racing Club; *b.* 27 June 1874; 4th *s.* of 1st Baron Ampthill; a godson of Queen Victoria and Emperor Frederick of Germany; *m.* 1909, Marjorie Gladys (*d.* 1949), *d.* of late Claude Hume Campbell Guinness (*b.* of late Lady Iveagh); two *s. Educ.:* Wellington; R.M.C. Sandhurst. Served South Africa 1899-1902 (despatches twice, Queen's medal six clasps, King's medal two clasps, Brevet Major); European War, 1914-18 (despatches three times, C.M.G.) Legion of Honour; Order of the Crown of Belgium; Order of the Crown of Prussia; Military Attaché, Berlin, 1910-14; special military mission to Chile, 1921; British Commissioner Hungarian-Roumanian Boundary Commission, 1922-24; retired pay, 1926. *Address:* Flat 6, 87 Cadogan Gardens, S.W.3. *T.:* Kensington 8371. *Clubs:* Guards, Brooks's. [*Died* 3 *Jan.* 1965.

RUSSELL, Sir Alexander (West), Kt., *cr.* 1937; *s.* of late William Russell, Grayshall, Bathgate; *b.* 27 Nov. 1879; *m.* Agnes Bunten (*d.* 1930), *d.* of late David Sturrock, Glasgow; one *s.* two *d. Educ.:* Bathgate Academy; Edinburgh University; M.A. Called to Bar, Middle Temple, 1920. M.P. (U.) Tynemouth, 1922-45. *Address:* 24 Hanover House, N.W.8 *T.:* Primrose 2658. *Clubs:* Athenæum, Royal Automobile.
[*Died* 22 *April* 1961.

RUSSELL, Sir Arthur Edward Ian Montagu, 6th Bt., *cr.* 1812; Lieut. late R.E.; *b.* 30 Nov. 1878; *s.* of 4th Bt. and Constance, *g.d.* of 4th Duke of Richmond; *S.* brother 1944; *m.* 1st, 1904, Aileen Kerr (*d.* 1920), *y. d.* of late Adm. M. R. Pechell; one *s.* one *d.*; 2nd, 1922, Cornélie (from whom he obtained a divorce, 1932), *d.* of Major Jacques de Bruijn, Amsterdam; one *s.*; 3rd, 1933, Marjorie Elisabeth Josephine, *d.* of Ernest Rudman, Foxhangers, Earley, Berks; one *s. Heir: s.* George Michael [*b.* 1908; *m.* 1936, Joy Francis Bedford, *d.* of late W. Mitchell, Irwin, W. Australia; one *d.*]. *Address:* Swallowfield Park, Reading.
[*Died* 23 *Feb.* 1964.

RUSSELL, Charles Pearce, C.V.O. 1953; J.P.; *b.* 1887; *s.* of H. C. Russell, Streatham; *m.* 1st, 1914, Marjorie May, *d.* of E. B. Warren, Streatham; 2nd, 1948, Evelyn May Victoria (who *m.* 1920, G. S. Simpson), *d.* of G. A. Shackles, Scarborough; two *s. Educ.:* Berkhampstead. Director, Nicholsons Ltd. Elected Westminster City Council, 1925, Alderman 1945, Mayor 1953-54. Commissioner for Income Tax; Dep.-Chm. Westminster Petty Sessional Bench; Member: Met. Water Board, Thames Conservancy. J.P. Co. London, 1940. *Address:* 41 Greencroft Gardens, N.W.6. *T.:* Maida Vale 5639. [*Died* 9 *Aug.* 1961.

RUSSELL, Sir (Edward) John, Kt., *cr.* 1922; O.B.E. 1918; F.R.S. 1917; D.Sc. Lond.; Hon. degrees: D.Sc. Wales, 1922; Manchester, 1922; Toronto, 1924; Maryland, 1927; South Africa, 1929; Rutgers, 1930; Oxford, 1932; Berlin, 1935; Durham, 1949; Vienna, 1949; Reading, 1951; Officer of the Order of the Crown of Belgium; Comdr., Order of Agricultural Merit, France; Foreign Associate of Academy of Science, Paris; member numerous foreign academies, etc.; Vice-Pres. Roy. Soc., 1941-42; Pres. of British Association for 1949; late Pres. Internat. Soc. of Soil Science; Hon. Fellow Queen Mary College, London, and Wye College, London University; *b.* Frampton, Glos, 31 Oct. 1872; *e. s.* of late Rev. E. T. Russell; *m.* 1903, Elnor, *y. d.* of late Walter Oldham, Manchester, formerly of Penang and Singapore; five *c. Educ.:* Univ. Coll. of Wales, Aberystwyth; Victoria Univ., Manchester. Lecturer and Demonstrator in Chemistry, Victoria University of Manchester, 1898-1901; Head of Chemical Dept., Agricultural College, Wye, 1901-7; Goldsmith Company's soil chemist, Rothamsted Experimental Station, 1907-12; Director of Rothamsted Experimental Station, Harpenden, 1912-43, and of the Imperial Bureau of Soil Science, 1928-43; Technical Adviser Food Production Dept.; Member of the Munitions Inventions Panel, and of the National Salvage Council, 1917. Adviser to the Soviet Relations Division, Ministry of Information; Chairman of Agriculture Sub-Committee of U.N.R.R.A., 1941-45. Kissenjoy Mookerjee Medal, Indian Assoc. for Cultivation of Science; Messel Medal, Society of Chemical Industry; Albert Medal, Royal Society of Arts; Gold Medal, Royal Agric. Soc.; Victoria Medal, R.G.S. *Publications:* The Fertility of the Soil; Soil Conditions and Plant Growth; Lessons on Soil; Soils and Agriculture of Kent, Surrey, and Sussex (with A. D. Hall); A Student's Book on Soils and Manures; Manuring for Higher Crop Production, 1916; Plant Nutrition and Crop Production, 1926; The Farm and the Nation, 1933; Artificial Fertilisers (Monograph of the Ministry of Agriculture); Fifty Years of Field Experiments at the Woburn Experimental Station (with J. A. Voelcker), 1936; English Farming, 1942; (Ed.) Agriculture Today and Tomorrow, 1945; World Population and World Food Supplies, 1954; Science and Modern Life, 1955; The Land Called Me (Autobiography), 1956; The World of the Soil, 1957. *Recreations:* gardening, travel, modern languages. *Address:* Woodstock House, Woodstock, Oxon. *T.A.* and *T.:* Woodstock 234. *Clubs:* Athenæum, Farmers'.
[*Died* 12 *July* 1965.

RUSSELL, George Clifford Dowsett; Director (Chm. and Man. Dir., 1962-65), Handley Page Ltd.; *b.* 30 December 1901; *s.* of George Blackburn Russell and Edith Blanche Russell; *m.* 1929, Winifred

Meads; no c. *Educ.:* St. Dunstan's College, Catford, London, S.E. Joined Handley Page Ltd. as an engineering apprentice, 1919; held a number of technical and administrative posts and during War of 1939-45 was personal Technical Assistant to Sir Frederick Handley Page; Secretary of Handley Page Ltd. and Handley Page (Reading) Ltd., 1947; Asst. Managing Director, 1953. Governor of Hendon College of Technology. F.R.Ae.S. *Address:* 59 Paines Lane, Pinner, Middlesex. *T.:* 01-868 5653. [*Died* 12 *June* 1970.

RUSSELL, Sir Guthrie; *see* Russell, Sir T. G.

RUSSELL, Gyrth, R.I.; R.O.I.; Member Royal Soc. Marine Artists; *b.* 13 April 1892; *s.* of Hon. Justice B. Russell, Supreme Court of Nova Scotia, and Louise Coleman Russell; *m.* 1911, Gladys Harman Webster; two *s.* one *d.*; divorced 1933; *m.* 1942, Ronagh Alexandra Slee. *Educ.:* Public Schools of Nova Scotia; studied Art in Boston and at Académie Julien and Académie Colarossi, Paris, 1913-14. Exhibited widely in Britain and America; represented in the Imperial War Museum, the National Gallery of Canada and the Nova Scotia Museum of Fine Arts; appointed Official War Artist for the Canadian Government, with hon. rank of Lieut., 1917; represented by eighteen works in the Canadian War Memorials Exhibition, Burlington House, 1919. Served in R.N. Patrol Service, 1940-43. *Publications:* See and Paint, 1957; (with L. du G. Peach) Unknown Devon, 1926; An Introduction to Oil Painting, 1959. Occasional contrib. to The Artist and The Studio. *Address:* 1 Kymin Terrace, Penarth, Glam. *T.:* Penarth 709362. [*Died* 8 *Dec.* 1970.

RUSSELL, Air Vice-Marshal Herbert Bainbrigge, C.B. 1945; D.F.C.; A.F.C.; *b.* 6 May 1895; 2nd *s.* of Herbert H. Russell, Hawkes Bay, New Zealand, and Wellswood, Torquay; *m.* 1926, Margaret Ann Bovill, Dinton, nr. Salisbury; one *s.* one *d.* *Educ.:* Wanganui College, New Zealand; R.M.A. Woolwich. Commissioned Royal Field Artillery Aug. 1914; transferred to R.F.C., 1915, in France; served in France till July 1916 (prisoner); Permanent Commission R.A.F. 1918; Sqn. Ldr., 1929; Wing Cdr., 1936; Air Staff (Operations) Air Ministry, 1935-38; Group Capt. 1940; Air Cdre. 1941; served in Western Desert and Persian Gulf, 1941-42; A.O.C. No. 70 Group, 1943-45; Air Officer i/c Administration, Headquarters Flying Training Command, 1946-Jan. 1949; retired as Air Vice-Marshal, 1949. *Recreations:* sailing and Southern Switzerland. *Address:* c/o Lloyds Bank Ltd., Cox & King's Branch, 6 Pall Mall, S.W.1. *Clubs:* R.A.F.; Royal Torbay Yacht. [*Died* 15 *June* 1963.

RUSSELL, Sir John; *see* Russell, Sir E. J.

RUSSELL, John Eaton Nevill; Registrar of Probate and Divorce Division of High Court of Justice since 1953; *b.* 27 Dec. 1911; *s.* of Major Leonard Russell (killed in action, 1915) and of Jenny Eleanor Russell (*née* Nevill); *m.* 1st, 1935, Elizabeth Frances Brodrick Birdwood (whom he divorced, 1946); one *s.*; 2nd, 1947, Hersey Constance Grenfell; one *s.* *Educ.:* Wellington; Queens' College, Cambridge. Called to Bar (Gray's Inn), 1935; practised at Probate and Divorce Bar and on South-Eastern Circuit. Royal Artillery, 1940; to India, 1942; G.H.Q., New Delhi, 1943; G.S.O. 2, S.E. Asia and India Commands, 1944-46. Mem., Civil Judicial Statistics Cttee., 1966-68. Consulting Editor, Tristram & Coote's Probate Practice. *Address:* Fairstow, West Byfleet, Surrey. *T.:* Byfleet 42842. *Club:* Athenæum. [*Died* 15 *July* 1970.

RUSSELL, Sir (Thomas) Guthrie, K.C.S.I., *cr.* 1943; K.C.I.E., *cr.* 1937; Kt., *cr.* 1932; Knight Order of St. John of Jerusalem; (Chancellor of Order in Scotland); B.Sc.; A.M.Inst.C.E.; M.Inst.E. (India); *b.* 19 January 1887; *s.* of late Rev. John Russell, Lochwinnoch, Scotland; *m.* Florence Heggie, *d.* of late Rev. Peter Anton, Kilsyth, Scotland; two *d.* *Educ.:* Glasgow Academy; Glasgow University. Graduated B.Sc., 1907; served engineering apprenticeship with Niven and Haddin, Civil Engineers, Glasgow, 1907-1910; joined staff of the North British Railway, 1910; Assistant Engineer, Great Indian Peninsula Railway, 1913; Resident Engineer, 1919; Asst. Secretary to the Agent, 1920; Officiating Dep. Agent, 1922; Controller of Stores, 1923; services lent to the Oudh and Rohilkhand Railway, 1925; Deputy Agent, 1925; Officiating Agent, 1926; Agent 1927; Member Engineering, Railway Board, 1928; Chief Commissioner of Railways, Railway Board, India, 1929-40; Member Council of State, 1930-40; Pres. War Transport Board, 1939-40; Director-General, Munitions Production, India, 1940-43. Regional Red Cross Comr. S. India, 1944-46; Dep. Chief, Disposals Group, C.C.G., 1948-52. President, Institution of Engineers (India), 1933-34. *Address:* 1A Westbourne Gardens, Glasgow, W.2. *Clubs:* Royal Over-Seas League; Royal Scottish Automobile. [*Died* 3 *Feb.* 1963.

RUSSELL, Hon. Victor Alexander Frederick Villiers, C.B.E. 1959 (O.B.E. 1919); J.P. Bedfordshire; Recorder of Bedford, 1926-49; *b.* 1874; 3rd *s.* of 1st Baron Ampthill; *m.* 1905, Annora Margaret Bromley (*d.* 1949), *y. d.* of late G. E. Martin, Ham Court, Worcs.; two *d.* (and one *d.* decd.). *Educ.:* Wellington; New College, Oxford; B.A. Bar, Inner Temple, 1899, Bencher 1934; served European War, 1914-18; Capt. Bedf. Militia, 3rd Bn. Bedf. Regt.; Lt.-Col. 25 Bedf. Regt. (despatches twice). *Address:* 22 Chelsea Square, S.W.3. *T.:* Flaxman 0256. [*Died* 11 *March* 1965.

RUSSON, Sir (William) Clayton, Kt. 1958; O.B.E. 1952 (M.B.E. 1946); *b.* 30 June 1895; *s.* of late William and Gertrude Emma Russon, Selly Park, Warwickshire *m.* 1931, Gladys, *d.* of Henry Markham, Dulwich; no *c.* *Educ.:* King Edward VI School, Birmingham. Chairman Merioneth National Savings Cttee., 1939-47; Founder Chm. N. Wales Industrial Assoc., 1944; Pres. Industrial Assoc. of Wales and Monmouthshire, 1947; High Sheriff, Merioneth, 1947-48. First Pres., Llangollen Internat. Musical Eisteddfod, 1947; Mem. Council for Wales and Monmouthshire, 1949-63; Mem. Devel. Corp. for Wales, 1958-63; Chairman: Ryder and Son (1920), 1962-; R. & G. Cuthbert Ltd., 1962-; David Miln & Co. (Seedsmen) Ltd.; George Bunyard & Co. Ltd.; International Seed Growers Ltd.; Phostrogen Ltd.; Glanavon Estates Ltd.; Carters Tested Seeds Ltd. Local Dir., Barclays Bank Ltd., Liverpool Bd.; Underwriting Mem. of Lloyd's. Master Worshipful Company of Fruiterers, 1957. Freeman of City of London. Pres. of Festival of Wales, 1958. K.St.J. 1968 (C.St.J. 1962). High Sheriff of Merioneth, 1965-66 (2nd term). *Recreations:* sketching, yachting, gardening. *Address:* Glanymawddach, near Barmouth, Merioneth. *Clubs:* Junior Carlton, Royal Automobile; Royal Welsh Yacht. [*Died* 16 *April* 1968.

RUSTON, Colonel Reginald Seward, C.B. 1918; *b.* 1867; *y. s.* of Alfred S. Ruston, J.P., of Chatteris, Cambs; *m.* 1st, 1896 Eva Mary (*d.* 1902), *yr. d.* of Major Justinian Armitage Nutt, late Inniskilling Fusiliers; two *d.*; 2nd, 1904, Marion, 2nd *d.* of Peter Addington; 3rd. 1928, Esmé, 2nd *d.* of Rev. J. Lister Coles; one *s.* *Educ.:* Bedford Modern School; Royal Military College, Sandhurst. Entered Devonshire Regt.

1885; transferred to Army Pay Dept., 1896; served Burmah, 1891-3, in command of Mounted Infantry of Devon Regt. (medal with clasp); European War as Lt.-Col. and Colonel (despatches twice, C.B.); retired with rank of Colonel, 1920. Home Guard, 1940-44; Defence Medal. *Recreations:* shooting, fishing, golf. *Address:* Tavy House, Mary Tavy, Devon.
[*Died* 22 *Nov.* 1963.

RUTHERFORD, James Rankin, C.B.E. 1945; J.P.; *b.* 1882; *m.* 1915, Helen, *d.* of late Timothy Warren, LL.D.; two *s.* two *d.* *Educ.:* Lenzie Academy. Town Council of Kirkintilloch, 1918-55 (Provost, 1931-33); Dunbarton County Council, 1930-51; Convener of County, 1939-45. Member War Damage Commission, 1948-59, and Central Land Board, 1947-59; Contested (Lib.) Northern Div. of Aberdeen, 1929, Kilmarnock Div. of Ayr & Bute, 1929. J.P. Co. Dunbarton, 1925; J.P. Co. of City of Glasgow, 1917; admitted as Hon. Burgess and given Freedom of Burgh of Kirkintilloch, 1955. Chm., Bd. of Management Kirkintilloch and Kilsyth Hosps., 1949-66. F.C.I.S. *Recreations:* golf and riding. *Address:* The Grange, Lenzi, Dunbartonshire; Ardnagag, Dunkeld, Perthshire. *Clubs:* National Liberal; Royal Scottish Automobile.
[*Died* 20 *Sept.* 1967.

RUTHERFORD, Sir John (George), Kt., *cr.* 1953; Partner, John Rutherford & Son, Marine Underwriters, since 1912; Chartered Accountant; *b.* 19 July 1886; *s.* of John and Mary May Rutherford; *m.* 1912; one *s.* *Educ.:* Argyle House, Sunderland: New College, Harrogate. Sunderland Town Council, 1922-Nov. 1931; Trustee, Sunderland Savings Bank, 1932; Commissioner for Income Tax, 1936; Local Representative, Royal Alfred Instn., 1940; Chm. Sunderland Conservative Assoc., 1941-50 (Pres., 1955-60, etc.); Chm. Conservative Northern Area Local Govt. Cttee., 1945-50; Pres. Sunderland Chamber of Commerce, 1953. *Address:* Red House, 46 Beechwood Terrace, Sunderland. *T.:* Sunderland 5593. *Club:* Sunderland.
[*Died* 6 *March* 1967.

RUTHVEN, Colonel Hon. (Christian) Malise Hore-, C.M.G. 1918; D.S.O. 1902; *b.* 1880; 3rd *s.* of 8th Lord Ruthven; *m.* 1925, Hon. Angela Margaret Manners, *d.* of 3rd Baron Manners; one *s.* two *d.* *Educ.:* Wellington. Joined Black Watch, 1899; A.D.C. to Viceroys of India and Ireland; Major, 1915; Lt.-Col. 1917; Col. 1928; served South Africa, 1899-1902 (despatches thrice, D.S.O.; Queen's medal, S.A. King's medal, S.A., five clasps); European War, 1914-18 (despatches, C.M.G.); G.S.O., 1st Grade, 3rd Canadian Division; commanded 1st Batt. The Black Watch; Commander 151st (Durham Light Infantry) Brigade (T.A.) 1929-33; A.D.C. to the King, 1932-33; retired pay, 1933; Secretary to Governor-General of Union of South Africa, 1933-36. *Recreation:* hunting. *Address:* 161 Ashley Gardens, S.W.1. *Club:* United Service.
[*Died* 3 *May* 1969.

RUTTLEDGE, Hugh, I.C.S. (retired); *b.* 24 Oct. 1884; *s.* of late Lieut.-Col. E. B. Ruttledge, I.M.S.; *m.* 1915, Dorothy Jessie Hair Elder; one *s.* two *d.* *Educ.:* Dresden; Lausanne; Cheltenham College; Pembroke College, Cambridge. Joined Indian Civil Service, 1909; Assistant Magistrate, Roorkee and Sitapur, 1909-13; City Magistrate, Agra, 1913-16; City Magistrate, Lucknow, 1917-19; Deputy Commissioner, Lucknow, 1919-20, and 1922-24; Deputy Commissioner Almora, 1925-1928; Settlement Officer, Almora, 1928-29; retired, Jan. 1932; Leader, Mount Everest Expeditions, 1933 and 1936; F.R.G.S.; Founder's Medallist, 1934; Tyneside Geographical Society Medallist, 1936. *Publications:* Everest, 1933; Everest: The Unfinished Adventure, 1937. *Address:* c/o Lloyd's Bank Ltd., 6 Pall Mall, S.W.1; The Grove, Stoke, Plymouth, S. Devon. *T.:* 53096. *Club:* Alpine.
[*Died* 7 *Nov.* 1961.

RYALLS, Hon. Capt. Harry Douglas, D.S.O. 1916; M.B.E. 1942; Cheshire Regt., Former Manager Export Dept. Meade-King, Robinson & Co. Ltd., Tower Building, Liverpool, now retired; *b.* 19 June 1887; *e. s.* of Henry John and Maud Ryalls, Birkenhead; *m.* 1924, Emmy Carla, *d.* of Dr. Raff, Frederikssund, Denmark; two *d.* *Educ.:* Birkenhead School. Secretary Ryalls & Jones Ltd., Birkenhead, 1903-11; Private Secretary to late Alfred Bigland, M.P. for Birkenhead, 1911-14; served in France, 1914-19, with 10th Battalion, King's Liverpool Regiment (Liverpool Scottish), later with 16th Cheshire Battalion as Lieut. and Captain (D.S.O., despatches); commercial appointments in Copenhagen, 1920; Rotterdam, 1924, and since 1934 in Liverpool. Chief Air Raid Warden of Birkenhead, 1938-1941. *Recreations:* reading, gardening, walking. *Address:* 34 Village Road, Oxton, Birkenhead. *T.:* Claughton 4163.
[*Died* 4 *June* 1964.

RYAN, Curteis Norwood, C.B. 1952; C.M.G. 1946; D.S.O. 1918; M.C. 1917; *b.* 2 Dec. 1891; *m.* 1919, Laura Elvira (*d.* 1966), *y. d.* of W. H. Impey, C.S.I.; two *d.* *Educ.:* King's School, Canterbury; City and Guilds Engineering College. Royal Engineers, and General Staff, Sept. 1914-July 1919. Treasury, Sept. 1919; Imperial Defence College, 1926; Asst. Sec. Committee of Imperial Defence, 1937-39; Principal Asst. Sec. Ministry of Food, 1939-41; Controller Ministry of Information, Middle East Services, Cairo, 1943-46; Under-Sec., Home Office, 1948; retired, 1955. *Recreations:* tennis, golf. *Address:* 19 Langside Avenue, S.W.15. *T.:* Prospect. 5820. *Clubs:* St. Stephens, Roehampton.
[*Died* 24 *June* 1969.

RYAN, Dr. James, M.B., B.Ch., B.A.O.; D.P.H.; D.Econ.Sc., National University of Ireland, 1964; Senator, 1965; Fianna Fáil member Dail for Wexford till 1965; Chief Medical Adviser to New Ireland Assurance Co., Dublin, 1948-51 and 1954-57; *b.* 6 December 1892; *m.* 1919, Mairin Cregan; two *s.* one *d.* *Educ.:* St. Peter's College, Wexford; Ring Irish College; National University. Junior Physician City Skin and Cancer Hospital, 1921-26; arrested 1916; M.P. for South Wexford, 1918; imprisoned on Spike Island, 1920-21; Vice-Chairman Wexford County Council, 1919-22; elected for County Wexford, 1921-23 and 1927; Minister for Agriculture, 1932-47; Minister for Health and Minister for Social Welfare, 1947-48, 1951-54. Director: New Ireland Assurance Co., Irish National Insurance Co. National Tanners Ltd.; Burnhouse (Ireland) Ltd., 1919-32, 1948-51, and 1954-57; Minister for Finance, Ireland, 1957-65; Senator, 1965-69; Member: Irish Delegation to Economic Conf., Ottawa, 1932; Delegation British-Irish negotiations, 1938. *Address:* Kindlestown House, Delgany, Co. Wicklow.
[*Died* 25 *Sept.* 1970.

RYAN, Mary, M.A.; D.Litt. (h.c.), 1952; Prof. of Romance Languages, University College, Cork, 1910-38; Chevalier de la Légion d'Honneur, 1935; *o. d.* of Edward Ryan, Ronayn's Court, Rochestown, Co. Cork. *Educ.:* Ursuline College, St. Angela's, Cork; Ursuline Convent, Berlin; Dominican Convent, Neuilly-sur-Seine. Exhibitioner and Gold Medallist, Intermediate Examinations; Exhibitioner and Student, Royal University of Ireland; Junior Fellow in Modern Literature, R.U.I., 1898-1901; Intermediate Examiner in French, 1902-8; Lecturer in German, University College, Cork, 1909. *Publications:* Our Lady's Hours, 1941 and 1946; Out of the Depths, 1942; Introduction to Claudel, 1950; articles in Irish Rosary, Month, Dublin Review, Studies, Blackfriars.

Recreations: music, travel. *Address:* Gortalough, Douglas, Cork. [*Died* 16 *June* 1961.

RYCROFT, Sir Benjamin William, Kt. 1960; Data Stia Negara Brunei (D.S.N.) 1964; O.B.E.; M.D., Ch.B., D.O.M.S., L.R.C.P., F.R.C.S., England; Consulting Ophthalmic Surgeon, Corneo-Plastic Unit, Queen Victoria Hosp., E. Grinstead, Kent County Ophthalmic and Aural Hosp., and Sussex Eye Hosp.; Clinical Director, Pocklington Research and Eye Transplantation Unit, R.C.S. of England; Hon. Consultant in Ophthalmology, Zoological Soc. of London; Civilian Consultant in Ophthalmology, Ministry of Aviation; Hon. Consulting Ophthalmic Surgeon, Royal National Institute for the Blind; *b.* 16 August 1902; *s.* of John Thomas and Annie Rycroft; *m.* 1925, Mary Elizabeth Rhodes; two *s.* *Educ.:* Univ. of St. Andrews; St. George's Hosp., London. Late Hunterian Prof., late Leverhulme Scholar, Royal College of Surgeons of England; Lang Research Scholar and Chief Assistant, Royal London Ophthalmic Hosp. (Moorfields); Middlemore Prizeman, British Medical Association and Drummond Exhibition; late Ophthalmic Surgeon to King's College Hospital Group (King's Coll. Hosp. and Royal Eye Hosp.), etc.; late Lieutenant-Colonel R.A.M.C. Adviser in Ophthalmology, Allied Force Headquarters, 1943-45; late External Examiner Queen's Univ., Belfast: Past Pres. Sect. Ophth. Roy. Soc. of Medicine; Vice-President, Faculty of Ophthalmology, 1966; Doyne Lectr., Oxford Ophthalmological Congress, 1965. Member Ophthalmic Society of Paris, United Kingdom, France, Italy, Belgium and Oxford: Hon. Member Ophthalmic Socs. of South Africa, Australia and N.Z.; President, Barraquer Institute of Opthalmology, Barcelona; Member, British Assoc. Plastic Surgeons. *Publications:* (jointly) Modern Trends in Ophthalmology; Br. Manual of Ophthalmology for Medical Officers; Corneo Plastic Surgery. Is also co-author of various essays and articles in British Medical Journal, British Journal of Ophthalmology, Transactions of Ophthalmological Society of United Kingdom. Editor: Corneal Grafts. *Recreation:* farming. *Address:* 35 Harley Street, W.1. *T.:* Langham 2863; Bishops Lodge, Oakley Green, Windsor. *T.:* Windsor 260. [*Died* 29 *March* 1967.

RYDE, John Walter, F.R.S. 1948; F.Inst.P.; F.R.A.S.; Chief Scientist, Research Laboratories of the General Electric Company, Ltd., Wembley, Middlesex; *b.* 15 April 1898; *o. s.* of W. W. Ryde, Brighton; *m.* 1930, Dorothy Ritchie; one *s.* *Educ.:* St. Paul's School; City and Guilds. Member of staff of General Electric Company Research Laboratories since 1919. *Publications:* Papers in Proceedings of the Royal Society, etc., principally on Spectroscopy, Scattering of Light, Electric Discharge Lamps, Luminescent Materials and on the Attenuation and Radar Echoes produced by Meteorological Phenomena at centimetre wavelengths. *Address:* Redhurst, 19 Elgood Avenue, Northwood, Middlesex. *T.:* Northwood 845; Research Laboratories of The General Electric Company, Ltd., Wembley, Middlesex. *T.:* Arnold 1262. *Club:* Athenæum. [*Died* 15 *May* 1961.

RYDER, Lady Frances, C.B.E. 1919; *b.* 7 Aug. 1888; *o. surv. d.* of 5th Earl of Harrowby. Organised Dominion Officers Hospitality Scheme, 1916-20; Director of Dominion Students Hospitality Scheme, 1920-1939, followed by the Dominion and Allied Services Hospitality Scheme until 1947. *Address:* Sandon Hall, Stafford. [*Died* 24 *Dec.* 1965.

RYLE, Herbert, C.V.O. 1939 (M.V.O. 1929); O.B.E. 1919; A.R.I.B.A.; (retd.); *b.* 1881; *s.* of John Thomas Ryle, Crook, Co. Durham; *m.* 1910, Mary (*decd.*), *d.* of George Weir Wilson; one *s.* Formerly Ministry of Works. *Address:* Vale Royal Hotel, Tunbridge Wells, Kent. [*Died* 14 *March* 1966.

RYMILL, John Riddoch; Grazier at Penola, South Australia; Commission in Roy. Australian Navy Volunteer Reserve, 1941; *b.* 13 March 1905; *yr. s.* of Robert Rymill and Mary Edith Riddoch; *m.* 1938, Eleanor Mary Francis; two *s.* *Educ.:* Melbourne Church of England Grammar School. Member of expedition of Cambridge University Museum of Archæology and Ethnology to Canada, 1929; Member of British Arctic Air Route Expedition to Greenland, 1930-31; Polar Medal in silver with Arctic bar, 1930-31; Member and subsequently leader of H. G. Watkins' expedition to Greenland, 1932-33; Murchison Grant from Royal Geographical Society, 1934; Leader of British Graham Land Expedition to the Antarctic, 1934-37; Founder's Medal of Royal Geographical Society, 1938; Antarctic Bar, 1934-37, to silver Polar Medal; David Livingstone Centenary Medal by American Geographical Society of New York for scientific achievement in the field of geography in the Southern Hemisphere, 1939. *Publication:* Southern Lights: the official narrative of the British Graham Land Expedition, 1934-37, 1938. *Recreation:* riding. *Address:* Old Penola Estate, Penola, South Australia. *Club:* Adelaide (Adelaide). [*Died* 7 *Sept.* 1968.

RYNER, Harry; Author, Lecturer, Inventor, Therapeutist, contributor to magazines, scientific and medical journals; *b.* 4 Aug. 1872; *s.* of David Reinheimer and Minna Somer; changed name by Deed Poll, 1935; unmarried. *Educ.:* London University. Devoted his life to the framing of a new organon of biology, adequate to the etiology of cancer and to the reversal of Darwinism; considers Selection far-fetched and little use; stresses instead mutual relations; here the master word is Co-operation, or Symbiosis, comprising ecological and moral factors—briefly; values; has marshalled a vast array of facts in support of Evolution by Symbiosis; Symbiosis, on the new interpretation, constitutes, not only the cardinal principle of progressive evolution and of organisation, but also that majestic principle of which disease, and especially cancer, are the infraction; it is shown that progress is a necessity, not an accident, and that all systems which regard evolution or disease as chapters of accident are founded upon error; Founder of Holopathy. *Publications:* Nutrition and Evolution, 1909; Evolution by Co-operation, 1913; Symbiogenesis, 1914; Symbiosis, a Socio-physiol. Theory of Evolution; Symbiosis v. Cancer, 1921; Evolution at the Crossways; Evolution Re-Interpreted; Cancer and Remedial Diet; Evolution by Symbiosis; Symbiosis, the Cure of Cancer and of Selectionitis; Synthetic Biology; Deliverance from Cancer; Science the Terrible; Darwin the Evi Genius of Science, 1933; Shall Cancer Conquer Unopposed, 1934; Cancer Expounded and Expunged, 1949; How to Live (in Aphorisms), 1954. *Recreations:* tennis, badminton, cycling, music. *Address:* c/o The National Bank Ltd., 13-17 Old Broad St. E.C.2. [*Died* 29 *Dec.* 1964.

S

SABELLI, Humbert Anthony, C.B.E. 1938; Hon. Life Counsellor of Internationa Lawn Tennis Federation; Hon. Life Vice-President of Lawn Tennis Association; *b.* 20 Dec. 1878; *m.* 1918, Agnes Octavia Swayne (*d.* 1958); *m.* 1959. Maud Fabian Brackenbury. *Educ.:* Marlborough Coll.

Zürich Univ. Foreign Sec. to Easton and Anderson, Erith, and Egyptian Engineering Co., Cairo, 1900-10; served European War, R.F.A., 1915-18, France and Italy; D.A.Q.M.G. Military Mission, Padua, 1918. Secretary of the Lawn Tennis Association, 1912-48. *Address:* 7 Langley Road, Surbiton, Surrey. *Clubs:* All England Lawn Tennis, Queen's, Senior Golfers' Society.
[*Died* 3 *May* 1961.

SACKVILLE, 4th Baron, *cr.* 1876; **Major-Gen. Charles John Sackville-West,** K.B.E., *cr.* 1919; C.B. 1921; C.M.G. 1915; *b.* 10 Aug. 1870; *s.* of Colonel Hon. W. E. Sackville-West, Grenadier Guards, and Georgina, *y. d.* of George Dodwell, Kevinsfoot, Co. Sligo; *S.* brother, 1928; *m.* 1st, 1897, Maude Cecilia (*d.* 1920), *d.* of late Captain Mathew John Bell of Bourne Park, Kent; one *s.* one *d.*; 2nd, 1924, Mrs. Anne Meredith Bigelow (*d.* 1961), New York Entered army, K.R.R.C., 1889; Captain, 1898; Major, 1905; Lt.-Col. 1914; Col. 1916; Maj.-Gen. 1919; served Manipur, 1891 (despatches); Burma, 1891-92; South Africa, 1899-1900 (despatches thrice, brevet of Major, Queen's medal 6 clasps); European War, 1914-18 (despatches five times, twice wounded, Bt. Col., prom. Maj.-Gen.); British Military Representative of Allied Military Committee of Versailles, 1918; and Military Attaché, Paris, 1920-24; Lieut.-Governor of Guernsey and its Dependencies, 1925-29; retired pay, 1929. *Heir:* *s.* Hon. Edward Charles Sackville-West, *q.v.* *Address:* Knole, Sevenoaks. *Club:* Army and Navy.
[*Died* 8 *May* 1962.

SACKVILLE, 5th Baron, *cr.* 1876; **Edward Charles Sackville-West;** *b.* 13 Nov. 1901; *o. s.* of 4th Baron Sackville, K.B.E., C.B., C.M.G., and Maude, *d.* of late Matthew Bell, Bourne Park, Kent; *S.* father, 1962; unmarried. *Educ.:* Eton; Christ Church, Oxford. *Publications:* Piano Quintet, 1925; The Ruin, 1926; Mandrake over the Water-Carrier, 1928; Simpson, 1931; The Sun in Capricorn, 1934; A Flame in Sunlight, 1936; The Rescue, 1945; Inclinations, 1949; The Record Guide (with Desmond Shawe-Taylor), 1951. *Heir:* *cousin,* Capt. Lionel Bertrand Sackville-West [*b.* 30 May 1913; *m.* 1953, Jacobine Hichens (*née* Menzies-Wilson); five *d.*]. *Address:* Long Crichel House, Wimborne, Dorset. *T.:* Tarrant Hinton 250; Cooleville House, Clogheen, Co. Tipperary, S. Ireland. *T.:* Clogheen 3; (Seat) Knole, Sevenoaks, Kent. *Clubs:* Savile; Kildare Street (Dublin).
[*Died* 4 *July* 1965.

SACKVILLE, Lady Margaret; 3rd *d.* of 7th Earl de la Warr. *Publications:* Poems, 1901; A Hymn to Dionysus, and other poems, 1905; Hildris the Queen, 1908; Fairy Tales for Old and Young (in collaboration), 1909; Bertrud and other Dramatic Poems, 1911; Lyrics, 1912; Songs of Aphrodite, 1913; The Dream-Pedlar and other Stories, 1914; The Travelling Companions, 1915; The Pageant of War, 1916; Selected Poems, 1919; Epitaphs, 1921; Poems, 1923; A Rhymed Sequence 1924; Three Fairy Plays, 1925; Epitaphs, 1926; Collected Dramas, 1926; Romantic Ballads, 1927; 100 Little Poems (collected), Alicia and the Twilight, 1928; Twelve Little Poems, 1931; Ariadne by the Sea, 1933; The Double House, 1936; Mr. Horse's New Shoes, 1937; Collected Poems, 1939; Tom Noodle's Kingdom, 1941; Return to Song, 1943; Poems and Paintings, Country Scenes and Country Verse, the Lyrical Woodland, 1945; Tree-Music, 1946; Miniatures, 1947 (also 2nd series); Country Verse, 1950; Floral Symphony, 1951; Quatrains, 1960. *Address:* 22 Lansdowne Terrace, Cheltenham.
[*Died* 18 *April* 1963.

SACKVILLE-WEST, Hon. V., C.H. 1948; D.Litt. (Durham and Newcastle) 1950; F.R.S.L.; J.P.; *b.* Knole, Sevenoaks, March 1892; *d.* of 3rd Baron Sackville; *m.* 1913, Hon. Sir Harold Nicolson, K.C.V.O., C.M.G.; two *s.* *Educ.:* home. *Publications:* Heritage, and other novels; Seducers in Ecuador; Knole and the Sackvilles; Passenger to Teheran; The Land (Hawthornden prize, 1927); Aphra Behn, 1927; Twelve Days, 1928; Andrew Marvell, 1929; The Edwardians, 1930; All Passion Spent, 1931; Sissinghurst, 1933; Collected Poems, 1933; The Dark Island, 1934; Saint Joan of Arc, 1936; Pepita, 1937; Some Flowers, 1937; Solitude, 1938; Country Notes, 1939; Country Notes in Wartime, 1940; Selected Poems, 1941; English Country Houses, 1941; Grand Canyon, 1942; The Eagle and the Dove, 1943; Another World Than This (anthology, with Harold Nicolson), 1945; The Garden, 1946 (Heinemann Prize, 1947); Nursery Rhymes, 1947; In your garden, 1951; The Easter Party, 1953; In your garden again, 1953; More for your garden, 1955; Even more for your garden, 1958; Daughter of France, 1959; No sign-posts in the sea, 1960; Faces: Profiles of Dogs (text for photographs by Laelia Goehr), 1961. *Address:* Sissinghurst Castle, Kent.
[*Died* 2 *June* 1962.

SACHS, Nelly (Leonie); poet and dramatist; *b.* Berlin, Germany, 10 Dec. 1891; *d.* of William Sachs and Margarete Karger. Literaturpreis des Jahresring, 1959; Annette Droste Preis, 1960; Friedenspreis, 1965; Nobelpreis, 1966. *Publications:* *poetry:* In den Wohnungen des Todes, 1947; Sternverdunkelung, 1949; Und Niemand weiss weiter. 1957; Flucht und Verwandlung, 1959; Fahrt ins Staublose, 1961; Späte Gedichte, 1965; Die Suchende, 1966; Glühende Rätsel, 1968; Selected Poems (translated), 1968; *drama:* Zeichen im Sand, 1962. *Address:* Bergsundsstrand 23, Stockholm, Sweden. [*Died* 12 *May* 1970.

SADD, Sir Clarence Thomas Albert, Kt., *cr.* 1945; C.B.E. 1938; D.L., J.P.; retired Bank General Manager; *b.* Anerley, Surrey, 8 Nov. 1883; *o. s.* of late Albert Gower Sadd, Kessingland House, Suffolk; *m.* Renee Georgette Elizabeth, *d.* of late Dr. Anth. Durand, Chevalier Légion d'Honneur, Lyons; three *s.* two *d.* *Educ.:* Fallowfield; Manchester University. Served European War, 1914-18 (despatches). Chief of Executive and Vice-Chairman Midland Bank, 1944-48; Vice-President of Institute of Bankers (President, 1947-48); Mem. Nat. Investment Council, 1945-48. Member of Royal Commission on Workmen's Compensations, 1938; Vice-President Football Assoc.; Life Vice-Pres.: Amateur Football Alliance, Lawn Tennis Assoc. (Hon. Treas. 1934-48); Hon. Treasurer: International Lawn Tennis Federation; The Friends of the Poor, 1939-1956 (now a Governor); London Homeopathic Hospital; British United Aid to China; Central Council of Physical Recreation; National Sports Development Fund; American Chapel Memorial Fund. President: British Chess Federation; Sussex Chess Association; Brighton Chess Club. Governor: Bristol University; City of London College. D.L. 1942; J.P. County of London. Légion d'Honneur (France), 1959. *Publications:* Carlyle's Influence on Ruskin; Credit and Industry; A Banker's View f Balance Sheets. *Address:* Hurst Farm, Ashurst Wood, East Grinstead, Sussex. *Clubs:* Athenæum, Royal Automobile, Reform; All England Lawn Tennis.
[*Died* 1 *Oct.* 1962.

SADLER, Arthur Lindsay, M.A.; Companion Imperial Order of Rising Sun; Professor of Oriental Studies, University of Sydney, 1922-47; retired Dec. 1947; Emeritus Professor, 1948; *b.* London, 1882; *s.* of William and Sara Ellen Sadler; *m.* Eva, *d.* of John Nicholson Seymour, B.A., M.B. *Educ.:* Dulwich College; Merchant Taylors' School; St. John's College, Oxford (Scholar); Pusey and Ellerton Hebrew Scholar, Kennicott Scholar Septuagint Prize, Honours in Oriental Languages. Lecturer in Higher College, Okayama 1909-19; in Peer's College, Tokyo, 1919-22. *Publications:* The Heike Monogatari, translation and notes, 1918-21; Trans. Ac. Soc. of Japan: Kócho, a drama by the Emperor Go-Mizu-no-o, translation and notes, 1922; The Ten Foot Square Hut, 1928; The Art of Flower Arrangement in Japan, 1933; Cha-no-yu, the Tea Philosophy of Japan, 1934; The Maker of Modern Japan, The Life of Tokugawa Ieyasu, 1937; Japanese Plays: No, Kyōgen, Kabuki, 1934; Short History of Japanese Architecture, 1941; Selections from the Confucian Texts, 1942; Three Military Classics of China, 1944; Short History of Japan, 1945. *Recreations:* books and art. *Address:* Buck's House, Great Bardfield, Braintree, Essex. *T.:* Great Bardfield 322. [*Died* 13 *July* 1970.

SAFFORD, Sir Archibald, Kt. 1957; M.C.; Q.C. 1946; Deputy Insurance Commissioner under the National Insurance and Industrial Injuries Acts, 1948-60; *b.* 17 July 1892; *s.* of late Frank Safford, sometime Recorder of Canterbury, and late Fannie Theresa Roberts; *m.* 1924, Nora Iris Leighton (*d.* 1949); one *s.* *Educ.:* St. Paul's School. Called to Bar, Middle Temple, 1913; Bencher Middle Temple, 1946. Served in Army, 1914-18 (M.C.). Dep. Chm. Courts of Referees under Unemployment Insurance Acts (East Kent), 1919-1923; Chairman (East Kent and later London district), 1923-30; Referee under Nat. Health Insurance Acts, 1922-48; Chairman of Inquiries Sub-Cttee. of Ophthalmic Benefit Approved Cttee., 1938-48; Referee under Contributory Pensions Acts, 1927-48; Senior Referee, 1930-48; Senior Referee under Family Allowances Act, 1946-48; Recorder of Faversham, 1934-48. *Publications:* Law of Town and Country Planning, etc. *Address:* 16 Berwyn Road, Richmond, Surrey. *T.:* Prospect 5179. *Clubs:* Junior Carlton; Richmond Golf. [*Died* 4 *May* 1961.

SAILANA, Raja of; H.H. Raja Sir Dileep Singh Bahadur, K.C.I.E., *cr.* 1936; Ruler of Sailana State, Madhya Pradesh, enjoying permanent salute of 11 guns; *b.* 18 March 1891; *s* of late Raja Sir Jeswant Singh Bahadur, K.C.I.E., of Sailana State; *m.* 1st, 1909, *d.* (decd.) of the Maharawat Sahib of Partabgarh; 2nd, *d.* of Rawatji Sahib of Meja (Mewar); two *s.* three *d.* *Educ.:* Mayo College, Ajmer. Made primary education compulsory but quite free; provided free medical aid throughout the State and a High School; a new Hospital with a separate Maternity Ward has been built; granted a democratic Constitution to the Local Municipality; established an Ayurvedic Dispensary, and Agricultural, Dairy and Poultry Farms in the Capital and an Industrial Free Mandi at Dileepnagar; constituted State Council consisting of 2 elected members. President of Kurukshetra Restoration Society and the Council of Shri Bharat Dharma Mahamandal, Benares; Member of General Council of the Mayo Coll., Ajmer, and Daly Coll., Indore. *Recreations:* music; shikar; agriculture; dairy; dogs; horses; cats; pigs. *Heir:* Maharaja Kumar Digvijaya Singhji, M.A., *b.* 15 Oct. 1918 *Address:* Sailana, Madhya Pradesh; India. [*Died* 8 *Feb.* 1961.

SAINT, Lawrence (Bradford); at present painting Biblical murals for Churches, and portraits; *b.* Sharpsburg, Pa., U.S.A., 29 Jan. 1885; *s.* of Joseph Alexander and Jennie Bradford Saint; *m.* 1910, Katharine Wright Proctor; seven *s.* one *d.* *Educ.:* Pennsylvania Academy of Fine Arts, Philadelphia; five trips for art and especially stained glass studies in England, France and Spain; spent one year copying stained glass windows in England and France. Began in stained glass as apprentice 1901; after working in four studios began working for Raymond Pitcairn, at the Bryn Athyn Cathedral, Philadelphia, and worked eleven years in research and experimenting and in designing and painting stained glass, completing six windows; rediscovered way to make medieval glass paint while there; Director of Department of Stained Glass of Washington Cathedral, 1928-35; established studio, glass making factory, invented two glass making furnaces, worked out with help of chemists and glass making experts over 1300 formulas for Stained Glass like medieval glass in colour and chemical composition, including striated ruby; designed, made full-sized figure cartoons, and directed the making of fifteen windows for Washington Cathedral, including North Transept Rose; represented: (by many drawings of mediæval stained glass) in the Victoria and Albert Royal Museum, London, and in Carnegie Institute, Pittsburgh; in Pepper Hall Free Library of Philadelphia by material from Washington Cathedral and by work in New York Public Library; also by collection in Corning Museum of Glass, Corning, New York. Large Mural of 23rd Psalm, Church of the Open Door, Philadelphia, Pa.; mural, David with the Sheep, Ebenezer M.B.C.C., Church, Bethlehem, Pa.; large mural, Walking with God, Kemble Park Church, Ogontz and Grange, Philadelphia; large Biblical mural, War Memorial Building, Bob Jones Univ., Greenville, S.C., also by portrait of Dr. Bob Jones, Sr. Rep. Dr. Alex. Silverman collection, Chemistry Dept., University of Pittsburg, Pennsylvania, by glassware. Made various Biblical oil paintings. Gave radio broadcast, Science Service program on subject of stained glass to over 65 stations. *Publications:* Author of fifty coloured illustrations of Stained Glass of the Middle Ages in England and France, text by Hugh Arnold; Author and illustrator of A Knight of the Cross; Author of Ponderin' Pete, and of technical stained glass articles. *Address*: Huntingdon Valley, Montgomery Co., near Philadelphia, Pennsylvania, U.S.A. *T.:* WI-7-0270. [*Died June* 1961.

SAINT-CLAIR, Georges; *see* Coudurier de Chassaigne, Joseph.

ST. ALBANS, 12th Duke of (*cr.* 1684), **Osborne de Vere Beauclerk,** Earl of Burford and Baron of Heddington, 1676; Baron Vere, 1750; Hereditary Grand Falconer of England; 2nd *s.* of 10th Duke of St. Albans, and 2nd wife, Grace, *d.* of late Ralph Bernal-Osborne, M.P.; *b.* 16 Oct. 1874; *S.* half-b. 1934; *m.* 1918, Lady Beatrix Frances Fitzmaurice, (*d.* 1953), G.B.E., *cr.* 1919, *d.* of 5th Marquess of Lansdowne, and *widow* of 6th Marquis of Waterford. Maj. South Notts. Hussars, 1902; late Capt. 17th Lancers; retired, 1902; Major, South Notts Yeomanry, 1904; served South Africa, 1899-1902 (despatches); European War, 1914-18. *Heir:* *kinsman* Charles Frederic Aubrey de Vere Beauclerk, O.B.E. *Address:* Newtown Anner, Clonmel, Co. Tipperary. *Clubs:* Brooks's, Turf; Kildare Street (Dublin). [*Died* 2 *March* 1964.

ST. AUBYN, Captain Hon. Lionel Michael, M.V.O. 1919; Captain, Reserve of Officers, late King's Royal Rifle Corps; *s.* of 1st Baron St. Levan; *b.* 1878; *m.* 1915, Lady Mary Theresa Parker (*d.* 1932), *d.* of 3rd Earl of Morley; one *s.* (and *e. s.* killed in action, 1944, and one *s.* decd. 1964). *Educ.:* Eton; Trinity College, Cambridge (B.A.); Hon. Attaché, Diplomatic Service, 1904; 1908; Equerry to Duchess of Albany, 1910-22; served European War, 1914-19 (despatches); Chevalier, Danish Order of Danebrog; Commander, Oaken Crown of Luxembourg. *Address:* Pound House, Yelverton, S. Devon. *Club:* Brooks's. [*Died* 17 *Sept.* 1965

ST. GEORGE, Frederick Ferris Bligh, C.V.O. 1953; *b.* 1908; 3rd *s.* of late Howard Bligh St. George; *m.* 1932, Meriel Margaret (*née* Radcliffe) (*d.* 1966); three *d. Educ.:* Eton. The Life Guards, 1927-36; Adjt. Royal Wiltshire Yeomanry, 1936-40; 1st Household Cavalry Regiment, 1940-45: The Life Guards, 1945-50 (3 years in command); Lieut.-Colonel, Household Cavalry, 1950-53; Commanding a Wing at Military College of Science, Shrivenham, 1953-55; R.A.R.O. 1955; Hon. Col. Royal Wilts. Yeomanry, 1956; County Comdt., Wilts. Army Cadet Force, 1956. High Sheriff of Gloucestershire, 1959. *Recreations:* yachting, shooting, hunting. *Address:* Flat 1, 23 Bruton Street, W.1. *T.:* 01-629 3542. *Clubs:* Turf, Cavalry, Buck's; Royal Yacht Sqdn.; Bembridge Sailing; Household Bde. Yacht. [*Died* 4 *April* 1970.

ST. JOHN-BROOKS, Ralph Terence, M.A., Sc.D. (h.c.), M.D., D.P.H. (Dubl.); D.T.M. and H. (Cantab.); F.L.S.; *b.* Dublin, 27 Oct. 1884; *y. s.* of Prof. Henry St. John-Brooks, University Anatomist, Dublin University, and Marion, *d.* of Aubrey Ohren; *m.* 1912, Julia Margaret, *y. d.* of John Gordon of Maryvale, Co. Down; two *s.* one *d. Educ.:* Erasmus Smith's School and Trinity College, Dublin; London School of Tropical Medicine. First of First Honours and Prize Natural Science, T.C.D., 1904; Haughton Medals and Prizes in Medicine and Surgery, Sir Patrick Dun's Hospital, 1908; M.B., B.Ch., B.A.O., *stip. cond.*, 1909; British Medical Association Research Scholar, 1911-13; Special Bacteriological Investigator, Local Government Board, 1911; Special Sanitary Investigator, Governments of Windward and Leeward Islands, 1912-14; Secretary, Commission for Plague Investigations in India, 1914-15; Temp. Captain R.A.M.C.; Specialist in Bacteriology, County of London War Hospital, Epsom, 1915-19; and to Royal Army Medical College, Millbank, 1919-20; Curator, National Collection of Type Cultures of Microorganisms (M.R.C., Privy Council), 1920-46; Secretary, Second International Congress for Microbiology, London, 1936, and President (Sec. 1) Third International Congress, New York, 1939; Hon. Secretary, Society for General Microbiology, 1944-46, Hon. Member, 1946; Secretary-General, International Association of Microbiologists, 1939-51; Collaborator, American Type Culture Collection and Inst. d'Hygiène, Lausanne. *Publications:* articles on Bacteriology and Serology in various scientific journals and in System of Bacteriology, Medical Research Council, 1929-31. *Recreations:* field natural history, gardening. *Address:* 15 Wilton Court, Wilton Place, Dublin, Ireland. *Club:* Cosmos (Washington, D.C., U.S.A.). [*Died* 27 *April* 1963.

SAINTHILL, Loudon; Designer (The Theatre); *b.* Tasmania, Australia, 9 Jan. 1919; *s.* of Willoughby A. Sainthill and Honora M. Sainthill (*née* Horder). *Educ.:* self-educated. Travelled with Col. de Basil Ballets Russe as Asst. Designer, 1938-41. Served A.I.F., Middle East, South Pacific, 1942-46. Exhibited Australia, 1947-49. Came to England, 1950, and has since designed for numerous productions at The Old Vic Theatre, Royal Shakespeare Theatre, Royal Opera House, Covent Garden, Sadler's Wells, Festival Ballet and West End Theatres; Royal Command Performance, Covent Garden, of opera Le Coq D'Or, 1954; also for American, Australian and Continental productions. *Publications:* Ed. (with H. Tatlock Miller): Royal Album, 1951; Undoubted Queen, 1958. *Recreations:* travel, swimming, sailing. *Address:* 8 Chester Street, Belgrave Square, S.W.1. *T.:* 01-730 6440. [*Died* 9 *June* 1969.

SALAZAR, Dr. Antonio de Oliveira; Grand Cross of Portuguese Orders of Torre e Espada, São Tiago da Espada, Império Colonial Português; Collar, Order of Infante Dom Henrique; economist and politician; President of the Council of Ministers, Portugal, 1932-68; *b.* 28 April 1889; *s.* of António de Oliveira and Maria do Resgate Salazar; unmarried. *Educ.:* Univ. of Coimbra. Doctor of Law. Prof. of Economic Sciences, Univ. of Coimbra, 1918; Mem. of Parliament; Min. of Finance, 1926 till few days after; and again, 1928-40; Minister for Colonies, *ad int.*, 1930, signed Portuguese Colonial Act; Prime Minister, 1932, presented to a national plebiscite the New Political Constitution of the Portuguese Republic now in force; Minister of War, ad int., 1936-44, reformer of the Portuguese Army; Minister for Foreign Affairs, 1936-47. Ex-officio Mem. Council of State; Pres. Nat. Union. Hon. D.C.L., Oxford Univ., 1941; Hon. LL.D. Fordham. Grand Cross of the following foreign Orders: St. Michael and St. George (Gt. Britain) (Hon. G.C.M.G.), Leopold (Belgium), Polonia Restituta (Poland), S. Mauricio e S. Lázaro (Italy), Boyaca (Colombia), Medhania (Morocco), Mérito (Chile), Service Fidèle (Rumania), Isabel a Católica (Spain), Cruzeiro do Sul (Brazil), Mérito Militar (Brazil), Mérito (Hungary), Salomon (Abyssinia). *Publications:* O ágio do ouro, 1916; Questão cerealífera do Trigo, 1916; Alguns aspectos da crise das subsistências, 1918; A minha resposta, 1919; O Centro Católico Português, 1922; Redução das despezas públicas, 1923: Discursos e notas politicas (5 vols.: I, 1928-1934; II, 1935-37; III, 1938-43; IV, 1943-1950; V, 1951-58). *Trans. into:* English: Doctrine and Action; The Road for the Future; French: Comment on relève un État, Une Révolution dans la paix, Le Portugal et la crise européenne; Dictionnaire Politique de Salazar; Spanish: El Pensamiento de la Revolución Nacional, El Estado Nuevo Português, Una Revolución Pacífica, Oliveira Salazar definido por si mismo; Italian: Il Portogallo d'oggi, Portogallo nella guerra e nella pace; German: Portugal—Das Werden eines neuen Staates; Rumanian: Oliveira Salazar—Doctrina si Organisarea Revolutici Portugheze; Hungarian: Békés Forradalom; Polish: Rewolucja Pokojawa; Bulgarian: Edna Mirna Revoliutsnia, etc. *Address:* Presidência do Conselho, Palácio de S. Bento, Lisboa, Portugal. [*Died* 27 *July* 1970.

SALBERG, Maj. Frank James, C.I.E. 1944; M.B.E. 1919; retired; Chartered Civil Engineer; M.Inst.C.E.; *b.* 20 Dec. 1884; *s.* of late Salis. E. Salberg, Clairville, Forest Hill; *m.* 1919, Janet Ruth Basker, R.R.C., 4th *d.* of John Anthony Basker, Ashbourne, Weston-super-Mare; one *s.* one *d. Educ.:* St. Dunstan's College, Catford City and Guilds of London Institute, S. Kensington. A.C.G.I. 1903; Civil Engineer with Assam Bengal Rly., 1905-41 (Chief Engineer, 1934-41); Civil Engineer with Dibru Sadiya Rly., 1941-44. Served with Auxiliary Forces, India, 1906-36, retd. Hon. Lt.-Col. (Maj.); I.A.R.O., attached 1st K.G.O.S. & M. and Royal Engineers,1915-19; service on N.W.F. India, Aden Expeditionary Force, Mesopotamian Expeditionary Force (despatches); Major in Indian Engineers in Defence of India Corps Rlys.; service in Upper Assam, 1942-1944. *Publications:* Plain Facts about Floods in Bengal and Assam, 1936; Practical Well Foundations and Girder Erection for the Lesser "Major Bridges" in India, 1938. *Recreations:* swimming and small boat sailing. *Address:* c/o Miss A. Salberg, 15 Northbrook Road, Lee, S.E.13. *Club:* Junior Army and Navy. [*Died* 28 *Sept.* 1964.

SALISBURY, Frank O., C.V.O. 1938; R.P., R.O.I., R.I.; LL.D. St. Andrews,

1935; Cavaliere of the Order of the Crown of Italy, 1936; Doctor of Fine Art (U.S.); Portrait and Figure Painter, Historical and Ceremonial subjects; *b.* 18 December 1874; *m.* 1901, Alice Maude (*d.* 1951), *e. d.* of C. Colmer Greenwood; twin *d.* *Educ.:* privately; Heatherley's and Royal Academy Schools; studied in Italy, Germany, and France; exhibited first picture at Royal Academy 1899, and Paris Salon (Gold Medallist). Most important works: *Portraits:* various members of the Royal Family; Archbishops of Canterbury; Prime Ministers (Winston Churchill, Field-Marshal Smuts, Mackenzie King); President Coolidge, President Hoover, President Roosevelt (the official portrait for the White House), President Truman, President Eisenhower, Signor Mussolini, Secretary Mellon, H.H. Pope Pius XII, Cardinal Hayes, Ambassadors (Myron Taylor, Joseph E. Davies), Mrs. Joseph Davies, J. Pierpont Morgan, John D. Rockefeller, Jun., Mrs. John D. Rockefeller, and many portraits of other Americans. *Historical subjects:* The Passing of Queen Eleanor and Edward I, in St. Albans Abbey (to commemorate the deliverance of Jerusalem); Katherine of Aragon before the Consistory Courts at Blackfriars; The Burial of the Unknown Warrior, Westminster Abbey, 11th Nov. 1920; The great Roof, Westminster Hall, Richard II; in the Houses of Parliament; Three panels: Alfred the Great rebuilding the walls of the City of London; King George V. and Queen Mary visiting the battle districts of France; and the National Thanksgiving Service on the steps of St. Paul's, 1919, in the Royal Exchange; John Travers Cornwell, V.C., in Battle of Jutland, painted for the Admiralty; border design in colour for the Queen's letter to the men of the Navy, Army, and Air Force, 1918; also Queen Mary's letter to the Nation, 1936; The All Indian Queen Victoria Memorial, Calcutta, twelve Panels for large hall; The Princess Mary's Wedding; The King's Offering, The Installation of the Order of the Bath; The Heart of the Empire, large painting of The Jubilee Thanksgiving Service in St. Paul's Cathedral, May 6th 1935, in Buckingham Palace; The Reception of King George and Queen Mary at St. Paul's at Jubilee Service; The official coronation picture presented to King George and Queen Elizabeth by the Dominions; Panel to commemorate King George VI visit to Chamber of Shipping; Picture commemorating the King and Queen's visit to Canada, for the Hall of Fame, Parliament House, Ottawa; A large picture presented by H.M. Govt. to the Govt. of the Union of the Soviet Republics to commemorate the signature of the Anglo-Soviet treaty in London, May 26, 1942; Picture for the Guildhall of the Freedom of the City of London being conferred on the Prime Minister, Sir Winston Churchill; The Royal Thanksgiving Service in Canterbury Cathedral; The Dedication of the American Roll of Honour, St. Paul's Cathedral, July 4, 1951 (present to America by British Memorial Cttee.); King George VI opening The Festival of Britain from the Steps of St. Paul's, 1951 (presented by British Pilgrims to Pilgrims of America). Other works in London Museum, St. Andrews Univ., and Provincial Galleries; Master of the Worshipful Company of Glaziers, 1933-34. President Atlantic Charter Brotherhood. *Publications:* Portrait and Pageant; Sarum Chase. *Recreations:* motoring, gardening, tennis. *Address:* Sarum Chase, West Heath Road, Hampstead, N.W.3. *T.:* Hampstead 2405. *Clubs:* Arts, Garrick, Devonshire, Knights of the Round Table, Pilgrims, Royal Society of St. George. [*Died* 31 *Aug.* 1962.

SALLES, Georges Adolphe; Commander, Legion of Honour; Croix de Guerre (twice); Conservateur des Musées Nationaux; Président du Conseil Artistique des Musées Nationaux since 1961; Director-General, Musées de France, 1944-59; *b.* Sèvres, Seine-et-Oise, 24 Sept. 1889; *s.* of Adolphe Salles and Claire Eiffel. *Educ.:* Lycée Condorcet; Sorbonne; Faculté de Droit, Paris (Licencié en Droit Diplômé d'Études Supérieures de Philosophie, Licencié ès Lettres). Rédacteur, Direction des Beaux-Arts, 1921-24; Attaché Musées Nationaux; Professor, École du Louvre, 1926; Keeper, Department of Asiatic Art, Musée du Louvre, 1932; Director, Musée Guimet, 1941; Editor Revue des Arts asiatiques; Hon. Pres., Internat. Council of Museums. Served European War, 1914-18, and War, 1939-44. Hon. K.B.E. 1953. *Publications:* Le Regard, Étude d'esthétique; Au Louvre—scènes de la vie d'un grand musée; numerous articles and studies on the history of art and aesthetics. *Address:* 3 Rue Auguste Comte, Paris 6e. [*Died* 20 *Oct.* 1966.

SALMON, Barnett Alfred; Chairman of J. Lyons & Company Ltd. since 1961; Director: Strand Hotel Ltd.; Palace Hotel Ltd.; Alliance Assurance Co. Ltd.: Sun Alliance Insurance Ltd.; Vice-Patron, London Hospital; *b.* 10 November 1895; *e. s.* of late Alfred and Frances Salmon; *m.* 1928, Molly, *o. d.* of Michael and Elizabeth Cohen; one *s.* one *d.* *Educ.:* St. Paul's School; Emmanuel Coll., Cambridge. Served European War, 1914-18, Captain London Regiment. *Address:* 53 Orchard Court, Portman Square, W.1. [*Died* 30 *May* 1965.

SALMON, Frederick John, C.M.G. 1937; M.C.; Hon. Director, Bath Citizens' Advice Bureau; Chairman S.W. Regional Advisory Cttee. National Council of Social Service; Member of Council, Order of St. John, Somerset; late Lieut.-Colonel Regular Army Reserve of Officers, Royal Engineers; *b.* 12 July 1882; *s.* of Charles Spencer Salmon, Colonial Administrative Service, and Antoinette Hubert; *m.* 1923, Dorothy Hoysted, Melbourne, Australia; one *d.* *Educ.:* University College School and Central Technical College, London. Transvaal mines, 1904-07; Survey Dept., Ceylon, 1908-30; Field Survey Battalions in France, 1915-19; Lt.-Col., R.E. (M.C., despatches thrice); Director, Land and Surveys, Cyprus, 1930-1933; Director of Surveys, Palestine, 1933; Commissioner for Lands and Surveys and Member of Advisory Council Palestine, 1935-1938; Divisional Petroleum Officer, Bristol, 1939-42; Regional Fire Prevention Officer, Regional Headquarters, Bristol, 1942-45. A.C.G.I.; Order of St. John of Jerusalem. *Publications:* various contributions to technical journals and to Cornhill Magazine. *Recreations:* mountaineering, sketching, and usual outdoor sports. *Address:* Court Leet, Bathampton, near Bath. *T.:* Bath 88295. [*Died* 8 *July* 1964.

SALMON, Rev. Prebendary Harold Bryant; Prebendary of Whitlackington in Wells Cathedral since 1963; *b.* 1891; *e.* and *o. surv. s.* of late Rev. William Bryant Salmon, Rector of Stoke Newington; *m.* 1924, Margaret Elsie, *d.* of William Hammon Devenish, Bath; two *s.* two *d.* *Educ.:* Haileybury; Jesus College, Cambridge. Second Class Classical Tripos, 1912; First Class Theological Tripos, 1914; B.A. 1913; M.A. 1919; served European War, Royal Artillery, 1916-19; ordained Curate of St. George, Barrow-in-Furness, 1919; Vice-Principal of Wells Theological College, 1921; Curate of St. Mary Redcliffe, Bristol, 1924; Vicar of St. Michael, Windmill Hill, Bristol, 1925; Vicar of Holy Trinity, Southport, 1930; Principal of Wells Theological College, 1931-47; Rector of Weston-super-Mare, 1947-51; Chancellor of Wells Cathedral, 1935-47, Sub-Dean, 1947-51; Prebendary of Taunton in Wells Cathedral, 1930-51; Canon Residentiary, 1931-47 and

1951-62; Archdeacon of Wells and Prebendary of Huish and Brent, 1951-62. *Address:* Eastfield, North Rd., Wells, Som. [*Died* 2 *Nov.* 1965.

SALMOND, Marshal of the Royal Air Force Sir John (Maitland), G.C.B. *cr* 1931 (K.C.B., *cr.* 1919); C.M.G. 1917; C.V.O. 1918; D.S.O. 1914; *b.* 17 July 1881; *s.* of late Maj.-Gen. Sir W. Salmond, K.C.B.; *m.* 1st, 1913, Helen Amy Joy Lumsden (*d.* 1916); one *d.*; 2nd, 1924, Hon. Monica Grenfell (author of Bright Armour, 1935), *er. d.* of Baron Desborough, K.G.; one *s.* one *d.* *Educ.:* Wellington, Sandhurst. Entered army, 1901; Captain, 1910; Bt. Maj. 1914; Major, 1916; Lieut.-Col. 1915; Bt. Col. 1917; Maj.-Gen. 1917; Air Marshal, 1923; Air Chief Marshal, 1929; Marshal of the Royal Air Force, 1933; Royal Flying Corps, 1912; Instructor, Central Flying School, 1912; Director-General of Military Aeronautics and on Army Council, 1917; Commanded R.F.C. and R.A.F. in the Field, 1918-19; Air Officer Commanding Inland Area, 1920-22; Air Officer Commanding British Forces in Iraq, 1922-24; Air Officer Commanding-in-Chief, Air Defence of Great Britain, 1925-29; Air Member for Personnel on Air Council, 1929-30; Principal Air A.D.C. to the King, 1925-30; Chief of the Air Staff, 1930-33; a Government Director, Imperial Airways, 1933; at request of the Governments of Australia and New Zealand, visited these countries in 1928 to make recommendations regarding the future development of their Air Forces; served South African War, 1901-2 (Queen's medal, 3 clasps); West African Frontier Force, 1903-05; European War, 1914-18 (despatches five times, D.S.O., C.M.G., Legion of Honour, Croix de Guerre (France and Belgian), Order of Leopold, Russian White Eagle); War of 1939-45, Director of Armament Production, Ministry of Aircraft Production: Director General Flying Control and Air Sea Rescue, Air Ministry. Hon. LL.D. Cambridge, 1919; Hon. D.C.L. Oxford. *Address:* The Old Inn, Keere St., Lewes, Sussex. *T.:* Lewes 4722. *Clubs:* Naval and Military, Bath, Royal Air Force. [*Died* 16 *April* 1968.

SALT, Sir Edward William, Kt., *cr* 1945; *b.* 18 May 1881; *s.* of Ashton Trow Salt and Emily Ward; *m.* 1910, Alice Elizabeth Edmunds (*d.* 1945); one *s.* three *d.* *Educ.:* Camp Hill Grammar School. In Paris business and educational, 1900-02; Chairman of Salt and Son Ltd., 5, 6 and 7 Cherry Street, Birmingham, 1903; during War joined Worcestershire Yeomanry; Chairman of British Artificial Limb Association, 1922; Birmingham City Council for Small Heath Ward, 1924; re-elected 1927 and 1930; Parliamentary Candidate for Unionist Party, Yardley Division, 1929; M.P. (U.) Yardley (Birmingham), 1931-1945; Chairman, The Parliamentary and Scientific Committee.; High Sheriff of Warwickshire, 1952. *Recreations:* golf, fishing. *Address:* Helston, Avenue Rd., Stratford-on-Avon, Warwicks. *T.:* Stratford-on-Avon 2728. *Club:* Midland Conservative (Birmingham). [*Died* 8 *Sept.* 1970.

SALT, Henry Edwin, M.A., LL.B. Cantab.; Q.C. 1946; Chancellor, County Palatine of Durham, 1960-69; *o. surv. s.* of late Henry Salt, Greystones, Leek, Staffs; *m.* 1926, Hope Mountfort, M.B., Ch.B., B.Sc., *o. d.* of J. Mountfort Johnson, M.D.; one *d.* (decd.). *Educ.:* Newcastle-under-Lyme; Trinity College, Cambridge. Entrance Scholar, 1915, Senior Scholar, 1920, Fellow, 1924, Law Lecturer, 1924-26, Trinity Coll., Cambridge. Served European War, 1914-18; Lieut. 5th North Stafford Regt., 1916-19; Western Front; War of 1939-45, Home Guard, 1940-44. Called to Bar, Gray's Inn, 1923 (Arden Prizeman, 1922); Bencher, 1943; Treasurer of Gray's Inn for 1959, Vice-Treasurer for 1960. Choate Fellow, Harvard Univ., 1923-24; Yorke Prizeman Cambridge, 1924; Lectr. Law Society's School of Law, 1926-31, and thereafter successively Assistant Reader and Reader to the Inns of Court; retd. 1968, now Senior Reader Emeritus (first conferment of this title); Member of Bentham Committee, and of Bar Council, 1942-46; Member Interdepartmental (Curtis) Committee (1945-46) on Care of Children; Member Prime Minister's (Nathan) Committee (1950-52) on Charitable Trusts and author of Minority Report; Chancellor of Diocese of Birmingham, 1957-70. Hon. D.C.L. Dunelm. *Publications:* The Local Ambit of a Custom (Cambridge Legal Essays), 1926; (with H. E. Francis) Eleventh Edition of Lindley on Partnership, 1951; Easement and Profits in Halsbury's Laws of England, Third Edition, 1955. *Recreations:* swimming, squash racquets. *Address:* 14 Park Lane, Southwold, Suffolk. *T.:* Southwold 3322. *Clubs:* Cambridge Union; Durham County. [*Died* 11 *June* 1970.

SALT, Lt.-Col. Sir Thomas Henry, 3rd Bt., *cr.* 1899; D.L., J.P.; late Duke of Cornwall's Light Infantry; County Commissioner for Boy Scouts in Dorset, 1945-55; *b.* 26 Nov. 1905; *s.* of Col. Sir Thomas A. Salt, 2nd Bt., D.S.O., and Elinor Mary, *d.* of Sir H. A. Wiggin, 2nd Bt.; *S.* father, 1940; *m.* 1943, Meriel Sophia Wilmot, *d.* of late Capt. Berkeley C. W. Williams and Hon. Mrs. Williams, Herringston, Dorchester; two *s.* two *d.* *Educ.:* Eton; R.M.C., Sandhurst. A.D.C. to Governor of Malta, 1931-34; Assistant Defence Security Officer, Malta 1934-36. Retired pay, 1948. D.L. 1949, J.P. 1952, High Sheriff, 1954-55, Dorset. *Heir:* *s.* Thomas Michael John, *b.* 7 Nov. 1946. *Address:* Shillingstone House, Shillingstone, Dorset. *T.:* Childe Okeford 259. [*Died* 15 *Aug.* 1965.

SALTER, Emma G.; *see* Gurney-Salter.

SALTER, Frank Reyner, O.B.E. 1944; Fellow, Magdalene College, Cambridge, since 1910; *b.* 7 May 1887; *s.* of William Henry Gurney Salter and Jane Reyner; *m.* 1923, Janie Eadie Barclay (*d.* 1967), *d.* of Rev. James Craig, Kirkpatrick-Durham, Kirkcudbrightshire; one *d.* *Educ.:* St. Paul's School; Trinity College, Cambridge (Scholar). 1st Class Historical Tripos Part I, 1907; and Part II, 1908. Magdalene Coll., Cambridge: Fellow, 1910, Tutor, 1927-45; Senior Tutor, 1940-45, Pres., 1951-57. Univ. Lectr. in History, 1926-52. Warden, Madingley Hall, Cambridge, 1954-61; Served European War, 1914-18: Rifle Brigade and later as Staff-Capt. and G.S.O. 3; War of 1939-45: Army Welfare Officer with Acting Rank (unpaid) of Lieut.-Col. (O.B.E.). County Welfare Officer for Cambridge, 1946. Chm. Camb. Univ. Bd. of Extra-Mural Studies, 1946-57; Mem. Council, City of Cambridge, 1953-65; Governor Thomas Wall Trust, 1947; Governor Gilchrist Trust, 1957-; Governor, St. Paul's Sch., 1954-67; Member Nat. Advisory Council on Educn. for Industry and Commerce, 1948; Vice-Chm., E. Anglian Regional Advisory Council for Further Educ., 1950-64; Mem. various Cttees. connected with Adult Education. Hon. Treas. Econ. Hist. Soc., 1941-54. Contested (L.) Cambridge, 1924; Pres. Camb. Borough Liberal Assoc., 1949-62. *Publications:* Karl Marx and Modern Socialism, 1921; Sir Thomas Gresham, 1925; Some early Tracts on Poor Relief, 1926; St. Paul's School, 1909-1959, 1959. Articles in Camb. Hist. Journal and Econ. Hist. Review. *Address:* 69 Storey's Way, Cambridge. *T.:* 52608; Broome House, Polseath, N. Cornwall. *Club:* Oxford and Cambridge. [*Died* 22 *Nov.* 1967.

SALUSBURY, Charles Vanne, C.S.I. 1946; C.I.E. 1942; V.D.; I.C.S., retired; *b.* 15 Feb. 1887; *s.* of Rev. Charles Thelwall and Florence Salusbury; *m.* 1929, Kathleen

Helen Esther Craik; two *s.* *Educ.:* Magdalen College School; Hertford College, Oxford. Indian Civil Service in Punjab, Bikanir, Kashmir State, North-West Frontier Province, Government of India. *Publications:* Settlement Reports of Hissar and Lyallpur Districts, Punjab. *Address:* St. Georges', Tidenham, Glos *T.* Chepstow 2409. [*Died* 13 *May* 1969.

SAMMONS, Herbert, C.B.E. 1952; *b.* 26 Feb. 1896; *s.* of Thomas Rotherham and Caroline Sammons; *m.* 1st; one *s.*; 2nd, 1951, Margery May Perrins, Melbourne, Australia; one *d.* *Educ.:* Bablake Secondary School, Coventry. Petters Ltd., Yeovil; Chief Designer, 1922-26, Chief Engineer, 1926-34. General Manager of a Works of Armstrong Whitworth (Engineers) Ltd., Newcastle upon Tyne, 1934-42; Chief Engineer of D. Napier & Son Ltd., 1942-49. Managing Dir., 1949-60, retd. (Jt.) George R. Henderson Medal of Franklin Inst., 1960. *Recreation:* golf. *Address:* Hope Cottage, Box, Nr. Stroud, Glos. [*Died* 23 *Sept.* 1967.

SAMPSON, Rev. Canon Christopher Bolckow; a Residentary Canon of Ripon Cathedral, 1961-66; Canon Emeritus, 1966; Chaplain to H.M. the Queen, since 1958; *b.* 9 Oct. 1903; *o. surv. s.* of late C. H. Sampson, M.A., Principal of Brasenose Coll., Oxford; *m.* 1928, Nancy José Fenton (*d.* 1966), *d.* of late Myles F. Davies, solicitor, Manchester; two *d.* *Educ.:* Bradfield College; Oriel College, Oxford (B.A. 1926; M.A. 1929); Wells Theological College. Deacon, 1927; priest, 1928; Curate of Armley, Leeds, 1927; Curate of Headingley, Leeds, 1930; Senior Curate of Leeds Parish Church, 1933; Vicar of Chapel Allerton, Leeds, 1937-47; Vicar of Maidstone, Kent, 1947-54; Rural Dean of Sutton (diocese of Canterbury), 1947-54; Hon. Canon of Canterbury, 1947-54; Vicar of Leeds and Hon. Canon of Ripon, 1954-61; Rural Dean of Leeds, 1954-61. Proctor in Convocation of Canterbury, 1950-52; Proctor in Convocation of York, 1954-61. *Recreation:* music. *Address:* c/o Westminster Bank Ltd., Park Row, Leeds 1. *Club:* Leeds (Leeds). [*Died* 21 *Nov.* 1967.

SAMPSON, Herbert E., Q.C.; Barrister-at-law, retired; *b.* 13 May 1871; *s.* of Thomas E. Sampson and Margaret A. McKee; *m.* 1899; two *s.* one *d.* *Educ.:* Public Schools, Toronto (Scholarship and Gold Medallist); Toronto Collegiate Institute (Scholarship and Head Boy); Toronto Univ. (Honour Graduate in Arts and Law); Osgoode Hall, Toronto (Scholarship and Gold Medallist); Q.C., Saskatchewan, 1916; sometime Pres. of the Law Society of Saskatchewan, and Bencher for life. Past Pres. Saskatchewan Div., Navy League of Canada. *Recreation:* mountain climbing. *Address:* 1820 College Avenue, Regina, Canada. *T.:* LA 2-4545. *Clubs:* Past Pres.: Canadian, Alpine of Canada, Tennis, Boat, Rotary, Wascana Winter (Regina). [*Died* 16 *Sept.* 1962.

SAMUEL, 1st Viscount, *cr.* 1937, of Mount Carmel and of Toxteth, Liverpool; **Herbert Louis Samuel,** P.C. 1908; G.C.B. 1926; O.M. 1958; G.B.E. 1920; M.A.; Hon. D.C.L. (Oxford); Hon. LL.D. (Camb. and Liverpool); Hon. Litt.D. (Leeds); Hon. Ph.D. (Jerusalem); Liberal Leader, House of Lords, 1944-55; *b.* Liverpool, 6 November 1870; *s.* of Edwin L. Samuel and Clara Yates; *m.* 1897, Beatrice (*d.* 1959), *y. d.* of Ellis A. Franklin; three *s.* one *d.* *Educ.:* University Coll. School; Balliol Coll., Oxford (Hon. Fellow, 1935; Visitor, 1946-57). First Class Hons., Oxford, 1893; contested (L.) S. Oxfordshire, 1895 and 1900; M.P. (L.) Cleveland Div., N. Riding, Yorkshire, 1902-18; M.P. (L.) Darwen division Lancs. 1929-35; Parliamentary Under-Secretary Home Dept. 1905-09; Chancellor of the Duchy of Lancaster (with a seat in the Cabinet), 1909-10 and 1915-16; Postmaster-General, 1910-14 and 1915-16; President of the Local Government Board, 1914-15; Secretary of State for Home Affairs, 1916; Chairman of Select Committee of House of Commons on National Expenditure, 1917-18; British Special Commissioner to Belgium, 1919; High Commissioner, Palestine, 1920-1925; Chairman, Royal Commission on Coal Industry, 1925; Chairman of the Liberal Party Organization, 1927-29; Leader of the Liberal Parliamentary Party, 1931-35; Secy. of State for Home Affairs, 1931-32. President: Royal Statistical Soc., 1918-20; Royal (formerly British) Inst. of Philosophy, 1931-59; Roy. Asiatic Soc., 1940-43; English Assoc., 1941; Classical Assoc., 1953. Lecturer: Herbert Spencer, Oxford, 1941; Romanes, Oxford, 1947; National Book League, 1949; Roscoe, Liverpool, 1952; Hibbert Trust Centenary, 1953; Eleanor Rathbone Memorial, Manchester, 1954. Hon. Fellow R.I.B.A., 1948; Hon. Freeman of the Metropolitan Borough of Paddington, 1951. Grand Officer of the Order of Leopold of Belgium, 1919; Assoc. Kt. of Order of St. John of Jerusalem, 1946. *Publications:* Liberalism: its Principles and Proposals, 1902; The War and Liberty, 1917; Philosophy and the Ordinary Man, 1932; The Tree of Good and Evil, 1933; Practical Ethics, 1935; Belief and Action: An Everyday Philosophy, 1937 (new edn. 1953); An Unknown Land, 1942; Memoirs, 1945; A Book of Quotations, 1947 (new edn. 1954); Creative Man, and Other Addresses, 1949; Essay in Physics, 1951; In Search of Reality, 1957; (with Prof. H. Dingle) A Threefold Cord: Philosophy, Science, Religion, 1961. *Relevant Publication:* Viscount Samuel, by Professor John Bowle, 1957. *Heir:* *s.* Hon. Edwin H. Samuel, C.M.G. *Address:* 32 Porchester Terrace, W.2. *T.:* Paddington 0040. *Clubs:* Reform, National Liberal. [*Died* 5 *Feb.* 1963.

SAMUEL, Sir Edward Louis, 3rd Bt., *cr.* 1898; late Captain R.F.A.; Major, R.A. (served, 1940-46, with R.F.A.); *b.* 6 Nov. 1896; *o. s.* of Sir Edward L. Samuel, 2nd Bt.; *S* father, 1937. *Educ.:* Repton. Served European War with R.F.A., 1914-18; Bursar, Prince of Wales Builder Fund of Toc H, 1928-40. *Recreations:* agriculture, hunting, tennis, music. *Heir:* cousin, John Oliver Cecil Samuel, *b.* 1916. *Clubs:* Junior Carlton, M.C.C. [*Died* 25 *April* 1961.

SAMUEL, John Augustus, C.I.E. 1943; B.A.; LL.B.; *b.* 3 Feb. 1887; *s.* of Charles Samuel and Clara Hasell; *m* 1910, Agnes Thirza Allerton; one *s.* two *d.* (and one *d.* decd.). *Educ.:* Queen's Royal College, Trinidad; Selwyn College, Cambridge. S.P.G. mission, Ranchi, India, 1914-17, as teacher in schools, legal adviser and organiser of co-operative village societies; Asst. Legal Remembrancer and Asst. Secretary of Bihar Legislative Council, 1917-21; Asst. Secretary, Legislative Dept., Bihar, 1922-24; Deputy Sec. 1924-38; Sec. 1939-43. Silver Jubilee Medal, 1935; Coronation Medal, 1937. *Publication:* The Bihar and Orissa Code, 3 vols., 1932-36. *Recreations:* golf, cricket, tennis. *Address:* 155 Great North Way, N.W.4. *T.:* Sunnyhill 3899. [*Died* 26 *Jan.* 1965.

SAMUEL, Sir John (Oliver Cecil), 4th Bt. *cr.* 1898; Company Director (private companies); *b.* 24 June 1916; *s.* of Lt.-Col. Henri Saul Samuel (3rd *s.* of 1st Bt.) and Eva, *d.* of late Joseph Fulton, The Glen, Renfrewshire; *S.* cousin, Sir Edward Louis Samuel, 3rd Bt., 1961; *m.* 1942, Charlotte Mary, *d.* of late Robert H. Hoyt, Calgary,

Alberta, Canada; one *s.* one *d.* *Educ.:* Radley. Served War as Flt./Lt. (Pilot) R.A.F.V.R., 1940-45. Racing Driver, 1935-1938; Life Mem., British Racing Driver's Club. *Recreations:* flying, motor racing, swimming, light railways. *Heir:* *s.* Jon Michael Glen Samuel, *b.* 25 Jan. 1944. *Address:* Greywood, Burwood Park, Walton-on-Thames, Surrey. [*Died* 24 *Oct.* 1962.

SANDBURG, Carl; *b.* Galesburg, Ill., 6 Jan. 1878; *s.* of August Sandburg and Clara Anderson; *m.* 1908, Lillian Steichen, Milwaukee; three *d.* *Educ.:* Lombard College, Galesburg. Secretary to Mayor of Milwaukee, 1910-1912; associate editor, System Magazine, Chicago, 1913; editorial writer, Chicago Daily News; Levinson Prize, Poetry Magazine, 1914; shared one-half prize of Poetry Society of America (Pulitzer award), 1919 and 1921; Pulitzer prize for Poetry, 1951. Amer. Acad. Arts and Letters Gold Medal for Hist. and Biog., 1952; Private, Co. C 6th Ill. Vols. 1898; active service in Porto Rico; Mem., editorial bd. Nat. Labor Defence Coun.; Stockholm Correspondent Newspaper Enterprise Assoc., 1918; Lecturer, University of Hawaii, 1934; writer of Commentary for U.S.A. Government film, Bomber, 1941, and of pamphlet, What Would Lincoln do Now?, for U.S.A. Department of the Treasury, 1942; 1941-45, weekly columnist syndicated by The Chicago Times in 22 newspapers. Holds several Honorary Doctorates. Commander, Order of the North Star, Sweden, 1953. *Publications:* Chicago Poems 1916; Cornhuskers 1918; The Chicago Race Riots 1919; Smoke and Steel, 1920; Slabs of the Sunburnt West, 1922; Rootabaga Stories, 1922; Rootabaga Pigeons, 1923; Abraham Lincoln: The Prairie Years: (2 vols.), 1926; The American Songbag, 1927; Good Morning, America, 1928; Steichen the Photographer, 1929; Potato Face; Early Moon, 1930; Mary Lincoln: Wife and Widow, 1932; The People, Yes, 1936; Abraham Lincoln: The War Years: (4 vols.), 1939; Storm Over the Land, 1942; Home Front Memo, 1943; The Photographs of Abraham Lincoln, 1944 (with Frederick H. Merserve); Remembrance Rock, 1948; Lincoln Collector, 1949; Complete Poems, New American Songbag, 1950; Always the Young Strangers, 1953; Abraham Lincoln: The Prairie Years, the War Years: (1 vol.), 1954; The Sandburg Range, 1957; Wind Song, 1960; Honey and Salt, 1963. *Address:* Flat Rock, North Carolina, U.S.A. [*Died* 22 *July* 1967.

SANDEMAN, Col. Donald George, C.I.E. 1926; late Q.V.O. Corps of Guides, Indian Army; *b.* Naini Tal, India, 14 Oct. 1884; *s.* of Colonel J. E. Sandeman, late Indian Survey Department, *nephew* of Sir Robert Sandeman, K.C.S.I., late Indian Political Department; *m.* 1st, 1920, Isabel Stella (*d.* 1941), *d.* of late John Cockburn, North Berwick; one *s.* two *d.*; *m.* 1946, Sophia Patricia, *widow* of Captain Godfrey Meynell, V.C., M.C., Q.V.O. Corps of Guides, Meynell Langley, Derby. *Educ.:* Haileybury; Sandhurst. Commissioned 1903; attached to 2nd Bn. Royal Irish Fusiliers, 1903-4; appointed to 25th Punjabis, Indian Army, 1904; transferred to Q.V.O. Corps of Guides, 1904; General Staff, Intelligence, Army Headquarters, 1919-24; Commandant Kitchener College, India, 1932-33; President Cantonment Board Secunderabad and Joint Secretary for Education, Hyderabad Administered Areas, 1933-34; Comdt. Mewar Bhil Corps and Assistant Resident in Mewar, 1935-36; served Zakka Khel Expedition, 1908; Mohmund Expedition, 1908; European War, North-West Frontier, 1915-16 (despatches); Mesopotamia, 1917; Palestine and Syria, 1918 (despatches); 3rd Afghan War, 1919; Waziristan, Razmak Field Force, 1922 (despatches); Brevet Col. 1931; Col. 1932; War of 1939-45; Home Guard, 1940; Chief Umpire, Orkney and Shetland Defences, 1941-43. *Address:* Meynell, Langley, Derby. [*Died* 13 *Sept.* 1965.

SANDERS, Alan; owner and editor of nine County of London weekly newspapers (The United Metropolitan Press, Ltd.); *b.* Leven, East Yorks, 28 Aug. 1878; *yr. s.* of Richard George Sanders, Leven, and Margaret Elinor Hudson, Catfoss Manor, Yorks; *m.* 1912, Elinor (*d.* 1960), *o. d.* of James Thomas Brennan, London; no c. *Educ.:* privately; Hull Gram. Sch. Started in journalism on Spalding Guardian, 1893; thence progressively Hull Daily News and Hull News 1896, Eastern Morning News and Hull Daily News 1898, Northants (Kettering) Evening Telegraph and Leader 1902, London Evening News 1904, London Daily Mirror 1905, London Evening News 1909-17; founded Marylebone Chronicle, Paddington News, and Westminster Chronicle, 1919; F.J.I.; Member of Newspaper Society. Has travelled extensively in Europe and America. *Publications:* A History of Albany, 1920; some two thousand poems, monologues, and songs, including The Sweetest Face, The Master to his Dog, Tommy Out East, Were I a Star, My Island of Wonderful Dreams, Farewell!, The Lily, etc.; has written largely on London antiquities under pen name of Civis, and contributed to principal magazines. *Address:* 6 Gardner House, Regent's Park, N.W.1. *Club:* National Liberal. [*Died* 1 *May* 1969.

SANDERS, Rev. Henry Martyn, M.A., Prebendary of St. Paul's, 1942-60, Emeritus, 1960; Priest in Ordinary to the Queen, 1962; Rector, All Hallows-on-the-Wall, E.C.2, 1933-54; *b.* 1869; *s.* of late Canon Lewis Sanders, Newcastle upon Tyne; *m.* Maude Mary (*d.* 1952), *d.* of late Canon J. G. Dixon, Roch; one *s.* *Educ.:* Royal Gram. Sch., Newcastle upon Tyne; Queens' Coll., Camb. (Schol., Hughes Prizeman). Ordained, 1892; Mem. of Council, Pan-Anglican Congress, 1906-8; Vicar of St. John's, Highbury, 1899-1911; H.C.F., 1915-18; S. Stephen, Twickenham, 1911-33; Editor of St. Paul's Review, 1930-37; of Teaching Church Review, 1943; (Hon.) Chaplain, Roedean School, 1934-38; London Area Rep. of C.C.M.F., 1942-, Oxford, 1959-; Select Preacher, Cambridge, 1942; Archbishops' Visitor to the Forces, 1944; Hon. Theological Adviser to R.F.C. and R.A.F. Chaplains; Gresham Professor in Divinity, 1946; Preacher, Lincoln's Inn, 1957; Hon. Chaplain to Archbishop of Canterbury, 1958. B.Sc. (Durham), 1959. *Publications:* The Message of the Church, 1909; works on Christian apologetics. *Club:* Oxford and Cambridge. [*Died* 28 *Jan.* 1963.

SANDERS, Sir Percy (Alan), Kt., *cr.* 1954; C.B.E. 1948 (O.B.E. 1918); D.L., J.P. (Essex); A.M.I.Mech.E.; Director, Davey, Paxman & Co. Ltd., Colchester; Chairman: E. N. Mason & Sons Ltd., Colchester; Criterion, Plates, Paper, Films Ltd., Birmingham; Director of other Companies; *b.* 7 May 1881; *s.* of E. J. Sanders, J.P., and E. F. Sanders. *Educ.:* Felsted; Union College, U.S.A. Engineer Apprenticeship, Davey, Paxman & Co. Ltd. 1898-1904; General Electric Co., U.S.A., 1904-06; British Westinghouse Co. Ltd., 1906-12; Davey, Paxman & Co. Ltd.: Director, 1912; Man. Dir. (25 yrs.). Chm. Assoc. Shell Boiler Makers (3 yrs.); Chm. Combustion Engineering Assoc. (2 yrs.); Pres. E. Anglian Assoc. Engineering Employers Fed. (many times); Mem. Nat. Council, 1914; Management Bd. and Policy Cttee., Eng. and Allied Employers Nat. Fedn. Commissioned and attached to Essex Regt., Sept. 1914-18. Colchester Borough Council, 1915-45: Alderman, 1930-45; Mayor, 1922-23 and 1939-43; Hon. Freedom of Colchester, 1944; High Steward, 1950-. C.C. Essex, 1919-59, C.A. 1946-59; J.P. Essex and Colchester, 1923-; D.L. Essex, 1942-; Chm. Colchester Justices, 1950-56: Chm.

Colchester Div. Conservative Assoc., 1918-48 (now Pres.). Hon. Freeman, City of London, 1946; Liveryman, Worshipful Company of Farriers, 1946. Chairman: Lord Roberts Workshops, Colchester, 1919-; Forces Help Soc. (Nat.) and Lord Roberts Workshops 1949-59; many County and local bodies *Recreation:* gardening. *Address:* Northwood, 82 Lexden Road, Colchester, Essex. *T.:* Colchester 3194. [*Died* 22 *Feb.* 1962.

SANDERSON, Sir Frank Bernard, 1st Bt., *cr.* 1920; Chairman, Humber Fishing Co. Ltd. since 1924; Director, Salts (Saltaire) Ltd. and J. & J. Crombie Ltd. (Chairman, 1923-58); a Member of Lloyd's; a Trustee Stowe School, Buckingham; President King Edward Memorial Hospital, W.13; Founder of Wray, Sanderson & Co. Ltd.; *b.* 4 Oct. 1880; 7th *s.* of late John Sanderson; *m.* 1st, 1904, Amy Edith (*d.* 1949), *d.* of late David Wing, Scarborough; two *s.* one *d.*; 2nd, 1951, Joan, *o. d.* of late H. Cubberley, Hill Court, W.5. Controller (unpaid) Trench Warfare National Shell Filling Factories and Stores, Ministry of Munitions, 1915-19; and of Aircraft Ammunition Filling, and Chemical Ammunition Filling, 1916-19. M.P. (C.) East Ealing, 1931-50; M.P. (C.) Darwen Div. (Lancs) 1922-23, and 1924-29; contested, May 1929; Member of the Parl. Delegation to Poland, 1925; Member of the Empire Parliamentary Delegation to Canada, 1928; Member of Inter-Parliamentary Union, British Group, Hague Conf., 1938, St. Moritz, 1946, Cairo, 1947, Member of Council, 1947, Vice-Chm. 1948-50; Vice-Pres. Rome Conf., 1948; Member of deleg. to Stockholm, 1949, Dublin, 1950, Berne, 1952, Washington, 1953, Vienna, 1954, Rome, 1955, Brussels, 1961; Chm. Standing Finance Cttee., Geneva, 1949; elected permanent Mem. Inter-Parliamentary Union, 1950; Member: Public Accounts Cttee. House of Commons, 1942-50; Council of Anglo-Egyptian Chamber of Commerce, 1940-, Chm., 1949-54; Vice-Pres. Anglo-Egyptian Soc. Diploma and Médaille de Vermeil de la Reconnaissance Française, 1949. *Heir: e. s.* Lt.-Commander Frank Philip Bryan Sanderson, R.N.V.R. [*b.* 18 Feb. 1910; *m.* 1933, Annette Irene Caroline, *d.* of late Korab Laskowski, Warsaw, and *g. d.* of late Gen. Count de Castellaz; two *s.* one *d.* *Educ.:* Stowe; Pembroke College, Oxford. Served War of 1939-45]. *Address:* 48 Grosvenor Square, W.1. *T.:* Grosvenor 1373. *Clubs:* 1900, Carlton. [*Died* 18 *July* 1965.

SANDERSON, Sir Harold Leslie, Kt., *cr.* 1946; D.C.M. 1914; *b.* 6 Sept. 1890; *s.* of Robert Alexander Sanderson and Elizabeth Smith; *m.* 1922, Maude Isolde Smieton; no *c.* *Educ.:* Blackheath School. 1st Bn. London Scottish, Belgium and France, 1914-1915 (D.C.M., wounded). Royal Commission on Wheat Supplies, 1918; partner Charles Wimble Sons & Co., 1921-53; Director of Rice, Ministry of Food, 1941-52; Chairman London Rice Brokers' Association, 1953. *Address:* c/o Midland Bank Ltd., 135 Fenchurch St., E.C.3. *Club:* Queen's. [*Died* 23 *July* 1966.

SANDERSON, William Allendale; Secretary, United Kingdom and British Commonwealth branch of the Calouste Gulbenkian Foundation, since 1956; *b.* 25 Jan. 1913; *o. s.* of late Robert Sanderson, C.I.E., and Mrs. Jean Sanderson; *m.* 1938, Evelyn Ioni, *o. d.* of Major G. J. R. Potter and Mrs. E. A. Potter; two *s.* two *d.* *Educ.:* Bow School, Durham; Clifton College, Bristol; St. John Baptist College, Oxford (open classical exhibitioner and M.A.). Messrs. Samson Clark & Co. Ltd., advertising agency, 1936-39; Intelligence Div., Naval Staff, Admiralty, 1940-43; Staff of Supreme Allied Commander South-East Asia, 1943-45; Lieut.-Comdr. (temp. Sub-Lieut.) R.N.V.R. Special Branch. Asst. Dir., Nuffield Foundation, 1945-57; Asst. Sec., Nuffield Provincial Hospitals Trust, 1945-55; Sec., Nat. Corp. for the Care of Old People, 1947-48; European Sec., Social Research Cttee., Internat. Assoc. of Gerontology. Hon. Member of Società Italiana di Gerontologia e Geriatria. Mem. editorial board of Twentieth Century. *Publications:* articles and reviews in Nature, Twentieth Century, etc. *Recreation:* gardening. *Address:* Bovingdon Ash, Bovingdon, Herts. *T.:* Bovingdon 2250. *Clubs:* Reform, R.N.V.R. [*Died* 21 *May* 1961.

SANDES, Alfred J. T. F.; *see* Fleming-Sandes.

SANDFORD, Brigadier Francis Rossall, C.B.E. 1941; M.C.; T.D.; M.B.; *b.* 2 Sept. 1898; 2nd *s.* of late Francis Berkeley Sandford, M.A., Roselands, Ambleside; *m.* 1925, Delphine Mary, *d.* of late Dr. Francis Richard Gibbs, Bourne End; one *s.* one *d.* *Educ.:* St. Bees School; Queens' Coll., Cambridge (Scholar); Middlesex Hosp., London (University Scholar). House Surgeon, Middlesex Hospital, 1924-25; served European War, 1917-19 in Royal Artillery, France and Belgium (M.C., despatches); served War of 1939-45 (despatches, C.B.E., Comdr. Roy. Order George I of Greece); A.D.M.S. 43rd (Wessex) Div., 1938-42 and 1947-50; D.D.M.S. 3rd Corps and Land Forces, Greece, 1942-45; Hon. Col. 43rd (Wessex) Div., R.A.M.C., 1946-51; Hon. Physician to the Queen, 1952-54 (to King George VI 1949-52). *Address:* 38 Barnfield Road, Exeter. *T.A.* and *T.:* Exeter 73743. [*Died* 28 *Oct.* 1962.

SANDFORD, Thomas Frederick, C.M.G. 1935; M.B.E. 1919; *b.* 7 Aug. 1886; *s.* of late Ven. Ernest Gray Sandford, Archdeacon of Exeter, and Ethel Maria Ruscombe Poole; *m.* 1912, Rachel Dorothy Foord; three *s.* one *d.* *Educ.:* Marlborough College; Oriel College, Oxford. Probationer N.E. Rhodesia, 1908; Private Sec., Administrator N.E.R., 1909; Native Comr., N. Rhodesia, 1913; E. Afric. Campaign, 1918-19, Capt.; Asst. Magistrate, 1924; Provincial Commissioner, 1932; Senior Prov. Comr. 1936; Member Exec. and Legislative Council, 1932, 1936-44; Chm. New Capital Construction Advisory Cttee. at Lusaka, 1933-35; Sec. for Native Affairs, N. Rhodesia, 1939-44; temp. Admin. Officer, C.O., 1944-1946; on special commission to British Honduras, 1947; Hon. Treas. Univs.' Mission to Cent. Africa, 1948-57; Hon. Lay Sec. Church Assembly Overseas Council, 1949-58; Hon. Treas. The Mothers' Union, 1950-57; Mem. Roy. Commonwealth Soc. *Recreation:* walking. *Address:* 60 High Street, Eaton Bray, Beds. [*Died* 21 *Sept.* 1963.

SANDHURST, 4th Baron, *cr.* 1871, **Ralph Sheldon Mansfield,** O.B.E.; late Capt. R.E.; *b.* 1892; *o. s.* of 3rd Baron and Edith Mary (*d.* 1939), *d.* of John Higson; *S.* father 1933; *m.* 1917, Victoria Morley (*d.* 1961), *o. c.* of Edward Berners Upcher of Kirby, Cane, Sheringham; two *s.* one *d.* *Educ.:* Winchester; Trinity College, Cambridge, B.A. Enlisted Royal Engineers (Signal Service), Aug. 1914; received commission, Sept. 1914 (despatches, O.B.E.); London Organising Secretary Royal National Lifeboat Institution, 1922-35. Employed Maj. Royal Corps of Signals, 1939; Lt.-Col. 1942; retired, 1945. Chairman British Road Federation, 1946-54. *Heir: s.* Hon. (John Edward) Terence Mansfield (now Lord Sandhurst), D.F.C. 1944; Man. Dir., Leslie Rankin, Ltd. [*b.* 4 Sept. 1920; *m.* 1st, 1942, Priscilla Ann (from whom he obt. a div., 1946), *yr. d.* of late J. Fielder Johnson; 2nd, 1947, Janet Mary, *er. d.* of late John E. Lloyd, New York; one *s.* one *d.*]. *Address:* Fairways, Worlington, Bury St. Edmunds. [*Died* 28 *Oct.* 1964.

SANDILANDS, George Sommerville; F.R.S.A.; Cav. della Corona d'Italia; Hon. A.R.C.A.; Art Critic; Governor Chelsea Polytechnic; *b.* Glasgow, 1889; *s.* of John Sandilands, Lanark, and Isabella Sinclair Sandilands, Caithness; *m.* 1921, Florence May Bonner; two *s.* *Educ.:* High School, Glasgow; Univ. Coll., London. Army, 1914-1919; Secretary Faculty of Arts French Institute, 1921-39; Registrar of Royal Coll. of Art S. Kensington, 1939-49; contested Harrow, 1931, Chelsea, 1935; Town Councillor Ealing, 1929-32; contributor to The Studio and to almost all the London dailies. Officier d'Académie, 1929; London County Council Lecturer. Exhibited paintings and etchings: Royal Academy, New English National Society, Royal Soc. of British Artists, R.Inst. of Oil Painters, etc. *Publications:* The Enthusiast, and other Poems; Atalanta, or The Future of Sport (To-day and To-morrow Series) (English and American editions); The Water-Colours of Frank Brangwyn, R.A.; The Water-Colours of W. Russell Flint, A.R.A.; The Water-Colours of J. M. W. Turner, R.A.; The Water-Colours of R. P. Bonington; Artists' Country, 1932; Studio Colour Plate Annual, 1937; The Lakes (An Anthology), 1947; Festival Play; Dangerous Drugs, 1950; Verse Play, Ruth; In Praise of the Lakes, 1953; In Praise of Rivers, 1955; Auction Sales, Ency. Brit. Year Book; over 59 radio scripts. *Recreations:* travel, painting, gardening. *Address:* Newlands Gate, Kingswood Way, Sanderstead, Surrey. *T.:* Sanderstead 2531.

[*Died* 6 *June* 1961.

SANDILANDS, Brig. Harold Richard, C.M.G. 1919; D.S.O. 1917; late Northumberland Fusiliers; *b.* 1876. *Educ.:* Harrow; Trinity College, Cambridge. Served South Africa, 1899-1902 (Queen's medal with two clasps, King's medal with two clasps, despatches); N.W. Frontier of India, 1908 (medal with clasp); European War, 1914-19 (despatches, D.S.O., Brevet Lt.-Col., C.M.G.); Commander Peshawar Brigade, 1929-32; retired pay, 1932. *Publications:* The 23rd Division, 1914-19, 1924; The Fifth in the Great War. *Address:* Drumalbin House, Camberley. *T.:* 559. *Club:* Royal Automobile.

[*Died* 16 *Sept.* 1961.

SANDLANDS, Paul Ernest, O.B.E. 1920; Q.C. 1935; D.L., Notts; retired; Bencher of the Inner Temple; *b.* 25 May 1878; *s.* of late Rev. John Poole Sandlands, M.A., Vicar of Brigstock, Thrapston, Northants, and late Janet Pitcairn, *d.* of late William Simpson, Airdrie; *m.* 1905, Laura (*d.* 1960), *d.* of late B. E. West, formerly of Flore Grange, Weedon; two *d.* *Educ.:* privately; Trinity College, Cambridge, B.A. (Law Tripos, 1898, 1899). Served in S. Africa, 1900, with the C.I.V. Mounted Infantry; was orderly to late General Sir James Grierson, and afterwards to Commander-in-Chief Lord Roberts (Queen's medal 5 clasps); Comdr. B Div. Birmingham Special Constabulary, 1916-19; called to Bar, Inner Temple, 1900; Bencher, 1928; Treas., 1950; joined the Midland Circuit, 1901; served as 1st Lieut. in 1st Cadet Batt. the Queen's (Royal West Surrey) Regt.; appointed a Revising Barrister, 1913; Recorder of Newark-on-Trent, 1915-32; of Leicester, 1932-44; of Birmingham, 1944-54; Chairman of the Committee appointed by the Notts Quarter Sessions for hearing of Rating Appeals, 1927-52; Chairman of Quarter Sessions for Newark and Retford Divisions of Notts, resigned 1954; Chairman Derbyshire Quarter Sessions, 1947-54; Chairman (Midland Region) of Medical Appeals Tribunal under National Insurance (Industrial Injuries) Act 1946, 1948-57; retd. 1958. Chairman of the Lindsey and Kesteven Agricultural Wages Cttee., 1933-37; Capt. H.Q. Staff V Sector Home Guard, 1942-44; Bd. of Management of Roy. Northern Hosp., and of Putney Hosp. till July 1948; Chairman: Workmen's Compensation (Supplementation) Bd., 1951-56; Pneumoconiosis and Byssinosis Benefit Scheme, 1952-56. *Publications:* (with His Honour Judge Amphlett, K.C.) Halsbury's Laws of England, Title Negligence. *Recreation:* music. *Address:* Ashmore Green Cottage, Ashmore Green, Newbury, Berks. *T.:* Thatcham 2349; 1 King's Bench Walk, Temple, E.C.4. *T.:* Central 8436.

[*Died* 8 *March* 1962.

SANDS, Ven. Haviland Hubert Allport; Retired; Archdeacon of Southwark, 1955-66; Vicar of St. Anselm, Kennington Cross, 1930-66; *b.* 26 March 1896; *s.* of Canon Hubert Sands of Birmingham. *Educ.:* King Edward's School, Birmingham; Oriel College, Oxford. Capt. Royal Warwickshire Regt., 1915-19. Ordained, 1922; Curate, St. John, Waterloo Rd., 1922-25; Priest-in-Charge, All Saints, Windsor, 1925-1930; Rural Dean of Lambeth, 1943-55; Hon. Canon of Southwark, 1951-55; Canon Emeritus, 1967. *Address:* Stibb East, Burbage, Marlborough, Wilts.

[*Died* 22 *March* 1970.

SANDWICH, 9th Earl of, *cr.* 1660, **George Charles Montagu,** Viscount Hinchingbrooke and Baron Montagu of St. Neots (1660); *b.* 29 Dec. 1874; *e. s.* of Admiral Hon. V. A. and Lady Agneta Montagu, *d.* of 4th Earl of Hardwicke; *m.* 1st. 1905, Alberta, (*d.* 1951), *d.* of William Sturges, New York; one *s.* two *d.*; 2nd., 1952, Ella, *d.* of George Sully. *Educ.:* Winchester; Magdalen College, Oxford, M.A. Assistant private secretary to President Board of Agriculture, 1898-1900; Private Secretary (unpaid) to President of Local Government Board, 1900-3; M.P. (C.) South Huntingdonshire, 1900-6; J.P., Alderman, and Chairman 1933-46, Lord-Lieutenant and custos rotulorum, 1922-46, Hunts; Chm. Hunts Territorial Army Association, 1922-46; Chairman of Bishop's Advisory Cttee. (Ely Diocese), 1931-46; Trustee of the Tate Gallery, 1934-41, and National Maritime Museum (Greenwich), 1937-46; Member of Committee of the British Council (Art Section) and of the Contemporary Art Society, 1946-; Dir. of the Exchange Telegraph Coy., 1902-61; Chairman Central Prisoners of War Committee, 1917-18. *Publications:* Ten Years of Locomotive Progress, 1907; Windows, 1924; The Bridle-Way, 1925; In a Green Shade, 1928; Flowers of Fancy, 1950; Boyhood, an autobiography, 1951; Gleanings, 1955; British and Foreign Naval Medals (Catalogue of collection at Greenwich Museum), 1937, Supplement, 1939, 2nd Edn., 1950. *Heir:* *s.* Viscount Hinchingbrooke, M.P. *Address:* The Cottage, Hinchingbrooke, Huntingdon. *T.:* Huntingdon 52.

[*Died* 15 *June* 1962.

SANDYS, 6th Baron (*cr.* 1802), **Arthur Fitzgerald Sandys Hill;** Lt.-Col., late R.E.; *b.* 4 Dec. 1876; *e. s.* of late Capt. A. B. G. Sandys Hill, R.B., and Helen Emily, 3rd *d.* of Richard Chenevix Trench, D.D., Archbishop of Dublin; *S.* cousin, 1948; *m.* 1924, Cynthia Mary, *o. d.* of late Col. F. R. T. T. Gascoigne, D.S.O.; one *s.* one *d.* (and one *d.* decd.). *Educ.:* Haileybury. Served Tibet Expedition, 1904 (medal); European War, 1914. *Heir:* *s.* Hon. Richard Michael Oliver Hill [*b.* 21 July 1931; *m.* 1961, Patricia Simpson, *er. d.* of late Lionel Hall and of Mrs. Hall, Parkgate, Lower Beeding, Sussex.]. *Address:* Himbleton Manor, Droitwich; Ombersley Court, Droitwich. *Club:* United Service.

[*Died* 24 *Nov.* 1961.

SANDYS, Oliver; novelist; *b.* Henzada, Burma; *d.* of Colonel Henry Pruce Jervis, I.M.S.; *m.* Caradoc Evans (*d.* 1945). *Educ.:* privately; Royal Academy of Dramatic Art. *Publications:* The Garment of Gold; The Green Caravan; Chappy—That's All; The

Pleasure Garden; Old Roses; The Crimson Ramblers; Sally Serene; Mr. Anthony; Tilly Make-Haste; Blinkeyes; The Curled Hands; The Sorceress; Mr. Scribbles; Bad Lad; Misty Angel; Vista the Dancer; Jinks; Mops; Squire; Butterflies; Just Lil; Happy Day; Spangles; Tiptoes; The Show Must Go On; The Curtain Will Go Up; The Happy Mummers; Angel's Kiss, Crinklenose; Mud on my Stockings, Whatagirl; Old Hat; Calm Waters; Singing Up Hill; Jack-be-Nimble; Wellington Wendy; Swell Fellows; No Faint Heart; Meadowsweet; Merrily all the Way; Deputy Pet, Miss Paraffin; Learn to Laugh Again; The Constant Rabbit; Dot on the Spot; Bachelor's Tonic; Shining Failure; Kiss the Moon; Let's All be Happy; Quaint Place; Shine my Wings; Suffer to Sing; The Happiness Stone; A New Day; Butterflies in the Rain; The Golden Flame; Laughter and Love Remain; The Happy Hearts; The Poppy and the Rose; Unbroken Thread (diary); Full and Frank (autobiography); Caradoc Evans (biography); Miracle Stone of Wales. *Films:* The Green Caravan; Mr. Anthony; Rose of the Sea; Jackie; Blink-eyes; Chappy—That's All; Born Lucky; as Countess Barcynska: Honeypot; Tesha; Under the Big Top; I Loved a Fairy; Exit Renee; Publicity Baby; Pick Up and Smile; God and Mr. Aaranson; Writing Man; That Trouble Piece; Let the Storm Burst; Black-out Symphony; The Wood is my Pulpit; Love Never Dies; Joy Comes After; Luck is a Lady; We Lost our Way; Gorgeous Brute; Conjuror; Yesterday is Tomorrow; These Dominant Hills; Bubble over Thorn; Sunset is Dawn; Beloved Burden; Miss Venus of Aberdovey; The Jackpot; Black Harvest; I was Shown Heaven; Smile in the Mirror. *Recreation:* anything to do with the countryside. *Address:* c/o Hurst and Blackett, 178/202 Great Portland Street, W.1.
[*Died* 10 *March* 1964.

SANGSTER, Hon. Sir Donald (Burns), K.C.V.O. 1967; Prime Minister, Jamaica, since Feb. 1967; Governor of the World Bank and International Monetary Fund since 1963; *b.* Jamaica, 26 Oct. 1911; *s.* of late W. B. Sangster, Commissioned Land Surveyor, St. Elizabeth, and Cassandra (*née* Plummer); unmarried. *Educ.:* Munro Coll., Jamaica. Solicitor, 1937. Mem. Parochial Bd., St. Elizabeth, 1933- (served as Chm. and Vice-Chm.). M.H.R., Jamaica, 1949-; Dep. Leader, Jamaica Labour Party, 1950-67; Leader, House of Representatives, 1953-55 and 1962-66; Minister of Social Welfare, 1950-53; Minister of Finance, 1953-55 and 1962-67; Dep. Prime Minister, 1963-65; Actg. Prime Minister, Actg. Minister of Defence, Actg. Minister of External Affairs, 1965-67. Chm., Commonwealth Parly. Assoc., 1964; Mem. numerous Boards and Cttees.; represented Jamaica abroad in several countries on different missions and subjects (incl. Commonwealth Prime Ministers' Confs.). *Recreations:* tennis, golf, cricket. *Address:* c/o Prime Minister's Office, Kingston, Jamaica. *T.:* 25451; Vale Royal, Kingston 10. *T.:* 76696. *Clubs:* Kingston Cricket, Constant Spring Golf.
[*Died* 11 *April* 1967.

SANGSTER, Leith; Sheriff-Substitute of Inverness, Elgin, and Nairn at Fort William, 1944-46; Sheriff-Substitute of Lanarkshire at Hamilton, 1946-59, retired. *Address:* 11, Belgrave Place, Edinburgh 4.
[*Died* 3 *May* 1962.

SANSOM, Sir George Bailey, G.B.E., *cr.* 1947; K.C.M.G., *cr.* 1935 (C.M.G. 1926); Consultant Professor, Stanford University, Cal. since 1955; Emer. Prof., Japanese Studies Columbia Univ., New York, 1954; Assoc. Fell. Berkeley Coll., Yale Univ.; *b.* 1883; *s.* of George William Morgan Sansom; *m.* 1928, Katharine Gordon, *e. d.* of W. Cecil Slingsby. *Educ.:* Palmer's School, Grays; Lycée Malherbe, Caen; Universities of Giessen and Marburg. Held various Consular posts in Japan from 1904; acting Japanese Counsellor to H.M. Embassy, Tokyo, in 1920 and 1924; Commercial Counsellor, British Embassy, Tokyo, 1925-40; retired 1940; served in Admiralty and Intelligence Directorate of War Office during War, 1914-18; Visiting Professor at Columbia Univ., New York, 1935-36 and 1940-41; Adviser to Far Eastern Mission, Ministry of Economic Warfare, at Singapore, 1941; Civilian Member of Far Eastern War Council, Singapore, 1941-42; attached to United Command Headquarters, Java, 1942; Minister, British Embassy, Washington, 1942-47; United Kingdom member of Allied Far Eastern Commission, 1946-47; Professor, 1947-53, and Director, East Asian Institute, Columbia Univ., 1949-53. Member of Japanese Academy, 1951. LL.D.: Columbia University, 1954, Mills Coll., California, 1964; Litt.D., Leeds University, 1960. *Publications:* Historical Grammar of the Japanese Language, 1928; A Short Cultural History of Japan, 1931; The Western World and Japan, 1950; History of Japan, Vol. I, 1958, Vol. II, 1961, Vol. III, 1964; papers on Japanese language, literature and history. *Address:* 672 Foothill Road, Stanford, California, U.S.A. *Clubs:* Athenæum; Century (New York).
[*Died* 8 *March* 1965.

SARA, Rt. Rev. Edmund Willoughby, M.A., D.D.; *b.* 1891; *s.* of William George Willoughby Sara; *m.* 1919, Meta Letitia, *d.* of William John Butler, M.A., Dun Laoghaire, Eire. *Educ.:* King's College, Taunton; Trinity Coll., Dublin; Salisbury Theological Coll. Curate of Holy Trinity, Weymouth, 1915-16; Gillingham, Dorset, 1917-19; Organising Sec. of Church of England Sunday School Institute, 1920-21; Secretary of Church of England Sunday School Institute, 1921-25; Director of Sunday Schools in the Diocese of London, 1925-26; Director of the London Diocesan Council for Youth, 1926-28; Vicar of St. John's, Walham Green, 1928-32; Canon Residentiary and Chancellor of Truro Cathedral and Examining Chaplain to the Bishop of Truro, Director of Religious Education in the Diocese of Truro, Chaplain to the Truro Diocesan Training College, 1932-37; Secretary of the Canterbury Provincial Council for Sunday Schools and Youth movements, 1926-37; Assistant Bishop of Jamaica, 1937-40; Assistant Bishop in Diocese of Bath and Wells, 1940-43; Prebendary of Holcombe in Wells Cathedral, 1941-44; Rector of Ludlow, 1944; a Prebendary of Hereford Cathedral, 1945, Assistant Bishop of Hereford, 1946; Retd. 1963. *Publications:* Teaching Method in the Sunday School; From Alban to Bede; Young Men and Maidens; Contributed to The Sunday School in the Modern World; Good Friday; The Teaching Church; An Introduction to Pastoral Theology. *Recreations:* novel reading and gardening. *Address:* Chy-an-Towan, Herkomer Cres., Llandudno, Wales.
[*Died* 18 *Sept.* 1965.

SARGENT, Sir (H.) Malcolm (W.), Kt. 1947; Mus.D. Dunelm, 1919; D.Mus. Oxon (Hon.), 1942; LL.D. Liverpool (Hon.), 1947; Hon R.A.M.; Hon. F.R.C.O.; F.R.C.M.; Hon. F.T.C.L.; F.R.S.A.; Chief Conductor B.B.C. Symphony Orchestra, 1950 until Sept. 1957 (subsequently Conductor-in-Chief of the Promenade Concerts and Chief Guest Conductor of the B.B.C. Symphony Orchestra); Conductor Orchestral Classes, and Professor Royal College of Music, since 1923; Conductor-in-Chief Royal Choral Society, 1928; Conductor: Huddersfield Choral Society since 1932; Liverpool Welsh Choral Union since 1941; Ceramic City Choir (Hanley) since 1942; Leeds Philharmonic Society since 1949; Hon. Adviser in Music to the Royal Marines since 1949; President of the National Youth Orchestra, 1957; President, R.S.P.C.A., 1958; Joint President, London Union of Youth Clubs, 1964; *b.* 29 April 1895; *s.* of Henry Edward Sargent, Stamford, Lincolnshire; *m.* 1923, Eileen Laura Harding, *d.* of Frederic Horne, Drinkstone, Suffolk; one *s.* *Educ.:* Stamford School. A.R.C.O. (Sawyer Prize), 1910. Articled Pupil Peterborough Cathedral, 1911-14; Mus.B. (Durham), 1914; Organist Melton Mowbray Parish Church, 1914-24; during War served 27th Durham Light Infantry; Pupil of Moiseiwitch, 1919-21. Conducted own composition, Impressions on a Windy Day, at Queen's Hall Promenade Concert, 1921, followed by Scherzo and Finale; 1st performance Vaughan Williams' Hugh the Drover and Holst's Boar's Head, 1924; 1st performance Walton's Troilus and Cressida, 1954; Hiawatha Productions, Royal Albert Hall, 1926; also at Covent Garden, 1936, 1954, 1955. London Music Festival, 1947; Promenade Concerts since 1947; Edinburgh Festival, 1947, 1948, 1953, 1955; Norwich Festival, 1947, 1951; Leeds Triennial Festival, 1947, 1953; conductor: B.N.O.C.; Hallé orchestra, 1939-43; Robert Mayer Concerts, 1924-40; British Women's Symphony Orch., 1925-38; Lord Palmer's Patron's Fund Concerts, 1924-39; Llandudno Orchestral Seasons, 1926-28; Diaghilef Season's Russian Ballet, 1927-30; Liverpool Philharmonic Orchestra, 1942-48; Gramophone Co. (H.M.V. Records); Musical Director and Conductor: Courtauld-Sargent Concerts, 1929-40; Leicester Symphony Orch. and Choral Soc. 1922-39; Bradford Festival Choral Society, 1928-51; London Season Gilbert and Sullivan Operas, 1926, 1929, 1951, 1961-62. Musical Director: Brit. Internat. Pictures, Carmen Prod., 1931. *Tours:* New Zealand, 1936; Australia, 1936, 1938, 1939, 1945, 1960, 1962; Coronation Concerts, Jerusalem, etc., with Palestine Orchestra, 1937, also 1938, 1939; National Broadcasting Company Concerts, New York, 1945; Vienna, 1946, 1947, 1958, 1959, 1960, 1962; Brussels, 1947; Oslo, 1947; Stockholm, 1943, 1945, 1956; Zürich, Rome, Johannesburg, Copenhagen, 1948; Madrid, Portugal, Gibraltar, Milan, Gothenburg, Oslo, 1949; Athens, Buenos Aires, Montevideo, Rio de Janeiro, Santiago 1950, Copenhagen, Buenos Aires, Santiago Lima, 1952; Malta, 1953; Paris, Düsseldorf, Hamburg, The Hague, Amsterdam, Maastricht, Brussels, Japan, 1954; Philadelphia, Washington, New York, Baltimore, Ascona, 1955; Caracas, Copenhagen, Bergen, Helsinki, Johannesburg, 1956; Houston, 1957, 1959, 1960, 1961; Moscow, Leningrad, Helsinki, Oslo, Canada, 1957; Czechoslovakia, Belgium, Buenos Aires, Lisbon, Yugoslavia, Canada, 1958; Berlin, 1959; Bonn, 1961, W. Germany, Far East, 1962; Canada and the U.S.A., 1963. Member of the B.B.C. Brains Trust, 1941; St. Olav medal, 1947; Member Roy. Swedish Acad. of Music, 1947; Hon. Freeman: London, 1935; Stamford, 1948; Huddersfield, 1961. Gold Medal, Roy. Philharm. Soc., 1959. Kt. Comdr. Order of Star of the North (Sweden), 1956; Star and Collar of Kt. Comdr. Order of the White Rose (Finland), 1965; Chevalier of Legion of Honour, 1967. *Relevant Publication:* Malcolm Sargent: a Biography, by Charles Reid, 1968. *Recreations:* riding, theatre, the Zoo. *Address:* 9 Albert Hall Mans., S.W.7. *Clubs:* Garrick, Beefsteak, White's, Pratt's. [*Died* 3 *Oct.* 1967.

SARGENT, Sir Orme, G.C.M.G., *cr.* 1948 (K.C.M.G., *cr.* 1937; C.M.G. 1925); K.C.B., *cr.* 1947 (C.B. 1936); J.P.; *b.* 31 Oct. 1884; *s.* of late H. Garton Sargent. *Educ.:* Radley. Entered the Foreign Office, 1906. Permanent Under-Secretary of State for Foreign Affairs, 1946-49; Church Commissioner; *Address:* Bathwick Hill House, Bath. *Club:* Brooks's. [*Died* 23 *Oct.* 1962.

SARJANT, Reginald Josiah, O.B.E. 1946; D.Sc. (Lond.); A.R.C.Sc., D.I.C., F.Inst.F., F.I.M., M.I.Min.E.; Consultant; *s.* of Dr. J. J. Sarjant, Worcester; *m.* 1919, Mary Evans, Machynlleth, Montgomeryshire; (one *s.* decd.). *Educ.:* Roy. Masonic Sch., Bushey, Hertfordshire; Imperial Coll. of Science and Technology, S. Kensington, Roy. Schol. Research asst. to late Prof. W. A. Bone at Imperial Coll. Fuel Officer Res. Dept., Hadfields Ltd., Sheffield, 1918, a pioneer appointment; scientific investigations in a wide range of fuel, furnace and metallurgical subjects; local Director, Hadfields Ltd., 1937; and later Head of Research Dept.; Professor of Fuel Technology, University of Sheffield, 1946-53, Emeritus, 1953. During War of 1939-45 and since has rendered service on many committees in the research and technological field, notably Fuel Efficiency Cttee. of Ministry of Fuel and Power, being Chm. of its Educ. Cttee., which produced a notable publication, The Efficient Use of Fuel. Melchett Medallist, Inst. of Fuel, 1950; Hon. Mem., Coke Oven Managers' Assoc., Junior Instn. of Engineers *Publications:* some 100 scientific papers on fuel technology metallurgy and allied subjects. Furnace Heating (Fuel Publications), 1925. *Recreations:* gardening, art. *Address:* 80 Totley Brook Road, Totley Rise, Sheffield. *T.:* Beauchief 71661. [*Died* 2 *April* 1965.

SARRAILH, Jean, Grand officier de la Légion d'Honneur, 1956; Hon. K.B.E. 1955; Honorary Rector of the University of Paris since 1961; *b.* 14 Oct. 1891. Formerly Professor: French Institute, Madrid; Univ. of Poitiers; Rector: University of Grenoble, 1937; Montpellier, 1941; Director-General at Ministry of Education, 1944-45. Doctor *h.c.* Univs. of Oxford London. Member, Institut de France. Président de la commission nationale française pour l'Unesco. *Publications:* many works on Spain, including L'Espagne éclairée de la seconde moitié du XVIIIe. siècle, 1954. *Address:* Monein, B. Pyr., France. [*Died* 29 *Feb.* 1964.

SASSOON, Sir (Ellice) Victor, 3rd Bt., *cr.* 1909; G.B.E. *cr.* 1947; *b.* 30 Dec. 1881; *s.* of 2nd Bt. and Leontine (*d.* 1955), *d.* of A. Levy; *S.* father, 1924; *m.* 1959, Evelyn Barnes, Dallas, Texas. *Educ.:* Harrow; Trinity Coll., Camb. Governing Dir. E. D. Sassoon Banking Co. Ltd.; late Capt. R.A.F.; Mem. of Legislative Assembly, India, 1922-23, 1926-29; Member of the Royal Commission for investigation of Labour Conditions in India, 1929. *Heir:* none. *Address:* 37 Upper Brook Street, W.1. *Clubs:* Carlton, St. James', Buck's, Royal Aero. [*Died* 12 *Aug.* 1961 (*ext.*).

SASSOON, Siegfried, C.B.E. 1951; Poet; *b.* 1886; *nephew* of Sir John Thornycroft, F.R.S., and Sir Hamo Thornycroft, R.A.; *m.* 1933, Hester, *d.* of late Sir Stephen Herbert Gatty, K.C.; one *s.* Hon. Fellow, Clare College, Camb., 1953; Hon.D.Litt. Oxford, 1965. Royal Gold Medal for Poetry, 1957. *Publications:* The Old Huntsman, 1917; Counterattack, 1918; Satirical Poems, 1926; The Heart's Journey, 1928; Memoirs of a Fox-Hunting Man, 1928 (awarded Hawthornden Prize, 1929); Memoirs of an Infantry Officer, 1930; Vigils, 1935; Sherston's Progress, 1936; The Old Century, 1938; Rhymed Ruminations, 1940; The Weald of Youth, 1942; Siegfried's Journey, 1916-20, 1945; Collected Poems, 1947; Meredith: a biography, 1948; Sequences, 1957; Collected Poems, 1908-1956, 1961. *Address:* Heytesbury House, Wiltshire. [*Died* 1 *Sept.* 1967.

SASSOON, Sir Victor; *see* Sassoon, Sir E. V.

SATOW, Sir Harold Eustace, K.C.M.G., *cr.* 1931; O.B.E. 1918; *b.* 10 July 1876; *e. s.* of late S. A. M. Satow and Kathrin Dakin; *m.* 1907, Ethel (*d.* 1968), *d.* of J. R. Hatherly; one *s.* *Educ.:* Berkhamsted School; Balliol College, Oxford. Entered Levant Consular Service, 1897; Vice-Consul at Uskub, 1904; Consul for Palestine, 1909; Trebizond, 1912; Acting Consul-General at Salonica, 1906, 1909, and 1915; Tripoli, 1912; employed in the Foreign Office, 1914-15; on Special Service in Albania, 1916; in Legation at Athens, 1916-1918; in Foreign Office, 1918-20; Consul-General at Beyrout, 1920-34; Tunis, 1934-37; retired, 1937; British Member of Assyrian Committee of Council of League of Nations, 1938; re-employed Foreign Office till 1944; again re-employed, 1946-47. *Address:* Flat 1, Avenue Court, Mount Avenue, Ealing, W.5. [*Died* 17 *July* 1969.

SATOW, Hugh Ralph, C.B.E. 1919; Chartered Accountant, 1905, retd. 1935; *b.* 1877; *s.* of late S. A. M. Satow, Master of Supreme Court; *m.* 1909, Gwynedd Anne (*d.* 1918), *d.* of Lieut.-Col. Eubule Thelwall; one *s.* (and one *d.* decd.). Served European War, 1914-1919 (despatches, C.B.E., Order of Crown of Belgium). War of 1939-45: Army Welfare Officer and Civil Defence. *Address:* Pyt House, Thornford, Sherborne, Dorset. [*Died* 24 *Sept.* 1967.

SATTERLY, John, A.R.C.Sc. (Lond.); D.Sc. (Lond.); M.A. (Cantab.); F.R.S.C.; F.P.S.L.; Prof. of Physics, Univ. of Toronto, 1925, retired 1950; *b.* 29 Nov. 1879; 3rd *s.* of John Satterly, Ashburton, Devon; *m.* 1905, May, *y. d.* of J. E. Randall, Loders, Dorset; one *s.* one *d.* *Educ.:* Ashburton Grammar School, Devon; Royal College of Science, South Kensington; St. John's College, Cambridge. Devon County Council Exhibitioner, 1895; National Scholar, 1898; Tyndall Prizeman, 1899; Royal Scholarship, 1899, 1900; University of London Scholar, 1901; Research student at the Cavendish Laboratory, Cambridge, under Professor Sir J. J. Thomson, 1903-12; Lecturer, University of Toronto, 1912-17; Assistant Professor, 1916-1921; Associate Professor, 1921-25; engaged in Admiralty Researches on Helium for use in Balloons, 1916-18; President, Devonshire Association, 1935. *Publications:* Experimental Researches on Radioactivity, Surface Tension, Mechanics of Vibrating bodies, Elasticity and Viscosity, published in the London Philosophical Magazine, Transactions of the Royal Society of Canada, Government Bulletins of Canada, American Journal of Physics, Transactions of the Devonshire Association, Eng. and Amer. High Sch. Jls. in Maths. and Physics, etc.; Text-books on Physics; Theory of Measurements (with L. Tuttle), 1925. *Address:* Physics Laboratory, Univ. of Toronto. *T.:* WA-2-7262. *Clubs:* Faculty Union, Univ. of Toronto, St. George's Society (Toronto). [*Died* 1 *Oct.* 1963.

SAUERWEIN, Jules Auguste; Journalist and novelist; *b.* Marseilles, 20 Jan. 1880; *s.* of Christian Alfred Sauerwein and Henriette Roux de la Jarriette; *m.* 1917, Agnès Compagnion de Wavrin; one *s.* *Educ.:* Lycée de Marseille; Sorbonne, Paris (L. ès L.). After few years in Vienna, Secretary of the French Ambassador; sub-editor of the paper l'Aurore and afterwards foreign editor of le Matin during 21 years; with Paris Soir, 1931-44, as foreign editor; lecturer in America and Europe; Commander Legion of Honour; Commander of St. Maurice and Lazare, of Order of Leopold of Belgium, of St. Jacques of Portugal; Grand Officer of St. Sava in Yugoslavia, of the White Lion of the Polonia Restituta. *Publications:* Où va l'Amérique, 1933; Mémoires d'un journaliste, 1933; Monarques d'hier ou de demain, 1951; translations of Rudolf Steiner's books; contributor to periodical publications in Europe and America (New York Tribune 6 years, New York Times 17 years). *Recreation:* piano. *Address:* 31 Quai de l'Horloge, Paris 1er. *T.:* Odeon 24.37. [*Died* 24 *June* 1967.

SAUL, Air Vice-Marshal Richard Ernest, C.B. 1941; D.F.C.; *m.* Claire Treleaven; one *s.* one *d.* *Educ.:* St. Andrew's College, Ross College, Dublin. Air Commodore, 1937; Senior Air Staff Officer, No. 11 Group (Fighter Command), 1937-1939; Air Vice-Marshal, comdg. No. 13 Group, 1939; A.O.C., Egypt, 1943; retired, 1944. [*Died* 30 *Nov.* 1965.

SAUNDERS, Colonel Alan, C.M.G. 1941; O.B.E. 1932; M.C.; *b.* 1886; *m.* 1920, Eva Helen (*d.* 1952), *e. d.* of Charles Worsley Strickland; one *s.* *Educ.:* Christ's Hospital. Indian Police, 1908-14; served European War, 1914-20, France, Flanders, and Palestine (wounded twice, despatches thrice); Palestine Police, Dist. Comdt., Jerusalem, 1920-1926; Deputy Inspector-General, 1926-35; Inspector-General, Nigeria Police, 1936-37; Inspector-General of Police and Prisons, Palestine, 1937; Mem. Advisory Council, 1937-43; M.L.C., 1943. King's Police Medal, 1929; retd. from Colonial Service, 1944; Chief Police Adviser, Allied Military H.Q. (Greece), 1944; Director (M.E.) Censorship, 1945-46. Commissioner Police, Tripolitania, 1946-52. O.St.J. 1946. *Address:* Rockhill, Thurlestone, S. Devon. *Club:* East India and Sports. [*Died* 26 *March* 1964.

SAUNDERS, Sir Alexander M. C.; *see* Carr-Saunders.

SAUNDERS, Sir Harold Leonard, Kt., *cr.* 1946; F.C.G.I., B.Sc.; Comptroller-General Patents, Designs and Trade Marks, and Comptroller Industrial Property Dept. of Board of Trade, 1944-49; *b.* 22 September 1885; *s.* of late Alfred Francis and Marie Saunders; *m.* 1911, Gertrude Florence, *d.* of late G. J. Dee; one *d.* *Educ.:* Bancroft's School; City and Guilds Engineering College. Barrister-at-Law, Middle Temple, 1923; Assistant Examiner, Patent Office, 1907. European War, 1915-19, Captain R.F.C. (despatches). Assistant Secretary, Board of Trade, 1940; Assistant-Comptroller, Patent Office, 1943; Member Patents Cttee., 1944; Chairman, Internat. Conf. on treatment of German Patents, 1946; British Delegate at Neuchatel Conf. of Internat. Union for Protection of Industrial Property, 1947, and at the Brussels Conf., 1948, for the revision of the Berne Copyright Convention; Member Monopolies and Restrictive Practices Commission, 1949-54. *Address:* 22 Lakeside Road, N.13. *T.:* Palmers Green 4565. [*Died* 23 *Nov.* 1965.

SAUNDERS, Ven. Harry Patrick; M.A. (Oxon); B.D.; Archdeacon of Macclesfield since 1965; Rector of St. James, Gawsworth, Cheshire, since 1964; *b.* 16 Mar. 1913; *s.* of William Percy and Helene Saunders. *Educ.:* The High School, Hanley; King's College, London; St. Catherine's Society and St. Stephen's House, Oxford. Chaplain and lecturer, St. Stephen's House, Oxford, 1936-1938, Vice-Principal, 1938-49; Chaplain, St. Edmund Hall, Oxford, 1936-46. Priest-in-charge, St. Peter's, Shrewsbury and O.C.F., R.A.F., 1939-45. Chaplain Magdalen Coll., Oxford, 1946-49; Vicar: St. Andrew's, West Bromwich, 1949-51; St. Mary's, Kingswinford, 1951-56; Lecturer, Queen's Coll., Birmingham, 1949-56; Canon Residentiary of Ely and Principal of Ely Theological College, 1956; Vicar of Holy Trinity, Oswestry, Shropshire, 1957-64. Examining Chaplain to: Bishop of Lichfield, 1964; Bishop of Chester, 1965. Director of Ordination and Post-Ordination Training, 1965. Fellow of the Woodard Corporation, 1959; Proctor in Convocation, 1960. *Recreations:*

theatre, travel. *Address:* Gawsworth Rectory, Macclesfield, Cheshire. *Club:* Athenæum. [*Died* 13 *May* 1967.

SAUNDERS, John Tennant, C.M.G. 1957; M.A. (Cambridge); *b.* 23 July 1888; *s.* of W. A. Saunders, Solicitor; *m.* 1919, Margaret, *d.* of A. C. Pearson, Regius Prof. of Greek, Cambridge; two *s.* one *d.* *Educ.:* Tonbridge; Christ's College, Camb. First Class Natural Sciences Tripos, Part I, 1910, and Part II, Zoology (1911); Frank Smart Prize for Zoology, 1910; Demonstrator in University of Toronto, 1911-12; Demonstrator of Animal Morphology, Cambridge, 1914-26; Univ. Lecturer in Zoology, 1926-34; elected Fellow of Christ's College, Cambridge, 1912; served during the War, 1914-18, with Durham L.I. Secretary-General of the Faculties in the University, 1935-53; Tutor 1923-35, and Vice-Master, 1950-53, of Christ's College, Cambridge; Principal of University College, Ibadan, Nigeria, 1953-56. Fellow of Christ's Coll., Camb. Hon. D.C.L., Oxford, 1954. Chairman of the West African Examinations Council, 1954-60. *Publications:* Manual of Practical Vertebrate Morphology (with S. M. Manton); various papers in scientific journals on experimental biology. *Address:* 25 Cavendish Avenue, Cambridge. *T.:* 47158. *Club:* Oxford and Cambridge University. [*Died* 28 *April* 1965.

SAUNDERS-PRYSE, Sir Pryse Loveden, 5th Bt., *cr.* 1866; *b.* 12 Nov. 1896; *o. s.* of Sir George Rice Pryse-Saunders, 4th Bt., and Geraldine Mabel, *d.* of late Conrade Abadam, Middleton Hall, Carmarthenshire; father assumed additl. surname of Saunders, 1932; changed name from Pryse-Saunders to Saunders-Pryse by deed poll, 1949; *S.* father, 1948; *m.* 1938, Emily G. H., *d.* of late Capt. Henry Cavendish, R.N., and late Lady Harriet Cavendish; no *c.* *Educ.:* Wellington College. Served European War, 1914-18, France, India and Mesopotamia; War of 1939-45, Royal Observer Corps. *Recreation:* reading. *Heir:* none. *Address:* Glanrhydw, Kidwelly, Carm. *T.:* Kidwelly 27. [*Died* 5 *Jan.* 1962 (*ext.*).

SAVAGE, Ernest A., LL.D. Edin.; *b.* Croydon, 30 Mar. 1877; *s.* of Albert E. Savage, Croydon; *m.* Beatrice Cattermole; one *s.* one *d.* Librarian, Bromley Public Library, 1904-6; Chief Librarian, Wallasey Public Libraries, 1906-15; City Librarian, Coventry, 1915-1922; Principal Librarian, Edinburgh Public Libraries, 1922-42; President of the Library Association, 1936; Hon. Secretary, 1928-34; President of the Scottish Library Association, 1929-30, 1930-31; Hon. Fellow, Library Association and Scottish Library Association; Hon. Member, Association of Music Libraries. President of the Edinburgh Bibliographical Society, 1929-30; Chairman, Chaucer House Building Committee, 1932-33; represented Library Association at Fiftieth Anniversary Conference of American Library Association, Philadelphia, 1926; surveyed Libraries of West Indies and British Guiana, 1933. *Publications:* Manual of Descriptive Annotation for Library Catalogues, 1906; Story of Libraries and Book Collecting, 1908; Old English Libraries, 1911; (with the late Walter Powell), Notes on Libraries visited in the United States and Canada, 1927; Early Monastic Libraries of Scotland, 1928; The Libraries of Bermuda, The Bahamas, the British W. Indies, British Guiana, etc. 1934 (report on which Central Library of Trinidad and Tobago and Eastern Caribbean Regional Library were founded). Special Librarianship in General Libraries, 1939; The Librarian and his Committee, 1942; Manual of Book Classification and Display, 1946; A Librarian Looks at Readers, 1947; A Librarian's Memories, Portraits and Reflections, 1952; numerous articles on bibliography and library technology. *Address:* 23 Braidburn Crescent, Edinburgh. *T.:* 2610 Morningside. [*Died* 4 *Feb.* 1966.

SAVAGE, John Percival; Chairman and Managing Director, Boots Pure Drug Co. Ltd. and Associated Companies 1954-61; *b.* 18 November 1895; *m.* 1922, Beatrice Maude Hodgson; one *s.* two *d.* *Educ.:* Mundella Gram. Sch., Nottingham. Joined staff of Boots Pure Drug Co. Ltd., 1911; Director, 1942; Vice-Chairman, 1951; retired, 1961. *Recreations:* golf, bowls. *Address:* 612 Derby Road, Nottingham. *Club:* Borough (Nottingham). [*Died* 22 *Feb.* 1970.

SAVAGE, Raymond; Managing Director Raymond Savage, Ltd., Literary Agents, from 1924; *s.* of late Canon Francis Forbes Savage, Canon Emeritus of Truro; *m.* 1947, Stella, *d.* of L. Dougal Callander, M.D., of Doncaster. *Educ.:* Kelly College, Tavistock; Keble College, Oxford, B.A. Served European War 2/4 Buffs, 1914; Captain and Adjutant 3/5 Durham L.I. 1915; Captain and Adjutant 6th Garrison Bn. R. Welch Fusiliers, 1916; Garr. Adjt. Citadel, Cairo, 1917-18; attached Staff Duke of Connaught, 1918; attached G.H.Q. Staff Palestine and acting Deputy Assistant Military Secretary to Field Marshal Viscount Allenby, 1918 (despatches); Staff Egypt, 1918-19; General Manager Curtis Brown, Ltd. 1921-24; War Office, Aug. 1939; Political Intelligence Dept. of Foreign Office, 1940-42; Pte. Home Guard, May-Dec. 1944; Director and Literary Adviser, Evans Brothers Ltd., Publishers, 1947-50. *Publications:* Allenby of Armageddon; a Record of the Career and Campaigns of F.M. Viscount Allenby, 1926; Barbados; British West Indies, 1937. *Address:* Hillside, Polperro, Cornwall. *T.:* Polperro 351. [*Died* 6 *Jan.* 1964.

SAVAGE, Rt. Rev. Thomas Joseph, M.A.; *b.* 5 February 1900; *s.* of Samuel Joseph Savage and Charlotte Stella Cunningham; *m.* 1937, Monica Olive Hill; one *s.* one *d.* *Educ.:* Chigwell and Highgate Schools; Peterhouse, Cambridge. Curate, St. John's, Waterloo Road, London, 1926-28; South African Church Railway Mission, 1928-31; Curate, All Hallows by the Tower, London, 1932-35; Toc H Padre, South Africa, 1935-1937; Rector of Springs, Transvaal, 1937-45; Vicar of Leominster, Herefordshire, 1945-49; Tait Missioner, Diocese of Canterbury, 1949-1954; Dean of Cape Town, S.A., 1955-58. Bishop of Zululand and Swaziland, 1958-66. Diocese of Zululand was re-named, Nov. 1960, as Zululand and Swaziland. *Address:* Bishopshurst, Eshowe, Zululand. [*Died* 22 *Oct.* 1966.

SAVAGE, Sir William George, Kt., *cr.* 1938; M.D.; M.R.C.S., L.R.C.P.; *b.* 1872; *s.* of John H. Savage and Alice, *d.* of Rev. Gardner, Jamaica; *m.* 1900, Mary Adele May, *d.* of E. D. Wilson; one *s.* one *d.* *Educ.:* private; University College, London; University College Hospital. B.Sc. (Lond.) 1894; M.B. (Honours in medicine, Gold Medal in Forensic Medicine), 1896; M.R.C.S., L.R.C.P., London, 1896; D.P.H. 1897; M.D. (Lond.) 1898; Hon. M.D. (Bristol); House Physician and Pathologist, Sussex County Hospital; Assistant Professor of Pathology, University College, London; Lecturer on Bacteriology and Public Health, University College, Cardiff, 1900-03; Medical Officer of Health and Public Analyst, Borough of Colchester, 1903-09; County Medical Officer of Health and School Medical Officer, Somerset, 1909-37; late Consultant County Medical Officer of Health, Somerset; Late Chairman of the Catering Trade Working Party (Ministry of Food); late Examiner in Public Health, Forensic Medicine, and State Medicine, London University; late Examiner in Public Health, University of Wales; late Examiner Sanitary Inspectors' Examination Board; late Examiner, Univ. of Reading for B.Sc.; Examiner in Public

Health and Forensic Medicine, University of Bristol; Milroy Lecturer, Royal College of Physicians, 1923; Sedgwick Memorial Lecturer (U.S.A.), 1932; Mitchell Lecturer Royal College of Physicians, 1933; President, Society Medical Officers of Health, 1935-36; Smith Award (1940) of Royal Institute of Public Health and Hygiene; Pres. Somerset Archæological Soc., 1945-46. *Publications:* The Bacteriological Examination of Water Supplies, 1906; Milk and the Public Health, 1912; Rural Housing, 1915; The Bacteriological Examination of Food and Water, 2nd edition, 1916; Food and The Public Health, 1919; Food Poisoning and Food Infections, 1920; Canned Foods in Relation to Health, 1923; The Prevention of Human Tuberculosis of Bovine Origin, 1929: Practical Public Health Problems, 1941, 2nd Ed., 1948; The Making of Our Towns, 1952; Many Scientific Papers and Reports. *Recreations:* history, archæology and gardening. *Address:* Edgehill, 20 Bereweeke Avenue, Winchester.
[*Died* 6 *April* 1961.

SAVATARD, Louis Charles Arthur; Hon. Consultant Dermatologist, 1950; formerly Hon. Physician, Manchester and Salford Hospital for Diseases of the Skin from 1907; Lecturer in Dermatology, Manchester University; retired from active practice; *b.* Leighton Buzzard, 26 Jan. 1874; *s.* of Rev. Louis Savatard, Vicar of Holy Trinity, Darwen, Lancs; *m.* 1st, 1906; no *c.*; 2nd, 1925, Judith E. M. Ormerod, M.B., B.S.; one *s.* two *d.* *Educ.:* St. John's School, Leatherhead. Appointed on the staff at Lloyd's, Royal Exchange, 1890; entered Guy's Hospital as a medical student, 1894; transferred to Owens College, Manchester, 1896; Medallist in Practical Anatomy, 1897-98; Prosector and Assistant Demonstrator in Anatomy and Morbid Histology, 1899-1900; Clinical Assistant, Cancer Hospital, 1900; Skin Hospital, 1901; Assistant Medical Officer with charge of Light Department, Skin Hospital, 1903-7. Hon. Mem.: Hungarian Derm. Soc., 1937; Brit. Assoc. Derm., 1952. Hon. M.Sc. Manch. Univ., 1945. *Publications:* Editor Manchester Med. Students' Gazette, 1900-2; contributions to medical literature in Lancet, British Medical Journal, British Journal of Dermatology. *Recreation:* golf. *Address:* Edenfield, Timperley, Cheshire. *T.:* Sale 3351.
[*Died* 18 *Jan.* 1962.

SAVERY, Frank, C.B.E. 1936; *b.* Huddersfield, 27 Sept. 1883; *s.* of late Frank P. Savery and Mary Hannah, *d.* of late George Brooke, Springwood, Huddersfield; unmarried. *Educ.:* Uppingham; Hertford College, Oxford (Classical Scholar). B.A. 1906; employed in British Legations, Munich and Berne, 1911-19; Consul at Warsaw, 1919, Consul-General, 1939; Counsellor, H.M. Embassy to Poland, 1939-45; employed in Foreign Office, 1945-49; retired, 1949. *Address:* Holmans, Silverton, nr. Exeter. *T.:* Silverton 227.
[*Died* 5 *June* 1965.

SAVILL, Agnes F., M.A. St. Andrews; M.D. Glasgow; F.R.C.P. Ireland; Dermatologist Royal Surrey County Hospital, Guildford (during wartime); formerly Physician, London Skin Hospital, Fitzroy Square, and Skin Department, South London Hospital for Women; Vice-President Electro-therapeutic Section, Royal Society of Medicine *b.* Dec. 1875; *d.* of Robert Blackadder, architect, Dundee, and Agnes Sturrock; *m.* 1901, Dr. Thomas D. Savill, M.D. (*d.* 1910). *Educ.:* Dundee; Glasgow, M.A. St. Andrews, 1895; M.B., Ch.B. Glasgow, 1898; M.D. Glasgow, 1901; F.R.C.P. Ireland, 1944; House Surgeon to Maternity Hospital, Glasgow, 1899; Belgrave Hospital for Children, 1900; Medical Officer, Toxteth Workhouse, Liverpool, 1901; formerly Physician St. John's Hospital for Skin Diseases and Skin Dept., South London Hospital for Women; Chief of Electro-therapeutic Dept. Scottish Women's Hospital, Royaumont, France, 1914-18. *Publications:* The Hair and Scalp, 5th edition 1962; Music, Health, and Character, 3rd edition, 1925; Alexander the Great and His Time, 1955, 3rd edn. 1959; Ed. Savill's Clinical Medicine, 1910-42; articles on Treatment of Pruritus, Eczema, Leukoplakia, and Kraurosis; Hypertrichosis; Electricity in Women's Diseases, 1938, Lancet, Brit. Med. Journal, Brit. Journ. Dermatology, 1940, Journal of Obstetrics, 1943, and Practitioner; articles on Alexander the Great, Encyclopædia Britannica. *Recreations:* music, gardening. *Address:* 7 Devonshire Place, W.1. *T.:* Welbeck 7380.
[*Died* 12 *May* 1964.

SAVILL, Lt.-Colonel Sydney Rowland, D.S.O. 1918; M.C., T.D.; late The Queen's Westminsters K.R.R.C.; *b.* 11 June 1891; *s.* of late P. R. Savill; *m.* 1928, Dora Helen, *d.* of late George H. Hampshire. *Educ.:* Wellington College. On active service in Queen's Westminsters, 1914-19 (D.S.O., M.C., 1914 Star, despatches four times); War of 1939-45: 12th Bn. K.R.R.C., seconded R.A.F. Regt. (G.S.O. 1), Civil affairs France and Holland, Military Government, Germany. *Address:* 1 Dorchester Mansions, Bournemouth, Hants. *Clubs:* United Service, Royal Automobile. [*Died* 16 *May* 1967.

SAVORY, Professor Sir Douglas (Lloyd), Kt., *cr.* 1952; M.A. Officer d'Académie; Officier de l'Instruction Publique; Officier de la Légion d'Honneur; Lieut; R.N.V.R., formerly attached to Naval Staff, Intelligence Division, Admiralty; Professor of French Language and Romance Philology at the University of Belfast, 1909-40, Professor Emeritus since 1941; Commissioner of Intermediate Education for Ireland, 1920-22; *b.* Palgrave Rectory, Suffolk, 17 August 1878; 2nd *s.* of late Rev. E. L. Savory, Rector of Palgrave; *m.* 1918, Madeline, *d.* of late James H. Clendinning, Lurgan, Co. Armagh. *Educ.:* Marlborough College; St. John's College, Oxford; Universities of Paris, Berne, Lausanne; Assistant Master at Marlborough College, 1902-5; French Lecturer at Goldsmiths' College, University of London, 1905-9; Lecturer on French Phonetics, and Examiner in French to L.C.C., 1906-7; on leave of absence from the Goldsmiths' College for one year in order to hold post as English Lecturer at the University of Marburg, Prussia, 1907-08; Phonetic Lecturer at Marburg University holiday course, 1907, 1908, 1909, 1910, 1913, and 1914; Lectr., Edinburgh Univ. holiday course, 1910 and 1911; Lectr., Bonn Univ., 1913 and 1914; Phonetic Lecturer to the Board of Education, 1914-15; Lecturer on French Literature to the London University Holiday Course, 1912 and 1913; Secretary to H.M. Minister at Stockholm, 1918-19; French Examiner and Inspector to the Oxford and Cambridge Schools Examination Board; French Examiner to the Civil Service Commission. M.P. (U.) Queen's University, Belfast, 1940-1950. South Antrim, 1950-55. Pres. Huguenot Society of London, 1946-48, President Emeritus, 1948-; President The Queen's University Club, London, 1949-50; jt. Vice-Pres. Franco-British Parl. Relations Cttee., 1953-55. *Publications:* Tercentenary Lecture on Racine, 1939; Racine and editions of Sainte-Beuve and Charles Nodier. *Recreation:* travelling. *Address:* Beechville, 33 Knockbreda Park, Belfast 6, Northern Ireland. *T.:* Belfast 641758. *Clubs:* Athenæum; Ulster (Belfast). [*Died* 5 *Oct.* 1969.

SAVORY, Sir William Borradaile, 3rd Bt., *cr.* 1890; *b.* 14 May 1882; *o. c.* of 2nd Bt. and Florence Julia (*d.* 1902), *d.* of late F. W. Pavy, M.D., F.R.S.; *S.* father, 1906; *m.* 1907, Argemone Margaret, *d.* of late C. Carruthers Johnstone; three *d.* M.A. Cantab., 1912; Rowed in the University Eight, 1905; Winning crew Ladies Plate

Henley, 1906. Member of M.C.C., 1923. High Sheriff, Buckinghamshire, 1923-24. K.J.St.J. 1920. *Heir:* none. *Address:* 1 Roehampton Lane, S.W.15. *T.:* Prospect 7862. [*Died* 16 *Sept.* 1961 (*ext.*).

SAWARD, Sidney Carman, C.M.G. 1946; M.C. 1916; M.M. 1916; *b.* 1889; *s.* of Frank Saward, Ipswich; *m.* 1919, Elizabeth Dorothy Harris (*d.* 1927); no *c.*; *m.* 1947, Florence L. Ascham (*d.* 1962). *Educ.:* Ipswich. Served European War, 1914-19 (despatches, M.M., M.C.); Surveyor, Gold Coast, 1919; field Supervisor, 1924; Assistant Surveyor-General, 1929; Director of Surveys, Gold Coast, 1938-47; retd. 1947. *Address:* Mill House, Burgh, Woodbridge, Suffolk. [*Died* 24 *Feb.* 1967.

SAYE and SELE, 20th Baron (*cr.* 1447 and 1603), **Ivo Murray Twisleton-Wykeham-Fiennes,** O.B.E. 1961; M.C. 1917; D.L.; High Steward of Banbury; Lt.-Col. R.A. (retd.); *b.* 15 Dec. 1885; 2nd *s.* of 18th Baron and Marion Ruperta Murray (*d.* 1946), *d.* of Major Lawes; *S.* brother, 1949; *m.* 1919, Hersey Cecilia Hester, *d.* of late Capt. Sir Thomas Dacres Butler, K.C.V.O.; two *s.* (and one *s.* killed in action, 1941). *Educ.:* Harrow; R.M.A., Woolwich. Served European War, 1914-18, Royal Horse and Field Artillery (despatches, M.C., French Croix de Guerre); served in War, 1939-41, commanding Light A.A. Regt., R.A. in England. Alderman Oxfordshire C.C.; D.L. Oxfordshire. *Heir: s.* Maj. (retd.) Hon. Nathaniel Thomas Allen Twisleton-Wykeham-Fiennes. Rifle Brigade [*b.* 22 Sept. 1920; *m.* 1958, Mariette, *d.* of Major-General Sir Guy Salisbury-Jones, G.C.V.O., C.M.G., C.B.E., M.C.; three *s.* one *d.* *Educ.:* Eton; New College, Oxford]. *Address:* Broughton Castle, Banbury, Oxon. *T.:* Banbury 2624. [*Died* 21 *Oct.* 1968.

SAYER, Brigadier Arthur Penrice, C.B. 1945; D.S.O. 1915; R.E.; *b.* 5 Nov. 1885; *s.* of William Feetham and Edith Alexandra Sayer; *m.* 1916, Blanche Mary, *y. d.* of late Dr. J. W. Leacroft and *widow* of Capt. David S. Dodgson, R.A. *Educ.:* Cholmeley School, Highgate; Woolwich. Entered Army, 1906; Bt. Major, 1919; Bt. Col. 1933; Col. 1934; Brig. 1938; served European War, 1915-16 (D.S.O., wounded); Vice-President R.E. Board, London, 1931; Assistant Director of Works, War Office, 1935-37; President Royal Engineer and Signals Board, 1937; retired, 1940; re-employed as Director of Radar, War Office; reverted to retired pay, 1945. *Address:* 54 Collington Avenue, Bexhill on Sea, Sussex. [*Died* 28 *April* 1962.

SAYERS, John Edward; Editor-in-Chief, Belfast Telegraph, since 1961; (Joint Managing Editor since 1953); a Director Belfast Telegraph Newspapers Ltd.; *b.* 13 July 1911; *s.* of John Sayers (Editor, Belfast Telegraph, 1937-39) and Elizabeth Lemon; *m.* 1945, Mrs. Daphne M. Godby (*née* Pannell); two *d.* *Educ.:* Methodist Coll., Belfast. Entered The Belfast Telegraph, 1930. R.N.V.R. 1935-45 (Lieut. Comdr.); H.M.S. Courageous, 1939, Ops. Div. Admty., on staff of First Lord's map room and Mr. Churchill's map room at Downing St., 1939-1945. Polit. corresp., Belfast Telegraph, 1945-53; Press officer to Prime Minister of Northern Ireland (Sir Basil Brooke) on tour of United States and Canada, 1950. Mem. N.I. Cttee., National Trust, 1952-; N.I. Adv. Council of B.B.C., 1958-65; Chm., Belfast Ophthalmic and Benn Hosp. Management Cttee., 1961-64; Mem., Belfast Hosps. Management Cttee., 1961-; Planning Cttee., N.I. Hosps. Authority, 1965-68; N.I. Rep. on Exec. British Council, 1966-; A Founder Mem. Protestant and Catholic Encounter. Hon. D.Lit., Queen's Univ., Belfast, 1964. *Publications:* Contrib. to Ulster Under Home Rule, 1955. *Recreations:* music, gardening. *Address:* Tara Cottage, The Spa, Ballynahinch, Co. Down, Northern Ireland. *T.:* Ballynahinch 445. *Club:* Ulster (Belfast). [*Died* 30 *Aug.* 1969.

SCALLAN, Eugene Kevin; diplomat, Union of South Africa; *b.* 2 January 1893; *s.* of Eugene Valentine Scallan; *m.* 1939, Helen, *d.* of J. O'Riordan, Senior Inspector of Schools, Dublin; no *s.* *Educ.:* Marist Brothers, Cape Town; School of Mines, Johannesburg; Pretoria University. B.A. University of Cape of Good Hope, 1916; entered Civil Service (Transvaal), 1909, Post Office, then in Treasury; Civil Service Commission, and Dept. of External Affairs; Secretary of Legation, Washington, 1929-34; Chargé d'Affaires, Lisbon, 1935, and Rome, 1936; Political Secretary, London, 1936-38; Union Consul-General at Lourenço Marques, 1939-43; Official Secretary, Office of High Commissioner for the Union of South Africa, London, 1943-47; Deputy High Commissioner, London, 1948; South African Minister in Brazil, 1948-51, in the Argentine and Chile, 1951-54. Gold staff officer at Coronation of King George VI; South African representative on Imperial Shipping Cttee., and on United Maritime Authority Executive Board, Chargé d'Affaires a.i. to the Netherlands and Belgian Govts. and South African rep. on Council of U.N.R.R.A. at 3rd Session, 1945, and 4th Session, 1946. 1914 Star, Gen. Service and Victory Medals, Coronation Medal. *Recreations:* golf, tennis, mountaineering. *Clubs:* Pretoria, Cape Mountaineering, Pretoria Country (Pretoria): Mowbray Golf, Owl (Cape Town), etc. [*Died* 1966.

SCARBROUGH, 11th Earl of (*cr.* 1690), **Lawrence Roger Lumley,** K.G. 1948; P.C. 1952; G.C.S.I. 1943; G.C.I.E. 1937; G.C.V.O. 1953; Royal Victorian Chain, 1963; Visc. Lumley in peerage of Ireland, 1628; Baron Lumley of Lumley Castle, Durham, 1681; Viscount Lumley, 1689; Earl of Scarborough, 1690, all in peerage of Great Britain; T.D.; D.L., J.P.; a Permanent Lord-in-Waiting to the Queen since 1963; Lord Chamberlain of H.M. Household, Oct. 1952-Jan. 1963, retd.; Lord-Lt., W.R., Yorks and City of York since 1948; High Steward of York Minster since 1967; *b.* 27 July 1896; 2nd and *o. surv. s.* of late Brig.-Gen. Hon. Osbert Lumley, C.M.G., and late Constance Eleanor, O.B.E., *e. d.* of Capt. Eustace John Wilson-Patten, 1st Life Guards, and Emily Constantia, *d.* of Rev. Lord John Thynne; *S.* uncle, 1945; *m.* 1922, Katharine Isobel (D.C.V.O. 1962; Kaisar-i-Hind Gold Medal, 1941, Extra Lady of the Bedchamber to Queen Elizabeth the Queen Mother since 1953 (Lady of the Bedchamber, 1947-53)), *d.* of late R. F. McEwen of Marchmont, Berwickshire, and Bardrochat, Ayrshire; one *s.* four *d.* *Educ.:* Eton; Royal Military Coll., Sandhurst; Magdalen Coll., Oxford. B.A. Oxford, 1921; Hon. D.C.L. (Durham), 1949; Hon. LL.D., Sheffield, 1951, Leeds, 1951, London, 1953. Chancellor, Durham University, 1958-. M.P. (C.) Kingston-upon Hull, East, 1922-29; York, 1931-37; Governor of Bombay, 1937-43; Parliamentary Under-Secretary for India and Burma, 1945; served with 11th Hussars, France, 1916-18, and Yorkshire Dragoons, 1921-37; acting Maj.-Gen. 1943-44. Chm. Interdepartmental Commn. on Oriental, Slavonic, East European and African Studies 1945; 1946; Pres. Royal Asiatic Society, 1946-49; Pres. East India Association, 1946-51; Pres. Roy. Central Asian Soc., 1954-60; Special Ambassador to Coronation of King of Nepal, 1956; Pro Grand Master, United Grand Lodge of Masons of England, 1967 (Grand Master, 1951-67; Dep. G.M., 1947-51; Chairman, Governing Body, School of Oriental and African Studies, 1951-59; President South Yorks County Scout Council); Chm., Commonwealth Scholarships Commn.,

1960-63. Hon. Master of Bench of Inner Temple, 1969. Hon. Col. Queen's Own Yorks. Yeo., 1956-62. Freeman of Doncaster, 1962. *Publication:* History of the Eleventh Hussars, 1936. *Heir:* *s.* Viscount Lumley. *Address:* Sandbeck Park, Rotherham, Yorks. *T.A.* and *T.:* Tickhill 210. *Clubs:* Carlton, White's. [*Died* 29 *June* 1969.

SCARFF, Robert Wilfred, C.B.E. 1960; M.B., B.S., F.R.C.S., F.R.S.E.; Emeritus Professor in Pathology, Univ. of London (Prof. 1946-66); Emer. Consultant in Pathology, Middlesex Hosp. (Dir., Bland-Sutton Inst. of Pathology, 1948-65); Consultant Adviser in Pathology to Minister of Health; *b.* 18 October 1899; *s.* of Robert William Scarff and Katherine Agnes (*née* Russell). *Educ.:* City of London School; Middlesex Hospital Medical School. Reader in Pathology, University of London, 1933-46; Consultant Pathologist, E.M.S., 1939-46; Hon. Scientific Sec. and Mem. Grand Council and other cttees., British Empire Cancer Campaign, 1936-. Editor British Journal of Cancer; Editor British Journal of Experimental Pathology, 1937-50. President Pathological Section, Royal Society Medicine, 1948-49; Liverymen, Society of Apothecaries; Freeman City of London; Examiner in Pathology, University of London; Secretary-General, VIIth Internat. Cancer Congress, London, 1958. *Publications:* numerous publications in scientific journals. *Recreation:* golf. *Address:* 170 Oakwood Court, W.14. *T.:* 01-937 5075. *Clubs:* Athenæum, Savage, Royal Automobile. [*Died* 19 *Jan.* 1970.

SCARFOGLIO, Carlo; literary and political writer; *b.* 16 Oct. 1887; *s.* of Edoardo Scarfoglio and Matilde Serao; *m.* Virginia Daleggio, Constantinople; one *s.* *Educ.:* Collegio Cicognini, Prato, Tuscany; Rome University. Started as foreign correspondent for the Mattino of Naples (his father's property); was in London, 1909-11; then was correspondent in the Tripoli and the Balkan Wars; specialised in Eastern and International affairs, always for the Stampa of Turin and the Mattino of Naples; was correspondent, European War, from the Anglo-French and from the Turkish front; assumed temporary editorship of the Mattino, and subsequently of the Nazione, of Florence; was Editor of last paper four years; left it to assume joint editorship of the Mattino until the sale of this family concern in 1928; left active journalism at that date, and has turned to literature and to political studies. After the fall of Mussolini (25 July 1943), called to the editorship of the Nazione of Florence. Left it within a month, in order to avoid collaborating with the Germans, who had occupied the town. Contributor to Milano-Sera, of Milan, also to Paese-Sera, of Rome, mainly on the Southern question and on foreign affairs; Editor of Il Rinnovamento d' Italia, weekly, Rome, and co-editor of La Pace, monthly, Rome. Now literary rather than journalistic. *Publications:* Idee Sulla Ricostruzione, 1920; Bidental, 1934; Russian Tour, 1934; England and the Continent, 1939; La Vera Croce, an historical novel (publ. in Eng. and Amer. as The True Cross); Ro-Ma, an inquiry on preolympic cults and civilisations, 1939; Davanti a questa guerra, 1941; Possiamo essere nazionalisti?; Il mezzogiorno e l' unità d' Italia, 1953; I Racconti della Torre, 1962; L'Antologia classica cinese (Ezra Pound), curata e volta in italiano, 1964; Le Memorie di un giornalista, 1964. *Recreations:* travelling, motoring, alpineering, swimming. *Address:* Viale Parioli 54, Rome. [*Died* 22 *April* 1969.

SCARTH, Lt.-Col. Robert, O.B.E. 1943; retired; Lord Lieutenant for the County of Orkney, since 1959; *b.* 24 July 1894; *e. s.* of Robert Scarth 2nd of Binscarth, and Emily Scott Abel; *m.* 1920, Hester V. W., *d.* of Rev. W. J. S. Dickey, D.D., T.D., Harray, Orkney; no *c.* *Educ.:* Aberdeen Grammar School; Aberdeen University. Served European War, 1914-19, 4th Gordon Highlanders; Lt. 1919; Orkney Home Guard, 1940-45; Lt.-Col. O.C. 1st Bn. 1944. D.L. 1944; J.P.; Hon. Sheriff Substitute. *Address:* Binscarth, Finstown, by Kirkwall, Orkney. *T.:* Finstown 200. [*Died* 18 *May* 1966.

SCHACHT, Dr. Hjalmar Horace Greely; Formerly Senior partner Schacht & Co., Bank, Düsseldorf; late Reichsminister without portfolio; former President of the Reichsbank, Berlin; *b.* Tingleff, 22 Jan. 1877; *s.* of William Schacht and Baroness Konstanze Eggers; *m.* 1st, 1903, Luise Sowa (decd.); one *s.* one *d.*; 2nd, 1941, Manci Vogler; two *d.* *Educ.:* University of Kiel (Ph.D. 1899), Berlin, Munich and Leipzig. Managing Secretary, Society of Commercial Treaties, 1900-03; Economist Dresdner Bank, 1903-03; Asst. Manager Dresdner Bank, 1908-15; Managing Partner National Bank für Deutschland and (after amalgamation 1922) in Darmstädter und National bank; Reich Currency Commissioner 1923; President of the Reichsbank under Dawes Plan, 1924; Delegate at Young Conference, Paris; Delegate Conference for constitution of Bank of International Settlements Baden-Baden; opposed adoption of Hague Agreement and resigned from Reichsbank, 1930; reappointed President, 1933; Reichsminister of Economics, 1934-37, when he was relieved of this position retaining position as Pres. of the Reichsbank till 1939. Acquitted at Nuremberg 1946, and by denazification court, 1948. *Publications:* The Stabilization of the Mark, 1927; The End of Reparations, 1931; Principles of German Economic Policy, 1932; Abrechnung mit Hitler, 1948; Mehr Geld, mehr Kapital, mehr Arbeit, 1951; 76 Jahre meines Lebens, 1953; Magie des Geldes, 1966; 1933: Wie eine Demokratie stirbt, 1968. *Address:* Muenchen 27, Kufsteiner Platz 2, Germany. [*Died* 4 *June* 1970.

SCHACHT, Prof. Joseph; Professor of Arabic and Islamics, Columbia University, New York, N.Y. 10027, since 1959; *b.* 15 March 1902; *s.* of Eduard Schacht and Maria Mohr; *m.* 1943, Louise Isobel Dorothy, *d.* of Joseph Coleman. *Educ.:* Univs. of Breslau and Leipzig. D.Phil. (Breslau) 1923; M.A. (Oxford) 1947; D.Litt. (Oxford) 1952. Lecturer, Univ. of Freiburg i. Br., 1925; Associate Prof., 1927; Prof., 1929; Univ. of Königsberg, 1932; Egyptian Univ., Cairo, 1934-39; Lecturer, Univ. of Oxford, 1946; Reader in Islamic Studies, 1948; Prof. of Arabic, Univ. of Leiden, 1954. Member: Arab Acad., Damascus, 1955; Royal Netherlands Acad., 1956. Hon. LL.D., Algiers, 1952. *Publications:* numerous edns. and trans. of Arabic texts; Esquisse d'une histoire du droit musulman, 1954; The Origins of Muhammadan Jurisprudence, 1950; Introduction to Islamic Law, 1964; The *Theologus Autodidactus* of Ibn al-Nafis, 1967. Joint Editor: Encyclopædia of Islam; Studia Islamica. *Recreation:* travel. *Address:* St. John's College, Oxford; 348 Ivy Lane, Englewood, N.J. 07631, U.S.A. *T.:* (201)568-1046. [*Died* 1 *Aug.* 1969.

SHAFER, Edward P. S.; *see* Sharpey-Schafer.

SCHÄRF, Adolf, Grand Star of Austrian Order of Merit, 1957; Federal President of Austria since 1957 (re-elected 1963); *b.* 20 April 1890; *s.* of Joseph Schärf and Magdalena (*née* Sitek); *m.* 1915, Hilda Hammer (*d.* 1956); one *d.* (one *s.* killed on active service). *Educ.:* Vienna Univ. (Doctor of Laws). Served European War, 1915-18 (first lieut.). Sec. to Socialist party in Parliament, 1919; Member Federal Council, 1933; arrested and imprisoned in concentration camp, 1934; Solicitor, twice arrested under National

Socialism, 1938-45; Secretary of State, Member of Political Cabinet, April 1945; Vice-Chancellor of Austrian Government, Chairman Austrian Socialist Party, Member of Parliament and Member Bureau of Socialist International, 1945-57. Dr. Karl Renner Award of City of Vienna, 1955; Hon. Citizen of Vienna and of numerous other Austrian places. Holds numerous foreign orders and awards. *Publications:* Lease Law and Tenants' Protection, 1925; Social Democracy and Country People, 1925 (pseudonym Schäfer); The Juridical Situation of Woman, 1925; April 1945 in Vienna 1948; Between Democracy and People's Democracy, 1950; Austria's Revival, 1945-55, 1955; Erinnerungen aus meinem Leben, 1963. *Recreation:* studies in history. *Address:* Hofburg, Vienna 1, Austria. [*Died* 28 *Feb.* 1965.

SCHICK, Béla; Discoverer of Schick test for diphtheria; Director Pediatric Service, Beth-El Hospital, Brooklyn, N.Y., U.S.A.; *b.* 16 July 1877; *s.* of Jacob and Johanna Schick; *m.* 1925, Catharine Fries. *Educ.:* Gymnasium and Karl Franzens Univ., Graz, Austria. Univ. children's clinic, Vienna: Asst. 1908; Privatdozent, 1912; Extraord. Prof., 1918. For several years Clinical Prof., Columbia Univ., New York; Attending Pediatrician, Mt. Sinai Hospital, 1923-42, then Consulting Pediatrician; Director Pediatric Dept., Sea View Hospital, 1928-42, afterwards Consulting Pediatrician; Consulting Pediatrician in several other hospitals. Visiting Professor, Dr. Albert Einstein University Coll. of Medicine, 1955. Hon-member of numerous medical societies includ. ing pediatric societies, etc., all over the World. Gold Medal, New York Acad. of Medicine, 1938; Addingham Medal, Leeds, 1938; Gold Medal, Forum of Allergy, 1941; John Howland Medal and Award, 1954; Semmelweiss Medal, 1955. *Publications:* many publications dealing with pediatric problems. *Relevant publication:* Béla Schick and The World of Children, by Antoni Gronowicz, 1954. *Recreations:* travel, music. *Address:* 1045 Park Avenue, New York, N.Y., U.S.A. *T.:* Rhinelander 4-3304. [*Died* 6 *Dec.* 1967.

SCHIPA, Tito; Grande Ufficiale SS. Maurizio e Lazaro, Italy, and of Crown of Italy; Commandeur of Order Alfonso XII Spain; Commandeur of S. Sepulcro, of S. Gregorio Magno; Grande Ufficiale Order of Mercede; Chevalier Légion d'Honneur, France; Commandeur Order of Christ (Portugal); Leading Lyric Tenor, Chicago Opera Co., Teatro Reale, Rome, etc. recitalist; *b.* Lecce, Italy, 2 Jan. 1890; *m.* 1920, Antoinette Michel (French); one *d.* *Educ.:* Seminary Lecce. Studied with Maestro Gerunda; appearances in Opera: La Scala Milano, Colon Buenos Aires, Central America, Havana, Cuba, Madrid, Barcelona, Lisbon, New York, and various cities U.S.A., etc. *Recreations:* golf, boxing, football, tennis, swimming, etc. *Address:* 4956 Los Feliz Blvd., Hollywood, California. *T.A.:* Schipatito, New York. *Clubs:* Lambs, Woodsmen of America, (New York); Southern California Athletics (Los Angeles). [*Died* 16 *Dec.* 1965.

SCHLAPP, Prof. Walter; Brackenbury Professor of Physiology, Manchester Univ. 1946-65 and Dean of Medical School, retd.; Professor Emeritus, since 1965; *b.* 14 Jan. 1898; *s.* of Prof. Otto Schlapp and Anna Lotze; *m.* 1925, Kathleen Dott; one *s.* *Educ.:* Edinburgh Univ. (B.Sc.). George Watson's College, Edinburgh, to 1916; served European War, 1916-19; Edinburgh Univ., 1919-23; Asst. in Physiology, Edin., 1924; Carnegie Research Fellow, 1925; Ph.D. 1927; medical study, 1927-30; M.B., Ch.B. 1930; Manchester University: Asst. Lecturer in Pharmacology, 1931, Lecturer in Physiology, 1932, and subsequently Reader; sometime Tutor to Faculty of Medicine. *Publications:* contributions to Jl. Physiol. and Quarterly Jl. Physiol. *Recreation:* playing viola in string quartets. *Address:* 13 Barcheston Road, Cheadle, Cheshire. [*Died* 1 *Oct.* 1966.

SCHLESINGER, Arthur Meier; Francis Lee Higginson Professor of History, Harvard University, 1939, Emeritus since 1954; *b.* 27 Feb. 1888; *s.* of Bernhard Schlesinger and Katharine Feurle; *m.* 1914, Elizabeth Bancroft; two *s.* *Educ.:* Ohio State Univ. (A.B.); Columbia (Ph.D.). Instr., asst. prof. and prof. of history, Ohio State Univ., 1912-1919; prof. Univ. of Iowa, 1919-24; prof. Harvard Univ. 1924-54; visiting prof. Univ. of London and Univ. of Edinburgh, 1934, and Univ. of Leiden, 1948-49. Member Committee on Records of War Administration (U.S. Govt.), 1942-46; Chairman, Social Science Research Council, 1930-33; Trustee, Radcliffe College, 1942-63; Pres., American Historical Assoc., 1942. Hon. degrees; Litt.D.: Beloit 1928; Rochester, 1948; Harvard, 1963; L.H.D.: Union, 1942; Chicago, 1951; Kenyon, 1954, Bucknell, 1957; LL.D., Brandeis, 1963; Member, Nat. Hist. Publications Commn., 1952-55, 1961-65; Mem. Commn. on The Rights, Liberties and Responsibilities of the American Indian, 1957-63. *Publications:* The Colonial Merchants and the American Revolution, 1918; New Viewpoints in American History, 1922; Political and Social History of the U.S. from 1829 (with revisions in 1933, 1941 and 1951); The Rise of the City, 1933; The New Deal in Action, 1939; Learning How to Behave, a Historical Study of American Etiquette Books, 1946; Paths to the Present, 1949; The American as Reformer, 1950; Prelude to Independence: The Newspaper War on Britain, 1764-76, 1958; In Retrospect: The History of a Historian, 1963; (ed.) F. L. Olmsted's The Cotton Kingdom, 1953. Co-author: The Reinterpretation of American Literature, 1928; Research in the Social Sciences, 1929; Historical Scholarship in America, 1932; Approaches to American Social History, 1937; A Free and Responsible Press, 1947; Harvard Guide to American History, 1954. Co-editor: A History of American Life, 13 vols., 1927-48. *Recreations:* gardening. Travelled round the world, 1933-34. *Address:* 19 Gray Gardens East Cambridge, Mass., U.S.A. *Club:* Faculty (Camb., Mass.). [*Died* 30 *Oct.* 1965.

SCHLINK, Sir Herbert (Henry), Kt., *cr.* 1954; Chairman Royal Prince Alfred Hospital, Sydney, since 1934; Hon. Gynaecological Surgeon since 1912; still on staff as Consultant; *b.* 28 March 1883; *s.* of Albert Schlink, Paderborn, and Franziska Schlink, Eversberg, who arrived in Australia in 1864; *m.* 1945, Dr. Margaret Mulvey, M.B., B.S., M.R.C.O.G. *Educ.:* University of Sydney (M.B., Ch.M.). Royal Prince Alfred Hospital: Junior R.M.O., 1907; Senior R.M.O., 1908; Deputy Medical Supt., 1909; Medical Supt., 1910-12. Patron Aust. Hosp. Assoc., 1946; Pres. Aust. Blue Cross Assoc., 1952. Mem. B.M.A. Aust. Br., 1908; F.R.A.C.S.; F.R.C.O.G.; F.R.G.S. (London). Hon. Mem. Amer. Hosp. Assoc., St. Louis, 1951. Jubilee Medal, 1935; Coronation Medals, 1937, 1953. *Publications:* Text Book of Gynaecology, 1st Edn. 1939, 2nd Edn. 1949, 3rd Edn. 1955. Contributions on cancer of the uterus, repair operations in gynaecology and pathological migration of the ovum. *Recreations:* rowing, ski-ing (Pres. Australian Ski Club, 1920-; Kosciusko Alpine Club, 1912; British Ski Club, 1912; Kandahar Club, Gold K. 1937); landscape gardening. *Address:* 185 Macquarie St., Sydney, N.S.W. *T.:* BW 5511; (country) Marara, Careel Bay. *T.:* Avalon Beach 2345 *Club:* Australian (Sydney). [*Died* 30 *Nov.* 1962.

SCHMITT, Bernadotte Everly, M.A. (Oxon); Ph.D. (Wisconsin); LL.D. (Western Reserve); Litt.D. (Pomona College); Hon.

DLitt., Oxford, 1967; Andrew MacLeish Distinguished Service Professor of Mod. History, Univ. of Chicago, 1939-46, Emeritus Prof. since 1946; *b.* 19 May 1886; *s.* of Cooper D. Schmitt, Prof. of Mathematics and Dean of the College, University of Tennessee; *m.* 1939, Damaris Ames, of Chicago, Illinois. *Educ.:* Universities of Tennessee, Oxford, Wisconsin. Rhodes Scholar from Tennessee, 1905; 1st Cl. Mod. His., Merton College, Oxford, 1908; Instructor in history, Western Reserve University, 1910-14, asst. prof., 1914-17, assoc prof. 1917-24; prof. 1924-25; professor of modern history University of Chicago, 1925-39; Chairman department of history, 1933-36; roundtable leader, Institute of Politics, Williamstown, Mass., 1925, 1932; Guggenheim Fellow, 1927; prof. at Institut Universitaire de Hautes Études Internationales, Geneva, 1931-32; Office of Strategic Service Dec. 1943-Apr. 1945; Special Adviser to the Secretary-General, United Nations Conference on International Organisation, San Francisco, April-June 1945; Special Adviser, Division of Research and publication, Department of State, Apr. 1945; Special Adviser, Division of Historical Policy Research, Department of State, Washington, D.C., 1946-49; Chief, German War Documents Project, Department of State, 1949-52; Editor of the Journal of Modern History, 1929-46; co-editor, Cambridge Mod. History, new series, 1935-49; Visiting Prof. of History, University of South Carolina, February-June 1956. Vice-Pres. Amer. Hist. Assoc., 1959, Pres. 1960. Hon. Fell., Merton Coll., Oxford, 1966. George Louis Beer Prize, Am. Hist. Assoc. 1930; Pulitzer Prize for History, 1931; 2nd Lt. F.A., U.S. Army, 1918. *Publications:* England and Germany 1740-1914, 1916; The Coming of the War 1914, 1930; Triple Alliance and Triple Entente, 1934; The Annexation of Bosnia 1908-1909, 1937; From Versailles to Munich 1918-1938, 1939; What shall we do with Germany?, 1943; The Origins of the First World War, 1958; The Fashion and Future of History, 1960; (Ed.) Some Historians of Modern Europe, 1942; Poland (United Nations Series), 1945; Ed. (with D. P. Myers), The Treaty of Versailles and After: Annotations of the Text of the Treaty, 1947. Contributor to Cambridge History of Poland, Am. Hist. Review, etc. *Recreations:* motoring and stamp collecting. *Address:* P.O. Box 324, Alexandria 22313, Virginia, U.S.A. *T.:* Temple 6-2981. *Clubs:* Cosmos, Literary Society (Washington); Chicago Literary.

[*Died* 22 *March* 1969.

SCHOFIELD, Herbert, C.B.E. 1946 (M.B.E.); formerly Chairman: J. A. Crabtree and Co. Ltd., Walsall; Crabtree Electrical Industries Ltd.; *b* Halifax, Yorks, 8 December 1883; *e. s.* of James Schofield, Mechanical Engineer, Halifax, and Alice Schofield; *m.* 1918, Clara (*d.* 1928), *y. d.* of late Henry Johns, London; one *s.* one *d.* *Educ.:* Trinity Higher Grade School, Halifax; The Municipal Technical College, Halifax; The Royal College of Science, London (University of London). Ph.D., B.Sc. (Hons.) London; A.R.C.Sc., Mechanics and Mathematics (1st in 1st Class and Mechanics Prizeman); A R.C.Sc., Physics (1st in 1st Class and Physics Prizeman); D.I.C. (Diploma of the Imperial College for original research); Whitworth Exhibitioner Carnegie Engineering Scholar; Royal Exhibitioner; Assoc.M.Inst.C.E.; M I Mech E; A.M.I.E.E.; M.Inst.Struct.E.; Past President Instn. of Production Engineers; F.Inst P.; Formerly Member of the National Trade Advisory Committee for Engineering and Shipbuilding; Past President of the Association of Principals of Technical Institutions; Past-Chm of Council of Assoc. of Technical Institutions; Past Chm. of the Council of the Association for the Advancement of Education in Industry and Commerce; Past President of Rotary International (Great Britain and Ireland) and Hon. Treasurer; Past Chm. European Economic Advisory Committee, Rotary International; formerly Principal, Loughborough Coll.; Past Member Consultative Committee of Ministry of Education; Past Pres. the Institute of Linguists; formerly Chm.: East Midlands Educational Union; Advisory Council for the organization of Further Education in East Midlands; Member, Nat. Advisory Council on Industry and Commerce; Mem. Council Production Engineering Research Association of Gt. Britain, Member, Brit. Assoc. for Commercial and Industrial Education. *Publications:* The Measurement of Air Supply to Internal Combustion Engines, Proc. Inst. of Mech. Eng.; Thermal and Combustion Efficiency Tests on a Daimler Sliding Sleeve Engine, Proc. Inst. of Automobile Eng.; Shell Turning for Munition Workers; Engineering for Munition Workers; Technical Education and its Relation to the Engineering Industry. *Recreations:* motoring, golf, tennis. *Address:* Iffley, Ashby Road, Loughborough. *T.:* Loughborough 2594.

[*Died* 18 *Sept.* 1963.

SCHOLEFIELD, Guy Hardy, C.M.G. 1948; O.B.E. 1919; *b.* Dunedin, N.Z., 1877; *s.* of John H. Scholefield; *m.* 1908, Adela L. S., *d.* of Miles R. Bree, of Southland, N.Z.; two *s.* one *d.* *Educ.:* Tokomairiro High School; Victoria College (Univ. of N.Z.), Bowen prizeman, 1903; Macmillan-Brown prizeman, 1904; on staff of Bruce Herald, 1896; N Z. Times, 1899; The Press, Christchurch, 1903-4; chief of staff N.Z. Times, 1906, London correspondent of New Zealand Associated Press, 1908-1919; Editor, Who's Who in N.Z., 1908-51. B.Sc. (Econ.) London Univ., 1915; D Sc. 1919; the first oversea correspondent at British front; Hon. Lieut. R.N.V.R. 1918; founder and honorary editor of The New Zealander, 1916-19, Member of Council of Empire Press Union (representing N.Z.), 1910-19; Editor and Director Wairarapa Age, 1921-26; Chairman Wairarapa High School Governors, 1924-1926; parliamentary librarian and Dominion Archivist, 1926-48; hon. secretary Institute of Pacific Relations (New Zealand branch), 1926-34, pres. P.E.N. (N.Z. Centre), 1934. 1937; of N.Z. Ex Libris Society; pres. N.Z. Library Assoc., 1940-41; F.L.A. 1939; Chairman, Advisory Committee, State Literary Fund, 1948-51. *Publications:* New Zealand in Evolution, 1909; Capt W. Hobson, R.N., first Governor of N.Z., 1934; New Zealand (International Information Series) The Pacific, 1919; Dictionary of N Z Biography, 1940; Notable N.Z. Statesmen, 1946; N.Z. Parliamentary Record, 1950; Newspapers in New Zealand, 1958; Richmond-Atkinson Papers, 1961. *Address:* 42 Watt Street, Wellington, N.Z.

[*Died* 19 *July* 1963.

SCHOLES, G. E., M.B.E.; M.Sc.; Professor of Mechanical Engineering, Liverpool University, 1926-46; Professor of Engineering, Thermodynamics of Heat Engines, 1920-26. *Address:* Well Close, Finsthwaite, Ulverston, Lancashire. *T.:* Newby Bridge 313.

[*Died* 29 *July* 1968.

SCHOLFIELD, Alwyn Faber; Fellow of King's College and Librarian to the University of Cambridge, 1923-49; *b.* 23 Feb. 1884; *s.* of late Robert Stanley Scholfield, J.P., of Sandhall, Howden, E. Yorks. *Educ.:* Eton; King's College, Cambridge. Keeper of the Records, Govt. of India, 1913-19; Librarian of Trinity College Cambridge, 1919-23. *Publications:* Bibliographies of W H. Frere, 1947, and M R. James, 1939; (joint editor with A. S. F. Gow), Nicander, 1953; Aelian (Loeb Class. Lib.). *Recreations:* painting cycling, swimming. *Address:* King's College, Cambridge *Club:* Athenæum.

[*Died* 19 *Oct.* 1969.

SCHONELL, Sir Fred Joyce, Kt. 1962; B.A., M.A., Ph.D., D.Lit.; Hon. D.Litt.; Hon. LL.D.; Hon. F.B.Ps.S.; F.A.C.E.;

F.A.Ps.S.; Vice-Chancellor, Univ. of Queensland, since 1960; *b.* Perth, W. Australia, 3 Aug. 1900; *s.* of Edward William Schonell, headmaster, and Agnes Mary Schonell; *m.* 1926, Florence Eleanor Waterman, M.A., Ph.D. (*d.* 1962); one *s.* one *d.* *Educ.:* Perth Modern School, Perth, W. Australia. B.A. Univ. of W. Australia; Post Graduate Research Scholar; full-time research educational psychology, King's Coll. and Institute of Education (Lond.), 1928-31; Ph.D. Univ. of London; Scholar and Tutor Geneva Sch. of Internat. Studies, 1932; Lectr., Educational Psychology, Goldsmiths' Coll. (Lond.), 1931-42; Hon. Sec. Brit. Psy. Soc. (Educ. Section), 1931-37; Sessional Lecturer Comparative Education, Institute of Education, 1940-45; Professor of Education, University College, Swansea, 1942; Prof. of Education and Head of Department of Education and Head of Remedial Education Centre, Univ. of Birmingham, 1946-50; Professor of Education and Dean of the Faculty of Education, 1950-59; Pres., Professorial Board, University of Queensland, 1956-59; D.Lit. (Lond.), 1943; M.A. (Birm.) 1947; Hon. D.Litt. (Univ. of W. Australia), 1963; Hon. LL.D. (Univ. of Sydney), 1965; Mackie Medal for outstanding work in education in Australia, 1962 (First Recipient); Joseph Bancroft Medal, 1962; Encyclopaedia Britannica Award for Education, 1965; Hon. Fellow, British Psych. Soc., 1966; Pres. Midland Branch Brit. Psy. Soc.; Council mem. British Psy. Soc. Admitted as Fell. Aust. Coll. of Educn., 1959; member Education Panel British Association, 1946; Staff Examiner Higher Degrees in Education for University of London, 1940-48. Consultant Australian Council of Organizations for Sub-Normal Children; Brit. Psychological Soc. (Australian Branch); Member of the Council, Australian Council for Educational Research; Chm., Qld. Cttee. and a Dir. of Aust. Elizabethan Theatre Trust; Hon. Pres., Qld. Sub-normal Children's Welfare Assoc., 1952-67; Pres., Australian and New Zealand Assoc. for the Advancement of Science, 1965-66; Chm., Queensland Regional Cttee. and Nat. Chm., Winston Churchill Fellowship Selection Committee, 1966-. *Publications:* Essentials in Teaching and Testing Spelling, 1932; Education of the 'C' Child, Year Book of Education, 1935; Diagnostic Tests, Year Book of Education, 1936; Diagnostic Arithmetic Tests, 1937; Essential Intelligence Test, 1940; Backwardness in the Basic Subjects, 1942; The Psychology and Teaching of Reading, 1945; Diagnostic and Attainment Testing, 1949; Essential Arithmetic Tests, 1946; Practice in Basic Arithmetic, 1954; A Study of the Oral Vocabulary of Adults, 1956; Diagnosis and Remedial Teaching in Arithmetic, 1957; The Subnormal Child at Home, 1959; Happy Venture Teacher's Manual, 1960; Essential Read-Spell Books, 1961; Promise & Performance—A Study of Student Progress at University Level, 1962; The Slow-Learner—Segregation or Integration, 1962; Failure in School, 1962; articles in British Journal of Educational Psychology, and educational journals; remedial material for backward and mal-adjusted children. *Recreations:* fishing, gardening. *Address:* University of Queensland, Brisbane, Australia. [*Died* 22 *Feb.* 1969.

SCHREIBER, Ricardo Rivera, G.B.E. (Hon.) 1962 (K.B.E. (Hon.) 1926); Member of Foreign Affairs Advisory Commission of Peru; *b.* Lima, Peru, 11 November 1892; *s.* of Ricardo Rivera Navarrete, Senator to the Republic, and Doña Matilde Schreiber de Rivera; *m.* 1940, Teresa Kroll; two *s.* *Educ.:* Sacred Heart College and Universidad Mayor de San Marcos of Lima (Dr. of Laws and Political Science). Consul and Sec. Peruvian Legation in Bolivia, 1917; Sec. Peruvian Deleg. to League of Nations, 1919; Second Sec., London, 1920; Chargé d'Affaires *ad interim*, London, 1921-26, *en titre* in Holland, 1926. Minister to Ecuador, 1928; Special Envoy to Ecuador, 1929; Member Foreign Affairs Advisory Commission of Peru and of Ecuadorian Commission, 1933; Peruvian Deleg. for Settlement of Peruvian-Colombian boundary dispute, 1934; Minister to Colombia, 1936, to Japan and China, 1938; Ambassador to Spain, 1943, to Italy, 1945. Pres. Peruvian Deleg. to Preparatory Commn. of U.N. and Vice-Pres. of its Legal Cttee., 1945-46; Ambassador of Peru to the Court of St. James's, 1949-52, and again Ambassador, 1954-62. Peruvian Minister for Foreign Affairs, 1952-54. Delegate to First Gen. Assembly of U.N.O., to 6th Assembly, 1951-1952; Pres. Delegation of Peru to 10th Inter-American Conf., Caracas, 1954. Especial Envoy to Celebrations of 4th Centenary of Henry the Navigator, Portugal, 1960. Member: International Law Assoc., London; International Diplomatic Academy, Paris; Royal Academy of Law and Jurisprudence, Madrid. Grand Cross of Order of El Sol del Peru; Grand Cross of the Pontifical Order of St. Sylvester; also Grand Cross etc. of various Orders from Spain, Chile, Colombia, Japan, China, Ecuador, Dominican Republic, Malta, Italy, Germany, Portugal, Brasil, Venezuela, Panama, Argentina, France, and Netherlands, etc. *Publications:* El Seguro de Vida, 1916; El Sentido Democrático de la Diplomacia Contemporanea, 1932; La Liga de las Naciones en la Historia, 1926; El Porvenir Internacional de América Latina, 1924; many contribs. to journals and magazines on international and juridical subjects. *Recreations:* golf and yachting. *Address:* Avenida del Golf 610, San Isidoro; Lima, Peru. *Clubs:* St. James', Travellers'; National (Lima). [*Died* 25 *July* 1969.

SCHRODER, Helmut William Bruno; Honorary President, Schroders Ltd. since 1966; *b.* 18 Jan. 1901; *s.* of late Baron Bruno Schroder and late Emma C. M. T. Deichmann; *m.* 1930, Margaret, *er. d.* of Col. Sir Lionel Edward Hamilton Marmaduke Darell, 6th Bt., D.S.O.; one *s.* one *d.* *Educ.:* Eton; Corpus Christi College, Oxford. Partner, J. Henry Schroder & Co., 1926, Senior Partner, 1950, Chairman until Dec. 1965. Order of Merit of Chile, 1954. Gr. Verdienstkreuz of Fed. Rep. of Germany, 1964. *Recreations:* farming, forestry, orchids. *Address:* Round Oak, Bishopsgate Road, Englefield Green, Surrey. *T.:* Egham 2030; Dunlossit, Port Askaig, Isle of Islay, Argyll. *T.:* Port Askaig 214 and 215; Flat 23, 51 South Street, W.1. *T.:* 01-499 4959. *Clubs:* White's, Bat. [*Died* 18 *June* 1969.

SCHRÖDINGER, Dr. Erwin, Dr. phil. (Vienna), M.A. (Oxon); Hon. Dr. (Ghent), Hon. D.Sc. (Univ. of Dublin. and N.U.I.); Hon. LL.D., University of Edinburgh; Professor, University of Vienna, 1956-58; Emeritus Professor, 1958; *b.* Wien, 12 Aug. 1887; *o. c.* of late Rudolf Schrödinger, botanist, Wien; *m.* 1920, Anna Maria Bertel, Salzburg; no *c.* Privat-dozent, Wien, 1914; Ausserordentlicher Professor, Stuttgart, 1920; o. Professor, Breslau, Zürich, 1921; Berlin, 1927; Fellow Magdalen College, Oxford, 1933-38; Fondation Francqui (Belgium), 1939; Professor, Royal Irish Academy, 1940; Senior Professor, Dublin Institute for Advanced Studies, 1940. Member of the Academies of Science in Berlin, Wien, U.S.S.R., Dublin, Madrid, Vatican-City, Rome (Lincei and Dei Quaranta), Boston, Brussels (Flemish Academy), Lima (Peru); Matteucci medallist; Planck medallist; Nobel Prize in Physics, 1933 (with P. A. M. Dirac). Foreign mem., Roy. Soc., 1949. Order of Merit (Germany); Litteris et Artibus (Austria). *Publications:* numerous

scientific papers in various physical journals and in the Proceedings of the Academies of Science of Wien, Berlin, Dublin, and the Vatican; collected papers on Wave Mechanics (trans. from the second German edn., 1928); four lectures on Wave Mechanics, 1928; Science and the human temperament, 1935; What is Life?, 1944; Statistical Thermodynamics; Space-Time Structure; Science and Humanism; Nature and the Greeks; Expanding Universes; Mind and Matter, 1958; many popular articles in newspapers and magazines. *Recreations:* formerly: skiing, cycling, swimming, mountaineering. *Address:* Wien IX, Pasteurgasse 4.
[*Died* 4 *Jan.* 1961.

SCHUMAN, Robert; French Statesman; Deputy of Moselle since 1919; barrister; *b.* 29 June 1886; unmarried. *Educ.:* Universities of Bonn, Munich, Berlin and Strasbourg (Docteur en Droit). Barrister, Metz, 1912. Minister of Finance, Bidault Government, 1946; Ramadier Government, Jan.-Nov. 1947; Prime Minister, 1947-48; Minister of Foreign Affairs: Marie Government, July 1948; Queuille Government, Sept. 1948-49; Bidault Government, 1949; Pleven Government, July 1950; Queuille Government, March 1951; Pleven Government, Aug. 1951; Faure Government, Jan. 1952; Pinay Government, March 1952; Minister of Justice, Faure Government, Feb. 1955. Leader French deleg., 3rd session of U.N. Gen. Assembly, 1948. Mem. Mouvement Républicain Populaire (M.R.P.). President, European Parliament, Strasbourg, March 1958 - March 1960, President of Honour, 1960-63; withdrew from parliamentary activities, there, Feb. 1963. Charlemagne Prize, 1958; Erasmus Prize, 1959. Dr. *h.c.* Univs. of: Edinburgh, Birmingham, Laval (Canada), Harvard (U.S.), Tilburg (Netherlands), Louvain (Belgium). Grand Cordon de l'Ordre de Léopold (Belgique); Grand Cross of numerous foreign orders. *Address:* 6 Rue de Verneuil, Paris 17e; Chazelles, par Moulins-les-Metz (Moselle), France; Chambre des Députés, Palais Bourbon, Paris, France.
[*Died* 4 *Sept.* 1963.

SCHUSTER, Sir (Felix) Victor, 2nd Bt., *cr.* 1906; *b.* 26 May 1885; *s.* of Sir Felix Schuster, 1st Bt. and Meta (*d.* 1918), *d.* of Sir Hermann Weber; *S.* father 1936; *m.* 1910, Lucy Edith (*d.* 1950), 3rd *d.* of late W. B. Skene, Hallyards and Pitlour, Fife; one *s.* two *d.* *Educ.:* Winchester; New College, Oxford. Served European War, 1914-18 (despatches). *Heir: s.* Felix James Moncrieff, O.B.E. 1955 [*b.* 8 Jan. 1913; *m.* 1937, Ragna, *d.* of Ole Sundø, Copenhagen]. *Club:* Boodle's.
[*Died* 22 *Dec.* 1962.

SCHWEITZER, Dr. Albert, Hon. O.M. 1955; Missionary surgeon, founder of Hospital at Lambaréné, French Equatorial Africa; *b.* 14 Jan. 1875, Kaysersberg, Upper Alsace; *s.* of Louis Schweitzer, Pastor of Günsbach, and Adèle Schillinger; *m.* 1912, Hélène (*d.* 1957), *d.* of Prof. Harry Bresslau, Strasbourg; one *d.* *Educ.:* Realschule, Munster; Gymnasium, Mulhouse; Univs. of Strasbourg (D.Phil., 1899; Licentiate of Theology, 1900; Doctor of Medicine, 1913), Paris and Berlin. Curate of St. Nicholas, Strasbourg, 1899; Privatdozent, Univ. of Strasbourg, 1902-12 and Principal of Theol. Coll. of St. Thomas, 1903-06; Organist of Société J. S. Bach, Paris, 1905-11; Organist of Orféo Català, Barcelona, 1905-11; founded Hospital at Lambaréné, 1913; at Lambaréné, 1913-17, 24-27, 29-32, 33-34, 35, 37-39, 39-48, 49-51, 51-52, 52-54, 54-55, 55-59, 59-; Hibbert Lecturer, Oxford and London, 1934; Gifford Lecturer, Edinburgh, 1934, 1935; Honorary degrees: D.D., Zürich, 1920; D.Phil., Prague, 1928; D.D. and Mus.Doc., Edinburgh, 1931; D.Phil., Oxford, 1932; LL.D., St. Andrews, 1932; LL.D. Chicago, 1949; LL.D., Cambridge, 1955. Elected Member of French Academy (Moral and Political Sciences), 1951. Awarded, in 1953, Nobel Peace Prize for 1952; also, since 1959, several national and international prizes and awards. *Publications:* Die Religionsphilosophie Kants, 1899; Geschichte der Abendmahlsforschung, 1901 (English: The Mystery of the Kingdom of God, 1914); Das Messianitäts - und Leidensgeheimnis Jesu; Eine Skizze des Lebens Jesu, 1901; J. S. Bach, le musicien-poète, 1905; Deutscher und französischer Orgelbau, 1906; Von Reimarus zu Wrede; Eine Geschichte der Leben-Jesu-Forschung, 1906 (English, The Quest of the Historical Jesus, 1910); J. S. Bach, German edn., 1908; (English, 1911); Geschichte der Paulinischen Forschung, 1911 (English, Paul and his Interpreters, 1912); Die psychiatrische Beurteilung Jesu, 1913; Zwischen Wasser und Urwald: Erlebnisse und Beobachtungen eines Arztes im Urwalde Aequatorial afrikas, 1921, (Swedish: Mellan Urskog och Vatten, 1921; English: On the Edge of the Primeval Forest, 1922, Danish edn., 1922; Dutch edn., 1922; Finnish edn., 1922; French edn., 1923; Spanish edn., 1932); Verfall und Wiederaufbau der Kultur (Kulturphilosophie, Erster Teil), 1923; Kultur und Ethik (Kulterphilosophie, Zweiter Teil), 1923; The English and Swedish edns. of these two vols. of the Philosophy of Civilisation, 1923; Christianity and the Religions of the World, 1923; Memoirs of Childhood and Youth, 1924; Mitteilungen aus Lambaréné, 1925-1928; Selbstdarstellung, 1929; Die Mystik des Apostels Paulus, 1930; (English: The Mysticism of Paul the Apostle, 1931); More from the Primeval Forest, 1931 (American title: The Forest Hospital at Lambaréné); Aus meinem Leben und Denken, 1931 (English edn., My Life and Thought, 1933); Die Weltanschauung der Indischen Denker Mystik und Ethik, 1935 (English edn., Indian Thought and its Development, 1936); From my African Notebook, 1939; Goethe, three addresses, 1949; The Problem of Peace in the World of Today (Nobel Prize address), 1954; A Declaration of Conscience, 1957; Peace or Atomic War?, 1958; many of the above also in various Indian vernacular, Japanese, Korean and other translations; The Teaching of Reverence for Life, 1966 (posthumous). *Relevant publications:* Albert Schweitzer, the Man and his Mind, by George Seaver, 5th edition, 1955; The Theology of Albert Schweitzer, by E. N. Mozley, 1950; Albert Schweitzer, his Work and his Philosophy, by Oskar Kraus, 1944; Music in the Life of Albert Schweitzer, ed. C. R. Joy, 1953; Albert Schweitzer: Christian Revolutionary, by George Seaver, 2nd edn., 1955; The World of Albert Schweitzer, by Erica Anderson, 1955; Days with Albert Schweitzer, by Frederick Franck, 1959; Albert Schweitzer, a Study of his Philosophy of Life, by Gabriel Langfeldt, 1960; Dr. Schweitzer of Lambaréné, by Norman Cousins, 1970. *Address:* Lambaréné, Gabon, Equatorial West Africa; Günsbach, près Munster, Hayt-Rhin, France.
[*Died* 4 *Sept.* 1965.

SCHWERDT, Captain Charles Max Richard, C.V.O. 1939; C.B.E. 1943; R.N. retd.; *b.* 3 Dec. 1889; *o. s.* of late C. F. G. R. Schwerdt, J.P.; *m.* 1928, Violet Vere Charlotte Dent; two *d.* *Educ.:* Twyford School, Winchester; H.M.S. Britannia. Served in Royal Navy, 1904-36; present at Heligoland Bight, and Dogger Bank actions in H.M.S. Lion (despatches); retired, 1936; Private Secretary to Governor of Newfoundland, 1936-39; rejoined R.N. at outbreak of war, 1939; lent to R.C.N. until end of war; King Haakon VII Liberty Cross. *Clubs:* United Service, Royal Automobile.
[*Died* 18 *Nov.* 1968.

SCOBIE, Lieutenant-General Sir Ronald MacKenzie, K.B.E., *cr.* 1945 (C.B.E. 1941); C.B. 1942; M.C.; *b.* 8 June 1893; *s.* of Mackay John Scobie of India P.W.D.; *m.* 1927, Joan Duncan, *d.* of W. H. Sidebotham, of Surrey; one *d.* *Educ.:* Cheltenham; R.M.A. Woolwich. 2nd Lt. R.E., 1914; Capt., 1917; Bt. Maj., 1919; Maj., 1929; Bt. Lt.-Col., 1934; Lt.-Col., 1937; Col., 1937; Maj.-Gen., 1941; Temp. Lt.-Gen., 1944; Director of Mil. Art., Royal Military College, Australia, 1932-35; Asst. Adjutant-General, War Office, 1938-39; Deputy Director of Mobilisation, War Office, 1939-40; Deputy Adjutant-General, May-Aug. 1940; Div. Comdr., 1941; G.O.C. Tobruk fortress, 1941; G.O.C. Malta, 1942; C.G.S. Middle East, 1943; G.O.C. Greece, 1944-46; served European War, 1914-18 (wounded, despatches twice, M.C., Bt. Maj.); War of 1939-45 (despatches, C.B.E., C.B., K.B.E., Czechoslovak Military Cross, Polish Virtuti Militari, Greek Grand Cross George I, Comdr. of Leopold, Belgian Croix de Guerre); retired pay, 1947; Col. Comdt., Royal Engineers, 1951-58; Lt., Tower of London, 1951-54; Vice-President, The Forces Aid Society; Lord Roberts' Workshops, 1965; Vice-Patron, Army Rugby Union, 1965. C.St.J. *Recreation:* played Rugby football for Scotland against England, Ireland and Wales, 1914. *Address:* Old Toll Gate, Mattingley, Nr. Basingstoke, Hants. *Club:* United Service. [*Died* 23 *Feb.* 1969.

SCOGGINS, Air Vice-Marshal Roy, C.B. 1964; C.B.E. 1953; *b.* 13 Mar. 1908; *er. s.* of F. J. D. Scoggins, Walthamstow, Essex; *m.* 1934, Edith Joyce, *yr. d.* of A. A. Maxwell, Walthamstow, Essex; two *s.* one *d.* *Educ.:* Sir George Monoux Grammar School; London Hospital. L.D.S., R.C.S. (Eng.) 1929. Joined R.A.F. Dental Branch, 1931; served War of 1939-45: Middle East and Italy (despatches); Q.H.D.S. 1952-64; Deputy Director of Dental Services, 1957; Director of Dental Services, R.A.F., 1958-64; retd., 1964. Air Commodore, 1957; Air Vice-Marshal, 1958. *Recreations:* cricket, tennis, gardening. *Address:* South Walk Cottage, South Walk, Middleton-on-Sea, Bognor Regis, Sussex. *T.:* Middleton-on-Sea 3371. *Club:* R.A.F. [*Died* 19 *Jan.* 1970.

SCOTHERN, Colonel Albert Edward, C.M.G. 1919; D.S.O. 1918; M.A.; *b.* 12 Sept. 1882 of British parents; *m.* 1919, Joyce E. S. Pilling, Tunbridge Wells; one *d.* *Educ.:* St. John's College, Oxford. Schoolmaster, 1906-14, Headmaster, High School, Redditch, Worcs. 1920-47; Army, Nov. 1914-Dec. 1919; served Gallipoli, Egypt, France, and Belgium (C.M.G., D.S.O., despatches five times). D.L. for County of Worcester, 1947-64. *Recreations:* golf, played Association football for Oxford University and England. *Address:* 53 Easemore Road, Redditch, Worcs. *T.:* Redditch 4349. [*Died* 20 *March* 1970.

SCOTT, A.; *see* Ritchie-Scott.

SCOTT, Adrian Gilbert, C.B.E. 1951; M.C.; F.R.I.B.A.; Architect; *b.* 6 Aug. 1882; *g.s.* of Sir G. Gilbert Scott; *m.* 1918, Barbara Agnes (*d.* 1957), *y. d.* of late Charles Napier Hemy, R.A.; two *s.* two *d.* *Educ.:* Beaumont College. Articled to late Temple Moore. *Principal works:* Cairo Cathedral; St. James's Church, Vancouver, B.C.; Farnborough Hill Convent Chapel and Hall; Mount St. Mary's College Chapel; Tower to Church of Holy Name, Manchester; Chesterton Memorial Tower, St. Teresa's Church, Beaconsfield; Our Lady's School, Dublin; Church of Our Lady and St. Joseph, Poplar; Church of Our Lady of Victories, Kensington; St. Anthony's Church, Manchester; Church of St. Rose of Lima, Birmingham; own house at Hampstead and various other churches, schools. Also House of Commons rebuilding (with brother, Sir Giles Gilbert Scott); Mt. Edgcumbe, Plymouth (rebldg.); St. Alban's Ch., Holborn (rebldg.); Parish Church, St. Leonard's (rebldg.). Served European War 1914-18, Major R.E. (SR), (M.C. and despatches); War of 1939-45, Dep. Controller, M.A.P., S.W. Div. *Recreations:* golf, tennis, shooting. *Address:* Shepherds' Well, Frognal Way, N.W.3. *T.:* Hampstead 7224; 11 South Square, Gray's Inn, W.C.1. *T.:* Holborn 5477. [*Died* 23 *April* 1963.

SCOTT, Vice-Admiral Albert Charles, C.B.E. 1918; F.R.Met.S.; retired; *b.* 1872; *s.* of late Maj.-General Charles Scott; *m.* Mary Louisa Harriett Knyvett (*d.* 1939). *Educ.:* Burgoyne House Academy. Commanded during World War H.M.S. Blonde up to March 1916, then H.M.S. Dublin; present at Battle of Jutland (despatches, Officer of the Legion of Honour). *Address:* Baroona Romsey, Hants. *T.:* Romsey 2186. [*Died* 16 *March* 1969.

SCOTT, Lt. Col. Archibald M. H.; *see* Henderson-Scott.

SCOTT, Cyril; Musical Composer, Librettist, and Author; *b.* Oxton, Cheshire, 1879; *s.* of Henry and Mary Scott; *m.* 1921, Rose Laure, novelist, *er. d.* of Cav. Uff. Robert Allatini. First Symphony performed in Darmstadt at age 20; orchestral and chamber works performed in Vienna, Berlin, Petrograd, Paris, Budapest, Brussels, New York, etc. *Publications:* numerous songs, piano works, violin works, chamber, choral, and orchestral works, including Neapolitan Rhapsody, 1960; concertos: Piano Concerto, Violin Concerto, Concerto for 2 Violins, Cello Concerto, Concertino for 2 Pianos; operas called The Alchemist, The Shrine, etc.; a ballet, The Incompetent Apothecary; Cantatas, Nativity Hymn, selected by the Carnegie Trust for publication; La Belle Dame sans Merci, first performed at Leeds Festival, 1934; Summerland; Mirabelle; Neptune, symphonic poem; Symphony entitled the Muses; 4 String Quartets, No. 4, 1968; *Poetry:* The Celestial Aftermath; The Vales of Unity; The Voice of the Ancient; *Prose:* Music: Its Secret Influence throughout the Ages; Memoirs, entitled My Years of Indiscretion; An Outline of Modern Occultism; The Ghost of a Smile; Doctors, Disease and Health; Victory Over Cancer; Cancer Prevention, 1968. *Recreations:* transcendental philosophy and mysticism, therapeutical research. *Address:* c/o Boosey & Hawkes, 295 Regent St., W.1; c/o Elkin & Co., 27 Soho Square, W.1. [*Died* 31 *Dec.* 1970.

SCOTT, Francis Reginald Fairfax, M.A.; Fellow since 1927 of Magdalene College, Cambridge; *b.* 10 September 1897; 2nd *s.* of late Reverend Reginald Fairfax Scott and Frances Louisa, *d.* of Rev. George Bridges Lewis; *m.* 1942, Louise Bywaters; two *s.* one *d.* *Educ.:* Lancing College; Magdalene College, Cambridge (Entrance Scholar). Served in R.A., 1916-1919; 1st Class Classical Tripos, Part I, 1921, Part II, 1923; Charles Kingsley Bye-Fellow, 1923; Assistant University Printer, 1923-1927; Tutor of Magdalene College, 1927; Temporary Administrative Officer, Air Ministry, 1940-44. Senior Tutor Magdalene Coll., 1945-64, President, 1962-67. *Recreations:* gardening, fishing. *Address:* 9A Cranmer Road, Cambridge. *Club:* Oxford and Cambridge University. [*Died* 30 *July* 1969.

SCOTT, George Walter, C.B.E. 1950; Chairman (late Managing Director), The United Molasses Co. Ltd.; Chairman, Athel Line Ltd., since 1953; *b.* 16 April 1896; *m.* 1923, Elsie Marion Taylor; two *s.* one *d.* *Educ.:* Liverpool. Joined predecessor of United Molasses Co. Ltd.,

1913; served European War, 1914-19, France. Went to U.S.A. 1928, and formed Amer. Subsidiary, Pacific Molasses Co. Ltd. (Pres. until 1936); returned to U.K. and was apptd. to Bd. of United Molasses Co. Ltd., 1936 (Jt. Man. Dir. 1944; Man. Dir. 1947). Rep. of Brit. Govt. on Raw Materials Mission and Food Mission, Washington, 1940-1945. *Recreation:* golf. *Address:* 13 Alexander Square, S.W.3. *T.:* Knightsbridge 2941. *Club:* West Indian.
[*Died* 30 *May* 1963.

SCOTT, Col. Gerald Bassett, C.B. 1930; D.S.O. 1915; Indian Army, retired; *s.* of late Lt.-Col. Hopton B. Scott; *b.* 1875; *m.* 1st, 1918, Blanche, *o. d.* of G. F. de Caen; one *d.*; 2nd, 1931, Brigid Mary, *d.* of Michael Lyons; one *s.* four *d.* *Educ.:* United Services College, Westward Ho! Entered Indian Army, 1896; Capt. 1905; Major, 1914; Lt.-Col. 1921; Col., 1926; served Waziristan, 1901-2; (medal and clasp); Somaliland, 1903-4 (medal and two clasps); European War, 1914-1918 (despatches, D.S.O.); N.W. Frontier India, 1931-32 (Medal and clasp); retd. 1931. *Address:* 4581 Pipeline Road, Royal Oak, Victoria, B.C., Canada.
[*Died* 1 *Sept.* 1964.

SCOTT, G(ilbert) Shaw, M.Sc. (Birmingham); F.Inst.Met.; F.C.I.S.; Secretary Emeritus of the Institute of Metals; *b.* Walsall, 29 June 1884; *o. c.* of late John Scott, J.P., Ashtead, Surrey, and Ellen, *y. d.* of late Joseph Shaw, Walsall; *m.* 1913, Christian Mary, B.Sc., *er. d.* of late Professor T. Turner; two *d.* (one *s.* decd.). *Educ.:* Queen Mary's School, Walsall; Birmingham University. President Guild of Undergraduates, 1905; first student to take Birmingham degree B.Sc. (Metallurgy), 1906; M.Sc. 1907; Bowen Research Scholar in Metallurgy, 1906-7. Secretary of the Institute of Metals, 1908-44. Editor of the Journal of the Institute of Metals, 1908-38; Motoring Correspondent of the Birmingham Post, 1907-50; Engineering Correspondent of the Daily Telegraph, 1912-18. Original Mem. of the Institute of Metals; Mem. of the Royal Institution; Vice-President of the Automobile Association; Past Pres., Birmingham University Guild of Graduates (London Branch); Member of Council, Chartered Inst. of Secretaries, 1937-1956; Original Member, Motor Volunteer Corps, 1903; Member, General Committee, Motor Union, 1908; Founder Member, Midland Aero Club and Member of Club's first Council, 1909; Member of the Circle of 19th Century Motorists. *Publications:* To the Alps and Back in a Small Car, 1910; numerous contributions to the technical press. *Recreations:* motoring and diary keeping (both since 1898), travel. *Address:* Gabledene, 25 Greville Park Road, Ashtead, Surrey. *T.A.:* Shawscott Ashtead. *T.:* Ashtead 2090. *Clubs:* Royal Automobile, Veteran Car.
[*Died* 3 *March* 1969.

SCOTT, Sir Harold (Richard), G.C.V.O., *cr.* 1953; K.C.B., *cr.* 1944 (C.B. 1933); K.B.E., *cr.* 1942; M.A.; *b.* 24 Dec. 1887; *y. s.* of late Richard Scott, Banbury; *m.* 1916, Ethel Mary, *d.* of late James Golledge, Bruton; one *s.* two *d.* *Educ.:* Sexey's School, Bruton; Jesus College, Cambridge (Scholar). Hon. Fellow, Jesus College, Cambridge, 1950. Entered Home Office, 1911; Foreign Trade Dept., 1916-18; Ministry of Labour, Secretary, Labour Resettlement Committee, 1918-19; rejoined Home Office, 1919; Assistant Secretary, 1932; Chairman H.M. Commissioners of Prisons for England and Wales, 1932-39; Dep. Sec., Ministry of Home Security, 1940-42; seconded for duty as Chief Administrative Officer, London Civil Defence Region, 1939-41; Secretary, Ministry of Home Security, 1942-43; Permanent Secretary, Ministry of Aircraft Production, 1943-1945; Commissioner of Police of the Metropolis, 1945-53; Lecture tours in N.Z. and U.S.A., 1955; Governor: Sexey's School, 1936-67; Sunny Hill Girls' School, Bruton, 1961-66. Member, Williton R.D.C., 1966-69. K.St.J. 1951. Commander Legion of Honour, Grand Officer Oranje Nassau, 1950; Kt. Commander Orders of Dannebrog and of St. Olaf, 1951. *Publications:* German Prisons, 1934; Belgian Prisons and Reformatory Institutions, 1936; Scotland Yard, 1954; Your Obedient Servant, 1959; From Inside Scotland Yard, 1963. *Recreations:* walking, gardening, painting. *Address:* Ellicombe, Minehead, Somerset. *T.:* Minehead 3674.
[*Died* 19 *Oct.* 1969.

SCOTT, Prof. James Henderson; Professor of Dental Anatomy, Queen's University of Belfast, since 1964; *b.* 8 Nov. 1913; *s.* of late John and Nell Scott, Dundalk, Ireland; *m.* 1945, Olive Marron; one *s.* three *d.* *Educ.:* Dundalk Gram. Sch.; Methodist Coll., Belfast. Joined R.C. Church, 1939. Lectr., 1946, Reader, 1956, Queen's Univ., Belfast. Lecture tours: S. Africa, 1957; U.S., 1960. Howard Mummery Prize for Dental Research, 1963. F.F.D. (Founder Mem.), R.C.S. Ire., 1963. *Publications:* The Christian Vision, 1964; (with A. D. Dixon) Anatomy for Students of Dentistry (2nd edn.), 1966; (with N. B. B. Symons) Introduction to Dental Anatomy (5th edn.), 1967; Essentials of Oral Anatomy, 1967; Dento-facial Development and Growth, 1967; contribs. to Jl. of Anatomical Soc., Trans. European Orthodontic Soc., Amer. Jl. of Orthodontics, Amer. Jl. of Physical Anthropology. *Recreations:* poetry, politics and polemics. *Address:* 3 Holyrood, Malone Rd., Belfast, N. Ireland. *T.:* Belfast 667144.
[*Died* 14 *Nov.* 1970.

SCOTT, Colonel Sir Jervoise (Bolitho), 1st Bt. *cr.* 1962; J.P., D.L., Hampshire; *b.* 3 Feb. 1892; *s.* of late Archibald Edward Scott, J.P., of Rotherfield Park, and Cecilia, *d.* of late William Bolitho of Polwithen, Cornwall; *m.* 1924, Kathleen Isabel, *yr. d.* of late Godfrey Walter of Malshanger, Basingstoke; three *s.* *Educ.:* Eton; Magdalen College, Oxford, B.A. 1913. Second Lieut. 4th Batt. The Hampshire Regt. (T.F.), 1911; 7th Q.O. Hussars, 1914; served with the Mesopotamia Expeditionary Force, 1917-19; retd., 1925; Joint Master of the Hampshire Hounds, 1925-29; Hampshire C.C., 1932; High Sheriff of Hampshire, 1936; C.A. 1949; B.E.F., France, 1939-40; R.A.C. 1940-42; Pioneer Corps, 1942; D.D.L. S.H.A.E.F., 1943-44; D.D.L. Eastern Command, 1944; D.D.L. Palestine, 1945. President, English Guernsey Cattle Soc., 1958; Chm. Hampshire Hunt, 1961. Official Verderer of the New Forest 1950-64. *Heir:* *s.* Major James Walter Scott, The Life Guards [*b.* 26 October 1924; *m.* 1951, Anne Constantia, *e. d.* of Lieut.-Col. Clive Austin, Roundwood, Micheldever, Hants; three *s.* one *d.*]. *Address:* Rotherfield Park, Alton, Hampshire. *T.:* Tisted 204. *Clubs:* Cavalry, Carlton.
[*Died* 21 *June* 1965.

SCOTT, John Alexander, O.B.E. 1941; M.D.; *b.* 8 Aug. 1900; *s.* of George Scott, Liverp.; *m.* 1927, Marjorie Mary Critchley; two *d.* *Educ.:* Liverp. Inst.; Liverpool Univ. M.B., Ch.B., Liverpool, 1924; D.P.H. 1926; M.D. 1927; M.R.C.P. Lond., 1951; F.R.C.P. 1957; Hon. Fell., Amer. Public Health Assoc., 1958. Asst. M.O.H., Surrey C.C., 1927-29; M.O.H., Shipley, 1929-32; Barnsley, 1932-35; Fulham, 1935-44; Prin. M.O., London C.C., 1945-48; Dep. M.O.H. and Dep. Sch. M.O., 1948-52. Medical Officer of Health and Principal School Medical Officer, London County Council, 1952-64. Examiner in Hygiene for M.B. and M.D. degrees, and D.P.H., Univ. of Lond., 1941-50; Examiner in Public Health, Univ. of Bristol, 1957-58. Lectr. in Hygiene, St. George's Hosp. Med. Sch., 1942-51. Member: Central Midwives Bd.; Training Council for

Teachers of the Mentally Handicapped; Bd. of Governors of Mandsley Hospital. Woodward Lectr., Yale Univ., 1958; Visiting Professor, Wayne Univ., Detroit, 1958. Q.H.P., 1956-59. *Publications:* (jointly) The National Health Service Acts, 1946 and 1949, 1950. Annual Reports and papers in Medical Journals. *Recreations:* gardening, motoring. *Address:* 64 Belvedere Court, Upper Richmond Road, S.W.15. *T.:* Putney 2701. *Club:* Athenæum. [*Died* 14 *March* 1965.

SCOTT, John William R.; *see* Robertson Scott.

SCOTT, Peter Heathcote Guillum, C.M.G. 1957; Ghana (1960) Census since 1959; *b.* 10 April 1913; *s.* of late Guy Harden Guillum Scott and Anne Dorothea Fitzjohn; *m.* 1959, Rekiya, *d.* of Alhaji Ibrahima. *Educ.:* King's School, Canterbury; Trinity College, Oxford. Administrative Officer, Nigeria, 1936; served with Nigeria Regt., Roy. W. African Frontier Force and M.O.I. (S.P.); War Office, Captain, 1940-43. Clerk, House of Assembly, N. Nigeria, 1946; Dep. Financial Secretary, 1951; Financial Secretary, Northern Nigeria, 1952-57; Member: House of Assembly, Executive Council, House of Chiefs, 1952. 1957; Chairman Diocesan Board of Finance, Diocese of N. Nigeria, 1952-57. *Recreations:* boxing, racing (Mem. Kaduna Turf Club). *Address:* Lower Farm House, Drayton Beauchamp, Aylesbury, Bucks. *Club:* Travellers'. [*Died* 8 *Feb.* 1961.

SCOTT, Rear-Admiral Richard James Rodney, C.B. 1944; A.M.; Rear-Adm. (retired); *b.* 21 April 1887; *s.* of R. J. H. Scott, F.R.C.S., Bath: *m.* 1923, Dorothy May (*d.* 1925), *d.* of E. T. Sturdy, Burton Bradstock; one *s.*; *m.* 1939, Ruth Margaret Macintyre, *d.* of late P. Macintyre Evans, C.B.E. *Educ.:* Bath College; H.M.S. Britannia. Joined R.N. 1902; served European War, 1914-19; Capt. 1929; Capt. of Fleet, Mediterranean Fleet, 1936-38; Director R.N. Staff College, Greenwich, 1939; Commodore, 11th Cruiser Squadron, 1939 (despatches); Flag Officer in Charge, Iceland, 1940; Rear-Adm. Training, South Africa, 1942; Flag Officer in Charge, Portland, 1944. J.P. Somerset, 1947; D.L. Somerset, 1950. *Address:* Winyatts, Freshford, nr. Bath. *Club:* Army and Navy. [*Died* 28 *Nov.* 1967.

SCOTT, Sir Robert, K.C.M.G., *cr.* 1954 (C.M.G. 1945); Kt., *cr.* 1953; Governor and C.-in-C. of Mauritius, 1954-59, retired; *b.* 10 Mar. 1903; *e. s.* of Dr. Robert Scott and M. C. S. Scott, J.P.; *m.* 1929, Barbara Maud (*d.* 1967), *d.* of P. Mitchell, J.P.; one *s.* one *d.* *Educ.:* Highgate Sch.; Balliol Coll., Oxford. Colonial Administrative Service: Cadet, 1928; Assistant District Officer, 1930-37, Uganda; Assistant Secretary, Palestine, 1937; Administrative Secretary, 1942; Financial Secretary, 1944-47; Colonial Sec., Gold Coast, 1947-50. Administrator, East Africa High Commission, 1950-54. K.St.J. *Publication:* Uganda (with H. B. Thomas, O.B.E.), 1936; Limuria: The Lesser Dependencies of Mauritius, 1961. *Recreations:* fishing, libraries. *Address:* Earles Court, Ide, Nr. Exeter. *T.:* Longdown 248. [*Died* 28 *May* 1968.

SCOTT, Sir Robert Claude, 7th Bt., *cr.* 1821; *b.* 25 Oct. 1886; *s.* of Bertie Charles Scott (3rd *s.* of 3rd Bt.) and Berthe Charlotte Ardin d'Eltheil; *S.* cousin, 1943; *m.* 1918, Janet Foster, *y. d.* of late John Turner, Dalmilling, Ayrshire; one *d.* *Educ.:* Merchiston Castle, Edinburgh. *Heir:* none. *Address:* 3 King's Gate, 48 Dowanside Road, Glasgow, W.2. *T.:* Glasgow Western 2367. *Club:* Royal Scottish Automobile (Glasgow). [*Died* 21 *Dec.* 1961 (*ext.*).

SCOTT, Sydney (Richard), M.B., M.S. Lond., F.R.C.S. Eng.; Governor of St. Bartholomew's Hosp. and of its Medical College, Consulting Aural Surgeon and late Lecturer on Aural Surgery, St. Bartholomew's Hospital; Consulting Surgeon for Diseases of the Ear, Nose, and Throat, National Hospital for Nervous Diseases, Queen Sq., St. Andrew's Hosp. and Red Cross; Hon. Life Mem. Collegium Oto-Laryng. Amicitiae Sacrum; late Consulting Surgeon British Post-Graduate Medical School; late Examiner for Diploma of Laryngology and Otology, R.C.S. of England; Ex-President, Section of Otology, Royal Society of Medicine; late Civil Surgeon, South African F.F., with Yorkshire Regt., 1900-1 (Queen's medal 3 clasps); temp. Major R.A.M.C. attached R.A.F. (France). Was Member Aeronautic Medical Investigation Committee, National Medical Research Council; investigated the problem of vertigo in relation to flying, 1918; late Hon. and Temp. Capt. R.A.M.C., B.E.F.; Duchess of Westminster's War Hospital, France (bronze star, 1914); Arris and Gale Lecturer, The Physiology of the Human Labyrinth, Royal College of Surgeons (1910), and late Senior Surgeon to Out-Patients and Aural Surgeon, Evelina Hospital for Sick Children; Hon. Sec. Section of Otology, 17th International Congress of Medicine, 1913; delegate for R.C.S. Internat. Congress Oto-Laryngology, Berlin, 1936; *m.* 1901, Ethel (*d.* 1958), 2nd *d.* of George Baker; three *s.* one *d.* *Educ.:* St. Bartholomew's Hospital. *Publications:* Operations of Aural Surgery (jointly); The Ear in relation to Certain Disabilities in Flying, Special Report Series No 37, National Health Insurance, M.R.C.; The Problem of Vertigo, Meningitis, Series No 37, National Health Insurance, Brain Abscess and other contributions (Proceedings of Royal Society Medicine); contributed to Official Medical History of the War (1914-18). *Address:* Newlands, Goodworth Clatford, Hants. *T.:* Andover 2647. [*Died* 4 *Feb.* 1966.

SCOTT, Major-General Thomas, C.B. 1947; *b.* 20 Feb. 1897; *s.* of Thomas Scott, Bonnyton, nr. Montrose, N.B.; *m.* 1922, Enid Pearl, *e. d.* of late Rev. Canon E. Sidney Savage, The Priory, Hexham, Northumberland; one *s.* *Educ.:* Montrose Academy, Montrose, N.B.; Edinburgh University. Commissioned into R.F.A. (S.R.), 1915; served European War, 1914-18, France and Belgium, 1915-18 (wounded twice, despatches thrice); transferred to 6th D.C.O. Lancers, I.A., 1927; served in Waziristan, N-W.F.P., 1927-29; graduated Staff Coll., Quetta, 1931; G.S.O. 2, H.Q. Peshawar District, 1933-36; Mohmand Ops. 1935 (despatches); G.O.S. 2, A.H.Q. New Delhi, 1937-38; War of 1939-45, commanded Skinner's Horse, 1940-41, Middle East in Sudan and Eritrea (wounded twice, despatches); G.S.O. 1, 6th Indian Div. 1941; G.S.O. 1, G.H.Q. Far East, 1941-42; B.G.S., Central Command, India, 1942-43; B.G.S. (Plans), S.E.A.C. 1943-44; Chief of Staff to C.-in-C., Ceylon, Jan.-June, 1944; Director of Manpower Planning, G.H.Q. India, 1944-1946; D.C.G.S. (B), G.H.Q. India, 1946-47; M.G.A., H.Q. Northern Command, India, 1947. Col. 1941 (seniority 1940); Brig. 1942; actg. Maj.-Gen. 1944; temp. Maj.-Gen. 1945; hon. Maj.-Gen., 1948; retired, 1948. *Recreation:* racing. *Address:* Grosvenor Square, College Road, Rondebosch, Cape, S. Africa. *T.:* 64755. *Clubs:* Civil Service, South African Turf (Steward), Milnerton Turf (Cape Town); Jockey (S. Africa). [*Died* 26 *Nov.* 1968.

SCOTT, Sir Walter, 3rd Bt., *cr.* 1907; Maj. late R.A.S.C.; *b.* 31 Mar. 1895; *s.* of late Joseph Samuel Scott, 2nd *s.* of 1st Bt.; *S.* uncle, 1922; *m.* 1st, 1915, Nancie Margaret (Margot) (*d.* 1944), *d.* of Samuel Herbert March, Châlet du Parc, Cannes; one *s.*; 2nd, 1949, Dorothea Cara, *widow* of John F. Crisp. *Educ.:* Charterhouse; Jesus College, Cambridge. *Heir:* *s.*, Walter Scott, Major (temp.) 1st Royal Dragoons [*b.* 29 July 1918; *m.* 1944, Diana Mary, *o. d.* of late J. R. Owen, Holly Hill, Coleman's Hatch, Sussex; one *s.* (*b.* Feb. 1948) one *d.*]. *Address:* Berry, Ardingly, Sussex. *Club:* Oxford and Cambridge. [*Died* 8 *June* 1967.

SCOTT, Sir William, Kt. 1957; O.B.E. 1946; Chairman, Armstrong Whitworth (Metal Industries) Ltd., Gateshead, since 1965 (Man. Dir., 1945-63); Chm., Thor Tools Ltd.; *b.* 12 Mar. 1898; *s.* of Watson Scott; *m.* 1924, Mary Gibson Wallace; two *s.* one *d.* *Educ.:* Manchester College of Technology. Apprenticeship began, 1912. Served European War, 1914-18, for short period in army. Works Manager of Armstrong Whitworth, 1929; General Manager and Director, of Armstrong Whitworth Group, 1938. M.I.Mech.E.; M.I.Prod.E., etc. *Recreations:* gardening, golf, fishing, music. *Address:* Aingarth, 34 Kenton Road, Gosforth, Newcastle, 3. *T.:* Gosforth 51293. *Club:* Royal Automobile. [*Died* 5 *April* 1965.

SCOTT, William Coxon, C.M.G. 1956; O.B.E. 1951; H.M. Diplomatic Service, retd.; *b.* 12 Dec. 1895; *s.* of late John Fenwick Scott and late Jane Ann (*née* Sayburn), Jarrow; *m.* 1932, Dorothy Fisk. *Educ.:* Carlton Grammar School, Bradford. Asst. Clerk, W.O., 1914; Second Div. Clerk, W.O., 1915; on active service in R.F.A., 1916-19. An Exec. Officer, Foreign Office, 1920; Accountant, Consulate-General, Shanghai, 1932; Sen. Accountant, Embassy, Ankara, 1943; transferred to Athens, 1946; Consul, Athens, 1947; Member of Foreign Service, 1948; Dep. Establishment Officer, Foreign Office, 1950. Grade 6 Officer in Sen. Branch of Foreign Service, 1954; Head of German Section Establishment and Organisation Dept., 1954-56; retired, 1956. Coronation Medal, 1953. *Recreations:* motoring, gardening; Director, Farnham Repertory Co. Ltd. *Address:* 3 Brambleton Ave., Farnham, Surrey. *T.:* 4430. [*Died* 13 *Nov.* 1968.

SCOTT, Sir William Dalgliesh, Kt., *cr.* 1946; C.B.E. 1924; Permanent Sec. to the Ministry of Finance and Head of the Northern Ireland C.S., 1944-53; *b.* 12 Nov. 1890; *m.* 1922, Val (*d.* 1964), *o. d.* of late Dr. A. M. Burn, Timaru, N.Z., and Harrow-on-the-Hill; two *s.* *Educ.:* Edinburgh Univ. (Thow Scholarship, two medals, Dalgety Prize); London School of Economics. Is a member of the English Bar; entered Inland Revenue Department, 1910; joined Chief Secretary's Staff in Ireland in 1920; Assistant Secretary, Ministry of Finance, 1921-24; Permanent Secretary to the Ministry of Commerce, 1924-44; Industrial Assurance Commissionerfor Northern Ireland, 1924-44; Chairman of the Electricity Commissioners for Northern Ireland, 1924-31; Member of Electricity Board for Northern Ireland, 1931-40; Coal Controller for Northern Ireland, 1939-42; Board of Trade Regional Representative in Northern Ireland, 1940-44; Regional Controller for Northern Ireland for Ministry of Supply, 1941-44; for Ministry of Production, 1942-44, and for Ministry of Aircraft Production, 1943-44. Governor of Ashleigh House School, 1946-61 (Chairman, 1958-61); Member of Joint Exchequer Board, 1949; Director Provincial Bank of Ireland Ltd., 1953. Chm. Cttee. on Teachers' Salaries, 1954; Member of two-man Economic Commission to Malta, 1956-1957; Chm. Ulster Scot. Historical Society, 1957; Chm. Central Council of Irish Linen Industry, 1957; Chm. Linen Industry Research Assoc., 1957-63. Hon. LL.D. (Belfast), 1953. *Recreations:* walking, reading. *Address:* Bryansburn House, Bangor, Co. Down. *Clubs:* Junior Carlton; Ulster (Belfast). [*Died* 15 *Oct.* 1966.

SCOTT HALL, Stewart, C.B. 1950; M.Sc., D.I.C., F.C.G.I., F.R.Ae.S., F.I.A.S.; Head of U.K. Defence Research and Supply Staff in Australia since 1959 and Scientific Adviser to U.K. High Commissioner; *b.* 23 March 1905; *s.* of Alfred Charles and Julia Richmond Hall; *m.* 1940, Margaretta Primrose (*née* Watson), *d.* of Captain J. C. Watson, R.N. (retd.). *Educ.:* Eastbourne Coll.; Imperial College of Science, London University. Busk Memorial Schol., 1925; joined Aerodynamics Dept. Royal Aircraft Establishment, Farnborough, 1927; Aeroplane and Armament Expntl. Estab., Martlesham Heath, 1929; Air Ministry Res. Tech. Officer, Vickers Supermarine Ltd., 1933; Head of Orfordness Ballistics Lab., 1937; Asst. to Dir. Gen. Aircraft Prod., Min. of Aircraft Prod., 1940; Head of Armament Research Dept., R.A.E., 1941; Supt. of Performance Testing, Aeroplane and Armament Exptl. Estab., Boscombe Down, 1944; Prin. Dir. Tech. Devel., Min. of Supply, 1946-49; Director-General of Technical Development (Air), Ministry of Supply, 1949-53; Head of Min. of Supply Staff, British Joint Services Mission, 1953-56; Scientific Adviser to the Air Ministry, 1956-1959. Mem. Council R. Aeronautical Soc. Founder member British Gliding Assoc. *Publications:* Aircraft Performance Testing, 1932; various scientific and technical papers. *Recreations:* sailing, entomology. *Address:* United Kingdom Defence Research and Supply, 339 Swanston Street, Melbourne, C.1, Vict., Australia. *Clubs:* Athenæum, Royal Aero. [*Died* 4 *Aug.* 1961.

SCOTT-HILL, Eng. Rear-Admiral Walter, C.B.E. 1945; M.Inst.Mech.E.; *b.* 2 Sept. 1873; *s.* of Walter and Mary Jane Cockey Hill, Rosebank, Peterborough; *m.* 1909, Helen Constance, *d.* of Joseph T. Ardron, Syston, Leicester; one *s.* one *d.* *Educ.:* The King's School, Peterborough; R.N.E. College, Devonport; R.N. College, Greenwich. Normal Naval Service, 1894-1904; lent to Egyptian Army for Service with Sudan Govt., 1904-14; H.M.S. Comus and H.M.S. Indomitable, 1914-18; H.M. Dockyard, Rosyth, Battle Cruiser Squadron, and H.M. Dockyard, Sheerness, 1918-27; Partner with Sir J. H Biles & Co., Naval Architects, 1927-39; Central Priority Dept., Ministry of Supply, 1939-41; Engineer Officer on Staff of Flag Officer, Greenock, 1941-45; Fourth Class Osmanieh; Third Class Nile; Third Class Stanislas; Second Class Boyaca (Columbia). *Publications:* sundry technical papers, Institute of Naval Architects, etc. *Address:* 105 Gloucester Court, Kew Rd., Kew, Surrey. *T.:* Richmond 0833. *Club:* Athenæum. [*Died* 18 *June* 1963.

SCOTT THOMSON, Gladys, M.A.; F.S.A.; (Scot.); *d.* of Walter Scott Thomson, M.D., M.R.C.S., and Elizabeth Stimpson. *Educ.:* City of London Sch. for Girls; Stuttgart; Somerville College, Oxford. Acting Head, Dept. of History, University College, Nottingham, 1916-20; Tutor, St. Hugh's College, Oxford, 1921-23; Archivist at Woburn Abbey, 1927-40. Member Council Society of Antiquaries, 1954-56. *Publications:* Lords Lieutenant in The Sixteenth Century, 1923; Life in a Noble Household, 1937; Russells in Bloomsbury, 1940; Letters of a Grandmother, 1943; Catherine the Great and the Expansion of Russia, 1948; Family Background, 1949. *Recreations:* music, walking. *Address:* 32 Drumsheugh Gardens, Edinburgh 3. *T.:* Caledonian 3448. *Clubs:* Ladies' Wing, Oxford and Cambridge University; Ladies' Caledonian (Edinburgh). [*Died* 5 *July* 1966.

SCRIVENER, Sir Patrick (Stratford), K.C.M.G., *cr.* 1952 (C.M.G. 1937); retd.; *b.* 22 Aug. 1897; *s.* of H. S. Scrivener; *m.* 1918, Margaret, 2nd *d.* of late Walter Dorling; one *s.* *Educ.:* R.N.C., Osborne; Winchester. Served Worcs. Yeomanry, 1915-19; Third Secretary in the Diplomatic Service, 1920, Warsaw; Second Sec., 1923; transferred to Cairo, 1923; Budapest, 1930; Foreign Office, 1932; First Secretary, 1932; Addis Ababa, 1933; Foreign Office, 1935; Angora, 1936; Rome, 1939-40; Lisbon, 1940-41; Acting Counsellor, 1941; Foreign Office, 1941-47; Counsellor, 1943; Minister to Syria, 1947; Deputy Special Commissioner in South-East Asia, 1947-48; Deputy Commissioner-General (Foreign Affairs) in South-East Asia, 1948-49; Ambassador at Berne, 1953 (Minister, 1950-53); retired 1954. *Recreations:* fishing, motoring. *Address:* Corner House, Great Bedwyn, Wilts. [*Died* 20 *Jan.* 1966.

SEAFIELD, Countess of (12th in line), *cr.* 1701, **Nina Caroline Ogilvie-Grant-Studley-Herbert;** Viscountess Seafield, 1698; Viscountess Reidhaven, Baroness Ogilvy, 1701; *b.* 17 Apr. 1906; *d.* of 11th Earl and Nina (*d.* 1962), *d.* of Dr. J. T. Townend, J.P., Christchurch, New Zealand; *S.* father, 1915; *m.* 1930, Derek Herbert Studley Herbert (marr. diss. 1957; he *d.* 1960), *s.* of late John Tatchell Studley, Seaborough Court, Dorsetshire; one *s.* one *d.* Pres. of League of Mercy (Banffshire); Vice-President of Red Cross, Cullen district, Banffshire. *Heir: s.* Viscount Reidhaven (Master of Seafield). *Address:* Cullen House, Banffshire; Kinveachy Forest, Boat of Garten, Inverness-shire. [*Died* 30 *Sept.* 1969.

SEAFORD, Sir Frederick Jacob, Kt., *cr.* 1949; C.B.E. 1944 (O.B.E. 1937); Director, Booker Bros. McConnell & Co., Ltd., Commonwealth Merchants and Sugar Producers, since 1949; *m.* 1949, Mrs. Noreen Tarrant. *Address:* c/o Booker Bros. McConnell & Co., Ltd., Bucklersbury House, 83 Cannon Street, E.C.4. [*Died* 24 *May* 1968.

SEALE, Sir John (Carteret Hyde), 4th Bt., *cr.* 1838; *b.* 23 July 1881; *s.* of 3rd Bt. and Mary, *d.* of A. H. Dendy, Rock House, Torquay and Parkfield, Paignton; *S.* father, 1914; *m.* 1917, Margaret (*d.* 1960), *d.* of late Lt.-Col. William Herring, 27th Inniskillings, of Narborough House, Narborough, Norfolk; two *s.* one *d.* *Educ.:* Eton; Christ Church, Oxford. Barrister, Inner Temple. *Heir: s.* John Henry [*b.* 3 March 1921; *m.* 1953, Ray Josephine, *d.* of R. G. Charters, Christchurch, New Zealand; one *s.* one *d.*]. *Address:* Slade, near Kingsbridge, S. Devon. *T.:* Loddiswell 226. [*Died* 22 *May* 1964.

SEAMER, Rev. Arthur John, C.M.G., 1949; Methodist Minister; *s.* of William and Jane M. Seamer (*nee* Townley), Victoria, Australia; *m.* 1907, Ida M., *d.* of Alex. Nisbet. *Educ.:* Tongala and Melbourne. Entered Maori Mission Work (N.Z.), 1897; served N.Z. Expeditionary Force, 1915-18; General Superintendent: of Maori Missions, 1919-22; of Home and Maori Missions Dept., 1923-39; Pres. Methodist Church of N.Z., 1933. *Address:* Te Rahui, Hamilton, New Zealand. [*Died* 18 *Sept.* 1963.

SEARLE, Alfred Broadhead; Consulting Technologist; Professional Arbitrator and Valuer; Past-Pres., Valuers' Institution; Past President, National Association of Industrial Chemists; Past Vice-President, Institution of Chemical Technologists; Vice-President of National Institute of Clay Technology; Fellow, Royal Society of Arts; Fellow and Maybury Gold Medallist of the Institute of Quarrying; Fellow of the Institute of Arbitrators and of the Institute of Ceramics; Lecturer on Brickmaking under Cantor Bequest, Royal Society of Arts; Lecturer on Colloids under the Chadwick Bequest; on Panel of Arbitrators of London Court of Arbitration; on Panel of Technical Assessors to assist H. M. Judges; in practice since 1900 as Consulting Chemist; specialising in Clays, Clay Products and Allied Materials; Technical Adviser on Clays and Clay Products, Refractory Materials, Sands, Concrete, Limestone and Lime Products; Founder and Principal (1913-54) of the Searle School of Clayworking; Member of various chemical, ceramic, and other learned societies; *b.* 4 May 1877; *m.* 1913; one *s.* one *d.* *Educ.:* Friends' Sch., Ackworth, Yorks; Sheffield and Leipzig Universities. *Publications:* The Chemistry of Clayworking; Abrasive Materials; The Clayworker's Handbook (4 edns.); Modern Brickmaking (4 edns.); British Clays, Shales, and Sands; Cement, Concrete and Bricks (2 edns.); Bricks and Artificial Stones of Non-Plastic Materials; The Natural History of Clay; Refractory Materials: their Manufacture and Uses (3 edns.); Refractories for Furnaces, Kilns, Retorts, etc.; Clays and Clay Products; Kilns and Kiln Building; Ceramic Industries Pocket Book; Chemistry and Physics of Clays and other Ceramic Materials (3 edns.); Sands and Crushed Rocks (2 vols.); Clay and What we Get from it; Uses of Colloids in Health and Disease; An Encyclopædia of the Ceramic Industries (3 vols.); Methods of Burning Continuous Kilns; Modern Tile Making; Sand and Gravel; Limestone and its Products; The Glazer's Book (3 editions); Romance of Refractories; Polishes, Manufacture and Uses of; Valuation of Industrial Properties; numerous papers in technical journals; Associate author of Bricks and Tiles (14 edns.); Cassell's Reinforced Concrete; Making and Burning of Glazed Ware; Roads Year Book; Foundrywork and Metallurgy; Sections on Colloidal Clay and Medicinal Colloids in British Association Report on Colloidal Materials; Kempe's Engineers Year Book; A New Dictionary of Chemistry; also several translations. *Address:* Conley Gate, Halifax. [*Died* 26 *Nov.* 1967.

SEARLE, Herbert Victor, C.B.E. 1957; V.D.; M.A. (Cantab.), M.Sc. (N.Z.); Headmaster of Nelson College, New Zealand, 1933-1956, retired; *b.* 6 Nov. 1892; *s.* of Walter Ernest and Mary Searle; *m.* 1931 Kathleen Hunter-Holmes Blaikie; two *s.* one *d.* *Educ.:* Waitaki (Junior and Senior Scholar); Otago University (Senior National Scholar, Sir George Grey Scholar); Christ's College, Cambridge (N.Z.E.F. Scholar); Coronation Medal, 1953. *Recreation:* bridge. *Address:* Fifeshire Crescent, Nelson, New Zealand. *Club:* Nelson (Nelson) [*Died* 20 *Sept.* 1968.

SECOMBE, Major-General (Hon. Lieut.-Gen.) Victor Clarence, C.B. 1955; C.B.E. 1941; Australian Staff Corps, retired; *b.* 1897. Adjutant, 5th Aust. Div. Engineers, A.I.F., 1919; joined Staff Corps, 1920; 6th and 3rd Military Districts, Royal Australian Engineers, 1920-25; Officer Commanding, Coast Defences, 5th Military District, 1926-28; Hon. A.D.C. to the Governor of Western Australia, 1926-28; Hon. A.D.C. to the Governor of New South Wales, 1931-32; Constructional Party, Darwin, 1932-33; Hon. A.D.C. to Governor of New South Wales, 1934-36; Instructor, Royal Military College, Duntroon, 1936-39; Commander, Royal Engineers, 7th Australian Division, Australian Imperial Forces, 1940-41; Assistant Adjutant and Quartermaster-General, 7th Australian Division, Syrian Campaign, May-Nov. 1941; Deputy Adjutant and Quartermaster-General, New Guinea Force, 1943; Deputy Adjutant and Quartermaster-General, Advanced L.H.Q., Hollandia, Morotai, Oct. 1944-Oct. 1945; Deputy Quartermaster-General, Army Headquarters, 1945-46; Master-General of Ordnance and Fourth Military Member, Department of the Army, 1946; Engineer in Chief, General Staff, Australian Headquarters, 1946; retired. *Address:* c/o The Department of the Army, Melbourne, Victoria, Australia. [*Died Feb.* 1962.

SECRETAN, Hubert Arthur, C.B.E. 1956 (O.B.E. 1919; M.B.E. 1918); J.P.; retired; *b.* 8 Aug. 1891; 3rd *s.* of W. B. Secretan, Croydon; unmarried. *Educ.:* Wellington; Balliol College, Oxford; London University, B.A. 1914, M.A. 1920, Oxford. Teachers' Diploma, 1920, London. Admiralty, 1915-1917; Min. of Shipping, 1917-19. Warden, Oxford and Bermondsey Club, 1922-26; Toc H.: Hon. Schools Sec., 1927-35; Hon. Administrator, 1935-40. Dep. Dir. Ports Div., Min. of War Transport, 1940-45. J.P. (London), 1950-. Governor, Borough Polytechnic, 1925 (Chm. 1954-); Governor, Nat. Coll. for Heating Ventilating, Refrigerating and Fan Engineering, 1948- (Chm. 1948-1962); Governor, St. Olave's Grammar School Foundation, 1926-; Pres. Toc H, 1957 (Chm. Central Exec., 1953-56); Vice-Pres. Nat. Assoc. of Boys' Clubs (Vice-Chm. 1948-); Pres. Oxford and Bermondsey Club: Estates Governor, Alleyn's College, 1962-. Chevalier Order of the Crown of Belgium, 1918. *Publications:* (with W. McG. Eagar) Unemployment Among Boys, 1925; London Below Bridges, 1931; Towards New Landfalls, 1936; The Road Ahead, 1947. *Recreations:* sea travel, motoring, reading. *Address:* Redriff 215 East Dulwich Grove, S.E. 22. *T.:* 01-693 1019. *Club:* United University. [*Died* 26 *June* 1969.

SECRETAN, Walter Bernard, M.B. (Lond.); F.R.C.S. (England); L.R.C.P.; Consulting Surgeon to R. Berks Hospital; retired from private practice; *b.* 1875; *e. s.* of Walter Secretan, Croydon, and Margaret Waters; *m.* 1914, Dorothy Crosse; one *d.* (one *s.* decd.). *Educ.:* Bradfield; Guy's Hosp. Capt. R.A.M.C. (T.), retd. Served European War, 1915-18, at Reading War Hosp. and in France; on Surgical Staff of Royal Berks Hospital, 1913-35. *Publications:* A Mixed Bag—Recollections and Reflections of a Surgeon, 1943; various articles on surgical subjects in medical journals. *Recreations:* country pursuits. *Address:* Upper House Farm, Hascombe, Nr. Godalming, Surrey. [*Died* 28 *Sept.* 1966.

SÉE, Peter Henri, C.B. 1952; Parliamentary Counsel to the Treasury since 1946; *b.* 31 Aug. 1910; *o. s.* of late Henri Sée; *m.* 1935, Margaret, *e. d.* of W. H. Wood. *Educ.:* Winchester; New College, Oxford. Called to the Bar, Middle Temple, 1935; Parliamentary Counsel Office, 1938. *Address:* Hill House, Westmead, S.W.15. *T.:* Putney 1923. *Clubs:* Garrick, Oxford and Cambridge. [*Died* 21 *Aug.* 1963.

SEFTON, Mrs. Walter; *see* Fish, Anne Harriet.

SEFTON-COHEN, Arthur; *see* Addenda: II.

SEGRAVE, Brig.-Gen. (William Henry) Eric, D.S.O. 1899; late Highland Light Infantry; *b.* 26 Nov. 1875; *s.* of late Captain W. F. Segrave, Highland Light Infantry; *m.* 1904, Nellie Borlase (*d.* 1957), *d.* of late Vice-Admiral J. J. Kennedy, C.B.; one *d.* Entered army, 1898; Captain, 1907; Lt.-Col., 1924; served Candia, 1898 (slightly wounded, despatches, D.S.O.); S. Africa, 1901-(Queen's medal with clasps); European War, 1914-18 (despatches seven times, Bt. Major, Bt. Lt.-Col., Legion of Honour, two bars to D.S.O.); retired pay, 1929. *Club:* Army and Navy. [*Died* 23 *Aug.* 1964.

SEITZ, John Arnold, C.M.G. 1949; M.A. (Oxon); B.C.E. (Melb.); J.P.; *b.* Carlton, Victoria, 19 Sept. 1883; *s.* of Edward Seitz, Civil Engineer, and Sophie Marie Elise (*née* Seyfarth); *m.* 1913, Eleanor Ida Agnes Dunn, M.B.E. 1956; no *c.* *Educ.:* Victorian State Schools; Hawthorn Coll.; Scotch Coll.; Melbourne University; Merton College, Oxford. Rhodes Scholar for Victoria, 1906; B.A. 1909; M.A. 1928; B.C.E. (Melb.), 1933. Appts. in Victoria, Australia: Master, Scotch Coll., 1910-14; Headmaster, Hamilton College, 1915-21; Master of Method, Teachers' Coll., 1921-24; Inspector of Secondary Schools, 1925-28, Chief Inspector, 1929-36; Director of Education, 1936-48; retired, 1949. Member, Melbourne Univ. Council, 1933-48; Member Council of Adult Education, 1947-; Chairman Soldiers' Children Education Board, 1945-. Fellow Inst. of Public Administration, 1938. J.P. 1942. Silver Jubilee Medal, 1935; Coronation Medals, 1937, 1953. *Publications:* educational articles in various books and pamphlets, mostly published by the Australian Council for Educational Research. *Recreations:* formerly cricket (Oxford and Melb. Univ. Blues; Interstate, Victoria, 1910-1914 (Capt. 1913-14); Pres. Victorian Cricket Assoc., 1947; ex-officio Trustee, Melbourne Cricket Ground, 1958); football (Melb. Univ. Blue); occasional golf. *Address:* 20 Gurner St., St. Kilda, S.2, Victoria, Australia. *T.:* XJ 2152. *Clubs:* (Vice-President) Public Schools Club of Victoria (Melbourne); Melbourne Cricket; Carlton Cricket (Vice-Pres. 1933-, Pres. 1959-). [*Died* 1 *May* 1963.

SELBY, Sir Walford Harmood Montague, K.C.M.G., *cr.* 1931; C.B. 1926; C.V.O. 1924 (M.V.O. 1911); *b.* 19 May 1881; *s.* of late Charles Edward M. Selby, 48 Sussex Square, Brighton; *m.* 1912, Dorothy, *d.* of late William Orme Carter of The Lodge, Hurst Green, Sussex, and The Rosary, Dean Park, Bournemouth. Attaché, 1904; 3rd Secretary, Berlin, 1906; The Hague, 1907-8; appointed a Member of the Secretariat of the Second Peace Conference at The Hague, 1907; resumed duty in Foreign Office, 1908; Secretary to Government Hospitality Fund, 1908; Secretary to Earl of Rosebery's Special Embassy to the Court of Vienna to announce Accession of King George V., 1910; Secretary to the Coronation (Executive) Committee, 1910-11; and Gold Staff Officer at the Coronation of King George V., 1911 (Coronation medal); Assist. Priv. Secret. to Viscount Grey, 1911-15; First Secretary, The Residency, Cairo, 1919-22; Principal Private Secretary to the Secretary of State for Foreign Affairs, 1924-32; Envoy Extraordinary and Minister Plenipotentiary in Vienna, 1933-37; Ambassador Extraordinary and Plenipotentiary in Lisbon, 1937-40. *Publication:* Diplomatic Twilight: 1930-1940, 1953. *Clubs:* Turf, Beefsteak. [*Died* 7 *Aug.* 1965

SELLAR, Harry Harpham, C.B.E. 1949; Civil Servant, retired; *b.* 28 December 1893; *s.* of late Henry Sellar; *m.* 1924, Brena Mary, *d.* of late T. Dodds, Mus. Doc. (Oxon); one *d.* *Educ.:* Merchant Taylors' School; St. John's College, Oxford (M.A.). Instructor Lieut., R.N., 1916-19; Asst. Principal, Inland Revenue Dept., 1919; Asst. Priv. Sec. to Rt. Hon. Margaret Bondfield and Sir Henry Betterton, Ministers of Labour, 1929-33; Priv. Sec. to Sir Thomas Inskip and Lord Chatfield, Ministers for Co-ordination of Defence, 1936-39; Priv. Sec. to Mr. Leslie Burgin and Mr. Herbert Morrison, Ministers of Supply, 1939-40; Secretary of Supply Council Ministry of Supply, 1940-45; Under-Secretary Ministry of Labour and National Service, 1953-57; retired, 1957. *Recreations:* philately, gardening *Address:* Hedges, Commander's Walk Fairlight, Sussex. *T.:* Pett 3312. [*Died* 15 *July* 1966.

SELLAR, Robert Watson, C.M.G. 1946; C.A.; retd. as Auditor General of Canada (1940-59); *b.* 6 August 1894; *s.* of Robert

Sellar; m. 1930, Gwendolyn B. Gauley; one s. one d. *Educ.:* Huntingdon Academy; Saskatchewan Law School. Printer and publisher to 1924; Private Secretary to Min. of Finance (Canada), 1924-30; Asst. Deputy Minister of Finance, 1930-32; Comptroller of the Treasury, 1932-40. *Address:* 28 Monkland Ave., Ottawa, Canada. *Clubs:* Rideau, Country (Ottawa).
[*Died* 3 *Jan.* 1965.

SELLS, Vice-Admiral William Fortescue, C.M.G. 1917; *b.* 1881; 2nd *s.* of late Rev. William Sells, Niton, Isle of Wight; *m.* 1908, Alice Augusta (*d.* 1943), *d.* of late J. F. Cornish, F.R.G.S.; one *s.* one *d.* *Educ.:* H.M.S. Britannia. Entered R.N. 1894; served in H.M.S. Aboukir, 1914, Commanding H.M.S. Sapphire, 1918; Naval Attaché, H.M.'s Legation at Athens, 1915-17; Capt. 1918; Deputy Director of Local Defence Division, 1921-23; Commanding H.M. Gunnery School, Devonport, 1923-25; H.M.S. Cleopatra, 1925-26; H.M.S. Emperor of India, 1928-29; Naval A.D.C. to the King, 1929-30; Rear-Admiral, and retired list, 1930; Vice-Adm., retired, 1935; Officer Legion of Honour; Officer White Eagle (Serbia). *Address:* Eyam, nr. Sheffield. *Club:* United Service.
[*Died* 31 *March* 1966.

SELSDON, 2nd Baron, *cr.* 1932, of Croydon, **Patrick William Malcolm Mitchell-Thomson,** D.S.C. 1943; Temp. Lieut. R.N.V.R.; *b.* 28 May 1913; *s.* of 1st Baron and Madeleine (*d.* 1946), *y. d.* of late Sir Malcolm M'Eacharn of Galloway House; *S.* father 1938; *m.* 1st, 1936, Phoebette (who obtained a divorce, 1944), *d.* of Crossley Swithinbank, Donnington Grove, Newbury; one *s.* one *d.*; 2nd, 1944, Dorothy Graham, *d.* of late Frederick John Greenish, Honnington Hall, near Grantham, Lincs.; one *d.* *Educ.:* Winchester. Served War of 1939-45 (D.S.C.). *Heir:* *s.* Hon. Malcolm McEacharn Mitchell-Thomson, *b.* 27 Oct. 1937. *Clubs:* Bath, Royal Thames Yacht.
[*Died* 7 *Feb.* 1963.

SELZNICK, David Oliver; American Film Producer; *b.* Pittsburgh, Pa., U.S.A., 10 May 1902; *s.* of Lewis J. Selznick and Florence A. Sachs; *m.* 1929, Irene Gladys Mayer (divorced, 1948); two *s.*; *m.* 1949, Phylis Isley Walker (Jennifer Jones); one *d.* *Educ.:* N.Y. City public schools; Hamilton Inst.; Columbia University (special courses). Apprenticeship in all departments of motion picture production, distribution and exhibition; producer of independent short subjects; production representative, Associated Exhibitors; reader, assistant story editor and associate producer, Metro-Goldwyn-Mayer; executive assistant to Man. Dir., later, associate producer and acting head, Paramount; vice-pres in charge of production, R.K.O.; vice-pres. and producer, Metro-Goldwyn-Mayer; organizer and president, Selznick International Pictures, Inc. to 1940; presently independent producer and executive head various motion pictures enterprises, including The Selznick Co., Inc., The Selznick Studio, The Selznick Studio, Releasing Division Ltd., etc. Also writer, including screenplays of Duel in the Sun, Since You Went Away, The Paradine Case. Productions include: (Paramount) Four Feathers, Street of Chance; (R.K.O.) A Bill of Divorcement, King Kong, Topaze, Bird of Paradise, Symphony of Six Million, What Price Hollywood, The Animal Kingdom; (M.G.M.) Viva Villa, Anna Karenina, David Copperfield, A Tale of Two Cities, Dinner at Eight, Night Flight, Dancing Lady; (Selznick International) A Star is Born, The Prisoner of Zenda, Nothing Sacred, The Adventures of Tom Sawyer, Gone with the Wind, Intermezzo, Rebecca, Little Lord Fauntleroy, Since You Went Away, Spellbound, Duel in the Sun, The Paradine Case, Portrait of Jennie; originated co-production between American and European producers, starting with The Third Man. Founder, 1950, of Golden Laurel Awards and Trophy for motion pictures made outside the U.S. contributing most to international understanding and goodwill, and presented each year at various film festivals. Many national and international awards, including: Academy Award for Best Production (twice); Irving Thalberg Memorial Award for the most consistent high quality of production; Venice Film Festival, best production (twice); League of Nations Medal; Fame Award for most successful production for each of 17 years, etc.; International Cinema Festival (Brussels); National Critics' Poll (twice). Various chairmanships have included: West Coast deleg. Repub. Nat. Convention; Nat. Co-Chm. Am. Brotherhood of Nat. Conf. of Christians and Jews; Chm. Freedom Train, Los Angeles Div. *Address:* Selznick Studio, Culver City, California, U.S.A.
[*Died* 22 *June* 1965.

SEMPILL, 19th Baron (*cr.* 1489), **Comdr. William Francis Forbes-Sempill;** Bt., *cr.* 1639; A.F.C.; F.R.Ae.S.; M.I.P.E.; a Representative Peer for Scotland, 1935-63; *b.* 24 Sept. 1893; *e. s.* of 18th Baron and Gwendolen (*d.* 1944), *d.* of Herbert ap Roger, Kington S. Michael, Wilts; *S.* father, 1934; *m.* 1st, 1919, Eileen Marion (*d.* 1935), *e. d.* of late Sir John Lavery, R.A.; one *d.* (and one killed on duty, 1941); 2nd, 1941, Cecilia Alice, *er. d.* of late B. E. Dunbar-Kilburn; three *d.* *Educ.:* Eton. Served engineering apprenticeship in the shops, 1910-13; joined R.F.C., Farnboro', Aug. 1914; Central Flying School, Upavon, Sept. 1914; Flight Commander, Feb. 1915; transferred from R.F.C. as Capt. and Flight Comdr. to R.N.A.S. as Flight Comdr., Jan. 1916; Sqdn. Comdr., Jan. 1917; Wing Comdr., Jan. 1918; transf. R.A.F. as Lt.-Col. and promoted to Col., Apr. 1918; Special Technical Mission to U.S.A., June-July 1918; retired from R.A.F., July 1919. Rejoined R.N.A.S., Sept. 1939, ret. 1941. Rep. of Air Ministry on Advisory Cttee. for Aeronautics and its Sub-Cttees., Advisory Council of D.S.I.R., Civil Aerial Transport Cttee., British Engineering Standards Assoc., and Timber Cttee. of Conjoint Board of Scientific Societies. Headed Mission to organize Imperial Japanese Naval Air Service. Air Force Cross; Order of the Crown of Italy; 3rd Order of the Rising Sun; 2nd Order of The Sacred Treasure; Special Medal of the Imperial Aero Society of Japan; Commander First Class of the Pole Star of Sweden. Lectured before German Aeronautical Society in Berlin, 1925 and 1928; competed in King's Cup Air Race round Britain, 1924, 1925, 1926, 1927, 1928, 1929, and 1930; visited Athens at the request of the Greek Government to report on reorganisation of Greek Naval Air Service, Jan. 1926; Chairman of the Royal Aeronautical Society, 1926-27; President, 1927-28, 1928-29, 1929-30; Deputy Chairman of the Council of the London Chamber of Commerce, 1931-34, Chairman 1934-35, now Vice-President; Vice-Pres. International Commission for the Study of Motor-less Flight, 1930; Pres. British Gliding Assoc., 1933-42; Institute of the Motor Industry, 1946-48; Member Advisory Committee of the Science Museum, 1930-42; of Advisory Committee for Aeronautics at Hull University, 1931; of Executive Committee of Navy League, Air League, Royal National Lifeboat Instn. (Vice-Pres.), and Roy. Soc. of Arts; President: Instn. of Production Engineers, 1935-37; Instn. of Engineers in Charge; Past Chairman: Anglo-Swedish Society (Pres.); Inst. of Advanced Motorists (Pres.). Late Aviation Editor of The Field. *Publications:* Wanderings along a Future Commercial Air Route; The British Aviation Mission to the Imperial

Japanese Navy; Aero Engine Fuels of To-day and To-morrow; The Air and the Plain Man, 1931. *Heir:* (to Barony only) *d.* Hon. Mrs. Chant [Ann Moira, *b.* 19 March 1920; *m.* 1st, 1941, Capt. Eric Holt (marriage dissolved); one *d.*; 2nd, 1948, Major Stuart Whitemore Chant, M.C., Gordon Highlanders and No. 5 Commando; two *s.*]. *Recreation:* farming. *Address:* East House, Dedham, Essex. *T.A.:* Sempleaero, London; Craigievar Castle, Aberdeenshire. *Club:* Athenæum.
[*Died* 30 *Dec.* 1965.

SEMPLE, Dugald; author and lecturer; *b.* Johnstone, 7 Feb. 1884; *s.* of Robert Semple, clothier, Johnstone; *m.* 1916, Catherine Amos Tuckwell, *d.* of late James Graham, Bridge of Weir. *Educ.:* Johnstone Public School; Paisley Grammar School. Trained as an engineer and draughtsman; began open-air life at Linwood Moss, 1907; camped near the river Gryfe, 1908; Secretary of the London Vegetarian Society, 1916; Hon. President of the Scottish Vegetarian Society. *Publications:* Simple Life Visitors, 1909; Living in Liberty, 1911; Fruitarianism, 1913; Diet in relation to Climate, 1914; Joys of the Simple Life, 1915; Simple Life Recipes, 1916; Life in the Open, 1919; Diet and Good Health, 1925; A Free Man's Philosophy, 1933; What to eat in War-Time, 1940; The Wheelhouse Nature Calendar, 1943; Nature Cure for Common Ailments, 1944; Looking at Nature, 1945; Health Cookery Book, 1948; The Nature Lover's Calendar, 1949; Round Kintyre, 1950; The Sunfood Way to Health, 1955; Joy in Living, 1957. *Address:* Rose Cottage, Fairlie, Ayrshire, Scotland.
[*Died* 19 *Jan.* 1964.

SEMPLE, John Edward; *b.* Budleigh Salterton, 18 Nov. 1903; *y. s.* of Henry Frederick Semple, Budleigh Salterton, *o. s.* of Henry Semple, Capt. 60th Rifles, and Charlotte Ellen Spencer, *d.* of Rev. E. Spencer, Tavistock; *m.* 1937, Wilhelmina, *y. d.* of William Miers, Scarcroft and Charlotte Thompson; one *s.* one *d.* *Educ.:* Rugby School; Corpus Christi College, Cambridge. B.A. (Hons.) 1925; M.A. 1933. Qualified, 1929; F.R.C.S. 1933; M.D. 1933. Raymond Horton-Smith Prize; Copeman Medal. Resident Assistant Surgeon, West London Hospital, 1935; Surgical Registrar, Hospital for Sick Children, Great Ormond Street, 1937; Surgeon, Battersea Gen. Hosp., 1937; Surgeon, St. Paul's Hospital, 1939. Consulting Urologist, Watford Peace Memorial Hosp., 1946; Consulting Genito-Urinary Surgeon, Bethnal Green Hosp., 1947. War of 1939-45: Surgical Specialist R.A.M.C., France and Egypt (dispatches). *Publications:* contrib. to numerous surgical textbooks and journals. *Recreations:* hunting, golf, ski-ing. *Address:* Moors House, W. Hendred, Berks. *T.:* East Hendred 383.
[*Died* 3 *Oct.* 1969.

SENCOURT, Robert; Critic, Biographer, Historian; *b.* N.Z., 1890; unmarried. *Educ.:* St. John's College, Tamaki, N.Z.; St. John's College, Oxford, M.A., B.Litt., 1918. Attached Central India Horse, 1915-16; General Staff, Simla-Delhi, 1917-18; India Office, 1919-20; has held Chairs of English at Lisbon and Lahore, India; Vice-Dean of the Faculty of Arts and Prof. of English Literature in the Univ. of Egypt, 1935-36; lectured throughout U.S.A., 1964; at Yale Univ., 1965; Catholic. *Publications:* Purse and Politics, 1921; Outflying Philosophy, 1924; India in English Literature, 1925; Life of George Meredith, 1929; Life of the Empress Eugenie, 1931; Spain's Uncertain Crown, 1932; Napoleon III: the Modern Emperor, 1933; (with Sir Victor Wellesley) Conversations with Napoleon III, 1934; The Genius of the Vatican, 1935; Spain's Ordeal, 1938; Italy (in Modern States Series), 1939; Winston Churchill, 1940; King Alfonso, 1942; Carmelite and Poet: St. John of the Cross, 1943; The Consecration of Genius: Studies in Religious Masterpieces, 1946; Life of Newman, 1947; St. Paul: Envoy of Grace, 1948; Heirs of Tradition: portraits of distinguished contemporaries, 1949; The Salvatorians and their Founder, 1953; Reign of King Edward VIII, 1961; many contributions to the Times Literary Supplement, Edinburgh Review, Quarterly Review, Tablet, XIX Century, Fortnightly, Contemporary, Discovery, Royal Geographical Journal, Pax, Eirenicon, Revue des Deux Mondes, Criterion, Times, Spectator, Cornhill, Hibbert Journal, Sunday Times, Sunday Telegraph, Daily Telegraph, etc., and leading American Revs. *Recreations:* tennis, swimming, riding, croquet, conversation. *Club:* Royal Automobile.
[*Died* 23 *May* 1969.

SENIOR, William Goodwin, C.B.E. 1953 (O.B.E. 1941); Ph.D.; Chief Dental Officer, Ministry of Health, 1947-61, retired; *b.* 8 Oct. 1894; *o. s.* of Fred Senior, Dewsbury, Yorks.; *m.* Janet Kyle Shirreff; one *d.* *Educ.:* Wheelwright Grammar School, Dewsbury; Leeds University. L.D.S. (Leeds) 1920; F.D.S.R.C.S. 1947. University Tutor in Dental Surgery, 1920-21; Public Dental Officer, Swansea County Borough, 1921-24; Senior Dental Surgeon, Croydon County Borough, 1924-31; Dental Sec., British Dental Assoc. 1931-47. Hon. Ph.D. Leeds, 1947. Hon. Mem. Pierre Fauchard Acad.; Hon. Mem. All India Dental Assoc.; Hon. Fell. Amer. Pub. Health Assoc.; Life Mem., Brit. Dental Assoc.; late F.R.Soc.Med. (Past Pres. Sect. Odontology, 1959-60); late Member Board of Faculty Dental Surgery, Royal Coll. of Surgeons; late Fellow Soc. Medical Officers of Health; Hon. Fellow Executive Vice-President and Member Council R.S.H. (Dep. Chm., 1961); late F.Z.S. Webb-Johnson Lectr., R.C.S., 1963-1964. *Publications:* communications in the British Dental Journal. *Recreations:* gardening, reading, theatre. *Address:* 54 Greenways, Court Moor, Fleet, Hants. *Clubs:* National Liberal, Arts Theatre.
[*Died* 27 *June* 1969.

SENTER, Sir John (Watt), Kt. 1958; Q.C. 1953; *b.* Edinburgh, 27 May 1905; *e.c.* of John Watt Senter (*b.* Kildrummy, Aberdeenshire; M.B., Ch.B. Edin.; killed in France, 1918), and Kate Cockburn Senter (*née* McIntyre), Edinburgh; *m.* 1st, 1928, Frances Knight Brand (marriage dissolved, 1961); no *c.*; 2nd, 1961, Anne Caroline Jarvis. *Educ.:* George Watson's Coll., Edinburgh; Edinburgh University. M.A., LL.B., Dalgety Prizeman in Jurisprudence, Vans Dunlop Law Scholar, President of the Union, etc., Edin. Univ. Called to Bar, Middle Temple, 1928; Bencher, 1961. Served with engineering company in Leicester, 1928-35. In chambers with Valentine Holmes, 1935-40. Mem. Army Officers' Emergency Reserve, 1938; Civilian Asst. attached Gen. Staff, War Office, 1940-41. Temp. Lt. (Sp.) R.N.V.R. addtl. for duty with N.I.D. outside Admlty., 1941; invalided, 1945, as Comdr. (Sp.) R.N.V.R. Resumed practice at Bar, 1945. Dep.-Chm. (London), Northern Assur. Co. Ltd. 1951-53. Mem. Gen. Council of the Bar, 1954-58; Hon. Treas. 1956-58. *Recreations:* fishing, reading, walking. *Address:* 1 Essex Court, Temple, E.C.4. *T.:* Central 9089; 6 King's Bench Walk, Temple, E.C.4. *T.:* Central 4606. *Clubs:* Brooks's; Army and Navy.
[*Died* 14 *July* 1966.

SETH-SMITH, David, F.Z.S., M.B.O.U.; late Curator of Mammals and Birds, Zoological Society, and Zoo Man of the B.B.C. Children's Hour; *b.* Tangley, Guildford, 1875; *e. s.* by 2nd marriage of late William Seth-Smith; *m.* 1st, 1901, Mary (*d.* 1945), *e. d.* of James Benjamin Scott; one *s.* two *d.*; 2nd, 1946, Heather Heydeman. Studied as civil engineer and architect, but devoted much time to natural history, especially Ornithology; served on Council of Zoological Society, 1906-9; went to Australia on behalf of Zoological Society, 1907; awarded Zoological Society's silver medal, 1908; Honorary Fellow, New York Zoological Society; Corresponding Fellow, American Ornithologists' Union; Honorary Member, Société Nationale d'Acclimation de France; Past Editor, Bulletin of British Ornithologists' Club and Avicultural Magazine. *Publications:* Monograph on Parrakeets; popular books on animals. *Recreations:* natural history, photography, gardening. *Address:* 3 St. Omer Road, Guildford. *T.:* Guildford 61068. [*Died* 30 *Oct.* 1963.

SETON, Sir Alexander Hay, 10th Bt. of Abercorn, *cr.* 1663; *b.* 14 August 1904; *s.* of late Sir Bruce Gordon Seton, 9th Bt. of Abercorn, C.B., and Elma (*d.* 1960), *d.* of Colonel Frank Armstrong, R.A.S.C.; *S.* father, 1932; *m.* 1st, 1927, Zeyla Daphne (who obtained a decree of divorce, 1939), *d.* of John Sanderson, Edinburgh; one *d.*; 2nd, 1939, Flavia *d.* of Lt.-Col. James Stewart Forbes, D.S.O.; 3rd, 1962, Julia Clements, Chelsea. *Educ.:* Glenalmond. Entered Army; served in Lothian and Border Horse (R.T.C.), 1924-26; gazetted 2nd Lieut. in Royal Scots, 1926; Lieut. 1929; seconded to Foreign Office as Hon. Attaché to H.B.M. Legation in Sofia, 1930; resigned commission, 1933; Carrick Pursuivant at Arms to the Lord Lyon, 1935-39; also Hereditary Armour Bearer and Squire to the Royal Body; Flight Lt. R.A.F.V.R., 1939; resigned commission with rank of Squadron Leader, 1943; Temp. Lt. (Sp.) R.N.V.R. 1944. *Recreations:* shooting, motoring, fishing, piping. *Heir:* *b.* Bruce Lovat Seton, Maj. (ret.) [*b.* 29 May 1909; *m.* 1st, 1937, Tamara Desni (from whom he obtained a divorce 1940), *d.* of Jacob Brodski; 2nd, 1940, Florence Antoinette Glossop Cellier; one *d.*]. *Address:* 122 Swan Court, S.W.3. *T.:* Flaxman 9039. [*Died* 7 *Feb.* 1963.

SETON, Sir Bruce Lovat, 11th Bt. of Abercorn, *cr.* 1663; Major (retd.) Cameronians (Scottish Rifles); Actor (as Bruce Seton) since 1932; *b.* 29 May 1909; *s.* of Sir Bruce Gordon Seton, 9th Bt. of Abercorn, C.B., and Ellen Mary Armstrong (*d.* 1960); *S.* brother, 1963; *m.* 1940, Antoinette Cellier; one *d.* *Educ.:* Edinburgh Academy; R.M.C. Sandhurst. Resigned commission 2nd Bn. The Black Watch, 1932. Studied music. Thereafter musicals and films (chorus to leading parts) until 1939. From 1945: stage, films, radio, TV; Sgt. Odd in Whisky Galore; P/O Tallow in The Cruel Sea; Fabian in TV series Fabian of the Yard. Served War of 1939-45; U.S. Medal of Freedom, 1945. *Recreations:* playing the pipes and composing pipe music. *Heir:* *cousin* Christopher Bruce Seton [*b.* 3 Oct. 1909; *m.* 1939, Joyce Vivian, S.R.N., S.C.M., *er. d.* of late Oliver George Barnard, Lynton House, Stowmarket; two *s.* two *d.*]. *Address:* 88 Redcliffe Gdns., S.W.10. *T.:* Fremantle 9506. [*Died* 28 *Sept.* 1969.

SEWELL, Arnold Edward, C.B.E. 1956; M.Inst.T.; Permanent Member, Transport Tribunal, 1949-56; *b.* 21 June 1886; *s.* of Joseph T. Sewell, J.P., Whitby; *m.* 1913, Marguerite E. Vatter, Geneva; two *s.* one *d.* *Educ.:* Ackworth School; Bootham School, York. Goods Manager (Scotland), L.N.E.R., 1934-42; Chm. (rail) Road-Rail Central Conf., 1939-47; Charges Adviser, British Transport Commn., 1947-49. *Publications:* various papers on transport economics. *Recreations:* gardening, walking. *Address:* Brambledown, Winscombe, Somerset. *T.:* Winscombe (Bristol) 3139. [*Died* 27 *March* 1969.

SEWELL, Lieut.-Colonel Robert Beresford Seymour, C.I.E. 1933; F.R.S. 1934; Sc.D.; I.M.S.; retired; Editor of the Fauna of India Series, 1933-63; *b.* 5 Mar. 1880; *s.* of Rev. Arthur Sewell; *m.* 1914, Dorothy Dean (*decd.*), *d.* of William and Matilda Dean, Chichester; two *d.* *Educ.:* Weymouth College; Christ's College, Cambridge; St. Bartholomew's Hospital, London. Entered I.M.S., 1908; retired 1935; Surgeon-Naturalist to Marine Survey of India, 1910-14; on Active Service, 1914-18 (despatches); Officiating Superintendent, Zoological Survey of India, 1919-1920; Surgeon Naturalist, 1920-25; Director, Zoological Survey of India, 1925-33; Leader of the John Murray Expedition, 1933-34; President, Royal Asiatic Society of Bengal, 1931-33; President, Indian Science Congress, 1931; Pres., the Ray Society, 1950-53; Pres. The Linnean Soc. of London, 1952-55; Corr. Member, Academy of Natural Sciences, Philadelphia, U.S.A.; Fellow, National Institute of Sciences, India; Hon. Fellow, Indian Assoc. for the Cultivation of Science; Hon. Fellow Indian Academy of Sciences, Bangalore; Hon. Fellow, Zoological Soc. of India. Hon. Mem. Marine Biological Assoc. of India. *Address:* 139 Huntingdon Road, Cambridge. *T.:* Cambridge 555431. [*Died* 11 *Feb.* 1964.

SEYMOUR, Charles, M.A., Ph.D., Litt.D., L.H.D.; LL.D.; Western Reserve 1920, Columbia University 1938; University of Lyon (France) 1947; LL.D., Trinity College 1922, Princeton Univ. 1937, Harvard Univ. 1938, Wesleyan Univ. (Conn.) 1939, Univ. of Penn. 1940, Williams Coll. 1943, Boston Univ. 1945, Cambridge Univ. (England) 1948, Univ. of Paris 1949, Yale Univ. 1950; L.H.D. Rollins Coll., 1939; Univ. of Hawaii, 1947; President Emeritus of Yale University; Hon. Fellow King's College, Cambridge University, 1937; Stanford Univ., 1941; *b.* 1 Jan. 1885; *s.* of Thomas D. Seymour, Professor of Greek at Yale University, and Sarah M. Hitchcock; *m.* 1911, Gladys M. Watkins; two *c.* *Educ.:* King's College, Cambridge; Yale University; Freiburg University; University of Paris. Instructor of History, Yale University, 1911-15; Assistant Professor, 1915-18; Prof., 1918-37; Sterling Prof. History, 1922-37; Provost of Yale Univ., 1927-37; Master of Berkeley Coll., Yale Univ., 1932-37; President of Yale Univ., 1937-50; Visiting Professor at Universities of Brussels, Liège, Louvain, Ghent, 1924; Special Assistant in Department of State, 1918-19; Member of American Commission to negotiate Peace at Paris, 1918-19; United States Delegate on Czecho-Slovak, Yugo-Slav and Roumanian Territorial Commissions; Director, Second National Bank, New Haven; Member Council on Foreign Relations, Am. Academy of Arts and Sciences, Am. Philosophical Society; F.R.Hist.S.; Commander Legion of Honour. *Publications:* Electoral Reform in England and Wales, 1915; Diplomatic Background of the War, 1916 (translated into French, 1920); How the World Votes (with D. P. Frary), 1918; Woodrow Wilson and the World War, 1921; The Intimate Papers of Colonel House, 4 vols., 1926-28; American Diplomacy in the World War, 1934; American Neutrality, 1914-17, 1935; Edited: What Really Happened at Paris (with E. M. House), 1921. *Address:* 223 Bradley Street, New Haven, Conn., U.S.A. *Clubs:* Graduates, Elizabethan (New Haven); Century (New York). [*Died* 11 *Aug.* 1963.

SEYMOUR SEYMOUR, Sir George, Kt., *cr.* 1952; O.B.E. 1934; engaged in penkeeping, planting and breeding of thoroughbred horses since 1915; Secretary Jockey Club of Jamaica since 1935 (Asst. Sec. 1917-22); *b.* St. Andrew, Jamaica, 30 Aug. 1880; *s.* of late Hon. George Solomon Seymour, Legislator, and Frederica Ann Seymour; *m.* 1919, Evelyn, *widow* of Thomas Milo Burke, and *d.* of late Col. James Ward; no *c.* *Educ.:* Kingston Collegiate and York Castle High Schools, Jamaica. Director of Knutsford Park Ltd., 1925-; Foundation

Director, Jamaica Banana Producers' Assoc., 1926; Mayor of Kingston, 1927-29, 1931-34; Chm. Assoc. of Parochial Boards, 1926-44 (retd.); Dir. Jamaica Mutual Life Assurance Soc., 1931-; Dir. Jamaica Co-operative Fire and Gen. Insurance Co., 1931-; first Vice-Pres., Jamaica Agric. Soc., 1936-44 (retd.); Member: cattle, banana, coconut, citrus industries, and agricultural policy cttees., 1944-. Custos (Senior Magistrate) parish of St. Andrew, B.W.I., 1940-; Chm. Water Commn., 1939-; Chm. Film Censorship Authority. *Recreations:* horse racing, reading, cricket. *Address:* Retreat, 19 Seymour Avenue, Liguanea, Jamaica, W.I.

[*Died* 30 *Sept*. 1962.

SHAFTESBURY, 9th Earl of (*cr.* 1672), **Anthony Ashley-Cooper**, Bt., 1622; K.P. 1911; P.C. 1922; G.C.V.O., *cr.* 1924 (K.C.V.O., *cr.* 1906); C.B.E 1919; Hon. LL.D. Queen's Univ., Belfast; Baron Ashley, 1661; Baron Cooper, of Paulet, 1672; H.M. Lieut. Co. Dorset, 1916-52; Chm. Dorset County Council, 1924-46; late Development Commissioner under the Development Fund Act 1910 (Chairman of the Commission, 1946-48); Younger Brother of Trinity House; Vice-Pres. Royal Choral Soc.; Provincial Grand Master of Dorset, 1902-1952; Pres., Shaftesbury Society; late President of the English Church Union, and Member National Church Assembly; late Chairman National Advisory Council to the Ministry of Labour for Juvenile Employment in England and Wales; Bailiff of Egle and Bailiff Grand Cross in the Order of St. John of Jerusalem; Brig.-General Commanding 1st South-West Mounted Brigade, 1913-16; served European War, 1914-18; retired with hon. rank of Brig.-Gen.; late Hon. Col. North Irish Horse; Lord Chamberlain to the Queen, 1910-22; Commissioner of Congested Districts Board for Ireland, 1902-14; Chancellor of Queen's Univ. of Belfast till 1923; H.M. Lieutenant for Co. of Antrim, 1911-16; Grand Officer Legion of Honour; *b.* 31 Aug. 1869; *s.* of 8th Earl and Harriet, *o. d.* of 3rd Marquess of Donegall, K.P. (*d.* 1898); *S.* father, 1886; *m.* 1899, Lady Constance Grosvenor (*d.* 1957), *e. d.* of late Earl Grosvenor, and *g.d.* of 1st Duke of Westminster; one *s.* two *d.* (and one *s.* one *d.* decd.). *Educ.:* Eton; Sandhurst. Entered army, 10th Hussars, 1890; Lieutenant, 1891; Mil. Sec. to Earl Brassey, Governor of Victoria, Australia, 1895-98; Captain, 1898; commanded North Irish Horse, 1902-12; H.M.'s Lieut. Belfast, 1904-11; Lord Mayor of Belfast, 1907; Lord Steward of H.M. Household, 1922-1936. *Recreations:* music, campanology. *Heir: g.s.* Lord Ashley. *Address:* St. Giles's, Wimborne, Dorset. *Clubs:* Carlton; Kildare Street (Dublin); Jockey (Newmarket); Royal Yacht Squadron (Cowes).

[*Died* 25 *March* 1961.

SHAIKH, Lt.-Colonel Abdul Hamid, C.I.E. 1942; I.M.S. retired; B.A. (Government College, Lahore), 1910; M.B., Ch.B. (Edin.), 1914; *b.* 5 Feb. 1890; *s.* of Shaikh Khan Mahamed, Khan Bahadur, Hon. magistrate, Rawalpindi; *m.* 1935, Constance Doreen, *d.* of late Dr. William Brady Sampson, Myono, Co. Clare; one *d.* Served Indian Expeditionary Force, France, 1914-1918; Egypt, Palestine, Syria, Turkey, 1918-20 (with 6th (K.E.O.) Cavalry); North-West Frontier of India, 1921-23, 1924-26; Shanghai Defence Force, 1927. Superintendent District and Central prisons, Agra and Lucknow, 1928-36; Deputy Director-General, I.M.S., 1937; Superintendent Juvenile Jail and Central Prison, Bareilly, 1938-40; Inspector-General of Prisons, United Provinces, 1940-46; retired from I.M.S., 1945. Adviser to H.E.H. the Nizam's Govt. on Jail Reforms, 1947; Office of Pakistan High Commissioner in London, 1949-54 Special Interest: Social Psychiatry. Studies were carried out in Maudsley Hospital and School of Medical Psychology, London, Vienna, Columbia Univ., New York. Member: Experts' Cttee. on Prison Reforms, U.P., 1937; Deptl. Cttee. on Prison Reforms, U.P., 1939; Sub-Cttee. (on Mental Health) of Bhore Cttee. on Health Survey of India, 1944; Inspector Generals of Prisons Conf., Nagpur, 1945; Delegate to: Internat. Diplomatic Conf., Geneva, 1949; 1st Internat. Biochem. Conf., Cambridge, 1949; Brit. Pharmaceutical Conf., Blackpool, 1949; Commonwealth Cttee. on Defence Science, 1950. *Publications:* Life History of Convict Sukha—a plea for introduction of psychiatric approach to criminal administration, 1939; Correctional and Rehabilitation Work, Juvenile Jail, Bareilly, 1942; Correctional and rehabilitation Work, Reformatory School, Lucknow, 1944; Prevention and Correction of Delinquency, Mental Disorder and Mental Deficiency, 1944; Fetters and Handcuffs, Past and Present, 1946; Irons Past and Present, Hyderabad State, 1947; Inspections: notes on Jails of Hyderabad State, 1947; Psychiatric Problems of Pakistan, 1949. *Address:* c/o Lloyds Bank, 6 Pall Mall, S.W.1. *Clubs:* Athenæum, Royal Commonwealth Society.

[*Died* 8 *April* 1963.

SHAKERLEY, Major Sir Cyril Holland, 5th Bt., *cr.* 1838; D.L., J.P.; *b.* 28 Feb. 1897; *s.* of Sir George Herbert Shakerley, 4th Bt., and late Evelyn Mary France-Hayhurst. *S.* father, 1945; *m.* 1928, Elizabeth Averil Eardley-Wilmot (M.B.E. 1955); two *s.* one *d.* *Educ.:* Harrow; R.M.C. Sandhurst. Served European War, 1st Bn. K.R.R.C., attached R.F.C. 1917 (prisoner); Capt. 4th Bn. Royal Sussex Regt., 1930-34; War of 1939-46, Royal Sussex Regt. J.P., D.L., Sussex. *Heir: s.* Geoffrey Adam Shakerley [*b.* 9 Dec. 1932; *m.* 1962, Virginia Elizabeth Maskell (*d.* 1968), two *s.*]. *Address:* Wyncombe Hill, Fittleworth, Sussex. *T.:* Fittleworth 373. *Club:* Naval and Military.

[*Died* 21 *Aug.* 1970

SHAKESPEAR, Brig. Arthur Talbot, D.S.O. 1918; M.C.; *b.* 15 Sept. 1884; *s.* of Col. A. B. Shakespear, R.M.A. and Egyptian Army; *m.* 1909, Sophie G. Eyndhoven; three *d.* *Educ.:* Monmouth; Cheltenham College. Service in the Royal Engineers and on the Staff of the Army in Ireland, Malta, War, 1914-18 (despatches, M.C., D.S.O.), Gibraltar, Singapore, and Egypt; A.A. and Q.M.G., Malaya, 1934-37; retired pay, 1937; A.R.P. Officer, Richmond, Surrey, 1938-39; A.A. and Q.M.G., Gibraltar, 1940; Comdt. R.E. Depot, 1941-42. *Recreations:* bowls and beekeeping. *Address:* 39 Christchurch Road, Winchester, Hants. *T.:* Winchester 4555.

[*Died* 5 *Sept*. 1964.

SHANAHAN, Foss, C.M.G. 1962; Deputy Permanent Head, Prime Minister's Dept., and Deputy Secretary, External Affairs Dept., New Zealand; *b.* 10 June 1910; *s.* of Thomas and Ethel Shanahan; *m.* 1938, Joan Katherine Mason McCormick; four *s.* one *d.* (and one *c.* decd.). *Educ.:* Christian Brothers Coll., Dunedin; Waitaki Boys' High School; Otago and Wellington Univs. Asst. Sec., Org. for Nat. Security, Prime Minister's Dept., 1938, Sec., 1940; later Sec. of War Council and Asst. Sec. of War Cabinet; Sec. of Cabinet, 1945-55; Asst. Sec. of Ext. Affairs, later Dep. Sec., 1948; Comr. for N.Z. in S.E. Asia (personal rank Amb.), 1955-58; N.Z. Council Rep., S.E.A.T.O., Bangkok, 1955-58; concurrently Amb. to Thailand and High Comr. to Malaya, 1956-1958; High Comr. to Canada and concurrently Permanent Rep. to U.N., 1958-61; Pres. Economic and Social Council, 1961. *Recreations:* swimming, fishing. *Address:* 40 Everest Street, Wellington, New Zealand.

[*Died* 13 *Sept*. 1964.

SHAND, Surgeon Rear-Admiral Jonathan, C.B. 1923; M.B.; Royal Navy; *b.* 9 Dec. 1865; *m.* 1897, Rosina; two *d.* *Educ.:* Aberdeen University; M.B., C.M., with hons., 1887. Entered Royal Navy 1887; Surgeon Commander, 1903; Surgeon Captain, 1918; Surgeon Rear-Admiral, 1920; retired list, 1923. *Address:* c/o Lloyds Bank, Palmerston Road, Southsea. [*Died* 25 *June* 1961.

SHANNON, 8th Earl of, *cr.* 1756, **Robert Henry Boyle;** Viscount Boyle, Baron of Castle-Martyr, 1756; Baron Carleton (U.K.), 1786; Captain Indian Army, 1940; Lieut. late Royal Fusiliers; late A.D.C., to Governor of Madras; *b.* 1 Feb. 1900; *s.* of 6th Earl and Nellie, *d.* of late Charles Thompson; *S.* brother, 1917; *m.* 1923, Marjorie, *d.* of S. A. Walker, of Ootacamund; one *s.* *Educ.:* Malvern; R.M.C., Sandhurst. *Heir: s.* Viscount Boyle. *Address:* c/o Lloyds Bank Ltd., 6 Pall Mall, S.W.1. [*Died* 29 *Dec.* 1963.

SHAPCOTT, Brig. Sir Henry, K.B.E., *cr.* 1955 (C.B.E. 1941; O.B.E. 1937); C.B. 1947; M.C. 1918; retired; *b.* 13 July 1888; *s.* of Capt. H. McKeever Shapcott; *m.* 1915, Rhoda, *d.* of Richard Sims; no *c.* *Educ.:* Plymouth College. Solicitor, 1909. Served European War, Roy. Artillery, 1915-18; Staff Capt., Southern Command, 1919; Ireland, 1921; Mil. Asst. Staff Capt., 1923, D.A.A.G., 1924, A.A.G., 1934, Judge Advocate-Gen.'s Dept., War Office; Col., 1939; Brig., 1941; Military Deputy of Judge Advocate-General and Brigadier-in-charge, Military Dept., Judge Advocate-General's Office, War Office, 1939-48; Director Army Legal Services, 1948-55; retired 1955. *Address:* 21 Penrith Road, Boscombe Manor, Bournemouth, Hants. *T.:* Bournemouth 36580. [*Died* 10 *July* 1967.

SHAPLEY, Rt. Rev. Ronald Norman, M.C. 1918; *b.* 16 July 1890; *s.* of Frank Shapley, M.R.C.S., L.R.C.P. and Edith Shapley (*née* Stockwood); unmarried. *Educ.:* King's College, London University. Commn. in 8th Battalion London Regiment, 1915; European War, 1914-18 (despatches, M.C.). A.K.C., 1919, F.K.C. 1950. Deacon, 1919; Priest, 1920; Asst. Curate of St. Clement's Notting Hill, London, 1919-23; Chaplain, Gordon Boys' Home (National Memorial to General Gordon), 1923-27. Entered Chaplains' Branch, R.A.F., 1927; served: Malta, 1927-31; Sealand, 1931-33; Boscombe Down and Netheravon, 1933-34; Calshot, 1934-36; Egypt, 1936-37; Palestine, 1937-39; War of 1939-45; Egypt, 1939-42; Senior Chaplain, Egypt, and Staff Chaplain; mentioned in despatches, 1942-43; Asst. Chaplain-in-Chief, Western Area, U.K., 1943; Asst. Chaplain-in-Chief, R.A.F., Middle East, 1945; Asst. Chaplain-in-Chief, Mediterranean and Middle East, 1946; Commandant, R.A.F. Chaplains' School, 1947; retired list, Nov. 1947. Chaplain, Gordon Boys' School (National Memorial to General Gordon), Nov. 1947-49; Bishop of the Windward Islands, 1949-62, resigned, Jan. 1962. *Address:* c/o Holy Trinity Rectory, Castries, St. Lucia, B.W.I. *Club:* Royal Air Force. [*Died* 27 *Dec.* 1964.

SHARMAN, Colonel Charles Henry Ludovic, C.M.G. 1919; C.B.E. 1918; I.S.O. 1946; *b.* England, 1881; *m.* 1905, Mabel, *d.* of I. Bettschen, Regina; one *s.* *Educ.:* St. Lawrence College, England. Royal North West Mounted Police, 1898-1904; South Africa (Canadian Mounted Rifles), 1902; Dept. of Agriculture, Ottawa, 1905-27; Chief Canadian Narcotic Service, 1927-46; Canadian Delegate Opium Advisory Committee, Geneva, 1934-46; Chm. U.N. Narcotics Commission, 1946-47, Cdn. Rep., 1948-53; Member Drug Supervisory Body, 1948, Chm. 1953-58. France 1st Canadian Div. 1914-18; North Russian Expeditionary Force, 1918-19. *Recreation:* golf. *Address:* 179 Carling Avenue, Ottawa, Canada. [*Died* 15 *May* 1970

SHARP, Gilbert Granville-, Q.C. 1948; A Commissioner in the Crown Courts, Manchester, 1963-67, and Liverpool, 1965-67, retired; *b.* 19 Feb. 1894; *s.* of late Reverend Alfred Spring Sharp, Methodist minister, Prestatyn, Flintshire; *m.* 1st, 1915, Margaret F. Kellett; one *d.*; 2nd, 1953, Eleanor Christina Brooke. *Educ.:* Kingswood; Fitzwilliam Hall Cambridge. Military Service, 1914-18, Public Schools Battalion and 2nd Border Regiment., Lieut., France, 1915-16 (wounded in Battle of Somme); Special Instructor of Signals, 1917. B.A., LL.B. Cambs., 1919; President of Union, 1921; President of Cambridge University Liberal Club, 1921; contested (L.) Epping Division, 1922, 1923, 1924, 1929, and 1935; Falmouth and Camborne, 1950. President Hardwicke Society, 1924. Called to Bar, Middle Temple, 1921; Member: Council of Liberal Party Organisation, 1941; General Council of the Bar, 1946-48; Chief of Legal and Advice Branch, Legal Division (British Section), Austrian Control Commn., 1944-45. Royal Commn. on the Press, 1947-1949. Recorder of King's Lynn, 1943-57; Justice of Appeal of the Supreme Court, Ghana, 1957-62. H.G., 1940, Lieut. E. Coy. 53rd East Surrey Battalion. *Publication:* (co-ed. with Brian Galpin), Maxwell on the Interpretation of Statutes, 10th edn., 1953. *Recreations:* angling, golf, cricket, painting, sailing. *Address:* The White House, Eastcombe, Glos. *T.:* Bisley 246. *Club:* Oxford and Cambridge University. [*Died* 1 *Nov.* 1968.

SHARPE, Sir William Rutton Searle, Kt., *cr.* 1936; former Chm., Bombay Port Trust; *b.* Dublin, 11 Dec. 1881; 3rd *s.* of W. D. Atkinson Sharpe; *m.* 1911, Kate (*d.* 1967), 3rd *d.* of T. Herbert Marsh, Porter's Hall, Essex; one *d.* *Educ.:* City of London Sch.; abroad. Joined Indian service of Grindlay & Co. Ltd., 1902; served in Calcutta, Bombay, and Simla; joined Bombay Port Trust, 1913; Chairman, 1931; retired, 1935; was for several years Chairman of Royal Bombay Seamen's Society, the Indian Sailors' Home, and the St. George's Hospital Nursing Assoc.; a Member of Bombay Municipal Corporation and Improvement Trust and of Advisory Committees of G.I.P. and B.B. and C.I. Railways; O.St.J. *Publication:* The Port of Bombay. *Address:* Skerries, Hertford. [*Died* 14 *Jan.* 1968.

SHARPEY-SCHAFER, Edward Peter; Professor of Medicine, London University, Director of Medical Division, St. Thomas's Hospital, since 1948; *b.* 22 Sept. 1908; *s.* of late Comdr. John Sharpey-Schafer, R.N., and Ruth Bateman Champain; *m.* Sheila Howarth; two *d.* *Educ.:* Winchester Coll. (Sch.); King's Coll., Cambridge (exhibitioner and Kitchener Scholar); Univ. College Hospital (Fellowes Gold and Silver medals). University College Hospital: House Physician, House Surgeon, Casualty Medical Officer. M.R.C.P. (Lond.) 1935; F.R.C.P. (Lond.) 1949. R.M.O., Heart Hospital, 1935; First Assistant and Senior Lecturer, Dept. of Medicine, Postgraduate Medical School, 1936-48. *Publications:* papers on circulatory dynamics and endocrinology. *Recreations:* childish pursuits; golf. *Address:* St. Thomas's Hospital, S.E.1. [*Died* 23 *Oct.* 1963.

SHARPLEY, Forbes Wilmot, B.Sc. Eng. (Lond.), Ph.D., F.R.S.E., M.I.E.E.; Head of Director's staff, Coal Research Establishment, National Coal Board, Cheltenham, 1952-62 retd.; *b.* Dublin, 7 Jan. 1897; *m.* Kathleen M. Kirkwood, Edinburgh, *grand-niece* of Robert and William Chambers, publishers, Edinburgh; no *c.* *Educ.:* Dublin; Edinburgh. Served with Dublin and Edinburgh engineering firms; apptd. first Prof. of Mechanical and Electrical Engineering, Indian School of Mines, Dhanbad, 1926. *Publications:* several papers on vision and illumination in coal-mines. *Recreations:* tennis, astronomy. *Address:* Morningside, Prestbury, Cheltenham, Glos. *Club:* Royal Over-Seas League. [*Died* 6 *Oct.* 1965.

SHASTRI, Shri Lal Bahadur; Prime Minister of India since June 1964; *b.* 2 October 1904; 2nd *s.* of Shri Sharda Prasad; *m.* 1928, Lalita Devi; four *s.* two *d.* *Educ.:* Harish Chandra School and Kashi Vidyapeeth, Varanasi (Benares). Joined non-violent non-co-operative movement and imprisoned for political activities; General Secretary, United Provinces Congress Committee, 1935-38; Member of U.P. Legislative Assembly, 1937; Secretary, U.P. Congress Parliamentary Board, 1945; Parliamentary Secretary to Chief Minister, U.P., 1946; Minister for Police and Transport, U.P., 1947-51; General Secretary, Indian National Congress, 1951; Member, Rajya Sabha, 1951; Minister for Railways, Government of India, 1952-56; Minister of Transport and Communications, 1957-58; Minister of Commerce and Industry, 1958-61; Minister of Home Affairs, 1961-63; Member of Congress Party Parliamentary Board, 1963-64; Minister without Portfolio, Jan.-June 1964; Minister for External Affairs, June-July 1964. *Publication:* Madame Curie (in Hindi). *Address:* Office of the Prime Minister, New Delhi, India; Mottial, Nehru Place, New Delhi. [*Died* 11 *Jan.* 1966.

SHATTOCK, Clement Edward, M.D., M.S., F.R.C.S.; retired; formerly Consulting Surgeon Royal Free Hospital, Royal Marsden Hosp. and Paddington Green Children's Hosp.; *b.* 2 Aug. 1887; *s.* of Samuel George Shattock, F.R.S., F.R.C.S., and Lucy Wood; *m.* 1918; one *s.* one *d.* *Educ.:* Wimbledon College. Late Examiner in Surgery London University, Member of Court of Examiners Royal College of Surgeons, Erasmus Wilson Lecturer Royal College of Surgeons, Examiner in Pathology, Conjoint Board. *Publications:* Handbook of Surgical Diagnosis; (joint author) Surgery for Dental Students. *Address:* The Chapel House, Wargrave, Berks. *T.:* Wargrave 3080. [*Died* 23 *Jan.* 1969.

SHAW, Colonel Francis Stewart Kennedy, C.B.E. 1919; *b.* 18 Sept. 1871; *s.* of Lt.-Col. G. K. Shaw 68th Light Infantry; *m.* Marion Isobel, *d.* of W. Boyd, J.P., of Longbenton, Northumberland; one *s.* *Educ.:* Charterhouse; R.M.C., Sandhurst. Served 2nd Hampshire Regt., 1890-1906; S. African War, 1900 (medal); Bde. Major, W. Riding Vol. Inf. Bde., 1906-8; Secretary, N. Riding Territorial Force Association, 1908-11; Remount Service, 1911-17; D.D. Remounts, First Army B.E.F., 1917-19 (despatches thrice, C.B.E.); D.L., J.P. Wiltshire. Vice-President Bath and West Agricultural Society. Past Pres. Arab Horse Society. *Recreation:* country life *Address:* Bathurst Cottage, Teffont Magna, nr. Salisbury, Wilts. *T.:* Teffont 288. [*Died* 8 *Nov.* 1964.

SHAW, Harold K.; *see* Knox-Shaw.

SHAW, Sir Havergal D.; *see* Downes-Shaw, Sir A. H.

SHAW, Helen Brown, M.B.E., J.P.; *d.* of late David Graham, J.P., Glasgow; *m.* late David P. Shaw, Major 6th Cameronians; one *d.* (one *s.* killed in action, 1943). *Educ.:* privately. M.B.E. 1920, for patriotic services during the War; elected to Lanarkshire Education Authority, 1920; member Lanark County Council, 1930-32; contested Bothwell Div., 1924, 1929, 1935 and 1945; M.P. (U.) Bothwell Division of Lanarkshire, 1931-1935. *Address:* Merchiston, Uddingston, Lanarkshire. *T.:* Uddingston 180. [*Died* 20 *April* 1964.

SHAW, Prof. John C. Middleton, M.A., B.Dent.Sc., D.Sc., F.R.S. (S.A.); Hon. F.D.S., R.C.S. (Eng.); Prof. Emer., lately Prof. of Human and Comparative Odontology, Univ. of the Witwatersrand, retd.; lately Mem. S.A. Med. Council; *b.* 5 Feb. 1901; 2nd *s.* of late John Palmer Shaw, J.P., and Mrs. Shaw, Ardandra, Rathfarnham, Dublin; *m.* 1st, Flora Cochrane, Londonderry; one *s.* one *d.*; 2nd, Lynette Coetzee, Johannesburg; no *c.* *Educ.:* St. Andrews College, Wesley College, and Trinity College, Dublin University. *Publications:* Taurodont teeth in S. African Races, 1928; The teeth and jaws of Bantu races of S. Africa, 1931; Benefactors of the Dental Profession, 1934; The dental problem, 1934; The teeth of fossil sharks, 1930; Composite odontomes, 1932; Growth changes and variations in wart hog third molars, 1939; The teeth of the South African fossil pig, *Notochoreus capensis* syn. *meadowsi*, 1938; A new primate from Sterkfontein, 1940; Further Pig Remains from the Vaal River Gravels, 1940, etc. *Recreations:* farming and reading. *Address:* c/o University, Johannesburg, South Africa. [*Died* 6 *Jan.* 1961.

SHAW, Sir John Houldsworth, Kt. *cr* 1927; Solicitor of Inland Revenue, 1921-39; *b.* 1874; *s.* of late Colonel Ed. Wm. Shaw, J.P., Indian Army; *m.* 1900, Elizabeth Dalrymple (*d.* 1932), *d.* of Charles George Shaw, Ayr; one *d.* Entered Inland Revenue Department, 1898. *Address:* Pathways, Cobham, Surrey. *T.:* Cobham 104. [*Died* 25 *July* 1962.

SHAW, Sir Robert de Vere, 6th Bt., *cr.* 1821; M.C.; Lt.-Col. late R.F.A.; *b.* 24 Feb. 1890; *er. s.* of 5th Bt. and Eleanor (*d.* 1946), *d.* of Major Horace de Vere, R.E., of Curragh Chase; *S.* father, 1927; *m.* 1923, Dorothy Joan Cross (*d.* 1967); two *s.* European War, 1914-18 (despatches, M.C.). *Heir:* *s.* Robert Shaw [*b.* 31 Jan. 1925; *m.* 1954, Jocelyn Mary, *d.* of late Andrew McGuffie; two *d.*]. *Clubs:* United Service; Kildare Street (Dublin). [*Died* 26 *March* 1969.

SHAW, Surgeon Rear-Adm. Thomas Brown, M.B., Ch.B.; R.N. retired; J.P.; *b.* 1879; *s.* of Thomas Shaw, J.P., The Glebe, Kircubbin, Co. Down; *m.* 1907, Ada Kathleen (*d.* 1944), *d.* of T. M. Watters, late of Nashville, Malone Park, Belfast; two *s.*; *m.* 1945, Maude Frances, *widow* of Frank Milton, Penzance. *Educ.:* Campbell College; Edinburgh University. M.B., Ch.B. with Honours, 1901; Allan Fellow in Clinical Medicine and Surgery; entered the Navy as Surgeon, 1901; Surg.-Commander, 1915; Haslar, 1901-2; H.M.S. Hyacinth, Flagship East Indies, 1903-1906; took part in Somaliland Campaign, 1904; Gunnery School, Sheerness, 1906-8; H.M.S. Inflexible, 1908-10; R.N. Hospital, Haslar, 1910-13, as assistant to lecturer in naval hygiene; served European War, 1914-1916, in North Sea in H.M.S. Falmouth; present at Battle of Heligoland Bight; afterwards, 1916-19, Medical Officer in charge of water supplies for H.M. ships; Fleet Medical Officer, Africa Station, in H.M.S. Birmingham, 1919-1921; R.N. Hospital, Plymouth, 1922-23; Professor of Hygiene and Director of Medical Studies, Royal Naval Medical School, Greenwich, 1923-29; Surg. Captain, 1926; Surg. Rear-Admiral, 1934. *Publications:* Textbook on Naval Hygiene, 1929; The Treatment of Syphilis with Salvarsan, Brit. Med. Journal, 1912; The Early Diagnosis of Syphilis, Journal of State Medicine, 1915; The Ships' Water Supply, R.N. Medical Journal, 1919; various other papers dealing with the prevention of disease in the Royal Navy. *Recreations:* tennis, golf, fishing, motoring. *Address:* Tudor House, Lee-on-Solent, Hants. *T.:* 79564. *Club:* Royal Naval (Portsmouth). [*Died* 17 *Jan.* 1961.

SHAW, Sir William Fletcher, Kt., *cr.* 1942; LL.D. (Hon.); M.D.; F.R.C.P.; F.R.C.O.G.; F.A.C.S. (Hon.); M.M.S.A. (Hon.); Emeritus Professor of Obstetrics and Gynæcology, Univ., Manchester; Hon. Consultant Gynæcological Surgeon, Manchester Roy. Infirmary; Hon. Consulting Surgeon, St. Mary's Hospital for Women, Manchester; Hon. Cons. Gynæcologist, Christie Hosp. for Cancer, Manchester; Consultant Adviser Gynæcology, North West Region, 1949-56; past Cons. Adviser for Gynæcology, Ministry of Health; 1st Hon. Sec., Roy. Coll. of Obstetricians and Gynæcologists, 1929-38; Pres. 1938-43; Hon. Fellow: Amer. Gyn. Soc.; Edinburgh Obst. Soc.; Canadian and N.Z. Obst. and Gyn. Socs.; Pres. Manchester Med. Soc., 1937-38 and 1951-52; *b.* 1878; *s.* of David Shaw, Manchester; *m.* 1st, Nora (*d.* 1934), *d.* of David Meredith Jones, Manchester; two *s.* (and one *s.* killed on active service, 1945); 2nd, 1939, Mabel Mary (*d.* 1947), *widow* of Archibald Campbell Stevenson, M.D., D.P.H. *Educ.:* Manchester University. M.B., Ch.B. Vict. 1903; Gold Medal, M.D. Thesis, 1906; Past President Obstetrical and Gynæcological Section, Royal Society of Medicine; late Chairman of Convocation, Manchester University; late President, Students Union, Manchester Univ.; Pres., 6th Congress of British Obstetrics and Gynæcology, 1927; Past Pres. Obst. and Gyn. Sect., B.M.A.; North of England Obst. and Gynæc. Society; Manchester Medical and Pathological Soc.; external examiner in Obstetrics and Gynæcology in the Universities of Liverpool, Leeds. Wales, Edinburgh, and Cambridge. *Publications:* Twenty-Five Years: The Story of the Royal College of Obstetricians and Gynæcologists, 1929-1954; numerous in medical periodicals. *Address:* 102 Rusholme Gardens, Manchester, 14. *T.:* Rusholme 4644. *Clubs:* Union: Union (Manchester). [*Died* 14 *Nov.* 1961.

SHAW, William Thomas; *b.* Finegand, Glenshee, 27 Feb. 1879; *s.* of William Shaw, o Milton and Westerton of Blacklunans, Forfarshire, and Jane, *d.* of James Robertson, Slochnacraig, Glenshee; *m.* 1908, Margaret Cassilis (*d.* 1949), *d.* of Dr. Charles Maclean, of Victoria, B.C.; three *d.* *Educ.:* Slochnacraig School; Dundee High School. Joined the London Stock Exchange, 1901; M.P. (U.). County of Forfar, Dec. 1918-22 and 1931-45: contested Dumbartonshire in the Unionist interest, Dec. 1910; served in the R.A.S.C., 1914-19. *Recreations:* shooting, fishing, golf. *Address:* Killiecrankie Cottage, Killiecrankie, Perthshire. *Club:* Carlton. [*Died* 20 *Oct.* 1965.

SHEA, Gen. Sir John Stuart Mackenzie, G.C.B., *cr.* 1929 (K.C.B., *cr.* 1923; C.B. 1915); K.C.M.G., *cr.* 1919 (C.M.G. 1918); D.S.O. 1901; p.s.c.; *b.* 17 Jan. 1869; *s.* of Col. H. J. F. Shea, R.A. of Avalon; *m.* 1902, Winifred Mary (*d.* 1938), *d.* of late William Congreve of Congreve and Burton; three *d.* (one *d.* decd.) *Educ.:* Sedbergh; Sandhurst. 2nd Lt. The Royal Irish Regt. 1888; Lt. 15th Lancers, 1891; Capt. 1899; Brevet Maj. 1902; Major, 1906; 35th Scinde Horse, 1912; Bt. Lt.-Col. 1912; Maj.-Gen. 1916; Lt.-Gen. 1921; General, 1926; served Chitral Relief Force, 1895 (medal with clasp); South Africa, 1900-02 (Queen's medal 4 clasps, King's medal 2 clasps, despatches, D.S.O., Brevet of Major, qualified for Staff); European War, 1914-18 (despatches, C.B., Bt. Col., Major-General, C.M.G., K.C.M.G.); Commander Legion of Honour; Order of the Nile; Officer of St. John of Jerusalem; G.O.C. Central Provinces District, 1921-23; A.D.C. General to H.M., 1924-28; Adjutant-General in India, 1924-28; G.O.C.-in C., Eastern Command, India 1928-32; retired, 1932; served War of 1939-45. Commissioner of London Scouts, 1936-48; Chief Scout's Commissioner, 1948; Pres. London Scouts, 1949-60; Pres. Roy. Central Asian Society, 1950-54. *Address:* 88 Rivermead Court, Hurlingham, S.W.6. *T.:* Renown 1723 [*Died* 1 *May* 1966.

SHEARER, Sir James Greig, Kt., *cr.* 1955; **President of the Supreme Court, Asmara, Eritrea, 1953-62; *b.* 9 Jan. 1893; *s.* of late James Shearer, merchant, Dundee; *m.* 1939, Helen Adair de la Nougerade, *d.* of B. A. de la Nougerade, engineer Indian Railways. *Educ.:* Dundee High School; Edinburgh University (Vans Dunlop scholar in classics); Christ Church, Oxford. Barrister-at-Law, Middle Temple. Indian Civil Service, 1917-53; Puisne Judge, High Court of Judicature, Patna, India, 1940-53. *Recreations:* shooting, golf. *Address:* Headley Lodge, 92 Surrey Rd., Branksome, Poole, Dorset. *Club:* East India and Sports.** [*Died* 29 *Dec.* 1966.

SHEARER, John Burt, C.M.G. 1952; C.I.E. 1947; O.B.E. 1944; *b.* 28 December 1904; *s.* of late William Ewing Shearer, Greenock; *m.* 1946, Ann Edith, *d.* of late Sir James M. Dunnett, K.C.I.E. *Educ.:* Greenock Academy; Glasgow Univ.; Trinity College, Oxford. Appointed to I.C.S. in 1929 and posted to Punjab; Under-Sec. to Govt. of India, Finance Dept., 1933; Dep. Sec. 1935; Comr. of Income-tax, 1939; Joint Sec., 1945; Member, Central Board of Revenue, Govt. of Pakistan, 1947; acting Finance Sec., 1949. Manager for Greece, Ionian Bank Ltd., 1950-57; Member, Nigerian Minorities Commission, 1957-58. *Recreations:* listening to music, hill walking. *Address:* West Poundgate Manor, Crowborough, Sussex. *Club:* Caledonian. [*Died* 25 *Aug.* 1962.

SHEARER, Lt.-Col. Magnus, O.B.E. 1937; T.D. 1945; J.P.; Chev. (1st Cl.) Roy. Order of Vasa, Sweden, 1946; Hon. Sheriff-Substitute of Caithness, Orkney and Shetland; Chairman: Shetland Cttee. Aberdeen Savings Bank, 1945; Br. Legion (Shetland Branch); Shetland (Lerwick) Local Employment Cttee., Min. of Labour and Nat. Service; Zetland Health Exec. Council, Dept. of Health for Scotland; T.A. Assoc. Co. Zetland; J.P. Zetland, 1949; President Unionist Assoc. (Chm. 1923-53). Member: N.E. Regional Cttee. for Physical Training, 1939; Playing Fields Assoc., Edinburgh; Scottish Tourist Assoc. (an Hon. Vice-Pres.); Vice-Consul for Sweden, at Lerwick; various positions as Trustee; *b.* 12 July 1890; *s.* of late Robert Shearer and Catherine Hughson; *m.* 1922, Flora Macdonald, *d.* of late Major Alex. Stephen, T.D.; one *s.* two *d.* *Educ.:* day school and privately. Served in Gordon Highlanders, T.F., 1912-19; commissioned during European War of 1914-18; served France, Flanders, etc.; again on service Gordon Highlanders, 1939-45. Business Interests: Managing Director of J. & M. Shearer, Ltd.; also Director other concerns; Convener of Zetland, 1929-35. Provost of Lerwick, 1941-46. *Recreations:* fishing, shooting, walking, etc. *Address:* Bayview Hse., King Harald St., Lerwick, Shetland I. *T.:* 139; office 56. *Club:* Zetland (Lerwick). [*Died* 8 *March* 1961.

SHEARMAN, Brig. Charles Edward Gowran, **C.B.E. 1940; D.S.O. 1918; M.C. 1914; *b.* 1889; *s.* of Ernest Charles Shearman, A.R.I.B.A.; *m.* 1924, Evelyn Winifred, *d.* of late Col. F. A. K. White, C.M.G., D.S.O.; one *s.* one *d.* *Educ.:* Westminster Sch. Served European War, 1914-18 (despatches, M.C., D.S.O., Legion of Honour); commanded 1st Bn. Bedfordshire and Hertfordshire Regt., 1933-37; A.Q.M.G. Northern Command,**

1937-39; War of 1939-45 (despatches twice); p.s.c., Camberley, 1926; retired pay, 1945. *Address:* The Old Orchard, Bembridge, I.W. *T.:* 358. [*Died* 10 *July* 1968.

SHEBBEARE, Edward Oswald; *b.* 8 March 1884; 5th *s.* (10th child) of Rev. C. H. Shebbeare, Vicar of Wykeham, Yorkshire; *m.* 1916, A. A. Cameron (*d.* 1962); one *d.* *Educ.:* Charterhouse; Coopers Hill. Indian Forest Service, 1906; Chief Conservator of Forests, United Provinces; Conservator of Forests, Southern Circle, C.P., 1937-38; Senior Conservator of Forests, Bengal, 1938; retired from Indian Forest Service, 1938, and became Chief Game Warden, Malaya; retired from Game Dept., Malaya, Dec. 1947. Prisoner in Singapore, Feb. 1942-Sept. 1945. Everest Expedition, 1924; Empire Forest Conf., Aust., 1929; 2nd in Command, Everest Expedition, 1933; Permanent Hon. Mem. of the Shikar Club, 1936. *Publications:* Soondar Mooni, 1958; a few technical papers on Forestry; (with G. E. Shaw) illustrated paper The Fishes of Northern Bengal, 1938; articles on botany, zoology, travel, etc., in local or club journals. *Recreations:* shooting, fishing, climbing. *Address:* The Sands House, South Newington, Banbury, Oxon. *Clubs:* Alpine, Royal Over-Seas League. [*Died* 11 *Aug.* 1964.

SHEEPSHANKS, Sir Thomas Herbert, K.C.B., *cr.* 1948 (C.B. 1941); K.B.E., *cr.* 1944; *b.* 10 Jan. 1895; *y. s.* of late Right Rev. John Sheepshanks, Bishop of Norwich; *m.* 1921, Elizabeth Creemer, *y. d.* of late James Calvert, J.P.; one *s.* (one *s.* killed in action, 1943; one *d.* decd. 1958). *Educ.:* Winchester College (Scholar); Trinity College, Oxford (Scholar). Joined Norfolk Regt. 1914; served in France attached to Suffolk Regiment; retired as Captain; entered Ministry of Health, 1919; Assistant Secretary, Ministry of Health, 1936; seconded to Home Office (A.R.P. Dept.), 1937; Assistant Under-Secretary of State, Home Office, 1938, and Principal Assistant Secretary, Ministry of Home Security, on establishment of that Ministry; Under-Secretary, 1941; Deputy Secretary, Ministry of Home Security, 1942; seconded to office of Minister of Reconstruction; Deputy Secretary, Ministry of National Insurance, 1944-45; Under-Secretary to the Treasury, 1945-46; Deputy Secretary, Ministry of Town and Country Planning, March-Aug. 1946; Permanent Secretary, 1946-51; Permanent Secretary, Ministry of Housing and Local Government, 1951-55, retired. *Recreation:* golf. *Address:* Broom House, Horsell, Woking. *T.:* Woking 1889. *Club:* Oxford and Cambridge [*Died* 1 *Feb.* 1964.

SHEIL, Charles Leo, Q.C. 1943; a Judge of the High Court of Justice, N. Ireland, since 1949; *b.* 11 April 1897; *yr. s.* of late Peter J. Sheil, J.P., Portadown; *m.* 1936, Elizabeth Josephine, *y. d.* of late James Cassidy, Ballyshannon, County Donegal; three *s.* *Educ.:* Clongowes Wood College; Queen's University, Belfast (Gold Medallist and Law Prizeman, LL.B.); King's Inns, Dublin. Called to Irish Bar, 1921; Crown Counsel, County Antrim, 1926-43; Senator, Queen's Univ., Belfast, 1943; County Court Judge of County Tyrone, 1943, resigned 1945; Senior Crown Counsel, City of Belfast, 1946; Bencher, 1946; Governor, Armagh Observatory. *Recreation:* golf. *Address:* 12 Bristow Park, Belfast 9. *T.:* 666839. [*Died* 5 *Sept.* 1968.

SHELDON, Christine Mary, C.B.E. 1955; First Headmistress, Benenden School, Cranbrook, Kent, September 1923-July 1954; *yr. d.* of John Sheldon. *Educ.:* Francis Holland School, N.W.1; Lady Margaret Hall, Oxford (M.A. Hons. Sch. Mod. Hist.). Asst. Mistress, Edgbaston High School, 1915-19; Assistant Mistress, Head of History Dept., Wycombe Abbey School, 1919-23. Mem. Exec. Cttee., Headmistresses' Assoc., 1946-1952; twice Pres. of Assoc. of Headmistresses of Boarding Schools; Chm. Board of Management, Girls' Common Entrance Examination, 1947-50 and 1953-54. *Address:* 703 Collingwood House, Dolphin Square, S.W.1. *T.:* 01-834 3800. *Club:* Sesame. [*Died* 7 *June* 1970.

SHELLEY, Sir James, K.B.E. *cr.* 1949; M.A. (Cantab.); retired; *b.* Coventry, 3 Sept. 1884; *m.* 1st, 1910, Mabel Winifred Booth; one *s.*; 2nd, 1952, Mary Willmott. *Educ.:* Bablake School, Coventry; Christ's College, Cambridge. Asst. Master, Heanor Secondary School, 1907; Tutor at the Training Coll., Chester, 1908; Lectr. in Education, Manchester Univ., 1910; 2nd Lt. R.F.A. 1917; Major, 1919; Chief Instructor, War Office School of Education, Newmarket; Prof. of Education, University College, Southampton, 1914-20; Professor of Education, Canterbury University College, Christchurch, New Zealand, 1920-36; Professor Emeritus, 1937; Director of the N.Z. Broadcasting Service, 1936-49. *Publications:* Speech, Poetry and Drama; articles on Art and Craft, etc., in Fielden Demonstration School Record, No. 2, and in The Uplands Circular etc. *Recreations:* art and drama—study of, in theory and practice; produced at Manchester Masefield's Pompey the Great, Milton's Comus, and Ibsen's Brand; Founder Christchurch Repertory Theatre. *Address:* 3 Bray's Close, Hyde Heath, Amersham, Bucks. *Club:* Authors'. [*Died* 18 *March* 1961.

SHELLEY, Kew Edwin, Q.C. 1937; Barrister-at-Law; *b.* 10 Nov. 1894; *m.* 1925, Lilian May Shrager; one *s.* one *d.* *Educ.:* Rugby School; New College, Oxford. Commissioned, 1914, 2/6th Bn. Royal Sussex Regt.; transferred R.F.C. 1916; served in India and Egypt with R.F.C. and R.A.F., 1916-19, with rank Flying Officer; called to Bar, 1921; Commissioned A.T.C., 1941. *Publication:* Terrell and Shelley on the Law of Patents. *Recreation:* croquet. *Address:* 11 Silver Street, Deal, Kent. *T.:* 2229. [*Died* 1 *May* 1964.

SHELLEY, Malcolm Bond, C.M.G. 1934; late Malayan Civil Service; *b.* 8 July 1879; *s.* of late Alfred Bond Shelley; *m.* 1913, Margaret Aileen (from whom he obtained a divorce, 1923), *d.* of late Geo. Caulfeild Prideaux Browne; two *d.* *Educ.:* Dulwich College; Christ's College, Cambridge. Held various appointments in the Malayan Civil Service from 1902, including those of Official Assignee and Public Trustee, Controller of Rubber, Treasurer, Straits Settlements, acting Director of Education and Pres. of Raffles College, acting Colonial Secretary, Straits Settlements, British Resident, Perak; Acting Chief Secretary to Goverment Federated Malay States; Captain in the Malay States Volunteer Rifles, 1915; retired, 1935. *Address:* 51D South Terrace, Littlehampton, Sussex. *T.:* Littlehampton 1057. [*Died* 27 *July* 1968.

SHELLEY, Sir Sidney Patrick, 8th Bt., *cr.* 1806; *b.* 18 Jan. 1880; *s.* of Sir Charles Shelley, 5th Bt., and Lady Mary Jane Jemima Stopford, 3rd *d.* of 5th Earl of Courtown; *S.* brother 1953. *Educ.:* Wellington College. Served South African War, 1900-01 (medal with four clasps); European War, 1914-18, Captain Hampshire Yeomanry. *Heir:* *kinsman*, 1st Viscount De L'Isle. *Club:* Sea View (Colombo 3, Ceylon). [*Died* 25 *July* 1965.

SHENTON, Sir William Edward Leonard, *kt.*, *cr.* 1933; J.P.; C.C.; *b.* 19 Mar. 1885; *s.* of William Shenton and Eleanor Johnson; *m.* 1913, Erica Lucy Denison, one *s.* one *d.* *Educ.:* Eastman's Royal Naval Academy, Northwood Park near Winchester; Heidelberg. Unofficial Member of the Executive and Legislative Councils of the Colony of Hong-Kong, 1927-36; Member of the Court of the University of Hong-Kong; Steward of the Hong-Kong Jockey Club; Wing Commodore Hong-Kong Flying Club; Knight of the Venerable Order of St. John of Jerusalem and member of Chapter General; Chairman St. John Planning Committee; Member of Council and Joint Treasurer Imperial Society of Knights Bachelor; Past Master of the Company of Pattenmakers; Governor: Birkbeck Coll., Lond. Univ.; Lond. Sch. of Hygiene and Tropical Medicine; Member Exec. Cttee. Governing Body Girls Public Schools. Chm. London Region Assoc. of Conservative Clubs. Hon. Col. 118th Field Regiment R.A.; Member of Lloyd's; Solicitor and Notary Public. *Recreations:* fishing, shooting. *Address:* The Old Rectory Cottage, Yarmouth, Isle of Wight. *T.:* Yarmouth, 567; 13 The Little Boltons, S.W.10. *T.:* Fremantle 6106. *Club:* Junior Carlton. [*Died* 20 *Nov.* 1967.

SHEPARDSON, Whitney Hart; *b.* Worcester, Mass., U.S.A., 30 October 1890; *s.* of Frank Lucius and Sarah Whidden Shepardson; *m.* 1921, Eleanor Macpherson Cargin; one *s.* *Educ.:* Colgate Univ.; Balliol Coll., Oxford; Harvard Law School (B.A., LL.B.). Attorney U.S. Shipping Board, 1917; Lt., U.S. Field Artillery, 1918; Member U.S. Commn. to Negotiate Peace, 1919; with P. N Gray & Co. N.Y., 1920-23; with Internat. Educn. Board, New York, 1923-27; Pres. Bates Internat. Bag Co., 1928-30; Vice-Pres. Internat. Railways of Central America, 1931-42; Special Asst. to U.S. Ambassador, London, 1942; in Washington, D.C. and overseas, 1943-46; Director British Dominions and Colonies Fund, Carnegie Corporation of N.Y., 1946-53; Pres. Free Europe Cttee., N.Y. City, 1953-56 (Dir., 1953-); Mem. Nat. Selection Cttee. for Fulbright Scholarship Awards; Mem. Mutual Security Agency Advisory Cttee. on Overseas Territories; Trustee: Council on Foreign Relations, New York; Clark Foundation, New York; Vice-Pres. and Trustee American Academy in Rome. Medal for Merit (U.S.), 1946; Chevalier Légion d'Honneur, Croix de Guerre with Palm (France), 1948; Commander Order Orange-Nassau (Netherlands), 1948. *Publications:* Agricultural Education in the United States, 1929; The United States in World Affairs (annually, with William O. Scroggs), 1934-40; The Interests of the United States as a World Power, 1942; Early History of the Council on Foreign Relations, 1960; contributions to Round Table (London), Foreign Affairs (New York). *Recreation:* golf. *Address:* 200 East 66th Street, New York 21, N.Y., U.S.A. *T.:* Templeton 8-7844. *Clubs:* Athenæum; Century (New York); Metropolitan (Washington, D.C.). [*Died* 29 *May* 1966.

SHEPHERD, Ven. Arthur Pearce, D.D., Archdeacon Emeritus of Dudley since 1951; Canon Emeritus of Worcester since 1965; *b.* 31 Dec. 1885; *s.* of Charles Carter and Katherine Gower Shepherd; *m.* 1912, Mary Elizabeth Rees; one *d.* (one *s.* decd.). *Educ.:* Cardiff High School; University of Wales; Jesus College, Oxford. Deacon, 1910, Priest, 1911; Assistant Curate at All Saints, Northampton, 1910-15; Assistant Secretary for Young People's Work at C.M.S. Salisbury Square, 1915-17; Vicar of S. James, Northampton, 1917-24; S. James the Greater Leicester, 1924-32; Vicar of Dudley, 1932-45; Canon Residentiary of Worcester, 1945-65; retired 1965; Archdeacon of Dudley, 1934-51; Proctor in Convocation for Diocese of Leicester, 1932-34, for the Diocese of Worcester, 1951-64. *Publications:* Arthur Neve of Kashmir; Tucker of Uganda Yarns on Brothers of All the World: Heroes of the Lone Trail, etc.; Sin, Suffering and God; The Eternity of Time; A Scientist of the Invisible; Marriage was made for Man. *Recreation:* golf. *Address:* Cottage Farm, Broome, Clent, Worcs. *T.:* Blakedown 584. *Clubs:* Royal Commonwealth Society; Union (Oxford). [*Died* 27 *Feb.* 1968.

SHEPHERD, Sir (Edward Henry) Gerald, K.C.M.G. 1946 (C.M.G. 1939); *b.* Torquay, 1886; *e. s.* of Edward Ernest Shepherd; *m.* 1927, Militza, *o. d.* of J. L. Meyer, formerly of Moscow; one *d.* (one *s.* decd.). *Educ.:* England, France, Germany. British Vice-Consul, New York, 1913-14; Philadelphia, 1915; New York, 1916-18; San Francisco, 1919-20; H.M. Consul-General, Liberia, 1921-23; Chargé d'Affaires there, and H.M. Consul for Fernando Po and Dependencies, 1922-23; Havre, 1924-1925; Riga, Latvia, 1926-28; New York, 1929-1937; Consul-General, Danzig, 1938-39; Amsterdam, 1939-40; Representative in U.S.A. of the Children's Overseas Reception Board, 1940-42. Special Ambassador at inauguration of the Republic of Iceland, June 1944; British Minister to Iceland, 1943-47; retired, 1947. Treatment of Offenders Commissioner, Bermuda, 1951-56; employed in Colonial Secretariat, Bermuda, 1952-60; Treasury, Bermuda, 1961-62; French Consular Agent in Bermuda, 1956-58. Officier, Légion d'Honneur (France), 1961. *Recreation:* philately. *Address:* Richmond Hill, R.R.1, Ontario, Canada; c/o Westminster Bank Ltd., 21 Lombard Street, E.C.3. *Club:* Royal Automobile. [*Died* 11 *Nov.* 1967.

SHEPHERD, Sir Francis Michie, K.B.E., *cr.* 1948 (O.B.E. 1941; M.B.E. 1932); C.M.G. 1946; *b.* 6 Jan. 1893; *s.* of late Francis Shepherd; *m.* 1960, Mrs. Barbara Bayntun Fairbairn-Crawford. *Educ.:* Univ. Coll. School; Grenoble Univ. Served European War, France, Mesopotamia, and India and Afghan Campaign, 1919, in R.F.A.; commissioned in Special Reserve, 1915; resigned, 1920, with rank of Captain; appointed to Consular Service, 1920, and served at San Francisco, Buenos Ayres, Lima, Antwerp and Hamburg; Chargé d'Affaires at Port-au-Prince, Hayti, 1932; in charge of the British Legation at San Salvador, 1934; Minister Resident and Consul to the Republic of Hayti, 1935-37; Acting Consul-General, Barcelona, March-May 1938; Consul at Dresden, 1938-1939; Acting Consul-General at Danzig, July-Aug. 1939; employed in Foreign Office, Oct. 1939-Feb. 1940; Counsellor of Legation and Consul-Gen. at Reykjavik, Iceland, 1940-42; at Leopoldville, Belgian Congo, 1942; British Political Representative in Finland, 1944-47; British Consul-General Netherlands East Indies, 1947-49; British Ambassador to Persia, 1950-52; British Ambassador to Poland, 1952-54, retired 1954. Grand Officer, Order of Hamayoun (Persia), 1951. *Recreations:* golf, fishing. *Address:* Culmer Firs, Wormley, Godalming, Surrey. *Club:* St. James'. [*Died* 15 *May* 1962.

SHEPHERD, Sir Gerald; *see* Shepherd, Sir E. H. G.

SHEPHERD, Brig. Gilbert John Victor, C.B.E. 1944; D.S.O. 1917; retired; late R.E.; *b.* 15 Feb. 1887; *s.* of late Rev. T. C. Shepherd, M.A., Chaplain Indian Government; *m.* 1915, Hermione (*d.* 1966), *d.* of L. G. Wingfield-Stratford; two *s.* one *d.* *Educ.:* Cheltenham College; R.M.A., Woolwich. Staff Coll., 1922-23; retired pay, 1939; recalled 1940; Deputy Director Quartering, W O., 1940-46; retired pay, 1946. Order of Crown of Italy, 1916. *Address:* Cooleen, Alexandra Road, Farnborough, Hants. *T.:* Farnborough 44972. [*Died* 9 *Jan.* 1969.

SHEPPARD, Sir John Tresidder, Kt., *cr.* 1950; M.B.E.; M.A.; Hon. Litt.D. (Universities of Manchester, Melbourne and New

Zealand); Hon. LL.D. (St. Andrews); Knight Commander of the Order of the Redeemer (Greece); Provost, King's College, Cambridge, and Senior Fellow of Eton College, 1933-54; Brereton Reader in Classics, 1931-47; Associate Fellow, Berkeley College, Yale; Hon. Fellow of New College, Oxford, and of Queen Mary College, London; *b.* 1881; *s.* of Alfred Henry Sheppard. *Publications:* Greek Tragedy (Cambridge Manuals); The Œdipus Tyrannus of Sophocles, translated and explained; The Pattern of the Iliad; Aeschylus and Sophocles, their work and influence; Æschylus, the Prophet of Greek Freedom; The Wisdom of Sophocles; Music at Belmont; Verse Translations of several Greek plays. *Address:* King's College, Cambridge. [*Died* 7 *May* 1968.

SHEPPARD, Vivian Lee Osborne, C.B.E. 1927; F.R.I.C.S.; F.R.G.S.; *b.* 9 Jan. 1877; 6th *s.* of late Osborne Sheppard; *m.* 1929, Lilian, *widow* of Lt.-Col. Ashton A. St. Hill, D.S.O., and *o. d.* of late Alfred Blakeney Carr, Sydney. *Educ.:* privately. Articled Dowlais Works (Guest, Keen, Nettlefolds), 1896-1902; Portland Breakwater, 1903; Gold Coast, 1904-5; entered the Egyptian Civil Service, 1902; Director Cadastral Survey, 1917; Surveyor-General of Egypt, 1924; advising the Government of Sarawak on settlement and registration of rights to land, 1932-33, and the Government of Uganda on the same problems, 1937-38; British Representative on and joint rapporteur of the permanent Cadastral Committee of the International Federation of Surveyors, 1934-40; Jt. Curator of Cadastral Survey and Land Records Office, 1931-55. 3rd Class Order of the Nile, 1920, 3rd Class Ismail, 1922. *Publications:* Jt. (with Sir Ernest Dowson) Land Registration; contribs. to the Empire Survey Review. *Address:* Eridge Cottage, Frant, Sussex. *Club:* Royal Societies. [*Died* 4 *Aug.* 1963.

SHEREK, Major Henry; Theatrical Producer; *b.* 23 April 1900; *m.* 1937, Hon. Kathleen Mary Pamela Corona Boscawen, *d.* of 7th Viscount Falmouth. *Educ.:* abroad. Joined the Rifle Brigade, 1915; retired 1919; re-employed 1940; retired 1944, with Hon. rank of Major. Presented or produced over 110 plays in the West End of London, New York and Paris since War of 1939-45. Main successes: Idiot's Delight (London); The First Gentleman (London); Edward, My Son (London and New York); The Cocktail Party (London and New York); Winter Journey (London); Escapade (London and New York); The Confidential Clerk (Edin. Fest., London, New York and Paris); Saint Joan (London); The Queen and the Rebels (London); Under Milk Wood (Edin. Fest., London and New York); Village Wooing and Fanny's First Play (Edinburgh and Berlin Festivals); Not in the Book (London); The Elder Statesman (Edin. Fest. and London); The Playboy of the Western World (London); The Affair (London and New York); Out of Bounds (London). *Publication:* Not in Front of the Children. *Address:* 82 Route de Florissant, Geneva. [*Died* 23 *Sept.* 1967.

SHERIDAN, Clare Consuelo; sculptor, painter, writer, traveller; *o. d.* of late Moreton Frewen and Clara (*d.* of Leonard Jerome, U.S.A.); *m.* (husband killed in France, Sept. 1915); one *d.* (one *s.* decd.). *Educ.:* Convent of the Assumption, Paris; Darmstadt, Germany. Portrait busts include; Senator Marconi, Lord Oxford and Asquith for the Oxford Union; Lord Birkenhead; Winston S. Churchill; Lenin, Trotzki, Kamenefe, Dsirjinski, etc., for the Soviet Govt.; The Archbishop of Galilee; The Mahatma Ghandi, Count Keyserling, etc.; European correspondent, New York World, 1922; interviewed Mustapha Kemal, Mussolini, Stamboulisky, Primo de Rivera etc. *Publications:* Russian Portraits, 1921; My American Diary, 1922; In Many Places, 1923; Across Europe with Satanella; The Thirteenth, 1925; A Turkish Kaleidoscope, 1926; Nuda Veritas, 1927; Arab Interlude, 1936; Redskin Interlude, 1938; My Crowded Sanctuary, 1943; To The Four Winds, 1954. *Recreation:* gardening. *Address:* M'cid, Biskra, Algeria, N. Africa. [*Died* 31 *May* 1970.

SHERIDAN, Sir Joseph, Kt., *cr.* 1932; *b.* 12 Nov. 1882; *s.* of late Joseph Sheridan, Spencer Park, Castlebar, Co. Mayo; *m.* 1913; Muriel, 4th *d.* of late Roger Macaulay, M.D., Ballina, Co. Mayo; two *s.* three *d.* *Educ.:* Christian Brothers, Castlebar; Castleknock College; Trinity Coll. Dublin. Called to Irish Bar, 1907; went Connaught Circuit; entered Colonial Service (Nyasaland), 1908; acted Attorney-General, Nyasaland, on many occasions, 1909-13; acted Judge of the High Court, Nyasaland, 1909-10; Asst. to Attorney-General, Nyasaland, 1912; Resident Magistrate, East Africa (now Kenya), 1913-20; acted Judge of the High Court, Kenya, and Judge of the Court of Appeal for Eastern Africa, 1919-20; Judge of the Supreme Court, Kenya, 1920-29; acted Chief Justice, Kenya, 1928-29; also acted Pres. Court of Appeal for Eastern Africa, 1928-29; Chief Justice Tanganyika Territory, 1929-34; Chief Justice of H.M.'s Supreme Court of Kenya, 1934-46; also Judge of the Court of Appeal for Eastern Africa, 1920-34, Pres. 1934-1946; Chairman Masai Riots Claims Commission, 1918-19. *Recreations:* tennis, squash racquets, billiards. *Address:* 11 Eaton Court, Eaton Gardens, Hove, Sussex. *Club:* East India and Sports. [*Died* 26 *Dec.* 1964.

SHERLOCK, David Thomas Joseph, M.B.E., 1919; Justice of Appeal until 1943; *b.* Dublin, 6 Sept. 1881; *s.* of Thomas Sherlock, Stillorgan Castle, Dublin, and Letitia Mary, *d.* of Sir John Nugent, Bt., Ballinlough Castle, Clonmellon; *m.* 1905, Augusta, *d.* of Sir F. R. Cruise, D.L.; four *d.* *Educ.:* Downside College; Trinity College, Dublin. Graduated Trinity College, Dublin, and called to Irish Bar, 1904; served European War, 1914-19, in Royal Irish Regiment (despatches, M.B.E.); called to the Inner Bar, Northern Ireland; Judicial Commissioner, British North Borneo, 1920; K.C. (N. Ire.) 1922; Chief Justice, British North Borneo, 1926-35; Justice of Appeal, Jamaica, 1935-43. Legal Adviser Brit. Mil. Admin., Cyrenaica, 1946-47. *Recreations:* racing and golf. *Address:* Balreask, Kells, Co. Meath. *Clubs:* Naval and Military; Kildare Street (Dublin). [*Died* 12 *Oct.* 1964.

SHERWILL, Sir Ambrose (James), K.B.E. 1960 (C.B.E. 1945); Kt. 1949; M.C.; *b.* 12 Feb. 1890; *s.* of James Edgar Sherwill, Les Landes, Castel, Guernsey; *m.* 1920, May de Beauvoir Clabburn; four *s.* one *d.* *Educ.:* Elizabeth College, Guernsey; Université de Caen, France (L. en D. 1914). Served with R.N.A.S. 1914-16, East Kent Regt. (The Buffs), 1916-18, Lieut. (wounded thrice); Royal Guernsey Militia, 1921-26, Major. Barrister-at-Law (Middle Temple), 1920; Advocate of the Royal Court, Guernsey, 1920; H.M. Comptroller (Solicitor-General), Guernsey, 1929; H.M. Procureur (Attorney-General), Guernsey, 1935; Bailiff of Guernsey, 1946-60. K.St.J. *Address:* Essex Castle, Alderney, C.I. *T.:* Alderney 31. [*Died* 25 *Sept.* 1968.

SHERWOOD, 1st Baron, *cr.* 1941, of Calverton; **Hugh Michael Seely;** 3rd Bt., *cr.* 1896; *b.* 2 Oct. 1898; *e. surv. s.* of Colonel Sir Charles Seely, 2nd Bt., and Hilda (*d.* 1939), *d.* of R. T. A. Grant; *S.* to father's baronetcy, 1926; *m.* 1st, 1942, Hon. Patricia Chetwode (marriage dissolved, 1948), *d.* of 1st Viscount Camrose, and *widow* of Roger Chetwode (she *m.* 3rd, 1958, Sir Richard Cotterell, 5th Bt.); 2nd, 1970, Mrs. Catherine Thornton Ranger. *Educ.:* Cheam; Eton. Lt. Grenadier Guards, 1917-19; South

Notts Hussars, 1920-23, contested East Norfolk, Nov. 1922; South Kensington, 1929; M.P. (L.) East Norfolk, Dec. 1923-Oct. 1924; Berwick-on-Tweed division of Northumberland, 1935-41; High Sheriff of Nottinghamshire, 1925; Squadron Leader commanding No. 504 (County of Nottingham) (Fighter) Squadron Auxiliary Air Force, 1937-40; Parl. Private Secretary to Secretary of State for Air, 1940-41; additional Parliamentary Under-Secretary of State, Air Ministry, 1941-45; J.P. Notts. *Heir:* (to Baronetcy only) *b.* Major Victor Basil John Seely. *Address:* 10 Berkeley Street, W.1. *T.:* 01-629 2541; Flat 1, Chichester House, Chichester Terrace, Brighton. *T.:* Brighton 21753. *Clubs:* White's, Beefsteak, Buck's. [*Died* 1 *April* 1970 (*ext.*).

SHEWELL, Brigadier Eden Francis, C.M.G. 1918; D.S.O. 1917; M.B.E. 1946, late Civil Defence Sub-Controller South Bucks Area; *b.* 1877; 2nd *s.* of late Rev. Frank Shewell of Loddiswell, S. Devon; *m.* 1st, 1903, Frances, *d.* of late John Greene, Newcastle on Tyne; one *s.*; 2nd, 1918, Dorothy, *twin-d.* of late Mrs. A. W. F. Baird; one *s.* *Educ.:* High Sch., Newcastle under Lyme; R.M.A. Woolwich. S. Af. War, 1899-1902 (Queen's medal and 3 clasps, King's medal and 2 clasps); European War (Mesopotamia), 1915-18 (despatches, C.M.G. D.S.O.); commanded Royal Artillery, 51st (Highland) Division, T.A., 1924-27; Royal Artillery Shanghai Defence Force, 1927; 1st Air Defence Brigade, 1928-31; Brigadier Commanding the Troops, Ceylon, 1931-34; retired pay, 1934. *Address:* 3 The Mount, Ifield, Crawley, Sussex. *T.:* Rusper 333. [*Died* 19 *June* 1964.

SHIELDS, John Veysie Montgomery, C.B.E. 1957 (O.B.E. 1946); Q.C. (Scot.) 1962; Sheriff Substitute of Lanarkshire, at Hamilton, since Oct. 1964; Senior Lecturer in Criminal Law and Criminology, University of Edinburgh, 1959-64; *b.* 27 Oct. 1914; *s.* of John Conynghame Shields; *m.* 1946, Grace Dalgety, *d.* of late George and Grace Wall Kerr, Virginia, U.S.A.; no *c.* *Educ.:* Dardenne Sch.; Univ. of Glasgow. M.A., LL.B. (with dist.), Glasgow, Faulds Fellow in Law. Admitted to the Faculty of Advocates, Scotland, 1938; Q.C. Aden, 1954. Military Service, 1939; gazetted Argyll and Sutherland Highlanders, 1940; regimental duty, 1940-41; thereafter Staff; Lieut. 1941; Capt. 1941; Major 1942; Lt.-Col. 1944; Col. 1945. Served in Middle East, E. Africa, Sicily, Italy, Malaya and attached British Mil. Mission, U.S.A., 1944 (despatches); Executive Sec., Brit. Section Caribbean Commission, 1946; Federal Counsel, Malaya, 1947; Attorney General, Aden, 1952-59. Chm. Commission of Inquiry into Labour Disputes, Aden, 1956; retired from Colonial Service, 1959. Member U.K. delegation, U.N. seminar on protection of human rights in criminal procedure, Vienna, 1960. Hon. Sheriff Substitute of the Lothians and Peebles, 1960 and of Selkirk, 1962; Mem. Scottish Probation Advisory and Training Council. *Publications:* Laws of Aden (Jt. revision Comr.), 1955; State of Crime in Scotland (with Judith A. Duncan), 1964; articles and reviews. *Address:* Grahne, 10 Holmwood Avenue, Uddingston, by Glasgow. *Clubs:* Royal Automobile; Honourable Company of Edinburgh Golfers; Western (Glasgow). [*Died* 16 *March* 1966.

SHILLIDY, George Alexander, C.I.E. 1931; *b.* 7 March 1886; *s.* of late Rev. John Shillidy, M.A., D.D., Surat, India; *m.* Mabel Catherine, *d.* of late Robert Steven J.P., Barnhill, Dundee; (one *s.* killed in action 1944) one *d.* *Educ.:* Campbell College, Belfast. Joined Indian Police, 1906; Assistant Inspector-General of Police, 1926; Deputy Inspector-General, 1929; Inspector-General of Police, Prov. Bombay, 1935-40; King's Police Medal, 1922. [*Died* 27 *June* 1968.

SHINER, Lieut.-Col. Sir Herbert, Kt., *cr.* 1950; D.S.O. 1918; M.C. 1918; D.L. 1949; *b.* 5 July 1890; *s.* of John Shiner, Somerset; *m.* 1921, Elizabeth (*d.* 1935). *Educ.:* privately. Served European War, 1914-19, with R.A.; 2nd Lt., 1915; Lieutenant-Colonel, 1942. C.C. 1928, C.A. 1934, West Sussex (Chairman, 1946-62). *Address:* Coldharbour, Sutton, Pulborough, Sussex. *T.:* Sutton, Sussex, 205. *Club:* Royal Automobile. [*Died* 1 *Aug.* 1962.

SHINER, Ronald Alfred; Actor Producer since 1928; *b.* 8 June 1903; *s.* of Alfred M. Shiner and Kathleen Way; *m.* 1932, Gladys Winifred Jones; one *s.* *Educ.:* Cathcart College, Tufnell Park; St. Aloysius, Highgate. N.W. Mounted Police, 1920-22; Roy. Corps of Signals, 1924-27. First appeared on stage, Hippodrome Theatre, Margate, 1928, in Dr. Syn. First appeared London, Q Theatre, 1929; Stage Director for Stage Soc., 1929-31; Down Our Street, Vaudeville, 1930; The Way to Treat a Woman, Duke of York's, 1930; Whitehall Theatre, 1931-34; Man and Superman, Cambridge Theatre, 1935; Hell for Leather, Phoenix, 1936; Amazing Dr. Clitterhouse, Haymarket, 1937; Third Party Risk, St. Martin's, 1939; served War of 1939-45, as full-time Special Constable 'A' Div., 1940-43; broadcasting to British Forces in Malta and films. Something in the Air, Palace, 1943; Worm's Eye View, Whitehall, 1945-50; Seagulls over Sorrento, Apollo, 1950-53; My Three Angels; The Lovebirds, Adelphi, 1957; Aladdin (Pantomime), Coliseum, 1959; You Prove It, St. Martin's Theatre, 1961. *Films:* Worm's Eye View; Reluctant Heroes; Top of the Form; Laughing Anne; Up to his Neck; Innocents in Paris; Aunt Clara; My Wife's Family; Dry Rot; Wanted on Voyage; Girls at Sea; Operation Bullshine; The Navy Lark; The Night We Got The Bird. Appears on Television. *Recreations:* riding, swimming, tennis. *Address:* Elmbrae Court, Denton Road, Meads, Eastbourne, Sussex. *T.:* 3215. *Clubs:* Savage, Green Room, Royal Automobile. [*Died* 29 *June* 1966.

SHINKWIN, Colonel Ion Richard Staveley, C.M.G. 1918, D.S.O. 1917; late R.A.S.C.; *b.* Agra, 29 Sept. 1875; *s.* of late Colonel R. Staveley Shinkwin, 59th Regiment, of Foot, of Limerick, Ireland, and *e. d.* of Rev. F. Wall, D.D., Heath House, Queen's County; *m.* Susan Digby (*d.* 1918), *y. d.* of late E. D. Berkeley, I.S.O.; one *s.* *Educ.:* Cheltenham College. Royal Sussex Regt.; Assistant Director of Supplies, War Office, 1925-29; retired pay, 1929. *Address:* Longley House, Rochester. *T.:* Chatham 42630. *Clubs:* United Service; Castle (Rochester). [*Died* 6 *Dec.* 1961.

SHINNIE, Andrew James, O.B.E. 1951; M.B., Ch.B., M.D., D.P.H.; Medical Officer of Health, City of Westminster, 1924-53, retd.; *b.* Aberdeen, 16 Feb. 1886; 2nd *s.* of James Foote Shinnie, manufacturer and Margaret Robb; *m.* 1914, Olive V. (*d.* 1921), *d.* of Arthur Lewis, Liverpool; one *s.* one *d.* *Educ.:* Aberdeen Grammar School; Aberdeen University; University College, London. Various hospital appointments attached to medical schools of Aberdeen, Glasgow and London Universities, 1908-13; M.B. (Aberd. Univ. 1908), M.D. with Commendation 1912; D.P.H. (London 1914); Entered Public Health Service, 1913; under Surrey County Council as Asst. Medical Officer and later under Westminster City Council. Late Lecturer in Public Health to Westminster Medical School (Univ. of London). Mem. of: Council Westminster Medical School; late Mem. Bd. of Governors and House Cttee. St. Peter's St. Paul's and St. Philip's Hosp.; Establishment Committee, Westminster Hospital; House Committee Westminster Children's Hospital; House Committee, Charing

Cross Hospital; Home Office Committee on Shop Hours Acts and Health and Welfare of Employees; Catering Trade Working Party, etc.; Fellow of Royal Inst. of Public Health and Hygiene and Mem. of Exec Council (Smith Award, 1952); Fellow, Soc. of Medical Officers of Health and Past President of Metropolitan Branch; late Fellow Royal Sanitary Institute and Mem. of Examining Board. *Publications:* Papers and Articles on Public Health subjects in technical and medical journals; Contributing Author to Principles and Practice of Public Health and Hygiene edited by Hutt and Thomson. *Address:* 34 Orleans Road, Twickenham, Middlesex. *Club:* Athenæum.
[*Died* 10 *May* 1963.

SHIPWAY, Sir Francis Edward, K.C.V.O., *cr.* 1929; M.A., M.D., B.Ch. (Cantab.); F.F.A.R.C.S.; Consulting Anæsthetist and late Lecturer on Anæsthetics to Medical School, late Lecturer on Anæsthetics to Dental School, Guy's Hospital; Consulting Anæsthetist St. Peter's Hospital for Stone; Hon. Member Assoc. Anæsthetists of Great Britain and Ireland; Fellow of Internat. Coll. of Anæsthesia; *b.* 6 Dec. 1875; *s.* of late Lt.-Col. R. W. Shipway, V.D., J.P.; *m.* 1912, Winifred Adine (*d.* 1955), *d.* of William Robert Biddell; two *d.* *Educ.:* Ipswich; Christ's College, Cambridge; St. Thomas's Hospital, Vienna. Held resident posts at St. Thomas's Hosp. and Hospital for Consumption, Brompton; late Fellow of Royal Society of Medicine; Vice-President, late President, Section of Anæsthetics, Royal Society of Medicine; President, Section of Anæsthetics. British Medical Association Centenary Meeting, 1932; Member of Anæsthetics Committee Medical Research Council and Royal Society of Medicine. Hon. Mem. Section of Anæsthetics, R.S.M.; Grand Officer of Order of King George I. of Greece. *Publications:* An Apparatus for the Administration of Warm Anæsthetic Vapours; An Apparatus for the Intratracheal Insufflation of Ether; Acetylene, Ethylene, Propylene; The Use of Avertin for Anæsthesia; various papers on anæsthetics in the medical journals. *Recreation:* photography. *Address:* 6 Wharfe Lane, Henley-on-Thames *T.:* 219
[*Died* 30 *Nov.* 1968.

SHIPWRIGHT, L. A. de L.; *see* de Lara, Adelina.

SHIRLAW, Matthew, D.Mus. (Edin.), F.R.C.O.; *b.* Ayrshire, 1873; *m.* 1894, Jessie Fenton, *y. d.* of late James Clark, Laird of Inverharity, Glenisla, Forfarshire; two *s.* one *d.* *Educ.:* Edinburgh University; privately. Assistant in Music, Edinburgh University, 1902; Lecturer Faculty of Music, Edinburgh University, 1914 (Senior Lecturer in Music, until 1939), also Lecturer in Theory of Music, Heriot Watt College, Edinburgh. Formerly took frequent part in Historical Concerts there under Professor Niecks; Examiner in Music, in schools, for Scottish Education Department. *Publications:* Theory of Harmony: An Enquiry into its Natural Principles, 1917; some vocal music; various articles dealing with musical and æsthetical subjects. *Recreation:* golf. *Address:* 94 Montpelier Park, Edinburgh. *T.:* Fountainbridge 5710. [*Died* 6 *June* 1961.

SHIRLEY, Rev. (Frederick) John, M.A. Oxon; D.D. Oxon; Ph.D. Lond.; F.S.A.; F.R.Hist.Soc. (formerly of the Hon. Society of Lincoln's Inn, Barrister-at-law); Headmaster, King's Sch., Canterbury, 1935-62, Sen. Canon Residentiary of Canterbury since 1935; *b.* 24 Feb. 1890; *y. s.* of William Shirley, Oxford; *m.* 1926, Dorothy, *d.* of late John Howard, Cruachan, Aberfeldy, Perthshire, and *niece* of 1st Baron Brocket; two *s.* one *d.* *Educ.:* City of Oxford School; S. Edmund Hall, Oxford; London University and Hon. Society of Lincoln's Inn. 2nd Class Honours in Modern History, Oxford; Preparatory Schoolmaster, and at Elstow School, Bedford, 1912-15; 2nd Lieut. R.M.L.I. and Sub.-Lieut. R.N.V.R., 1915-Jan. 1919; called to the Bar (Lincoln's Inn), 1919; LL.B. Lond. (2nd Class Honours), 1920; VI. Form and Housemaster at Framlingham College, Suffolk, 1919-25; Ordained, 1920; Curate of Framlingham with Saxtead, 1920-1923; Rector of Sternfield, 1923-25; Headmaster, Worksop College, 1925-35; Member H.M.C., I.A.H.M.; Liveryman, and Hon. Chaplain to Worshipful Company of Glaziers, 1939, Freeman of the City of London, 1939; Select Preacher: Cambridge, 1950; Oxford, 1950, 1951; Treasurer of Canterbury Cathedral. Hon. Fellow, St. Edmund Hall, Oxford, 1963. *Publications:* God my Father, 1936; edited A Public School Psalter 1929, also Macbeth, 1926, Hamlet, 1932, Memorabilia Latina, 1933, ed. Acting Edition of Sir Thomas More, 16th c. anonymous play, partly attributed to Shakespeare, 1939; Reminiscences of George Gilbert, 1939; Canterbury Prayer Book, 1940; Canterbury Hymn Book, 1960; Elizabeth's First Archbishop, 1948; Richard Hooker and Contemporary Political Ideas, 1949. Contrib. Enc. Brit. *Recreation:* walking. *Address:* 15 The Precincts, Canterbury. *Clubs:* Oxford and Cambridge, Public Schools, Brooks's. [*Died* 19 *July* 1967.

SHOENBERG, Sir Isaac, Kt. 1962; M.I.E.E.; Director of Electric & Musical Industries Ltd. (E.M.I.), 1955; Adviser to Board of E.M.I. since 1952; *b.* 1 March 1880; *m.* 1903; three *s.* two *d.* *Educ.:* Polytechnical Institute, Kiev; Royal College of Science, London. Between 1905 and 1931 was for various periods Chief Engineer, Russian Wireless Telegraph and Telephone Co.; Consultant, in charge of Patent Dept., and Jt. General Manager, Marconi's Wireless Telegraph Co. Ltd., and Jt. Gen. Man., Columbia Graphophone Co. Ltd. Appointed Director of Research of Electric & Musical Industries Ltd., 1931. Faraday Medal, 1954. *Address:* 203 Willesden Lane, N.W.6.
[*Died* 25 *Jan.* 1963.

SHONE, Sir Terence Allen, K.C.M.G., *cr.* 1947 (C.M.G. 1943); *b.* 4 Sept. 1894; *s.* of late Lieut.-Gen. Sir William Terence Shone, K.C.B., D.S.O., and Janet, *d.* of late Rt. Hon. Gerald Fitzgibbon, Lord Justice of Appeal in Ireland; *m.* 1927, Sophie Marie, 2nd *d.* of Herman Andreae, Moundsmere Manor, Basingstoke, Hants.; one *s.* *Educ.:* Winchester; University College, Oxford. Served European War, 1914-18 (despatches), Capt. 10th Bn. Hampshire Regt. and Intelligence Corps; 3rd Secretary Diplomatic Service, 1919; 2nd Secretary, 1920; 1st Secretary, 1927; Counsellor of Embassy, 1940; British Minister, Cairo, 1940; Minister to Republics of Syria and Lebanon, 1944-46; High Commissioner for the U.K. in India, 1946; Deputy to the Permanent Representative of the U.K. and the U.N., 1948. In addition to Foreign Office has served at Lisbon, Oslo, Washington, Berne, and Belgrade; retired 1952. *Address:* 38 Cadogan Place, S.W.1. *Clubs:* St. James', Brooks's.
[*Died* 29 *Oct.* 1965.

SHOOBERT, Sir (Wilfred) Harold, Kt. 1946; C.I.E. 1943; E.D. 1939; S. Pk. (Sitara-i-Pakistan) 1960; late I.C.S.; Hon. ecretary, The Pakistan Society, since 952; *b.* 7 June 1896, *s.* of Joseph Cornelius Shoobert, Twickenham, and Sarah Elizabeth White; *m.* 1920, Suzanne Mary Marshal Ellis; no *c.* *Educ.:* St. Paul's School, London; Christ Church, Oxford. Inns of Court Rifles (T.F.), 1915; Rifle Brigade, 1915-19 (twice wounded); Capt. A.I.R.O. 1927: Major A.I.R.O. 1929; commanded Nagpur Rifles A.F.(I.), 1938-38; Hon. A.D.C. to Viceroy, 1933-39, Hon. Lt.-Col. Indian Civil Service, 1919; Asst. Commissioner, Central Provinces, 1920-23; Supervisor Assam Labour Board, 1923-25, officiat-

ing Chairman 1924; Deputy Commissioner in C.P. 1925-30; Provincial Supt. of Census Operations, C.P. and Berar, 1930-33; Deputy Commissioner, Nagpur, Settlement commr., Excise commr. etc., 1934-37; Posts and Telegraphs Dept. 1937; Postmaster-General U.P. Circle, 1938-40; Senior Deputy Director-General, 1940-41; Director-General, Indian Posts and Telegraphs, 1941-46. Visited Persia and Iraq Forces and Middle East Forces, 1941; Burma front, 1943; C.M.F., M.E.F., and Paiforce, 1945; Offg. Sec. to Govt. of India, Posts and Air Dept., 1945; Sec. Govt. of India, Dept. of Communications, 1946; Member Central Legislative Assembly; Leader Indian Deleg. to Postal Experts Conf., Lake Success, 1946; Chm. Indian Deleg. to Internat. Telecommunications Conf., Atlantic City, 1947; Chm. of Cttee. of Internat. Telecommunications Union, which negotiated relationship agreement with U.N.; Sec. to Govt. of Pakistan, Min. of Food, Agric. and Health, 1948, Sec., Min. of Communications, 1950-51. F.R.S.A. *Recreation:* horticulture (Vice-Pres. Hort. Assoc. of Pakistan). *Address:* Sunnybrook, Holmbury St. Mary, Dorking, Surrey. *T.:* Forest Green 353; The Pakistan Society, 17 Lowndes St., S.W.1. *Clubs:* East India and Sports, Royal Commonwealth Society.
[*Died* 6 *Nov.* 1969.

SHOOBRIDGE, Hon. Sir Rupert Oakley, Kt., *cr.* 1947; President Legislative Council, Tasmania, 1946-55, retd.; M.L.C. for Derwent since 1937; *b.* Hobart, 25 Jan. 1883; *s.* of Hon. L. M. Shoobridge, Hobart; *m.* 1st, 1906, Muriel, *d.* of late C. E. Walch; three *s.* two *d.*; 2nd, 1930, Sara, *d.* of late A. E. Walkeden, Melbourne. *Address:* Glenora, Tasmania. *Clubs:* Royal Over-Seas League; Tasmanian (Hobart).
[*Died* 6 *Nov.* 1962.

SHORT, Herbert Arthur, C.B.E. 1946; M.C.; E.R.D.; M.Inst.T.; former General Manager, North Eastern Region, British Railways; Colonel, R.E. (T.A.); *b.* 22 March 1895; *s.* of late George Short, Bournemouth; *m.* 1921, Gladys May, *d.* of late Horace John Paul, Waterson, nr. Dorchester; one *s.* *Educ.:* Bournemouth School. Joined former London & South Western Railway, 1913. Served Suffolk Regt., European War, 1914-18 (despatches, M.C.). Various appointments with Southern Railway Co., including Docks & Marine Manager; former Chm. Southampton Harbour Bd., Docks Cttee. of Railway Executive, Southampton Port Emergency Cttee., and Southampton Dock Labour Bd., etc., during period of despatch of troops and equipment from Southampton for D-Day operations. Commanded Southern Railway Gp., R.E. (Supp. Res.), 1925-37. Dep. Traffic Manager Southern Railway, 1945; Chief Officer, Railway Exec., 1948; Chief Regional Officer, N.E. Region, British Railways, 1950. Loaned by Southern Railway Co. to Colonial Office and Argentine Govt. to advise on transport problems in Malaya, 1946, and in Argentine, 1947 and 1948. Mem. of Brit. Transport Commn. team to U.S.A., 1957, to study U.S. railroads. Former Chm.: Associated Humber Lines, Ltd. (now Dir.); Wilsons & N.E. Shipping Company Ltd.; Director: E. Yorks. Motor Services, Ltd.; Atlantic Steam Navigation Co. Ltd.; Frank Bustard & Sons, Ltd.; Ravenshall (Bournemouth) Maintenance Co. Ltd.; Ravenshall (Bournemouth) Freehold Co. Ltd.; Past Vice-Pres. Inst. of Transport; former Mem. Council of Chamber of Shipping. Medal of Freedom, Silver Palm (U.S.). C.St.J. *Recreations:* interested in all sports, especially Association football. *Address:* 1 Ravenshall, West Cliff Road, Bournemouth. *T.:* Westbourne 63192. [*Died* 15 *Nov.* 1967.

SHORT, Professor John; Professor Emeritus; Professor and Director Dept. of Anatomy, Durham Univ., 1947-60; *b.* 10 Dec. 1894; *o. s.* of S. A. Short and Isabella Amelia Short (*née* Forster), Newcastle upon Tyne; unmarried. *Educ.:* privately; Christ Church, Oxford; Medical School, Durham University. B.A. Oxon 1924, M.A. 1929; M.B., B.S., Dunelm., 1932. Partner in S. A. Short & Son, Iron Merchants, Newcastle upon Tyne, 1924-29; Demonstrator and lecturer on Anatomy, Medical School, King's Coll., Newcastle, 1932-42; Deputy-Director of Anatomy, 1943. Captain R.A.M.C. (T.A.); seconded to Durham University Senior Training Corps, 1942-45. J.P. City and Co. of Newcastle upon Tyne, 1947; Chairman, Juvenile Court, 1957-59; Chairman of Magistrates, 1961-64. *Recreation:* fishing. *Address:* 14 Southwood Gdns., Kenton, Newcastle upon Tyne 3. *T.:* Newcastle 57761.
[*Died* 30 *April* 1967.

SHOTWELL, James Thomson, B.A., Ph.D., LL.D.; President, Carnegie Endowment for Internat. Peace, 1948-50; Pres. Emeritus, 1950-; Chm. Nat. Cttee. of the U.S.A. on Internat. Intellectual Co-operation of League of Nations, 1932-43; Pres. League of Nations Assoc., 1935-39; Chairman, Commission to Study the Organization of Peace, 1939-; State Dept. Consultant: on Post-War Planning, State Department, 1942-44; to Office of War Information, 1945; Chairman Consultants at San Francisco Conf., 1945; Chm. Carnegie Endowment Cttee. on Atomic Energy, 1946; Prof. of History, Columbia Univ., New York, 1908-42; Prof. Emeritus since 1942; *b.* 6 Aug. 1874; *s.* of John B. Shotwell of Strathroy, Ontario, Canada, and Anne Thomson; *m.* 1901, Margaret, *d.* of Albert Harvey, M.D., of Wyoming, Ontario, Canada; two *d.* *Educ.:* Strathroy Collegiate Institute; Toronto Univ. (B.A.1898); Columbia Univ. (Ph.D. 1903); LL.D. Univ. of Western Ontario, 1922; Toronto, 1926; Dartmouth, 1926; McGill, 1927; Columbia, 1929; Budapest, 1935; Queen's Univ. (Ontario), 1937; Johns Hopkins Univ., 1939; St. Lawrence Univ., 1940; Univ. of Maine, 1945; D.Sc. S. et P., Montreal, 1941; Asst. General Editor Encyclopædia Britannica, in London, 1904-05; Chm. Nat. Bd. for Historical Service, Washington, 1917; Chief of History Div., Amer. Commn. to negotiate Peace, Paris, 1918-19; Member Internat. Labor Legislation Commission at Peace Conf., 1918-19; American rep. Organising Cttee. Internat. Labour Conf., London, 1919; Director div. of Internat. Relations of Social Science Research Council, 1931-33; American rep. Union Académique Internationale, 1919-23; (American) Pres. Fifth Internat. Congress of Historical Sciences, Brussels, 1923; Lecturer to the Nobel Institute, Christiania, 1923; Marfleet Lectures, Univ. of Toronto, 1934; Meier Katz Memorial Lectures, Johns Hopkins, 1939; James Gould Cutler Lecturer, College of William and Mary, 1942; Research Director, Institute of Pacific Relations, 1927-30; Associate Member, Belgian Academy of Science, Letters and Fine Arts, 1929. Comdr., Legion of Honour, France; Comdr., Order of the Crown, Belgium; Comdr., Order of the Saviour, Greece; Comdr., Order of St. Sava, Yugoslavia. *Publications:* The Religious Revolution of To-day, 1913; Labor Provisions in the Peace Treaty, 1919; History of the Peace Conference of Paris (joint), 1920; The History of History, 1921 and 1939 (Chinese ed. 1929; Spanish ed. 1940); The See of Peter (joint), 1927; War as an Instrument of National Policy, 1929 (French and German translations); The Heritage of Freedom, 1934; On the Rim of the Abyss, 1936; At the Paris Peace Conference, 1937; What Germany Forgot, 1944; Turkey at the Straits (joint), 1940; The Great Decision, 1944 (French trans.); Poland and Russia (joint), 1945; Robinson's History of Western Europe, rev. and enlarged, 1946; (joint)

Lessons on Security and Disarmament from the League of Nations, 1949; A Balkan Mission, 1949; Editor, Records of Civilization, Sources and Studies (5 vols.), 1915-21; European History Series College Textbooks (10 vols.); Economic and Social History of the World War (150 vols.), 1919-29; The Paris Peace Conference, History and Documents, 7 vols., 1934-41; Canadian-American Relations (25 vols.), 1936-45; Governments of Continental Europe, 1940 (revised edn., 1952); Poems, 1954; The United States in History, 1956; The Long Way to Freedom, 1959; Autobiography, 1961. *Address:* U.N. Plaza, 345 East 46th St., New York 17.

[*Died* 16 *July* 1965.

SHOVE, His Honour Ralph Samuel, J.P.; County Court Judge, Circuit 17 (Lincolnshire), 1945-60, retd.; Chairman Quarter Sessions, Parts of Kesteven, from 1946, and Chairman Parts of Holland from 1946; Vice-Chairman Quarter Sessions, Parts of Lindsey, from 1945; *b.* 31 May 1889; 3rd and *y. s.* of Herbert Samuel Shove and Bertha Millen, Ospringe, Faversham, Kent; *m.* 1928, Evelyn (*d.* 1963) (*widow* of Henry Sneyd, Ashcombe, Staffs) *d.* of Rev. Charles Forster, Holne Chase, Ashburton, Devon; no *c.* *Educ.:* Uppingham; Trinity College, Cambridge. Class II Classical Tripos, 1911; served in R.F.A. in European War, 1914-18, retired 1919 with rank of Major. Called to Bar, 1918. *Recreations:* none in particular; rowed in University VIII, 1912 and 1913. *Address:* The Old Hall, Washingborough, Lincoln. *Clubs:* United Service, Leander; Pitt, Hawks (Cambridge).

[*Died* 2 *Feb.* 1966.

SHOVELTON, Sydney Taverner, C.B.E. 1948; *b.* 17 Nov. 1881; *e. s.* of J. W. Shovelton, Eccles; *m.* 1907, Mary Catherine Kelly (*d.* 1958); one *s.* two *d.* *Educ.:* Manchester Gram. Sch.; Corpus Christi Coll., Oxford (Math. Schol. and Univ's. Jun. and Sen. Math. Schols.). Fellow, Merton Coll., Oxford, 1903-10; Lecturer, King's Coll., London, 1904-19; Secretary, King's Coll., London, 1919-47. Chm. Central Council Federated Superannuation System for Universities, 1938-55; Chm. and Hon. Director, Thomas Wall Trust, 1952-61; Chm. Covenanters' Educational Trust, 1953-61; Sec. Gilchrist Educational Trust, 1948-61; Treas., London Mathematical Soc., 1950-60; Vice-Chm. Finance Cttee., City Parochial Foundation, 1950-58; Gov. Old Vic and Sadler's Wells, 1950-56; Chm. Bishopsgate Institute, 1952-55. *Publications:* (jointly) Caliban's Problem Book, 1933. Papers in mathematical and actuarial jls. *Recreation:* golf. *Address:* 22 Friern Watch Avenue, N.12. *T.:* Hillside 2650.

[*Died* 28 *June* 1967.

SHVERNIK, Nikolai Mikhailovich; Order of Lenin, 1938 and 1946; Soviet politician and trade union leader; Chairman of All-Union Central Council of Trade Unions since 1953; Member of Supreme Soviet of U.S.S.R. since 1937 (Chm., Soviet of Nationalities, 1938-46; Pres. Presidium of Supreme Soviet, 1946-53); Mem. Central Cttee. of Communist Party of Soviet Union since 1925 and alternate mem. of its Presidium since 1953; *b.* 1888. Joined Bolshevik Party, 1905; Chm. Central Cttee., Metal Workers' Union, 1929; First Sec., All-Union Central Council of Trade Unions, 1930-44 Alternate Mem., Political Bureau, 1939; led Soviet Trade Union Delegation to Great Britain, 1942; attended T.U.C. Congress, 1943; First Vice-Pres. Presidium of U.S.S.R. Supreme Soviet, and Pres. Presidium of R.S.F.S.R. Supreme Soviet, 1944. *Address:* All-Union Central Council of Trade Unions, Kaluzhskoe Chaussée 66, Moscow U.S.S.R.

[*Died Dec.* 1970.

SIBBETT, Cecil James, J.P.; Hon. Colonel, The Cape Town Rifles; Chairman and founder, South African National Savings Organisation; Past Provincial Grand Master I.C., Southern Cape Province; Hon. President, 1820 Memorial Settlers' Association; Trustee: South African Library; South African National Gallery; South African Museum; Vice-President, The Cape Horticultural Soc.; Director of Companies; *b.* Belfast; *m.* 1910, Cecil Mary Poole, goddaughter of Cecil Rhodes. Went to South Africa, 1897; War Correspondent, South African War, 1899-1900; Assistant Political Secretary, Cecil Rhodes, 1901-02; Special Correspondent, Daily Express, with Mr. Chamberlain's South African Tour, 1902-1903; Ex-Member Provincial Council of the Cape Province; Ex-Member Cape Town City Council; Member of the Civilian War Losses Commission in South Africa 1926-27. Member S.A. P.E.N. Centre. King's Commendation for services during War of 1939-45. *Publications:* The Odyssey of a District Governor of Rotary; A Noodle's Orations; The Rubáiyát of Bridge. *Recreation:* gardening. *Address:* Hof-Park, Cape Town, South Africa. *Club:* City (Cape Town).

[*Died* 23 *Nov.* 1967.

SICHEL, Alan William Stuart, M.D. (Ed.); Past Chairman of Federal Council, Medical Association of South Africa (Member: Federal Council, 1935-63; Exec. Committee, 1941-60; Past Chairman Head Office and Journal Committee, 1949-63); Vice-President British Medical Association, 1955 (Past Pres.); Vice-Pres., Medical Association of S.A. (Past Pres.); *b.* Claremont, Cape Province, 10 October 1886; *s.* of Godfrey Sichel and Charlotte Stuart; *m.* 1914, Elizabeth, *d.* of Thomas Allen, Newport, Scotland; one *s.* two *d.* (and one *s.* decd.). *Educ.:* Diocesan College, Rondebosch, Cape, S. Africa. B.A. (Classics), Univ. of Cape Town, 1906; M.B., Ch.B. (1st Cl. Hons.), Univ. of Edin., 1912, M.D. 1920, Conan Doyle Prizeman, 1912; Murchison Memorial Scholar, 1913. Res. Phys. to late Sir Thos. Fraser, Roy. Infirmary, Edin., 1912-13; selected by late Sir John Murray to investigate outbreak of trachoma in Christmas Island Indian Ocean, 1913-15. Served European War, 1914-18, temp. Capt. R.A.M.C., 1915-1918; Ophth. Specialist, B.E.F. France, 1918. Resident Surgical Officer Birm. and Midland Eye Hosp., Birmingham, 1919-20. D.O., Univ. of Oxford, 1920; D.O.M.S., Roy. Coll. Phys. and Surg., Lond., 1920; Hon. LL.D. Nat. Univ. of Ireland, Univ. of the Witwatersrand, Johannesburg, 1952. Late Pres. S.A. Students Union, Edin. Practice as Ophth. Surg., Cape Town, 1921; Non-Res. Life Mem. Ophth. Soc. of U.K.; late Pres.: Ophth. Soc. of S. Africa; South Peninsula Med. Soc.; Cape Western Branch, Med. Assoc. S. Africa, 1941; Organising Sec., S.A. Med. Congress, Cape Town, 1933; Cons. Ophth. Surg., Groote Schuur Hosp.; late Lect. in Ophth., Univ. of Cape Town; Cons. Ophth. Surgeon, Victoria Hosp., Wynberg; late Mem., Consultative Council to D.G.M.S.; Cons. Ophth. Surg., Dept. of Defence, 1941-46; late Ophth. Surg. S.A. Rail and Harbours Sick Fund; Chm., Steering Cttee., Coll. Phys. Surgs. and Gynæcologists of S.A., 1953-56, Mem. Council, 1956-59; Mem. S.A. Medical and Dental Council, 1958-63. Coronation Medal, 1953. *Publications:* articles to medical journals. *Recreations:* formerly Rugby football (played for Edinburgh University 1st XV, 1908-1911, Scottish Trial International 1909); photography and mountaineering. *Address:* 11 Cumbury Court, Cumnor Ave., Kenilworth, Cape, S. Africa. *T.:* 77-2996 and 3-6608. *Clubs:* Civil Service (Cape Town); Mountain Club of S. Africa.

[*Died* 17 *May* 1966.

SIDGWICK, Ethel; novelist; *b.* Rugby, 20 Dec. 1877, *o. surv. d.* of late Arthur and

Charlotte S. Sidgwick, Oxford. *Educ.:* Oxford High School; studied music and literature. *Publications:* Promise, 1910; Le Gentleman, 1911; Herself, 1912; Succession, 1913; Four Plays for Children, 1913; A Lady of Leisure, 1914; Duke Jones, 1914; The Accolade, 1915; Hatchways, 1916; Jamesie, 1917; Madam, 1921; Plays for Schools, 1922; Restoration, 1923; Laura, 1924; Fairy-tale Plays, 1926; The Bells of Shoreditch, 1928; Dorothy's Wedding, 1931; Mrs. Henry Sidgwick, a Memoir, 1938. *Address:* Woodlands Nursing Home, Durham Avenue, Bromley, Kent. [*Died* 29 *April* 1970.

SIEPMANN, Harry Arthur; Director, Mocatta and Goldsmid; *b.* 1 October 1889; *e. s.* of Otto Siepmann, Clifton College; *m.* 1936, Doris Banfather; one *s.* one *d.* *Educ.:* Cargilfield; Rugby; New College, Oxford. H.M. Treasury, 1912-19; European War, 1915-19, Captain 14th Brigade R.H.A. (despatches). Peace Conference, 1919; India, 1923-24, as Asst. to Finance Member of Viceroy's Council; Hungary, 1924-26, as Adviser to National Bank; Bank of England, 1926, as Adviser to the Governors. Executive Dir. Bank of England, 1945-54. *Publication:* Verse in Translation. *Address:* Lostwithiel, Fleet Road, Fleet, Hants. *Club:* Athenæum. [*Died* 16 *Sept.* 1963.

SIFTON, John William; President: F.P. Publications Ltd.; Winnipeg Free Press Co. Ltd.; Free Press Weekly Ltd.; Jactor Ltd.; Vice-President, Invictus Ltd.; *b.* 22 Oct. 1925; *s.* of Victor Sifton and Louise C. MacDonald; *m.* 1952, Nancy Gloria Dailey; one *s.* *Educ.:* Upper Canada College; University of Manitoba; Queen's University. Director: Free Press Weekly Ltd., 1955- (Pres., 1955-); Winnipeg Free Press Co. Ltd., (Gen. Manager, 1960-, Pres., 1961-); Jactor Ltd., 1953- (Pres., 1954-); Invictus Ltd., 1959- (Vice-Pres., 1961-); F.P. Publications Ltd., 1961- (Pres., 1961-). *Recreations:* breeding and showing horses, golf. *Address:* R.R. 5, Winnipeg, Manitoba. *T.:* (office) Whitehall 3-9331. *Clubs:* Assiniboia Downs Turf, Manitoba, St. Charles Country (Win.). [*Died* 10 *June* 1969.

SIFTON, Victor, C.B.E. 1944; D.S.O. 1918; LL.D. Univ. of Manitoba, 1952; Publisher Winnipeg Free Press since 1945; Vice-President of the Great-West Life Assurance Co.; *b.* 17 March 1897; *s.* of late Hon. Sir Clifford Sifton, K.C.M.G., K.C., P.C.; *m.* 1925, Louise, *d.* of Brig.-Gen. W. C. Macdonald, Toronto; one *s.* two *d.* *Educ.:* Ottawa Public School and Collegiate Institute; Univ. of Toronto. Served European War, Canadian Forces, 1915; demobilised with rank of Major, 1919. Master-General of Ordnance, Canadian Army, 1940-42. *Address:* 514 Wellington Cr., Winnipeg; Assiniboine Lodge, Mallorytown, Ontario. *T.A.:* Free Press, Winnipeg. *T.:* Grover 5-6814. *Clubs:* Manitoba, Winter (Winnipeg); University, Royal Canadian Yacht (Toronto). [*Died* 21 *April* 1961.

SIKKIM, Maharaja of, H.H. Maharaja Sir Tashi Namgyal, K.C.S.I. *cr.* 1939; K.C.I.E., *cr.* 1923 (C.I.E. 1918); *b.* 26 Oct. 1893; *s.* of His late Highness Maharaja Sir Thotub Namgyal, K.C.I.E., of Sikkim, and second wife, Yeshe Dolma; *S.* brother Sidkeong Namgyal, C.I.E., 1914; *m.* 1918, Kunzang Dechĕn, *d.* of Depon Medrak, General Ra-ka-shar, Tibetan Army; two *s.* (and *e. s.* Pilot Officer, killed in action 1941) three *d.* *Educ.:* Mayo Chief's College, Ajmere; St. Paul's School, Darjeeling. *Recreations:* painting and photography. *Heir:* *s.* Maharaj Kumar Palden Thondup Namgyal, O.B.E. 1947; Hon. Lt.-Col. 8th Gurkha Rifles [*b.* 22 May 1923; *m.* 1st 1950, Sangey Deki (*d.* 1957), *d.* of Theiji Tsewang Rinzing Namgyal of Yapshi Samdup Phodrang, Lhasa; two *s.* one *d.*; 2nd, 1962, Hope Cooke, Seal Harbour, Maine, U.S.A.; one *s.* *Address:* The Palace, Gangtok, Sikkim. *T.:* Gangtok 1 and 2. [*Died* 2 *Dec.* 1963.

SILCOCK, Henry Thomas, M.A.; retired; *b.* 1882; *e. s.* of late T. B. Silcock, J.P., Bath; *m.* Margaret, *d.* of H. F. Standing, D.Sc., formerly of Tananarive; three *s.* one *d.* (one *d.* decd.). *Educ.:* Bath College; Fettes College, Edinburgh; Oriel College, Oxford (Scholar). Travelling Secretary Student Christian Movement; Dean of Faculty of Education and Vice-President of West China Union University, Chengtu, China; General Secretary Friends Foreign Mission Association; Joint General Secretary Friends Service Council; Director and Adviser to Chinese students, Universities' China Committee in London. Secretary of Friends Centre, Shanghai; and Hon. Secretary National Christian Council of China; Secretary Friends World Committee for Consultation. *Publication:* Christ and the World's Unrest (Swarthmore Lecture, 1927). *Address:* 12 Ajax Avenue, The Hyde, N.W.9. *T.:* 01-205 2339. [*Died* 7 *Feb.* 1969.

SILLITOE, Sir Percy (Joseph), K.B.E., *cr.* 1950 (C.B.E. 1936); Kt., *cr.* 1942; D.L. Glasgow; *b.* 22 May 1888; *m.* 1920, Dorothy Mary, *o. d.* of late John Watson, M.B.E., J.P., Hull; two *s.* (one *d.* decd.). *Educ.:* privately. Joined British S.A. Police, 1908; gazetted Northern Rhodesia Police, 1911; served German East Africa Campaign, 1914-18; Actg. Dist. Political Officer, Dodoma, 1919; transferred Colonial service, Tanganyika Territory, 1920; resigned appointment Administrative officer, first grade, 1923; Chief Constable of Chesterfield, 1923-25; East Riding of Yorks, 1925-1926; Sheffield, 1926-31; Glasgow, 1931-43; Chief Constable of Kent, March 1943 and of the combined Police Forces (10) of Kent, April 1943-46; Director-General, Security Service, 1946-53. *Publication:* (Autobiography) Cloak without Dagger, 1955. *Address:* 50 St. John's Road, Eastbourne. *T.:* Eastborne 6406. [*Died* 5 *April* 1962.

SILVERMAN, (Samuel) Sydney, B.A., LL.B.; M.P. (Lab.) Nelson and Colne since 1935; Member, National Executive Committee, Labour Party, since 1956; *b.* 8 October 1895; *s.* of late M. Silverman, Liverpool; *m.* 1933, Nancy, *d.* of late L. Rubinstein, Liverpool; three *s.* *Educ.:* Liverpool Institute; Liverpool University. Admitted Solicitor, 1927; formerly University Lecturer, National University of Finland. *Publication:* (with R. T. Paget, Q.C., M.P.) Hanged—and Innocent? *Address:* 122c Finchley Road, N.W.3; 4 Essex Court, Middle Temple, E.C.4 [*Died* 9 *Feb.* 1968.

SILVESTRI, Constantin; Principal Conductor, Bournemouth Symphony Orchestra, since 1961; Pianist; Composer; *b.* Bucharest, 1913. *Educ.:* Bucharest Conservatoire. Made debut as pianist, 1924; début as conductor, 1930. Conductor: Bucharest Opera, 1935; Bucharest Philharmonic Orchestra, 1945 (former General Manager). Has toured widely. *Compositions include:* Two Sonatas for Violin, op. 19 nos. 1 and 3; Two String Quartets, op. 27; Prelude and Fugue, op. 17 no. 2; Music for Strings, op. 27 no. 2; Three Pieces for String Orchestra, op. 4 no. 2; sonatas for harp, flute, clarinet, bassoon, etc. *Address:* Flat 4, Addiscombe, Cranborne Rd., Bournemouth, Hants. [*Died* 23 *Feb.* 1969.

SIMEY, Baron *cr.* 1965 (Life Peer); **Thomas Spensley Simey;** Charles Booth Professor of Social Science, University of Liverpool, since 1939; *b.* 25 November 1906; 3rd *s.* of G. I. Simey, Clerk of the Peace and of the County Council, Somerset; *m.* 1935, Margaret

Bayne Todd; one *s.* *Educ.:* Balliol College, Oxford. Honour School of Philosophy, Politics and Economics 1st Class 1928; Solicitor, 1931; Lecturer in Public Administration, University of Liverpool 1931-39; Adviser on social welfare to Comptroller for Development and Welfare in the West Indies, 1941-45; Member, Governing Body of William Temple College, 1948-67; Director, Liverpool Repertory Theatre Ltd. 1947-; Chm. Joint Univ. Council for Social Studies, 1948-51; Central Advisory Cttee., Min. of Educn., 1956-60; Pres. Nat. Fedn., Community Assocs., 1961-64 (Vice Pres. 1965); Treas. Brit. Sociological Assoc., 1949-50 (Mem., Exec. Cttee., 1960-64; Chm., 1963-64). *Publications:* Principles of Social Administration, 1937; Welfare and Planning in the West Indies, 1946; The Concept of Love in Child Care, 1960; Charles Booth, Social Scientist (with Mrs. M. B. Simey), 1960; Social Science and Social Purpose, 1968. *Recreation:* systematic idleness, preferably in mountainous country, or in the theatre. *Address:* 3 Blackburne Terrace, Liverpool 8. *T.:* Royal 5762 [*Died* 27 *Dec.* 1969.

SIMKIN, Rt. Rev. William John, C.M.G. 1965; *b.* 15 June 1883; *e. s.* of William Butler and Lucy Elizabeth Simkin, Rugeley, Staffs.; *m.* 1919, Florence, *d.* of Thomas Emberton, Stafford; no *c.* *Educ.:* Prince of Wales Sch., Rugeley; S. Oswald's Coll., Ellesmere; Lichfield Theological College. Law Office, 1897-1904; 1st Cl. Universities Preliminary Theological Exam., 1907; L.Th. University of Durham, 1908; Deacon, 1908; Priest, 1909; Curate of Christ Church, Stafford, 1908-11; Vicar of Wairoa, N.Z., 1911-1918; Secretary, Treasurer, and Mission Chaplain, Diocese of Waiapu and Private Chaplain to Bishop of Waiapu, 1918-26; Archdeacon of Hawke's Bay and Superintendent of Maori Mission, 1919-26; Provincial Secretary of Church of Province of New Zealand and Private Chaplain to Archbishop of New Zealand, 1926-40; Bishop of Auckland, 1940-60, retired. *Publications:* History of The College of Saint John The Evangelist, Auckland, N.Z., 1938; (with Rt. Rev. H. W. Williams) The Dioceses of the Church of the Province of New Zealand and the Associated Missions, 1934. *Recreations:* gardening, fishing. *Address:* Bishop's Lodge, 9 Kaka Road, Taupo, N.Z. [*Died* 8 *July* 1967.

SIMMONDS, Arthur, O.B.E. 1954; M.C. 1918; Secretary, The Royal Horticultural Society, 1956-62; *b.* 25 Feb. 1892; *y. s.* of Frederick Maurice and Caroline Simmonds; *m.* 1st, 1920, Doris Moorhouse Dean (*d.* 1944); one *d.*; 2nd, 1945, Grace Ellen Harrison. *Educ.:* Farnham Grammar School. Served European War, 1914-18, in The Queen's and Machine Gun Corps, Major 1918 (despatches twice, M.C.). Asst. Director, The Royal Horticultural Society's Gardens, Wisley, 1922-25; Asst. Secretary, R.Hort.S., 1925-1946; Dep. Secretary, 1946-56. V.M.H., 1947. *Publications:* articles on horticultural biographies and history in R.H.S. Journal. *Address:* 52 St. Margarets, London Road, Guildford. *T.:* Guildford 63316. [*Died* 16 *March* 1968.

SIMMONDS, William George; R.W.A.; Sculptor, Woodcarver, Painter; Past Pres., Cheltenham Group of Artists; *b.* Constantinople, 3 March 1876; *s.* of John Simmonds, Architect and Martha Simmonds; *m.* 1912, Eveline, *d.* of Benjamin Peart. *Educ.:* Privately; Royal Coll. of Art; Royal Academy Painting School. Exhibited at R.A. and Arts and Crafts Exhibition Society (London), Theatre Arts, Victoria and Albert Museum and Provincial Galleries; assisted Edwin Abbey, R.A., 1906-10, with mural paintings for Pennsylvanian State Capital; during war 1914-18 mechanical draughtsman with Col. R. E. Crompton, C.B., on Tank Designs and Capt. de Haviland on aircraft design; Official Purchases: Water colour (Chantrey Bequest, 1907), Tate Gallery; Horses Grazing, wood (National Arts Collection Fund, 1925), Leicester Art Gallery; Farm Team, wood (Lewis "A" Fund, 1929), Tate Gallery; Cat, wood, Carlisle Art Gallery, 1936; Old Horse, wood (Chantrey Bequest, 1937), Tate Gallery; Cart Horse Foal, alabaster, Sheffield Art Gallery, 1938; Autumn Calf, painted oak, Cheltenham Art Gallery, 1952; other principal works: Ducks, wood, Charles Rutherston Collection, Manchester; Black Mare, wood lacquered, George Eumorphopoulos Collection; White Calf, marble. Several works, in private collections, bought, 1954-64. Regular exhibitor at R.A. until 1967; retrospective exhibition (1879-1966), Painswick, Glos., 1966. Young Donkey (oak), R.A. 1967. *Recreations:* mario ettes and amateur drama. *Address:* Oakridge Lynch, Stroud, Glos. [*Died* 23 *Aug.* 1968.

SIMMONS, Mrs. Amy; Master of South Hereford Foxhounds, 1931-51 and 1959-61 (Joint-Master, 1956-59); *d.* of late J. A. Fairhurst, J.P., T.D., M.A., Arlington Manor, Newbury, Berks. Served in France, European War, 1914-19 (despatches); Master Tedworth Foxhounds, 1921-24; Master Quarme Harriers, 1928-31. *Recreations:* hunting, shooting. *Address:* Gillow Manor, St. Owen's Cross, Hereford. *T.:* Harewood End 216; Garinish Island, Sneem, Co. Kerry. [*Died* 21 *Nov.* 1964.

SIMMS, Captain Charles Edward, D.S.O. 1940; R.N., retired; Director, C. & A. Simms (Engineers) Ltd., 4 Station Rd., Maidstone; *b.* 25 May 1900; *s.* of late James Simms, owner of the firm of Troughton and Simms, Scientific Instrument Makers; *m.* 1st, 1924, Mary Pauline Howard Tutton (who obtained a divorce, 1948); one *s.* two *d.*; 2nd, 1948, Minetta Gunn; one *d.* *Educ.:* King's School, Canterbury; H.M.S. Conway; Royal Naval College, Dartmouth. After leaving Dartmouth in 1917 joined the Battle Cruiser Force, H.M.S. Repulse, and saw active service until end of war; turned over to engineering branch and went to R.N.E.C. Keyham 1922, where qualified in 1923; on the Staff at R.N.C., Dartmouth, 1925-27; Commander, 1934; lent to Royal Australian Navy in flagship, H.M.A.S. Canberra, 1935-1937; H.M.S. Exeter, South American Division, 1937-40 (D.S.O.); sent to Narvik as Base Engineer Officer, 1940; attached to Royal Canadian Navy as Chief Engineer at St. John's, Newfoundland, 1941; at Admiralty, 1944; Captain (E)-in-Command, H.M.S. Imperieuse, Stokers Training Estab. Devonport; Fleet Engineer Officer, Mediterranean Fleet, 1947; Admiralty Engineer and overseer, Southern Area, 1950-51; retired list, 1951. *Address:* Pilgrims' Way, Broad Street, Hollingbourne, Kent. *Club:* Golfers'. [*Died* 30 *Dec.* 1963.

SIMNER, Colonel Sir Percy Reginald Owen Abel, K.C.B., *cr.* 1947 (C.B. 1934); D.S.O. 1917 and bar, 1919; T.D.; D.L.; sometime Senior Master of the Supreme Court and King's Remembrancer; *b.* 1878; *o. s.* of late A. Simner of Grosvenor Court, S.W., and Friog, Merionethshire; *m.* 1948, Irene, *widow* of Kenelm Preedy. *Educ.:* Pocklington; Exeter Coll., Oxford. M.A.; called to Bar, Lincoln's Inn, 1903; joined Western Circuit; Dep.-Lieut. for the Co. of London; was a member of the Westminster City Council for 16 years; represented West Woolwich on London County Council; contested (C.) Gower Division of Glamorganshire, 1910; was a founder and Vice-Chairman of Junior Imperial League; Chairman of the Governors of Welsh Girls' School, Ashford; served European War, 1914-18; Commanded a Bn. of the West Yorkshire Regt. from 1916 (despatches four times, D.S.O. and bar); Col. (T.A.) 1925; Commanded 10th London Regt. (T.A.), 1921-27, and 168th Infantry Brigade, 1927-1931; Hon. Colonel 5th Bn. the Royal Berkshire Regiment (T.A.), 1934-48; served War of 1939-45, in Home Guard as Zone Weapon-training Officer; Chairman T. and A.F.A. for the County of London, 1942-48; County Commandant of Army Cadets for the County of London, 1932-46; Prime Warden of the Fishmongers' Company, 1951. *Recreations:* shooting, fishing. *Address:* 120 Rivermead Court, S.W.6. *T.:* Renown 5554; Friog, Merionethshire. *Club:* Athenæum. [*Died* 11 *Jan.* 1963.

SIMON, André Louis; President Wine and Food Society; *b.* Paris, 28 Feb. 1877; *s.* of Ernest Constant Simon and Jeanne Dardoize; *m.* 1900, Edith Winifred Symons (*d.* 1963); two *s.* three *d.* *Educ.:* Paris. Hon. C.B.E. 1964. *Publications:* History of the Champagne Trade in England, 1905; History of the Wine Trade in England previous to the Fifteenth Century, 1906; History of the Wine Trade in England during the 15th and 16th Centuries, 1907; History of the Wine Trade in England during the 17th Century, 1909; The Search after Claret, 1912; In Vino Veritas, 1913; Bibliotheca Vinaria, 1913; Wine and Spirits—The Connoisseur's Textbook, 1919; The Blood of the Grape—The Wine Trade Text Book, 1920; Wine and the Wine Trade, 1921; The Supply, the Care and the Sale of Wine, 1923; Bottlescrew days: Wine drinking in England during the 18th Century, 1926; Bibliotheca Bacchica, Vol. I. 1927, Vol. II. 1932; The Bolton Letters, 1928; The Art of Good Living, 1929; Tables of Content, 1933; Madeira Wine, 1933; Champagne, 1934; Port, 1934; A Dictionary of Wine, 1936; A Concise Encyclopædia of Gastronomy, 9 vols., 1939-46; Vintagewise, 1945; English Wines and Home-made Cordials, 1946; A Wine Primer, 1946; Drink, 1948; A Dictionary of Gastronomy, 1949; Food, 1949; In Praise of Good Living, 1950; Mushrooms Galore, 1951; The Wines of the World Pocket Library: First Series 1950, Second Series 1951; The Gourmet's Weekend Book, 1952; Bibliotheca Gastronomica, 1953; What About Wine?, 1953; English Fare and French Wines, 1955; Cheeses of the World; Know your Wines; Wine and Food Menu Book, 1956; By Request: an autobiography; The Noble Grapes and the Great Wines of France, 1957; The Star Chamber Dinner Accounts, 1959; Champagne and its history, 1962; Wine in Shakespeare's Days and Shakespeare's Plays, 1964; The Commonsense of Wine, 1966; The Wines, Vineyards, and Vignerons of Australia, 1967; (ed.) Wines of the World, 1967; In the Twilight, 1969. *Recreations:* books and gardening. *Address:* Little Hedgecourt, Felbridge, East Grinstead, Sussex. *T.:* East Grinstead 23898. [*Died* 5 *Sept.* 1970.

SIMON, George Percival; Managing Director, Daily Telegraph, since 1962; *b.* 3 March 1893; *s.* of John Simon, Newton-by-Toft, Lincolnshire, and Ellen Forman, Theddlethorpe, Lincolnshire; *m.* 1924, Elsie Kate, *d.* of Captain H. Branton, Flamboro', Yorkshire; two *d.* *Educ.:* St. Boniface College, Warminster; Selwyn College, Cambridge (M.A.). Lieut. R.A. 1914-16; Flying Officer, R.F.C., 1916; Prisoner of War, Germany, 1917; E.R.Y. Yeo. (Capt.); Cambridge, 1919-22; Journalism, Hull, 1923; London Press Exchange, 1925; Advertising Director, Daily Telegraph, 1929, General Manager, 1939-62. Chairman, Education Committee, Advertising Association, 1936-1942; President The Thirty Club, 1948-49. Broadcasting tour U.S.A., 1939, Advertising and the Press. Master, Worshipful Company of Stationers and Newspaper Makers, 1958-59. *Recreations:* golf, riding. *Address:* Brackenwood, Oxshott, Surrey. *T.:* Oxshott 2505. *Clubs:* Carlton, Garrick, Royal Automobile. [*Died* 29 *April* 1963.

SIMON, Sir Leon, Kt., *cr.* 1944; C.B. 1931; *b.* Southampton, 11 July 1881; *s.* of Rev. I. Simon, later of Manchester; *m.* 1916, Nellie, 2nd *d.* of Dr. M. Umanski, Leeds; two *d.* *Educ.:* Manchester Grammar School; Balliol Coll., Oxford (Senior Classical Scholar); 1st Class Honour Moderations, 1902; Ireland and Craven Scholar, 1902, 2nd Class Lit. Hum., 1904; Civil Service Open Competition, 1904; Entered G.P.O., 1904; Head of Commission of Enquiry into American Telegraph Methods, 1928; Member of Zionist Commission to Palestine, 1918; Director of Telegraphs and Telephones, G.P.O., 1931-35; Director of Savings, G.P.O., 1935-44. Member of Commission of Enquiry into Jewish Education in Palestine, 1945-46; Chairman Exec. Council of Hebrew University of Jerusalem, 1946-49, and of its Bd. of Governors, 1949-50; President of Israel Post Office Bank, 1950-53. Hon. Ph.D. Hebrew Univ. of Jerusalem, 1964. *Publications:* Studies in Jewish Nationalism; Ahad-Ha-Am (Asher Ginzberg), a Biography; Essays on Ancient Greek Literature (in Hebrew); translator of Essays of Ahad-Ha-Am into English and of some of Plato's Dialogues, Xenophon's Memorabilia and Mill's Liberty into Hebrew; editor of Aspects of the Hebrew Genius; joint editor of Awakening Palestine; contributor to English and Hebrew publications on Zionist questions. *Recreations:* chess, music. *Address:* 7 Briardale Gardens, N.W.3. *T.:* Hampstead 3313. [*Died* 27 *April* 1965.

SIMON, Walter, C.M.G. 1948; *s.* of Charles Moncrieffe Simon; *m.* Delia Steel. Retired Director of Wm. and Jno. Lockett Ltd. Former President Chilean Nitrate Association. Member of Blockade Committee, 1940-41; Financial Adviser and 1st Sec. H.M. Embassy, Buenos Aires; also representative of Ministry of Economic Warfare in Argentina, 1941-43; Treasury, 1944-46 (Temp. Asst. Sec.); Member Economic and Financial Mission to Argentina, 1946; head of Economic and Financial Mission to Uruguay, 1947, to Mexico, 1948. *Address:* Rock Hotel, Gibraltar. *Club:* Reform [*Died* 18 *Dec.* 1967.

SIMONDS, Most Rev. Justin Daniel, D.D., Ph.D.; *b.* Glen Innes, N.S.W., 22 May 1890; *s.* of Peter Simonds and Catherine Troy. *Educ.:* St Patrick's College, Manly, N.S.W.; Catholic University of Louvain, Belgium. Priest, 1912; Professor of Sacred Scripture and Dean of Discipline in St. Patrick's College, Manly, and subsequently Rector of St. Columba's College, Springwood; Archbishop of Hobart, 1937-42; Coadjutor Archbishop of Melbourne, 1942-63; Archbishop of Melbourne, (R.C.), 1963-67, retired. *Publication:* The Influence of the Alexandrian Philosophy on the Thought of the Apologists. *Address:* St. Patrick's Cathedral, Melbourne, C.2. [*Died* 3 *Nov.* 1967.

SIMONSON, Lee; author and designer; *b.* New York City, 26 June, 1888; *s.* of Augusta Goldenberg and Sali Simonson; *m.* 1st, 1916, Helen Strauss; divorced 1926; 2nd, 1927, Carolyn Hancock (*d.* 1951); one *s.* one *d.* *Educ.:* Harvard University, Cambridge, Mass., A.B., 1909. Designer, principally scenic, author and lecturer; one of the founders of the Theatre Guild in 1919; a director of the Theatre Guild, New York, from its inception until Jan. 1941; designed many of its productions, including Heartbreak House, Back to Methuselah, Liliom, Marco Millions, Volpone, Dynamo, Elizabeth the Queen, Apple Cart, Idiot's Delight, Amphytrion 38; Ring of the Niebelungen (Metropolitan Opera Association N.Y., 1948); Director of International Exhibition of Theatre Art, Museum of Modern Art, New York City, 1934; Editor of Creative Art (the American edition of the London Studio), 1928-29; consultant on Theatre Construction and Equipment for Wis-

consin Memorial Theatre, Univ. of Wisconsin, 1939; Theatre at Hunter College, New York City, 1940; Hall of Music and Student Theatre, University of Indiana. 1941; Guest Lecturer on the Theatre and on Art at the leading American colleges, universities, and art museums; Special consultant to Metropolitan Museum of Art, Gillender Lecturer, 1944-45. *Publications:* Minor Prophecies, 1927; The Stage is Set, 1932; Theatre Art, 1934; Co-Editor, Settings and Costumes of the Modern Stage, 1933; Part of a Lifetime, 1943; Untended Grove, 1946; The Art of Scenic Design, 1950; Articles on Scenic Design and Stage Equipment in Oxford Companion to the Theatre, 1948; Encyclopædia Britannica. *Address:* 411 E. 50th Street, New York City. *T.:* Eldorado 5-2123. *Club:* Harvard (New York City).
[*Died* 23 *Jan.* 1967.

SIMPSON, Sir Basil Robert James, 2nd Bt., *cr.* 1935; O.B.E. 1954; D.L.; *b.* 13 Feb. 1898; *s.* of Col. Sir Frank Robert Simpson, 1st Bt., C.B., and of Alice Matilda (*d.* 1950), *d.* of late James Finucane Draper; *S.* father, 1949. *Educ.:* Rugby School; Queen's College, Oxford. Formerly Lieut. Durham Light Infantry; served European War, 1914-18, in France and Belgium, 1917-18 (wounded). J.P. 1953, D.L. 1956, Durham. High Sheriff, Co. Palatine of Durham, 1955. *Heir: b.* John Cyril Finucane Simpson [*b.* 10 Feb. 1899; *m.* 1st, 1936, Betty (Mrs. Miesagaes) (marriage dissolved, 1944), *o. c.* of Frank J. Lambert, Newcastle upon Tyne; 2nd, 1945, Maria Teresa, *d.* of John Sutherland Harvey, Romerillo, Biarritz]. *Address:* Bradley Hall, Wylam, Northumberland. *T.:* 2246. *Clubs:* Bath; Northern Counties; Durham County. [*Died* 19 *Aug.* 1968.

SIMPSON, Very Rev. Cuthbert Aikman, D.D.; Dean of Christ Church, since 1959; *b.* 24 May 1892; *s.* of James Simpson and Alice Maude Susan Simpson; *m.* 1918, Jessie Catherine Matheson Kemp (*d.* 1961); no *c.* *Educ.:* St. Peter's School, Charlottetown, P.E.I.; King's Univ., Windsor, N.S.; Christ Church, Oxford. King's B.A. 1915, M.A. 1918; Captain, Canadian Army Pay Corps, 1916-19; Oxford, B.A. 1921; Diploma in Theology, 1922; M.A. 1939; B.D. and D.D. 1945; G.T.S., S.T.B. 1929; S.T.M. 1932; D.Th. 1935. Deacon, 1920; priest, 1921. Rector, St. Alban's Church, Woodside, N.S., 1922-28; Fellow and Tutor, Gen. Theol. Seminary, N.Y. City, 1928-30; Instructor in Old Testament, 1930-34; Asst. Professor O.T., 1934-40; Prof. of O.T., 1940-54; Sub-Dean, 1948-54; Canon of Christ Church and Regius Professor of Hebrew, Oxford University, 1954-59. Naturalized as citizen of U.S.A., 1937. Hon. D.D.: King's Univ., N.S., 1939; St. Andrews, 1967; Hon. D.C.L. Bishop's Univ., Lennoxville, Quebec, 1947; Hon. L.H.D. Simpson College, Iowa, 1962. *Publications:* Revelation and Response in the Old Testament, 1947; Jeremiah, The Prophet of "My People", 1947; The Early Traditions of Israel, 1948; The Composition of the Book of Judges, 1958; (with B. I. Bell) Course on Old Testament in St. James Lessons, 1946. *Address:* Christ Church, Oxford. *T.:* Oxford 43815.
[*Died* 30 *June* 1969.

SIMPSON, Sir George (Clarke), K.C.B., *cr.* 1935 (C.B. 1926); C.B.E. 1919; F.R.S, 1915; D.Sc. (Manchester and Sydney); Hon. LL.D. (Aberdeen); Hon. F.R.S.E.; Corr. Member Preussische Akademie der Wissenschaften, Akademie der Wissenschaften, Vienna, Gesellschaft der Wissenschaften, Göttingen; *b.* Derby, 1878; 2nd *s.* of Arthur Simpson, Derby; *m.* 1914, Dorothy, *d.* of Cecil Stephen, Sydney; three *s.* one *d.* *Educ.:* Diocesan School, Derby; Owens College, Manchester; University of Göttingen. Fellow, Manchester University, 1901; 1851 Exhibition Scholar, 1902-5; investigated electrical state of atmosphere, Lapland, 1903-4; Scientific Assistant, Meteorological Office, London, 1905; Lecturer on Meteorology, Manchester, 1905-6; joined staff of Indian Meteorological Department, 1906; Physicist British Antarctic Expedition, 1910-12; Indian Munitions Board, 1917-19; Director of Meteorological Office, 1920-38; President, Section A, British Association, 1925; awarded Symons Gold Medal by the Royal Meteorological Society, 1930, and Chree Medal by the Physical Soc. 1951; President, Royal Meteorological Society, 1940-42, *Publications:* scientific articles. *Address:* Cote, Westbury-on-Trym, Bristol. *Club:* Athenæum. [*Died* 1 *Jan.* 1965.

SIMPSON, Sir James Fletcher, Kt., *cr.* 1922; Director, Gordon Woodroffe & Co., Ltd., London, upon retirement from Gordon Woodroffe and Co. (Madras), Ltd., Madras; Vice-President, Trustee Savings Bank Association; Member Scottish Savings Committee; *b.* 24 Oct. 1874; *m.* 1905, Isabel Talbert (*d.* 1948), *d.* of P. C. Brooks Hatton of Ardoyne, Insch, Aberdeenshire; two *s.* *Educ.:* High School, Falkirk; Glasgow. Represented the Associated Chambers of Commerce of India, Burma and Ceylon on the Legislative Assembly of India, 1928-29; Chairman Chamber of Commerce, Madras, 1920-22; Member Madras Legislative Council; Member Madras Port Trust; Governor of Imperial Bank of India; Consul for Norway at Madras; Chevalier of the Order of St. Olav, 1st Class. *Address:* Woodthorpe, Bieldside, Aberdeen. *T.:* Aberdeen 47717. *Clubs:* Royal Over-Seas League; Scottish Conservative (Edin.); Royal Scottish Automobile (Glasg.)
[*Died* 29 *Aug.* 1967.

SIMPSON, Rev. John E., M.A. (Cantab.), B.Sc. (London); Rector of Tingewick with Water Stratford, Buckinghamshire, since 1966; *b.* 25 Feb. 1905; *m.* 1930, M. V. Erskine Stuart; one *s.* *Educ.:* Morpeth Gram. Sch.; Corpus Christi Coll., Cambridge; Westcott House, Cambridge. Deacon, 1945; Priest, 1945; Geography Master, Morpeth Grammar School, 1927-30; Geography Master, Pocklington School, 1930-32; Headmaster, Junior School, Hymers College, Hull, 1932-35; Headmaster, Dr. Challoner's Grammar School, Amersham, Bucks, 1935-37; Headmaster, Scarborough College, 1937-42; Headmaster, Heanor Grammar School, 1942-1945; Vice-Principal, St. Paul's College, Cheltenham, 1945-49; Headmaster Canon Slade Grammar School, Bolton, Lancs, 1949-1953; Rector of Denham, Buckinghamshire, 1953-62; Senior Lectr., Divinity and Education, Newland Park Coll., 1962-66. *Address:* Tingewick Rectory, Buckingham. *T.:* Finmere 273. [*Died* 20 *Jan.* 1970.

SIMPSON, Air Cdre. John Herbert Thomas, D.S.O. 1942; A.F.C. 1947; Commandant Royal Observer Corps, 1954-59; retd.; *b.* 26 Mar. 1907; *s.* of late Herbert William Simpson, Madrid, Spain; *m.* 1939, Charlotte Eleanor, *d.* of late R. Brandon Trye, Sutton Coldfield, Warwicks.; four *s.* one *d.* *Educ.:* West Buckland Sch., Devon. Joined R.A.F. 1927; squadron leader, 1937; served War of 1939-45: Middle East, N. Africa and Italy; group capt., 1946; air commodore, 1951; Senior Air Staff Officer 22 Group, Technical Training Command, 1951-54. Commander U.S. Legion of Merit. *Address:* Fairacre, Lea, Malmesbury, Wilts. *T.:* Malmesbury 2248. [*Died* 26 *Aug.* 1967.

SIMPSON, Sir John Hope, K.B.E., *cr.* 1937; Kt., *cr.* 1925; C.I.E. 1913; Grand Cross of the Order of the Phœnix (Greece), 1930; Order of the Brilliant Jade (China), 1936; *b.* 23 July 1868; *s.* of late John Hope Simpson of Sefton Park, Liverpool; *m.* 1st, Quita (*d.* 1939), *d.* of late Robert Barclay, J.P., of Sedgley New Hall, Prestwich, Manchester; two *s.* three *d.*;

2nd, 1941, Evelyn, *widow* of W. H. Brookes and *yr. twin d.* of late J. Forster Hamilton. *Educ.:* Liverpool College; Balliol College, Oxford; M.A. Joined the I.C.S. as Assistant Magistrate and Collector, 1889; Magistrate and Collector, 1897; Joint Secretary, Board of Revenue, U.P. 1902; Registrar of Co-operative Credit Societies, U.P. 1904; President, Municipal Taxation Committee, U.P. 1908; Magistrate and Collector, 1st grade, 1909; Acting Chief Commissioner, Andaman and Nicobar Islands, 1914 and 1916; retired, 1916; M.P. (L.) Taunton Division, 1922-24; Chairman, India Colonies Committee, 1924; Vice-President, Refugee Settlement Commission, Athens, 1926-30; special mission to Palestine for British Government, 1930; Director-General, National Flood Relief Commission, China, 1931-33; Commissioner for Natural Resources, Commission of Government of Newfoundland, 1934-36. *Publications:* Refugees: Preliminary Report of a Survey, 138; The Refugee Problem, 1939. *Address:* 24 Rosebery Avenue, Worthing. *T.:* Goring-by-Sea 42402. [*Died* 10 *April* 1961.

SIMPSON, Sir Joseph, K.B.E. 1959 (O.B.E. 1946); Commissioner, Metropolitan Police, since 1958; *b.* 1909; *s.* of late Joseph Simpson, Horsehay and Lawley, Salop; *m.* 1936, Elizabeth May, *d.* of late Percy Bowler; two *s.* *Educ.:* Ashdown House; Oundle; Manchester Univ. Technical Coll. Member Metropolitan Police, 1931-37; Asst. Chief Constable of Lincolnshire, 1937-43 (seconded to Regional Commissioners Offices, 1939-43); Chief Constable, Northumberland, 1943-46; Chief Constable, Surrey, 1946-56, Asst. Comr. Metropolitan Police, 1956; Deputy Comr., 1957. Barrister, Gray's Inn, 1937. *Recreations:* formerly: athletics, Rugby football, cricket, game and rifle shooting, working dogs; now: supporting games and sports which formerly provided so much pleasure, exercise and comradeship. *Address:* New Scotland Yard, S.W.1. *Clubs:* Reform, Kennel. [*Died* 20 *March* 1968.

SIMPSON, Percy, M.A. (Oxford and Cambridge), D.Litt. (Oxford); Hon. Litt.D. (Camb.); Hon. LL.D. (Glasgow); *b.* 1 Nov. 1865; *s.* of late John Simpson, Lichfield; *m.* 1921, Evelyn Mary, *d.* of late James Spearing, Great Shelford, Cambridge; one *d.* (one *s.* decd.). *Educ.:* Denstone Coll.; Selwyn Coll., Cambridge (Classical Scholar). Master at Denstone College, 1887-95; at St. Olave's Grammar School, 1899-1913; English Lecturer at Oxford, 1913; Reader in English Textual Criticism, 1927; Goldsmiths' Reader in English, 1930-35; Librarian of the English School, 1914-34; Fellow of Oriel, 1921-1936, Hon. Fellow, 1943; Leverhulme Research Fellow, 1935-37; Hon. Fellow of Selwyn College, Cambridge, 1951. *Publications:* Shakespearian Punctuation, 1911; The Life of Sir John Oldcastle, Fidele and Fortunio (Malone Society), 1907-09; Actors and Acting The Masque, in Shakespeare's England, 1916; Ben Jonson's Every Man in his Humour, 1919; Designs by Inigo Jones for Masques and Plays at Court (with C. F. Bell), 1924; Ben Jonson (with C. H. Herford), vols. I-V, 1925-37, (with E. M. Simpson) vols. VI-XI, 1938-52; The Bibliographical Study of Shakespeare (Oxford Bibliographical Society), 1927; The Theme of Revenge in Elizabethan Tragedy (Shakespeare Lecture to the British Acad.) 1935; Proof-Reading in the Sixteenth, Seventeenth and Eighteenth Centuries, 1935; Studies in Elizabethan Drama, 1955; editor, Essays and Studies of the English Association, vol. xxv. 1940; (included in) A List of the Published Writings of Percy Simpson, 1951. *Recreation:* walking. *Address:* 10 Town Close Road, Norwich. [*Died* 14 *Nov.* 1962.

SIMPSON, Air Vice-Marshal Sturley Philip, C.B. 1944; C.B.E. 1942; M.C.; Divisional Controller, London and South-Eastern Division of Ministry of Transport and Civil Aviation, 1953-56, retired (Ministry of Civil Aviation, 1950-53); *b.* 1896; *m.* 1923, Hilda Marion Drabble. A.O.C., R.A.F. Gibraltar, 1941-44; A.O.C. 18 Group, Coastal Command, 1944-47; retired, 1947 Commandant Northolt Civil Aerodrome, 1947-50. *Address:* The Cedar Cottage, Bridle Way, Goring-on-Thames, Oxon. [*Died* 28 *April* 1966.

SIMPSON, Thomas, M.A., Barrister-at-law, Inner Temple, Golf Course Architect; *b.* 1877; *o. s.* of W. W. Simpson, of Winkley Hall, Lancs.; *m.* 1903, Edith Mary (*d.* 1961), *d.* of late Frederick Baynes; one *s.* *Educ.:* Trinity Hall, Cambridge. Called to the Bar, 1905; Practised at the bar for five years and then became a Golf Course Architect. *Publications:* Modern Etchings and Their Collectors, 1919; The Architectural Side of Golf, 1929 (with H. N. Wethered); (joint author with four others) The Game of Golf, 1931, and Golf Courses: Design, Construction, and Upkeep, 1933 and 1950. *Recreations:* Rhine Wines; was responsible for drafting in Chambers the rule which removed from the hands of a cttee. of a Proprietary Club all power of management; has always had a great objection to be taken seriously except in his lighter moments. *Address:* Humbly Grove, South Warnborough, Basingstoke, Hants. *T.:* Long Sutton 26. *Club:* Carlton. [*Died* 10 *May* 1964.

SIMPSON, Thomas Young, C.B.E. 1919; M.D., M.S., F.R.C.S., L.R.C.P. (Lond.); *b.* Dungannon, Co. Tyrone; *s.* of John Simpson and Julia Young; *m.* Rosalie Florence Tall; no *c.* *Educ.:* Bristol Grammar School (Prizeman Chemistry); Cooke's School of Anatomy (Bland Sutton Scholar); Middlesex Hospital (Prizeman Materia Medica, Pharmacy, and Therapeutics); London Hospital (Prizeman Surgery); Durham University (Honours in Anatomy, Physiology, Materia Medica, Pharmacy, and Therapeutics); Royal Infirmary, Newcastle and Edinburgh; attended French wounded after Verdun, 1916; late Chirurgien Chef and Administrator, Hôpital Anglais, Lyons; Temp. Surg., V.D. Dept., Royal Sussex County Hospital, Brighton, and Worthing Hospital, 1930-39, and Middlesex, Shenley and Banstead Hosps., 1939-45; Temp. Casualty Surgeon, West London Hosp., 1931-34; Consulting and Operating Surgeon Ford House Hosp., Devonport, Plymouth City Hosp., Totnes, Saltash, and Okehampton Hosps., and Southern Railway Co.; late Surgeon Specialist, 4th Southern General Hospital, Ford House, Devonport, and Military Families Hospital, Devonport; Gynæcologist, Ministry of Health. *Publications:* Cartilage Grafts to close Cranial Defects, British Medical Journal, 21 April 1917; and other articles of surgical interest; The Treatment of Ectopia Vesicæ by Grafting the Ureters into the Bowel extra-peritoneally; Simpson's Improved Lithotomy Straps; Dangers of Flute Key Flask in Administration of Ethyl Chloride, Lancet, 1906; Simpson's Automatic Apparatus for Analgesia and Anæsthesia during labour, B.M. Journal, 4 July 1936 and Med. Annual, 1937. *Address:* 114 Gloucester Road, S.W.7 *T.:* Fremantle 2608. [*Died* 2 *March* 1963.

SIMPSON, William Douglas, C.B.E. 1962 (O.B.E. 1954); M.A., D.Litt., LL.D.; retired as Librarian, Clerk of the General Council and Registrar of the University of Aberdeen (1926-66); *b.* Aberdeen, 1896; *s.* of late Henry F. Morland Simpson, M.A., LL.D., and late Jenny F. Dohm; *m.* 1935, Dorothy, *e. d.* of late J. R. Mason, Dundee; one *d.* *Educ.:* Grammar School and University of Aberdeen, 1st Class Hons. in History. Caithness Prizeman and Forbes Gold Medallist, 1919. In charge of Boy Scouts on Admiralty Coastwatching Service in Scotland, 1917-18; on Secretariat, Ministry of Nat. Service, 1918; Assistant to Professor of

History, 1919-20; Lecturer in British History, 1920-26. F.S.A.Scot.; F.S.A.; Hon. F.R.I.A.S.; Chairman, Ancient Monuments Board for Scotland; Member Royal Commission on the Ancient Monuments of Scotland; Member Scottish National Portrait Gallery Advisory Board and Scottish Records Advisory Council, 1938-55; Pres. Scottish Ecclesiological Soc., 1954-55; Pres. Scottish History Society, 1966. Rhind lecturer in Archæology, 1941; Dalrymple lecturer in Archæology (Glasgow University), 1950; directed excavations at Kildrummy Castle, 1919-39; at Coull Castle 1923; at Kindrochit Castle, 1925-27; at the Doune of Invernochty, 1935; at Esslemont Castle, 1938; at Dundarg Castle, 1950-51; at Finavon Castle, 1952-53. Hon. LL.D., Aberd. Comdr., Royal Order of St. Olaf, Norway, 1964. *Publications:* Huntly Castle, 1922; The Castle of Kildrummy, its place in Scottish History and Architecture, 1923; Dunnottar Castle (11th edn., 1968); The Scottish Castle (Hist. Association, Scotland, Publications), 1924; The Origins of Christianity in Aberdeenshire 1925; Aberdeenshire (official guide), 1927; The Historical Saint Columba, 3rd edn. 1963; The Palace of the Bishops of Moray at Spynie, 1927; On Certain Saints and Professor Watson, 1927; Stirlingshire (Camb. County Geography), 1928; Urquhart Castle, 1929; Julian the Apostate, 1930, Lochindorb Castle, 1932; Skye (official guide), 1934; The Celtic Church in Scotland, 1935; Ravenscraig Castle, 1938; Dunvegan Castle, 15th edn. 1965; St. Ninian and the Origins of the Christian Church in Scotland, 1940; The Province of Mar, 1943; The Earldom of Mar, 1949; Castles from the Air, 1949; Dundarg Castle, 1954; A Short History of Tarves, 1954; Exploring Castles, 1957; Dunstaffnage Castle and the Stone of Destiny, 1958; A Short History of St. John's Kirk of Perth, 1958; Scottish Castles, 1959; The Building Accounts of Tattershall Castle, 1960; The Castle of Bergen, 1960; Doune Castle, 2nd edn. 1966; The Ancient Stones of Scotland, 2nd edn. 1968; Castles in Britain, 2nd edn. 1967; The Church of the Holy Rude, Stirling, 1967; Portrait of Skye and the Outer Hebrides, 2nd edn. 1968; Portrait of the Highlands, 1968; numerous papers on historical and archæological subjects. *Recreation:* shooting. *Address:* The Wallace Tower, Tillydrone, Old Aberdeen. *Club:* Scottish Conservative (Edinburgh).

[*Died* 9 *Oct.* 1968.

SIMPSON, Colonel William George, C.M.G. 1916; D.S.O. 1918; T.D; Captain, retired; *b.* 1876; *s.* of late Colonel S. Simpson, R.A.; *m.* 2nd, 1934, Hermenie Hilda, *d.* of late Rev. E. F. Felton, Milverton, Somerset. Joined Royal Marines, 1895; served North China, 1900 (China medal); Adjutant 1st V.B. Northamptonshire Regiment, 1907-9; retired, 1910; Lt.-Col. 24th London Regt., The Queen's, 1910-18; Colonel 1917; Hon. Colonel 1/7th (Southwark) Battalion the Queen's, 1920-46; served European War, 1915 (despatches 4 times, C.M.G., D.S.O., Comendador da Ordem Militar da Avis). *Address:* 29 Highworth Avenue, Cambridge.

[*Died* 10 *June* 1961.

SIMPSON-HINCHLIFFE, William Algernon, J.P.; *b.* 1880; *m.* 1902, Helen, *d.* of Hinchliffe Hinchliffe, of Cragg Hall, Yorks. M.P. (U.) Sowerby Div. Yorks, 1922-1923. *Address:* Daleside, Harrogate, Yorks.

[*Died* 8 *June* 1963.

SIMS, Sir Arthur, Kt., *cr.* 1950; M.A.; Industrialist having land and business interests in Rhodesia, also land interests in Africa south of Zambesi River, timber interests in New Zealand, and large interest in North Canterbury Sheepfarmers' Co-operative, Freezing, Export & Agency Co. Ltd., N.Z.; Amalgamated Holdings Ltd., N.Z., etc. Director: Davis Gelatine interests in Australia and various Dominions: Yanga Pty. Ltd.; Cooper, Triffitt & Co. Ltd., Bradford; London Produce Co. Ltd., London; timber interest, etc.; *b.* 27 July 1877; *s.* of Samuel Sims, Lincs.; *m.* 1909, Agnes Marian Todd; one *d.* (and one *d.* decd.). *Educ.:* Christchurch Boys' High Sch., Canterbury Coll., Christchurch, N.Z. (M.A.). Endowed Rutherford Memorial Sch., Canterbury Coll., N.Z., also Commonwealth Travelling Professorship. R.C.S. of Eng.; a trustee Empire Grad. Research Scholar, Canada, Australia and New Zealand. Hon Medallist R.C.S. of Eng.; Hon. F.R.A.C.S.; Hon. F.R.A.C.P.; Hon. F.R.C.O.G.; Hon. F.R.C.S.; Hon. F.R.C.P. (Can.); Hon. F.R.C.S. (Can.). Hon. LL.D. New Zealand Univ. *Recreations:* cricket (Capt. New Zealand team, 1905), etc. *Address:* London Produce Co. Ltd., Terminus Chambers, 6 Holborn Viaduct, E.C.1. *T:* City 7106; c/o Messrs. Sims, Cooper & Co. (Australia) Pty. Ltd., Almora House, 522 Little Collins St., Melbourne; Merivale, Christchurch, N.Z. *Clubs:* Carlton; Canterbury (Christchurch).

[*Died* 27 *April* 1969.

SIMSON, Captain Sir Donald (Petrie), K.B.E., *cr.* 1939 (C.B.E. 1937; O.B.E. 1934); a Founder British Legion; Hon. Organiser Earl Haig's Tours of Newfoundland, South Africa, Canada; Foundation Hon. Sec. British Empire Service League (under late Field Marshal Earl Haig); Founder and First Pres. New Zealand Services Assoc.; one of Founders Comrades of the Great War Boer War with N.Z. Contingent; Staff, Thorneycrofts Column; European War, 1914-18, with New Zealanders, Egypt and Gallipoli. Member: Council, Royal Over-Seas League; Cttee., Empire Day Movement, Not-forgotten Assoc., South Africa Soc., Compatriots Club. Man. Dir., Empire Service Publications Ltd. F.Z.S. *Recreations:* Empire service, racing, deep-sea fishing. *Address:* 14 Dilworth Ave., Remuera, N.Z. *Clubs:* English-Speaking Union, Royal Over-Seas League, Royal Commonwealth Society, Compatriots.

[*Died* 20 *Jan.* 1961.

SINCLAIR, Arthur Henry Havens, M.B., C.M., M.D.(Edinburgh), F.R.C.S.Ed., F.R.S.Ed.; retd., Cons. Ophthalmic Surgeon to Department of Health for Scotland, Royal Infirmary, Edinburgh, Royal Hospital for Sick Children, Edinburgh, and Leith Hosp.; formerly Lecturer on Diseases of the Eye, University of Edinburgh; *b.* Kenmore, Perthshire, Feb 1868; *y. s.* of Rev Allan Sinclair and Sarah Fraser; *m.* 1898, Mabel Kennedy (*d.* 1947), *y. d.* of Andrew Tod and Mary Kennedy; two *s.* one *d.* *Educ.:* Edinburgh; London; Utrecht. President, Ophthalmological Section, B.M.A., Edinburgh Meeting, 1927; Pres., Ophthalmological Society of U.K., 1931-33; President, Royal College of Surgeons, Edinburgh, 1933-1935; International Society for Prevention of Blindness, and of the Medical Society of Copenhagen; temporary Captain R.A.M.C., 1916-17, Salonika Expeditionary Force; Member of Royal Company of Archers, Queen's Bodyguard for Scotland. *Publications:* contributions to ophthalmic literature. *Recreations:* fishing, shooting, golf. *Address:* 22 Rothesay Terrace, Edinburgh. *T.:* Caledonian 4250. *Clubs:* Caledonian; New (Edinburgh); Hon. Company Edinburgh Golfers (Muirfield).

[*Died* 30 *June* 1962.

SINCLAIR, John Alexander; retired as Joint Managing Director, Carreras Ltd., London, 1955; *b.* Newcastle upon Tyne, 22 May 1885; *e. s.* of John Sinclair; *m.* 1909, Hester Heywood, *d.* of Samuel M. Anglin, Stockton-on-Tees; three *s.* four *d.* *Address:* 30 South Grove House, N.6. *T.:* Mountview 8140.

[*Died* 2 *May* 1961.

SINCLAIR, John Houston, C.M.G. 1915; C.B.E. 1919; Order of Brilliant Star of Zanzibar, 1st class, 1923; King George V Silver Jubilee Medal, 1935; *b.* 1871; *y. s.* of late W. H. Sinclair of Morton, Brading, Isle of Wight; *m.* 1902, Muriel Eveleen Kathleen, M.B.E. 1918 (*d.* 1952), *y. d.* of Col. Cockburn, Black Watch; one *d.* H.M. Vice-Consul, 1899; H.M. Consul, 1906; Chief Sec. to the Government, Zanzibar, 1914-21, and British Resident, 1921-24; Actg. High Commissioner in 1922-23; retired, 1924; Commanded Zanzibar Defence Force during European War. *Publication:* Laws of Zanzibar, 1863-1911. *Recreations:* golf and polo. *Address:* Dar el Huari, Tanger Socco 2011, Tangier. *Club:* Caledonian.

[*Died* 17 *Aug.* 1961.

SINCLAIR, Meurice, C.M.G. 1918; Major R.A.M.C.; retired, July 1924; M.B., Ch.B. Edinburgh University, 1903; *b.* 30 Dec. 1878; *s.* of late Surgeon-General D. Sinclair, C.S.I., I.M.S.; *m.* 1908, Mary Margaret Best, *widow* of Major Sellick, I.M.S.; two *d. Educ.:* Clifton Coll. Served European War in France: mobilised with the 2nd Coldstream Guards, 1914-15; prisoner 1 September 1914, Vivières retaken by French, released 15 September 1914; Surgeon in charge of fractures at No 8 Stationary Hospital, Wimereux, near Boulogne, France, 1916, until the Armistice; demonstrations in the treatment of fractures given to all the Allies and to many military orthopaedic hospitals in Great Britain and Ireland (despatches thrice, C.M.G.); late orthopædic and limb-fitting surgeon to the Army; member of Committee of Enquiry on Artificial Limbs in 1921 and 1925; specialist in orthopædic surgery and fractures to St. Luke's Hospital, Sydney Street, S.W.3.; St. Stephen's Hospital, 369 Fulham Road, S.W.10, and Dulwich Hospital, East Dulwich Grove, S.E.22; sundry inventions for the treatment of fractures. *Publications:* The Thomas Splints and its Modifications; Fractures; several articles on treatment of fractures. *Recreations:* shooting, motoring, and tennis. *Address:* 29 Westleigh Avenue, Putney, S.W.15. *T.:* Putney 4021.

[*Died* 18 *April* 1966.

SINCLAIR, T(homas) Alan, M.A.; Hon. D.Litt.; Professor of Greek in the Queen's University of Belfast since 1934; *b.* 9 April 1899; *s.* of late Samuel Sinclair, Belfast; *m.* 1931, Sally, *d.* of late Stanley Ferguson, Belfast. *Educ.:* Royal Belfast Academical Institution; Queen's Univ., Belfast; St. John's Coll., Camb.; Ecole des Hautes Etudes and Univ. of Paris. Lecturer in Classics, University College, Southampton, 1923-26; Reader in Classics in the University of London (Birkbeck College), 1926-1934; Fellow of St. John's College, Cambridge, 1926-29. *Publications:* (with F. A. Wright) A History of Later Latin Literature, 1931; Hesiod: Works and Days, Text and Commentary, 1932; A History of Classical Greek Literature, 1934; A History of Greek Political Thought, 1952. [*Died* 10 *Oct.* 1961.

SINCLAIR, Upton; author; *b.* Baltimore, Maryland, 20 Sept. 1878; *s.* of Upton Beall and Priscilla Harden; *m.* 1st, 1901, Meta H. Fuller (divorced, 1912); one *s.*; 2nd, 1913, Mary Craig Kimbrough; 3rd, 1961, at Claremont, California, Mrs. Mary Hard Willis (*d.* 1967). *Educ.:* College, City of New York; Columbia University. Exposed conditions in American meat-packing industry, and assisted President Roosevelt in investigations which led to reforms; founded Intercollegiate Socialist Soc., 1905, now League for Industrial Democracy; Socialist candidate for Congress, 1906 and 1920; Socialist Party candidate for U.S. Senate, California, 1922; arrested, 1923, for attempting to read the Constitution of the U.S.A.; Socialist candidate for Governor of California, 1926, 1930; Democratic Candidate for Governor of California, with program to End Poverty, 1934. Page One Award, by American Newspaper Guild, 1962; Social Justice Award, by United Automobile Workers, 1962. The Sinclair Archives are at Indiana Univ. *Publications:* Springtime and Harvest, 1901; King Midas, 1901; The Journal of Arthur Stirling, 1903; Prince Hagen: a Fantasy, 1903; Manassas: a Novel of the War, 1904; The Jungle, 1906; A Captain of Industry, 1906; The Industrial Republic, 1907; The Overman, 1907; The Metropolis, 1908; The Moneychangers, 1908; Samuel the Seeker, 1910; Love's Pilgrimage, 1911; The Fasting Cure, 1911; Plays of Protest, 1912; The Millenium: A Comedy of the Year 200, 1912; Sylvia, 1913; Damaged Goods, 1913; Sylvia's Marriage, 1914; The Cry for Justice, 1915; King Coal, 1917; The Profits of Religion, 1918; Jimmie Higgins, 1919; The Brass Check, 1919; 100%: The Story of a Patriot, 1920; The Book of Life, 1921; They Call Me Carpenter, 1922; The Goose-step, 1923; Hell: a Verse Drama, 1923; The Goslings, 1924; The Pot Boiler, 1924; Singing Jail-birds, 1924; Mammonart, 1925; Bill Porter, 1925; Letters to Judd, 1926; The Spokesman's Secretary, 1926; Oil!, 1927; Money Writes!, 1927; Boston, 1928; Mountain City, 1930; Mental Radio, 1930; Roman Holiday, 1931; The Wet Parade, 1931; Candid Reminiscences (American Outpost), 1932; Upton Sinclair Presents William Fox, 1933; The Way Out, 1933; I, Governor of California, 1933; I, Candidate for Governor: And How I got Licked, 1934; The Epic Plan for California 1934; We People of America: And How We Ended Poverty, 1935; Depression Island, 1935; What God Means to Me, 1936; The Gnomobile, 1936; Co-op. 1936; Wally for Queen, 1936; No Pasaran, 1937; The Flivver King, 1937; Our Lady, 1938; Little Steel, 1938; Terror in Russia, 1938; Marie Antoinette, a play, 1939; Your Million Dollars, 1939; Expect No Peace, 1939; Letters to a Millionaire, 1939; Telling the World, 1939; World's End, 1940; Between Two Worlds, 1941; Peace or War in America, 1941; Dragon's Teeth, 1942 (Pulitzer Prize); Wide is the Gate, 1943; Presidential Agent, 1944; Dragon Harvest, 1945; A World to Win, 1946; Presidential Mission, 1947; A Giant's Strength, 1948; One Clear Call, 1948; Limbo on the Loose, 1948; To the Editor, 1948; O Shepherd Speak!, 1949; Another Pamela, 1950; The Enemy Had It Too, 1950; A Personal Jesus, 1952; The Return of Lanny Budd, 1953; What Didymus Did, 1955; The Cup of Fury, 1956; It Happened to Didymus, 1958; Their's Be the Guilt, 1959; My Lifetime in Letters, 1960; Cicero, 1960; Affectionately, Eve, 1961; Autobiography of Upton Sinclair, 1962. *Address:* Post Office Box 84, Martinsville, New Jersey 08836, U.S.A.

[*Died* 26 *Nov.* 1968.

SINCLAIR-BURGESS, Maj.-Gen. Sir William Livingstone Hatchwell, K.B.E., *cr.* 1935; Kt., *cr.* 1934; C.B. 1919; C.M.G. 1918; D.S.O. 1916; *b.* 18 Feb. 1880; *s.* of late Rev. George Burgess, F.R.A.S., Auckland, N.Z. *Educ.:* England. Served European War, 1914-1918 (despatches six times, C.B., C.M.G., D.S.O., Officer Legion of Honour, American Distinguished Service Medal); Chief of the General Staff, New Zealand, 1924-37; G.O.C., N.Z. Military Forces, 1931-37. *Address:* Mahina Bay, Eastbourne, Wellington, N.Z.

[*Died* 3 *April* 1964.

SINCLAIR-LOCKHART, Sir John Beresford, 13th Bt. of Murkle and Stevenson, *cr.* 1636 (N.S.); E.D.; *b.* 4 November 1904; 2nd *s.* of Sir Robert Duncan Sinclair-

Lockhart, 11th Bt. (*d.* 1918), of Cambusnethan Priory, Lanarks., Scotland, and Auckland, N.Z.; *b.* of Sir Graeme Duncan Power Sinclair-Lockhart, 12th Bt.; *S.* brother 1959; *m.* 1949, Winifred Ray, 4th *d.* of late Tom Ray Cavaghan, Aglionby Grange, Carlisle. *Educ.:* King's College, Auckland; University of New Zealand; Sidney Sussex College, Cambridge. B.E. (Civil), B.Sc. (Physics). Kenya Administration, 1934-63. Served War of 1939-1945, as Major, R.A. *Heir: b.* Muir Edward Sinclair-Lockhart [*b.* 23 July 1906; *m.* 1940, Olga Anne, *d.* of Claude Victor White-Parsons, Waipawa, Hawkes Bay, New Zealand; one *s.* one *d.*]. *Address:* Moray House, Ventnor, Isle of Wight. *Clubs:* Mombasa; Royal Over-Seas League.

[*Died* 11 *March* 1970.

SINGER, Dorothea Waley; author and social worker; *b.* London, 1882; *d.* of Nathaniel L. Cohen, L.C.C., and of Julia M. Waley; *m.* 1910, Prof. Charles Singer (*d.* 1960); one *s.* one *d.* *Educ.:* Queen's Coll., London; British Museum. Former Vice-Pres.: Académie Internationale d'Histoire des Sciences; Union Internat. d'Histoire des Sciences; former Chm. of its Bibliographical Commission; former Vice-Pres. British Soc for the History of Science; former Member Council and Vice-Pres., Hist. Section of R.S.M.; Life Mem., Institute of Historical Research; Life Member Royal Institute of International Affairs; Corr. Fellow Mediæval Acad. of Amerca, 1961. Sarton Medal (jointly with Charle Singer) History of Science Society, 1956. *Publications:* Catalogue of Greek Alchemical Manuscripts in British Isles, 1921; Catalogue of Latin and Vernacular Alchemical Manuscripts in British Isles, 3 vols., 1926-31; Ambroise Paré, 1929; Introduction to the *Philobiblon* of Richard de Bury, 1933; Comeniius and Confidence in the Rational Mind in J. Needham, Comenius, Teacher of Nations, 1942; Giordano Bruno, his Life and Thought; with translation of his work De l'infinito universo et mondi, 1950; Plague Texts in Great Britain and Eire in MSS. before the 16th Century, 1950; Margrieta Beer, a Memoir, 1955; Card Handlist of Greek, Latin and Vernacular Scientific MSS. in Gt. Brit. and Eire written before XVI century, with Indexes of Names, Places, Libraries and Catalogues; deposited in MS. Dept. of Brit. Mus., microfilm in Warburg Inst., Univ. London, in Lib. of Congress, U.S.A., in Cornell Univ., etc.; numerous articles on the History of Science. *Recreations:* conversation and travel. *Address:* Kilmarth, Par, Cornwall. *T.:* Par 2056. *Club:* Lyceum

[*Died* 24 *June* 1964.

SINGH ROY, Sir Bijoy Prosad, K.C.I.E. 1943; Kt. 1933; M.A., LL.B., M.L.C.; *b.* 12 Jan. 1894; *s.* of Rajani Lall Singh Roy and Srimati Binoylata Debi; *m.* Bilwabasini Debi; two *s.* two *d.* *Educ.:* Chakdighi Sarada Prasad Institution; Hindu School, Presidency College and University Law College, Calcutta. Hon. 2nd Lieutenant, 1918; Member of the Calcutta Volunteer Rifles, 2nd Bn., 1913-18; Advocate, High Court, Calcutta; Member, Bengal Legislative Council, since 1921, Pres. 1943; Minister, Local Self-Govt., Bengal, 1930-37; Minister in charge of the Revenue Dept., Bengal, under the new constitution, 1937-41; Councillor of the Calcutta Corporation, 1924-30; Trustee of the Calcutta Improvement Trust, 1924-30; Member of the British Indian Association, its Honorary Asst. Sec., 1925-28, Trustee and a Vice-President; represented the Landlords of Bengal before the Simon Commission, 1926; Member of the Bengal Provincial Franchise Cttee., 1932; President, All-India National Liberal Federation, 1941. Trustee, Victoria Memorial. President, All-India Kshatriya (Rajput) Mahasava, 1939; Sheriff of Calcutta, 1952; President, Indian Chamber of Commerce; Fellow of the Senate, Calcutta University. Chairman: Basanti Cotton Mills Ltd., Insulated Cable Co. Ltd.; Director: Alkali Chemical Industries Ltd., The Imperial Bank of India, Lionel Edwards Ltd., Calcutta, Belvedere Jute Mills Ltd., Budge Budge Jute Mills Ltd., India Steamship Co. Ltd.; Reserve Bank of India, etc. *Publications:* Annotated Edition of the Bengal Municipal Act. Parliamentary Government in India. *Recreations:* shooting and tennis. *Address:* Major's Hall, Chakdighi, Burdwan; 15 Lansdowne Road, Calcutta, India. *T.:* 47-1230; 5/1A Hungerford Street, Calcutta 16. *T:* 44-5648; Manjusree, Altamont Site, Darjeeling. *Clubs:* Calcutta, Royal Calcutta Turf (Calcutta); Darjeeling Gymkhana.

[*Died* 23 *Nov.* 1961.

SINHA, 2nd Baron of Raipur, *cr.* 1919; **Aroon Sinha,** Barrister-at-law; *b.* 22 Aug. 1887; *e. s.* of 1st Baron; *S.* father, 1928; *m.* 1st, 1916, Pryatama (*d.* 1920), *e. d* of Rai Bahadur Lalit Mohan Chatterjee; two *d.*; 2nd, 1920, Nirpuama, *yr. d.* of Rai Bahadur Lalit Mohan Chatterjee; two *s.* *Educ.:* Worcester Coll., Oxon.; Lincoln's Inn. *Heir: s.* Hon. Sudhindro Prosanno Sinha [*b.* 29 Oct. 1920. *Educ.:* Bryanston School, Blandford]. *Address:* National Liberal Club, Whitehall Place S.W.1; 7 Lord Sinha Road, Calcutta, India *Clubs:* National Liberal; Calcutta, Royal Calcutta Turf (Calcutta).

[*Died* 11 *May* 1967.

SINNATT, Oliver Sturdy, M.C., D.Sc. (Lond.), M.Sc. (Manc.); A.F.R.Ae.S.; *b.* Liverpool, 6 Sept. 1882; *s.* of late Francis Sinnatt; *m.* 1920, Marjorie Helen (*d.* 1964), *o. d.* of late W. R. Randall, solicitor, Bridgend, Glam.; two *s.* (*e. s.* killed in action, 1944). *Educ.:* College of Technology, Manchester; The Owens College, Manchester University. On staff of King's College, London, 1905-20; in succession Demonstrator, Senior Demonstrator and Lecturer in Civil and Mechanical Engineening Dept.; conducted researches on Thermo-dynamics of Metals; Captain in University of London O.T.C. from 1909; served with 2/2nd London Regiment in France (severely wounded at Poelcappelle, Oct. 1917); M.C.; attached Air Ministry as Technical Officer till 1919; Professor of Aeronautical Science, Royal Air Force College, Cranwell, Sleaford, 1920-42. *Recreation:* golf. *Address:* 140 Poplar Av., Hove 4, Sx. *T.:* 38130.

[*Died* 28 *May* 1965.

SINNOTT, Colonel Edward Stockley, C.M.G. 1916; V.D.; T.D.; D.L. (1919); J.P. (1936); M.I.C.E.; *b.* 1868; *e. s.* of late James Sinnott, Brislington, nr. Bristol; *m.* 1st, 1905, Violet Carew (*d.* 1920), *d.* of late Rev. P. Potter, Rector of Bishopston; (one *s.* decd., one killed in action, 1941); five *d.*; 2nd, 1922, Violet Adela (*d.* 1943), *d.* of late Col. Frederick Peel, Royal Engineers. *Educ.:* Clifton College. Chartered civil engineer engaged principally on railway and dock construction, 1886-1907; County Surveyor, Glos. 1907-35; Lieut. 2nd Glos. R.E. Vols. (later S. Midland R.E., T.A.), 1885; Capt. 1893; Major, 1901; Lt.-Col. 1912; Col. 1918; served S. Africa, 1900 (Queen's medal 3 clasps); European War, 1914-18, France and Belgium (despatches, C.M.G.). *Address:* Beacon Cottage, Trelleck, Monmouth.

[*Died* 8 *Aug.* 1969.

SISSON, Charles Jasper, M.A., D. ès. L., D.Lit.; *b.* 1885; 12th *s* of late George Sisson and Amelia Sisson of Plawsworth Grove, Co. Durham; *m.* 1916, Vera Kathleen, *y. d.* of David George and Anna Mara Ginn; two *d.* *Educ.:* Rutherford Coll.; Univ. of Edinburgh (Heriot Fellow, 1907); France and Germany. Lecturer in English, University of Dijon, France, 1907-9; Lecturer in English Literature, Egyptian University, Cairo, 1909-10; Professor of English Literature, Elphinstone College, Bombay, 1910-1921; Principal, Karnatak College, Bombay, 1922; Principal, Elphinstone College, Bombay,

1923; University Reader in English Literature, University Coll., London, 1923-28; Lord Northcliffe Professor of Modern English Literature, University College, London, 1928-51; Emeritus Professor University of London, 1951; Assistant Director and Senior Fellow, Shakespeare Institute in the University of Birmingham, Stratford-on-Avon, 1951-59. Editor Modern Language Review, 1927-55; Lecturer in Poetics, Royal Academy of Music, London, 1926-39; Visiting Professor of English, University of Wisconsin, U.S.A., 1925-26, and University of Utah, summer, 1926; Member of Personal Board Civil Services Commission, 1927; Member of College Committee, University College, 1928-31 and 1941-46; Visiting Professor of English, Harvard University, winter, 1928-29, and summer, 1930; External Examiner, University of Edinburgh, 1929-34, Cambridge, 1938-1939, Glasgow, 1939-47; Sanders Reader in Bibliography, University of Cambridge, 1938. Member of Senate, University of London, 1932-40; Dean of Faculty of Arts, University of London, 1934-38; Governor of Cheltenham Ladies' College since 1939; 2nd Lieut. Home Guard, 1939-41, Capt., T.A., General List, since 1941. Pro-Provost, University College, London, at Aberystwyth, 1943-1944. Member Advisory Board of Shakespeare Survey, 1947-. Hon. Member, Modern Language Association of America, 1949; Visiting Prof. of English, Univ. of North Carolina, 1949; Turnbull Lecturer, Johns Hopkins Univ., 1949; Pres. Modern Humanities Research Assoc.; Pres. Shakespeare Club, Stratford-on-Avon, 1951; Hon. Mem., Elizabethan Club, Yale Univ., 1953. Lord Northcliffe Lectr., Univ. Coll., London 1956. *Publications:* Nineteenth Century Speeches, 1916; Le Goût Public et le Théâtre Elisabéthain, 1922; Shakespeare in India, 1925; Keep the Widow Waking, a Lost Play by Dekker, 1927; Believe as you List (Malone Society), 1928; Marks as Signatures (Bibliographical Society), 1928; Grafton and the London Greyfriars (Bibliographical Society 1930); Thomas Lodge and other Elizabethans, 1933; Lost Plays of Shakespeare's Age, 1936; The Judicious Marriage of Mr. Hooker 1940; William Shakespeare: Complete Works, 1954; Shakespeare, 1954; New Readings in Shakespeare, 1956; Shakespeare's Tragic Justice, 1962; Gabriel, 1965; articles and reviews in Modern Language Review, Review of English Studies, Library, Life and Letters To-day. *Recreations:* the Record Office and detective stories, playing the piano. *Address:* 167 New King's Road, Parsons Green, S.W.6. *Clubs:* Athenæum; Elizabethan (Yale).

[*Died* 28 *July* 1966.

SISSONS, Charles B., B.A., LL.D., F.R.S.C.; Professor Emeritus of Ancient History, Victoria College, University of Toronto; *b.* 4 Sept. 1879; 3rd *s.* of late Jonathan Sissons and Margaret Ann Shaver; *m.* 1913, Anna R. Normart, Glenolden, Pennsylvania; four *s.* *Educ.:* Barrie Collegiate Institute and University of Toronto. Entered University after a year spent in teaching; graduated in 1901 Edward Wilson medallist in Classics; taught in Chatham Collegiate Institute, 1902-4; Principal, High School at Revelstoke, B.C., 1904-8; recalled after a year at Oxford to his own college in 1909; Secretary of the Ontario Housing Committee, 1918-19. *Publications:* Bi-lingual Schools in Canada, 1917; Egerton Ryerson, His Life and Letters, vol. i, 1937, vol. ii, 1947; A History of Victoria University, 1952; My Dearest Sophie, Letters from Egerton Ryerson to His Daughter 1955; Church and State in Canadian Education, An Historical Study, 1959; The Memoirs of C. B. Sissons, 1964. *Recreations:* tennis, mountaineering, farming. *Address:* Newcastle, Ontario, Canada. [*Died* 27 *May* 1965.

SITWELL, Dame Edith, D.B.E. *cr.* 1954; Hon. Litt.D. (Leeds), 1948, Hon. D.Litt. (Durham), 1948, (Oxford), 1951, (Sheffield), 1955, (Hull), 1963; Hon. Associate, American Inst. of Arts and Letters, 1949; Visiting Professor Inst. Contemporary Arts, 1957; Vice-Pres., Royal Society of Literature, 19 8; C.Lit., 1963; *b.* Scarborough, *sister* of Sir Osbert Sitwell, 5th Bt., *q.v.*, and of Sacheverell Sitwell. *Educ.:* privately. Editor of Wheels, an annual anthology of modern verse, 1916. *Publications:* The Mother and other Poems, 1915; Clowns Houses; Bucolic Comedies; Sleeping Beauty; Wheels, 1916, 1917, 1918, and 1921; Elegy on Dead Fashion, 1926; Gold Coast Customs, 1929; Alexander Pope, 1930; Collected Poems, 1930; The Pleasures of Poetry, An Anthology, 2nd series, 1931; Bath, 1932; The English Eccentrics, 1933; Aspects of Modern Poetry, 1934; Victoria of England, 1936; I Live Under a Black Sun, 1937; (with Osbert Sitwell) 20th Century Harlequinade and other Poems; (with Osbert and Sacheverell Sitwell) Trio, 1938; Street Songs, 1942; A Poet's Notebook, 1943; Green Song, 1944; A Song of the Cold, 1945; Fanfare for Elizabeth, 1946 (film script, 1953); A Notebook on William Shakespeare, 1948; The Canticle of the Rose, 1949; Gardeners and Astronomers (poems), 1953; Collected Poems, 1954 (New York); Collected Poems, 1957; The Atlantic Book of English and American Poetry (anthology), 1958 (America), 1959 (England); Swinburne: A Selection, 1960; The Outcasts (poems), 1962; The Queens and the Hive, 1962. *Relevant publication:* Edith Sitwell: the Hymn to Life, 1961; *Posthumous publications:* Autobiography: Taken care of, 1965; Selected letters, 1970. *Recreations:* listening to music; silence. *Address:* c/o Macmillan & Co., Ltd., St. Martin's St., W.C.2.

[*Died* 9 *Dec.* 1964.

SITWELL, Sir Osbert, 5th Bt., *cr.* 1808; C.H. 1958; C.B.E. 1956; C.Lit. 1967; Hon. LL.D. St. Andrews, 1946; Hon. D.Litt. Sheffield, 1951; Hon. Associate of A.I.A.L., 1950; Hon. F.R.I.B.A. 1957; F.R.S.L.; poet, essayist, novelist, and writer of short stories and art criticism; a Trustee of the Tate Gallery, 1951-58; *b.* 3 Arlington Street, W., 6 Dec. 1892; *e.s.* of Sir George Sitwell, 4th Bt., and Lady Ida Emily Augusta Denison (*d.* 1937), *d.* of 1st Earl of Londesborough; *S.* father, 1943. *Educ.:* during the holidays from Eton. Grenadier Guards, 1912-19. For the past 30 years has conducted, in conjunction with his brother and sister, a series of skirmishes and hand-to-hand battles against the Philistine. Though outnumbered, has occasionally succeeded in denting the line, though not without damage to himself. Advocates compulsory Freedom everywhere, the suppression of Public Opinion in the interest of Free Speech, and the rationing of brains without which innovation there can be no true democracy. Chm. Management Cttee., Society of Authors, 1944-45, 1946-48 and 1951-52. Received the first Annual Award of the Sunday Times Prize and Gold Medal for literature for 1946-47. Has lectured extensively in public and private. *Publications:* Twentieth Century Harlequinade and other Poems (with Edith Sitwell), 1916; Argonaut and Juggernaut, 1919; The Winstonburg Line, 1919; Who Killed Cock Robin?, 1921; Out of the Flame, 1923; Triple Fugue, and other Stories, 1924; Discursions on Travel, Art and Life, 1925; Before the Bombardment, 1926; England Reclaimed, 1927; All at Sea (a play, with Sacheverell Sitwell), 1927; The People's Album of London Statues (with illustrations by Nina Hamnett), 1928; The Man who lost Himself, 1929; Sober Truth (with Margaret Barton), 1930; Dumb Animal and other stories, 1930; Victoriana (with Margaret Barton), 1931; Portrait of Michael Arlen, 1931; Collected Poems and Satires, 1931; Winters of Content, 1932; Dickens, 1932; Miracle on Sinai, 1933; Brighton (with Margaret Barton), 1935; Penny

Foolish, 1935; Those Were the Days, 1938; Trio (with Edith and Sacheverell Sitwell), 1938; Escape with Me, 1939; Two Generations, 1940; Open the Door, 1941; A Place of One's Own, 1941 (Filmed Gaumont British, 1944); Gentle Caesar (a play, with R. J. Minney); Selected Poems, 1943; Sing High! Sing Low!, 1944; A Letter to My Son, 1944. Autobiography: Vol. 1, Left Hand, Right Hand!, 1945; Vol. 2, The Scarlet Tree, 1946; Vol. 3, Great Morning, 1948; Vol. 4, Laughter in the Next Room, 1949; Vol. 5, Noble Essences, 1950. The True Story of Dick Whittington, 1946; Ed.: A Free House (The Writings of Walter Richard Sickert), 1947; Demos the Emperor (Poems); Death of a God (short stories), 1949; Wrack at Tidesend (Poems), 1952; Collected Short Stories, 1953; Four Continents, 1954; On the Continent (Poems), 1958; Fee Fi Fo Fum (modern Fairy Stories), 1959; Tales My Father Taught Me, 1962; Pound Wise (Collected Essays), 1963; Portraits of People, of England Reclaimed, 1965; and innumerable contributions to newspapers. *Recreations:* listening to the sound of his own voice, preferably on gramophone records and not answering letters *Heir:* b. Sacheverell Sitwell. *Address:* Castello di Montegufoni, 50020 Montagnana, Val di Pesa, Florence, Italy. *Club:* St. James'. [*Died* 4 *May* 1969. *See also Dame Edith Sitwell.*

SKELMERSDALE, 5th Baron, *cr.* 1828, of Skelmersdale; **Arthur George Bootle-Wilbraham,** M.C., late Captain R.E.; *b.* 21 May 1876; *s.* of late Arthur Bootle-Wilbraham and Elizabeth Jane, *e. d.* of John Jardine, Rockhampton, Qld.; *S.* to Barony of *cousin*, 3rd Earl of Lathom, 1930. Served European War, 1914-19 (M.C.). *Heir:* c. Brigadier Lionel Bootle-Wilbraham, D.S.O., M.C. *Address:* Greenacres, Anstye, Nr Haywards Heath, Sussex. [*Died* 9 *Feb.* 1969.

SKELTON, Major-General Dudley Sheridan, C.B. 1936; D.S.O. 1916; late R.A.M.C.; *b.* 1878; *s.* of George William Skelton; *m.* Charlotte Nancy (*d.* 1944), *d.* of M. G. Rooper, The Grange, Goring-on-Thames; one *s.*: *m.* 1948, Ursula Joyce, 2nd *d.* of late G. L. Shepherd, Nottingham. *Educ.:* Shrewsbury School; Bonn; London Hospital. M.R.C.S. (Eng.); L.R.C.P. (Lond.); D.P.H. (Lond.); Lieut. R.A.M.C. 1902; Capt. 1905; Major, 1914; Lt.-Col. 1924; Col. 1930; Maj.-Gen. 1933; Demonstrator, Adv. Bacteriology, Univ. Coll., London; Acting Sanitation Officer, Sierra Leone; Med. Officer Political Dept., Somaliland; Health Officer, Zanzibar; Medical Officer in charge anti-plague measures, Mombasa; Senior Sanitation Officer, Tanganyika Territory; Senior Medical Officer, Irak levies; served South Africa (Queen's medal and 5 clasps); Somaliland, 1908-10 (medal and clasp); served European War, 1914-18 (despatches, D.S.O., Bt. Lieut.-Colonel); operations in Kurdistan, 1925-26 (medal); Officiating Director of Medical Services in India, 1937; late Hon. Surg. to the Viceroy; Hon. Surgeon to the King, 1935-37; retired pay, 1937; re-employed in 1940 with rank of Colonel; War of 1939-44; Operations in Palestine, 1945-47 (Medal and clasp); retired finally 1947. A Senior Surgeon, P. & O. S.N. Co., 1938-40; acting Med. Supt. P. & O., Bombay, 1948-49; Surgeon Brit. India S.N. Co., 1949-1953; Clan Line, 1953-56. *Publications:* By Motor through Ceylon, 1903; This Amazing India, 1904; sundry professional papers. *Recreation:* travel. *Address:* Philpots Manor, Hildenborough, Kent. *Club:* Royal Bombay Yacht. [*Died* 2 *March* 1962.

SKIFFINGTON, Sir Donald Maclean, Kt., *cr.* 1949; C.B.E. 1939; J.P.; late Director, John Brown & Company, Ltd.; *b.* 1880; *s.* of James Skiffington, Kintyre; *m.* Jessie (*d.* 1955), *d.* of William Mackay, Kilbowie, Clydebank; one *s.*; *m.* Margaret, *d.* of Robert Douglas Thompson, Carlisle, Cumberland, and Johannesburg, S.A. *Educ.:* Clydebank High School; Glasgow Royal College of Science and Technology. Member Institution of Naval Architects and Institution of Engineers and Shipbuilders in Scotland. *Recreations:* music, natural history, fishing, motoring. *Address:* Whittingehame Gardens, Glasgow, W.2. *T.:* Western 1822. [*Died* 18 *Nov.* 1963.

SKINNER, Hon. Clarence Farringdon, M.C.; M.P. (N.Z.); Deputy Prime Minister of New Zealand and Minister of Agriculture and Lands, 1957-60; *b.* Melbourne, 19 Jan. 1900; *s.* of T. W. F. Skinner; *m.* 1924 (wife *d.* 1957); two *s.*; *m.* 1958. *Educ.:* Parnell School; Seddon Technical College, Auckland. Career in farming, contracting and bridge-building. M.P. Labour, Motueka, 1938-46, Buller, 1946-; Minister of Rehabilitation and Lands and Commissioner of State Forests, 1943-49; Deputy Leader of Opposition, 1951-. Served 2nd N.Z. Expeditionary Force, Middle East, 1940-43 (wounded, despatches, Major, M.C. 1943). *Address:* Parliament Buildings, Wellington, New Zealand. [*Died* 26 *April* 1962.

SKINNER, Colin Marshall, C.B.E. 1953; retired; until Sept. 1957, Senior Partner Jones, Crewdson & Youatt, Chartered Accountants, Manchester; *b.* 21 July 1882; 4th *s.* of Charles Gordon Lennox Skinner, M.D.; *m.* 1910, Martha Duckworth Shepherd; no *c.* *Educ.:* Manchester Gram. Sch. Hon. Treas., Manchester Royal Infirmary, 1929-48; Chairman United Manch., Hosps., 1948-53; Mem. Manch. Reg. Hosp. Bd., 1948-53; Mem. of Court, Manch. Univ., 1937-. Hon. LL.D. (Manchester) 1953. *Address:* Bentley House, Nether Alderley, Macclesfield, Cheshire. *T.:* Alderley Edge 2274. *Clubs:* Union; St. James's (Manchester). [*Died* 14 *Jan.* 1968.

SKINNER, Sir (Thomas) Hewitt, 2nd Bt., *cr.* 1912; President, Thomas Skinner & Co. (Publishers) Ltd. (Chm. of the company until Sept. 1964); *b.* 12 June 1875; *e. s.* of 1st Bt. and Sarah Margaret (*d.* 1902), *d.* of Jonas D. Hewitt; *S.* father, 1926; *m.* 1899, Nellie Constance (*d.* 1955), *d.* of James Hay Hall; one *s.* (and one killed in action Dieppe raid, 1942, S. H. Skinner, Wing Commander R.A.F.), two *d.* *Heir:* *s.* Thomas Gordon Skinner [*b.* 29 Dec. 1899; *m.* 1st, 1926, Mollie Barbara (marr. diss. 1953; she *d.* 1965), *d.* of H. W. Girling; three *s.*; 2nd, 1953, Jeanne Marie Louise, *d.* of François de Launoit, Brussels]. *Address:* Laburnum Cottage, The Common, Southwold, Suffolk. *Club:* Gresham. [*Died* 4 *Oct.* 1968.

SKIPWITH, Col. Frederick George, C.M.G. 1919; retired; *b.* Wokingham, Berks, 31 Aug. 1870; *s.* of Captain Grey Skipwith, R.N., and Fanny Elizabeth Tudor; *m.* 1903, Bertha Sylvia Chapman (*d.* 1944), Highland Park, near Chicago; no *c.*; *m.* 1954 Nora; (*widow* of Major Charles Hacket) (she *d.* 1958); *m.* 1963, Dorothea, (*widow* of Captain Arthur Townley Fulham), *Educ.:* Evelyns; Wellington Coll. Joined 4th Bn. Royal Warwickshire Regt., 1889; 1st Battalion, 1892; served Sudan Campaign, 1898; South African War and European War (despatches, C.M.G.). *Recreation:* fishing. *Address:* c/o Glyn, Mills & Co., Whitehall, S.W.1. [*Died* 29 *Jan.* 1964.

SKYRM, Llewellyn Sidgwick M., M.A.; C.A. (Dorset); *s.* of Thomas Skyrm, Pembroke, and Ellen Sidgwick, Grassington, Skipton, Yorks; *m.* Alice, *d.* of Thomas R. Hill, Bradford. *Educ.:* Skipton School; Trinity College, University of Dublin (M.A.). Assistant Master at Skipton School; Heckmondwike School; King Edward VII School, Sheffield; Headmaster, The Grammar School, Beaminster, 1916-33; Dorset C.C., 1929-52, C.A. 1952-64. Member, Incorporated Assoc. of

Headmasters; Licentiate, Coll. of Preceptors. *Recreation:* dialect. *Address:* Middlebrook, Beaminster, Dorset; Grassington, Skipton, Yorks. *T.A.:* Beaminster. *T.:* Beaminster 229. *Club:* County (Dorchester).
[*Died* 18 *Nov.* 1964.

SLADE, Sir Gerald Osborne, Kt., *cr.* 1948; **Hon. Mr. Justice Slade;** Judge of the High Court of Justice, King's Bench Division, since 1948; *b.* 14 Oct. 1891; *yr. s.* of late Sir James Benjamin Slade; *m.* 1917, Phyllis Mary, *y. d.* of Dr. John Wesley-Smith, Harrogate; four *d. Educ.:* Lindisfarne College, Westcliff; Bedford School; Trinity College, Cambridge. B.A. 1912; M.A. 1919; K.C. 1943. Bencher of the Middle Temple, 1948. Chairman of the General Council of the Bar, 1946-48; Chancellor of Diocese of Chelmsford, 1934-48, and of Southwark, 1944-48; Recorder of Tenterden, 1942-48. Member of Lord Chancellor's Committee on the Law of Defamation, 1939; Chairman of Legal Cttee. on Medical Partnerships appointed by Minister of Health, 1948. *Recreations:* tennis, golf, swimming. *Address:* Royal Courts of Justice, Strand, W.C.2. *T.:* Holborn 7641; The Close, St. Saviour's, Eastbourne. *T.:* Eastbourne 514.
[*Died* 10 *Feb.* 1962.

SLADE, Sir Michael Nial, 6th Bt., *cr.* 1831; Managing Director, Starkey, Knight & Ford, Ltd., since 1960; *b.* 30 July 1900; *S.* brother, Sir Alfred Slade, 5th Bt., 1960; *m.* 1928, Angela Clare Rosalind Chichester (*d.* 1959); one *s.* one *d.* (and *er. s.* decd.). *Educ.:* Cheltenham College; R.M.C., Sandhurst. Captain (retired), Somersetshire Light Infantry. *Recreations:* field sports. *Heir: s.* Benjamin Julian Alfred Slade, *b.* 22 May 1946. *Address:* Maunsel, North Petherton, Somerset. *T.:* North Petherton 500. *Club:* Somerset County (Taunton).
[*Died* 15 *April* 1962.

SLADE, Roland Edgar, M.C., D.Sc. (Victoria); Hon. D.Sc. (Dunelm); F.R.I.C.; *b.* 23 May 1886; *s.* of late Arthur Edgar and Ellen Slade; *m.* 1914, Muriel Alice, *d.* of late Joseph Phillips Bedson, M.I.C.E.; one *s.* two *d. Educ.:* Sandbach School; Manchester University. Lecturer in Physical Chemistry at Liverpool Univ., 1909-1913, at University Coll., London, 1914-18 Served European War, Royal Engineers (Capt.). Director of British Photographic Research Association, 1918-20; joined Brunner Mond & Co., 1920; Managing Director of Synthetic Ammonia & Nitrates Ltd., 1927-34, and Director of other subsidiary companies of I.C.I.; Controller of Research, I.C.I., 1935-45. Member Chemical Board, Min. of Supply, 1939-46; Treasurer of Faraday Society, 1939-49; Member Technical Committee for Atomic Energy, 1942-46; Sec. Chemical Council, 1944-45; Treasurer Royal Institution, 1946-52; Member Carpet Working Party of Board of Trade, 1946; Member of Steel Scrap Investigation Cttee., Ministry of Supply, 1948. Roy. Soc. of Arts Centenary Prize and Gold Medal, 1951; Pres., Section M., British Association, 1954. *Publications:* papers on chemistry and agriculture; (with Prof. S. J. Watson) The Feeding of Cattle, 1942. *Address:* Campions, Sheering Road, Harlow, Essex. *T.:* Old Harlow 2028. *Club:* Athenæum.
[*Died* 2 *Feb.* 1968.

SLADEN, Francis Farquhar, C.I.E. 1923; J.P. (Herts), 1928; Indian Civil Service (retired); *b.* 1875; 2nd *s.* of late Joseph Sladen, B.C.S., and late Mrs. Sladen, Wellbank, Sandbach, Cheshire; *m.* 1906, Mary (*d.* 1948), *d.* of Maj.-Gen. Bainbridge, I.S.C.; one *s. Educ.:* Charterhouse; Balliol College, Oxford. Joined Indian Civil Service, 1899; served in the United Provinces, 1899-1922; retired, 1925. *Address:* Town Farm, Wheathampstead, Herts. *T.:* Wheathampstead 2131.
[*Died* 17 *Sept.* 1970.

SLADEN, Commissioner Hugh Alfred Lambart; *b.* 9 Dec. 1878; *s.* of late Col. Joseph Sladen, R.A., and Lady Sarah Sladen, Ripple Court, Deal, and *g.s.* of 8th Earl of Cavan; *m.* 1916, Motee Booth Tucker, *d.* of late Frederick St. George de Latour Booth Tucker, and *g.d.* of Founder of the Salvation Army; one *s.* one *d.* (and one *s.* decd.). *Educ.:* Home, under tutorship of Prof. of Mathematics and Prof. of Classics. Entered Salvation Army as an Officer, 1897; inaugurated boys' organisation known as The Life Saving Scouts of the World, 1914; Freeman City of London, 1930; National Young People's Sec. for Great Britain, 1931; served in Finland as Territorial Comdr., 1939-42, during which period his wife was awarded White Rose of Finland in recognition of Relief Work. Director of European Relief Work of The Salvation Army under the British Red Cross, 1943; awarded Médaille de la Reconnaissance Française in recognition of Relief Work; Secretary of International Public Relations Bureau of the Salvation Army, 1946-48. World tour, Autumn 1948 - Spring 1949; tour Canada, United States, 1956. Is actively interested in Boy Scout work. *Recreations:* lectures on travel, Youth Welfare. *Address:* 44 Grove Way, Esher, Surrey. *T.:* Emberbrook 1908. *Club:* English-Speaking Union.
[*Died* 6 *May* 1962.

SLANEY, Major Robert O. R. K.; *see* Kenyon-Slaney.

SLANEY, Sybil A. K.; *see* Kenyon-Slaney.

SLATER, Samuel Henry, C.M.G. 1923; C.I.E. 1919; I.C.S., retired; *b.* 12 Jan. 1880; *s.* of late Rev. S. Slater, D.D.; *m.* 1st. 1904, Muriel Agnes, *d.* of late Canon. H. B. Streatfield (divorced, 1923); three *s.* one *d.*; 2nd, 1935, Violet, *d.* of Rev. F. H. Roach; one *d. Educ.:* King Edward VI Grammar School, Louth; Oxford Univ. (unattached). Entered the Indian Civil Service, 1904, and posted to Madras Presidency; Under-Secretary to the Govt. of Madras, 1910-1913; to Govt. of India, 1913-16; Deputy Secretary, 1917; Military Service, M.E.F., 1918; Financial Secretary to Civil Commissioner of Mesopotamia, 1919-1920; on loan to the Government of Iraq as Financial Adviser, 1921-24; Secretary to the Govt. of Madras Public Works Dept., 1926; Commissioner of Labour, Madras, 1927; Secretary to Govt., Madras, Development Dept., 1932; retired, 1935. *Address:* Beech Lawn, Guildford, Surrey. [*Died* 24 *Dec.* 1967.

SLATER, William Henry; Textile Technologist and Consultant; Publisher; Director of The Textile Weekly, Manchester, retd.; *b.* 26 May 1896; *s.* of Thomas Whittaker Slater and Sarah Ann Wood; unmarried. *Educ.:* Manchester University (B.Sc.); Municipal Technical College, Oldham. Licentiate of the Textile Institute (L.T.I.). Formerly Assistant to Sir C. W. Macara, Bt.; Statistician to the Cotton Yarn Association Ltd., Manchester; seven years' evening teaching experience (cotton spinning) at Oldham Municipal Technical College. *Publications:* Statistical Methods for Forecasting Raw Cotton Prices; numerous economic pamphlets in connection with the cotton trade. *Recreations:* Statistics and the Trade Cycle, motoring, reading. *Address:* Oberlin Cottage, Greenacres, Oldham. *T.:* Main 1117; 33 Blackfriars Street, Manchester 3. *Club:* Lyceum (Oldham).
[*Died* 31 *July* 1962.

SLATER, Sir William (Kershaw), K.B.E., *cr.* 1951; F.R.S. 1957; D.Sc., F.R.I.C.; retired; *b.* 19 Oct. 1893; *s.* of late James

Slater, Shaw, Lancs; *m.* 1921, Hilda (*d.* 1966), *e. d.* of late A. Whittenbury, Brooklands, Cheshire; two *s.* one *d.* *Educ.:* Hulme Gram., Sch., Oldham; Manchester Univ. (D.Sc.); University College, London; Hon. D.Sc. Belfast, 1952. Beit Memorial Medical Research Fellow, 1923; Senior Beit Fellow, 1927. Director of Research and of Agricultural Industries, Dartington Hall, Devon, 1929-42; seconded to Ministry of Agriculture, 1942-44; Senior Advisory Officer, Ministry of Agriculture, 1944-49. Sec., Agricultural Improvement Council, 1944-49; Sec., Agricultural Research Council, 1949-60; Pres., Royal Institute of Chemistry, 1961-1963; U.K. Representative on C.E.N.T.O. Scientific Council, 1961-; Chm. Colonial Development Corporation, Panel of Scientific Advisors, 1960-65; U.K. Co-ordinator for the U.N Confs. on the application of Science and Technology in the Less Developed Areas, 1960-63. Gen. Sec., British Assoc., 1962-65 Regent's Lectr., Davis Campus, Univ. of California, 1963; Cyril Foster Lecture, 1968; Spooner Lecture, 1969. *Publications:* Man Must Eat; various agricultural and scientific papers. *Recreation:* painting. *Address:* Two Oaks, Fittleworth, Sussex. *T.:* Fittleworth 332. *Club:* Athenæum. [*Died* 19 *April* 1970.

SLATOR, Instructor Captain Thomas, C.B. 1927; R.N. retired; *e. s.* of late Thomas Slator, Boston; *m.* 1918, Katherine, *d.* of late William Thatcher of Midsomer Norton, Somerset; two *s.* *Educ.:* Boston Grammar School; Pembroke College, Oxford (Scholar). Received commission as Naval Instructor in R.N., 1896; at sea, 1896-1901; H.M.S. Britannia, 1902-5; at sea, 1905-8; H.M.S. Cornwall, 1908-13; R.N. College, Greenwich, 1913-14; R.N. College, Osborne 1914-15; R.N.A.S., 1915-18; Admiralty, 1919-27; Deputy Inspector of Naval Schools, Admiralty, 1922-27; recalled for service, 1941-1945. *Recreation:* cycling. *Address:* Arrochar, Holt, Norfolk. [*Died* 20 *Dec.* 1961.

SLATTER, Air Marshal Sir Leonard Horatio, K.B.E., *cr.* 1942 (O.B.E. 1920); C.B. 1941; D.S.O. and bar; D.F.C.; D.L.; retd.; *b.* Durban, S.A., 8 Dec. 1894; *m.* Cecil Nancy Ashwin, *e. d.* of Col. C. M. Davies, D.S.O., Harlow, Essex; two *s.* one *d.* *Educ.:* Dale College, S. Africa. Formed and commanded R.A.F. High Speed Flight, 1926-1927, captaining R.A.F. team Schneider Race, Venice, 1927; flew Solo England-S. Africa, 1929; commanded Nos. 19, 111, and 43 Fighter Squadrons, 1929-31; Senior R.A.F. Officer H.M.S. Courageous, 1932-35; served War of 1939-45 (C.B., K.B.E.); commanded R.A.F. in Eritrea/Abyssinia Campaign, 1940-41; commanded No. 201 (Naval Co-operation Group), Middle East, 1942; commanded No. 15 Group, 1943; A.O.C.-in-C. Coastal Command, 1945-48. D.L. (Bedfordshire), 1951. 2nd Class, Order of St. Stanislaus (Russia), 1919; 1st Class, Order of St. George (Greece), 1946. *Address:* The Mallowry, Riseley, Beds. *Club:* International Sportsmen's. [*Died* 14 *April* 1961.

SLAUGHTER, Lieut.-Col. Reginald Joseph, C.M.G. 1919; D.S.O. 1916; *b.* 28 April 1874; 3rd *s.* of William Edmund Slaughter; *m.* 1927, Gladys Elizabeth, *o. d.* of T. W. Pessell of Crapstone, Yelverton. *Educ.:* St. Augustine's Coll., Ramsgate; St. Mary's College, Oscott. Commissioned from Lt. Volunteer Service Coy. of the "Buffs" into S. Lancashire Regt. 1900; Lt., 1901; Capt., 1905; Maj., 1914; Lt.-Col., 1922; Adj. T.F. 1912-14; D.A., Q.M.G. 42nd Div., 1914-15; D.A.A. and Q.M.G. 8th Army Corps, 1915; A.A. and Q.M.G. 42nd Div., 1915-1919; A.A. and Q.M.G. Midland Div., 1919; rtd. pay, 1923; served S. African War, 1900-2 (King's and Queen's S. African medal); served European War, 1914-19 (despatches six times, D.S.O., C.M.G., Bt. Lt.-Col.); Egyptian Expeditionary Force, 1916; operations in France, 1917-18 *Address:* Flat 2, Winchester House, Folkestone, Kent. [*Died* 8 *March* 1968.

SLEE, Frederick Abraham, C.B. 1938; late Commissioner of Inland Revenue; late Secretary, Board of Inland Revenue; *b.* 1882; *s.* of late Charles Slee, Manchester; *m.* 1914, Elaine, *d.* of late James Fleming, I.S.O. Hampstead; two *d.* *Educ.:* Manchester Grammar School; Pembroke College, Oxford. Entered Civil Service, 1906; retired, 1945. *Address:* 3 Heath Close, Hampstead Way, N.W.11. [*Died* 6 *Oct.* 1963.

SLEEMAN, Col. Sir James Lewis, Kt. 1946; C.B. 1936; C.M.G. 1921; C.B.E. 1919; M.V.O. 1920; T.D. 1944; D.L. 1953; Kt. Sovereign Mil. Order of Malta; K.J.St.J. Ven. Order; Kt. Comdr. Equestrian Order of the Holy Sepulchre, with star, 1933; Orders of: Sacred Treasure of Japan; Excellent Crop of China; Order of Mercy and Bar; Service Medal of the Order of St. John; for Conspicuous Service, Freedom of the City of London; M.A. (Hon.); F.R.G.S.; J.P.; late Royal Sussex Regt.; Comdr. of 160th (South Wales) Inf. Brigade T.A. 1931-35; *s.* of Capt. H. A. Sleeman, 16th (Queen's) Lancers, Pool Park, St. Tudy, Cornwall, and *g.s.* of Major General Sir William Sleeman, K.C.B., Suppressor of Thuggee in India; *b.* 7 Mar. 1880; *m.* 1908, Frances Mary, D.St.J., Order of Mercy and Bar (*d.* 1960), *o. c.* of David Howell, J.P.; two *s.* one *d.* (and one *s.* decd.). Entered Army, 1899; Lt.-Col. 1917; Col. 1930; Brigade Comdr. 1931; served South African War; European War in France and Flanders; Attaché to Japanese Fleet on War Service, 1916-18 (despatches twice); Imperial General Staff and Dir. Military Training, 1916-18, N.Z. Forces and Lieut.-Col. on Imperial General Staff, 1916-1921; Chief of Staff N.Z. Forces, 1919-21; Officer-in-Charge, Air Services, N.Z. Forces, 1916-19; on General Staff, and formed first contingents of O.T.C. in Ireland, 1909-20; on personal staff Prince of Wales throughout N.Z. visit, 1920; rep. Duke of Connaught on Visitation to Order of St. John Establishments in South Africa, Rhodesia, New Zealand, and Australia, 1935-36; also during inspectional tour of Canada, 1929, and India, Burma, Malaya, Hong Kong, Ceylon, Kenya, Uganda, Tanganyika, Zanzibar, South Africa, Malta and St. Helena, 1936-38, and the Order of St. John in West Indies, Bermuda, West Africa, Egypt, Palestine and Cyprus during 1945: Malta and Gibraltar, 1947; Hong Kong, Malta, Singapore and Malaya, 1949. County Commissioner Boy Scouts Herefordshire (silver wolf and Belgian medal); Chief Commissioner St. John Ambulance Brigade Overseas, 1930-50. County Comr., Gloucestershire, Order of St. John, until 1960. Hon. Colonel 602, H.A.A. Regiment, Royal Artillery, 1935-50. Commandant Gloucestershire Special Constabulary, 1939-48; Member Joint War Organisation Red Cross Society and Order of St. John, 1941-45. *Publications:* Tales of a Shikari; Thug or a Million Murders; La Secte secrète des Thugs; From Rifle to Camera; various books on Military Training. *Address:* Ludloes, Painswick, Gloucestershire. *T.:* Painswick 3253. [*Died* 4 *Nov.* 1963.

SLEEMAN, John Herbert, M.A. (Cantab.); Professor Emeritus of Classics in London Univ. (Prof., 1922-46); *b.* Bristol, 4 Feb. 1880; *m.* 1918, Dorothy, B.A., *y. d.* of Mrs. William Thorpe, of Chesterfield, Derbyshire; no *c.* *Educ.:* Bristol Grammar School; Sidney Sussex College, Cambridge. Stewart of Rannoch University Scholar, 1898; First Class Classical Tripos, Part I., 1901; Part II. (Ancient Philosophy), 1902; Fellow Sidney Sussex Coll. 1903; Sec. Classical Assoc. 1908-13; Examiner for

Classical Tripos, 1909-12; Lecturer in Latin at Sheffield University, 1909; Lecturer in Philosophy, 1915; Lecturer in Classics at the Royal Holloway College for Women, 1918. *Publications:* Herodotus, Book I., 1909; Cæsar in Britain and Belgium (simplified text), 1912; Tacitus, Agricola and Germania, 1914; contributions to the Year's Work in Classical Studies, the Classical Quarterly, the Classical Review, Journal of Hellenic Studies and Trans. of Society for the Study of Religions. *Address:* 3 Chywoone Grove, Newlyn, Penzance, Cornwall. *T.:* Mousehole 295. [*Died* 4 *Jan.* 1963.

SLIM, 1st Viscount, *cr.* **1960; Field-Marshal William Joseph Slim,** K.G. 1959; G.C.B. 1950 (K.C.B. 1944; C.B. 1944); G.C.M.G. 1952; G.C.V.O. 1954; G.B.E. 1946 (C.B.E. 1942); D.S.O. 1943; M.C.; LL.D. (Hon.) Leeds, Birm., Cantab., Sydney, Adelaide, Melbourne; D.C.L. (Hon.) Oxon.; D.Lit. (Hon.) New England, N.S.W.; D.Sc. (Hon.) N.S.W.; F.R.A.C.P. (Hon.); F.R.C.S. Ed. (Hon.); late I.A.; Constable and Gov. of Windsor Castle, 1964-70 (Lieut.-Gov., 1963-1964); *b.* 6 Aug. 1891; *s.* of John Slim, Bristol; *m.* 1926, Aileen, *d.* of Rev. J. A. Robertson, M.A., Edinburgh; one *s.* one *d.* *Educ.:* King Edward's Sch., Birmingham. Served European War, R. Warwickshire Regt., Gallipoli (wounded), France, Mesopotamia (wounded, M.C.); joined 6th Gurkha Rifles, Indian Army; Instructor Staff College, Camberley, 1934-36; Imperial Defence College; Commandant 2nd Bn. 7th Gurkha Rifles; Commandant Senior Officers School, India; War of 1939-45 commanded 10th Infantry Brigade, Sudan, Eritrea (wounded); 10th Indian Division Syria-Persia-Iraq (D.S.O.); commanded 1st Burma Corps, Burma (C.B.E.); commanded 15 Indian Corps (C.B.); commanded Fourteenth Army (K.C.B.); C.-in-C. Allied Land Forces, S.E. Asia, 1945-46; Commandant Imperial Defence College, 1946-47; Chief of Imperial General Staff, 1948-52; Governor-General and Commander in Chief of Australia, 1953-60. Colonel: 7th Gurkha Rifles, 1944-1956; The West Yorkshire Regt., 1947-56; 1st Gurkha Rifles (Indian Army), 1949-56. Deputy Chairman, Railway Executive, 1948. Dep. Chm., Railway Executive, 1948. Director: London Assurance; Dalgety and New Zealand Loan Ltd. (President, 1965); Edger Investments (Dep. Chm.); Imperial Chemical Industries, 1960-66; Mem., London Board of Advice, National Bank of Australasia, 1960; Chairman: British Home Entertainment Ltd.; British Australian Investment Trust Ltd. *Publications:* Defeat into Victory, 1956; Courage and Other Broadcasts, 1957; Unofficial History, 1959. *Relevant Publication:* Slim as Military Commander, by Sir G. C. Evans, 1969. *Heir:* *s.* Lt.-Col. Hon. John Douglas Slim [*b.* 20 July 1927; *m.* 1958, Elizabeth, *d.* of Rawdon Spinney; two *s.* one *d.*]. *Address:* c/o Lloyds Bank Ltd., 6 Pall Mall, S.W.1. *Clubs:* Athenæum, Naval and Military. [*Died* 14 *Dec.* 1970.

SLOAN, Alfred Pritchard, Jun.; Honorary Chairman, General Motors Corporation, New York, 1937-56; President Alfred P. Sloan Foundation, New York; *b.* New Haven, Connecticut, 23 May 1875; *s.* of Alfred Pritchard and Katherine Mead; *m.* 1898, Irene Jackson; no *c.* *Educ.:* Massachusetts Institute of Technology, Cambridge, Mass. Engineer B.Sc. Mass. Inst. Tech., 1895. President and General Manager Hyatt Roller Bearing Co., 15 yrs.; Pres. United Motors Corp., 3 yrs.; Pres. General Motors Corp., 12 yrs.; Chairman, General Motors Corp., 1937-56; Chairman, Sloan-Kettering Institute for Cancer Research, 1945-58. Politics: Republican. LL.D. Princeton Univ., 1946. Holds 12 other hon. degrees from Universities and Colleges in the U.S.A. *Address:* (home) 82 Fifth Avenue, New York, N.Y., U.S.A. *T.:* Templeton 8-1810, N.Y. *Clubs:* Knickerbocker, University, Metropolitan Union (N.Y.); Turf and Field (L.I.). [*Died* 17 *Feb.* 1966.

SLOANE, Mary Annie, A.R.E.; Member of the Leicester Society of Artists; President Women's Guild of Arts, 1953. Studied art at Leicester, at Bushey under Prof. Herkomer, R.A., and Royal College of Art under Sir Frank Short, R.A. Painter of portraits, landscapes, gardens, children, old-time cottage craft workers—Huguenot silk weavers at Bethnal Green, Leicestershire stockingers, Buckinghamshire pillow lace makers, and others; Painter-etcher; hon. mention Paris Salon, 1903; Exhibitor, R.A. Salon, etc. *Publications:* contributor to English Illustrated Magazine, Reliquary, etc. *Address:* 8 Hammersmith Terrace, W.6. *T.:* Riverside 4823; The Nook, Enderby, Leicestershire. *T.:* Narborough 3335. [*Died* 29 *Nov.* 1961.

SLOCOMBE, George Edward; author, journalist and war correspondent; *b.* 8 March 1894; *e. s.* of Edward John and Esther Ann Slocombe; *m.* Marie Karlinskaya; one *s.* two *d.* *Educ.:* Merchant Venturers Tech. College, Bristol. Joined editorial staff Daily Herald, 1912, Daily Chronicle, 1914; served with R.A.F. 1916-1919; News Editor, Daily Herald, 1919, subsequently Chief Foreign Correspondent until 1931; Pres. Anglo-American Press Association of Paris, 1927; publicly commended by three British Cabinet Ministers for despatches from Hague Conference, 1929; mentioned in Govern. White Paper, 1930, for having initiated gaol negotiations with Gandhi which led to Irwin-Gandhi Pact of Delhi and subsequent appearance of Gandhi at Second Round Table Conference; Special Correspondent of Evening Standard, 1931; Foreign Editor, 1932-34; Commentator on foreign affairs for Sunday Express, 1940-44, subsequently war correspondent; joined Daily Mail as Special correspondent, 1945; news commentator in B.B.C. Empire Service; has frequently lectured in America on world affairs. *Publications:* A History of Poland, 1916 (reprinted 1939); Gaucheries (verse), 1922; Paris in Profile, 1928; Henry of Navarre, 1931; Dictator (novel), 1932; The Heart of France, 1934; Crisis in Europe, 1934; Don John of Austria, 1935; The Tumult and the Shouting (autobiography), 1936; Men in Arms (novel), 1936; The Dangerous Sea: a Study of the Mediterranean, 1936; A Mirror to Geneva, 1937; Rebels of Art: Manet to Matisse, 1939; Escape into the Past (novel), 1943; Conquest of the Mediterranean, 1943; William the Conqueror, 1959; Sons of the Conqueror, 1960. Contributor to Saturday Evening Post, Esquire and other periodicals. *Recreation:* landscape painting. *Clubs:* Savage, Press. [*Died* 19 *Dec.* 1963.

SLOMAN, Harold Newnham Penrose, M.C., M.A. Oxon; J.P. (ret.); *b.* 22 Apr. 1885; *s.* of late Rev. A. Sloman, M.A., Headmaster of Birkenhead Sch., later Hon. Canon of Ely; *m.* 1912, Mary (*d.* 1959), *er. d.* of A. Probus Trinder, M.R.C.S., L.R.C.P.; one *s.* *Educ.:* Rugby Sch. (Classical Schol.); Balliol College, Oxford (Classical Scholar). 1st Class Classical Moderations, 1906; 1st Class Literae Humaniores, 1908; Classical Fifth and Sixth Form Master, Radley College, 1908-12; Headmaster of the Sydney Grammar School, 1913-20; head of Modern Side and Modern Sixth Form Master, Rugby School, 1921-22; Headmaster Tonbridge School, 1922-39; work in Sydney on the Censorship Staff, 1916; Active Service (The Rifle Brigade), 1916-19 (wounded Aug. 1917, M.C.); work in Ministry of Economic Warfare, 1940-41; Home Guard, 1940; temp. Assistant Master, St. Paul's School, 1941-

1947; Educational Adviser to the British Council and the British Community Council of Argentina, 1947-49; temp. Assistant Master, Charterhouse, 1950-54. *Publications:* Six Contes: G. de Maupassant, 1914 (Cambridge Modern French Series); Boule de Suif and other Stories of Guy de Maupassant (Penguin Classics), 1946; Miss Harriet and other stories of Guy de Maupassant (Penguin Classics), 1951; The Monuntain Inn and other stories of Guy de Maupassant (Penguin Classics), 1955; Bel-Ami, Guy de Maupassant (Penguin Classics), 1961; Cæsar's Civil War, Books I and II, 1923; contributor to The Headmaster Speaks, 1936. *Recreations:* tennis, racquets, fives, cricket, mountaineering. *Address:* 13 Priory Mansions, Drayton Gardens, S.W.10. *Clubs:* Athenæum, Alpine. [*Died* 25 *July* 1965.

SMAIL, James Cameron, O.B.E.; LL.D.; D.Sc.; F.H.W.C.; F.R.S.E.; F.R.S.G.S.; Comp. I.E.E.; Hon. Member Merchant Company and Chamber of Commerce, Edinburgh; *b.* Edinburgh, 1880; 2nd *s.* of late Adam Smail, Edinburgh; *m.* 1908, Louisa Florence, *e. d.* of late Alexander Davidson, Winnipeg; one *s.* two *d.* *Educ.:* Daniel Stewart's College, Edinburgh; Heriot-Watt College, Edinburgh; Royal College of Science, London; London School of Economics. Brush Electrical Engineering Co., Ltd; Carrick and Ritchie, Ltd., Engineers; Whitworth Exhibitioner; Royal Exhibitioner; Inspector Dept. of Agriculture and Technical Instruction (Ireland), 1902-1911; Organiser of Trade Schools, L.C.C., 1911-1919; Head of Technology Branch, and Asst Education Officer (Technology), L.C.C., 1919-28; Dist. Manager Metropolitan Munitions Cttee., 1915-18; Manager for L.C.C. manufacture of munitions and training of munition workers, 1915-18; Principal Heriot-Watt College, Edinburgh, 1928-50; Chairman of Council, Assoc. of Technical Institutions, 1931-32; Member of Departmental Committee on Overseas Students, 1933-34; Chairman of Council, Royal Scottish Geographical Society, 1934-38; President of Association of Principals of Technical Institutions, 1938-39; Vice-Pres. Royal Society of Edinburgh, 1937-40; Member of Advisory Council of Scottish Education Department, 1930-46; Hon. Mem. Royal Scottish Soc. of Arts (Pres. 1950-53); Member Royal Fine Art Commission for Scotland, 1944-64. *Publications:* Reports and papers on Technical Education etc. *Address:* 1 Grange Terrace, Edinburgh. [*Died* 26 *April* 1970.

SMALL, Professor James, D.Sc., Ph.D., M.I.C.E., M.I.Mech.E.; James Watt Professor of Mechanical Engineering, 1951-65 (formerly of Theory and Practice of Heat Engines, from 1938) in the University of Glasgow; Professor Emeritus; Director, James Watt Laboratories, 1953-65; *s.* of Alexander C. D. Small and Mary Wilkie; *m.* 1942, Eleanor R. Weir, M.A., *d.* of Rev. Dr. T. H. Weir; one *s.* one *d.* *Educ.:* Allan Glen's School; University of Glasgow. B.Sc., 1920 (Glasgow); Lecturer in Engineering, University of Glasgow, 1920; Professor of Theory and Practice of Heat Engines, 1938; Member Glasgow University Court, 1953-61; Past Pres., The Royal Philosophical Soc. of Glasgow; Past Pres. Instn. of Engineers and Shipbuilders in Scotland; Moderator in Mechanical Engineering for the University of London 1959-64; Past Dir., Laurel Bank Sch. *Address:* 245 Wilton St., Glasgow, N.W. *T.:* 946 5316. [*Died* 9 *Jan.* 1968.

SMALLWOOD, Oliver Daniel, C.B.E. 1938; T.D.; D.L. Warwick; Hon. Air Commodore, A.A.F.; Hon. Brigadier T.A.; *b.* 23 May 1889; *m.* 1920, Gladys Maude, *d.* of G. W. Parker; two *s.* *Educ.:* Blanquettes, Worcester. *Address:* Amesbury Road, Moseley, Birmingham. *T.:* South 3622. [*Died* 4 *June* 1962.

SMART, Archibald Guelph Holdsworth, C.M.G. 1941; M.B.E.; M.D.; D.P.H.; *b.* 13 Feb. 1882; *s.* of late Andrew Smart, LL.D., M.D., Edinburgh, and late Clara Wellington Holdsworth, Worcester; *m.* 1921, Ina Fanny Dickin, *d.* of late Albert Victor Cowley, Felbridge, Sussex; no *c.* *Educ.:* George Watson's College; Edinburgh University. House Surgeon, Royal Infirmary, Edinburgh; Colonial Medical Service, in Malaya, 1912-34, and in the British West Indies, 1935-38; served European War in France, 1915-19 (M.B.E., Croix de Guerre); Assistant Medical Adviser to Sec. of State for Colonies, 1938-40; U.K. Representative on U.N.R.R.A. Far Eastern Sub-Committee on Health, 1944; on a special mission to British Far Eastern territories on behalf of the Colonial Office, 1945-46; late Medical Adviser to Sec. of State for the Colonies; Vice-Chm., Colonial Advisory Medical Committee; F.R.S.H. *Publications:* various scientific articles. *Recreations:* golf, fishing, bowls. *Address:* P.O. Box 81, Richmond, Natal, South Africa. *Club:* Victoria (Pietermaritzburg). [*Died* 20 *May* 1964.

SMART, D. I.; *see* Addenda: II.

SMART, Lt.-Gen. Edward Kenneth, D.S.O. 1919; M.C.; Company Director; *b.* 23 May 1891; *s.* of E. A. Smart, St. Kilda, Melbourne; *m.* 1915, Phylis Evelyn (*decd.*), *d.* of Lt.-Col. J. E. Robertson; one *s.* one *d.*; *m.* 1953, Marjorie, *d.* of Dr. Charles W. Gordon, Winnipeg. *Educ.:* Melbourne Church of England Grammar School. Served European War, France and Flanders, 1915-18 (despatches, M.C., D.S.O.); Director of Ordnance Services, 1933-35; Military Liaison Officer, High Commissioner's Office, London, 1936-39; Quartermaster-General, A.M.F. 1939-40; G.O.C. Southern Command, Australia, 1940-41; head of Australian Military Mission to U.S.A., 1942; Australian Army Representative in U.K., 1942-46; Australian Consul-General in San Francisco, 1946-49; Australian Consul-General in New York, 1949-54, retired. *Address:* Banff, 3 Charnwood Crescent, St. Kilda, Melbourne, Victoria, Australia. *Club:* Naval and Military (Melbourne). [*Died* 2 *May* 1961.

SMART, Sir Walter Alexander, K.C.M.G., *cr.* 1942; *b.* 12 Nov. 1883; *s.* of late Col. A. W. Smart and Fanny Kairns; *m.* 1931, Amy, *d.* of Dr. Fares Nimr Pasha. *Educ.:* Clifton College; Jesus College, Cambridge. Entered Levant Consular Service, 1903; served in Persia, Morocco, U.S.A., Greece, Syria, Egypt; Oriental Secretary at Tehran, 1920-22; Oriental Secretary, Cairo, 1926; Oriental Counsellor, Cairo, 1929-1945; Oriental Minister to British Embassy, Cairo, 1945; ret. Silver Jubilee Medal, 1935. *Clubs:* St. James'; Mohamed Aly (Cairo). [*Died* 11 *May* 1962.

SMART, Wilfred Wilmot, C.I.E. 1935; B.A. (Oxon.); *b.* 10 Jan. 1876; *s.* of John Smart and Emma Jane Dallow; *m.* 1906, Katie Sybil Sutherland; one *s.* *Educ.:* Dulwich College; New College, Oxford. 1st cl. Litt. Hum. Oxon, 1899; Dipl. of Agriculture (Cantab.); appointed Assistant Collector and Magistrate, Bombay Presidency, 1900; Assistant Political Agent, Baluchistan, 1905; Director of Agriculture, Bombay Presidency, 1911; Collector and District Magistrate, 1915; Commissioner of Revenue, 1928-35; retired. Fell. Roy. Commonwealth Society. *Recreation:* golf. *Address:* Flat 12, 31 St. Peter's Cres., Bournemouth, Hants. *Club:* Roy. Over-Seas League. [*Died* 18 *Oct.* 1961.

SMELLIE, Elizabeth Lawrie, C.B.E. 1934; R.R.C.; retd. 1948; *b.* 22 March 1884; *d.* of Thomas Stuart Traill Smellie and Janet Eleanor Lawrie. *Educ.:* Port Arthur High School; St. Margaret's College, Toronto. Graduate Johns Hopkins Training School for Nurses, Baltimore, U.S.A.; Overseas Canadian

Army Nursing Service, 1915; returned to Canada, 1918, as Asst. to Matron-in-Chief in the Director-General's Office; Post-graduate training Public Health Nursing, Simmons Coll., Boston, 1920-21; Assistant to Director School for Graduate Nurses McGill University, Montreal, part time with Montreal Branch Victorian Order, 1921-24; to Europe under auspices Rockefeller Foundation to study Maternal Welfare, 1932; Mary Agnes Snively Memorial Medal, 1938. Col. (Matron-in-Chief), Royal Canadian Army Medical Corps Nursing Service, 1940-44; assisted in organising Canadian Women's Army Corps, 1941; Chief Superintendent Victorian Order of Nurses for Canada, 1924-47; Dept. Veterans' Affairs, 1947-1948; former Member Dominion Council of Health. Hon. LL.D. Univ. of Western Ontario, 1942. *Address:* Central Park Lodge, 10 William Morgan Drive, Toronto 17, Ont., Canada. *Clubs:* Chelsea (Ottawa); Toronto Ladies (Toronto).

[*Died March* 1968.

SMELLIE, Professor James Maclure, O.B.E. 1944; T.D. 1950; M.D., F.R.C.P.; Emeritus Professor of Pædiatrics and Child Health, Birmingham University, 1958 (Professor, 1946-58); Consultant in Child Health, Birmingham Regional Hospital Board, 1959; Member Midland Region Medical Appeal Tribunal; Honorary Consulting Pædiatrician, Birmingham United Hosp., 1959; Col. R.A.M.C. (T.A.R.O.) ret.; *b.* 19 May 1893; *s.* of late Alderman J. Smellie, M.B.E., J.P.; *m.* 1929, Kathleen Lamsdale; two *s.* *Educ.:* Dumfries Acad.; Edinburgh Univ. M.B., Ch.B. Edin. 1916; M.D. Edin. 1920; F.R.C.P. Lond. 1932. Captain R.A.M.C., 1916-20; Physician, Birmingham Children's Hospital, 1922-52; Physician, Birmingham General Hospital, 1924-46; Consulting Physician, Roy. Cripples' Hosp., Birmingham, 1930; Lecturer, Pharmacology and Therapeutics, 1925-46, and Lecturer Clinical Med. and Diseases of Children, 1924-1946, Birmingham Univ.; Lt.-Col. R.A.M.C. (T.A.), 1939; Colonel A.M.S., 1944; Brig., Cons. Physician, India, 1944. Pres., Sect. of Pædiatrics, Roy. Soc. Med., 1948; Pres. Brit. Pædiatric Assoc., 1952-53; Member Bd. of Govs., Birmingham United Hosps., 1953-58; Chm., Birmingham Area Nurse Training Cttee., 1952-60; Life Governor, Univ. of Birmingham, 1960. *Publications:* Ingleby Lectures (Birmingham Univ.), 1939. Contrib. to: Parsons and Barling, Diseases of Children, 1933; Modern Trends in Pædiatrics, 1950. Papers to Lancet, Proc. Roy. Soc. Med., Archives of Disease in Childhood, etc. *Recreation:* golf. *Address:* Wood End Lodge, Hockley Heath, Solihull, Warwickshire. *T.:* Tanworth-in-Arden 234.

[*Died* 3 *April* 1961.

SMETERLIN, Jan; Concert Pianist; *b.* Bielsko, Poland, 7 Feb. 1892; *m.* 1925, Edith Mannaberg. *Educ.:* Vienna Masterschool and University. Has toured Europe, United States, S. America, Far East, Australia, New Zealand. First performances of Szymanowski (including Symphonie Concertante with Royal Philharmonic Society, 1933), Dukas, Koechlin, Mompou, etc. Recent appearances Festival Hall, Chopin Recital, Feb. 1958 and May 1959; Recitals in Lincoln Center, New York City, Holland, Germany, London Festival Hall, 1963-64; Concerts in Holland, Switzerland, England, 1965; London Festival Hall, Chopin recital, 1966; Geneva 3 times; Zurich; Lincoln Center, N.Y.C., Boston, Mass.; Holland; Pitlochry Festival. *Address:* 7 St. Mary Abbots Place, W.8. *T.:* Empress 7046.

[*Died* 18 *Jan.* 1967.

SMIDDY, Professor Timothy A., M.A.; D.Econ.Sc.; Director, Central Bank of Ireland, 1943-55; Chairman of Free State Trade Loans Committee, 1933-57; Chm. of Cttee. of Inquiry in Post-Emergency Agricultural Policy, 1947-57; member of Institute for Industrial Research and Standards, 1946-55; Chairman and Managing Director of the Arklow Pottery, Ire., 1946-59; *b.* Cork, 30 Apr. 1875; *s.* of William Smiddy, Kilbarry House, Cork; *m.* 1900, Lilian, *d.* of Cornelius O'Connell, Cork; one *s.* five *d.* *Educ.:* St. Finbarr's College, Cork; Queen's College, Cork; St. Sulpice, Issy-sur-Seine; Paris; Handelshochschule, Cologne. M.A., R.U.I. Professor of Economics, Warden, Honan Hostel, and Dean of the Faculty of Commerce, University College, Cork, 1909-24; Hon. Professor of University College, Cork; sometime appointed Member of Trade Boards, Ireland; Economic Adviser to Irish Plenipotentiaries, Anglo-Irish Treaty, Dec. 1921; Envoy and Fiscal Agent of Dail Eireann to the United States, 1922-24; Chairman of the Fiscal Committee, Irish Free State, 1923; Envoy Extraordinary and Minister Plenipotentiary of the Irish Free State at Washington, D.C., 1924-29; High Commissioner for the Irish Free State in London, 1929-30; Delegate from Irish Free State to London Naval Conference, 1930; member of Irish Free State Tariff Commission, 1930-33; Chairman of Commission on Agriculture, 1939-45; Chairman of: Summer Time Cttee., 1940-56. *Publications:* various contributions on educational and economic subjects. *Recreation:* music. *Address:* 81 Merrion Road, Dublin. [*Died* 9 *Feb.* 1962.

SMILEY, Norman Bryce; Managing Director, Arthur Guinness Son & Co. Ltd., since 1967; *b.* 30 March 1909; *s.* of Thomas Bryce Smellie and Edith Anne (*née* Bardsley); *m.* 1936, Elsie Marion Steen; two *s.* two *d.* *Educ.:* Denstone; New Coll., Oxford (Open Schol.). Joined Guinness, 1931; Exec. Dir., 1942; Jt. Man. Dir. (Park Royal Co.), 1956. Governor: Sir John Cass Foundn., 1950-; Ashridge Management College, 1964-. Mem. Coun., London and S.E. Region of F.B.I., 1947-65 (Chm., 1964-65); Chm., London and S.E. Regional Coun. of C.B.I., 1965-66; Mem. Coun., C.B.I., 1965-. Mem., British Egg Marketing Bd., 1957-; Mem. Coun., Brewers' Soc., 1944-; Chm. Research Bd., Inst. of Brewing, 1952-62; Pres., Inst. of Brewing, 1966-68; Vice-Pres., European Brewing Convention, 1963- (Mem. Coun., 1948-); Mem., Arton Wilson Cttee. (Min. of Agric.), 1954-1956. *Recreations:* golf, tennis, swimming, ski-ing, reading. *Address:* Upton Leigh, Beaconsfield, Bucks. *Club:* Athenæum.

[*Died* 8 *Oct.* 1968.

SMITH, Sir Alan R.; *see* Rae Smith.

SMITH, Prof. Albert Hugh, O.B.E. 1947; B.A., Ph.D., D.Lit.; F.S.A.; Quain Professor of English Language and Literature, University College, London, since 1949; *b.* 24 Feb. 1903; *s.* of late A. J. Smith and late Anne Smith, Sowerby, Yorks; *m.* 1928, Helen Penelope, *d.* of late C. H. Tomlinson and late Lucy Tomlinson; one *s.* one *d.* *Educ.:* Rishworth School, Yorks; University of Leeds. B.A. (Leeds) 1924, Ph.D. (Leeds) 1926, D.Lit. (Lond.) 1937. Vaughan Fellow, Univ. of Leeds, 1924-26; Lectr. in English, Saltley Coll., Birmingham, 1926-28; English Lecturer, Uppsala Univ., 1928-30; Lecturer, 1930-34, Reader in English, 1934-1949, Dir. of Scandinavian Studies, 1946-63, Univ. Coll., London; Dir. of the English Place-Name Society, 1951-; President: Internat. Conf. of Scandinavian Literature, 1963-66; Internat. Cttee. of Onomastic Sciences, 1966-67; Corresp. Mem. Medieval Acad. of America, 1954; Mem. of Royal Gustav Adolf Academy of Sweden, 1955; Mem. Svenska Vitterhets Akademien, 1963; Hon. Mem. Viking Society, 1963 (Pres. 1956); Mem. Danish Academy of Sciences, 1964. Hon. Fil. Dr. (Uppsala), 1962; Hon. D.Litt. (Sheffield), 1963. Sir

Israel Gollancz Memorial Prize, British Academy, 1965. Chevalier: Swedish Order of the Royal North Star, 1954. Icelandic Order of the Falcon, 1956, and Danish Order of the Dannebrog, 1963. *Publications:* Place-Names of the East Riding, 1937 (English Place-Name Society); Three Northumbrian Poems, 1933; The Parker Chronicle, 1936; Facsimile of the Parker Chronicle, 1940 (Early English Text Society); Description of the Hand-Press at University College, London, 1934; The Heimskringla, 1932; Odham's English Dictionary, 1946; The Photography of Manuscripts, 1938; The Preparation of County Place-Name Surveys, 1954; English Place-Name Elements (2 vols. English Place-Name Soc.), 1955; Aspects of Translation (ed.), 1958; The Teaching of English (jt. ed.), 1959; Place-Names of the West Riding, 1961 (8 vols.); Place-Names of Gloucestershire, 1964 (4 vols.); Jt. Editor of Namn och Bygd, (with F. Norman) of Methuen's Old English Library, and (with F. Norman and G. Kane) of London Mediæval Studies. Many articles in Viking Society Saga Book, London Mediæval Studies, etc. *Recreations:* cricket, horology, light engineering. *Address:* Alderton, nr. Tewkesbury, Glos. *T.:* Alderton (via Cheltenham) 204; 37 Nevern Sq., S.W.5. *T.:* Fremantle 0593. *Club:* Athenæum [*Died* 11 *May* 1967.

SMITH, Major-Gen. Alfred Travers Fairtlough, C.B.E. 1943; M.C.; I.A. (retd.); *b.* 29 Sept. 1890; *s.* of Capt. C. J. Smith, late Royal Berks Regt.; *m.* 1914, Kate Bennett Wood; one *s.* one *d.* *Educ.:* Univ. Coll., London. 2nd Lt. 3rd Lancashire Fusiliers, 1910; transferred to R.A.S.C. 1914; to Indian Army, 1931. B.Sc. (Engineering) London; A.M.Inst.C.E. *Recreations:* golf, fishing, shooting. *Address:* Kendal Cottage, Bourne, Farnham, Surrey. [*Died* 20 *Oct.* 1965.

SMITH, Sir Andrew, Kt. 1960; C.B.E. 1951; Chm., Lancashire County Council Education Committee, 1964; Chairman Lancashire County Council, 1952-55 and 1958-61; *b.* 11 March 1880; *s.* of William and Dinah Smith; *m.* 1922, Bertha Lonsdale; one *s.* one *d.* *Educ.:* various Elementary Schools. *Recreations:* reading and motoring. *Address:* 356 Railway Street, Nelson, Lancs. *T.:* Nelson 62108. [*Died* 22 *Aug.* 1967.

SMITH, (Arnold) John Hugh, M.C.; *b.* 4 April 1881; *s.* of late Hugh Colin Smith and Constance *d.* of Henry J. Adeane, M.P., of Babraham and Maud, *d.* of 1st Baron Stanley of Alderley; *m.* 1941, Mrs. Adriana Hewitt (*née* Pellicioni) (*d.* 1962). *Educ.:* Eton; Trinity College, Cambridge. 1st Class Honours, Pt. I. and Pt. II., History Tripos; Major Scholar Trinity College; Gladstone Prizeman, 1902. 2nd Lieut. 5th Batt. Yorkshire Regt., Aug. 1914; 2nd Lieutenant Coldstream Guards, 1915; G.S.O. 3, 1917; Brigade Major, 1918; G.S.O. 2, British section Supreme War Council, 1918 (M.C., French Croix de Guerre, despatches, wounded); Treasurer and Member of Executive Committee, National Art Collections Fund. Past Dir., Hambros Bank, Ltd.; F.S.A. *Address:* 64 Park St., W.1. *T.:* Mayfair 8796; 41 Bishopsgate, E.C. *T.:* London Wall 2851. *Clubs:* Athenæum, Brooks's, Beefsteak. [*Died* 14 *Jan.* 1964.

SMITH, Arthur William, C.B.E. 1943; F.C.I.S. 1928; Hon. M.Inst.Gas.E. 1936; Director Glover & Main Ltd. and Midland Tar Distillers Ltd.; General Manager and Secretary, City of Birmingham Gas Department, 1919-45; *b.* 18 March 1880; *s.* of late William Potter Smith and Emma Elizabeth Platt; *m.* 1909, Louisa Gertrude Parsons (*d.* 1944); one *s.* two *d.* *Educ.:* Stratford Road School and George Dixon School, Birmingham. Commenced with Birmingham Gas Department as Apprentice, 1895; Assistant Secretary, 1912; Secretary, 1918. Member of Central Executive Board, National Gas Council, 1917-45, Chairman British Commercial Gas Association, 1937; Chairman Conjoint Conference of Public Utility Associations, 1940-41. Member of Fuel Research Board, D.S.I.R., 1941-45; also of Advisory Committees to Mines Dept. and Min. of Fuel and Power; Member West Midland Gas Board, 1949-51. *Recreations:* golf, fishing. *Address:* 39 Reddings Road, Moseley, Birmingham 13. *T.:* South 0644 (Birmingham). *Clubs:* Midland. Moseley Golf (Birmingham. [*Died* 9 *June* 1961.

SMITH, Rev. Canon Basil Alec; Canon and Treasurer of York Minster since 1963; *b.* 11 June 1908; *s.* of Samuel George and Margaret Smith; *m.* 1935, Phillis Eva Guy; no *c.* *Educ.:* Wheelwright Grammar School; Bede College, University of Durham. Tutor, Bede College, 1931; Assistant Curate: St. Chad's, York, 1938; Fulford, 1940; Vicar of Poppleton, York, 1943; Rector of Holy Trinity, Micklegate, City of York, 1947; Proctor in Convocation, 1955-; Prebendary of Ulleskelf in York Minster, 1961-. *Publication:* Dean Church, 1958. *Address:* 10 Precentor's Court, York. *Club:* National Liberal. [*Died* 9 *Dec.* 1969.

SMITH, General Bedell; *see* Smith, General W. B.

SMITH, Rt. Hon. Sir Ben, P.C. 1943; K.B.E., *cr.* 1945: *b.* 1879; *s.* of Richard Smith; *m.* 1st, 1899, Mildred Ellen (*d.* 1959), *d.* of Charles Edison, Peckham; two *s.*; 2nd. 1961, Gertrude Elizabeth, *d.* of late E. A. Lacey. Organiser of Transport and Gen. Workers' Union; M.P. (Lab.) Rotherhithe Div. of Bermondsey, 1923-31 and 1935-46; Labour Whip, 1925; Treasurer of the Household, 1929-31; Parl. Sec. Ministry of Aircraft Production, 1942; Minister Resident in Washington for Supply, 1943-45; Minister of Food, 1945-46; Chairman of West Midlands Divisional Coal Board, 1946-50; U.N.R.R.A. Cttee. for Far East, Washington, 1944. Associate Institute of Transport; Liveryman of City of London, Bakers' Company; Alderman Bermondsey Borough Council; Carmen's Company; Member of London Traffic Advisory Committee Retired. *Address:* Hazeldene, Coombe Cross, Bovey Tracey, Devon. *T.:* Bovey Tracey 2158. *Club:* Royal Automobile. [*Died* 5 *May* 1964.

SMITH, Sir Bracewell, 1st Bt., *cr.* 1947; K.C.V.O., *cr.* 1948; Kt., *cr.* 1945; B.Sc.; Under-writing Member of Lloyd's; Sheriff, 1943-44; Lord Mayor of London, 1946-47; Chairman, Arsenal Football Club, 1948-61 (Life Pres.); *b.* 1884; *s.* of Samuel Smith, Keighley; *m.* Edith (*d.* 1953), *d.* of George Whitaker, Keighley; one *s.* one *d.* *Educ.:* privately; Univ. of Leeds. Hon. Doctor of Laws (Leeds); M.P. (U.) Dulwich Div. of Camberwell, June 1932-45; Councillor and Alderman Holborn Borough Council, 1922-37; Mayor of Holborn, 1931-32; L.C.C., Holborn, 1925-28. Lieutenant, City of London. Past Master of Worshipful Companies: Bakers, 1946; Spectacle-Makers, 1946; Glaziers, 1949; Framework Knitters, 1949; Member of Court of Carmen's Company. President: London Schools Athletic Assoc., 1948-; Past Pres. Soc. of Yorkshiremen in London, 1949. Hon. Treasurer, Reedham School; Hon. Freeman, Borough of Keighley, Yorks., 1957; Chairman: Park Lane Hotel, Ltd.; Ritz Hotel, Ltd.; Carlton Hotel, Ltd.; Ritz Development Co. Ltd.; Practical Press Ltd.; Director: Parkland Mfg. Co. Ltd.; Ritz Hotel (Paris), Ltd. *Recreations:* golf, motoring. *Heir:* *s.* George Bracewell [*b.* 5 Nov. 1912; *m.* 1951, Helene Marie Hydock, Philadelphia; two *s.*]. *Address:* Park Lane Hotel, Piccadilly, W.1. *Clubs:* Carlton. Royal Automobile; Royal and Ancient (St Andrews). [*Died* 12 *Jan.* 1966

SMITH, Charles Henry C.; *see* Chichester-Smith.

SMITH, Sir Clifford E. H.; *see* Heathcote-Smith.

SMITH, David Nichol, M.A.; Hon. D.Litt. Durham, Princeton, Adelaide; Hon. LL.D. Glasgow, Edinburgh; Hon. Litt.D. Cambridge; Hon. Dr., University of Lyons; Hon. Fellow of Merton Coll., Oxf.; F.B.A.; *b* Edinburgh, 16 Sept. 1875; *s.* of late Henry G. C. Smith, Edinburgh; *m.* 1915, Mary, *d.* of late Rev. Canon Harford; three *d.* (one *s.* fell in action, 1942). *Educ.:* University of Edinburgh; the Sorbonne. Assistant and Lecturer in English in the University of Glasgow, 1902-04; Professor of English Literature, Armstrong College, Newcastle on Tyne, 1904-08; Goldsmiths' Reader in English, Univ. of Oxford, 1908-29; Fellow of Merton Coll., 1921-46; Merton Prof. of English Literature, Oxford, 1929-46; Visiting Scholar, Huntington Library, 1936-37; W. A. Neilson Visiting Prof., Smith Coll., Mass., U.S.A., 1946-47; Frederic Ives Carpenter Visiting Prof., Univ. of Chicago, 1947; Clark Lecturer, Trinity Coll., Cambridge, 1948; Visiting Professor Fuad I Univ., Cairo, 1949; Sir Walter Scott Lecturer, Univ. of Edinburgh, 1950; Prof. of English, Univ. of Adelaide, 1950-51; Nuffield Lecturer, Univ. of N.Z., 1951. *Publications:* Brunetière's Essays in French Literature (translation), 1898; Boileau's Art Poétique, 1898; Dryden's Essay of Dramatic Poesy, 1900; Hazlitt's Essays on Poetry, 1901; Eighteenth Century Essays on Shakespeare, 1903; The Functions of Criticism, 1909; Jeffrey's Literary Criticism, 1910; Letters of Thomas Burnet to George Duckett (Roxburghe Club), 1914; Shakespeare Criticism, 1916; Characters from the Histories and Memoirs of the Seventeenth Century, 1918; Swift's A Tale of a Tub (with A. C. Guthkelch) 1920, rev. 1958; Wordsworth 1921, and Dryden, 1925, in the Clarendon English Series; The Oxford Book of Eighteenth Century Verse, 1926, Shakespeare in the Eighteenth Century, 1928; Johnson's Revision of his Publications (in Johnson and Boswell Revised), 1928; Samuel Johnson's Irene, 1929; Warton's History of English Poetry (Warton Lecture), 1929; Percy's Ancient Songs on Moorish Subjects, 1932; The Letters of Jonathan Swift to Charles Ford, 1935; Some Observations on Eighteenth Century Poetry, 1937; The Poems of Samuel Johnson (with E. L. M'Adam), 1941; John Dryden (Clark lectures), 1949; Johnsonians and Boswellians, 1950; contributions to the Cambridge History of English Literature, Shakespeare's England, Johnson's England, Dictionary of National Biography, etc. *Address:* 20 Merton Street, Oxford. *Club:* Athenæum.

[*Died* 18 *Jan.* 1962.

SMITH, David S.; *see* Seth-Smith.

SMITH, Sir Dermot C.-; *see* Cusack-Smith, Sir W. R. D.

SMITH, Ean K. S.; *see* Stewart-Smith.

SMITH, Edward Percy; *b.* 5 Jan. 1891; *y. s.* of Benjamin Figgis Smith, Streatham; *m.* 1918, Gertrude Ethel (marriage dissolved, 1951), *e. d.* of late Sir Richard Glazebrook, K.C.B., K.C.V.O.; one *d.*; *m.* 1951, Lilian Mary Denham. *Educ.:* Haileybury Coll.; in France. In East Indian and Colonial Commerce, 1909-30; President General Produce Brokers' Assoc. of London, 1924; a Dramatist under the pen-name of Edward Percy. Served 1915-17 as A.B. in R.N.V.R., 1917-19 as officer in the Labour Corps. Freeman of City of London, of Bakers' Company. M.P. (C.) Ashford Div. of Kent, 1943-50. *Publications: novels:* Eastward Drift; Cowferry Isle; We Shall Ne'er Be Younger (Verses of a Dramatist); *plays:* Joseph of Arimathaea, If Four Walls Told, Trespasses, The Rigordans, Dr. Brent's Household, The Wintry Bough, The Misdoings of Charley Peace, The House on the Bridge, The Shop at Sly Corner, My Wives and I, The Old Gentleman; also many one-act plays. With Reginald Denham: Suspect, Trunk Crime, Give Me Yesterday, The Man They Acquitted, Ladies in Retirement; with Lilian his wife: The Man with Expensive Tastes; A Stranger in the Tea; Major Road Ahead. *Recreations:* gardening, fishing, cooking. *Address:* Selmeston House, Selmeston, Sx. *T.:* Ripe 323.

[*Died* 27 *May* 1968.

SMITH, Col. Edwin C.M.; *see* Montgomery-Smith.

SMITH, Ellis, J.P.; *b.* Eccles, 1896. *Educ.:* Green Lane Council School, Patricroft. First class Certificate Advanced Economics, Co-operative College; Secretary Eccles Trades Council, 1925-1935; contested Parliamentary Election, 1931; President Lancashire and Cheshire Trades Councils, 1931-64; M.P. (Lab.) Stoke-on-Trent, 1935-50; Stoke-on-Trent South, 1950-66. Parliamentary Secretary, Board of Trade, 1945-1946; Gen. President United Patternmakers Assoc., 1946-50, 1952, 1958-64. J.P. Lancs. 1944; *Publications:* several Industrial Pamphlets. *Address* 61 Grasmere Crescent, Westwood Park, Eccles, Manchester.

[*Died* 7 *Nov.* 1969.

SMITH, Francis Jagoe, C.M.G.; M.A. Oxon; Ceylon Civil Service, retired; *b.* Barnet, 9 Sept. 1873; *s.* of Henry Francis Smith and Anna M Jagoe; *m.* 1908, Eleanor Margaret, *d.* of Leonard W. Booth, C.M.G., Ceylon Civil Service; one *s.* (*yr. s.* a Spitfire Pilot Officer killed in action, Oct. 1941). *Educ.:* Merchant Taylors' School, London; St. John's College, Oxford (Classical and Mathematical Scholar). First selected candidate after Colonial Civil Service Examination, 1896; appointed to Ceylon; held various revenue and judicial appointments, 1896-1911; Government Agent, Province of Uva, 1912; Postmaster Gen., Ceylon, 1913-20, and 1921-23; Director of Food Production, 1920; acting Colonial Treasurer, 1923 and 1927; Govt. Agent Northern Province, and Superintendent Pearl Fishery Camp, 1924-26; Acting Controller of Revenue, 1928; member of Executive and Legislative Councils, 1923, 1927, 1928; retired, 1928. *Publication:* Joint Editor of Ceylon Ordinances, 1907 edition. *Address:* 20 Ernle Road, S.W.20. *T.:* Wimbledon 5731.

[*Died* 1 *April* 1969.

SMITH, Francis William Head, C.I.E 1929; *b.* 18 Aug. 1886. *Educ.:* Tonbridge School; Christ Church, Oxford. Entered India Office, 1909; Assistant Secretary to Indian Finance and Currency Commission, 1913-14; Joint Secretary to Indian Agricultural Commission, 1926-28; Assistant Under-Secretary of State, Burma Office, 1944-47; retired, 1947. *Address:* Farm Cottage, Greatham, Liss, Hants.

[*Died* 4 *March* 1964.

SMITH, Sir Frank Edward, G.C.B., *cr.* 1942 (K.C.B., *cr* 1931; C.B 1926); G.B.E., *cr.* 1939 (C.B.E. 1922; O.B.E. 1918); F.R.S. 1918; A.R.C.Sc., D.Sc. (Oxon); LL.D. (Birmingham); LL.D. (Aberdeen); D.Sc. (Sheffield); Fellow of Imperial College of Science, 1937; Director of Research to Anglo-Iranian Oil Co., 1939 55; ex-Dir., Birmingham Small Arms Co. Ltd.; *b.* Aston, Birmingham, 14 Oct. 1879; *s.* of late Joseph Smith; *m.* May (*d.* 1961), *d.* of Thomas B. King, Birmingham; one *d.* *Educ.:* Royal College of Science (National Scholar in Physics). Superintendent of Electrical Dept., National Physical Laboratory, 1901-20; Director of Scientific Research, Admiralty, 1920-29; Secretary, Department of Scientific and Industrial Research, 1929-39; Controller of Telecommunications Equipment, Ministry of Aircraft Production, 1940-42; Dir. Instrument Production, Min. of Supply, 1939-42; Controller of Bearings Production, Min. of Supply, 1939-43; Chairman: Technical Defence Cttee., M.I.5, 1940-46; Scientific Advisory Council, Min. of Supply, 1941-47; Road Research and Safety Research Board, 1945-54; Hon. Secretary, British Association for Advancement of Science, 1922-29; Secretary of Royal Society, 1929-38; President Phys. Soc., 1924-1927; Pres. Junior Institution of Engineers, 1935-36; President Institute of Physics, 1943-46; awarded the Hughes Medal by the Royal Society, 1925, the Duddell Medal by the Council of the Physical Society, 1927, the Faraday Medal by the Institution of Electrical Engineers, 1934, and Gustave Canet Medal by the Jr. Institution of Engineers, 1934, the Charles Parson's Memorial Medal by North East Coast Engineers and Shipbuilders, 1936. U.S.A. Medal of Freedom with Silver Palm, 1947. *Publications:* a large number of scientific papers, mostly on electrical and magnetic subjects, in Phil. Trans. and Proc. Royal Society and Physical Society. *Address:* Dunrovin, Minehead, Somerset. *Club:* Athenæum. [*Died* 1 *July* 1970.

SMITH, Frederic G.; *see* Gordon-Smith.

SMITH, Geoffrey R. H.; *b.* 1901; *o. s.* of late Samuel Smith, Oxton Hall, Tadcaster, Yorkshire; *m.* 1942, Rosamond Margaret Stirling, 3rd *d.* of late Bishop Woollcombe, D.D.; two *s.* two *d.* *Educ.:* Eton; Magdalene College, Cambridge. Barrister, Middle Temple, 1925; High Sheriff of Yorks, 1946; J.P. (W.R. Yorks), 1935. *Recreation:* breeder of pedigree dairy shorthorns. *Address:* Oxton Hall, Tadcaster, Yorkshire. *T.:* Tadcaster 3121. *Clubs:* Boodle's; Yorkshire (York). [*Died* 9 *May* 1964.

SMITH, Air Vice-Marshal Gilbert H.; *see* Harcourt-Smith.

SMITH, Col. Sir Harold C. T.; *see* Templar-Smith.

SMITH, Ven. (Harry Kingsley) Percival; Adviser on Christian Stewardship to the Diocese of Norwich since 1961; *b.* 5 June 1898; *s.* of Reverend Harry Percival Smith; *m.* 1922, Francis Isabel, *o. d.* of late R. L. Halstead, Cleveland Lodge, Dorking; two *s.* two *d.* *Educ.:* Haileybury; Gonville and Caius College and Westcott House, Cambridge. Curate of Holy Trinity, Cambridge, 1921; Chaplain of Gonville and Caius College, Cambridge, 1922-23; Assistant master at Haileybury College, 1923; Chaplain to the Forces, 1925; Head of Cambridge House, Camberwell, 1927; Curate, St. George's, Queen's Square, London, 1930; Curate, Holy Trinity, Maidstone, 1932; Priest in charge, St. Mary of Nazareth, West Wickham, Kent, 1935; Vicar of Yaxley, Peterborough, 1941; Vicar of Fenstanton, Hunts, 1943; Rector of Blofield, Norwich, 1947; Rector of Foulsham, 1955-61; Archdeacon of Lynn, 1956-61; Archdeacon emeritus, 1961. *Address:* The Gatehouse, St. Martin-at-Palace Plain, Norwich, NOR 20P. [*Died* 27 *Jan.* 1965.

SMITH, H(enry) Norman; *b.* 31 Jan. 1890; *y. s.* of late Enoch Smith, Swindon, Wilts; *m.* 1922, Clare Louise, 2nd *d.* of late Joseph Ody, farmer, Eastcourt, Wilts; one *d.* *Educ.:* Swindon High School; The College, Swindon. Editorial staff of Daily Herald, 1919-30; accompanied Prime Minister MacDonald to U.S.A. and Canada for the naval conversations, 1929. Later associated with Reynolds News, Illustrated and John Bull. Contested Faversham, Kent, 1931 and 1935. M.P. (Lab.-Co-op.) Nottingham South, 1945-55. Active in monetary reform movement since 1926. *Publication:* The Politics of Plenty, 1944. *Recreations:* astronomy, gardening. *Address:* 6 Dolphin Way, Rustington, Sussex. *T.:* Rustington 2303. [*Died* 21 *Dec.* 1962.

SMITH, Sir Herbert, 2nd Bt., *cr.* 1920; Company Director, Engineer; *b.* 26 Sept. 1903; *s.* of Sir Herbert Smith, 1st Bt.; *S.* father, 1943; *m.* 1929, Eileen Norton (*d.* 1955); two *d.* *Educ.:* Rossall. *Heir:* none. *Address:* Oldbury Grove, Bridgnorth, Shropshire. *T.:* Bridgnorth 3114. [*Died* 12 *July* 1961 (*ext.*).

SMITH, Herbert Arthur, D.C.L.; Prof. of International Law in the University of London, 1928-46; Professor Emeritus, 1948; Lecturer at Royal Naval War and Staff Colleges, Greenwich, 1935-39; *b.* Basti, U.P. India, 4 Aug. 1885; 3rd *s.* of Vincent Arthur Smith, C.I.E., M.A., D.Litt., Indian Civil Service; *m.* 1912, Mora Stewart (*d.* 1936), 2nd *d.* of late Dugald Stewart Macphee, Helensburgh, Scotland; one *s.* one *d.* (and two *s.* decd.). *Educ.:* Cheltenham College; St. John's College, Oxford (Scholar); B.A. 1908; Chancellor's Essayist, 1909. Called to Bar, 1909; M.A. 1911; D.C.L., 1933; Fellow and Law Tutor of Magdalen College, Oxford, 1911-19; on military service, 1914-19; member of the British Mission to the United States, 1918; Professor of Jurisprudence, McGill University, 1919; Professor of Constitutional Law, 1924; official War work 1939-45; Col., G.S., 1944-45, at H.Q. of 21st Army Group (despatches). Officer of the Order of Leopold. *Publications:* The Law of Associations, Corporate and Unincorporate, 1914; The American Supreme Court as an International, Tribunal, 1920; Federalism in North America, 1923; The Economic Uses of International Rivers, 1931; Great Britain and the Law of Nations, vol. i. 1932, vol. ii. 1935; Le Développement Moderne des Lois de la Guerre Maritime, 1938; The Crisis of the Law of Nations, 1947; The Law and Custom of the Sea, 1948, 3rd edn., 1958; numerous articles in legal and other reviews. *Recreations:* painting, miscellaneous. *Address:* Les Avants sur Montreux, Vaud, Switzerland. *T.:* 021/6-47-46. *Club:* Royal Commonwealth Society. [*Died* 16 *April* 1961.

SMITH, Hugh A. M.; *see* McClure-Smith.

SMITH, Lt.-Col. Sir Hugh B. P.; *see* Protheroe-Smith.

SMITH, James David Maxwell, C.M.G. 1949; *b.* 25 Jan. 1895; *s.* of James Smith, Clergyman; *m.* 1937, Katharine Elizabeth Miller; one *s.* one *d.* *Educ.:* Robert Gordon's College, Aberdeen; Aberdeen University. M.A. 1920. Served European War, 1914-18, Army and Royal Marines, 1914-19. Malayan Civil Service from 1920; retd., 1951. Financial Secretary, Singapore, 1947-51; Salaries Commissioner, Mauritius, 1951; U.N. Technical Assistance Administration, Nicaragua, 1953-55, Chile, 1956-57, Brazil, 1957-58, Venezuela, 1959-61. *Address:* 18 Braid Mount, Edinburgh 10. *Clubs:* Royal Commonwealth Society; Royal Over-Seas Legaue; Singapore (Singapore). [*Died* 5 *March* 1969.

SMITH, John, O.B.E. 1933; M.R.C.V.S., D.V.H.; *b.* 4 May 1883; *y. s.* of late John Smith, Wigan; *m.* 1917, Beryl, *d.* of late C. E. Paterson, M.D., and Mrs. Paterson, Farnborough, Hants; one *s.* one *d.* *Educ.:* privately; New Veterinary College, Edinburgh; Liverpool University. Veterinary Officer, N. Rhodesia, 1913; with Forces, 1916-19 (despatches); Chief Veterinary Officer, N. Rhodesia, 1921; Member of Legislative Council and head of agricultural, veterinary, and forestry services, 1924; Chairman European Settlement Board; Member Victoria Falls Conservancy Board; Member Native Education Board; retired 1933; Member Colonial Advisory Council of Agriculture and Animal Health, 1933, and

Chairman of its standing committee on Animal Health, 1937; Member Agricultural Research Council, 1934-45; Member departmental committees to investigate veterinary education and the poultry industry, 1937; Chairman Army Veterinary Service Selection Committee, 1943; Adviser on Animal Health to Secretary of State for the Colonies, 1940-1948; Trustee and Member of Council, Animal Health Trust. *Publications:* various technical. *Recreation:* golf. *Address:* Rocklands, Littlewick Road, Knaphill, Surrey. [*Died* 5 *Nov*. 1964.

SMITH, Sir John A. L.; *see* Lucie-Sm th.

SMITH, John George, O.B.E. 1946; M.A.; M.Com.; LL.D.; D.Litt.; formerly Mitsui Professor of Finance, Dean, Faculty of Commerce, and Vice-Principal, Univ. of Birmingham; *b.* Dunmanway, Co. Cork, 13 Oct. 1881; *m.* Mary Gibson (*d.* 1967), M.A., B.Litt., Ph.D., Greystone Hall, Co. Durham; one *s.* one *d.* *Educ.:* Portora Royal Sch., Enniskillen; Trinity Coll., Dublin. Lecturer in Pure and Applied Mathematics, Univ. Coll. of South Wales and Monmouthshire, 1905-18; Acting Professor of Economics and Political Science, Queen's University of Belfast, 1918-19; Assistant Professor of Commerce, University of Birmingham, 1919-23; Sponsor North Staffordshire University College, 1949-62; Member of Fiscal Inquiry Committee of Irish Free State, 1923; Appointed Member of Warwickshire Agricultural Wages Committee, 1924-59; formerly Chairman of several Wages Councils; Member Conscientious Objectors' Midland Tribunal Military Service Act, 1939-58; Chairman Midland Region Price Regulation Committee, 1939-53; Mem. Departmental Committee on Commercial Education, 1946; Independent member of Jewellery and Silversmiths' Working Party, Board of Trade, 1946; Mem. Cttee. of Inquiry into Dock Workers (Regulation of Employment) Scheme, 1955. President, Section F, British Association Norwich Meeting, 1935; Member of Council, 1937-47. *Publications:* papers and reviews in economic periodicals; articles and discussions in actuarial and statistical publications; Organised Produce Markets. *Recreation:* gardening. *Address:* 21 Woodlands Park Road, King's Norton, Birmingham, 30 *T.:* King's Norton 1500. [*Died* 14 *Dec*. 1968.

SMITH, John H.; *see* Smith, Arnold J. H.

SMITH, John H. W.; *see* Wardle-Smith.

SMITH, Sir Jonah W.; *see* Walker-Smith.

SMITH, Louis L.; *see* Laybourne-Smith.

SMITH, Marcella, R.I., R.B.A.; Vice-President Society of Women Artists; *b.* East Molesey, Surrey; *e. d.* of Rev. Dr. C. Ernest Smith, Washington, D.C., U.S.A. *Educ.:* The Corcoran School of Art, Washington; School of Design, Philadelphia; Paris. Exhibited at Royal Academy and all chief Provincial Exhibitions. *Publication:* Flower Painting in Water Colour, 1955. *Recreation:* gardening. *Address:* 32B Blomfield Road, W.9. [*Died* 10 *Oct*. 1963.

SMITH, May, O.B.E. 1945; M.A. (Manch.); D.Sc. (Lond.); Senior Investigator to Industrial Health Research Board, 1920-44, formerly Lecturer in Applied Psychology at Birkbeck College, retired 1955; Visiting Professor Women's College, Cairo, 1947 and 1948; *b.* 29 Aug. 1879; *d.* of Thomas Smith and Augusta Mathews. *Educ.:* Manchester Science School; Manchester University; Oxford Psychological Laboratory. Assistant Mistress at Practising School in connection with the Education Dept. of the Manchester University, 1903-5; Lecturer in Psychology and Senior Tutor at Cherwell Hall, Oxford, 1906-20; F.R.S.M.; F.B.Ps.S.; Hon. Member of Medical Women's Federation, 1949. *Publications:* A Contribution to the Study of Fatigue, British Journal of Psychology, 1916; (with Wm. McDougall) The Effects of Alcohol and some other Drugs during Normal and Fatigued Conditions (Med. Research Council Special Report No. 56); Studies in the Laundry Trade, Industrial Health Research Board, Report 22; Industrial Psychology, Article in Ency. Brit.; The Nervous Temperament, British Journal of Medical Psychology, 1930; Some Pioneers of Medical Psychology, Br. J. of Medical Psy. 1934 (with Professor Greenwood); An Introduction to Industrial Psychology, 1943; (with H. Maule) Industrial Psychology and the Laundry Trade, 1947. *Recreation:* walking. [*Died* 22 *Feb*. 1968.

SMITH, Naomi G. R.; *see* Royde Smith.

SMITH, Nevil D. B.; *see* Bosworth-Smith.

SMITH, Noel James Gillies, M.A.; B.Sc., Ph.D.; formerly Plant Pathologist, South African Government Division of Botany; *b.* 25 Dec. 1899; *e. s.* of late Dr. W. G. Smith, Edinburgh, and Elizabeth M. Gillies; *m.* 1934, Frances Isabel (*d.* 1960), *o. d.* of late F. C. Church, Blackheath. *Educ.:* George Watson's Coll., Edinburgh; Univs. of Edinburgh and Cambridge. Temporary 2/Lieutenant R.F.A. 1918; Sibbald Bursar, Vans Dunlop Scholar, and J. H. Balfour gold medallist, University of Edinburgh; Carnegie research scholar and Demonstrator in Botany School, University of Cambridge, PhD. (Cambridge) 1926; was assistant in Botany, University of Aberdeen, 1925-26; Professor of Botany, Rhodes University College, Grahamstown, Cape, 1926-1948; has acted as examiner in the Universities of Cape Town, Pretoria, Stellenbosch, and S. Africa; has been chairman of the botanical studies committee of the University of S. Africa; was president (1931) of the botanical section of the S. African Association for the Advancement of Science; has taken part in expeditions for botanical exploration, the longest being (1933) into little-known parts of the Namib Desert; served with South African Artillery, 1940-41, and South African Medical Corps, 1941-42, in Africa. F.L.S. 1934-41; F.R.S.S.A. 1936. *Publications:* Has published, from 1924 onwards, in various botanical and agricultural periodicals, a series of articles on diseases of cereals and grasses caused by fungi of the genus Helminthosporium, the most important being Leaf-stripe disease of Barley and Foot-rot of Wheat, and the longest papers being in the Annals of Applied Biology, and the South African Journal of Science; has also, from 1934 onwards, published a series on S. African Gasteromycetous fungi; has also reported more general botanical results of explorations *e.g.* some results of Namib Desert expedition in Proceedings Linnean Soc. (1934). *Address:* c/o Barclays Bank Ltd., 1 Cockspur Street, S.W.1. [*Deceased*.

SMITH, Norman; *see* Smith, H. N.

SMITH, Norman, LL.D. (Hon.), D.Sc. (Manchester); Registrar, the University of Manchester, 1920-45; *b.* Bury, Lancs, 1877; *s.* of Samuel Smith, Bury; *m.* 1902, Elsie, *d.* of John Hollingworth, Bury; one *d.* *Educ.:* Ashville College, Harrogate; University of Manchester University of Berlin; late University Fellow (Manchester); late 1851 Exhibition Scholar. *Publications:* various publications in the Journal of the Chemical Society on Inorganic Chemistry. *Address:* 104 Mt. Pleasant Rd., Wallasey, Cheshire. *T.:* New Brighton 1769. [*Died* 1 *May* 1963.

SMITH, Norman Lockhart, C.M.G. 1937; *b.* 29 May 1887; 3rd *s.* of late Hugh Crawford Smith, M.P., Newcastle on Tyne; *m.* 1914, Maud Violet, *o. d.* of late W. Banister, D.D., Bishop of Kuangsi-Hunan; three *s.* two *d.* *Educ.:* Sedbergh; Queen's

College, Oxford (Hastings Exhibitioner). Entered Hong Kong Civil Service, 1910; various administrative posts since that date; Colonial Secretary, Hong Kong, 1936-41; Acting Governor, 1935, 1937, 1940, 1941. *Address:* Flat 2, Ebernoe House, Petworth, Sussex. *T.:* North Chapel 353. *Club:* Royal Societies. [*Died* 26 *Jan.* 1968.

SMITH, Sir Norman Percival Arthur, Kt., *cr.* 1947; C.I.E. 1944; O.B.E. 1941; *b.* 30 Nov. 1892; *m.*, *d.* of Thomas Martin; three *s.* one *d.* *Educ.:* Dulwich College. Joined Indian Police, 1912; Commissioner of Police, Bombay, 1939; Joint Secretary to Government of Bombay, Home Dept., Oct. 1939-Feb. 1941; Inspector General of Police, Bombay, 1942-44; Director Intelligence Bureau, 1945-47; retd. 1947. King's Police Medal, 1938. *Address:* Ground Floor Flat, Lynmead, Darley Road, Meads, Eastbourne, Sussex. *T.:* Eastbourne 5420. [*Died* 25 *July* 1964.

SMITH, Nowell (Charles); *b.* 24 Feb. 1871; *s.* of late Horace Smith; *m.* 1901, Cecil Violet, 3rd *d.* of A. G. Vernon Harcourt; two *s.* four *d.* *Educ.:* Temple Grove; Winchester; New Coll., Oxford. 1st Class Classical Moderations and Final School (Literæ Humaniores); Fellow of Magdalen Coll., 1894-97; Fellow and Tutor of New College, 1897-1905, Hon. Fellow, 1953; House Master at Winchester Coll., 1905-1909; Headmaster of Sherborne School, 1909-1927; Chm. Committee Council for Education in World Citizenship, 1939-46; Chairman, English Association, 1941-43. *Publications:* editor of Selections from Wordsworth's Poetry; Wordsworth's Critical Prose; Wordsworth's Poetical Works; Lord Brooke's Life of Sir Philip Sidney; Sermons at Sherborne; Notes on The Testament of Beauty; The Dawn of World-Order, 1932; Sydney Smith's Letters, 1953; pamphlets and contributions to periodicals. *Address:* Thames Bank, Goring-on-Thames, Oxon. *Club:* Public Schools. [*Died* 21 *Jan.* 1961.

SMITH, Very Rev. Oswin H. G.; *see* Gibbs-Smith.

SMITH, Ven. Percival; *see* Smith, Ven. H. K. P.

SMITH, Major Percy G. D.; *see* Darvil-Smith.

SMITH, Brig. Philip W. L. B.; *see* Broke-Smith.

SMITH, Ralph H. H.; *see* Hammersley-Smith.

SMITH, Reginald Eccles, O.B.E., M.B.; F.R.C.S.Ed.; retired; formerly: Hon. Surgeon to Corbett Hospital, Stourbridge; Chairman of B.M.A. (Dudley Division); President, Dudley Medical Society; *b.* Driffield, E. Yorks, 11 Feb. 1887; *s.* of Charles Smith, J.P.; *m.* 1918, Marjorie, *d.* of Cecil Turner, Twickenham. *Educ.:* Bridlington Grammar School; Leeds University; M.B., Ch.B., with honours, 1909, Prizeman in Practical Surgery. House Surgeon at the Leeds Gen. Infirmary, 1910; Asst. M.O. at the Leeds City Fever Hospital; Resident Surgeon, Stockton-on-Tees, 1911-13; Temporary House Surgeon, Nottingham General Hospital, 1914; served in H.M. Royal Navy, 1914-19; Gallipoli and early part of the Salonika Campaign; torpedoed in H.M.H.S. Rewa, 4 Jan. 1918; acted as surgical specialist in H.M. Navy; member of the British Medical Association, member of the Cardiff Medical Society. Battalion M.O. to 7th Worcs. Home Guard, War of 1939-45. *Publications:* Influenzal Intra-Abdominal Catastrophes, Lancet, 1918; Intra-Cranial Lesions, Lancet, 1919; Full-time Tubal Pregnancy, Lancet, 1920, etc. *Recreations:* shooting, fishing. *Address:* Rewa, Chantry Road, Stourbridge, Worcs. [*Died Sept.* 1963.

SMITH, Reginald Henry M. A.; *see* Abel Smith.

SMITH, Rennie, B.Sc. (Econ.); Lecturer and Journalist; *b.* 14 April 1888; *s.* of Ben Smith, Nelson; *m.* 1922, *d.* of Otto Peemueller. *Educ.:* Nelson Schools; Graduate in Economics and Political Science, London University. W.E.A. Tutor, Sheffield University; Joint Principal, International People's Coll. 1922-23; Lecturer under Miners' Welfare Scheme, and Tutor for Iron and Steel Trades Confederation; contested Penistone Division, 1923; M.P. (Lab.) Penistone Division, 1924-31; Parliamentary Private Secretary to Under Secretary for Foreign Affairs; Secretary, British Group, Interparliamentary Union, 1929-32. Secretary, Friends of Europe, 1933; Joint Editor Central European Observer, 1940-46; Civilian Officer, Germany, 1946-49; Lecturer on Christianity and International Affairs, 1950. *Publications:* General Disarmament or War?, 1927; Peace Verboten, 1943. *Address:* The Moorings, 9 Fieldway, Ringwood, Hants. [*Died* 25 *May* 1962.

SMITH, Rev. Prof. Ronald Gregor, M.A., B.D. (Edin.); D.D. (Edin.), D.Theol. (Marburg); Primarius Professor of Divinity, University of Glasgow, since 1956; *b.* 17 April 1913; 2nd *s.* of George Henry and Helen Wilson Smith; *m.* 1947, Käthe Wittlake, Ph.D. (Marburg), *yr. d.* of Otto and Elisabeth Wittlake. *Educ.:* Universities of Edinburgh, Munich, Marburg and Copenhagen. Minister of Lawson Memorial Church, Selkirk, 1939-44; C.F., 1944-46; Control Officer, Bonn Univ., C.C.G., 1946-47; Assoc. Editor, S.C.M. Press, 1947-50, Man. Dir. and Editor, 1950-56. Love Lectr., Ormond Coll., Melbourne, 1955; F. D. Maurice Lectr., King's Coll., London, 1958; Visiting Professor: McCormick Theol. Seminary, Chicago, 1964, 1969; Heidelberg Univ., 1967; Colgate Rochester Divinity Sch., 1969; Warfield Lectr., Princeton Theological Seminary, 1968-69. *Publications:* Still Point, 1943; (jt. author) Back from the Front, 1946; The New Man, 1956; J. G. Hamann, 1960; (Trans.) of I and Thou, 1937, Between Man and Man, 1947; Kierkegaard's Journals: The Last Years, 1964; Secular Christianity, 1966; Martin Buber, 1966; The Free Man, 1969; The Doctrine of God, 1969, etc.; (Ed.) I Knew Dietrich Bonhoeffer, 1966 (Ed.) World Come of Age, 1966; contrib. to: Zeit und Geschichte, Festschrift für Rudolf Bultmann, 1964; Kierkegaardiana, 1964; Conflicting Images of Man, 1966; Jewish Jl. of Sociology, Theology, Hibbert Journal, Listener, Zeitschrift für Theologie und Kirche, etc. *Address:* 5, The University, Glasgow. *T.:* (Glasgow) Western 6265. *Club:* Athenæum. [*Died* 26 *Sept.* 1968.

SMITH, Sir Sydney Alfred, Kt., *cr.* 1949; C.B.E. 1944; F.R.S.E., LL.D., M.D., Edin., F.R.C.P.Edin.; D.P.H.; M.D. (Louvain); Emeritus Professor of Forensic Medicine, Edinburgh University, since 1953; *m.* 1912, Catherine Goodsir Geleneck; one *s.* one *d.* *Educ.:* Victoria Coll., Wellington; Univ. of New Zealand; Edinburgh Univ Formerly Medical Officer of Health, N.Z. Government; Principal Medico-legal Expert to Egyptian Government and Professor of Forensic Medicine, University of Egypt; Regius Professor of Forensic Medicine, Edinburgh University, 1928-53; Dean of the Faculty of Medicine, 1931-53; Consultant in Forensic Medicine, World Health Organization, 1953; Rector of Edinburgh University, 1954-57; Member, General Medical Council, 1931-56, resigned. Hon. Mem. Royal Society of New Zealand, 1956. Order of the Nile, 3rd class: Polonia Restituta, 3rd class.

Publications: Text-Book of Forensic Medicine 1925 (now in 10th edn.); Mostly Murder, 1960. *Address:* Rhycullen, Oswald Road, Edinburgh. *T.:* Newington 3156. *Club:* New (Edinburgh). [*Died* 8 *May* 1969.

SMITH, Sydney William, C.B.E. 1933; D.Sc. (Lond.), Hon. D.Sc. (Witwatersrand), A.R.S.M., Hon. M.Inst.M.M., F.R.I.C., F.C.S., F.R.G.S.; *b.* 18 March 1878; unmarried. *Educ.:* Taunton's Sch. and Hartley Coll., Southampton; Royal School of Mines. Private Assistant to the late Sir William Roberts-Austen at the Royal Mint, 1899-1902; Assistant Assayer at the Royal Mint, 1902-26; Chief Assayer, 1926-38; Lecturer, Royal School of Mines, 1940-45. President of the Institution of Mining and Metallurgy, 1932-33; Hon. Fellow Imperial College of Science and Technology, 1941. *Publications:* Roberts-Austen: a Record of his Work, 1914; numerous scientific papers, addresses and contributions to discussions. *Recreation:* golf. *Address:* 10 Queensberry Place, South Kensington, S.W.7. *Clubs:* Royal Commonwealth Society, Roehampton. [*Died* 30 *Jan.* 1963.

SMITH, Sir Thomas, Kt., *cr.* 1921; *b.* 28 August 1875; *s.* of late Thomas Smith, Haddington; *m.* 1907, Elsie Maud, *d.* of late Sir Henry Ledgard; two *s.* one *d.* Royal Bank of Scotland, 1891-95; served in India, 1895-1935; Allahabad Bank Ltd. 1895-1913 and a Director of same, 1929-1935; Muir Mills Co. Ltd., Cawnpore, 1913-1935, of which Managing Director and Chairman, 1915-35; Deputy Chairman of the Mercantile Bank of India Ltd., 1935-1951; President, Upper India Chamber of Commerce, 1918-21; apptd. Hon. Mem. of the same, 1932; Member United Provinces Legislative Council, 1918-26; Commandant Cawnpore Rifles, 1913-20; Member of Hunter Committee on Punjab Disorders, 1919; Member New Delhi Capital Enquiry Committee, 1922; Delegate representing employers of labour in India at Geneva, 1925; Chevalier of the Order of the Crown, Belgium, 1919; Volunteer Decoration, 1914. *Address:* Westfield, Virginia Water, Surrey. *T.:* Wentworth 2129. *Club:* Oriental. [*Died* 15 *Nov.* 1963.

SMITH, Thomas, F.R.S. 1932; Consulting Physicist; lately Superintendent of Light Division, National Physical Laboratory; *b.* 1883; *s.* of W. E. and D. A. Smith, Leamington Spa; *m.* 1913, Elsie Muriel, *d.* of late E. M. Elligott; two *s.* three *d.* *Educ.:* Warwick School; Queens' College, Cambridge (Scholar). Past President, Physical Soc.; Past President, Optical Society; Past Pres., Internat. Commission of Optics; Hon. Mem. Optical Soc. of America, 1957. *Publications:* Many papers, mainly on optical and mathematical subjects, in Trans. Opt. Soc., Proc. Phys. Soc., Dictionary of applied Physics, and elsewhere. *Address:* Buxhall, Prospect Rd., Heathfield, Sussex. *T.:* Heathfield 2857. [*Died* 28 *Nov.* 1969.

SMITH, Sir Thomas D. S.; *see* Straker-Smith.

SMITH, Major Sir Thomas G. L.; *see* Lumley-Smith.

SMITH, Thomas James; Joint General Secretary, Society of Graphical and Allied Trades, 1966-70; *b.* 20 November 1905; British; *m.* Eileen Blackburn (decd.); one *d.*; *m.* 1950, Ellen Mary Lawrence. *Educ.:* L.C.C. and Shoreditch Techn. Institute. National Union of Printing, Bookbinding and Paper Workers: Sec., London Central Br., 1951-61; Gen. Sec., 1961; Union amalgamated to form S.O.G.A.T.; Exec. Mem., Internat. Graphical Fedn.; Printing Kindred Trades Fedn.; Mem., Nat. Economic Development Councils for Paper and Board and for Newspapers, Printing and Publishing; Cttee. Trade Union Unit Trust. *Recreations:* motoring, travel. *Address:* 28 Crown Lane, Southgate, N.14. [*Died* 3 *Aug.* 1970.

SMITH, Sir Thomas (Turner), 3rd Bt., *cr.* 1897; *b.* Hindhead, Surrey, England, 28 June 1903; *e. s.* of Gilbert Smith, M.D., F.R.C.S. (*d.* 1950) (2nd *s.* of 1st Bt.); *S.* uncle (Sir Thomas Rudolph Hampden Smith, Bt.), 1958; *m.* 1935, Agnes, *o. d.* of Bernard Page, Wellington, New Zealand; two *s.* two *d.* *Educ.:* Oundle. *Heir:* *s.* Thomas Gilbert Smith, *b.* 2 July 1937. *Address:* 27 Bond Street, Marton, New Zealand. [*Died* 11 *May* 1961.

SMITH, Vivian Francis C.; *see* Crowther-Smith.

SMITH, General (Walter) Bedell, Hon. G.B.E., *cr.* 1945; Hon. K.C.B., *cr.* 1944; D.S.M. (2 oak leaf clusters), D.S.M.-Navy, Legion of Merit, Bronze Star Medal, National Security Medal, and numerous foreign decorations; Vice-Chm., Board of Directors, American Machine & Foundry Co., since 1954; *b.* Indianapolis, 5 Oct. 1895; *e. s.* of William Long Smith and Ida Frances Bedell; *m.* 1917, Mary Eleanor Cline, Indianapolis, Indiana, U.S.A.; no *c.* *Educ.:* St. Peter and Paul's and Rensslear Polytechnic Inst., U.S.A. Private, Indiana Nat. Guard, 1910; 2nd Lieut. of Inf. U.S.A. 1917; France, 1918; served in the various grades as an Infantry and General Staff Officer; Maj.-Gen. Regular Army, 1942; General, 1951. Graduated Army War Coll., 1937; Command and Gen. Staff School, 1935, Inf. School (Advanced Course), 1932. Assistant to Chief Co-ordinator (U.S.), and later Exec. Officer and Dep. Chief Co-ordinator, Bureau of Budget, 1926-29; Asst. Sec. and Sec., War Dept. Gen. Staff, 1939-42; First U.S. Secretary, Combined Chiefs of Staff, 1942; Chief of Staff Allied Forces, during the campaigns in N. Africa, Sicily and Italy, 1942-44; Chief of Staff, Allied Expeditionary Forces in Europe, 1944-45; on behalf of Gen. Eisenhower signed formal unconditional surrender of Italy, 1943, and Germany, 1945; U.S. Ambassador to Soviet Union, 1946-49; Commanding General 1st Army, Governor's Island, New York, April 1949-Oct. 1950; Director Central Intelligence Agency, Oct. 1950-Jan. 1953. Army Retired List, 1953, as General; Under-Secretary of State, U.S., Jan. 1953-Sept. 1954. Holds many Hon. degrees from American and foreign Universities. *Publications:* Eisenhower's Six Great Decisions (Sat. Ev. Post), 1945; My Three Years in Moscow, 1950. *Recreations:* fishing and shooting. *Address:* American Machine & Foundry Co., 1701 K. St., N.W., Washington 6, D.C., U.S.A. *Clubs:* Army and Navy (Washington); Union, Links and Metropolitan (New York); Rockaway Hunting (Long Island). [*Died* 9 *Aug.* 1961.

SMITH, Walter Robert George, C.I.E. 1937; Barrister-at-law, Gray's Inn; *b.* 5 Nov. 1887; *m.* 1913, Ellen, *d.* of late John Cochrane. *Educ.:* Grove Park School, Wrexham. Joined Indian Police, 1908; District Superintendent, 1921; Deputy Commissioner of Police, Bombay, 1932; Commissioner of Police, Bombay, 1933-42; King's Police Medal, 1933; Member, Federal Public Service Commission, Govt. of India, 1942-47. *Recreation:* photography. *Address:* c/o National and Grindlay's Bank Ltd., 13 St. James's Square, S.W.1. *Club:* Royal Over-Seas League. [*Died* 23 *June* 1966.

SMITH, Vice-Admiral William B.; *see* Bowden Smith, Vice-Adm. W.

SMITH, William Henry, C.B.E. 1953; President: Welsh National Opera Co. Ltd. since 1968 (Chairman, 1948-68); Guild of

Welsh Playwrights; *b.* 9 Oct. 1894; *s.* of William Henry and Eliza Smith; *m.* 1924, Elsie, *d.* of William Alexander and Dinah Dugard Allan. *Educ.:* Albany Road Sch. and Technical Coll., Cardiff. Served European War, 1914-18, with R.A., in Serbia, Egypt and Palestine; subsequently joined Stratton Instone Ltd., London; started in retail car business on own account, 1932. Chairman, Welsh Centre of Motor and Cycle Trades Benevolent Fund, 1934-50 and of E. Wales Div. of Motor Agents Assoc., 1935-37 and 1943-44. Member: Cardiff New Theatre Trust; Court of Governors, Univ. Coll. of S. Wales and Mon. Hon. LL.D. University of Wales, 1961. F.I.M.I. *Recreations:* music, golf, football. *Address:* Little Mead, Cefn Mount, Dinas Powis, Glam. *T.:* Dinas Powis 3172. *Clubs:* Royal Over-Seas; Cardiff and County, Cardiff Exchange (Cardiff); Swansea Exchange and County. [*Died* 9 *June* 1968.

SMITH, Sir William P., Bt.; *see* Prince-Smith.

SMITH, Sir William P(roctor), Kt. 1959; J.P.; President, Refuge Assurance Co. Ltd., since 1962 (Chm. 1952-62); Director District Bank Ltd.; *b.* 20 Dec. 1891; *s.* of late Philip Smith, Sale, and late Margaret Smith (*née* Proctor), Hale; *m.* 1925, Ailsa Mary, *d.* of late William Cooke, Putney; one *s.* one *d.* *Educ.:* Bowdon College. Served European War, 1915-18, with Artists' Rifles and Manchester Regiment. J.P. Cheshire, 1933. *Recreations:* reading, gardening and sport. *Address:* Bexton House, Knutsford, Cheshire. *T.:* Knutsford 3523. *Clubs:* Royal Automobile, Kennel; St. James's (Manchester). [*Died* 11 *Dec.* 1963.

SMITH, Wilson, F.R.S. 1949; M.D.; F.R.C.P.; Dipl. Bact.; Consultant and Adviser, Microbiological Research Establishment, Porton, 1960-64, retd.; Professor Emeritus of Bacteriology, Univ. of London, since 1960; Hon. Consultant Bacteriologist, Univ. Coll. Hospital, since 1960; Member, Medical Research Council, since Oct. 1961; *b.* 21 June 1897; *s.* of late John Howard and Nancy Smith; *m.* 1927, Muriel Mary Nutt; two *d.* *Educ.:* Accrington Gram. Sch.; Manchester University, M.B., Ch.B. 1923; Diploma Bacteriology, Manchester, 1927; M.D. (Commendation) Manchester, 1929. Served European War, 1915-19, 107th Field Amb. Research Assistant, National Institute Medical Research, 1927; Member of Scientific Staff, National Institute Medical Research, 1929-39; Professor of Bacteriology, University of Sheffield, 1939-46; Professor of Bacteriology, Univ. Coll. Hosp. Medical School, Univ. of London, 1946-60; Consultant Bacteriologist, Univ. Coll. Hosp., 1950-60. Leeuwenhoek Lectr., Roy. Soc., London, 1957; Ambuj Nath Bose Prize, Roy. Coll. of Physicians, 1959; Graham Gold Medal, Univ. Lond.,1960. Chairman, Governing Body, Foot and Mouth Disease Res. Institute, 1952-55; Advisory Editor, Brit. Jl. Experimental Pathology; Member: Pathological Soc. Gt. Brit. and Ireland; Medical Research Club; Soc. General Microbiol.; Brit. Soc. Immunol.; Governing Body, Lister Inst.; Hon. Mem. Pathological Soc. of Manch. Hon. Mem. New York Acad. of Sciences. *Publications:* numerous papers on Influenza, Poliomyelitis, Viruses and Bacteriological subjects; ed., Mechanisms of Virus Infection, 1963. *Recreations:* music, carpentry. *Address:* 69 St. Francis Road, Salisbury, Wilts. *T.:* 4518. *Club:* Athenæum. [*Died* 10 *July* 1965.

SMOUT, Sir Arthur John Griffiths, Kt., *cr.* 1946; J.P.; LL.D.; C.G.I.A.; Chairman of Murex Ltd. and Murex Welding Processes Ltd. since 1953; *b.* 18 Nov. 1888; *e. s.* of Thomas and Mary Smout, Birmingham; *m.* 1918, Annie Hilda, *er. d.* of Arthur John Follows, J.P., Metchley Park, Edgbaston; five *s.* Formerly: Director-General of Ammunition Production, Ministry of Supply; Executive Director, I.C.I. *Address:* Sheriff's Lench, Evesham. *T.:* Harvington 371. *Club:* Union (Birmingham). [*Died* 21 *Feb.* 1961.

SMYLIE, Air Commodore Gilbert Formby, C.B. 1946; D.S.C. 1915; M.A. (Cantab.), M.I.M.E.; A.M.I.E.E.; R.A.F. (retd.); *b.* 22 Aug. 1895; *y. s.* of James Smylie, Manchester; *m.* 1916, Juliet, *d.* of E. C. Hoegerstaedt; two *d.* *Educ.:* King William's College; Downing College, Cambridge. Royal Naval Air Service (Pilot), 1915-18; served Dardanelles, Eastern Mediterranean and with Home Fleet; graduate of R.A.F. Staff College; served in England, Egypt and Italy, 1939-44; Director of Technical Training, Air Ministry, 1945-47; Sen. Tech. Staff Officer, H.Q. Flying Training Command; retired, 1949. *Address:* c/o Glyn, Mills & Co., Kirkland House, Whitehall, S.W.1. *Club:* R.A.F. [*Died* 5 *July* 1965.

SMYTH, John William, C.S.I. 1937; C.I.E. 1932, M.A. Cantab.; I.C.S., retired; *b.* London, 13 May 1880; *s.* of late F. H. Smyth, London; *m.* 1936, Muriel (*d.* 1948), *d.* of late John Cathie, Carshalton, and *widow* of Eric Russell, Ceylon. *Educ.:* Clare College Cambridge. Joined Indian Civil Service 1904; Deputy Commissioner, Upper Sind Frontier, 1911-12-1916-20; Assistant Commissioner in Sind, 1912-1916; Member of Council of State, 1926; Revenue Secretary to the Government of Bombay, 1926-30; Chief Commissioner, Andaman and Nicobar Islands, 1931-35; Commissioner, Poona, 1936-39. *Address:* Westbourne, Riseley, Reading. *T.:* Reading 83450. *Clubs:* East India and Sports; Royal Bombay Yacht; Sind (Karachi). [*Died* 2 *Feb.* 1968.

SMYTH, Michael Joseph, M.Ch., B.Sc. (N.U.I.); F.R.C.S. (Eng.); Surgeon, Westminster Hospital (Gordon Hospital); Senior Hon. Surgeon, Hosp. of St. John and St. Elizabeth; Consulting Surgeon: King Edward VII's Hospital for Officers; Queen Mary's (Ministry of Pensions) Hospital, Roehampton (abdominal diseases); Beckenham Hospital and St. Anthony's Hospital, Cheam; Jockey Club and National Hunt; *yr. s.* of late Patrick Smyth, J.P., Castleblayney, Co. Monaghan; *m.* Esther Mary, *er. d.* of late Hugh Kennedy, The Donahies, Raheny, Co. Dublin; three *s.* two *d.* *Educ.:* St. Vincent's College, Castleknock; St. Vincent's Hospital, Dublin; St. Bartholomew's and London Hospitals. 1st, 2nd, 3rd, 4th and final year Exhibitioner and Scholar, Univ. Coll., Dublin. M.B., B.Ch., B.A.O. First Hons., Special Distinction with Gold Medal, 1917. Flight-Lieut. R.A.F. Medical Service, 1918-20; Surgeon to Z. Royal Air Force Expedition, Somaliland, 1919; Resident Surgeon North Middlesex Hospital, 1921-25; First Surgical Assistant and Registrar, London Hospital, 1925-30. Fellow of: Assoc. of Surgeons of Gr. Brit. and Ireland; Internat. Soc. of Surgery; Roy. Soc. of Medicine (Member of Council and Ex-Pres., Section of Proctology); Med. Soc. of London (Ex-Sec. and Ex-Vice-Pres.); Mem. Council British Empire Cancer Campaign; Roy. Acad. of Med., Ireland; Member B.M.A. K.S.G. *Publications:* various articles in medical journals of Gt. Britain and Ireland. *Recreations:* golf, fishing. *Address:* 82 Harley Street, W.1. *Clubs:* Garrick; Sunningdale Golf; Royal St. George's Golf (Sandwich); Portmarnock Golf. [*Died* 15 *Sept.* 1964.

SMYTH, Montague, R.O.I.; *b.* St. Pancras 1863; *o. s.* of John Smyth, Barrister; *m.* 1891; one *s.* *Educ.:* Leamington College; Magdalene College, Cambridge. Went round the world at an early age to New Zealand in a sailing ship. Later studied in Germany for the army but eventually took up painting, and studied in Italy and Holland. Has exhibited many years in Royal Academy and other galleries. Sold, a few years ago, 4 pictures to Queen Mary. Served in Artists' Rifles and R.N.V.R. (commission) in European War, 1914. Went to China and Japan in 1905. *Publications:* Illustrated: Side Lights on Chinese Life; Old and New Japan. *Recreations:* golf and travel. *Address:* 10 Primrose Hill Studios, Fitzroy Road, N.W.1. *T.:* Primrose 3013. [*Died* 28 *Feb.* 1965.

SMYTH-OSBOURNE, Air Commodore Sir Henry Percy, Kt. 1959; C.M.G. 1919; C.B.E. 1945; D.L. and J.P., Devon; late R.A.F.; *b.* 28 Jan. 1879; *s.* of late J. S. Smyth-Osbourne, D.L., J.P., of Ash, Iddesligh, N. Devon, and Mrs. E. C. Smyth-Osbourne, *d.* of Gen. Prior; *m.* 1913, Elaine Mabel Cecily Katherine (*d.* 1964), *d.* of late Sir Martin le M. Gosselin and Hon. Lady Gosselin of Blakesware, Herts; two *d.* *Educ.:* Pencarwick, Exmouth; Littlejohns; H.M.S. Britannia. Served as Midshipman in North America and West Indies in the corvette, H.M.S. Cordelia; later in H.M. Frigate Raleigh, Sub-Lieut. 1899; as a Lieut. served as Flag-Lieut. in Channel Fleet, China Fleet, Cruiser Squadron, and Mediterranean Fleet; Comdr. 1913; Wing Commander R.N.A.S., 1915; Wing Captain R.N.A.S., 1917; Brig.-General R.F.C., 1918; served in France in command of H.Q. Brigade R.F.C.; Air Sec. to Sec. of State for War (Sir Winston Churchill), and Dep. Dir. Air Ministry; Regional Controller Air Defence Cadet Corps for S.W. England and Wales, 1938-41; Commandant Air Training Corps, S.W. Command, 1941-45; was Joint-Master of Eggesford Hounds; J.P., D.L. Devon; Hon. Air Commodore Nos. 3512 and 3513 Fighter Control Units, R.A.A.F.; former Pres. Torrington Div. Conservative and Unionist Assoc.; President Okehampton R.A.F. Assoc. *Recreations:* shooting and fishing. *Address:* Holmedown, Exbourne, North Devon. *T.:* Exbourne 241. *Club:* Army and Navy. [*Died* 28 *March* 1969.

SMYTHE, Canon Francis Henry Dumville, M.A.; Canon Emeritus; Proctor in Convocation, 1937; *b.* Jan. 1873; *s.* of Francis Cooper Dumville Smythe, solicitor of Staple Inn and Girdlers Hall; *m.* 1st, Angelina (*d.* 1960), *d.* of D. Busby; two *d.*; 2nd, 1960, Phyllis Violet, B.A. Hons. Lond., *d.* of E. H. Phillips, Hove. *Educ.:* Haileybury; Emmanuel Coll., Camb. Rector of Horsted Keynes, Sx., 1900-09; Vicar of St. Barnabas, Hove, 1909-29; Vicar of Eastbourne, 1929-30; Prebendary of Hova Villa in Chichester Cathedral, 1929; Rural Dean of Eastbourne; Archdeacon of Lewes, 1929-46; Canon Emeritus, 1946. *Publications:* Guide to the King's Highway: The Choir Psalter; St. Mary's Book; The Christian's Stewardship; Christian Giving, etc. *Address:* Moorcroft, Birtley Road, Bramley, Nr. Guildford, Surrey. [*Died* 8 *Oct.* 1966.

SNEDDEN, Sir Richard, Kt., *cr.* 1951; C.V.O. 1967; C.B.E. 1942; M.A., LL.B.; Barrister-at-Law; Hon. Capt. Royal Naval Reserve; Hon. LL.D. (Edin.); *b.* 1900; *e. s.* of late George Snedden, Edinburgh; *m.* 1926, Janet Catherine, *o. d* of late Duncan MacDougall, Kilchoman, Islay; one *s.* *Educ.:* George Watson's College; Edinburgh University (President of Students' Representative Council). First Life Mem. Exec. Council of Shipping Fedn. (Chief Exec., 1936-1962; Sec., 1933-36; Asst. Sec., 1929-33); Dep. Chm., King George's Fund for Sailors (Chm., Merchant Navy Cttee., 1946-62); Mem., Nat. Insce. Adv. Cttee., 1955-65, and Railway Staff Nat. Tribunal, 1958-65; Gen. Manager, Internat. Shipping Fedn. and Chm. of Shipowners' Gp. at Internat. Maritime Confs. and Jt. Maritime Commn.; Director: Consolidated Gold Fields; Monotype Corp.; Aldershot Traction; Amalgamated Roadstone Corp.; Chm, National Sea Training Schools, 1944-60; Vice-Chm., M.N. Training Board. 1936-62; Chairman, Industrial Relations Committee of British Employers' Confederation, 1942-62; Member, National Maritime Board, 1936-62; Member, M.N. Welfare Board, 1948-62; Member, Minister of Labour's National Advisory Cttee., 1940-1962; Mem., Colonial Labour Adv. Cttee., 1952-60; Mem., Sea Cadet Council and Exec. of Navy League, 1943-62; Mem., Brit. Delegn. to Internat. Labour Confs., 1923-(Vice-Pres., 1955 Conf.) and Vice-Chm., Employers' Group, 1953-60; Mem., Govg. Body of I.L.O., 1952-60; Pres., Internat. Organisation of Employers, 1957-58 (Vice-Pres., 1955-56); Sec., Brit. Employers' Confedn., 1926-29. Member of the Queen's Body Guard for Scotland; Grand Officer of the Order of Christ (Portugal). Commander of: Order of Dannebrog (Denmark); Order of the Lion of Finland; Order of St. Olav (Norway); Order of Vasa (Sweden); Order of the Crown (Belgium); Order of Orange-Nassau (Netherlands). *Recreation:* heraldry. *Address:* Aldwick Grange, Boar's Head, Crowborough, Sussex. *T.:* Crowborough 2851. *Clubs:* Athenæum, Junior Carlton, Pratt's. [*Died* 9 *March* 1970.

SNELL, Harvie Kennard; C.B.E. 1961; Q.H.P. 1959-62; Director of Medical Services, Prison Commission, 1951-63, retd.; *b.* 25 Apr. 1898; *s.* of late William Kennard Snell, Okehampton, Devon; *m.* 1926, Eileen Mary Chalker; one *s.* *Educ.:* Alleyn's School, Dulwich; King's College, London Univ.; King's College Hospital, London. Appointments at K.C.H., 1921-23. Joined Prison Medical Service, 1924, and served in various prisons; seconded to Broadmoor as Medical Officer, 1926-28; Principal Medical Officer, Wormwood Scrubs Prison, 1947-50. Inspector of Retreats under Inebriates Acts, 1951. *Publications:* contrib. to professional journals. *Address:* Westwinds, Green End, Comberton, Cambridge. [*Died* 9 *March* 1969.

SNELLING, Major-Gen. Arthur Hugh Jay, C.B. 1945; C.B.E. 1945 (O.B.E. 1943); *b.* 30 Sept. 1897; *s.* of Arthur Thomas Snelling, Norwich; *m.* 1919, Helen Elizabeth, *d.* of Captain E. J. W. Reader, O.B.E., Queen's Royal Regiment; one *s.* two *d.* *Educ.:* Gresham's School, Norfolk. Commissioned into Indian Army, 1915, 4 P.A.V. Rajputs; European War, Mesopotamia, Aug. 1916-May 1918; North West Frontier, 1919-23, 1932-33; Staff College, Camberley, 1930-1931; War of 1939-45, A.A. and Q.M.G. 10 Ind. Div., 1941-42, operations Iraq, E. Syria and Persia (O.B.E.); Brigadier i/c Administration Ceylon, 1942-43; Maj.-Gen. i/c Admin. Fourteenth Army, 1943-45, Campaign in E. Bengal, Burma and Arakan (C.B.E., C.B.); Commander 505 (North and Central Burma) District, Apr.-Nov. 1945; Major-General i/c Administration Southern Commd., India, 1945; retd., 1948. Ministry of Defence, 1949-58. *Address:* Tamia Ridge, Camberley Sy. *T.:* 4720. *Club:* United Service. [*Died* 30 *Dec.* 1965.

SNOW, (George) Robert Sabine, F.R.S. 1948; B.Sc., M.A.; *b.* 19 Jan. 1897; *s.* of Thomas Snow and Edith (*née*)Banbury; *m.* 1930, Christine Mary Pilkington. *Educ.:* Winchester; New College, Oxford. Fellow of Magdalen College, Oxford, 1922-60. *Publications:* Papers in Proc. and Trans. of Roy. Soc., New Phytologist, etc. *Address:* Villa Roca-Rosa, Ave. Clemenceau, 66, Vernet-les-Bains, Pyr.-Or., France. [*Died* 1 *Aug.* 1969.

SNOW, Lieut.-Col. Humphry Waugh, C.M.G. 1919; D.S.O. 1916; late Royal West Kent Regiment Reserve of Officers; *b.* 10 April 1879 *s.* of late Andrew Waugh Snow, Kingsmill House, Nutfield, Surrey; *m.* 1914, Jean Bouverie, *y. d.* of late Colonel

W. T. MacLeod, of Raasay. *Educ.:* Radley College. Joined Regiment, 1899; Adjutant, 1906-09; attached Egyptian Army, 1910-14 (4th class Medjidie); European War, 1914-18 D.A.A. and Q.M.G. 15th Division, A.A.G. 3rd Army, A.A. and Q.M.G. Royal Tank Corps (despatches five times, C.M.G., D.S.O., Officer Legion of Honour, Bts. Major and Lieut.-Col.); Private Secretary and Comptroller of the Household to Viscount Byng of Vimy, Governor-General of Canada, 1924-26; Comptroller of the Household to Viscount Willingdon, 1926-31; and to the Earl of Bessborough, 1931. *Address:* Old Swan Cottage, Wilton, near Marlborough, Wilts *T.:* Great Bedwyn 252. [*Died* 22 *May* 1969.

SNOW, Robert S.; *see* Snow, G. R. S.

SOAR, Leonard Charles; Headmaster, Enfield Grammar School, Middlesex, 1934-64; *b.* 26 Feb. 1899; *s.* of late William Edward Soar, Sidmouth; *m.* 1926, Margaret Mary, *y. d.* of late T. B. Ellery, Dulwich; two *s.* *Educ.:* Alleyn's School, Dulwich; St. John's College, Cambridge. Assist. Master, Whitgift Grammar School, 1923-31; Chief Physics Master, Whitgift Grammar School, 1927-31; Headmaster, The Grammar School, Henley-on-Thames, 1931-34; Member I.A.H.M., A.S.E. and Maths. Assoc. *Address:* 2 Bycullah Road, Enfield, Middx. *T.:* Enfield 1782. [*Died* 14 *Feb.* 1969.

SOLE, Brig. Denis Mavesyn Anslow, D.S.O. 1917; *b.* 3 May 1883; *m.* 2nd, Lilian May, *d.* of R. H. Story; one *s.* one *d.* *Educ.:* Cheltenham College. Served S. Africa, 1901; European War, 1914-19 (despatches five times, D.S.O. and bar, Bt. Major, Legion of Honour); commanded 1st Bn. The King's Regt. 1932-36; Commander 148th (North Midland) Infantry Brigade, T.A., 1936; retd., 1939. *Address:* Arnfield, Warminster, Wilts. *T.:* Warminster 2400. [*Died* 27 *March* 1962.

SOLLEY, Leslie Judah, B.Sc.; Barrister; *b.* 15 Dec. 1905; *e. s.* of Emmanuel Solley, London; *m.* 1944, José Olga Fisher (marr. diss. 1964); two *s.* one *d.* *Educ.:* Davenant Foundation Sch., London; London Univ (B.Sc.). Originally intended to take up science as a career; called to Bar, Inner Temple, 1934 (Profumo Prize and Yarborough-Andersen Scholarship); Member S.E. Circuit and Herts and Essex Sessions. Practises at Common Law Bar. Member Labour Party, 1923-49; M.P. (Lab. Ind.), 1949-50, Thurrock Div. of Essex (Lab., 1945-1949, when expelled from Labour Party); subsequently re-admitted to Labour Party. Member Performing Rights Society; Vice-Pres., Songwriters' Guild of Great Britain Ltd. *Publications:* pamphlets and articles on legal, political and industrial matters. *Recreation:* music, composer and pianist. *Address:* 16 Woodstock Avenue, N.W.11. [*Died* 8 *Jan.* 1968.

SOLOMON, Captain William Ewart Gladstone; Kaiser-i-Hind Medal (First Class); Fellow, Royal Society of Arts; *b.* Sea Point, Cape Town, 1880; *s.* of late Saul Solomon, M.L.A.; *m.*; one *s.* Studied Royal Academy Schools, London; took highest prizes and medals including Gold Medal and Travelling Studentship in Painting; exhibited Royal Academy, Paris Salon, etc.; military service Gallipoli, Mesopotamia, and India, 1914-19; Principal, Government School of Art, Bombay, 1919, Director 1929-1937; Curator, Prince of Wales Museum of Western India, 1919-37, and Member of the Board of Trustees; reorganised curriculum of Bombay School of Art, introducing Mural Painting, Life Classes, Indian Design, etc. Exhibited his own paintings of India at Walker's Galleries, London, 1938; lectured on Indian Art, London, Oxford and Paris (Musée Guimet). He resided in Johannesburg, formerly, where he held several one-man exhibitions. *Publications:* Mural Paintings of the Bombay School; "Essays on Mogul Art"; "Saul Solomon, the Member for Cape Town" etc. *Address:* Riviera, Pentrich Rd., St. James, Cape, South Africa. *Club:* Arts. [*Died* 18 *Dec.* 1965.

SOLOMONS, Bethel, M.D., B.Ch., B.A.O. (University, Dublin), F.R.C.P.I.; M.R.I.A.; F.R.C.O.G.; F.A.C.S. (Hon.); Inspector of Qualifying Examinations and Visitor of Medical Schools in Midwifery for G.M.C.; late Gynæcologist to Dr. Steevens Hospital, Dublin; Master Rotunda Hospital, Dublin, 1926-1933; Vice-Pres. British College of Obstetricians and Gynæcologists; Pres. Royal College of Physicians, Ireland; Gynæcologist Mercers Hosp., Dublin; Consulting Gynæcologist, Countess of Wicklow Hospital, Arklow, and Newcastle Sanatorium; *s.* of late Maurice E. Solomons, J.P.; *m.* Gertrude, *d.* of Joseph Levy, Manchester; two *s.* one *d.* *Educ.:* Trinity College, Dublin (B.A.); Paris, Vienna, Berlin, Leipzig, Dresden, Munich, etc. L.M. Rotunda Hospital, 1908; F.R.C.P.I. 1914; Extern Maternity Assistant Rotunda Hospital, 1908, Assistant Master, 1908; President Obstetrical Section, B.M.A., 1933; President: Obstetrical Section, Royal Academy of Medicine, Ireland (late Secretary Obstetrical Section; Member of Council Pathological Section); President Dublin University Biological Association, 1919-20; Hon. Secretary: Obstetrical and Gynæcological Section B.M.A. 1910; British Gynæcological Congress; Hon. Fellow: American Assoc. Obstetricians and Gynæcologists; Central Association of Gynæcologists of America; Hon. Member: Société Française de Gynécologie, Sociedade Brasileira de Ginecologia. *Publications:* Handbook of Gynæcology, 4th edition, 1944; Seventh Edition Tweedy's Obstetrics; Practical Midwifery for Nurses, 1931; Epitome of Obstetrical Diagnosis and Treatment in General Practice, 1934; One Doctor in his Time, 1956; many original papers on Gynæcology and Obstetrics, published in Surgery, Gynæcology, and Obstetrics; Transactions, Royal Academy of Medicine, Ireland, Medical Press, etc. *Recreations:* hunting, etc. *Address:* Laughton Beg, Rochestown Avenue, Dun Laoghaire, Co. Dublin. *T.:* Dublin 83192. *T.A.:* Dr. Bethel Solomons, Dublin. *Clubs:* Savage; St. Stephens Green (Dublin). [*Died* 11 *Sept.* 1965.

SOLOMONS, Estella Frances, H.R.H.A. *Educ.:* Metropolitan School of Art, Dublin; Royal Hibernian Academy; Chelsea Art School. Portraits in Dublin and Belfast Municipal Galleries and Armagh Gallery. *Publications:* Illustrations in: Mud and Purple, by Seumas O'Sullivan, 1918; The Glamour of Dublin, by D. L. Kelleher, 1929; The Road Round Ireland, by Padraic Colum, 1926; Portraits of Patriots, by Hilary Pyle, 1966, etc. *Address:* 2 Morehampton Road, Dublin. *T.:* 684140. [*Died* 2 *Nov.* 1968.

SOLOMONS, Henry; M.P. (Lab.) Kingston upon Hull North since 1964; *b.* 7 Nov. 1902; *e. s.* of Benjamin Solomons and late Elizabeth Solomons; *m.* 1939, Anne Bass. *Educ.:* L.C.C. Schools. Miscellaneous commercial appointments until 1938. Staff, Board of Deputies of British Jews, 1938-39. Served Army, 1939-45 ("Labour Prime Minister" in "Cairo Forces Parliament"). Organising Sec., Union of Liberal and Progressive Synagogues, 1946-54; Officer, Union of Shop, Distributive and Allied Workers, 1954-64. *Recreations:* politics, listening to others' speeches and sermons. *Address:* 9 Flanchford Road, Stamford Brook, W.12. [*Died* 7 *Nov.* 1965.

SOMERS, Thomas Peter Miller, C.B.E. 1938; J.P., Glasgow; M.Inst.Mun.E.; *b.* 14 June 1877; *m.* 1909, Mary Crawford Lindsay; no *c.* *Educ.:* Woodside

Public School; Royal Technical College. City Engineer, Corporation of Glasgow; Chief Asst., 1912-24; Master of Works and City Engineer, Glasgow, 1924-42; retired; late Chairman, Clyde Valley Regional Town Planning Committee. *Club:* Art (Glasgow). [*Died* 21 *Nov.* 1965.

SOMERS COCKS, John Sebastian, C.B.E. 1959; C.V.O. 1961; H.M. Consul-General, Naples, since 1959; *b.* 6 Feb. 1907; *s.* of late Philip Alphonso Somers Cocks, C.M.G., and late Gwenllian Blanche Williams; *heir-pres.* to 8th Baron Somers; *m.* 1946, Marjorie Olive Weller: one *s.* two *d.* *Educ.:* Ampleforth College; Balliol College, Oxford. Laming Trav. Fell. of The Queen's Coll., Oxf., 1929. H.M. Foreign Service, 1930; Brussels Embassy, 1930-33; Foreign Office, 1933-37; Bagdad Embassy, 1937-39; Budapest Legation, 1939-40; Helsinki Legation, 1940-41; Foreign Office, 1941-43; Tehran Embassy, 1943-47; Holy See Legation, 1947-52; Foreign Office, 1952-54; Munich, 1954-59. *Recreations:* music, literature, ski-ing, climbing, sightseeing. *Address:* British Consulate-General, Naples, Italy. *Clubs:* St. James', Challoner [*Died* 25 *May* 1964.

SOMERSET, Henry Robert Somers Fitzroy de Vere, D.S.O. 1917; late Coldstream Guards; *b.* 3 March 1898; *s.* of late H. C. Somers Somerset; *heir-pres.* to 10th Duke of Beaufort, K.G., P.C., G.C.V.O.; *m.* 1922, Bettine, *d.* of late Hon. Mrs. Sopwith and late Major C. E. Malcolm; one *s.* one *d.* (and *er. s.* killed in action, 1945). *Educ.:* Eton; Sandhurst. Served European War (despatches, D.S.O.); War of 1939-45, R.N.V.R. *Clubs:* Beefsteak, White's, Royal Ocean Racing. [*Died* 27 *Feb.* 1965.

SOMERVELL, David Churchill, M.A. Oxon; *b.* 16 July 1885; *s.* of late Robert Somervell, bursar of Harrow School; *m.* 1918, Dorothea, *d.* of Rev. D. Harford; one *s.* one *d.* *Educ.:* Harrow; Magdalen College, Oxford. Assistant Master at Repton School, 1909-18 and at Tonbridge School, 1919-50. *Publications:* A Short History of our Religion, 1922; Disraeli and Gladstone, 1925; English Thought in the Nineteenth Century, 1928; The British Empire, 1930; The Reign of King George the Fifth, 1935; Robert Somervell of Harrow, 1935; Livingstone, 1936; A History of the United States, 1942; A History of Tonbridge School, 1947; British Politics since 1900, 1950; Stanley Baldwin, 1953. *Recreations:* walking, bicycling, music. *Address:* Russetts, Benenden, Cranbrook, Kent. *T.:* Benenden 2114. [*Died* 17 *Jan.* 1965.

SOMERVELL, Rupert Churchill Gelderd, C.B. 1942; *b.* 24 April 1892; *s.* of Frederick Gelderd Somervell and Emma Churchill; *m.* 1st, 1918, Olive Winifred Naylor (*d.* 1957); one *d.*; 2nd, 1962, Mrs. Effie C. Inskipp, London, *widow* of Wilson Inskipp. *Educ.:* Eton; Magdalen College, Oxford. Served European War, 1914-18, 60th Rifles and R.F.C.; Ministry of Labour, 1919-37; seconded for service under League of Nations as adviser to Chinese Govt., 1933-1935; transferred to Board of Trade (Industries and Manufactures Dept.), 1937; Under-Secretary, 1941, retired 1952. *Recreations:* sailing and riding. *Address:* 33 Gallis Flats, Hughes-Hallet St., Sliema, Malta G.C. *Club:* Royal Thames Yacht. [*Died* 10 *Aug.* 1969.

SOMERVILLE, Sir John Livingston, Kt., *cr.* 1954; F.R.S.E.; *b.* 1 Aug. 1885; 2nd *s.* of George Somerville, Procurator Fiscal, Edinburgh; *m.* 1926, Frances Agnes Dalrymple, *d.* of late R. P. Wilson, Markinch, Fife; one *d.* *Educ.:* George Watson's College; Edinburgh University. Chartered Accountant senior partner, Wallace & Somerville, C.A., Edin.; Pres. Inst. of Chartered Accountants of Scotland, 1953-55. Served European War, 1914-18 (wounded); Major R.G.A.T.F.; Staff Captain, R.A. VII Corps. *Recreations:* golf, fishing, shooting. *Address:* 8 Ravelston Park, Edinburgh. *T.:* Dean 1928. *Clubs:* Caledonian United Service (Edinburgh); Royal and Ancient Golf (St. Andrews). [*Died* 31 *Aug.* 1964.

SOMERVILLE, Mary; O.B.E. 1935; Hon. M.A. Manchester, 1943; *b.* N.Z., 1 Nov. 1897; *e. d.* of late Rev. J. A. Somerville; *m.* 1928, Ralph Penton Brown (whom she divorced, 1945); one *s.*; *m.* 1962, Eric Rowan Davies. *Educ.:* privately; Somerville College, Oxford (B.A. 1925). Experimental talks for schools broadcast during 1924; joined B.B.C. in 1925 as Schools Assistant to the late J. C. Stobart, then Education Director; Director of School Broadcasting, B.B.C., 1929-47; Secretary Central Council for School Broadcasting, 1929-35; Asst. Controller, Talks Division, 1947-50; Controller of Talks Division, 1950-1955, retired. *Publications:* Short stories and articles contributed to various English and American periodicals. *Address:* 5 Macaulay Buildings, Bath. *T.:* 5836. [*Died* 1 *Sept.* 1963.

SOMERVILLE SMITH, Herbert, C.M.G. 1953; D.S.O. 1918; O.B.E. 1937; M.C. 1917; *b.* 1890; *e. s.* of Wm. Smith, I.S.O., Ottawa; *m.* 1936, Anne John, *d.* of L. H. Montgomery, Selma, Ala. *Educ.:* Queen's Univ., Kingston, Ontario; New College, Oxford. Rhodes Scholar, 1912-14. Served European War, R.F.A., 1914-19; Reparation Commission, Paris, 1920-30; Export Credits Guarantee Dept., 1930-40; Chief Civil Adviser on Spears Mission to Free French, 1940-42; Chairman, British American Coordinating Cttee., Turkey, 1942-45; Overseas Finance Dept., H.M. Treasury, 1946-49; Comptroller General Export Credits Guarantee Dept., 1949-52. Governor, Milton Abbey School, Dorset; Councillor, Anglo-Turkish Society. *Recreation:* golf. *Address:* Lista de Correos Plaza Corsini, Tarragona, Spain. [*Died* 4 *March* 1967.

SOMMERVILLE, Vice-Admiral Frederick Avenel, D.S.O. 1918; *b.* 1883; 3rd *s.* of late William Sommerville, Bitton, Glos.; *m.* 1st, 1912, Gladys Rothes (*d.* 1943), 3rd *d.* of late Col. J. A. Barlow, Manchester Regt.; two *s.*; 2nd, Elizabeth Hay M'Whirter. Served European War, 1914-18 (despatches, D.S.O., promoted, Legion of Honour, Siamese Order of the Crown); commanded Submarine Depôt, Fort Blockhouse, 1921; Chief Staff Officer, New Zealand Division Navy Office, Wellington, 1925; Inspecting Captain, Mechanical Training Establishments, 1927; Flag Captain, H.M.S. Emperor of India, 1929-30; H.M.S. Valiant, 1930-31; Ceres, 1931; Rear-Admiral and retired list, 1931; Vice-Adm., retd., 1935. War of 1939-45, served as Commodore of Convoys and in the Ministry of Aircraft Production. *Address:* Sevens, St. Catherine's Road, Hayling Island. *T.:* Hayling Island 77464. *Club:* United Service. [*Died* 15 *July* 1962.

SONDES, 4th Earl (*cr.* 1880), **George Henry Milles-Lade;** Baron Sondes, 1760; Viscount Throwley, 1880; *b.* 8 Feb. 1914; *o. s.* of Hon. H. A. Milles-Lade, 4th *s.* of 1st Earl and Esther, *d.* of late Col. J. S. Benyon, Islip House, Thrapston; *S.* uncle, 1941; *m.* 1939, Pamela (*d.* 1967), *d.* of Col. H. McDougall, Cawston Manor, Norfolk; one *s.* *Educ.:* Eton Coll. Landowner. *Recreations:* all sports; shooting, cricket, golf, tennis, etc. *Heir:* *s.* Viscount Throwley. *Address:* Lees Court, Faversham, Kent. *T.:* Faversham 2615. *Club:* Junior Carlton. [*Died* 30 *April* 1970.

SOPWITH, Douglas George, C.B.E. 1957; J.P.; D.Sc., Wh. Sch., F.I.Mech.E., F.R.S.E.; Director, 1951-66, Special Adviser, 1967-68, National Engineering Laboratory (formerly Mechanical Engineering Research Laboratory), Ministry of Technology (formerly Department of Scientific and Industrial Research); Vis. Prof. of Mechanical Engineering, Univ. of Strathclyde; *b.* 13 Nov. 1906; *s.* of Joseph Douglas and Olga Alexandra Sopwith. *Educ.:* Manchester Grammar School; Manchester University. Practical training, Manchester Dry Docks Co. Ltd., 1922-25; Manchester Univ., 1925-28; B.Sc. Tech. (Mech. Eng.) 1st Cl. Hons., 1928; Whitworth Schol., 1928; D.Sc., 1948. Joined Scientific Staff of Engineering Dept., Nat. Physical Laboratory, 1928 (Supt. Engineering Div., 1948). Instn. of Mech. Engrs. prizes: Thomas Lowe Gray, 1934, T. Bernard Hall, 1949. Member various scientific and technical cttees. and of British delegations to internat. confs. on engineering standards, etc.; Pres. Whitworth Soc., 1963-64; Member of Court of Governors, Manchester College of Science and Technology; Chm., Scottish Branch, I.Mech.E.; Mem. Council, R.S.E. *Publications:* numerous papers in Proc. Roy. Soc., Instn. of Mech. Engrs., etc. *Address:* 45 Whitemoss Road, East Kilbride, Glasgow. [*Died* 20 *Oct.* 1970.

SORLEY, Herbert Tower, C.S.I. 1946; C.I.E. 1939; M.A., D.Litt.; F.R.S.A. 1950; I.C.S. (retd.); Member Central Board of Revenue, Pakistan Government, Karachi, until 1952; *b.* 12 April 1892; *e. s.* of late J. T. Sorley, M.A., Ardgay, Milltimber, Aberdeenshire; *m.* 1920, Marjorie Davidson, *o. d.* of late George Niven, Physician, West Didsbury, Manchester; two *d.* *Educ.:* Aberdeen Grammar School; Aberdeen Univ.; Christ Church, Oxford. Entered I.C.S. in 1914; India, 1915, Bombay Presidency; served in various capacities in revenue and magisterial appointments; Member Legislative Assembly of the Governor General, 1930-32 (Central Government); President Anthropological Society of Bombay, 1938-39; Chief Sec. to Govt. of Bombay Political and Services Dept., 1946. *Publications:* The Census Volumes relating to Bombay Presidency and Sind, 1931 (with A. H. Dracup), 1932; The Marine Fisheries of the Bombay Presidency, 1933; Shah Abdul Latif of Bhit, 1940; Light verse for private circulation, 1945; Musa Pervagans: translations of lyric poetry, 1953; Exile: studies of: Ovid, Prince Charles Edward, and Victor Hugo, 1964. Editor-compiler of Sind Gazetteers (for W. Pakistan Govt.), 1956. *Recreations:* literature, art. *Address:* 3 Taormina Avenue, Marlborough, Salisbury, Rhodesia. [*Died* 7 *Aug.* 1968.

SOROKIN, Pitirim Alexandrovitch, LL.M., Dr.Soc. hon. Ph.D.; Professor of Sociology, Harvard University, since 1930; Director, Harvard Research Center in Altruism since 1949; *b.* Turia, Russia, 21 Jan. 1889; *s.* of Alexander P. Sorokin and Pelageia V. Rymskich; *m.* 1917, Elena P. Baratynskaia; two *s.* *Educ.:* Night School; Teacher College; Psycho-Neurol. Inst.; University of St. Petersburg. Itinerant artisan and farm-boy; factory hand and tutor; journalist; Privatdozent: Psycho-Neurol. Inst., 1914-16; Univ. of St. Petersburg, 1916-17. Prof. of Sociol., 1919-22; Univ. of Minnesota, 1924-30; Founder and Prof. of Sociology Dept., Harvard Univ., 1930-49. Co-editor of the New Ideas in Sociol., Editor-in-chief of Volia Naroda, newspaper, 1917. Member: exec. cttees., All-Russian Peasant Soviet; Council of Russian Rep., 1917; Kerensky's Cabinet, 1917; Russian Contl. Assembly, 1918; Amer. Acad. of Arts and Sciences; Roumanian Royal Acad. of Sciences; Royal Acad. of Arts and Sciences of Belgium; Czechoslovak Academy of Agriculture; of American, German, Czech, and other scientific societies. Religion: Russian Orthodox. Ancestry: Russian-Ugro-Finnish. Condemned to death by Soviet Govt., 1917, banished 1922. Pres. Internat. Congress and Inst. of Sociology, 1937, also Amer. Sociol. Assoc., Internat. Society for Comparative Study of Civilisations. *Publications:* Crime and Punishment, 1914; Leo Tolstoi as a Philosopher, 1915; System of Sociology (2 vols.), 1920-21; General Theory of Law, 1920; Leaves from a Russian Diary, 1924; Sociology of Revolution, 1925; Social Mobility, 1927; Contemporary Sociological Theories, 1928; Principles of Rural-Urban Sociology, 1929; A Source Book in Rural Sociology (3 vols.), 1930-31; Social and Cultural Dynamics (4 vols.), 1937-41; Time-Budgets of Human Behaviour, 1939; Crisis of Our Age, 1941; Man and Society in Calamity, 1942; Socio-cultural Causality, Time, Space, 1943; Russia and the United States, 1944; Society, Culture and Personality: Their Structure and Dynamics, 1947; Reconstruction of Humanity, 1948; Altruistic Love, 1950; Social Philosophies of an Age of Crisis, 1950; Explorations in Altruistic Behaviour, 1950; S.O.S. Meaning of Our Crisis, 1951; The Ways and Power of Love, 1954; Factors and Techniques of Altruistic and Spiritual Growth, 1954; Fads and Foibles of Modern Sociology, 1956; American Sex Revolution, 1957; Power and Morality, 1959; A Long Journey, 1963; Basic Trends of Our Time, 1964; Sociological Theories of Today, 1966. *Recreations:* music, gardening, fishing, camping, mountain climbing, etc. *Address:* 8 Cliff St., Winchester, Mass., U.S.A. *T.:* Winchester PA-9-3486. *Club:* Faculty (Harvard). [*Died* 10 *Feb.* 1968.

SOULSBY, Sir Llewellyn T. G., Kt. 1944; J.P.; retired 1961, as Chairman, Mountstuart Dry Docks Ltd., and as Director: Stothert & Pitt Ltd. (Chm. 1946-59, resigned), Bristol Channel Employers' Accident Indemnity Assoc.; *b.* 24 Jan. 1885; *s.* of late J. C. Soulsby, Marine Surveyor, Cardiff; *m.* 1911, Margaret Dickinson; no *c.* *Educ.:* Jarrow-on-Tyne. Apprenticed as Naval Architect at Palmers Shipbuilding Co., Jarrow, 1900; afterwards in Scott's Shipbuilding Co., Greenock; Works Manager of Cardiff Channel Dry Docks, 1912; Manager C. H. Bailey Ltd., Newport, 1919; General Manager Channel Dry Dock Co. of Cardiff, Newport and Barry, 1928; on amalgamation of Channel Co. with Mountstuart Co. became Commercial Manager of Mountstuart Dry Docks Ltd. 1931, and Managing Director, 1937-47; also Regional Director Merchant Shipbuilding and Repairs for Bristol Channel and N.W. England, 1941-47. *Address:* 77 Roath Court Road, Cardiff. *T.:* Cardiff 4673. *Clubs:* Cardiff and County, Exchange (Cardiff). [*Died* 9 *Jan.* 1966.

SOUTER, Sir William A(lfred), Kt. 1951; *b.* 24 Feb. 1879; *s.* of Charles William and Clara Souter; *m.* 1909, Madalene, *d.* of J. W. Robson, J.P.; two *s.* one *d.* (and one *s.* killed on active service, 1941). *Educ.:* Sheffield Royal Grammar School. Shipowner; Director (formerly Chairman): W. A. Souter & Co. Ltd.; Hebburn S.S. Co. Ltd.; Sheaf Steam Shipping Co. Ltd.; Bamburgh Shipping Co. Ltd.; Chairman: Tyne Mariners Benevolent Instn., 1943-67; Tyne Improvement Commn., 1945-50; Wireless Cttee. Internat. Shipping Conference at International Telecommunications Confs.: Washington, 1927; Madrid, 1932; Cairo, 1938; President: Baltic and Internat. Maritime Conf., 1929-33; Chamber of Shipping of U.K., 1938; Internat. Shipping Conf., 1938. Served European War, 1914-18. *Recreations:* golf, bird-watching. *Address:* Dursley, Fencer Hill Park, Gosforth, Newcastle upon Tyne 3. *T.:* Wideopen 2624. [*Died* 22 *Dec.* 1968.

SOUTHALL, Reginald Bradbury, C.B.E. 1953; J.P.; Director since 1950 and General Manager since 1942, BP Refinery (Llandarcy) Ltd.; Director, British Hydrocarbon Chemicals Ltd., since 1960; *b.* Bollington, Cheshire, 5 June 1900; *s.* of late Rev. George Henry and Harriette Southall; *m.* 1925, Phyllis May Hemming; one *d.* *Educ.:* West Monmouth School. Joined The British Petroleum Company Group, 1921. U.K. delegate, I.L.O. Petroleum Cttee., 1947-60; Vice-President Univ. Coll. of Swansea, 1956-64; Mem., Milford Haven Conservancy Bd., 1958-64; Dir. Development Corp. for Wales, 1958-64; Mem. Cttee. on Higher Education (Robbins), 1961-63; Mem. British Transport Docks Bd., 1963-65; Mem. Central Training Coun., 1964. J.P. Swansea, 1954. C.G.I.A. 1952; Hon. LL.D. (Wales), 1962. *Publications:* various articles. *Recreations:* golf, etc. *Address:* The Meadows, Bishopston, Swansea. *T.:* Bishopston 408 *Clubs:* Reform; Bristol Channel Yacht (Swansea). [*Died* 1 *Dec.* 1965.

SOUTHALL, His Honour Judge Thomas Frederick; Judge of County Courts, Circuit 33 (Suffolk and Essex), 1954-1965; Chairman, East and West Suffolk Quarter Sessions, 1961-65; D.L.; *b.* 15 March 1898; 2nd *s.* of late Charles Henry Southall, Norwich, and Alice Lucy Southall (*née* Boswell); *m.* 1st, 1922, Phyllis Wharton (*d.* 1927), *d.* of late Ernest Kent, F.S.A.; one *d.*; 2nd, 1931, Rosalie Mary, *d.* of late Walter Francis, I.C.S.; one *s.* one *d.* *Educ.:* Charterhouse. Served European War, 1915-1918, The Norfolk Regt. and R.F.C. Sheriff of Norwich, 1927-28; Barrister, Gray's Inn, 1931. D.L. Suffolk, 1964. *Address:* Hill House, Nayland, Colchester, Essex. *T.:* Nayland 276. *Club:* Reform. [*Died* 6 *April* 1965.

SOUTHBY, Commander Sir Archibald Richard James, 1st Bt., *cr.* 1937; R.N.; *b.* 1886; *m.* 1st, 1909, Phyllis Mary (marriage dissolved, 1962), *er. d.* of late Charles H. Garton, Banstead Wood, Surrey; two *s.*; 2nd, 1962, Noreen Vera, *o. d.* of late B. Compton Simm, Ashbourne, Derbyshire, and of Mrs. Simm, Parkstone, Dorset. *Educ.:* Brandon House School, Cheltenham; H.M.S. Britannia, 1901. Lt. Royal Navy, 1908; Flag Lt. and Flag Lieutenant-Commander to Admiral Sir Montague Browning, Grand Fleet and North America and West Indian Station, 1913-18; Member, Naval Armistice Commission, 1918-19; Naval Inter-allied Commission of Control, 1919-1920; Commander, 1919; retired 1920; Assistant Government Whip, 1931-35; Junior Lord of the Treasury, 1935-37. Was Member, L.D.V. and Home Guard. Member, Parliamentary Delegation to Buchenwald Concentration Camp, Apr. 1945; Chevalier Legion of Honour; Younger Brother, Trinity House, 1944; D.L. Surrey and J.P. Surrey and Oxon. until 1946; M.P. (C.) Epsom Div., 1928-47. *Heir:* *s.* Archibald Richard Charles Southby, Lt.-Col. Rifle Brigade, O.B.E. [*b.* 18 June 1910; *m.* 1935, Joan Alice, *o. d.* of Reginald Balston, 105 Onslow Square, S.W.; *m.* 1947, Olive Marion (who *m.* 1928, J. N. R. Moore), *d.* of late Sir Thomas Bilbe-Robinson, and Lady Bilbe-Robinson, Upper Sorrels, Fittleworth, Sussex; one *s.*; *m.* 1964, Hon. Ethel Peggy, *d.* of 1st Baron Cunliffe, and *widow* of Brig. Bernard Lorenzo de Robeck, M.C., R.A.]. *Address:* 18 Harbour View Road, Parkstone, Dorset. *T.:* Parkstone 1720. *Clubs:* Carlton; Royal Yacht Squadron (Cowes); Parkstone Yacht. [*Died* 30 *Oct.* 1969.

SOUTHEE, Ethelbert Ambrook, O.B.E.; M.A. (Oxon); B.Sc., B.Sc.Agr. (Syd.); Principal, Hawkesbury Agricultural College, Richmond, N.S.W., 1921-54, retired; *b.* Cootamundra, N.S.W., 6 Aug. 1890; *s.* of Frederick Robert Southee, Herne Bay, Kent, and Catherine Charlotte McCutcheon; *m.* 1918, Charlotte Elizabeth Lappin (*d.* 1944); one *s.* one *d.* (and one *d.* decd.). *Educ.:* Cootamundra Superior Public School; Sydney Boys' High School; Sydney University; Oxford University; Cornell University. Rhodes Scholar for N.S.W., 1913; double blue—athletics and Rugby football—of Sydney University and Oxford University; War service, 1914-19 (gazetted 2nd Lieut. 7th Oxford and Bucks L.I.; transferred to Army Service Corps); on active service with 23rd Divisional Train in France and Italy; attained rank of temp. Major (despatches twice, O.B.E.); elected to Council of Royal Agricultural Society of N.S.W., 1922, Vice-Pres., in 1939. Farrer Memorial Medal "for distinguished service in agricultural science", 1955. *Publications:* articles on agricultural subjects. *Address:* Unit 3, 71 Foamcrest Ave., Newport Beach, N.S.W., 2106, Australia. [*Died* 26 *Dec.* 1968.

SOUTHERN, Ralph Lang; *see* Addenda: II.

SOUTHGATE, Margaret Cecil Irene, M.A.; Headmistress of St. James's, West Malvern, since Sept. 1960; *b.* 5 Oct. 1918; *d.* of George Walter and Ethel Winifred Southgate; unmarried. *Educ.:* Newnham College, Cambridge. B.A. (Classical Tripos) 1941, M.A. 1944. Classics mistress: St. James's, West Malvern, 1942-45; Burlington School, London, 1945-46; St. Monica's School, Clacton-on-Sea, 1946-60, and Housemistress there, 1949-60. Member of Church Assembly, 1965. *Recreation:* church embroidery. *Address:* St. James's, West Malvern, Worcs. *T.:* Malvern 3129. *Club:* Royal Over-Seas League. [*Died* 3 *Jan.* 1970.

SOUTHWELL, Sir Richard Vynne, Kt., *cr.* 1948; F.R.S.; M.A., LL.D. (St. Andrews, Glasgow), D.Sc. (Belfast, Bristol, Brussels); D.Eng. (Sheffield); Hon. M.I.Mech.E.; Hon. F.R.Ae.S., Hon. F.I.Ae.S. For. Assoc. U.S. National Acad. Sci.; Hon. Fellow of Brasenose Coll., Oxford, and Trinity Coll. Cambridge; Fellow of Imperial Coll., London; *b.* 2 July 1888; *s.* of Edwin B. and Annie Southwell, Bracondale, Norwich; *m.* 1918, Isabella Wilhelmina Warburton, *d.* of W. W. Wingate, Scroope House, Cambridge; four *d.* *Educ.:* Norwich School; Trinity Coll., Cambridge. Fellow and Lecturer in Mechanical Sciences, Trinity Coll., Cambridge, 1912-20; served in R.A.S.C. 1914-15, R.N.V.R. 1915-18, and R.A.F. 1918-19; Superintendent of the Aerodynamics Dept., Nat. Physical Laboratory, 1920-25; Univ. Lecturer in Mathematics and Fellow of Trinity Coll., Cambridge, 1925-29; Prof. of Engineering Science and Fellow of Brasenose College, Oxford, 1929-42; Rector of Imperial College of Science and Technology, London, 1942-48; Member of Bridge Stress Comm., 1923-28; of Aeronautical Research Comm., 1927-30, 1931-34, 1935-38, 1940-43; Steel Structures Research Comm., 1929-30; Comm. of Award for Commonwealth Fund Fellowships, 1930-38; Lord Privy Seal's (Hailey) Conference on Air Raid Shelters Policy, 1939; Civil Defence Research Comm., 1939-48; Scientific Advisory Council, Ministry of Supply, 1940-43; Ministry of Labour Higher Appointments (Hankey) Comm. 1943-1944; Colonial Office (Asquith) Commission on Higher Education in the Colonies, 1943-45; Board of Education (Percy) Committee on Technological Education, 1944-45; Standing Commission on Museums and Galleries, 1946-1950; Pres. Sect. G. (Engineering), 1938, and a Gen. Sec., 1947-55, of British Assoc.; Pres. International Union Theoretical and Applied Mechanics, 1946-48; Pres. VII. International Congress of Applied Mechanics, 1948-52, Treasurer 1952-56; Worcester Reed Warner medal (Am. Soc. M.E.), 1941; James Alfred Ewing medal (Inst. C.E.), 1946; Clayton Prize (Inst. M.E.) and U.S. Medal of Freedom with Silver Palm, 1947; Timoshenko Medal (Amer. Soc. M.E.). 1959; Elliott Cresson

Medal (Franklin Inst.), 1964. *Publications:* Introduction to the Theory of Elasticity, for Engineers and Physicists, 1936; Relaxation Methods in Engineering Science, 1940; Relaxation Methods in Theoretical Physics, Vol. I, 1946, Vol. II, 1956; Papers on Elasticity, Theory of Structures, Hydrodynamics, etc. in Transactions of Royal Soc., Philosophical Magazine, etc. *Address:* The Old House, 20 Church Lane, Trumpington, Cambridge. *T.:* Trumpington 3289. *Club:* Athenæum. [*Died* 9 *Dec.* 1970.

SOUTTAR, Sir Henry, Kt., *cr.* 1949; C.B.E. 1919; Officer Order of the Crown of Belgium, 1917; Officer Legion of Honour of France, 1937; D.M., M.Ch.(Oxon), F.R.C.S.(Eng.); Hon. M.D. Trinity College, Dublin; Hon. F.R.C.S. Australasia; Hon. F.A.C.S.; Hon. F.R.S.M.; Consulting Surgeon; Consulting Surgeon, London Hospital; Past President B.M.A.; Past Chairman, Central Medical War Committee; Past Vice-Pres. Royal College of Surgeons of England; Past Pres. Institute of British Surgical Technicians; Past Fellow R.S.M.; Fellow Association of Surgeons of Great Britain; late Chairman of Representative Body, and of Council, B.M.A.; late Examiner in Surgery, R.C.S. of England, Universities of Oxford, London, Aberdeen, and Liverpool; late Chm., Medical Personnel (Army in India) Mission, 1942; late Deputy Chairman, Inter-departmental Committee on Nursing Services; Chm. Medical Planning Commission; Chm. Radium Technical Committee of Royal Colleges of Physicians and Surgeons; Director of Surgical Unit, London Hospital; *b.* 1875; *s.* of Robinson Souttar, formerly M.P. for Dumfriesshire; *m.* 1st, 1904, Catharine (*d.* 1959), *d.* of late R. B. Clifton, F.R.S., Professor of Physics, Oxford; one *s.* one *d.*; 2nd, 1963, Amy Bessie Wigdahl, *widow* of Harry Douglas Wigdahl, Walberswick, Suffolk. *Educ.:* Oxford High School; Queen's College, Oxford (Scholar, Double First Class Honours Mathematics); London Hospital. Entered London Hospital, 1903; appointed Surgical Registrar, 1910; Assist. Surg., West London Hospital, 1912 and London Hospital, 1915; Surg.-in-Chief of Belgian Field Hospital at Antwerp and at Furnes, 1914; Maj., R.A.M.C., and Senior Surgeon, British Red Cross Hospital, Netley, 1916; Dep. Consulting Surg., Southern Command, 1918. Hon. Freedom, Soc. of Apothecaries, 1958. *Publications:* A Surgeon in Belgium; Injuries of Peripheral Nerves: The Art of Surgery; Radium and its Surgical Application; Radium and Cancer, 1934; Physics and the Surgeon, 1948; article, Oesophagus in Choyce's System of Surgery; articles on Tongue, Mouth and Pharynx, in Hutchison's Index of Treatment; and on Tongue and Oesophagus in Tidy's Index of Symptomatology; numerous professional articles, chiefly on Nerve Injuries, Cerebral Surgery, Thoracic Surgery, the Oesophagus, and Radium. (Ed) Textbook of British Surgery, 1956. *Address:* 9 Cambridge Gate, N.W.1. *T.:* Welbeck 9617. *Clubs:* Athenæum, London Rowing, Leander, English-Speaking Union. [*Died* 12 *Nov.* 1964.

SOVEREIGN, Rt. Rev. Arthur Henry; *see* Addenda: II.

SOWERBY, Katherine Githa (Mrs. John Kendall); 2nd *d.* of John Sowerby; *m.* J. K. Kendall (*d.* 1952); one *d.* *Publications: plays:* Rutherford & Son, 1912, has been translated into nearly every European language; Before Breakfast, 1912; A Man and Some Women, 1914; Sheila, 1917; The Stepmother, 1924; The Policeman's Whistle, 1934; a considerable number of books for children (Childhood, Yesterday's Children, The Bumbletoes etc.) with her sister, Millicent Sowerby. *Address:* 11 Campbell Court, Gloucester Road, S.W.7. *T.:* Knightsbridge 0872. *Club:* Dramatists' [*Died* 30 *June* 1970.

SOWLER, Col. Harry; 2nd and *e. surv. s.* of Sir Thomas Sowler; *m.* Hon. Eirene Holland (*d.* 1947), *e. d.* of 1st Baron Rotherham; one *s.* three *d.* *Educ.:* Harrow; University College, Oxford (B.A. 1891, Hons. School of Modern History, M.A. 1899). Was a journalist and worked as leader-writer, sub-editor, and on the business side of newspaper management. Was Managing Director of Manchester Courier, 1900-05; was Director of that paper under late Lord Northcliffe until Aug. 1914. Takes an active part in political work in Lancashire and Derbyshire; contested (C.) North Manchester, 1906; commanded the 52nd Field Regiment R.A. (The Manchester Artillery); served throughout European War, 1914-18, in Egypt, Palestine, and France; D.L. Lancs.; J.P. city of Manchester. *Address:* King Sterndale, Buxton, Derbyshire. [*Died* 15 *Jan.* 1962.

SOWREY, Group Captain Frederick, D.S.O. 1916; M.C.; A.F.C.; late R.A.F.; late Royal Fusiliers; *b.* 25 Aug. 1893; 2nd *s.* of John Sowrey, Yeoveney Manor, Staines; *m.* 1921, Margarita Beatrice (Rita), *d.* of late Herbert White and Mrs. White, The Poplars, Maidstone, Kent; one *s.* one *d.* *Educ.:* King's College School, Wimbledon; King's Coll., London University; Caius College, Cambridge, Inter. B.Sc. 1910. Commissioned in Royal Fusiliers, 1914; active service in France during 1915; seconded to R.F.C. Jan. 1916; brought down Zeppelin L32 in flames at Billericay, 23 Sept. 1916 (D.S.O.). *Recreation:* golf. *Address:* 1 Priory Court, Eastbourne, Sussex; Brookfields, Warsash, Hants. *Clubs:* Bath; Cooden Beach Golf, Royal Eastbourne Golf. [*Died* 21 *Oct.* 1968.

SOWREY, Air Commodore William, C.B.E. 1941; D.F.C.; A.F.C.; R.A.F., retd.; *b.* 9 Aug. 1894; 3rd *s.* of J. W. Sowrey, Yeoveney Lodge, Staines; *m.* 1918, Daisy Maud Standish (*d.* 1951), *e. d.* of T. W. Smith, East View, Acton; one *d.* *Educ.:* King's College School and King's Coll., London. Transferred from R. Berkshire Regt. to R.F.C., 1915; served with R.F.C. and R.A.F., France, 1916-1918; Iraq, 1920-22, and 1934-36; China, 1927; A.O.C. East Africa, 1940-42, during Abyssinian Campaign; retired list, 1942. *Recreations:* yachting, shooting, golf. *Address:* Standish, East Mersea, Essex. *T.:* East Mersea 205. *Clubs:* R.A.F. Yacht: West Mersea Sailing. [*Died* 15 *Feb* 1968.

SPACKMAN, Cyril Saunders, R.B.A., A.R.Cam.A., L.R.I.B.A., R.M.S., F.R.S.A.I., F.S.A.Scot., F.R.S.A., A.I.A.L.; sculptor; painter-etcher; architect; *b.* Cleveland, U.S.A., 15 Aug. 1887; *o. s.* of Rev. John and Adelaide Saunders Spackman; *m.* 1922, Ada Victoria (Queenie), *yr. d.* of Richard Joseph and Alice Sadleir; one *s.* one *d.* *Educ.:* public schools, Cleveland; Central Foundation School, London; King's Coll., London. F.R.N.S. Vice - President South - Eastern Society of Architects, Hon. Member Cleveland Society of Artists, Chicago Society of Etchers, etc., exhibited at Royal Academy, Paris Salons, Royal Cambrian Academy, Roy. Soc. of British Artists, Roy. Soc. of Miniature Painters, Roy. Inst. of Oil Painters, Roy. Inst. of Painters in Watercolours, Roy. Birmingham Soc. of Artists, Roy. Scottish Soc. of Painters in Water-colours, Roy. West of England Academy, Walker Art Gallery, Liverpool; Internat. Soc. of Sculptors, Painters, and Gravers; National Portrait Society; the Carnegie Institute, Pittsburg; the Art Institute, Chicago; Corcoran Gallery, Washington; Pennsylvania Academy of Fine Art; Hull and Doncaster Municipal Art Gallery, etc., etc. Designer of the Masonic Million Memorial Medal (exhibited Royal Academy and R.M.S., 1922); Medals for the Corporation of Croydon and the Incorporated Association of Architects and Surveyors; Medal of Harding Award for Selhurst Grammar School; The

Nativity, The Crucifixion, The Ascension, Altar Panels in Grosmont Church, Monmouthshire; Crucifix in Hoptonwood stone in All Saints at Selhurst; Large Relief, St. George and the Dragon, Clipsham stone, Ashburton Sec. Mod. Sch., Croydon; filmed by Br. Paramount News and Wallace Productions Ltd. carving bust of Wendy Newbury; Emancipation, in Belgian Black Marble; (Hon. Mention Salon, Paris, 1952), **Duke of Devonshire, K.G., in Hadene Marble; The Hall Stone Medal for United Grand Lodge of England; Black Marble Head (in the Municipal Museum Art Gallery, Arnheim). Collection of Works at National Museum of Wales.** Late Art Editor of The Parthenon. Chairman, Croydon Univ. Extension Cttee.; Hon-Vice-President Croydon Symphony Orchestra; Member Cttee. Croydon Writers' Circle; Vice-Pres. Croydon Camera Club. Works in public and private collections in Gt. Britain, America, Sweden, France, Holland; Freeman and a Citizen of London; Freedom and Livery of The Company of Masons. *Publications:* Colour Prints of a Dream Garden, and an Old-World Garden, from the original paintings exhibited at the R.B.A.; contributor to the Architectural Review, etc. *Address:* The Studio, Edridge Road, Croydon. *T.:* 2008. *Club:* Rotary (No. 62). [*Died* 16 *May* 1963.

SPAHLINGER, Henry; past Director, Institut Bactériothérapique, Geneva, and the Research Institute for Endocrine Glands, 38 Pont St., Knightsbridge, S.W.1; *b.* Geneva, 8 Aug. 1882; *m.* Countess Charlotte Gandolfi Hornyold, *d.* of late Duke Gandolfi Hornyold, Blackmore Park, Worcester. *Educ.:* Geneva University: science, medicine, law. Bacteriologist; has occupied himself mostly with the study of tuberculosis, its therapy and prevention; his bovine Anti-Tuberculous Vaccine has been successfully tested in Switzerland, England, and officially by the Government of Northern Ireland; has of late years devoted his researches to the study of endocrine glands as a means of increasing vitality, longevity and resistance to disease; his new hormone complex for treatment of inoperable cases of cancer of prostate has been tested at Univ. of Geneva and by Swiss biologists who published successful results, 1956. *Publications:* various contributions on tuberculosis and tetanus; contrib. to Swiss medical papers on cancer. *Recreations:* rowing, gardening, riding, skating, reading. *Address:* Alde, Charters Road, Sunningdale, Berks. [*Died* 10 *April* 1965.

SPAIGHT, James Molony, C.B. 1936; C.B.E. 1927 (O.B.E. 1918); *b.* Ireland, 1877; *y. s.* of Robert Spaight, J.P.; *m.* 1907, Dolly (*d.* 1962), *y. d.* of Col. W. F. Spaight, J.P., R.E. (retired); one *d.* *Educ.:* Dublin University (Trinity) (Scholar). Double Senior Moderator, 1900; LL.B. and LL.D., 1905 (first place in both, together); Member of Senate, 1905; entered higher division of Civil Service, 1901; Director of Accounts, Air Ministry, 1930-34; Principal Assistant Secretary, Air Ministry, 1934-37. *Publications:* War Rights on Land, 1911; Aircraft in War, 1914; Aircraft in Peace and the Law, 1919; Air Power and War Rights, 1924; Aircraft and Commerce in War, 1926; Beginnings of Organised Air Power, 1927; Pseudo-Security, 1928; Air Power and the Cities, 1930; An International Air Force, 1932; Air Power in the Next War, 1938; The Sky's the Limit, 1940; The Battle of Britain, 1941; Blockade by Air, 1942; Volcano Island, 1943; Bombing Vindicated, 1944; The Atomic Problem, 1948; Air Power Can Disarm, 1948; papers in Quarterly Review, etc. *Address:* 35 Forester Road, Bath. [*Died* 8 *Jan.* 1968.

SPAIN, Lieut.-Colonel George Redesdale Booker, C.M.G. 1916; T.D. 1918; F.S.A. 1924; late 6th Batt. Northumberland Fusiliers (T.); Land Agent to the Public Trustee; *b.* 23 June 1877; 2nd *s.* of late George Spain, of Hacklinge, Kent, and of late Georgiana Louisa Stewart, of Sandwich; *m.* 1910, Norah Elizabeth, *d.* of late W. H. Smiles, of Belfast; two *d.* *Educ.:* Eastbourne College. Succeeded father as Land Agent to Lord Northbourne, 1906; 2nd Lieut. 3rd V.B.N.F., 1898; commanded 4th Volunteer Service Company, Northumberland Fusiliers, as Captain during the South African War, 1901-1902 (Queen's medal 5 clasps); Lieut.-Col. 6th Batt. 1912-18; served European War in France, 1915-18, including second battle of Ypres and first Somme battle (despatches twice, C.M.G.); Fellow of the Huguenot Society of London; Past Pres. Society of Antiquaries of Newcastle upon Tyne, 1940-41; Hon. Freeman, City of Newcastle, 1902; occasional contributor to Punch, Cornhill, and other periodicals; *Recreations:* fishing, shooting, and archæology, collector of topographical prints of Northumberland and Newcastle, tokens and medals. *Address:* 7 Tankerville Place, Newcastle upon Tyne. [*Died* 12 *Oct.* 1961.

SPAIN-DUNK, Susan, F.R.A.M. 1927; late Professor at Royal Academy of Music; *b.* 22 Feb. 1880; *d.* of Alderman W. Dunk, J.P., Folkestone. *Educ.:* Royal Academy of Music., Conducted her own works for orchestra at the Queen's Hall Promenade Concerts for four successive years; after the production of her String Suite in the first year, was invited by Sir Henry Wood to write a work specially for these concerts, and her Idyll for Strings was accordingly performed the following year, and was followed by an overture, Kentish Downs, and a symphonic poem, Elaine; conducted two of her own works for orchestra at the Bournemouth Festival, 1927; has won various prizes at the R.A.M. and the Cobbett competition for chamber music; other compositions for orchestra; overture, Andred's Weald, broadcast in 1927, which she conducted in March 1932 at the R.A. Theatre, Woolwich, being the first woman to conduct a military orchestra; symphonic-poem, Stonehenge; Cantiléna for clarinet and orchestra; instrumental trios and quartettes. *Publications:* Overtures, etc., for orchestra; pieces for violin, flute and piano, etc.; overture, Kentish Downs; Phantasy String Quartet; Two Overtures for Military Band; Quintet for Wind instruments. *Recreation:* French and German study. *Address:* 24 Lansdowne Crescent, W.11. *Club:* R.A.M. [*Died* 1 *Jan.* 1962.

SPALDING, Kenneth Jay, M.A.; Fellow of Brasenose College, Oxford, since 1928; *b.* 17 March 1879; *s.* of late H. B. Spalding of Eastbourne; *m.* Amy Katherine (*d.* 1932), *d.* of A. H. Baynes; one *s.* one *d.* *Educ.:* Collège de St. Servan, France; Eastbourne College; Balliol College, Oxford. Lecturer in French, Culham College, 1903-5; Lecturer in Logic and Philosophy, King's College, London, 1905-12; Professor of Classical Literature and Philosophy, Queen's College, London, 1909-28. *Publications:* Desire and Reason; Talks on Philosophy; Three Chinese Thinkers; the Philosophy of Shakespeare; Essays on the Evolution of Religion; articles in Mind and other periodicals. *Address:* Brasenose College, Oxford. [*Died* 20 *Jan.* 1962.

SPALDING, William F.; Capt. (Hon.) F.Inst.B.; Author, Retired Banker; Associate City of London College; Fellow Royal Economic Society; Chaplain and P.M., Authors Lodge; Hon. Fellow Grand College of Rites (U.S.A.); *b.* Highgate, 7 Oct. 1879; *s.* of Walter and Elizabeth Spalding; *m.* 1903, Lily Rosina (*d.* 1962), *d.* of John Bradbury; two *s.* one *d.* Was in the service of Hong-Kong and Shanghai Banking Corporation for 36 years; Associate of Institute of Bankers, by examination, 1911 (now Fellow); gained first and only essay prize awarded by English Institute of Bankers, 1912; Premier Gilbart Prizeman, 1912 and 1913, in Banking at King's College (Univ. of London); Hon. Moderator in Banking and Currency to the London Chamber of Commerce; late Examiner in For. Exchange to the Institute of Bankers, London; late Examiner in Banking and Exchange to the Chartered Institute of Secretaries. *Publications:* Foreign and Colonial Banking Appointments; Foreign Exchange and Foreign Bills in Theory and in Practice; Eastern Exchange Currency and Finance; A Primer of Foreign Exchange; The Functions of Money; Bankers' Credits; The London Money Market; Banking and International Exchange; The Finance of Foreign Trade; The Banker's Place in Commerce; Tate's Modern Cambist; A Dictionary of the World's Currencies and Foreign Exchanges; The Centenary Edition Tate's Cambist; A Money Manual, Vol. I., Vol. II.; An Introduction to the Study of the Foreign Exchanges, 1935; A Key to Money and Banking; First Impressions of the Royal Arch; chapter on Education for Banking in Education Year Book, 1934-1935; author British Banking article, Ency. Brit., 12th ed., and of Overseas Banking and its Organization in Handwörterbuch des Bankwesen; Editor, Authors Lodge Transactions, Vol. VII, 1946, Vol. VIII, 1955; articles in Hutchinson's Pictorial Encyclopaedia, 1947, etc. *Recreation:* gardening. *Address:* Aylmerton, 123 The Chine, Grange Park, N.21. *T.:* Laburnum 4518. *Club:* Middlesex Regt. Officers'. [*Died* 6 *Jan.* 1963.

SPARGO, John; author, and retired museum official; *b.* Stithians, Cornwall, 31 Jan. 1876; *s.* of Thomas Spargo and Jane Hocking Spargo; *m.* 1st, 1901, Prudence Edwards (*d.* 1904), at Cardiff; 2nd, Mary Bennetts, Yonkers, N.Y.; one *s.* one *d.* *Educ.:* Elementary Schools, supplemented by University Extension (Oxford and Cambridge); one of founders of Federation of Trades and Labour Councils, and President Barry (S. Wales) Council; for several years on National Executive of S.D.F. (later National Socialist Party); went to United States in 1901; has travelled in Europe and America lecturing and studying social problems; one of the founders of Prospect House Settlement, Yonkers, N.Y.; Editor of the Comrade, New York, 1901-4; Member National Executive Socialist Party of America for some years, but resigned as protest against anti-war policy of party. With others founded Social Democratic League of America; visited England, France, and Italy on war mission in 1918, and served some time U.S. Committee on Public Information in Rome; went to Sweden on special confidential mission for President Wilson, 1920; appointed by President Wilson to represent public at First Industrial Relations Conference, Washington, 1919; Chairman U.S. Vermont Sesqui-Centennial Commission (appointed by President Coolidge); Chairman Vermont State Sesqui-Centennial Commission, 1925-27; Member American Friends of Lafayette; President Vermont George Washington Bicentennial Commission, 1932; Chairman Vermont State Commission on Early Records. Various interests in Bennington, Vt. Freemason (33°), etc.; Member Royal Order of Scotland; Grand Commandery Knights Templar; Episcopalian, active in Diocese of Vermont; Member of Newcomen Society in America, etc. Founded, 1927, Bennington Vt., Historical Mus. and Art Gall., was Dir. and Curator until 1954, retiring with title Director-emeritus; at same time resigned all Civic and diocesan offices; retd., 1964, from all offices in Masonic grand bodies with title emer. in each case. *Publications:* The Bitter Cry of the Children; Socialism, a Summary and Interpretation; The Socialists: Who they Are and what they Stand For; Forces that make for Socialism in America; Capitalist and Labourer; The Common Sense of the Milk Question; The Common Sense of Socialism; The Spiritual Significance of Modern Socialism; Socialist Readings for Children; The Substance of Socialism; Karl Marx: His Life and Works; Sidelights on Contemporary Socialism; The Marx he Knew; Elements of Socialism (with Prof. G. L. Arner), Applied Socialism; Syndicalism, Industrial Unionism, and Socialism; Socialism and Motherhood; Marxian Socialism and Religion; Social Democracy Explained; Americanism and Social Democracy; Bolshevism; The Psychology of Bolshevism; Russia as an American Problem; The Greatest Failure of all History; The Jew and American Ideals; A Memorandum on Trade with Soviet Russia; The Problem of Trading with Soviet Russia; The Battle Monument and its Story; Anthony Haswell, Patriot, Printer, Poet; The Potters and Potteries of Bennington; Early American Pottery and China; The Stars and Stripes in 1777; The Legend of Hoover Who Did Nothing; The A.B.C. of Bennington Pottery Wares; Iron Mining and Smelting in Bennington, Vermont, 1786-1842; Lt.-Col. Joseph Wait of Rogers Rangers and the Continental Army, Freemason and Pioneer Vermont Settler, 1942; Rise and Progress of Freemasonry in Vermont, 1944; Notes on the Name and Family of Spargo of the Parish of Mabe in Cornwall, 1945; The Return of Russell Colvin, 1945; David Redding, Queen's Ranger, who was hanged in Bennington, Vermont, June 11, 1778, 1946; Verses Grave and Gay, 1946; Two Bennington-Born Explorers and Makers of Modern Canada, 1950; Faith and Fun at Sunset, 1951; The Constitution and the Supreme Court, 1963; articles, poems, and pamphlets. *Address:* Old Bennington, Vermont, U.S.A. [*Died* 17 *Aug.* 1966.

SPARKE, George Archibald, Hon. M.A. (Manchester); Hon. F.R.S.L., F.L.A.; Hon. Secretary Lancashire Parish Register Soc., 1931-57; *b.* 19 July 1871; *o. surv. s.* of late Edward Sparke, Cardiff; *m.* 1896, Beatrice (*d.* 1948), *e. d.* of James Andrews, Roath Park, Cardiff; one *d.* (and one *d.* decd.). *Educ.:* Tredegarville School, Cardiff; private tutors. Formerly Librarian of Kidderminster, Carlisle, Bury, and Bolton; retired, 1931. Freeman of City of Exeter; Ex-Member Council Library Association; past President North-West Branch Library Association: Hon. Fellow of Library Assistants' Association; Lecturer (extra mural), Victoria University, Manchester. *Publications:* The Uses of Public Libraries, 1895; Handbook to Turner's Liber Studiorum, 1902; The Index to the first 16 Vols. of Transactions of the Cumberland and Westmorland Antiquarian and Archæological Society (1866-1900), 1901; John Kay, Inventor: an appreciation, 1904; The Bury Art Gallery and the Wrigley Collection of Pictures, 1904; A Bibliography of the Dialect Literature of Cumberland, Westmorland, and Lancashire North of the Sands, 1907; Bibliography of Walt Whitman, 1931; editor and transcriber of The Bury Parish Registers (1647-98), 1905; The Newchurch in Rossendale Parish Registers (1653-1723), 1913; Warrington Parish Registers (1591-1653), 1933; The Township Booke of Halliwell (1640-1762), 1911; Bibliographia Boltoniensis, 1913; The Bolton Parish Registers (1573-1660), 1914; (with A. R. Corns) A Bibliography of Unfinished Books, 1915, 2nd edn., Detroit, 1968; The Deane Parish Registers (1604-1750), 2 vols., 1917, Vol. 3 (1751-1812), 1940; Great Harwood Parish Registers (1547-1812), 1937; How the Public Library can help the Business Man, 1917, 3rd edition, 1919; Broken Arcs, 1918; The Bowyer Bible, 1920; Town Bibliographies 1913; (with H. Hamer) The Book of Bolton, 1930; Index to Garstang Parish Registers (1660-1734), 1932; North Meols Parish Registers (1732-1812), 1935; Guide to Iwerne Minster, 1934; 2,000 Items in Notes and Queries (1905-31); Turton Parish Registers (1720-1812), 1943; Leigh Parish Registers (1626-1700), 1948; Warrington Parish Registers (1653-80), 1955, (1681-1700), 1962; Notes from my Memory Box, 1963; many pamphlets and articles on librarianship and bibliography in professional jls. *Recreation:* ergophobia even in retirement. *Address:* 11 Conyers Ave., Birkdale, Southport, Lancs. *T.:* Southport 67313. [*Died* 28 *Nov.* 1970.

SPARKS, Sir Ashley, K.C.M.G., *cr.* 1941; K.B.E., *cr.* 1919; Resident Director, Cunard Steamship Co. in U.S.A., 1917-50, Deputy Chm., 1947-52; *b.* 23 March 1877; *s.* of John Ashley Sparks, Sutton, Surrey; *m.* 1900, Mina Jane (*d.* 1958), *d.* of James Roberts, New York; two *d.* *Educ.:* Barnet Grammar School; Denstone College; Hurstpierpoint. Director-General of British Ministry of Shipping in U.S.A., 1918-19; Representative in U.S.A., British Ministry of Shipping, 1939-41; Ministry of War Transport, 1941-45. *Address:* Syosset, Long Island, N.Y., U.S.A. *Clubs:* Racquet and Tennis, Recess, Piping Rock (New York); Harford Hunt (Baltimore). [*Died* 21 *May* 1964.

SPEAKMAN, Prof. John Bamber, C.B.E. 1963; D.Sc.; Emeritus Professor; Professor and Head of the Department of Textile Industries, Univ. of Leeds, 1939-63; *b.* 23 Oct. 1897; *s.* of Peter and Elizabeth Speakman, Atherton, Manchester; *m.* 1924, Gertrude Hughes Trafford; one *s.* one *d.* *Educ.:* Leigh Grammar School; Manchester University, B.Sc. Manch., 1920; Mercer Graduate Schol.; M.Sc. Manch., 1921; Research Chemist, Chemical Warfare Cttee., War Office, 1921-24; Lecturer in Textile Chemistry, 1924, Reader, 1936, Leeds University. D.Sc. Manch., 1931; F.T.I., 1931 (Hon. Fellow, 1951); Warner Memorial Medal, Textile Inst., 1931; Worshipful Company of Dyers Research Medal, 1933, 1937, 1938; Hon. Freeman, Worshipful Company of Clothworkers, 1944; Perkin Medal, Society of Dyers and Colourists, 1950; Grand Prix Littéraire, Internat. Wool Textile Organization, 1952; Gold Medal of Honour, Verein der Textilchemiker und Coloristen, Germany, 1957; Literature Award, Soc. of Cosmetic Chemists, New York, 1967. Visited Australia, 1945, and South Africa, 1947, as adviser on wool research; Textile Inst.; Fellow, 1931; Hon. Fellow, 1951; Pres., 1962-64; President, Bradford Textile Soc., 1965-66. *Publications:* numerous in Proc. Roy. Soc., Transactions of Faraday Soc., etc. *Recreation:* travel. *Address:* 181 Otley Road, Leeds 6, Yorkshire. *T.:* 53358. [*Died* 5 *July* 1969.

SPEARES, Denis James, C.M.G., 1970; Head of North African Department, Foreign and Commonwealth Office, since 1968; *b.* 27 Sept. 1922; *s.* of late John Speares, M.D., F.R.C.P.I. and Mrs. E. E. Speares; unmarried. *Educ.:* Harrow; Pembroke College, Oxford. Served with R.A.F., 1940-46 (despatches). Pembroke Coll., Oxford, 1946-48. Member of H.M. Diplomatic Service, 1948-. Served: London, 1948-51; Bonn, 1951-53; London, 1953-58; Tehran, 1958-60; Washington, 1960-63; London, 1963-64; Nicosia, 1964-65; London 1965-. *Recreations:* golf, ski-ing. *Address:* 4 Kingsley Mews, Stanford Road, W.8. *T.:* 01-937 2041. *Club:* Travellers'. [*Died* 24 *March* 1970.

SPEARS, Lady; *see* Borden, Mary.

SPELLMAN, Cardinal, His Eminence Francis J., D.D., LL.D.; Archbishop of New York since 1939; *b.* Whitman, Mass., 4 May 1889; *s.* of late William Spellman and late Ellen Conway. *Educ.:* Whitman Gram. and High Schools; Fordham Univ., A.B. 1911; Urban Univ. in Rome, S.T.D., 1916. Ordained, Rome, 1916; Asst. All Saints' Church, Roxbury, Massachusetts, 1916-18; Ed. Staff, Boston Pilot, 1918-22; Assistant Chancellor Archdiocese of Boston, 1922-25; Attaché to the Secretary of State's Office in the Vatican, 1925-32; Titular Bishop of Sila, 1932; Auxiliary Bishop of Boston, 1932-1939; Pastor of Sacred Heart Church, Newton Center, Mass., 1933-39. Military Vicar for the United States, 1939; Cardinal, 1946. Has numerous hon. degrees from Univs. in North and South America, and in Europe. *Publications:* The Word of God, 1921; In the Footsteps of the Master, 1924; The Road to Victory, 1942; Action This Day, 1943; The Risen Soldier, 1944; No Greater Love, 1945; Prayers and Poems, 1946; Heavenly Father of Children, 1947; The Foundling, 1951; Cardinal Spellman's Prayer Book, 1952; What America Means to Me and Other Poems and Prayers, 1953. *Address:* 452 Madison Avenue, New York, N.Y., U.S.A., [*Died* 2 *Dec.* 1967.

SPENCE, Sir George Hemming, K.C.S.I., *cr.* 1947 (C.S.I. 1937); K.C.I.E., *cr.* 1943 (C.I.E. 1931); Kt., *cr.* 1939; I.C.S. (retired); *b.* Nov. 1888; *s.* of late James Knox Spence, C.S.I., Indian Civil Service; *m.* 1923, Constance Isabel, *d.* of late Rev. T. N. H. Smith-Pearse; one *s.* two *d.* *Educ.:* Marlborough; Trinity College, Oxford. Entered Indian Civil Service, 1912; served in Punjab till 1919, thereafter under Govt. of India; Secretary, Government of India, Legislative Department, 1935-47 (Law and Education Member in "Caretaker" Government, India, July-Aug. 1946); on special duty in Reforms Secretariat, India, June-Aug. 1947; retired; Legal Adviser to Govt. of Hyderabad (Deccan), 1949-50. *Address:* Yew Tree Cottage, Beadles Lane, Oxted, Surrey. *T.:* Oxted 3062. [*Died* 3 *Dec.* 1962.

SPENCE, Sir Reginald, Kt., *cr.* 1926; *b.* 1880; *s.* of late Robert Spence of Bickley, Kent, and Alice, *d.* of Thomas Layton of Culverwood, Cross-in-Hand, Sussex; unmarried. *Educ.:* Christ's Hospital. Arrived in India as Assistant, Phipson & Co., Bombay, 1901; served in Bombay Light Horse, 1901; retired (Lieutenant), 1922; Captain, Home Guard, 1940-45; Editor, Bombay Natural History Society's Journal, and Honorary Secretary, 1920-33; Member Legislative Assembly, India, 1921-23; Council of State, 1930; Bombay Legislative Council, 1931-33; Sheriff of Bombay, 1929; Chairman, R.D.C., Uckfield, 1947-49; J.P. and Hon. Presidency Magistrate, Bombay; Past District Grand Craft and Mark Master, and District Grand Superintendent Royal Arch Masons English Constitution, Bombay; Past Provincial Grand Mark Master, Sussex; late Chairman, Bombay Education Society; Governor of Christ's Hospital. Master Worshipful Company of Distillers, 1949-50. C.St.J. *Address:* Pear Tree Cottage, Blackboys, Sussex. [*Died* 13 *Sept.* 1961.

SPENCE Robert, R.E. 1901; *b.* 6 Oct. 1870; *s.* of Charles James Spence and Alice Clibborn. Studied Newcastle School of Art; Slade School of Art; Atelier Julien; Atelier Cormon. Associate Société National des Beaux-Arts, 1905. Fellow of Roy. Soc. of Painter Etchers. Croix de Guerre, 1918. *Publications:* etched plates to life of G. Fox. *Recreations:* mountaineering, ski-ing, skating. *Address:* 9 Frognal Gardens, Hampstead, N.W.3. *T.:* Hampstead 5115. *Club:* Arts. [*Died* 22 *May* 1964.

SPENCE, Robert; late Resident Secretary (Aberdeen Council), and Parliamentary Agent, Scottish Temperance Alliance (retired, Dec. 1946); Past President National Association of Temperance Officials; *b.* Airdrie, Lanarkshire,

1879; *s.* of Thomas Spence and Margaret Fullarton; *m.* 1899, Jane Mossman Niven; two *s.* two *d.* *Educ.:* M'Intyre's School and Scottish Labour College, Glasgow. Contested E. Renfrew, 1918; Berwick and Haddington, 1922; M.P. (Lab.) Berwick and Haddington, 1923-24. *Address:* Marclann, George Street, Hunters Quay, Argyllshire, Scotland.
[*Died Feb.* 1966.

SPENCER, Dorothy, C.B.E. 1939; M.A. (Oxon); formerly Deputy Chief Organisation Officer, Conservative and Unionist Party Organisation; *d.* of Thomas William and Rachel Spencer. *Educ.:* Manchester High School; Somerville College, Oxford. Official at headquarters of Conservative and Unionist Party Organisation, 1923-56, retired 1956. *Address:* Flat 3, 17 Onslow Square, S.W.7.
[*Died* 3 *Aug.* 1969.

SPENCER, Air Vice-Marshal Geoffrey Roger Cole, C.B. 1952; C.B.E. 1946 (O.B.E. 1941); p.s.a.; R.A.F. retd.; *b.* 23 Nov. 1901; *s.* of late Colonel Maurice Spencer, C.M.G., J.P.; *m.* 1st; two *s.*; 2nd, 1939, Juliet Mary, *d.* of Col. H. B. Warwick, Coddington, nr. Newark, Notts.; one *s.* two *d.* *Educ.:* R.N. Colleges, Osborne and Dartmouth; R.A.F. College, Cranwell. Served European War, 1914-19, Midshipman, R.N., 1917-19; joined R.A.F., 1920; R.A.F. Coll., Cranwell, 1920; Wing Commander, 1939; Group Captain, 1940; Air Commodore, 1943; Air Vice-Marshal, 1950. War of 1939-45 (O.B.E., C.B.E.); Bomber Command: Air Staff, 1940; Station Commander, 1940-42; North African Air Staff, 1943; 2nd Tactical Air Force; Bomber Command Headquarters Staff, 1945; Commandant, Central Bomber Establishment, 1946-47; Director, Air Force Welfare, 1948; A.O.C., R.A.F. Gibraltar, 1949; A.O.C., 19 Group, Mount Batten, Royal Air Force, 1950-52; S.A.S.O., H.Q., M.E.A.F., 1952-54; Air Officer i/c Administration, H.Q. Technical Training Command, 1954-56, retired. A.R.Ae.S., 1960. Commander Order of Leopold II and Croix de Guerre with Palms (Belgium), 1946. *Recreation:* sailing. *Address:* Heath Cottage, Church Crookham, Aldershot, Hants. *T.:* Fleet 5614. *Clubs:* Royal Air Force, Royal Aero; R.A.F. Yacht.
[*Died* 7 *Dec.* 1969.

SPENCER, Sir Henry (Francis), Kt. 1963; Managing Director, Richard Thomas & Baldwins Ltd., since 1952; *b.* 8 April 1892; *s.* of late Henry Francis and Alice Spencer; *m.* 1916, Ethel May, *o. d.* of late William and Louise Southall; one *d.* *Educ.:* informally. Chairman: H. F. Spencer & Co. Ltd.; S. J. & E. Fellows; Director: Monks, Hall & Co. Ltd.; Bitmac Ltd.; The Whitehead Thomas Bar & Strip Co. Ltd.; B.I.S.C. (Ore) Ltd.; Development Corporation for Wales; British Iron & Steel Corp.; British Ore Investment Corp. Ltd.; and several other cos. Vice-Pres., British Inst. of Management. *Recreations:* golf, gardening and stamp collecting. *Address:* Briar Croft, Sytch Lane, Wombourn, Nr. Wolverhampton. *T.:* Wombourn 3144. *Clubs:* Garrick, Royal Automobile; Royal Thames Yacht.
[*Died* 31 *May* 1964.

SPENCER, Lieut.-Col. Rowland Pickering, T.D.; M.A.; *b.* 27 Feb. 1892; *s.* of C. A. Spencer, Stoughton Lane, Leicester; *m.* 1932, Lexie Wilson (*d.* 1959); one *d.* *Educ.:* Charterhouse; Brasenose College, Oxford. Served European War, 1914-18; 12th Royal Lancers and Leicestershire Yeomanry; continued T.A. service till appointed C.O. Leicestershire Yeomanry, 1938. War of 1939-45; Light Anti-Aircraft A.D.G.B. Farmer since 1921. Leicestershire and Rutland T.A. Assoc., 1945-57; Rutland C.C. 1945-58; High Sheriff of Rutland, 1948-49. *Recreations:* hunting, gardening. *Address:* Braunston, Oakham, Rutland. *T.A.:* Braunston, Rutland. *T.:* Oakham 2073.
[*Died* 15 *Jan.* 1965.

SPENCER-CHURCHILL, Capt. E. G.; *see* Churchill.

SPENCER-NAIRN, Sir Douglas L.; *see* Nairn.

SPENS, Janet; *b.* 1876; *d.* of Walter Spens, Sheriff Substitute of Lanarkshire, and Helen, *d.* of Sir John Gillespie. *Educ.:* Privately; Glasgow University. Joined in founding Laurel Bank School, 1903; Tutor to Women Students in Arts and Asst. to Professor of English at Glasgow University; M.A., D.Litt. and Hon. LL.D., 1944; of Glasgow University; Tutor, and afterwards Fellow, of Lady Margaret Hall, Oxford, 1911-36; M.A. of Oxford by Decree. *Publications:* Two Periods of Disillusion; Shakespeare and Tradition; Elizabethan Drama; Spenser's Faerie Queene (An Interpretation); Editor of Terms and Vacations, by Eleanor C. Lodge; articles on Rossetti's Ethical Thought, Chapman's Ethical Thought, Charlotte Brontë; Study of Keats's Ode to a Nightingale; reviews. *Address:* 5 Fyfield Road, Oxford. *T.:* Oxford 57559. *Club:* University Women's.
[*Died* 14 *Jan.* 1963.

SPENS, J(ohn) Ivan, O.B.E. 1919; Senior Partner in Brown, Fleming and Murray, 175 West George St., Glasgow, and 4b Frederick's Place, Old Jewry, E.C.2; *b.* 22 Feb. 1890; 3rd *s.* of late John Alexander Spens and Sophie Nicol Baird; *m.* 1915, Gwendoline Helen Donaldson; one *s.*; *m.* 1928, Frances May (Lidiard) Murdoch. *Educ.:* Cargilfield; Rugby. Admitted Member of Institute of Accountants and Actuaries in Glasgow, 1914, and Partner in Brown, Fleming and Murray, 1919; Director, Union Discount Company of London Ltd., and other Companies; Extraordinary Director and a Vice-President of Scottish Amicable Life Assurance Society; Ministry of Supply, Accountant-General, 1939-41; Deputy Director-General of Finance and Accountant-General, 1941-42; Head of Industrial Division of Ministry of Production, 1942-43; an Adviser to Minister of Production, 1943-45; served European War 5th Bn. The Cameronians (Scottish Rifles) (1914 Star, despatches, O.B.E.); Member Queen's Body Guard for Scotland, Royal Co. of Archers (retired). *Recreation:* golf. *Address:* 4b Frederick's Place, Old Jewry, E.C.2. *Clubs:* City of London, Carlton, Pratt's, Buck's, Western (Glasgow); Royal and Ancient Golf.
[*Died* 19 *Jan.* 1964.

SPENS, Sir Will, Kt., *cr.* 1939; C.B.E. 1918; M.A.; Hon. LL.D. (Columbia and St. Andrews); High Steward of Great Yarmouth; Steward of the Chapter of Ely; Hon. Fellow Corpus Christi College, Cambridge (Master 1927-52); *b.* 1882; *e. s.* of John A. Spens; *m.* 1912, Dorothy Theresa, *d.* of late J. R. Selwyn, Bishop of Melanesia, and Master of Selwyn College; two *s.* one *d.* *Educ.:* Rugby (leaving exhibitioner); King's College, Cambridge (Scholar). Fellow (1907), Tutor (1912), Corpus Christi College, Cambridge; temporary work at the Foreign Office, 1915; Secretary of the Foreign Trade Department of that Office, 1917; Chevalier of the Legion of Honour, and Officer of the Order of the Crown of Italy, 1919; Statutory Commission for Cambridge University, 1923; Vice-Chancellor 1931-33; Regional Commissioner for Civil Defence, Eastern Region, 1939-45. Chairman Governing Body of Rugby School, 1944-58. *Publications:* Belief and Practice, 1915; 2nd ed. 1917; occasional articles on theology and the philosophy of religion. *Address:* The

Old Sacristy, The College, Ely. *T.:* Ely 2429. *Club:* United University. [*Died* 1 *Nov.* 1962.

SPERLING, Sir Rowland Arthur Charles, K.C.M.G., *cr.* 1934 (C.M.G. 1921); C.B. 1924; *b.* 4 January 1874; *s.* of late Commander R. M. Sperling, R.N.; *m.* 1905, Dorothy Constance (*d.* 1951), *e. d.* of late W. H. Kingsmill, of Sydmonton Court, Newbury; one *s.* one *d.* (and one *s.* killed on active service, 1940). *Educ.:* Eton; New College, Oxford. Clerk in Foreign Office, 1899; Senior Clerk, 1913; Assistant Secretary, Foreign Office, 1919; Minister at Berne, 1924-27; Sofia, 1928-29; Helsingfors, 1930-35. High Sheriff for Hants, 1945-46; Hants C.C., 1936-49. *Address:* Chetcombe House, Mere, Wilts. [*Died* 8 *Jan.* 1965.

SPERRING, Digby; Editor, The Tobacco World, until 1962, now retired; Editorial adviser Confectionery News; *b.* 12 March 1897; *s.* of A. E. Ormen and Eola Catherine Sperring; *m.* 1934, Iris N. Culver. *Educ.:* Christ's College; Finchley. R.A.F., 1917-1919, journalism since. *Publications:* Articles on Empire tobacco, in Times Trade and Engineering; Cigars, Encyclopædia Britannica. *Recreations:* anything to do with country life. *Address:* c/o Confectionery and Tobacco News, 33-39 Bowling Green Lane, E.C.1. [*Died* 27 *Oct.* 1969.

SPICER, Sir (Albert) Dykes, 2nd Bt., *cr.* 1906; *b.* 27 November 1880; *s.* of Right Honourable Sir Albert Spicer, 1st Bt., and Jessie Stewart Dykes; *S.* father 1934; *m.* 1910, Alice Frances Mary (*d.* 1963), *d.* of late Rev. W. D. Morrison, LL.D.; three *d.* *Educ.:* Mill Hill School; Univ. Coll., Oxford. *Heir:* *b.* Captain Stewart Dykes Spicer, R.N., retired, *b.* 1888, *q.v.* *Address:* 90 Albion Gate, Hyde Park, W.2. *T.:* Paddington 5700. *Club:* Athenæum. [*Died* 27 *Oct.* 1966.

SPICER, Capt. Sir Stewart Dykes, 3rd Bt. *cr.* 1906; R.N. retd.; *b.* 2 Nov. 1888; *s.* of Rt. Hon. Sir Albert Spicer, 1st Bt., P.C. (*d.* 1934); *S.* brother, Sir Dykes Spicer, 2nd Bt., 1966; *m.* 1917, Margaret Grace (*d.* 1967), *d.* of late Thomas Paterson Gillespie, Linlithgow; one *s.* three *d.* *Educ.:* Clifton Coll. Royal Navy, 1903; served War of 1914-18: Jutland (despatches); Comdr., 1921; Capt. (retd.), 1933; War of 1939-45 (recalled): on staff of C.-in-C., Western Approaches, 1939-1941; Naval Asst. to Vice-Chief of Staff, 1941-45. With B.B.C. Talks Division, 1935-1951. *Recreations:* music, reading Shakespeare. *Heir:* *s.* Peter James Spicer [*b.* 20 May 1921; *m.* 1949, Margaret Wilson; one *s.* three *d.*]. *Address:* Salt Mill House, Fishbourne, Chichester, Sx. *T.:* Chichester 82825. *Club:* Army and Navy. [*Died* 11 *Jan.* 1968.

SPIELMANN, Percy Edwin, Ph.D. (Bâle), B.Sc. (Lon.), F.R.I.C., A.Inst.P., A.R.C.S.; F.Inst.Pet.; F.R.S.L.; chemist; *b.* London, 26 Sept. 1881; *s.* of late M. H. Spielmann. *Educ.:* St. Paul's School; Royal College of Science, South Kensington; University College, London; Polytechnic, Zürich. Head of Coal Tar Analytical Laboratory of the Department of Explosives Supply, Ministry of Munitions of War, 1914-19; Head of the Technical Section, Highways Construction, Ltd., 1919-22; British representative at International Committee on the Nomenclature and Standardisation of Tests of Road-making Materials (Permanent International Association of Road Congresses) 1927 onwards; served and serving as Chairman and Member on many Standardization Committees in connection with road materials, coal tar, and petroleum. Head of organisation associated with Board of Trade to index British and American Reports and German Documents relating to German Chemical Industries, 1947-49; Liveryman Worshipful Company of Paviors, 1950. *Publications:* edited and translated the first English edition of Richter's Organic Chemistry, vol. i. 1915; Tables of Chemical and Physical Constants, of special interest to the Light Naphtha Section of the Coal Tar and Coke Oven Industries (in part with E. G. Wheeler), 1918; The Genesis of Petroleum, 1923 (French translation by E. Wiener, 1926); The Constituents of Coal Tar, 1924; Bituminous Substances, 1925; Chemistry, 1927; Editor, Roadmakers' Library, including Road Making and Administration (with E. J. Elford), 1934, 2nd ed. 1948; Asphalt Roads (with Brig. A. C. Hughes), 1936. Editor: Transactions of 9th Internat. Congress of Pure and Applied Chemistry, 1947. Contributions to scientific and technical journals. *Recreation:* collecting miniature books. *Address:* 76 Cranmer Court, Sloane Avenue, S.W.3. *T.:* Kensington 8316. *Club:* Athenæum. [*Died* 2 *Jan.* 1964.

SPINKS, Major John Thomas, C.B.E. 1959; D.L.; J.P.; *b.* 4 October 1889; *s.* of late John T. Spinks, Cardiff; *m.* 1919, Anne May Jones, *d.* of late G. Watkin Jones, Marshfield; three *d.* (one *s.* decd.). *Educ.:* Howard Gardens High School and University College, Cardiff. Served War, 11th Welch Regt., Special Bde., R.E. France, 1914-19; Royal Pioneer Corps, N. Africa and Italy, 1940-45 (despatches); Maj. 1941. J.P. 1950, D.L. 1956, Monmouthshire. National Chairman, British Legion, 1956-59. *Address:* 141 Stow Hill, Newport, Mon. *T.:* Newport 65033. *Clubs:* National Liberal, Royal Commonwealth Society. [*Died* 23 *Nov.* 1969.

SPITTEL, Richard Lionel, C.M.G. 1950; C.B.E. 1942; F.R.C.S. (Eng.); Consulting Surgeon, General Hospital, Colombo, 1935 (Retd.); Chm. Colombo Group of Hospitals, 1955 (Retd.); *b.* 9 Dec. 1881; *m.* 1911, Claribel Frances van Dort; one *d.* *Educ.:* Colombo and London. F.R.C.S. Eng., 1909; Surgeon, General Hospital, Colombo, 1910-35, when retired. Member Wild Life Protection Soc., Ceylon. *Publications:* *literary:* Wild Ceylon, 1924; Far-off Things, 1933; Savage Sanctuary, 1941; Vanished Trails, 1950; Where the White Sambur Roams (novel), 1951; Wild White Boy (novel), 1957; Brave Island (with Christine Wilson), 1967; *surgical:* Essentials of Surgery, 1932; Framboesia Tropica, 1923. *Recreations:* Jungle travel, anthropology, wild life preservation. *Address:* Wycherley, Buller's Road, Colombo, Ceylon. *T.:* 8743. *Club:* Eighty (Colombo). [*Died* 3 *Sept.* 1969.

SPOONER, Rt. Hon. Sir William Henry, P.C. 1966; K.C.M.G. 1963; M.M.; Director: Mercantile and General Reinsurance Co. Ltd.; The Mutual Acceptance Co. Ltd.; Duly and Hansford Ltd.; Hoechst Chemicals (Aust.) Ltd.; Minister for National Development, Australia, 1951-64; Vice-President of Executive Council, 1958-64; Leader of Government in the Senate, 1958-1964; *b.* 23 Dec. 1897; *s.* of William Henry Spooner, Sydney, N.S.W., and Maude Ann Dubois, Sydney, N.S.W.; *m.* 1924, Catherine Frier Vera Bogle; one *s.* two *d.* *Educ.:* Christ Church School, Sydney; Sydney University. Chartered Accountant, Hungerford, Spooner & Kirkhope, Sydney. Senator for N.S.W., 1949-65; Minister for Social Services, 1949-51; Minister in charge: Snowy Mountains Authority, Joint Coal Board, Australian Atomic Energy Commission, War Service Homes, and Pres., River Murray Commn., 1951-64; Acting Prime Minister, Sept. 1962. *Recreation:* golf. *Address:* 1 West Street, Balgowlah, N.S.W., Australia. *T.:* XJ 1032. *Clubs:* New South Wales, National, Manly Golf (N.S.W.). [*Died* 15 *July* 1966.

SPOWERS, Colonel Allan, C.M.G. 1956; D.S.O. 1916; M.C. 1916: Director: Capel

Court Group of Investment Companies; Moran and Cato Ltd.; *b.* Melbourne, 9 July 1892; *s.* of late W. G. L. Spowers; *m.* 1922, Rosamond, *d.* of Reverend E. S. Lumsdaine; two *s.* one *d.* *Educ.:* Geelong Grammar School; Trinity College, Melbourne. Served as Lieutenant, East Lancashire Regiment, European War, 1914-1918; in command 2/24 Australian Battalion, War of 1939-45. Chairman, Victorian Division, Australian Red Cross Society, 1951-59. *Address:* Everton, Victoria, Australia. [*Died* 4 *May* 1968.

SPRECKLEY, Air Marshal Sir Herbert (Dorman), K.B.E. 1960 (O.B.E. 1942); C.B. 1952; M.I.Mech.E., F.R.Ae.S.; p.s.a.; retd.; Military Adviser to Smith's Aviation Division, since 1962; *b.* 1 Dec. 1904; *s.* of A. H. Spreckley, Bristol; *m.* 1931, *y. d.* of F. N. Teague, J.P., Worcester; one *s.* *Educ.:* Aircraft Apprentice, Halton; Royal Air Force College. Commissioned December 1925. North West Frontier, India, Campaign 1930 (despatches); 2 yr. Armament Course, 1932; Royal Air Force Staff College, 1935; subseq. Research and Development at Air Ministry; Ministry of Aircraft Production and Ministry of Supply on Armament Research and Development, 1937-45. A.O.C. and Commandant, Empire Air Armament School, 1946-48; i.d.c. 1949; subsequently Director of Operational Requirements (B), 1950-52; Air Officer Commanding and Commandant, R.A.F. Technical College, Henlow, Bedfordshire, 1952-54; Director-General of Technical Services, Air Ministry, 1954-57; A.O.C. No. 24 (Training) Group, Technical Training Command, R.A.F., 1957-59; Controller of Engineering and Equipment, Air Ministry, 1959-62. U.S. Legion of Merit (Degree of Commander), 1947. *Recreations:* various. *Address:* 8 Church Close, Kensington Church St., W.8. *T.:* Western 3355. *Club:* Army and Navy. [*Died* 29 *Aug.* 1963.

SPRIGGS, Sir Frank Spencer, K.B.E. 1948; Kt., 1941; retired as Managing Director of the Hawker Siddeley Group Ltd., (1936-58); *b.* 29 Mar. 1895; *s.* of late William Samuel and Katherine Spriggs; *m.* 1920, Gladys Amy Spratlea (*d.* 1967); two *d.* *Educ.:* Westbourne. Sopwith Aviation Co. Ltd., 1913-20. Formerly Chairman of: Armstrong Siddeley Development Co. Ltd., Sir W. G. Armstrong Whitworth Aircraft, Ltd., Armstrong Siddeley Motors, Ltd., A. V. Roe & Co., Ltd., Air Service Training, Ltd., Hawker Aircraft, Ltd., and Gloster Aircraft Co. Ltd., Hawker Aircraft (Blackpool), Ltd., Hawkeley Constructions, High Duty Alloys Ltd., Self-Changing Gears Ltd., Hawker-Sanders Ltd., Kelvin Constructions Co. Ltd., Gears Investment Trust, Ltd., Self Changing Gear Co. Ltd., M. & W. Patents Ltd.; Director of: A. V. Roe (Canada) Ltd., Brush Group, Canadian Car Co. Ltd., Hawksley S.M.E. Ltd., Brockworth Building Co. Ltd., Racair Ltd., Society of British Aircraft Constructors Ltd.; Pres. Soc. of British Aircraft Constructors, Ltd., 1939-41. Hon. F.R.Ae.S. *Publications:* Papers on various aspects of aviation. *Recreations:* yacht racing, golf. *Address:* Steepway, Broom Close, Esher, Surrey. *T.:* Esher 62671. *Clubs:* Royal Aero, Royal Automobile. [*Died* 11 *June* 1969.

SPRING, Brig.-Gen. Frederick Gordon, C.B. 1934; C.M.G. 1919; D.S.O. 1917; late The Royal Lincolnshire Regt.; *b.* 1878; *s.* of late Col. F. W. M. Spring, R.A., of Midhurst, Sussex; *m.* 1919, Violet Maud, *d.* of late A. Charles Turnbull, formerly of Witley, Surrey; (two *s.* decd.). *Educ.:* Blundell's School, Tiverton; R.M.C., Sandhurst; Staff College, 1914. Served South African War, 1900-2 (Queen's medal and three clasps, King's medal and two clasps); with 2nd Bn. Lincolnshire Regt. and 2nd Mounted Infantry Battalion; European War, 1914-18 (despatches five times, D.S.O., C.M.G., Bt. Lieutenant-Colonel, temporary Brig.-Gen.); commanded 11th Bn. Essex Regt., 1916-17, and 33rd Inf. Bde., 1917-19; commanded 52nd Bn. Sherwood Foresters, 1919-20; Chief Instructor Senior Officers School, Belgaum, 1921-22; commanded 1st Bn. Lincolnshire Regt., 1923-27; A.Q.M.G. Southern Command, 1927-31; Commander Poona Independent Brigade Area, India, 1931-35; retired pay, 1935; Inspector of Recruiting, 1935-39. Served with 25th Hampshire Home Guard Battalion, 1940-44, and as H.G. Adviser to Aldershot District. *Address:* Birchdene, Fleet, Hants. *Club:* United Service. [*Died* 24 *Sept.* 1963.

SPRING, Howard; author; *b.* Cardiff, 1889; *m.* Marion Ursula, *d.* of late G. W. Pye; two *s.* Worked successively on the staffs of the South Wales Daily News, the Yorkshire Observer, the Manchester Guardian, Evening Standard. *Publications: for children:* Darkie and Co., 1932; Sampson's Circus, 1936; Tumbledown Dick, 1939; *novels:* Shabby Tiger, 1934; Rachel Rosing, 1935; My Son, My Son!, 1938; Fame is the Spur, 1940; Hard Facts, 1944; Dunkerley's, 1946; There is No Armour, 1948; The Houses in Between, 1951; A Sunset Touch, 1953; These Lovers Fled Away 1955; Time and the Hour, 1957; All the Day Long, 1959; I Met a Lady, 1961; Winds of the Day, 1964; *Relevant publication:* Howard, by Marion Howard Spring, 1967; *autobiography:* Heaven Lies About Us, 1939; In the Meantime, 1942; And Another Thing, 1946; *criticism:* Book Parade, 1938; *plays:* Three Plays (Jinny Morgan, The Gentle Assassin, St. George at the Dragon), 1954. *Address:* The White Cottage, Fenwick Road, Falmouth. [*Died* 3 *May* 1965.

SPRINGHALL, Brig. Robert John, C.B. 1955; O.B.E. 1943; retired from Army September 1954; *b.* 23 September 1900; *s.* of Lieut.-Colonel John Winchester Springhall, O.B.E.; *m.* 1940, Emilie Evelyn Pritchard, *d.* of Maj.-Gen. H. L. Pritchard, C.B., C.M.G., D.S.O.; one *s.* decd. *Educ.:* Christ's Hosp.; Wellington (Som.). Commissioned East Yorkshire Regt. (Duke of York's Own), 1920; served in Egypt, Turkey, N. China and India, 1922-39; Staff College, 1934 and 1935; Waziristan, 1936-38 (despatches). Served War, 1939-45 (despatches): D.A.A.G. War Office, 1939-40; G.S.O.1, Middle East and Malta, 1941-43; B.G.S. 3 Corps, 1943-45. Commanded 1st E. Yorks Regt., Burma, Austria, 1946-47; A.A.G., War Office, 1947-48; Brig. A/Q Northern Command, 1948-51; Commander, East and West Ridings Area, 1951-54. Colonel, East Yorkshire Regt., 1950-58; Colonel, The Prince of Wales's Own Regiment of Yorkshire, 1958-60. Commander, Order of King George of the Hellenes. *Address:* 9 Dorchester Court, Sloane St., S.W.1. *T.:* Belgravia 6203. [*Died* 30 *Dec.* 1965.

SPROULL, Maj.-Gen. Alexander Wallace, C.B. 1947; C.B.E. 1944; F.C.G.I.; B.Sc. (Eng.); M.I.Mech.E., M.I.E.E.; *b.* Honolulu, 24 Dec. 1892; *s.* of A. M. Sproull, B.E.; *m.* 1918, Adeline Frances Godby. *Educ.:* St. Lawrence College, Ramsgate; City and Guilds College. In ranks, King Edward's Horse, 1914; commission, R.E. (S.R.), 1914; served European War, 1914-18 (wounded); (Regular) 1921; Staff Captain, War Office, 1919-23; Assistant Inspector Engineer Stores, 1926-31; Dep. Asst. Dir., W.O., 1933-37; Inspector Engineer and Signal Stores, 1937; Dep. Chief Insp., 1937-40; special appt. Air Ministry (Radar), 1940; Chief Inspector Engineer and Signal Stores, 1940-42; Chief Inspector Electrical and Mechanical Equipment, 1942-1946; Dir.-Gen. of Armament Production, Ministry of Supply, 1946-47. Pres. Institution of Engineering Inspection, 1943-44; Pres. Junior Institution of Engineers, 1946-1947. Captain, R.E., 1924; Bt. Major 1931; Major, R.E., 1933; Bt. Lt.-Col. 1936; Lt.-Col. 1939; Col. 1939; Actg. Brigadier 1942; Temp. Brigadier 1943; Actg. Major-General 1944; Temp. Maj.-Gen. 1945; retired from Army, 1947. Special Appointment Ministry of Supply, 1947; relinquished appointment, 1948. Director British Photographic Industries, Ltd. and associated companies, 1948-54; Deputy Chm. Ross Ltd., 1948-51, Chairman, 1952, Director 1953-54; Director: Phoenix Telephone and Electric Holdings Ltd., 1950-; Sewell & Hulton, Ltd., 1952-; John Oakey & Sons Ltd., 1954-. *Recreations:* golf, tennis, rifle shooting (Army XX, 1939-46). *Address:* Lamarsh, Wilderness Road, Chislehurst, Kent. *T.:* Imperial 1660. *Club:* Army and Navy. [*Died* 12 *March* 1961.

SPURLING, Sir Stanley, Kt., *cr.* 1934; C.M.G. 1925; O.B.E. 1918; Director, Bank of Bermuda; President, Bermuda Fire and Marine Insurance Co.; Director, Bermuda Telephone Co.; President, Salisbury Construction Co.; *b.* 1879; *s.* of late George Spurling; *m.* 1904, Frances Ellen, *d.* of John Gush, Taunton, Somerset; two *s.* two *d.* *Address:* Haslemere, St. George's, Bermuda. *Club:* Royal Bermuda Yacht. [*Died* 11 *Jan.* 1961.

SPURRELL, Walter Roworth, M.S., F.R.C.S., M.Sc.; Emeritus Prof. of Physiology, Guy's Hosp. Medical School, London Univ. (Prof., 1946-62); *b.* 24 June 1897; *m.* 1927, Dorothy Gwynne Griffith; one *s.* two *d.* *Educ.:* Llandovery College; Guy's Hospital. Served European War in R.F.A., 1915-18. Qualified, 1924; House Appointments, Guy's Hospital, 1924-26; Experimental Pathology, Leeds Univ., 1929; Physiology Dept., Leeds Univ., 1931; Physiology Dept., Guy's Hospital, 1933-. *Publications:* scientific papers in Journal of Physiology from 1931 onwards. *Recreation:* gardening. *Address:* Rivendell, 107 Orchard Avenue, Parkstone, Poole, Dorset. *T.:* Parkstone 2464. [*Died* 7 *June* 1966.

SPURRIER, Sir Henry, Kt. 1955; President, Leyland Motors Ltd., since June 1963 (Chm., 1957-63; Man. Dir., 1947-62); Chairman, Albion Motors Ltd.; Director: Associated Commercial Vehicles; Scammell Lorries Ltd.; District Bank Ltd.; Pt.-time Mem. Iron and Steel Bd. since 1958; *b.* 16 June 1898; *m.* 1920, Winifred Mary Cope; two *d.* *Educ.:* Repton. Served European War: Royal Flying Corps, Lieut. pilot; overseas service, Mesopotamia, India, Middle East; demobilised 1919. Joined Leyland Motors, 1920; Asst. to General Manager, 1925-30; Asst. General Manager, 1930-42; General Manager, 1942-1947; Chm. Standard Triumph Internat. Ltd., 1961-63. Coronation Medal, 1953. *Recreations:* sailing and shooting. *Address:* Ingol Cottage, Walker Lane, Preston, Lancs. *T.:* Preston 77313; Sowley House, Lymington, Hants. *T.:* East End 231. *Clubs:* Royal Automobile, Royal Thames Yacht; Royal Clyde Yacht. [*Died* 17 *June* 1964.

SPURRIER, Steven, R.A. 1952; R.B.A. 1934; *b.* and *Educ.:* London. Was for many years special artist on the Illustrated London News, and has made drawings for the principal periodicals in England, France, America, Holland and Germany; exhibits at most of the Galleries in London and the provinces and at International Exhibition, Pittsburg. *Publications:* Black and White, 1909; Illustration, 1933. *Address:* 33 Abercorn Place, N.W.8. *Club:* Arts. [*Died* 11 *March* 1961.

SPYERS, Roper, M.A.; *e. s.* of T. C. Spyers, M.D., Faversham; *b.* 7 December 1868; *m.* Margaret (*decd.*), *d.* of H. Nye, Kircudbright; one *s.* two *d.*; *m.* 1943, Enid (*d.* 1955), *o. c.* of late Col. Ernle Amyatt-Burney, 3rd Dragoon Guards. *Educ.:* Radley Coll. (Scholar and prizeman); Keble College, Oxford (Racquets Blue). 2nd Class Mods.; B.A. 1891; M.A. 1892; Barrister, Inner Temple, 1891; studied music, Paris, 1895; actor, 1896; with Beerbohm Tree, F. R. Benson, Sarah Thorne's companies: produced and played in My Soldier Boy, Criterion Theatre, 1899; Assist. Master, Radley Coll., 1901-3; produced Aristophanes Frogs in Greek; Hon. Secy. Radleian Soc., 1901-7. Ordained Deacon, 1901; returned to stage, rejoined Benson, and later Oscar Asche: Taming of the Shrew, Prayer of the Sword; Headmaster, Preparatory School, Weybridge, 1906-18; opened and managed Willow Hayne Hotel, Angmering-on-Sea, 1919-29; Proprietor Newlands Corner Hotel, 1930-39. *Recreations:* reading, gardening. *Address:* Flat I, 23 Randolph Crescent, W.9. *T.:* Cunningham 2986. *Clubs:* Reform, Green Room, M.C.C. [*Died* 19 *Feb.* 1961.

SQUIRE, Prof. Herbert Brian, F.R.S. 1957; Zaharoff Professor of Aviation, Imperial College, Univ. of London, since 1952; *b.* 13 July 1909; *m.* 1937, Winifred Fenney; one *s.* one *d.* *Educ.:* Bedford School; Balliol College, Oxford. On scientific staff: R.A.E., Farnborough, 1934-38 and 1939-49; Nat. Physical Laboratory, 1949-52. Director, Hovercraft Development Ltd., 1961-. *Publications:* papers and reports on aerodynamics. *Address:* 8 Hersham Road, Walton-on-Thames, Surrey. *T.:* Walton 25443. [*Died* 22 *Nov.* 1961.

SQUIRE, Professor John Rupert, M.D.; F.R.C.P.; Leith Professor of Experimental Pathology and Director of Division of Pathological Studies, Univ. of Birmingham, since 1948; Deputy-Dean, Faculty of Medicine, 1959-61; Director-Designate, Clinical Research Centre (Medical Research Council); *b.* 20 August 1915; *s.* of A. E. Squire; *m.* 1940, Marguerite Mary, *d.* of George Lewtey; two *d.* *Educ.:* Westminster School; Trinity College, Cambridge; University College Hospital Medical School. Various appointments with U.C. Hosp., including assistant to Sir Thomas Lewis, 1939-42. Service with R.A.M.C.: Operational Research, and Officer Commanding, Biological Research Unit, A.L.F.S.E.A., 1942-45. Director, Medical Research Council Industrial Medicine and Burns Research Units, Birmingham Accident Hospital, 1946-48. Hon. Director, Medical Research Council Unit for Research on the Experimental Pathology of the Skin, 1953-62. Oliver-Sharpey Lecturer, 1957. Governor, King Edward VI Schools, Birmingham. *Publications:* various publications dealing with allergy, skin and renal disease in Clinical Science and other med. jls.; co-author, Dextran, 1955. *Recreations:* painting and most things out-door. *Address:* 47 Church Hill Road, Solihull, Warwickshire. *T.:* Solihull 2940. [*Died* 6 *Jan.* 1966.

SQUIRE, William Henry; violoncellist and composer; *b.* Ross, Herefordshire, 8 Aug. 1871; *e. s.* of John Squire, Camborne. *Educ.:* Kingsbridge (Devon) Grammar School; Royal College of Music (Scholar); pupil of Edward Howell, Sir C. H. H. Parry, Sir C. V. Stanford, and Sir Fred. Bridge. London début, St. James's Hall, 1890; Crystal Palace, 1891; solo 'cellist, R.I. Opera, 1894-97; Queen's Hall Orchestra, 1897-1901; professor Royal College of Music, 1898-1917, and Guildhall School of Music, 1911-17. Now retired; last public appearance, Festival of Arts, Exeter Cathedral, Oct. 1941. Director, Performing Rights Soc., 1926-Nov. 1953; 1st hon. mem., Gen. Council, Nov.

1953-. *Publications:* compositions for 'cello also for piano, violin, and orchestra. Popular song writer. *Address:* 28 Queen's Grove, N.W.8. *T.:* Primrose 1745. [*Died* 17 *March* 1963.

SQUIRES, Herbert Chavasse, C.M.G. 1930; M.A.; D.M. Oxon.; F.R.C.P.Lond.; D.P.H.; *b.* 1880; *s.* of late Rev. Henry Charles Squires, M.A.; *m.* 1916, Hilda Margaret, *y. d.* of late Sir Henry Norbury, K.C.B., R.N.; two *d.* *Educ.:* St. Paul's School (Foundation Scholar); Hertford College, Oxford (Exhibitioner); Abbot (Oxford University) Scholar. House Physician, Medical Registrar Demonstrator Practical Medicine St. Thomas' Hospital; Clinical Assistant Brompton Hospital; Medical Inspector and Senior Medical Inspector, Sudan Medical Service; Director Khartoum Hosp., and Lecturer in Medicine, Kitchener Medical School, Khartoum; Consulting Physician to Sudan Govt. in London, 1938-51; Medical Inspector in Nullity, 1943-55; Physician to Cent. Advisory Council of Training for Ministry of the Church of England, 1943-56. Fellow Royal Society of Medicine; Fellow Royal Society Tropical Medicine and Hygiene. Chm. Med. Soc. of Individual Psychology, 1937-38. (Ed. Society's Proceedings, 1935-1943.) Commander of the Order of the Nile. *Publication:* The Sudan Medical Service, 1958. *Recreations:* formerly Rugby football, boxing and rowing. (Rugger Caps school, college and hospital. Rep. Oxford Middle weights 1900 and 1901: Capt. College Boat Club.) *Address:* 2 Northaw, Wych Hill Lane, Woking, Surrey. *Club:* Athenæum. [*Died* 17 *Feb.* 1964.

STACTON, David Derek; *b.* Nr. Minden, Nevada, 25 April 1925; *s.* of David Stacton and Dorothy Green. *Educ.:* Stanford University; University of California at Berkeley (B.A. 1950). Guggenheim Fellow, 1960-61 and 1966-67. Vis. Glasgow Prof., Univ. of Washington and Lee, 1965-66. *Publications: novels:* Remember Me, 1957; On a Balcony, 1958; Segaki, 1958; A Signal Victory, 1960; The Judges of the Secret Court, 1961; Tom Fool, 1962; Old Acquaintance, 1962; Sir William, 1963; Kaliyuga, 1965; People of the Book, 1965; *non-fiction:* A Ride on a Tiger, 1954; The World on the Last Day, 1965; The Bonapartes, 1967. *Recreations:* painting, travel. *Address:* c/o Faber & Faber, 24 Russell Square, W.C.1. [*Died* 19 *Jan.* 1968.

STAIR, 12th Earl of (*cr.* 1703), **John James Hamilton Dalrymple,** K.T. 1937; D.S.O. 1919; Bt. 1664 and (Scot.) 1698; Viscount Stair, Baron Glenluce and Stranraer, 1690; Bt. (Scot.), 1698; Viscount Dalrymple, Baron Newliston, 1703; Baron Oxenfoord (U.K.), 1841; Lord Lieutenant of Wigtownshire since 1935; Lt.-Col. (retd.) Scots Guards; Captain-General Royal Company of Archers, Queen's Body Guard, Scotland; Convener Wigtownshire C.C.; *b.* 1 Feb. 1879; *s.* of 11th Earl and Susan Harriett (*d.* 1946), *d.* of Sir James Grant Suttie, 6th Bt.; *S.* father, 1914; *m.* 1904, Violet Evelyn, *o. d.* of Col. Harford; three *s.* (and one killed on active service 1945) two *d.* *Educ.:* Harrow; Sandhurst. Entered Scots Guards, 1898; served S.A., 1900-1902; European War, 1914-19 (despatches, D.S.O.); J.P., D.L. Wigtownshire and Midlothian. M.P. Wigtownshire, 1906-14; Grand Master Mason Scottish Constitution, 1924-25; Lord High Commissioner, Church of Scotland, 1927 and 1928; Vice-Lt. of the County of Wigtown, 1928; Hon. Air Cdre., 603 Sqdn., Edinburgh T.A.F., 1930-39; Hon. Col. 5th Bn., K.O.S.B., 1936-49. *Heir: s.* Viscount Dalrymple, M.B.E. (now 13th Earl of Stair. His *s.*, John David James Dalrymple, *b.* 4 Sept., 1961, is now Viscount Dalrymple). *Address:* Lochinch Castle, Stranraer, Wigtownshire. *Clubs:* Guards, Carlton, Turf; New (Edin.); Western (Glasgow). [*Died* 4 *Nov.* 1961.

STALLARD, Brig.-General Stacy Frampton, C.M.G. 1917; D.S.O. 1916; *b.* 1873; *y. s.* of late Major-General S. Stallard and late Mrs. Stallard, Redhearn, Churt, nr. Farnham; *m.* Violet Kathleen (*d.* 1931), *d.* of late Brooke Mockett, Prescott House, Ealing; one *s.* one *d.* *Educ.:* abroad. Entered Royal Artillery, 1893; served South African War (Queen's S.A. medal), European War, both in France and Mesopotamia (despatches twice, C.M.G., D.S.O., Croix de Guerre, 1914 Star); retired pay, 1923. *Address:* 21 Cambridge Road, Colchester. *Club:* Army and Navy. [*Died* 30 *Sept.* 1961.

STAMER, Major-General William Donovan, C.B. 1948; C.B.E. 1941; D.S.O. 1938; M.C. 1918; *s.* of Rev. F. C. Stamer; *g.s.* of Sir Lovelace Stamer, 3rd Bart., Bishop of Shrewsbury; unmarried. *Educ.:* Rugby School; R.M.C., Sandhurst. Served European War, 1914-18 (despatches, M.C.), North Staffordshire Regiment, Palestine, 1936-38 (despatches, D.S.O.); War of 1939-45 (despatches, C.B.E., American Legion of Merit); G.O.C. Sudan and Eritrea, 1945; retired pay, 1948. Col. The North Staffordshire Regt., 1945-55. *Address:* 1 The Moorings, St. John's Road, Eastbourne. [*Died* 21 *Sept.* 1963.

STAMP, Professor Sir (Laurence) Dudley, Kt. 1965; C.B.E. 1946; Director of the World Land-Use Survey (Int. Geog. Union); University Professor of Social Geography, London Univ., at London School of Economics and Political Science, 1948-58 (Professor of Geography in the Univ. 1945-48), retired; Professor Emeritus and Honorary Lecturer since 1958; *b.* 9 March 1898; *y. s.* of late Charles Stamp, Bexley; *m.* 1923, Elsa Clara (B.A. Lond.) (*d.* 1962), *d.* of late A. U. Rea, Bude, Cornwall; one *s.* *Educ.:* King's College, London (Fellow, 1949; President K.C.L. Association, 1952-1958); B.Sc., 1st Cl. Hons. (Geology), 1917; M.Sc., 1918; D.Sc. 1921; B.A., 1st Cl. Hons. (Geography), 1921; D.Lit. 1949. Served R.E. 1917-19; Demonstrator, 1920-21; Daniel Pidgeon Award Geological Society, 1920; Geological Adviser to Indo-Burma Petroleum Co., 1922; Gold Medal from Mining and Geological Institute of India, 1922; Médaille Gosselet, Société des Sciences (Lille), 1923; Professor of Geology and Geography, Rangoon Univ., 1923-26; Sir Ernest Cassel Reader in Economic Geography, Univ. of London, 1926-1945; Represented India, Science Congress, Russia, 1925; Pres., Ind. Science Congress (Geology), Lahore, 1927; Maiben Lecturer, American Association for the Advancement of Science, California, 1934; British Delegate Indian Science Congress Jubilee, 1937-38; Soil Erosion research, N. and S. America, 1933-34, West Africa, 1937, Burma, 1938; Mem. C.P.R.E. Exec.; Mem. Farm Survey Cttee. (Min. of Agriculture), 1940; Vice-Chm. of Lord Justice Scott's Committee on Land Utilisation in Rural Areas, 1941-42; Chief Adviser on Rural Land Utilisation to the Ministry of Agriculture, 1942-55; Member Royal Commission on Common Land, 1955-58; U.K. Delegate on Land Use, to F.A.O., 1955-; Member, Nature Conservancy, 1958- (Chairman, England, 1963-); Research Committee, Min. of Town and Country Planning, 1943; The Lord Chancellor's Committee on Land Transfer, 1943; Hon. M.T.P.I. 1944; Pres., Section E British Assoc., 1949; Pres., Geog. Assoc., 1950; Pres. The International Geographical Union, 1952-56; Vice-Pres., Roy. Soc. of Arts, 1954-56; Pres. Inst. Brit. Geographers, 1956; Pres., R.G.S., 1963-; Pres., Inst. of Grocers, 1960-63; Chm. Natural Resources Advisory Committee (Ministry of Land), 1965; Founder's Medal, Roy. Geog. Soc., 1949; Daly Medal, Amer. Geog. Soc., 1950; Vega Medal, Sweden, 1954; Tokyo Geog. Soc. Medal, 1957; Scottish Geographical Medal, R.S.G.S., 1964. Hon. LL.D.: Clark Univ., Mass., U.S.A., 1955; Edinburgh, 1963; Hon. Ekon.D. Stockholm, 1959; Hon. D.Sc., Univ. of Warsaw, 1962; Exeter, 1965. *Publications:* An Introduction to Stratigraphy, 1923; The Vegetation of Burma, 1925; A Handbook of Commercial Geography, 18th edition, 1966; Asia, a Regional and Economic Geography, 1929, 11th Edition, 1962; The British Isles: a Geographic and Economic Survey, 5th ed., 1963; Editor, The Land of Britain, 1936-44; The Face of Britain, 1940; Britain's Structure and Scenery, 1945; The Land of Britain, its Use and Misuse, 1948, 1962; Our Undeveloped World, 1953; Africa (2nd Edn.), 1964; Man and the Land, 1955; Our Developing World, 1960; Applied Geography, 1960; Glossary of Geographical Terms, 1961; Some Aspects of Medical Geography, 1964. Editor, U.N.E.S.C.O. History of Land Use in Arid Lands, 1961. Text-Books of Geography; papers in geological, geographical, and botanical jls. *Recreations:* travelling, philately. *Address:* Ebbingford Manor, Bude Haven, Cornwall. *T.:* Bude 2045; 93 Sloane St., S.W.1. *T.:* Belgravia 7659. *Club:* Athenæum. [*Died* 8 *Aug.* 1966.

STANDEN, Rev. Canon Aubrey Owen; Canon Residentiary of Canterbury Cathedral since 1946; *b.* 14 Feb. 1898; *s.* of late Canon James Edward Standen and late Mrs. H. E. Standen; unmarried. *Educ.:* Merchant Taylors' School, London; St. John's College, Oxford. Served European War, 1914-18, Lt. R.F.A., 1917-19; prisoner of war (Germany), 1918; Exhibitioner and Prizeman, St. John's Coll., Oxford, 1920; Pusey and Ellerbon Hebrew Scholar, 1920; B.A. 1922, 2nd class Hon. School of Theology; Senior Fish Exhibitioner, 1924; 2nd class Hon. School of Oriental Languages, 1924; Houghton Syriac Prizeman, 1925; M.A. 1926; Lecturer in Hebrew, Cuddesdon Coll., 1922-24; deacon and priest, 1925; Curate of St. Margaret, Rochester, 1925-28; Sub-Warden Lincoln Theol. Coll., 1928-29; Examining Chaplain to Bishop of Lincoln, 1927-32, to Bishop of Rochester, 1932-40, to Archbishop of Canterbury, 1947-; Rector of Chatham, 1929-35; Vicar of Maidstone and Rural Dean of Sutton, 1935-47. Surrogate 1932-; Hon. Canon of Canterbury, 1941; Proctor in Convocation for Diocese of Canterbury, 1940-. Select Preacher, Univ. of Cambridge, 1950-51; Select Preacher, Univ. of Oxford, 1955-56, 1957. *Recreations:* riding and golf. *Address:* The Precincts, Canterbury. *Clubs:* Royal Commonwealth Society, Royal Over-Seas League; East Kent (Canterbury). [*Died* 25 *Oct.* 1961.

STANDING, Rev. George, C.B.E. 1933; D.S.O. 1918; M.C.; Officer of the Order of the Crown of Italy; *b.* 11 Nov. 1875; *s.* of late G. R. Standing, J.P. Havant, Hants; *m.* 1905, K. Ella, *d.* of A. Fielder, Purbrook, Hants; two *s.* *Educ.:* Havant School; Hartley College, Manchester. Primitive Methodist Minister at Chipping Norton, Ventnor, Bournemouth, Reading, Aldershot, 1900-14; commissioned temp. C.F. Oct. 1914; served European War, France and Italy, 1915-21; A.P.C. 2nd Army, 1916-18; A.P.C. 3rd Army, 1918; A.P.C. British Troops, France and Flanders, 1919-21 (despatches 4 times); C.F. 1st Class, 1 Jan. 1921; S.C.F. (United Board) Aldershot, 1921-26; Assistant Chaplain General, Western Command, 1926-28; Deputy Chaplain-General to H.M. Forces, 1929-32; Hon. Chaplain to the King, 1930-32; retired pay, 1932. *Address:* 21 Grove Road, Havant, Hants *T.:* Havant 4777 [*Died* 6 *Jan.* 1966.

STANDISH, Colonel Ivon Tatham, C.M.G. 1917; D.S.O. 1915; late Royal N.Z. Artillery; *b.* 31 Dec. 1883; *m.* 1908, Eleanor Gifford Wordsworth. Served European War, Gallipoli, 1915 (despatches, D.S.O.), elsewhere 1916-17 (C.M.G.); A.A. and Q.M.G., Northern Command, N.Z., 1923-27, and Artillery Staff Officer, 1924-27; Chief Staff Officer, Central Command, 1928-31; Q.M.G. General Headquarters, Wellington, New Zealand, 1931-34; Adjutant-General and Assistant Director of Artillery, G.H.Q., 1934-35; Officer Commanding Central Command, Wellington, 1935-39; Additional A.D.C. to the King, 1938-39; Adj.-Gen., Army H.Q., Wellington, 1940. *Address:* 69 Nicholson Road, Khandallah, Wellington, N.5, New Zealand. [*Died* 11 *Sept.* 1967.

STANDISH-WHITE, Robert, C.B.E. 1945 (O.B.E. 1919); F.R.C.S.I.; Hon. Consulting Surgeon, Bulawayo General Hospital, 1924-1954; Emeritus Surgeon, 1954; *b.* 1 May 1888; *s.* of Hugh Robert White and Ada Louisa Moyers; *m.* 1923, Winifred Kellman, *d.* of Sir William Chandler, K.C.M.G., Barbados, B.W.I.; three *s.* *Educ.:* Corrig School, Kingstown; Presbyterian College, Dublin; Royal College of Surgeons. L.R.C.P. and L.R.C.S. Ireland, 1909; L.M. (Rot.) 1909; F.R.C.S.I. 1914. Surgeon British S. African Co., N. Rhodesia, 1911-20; Major N. Rhodesian Medical Corps, E. Africa, 1914-18; Major R.A.M.C., 1918-20; Major S.R.M.C., Consultant Surgeon, R.A.F., 1939-46. Pres. Med. Council, S. Rhodesia, 1941-54. *Address:* Rathbeggan, 3rd Street, Heyman Road, Bulawayo, S. Rhodesia. *Clubs:* Naval and Military; Bulawayo (Bulawayo, S. Rhodesia). [*Died* 14 *Oct.* 1961.

STANFORD, Ernest, C.B.E. 1938; *b.* 27 Nov. 1894; *s.* of Edwin Stanford and Anne Wells; unmarried. *Educ.:* Church of England School, Crawley. Contested Horsham and Worthing (Lab.), 1923 and 1924; W. Wolverhampton (Nat. Lab.), 1931, but withdrew on nomination day to avoid split in national vote; contested Central Southwark (Nat.) 1935; played an active part in the Premier's election campaign at Seaham, 1931, after withdrawing from Wolverhampton; National Appeals Organiser, British Empire Cancer Campaigns, 1932-39; Appeals Organiser St. Dunstan's, 1939-59; Dep. Chm., Crawley Development Corporation; Crawley Parish Council, 1947 (Chairman); Chairman Weir Wood Water Bd.; Governor, St. Dunstan's, 1959-. Served European War in the Royal Army Medical Corps, seeing service with the Dardanelles Force from which he was invalided home with enteric fever; was connected with the Salonica and Egyptian Expeditionary Forces and the last year of the War with the Western Front Expeditionary Force. O.St.J. 1962. *Recreations:* golf and gardening. *Address:* Stanwells, Seaview Avenue, Angmering-on-Sea, Sussex. *T.:* Rustington 5582. [*Died* 14 *April* 1966.

STANFORD, Rt. Rev. Frederic; *b.* 1883. *Educ.:* King's College, London; St. Stephen's House, Oxford. Deacon, 1907; priest, 1908; Curate of All Souls, Grosvenor Park, Camberwell, 1907-12; St. Chad's, Regina, 1912-1913; Rector of St. Peter's, Regina, 1913-28; Principal of Gordon's Indian School, Punnichy, 1928-31; Vicar of Windermere, Dio. of Kootenay, 1931-42; Rector of Barkerville-Wells, 1942-43; Bishop of Cariboo, 1943-53. *Address:* Bishop's Retreat, Oliver, B.C., Canada. [*Died* 3 *Jan.* 1964.

STANFORD, Ven. Leonard John, M.A.; Archdeacon of Coventry, 1946-65, Archdeacon Emeritus since 1965; Vicar and Rector of Great with Little Packington, Coventry, 1959-66; *b.* 26 Sept. 1896; *s.* of late Ephraim Stanford, Barnsbury; *m.* 1st, 1927, Dora Kathleen Timms (*d.* 1939); three *s.* one *d.*; 2nd, 1941, Hilda Kathleen Cooke. *Educ.:* St. Clement's, Barnsbury; County Secondary School,

Holloway; Merton College, Oxford (B.A. 1922, M.A. 1925); Cuddesdon College. Lieut. 8th London Regt., attached 4th North Staffordshire Regt., European War, 1914-18 (severely wounded); invalided, 1919. Deacon, 1925; Priest, 1926; Curate of Royston, Yorkshire, 1925; Priest-in-Charge, Brierley, Yorkshire, 1929; Rector of Wolverton with Norton Lindsey and Langley, 1931-1940; Sec. S.P.G. for Coventry and Warwick Archdeaconries, 1933-36; Sec. The Bishop's Appeal, Coventry, 1936-40; Proctor in Convocation since 1937; Hon. Canon of Coventry, 1939-46; Vicar of Newbold-on-Avon with Long Lawford, 1940-47; Hon. Chaplain, R.A.F., 1941-45; Rector of St. Mark's, Bilton, 1947-59. *Address:* The Old School, Shabbington, Aylesbury, Bucks. *T.:* Ickford 623. [*Died* 20 *Nov.* 1967.

STANHOPE, 7th Earl (*cr.* 1718), **James Richard Stanhope;** (The Earldom of Chesterfield *cr.* 1628 devolved upon him on the death of 12th Earl but was not used and became extinct at his death); Visc. Stanhope of Mahon, Baron Stanhope of Elvaston, Co. Derby, 1717; K.G. 1934; P.C. 1929, D.S.O. 1917; M.C. 1916; D.L. and J.P. for Kent; *b.* 11 Nov. 1880; *e. s.* of 6th Earl and Evelyn, *o. d.* of late Richard Pennefather and late Lady Emily Hankey; *S.* father, 1905; *m.* 1921, Lady Eileen Browne (*d.* 1940), *e. d.* of 6th Marquess of Sligo. *Educ.:* Eton; Magdalen College, Oxford. Grenadier Guards 1901-8; served South African War, 1902; Lt.-Col. Reserve of Officers (Grenadier Guards), 1909-35; Major 4th Batt. Royal West Kent Regt., 1909-20; London County Council (Lewisham), 1910-13; served with 1st Batt. Grenadier Guards in France from Nov. 1914; General Staff Officer, Mar. 1915-May 1918 (despatches twice, M.C., D.S.O. Chevalier Légion d'Honneur); Parliamentary Secretary to War Office, 1918; Chairman Joint Substitution Board, 1923-24; Civil Lord of the Admiralty, 1924-29; Parliamentary and Financial Secretary to the Admiralty, Sept.-Nov. 1931; Under-Secretary of State for War, 1931-34; Parliamentary Under-Secretary of State for Foreign Affairs, 1934-36; First Commissioner of Works with a seat in the Cabinet, 1936-37; President of Board of Education, 1937-38; First Lord of the Admiralty, 1938-39; Lord President of the Council, 1939-40; Leader of House of Lords, 1938-40; Trustee of National Portrait Gallery, 1930-60; Chairman of Trustees of National Maritime Museum, 1934-59; Chairman Standing Commission on Museums and Galleries, 1941-48; Pres. Navy Records Soc., 1948-58; Conservative. *Recreation:* shooting. *Heir:* (to Earldoms) none; (to Viscountcy and Barony) 11th Earl of Harrington. *Address:* Chevening, near Sevenoaks. *Clubs:* Travellers', Carlton, Leander. [*Died* 15 *Aug.* 1967 (*ext.*).

STANIER, Sir William Arthur, Kt., *cr.* 1943; F.R.S. 1944; D.Sc. (Clarkson); Hon. Member American Society Mechanical Engineers; Hon. M.I.Mech.E.; M.I.Loco.E.; Chief Mechanical Engineer, London, Midland and Scottish Railway Co., 1932-44; Member of Research Council, B.T.C.; Director (past Chairman), Power Jets (Research and Development) Ltd., since 1950 (Director, 1944-50); *b.* 27 May 1876; *s.* of W. H. Stanier, Stores Superintendent, G.W.R., Swindon; *m.* 1906, Ella Elizabeth, (*d.* 1957), *d.* of L. L. Morse; one *s.* one *d.* *Educ.:* Wycliffe Coll., Stonehouse, Glos. Apprenticeship G.W.R., Swindon; Divisional Locomotive Supt., Swindon, 1906-12; Assistant Locomotive Works Manager, 1912-1919; Works Manager, 1920-22; Principal Assistant to Chief Mechanical Engineer, 1922-31. Scientific Adviser, Ministry of Production, 1942-48. President Production Engineers Research Association. Gold Medal of Institution of Locomotive Engineers 1957; International James Watt Medal, 1963. *Address:* Newburn, Chorleywood Road, Rickmansworth, Herts. *T.:* 72131. *Club:* Athenæum. [*Died* 27 *Sept.* 1965.

STANLEY, Col. Hon. Algernon Francis, D.S.O. 1914; *b.* 8 Jan. 1874; 7th *s.* of 16th Earl of Derby; *m.* 1918, Lady Mary Grosvenor, (*d.* 1959), *d.* of 1st Duke of Westminster and *widow* of Viscount Crichton; one *d.* (one *s.* killed on active service, 1943). *Educ.:* Wellington College. Entered 1st Life Guards, 1899; Captain, 1906; Major, 1914; Bt. Lt.-Col. 1915; Col. 1921; served South Africa, 1900 (Queen's medal 2 clasps); European War, 1914-18 (despatches 4 times, D.S.O.); Colonel-Commandant 159th Welsh Brigade, 1923-27; retired pay, 1927. *Address:* The Cottage, Badminton, Glos. *T.:* Badminton 289. [*Died* 10 *Feb.* 1962.

STANLEY, Arthur; *see* Megaw, A. S.

STANLEY-WRENCH, Mollie (Louise), F.R.H.S.; writer; *b.* Banbury; *e. d.* of John Kennedy Gibbs; *m.* 1902, William Stanley-Wrench (*d.* 1951), *e. s.* of Wm. Thomas Wrench and Dinah Stanley, Banbury; one *d.* *Educ.:* privately. Has written short stories, serials, articles, and verse for many magazines and newspapers; made a study of folk-lore and country customs and is an authority on folk-cookery and dishes of the countryside. *Publications:* Love's Fool, 1908; Burnt Wings, 1909; A Perfect Passion, 1910; A Priestess of Humanity, 1911; Pillars of Smoke, 1912; Ruth of the Rowldrich, 1912; Court of the Gentiles, 1913; Potter and Clay, 1914; Lily Louisa, 1915; Beat, 1917; Devil's Stairs, 1918; Stories of the Operas, 1924; Cupboard Love, 1926; More Stories of the Operas, 1926; Divorced Love, 1927; Strange Lovers, 1933; Sing for the Moon, 1934; Bachelor Woman's Cookery, 1934; Green Pleasure, 1934; Long Harvest, 1935; No Fixed Abode, 1936; The Rose dies Hard, 1938; Home Management, 1934; Complete Home Cookery Book, 1938; Good Things in Kitchen, 1946; A Winter's Tale, 1946; Brides' Cook Book, 1946; A Book of hors-d'œuvres, Cocktail Canapes and Snacks, 1952; Garden Patchwork, 1954; compiled and edited The Lyceum Book of Verse, 1931. *Recreations:* gardening, cooking, inventing new recipes. *Address:* 4 Love Walk, Denmark Hill, S.E.5. *Club:* P.E.N. [*Died* 27 *Oct.* 1966.

STANTON, Hon. Sir Joseph, Kt. 1957; lately Third Puisne Judge of Supreme Court, Wellington, New Zealand; *b.* 1884; *s.* of A. Stanton; *m.* 1911, Marjorie A., *d.* of T. McMaster; one *s.* three *d.* *Educ.:* Auckland Grammar Sch.; Auckland Univ. Coll. (LL.B.). Barrister and Solicitor, 1907; City Solicitor, Auckland, 1914-48; Judge of Supreme Court, Auckland, 1948-57. *Address:* 88 Mountain Road, Auckland, S.E.3, New Zealand. [*Died* 9 *Oct.* 1963.

STANYFORTH, Lieut.-Col. Ronald Thomas, C.V.O. 1937 (M.V.O. 1930); M.C.; *b.* 1892; *o. s.* of late Lieut.-Col. E. W. Stanyforth, C.B.; *m.* 1941, Prudence Elizabeth, *o. d.* of late David Daniel, Alltyferin, Nantgaredig, Carmarthenshire. *Educ.:* Eton; Christ Church, Oxford; B.A. Served 17th Lancers, 1914-18 (despatches, M.C.); retired, Major 1930; re-employed, 1939; served B.E.F., 1939-40; Personal Assistant to C.-in-C. Home Forces, 1940-41; G.S.O. 1 8 Corps, Northumbrian District, 21 Army Group H.Q., 1941-45; retired, 1946. Equerry to Prince Henry, 1921-24; Comptroller of the Household, to the Duke of Gloucester, 1930-39, Extra Equerry, 1947-. Captained the M.C.C. team which went to South Africa, 1927-28. Trustee M.C.C. *Publication:* Wicket Keeping, 1935. *Recreations;* shooting and fishing. *Address:* Kirk Hammerton Hall, York. *T.:* Green Hammerton 202. *Clubs:* Cavalry, White's. [*Died* 20 *Feb.* 1964.

STAPLES, Sir Robert George Alexander, 13th Bt., *cr.* 1628; *b.* 21 Sept. 1894; *o. s.* of Sir Robert Ponsonby Staples, 12th Bt., and Ada Louise, *d.* of H. Stammers, London; *S.* father 1943; *m.* 1922, Vera Lilian, *y. d.* of John Jenkins, Dulwich Wood Park, London; two *d.* *Educ.:* Campbell College, Belfast; Trinity College, Dublin. Served European War, Lt. R.A.S.C., 1916-1919; service in German East Africa. Entered business, 1926, and has been entirely employed in Sales Promotion and Management; joined staff of Kelvinator, Ltd., 1923; Sales Manager, Kelvinator Ltd., 1940-48; Director, Peter Marsh & Sons (N.I.) Ltd., 1961. *Recreations:* contract bridge, poker and a good argument. *Heir:* John Richard Staples [*b.* 5 April 1906; *m.* 1933, Sybella, *d.* of late Dr. Charles Henry Wade, two *d.*]. *Address:* Lissan, Cookstown, Co. Tyrone, Ireland. *T.:* Cookstown, 2315. *Club:* Killymoon Golf. [*Died* 9 *Dec.* 1970.

STAPLETON, Henry Ernest, D.Litt.; M.A.; B.Sc.; F.A.S.; Fellow of the Chemical Society and the Society of Genealogists; Member of the Royal Asiatic Society, the Asiatic Society of Bengal (Vice-President, 1930) and Numismatic Society of India (Pres. 1930); Membre de l'Académie Internationale d'Histoire des Sciences; Hon. Member, Kamrup Anusandhan Samiti; *b.* 3 May 1878; *e. s.* of late Rev. Henry Stapleton, Vicar of Kirkby Hill, Boroughbridge, Yorks, and Rural Dean; *m.* 1911, Eleanor Neste, 2nd *d.* of late Rev. J. J. Evans, Cantreff Rectory, Brecon; two *s.* one *d.* *Educ.:* Bradford Grammar School; St. John's College, Oxford (Scholar); 1st class, Honours School of Natural Science, 1899; also worked at the Caius College Laboratory, Cambridge, 1899-1900, for research degree. Appointed to Indian Educational Service as Professor of Chemistry, Presidency College, 1900; Officiating Principal, Calcutta Madrasah, 1903-4 (twice) and Inspector of European Schools, 1904; Inspector of Schools, Dacca Division, 1905-15; Officiating Director of Public Instruction, Eastern Bengal and Assam, 1909; Hon. Numismatist to the Government of Eastern Bengal and Assam, 1908-12; and to the Government of Bengal, 1928-33; appointed to I.A.R.O., May 1915, (123rd Outram's Rifles); September 1915, took draft to Mesopotamia to join the 24th Punjabis; action of Ummu-t-Tubul and retreat from Ctesiphon to Kut el Amarah, November 1915; prisoner of war in Turkey from surrender of Kut, 29 April 1916 till Armistice; on return to India at end of 1919 appointed Special Officer in connection with the starting of Dacca University; Divisional Inspector of Schools, Dacca, 1922-24; Principal, Presidency College, Calcutta, 1924; Bengal Government delegate to the Imperial Educational Conference, 1927; Director of Public Instruction, Syndic of Calcutta University and M.L.C., 1926, and from 1928; retired, 1933. Since 1935 (and during the German occupation of Jersey, 1940-45) has bred Jersey cattle experimentally with the aim of increasing the Butter Fat content of their milk. *Publications:* Papers in Journal of Chemical Society, Journal and Memoirs of A.S.B., etc. *Recreations:* genealogy, numismatics, arboriculture, and cattle breeding. *Address:* Sands, St. Brelade, Jersey, C.I. *T.:* Southern 133. *Club:* East India and Sports. [*Died* 12 *Feb.* 1962.

STAPYLTON, G. B. C.; *see* Chetwynd-Stapylton.

STARKIE, Enid Mary, C.B.E. 1967; M.A., D.Litt. Oxon; Member of the Irish Academy of Letters; F.R.S.L.; Docteur de l'Université de Paris, Lauréate de l'Académie Française; Reader Emeritus in French Literature at the University of Oxford; Fellow of Somerville College, Oxford, 1934-65, Honorary Fellow since 1965; *d.* of late Right Honourable W. J. M. Starkie, P.C., Litt.D., Resident Commissioner of National Education for Ireland. *Educ.:* Alexandra School and Alexandra College, Dublin (Scholar); Royal Irish Acad. of Music (Scholar), pupil of Michele Esposito; Somerville Coll., Oxford (Scholar); La Sorbonne, Paris. For two years asst. lecturer in Modern Languages at University College, Exeter; then appointed to lectureship in French literature at Somerville College, Oxford; later to a University lectureship in French literature at Oxford; Reader in French Literature at Univ. of Oxford, 1945-1965. Visiting Professor in French Literature, Berkeley University, Calif., U.S.A., Seattle University, Washington, U.S.A., 1951, Virginia, U.S.A., 1959, Columbia Univ., 1968; Zaharoff Lecturer, Univ. of Oxford, 1954; lectured at Univs. of Paris, Strasbourg, Lyon and Lille, 1951; Brussels, 1955; Aix, 1963; Ghent, 1964. Mem. Anglo-French Jt. Govt. Cultural Commn., 1955-. Hon. D. ès Lettres, Aix; Hon. Litt.D., Dublin; Hon. D.Litt., Exeter. Hollins Medal, 1967. Officier de la Légion d'Honneur; Chevalier du Tastevin. *Publications:* Émile Verhaeren, Paris, 1928, couronné par l'Académie Française; Baudelaire, 1933; Rimbaud in Abyssinia, 1937; Arthur Rimbaud, 1938; Rimbaud en Abyssinie, Paris, 1938; A Lady's Child, 1941; A Critical Edition of Les Fleurs du Mal of Baudelaire, 1942; Arthur Rimbaud, 1947; The God that failed, 1948; Petrus Borel en Algérie 1950; Andre Gide, 1953; Arthur Rimbaud, 1854-1954, 1954; Petrus Borel, 1954; Baudelaire, 1957; From Gautier to Eliot, 1960; Arthur Rimbaud, 1961; Flaubert: The Making of the Master, 1967; Flaubert: The Master, 1971 (posthumous). *Recreation:* music. *Address:* 23 Walton St., Oxford. *T.:* 57110. [*Died* 22 *April* 1970.

STARLING, Frederick Charles, C.B. 1947; C.B.E. 1939; Hon. M.Inst.Pet.; *b.* Sept. 1886; *er. s.* of Harvey Starling, Elsenham; *m.* 1911, Laura Mary Gray (*d.* 1958), *e. d.* of Reuben Stubbings; one *s.* one *d.* *Educ.:* Bigods School, Essex. Entered Civil Service, 1903; Board of Trade, 1910; Mines Dept., 1920; Secretary to Coal Advisory Committee and Metalliferous Advisory Committee, 1921-27; Asst. Sec. to Royal Commission on the Coal Industry, 1925; Joint Secretary to Standing Committee on Mineral Transport, 1927-30; Principal Asst. Secretary and Director of Petroleum Supplies, 1940-1946; Under Secretary (Petroleum Division), Ministry of Fuel and Power, Jan.-Oct. 1946; Member of four special Missions to U.S.A. on oil questions, 1941-44; U.S. Medal of Freedom with Silver Palm, 1946. *Address:* 4 Bromley Court, Bromley Grove, Shortlands, Kent. *T.:* Ravensbourne 4179. [*Died* 26 *Aug.* 1962.

STARLING, John Henry, C.M.G. 1925; O.B.E. 1920; *b.* Greensborough, Victoria, Australia, 15 Jan. 1883; *s.* of late J. H. Starling; *m.* 1911, May, *d.* of late A. H. Price, J.P.; two *s.* one *d.* A.A.S.A., A.C.I.S.; Licensed Company Auditor, Vic. Official Sec. to Governor-General of Australia, 1919-28; Secretary Prime Minister's Dept. and Secretary Dept. of External Affairs, 1933-35; Commonwealth 1st Asst. Public Service Commissioner, 1935-48. *Address:* 66 Dominion Circuit, Forrest, Canberra, Australia. [*Died* 5 *April* 1966.

STARTE, Oliver Harold Baptist, C.B.E. 1932; Indian Civil Service, retired; *b.* 23 Jan. 1882; *s.* of Henry Starte, Cambridge; *m.* 1920, Frances Mary Bushill; two *s.* one *d.* *Educ.:* Perse School; Clare College, Cambridge. *Address:* 7 Athelstan Road, Worthing, Sussex. *T.:* 1474. [*Died* 22 *Jan.* 1969.

STATHAM, Ira Cyril Frank, C.Eng.; M.Eng. (Sheffield); M.Inst. Min. Eng.; F.G.S.; F.R.S.A.; F.R.I.C.S.; formerly Professor of Mining, Dean of the Faculty of Engineering, University of Sheffield, retired from Professorship 1954; Consulting Mining Engineer; *b.* 29 Nov. 1886; *y. s.* of James Statham of Clayhanger, nr. Walsall; *m.* Minnie, *d.* of David Bradbury, Brownhills, nr. Wallsall; one *s.* one *d.* *Educ.:* Brownhills Central School; Walsall Municipal Technical Institute; University of Birmingham. Mining experience in South Staffs and S. Yorkshire; various official positions, including Assistant Manager, Brownhills Collieries; Assistant Manager and Surveyor, Hoyland Silkstone Colliery, Yorkshire; Lecturer in Surveying and allied subjects, S. Staffordshire Mining Schools, 1909-11; Lecturer in Mining and Surveying, Wigan Mining and Tech. Coll., 1911-13; Lecturer in Mining, Univ. of Sheffield, 1919-25; Past Pres. and Peake Medallist, Midland Instn. Mining Engineers; Past Vice-Pres., Institution and Hay Medallist, Instn. of Mining Engineers; Past Pres.: Institute of Mine Surveyors of Gt. Britain; Yorks Branch, Nat. Assoc. of Colliery Managers; Gold Medallist, Nat. Assoc. of Colliery Managers; Fellow and Thornton Medallist, Assoc. Min. Elec. and Mech. Engineers; Member Yorks. Dist. Valuation Board; active service in France in War of 1914-18 with Royal Engineers, field survey. *Publications:* Winning and Working of Coal; Coal Mining; (Joint) Mine Atmospheres; Firedamp Explosions and their Prevention; A Textbook on Coal Mining; Coal Mining Practice, four Vols.; papers and articles in technical Jls. on Mining Subsidence, Flameproof Electrical Apparatus for use in Mines, Utilization of Waste Heat and Surplus Gases from Coke Ovens, Haulage Accidents, Mine Ventilation, Safety Developments, Coal Mining in India, Power Loading, etc. *Recreation:* gardening. *Address:* Parkside, 37 Bramhall Park Road, Bramhall, Nr. Stockport. *T.:* Bramhall 2229. [*Died* 15 *Nov.* 1967.

STAUDINGER, Professor Hermann, Dr.phil.; German chemist; Nobel Prize for Chemistry, 1953; *b.* Worms (Rhein), 23 March 1881; *m.* 1928, Magda (*nee* Woit) Dr.phil., Mag.rer.nat., *d.* of His Excellency Dr. Oskar Woit, formerly Latvian Ambassador in Germany. *Educ.:* Halle; Darmstadt; Munich. Lecturer in Chemistry, Strassburg Univ., 1907-8; Extra Prof., Karlsruhe Tech. High Sch., 1908-12; Ord. Prof.: Federal Technical High School Zürich, 1912-26: University of Freiburg-im Breisgau, 1926-51; Prof. Emeritus, member: Göttingen, Heidelberg, Halle und Munich Acads. of Sciences; Institut de France, 1959; Frankfurt and Zürich Phys. Socs., Royal Physiographical Soc., Lund.; Hon. mem.: Union of Finnish Chemists; Soc. Polymer Science, Japan; French Chem. Soc.; German Chem. Soc.; Japanese Chem. Soc.; Corresponding member Naturforschende Gesellschaft, Zürich. Leblanc medal, French Chemical Society, 1931; Cannizzaro Prize, Rome, 1933; Goldene Ehren-Medaille des Vereins der Textilchemiker und Coloristen, 1962. Hon. citizen, Freiburg, 1955. Hon. degrees: Dr.Ing. (Karlsruhe) 1950; Dr.rer.nat. (Mainz), 1951; Dr. (C) (Salamanca), 1954; Dr. chem. (Torino), 1954; Dr. sc. techn. (Zürich). 1955; Dr. *h.c.* (Strassburg), 1959. Grosses Verdienstkreuz mit Stern und Schulterband des Verdienstordens der Bundesrepublik Deutschland, 1965. *Publications:* Die Ketene, 1912; Die hochmolekularen organischen Verbindungen, 1932, new edn., 1960; Vom Aufstand der technischen Sklaven, 1947; Makromolekulare Chemie und Biologie, 1947; Tabellen für allgemeine und anorganische Chemie, 1947; Organische Kolloidchemie, 1950; Organische qualitative Analyse, 1955; Arbeitserinnerungen, 1961. *Address:* Lugostrasse 14, Freiburg-im-Breisgau, Germany. *T.:* Freiburg i.Br. 32874. *Club:* Rotary (Freiburg i.Br.). [*Died* 8 *Sept.* 1965.

STAUNTON, Most Rev. James, D.D.; Bishop of Ferns (R.C.), since 1939; *b.* 1889. *Educ.:* St. Kieran's College, Kilkenny; Maynooth. B.A. (R.U.I.), 1909; B.C.L. 1911; B.D. 1913; priest, 1913; Professor of Dogmatic Theology, St. Kieran's College, 1913-1918; subsequent studies at University of Freiburg, 1918-21; D.D. 1921. Professor of Sacred Scripture, St. Kieran's College, 1921-1923; Junior Dean of Maynooth College, 1923-28; President of St. Kieran's College, 1928-38; Canon of Ossory, 1932. Freedom of Kilkenny, 1939. *Address:* Summerhill, Wexford, Eire. [*Died* 27 *June* 1963.

STAVELEY, Brig. Robert, D.S.O. 1914; late R.A.; *b.* 28 Feb. 1892; *o. s.* of late Robert Staveley, Merton Lodge, Headington, Oxford; *m.* 1923, Ilys Evelyn, *er. d.* of D. A. Sutherland, Fairfield Lodge, Twickenham; one *s.* one *d.* Entered Army, 1911; Captain, 1916; served European War, 1914-1918 (despatches five times, D.S.O.); Arab Rebellion and operations in N.W. Persia, 1920; p.s.c. 1927; Col. 1941; Operations France and Belgium, 1939-40; North Africa and Italy, 1943; retired pay, 1946. *Address:* c/o Lloyds Bank, Ltd., 6 Pall Mall, S.W.1. *Club:* Army and Navy. [*Died* 23 *Nov.* 1968.

STEACIE, Dr. Edgar William Richard, O.B.E. 1946; F.R.S. 1948; F.R.S.C. 1934; Ph.D., D.Sc., LL.D., D. de l'U.; President of the National Research Council, Ottawa, since 1952 (Director of the Division of Chemistry, 1939-52, Vice-Pres., 1950); *b.* 25 December 1900; *s.* of Capt. Richard Steacie and Alice Kate McWood; *m.* Dorothy C. Day; one *s.* one *d.* *Educ.:* McGill University. B.Sc. 1923, M.Sc. 1924, Ph.D. 1926, McGill; also studied at Frankfurt, Leipzig, and King's College, London. Hon. D.Sc. (McMaster) 1946, (New Brunswick) 1950, (Laval) 1952, (Manitoba and Toronto) 1954, (Ottawa) 1956, (British Columbia, St. Lawrence, St. Francis-Xavier) 1957; LL.D. (Queens) 1952, (Dalhousie) 1952, (McGill) 1953, (Western Ontario) 1958; D. de l'U. (Montreal), 1956; D.Sc. (Oxford), 1960. D.Sc.: (Royal Military College), 1960; (Memorial), 1961; (Saskatchewan), 1962. Lecturer in Chemistry, 1926-30, Asst. Prof. 1930-37, Assoc. Prof., 1937-39, McGill. Mem. Atomic Energy Control Board Defence Research Bd. Chm., Bd. of Govs., Carleton Univ.; Chm., Adv. Cttee. for Science, Univ. of Ottawa; Hon. Member: Canadian Physiolog. Soc.; Enginrg. Inst. of Can.; Agric. Inst. of Can.; also of foreign Chem. Socs. Past-President Chemical Inst. of Canada; Baker Non-Resident Lectr. in Chemistry, Cornell Univ., 1953; Vice-Pres., Internat. Union of Pure and Applied Chemistry, 1951-53; President Royal Soc. Can., 1954-55; Liversidge Lectr., Chemical Society of London, 1955; Hon. Fell., Chem. Soc., London, 1957; President Faraday Soc., 1959; Foreign Assoc., Nat. Acad. of Sciences (U.S.A.), 1957; For. Mem. Acad. of Sciences of U.S.S.R., 1958. Mem., Internatl. Adv. Cttee. on Research in the Natural Sciences Programme of Unesco, 1958-61; Canadian Rep., N.A.T.O. Science Cttee., 1958-61; Pres., Internat. Council of Scientific Unions, 1961-. Pres., XVIIIth Internat. Congress of Pure and Applied Chemistry, 1961. Chem. Inst. of Canada Medal, 1953; Tory Medal, Roy. Soc. of Canada, 1955; Bennett Prize, Roy. Soc. of Arts, 1960. *Publications:* books and papers on photochemistry and rates of gaseous chemical reactions. *Address:* 275 Hillcrest Road, Rockcliffe Park, Ottawa, Canada. *Club:* Rideau (Ottawa). [*Died* 28 *Aug.* 1962.

STEAD, Sir Charles, Kt., *cr.* 1931; C.B.E. 1922 (O.B.E. 1921); M.V.O. 1912; King's

Police Medal, 1915; *b.* 30 Aug. 1877; *s.* of late Arthur C. Stead; *m.* 1st, Louisa Cecily Waldron (*d.* 1934), *er. d.* of late Rev. J. C. Witton, Headmaster of Andover Grammar School; two *s.* one *d.*; 2nd, 1941, Helen Maud, M.B.E., *d.* of late W. E. Hewitt, A.R.I.B.A., Wimbledon. *Educ.:* Elmham; Mason Coll., Birmingham. Indian Police, 1898, after open competition and was attached to the Punjab; Principal Police Training Sch. and in charge Finger Print Bureau, Punjab, 1909; Asst. to Deputy Inspector-Gen. C.I.D., Punjab, 1911; on special C.I.D. duty in connection with Their Majesties' visit to India, 1911-12; on special duty with Govt. of India C.I.D., 1913; personal assistant to Inspector-General of Police, Punjab, 1913-1919; Assistant Inspector-General Railway Police, 1920; on special duty in connection with the Prince of Wales' tour in India, 1921-1922; Deputy Inspector-Gen. of Police, Punjab, 1924; Inspector-Gen. of Police, North West Frontier Province, 1927; Inspector-General of Police, Punjab, 1928-32; retired 1932; Acting Inspector of Constabulary (Home Office), 1940-45. *Address:* c/o National and Grindlay's Bank Ltd., 54 Parliament Street, S.W.1. *Club:* Athenæum. [*Died* 8 *Feb.* 1961.

STEDMAN, Ralph Elliott, C.M.G. 1960; Executive Director, International Sugar Council; *m.* Helena Margaretta, *d.* of Rev. Canon H. Underhill, Vancouver, British Columbia; three *s.* *Educ.:* Brighton Grammar School; University of British Columbia; Edinburgh University. Asst. to Prof. of Logic, Edinburgh, 1928-32; Lectr. in Philosophy, Univ. Coll. of Swansea, 1932-37; Lecturer and Head of Dept. of Logic, Univ. Coll., Dundee, in Univ. of St. Andrews, 1937-1945; Assistant Secretary, Ministry of Food, 1947-51; Under-Secretary, Ministry of Agriculture, Fisheries and Food, 1951-59. *Publications:* contrib. to philosophical journals. *Recreation:* painting. *Address:* 11 Bloomfield Road, Highgate, N.6. *T.:* Mountview 1468. [*Died* 1 *Feb.* 1964.

STEEGMAN, John E. H., O.B.E. 1952; M.A.; Writer on art and architecture; *b.* 10 Dec. 1899; *er. s.* of late Fleet Surgeon E. J. Steegman, R.N.V.R., O.B.E., M.D., D.P.H., and Mabel, *d.* of Rear-Adm. Barnet. *Educ.:* Clifton College; King's College, Cambridge, Officer-Cadet, R.F.A., 1918. Assistant in National Portrait Gallery, 1929-45 (seconded for other duties, 1939-44). Organised the Sala de l'Aliança at the Lisbon Centenaries Exhibition, 1940. Keeper of the Department of Art, National Museum of Wales, 1945-52; Director of the Museum of Fine Arts, Montreal, 1952-59. Visiting Professor, University of Chicago, 1950. Member of Fine Arts Advisory Panel, British Council. Member Council of the Georgian Group since its foundation. Lectured in: Europe, Mid. East, U.S.A., Canada, Austr., N.Z. Water-colour painter. *Publications:* Hours in the National Portrait Gallery, 1928; Sir Joshua Reynolds, 1933; Iconography of the Duke of Wellington, 1935; The Rule of Taste, 1936; Cambridge, 1940; The Artist and the Country House, 1949; Consort of Taste, 1950; Survey of Portraits in N. Wales Houses, 1955; Survey of Portraits in S. Wales Houses, 1961; articles and reviews. *Clubs:* Reform; National Arts (New York). [*Died* 15 *April* 1966.

STEEL, Gerald Arthur, C.B. 1919; *yr. s.* of C. G. Steel, M.A., J.P., of Rugby School, and Amy Maud Price, Oxford; *m.* 1913, Ellen, *d.* of late Edward Price Edwards, Secretary of the Trinity House; one *s.* *Educ.:* Rugby School; University College, Oxford. Entered Civil Service by the Higher Division Examination, 1907; appointed First Division Clerk, Admiralty; Assistant Private Secretary to First Lord of the Admiralty, 1911-1915; Private Secretary, 1915-18, Assistant Secretary, Ministry of Transport, 1919-21; Secretary of the Geddes Committee on National Expenditure, 1921-22; Assistant Secretary Scottish Office, 1922-25; resigned from Civil Service, 1925. General Manager and Director, British Aluminium Co., 1925-52. A Governor of Rugby School; Legion of Honour; Order of St. Maurice and Lazarus. *Address:* 14 Dover Park Drive, Roehampton, S.W.15. *T.:* Putney 2131. *Clubs:* Brooks's, Alpine. [*Died* 14 *Dec.* 1963.

STEEL, Air Chief Marshal Sir John Miles, G.C.B., *cr.* 1937 (K.C.B., *cr.* 1935; C.B. 1922); K.B.E., *cr.* 1926 (C.B.E. 1919); C.M.G. 1919; *b.* 1877; *s.* of late Col. J. P. Steel, R.E.; *m.* 1909, Kathleen, (*d.* 1956), *d.* of late Wm. Sinclair Thomson; three *s.* one *d.* *Educ.:* Stubbington House; H.M.S. Britannia. Naval Cadet, 1892; Sub-Lieut., 1897; served S.A. War with Naval Brig. for relief of Ladysmith and subsequent operations (wounded Elandslaagte, medal and five clasps); Expedition Gambia River (medal, despatches); Commander, 1912; served in Grand Fleet, 2nd in Command, H.M.S. Conqueror (despatches, Jutland, awarded Russian Order of St. Stanislas); Captain, 1916; appointed R.N. Air Service; Temp. Brig.-General, 1918, R.A.F.; Director of Air Division Admiralty; transferred to R.A.F., Air Commodore, 1919; Air Vice-Marshal, 1925; Air Marshal, 1932; Air Chief Marshal, 1936; Deputy Chief of the Air Staff, Air Ministry until May 1926; additional member of the Air Council, 1923-26; Air Officer commanding Wessex Bombing Area, 1926-31; Air Officer Commanding R.A.F. in India, 1931-35; Air Officer Commanding-in-Chief Air Defence of Great Britain, 1935-36; Bomber Command, 1936-37; retired list, 1937; Air Officer Commanding Reserve Command, 1939-40; Controller-General of Economy, Air Ministry, 1941-45. *Address:* 9 Nevern Mansions, S.W.5. *Club:* United Service. [*Died* 2 *Dec.* 1965.

STEEL, Major Sir Samuel Strang, 1st Bt., *cr.* 1938; Forestry Commissioner, 1933-1949; Director, Bank of Scotland; *b.* 1882; *o. s.* of late W. Strang Steel, of Philiphaugh; *m.* 1910, Vere Mabel, *d.* of 1st Baron Cornwallis, Linton Park, Kent; three *s.* one *d.* *Educ.:* Eton; Trinity College, Cambridge. Served in France and Salonika and Mesopotamia in European War; Lieut. Royal Company of Scottish Archers; Convener, Selkirkshire County Council; M.P. (U.) Ashford Division of Kent, Dec. 1918-29; was Parliamentary Private Secretary to Rt. Hon. Sir Robert Sanders, Bart., M.P., Minister of Agriculture, 1923, and to Rt. Hon. Ronald McNeill, Parliamentary Secretary to the Treasury, 1925. President Scottish Unionist Association, 1937-38 and 1942-43. H.M. Lieutenant for County of Selkirk, 1946-58. *Heir:* *s.* Major Fiennes William Strang Steel, 17/21st Lancers, *b.* 1912. *Address:* Philiphaugh, Selkirk. *Clubs:* Carlton; New (Edinburgh). [*Died* 14 *Aug.* 1961.

STEEL-MAITLAND, Sir Keith (Richard Felix) Ramsay-, 3rd Bt. *cr.* 1917; Chairman and Managing Director, Barnton Sauchie and Bannockburn Estates Company; *b.* 6 May 1912; *yr. s.* of Rt. Hon. Sir Arthur Steel-Maitland, 1st Bt., M.P.; *S.* brother (Sir James Ramsay-Steel-Maitland, 2nd Bt.) 1960. *Educ.:* Winchester College; Balliol College, Oxford. President Oxford Union Society, 1934. Chairman West Stirlingshire Unionist Association, 1948-64, Pres., 1964-. *Recreations:* photography, golf, tennis. *Heir:* none. *Address:* Sauchieburn, Stirling. *T.:* Bannockburn 2233. *Clubs:* Carlton; Western (Glasgow). [*Died* 4 *April* 1965 (*ext.*).

STEELE, Sir Henry, Kt., cr. 1941; D.L., LL.D., J.P.; Senior Partner of Steele Bros. and Sons, Ltd., Enamelled Sanitary Fireclay Manufacturers, Niddrie, Portobello, Midlothian; *b.* 1879; *s* of Henry Steele, Perceton, Dreghorn, and Sarah Cairns, Dreghorn; *m.* 1906, Elizabeth Gallacher, Dreghorn; one *s.* two *d.* *Educ.:* Dreghorn. Entered Edinburgh Town Council, 1932; Magistrate, 1935; Lord Provost of Edinburgh, 1938-41. *Recreations:* curling, bowling, golf, fishing, motoring. *Address:* Ormelie, Joppa, Midlothian. *T.:* 81662. *Club:* Scottish Conservative. [*Died* 24 *April* 1963.

STEENBOCK, Harry; Emeritus Professor of Biochemistry, University of Wisconsin, since 1956 (Prof. 1938); *b.* Charlestown, Wis., 16 Aug. 1886; *s.* of Henry Steenbock and Christine Margaretha Oesau; *m.* 1948, Evelyn Carol Van Donk. *Educ.:* University of Wisconsin; Yale University; University of Berlin. B.S. 1908, M.S. 1910, Ph.D. 1916, Sc.D. 1938, Univ. of Wisconsin; Sc.D. Lawrence Coll., 1947. Univ. of Wisconsin, Agricultural Chemistry, Asst. 1908, Instructor 1910, Asst. Prof. 1916, Associate Prof. 1917, Prof. 1920. Fellow, Am. Assoc. for The Advancement of Science; Fellow, Am. Institute of Nutrition; Member: Am. Chemical Soc.; Am. Soc. of Biological Chemists; Biochem. Soc. Wisconsin Acad. of Science; German Acad. of Naturalists (Leopoldina); Madison Art Foundation; Madison Civic Music Association; Jackson Foundation; Audubon Society; Madison Art Assoc.; Wisconsin Historical Soc. Founder Wisconsin Alumni Research Foundation; inventor irradiated and vitamin D enriched foods. *Publications:* numerous papers in Jl. of Biological Chemistry, Jl. of Nutrition, etc. *Recreations:* golf, photography. *Address:* 809 Ottawa Trail, Madison, Wisconsin 53711, U.S.A. *T.:* 233-0265. *Clubs:* University (Chicago), Black Hawk Country, Madison [*Died* 25 *Dec.* 1967.

STEFANSSON, Vilhjalmur; *b.* Arnes, Manitoba, 3 Nov. 1879; *s.* of Johann Stefánsson and Ingibjörg Jóhannesdóttir; *m.* 1941, Evelyn Baird. *Educ.:* University of North Dakota; University of Iowa (A.B. 1903); Harvard Divinity School (1903-4); Harvard Graduate School (1904-6); A.M. Harvard University; LL.D. Univ. of Michigan, 1921; of Iowa, 1922; of North Dakota, 1930; of Manitoba, 1937; of Pittsburgh, 1938; Ph.D., Univ. of Iceland, 1930; Litt.D. Florida Southern College, 1945; Litt.D., Dartmouth College, U.S.A., 1959. Reporter on daily paper (Evening Transcript, Boston, Mass.), City Editor (Daily Plain-dealer, Grand Forks, N.D.), Assistant Instructor in Anthropology, Harvard University (M.A.); Private Expedition to Iceland, 1904; Archæological Expedition to Iceland for Harvard University, 1905; Ethnological Expedition to Eskimo of mouth of Mackenzie River and northern Alaska, for Harvard University and University of Toronto, 1906-7; Arctic Expedition under auspices of American Museum of Natural History and Geological Survey of Canada, 1908-12; Commander Canadian Arctic Expedition, 1913-18; journey to centre of Australia (Macdonnell Ranges), 1924; Founder's Medal of Royal Geographical Society, and several other gold medals and honours from learned societies; Associate in Anthropology, Harvard University; Lecturer on Religions, Crane Theological School of Tufts College, Boston, Mass.; Lecturer on History of Geographic Discovery, University of Cambridge, England; Adviser on northern operations to Pan-American Airways, 1932-45; Arctic Consultant, Northern Studies Program of Dartmouth College, 1953-. *Publications:* My Life with the Eskimo, 1913; Anthropological Report, 1914; The Friendly Arctic, 1921; The Northward Course of Empire, 1922; Hunters of the Great North, 1922, The Adventure of Wrangel Island, 1925; The Standardization of Error, 1927; Adventures in Error, 1937; Three Voyages of Martin Frobisher, 1938; Unsolved Mysteries of the Arctic, 1938; Iceland: The First American Republic, 1939; The Problem of Meighen Island, 1939; Ultima Thule, 1940; Greenland, 1942; Arctic Manual, 1944; Compass of the World, 1944; The Arctic in Fact and Fable, 1945; Not by Bread Alone, 1946; Great Adventures and Explorations, 1947; New Compass of the World, 1949; The Fat of the Land, 1956; Northwest to Fortune, 1958; Cancer: Disease of Civilization, 1960; many scientific articles. Editor of Encyclopedia Arctica project for Office of Naval Research U.S. Navy, 1947-51. *Address:* Dartmouth College Library, Hanover, New Hampshire, U.S.A. *Clubs:* Athenæum; Canadian, Century, Explorers', Harvard (New York City); Faculty (Cambridge, Mass.); Cosmos (Washington); Rideau (Ottawa). [*Died* 26 *Aug.* 1962.

STEINBECK, John Ernst; writer; *b.* Salinas, California, 27 Feb. 1902; *s.* of John Ernst Steinbeck and Olive Hamilton; *m.* 1st, 1930, Carol Henning (divorced 1943); 2nd, 1943, Gwyn Conger; 3rd, 1950, Elaine Anderson. *Educ.:* Salinas High School; Stanford University. Awarded Pulitzer prize, 1940. War columnist overseas, 1943. Nobel prize for Literature, 1962. *Publications:* Cup of Gold, 1929; Pastures of Heaven, 1932; To a God Unknown, 1933; Tortilla Flat, 1935; In Dubious Battle, 1936; Of Mice and Men, 1937; Red Pony, 1937; dramatization of Of Mice and Men, 1937; Grapes of Wrath, 1939; The Moon is Down, 1942; Cannery Row, 1944; The Wayward Bus, 1947; A Russian Journal, 1949; Burning Bright, 1951; East of Eden, 1952; Sweet Thursday, 1954; The Short Reign of Pippin IV, 1957; Once There Was a War, 1958; The Log from the Sea of Cortez, 1958; Winter of Our Discontent, 1961; Travels with Charley, 1962; America and the Americans, 1966. *Address:* c/o McIntosh & Otis, 18 East 41st Street, New York, N.Y., U.S.A. [*Died* 20 *Dec.* 1968.

STEINBERG, Sigfrid Henry, Ph.D., F.R.Hist.S.; Editor, The Statesman's Year-Book, from 1946; *b.* 3 Aug. 1899; *m.* 1923, Christina Constance von Pape; one *s.* Assistant Master, Sedbergh School, 1941-44; Assistant Editor, Chambers's Encyclopædia, 1945-49; Editor, Cassell's Encyclopædia of Literature, 1953; Editor, Dictionary of British History, 1963 (rev. edn., 1964). *Publications:* Historical Tables, 1939, 8th edn., 1966; Short History of Germany, 1944 (Amer., Cdn., Spanish and German edns.); Five-hundred Years of Printing, 1955, 3rd edn. 1966 (German, Italian, Spanish, Danish edns.); The Thirty Years War, 1966 (German edn.). *Recreation:* gardening. *Address:* 182 Stoneleigh Pk. Rd., Ewell, Surrey. *T.:* 01-393 6934. [*Died* 28 *Jan.* 1969.

STENNING, Ven. Ernest Henry, M.B.E. 1956; T.D. 1931; Archdeacon of the Isle of Man since 1958; *b.* 27 Jan. 1885; *s.* of Henry Parsons Stenning, Shermanbury, Sussex; *m.* 1912, Margaret Louisa (*d.* 1958), *d.* of Rev. H. C. Bartlett, Vicar of Westerham, Kent; no *c.* *Educ.:* St. Mark's Coll., Chelsea; Downing Coll., Cambridge. B.A. Nat. Sciences Tripos, Class II, 1909, M.A. 1911. Science Master, King William's Coll., Isle of Man, 1909. Deacon, 1911; Priest 1912. Chaplain of King William's Coll., 1911; Housemaster of Junior House, 1911-39; Sen. Science Master, 1916-53; Vice-Principal, 1945-53; Trustee, 1958. Examining Chaplain Sodor and Man, 1943-; Canon, 1944-58. Chaplain to the Queen, 1959; Dio. Director of Education, 1916-; Chm. Governors Buchan School, 1954-. Hon. Mem. Auto-Cycle Union, 1930; President Manx Motor Cycle Club, 1923-; Co-founder of the Manx Grand Prix Motorcycle Race. *Publications:* The Isle of Man (County Books), 1950; Portrait of the Isle of Man, 1958. Contrib. articles to: Isle of Man; Sodor and Man; Encyclopædia Britannica. *Recreations:* motor-cycling races, motor touring, photography. *Address:* Hosey, Castletown, Isle of Man. *T.:* Castletown 3203. *Club:* National Liberal. [*Died* 2 *Feb.* 1964.

STENT, Percy John Hodsoll, C.I.E. 1938; Indian Civil Service, retd.; *b.* 24 Nov. 1888; *s.* of William Kitson Stent; *m.* 1922, Pamela Margaret Anstice, *d.* of Francis Winckworth Anstice Prideaux; one *d.* *Educ.:* King's College School; Pembroke College, Oxford, B.A. Entered I.C.S. 1913; Army Service, 1916-19; Staff Capt. Bushire Force (despatches), 1918-19; Sec. to Govt. Revenue Dept. 1933; Commissioner Nagpur, 1933. Chairman Nagpur Improvement Trust in addition, 1937-38; retired, 1939 and temp. employed Home Office; Senior Regional Officer, London, 1939; Asst. Chief Admin. Officer, London, Ministry of Home Security, 1942; 1st Secretary (temp.) Foreign Office, 1943; Counsellor (temp.), 1946; U.K. Representative, Economic Commission for Asia and the Far East, 1948-51. *Recreation:* bookbinding. *Address:* Lyndhurst, 9 Murdoch Rd., Wokingham, Berks. *T.:* Wokingham 425. [*Died* 18 *April* 1962.

STENTON, Sir Frank Merry, Kt., *cr.* 1948; F.B.A. 1926; Professor of Modern History, Univ. Coll., afterwards Reading Univ., 1912-46; Deputy Vice-Chancellor, 1934-46; Vice-Chancellor, 1946-50; *b.* 17 May 1880; *s.* of Henry Cawdron Stenton, Southwell; *m.* 1919, Doris Mary (F.B.A., 1953; author of The English Woman in History, 1957), *d.* of J. Parsons, Woodley. *Educ.:* Southwell Grammar School; Univ. Coll., Reading; Keble Coll., Oxford (scholar, 1899, hon. fellow, 1947). 1st class Honours Modern History, 1902; Hon. D.Litt. (Oxford) 1936, (Manchester) 1944, (Nottingham) 1951, (Reading) 1951; Hon. Litt.D. (Leeds) 1939, (Cambridge) 1947; Hon. D.Lit. (London), 1954; Hon. LL.D. (Sheffield), 1948. Corresp. de l'Acad. des inscriptions et Belles-Lettres in the Institut de France, 1947; Hon. Member, Royal Flemish Acad. for Lang. and Lit., 1949; Member Council British Acad., 1927-36; Pres. R.Hist.Soc., 1937-45; Raleigh Lecturer, British Acad., 1927; Ford's Lecturer in English History, Oxford Univ., 1928-29; Creighton Lecturer, London Univ., 1937; Jt. Ed. Survey of English Place-Names, 1924-42, Director, 1942-46, Pres., 1946-; Pres., Lincoln Record Soc., 1942-; Pres. Hist. Assoc., 1949-52; Vice-Pres. Northants Record Soc., 1921-; Trustee Nat. Portrait Gallery, 1948-65; Chm. Editorial Bd., History of Parliament, 1951-. *Publications:* William the Conqueror, 1908; Types of Manorial Structure in the Northern Danelaw, 1910; Place Names of Berkshire, 1911; Early History of the Abbey of Abingdon, 1913; Documents illustrative of the Social and Economic History of the Danelaw, 1920; Gilbertine Charters, 1922; The Danes in England, 1927; Facsimiles of Early Charters from Northamptonshire Collections, 1930; The First Century of English Feudalism, 1066-1166, 1932; Norman London, 1934; Anglo-Saxon England, 1943 (2nd Ed., 1947); The Latin Charters of the Anglo-Saxon Period, 1955; (General Editor and part author) The Bayeux Tapestry, 1957; (with Sir A. Mawer) The Place Names of Buckinghamshire, 1925, etc.; contributions to Victoria History of Counties of England, English Historical Review, History, etc. *Recreation:* music. *Address:* Whitley Park Farm, Reading. *T.:* Reading 81585. [*Died* 15 *Sept.* 1967.

STEPHENS, Brigadier Frederick, C.B.E. 1959; D.S.O. 1942; *b.* 19 June 1906; *e. s.* of late General Sir Reginald Byng Stephens, K.C.B., C.M.G. and Lady Stephens; *m.* 1936, Esme, *d.* of late Col. Mackenzie Churchill, Withyclose, Bagendon, Glos.; one *s.* one *d.* *Educ.:* Winchester; Royal Military College, Sandhurst. 2nd Lieutenant, The Rifle Brigade, 1925; served in India, 1926-31; British Somaliland, 1931-36; France and Flanders, 1940; Western Desert, 1941-43; U.S.A., 1944-45; comd. 1st Bn. The Rifle Brigade, 1948-50; 31st Infantry Brigade, 1950-52; British troops, Berlin, 1952-54; Port Said Base, 1956 (despatches 1957); A.D.C. to the Queen, 1958-59; retd. 1959. *Recreations:* hunting and fishing. *Address:* Ivy Farm, Farringdon, Alton, Hants. *Clubs:* Greenjackets; I Zingari. [*Died* 9 *Nov.* 1967.

STEPHENS, Captain Richard Markham Tyringham, C.M.G. 1915; R.N., retired; *b.* 13 Nov. 1875; *s.* of Capt. Prescot W. Stephens, R.N.; *m.* 1913, Frances R. (*d.* 1945), *d.* of Rev. S. Schor; one *s.* *Educ.:* Abbey School, Beckenham; Stubbington House, Fareham. Joined Britannia, 1889; Lieut., 1896; served on staff of Sheerness Gunnery School, 1900-1; S. African War, Gunnery Lieutenant of Monarch, 1901-3; 1st Gunnery Lieut. Formidable, 1904-6; H.M.S. London, 1906-8; Director of Naval Gunnery, Canadian Navy, 1909; Chief of Staff, 1914; Assist. Director Naval Service of Canada, 1919-22; Consular Shipping Adviser, Santos, 1941, Istanbul, 1945. *Address:* 190 Cooden Drive, Bexhill-on-Sea. *T.:* Cooden 2398. [*Died* 12 *Dec.* 1967.

STEPHENS, Lieutenant-Colonel Rupert, J.P. Wilts; late Oxfordshire L.I.; *b.* 28 March 1884; *s.* of late Harold Stephens, of South Africa, and nephew of late H. C. Stephens of Cholderton; *m.* 1926, Kate May, *d.* of late Douglas Howard Harris: one *d.* *Educ.:* Harrow: R.M.C. Sandhurst. Entered Army, 1903; Captain, 1914; Major, 1918; retired, 1920; Lieut.-Colonel (R. of O.), 1928; A.D.C. to Commander in Chief, India, 1912-13; A.D.C. to Viceroy, India, 1914; served European War; Mesopotamia, 1914-16 (despatches); France, 1917-18, Acting Lt.-Col., Commanded 4th Gloucesters and 4th Oxf. and Bucks. Lt. Infantry (wounded); Staff Captain G.H.Q.; Instructor R.M.C. 1919; Major 4th Wilts. (T.F.), 1921-24; High Sheriff of Wiltshire, 1940. *Recreations:* shooting, fishing, gardening. *Address:* Broadway, The Cotswolds, Kenilworth, Cape of Good Hope, South Africa. *Clubs:* Army and Navy, Flyfishers'. [*Died* 5 *Oct.* 1970.

STEPHENS, William Francis, C.B.E. 1937; Planter; *b.* London, 10 June 1869; *s.* of John Samuel and Emma Stephens, London; *m.* 1st, 1911, Hélène Vielle (*d.* 1915); 2nd, 1926, Augusta Pillieron; no *c.* *Educ.:* Central Schools, Finsbury; Birkbeck College. Gas Light and Coke Company, London, 1887; Sudan Exploration Company, 1902-4; Syria, Palestine and Trans-Jordan, 1904-5; arrived Seychelles, 1906, to manage exploitation of guano deposits; planting in Seychelles from 1924; served 1917-1918 on Western Front in 10th Section British Red Cross attached to French Army; President Seychelles Planters Association, 1927-35; unofficial member of Executive and Legislative Councils of Seychelles, 1924-48; Rep. of Seychelles Colony at the Coronation, 1937. *Recreation:* reading. *Address:* Anse Nord Est, Mahé, Seychelles Colony. [*Died* 7 *July* 1963.

STEPHENSON, Sir Arthur (George), Kt., *cr.* 1954; C.M.G. 1953; M.C. 1917; Senior partner Stephenson & Turner, architects, Melbourne, Sydney, Adelaide, and Wellington (N.Z.); Trustee of the National Museum of Victoria since 1956;

b. 7 April 1890; *s.* of Rev. A. R. Stephenson, M.A., and Sarah Anne Stephenson (*née* Chewings), Adelaide; *m.* 1915, Evelyn May Stephenson (*née* MacKay), Melbourne: one *s.* two *d.* *Educ.:* Melbourne Church of England Gram. Sch. Architectural educn., Melbourne and Sydney. Served in War, C.M.F.; retained on instructional duties, 1915; transf. A.I.F. as Capt., 3rd Pioneer Bn., 1916; France, 1916-18. Architectural Assoc. Schools, London, 1919-1920. Assoc. R.I.B.A. and Assoc. Mem. T.P.I., 1920; F.R.I.B.A., F.R.A.I.A., 1933. Practice in Melbourne, 1921-; specialised in institutional and hosp. work from 1924. Assisted Commonwealth in building mil. hosps. and other defence projects during war years, 1939-45. R.I.B.A. Royal Gold Medal for Architecture, 1954. Hon. Citizen of City of New York. Hon. Fell., Amer. Coll. of Hosp. Administrators, 1958. Gold Medal R.A.I.A., 1963. Hon. Fell. A.I.A. 1964. *Recreations:* golf, reading and fishing. *Address:* 400 St. Kilda Road, Melbourne, Australia. *T.:* 26-6611; 42 Walsh Street, South Yarra, Melbourne. *T.:* 26-3835. *Clubs:* Melbourne, Athenæum, Metropolitan Golf (Melb.); Union, Royal Sydney Yacht Squadron, Royal Sydney Golf (Syd.).
[*Died* 18 *Nov.* 1967.

STEPHENSON, Joseph, O.B.E. 1920; Chartered Accountant in practice; *b.* 9 May 1882; *m.* 1905, Emmeline Louise Bailey; three *s.* one *d.* Chartered Sec. Mem. of Council of Chartered Institute of Secretaries. High Sheriff Cambs and Hunts, 1944. *Recreations:* shooting and golf. *Address:* Priors Gate, Peterborough. *T.:* Peterborough 2406. *Club:* City and Counties (Peterborough).
[*Died* 17 *July* 1965.

STEPHENSON, Rt. Rev. Percival William, D.D. (Hon.) St. John's College, Winnipeg; *b.* 5 May 1888; *s.* of Arthur Henry Stephenson, Malmsbury, Victoria, Australia; *m.* 1913, Grace Ermyntrude Lavender; two *s.* one *d.* *Educ.:* Caulfield Grammar School, Melbourne; Ridley College, Melbourne; Trinity College, Melbourne; University of London; University of Melbourne, B.A. 1912, M.A. 1915; University of London, B.D. 1917. Th.L. Australian College of Theology; Deacon, 1913; Priest, 1914; Missionary of Church Missionary Society, Peshawar, N.-W. India, 1914-24; Tutor at Edwardes College, Peshawar, 1914-1921; Principal, 1921-24; Professor of Exegetical Theology, St. John's College, and Canon of St. John's Cathedral, Winnipeg, 1924-28; Federal Secretary of Church Missionary Society of Australia and Tasmania, 1928-37; Head Master, Trinity Grammar School, Sydney, 1935-37; Commonwealth Secretary, British and Foreign Bible Society, 1938-40; Bishop of Nelson, N.Z., 1940-54, retd. *Address:* 69 Ruthven Way, Ringwood East, Vic., Australia.
[*Died* 29 *May* 1962.

STEPHENSON, Thomas Alan, F.R.S. 1951; D.Sc. (Wales); Professor of Zoology in the University of Wales since 1940; painter of zoological and other subjects; *e. s.* of Dr. Thomas Stephenson and Margaret Ellen Fletcher; *m.* 1922, Anne Wood, *d.* of Joseph Dore Wood, Barry; no *c.* *Educ.:* Kingswood School, Bath. Research work under Dept. of Scientific and Industrial Research, 1919-22; Lecturer in Zoology, University College, London, 1922-30; Fisheries Research for the Island of Guernsey, 1923; in charge of Reef section of the Great Barrier Reef Expedition of 1928-29; Prof. of Zoology, University of Cape Town, 1930-40; Marine ecological work in North America, 1947-48; study of coast of Bermuda, 1952. *Publications:* various papers in a number of scientific journals or other publications; Journal of the Marine Biological Association; Quarterly Journal of Microscopical Science; Transactions of the Royal Society of Edinburgh; Reports of the Terra Nova Expedition (British Museum); Reports of the Great Barrier Reef Expedition (British Museum); Journal of Ecology, etc.; Monograph on the British Sea Anemones in the Ray Society's series, 2 vols. 1928 and 1935; papers recording the results of a survey of the South African coast from Port Nolloth to Durban in Linnaean Society's Journal and in South African Journals; Seashore life and pattern, 1944 (Penguin). *Recreation:* gardening. *Address:* Zoology Department, University College of Wales, Biology Block, Penglais, Aberystwyth.
[*Died* 3 *April* 1961.

STEPHENSON, William Lawrence; farming 2500 acres; *b.* 13 Jan 1880; *s.* of Frederick James Stephenson and Jessie Toder; *m.* 1909, Lilian Drake; one *s.* three *d.* *Educ.:* Hull; Birmingham. Entered Merchants Business as apprentice, finally chief buyer; late Chairman, F. W. Woolworth and Co. Ltd.; late Director of Phoenix Assurance Company; retired. President: Blandford Young Farmers; Parkstone Sea Cadets. *Recreations:* yacht racing, golf, fishing, and stock breeding. *Address:* Rudleigh, Canford Cliffs, Bournemouth. *Club:* Royal Motor Yacht (Commodore).
[*Died* 7 *May* 1963.

STERLING, Thomas Smith, M.B.E.; M.A. (Cantab.); *b.* 13 April 1883; *e. s.* of late John and Mrs. Sarah J. Sterling. *Educ.:* Downing Coll., Camb. (Mediaeval and Modern Languages Tripos); Geneva. First Charles Oldham Shakespeare Scholar in University of Cambridge; Pres., Mermaid Literary Club (Undergraduate), Cambridge; Lectr. in English, University College, Southampton; Indian Educational Service, Professor of English Language and Literature, Presidency College, Calcutta, 1909-27; Principal, Presidency College, 1926; Fellow of University of Calcutta, 1914-27; Adviser, Students' Information Bureau, Calcutta, 1923-27; during European War, 1914-18, raised and for a time commanded the first O.T.C. in India, the Calcutta Univ. Training Corps; retired, 1928; Asst. Secretary and Secretary, Universities Bureau of the British Empire, London, 1927-1929; Professor of English Literature and for some time Dean of the Faculty of Arts, Egyptian University, Cairo, 1929-33; tours in America, Australia and New Zealand in connection with Empire Migration, 1934-37; held a post as a principal in Information Department of India Office, April 1940-Sept. 1941; Secretary, School of Oriental and African Studies, Univ. of London, Sept. 1941-Oct. 1945. *Publications:* text-books for students. *Recreations:* travelling, tennis, walking. *T.A.:* c/o Ejus London. *T.:* Whitehall 1000. *Clubs:* East India and Sports, Authors' (Life mem.; Chm., 1948-51).
[*Died* 19 *Dec.* 1970.

STERN, Lieut.-Colonel Sir Albert, K.B.E., *cr.* 1918; C.M.G. 1917; D.L. Kent; Officer Legion of Honour; *b.* 24 Sept. 1878; 2nd *s.* of late James Stern, 25 Prince's Gate, S.W.; *m.* 1922, Helen, *er. d.* of late Sir Frederick Orr-Lewis, 1st Bt.; two *s.* two *d.* *Educ.:* Eton College; Christ Church, Oxford (M.A.). Head of the firm of Stern Bros.; formerly Director, The Midland Bank Ltd. (retired 1939); Director, Clydesdale Bank; Member of London Committee of the Ottoman Bank, 1921-64; Lieutenant R.N.V.R. Armoured Car Division, 1914; Secretary Landship Committee, Admiralty, 1915; Chairman Tank Committee, 1916; Ministry of Munitions, Director Tank Supply Dept., 1916; Major Machine Gun Corps, Heavy Branch, 1916; Director-General Mechanical Warfare Dept. 1916; Lt.-Col. 1916; Commissioner (Mechanical

Warfare, Overseas and Allies Dept.), 1917; Brit. Commissioner (Anglo-Amer. Commission), 1918; Chairman Special Vehicle Development Committee, Ministry of Supply, 1939-43; Member of Tank Board, 1941. Chairman of Governors, Queen Mary Coll. (London Univ.), since 1944 Vice-Patron London Hosp. (50 years on House Cttee.) 1957-. High Sheriff of Kent, 1945-1946. Master of Drapers' Company, 1946-47. Hon. Fell.: King's Coll., Queen Mary Coll., London Univ. O.St.J. *Publications:* Tanks, 1914-18; The Log-Book of a Pioneer, 1919. *Address:* Barham Court, Maidstone. *T.:* Wateringbury 82219. *Clubs:* Carlton, Garrick, City of London, Union; County of Kent (Maidstone). [*Died* 2 *Jan.* 1966.

STERN, Col. Sir Frederick Claude, Kt., *cr.* 1956; O.B.E. 1919; M.C. 1917; *b.* 8 April 1884; *y. s.* of late James Stern, 25 Princes Gate, S.W.7; *m.* 1919, Sybil Alice, J.P., *er. d.* of late Sir Arthur Lucas, 27 Bruton Street, W.1. *Educ.:* Eton; Christ Church, Oxford. Joined 2nd Co. of London Yeomanry, 1905; served European War, 1914-18, Gallipoli, Egypt and Palestine (despatches twice); War of 1939-45, Group Comdr. W. Sussex H.G., 1941-45. Chm. Council John Innes Hort. Inst., 1947-61; Vice-Pres., 1941-58, Treasurer, 1941-58, Linnean Soc.; Master of Drapers' Co., 1954-55; Vice-Pres. Royal Horticultural Soc., 1962; Hon. Col., 1945. *Publications:* Study of Genus Paeonia, 1946; Study of Genera Galanthus and Leucojum, 1956; A Chalk Garden; articles in botanical and horticultural journals. *Recreations:* gardening and botany. *Address:* Highdown, Goring-by-Sea, Sussex. *T.:* Worthing 41110. *Clubs:* Athenæum, City of London. [*Died* 10 *July* 1967.

STEVEN, Emer. Prof. Henry Marshall, C.B.E. 1959; B.Sc., Ph.D. (Edin.); Hon. LL.D. (Aber.); Hon. M.A. (Oxon); F.R.S.E.; Professor of Forestry, Univ. of Aberdeen, 1938-63; *b.* 24 June 1893; *s.* of Robert and Mary Steven; *m.* 1922, Clementina Macdonald, *d.* of late Rev. Prof. A. F. Findlay, D.D.; three *s.* *Educ.:* Bathgate Acad.; Univ. of Edinburgh. Research and executive posts in Forestry Commission, 1919-38; Lecturer in Silviculture, Imperial Forestry Institute, Oxford, 1924-30. Member of staff of Ministry of Supply, Timber Production Department, 1939-43. Editor of Forestry, the Journal of the Society of Foresters of Great Britain, 1926-45. President, Soc. of Foresters of Great Britain, 1950, 1951. Chairman, Home Grown Timber Advisory Cttee., Forestry Commn., 1963-65. Medal of Soc. of Foresters of Gt. Britain, 1954. *Publications:* (in collab.) Native Pinewoods of Scotland, 1959; numerous contributions to forestry and other scientific jls. *Address:* 8 Gladstone Place, Queens Cross, Aberdeen. *T.:* Aberdeen 51295. [*Died* 15 *Feb.* 1969.

STEVENS, Col. Arthur Borlase, C.M.G. 1917; D.S.O. 1915; V.D.; *b.* 26 June 1881; *s.* of William Borlase Stevens, Sydney, N.S.W.; *m.* 1903, Vera Proctor, Newcastle, N.S.W. *Educ.:* Collegiate School, Summerhill, N.S.W. Served European War, 1914-19 (despatches twice, D.S.O., C.M.G.). *Address:* 42 Hay Street, Collaroy, N.S.W., Australia [*Died* 1965.

STEVENS, Colonel Arthur Cornish Jeremie, C.B.E. 1922; D.S.O 1917; late R.E.; *b.* 1875; *s.* of late Sir Charles Cecil Stevens, K.C.S.I.; *m.* 1907, Nancy, *d.* of late J. W. Morison, J.P., of Portclew, Lamphey, Pembrokeshire; three *d.* Served China, 1900 (medal); European War, 1914-17 (despatches, D.S.O.); Chief Engineer Scottish Command, 1928-32; retired pay, 1932. *Address:* Glan-y-mor, 55 Marine Parade West, Lee-on-the-Solent, Hants. *Club:* Lee-on-the-Solent Sailing. [*Died* 5 *Jan.* 1962.

STEVENS, Colonel Harold Raphael Gaetano, C.M.G. 1946; D.S.O. 1917; *b.* 1883; *m.* 1905, Bertha Gordon (*d.* 1947); three *s.* one *d.*; *m.* 1948, Helen Gordon. *Educ.:* Beaumont; R.M.A., Woolwich; Staff College. Served European War, 1914-18 (despatches, D.S.O., Croix de Guerre, Brevet Lieut.-Colonel, 3rd Class Greek Order of Military Merit, Officer of Order of Redeemer of Greece); Military Attaché, Rome and Durazzo, 1931-35; Commander R.A. 56th (1st London) Division, T.A., 1935; retired pay, 1936; A.R.P. Department, Home Office 1937-39; Italian Commentator, B.B.C., 1940-45. *Recreation:* travel. *Club:* United Service. [*Died* 1 *Jan.* 1961.

STEVENS, Sir Harold Samuel Eaton, K.C.I.E., *cr.* 1947 (C.I.E. 1938); C.S.I. 1944; M.C.; late Chief Secretary, Govt. of Bengal; *b.* 29 Nov. 1892; *s.* of late Capt. H. G. R. Stevens, Cheltenham; *m.* 1st, 1920, Mona McGregor (*d.* 1931); one *d.*; 2nd, 1935, Cecilia Iris Brown. *Educ.:* George Heriot's School; Edinburgh University. Served European War, France, 1914-18, with The Royal Scots; joined I.C.S., 1920. Chevalier, Legion of Honour, 1918; Croix de Guerre avec palme, 1918. *Address:* 11 Cooden Drive, Bexhill-on-Sea, Sussex. [*Died* 23 *July* 1969.

STEVENS, Henry, C.M.G. 1948; O.B.E. 1936; *b.* 27 July 1885; *s.* of William Stevens, Cornwall and Johannesburg; unmarried. *Educ.:* High School, Penzance, Cornwall, and privately. Entered Civil Service as Second Division Clerk, 1905; Regional Controller, North Midlands, 1939-1945; in Turkey as Labour Adviser to Turkish Government in Ankara, Jan. 1946-Oct. 1947; Regional Controller Ministry of Labour and National Service, East and West Ridings Region, 1947-50; retired, April 1950. *Recreation:* golf (Captain Southport and Ainsdale G. C., 1929 and 1930). *Address:* 31 Hartley Road, Birkdale, Southport, Lancs. [*Died* 28 *Dec.* 1963.

STEVENS, Major-General Sir Jack (Edwin Stawell), K.B.E., *cr.* 1955; C.B. 1946; D.S.O. 1941; E.D.; Director: Mt. Isa Mines Limited; Commonwealth Industrial Gases; Development Underwriting Ltd. (Chm.); Custom Credit Corporation Ltd.; Advance Industries Ltd.; New South Wales Board of Trustees Executors and Agency Company Ltd.; N.S.W. Board, National Bank; Chairman, Brit. Automotive Industries Pty. Ltd.; *b.* 7 September 1896; *s.* of Herbert and Violet Stevens; *m.* 1920, Catherine Macdonald; one *s.* *Educ.:* Daylesford, Victoria. Commonwealth Public Service; Assistant Commissioner Commonwealth Public Service, 1945; General Manager, Overseas Telecommunications Commission (Aust.), 1946-50; Secretary, Ministry of National Development, 1950; Secretary, Department of Supply, 1951-53; Chm. Australian Atomic Energy Commission, 1953-56. Fell. Australian Soc. of Accountants. Served European War 1914-18, with Australian Corps of Signals; in War of 1939-45, served in Middle East and New Guinea; commanded 21st Aust. Inf. Bde. and, later, 4th Aust. Div., Northern Territory Force, and 6th Aust. Div. A.I.F. Colonel Comdt. Royal Australian Corps of Signals, 1955-60. *Recreation:* golf. *Address:* Box 4954, G.P.O. Sydney, Australia. *Clubs:* Australian (Sydney), Royal Sydney Golf. [*Died* 20 *May* 1969.

STEVENS, Rt. Rev. Percy; *b.* 21 May 1882; *s.* of John Medhurst and Jane Emma Stevens; *m.* 1911, Norah Annie Prowse (*d.* 1960), Plymouth; one *d.* *Educ.:* Winchester House, Bristol; St. Aidan's Theological Coll. Deacon 1906; Priest, 1907; Curate of St. Jude's, Plymouth, 1906-8; C.M.S. Missionary in Kwangsi-Hunan, 1909-24; Organising Secretary for C.M.S. in North Ireland, 1926-33; Bishop of Kwangsi-Hunan, 1933-50. *Recreations:* normal, nothing special. *Address:* 45 Downs Cote Drive, Bristol 9. [*Died* 7 *July* 1966.

STEVENS, Lieut.-Col. Thomas Harry Goldsworthy, O.B.E. 1919; *b.* 27 Jan. 1883; *s.* of late Marshall Stevens, M.P., promoter of Manchester Ship Canal and Trafford Park Estates Ltd. *Educ.:* King William's College; Royal Indian Engineering College, Coopers Hill. Public Works Dept., Burma, 1903-21; Lt.-Col. Indian Army Reserve of Officers (retd.); Active Service R.E.'s Mesopotamia (O.B.E., despatches thrice); Master of Worshipful Company of Glaziers, 1939; *Publication:* Trees and Shrubs in my Garden, 1939; Manchester of Yesterday, 1959. *Recreation:* gardening. *Address:* Dingle Bank, Bowdon, Cheshire. *T.:* Altrincham 1441. [*Died* 12 *Dec.* 1970.

STEVENSON, Hon. Lord; James Stevenson, O.B.E. 1919; B.L. (Glasgow Univ.); *b.* Glasgow; *s.* of late William Stevenson, writer, Glasgow; *m.* 1919, Sophronia Reynolds Gleeson, Toronto, Canada; one *d.* *Educ.:* Kelvinside Academy, Glasgow; Glasgow University. Called to Bar, Scotland, 1908; K.C. 1931; served European War, France, 1915-19, in Signal Service; retired with rank of Lt.-Col.; Political: M.P. (C.) Camlachie Division of Glasgow, 1931-35; contested (C.) Camlachie Division of Glasgow, 1929 and 1935; Senator of College of Justice for Scotland, 1936-48, resigned 1948. *Address:* Gateside, Gullane, East Lothian. *T.:* Gullane 3139. *Club:* New (Edinburgh). [*Died* 3 *March* 1963.

STEVENSON, Adlai Ewing; Distinguished Service Award, U.S. Navy, 1945; U.S. Ambassador to U.N. since 1961; *b.* 5 Feb. 1900; *s.* of Lewis Green Stevenson and Helen Louise Stevenson (*née* Davis); *m.* Ellen Borden (marriage dissolved); three *s.* *Educ.:* The Choate School, Wallingford, Conn.; Princeton Univ. (A.B.); Northwestern Univ. Law School (J.D.). Asst. Man. Editor Daily Pantagraph, Bloomington, Ill., 1924-25; admitted to Illinois Bar, 1926; Assoc. Cutting, Moore & Sidley, lawyers, Chicago, 1927-33; special counsel Agric. Adjust. Adm. Washington, D.C., 1933-34, partner in firm of Sidley, Austin, Burgess & Harper, Chicago, 1935-41; Asst. to Sec. of Navy, Washington, D.C., 1941-44; Chief Foreign Econ. Administration's Italy Mission, 1943; War Dept. Mission to Europe, 1944; Asst. to Sec. of State, Washington, D.C., 1945. Advisor U.S. deleg., Conf. on Internat. Orgn., San Francisco, 1945; U.S. Delegate, U.S. Minister and Chief U.S. deleg. to Preparatory Commn. of U.N., London, 1945; Sen. advisor U.S. deleg. Gen. Assembly of U.N., London, 1946; U.S. deleg. Gen. Assembly of U.N., N.Y., 1946 and 1947. Governor of Illinois, 1949-53. Democratic nominee for President, U.S.A., 1952 and 1956. Sr. partner, Stevenson, Rifkind & Wirtz, 1957-60. Holds several hon. degrees. *Publications:* Speeches, 1953; (all the following publ. in U.S.A. and Eng.) Call to Greatness, 1954; What I Think, 1956; The New America, 1957; Friends and Enemies: What I Learned in Russia, 1958; Putting First Things First, 1960; contrib. Foreign Affairs, Harper's, Atlantic Monthly. *Relevant publication:* Adlai Stevenson: A Study in Values, by Herbert J. Muller, 1968. *Recreations:* tennis, golf, swimming. *Address:* 799 U.N. Plaza, New York, N.Y., U.S.A. *Clubs:* Chicago, Commercial, Attic (Chicago); Onwentsia (Lake Forest); Metropolitan (Washington, D.C.); Century, River (New York). [*Died* 14 *July* 1965.

STEVENSON, Sheriff Alexander James; Sheriff Substitute of the Lothians at Edinburgh, 1953-69; *b.* 15 July 1901; 2nd *s.* of Rev. William Black Stevenson, D.D., and Jane Lilias Dennistoun Brown; *m.* 1944, Sylvia Florence, 2nd *d.* of Clement Rolfe Ingleby, Sedgeford Hall, Norfolk; three *s.* *Educ.:* Edinburgh Acad., King's Coll., Cambridge (B.A. Eng.); Edinburgh Univ. (LL.B.). Called to Scots Bar, 1927. Colonial Service (Administration), Kenya, 1928; invalided out, 1933; Organiser, Scottish Country Industries Development Trust, 1937; Carrick Pursuivant, 1939-46; served War of 1939-45, R.A.F. (despatches); Wing Comdr. 1943; Sheriff Substitute of Lanarkshire, 1946-53; Chm., Gogarburn Hosp. Bd. of Management, 1960-68. Mem., Queen's Body Guard for Scotland (Royal Company of Archers). *Recreations:* various games (played cricket for Scotland, 1925-28). *Address:* Westfield House, West Calder Midlothian. *T.:* West Calder 325. *Clubs:* M.C.C.; New (Edinburgh). [*Died* 2 *Sept.* 1970.

STEVENSON, Air Vice-Marshal Donald Fasken, C.B. 1946; C.B.E. 1942 (O.B.E. 1937); D.S.O. 1918; M.C. and bar; i.d.c.; p.s.a.; R.A.F. retd.; Chairman and Company Director; *b.* 7 April 1895; *s.* of Lt.-Col. John Stevenson; *m.* 1917, Janet Mary, *d.* of John Henson, Hull; one *s.* one *d.* European War, 1914-18 (despatches, M.C. with Bar, D.S.O.); R.F.C. 1916; Staff College, 1923; Naval Staff College, 1927; Imperial Defence College, 1929; Palestine, 1936 (O.B.E.); War of 1939-45 (despatches, C.B.E., C.B.); Director of Home Operations, Air Ministry, 1938-41; A.O.C. No. 2 Bomber Group 1941; Burma, 1942; Bengal Command, 1943; Northern Ireland, 1944; No. 9 Fighter Group, 1944; High Commissioner, Roumania, 1944-47; retd. 1948. Air A.D.C. to the King, 1939-40. *Recreations:* shooting, fishing, golf. *Clubs:* United Service, International Sportsmen's, Roehampton; York (Toronto). [*Died* 10 *July* 1964.

STEVENSON, Brig.-General Edward Hall, C.M.G. 1918; D.S.O. 1900; *b.* 21 July 1872; *m.* 1st, 1917, Ethel Vaughan (*d.* 1944), *widow* of Leopold Hudson, F.R.C.S.; 2nd, 1945, Daisy May, *widow* of Major E. J. Hudson, O.B.E. Entered R.A. 1892; Captain, 1900; Major, 1910; served South Africa, 1899-1902 (despatches, Queen's medal 6 clasps, King's medal 2 clasps, D.S.O.); European War, 1914-18 (despatches, Bt. Lt.-Col. and Col., C.M.G.); J.P. Wilts., 1920-34. *Address:* The Hill, Bickwell Valley, Sidmouth. *T.:* Sidmouth 530. [*Died* 3 *Jan.* 1964.

STEVENSON, Ralph Cornwallis, C.B.E. 1937; *b.* 25 July 1894; *s.* of late Charles Cornwallis Stevenson and Madeleine Marie Boutry; *m.* 1926, Ilse Christina Dinklage; two *d.* *Educ.:* Gymnasium in Hanover; Hurstpierpoint College, Sussex; London School of Economics. Served European War, France and Belgium, 1915-18. Entered Consular Service, 1920; Cologne, 1921-23; Monrovia, 1924-25; Milan, 1926-28; Lima, 1929-33; Buenos Aires, 1934-36; Bilbao, 1936-37; i.d.c. 1938; Moscow, 1939; Rio de Janeiro, 1939-47; Zagreb, 1947-52; Naples, 1952-54; retired, 1955. *Address:* Long Rock, Aldington, Kent. *T.:* Aldington 243. [*Died* 10 *Dec.* 1967.

STEVENSON, Robert Scott, M.D., F.R.C.S. Edin.; Medical Administrator, 1961-64; Consultant Ear, Nose and Throat Surgeon, Colonial Hospital, Gibraltar, since 1954; Hon. Consulting Surgeon, Metropolitan Ear, Nose and Throat Hospital, London; late Laryngologist to Colindale, Preston Hall and High Wood (Brentwood) Hospitals; Chairman, National Institute for the Deaf, 1945-54; Fellow Royal Soc. Med. (Pres., Sect. Otology, 1948-49); Hon. Fell., Amer. Laryngological, Rhinological and Otological Soc.; Hon. Mem.,

Scottish Otolaryngological Soc.; Corresponding Member, Société Française d'Oto-Rhino-Laryngologie; Vice-President, Section of Laryngology and Otology, 1939 and late Member of Council, British Medical Association; *b.* Edinburgh, 11 June 1889; *e. s.* of late W. Scott Stevenson, Edinburgh College of Agriculture; *m.* 1915, Gertrude (author of The Letters of Madame; Charles I. in Captivity, etc.) *e. d.* of late F. Ferguson Kerr, M.D., Manchester; two *d.* *Educ.:* Royal High School, George Watson's College, and University, Edinburgh; M.B., Ch.B., Edin. 1912; late First Assistant, Ear, Nose and Throat Department, University College Hospital; Assistant Surgical Officer, Ear, Nose and Throat Department, Manchester Royal Infirmary; Editor and Associate Editor of The Practitioner, 1924-36; Sub-Editor, British Medical Journal, 1921-23; Asst. Ed., Jl. of Laryngology and Otology, 1950-53. Served R.A.M.C. 1916-18 (Capt.) and 1940-1945 (Maj., acting Lt.-Col.). William W. Root Lectr., Chicago, 1948; Guest Lectr. Triological Soc., Toronto, 1952; Watson-Williams Memorial Lecturer, Bristol University, 1955; James Yearsley Lecturer, London, 1956; Kate Hurd Mead Lecturer, Philadelphia, 1957; Beaumont Lecturer, Yale University, 1957. Contested (L. Nat.) West Fife, 1945, and Scottish Universities, 1946. *Publications:* Famous Illnesses in History; Goodbye Harley Street; In a Harley Street Mirror; In Search of Spanish Painting; Morell Mackenzie (biog.); (with D. Guthrie) A History of Oto-laryngology; Recent Advances in Oto-laryngology, 1935 (2nd edn. 1949); Hearing and not Hearing; The Ear, Nose and Throat in the Services; trans. Portmann's Ear, Nose and Throat Treatment; articles in Brit. and Amer. med. jls. *Recreation:* Pres., Calpe Artists Soc. (Gib.). *Address:* 15 Rodger's Rd., Gibraltar. *Club:* Athenæum. [*Died* 22 *March* 1967.

STEVENSON, Sir Roy (Hunter), Kt. 1961; M.B.E. 1955; Chairman and Managing Director, Dunedin Engineering and Steel Co. Ltd., Dunedin, N.Z., since 1933; *b.* 17 July 1892; *s.* of John Stevenson; *m.* 1917, Alicia Newnham Howes; one *s.* two *d.* *Educ.:* Otago Boys' High School (N.Z.); Otago University (N.Z.); Sheffield University (Eng.). Served 1914-18 and 1939-45 Wars. Director: Otago Daily Times and Witness Co. Ltd., 1946; National Insurance Co. of New Zealand Ltd., 1947; Perpetual Trustees Estate and Agency Co. Ltd., 1950. Past Pres., Dunedin Club. Pres., Vice-Pres., or Exec. Mem. welfare and cultural societies. Chartered Mechanical Engineer. M.I.Mech.E. *Recreations:* golf, bowls. *Address:* 330 Stuart St., Dunedin, N.Z. *Clubs:* Dunedin, Officers, Otago (N.Z.). [*Died* 10 *May* 1963.

STEWARD, Colonel Godfrey Robert Viveash, C.B. 1932; C.B.E. 1919; D.S.O. 1914; late the Royal Inniskilling Fusiliers; *b.* 2 Aug. 1881; *s.* of Major-General E. H. Steward; *m.* 1919, Madeleine Janssens (*d.* 1949); one *d.* Entered Army, 1899; Capt., 1905; Major, 1915; Col. 1921; served S. African War, 1899-1902 (severely wounded; Queen's medal 3 clasps, King's medal 2 clasps); European War, 1914-18 (very severely wounded, despatches, C.B.E., D.S.O. Bt. Lt.-Col.); Military Attaché H.B.M. Legation, Peking, 1924-28; G.S.O.1. British Troops in China, 1929-36; retired pay, 1936; recalled, 1939; Gen. Staff, War Office, 1939-46; Foreign Office, German Section, 1946-1948. *Club:* United Service.
[*Died* 24 *March* 1969.

STEWART, Lieut.-Colonel Alexander Dron, C.I.E. 1934; LL.D.; F.R.S.E.; M.B.; F.R.C.P.E.; F.R.C.S.E.; D.P.H.; D.T.M. and H.; late Superintendent Royal Infirmary, Edinburgh; late Director of All India Institute of Hygiene, Calcutta; *b.* 22 June 1883; *s.* of late William Stewart, Blairgowrie; *m.* *d.* of late Alexander Mann, Edinburgh; two *s.* *Educ.:* Edinburgh University. Joined I.M.S., 1906; military employment, 1907-14 and 1914-19; School of Tropical Medicine, Calcutta; Order of St. John of Jerusalem, 1934. *Address:* 7 Elliot Place, Edinburgh. *T.:* Colinton 8137.
[*Died* 16 *Aug.* 1969.

STEWART, Andrew Graham; Chairman and General Managing Director, Stewarts & Lloyds Ltd.; *b.* 22 August 1901; *s.* of late John Graham Stewart; *m.* 1929, Barabel Greig; three *s.* two *d.* *Educ.:* Winchester; Pembroke College, Cambridge (B.A.). Director: Oxfordshire Ironstone Co. Ltd.; Stewarts & Lloyds of South Africa Ltd.; United Steel Companies Ltd. Past Pres. British Employers' Confederation; Past Pres., and Pres. Elect 1963, British Iron and Steel Federation. *Address:* Stewarts & Lloyds Ltd., Brook House, Upper Brook St., W.1; Corsliehill, Houston, Renfrewshire. [*Died* 7 *May* 1964.

STEWART, Commander Archibald Thomas, O.B.E. 1918; R.N.; *b.* 1876; *e. s.* of late Col. T. B. Stewart, 30th Regt. and R.A.S.C.; *m.* 1913, Agnes Herbert, O.B.E. (*d.* 1960). *Educ.:* Dover Coll.; H.M.S. Britannia; R.N. College. Stations served on: East Indies, Training Squadron, North America and West Indies, Home, Australia, Mediteranean: War Service: Channel, Eastern Mediterranean in H.M.S. Cornwallis throughout Dardanelles campaign; fired first shot of opening bombardment, 19 Feb. 1915; Suez Canal, 1916; Cornwallis sunk by torpedo, 9 Jan. 1917; Staff of Admiral Commanding, Malta; Port Convoy Officer and Senior British Naval Officer Bizerta, 1917-19; mention for War services, 1919; Commander Order of Nichan Iftikar (Tunisia), 1918; Chevalier Legion of Honour, 1919; retired, 1920; served Admiralty, Historical Section, 1941-48. *Publications:* part author The Immortal Gamble, 1917; articles on nautical subjects; book reviews. *Recreation:* golf. *Address:* c/o Westminster Bank, 26 Haymarket, S.W.1.
[*Died* 19 *March* 1968.

STEWART, Lady (Frances Henrietta), O.B.E. 1939; *b.* 1883; *d.* of late Arthur G. Rickards, K.C.; *m.* 1906, Sir Francis Hugh Stewart, C.I.E. (*d.* 1921); three *s.* four *d.* *Educ.:* privately. In India, 1906-19; contested North Kensington (Liberal), 1929. *Recreations:* music, reading, grandchildren. *Address:* Hammer Hill, Abinger Hammer, Surrey. *T.:* Abinger 151.
[*Died* 26 *Sept.* 1962.

STEWART, Francis William, C.I.E. 1931; M.C.; M.A.; Indian Civil Service (retired); *b.* 1885; *e. s.* of late Chief Engineer W. F. Stewart, R.N.; *m.* 1923, Florence Campbell, *d.* of Hugh Macnish, Campbeltown, Argyll; one *s.* (and one *s.* decd.). *Educ.:* Christ's Hospital; Trinity College, Cambridge. Bracketed 6th Wrangler, 1907; entered Indian Civil Service, 1908; Capt. Indian Army Reserve of Officers; served with 19th Punjabis, 1916-19; Member, Council of State, India, 1934-35; First Member, Board of Revenue, Madras; retired, 1944. *Address:* 2 Broomfield Road, Kew Gardens. *Club:* Athenæum. [*Died* 29 *Dec.* 1963.

STEWART, Frank Ogilvie, C.B.E. 1948; *b.* 2 January 1893; *s.* of late Francis and Margaret Stewart; *m.* 1934, Jeanne Marguerite Bradley; three *s.* *Educ.:* Lasswade; Royal High School; Edinburgh and Oxford Universities. Secretariat, Board of Customs and Excise, 1916-17; Ministry of Food, 1917-19; Deputy Director of Milk Products, 1919; Scottish Office, Assistant Principal, 1920; Private Secretary to Secretary for Scotland, 1923-25; Assistant

Secretary, 1934-48; Under-Secretary Scottish Home Department, 1948-53; retired Jan. 1953. *Recreations:* reading, gardening. *Address:* Invercoe, Churston Ferrers, Devon. [*Died* 9 *Dec.* 1964.

STEWART, Hon. Sir Frederick Harold, Kt., *cr.* 1935; former M.H.R. for Parramatta, Australia, 1931-46; Proprietor Dundas Woollen Mills, Sydney, Australia; Founder Metropolitan Transport Company, Sydney; Founder of CH Broadcasting Station; Foundation Chm. of Australian National Airways, the first Commercial Airlines in Australia; Director, Associated Newspapers, Sydney; Director, John Herford, Tanners; Public Works Contractor (road building and developing); Proprietor of St. Cloud Jersey Cattle Stud; Treasurer N.S.W. Adult Deaf and Dumb Society; *b.* 14 Aug. 1884; *m.* 1st, Lottie (*d.* 1943), *d.* of William Glover; three *s.* three *d.*; 2nd, 1945, Marjorie, *d.* of Rev. Frederick Dixon. Minister for Commerce and Industry, Australia, 1932-1934; Parliamentary Under-Secretary for Employment, 1934-36; Minister for Health, 1939-40; Minister for the Navy, 1939-1940; Minister for Social Services, 1939-1941; Minister for Supply and Development, 1940; Minister for External Affairs and Health, 1940-41; Member Australian War Cabinet, 1939-41; represented Australia in trade negotiations in N.Z., 1934, and at International Labour Conference, Geneva, 1935. Has made various benefactions to hospitals, and to homes for children. *Recreation:* bowls. *Address:* Kalang Street, Elanora Heights, Narrabeen, N.S.W., Australia. [*Died* 30 *June* 1961.

STEWART, George Innes, C.B.E. 1957; M.C. 1918; Senior Partner, Martin, Currie and Company, Chartered Accountants, Edinburgh; *b.* 27 June 1896; *s.* of late George Stewart, J.P., S.S.C., and Flora Philip, M.A.; *m.* 1929, Josepnine Frances Doreen Shaen-Bingham; one *s.* two *d.* *Educ.:* Daniel Stewart's College, Edinburgh; Edinburgh University. Chartered Accountant, 1922. Pres. Inst. of Chartered Accountants of Scotland, 1956-57. War service, 1914-19, with Black Watch, 9th Scottish Div. (wounded, Italian Silver Medal for Military Valour, M.C.). Acted as Canadian Agent of Bank of England, Ottawa, 1940-41, in repatriation of British-owned Canadian Securities. Mem., The Church of Scotland General Trustees. H.M. Commissioner, Queen Victoria School, Dunblane. *Recreations:* golf, fishing. *Address:* 16 Belgrave Crescent, Edinburgh 4. *T.:* Dean 3009; (office) 29 Charlotte Square, Edinburgh. *Clubs:* Royal Automobile; New (Edinburgh); Honourable Company of Edinburgh Golfers (Muirfield); Senior Golfers. [*Died* 8 *Aug.* 1968.

STEWART, Howard Hilton, M.D., M.R.C.P. Lond.; F.R.C.P. Lond. 1951; Senior neurologist, Claremont St. Hospital, Belfast; Neurologist, Royal Victoria Hosp.; Belfast City Hosp.; Consulting Physician, Ulster Hosp. for Children and Women, Belfast; *b.* 30 Dec. 1900; *s.* of Andrew William and Marie Hilton Stewart; *m.* 1930, Clara Maria Luiza dos Santos (*d.* 1955); no *c.* *Educ.:* Royal Belfast Academical Institution. M.B., B.Ch., B.A.O. Belfast, 1923; Resident Med. Officer Roy. Victoria Hosp., 1923-24; Ulster Hospital, 1924-25; House Physician, Hospital for Epilepsy and Paralysis, Maida Vale, 1925-26; M.D. Belfast, 1926; a Member of the Royal College of Physicians, London, 1928; Medical Staff Ulster Hospital, 1928; Medical Registrar Royal Victoria Hospital, 1928-31; Member of British Pædiatric Assoc., 1934-52; Member of the Association of British Neurologists, 1935; Member of Association of Physicians of Great Britain and Ireland, 1937; Trustee, Whitla Medical Institute, 1933; Fellow Ulster Medical Soc.; Chairman, Claremont Street Hospital, 1948-; President Ulster Neuro-Psychiatric Soc., 1959. *Recreations:* golf, motoring. *Addess:* 18 Malone Road, Belfast 9. *T.:* Belfast 666265. *Club:* Royal Co. Down Golf (Newcastle). [*Died* 25 *Nov.* 1961.

STEWART, Sir James H.; *see* Henderson-Stewart.

STEWART, Brig.-Gen. John Smith, C.M.G. 1918; D.S.O. 1917; E.D.; *b.* Brampton, Ont., 18 May 1877; *m.* 1907, Jean Chesney M'Clure (*d.* 1944); no *c.*; *m.* 1946, Ella Whitson Paterson Greenock. *Educ.:* Brampton Public and High Schools; Honour Graduate, Trinity University, Toronto. Went Edmonton, 1896; served as private, Strathcona's Horse, S. Africa, 1900-01 (Queen's medal 4 clasps); went Lethbridge, 1902; raised and commanded 25th Battery C.F.A. (Militia), 1908; raised 20th Battery, C.F.A., for Overseas, Nov. 1914; appointed O.C. 7th Brigade, C.F.A., 10 Mar. 1915; came to France, Jan. 1916 (wounded twice); O.C. 4th Brigade, March, 1917; C.F.A. France (D.S.O., C.M.G., despatches, Fr. Croix de Guerre); Brig.-Gen., Dec. 1917; C.R.A., 3rd Canadian Division; with other World War I Canadian Veterans, attended as Sen. Officer in rank and age the Pilgrimage to Battlefields of Europe to celebrate 50th Anniversary of Armistice 11 Nov. 1918. Elected Legislative Assembly (C.) for Lethbridge City, 1911, 1913, 1917, 1921; resigned, 1925; elected House of Commons, 1930; defeated, 1935; Conservative; practised dentistry, Lethbridge, from 1902 (L.D.S., D.D.S.). LL.D. *h.c.* Alberta Univ., 1957. *Address:* Lethbridge, Alberta, Canada. [*Died* 14 *Aug.* 1970.

STEWART, Joseph Francis; Nationalist Member of Northern Ireland Parliament since 1929; Wine and Spirit Merchant; auctioneer; *b.* 1889; *s.* of Robert Stewart, Builder and Contractor; *m.* 1915; three *s.*; *m.* 1941; one *s.* two *d.* *Educ.:* Convent; Christian Bros.; M.P. (Nat.) Fermanagh and Tyrone, 1934-35. *Address:* Irish Street, Dungannon, Co. Tyrone. *T.:* Dungannon 2784. *Club:* Catholic (Dungannon). [*Died* 6 *May* 1964.

STEWART, Sir Robert Sproul, Kt., *cr.* 1955; C.B.E. 1938; *b.* 14 Jan. 1874; *s.* of John Stewart, Barrhead; *m.* 1909, Margaret Heys Frame, *d.* of Thomas Frame, Glasgow; one *s.* one *d.* *Educ.:* Hutcheson's Grammar School, Glasgow; Glasgow University. Admitted a solicitor, 1898; Chairman, Glasgow Unionist Assoc., 1934-37; President, Scottish Unionist Assoc., 1946-47; Chairman, Royal Scottish Academy of Music, 1951-54. *Address:* Little Rais, Barrhead, Renfrewshire. *T.:* Barrhead 1426. *Club:* Conservative (Glasgow). [*Died* 7 *May* 1969.

STEWART, Sir Thomas Alexander, K.C.S.I., 1939 (C.S.I. 1935); K.C.I.E. 1937; M.A., B.Sc.; I.C.S. (Retd.) *b.* 26 February 1888; *m.* 1914, Elsie (*d.* 1961), *d.* of Crandon Gill; one *s.* two *d.* *Educ.:* George Heriot's School, Edinburgh; Edinburgh University. Entered Indian Civil Service, 1911; served in U.P. 1912-18; Asst. Collector, Imperial Customs Service, Rangoon, 1919; Deputy Rice Commissioner, Rangoon, 1920; Rice Commissioner, 1921; Collector of Customs, Rangoon, 1923, Madras, 1925, and Bombay, 1928; Collector of Salt Revenue, 1932; Additional Secretary, Commerce Dept. Government of India, 1932; Secretary, Commerce Dept., 1934; Member of Viceroy's Executive Council, 1937; Acting Governor of Bihar, 1938; Governor of Bihar, 1939-43. Kt. St. John, 1940. *Address:* 27 Roehampton Close, S.W.15. *T.:* Prospect 2941. *Club:* Roehampton. [*Died* 11 *May* 1964.

STEWART, Rt. Rev. Weston Henry, C.B.E. 1951; D.D. (Lambeth), 1943; Assistant Bishop of Peterborough and non-residentiary Canon of Peterborough since 1957; Rural Dean of Oakham, 1967; *b.* 15 March 1887; *y. s.* of late Ven. Ravenscroft Stewart (Archdeacon of N. Wilts); *m.* 1932, Margaret Alison, M.B.E. 1950, *e. d.* of late Sir J. H. Clapham, C.B.E. *Educ.:* St. Paul's School; Oriel College, Oxford (Foundation Scholar and Bishop Fraser's Scholar); B.A. 1909; M.A. 1912. Deacon 1910; Priest, 1911; Assistant Curate, St. Luke's, Chelsea, 1910-16; Incumbent, Chelsea Old Church, 1916-26; Employed in Home Office, 1917-18; Chaplain, St. George's Cathedral, Jerusalem, 1926-28; Archdeacon in Palestine, Syria, and Transjordan, 1928-43; Seconded, S. George's, Baghdad, 1939-40, Chaplain, Iraq Petroleum Co., 1940-41, S. Peter's, Basra, 1941-42; Examining Chaplain to Bishop in Jerusalem, 1932-42; Hon. Chaplain, Palestine Police, 1938-48; Bishop in Jerusalem, 1943-57, resigned; Rector of Cottesmore with Barrow, Oakham, 1957-64. O.St.J. (Sub-Chaplain), 1938; Chaplain and Sub-Prelate, 1943-. *Publication:* Chelsea Old Church, 1926. *Address:* Top House, Exton, Oakham, Rutland. *T.:* Cottesmore 237. *Club:* Athenæum.

[*Died* 30 *July* 1969.

STEWART, His Honour William; Judge of County Courts, Circuit No. 15 (N. Yorkshire), 1933-36, Circuit No. 14 (Leeds, etc.) 1936-52; Chairman of the National Service Tribunal for the N.E. Div., 1939-52; Chairman of the Quarter Sessions of West Riding of Yorkshire, 1942-55; Barrister-at-law, Middle Temple; *b.* 16 Dec. 1879; *s.* of William Henry Stewart; *m.* 1910, Jessica Beaumont Beaumont; two *d.* *Educ.:* Charterhouse. Mining Engineering, 1898-1905; 1st Class Certificate, 1903; called to Bar, 1908; Practice N.E. Circuit; Recorder of Doncaster, 1933. Reg. Controller, N. Eastern Region, Ministry of Fuel and Power, Jan. 1944-Sept. 1946. *Address:* Cross-in-Hand, Heathfield, Sussex.

[*Died* 27 *April* 1964.

STEWART, William James, C.B.E. 1935; C.D.; Chairman, Select Committee on Reform Institution of Ontario Legislature, from 1953; former Hon. Col. Queen's York Rangers 1st American Regiment Reserve Battalion; *b.* 13 Feb. 1889; *s.* of Albert Duncan Stewart and Sarah Maria Hughes; *m.* 1910, Ethel Leah Huff (*d.* 1955); two *s.* three *d.*; *m.* 1957, Thelma Jean Standeaven. *Educ.:* Toronto. Elected to Ontario Legislature, 1938; Speaker 1944-47; defeated in Ontario elections, 1948; re-elected 1951. Alderman Toronto, 7 years; Mayor Toronto, 4 terms; Chairman several Civic Committees; Chairman: first Board Trustees first Canadian College Embalming to be established at Toronto, resigned 1949; Chairman, Toronto Historical Board; Greater Toronto Veterans Hospital Committee; Mem. Bd. of Governors, Toronto Arts Foundn.; Life Dir., Runnymede Hosp.; Past Master Ulster Masonic Lodge; P.G.S. Deacon Grand Lodge Masons, P.D.M. Orange; Oddfellow; United Church; Conservative. Coronation Medals, 1935, 1953; Canada Centennial Medal, 1967. *Address:* 361 Ellis Park Rd., Toronto, Canada. [*Died* 28 *Sept.* 1969.

STEWART, Air Vice-Marshal William Kilpatrick, C.B. 1964; C.B.E. 1953; A.F.C. 1941; Senior Consultant in Physiology, R.A.F., since 1962; *b.* 28 June 1913; *s.* of Dr. John and Penelope S. Stewart; *m.* 1941, Audrey Wentworth Tyndale; one *s.* three *d.* *Educ.:* Hamilton Acad.; Glasgow Univ. B.Sc. 1934; M.B., Ch.B. 1936; M.R.C.P. 1964; Residencies in Western Infirmary, Glasgow, 1937; M.R.C. Research Fellow, 1938-39; Flying Officer, R.A.F.V.R., 1939; Commanding Officer, R.A.F. Inst. of Aviation Medicine, 1946; Associate Research Fellow, McGill Univ., Montreal, 1957-1958; Commanding Officer, Inst. of Aviation Medicine, 1958-64; Chief Exec. Officer, Flying Personnel Research Cttee., 1960-63. Q.H.P., 1966-. Wakefield Gold Medal, R.Ae.S., 1956; Theodore C. Lyster Award, Aerospace Medical Assoc., 1961. *Publications:* papers in physiological and neurological jls. *Recreation:* golf. *Address:* c/o Bank of Scotland Ltd., 332 Oxford St., W.1. *Club:* Royal Air Force.

[*Died* 1 *May* 1967.

STEWART, Major-General William Ross, C.B. 1945; C.I.E. 1936; F.R.C.S.E.; I.M.S., retd.; K.H.P. since 1943; *b.* 16 March 1889; *s.* of David Ross Stewart, M.A., LL.B., Advocate, Edinburgh, and Elizabeth Catherine Dobie, Ladykirk, Berwickshire; *m.* Margaret Jean Denholm Fraser; one *s.* one *d.* *Educ.:* Edinburgh Academy; Edinburgh University. M.B., Ch.B., 1912; entered I.M.S. as Lieutenant, 1914; Brevet-Major, 1919; F.R.C.S.E. 1921; Surgeon to Gov. of Bombay, 1919-20; Surgeon to C.-in-C. in India, 1931; Surgeon to the Viceroy of India, 1933-36; Col. 1941; Temp. Brig. 1942; served European War; N.W. Frontier, 1930-31; A.D.M.S. with 10th Indian Division in Iran and Iraq, 1939; D.D.M.S. Ceylon Command H.Q., 1942-44; D.D.M.S. Northern Command, India, 1945-1946; retired 1947. *Publications:* Indian Supplement to First Aid to the Injured, St. John's Ambulance Association. *Recreations:* fishing, golf. *Address:* Blakehope, Caddonfoot, Galashiels, Selkirkshire.

[*Died* 1 *June* 1966.

STEWART-BROWN, Ronald David, Q.C. 1957; *b.* 5 Dec. 1911; 2nd *s.* of Ronald Stewart-Brown; *m.* 1946, Mrs. Esther Lynette Sutherland Stuart-Hamilton, widow (*née* Mackay); two *s.* one *d.* *Educ.:* Harrow; Trinity College, Cambridge. Called to Bar, 1934. Supplementary Reserve Commission, Welsh Guards, 1939; served with 2nd Bn., Boulogne, 1940; France and Germany, 1944-1945 (despatches, wounded); G.S.O.2 H.Q. Second Army, 1943-44. Q.C. 1957. *Publications:* Editor of Encyclopædia of the Law of Compulsory Purchase and Compensation, 1960; Guide to Compulsory Purchase and Compensation, 1962. *Recreations:* fishing, golf. *Address:* 22 Cliveden Place, S.W.1. *Club:* St. Stephen's.

[*Died* 10 *Oct.* 1963.

STEWART-RICHARDSON, Major Sir Ian Rorie Hay, 16th Bt., *cr.* 1630; late Irish Guards; Chairman: Bulmer & Lumb, 1936-68; Vokes Ltd., etc.; *b.* 25 Sept. 1904; *e. s.* of 15th Bt. and Lady Constance Mackenzie (*d.* 1932), *sister* of The Countess of Cromartie (3rd in line, *cr.* 1861; *d.* 1962); *S.* father, 1914; *m.* 1944, Audrey Meril, *er. d.* of Claude Odlum, Leinster Grove, Co. Kildare; two *s.* two *d.* Served War of 1939-45, Africa, Italy, (wounded, despatches). *Heir: s.* Simon Alaisdair Stewart-Richardson, *b.* 10 June 1947. *Address:* Lynedale, Longcross, Surrey; 50 St. James's Street, S.W.1. *Clubs:* Devonshire, White's; Kildare St. (Dublin).

[*Died* 16 *June* 1969.

STEWART-RICHARDSON, Violet Roberta, M.V.O. 1941; O.B.E. 1938; *b.* 3 Feb. 1882; *y. d.* of late Henry Gresham Stewart-Richardson, 2nd *s.* of 13th Baronet of Pitfour; unmarried. *Educ.:* Edinburgh. Temp. appointment H.M. Treasury, 1917-22; Assistant to Establishment Officer and later Establishment Officer in H.M.'s Household, 1922-42. Jubilee Medal, 1935; Coronation Medal, 1937. *Address:* Lingfield Lodge, East Grinstead, Sussex. *T.:* East Grinstead 23915. [*Died* 13 *Feb.* 1967.

STEWART-SMITH, Ean Kendal, M.B.E. 1940; Chamberlain of London since 1962; *b.* 10 Jan. 1907; *s.* of late Sir Dudley Stewart-Smith, K.C., Vice-Chancellor of Duchy of Lancaster, and Katherine Cautley; *m.* 1934, Edmée von Wallerstain und Marnegg; two *s.* one *d.* *Educ.:* Winchester College; New College, Oxford. Barclay's Bank, 1933-62: Asst. General Manager, 1948-53; Local Director, 1953-62; Director of Barclay's Bank (France) Ltd., 1955-62. Member of Eastern Gas Board, 1956-62. Military service, 1939-45; released with rank of Lieut.-Colonel. *Recreations:* tennis, shooting, drawing. *Address:* Stanley Hall, Halstead, Essex. *T.:* Halstead 2315. *Club:* Brooks's. [*Died* 12 *Jan.* 1964.

STEWART-WALLACE, Sir John Stewart, Kt., *cr.* 1931; C.B. 1926; Barrister of Inner Temple; Chief Land Registrar, H.M. Land Registry, for England and Wales, 1923-41; Chairman Organisation Department, Liberal Party, 1945-47; Hon. Sec. Liberal Parliamentary Party, 1941-45; Chm. Samaritan Hosp. for Women till 1948; Vice-Chm. of General Purposes and Finance Committee, Charing Cross Hospital till 1955; Member N.W. Appeals Committee for Health Services; Vice-President and Ex-Chairman, World Congress of Faiths; Vice-President, National Society Colony, Bucks.; a Gov., Ramakrishna Vedanta Centre, London; *s.* of late J. S. Stewart-Wallace, M.P., J.P.; *m.* 1908, Edith Lillian (*d.* 1961), *d.* of late H. W. Lee; two *s.* two *d.* *Educ.:* Queen's, Ireland (1st Cl. Exhibitioner, triple First Prizeman and First of 1st Cl. Hons. in Political and Constitutional History and Political Economy); Lincoln Coll., Oxford (Carrington Legal Essay Prizeman, First Class Honours in Law, and Vinerian Scholar in the Univ.); Heidelberg Univ. Volunteered for active service, 1914; served in France on Staff of 25th Div., then as Assistant Director of Ordnance Services (Lieut.-Col., despatches). *Publications:* Principles of Land Registration; Joint author Land Charges Act, 1925; Joint editor (with Sir Charles Fortescue-Brickdale) Land Registration Act, 1925; Titles on registration of title and land charges in Halsbury's Laws of England; contributions to leading literary and law reviews. *Recreations:* cruising, sea-sickness, and unskilled labour. *Address:* 2 Ethorpe Crescent, Gerrards Cross, Bucks. *Club:* Reform. [*Died* 14 *April* 1963.

STILES, Walter, Sc.D. (Cambridge), 1922; M.Sc. (Birmingham); F.R.S 1928; F.L.S.; Emeritus Professor of Botany and Life Governor, Birmingham University; *b.* London, 23 Aug. 1886; *s.* of Walter and Elizabeth Sarah Stiles; *m.* 1920, Edith Ethel May Harwood; one *s.* one *d.* *Educ.:* Latymer Upper School; Emmanuel College, Cambridge (Exhibitioner, 1905; scholar, 1907); 1st Class Natural Sciences Tripos, Parts I. and II., 1907-09; Walsingham Medallist, 1911, M.A., 1912. Assist. Lecturer in Botany, Univ. of Leeds, 1910-19; Professor of Botany in Univ. College, Reading, 1919-26; University of Reading, 1926-29; Mason Professor of Botany, University of Birmingham, 1929-51; research worker, Food Investigation Board, 1918-20; Dean of the Faculty of Science, Univ. of Birmingham, 1932-35. Corresp. mem., Amer. Soc. Plant Physiologists. Hon. D.Sc. (Nottingham Univ.), 1963. *Publications:* Carbon Assimilation (with I. Jorgensen), 1917; The Preservation of Food by Freezing, 1922; Permeability, 1924; Photosynthesis, 1925; Respiration in Plants (with W. Leach), 1932, 4th edn. 1960; An Introduction to the Principles of Plant Physiology, 1936, 2nd edn., 1950; Trace Elements in Plants, 1946, 3rd edn., 1961; numerous Botanical, Physiological, and Biochemical papers in Annals of Botany, New Phytologist, Biochemical Journal, Science Progress, Proceedings of the Royal Society, etc. *Recreations:* walking, gardening, photography. *Address:* 21 Elsley Road, Tilehurst on Thames, Reading. [*Died* 19 *April* 1966.

STIRLING, Brigadier Alexander Dickson, D.S.O. 1918; R.A.M.C. retired; *b.* 8 June 1886; 2nd *s.* of late Rev. Alexander Stirling, Arbroath, Angus, and late Mrs. Stirling; *m.* 1925, Isobel, *o. surv. d.* of Rev. J. C. Matthew, M.A., B.D., late Senior Presidency Chaplain, Bombay; two *s.* two *d.* *Educ.:* Arbroath High School; University College, Dundee; M.B., Ch.B. (with distinction), St. Andrews University, 1907; D.P.H. St. Andrews, 1911; House Physician and Senior House Surgeon, Dundee Royal Infirmary, 1907-08; entered R.A.M.C., 1909; Captain, 1912; Major, 1921; Bt. Lt.-Col. 1933; Lt.-Col. 1934; Col. 1937; served in Egypt, 1911-14; S.M.O. British Troops, Khartoum, 1913; served European War, France and Italy, 1914-19; D.A.D.M.S., Boulogne Base, 1918-19 (D.S.O., wounded, despatches four times); awarded Military Order of Avis by Portuguese Government; D.A.D.G. Army Medical Service War Office, 1919-23; D.A.D.M.S., H.Q. Northern Command, India, 1925-28; Deputy Assistant Director-General, Army Medical Services, War Office, 1930-34; D.D.M.S., H.Q. L. of C., B.E.F., 1940; D.D.M.S., H.Q. 1 Corps, 1940-1941, Brigadier; O.C. Troops, Netley, and O.C. Royal Victoria Hospital; Hon. rank of Brig. on retirement. Member of Council U.S. Section, Royal Society of Medicine; Member of Lord Southborough's War Office Committee on Shell Shock; Member of Permanent Committee of the International Congress of Military Medicine and Pharmacy; Secretary 5th International Congress of Military Medicine and Pharmacy, War Office; F. R. Hort. S. *Publication:* a short article with the late Dr. A. J. Chalmers on a tropical skin disease. *Recreations:* horticulture, photography, modern languages, travel. *Address:* c/o L. & J. McLaren, W.S., 14 Alva Street, Edinburgh. [*Died* 2 *May* 1961.

STIRLING, Mrs. A. M. W.; *y. d.* of Percival Andrée Pickering, Q.C., Recorder of Pontefract and Attorney-General for the County Palatine of Lancaster, and Anna Maria Wilhelmina, *d.* of Mr. and Lady Elizabeth Spencer-Stanhope of Cannon Hall, Yorkshire, and *g.d.* of Coke of Norfolk, first Earl of Leicester; *m.* 1901, Charles G. Stirling, M.A.; no *c.* Has inaugurated and endowed the De Morgan Collection shown at Old Battersea House. *Publications: fairy tales:* The Adventures of Prince Almero, 1890; The Queen of the Goblins, 1892; *novels:* as *Percival Pickering:* A Life Awry, 1893 (afterwards dramatised and performed at the Prince of Wales's Theatre, 1906); Toy Gods, 1904; A Pliable Marriage 1895; The Spirit is Willing, 1898; *biographies:* under the name of Mrs. A. M. W. Stirling: Coke of Norfolk and his Friends; The Life of the 1st Earl of Leicester, 1908; Annals of a Yorkshire House, 1911; The Letter-Bag of Lady Elizabeth Spencer-Stanhope, 1913; Macdonald of the Isles, 1913; A Painter of Dreams, 1916; The Hothams, 1918; Pages and Portraits from the Past (Memoirs of Admiral Sir William Hotham, G.C.B.), 1919; William De Morgan and his Wife, 1922; Life's Little Day, 1924; The Richmond Papers, 1926; Fyvie Castle, Its Lairds and their Times, 1928; The Ways of Yesterday, Being Chronicles of the Way Family, 1930; Life's Mosaic: Memories Canny and Uncanny, 1934; The Diaries of Dummer, 1934; Victorian Sidelights, 1954; The Merry Wives of Battersea, 1956; Ghosts Vivisected, 1957; Odd Lives, 1958; A Scrap heap of Memories, 1960; Stirling Tales, 1961; Why?, 1964; Unlikely Tales, 1964. Articles in the Nineteenth Century and After, etc. *Recreations:* motoring and reading. *Address:*

Old Battersea House, S.W.11. *T.:* Battersea 2773. [*Died* 11 *Aug.* 1965.

STIRLING, Brig. James Erskine, D.S.O. 1943; T.D.; Lord-Lieutenant of Nairnshire since 1958; *b.* 27 April 1898; *s.* of late Major William Stirling, Fairburn, Muir-of-Ord, Ross-shire; *m.* 1924, Evelyn Alice Beatrix, *d.* of Captain Henry Cavendish, R.N.; one *s.* three *d.* *Educ.:* Harrow; Royal Military College. Served European War, 1914-19, Seaforth Highlanders; served War of 1939-45; Lt.-Col. 1941; Middle East, 1942-43 (despatches); acting Brig. 1943. D.L. Nairnshire, 1954, Vice-Lieut., 1957. *Address:* Holme Rose, Gollanfield, Inverness-shire. *Club:* United Service. [*Died* 20 *Dec.* 1968.

STIRLING, John Ashwell, C.M.G. 1943; O.B.E. 1931; *b.* 16 Oct. 1891; *y. s.* of late Hugh Stirling, Aberdeen and Blackheath; *m.* 1st, 1920, Gladys Margaret (*d.* 1948), *o. d.* of late William Vivian Oporto; no *c.*; 2nd, 1952, Olive Joan, 2nd *d.* of late A. Clifton Stock and of Mrs. J. Beloe, Lisbon. *Educ.:* Rugby School. Cockburn, Smithes & Co., Wine Shippers, Oporto, 1911-14; Lieut. 7th Border Regt., Flanders (invalided), 1914-16; Dept. of Overseas Trade, 1917-27; Export Credits Guarantee Dept., 1927-35; Commercial Relations and Exports Dept., Board of Trade, 1935; Assistant Secretary, Board of Trade; visited Trade Commissioner Offices throughout Commonwealth, 1949-51; retired, 1951. *Recreations:* golf, gardening, photography. *Address:* Hunter's Piece, Southgate, Swansea. [*Died* 6 *Oct.* 1965.

STOCK, Ralph; Writer; *s.* of Elliot Stock, publisher; *m.* 1939, Elwyn Freda Rhys Williams; one *d.* *Educ.:* Nowhere. World travel, including crossing of Atlantic and Pacific Oceans in 47-ft. sailing boat. *Plays:* (among others) Quest; Out of the Frying Pan; Always Afternoon; Chinook; The Day Before Yesterday. Short stories, journalism and films for England and U.S.A. *Publications:* (among others) The Cruise of the Dream Ship; Confessions of a Tenderfoot; Marama; Uncharted Waters; South of the Line. *Recreations:* boats, painting. *Address:* c/o Barclays Bank Ltd., 52 Regent Street, W.1. [*Died* 30 *April* 1962.

STOCKS, Sir (Andrew) Denys, Kt., *cr.* 1945; C.B. 1932; O.B.E. 1919; *b.* Market Harborough, 2 Dec. 1884; 7th *s.* of late John Edward Stocks, D.D., Archdeacon of Leicester, and Canon of Peterborough; *m.* 1922, Margaret, *er. d.* of late John McKane; two *s.* one *d.* *Educ.:* Loretto School. Joined the staff of the Solicitor to the Board of Customs and Excise, 1910; transferred to Treasury Solicitors Dept., 1914; Assistant Legal Adviser and Solicitor to the Ministry of Agriculture and Fisheries, and the Commissioners of Crown Lands, 1920-25; Legal Adviser and Solicitor to the Ministry of Agriculture and Fisheries, the Commissioners of Crown Lands, Tithe Redemption Commission and Forestry Commission, 1925-49. Member: New Romney Borough Council since 1951; Kent County Council since 1955. *Recreations:* golf and gardening; played hockey for England, 1908-21; ex-Pres. Hockey Assoc. and Chm. of Internat. Hockey Board. *Address:* Gunwalloe, Littlestone-on-Sea, New Romney, Kent. *T.:* New Romney 2321. *Club:* Union. [*Died* 27 *April* 1961.

STOCKWELL, Captain (Commodore 2nd Class) Henry, C.B. 1931; D.S.O 1917; R.D.; *b.* 21 Jan. 1875; *s.* of late Frederick Stockwell, M.D. (London), Bruton, Somerset; *m.* 1899, Laura Fanny, *d.* of Dillon-Trenchard, Lytchett-Matravers, Dorset; no *c.* *Educ.:* King's School, Bruton; H.M.S. Worcester. Served European War, 1914-18 (D.S.O., despatches); R.N.R. A.D.C. to the King, 1928-30; retired list, 1930; Commodore 2nd Class, 1929; commanded the British Indian Steam Navigation Co.'s. S.S. Mandala; retired, 1932. *Address:* c/o Westminster Bank, Bruton, Somerset. [*Died* 27 *Nov.* 1962.

STOCKWELL, Colonel Hon. Ralph Frederick, Q.C. (Can.); B.A., B.C.L., V.D.; Reserve of Officers; *b.* 21 Nov. 1885; *s.* of Charles Frederick Stockwell and Joséphine Roy; *m.* 1916, Jane Elizabeth, *d.* of late W. S. Cotton, Cowansville, Quebec; one *s.* one *d.* *Educ.:* Danville Academy (Associate in Arts); McGill University (B.A., 1908; B.C.L., 1911). Admitted to practice of Law as Member Bar Assoc. of City of Montreal; K.C. 1922; at outbreak of Great War was Major, Second in Command of 11th Hussars; organised a squadron of Mounted Rifles, 1914; enlisted in 5th Canadian Mounted Rifles, 1915; served in France and Flanders as a Company Commander; subseq. held various appointments in England; resumed practice of Law, 1919; Crown Prosecutor, District of Bedford, 1929-31; M.L.A. 1931-1936; Treasurer of Province of Quebec, 1932-1936; Gov. of Brome-Missisquoi-Perkins Hospital. *Recreations:* riding, fishing, and golf. *Address:* P.O. Box 389, Cowansville, Quebec, Canada. *Club:* Reform (Montreal). [*Died* 15 *Oct.* 1962.

STOKER, Captain Hew Gordon Dacre, D.S.O. 1919; R.N.; *b.* 2 Feb. 1885; *s.* of late William Stoker, F.R.C.S.I.; *m.* 1925, Dorothie Margaret, *d.* of late Rev. L. G. Pidcock. Joined Navy, 1900; submarines, 1906; commanded first submarine to voyage half-way round the world, 1914, and first submarine to dive through Dardanelles, 1915; Prisoner of War in Turkey, 1915-18; Commander, 1919; retired at own request, 1920. Became actor and theatrical manager, appearing in numerous plays in London and New York, and on Television and Radio. Collaborated in writing several plays for stage and television, including Below the Surface, Morning Departure, Deep Waters. Rejoined Navy, 1939, serving in various commands and staff appointments; reverted to retired list Jan. 1946 with rank of Captain. Pres. R.N. Lawn Tennis Assoc., 1953-63. Winner Croquet Championship of Ireland, 1962. *Publications:* Straws in the Wind (autobiography), 1925. *Address:* 11 Astell St., S.W.3. *Club:* Garrick. [*Died* 2 *Feb.* 1966.

STOKES, Rear-Admiral Graham Henry, C.B. 1942; D.S.C.; R.N. retd.; *b.* 8 Sept. 1902; *s.* of late Graham Stokes and Mrs. Esther F. Magniac, The Glen, Buckland Brewer, Bideford; *m.* 1941, Wendy, *d.* of late William Brice, Mockbeggar, Higham, Kent; one *s.* one *d.* *Educ.:* R.N.C., Dartmouth. Went to sea as Naval Cadet, 1919; Lieut., 1925; Commander, 1938; commanded various destroyers from 1933 onwards; commanded H.M.S. Sikh in operations against German Battleship Bismarck (D.S.C.); also when leading a division of 4 destroyers in a night action resulting in destruction of Italian Cruisers Alberto di Guissano and Alberico Da Barbiano (C.B.); Captain, 1942; in command of H.M.S. Devonshire, 1950; Rear-Admiral, 1952; Senior British Naval Officer and Flag Officer (Liaison) Middle East, 1952-54, retired 1954. *Recreations:* fishing, painting. *Address:* Little Marsh, Buckland Brewer, Bideford, N. Devon. *T.:* Torrington 2179. [*Died* 22 *Aug.* 1969.

STONE, Christopher Reynolds, D.S.O. 1918; M.C.; author; Joint Founder of The Gramophone; *b.* Eton, 19 Sept. 1882; *y. s.* of late Rev. E. D. Stone; *m.* 1908, Alice (*d.* 1945), *d.* of James Wilson, and *widow* of W. M. Chinnery. *Educ.:* Eton; Christ Church, Oxford. Private 16th Middlesex, 1914; Commission 22nd Royal Fusiliers, 1915; Major, 2nd in command, 1917; A.D.C. to G.O.C. 2nd Division, 1918 (despatches 3 times, D.S.O., M.C.). *Publications:* Christopher Stone Speaking, 1933; Novels: Scars, Valley of Indecision, Rigour of the Game, etc.; books about Eton; edited several books for the Clarendon Press. [*Died* 22 *May* 1965.

STONE, Sir Gilbert, Kt., *cr.* 1936; **Hon. Mr. Justice Stone;** *b.* 1886; *s.* of Richard and Elizabeth Stone; *m.* 1912, Elsie Lawton Scott; one *s.* *Educ.:* Wrekin College; Caius College, Cambridge; Lincoln's Inn, London. Barrister, 1911; Parliamentary Candidate, 1922-1923-24; Judge, High Court of Judicature, Madras, India, 1930-35; Chief Justice, High Court, Nagpur, 1936-43. *Address:* 28 Millington Road, Cambridge. [*Died* 14 *May* 1967.

STONE, Air Vice-Marshal James Ambrose, C.B. 1944; Officer American Legion of Merit, 1946; *b.* 20 Mar. 1885; *s.* of James Ambrose Stone; *m.* 1915, Agnes Wallace Allport; one *d.* *Educ.:* King's College, London. Army and R.A.F.; retired, 1945. *Recreations:* cricket and golf. *Address:* Apple Tree, Winchelsea, Sussex. *T.:* Winchelsea 288. [*Died* 14 *Jan.* 1966.

STONE, Thomas Archibald; Special Assistant to the President of The International Nickel Company of Canada since 1959; *b.* Chatham, Ontario, Canada, 12 Dec. 1900; *s.* of Spencer Stone and Flora Maud Campbell; *m.* 1934, Alexandra Ewing (*d.* 1961); one *d.*; *m.* 1962, Emily Coolidge. *Educ.:* University of Toronto, Toronto, Ontario, Canada; l'École Libre des Sciences Politiques, Paris, France. Joined Canadian Dept. of External Affairs, 1927, and posted to Washington with rank of Third Sec.; transferred to Paris, 1932, with rank of Second Sec. Retired from diplomatic service, 1935, to take up farming in S. Carolina; returned to External Affairs at outbreak of war as First Sec. at Ottawa. Special mission to England and North Africa, 1943; Counsellor, staff Canadian High Commissioner in U.K., 1944; Chargé d'Affaires of Canadian Legation to Allied Govts. in U.K., 1944; transferred to Washington as Counsellor, Canadian Embassy, 1945; Minister, 1946-1949; Canadian Minister, Sweden, 1949-52; Ambassador, Netherlands, 1952-58. *Recreations:* fishing and carpentry. *Address:* The International Nickel Co. of Canada, Ltd., 67 Wall Street, New York 5, N.Y., U.S.A.; (home) Snee Farm, Mount Pleasant, S.C. *Clubs:* Brook (New York); Country (Ottawa); Travellers' (Paris). [*Died* 26 *July* 1965.

STONEHAM, Sir Ralph Thompson, K.B.E., *cr.* 1947; *b.* 29 June 1888; *s.* of Robert Thompson Henry Stoneham; *m.* 1930, Vera Dorothea Frances, *d.* of Malcolm Beckett Nicholson; two *d.* *Educ.:* Brentwood School; Peterhouse, Cambridge. Served as Asst., Manager and Managing Director with Foucar & Co. Ltd., Teak Lessees and Merchants, Burma, 1912-43; during this period was member of Burma Legislative Council and other local bodies. Additional Secretary, Govt. of Burma (temp. Government servant), 1943-45; Government Project Financial Representative, 1945-47. Director of Welfare, Cameroons Development Corporation, 1947-52. *Recreations:* interested in riding, hunting and racing, also in Rugby football and other games. *Address:* Danesmount, Longdown Lane, Epsom. *Club:* Pegu (Rangoon). [*Died* 6 *Sept.* 1965.

STONEHAM, Robert Thompson Douglas, C.B.E. 1951; Senior partner, Stoneham & Sons, Solicitors, since 1917; *b.* 10 March 1883; *e. s.* of late Robert Thompson Henry Stoneham; *m.* 1906, Mary Emily, *d.* of Robert William Cowell; one *s.* two *d.* (and one *s.* decd.). *Educ.:* Brentwood School, Essex. Admitted a Solicitor, 1904; Master, City of London Solicitors' Company, 1956-1957; Past-Master Needle-makers' Company, 1949; Member of Corporation of City of London, 1930-; Chief Commoner, 1949; Deputy for Candlewick Ward. Chairman of Brentwood School, Essex, 1955-62; Past Chm. City of London School and City of London School for Girls. One of H.M. Lieutenants for City of London. Officier de la Légion d'Honneur, 1950. *Address:* 108A Cannon Street, E.C.4. *T.:* Mansion House 8656. *Clubs:* Royal Automobile; Royal British (Lisbon and Oporto). [*Died* 21 *Aug.* 1962.

STONER, Edmund Clifton, F.R.S. 1937; Sc.D. (Cambridge); F.Inst.P.; Emeritus Professor of Physics in the University of Leeds; *b.* East Molesey, Surrey, 1899; *s.* of late Arthur Hallett Stoner, and late Mary, *d.* of late Thomas Roberts Fleet; *m.* 1951, Jean Heather, *d.* of late Herbert Crawford. *Educ.:* Bolton School; Emmanuel College, Cambridge (Scholar.) Natural Sciences Tripos Parts I and II, B.A., 1921; Research at Cavendish Laboratory; Ph.D., 1925; Research Fellow of Emmanuel Coll., Camb., 1928-31; Lecturer in Physics, University of Leeds, 1924; Reader, 1927; Professor of Theoretical Physics, 1939-51; Cavendish Professor of Physics, 1951-63. *Publications:* Magnetism, and Atomic Structure, 1926; Magnetism, 1930 revised 1936, 1946, 1949; Magnetism and Matter, 1934; Papers on theoretical physics in various journals. *Recreations:* music, sight-seeing, gardening. *Address:* 12 St. Chad's Drive, Leeds 6, Yorks. *T.:* Leeds 53927. [*Died* 27 *Dec.* 1968.

STONES, Hubert Horace, M.D. (Commend.), M.B., Ch.B., M.D.S. (Commend.), B.D.S. (1st cl. Hons.) (Manc.), F.D.S.R.C.S. (Eng.); L.D.S. (Eng.); retired as Professor of Dental Surgery and Director of Dental Education, Univ. of Liverpool, Director and General Consultant, Liverpool Dental Hospital, Consultant, maxillo-facial centre, Broad Green Hospital, Liverpool, 1957; Hon. Consultant Dental Surgeon, Liverpool Regional Board Hospitals and Dental Hospital; Editor-in-Chief (first) of Journal Official de la Fédération Dentaire Internationale; *b.* 1892; *s.* of Thos. Stones, Shrewsbury, and Sibylla Tennant, Settle; *m.* Frances Freida, *d.* of Edward Allen, Bowden and Anglesea, and Sara A. Warburton, Warburton, Cheshire. *Educ.:* University of Manchester; Dublin; London. Many prizes; Capt. late R.A.M.C.; Hon. Dental Surgeon University College Hospital Dental Dept. London, 1932-1935; Research Worker, Roy. Dental Hosp., London, 1929-35; formerly: Vice-Dean, Board of Faculty of Dental Surgery, R.C.S. (Eng.); Examiner for Primary Examination, Fellowship in Dental Surgery, R.C.S. (Eng.) and External Examiner in Dental subjects to Universities of Birmingham, Bristol, Cambridge, Durham, Edinburgh, Glasgow, Leeds, Manchester and St. Andrews; formerly External Expert in Dentistry to University of London; formerly Member Liverpool Regional Hospital Board, Bd. of Governors, Liverpool United Teaching Hosps., Gen. Dental Council and Dental Cttee., Medical Research Council. Howard Mummery Prize, 1936; John Tomes Prize of R.C.S. (Eng.), 1945-47; Charles Tomes Lectr. of R.C.S. (Eng.), 1951; first Evelyn Sprawson Lectr. of London Hosp. Med. College Dental School, 1961; F.R.S.M. (Past Pres. and Hon. Mem. Section of Odontology); F.A.C.D.; Vice-Pres., List of Honour of Fédn. Dent. Internat.; Hon. Member of many dental socs. (including foreign) and Mem. medical societies. *Publications:* Oral and Dental Diseases, 3rd edn., revised reprint, 1957, 5th edn. (with co-authors), 1966; Dental Health (ed.), 1956; Your Child's Teeth (anglicized and ed.) 1957; many papers on scientific and dental subjects. *Address:* Curzon Mews, Howe Rd., Curzon Park, Chester. *Club:* University (Liverpool). [*Died* 28 *Sept.* 1965.

STONES, William; *b.* 2 Oct. 1904; *s.* of Thomas and Margaret Stones; *m.* 1926; one *d.* *Educ.:* elementary school; National Council of Labour Colleges. Secretary, Stanley Labour Party, 1940-55. A Mines Inspector, 1950-55; M.P. (Lab.) Consett Division of Durham, 1955-66; retired. Formerly: Mem. National Union of Mineworkers; President District Nursing Association. *Address:* 26 Tweed Terrace, Stanley, Co. Durham. [*Died* 2 *July* 1969.

STONEY, Richard Atkinson, M.B., M.Ch. (*h.c.*), B.A.O. (Univ. Dublin), F.R.C.S.I., L.M. Rotunda; Late Consulting Surgeon to Royal City of Dublin Hospital; Late Hon. Surgeon Masonic Boys' Sch.; Late Consulting Surgeon, Ministry of Pensions Hospital, Leopardstown; Consulting Surgeon, Incorporated Dental Hospital; Late Mem. of Gen. Med. Coun. and Gen. Dental Council; Mem. of Medical Registration Council and Member Dental Board of Ireland; Vice-Pres. Royal Zoological Society, Ireland; late Médecin Major 2ème Class Armée Française; Médecin Chef Hôpital de Lamothe, Villeneuve sur Lot. Chirurgien du 5ème Secteur du 17ème Région, 1915-18; ex-Examiner in Surgery Conjoint Board, R.C.P.I. and R.C.S.I.; Ex-President, R.C.S.I., 1931 and 1932; Ex-President Royal Academy of Medicine in Ireland; Ex-President, Association of the Royal College of Surgeons in Ireland; *b.* Dublin, 13 May 1877; *s.* of Canon R. B. Stoney, D.D., late Rector of Holy Trinity Church, Killiney, Co. Dublin, and Kate Mabel Atkinson, Gortmore, Dundrum, Co. Dublin; *m.* 1915, Gladys Enid, *d.* of late A. Lenox Figgis, Gorse Hill, Greystones, Co. Wicklow; two *d.* *Educ.:* St. Helen's School and Trinity College, Dublin. Entered Medical School, 1896; Medical Scholarship, 1899; Travelling Prizes in Surgery and Medicine; attended Royal City of Dublin Hospital as a student (Wheeler medal in Medicine, 1901). Past President and Vice-Pres. Biological Association T.C.D.; past Pres. Surgical Section Academy of Medicine in Ireland; Chevalier of the Legion of Honour. *Publications:* chapter in Surgery of Modern Warfare on methods of removing projectiles and kindred foreign bodies; articles in Medical Journals. *Recreation:* motoring. *Address:* 56 Fitzwilliam Square, N. Dublin. *T.:* Dublin 61397. *Club:* St. Stephen's Green (Dublin). [*Died* 2 *May* 1966.

STONHOUSE, Sir Arthur Allan, 17th Bt., *cr.* 1628, and 13th Bt., *cr.* 1670; Rancher; Reeve, Municipal District, Pine Lake, Alberta; *b.* 24 Feb. 1885; *s.* of George Arthur Stonhouse; *S.* cousin 1937; *m.* 1914, Beatrice, *d.* of late T. Feron, Santa Monica, California; one *s.* two *d.* (and one *d.* decd.). *Educ.:* St. Paul's School, London. Has engaged in mining in Mexico; ranching in Canada. *Recreations:* hunting, shooting, tennis. *Heir:* *s.* Philip Allan Stonhouse [*b.* 24 Oct. 1916; *m.* 1946, Winnifred Emily, *d.* of J. M. Shield, Lethbridge, Alberta; two *s.*]. *Address:* 4574 Waskasoo Crescent, Red Deer, Alberta, Canada.

[*But his name did not appear on the Official Roll of Baronets.* [*Died* 22 *Nov.* 1967.

STOPFORD OF FALLOWFIELD, Baron *cr.* 1958 (Life Peer), of Hindley Green; **John Sebastian Bach Stopford,** K.B.E. 1955 (M.B.E. 1920); Kt. 1941; F.R.S. 1927; M.D. (gold medal); Hon. Sc.D. (Cambridge and Dublin); Hon. D.Sc. (Leeds); Hon. LL.D. (Manchester and Liverpool); Hon. D.C.L. (Durham); F.R.C.P.; Hon. F.R.C.S. (Eng.); Vice-Chancellor, Univ. of Manchester, 1934-1956; Professor of Experimental Neurology 1938-56, Emeritus Professor since 1956; Hon. Fellow of Manchester College of Science and Technology, 1957; *b.* Hindley Green, nr. Wigan, 25 June 1888; *e.* *s.* of Thomas Rinck Stopford; *m.* 1916, Lily Allan, M.B., Ch.B., Hon. M.A., J.P.; one *s.* *Educ.:* Liverpool Coll.; Manchester Gram. Sch.; University of Manchester. Late Demonstrator and Lecturer in Anatomy, University of Manchester; Professor of Anatomy, 1919-1938 and late Dean of Medical School, University of Manchester; late Pro-Vice-Chancellor; Hon. Fellow Brit. Orthop. Assoc.; late Ext. Examiner, Univs. of Bristol, Camb., Leeds, Liverpool, Wales, and T.C.D.; late Vice-President Anatomical Society of Great Britain and Ireland; late Pres. Manchester Medical Soc.; Mem. Amer. Assoc. of Anatomists; late Hon. Advisory Anatomist, Manchester Royal Infirmary; late Member British Elective Cttee. of Commonwealth Fund; late Member of Council of Royal Coll. of Physicians; late Chairman Universities Bureau of the British Empire; late Member and Chairman of Business of General Medical Council; late Mem. Cttee. on Higher Agricultural Education (Min. of Agric.); late Vice-Chairman Committee of Principals and Vice-Chancellors; Vice-Chairman, Managing Trustees of Nuffield Foundation; late Chairman of Council (remains a trustee), John Rylands Library, Manchester and Manchester R.C.M.; Chairman Manchester Regional Hospital Bd., 1947-1953; late mem. Bd. of Governors, United Manchester Hosps. Formerly Vice-Chm. Interdepartmental Cttee. on Medical Schools; mem. Medical Advisory Cttee. University Grants Cttee.; Court of Governors, Univ. Coll. of North Staffs.; Chm. Manchester, Salford and Stretford Joint Hosp. Advisory Bd.; Chm. Cttee. on Admin. Officers (Min. of Health); Member of Court of Governors University of Manchester; Member Lancaster and Kendal Hospital Management Cttee., 1957-. Mem. Westmorland Education Cttee. Hon. Freeman of City of Manchester, 1956. *Publications:* Sensation and the Sensory Pathway, 1930; Papers on anatomical, educational and neurological subjects. *Recreations:* gardening and walking. *Address:* Knott Lea, New Barnes Rd., Arnside, via Carnforth, Lancs. *T.:* Arnside 410. *Club:* Athenæum. [*Died* 6 *March* 1961.

STOPFORD-TAYLOR, Richard, D.S.O. 1917; Hon. Consulting Dermatologist to Royal Liverpool United Hosp. and Roy. Liverpool Children's Hosp.; retired, 1955; *b.* Liverpool, 7 March 1884; 2nd *s.* of late G. G. S. Stopford-Taylor, M.D., and Ann Alice Stopford-Taylor, Liverpool; *m.* 1916, Marion Gertrude, *d.* of late William Buckley, J.P., Blundellsands, Liverpool; no *c.* *Educ.:* Epsom College. Qualified as M.B., Ch.B., Liverpool University, 1907; F.R.C.S.E. 1910; Thelwall Thomas Fellow and Holt Fellow in Pathology, Liverpool University, 1910-12. Mobilised Aug. 1914; 1/1 West Lancs. Fd. Amb. (T.F.), Gallipoli, Egypt, France, 1915-18; with 29th Div., rank Capt. to acting Lieut.-Col. (despatches, D.S.O.). late Consulting Dermatologist Clatterbridge General Hospital and the Open-Air Hospital for Children, Leasowe. President British Association of Dermatology and Syphilology, 1943; President Liverpool Medical Institution, 1944. *Recreations:* motoring and walking. *Address:* Alton House, 63 Mersey Road, Liverpool 17. *T.:* Cressington Park 2113. *Club:* University (Liverpool). [*Died* 4 *Dec.* 1964.

STOPP, Eric John Carl, C.M.G. 1953; M.B.E. 1941; Consul for the Netherlands in Tasmania, since 1961; *b.* Gawler, S.A., 1894; *o.* *s.* of Richard and Janet Stopp; *m.* 1927, Eileen, *e.* *d.* of S. T. Chancellor, Hobart, Tasmania; two *s.* *Educ.:* Pulteney Grammar School and St. Peter's College, Adelaide. Served in War, 1914-18. Private Secretary

and A.D.C.: to Governor, Tasmania, 1918-1920; to Administrator of Tasmania, 1923-1924; to Governor of Tasmania, 1924-27; Priv. Sec. to Administrator, Norfolk Island, 1927; Official Secretary, 1935-41; Dep. Administrator, 1937-41; Asst. Director of Civil Defence, Tasmania, 1942-44; Official Secretary to Governor of Tasmania, 1944-59. *Recreations:* golf, bowls. *Address:* 19 Beechworth Road, Lower Sandy Bay, Hobart, Tasmania. *T.:* 51662. *Clubs:* Tasmanian, Naval Military and Air Force (Hobart).
[*Died* 1 *Dec.* 1967.

STOREY, Charles Ambrose, M.A.; *b.* Blackhill, Durham, 21 Aug. 1888; *er.* and *o. surv. s.* of late Rev. Thomas Jackson Storey, Vicar of Blackhill; unmarried. *Educ.:* Rossall; Trinity College, Cambridge (Major Scholar). Porson Prize, 1908; Bell Scholar, 1908; Jeremie LXX Prize, 1912; Allen Scholar, 1913; Tyrwhitt Hebrew Scholar, 1914; Mason Hebrew Prize, 1914; 1st Class (Div. I.) Classical Tripos, 1910; 1st Class Oriental Languages Tripos, 1912; Professor of Arabic at the Muhammadan College, Aligarh, India, 1914-19; Assistant Librarian to the India Office, 1919-27; Librarian, 1927-1933; Sir Thomas Adams's Professor of Arabic, Cambridge, 1933-47; Examiner at Cambridge for the Oriental Languages Tripos, 1921, 1934-35, 1940, and for the Ph.D., 1925, and at Oxford, for the B.Litt., 1923. *Publications:* The Fâkhir of Al-Mufaddal, 1915; Persian Literature, a bio-bibliographical survey (in progress), 1927- ; Catalogue of Arabic MSS. in the India Office Library, vol. ii. pt. i., 1930; articles and reviews in Orientalist publications. *Address:* 13 Lawrence Road, Hove 3, Sussex. [*Died* 24 *April* 1967.

STOREY, Harold Haydon, C.M.G. 1948; F.R.S. 1946; M.A., Ph.D. (Cantab.); Retired Research worker; *b.* 10 June 1894; *s.* of Henry and Mary Louisa Storey; *m.* 1930, Molly Everitt; one *d.* *Educ.:* King Williams College, Isle of Man; Gonville and Caius College, Cambridge. Served in Royal Engineers and Royal Air Force, 1914-19; Plant Pathologist in Dept. of Agriculture, Union of South Africa, 1922-28; Plant Pathologist, East African Agricultural Research Institute, Amani, 1928-41; service in various civilian capacities in organising research on war supplies in East Africa, 1941-46; Chairman, E. A. Industrial Research Board, 1944-46; Secretary for Colonial Agricultural Research in the Colonial Office, 1946-48; Dep. Dir. E. African Agriculture and Forestry Research Organisation, 1948-1955; Actg. Dir., 1954-55; Assoc. Mem. Scientific Council for Africa, 1950-54; Member, 1954-56. *Publications:* scientific contributions to British and American journals. *Recreation:* trout fishing. *Address:* P.O. Box 21007, Nairobi, Kenya.
[*Died* 5 *April* 1969.

STORKEY, Percy Valentine, V.C. 1918; LL.B.; Barrister-at-law; Judge, District Court, Northern Circuit, N.S.W., Australia, retired Dec. 1955; *b.* Napier, New Zealand, 9 Sept. 1893; *s.* of Samuel James and Sarah Edith Storkey; *m.* *Educ.:* Boys' High School, Napier; Victoria College, Wellington; Sydney University. Joined 19th Battalion A.I.F. (wounded Fleurs Nov. 1916, and Passchendale, Oct. 1917; Villers Bretonneaux, V.C., 8 April 1918); returned Australia December 1918; admitted student at law, Sydney University, 1913; re-admitted, 1919. *Address:* 20 Trowlock Av., Teddington, Middlesex. *T.:* 01-977 2303.
[*Died* 3 *Oct.* 1969.

STORRAR, Air Vice-Marshal Sydney Ernest, C.B.E. 1944; *b.* 1895; *s.* of Ernest W. Storrar, Leigh-on-Sea, Essex; *m.* 1920, Hilda, *d.* of Jesse Young, J.P., Poole, Dorset; one *d.* European War, 1914-19. Oxford and Bucks Light Infantry, 1916; transferred R.F.C. 1917; R.A.F. 1918; Wing Comdr. 1938; Group Capt. 1940; Air Commodore, 1943; Acting Air Vice-Marshal, 1944. Director of Organisation (Establishments) at Air Ministry, 1942-1944; A.O. i/c Admin. Transport Comd., 1944-47; retired, 1947. Formerly Director of Civil Aviation, Palestine and Malaya. *Address:* Little Wales, Queen Camel, Yeovil, Somerset. *T.:* Marston Magna 205.
[*Died March* 1969.

STORRS, Rear-Adm. (Retd.) Robert Francis, C.B. 1960; *b.* 14 July 1906; *s.* of late Lieutenant-Colonel R. Storrs, R.A.M.C., Lion House, Teddington; *m.* 1934, Olivia Hope, *d.* of Lieut.-Colonel H. S. White, London; one *s.* two *d.* *Educ.:* Newton College, Devon; Royal Naval Colleges, Osborne and Dartmouth. Joined Royal Navy, 1920. Served War of 1939-45, Submarine H.Q., H.M.S. Foxhound; Underwater Weapons Design. Captain, 1950; Rear-Admiral, 1958. Chief Staff Officer (Technical) and Command Engineer Officer, Staff of Commander-in-Chief, Plymouth, 1958-60. *Recreations:* model railways, photography, gardening. *Address:* Westhayes, Halse, Taunton, Som. *T.:* Bishop's Lydeard 315. *Club:* Somerset County.
[*Died* 23 *Aug.* 1968.

STORRS, William Hargrave, J.P.; *b.* 6 Aug. 1880; *e. s.* of James Storrs, J.P., C.C., Stalybridge; *m.* 1907, Emily Gertrude Pratt; one *d.* *Educ.:* Dinglewood, Colwyn Bay. High Sheriff for County of Denbigh, 1941. *Address:* Bryn-Eithin, Colwyn Bay. *T.:* Colwyn Bay 2754. [*Died* 21 *Aug.* 1964.

STOTT, Major-Gen. Hugh, C.I.E. 1941; O.B.E. 1918; C.St.J. 1940; I.M.S., retd.; *b.* 18 July 1884; *s.* of Dr. Hugh Stott, M.O.H., East Sussex; *m.* 1911, Ethel, *d.* of Fred Crisp, J.P., D.L. Cambs., Friern Barnet, N.; one *s.* one *d.* *Educ.:* Mercers' School; London University. M.D. (London), Gold Medal, 1920; F.R.C.P. (Lond.), 1920; D.P.H. (Lond.), 1920; Indian Medical Service, 1908; Surgeon to Governor of Madras, 1913-14; served European War (1914-15 Star, British War Medal, Victory Medal); Afghanistan, 1919 (Indian General Service Medal with clasp); Persia, 1920 (General Service Medal with clasp); War of 1939-45 (British War Medal, Indian Service Medal); Principal, Professor of Pathology and Physician, King George's Medical College and Hospital, Lucknow, India, 1922-37; Inspector-Gen. Civil Hosps., Bihar Province, 1937-41; Surgeon-Gen. with Govt. of Madras; K.H.P. 1943; retired, 1944; Health Branch, Allied Commission, Austria, 1945-46; Fell. Vienna Univ., 1946; Ministry of Pensions, 1947; Councillor, Eastbourne County Borough, 1950. Silver Jubilee Medal, 1935; Coronation Medal, 1937. *Address:* Skye, The Avenue, Chobham, Nr. Woking, Surrey. *Club:* East India and Sports. [*Died* 23 *May* 1966.

STOURTON, Colonel Hon. Edward Plantagenet Joseph Corbally, D.S.O. 1917; *b.* 24 Mar. 1880; 4th *s.* of 23rd Baron Mowbray and Stourton; assumed additional name of Corbally in 1927, by Deed Poll; *m.* 1934, Beatrice (Bey), *o. d.* of H. E. Page, Wragby, Lincs, and Titchwell, Norfolk; one *s.* one *d.* *Educ.:* Beaumont; Ampleforth. Served South Africa, 1900-1902 (Queen's medal 3 clasps King's medal 2 clasps); European War, 1914-18 (wounded twice, despatches four times, D.S.O.); comd. 1st Bn. K.O.Y.L.I., 1929-32; half pay, 1932; Col. 1933; ret. pay, 1933. *Address:* Arlonstown, Dunsany, Co. Meath. *Clubs:* Boodle's; Kildare St. (Dublin).
[*Died* 6 *March* 1966.

STOW, Vincent Aubrey Stewart, C.I.E. 1934; M.A., I.E.S. (retired); *b.* 27 July 1883; *s.* of late Stewart Smith Stow; *m.* 1912,

Marie Elinor Morler; two *d.* *Educ.:* Winchester College (scholar); Exeter College, Oxford (Classical scholar). Literæ Humaniores, 1906; Assistant Master, Marlborough College, 1906; The Daly College, Indore, 1907; Principal Rajkumar College, Raipur, 1912; Served (Mesopotamia) M.E.F. in I.A.R.O., 1918-19; Principal Rajkumar College, Raipur, 1919-31; Principal The Mayo College, Ajmer, 1931-43; *Publications:* Educational Works, Historical and Geographical. *Recreations:* gardening and bridge. *Address:* The Grange, Goring-on-Thames, Oxon. *T.:* Goring 2628.
[*Died* 21 *April* 1968.

STOWELL, Thomas Edmund Alex., C.B.E. 1949; M.D., F.R.C.S., etc.; Consulting Surgeon, E.M.S.; F.R.S.M.; F.R.I.P.H.H.; Diploma, Industrial Diseases (h.c.), Buenos Aires; Diploma in Industrial Health (h.c.), Soc. of Apothecaries; Hon. Surgeon, Victoria Infirmary, Northwich; Senior Hon. Surgeon and Radiologist, Mid-Cheshire Orthopædic Clinic, Northwich; Traumatic Surgeon Messrs. Brunner Mond & Co. Ltd.; formerly Surgeon, Queen Mary's Hosp., Sidcup; Chm. of British Committee of International Congresses on Industrial Health and Safety; Lecturer and Examiner, St. John Ambulance Association and B.R.C.S.; Member British Social Hygiene Council; Member of House of Laity National Church Assembly; Member of Ministry of Pensions Cttee. on rates of compensation for specific injuries sustained by members of H.M. Forces; *m.* 1913, Lilian, *er. d.* of W. Wagner, Hayle, Cornwall: one *s.* (one *d.* decd.). *Educ.:* St. Paul's; St. Thomas' Hospital, (Tite Scholar); Leeds, Manchester, Liverpool, Newcastle, Zürich, Vienna and Harvard. Held appointments at St. Thomas's Hospital, Royal Southern Hospital, Liverpool, etc.; formerly Lecturer London School of Economics, University of London; formerly Asst. Ophthalmic Surgeon: St. Andrews Hosp., Bromley-by-Bow; Battersea Gen. Hosp.; formerly Chief Medical Officer to Imperial Chemical Industries, Ltd. A founder of Assoc. of Industrial Medical Officers; Chm. of Council of Industrial Medicine, and of Medical Advisory Cttee. of Industrial Welfare Soc.; Hon. Member of American Union of Industrial Medicine; Member of Court of Examiners for Diploma of Industrial Health; Surgeon Specialist, B.E.F.; Surgeon, The Ley and Numsmere Red Cross Hospitals; Member Ross Institute Cttee. on Tropical Diseases; Medical Referee Standard and other Assurance Cos.; Member of Industrial Diseases Sub-Committee, Chemical Employers Federation; Senior Vice-Pres. Congrès International de Sauvetage et de Premier Secours en Cas d'Accidents; Chairman of Children's Committee of London Diocesan Council of Moral Welfare; Chm. British Organising Council for IX International Council Industrial Health, 1948; President Commission Internationale Permanente (Malades de Travail); Vice-President Casualties Union. *Publications:* Some Thoughts and Doubts on the Etiology of Dupuytren's Contracture (Proceedings of XIII International Congress on Occupational Health, New York), 1960; (co-editor) Archiv für Gewerbepathologie und Gewerbehygiene; chapters on injuries to the elbow and injuries to lower extremity in Injuries in Sport; papers to B.M.J., etc., and Proc. of the National Safety First Congress, 1935. *Address:* B3 Archers, Archers Road, Southampton SO1 2ND. *T.:* Southampton 26000. *Club:* Athenæum.
[*Died* 8 *Nov.* 1970.

STRACHAN, Gilbert Innes, C.B.E. 1953; M.D. Glas., Hon. LL.D. Glas. 1954; F.R.C.P. Lond., F.R.C.S. Eng. and Ed., F.R.C.O.G. Emeritus Professor of Obstetrics and Gynæcology, University of Wales; Hon. Consulting Obstetrn. and Gynæcol., United Cardiff Hospitals; *b.* 7 Aug. 1888; *s.* of James Strachan and Agnes Todd; *m.* 1920, Olive, *o. d.* of late F. E. Andrews; one *s.* *Educ.:* Glasgow High School; Glasgow University; London Hospital. Vice-Chm., Board of Governors, United Cardiff Hosps. and Chm. Nursing Cttee., 1948-58; Chm. Medical Advisory Cttee. and Obstetric Advisor, Welsh Regional Hospital Board; President XVth British Congress of Obst. and Gynæcols., Cardiff, 1959; Senior Vice-Pres., R. Coll. of Obstetricians and Gynæcologists, 1952-55; Past Pres., Sect. of Obstet. and Gyn., Roy. Soc. Med; Vice-Pres. B.M.A.; a Vice-Pres. Medical Defence Union; Member Central Consultants' and Specialists' Cttee. and Chm., Hospital Staffing Subcttee., B.M.A.; Member Joint Consultants' Committee; Vice-President, Royal College of Nursing; late Examiner in Obstetrics and Gynæcology to: Univs. of Wales, Birmingham, Bristol and Oxford; Conjoint Bd. in Eng. and R.C.O.G. Capt. R.A.M.C.T.F., 1915-19. *Publications:* Textbook of Obstetrics, 1947; articles in Jl Obstetrics and Gynæcology of the Brit. Empire, B.M.J., Lancet, Proc. Roy. Soc. Med., Indian Med. Jl., Practitioner, Acta Radiologica, Post-Grad. Med. Jl. *Recreations:* music, literature and fine art collecting. *Address:* 29 Cathedral Road, Cardiff. *T.:* Cardiff 29525; Innes, Pwllheli, North Wales. *T.:* Pwllheli 2297.
[*Died* 9 *Dec.* 1963.

STRACHEY, Rt. Hon. (Evelyn) John (St. Loe), P.C. 1946; M.P. (Lab.) West Dundee since 1950 (Dundee, 1945-50); Wing Comdr. R.A.F.V.R.; author; *b.* 21 Oct. 1901; *o. surv. s.* of late John St. Loe Strachey; *m.* 1st, 1929, Esther (who obtained a divorce 1933), *o. d.* of P. F. Murphy, New York; 2nd, 1933, Celia, 3rd *d.* of Rev. A. H. Simpson; one *s.* one *d.* *Educ.:* Eton College; Magdalen College, Oxford. Contested Aston Manor Division of Birmingham, 1924; M.P. (Lab.) Aston Division of Birmingham, 1929-1931; resigned from Parliamentary Labour Party 1931; contested Aston (Ind.) 1931; adopted Labour Candidate for Dundee, 1943; Parliamentary Under-Secretary of State, Air Ministry, 1945-46; Minister of Food, 1946-1950; Secretary of State for War, 1950-1951. *Publications:* The Coming Struggle for Power, 1932; The Menace of Fascism, 1933; The Nature of Capitalist Crisis, 1935; The Theory and Practice of Socialism, 1936; What Are We to Do?, 1938; A Programme for Progress, 1940; A Faith to Fight For, 1941; Post D, 1941; Arise to Conquer, 1944; Contemporary Capitalism, 1956; The End of Empire, 1959; The Strangled Cry, 1962; On the Prevention of War, 1962, etc. *Recreations:* tennis, walking, cricket. *Address:* 12 Wellington Square, S.W.3.
[*Died* 15 *July* 1963.

STRACHEY, Philippa, C.B.E. 1951; Hon. Secretary, The Fawcett Society, 27 Wilfred Street, S.W.1; Governor of Bedford College for Women, Univ. of London; *b.* 1872; *d.* of late Lt.-Gen. Sir Richard Strachey, R.E., G.C.S.I., F.R.S., LL.D. *Address:* Lord's Wood, Marlow, Bucks. [*Died* 23 *Aug.* 1968.

STRAFFORD, Air Marshal Stephen Charles, C.B. 1944; C.B.E. 1941; D.F.C. 1918; retired; *b.* 21 Nov. 1898; *s.* of late John Harrison Strafford; *m.* 1923, Nora Edna, *d.* of W. J. H. Whittall, and *g. d.* of late Sir James Whittall; one *s.* one *d.* *Educ.:* Thames Nautical Training College, H.M.S. Worcester. Served European War, 1914-18, R.N.A.S. and Royal Air Force, Italy and Albania (despatches, D.F.C. and Al Valore Militare); Peace service Mediterranean, Black Sea, Palestine, Egypt, Air Ministry, Staff College, Imperial Defence College; War of 1939-45, No. 2 Mission in France, commanded advanced operational Headquarters (North), British Air Forces in France (despatches, C.B.E.), 1939-40; Air

Staff, Plans and Operations, Jt. Staff, Anti-Invasion H.Q., Home Forces, 1940; Dep. Dir. of Plans, Air Ministry, 1940-41; Head British Air Planner, Combined Chiefs of Staff, Washington, D.C., 1941-42; Combined Planning Staff, COSSAC, 1943; Chief of Operations and Plans, H.Q., Advanced A.E.A.F., 1944 (C.B., despatches, Legion of Honour, Croix de Guerre with Palm); Air Officer in Charge Administration Middle East, 1944-45; A.O.C., R.A.F. in Iraq and Persia, 1945-47; Senior Air Staff Officer, H.Q. Bomber Command, 1947-50; Commandant-General of the R.A.F. Regiment, 1950-52; Inspector-General of the R.A.F., 1952-54. Founder Chairman, R.A.F. Equitation Association. *Address:* Dragon Close, Haddenham, Bucks. *T.:* Haddenham 265. *Club:* United Service. [*Died* 18 *May* 1966.

STRAKER-SMITH, Sir Thomas D., Kt. *cr.* 1953; *b.* Hawkes Bay, New Zealand, 3 March 1890; *e. s.* of late W. H. Smith, Rotorua, New Zealand; *m.* 1920, Edith Helen, *d.* of late J. H. Straker, Howden Dene, Corbridge, Northumberland; took name of Straker-Smith by deed poll, 1920; one *s.* one *d.* *Educ.:* Canterbury College, N.Z. Bachelor of Engineering N.Z. University, 1913; came to England, 1914; served European War with Northumberland Hussars, and on staff of 3rd Div. B.E.F., 1914-18 (despatches). Alderman, Northumb. C.C.; J.P. and High Sheriff, 1938; D.L. 1953. *Address:* Carham Hall, Cornhill-on-Tweed, Northumberland. *T.:* Birgham 210. *Clubs:* M.C.C.; Northern Counties (Newcastle upon Tyne). [*Died* 6 *April* 1970.

STRANG, John Martin, C.B.E. 1966; D.Sc. (Glasgow); Chairman and Managing Director, Barr and Stroud Ltd., Glasgow, 1965-1968; *b.* 12 Jan. 1888; *s.* of Matthew William Strang; *m.* 1913, Margaret May MacLeod Harvey; one *s.* two *d.* *Educ.:* Allan Glen's School, Glasgow; Glasgow University. Director of Barr and Stroud Ltd., Glasgow, 1917-; Jt. Man. Director and alternate Chairman, 1950-65. Member of Court, Glasgow Univ., 1953-, Strathclyde Univ., 1964-67; Governor, Royal Coll. of Science and Technology, 1950-64; Mem. Gov. Body, Boys' Brigade, 1929-67 (Vice-Pres., 1947-67). J.P., County of Dunbarton. *Recreations:* walking, bird-watching. *Address:* 18 Ledcameroch Road, Bearsden, by Glasgow. *T.:* 041-942 0177. *Clubs:* Conservative, Royal Scottish Automobile (Glasgow). [*Died* 28 *Jan.* 1970.

STRANGE, Lieut.-Col. Louis Arbon, D.S.O. 1919; O.B.E. 1945; M.C., D.F.C. R.A.F., retired; Actg. Group Capt. R.A.F.V.R.; a Director of Spartan Aircraft; *b.* 1891. Served European War, 1914-19 (despatches, D.S.O., D.F.C., M.C.); War of 1939-45 (Bar to D.F.C.). *Publication:* Recollections of an Airman, 1933. *Address:* c/o R.3 Section, Lloyds Bank, Cox & Kings, 6 Pall Mall, S.W.1. [*Died* 15 *Nov.* 1966.

STRATHALMOND, 1st Baron, *cr.* 1955, of Pumpherston, Co. Midlothian; **William Fraser,** Kt., *cr.* 1939; C.B.E. 1918; Chairman of British Petroleum Co. Ltd., 1941-56 (Director, 1923. Deputy Chairman, 1928); *b.* 3 November 1888; *s.* of William Fraser; *m.* 1913, Mary (*d.* 1963), *d.* of Thomson McLintock, Glasgow; one *s.* one *d.* *Educ.:* Glasgow Acad.; Royal Technical Coll., Glasgow. Hon. LL.D. (Birmingham Univ.). K.St.J. Officer of the Legion of Honour 1953. *Heir:* *s.* Hon. William Fraser, C.M.G., O.B.E., T.D. *Address:* 42 Cumberland Terrace, N.W.1. *Club:* White's. [*Died* 1 *April* 1970.

STRAUSS, Eric Benjamin, M.A., D.M., B.Ch. (Oxon); F.R.C.P.; Hon. D.Sc. (Frankfurt); Consulting Physician for Psychological Medicine, St. Bartholomew's Hospital; late Lecturer in Psychological Medicine, St. Bart's Medical College (London University); Consulting Physician for Psychological Medicine, Northern Middlesex Hospital; Consultant Psychiatrist, Besford Court Catholic Residential Special School and Certified Institution; Hon. Cons. Psychiatrist, Hospital of St. John of God, Stillorgan; Phys. for Psych. Med., St. Andrew's Hospital, Dollis Hill; late Pres., British Branch International Gen. Medical Soc. for Psychotherapy; F.B.Ps.S., President 1956-57; late Chm., Medical Sect., and Member, Council, F.R.Soc. Med. (President Sect. of Psychiatry, 1953-54); Fellow Med. Soc. of London; Hon. Sec. to Cttee. of Psycholog. Med., and Croonian Lecturer for 1952, R.C.P.; Corresp. Mem., Assoc. German Neurologists and Psychiatrists; *b.* London, 18 Feb. 1894; *y. s.* of late Siegfried Strauss and late Elizabeth Berens; unmarried. *Educ.:* Cothill House, nr. Oxford; Oundle; Univ. Coll. School; New Coll., Oxford. After leaving school, travelled abroad to study foreign languages; served in Infantry during European War of 1914-18 at home and in the field (Captain, D.C.O. Middlesex Regt.); read Mediæval and Modern Languages and later Medicine at Oxford Univ. after war; later proceeded to King's College Hospital; M.A., 1930; B.A., 1921; D.M., 1930; B.M., B.Ch., 1924; F.R.C.P., Lond., 1939; M.R.C.P., 1926; studied psychological medicine at Marburg Univ., 1930-31; Examiner (D.P.M.), R.C.P., 1939-43; Ext. Examiner in Psychological Medicine, Nat. University of Ireland. *Publications:* Reason and Unreason in Psychological Medicine, 1953; Psychiatry in the Modern World, 1958; (with W. Russell Brain) Recent Advances in Neurology, 1929, 3rd ed. 1934, 5th edn. 1945, 6th edn. 1955; The Psychology of Character (Translated and Introd.), 1930; A Textbook of Medical Psychology (Trans. and Introd.), 1934, revised edn., 1952; (jointly) Sexual Disorders in the Male, 1954; Hypnotism, in Encyclopædia of Medical Practice (Ed. Sir Humphrey Rolleston), 1938; Psychotherapy, Religion and Science, 1940; papers to B.M.J., Lancet, Month, Dublin Review, etc. *Recreations:* music, foreign travel, mountain-walking. *Address:* 45 Wimpole St., W.1. *T.:* Welbeck 3676. *Clubs:* Savile, Royal Automobile. [*Died* 11 *Jan.* 1961.

STREET, Arthur George; Farmer, Author, and Journalist; *b.* 7 Apr. 1892; *s.* of late Henry and Sarah Anne Street, Ditchampton Farm, Wilton, Salisbury, Wilts; *m.* 1918, Vera Florence Foyle; one *d.* *Educ.:* Dauntsey's Sch., West Lavington, Devizes. Farmed at home until eighteen years old; emigrated to N.W. Manitoba, September 1911; worked there as farm labourer until 1914; came home rejected for army, farmed with father until his death in 1917; took over farm 1918; began writing 1931 as hobby; lectures on Agricultural policy at leading universities and political colleges; Hon. Pres., Edinburgh Univ. Agricultural Society, 1935; Lecture tour through Canada and Western States of America, 1937; Broadcasts talks on countryside. Also television programmes. *Publications:* Farmer's Glory, 1932; Strawberry Roan, 1932; Hedge Trimmings, 1933; Land Everlasting, 1934; Country Days, 1933; Endless Furrow, 1934; Thinking Aloud, 1934; To be a Farmer's Boy, 1935; Country Calendar, 1935; The Gentleman of the Party, 1936; Moonraking, 1936; Farming England, 1937; Already Walks Tomorrow, 1938; A Year of my Life, 1939; A Crook in the Furrow, 1940; Wessex Wins, 1941; From Dusk Till Dawn, 1943; Hitler's Whistle, 1943; Ditchampton Farm, 1946; Holdfast, 1946; Landmarks, 1949; In His Own Country, 1950; Shameful Harvest, 1952; Kittle Cattle, 1954; Feather-Bedding, 1954; Sweetacres, 1956; Master of None

1956; Bobby Bocker, 1957; Cooper's Crossing, 1962; Fish and Chips, 1964; Johnny Cowslip, 1964; as James Brian (Pen-name) Fair Enough, 1962. *Recreations:* shooting, contract bridge, salmon and trout fishing. *Address:* Mill Farm, South Newton, Salisbury, Wilts. *T.A.:* Street, South Newton. *T.:* Wilton 3153. *Clubs:* Savage, Farmers'. [*Died* 21 *July* 1966.

STREET, Fanny, M.A. Lond.; *b.* 21 Nov. 1877; *e. d.* of late Henry and Sarah Anne Street of Wilton, Wiltshire. *Educ.:* Salisbury and Whitelands Training Colleges; Royal Holloway College, University of London. Junior Lecturer, Whitelands College, Chelsea, 1900-02; Lecturer in History and Assistant Mistress of Method, Salisbury Training College, 1902-05; Head of Staff and Mistress of Method, Barnard's Cross, Salisbury, T.C., 1907-11; Staff Lecturer in History, Royal Holloway College, University of London, 1911-17; Assistant Administrative Officer, Ministry of Food, 1917-1918; Organising Secretary, Teachers' Christian Union, 1918-20; Principal, Residential College for Working Women, Hillcroft College, Surbiton, 1920-33; Acting Principal of Royal Holloway College, University of London, Session 1944-45; Member: British Federation of University Women; National Trust. *Publications:* Relations of Bishops and Citizens of Salisbury, reprinted from the Wilts Archæological Journal; The Faith of a Teacher; The Creative Life; various articles on Education and Religion. *Recreations:* gardening, music. *Address:* 70 Lynch Road, Farnham, Surrey. [*Died* 20 *March* 1962.

STREET, Reginald Owen, M.A., M.Sc.; Professor Emeritus, 1951; *b.* Christchurch, Hants, 1 Jan. 1890; 2nd *s.* of late Alfred James Street; *m.* Alice Emily, 2nd *d.* of late Henry Taylor, Cudworth, Yorkshire. *Educ.:* Bournemouth School; St. John's College, Cambridge (Fellow). Lecturer Univ. Coll., Southampton and University of Liverpool; Professor of Mathematics, The Royal Technical College, Glasgow, 1934-51. *Publications:* contributions to scientific journals. *Address:* 12 Lombard Avenue, Southbourne, Bournemouth. *T.:* Bournemouth 48432. [*Died* 24 *Aug.* 1967.

STREET, Maj.-Gen. Vivian Wakefield, C.M.G. 1962; C.B.E. 1958 (O.B.E. 1941); D.S.O. 1944; M.C. 1938; J.P.; *b.* 24 Oct. 1912; *s.* of late Col. Harold Street, D.S.O., Hythe, Kent; *m.* 1945, Annette Mary Lever, *d.* of John Fitzgerald Crean, Gateacre, nr. Liverpool; three *d.* *Educ.:* Wellington; R.M.C. Sandhurst. Commissioned 2nd Lieut., Devon Regt., 1932. Served Palestine, 1938 (M.C.). Served War of 1939-45 (O.B.E., D.S.O., P.O.W.): Rifle Bde. and S.A.S. Regt., Greece, Africa, and Special Forces, Yugoslavia. Mil. Adviser to King Hussein of Jordan, 1959-61; G.O.C. 3 Div., 1961-62; retired, 1963. Lieut.-Col. 1942; Brigadier, 1954; Maj.-Gen. 1961. Mem., Nat. Hunt Cttee., 1967; Chm. Save the Children Fund, 1967. J.P. 1966. C.St.J. 1960. Star of Jordan, 1961. *Recreations:* fishing, racing. *Address:* White House, East Claydon, Bletchley, Bucks. *T.:* Winslow 2559. *Club:* Boodle's. [*Died* 4 *April* 1970.

STREETER, Wilfrid A., D.O.; osteopathic specialist; *b.* Sturbridge, Mass., U.S.A., 25 Oct. 1877; *s.* of Emory Smith Streeter and Hannah Redding. *Educ.:* Worcester Academy, Worcester; Worcester Polytechnic; Brown Univ., U.S.A.; American School of Osteopathy, Kirksville, Missouri. Practised in Worcester and Boston, Mass., U.S.A., 1902-7; as Chairman of the Legislative Committee of the Massachusetts Osteopathic Association, 1904-5; was instrumental in promoting first law for legal regulation of osteopathy in that State, and legalising the degree of D.O.; came to Great Britain in 1907 and settled in Glasgow, where he conducted for seventeen years the pioneer practice of osteopathy in Europe; initiated Parliamentary discussion of the legal status of Osteopathy in Britain, March 1925; founded Osteopathic Defence League, 1929, initiated first Bill in House of Commons, 1931; leading witness before Select Committee of House of Lords on Osteopaths Registration Bill, 1935; First Chairman, General Council and Register of Osteopaths, 1936. *Publications:* The New Healing, 1929; Ambulant Proctology, 1932; numerous articles on the cure of deafness by finger surgery, hay fever, asthma, and allied catarrhal affections, also on the legal recognition of osteopathy. *Recreations:* golf, fishing, motoring. *Address:* c/o Lloyds Bank Ltd., St. Helier, Jersey, Channel Islands. [*Died* 16 *April* 1962.

STRETTON, His Honour Judge Leonard Edward Bishop, C.M.G. 1956; Senior Judge, County Courts, Victoria, and Chairman, Courts of General Sessions, Victoria, Australia; *b.* Brunswick, Vic., 10 Oct. 1893; *m.* Norah Helen, *d.* of Rev. E. A. Crawford, Brighton, Vic.; two *s.* one *d.* *Educ.:* Melbourne University. Admitted to Bar, 1919; partner, Herman and Stretton, Solicitors; Judge, 1937. Royal Commissioner on Bush Fires, Victoria, 1939. Sometime President of Industrial Appeals, Judge of Marine Courts, Chairman of Workers' Compensation Board, Victoria. *Address:* Broad Gully Road, Diamond Creek, Victoria, Australia. [*Died* 16 *May* 1967.

STRIBLING, Thomas Sigismund; Novelist; *b.* Clifton, Tennessee, 4 March 1881; *s.* of Christopher C. Stribling and Amelia Waits; *m.* 1930, Louella Kloss. *Educ.:* Normal College, Florence, Alabama. Taught novel-writing in Columbia University in 1936 and in 1940. *Publications:* Birthright; Teeftallow; Bright Metal; Red Sand; Fombombo; Clues of the Carribees; Strange Moon; The Forge; The Store (Pulitzer Prize, 1932); Unfinished Cathedral, 1934; The Sound Wagon, 1936; These Bars of Flesh, 1938. *Recreations:* tennis, chess. *Address:* Clifton, Tennessee, U.S.A. [*Died* 8 *July* 1965.

STRICKLAND, Claude Francis, C.I.E. 1930, Indian Civil Service (retired); *b.* 19 Dec. 1881, *s.* of late Robert Strickland, Gerrards Cross, Bucks; *m.* Dorothy, *d.* of late George Branson, F.R.C.S., The Manor House, Rockingham, England; two *d.* *Educ.:* Winchester; New College, Oxford. Indian Civil Service, 1905-30; Registrar of Co-operative Societies, Punjab, 1915-20 and 1922-27; Commissioner of Northern India Salt Revenue, 1921-1922; Economic duty in British Malaya, 1929; Palestine, 1930; East Africa, 1931; West Africa, 1933; China, 1934; Delegate to International Institute of Agriculture, 1926: Lecturer for Foreign Policy Association U.S.A. 1930; Lecturer in Indian Social Welfare, Oxford, 1937-41. *Publications:* Introduction to Co-operation in India, 1922; Studies in European Co-operation, 1925; Co-operation for Africa, 1933; Rural Welfare in India, 1936. *Address:* Goldhill Manor, Lower Bourne, Farnham, Surrey. *T.:* Frensham 528. [*Died* 30 *Jan.* 1962.

STRICKLAND, Hon. Mary C. E. C.; *see* Hornyold-Strickland.

STRICKLAND, Captain Paul Sebring, C.B.E. 1941; R.N retd.; *b.* 25 Nov. 1885; *y. s.* of Manuel P. Strickland; *m.* 1916, Janet Margaret (*d.* 1961), *e. d.* of John Alexander Hodgson, O.B.E.; one *d.* *Educ.:* Montpelier School, Paignton; Newton College. Joined R.N. as Assistant Clerk R.N. 1903; Paymaster Commander, 1924; Paymaster Captain, 1935; retired, 1940; Port Accountant Officer, The Nore, 1939-1940; Command Accountant Officer Western Approaches, 1941-43; Supply Officer R.N. College, Eaton Hall, 1943-45. *Address:*

29 Manor Road, Henley-on-Thames, Oxon. *T.:* Henley 1652. [*Died* 9 *May* 1964.

STROHMENGER, Sir Ernest John, G.B.E., *cr.* 1937 (K.B.E., *cr.* 1927); C.B. 1919, Officer, Legion of Honour; Officer, Crown of Italy; *b.* 13 Jan. 1873; 2nd *s.* of late Henry Charles Strohmenger; *m.* Constance Mary Rumbold (*d.* 1960), one *s.* one *d.* Entered Civil Service, 1893; Deputy Comptroller National Health Insurance Commission, 1913; Dep. Accountant-General Ministry of Shipping, 1917; Accountant Gen., Ministry of Health, 1919-30; Deputy Secretary, Ministry of Health, 1930-32; Under Secretary, Treasury, 1932-34; Deputy Chairman Unemployment Assistance Board 1934-37; retired 1937. Member, Expert Cttee., Defence of India, 1938-39. *Recreation:* gardening. *Address:* Elbourne House, Washington, Sussex. [*Died* 17 *June* 1967.

STRONACH, Catherine Geddes, C.B.E. 1928; R.R.C; late Principal Matron of Queen Alexandra's Imperial Military Nursing Service. Served S. Africa, 1900 (Queen's Medal); European War, 1914-19 (despatches twice, R.R.C., and Bar, 1914 star, two medals). *Address:* Fieldcroft, Fairford, Glos. [*Died* 16 *Feb.* 1962.

STRONACH, John Clark, C.M.G. 1942; *b.* 11 Oct. 1887; *s.* of late C. M. Stronach and late Ruth Fairbairn; *m.* 1915, Madge Helen Hemsworth; two *s.* four *d.* *Educ.:* St. Andrew's College and Trinity College, Dublin. Joined Indian Public Works Dept., 1911; Asst. Engineer and Executive Engineer, New Delhi Works, 1913-26; seconded Kenya P.W.D., 1926-30, as Superintending Engineer; transferred Kenya P.W.D. 1930; Director of Public Works, Kenya, 1936; retired, 1946. *Recreation:* gardening. *Address:* Carrig, Killincarrig Delgany, Co. Wicklow. *T.:* Greystones 874121. [*Died* 23 *Feb.* 1967.

STRONGE, Sir Herbert (Cecil), Kt., *cr.* 1930; *b.* Kilkee, Co. Clare, Ireland, 3 Jan. 1875; *er. s.* of S. E. Stronge, M.A., I.S.O., and Minnie L. Stronge; *m.* 1913, Louise, *d.* of R. Harvey, Belfast; two *d.* *Educ.:* Falmouth School; Trinity College, Dublin; Prizeman in Classics and English Literature, B.A. Barrister, Ireland, 1900; joined North-East Circuit, 1901; stipendiary magistrate, Bahamas, 1911; acted as Attorney-General, Bahamas, 1914 and 1915; Chief Justice, Tonga Protectorate, 1917-25; Leeward Islands, 1925-31; Chief Justice of Cyprus, 1931-38. Q.C. (Ire.). *Address:* Fernleigh Hotel, Lambert Rd., Durban, South Africa. [*Died* 22 *Aug.* 1963.

STROSS, Sir Barnett, Kt. 1964; D.Sc., M.B., Ch.B.; retired; Honorary Medical Adviser North Staffordshire Miners Federation and Pottery Workers Society of Great Britain; *b.* 25 December 1899; *s.* of Samuel and Celia Stross; *m.* 1st, 1922, Olive Marion Reade (*d.* 1961); no *c.*; 2nd, 1963, Gwendolen Chesters. *Educ.:* Leeds Grammar School; Leeds University and Medical School. Practised Medicine since 1926 in Stoke-on-Trent. Lectured for Ministry of Food, 1940-44. M.P. (Lab.) Hanley Division, 1945-50, Stoke-on-Trent Central, 1950-66. Parliamentary Secretary, Min. of Health, 1964-65. Hon. D.Sc. University of Keele, 1965. Honorary Citizen of Lidice, Czechoslovakia, 1957. Commander Order of White Lion of Czechoslovakia. *Recreations:* chess, music, the fine arts. *Address:* Flat 11A, Thorney Court, Palace Gate, Kensington, W.8. *T.:* Knightsbridge 7411. [*Died* 13 *May* 1967.

STRUGNELL, Surgeon Rear-Admiral (retd.) Lionel Frederick, C.B. 1949; *b.* 1 Oct. 1892; *s.* of W. T. Strugnell, M.D; *m.* 1924, Edythe May Mitchell; one *s.* one *d.* *Educ.:* St. Bartholomew's Hospital, London. M.R.C.S., L.R.C.P., 1915; Royal Navy, 1915; M.B., B.S., London, 1921; Surgeon Lieut.-Comdr., 1921; Gilbert Blane Medal, 1925; Surgeon Comdr., 1926; Surgeon Capt., 1941; Surgeon Rear-Adm., 1947. O.St.J. 1947; K.H.P. 1948-51; Deputy Medical Director-General of the Navy, 1947-51; retired list, 1951. *Recreations:* nothing outstanding. *Address:* Lavender Cottage, Sinah Lane, Hayling Island, Hants. *T.:* Hayling Island 77429. [*Died* 3 *Feb.* 1962.

STRUVE, Dr. Otto; Member, Institute of Advanced Study, Princeton, N.J., since 1960; A. W. Greenway Visiting Professor of Astronomy, California Institute of Technology and Mt. Wilson-Palomar Observatory since 1962; *b.* Kharkov, Russia, 12 Aug. 1897; *s.* of Ludwig Struve; naturalised U.S.A. citizen, 1927; *m.* 1925, Mary Martha Lanning; no *c.* *Educ.:* University of Kharkov, Russia; University of Chicago. Junior Instructor, University of Kharkov, 1919; Assistant, Yerkes Observatory, Univ. of Chicago, 1921; Instructor, Asst. Prof., Assoc. Prof. and full Professor of Astrophysics, 1923-50; Director Yerkes Observatory, Univ. of Chicago and McDonald Observatory, Univ. of Texas, 1932-47; Chairman Astronomy Dept., Univ. of Chicago, 1947-50; Professor of Astrophysics, Chairman of Astronomy Department and Director of Leuschner Observatory, University of California, Berkeley, Calif., 1950-59; Director of National Radio Astronomy Observatory, W. Va., U.S., 1959-1962. Editor, Astrophys. Journal, 1932-1947. Michael Artillery School, Petrograd, Russia, 1916-17; served as Lieut., Field Artillery, Russian Army and White Army, 1917-20. Mem. Nat. Acad. of Sciences, Washington; Pres., Internat. Astronomical Union, 1952-55; For. mem., Royal Society (London and Edin.). Corresp. mem. Paris Acad. Sci.; Roy. Belgian Acad. Sci., etc. Ordre de la Couronne, Belgium, Chevalier, 1939; Commandeur, 1950. Gold Medals: Royal Astronomical Soc., London, 1944; Astr. Soc. Pacific, San Francisco, 1948; Janssen Medal, Paris, 1954. Rittenhouse Medal, Philadelphia, 1954. *Publications:* Stellar Evolution (Princeton), 1950; Elementary Astronomy, 1959; The Universe, 1961; Astronomy of the 20th Century, 1962; about 600 articles in Astrophysical Journal, etc. *Address:* (home) 853 Station Place, Berkeley 7, California, U.S.A. *Club:* Faculty (Univ. of California). [*Died* 6 *April* 1963.

STUART, Rear-Admiral Charles Gage, D.S.O. 1920; D.S.C.; *b.* 2 Feb. 1887; *s.* of William Stuart, Ballyhivistock, Dervock, Co. Antrim, N. Ireland, and Barbara Frances, *d.* of Lt.-Col. Gardiner Harvey; *m.* 1916, Elizabeth, *d.* of Ernest Buckland, Hurlingham, Buenos Aires; two *s.* two *d.* Served European War, 1914-19 (despatches, D.S.O., D.S.C.); Commanded H.M.S. Curlew, 1930-32; Captain of Dockyard, Malta, 1932-35; Captain of Chatham Dockyard, 1935-37; Captain-in-charge, H.M. Dockyard, Simonstown, S. Africa, 1937-40; Rear-Admiral, 1940; Flag Officer-in-charge, Invergordon, 1940; Flag Officer-in-charge, Aberdeen, 1941; Flag Officer, East Africa, 1942-44; Senior Naval Officer of the Channel Islands Relief Force, 1945. *Address:* Ballyhivistock, Plettenberg Bay, Cape Province, S.A. [*Died* 2 *July* 1970.

STUART, Dorothy Margaret; author; *o. d.* of David Browne J.P., and Georgina Grace, *y. d.* of George Gordon Stuart, Ballindalloch, Banffshire; assumed her mother's maiden name of Stuart by deed-poll, 1933; unmarried. *Educ.:* at home, mainly by her mother. Began to write lyrics and romances (of sorts) in the nursery, and to contribute verse to leading periodicals at a very early age; by her cycle of Sword Songs won for Great Britain the silver medal of the International Literary Contests of the Eighth Olympiad, 1924; F.R.S.L. Contributor (1938-51) to the Year's Work in English Studies. Giff Edmonds Memorial Lecturer, R.S.L., 1949. *Publications:* Beasts Royal and other Poems, 1923; Historical Songs and Ballads, 1925; Sword Songs, 1925; The Boy through the Ages, 1926; Horace Walpole (English Men of Letters), 1927; Men and Women of the Middle Ages, 1928; England's Story, 1929; Christina Rossetti (English Men of Letters), 1930; Men and Women of Plantagenet England, 1931; The Girl through the Ages, 1933; Molly Lepell, Lady Hervey, 1936; An Interlude in Porcelain (with E. V. Davenport); King George the Sixth, 1937; The Daughters of George III, 1939; A Child's Day, 1941; The Mother of Victoria, 1942; Historic Cavalcade, 1942; Regency Roundabout, 1943; The Children's Chronicle, 1944; The English Abigail, 1946; The Young Clavengers, 1947; The Five Wishes, 1950; Daughter of England, 1951; The Mysterious Mamma, 1951; The Story of William the Conqueror, 1952; Portrait of the Prince Regent, 1953; Dearest Bess: the Life and Times of Lady Elizabeth Foster, afterwards Duchess of Devonshire, 1955; London Through the Ages, 1956; A Book of Birds and Beasts, 1957; The Young Rider through the Ages, 1958; A Book of Cats, 1959; The Young Londoner Through the Ages, 1962. Collector, English Association Essays and Studies, 1959. *Recreations:* music, antiquarian pottering, cooking, good company. *Address:* 132 Gloucester Court, Kew, Surrey. *T.:* Richmond 2105. [*Died* 14 *Sept.* 1963.

STUART, Ian Malcolm Bowen; Assistant to President Jefferson Savings & Loan Assoc.; *b.* 18 Sept. 1902; *s.* of late William Henry Stuart (Estates Commissioner for Ireland, 1911-21) and Florence Ann Bowen; *m.* Barbara, *d.* of Reginald Millar, C.B.E., Weybridge, Surrey; one *s.* two *d.* *Educ.:* Malvern Coll.; Trinity Coll., Dublin. M.A., M.R.S.T.; Moderator and Medallist, History and Political Science, 1924; Asst. Master, St. Paul's School, 1925-27; Harrow School, 1927-31 (introduced Rugby Football to Harrow, 1927); Joint Prin., Marcy's, Chancery Lane, 1931-33; Headmaster, Beaminster Grammar School, 1933-35; Headmaster, Portora Royal School, 1935-45; Director of Student Guidance, Mercersburg Academy, Pennsylvania, 1947-49; Dir. Alabama Educational Foundation, U.S.A., 1949-53; Director Public Relations and Education for Southern States Industrial Council, U.S.A., 1953-57; Dir., Community Relations, of the Florists' Telegraph Delivery Association, 1957-64. Member Senate (1936-45) of Queen's University, Belfast; Life Member Headmasters' Conference; Free Lance Journalist leading London papers, 1925-32; Radio News Commentator; Radio Program over many stations; Hon. Sec. to Headmasters' Conference (Southern and Ulster Headmasters' Association); Royal Humane Society Parchment for gallantry; Freedoms Foundn. Award, 1960; Douglas MacArthur Medal, 1964; Daughters of American Revolution and Congress of Freedom Medals, 1966. *Publications:* A Text Book on Rugby Football; Theory of Modern Rugby Football; Reminiscences of a Public Schoolboy; Matriculation English History; Scenes from Shakespeare: Editor of The Simplified Shakespeare Series (8 Volumes); Thoughts for Johnny. *Recreations:* The Georgian Period; collecting Sheraton furniture; represented University in Rugby football, running, and tennis; Irish Rugby football International, 1924; and running International, 1923; selected for British Rugby Tour in S. Africa, 1924. *Address:* 312 Montgomery Highway, Birmingham, Ala., U.S.A. *Club:* Million Miles Flying. [*Died* 3 *Aug.* 1969.

STUART, Captain Murray, D.Sc. Birm.; Ph.D. London; B.Sc. (Rsch.) London; *b.* Liverpool, 5 Nov. 1882; *s.* of George Stuart Wordsley, Staffs.; *m.* Katherine (*d.* 1943), *widow* of Maj. T. Assheton Smith, M.R.C.V.S., R.A.V.C.; one *s.*; 1946, May Howell, late W.A.A.F., Balloon Command; two *s.* *Educ.:* King Edward VI High School, Birmingham (Gymnasium Championship, 1901); Birmingham Univ. Chemist in City of Birmingham Corporation Gasworks, 1905; Acting Lecturer and Demonstrator in Geology in the South Wales University College, Cardiff, 1906; Assistant Superintendent, Geological Survey of India, 1907-11; Indian Education Service as Professor of Geology, Presidency College, Madras, 1911-14; Univ. Lecturer on Oil Geology in Madras Univ., 1913-14; Geological Survey of India, 1914-21; Professor of Geology in the Poona College of Engineering, Bombay, in addition to other duties, 1916-17; Chief Geologist Indo Burma Oilfields (1920), Ltd., 1921-24; Chief Chemist to Improved Hydrocarbon Processes, Ltd., 1929-31; Chief Geologist in Germany to British Borneo Petroleum Syndicate, Ltd., 1932-33; Consultant Wankie Colliery Co. Ltd., 1934-45; Postal Censorship Department, Ministry of Information, 1940; Deputy Asst. Censor, Telegraph Censorship Dept. (C.T.O.), 1941-1945; Temp. Exec. Officer, Foreign Office, 1946-50; Consulting mining and oil geologist; Consultant in the low-temperature treatment of coal and oil-shales. 1st V. B. Royal Warwickshire Regt., 1901-4; Lieut. 1st Calcutta Volunteer Rifles, 1914; Capt. Indian Defence Force, 1917; transferred to 35th Poona Rifles, 1917; transferred to 44th Calcutta Scottish, 1918; served India, 1914-18; Waziristan Campaign, 1919-21; Mahsud Expedition, 1919-20 (despatches); retired with rank of Captain, 1920; Army Officers' Emergency Reserve, 1939. *Publications:* memoirs and papers in publications of Geological Survey of India, Institution of Petroleum Technologists, etc.; The Geology of Oil, Oil-Shale, and Coal, 1926; Low-Temperature Carbonization Explained, 1929; Tin, Salient Facts and Opinions, 1929; The Oil Resources of Germany, 1940. *Recreations:* big-game shooting and fishing. *Address:* Rhyd Dafydd, Rhosgoch, Anglesey. [*Died* 26 *Nov.* 1967.

STUART, Brig.-Gen. W. V.; *see* Villiers-Stuart.

STUBBS, Albert Ernest; Labour Party organiser; Chairman of workers' side of Agricultural Wages Committee; *b.* 1877. Formerly Machinist on a daily paper; Pres. Cambridge Trades Council and Labour Party, 1916; Alderman Cambridge Borough and County, 1942. Contested Cambridgeshire, 1918, 1922 and 1923; M.P. (Lab.) Cambridgeshire, 1945-50. *Address:* 5 Arbury Road, Cambridge. [*Died Feb.* 1962.

STUBBS, William, C.B.E. 1960; M.C. 1942; Sec.-General, Commonwealth Telecommunications Bd., since 1961; *b.* 26 Oct. 1911; *s.* of William James Stubbs and Mary Marsland Stubbs (*née* Stelfox); *m.* 1947, Susan Mary Murless, *d.* of Robert Murless, M.R.C.V.S.; one *s.* one *d.* *Educ.:* Royal Wolverhampton Sch. Engineer, Posts and Telegraphs Dept., S.S. and F.M.S., 1935; Asst. Controller of Telecommunications, 1940; Military Service, 1941-46: Major (M.C.). Controller of Telecommunications, 1949; Dep. Dir.-Gen. of Telecommunications, Fedn. of Malaya and Singapore, 1952-57; Director-General, 1957-1959; a Director, Internat. Automatic Telephone and Electric Co. Ltd., 1960-61. C.Eng.; M.I.E.E.; M.I.E.R.E. Order of Johan Mangku Negara (Malaya), 1958. *Recreations:* tennis, flying, photography. *Address:* The Old Forge Cottage, Winkfield, Nr. Windsor, Berkshire. *T.:* Winkfield Row 2232. *Clubs:* Royal Aero, Royal Commonwealth Society. [*Died* 3 *July* 1967.

STUDDERT, Major-General Robert Hallam, C.B. 1946; D.S.O. 1917; M.C.; *b.* Nov. 1890; *e. s.* of Hallam G. Studdert, Hazelwood, Quin, Co. Clare; *m.* 1930, Maud Lettice Mary, *y. d.* of late Col. Lord John Joicey-Cecil; one *s.* one *d.* *Educ.:* Mostyn House, Parkgate; Clifton College; R.M.A., Woolwich. Entered R.A. 1910; Captain, 1916; Major, 1928; Bt. Lt.-Col. 1932; Lt.-Col. 1937; Brig. 1939; Acting and Temp. Maj.-Gen. 1942-46; served European War, 1914-18 (despatches five times, wounded three times, Bt. Major, 1917, D.S.O., M.C.); Dep. Assistant Director of Mechanisation, War Office, 1932-36; Commanded 4th Field Regiment, R.A., 1937-39; Waziristan Operations, 1937 (despatches); War of 1939-45; Commander R.A. of a Div. 1939-40; Commander Royal Artillery of a Corps, 1940-42; Additional Deputy Master General of the Ordnance in India, 1942-45; A.D.C. to the King, 1944-46; retired, 1946, with hon. rank of Maj.-Gen.; Temp. Civil Servant Board of Trade, 1946-49. *Address:* Clonderlaw, Enniskerry, Co. Wicklow, Ireland. *T.:* Dublin 863533. *Club:* Army and Navy.
[*Died* 2 *Oct.* 1968.

STUDHOLME, Sir Richard Home, Kt. 1962; O.B.E. 1945; Solicitor since 1929; one of H.M.'s Lieutenants for City of London since 1954; Alderman (1954) and Sheriff (1960-61), of City of London; *b.* 7 November 1901; *e. surv. s.* of late Lieut.-Colonel John Studholme, C.B.E., D.S.O., of Coldstream and Middleton, N.Z., and of Alexandra, 4th *d.* of late William Thomson, D.D., Archbishop of York; *m.* 1927, Alice Rosemary, 4th *d.* of late Cecil Wilson, D.D., Bishop of Melanesia; one *s.* one *d.* *Educ.:* Eton; Trinity College, Cambridge (M.A.). Farmed, New Zealand, 1924-26. Served War of 1939-45 in London Scottish and Royal Artillery, 1939-46; Colonel, 1944. O.St.J. 1961; Order of Three Divine Powers (Nepal) 1960; Order of the Lion (Finland) 1961; Order of the Republic (Tunisia) 1961. *Publications:* Electricity Law and Practice, 1934, etc. *Recreations:* fly-fishing, travel. *Address:* 380 Gresham House, Old Broad Street, E.C.2; Pembroke House, Send, Surrey. *Clubs:* Travellers', City University, City Livery, M.C.C. [*Died* 2 *May* 1963.

STURDEE, Rear-Admiral Sir Lionel (Arthur Doveton), 2nd Bt., *cr.* 1916, of the Falkland Isles; C.B.E. 1946; *b.* 3 Sept. 1884; *o. s.* of Admiral of the Fleet Sir Doveton Sturdee, G.C.B., K.C.M.G., C.V.O., L.L.D., 1st Bt. and Marion Adela, *d.* of W. J. Andrews; *S.* father, 1925; *m.* 1910, Dorothy Mary Mowbray (*d.* 1966), *d.* of W. F. Sayer; one *d.* *Educ.:* Stanmore Park; H.M.S. Britannia. Lieut. R.N. 1906; Lieut.-Comdr. 1914; Comdr. 1919; Captain, 1926; Rear-Adm., 1938; served European War, 1914-19; in command of H.M. Ships Forth and Hazard of Dover Patrol (was present in latter when H.M. Hospital Ship Anglia was mined, and received thanks of Army Council for saving life) and later in Grand Fleet; comd. H.M. Ships Calliope, Assistance and Defiance, 1927-32; Flag Captain and Chief Staff Officer, Malta, 1932-34 (Member of Governor's Nominated Council, 1933-34); commanded H.M. Ships Dauntless, 1936, and Resolution, in Home Fleet, 1936-38; Naval A.D.C. to King, 1936-38; retired, 1938; Hon. Wing Commander, General Duties Branch and Commandant, R.A.F.V.R. Cambridge District, 1939; Rear-Admiral (retired) H.M.S. President for special service under the War Office and later under the Ministry of Information as Chief Telecommunications Censor, 1940-45. King Haakon VII Liberty Cross (Norway), 1947. *Heir:* none. *Address:* Brendon, Park Road, Winchester, Hants. *T.:* Winchester 4731. *Clubs:* United Service; Hampshire (Winchester). [*Died* 19 *Dec.* 1970 (*ext.*).

STURDEE, Lt.-Gen. Sir Vernon Ashton Hobart, K.B.E., *cr.* 1951 (C.B.E. 1939; O.B.E. 1919); C.B. 1943; D.S.O. 1916; retd.; Director of Standard Telephones & Cables Pty. Ltd., Sydney, since 1950; *b.* Frankston, Victoria, 16 April 1890; *o. s.* of late Col. A. H. Sturdee, C.M.G.; *m.* 1913, Edith Georgina, *o. d.* of late F. J. Robins, Melbourne; one *s.* one *d.* *Educ.:* Church of England Grammar School, Melbourne. Served articles as Mechanical Engineer; 2nd Lieut. Australian Engineers (Militia), 1908; transferred to Royal Australian Engineers (Regular), 1911; European War, 1914-18, Egypt, Landing and Evacuation Gallipoli, Sinai, France, and Belgium; Staff College, Quetta, 1922-23; General Staff Officer, 2nd Grade, War Office, 1929-31; Imperial Defence College, 1931; Army Representative, Australia House, 1932; Director of Military Operations and Intelligence, 1933-37; Director of Staff Duties, Army Headquarters 1937-39; G.O.C. Eastern Command, Australia, 1939-40; Local Maj.-Gen. and Temp. Lt.-Gen. 1939; Commander 8th Div. A.I.F. 1940; Lieut.-Gen. 1940; Chief of the General Staff, Australia, 1940-42; Head of Australian Military Mission to Washington, 1942-44; Commanded First Australian Army, 1944-45; Chief of General Staff, A.M.F., 1945-50. Retired list, 1950. *Address:* 13 Mernda Road, Kooyong, Melbourne, Australia.
[*Died* 25 *May* 1966.

STURGES, Lieut-Gen. Sir Robert Grice, K.B.E., *cr.* 1945; C.B. 1942; D.S.O. 1943; late Royal Marines (retd.); farming; *b.* 14 July 1891; *s.* of late E. M. Sturges, Barkham, Wokingham; *m.* 1927, Leslie Grace (*d.* 1969), *d.* of late Harry Wiggett, Allanbay Park, Binfield; one *s.* one *d.* *Educ.:* Royal Naval Colleges, Osborne and Dartmouth. Entered Royal Navy, 1908; transferred R.M.L.I. 1912; served European War, 1914-18 at sea and at Gallipoli with R.N. Div.; in command operations 1st occupation of Iceland, 1940, Madagascar, 1942; Commando Group, 1943 (wounded, despatches twice, C.B., D.S.O.); A.D.C. to the King, 1942-43; Lt.-Gen. 1945; retired list, 1946; Hon. Col. Commandant, Plymouth Group, R.M., 1949-53. Commander, with Star, Royal Order of St. Olaf (Norway). *Recreation:* shooting. *Address:* Clyston, Broadclyst, near Exeter, Devon. *Club:* Naval and Military.
[*Died* 12 *Sept.* 1970.

STYLES, (Herbert) Walter; *b.* 4 Apr. 1889; *s.* of Frederick Styles; *m.* 1922, Violet, *o. d.* of Major H. Hawkins, Everdon, Northants; one *d.* *Educ.:* Eton; Exeter College, Oxford. M.P. (U.) Sevenoaks, 1924-29. *Address:* Old Farmhouse, Rodmell, Lewes, Sussex.
[*Died* 5 *Oct.* 1965.

SUDBOROUGH, Professor John Joseph, Ph.D., D.Sc., F.R.I.C.; *b.* Birmingham, 1869; *m.* 1st, Jint, *d.* of W. Hunter, Belfast; 2nd, Elsie Dora, *d.* of A. Bean, formerly Postmaster General, Punjab, India. *Educ.:* King Edward's School, Camp Hill, Birmingham; Mason College, Birmingham; University of Heidelberg; Owens College, Manchester; D.Sc. London; Double First-Class Honours at B.Sc.; Ph.D. Heidelberg. Late Head of Department of General and Organic Chemistry, Indian Institute of Science; Prof. of Chemistry, Director of the Edward Davies Chemical Laboratories and Dean of the Faculty of Science, Univ. Coll. of Wales, Aberystwyth; Senior Lecturer and Demonstrator, Nottingham University College. Pres. Torquay Natural History Society, 1951-53. Hon. Fell. Indian Inst. of Science. *Publications:* Practical Organic Chemistry, various papers of English and foreign journals; Editor in new edition of Bernthsen's Organic Chemistry; Practical Organic Chemistry. *Address:* 2 Georgian Court, Babbacombe Road, Torquay, S. Devon. *T.:* Torquay 3412. [*Died* 25 *July* 1963.

SUGDEN, Gen. Sir Cecil (Stanway), G.B.E. 1960 (C.B.E. 1944; O.B.E. 1940); K.C.B. *cr.* 1955 (C.B. 1946); *b.* 4 December 1903; *s.* of Captain A. Sugden; *m.* 1934, Diana Primrose, *d.* of late General Sir Richard Ford, K.C.B., C.B.E.; two *d.* *Educ.:* Brighton College; Royal Military Academy, Woolwich. Commissioned R.E. 1923; Major, 1940; Major-General 1949; Lieut.-General 1954. Served North Africa, 1942-43 (U.S.A. Legion of Merit, 1943). Dir. of Plans, War Office, 1943-45; Dir. of Military Operations, War Office, 1945-46; Chief of Staff, H.Q., British Troops in Egypt, 1948-49; Director of Personnel Administration, War Office, 1949-51; Chief of Staff, B.A.O.R., 1951-53; Comdr. Brit. Forces, Hong Kong, 1954-55; C.-in-C., Allied Forces, Northern Europe, 1956-58; Quarter-Master-General to the Forces, 1958-61; Master General of the Ordnance, War Office 1962; A.D.C. General to the Queen, 1960-61, retd.; Col. Comdt. R.E. 1960; Col. Comdt. R.A.O.C., 1962. *Address:* 45 Ovington St., S.W.3. *Club:* United Service. [*Died* 25 *March* 1963.

SUGDEN, Kaye Aspinall Ramsden, Barrister-at-law; M.A. (Oxon); *b.* 5 Sept. 1880; *y. s.* of late Richard Sugden, Brighouse, Yorks. *Educ.:* Bradford School; Magdalen College, Oxford (Demy; Akroyd Scholar; 1st Class Classical Moderations). Has been a master at Rugby and other schools. *Publications:* A Short History of the Brontës, 1929; A History of Wantage School. *Recreation:* palaeography. *Address:* c/o Westminster Bank, Wantage, Berks. *Club:* Union (Oxford). [*Died* 3 *Nov.* 1966.

SUHRAWARDY, Huseyn Shaheed, M.A.; *b.* 8 Sept. 1893; *yr. s.* of Sir Zahid Suhrawardy and Khujesta Akhtar Banu Begum; *m.* 1919, *e. d.* of Sir Abdur Rahim (she *d.* 1922); one *d.* (one *s.* decd.); *m.* 1940, Vera Tiscenko (marr. dissolved); one *s.* *Educ.:* Calcutta Madrasah; St. Xavier's College, Calcutta; Oxford University; Gray's Inn. Formerly Dep. Mayor, Calcutta Corp.; Sec. Bengal Provincial Muslim League; member First Bengal Legislative Council, remained a mem. until partition of Indo-Pakistan subcontinent; was a prominent Muslim Leaguer in undivided Bengal. Has held portfolios of Labour, Commerce, Rural Reconstruction, Finance, Public Health and Local Self Government; Food Minister, 1943-45; Chief Minister of undivided Bengal, 1946-47; Organiser and Convenor of Awami League in Pakistan; Minister of Law, Federal Cabinet, Dec. 1954, resigned Aug. 1955; Leader of the Opposition in the National Assembly; Prime Minister of Pakistan, Sept. 1956-Oct. 1957. *Publications:* many political pamphlets. *Recreations:* music, photography, golf, gardening and bridge. *Address:* Lakham House, Karachi, Pakistan. [*Died* 5 *Dec.* 1963.

SULIVAN, Vice-Admiral Norton Allen, C.V.O. 1927; *b.* 23 Jan. 1879; *s.* of late H. N. Sulivan, *s.* of Adm. Sir Bartholomew James Sulivan, K.C.B.; *m.* 1912, Gladys Eva, *yr. d.* of late Leonard James Maton; two *d.* *Educ.:* H.M.S. Britannia. Five first-class certificates in passing for Lieutenant R.N.; Torpedo Lieutenant of H.M.S. Dreadnought in her first commission; Commanded H.M. ships Hope, Moon, and Marksman in Grand Fleet Flotillas during European War, and present at Jutland in last named (despatches); Order St. Stanislaus 2nd Class with Swords, 1917; Commanded H.M.S. Cordelia, Atlantic Fleet, 1919-1921; Director of Torpedo Division, Naval Staff, 1924-2 ; Comd. H.M.S. Renown, 1926-1927, in Atlantic Fleet and during tour round world, and to Australasia of King George VI and Queen Elizabeth when Duke and Duchess of York (C.V.O.); A.D.C. to King George V, 1928; Rear-Admiral and retired, 1928; Vice-Adm., retired, 1932; Lieut.-Col., Comdg. 18th Bn. Hampshire Home Guard, 1941. *Address:* 2 Rectory Close, Alverstoke, Hants. [*Died* 30 *Sept.* 1964.

SULLIVAN, Hon. Sir William, K.C.M.G. 1957; Merchant and Company Director; *b.* 8 Dec. 1891; *s.* of S. J. Sullivan; *m.* 1916, Elvina C. (*d.* 1963), *d.* of J. W. Brayshaw; one *s.* three *d.* (and three *s.* decd.). *Educ.:* Taranaki; I.C. School. Building Contractor and Timber Merchant, Whakatane, 1913-. Served European War, 1916-18, as N.C.O., N.Z. Camp. Chm. Whakatane Harbour Board, 1923-26; Mayor of Whakatane, 1925-38; Borough Councillor, 1938-50; Chm. Unemployment and Relief Organisation, 1930-35. Past Pres. Chamber of Commerce; Past Pres. Winter Show Association. Contested Tauranga seat, 1931; M.P. (National) Bay of Plenty, 1941-57. Minister in Nat. Govt., 1949-57, holding portfolios of Labour, Mines, Immigration, Housing, and Minister in Charge State Advance Corporation. *Recreations:* shooting, fishing. *Address:* McAllister St., Whakatane, N.I., N.Z. *T.:* (private) 59; (business) 819. [*Died* 16 *March* 1967.

SULZBERGER, Arthur Hays; Publisher of The New York Times, 1935-61; President of The New York Times Company, 1935-57; Director since 1935, and Chairman of the Board since 1957, of The New York Times Company, Interstate Broadcasting Company; Director and Chairman of the Board of the Times Printing Company (Chattanooga, Tennessee) since 1957; Chairman of the Chattanooga Publishing Company; *b.* New York, N.Y., 12 Sept. 1891; *s.* of Cyrus L. Sulzberger and Rachel Peixotto Hays; *m.* 1917, Iphigene B. Ochs, New York; one *s.* three *d.* *Educ.:* Public Schools 166 and De Witt Clinton and Horace Mann High School, New York. B.S., Columbia Univ., 1913. Holds numerous honorary doctorates in Laws, Letters, Humanities, Public Service, etc., awarded, 1939-, by Universities, Colleges and Institutions. Started work in a textile business in New York; Second Lieut., Field Artillery, 1st Plattsburg Camp, 1917 In newspaper business since 1919. Director: Amer. Red Cross, New York Central Cttee. (1942-45) and Nat. Bd. of Govs. (1951-52); Spruce Falls Power and Paper Co. Ltd., Toronto (1926-61); The Associated Press (1943-52); The Woodrow Wilson Foundation (1954-57); Soc. of Friends of Touro Synagogue (Nat. Historic Shrine at Newport, R.I.); Amer. Arbitration Soc.; Acad of Polit. Science; American-Korean Foundation; Netherland-America Foundation; Trustee Emeritus: Columbia Univ.; New York Foundation (1932-60); Trustee: The Rockefeller Foundation (1938-57); Metropolitan Museum of Art, etc Fellow, New York Academy of Sciences; Governor, Thomas Jefferson Memorial Foundation; Member: Sons of the American Revolution; Pilgrims of the United States, etc. *Address:* (home) 1115 Fifth Ave., New York, N.Y. 10028; Hillandale, 1233 Rock Rimmon Rd., Stamford, Conn. 06903, U.S.A.; (office) The New York Times, 229 West 43rd St., New York 36, N.Y., U.S.A. *Clubs:* Advertising, Century Association, Columbia, Economic, Grolier, Metropolitan (Washington, D.C.); Mountain City (Chattanooga, Tenn.); Athenæum (London, Eng.). [*Died* 11 *Dec.* 1968.

SUMMERFORD, Engineer Rear-Admiral Horace George, C.M.G. 1919; C.V.O. 1923; *b.* 1872; *s.* of J. S. Summerford; *m.* Ethel (*d.* 1950), 2nd *d.* of Inspector of Machinery John Johnson, R.N.; one *s.* one *d.*; 1951, Mrs. Dorothy Pera Ross, *widow* of William Ewart Ross, Toronto, Canada. *Educ.:* privately, and at Keyham College. Served China War, 1900 (medal); European War, H.M.S. Royal Sovereign, 1914-19 (C.M.G., two medals); H.M. Yacht

Victoria and Albert, 1912-14 and 1919-23; Engineer Captain, 1919; Fleet Engineer Officer, Atlantic Fleet, 1923-25; Eng. Rear-Adm., 1925; Eng. Rear-Adm. on the Technical and Administrative Staff at the Nore, 1925-29; retired, 1929. *Recreation:* golf. *Address:* The Barn, 74 Elm Close, Hayling Island, Hants. [*Died* 22 *Aug.* 1963.

SUMMERSBY, Charles Harold, J.P.; *b.* 1882; *s.* of Rev. B. J. Summersby, Oxfordshire; *m.*, two *s.* one *d.* Mayor of Hornsey, 1930-31; M.P. (L.Nat.) Shoreditch, 1931-35. *Address:* Red Lion Hotel, Henley-on-Thames. *Club:* National Liberal. [*Died* 13 *Aug.* 1961.

SUNLEY, Bernard; Chairman of Blackwood Hodge Ltd. since 1953; Chairman of Bernard Sunley Investment Trust since 1940; *b.* 4 Nov. 1910; *y. s.* of John Sunley and Emily Martha (*née* Coppins); *m.* 1931, Mary Goddard; one *s.* two *d.* *Educ.:* St. Ann's School, Hanwell, Middx. Chairman and Founder: Blackwood Hodge Ltd., 1953 (John Blackwood Hodge, 1939); Bernard Sunley Investment Trust Ltd., 1944; Chairman, Bernard Sunley & Sons Ltd., 1940; Director, Bank of Nova Scotia Trust Co. (Bahamas) Ltd., 1961. Mem. Council, Royal Society of St. George. *Recreations:* golf, horse-racing, swimming. *Address:* 26 Harley Road, N.W.3; 25 Berkeley Square, W.1. *T.:* Mayfair 9090; Vale Farm, Ashton, Nr. Roade, Northants; 1 The Dunes, Sandwich Bay, Kent. *Clubs:* Devonshire, United and Cecil, M.C.C.; Princes Golf; Royal Cinque Ports; Sky Club (New York). [*Died* 20 *Nov.* 1964.

SUTHERLAND, 5th Duke of (*cr.* 1833), **George Granville Sutherland-Leveson-Gower,** K.T. 1929; P.C. 1936; Earl of Sutherland, Baron Strathnaver, 1235; Bt. 1620; Baron Gower, 1703; Earl Gower, Viscount Trentham, 1746; Marquis of Stafford (county), 1786; Lord-Lt. Sutherland, 1913-45; former Hon. Col. 5th Seaforth Highlanders; former Pres. Sutherland T.A. Assoc.; former President British Olympic Association; First President (now Vice-President) National Playing Fields Associations; former President British Group Inter-parliamentary Union; *b.* 29 Aug. 1888; *s.* of 4th Duke and Millicent, Duchess of Sutherland (*d.* 1955); *S.* father, 1913; *m.* 1st, 1912, Lady Eileen Butler (*d.* 1943), *e. d.* of 7th Earl of Lanesborough; 2nd, 1944, Mrs. Clare Josephine Dunkerly. Commander, R.N.R.; served in command of H.M.Y. Catania, North Sea, 1914, and with British Military Mission, Belgium, 1914-15; in command Motor Boat Flotillas, Egypt and Adriatic, 1915-17; represented Colonies in House of Lords, 1921-22; Under-Sec. of State for Air, 1922-23; Lord High Commissioner to the General Assembly of the Church of Scotland, 1921-22; Paymaster-General to H.M.'s Government, 1925-1928; Parliamentary Under-Secretary of State for War, 1928-29; Lord Steward of H.M. Household, 1936-37; President: Air League of the British Empire, 1922-44; Navy League, 1922-24; Grand Prior of the Primrose League, 1922-44; Chm. of Royal Aero Club, 1924-25 (now Vice-Pres.); Pres. Royal Counties Agricultural Soc. Show, Guildford, 1952, Vice-Pres. 1953; High Steward of Roy. Borough of Kingston-upon-Thames, 1953-. Order of the Crown of Italy *Publications:* The Story of Stafford House, 1935; Looking Back (autobiography), 1958. *Heir: kinsman* 5th Earl of Ellesmere, T.D.; (to Sutherland Earldom) *niece* Elizabeth Millicent Janson [*b.* 30 March 1921; *d.* of late Lord Alastair Sutherland-Leveson-Gower]. *Address:* Thatched House Lodge, Richmond Park, Surrey. *T.:* Kingston 6316; Dunrobin Castle, Golspie, and House of Tongue, Sutherland. *Clubs:* Carlton, Turf, Royal Automobile; Royal Yacht Squadron. [*Died* 1 *Feb.* 1963.

SUTHERLAND, George Arthur, M.A. (Cantab.); Principal of Dalton Hall, University of Manchester, 1924-58, retired; late Examr. in Physics to Pharmaceutical Society; *b.* New Deer, Aberdeenshire, 6 Feb. 1891; *s.* of late John Sutherland, M.A.; *m.* 1st, 1916, Christine (*d.* 1941) 2nd *d.* of late W. G. Bell, Trinity Hall, Cambridge; one *s.* two *d.*; 2nd, 1943, Mary Sanders, 5th *d.* of late Frederick Lakeman; one *d.* *Educ.:* Rhodes College, Grahamstown, S. Africa; St. John's College, Cambridge. Lecturer in Physics, University of the Cape, 1913-15; Master at Harrow School, 1915-16; Lecturer in Physics, University College, London, 1919-1924; Special Lecturer in Physics, University of Manchester, 1927-58; sometime Member: Court of Governors of University of Manchester; Privy Council Advisory Committee on Architectural Acoustics; Pres. of Section V. (Acoustics) of the 12th International Congress of Architects at Budapest, 1930; sometime Acoustic Consultant: Wembley Exhibition Concert Hall, Legislative Chamber, New Delhi, Friends' House, London, etc.; Ex-Clerk (Chairman) to Meeting for Sufferings (Executive of the Society of Friends); Ex-Chairman, Society of Friends Education Council; Ex-Pres. Manchester University Mountaineering Club. *Publications:* Dalton Hall, a Quaker Venture, 1963; Papers on Physical Subjects, especially Auditorium Acoustics. *Recreations:* mountaineering, travel. *Address:* Windy How, Colthouse, Hawkshead, Ambleside, Westmorland. *T.:* Hawkshead 282. (*Died* 1 *March* 1970.

SUTHERS, Rev. Canon George; Canon Residentiary of Newcastle Cathedral and Director of Religious Education, Diocese of Newcastle, since 1962; *b.* 3 March 1908; *s.* of William and Mary Suthers; *m.* 1939, Susie Mary Jobson; one *s.* one *d.* *Educ.:* Todmorden Grammar School; Christ's College, Cambridge; Ely Theological College. B.A. 1930, M.A. 1934; Dipl. in Education, 1931. Asst. Master, Oswestry School, 1931-1933; Deacon, 1934; Priest, 1935; Asst. Curate, St. Mark's, Swindon, 1934-37; Chaplain and Lecturer, King Alfred's College, Winchester, 1937-40. C.F. 1940-45. Secretary, Church of England Adult Education Council, 1945-56; Rector of Kegworth, 1956-62. *Recreations:* cricket, music. *Address:* 50 Two Ball Lonnen, Newcastle upon Tyne. *T.:* 33822. *Club:* United University. [*Died* 24 *Dec.* 1965.

SUTTON, Engineer Rear-Adm. Charles Edwin, M.V.O. 1927; *b.* Dec. 1880; *m.* 1st, 1907, Ellen (*d.* 1950), 2nd *d.* of George Cole, Plymouth; one *s.* one *d.*; 2nd 1951, Ruth, *d.* of Robert Hutton Newcastle upon Tyne; one *s.* *Educ.:* R.N.E. College, Devonport. Entered Royal Navy, 1897; Engineer Commander, 1919; Engineer Captain, 1928; Engineer Rear-Admiral and retired list, 1934; served in H.M.S. Indomitable during visit of King George V. to Canada, 1908; European War, 1914-18; served in H.M.S. Renown during visit of Duke and Duchess of York to Australia and New Zealand, 1927; Naval A.D.C. to the King, 1934; War of 1939-46, served on staff of Flag Officer in Charge North East England. *Address:* The Drift Cottage, Park Crescent, Emsworth, Hants. *T.:* Emsworth 2962. [*Died* 15 *Nov.* 1968.

SUTTON, Major-General Evelyn Alexander, C.B. 1947; C.B.E. 1943 (O.B.E. 1941); M.C.; *b.* 14 Sept. 1891; *yr. s.* of late Major-General A. A. Sutton, C.B., D.S.O.; *m.* 1915, Gladys, *d.* of late J. A. Dolton; two *d.* *Educ.:* Berkhamsted School; Charing Cross Hospital, London (Huxley Scholar). M.R.C.S. (England), L.R.C.P. (Lond.), 1914. Served European War, 1914-18, Lieut., 1914; Captain, 1915; Brevet Major, 1919; Major, 1926; Lieut.-Col., 1935; Colonel, 1941; Maj.-Gen., 1945;

France, Belgium and East Africa (wounded, despatches twice. M.C.); War of 1939-45, D.M.S., East Africa Command and Allied Armies in Italy; Dep. Chief Surgeon, S.H.A.E.F.; K.H.S., 1946; late D.D.M.S., H.Q., Northern Command, York; retired, 1948. *Address:* Fairfield, Elphinstone Rd., Highcliffe-on-Sea, Hants.
[*Died* 8 *Jan.* 1964.

SUTTON, George Lowe, C.M.G. 1951; Director of Agriculture, Western Australia, retired; Chairman: Dairy Products Marketing Board, 1936-63, retd.; Merchants' Agricultural Research Trust, 1938-62, retd.; *b.* 23 Oct. 1872; *s.* of Henry Hall Sutton and Ellen Lowe; *m.* 1896, Ada Alice Everington (*d.* 1960); two *s.* four *d.* *Educ.:* Fort St. State Sch., Sydney; Sydney High School. Experimentalist, Hawkesbury Agric. Coll., 1900-05; Manager Cowra Research Station, 1905, and N.S.W. Wheat Experimentalist, 1906-11; Comr. Wheat Belt, W. Australia, 1911-22; Director of Agriculture, W.A., 1922-37. Pres. Roy. Soc. of W.A., 1920; Pres. W.A. Branch Australian Inst. of Agric. Science, 1938; Chm. Grain and Foodstuffs Board in European War, 1914-18; Scientific Liaison Officer, War of 1939-45. Mem. Advisory Cttee., Faculty of Agric., Univ. of W. Australia until 1962, retd. Hon. D.Sc. (Agric.), Univ. of W. Australia, 1937. Hon. Life-mem., Austr. Inst. of Agric. Science, 1953; Hon. mem. Mt. Lawley Rotary of W.A., 1953. *Publications:* Comes the Harvest, 1952; The Basic Principles of Wheat Marketing, 1953; The Modernisation of the F.A.Q. Wheat Marketing System, 1957; Australian Strong White Wheat, 1956; contrib. many articles to Agric. Gazette of N.S.W. and to Agric. Jl. of W. Australia; one article to Economic Record of Australia and N.Z. *Recreations:* reading, photography. *Address:* Riverview, 5 Ellesmere Road, Mount Lawley, Western Australia. *T.:* 71.1161.
[*Died* 11 *Jan.* 1964.

SUTTON NELTHORPE, Colonel Oliver, C.B.E. 1942; D.S.O. 1919; M.C.; D.L., J.P.; *b.* 5 June 1888; *s.* of late R. N. Sutton Nelthorpe; *m.* 1914, Marjorie Elspeth Constable Curtis; two *s.* one *d.* *Educ.:* Eton; R.M.A., Woolwich. Joined Rifle Brigade, 1906; to France with regiment, Aug 1914; served on General Staff in France, 1915-18 (despatches thrice, Brevet-Major, D.S.O., M.C., French Croix de Guerre with 2 palms); served on Gen. Strickland's staff at Cork, 1919-20; retired with rank of Lieut.-Col., 1920; Lt.-Col. 5th Batt. Lincoln Regiment, 1929-33; Colonel 1933; recalled for service on General Staff, 1941-45. *Address:* Scawby, Brigg, Lincolnshire. *T.A.:* Scawby. *T.:* Scawby 205. *Club:* Naval and Military.
[*Died* 25 *May* 1963.

SUTTON-PRATT, Brigadier Reginald, C.M.G. 1946; O.B.E. 1939; Military Attaché, British Embassy, Stockholm, 1939-47; retd. 1948; *b.* 23 April 1898; *s.* of W. Sutton-Pratt, F.R.C.S., L.R.C.P.; *m.* 1922, Mary, *d.* of Col. H. McRae, C.B., A.D.C.; one *s.* *Educ.:* Charterhouse. Commissioned Royal Artillery, 1916; B.E.F. France, 1917-18; transferred Royal Signals, 1923; Assistant Military Attaché, Czechoslovakia, 1938. *Recreations:* golf, tennis, sailing. *Address:* Granen, Belton Rd., Camberley.
[*Died* 1 *Dec.* 1962.

SWAFFER, Hannen; Journalist and dramatic critic; *b.* Lindfield, Sussex, 1 Nov. 1879. *Educ.:* Stroud Green Grammar School. Joined Daily Mail, 1902; sometime Editor of Weekly Dispatch; ten years on Daily Mirror; invented Mr. Gossip for Daily Sketch, 1913; joined Daily Graphic (Mr. London); contributed Plays and Players to Sunday Times; Dramatic Critic to Daily Express, 1926; joined Daily Herald, 1931. *Publications:* Northcliffe's Return; Really Behind the Scenes, 1928; Hannen Swaffer's Who's Who, 1929; Inspiration, 1929. *Address:* c/o Daily Herald, 12 Wilson Street, W.C.2.
[*Died* 16 *Jan.* 1962.

SWAINSON, Major-General Frederick Joseph, C.B. 1965; O.B.E. 1956; Signal Officer in Chief, 1962-65; retd.; *b.* 2 Sept. 1911; *m.* 1938, Agnes (*née* Hendrie); one *s.* *Educ.:* Oldershaw Grammar School, Wallasey. Joined Army (Royal Signals) in ranks, 1929. Served in India, 1931-36; commissioned, 1941. Served in Northwest Europe, Burma, French Indo-China, Malaya and Egypt. Attended Camberley Staff College, 1947. Col. 1958; Brig. 1960; Maj.-Gen. 1962. Col. Comdt., Royal Corps of Signals, 1965-. *Recreations:* riding, golf, music, photography. *Address:* c/o Ministry of Defence, Whitehall, S.W.1; West Court, Westcourt Drive, Bexhill-on-Sea, Sussex. *T.:* Bexhill 5572. *Club:* Junior Army and Navy.
[*Died* 28 *Nov.* 1965.

SWAINSON, Willan, M.A., F.R.C.O., A.R.C.M.; Lecturer in Music, Univ. of Aberdeen, 1925-56, retired; and Director of the Dept. of Music, 1942-56; Reader in Music, 1949-56; *b.* Harrogate; *s.* of William and Mary Swainson; *m.* 1916, Grace Robertson, Newport, Fifeshire; two *s.* one *d.* *Educ.:* Privately. Sub-organist St. Peter's, Harrogate, 1903-6; Organist, Bilton Parish Church, Harrogate, 1906-16; Conductor: Aberdeen Bach Choir, 1917-22; Peterhead Choral Society, 1917-24; Aberdeen Oratorio Choir, 1923-42; Organist and Director of the Choir, West Church of St. Nicholas, Aberdeen, 1937-44; Queen's Cross Church, Aberdeen, 1916-37. *Publications:* numerous articles on music including that on The Use of the Organ in the Church Service (Church of Scotland Praise Manual). *Address:* 12 Fonthill Road, Aberdeen. *T.:* 21886.
Died 28 *Sept.* 1970.

SWAN, Lionel Maynard, C.B.E. 1926; *b.* 11 Jan. 1885; *s.* of late Edgar Augustine Swan, Barrister-at-law; *m.* Margaret Mabel, 2nd *d.* of late Cameron Brodie; one *s.* one *d.* *Educ.:* Christ's Hospital; London University, B.Sc. (Econ.). Served European War, 1914-18; Mesopotamia, 1917-18; Captain 4th Dorsets Territorial (despatches): late Adviser, Ministry of Finance, Iraq; Order of the Rafidain (3rd Class). *Address:* 26 Fairways Road, Seaford, Sussex.
[*Died* 16 *Nov.* 1969.

SWANN, Rev. Canon Alfred, M.A., D.S.C.; Canon Emeritus of Salisbury Cathedral since 1952; *s.* of late Rev. Sidney Swann; *m.* 1923, Katharine Nona, *d.* of late Bishop C. T. Abraham; two *s.* two *d.* *Educ.:* Rugby Sch.; Trinity Hall, Camb. C.U.A.C. Half Blue, 1913; won Colquhoun Sculls, 1920; President C.U.B.C., won University Boat Race; Henley Regatta, won Silver Goblets, 1913 and 1914, and Stewards Challenge Cup, 1914; A.B., R.N.R. (T), Aug. 1914; Sub-Lieut. R.N.V.R., 1915; Lieut. R.N.V.R., H.M. Coastal Motor Boats, 1916; in Zeebrugge Raid, 1918; Assistant Curate, Kirkburton, Yorks, 1921: Vicar of Liversedge, Yorks, 1924; Dean of Hong-Kong, 1928-35; Vicar and Rural Dean of Potterne, Wilts, 1936-41; Rector and Rural Dean of Marlborough, 1941-52; Prebendary in Salisbury Cathedral, 1941-52; Acting Dean of St. John's Cathedral, Newfoundland, 1955; Vicar of Bicknoller, Somerset, 1956-58. *Recreation:* painting. *Address:* The Old Manor House, Combe Florey, Taunton, Somerset. *Club:* Leander.
[*Died* 7 *Oct.* 1961.

SWANN, Rev. Cecil Gordon Aldersey, M.A.; Retired; *b.* 27 May 1888; *s.* of Rev. H. A. Swann; *m.* 1927, Hilda, *y. d.* of late Archdeacon E. O. McMahon, of Madagascar; three *s.* Archdeacon of East Coast, Madagascar, 1924-36; Archdeacon of Imerina, Madagascar, 1936-39; Rector of Rivenhall, 1939-52; Rector of Quendon with Rickling,

1952-59; Asst. Priest, All Saint's, Birchington, 1959-64. *Address:* 15 St. Mildred's Avenue, Birchington, Kent. [*Died* 28 *March* 1969.

SWANN, Sir (Charles) Duncan, 2nd Bt., *cr.* 1906; *b.* 27 Jan. 1879; *e. s.* of Rt. Hon. Sir C. E. Swann, 1st Bart., and Elizabeth (*d.* 1914), *d.* of David Duncan, Manchester; *S.* father 1929; *m.* 1909, Dorothy Margaret, *d.* of late Capt. R. H. Johnson; one *s.* *Educ.:* Eton; Balliol College, Oxford (M.A.). Barrister-at-law; called to Bar, Inner Temple, 1904; M.P. (L.) Hyde Division of Cheshire, 1906-9. *Publications:* The Book of a Bachelor, 1910; The Magic of the Hill, 1911; Molyneux of Mayfair, 1912; A Country House Comedy, 1914; A Villa in the South, 1919; The Book of a Benedict, 1923. *Recreations:* travel and reading. *Heir: s.* Anthony Charles Christopher Swann, C.M.G., O.B.E [*m.* 1940, Jean Margaret Niblock-Stuart; one *s.*]. *Address:* Rudge Hall, Pattingham, Wolverhampton. *Clubs:* Carlton, Beefsteak. [*Died* 10 *March* 1962.

SWANN, William Francis Gray, D.Sc. 1910; A.R.C.S., 1906; Director of Bartol Research Foundation of the Franklin Institute 1927-59 (Emer. 1959); *b.* 29 Aug. 1884; *s.* of William Francis and Anne Evans Swann; *m.* 1st, 1909, Sarah Frances Mabel Thompson; two *s.* one *d.*; 2nd, 1955, Helene Laura Diedrichs. *Educ:* Technical Coll., Brighton; Roy. College of Science; University College, King's College, City and Guilds of London Institute. Junior demonstrator in physics at the Royal College of Science, 1905-07; assistant lecturer and demonstrator in physics at the University of Sheffield, 1907-13; came to United States in 1913; chief of physical division of the Department of Terrestrial Magnetism, Carnegie Institution of Washington, 1913-18; professor of physics at the University of Minnesota, 1918-23; at the University of Chicago, 1923-24; at Yale University, 1924-1927; director of the Sloane Laboratory, Yale University, 1924-27; chairman of the advisory research committee of the Bartol Research Foundation of the Franklin Institute, 1924-27; Senior Consultant for Research and Development Laboratories of Franklin Institute, 1945- ; Pres. American Physical Soc., 1931-33; Sec. American Philosophical Soc., 1939-46, Councillor, 1939-42; Mem. numerous scientific philosophical and geophysical socs.; Elector, Hall of Fame, N.Y. Univ., Gamma Alpha, Sigma Xi, Sigma Pi Sigma; Tan Beta Pi; Associate Editor of Jl. of Franklin Inst. Hon. M.A., Yale, 1924; Hon. D.Sc., Swarthmore, 1929; Hon. D.Litt., Temple, 1954; Fell. Imperial Coll. of Sci. and Tech., London; Hon. F.T.C.L. Elliot Cresson Gold Medal, Franklin Inst., 1960. *Publications:* The Story of Human Error (joint), 1936; The Architecture of the Universe, 1934; Physics, 1941; numerous publications in various scientific journals; also three articles to Encyclopedia Britannica. *Recreations:* music, 'cellist, former Conductor, Swarthmore Symphony Orchestra, tennis, golf. *Address:* 609 Ogden Avenue, Swarthmore, Pa., U.S.A.; Bartol Research Foundation, Whittier Place, Swarthmore, Pa., U.S.A. *T.:* Kingswood 3-1539. *Clubs:* Cosmos (Washington); Explorers', Yale (New York); Art Alliance (Philadelphia, Pa.); Great Chebeaque Golf (Maine). [*Died* 29 *Jan.* 1962.

SWARBRICK, John, F.S.A.; F.R.I.B.A.; M.I.Struct.E.; *b.* 22 May 1879; *o. s.* of late Alderman Joseph Swarbrick, F.R.I.B.A., M.Inst.C.E., Manchester; *m.* 1926, Beatrice, *d.* of Alfred Neill, Colwyn Bay. *Educ.:* Manchester University; Royal Academy of Arts, London, etc. Practising as an architect and specialist in the measurement of daylight in London and the provinces; Inventor of the Radial Calculating Sheets, the Daylight Factor Phototheodolite, and grilles; Member of Council R.I.B.A., 1939-49, and their representative on Joint Committee on School Lighting, 1930-31; at the International Illumination Congress in 1931; and on Cttee. on the Law of Ancient Light, 1932; Formerly: Vice-Pres. Ancient Monuments Soc.; Dir., National Home Industry Council; Member Ancient Monuments Committees for Lancashire and Cheshire under H. M. Ancient Monuments Board (England); Hon. Sec. National Amenities Council; Past Pres. Lanc. and Ches. Antiqn. Soc., Emergency Works Officer, Ministry of Works and Buildings, 1941; Chief Technical Officer, Factory Control, Bd. of Trade, 1942-43. Codes of Practice Council (Dept. of Sci. and Indust. Research), 1945-47. F.R.S.A. *Publications:* Robert Adam and his Brothers, 1915; Easements of Light, 1930-33 (2 vols.); Synopsis of modern practice, 1938, Daylight, 1953; England's Tribute to the Architects and Craftsmen of France; The Dawn of Civilisation, etc.; articles on architecture, measurement of daylight, craftsmanship, and social welfare; formerly Editor of the National Ancient Monuments Handbook, The National Ancient Monuments Review, etc. *Address:* Harlyn, 206 Dinerth Road, Rhos-on-Sea, Colwyn Bay, N. Wales. *Clubs:* National Liberal; Reform (Manchester). [*Died* 19 *Oct.* 1964.

SWARBRICK, Thomas, C.B.E. 1964; Director, Scottish Horticultural Research Institute, Invergowrie, Dundee, since 1951; *b.* 8 Jan. 1900; *s.* of William Swarbrick and Margaret (*née* Lawrenson); *m.* 1924; three *s.* one *d.* *Educ.:* Leeds University (B.Sc. 1st Cl. Hons., M.Sc., Ph.D.). Physiologist and Pomologist, Long Ashton Agricultural and Horticultural Research Inst., 1926-45; Research and Development Dept., Royal Dutch Shell, The Hague, 1945-51. *Publication:* Harnessing the Hormone, 1933. *Address:* The Director's House, Scottish Horticultural Research Institute, Invergowrie, Dundee, Angus. *T.:* Invergowrie 592. [*Died* 26 *Nov.* 1965.

SWAYNE, Lieut.-Gen. Sir John George des Réaux, K.C.B., *cr.* 1944 (C.B. 1942); C.B.E. 1940; Regular Army (retired); *b.* 3 July 1890; *s.* of late Rt. Rev. Bishop W. S. Swayne; *m.* 1919, Edna Winifred, *d.* of late Lt.-Col. E. H. Swayne, Somerset L.I.; one *d.* *Educ.:* Charterhouse; Trinity College, Oxford. Served France and Belgium, 1914-18 (Prisoner); Adjutant, Somerset L.I., 1924; Brigade-Major 7th Infantry Brigade, 1929-1930; Military Assistant to Chief of Imperial General Staff, 1931-33; Chief of Staff of International Force for Saar Plebiscite, 1934-1935; commanded 1st Bn. Royal Northumberland Fusiliers, 1935-37; Chief Instructor Staff College, Camberley and Minley, 1937-1939; Head of British Military Mission to French G.Q.G. 1939-40; G.O.C. 4th Division, 1940-42; Chief of General Staff, Home Forces, 1942; G.O.C.-in-C. South Eastern Command, 1942-44; Chief of General Staff, India, 1944-46; retired 1946. Colonel, Somerset, L.I., 1947-53. *Address:* 179 Chatsworth Court, Pembroke Road, W.8. *T.:* Western 4961. [*Died* 16 *Dec.* 1964.

SWEET, Lieutenant-Colonel Edward Herbert, C.M.G. 1919; D.S.O. 1917; 2nd King Edward's Own Gurkha Rifles; retired, 1922; *b.* 1 June 1871; *y. s.* of late Rev. George Sweet, Broadleigh, Wellington, Soms.; *m.* 1906, Hilda Margaret (*d.* 1941), *yr. d.* of John Boyall, 36 Hamilton Road, Ealing, W.5; one *s.* one *d.* *Educ.:* Blundell's School, Tiverton; Haileybury College. Joined 3rd Bt. Gloucester Regt. 1889; transferred to 18th Royal Irish Regt. 1892; to 27th Punjabis, 1896; to 2nd P.W.O. Gurkha Rifles, 1897; served Tirah Expedition, 1897-8; Tutor and guardian to Hari Singh of Jammu and Kashmir, 1907-08; served Abor Expedition, 1911-12 (despatches); Tutor and guardian to Maharaja of Bharatpur, 1912-1914; served European War, 1914-18, in France, Egypt, Mesopotamia, and in N.W. Persia, 1918-1920 (despatches four times, C.M.G., D.S.O.); commanded Indian Representatives Camp at Delhi for the Duke of Connaught's visit, Jan.-Feb. 1921; Secretary to Organise Ex-Services Association in India, Jan.-Dec. 1921; Head Warden A.R.P., 1937; Councillor for Wokingham Rural District, 1930-45. *Address:* Green Hedges, Crowthorne, Berks. *T.:* Crowthorne 2685. [*Died* 15 *Sept.* 1966.

SWIFT, Sir Brian (Herbert), Kt., *cr.* 1954; M.C. 1918; M.D.; F.R.C.S. (Edin.); F.R.A.C.S.; F.R.C.O.G.; Obstetrician and Gynæcologist; *b.* 2 February 1893; *s.* of late Harry Swift, M.D.; *m.* 1934, Joan Royal, *d.* of John Tennant, Princess Royal Station, Burra, S.A.; one *d.* (one *s.* decd.). *Educ.:* St. Peter's Coll. Adelaide, S.A.; Caius Coll., Cambridge. Hon. Gynæcologist, Roy. Adelaide Hosp., 1938-53; Hon. Cons. Obstetrician Queen Victoria Maternity Hosp., Adelaide, 1935-69; Lectr. in Gynæcology, Univ. of Adelaide, 1947-52. Chairman, Australian Regional Council, Royal College of Obstetricians and Gynæcologists, 1953-56. Served European War, 1916-1918; Captain R.A.M.C., France; served 1941-42, Major, A.A.M.C., Middle East. *Recreations:* golf and fishing. *Address:* 6 The Avenue, Medindie, South Australia. *T.:* M.L. 1828. *Club:* Adelaide (Adelaide, S.A.). [*Died* 19 *May* 1969.

SWINBURNE, Sir Spearman (Charles), 10th Bt. *cr.* 1660; retired; *b.* 8 Jan. 1893; *s.* of Sir James Swinburne, 9th Bt., F.R.S., and Ellen, *d.* of R. H. Wilson, M.D.; *S.* father 1958; *m.* 1935, Millicent, *widow* of G. R. Fenton, The Connaught Rangers, and *er. d.* of late Lieut.-Col. E. H. Montrésor, Royal Sussex Regt.; no *c.* *Educ.:* Tonbridge; Univ. of Edinburgh; School of Medicine of Royal Colleges, Edinburgh; King's College Hospital. M.R.C.S. Eng., L.R.C.P. Lond., 1920; L.R.C.P., L.R.C.S. Edin., L.R.F.P.S. Glas., 1916. Served in Lady Paget's Unit, Serbia, 1914; Lieut. R.A.M.C. Special Reserve, 1916, Capt. 1917; served in Mesopotamia. Capt. R.A.M.C., T.A.R.O., 1939, Maj. 1940; home service. Physician and Surgeon, firstly at Hampton Court, secondly at Hawkhurst, Kent. Croix de la Société Serbe de La Croix Rouge, 1915; Croix de Charité de St. Pierre de Serbie, 1915. *Recreations:* trout fishing, gardening, heraldry. *Address:* Great Maytham, Rolvenden, Kent. *T.:* Rolvenden 384. [*Died* 1 *March* 1967 (*ext.*).

SWINBURNE-WARD, Colonel Henry Charles, C.I.E. 1920; O.B.E. 1919; *b.* 12 June 1879; *m.* 1924, Lorna, *d.* of Brig.-Gen. Sir Robert Colleton, 9th Bt., and *widow* of Lt.-Col. A. H. Bowring, R.F.A. *Educ.:* Winchester; R.M.C., Sandhurst. Served European War, 1914-18 (despatches); 3rd Afghan War, 1919 (despatches); A.Q.M.G., Southern Command, India, 1926-27; ret., 1927; re-employed, 1940-44. *Address:* 44 Rivermead Court, Hurlingham, S.W.6. *Club:* United Service. [*Died* 28 *Dec.* 1966.

SWINEY, Maj.-Gen. Sir (George Alexander) Neville, K.B.E. 1955 (C.B.E. 1946); C.B. 1951; M.C. 1918; retired; *b.* 10 June 1897; *s.* of late Brigadier-General A. J. H. Swiney, C.B., C.S.I., C.M.G. and late M. M. G. Swiney (*née* Bishop); *m.* 1923, Ena Margery le Poer Power; three *s.* *Educ.:* Cheltenham Coll.; R.M.A., Woolwich. 2nd Lt. R.A., Nov. 1916; transferred to R.A.O.C. 1925 (1922); Adjutant H.Q. Depot, R.A.O.C., 1924-28; Major 1933; Lt.-Col. 1939; Temp. Col. 1940; Temp. Brig. 1941; D.D.O.S. War Office; Col. 1945; D.D.O.S., B.T.E., 1944; D.O.S., G.H.Q., M.E.L.F., 1944; D.D.O.S., Southern Comd., 1947; Temp. Maj.-Gen. and Comd. M.T. Organisation, R.A.O.C., 1948; A.D.C. to the King, 1949-50; Maj.-Gen. 1950; Director of Ordnance Services, War Office, 1951-55; retd. 1955. Col. Comdt. R.A.O.C., 1954-62. *Recreations:* shooting, fishing, all games, gardening. *Address:* Little Summeries, Whielden Street, Amersham, Bucks. *T.:* Amersham 5120. [*Died* 21 *May* 1970.

SWING, Raymond; Journalist, Writer, and Broadcaster; *b.* Cortland, New York, 25 March 1887; *s.* of Rev. Albert Temple Swing and Alice Mead; *m.* 1st, 1913, Suzanne Morin; 2nd, 1921, Betty Gram; three *s.* two *d.*; 3rd, 1945, Mary Hartshorne; 4th, 1957, Meisung Euyang Loh. *Educ.:* Oberlin (Ohio) College (non-graduate). Began newspaper work in Cleveland, Ohio, 1906; on Middle-Western papers to 1913; Correspondent of Chicago Daily News in Berlin, 1913-17; Examiner War Labour Board, 1918; Berlin Correspondent New York Herald, 1919-1922; Director Foreign Service Wall St. Journal, 1924; London Correspondent Philadelphia Public Ledger and New York Evening Post, 1924-34; on board of editors The Nation (N.Y.), 1934-36; New York Correspondent, London, News Chronicle, 1936-37; Commentator on American affairs for British Broadcasting Corpn., 1935-45; Commentator for Columbia Broadcasting System, 1935-36; for Mutual Broadcasting System, 1936-42; for Blue Network, 1942-46; for Liberty Network, 1950-51; for Voice of America, 1951-53, 1959-64; (ed.) This I Believe, Columbia Broadcasting System, 1953. *Publications:* Forerunners of American Fascism, 1935; How War Came, 1940; Preview of History, 1943; In the Name of Sanity, 1946; Good Evening, 1964. *Address:* 3116 Rodman St. N.W., Washington, D.C., U.S.A. [*Died* 22 *Dec.* 1968.

SWINGLER, Rt. Hon. Stephen Thomas, P.C. 1969; M.P. (Lab.) Newcastle-under-Lyme since October 1951; Minister of State, Dept. of Health and Social Security, since 1968; *b.* 2 March 1915; *s.* of late Rev. H. T. C. Swingler, Nottingham; *m.* 1936, Anne Matthews; three *s.* one *d.* *Educ.:* Stowe School; New College, Oxford. W.E.A. Lecturer in North Staffs, 1936-39; Lectr. to H.M. Forces under Oxford University Regional Committee on Education in H.M. Forces, 1939-41; joined Royal Armoured Corps, 1941; commissioned at Sandhurst R.M.C., 1943; served in Royal Tank Regt., 1943-45, in B.L.A. as a Capt., 1944-45. M.P. (Lab.) Stafford, 1945-50; Jt. Parly. Sec., Min. of Transport, 1964-67, Minister of State, 1967-68. *Publication:* Outline of Political Thought since the French Revolution, 1938. *Recreations:* rowing, travelling. *Address:* 6B Belsize Pk. Gdns., N.W.3. *T.:* Primrose 3453. [*Died* 19 *Feb.* 1969.

SWINNERTON, Henry Hurd, C.B.E. 1950; D.Sc., F.Z.S., F.G.S., A.R.C.S.; Emeritus Professor, University of Nottingham, 1946; *b.* 17 Sept. 1875; *s.* of Rev. G. F. Swinnerton, Wesleyan minister; *m.* Florence Daisy, *o. d.* of Joseph Bennett, Nottingham; three *d.* *Educ.:* Woodhouse Grove School, nr. Leeds; Kingswood School, Bath. Assistant Master, Trowbridge High School, 1894-97; Student and Demonstrator Royal College of Science, 1897-1901; First Class Hon. B.Sc., qualifying for University Scholarship, London University, 1898; Marshall Scholar in Huxley Research Laboratory; Science Master, Kingswood School, 1901-2; Lecturer and Demonstrator in Natural Science Department, University College, Nottingham, 1902-12; Professor of Geology, University College, Nottingham, 1912-46; D.Sc. (*h.c.*) Nottingham, 1961; on Council of Geological Soc., 1918-20, 1927-32, 1935, 1936; Vice-President, 1936-38, 1940-41, President, 1938-40; Murchison Medallist, 1942. *Publications:* Geography of Nottinghamshire (Cambridge County Geog.); The Lands Behind the Bible Story; Outlines of Palæontology; The Growth of the World and its Inhabitants; Solving Earth's Mysteries; The Earth beneath Us; Fossils. *Researches:* Development; of Skeleton of Sphenodon; of Head Skeleton of Gasterosteus; Morphology of Pectoral Skeleton of Teleosts; a number of minor papers on Teleosts; a number of papers on Geology of Lincolnshire, of country round Nottingham, and on Palæontological subjects in various geological journals and Biological Reviews. *Address:* Headmaster's House, Haberdashers' Aske's School, Elstree Hertfordshire. [*Died* 6 *Nov.* 1966.

SWORDS, William Francis, Q.C. 1930; B.A., LL.B.; *b.* 1873; *s.* of John George Swords, Woolston, Southampton; *m.* 1914, Lillie St. Patrick Fern (*d.* 1940); one *d.* *Educ.:* Hartley College, Southampton; Royal College of Science; St John's College, Cambridge. Called to Bar. Middle Temple, 1909. *Address:* 26 Fourth Avenue, Hove. *T.:* Hove 32260. [*Died* 4 *March* 1964.

SYKES, Brigadier Arthur Clifton, O.B.E. 1940 (O.B.E. 1919); D.S.O. 1918; American Legion of Merit, 1946; *b.* 26 May 1891; *e. s.* of late Adam Sykes and late Mrs. Sykes of Wadbury, nr. Frome; *m.* 1919, Lorna Evelyn, *e. d.* of Ernest Stanier, Elmhurst, Isleworth; two *s.* *Educ.:* Wellington College; Royal Military Academy, Woolwich. 2nd Lieut. Royal Engineers, 1910; Lieut. 1912; Captain, 1916; Mesopotamian Campaign, 1914-18, temp. Maj. 1917 (despatches 5 times, D.S.O., O.B.E.); transf. to Royal Corps of Signals, 1921; Maj., 1926; Lt.-Col. 1933; Col. 1936; Brig. 1941; served with B.E.F. in France from outbreak of war until evacuation from Dunkirk, 1940, where was in charge of La Panne beach for evacuation of 2nd Corps of B.E.F. (despatches, C.B.E.); a Chief Signal Officer, 1938-42; Chief Signal Officer, British Army Staff, and senior British member of Combined Communication Board of Combined Chiefs of Staff, Washington, and representative in Washington of Dir. of Signals, War Office, 1942-46; retired from Army, 1946. Hon. Member Wilts and Dorset Society of Architects. F.R.G.S.; C.Eng.; M.I.E.E. *Recreations:* fishing; the study of painters and painting. *Address:* The Grange, Edington, Nr. Westbury, Wilts. *T.A.:* Sykes Edington. *T.:* Bratton 219. *Club:* Army and Navy. [*Died* 26 *Jan.* 1967.

SYKES, Joseph, O.B.E. 1955; Ph.D., M.A., M.Com.; Special Lecturer, University of Manchester, 1964-66; formerly Deputy Vice-Chancellor and Professor of Economics, University, Exeter; *b.* 14 April 1899; *s.* of Joseph and Emma Sykes; *m.* 1923, Phyllis Mary Greenwood; one *s.* one *d.* *Educ.:* Univs. of Manchester and Leeds. Naval service, 1917-18; Economic Adviser, National Savings Cttee., 1940-41; Asst. Regional Controller, Ministry of Labour and National Service, 1941-43; Member, China Clay Working Party; Adviser, Economic Research, Board of Trade, 1946-55; sometime Managing Editor, The Banker; Leverhulme Research Fellowship in Economics, 1933; Council of Europe Research Fellow, 1954; Warden Astor Hall of Residence, 1929-34. *Publications:* The Amalgamation Movement in English Banking, 1926; The Present Position of English Joint Stock Banking, 1928; The Coal Industry of the Eighteenth Century (with T. S. Ashton), 1929; British Public Expenditure, 1933; A Social Survey of Plymouth, 1935; National and Local Finance (Britain in Depression), 1935; A Study of English Local Authority Finance, 1939; (joint author) Devon and Cornwall: a preliminary survey, 1947; Section F, British Association, Paper on The Effects of the Distribution of Industry Act, 1945; various articles, etc. *Recreations:* cricket, swimming. *Address:* 19 Riverside Road, Topsham, Exeter. *T.:* Topsham 3851. [*Died* 16 *June* 1967.

SYKES, Very Rev. Norman, F.B.A. 1951; M.A., D.Litt.; Hon. D.D. (Glasgow, 1949, Edinburgh, 1960); Hon. D.Litt. (Leeds, 1959); Dean of Winchester since 1958; *b.* 17 May 1897; *s.* of late Percy and Eliza Sykes, Liversedge, Yorks.; *m.* 1927, Betsy Farrow, M.A., *d.* of late Edmund and Elisabeth Farrow, Newbold, Rochdale. *Educ.:* Leeds University (1st class Honours History); Queen's College, Oxford (Scholar). B.A. (1st class Honours Theology), M.A., D.Phil., 1923; Lecturer in History, King's College, University of London, 1924-31; Professor of History, University College of the South-West, Exeter, 1931-33; Birkbeck Lecturer in Ecclesiastical History, Trinity College, Cambridge, 1931-33; Professor of History in the University of London, Westfield College, 1933-44; Dixie Professor of Ecclesiastical History in University of Cambridge and Fellow of Emmanuel College, 1944-58; Proctor in Convocation for Cambridge University 1945-58; Hon. Fellow of Emmanuel Coll., Camb. 1958. Canon Theologian of Liverpool, 1937-43; Fellow and Praelector in Theology and Modern History, Queen's College, Oxford, 1943-45; Examining Chaplain to the Bishops of Chichester since 1929, and of Exeter, 1932-45; Select Preacher, Cambridge, 1933 and 1941; Oxford, 1942-44; Gunning Lectr., Univ. of Edin., 1953-54; Edward Cadbury Lectr., Birmingham Univ., 1954-55; Ford's Lecturer, Oxford Univ., 1957-58; Wiles Lecturer, Queen's Univ., Belfast, 1959. *Publications:* Edmund Gibson, Bishop of London, 1669-1748, 1926; Church and State in England since the Reformation, 1929; Church and State in England in the Eighteenth Century (Birkbeck Lectures), 1934; The Crisis of the Reformation, 1938; The Study of Ecclesiastical History (Inaugural Lecture), 1945; The Church of England and Non-Episcopal Churches in the 16th and 17th Centuries, 1947; Daniel Ernst Jablonski and the Church of England, 1950; The English Religious Tradition, 1953; Old Priest and New Presbyter (Gunning and Cadbury Lectures), 1956; William Wake, Archbishop of Canterbury, 1657-1737, 1957; From Sheldon to Secker (Ford Lectures); 1959; Man as Churchman (Wiles Lectures), 1960. *Recreations:* cycling, music. *Address:* The Deanery, Winchester. *T.:* 3137. *Club:* Athenæum. [*Died* 20 *March* 1961.

SYKES, Commander Percy Stanley, C.M.G. 1944; O.B.E. 1919; R.D.; R.N.R.; *b* 26 Mar. 1878; *s.* of Joseph Sykes, Alderley Edge, Cheshire; *m.* 1942, Diana Ellen, *d.* of A. H. Croft Ansty; no *c.* *Educ.:* King's Coll. School and King's Coll., London. Articled to W. W. Wright, F.C.A., Chartered Accountant, 1897; A.C.A. 1902; F.C.A. 1960; practised as partner in firm of W. W. Wright & Sykes. Joined R.N.R. as Asst Paymaster, 1904; served European War, 1914-18, afloat until 1915. Attached R.N. Armoured Car Div. Transferred to a Dept. of Foreign Office, *Recreations:* fishing, reading, gardening, sketching. *Address:* Alderley, Wherwell, nr. Andover, Hants. *T.:* Chilbolton 270. *Club:* Devonshire. [*Died* 27 *Dec.* 1966.

SYKES, Sir William (Edmund), Kt. 1959; M.C. 1917; Director of Companies; Chartered Accountant (not in practice); *b.* 12 June 1884; *m.* 1913, Edith (*d.* 1950), *d.* of D. W. James, Abercarn, Mon.; three *d.* *Educ.:* Rydal School, Colwyn Bay. Member of Court of Common Council, City of London, 1937 (Chm. Coal and Corn and Finance Cttee. 1952-59, Chm. Rates Finance Cttee., 1941-43; Rep. on Bd. of Thames Conveyancy, 1948-1960). Mem. of London Court of Arbitration. J.P. Hampstead, 1945-59 (Dep. Chm. of Bench, 1954-58). Dep. Governor the Hon.

the Irish Society, 1945. *Address:* Colebrooke, Red Road, Boreham Wood, Herts. *T.:* Elstree 1940. *Clubs:* Junior Carlton, Guildhall, City Livery. [*Died* 21 *Jan.* 1961.

SYKES, William Stanley, M.B.E.; retd.; late Anæsthetist to the Gen. Infirmary, the Hosp. for Women, Leeds, St. James' Hosp., Leeds, and the Dewsbury Infirmary; *b.* 5 Aug. 1894; *s.* of late Arthur Stanley Sykes; *m.* 1921, Ella Barbara Clarke; *m.* 1952, Nancy Pickard. *Educ.:* Rossall; Emmanuel College, Cambridge. Late Surg. Sub. Lieut. R.N.V.R.; joined R.A.M.C. 26th General Hospital, 1940, Major (prisoner). *Publications:* The Missing Money Lender; The Harness of Death; The Ray of Doom; A Manual of General Medical Practice; Anæsthesia; Essays on the first Hundred Years of Anæsthesia, Vol. I 1960, Vol. II 1961. *Address:* Glenholme, Morley, nr. Leeds. *T.:* Morley 4180. [*Died* 31 *March* 1961.

SYLVESTER, Sir (Arthur) Edgar, K.B.E., *cr.* 1949; F.C.A.; *b* 1891, *s.* of Arthur John Sylvester, Nottingham; *m.* 1916, Hilda May, *d.* of Rev. E. A. Simms; four *s.* one *d.* Chartered Accountant; Partner in Barton Mayhew & Co., 1920-34. Served European War, 1914-18, Sherwood Foresters and Machine Gun Corps. Gas Light & Coke Co., Comptroller, 1934, Gen. Manager, 1941, Managing Director, 1942, Governor, 1945; Chairman, South-Eastern Gas Corporation, 1945-49; Chairman, Gas Council, 1948-51; Pres. National Benzole Association, 1949-1952. *Recreation:* music. *Address:* White House, Maplefield Lane, Chalfont St. Giles, Bucks. *T.:* Little Chalfont 2190. [*Died* 11 *Oct.* 1969.

SYLVESTER, George Oscar; M.P. (Lab.) Pontefract since 1950, Normanton, 1947-50; *b.* 14 Sept. 1898; *m.* 1922, Mildred Arnold. *Educ.:* Normanton Common Council School. Local Miners' Official, 1925-47; Urban Councillor, Normanton, 1927-47; C.C., W.R. Yorks for 1 year. *Address:* 70 Firville Avenue, Normanton, Yorks. *T.:* Normanton 2140. [*Died* 26 *Oct.* 1961.

SYMES, Lt.-Col. Sir (George) Stewart, G.B.E. *cr.* 1939 (K.B.E., *cr.* 1928); K.C.M.G., *cr.* 1932 (C.M.G. 1917); D.S.O. 1904; Governor-General of the Sudan, 1934-40; *b.* 29 July 1882; *o. s.* of late Lieutenant-Col. W. A. Symes, 71st Highland Light Infantry, and Hon. Emily Catherine Shore; *m.* 1913, Viola Colston (*d.* 1953), *y. d.* of late J. Felix Broun; one *d.* (one *s*, decd.) Entered Army, 1900; Capt. 1907; Maj., 1915; Bt. Lt.-Col. 1917; served S. Africa, 1902 (Queen's medal two clasps); Aden Hinterland, 1903-4 (despatches, D.S.O.); Blue Nile Expedition, Sudan, 1908 (medal); European War (despatches, medal, Bt. Lt.-Col.); A.D.C. to Sirdar; Assistant Director of Intelligence, Sudan Government; Private Secretary to Sirdar and Governor-General of the Sudan; G.S.O. 1, attached to staff of High Commissioner in Egypt; Governor of Northern District in Palestine, 1920-25; Chief Secretary to Government of Palestine, 1925-28; Resident and Comdr.-in-Chief at Aden, 1928-31; Governor and Comdr.-in-Chief of Tanganyika Territory 1931-33; accredited representative to Permanent Mandates Commission, Geneva, June 1926, 1928 and 1933; 4th class Osmanieh, 1912, 3rd class Nile, 1915; Nahda (Hedjaz); Grand Cordons Star of Ethiopia, and Order of Ismail (Egypt). *Publication:* Tour of Duty, 1946. *Address:* Princes Hotel, Folkestone, Kent. [*Died* 5 *Dec.* 1962.

SYMINGTON, Hon. Herbert James, P.C. (Can.) 1956; C.M.G. 1944; Q.C. (Can.); *b.* 22 Nov. 1881; Scottish Canadian; *m.* 1910, Fay Christie; two *d.* (one *s.* decd.). *Educ.:* Sarnia Collegiate; Univ. of Toronto (B.A.); Osgoode Hall. Practised law in Winnipeg, Manitoba, 1905-28. Moved to Montreal in 1929 and became Executive Counsel for various industrial and power concerns. Director: International Power Company, Limited; Federal Grain Limited. Represented Canada in International Air Conferences. *Recreations:* golf and fishing. *Address:* 3940 Cote des Neiges Road, Montreal. *Clubs:* Mount Royal, St. James's, Mount Bruno (Montreal); Rideau (Ottawa); Manitoba (Winnipeg). [*Died* 28 *Sept.* 1965.

SYMINGTON, John Alexander; Librarian, Bibliographer (Brotherton Librarian); *b.* Leeds, 4 July 1887; *s.* of J. Simpson Symington, Bookseller; *m.* 1st, 1915, Eliz. Fitzgerald Flower (*d.* 1927), Beverley; five *s.*; 2nd, 1928, Beatrice Thornton-Lambert, East Molesey, Surrey. *Educ.:* Leeds University. Assistant Librarian Leeds Public Reference Library to 1910; The University Library to 1912; Ministry of Labour N.E. Division, 1912-30; Private Librarian to Lord Brotherton, 1923-30; Brotherton Librarian, 1930-38; entrusted with the creation of the Brontë Parsonage Museum, Haworth by Sir James Roberts, 1928; Hon. Curator and Bibliographical Secretary of the Brontë Society for many years; Queen's Messengers Convoy Officer N.E. Div. (Yorks), Ministry of Food, 1941-42. *Publications:* Old Leeds Charities, 1926; The Leyland Manuscripts, 1926; Brontë Museum Catalogue, 1927; Ancient Manuscripts and Early Printed Books, Brotherton Library Catalogue, 1931; Editor, Shakespeare Head edition of the Works of the Brontës, with T. J. Wise, M.A., 20 Vols., 1932-39; Some unpublished Letters of Sir Walter Scott, 1932; Fairfax Library Catalogue and Publications, 1939. *Recreations:* bibliography, autograph collecting. *Address:* 40 Newlaithes Rd., Horsforth, Leeds. *T.:* Horsforth 2615. [*Died* 19 *May* 1961.

SYMON, Rev. Dudley James; Hon. Canon of St. Edmundsbury, 1943; *b.* London, 19 Aug. 1887; *s.* of James Sutherland Symon, Civil Servant, and Sarah Charlotte Symon; *m.* 1917, Elsie Ellen Maisey; one *s.* two *d.* *Educ.:* Merchant Taylors' School; St. John's Coll., Oxford (Schol.). Asst. Curate St. Mark's, Leicester, 1911-15; Assistant Master and Chaplain, Chigwell School, Essex, 1915-17; Sixth Form Tutor, Lancing College, 1917-19; Assistant Master, Rugby School, 1919-21; Headmaster, Woodbridge School, Suffolk, 1921-47; Warden, St. Anne's House, Soho, 1948-50; Chaplain to the Sisters of the Church, Ham Common, Surrey, 1952-56; Bursar, Society of the Faith, 1953-60. *Publications:* Doubts and Desires, 1933; Thanks to Vergil, 1935; Lambeth Questions, 1948; Roman and Uncondemned?, 1959. *Recreation:* bridge. *Address:* College of St. Mark, Audley End, Essex. *Club:* United University. [*Died* 16 *Nov.* 1961.

SZLUMPER, Gilbert Savil, C.B.E. 1925; T.D.; *b.* Kew, 18 Apr. 1884; *o. surv. s.* of late Alfred Weeks Szlumper, C.B.E.; *m.* 1913, Jessie Margaret (*d.* 1968), *d.* of James O. Salter, Aldershot; one *d.* *Educ.:* King's College School, Wimbledon; King's Coll. (London). Pupil in Engineers' Dept., L. and S.W. Rly., 1902-5; Engineering Assistant, L. and S.W. Rly., 1905-13; Assistant to the General Manager, 1913; Secretary to the Railway Executive Committee and Senior Railway Transport Officer of the British Army, 1914-1919; Major in the Engineer and Railway Staff Corps (T.A.) Jan. 1916; Lieut.-Colonel, 1928; Colonel, 1937; Major-General, 1939; Docks and Marine Manager, L. and S.W. Railway, 1920; Assistant General Manager Southern Railway (Waterloo Station), 1925-37; General Manager Southern Railway, 1937-42; Director-General of Transportation and Movements at the War Office, 1939-40; Railway Control Officer, Ministry of Transport, 1940-41; Director-General of Supply Services, Min. of Supply; 1942-45; one of H.M.'s Lieutenants of City of London; K.St.J.; Officer, Légion d'Honneur,

Commander, Leopold II. *Address:* 18 Cranmer Court, S.W.3. *T.:* Knightsbridge 4949. *Clubs:* Royal Automobile, City Livery. [*Died* 19 *July* 1969.

T

TACHIE-MENSON, Sir Charles (William), Kt. 1960; C.B.E. 1955 (O.B.E. 1947); *b.* 12 Feb. 1889; *s.* of Robert Menson, merchant; *m.* 1927, Maria Joyce, *d.* of Harry Reginald Amonoo, merchant; three *s.* three *d.* *Educ.:* Methodist School and privately. Member Sekondi-Takoradi Municipal Council, 1936-49; M.L.A. and M.L.C., Gold Coast, 1944-51; Director, W. African Airways Corp., 1946-52; Member: Town and Country Planning Bd., 1945-54; Central Advisory Cttee. on Educn., 1948-52; Higher Educn. Cttee., 1946; Exec. Council, 1946-51; Industrial Development Corp., 1948-51; Coussey Constitutional Cttee., 1949; Chm. Achimota Constitutional Conf., 1956; rep. Gold Coast several Internat. Confs. and at Sec. of State's Afr. Conf., 1948; First Gold Coast rep. to Commonwealth Parliamentary Assoc. Conf., 1948; Member Ghana Public Service Commn., 1951-56, Chairman, 1957-62. Dir. Ghana Nat. Red Cross Soc., 1959-60, Vice-Pres., 1961-62. *Recreations:* cricket and tennis. *Address:* P.O. Box 1618, Accra, Ghana. *Clubs:* Royal Commonwealth Society; Optimism (Sekondi, Ghana). [*Died* 17 *Oct.* 1962.

TAFAWA BALEWA, Alhaji Rt. Hon. Sir Abubakar, P.C. 1961; K.B.E. 1960 (C.B.E. 1954: O.B.E. 1951); M.P.: Prime Minister of the Federal Republic of Nigeria since 1957, and Minister of External Affairs since 1965; Chancellor, University of Ibadan, since 1963; *b.* 1912; *m.* 1934; has *c.* *Educ.:* Katsina Higher College, London University (Institute of Education). Teacher, 1933-43; Headmaster, 1943-47; Provincial Education Officer, 1949-51; General President, Northern Teachers' Assoc.; Federal Minister of Works, 1952-54; Federal Minister of Transport, 1954-57; Deputy President-General, Northern Peoples' Congress. Trustee, Boy Scouts Association of Nigeria. Hon. LL.D. Univs.: Sheffield, 1960; New York, 1961; Dublin, 1962; Nigeria (Nsukka), 1962; Ibadan, 1963; Ahmadu Bello, 1963. Holds highest State award of Republic of Niger, 1962, and several foreign orders, awards and hon. citizenships. *Publications:* Shaihu Umar, 1934; Nigeria Speaks, 1964. *Recreations:* cricket, athletics, Association football. *Address:* Cabinet Office, Lagos, Nigeria; (residence) 5 King George V Road, Onikan, Lagos, Nigeria. *Club:* Travellers' (Hon. Mem.). [*Died Jan.* 1966.

TAFFRAIL; *see* Dorling, Capt. Henry T.

TAIT, Sir Frank (Samuel), Kt. 1956; Managing Director J. C. Williamson Theatres, Australia; *b.* 12 Nov. 1883; his father came from the Shetland Islands and his mother from London, England; *m.* 1st, 1913; three *d.* (one *s.* decd.); 2nd, 1941, Viola Wilson Hogg; three *d.* *Educ.:* Melbourne Grammar School. Has had long career as theatrical and concert manager. *Recreation:* golf. *Address:* 32 Hopetoun Road, Toorak, Melbourne, Australia. *T.:* 50-1089. *Clubs:* Athenæum (Melbourne); Metropolitan Golf. [*Died* 24 *Aug.* 1965.

TALBOT, Vice-Admiral Sir Cecil Ponsonby, K.C.B., *cr.* 1947 (C.B. 1934); K.B.E., *cr.* 1939; D.S.O. 1915, and Bar, 1917; R.N., retd.; *b.* 1884; *s.* of Major F. Talbot; *m.* 1912, Bridget (*d.* 1960), *d.* of R. B. D. Bradshaw; one *s.* one *d.* (and two *s.* killed on active service). Has Royal Humane Society's medal for saving life at sea; served European War, 1914-16 (despatches, promoted Comdr., D.S.O. and bar); Director of Naval Equipment, Admiralty, 1932-34; Rear-Adm. Submarines, 1934-36; retired list, 1936; Director of Dockyards, Admiralty, 1937-46; is a Chevalier of the Legion of Honour and Grand Officer of Orange Nassau. *Address:* Penberth, St. Buryan, Cornwall. *Club:* United Service. [*Died* 17 *March* 1970.

TALBOT, John Ellis; M.P. (C.) Brierley Hill Division of Staffordshire since Oct. 1959; Solicitor since 1929; Joint Manager Kidderminster Permanent Benefit Bldg. Soc., 1938-1961; Chm. Kidderminster Equitable Bldg. Soc., 1961; *b.* 24 April 1906; *s.* of Major Ellis W. Talbot, T.D.; *m.* 1930, Sabina Emily Wood, *d.* of Joseph Perrins, Chaddesley Corbett, Kidderminster; two *s.* *Educ.:* Stubbington House, Fareham; Rossall. Served War, 1941-45, Capt. R.A.O.C. Kidderminster Borough Council: Councillor, 1936; Mayor, 1947-49; Alderman, 1952-63; Councillor, Worcestershire County Council, 1952-55. Master Worshipful Company of Gardeners, London, 1962. Chm. Gardeners' Royal Benevolent Soc., 1964. *Recreations:* bowls, travel. *Address:* 6 Wedderburn House, 95 Lower Sloane St., S.W.1; Villa Sabina, Great Witley, Worcs. *Clubs:* Junior Carlton, City Livery. [*Died* 9 *Jan.* 1967.

TALLENTS, Philip Cubitt, C.S.I. 1934; C.I.E. 1929; *b.* 13 Apr. 1886; *s.* of late George William Tallents, Barrister-at-Law. *Educ.:* Harrow; Magdalen College, Oxford, M.A. Entered Indian Civil Service, 1909; retired, 1939. *Address:* The Cottage, Great Bealings, Woodbridge, Suffolk. *T.:* Grundisburgh 224. [*Died* 4 *Nov.* 1962.

TANCOCK, Lieut.-Colonel Alexander Charles, C.I.E. 1927; Indian Army, retired; 3rd *s.* of late Rev. Canon O. W. Tancock. *Educ.:* King Edward VI. School, Norwich; R.M.C., Sandhurst. Gazetted to the Royal Sussex Regt., 1899; transferred to Indian Army, 1901; China Expeditionary Force, 1902; seconded to Khyber Rifles, 1903; to Kurram Militia, 1911; Commandant Kurram Militia, 1916; Commandant, Mohmand Militia, 1918; appointed Inspecting Officer, Frontier Corps, 1920 (Indian Frontier Medal four clasps); President Board of Examiners in Pushtu, Peshawar, 1920-26; retired, 1928; passed Government Examination Modern Greek, Nicosia, Cyprus, 1935; travelled extensively in Near, Middle and Far East. *Recreations:* usual. *Address:* c/o National and Grindlay's Bank Ltd., 13 St. James's Square, S.W.1. *Clubs:* Athenæum, East India and Sports, M.C.C. [*Died* 23 *March* 1966.

TANDY, Sir Arthur (Harry), K.B.E. 1962 (C.B.E. 1950); retired; *b.* 11 May 1903; *e. s.* of late H. Tandy; *m.* 1931, Lilian, *d.* of J. S. Tattersfield; two *d.* *Educ.:* Christ's Hosp. (Grecian 1919-22, Exhibitioner 1922); Magdalen College, Oxford (Demy 1922; Goldsmiths' Exhibitioner 1923; B.A. 1926). Entered H.M. Diplomatic Service, 1927; Vice-Consul: Bangkok, 1927, Barcelona, 1928, Philadelphia, 1929, Los Angeles, 1933, Valparaiso, 1937; Consul: New York, 1939, Cincinnati, 1943; First Secretary, Washington, 1945; Commercial Counsellor, Paris, 1947; seconded to O.E.E.C., 1948; Commercial Counsellor, Brussels, 1949; Minister, British Embassy, Buenos Aires, 1955; Ambassador to the European Communities, 1958-63. *Address:* Broadways, Selsey, Sussex. *Club:* Canning. [*Died* 20 *Oct.* 1964.

TANGYE, Captain Sir Basil Richard Gilzean, 2nd Bt., *cr.* 1912; Chairman (late Managing Director) Tangyes Ltd., Cornwall

Works, Birmingham; *b.* 27 July 1895; *o. s.* of Sir Lincoln Tangye, 1st Bt., and Annie Gilzean, *e. d.* of late Sir Hugh Gilzean-Reid, LL.D., of Tenterden Hall, Hendon; *S.* father, 1935; *m.* 1924, Clarisse, *o. d.* of Baron Victor Schosberger, of Tura, Hungary; one *d.* *Educ.:* Harrow. *Heir:* none. *Address:* 55 Park Lane, W.1. *Club:* Junior Carlton.
[*Died* 19 *Dec.* 1969 (*ext.*).

TANNER, Lieut.-Colonel Frederick Courtney, C.M.G. 1919; D.S.O. 1914; late The Royal Scots; *b.* 2 Dec. 1879; *s.* of C. F. Tanner; *m.* 1911, Ethelwyn F. Mourilyan (*d.* 1965); two *s.* one *d.* *Educ.:* Marlborough Coll.; R.M.C., Sandhurst. Entered army (Lancs Fus.), 1899; Capt., 1904; Capt. Royal Scots, 1908; Major, 1915; Lt.-Col., 1926; served European War, 1914-18 (despatches, D.S.O., Bt. Lt.-Col., C.M.G., Officer Crown of Italy, Sacred Treasure 3rd Class, Croix de Guerre); retired, 1930; re-employed 1939-44. *Address:* Rosehill, Cefnlys Road, Llandrindod Wells, Radnorshire.
[*Died* 14 *July* 1965.

TANNER, Jack, (Frederick John Shirley Tanner), C.B.E. 1954; President Amalgamated Engineering Union, 1939-54; *b.* Whitstable, Kent, 28 April 1889. Member of T.U.C. General Council, 1943 (President, 1953-54). *Address:* Farmcote, Sapperton, Heathfield, Sussex. [*Died* 3 *March* 1965.

TAPP, Percy John Rutty, C.B.E. 1946; M.C. 1917; Chairman, County Commercial Cars Ltd., also of several Engineering Cos.; *b.* 4 Sept. 1886; *m.* 1922, Maud Mary Pool; one *s.* two *d.* Director of Govt. Road Haulage Organisation at Ministry of War Transport, 1943-46. Member Road Haulage Executive, 1947-51. Served European War, 1914-18, in 19th Div. in France. *Address:* Shermanbury, Hartley Wintney, Hants. *T.:* Hartley Wintney 2342. [*Died* 22 *March* 1964.

TARDREW, Rev. Canon Thomas Hedley; Canon Residentiary and Precentor of York Minster since 1954; *b.* 12 Dec. 1889; *s.* of late Thomas Hedley and late Edith Steward Tardrew, Liverpool; *m.* 1913, Kate Elizabeth (*d.* 1958), *d.* of late Frederick and late Annie Barker Allison, Bridlington; three *s.* one *d.* (one *s.* decd.); *m.* 1959, Dorothy, *d.* of late Joseph Thwaites Coulthard and Susan Nutt, Keighley. *Educ.:* Liverpool Coll.; Liverpool University (LL.B.). Articled to Messrs. Clancey, Sons & Tardrew (Average Adjusters), 1908-13. Deacon, 1913; Priest, 1914; Asst. curate: Spalding, 1913-15; Grimsby, 1915-22; Vicar of Newington, Hull, 1922-33; Vicar of St. Mary's, Beverley, 1933-54. Proctor in Convocation, 1943-54; Canon and Prebendary of Strensall in York Minster, 1944-54. *Publication:* contrib. to The Anglican Pulpit To-day, 1953. *Recreations:* trying to: recall the past; remind myself; reform the present; reface the future. *Address:* 2 Minster Court, York.
[*Died* 28 *Feb.* 1966.

TARGETT, Sir Robert William, Kt., *cr.* 1945; C.I.E. 1942; *b.* 23 Feb. 1891; *m.* 1947, Mrs. R. E. Mackessack, *yr. d.* of Sir Henry Craik, 3rd and last Bt., G.C.I.E., K.C.S.I. *Address:* La Cible, Rozel, Jersey.
[*Died* 1 *Dec.* 1965.

TASCHEREAU, Rt. Hon. Robert, C.C. (Canada), 1967; P.C. (Canada) 1963; LL.D.; Chief Justice of Canada, 1963-67, retd.; *b.* Quebec, 10 Sept. 1896; *s.* of Louis Alexandre Taschereau, former Prime Minister of Quebec, and Adine Dionne; *m.* 1926, Elleen Donohue; two *d.* *Educ.:* Quebec Seminary (B.A.); Laval Univ. (LL.L. 1920). Admitted to Bar, Province of Quebec, 1920; practised law in Quebec, 1920-40; K.C. 1930. Apptd. to Supreme Court, Canada, 1940. Prof. of Criminal Law, Laval Univ., 1929-40; now Prof. of Civil Law and Private Internat. Law, Univ. of Ottawa. Elected (Liberal) for Bellechase County to Quebec Legislature, 1930, re-elected 1931 and 1935. Mem. Canadian Bar Assoc. (Hon. Sec., 1934-41); Mem. Royal Commn. on Espionage, 1946. Pres. l'Alliance Française many years; Mem. Comité France-Amérique. Medal 'La gloire de l'Escole', Laval, 1965. Dr. of Law (*h.c.*): Ottawa, 1942; Laval, 1944; Montreal, 1947; McGill, 1967. Chevalier, Légion d'Honneur, 1947. *Recreations:* fishing, travel, photography. *Address:* Apt. 805, 4300(W) Boulevard de Maisonneuve, Westmount, Montreal 6, Quebec, Canada. *Club:* Garrison (Quebec).
[*Died* 26 *July* 1970.

TATCHELL, Sydney Joseph, C.B.E. 1946; F.R.I.B.A. (Retd.); F.R.S.H.; Senior Partner and Consultant, Sydney Tatchell, Son & Partners; *b.* 1887; *er. s.* of late Joseph Veale Tatchell; *m.* Edith Evelyn (*d.* 1957), *d.* of late Jacob Myring, Richmond; one *s.* two *d.* (and one *d.* decd.). *Educ.:* privately. Articled to late Thomas Henry Watson, F.R.I.B.A., and at the Architectural Association. Commenced practice in Westminster, 1905; Vice-Pres. R.I.B.A. 1931-33, Mem. of Council 1928-39; Chm. of Practice Standing Cttee., 1928-31; Mem. of Bd. of Architectural Education, 1935-45 (Chm. Bd. of Moderators, 1939-45); External Examiner and member of Board of Studies U.C., London, and the Regent St. Polytechnic; formerly: Mem. of governing Body of the Northern Polytechnic; Mem. of the Tribunal of Appeal under the London Building Acts; Chairman: Architects' Registration Council of the U.K., 1935-1951; Joint Tribunal on the Building Contract, 1929-56; Standards and Plumbing Committees of Ministry of Works; Past-Pres. Building Industries National Council; Chairman of Building Divisional Council and member of Executive of British Standards Institution, 1945-48; Surveyor to Worshipful Company of Ironmongers, 1921-1953 (now Freeman and Liveryman). Surveyor to 5 of the City Churches. *Principal works include:* Stowell Park, Gloucestershire; Ironmongers' Hall, Aldersgate; St. Dionis Hall, City; reconditioning the Mansion House, Barber-Surgeons' Hall, and Bakers' Hall in the City of London; Niblett Hall, Inner Temple; the National Library for the Blind; Imperial H.Q. Girl Guides Assoc.; Surrey County Sanatorium, Milford; Hall of the Chartered Institute of Secretaries; Science Workshops, Great and Dominions Libraries and New Quad Christ's Hospital, Horsham, and Art School and Domestic Science Laboratories, Christ's Hospital, Hertford; (and with his son, Rodney), The Village, Entrance Gates and Lodges to Royal Lodge, Queen's Gate Cottages for Crown pensioners, The Garden House, and various other works in Windsor Great Park; also town and country houses. Lectures given at London Univ., Sheffield Univ. and elsewhere, on: Professional Practice; The Building Contract; Arbitration. *Address:* Clifford's Inn, Fleet Street, E.C.4. *T.:* Holborn 7983. *Club:* Athenæum.
[*Died* 7 *July* 1965.

TATTERSALL, Lieut.-Colonel Edmund Harry, D.S.O. 1918; soldier, author and journalist; *b.* 1897; *o. s.* of late Harry George Tattersall; *m.* 1st, 1925, Mona (*d.* 1928), *e. d.* of Sir James H. Dunn, 1st Bart; one *d.*; 2nd, 1932, Ruby Carol Jevons (who obtained a divorce); 3rd 1948, Monica Katharine Mary Hodsoll (who obtained a divorce); two *s.* *Educ.:* Uppingham; Sandhurst. 2nd Lieutenant 5th Dragoon Guards, 1916; Lt. 1917; served in France, 1916-18 (D.S.O., despatches, wounded); A.D.C. to I.G.C. Italy, 1919; retired pay, wounds, 1924; re-employed Oct. 1939, Major, G.S.O.2 Public Relations Directorate,

War Office; Lt.-Col. 1941; retired, Oct. 1945. Fellow Royal Philharmonic Society. *Publication:* Europe at Play. *Recreations:* travelling, fishing, shooting. *Address:* Scio House Hospital, Putney Heath, S.W.15. *Clubs:* Buck's, I Zingari, Free Foresters. [*Died* 12 *Dec.* 1968.

TAWNEY, Prof. Richard Henry; F.B.A.; lecturer and author; Professor of Economic History, University of London, 1931-49, Professor Emeritus since 1949; *b.* Calcutta, 1880; *s.* of late C. H. Tawney, C.I.E., and Constance Catherine Fox; *m.* 1909, Annette Jeanie (*d.* 1958), *d.* of late Henry Beveridge, I.C.S. *Educ.:* Rugby; Balliol Coll., Oxford (Fellow, 1918-21). Assistant at Glasgow University, 1906-08; Teacher for Tutorial Classes Committee of Oxford Univ., 1908-14; Member of Executive of Workers' Educational Association, 1905-47, and President, 1928-44; Director of Ratan Tata Foundation, University of London, 1913-1914; Member of Consultative Committee of Board of Education, 1912-31; Member of Coal Industry Commission, 1919; Member of Chain Trade Board, 1919-22; Member of Cotton Trade Conciliation Comm., 1936-39; Adviser, British Embassy, Washington, 1941-42; Member of Univ. Grants Cttee., 1943-48. F.B.A., 1935; Hon. Fell. of Balliol Coll., Oxford, 1938; Hon. Fell. of Peterhouse, Cambridge, 1946; Mem. of Amer. Philosophical Soc., 1942; Hon. Dr. Univs. of Oxford, Glasgow, Manchester, Birmingham, Sheffield, London, Chicago, Melbourne and Paris. *Publications:* The Agrarian Problem in the Sixteenth Century; English Economic History, Select Documents (in co-operation with Bland and Brown); Studies in the Minimum Wage: 1. Chain-making industry, 2. Tailoring industry; Tudor Economic Documents (with Prof. E. Power); The Acquisitive Society; Education, The Socialist Policy; Thomas Wilson, A Discourse of Usury; Religion and the Rise of Capitalism, 1926; Equality, 1931; Land and Labour in China, 1932; The Attack and other Papers, 1953; Business and Politics under James I, 1958; The Radical Tradition, edited R. Hinden (posthumous), 1964. *Address:* 21 Mecklenburgh Square, W.C.1. [*Died* 16 *Jan.* 1962.

TAYLOR, Captain Arthur Lombe; late Norfolk Regiment; Barrister, Inner Temple; South-Eastern Circuit; retired; *b.* 15 Feb. 1882; *e. s.* of late Alfred Taylor and Anna Enfield Taylor of Starston Place, Norfolk; *m.* 1918, Sybil Isobel Gordon, *d.* of late Alexander Gordon McKenzie; one *s.* two *d.* *Educ.:* Charterhouse; Trinity Coll., Camb. Called to Bar, Inner Temple, 1906; served European War in France, 1915-19; J.P. Norfolk; Chairman Norfolk Quarter Sessions, 1945-57; Recorder of Thetford, 1927-1951. *Address:* Starston Place, Harleston, Norfolk. [*Died* 8 *Dec.* 1968.

TAYLOR, Rear-Adm. (retd.) Bertram Wilfrid, C.B. 1959; D.S.C. 1945; *b.* 23 Mar. 1906; *s.* of John Mathews and Bertha Hall Taylor, Clifton, Bristol; *m.* 1934, Frances Louisa Stevenson; one *s.* one *d.* (one *s. decd.*). *Educ.:* R.N. Colleges Osborne and Dartmouth. Joined R.N. Coll., Osborne, 1919; specialised in Submarines, 1928; in command H.M. Submarine Severn, 1939-40 (despatches). Comdr. 1941; Staff of Flag Officer Submarines and C.-in-C. Western Approaches, 1942-43; in command 5th Frigate Squadron, 1944-45; Admiralty, Naval Staff, 1946-47; Capt. 1947; in command 1st Submarine Squadron, 1948-50; Chief of Staff to Flag Officer Submarines, 1950-52; i.d.c. 1953; Captain of Fleet, Home Fleet, 1954-57; Rear-Admiral, 1957; Flag Officer (Submarines), 1957-59, retired 1960. *Recreations:* gardening, golf and shooting. *Address:* Mulberry Cottage, Wrington, nr. Bristol, Somerset. *Club:* Army and Navy. [*Died* 30 *Sept.* 1970.

TAYLOR, Charles Allison, C.B. 1941; M.C.; *b.* 12 Oct. 1885; *s.* of late William Taylor and Margaret Whitson Allison; *m.* 1st, 1912, Agnes Dickie Lochhead (*d.* 1933); one *s.* one *d.*; 2nd, 1940, Isabella Cassells Marr Eadie. *Educ.:* Glasgow University. Civil and Electrical Engineer. Entered Post Office, 1907; Engineering Department, 1907-35; Deputy Regional Director, Scottish Region, G.P.O., 1935-39; Regional Dir., London Telecomm., G.P.O., 1939-48. *Recreation:* golf. [*Died* 28 *Oct.* 1965.

TAYLOR, Professor Eva Germaine Rimington, D.Sc. (Lond.); LL.D. (Aberdeen); F.R.G.S., F.R.Hist.Soc.; *d.* of late Charles Richard Taylor, M.A., LL.D. *Educ.:* North London Collegiate Sch. for Girls; Universities of London and Oxford. Private Assistant to Professor A. J. Herbertson (Oxford School of Geography); Lecturer in Geography at Clapham and Furzedown Training Colleges (L.C.C.); Lecturer in Geography at Birkbeck College, 1921-30; Professor and Head of Department of Geography, 1930-44; Emeritus Professor of Geography in the University of London, 1944; Fellow of Birkbeck College; Victoria Medallist of R.G.S., 1947. Hon. Member: Inst. of Navigation; Society for Nautical Research. Vice-Pres., Hakluyt Society. *Publications:* Barlow's Brief Summe of Geographie; Tudor Geography; Late Tudor and Early Stuart Geography; Writings of the Two Richard Hakluyts; Sketch Map Geography; Geography of an Air Age; Ideas on the Shape, Size and Motions of the Earth; Mathematical Practitioners of Tudor and Stuart England; The Haven-finding Art; Voyage of Edward Fenton; Writings of William Bourne; The Geometrical Seaman (with M. W. Richey); Contribs. to Geographical Journal, Journal of the Institute of Navigation. *Address:* Ralph's Ride, Bracknell, Berks. *T.:* Bracknell 629. [*Died* 5 *July* 1966.

TAYLOR, Fred, R.I.; R.D.I.; Artist, Water Colour and Posters; *b.* London, 22 March 1875; *s.* of William and Charlotte M. Taylor; *m.* 1904, Florencia Rosamond Sarg; one *s.* one *d.* *Educ.:* Académie Julien; Goldsmiths' College. Gold medal, Travelling Scholarship to study decoration (Italy); exhibits water colours at R.I. (principally architectural); exhibited R.A., R.I., R.W.A., Glasgow, Liverpool; official purchasers: Bristol, Liverpool, Toronto, N.S.W.; decorations at Lloyd's; long series of posters for the L.N.E.R. War Work—Camouflage. *Address:* 19 Clarendon Rd., W 11 *T.:* Park 6829. [*Died* 29 *Jan.* 1963.

TAYLOR, Right Rev. Frederick Adrian, O.S.B.; F.R.Hist.S.; *b.* 28 Mar. 1892; *s.* of Lewis Charles Taylor and Camille Victoire Eugénie Soulard. *Educ.:* Grocers' Company's School, Hackney Downs; St. John's College, Cambridge (B.A. 1914, M.A. 1918). Successively Private, 2nd Lieut., Lieut., and Captain, Royal Fusiliers, 1914-19; Active Service in France, 1915-18 (M.C. 1917); Gladstone Memorial Prize and Prince Consort Medal for Historical Research, Cambridge University, 1920; entered St. Augustine's Abbey, 1920; Head Master of the Abbey School, 1924-34; Abbot of St. Augustine's, Ramsgate, 1934-54; retired. *Publications:* The Art of War in Italy, 1494-1529, 1921; occasional articles. *Address:* St. Michaels' Abbey, Farnborough, Hants. *T.:* 5. [*Died* 31 *July* 1961.

TAYLOR, Sir George L.; *see* Langley-Taylor.

TAYLOR, George Reginald Thomas; *b.* 6 July 1876; *s.* of T. A. O. Taylor, Buckingham House, Headingley, Leeds; *m.* (wife *d.* 1954); two *s.* two *d.* *Educ.:* Uppingham. President (late Consultant), International Combustion (Holdings) Ltd. *Address:* c/o

Mrs. A. W. Richardson, Quarndon Hall, Nr. Derby. [*Died* 8 *June* 1965.

TAYLOR, Rear-Admiral George William, C.B.E. 1946; retired; *b.* 10 May 1883; *s.* of late G. E. M. Taylor, Link Elm, Malvern Link, Worcs.; *m.* 1918, Eileen Norah Boyce; one *s.* *Educ.:* H.M.S. Britannia. Joined H.M.S. Orlando as a naval cadet, 1899; served European War, 1914–18, in destroyers, Harwich Force. Retired with rank of Rear-Adm., 1934; War of 1939-46, service in convoys, at the Admiralty and Bermuda, ending up as Commodore Superintendent, Ceylon. *Address:* c/o The Midland Bank Ltd., Canford, Cliffs, Poole, Dorset. [*Died* 21 *Oct.* 1964.

TAYLOR, Professor Griffith; *see* Taylor, Professor T. G.

TAYLOR, Herbert; *see* Addenda: II.

TAYLOR, Rev. Harold Milman Strickland, O.B.E. 1919; M.A.; *b.* 4 Aug. 1890; *s.* of late Rev. John Charles Taylor, M.A., Vicar of Harmondsworth and Charlotte Katherine Strickland; *m.* 1918, Violet Ursula, *d.* of Gerald Hunnybun, Godmanchester; three *s.* *Educ.:* Sandroyd School, Cobham; Marlborough College; Trinity College, and Ridley Hall, Cambridge. B.A. 1912 Honours Degree in Classics; M.A. 1915; Deacon, 1913; Priest, 1914; Curate of St. James, Shirley, Southampton, 1913-15; Chaplain to B.E.F., 1916-18, with 21st Div. Art. and 6th Corps in France (despatches, O.B.E.); Assistant Master, Housemaster, and Assistant Chaplain at Dean Close School, Cheltenham, 1919-20; Headmaster of Cheam School, 1920-47. In 1934 transferred school from Cheam (Surrey) where it had existed since 1646, to Headley (Hants) where it has since been established. Raised Headley Platoon, H.G., in 1940 and commanded it until 1945. Patron of Harmondsworth Church, 1920-. Chairman of Boscombe Printing Co., 1948-; Chairman Industrial and Commercial Publications Ltd., 1958; Member of Dorset County Education Cttee., 1950-52. Member Institute of Directors; Fellow, Ancient Monuments Society. *Recreation:* golf. *Address:* 2 Porchester Gate, W.2. *T.:* Bayswater 2839. *Club:* M.C.C. [*Died* 4 *Jan.* 1966.

TAYLOR, Harold Victor, C.B.E. 1948 (O.B.E. 1928); D.Sc.; A.R.C.S.; *s.* of Albion Taylor, farmer, Taunton, Somersetshire; *m.* Dorothy (*d.* 1962), *d.* of Frederick Speedy, 76 Tulse Hill, S.W.2; no *c.* *Educ.:* Huish Sch., Taunton; The Roy. Coll. of Science, S. Kensington, Prizeman for Chem.; 1st class Hons. B.Sc. and D.Sc., Univ. of London. Diploma Royal Coll. of Science; Science Master Huish School, Taunton, 1906-09; joined the Ministry of Agriculture as Inspector in Horticulture, 1912; Deputy Controller of Horticulture, 1920-27; Commissioner of Horticulture and Chairman Horticulture Advisory Council, 1927; Senior Advisory Officer, National Advisory Service, 1945; retd., 1948. Council mem. of Royal Horticultural Soc.; Chm. Governors, Nat. Vegetable Research Station, 1951-57. Governing Member, East Malling Research Station. Victorian Medal of Honour in Horticulture, 1938. *Publications:* The Apples of England, 1936; The Plums of England, 1949. *Recreation:* gardening. *Address:* Preston Grange, Potters Bar, Herts. *Clubs:* Athenæum, Farmers'. [*Died* 14 *Nov.* 1965.

TAYLOR, Harry W. O.; *see* Oddin-Taylor.

TAYLOR, Col. Jack H.; *see* Hulme-Taylor.

TAYLOR, Prof. James Haward, F.R.S. 1960; Professor of Geology in the University of London, King's College, since 1949; *b.* 24 Feb. 1909; *o. s.* of late James Taylor, Milngavie, Dunbartonshire, and Lilian Dudley Ward Haward; unmarried. *Educ.:* Clifton College; King's College, University of London; Harvard University. B.Sc. (London) with 1st Class Hons., A.K.C., Jelf Medal (Natural Science), 1931. Henry Fellowship, Harvard Univ., 1933-34; A.M. (Harvard), 1934; Ph.D. (London), 1936. Joined Geological Survey of Great Britain, 1935; Principal Geologist, 1946. M.I.M.M. (Vice-Pres. 1962-65); Pres. Mineralogical Society, 1963-65; F.G.S., F.K.C. 1962; Mem. Natural Environment Research Council. *Publications:* various scientific papers, especially on geology of mineral deposits and on sedimentation. *Recreations:* golf, fishing, geology in the field. *Address:* Department of Geology, King's Coll., Strand, W.C.2; 18 Kingsdowne Rd., Surbiton, Surrey. *Club:* Bath. [*Died* 25 *Jan.* 1968.

TAYLOR, John, J.P.; M.P. (Lab.) West Lothian since 1951; Deputy Chief Opposition Whip since Oct. 1959; *b.* 22 July 1902; *e. s.* of John Taylor and Maud Wilson, Edinburgh; *m.* 1930, Olive, *d.* of Councillor J. K. Fox, ex-Mayor of Lincoln; two *s.* *Educ.:* Sciennes Sch., Edinburgh. Docker, Journalist and Organiser. Member Reading County Borough Council, 1933-35. Eastern Counties Organiser, The Labour Party, 1935-39; Scottish Secretary, The Labour Party, 1939-50. J.P. 1944. *Publications:* several political pamphlets. *Address:* House of Commons, S.W.1; 68 Ellingham Road, Hemel Hempstead, Herts. [*Died* 1 *March* 1962.

TAYLOR, Rev. John Edward, M.A., B.Litt. (Oxon.); Headmaster of Bedford Modern School 1946-65; *b.* 1899; *s.* of late Dr. J. G. Taylor, F.S.A., Headmaster of Sir Walter St. John's School (1907-32); *m.* 1st, 1939, Francesca (*d.* 1959), *d.* of late Dr. F. J. Sadler; one *s.* 2nd, 1961, Margaret Patricia Gordon, *d.* of late Capt. Adam Kerr. *Educ.:* Merchant Taylors'; St. John's College, Oxford (Schol.). 1st Cl. Classical Mods, 1920; 2nd Cl. Lit. Hum., 1922; B.Litt., 1924; Bishops' College, Cheshunt, 1961; Classical Upper Sixth Form Master, Tonbridge Sch., 1923-32; Headmaster of Sir Walter St. John's School, S.W.11, 1932-1946. Ordained deacon, 1961, priest, 1962 (St. Albans); Hon. Priest Vicar of Exeter Cathedral, with permission to officiate in dio. Exeter, 1965-. *Address:* 24 Denmark Rd., Exeter, Devon. [*Died* 19 *Jan.* 1966.

TAYLOR, Rt. Rev. John Ralph Strickland, M.A., D.D.; *b.* 13 Dec. 1883; *s.* of Rev. John Charles Taylor, M.A., Vicar of Harmondsworth, and Charlotte Catherine Strickland, a great-niece of Agnes Strickland the historian; *m.* 1913, Margaret Irene, *d.* of Lieutenant-Colonel R. V. Garrett, late of the Indian Army; two *s.* two *d.* *Educ.:* Elstree Preparatory School; Marlborough College; Pembroke College and Ridley Hall, Cambridge. First-class Honours in Classics; Second-class in Theological Tripos, Part I.; ordained, 1910, as Chaplain of Ridley Hall, Cambridge; Tutor, 1911; Vice-Principal, 1913; Examining Chaplain to the Bishop of Norwich, 1911-42; became temporary Chaplain to the Forces, March 1917; for 18 months was Chaplain at the Royal Military Academy, Woolwich; Headmaster of St. Lawrence College, Ramsgate, 1918-28; Rector of Hodnet with Weston-under-Redcastle, 1928-32; Rural Dean of Hodnet, 1930-32; Principal of Wycliffe Hall, Oxford, 1932-42; Bishop of Sodor and Man; 1942-54; Hon. Canon of Norwich, 1938-42; Examining Chaplain to Bishop of Ripon, 1932-34, and to Bishop of Lichfield, 1935-42. President of the London College of Divinity since 1945. *Recreation:* gardening. *Address:* The Lodge, Pembury, Nr. Tunbridge Wells. [*Died* 13 *Dec.* 1961.

TAYLOR, Julian, C.B.E. 1946; M.S., F.R.C.S.; *b.* 26 Jan. 1889; *s.* of Edward Ingram Taylor and Margaret, *d.* of George Boole; *m.* 1926, Margaret (*d.* 1955), *d.* of Dennis Ross-Johnson; two *s.* *Educ.:* University College School; University College, London; University College Hospital. F.R.C.S. Eng. 1914; M.S. Lond. 1920; 85th Field Ambulance, France and Macedonia, 1914-19; Consulting Surgeon to Malayan Command, Singapore, 1941-45, etc. Prof. Surg., Univ. of Khartoum. Consulting Surgeon: University College Hosp.; the National Hosp., Queen Square, London; Member of Council, Royal College of Surgeons. *Publications:* various publications on surgical subjects. *Recreation:* sailing. *Address:* The Old Rectory, Bepton, Nr. Midhurst, Sussex. *T.:* Midhurst 215. *Club:* Athenæum. [*Died* 15 *April* 1961.

TAYLOR, Most Rev. Leo Hale, C.B.E. 1944; S.M.A., D.D.; *b.* 27 Sept. 1889; *s.* of Joseph Francis Taylor and Caroline Hale, both of Pontefract, Yorks. *Educ.:* African Missions and National University, Cork. Ordained Priest of the Society of African Missions, 1914; taught in Society's Seminary in Cork; first Editor of the African Missionary; went to W. Africa, 1920; Principal of St. Gregory's College, Lagos, 1928-34; Vicar Apostolic of Western Nigeria (now Benin Dio, 1934, Vicar Apostolic of Lagos (formerly Bight of Benin, changed to Lagos by Holy See in 1943), 1939, also titular Bishop of Vartana until 1950; Archbishop of Lagos (R.C.), 1950-65. *Address:* Catholic Mission, Lagos, Nigeria. *T.:* Lagos 20815. [*Died* 27 *Oct.* 1965.

TAYLOR, Leonard Campbell, R.A. 1931 (A.R.A. 1923); *b.* Oxford, 12 Dec. 1874; *s* of James Taylor, Mus.Doc., organist of New Coll. and to Univ. of Oxford, and Eliza Ann, *d.* of John Stone, D.L., J.P., of the Prebendal Thame, Oxon, and Long Crendon, Bucks; *m.* 1st, 1920, Katharine Elizabeth (*d.* 1933), *widow* of Frank Craig; 2nd, 1935, Audrey Brenda, *d.* of late J. C. Moore; one *d.* *Educ.:* Dragon School, Oxford; Cheltenham College (scholar). Studied art at Ruskin School Oxford, St. John's Wood Art School and at Royal Academy Schools; among exhibits are The Rehearsal, now in Chantrey Collection at National Gallery of British Art, Bed-time (purchased by Italian Govt. for National Gallery, Rome), Piquet (in National Gallery, Sydney), The Harpist (National Gallery, Cape Town), Portrait of H.M. Queen Mary; The Coronation of their Majesties King George VI and Queen Elizabeth (now in Royal Collection), 1938; exhibited also in Provinces, Paris Salon, Venice International Exhibition, Carnegie Institute, Pittsburgh, U.S.A., and Ghent; represented in Public or Corporation Galleries: Birkenhead, Toronto, San Francisco, Southampton, Rochdale, Port Sunlight, Bradford, Hull, Cheltenham, Manchester, Bristol, Merthyr Tydfil; sometime Trustee Whitechapel Art Gallery. Bronze medal, 1912, gold medal, 1931, Paris Salon, Société des Artistes Français. Lieut. 1916; Capt. 1917, Surrey Vol. Regiment; Lieut. 1918, R.N.V.R. *Relevant publications include:* L. Campbell Taylor, R.A., His Place in Art (Herbert Furst, 1945); Leonard Campbell Taylor, R.A. (Cyril G. E. Bunt, 1949). *Address:* Pampisford Mill, Cambridge. *T.:* Sawston 3205. *T.A.:* Campbell-Taylor, Pampisford Mill, Cambridge. [*Died* 1 *July* 1969.

TAYLOR, Sir Lionel Goodenough, Kt., *cr.* 1927; *b.* London, 16 July 1871; *s.* of John Howell Goodenough Taylor; *m.* 1st, 1901, Edith, *d.* of H. W. Banks-Davis, R.A.; one *s.* one *d.*; 2nd, 1920, Hilda Paulina (*d.* 1936), *d.* of Arthur Tanner of Frenchay, Bristol; one *s.* one *d.*; 3rd, 1943, Eileen, *widow* of Capt. George Edward Hill, M.C., Intelligence Corps, and *er. d.* of Col. A. C. Ellis, C.B.E. *Educ.:* Blundell's, Tiverton; Exeter College, Oxford, M.A. Captain of College VIII, 1892; rowed bow of winning Trial VIII, same year; London Letter and Political lobbyist, 1896-1907; Sheriff of Bristol, 1925-26; Master of Society of Merchant Venturers of Bristol, 1926-27. *Address:* Lye Hole, Wrington, Bristol. *T.:* Wrington 371. [*Died* 25 *May* 1963.

TAYLOR, Gen. Sir Malcolm C. C.; *see* Cartwright-Taylor.

TAYLOR, Air Vice-Marshal Malcolm Lincoln, C.B.E. 1943; A.F.C. 1918; *b.* 15 Nov. 1893; 2nd *s.* of late Leo Taylor, O.B.E., F.I.C., Kingswood, Surrey; *m.* 1st, 1917, Gwendolen Dewberry; one *d.*; 2nd, 1946, Pamela Susan Mary, *o. c.* of late Major D. R. Ewing, Cameronians. *Educ.:* Churchfields, Margate; Louth School. Served European War, 1914-18, in France in R.E., R.F.C., and R.A.F. (A.F.C.); commanded No. 29 Squadron, 1927-29; Chief Instructor, School of Photography, 1930; commanded No. 40 Squadron, 1931-1934; Wing Comdr., 1934; commanded School of Photography and R.A.F. Station, Farnborough, 1934-36; commanded R.A.F. Station Hal Far, Malta, 1936-38; Group Capt., 1938; Organisation Staff H.Q. Bomber Command, 1938-39; commanded R.A.F. Station, Bassingbourne, 1939-41 (despatches); Acting Air Commodore and Air Officer i/c Administration, Malta, 1941-42 (despatches twice, C.B.E.); Air Commodore, 1942; A.O.C. East Africa, 1942 (despatches); Levant, 1943; Acting Air Vice-Marshal, 1943-45, and again, 1945-46; A.O.C. No. 203 Group, Middle East, 1943-45; S.A.S.O. Flying Training Command, 1945-46; retired list, 1946. Hon. Freeman City of London, 1918. *Recreations:* tennis, golf. *Address:* Oldner House, Chipping Norton, Oxon. *T.:* Chipping Norton 2696. [*Died* 24 *Dec.* 1970.

TAYLOR, The Hon. Mrs. (Margaret Sophia); *b.* 16 April 1877; 2nd *d.* of Hon. Conrad Dillon and Ellen, *d.* of Sir Henry Dashwood, Bart.; *m.* 1907, Rev. Charles Taylor, D.D., LL.D., J.P., Master of St. John's College, Cambridge (*d.* 1908); no *c.* *Educ.:* St. Winifred's, Eastbourne. Representative of Southwark on Church Assembly, 1925-45; Member of Central Board of Finance; Head of Talbot Settlement, 1918-26. Fell. Roy. Commonwealth Soc., 1959. *Address:* Orchard Cottage, Lower Farm, Madehurst, Arundel, Sussex. *T.:* Slindon 288. [*Died Feb.* 1962.

TAYLOR, Margerie Venables, C.B.E. 1948; M.A.; F.S.A.; Editor of Journal of Roman Studies since 1923; *b.* 20 Jan. 1881; 2nd *d.* of Henry Taylor, F.S.A., Curzon Park, Chester and Agnes Taylor (*née* Venables). *Educ.:* Queen's School, Chester; privately; Somerville College, Oxford. Secretary, Society for Promotion of Roman Studies, 1923-1954, Vice-President, 1954, Pres., 1955. F.S.A. 1925, a Vice-Pres. (first woman), 1944-1948; Hon. Res. Fell. of Somerville Coll., 1946, Hon. Fellow, 1962; Hon. member of Soc. of Antiquaries of Newcastle upon Tyne, 1947; Corr. mem. German Archæological Institute, 1937. *Publications:* contributions on Roman Britain to The Victoria County Histories, Antiquaries Journal, Oxoniensia and other local archæological journals. *Address:* 45 Woodstock Road, Oxford. *T.A.* and *T.:* Oxford 57431. [*Died* 24 *Dec.* 1963.

TAYLOR, Capt. Sir Patrick Gordon, G.C. 1942; Kt. 1954; M.C.; Australian air pilot and navigator; *m.* 1st, 1938, Eileen J. Broadwood (*d.* 1950); two *d.*; *m.* 1951, Joyce A., *d.* of W. Kennington; one *s.* two *d.* Served European War, 1914-18; with Royal Flying Corps; since then engaged in Australian civil aviation as airline Captain.

Pacific flight with late Sir Charles Kingsford-Smith, 1934; saved Southern Cross and crew in Australia-New Zealand flight, 1935 (G.C.); made first air-crossing of Indian Ocean, and survey of air route for British and Australian governments, 1939; first crossing of Central Pacific and survey of air route for Royal Air Force, 1944. Served War of 1939-45 as aircraft Captain with R.A.F. Transport Comd. First crossing of South Pacific, Australia-Chile, 1951. *Publications:* Pacific Flight; VH-UXX; Call to the Winds; Forgotten Island; Frigate Bird; The Sky Beyond; Bird of the Islands. *Address:* 141 York St. Sydney, N.S.W. [*Died* 14 *Dec.* 1966.

TAYLOR, Rear-Admiral Philip Cardwell, C.B. 1955; Deputy Engineer in Chief (Personnel), Admiralty, 1955-56, ret.; (Extra Naval Assistant to Second Sea Lord, 1953-55); *b.* 12 Oct. 1902; *s.* of late Eng. Capt. C. G. Taylor, M.V.O., R.N.; *m.* 1931, Irene May Scott; one *s.* one *d.* *Educ.:* R.N. Colleges Osborne and Dartmouth. Commander (E), 1936; Engineer Officer, H.M.S. Duncan, 1937-39; Asst. to Extra Naval Asst. to 2nd Sea Lord, Admiralty, 1939-42; Engineer Officer, H.M.S. Kenya, 1942-44; H.M. Dockyard, Portsmouth, 1944-46; Capt. (E), 1946; H.M.S. Imperieuse, 1947; H.M.S. Raleigh, 1948; Chief Engineer, H.M. Dockyard, Gibraltar, 1949-52; Asst. Engr.-in-C., Admty., 1952-53; Rear-Adm., 1953. *Address:* The Old Farm House, Monxton, Nr. Andover, Hants. [*Died* 13 *Nov.* 1965.

TAYLOR, Richard S.; *see* Stopford-Taylor.

TAYLOR, Robert; Actor; Lieut. U.S.N.R. until Nov. 1945; *b.* 5 Aug.; *s.* of S. A. Brugh, M.D.; *m.* 1st, 1939, Barbara Stanwyck (marr. diss., 1951); 2nd, 1954, Ursula Thiess; one *s.* one *d.* *Educ.:* Doane Coll., Nebraska; Pomona Coll., Cal. (Liberal Arts degree). Films, starred in, include: Broadway Melody of 1936, Magnificent Obsession, Small Town Girl, His Brother's Wife, Camille, Personal Property, Broadway Melody of 1938, Yank at Oxford, Three Comrades, Flight Command, Escape, Billy the Kid, Waterloo Bridge, Johnny Eager, Bataan, Song of Russia, Undercurrent, High Wall, Quo Vadis, Ivanhoe, Knights of the Round Table, Rogue Cop, Quentin Durward, The Power and the Prize, Guns of Wyoming, The Sixth of June, Tip on a Dead Jockey, Party Girl, The Law and Jake Wade, Saddle the Wind, The Hangman, Killers of Kilimanjaro, House of Seven Hawks, Cattle King, Miracle of the White Stallions, A House is Not a Home, The Night Walker, Johnny Tiger; The Savage Pampas; Return of the Gunfighter; The Glass Sphinx; Hondo; The Day the Hot Line got Hot; Where Angels Go . . .Trouble Follows. TV: 1959-62, 1966-, inc. series Death Valley Days, Hondo. *Recreations:* fishing, hunting. *Address:* c/o Suite 11-K, 400 South Burnside Ave., Los Angeles, California 90036. [*Died* 8 *June* 1969.

TAYLOR, Stanley Shelbourne, C.M.G. 1918; D.S.O. 1917; *b.* 1875. *Educ.:* Pembroke College, Cambridge (Scholar); First Class Classical Tripos, 1897. Called to Bar, Inner Temple, 1901; K.C. (South Africa), 1919; served Transvaal Horse Artillery and South African Field Artillery, West Africa, East Africa and Palestine, 1914-18 (despatches, C.M.G., D.S.O., Croix de Guerre, Order of St. Stanislaus); formerly Director Anglo-American Corp. of S. Africa Ltd., De Beers Consolidated Mines Ltd. *Club:* United University, [*Died* 22 *July* 1965.

TAYLOR, Professor (Thomas) Griffith, D.Sc., B.E. (Sydney), B.A. (Cantab.), F.G.S, 1910; F.R.S.C. 1942; F.A.A. 1954; F.R.G.S.; Prof. of Geography, Univ. of Toronto, 1935-51. Emeritus, 1951; *b.* Walthamstow, Essex, 1 Dec. 1880; *s.* of James Taylor, B.Sc., late Government Metallurgist of N.S. Wales; *m.* Doris, *d.* of Joseph Priestley, of Tewkesbury; two *s.* (one *d.* decd.). *Educ.:* University of Sydney; Deas-Thomson Scholar in Physics, also in Geology; 1851 Exhibition Science Research Scholar; Emmanuel College, Cambridge, Sudbury-Hardyman Prizeman; Physiographer Commonwealth Weather Service, 1910; Senior Geologist Scott's Last Expedition, 1910; Leader of Western Parties in the Antarctic, 1911-12; Lecturer in Physiography, Melbourne University, 1917-18; Associate-Professor of Geography, University of Sydney, 1920-1928; Professor of Geography, University of Chicago, 1929-35; Acting Commonwealth Geologist at Canberra; Honorary Lecturer in Meteorology at Commonwealth Flying School, 1914-18; Foundation Member of Australian National Research Council, 1919; Livingstone Lecturer, Sydney, 1928; Messenger Lecturer, Cornell, 1944; Co-Editor, Zeitschrift fur Rassenkunde; Commonwealth Education Commn., Canberra, 1948. Co-Editor, Economic Geography; Pres. of Section E. (Geog.) British Assoc. for the Advancement of Science, 1938; Pres., Assoc. of American Geographers, 1941; Pres. Australian Inst. of Geographers, 1959. Hon. Dr. of Letters, Univ. of Sydney, 1959. Medals: King's Polar, Syme, Thomson, Johnston, also of R.G.S. Queensland and American Geog. Soc. and of Roy. Soc. (N.S.W.). *Publications:* Australia Physiographic and Economic, 1911; With Scott, The Silver Lining, 1916; Australian Environment, 1918; Australian Meteorology, 1920; Antarctic Physiography, 1922. Environment and Race, 1927 (Japanese ed. 1931, Chinese ed. 1939); Antarctic Adventure and Research, 1930; Australia, a descriptive geography, 1931; Australian Climatology, 1932; Atlas of Environment and Race, 1933; Environment and Nation, 1936; Environment, Race and Migration, 1937; Geographical Laboratory for Americans, 1938; Australia, a University text book, 1940 (Spanish edn. 1954); Newfoundland, 1946; Our Evolving Civilization, 1947; Canada, University Text, 1947; Urban Geography, 1948 (Spanish edn. 1954); (ed.) Geography in the Twentieth Century, 1951 (revised edn. 1953); Journeyman Taylor (biography) 1958; Sydneyside Scenery, 1958; Mawson (biog.), 1962; 150 Memoirs on Canada, Australia, Antarctica, World Climatology and Ethnology. *Recreations:* travelling, bridge. *Address:* 28 Alan Ave., Seaforth, New South Wales, Australia. [*Died* 5 *Nov.* 1963.

TAYLOR, Sir Thomas Murray, Kt., *cr.* 1954; C.B.E. 1944; Q.C. (Scot.) 1945; M.A., LL.B.; D.D. (Edinburgh); LL.D. (St. Andrews and Glasgow); Principal and Vice-Chancellor of the University of Aberdeen since 1948; *b.* 27 May 1897; *o. s.* of John Taylor, The Knowe, Keith, Banffshire; *m.* 1939, Helen Margaret Jardine, M.D., M.M.S.A.; one *s.* one *d.* *Educ.* Keith Grammar School; Aberdeen University, M.A. 1st Class Hons. Classics, 1919; Fullerton, Scholar in Classics, and Ferguson Scholar in Classics, 1919; LL.B. 1922; called to Scottish Bar, 1924; Advocate-Depute, 1929; Home Advocate-Depute, 1934. Chairman or member of various departmental cttees.; member Executive Cttee., World Council of Churches, 1948-54. Prof. of Law in the Univ. of Aberdeen, 1935-1948; Sheriff of Renfrew and Argyll, 1945-48. Riddell Lecturer, Univ. of Durham, 1954. Commander, Royal Order of the North Star (Sweden), 1954. *Publications:* The Discipline of Virtue; Where One Man Stands. *Recreations:* golf, cinephotography. *Address:* Chanonry Lodge, Old Aberdeen. *T.:* Aberdeen 43074. *Clubs:* New (Edinburgh); University (Aberdeen). [*Died* 19 *July* 1962.

TAYLOR, Right Rev. Mgr. Thomas N., Hon. Canon of Glasgow Archdiocese and also of Motherwell Diocese; Domestic Prelate to H.H. the Pope · Parish Priest, Carfin, 1915-60; in charge of Carfin Grotto, from erection, 1922-60; retd. Oct. 1960. *Educ.:* St. Aloysius Coll., Glasgow; Blairs Coll., Aberdeen; St. Sulpice and Catholic Univ., Paris, 1893-97. Prof. of Sacred Scripture and Ecclesiastical History in St. Peter's Coll., New Kilpatrick, Glasgow, 1900-15. *Publications:* Lourdes and its Miracles, 1911 (2nd ed. 1919); Sœur Thérèse of Lisieux, 1912; A Little White Flower, 1915 (Golden Jubilee edition, 1947, 130th thousand, Diamond Jubilee edition, 1957); Saint Thérèse of Lisieux, 1927 (110th thousand); The Carfin Grotto, 1930; The Carfin Grotto: Fifteen Years After, 1938; First Thirty Years: Carfin Grotto, 1954. *Address:* St. Francis Xavier's, Carfin, Motherwell. *T.:* Motherwell 3308. [*Died* 1 *Dec.* 1963

TAYLOR, Rev. Vincent, Ph.D., D.D. (Lond.); F.B.A. 1954; formerly Principal of Wesley College, Headingley, Leeds, and Ferens Professor of New Testament Language and Literature, 1930-53, retired; *b.* 1 Jan. 1887; *s.* of Benjamin Taylor and Margaret Emmett; *m.* 1914, Elizabeth Alice Harrison; one *d.* *Educ.:* Accrington Grammar School; Divinity School of University of London, Richmond College, Surrey. B.D. (Lond.) 1911; B.D. Hons. (Lond.), 1st class in Greek New Testament and Apocrypha, 1924; Ph.D. (Lond.) 1922, D.D. (Lond.), 1926; entered Wesleyan Methodist Ministry, 1909; Pastoral Charges at Mansfield, Carmarthen, Bath, Keighley, Aberdeen, Lytham St. Annes; Examiner in Biblical Languages in the London University, 1931-34; Examiner in Theology, London University, 1942-43; Examiner in New Testament Greek in the University of Wales, 1937-42; Associate Lecturer in New Testament Greek, 1948-53. Select Preacher, Cambridge, 1945-46; Member of Board of Arts, Leeds University, 1950-1953; Speaker's Lectureship, Oxford, 1951-1956; Visiting Professor in New Testament Studies, Drew Univ., New Jersey, U.S.A., 1955-56. Hon. D.D.: Leeds, Dublin, Glasgow. Burkitt Medal for Biblical Studies, British Acad., 1960. *Publications:* The Historical Evidence for the Virgin Birth, 1920; Behind the Third Gospel, 1926; The First Draft of St. Luke's Gospel, 1927; The Gospels: A Short Introduction, 1930; The Formation of the Gospel Tradition, 1933; Jesus and His Sacrifice: A Study of the Passion-sayings, 1937; The Atonement in New Testament Teaching, 1940 (Fernley-Hartley Lecture); Forgiveness and Reconciliation, 1941; The Gospel according to St. Mark, 1952; The Names of Jesus, 1953; The Life and Ministry of Jesus, 1954; The Epistle to the Romans, 1955; The Cross of Christ, 1956; The Person of Christ in New Testament Teaching 1958; The Text of the New Testament, 1961; New Testament Essays, 1969. *Address:* Otterbourne Grange, Otterbourne, Nr. Winchester, Hants. *T.:* Chandler's Ford 5518. [*Died* 28 *Nov.* 1968.

TAYLOR, William Ernest, C.B.E. 1957; Counsellor, British Embassy, Washington, since 1951; *b.* 16 Oct. 1900; *s.* of Ernest Taylor; *m.* 1930, Winifred Marjorie, *d.* of W. G. K. Ridley, Staines, Middlesex; one *s.* one *d.* *Educ.:* Cranbrook, Kent. Various posts at Air Ministry, from 1918. Served in U.S.A., 1941-45. *Recreations:* music, sport. *Address:* British Embassy, Washington, D.C., U.S.A. [*Died* 30 *Oct.* 1965.

TAYLOR, Sir William (Ling), Kt. 1949; C.B.E. 1945; Fellow and Dip. Forestry, R.I.C.S.; Chairman, Standing Adv. Cttee. on Planting in the Royal Parks, Ministry of Works, 1954-67; *b.* 29 May 1882; *er. s.* of G. L. Taylor and Emily Mary Brooke; *g.s.* of George Taylor, Park Vale, Warwicks; *m.* 1911, Muriel (*d.* 1967), M.B.E. 1951, 3rd *d.* of Richard Savage Woollatt. Land agency, 1901-09. Served in Imperial Yeomanry, 1902-07. Entered Public Service, 1910; Timber Directorate, 1916-19: Forestry Commission, 1919; Deputy Surveyor Forest of Dean and Steward of the Royal Manors, 1931; Assist. Forestry Commissioner for England and Wales, 1932-38; Enclosure Commissioner, Forest of Dean, 1934-38; Pres. Soc. of Foresters of Great Britain, 1936-38; Vice-Pres. Soc. for Promotion of Nature Reserves, 1938-.; Commissioner in charge Home Timber Production, England and Wales and N. Ireland, 1939-42; Forestry Commissioner, 1938-49; late Dir.-Gen. Forestry Commission; U.K. delegate to Forestry Confs. at home and abroad; Member of Home Office Advisory Committee on Wild Birds Protection, 1945-54; National Parks Commission, 1951-54; Charter Member Nature Conservancy, 1949-58; Member of Nature Conservancy Committees (Scientific Policy), 1949-64; Member, University Grants Sub-Committee, 1951-64; Mem. of Coun., Wycombe Abbey School, 1952-62. Hon. Fell., Soc. of Foresters of Gt. Britain, 1965. *Publications:* Forests and Forestry in Great Britain, 1945; Estate Forestry, 1951; numerous contributions to technical and other periodicals. *Recreations:* natural history and shooting. *Address:* 40 Abingdon Ct., W.8. *Club:* United Service. [*Died* 5 *Jan.* 1969.

TEACHER, Anthony Donald Macdonald, C.B.E. 1955; D.L.; Brig. (retd.); Inspector of Courses (National Hunt), since 1960; *b.* 29 Oct. 1905; *s.* of late Donald Teacher, Hawick, Roxburghshire; *m.* 1936, Audrey Clarisse, *d.* of late Brig.-Gen. Ernest B. Macnaghten, C.M.G., D.S.O.; two *s.* *Educ.:* Rugby; R.M.A., Woolwich. 2nd Lt. R.A., 1925. Served War of 1939-45, France, U.K. and N.W. Europe. Lt.-Col. 1942; Brig. 1948; C.R.A. 16 Airborne Div. (T.A.), 1948-51; B.G.S., H.Q. Southern Command, 1951-54; B.R.A., H.Q. Scottish Comd., 1955-58; retd. 1958. D.L. City and County of the City of Edinburgh, 1963. Bronze Medal, Royal Humane Society. *Recreation:* gardening. *Address:* Church Hill House, Potterne, Devizes, Wilts. *Club:* Army and Navy. [*Died* 18 *Sept.* 1969.

TEAGO, Frederick Jerrold, D.Sc., M.I.E.E.; Robert Rankin Prof. of Electrical Machinery and Electrical Engineering Electrotechnics in the Univ. of Liverpool, 1926-52; Professor Emeritus since 1952; *b.* 11 Nov. 1886; *s.* of Jerrold Teago and Ellen Matthews; *m.* 1913, Anne Middlemiss; one *s.* *Educ.:* Armstrong College, Newcastle upon Tyne; Durham University. Apprenticed with C. A. Parsons & Co., Heaton Works, Newcastle upon Tyne, on Design Staff of C. A. Parsons & Co. and Metropolitan Vickers Co., Manchester; Assistant Manager, H.M. Steel Billet Plant, Trafford Park, Manchester; Lectr. in Electrical Engineering, Liverpool Univ., 1912-25. Visiting Prof. Electrical Engineering, U.C. Cork, 1953-1961. Chairman Wallasey Embankment Commission, 1947-52. Hon. LL.D., N.U.I., 1960. *Publications:* Air Blast Cooling of Transformers; Heating of Buried Cables. Nature of Magnetic Field in Induction Motors; Three-Phase Shunt Commutator Motor; Atkinson Repulsion Machine as a Motor and Generator; Electric Traction, 1937, Journal of the Institution of Electrical Engineers; The Dimensions of a Transformer and the Output, World Power; The Commutator Motor 1952; Examples in Electrical Engineering; Electric Traction, 1948; Mercury Arcs 1961. *Recreation:* gardening. *Address:* University College, Cork. [*Died* 4 *Oct.* 1964.

TEASDALE, Sir John Smith, Kt., *cr.* 1951; C.B.E. 1948; Chairman, Australian Wheat Board, since 1950 (Member since 1939); *b.* 28 June 1881; *s.* of James Teasdale, late of Alston and Carlisle, Cumberland; *m.* 1930, Luita Christina Waldeck; one *d.* *Educ.:* Alston High School; Cockermouth; Rutherford College, Newcastle upon Tyne. Apprenticed R. Stephenson & Co., Newcastle, 1897-1902; John Liddell & Sons, Haltwhistle, 1902-06; Trustee Wheat Pool, 1921; Pres. Primary Producers of W.A. (8 yrs.; 16 yrs. Vice-Pres.); Council Royal Agric. Soc. of W.A. (10 yrs.); Director Co-operative Bulk Handling, 1935 (Chm. 1940); Chm. Nicholls Pty. Ltd., Stevedores, Fremantle; Chm. Royal Commn. on Wheat Marketing, 1948. *Recreation:* bowls. *Address:* 367 Cotham Road, Kew, E.5, Victoria, Australia. *T.:* WY 1998. *Club:* West Australian (Perth). [*Died* 2 *July* 1962.

TEDDER, 1st Baron, *cr.* 1946, of Glenguin; **Marshal of the Royal Air Force Arthur William Tedder,** G.C.B., *cr.* 1942 (K.C.B., *cr.* 1942; C.B. 1937); i.d.c.; Chancellor of the University of Cambridge since 1950; President Royal Air Force Association, 1952-67; Vice-President Surrey County Cricket Club, since 1959 (President, 1953-59); *b.* 1890; *yr. s.* of late Sir Arthur John Tedder, C.B.; *m.* 1st, 1915, Rosalinde (*d.* 1943), *d.* of W. M. Maclardy, Sydney, N.S.W.; one *s.* (and one killed on active service) one *d.*; 2nd, 1943, Marie De Seton Black (*d.* 1965), *yr. d.* of Col. Sir Bruce Seton, 9th Bt. of Abercorn, C.B.; one *s.* *Educ.:* Whitgift; Magdalene College, Cambridge. B.A. (Historical Tripos) 1912; Prince Consort Prize, 1913; Colonial Service, 1914 (Fiji); commissioned Dorsetshire Regiment, 1914; seconded to R.F.C., 1916; service in France, 1915-17, and Egypt, 1918-19 (despatches thrice); Italian Médaille Militaire, 1916; transferred to R.A.F., 1919; commanding 207 Squadron, Constantinople, 1922-23; Royal Naval Staff College, 1923-1924; commanding No. 2 Flying Training School, 1924-26; Air Ministry, 1926-27; Imperial Defence College, 1928; Directing Staff, R.A.F. Staff College, 1929-31; commanding Air Armament School, Eastchurch, 1932-33; Director of Training, Air Ministry, 1934-36; Air Officer Commanding Royal Air Force, Far East, 1936-38; Director-General of Research and Development, Air Ministry, 1938-40; Deputy Air Officer Commanding in Chief, R.A.F., Middle East, 1940-41; Air Officer Commanding in Chief, R.A.F., Middle East, 1941-43; Air Commander-in-Chief, Mediterranean Air Command, 1943; Deputy Supreme Commander under General Eisenhower, 1943-45; Chief of the Air Staff and First and Senior Air Member, Air Council, 1946-50; Chairman of British Joint Services Mission, Washington, and U.K. representative on the standing group of the Military Committee of the North Atlantic Treaty Organisation, 1950-51. A Governor of the B.B.C. (Vice-Chm.), 1950. President (formerly Chairman) Standard Triumph-International Ltd. Deputy President, National Rifle Association. *Publications:* The Navy of Restoration, 1915; Air Power in War, 1948; With Prejudice, 1966. *Heir:* *s.* Hon. John Michael Tedder [*b.* 4 July 1926; *m.* 1952, Peggy, *yr. d.* of S. C. Growcott; two *s.* one *d*]. *Address:* Well Farm, Banstead, Surrey. *T.:* Burgh Heath 56677. *Clubs:* Royal Air Force, Athenæum, Oxford and Cambridge, Savage. [*Died* 3 *June* 1967.

TEICHMAN-DERVILLE, Major Max, O.B.E. 1919; D.L.; J.P. County of Kent; *b.* Eltham, Kent, 187; *s.* of E. Teichman, Chislehurst, Kent; assumed additional name of Derville, 1922; *m.* 1907, Leonore Derville Curle (*d.* 1951); two *s.* one *d.* *Educ.:* Repton; Trinity College, Oxford. M.A. Oxford, 1903; served European War, 1914-19 (O.B.E.); late Major, R.A.R.O.; County (Council) Alderman; Bailiff of Romney Marsh; Mayor of New Romney, 1926-38; Baron of Cinque Ports for New Romney, 1937; Speaker of the Cinque Ports, 1930 and 1937; High Sheriff of Kent, 1938-39; F.S.A.; F.R.Hist.S.; late Pres. Kent Archæological Soc.; Freeman of New Romney; Lord of the Manors of Eastbridge and Snave. *Publications:* The Town and Port of New Romney; The Level and Liberty of Romney Marsh. *Recreations:* fishing, shooting. *Address:* The Red House, Littlestone, New Romney, Kent. *T.:* New Romney 2333. *Club:* Royal St. George's (Sandwich). [*Died* 11 *May* 1963.

TEIGNMOUTH, 6th Baron, *cr.* 1797; **Hugh Aglionby Shore,** 5th Bt., 1792; late India, P.W.D.; *b.* 12 July 1881; *s.* of 5th Baron and Mary Aglionby (*d.* 1934) *d.* of Rev. Canon Porteus; *S.* father, 1926; *m.* 1915, Caroline, *d.* of Col. Marsh, R.E.; one *s.* (*er. s.* killed in action, Italy, July 1944) one *d.* *Educ.:* Wellington College; Coopers Hill. Retired from Indian Public Works Department, 1917; held commission in Royal Marine Engineers, 1918; J.P. 1940; Somerset C.C. 1946-50; Pres. Y.M.C.A. W. Div.; District Commissioner Scouts for N. Somerset, 1939-50. *Recreations:* shooting, fishing, water-colour painting. *Heir:* *s.* Hon. Frederick Maxwell Aglionby Shore, D.S.C. and Bar 1944, Lieut. R.N.V.R., *b.* 2 Dec. 1920. *Address:* Brownsbarn, Thomastown, Co. Kilkenny, Eire. [*Died* 13 *Aug.* 1964.

TEK CHAND, Sir, Kt., *cr.* 1942; Hon. LL.D. Punjab Univ.; *b.* 1883; Puisne Judge, High Court, Lahore, 1927-43; Senior Advocate, Supreme Court of India; Member Parliament of India, 1950-52. *Address:* 1 Albuquerque Lane, New Delhi, India. [*Died* 28 *Aug.* 1962.

TELFER, Rev. Canon William, M.C. 1916; D.D., M.A. (Cantab.); Hon. Fellow of Clare College, and Fellow of Selwyn College, Cambridge; *b.* 16 January 1886; *s.* of Andrew Telfer and Annie Emily Bayly; unmarried. *Educ.:* The King's School, Canterbury; Clare and Jesus Colleges, Cambridge. Deacon, 1909; Priest, 1910; at Clare College Mission, 1909-1914 and 1917-18; Temp. Chaplain to Forces, 1914-17 (M.C.); Combatant service, 1918-19; Vicar of All Saints, Rotherhithe, 1919-21; Fellow of Clare College, Cambridge, 1921-46; Dean, Praelector and Assistant Tutor of Clare College, 1923-46; Univ. Lecturer, Faculty of Divinity, 1926-51; Ely Prof. of Divinity, 1944-46, Professor Emeritus, 1967-; Canon-residentiary of Ely Cathedral, 1944-46; Canon emeritus, 1948-; Hon. Canon, 1950-56; Master of Selwyn College, Cambridge, 1947-56; retired. *Publications:* The Treasure of São Roque, 1932; Cyril of Jerusalem and Nemesius of Emesa (Christian Classics Vol. IV), 1955; The Forgiveness of Sins, 1959; The Office of a Bishop, 1962. Contribs. on subjects of Christian history to various learned jls., English and foreign, from 1927, and concurrently. *Recreation:* travel. *Address:* Langton, Upper St. Ann's Road, Faversham, Kent. *T.:* Faversham 2542. [*Died* 13 *Jan.* 1968.

TELFORD, Evelyn Davison, M.A., B.C. (Cantab.), F.R.C.S. (Eng.); M.Sc (Manch.); Surgeon Manchester Royal Infirmary; Professor of Systematic Surgery, Manchester Univ., 1922-36, now Emeritus; late Surgeon Manchester Education Com.; *b.* 16 June 1876; *m.* 1909, Sarah, *d.* of A. Waterhouse. *Educ.:* Manchester Grammar School; Caius College, Cambridge (Foundation Scholar). First Class, Pt. I., Natural Science Tripos, 1897; House Surgeon, Surgical Registrar, Resident Surgical Officer, Surgical Tutor, Assistant Surgical Officer at the Manchester Royal Infirmary; also Surgeon the Manchester Hospital for Sick Children and Assistant Surgeon the Salford Royal Hospital; Lecturer in Surgery, University of Manchester; in practice as Consulting Surgeon since 1904. *Publications:* The Problem of the Crippled School Child; numerous articles in the Medical Journals. *Address:* 7 Aberconway Road, Prestatyn, Flintshire. *T.:* Prestatyn 323. [*Died* 26 *March* 1961.

TELLING, Harry George, F.C.S., F.Inst.P.I.; Managing Director Amalgamated Code Compilers Ltd., London Bridge Street, S.E.1; *b.* 1 Sept 1880; *s.* of Henry Thomas Telling, Winterdyne, Beckenham, Kent, and Esther Elizabeth Telling; *m.* 1910, Edith Willis; one *s.* two *d.* *Educ.:* Wilson's Grammar School. Managing Director, Adaptable Code Condensers Ltd.; Manager, Marconi International Code Co. Ltd.; Managing Director, Stenocode Exploitation Syndicate. *Publications:* New Standard Half Word and Three Letter Codes, Private Banking, Commercial and Shipping Codes; Secret and Automatic Coding Devices; Treatise on Telegraphic Codes *Recreations:* rock gardening, philately. *Address:* c/o Amalgamated Code Compilers Ltd., London Bridge Street, S.E.1. *Clubs:* Royal Societies, Aldwych. [*Died* 26 *Dec.* 1961.

TEMPLAR-SMITH, Col. Sir Harold (Charles), K.B.E. 1953 (C.B.E. 1944); D.L.; LL.D.; C.Eng., F.I.C.E., Hon. F.I.GasE.; Past Chairman of the Gas Council (1952-60); *b.* 1890; *s.* of William Henry Smith, Birmingham; name changed to Templar-Smith by deed poll, 1967; *m.* 1917, *d.* of Reuben Heaton, Birmingham; two *d.* *Educ.:* King Edward VI School, Aston. Served in Royal Field Artillery, 1914-19. C.St.J. 1957. Hon. LL.D. Leeds, 1959. *Recreations:* yachting, shooting. *Address:* Cowslade Farm, Hartley Wintney, Hampshire. *T.:* 2461. *Clubs:* Royal Thames Yacht; Royal Lymington Yacht. [*Died* 6 *Sept.* 1970.

TEMPLE of STOWE, 6th Earl (*cr.* 1822); Chandos Grenville Temple-Gore-Langton; *b.* 13 July 1909; *s.* of late Capt. Hon. Chandos Graham Temple-Gore-Langton (2nd *s.* of 4th Earl) and late Frances Ethel, *d.* of late Rev. Arthur Gore; *S.* uncle, 1940; *m* 1st, 1934, Frances Vauriel Fenton (who obtained a divorce, 1940), *o. d.* of Major F. V. Lister, Ashwick Grove, Oakhill, Somerset; 2nd, 1943, Joan Helen Abbott. *Heir:* *b.* Hon. Ronald Stephen Brydges Temple-Gore-Langton, *b.* 1910 *Address:* Burrow Hall, Carnforth, Lancs *Club:* Junior Carlton. [*Died* 14 *April* 1966.

TEMPLE, Commander Grenville Mathias, D.S.O. 1940; D.S.C.; R.N. (retd.); *b.* 31 July 1897; *s.* of late Col. John Alexander Temple and Elizabeth Mathias; *m.* 1945, Meriol Hendry Wratislaw, *widow* of Lt. R. J. M. Wratislaw, R.N., and *o. c.* of late Capt. Sir Maxwell H. Maxwell-Anderson, C.B.E.; one *s.* one *d.* *Educ.:* Osborne; Dartmouth. H.M.S. Cumberland, 1914; served as Midshipman in H.M.S. Collingwood with King George VI; served European war, 1914-18, Jutland, Zeebrugge, Ostend; in Minesweepers and Destroyers until end of war; lent to R.A.N. for 2 years and retired in 1924; ranching in Australia (Queensland and N.S.W.) until 1929; settled in Kenya, dairy farming until 1936; returned to England, Hotel-keeping and real Estate; rejoined Navy, Jan. 1939; Acting Commander 1940 (Commander retired 1936); Evacuation of Dunkirk, 1940, and mine-sweeping later (D.S.O. and Bar); mine-sweeping operations at Malta, 1944 (D.S.C.), farming Trans-Nzoia, Kenya, 1946. *Recreations:* polo, shooting, golf, squash. *Address:* Box 49, Kitale, Kenya. *Clubs:* Naval and Military; Muthaiga Country (Nairobi). [*Died* 26 *July* 1965.

TEMPLE, Colonel (retd.) Sir Richard Durand, 3rd Bt., *cr.* 1876; D.S.O. 1918; late 60th Rifles; late commanding 5th Batt. Worcesters. Regt. (S.R.); *b.* 27 Dec. 1880; *o. s* of Lt.-Col. Sir R. C. Temple, 2nd Bt., and Agnes Fanny, 2nd *d.* of Maj.-Gen. G. A. Searle, M.S.C.; *S.* father, 1931; *m.* 1st, 1912, Katherine Marjorie (*d.* 1932), *d.* of late F. de la F. Williams, and *widow* of F. S. B. Anderton, Bolton Royd, Bradford; one *s.*; 2nd, 1939, Marie Wanda, *d.* of late F. C. Henderson, and of Mrs. Henderson, Bombay; two *s.* *Educ.:* Harrow; Royal Military Coll., Sandhurst. Entered Army, 1900; served S.A. War, 1901-2 (Queen's medal and four clasps); European War, 1914-18 (despatches six times, D.S.O., Croix de Guerre with Palm, 1914 Star, Bt. Major and Bt. Lt.-Col.). *Heir:* *s.* Major Richard Antony Purbeck, M.C. 1941, K.R.R.C. [*b.* 19 Jan. 1913; *m.* 1st, 1936, Lucy Geils (marriage dissolved, 1946), 2nd *d.* of Alain Joly de Lotbinière, Montreal; two *s.*; 2nd, 1950, Jean, *d.* of late James T. Finnie; one *d.* *Educ.:* Stowe School; Trinity Hall, Cambridge]. *Address:* 159 Colaba Rd., Bombay, India. [*Died* 15 *Sept.* 1962.

TEMPLETON, Archibald Angus, C.B.E. 1951 (M.B.E. 1918); D.L., Solicitor since 1914; Commissioner of General Board of Control for Scotland, 1955-62; *b.* 22 Aug. 1893, *er. s.* of William Templeton of Torland, J.P., Dalserf, Lanarkshire; *m.* 1927, Anna Kinloch, *d.* of H. Yeudall, Dumbarton; one *s.* two *d.* *Educ.:* Hamilton Academy; Glasgow Univ. County Clerk and Treasurer of Dunbartonshire, 1929-53; J.P. (Dunbartonshire) 1939; Hon. Sheriff Substitute at Dumbarton, 1950; Past Member Council of Law Society of Scotland; Mem. Scottish Probation Advisory and Training Council, 1942-65; Scottish Local Government Law Consolidation Committee, 1948; Chairman Building Materials Committee of Scottish Council (Development and Industry), 1949-65; Member: Historic Buildings Council for Scotland, 1953; Dunbartonshire Exec. Council (Nat. Health Service) 1954. Served European War, 1914-18, in France with 1st Black Watch (wounded); retired with rank of Capt.; War of 1939-45, Civil Defence Controller for Dunbartonshire. D.L., Dunbartonshire, 1968. *Publication:* (with Margaret S. Dilke) Third Statistical Account (Dunbartonshire) of Scotland, Vol. II, 1959. *Address:* Grendon, Helensburgh, Dunbartonshire. *T.:* 2575. *Clubs:* Scottish Conservative (Edinburgh); Royal Scottish Automobile (Glasgow). [*Died* 1 *May* 1969.

TENBY, 1st Viscount *cr.* 1957, of Bulford; **Gwilym Lloyd George,** P.C. 1941; T.D. 1952; J.P.; Chairman, Council on Tribunals since 1961; *b.* 4 Dec. 1894; *s.* of 1st Earl Lloyd-George of Dwyfor, P.C., O.M.; *m.* 1921, Edna Gwenfron, *d.* of David Jones, of Gwynfa, Denbigh; two *s.* *Educ.:* Eastbourne College; Jesus College (Hon. Fellow, 1953), Cambridge. Served European War, 1914-18, France; Major R.A. (despatches). M.P. (L.) Pembrokeshire, 1922-24 and 1929-1950 (L. and C.) Newcastle upon Tyne North, 1951-57. Parliamentary Sec.: Board of Trade, 1931 and 1939-41; Min. of Food, 1941-42; Minister of Fuel and Power, 1942-1945; Minister of Food, 1951-Oct. 1954; Secretary of State for the Home Department and Minister for Welsh Affairs, Oct. 1954-Jan. 1957. Freeman: City of London; Cardiff; Haverfordwest; Pembroke. Chm., Governing Body, Eastbourne Coll.; Past Pres., Univ. Coll. of Swansea. J.P. Pembrokeshire, 1938; Haverfordwest, 1934. Hon. LL.D. (Wales). *Heir:* *s.* Hon. David Lloyd-George, *b.* 4 Nov. 1922. *Address:* 231 St. James' Court, Buckingham Gate, S.W.1. *T.:* Victoria 2360. *Clubs:* Buck's, Reform. [*Died* 14 *Feb.* 1967.

TENGBOM, Ivar Justus; Hon. R.A. 1947; professor, architect; practising architect since 1906; *b.* 7 April 1878; *s.* of Captain J. Tengbom and Agnes Almqvist; *m.* 1st, 1905, Hjördis Nordin; 2nd, 1931, Madeleine Douglas; one *s.* two *d.* (and one *s.* decd.). *Educ.:* Chalmers Technical Institute, Göteborg; Academy of Art, Stockholm. Received the King's Medal at the Academy of Art in Stockholm, 1901; Professor at Architectural

School of the Academy, 1916-20, 1922-58; Architect at the Royal Palace at Stockholm and Drottningholm, 1922-61; General Director and Head of the Royal Board of public buildings, 1924-36; President of the Academy of Art, Stockholm, 1943-53; Royal Swedish Institute for Engineering Research; Royal Acad. of Letters, Hist. and Antiq. Member or Corr. Member of numerous Academies, etc. in Europe, Russia and America; Hon. Dr. at the Technische Hochschule, Stuttgart, Darmstadt, Wien and Gothenburg; The Roy. Gold Medal at R.I.B.A., 1938; Hon. Academician Roy Acad., London; Accademia di San Luca, Rome; The American Institute of Architects, Academy of Art, Copenhagen. Architectural works; many public buildings, schools, and private residences. *Publications:* Stockholms Enskilda Bank, 1916, Stockholms Konserthus, 1926; Högalid-skyrkan, 1923; The Swedish Match Company's Head Office, Stockholm 1931; Atvidabergshuset, 1944. *Address:* Korn hamnstorg 6, Stockholm.

[*Died* 6 *Aug.* 1968.

TENNANT, Admiral Sir William George, K.C.B. *cr.* 1945 (C.B. 1940); C.B.E. 1944; M.V.O. 1925; Lord Lieutenant of Worcestershire since 1950; *b.* 2 Jan. 1890; *e. surv. s.* of late Lt.-Col. E. W. Tennant of the Eades, Upton-on-Severn; *m.* 1919, Catherine *d.* of late Major C. H. Blount, R.H.A. *Educ.:* Joined H.M.S. Britannia, 1905. Lieut. 1912; Commander, 1925; Capt. 1932; Rear-Adm. 1942; Vice-Adm. 1945; served Dunkirk, 1940 (C.B.); Invasion of Normandy, 1944 (C.B.E.). For services in the War in Europe K.C.B. Flag Officer Levant and E. Mediterranean, 1944-46; Admiral, 1948; Commander-in-Chief America and West Indies Station, 1946-49; retired, 1949. Past Chm., King George's Fund for Sailors; K.St.J., 1950. Hon. Freeman of Worcester, 1958. Legion of Honour and Croix de Guerre (France); Legion of Merit (U.S.A.); Grand Cross of St. George of Greece. *Address:* The Eades, Upton-on-Severn, Worcestershire. *Club:* United Service. [*Died* 26 *July* 1963.

TENNANT, Sir William Robert, Kt., *cr.* 1947; C.I.E. 1941; late Deputy Auditor-General of India; *b.* 26 Sept. 1892; *m.* 1925, Isabel, *d.* of Rev. Hector Adam; one *s.* one *d.* *Educ.:* Aberdeen Grammar School and Univ. M.A., LL.D. Served British and Indian Armies, 1915-19; entered Indian Civil Service, 1919 (1916), retired 1949; served Indian Audit Dept., 1923-27 and 1934-47; Finance Dept., 1927-33. C.St.J., 1944; Kaisar-i-Hind Gold Medal, 1947. *Address:* 5 Gillespie Terrace, St. Andrews, Fife. *T.:* 475. *Club:* Royal and Ancient

[*Died* 4 *May* 1969.

TENNENT, Thomas, M.D. (Glasgow), F.R.C.P. (London), D.P.H. (London), D.P.M (London); Medical Superintendent St. Andrew's Hospital, Northampton; Examiner in Psychological Medicine, University of London; Chief Consultant Ex-Services Welfare Society; Physician in Psychological Medicine, Miller Hospital, Greenwich; Physician in Psychological Medicine, Northampton General Hospital; *b.* Kirkintilloch, Dunbartonshire, 1900; *s.* of Thomas Tennent; *m.* 1931, Mildred Evelyn Gale; one *s.* two *d.* *Educ.:* Lenzie Academy; Universities of Glasgow, London and Johns Hopkins, Baltimore, U.S.A. House Surgeon and House Physician, Western Infirmary, Glasgow, 1922-23; Assistant Medical Officer, Dykebar Mental Hospital, Paisley, 1924-26; Assistant Medical Officer, Maudsley Hospital, London 1926-31; Clinical Assistant, National Hospital for Nervous Disorders, Queen Square, 1927; Rockefeller Medical Fellow, Phipps Psychiatric Clinic, Johns Hopkins Hospital, Baltimore, U.S.A. 1927-28; Deputy Medical Superintendent, Maudsley Hospital, 1931-38; Lecturer in Psychological Medicine, Maudsley Hospital Medical School; Senior Assistant, Department of Psychological Medicine, King's College Hospital, 1931-36; Assistant Physician in Psychological Medicine, King's College Hospital, 1936-38. *Publications:* Section on Psychological Medicine in Saville Textbook of Medicine, 1950; Papers on neurological and psychological subjects in scientific journals. *Recreations:* golf, fishing. *Address:* 55 Harley Street, W.1. *T.:* Langham 4031; Priory Cottage, Northampton. *T.:* Northampton 4354. *Club:* Bath.

[*Died* 28 *Jan.* 1962.

TERRINGTON, 3rd Baron, *cr.* 1918, of Huddersfield, **Horace Marton Woodhouse,** K.B.E., *cr.* 1952 (C.B.E. 1919); *b.* 27 Oct. 1887; 2nd *surv. s.* of 1st Baron and Jessie (*d.* 1942), *d.* of W. J. Reed, of Skidby, Yorks; *S.* brother 1940; *m.* 1st, 1914, Valerie, (*d.* 1958), 2nd *d.* of late G. A. Phillips, Leyden's Hse., Edenbridge, Kent; two *s.*; 2nd, 1959, Mrs. Phyllis Mary Haggard, *d.* of late W. W. Drew, I.C.S. *Educ.:* Winchester; New College, Oxford. Called to Bar, Inner Temple, 1911; Chairman Industrial Disputes Tribunal (formerly National Arbitration Tribunal), 1944-59; Assistant Secretary, Ministry of Food, 1918-21; Principal Asst. Secretary, Ministry of Labour and National Service, 1941-44; Chairman Industrial Court, Air Transport Licensing Board, Cotton Conciliation Committee; Dep. Chm. London Theatres Council and Provincial Theatres Council; Deputy Speaker and Deputy Chairman of Committees, House of Lords, 1949-. *Heir: s.* Hon. (James Allen) David Woodhouse [*b.* 30 Dec. 1915; *m.* 1942, Suzanne, *d.* of Col. T. S. Irwin, Justicetown, Carlisle; three *d.* *Educ.:* Winchester; Sandhurst. Member Stock Exchange]. *Address:* 44 Hornton Court, W.8. *T.:* Western 7902. *Clubs:* Reform, Bath. [*Died* 7 *Jan.* 1961.

TERRY, Captain Frederic Bouhier Imbert-, M.C.; J.P. County of Devon; late Devonshire Regiment; *b.* 1887; *yr. s.* of Sir H. M. Imbert-Terry, 1st Bt.; *m.* 1917, Lilian Frederica Violette Lucy (*d.* 1949), *d.* of Sir Alfred Hickman, 1st Bt. Served European War, 1914-18 (despatches, M.C.); High Sheriff of Devon, 1928. *Address:* Birnam, 5 Laureston Road, Wolborough Hill, Newton Abbot, Devon *T.:* Newton Abbot 2518. *Club:* Carlton.

[*Died* 20 *Jan.* 1963.

TERRY, Lt.-Col. Sir Henry B. I.; *see* Imbert-Terry.

TEVIOT, 1st Baron, *cr.* 1940, of Burghclere; **Lt.-Col. Charles Iain Kerr,** D.S.O. 1919; M.C.; Member of Council of St. Dunstan's; Past Director: G. D. Peters and Co. (Dep. Chm. resigned 1963); Lloyds Bank Ltd. (retd. 1951); General Accident Fire and Life Assce. Corp. Ltd.; National Bank of Scotland (retd. 1959); Andrew Weir & Co. (London); Bank Line (Shipping); Past Chm., Nat. Jt. Council of Scotland; Past Hon. Treasurer, Association of British Chambers of Commerce; *b.* 3 May 1874; *e. s.* of late C. W. R. Kerr; *m.* 1930, Florence Angela, *d.* of late Lt.-Col. Charles Walter Villiers, C.B.E., D.S.O.; one *s.* M.P. (L. Nat.) Montrose Burghs, 1932-40; Lord Commissioner of the Treasury and Chief Whip Liberal National Party, 1937-39; Chairman, 1940-56; Comptroller of H.M. Household, 1939-40. Chairman of Lloyds Bank, Western Board, Salisbury, 1953-56. Ensign, Queen's Body Guard for Scotland, 1945. *Heir: s.* Hon. Charles John Kerr [*b.* 16 Dec. 1934; *m.* 1965, Mary, *d.* of the late Alexander Harris and Mrs. Harris]. *Address:* 9 North Audley Street, W.1.

[*Died* 7 *Jan.* 1968.

TEW, Sir Mervyn Lawrence, Kt., *cr.* 1932; *b.* 1876; *s.* of E. L. H. Tew, Vicar of Hornsea and Rector of Long Riston, East Yorks, and afterwards Rector of Upham, Hants, and Jane, *d.* of Rev. Thomas Henderson, Vicar of Messing, Essex; *m.* 1st, 1911, Muriel Ramsbotham (*d.* 1941), *d.* of Capt. R. W. Davies, R.N.; one *s.*; 2nd, Sadie, *y. d.* of late Thomas Houston of Tyrone, N. Ireland. *Educ.:* Marlborough; Hertford College, Oxford; B.A. 1899; M.A. 1902. Served South African War, 1900-1; Assistant District Commissioner, Southern Nigeria, 1904; District Commissioner, 1909; Crown Solicitor, 1911; called to Bar, Lincoln's Inn, 1913; Acting Attorney-General, Northern Nigeria, 1913; Legal Adviser, Nigeria, 1914; Solicitor-General, 1920; Puisne Judge, 1923; Chief Justice of Sierra Leone, 1929-32; retired, 1932; Chairman, Pensions Appeal Tribunals, 1944-56. *Address:* 301 Grove End Gdns., N.W.8. *T.:* Cunningham 4776. [*Died* 27 *Dec.* 1963.

te WATER, Charles Theodore, B.A., LL.B.; *b.* 1887; *s.* of Dr. Hon. T. te Water; *m.* 1916, E. M. Marais, Pretoria; one *s.* one *d. Educ.:* Normal College, Cape; Bedford Grammar School; Cambridge. Barrister-at-Law of the Inner Temple, and Member of the Pretoria Bar; Represented Pretoria (Central) in the Union Parliament, 1924-29; High Commissioner for the Union of South Africa in London, 1929-39. Ambassador at large of S. Africa, 1948-49. President of Assembly of League of Nations, 1933; Patron and Ex-President South African Association of Arts; Trustee for the Lord Nuffield Fund for Cripples in South Africa; Deputy Chairman National Council for the care of cripples in South Africa; Hon. Life Pres., National Veld Trust; Chm. Citizens Housing League Utility Company, 1940-46; Past Dir., South African Reserve Bank. Chancellor of Pretoria University. Hon. LL.D., Witwatersrand University. *Recreations:* golf, fishing. *Address:* Môreson, St. James, Capetown, S. Africa. *Clubs:* Pretoria (Pretoria); Civil Service (Capetown). [*Died* 6 *June* 1964.

THACKER, Ransley Samuel, Q.C., Fiji, 1937; *b.* 17 March 1891; *s.* of late Henry Ransley Thacker; *m.* 1915, Olive Frances Braithwaite (*d.* 1948), London; two *s.* one *d.*; *m.* 1961, Mary Laugharne. *Educ.:* Choir School of H.M. Chapels Royal, St. James; Dulwich Coll. Called to Bar, Gray's Inn, 1913; practised at Bar, England, 1913-. Asst. to Sec. Brit. Metal Corp. Ltd., London, 1923-27; Sec., Financial Assistant, to Corporations, London, 1927-29. H.M. Colonial Legal Service 1930; Chief Justice, St. Vincent, B.W.I., 1930; H.M. Attorney-General, Fiji 1933-38; Mem. of Legislative Council; Mem. of Exec. Council; Chm. of Native Regulations Bd.; Chm. of Board of Visitors, Colonial War Memorial Hospital; Chairman of Board of Visitors, Public Lunatic Asylum; Chairman of War Pensions Board; Member of Tender Committee; Acting Chief Justice of Fiji and Acting Chief Judicial Commissioner for the Western Pacific, Sept. 1935-July 1936; Q.C., Fiji, 1937; Puisne Judge of H.M. Supreme Court of Kenya, and Member Court of Appeal for Eastern Africa, 1938-1952; retired 1952. Now farming, and is Chairman of various (Government) Industrial Boards, in Rhodesia. Formerly (in Kenya): Chm., Farmers Conciliation Board, 1938-40; Chm., War Compensation Board, 1939-40; President Trade Disputes Tribunal, 1947; President Ginnery Arbitration Tribunal, Uganda, 1952; Chairman, Court of Review, Kenya, 1952. Acting Chief Justice on several occasions. Editor of Law Reports of H.M. Court of Appeal for Eastern Africa, 1942-43. Coronation medals, 1902, 1937, 1953. *Address:* Umdala, P.O. Box 50, Chipinga, Rhodesia. *T.:* Chipinga 40; Silverlands, Sutton Avenue, Seaford, Sussex. *T.:* Seaford 3459. *Club:* Umtali (Rhodesia). [*Died* 27 *Dec.* 1965.

THACKSTONE, Howard Harrison; Chief General Manager, Midland Bank Ltd., 1962-1968, Senior Executive Director, 1968; Director since 1966; Vice-Chairman, Midland Bank Finance Corporation, since 1967; *b.* 21 Oct. 1905; *o. s.* of William Edward and Eliza Thackstone; *m.* 1932, Amelia Hearn; two *d. Educ.:* Archbishop Holgate's Grammar School, Barnsley. Entered Midland Bank, Barnsley, 1920; transferred to London, 1929; Secretary to Frederick Hyde, Managing Director, 1929-33; Asst. Secretary of Bank, 1933-37; Dep. Asst. Manager, Threadneedle Street, 1937-40; Asst. Chief Accountant, 1940-44; Chief Foreign Manager, 1947; Asst. General Manager, 1953; Jt. Gen. Manager, 1955; Asst. Chief Gen. Manager, 1958; Chief Gen. Manager, 1962; Director, 1966. Fellow Inst. of Bankers; Chm. Chief Exec. Officers; Cttee., of London Clearing Bankers, 1964-66; Director: Midland Bank Finance Corporation Ltd.; Midland Bank Executor and Trustee Co.; Standard Bank; Bank of W. Africa; Montagu Trust Ltd.; European-American Banking Corp.; British Export Trade Research Organisation (1952) Ltd.; Member, Export Credits Guarantee Department Advisory Council, 1962-66. Mem. Council, B.I.M., 1967. Governor, St. Helen's School for Girls, Northwood. *Recreations:* cricket, golf. *Address:* Oriel House, Main Avenue, Moor Park, Northwood, Middlesex. *T.:* Northwood 25386. *Clubs:* Overseas Bankers; Sandy Lodge Golf. [*Died* 25 *Jan.* 1969.

THAKURDAS, Sir Purshotamdas, K.B.E., *cr.* 1944 (M.B.E. 1917); Kt., *cr.* 1923; C.I.E.; *b.* 30 May 1879. *Educ.:* Elphinstone College, Bombay. Merchant; ex-Pres. East India Cotton Assoc. Ltd., Bombay; Director, Tata Locomotive & Engineering Co. Ltd., etc. *Address:* Ridge Road, Mabar Hill, Bombay. [*Died* 4 *July* 1961.

THAPA, Hon. Captain Lalbahadur, V.C. 1943; O.B.I.; Sardar Bahadur, retd.; 4th Class Order of the Most Refulgent Order of the Star of Nepal; is farming in Nepal; *b.* 1907; Gurkha, Hindu; *m.* 1932, Hasti; four *s.* two *d.* Rifleman, I.A., 1925; Lance-Naik, January 1930; Subadar Major, 1944; retired, 1949 (granted hon. rank of Capt.). 2nd K.E. VII's O. Gurkha Rifles, The Brigade of Gurkhas, Malaya. *Recreations:* hunting boars and tigers; gardening. *Address:* Sumsa, Thantap, 4000 Parbat, Baglung, Nepal. [*Died* 19 *Oct.* 1968.

THATCHER, William Sutherland, M.C., M.A., Censor Emeritus of Fitzwilliam House, Univ. of Cambridge, 1924-54; Senior Tutor, 1954-55; *b.* Dec. 1888; *s.* of late Rev. W. Thatcher, Vicar of All Saints' Church, Gt. Nelson St., Liverpool; *m.* 1917, Thelma, *y d.* of Mark William Hydes, merchant; one *d. Educ.:* Farnworth Grammar School; Liverpool College Middle School, Fitzwilliam House, Cambridge; Professor (Lecturer) in Economics in the Agra College. University of Allahabad; Member of Faculty of Economics, 1912-14; joined I.A.R.O. attached 129th Baluchis, I.A.; served in Flanders, (wounded); East Africa (twice wounded, M.C.); resigned appointment in Agra owing to wounds; returned to Cambridge 1918; formerly Lecturer in Faculty of Geography. *Publications:* 4/10 Baluch Regiment in the Great War; Economic Geography. *Recreation:* walking. *Address:* 9 Little St. Mary's Lane, Cambridge. *T.:* Cambridge 50596. [*Died* 12 *Dec.* 1966.

THEIS, Otto Frederick; editor; *b.* Germania, Pennsylvania, U.S.A., 16 Dec. 1881; *e. s.* of Henry J. and Virginia Theis; *m.* Louise Morgan Fulcher (*d.* 1964); one *s. Educ.:* privately; Lafayette College, first honours. In newspaper work, Philadelphia; on staff of several works of reference; with various American publishers, scientific and general, in an editorial capacity; associate and literary editor, The Outlook, London, 1922-28; has represented various American publishers in England. *Publications:* contributions to various periodicals; translator Gauguin's Noa Noa, Schnitzler's Shepherd's Pipe, Zweig's Verlaine, Przybyszewski's Snow, Gudmundsson's The Bridal Gown, Kaus's Luxury Liner, etc. *Address:* West Beam, Henley's Down, Nr. Catsfield, Battle, Sussex. *T.:* Crowhurst 355. [*Died* 4 *Dec.* 1966.

THELWELL, Sir Arthur (Frederick), Kt. 1962; C.B.E. 1951 (O.B.E. 1945); J.P.; Chairman, Christiana Area Land Authority since 1955; *b.* 17 Nov. 1889; *s.* of H. N. and Agnes Jane Thelwell; *m.* 1943, Mary Pawsey; three *d.* *Educ.:* Mico Coll., Jamaica. Superintendent of Agriculture, Jamaica, 1935-37; Senior Agriculture Officer, 1943-1946; Deputy Director of Agriculture, 1946-1947; Commissioner of Lands, 1947-51. M.L.C. Jamaica, 1948-51. Co-ord. Officer, Jamaica Banana Growers Assoc., 1951-54. Served European War, France and Italy, 1916-19. Capt. (retd.), B.W.I. Regt. *Recreations:* golf, fishing. *Address:* Braemar, Mandeville, Jamaica. *T.:* Mandeville 2072. *Clubs:* Manchester, Jamaica, Kingston Cricket, Constant Spring Golf (all in Jamaica). [*Died* 30 *Nov.* 1966.

THERON, Maj.-Gen. François Henri, C.B. 1944; C.B.E. 1942; South African Forces, retired; *b.* 1891; *s* of S. W. Theron; *m.* 1920, Audrey Baillie, *d.* of late Barham Molyneux Noel; one *s.* one *d.* *Educ.:* St. George's Cathedral Grammar School, Cape Town. Served 1914-18 War, in S.W. and East Africa, and France; War of 1939-1945 in Middle East (despatches, C.B.E., C.B.). Sometime Minister of Union of S. Africa in Rome; Minister, Cairo and Athens, 1946-51. *Address:* Vrede Vlei, Milnerton, C.P., S. Africa. [*Died* 28 *July* 1967.

THESIGER, His Honour Arthur Lionel Bruce; *b.* 19 Oct. 1872; *e. s.* of late Hon. Sir Edward P. Thesiger, K.C.B., and Georgina Mary Stopford; *m* 1902, Florita Maria-Engracia (*d.* 1966), *d.* of Edward Knight, Pencoed, Glamorgan; one *s.* one *d.* *Educ.:* Winchester; New Coll., Oxford. 14 yrs. in the Insurance profession; called to Bar, Inner Temple, 1899, but did not begin to practise until 1907, joined South Eastern circuit; County Court Judge, Circuit No. 1, 1931-37; No. 57, 1938-47; retd., 1947; formerly Dep. Chm., Devon Quarter Sessions, and Governor Blundell's School. *Address:* Eleven Plus, Hungershall Park, Tunbridge Wells. *T.:* Tunbridge Wells 26601. [*Died* 20 *Feb.* 1968.

THESIGER, Admiral Sir Bertram Sackville, K.B.E., *cr.* 1942; C.B. 1916; C.M.G. 1911; *b.* 14 January 1875; 2nd *s.* of late Hon. Sir Edward Thesiger, K.C.B.; *m.* 1921, Violet, *widow* of W. Brodrick Cloete, and *d.* of late J. A. Henley, Waterperry, Oxford. Entered R.N., 1887; Lieut., 1895; Comdr., 1905; Capt., 1912; Rear-Adm., 1922; Vice-Adm., 1928; Adm., 1932; served European War, Battle of Jutland, 1914-1918 (despatches, C.B.); Admiral-Supt. of Portsmouth Dockyard, 1925-27; Com.-in-Chf., East Indies Station, 1927-29; A.D.C. to the King, 1922; retired list, 1932; served as Commodore R.N.R., 1940-42; Flag Officer in Charge, Falmouth, 1942-44. Has been connected with Boy Scout Movement for 46 years; was County Comr. for Hampshire for 15 years. 2nd Class Order of St. Anne of Russia with crossed swords; St. Vladimir, Russia, with crossed swords; Legion of Merit, U.S.A. *Publication:* Queries in Seamanship. *Address:* 21 De Vere Gardens, W.8. *T.:* Western 5760. *Clubs:* United Service, I Zingari. [*Died* 12 *May* 1966.

THESIGER, Ernest, C.B.E. 1960; actor; *b* 15 January 1879; *s.* of late Hon. Sir Edward Thesiger, K.C.B.; *m.* 1917, Janette Mary Fernie Ranken. *Educ.:* Marlborough. Studied at the Slade School of Art as a painter; first appeared on the stage with Sir George Alexander at the St. James' Theatre, 1909. Served European War: joined the Queen Victoria Rifles, 1914; wounded, 1 Jan. 1915; discharged, May 1915. Returned to the stage in A Little Bit of Fluff, playing in it for 1300 performances; other parts, Cameron in Mary Rose, the Dauphin in St. Joan, Dr. Marshall in A Sleeping Clergyman, Sir Orpheus Midlander in Geneva, King Charles II. in In Good King Charles's Golden Days, etc.; Voltaire, in Crisis in Heaven; The Chief Statistician, in Under the Sycamore Tree; John Cadmus in Marching Song; Polonius, 1955 (on tour, Russia, London); in the Hidden King, Edinburgh Fest., 1957; Talbot, in Mary Stuart, Edinburgh Fest., and Old Vic, London, 1958; Vigeon, in The Edwardians, Saville, 1959; The Last Joke, 1960. *Films:* The Old Dark House, The Night of the Party, The Bride of Frankenstein, The Miracle Man, They Drive by Night, The Lamp still Burns, Henry V, Caesar and Cleopatra, Beware of Pity, The Winslow Boy, Quartet The Man in the White Suit, Laughter in Paradise, The Robe, Value for Money, Who dun it, Three Men in a Boat, The Horse's Mouth, Battle of the Sexes, Sons and Lovers. *Publications:* Practically True, 1927; Adventures in Embroidery, 1941. *Recreation:* painting. *Address:* 8 St. George's Ct., Gloucester Rd., S.W.7. *T.:* Knightsbridge 8580. [*Died* 14 *Jan.* 1961.

THEUNIS, Georges; *b.* 28 Feb. 1873; *s.* of Emile Theunis and Georgine Renson; *m.* 1898, Louise Brasseur (*d.* 1964); no *c.* *Educ.:* Ecole Militaire (Artillerie) Brussels; Institut Electrotechnique Montefiore, Liége. Artillery Officer; left the Army to be engineer and later on a Director of electrical engineering and distribution companies; during war, 1914-18, Lt.-Colonel, Head of the Belgian Commission for war supplies in London; First Belgian Delegate at the Reparations Commission 1919; Minister of Finance 1920; Prime Minister and Minister of Finances, 1921-25; Minister of State, 1925; President of the International Economic conference in Geneva, 1927; President of the International Chamber of commerce 1929-31; Ministre de la Défense Nationale Oct.-Dec. 1932; Premier Ministre Nov. 1934-Mars 1935; Belgian Ambassador-at-large in U.S.A., Oct. 1939-Nov. 1944. President of Oeuvre Nationale de l'Enfance and of the Fondation Médicale Reine Elisabeth. *Address:* 2 rue des II Eglises, Brussels. [*Died* 4 *Jan.* 1966.

THIRKELL, Angela Margaret, F.R.S.L.; **(Mrs. G. L. Thirkell);** *b.* 30 Jan. 1890; *d.* of late J. W. Mackail, O.M., and Margaret Burne-Jones; *m.* 1st, 1911, J. Campbell MacInnes (whom she divorced 1917); two *s.*; 2nd, G. L. Thirkell; one *s.* Born and lived in London till second marriage when she went to Australia for some years; in Melbourne, Australia, did broadcasting and some journalism and began to contribute to English magazines; has lived in England since 1930. *Publications:* Three Houses; Ankle Deep; High Rising; Wild Strawberries; The Demon in the House; O, These men, these men!; The Grateful Sparrow; The Fortunes of Harriette; August Folly, 1936; Coronation Summer, 1937; Summer Half, 1937; Pomfret Towers, 1938; The Brandons, 1939; Before Lunch, 1939; Cheerfulness Breaks in, 1940; Northbridge Rectory, 1941; Marling Hall, 1942; Growing Up, 1943; The Headmistress, 1944; Miss Bunting, 1945; Peace Breaks Out, 1946; Private Enterprise, 1947; Love Among the Ruins, 1948; The Old Bank House, 1949; County Chronicle, 1950; The Duke's Daughter, 1951; Happy Returns, 1952;

Jutland Cottage. 1953; What Did it Mean?, 1954; Enter Sir Robert, 1955; Never Too Late, 1956; A Double Affair, 1957; Close Quarters, 1958; Love at All Ages, 1959; Three Score and Ten, 1961 (posthumous; finished by C. A. Lejeune); contributed to Times, News Chronicle, Cornhill, National Mercury, Fortnightly, Spectator, etc. *Address:* c/o Barclay's Bank, 276 Kensington High Street, W.8. [*Died* 29 *Jan.* 1961.

THODAY, David, F.R.S. 1942; F.R.S.S.Af.; Sc.D.; Emeritus Professor in the University of Wales, 1949; *b.* Honiton, 5 May 1883; *s.* of David Thoday and Susan E. Bingham; *m.* Mary Gladys (Girton College and sometime Fellow of Newnham College, Cambridge, *d.* 1943), *e. d.* of J. Thorley Sykes, of Rossett, Denbighshire; four *s.* *Educ.:* Trinity College, Cambridge. Walsingham Medallist, 1908; University Demonstrator in Botany at Cambridge, 1909-1911; Lecturer in Plant Physiology, University of Manchester, 1911-18; Prof. of Botany, University of Cape Town, S.A., 1918-22; Professor of Botany, Univ. Coll. of North Wales, Bangor, 1923-49; Professor of Plant Physiology, University of Alexandria, 1950-1951; Visiting Professor in the University of Leeds, 1951-52; President of Section K, British Association, 1939. Hon. D.Sc. (Wales) 1960. *Publications:* Botany, 1915; botanical papers in scientific journals. *Address:* c/o Botany Dept., University College of N. Wales, Bangor, Caerns.
[*Died* 30 *March* 1964.

THOMAS, Alan Ernest Wentworth, D.S.O. 1917; M.C.; Editor of The Listener, 1939-58; *b.* 21 Aug. 1896; *o. surv. s.* of late Ernest and Jessie Thomas, London; *m.* 1927, Elsa Dorothy, 2nd *d.* of W. G. Auger; two *s.* *Educ.:* Malvern (Classical Scholar); Clare College, Cambridge (Classical Scholar, Choral Scholar); 2nd class honours Law Tripos, M.A., LL.B. Served European War, 1915-19, Captain Royal West Kent Regiment (despatches, D.S.O., M.C., four times wounded); Barrister-at-law, Gray's Inn, 1920; on the staff of League of Nations Union, 1921-36. *Publications:* The Death of Laurence Vining; The Tremayne Case; Daggers Drawn; The Lonely Years; The Stolen Cellini; Summer Adventure; Death of the Home Secretary; That We Might Live: The Mask and the Man; The Fugitives; The Director; The Governor; The Surgeon; The Judge; (autobiog.) A Life Apart, 1968; The Professor, 1969; The Calverston Story, 1970. *Address:* 3 Montpelier Villas, Brighton 1, Sussex. *T.:* Brighton 27939. *Clubs:* United University, M.C.C., P.E.N.
[*Died* 23 *Nov.* 1969.

THOMAS, Bert; Black and White and Poster Artist; Member of Pastel Society; *b.* Newport, Mon.; 3rd *s.* of Job Thomas, sculptor; *m.* 1909, Elizabeth Bowen (*d.* 1949); two *s.* (and two decd.); two *d.*; *m.* 1950, Mrs. F. A. Corrie. Served European War 1914-18: Artists' Rifles; official artist to War Bonds Campaign, March 1918. Contributor to most humorous periodicals. *Recreations:* field sports. *Address:* 33 Inverness Terrace, W.2. *Clubs:* Savage, Chelsea Arts, London Sketch (Hon.).
[*Died* 6 *Sept.* 1966.

THOMAS, Professor David Winton; F.B.A. 1966; M.A. (Oxford, Cambridge); Regius Professor of Hebrew in the University of Cambridge, 1938-68; Fellow of St. Catharine's College, Cambridge, 1943, President, 1965-1968, Emeritus Fellow since 1968; *b.* London, 26 January 1901; *s.* of late Rev. David John Thomas; *m.* 1932, Edith Marion Higgins, *y. d.* of Arthur Higgins, Meols, Cheshire; two *s.* one *d.* *Educ.:* Merchant Taylors' School; St. John's Coll., Oxford; First Class Honours in the Final School of Oriental Languages; Junior Septuagint Prize; Pusey and Ellerton Hebrew Scholarship; Houghton Syriac Prize; James Mew Rabbinical Hebrew Scholarship; Junior Kennicott Hebrew Scholarship; Senior Kennicott Fellowship; Examiner to the University for the Hall and Hall-Houghton Syriac and Septuagint Prizes and for the Pusey and Ellerton and Kennicott Hebrew Scholarships; Special Assistant in the Oriental Department of the Bodleian Library, Oxford; Senior Scholar and Lecturer in Oriental Languages at St. John's College, Oxford; Lecturer in Arabic to the Gordon College, Khartoum, Sudan; Student, University of Marburg, Germany; Professor of Hebrew and Oriental Languages in the Univ. of Durham, 1930-38; External Examiner for the Univs. of Oxford, Manchester, Leeds, Durham, Birmingham, Edinburgh, Liverpool, Bristol and London; President of the Society for Old Testament Study, 1953; Member Council of the Senate, 1955-58; Member Archbishops' Commission on the Revision of the Psalter; Executive Officer Cambridge University A.R.P. Organ., 1941-45, and N.F.S., 1943-44. Hon. Curator, Geniza Collection, Univ. Library, Cambridge, 1965-69. Hon. D.D. Durham and Wales. Burkitt Medal, 1969. *Publications:* The Language of the Old Testament (in Record and Revelation, ed. H. Wheeler Robinson); The Recovery of the Ancient Hebrew Language; Ed. Essays and Studies presented to S. A. Cook; The Textual Criticism of the Old Testament (in The Old Testament and Modern Study, ed. H. H. Rowley); Ed. (with M. Noth) Wisdom in Israel and in the Ancient Near East; Ed. Documents from Old Testament Times; Ed. (with W. D. McHardy) Hebrew and Semitic Studies presented to Godfrey Rolles Driver, 1963; The Text of The Revised Psalter, 1963; Ed. Archaeology and Old Testament Study, 1967; Liber Jessaiae in Biblia Hebraica Stuttgartensia, 1968; contributor to various learned journals. *Recreations:* Rugby football, music. *Address:* 4 Grantchester Road, Cambridge. *T.:* Cambridge 54640.
[*Died* 18 *June* 1970.

THOMAS, Edgar William, C.B.E. 1919; *b.* 30 April 1879; *o. surv. s.* of late George Thomas, Croydon; *m.* 1911, Phyllis Annette, *y. d.* of late T. H. Whitmore, East Grinstead, Sussex; one *s.* two *d.* (and one *s.* decd.). *Educ.:* Christ's Hospital. Entered Public Trustee Office, 1908; resigned position of Financial Adviser to Public Trustee, 1919, to become a member of the London Stock Exchange; retired, 1930. *Address:* 131 Cranmer Court, S.W.3. *T.:* Kensington 1366.
[*Died* 1 *Jan.* 1963.

THOMAS, Hon. Sir Eric; *see* Thomas, Hon. Sir W. E.

THOMAS, Wing Comdr. Forest Y.; *see* Yeo-Thomas.

THOMAS, Frederic W. W.; *see* Watkyn-Thomas.

THOMAS, Sir George Hector, Kt., *cr.* 1941; *b.* 23 June 1884. Called to Bar, Middle Temple, 1905; Government Advocate, Chief Court, Lucknow, 1925; Judge, Chief Court, Oudh, 1934; Chief Judge, Chief Court, Oudh, 1938-46. *Address:* 104 Mahatma Gandhi Road, Lucknow, India.
[*Died* 11 *April* 1965.

THOMAS, Rt. Hon. Sir Godfrey (John Vignoles), 10th Bart., *cr.* 1694; P.C. 1958; G.C.V.O., 1948 (K.C.V.O., 1925; C.V.O. 1920); K.C.B., 1937; C.S.I. 1922; *b.* 14 April 1889; *o. s.* of Brigadier-General Sir Godfrey Thomas, C.B., C.B.E., D.S.O., 9th Bart; *S.* father, 1919; *m.* 1924, Diana, *d.* of late Ven. B. G. Hoskyns, Archdeacon of Chichester; one *s.* *Educ.:* Harrow. Diplomatic Service, 1912; Third Secretary, Berlin, 1913-14; Private Secretary to the

Prince of Wales, 1919-36; Asst. Private Secretary to the King, 1936; Private Secretary to the Duke of Gloucester, 1937-57; Extra Equerry, 1958-; employed F.O., 1939-44. *Heir:* *s.* Godfrey Michael David Thomas, Capt. The Rifle Bde. [*b.* 10 Oct. 1925; *m.* 1956, Margaret, *yr. d.* of John Cleland, Sevenoaks]. *Address:* Royal Cottage, Kew, Surrey. *T.:* Richmond 0711. *Clubs:* Boodle's, M.C.C.

[*Died* 4 *March* 1968.

THOMAS, Henry Hugh, C.B.E. 1949; retd.; *b.* 19 April 1904; *s.* of H. C. Thomas; *m.* 1932, Rhona Cecilia Clark; three *d.* *Educ.:* Alleyn's School, Dulwich; Sidney Sussex College, Cambridge; Yale University. Entered H.M. Consular Service (Japan), 1927; Vice-Consul, 1932; Consul, Grade II, 1938, Consul, 1942; seconded to H.M. Treasury, 1944; appointed Counsellor (Financial) of H.M. Embassy, China, 1946, and (concurrently) Financial Adviser, U.K. Liaison Mission, Tokyo, 1947; Economic Counsellor, British Embassy, Libya, Oct. 1953; H.B.M. Consul-General, Valparaiso, 1956; retired, 1959. *Recreation:* motoring. *Address:* Little Broome, Rudgwick, Sussex. [*Died* 16 *Dec.* 1967.

THOMAS, Hugh Hamshaw, M.B.E.; F.R.S. 1934; Sc.D.; F.L.S.; F.G.S.; Wing-Comdr. R.A.F.V.R., retd.; Reader Emeritus in Plant Morphology, University of Cambridge, since 1950; Hon. Fellow of Downing College; *b.* 29 May 1885; *s.* of W. Thomas, Wrexham; *m.* 1923, Edith Gertrude, *d.* of J. Torrance, Cape Town; one *s.* one *d.* *Educ.:* Grove Park School, Wrexham; Downing College, Cambridge. Walshingham Medallist, 1909; Curator of the Univ. Botanical Museum, 1909-23; served as Lieut. R.F.A. 1915-16 in France and Egypt; Captain, R.F.C. and R.A.F. 1917-19; developed and directed air photography and aerial survey of Palestine (despatches twice, M.B.E., Order of the Nile); Fellow of Downing College, 1914-50, Dean 1920-1927; Steward of the College, 1920-37; Pres. Downing College Assoc., 1938; University Lecturer in Botany, 1923-37; Reader, 1937-50; Secretary, Botanic Garden Syndicate, 1920-51; President Linnean Soc. of London, 1955-58. Sedgwick Prizeman, Univ. of Cambridge, 1924; has devoted much time to research on fossil plants, discovered and described several groups hitherto unknown; Recorder for Palæobotany at 5th International Botanical Congress; Secretary International Committee for nomenclature of fossil plants, 1930-54; Pres. Palæobotany Section, 7th Internat. Botanical Congress, Stockholm, 1950. Served in R.A.F.V.R. as Intelligence Officer, 1939 to end of 1943, taking part in the reorganisation of the photographic intelligence service (despatches); later responsible for photo-intelligence on enemy industry and rocket preparations. Pres. Medmenham Club, 1946-; Member Council British Association for the Advancement of Science, 1947-53; Pres. Botanical Sect. of Assoc., 1947; Pres. Brit. Soc. for Hist. of Science, 1953-55, Hon. Mem. 1961-; Corr Mem. Bot. Soc. Amer.; Darwin-Wallace Commemorative Medal, Linnean Soc., 1958; Linnean Gold Medal, 1960. *Publications:* numerous papers on Fossil Plants and other botanical subjects in scientific journals; articles on Aerial Survey and the History of Science. *Address:* Millington Lodge, Cambridge. *T.:* 50160. *Club:* Athenæum.

[*Died* 30 *June* 1962.

THOMAS, Iorwerth Rhys; M.P. (Lab.) Rhondda West since 1950; Member South Wales Electricity Bd. since 1947; *b.* 1895; *m.*; one *s.* one *d.* *Educ.:* Elementary Sch. Colliery checkweighman, 1922. Joined Lab. Party, 1918; Member: Rhondda Urban Council since 1928; National Union of Mineworkers and has held various positions in local branch; has served on joint industrial councils for Wales and Monmouthshire. *Address:* 94 Park Road, Cwmpark, Glam., S. Wales. *T.:* Pentre 3177; Willesden 2084; House of Commons, S.W.1.

[*Died* 3 *Dec.* 1966.

THOMAS, John Richard; Retd. Fell. Inst. Chartered Accountants; *b.* 9 March 1897; *s.* of late Richard and Kathleen Thomas, Wrexham, North Wales; *m.* 1920; two *s.* *Educ.:* Private. M.P. (Lab.) Dover Division of Kent, 1945-50. Served 4th Gloucestershire Regiment, European War. R.A.F., 1924-28. *Address:* The Spinney, Links Road, Worthing. *T.:* Swandean 1233. *Club:* Royal Air Force.

[*Died* 4 *July* 1968.

THOMAS, His Honour Leonard Charles; a Judge of County Courts (Circuit 24, Cardiff, etc.), 1926-53; retired 1953; *b.* 18 Oct 1879; 3rd *s.* of John Henwood and Elizabeth Thomas; *m.* 1906, Gertrude (*d* 1948), *d.* of J. C. Horsfield, Brockley; one *s.* two *d.* (and one *s.* decd.). Called to Bar, Middle Temple, 1905; Revising Barrister, Western Circuit, 1914; Directorate of Military Intelligence (Censorship), 1914-18; Aliens Tribunal, 1939; formerly: Indep. Chm. Pneumoconiosis Bd. for Gt. Brit.; Chm. Cttee., Cwmbran New Town. *Address:* Kensington Close Hotel, W.8. *Club:* Athenæum. [*Died* 16 *Nov.* 1964.

THOMAS, Sir Percy Edward, Kt., *cr.* 1946, O.B.E.; J.P.; D.L.; LL.D.; R.I.B.A. (Past Pres.); Chm. Welsh Board for Industry, 1942-55; Regional Controller for Wales, M.O.P. 1942-45; late Lt.-Col., 22nd Battalion, Glamorgan (Cardiff) Home Guard; *b.* 13 Sept 1883; *s.* of Christmas and Cecilia Thomas; *m.* 1906, Margaret Ethel Turner (*d.* 1953); one *s.* three *d.* *Educ.:* Private Schools. Articled to E. H. Bruton, F.R.I.B.A., of Cardiff; Asst in Lancashire Offices until 1911 when he won Cardiff Technical College in Open Competition; responsible for many public buildings, business premises, and private houses including Swansea Civic Centre; Bristol Police and Fire Station; Carmarthen County Offices; Accrington Police and Fire Station; Glamorgan County Offices, Cardiff; Temple of Peace, Cardiff; etc. A.R.I.B.A., 1919; Vice-Pres. R.I.B.A., 1927-28; President, 1935-37 and 1943-46; was three times President of the South Wales Institute of Architects. Honorary Member, American Institute of Architects. Consulting Architect for re-building of Euston Station, 1936. Royal Gold Medal, 1939; Artists' Rifles Royal Engineers, Staff Officer to C.E. XIIIth Army Corps; Hon. Col. 109 Regt. R.E. (T.A.); High Sheriff of Glamorgan, 1949. *Address:* Tregenna, Llanishen, Nr. Cardiff. *T.:* Cardiff 753045. *Club:* Cardiff and County (Cardiff).

[*Died* 17 *Aug.* 1969.

THOMAS, Philip Martin; Chief Executive Officer, Cooperative Wholesale Society Ltd., since 1967; *b.* 12 Feb. 1924; *s.* of Harold Beken Thomas, O.B.E., and Kathleen Jessie Taylor; *m.* 1952, Elise Berbuto (*d.* 1968); one *d.* *Educ.:* Tonbridge; Hertford Coll., Oxon. (M.A. (Oxon.) 1st class Hons. Jurisprudence). Served Indian Army, 1942-1946 (Capt. and Adjt., 15th Baluch. Regt.; Major, D.A.J.A.G. in India; War Crimes Prosecutor, Malaya). Called to the Bar, Middle Temple, 1948; Director and Secretary, Associated British Foods Ltd., 1959-1966; Director: Premier Milling Co. Ltd. (of South Africa), 1964-66; Wood Hall Trust Ltd., 1966-67; C. Lindley & Co. Ltd., 1966-. Genealogist and Dynastic Lawyer. Proprietor, Grand Album des Maisons Royales et Médiatisées. *Publications:* many contributions on Dynastic Law in jls. in U.K. and Europe and in particular Burke's Peerage, 1953-. *Address:* Charlton House, Davey Lane, Alderley Edge, Cheshire.

[*Died* 20 *April* 1968.

THOMAS, Robert Clifford Lloyd, M.C. 1917; T.D. 1930; *b.* 1893; *s.* of late W. Calvin Thomas, Park Square, Newport, Mon.; *m.* 1922, Ethel Theodora, 5th *d.* of Alderman F. Phillips, J.P., Nant Coch, Newport, Mon.; three *d.* *Educ.:* Taunton School. Partner in Walter Hunter, Bartlett Thomas & Co., Chartered Accountants, Newport, 1919-63 (Retd.; Consultant, 1963-). Commissioned 1st Monmouthshire Regiment Territorial Army 1913; retired, 1936, with rank of Bt.-Col. In War of 1939-1945 was with 45th A.A. Bde. in Cardiff gun operation room: subsequently commanded 27th Home Guard A.A. Regiment. Chairman (1955-58) Mon. T. & A.F.A. J.P. Newport, Mon., 1942; D.L. Monmouthshire, 1936; High Sheriff of Monmouthshire, 1949. *Recreation:* golf. *Address:* The Shrubbery, 224 Stow Hill, Newport, Mon. *T.:* 63440. *Club:* Monmouthshire County (Newport, Mon.). [*Died* 21 *July* 1969.

THOMAS, Sir (Thomas) Shenton (Whitelegge), G.C.M.G., *cr.* 1937 (K.C.M.G., *cr.* 1930; C.M.G. 1929); O.B.E. 1919; K.St.J.; *b.* 1879; *e. s.* of late Rev. T. W. Thomas, M.A., Rector of Newton-in-the-Isle, Cambs.; *m.* Lucy Marguerite, *d.* of late Col. J. A. L. Montgomery, C.S.I., C.B.E., of Moville, Co. Donegal; one *d.* *Educ.:* St. John's, Leatherhead; Queens' Coll., Cambridge (Hon. Fellow, 1936). Entered Colonial Civil Service as Assistant District Commissioner East Africa Protectorate, 1909; Assistant Chief Secretary, Uganda, 1918; Principal Assistant Secretary, Nigeria, 1921; Deputy Chief Secretary, 1923; Colonial Secretary, Gold Coast Colony, 1927; Governor Nyasaland Protectorate, 1929; of Gold Coast, 1932; Governor of Straits Settlements and High Commissioner for the Malay States, 1934. Interned by the Japanese Feb. 1942-Aug. 1945; retired 1946. Vice-President: Brit. Empire Leprosy Relief Assoc. (Chm., 1949-55); Fauna Preservation Soc.; Overseas League (Chm., 1946-49). *Recreations:* cricket, lawn tennis, golf. *Address:* 28 Oakwood Court, W.14. *Club:* M.C.C. [*Died* 15 *Jan.* 1962.

THOMAS, Hon. Sir (Walter) Eric, Kt., *cr.* 1954; C.M.G. 1950; O.B.E. 1939; M.C.; Q.C.; *b.* 16 July 1889; *s.* of William Elliott Thomas, J.P., and Helen Poulteney; *m.* 1925, Margaret Halcro Fairbairn; one *s.* one *d.* *Educ.:* South African College, Capetown; Brasenose College, Oxford. Rhodes Scholar, 1910; Played for Oxford *v.* Cambridge, Rugby, 1911-13; joined Rhodesian Civil Service, 1914; 2nd Rhodesian Regiment, 1914; East African Campaign, 1915-1917; served with 1st Battalion K.R.R.C. in France as Captain, 1917-18; Legal Adviser, S. Rhodesia Govt., 1928; Solicitor General, 1933; Attorney General, 1934; Judge of the High Court, S. Rhodesia, 1944-54. *Club:* Salisbury (Rhodesia). [*Died* 18 *Jan.* 1963.

THOMPSON, Capt. Sir Algar de C. C.; *see* Meysey-Thompson.

THOMPSON, Commander Charles Ralfe, C.M.G. 1945; O.B.E. 1939; Royal Navy; *b.* 22 Nov. 1894; 2nd *s.* of late R. C. Thompson, Fencehouses, Co. Durham. *Educ.:* R.N. Colleges, Osborne and Dartmouth. Midshipman, H.M.S. Monarch, 1912; served mainly in Submarines, China and Mediterranean, 1915-31; in command from 1918; Flag Lieutenant to Admiral Sir Arthur Waistell and Admiral of the Fleet Sir John Kelly (Commanders-in-Chief, Portsmouth), 1931-36; Flag Lieutenant and Flag Commander to the Board of Admiralty, 1936-40; retired with rank of Commander, 1939; Personal Assistant to Minister of Defence, 1940-45. Chevalier, Legion of Honour, France, 1946. *Address:* 14 Pont Street Mews, S.W.1. *T.:* Kensington 2386. *Club:* Bath. [*Died* 11 *Aug.* 1966.

THOMPSON, Dorothy; Journalist and writer; *b.* Lancaster, New York, N.Y., 9 July 1894; *d.* of Peter Thompson and Margaret Grierson; *m.* 1st, 1923, Josef Bard (marriage dissolved); 2nd, 1928, Sinclair Lewis (marriage dissolved, 1942; he died 1951); one *s.*; *m.* 3rd, 1943, Maxim Kopf (*d.* 1958). *Educ.:* Lewis Institute, Chicago; Syracuse Univ. New York Speaker in up-state New York Woman Suffrage campaign, 1915-17; social work, 1917-20; foreign correspondent Curtis-Martin Newspapers, Inc. (Phila. Public Ledger and N.Y. Evening Post), 1920-28; at Vienna, 1920-24; at Berlin, Chief of Central European Service, 1924-28. Member: American Acad. of Political and Social Science; Amer. Academy of Arts and Letters; Honorary doctorates: Russell Sage, Syracuse, St. Lawrence, Tufts, Dartmouth, Columbia, Oberlin, McGill (Canada). *Publications:* I Saw Hitler; The New Russia; Refugees: Anarchy or Organization?; Political Guide; Once on Christmas; Let the Record Speak; Listen, Hans; The Courage to be Happy; Monthly editorial for Ladies' Home Journal. *Recreation:* gardening. *Address:* Twin Farms, South Pomfret, Vermont, U.S.A. *Clubs:* P.E.N., Cosmopolitan (New York). [*Died* 31 *Jan.* 1961.

THOMPSON, Edith Marie, C.B.E. 1920 (O.B.E. 1918); *o. d.* of late W. F. Thompson, J.P. *Educ.:* Cheltenham Ladies' Coll.; King's College, University of London. Controller of Inspection, Queen Mary's Army Auxiliary Corps, 1917-20; Headquarters Organizer, Women's Land Army, 1939-40; Liaison Officer, Children's Overseas Reception Board in South Africa, 1940-45; Chairman of Executive Oversea Settlement for British Women, 1936-46; President All England Women's Hockey Association, 1946-47 and 1924-29; Governor: Bedford College, Univ. of London and St. Felix School, Southwold. *Address:* Gables, Aldeburgh, Suffolk. *Clubs:* Royal Commonwealth Society, Service Women's. [*Died* 25 *Aug.* 1961.

THOMPSON, Edwin, J.P.; late Chairman of Thompson & Capper Ltd., Liverpool, Manufacturing Chemists; *b.* 1881; *s.* of late Isaac Cooke Thompson, Liverpool; *m.* 1906, Marie Louise (*d.* 1959), *d.* of late H. J. Decker, Liverpool; one *s.* (younger son killed in action, R.A.F., 1944) four *d.* *Educ.:* Sedbergh. Lord Mayor of Liverpool, 1930-1931; High Sheriff of Lancashire, 1944-45. Pres. British Waterworks Assoc., 1931-32; Pres. Soc. of Chemical Industry, 1934-35; Chairman Liverpool Red Cross Penny-a-Week Fund, 1941-44. Member of Council of Duchy of Lancaster, 1950-56; Representative of Chancellor of the Duchy of Lancaster to the Court of Univ. of Liverpool. Vice-President, Liverpool Repertory Theatre; Member of Pilgrims Society; a Governor of Liverpool Blue Coat School. F.C.S. *Address:* 7 Fulwood Park, Liverpool, 17. *Clubs:* Royal Automobile; Athenæum (Liverpool). [*Died* 3 *Oct.* 1967.

THOMPSON, Edwin R. R.; *see* Roe-Thompson.

THOMPSON, Eric, C.B.E. 1964; Emeritus Professor, University of Strathclyde, since 1965; *b.* 15 July 1905; *s.* of James Thompson, F.R.C.O., and Annie Clark; *m.* 1932, Phyllis Slater; one *d.* *Educ.:* Stand Grammar School; Manchester Univ. (B.A. Com., M.A. Com.); Univ. of London (B.Sc. Econ., Ph.D.). Head of Dept. of Commerce, Wolverhampton and Staffs. Technical College, 1938-42; Head of Dept. of Commerce, Welsh College of Advanced Technology, 1942-46; Principal, Scottish College of Commerce, 1946-64; Deputy to Vice-Chancellor, Univ. of Strathclyde, 1964-66. Secretary, National Committee for Commercial Education (Scotland), 1946-61: Member: British

Specialist Team on Education for Management to U.S.A., 1951; Annan Committee on the Teaching of Russian, 1960-62; Standing Adv. Committee on Grants to Students, 1961-63; Scottish Coun. for Commercial Educn., 1961-; Exec. Cttee., Scottish Coun. (Development and Industry), 1961-66; Coun. for Technical Educn. and Training for Overseas Countries, 1962-66; Deputy Chairman, Various Wages Councils, 1959-65. F.B.I.M. 1961. *Publications:* Popular Sovereignty and the French Constituent Assembly, 1952; (part author) Technical Education, 1955; articles in various jls. *Recreations:* gardening, hill walking. *Address:* 14 Iain Road, Bearsden, Glasgow. *T.:* 041-942 2929. [*Died* 15 *Oct.* 1969.

THOMPSON, Sir Geoffrey Harington, G.B.E. 1957; K.C.M.G. 1949 (C.M.G. 1933); H.M. Diplomatic Service, retired; Director Atlas Assurance Co.; *b.* 12 Mar. 1898; *s.* of late Lt.-Col. Croasdale Miller Thompson, I.M.S., and Ella Dalziel Harington; *m.* 1926, Louise Sewall (marriage dissolved 1943), Englewood, N.J.; one *s.* one *d.*; *m.* 1943, Hilda Alice, *d.* of the Rev. D. Westcott, D.D. *Educ.:* Eastmans, Southsea; Westminster. Second Lt. R.F.A. (S.R.), 1917; served France and Flanders, 1917-1918 (wounded), and Rhine, 1919; Third Secretary H.M. Diplomatic Service, 1920; transferred Rio de Janeiro, 1920, and to Washington, 1922; Second Secretary, 1923; transferred to Foreign Office, 1927, and to Santiago, 1931; Chargé d'Affaires, 1932 and 1933; transferred to Foreign Office, 1934, and to Embassy in Spain (Valencia) January 1937 and from there to Hendaye, June 1937, and was Chargé d'Affaires there in Sept. and Jan.-July 1938, transferred to Foreign Office, Sep. 1938; attached Imperial Defence College, 1939; Foreign Office, 1939; Ankara (Actg. Counsellor), 1941; Baghdad, 1942; Chargé d'Affaires; 1942, '43, '44, '45; Counsellor, 1943. British Ambassador in Bangkok, 1947-50 (Minister, 1946-47); Civilian Instructor, Imperial Defence College, 1950-51; British Ambassador to Brazil, 1952-56. *Publication:* Front Line Diplomat, 1959. *Address:* 4 Pelham Gardens, Folkestone, Kent. *T.:* Folkestone 52734. *Club:* White's. [*Died* 26 *Jan.* 1967.

THOMPSON, Harry Sydney, C.B.E. 1943; M.I.E.E.; retired as Regional Director, G.P.O., N. Ireland; *b.* 1 Sept. 1878; *s.* of late George Thompson, Birmingham; unmarried. *Educ.:* King Edward VI. Grammar School and Mason College, Birmingham. With late National Telephone Co., 1896-1912; with G.P.O., 1912-44. *Recreation:* golf. *Address:* Ryon Hill House, Warwick Road, Stratford-on-Avon, Warwickshire. [*Died* 24 *May* 1966.

THOMPSON, Sir Ivan, Kt. 1955; Commodore, Cunard Steamship Co., 1954-57; retired; *b.* 1 Nov. 1894; *s.* of Charles Edward Thompson and Hannah (*née* Tracey); *m.* 1926, Eileen Smallwood; two *s.* two *d.* *Educ.:* St. Francis Xavier's, Liverpool; Xaverian College, Bruges, Belgium. Joseph Chadwicks-Drum Line, 1910; The Harrison Line, 1911-16. *Recreations:* football, baseball. *Address:* Holmrook, Aigburth Hall Road, Liverpool 19. *T.:* 051-427 1396. *Club:* Old Xaverians (Liverpool). [*Died* 22 *July* 1970.

THOMPSON, Dr. John Fairfield, Hon. Chairman: The International Nickel Co. of Canada, Ltd., since 1960; International Nickel Co. Inc., since 1960; *b.* Portland, Maine, 8 Mar. 1881; *s.* of Frank E. and Mary J. Clarke Thompson; *m.* 1911, Elizabeth Fisher Wheeler (*d.* 1947); one *s.* one *d.* *Educ.:* Sch. of Mines, Columbia Univ. B.S. 1903; Ph.D. 1906; Asst. in Metallurgy, School of Mines, Columbia Univ. International Nickel Co. of Canada Ltd.: metallurgist, Orford Works, 1906; in charge of research and technical activities and head of all field and outside plant operations, 1906-1918; established and became manager of first Technical Dept.; Manager of Operations, 1921; supervised construction and initial operations of Company's Huntington Works, West Va., founded for production of high-nickel alloys; Asst. to President (present company), 1928; Director and member Exec. Cttee., 1931; Vice-President 1932; Exec. Vice-President, 1936; President, 1949-52; Chairman 1951-60. Director: Amalgamated Metal Corporation Ltd.; Henry Gardner & Co. Ltd.; Trustee: Packer Collegiate Inst.; Nat. Safety Council; Member: Amer. Soc. for Testing and Materials; Mining and Metallurgical Soc. of America (Past Pres.); Hon. Mem.: Amer. Inst. of Mining, Metallurg. and Petroleum Engrs., etc.; Inst. Met. (Gt. Brit.); Copper Develt. Assoc. (Gt. Brit.). Hon. Sc.D., Columbia 1950 (Egleston Medal, 1955); Hon. LL.D., Queen's Univ., 1954; Hon. LL.D., Bowdoin Coll., 1959; Hon. L.H.D. Marshall College, Huntington, W.Va., 1960. Hon. Mem. Inst. of Metals (G.B.); Gold Medal of Inst. M.M. (Gt. Brit.), for 1958; Rand Memorial Medal, Amer. Inst. of Mining, Metallurgical and Petroleum Engineers, 1958; Commander Order of White Rose (Finland). *Address:* (business) 67 Wall Street, New York, N.Y. 10005, U.S.A. *T.:* Whitehall 4-1000; New York, N.Y., U.S.A. *Clubs:* City Midday, Columbia University, University and Down Town Association (New York); New Canaan Country; Toronto (Toronto). [*Died* 13 *July* 1968.

THOMPSON, Merrick A.B.D.; *see* Denton-Thompson.

THOMPSON, Piers Gilchrist; *b.* 10 May 1893; *s.* of late Rev. Canon H. P. Thompson; *m.* Hester M. Barnes; two *s.* one *d.* *Educ.:* Winchester; Brasenose College, Oxford; M.A. M.P. (L.) Torquay 1923-24. *Address:* The Wood House, Shipbourne, nr. Tonbridge, Kent. *T.:* Plaxtol 354. [*Died* 7 *Feb.* 1969.

THOMPSON, Robert Cyril, C.B.E. 1941; M.A.; Director and Deputy Chairman, Doxford and Sunderland Shipbuilding and Engineering Company Ltd., and subsidiary companies, since 1965; Joint Chairman, Technical Committee, Lloyd's Register of Shipping, 1965; *b.* 31 May 1907; *s.* of late Sir Robert Norman Thompson; *m.* 1934, Doreen Hermine Allan; one *s.* one *d.* *Educ.:* Marlborough College, Wilts; Pembroke College, Cambridge. Served apprenticeship with Sir James Laing and Sons, Shipbuilders, Sunderland, 1925-30; Director of Joseph L. Thompson and Sons Ltd., 1931; served in various positions abroad; Director, Sir James Laing and Sons Ltd., 1934; went to U.S.A., and Canada as Leader of Admiralty Merchant Shipbuilding Mission, 1940; went to U.S.A. as Shipbuilding Adviser to Sir Arthur Slater, K.C.B., M.P., Head of British Merchant Shipping Mission, 1941; Director: The Sunderland Forge & Engineering Co. Ltd.; T. W. Greenwell & Co. Ltd.; Sunderland & South Shields Water Co.; The Wolsingham Steel Co. Ltd.; Sunderland Engineering Equipment Co. Ltd.; Fortis Tools Ltd.; St. Helen's Shipping Co. Ltd.; British Employers Mutual Accident Indemnity Assoc. Ltd.; Joseph L. Thompson & Sons (Trustees) Ltd.; The Sunderland Shipbuilding Dry Docks & Engineering Co. Ltd.; The Wear Winch Foundry Co. Ltd.; John Lynn & Co. Ltd.; The Bishopsgate Shipping Co. Ltd.; The Sheaf Steam Shipping Co. Ltd.; The Doxford & Sunderland Shipbuilding & Engineering Co. Ltd.; William Doxford & Sons (Shipbuilders) Ltd.; Past President and Fellow, N.E. Coast Instn. of Engineers and Shipbuilders; Pres. Shipbuilding

Employers' Fedn., 1961-62. *Address:* South Lodge, East Boldon, Co. Durham. *Clubs:* City of London, Royal Automobile. [*Died* 9 *March* 1967.

THOMPSON, Sylvia, (Mrs. Peter Luling); Novelist and Speaker; *b.* 4 Sept. 1902; *d.* of Norman Thompson; *m.* 1926, Theodore Dunham (Peter) Luling; two *d.* (and one *d.* decd.). *Educ.:* assorted schools; Somerville College, Oxford. Left Oxford, 1923; American Lecture Tour, 1932. *Publications:* The Rough Crossing, 1918; The Hounds of Spring, 1925; Winter Comedy; Summer's Night, 1932; Helena, 1933; Breakfast in Bed, 1934; (with Victor Cunard) Golden Arrow, 1935; A Silver Rattle, 1935; Third Act in Venice, 1936; Recapture the Moon, 1937; The Adventure of Christopher Columin, 1939; The Gulls Fly Inland, 1941; The People Opposite, 1949; The Candle's Glory, 1953. *Recreations:* reading, dogs, variety shows. *Address:* Heath Farm, Reigate Heath, Surrey. [*Died* 27 *April* 1968.

THOMPSON, Lieut.-Colonel Sir Thomas (Raikes Lovett), 4th Bt., *cr.* 1806; M.C.; formerly in the Royal Engineeers, 7th Hussars, 18th Hussars, and 3rd Hussars; *b.* 12 May 1881; *e. s.* of 3rd Bt. and Alice Maude Lovett, *d.* of William Lochiel Cameron, E.I.C.S.; *S.* father, 1904; *m.* 1st, 1914, Milicent Ellen Jean (marriage dissolved, 1936), 2nd *d.* of late Edmund Tennyson-d'Eyncourt of Bayons Manor, Lincolnshire; one *s.* (and one killed on active service, 1945) one *d.*; 2nd, 1943, Ellinor Mary, *o. d.* of late Major H. O. Pugh, D.S.O., D.L., Cymmerau, Glandyfi, Cardiganshire. *Educ.:* Rugby; R.M.A., Woolwich. Received Commission in R.E. 1899, transferred to 7th Hussars, 1914; promoted into 18th Royal Hussars, 1920; transferred to 3rd Hussars, 1922; served South African War, 1901-2; European War, 1914-18 (M.C., Brevet Major, despatches twice); retired, 1933. Recalled to service on staff, June 1940-Nov. 1941. *Recreations:* hunting and shooting. *Heir: s.* Thomas Lionel Tennyson, barrister-at-law, late Flying Officer, R.A.F.V.R., *b.* 19 June 1921. *Address:* Merry Gardens, Burley, nr. Ringwood, Hants. *T.:* Burley 2127. *Club:* United Service. [*Died* 17 *Sept.* 1964.

THOMPSON, Walter Scott, C.B.E 1946; *b.* 22 Oct. 1885; *s.* of John Thompson and Isabella Stenhouse; *m.* 1913, Grace Baylis; no *c.* *Educ.:* English elementary schools. Newspaper reporter in London and Australasia; City Editor of The Witness, Montreal, 1911; News Editor of Montreal Herald; entered Grand Trunk and Grand Trunk Pacific Railways, 1914; Director of Public Relations: Trans-Canada Air Lines, 1937-49; Canadian National Railways, Steamships, Hotels, Telegraphs, Express, 1922-50 (retired, 1950). Director of Censorship, 1939; Director of Public Information, Ottawa, 1940. *Recreations:* friendship and fellowship. *Address:* 6955 Fielding Ave., Montreal 39, Canada. *Clubs:* Press (London); Men's Press (Montreal) [*Died* 25 *June* 1966.

THOMPSON, William Hugh, C.S.I. 1936; *b.* 9 Aug. 1885; *s.* of late Rev. Dr. G. A. Thompson; *m.* 1914, Norah Edmée Dickinson; two *s.* *Educ.:* Clifton; Jesus College, Cambridge. 14th Wrangler; 1st Class Nat. Science Tripos, Cambridge; Indian Civil Service; Settlement Officer, Bengal; Superintendent 1921 Census Bengal: Retired, 1922; General Manager Bengal Telephone Corporation; Member Legislative Council Bengal representing Bengal Chamber of Commerce, 1928-36; Secretary, Calcutta Electric Supply Corporation Ltd. London, 1936; Assistant Secretary Ministry of Home Security in charge of Air Raid Warning System, 1941-45; Director Calcutta Electric Supply Corp. Ltd., 1945. *Publications:* Settlement Reports of Districts of Tippera and Noakhali, Bengal; Census Report Bengal, 1921. *Address:* Comilla, 3 Whitehouse Gardens, Beccles, Suffolk. *T.:* Beccles 3076. *Clubs:* Oriental, East India and Sports, Leander. [*Died* 26 *July* 1966.

THOMSON, Lord; Rt. Hon. George Reid Thomson, P.C. 1945; Lord Justice Clerk of Scotland since 1947; Hon. Fellow, Corpus Christi College, Oxford; *b.* 1893; *s.* of Rev. W. R. Thomson; *m.* 1925, Grace Georgeson; no *c.* *Educ.:* South African College, Cape Town: Corpus Christi College, Oxford (Rhodes Scholar); Edinburgh University. Served European War, 1914-18, Captain 5th Argyll and Sutherland Highlanders; called to the Scottish Bar, 1922; K.C. at the Scottish Bar, 1936; Advocate Depute, 1940-45; Lord Advocate, 1945-47; M.P. (Lab.) East Edinburgh, 1945-47. Hon. LL.D. Edinburgh, 1957. *Recreations:* golf, fishing. *Address:* 22 Craigleith View, Edinburgh. *T.:* Donaldson 4039. *Club:* New (Edinburgh). [*Died* 15 *April* 1962.

THOMSON, Engineer Captain Alan Leslie, C.B.E. 1943; R.N. retired; *b.* 12 May 1890; *er. s.* of John Harding Thomson, Brighton; *m.* 1918, Rosa Marie Louise, *er. d.* of Bennet Greet; three *s.* *Educ.:* Brighton Grammar School. Entered Navy, 1906. *Address:* Springhead, Kilmington, Axminster, Devon. *T.:* Axminster 3336. [*Died* 16 *March* 1970.

THOMSON, David, M.A. 1938; Ph.D. 1938; F.R.Hist.S.; Master of Sidney Sussex Coll., Cambridge, since 1957; *b.* 13 Jan. 1912: *s.* of Robert and late Isabella Thomson, Edinburgh, Scotland; *m.* 1943, Margaret Gordon Dallas; two *s.* *Educ.:* Sir George Monoux Gram. Sch. and Sidney Sussex Coll., Cambridge. Open Schol., Sidney Sussex Coll., 1931-34; 1st Cl. Historical Tripos, 1933 and 1934; Gladstone Memorial Prize, 1937; Research Fellow of Sidney Sussex Coll., 1938-45, Fellow, 1945-57 and Sen. Tutor, 1945-53; Univ. Lecturer in History, Cambridge, 1948-68, Reader in Modern French History, 1968-. Visiting Professor in Public Law and Government, Columbia Univ., New York, 1950 and 1953. Member of Inst. for Advanced Study, Princeton, 1950. Member of Council of Senate of Cambridge Univ., 1950-58; Chm. Faculty Board of History, 1958-60; Chm. of Governors, Cambridge Inst. of Education, 1962-. *Publications:* Personality in Politics, 1939; The Democratic Ideal in France and England, 1940; Democracy in France since 1870, 1946 (5th edn., revised, 1969); The Babeuf Plot, 1947; Equality, 1949; England in the Nineteenth Century, 1950; Two Frenchmen: Pierre Laval and Charles de Gaulle, 1951; World History from 1914 to 1968, 1969; Europe since Napoleon, 1957 (2nd edn., 1962); (Ed.) Vol. XII New Cambridge Modern History, 1960; England in the Twentieth Century, 1964; (Ed.) Political Ideas, 1966; The Proposal for Anglo-French Union in 1940, 1966, (Ed.) France: Empire and Republic 1850-1940, 1968; The Aims of History, 1969. *Recreation:* gardening. *Address:* The Master's Lodge, Sidney Sussex Coll., Cambridge. *T.:* Cambridge 55860. [*Died* 24 *Feb.* 1970.

THOMSON, David Landsborough, M.A., B.Sc., Ph.D.; Hon. LL.D. (Middlebury, Aber.); Hon. D.Sc. (Colby, McMaster, Man., Sask.); F.R.S.C., F.C.I.C.; Gilman Cheney Prof. of Biochemistry, 1937-60; Dean, Faculty of Graduate Studies and Research, 1942-63, and Vice- Principal, McGill Univ., Montreal, from 1955; *b.* Aberdeen, 1901; *s.* of late Professor Sir Arthur Thomson, LL.D.; *m.* 1928, Marian Stancliffe, *d.* of late A. Collingwood, F.R.C.O.; one *s.* *Educ.:* Aberdeen Grammar School; Univ. of

Aberdeen, Grenoble, Graz; Gonville and Caius College, Cambridge. 1851 Exhibition Senior Student, 1925; lecturer in biochemistry, McGill University, 1928. *Publications:* The Life of the Cell, 1928; many scientific papers and reviews. *Address:* 3521 University Street, Montreal, Canada. *Club:* University (Montreal). [*Died* 20 *Oct.* 1964.

THOMSON, Major George, C.B.E. 1952; D.S.O. 1919; M.A. (Hons. Queen's University, Belfast); Clerk of the Parliaments of Northern Ireland, and Clerk of the Senate, retd. 1962; *b.* 10 Jan. 1889; *e. s.* of George Thomson, Man. Dir. of Broadway Damask Co., Ltd.; *m.* 1921, Maud, *e. d.* of J. H. McIlveen, of W. R. Young & Co., Limited; one *s.* *Educ.:* Royal Belfast Academical Institution; Queen's University, Belfast; Assembly's Coll., Belfast. Commissioned 12th (S.) Batt. Royal Ulster Rifles, 17 Sept. 1914; Captain, 1915; Adjutant, 1915; Major and 2nd in command, 1917; Lt.-Col., 1918; Croix de Guerre with palm; Cashier and Assistant General Manager, Larne Shipbuilding, Ltd., 1919-21. *Recreations:* golfing, fishing, and sailing. *Address:* 13 Brerton Crescent, Newtownbreda Road, Belfast 8, N.I. [*Died* 16 *Oct.* 1970.

THOMSON, Rear-Adm. Sir George (Pirie), Kt. 1963; C.B. 1946; C.B.E. 1939 (O.B.E. 1919); *b.* 1887; *g. s.* of late Principal W. R. Pirie; two *d.* *Educ.:* George Watson's College, Edinburgh. Capt., Royal Navy, 1927; Second Member Naval Board, Australia, 1937-39; Rear-Adm. 1939; retired list, 1939; Chief Press Censor, Ministry of Information, 1940-45. *Publication:* Blue Pencil Admiral, 1947; Submarines, 1959. *Address:* 2 Heath Rise, Putney Hill, S.W.15. *Club:* Press. [*Died* 24 *Jan.* 1965.

THOMSON, Henry John, M.A. (Oxon), D.Litt. (St. And.); Professor of Latin, University College of North Wales, Bangor, 1924-1948, now Emeritus. Assistant, Edinburgh University, 1906; Lecturer in Latin, St. Andrews, 1908. *Publications:* Ancient Lore in Mediæval Latin Glossaries (with W. M. Lindsay); edition of the Abstrusa Glossary; Prudentius, with an English translation; articles in classical journals. [*Died* 29 *March* 1966.

THOMSON, Professor Mark Alméras, M.A., D.Phil. (Oxon.); Astor Professor of English History, University College, London University, since 1956; *b.* 4 June 1903; *s.* of late Reverend A. S. Thomson; *m.* 1940, Helen Katherine, *d.* of late John Gaston Leathem. *Educ.:* Plymouth College; Exeter and Magdalen Colleges, Oxford. Scholar of Exeter Coll., Oxford, 1922; 1st Cl. Hon. Mods., 1924; 1st Cl. Lit. Hum., 1926; 1st Cl. Mod. Hist., 1927; Univ. Sen. Studentship, 1927-29; Sen. Demy of Magdalen Coll., 1928-30; Passmore Edwards Schol., 1928. On staff of History Dept., Univ. Coll., London, 1930-39; Asst. Lecturer, 1930; Lecturer, 1933-38; Reader, 1938-39. Foreign Office, 1939-45. Andrew Geddes and John Rankin Professor of Modern History in the Univ. of Liverpool, 1945-56. *Publications:* The Secretaries of State, 1681-1782, 1932; A Constitutional History of England, 1642-1801, 1938. Some Developments in English Historiography during the Eighteenth Century, 1957; Macaulay, 1959. Articles and reviews in learned journals. *Recreations:* bibliophily, conversation, walking. *Address:* 160 Oakwood Court, W.14. *T.:* Western 0706. *Club:* University (Liverpool). [*Died* 4 *Jan.* 1962.

THOMSON, (Matthew) Sydney, M.A., M.D., F.R.C.P., F.R.S.E.; Hon. Consulting Physician to King's College Hospital and Camberwell Group of Hospitals; Emeritus Lecturer, King's College Hospital; retired as Physician for Diseases of the Skin, King's College Hosp., Belgrave Hosp. for Children, Dulwich, Fulham and St. Giles Hosps.; was Consulting Dermatologist to the London County Council, E.M.S., R.M.I.G., St. Dunstan's, Star and Garter Home, Booksellers' Prov. Inst., etc.; *b.* 7 Nov. 1894; *s.* of Matthew and Emilie Thomson; *m.* 1922, Dora Alice, *d.* of Chas. E. Wallis, Pinner; two *d.* *Educ.:* Merchant Taylors' School (Stuart Exhibitioner); Downing Coll., Cambridge (Foundation Scholar); King's College Hospital (Burney Yeo Scholar). Lieutenant R.A.M.C. (S.R.) 1918-19; Past Pres. and Hon. Mem. British Assoc. of Dermatology; Lectr. St. John's Hosp. for Diseases of the Skin and King's Coll. Hosp.; Past Pres. and Hon Mem. Dermatological Section R.S.M. and Vice-Pres. Section of Dermatology, B.M.A.; Hunterian Professor, R.C.S., 1957. Mem. Bd. of Governors, King's Coll. Hosp., 1950-59; Watson Smith Lectr., R.C.P., 1958; Hon. Mem. Derm. Socs. of Britain, Denmark, France, Holland and Hungary. *Publications:* numerous papers on Skin Diseases in medical journals. *Recreation:* shooting. *Address:* 5 Hartington Mansions, Hartington Place, Eastbourne, Sussex. *T.:* Eastbourne 28460. [*Died* 26 *April* 1969.

THOMSON, Lieut.-Gen. Sir William (Montgomerie), K.C.M.G., *cr.* 1919 (C.M.G. 1919); C.B. 1917; M.C.; *b.* 2 Dec. 1877; 4th *s.* of late Captain William Thomson, 78th Highlanders, and Alice, *d.* of late Captain William Broughton, R.N.; *m.* 1st 1919, Ethel Violet (*d.* 1927), *d.* of late Duncan Davidson of Inchmarlo, Aberdeenshire; two *d.*; 2nd, 1928, Mai, sister of first wife. Joined Seaforth Highlanders, 1897; Capt. 1901; Major, 1915; Bt. Lt.-Col. 1916; Bt. Col. 1916; Maj.-Gen. 1923; Lt.-Gen. 1931; served Soudan Expedition, 1898; European War: commanded 1st Seaforth Highlanders in France and Mesopotamia, 1915-1916, a Brigade 1916-17, a Division 1917-1918; subsequently commanded North Persian Force Sept. 1918, and later British troops in Trans-Caucasia up to May 1919 (wounded twice, despatches eight times M.C., C.B., K.C.M.G., 3rd Class Serbian Order of White Eagle, Commander Legion of Honour); retired, 1934; Hon. Colonel 8th Bn. Argyll and Sutherland Highlanders, 1935-40. Colonel of The Seaforth Highlanders, 1939-47. *Address:* Milton Brodie, Forres, Scotland. *Club:* United Service. [*Died* 23 *July* 1963.

THORLEY, Wilfrid; poet and translator; *b* Southport, Lancs, 31 July 1878; *s* of late John Thorley J.P.; *m.* 1st, 1914, Katherine Elizabeth Dunn (*d.* 1925); 2nd, 1937 Gertrude Margaret Neville. *Educ.:* privately; Liverpool Institute; Grenoble University. Learnt most while teaching English to foreign students in Sweden, Belgium, France, and Italy, during the ten years preceding 1st Great War. *Publications:* A Primer of English for Foreign Students, 1910; an English Reader for Foreign Students, 1913; Cloud-Cuckoo-Land: a Child's Book of Verses, 1923; Confessional, and other Poems, 1911; Paul Verlaine 1914; Fleurs-de-Lys, 1920; The Londoner's Chariot, and other Poems, 1925; A Bouquet from France, 1926; Maypole Market: a Child's Book of Verses, 1927; Cartwheels and Catkins: Verses for Girls and Boys, 1930; A Year in England for Foreign Students, 1930; The Happy Colt, and other verses, 1940; Barleycomb Billy, and other rhymes, 1943; The French Muse, 50 Examples, 1945. As Harley Quinn: A Caboodle of Beasts, 1945; Quinn's Quiz: rhymed riddles on a variety of subjects for children or their parents, 1957. *Address:* 16 Circular Drive, Greasby, Wirral, Cheshire. *T.:* Arrowebrook 1409. [*Died* 28 *Jan.* 1963.

THORNE, General Sir (Augustus Francis) Andrew (Nicol), K.C.B., *cr.*

1942 (C.B. 1939); C.M.G. 1919; D.S.O. 1916; D.L. Berks; *b.* 20 September 1885; *e. s.* of late Augustus Thorne, D.L., J.P., London, W.1; *m.* 1909, Hon. Margaret Douglas Pennant (*d.* 1967), *d.* of 2nd Baron Penrhyn; three *s.* three *d. Educ.:* Mulgrave, nr. Whitby; Eton; R.M.C., Sandhurst. Joined Grenadier Guards, 1904; served European War (despatches 7 times, D.S.O. and two bars); commanded 3rd Battalion Grenadier Guards, Sept. 1916-Sept. 1918 and Sept. 1927-Jan. 1931; 184th Infantry Brigade, Oct. 1918-March 1919; Assistant Military Attaché to Washington, U.S.A., 1919-20; Military Assistant to the C.I.G.S., 1925-26; Military Attaché, Berlin, 1932-35; commanded 1st (Guards) Brigade, 1935-38; A.D.C. to the King, 1936-38; G.O.C. London District and Major-General commanding the Brigade of Guards, 1938-39; Commander 48th Div. B.E.F., 1939-40 (despatches); XII Corps (Kent), 1940-41; G.O.C.-in-C. Scottish Command and Governor of the Castle of Edinburgh, 1941-45; C.-in-C. Allied Land Forces, Norway, and Head of the S.H.A.E.F. mission to Norway, 1945; retired pay, 1946; returned to active list, 1950-51, for work with the Norwegian Ministry of Defence. Member T.A.A. Berks, 1949-54; Pres. Old Etonian Association, 1949-50. Master, Worshipful Company of Cordwainers, 1954-55. Chm., Cttee. of Visitors, Broadmoor Hosp., 1949-64. Polonia Restituta (2nd class), 1943; Comdr. Legion of Honour (France), 1939, Chevalier, 1917; Comdr. U.S. Legion of Merit, 1945; Grand Cross St. Olaf (Norway); Freedom Medal (Norway), 1945. *Address:* Knowl Hill House, nr. Reading. *T.:* Littlewick Green 2906. *Clubs:* Guards; New (Edinburgh). [*Died* 25 *Sept.* 1970.

THORNE, Gordon, M.A., Mus.B. (Cantab.), F.R.C.O., L.R.A.M.; Principal, Guildhall School of Music and Drama, since 1959; *b.* 29 Dec. 1912; *s.* of Leonard Thorne (Engineer, Metropolitan Water Board), and Nellie Louise Thorne (*née* Maxwell); *m.* 1936, Sheila Collins, Johannesburg; one *s.* two *d. Educ.:* City of London School; Christ's College, Cambridge. Asst. Organist, St. Margaret's, Westminster, 1929-30; Organ Scholar, Christ's College, Cambridge, 1930-1934; Director of Music, Bradfield College, Berkshire, 1934-37; Senior Music Asst., B.B.C. North Region and Deputy Conductor, B.B.C. Northern Orchestra, 1938-40 and 1946-53. War Service: Flying Instructor and Transport Command Pilot, R.A.F., 1941-46. Head of Music, B.B.C. North Region, 1953-59. Guest Conductor, Hallé, Royal Liverpool Phil., Sheffield Phil. orchestras, etc., 1954-; Adjudicator, British and Canadian Festivals, 1948-. Hon. F.T.C.L. 1959. Hon. R.A.M., F.G.S.M., F.R.C.M., 1961. *Recreations:* motoring, woodworking, etc. *Address:* 33 Queen's Rd., Richmond, Surrey. *T.:* Richmond 7222. [*Died* 19 *May* 1965.

THORNE, Sir John (Anderson), K.C.I.E., *cr.* 1942 (C.I.E. 1931); C.S.I. 1938; *b.* 17 Oct. 1888; *s.* of James Cross Thorne, of Madagascar; *m.* 1914, Dorothy Horton (*d.* 1944); one *s.* one *d. Educ.:* Blundell's School, Tiverton; Balliol College, Oxford. Indian Civil Service, 1911; served in various posts in Madras Presidency, 1912-34; Joint Secretary then Secretary Home Department, Government of India, 1935-38; Secretary to Governor-General (Public), 1938-45; Officiating Member Governor-General's Executive Council, June-Oct. 1939; Temp. Member Governor-General's Executive Council, April-July 1944; Home Member of Governor-General's Executive Council, 1945; retired, 1946. Director, Peirce, Leslie & Co. Ltd. *Address:* Sherrald, Sedlescombe, Sussex. *T.:* Sedlescombe 323. *Club:* East India and Sports. [*Died* 29 *April* 1964.

THORNEYCROFT, Thomas Hamo; Chairman, Harland Engineering Co. Ltd.; Director: William Baird & Co. Ltd.; Bank of Scotland; Sierra Leone Development Co. Ltd.; Monkland Finance Ltd.; Western Reversion Trust Ltd. Member of the Institute of Directors. *Address:* William Baird & Co. Ltd., 168 West George Street Glasgow, C.2. [*Died* 5 *March* 1970

THORNHILL, Arthur H(orace); Chairman of the Board, Little, Brown & Co., since 1962 (Pres. and Chm. of Bd., 1948-62); Director: Atlantic Monthly Co., Boston; *b.* Hyde Park, Mass., 25 Feb. 1895; *s.* of Joseph Thornhill and Eliza (*née* Jones); *m.* 1922, Mary J. Petersen; one *s. Educ.:* Public Schools of Hyde Park, Mass. Joined Little, Brown & Co., 1913; Manager of New York Office, 1935-48; Director, 1938-1941; Vice-Pres., 1941-48. *Address:* Washington Street, Duxbury, Mass., U.S.A.; 34 Beacon Street, Boston 6, Mass., U.S.A. *Clubs:* Publishers' Lunch (New York); Union (Boston). [*Died* 9 *Jan.* 1970.

THORNHILL, Dame Rachel; *see* Crowdy, Dame R. E.

THORNLEY, Sir Hubert (Gordon), Kt. 1958; C.B.E. 1949 (O.B.E. 1919); D.L.; retired as Clerk of the Peace and Clerk of N. Riding of Yorkshire County Council (1916-1960); *b.* 16 Jan. 1884; *s.* of Robert Thornley, The Clevelands, Bishop's Cleeve, Cheltenham. Admitted a Solicitor, 1906; Dep. Clerk, Worcestershire Co. Council, 1908-12; Asst. Solicitor, Essex C.C., 1913-15; County Controller, N.R. (Yorks.) for A.R.P., 1939-1945; Vice-Chm. N.R. (Yorks.) T. and A.F.A., 1941-46; Asst. Comr. Local Govt. of Boundary Commission, 1947; Chairman, Society of Clerks of the Peace and Clerks of County Councils, 1947-50. D.L. North Riding of Yorkshire, 1941. *Address:* The Register House, Northallerton, Yorkshire. *T.:* Northallerton 91. *Club:* National [*Died* 10 *Sept.* 1962.

THORNTON, Edna; contralto vocalist; *b.* Bradford, Yorkshire. *Educ.:* Manchester Royal College of Music, under Madame Lemmens Sherrington; came to London, 1900; and studied under Sir Charles Santley, also coached with Marguerite Swale. First operatic work at Daly's Theatre in Ib and Little Christina, then to Covent Garden Grand Season; toured the world with the Quinlan Opera Co., and afterwards with Sir Thomas Beecham's Opera Co. as premier contralto operatic rôles include Amneris in Aïda, Delilah in Samson and Delilah, Brangäna in Tristan and Isolda, Ortrude in Lohengrin, Azucena in Il Trovatore, La Cieca in La Gioconda, Erda, Waltraute, Fricka, in The Ring, etc. *Recreations:* motoring, gardening. [*Died July* 1964.

THORNTON, Rev. George Ruthven, M.A.; retired; *b.* 30 Sept. 1882; *s.* of late Rev. George R. Thornton, M.A., S. Barnabas, Kensington, W.; *m.* 1908, Frances Penelope Phillipps; one *d. Educ.:* Haileybury College; Trinity College, Cambridge. Vicar of S. Anne's, Bermondsey, S.E.; 4th Class Army Chaplain, 1916-18; Vicar of Woodford Bridge; Vicar of Christ Church, Blacklands, Hastings; Archdeacon of Stanley, Falkland Isles, 1927-31; Vicar of Badby-cum-Newnham, Daventry, 1932-34; Rector of Cheadle, 1936-41; Vicar of St. Mathias, Preston, Brighton, 1941-46; Vicar of All Saints, Laughton, nr. Lewes, 1946-50; Assistant Priest, St. Clements, Fulham Palace Road, 1951-53. *Address:* 76 Hazlewell Road, Putney, S.W.15. *T.:* Putney 0441. [*Died* 18 *June* 1964.

THORNTON, Hugh Aylmer, C.S.I. 1930; C.I.E. 1916; late I.C.S.; *b.* 1872; 3rd *s.* of late

Thomas Thornton of Wolferton House, Sporle, Norfolk, and Katharine Ellen, *e. d.* of late Hugh Aylmer, of The Abbey, West Dereham; *m.* 1908, Mary Elizabeth, *e. d.* of late N. N. Cookman, D.L., of Monart House, Monart, Co. Wexford. *Educ.:* Cheltenham; Christ Church, Oxford (B.A.). Entered I.C.S. 1895; Commissioner Burma, 1922; retired, 1931. *Address:* c/o Westminster Bank, 46 Notting Hill Gate, W.11; Onslow Court Hotel, Queen's Gate, S.W.7. [*Died* 8 *April* 1962.

THORNTON, Sir Hugh Cholmondeley, K.C.M.G., *cr.* 1943 (C.M.G. 1920); C.V.O. 1920; *b.* 16 May 1881; *e. s.* of late Rev. Canon A. V. Thornton; *m.* 1st, 1921, Margaret Florence (*d.* 1930), *widow* of Arnold Harris Mathew; 2nd, 1946, May Louisa, *d.* of late J. A. Macdonell Bonar; no *c.* *Educ.:* Kelly Coll., Tavistock; Christ Church, Oxford, B.A. Conservative Central Office, 1907-14; Military Service, 1914-16; Private Secretary to Viscount Milner, as Member of the War Cabinet, 1916-18; as Secretary of State for War, 1918-19; as Secretary of State for the Colonies, 1919-20; Second Crown Agent for the Colonies, 1920-43; Director of Colonial Scholars, 1940-42; Senior Crown Agent for the Colonies, 1943; retired, 1943. *Address:* 62A St. John's Wood High Street, N.W.8. *Club:* Travellers'. [*Died* 8 *March* 1962.

THORNTON, James Cholmondeley; Director, United Kingdom and British Commonwealth Branch, Calouste Gulbenkian Foundation, since 1966 (held same post, as Secretary, 1961-66); *b.* 22 Dec. 1906; *o. s.* of late Horace George Thornton and Lucy (*née* Baker); *m.* 1938, Marjorie Joan, *d.* of late Augustus Burnand; two *s.* *Educ.:* Christ's Hospital; Corpus Christi College, Cambridge (1st Cl. Hons. English; M.A.). Reviewing; reading and editing for J. M. Dent & Sons and other publishers; indexed centenary edition of Hazlitt's Works, 1934. Joined B.B.C. staff, 1936; Asst. Director, Secretariat, 1941. Served R.E., 1943; Major, Civil Resettlement H.Q., 1945. Returned B.B.C., 1946; Asst. Controller, Talks Div., 1953; Dep. Secretary B.B.C., 1959. Chm., Society of Indexers, 1959-62, Pres., 1966-; a Trustee of the Farquharson Charity; Member, Editorial Cttee., Pilgrim edition of Letters of Charles Dickens, 1949-. *Address:* 1 Kent Terrace, Regent's Park, N.W.1. *T.:* 01-262 4107. *Club:* Athenæum. [*Died* 4 *May* 1969.

THORNTON, Major Roland Hobhouse, M.C. 1916; Partner, Alfred Holt & Co., Liverpool, shipowners, 1927-53; *b.* 19 June 1892; *s.* of Canon A. V. Thornton, Roche, Cornwall; *m.* 1933, Dorothy, *widow* of Herbert Leith Murray, Professor of Gynæcology and Obstetrics, Liverpool University; no *c.* *Educ.:* Marlborough; Balliol College, Oxford (M.A.). Served European War, 1914-18, Rifle Brigade and General Staff; War Office, 1918-19. Alfred Holt & Co., shipowners, 1919-53. Founder Member, Air Registration Board, 1937; Member of: various Govt. Cttees. on Civil Aviation, 1937-44; Bd., B.O.A.C., 1946-55; Dep. Chm. Mersey Docks and Harbour Board, 1950-53; Director, Martin's Bank, 1948-53. *Publication:* British Shipping, 1959. *Address:* Sheep St., Burford, Oxon. *T.:* Burford 2196. *Clubs:* Oxford and Cambridge, Royal Aero. [*Died* 12 *April* 1967.

THORNTON, Russel William, C.M.G. 1947; C.B.E. 1936; retd. J.P., Dep. Mayor of Bathurst; Agricultural Adviser to High Commr. for Swaziland, Bechuanaland Prot. and Basutoland, and Director of Native Land Settlement, Swaziland, 1943-47; retd. 1947; *b.* 25 Dec. 1881; *s.* of late William Thornton, landowner and farmer; *m.* 1907, Harriette Demaine Thornton; two *d.* *Educ.:* Graaff Reinet College; Stellenbosch-Elsenberg College. Agricultural Assistant in Agricultural Department, Cape Colony, 1905-7; Officer-in-Charge of Agricultural Research Branch, 1908-10; Principal, Middelburg Agriculture School, Union Department of Agriculture, 1911-23; Director of Field and Animal Husbandry, Union Dept. of Agriculture, 1924-28; Director of Agriculture, Native Affairs Dept. for The Union, 1928-34; Director of Agriculture, Basutoland, 1934-41. Dir. Peak Timber Ltd.; Mem. of Bd. S. African Veldt Trust; Exec. Mem.: Bathurst Agric. Soc. and Farmers' Assoc.; Farm Property Valuer, Union Govt. Land Bank. *Publications:* The Origin and History of the Basuto Pony, 1936; A Contribution to the Study of African Native Cattle, 1937; 17 other publications prior to 1936. *Recreations:* tennis and golf. *Address:* Wedgelands, Bathurst, C.P., S. Africa. [*Died* 14 *Aug.* 1966.

THORNTON-BERRY, Trevor, M.A. (Oxon); *b.* 1895; *s.* of late Edward Thornton Berry, Worksop, Nottinghamshire; assumed surname of Thornton-Berry by deed poll, 1921; *m.* 1922, Sylvia Mary Talbot, *yr. d.* of Rev. G. T. Whitehead, Flanders Hall, Leyburn, Yorks; one *s.* three *d.* (and one *s.* decd.). *Educ.:* Privately; Oriel College, Oxford. Served European War, 1915-19 with Somerset L.I. (Lieutenant, 2 service medals); graduated in Jurisprudence at Oxford, 1920, M.A. 1921; called to Bar, Inner Temple, 1922. Pres., Aysgarth Br., British Legion, 1930-61 (Long Service Cert.). High Sheriff of Yorks., 1937 (Coronation Medal, 1937); A.R.P. Service, 1939-42; R.O.C., 1942-45 (Defence Medal). F.R.S.A. 1948; J.P. North Riding of York, 1930. Income Tax Commissioner. *Publications:* The Hope of the World (an appreciation of the League of Nations Scheme), 1919; A forgotten View of War (pamphlet), 1920; Stray Leaves, 1929; various articles. *Recreations:* shooting, fishing, lawn tennis, cricket, and golf. *Address:* Swinithwaite Hall, Leyburn, Yorks. *Club:* Junior Carlton. [*Died* 13 *Oct.* 1967.

THOROGOOD, Horace Walter; author and journalist; *b.* Epping, Essex; *m.* 2nd, Helen, *d.* of late John Macdonald, Glasgow; one *s.* one *d.* Literary Staff of Evening Standard, 1927-47; Literary Editor, Star, 1915-27. *Publications:* Low and Terry, 1934; East of Aldgate, 1935. *Recreation:* walking. *Address:* 14 Hill Road, St. John's Wood, N.W.8. *T.:* Cunningham 0621. *Club:* Press. [*Died* 6 *Feb.* 1962.

THOROLD, Sir Guy Frederick, K.C.M.G. 1959 (C.M.G. 1945); *b.* 21 July 1898; *s.* of late Commander H. G. Thorold, Royal Navy, and Lora Marsh Thorold; *m.* 1928, Mary Wilder (*d.* 1963), *d.* of H. Husey; two *s.* *Educ.:* Winchester; New College, Oxford. Served R.F.A. (Lieut.), 1917-19; Min. of Economic Warfare, 1939-45; Assistant Secretary, 1944; attached to U.K. Delegation to Organization for European Economic Co-operation, Paris, 1948. Head of Treasury Delegation and Economic Minister, Washington Embassy, 1957-59; U.K. Exec. Director, Internat. Monetary Fund and Internat. Bank for Reconstruction and Development 1957-59. Dir., Agric. Mortgage Corp., 1963-68. *Address:* Stanton Court, nr. Broadway, Worcs. *Club:* Brooks's. [*Died* 16 *Jan.* 1970.

THOROLD, Air Vice-Marshal Henry Karslake, C.B. 1945; C.B.E. 1942; D.S.C. 1916; D.F.C. 1921; A.F.C. 1918; *b.* 11 May 1896; *e. s.* of late John Leofric de B. Thorold and Jane Preston Thorold. *Educ.:* Marlborough College. Entered R.N.A.S. as Flight Sub-Lieut., 1915; served European War, 1915-18, Eastern Mediterranean and France; Iraq (No. 84 Sqdn.), 1920-22; Squadron Leader, 1924; R.A.F. Staff College, 1926-27; No. 58 (B) Sqdn., 1928-29; Air Ministry (Dep. Direc-

torate of Staff Duties), 1929-32; Imperial Defence College, 1932-33; Wing Comdr., 1932; comd. No. 10 (B) Squadron, Boscombe Down, 1933-34; comd. No. 70 (BT) Squadron and at Air Headquarters, Iraq, 1934-36; Gp. Capt. 1937; comd. R.A.F. Station, Mildenhall, 1937-38; Air Ministry (Dep. Dir. of Equipment), 1938-39; H.Q. British Air Forces in France, 1940; Gold Coast (Takoradi) (West African Reinforcement Route), 1940-42; Air Commodore, 1941; S.A.S.O., General Headquarters, Home Forces, 1942-43; A.O.C. No. 92 Group, Bomber Command, 1943-45; Air Vice-Marshal, 1943; Head of Air Section, British Military Mission in Moscow, 1945; S.A.S.O. H.Q., Flying Training Command, 1946-47. Polish Order of Polonia Restituta (3rd Class) 1942. Retired 1947. *Clubs:* Royal Aero, Public Schools.
[*Died* 10 *April* 1966.

THOROLD, Sir James (Ernest), 14th Bt., *cr.* 1642; Fellow, Land Agents' Society; *b.* 27 Jan. 1877; *o. surv. s.* of 12th Bt. and Hon. Henrietta Alexandrina Matilda Willoughby, *e. d.* of 8th Baron Middleton; *S.* brother, 1951; *m.* 1902, Katharine Isabel Mary (*d.* 1959), *e. d.* of late Rev. William Rolfe Tindal-Atkinson; two *s.* two *d.* *Educ.:* Winchester; S. Eastern Agricultural Coll., Wye, Kent. Sub-agent to Marquess of Exeter, 1900-02; Agent to: Earl of Harrowby, 1902-1907; Sir George Cooper, Bt., 1907-19; Lady Wantage, 1919-21; A. Thomas Loyd, 1921-23. *Recreations:* bee-keeping and gardening. *Heir: s.* Anthony Henry Thorold, O.B.E., D.S.C. and Bar. *Address:* The Old Hall, Syston, Grantham.
[*Died* 27 *July* 1965.

THORP, Sir John (Kingsmill Robert), Kt. 1959; C.M.G. 1957; M.B.E. 1949; Governor and C.-in-C., Seychelles, since 1958; *b.* 13 June 1912; *er. s.* of late Samuel R. Thorp, Tullow, Co. Carlow, and Mary (*née* Williams), Mallow, Co. Cork; *m.* 1939, Doreen Mary, *o. d.* of Harold D. Hill, Machakos, Kenya; one *s.* one *d.* *Educ.:* Campbell Coll., Belfast; Univ. of Dublin; Univ. of Cambridge (Colonial Service Course). Foundation Scholar, T.C.D., 1932; B.A. (Dublin), 1st Cl. Moderatorship and Gold Medal, Mental and Moral Science, 1933; Hon. LL.D. (Dublin) 1960. Lecturer in Logic, T.C.D., 1934; Cadet, Colonial Admin. Service, Kenya, 1935; served in the Kitui, Machakos, Turkana, Mombasa, Digo, Isiolo, Marsabit, Fort Hall and Nandi Districts. Mil. Service, Northern Frontier Admin., Capt. (Hon.), 1940-43; Actg. Secretary, Development and Reconstruction Authority, 1951; Administrator of St. Lucia, 1953 - 57. Lecture tour to American Universities and for Canadian Inst. of International Affairs (Ontario and Quebec), 1950. K.St.J. 1958. *Publications:* articles in Journal of H.M.'s Overseas Service, Jl. of E. African Nat. Hist. Soc., and sundry periodicals. *Recreations:* painting, tennis. *Address:* Government House, Seychelles; c/o Barclay's Bank Ltd., 52 Regent St., W.1. *Clubs:* East India and Sports; Nairobi (Kenya).
[*Died* 13 *Aug.* 1961.

THORP, Joseph Peter; journalist and designer of printing; *b.* 1873; *s.* of Rev. William Thorp, B.D.; *m.* 1905, Helen Syrett. *Educ.:* Stonyhurst. Entered Jesuit Order, 1891; left, 1901; studied Theology, Oscott, 1901-3; did not proceed to Holy Orders; joined W. H. Smith & Son as printers' traveller, 1905; organised Agenda Club, 1910; Member H.M. Stationery Office special committee *re* type faces, etc.; Dramatic Critic Punch, 1916-34. *Publications:* Verses: Open Letter to English Gentlemen; The Other War; Printing for Business; Broken Bridges; Design in Modern Printing, 1928; Eric Gill, 1929; Friends and Adventures, 1931; Design for Transition, 1935; Bernard Newdigate: Scholar-Printer, 1950. *Address:* Nazareth House, Criccieth, Caerns.
[*Died* 23 *Feb.* 1962.

THORP, Brig. Robert Allen Fenwick, O.B.E. 1941; *b.* 1900; *o. surv. s.* of late Thomas Alder Thorp, Bondgate Hall, Alnwick, Northumberland; *m.* 1939, Sybil May, 2nd *d.* of Francis William Morton-Hall, Quorn, Leicestershire, and Villa Rema, Durban, South Africa. *Educ.:* Charterhouse; Royal Military College, Quetta. 3rd Skinner's Horse, 1919; served on N.W. Frontier, 1919-21; trans. to 1st Life Guards, 1921; Adjt. Northumberland Hussars Yeomanry, 1929-34; Staff College Camberley, 1936-37, p.s.c.; 2nd i/c Life Guards, 1937-39; G.S.O. 2 3rd Div. France, 1939; D.A.Q.M.G. 1st Cav. Div. Palestine, 1940; A.A.Q.M.G. 11th Div. during the Abyssinian Campaign and capture of Addis Ababa, 1941; G.S.O. 1 H.Q. District, East Africa, 1941; Full Col. in com. district Northern Rhodesia, 1942; Brig. com. 31st Bde. Abyssinian Frontier, 1943-45. M.P. (C.) for Berwick-on-Tweed Division, 1945-51. *Address:* Hedgehope Edge Hill, Ponteland, Northumberland. *Club:* Conservative (Newcastle).
[*Died* 5 *May* 1966.

THORPE, Frank Gordon, C.M.G. 1939; M.B.E. 1936; Commonwealth Public Service Commissioner, Canberra, Australia, 1937-1947; *b.* 15 Feb. 1885; *s.* of late W. J. and Mrs. Thorpe, Kooreh, Victoria, Australia; *m.* 1st, 1917, Elsie Leake; (one *s.* killed in R.A.A.F. in India 21 Apr. 1943); 2nd, 1926, Vera Donaldson. *Educ.:* Public Schools, St. Arnaud and Warrnambool, Victoria. Entered public service as Telegraph Messenger, 1898; served in various capacities in the Postal Department; in 1914-18 war served in Australian Army Pay Corps, with rank of Lieut.-Colonel; Senior Clerk in Prime Minister's Dept., 1920-23; Public Service Inspector, Secretary to Public Service Board, and Assistant Commissioner, 1923-37. Retired, 1947. *Recreations:* horticulture, bowls. *Address:* Dominion Circuit, Canberra, A.C.T.
[*Died* 30 *March* 1967.

THORPE, Col. Sir Fred (Garner), Kt., *cr.* 1952; M.C. 1917; E.D. 1937; Trustee of the Museum of Applied Science of Victoria, since 1950; Trustee, National Museum of Victoria, since 1945; *b.* Macorna, Victoria, 25 Dec. 1893; *s.* of James and Dorothy Thorpe; *m.* 1918, Myrtle, *d.* of John and Mary Bishop; one *s.* *Educ.:* State School, Melbourne; Melbourne Technical College. Diplomas in Mechanical and Electrical Engineering. Engineering Assistant, Victorian Rlys., 1919-20; Sales Engineer in Machine Tools, 1920-24; Manager, E. P. Bevan & Sons, Melb., Machine Tools Merchants, 1924-38; Manager Machinery Depts., McPherson's Ltd., Melbourne, 1939 - 48, Technical Director, 1948 - 53 M.I.Prod.E. 1945; A.M.I.E.A. 1925. Served overseas, Suez Canal Zone and France, with Field Engineers, A.I.F., 1915-19; served continuously with Australian Citizen Mil. Forces, 1920-50, to rank of Col. and was Chief Engineer Southern Command at outbreak of War of 1939-45; seconded as Director of Machine Tools and Gauges with Munitions Dept., Commonwealth of Australia, on its formation in 1940 until June 1945. *Recreation:* gardening. *Address:* 28 Odenwald Road, Heidelberg, Vic., Austr. *T.:* 45-1002. *Club:* Naval and Military (Melb.).
[*Died* 29 *March* 1970.

THORPE, Major-General Gervase, C.B. 1931; C.M.G. 1918; D.S.O. 1915; *b.* 10 Aug. 1877; *s.* of late Col. James Thorpe of Coddington Hall, Nottinghamshire, and Ardbrecknish, Argyllshire; *m.* 1917, Margaret, *y. d.* of late James Burt-Marshall, Luncarty, Perthshire; *er. s.* killed in action, 1944, *yr. s. d.* 1958.

Educ.: Eton. Entered Army, 1897; Captain, 1904; Major, 1915; Bt. Lt.-Colonel, 1917; Bt. Colonel, 1919; Colonel, 1920; Maj.-General, 1931; served South African War, 1899-1902 (Queen's medal 3 clasps, King's medal 2 clasps); European War, 1914-18 (despatches eight times, D.S.O. and bar, C.M.G., Bt. Lt.-Col., and Bt. Col.); Brigade Commander 3rd Infantry Brigade, 1927-31; Deputy Adjutant-Gen., Army Headquarters, India, 1931-35; Comdr. 53rd (Welsh) Division T.A., 1935-39; Colonel Argyll and Sutherland Highlanders, 1937-45; retired pay, 1939; re-employed, 1940 (despatches). *Address:* Northbeck House, Hundleby, Spilsby, Lincs. *Club:* Caledonian. [*Died* 4 *Oct.* 1962.

THORVALDSON, Hon. Gunnar S., Q.C. (Can.); Senator of the Dominion of Canada, since 1958; senior partner in legal firm of Thorvaldson & Company, 209 Bank of Nova Scotia Building, Winnipeg; *b.* 18 March 1901; *s.* of Sveinn Thorvaldson and Margaret Solmundson; *m.* 1926, Edna E. Schwitzer; three *d.* *Educ.:* Univ. of Saskatchewan (B.A. 1922); Univ. of Manitoba (LL.B. 1925). Called to Manitoba Bar, 1925; K.C. (Can.), 1943. Mem. of Legislature of Manitoba, 1941-49; Mem., Canadian Delegn. to U.N., N.Y., 1958; Inter-Parliamentary Union: Head, Canadian Parly. Delegn., Tokyo, 1960, Brussels, 1961, Brasilia, 1962; Mem. Council, 1960-1962. President: Law Society of Manitoba, 1956-57 (Life Bencher); Progressive Conservative Assoc. of Canada, 1959-61; Winnipeg Chamber of Commerce, 1952-53; Canadian Chamber of Commerce, 1954-55. Director: Western Gypsum Ltd.; North Canadian Trust Co.; Gamble Macleod Ltd.; Canadian Premier Life Insurance Co.; Anthes-Imperial Ltd.; Canadian Aviation Electronics Ltd.; Canada Security Assurance Co. *Recreations:* golf, game bird hunting. *Address:* 1009 - 99 Wellington Crescent, Winnipeg, Man., Canada. *Clubs:* Manitoba, St. Charles Country, Winnipeg Conservative, Winnipeg Winter, Optimist (Winnipeg); Rideau (Ottawa); Seigniory (Montebello, P.Q.). [*Died* 2 *Aug.* 1969.

THRING, Captain Ernest Walsham Charles, C.B. 1919, R.N. (retd.); *b.* 22 Feb. 1875; 5th *s.* of Rev. John Charles Thring; *m.* 1906, Bertha Marjory Langley (*d.* 1953). *Educ.:* Bath Grammar School; Dunstable School. Admiralty War Staff, 1910-20 and 1939-45; Mem. Committee on Breaches of Laws of War, 1919-20. *Address:* Riverside, Heytesbury, Wilts. *T.:* Sutton Veny 203. [*Died* 17 *March* 1970.

THURBER, James Grover; *b.* 8 Dec. 1894; *s.* of Charles L. and Mary Fisher Thurber; *m.* 1921, Althea Adams; one *d.*; *m.* 1935, Helen Wismer; no *c.* *Educ.:* Ohio State University. Code Clerk, American Embassy, Paris, 1918-20; Reporter: Columbus, O., Dispatch, 1920-24, Chicago, Ill., Tribune, Paris ed., 1924-26, New York Evening Post, Sept. 1926-March 1927; on staff of The New Yorker since 1927. Honorary Degrees: Litt.D., Kenyon College, 1950; Yale Univ., 1953. L.H.D., Williams College, 1951. *Publications:* (with E. B. White) Is Sex Necessary? (drawings first appeared in this book), 1929; The Seal in the Bedroom, 1931; The Owl in the Attic, 1932; My Life and Hard Times, 1933; The Middle-Aged Man on the Flying Trapeze, 1935; Let Your Mind Alone, 1937; The Last Flower, 1940; (with Elliott Nugent) The Male Animal (play), 1940; Fables for our Time, 1941; Men, Women and Dogs, 1943; Many Moons, 1943; My World and Welcome To It, 1944; The Great Quillow, 1944; The Thurber Carnival, 1945; The White Deer, 1945; The Beast in Me, and other Animals, 1948; The Thirteen Clocks, 1950; Fables for Our Time, 1951; The Thurber Album, 1952; Thurber Country, 1953; Thurber's Dogs, 1955; A Thurber Garland, 1955; Further Fables for Our Time, 1956; Alarms and Diversions, 1957; The Wonderful O, 1958; The Years with Ross, 1959; Lanterns and Lances, 1961; Credos and Curios, 1962 (posthumous). A Thurber Carnival (show), Anta Theatre, Broadway, New York, 1960 (appeared, himself, in a sketch: File and Forget); London 1962. *Address:* West Cornwall, Connecticut, U.S.A. *T.:* Cornwall Orleans 2-6557. *Clubs:* Phi Kappa Psi, Sigma Delta Chi (New York). [*Died* 2 *Nov.* 1961.

THURSFIELD, (Edward) Philip; *b.* 26 June 1876; 3rd *s.* of Thomas William Thursfield, M.D., F.R.C.P. (Lond.), Leamington, Warwickshire; unmarried. *Educ.:* Tonbridge School; Brasenose College, Oxford. Called to Bar, Inner Temple, 1904; Midland Circuit; since 1925 has lived in Somerset; Alderman Somerset County Council, 1943-60, and J.P. for Somerset since 1928; High Sheriff of Somerset, 1941-42; Dep. Chairman of Quarter Sessions, 1932-45, Chairman, 1945-52. *Recreations:* chiefly living in the country. *Address:* Chilcote Manor, Wells, Somerset. *T.:* Wells 2104. [*Died* 13 *March* 1962.

THURSFIELD, Rear-Admiral Henry George; Editor of Brassey's Annual since 1936; F.S.A.; *b.* May 1882; *o. s.* of late Sir James R. Thursfield; *m.* 1923, Celia (*d.* 1956), *d.* of late A. S. Taylor, F.R.C.S., M.D.; one *s.* (and *yr. s.* died on active service, 1946). *Educ.:* Berkhamsted School; H.M.S. Britannia. Lieut. 1902; Captain, 1920; Asst. Director of Naval Staff College, 1920; Commanded ships in Med. Fleet, 1922-24 and 1930-32; Naval Mission to Greece, 1925; Director of Tactical Division, Admiralty Naval Staff, 1928; A.D.C. to King George V, 1932; Rear-Admiral, 1932; retired, 1932; Naval Correspondent of The Times, 1936-52. Trustee, National Maritime Museum, 1948-55; Councillor or Vice-President Navy Records Society, 1929-; Trustee of Soc. for Nautical Research; a Treasurer, Royal Literary Fund, 1951-57; Vice-Pres. Norfolk and Norwich Archæological Soc. *Publications:* Action Stations, 1941; Five Naval Journals, 1950; Essays on Naval subjects in Brassey's Annual, National Review, Army Quarterly, and other periodicals. *Recreation:* gardening. *Address:* The Ship House, Burnham Overy Staithe, King's Lynn, Norfolk. *T.:* Burnham Market 244. *Clubs:* Athenæum; Norfolk (Norwich). [*Died* 23 *Oct.* 1963.

THURSFIELD, Philip; *see* Thursfield, E. P.

THURSO, 1st Viscount, *cr.* 1952, of Ulbster; **Archibald Henry Macdonald Sinclair,** 4th Bt., *cr.* 1786, of Ulbster, Caithness; K.T. 1941; P.C. 1931; C.M.G. 1922; President Scottish Liberal Party; Chevalier Légion d'Honneur; J.P.; Lord-Lieutenant of Caithness, 1919-64; LL.D. Edinburgh University, 1932; Glasgow University, 1940; *b.* 22 Oct. 1890; *s.* of Clarence Granville Sinclair, *e. s.* of 3rd Bt. and Mabel, *d.* of M. Sands, New York; *S.* grandfather, 1912; *m.* 1918, Marigold, *d.* of Col. J. S. Forbes, D.S.O.; two *s.* two *d.* *Educ.:* Eton; Sandhurst. Entered Army, 1910; Personal Military Secretary to Secretary of State for War, 1919-21; Private Secretary to Secretary of State for Colonies, 1921-22; M.P. (L.) Caithness and Sutherland, 1922-45; Temp. Chairman of Committees, House of Commons, 1925-30; Member of Empire Marketing Board, 1927-30; Chief Liberal Whip, 1930-31; Secretary of State for Scotland, 1931-32; Secretary of State for Air, 1940-45; Leader, Liberal Parliamentary Party, 1935-45; Hon. Air Commodore A.A.F., 1942-49. Lord Rector of Glasgow University, 1938-45. Pres., Eighty Club,

1953-68; Pres., Air League of British Empire, 1956-58. Mem. Political Honours Scrutiny Cttee., 1954-61. *Recreations:* fishing, shooting. *Heir: s.* Hon. Robin Macdonald Sinclair. *Address:* Fotheringay House, Montpelier Row, Twickenham, Middlesex. *Clubs:* National Liberal, Royal Automobile. [*Died* 15 *June* 1970.

THURSTON, Albert Peter, M.B.E. **1919;** D.Sc. (Lond.) 1913 (first Dr. of Science in Aeronautics in Gt. Brit.); M.I.Mech.E., M.I.E.E., F.R.Ae.S., F.C.I.P.A.; Consulting Aeronautical Engineer; *b.* 31 Oct. 1881; *s.* of Peter and Elizabeth Thurston; *m.* Susan, *d.* of Clair Grece, LL.D., Reigate; no *c. Educ.:* Queen Mary College, London University (Drapers' Schol.); S. H. Johnson & Co. Pioneer in Aeronautics; Chief Asst. to Sir Hiram Maxim in aeronautical expts, and design of aeroplanes, 1903 - 10; discoverer of use of " Rider " planes to control air-flow over main planes, 1912-14; founded first Univ. Aeronautical Lab. in Gt. Brit. (Queen Mary College), 1909; in charge of Aeronautical Dept., Q.M. Coll., 1909-14; Lecturer in Aeronautics, University of Sheffield, 1910; examining staff, Patent Office, 1905-14. Univ. of London O.T.C., 1914; London Electrical Engineers, 1914; Special Res., R.F.C., 1915; Inspector of Aeronautics (A.I.D.), 1915; in charge of safety of design (Military Aeronautics Directorate) and Air Board, 1915-17; of metal construction of aircraft (Air Board), 1917-18. Consultant in Patents & Trade Marks and the protection of industrial property, 1920-; acted for Major J. Coats in developing Hafner Gyroplane and Helicopter, 1930-1945; President Northern Heights Model Flying Club; Inaugurator of Wakefield Cup and Queen Elizabeth's Cup, both for model flying; Member Council International Association for Protection of Industrial Property (Brit. Gp.) Incorp.: Mem. Camp 1 of Engineers of Toronto Univ.; for many years Pres. or Vice-Pres. Soc. of Model Aeronautical Engineers; Past Member Council R.Ae.S., Past Member Council Instn. of Aeronautical Engineers. Pres. Newcomen Soc., 1947-48, 1948-49; Adviser on Patents Assoc. Supervising Electrical Engineers, 1925-; Liveryman Worshipful Company of Patternmakers. *Publications:* Text Book of Aeronautics, 1911; The Future of Aerial Transport, Reconstruction Problems 34, Ministry of Reconstruction, 1919. Ed. Molesworth's Pocket Book of Engineering Formulae; Molesworth's Aeronautical Engineer's Pocket Book. *Recreations:* flying, model flying, yachting, shooting. *Address:* Petersbank, Bidborough, Kent. *T.:* Penshurst 243. *Clubs:* Author's, Royal Aero; Surrey and Kent Flying (Pres.); (Hon.) Aero Club de Basse-Normandie. [*Died* 17 *April* 1964.

THYATEIRA, Archbishop of; *see* Athenagoras, Archbishop.

TICHBORNE, Sir Anthony Joseph Henry Doughty Doughty-, 14th Bt., *cr.* 1620; Major, 4th County of London Yeomanry R.A.C.; Privy Chamberlain to H.H. The Pope; *b.* 29 June 1914; *s.* of 13th Bt. and Denise, *o. d.* of Lt.-Col. Henry F. Greville; *S.* father, 1930; *m.* 1936, Antonia (*d.* 1966), twin *d.* of late Sir Harold Snagge, K.B.E.; three *d.* Legion of Honour, Croix de Guerre, Knight of Malta. *Heir:* none. *Address:* Tichborne Park, Alresford, Hants. [*Died* 18 *July* 1968 (*ext.*).

TILLEY, George Reginald Louis; Company Director; *b.* 19 Sept. 1904; *s.* of late Sir George Tilley; *m.* 1931, Lewis (*d.* 1942), *d.* of late Sidney Bacon. *Educ.:* Dover Coll.; Jesus Coll., Cambridge (M.A.). Chancery Bar, 1928. Chairman: British Combined Investors Trust Ltd.; London Border & General Trust; Director: Abbots Investment Trust Ltd.; City & International Trust Ltd.; Southern Stockholders Investment Trust Ltd.; Cable & Wireless (Holding) Ltd. Freeman of City of London; Liveryman of Merchant Taylors' Company; Liveryman, Worshipful Company of Farmers. Fellow of the Chartered Institute of Secretaries (Council). *Address:* 17 Lowndes Square, S.W.1. *Clubs:* Carlton, Bath, Royal Thames Yacht. [*Died* 28 *May* 1963.

TILLICH, Professor Paul; John Nuveen Prof., Univ. of Chicago Divinity School, 1962; University Prof., Harvard, 1955-June 1962, retired; *b.* 20 August 1886; *s.* of Johannes Tillich and Mathilde (*née* Duerselen); *m.* 1924, Hannah (*née* Werner); one *s.* one *d. Educ.:* Universities of Berlin, Tübingen and Halle. Privatdozent, Univ. of Berlin, 1919-24; Prof. Extraord., Marburg, 1924-25; Prof. Ord., Dresden, 1925-29; Hon. Prof., Leipzig, 1926-29; Prof. Ord., Frankfurt-am-Main, 1929-33; Prof. of Philosophical Theology, Union Theological Seminary, New York, 1933-55. Hon. Degrees: D.Theol. (Halle), 1926; D.D. (Yale), 1940; D.D. (Glas.), 1951; D.Lit. (Princeton), 1953; D.Theol (Harvard), 1954; D.Phil. (Free University of Berlin), 1956. Grosse Verdienstkreuz, West German Republic, 1956; Goethe Medal, Frankfurt, 1956; Goethe Prize, Hamburg, 1958. *Publications:* The Interpretation of History, 1936; The Protestant Era, 1951 (in England); The Shaking of the Foundations, 1951; The Courage to Be, 1953 (Eng.); Systematic Theology, Vol. 1, 1953 (Eng.), Vol. 2, 1957, Vol. 3, 1963; Love, Power and Justice, 1954; The New Being, 1955; Biblical Religion and the Search for Ultimate Reality, 1955; Dynamics of Faith, 1957 (U.S.); Theology of Culture, 1959 (Eng.); Frühe Hauptwerke Gesammelte Werke, Band I, 1959 (Stuttgart). *Address:* c/o Divinity School, The University, Chicago, U.S.A. [*Died* 22 *Oct.* 1965.

TILLOTSON, Prof. Geoffrey, F.B.A.1967; M.A., B.Litt.; Prof. of English Literature in the Univ. of London, Birkbeck Coll., since 1944; *b.* 30 June 1905; *e. s.* of John Henry and Annie Tillotson, Bradford, Yorks; *m.* 1933, Kathleen Mary Constable (*see* K. M. Tillotson); two adopted *s. Educ.:* Keighley Trade and Grammar School; Balliol College, Oxford. B.A. Hons. School of English Language and Literature, 1927; B.Litt. 1930; teaching Leicester Technical Coll., 1928-29; teaching Castleford secondary school, 1930; sub-librarian English School Library, Oxford, and War Memorial Student, Balliol Coll., 1930-31; Asst. Lecturer, Lecturer, and Reader in English Literature, Univ. College, London, 1931-44; Ministry of Aircraft Production, 1940-44; Visiting Lecturer, Harvard University, 1948; Governor of City Lit. Inst., 1952-; Pres. Charles Lamb Society, 1955-. Foreign Hon. Member, Amer. Acad. of Arts and Sciences, 1960; Governor of Dr. Johnson's House Trust, 1961-, Trustee, 1968-. *Publications:* On the Poetry of Pope, 1938; Twickenham Edition of Poems of Pope, Vol. II, 1940 (revised, 1962); Pope's Rape of the Lock, 1941; Bibliography of Michael Drayton, 1941; Essays in Criticism and Research, 1942 (repr. 1967); Criticism and the Nineteenth Century, 1951 (repr. 1967); Thackeray the Novelist, 1954; Newman (Reynard Library), 1957; Pope and Human Nature, 1958; Augustan Studies, 1961; Vanity Fair (ed. with K. Tillotson), 1963; Mid-Victorian Studies (with K. Tillotson), 1965; The Continuity of English Poetry from Dryden to Wordsworth (Byron Foundation Lecture, Nottingham Univ.), 1967; Thackeray (with D. Hawes), in Critical Heritage Series, 1967; Eighteenth Century English Literature (anthology), 1969; (ed.) Rasselas, 1970; (ed. with D. Harvey) Villette, 1970; contributions to periodicals. *Address:* 23 Tanza

Road, Hampstead, N.W.3. *T.:* 01-435 5639. [*Died* 15 *Oct.* 1969.

TILLYARD, Eustace Mandeville Wetenhall, O.B.E., Litt.D., F.B.A., 1952; F.R.S.L.; Hon. Member, Mod. Lang. Assoc. of America; Master of Jesus College, Cambridge, 1945-59; University Lecturer in English, 1926-54; *b.* 1889; *s.* of late Alfred Isaac Tillyard, M.A., J.P., and Cath. S. Wetenhall; *m.* 1919, Phyllis, *d.* of Henry M. Cooke; one *s.* two *d. Educ.:* College Cantonal, Lausanne; Perse, Cambridge; Jesus Coll., Camb. (Schol.). 1st class both parts of Classical Tripos, Craven Student; Student of British School of Archæology, Athens, 1911; Fell. of Jesus Coll., Cambridge, 1913-1915, 1934-45, 1959-; commn. in 4th R. Lanc. Regt. (T.F.), 1914-19; Captain, 1915; served with regiment, B.E.F. France, 1915-1916; seconded to Salonica Force, 1916-19; Intelligence Corps, 1917-18; British Liaison Officer with Greek G.H.Q., 1918-19 (O.B.E., Greek M.C., despatches thrice). Alexander Lecturer at the University of Toronto, 1948; Turnbull Memorial Lecturer at Johns Hopkins University, 1951; President, International Association of University Professors of English, 1953-56; Walker-Ames Lecturer, University of Washington, 1955. *Publications:* The Hope Vases, 1923; Lamb's Criticism, 1923; The Poetry of Sir Thomas Wyatt, a Selection and a Study, 1929; Milton, 1930; Milton's Correspondence and Academic Exercises, 1932; Poetry Direct and Oblique, 1934 and 1945; Shakespeare's Last Plays, 1938; The Miltonic Setting, 1938; The Personal Heresy (with C. S. Lewis), 1939; The Elizabethan World Picture, 1943; Shakespeare's History Plays, 1944; Five Poems, 1470-1870, 1948; Shakespeare's Problem Plays, 1950; Studies in Milton, 1951; The English Renaissance, Fact or Fiction, 1952; The English Epic and its Background, 1954; The Metaphysicals and Milton, 1956; The Epic Strain in the English Novel; The Muse Unchained, 1958; Some Mythical Elements in English Literature, 1961; Shakespeare's Early Comedies, 1965 (posthumous). *Recreations:* walking, cycling, travel. *Address:* 4B Millington Road, Cambridge; Jesus College, Cambridge. [*Died* 24 *May* 1962.

TILLYARD, Sir Frank, Kt., *cr.* 1945; C.B.E. 1929; M.A., M.Com.; Emeritus Professor of Commercial Law, University of Birmingham; *b.* 1865; *y. s.* of Isaac Tillyard of Norwich; *m.* 1891, E. Katharine (*d.* 1952), *y. d.* of Edwin Ridley of Finchley; two *d. Educ.:* City of London School; Balliol College, Oxford. First class Final School of Maths., 1886; Vinerian Law Scholarship, 1888; first class Final School of Jurisprudence, 1888; called to the Bar, 1890; engaged in social work, Mansfield House University Settlement, Canning Town, 1891-96, where he was the founder of the Poor Man's Lawyer Movement; Head of the Shalesmoor Neighbour Guild, Sheffield, 1896-1904; Organising Secretary Birmingham C.O.S., 1904-13; Lecturer, 1904-13; Professor of Commercial Law, 1913-30, and Warden of Chancellor's Hall, 1928-30, at the University of Birmingham; Chairman of Court of Referees for Birmingham, 1912-28, and for the Metropolitan Area, 1931-37; Appointed member of Trade Boards, 1910-44, and Chairman of several Trade Boards, mostly in the Midlands; Chairman of the Birmingham Copec House Improvement Society Ltd., 1926-41. *Publications:* Law of Banking and Negotiable Instruments (6th edition); Introduction to Commercial Law (2nd edition); Industrial Law (2nd edition); The Worker and the State (3rd edition); (joint) Goodwill and its Treatment in Accounts; (joint) Unemployment Insurance, 1911-48; occasional papers in various journals. *Recreation:* chess. *Address:* 6 Church Road, Highgate, N.6. *T.:* Mountview 5445. [*Died* 10 *July* 1961.

TILLYARD, Henry Julius Wetenhall, M.A., D.Litt.; *e. s.* of Alfred Isaac Tillyard, M.A., J.P., and Cath. S. Wetenhall; *b.* Cambridge, 18 Nov. 1881; *m.* 1913, Wilhelmina, *d.* of Theo. Kaufmann, Lahr, Baden. *Educ.:* Tonbridge School; Gonville and Caius College, Cambridge. Member of British School at Athens, 1904-12; Research Fellow of Edinburgh University with grant from Carnegie Trust; Lecturer in Greek at Edinburgh University, 1908-17; civil prisoner at Ruhleben, 1914-15; Professor of Latin at University College, Johannesburg, 1919-21, Professor of Russian, Birmingham University, 1921-26; Professor of Greek, University College, Cardiff, 1926-46; Temp. Lecturer in Classics, Rhodes University, Grahamstown, 1947-49; Corr. Member Am; Musicol. Soc.; Member Royal Danish Acad.; joint editor of Monumenta Musicæ Byzantinæ. *Publications:* Agathocles (Prince Consort Prize); Greek Literature (People's Books); Byzantine Music and Hymnography (Faith Press); Roswitha (trans.) (Faith Press); articles on Greek Epigraphy, Greek and Byzantine Music in Annual of British School at Athens, Laudate, Byz. Zeitschr., etc.; Russian Poetry Reader (in collaboration); Handbook of Middle Byzantine Musical Notation (Copenhagen, 1935); Hymns of Sticherarium for November (*ibid.* 1938); Octoechus, Pt. I (*ibid.* 1941), Pt. II. 1949; Twenty Canons fr. Trinity Hirmologium (Oxford), 1951; Pentecostarium, 1958. *Address:* Castle End, Saffron Walden, Essex. [*Died* 2 *Jan.* 1968.

TIMMIS, Colonel Reginald Symonds, D.S.O. 1918; J.P.; Royal Canadian Dragoons; *b.* 16 Oct. 1884; *s.* of late Illius Augustus Timmis and Honoria Udal, Stone Hall, Oxted, Surrey. *Educ.:* Charterhouse; King's College, London; Toronto University. Five years Imperial Yeomanry; Canadian Army, 1911; served with R.C.D., European War, 1914-18, over 4 years in France and Belgium (D.S.O., despatches, twice wounded); served overseas in War of 1939-45, 1942-45. Commanded R.C.D., 1931-36. Former President Toronto Humane Society; Member Canadian Army International Jumping Team, 1926 to War of 1939-45; Past Pres. Canadian Hunter and Light Horse Improvement Society, and Canadian Arabian Horse Assoc.; Hon. Chm. and Founder, Canadian Pony Club Board. *Publications:* Modern Horse Management, Riding and Schooling, Driving and Harness, etc. *Recreations:* Association football, hunting, driving, diving, photography. *Address:* 3000 Yonge St., Toronto 12. *Club:* Cavalry. [*Died* 10 *June* 1968.

TIMOSHENKO, Marshal Semyon Konstantinovich; Orders of Lenin and of Suvarov; Order of Victory; Hero of the Soviet Union; 2 Gold Star Medals; Marshal of the Soviet Union, 1940; *b.* Furmanka village, Bessarabia, 18 Feb. 1895; *s.* of peasant parents. Conscripted into Tsarist Army, 1915; Civil War, 1918-1921, guerilla fighter and cavalry leader; 8th Congress of Soviets, 1920; graduated from Higher Military Academy, 1922; Commander-Commissar of Third Cavalry Corps, 1925; graduated from Courses for Higher Command, 1927; Asst. Commander, Byelo-Russian Military District, 1933; travelled abroad to study foreign armies; Asst. Commander of Kiev Mil. Dist.; Commander: N. Caucasus Mil. Dist., 1935-37; Kharkov Mil. Dist., Kiev Special Mil. Dist., 1937-38; ops. in W. Ukraine, 1939, in Finland, 1940; Bessarabia, 1940; People's Commissar of Defence, May 1940-June 1941; C.-in-C. Western (Central) Front, July-Nov. 1941; in comd. ops. S.W. and S. Fronts, 1941-42; ops. N. Front, 1943; 2nd and 3rd Ukrainian 1944; subseq. Comdr. Byelo-Russian Dist., retd. 1960. Mem. Central Cttee. Communist

Party, 1939-52; Deputy to Supreme Soviet. *Address:* Chamber of the Supreme Soviet, Moscow, U.S.S.R. [*Died* 1 *April* 1970.

TINDAL, Rev. Professor William Strang, O.B.E. 1946: M.A., Hon. D.D.; Hon. Chaplain to H.M. Forces; Professor of Christian Ethics and Practical Theology, New College, Edinburgh University, since 1945; *b.* 25 Jan. 1899; *e. surv. s.* of late James A. Love Tindal, Glasgow, and late Maggie Strang; *m.* 1929, Elfrida (*d.* 1963), *yr. d.* of late Jurat Arthur Dorey, Guernsey, C.I.; four *d.* *Educ.:* Glasgow High Sch.; Glasgow Univ.; Trinity Coll., Glasgow; Universities of Marburg and Tübingen. Kerr Travelling Scholarship and Brown Downie Fellowship, 1926-27; ordained 1927; Study Secretary of Student Christian Movement of Gt. Britain and Ireland, 1927-32; Minister of Lindowan Church, Cove and Kilcreggan, 1932-36; Minister of Pleasance Church, Edinburgh, Warden of New College Settlement, and Lecturer in Christian Sociology, New College, Edinburgh, 1936-45. C.F., 52 Lowland Div., 1940-43; staff chaplain, H.Q. 21 Army Group, 1944-45 (despatches twice, O.B.E.). Hon. Sec. Inter-Church Relations Cttee. of Church of Scotland, 1950-1959; Convener, 1959-63. Mem. of Central Committee, World Council of Churches, 1954-. Hon. D.D. Glasgow University, 1949. *Publications:* articles in composite works and religious journals. *Recreation:* golf. *Address:* 16 Lauder Rd., Edinburgh 9. *T.:* Newington 3998. *Club:* New (Edinburgh). [*Died* 11 *Sept.* 1965.

TINDALL, Hon. Benjamin Arthur, Q.C.; 4th *s.* of late Rev. Henry Tindall, Cape Colony; *m.* 1912, Geraldine (*d.* 1950), *e. d.* of E. Lomax, England; one *s.* one *d.* *Educ.:* Victoria College, Cape Province. Practised at the Bar in Pretoria, 1903-22; Judge, 1922; Judge President of Supreme Court of South Africa, Transvaal Provincial Division, 1937-1938; Judge of Appellate Division of Supreme Court, South Africa, 1938-49 (acted as Chief Justice, Feb.-June 1948); Chairman of the Joint Committee for Professional Examinations, 1925-37; Chairman of the Southern Africa Customs Union Council, 1949-51. *Clubs:* Civil Service (Capetown); Pretoria. [*Died* 3 *Feb.* 1963.

TINDALL, Rt. Rev. Gordon Leslie; Bishop of Grahamstown since 1964. *Educ.:* St. Paul's College, Burgh; Hatfield College, Durham. L.Th. 1934; B.A. 1935; Deacon 1935; Priest 1936. Curate of: Swinton, 1935-37; Motito, 1937-39; Vryburg, 1939; Rector of Vryburg and Director of Vryburg and Ganesa Mission, 1939-47; Director of South Bechuanaland Mission, 1942-50; Priest in charge of Warrenton, 1947-50; Archdeacon of Bechuanaland, 1945-50; Rector of St. Saviour, East London, C.P., 1950-60; Canon of Grahamstown Cathedral, 1952-64; Chancellor, 1952-57; Archdeacon of: King William's Town, 1957-64; Queenstown, 1960-62; Rector of Peddie, 1960-64; Director of Religious Education, Grahamstown, 1962-64. *Address:* Bishopsbourne, P.O. Box 162, Grahamstown, Cape Province, South Africa. [*Died* 24 *June* 1969.

TINKER, Chauncey Brewster, Litt.D. Princeton; Professor Emeritus of English Literature, Yale University; *b.* Auburn, Maine, U.S.A., 22 Oct. 187; *s.* of Rev. Anson Phelps Tinker and Martha Jane White; unmarried. *Educ.:* Yale University, B.A., 1899; Ph.D. 1902. Associate in English, Bryn Mawr College, 1902-03; Instructor, Assistant Professor, and Professor of English Literature, Yale University, 1903-46; Visiting Professor, Harvard University, 1930; Norton Professor of Poetry, Harvard University, 1937-38; Captain, Military Intelligence Division, U.S. Army, 1918; American Academy of Arts and Letters; Chancellor, 1949. Keeper of Rare Books, Yale University Library; has several hon. degrees. *Publications:* Beowulf, 1902, a translation; Select Translations from Old English Poetry (with A. S. Cook), 1902; Dr. Johnson and Fanny Burney, 1908; Nature's Simple Plan, 1922; Young Boswell, 1922; Letters of James Boswell, 2 vols., 1924; Good Estate of Poetry, 1929; Poet and Painter, 1938; The Poetry of Matthew Arnold. A Commentary (with H. F. Lowry), 1940; Essays in Retrospect, 1948; The Complete Poetical Works of Matthew Arnold (edited with H. F. Lowry), 1950. Hon. medal for service, Yale Univ., 1955. *Address:* Yale University, New Haven, Connecticut, U.S.A. *Clubs:* Century, Grolier (N.Y.). [*Died* 16 *March* 1963.

TINTON, Major Ben Thomas, J.P. Warden and Head of the Dockland Settlements, 1937-47; *b.* 2 Jan. 1897; *s.* of late H. Tinton, London and Howe, Cambridge; *m.* 1918, Violet Lilian Butcher; one *s.* *Educ.:* privately. Served in the European War, going overseas October 1914 (despatches); transferred Indian Army, 1918, and served in North Western Front Province; from 1919 with Sir Reginald Kennedy-Cox, built up chain of Dockland Settlements in London Docks, Millwall, Dagenham, Rotherhithe, Poplar, Bristol, and Southampton; serves on Juvenile panel at West Ham Court; F.R.S.A.; Public Schools Art Exhibition Committee; holds Diocesan Readership of Chelmsford; Chairman R.S.P.C.C. (West Ham and District); President South West Ham British Legion; Hon. Treas. British Legion and United Services Fund (South West Ham); various Welfare Committees; late Welfare Officer to the Troops; Chairman of Advisory Committee to the Lord Chancellor; Fellow of Institute of Welfare. *Publications:* War Comes to the Docks; 25 years in Dockland; Short Stories, and Articles dealing with Social and Spiritual problems. *Recreations:* gardening (Fellow Royal Horticultural Soc.), art and travel. *Address:* 6 Longwood Gardens, Ilford, Essex. *Club:* Royal Societies. [*Died* 16 *May* 1966.

TIRIKATENE, Hon. Sir Eruera (Tihema), K.C.M.G. 1960; Politician, New Zealand; *b.* Kaiapoi, N. Canterbury, N.Z., 5 Jan. 1895; *e. s.* of Captain John Driver Tregarthyn (Tirikatene), R.N., and Tini Tuhuru Arapata (*née* Horau); *m.* 1920, Ruti Matekino Solomon Horomona of Canterbury, N.Z., Chieftainess of Ngati Pahauwera and Ngati Kahungunu tribes; six *s.* three *d.* *Educ.:* Tuahiwi Primary School, Kaiapoi District High School, N. Canterbury, N.Z. Stock-dealer and timber-miller, working with father, 1911-14. Served European War of 1914-18: Soldier; Member, Te Hokowhitu-a-Tu, Maori Bn. of 1st N.Z.E.F. Dairy farmer, 1919-20; certificated oil, gas, electrical and fluid marine engineer; Proprietor and Master of sea-going ferry service and fishing craft, 1920-23; Mission work with Ratana Church, Ratana Pa, as Dir. of Farming Ops. and Engineering, 1923-32; elected to N.Z. House of Reps. as Ind.-Ratana Mem. for Southern Maori, 1932; J.P., 1932; elected Mem. Maori Affairs Cttee., N.Z. House of Reps., also Maori Purposes Bd., 1932; with other Ind.-Ratana candidates, allied with N.Z. Lab. Party by contesting Gen. Election as official Lab. candidate for Southern Maori electorate, re-elected, 1935; Pres., Maori Advisory Council and Policy Cttee. of N.Z. Labour Party, 1935-58; Minister of Forests; Minister i/c Printing and Stationery; Associate Minister of Maori Affairs, 1957-60. Senior Maori Representative, N.Z. contingent to coronation of King George VI, 1937; attended Commonwealth Parl. Assoc., England, 1937. During War of 1939-45: Mem. N.Z. War Council; Chm. Maori War

Effort Organisation; Rep. of Maori Race on N.Z. Exec. Council. 1st Pres. Ngaitahu Trust Bd. and Mem. Ngarimu Scholarship Bd., 1946; represented N.Z. at centennial celebrations of France's occupation of New Caledonia, Noumea, 1933; Leader N.Z deleg. to 5th Session of Asia-Pacific Forestry Commn. of F.A.O., New Delhi, 1960. Member: numerous sports and cultural groups, Historical Assocs., etc. A registered Minister of the Ratana Church since 1939; was appointed Te Koata (one of highest positions in Ratana Church and Political Movement) by founder, T. W. Ratana, 1937, and is o. surv. Mem. of this hierarchy. Rangatira (Chief) of the Ngaitahu tribe. Received life-title of Honourable for services on Exec. Council, 1950. *Recreations:* football, athletics, wrestling, boxing, swimming, motor-cycling, speedboat racing, horse-riding. *Address:* Te Hiwi Marama, Kaiapoi, North Canterbury, N.Z. *T.:* Kaiapoi 48. *Clubs:* sundry golf. [*Died* 11 *Jan.* 1967.

TITCHMARSH, Edward Charles, F.R.S. 1931; M.A. (Oxon); Hon. D.Sc. (Sheffield); Savilian Professor of Geometry, Oxford University, and Fellow of New College since 1931; *b.* Newbury, Berks, 1 June 1899; *e. s.* of Rev. E. H. Titchmarsh, M.A.; *m.* 1925, Kathleen, *d.* of A. Blomfield, J.P.; three *d.* *Educ.:* King Edward VII School, Sheffield; Balliol College, Oxford. War Service, 1917-1918; Lecturer at University College, London, 1923-29; Fellow of Magdalen College, Oxford, 1923-30; Professor of Pure Mathematics in the University of Liverpool, 1929-1931; President London Mathematical Soc., 1945-47. De Morgan medallist, 1953; Sylvester medallist, Roy. Soc., 1955. *Publications:* The Zeta-Function of Riemann; The Theory of Functions; Introduction to the Theory of Fourier Integrals; Eigenfunction Expansions associated with Second Order Differential Equations; Mathematics for the General Reader; mathematical papers, mainly in the Proceedings of the London Mathematical Society and Quarterly Journal of Mathematics. *Address:* 4 Capel Close, Oxford. *T.:* Oxford 58063. [*Died* 18 *Jan.* 1963.

TITHERADGE, Madge; *b.* Melbourne, Australia; *d.* of G. S. Titheradge; *m.* 1928, Edgar Park (*d.* 1938), New York. *Educ.:* Private School, Hampstead. Made stage debut at Garrick Theatre, London, 1902, playing a child's part in Kingsley's Water Babies; has since that time played leading parts in most of the London theatres. *Recreations:* fishing, swimming, and gardening. *Address:* Orchard Walls, The Street, Fetcham, Surrey. *T.A.:* Madgedgar, Leatherhead. *T.:* Leatherhead 2366. [*Died* 14 *Nov.* 1961.

TITTLE, Walter (Ernest); artist, painter of portraits; *b.* Springfield, Ohio, U.S.A., 9 Oct. 1883; *s.* of Levi Henry Tittle and Mary Elizabeth Tittle (*née* Buck); *m.* 2nd, 1933, Helen Salisbury Carr. *Educ.:* Public and High Schools, Springfield. Studied art in N.Y. under William M. Chase, Robert Henri, and Kenneth Hays Miller; took up etching and dry-point, 1917; as official U.S. artist, produced Washington Arms Conference Memorial Portfolio of portraits in dry-point of 25 leading statesmen attending Naval Disarmament Conf., Washington, 1920-21 (sets of these prints acquired by Brit. Govt. for British Museums); exhibited first in London, Leicester Galleries, 1922; exhib. Galerie Devambez, Paris, 1923; Roy. Acad. London, 1932; produced forty portraits in lithograph of leading literary men of Britain; executed series of 15 dry-point plates of Art Gallery interiors, and portraits for Lord Duveen of Millbank, 1930-36; engaged in making portraits in dry-point of President Roosevelt, from personal sittings, 1942-43; portrait of Lord Duveen of Millbank (City of Hull Guildhall), 1951. Oil portrait of Joseph Conrad acquired by National Portrait Gallery, London, 1932, also portrait of Arnold Bennett purchased 1934; lithograph portrait of Henry Arthur Jones, 1961; oil portraits from life of Joseph Conrad, purch. Yale Univ., 1949; of George Bernard Shaw, 1949, and oil portrait of Professor Archibald Henderson, purch. Univ. of Carolina; Arms Conference Memorial Portfolio acquired by Bibliothèque Nationale, Paris, 1957. Rep. in many Art Museums in Brit. and U.S.; rep. for 12 consesl yrs. in internat. publication Fine Princ. of the Year; contrib. illustrations and cartoons for many years to Harper's Magiazine, Scribner's, Century, Life, etc. Prze-National Arts Club, New York, 1931; Silver Medal, Calif. Printmakers International, 1932; Prize, Chicago Soc. of Etchers, Century of Progress Exposition, 1934. 1st gold medal for dry-point, Amer. Artist Professional League, New York, 1961. Member: Soc. Amer Etchers; Chicago Soc. Etchers; Printmakers of Calif. *Publications:* The First Nantucket Tea-Party, 1907; Colonial Holidays, 1910; My Country, 1911; Roosevelt as an Artist Saw Him, 1948. *Address:* Box 4203, Carmel, California, U.S.A. *Club:* Dutch Treat (New York). [*Died* 27 *March* 1966.

TITUS, Rev. Murray Thurston; retired; *b.* Batavia, Ohio, 5 November 1885; *s.* of Frank M. Titus and Lottie Harrison; *m.* 1910, Olive McIntire Glasgow, Seaman, Ohio; one *d.* *Educ.:* High School, Batavia, O.; Ohio Wesleyan Univ., B.Litt., 1908; Hon. D.D. 1926; Hartford (Conn.) Seminary Foundation, Ph.D., 1927. Principal, High School, Sleepy Eye, Minn., 1908-1910; teacher philosophy, Lucknow Christian Coll., 1910-13; dist. supt. N. India Conf., M.E. Church, 1916-41; Principal, Lucknow Christian Coll., 1941-43; Sec. Bd. of Missions, N.Y., 1943-45; Associate Sec. National Christian Council, India, Burma, Ceylon, 1945-47; Mission Treas., N. India Conf. Methodist Church, 1948-50. Dist. Supt., Methodist Church, 1948-50; Prof. of Missions, Westminster Theol. Sem., Westminster, Maryland, U.S.A., 1951-55; retired 1957. Member International Committee which prepared Survey of Christian Literature in Moslem Lands, Cairo, 1932; deleg. to Conference on mission work in Moslem lands, Jerusalem, 1924; Secretary for work among Moslems, National Christian Council of India, Burma and Ceylon, 1927-31; Associate Editor, Moslem World Quarterly; Associate Editor, Religious Quest of India Series; Lecturer on Islam, Sat. Tal Ashram, since 1930 and at Henry Martyn School, Islamic Studies, Landour; member Phi Delta Theta; Phi Beta Kappa. *Publications:* Indian Islam, 1930; Islam for Beginners, 1931 (also translated into six Indian languages); Chapters in various publications; Ikhtisar-ul-Islam, 1934; The Young Moslem Looks at Life, 1937; Islam in India and Pakistan, 1959; contrib. religious and historical periodicals. *Address:* The Methodist Home, 807 West Avenue, Elyria, Ohio, U.S.A [*Died* 31 *Oct.* 1964.

TIVEY, Sir John (Proctor), Kt., *cr.* 1955; *b.* 1882; *s.* of Samuel and Margaret Tivey; *m.* 1910, Lorna, *d.* of James Henderson; two *d.* Formerly President of Associated Chambers of Manufacturers of Australia; Past Pres., Instn. of Engrs., Australia; Mem., C.S.I.R., 1937-46. *Address:* 59 Ashley St., Chatswood, Sydney, N.S.W., Australia. [*Died* 5 *Nov.* 1968.

TOCKER, Prof. Albert Hamilton, C.B.E. 1952; M.A.; President of Canterbury Chamber of Commerce, 1951 (Vice-Pres., 1950); Professor of Economics, Dean of Faculty of Commerce, 1926 - Feb. 1950, Rector, 1943 - 1948, Canterbury University College, Christchurch, N.Z.; retired 1950; *b.* N.Z., 1884; *s.* of John Tocker and Annie Baillie; *m.* 1920, Mary Helen Sievwright, B.A., Wellington, New Zealand; three *s.* *Educ.:* Victoria College, Wellington; Birmingham University. B.A. 1915; M.A. 1917, University of New Zealand, Post-graduate study at Birmingham University; served overseas in N.Z.E.F., 1917-19; Lecturer in Economics, Canterbury College, 1920-26; N.Z. representative at International Labour Conference, Geneva, 1930; and Adviser at World Economic Conference, 1933; Member of Government Committee of Economists, 1931-1932 and 1932-33. *Publications:* numerous articles on economic and financial subjects in journals. *Recreations:* shooting and fishing. *Address:* 68 Murray Place, Christchurch, C.1, N.Z. *T.:* 56687. *Club:* Canterbury (Christchurch). [*Died* 14 *July* 1964.

TOD, Sir Alan Cecil, Kt., *cr.* 1953; C.B.E. 1943 (O.B.E. 1918); T.D.; D.L. County Palatine of Lancaster; J.P. Liverpool; *b.* 10 August 1887; *er. s.* of Archibald James Tod; *m.* 1914, Helen Marjorie, 3rd *d.* of James Edgar Gordon; two *d.* *Educ.:* Wellington. T.A., 1908-28 (despatches, O.B.E., Belgian Croix de Guerre); Commanded 59th Medium Brigade, 1924-28; Director, Liner Holdings; President, Liverpool Cathedral Exec. Cttee. (Chm., 1934-61). High Sheriff of Lancashire, 1939-40; Treasurer Liverpool Bluecoat School; Zone Commander Home Guard. Hon. LL.D. Liverpool University, 1954. Commander Order of Orange-Nassau, 1951. *Recreation:* shooting. *Address:* Maryton Grange, Mossley Hill, Liverpool 18. *T.:* 051-428 1010. *Clubs:* Liverpool Racquet, Palatine (Liverpool). [*Died* 7 *Sept.* 1970.

TODD, Lt.-Col. Alfred John Kennett; *b.* 13 April 1890; *s.* of late George Todd; *m.* 1920, Edith Mary, *o. c.* of late William Ernest Gray, Blackheath; two *s.* one *d.* *Educ.:* Rugby. Served in France, 1915-18 (wounded, despatches); Captain, The Queen's Bays, Seconded to Remount Service, 1918-21; M.P. (C.) Berwick-upon-Tweed, 1929-35; commanded 7th Bn. Northumberland Fusiliers, 1932-36. J.P., Northumberland, 1930-1936. Served G.H.Q. M.E.F., 1940-44. Chm. Hartley Wintney R.D.C., 1949-50; C.C. Hants, 1949-53; Mem. Bath City Council, 1957-63. *Address:* Bathwick Hill House, Bath. *T.:* Bath 64698. *Clubs:* Cavalry; Bath and County (Bath). [*Died* 27 *Aug.* 1970.

TODD, Arthur Ralph Middleton, R.A. 1949; R.W.S. 1937; R.P. 1958; N.E.A.C. (Hon. Mem.); Painter; *b.* Cornwall. Studied Art at Slade School of Fine Art, also in Italy, France and Holland. *Works:* at Tate Gall. (Chantry Collection), Diploma Gall., Burlington House (Edward Stott Collection). Colonial and Provincial City Art Galls., National War Records Collection, Contemporary Art Soc., etc. Served European War, 1914-18, in Motor Transport section, R.A.S.C. Instructor in Drawing and Painting, Royal Academy Schools, 1945-49, City and Guilds of London Art School. Member of Royal Academy Council, 1949-51, 1958-59. *Address:* 71 Campden Street, W.8. *T.:* Park 8403. [*Died* 21 *Nov.* 1966.

TODD, Sir Desmond Henry, Kt. 1968; Chairman, Todd Motor Corporation and associated companies; *b.* 1 July 1897; *s.* of Charles and Mary Todd; *m.* 1925; one *s.* two *d.* *Educ.:* Heriot and Tapanui, New Zealand. Associated with Todd family companies all his life. *Recreation:* water sports. *Address:* 37 Salamanca Road, Wellington, New Zealand. *T.:* 45 318. [*Died* 5 *Aug.* 1970.

TOFT, Alfonso, R.O.I.; landscape painter in oil and water-colour; *b.* Birmingham. *Educ.:* privately; Art Schools at Birmingham and Hanley; National Scholar at Royal College of Art. Exhibited at Royal Academy, Royal Institute, International, New Gallery, Glasgow, Liverpool, Manchester, Birmingham, International Exhibition at Venice, Carnegie Institute, Pittsburg, etc.; at the Cardiff Art Gallery is The Investiture of the Prince of Wales at Carnarvon Castle, 1911. *Recreation:* cycling. *Club:* Chelsea Arts. [*Died* 10 *Feb.* 1964.

TOLLEMACHE, Sir (Cecil) Lyonel (Newcomen), 5th Bt., *cr.* 1793; *b.* 14 March 1886; *e. s.* of Sir Lyonel Felix Carteret Eugene Tollemache, 4th Bt. and Hersilia Henrietta Diana, *d.* of late Joseph Collingwood; *S.* father 1952. *Heir:* *b.* Maj.-Gen. Humphry Thomas Tollemache, C.B., C.B.E. [*Died* 31 *March* 1969.

TOLLEMACHE, Lyonulph De Orellana, M.A.; Tutor at Stafford House College; *b.* 11 January 1892; *s.* of Rev. R. W. L. Tollemache; *m.* Lilian May, *d.* of E. T. W. Pearse, Government Agent, Kamloops, B.C., Canada; one *s.* *Educ.:* Winchester College; New College, Oxford. Assistant Master, Wellington College, Berks, 1915; Bradfield College, Berks, 1916-33; Housemaster, 1920-33; Officer commanding Bradfield College O.T.C., 1926-33; Headmaster of Wellingborough School, Northamptonshire, 1933-35; Headmaster of Imperial Service College, Windsor, 1935-41; Ministry of Home Security (Midland C.D. Region), 1941-44; (Southern C.D. Region), 1944-45; Home Office (Departmental Training Officer), 1945-52. *Recreation:* walking. *Address:* 58 St. Helen's Gardens, W.10. *T.:* Ladbroke 5026. [*Died* 30 *Nov.* 1966.

TOLLER, William Stark, C.M.G. 1941; O.B.E. 1935; retired; *b.* 3 March 1884; *m.* 1910, Rose Florence, *née* Murray (*d.* 1946), *widow* of Rev. Arthur Lawrence; one *s.* one *d.* (and one *s.* killed on active service, 1944). *Educ.:* Huish Grammar School, Taunton; King's Coll., London. Student Interpreter in China, 1907; one of H.M. Vice-Consuls in China, 1925; one of H.M. Consuls in China, 1929; Burma-Yunnan Boundary Commission, 1936-37; one of H.M. Consuls-General in China, 1937; retired, 1941. *Publication:* Handbook of Company Law in China, 1923. *Address:* Raglans Hotel, Reigate, Surrey. *T.:* Reigate 43052. [*Died* 6 *Jan.* 1968.

TOMBLINGS, Douglas Griffith, C.M.G. 1939; *b.* Canterbury, Kent, 24 Sept. 1889; *y. s.* of late Lt.-Col. E. G. Tomblings; unmarried. *Educ.:* King Edward VI's School, Stratford-on-Avon; King's School, Ely; Selwyn College, Cambridge. B.A. 1911, M.A., 1920; Asst. District Commissioner Uganda, 1912; Secretariat and Private Secretary to the Governor to 1917; served European war, East Africa, 1917-19 (despatches); District Commissioner, Lango, Uganda, 1920-23; Makerere College, Uganda, 1924; Prin., 1924-39; Headmaster: Queen Victoria School, Fiji, 1940-47; Nyakasura School, Toro, Uganda, 1947-48; Masaba School, Bugisu, Uganda, 1953-56. Hon. Fellow, Makerere University College, 1964; Hon. LL.D., Univ. of East Africa, 1967. *Publications:* African Native Medical Corps in the E.A. Campaign (with Major Keane, C.M.G., D.S.O.), 1920; Physical Training for Boys' Schools (Uganda), 1926. *Address:* Gangu, P.O. Box 404, Kampala, Uganda, East Africa. *Clubs:* Royal Societies, Royal Commonwealth Society, Royal Over-Seas League; Uganda (Uganda). [*Died* 29 *Nov.* 1970.

TOMKINSON, Rev. Cyril Edric; *b.* 15 May 1886; 2nd *s.* of late Frederick Tomkinson. *Educ.:* Dulwich College; Sidney Sussex College, Cambridge. B.A. (3rd cl. Cl. Trip.), 1908; Geo. Williams Prize, 1909; 3rd cl. Th Trip., pt. II. 1910; M.A., 1912; Wells Th. Coll., 1910; Deacon, 1910; Priest, 1911; Vicar of St. Stephen's, Lewisham, 1930-34; Vicar of St. Bartholomew's, Brighton, 1934-37; permission to officiate in Dioceses of London and of Bath and Wells, 1938-39; Vicar of All Saints, Clifton, Bristol, 1939-43; Vicar of All Saints, Margaret Street, W.1, 1943-51; permission to officiate in dioceses of Canterbury and Worcester, 1951-54; licensed under Seal, Diocese of Ely, 1954. *Address:* c/o Trustee Dept., Westminster Bank, 28 Market Hill, Cambridge. [*Died* 5 *June* 1968.

TOMKINSON, Sir Geoffrey (Stewart), Kt., *cr.* 1955; O.B.E. 1919; M.C. 1916; J.P.; M.A.; President (formerly Managing Director), Tomkinsons Ltd., Carpet Makers; *b.* 7 November 1881; 7th *c.* of Michael Tomkinson, D.L., J.P., and Annie Tomkinson, Wakefield; *m.* 1912, F. Murielle Fenton; three *s.* one *d.* *Educ.:* Winchester; King's College, Cambridge. B.A. (Mech. Sciences) 1905; M.A. 1919. Platt Bros., Oldham, 1900-02. Constructional Engineer, Great Western Brazil Railway, 1905-14. Tomkinsons Ltd., 1919-. Member Kidderminster Town Council, 1924-36 and 1944-45; Mayor, 1929; Pres. Chamber of Commerce, 1926, 1927; Mem. Worcestershire Agric. Wages Bd., 1930-50 (Chm. 1945-50); Chm. Arbitration Tribunal, 1945-50; Income Tax Comr., 1938-; formerly Mem. Worcester Regional Bd. for Industry; County Chm. Worcestershire Assoc., 1955; J.P. Worcs. 1940. Formerly Pres. Kidderminster Conservative Club and Leader of Parlty. Divl. Party. Served European War, 1914-18 (twice wounded, despatches, O.B.E., M.C.); Private, Inns of Court, 1914; commissioned, Worcs. Regt., Nov. 1914; went to France, Mar. 1915; Lt.-Col. 1918; War Office, Dec. 1918-July 1919. War of 1939-45, Principal, Min. of Supply; Regional Recovery Officer for Midlands; Comdr. Kidderminster Special Constab., 1937-49. *Publications:* Bibliography of Modern Presses; Those d . . . . d Tomkinsons; Memorable Cricket Matches. *Recreations:* cricket (President Worcestershire County Cricket Club, 1956), Rugby football, rackets, fishing. *Address:* (home) Whitville, Kidderminster. *T.:* Kidderminster 2151; (business) Church Street, Kidderminster. *T.:* Kidderminster 2207. *Clubs:* Lansdowne, M.C.C.; Jesters; Leander (Henley on Thames). [*Died* 8 *Feb.* 1963.

TOMLINSON, Sir George (John Frederick), K.C.M.G. 1934; C.B.E. 1928; Hon. Fellow of School of Oriental and African Studies; *b.* 1876; *e. s.* of G. W. Tomlinson, F.S.A.; *m.* 1914, Beatrix Violet Headlam (*d.* 1962), *y. d.* of F. H. Keenlyside, Barrister-at-law; one *d.* (one *s.* decd.). *Educ.:* Charterhouse; University College, Oxford. M.A. President Oxford Union; Barrister-at-law; Transvaal Education Department, 1903-4; Nigerian Administrative Service, 1907-28; seconded to Gold Coast as Director of Education, 1910-11; Acting Secretary for Native Affairs, Nigeria, 1925-27; Lecturer in Hausa, School of Oriental Studies, 1928-1930; Member of Committee on Colonial Appointments, 1929-30; Assistant Under-Secretary of State, Colonial Office, 1930-39; Temp. Clerk, House of Commons, 1940-44. Member of the Governing Bodies of Charterhouse School, 1936-54, and of the School of Oriental and African Studies, 1940-57. *Address:* Brunger, Tenterden, Kent. *T.:* Tenterden 463. *Club:* Union. [*Died* 23 *Jan.* 1963.

TOMLINSON, Sir Thomas (Symonds), Kt., *cr.* 1925; J.P., Lancashire; *b.* 2 November 1877; *s.* of Rev. A. R. Tomlinson; *m.* Diana (*d.* 1956), *d.* of P. J. Hibbert, J.P., D.L., Hampsfield, Grange-over-Sands; one *s.* four *d.* *Educ.:* Marlborough; Trinity College, Cambridge, Called to Bar of Inner Temple, 1901; Town Magistrate, Zanzibar, 1907; Assistant Judge H.B.M.'s Court for Zanzibar, 1911; Judge, 1919; seconded as Legal Adviser and Member of Executive Council of the Tanganyika Territory, 1918-21; Chief Justice, H.B.M.'s Court for Zanzibar, 1925-28. *Address:* Honeywood House, Rowhook, Nr. Horsham, Sussex. *T.:* Oakwood Hill 389. [*Died* 18 *April* 1965.

TOMORY, Major-General (retd.) Kenneth Alexander Macdonald, C.B. 1949; O.B.E. 1944; *b.* 15 November 1891; *s.* of Rev. Alexander Tomory, M.A., and Mrs. Mary Campbell Tomory, Scottish Churches College, Calcutta; *m.* 1st, 1919, Evelyn Cowe (*d.* 1934); 2nd, 1936, Evelyn Frances, *d.* of J. A. McGuinness, Londonderry; two *s.* one *d.* *Educ.:* Aberdeen Grammar School; Edinburgh University. M.B., Ch.B., Edin., 1914; joined Army, Nov. 1914; served European War; India, Mesopotamia, N.W. Persia Force, till 1919; Hong Kong, 1919-23; India, 1925-30; Major, 1926; specialist in anæsthetics, 1931; India, 1933-38; Lieut.-Col., 1939. War of 1939-45; B.E.F., France, 1939-40; West Africa Force, 1940-42; A.D.M.S. 43 (Wessex) Div., 1942-44; B.L.A., 1944-45; Col. 1944; D.D.M.S., Paiforce, 1945; Brig., 1947; D.D.M.S., British Troops, Egypt, 1946-47; D.D.M.S., Scottish Command, 1948-49; Major-Gen., 1949; Deputy Director Medical Services, Eastern Command, Hounslow, 1949-51; K.H.P. 1949-Nov. 1951; retired, 1951; Col. Comdt., R.A.M.C., 1951-55. *Recreations:* golf, climbing. *Address:* 104 Findhorn Pl., Edinburgh 9. [*Died* 16 *Dec.* 1968.

TONGA, H.M. the Queen of; Queen Salote Tupou, Hon. G.C.M.G. 1965; Hon. G.C.V.O., 1953; Hon. G.B.E., 1945 (Hon. D.B.E., 1932); *b.* 13 March 1900; *d.* of King George Tupou II and *g.g. gr. d.* of King George Tupou I; *m.* 1917, Prince Uiliami Tupoulahi Tungi, C.B.E. (Hon.) 1937 (*d.* 1941), a Tongan Chief; two *s.* (and one *s.* decd.). *Educ.:* Diocesan High School, Auckland, N.Z. D.St.J. *Heir:* *s.* Crown Prince Tungi, Hon. K.B.E. 1958. *Address:* Palace, Nukualofa, Tonga. [*Died* 15 *Dec.* 1965.

TONNOCHY, Alec Bain, M.A., F.S.A.; Keeper of British and Medieval Antiquities, British Museum, 1950-54 (Deputy Keeper, 1945-50). *Address:* c/o British Museum, W.C.1. [*Died* 13 *July* 1963.

TOOGOOD, Colonel Cyril George, C.I.E. 1938; D.S.O. 1917; Indian Army retd.; *b.* 23 Aug. 1894; *m.* Peggy, *d.* of late Captain Page, R.E.; one *s.* one *d.* (one *d.* decd.). Military Secretary to: G.O.C.-in-C. Eastern Comd. (India), 1928-32; Governor of Bombay, 1935-37; Viceroy of India, 1938-39 and 1942-1943. Served European War, 1914-18, Egypt, Gallipoli, Mesopotamia, Persia (wounded, despatches twice); War of 1939-1945, Mideast, Italy, Burma (despatches); retired, 1947. Chief of Staff, Bhopal State Forces, 1947-49. *Address:* Terrington, Highfield Close, Canterbury. [*Died* 22 *Oct.* 1962.

TOPE, Major-General Wilfrid Shakespeare, C.B. 1945; C.B.E. 1943; Director of Assoc. Brit. Oil Engines Ltd.; Col. Commandant R.E.M.E., 1950-57; Rep. 1951, 1953 and 1956; *b.* 19 Aug. 1892; *s.* of late W. S. Tope and Helen Spooner; *m.* 1st, 1916, Doreen Alice Wykeham Jollye; two *d.*; 2nd, 1954, Doreen Olive Jubb; two *d.* *Educ.:* Whitgift. In the City, 1908-14, studying for Institute of Actuaries degree; T.A., London

Rifle Brigade, 1909-14; Commissioned Regular Army, 1915, R.A.S.C.; 1914-18, France, Belgium, Salonika, and Caucasus (despatches twice, wounded). Instructor R.A.S.C. Training Centre, 1925-27; War Office, 1927-32; Instructor R.M.C., Sandhurst, 1937-39. Acting Lt.-Col. 1939; Acting Col. 1940; Acting Brig. 1942; Acting Maj.-Gen. 1943; Subst. Col. and Temp. Maj.-Gen. 1944; Director of Mech. Engineering, W.O., 1946-50; retd., 1950. War of 1939-45 (despatches, C.B.E., C.B.). *Recreations:* shooting, golf. *Address:* Hermitage West, High Hurstwood, nr. Uckfield, Sussex. *T.:* Buxted 2170. *Club:* United Service. [*Died* 28 *Feb.* 1962.

TOPLIS, James, C.B.E. 1920; M.A.; *b.* Charlton, Kent, 12 July 1876; *s.* of late Frederick and Elizabeth Toplis; *m.* 1906, Ellen Kate Jameson (*d.* 1946); one *s.* one *d.* *Educ.:* St. Paul's School; Trinity College, Cambridge (Classical Tripos). Passed Higher Division Examination for the Home Civil Service, and posted to the War Office, 1899; Assistant Financial Adviser to the G.O.C.-in-C. British Forces in France, 1915-18; Financial Adviser to the G.O.C.-in-C. British Forces in Italy, 1918-19; Financial Adviser to the G.O.C.-in-C. British Forces in Iraq, 1920-22; Assistant Director of Army Contracts, War Office, 1923-36; retired, 1936; Assistant Director of Supply, Ministry of Home Security, 1936-45. *Address:* 15 King Charles Road, Surbiton, Surrey. [*Died* 8 *Aug.* 1961.

TOPPIN, Aubrey John, C.V.O. 1961 (M.V.O. 1946); F.S.A. 1922; *b.* Twickenham, 1881; 2nd *s.* of late Percy Toppin, Ellerslie, Shankill, Co. Dublin; *m.* 1908 Agnes Louise (*d.* 1951), 2nd *d.* of late Samuel A. Johnston, J.P., Dalriada, Whiteabbey, Co. Antrim; three *s.* one *d.* Employed Science and Art Museum, Dublin, from 1901: in charge of Educational Sections, Cork International Exhibition, 1902; Universal Exposition, St. Louis, U.S.A., 1904 (under Dept. of Agriculture and Technical Instruction for Ireland), and Historical Section, Irish International Exhibition, Dublin, 1907. Appointed first assistant to Keeper of Irish Antiquities, National Museum of Ireland, 1906; Assistant Keeper, Art and Antiquities Division, 1907 until retirement, 1923. Served in 3rd Special Reserve Bn. Royal Irish Rifles, 1915-19 (Captain and Adjutant 1st Garrison Bn. in India, 1916-19). Bluemantle Pursuivant of Arms, 1923-1932; York Herald, 1932-57; Norroy and Ulster King of Arms, and Registrar and Knight Attendant of the Order of St. Patrick, 1957 until retirement, Oct. 1966, having served over 65 years and eight months under the Crown; Maltravers Herald of Arms Extraordinary, 1966-. Fell. Roy. Soc. of Antiquaries of Ireland; Pres. English Ceramic Circle, 1946-53; member Cttee. Internat. Museum of Ceramics, Faenza, Italy; Fell. Soc. of Genealogists: Hon. Fell. Heraldry Soc.; Vice-Pres. Oxford University Heraldry Soc.; Hon. Mem. Ulster-Scot Histor Soc.; Vice-Pres. (and a Founder) Irish Genealogical Research Society. Freeman of the City of London; Liveryman of the Scriveners' Company. *Publications:* Articles in Dublin Museum Bulletin, Burlington Magazine, and Trans. English Ceramic Circle. *Address:* 45 Palace Gdns. Tce., Kensington, W.8. *T.:* Park 7994. *Clubs:* Athenæum; Kildare Street (Dublin); Royal Irish Yacht (Dun Laoghaire). [*Died* 7 *March* 1969.

TORR, Brig. (William) Wyndham (Torre), C.M.G. 1942; D.S.O.; M.C.; Croix de Guerre; *b.* 7 July 1890; *s.* of late Rev. Canon W. E. Torr; *m.* 1917, Enid Milnes (*d.* 1950), *d.* of late Rev. Canon H. D. Burton, O.B.E.; one *d.* *Educ.:* Harrow; Sandhurst. Joined The Prince of Wales' Own W. Yorks Regt. 1910; served with 2nd Batt. in Albania, 1913; Adjutant Albanian Gendarmerie Scutari, 1913; A.D.C. to G.O.C., Straits Settlements, 1914; on active service in France, 1915-18, with 2nd Batt. West Yorks Regt. and on Staff (despatches four times, M.C., D.S.O., Croix de Guerre); p.s.c. Camberley, 1921-22; Bde. Major 2nd Rhine Bde., 1924-25; Military Attaché, Madrid and Lisbon, 1925-28; G.S.O. 2, War Office, 1929-1933; Bt. Major, 1917; Bt. Lt.-Col. 1931; Bt. Col. 1934; Col. 1935; Military Attaché, Washington and Central American Republics, 1934-38; Military Attaché, Spain, 1939-46; Master Staff College Hunt, 1921-22; Member Thoroughbred Breeders Association and of National Horse Assoc. of Great Britain, and of Hunters Improvement and National Light Horse Breeding Soc. *Recreations:* racing, shooting. *Address:* Sandleford Place, Newbury, Berks. *Club:* Turf. [*Died* 30 *Oct.* 1963.

TORRINGTON, 10th Viscount (G.B., *cr.* 1721); **Arthur Stanley Byng;** 10th Bt., *cr.* 1715: Baron Byng of Southill, 1721; *b.* 23 July 1876; *e. s.* of late Hon. Sydney Byng; *S.* cousin, 1944; *m.* 1st, 1909, Louise Annette, *d.* of Joseph Rawlins, of Cirencester; (*s.* died on active service, 1944) three *d.*; 2nd, 1936, Rosamond Ella, *d.* of late Vice-Adm. A. P. Davidson, D.S.O., R.N.; one *d.* Served South African War in East Kent Yeomanry and R.A.S.C., 1899-1902 (despatches, D.C.M., Queen's Medal 3 clasps, King's Medal 2 clasps); attached Indian Army as Supply and Transport Officer Khyber Moveable Column and Transport Adjutant 3rd (Lahore) Division, 1904-8; European War, 1914-18, Adjutant, 1st Divisional Train, retreat from Mons (despatches, Officer Legion of Honour), O.C. 16th (Irish) Divisional Train, 1915-16; O.C., R.A.S.C. Bedford and Belfast Districts, 1917-20; retired, 1920 (ill-health). Conservative. *Heir: g.s.* Timothy Howard St. George Byng [*b.* 13 July 1943; *s.* of Paymaster Lieut. Hon. George Byng and Anne Yvonne, *d.* of late Capt. R. G. P. Wood, 7th Dragoon Guards]. *Address:* 7 Montague Street, W.1. [*Died* 28 *Nov.* 1961.

TOTHILL, Dr. John Douglas, C.M.G. 1938; D.Sc.; *b.* 9 Feb. 1888; *s.* of Walter Tothill, L.D.S., R.C.S. Eng. and Frances Louisa Tothill; *m.* 1916, Ruby Beatrice Hughes (*d.* 1966), Gurnee, Illinois; two *s.* one *d.* *Educ.:* Blundell's School; Toronto, Cornell and Harvard Universities. U.S. Govt. Service, 1911-12; Canadian Civil Service, 1912-26; seconded to Fiji from Canada, 1924-26; Colonial Civil Service, 1926-39; Director of Levuana Campaign, Fiji, 1924-29; Director of Agriculture, Fiji, 1926-29; Uganda, 1929-39; Director of Agriculture and Forests, Anglo-Egyptian Sudan, 1939-44; Principal Gordon Memorial Coll., Khartoum, 1944-47; retired 1947. *Publications:* The Natural Control of the Hyphantria Moth; The Coconut Moth in Fiji; Editor, Agriculture in Uganda, 1940; Editor, Agriculture in the Sudan, 1947; many shorter entomological papers and papers and reports on agricultural subjects. *Recreations:* sailing, fishing, etc. *Address:* Lochiel, 14 Shore Road, W. Anstruther, Fife. *Club:* Royal Commonwealth Society. [*Died* 16 *July* 1969.

TOTTENHAM, Admiral Sir Francis Loftus, K.C.B., *cr.* 1937 (C.B. 1933); C.B.E. 1919; R.N.; *b.* 17 Aug. 1880; 2nd *s.* of late Captain Francis Loftus Tottenham and Cicell, *d.* of Col. C. Grimston; *m.* 1932, Evelyn, *widow* of Captain Herbert Street, and *o. d.* of H. E. Prescott; one *d.* Entered Navy, 1895; Lieutenant, 1903; served on Staff of Rear-Admiral Sir Douglas Gamble for re-organisation of Turkish Navy, 1909-11 (Order of Osmanieh 3rd Class); Commander, 1914; served European War, 1914-1918 (C.B.E.); Captain, 1918; Inter-Allied Naval Armistice Commission and Commission of Control in Germany, 1918-20; Commanding H.M.S. Delhi, 1920-22; Naval

Attaché, Washington, 1922-25; Commanding H.M.S. Excellent 1926-27; H.M.S. Rodney, 1928-29; A.D.C. to H.M. 1930; Rear-Admiral, 1930; Rear-Adm. commanding 3rd Cruiser Squadron, 1932-33; Vice-Admiral, 1935; Commander-in-Chief, Africa Station, 1935-38; Admiral, 1939; retired, 1940. *Address:* Westhill, Bembridge, Isle of Wight. *Club:* United Service. [*Died* 9 *Nov.* 1967.

TOURS, Frank E.; composer and conductor; *b.* London, 1 Sept. 1877; *s.* of late Berthold Tours; *m.* 1920, Helen, *e. d.* of late Elliott B. Clark, New York; two *s.* three *d.* *Educ.:* privately; Royal College of Music by Sir C. Stanford, Parratt, and Bridge. Organist at St. John's, Hammersmith; Conductor of Stanford's opera, Shamus O'Brien-1897; six years Conductor for George Edwardes at Daly's, Prince of Wales, Gaiety, and three years for Chas. Frohman and Seymour Hicks at the Aldwych and Globe Theatres, and toured round the world in 1903-4; Musical Director of the de Koven Opera Company, Winter Garden, Century Theatre, New Amsterdam Theatre, Ziegfeld Follies, New York; Music Box Theatre, New York; Famous Players-Lasky Co. at the Plaza Theatre, London. Paramount Picture Corp., N.Y., 1929-32; 15 yrs. Hollywood, Calif., composing and directing pictures and 8 yrs. conductor of summer season Light Opera at Philharmonic Auditorium and Greek Theatre, Los Angeles. Numerous radio programmes. Connected with Irving Berlin Publishing Co., N.Y. *Compositions:* Comic Opera Melnotte, 1901; The Dairymaids and The Hoyden, with Mr. Paul Rubens; part composer of The Little Cherub, See-See, and The New Aladdin. Songs: Mother o' Mine, Red Rose, A Meeting, A Rose Romance, Beyond the Sunset, A Year Ago, In Flanders Fields, Trees, Fury of the Sea, etc. Light Operas: The Dashing Little Duke, Girl O' Mine. *Address:* West Los Angeles 25, Cal., U.S.A. *Clubs:* Savage; Lambs (New York). [*Died* 2 *Feb.* 1963.

TOVELL, Brig. the Hon. Raymond Walter, C.B.E. 1943; D.S.O. 1918; E.D.; M.L.A. Victoria, 1945-55; Minister of Education, Victoria, Aust., 1948-50, 1952; A.I.F.R. of O.; Chartered Accountant (Australia) in practice; *b.* 9 March 1890; *s.* of Charles Edward Tovell and Mary Annie Mitchell; *m.* 1924, Madeleine Dubrelle Guthrie; two *d.* *Educ.:* Brighton Grammar School, Victoria, Australia. Qualified as Public Accountant, 1911; continued studies in London, 1912-13; European War, enlisted as private 1915, rose to rank Lieut.-Col. (D.S.O.); resumed practice as Chartered Accountant (Aust.), 1919, firm Tovell and Lucas; commanded 14 Bn. The Prahran Regt. 1924-29, and 46 Bn. 1932-38; served Middle East and Pacific Area, War of 1939-45, commanded an Infantry Bde. and D.A.G. H.Q., A.M.F. (despatches thrice, Bar to D.S.O., C.B.E.). *Recreation:* horticulture. *Address:* Charter House, 4 Bank Place, Melbourne, Australia; Indl, 336 New Street, Brighton, Victoria, Australia. *T.:* Melbourne 67.7088 and 96.3581. *Club:* Naval and Military (Melbourne).
[*Died* 18 *June* 1966.

TOWER, Vice-Admiral Sir Francis Thomas Butler, K.B.E., *cr.* 1942 (O.B.E. 1919); C.B. 1937; *b.* Dec. 1885; *s.* of late Francis Fitzpatrick Tower, Upper Holmewood, Cowes, I. of W.; *m.* 1937, Mary Estelle Clayton, *d.* of late Robert Clayton Swan. *Educ.:* H.M.S. Britannia, Dartmouth. Joined R.N. 1902; served European War, 1914-19; Captain, 1923; Director of Naval Ordnance, 1931-33; A.D.C. to the King, 1935; Rear-Adm. 1935; Director of Naval Equipment, Admiralty, 1936-39; Vice-Adm. 1939. Retired and re-apptd. Vice-Controller Admiralty, 1939-44. Officer Legion of Merit (U.S.). *Address:* Spindles, Sway, Hants. *T.:* 445. [*Died* 19 *July* 1964.

TOWER, Rev. Henry Bernard, M.A.; Hon. Treasurer, National Society, since 1948; *b.* 21 Nov. 1882, *s.* of late Rev. Charles M. A. Tower and Henrica Watson; *m.* 1912, Stella Mary Hodgson, *d.* of first Lord Bishop of St. Edmundsbury and Ipswich; (one *s.* killed on active service) one *d.* *Educ.:* Marlborough College; St. Catharine's College, Cambridge. Curate of Berwick-on-Tweed, 1905-10; Senior Curate of Benwell and Vice-Principal Bishop Jacob Hostel, Newcastle on Tyne, 1910-11; Minor Canon of Worcester Cathedral and Lower VIth Form Master, King's School, Worcester, 1911-14; Domestic Chaplain to first Bishop of St. Edmundsbury and Ipswich, 1914-16; Examining Chaplain to Bishop of St. Edmundsbury and Ipswich, 1914-27; Headmaster Junior King's School and Second Master King's School, Canterbury, 1916-19; Headmaster, Churcher's College, Petersfield, 1919-23; Headmaster Hurstpierpoint College, 1924-37; Appeal Secretary for London Diocesan Fund and Organizing Director of the Friends of the Diocese of London, 1937-39; Rector of Much Hadham, Herts, 1939-48; Rural Dean of Bishop's Stortford, 1945-48; Vicar of Swinbrook with Widford, 1951-55; Director of Studies, Church of England Board of Education Study Centre, 1949-61. Hon Chap. to the Bishop of London, 1961. *Publications:* Devotion and Doctrine; Sheshbazzar to Ezra; Daniel and I. Maccabees; Short introductions to the Revised Lectionary. *Address:* Teffont Manor, Salisbury, Wilts. *T.:* Teffont 226; 607 Hood House, Dolphin Sq., S.W.1. *T.:* Victoria 3800.
[*Died* 21 *June* 1964.

TOWLE, Mrs. Arthur; *see* Lawrence, Margery.

TOWNLEY, Athol Gordon; Minister for Defence, Commonwealth of Australia, since 1958; *b.* 3 Oct. 1907; *m.* 1934, Hazel, *d.* of Oliver Y. Greenwood; one *s.* *Educ.:* Hobart High and Technical Schools; University of Tasmania. Pharmaceutical and Cereal Chemist; Gen. Manager of Sidwell and Townley, Chemists, Hobart, Tasmania. Served War of 1939-45, Hon. Comdr., R.A.N.R. M.H.R. for Denison, Tasmania, 1949-; Minister for: Social Services, 1951-1954; Air and Civil Aviation, 1954-56; Immigration, 1956-58; Supply and Defence Production, Feb.-April 1958; Supply, April-Dec. 1958. *Recreations:* flying, fishing, cricket, football. *Address:* Grange Avenue, Taroona, Tasmania. *Clubs:* United Service, Naval and Military, Tasmanian, Legacy (all in Tasmania). [*Died* 24 *Dec.* 1963.

TOWNROE, Bernard Stephen, C.B.E. 1957 (O.B.E. 1952); M.A.; Hon. A.R.I.B.A.; D.L., J.P. County of Southampton; Commander Legion of Honour; Officier d'Académie; Grand Officier de l'Étoile Noire; Member Church Information Board; Chairman Deputy-Lieutenant's Committee, Paddington; *b.* Nottingham, 1885; *e. s.* of late C. E. Townroe; *m.* 1910, Marjory, *d.* of late Sir William Collingwood, K.B.E.; three *s.* one *d.* *Educ.:* St. John's College, Oxford. Served European War, 1914-19; Personal Military Asst. to Lord Derby; Min. of Health, 1919-22; Mayor of Hampstead, 1934-36; Director of Censorship, Ministry of Information, 1939-40. Contested (C.) West Nottingham, 1945; Secretary-General: United Assoc. of Great Britain and France, 1924-44; Franco-British Soc., 1944-58. *Publications:* A Handbook of Housing; A Wayfarer in Alsace; A Pilgrim in Picardy; Nottingham University College; The Slum Problem; Britain Rebuilding; Reconstruction of Bombed Buildings; The Building of a New Britain: A Policy for the Building Industry;

The Village of 13 Names. *Address:* Maresfield, Yateley, Hants. *T.:* Yateley 2170. [*Died* 22 *July* 1962.

TOWNSEND, Alexander Cockburn, O.B.E. 1965; M.A.; Librarian, British Museum (Natural History), since 1930; *b.* Moseley, Warwicks., 1 Nov. 1905; *o. s.* of late B. R. Townsend and Phyllis Kathleen Band; *m.* 1936, Ruth Emmerton, *d.* of late Montagu Pasco, Toowoomba, Queensland. *Educ.:* The Grammar School, Shaftesbury, Dorset; St. Paul's School; Magdalene College, Cambridge (Scholar). Entered British Museum (Natural History), 1930. Attached to Foreign Office, 1941-45. Hon. Sec. and Ed., Soc. for the Bibliography of Natural History, 1948-. Treasurer Ray Society, 1962-. *Address:* 1 Little Youngs, Welwyn Garden City, Herts. *T.:* Welwyn Garden 23795. *Club:* United University. [*Died* 31 *Dec.* 1964.

TOYE, Dudley Bulmer, C.B. 1945; O.B.E. 1920; *b.* 25 Nov. 1888; *o. s.* of late Henry Toye, Greenwich and Redhill, and Mary Forsyth, *e. d.* of late John Bulmer, J.P., Hove; *m.* 1931, Irene Adelaide, *yr. d.* of late Joseph Candelent, Solihull, Warwickshire; one *d.* *Educ.:* Blackheath; King's Coll., Univ. Coll. London; Honours in History and Law; LL.D. 1925. Barrister-at-Law, Gray's Inn and Middle Temple. Prizeman and Research Scholar of the Middle Temple. F.R.Hist.S. Fellow, Hugenot Soc. of London. Entered C.S., 1907; Min. of Agriculture and Fisheries, 1908-16; Min. of Blockade, 1916-19; Private Sec. successively to Chief Scientific Adviser, Parliamentary Sec. and Permanent Sec., Ministry of Agriculture and Fisheries, 1920-30; Principal Private Secretary to the Minister, 1934-36; Secretary to the Agricultural Tribunal of Investigation, 1922-24; Secretary to Royal Commission on Land Drainage, 1927; Asst. Secretary, Ministry of Agriculture and Fisheries, 1936-41; Principal Establishment Officer, 1936-43; Principal Asst. Secretary, 1941-45; retired, 1945; Governor of the Royal Veterinary Coll., 1946-59. *Publications:* various articles on historical and legal subjects. *Address:* Berryknowle, 21 Lady Park Road, Livermead, Torquay, Devon. *Club:* Athenæum. [*Died* 9 *July* 1968.

TOYE, Francis; *see* Toye, J. F.

TOYE, Herbert Graham Donovan; Chairman, Toye Group of Companies, including: Toye & Co. Ltd.; Toye, Kenning & Spencer Ltd.; W. J. Dingley Ltd.; Oakey & Cox Ltd.; George Kenning (Bedworth) Ltd.; John Taylor (Silversmiths) Ltd.; John Taylor (Wholesale) Ltd.; Toye & Co. (S.A.) Pty. Ltd., Johannesburg; Mayer & Toye Ltd., Wellington, N.Z.; *b.* 6 Oct. 1911; 2nd *s.* of Frederick Ernest Toye and Edith May (*née* Ransome); *m.* 1934, Marion A., *d.* of William C. Montignani, Edinburgh and U.S.A.; two *s.* *Educ.:* Magdalen Coll. Sch. 3rd County of London Yeomanry (T.A.), 1937-40 (invalided); Home Guard, 1940-45 (Capt.). Entered family business, 1929; Dir. 1933; Man. Dir. 1945; Chm. 1963. Dir. and Founder, Gold Lace and Embroiderers Assoc.; Royal Warrant Holder to the Queen for Gold and Silver Laces and Embroidery, also Orders of Chivalry, Robes and Decorations; Mem. Exec. Coun. and Cttee. of Management, Royal Sch. of Needlework. Past Master and Liveryman, Gold and Silver Wyre Drawers' Co., 1961; Mem. Court and Liveryman, Broderers' Co.; Sheriff, City of London, 1966-67, Mem., Court of Common Council, 1968. F.R.P.S.L., F.Inst.D.; O.St.J. 1959; Comdr., Order of St. Lazarus of Jerusalem, 1963. *Recreations:* golf (Pres. Gold and Silver Wyre Drawers' Golfing Soc.); Rugby football (Vice-Pres. Wasps Club); cricket; philately; veteran cars; freemasonry. *Address:* 3 Wyndham Mews, W.1. *T.:* Ambassador 6464. *Clubs:* City Livery, Cripplegate Ward, United Wards. [*Died* 5 *Jan.* 1969.

TOYE, (John) Francis, C.B.E. 1954; retired as Director of British Institute of Florence (1939-58); *b.* Winchester, 27 Jan. 1883; *e. surv.* *s.* of late Arlingham James Toye, Housemaster at Winchester College; *m.* 1914, Ann Huston, *e. d.* of Benjamin Huston Miller, Germantown, Philadelphia, U.S.A.; no *c.* *Educ.:* Winchester College; Trinity College, Cambridge. Passed Foreign Office Examination for Student Interpretership in the Levant, 1904; resigned, 1906; studied singing for two years and worked at composition with E. J. Dent and S. P. Waddington, travelling also extensively abroad for musical purposes; started musical criticism in Vanity Fair, 1908; entered employment of War Office, under which served in various capacities, 1914-17, when transferred to the Intelligence Dept. of Admiralty, where served in London and at Scapa Flow; Manager of the Coinage Dept. of the Mond Nickel Co., 1920-22; subsequently joined the Staff of the Daily Express as leader-writer, and later, music critic; Music Critic of The Morning Post, 1925-37; Managing Director of Restaurant Boulestin, 1933-39. Director of the Sociedade Brasileira de Cultura Inglesa, Rio de Janeiro, 1941-45 (and 1943-45 acting British Council Representative in Brazil). *Publications:* Diana and Two Symphonies, a novel, 1913; The Well-Tempered Musician, 1925; Giuseppe Verdi, 1931; Rossini, 1934; For what we have received: Autobiog. (U.S.A.) 1948, (Eng.) 1949; Truly Thankful;: A Sequel, 1957; Italian Opera, 1952; songs; articles on musical and allied subjects. *Recreations:* talking, sea-and-sun-bathing, riding, various games, and song-writing. *Address:* Vessinaro, Portofino, Genova, Italy. *Club:* Garrick. [*Died* 13 *Oct.* 1964.

TOYNE, Stanley Mease, M.A., F.R.Hist.S.; *s.* of Rev. Canon Toyne; *m.* *d.* of Col. Young, R.E.; three *d.* *Educ.:* Haileybury College; Hertford Coll. Oxford (Classical Exhibitioner). History Honour School, 1905; Assistant Master at Haileybury, 1906-13; Headmaster of St. Peter's School, York, 1913-1936. Chm. Hist. Assoc. Council, 1946, 1947 and 1948. *Publications:* Albrect von Wallenstein; The Race; Source Book of English History; The Scandinavians in History; Brunel, I. K., a Great Engineer; Sark, a Feudal Survival; articles in History To-Day. *Recreations:* cricket, football, hockey (for Herts and Yorkshire, 1919-20), racquets (Public School Finals 1901, Amateur Championship Final 1911); Captain British Squash Racquet Team in America, 1924. *Address:* Little Acres, Ware, Herts. *T.:* 2347. *Clubs:* United University, M.C.C. [*Died* 22 *Feb.* 1962.

TOZER, Major Sir James Clifford, Kt., *cr.* 1939; *b.* 1889; *m.* 1918, Gwendoline Mary Shannon; one *s.* one *d.* *Educ.:* Sherborne Sch. Served European War, 1914-19; Councillor and Alderman of Plymouth City Council, 1921-67; President Devonport Conservative Association; J.P. Plymouth City; Mayor of Plymouth, 1930; Lord Mayor of Plymouth, 1953; Freedom of City of Plymouth, 1952. *Recreation:* golf. *Address:* 4 Delgany Villas, Crownhill, Plymouth. *T.:* Plymouth 71653. *Clubs:* Constitutional; Royal Western Yacht (Plymouth). [*Died* 8 *June* 1970.

TRACY, Spencer; American Actor, stage and films; *b.* Milwaukee, Wisc., 5 Apr. 1900; *s.* of John Edward Tracy and Carrie Brown; *m.* 1923, Louise Treadwell; one *s.* one *d.* *Educ.:* Ripon College. Began acting at age of 18 in Stock company and subsequently successful on New York stage. Entered films, 1930. Films include: The Power and the

Glory; The Show-Off; Captains Courageous; Northwest Passage; Tortilla Flat; Keeper of the Flame; A Guy Named Joe; The Seventh Cross; Thirty Seconds over Tokyo; Without Love; Sea of Grass; Cass Timberlane; State of the Union; Edward My Son; Adam's Rib; Father of the Bride; Father's Little Dividend; The People Against O'Hara; The Actress; Broken Lance: Bad Day at Black Rock; His Other Woman; The Old Man and the Sea; Inherit The Wind; The Devil at Four O'Clock; Judgment at Nuremberg; Guess Who's Coming to Dinner. *Address:* c/o Metro-Goldwyn-Mayer Studio, Culver City, California, U.S.A.
[*Died* 10 *June* 1967.

TRAGETT, Mrs. M. R.; *see* Larminie, Margaret Rivers.

TRAILL, Major Cecil James, M.C.; *b.* 1888; *e. s.* of late Major J. W. Traill, D.L., J P., Rattar, Co. Caithness, and Hobbister, Isle of Orkney; *m.* 1946, Mary, *widow* of Lt.-Col. Alan Murdoch and *d.* of late Harry Manders, Co. Dublin. *Educ.:* Repton. Joined Seaforth Highlanders, 1911; served European War, 1914-18; Capt. Seaforth Highlanders; A.D.C. to Gov.-Gen. and C. in C. Australia, Lord Forster, 1920-1923; Private Sec. to Gov. of Trinidad, 1924-29; Member, Royal Company of Archers, Queen's Body Guard for Scotland; Master of Goathland Foxhounds, 1934-36. Gold Staff Officer, Coronations of 1937 and 1953. *Recreations:* hunting, fishing, shooting, travelling. *Address:* Brook Cottage, South Cerney, Glos. *Clubs:* Boodle's, M.C.C.; Melbourne (Melbourne)
[*Died* 31 *March* 1968.

TRAILL, Peter; *see* Morton, Guy Mainwaring.

TRAIN, Sir (John) Landale, Kt. 1957; C.B.E. 1952; M.C.; F.Inst.C.E.; *b.* 10 November 1888; *s.* of Rev. J. G. Train, Southend, Kintyre, Argyll and Julia Landale Train (*née* Watt), Woodbank, Cameron Bridge, Fife; *m.* 1916, Eileen (*d.* 1966), *d.* of Matthew Patteson, Dundalk (Megaw, Norton & Co); two *d. Educ.:* Dulwich Coll.; Hull and Glasgow Tech. Colleges. Entered North Brit. Rly., Edinburgh, as Apprentice, 1908; Enlisted Infantry, Aug. 1914; served European War, Major, R.E. Field Company; returned to G.N.R. 1919; Asst. to Sir Ralph Wedgwood, 1926; Dist. Engineer, Glasgow, 1929; Asst. Engineer (Maintenance) L.N.E.R. (Southern Area), 1934; Engineer (Scotland), L.N.E.R. 1938; Chief Engineer, L.N.E.R. 1942-47; Mem. Railway Executive, 1947-53; Mem. British Transport Commission, 1953-1958, Retd. Mem. Highland Soc. of London. Pres. London Argyllshire Assoc., 1960-1963. *Publications:* papers on Mechanisation, Human Relations, etc., in Journals. *Recreations:* swimming, shooting, golf. *Address:* Little Mill Brook, Nutley, Sussex.
[*Died* 30 *Dec.* 1969.

TRAPPES-LOMAX, Brigadier Thomas Byrnand, C.B.E. 1947; J.P.; D.L.; *b.* 7 Sept. 1895; *s.* of late Richard Trappes-Lomax, Allsprings, Great Harwood, Lancashire and late Hon. Alice Fitzherbert, *d.* of Basil Fitzherbert, Swynnerton, Staffs., and sister of 13th Lord Stafford; *m.* 1933, Dorothy Evelyn, *d.* of Major Edward Herbert, Upper Helmsley Hall, York; no. *c. Educ.:* Stonyhurst. Brigade Major 1 Guards Brigade, 1927-29; Chief Instructor R.M.C. Sandhurst, 1935-39; Comdg. 1 Bn. Scots Guards, 1939-40; B.G.S., Southern Army, India, 1942-45; Brig. i/c Administration London Dist., 1945-48. Pres. Stonyhurst Association, 1939-45. Pres. Emeriti Cricket Club and Vice-Pres. Catholic Record Soc. Civil Defence Controller, South Norfolk Area. D.L. Norfolk, 1954. *Address:* Great Hockham Hall, Thetford, Norfolk. *T.A.* and *T.:* Great Hockham 209. *Clubs:* Guards; Norfolk (Norwich).
[*Died* 1 *Feb.* 1962.

TRAVERS, Morris William, D.Sc. (Lond.) 1898; D.Sc. (Bristol) 1912; F.R.S. 1904; Professor emeritus, University of Bristol 1937; Fellow of the University College, London; *b.* 24 Jan. 1872; *s.* of late Wm. Travers, M.D., F.R.C.S., London; *m.* 1909, Dorothy, *d.* of Robert J. Gray, of London; one *s.* one *d. Educ.:* Blundell's School, Tiverton; Univ. College, London; University of Nancy. Assistant Professor, University College, London, 1898; Professor of Chemistry, University College, Bristol, 1904; Director, Indian Institute of Science, 1906-14; Scientific Director, Duroglass, Ltd., 1914-19; Hon. Professor, Fellow and Nash Lecturer in the Univ. of Bristol, 1927-37; Pres., Society of Glass Technology, 1922, Hon. Fellow, 1930; Vice-President and Melchett Medalist Institute of Fuel, 1930, Hon. Member, 1933; Member Fuel Research Board, 1929-32; President Faraday Society, 1936; Technical Consultant, Ministry of Supply, 1940-45. *Publications:* The Experimental Study of Gases; The Discovery of the Rare Gases, 1928; A Life of Sir William Ramsay, K.C.B., F.R.S., 1956; papers to Phil. Trans., etc. *Recreations:* mechanical work, reading, writing. *Address:* Roadways, Bussage, Stroud, Glos. *Club:* Authors' (Hon. Mem.). [*Died* 25 *Aug.* 1961.

TREACHER, Rev. Preb. Hubert Harold; Prebendary of Oxgate in St. Paul's, 1945-60; Prebendary Emeritus, 1960; Chaplain to H.M. Household since 1946; Rector St. Botolph, Bishopsgate, 1954-60 (Assistant Rector, 1950-54); *b.* 12 September 1891; *s.* of Allen Samuel Treacher; *m.* 1920, Hilda Pettman; two *d. Educ.:* Wesleyan Higher Grade School, Gillingham, Kent; H.M. Dockyard School, Chatham. Apprenticed H.M. Dockyard, Chatham, 1906; S. Augustine's College, Canterbury, 1914; Private, The Buffs, 1915; 2nd Lieutenant, Bedfordshire Regiment, 1915; service in France, Singapore, India, and Mesopotamia; Lincoln Theological College, 1919; ordained, 1920; Vicar of S. Mary's, Strood; S. Barnabas, Gillingham; Christ Church, Gravesend; Rector of Hanley and Rural Dean of Stoke-on-Trent; General Secretary and Head of Church Army, 1942-49. *Recreations:* reading, indoor flower cultivating and pewter work. *Address:* Chapel House, Buckland, Nr. Aylesbury, Bucks.
[*Died* 26 *Nov.* 1964

TREADWELL, Brigadier John William Ferguson, C.B.E. 1957; National Vice-President of the English-Speaking Union of the United States since 1949 (Acting President, 1959-61); Sec.-Treas. and Mem., Bd. of Govs., Amer. Soc. of Order of St. John of Jerusalem; Trustee, St. Luke's Hospital, New York; Member, Council of American Museum in Britain; *b.* 14 July 1901; *o. s.* of late Rev. Frederick William Treadwell and late Isabel Marian Ferguson; *m.* 1939, Susan Vanderpoel, *o. d.* of late Joseph P. Ord and Susan V. Ord, Albany, New York; two *s. Educ.:* Eton; Christ Church, Oxford. M.A. Honours School of Modern History. Joined 2nd Bn. Scots Guards as 2nd Lieut., 1924; served Shanghai Defence Force, 1927; Adjt. Guards Depôt, 1930; A.D.C. to G.O.C.-in-C. Aldershot Comd., 1933; Adjt. Eton Coll. O.T.C., 1934; Student, Staff College, Camberley, 1936; G.S.O. 3 Aldershot Comd., 1938; Bde. Major, First Guards Bde., 1939; G.S.O. 2, H.Q. London Dist., 1940; G.S.O. 1, War Office, 1942; Director-Gen. Public Relations, Control Commission for Germany (B.E.), 1945. Retired from Army, 1947. K.St.J. 1959. *Recreations:* dairy farming, tennis, golf. *Address:* Bessboro Farm, Westport-on-Lake Champlain, Essex County, New York, U.S.A.; 47 East 87th Street, New York 28, N.Y., U.S.A. *Clubs:* Guards, Travellers' (London); Century, Brook, Racquet, River (New York). [*Died* 10 *Dec.* 1968.

TREDEGAR, 6th Baron, *cr.* 1859; **Frederic Charles John Morgan;** Bt., *cr.* 1792; *b.* 26 Oct. 1908; *o. s.* of 5th Baron and Dorothy Syssyllt, *d.* of Ralph Thurston Bassett; *S.* father 1954; *m.* 1954, Mrs. Joanna Russell. *Educ.:* Eton. Served War of 1939-45, with King's Own Scottish Borderers, and on staff, U.K. and Middle East. *Recreations:* yachting, golf. *Address:* 115 Ave. Henri Martin, Paris 16e, France; (Seat) Tredegar Park, Newport, Monmouthshire. [*Died* 17 *Nov.* 1962 (*ext.*).

TREE, Ven. Ronald James, M.A., B.Lit.; Archdeacon of St. David's, since 1968; Canon of Mydrim, since 1968; Diocesan Director of Religious Education, since 1966; *b.* 30 March 1914; *s.* of Frederick George and Susan Maud Tree, Garnant, Carms; *m.* 1944, Ceredwen, *d.* of G. C. Thomas, Gwaun-Cae-Gurwen, Glamorgan; one *s.* one *d.* *Educ.:* University College of Wales, Swansea; New College, Oxford; St. Michael's Theological College, Llandaff. 1st Class Hons. Philosophy, B.A. 1937, M.A. 1939 (Wales); B.Litt. 1941 (Oxon.). Curate: of Cwmamman, 1941; of Aberystwyth, St. Michael's, 1944 Lecturer in Philosophy, St. David's Coll., Lampeter, 1946; Professor of Philosophy, 1950; Senior Tutor and Bursar, 1956; Warden and Headmaster, Llandovery College, 1957-66; Vicar of St. Mary's, Haverfordwest, 1966-68. Member, Governing Body, Church in Wales. Canon of Mathry in St. David's Cathedral, 1961. *Publications:* contributor: Efrydiau Athronyddol; Theology; Journal of the Historical Society of the Church in Wales. *Recreation:* carpentry. *Address:* The Archdeaconry, St. David's, Pembs. [*Died* 28 *Nov.* 1970.

TREHARNE, Reginald Francis; Professor of History, University College of Wales, Aberystwyth, since 1930, and Vice-Principal, 1952-54 and 1957; *b.* 21 November 1901; *s.* of Lewis Treharne, Merthyr Tydfil, Glamorgan, and Ethel Mary Hill, Melksham, Wilts; *m.* 1928, Ellen, *d.* of Arthur Roberts, Tyldesley, Lancs.; one *d.* *Educ.:* Grammar School, Ashton in Makerfield, Lancs.; University of Manchester (Scholar). B.A. and University Postgraduate Prize and Studentship, 1922; M.A. and Langton Fellowship, Univ. of Manchester, 1923; Ph.D. 1925; Asst. Lecturer in History, 1925; Lecturer in History, 1927, Univ. of Manchester; F.R.Hist.S. 1932; President of Historical Association, 1958-61; Leverhulme Research Fellow, 1946-47; Raleigh Lecturer to British Academy, 1954; Visiting Professor of History, Universities of Otago and Canterbury (N.Z.), 1965. Editor of History (journal of Hist. Assoc.), 1947-56. *Publications:* The Baronial Plan of Reform 1258 to 1263, 1932; The Battle of Lewes in English History, 1964; The Glastonbury Legends: St Joseph of Arimethea and King Arthur, 1967; Bibliographer of Historical Atlases, 1939; Handlist of Historical Wall-Maps, 1945; current editions of Ramsay Muir's Historical Atlas, Medieval and Modern and New School Atlas of Universal History; occasional articles in English Historical Review, etc. *Recreation:* walking. *Address:* Hillside, Bryn-y-Mor Road, Aberystwyth. *T.:* Aberystwyth 7324. *Club:* Sesame. [*Died* 3 *July* 1967.

TREHEARNE, Alfred Frederick Aldridge, F.R.I.B.A., F.R.I.C.S.; F.R.S.A.; formerly senior partner of the firm of Trehearne and Norman, Preston and Partners, architects, Windsor House, Kingsway, W.C.; *b.* 22 April 1874; *e. s.* of late Alfred Thomas Trehearne, solicitor, London, and Helen, 3rd *d.* of late Edward H. Aldridge, Putney; *m.* Gladys Mary, 4th *d.* of late Daniel Crawley; one *s.* one *d.* *Educ.:* Merchant Taylors' Sch. Mem. of Council of Soc. of Architects, 1918-23. *Recreations:* yachting, golf, and travelling. *Address:* Little Heath House, Limpsfield, Surrey; Aldwick, Sussex. *Clubs:* Carlton, Junior Carlton, Royal Automobile. [*Died* 28 *Sept.* 1962.

TRENCH, Col. Arthur H. C.; *see* Chenevix-Trench.

TRENCH, Charles Godfrey C.; *see* Chenevix-Trench.

TRENTHAM, Everard Noel Rye, C.M.G. 1938; *b.* 24 Dec. 1888; *s* of late William Henry Trentham and Constance Eveline Bond Rye; *m.* 1937, Mary, *d.* of late J. J. Dobbin; two *d.* *Educ.:* Westminster; Christ Church, Oxford. A Master at Rugby, and Inspector of Schools in Yorkshire, 1910-13; entered Board of Education, 1913; War Office, Ministry of Munitions, War Cabinet Staff, Ministry of Food (Assistant Secretary), 1914-19; Food Mission to Czechoslovakia, 1919; appointed to H.M. Treasury, 1919, British Finance Member of Inter-allied Plebiscite Commission, Upper Silesia, 1920-22; Reparation Commission, Berlin, 1922-24; Member of Imperial Defence College, 1931; Controller of Treasury and Commissioner for Finance, Newfoundland Govt., 1932-37; Financial Adviser, British Embassy, Washington, 1937-38; Financial Adviser, British Embassy in Berlin, 1939; British War Purchasing Mission in Canada and United States, 1939; Imperial censorship, Bermuda and B.W.I., 1940, Financial Adviser, British Embassy, Tehran, 1944; Treasury Establishment Representative, North America, 1945-50; has Order of St. Anne. *Address:* Somerset, Bermuda. [*Died* 9 *May* 1963.

TRESIDDER, Lieut.-Col. Alfred Geddes, C.I.E. 1927; M.D., M.S. (Lond.); F.R.C.S. (Eng.); Lieutenant-Colonel I.M.S., retd.; late Ear, Nose and Throat Surgeon to St. Helier Hospital, Surrey, and to Memorial Hospital, Woolwich; *b.* 1881; *s.* of Samuel Tresidder, Falmouth; *m.* 1909, Lilian Annie (*d.* 1969), *d.* of late Thomas Henry Trelease, J.P., Falmouth; one *s.* two *d.* *Educ.:* London University. Late Major R.A.M.C., Specialist in Diseases of Ear, Nose and Throat to a Military Hospital; Laryngologist Blackheath and Charlton Hospital; Clin. Asst. Central London Throat, Nose and Ear Hospital; Clinical Asst. to Throat, Nose and Ear Dept., Queen's Hospital for Children; Surgeon Ear, Nose and Throat Department, G.T. Hospital, Bombay; Surgeon to Governor of Bombay; Civil Surgeon, Karachi and Hyderabad. Served European War, 1914-1919 (despatches); retired, 1931. *Publications:* papers to the Lancet. *Address:* c/o National and Grindlay's Bank Ltd., 13 St. James's Square, S.W.1; 2 Lyndhurst Terrace, Hampstead, N.W.3. *T.:* 01-435 6682. [*Died* 9 *July* 1970.

TRESTON, Col. Maurice Lawrence, C.B.E. 1944; F.R.C.S.; F.R.C.O.G.; I.M.S., retired; *b.* 9 Feb. 1891; *s.* of late James and Mary Treston, Mayo, Ireland; *m.* 1914, Isobel (decd.), *d.* of Reverend D. F. Mackenzie, Tain, Ross-shire; two *d.*; *m.* 1947, Daphne, *g.d.* of Alice Perrin. *Educ.:* Pittsfield, Mass., U.S.A.; Rockwell College, Cashel; Hartley Univ. Southampton; London Hospital. Clinical Asst., Out-Patients' Dept., and Emergency Officer *In Patients*, London Hospital, and House Surgeon, Essex County Hospital, Colchester; I.M.S. 1914. Surgical Specialist, I.A., N.W.F.P., India, Mesopotamia, 1914-23 (despatches); Civil, Burma, 1923; Medical Supt. Dufferin Hosp., Rangoon, and Professor of Obstetrics and Gynæcology, University of Rangoon, 1928-1941; Inspector-General of Civil Hospitals, Burma, 1941-47. *Publications:* A Handbook on Difficult Labour, 1943; Health Notes, 1944; various publications in medical journals since 1914. *Recreations:* golf, tennis, swimming. *Address:* Croaghmere, Greystones, Co. Wicklow. [*Died* 14 *April* 1970.

TREVASKIS, Rev. Hugh Kennedy, O.B.E. 1920; F.R.S.A.; F.R.E.S.; Indian Civil Service (retired); M.A.; Chaplain, R.A.F., 1940; *b.* 14 June 1882; *s.* of Rev. Dr. James Trevaskis, Kilkhampton, Cornwall, and Mary Janet Kennedy, Ailsa, Ayrshire; *m.* 1913, Eva Myfanwy, *e. d.* of Capt. A. E. Tizard, R.N., Radipole, Dorset; one *s.* two *d.* *Educ.:* Marlborough (scholar); King's College, Cambridge (scholar). Wrangler 1904; I.C.S., 1905; District Judge, Ambala, 1913, Deputy Commissioner, Rohtak, 1914; Hissar, 1916; Capt., I.A.R.O., 1917; on recruiting duty in India, 1917-18 (despatches); retired rank, Captain; Deputy Commissioner, Gurgaon, 1919; Sialkot, 1919; Ludhiana, 1920; Mianwali, 1921; Inspector-General of Registration and Director of Land Records, Punjab, 1923; retired from I.C.S. and entered Westcott House, Cambridge, 1928; Deacon, 1929; Priest, 1930; Curate in charge St. John's, Farnham Common, Bucks., 1929. Rector of Rusper, Sussex, 1933-48; retired, 1948. *Publications:* Land of the Five Rivers; Punjab of To-day; Indian Babel; Christianity and the Atom. *Recreations:* reading, tennis walking. *Address.* Tymperleys, 50 King's Road, Horsham, Sussex. *Club:* Royal Commonwealth Society.

[*Died* 14 *Oct.* 1962.

TREVELYAN, George Macaulay, O.M. 1930; C.B.E. 1920; F.R.S. 1950; F.B.A.; Hon. D.C.L., Oxford; Hon. LL.D., St. Andrews, Edinburgh, Sheffield, Liverpool; Hon. Litt.D. Cambridge, London, Harvard, Yale, Manchester, Durham Nottingham, Turin; Hon. Fellow of Oriel College, Oxford; C.Litt. 1961; Master of Trinity College, Cambridge, 1940-June 1951; formerly Trustee, National Portrait Gallery; High Steward, Borough of Cambridge, since 1946; Chancellor of Durham University, 1949-1957; *b.* 16 Feb. 1876; 3rd *s.* of Sir G. O. Trevelyan, 2nd Bt., O.M.; *m.* 1904, Janet Penrose, C. H. (*d.* 1956), *d.* of late T. Humphry Ward; one *s.* one *d.* *Educ.:* Harrow; Trinity College, Cambridge. Regius Prof. of Modern History, Cambridge Univ., 1927-40. War Service, 1915-18; Cmdt. 1st British Ambulance Unit for Italy. Pres., Youth Hostels Association, 1930-50; formerly Trustee of British Museum; late Chm. Estates Cttee. National Trust. *Publications:* England in the Age of Wycliffe; England under the Stuarts; The Poetry and Philosophy of George Meredith; Garibaldi's Defence of the Roman Republic, 1907; Garibaldi and the Thousand, 1909; Garibaldi and the Making of Italy, 1911; The Life of John Bright, 1913; Recreations of an Historian, 1919; Scenes from Italy's War, 1919; Lord Grey of the Reform Bill, 1920; British History in the Nineteenth Century (1782-1901), 1922; Manin and the Venetian Revolution of 1848, 1923; Romanes Lecture, Oxford, 1926; History of England, 1926; Must England's Beauty Perish? 1929 (for National Trust); England under Queen Anne: Blenheim, 1930; Ramillies and the Union with Scotland, 1932; The Peace and the Protestant Succession, 1934; Sir George Otto Trevelyan: A Memoir, 1932; Grey of Fallodon, 1937; The English Revolution, 1688 (Home University Library), 1938; English Social History, A Survey of Six Centuries, 1944; An Autobiography and Other Essays, 1949; The Seven Years of William IV, 1952; A Layman's Love of Letters (Clark Lectures, 1953), 1954; A Shortened History of England, 1959. *Recreations:* shooting, cross-country walking. *Address:* 23 West Road, Cambridge. *T.:* Cambridge 56704. *Club:* Athenæum.

[*Died* 21 *July* 1962.

TROLLIP, Arthur Stanley, C.I.E. 1941; *b.* 1888, of British parents; *m.* Margaret (*d.* 1952); two *d.* *Educ.:* Dale College, King Williamstown, S. Africa; Univ. of Birmingham (Engineer). Late General Manager, Bombay Electric Supply and Tramways Co. Ltd.; Ed., Efficiency News. *Publications:* If India is Attacked; Stop-Look-Listen, a primer on Road Safety; Road Transport in India. *Address:* 1 Banstead Road South, Sutton, Surrey. *Club:* Royal Automobile.

[*Died* 22 *Oct.* 1963.

TROTMAN, Arthur Edwin, C.M.G. 1954; Secretary, Commonwealth Agricultural Bureaux, since 1961; *b.* 23 May 1906; *s.* of Thomas and Emily Trotman; *m.* 1931, Vera Appleby; two *s.* *Educ.:* Chipping Sodbury Grammar School; Harper Adams Agricultural College; Queen's College, Oxford; Imperial College of Tropical Agriculture, Trinidad. Agricultural Officer, Nigeria, 1929-41; Marketing and Co-operative Officer, Trinidad, 1941-47; Deputy Director of Agriculture (Research), Jamaica, 1947-49; Director of Agriculture, Jamaica, 1949-51; Mem. for Agriculture and Nat. Resources, Tanganyika, 1951-57; Minister for Natural Resources, Tanganyika, 1957-1960. *Address:* Farnham House, Farnham Royal, Bucks. *T.:* Farnham Common 781.

[Kt. *cr.* 1961, *but he died before letters patent issued; his widow was granted permission to be styled Lady Trotman.*]

[*Died* 14 *Jan.* 1961.

TROTTER, Edith, C.B.E. 1920 (O.B.E. 1918); *d.* of late Rev. H. E. Trotter, Hon. Canon of Christ Church, Oxford. Served in Queen Mary's Army Auxiliary Corps, 1917-19 successively as Deputy Section Controller, H.Q., Recruiting Controller for South Western England, and Controller of Personnel. *Address:* Flat 2A, Bransgore House, Bransgore, Christchurch, Hants. *T.:* Bransgore 441.

[*Died* 15 *July* 1962.

TROTTER, Hugh, C.I.E. 1943; O.B.E. 1948; *b.* 16 Aug. 1890; *s.* of late Stuart Trotter, J.P., Broomfield Lodge, Chelmsford; *m.* 1919, Kathleen Norah, *d.* of Arthur A. Muller, Oak Cottage, Lymington; two *s.* *Educ.:* Repton; Oxford. Joined Indian Forest Service, 1913; served European War as Capt. in 2nd K.E.O. Gurkhas and Adjutant of Anti-Aircraft Defence Command, Chelmsford. Returned to Indian Forest Service in 1921 as Asst. Forest Economist at Forest Research Institute, Dehra Dun; Forest Economist, 1927; later Utilisation Officer to Govt. of India until 1943; retired, 1943; Comptroller of Nuffield Centre for H.M. Forces, Adelaide Street, W.C.2, 1946-50. *Publications:* The Common Commercial Timbers of India and their Uses, 1930, 3rd ed. 1943; A Manual of Indian Forest Utilization, 1941. *Address:* Villa Annunciata, Avenue Roi Albert, Cannes, A.M., France.

[*Died* 26 *July* 1965.

TROTTER, Captain Richard Durant; late Rifle Brigade; *b.* 1887; *e. s.* of John Trotter, Brickendon Grange, Hertford, and Louisa, *d.* of Richard Durant, Sharpham, Devon, and High Cannons, Herts; *m.* 1927, Dorothy Clementina (*d.* 1966), *o. d.* of Edward Lee Rowcliffe of Hall Place, Cranleigh, Surrey; one *s.* two *d.* *Educ.:* Eton; Trinity College, Cambridge. Member of the Royal Company of Archers (Queen's Body Guard for Scotland). Served European War. Victoria Medal of Honour, Royal Horticultural Society, 1953. *Recreations:* gardening, shooting. *Address:* Brin House, Flichity, Inverness. *T.:* Farr 211. *Clubs:* United University; Highland (Inverness).

[*Died* 20 *March* 1968.

TROUBRIDGE, Lt.-Col. Sir (Thomas) St. Vincent (Wallace), 5th Bt., *cr.* 1799; M.B.E. 1919; an Examiner of Plays in the Lord Chamberlain's Office since 1952; *b.* 15 Nov. 1895; *o. s.* of Sir Thomas Troubridge, 4th Bt., and Laura (*d.* 1946), *d.* of Charles Gurney; *S.* father, 1938; *m.* 1939, Pamela, *d.* of Percy Clough, Keighley, Yorks. *Educ.:* Wellington College; Sandhurst. King's Royal Rifle Corps, 1914; Captain, 1921; retired, 1922; served European War (wounded, M.B.E., Croce di Guerra, Order of the Crown of Italy); served in War of 1939-45 on General Staff (despatches). *Recreation:* the drama. *Heir:* cousin, Lieut.-Comdr. Peter Troubridge, R.N. [*b.* 6 June 1927; *m.* 1954. Venetia Daphne, *yr. d.* of 1st Baron Weeks, K.C.B., C.B.E., D.S.O., M.C., T.D.; one *s.* two *d.*]. *Address:* Ivy Cottage, Longstock, Hants. *T.:* Stockbridge 101. *Clubs:* White's, Garrick. [*Died* 16 *Dec.* 1963.

TROWER, John Henry Peter, C.B.E. 1963 (O.B.E. 1954; M.B.E. 1950). F.C.A.; Director, Procter & Gamble Limited; a Governor, British Broadcasting Corporation, since 1966; *b.* 30 January 1913; *s.* of late John Trower; *m.* 1943, Elizabeth Kelly; one *s.* one *d.* *Educ.:* Royal Masonic School, Herts. Chartered Accountant, 1934, F.C.A. 1957; Deloitte, Plender, Griffiths & Company, 1934; joined Procter & Gamble Limited 1935, Director, 1965. Member of North Region B.B.C. Appeals Committee, 1965-66; National Savings Movement; Regional Mem., 1954-; Newcastle upon Tyne Savings Cttee. Chm., 1950-66; Vice-Pres., 1966-; Mem. Council, Soc. of British Soap Makers, 1954-; C.B.I.: Northern Region Elected Mem. 1965-; Co-opted Mem. of Nat. Grand Council, 1965-67; Mem., Northern Br. Cttee., Nat. Assoc. of British Manufacturers (Chm., 1962-64); Mem. of Council, Industrial Co-Partnership Assoc., 1957-; Vice-Pres., Tyneside Chamber of Commerce, 1963-; Mem., North East Development Council 1961-; Mem., Exec. Cttee., North Eastern Assoc. for the Arts, 1961-; Newcastle upon Tyne People's Theatre Arts Group: Mem., Management Cttee. 1940-; Chm. New Building Fund, 1959-; Chm., Newcastle upon Tyne World Refugee Appeal, 1962-63. Local Director, Sun Alliance & London Insurance Group, 1967-; Chm., Marshall Branson Ltd., 1951-. *Recreations:* theatre, music, fell-walking. *Address:* Denewood, Clayton Road, Newcastle upon Tyne 2. *T.:* Newcastle upon Tyne 81-2137. *Clubs:* Royal Automobile; Royal Commonwealth Society. [*Died* 30 *Jan.* 1968.

TROWER, Sir William (Gosselin), Kt. 1957; Solicitor, Trower Still & Keeling, since 1919; *b.* 15 May 1889; *s.* of late Sir Walter Trower and Emma Mabel, *d.* of Henry Plantagenet Phelips; *m.* 1920, Hon. Joan Olivia Tomlin, *e. d.* of Baron Tomlin of Ash; two *s.* two *d.* *Educ.:* Eton; New College, Oxford. Served European War, 1914-18 (despatches). *Recreation:* fishing. *Address:* Stansteadbury, Ware, Hertfordshire. *T.:* Roydon 3171; (professional) 5 New Square, Lincoln's Inn, W.C.2. *Club:* Buck's. [*Died* 27 *Aug.* 1963.

TROYTE, Lt.-Col. Sir Gilbert John A.; *see* Acland-Troyte.

TRUMPLER, Stephen Alfred Herman, M.A. Oxon.; *b.* 10 May 1879; *s.* of late W. H. Trumpler, Ashley House, Tiverton, and Julia Craven; *m.* 1916, Muriel, *y.d.* of late Lt.-Col. G. W. Addison, R.E.; two *d.* *Educ.:* Blundell's School; Merton Coll., Oxford. Admitted Solicitor 1905; Master of the Supreme Court of Judicature, 1933-52. Served in European war, 1915-19, and with Salonika Army, 1917-19. *Address:* Batsford, Beaconsfield. *T.:* Beaconsfield 303. [*Died* 6 *Dec.* 1963.

TRUNINGER, Lionel, C.I.E. 1904; *b.* 29 Sept. 1870; *s.* of late J. Ulrich Truninger; *m.* 1908, Ann Catharine, *d.* of late Andrew B. Bell. *Educ.:* Winchester; Coopers Hill College. Assistant Superintendent of Indian Govt. Telegraphs, 1891; Superintendent, 1904; Director of Telegraphs and Postmaster-General, U.P., 1915; retired 1920; served Tirah, 1897-98 (medal with three clasps); Thibet, 1903-4 (medal with clasp, C.I.E.). *Address:* Braemore, Gullane, East Lothian. [*Died* 22 *Feb.* 1961.

TRUSTAM, Sir Charles (Frederick), Kt. 1960; M.A., F.I.A., F.C.I.I., F.S.S.; retired as Chief General Manager of Royal Insurance Co. Limited and The Liverpool & London & Globe Insurance Co. Limited, December 1962; *b.* 5 July 1900; *e. s.* of late Charles Frederick Trustam and of Emma Elizabeth Trustam (*née* Johnson); *m.* 1926, Gwendoline Firkin; two *d.* *Educ.:* Hymers College, Hull; Trinity College, Cambridge. Entered service of Royal Insurance Company Ltd., 1921. Travelled extensively in U.S., Canada and Australasia. Chairman, Fire Salvage Assoc. of Liverpool, 1948-49; Pres. Insurance Inst. of Liverpool, 1949-50; Pres. Chartered Insurance Inst., 1953-54; Chairman, British Insurance Assoc., 1957-59. Director of Liverpool Repertory Theatre Ltd.; Trustee, Yvonne Arnaud Theatre, Guildford. Member University Court of Liverpool. *Address:* Broad Eaves, Mizen Way, Cobham, Surrey. *T.:* Cobham 2771. *Club:* Pilgrims. [*Died* 10 *Jan.* 1964.

TUBBS, Rt. Rev. Norman H., M.A.; D.D.; *b.* 5 July 1879; *s.* of Alfred T. Tubbs, Highgate; *m.* 1918, Norah E., *y. d.* of late Prebendary Lunt, Rector of Walcot, Bath Diocese; three *s.* one *d.* *Educ.:* Highgate School; Caius College, Cambridge. 3rd Class Classical, 2nd Class Theological Triposes, Cambridge; Curate, Whitechapel Parish Church, 1902-5; C.M.S. Missionary, 1905-17; Sub-Warden, Oxford and Cambridge Hostel, Allahabad, 1905-8; Principal, St. John's School, Agra, 1908-17; Principal, Bishop's College, Calcutta, and Hon. Sec. S.P.G., Calcutta Diocese, 1917-23; Bishop of Tinnevelly, 1923-28; Bishop of Rangoon, 1928-34; Archdeacon of Chester, and Canon Residentiary of Chester Cathedral, 1934-37; Assistant Bishop, 1934-48; Dean of Chester, 1937-53; Vicar of Patshull, 1953-61, retired. *Publication:* A Modern Pilgrim's Progress. *Recreations:* Association football (blue), Corinthian Football Club. *Address:* Vicarage Cottage, Scalby, Scarborough, Yorks. [*Died* 2 *Sept.* 1965.

TUCK, Col. Gerald Louis Johnson, C.M.G. 1919; D.S.O. 1918; *b.* 26 Nov. 1889; *e. s.* of late Rev. F. J. Tuck; *m.* 1925, Marion (*d.* 1951), *d.* of late R. Tunstall Smith, Baltimore, U.S.A.; two *s.* *Educ.:* Eton; King's College, Cambridge (M.A.). Served European War with 11th (S) Batt. Suffolk Regt. (Cambs.), 1914-19; commanded Batt. 1918-19; France, 1916-19 (despatches four times, wounded twice, D.S.O. and bar, C.M.G., Chevalier of Legion of Honour); France, 1939-40 (despatches); served War of 1939-45 with Pioneer Corps and Staff. Master Worshipful Co. of Poulters, 1957-58. Mayor of Sudbury, Suffolk, 1959-60 and 1960-61. *Address:* Stour Hall, Sudbury, Suffolk; 14 Lincoln Street, S.W.3. *Clubs:* Royal Aero, M.C.C. [*Died* 1 *Jan.* 1966.

TUCKER, Sir Edward (George), Kt. 1960; *b.* 22 June 1896; *s.* of William Sidney Tucker and Mary Tucker, Lewes, Sx.; unmarried. *Educ.:* Lewes Gram. Sch.; Brighton Gram. School. Entered Civil Service, 1913; assigned to Estate Duty Office, 1915; Asst. Controller of Death Duties, 1950; Dep. Controller of Death Duties, 1955; Controller of Death Duties, 1957-60. LL.B. (Lond.) 1920. Barrister, Lincoln's Inn, 1928 (Certificate of Honour, Trinity Term, 1928). *Recreations:* walking, travelling. *Address:* Kenwyn, Ferrers Road, Lewes. [*Died* 3 *June* 1961.

TUCKER, His Honour Howard Archibald; retd. Judge of Circuit 26 (Hanley, Stoke-upon-Trent, Stafford, etc.) and additional Judge of Circuit 21 (Birmingham) (1944-61); *b.* 1889; *m.* 1927, Margaret Minton, *d.* of H. S. Thacker, Walsall; one *s.*

one *d.* Called to Bar, Middle Temple, 1922; Recorder of Worcester, 1937-41; Recorder of Stoke-on-Trent, 1941-43; Judge of Circuit 18 (Nottingham, Doncaster, etc.), 1943-44. Chairman of Staffordshire Quarter Sessions. 1949-63. *Address:* Leycroft, 60 Mellish Road, Walsall. *T.:* Walsall 22473.
[*Died* 5 *Sept.* 1963.

TUCKER, Sir James (Millard), Kt., *cr.* 1955; Q.C. 1932; Director, Prudential Assurance Co. Ltd.; Chairman, Treasury Advisory Panel (Section 468, Income Tax Act, 1952); *b.* 14 October 1892; *e. s.* of late W. I. Tucker, of Bishops Stortford and Ilford; *m.* 1st, Cecily (*d.* 1938), *y. d.* of late John Rylands, J.P., The Grange, Thelwall, Cheshire; 2nd, 1947, Molly Cooper, *yr. d.* of late J. H. Woodham, Cheam. Formerly Chartered Accountant (B.C.); called to Bar, Middle Temple, 1920; Bencher, 1938, Treasurer, 1957; Freeman of City; Master, 1949, Worshipful Company of Glaziers. Enlisted 1914, 29th (Vancouver) Bn. C.E.F.; 2nd Lt., 6th Bn. Essex Regt., 1915; in France 1916-17, attached Bucks Bn. O.B.L.I.; contested (L.) Tonbridge, Kent, Div., 1924, (L.Nat.) Bosworth Division of Leicestershire, 1945. Chairman Government Cttee.: on taxation of trading profits, 1949; on Taxation of Pensions, etc., 1950; Vice-Chm. Roy. Commn. on Income Tax, 1950. *Address:* Bowood, Bashurst Copse, Itchingfield, nr. Horsham, Sussex. *T.:* Slinfold 282. *Club:* National Liberal.
[*Died* 9 *Sept.* 1963.

TUCKER, Keith Ravenscroft, C.B.E. 1932; retd.; Economic Secretary, N. Rhodesia, 1944-45, and Chairman of the War Supply Board; ex-Member Legislative and Executive Councils; *b.* 1 May 1890; *s.* of Henry Oliver Tucker and Anne Lewis; *m.* Marcella MacDonogh; one *s.* *Educ.:* Sandwich and Plymouth Colleges. Auditor, Colonial Audit Dept., 1913; served in Gold Coast, West Africa; attached to Gold Coast Regt.; served in German Togoland, Aug. 1914; Captain, Nyasaland Field Force, 1916; Deputy Treasurer, Nyasaland, 1921; Treasurer, Nyasaland, 1924; Financial Secretary, N. Rhodesia, 1938. *Recreations:* golf, fly fishing. *Address:* c/o The Crown Agents for Oversea Governments and Administrations, 4 Millbank, S.W.1. *Clubs:* Royal Societies, St. James'.
[*Died* 7 *May* 1963.

TUCKER, Sir Norman (Sanger), Kt. 1963; O.B.E. 1959; Gen. Secretary, National Council of Y.M.C.A. since 1956; *b.* 14 Nov. 1895; *s.* of Edward John Sanger Tucker and Sarah Anne Tucker; *m.* 1920, Mabel, *d.* of Albert and Caroline Burnell; no *c.* *Educ.:* privately. Local Y.M.C.A. secretaryships, 1913-28; in charge of Y.M.C.A. Service to Mediterranean Fleet, 1928-33; Y.M.C.A. Regional Sec. for Western Region, 1933-39; Y.M.C.A. H.Q. Administration, 1939-44; Asst. Gen. Sec., Nat. Council of Y.M.C.A., 1944-55. Chevalier of the Order of Orange Nassau (Holland), 1952. *Address:* 112 Great Russell Street, W.C.1. *T.:* Museum 8954.
[*Died* 28 *March* 1965.

TUDOR, Major-Gen. Sir H. Hugh, K.C.B., *cr.* 1923 (C.B. 1918); C.M.G. 1916; *o. surv. s.* of late Rev. Harry Tudor, Sub-Dean of Exeter Cathedral; *b.* 1871; *m.* 1903, Eva (*d.* 1958), *o. d.* of L. P. Edwards; one *s.* three *d.* Brig.-Gen. 1916; C.R.A. 9th Division; Major-General, 1919; commanded 9th Division, 1918; Chief of Police, Ireland, 1920; Inspector General Police and Prisons, Temp. Air Vice-Marshal, and G.O.C. Palestine, 1922; served S. Africa, 1899-1902 (wounded, despatches, Queen's medal 4 clasps, King's medal 2 clasps); European War, 1914-18 (wounded, despatches); retired, 1925. *Address:* 19 Churchill Sq. Apts., St. John's, Newfoundland. *Club:* Army and Navy. [*Died* 25 *Sept.* 1965.

TUDSBERY, Sir Francis (Cannon Tudsbery), Kt., 1954; C.B.E. 1920; M.A., LL.M.; Hon. President, Scottish Tar Distillers, Ltd., and assoc. companies; Founder and Hon. President of The Thistle Foundation (for disabled Scottish ex-service men); *b.* 1888; *s.* of late J. H. T. Tudsbery; *m.* 1914, Isabella Fleming, *d.* of late R. M. Sutherland of Solsgirth, Dollar; (one *s.* killed in action, 1945). *Educ.:* Dulwich; King's College, Cambridge (Yorke Prizeman). Called to bar, Middle Temple, 1911. Served European War of 1914-18. Secretary of the Surplus Government Property Disposal Board, 1918-20. *Publications:* The Glory of Discontent, 1928; (with J. W. Herries) The Robin Chapel, 1956; essays and papers on legal and other subjects. *Recreation:* played Rugby football for Cambridge University, 1907-1909. *Address:* Champfleurie, Linlithgow, West Lothian. *Club:* Athenæum.
[*Died* 23 *Sept.* 1968.

TUFF, Sir Charles, Kt. 1953; D.L., J.P., C.A.; President Folkestone and Hythe Conservative Association, 1947-58; *b.* 16 May 1881; *s.* of late Charles Tuff, M.P. for Rochester; *m.* 1904, Helen Constance, *d.* of late Thomas Denne, Walmer, Kent; one *s.* *Educ.:* Malvern College. Member Kent County Council, 1922-, Alderman 1939-; J.P. Kent, 1927-; D.L. Kent, 1940-. Served European War, 1914-19, with Queen's Own Royal West Kent Regt. Captain Special Reserve; served overseas, Mesopotamia and France; War of 1939-45; Major in The Buffs, 1939-41. *Recreation:* shooting. *Address:* Norrard, Godwyn Road, Folkestone, Kent. *T.:* Folkestone 2167. *Club:* Junior Carlton. [*Died* 3 *Sept.* 1961.

TUITE, Sir Brian Hugh Morgan, 12th Bt., *cr.* 1622; *b.* 1 May 1897; *s.* of late Capt. Hugh G. S. Tuite and late Eva Geraldine, *d.* of Peter Valentine Hatton; *S.* uncle, 1946; unmarried. *Educ.:* Kelvinside Academy; Highgate School. European War, 1914-18. Lieutenant, Royal Northumberland Fusiliers; served with Queen Victoria's Rifles (wounded). On staff of Standard Telephones and Cables, Ltd., 1922-1934; with Associated Newspapers, 1934-40; Charrington & Co. (S.E.) Ltd., 1953-64 (retd.). Major Royal Pioneer Corps, 1940. *Address:* 116 Saltdean Vale, Saltdean, Brighton, Sussex BN2 8HF. *T.:* Brighton 33890.
[*Died* 26 *Aug.* 1970.

TUKER, Lieut.-Gen. Sir Francis Ivan Simms, K.C.I.E., *cr.* 1946; C.B. 1943; D.S.O. 1943; O.B.E. 1937; F.R.S.A. 1950; *b.* 14 July 1894; *s.* of late W. J. Sanger Tuker, Butts Green Hall, Sandon, Essex, and Katherine Louisa Simms, Yew House, Twickenham; *m.* 1st, 1923, Catherine Isabella Bucknall (*d.* 1947), Copsale Court, Horsham; two *d.* (and one *d.* decd.); 2nd 1948, Cynthia Helen Fawcett (*née* Gale), M.A. (Cantab.), Kaisar-i-Hind, *widow* of Lt.-Col. R. B. Fawcett, M.C., 9th Gurkha Rifles. *Educ.:* Hillside, Brighton; Brighton College; R.M.C., Sandhurst. 2nd Lt. attached R. Sussex Regt., 1914; I.A., 2nd Goorkhas, 1914; Lt.-Col. Commanding 1/2nd Goorkhas, 1937-39; Bt. Lt.-Col. 1933; Col. 1936; Brig. 1940; Acting Maj.-Gen. 1941; Maj.-Gen. 1943; acting Lt.-Gen. 1945; Lt.-Gen. 1946. Staff College, Camberley, 1925-26; Director of Military Training, G.H.Q., India, 1940-41; Comd. 34 Ind. Div., 1941; Comd. 4 Ind. Div., 1942-44; Chm., Frontier Cttee., India, 1944; G.O.C. Ceylon, 1945; Comd. 4 Ind. Corps 1945. Served European War, 1914-18 (wounded); Kuki Punitive Expedition, 1918-19; N.W. Persia Operations, 1920-1921; N.W. Frontier, India, 1937-38 (despatches, O.B.E.); War of 1939-45 N. Africa (despatches twice, C.B., D.S.O.); Italy; Burma (despatches); G.O.C.-in-C. Eastern Command, India, 1946-47; Colonel, 2nd

Goorkhas, 1946-56; retired, April 1948. *Publications:* The Pattern of War, 1948; While Memory Serves, 1949; Does Stalin Mean War?, 1952; Private Henry Metcalfe, H.M. 32nd, 1952; Gorkha, 1957 (Sir Percy Sykes Memorial Medal, Royal Central Asian Society); The Yellow Scarf, 1961; Approach to Battle, 1963; book of verse, The Desert Rats; several art exhibits in India; two librettos for operetta, 1965; articles in Military Journals; contributor to Civil Journals and newspapers. *Recreations:* writing, sailing. *Address:* Bosilliac, Mawnan Smith, Cornwall. [*Died* 7 *Oct.* 1967.

TULLOCH, William John, O.B.E.; M.D., D.Sc.; Prof. of Bacteriology, St. Andrews Univ., 1921 retd. 1962; *b.* 12 Nov. 1887; *s.* of Henry Tulloch, Dundee; *m.* Miss Sheridan, Newcastle on Tyne; one *s.* two *d.* *Educ.:* St. Andrews. *Address:* 22 Glyn Way, Stubbington, Fareham, Hants. [*Died* 26 *Aug.* 1966.

TUNSTALL, (William Cuthbert) Brian, F.S.A.; *b.* 23 April 1900; *s.* of late Frederick William Whitelock Tunstall; *m.* 1928, Gillean Elizabeth, *d.* of late Sir Julian Stafford Corbett; three *s.* one *d.* *Educ.:* Haileybury Coll.; St. John's Coll., Cambridge. 2nd Lt. Coldstream Guards, 1919; Assistant Master, Weymouth College, 1922; Assistant Master, Oundle School, 1922-25; Lecturer in History and English, Royal Naval College, Greenwich, 1925-37; Hon. Secretary of Navy Records Society, 1931-37; Member of B.B.C. Research Unit (Overseas), 1941; Naval Correspondent, B.B.C. European Services, 1942-45. Lecturer and Senior Lecturer in International Relations, London School of Economics, 1945-64; Visiting Professor, R.M.C., Kingston, Ont., 1965-66; Raffles Lecturer, Queen's Univ., Ontario, 1970. Chm. Chichester Centre, National Trust; Hon. Sec. Friends of Southwark Cathedral, 1958-64. *Publications:* Admiral Byng and the Loss of Minorca, 1928; Flights of Naval Genius, 1929; The Byng Papers, 1930-33; Nelson, 1933; The Realities of Naval History, 1936; The Anatomy of Neptune, 1936; Eagles Restrained, 1936; The Book of Naval Adventures, 1937; William Pitt, Earl of Chatham, 1939; World War at Sea, 1942; Ocean Power Wins, 1944; The Commonwealth and Regional Defence, 1959; The Pictorial History of Southwark Cathedral, 1961; Contributor to Cambridge History of the British Empire. *Address:* Coaters, Bignor, Pulborough, Sussex. *T.:* Sutton (Sussex) 262. [*Died* 27 *Sept.* 1970.

TUPOU, Queen Salote; *see* Tonga, H. M. the Queen of.

TUPPER, Sir Charles, 3rd Bt., *cr.* 1888, of Armdale, Halifax, Nova Scotia; Major (retired) Canadian Militia; Civil Engineer, retired, 1957; *b.* 10 Dec. 1880; *s.* of late Hon. Sir Charles Hibbert Tupper, K.C.M.G., K.C., and Janet (*née* Macdonald); *S.* cousin, Sir Charles (Stewart) Tupper, 2nd Bt., 1960; *m.* 1910, Mary Myra Dickey; two *d.* *Educ.:* Ashbury College, Ottawa; McGill University, Montreal (B.Sc.). Railway construction, 1900-14. Canadian Corps and Canadian Railway Troops, 1914-18 (despatches, 1919). Railway, canal and highway construction, 1918-57. *Heir: b.* James Macdonald Tupper [*b.* 22 Dec. 1887; *m.* 1928, Agnes Collins; one *s.* one *d.*]. *Address:* 8 Meredith Crescent, Toronto 5, Canada. *T.:* 924 1266. [*Died* 19 *June* 1962.

TUPPER, Sir James Macdonald, 4th Bt. *cr.* 1888, of Armdale, Halifax, Nova Scotia; *b.* 22 Dec. 1887; *s.* of Hon. Sir Charles Hibbert Tupper, K.C.M.G., K.C. (2nd *s.* of 1st Bt.) and Janet (*née* Macdonald); *S.* brother, Sir Charles Tupper, 3rd Bt., 1962; *m.* 1928, Agnes Collins; one *s.* one *d.* Formerly Asst. Comr., Roy. Can. Mounted Police and Hon. Lt.-Col., Can. Militia. *Heir: s.* Charles Hibbert Tupper [*b.* 4 July 1930; *m.* 1959, Bernice Yvonne Quinn; one *s.*]. *Address:* 1266 West 26th Avenue, Vancouver, B.C. [*Died* 23 *June* 1967.

TURGEON, Hon. William Ferdinand Alphonse, P.C. Canada, 1941; Q.C.; LL.D.; *b.* Bathurst, New Brunswick, 3 June 1877; *m.* 1901, Gertrude, *d.* of Jerome Boudreau of Petit Rocher, N.B.; two *s.* three *d.* *Educ.:* New York City; Levis Coll., Quebec. B.A. Laval Univ. 1899. Admitted New Brunswick Bar, 1902; moved to Prince Albert, Sask., 1903; Attorney-General for the Province of Saskatchewan, Canada, 1907-21; Member of Provincial Parliament for Prince Albert and afterwards for Humboldt; Chief Justice of Saskatchewan, 1938-41; Canadian Minister to Argentina and Chile, 1941-44; Canadian Ambassador to Mexico, 1944; Canadian Ambassador to Belgium, 1944-46; Canadian Ambassador to Republic of Ireland, 1950-55 (Canadian High Commissioner in Eire, 1946-50); Canadian Ambassador to Portugal, 1955-57 (Canadian Minister, 1952-55). *Address:* 221 21st St. E., Prince Albert, Saskatchewan, Canada. [*Died* 11 *Jan.* 1969.

TURING, Sir Robert Andrew Henry, 10th Bt., *cr.* 1638; *b.* 13 Sept. 1895; *s.* of 9th Bt. and Mabel Rose, *d.* of Andrew Caldecott, of Pishiobury, Sawbridgeworth; *S.* father, 1928. *Educ.:* Eton; R.M.C., Sandhurst. Late Capt. The Rifle Brigade (Prince Consort's Own); served European War, 1914-18 (wounded, despatches, 1914-15 star, two medals). *Heir: twin-b.* John Leslie Turing [M.C., late Seaforth Highlanders; *b.* 13 Sept. 1895; served European War, 1916-18 (wounded, M.C.)]. *Address:* The Warren, Chichester. *T.:* Chichester 7168. *Club:* Naval and Military. [*Died* 6 *Jan.* 1970.

TURLE, Rear-Adm. Charles Edward, C.B.E. 1945; D.S.O. 1918; R.N.; *b.* 1883; *s.* of E. Turle; *m.* 1938, Jane Gillies, *d.* of late James Gray, D.L., J.P., Wemyss Bay, Renfrewshire; two *s.* *Educ.:* Wellington College. Served European War, 1914-19 (despatches, D.S.O., Italian Order of St. Maurice and St. Lazarus); Mine Clearance Officer for Aegean and Black Seas, 1919; Head of British Naval Mission to Greece, 1927-29 (Commander of the Order of the Redeemer, 1st Class of Greek Order of Military Merit); Rear-Adm. and retired list, 1934. Served European War, 1939-45 (despatches); C.B.E. for work in Greece, 1944-45. Grand Officer, Order of George I of Greece with Swords. *Address:* 26 Trevor Square, S.W.7. [*Died* 16 *March* 1966.

TURNBULL, Colonel Alan William, C.B. 1945; M.C.; T.D.; D.L. Shropshire; Colonel T.A. (retired), and Hon. Col. 4th Bn. K.S.L.I. (T.A.), 1939-49; Partner in Sprott Stokes & Turnbull, Solicitors, Shrewsbury; *b.* 18 Nov. 1893; *s.* of William Peveril Turnbull and Fanny Hayes, late of Church Stretton, Shropshire; *m.* 1924, Violet May Rushton. *Educ.:* Giggleswick, Yorks. Served with B.E.F. in France and Flanders in 8th Bn. Seaforth Highlanders in European War, 1914-18, attaining rank of Lt.-Col.; admitted Solicitor, Dec. 1920. Joined 4th Bn. K.S.L.I. (T.A.), 1920; commanded 4th Bn. K.S.L.I. (T.A.), 1925-33. Col., T.A. 1933. Vice-Chairman, Shropshire T.A. Assoc., 1938-47; Chm. Shropshire T. & A.F.A., 1947-58; President, Shropshire Law Society, 1947 and 1948; Clerk to the Justices for the Division of Condover, Shropshire, 1937-59. *Recreations:* hill-walking and gardening. *Address:* 12 Port Hill Gardens, Shrewsbury. *T.:* 3962. [*Died* 14 *Dec.* 1964.

TURNBULL, Sir Alfred Clarke, K.B.E., *cr.* 1946; *b.* Balclutha; *s.* of John Turnbull;

m. 1921, Grace, *d.* of W. Moncrieff, Wellington; one *d.* Secretary and Deputy Administrator, Western Samoa, 1930; acting Administrator, 1935; Administrator, 1943-1946; retired. *Address:* 21 Strawberry Hill Ave., Stamford, Conn. [*Died Sept.* 1962.

TURNBULL, Edwin Laurence, C.B.E. 1942; B.A., LL.B.(Cantab.); *b.* 25 Jan. 1888; *s.* of late W. P. Turnbull; *m.* May Eileen Nye. *Educ.:* Giggleswick School; Christ's Coll., Cambridge. Solicitors' Final Examination (Hons.), 1913; Junior Examiner, 1913. Sec. Juvenile Organisation Committee, 1935; Deputy Accountant-General, 1937, Board of Education; Principal Officer North Eastern Civil Defence Region, Ministry of Home Security, 1939; Principal Establishment Officer Home Office and Ministry of Home Security, 1942; Under-Secretary, Ministry of Education, 1946; Deputy Secretary, National Coal Board, 1946-54; Chairman, Auxiliary Hospitals Cttee., King Edward's Hospital Fund; Governor, Hammersmith Hospital, 1958-64. *Address:* 7 De Vere Cottages, W.8. *T.:* 01-937 7866. *Club:* United University. [*Died* 31 *July* 1968.

TURNBULL, Mrs. George; (Patricia Wentworth); Dora Amy, *d.* of late Lt.-General Sir Edmund Roche Elles, G.C.I.E., K.C.B.; *m.* 1st, Lt.-Colonel George Dillon, C.B. (*d.* 1906); 2nd, 1920, Lt.-Col, G. O. Turnbull, D.S.O.; one *d.* *Educ.:* privately; Blackheath High School. *Publications:* Verse, Historical Romances and a number of Mystery Novels under the pen-name of Patricia Wentworth. *Recreations:* reading, gardening, music, motoring. *Address:* Rule, Camberley. *T.:* Camberley 241. [*Died* 28 *Jan.* 1961.

TURNBULL, George Henry, M.A. (Liverpool), Ph.D. (Bonn); Professor Emeritus, Sheffield Univ., 1954; *b.* 27 May 1889; 4th *s.* of late R. J. Turnbull, Berwick-on-Tweed; *m.* Gwladys Elizabeth, *widow* of Morrice Greer. *Educ.:* Berwick Grammar School; Universities of Liverpool and Bonn. Assistant Master, March Grammar School, Cambs., 1910-12; Lecturer in Education in the University of Liverpool, 1914-22; served with the Liverpool Scottish, 1914-18; very severely wounded near St. Julien, 31 July 1917; Senior Warden of Liverpool University Halls of Residence for men, 1919-21; Professor of Education, Univ. of Sheffield, 1922-54; Dean of the Faculty of Arts, Univ. of Sheffield, 1930-33; Director of Sheffield University Institute of Education, 1948-49; Hon. Freeman of Berwick-upon-Tweed; Chairman of the Educational Handwork Assoc., 1936-46; Pres. of Educational Development Assoc. (formerly Educational Handwork Assoc.). Comenius Medal, 1957. *Publications:* Samuel Hartlib, 1920; Fichte's Addresses to the German Nation (with R. F. Jones), 1922; The Educational Theory of J. G. Fichte, 1926; Hartlib, Dury and Comenius: Gleanings from Hartlib's Papers, 1947; Two Pansophical Works by J. A. Comenius, ed. for Czech Acad. of Arts and Sciences, Prague, 1951; contributions to philosophical and educational journals. *Recreation:* fishing. *Address:* Careglefn, 21 Bryntirion Drive, Prestatyn. *T.:* Prestatyn 786. [*Died* 23 *Sept.* 1961.

TURNBULL, Herbert Westren, F.R.S. 1932; M.A. Camb., Oxon.; Professor Emeritus and Hon. LL.D. St. Andrews, 1952; F.R.S.E.; *b.* Tettenhall, Wolverhampton, 31 August 1885; *s.* of late W. P. Turnbull, H.M. Inspector of Schools, Wolverhampton and Sheffield; *m.* 1911, Ella Drummond, *d.* of late Rev. Canon H. D. Williamson; one *s.* *Educ.:* Sheffield Grammar School; Trinity College, Cambridge (Scholar). M.A. Camb. 1911, Oxford, 1920; Second Wrangler, 1907; 1st Cl. (1st div.) Math. Tripos, Part II. 1908; Smith's Prizeman, 1909; late Fereday Fellow of St. John's College, Oxford, 1919; Mathematical Lecturer in Cambridge, Liverpool, and Hong-Kong, 1909-13; Acting Warden C.M.S. Hostel, Hong-Kong University, 1913-15; Assistant Mathematical Master, Repton, 1916-19; H.M. Inspector of Schools, 1919-1921; Regius Professor of Mathematics at United College, University of St. Andrews, 1921-50. *Publications:* Memories of W. P. Turnbull, 1920; Theory of Determinants, Matrices and Invariants, 1928; The Great Mathematicians, 1929; Canonical Matrices, 1932 (with Dr. A. C. Aitken); James Gregory Memorial Volume, 1939; Theory of Equations, 1939; Mathematical Discoveries of Newton, 1945; The Correspondence of Isaac Newton, Vol. I, 1959, II, 1960; various papers in mathematical journals. *Address:* 1 Red Hills, Skelsmergh, Kendal, Westmorland. *Club:* Alpine. [*Died* 4 *May* 1961.

TURNBULL, Commodore James, C.B.E. 1919; R.D. 1917; R.N.R. (retired list); late commanding in the Canadian Pacific Steamships Ltd.; *b.* 1874; widower; one *s.* Served European War, 1914-19 (despatches, C.B.E.); R.N.R. A.D.C. to the King, 1927-1929; Younger Brother of Trinity House; a Freeman of the City of London. *Address:* 68 Sherborne Court, Anerley, S.E.20. *T.:* Sydenham 8713. [*Died* 16 *Oct.* 1964.

TURNER, Lady; *see* Robertson, E. Arnot.

TURNER, Miss Beatrice (Ethel), O.B.E. 1943; F.R.C.S. Ed., F.R.C.O.G.; Hon. Cons. Obstetric Surgeon, Elizabeth Garrett Anderson Hospital; Hon. Cons. Gynæcologist, St. Mary's Hospital, Plaistow; *b.* 23 Jan. 1891; 2nd *d.* of Edward Beadon Turner, F.R.C.S. *Educ.:* St. Mary's College, Paddington; Bedford College, University of London; London School of Medicine for Women. V.A.D. Nurse (despatches), France, 1915-19. M.B., B.S. Lond. 1925; F.R.C.S.Ed., 1928; M.R.C.S.Eng., L.R.C.P. Lond., 1925; F.R.C.O.G., 1939. F.R.Soc. Med. (Vice-President Sect. Gyn. and Obst.); Mem. B.M.A. (Ex-Vice-Pres. Metrop. Cos. Br.); Ex-Vice-Pres. Med. Wom. Federat. Formerly Sen. Asst. Gyn. and Obst. Unit, Gyn. and Obst. Regist. and Ho. Surg. Roy. Free Hosp.; Jun. Asst. Obst. Elizabeth Garrett Anderson Hosp.; Ho. Surg. Cancer Hosp., Fulham Rd. Late Senior Obstetric Surgeon, Elizabeth Garrett Anderson Hospital (Royal Free Hosp. Group); Vice-Dean, Roy. Free Hosp. School of Medicine; Consulting Obstetrician and Gynæcologist, Amersham Gen. Hosp.; Cons. Gynæcologist, St. Mary's Hosp., Plaistow; Cons. Obstetrician, Bucks C.C.; Teacher and Examiner Univ. of Lond.; Retired, 1956. *Recreations:* sport, motoring, music. *Publications:* contributions to B.M.J., Lancet, Proc. Roy. Soc. Med., Medical Press. *Address:* Aros, Isle of Mull, Scotland. [*Died* 25 *Dec.* 1964.

TURNER, Col. Charles Edward, C.B.E. 1943; D.S.O. 1916, T.D., D.L., J.P.; *b.* 1876; *s.* of F. J. Turner, Mansfield Woodhouse, Notts; *m.* 1904, Isabella (*d.* 1955), *d.* of Alexander Walker, Kilmarnock; one *s.* one *d.* (and one *s.* decd.). *Educ.:* Sedbergh School. Served S. African War, 1900-1 (Lumsden's Horse) (despatches); European War, 1914-19 (R. Glos. Hussars) (despatches, D.S.O.); commanded (21st) R. Glos. Hussars Armoured Car Co., 1923-26 (Bt. Lt.-Col 1923). Glos. C.C., 1910-19 and 1942-46. Commanded Gloucestershire Home Guard, Aug. 1940-Nov. 1944; Joint Master Berkeley Hounds, 1928-41; Sheriff of Gloucestershire, 1940. *Address:* The Brake, Old Down, Tockington, nr. Bristol. *T.A.:* Tockington. *T.:* Almondsbury 2151. *Club:* Cavalry. [*Died* 7 *Dec.* 1961.

TURNER, Ernest James, C.B. 1937; C.B.E. 1918; *b.* 1877; *s.* of Arthur James

Turner; *m.* 1908, Minnie Florence, *d.* of John Bulgin. *Educ.:* St. Paul's School; Trinity College, Cambridge. Entered Military Department, India Office, 1900; Sec. Economic and Overseas Depart. India Office, 1921-37. *Address:* 22 Grosvenor Court, Acton, W.3. *T.:* Acorn 4711. [*Died* 2 *April* 1966.

TURNER, Eustace Ebenezer, F.R.S. 1939; F.R.I.C.; M.A. (Cantab.), D.Sc. (Lond.); Research Director, Biorex Laboratories, Ltd., since 1960; Head of Dept. of Chemistry at Bedford College, 1946-60, and Professor of Chemistry in the University of London 1944-60, Professor Emeritus, 1960; Fellow of Queen Mary College; *b.* London, 22 May 1893; *s.* of John and Annie Elizabeth Turner; *m.* 1921, Beryl Osborne, *d.* of Reginald Wyndham of New South Wales; one *d.* *Educ.:* Coopers' Company's School; Queen Mary College, University of London; Sidney Sussex College, Cambridge. Lecturer in Chemistry, Goldsmiths' College, University of London, 1914-15; Research Assistant to Sir William Pope, Chemical Laboratory, Cambridge, 1916-19, mainly in connexion with chemical warfare research; Lecturer in Organic Chemistry, University of Sydney, 1919-21; Chemist in Research Department, Royal Arsenal, Woolwich, 1921-23; Senior Lecturer in Chemistry, Queen Mary College, 1923-28; Head of Dept. of Organic Chemistry, Bedford College, and University Reader, 1928-44. Freeman of City of London; Liveryman of Coopers' Company. *Publications:* Organic Chemistry (with Dr. M. M. Harris), 1952; numerous scientific papers mainly in Journal of the Chemical Society since 1914. *Address:* 47/51 Exmouth Market, E.C.1; Ridge End, 30 The Ridgeway, Tonbridge, Kent. *T.:* Tonbridge 2421.
[*Died* 8 *Sept.* 1966.

TURNER, Frederick Bancroft, B.A., LL.B.; Stipendiary Magistrate of the City of Manchester since 1951; Barrister-at-Law. Called to the Bar, Middle Temple, June 1918. Stipendiary Magistrate of Salford City, 1938-51. *Address:* 14 Riddings Road, Hale, Cheshire; c/o City Police Court, Manchester.
[*Died* 20 *Aug.* 1966.

TURNER, George Charlewood, C.M.G. 1945; M.C.; *b.* 27 March 1891; 4th *s.* of late Charles Henry Turner, D.D., Bishop of Islington, and Edith Emma, *d.* of late Bishop McDougall. *Educ.:* Marlborough College; Magdalen College, Oxford (Classical Demy); B.A. 1914; M.A. 1918. Served with 23rd London Regt. and General Staff, 47th (London) Division, 1914-19; Assistant Master, Marlborough College, 1919-26; Master of Marlborough College, 1926-39; Principal of Makerere College, Kampala, Uganda, 1939-46; Headmaster of Charterhouse, 1947-52. Dep. Chm., Governing Bodies Assoc. Hon. Fellow, Makerere University Coll., 1964. *Address:* 1 St. Martin's Square, Chichester, Sussex. *T.:* Chichester 2715. *Club:* Athenæum. [*Died* 11 *April* 1967.

TURNER, Rt. Rev. Gilbert Price Lloyd, O.B.E. 1959; *b.* Wrexham, Denbigh, 8 May 1888; *s.* of Major George Henry and Frances Turner; unmarried. *Educ.:* Collegiate Sch., Vict., B.C.; St. Augustine's Coll., Cant. L.Th. Durh. Priest, 1913; S.P.G. Mission, Sarawak, Borneo; Chaplain to the Forces in Salonika and Constantinople; Priest in Diocese of Capetown and Rector of St. Paul's, Bree Street, Capetown; Archdeacon of St. Helena, 1938-39; Bishop of St. Helena, 1939-60 (Dio. incl. Ascension Is.); Chap., Ch. of the Holy Family, 1961-64, retd.; Hon. Chap. to the Forces. *Address:* c/o Canon D. H. Cumming, Muizenberg Rectory, C.P., S.A. [*Died* 3 *Nov.* 1968.

TURNER, Maj.-Gen. Guy Roderick, C.B. 1943; M.C. 1916; D.C.M. 1915; C.D.; i.d.c., p.s.c.; *b.* 13 December 1889; *s.* of Francis Turner and Annie Peat; *m.* 1916, Margaret Osborne; one *s.* Officer, Canadian Regular Army; served European War, Royal Canadian Engineers, 1914-18 (D.C.M., M.C. and Bar); School of Military Engineering, Chatham, England, 1920-22; Staff Coll., Quetta, 1925-26; Imperial Defence College, 1938; War of 1939-45: G.S.O. 1, 1st Canadian Div., 1939; B.G.S., 7th Corps (Brig.), July 1940; D.A. & Q.M.G., 1st Cdn. Corps, Dec. 1941; Maj.-Gen. 1942; Deputy Adjutant and Quartermaster-General, First Canadian Army, 1942; Inspector-General, Western Canada, 1945; retired, 1946. C.St.J. 1959. *Address:* 260 Metcalfe Street, Ottawa, Canada. *Club:* Rideau (Ottawa). [*Died* 22 *Feb.* 1963.

TURNER, Sir Henry (Ernest), Kt., *cr.* 1951; C.B.E. 1935; General Secretary of Commonwealth Press Union (formerly Empire Press Union), 1919-56; *m.* E. Arnot Robertson, *q.v.*; one *s.* Organised Commonwealth Press Confs. held in Britain, Canada, Australia, New Zealand and S. Africa; Member of Council, Royal Empire Society, 1952-56. Served (infantry), 1914-19. *Address:* 98 Heath St., Hampstead, N.W.3. *Club:* Savile. [*Died* 21 *April* 1961.

TURNER, Rt. Rev. Herbert Victor; retired as Suffragan Bishop of Penrith and Archdeacon of Furness (1944-58); *b.* 1888; *m.* Mildred Aline, *d.* of A. H. Bonser; two *d.* *Educ.:* Merton Coll., Oxford (Exhibitioner); Cuddesdon Coll., Oxford. B.A. 1911; M.A. 1914; deacon, 1913; priest, 1914; Archdeacon of Nottingham, 1936-44; Vicar of Radcliffe-on-Trent, 1940-44; Canon of Southwell, 1937-44, and Examining Chaplain to Bishop of Southwell; Vicar of Hawkshead, 1944-55. *Address:* Copt Hill, Windermere, Westmorland. *T.:* 3789.
[*Died* 10 *March* 1968.

TURNER, Rear-Admiral Laurence, C.B. 1938; *b.* 1882; *m.* 1917, Marian Edith, *d.* of late P. W. Gilbert, Shanklin; one *s.* *Educ.:* Bloxham; Royal Naval Engineering College, Keyham. Entered R.N., 1898; retired list, 1939; Regional Controller, North West, Ministry of Supply, 1939-45. *Address:* Langdale, Riverside Rd., Dittisham, S. Devon. *Club:* R.N. (Portsmouth).
[*Died* 27 *Jan.* 1963.

TURNER, Laurence Beddome, M.A., Sc.D., M.I.E.E., Fellow of King's College, and Reader Emeritus in Engineering, Cambridge; *b.* Charlton, Kent, 6 April 1886; *s.* of George Turner, M.A., J.P., O.B.E., Cambridge; *m.* 1st, 1914, Katharine (*d.* 1928), *d.* of Dr. Evan Morgan, Shanghai; 2nd, 1930, Margaret, *d.* of Mrs. Bernard Turner, Godstowe School, High Wycombe; three *s.* one *d.* *Educ.:* Bedford School; King's College, Cambridge (Foundation scholar); John Winbolt University prizeman. After a year in works of Siemens Bros., London, and Siemens und Halske, Berlin, entered Post Office as Assistant Staff Engineer; during European War, 1914-18 at Signals Experimental Establishment (Captain Special List), developing wireless apparatus for army; 1919, retired from Post Office, and elected Fellow and Director of Studies in Engineering at King's College, Cambridge; during War of 1939-45, engaged on radar at Admiralty Signals Establishment. *Publications:* Outline of Wireless, 1920; Wireless: a treatise on the theory and practice of high-frequency electric signalling, 1931; Contributions on engineering subjects to societies and journals. *Address:* 3 Burlington House, King's Road, Richmond, Surrey. [*Died* 28 *Jan.* 1963.

TURNER, Lt.-Gen. Sir Richard Ernest William, V.C. 1900; K.C.B., *cr.* 1918; K.C.M.G., *cr.* 1917; D.S.O. 1900;

b. 25 July 1871; *e. s.* of Richard Turner, M.L.C.; *m.* 1900, Harriet Augusta, *e. d.* of Horace George Goodday of London; one *s.* two *d. Educ.:* Quebec, Canada. Served S. Africa, 1900 (despatches thrice, Brevet Lt.-Col., Queen's medal 6 clasps, D.S.O., V.C.). Comd. Canadian Brigade of Infantry, European War, 1914-18, also 2nd Canadian Division (despatches, C.B., K.C.M.G., K.C.B.; Commander Legion of Honour, Croix de Guerre of France with Palms); G.O.C. Canadian Forces in England, 1916-18. *Address:* The Claridge, Grande Allée, Quebec, Canada. *Clubs:* Garrison (Quebec); United Services (Montreal); Canadian Military Institute (Toronto). [*Died* 20 *June* 1961.

TURNER, Sir Sidney, Kt., *cr.* 1942; C.B.E. 1927; *b.* 18 Jan. 1882; *s.* of late Charles Turner; *m.* 1917, Doris Muriel, *d.* of F. W. Spencer; one *s.* one *d. Educ.:* Sherborne School; Gonville and Caius College, Cambridge. Entered India Office, 1905; Accountant - General, 1921; retired 1945. *Address:* Two Elms, Old Bath Road, Sonning, Berks. *T.:* Sonning 3310. [*Died* 5 *July* 1966.

TURNER, Sydney George, C.B.E. 1956 (O.B.E. 1920); Q.C. 1931; *b.* 5 Oct. 1880; *y.s.* of Arthur James Turner, Kensington; *m.* Alice Edith (*d.* 1965), *d.* of George Andrew Matzinger; two *d. Educ.:* Westminster City School. Barrister, 1906, Master of the Bench, 1937, Middle Temple; Autumn Reader, 1948; Master Treasurer, 1955; Master Emeritus, 1963. Practised at Parliamentary Bar until retirement in 1947, except for period of service as head of legal section of Lands Directorate, War Office, 1915-23. Recorder of Sandwich, 1942-51. Dep. Chm., Essex Court of Quarter Sessions, 1947; Chm. 1950-55; Member of General Claims Tribunal under Compensation (Defence) Act 1939, 1948-58; Chairman of Hospital Management Committee for Battersea and Putney Group under National Health Service Act, 1948-59. *Address:* Rose Cottage, Longcross Farm, Headley, Nr. Newbury, Berks. *T.:* Headley 370; 1 Brick Court, Temple, E.C.4. *T.:* Central 0777. [*Died* 5 *Jan.* 1967.

TURNER, Sir Walford (Hollier), Kt. 1952; J.P.; President: Wright's Ropes Ltd. since 1957 (Director, 1908-Nov. 1959, Chm., 1934-57); Guardian of the Standard of Wrought Plate in Birmingham since 1937; *b.* 8 Jan. 1881; *s.* of George Turner, Edgbaston; *m.* 1909, Elsie Rose, *d.* of John Walsh; one *s. Educ.:* King Edward's High School, Birmingham. Chairman: The Rollason Wire Co. Ltd., 1937-57; W. & T. Avery Ltd., 1940-55 (Director, 1919); Avery-Hardoll Ltd., 1933-55; Parnall & Sons Ltd., 1941-55; Birmingham Local Board, Barclays Bank Ltd., 1951-53 (Director, 1929); Director: Wellington Tube Works Ltd., 1907-60; Mitchells & Butlers Ltd., 1943-56; Member of Council: Univ. of Birmingham, 1942-56; Finance Cttee., 1944-56; Hon. Treas., Birmingham Conservative and Unionist Assoc., 1940-54; Regional Controller, Ministry of Supply, West Midlands, 1941; Comr. of Taxes, Div. of Hundred of Hemlingford, Warwickshire, 1937-53; High Sheriff of Warwickshire, 1951-52; *Recreations:* golf, shooting and yachting. *Address:* Holmwood, Somerset Road, Edgbaston, Birmingham. *T.:* Edgbaston 0366. *Clubs:* Conservative (Birmingham); Edgbaston Golf; Mosley Golf. [*Died* 8 *Aug.* 1962.

TURNER, William Ernest Stephen, OB.E.; D.Sc. (Lond.), M.Sc. (B'ham), Hon. D.Sc.Tech. (Sheffield), F.R.S. 1938; F.S.A.; F.Inst.P.; F.S.G.T.; Commendatore al Merito, Republic of Italy, 1954; Professor of Glass Technology, Univ. of Sheffield, 1920-45; now Emeritus Professor; Visiting Prof., University of Illinois, Ill., 1946-47; *b.* 22 Sept. 1881; *s.* of W. G. Turner, Smethwick, Staffs; *m.* 1st, Mary I. (*d.* 1939), *d.* of John Marshall, Birmingham; two *s.* two *d.*; 2nd, 1943, Annie Helen Nairn Monro, M.A. (Edin.), *er. d.* of D. L. Monro, Edinburgh. *Educ.:* King Edward VI. School, Birmingham; University of Birmingham. University Research Scholar in Chemistry and Ehrhardt Research Prizeman; Lecturer in Physical Chemistry, Univ. of Sheffield, 1904; Organiser of Department of Glass Technology, 1915; Hon. Sec. Society of Glass Technology, 1916-22, 1924-37, 1938-46; Pres. 1922-24 and 1937-1938; Hon. Fellow Society of Glass Technology; Hon. Fellow of Institute of Ceramics; Hon. Member Deutsche Glastechnische Gesellschaft and of American Ceramic Soc.; For-Member Masarykova Akademie Prace, Czechoslovakia; Hon. Freeman, Glass Sellers Company; Hon. Mem. of Keramos; Life Member Univ. Court, Sheffield; President Internat. Commn. on Glass, 1933-53, now Hon. President; Vice-President, Circle of Glass Collectors; Silver medal, Royal Society of Arts, 1943; Otto Schott Commemoration Medal, Deutsche Glastechnische Gesellschaft, 1955; Silver medal City of Paris, 1956. *Publications:* Molecular Association, 1915; Introduction to Modern Inorganic Chemistry (in collab.), 1914; more than 400 scientific papers dealing with problems in Physical Chemistry, and Glass Technology and History in British, American, German, French, Belgian, Italian, Czech, Indian and Japanese Journals; founder and editor, 1917-51, of Journal of Society of Glass Technology, and founder and editor (1925-45) of Glass Review. *Recreations:* walking, mountaineering, travel. *Address:* c/o Society of Glass Technology, 20 Hallam Gate Road, Sheffield 10. *Club:* Athenæum. [*Died* 27 *Oct.* 1963.

TURNER, William Percy Whitford, C.M.G. 1932; O.B.E. 1927; *b.* 23 Feb. 1884; *s.* of late John Whitford Turner, London; *m.* 1913, Rosina Elisabeth (*d.* 1958), *d.* of late James Saker, tea planter, Assam. *Educ.:* Owens School, London; abroad. Student Interpreter in China, 1905; Vice-Consul, Peking, 1916; Consul, 1928; Consul, Honolulu, 1934-35; Consul-General, Yunnanfu, 1936; Manila, 1937-1938; retired, 1938. *Recreations:* cricket, tennis, bridge. *Address:* Kazaphani House, Karakoumi, Kyrenia, Cyprus. *Clubs:* Junior Carlton, Royal Automobile; Bournemouth. [*Died* 1 *Aug.* 1962.

TURRILL, William Bertram, O.B.E. 1955; F.R.S. 1958; D.Sc. (Lond.), F.L.S.; V.M.H.; formerly Keeper of Herbarium and Library, Royal Botanic Gardens, Kew, 1946-1957; *b.* Woodstock, Oxf., 14 June 1890; *e.s.* of William Banbury Turrill; *m.* 1918, Florence Emily Homan. *Educ.:* Oxford High Sch.; Chelsea Polytechnic. Entered Kew, as Technical Assistant, 1909; Assistant in Herbarium, 1914; Senior Principal Scientific Officer, 1946. Editor of Botanical Magazine for Royal Horticultural Society, 1947-. V.M.H. (Royal Horticultural Society); Linnean Gold Medal, 1958. *Publications:* Plant Life of the Balkan Peninsula, 1929; British Plant Life, 1948; Pioneer Plant Geography, 1953; The Royal Botanic Gardens, Kew, 1959; (ed.) Vistas in Botany, 1959; papers in Kew Bulletin, Botanical Review, Journ. Ecology, Journ. Genetics, New Phytologist, etc. *Recreations:* gardening and walking. *Address:* 26 Ennerdale Road, Richmond, Surrey. [*Died* 15 *Dec.* 1961.

TUSHINGHAM, Sidney, A.R.C.A. (Lond.), A.R.E. 1915; member of the Society of Graphic Art, 1920; a portrait painter and etcher; *m.* Ella (*d.* 1967), *d.* of Henry Westlake, Othery, Som. *Educ.:* Sch. of Art, Burslem, Staffs; Royal College of Art, South Kensington, S.W. (National and R.C.A. Scholar, full diploma, 1910); abroad. Art Supervisor, L.C.C. School of Photoengraving, 1940-50. Exhibitor in Europe and America; one-man shows in London, Glasgow, New York, Cardiff, Sydney; works purchased by City Corp., Liverpool; Glasgow City Corp. Art Gallery; Corporations of Derby, Southport, and Stoke-on-Trent; and for various collections in America. Etchings and Dry Points in Print Dept., British Museum, Budapest, National Museum of Wales, Cardiff, New York Public Library, Californian State Library, etc. *Recreations:* music, travel, reading, genealogy. *Address:* 18 Ormerod Court, Haywards Heath, Sussex. *T.:* Haywards Heath 2203. *Club:* Garrick. [*Died* 23 *Aug.* 1968.

TUSON, Alan Arthur Lancelot, O.B.E. 1946; *b.* 17 Aug. 1890; *s.* of late F. E. Tuson, I.C.S., and of late K. S. Tuson; *m.* 1920, Gwendoline Dorothy Innocent; three *s.* *Educ.:* Haileybury; Jesus College, Cambridge. China Consular Service, 1913-42 in Peking, Tientsin, Wei-hai-wei, Canton, Nanking, Honolulu, and Shanghai; Envoy Extraordinary and Minister Plenipotentiary, Port-au-Prince, Haiti, 1943-46; retired, 1946. *Recreation:* gardening. *Address:* Nyton Cottage, Aldingbourne, Sx. *T.:* Eastergate 2286. [*Died* 29 *Dec.* 1968.

TUTTLE, Wilbur C.; author, U.S.A.; *b.* 11 Nov. 1883; *s.* of Henry C. Tuttle and Anna Dineen; *m.* 1917, Bertha M. Stutes (*d.* 1963); one *s.* *Publications:* approximately 120 books, novels on Western subjects, since 1931. *Recreations:* fishing, hunting, golf. *Address:* c/o Laurence Pollinger Ltd., 18 Maddox Street, W.1. [*Died* 6 *June* 1969.

TWEEDDALE, 11th Marquess of (*cr.* 1694), **William George Montagu Hay,** Baron 1488; Earl of Tweeddale, 1646; Earl of Gifford, Viscount Walden, 1694; Baron (U.K.), 1881; Hereditary Chamberlain of Dunfermline; Lord Lieutenant of East Lothian since 1944; *b.* 4 Nov. 1884; *s.* of 10th Marquess and Candida (*d.* 1925), C.B.E., *d.* of Vincenzo Bartolucci of Cantiano, Rome; *S.* father, 1911; *m.* 1st, 1912, Marguerite (*d.* 1944), *d.* of Mrs. Lewis Einstein; four *d.*; 2nd, 1945, Mrs. Marjorie Nettlefold, *d.* of H. Wagg. *Educ.:* Eton; Oxford. Retired Major R.F.A. and 1st Life Guards; served European War, 1914 (wounded). Major Home Guard, 1939-45; Ensign, Queen's Body Guard for Scotland, Royal Company of Archers. Owns about 40,000 acres. *Heir:* *n.* David George Montagu, Lt. R.N.R. [*b.* 1921; *s.* of late Lord Edward Hay and Bridget, *o. d.* of Major Cameron Barclay, 10th Royal Hussars; *m.* 1946, Hon. Sonia Mary Peake (marriage dissolved, 1958), *d.* of Viscount Ingleby; three *s.*]. *Address:* Yester House, Gifford, East Lothian. *T.:* Gifford 241. [*Died* 30 *March* 1967.

TWEEDIE, Mary, M.A., F.E.I.S.; *b.* 19 Nov. 1875; *d.* of late William Tweedie, Edinburgh, and Mary Porteous. *Educ.:* The Edinburgh Ladies' College; Germany; Universities, Edinburgh, Montpellier, Geneva. Franco-Scottish Scholar, Edinburgh, 1898; Heriot Travelling Scholar, 1900; M.A. (Hon. First Class), 1901; Head of Modern Languages Department in various schools; Headmistress, The Edinburgh Ladies' College, 1924-37; studied educational systems in France, Germany, Switzerland, Scandinavia, Canada and U.S.A.; External Examiner for degrees (French), Edinburgh University, 1920-1922; President Educational Institute of Scotland, 1924-25; Director, World Federation Educational Associations, 1925-29; Member National Advisory Committee to the Scottish Education Dept., 1922-30; Member East of Scotland Prov. Committee for the Training of Teachers, 1925-34; one of the 12 British Headmistresses sent by the Overseas Dept. to study and report on Canadian Universities, 1931. *Publications:* Introductory French Course; numerous articles; (in collaboration) Prospects for British Girls in Canada. *Recreations:* travel, walking, swimming. *Address:* 29 Colinton Road, Edinburgh. *T.:* 52206. *Clubs:* University Women's, English-Speaking Union, Ladies Caledonian. [*Died* 16 *Nov.* 1961.

TWIGG, Surgeon Rear-Admiral Francis John Despard, C.B.E. 1946; *b.* 22 Jan. 1888; *s.* of William Robert Twigg, Limerick, Ireland; *m.* 1913, Esther Josephine Greene (*d.* 1942); no *c.*; *m.* 1948, Florence M. Cook; one *s.* *Educ.:* Queen's College, Cork. Surgeon R.N., 1912; Surgeon Lieutenant-Commander, 1918; R.N. Hospital, Chatham, 1921-23; H.M.S. Revenge, 1923-25 (Surgeon Cmdr., 1924); H.M. Hospital Ship Maine, 1925-27; R.N. Hosp., Haslar, 1927-30; H.M.S. Nelson, 1930-31; R.N. Hospitals: Cape of Good Hope, 1931-34 (Surg.-Capt., 1934); Haslar, 1935-38; Bermuda, 1938-41; Plymouth, 1942-45 (Surgeon Rear-Adm. 1942); Seaforth, 1945; Sherborne, Dorset, 1945-46; retired, 1946. *Recreations:* tennis, golf. *Address:* Nyeri, Kenya, East Africa. [*Died* 3 *July* 1962.

TWINING, Baron *cr.* 1958 (Life Peer), of Tanganyika and of Godalming; **Edward Francis Twining,** G.C.M.G. 1953 (K.C.M.G. 1949; C.M.G. 1943) M.B.E. 1923; *b.* 1899; *s.* of late Rev. W. H. G. Twining, St. Stephen's, Westminster; *m.* Helen Mary (O.B.E. 1944, M.R.C.S., D.P.H., C.St.J.), *d.* of late A. E. DuBuisson, Glynhir, Carms.; two *s.* *Educ.:* Lancing College; R.M.C. Sandhurst. Commissioned Worcestershire Regt., 1918; served 4th King's African Rifles, 1923-28; retired, 1930. Joined Colonial Administrative Service in Uganda, 1929; Deputy Director of Labour, Mauritius, 1939, Director, 1939-43; Administrator, St. Lucia, Windward Islands, 1944-1946 (Actg. Gov. and C.-in-C., 1946); Governor and C.-in-C., North Borneo, 1946-1949; Governor and C.-in-C., Tanganyika, 1949-58. Hon. Col. to 6th Bn. King's African Rifles, 1955-58. Chairman: Ross Institute of Tropical Hygiene; Business Archives Coun.; Director: National & Grindlay's Bank Ltd.; Smith Mackenzie Ltd. Chm., Victoria League. K.St.J. 1950. *Publication:* A History of the Crown Jewels of Europe, 1960. *Address:* Lloyds Bank, 222 Strand, W.C.2. *Clubs:* Athenæum, United Service. [*Died* 21 *June* 1967.

TWISS, Maj.-Gen. Sir William Louis Oberkirch, K.C.I.E., *cr.* 1938; C.B. 1930; C.B.E. 1919; M.C.; F.R.G.S.; Col., 9th Gurkha Rifles, 1930-49; Col., 5/1st Punjab Regt. (formerly 82nd Punjabis), 1932-47; Col. 4th Burma Rifles, 1938; *b.* 18 Jan. 1879; *s.* of Rev. William Christopher Twiss, M.A., and Baroness Marie Elizabeth d'Oberkirch; *m.* 1st, 1915, Nora Muriel (*d.* 1929), *d.* of J. E. Wasfield, J.P.; *s* 2nd, 1932, Isabel Vivien, *d.* of T. C. Drake. *Educ.:* Bedford School; R.M.C. Sandhurst. First commission, 1898; appointed 9th Gurkha Rifles, 1901; Staff College, Camberley, 1906-07; War Office (Gen. Staff), 1908-12 and 1919-21; Brigade-Maj., Nowshera Brigade, 1913-14; Deputy Director of Military Intelligence, Army Headquarters, India, 1917-19; commanded 2/9th Gurkha Rifles, 1921-23; Director of Military Intelligence, Army Headquarters, India, 1923-24; Director of Military Operations, Army Headquarters, India, 1924-1927; Commander Jullundur Brigade, Punjab, India, 1927-31; Major-General, 1929; Military Secretary, Army Headquarters, India, 1932-36; G.O.C. Burma Independent District, 1936-37; G.O.C. Army in Burma, 1937-39; retired, 1939; Observer Comdr. and Group Comdt., No. 3 Group, Royal Observer Corps, 1943-48 (Observer Group Officer, 1939-43). Served Boxer (N. China) Expedition, 1900-01 (medal and clasp, despatches); Tibet Expedition, 1903-04 (medal); North-West Frontier of India; European War in

France, 1914-17 (C.B.E., M.C., Legion of Honour; Order of Sacred Treasure (Japan), despatches five times, Brevet of Lieut.-Col.); bronze medal of Royal Humane Society, 1903; Officer of Norwegian Order of St. Olaf, 1909; member of Military Order of the Dragon, U.S.A., 1901; Founder Member of Royal Institute of International Affairs (Chatham House); Founder Member of Himalayan Club; Member of British Empire League and English-Speaking Union. *Recreations:* (formerly) cricket, tennis, golf, swimming, shooting, etc. *Address:* Chilland Barn, Martyr Worthy, Winchester, Hants. *Clubs:* United Service, English-Speaking Union, Free Foresters. [*Died* 13 *Oct.* 1962.

TWYFORD, Sir Harry Edward Augustus, K.B.E., *cr.* 1938; Kt., *cr.* 1935; Lieutenant, City of London; Past Master Masons Co., Framework Knitters Co., Parish Clerks Co.; *b.* 1870; *s.* of late Augustus S. Twyford; *m.* 1st, 1900, Ethel Rose (*d.* 1948), *d.* of Richard Honey, Adelaide, S. Australia; one *s.* one *d.*; *m.* 2nd, 1950, Ida Marks. *Educ.:* privately. Alderman City of London, 1930-48; Sheriff, 1934-35; Lord Mayor of London, 1937-38. Hon. Vice-Pres. Cables & Wireless Holdings Co. Ltd.; Grand Cross of Leopold of Belgium; Order of White Lion (Czechoslovakia). *Address:* High Knowle, Muttersmoor Road, Sidmouth, Devon. *Club:* Royal Thames Yacht [*Died* 10 *Jan.* 1967.

TWYNAM, Sir Henry Joseph, K.C.S.I., *cr.* 1940 (C.S.I. 1937); C.I.E. 1934; late I.C.S.; *b.* 24 April 1887; *s.* of Charles Henry Twynam, The Grange, Old Portswood, Hants, and Mary Sophia Piggott; *m.* 1915, Muriel Hearson (Kaisar-i-Hind gold medal, 1944); two *d.* (and one *s.* killed in action). *Educ.:* Ratcliffe College; Rouen; Universities of Manchester (B.A. Hons.), London, Lausanne. Entered Indian Civil Service, 1909; Assistant Magistrate East Bengal and Assam, 1910; Political Department Government of Bengal, 1914; I.A.R.O., 1915-18 (Capt. and Adjutant 2/123rd Outram's Rifles); Vice-President Cooch-Behar State Council, 1920-24; District Magistrate Mymensingh, 1925-27; Revenue and Irrigation Sec. Govt. of Bengal, 1929-31; M.L.A. Additional Secretary Political Dept. and Officiating Chief Secretary, 1932, 1936-40; Commissioner, Presidency and Chittagong Divisions of Bengal, 1933-34; Acting Governor of Assam, 1939; Governor of the Central Provinces and Berar, 1940-46; Acting Governor of Bengal, 1945; retd. 1946. *Recreations:* golf, riding. *Address:* Holm Farm, Sway, Hants. *Club:* Roy. Over-Seas League. [*Died* 21 *Oct.* 1966.

TWYSDEN, Sir William Adam Duncan, 12th Bt., *cr.* 1611; Lt.-Comdr. R.N., retd.; *b.* 6 April 1897; 2nd *s.* of Capt. James Stevenson Twysden, R.N. and Aileen Frances Mary, *d.* of Sir William Henry Wilson-Todd, 1st Bt.; *S.* nephew 1946; *m.* 1949, Isla Grey, *d.* of late A. E. Howlett and Mrs. H. M. Howlett, Rye, Sussex. *Educ.:* Haileybury. *Recreations:* yachting, shooting, motor travelling. *Address:* Merida, Park Hill Road, Torquay. *T.:* Torquay 227371. *Clubs:* United Service, American; Royal Yacht Squadron (Cowes); Royal Western Yacht Club of England (Plymouth); Royal Torbay Yacht (Torquay). [*Died* 17 *Feb.* 1970 (*ext.*).

TYLECOTE, Frank Edward, C.B.E. 1956; M.D., F.R.C.P. (Lond.); J.P. City of Manchester, 1934; Professor Emeritus of Medicine, Univ. of Manchester; Hon. Alderman, City of Manchester; Mem. Coun., Roy. Coll. of Physicians of London, 1938-41; Hon. Consulting Physician, Manchester Royal Infirmary and Macclesfield General Infirmary; Consulting Medical Officer, Williams Deacons Bank; Ex-Member Byssinosis Medical Bd.; and pneumoconiosis and silicosis panels; ex-President National Smoke Abatement Society; Governor and Member of Council Whitworth Art Gallery Manchester; Court of Governors, Manchester Univ.; Medical Advisory Committee Asthma Research Council; Health Centres Sub-Cttee. of Central Health Services Council of Ministry of Health; Standing Conference on investigation of atmospheric pollution; *b.* Cannock, Staffs; *s.* of Frank Tylecote, bank manager; *m.* 1st, 1915, Charlotte Dora (*d.* 1930), *d.* of John Boddan; one *s.* one *d.*; 2nd, 1932, Mabel Phythian, Ph.D., *yr. d.* of late J. Ernest Phythian; one *s.* *Educ.:* King Edward VI School, Macclesfield; Victoria University, Manchester; Heidelberg. University Medallist in Practical Anatomy, Hygiene and Public Health, Forensic Medicine and Toxicology, and in Systematic Medicine; Turner Scholar in Medicine; Sidney Renshaw Exhibitioner in Physiology; M.B., Ch.B. 1902; M.D. 1904; D.P.H. 1906; M.R.C.P. Lond. 1907; F.R.C.P. Lond. 1923; Prof. of Medicine Manchester University, 1929-40; formerly Member of Nurses Whitley Council and of Rushcliffe Cttee.; late R.M.O., Royal Infirmary, Manchester; late Chm., Manchester Public Health Cttee.; ex-Chm., Manchester City Libraries Committee; ex-Pres., Royal Manchester Institution; late Treasurer, Manchester and Salford Council of Social Service; ex-Chairman, Manchester City Art Galleries Cttee.; Major R.A.M.C. (B.E.F.), 1917; Examiner in Medicine to Conjoint Bd., 1937-41; Chesterfield Medallist in Dermatology, London. F.R.S.H., 1958. *Publications:* (with G. Fletcher) Diagnosis and Treatment in Diseases of the Lungs, 1927; articles in various medical journals. *Address:* Heaton Lodge, Heaton Mersey, Stockport, Ches.; Smeaton Cottage, St. Ives, Cornwall. *Club:* St. James's (Manchester). [*Died* 7 *Oct.* 1965.

TYLER, Sir Henry H. F. M.; *see* Macdonald-Tyler.

TYLOR, Sir Theodore (Henry), Kt. 1965; Fellow and Tutor in Jurisprudence at Balliol College, Oxford, 1929-67; Jowett Fellow, 1944-59; Blanesburgh Fellow, 1962-1967, Hon. Fellow 1967; Estates Bursar, 1947-65; Lecturer in Jurisprudence to Corpus Christi College, Oxford, 1931-67; retired, 1967; *b.* Bournville, 13 April 1900; *s.* of Henry Bedford Tylor, A.R.I.B.A.; unmarried. *Educ.:* Coll. for the Blind, Worcester; Balliol College, Oxford (Hon. Scholar). B.A. in Jurisprudence (Class I), 1922; B.C.L. 1923; M.A. 1925; of the Inner Temple, Barrister-at-Law, 1928 (Class I with special prize); Asst. Lecturer in Jurisprudence at Balliol College, Oxford, 1924, Tutor and Lecturer, 1926. Member Executive Council of Roy. Nat. Institute for the Blind, 1925, Chm. of its Educ. and Research Cttee., 1936-46, Vice-Chm. of its Council, 1952-61, Chm., 1962; Vice-Chairman Worcester Coll. for the Blind; Member: Min. of Health Advisory Cttee. on Handicapped Persons, 1962; Council of St. Dunstan's, 1962. *Publications:* notes and articles in journals dealing with Law, Blind Welfare, and Chess. *Recreations:* chess—Midland champion 1925-26, British Championship 2nd 1933, B.C.F. 4th 1949 and 1951, Correspondence Champion, 1933-35, Nottingham Masters' Tournament, 1936, British Chess Master for life, 1955; bridge. *Address:* 2 Rawlinson Rd., Oxford. [*Died* 23 *Oct.* 1968.

TYNDALE, Geoffrey Clifford, Q.C. 1943; M.A. Oxon., LL.B. (London); a Master of the Bench, Inner Temple, 1950; *b.* 19 Feb. 1887; 2nd *s.* of late Walter Tyndale; *m.* 1st, 1921, Adelaide, *d.* of John Citron; (one *s.* killed in action 24 March 1944); 2nd, 1923, Mary Winifred (*d.* 1950), *d.* of late

George Pitt-Lewis, K.C., M.P. *Educ.:* Epsom College; Keble College, Oxford, B.A., 1909, 2nd Class Hons. History; M.A. 1932; LL.B. (London). Called to Bar, Inner Temple, 1913; some time on Teaching Staff of Incorporated Law Society; practises in Probate and Divorce Division, has sat as Special Commissioner in Divorce; Ex-Pres. Hardwicke Society. *Recreations:* travel, reading history. *Address:* 76 Kensington Church Street, W.8. *T.:* Bayswater 1614. *Club:* Reform. [*Died* 6 *May* 1966.

TYNDALE, Lieut.-Col. Wentworth Francis, C.M.G. 1902; D.S.O. 1918; M.D. (London); M.R.C.S., L.R.C.P.; D.P.H. Lond., 1907; late R.A.M.C.; *b.* 11 May 1874; *s.* of Wentworth R. Tyndale, M.B.; *m.* 1912, Ethel Margaret McEwan; three *s.* two *d.* *Educ.:* St. George's Hospital. Served S. Africa, 1899-1902 (despatches, Queen's medal three clasps, King's medal two clasps); European War, 1914-18 (despatches; D.S.O., Bt. Lt.-Colonel); retired pay, 1929. Late Medical Instructor, Home Office (A.R.P. Dept.). Retired J.P. *Address:* The Laurels, Bishopthorpe, York. [*Died* 20 *Sept.* 1964.

TYNDALL, Arthur Mannering, C.B.E. 1950; F.R.S. 1933; D.Sc. (Bristol and London); Emeritus Professor and Honorary Fellow, Univ. of Bristol; *b.* 18 Sept. 1881; *s.* of Henry Augustus Tyndall and Hannah Mannering; *m.* Lilly Mary Gardner; one *s.* two *d.* *Educ.:* University College, Bristol. Henry Overton Wills Prof. of Physics, Univ. of Bristol, 1919-48; Director of the Henry Herbert Wills Physical Lab., 1927-48; Acting Vice-Chancellor Univ. of Bristol, 1944-45; Pro-Vice-Chancellor, 1940-47. Hon. LL.D. (Bristol) 1959. President Inst. of Physics, 1946-48, Hon. Fellow, 1953. Chairman Executive Committee National Physical Laboratory, 1946-49. *Publications:* Mobility of Positive Ions in Gases; papers to Proc. Roy. Soc., etc. *Address:* 9 Henleaze Gardens, Westbury-on-Trym, Bristol. *Club:* Athenæum. [*Died* 29 *Oct.* 1961.

TYRER, (Frank) Anderson, F.R.M.C.M., F.T.C.L.; Composer, Conductor; *s.* of Arthur and Jane Ann Tyrer; *m.* 1921, Laura Nanette Evans, Violinist. *Educ.:* Royal Manchester College of Music (Scholar). Made debut at the Hallé Promenade Concerts in 1914; in 1915 joined the Army and was later discharged owing to a nervous breakdown; made his London debut 11th Nov. 1919 in the Queen's Hall. Musical Adviser and Conductor to the New Zealand Government for the Centennial Music Celebrations in 1940. Has appeared frequently as Guest Conductor, solo pianist, and Composer with Australian, Canadian, South African, New Zealand Broadcasting Commissions. In 1946 was invited by New Zealand Government to form, organise and conduct first National Symphony Orchestra. Has been associated with the Trinity College of Music as Examiner since 1925. Has composed many works for Orchestra, Chorus and Piano. *Recreations:* bowling, golfing. *Address:* c/o Trinity College of Music, Mandeville Place, W.1. [*Died* 16 *Dec.* 1962.

TYRRELL, Sir Francis Graeme, K.B.E., *cr.* 1934; C.M.G. 1928; Ceylon Civil Service, retired; *s.* of General Francis Hardinge Tyrrell, I.A.; *m.* Marian Frances (*d.* 1953), *d.* of Joseph Brutton, Yeovil, Somerset; no *c.* *Educ.* King's College School, London; Pembroke College, Oxford. Cadet, Ceylon Civil Service, 1900; Govt. Agent N.C. Province, 1919; N.W. Province, 1921; Chairman Port Commission and Principal Collector of Customs, Colombo, 1926; Controller of Revenue, 1927; Deputy Chief Secretary, 1931-32; Chief Secretary, 1932-1937; temporary Captain 6th Yorkshire Regt.; served in Gallipoli, France, and N. Russia (despatches). [*Died* 18 *July* 1964.

TYRRELL, George Walter, A.R.C.Sc., D.Sc. (Glasgow); F.G.S., F.R.S.E.; Hon. Research Fellow, University of Glasgow; formerly Senior Lecturer in Geology; *b.* 1883; *s.* of George Tyrrell and Annie Tyrrell, Watford; *m.* 1906, Alice Annie Williman; three *d.*; *m.* 1950, Ursula Joan Demont. *Educ.:* Watford Grammar School; Imperial College of Science and Technology. Demonstrator in Geology, Royal College of Science, 1905; Assistant to Prof. of Geology, Glasgow University, 1906; Lecturer, 1911; Senior Lecturer, 1919; Murchison Fund (Geological Soc.), 1916; Chief of Scientific Staff, Scottish Spitsbergen Syndicate Expedition, 1919; Chief Geologist on 1920 Expedition; Leader of Expedition to Iceland, 1924; Fellow Royal Society of Edinburgh, 1918, Member of Council, 1927-29, Vice-President, 1940-43; President, Glasgow Geological Society, 1924-26; Murchison Medal (Geological Society), 1931; Neill Gold Medal and Prize (Royal Society, Edinburgh), 1934; Clough Medal (Geol. Soc. Edin.), 1952. *Publications:* The Principles of Petrology, 1926, 11th Ed. 1950; The Geology of Arran (H.M. Geological Survey), 1928; Volcanoes (Home University Library), 1931; The Earth and Its Mysteries, 1953; about 90 original memoirs and papers on the geology and petrology of the West of Scotland, North and South Polar Regions, West Africa, etc., and on the glaciers of Spitsbergen. *Recreations:* walking, motor camping, music. *Address:* 26 Canniesburn Road, Bearsden, Glasgow. *T.:* Bearsden 1707. [*Died* 20 *July* 1961.

TYRRELL, Air Vice-Marshal Sir William, K.B.E., *cr.* 1944 (C.B.E. 1942); D.S.O. and Bar, 1918; M.C. 1914; Croix de Guerre (Belgium), 1918; K.St.J. 1947; M.B., B.Ch., D.P.H., LL.D. (h.c.) Queen's Univ., Belfast, 1947; Royal Air Force Medical Services, retired; *b.* 20 Nov. 1885; *s.* of John Tyrrell, Belfast and Bangor, Co. Down; *m.* 1929, Barbara, *d.* of M. J. Coleclough, Romsey, Hants; two *s.* one *d.* *Educ.:* Royal Belfast Academical Institution; Queen's University, Belfast. R.A.M.C. (Spec. R.), 1912; served European War, 1914-18 (despatches six times, D.S.O. and Bar, M.C., Croix de Guerre); R.M.O. 2nd Lancashire Fusiliers, 1914-15; O.C. No. 1 M.A.C., 1915-16; D.A.D.M.S. VIII Corps B.E.F., 1916; O.C. 76 Field Ambulance, 1917-18; Assistant Commandant and O.C. R.A.M.C. School of Instruction, 1918; seconded as P.M.O. H.Q. R.A.F. with Army of Occupation, 1918-19. P.M.O. Z Expedition Somaliland, 1919-20; transferred to R.A.F., 1920; S.M.O. Basrah, 1922-23; P.M.O. Palestine, 1923-26, Cranwell, 1927-31; P.M.O. Iraq and Middle East, 1932-35; Inland Area, Trng. and Tech. Trng. Command, 1935-1944. Air Commodore, 1935; Air Vice-Marshal, 1939; retired, 1944. K.H.S., 1939-1943. D.M.S., B.O.A.C., 1945-47. *Recreations:* walking, swimming. *Address:* c/o Glyn, Mills & Co., Whitehall, S.W.1. *Clubs:* Royal Ulster Yacht (Bangor, Co. Down); Ulster Reform (Belfast). [*Died* 29 *April* 1968.

TYRRELL, Brigadier William Grant, D.S.O. 1917; *b.* 6 June 1882. Served European War 1914-18 (D.S.O., despatches twice, Bts. Major and Lt.-Col., 1914-15 star, two medals); Assistant Director of Transportation, War Office, 1933-37; retired pay, 1937; re-employed 1939-40. *Address:* 119 Norbiton Hall, Kingston, Surrey. [*Died* 18 *Aug.* 1961.

TYRWHITT, Admiral Sir St. John (Reginald Joseph), 2nd Bt., *cr.* 1919; K.C.B. 1961 (C.B. 1957); D.S.O. 1943; D.S.C. 1942, Bar, 1944; a Lord Commissioner of the Admiralty, Second Sea Lord and Chief of Naval Personnel, 1959-61; *b.* 18 April 1905; *o. s.* of Admiral of the Fleet Sir Reginald Tyrwhitt, 1st Bt., G.C.B., D.S.O., and Angela, *d.* of late Matthew Corbally, J.P., D.L., Rathbeale Hall, Swords; *S.* father 1951; *m.* 1944, Nancy Veronica, *o. d.* of Captain Charles Newman Gilbey, Gibsons, Hatfield Heath, Essex; two *s.* one *d.* *Educ.:* R.N. Colleges, Osborne and Dartmouth. Joined R.N., 1919; Lt., 1927; served War of 1939-45 (D.S.C. and bar, D.S.O.), commanded H.M. ships Defender, Juno, Tartar, 1939-44; A.D.C. to the Queen, 1955; Comdr., 1940; Capt., 1945; Rear-Adm., 1955; Vice-Adm., 1958; Chief of Staff to Commander-in-Chief, Allied Forces, Mediterranean, 1958-59; Adm. 1961. Younger Brother of Trinity House. *Heir: s.* Reginald Thomas Newman, *b.* 21 Feb. 1947. *Address:* 40 Bathgate Rd., Wimbledon, S.W.19. *T.:* 3613. *Club:* United Service.

[*Died* 10 *Oct.* 1961.

TYRWHITT-DRAKE, Sir Garrard; *see* Drake, Sir H. G. T.

TYSER, Granville; Director, Lazard Brothers & Co. Ltd., 1920-60; *b.* 29 Nov. 1884; *m.* 1st, 1913, Constance Evelyn (*d.* 1922), *d.* of George Wood, J.P., Brandon, Suffolk; one *s.* two *d.*; 2nd, 1957, Elsie, *d.* of late Edward and Jane Selwood. *Educ.:* Highgate School; London Univ. (LL.B.). Solicitor, 1907-19 (John Mackrell Prizeman Solicitors' Final); Partner in Paines Blyth & Huxtable (now Linklaters & Paines). A Managing Dir. of Lazard Brothers & Co. Ltd., 1920-50. Director Mercantile Group of Investment Trust Companies, 1948-60; Director, Phoenix Assurance Co., 1935-61; Director, Colonial Development Corporation, 1951-57. *Address:* 53 Fountain House, Park Lane, W1Y 3WB. *T.:* 01-499 2396. *Clubs:* City of London, Travellers'.

[*Died* 18 *Nov.* 1970.

TYSON, Moses, M.A., Ph.D.; retired as Librarian of the University of Manchester (1935-65); *b.* 24 December 1897; *s.* of John Dixon Tyson; unmarried. *Educ.:* Kelsick Gram. Sch., Ambleside; Univ. of Manchester (M.A., Ph.D.). Univ. of Manchester: Jones Fellow, 1924, 1926; Keeper of Western Manuscripts in John Rylands Library, 1927-1935; Lecturer in Palæography, 1929-56; Reader in Palæography, 1956-65. Emeritus Librarian, Manchester Univ., 1965. *Publications:* The French Journals of Mrs. Thrale and Dr. Johnson (ed. with H. Guppy), 1932; various catalogues of MSS. in the John Rylands Library; articles in learned periodicals, etc. *Recreations:* hill walking, golf. *Address:* Busk House, Ambleside, Westmorland. *T.:* Ambleside 3217.

[*Died* 3 *Feb.* 1969.

TYTLER, Lt.-Col. Sir William K. F.; *see* Fraser-Tytler.

U

UDAL, (Nicholas) Robin, C.B.E. 1929; Secretary of the Athenæum, 1936-51; *b.* Richmond, Surrey, 16 October 1883; *y. s.* of late his Hon. J. S. Udal, formerly Chief Justice of the Leeward Islands; *m.* 1920, Margaret Ruth, *yr. d.* of late Roderic Oliver, of Orlestone, Kent; two *s.* *Educ.:* Winchester College; New College, Oxford. Honours Mods, 1904; Honours History, 1905; B.A. 1905; Honours Arabic, 1906; Oxford University Cricket XI, 1905 and 1906; Sudan Civil Service, 1906; Chief Inspector of Education, Sudan Government, 1915; Assistant Director of Education, Sudan Government, 1918-30, and Warden of Gordon College, Khartoum, 1927-30; Secretary and Bursar, Clifton College, 1930-36; 4th class Order of the Nile, 1919; 3rd class, 1926. *Club:* Athenæum.

[*Died* 27 *Feb.* 1964.

UNDERHILL, Rev. Percy Cyril, O.B.E. 1956; *b.* 8 June 1883; *s.* of late Rev. P. L. Underhill, M.A.; formerly Rector of Bletsoe, Beds; *m.* 1914; two *s.* one *d.* *Educ.:* St. Edward's School and Brasenose College, Oxford. B.A. 1906, M.A. 1915. Asst. Master, Stone House, Broadstairs, 1906-8; Asst. Master, Heatherdown, Ascot, 1908-12; Headmaster (joint) Northaw Place, Potters Bar, 1912-19; Headmaster, Wellington House, Westgate-on-Sea, 1919-38: Chairman Incorporated Association of Preparatory Schools, 1933; Sec. Incorporated Assoc. of Preparatory Schools, 1938-57; Secretary Common Examination for Entry to Public Schools, 1938-61. Rector of Checkendon, nr. Reading, 1945-49. Vicar of Kingston-cum-Iford, nr. Lewes, 1949-52. Rector of Swyncombe, Oxon., 1952-55. *Recreation:* rowing. *Address:* Braybrooke Road, Wargrave, Berks. *Clubs:* Leander, English-Speaking Union.

[*Died* 2 *April* 1963.

UNGER, Professor Josef, LL.M.; Barber Professor of Law in the University of Birmingham since 1960; *b.* 9 Aug. 1912; *s.* of Abraham and Adele Unger; *m.* 1960, Elisabeth (*née* Heber). *Educ.:* Oberrealschule, Hannover; Universities of Leipzig, Berlin, Heidelberg, London. LL.B. (Lond.), 1st cl. hons., Univ. Schol., 1936; Holker Schol., 1936; LL.M. (Lond.), 1937; Barstow Schol., 1939; Barrister, Gray's Inn (Certificate of Honour), 1940. Lecturer in Law, Univ. Coll. of Wales, Aberystwyth, 1941; Reader in Internat. Law, Birmingham, 1949. Co-editor, Modern Law Review. *Publications:* contrib. to English and foreign legal periodicals. *Recreations:* music, travel, tennis. *Address:* 5 Church Street, Warwick.

[*Died* 20 *Oct.* 1967

UNWIN, Rear-Adm. John Harold, C.B. 1959; D.S.C. 1941; Retired 1961; Joint Man. Dir., Furness Shipbuilding Co., 1961-64; Managing Director, Product Knowledge Ltd., 1964; *b.* 13 Nov. 1906; *s.* of G. H. Unwin and S. P. Unwin (*née* Hallowes); *m.* 1939, Elizabeth Strong, *d.* of late Prof. Sir David Kennedy Henderson; three *s.* one *d.* *Educ.:* Preparatory School; R.N. Colleges Osborne and Dartmouth. R.N. Coll., Osborne, 1920; H.M. Ships: Marlborough, 1924, Versatile, 1928, Queen Elizabeth, 1930, Devonshire, 1934, Douglas, 1938, Valiant, 1939-42, Dido, 1942; C.O., H.Q., 1942-44; H.M.S. Indefatigable, 1946-47; Captain, 1948; H.M.S. Mounts Bay, 1949-50; Admiralty, 1951-53; Portsmouth Dockyard, 1953-55; Commodore, Hong Kong, 1955-57; Rear-Admiral 1957; Admiral Superintendent, H.M. Dockyard, Portsmouth, 1957-61. Legion of Merit (U.S.A.), 1950. *Recreations:* gardening, golf. *Address:* The Manor House, Burghfield, Reading, Berkshire. *T.:* Burghfield Common 204. *Club:* United Service.

[*Died* 31 *Dec.* 1970.

UNWIN, Sir Stanley, K.C.M.G. 1966; Kt., 1946; Hon. LL.D. (Aberdeen); Publisher; Chairman: George Allen & Unwin Ltd.; Elkin Mathews and Marrot, Ltd.; *b.* 19 December 1884; *s.* of late Edward Unwin and Elizabeth Spicer; *m.* Mary, *d.* of late Rayner Storr; two *s.* one *d.* *Educ.:* Abbotsholme; Haubinda. Member Executive, The British Council; Life Member R.I.I.A.; M.R.I.; F.R.S.L.; Chairman, Sir Halley Stewart Trust; President Publishers' Association of Great Britain, 1933-35; President International Publishers' Association, 1936-38, 1946-54. Has Palm in Gold of the

Order of the Crown of Belgium; Officier d'Académie, France; Order of White Lion of Czecho-Slovakia; Officer in the Order of Orange Nassau; Knight Commander of the Order of the Falcon (Iceland). *Publications:* The Truth about Publishing; (joint) Two Young Men see the World; Best Sellers: Are they Born or Made? How Governments Treat Books; The Truth about a Publisher. *Recreations:* foreign travel, walking, tennis. *Address:* 4 Oak Hill Park, Hampstead, N.W.3. *T.A.:* Deucalion. *Club:* Reform.

[*Died* 13 *Oct.* 1968.

UPCOTT, Sir Gilbert Charles, K.C.B., *cr.* 1933 (C.B. 1919); *b.* Cullompton, Devon, 25 Feb. 1880; *s.* of late Charles John Upcott; *m.* 1st. 1908, Blanche (*d.* 1928), *d.* of H. Brodmeier, three *d.*; 2nd, 1929, Kathryn, *d.* of late Rev. De Lancey Townsend, D.D., New York. *Educ.:* Marlborough; Corpus Christi College, Oxford (Scholar); 1st Cl. Classical Mods., 1901; 1st Cl. Lit. Hum., 1903. Hon. Fellow of Corpus Christi College, 1942; Civil Servant (entered Treasury, 1903); Deputy Controller, Treasury, 1921-31; Comptroller and Auditor General, Exchequer and Audit Department, 1931-46. *Address:* 28 Cholmeley Crescent, Highgate, N.6. *T.:* Mountview 6260.

[*Died* 26 *June* 1967.

UPSON, Rt. Rev. Dom Wilfrid, O.S.B., Abbot of Prinknash (Abbey of St. Mary and St. Peter, Prinknash, Gloucester) since 1938; *b.* 1880. Before joining the Anglican community at Caldey Island, did lay mission work at Stepney and Poplar; also did considerable work with Boys' clubs; assisted R. Wilson in the beginning of his work on the Kent hopfields; was received into Catholic Church with the Anglican community of Caldey, 1913; priest, 1915; claustral prior, 1917; superior of Caldey, 1921; parish priest of Westgate-on-Sea, 1932; resigned from the active administration of the Abbey, 1961, whilst retaining the title. *Address:* Prinknash Abbey, Gloucester.

[*Died* 26 *Oct.* 1963.

URE, Professor Peter; Joseph Cowen Professor of English Language and Literature, University of Newcastle upon Tyne since 1960; *b.* 1919; 2nd *s.* of James Matthew Ure and Elsie Mai (*née* Overton). *Educ.:* Birkenhead School; Liverpool University. B.A. 1940, M.A. 1944. Mem. of Friends' Ambulance Unit, 1942-46. Welfare Officer, U.N. Relief and Rehabilitation Administration, 1946; Graduate Research Fellow, Univ. of Liverpool, 1947; Lecturer in English Language and Literature, 1947-58, Sen. Lecturer, 1958-1960, King's Coll., Newcastle, Univ. of Durham; Vice-Pres., Senior Common Room, Newcastle Univ., 1963-64. Vice-Pres., Newcastle Literary and Philosophical Soc., 1967-. *Publications:* Towards a Mythology: Studies in the Poetry of W. B. Yeats, 1946; Seventeenth-Century Prose, 1956; King Richard II (Arden Shakespeare), 1956; Mr. Hobb's State of Nature Discovered, 1958; Shakespeare and the Inward Self of the Tragic Hero, 1961; Shakespeare: the Problem Plays, 1961; Yeats the Playwright, 1963; Yeats (Writers and Critics Series), 1963; Perkin Warbeck (Revel Plays), 1968; contributor to: Stratford-upon-Avon Studies, Review of Eng. Studies, Mod. Lang. Review, Philological Quarterly, etc. *Address:* The University, Newcastle upon Tyne, 1. *T.:* Newcastle 28511. [*Died* 30 *June* 1969.

URQUHART, Major-General Ronald Walton, C.B. 1957; D.S.O. 1944; D.L.; retired; Colonel Commandant, Royal Engineers, since 1964; *b.* 26 Mar. 1906; 3rd *s.* of late W. L. A. Urquhart, Montevideo, Uruguay; *m.* 1942, Jean Margaret, *d.* of W. Moir, formerly of Colombo, Ceylon; three *s.* one *d.* *Educ.:* Bedford; Royal Military Academy; Pembroke College, Cambridge. 2nd Lieut. Royal Engineers, 1925. Served War: Palestine, 1938-39; Norway, 1940 (despatches); Europe, 1944-45 (despatches). Director of Combined Operations, 1947-49; Commander 35 Inf. Bde., 1953-54; Chief of Staff, Western Command, 1956; Commandant Royal Military Academy, Sandhurst, 1957-60; Temp. Brig., 1947; Temp. Maj.-General, 1956; Major-General, 1957. Chairman, Glos. S.S.&A.F.A., 1966-. D.L. Gloucestershire, 1965. Chevalier, Order of Leopold II with palm and Croix de Guerre with palm, 1940 (Belgium). *Address:* Meredith, Tibberton, Glos. *T.:* Tibberton 221. *Club:* United Service.

[*Died* 19 *April* 1968.

URQUHART, Rev. William Spence, M.A., D.Litt., D.D., D.L., LL.D.; Principal Emeritus of the Scottish Church College, Calcutta; *b.* 8 May 1877; *s.* of late Rev. Robert Urquhart, Oldmeldrum, Aberdeenshire; *m.* 1905, Margaret (authoress of Women of Bengal, 1926), 4th *d.* of late Rev. Murdoch Macaskill, Dingwall; no *c.* *Educ.:* Grammar School, Old Aberdeen; Gordon's College, Aberdeen; University of Aberdeen; New College, Edinburgh; Universities of Marburg and Göttingen. M.A. with 1st Class in Mental and Moral Philosophy, Aberdeen, 1897; Professor of Philosophy in Duff College, Calcutta, 1902; Professor in Scottish Churches College, Calcutta, 1908; D.Litt. University of Aberdeen, 1916; Member of Congress of Universities, 1921 and 1948; Member of Indian Universities Congress, 1924 and 1929; Principal of the Scottish Church College, Calcutta, 1928-38; Vice-Chancellor of the University of Calcutta, 1928-30; Dean of the Faculty of Arts, 1927 and 1930; Chairman of Inter-University Board, India, 1931-32; Temporary Professor of Christian Dogmatics, University of Aberdeen, 1937; Temporary Professor of Systematic Theology, Knox College, Toronto, 1938-39; Croall Lecturer, University of Edinburgh, 1938-39; Wilde Lecturer Univ. of Oxford, 1942-45; Riddoch Lecturer, Univ. of Aberdeen, 1944 and 1946. Hon. D.D. Univ. of Aberdeen, 1930; Hon. D.L. University of Calcutta, 1930; Hon. LL.D. University of St. Andrews, 1937. *Publications:* The Historical and the Eternal Christ, 1916; The Upanishads and Life, 1917; Pantheism and the Value of Life, 1919; Theosophy and Christian Thought, 1922; The Vedānta and Modern Thought, 1928; Humanism and Christianity, 1945. *Recreations:* walking, gardening. *Address:* Rowanlea, Torphins, Aberdeenshire. *T.:* Torphins 330. [*Died* 16 *July* 1964.

USHER, Sir George Clemens, Kt., *cr.* 1942; M.Am.Soc.M.E.; F.Inst.F.; *b.* 20 Dec. 1889; *s.* of Thomas Clemens and Mary Usher; *m.* 1st, Constance, *d.* of Dr. J. H. Woods; two *s.* one *d.*; 2nd, Nora Kathleen, *d.* of Charles A. Bates. *Educ.:* Malvern College; France and Germany. After studying engineering in Germany went to U.S. to become General Manager of Green Fuel Economiser Co.; returned to England, 1921, and was associated with founding of well-known firm of International Combustion, Ltd., of which Company he was formerly Man. Dir.; in 1937 founded Aberdare Cables, Ltd., as a successful pioneer effort to relieve unemployment in a Distressed Area. Controller of Light Alloys and Magnesium for Ministry of Aircraft Production; Director-General of Material Production for same Ministry; subsequently Director-General of Tank Supply, and in this capacity visited U.S. and Canada, 1942, as Member of British Tank Mission. *Recreations:* farming, fishing, shooting, etc. *Address:* Fordoun, Nottingham Road, Natal, South Africa. *T.:* Nottingham Road 23. *Clubs:* Flyfishers'; Port Elizabeth (South Africa; Victoria Club (Pietermaritzburg).

[*Died* 6 *Oct.* 1963.

USHER, Herbert Brough, C.B. 1948; Deputy Secretary, War Damage Commission, 1946-57; Central Land Board, 1948-57; *b.* 5 Oct. 1892; *o. c.* of late Herbert Usher, Market Weighton, Yorks; *m.* 1923, Grace, *d.* of Robert Barker, Todmorden; three *d.* *Educ.:* Haileybury; Trinity Hall, Cambridge. 1st Cl. Historical Tripos, Part I, 1914; served European War, France and Mesopotamia, Middlesex Regt. 1914-18, Captain. B.A. 1919; Assistant Editor, Westminster Gazette, 1919; Candidate (Labour) South Leicester, 1924 and 1929; Personal Private Sec. to Prime Minister, 1929-35; Treasury, 1936; Principal, 1938; Assistant Secretary, 1940; Under-Secretary, War Damage Commn. 1946. *Address:* 85 Riverview Gardens, Barnes, S.W.13. *T.:* Riverside 1143. *Club:* Oxford and Cambridge. [*Died* 6 *April* 1969.

USHER, Sir (Robert) Stuart, 4th Bt., *cr.* 1899, of Norton, Midlothian, and Wells, Roxburgh; Farming 640 acres; *b.* 19 April 1898; 3rd *s.* of Sir Robert Usher 2nd Bt. and late Katharine Scott, *d.* of James Turnbull, of Edinburgh; *S.* brother 1951; *m.* 1930, Gertrude Martha, 2nd *d.* of Lionel Barnard Sampson, Los Tres Montes, Villa Valeria, Prov. Cordoba, Argentina; two *s.* *Educ.:* Uppingham; R.M.C. Sandhurst. Inniskilling Dragoons, 1917-22; Cattle ranching in Argentina, 1924-47. *Recreations:* hunting and shooting. *Heir:* *s.* Peter Lionel, *b.* 1 Oct. 1931. *Address:* Hallrule, Hawick, Roxburghshire. *T.:* Bonchester Bridge 216. *Clubs:* Cavalry; Scottish Conservative (Edinburgh). [*Died* 10 *Nov.* 1962.

USHERWOOD, John F., M.A. Oxon; *e. s.* of George Usherwood, formerly of Ightham, Kent, and Blackheath, S.E.; *m.* *y. d.* of late William Crush, of Blackheath and Glasgow; two *s.* one *d.* *Educ.:* The Roan School, Greenwich; St. John's College, Oxford (History Exhibitioner). Assistant Master, Roan School, 1899 1902; St. Dunstan's College, Catford, 1902-27; Headmaster, the Brockley County School, S.E.4, 1927-31; Headmaster, St. Dunstan's College, Catford, S.E.6, 1931-38. Member, Modern Churchmen's Union. *Address:* Oakdene, Speldhurst, Kent. *T.:* Speldhurst 109. [*Died* 6 *Dec.* 1964.

UVAROV, Sir Boris (Petrovitch), K.C.M.G. 1961 (C.M.G. 1943); F.R.S. 1950; D.Sc.; Director Anti-Locust Research Centre, London, 1945-59, retd.; Consultant 1959; Pres., Royal Entomological Soc. of London, 1959-61; *b.* 5 Nov. 1889; *s.* of P. P. and A. V. Uvarov; *m.* 1910, Anna (decd.), *d.* of F. and E. Fedorov; one *s.* *Educ.:* St. Petersburg University. Entomologist, Crown Cotton Estate, Bairam-Ali, Transcaspia, 1911; Entomologist, Department of Agriculture, St. Petersburg, 1911-12; Director, Bureau of Entomology, Stavropol, 1912-15; Director, Bureau of Plant Protection, Tiflis, 1915-20; Lecturer in Zoology and Entomology, State University, Tiflis, 1919-20; Assistant Entomologist, Imperial Institute of Entomology, 1920; Senior Entomologist, 1927. *Publications:* Locusts and Grasshoppers, 1928; Insect Nutrition and Metabolism, 1928; Insects and Climate, 1931; Acrididae of European Russia, 1925; Acrididae of Central Asia, 1927; Anatomy and Physiology of Acrididae, 1948; Locust Research and Control, 1929-50, 1951; Grasshoppers and Locusts, 1966; about 400 articles and papers. *Address:* c/o Anti-Locust Research Centre, College House, Wright's Lane, W.8. *T.:* 01-937 8191. [*Died* 18 *March* 1970.

UZIELLI, Herbert Rex, C.I.E. 1931; J.P. Surrey; I.C.S., retired; *b.* 31 Aug. 1890. *Educ.:* Marlborough; Pembroke College, Cambridge. Secretary to Government Revenue Dept., Madras, 1934; Home Dept., 1938; retired, 1940. *Address:* Heathercroft, Totland Bay, Isle of Wight. [*Died* 20 *Jan.* 1961.

V

VACHELL, Benjamin G. L.; *see* Lampard-Vachell.

VAILLAND, Roger; writer; *b.* 16 Oct. 1907; *m.* 1952, Elisabeth Naldi; no *c.* *Educ.:* Sorbonne. Awarded Prix Interallié, 1945, Prix Goncourt, 1957. *Publications:* novels: Drôle de Jeu, 1945 (Eng. trans. Playing with Fire, 1948); Les Mauvais Coups, 1948 (Eng. trans. Turn of the Wheel, 1962); Bon pied Bon œil, 1950; Un jeune homme seul, 1952; Beau Masque, 1954; 325,000 francs, 1955; La Loi, 1957 (Eng. trans. The Law, 1958; filmed as Where the Hot Wind Blows, 1961); La Fête, 1960 (Eng. trans. The Sovereigns, 1960); La Truite, 1964 (Eng. trans. The Young Trout, 1965); play: Heloïse et Abelard, 1952. *Address:* Meillonnas (Ain), France. *T.:* Meillonnas 19. [*Died* 11 *May* 1965.

VAISEY, Dame Dorothy (May), D.C.V.O. 1962; O.B.E. 1955; General Secretary of Friends of the Poor and Gentlefolks Help, 1938-69; *o. d.* of Charles Arthur Whatmore; *m.* 1917, Rev. Francis Dent Vaisey (*d.* 1933); two *d.* *Educ.:* Ravenscroft, Eastbourne; also privately. *Address:* Middle School, Coldharbour, Nr. Dorking, Surrey. [*Died* 20 *Nov.* 1969.

VAISEY, Hon. Sir Harry Bevir; Kt. 1944; Judge of Chancery Division, High Court of Justice, 1944-60, retired; D.C.L. (Lambeth) 1939; *b* 22 June 1877; *e s.* of late Arthur William Vaisey Tring, Herts, *m* 1903, Eleonora Mary, *o. c* of Rev. Canon William Quennell; one *s* (one *d* decd.). *Educ:* Shrewsbury School; Hertford College, Oxford (M.A.); 1st class Classical Mod. 1898; 1st class Lit. Hum. 1900; Bar, Lincoln's Inn, 1901; K.C. 1925; Bencher, 1929; Vicar-General of Province of York, 1934-44; Chancellor of Derby and Wakefield Dioceses, 1928-44, of Diocese of Carlisle, 1930-44, and of York Diocese, 1934-44; Commissary-General of Diocese of Canterbury, 1942-44; Chm., London Diocesan Fund; Mem. Council, Keble College, Oxford, 1939-51; Chm., Herts Quarter Sessions, 1946-58; Treasurer Lincoln's Inn, 1950; Hon. Fellow, Hertford Coll. *Address:* 11 Ashley Gardens, S.W.1. [*Died* 24 *Nov.* 1965.

VAITHIANATHAN, Sir Kanthiah, Kt., *cr.* 1950; C.B.E. 1949; now retired; *b.* 23 July 1896; *s.* of Velauther Kanthiah, Kopay, and Thaiyalnayaki (*née* Chinniah); *m.* 1926, Puvaneswari (*née* Sanmugam); two *s.* two *d.* *Educ.:* St. Joseph's Coll., Colombo; King's College, London. Ceylon Civil Service, 1923; held several judicial appointments under Ceylon Govt.; Secretary to Minister of Home Affairs, 1931; Secretary to Minister of Communications and Works, 1936; Commissioner of Ceylon Government Supplies in India, 1942, and represented Ceylon Govt. in India; Government Agent, Central Province, Ceylon, 1947; Permanent Sec., Min. of Defence and External Affairs, Oct. 1947-53; Minister of Industries, Housing and Social Services, 1953-56, also Senator. *Recreations:* travel; archæology; Hindu philosophy. *Address:* Senthil, Pedris Road, Colombo 3, Ceylon. *T.:* Colombo 4978. *Club:* Orient (Colombo). [*Died* 27 *Aug.* 1965.

VALE, (Henry) Edmund (Theodoric), M.A.; Author and Topographer; *b* 1888; *s.* of Rev. W. T. Vale and Catharine Emma, *d.* of

Edmund Charles Buxton; *m.* 1924, Ruth Madeline Hutchings; one *s.* two *d.* *Educ.:* privately; St. John's College, Cambridge. Organising Secretary Toys Hill Farm School Experiment, 1913; served 1914-18, R.E. Signals; 1939-45, Royal Signals. *Publications:* Pixie Pool, 1911; Elfin Chaunts and Railway Rhythms, 1914,; By Shank and by Crank, 1924; Porth Smuggler, 1926; Roc, a dog's-eye view of war, 1930; Shipshape, 1931; The Offing, 1932; See for Yourself, 1933; Local Colour, 1934; The World of Wales, 1935; The Seas and Shores of England, 1936; North Country, 1937; How to See England, 1937; The Way of Ships, 1938; Straw into Gold, 1939; How to look at old Buildings, 1940; Curiosities of Town and Countryside, 1940; Ancient England, 1941; Shropshire, 1948; The World of Cotton, 1950; Churches, 1954; Abbeys and Priories, 1955; Cathedrals, 1956; Cambridge and its Colleges, 1958; The Mail-coach Men, 1960; An Outline of English Architecture, 1966; The Harveys of Hayle, 1966. Contributions to numerous periodicals; Local Information-sheets. *Address:* Nant Ffrancon Pass, Bangor, N Wales. *T.:* Bethesda 254. [*Died* 13 *March* 1969.

VALENTINE; *see* Pechey, Archibald T.

VALENTINE, Alfred Buyers, C.B. 1949; Under Secretary, Ministry of Housing and Local Government, 1951-56 (retd.) (Ministry of Town and Country Planning, 1946-51); *b.* 15 June 1894; *s.* of late Robert and Hannah Valentine, Aberdeen; *m.* 1924, Violet Elise, *d.* of late Thomas and Marie Chegwidden, Bournemouth; one *s.* one *d.* *Educ.:* Aberdeen Grammar School; Aberdeen Univ. M.A. 1919 (Hons. Classics Cl. I). Served European War, 1914-18, France, German and Portuguese East Africa, Lieut. Gordon Highlanders; entered Home Civil Service, 1920; Secretary, British Deleg., Internat. Labour organisation, 1921-23; Private Secretary to late Sir David Shackleton and to late Lord Rushcliffe, 1923-28; i.d.c., 1932; Assistant Commissioner for Special Areas in Scotland, 1937-40; principal assistant secretary Ministry of Supply, 1940-41, Ministry of Home Security, 1941-45. *Recreations:* gardening, family bridge, varied voluntary social work. *Address:* 40 Clifford Manor Rd., Guildford, Sy. *T.:* 5099. [*Died* 21 *Feb.* 1970.

VALENTINE, Charles Wilfrid, M.A. (Cantab.), D.Phil. (St. Andrews); Hon. F.B.Ps.S.; Professor of Education, Univ. of Birmingham, 1919-46, now Emeritus; Editor of the British Journal of Educational Psychology, 1931-55; *b.* 1879; *s.* of Rev. Henry Valentine; *m.* 1911, Ethel Rothwell (*d.* 1956), *d.* of Arthur Jackson, Moss Side, Southport; three *s.* one *d.* *Educ.:* Nottingham High School; Preston Grammar School; University College, Aberystwyth (Exhibitioner), graduating B.A. at London University; Downing College, Cambridge (Foundation Scholar in Moral Sciences), double first-class honours (Philosophy and Psychology). Seven years' teaching experience in various secondary schools in England and Wales (including St. Olave's, Southwark); five years Lecturer in Psychology to St. Andrews Provincial Committee, and four years (concurrently) Assistant in Education in the University of St. Andrews; five years Professor of Education in the Queen's University of Belfast. Chairman of the Birmingham Higher Education Sub-Committee, 1919-25; Pres. of Psychology Section, British Association, 1930; President British Psychological Soc., 1947, 1948. *Publications:* Experimental Psychology of Beauty, 1962; The Normal Child and Some of His Abnormalities, 1956; Reasoning Tests for Higher Levels of Intelligence, 1954; Parents and Children, 1953; Abnormalities in Normal Children, 1951; Psychology: and its Bearing on Education, 1950, 2nd edn., 1960; Latin through English: a Basic Vocabulary, 1948; Psychology and Mental Health, 1947; Intelligence Tests for Children, 6th edn. (revised), 1958; The Human Factor in the Army, 2nd edn. 1953; Principles of Army Instruction, 1942; The Psychology of Early Childhood, 3rd edn. 1946; The Difficult Child and the Problem of Discipline, 4th edn. revised, 1947; Examinations and the Examinee, 1938; Latin: its Place and Value in Education, 1935; The Reliability of Examinations: An Enquiry, 1932 (out of print); Dreams and the Unconscious, 1921; second edition, 1928, under new title, The New Psychology of the Unconscious; Introduction to Experimental Psychology, 5th edn. enlarged, 1953; Theological Aspects of Lotze's Philosophy (St. Andrews Quincentenary Essays), 1911; articles. *Address:* The White House, Wythall, Worcs. *T.:* Wythall 3154. [*Died* 26 *May* 1964

VALLERY-RADOT PASTEUR, Louis; Grand Croix de la Légion d'Honneur; Croix de Guerre, 1914-18; Médaille de la Résistance (avec rosette) 1944; Medal of Freedom (with palm); Medal for distinguished achievements (New York University); Member of the French Academy; Member of the Acad. of Med.; Professor honorarius of Clinical Medicine, Faculty of Medicine, Paris; *b.* Paris, 13 May 1886; *s.* of René Vallery-Radot and Marie-Louise Pasteur; *m.* 1937, Jacqueline de Longchamps. *Educ.:* Lycée Louis-le-Grand, Paris. *Publications:* Mémoires d'un non-conformiste; Pasteur inconnu; Science et humanisme; Médecine à l'échelle humaine; Médecine d'hier et d'aujourd'hui; Lettres de Claude Debussy à sa femme Emma; Tel était Debussy; Héros de l'esprit français; Quelques grands problèmes de la médecine contemporaine; Pour la terre de France par la douleur et la mort; articles, in particular on kidney diseases and on allergic diseases. Publisher of Pasteur's complete works. *Address:* 24 Avenue Gabriel, Paris 8e. *T.:* Elysées 21.16. *Clubs:* Automobile Club de France, Maison de l'Amerique Latine (Paris). [*Died* 9 *Oct.* 1970.

VALLUY, Général d'Armée Jean Étienne; French Army, retd.; Grand Croix de la Légion d'Honneur, 1948; Croix de Guerre, 1914-18 and 1939-45; Croix de Guerre des Théâtres d'Opérations Extérieures; Médailles Coloniales; *b.* Rive-de-Gier (Loire), France, 15 May 1899; *m.* 1931, Marie Bourdillon; one *s.* three *d.* *Educ.:* Saint-Cyr Military Academy. War College, 1927. Captain 1929; Major 1937; Lt.-Col. 1941; Colonel 1942; Brig.-Gen. 1944; Maj.-Gen. 1946; Lt.-Gen. 1947; Gen. 1955. Appointments in: Syria, China, Morocco, French W. Africa, Algeria, Indo-China, U.S.A. C.-in-C. and High Comr. in Indo-China, 1946-1948; Inspector Colonial Troops, 1948-52; Dep. Chief of Staff to Supreme Allied Commander Europe, 1952-53; French Rep. to Standing Group N.A.T.O., Sept. 1953-Oct. 1956; Commander-in-Chief, Allied Forces, Central Europe, 1956-60. D.S.O., Gt. Britain; Legion of Merit, U.S.A. (Comdr.). *Address:* 56 rue de la Rochefoucauld, Paris 9e, France. [*Died* 4 *Jan.* 1970.

VANCE, Right Rev. Dr. John Gabriel; Hon. Canon of Westminster since 1933; Domestic Prelate to the Pope, 1938; *b.* 12 Nov. 1885; *s.* of Thomas Vance, of the ancient family of Vaux, and Margaret Casey. *Educ.:* St. Edmund's College; Cambridge and Louvain. Studied at Institute of Actuaries, 1902-4; at St. Edmund's (Theological) College, 1904-7; at Cambridge, 1907-10 (M.A. 1913); Louvain, degree of D.Ph. (avec la plus grande distinction), 1912; Thesis on experimental psychology; F.B.Ps.S.; Priest, 1911; Visit to the German Univs.; Professor of Philosophy, Old Hall, 1912; Vice-President of St. Edmund's College,

1919-26; Chaplain to the Forces, 1917-19 (despatches); special mission to Czecho-Slovakia, 1919-20; Consultor of the Metropolitan Consistory of Prague, May 1920; Second Mission to Czechoslovakia, 1920-21; Burge Lecturer, 1934; Chairman of Finance Board and Schools' Commission of the Archdiocese of Westminster, 1935-44. *Publications:* Reality and Truth, 1917; Adrian Fortescue: a Memoir (with Hon. Sir John Fortescue), 1924; A Mirror of Personality, 1927; Honour: The Sovereignty of God; Leadership and Life; numerous articles on philosophy. *Address:* Crawley St. Mary, Crawley Down, Sussex. *T.:* Copthorne 2505. *Club:* Athenæum. [*Died* 29 *March* 1968.

VANDEN HEUVEL, Frederick, C.M.G. 1945; O.B.E. 1918; *b.* 24 Nov. 1885; *s.* of late Count William Vanden Heuvel; *m.* 1927, Katherine O'Leary Colbert, M.A.; no *c.* *Educ.:* Privately; Univ. Coll. London. Various Directorships; formerly Managing Director J. C. Eno, Ltd. Served European War, 1914-18, retired with rank Major; Attaché British Legation, Berne, 1940-45; British Embassy, Rome, 1947. *Recreations:* golf, travel. *Address:* Beaufortwood, Sunningdale. *T.:* Ascot 62. *Clubs:* Bath, Garrick; Sunningdale. [*Died* 25 *April* 1963.

VANDEPEER, Sir Donald (Edward), K.C.B., *cr.* 1946; K.B.E., *cr.* 1941; *b.* 21 Sept. 1890; *s.* of Thomas E. Vandepeer; *m.* 1915, Florence Scott; two *d.* *Educ.:* Strand School, King's College; London Univ. (B.Sc.). Entered Civil Service, 1908; served European War, 1914-18, Civil Service Rifles, Worcestershire Regiment, West African Frontier Force, Cameroons, 1915-16; German East Africa, 1916-18; Private Secretary to Permanent Secretaries and successive Ministers of Agriculture, 1922-34; participated in Ottawa Conf., 1932, League of Nations Assembly (Geneva), 1936; led U.K. Deleg. to F.A.O. Conf., 1947 (Geneva), 1949 (Washington), 1953 and 1955 (Rome), and World's Poultry Congress, 1948 (Copenhagen). Permanent Sec., Min. of Agric. and Fisheries, 1945-52; retired, 1952. *Address:* 15 Marina Court, Exmouth, Devon. [*Died* 6 *Oct.* 1968.

VANDRY, Rt. Rev. Mgr. Ferdinand; *see* Addenda: II.

VANIER, General the Rt. Hon. Georges Philias, P.C. 1963; D.S.O. 1919; M.C. and Bar; Hon. LL.D.: Governor General of Canada since 1959; *b.* 23 April 1888; *s.* of Philias Vanier and Margaret Maloney, both of Montreal; *m.* 1921, Pauline, *d.* of Hon. Mr. Justice Charles Archer; four *s.* one *d.* *Educ.:* Loyola College, Montreal; Laval University (B.A. 1906, LL.B. 1911). Called to Bar, Quebec, 1911: served European War, 1915-18 (wounded, despatches, D.S.O., M.C. with Bar, 1915 Star, Chevalier of the Legion of Honour); A.D.C. to Governor-General of Canada, 1921-22 and 1926-28; commanded Royal 22nd Regiment, Citadel, Quebec, 1925-28; Canada's Representative on Permanent Advisory Commission for Military, Naval and Air Questions, and on Preparatory Disarmament Commission, League of Nations, 1928-31; Canadian delegate to diplomatic Conf. for revision of Geneva (1906) Red Cross Convention, 1929; Member Canadian Delegation London Naval Conference, 1930; one of the Canadian Delegates to the Assembly of the League of Nations, Sept. 1930; Secretary, Office of High Commissioner for Canada, London, 1931-38; Technical Adviser to the Canadian Delegation to the Assembly of the League of Nations, Sept. 1936; a Canadian member of the Coronation Commissions appointed to consider arrangements of common interest to the British Commonwealth of Nations in connection with the Coronation ceremonies of King Edward VIII and of King George VI, July and Dec. 1936; Canadian Minister to France, 1939-40; Member Joint Board on Defence, United States—Canada, 1940-42; Officer Commanding Quebec Military District, 1941-42; Canadian Minister to the Allied Governments established in the United Kingdom, 1943; Canadian Representative to the French Committee of National Liberation, London, 1943; Algiers, 1944; Canadian Ambassador to France, 1944-53; retired from Diplomatic Service, 1953. Canadian deleg. to Peace Conf., Paris, 1946, to draft Treaties with Italy, Roumania, Hungary, and Finland, and signatory for Canada, Paris, February 1947; one of Canadian delegates to Assembly of U.N.O., Paris, September 1948; Mem. Académie des Sciences Morales et Politiques de l'Institut de France; Member, The Canada Council, 1957-59; Membre Académie des Belles Lettres et Arts (Rouen); Director: The Bank of Montreal, 1954-59; Crédit Foncier Franco-Canadien, 1954-59. Colonel Royal 22e Regt., 1958-64. Freeman, citoyen d'honneur: Lille, 1945; Dieppe, 1946; Dijon, 1947; Honfleur, 1949; Douai, 1951; Caen, 1954; Citoyen de Paris, 1955; Granby, 1959. Hon. LL.D.: Univs.: Ottawa, 1945, Laval, Lyon, 1946, Montreal, 1955, Toronto, B.C., McGill, 1960; St. Joseph's, Moncton, 1961; Laurentian Univ., Sudbury, 1961; Assumption Univ., Windsor, 1961; Saint Mary's Univ. Halifax, 1966; Univ. of New Brunswick, Fredericton, 1966; Memorial Univ., St. John's, Nfld., 1966; Hon. D.M.Sc., R.M.C., Kingston, Ont., 1961; Hon. D.C.L., Univ. of Western Ont., London, Ont., 1960. K.St.J.; Prior of the Order of St. John of Jerusalem in Canada. Knight Grand Cross of Order of Malta. Chevalier Legion of Honour, 1917; Commander Legion of Merit (U.S.), 1946. *Address:* Government House, Ottawa, Canada. *Clubs:* Mount Royal, University (Montreal); York (Toronto); Rideau (Ottawa). [*Died* 5 *March* 1967.

VAN LARE, William Bedford; C.M.G. 1960; G.M. 1968; LL.B. (Lond.); High Commissioner for the Republic of Ghana in Canada, since 1966; *b.* 7 Sept. 1904; *y. s.* of late W. L. Van Lare, Mercantile Agent, Legion of Honour (France), and late Wilhemina Fiawonu Amegashie, *d.* of Chief Amegashie Aweku I of Keta; *m.* 1953, Aline, *o. d.* of late Fernd. Brandenbourger, Bar-le-duc, and of late Eva Brandenbourger, Accra. *Educ.:* Mfantsipim Sch., Cape Coast; Univ. College, University of London. Master, Mfantsipim School, Cape Coast, 1925-27; School Teacher, Education Dept., Gold Coast, 1928-32. Called to the Bar, Lincoln's Inn, 1937. Gold Coast: Legal Practitioner, Supreme Court, 1937-43; District Magistrate, 1943-52; Actg. Chief Registrar, Supreme Court, and Actg. Registrar, W. Af. Court of Appeal, 1948, 1950; Actg. Puisne Judge, 1950-51; Puisne Judge, 1952-57; Judge of the Supreme Court of Ghana, 1957-63; Chairman: Committee of Enquiry, Constitutional Matter, Akwapim State and Western Nzima. 1952; Representational and Electoral Reform Commn., 1953. Cons. Ed. and Chm. Editorial Bd., West African Law Reports, 1955-60; Chairman: Cttee. of Enquiry, Status of Chiefs and Composition House of Chiefs, Trans-Volta/Togoland, 1956-57; Regional Constitutional Commn., Ghana, 1957-1958; Actg. Chief Justice, 1957-58 and on occasions, 1959-63; Actg. Gov.-General and C. in C., Ghana, Jan. 1958. Leader, Goodwill Mission to neighbouring French-speaking states, after Feb. 1966; Chm., Conf. of neighbouring states for re-establishment of friendly relations and re-opening of borders, May 1966; Mem., Ghana delegns.: to U.N. Gen. Assembly, 1966-67; to Special Cttee. of U.N. on Friendly Relations, etc., Geneva, 1967 (Vice-Chm., 1968). Foundation Mem. and Treasurer, Ghana Acad. of Sciences, 1959-62 (Elected Fellow, 1963). *Recreations:* golf and gardening. *Address:* Ghana High Commission, 85 Range Road, Ottawa, Canada. [*Died* 3 *Sept.* 1969.

VAN MILTENBURG, Most Rev. Mgr. Alcuin, O.F.M.; Archbishop-Bishop of Hyderabad (R.C.), since 1958; *b.* Harmelen, Utrecht, Holland, 14 Sept. 1909. *Educ.:* Franciscan Mission College, Sittard, Holland. Ordained Priest, 1935; Asst. Chaplain, St. Patrick's, Karachi, 1935; Parish Priest, Nawabshah, 1940; First Chaplain, St. Patrick's, Karachi, 1941; Superior of the Mission, 1943, Bishop, 1948; Archbishop and Apostolic Delegate for Pakistan, 1950, Chargé d'Affaires of the Holy See in Pakistan, 1952. *Address:* St. Francis Xavier's Cathedral, near Tilak Incline, Hyderabad (Sind), Pakistan. [*Died* 14 *March* 1966.

VANNECK, Hon. Andrew Nicolas Armstrong, M.C.; *b.* 21 July 1890; *s.* of late Hon. W. A. Vanneck; *m.* 1939, Britta, *o. d.* of late Count Nils Bonde, Stockholm; one *s.* one *d.* *Educ.:* Harrow. Scots Guards; served European War, 1914-18 (M.C.). Governor of Framlingham College, Suffolk. *Address:* Heveningham Hall, Halesworth, Suffolk. *T.:* Ubbeston 355. *Club:* Turf. [*Died* 20 *Feb.* 1965.

VAN NECK, Capt. Stephen Hugh, C.V.O. 1948 (M.V.O. 1938); M.C. 1917; Chief Constable of Norfolk, 1928-56; *b.* 23 Nov. 1889; 3rd *s.* of late Charles Van Neck, Lily Hill, Bracknell, Berks; unmarried. *Educ.:* Wellington. Served on Great Eastern Railway, North-Western Rly. (India), Canadian Pacific Rly., 1908-14; served European War and Army of the Rhine, 1914-21; Reserve of Officers, 1921; attached Surrey Constabulary, 1921-25; raised, trained and organised War Dept. Constabulary as First Chief Constable, 1925-28; Major, 1927; returned to H.M. Forces, 1940. D.L. Norfolk, 1956. *Recreation:* shooting. *Address:* Overbury House, Wroxham, Norfolk. *T.:* Wroxham 251. *Clubs:* International Sportsmen's; Norfolk County (Norwich). [*Died* 30 *April* 1963.

VAN ROEY, His Eminence Joseph Ernest; Cardinal-Archbishop of Malines since 1926; Primate of Belgium; *b.* Vorsselaer, Province Antwerp, 13 Jan. 1874. *Educ.:* Herenthals College; Malines Seminary. Priest, 1897; Doctor and Master of Theology, Louvain University, 1903; Professor Louvain University, 1901; Hon. Professor, 1907; Vicar-General, Archdiocese of Malines, 1907; Apostolic Protonotary, 1924; Cardinal Priest, 1927. *Address:* Archevêché, Malines, Belgium. *T.A.:* Malines. *T.:* 015-16501. [*Died* 6 *Aug.* 1961.

VAN VECHTEN, Carl; author; *b.* Cedar Rapids, Iowa, 17 June 1880; *s.* of Charles Duane Van Vechten and Ada Amanda Fitch; *m.* 1st 1907, Anna Elizabeth Snyder; divorced, 1912; 2nd, 1914, Fania Marinoff, Russian actress. *Educ.:* University of Chicago; Ph.B. 1903. Assistant musical critic, New York Times, 1906-7, 1910-13; Paris Correspondent New York Times, 1908-1909; editor of Programme Notes Symphony Society of New York, 1910-11; dramatic critic New York Press, 1913-14; contributor, musical biographies to revised edition Century Dictionary, 1911; Member Art Commission, Fisk University; Member of Board: Cosmopolitan Symphony Orchestra; W.C. Handy Foundation for the Blind, 1952; Life Member Negro Actor's Guild; Founder of the James Weldon Johnson Memorial Collection of Negro Arts and Letters at Yale Univ. Library, 1941 (awarded title of Hon. Curator 1946); Founder: Carl Van Vechten Collection of Books and Manuscripts at the New York Public Library, 1941; George Gershwin Memorial Collection of Music and Musical Literature at Fisk Univ. Library, 1944; Founder of Jerome Bowers Peterson Memorial Collection of Photographs of Celebrated Negroes by Carl Van Vechten, at Jonson Gallery, University of New Mexico, 1955; Rose McClendon Memorial Collection of Photographs of Celebrated Negroes by Carl Van Vechten, at Howard University, 1946; Anna Marble Pollock Memorial Library of Books about Cats, at Yale University Library, 1947; Florine Stettheimer Mem. Lib. of books about the Fine Arts at Fisk Univ., 1949. Captain at American Theatre Wing Stage Door Canteen in New York, 1942-45, and at their Merchant Seamen's Club, 1943-45. Hon. Doctor of Litt. Fisk Univ., 1955. Mem. Nat. Inst. of Arts and Letters, 1961. *Publications:* Composer: Five Old English Ditties, 1904. Author: Music after the Great War, 1915; Music and Bad Manners, 1916; Interpreters and Interpretations, 1917; The Merry-go-round, 1918; The Music of Spain, 1918; In the Garret, 1920; A Letter by Morgan Lewis Fitch, 1920; Interpreters, 1920; The Tiger in the House, 1920; Lords of the Housetops, 1921; Peter Whiffle—His Life and Works, 1922; The Blind Bow-Boy, 1923; The Tattooed Countess, 1924 (made into musical by Coleman Dowell, prod. New York, 1961); Red, 1925; Firecrackers, 1925; Excavations, 1926; Nigger Heaven, 1926; Spider Boy, 1928; Feathers, 1930; Parties, 1930; Sacred and Profane Memories, 1932; Nijinsky, 1946; Isadora Duncan, 1947; Pavlova, 1947; Alfred A. Knopf at 60, 1952; Fragments from an Unwritten Autobiography, 1955; Gardenias for Alicia, 1960; Between Friends, 1961; editor Selected Writings of Gertrude Stein, 1946; editor Last Operas and Plays by Gertrude Stein, 1949; Photographer, 1932-64; (editor) Two: Gertrude Stein and her brother, 1951; Mrs. Reynolds, 1952; Bee-Time Vine, 1953; As Fine as Melanctha, 1954; Painted Lace, 1955; Stanzas in Meditation, 1956; Book of Alphabets and Birthdays, 1957. *Relevant publications:* A Bibliography of the Writings of Carl Van Vechten, Scott Cunningham, 1924; Carl Van Vechten and the Twenties, Edward Lueders, 1955; Carl Van Vechten, a Bibliography, Klaus W. Jonas, 1955; Carl Van Vechten, a critical biography by Dr. Edward Lueders, 1964. *Address:* 146 Central Park West, New York City 23. [*Died* 21 *Dec.* 1964.

VARCOE, Frederick Percy, C.M.G. 1946; Q.C.; LL.D.; lately Deputy Minister of Justice and Deputy Attorney-General of Canada; *b.* Toronto, Canada, 1 Oct. 1889; *s.* of Frederick Richard and Charlotte Varcoe; *m.* 1928, Helen, *d.* of Robert Stewart, Ottawa; two *s.* *Educ.:* Harbord Collegiate; University of Toronto; Osgoode Hall. *Publication:* Constitution of Canada, 1965. *Recreation:* golf. *Clubs:* University (Ottawa), Royal Ottawa Golf. [*Died* 15 *Oct.* 1965.

VASKESS, Henry Harrison, C.M.G. 1946; O.B.E. 1938; *b.* 15 July 1891; *m.* 1922; two *s.* Entered Colonial Service, 1911; Chief Secretary, Western Pacific High Commission, 1929-48; Second Commissioner for the U.K. on the South Pacific Commission, 1948-59; retired, 1959. *Address:* 15 Des Vœux Road, Suva, Fiji. [*Died* 7 *July* 1969.

VASSE, Air Commodore Gordon Herbert, C.B.E. 1945; Retired, 1954, as Commandant Royal Observer Corps; *b.* 23 Apr. 1899; *s.* of H. A. Vasse and K. Vasse (*née* Hill), Herne Bay, Kent; *m.* 1922, Kathleen Sophia Igglesden, Dover; one *s.* one *d.* (and one *d.* decd.). *Educ.:* Goudhurst, Kent. R.N.A.S., R.A.F., 1916-19; R.A.F., 1921-54; O.C. Air Fighting Devel. Unit, 1937-41; Gp. Capt., 1940; O.C. R.A.F., Duxford, 1941; Dir. of Air Tactics, Air Min., 1941-44; Air Cdre. 1942; Dep. S.A.S.O., Air Command, South East Asia, 1944; S.A.S.O.: No. 221 Gp., 1944-45; S.A.S.O., R.A.F. Burma, 1945-46; Air Cdre.

Comdg. R.A.F. Seleter, 1946; A.O.C.: No. 21 Gp., 1946-47; No. 25 Gp., 1947-48; No. 63 Gp., 1948-51; Comdt., Royal Observer Corps, 1951-54. *Address:* Kearsney, 15 Castle La., Chandler's Ford, Hants. *T.:* 3909. [*Died* 26 *March* 1965.

VAUCHER, Paul; Professor of Modern History at the Sorbonne, 1945-56; Chevalier de la Légion d'Honneur; *b.* 1887; *s.* of Professor E. Vaucher, Dean of the Faculty of Theology, Paris; *m.* Antoinette Lauth (*d.* 1964). *Educ.:* Sorbonne; École libre des Sciences Politiques. Licencié de Philosophie, 1906; agrégé d'histoire et de géographie, 1912; docteur ès lettres, Paris 1925; teacher at schools in Niort, Mulhouse, Strasbourg, Prytanée Militaire de la Flèche, 1913-20; lecturer at the University of Lund, Sweden, 1918; lauréat de l'Institut; Professor of Modern French History, and Institutions, University of London, 1922-42: Secretary to the Council for Social Research (University of Paris); lecturer at the New School for Social Research, New York, 1941; head of the Educational Services and Conseiller Culturel at the French Embassy, London, 1942-45. *Publications:* Robert Walpole et la politique de Fleury, 1925; La Crise du ministère Walpole, 1733-34, 1925; Le Monde anglo-saxon au XIXe siècle, 1927; Post-War France, 1934; L'Opinion britannique et la guerre italo-éthiopienne, 1936; Contribution to History of England in the XIXth Century, by Élie Halévy, vol. iv, 1947; The XVIIIth Century in the European Inheritance, vol. iii, 1954; Recueil des Instructions aux Ambassadeurs et Ministres de France en Angleterre, 1697-1791, 1965; also articles in Revue des Sciences Politiques, etc. *Address:* 180 rue de Grenelle, Paris. [*Died* 11 *Oct.* 1966.

VAUGHAN, Dame Helen C. I. G.; *see* Gwynne-Vaughan.

VAUGHAN, John Henry, M.C. 1917; retired; *b.* 9 Feb. 1892; *s.* of late Herbert Vaughan, Wooburn, Bucks; *m.* 1925, Thelma Collingridge, 3rd *d.* of Roland Green; three *s.* *Educ.:* Eastbourne College; Corpus Christi Coll., Cambridge. Served H.M. Military Forces Sept. 1914-April 1921; Administrative Officer, Zanzibar, 1921. Called to Bar, 1929. Resident Magistrate, Zanzibar, 1929; Asst. Attorney-General, 1933; Solicitor-General, Tanganyika, 1936. Temp. Lieut.-Colonel, Occupied Enemy Territory Admin., as Dep. Legal Adviser, 1941; Pioneer Corps (E.A.), 1942. Legal Adviser, Cyrenaica, 1944. Attorney-General, Fiji, 1945; K.C. (Fiji), 1948; Chief Justice, Fiji, 1949-52. *Publications:* Dual Jurisdiction in Zanzibar, 1935. Papers in Ibis, on Zanzibar birds. *Recreations:* riding, ornithology, gardening. *Address:* Dell House, Wooburn, High Wycombe, Bucks. [*Died* 16 *April* 1965.

VAUGHAN, Robert Charles, C.M.G. 1946; Dr.Sc.; Chairman, 1942-50 and President, 1941-50, Canadian National Rlys., retd. 1950; Director: Belding-Corticelli Silk Co., Ltd.; Provincial Transport Co.; Sherwin-Williams Co. of Canada; Commonwealth Internat. Corp.; Leverage Fund of Canada; Canadian Internat. Growth Fund; *b.* Toronto, 1 Dec. 1883; *s.* of Robert Crawford Vaughan and Blanchard McCarthy; *m.* Henriette Rosalie Cheadle; two *s.* two *d.* *Educ.:* Toronto Public Schs., High Schs. and Business College, 1898, messenger, railway service-clerk and stenographer; worked in Grand Trunk Railway freight sheds, 1902; joined Canadian Northern Railway, 1902; Secretary and Chief Clerk to Vice-President and General Manager, 1903; Assistant to Vice-President and General Manager, 1910, also had charge Royal Line Steamers from Montreal to United Kingdom; Asst. to President, Canadian National Railways and Canadian Government Merchant Marine at Toronto, 1918; Vice-President in charge of purchases and stores and steamships, 1920; Chairman Defence Purchasing Board at Ottawa, 1939; President, Canadian National System, Central Vermont Railway, Grand Trunk Western Railroad, Canadian National (West Indies) Steamships; ex-Director Trans-Canada Air Lines; ex-Pres., Railway Association of Canada; Governor Montreal General Hosp. K.G.St.J., 1947. *Address:* 1460 McGregor Avenue, Montreal 1, Canada. *Clubs:* Granite, National (Toronto); St. James's, Royal Montreal Golf (Montreal, P.Q.). [*Died* 5 *Jan.* 1966.

VAVASOUR, Captain Sir Leonard (Pius), 4th Bt., *cr.* 1828; late R.N.; *b.* 22 Sept. 1881; *s.* of 3rd Bt. and Mary Teresa, *d.* of Edward J. Weld, Lulworth Castle, Wareham, Dorset; *S.* father, 1915; *m.* 1913, Ellice Margaret, *e. d.* of Henry Ellis Hay Nelson; one *s.* two *d.* *Educ.:* Downside. Joined Royal Navy, 1895, Commander, 1915; Captain, retired list, 1927. *Heir:* *s.* Geoffrey William, D.S.C. 1944, Commander R.N. retd. [*b.* 5 Sept. 1914; *m.* 1940, Joan Millicent Kirkland (marriage dissolved, 1946), *d.* of Arthur John Robb; two *d.*]. *Address:* 15 St. Mark's Road, Alverstoke, Hants. *T.:* Gosport 81857. *Club:* Naval and Military. [*Died* 14 *Sept.* 1961.

VAWDREY, Colonel George, C.B. 1926; C.M.G. 1916; C.B.E. 1919; *b.* 6 July 1872; *s.* of Dr. George Vawdrey of Hayle, later of Farnborough, Hants. *Educ.:* Mannamead School, Plymouth; R.M.C., Sandhurst. 2nd Lieut. Leicestershire Regiment, 1892; Army Service Corps, 1894; served South African Campaign (Queen's medal with 5 clasps, King's medal with 2 clasps, despatches, Bt.-Major); Occupation of Crete, 1897-98; European War, 1914-18 (despatches four times, C.M.G., C.B.E., Order of the Crown of Italy, 3rd Class); retired pay, 1926. *Address:* Crill House, Budock, Falmouth, Cornwall. *T.:* Falmouth 994. [*Died* 28 *July* 1961.

VEITCH, William, C.B.E. 1955; J.P. County of the City of Aberdeen; Chevalier Legion of Honour; Dir. Aberdeen Jls. Ltd.; *b.* Edinburgh, 5 Mar. 1885; *m.* 1911, Jean Grant Blair; one *d.* *Educ.:* George Watson's College, Edinburgh. Edinburgh Evening Dispatch; London Editor, Aberdeen Daily Journal, 1910-22; Press and Journal, 1923-1927; Editor-in-Chief and Managing Dir. Aberdeen Jls. Ltd., 1927-57; Dir. Kemsley Newspapers Ltd., 1937-57; Hon. General Treasurer National Union of Journalists, 1917-23; Chairman Parliamentary Press Gallery, 1923. President Scottish Daily Newspaper Society, 1942-45. *Recreation:* motoring. *Address:* 7 Royal Court, Aberdeen. *T.:* Aberdeen 37376. [*Died* 12 *Aug.* 1968.

VEITCH, Maj.-Gen. (Hon.) William Lionel Douglas, C.B. 1952; C.B.E. 1944 (O.B.E. 1938); R.E. (retd.); *b.* 21 Nov. 1901; *s.* of William Veitch, M.A., T.D., and Helen Flowerdew Lowson. *Educ.:* Edinburgh Academy; Royal Military Academy, Woolwich. Commissioned in Royal Engineers, 1921; joined K.G.O. Bengal Sappers and Miners, 1924; commanded Bengal Sappers and Miners, 1944-46; Dep. Engineer-in-Chief, Pakistan, 1947-50; operations in N.W. Frontier, 1931 and 1937 (despatches twice, medal and clasps); served War of 1939-45: C.R.E. 19 Indian Division, 1941; S.O., I.A.H.Q. 1942. Col. Commandant, Royal Pakistan Engineers, 1952-1959; Engineer-in-Chief, Pakistan Army, 1950-53; retd. 1953. *Recreation:* fishing. *Address:* Tweedside, St. Boswells, Roxburghshire. *Clubs:* Naval and Military; Punjab (Lahore). [*Died* 13 *Dec.* 1969.

VELÁZQUEZ, Dr. Carlos María; Ambassador of Uruguay to the U.S.S.R., since 1969; *b.* 29 Nov. 1918; *s.* of Conrado Velázquez and Aurea Rodríguez Pintos; *m.* 1955, Blanca Lis García de Velázquez; five *s.* two *d.* *Educ.:* Univ. of the Republic, Montevideo, Uruguay. Dr. in Law and Social Sciences. Prof. of History, High Sch., 1941-58; Prof. of Internat. Law, Mil. Sch., 1960-61; Legal Advisor, Nat. Inst. of Pensions, 1959-61; Permanent Representative of Uruguay to the U.N., 1961-65; Ambassador to the Court of St. James's, 1965-69. Holds foreign decorations. *Publications:* La Protección Internacional de la Libertad de Enseñanza, 1957; El Derecho Natural y la Misión del Jurista, 1957; La Invalidez de los Tratados Inconstitucionales, 1960; Las Naciones Unidas y la Descolonización, 1964. Contrib. learned jls. in Uruguay and abroad. *Recreations:* golf, tennis. *Address:* Embassy of Uruguay, Ulitsa Zholtovskogo 28, Moscow, U.S.S.R. *Clubs:* Travellers', Hurlingham, Canning.
[*Died* 3 *July* 1970.

VELLA, Col. Victor George, C.M.G. 1960; C.V.O. 1954; O.B.E. 1946; E.D.; *b.* 4 August 1901; *s.* of late Lieut.-Colonel Alfred Vella, O.B.E., R.M.A.; *m.* 1928, Maud, *d.* of late His Honour Sir Michael Angelo Refalo, C.B.E., LL.D. *Educ.:* privately. Joined Civil Service, Malta, 1922; later enrolled in H.M. Overseas Civil Service. Served War of 1939-45 (O.B.E.), Lt.-Col. Clerk to Exec. Council and Council of Govt., Malta, 1945-46; Asst. Sec., Lieut.-Governor's Office, 1946-47; Private Sec. to Prime Minister and Sec. to Cabinet, 1947-49; Civil Defence Planning Officer, 1949-50; Sec., Maltese Imperial Government, 1950-58 (Governor's Deputy, 1953, 1955, 1957, 1958); Commissioner-General for Malta in London, 1958-61. O.St.J. *Recreation:* photography. *Address:* 6 Sutherland House, Marloes Road, W.8. *Clubs:* Travellers'; Union, Casino Maltese (Malta).
[*Died* 12 *April* 1963.

VENMORE, Arthur; J.P. Liverpool; Senior Partner, W. and J. Venmore, Estate Agents and Surveyors, Liverpool, and Director of various companies; *b.* 14 July 1883; *e. s.* of James and Margaret Venmore, Liverpool; *m.* 1922, Muriel Irene, *d.* of Walter E. Lloyd, formerly of Liverpool and Stockyn Hall, Flintshire; three *d.* *Educ.:* Liverpool College. High Sheriff of Anglesey, 1941-42; holds many important offices, Presbyterian Church of Wales; served with Mesopotamian Expeditionary Force, 1914-18; War of 1939-45, Army Welfare Officer (Capt.) for Anglesey. *Recreations:* fishing and shooting. *Address:* 31 North John Street, Liverpool 2; Bronydd, Cemaes Bay, Anglesey. *T.:* Cemaes Bay 256. *Club:* Athenæum (Liverpool).
[*Died* 18 *June* 1961.

VENNING, Brigadier Francis Esmond Wingate, C.B. 1932; C.B.E. 1925; D.S.O. 1917; Indian Army, retired; *b.* Opalgalla, Matale, Ceylon, 26 Jan. 1882; *s.* of late Alfred Reid Venning, I.S.O., Federal Secretary, Federated Malay States; *m.* 1907, Edith Lucy (*d.* 1967), *d.* of late Dr. A. H. Twining, Salcombe Devonshire; one *s.* two *d.* (and one *d.* decd.). *Educ.:* Bath Coll., Bath; R.M.C., Sandhurst. Attached 1st Bn. The Wiltshire Regt., 1901-2; entered Indian Army, 31st Punjab Infantry, 1902; served Peshawar, 1901-2; Rawalpindi, 1902-5; Bannu, 1905-7; Burma Military Police, 1907-14; European War, Mesopotamia, 1915-20 (D.S.O., Bt. Lt.-Col., despatches five times, three War medals); Staff College, Camberley, 1921; on staff Waziristan, 1922-23 (Frontier medal, C.B.E., despatches twice); on staff Meerut District, 1924-28; Brigadier, Multan Brigade, 1929-32 (C.B.); Brigadier, Peshawar Brigade, 1932-33; served Chitral Reliefs, 1932 (despatches); retired, 1933. Supt. A.F.S. New Forest Rural Dist., 1939-40; Chief Warden, A.R.P., New Forest, 1939-40; Comd. 9th Forest Bnt. Hampshire H.G., 1940-44. Pres. Southampton Natural History Soc., 1947-. *Recreation:* natural history. *Address:* Butts Ash, Hythe, Southampton
[*Died* 28 *Aug.* 1970.

VENNING, General Sir Walter King, G.C.B., *cr.* 1942 (K.C.B., *cr.* 1939; C.B.1935); C.M.G. 1918; C.B.E. 1926; M.C.; *b.* 17 Jan. 1882; *s.* of late E. Venning, Ceylon Civil Service; *m.* 1st, 1912, Marcia (*d.* 1946), *d.* of late Surg.-Gen. J. C. Dorman, C.M.G.; two *s.*; 2nd, Vera (who *m.* 1928, Roland Cephus Weightman; he *d.* 1944), *d.* of A. E. Thomas-Haime. *Educ.:* Clifton College; Royal Military College, Sandhurst. Commissioned Duke of Cornwall's Light Infantry, 1901; served European War, 1914-18; Instructor, Staff College, 1919-21; Colonel, 1921; D.A. and Q.M.G. Eastern Command, India, 1929-31; Commander 2nd (Rawalpindi) Infantry Brigade, India, 1931-34; Maj.-Gen., 1933; Director of Movements and Quartering, War Office, 1934-38; Lt.-Gen., 1938; Quarter-Master-Gen. to the Forces, 1939-42; General, 1940; A.D.C. General to the King, 1941-42; retired pay, 1942; Director-General of British Supply Mission in Washington, 1942-46; Colonel Duke of Cornwall's Light Infantry, 1935-47; Colonel Comdt. Army Catering Corps, 1941-45; Colonel Comdt. Royal Electrical and Mechanical Engineers. 1942-50. Legion of Merit (Commander) U.S. Army, 1946. *Recreations:* golf, gardening. *Address:* Wyke House, Gillingham, Dorset. *T.:* Gillingham (Dorset) 426. *Club:* United Service.
[*Died* 19 *June* 1964.

VEREY, Lt.-Col. Henry Edward, D.S.O. 1918; Solicitor (retd.); *b.* 8 May 1877; *o. s.* of late Sir Henry William Verey and late Henrietta Maria, 5th *d.* of Edward W. Hasell of Dalemain, Penrith; *m.* 1907, Lucy Alice (*d.* 1968), *er. d.* of late Judge Amyas Philip Longstaffe and late Lady Tindal Atkinson; two *s.* one *d.* *Educ.:* Eton; Trinity College, Cambridge, M.A., LL.B. Served European War (D.S.O. despatches. Cavaliere Uff. Crown of Italy); O.C.St.J. *Recreations:* gardening, travel. *Address:* Bridge House, Twyford, Berks. *T.:* Twyford 7. *Clubs:* United University, Leander.
[*Died* 23 *Nov.* 1968.

VEREY, Rev. Lewis, M.V.O. 1947; *b.* 1874; *s.* of late Capt. Charles Verey, J.P., The Buffs, and Jane Mary Wynter, Brecon. *Educ.:* Bedford School; Trinity Hall, Cambridge; Cuddesdon College, Oxford. B.A. 1898, M.A. 1901, Cambridge; Deacon, 1898, Priest, 1900, St. Albans; Curate of Plaistow, E., 1898-1902, Westminster, 1903-08; Chaplain to King Edward VII at Sandringham, 1908-11; Rector of Carlton, 1911-17; Vicar of Rottingdean, 1917-35; Chaplain to King George VI, Chapel Royal, Hampton Court Palace, 1940-47; Chaplain at Royal Memorial Church, Cannes, France, 1930-39. *Address:* 46 Ennismore Gardens, S.W.7. *T.:* Knightsbridge 0143. *Club:* Sion College.
[*Died* 18 *Feb.* 1961.

VERITY, Sir John, Kt. 1943; Chief Justice of Nigeria, 1946-54, retired; *b.* 1892; *s.* of late Canon H. B. Verity; *m.* 1918, Grace Elizabeth Rochat (*d.* 1967); two *d.* Entered Col. Service, Brit. Honduras, 1908; resigned, 1913; called to Bar, Middle Temple, 1918; Deputy Clerk of Courts, Jamaica, 1918; Clerk of Courts, 1920; Resident Magistrate, 1925; Chairman, Lands Department Commission of Enquiry, 1935; Second Puisne Judge, British Guiana, 1936; First Puisne Judge, 1937; Chief Justice of Zanzibar, 1939-42; Chief Justice of British Guiana, 1942-46. Chairman Leonora Riot Commission of Enquiry, 1939; Chancellor of Diocese of Guiana, 1937-39 and

1942-45; Chairman: Advisory Social Welfare Committee, British Guiana, 1943-45; Fiji Police Commn. of Enquiry, 1955; Comr., Law Revision, W. Region, Nigeria, 1955-59. *Address:* Lushoto, Tanzania.
[*Died* 9 *April* 1970.

VERNEY, Prof. Ernest Basil, F.R.S. 1936; M.A., M.D., B.Ch., F.R.C.P.; retired; Emeritus Professor of Pharmacology, University of Cambridge; Hon. Fellow, Downing College, 1961; *b.* 22 Aug. 1894; 4th *s.* of late Frederick Palmer Verney; *m.* 1923, Ruth Eden, *e. d.* of late Professor R. S. Conway; two *s.* one *d.* *Educ.:* Judd School, Tonbridge; Tonbridge School; Downing College, Cambridge (Scholar); St. Bartholomew's Hospital, London (Shuter Scholar); Freiburg im Breisgau. 1st Class Natural Science Tripos, Part I, 1916; served in the R.A.M.C. (S.R.), Lieut. and Capt., 1918-20; Assistant in the Dept. of Physiology, University College, London, 1921-24; Beit Fellow, junior 1922-25, 4th year 1925-26, senior 1926; Assistant in the Medical Unit, University College Hospital Medical School, London, 1924-26; Professor of Pharmacology, Univ. Coll., London, 1926-34. Reader in Pharmacology, University of Cambridge, 1934-46; Sheild Professor of Pharmacology, University of Cambridge, 1946-61; Research Professor in Physiology, University of Melbourne, 1961-1964; Fellow of Downing College, 1934-1961. Sharpey-Schafer Lectr., Univ. of Edinburgh, 1945; Croonian Lectr., Royal Soc., 1947; William Withering Memorial Lectr., Univ. of Birmingham, 1949; Dunham Lectr., Univ. of Harvard, 1951; John Malet Purser Lectr., T.C.D., 1954; Louis Abrahams Lectr., R.C.P., 1954; Baxter Lectr., Amer. Coll. of Surgeons, 1957; Hon. Fellow Society Reg. Med. Budapest, 1938; For. Mem. Finnish Med. Society, 1949; Hon. Mem. Aust. Physiol. Society, 1962; Hon. Mem. Med. Research Society, 1963; Hon. D.Sc. (Melb.), 1956; Baly Medal, R.C.P., 1957. *Publications:* Physiological Papers in scientific journals. *Recreations:* reading and carpentry. *Address:* 33 Sherlock Close, Cambridge. *T.:* Cambridge 54336.
[*Died* 19 *Aug.* 1967.

VERNON, 9th Baron, *cr.* 1762; **Francis William Lawrance Venables-Vernon,** Commander R.N.; retired, March 1919; *b.* 6 Nov. 1889; *s.* of 7th Baron, and Frances, *d.* of Francis C. Lawrance, New York; *S. bro.*, 1915; *m.* 1915, Violet, *d.* of Colonel Clay; one *s.* one *d.* *Heir: s.* Hon. John Lawrance Vernon [*b.* 1 Feb. 1923; *m.* 1955, Sheila Jean, *yr. d.* of W. Marshall Clark, Johannesburg]. *Address:* Sudbury Hall, Derby.
[*Died* 18 *March* 1963.

VERNON, Air Commodore Frederick Edward, C.B. 1946; O.B.E. 1941; *b.* 17 Nov. 1899; *s.* of late James Lewin Frederick Vernon; *m.* 1927, Hilda Ivy, *d.* of late John Willson; three *s.* *Educ.:* Loughborough College (D.L.C.); St. Catharine's College, Cambridge (M.A.). Imperial College of Science and Technology, London (D.I.C.). Joined Royal Flying Corps, 1917; served European War, 1917-18; Group Capt. 1940; Air Commodore, 1943. Deputy Director Technical Development, M.A.P., 1942-43; Middle East Forces, Air Officer Cmdg. Maintenance Group, 1943-46; S.A.S.O., Technical Training Comdt., 1946-48; Senior Technical Staff Officer Air Headquarters, B.A.F.O., R.A.F., 1948-50; retired, 1950; Director of Studies, Air Service Training Ltd. in Pakistan, 1950-55. *Address:* Hillside House, Baltonborough, Somerset *Club:* Royal Over-Seas League.
[*Died* 15 *July* 1963.

VERNON, Rt. Rev. Gerald Richard; Dean of Belize, British Honduras, since 1957; *b.* 13 Feb. 1899; *s.* of late Rev. H. R. C. Vernon and Jessie Georgiana Paul. *Educ.:* Winchester College; Magdalen College, Oxford; Cuddesdon Theological College. Assistant Priest, Christ Church, St. Leonards-on-Sea, 1923-32; Rector of Christ Church, St. Leonards, 1932-40; Bishop in Madagascar, 1940-50; Vicar of Finedon, Northants, and Assistant Bishop of Peterborough, 1952-1957; Canon of Peterborough Cathedral, 1957. *Recreation:* golf. *Address:* The Deanery, Belize, British Honduras. *Club:* Royal Automobile.
[*Died* 12 *May* 1963.

VERNON, Sir Norman; *see* Vernon, Sir W. N.

VERNON, Sir Sydney, Kt., *cr.* 1955; Solicitor; *b.* 26 May 1876; *s.* of William Frederick Vernon; *m.* 1903, Mira Horton (*d.* 1959); one *s.* *Educ.:* Oliver's Mount Sch., Scarborough. LL.B. London; admitted Solicitor, 1898. Clerk to Oldbury U.D.C., 1912-24; Borough Coroner for Smethwick, 1924-46; Chairman Birmingham Hospitals Council, 1937-47; Pro-Chancellor, Birmingham University, 1947-55. LL.D. Birmingham University (*Honoris causa*). *Address:* 36 Westfield Road, Birmingham 15. *T.:* Edgbaston 2722. *Club:* Union (Birmingham).
[*Died* 8 *Sept.* 1966.

VERNON, Sir (William) Norman, 3rd Bt., *cr.* 1914; Dep. Chm. and Managing Director Spillers Ltd., 1929-49; *b.* 19 Apr. 1890; *s.* of Sir John Herbert Vernon, 2nd Bt., and Elizabeth Bagnall; *S.* father, 1933; *m.* 1921, Caroline Janet Robertson-Macdonald; one *s.* one *d.* *Educ.:* Mostyn House, Parkgate, Cheshire; Charterhouse; Magdalen College, Oxford, M.A. Served apprenticeship in flour milling at Birkenhead after leaving Oxford; eventually Manager, W. Vernon & Sons, flour millers, Birkenhead; became partner after four years in W. Vernon & Sons, Liverpool and London; Director of W. Vernon & Sons Ltd., when the company amalgamated with Spillers Milling and Associated Industries, branch Director in Liverpool; elected on the Board of the parent company in 1926 in London; Official Examiner in Milling Technology for three years; President of North-Western Flour Millers' Association, 1923, 1924; President of North-Western Flour Millers' Federation, 1924; President of National Flour Milling Federation, 1925, 1926; presided over a Committee appointed to reorganise the Whitley Scheme for the industry; Member of National Joint Industrial Executive Committee for the flour millers' industry, 1922-49; President Birkenhead Chamber of Commerce, 1924, 1925-1926; Chairman Finnish Section London Chamber of Commerce; Pres. National Assoc. of British and Irish Millers for two years, 1931-32; went as one of Government Trade Mission to Finland, 1933; led Cttee. which negotiated Wheat Act of 1932 with Govt.; Member: Agricultural Marketing Facilities Cttee., 1933-1958 (Chm. 1956-); Tithe Redemption Commn., 1936-55; Cereals Control Board, 1939; Director of Flour Milling, Ministry of Food, 1940-41; Flour Mills Advisory Committee, 1939-47; Head of Food Mission to occupied Germany, Nov. 1945; Dir. Baltic Exchange, 1944 (Chm. 1946 and 1947). Joined Allied Bakeries, 1950 (Dir., 1952-57), now retired. F.R.S.A. 1943; Order of a Knight of the White Rose of Finland, 1934. *Recreations:* cricket, golf, tennis. *Heir: s.* Nigel John Douglas [*b.* 2 May 1924; *m.* 1947, Margaret Ellen, *e. d.* of R. Lyle Dobell, The Mount, Waverton, nr. Chester; two *s.* Joined Royal Navy, 1942; Lieut. 1945]. *Address:* The Deer Tower, Shillinglee Park, Chiddingfold Surrey. *T.:* Northchapel 234; 16 Stanford Court, Cornwall Gardens, S.W.7. *T.:* Western 4006. *Clubs:* Bath; Vincent's (Oxford).
[*Died* 12 *April* 1967.

VERPILLEUX, Antoine Emile, M.B.E.; artist (signing earlier works E. A. Verpilleux and later ones A. E. Verpilleux), portrait and landscape painter, illustrator, engraver; *b.* Kensington, London, 3 Mar. 1888; *s.* of Antoine Verpilleux, St. Etienne, France, and Edith Beard, London; *m.* 1910, Grace Newsom; four *d.*; *m.* 1936, Carolyn Putnam. *Educ.:* Philological School, London; St. Genis, France; Institut Superieur des Beaux Arts, Antwerp. Studied art in England, France, Belgium, Holland; during early years illustrated for principal periodicals, press, and poster work; producer of original colour prints and many portraits in England and U.S. America; served European War in R.F.C. and R.A.F., Captain (despatches, M.B.E.); exhibitor at Salon, R.A., New English Art Club, International Society, etc.; works in public galleries: British Museum, South Kensington, and in Paris, New York, Ottawa, Rome, Moscow, Liverpool, Manchester, Sweden, Japan, etc. *Recreations:* sailing, fencing, gardening. *Address:* Charlton, Pembroke, Bermuda. *Club:* Royal Air Force. [*Died* 10 *Sept.* 1964.

VERSCHOYLE, Beresford St. George, C.B.E. 1918; M.I.C.E.; General Manager, Egyptian State Railways, retired; 4th *s.* of Rev. Prebendary Richard Verschoyle, M.A.; *m.* Ethel Janet Plews (*d.* 1941). *Educ.:* Royal Naval Academy, Southsea; Portora Royal School. Engineering Staff, Buenos Aires and Rosario and Central Argentine Railways, Argentine Republic. *Recreations:* golf, small boat sailing. *Address:* 180 Heene Road, Worthing. *Club:* West Worthing. [*Died* 20 *Dec.* 1962.

VERSCHOYLE-CAMPBELL, Major-Gen. William Henry McNeile, C.I.E. 1941; O.B.E. 1919; M.C.; *b.* 28 May 1884; *s.* of Very Rev. R. S. D. Campbell, D.D., Dean of Clonmacnoise, and S. W. Verschoyle; *m.* 1910, Ethel Mary Pilkington, Cape Town, South Africa. *Educ.:* Marlborough College, R.M.A., Woolwich. 2nd Lt. R.A., 1903; Army Ordnance Dept., 1912; Capt., 1914; Brevet Major, 1917; Major, 1922; Lt.-Col., 1929; Col., 1935; Brig., 1936; Major-General, 1938; A.D.O.S. War Office, 1935; Director Ordnance Services, India, 1936-40; Deputy Master General of Ordnance, India, 1938-40; retired 1941; served European War, France and Belgium, 1914-16; Greek Macedonia, Serbia, Bulgaria, European Turkey and the Islands of the Aegean Sea, 1916-18 (despatches four times, Brevet of Major, 1914 Star and Clasp, British War Medal, Victory Medal, O.B.E., M.C.). *Recreations:* usual games and sports. *Address:* Shanet, Baily, Co. Dublin, Eire. *lubs:* United Service; Kildare Street (Dublin). [*Died* 17 *June* 1964.

VERWOERD, Dr. Hendrik Frensch, M.A., D.Phil.; Prime Minister and Leader of the National Party, of the Republic of South Africa, since 31 May 1961 (of Union of South Africa, 1958-61); Farmer; M.P. for Heidelberg, Transvaal since 1958; Leader and Chairman, National Party of Transvaal; Chairman, Federal Council of National Party in South Africa; *b.* 8 Sept. 1901; *s.* of late Wilhelm Johannes Verwoerd, Brandfort, O.F.S.; *m.* 1927, Elizabeth, *d.* of Wynand Johannes Schoombee, Middelburg, C.P.; five *s.* two *d.* *Educ.:* Wynberg High Sch. and Milton High Sch., Bulawayo, S.R.; Brandfort, O.F.S.; Stellenbosch University; several overseas Univs. in Germany and U.S.A. Formerly Chief Organiser of Nat. Conf. on Poor White Problem, Kimberley, 1936, and Chairman of its Continuation Cttee. Began career as Lecturer in Logic and Psychology; Prof. of Applied Psychology, Univ. of Stellenbosch, 1927-32; Prof. of Sociology and Social Work, Univ. of Stellenbosch, 1933-37; Chief Editor, "Die Transvaler", Johannesburg, 1938-48; Senator, Parliament Union of S.A., 1948-58; Minister of Native Affairs in Parliament of Union of S.A., 1950-58; Prime Minister, 1958-. D.Phil (*h.c.*) Stellenbosch University. *Publications:* The Blunting of the Emotions (Afstomping van die Gemoedsaandoeninge); An Experimental Study on the Thinking process; and many pamphlets and articles on cultural, scientific, social and political subjects. *Address:* Union Buildings, Pretoria; (official residence during session) Groote Schuur, Cape Town; (official residence during recess) Libertas, Pretoria. [*Died* 6 *Sept.* 1966.

VEVERS, Geoffrey Marr, F.R.C.S. (Eng.), L.R.C.P.(Lond.); F.Z.S.; Honorary Consultant to the Zoological Society of London; *b.* Hereford, 20 Sept. 1890; *y. s.* of late Henry Vevers, surgeon, of Hereford. *Educ.:* Hereford; St. Thomas's Hospital. Supt. to Zoological Society of London, 1923-1948. Editor of Anglo-Soviet Journal, 1939-1946; Assistant Helminthologist, London School of Tropical Medicine, 1919-23; Hon. Parasitologist to the Zoological Society of London, 1919-21; Beit Memorial Research Fellow, 1920-22; Member of the Filariasis Commission to British Guiana, 1921; served European War, 1914-15, as Dresser B.R.C.S.; Capt. R.A.M.C., 1916-19 (1914-15 Star). Silver Medallist Zoological Soc. of London, 1942; Gold Medallist Zoological Soc. of Glasgow & West of Scotland, 1947. Hon. Member Zool. Soc. Philadelphia; Corr. Member Royal Zool. Soc. Ireland. *Publications:* numerous scientific papers and children's books on natural history. Regular broadcasts in B.B.C. Children's Hour on Zoological subjects, 1946-47. *Recreation:* the contemplation of nature. *Address:* Springfield, Whipsnade, Beds. *T.:* Whipsnade 238. [*Died* 9 *Jan.* 1970.

VIAN, Admiral of the Fleet Sir Philip, G.C.B., *cr.* 1952 (K.C.B., *cr.* 1944; C.B. 1944); K.B.E., *cr.* 1942; D.S.O. 1940, and Bars 1940, 1941; Director, Midland Bank, since 1952; Director, North British and Mercantile Insurance Co.: *b.* 1894; *s.* of late Alsager and Ada Vian, Gilridge, Cowden Pound, Kent; *m.* 1929, Marjorie, *d.* of late Col. David Price Haig, O.B.E., Highfields Park, Withyham, Sussex; two *d.* *Educ.:* Dartmouth. *Publication:* Action This Day, 1959. *Address:* Pitt House Farm, Ashford Hill, Nr. Newbury. *T.:* Kingsclere 250. *Club:* White's. [*Died* 27 *May* 1968.

VIANT, Samuel Philip, C.B.E. 1948; J.P.; M.P. (Lab.) West Willesden, 1923-31 and 1935-59; *b.* Plymouth, 1882; *s.* of Daniel Viant, Plymouth; *m.* 1911, Emily (*d.* 1956), 2nd *d.* of John Harvey, Plymouth; one *s.* (one *d.* decd.). *Educ.:* Devonport Higher Grade School. Ruskin Coll. Correspondence Student. Asst. Postmaster-General, 1929-31; late Vice-Chm. of National Conciliation Board for Building Industry; Member Select Cttee. on Procedure, 1945-46; Chm. Select Cttee. on the revision and amendment of rules governing the Member's Fund, 1947; Chm. Trustees of the Members' Fund, 1955-1957; Member, Cttee. of Privileges, 1953-57. J.P. Middlesex 1928. Co-opted as Mayor of Willesden, May 1960-61; Freeman of Borough, 1961. *Recreations:* ex-Rugby player, bowling and walking. *Address:* 94 Doyle Gardens, N.W.10. *T.:* Elgar 6624. *Club:* Labour. [*Died* 19 *May* 1964.

VICKERS, Dr. Allan Robert Stanley, C.M.G. 1955; O.B.E. 1951; Medical Superintendent, Royal Flying Doctor Service of Australia (Qld. Section) since 1952; *b.* 3 June 1901; *s.* of Robert Vickers, Albury, N.S.W.; *m.* 1934, Lilias, *d.* of James Litton Whitman, Cloncurry, Queensland; two *s.* *Educ.:* University of Sydney. M.B., Ch.M. 1926. Medical Officer of Royal Flying Doctor Service of Australia in many parts of Australia, 1931-; Resident Magistrate, Port Hedland, 1935-39. Served War, 1939-43:

Lieut.-Col. A.A.M.C. (retd.); C.O. 110 Aust. General Hospital, 1941-43. Duty with Flying Doctor Service, at Charleville, Qld., 1943-52. Visited U.K. under auspices of Nuffield Foundation, 1954. C.St.J. 1946. *Recreations:* fishing, golf. *Address:* 20 Welwyn Crescent, Coorparoo S.E.2, Queensland, Australia. *T.:* XU 2385; c/o The Royal Flying Doctor Service of Australia, Queen Street, Brisbane, Queensland, Australia. *T.:* F.A. 1504. *Club:* United Service (Brisbane). [*Died* 31 *Oct.* 1967.

VICKERS, Harold James, C.B.E. 1936; *b.* 1 June 1895; *m.* 1922, Mabel Mary Langley; two *s.* one *d.* *Educ.:* Liverpool Institute. Indian Police, 1914, retired, 1948. Served War, 1914-18, in Infantry, Cavalry and Royal Air Force; Special War Service Italy, 1944; also in India (dangerously wounded and captured by tribesmen); despatches thrice. Dep. Director, Intelligence, Government of India, Peshawar, 1933-1940; Deputy-Inspector-General of Police, N.W.F.P., 1940-45; Inspector-General of Police, N.W.F.P., India, 1945-46; Civil Assistant War Office, 1947-49. King's Police Medal, 1926; Indian Police Medal, 1944. *Recreation:* walking. *Address:* Allerton, West Mersea, Colchester, Essex. [*Died* 22 *Sept.* 1970.

VICKY; *see* Weisz, Victor.

VIGNOLES, Charles Malcolm, C.B.E. 1957 (O.B.E. 1946); Chairman, Evershed & Vignoles Ltd.; Director, Remploy Ltd.; *b.* 2 May 1901; *m.* 1928, Frances Beatrice Macartney; two *s.* one *d.* *Educ.:* Sedbergh Sch.; Magdalene Coll., Cambridge (M.A., Mech. Sci. Tripos). Joined Shell group of oil companies, 1924; served Asiatic Petroleum Co., Malaya, 1924-32; Fuel Oil Dept., Shell Petroleum Co., 1932-40; Jt. Sec., Overseas Supply Cttee., Petroleum Board, 1940-46; Eastern Area Manager, Shell Petroleum Co., 1946-50; Managing Director, Shell Mex and B.P., 1951-61. Pres. of Inst. of Petroleum, 1958-60. Member, Council Royal Society of Arts. Chairman of Governors, Sedbergh School. Master of Worshipful Company of Turners, 1957. *Recreations:* travel and interest in English history and countryside. *Address:* Pear Tree House, Chertsey Road, Chobham, Surrey. *T.:* Chobham 42. *Clubs:* Garrick. East India and Sports, Royal Automobile. [*Died* 23 *Sept.* 1961.

VILLAR, Captain George, C.B.E. 1954; Royal Navy retired; *b.* 30 May 1887; *m.* 1919, Monica Estelle (*née* Cook); one *s.* two *d.* *Educ.:* R.N.E.C., Devonport; R.N.C. Greenwich. Engineer Cadet, 1903-7; Engineer Officer, 1907-39. With John I. Thornycroft, 1939-59. Commander of Order of Orange Nassau, 1946. *Recreations:* sailing, gardening. *Address:* Elms, Warsash, Hants. *T.:* Locksheath 2233. [*Died* 18 *April* 1970.

VILLIERS, Hon. Arthur George Child, D.S.O. 1917; late Oxfordshire Yeomanry; D.L. County of Oxford; *b.* 24 Nov 1883; 2nd *s.* of 7th Earl of Jersey. *Educ.:* Eton; Oxford. Served European War, 1914-18 (D.S.O., Bar, and Croix de Guerre). Received Freedom of Leyton, 1951; Freedom of Hackney, 1955. *Club:* Bath. [*Died* 7 *May* 1969.

VILLIERS, Sir (Francis) Edward Earle, Kt., *cr.* 1936; Easter (Chick) Hatchery, Conon Bridge, Ross-shire; *b.* 1 Jan. 1889; *s.* of Rev. Preb. H. Montagu Villiers, of St. Paul's, Knightsbridge, and 2nd wife, Charlotte Louisa Emily, *d.* of Hon. F. W. Cadogan; *m.* 1933, Katharine Mary Wakefield (*d.* 1965), *o. d.* of Hugh White, Baltic Exchange, attached Grenadier Guards. *Educ.:* Harrow; Christ Church, Oxford. Served R.F.C. and R.A.F. in European War, and in R.A.F. in 1919 Afghan War; Member Bengal Legislative Council, 1924-26; President European Assoc. of India, 1931 and 1932; Vice-Chairman Union of Britain and India, 1933-35. *Publication:* Help For The Asking. *Recreation:* fishing. *Address:* Easter Hatchery, Conon Bridge, Ross-shire. *T.:* 258. [*Died* 20 *March* 1967.

VILLIERS-STUART, Brigadier-General William, C.B.E. 1919, D.S.O. 1925; late 5th Royal Gurkhas; *b.* 1872; *e. s.* of late Lt.-Col. H. J. R. Villiers Stuart; *m.* 1926, Erica Cecil, *yr. d.* of R. Shepley-Shepley, of Troquhain, Balmaclellan, Scotland. Served N.W. Frontier of India, 1897-98 (medal and two clasps); Tirah Expedition, 1897-98 (dangerously wounded, clasp); Waziristan Expedition, 1901-02 (clasp); commanded 9th Batt. Rifle Brigade in France and Flanders, 1914-15 (1914-15 Star); commanded 1/5th Royal Gurkhas in Egypt and India, 1916; Comdt. Mountain Warfare School, India, 1916-18 and 1920; in charge Nepalese Allied Contingent, 1916-17 (2nd Class Order of Star of Nepal); raised 3rd Batt. Q.V.O. Corps of Guides, 1917-18; Brig.-General Inspector of Infantry, 1918-20 (War and Victory Medals, C.B.E., brevet of Lieut. Col.); N.W.F. India, 1920 (medal and two clasps); commanded 1/5 Royal Gurkhas, 1920-24, during which period served with above battalion through Razmak and Makin operations, 1922-1923 (clasp to N.W.F. India medal and D.S.O., brevet of Colonel); retired, 1924. *Address:* Hazelrigg, Balmaclellan, by Castle Douglas, Scotland. [*Died* 25 *Jan.* 1961.

VINCENT, Sir Alfred, Kt. 1946; *b.* 1891; *s.* of late H. A. Vincent, Batavia, Bushey Hall Rd., Bushey, Herts.; *m.* 1st, 1928, Annie (*d.* 1960), *d.* of Alfred Mortimer, Shipley, Yorks.; four *s.* one *d.*; 2nd, 1961, Francis Belmont Ahrens, Westcliff, Johannesburg. *Educ.:* Russell Hill, Purley. Member Kenya Executive Council, 1944-48 and Kenya Legislative Council, 1942-48; Leader and Chairman, European Elected Members, 1944-48; Mem. East African Civil Defence and Supply Council, 1942-45; Director of Road Transport, Controller of Petroleum Products and Mem. E. A. Production and Supply Council, 1942-56; Mem. Kenya Development and Reconstruction Authority, 1945-53; Mem. Kenya Road Authority, 1953-57; Corporate Mem. Kenya Legislative Council and Chm. of European Elected Members Organisation, 1957-61; Mem. East Africa Central Legislative Assembly and Chm., Members Organisation; Mem. E.A. Transport Advisory Council, E.A. Air Advisory Council, 1947-61; Mem. Council Roy. Agricultural Society of Kenya; President of the Kenya Wild Life Society; Chairman: Greenham (E.A.) Ltd.; Leyland Paint (E.A.) Ltd.; Murphy Chemicals (E.A.) Ltd.; Royal National Parks of Kenya; Savings and Loan Society Ltd.; South African Mutual Life Assurance Society (E.A. Board). *Address:* c/o Barclays Bank D.C.O., 33 Old Broad St., E.C.2; Rhino Park, P.O. Box 24826, Karen, Kenya, E. Africa. [*Died* 4 *May* 1967.

VINCENT, Brig.-General Sir Berkeley, K.B.E., *cr.* 1924; C.B. 1919; C.M.G. 1916; *b.* 4 Dec. 1871; *e. s.* of late Col. A. H. Vincent, 3rd (K.O.) Hussars, of Summerhill, Co. Clare; *m.* 1st, 1906, Lady Kitty Ogilvy (marriage dissolved, 1925; she *m.* 2nd, 1926, Lieut.-Col. Ralph Gerald Ritson), *d.* of 8th Earl of Airlie; 2nd, 1925, Ellaline, *d.* of Dr. Esmonde Bramley-Moore; three *s.* *Educ.:* Wellington College; R.M.A., Woolwich; passed Staff College. Served China, 1900 (medal); South Africa, 1901-02 (Queen's medal 5 clasps); Russo-Japanese War, 1904-05, attached to Japanese army in Manchuria (Japanese war medal, Order of Sacred Treasure, 4th Class); European War, 1914-18 (wounded, despatches 5 times, C.M.G., C.B., Bt. Lt.-Col., Bt.-Col., Officier Légion d'Honneur, 1914 Star, G.S. and Victory medals); operations in Kurdistan, 1923 (despatches, medal and clasp); commanded The Inniskillings (6th Dragoons); formerly Capt. in R.H.A.; Colonel Commandant Military Forces Iraq, 1922-24; retired pay, 1924. *Address:* Bridge House, Sandbanks, Bournemouth. *T.:* Canford Cliffs 77860. [*Died* 29 *Jan.* 1963.

VINCENT, Air Vice-Marshal (Retd.) Claude McClean, C.B. 1946; C.B.E. 1952; D.F.C and Bar; A.F.C.; *b.* 21 Jan. 1896; *s.* of Harry Vincent of Thame, Oxon, and Trinidad, British West Indies, and Clarica Jane Herd McClean; *m.* 1922, Louise Anita Evelyn, *d.* of Col. E. F. L'Estrange; one *s.* *Educ.:* Queen's Royal College, Trinidad. Army, 1915 - 17, Salonika; R.F.C. 1917-18, Middle East; Royal Air Force, 1919-23, India; Royal Aircraft Establishment, 1924-36, as Experimental Pilot; O.C. Pilotless Aircraft Development Unit, 1936-39; R.A.F. Station, Locking, 1939-40; Aden, 1940-42; Middle East, 1942-43 (despatches twice); Commandant Empire Central Flying School, 1944-47; Director of Flying Training, Air Ministry, 1947-49; Air Officer in Charge of Administration, Fighter Command, 1949-52. Pres. R.A.F. Assoc. (Trinidad and Tobago Branch); Cdre. Trinidad Yacht Club; Colony Director, Brit. Red Cross Soc., Trinidad and Tobago Branch, 1953-63; inaugural Chm. Coun., Red Cross Soc. of Trinidad and Tobago on formation as a Nat. Soc., 1963. Chairman, Air Licensing Authority, Trinidad and Tobago; Member, Commission of Enquiry into Civil Aviation in The West Indies, Brit. Guiana, and Brit. Honduras, 1960. *Recreations:* fishing, Rugby, polo, sailing. *Address:* 3 Third Ave., Cascade, Port of Spain, Trinidad, W.I. *T.:* 41025. *Club:* R.A.F. [*Died* 8 *Aug.* 1967.

VINCENT, Lady Kitty; *see* Ritson, Lady Kitty.

VINCENT, Sir Lacey Eric, 2nd Bt., *cr.* 1936; Chairman L. E. Vincent & Partners Ltd. and other Companies; *b.* 13 Jan. 1902; *o. s.* of Sir Percy Vincent, 1st Bt., and Christine Emily, *d.* of George Horatio Board; *S.* father, 1943; *m.* 1938, Helen Millicent, *yr. d.* of late Field Marshal Sir William Robert Robertson, 1st Bt., G.C.B., G.C.M.G., G.C.V.O., D.S.O.; one *s.* one *d.* *Educ.:* Mill Hill. Spent many years in South Africa and Rhodesia in development of British Overseas Trade. Joined Officers Emergency Reserve, 1939; 2nd Lt. R.A.S.C. 1940; invalided out, 1941. *Recreations:* travel, yachting. *Heir:* *s.* William Percy Maxwell Vincent, *b.* 1 Feb. 1945. *Address:* 17 Eresby House, Rutland Gate, S.W.7. *Club:* Buck's. [*Died* 21 *Oct.* 1963.

VINCENT-GOMPERTZ, Frank Priestly, C.I.E. 1927; late Revenue Survey Dept., Madras. Joined service, 1893; Director of Revenue Survey, Madras, 1922; retired, 1928. *Address:* The Briers, St. Leonards-on-Sea, Sussex. [*Died* 13 *Jan.* 1968.

VINE, Francis Seymour, C.M.G. 1957; Managing Director James Miller and Company Pty. Ltd., since 1947; President of Victoria Chamber of Manufacturers; Member, Commonwealth Hard Fibres and Allied Materials Advisory Committee, and Consultant on Cordage to the Commonwealth, 1953; Vice-President of Association of Chambers of Manufacturers of Australia, 1954; Chairman Australian Rope, Cordage and Twine Manufacturers' Association, 1945; *b.* 1 Nov. 1904; *s.* of W. P. Vine, St. Kilda; *m.* 1929, Elizabeth S., *d.* of William Henry Cuming; one *s.* one *d.* *Educ.:* Melbourne Grammar School. Commonwealth Controller of Fibres and Cordage; Member Commonwealth Raw Jute Purchasing Committee, 1941-54. Director: Downs and Son Pty. Ltd.; W. A. Rope and Twine Co. Pty. Ltd.; Jarke Pty. Ltd.; Fibre Plantations, Ltd.; The Commercial Bank of Aust. Ltd.; The Union Trustee Co. of Aust. Ltd.; Preston Motors Holdings Ltd. *Address:* James Miller & Co. Pty. Ltd., Toorak, Victoria, Australia; 9 Myrnong Crescent, Toorak, Vic. *Clubs:* Athenæum, Yorick (Melbourne); Amateur Sports, V.R.C., M.C.C., Davey's Bay Yacht, Peninsula Golf, Commonwealth Golf. [*Died* 6 *Oct.* 1961.

VINE, Norman Douglas; Chartered Accountant; *b.* 2 March 1890; s. of John William Vine; *m.* 1913, Florence, *d.* of Thomas Leaverland; one *s.* one *d.* *Educ.:* Belle Vue Road Council School; Leeds Modern School. Articled, 1906 - 11, to Atkinson Smith & Atkinson, Chartered Accountants, Leeds; became Chartered Accountant, and started in Practice on own account 1911, at 21 years of age; F.C.A. 1916. Member Leeds City Council, 1928; Alderman, 1935; Deputy Lord Mayor, 1944-1945; Lord Mayor of Leeds, 1949-50. Member Leeds Provincial Building Society Board, 1944; President Leeds Chamber of Commerce, 1948; North-Eastern Zone Board of Friends' Provident & Century Life Office, 1949. *Recreations:* cricket, football, tennis, squash. *Address:* Lane House, Drury Lane, Pannal, Nr. Harrogate. *T.:* Harrogate 81919, Leeds 24607. *Club:* Leeds and County Conservative (Leeds) [*Died* 25 *Nov.* 1966.

VINES, Col. Clement Erskine, C.I.E. 1935; late Indian Army; *b.* 9 June 1878; *y. s.* of Canon T H. Vines, Prebendary of Lincoln, and Catherine Maria Stuart Menteth; *m.* 1906, Jenny Bonney Bamberger (*d.* 1958); two *d.* *Educ.:* Rossall Sch.; Central Technical Coll 1st Class Certificate Electrical Engineering, 1900; Entered Royal Artillery, 1900; passed Advanced Class Military College of Science, 1904; Assist. Proof and Expr. Officer, 1905-07; joined Indian Ordnance Dept., 1908; served under Ministry of Munitions as Deputy Director of Munition Inspection in U.S.A., 1916-17; Superintendent Ammunition Factory, Dum Dum, 1920-21; Assist. Director of Artillery, A.H.Q., India, 1922-26; Inspector of Guns and Rifles, 1927-28; Ordnance Consulting Officer, India Office, 1929-35; retired, 1935. *Address:* Tremichael, Upper West Terrace, Budleigh Salterton, Devon. *T.:* Budleigh Salterton 228. *Club:* Army and Navy. [*Died* 5 *Jan.* 1964.

VISVESVARAYA, Sir Mokshagundam, K.C.I.E., *cr.* 1915; M.I.C.E.; late Dewan of Mysore; *b.* 15 Sept. 1861. *Educ.:* Central Coll., Bangalore; Coll. of Science, Poona. Hon. D.Sc.: Calcutta, Patna, Allahabad; Hon. LL.D.: Bombay, Mysore; Hon. D.Litt. Benares. Asst. Engineer, Public Works Dept., Bombay, 1884; Exec. Engineer, 1899; Suptg. Engineer, 1904; retd. from Bombay P.W.D., 1908; Special Cons. Engineer to the Nizam's Govt. in connection with Flood Prevention and Drainage of Hyderabad City, Apr.-Oct. 1909; Chief Engineer and Secretary, Public Works and Railway Departments, Government of Mysore, 1909; Dewan (Prime Minister) of Mysore State, 1912-18; Chairman, Bombay Technical and Industrial Education Committee (appointed by the Government of Bombay), 1921-22; Member, New Capital Enquiry Committee, Delhi, 1922; Chairman, Indian Economic Enquiry Committee, 1925; Member, Bombay Back Bay Enquiry Committee, 1926; Chairman, Irrigation Inquiry Committee, 1938; President All-India Manufacturers' Organization, Bombay, since 1941. *Publications:* Reconstructing India, 1920; Planned Economy for India, 1934; Memoirs of My Working Life, 1951. *Recreations:* walking and travel. *Address:* 5 Cubbon Road, Bangalore, India. [*Died* 14 *April* 1962.

VISWA NATH, Rao Bahadur Bhagavatula, C.I.E. 1943; Indian Soil Scientist; *b.* 1 Jan. 1889; *s.* of Joga Rao B.; *m.* 1905, Venkata Lakshmi; six *s.* three *d.* *Educ.:* Maharaja's College of Vizianagram; Andra University (D.Sc.). Served in Agricl. Research Inst. of Iraq Govt., 1919-21; in Coimbatore, 1921-23; Chief Chemist, Agricl. Research Inst. of Coimbatore, 1923-34; Imperial Agricl. Chemist, Imp. Agricl. Research Inst., New Delhi, 1934-44, Dir., 1935-44; Dir. of Agriculture for Madras Govt., 1944-47; Member F.A.O. Rice Study Group, 1947; Principal and Univ. Prof. of Agricultural Science, Benares Univ., 1947-48; Member F.A.O., E.C.A.F.E. Mission, Shanghai, China, 1948; Food Comr. and Dir. of Agriculture, Rajasthan, 1949; Regional Agricl. Production Comr., Min. of Food and Agriculture, Govt. of India, New Delhi 1950 and 1951; Adviser, Agricultural Programmes, Planning Commission, Govt. of India, 1951, 1952; Pres. Agricl. Sect., Indian Science Congress, 1937; Member, Imp. Council of Agricl. Research, 1935-; Fellow: Roy. Inst. of Chemistry of London; Indian Soc. of Soil Science (Past Pres.); Nat. Inst. of Sciences; Indian Acad. of Sciences; Indian Chemical Soc.; Vice-Pres. Soc. of Biological Chemists. Rao Bahadur, 1929; Coronation and Silver Jubilee Medals. *Publications:* articles in scientific journals. *Address:* 8A/85 Western Extension Area, Pusa Road, Karolbagh, New Delhi, India. [*Died* 1 *Feb.* 1964.

VIVIAN, Vice-Admiral John Guy Protheroe, C.B. 1941; *b.* 1887; *s.* of C. H. G. Vivian; *m.* 1919; one *d.* *Educ.:* H.M.S. Britannia. Served European War, 1914-19; War of 1939-45, Admiral Commanding A/A Ships, 1939-41; Admiral Commanding Reserves, 1941-45. *Address:* Culverhays, Bicknoller, Taunton, Somerset. [*Died* 10 *April* 1963.

VIVIAN, Lieut.-Colonel Valentine Patrick Terrel, C.M.G. 1947; C.B.E. 1923 (O.B.E. 1918); Indian Police Service, retired; *b.* 17 Mar. 1886; *s.* of late Comley Vivian, Portrait Painter, Bath and Kensington; *m.* 1911, Mary Primrose, *e. d.* of late Ven. E. J. Warlow; two *s.* one *d.* *Educ.:* St. Paul's School. Entered Indian Police (Imperial Service) 1906; retired 1925; attached Foreign Office, 1923; retired 1951. Served European War (Major, Indian Army Reserve of Officers) in Palestine and Turkey (despatches); re-commissioned (Officers' Emergency Reserve, General List) 1939-46. Officer Legion of Merit (U.S.), 1946. *Address:* Closeburn, 29 Southlands, Pennington, Lymington, Hants. *T.:* Lymington 2414. *Club:* Brokenhurst Manor Golf (Brockenhurst, Hants.) [*Died* 15 *April* 1969.

VIZIANAGRAM, Rajkumar of; Sir Gajapatatiraj Vijaya Ananda, Kt., cr. 1936; *b.* 1905; *s.* of Sri Rajah Pusapati Viziaram, Maharaj of Vizianagram; *m.* 1922, Bhagirathi Devi, *d.* of Raja of Kashipur. Member of Indian Legislative Assembly. *Address:* Vizianagram Palace, Benares, India. [*Died* 2 *Dec.* 1965.

von ANREP, Boris; mosaicist; *b.* St. Petersburg, 28 Sept. 1883; *s.* of Vassili Konstantinovich von Anrep and Paraskeva Mikhailovna Zatzepina; *m.* 1918, Helen Ann Maitland (decd.); one *s.* one *d.* *Educ.:* Imperial School of Law, St. Petersburg. Settled in Paris in 1908 as an artist painter; attended Académie Julien. Served as Captain in Russian Army in Galicia, 1914-16, when was appointed to Russian Govt. Cttee. in London as Military Secretary and Assistant Legal Adviser. Returned to Paris in 1926 and devoted himself to revival of mosaic as an independent art. Chief works in Britain are in: Royal Military College Chapel, Sandhurst, Tate Gallery; Chapel of Keir, Scotland; National Gallery; Bank of England; Greek Cathedral, London; Westminster Cathedral. *Address:* 65 Boulevard Arago, Paris XIII. [*Died* 7 *June* 1969.

von KARMAN, Theodore, Ph.D.; Medal of Merit (U.S.), 1946; Medal of Freedom (U.S.), 1956; Gold Medal (U.S.A.F.), 1956, etc.; Chairman, Advisory Group for Aeronautical Research and Development, N.A.T.O., since 1952; Chief Consultant and Chairman of Technical Advisory Bd. of Aerojet-Gen. Corp., Azusa, Calif.; Scientific Dir. and Hon. Chm. of Bd., Gen. Applied Science Laboratories, Inc., Westbury, L.I., New York (formerly Gruen Applied Sci. Lab., Inc.) since 1955; Chm., Bd. of Direction, Trg. Center for Expertl. Aerodynamics, Rhode-Saint-Genèse, Belgium; Director, Internat. Acad. of Astronautics; Editor-in-Chief of Astronautica Acta; *b.* 11 May 1881; *s.* of Prof. Maurice de Kármán and, Helène (*née* Konn); Naturalised Citizen of U.S.A., 1936; unmarried. *Educ.:* Royal Technical Univ., Budapest; Univ. of Göttingen (Ph.D., M.E.). Research Engineer, Ganz & Co., Germany, 1903-06; Asst. Prof., Roy. Tech. Univ., Budapest, 1903-06; Prof. Univ. of Göttingen, 1909-12; Director, Inst. for Aeronautics, Tech. Univ., Aachen, 1912-29 (Officer, Austro-Hungarian Air Corps, 1914-18); Consultant to Junkers Airplane Works, Germany, 1912-1928; to Kawanishi Airplane Co., Japan, 1927-29; Director: Guggenheim Aeronautical Laboratories, Cal. Inst. of Tech., 1930-49; Jet Propulsion Lab., Cal. Inst. of Tech., 1938-45; Consultant to: Ballistic Research Lab., Dept. of Ordnance, U.S. Army, 1938-1952; General Electric Co., N.Y., 1940-60; Northrop Aircraft Co. Cal., 1941-49. Founder, Aerojet Engineering Corp. (now Aerojet Gen. Corp.), 1942; Chm. Scientific Advisory Board to Chief of Staff, U.S.A.F., 1944-55 (Chairman Emeritus of U.S.A.F.). Consultant in various schemes and mem. special Cttees. Holds numerous hon. degrees in Engineering, Science, Law and Philosophy. Hon. Prof. Columbia Univ., N.Y., 1948-; Prof. Emeritus, Cal. Inst. of Tech., 1949. Several Gold Medals, etc., from 1941, including Gold Medal, Roy. Aeronautical Soc., 1952. Rouse Ball Lecturer, Cambridge Univ., 1937; Wilbur Wright Lectr., Roy. Aeronautical Soc., 1937, etc. Hon. Member, Member, Hon. Fellow, or Fellow of many American and foreign societies; Foreign Mem., Royal Society (London), 1946; Hon. Fell., Royal Aeronautical Soc., London. Commandeur de la Légion d'Honneur, 1955, and holds several other foreign decorations. *Publications:* General Aero-dynamic Theory (with J. M. Burgers) 2 vols., 1924; Mathematical Methods in Engineering (with M. A. Biot), 1940 (trans. into several langs.; Aerodynamics—selected topics in light of their historical development, 1954 (trans. into several langs.); Collected Works of Dr. Theodore von Kármán, 4 vols. (England). *Address:* (home) 1501 South Marengo Ave., Pasadena 5, Cal., U.S.A. *T.:* Sycamore 9-3410; Advisory Group for Aeronautical Research and Development (AGARD), Palais de Chaillot, Paris. *Clubs:* Men's Faculty (of Columbia Univ.); Athenæum (of Calif. Inst. of Tech.); Princeton (S. Cal.). [*Died* 7 *May* 1963.

VOROSHILOV, Kliment Efremovich; Order of Lenin (8 times); Order of the Red Banner (6 times); Hero of the Soviet Union, 1956; Hero of Socialist Labour, 1960; Praesident of the Praesidium of the Supreme Soviet of the U.S.S.R., 1953-60; Member, Praesidium of the Supreme Soviet, since 1960; Marshal of the Soviet Union since 1935; Mem. of Political Bureau of Central Cttee. of Communist Party of Soviet Union, 1926-52, and of its Praesidium 1952-60; *b.* Dnepropetrovsk (then Eka-

terinoslav) Region, 4 Feb. 1881; *s.* of a railway worker. Worked in mines, ironworks, etc. from age of six; began work as fitter, at Alchevsk, 1896; led strike, 1899; joined Bolshevik group of Russian Social Democratic Labour Party, 1903; led underground work in Lugansk, 1903-07; leader of Lugansk workers in 1905 Revolution; delegate to Stockholm Congress of Bolshevik Party, meeting Lenin and Stalin, 1906; delegate to London Congress of Bolshevik Party, 1907; arrested, exiled, and escaped, each on several occasions, 1907-14; active underground political work in Petrograd, Baku and Tzaritsyn, 1908-17; after Feb. Revolution, 1917, returned to prepare Lugansk workers for Oct. Revolution; Mem. Petrograd City Council, 1917; organised and led Lugansk Socialist Partisan detachment against German occupationists, 1918; military commander in defence of Tzaritsyn, 1918-19; People's Commissar for Home Affairs in Ukraine, Commander of Kharkov military district and of Fourteenth Army, operations against Denikin, Wrangel, etc., 1919-20; member of Central Committee of Communist Party, 1921; suppression of Kronstadt counter-revolutionary rising, and operations in the Soviet Far East, 1921; Commander, N. Caucasus Military Area 1921-24; Moscow Military Area, 1924-25; People's Commissar for Military and Naval Affairs of U.S.S.R. and Chm. Revolutionary Military Council, 1925-1934; U.S.S.R. People's Commissar for Defence, 1934-40; elected to Supreme Soviet of U.S.S.R., 1937-; Vice-Chairman, U.S.S.R. Council of People's Commissars, 1940; Member State Defence Committee, 1941-45; Commander-in-Chief, North Western Front. Took part in Moscow Conference with British and U.S. representatives, 1941, and Teheran Conference 1943; Chairman, Allied Control Commission, Hungary, 1945-47; Vice-Chm. U.S.S.R. Council of Ministers, 1946-53. *Publications:* Life Stories (Memoirs), 1968; books on military science and history. *Address:* Praesidium, U.S.S.R. Supreme Soviet, Kremlin, Moscow, U.S.S.R.
[*Died* 3 *Dec.* 1969.

VULLIAMY, Edward, M.A.; *b.* 1 Jan. 1876; *s.* of Theodore Vulliamy, Nonancourt, Eure, France, and Hélène Réal de Champlouis; *m.* 1901, Katherine Tite; three *s.* one *d.* *Educ.:* Chigwell; King's College, Cambridge (Classics and Modern Languages). Late Cambridge Univ. Lecturer (French); and Assist. Lecturer Modern Languages, Pembroke College. Watercolour painter; exhibitor N.E.A.C., etc.; Honorary Keeper of the Pictures, Fitzwilliam Museum, Cambridge, resigned 1955; Musketry Instructor, Wareham, Cambridge, 1915; Intelligence Corps, B.E.F., France, 1918; Special Constable, 1939-45. *Address:* 19 Millington Road, Cambridge. *T.:* Cambridge 50748. [*Died* 6 *Jan.* 1962.

VYSE, Major-General Sir Richard G. H. H.; *see* Howard-Vyse.

W

WACE, Sir Blyth; *see* Wace, Sir F. B.

WACE, Brig.-General Edward Gurth, C.B. 1919; D.S.O. 1916; late R.E.; *b.* Poona, 19 Nov. 1876; *s.* of late Major-Gen. R. Wace, C.B., R.A.; *m.* Evelyn Mabel Hayward, *d.* of late Col. G. H. Sim, C.B., C.M.G.; one *s.* three *d.* *Educ.:* Marlborough; R.M.A., Woolwich. Adjutant Service Batt, R.E. 1903-04; Adjt. Training Batt. R.E., 1904-07; Staff Capt. Army Hdqrs., 1907-10; General Staff Officer, War Office, 1912-15; General Staff, with B.E.F. 1915-16 (Bt. Lt.-Col.); Controller of Labour, B.E.F. 1918-19; British Commissioner and President of the Saar Basin Delimitation Commission, 1920-21; retired pay, 1926. *Address:* 10 Watchbell Street, Rye. *T.:* Rye 2307. [*Died* 1 *June* 1962.

WACE, Sir (Ferdinand) Blyth, K.C.I.E., *cr.* 1947 (C.I.E. 1939); C.S.I. 1943; late I.C.S., Punjab; *b.* 21 Feb. 1891; *s.* of Herbert Wace, C.M.G., Ceylon Civil Service; *m.* 1917, Mary Alice Graveley Morritt; one *s.* two *d.* *Educ.:* Cheltenham; Brasenose College, Oxford. I.C.S., 1914; war service in India, 1916-18; has held posts of Deputy Commissioner, Colonisation Officer, Registrar of Co-operative Societies, Comr. and Secy. to Govt. in the Punjab; retired, 1946. County Councillor, West Sussex, 1949-, Alderman, 1958. *Address:* The Orchard, S. Harting, Petersfield, Hants. *T.:* Harting 264.
[*Died* 23 *March* 1964.

WADDELL, Gilbert, C.I.E. 1946; Indian Police, retired; *b.* 24 October 1894; *s.* of George Waddell, Drumcro House, Magheralin, County Down, Ireland; *m.* 1925, Winifred Mary, *d.* of C. P. Charlesworth, J.P., Skipton, Yorkshire; no *c.* *Educ.:* Victoria Coll., Jersey. Indian Police, 1914; seconded to Indian Army Reserve, 1918-19; Supt., Indian Police, 1924; Dep. Insp.-Gen., 1940; Insp.-Gen., Rajputana States, 1947; retd. from Indian Police, 1947. Served in British Police Mission to Greece with rank of Deputy Chief, 1948-50, employed on post-war re-organisation of Royal Greek Gendarmerie. Sec. of the Ceylon Planters' Society, 1952-1958, retd. King's Police and Fire Services Medal, 1943. *Recreations:* big game and other photography, fishing, philately. *Address:* c/o National and Grindlay's Bank, 13 St. James's Sq., S.W.1. *Club:* Royal Commonwealth Society.
[*Died* 11 *June* 1967.

WADDELL, Helen, M.A., Hon. D.Litt. Durham, Belfast, Columbia; Hon. LL.D. St. Andrews; *b.* Tokio, 31 May 1889; *d.* of Rev. Hugh Waddell of Manchuria and Japan. *Educ.:* Victoria College and Queen's University, Belfast. Member of Somerville College, Oxford, 1920-22; Cassell Lecturer for St. Hilda's Hall, Oxford, 1921; Lecturer Bedford College, London, 1922-23; held Susette Taylor Fellowship from Lady Margaret Hall, Oxford, in Paris, 1923-25; awarded A. C. Benson Silver Medal by the Royal Society of Literature, 1927; Member of the Irish Academy of Letters, 1932; Corresponding Fellow of Medieval Academy of America, 1937. *Publications:* The Wandering Scholars, 1927; Mediæval Latin Lyrics, 1929; John of Salisbury in Essays and Studies, 1928; Peter Abelard: The Abbé Prévost, 1933; Lyrics from the Chinese, 1913; A Book of Medieval Latin for Schools; Introduction to the Paris and Blecheley Diaries of Rev. William Cole; Translation of Manon Lescaut, 1931; Beasts and Saints, 1934; The Desert Fathers, 1936; Stories from Holy Writ, 1949. *Address:* c/o Constable & Co., 10 Orange Street, W.C.2.
[*Died* 5 *March* 1965.

WADDY, Dorothy Knight, Q.C. 1957; **Her Honour Judge Waddy;** a County Court Judge since 1968; *b.* 8 Sept. 1909; 2nd *d.* of late William Knight Dix and late Jane (*née* l'Anson); *m.* 1947, Bentley H. Waddy, M.C., Q.C. (*d.* 1956); one *d.* *Educ.:* St. Christopher's School, Hampstead; Lausanne University; University College, London. B.A. (Hons.) English, London Univ., 1931; called to Bar, Inner Temple, 1934; Member of South-Eastern Circuit and Kent Sessions. Deputy-Recorder of Deal, 1946, during absence of T. Christmas Humphreys at the Tokyo War Trials; Deputy-Recorder of Margate, 1949-50, during illness of Recorder; member General

Council of the Bar, 1953-57; member Legal Aid Area Cttee. (No. 2), 1956-61; Chm. West Kent National Assistance Appeal Tribunal, 1959-61; Legal member, Mental Health Review Tribunal, South East Metropolitan Area, 1960-66; Temp. Dep. Chm., S.E. London Q.S., 1965-67. *Publications:* In The Eyes of the Law (with G. Evelyn Miles), 1937 (Third edition, solely, 1962); The Law Relating to Competitive Trading, 1938; Medical Evidence in Personal Injury Cases (with A. H. Todd, F.R.C.S.), 1961; Contracts of Employment, 1963. *Recreations:* travel, music, gardening. *Address:* The Vane, 7 Bickley Rd., Bickley, Kent. *T.:* 01-467 1174. [*Died* 8 *Jan.* 1970.

WADE, Sir Armigel de Vins, Kt., *cr.* 1937; C.M.G. 1935; O.B.E. 1931; *b.* 14 Oct. 1880; *s.* of Charles Aubrey Wade and Sarah Crouch; *m.* 1917, Constance Marianne Douglas Fox (*d.* 1938); *m.* 1947, Monica (Mona) Mary, *yr. d.* of late Donald Galbally. *Educ.:* Lancing; Keble Coll., Oxford Senior Classical Master, Worksop Coll., Notts, 1906-1909; Forest School, 1909-11; Assistant District Commissioner, East Africa Protectorate, 1912; Chief Native Commissioner, Kenya Colony, 1932 Chief Secretary to the Government of Kenya, 1934-39; Acting Governor and Commander-in-Chief, March-Aug. 1935, Dec. 1936-April 1937 *Recreations:* water-colour painting, cricket, tennis, golf, fishing; was Colony Commissioner for B.P. Boy Scouts (Silver Acorn, 1936). *Address:* West Chiltington, Pulborough, Sussex. *T.:* West Chiltington 3230. [*Died* 4 *Dec.* 1966.

WADE, Brigadier Ernest Wentworth, D.S.O. 1918; O.B.E. 1940; late R.A.M.C.; *b.* 14 Oct. 1889; *s.* of late Major George Augustus Wade, R.A.M.C., and Caroline Oram Ada Corrall; *m.* 1st, 1918, Winifred (*d.* 1939), *d.* of D. McG. Alexander, Rathgar, Dublin; one *s.* (two *d.* decd.); 2nd, 1940, Anna Reaveley, *d.* of late T. R. Glover. *Educ.:* Stubbington House, Fareham; Univ. College, Bristol (Medical Entrance Scholarship). Augustin Pritchard Anatomy Prize 1910; 1st Place R.A.M.C. Entrance Examination, July 1913; M.B. B.S. Lond. 1913, M.D. Lond. 1921, D.P.H., R.C.S. 1924, D.T.M. and H. R.C.S. 1924; Specialist in Hygiene, 1925; House Physician, Bristol General Hospital, 1913; House Surgeon, Bristol Royal Infirmary, 1914; Joined R.A.M.C. 1913; Captain, 1915, Major, 1923; Instructor, Army School of Hygiene, Aldershot, 1925; D.A.D.H. Lucknow and P. and A. Districts, India, 1927-1930; D.A.D.H. Army Headquarters, India, 1931; D.A.D.H. South Western Area, Portsmouth, 1932-34; Lt.-Col., 1935; Assistant Director of Hygiene, Southern Command, India, 1935-39; A.D.H. Scottish Command, 1939; Colonel, 1938; A.D.M.S Orkney and Shetland Defences, May-Sept. 1940; A.D.M.S. 52nd (L) Division, 1940-41; D.D.M.S. 3 Corps, Aug.-Dec. 1941; D.D.M.S. E.F. Home Forces, Jan.-June 1942; D.D.M.S. 1st Army, June 1942-July 1943; Inspector of Medical Services, War Office, Aug. 1943-Apr. 1944; O.C. 111 General Hospital, May-Sept. 1944; D.D.M.S. Control Commission for Germany, Oct. 1944; retired pay, 1946. Served European War, B.E.F., Aug. 1914-Oct. 1919, Acting Lieut.-Colonel, May 1917-Oct. 1919 (D.S.O., 1914 star, General Service and Victory Medals); Coronation Medal, 1937; War of 1939-45 (O.B.E., 1939-45 Star, Africa Star 1st Army, Defence Medal, War Medal). *Address:* c/o Glyn, Mills and Co., Holt's Branch, Kirkland House, Whitehall, S.W.1. [*Died* 4 *Dec.* 1970.

WADE, Major George Frederick Dennis, C.B.E. 1956; D.L.; J.P.; *b.* 14 June 1899; *m.* 1922, Beryl, *yr. d.* of late C. A. and Mrs. Vicarino, Knowle; four *d.* *Educ.:* Wellington; R.M.A. Woolwich. 2nd Lt. R.H.A. and R.F.A., 1917; served in France and Belgium; transferred R.A.R.O., 1919; rejoined, 1939; served War of 1939-45, Holland and Germany. J.P. Warwickshire, 1949; High Sheriff of Warwickshire, 1956-1957; D.L. Warwickshire, 1959. *Address:* Pinley Hill, Hatton, Warwick. *T.:* Claverdon 245. *Club:* Conservative (Birmingham). [*Died* 14 *May* 1968.

WADE-EVANS, Rev. Arthur Wade; *b.* Fishguard, 31 Aug. 1875; *s.* of Titus and Elizabeth Evans; *m.* 1899, Florence May Dixon (*d.* 1953); one *d.* (and *er. d.* decd.). *Educ.:* Jesus Coll., Oxford. Vicar of France Lynch, Glos., 1909-26, of Potterspury, 1926-1932; Rector of Wrabness, 1932-57. *Publications:* Welsh Medieval Law, 1909; Life of St. David, 1923; Welsh Christian Origins, 1934; Nennius's History of the Britons, 1938; Vitae Sanctorum Britanniae, 1945; Coll Prydain, 1950; The Emergence of England and Wales, 1956 (Belgium), 1959 (Cambridge); contributor to the Encyclopædia Britannica (last edition). *Address:* Iona, Upper Third Avenue, Frinton-on-Sea, Essex. [*Died* 4 *Jan.* 1964.

WADELY, Frederick William, O.B.E. 1955; M.A., Mus.D. (Cantab.), F.R.C.O.; Hon. A.R.C.M.; Hon. R.A.M.; Organist and Master of the Music, Carlisle Cathedral, 1910-60; *b.* Kidderminster, 30 July 1882; *e. s.* of William Edward and Zoë Wadely; *m.* 1910, Ethel Muriel, 3rd *d.* of Charles Berners Stokes of Lloyds Bank, Malvern; one *s.* two *d.* *Educ.:* Charles I.'s School, Kidderminster; Selwyn College, Cambridge; Royal College of Music. A pupil of his father; appointed at the age of 13 Organist of Wolverley Parish Church; Organ Scholar at Selwyn College, Cambridge, 1900; Stewart of Rannoch Scholar, 1901-3; B.A., Mus.B., Cambridge, 1903; while at the Royal College of Music, where he studied under Sir Charles Stanford, Sir Walter Parratt, and Dr. Charles Wood, he was Organist and Choirmaster at St. Andrew's, Uxbridge; Organist and Choirmaster, Malvern Priory Church, 1904; formed the Malvern Choral Union, 1906; conductor till 1910; conductor Carlisle Symphony Concerts, 1912, 1913, and 1914; conductor of the Carlisle Musical Society, 1914; Conductor of the Carlisle Choral Society, 1919; M.A. 1907; D.Mus., 1915. Examiner: Royal College of Organists, 1934; Royal Schools of Music, 1943; Cambridge Univ., 1948; Durham Univ. 1957. Fellow of the Royal School of Church Music, 1947. Chairman, Carlisle and District Musical Festival. Hon. Freeman, City of Carlisle, 1966. *Publications:* part-songs, anthems, carols, etc.; larger compositions include settings for chorus and orchestra of Longfellow's Norman Baron; Tennyson's Merman and Mermaid; Shelley's three lyrics, To the Night, Proserpine, and Serenade—from the Arabic; The Music to the Carlisle Historical Pageant, 1928, 1951; Christ is our Corner Stone, for Festival of the Sons of the Clergy, 1936; Christmas Carol (Dickens); Scenes from Pickwick Papers (Dickens); The Holy Birth, a Nativity Play; also two concert overtures, three light operas, an Irish suite, Old English Suite (chorus and orchestra), and a set of symphonic variations. *Address:* 11 Longlands Rd. South, Carlisle. *T.:* 25044. [*Died* 28 *May* 1970.

WADIA, D. N., F.R.S. 1957; M.A., D.Sc., F.G.S.; Dept. of Atomic Energy of India since 1954; Geological Adviser to Govt. of India; *b.* 23 Oct. 1883; *m.* 1940, Meher G. Mediwala. *Educ.:* Baroda Coll.; Bombay Univ. Prof. of Geology, Prince of Wales Coll., Jammu, Kashmir State, 1907-20; Geological Survey of India, 1921; carried out the Geological Survey of the Pir Panjal Range, Hazara and Kashmir Himalaya; N.W. Punjab and parts of Waziristan; President, Indian Science Congress, 1942; Pres. (1945-1946), Nat. Inst. of Sciences, India; Lyell Medallist, Geol. Soc. London. *Publications:* Geology of India, 5th Edition, 1961; also

Papers. *Address:* 10 King George's Avenue, New Delhi, India. [*Died* 15 *June* 1969.

WAGER, Lawrence Rickard, F.R.S. 1946; F.G.S., F.R.G.S.; Sc.D. (Cantab.); Professor of Geology, Oxford University, since 1950; Fellow of University College, Oxford; *b.* 5 Feb. 1904; *s.* of Morton E. Wager; *m.* 1934, Phyllis Margaret, *d.* of Edgar Worthington; two *s.* three *d.* *Educ.:* Leeds Grammar School; Pembroke College, Cambridge. Goldsmiths' Company's studentship for research in geology at Cambridge, 1926-29; Lecturer in Mineralogy and Petrology at Reading University, 1929-43; Professor of Geology at the Durham Colleges in Univ. of Durham, 1944-50. Geologist to British Arctic Air-Route Expedition, 1930-1931; Member of Mount Everest Expedition, 1933; Leader of British East Greenland Expedition, 1935-36; served in R.A.F.V.R., 1940-44 (despatches); Leverhulme Fellow, 1935-36; Arctic Medal, 1933; Mungo Park Medal, 1936; Bigsby Medal Geological Soc. of London, 1945; Spendlarov Prize, International Geological Congress, 1948. Correspondent of Geological Soc. of America. President of geological section, British Association, 1958. Pres. Mineralogical Soc. of London, 1960-63. Lyell Medal, Geological Soc. of London, 1962. *Publications:* Chapters in Everest, 1933; geological and petrological papers. *Recreation:* mountaineering. *Address:* Stone Croft, South Hinksey, Oxford. [*Died* 20 *Nov.* 1965.

WAGG, Alfred Ralph, C.B.E. 1957; for many years Director and Chairman Helbert, Wagg & Co., Ltd., merchant bankers, retired, 1959; *b.* 14 March 1877; *s.* of Arthur and Mathilde Wagg. *Educ.:* Eton; King's College, Cambridge. Member of Court of the Fishmongers' Company (Prime Warden, 1945). *Address:* The Hermitage, East Grinstead, Sussex. *T.:* East Grinstead 23129. *Clubs:* Brooks's, St. James'. [*Died* 30 *May* 1969.

WAGNER, Wieland (Adolf Gottfried); Co-Director of the Bayreuth Festival; Operatic Producer; *b.* Bayreuth, 5 Jan. 1917; *s.* of late Siegfried Wagner and of Winifred (*née* Williams); *g.s.* of Richard Wagner and *g.g.s.* of Franz Liszt; *m.* Gertrud Wagner; one *s.* three *d.* Has produced all the works of Richard Wagner from Der fliegende Holländer to Parsifal at Bayreuth, and Rienzi at Stuttgart. Has also, as Guest Producer, presented Wagner's work in Berlin, Vienna, Paris, Brussels, Copenhagen, Geneva, Milan, Rome, Venice, Naples, etc. Other productions include Gluck's Orpheus, Beethoven's Fidelio, Bizet's Carmen, Orff's Antigonae, Verdi's Aida and Othello, Berg's Lulu and Wozzeck, etc. *Address:* c/o Bayreuther Festspiele, 8580 Bayreuth, Bavaria, Germany. [*Died* 16 Oct. 1966.

WAGSTAFF, Professor John Edward Pretty, M.A., D.Sc.; Professor of Physics in the University of Durham, 1924-55; *b.* 11 Aug. 1890; *o. s.* of D. Wagstaff, Leicester; *m.* Dorothy Margaret, 2nd *d.* of George Greig McRobie, J.P., Portsoy; one *s.* one *d.* *Educ.:* Alderman Newton's School, Leicester; St. John's College, Cambridge (scholar), 1st Class, Part I Mathematical Tripos, 1912, 1st Class, Part II Natural Sciences Tripos, 1915. Fellow of St. John's College, 1922; Research Physicist at Research Department, Royal Arsenal, Woolwich, 1916-19; lecturer in Physics (University of Leeds), 1920-24. *Publications:* papers on physical subjects in scientific journals. *Recreations:* motoring and golf. *Address:* Dovern, Observatory Road, Durham. [*Died* 2 *Aug.* 1963.

WAHBA, Sheikh Hafiz, Hon. K.C.V.O. 1947; Order of the Nile; Order of Rhafdein, 1937; Political Adviser to H.M. The King of Saudi Arabia; Ambassador of Saudi Arabia to the Court of St. James's, 1963-66 (also 1948-56) (Min., 1930-48); Dir., Arabian American Oil Company (Aramco), since 1959; *b.* 1889; *m.*; two *s.* four *d.* *Educ.:* Azhar University; Muslim Jurisprudence College, Cairo. In pearl business until 1920; Counsellor to King Ibn Saud when Sultan of Nejd; Governor of Mecca, 1924-1926; Minister of Education and Assistant to Viceroy of Hejaz, 1926-29. *Publications:* Arabia in the 20th Century, 1934; Fifty Years in Arabia, 1962; Arabian Days, 1964; articles on Arabia and Arab History. *Address:* Al Dewan, Al Malaki Riad, Saudi Arabia. [*Died* 23 *Nov.* 1967.

WAIGHT, Leonard, C.M.G. 1951; *b.* 1 October 1895; *s.* of Frank Herbert Waight, Welwyn, Hertfordshire; *m.* 1948, Aïda Violet, *d.* of S. Räaman. *Educ.:* Hillmartin College, Highgate. Served European War, 1914-18, Canadian Mounted Rifles, Royal Flying Corps, Royal Air Force, Intelligence Corps (despatches twice). Morgan Grenfell & Co. Ltd., 1919-39. Occupied Enemy Territory Administration, 1941-1943, Controller of Finance and Accounts, 1943-44 (despatches); Financial Adviser to the Governor of Burma, 1944-47; British Treasury Representative in the Middle East, 1947-51; U.K. Member on International Materials Conference, Washington, 1951-53, Vice-Chm., 1953; U.K. Delegate Internat. Cotton Advisory Cttee., 1953; U.K. Alternate Director Internat. Bank for Reconstruction and Development, 1953; U.K. Treasury Representative in South Asia, New Delhi, 1953-57; Chief of Finance and Establishments, I.T.A., 1957-63. *Publications:* History and Mechanism of the Exchange Equalisation Account, 1938; British System of Exchange Control, 1939. *Address:* 4 Netherton Grove, Chelsea, S.W.10. [*Died* 15 *Jan.* 1970.

WAINEWRIGHT, Brig.-Gen. Arthur Reginald, C.M.G. 1919; D.S.O. 1918; late R.A.; *b.* 1874; *s.* of late J. H. Wainewright, Hove, Sussex. *Educ.:* Rugby School; R.M.A., Woolwich. Served S. Africa, 1899-1902 (Queen's medal with two clasps, despatches); European War, 1914-19 (despatches, D.S.O., C.M.G., Croix de Guerre). *Address:* Springs Farm, P.O. Box 139, Limuru, Republic of Kenya. *Clubs:* Naval and Military, Cavalry. [*Died* 23 *July* 1970.

WAINWRIGHT, Major-Gen. Charles Brian, C.B. 1946; Director Duck Ringing Research Station since 1949; *b.* 17 Aug. 1893; *s.* of C. H. Wainwright, J.P.; *m.* 1917, Violet Myfanwy, *d.* of W. J. Foster, M.R.C.S., L.R.C.P.; one *d.* (one *s.* decd.). *Educ.:* Wellington College, Berkshire; Lincoln College, Oxford. Retired, 1948. *Address:* Hill Farm Malting Green Layer-de-la-Haye, Colchester. *Club:* Army and Navy. [*Died* 23 *Oct.* 1968.

WAINWRIGHT, Elsie, M.A. (Lond.); *d.* of Rev. A. Wainwright. *Educ.:* North London Collegiate School; Bedford High School; Bedford College (University of London). Lecturer in English at Southlands College, London, 1919-26. Headmistress of Jersey College for Girls, 1926-28; Headmistress of Penrhos College, Colwyn Bay, 1928-38; Assistant Examiner to University of London, in English, 1921-26; Governor of Battersea County School, 1924-26; Member of the Court of Governors of the University of North Wales, 1928; Governor of Colwyn Bay Secondary School, 1935; District President National Council of Women, 1934; Educational administrative work in Notts, 1938; Schools Adviser, Lincolnshire-Kesteven, 1948; Acting Principal, Kesteven Training Coll. for Women Teachers, 1953-54; Asst. Education Officer, Kesteven, 1958-60. Methodist Local Preacher.

Governor of: Clacton County High School; Clacton County Secondary School for Girls. *Address:* Eslaford, 12 Cherry Tree Avenue, Clacton-on-Sea, Essex. [*Died* 23 *Aug.* 1964.

WAIT, Walter Ernest, C.M.G. 1930; F.Z.S.; Ceylon Civil Service; retired, 1934; *b.* 1878; 2nd *s.* of William George Wait, Coonor, Nilgiris, S. India; *m.* 1910, Elizabeth Winchester, *d.* of Rev. William Aitken; one *s.* two *d.* *Educ.:* Fettes College, Edinburgh; Edinburgh University, M.A., 1st class Honours Classics, 1902; Entered Ceylon Civil Service, 1902; Assistant Settlement Officer, 1905; Police Magistrate, Colombo, 1915; Settlement Officer, 1920; Principal Collector Customs, 1927; Deputy Chief Secretary, 1932; served S. African War, 1900-1, in Volunteer Service Company, 1st Bn. Royal Scots (medal, 4 clasps). *Publication:* Manual of the Birds of Ceylon, 1925; 2nd, ed. 1931. *Recreations:* ornithology, gardening. *Address:* Applegarth, Aldbury, Tring, Herts. [*Died* 3 *Jan.* 1961.

WAITE, Herbert William, C.M.G. 1954; C.I.E. 1938; Principal, Punjab (Pakistan) Police Training School, Sargodha, 1949-54; *b.* 30 June 1887; *er. s.* of late Henry Waite; unmarried. *Educ.:* Leamington College; Sutton Valence School. Assistant Superintendent, Indian Police, Punjab, 1907; Superintendent, 1917; Personal Assistant to Inspector-General of Police, Punjab, 1919-1921; Principal, Police Training School, Phillaur, 1926-27; Deputy Inspector-General Indian (Imperial) Police, Punjab, 1933; retired, 1942; Emergency Commission, Indian Army, 1941-46. *Recreations:* shooting, travel, ornithology. *Address:* c/o National and Grindlay's Bank Ltd., 13 St. James's Sq., S.W.1. *Club:* Punjab (Lahore). [*Died* 23 *July* 1967.

WAKE, Maj.-Gen. Sir Hereward, 13th Bt. of Clevedon, *cr.* 1621; C.B. 1933; C.M.G. 1918; D.S.O. 1901; *b.* 11 Feb. 1876; *e. s.* of 12th Bt. and Catherine (*d.* 1944), *d.* of Sir Edward St. Aubyn, 1st Bt., St. Michael's Mount, Cornwall, and *sister* of 1st Lord St. Levan; *S.* father, 1916; *m.* 1912, Margaret Winifred, *e. d.* of late Robert H. Benson; three *s.* three *d.* (and one *d.* decd.). *Educ.:* Eton; Royal Military Coll., Sandhurst; Staff Coll. Entered army, 1897; served South Africa, 1899-1902 (once wounded, despatches four times, Queen's medal 5 clasps, King's medal 2 clasps, D.S.O.); European War, 1914-18 (despatches, Bt. Lt.-Col., C.M.G.); Brig.-Gen. Dec. 1917; Commanded 4th Batt. K.R.R.C., in India, 1920-23; 162nd (East Midland) Territorial Infantry Brigade, 1928-29; A.D.C. to the King, 1931-32; Commanded 12th Infantry Brigade, Dover, 1929-32; Maj.-Gen. 1932; Commander 46th (North Midland) Division T.A., 1934-37; retired pay, 1937; served again 1939-40, and Commander Northants Home Guard, 1940-43; D.L., J.P. Northants; Colonel Commandant, 1st Bn. K.R.R.C., 1938-46; Colonel Comdt. Northants Army Cadet Force, 1943-45; a Freeman of town of Dover; High Sheriff of Northants., 1944; holds bronze medal of Roy. Humane Soc.; Comdr. Légion d'Honneur and Order of Crown of Italy. *Publication:* Ed. (with W. F. Deedes) Swift and Bold, 1949. *Heir:* *s.* Major Hereward Wake, M.C. *Address:* Courteenhall, Northampton; Axford Lodge, Basingstoke, Hants. *Club:* Brooks's. [*Died* 4 *Aug.* 1963.

WAKEFIELD, Sir Edward (Birkbeck) 1st Bt. *cr.* 1962; C.I.E. 1945; *b.* 24 July 1903; 3rd *s.* of late Roger William Wakefield, M.B., B.Ch., J.P., Birklands, Kendal, Westmorland; *m.* 1929, Constance Lalage, *e. d.* of late Sir John Perronet Thompson, K.C.S.I., K.C.I.E., I.C.S.; two *s.* (two *d.* decd.). *Educ.:* Haileybury; Trin. Coll., Camb. M.A. (1st class Classical Tripos, parts I and II); joined Indian Civil Service, 1927; Political Department 1930; served in Punjab, Rajputana, Kathiawar, Baluchistan, Central India, Tibet and Persian Gulf; Chief Minister, Kalat State 1933-36, Nabha State 1939-41 and Rewa State 1943-45; Joint Secretary, Political Dept., Delhi, 1946-47; M.P. (C.) West Derbyshire, 1950-62; Assistant Whip, 1954-56; a Lord Comr. of the Treasury, 1956-58; Comptroller of H.M. Household, 1958-59; Vice-Chamberlain, 1959-60; Treasurer of H.M. Household, 1960-62; Commissioner for Malta, 1962-64, High Commissioner, 1964-65. First Crossing of Laji La (W. Tibet), 1929. Joined Sir Tom Hickinbotham, K.C.M.G., in his circumnavigation of Warbah Island, 1942. Bronze Medal, Royal Humane Society, 1936. *Publication:* Past Imperative: My Life in India, 1927-47, 1966. *Recreation:* shooting. *Heir:* *s.* Edward Humphry Tyrrell Wakefield [*b.* 11 July 1936; *m.* 1st, 1960, Priscilla (marr. diss., 1963), *e. d.* of O. R. Bagot; 2nd, 1966, Hon. Mrs. Colthurst, *e. d.* of 1st Viscount De Lisle]. *Address:* Williamsbrook House, Birr, Co. Offaly, Eire. *T.:* Birr 131. *Clubs:* Bath, Farmers'. [*Died* 14 *Jan.* 1969.

WAKEFIELD, Major-Gen. Hubert Stephen, C.B. 1945; O.B.E. 1919; Major-General (retd.) S. African Staff Corps; *b.* 26 Dec. 1883. Enlisted Cape Mounted Riflemen, 1901; served South African War, 1901-1902; Corporal 1907; Lieutenant 1912; transf. to 1st Regt. S.A. Mounted Riflemen, 1913. Served European War: in S.W. Africa, 1914-16 (wounded, P.O.W.); France and Flanders, Staff Capt. 1st S.A. Infantry Bde., 1917-18; in Persia, 1918-19; Major, D.A.A. & Q.M.G. Resumed rank of Lt. (S.A.M.R.), 1919; Capt., D.A.A.G. Defence H.Q., 1921; S.A. Staff Corps, 1923; Maj. 1929; Lt.-Col.; O.C. No. 1 Mil. Dist. Cape Town, 1931; O.C. No. 4 Mil. Dist. Johannesburg, 1933; Adj.-Gen. Union Defence Force, 1934-39; Colonel, 1935; Brig.-Gen. 1937; retired on pension, 1939. Recalled for service, 1939. Served War of 1939-45: Dep. Adj.-Gen. 1940; Deputy Chief of Staff, 1944; Adj.-Gen., 1945. Major-Gen., 1945. Released from service, 1946. *Address:* 702 Grand National Building, Johannesburg. *Clubs:* Rand, Country (Johannesburg). [*Died* 16 *April* 1962.

WAKEHURST, 2nd Baron, *cr.* 1934, of Ardingly; **John de Vere Loder,** K.G. 1962; K.C.M.G. 1937; Governor of Northern Ireland, 1952-64; *b.* 5 February 1895; *o. s.* of 1st Baron and of late Lady Louise de Vere Beauclerk, *e. d.* of 10th Duke of St. Albans; *S.* father, 1936; *m.* 1920, Margaret (*see* Lady Wakehurst), *d.* of late Sir Charles Tennant, Baronet; three *s.* one *d.* *Educ.:* Eton. 4th Royal Sussex Regiment and Intelligence Corps, 1914-19; served in Gallipoli, Egypt, and Palestine (despatches); Clerk in Foreign Office, 1919-1921; M.P. (C.) East Leicester, 1924-29, Lewes, E. Sussex, 1931-36; Governor of N.S.W., 1937-46; Prior of the Order of St. John of Jerusalem, 1948-69; a Trustee, Royal Opera House, Covent Garden, 1949-57; Governor, The Royal Ballet, 1957-. *Publications:* The Truth about Mesopotamia, Syria, and Palestine, 1923; Industry and the State, 1927; Bolshevism in Perspective, 1931; Colonsay and Oronsay, 1935; Our Second Chance, 1944; Preparation for Peace, 1945. *Recreations:* golf, tennis. *Heir:* *s.* Hon. (John) Christopher Loder [*b.* 23 September 1925; *m.* 1956, Inge Hess, *d.* of Mrs. Walther Hess and *step d.* of Dr. Walther Hess; one *s.* one *d.*]. *Address:* 31 Lennox Gdns., S.W.1. *Club:* Travellers'. [*Died* 30 *Oct.* 1970.

WAKELAM, Lieut.-Col. Henry Blythe Thornhill, T.D.; B.A., R.E.; Journalist, Author and Rugby and Lawn Tennis Commentator to the B.B.C.; *b.* 8 May 1893; *s.* of Henry Titus Wakelam and Mary Whitfield; *m.* 1922, Vera Harriet Greenhill; one *d.* *Educ.:* Marlborough Coll.; Pembroke Coll.,

Cambridge. 2nd Lieut. 2nd C.O.L. Regt. Royal Fusiliers, Aug. 1914; Malta, France, and Belgium, 6th Division; Royal Artillery, March 1915, Gallipoli, Egypt. Palestine, France, 29th and 74th Divisions (despatches twice, wounded); Foch special mission transporting General Haller's Polish Army from France, through Germany to Poland, 1919; resigned commission, 1921; Major R.E. (T.A.), 1936; War Office Lecturer (A.A.G., T.A.), 1936-39; A.D.G.B. 1939; G.S.I., G.H.Q. Middle East, 1940; Propaganda Officer (M. of I.), N. Syria, 1942 (African Star); invalided 1944. Gave first running commentary ever broadcast in this country—England *v.* Wales, Twickenham, 1927; since has carried out all big Rugby matches, Lawn Tennis Championships from Wimbledon, Davis Cup from Wimbledon and Paris and cricket Test Series, including first Television Commentary of Test Match, England *v.* Australia, Lords, 1938; joined Morning Post, 1928, as Rugby Correspondent. President British Legion Dedham and District Branch; Pres. Colchester R.F.C. *Publications:* Twickenham Calling; And the Whistle's Gone; The Game goes on; Half time or the Microphone and Me; Rugby Football; and Lawn Tennis (with L. A. Godfree), 1937 (for the Modern Library of Sport); Rugby Football: How To Succeed; Harlequin Story. *Recreations:* cricket, tennis, swimming, bridge. *Address:* Inverness, Dedham, Essex. *T.:* Dedham 3144. *Club:* Royal Automobile.
[*Died* 10 *July* 1963.

WAKELY, Sir Leonard Day, K.C.I.E., *cr.* 1935; C.B. 1924; *b.* 1880; *s.* of Charles Wakely; *m.* 1908, Florence Dean (*d.* 1947), *d.* of late William Titley; two *s.* one *d.* *Educ.:* St. Olave's School; St. John's Coll., Cambridge. Entered India Office, 1902; Secretary, Political Department, 1924-30; an Assistant Under-Secretary of State, India Office, and Clerk to the Council of India, 1930-34; Deputy Under-Secretary of State for India, 1934-41. *Address:* 37 Marryat Road, S.W.19. *Club:* Oxford and Cambridge. [*Died* 27 *Feb.* 1961.

WALBROOK, Anton; actor; *b.* Vienna, 19 Nov. 1900; *s.* of Adolph Wohlbrück; became naturalized British subject, 1947. Fifteen years on stage; played in Max Reinhardt productions; then on German and English screens; first stage appearance, 1920; entered films, 1931. First London stage appearance as Otto in Design for Living, Haymarket, 1939; Kurt Müller in Watch on the Rhine, Aldwych, Apr. 1942; Michael Fox in Another Love Story, Phœnix, Dec. 1944; Hjalmar Ekdal in The Wild Duck, St. Martin's, Nov. 1948; Hugo Möbius in Man of Distinction, Edinburgh, 1957, etc.; musical plays: Call Me Madam, 1953; Wedding in Paris, 1954. Films include: Victoria the Great, Sixty Glorious Years, Dangerous Moonlight, The Rat, Gaslight, 49th Parallel, Colonel Blimp, The Man from Morocco, La Ronde, Rosalinda, Lola Montez, I Accuse. *Address:* c/o Christopher Mann, 140 Park Lane, W.1. [*Died* 9 *Aug.* 1967.

WALBY, Herbert Charles, D.S.O. 1918; M.C.; M.A. (Cantab.); retired; *b.* 27 June 1897; *e. s.* of late Charles Percy Walby and Catherine Jane Stephens; *m.* 1925, Marie-Magdeleine Yvonne, *d.* of late Emmanuel Ville de Castaigner; one *s.* two *d.* *Educ.:* Perse School; Emmanuel College, Cambridge. 2nd Lieut., 1916; Lieut., 1917; Captain, 1918; Captain and Adjutant, 1918; Staff Capt. 64th Infantry Brigade, 1918; served European War with K.O. Yorkshire L.I., 1916-18 (M.C. and bar, despatches, D.S.O.). Emmanuel College, 1919-20; International banking and industrial studies, France, 1921-1923; Emmanuel College, 1924; Director and Treasurer, Chrysler Corporation, Antwerp, 1925-30; Export Market Research, Jas. Williamson & Son Ltd., 1931-35; General Manager, Jenson & Nicholson (India) Ltd. (Calcutta), 1936-50. War services: Calcutta and Presidency Battn. Armoured Car Co.; Group Leader, Calcutta Special Constabulary; political broadcasts, All India Radio; lectures to British and Allied Forces, 1939-45; Vice-Chm. European Assoc. (Calcutta Br.), 1946-47; Counsellor, O.E.E.C., Paris, 1951-60; Member Kent C.C. for Eastry North Division, 1961-65. Travelled extensively on missions or pleasure throughout Europe, North America, the Mediterranean Countries, Near and Far East. *Publications:* contributions to social and political reviews. *Address:* Candleriggs, Sandwich, Kent. *T.:* Sandwich 2215; Vengeau, Pouancé, M. et L., France. *T.:* Pouancé 52. *Clubs:* Royal Automobile; Bengal; Tollygunge (Calcutta).
[*Died* 31 *Jan.* 1966.

WALCOTT, Captain Colpoys Cleland, C.B.E. 1920; *b.* Maidenhead, 31 July 1878; *s.* of Lyons Roden Sympson Walcott and Jean Cleland Hussey; *m.* 1st, 1913; two *d.*; 2nd, 1933; 3rd, 1939, Idonea Cynthia, *d.* of late Henry Hutchinson, Brougham, Westmorland. *Educ.:* Eastman's, Southsea; H.M.S. Britannia. Naval Cadet, 1892-95; Midshipman, 1895-98; Sub-Lieut., 1898-1900; Lieutenant, 1900; Commander, 1912; retired, 1914; Captain (retired), 1918; served China, 1900; European War, 1914-18; India and N.W. Frontier, 1922-35; Haifa, Palestine, 1935-36; Gold Rod, Coronation of King George VI, 1937; Naval Observer, Spain, 1937-38; War of 1939-45, Aberdeen, Invergordon, Admiralty, Salcombe, Exmouth (L. Barges). *Recreations:* writing (Cleland); interested in all sports. *Address:* 4 Bank Close, Christchurch, Hants.
[*Died* 29 *April* 1961.

WALDEN, Alfred Edward, B.Sc., A.R.I.C.; Principal, Dombodema Teacher-Trg. Sch., retd. 1959; *b.* 10 Jan. 1893; *e. s.* of H. E. Walden, Slough, Bucks; *m.* 1919, Ella Howison, *y. d.* of late James A. Henderson, Aberdeen, and Mrs. Henderson, Nottingham; five *d.* Professor of Chemistry, Wilson College, Bombay, 1919-26; Principal London Mission High School, Bangalore, S. India, 1926-35; Vice-Principal, United Mission High School, Bangalore City, 1935-1937. Principal Inyati Bantu Boys' Institution, near Bulawayo, 1939-54. *Address:* The Knowle, Stakes Hill Rd., Waterlooville, Hants. [*Died* 24 *May* 1968.

WALERAN, 2nd Baron (*cr.* 1905), of Uffculme; Bt., *cr.* 1876; **William George Hood Walrond;** *b.* 30 Mar. 1905; *s.* of late Hon. W. L. C. Walrond, M.P. for Tiverton till his death in 1915, of Bradfield, Cullompton, Devon, and Hon. Charlotte Coats (who *m.* 2nd, 1920, Comdr. H. W. A. Adams, R.N., retd.; he *d.* 1962), *er. d.* of 1st Baron Glentanar; *S.* grandfather, 1925; *m.* 1st, 1932, Margaret Patricia Blackader (from whom he obtained a divorce, 1934); 2nd, 1936, Betty (marriage dissolved, 1952), *yr. d.* of late Sir Emsley Carr; 3rd, 1954, Mrs. Valentine Rothwell, *er. d.* of late E. O. Anderson, C.B.E., of Bleek House, St. Albans, and Mrs. E. O. Anderson, 20 Victoria Grove, W.8. *Educ.:* Eton; Trinity Coll., Oxford. Assistant Private Secretary to Governor-General of New Zealand, 1927-30; joined R.A.F.V.R. 1939; Wing Commander, 1944 (despatches). Director, Ekco Electronics Ltd. *Address:* 22 Launceston Place, W.8; Bradfield Cottage, Cullompton, Devon. *Clubs:* Carlton, Savage, Royal Automobile; Royal Yacht Squadron.
[*Died* 4 *April* 1966 (*ext.*).

WALES, Sir (Alexander) George, Kt., *cr.* 1937; Director of several companies; *b.* Richmond, Melbourne, 11 Oct. 1885; *s.* of Alexander Wales, Melbourne; *m.* 1911, Ethel May, *y. d.* of Judah Bromet, Brunswick; one *d.* Lord Mayor of Melbourne, 1934-37; M.L.C.

Victoria, 193-38; Pres. Melbourne Chamber of Commerce, 1947. *Address:* 7 Martin Court, Toorak, Melbourne, Australia.
[*Died* 31 *May* 1962.

WALES, Rev. Arthur Philip, R.D.; Rector of Warmington and Vicar of Shotteswell since 1945; Rural Dean of Dassett Magna since 1950; *b.* 19 March 1896; *s.* of James Wales, Hampshire; *m.*; two *d.* *Educ.:* Coll. of Resurrection, Mirfield, Yorks. Curate of Liversedge, Yorks, 1921; Rector of Coonamble, N.S.W., 1923; Canon Residentiary of Goulburn Cathedral, Vice-Dean and Rector of Goulburn, 1927-32; Vicar of St. Mark's Coventry, 1932-45; Chaplain Poor Law Institution, Coventry, 1937-45; Hon. Chaplain Coventry and Warwickshire Hospital, 1938-45. *Publications:* various short stories. *Address:* Warmington Rectory, Banbury.
[*Died Nov.* 1964.

WALES, Sir George; *see* Wales, Sir A. G.

WALEY, Arthur David, C.H. 956; C.B.E. 1952; F.B.A.; translator of Chinese literature; late Assistant-Keeper in the Department of Prints and Drawings, British Museum; *b.* 1889. *Educ.:* Rugby; King's Coll., Cambridge. Hon. Fellow: King's Coll., Cambridge; School of Oriental and African Studies, London. Hon. LL.D., Aberdeen; Hon. Lit.D., Oxf. Queen's Medal for Poetry, 1953. *Publications:* 170 Chinese Poems, 1919; More Translations; The Temple; Japanese Poetry; The Nō Plays of Japan; Introduction to the Study of Chinese Painting; The Tale of Genji (6 vols.); The Pillow-book of Sei Shonagon; The Way and Its Power; The Book of Songs; The Analects of Confucius; Three Ways of Thought in Ancient China; Monkey (a Chinese novel); Chinese Poems, 1946; The Life and Times of Po Chü-i, 1948; The Poetry and Career of Li Po, A.D. 701-762, 1951; The Real Tripitaka, 1952; Yuan Mei: Eighteenth Century Chinese Poet, 1957; The Opium War through Chinese Eyes, 1958; Ballads and Stories from Tun-Huang, 1960; The Secret History of the Mongols, 1963. *Recreation:* ski-ing. *Address:* 22 Great James Street, W.C.1. [*Died* 27 *June* 1966.

WALEY, Sir (Sigismund) David, K.C.M.G., *cr.* 1943; C.B. 1933; M.C.; Director of: Ashanti Goldfields Corporation since 1948; International Paints (Holdings) since 1949; W. African Finance Corporation since 1950; Ashanti-Obuasi Trading Co., since 1950; Chairman Export Facilities Ltd. since 1956; Sadler's Wells Trust since 1957; Mercury Theatre Trust since 1957; *b.* 19 March 1887; *s.* of David Frederick Schloss and Rachel Sophia Waley; assumed name of Waley by deed poll, 1914; *m.* 1918, Ruth Ellen, *d.* of Montefiore Simon Waley and Hon. Florence Waley; two *s.* *Educ.:* Rugby; Balliol College, Oxford. Entered Treasury, 1910; Military Service, Aug. 1916-Jan. 1919; 2nd Lieut., 22nd Batt. London Regiment, Aug. 1917 (M.C.); Assistant Secretary, 1924; Principal Asst. Secretary, 1931; Third Secretary, H.M. Treasury, 1946-47; European Recovery Dept., Foreign Office, 1948; Chairman, Furniture Development Council, 1949-57; Chairman, Capital and Provincial News Theatres Ltd., 1952-57. Alternate U.K. delegate Tripartite Commission on German Debts, 1951-52. *Address:* 25 Holland Villas Road, W.14. *T.:* Park 6244.
[*Died* 4 *Jan.* 1962.

WALKDEN, Evelyn; *b.* 1893; *s.* of Lancashire Miners' Leader; *m* 1916, Margaret Croston, O.B.E., J.P. (*d.* 1968), County Alderman; two *s.* one *d.* *Educ.:* St. Peter's Elementary, Bryn; Wigan; Lancs. Evening Insts.; Workers' Educational Assocn. and N.C.L.C. student. Served with 1st Battn. York and Lancasters; joined Lancashire Hussars in 1914; in Salonica, 1916-19; organiser N.U.D.A.W., 1928-41; Founder Sutton Municipal Open-Air Theatre; co-opted member L.C.C. Hospital and Education Sub-Committees; Parliamentary Candidate Rossendale, 1935. M.P. (Ind.) Doncaster Division of Yorkshire, 1947-50 (Lab. 1941-47); Parliamentary Private Secretary Minister of National Insurance (Sir William Jowett), 1944-45; Parliamentary Private Secretary Minister of Food (Sir Ben Smith), 1945-46; All-Party Parliamentary Mission, Greece, 1946. *Recreations:* cricket and Rugby (regular watcher for 60 years). *Address:* 42 All Saints Road, Sutton, Surrey. *T.:* 01-644 5451. [*Died* 12 *Sept.* 1970.

WALKER, Sir Arnold (Learoyd), Kt. 1966; C.B.E. 1953; M.A., M.B., B.Ch., F.R.C.S., F.R.C.O.G.; Cons. Obst. Surgeon, City of London Maternity Hospital; Cons. Gynæcological Surgeon, West London Hospital; Chm., Central Midwives Board, 1946-67; 2nd *s.* of Edward Walker, M.D., Huddersfield; *m.* Gwenville (*d.* 1966), *d.* of late John Clouston, Middlesbrough; no *c.* *Educ.:* Oundle School; Pembroke College, Cambridge; Middlesex Hospital. Served European War (France), 1915-19; Lieut., R.G.A.; wounded 1918 and invalided out of Army; Senior Broderip Scholar (Middlesex Hospital); Obstetric and Gynæcological Registrar and Tutor, Middlesex Hospital, 1925-28; Examiner to the Maternal Mortality Committee, the Ministry of Health. *Publications:* Berkeley's Handbook of Midwifery, 1953; several articles on Obstetric and Gynæcological subjects in medical papers. *Address:* Harewood, Thornton Grove, Hatch End, Middx. *Club:* United University.
[*Died* 14 *Sept.* 1968.

WALKER, Augustus Merrifield; *b.* 11 Feb. 1880; *yr. s.* of late George Booth Walker, Bridge House, Wainfleet, Lincolnshire; *m.* 1910, Frances Katharine, *y. d.* of late Hugh Mortimer Rowland, M.D.; one *s.* one *d.* *Educ.:* Magdalen College School, Oxford. Entered service of Bank of England in 1899; Chief Accountant of the Bank of England, 1921-45. *Recreation:* shooting. *Address:* Ballards, Wickham Bishops, Witham Essex. *T.:* Wickham Bishops 218. [*Died* 15 *Jan.* 1965.

WALKER, Bernard F.; *see* Fleetwood-Walker.

WALKER, Major Sir Cecil Edward, 3rd Bt., *cr.* 1906; D.S.O. 1919; M.C.; *b.* 6 Aug. 1882; *y.* and 3*rd s.* of late Sir Samuel Walker, Bart., Lord Chancellor of Ireland; *S.* half-b. 1932; *m.* Violet (*d.* 1961), *y. d.* of late H. D. McMaster, Gilford, Ireland; one *s.* one *d.* *Educ.:* Rugby. Entered R.A. 1901; retired, 1926; served European War in Royal Horse and Royal Field Artillery, B.E.F. and E.E.F. (despatches, D.S.O., M.C., Legion of Honour). *Heir:* *s.* Hugh Ronald, Major R.A.; *b.* 13 Dec. 1925. *Address:* Ballinamona Hospital, Kilmallock, Co. Limerick, Eire; Pitt Farm, Odcombe, Somerset. [*Died* 2 *July* 1964.

WALKER, Charles Alfred le Maistre, C.B.E. 1920 (M.B.E. 1916); Médaille du Roi Albert (Belgium); F.C.A. (Aust.); J.P. (N.S.W. and Qld.): retired as Senior Partner, C. A. Le Maistre Walker, Son & Co., Chartered Accountants, and as Director of Australian Record Co. Pty. Ltd., 1958; *b.* Melbourne, 27 Mar. 1873; *s.* of Alfred Thomas Walker, Orange, N.S.W., and Marie Elizabeth Journeaux, of Jersey, Channel Islands; *m.* 1st, 1900, Edith Gertrude (*decd.*), *widow* of Alex. Wilson, *d.* of Wm. Wood Cater; two *s.*; 2nd, 1936, Nedda Sedley Bray, *widow* of Leslie Bray, *d.* of late Fred Futter. *Educ.:* State High Schools, Victoria; private tuition. Employed in various commercial firms in Melbourne and Sydney, 1889-1906; partner in firm Fred S. Willis & Co., Public Accountants,

Sydney, Sept. 1906; founded Citizens' War Chest Fund of N.S.W., 1914; Hon. Secretary for duration of war; Hon General Secretary, Australian Comforts Fund, 1916; organised the formation of French Australian League of Help; organised, N.S.W. Returned Soldiers' Association, 1916; served on Seventh War Loan Committee, 1918, Peace Loan Committee, 1919; Second Peace Loan Committee, 1920; Nationalist; Anglican. Jubilee Medal 1935; Coronation Medals, 1937, 1953. *Recreation:* bowls. *Address:* Coolagalla, Pymble, Sydney, N.S.W. *T.A.:* Fidelis, Sydney. *T.:* B.L. 1011 (Sydney Exchange). *Club:* Warrawee Bowling (Life Member, 1960) (Sydney).
[*Died* 4 *Jan.* 1961.

WALKER, Charles Clement, C.B.E. 1947; A.M.Inst.C.E., Hon. F.R.Ae.S., Hon. F.I.Ae.S.; a director of The de Havilland Aircraft Co Ltd., Hatfield, 1920-Jan. 1955, retired; *b.* 25 Aug. 1877; 2nd *s.* of W. T. and Claudia Ann Walker; *m.* 1916, Eileen Kenneth Hood. *Educ.:* Highgate School; Univ. Coll., London. General Civil Engineering; before 1920 chief technical asst. at Aircraft Manufacturing Co., Hendon. *Publications:* miscellaneous articles in aeronautical technical press. *Recreations:* Natural Science, Physics, etc. *Address:* Foresters, Stanmore Common, Middlesex. *T.:* Bushey Heath 1157. [*Died* 30 *Sept.* 1968.

WALKER, Cyril Herbert, C.B.E. 1952 (O.B.E. 1945); M.C. 1918; F.R.I.B.A.; F.R.I.C.S.; in consultant practice; *b.* 12 December 1888; 2nd *s.* of Plumer Cosby Walker; *m.* 1918, Mary Beevers Hirsch, Leeds; two *s.* *Educ.:* Leeds Modern School. Served European War, 1914-1918: Derbyshire Yeomanry, 1914-15; commissioned to 5th Norfolks, 1915-18 (despatches). City Engineer's Department, Leeds, 1919-24; Chief Estate and Town Planning Asst. to Borough Engineer, Preston, 1924-25; City Estates Surveyor, Norwich, 1925-30; Director of Housing, Bolton, 1930-1935; Borough Valuer, Croydon, 1935-45; Director of Housing, 1946-54, also Valuer, 1945-54, London County Coun.; Chairman: Building Industry Youth Trust; Croydon Br., Royal Assoc. in aid of Deaf and Dumb; Pres., Croydon and Dist. Assoc. for Mentally Handicapped Children. M.I.Mun.E.; Past Pres., Institute of Housing; Past Pres., Assoc. Local Authority Valuers and Estate Surveyors. *Recreations:* golf, gardening. *Address:* 4A Bramley Close, Bramley Hill, South Croydon. *T.:* Croydon 1002. *Club:* Farmers'. [*Died* 5 *Sept.* 1970.

WALKER, David Esdaile; Public Relations Executive, W. S. Crawford Ltd.; *b.* 15 September 1907; *o. c.* of late Maj.-Gen. Sir Ernest Walker, K.C.I.E., C.B., I.M.S., and Lady Walker; *m.* 1943, Rosalys Amy Campbell; one *s.* *Educ.:* Ampleforth; Christ Church, Oxford. Joined Daily Mirror, 1932; (Foreign Corresp., 1938-52); Acting Correspondent: Reuters, Balkans, 1939-41; The Times, Christian Science Monitor, Lisbon, 1943-44; News Chronicle, 1953-60, Daily Herald to Feb. 1961. *Publications:* Eat, Drink and Be Merry (as David Esdaile), 1932; Religion in the Reich (as Michael Power), 1939; Death at my Heels, 1942; The Greek Miracle (trans.), 1943; Civilian Attack, 1943; We Went to Australia, 1949; I Go Where I'm Sent, 1952; Diamonds for Moscow, 1953; The Rigoville Match, 1955; Adventure in Diamonds, 1955; Lunch With a Stranger, 1957; The Fat Cat Pimpernel, 1958; Pimpernel and the Poodle, 1959; The Modern Smuggler, 1960. *Recreations:* fishing, travel. *Address:* 50 Warwick Square, S.W.1. *Club:* Press. [*Died* 24 *Oct.* 1968.

WALKER, Douglas Learoyd, C.B.E. 1948; Vice-President and Member, Grand Council, Federation of British Industries, since 1959; Director: British Plaster Board (Holdings) Ltd.; Triplex (Holdings) Ltd.; *b.* 7 June 1894; *s.* of Dr. Edward Walker, M.B.E., M.D., Spring Bank, Huddersfield. *Educ.:* Oundle; Pembroke Coll., Cambridge. Served European War, France, 1915-16; Foreign Office, 1916-17; Federation of British Industries, 1917, General Secretary, 1921-59. *Address:* Flat 12, 85 Cadogan Gardens, S.W.3. *T.:* Knightsbridge 4592. *Club:* United University.
[*Died* 12 *Feb.* 1962.

WALKER, Sir Francis William, Kt. 1961; C.B.E. 1957; J.P.; C.C.; *b.* 1887; *s.* of late William Walker, North Bog, Aberdeenshire; *m.* 1912, Elizabeth Frances, *d.* of late Frederick C. Burfitt, Derby; two *s.* two *d.* *Educ.:* Derby. Served European War, 1914-18, with Army Service Corps (M.T.). County Councillor, 1929, Vice-Convener of Council, 1949, Convener, 1951-, Inverness-shire; J.P. 1935. Member: Advisory Panel on Highlands and Islands (Chairman, Road, Rail and Air Transport and Industries Group); Executive Committee, Scottish Council (Development and Industry); Scottish Housing Advisory Committee, 1948-54; County Councils' Association, 1951; Chairman: Kinlochleven Village Improvement Society Limited, 1948; Inverlochy Village Society Limited, 1948. *Address:* Leys Castle, Inverness-shire. *T.:* 394. *Clubs:* Carlton, Conservative (Edinburgh); Highland (Inverness).
[*Died* 19 *May* 1968.

WALKER, Sir Hubert (Edmund), Kt. 1947; C.B.E. 1943 (O.B.E. 1935); *b.* 31 May 1891; *s.* of Edmund Walker; *m.* 1924, Dorothy Gladys Turley; no *c.* *Educ.:* Bromsgrove School, Worcs. Served European War, 1914-18, R.N. Divisional Engineers and Royal Engineers, Gallipoli and France. Director of Public Works and Controller of Civil Aviation, Nigeria, retired 1948; Chairman West African Airways Corporation, 1946-54; Adviser on Engineering Appts. Colonial Office, 1954-58; Mem. of Council, Inst. of Civil Engineers, 1949-52, 1955-58. *Recreations:* fishing, golf. *Address:* Chalgrove Cottage, 9 Marine Drive, Rottingdean, Sussex BN2 7HJ. *T.:* Brighton 32522.
[*Died* 29 *Dec.* 1969.

WALKER, John, C.B.E. 1963; Keeper of Coins and Medals, British Museum, since 1952; *b.* 4 Sept. 1900; *y. s.* of John Walker and Isabella Watson, Glasgow. *Educ.:* Univ. of Glasgow. M.A. (First Cl. Hons. in Semitic Langs.) 1922; D.Litt. 1942; Lanfine Bursar, 1919-22; John Clark Schol., 1922-26; Asst. Lectr. in Arabic, 1927-28; Min. of Education, Egypt, 1928-31; Asst. Keeper, British Museum, 1931, Dep. Keeper, 1949. Air Staff Intelligence, 1941-45. Additional Lectr. in Arabic and Arabic Epigraphy at Sch. of Oriental and African Studies, 1937-47. F.B.A., 1958; M.R.A.S., F.S.A.; a Sec. of Roy. Numismatic Soc., 1948-64; an Editor Numismatic Chronicle, 1952-64. Corresp. Mem. Kungl. Vitterhets Akad., Sweden. Mem. de l'Institut d'Égypte. Huntington Medallist American Numismatic Society, 1955; Medallist of Royal Numismatic Society, 1956. *Publications:* Bible Characters in the Koran, 1931; Folk-Medicine in Modern Egypt, 1934; Catalogue of the Muhammadan Coins in the British Museum, vol. I, 1941, vol. II, 1956; Coinage of the Second Saffārid Dynasty in Sistān, 1936. Contrib. to Encyclopædia of Islam and various oriental periodicals. *Address:* Mill Cottage, Little Baddow, Essex. *Club:* Athenæum. [*Died* 12 *Nov.* 1964.

WALKER, Kenneth Macfarlane, M.A., M.B., B.Ch. (Cantab.), F.R.C.S.(Eng.); F.I.C.S.; Consulting Surgeon; Emeritus

Surgeon, Royal Northern Hospital; Medical Secretary British Social Hygiene Council; *s.* of late W. J. Walker, Hampstead; *m.* 1926, Eileen Marjorie, *o. d.* of Frederick H. Wilson; one *s.* one *d.*; *m.* 1944, Mrs. Mary Piggott (*née* Ginnett), Little London, Ambersham, Midhurst, Sussex. *Educ.:* Cambridge; St. Bartholomew's; Buenos Aires. Jacksonian Prizeman, Royal College of Surgeons, 1910; Hunterian Professor, 1911, 1922, 1924; Captain R.A.M.C. 1915-19 (despatches thrice); Fellow of Royal Society of Medicine and other societies. *Publications:* Tubercle of the Bladder and Male Genitalia (Prize Essay, 1910); Hunterian Lectures on the Cause and Nature of Old Age Enlargement of the Prostate; Paths of Infection in Genito-urinary Tuberculosis; Testicular Grafts; Diseases of the Male Organs of Generation, 1923; The Enlarged Prostate; Male Disorders of Sex; Editor of Sir J. Thomson-Walker's Genito-Urinary Surgery; numerous contributions to scientific journals; The Log of the Ark, 1923; The Physiology of Sex, Sex and Society (Special Pelican Series), 1940; Diagnosis of Man, 1942; Meaning and Purpose, 1944; I Talk of Dreams, 1946; A Doctor Digresses, 1950; Venture with Ideas, 1951; Only the Silent Hear, 1953; The Story of Medicine, 1954; A Study of Gurdjieff's Teaching, 1957; So Great a Mystery Life's Long Journey, 1959; The Unconscious Mind, 1961; The Conscious Mind, 1962; The Making of Man, 1963. *Recreation:* journalism. *Address:* Little London, Ambersham Common, Nr. Midhurst, Sussex. *T.:* Midhurst 446. *Club:* Savile. [*Died* 22 *Jan.* 1966.

WALKER, Leonard, R.I.; Designer and worker in stained glass, and water colour painter. *Educ.:* King Edward's School, Bromsgrove. Apprenticed to stained glass; studied art at St. John's Wood Art Schools; eventually became a Principal for some years of these schools; exhibited designs and pictures at the R.A.; stained glass work in many churches, municipal, and private buildings. Commissioned to design and execute the Victory and Thanksgiving stained glass windows for Royal Academy of Music, London; commemorative windows for Stoke on Trent Town Hall; exhibited large East Window, Royal Exchange, City of London, 1954. Awarded a Diplôme d'Honneur by the French Government for glass at the Decorative Art Exhibition, Paris, 1925; Freeman of City of London; Liveryman of Worshipful Company of Glaziers; Master of the Art Workers Guild, 1950. *Publications:* articles on Stained Glass and Water Colour Painting for the Press and magazines; also Lectures on Art Matters. *Address:* Studio, 151A King Henry's Road, N.W.3. *T.:* Primrose 4110. [*Died* 13 *June* 1964.

WALKER, Norman; Professor of Singing and Examiner, Guildhall School of Music, London, since 1951; *b.* Shaw, nr. Oldham, Lancs., 28 Nov. 1907; *s.* of John R. and Bertha A. Walker; *m.* 1938, L. Merle, *d.* of M. J. Miller, Christchurch, N.Z.; two *s.* one *d.* (and one *s.* decd.). *Educ.:* Shaw National Sch.; Roy. Manchester Coll. of Music (Sarah Andrew Schol.); Guildhall Sch. of Music (Heilbut Major Schol.). Made London Début, 1935, Roy. Philharmonic Concert. Hallé Concerts, 1933; Internat. Opera Season, 1935, 1936; Glyndebourne Opera, 1937; Internat. Opera Season, 1938-1939. Served as officer, R.A.F., 1941-46. Sadler's Wells Opera, 1946; Glyndebourne Opera, 1946; Promenade Seasons, 1936-54; Three Choir Festivals, 1947-51 and 1953-54. Has sung with principal choral and orchestral societies; Royal Opera House, Covent Garden, 1948-52; Australian and New Zealand tour, 1952; Rhodes Centennial Exhibition, Bulawayo, 1953. Has sung in Germany and Holland. Fellow: Roy. Manchester Coll. of Music, 1941; Guildhall Sch. of Music, 1946. *Recreations:* typography and printing. *Address:* 15 Rodway Rd., Roehampton, S.W.15. *T.:* Putney 8252. [*Died* 5 *Nov.* 1963.

WALKER, Professor Thomas Kennedy, D.Sc., Ph.D. (Manchester), F.R.I.C.; Emer. Prof. of Industrial Biochemistry, Univ. of Manchester (Prof., 1956-58); *b.* 21 Feb. 1893; *er. s.* of late John Reece Walker and Mary Walker (*née* Kennedy); *m.* 1922, Laura May Saunders. *Educ.:* The Grammar School, Mottram-in-Longdendale; Glossop Grammar School; University of Manchester. B.Sc. (Manch.), 1915, M.Sc. (Manch.), 1919, Ph.D. (Manch.), 1921, D.Sc. (Manch.), 1931. Asst. chemist, Roy. Naval Cordite Factory, Holton Heath, and Roy. Arsenal, Woolwich, 1915-19. Engaged in research in organic chemistry and biochemistry, Univ. of Manchester, 1919-1925; Lecturer in Fermentation Processes in Univ. and in Coll. of Technology, Manchester, 1925-40, Sen. Lecturer, 1940-51, Reader, 1951-56. *Publications:* papers in Jl. of Chem. Soc., Biochemical Jl. and other scientific jls. *Recreations:* gardening, painting. *Address:* Delamere, 25 High Grove Road, Cheadle, Cheshire. *T.:* Gatley 2907. [*Died* 29 *June* 1970.

WALKER, Sir William, Kt., *cr.* 1945; Lord Mayor of Manchester, 1932-33; Alderman, Manchester; LL.D.; J.P.; M.I.E.E.; M.I.Mech.E.; chartered electrical and mechanical engineer; Member of the Council, Victoria University, Manchester; *m.* Priscilla (*d.* 1945), *d.* of Richard Stothert; two *d.* *Educ.:* Grammar School, Farnworth; Farnworth and Bolton Technical Schools. Has served on national committees dealing with Chimney Emissions, electrical distribution, etc. Hon. LL.D. Manchester. *Publications:* papers on technical and industrial subjects. *Recreations:* mountaineering and photography. *Address:* Naddle Gate, Burn Banks, by Penrith. *T.* and *T.A.:* Bampton 231 Penrith. *Club:* Engineers (Manchester). [*Died* 13 *March* 1961.

WALKER, William Anderson Macpherson, C.B.E. 1942; retired East India merchant; *b.* 24 July 1891; *o. s.* of William and Margaret Walker; unmarried. *Educ.:* privately. After working on London Stock Exchange, came to India in 1913 to join firm of Barry and Co., Merchants; made partner in 1933. Adviser to Govt. of India on Jute Supplies, 1940-45; Chairman Indian Jute Mills Assoc., 1940-45; Member Bengal Legislative Assembly, Jute Mills Constituency, 1934 and 1937-45. Was leader European Party in Bengal legislature, 1939-41. Pres. Calcutta Hospital Nurses Institution, 1940-45; Vice-Pres. Indian Central Jute Committee, 1940-43; etc. *Address:* c/o Chartered Bank, 2 Regent Street, S.W.1. *Club:* Royal Automobile. [*Died* 10 *June* 1962.

WALKER-SMITH, Sir Jonah, Kt., *cr.* 1925; *b.* Watford, 1874; *s.* of late I. Jonah Smith; *m.* 1905, Maud Coulton, *d.* of late Coulton Walker Hunter, of Barrow-in-Furness and Barton Hall, Yorks; two *s.* (one *d.* decd.). *Educ.:* privately; King's Coll. City Engineer of Edinburgh; Dir. of Housing and Town Planning, Local Government Bd. of Scotland and Consulting Engineer in Scotland to the Road Board; subseq. Dir. Housing, Ministry of Health, 1919-25; Barrister-at-Law; M.I.C.E.; M.I.Mech.E.; F.R.I.C.S.; Hon. A.R.I.B.A.; M.P. (C.) Barrow-in-Furness, 1931-45. Chairman and Managing Director of Engineering and other cos. *Publications:* Technical Books and contributions upon engineering subjects. *Address:* 8 Heath Close, N.W.11. *T.:* Speedwell 4572. *Club:* Carlton. [*Died* 23 *Feb.* 1964.

WALKEY, Rear-Adm. Howarth Seymour, C.B.E. 1956; retd.; *b.* 13 May 1900; *s.* of Samuel Walkey, Dawlish, Devon: *m.* 1923, Marjory Edith Awdry Burnard; one *s.* *Educ.:* Dartmouth College. Entered Osborne, 1913; served H.M.S. Queen Elizabeth, 1916-1919; specialised in Gunnery, 1924; served in West Indies, Mediterranean and Far East. Joined Naval Ordnance Dept., 1935; Commander 1940; Captain 1947; Rear-Adm., 1956; Vice-Pres. Ordnance Bd., 1956-58; President, 1958-59, retired, 1959. *Recreation:* golf. *Address:* Lowdon Lodge, Chippenham, Wiltshire. *T.:* Chippenham 3038; Treworrick, St. Cleer, Liskeard, Cornwall. *T.:* Liskeard 2094.
[*Died* 20 *Aug.* 1970.

WALKINTON, John James Gordon, O.B.E. 1950; M.A.; Headmaster, Beverley Grammar School, 1934-60; *b.* 2 Feb. 1895; *s.* of Edwin Walkinton and Emma Stones; *m.* 1926, Marjorie, 2nd *d.* of G. E. Hubbard, J.P., Leicester; one *d.* *Educ.:* Sutton-on-Sea Council School; Louth, Grammar School; St. Edmund Hall, Oxford. Business career in London, 1911-14; enlisted Queen's Westminster Rifles, August 1914; served in France and Ireland throughout the war; Captain and Adjutant 6th Lincolnshire Regt.; Oxford 1919-22, 2nd Class Honours, Modern History, 1922; Vacation Course, Grenoble Univ., 1921; Senior History and English Master, Weymouth College, 1922-34; Commanded Weymouth College O.T.C., 1923-31; Lt.-Col. retd late Comdg. 2nd Cadet Bn., East Yorkshire Regt. *Recreations:* golf, walking. *Address:* 7 Great Austins House, 90 Tilford Road, Farnham, Surrey. *T.:* Farnham 3602. [*Died* 27 *June* 1968.

WALL, Arnold, C.B.E. 1956; M.A., Professor of English Language and Literature in Canterbury College, University of New Zealand, 1898-1932; now Emeritus Professor; *s.* of late George Wall; *m.* Elsie Kent Monro Curnow (*d.* 1924); one *s.* two *d.* The University appointment included History until 1906. *Publication:* The Queen's English, 1959. *Address:* 51 Arnold Street, Sumner, Christchurch, N.Z.
[*Died* 29 *March* 1966.

WALLACE, Major David Johnston, C.M.G. 1938; O.B.E.; T.D.; *b.* 1 Aug. 1886; *s.* of late J. Wilson Wallace, J.P.; *m.* 1925, Elizabeth Marie Louise, *d.* of late Ernest H. Saniter; two *d.* *Educ.:* Kilmarnock Academy; Glasgow University (M.A., LL.B.). 2/Lieut. 4th Royal Scots Fusiliers 1909; served European War, Staff Capt., Major 1917; joined Egyptian Frontiers Administration 1918 as Staff Officer; Legal Secretary, 1919; Civil Secretary, 1923; Deputy Director General, 1927; Rank of Miralai in Egyptian service; retired, 1938; Upper Thames Patrol, Home Guard; Order of Nile 3rd Class; Egyptian Order for Meritorious Services (Gold); Order of Crown of Italy (Commendatore); Greek Order of Phoenix (3rd Class). *Recreations:* golf and shooting. *Address:* 10 Perth Road, Dundee. *T.:* Invergowrie 593.
[*Died* 1 *July* 1965.

WALLACE, Harold Frank; author and artist; Deer Control Officer for Scotland, 1939-46; *b.* 21 March 1881; *s.* of late Edward James Wallace, M.D., J.P., and late Constance A. Wallace, 17 Stratton Street, W.1, and Bearnock, Glen Urquhart; *m.* 1912, Elizabeth A., *e. d.* of late Lachlan A. Macpherson of Corriemony, Inverness, and Little Wyrley Hall, Staffs; one *s.* one *d.* *Educ.:* Eton; Christ Church, Oxford (B.A.). Called to Bar, Inner Temple, 1908; has travelled extensively and shot in many parts of the world; journeyed in search of unknown species of Chinese big game; held shows of Water Colour Drawings, Sporting and Landscape, Scotland and London; organised British Section: Internat. Hunting Exhibn., Berlin, 1937, Düsseldorf, 1954. Hon. Vice-Pres. Conseil International de la Chasse. *Publications:* Stalks Abroad, 1908; The Big Game of Central and Western China, 1913; British Deer Heads, 1914; contributed chapters and drawings on shooting in China and New Zealand and on Asiatic deer to The Gun at Home and Abroad and British Sports and Sportsmen; Hunting and Stalking the Deer (with Lionel Edwards), 1927; A Highland Gathering, 1932; A Stuart Sketch Book, 1542-1746, 1933; Big Game, 1934; Happier Years, 1945; Hunting Winds, 1949; Please Ring the Bell, 1952; many articles. *Recreations:* deer-stalking, shooting, fishing, natural history, and archery. *Address:* Little Wyrley Hall, Pelsall, Staffs. *T.:* Pelsall 210; Old Corriemony, Glen Urquhart, Inverness. *T.:* Cannich 207. *Clubs:* Brooks's, Pratt's, Shikar (Hon. Sec.); (Assoc. Mem.) Boone and Crockett (New York).
[*Died* 16 *Sept.* 1962.

WALLACE, Henry Agard; author, editor and statesman; Research Worker in Plant and Poultry Breeding; *b.* 7 Oct. 1888; *s.* of Henry C. Wallace and May Brodhead; *m.* 1914, Ilo Browne; two *s.* one *d.* *Educ.:* B. S. Iowa State College, 1910 (hon. M.S. in agriculture, 1920). Associate editor Wallaces' Farmer, 1910-24; editor, 1924-29; editor Iowa Homestead and Wallaces' Farmer (merged), 1929-33; Secretary of United States Department of Agriculture, 1933-40; Vice-Pres. of the United States, 1941-45; Secy. of Commerce, U.S.A., 1945-46. Progressive Party Candidate for President 1948. *Publications:* Agricultural Prices, 1920; Corn and Corn Growing, 1923; Correlation and Machine Calculation, 1924; America Must Choose, 1934; New Frontiers, 1934; Whose Constitution, An Inquiry into the General Welfare, 1936; Democracy Reborn, 1945; Sixty Million Jobs, 1946; Toward World Peace, 1949; Corn and its Early Fathers, 1956. *Address:* South Salem, N.Y., U.S.A. [*Died* 18 *Nov.* 1965.

WALLACE, Captain Henry S. M. H.; *see* Harrison-Wallace.

WALLACE, Sir John S. S.; *see* Stewart-Wallace.

WALLACE, Rear-Admiral Richard Roy, C.B.E. 1949; R.N. retired; *b.* 14 Dec. 1895; *m.* 1st, 1924, Frances G. Canton; one *s.* one *d.*; 2nd, 1950, Nancy Stuart Alexander. *Educ.:* Hurstpierpoint College. Royal Navy, 1913-51; retired, 1951. *Address:* 41 Chiltley Way, Liphook, Hants. *T.:* Liphook 3045. [*Died* 24 *Jan.* 1963.

WALLACE of that Ilk, Colonel Robert Francis Hurter, C.M.G. 1919; retd. pay, 1923; *b.* 1880; *e. s.* of late Col. C. T. Wallace, H.L.I.; *m.* 1920, Euphemia, *e. d* of Col. Sir Chandos Hoskyns, 10th Bart., R.E.; two *s.* (and one killed in action). *Educ.:* Charterhouse; New College, Oxford, M.A. Gazetted the Black Watch, 1902; gained rank Maj., 1917; passed Staff College, 1910; served European War, France, 1914, Brigade-Major 18th Infantry Brigade (severely wounded); War Office, 1916-17, and G.H.Q., France, 1917-19, on General Staff; temp. Colonel, 1918-19 (French Croix de Guerre avec palme; Officier Ordre de Léopold and Belgian Croix de Guerre; despatches thrice; Bt. Lt.-Col.; C.M.G.; 1914 Star, British War Medal, Victory Medal); Officer in Charge Records, Highland Area, 1920-22; attached Egyptian Army, 1922-25; Order of the Nile, 4th class. A.R.P. and Home Guard, 1938-44; Defence Medal. *Address:* Corsee, Nairn.
[*Died* 1 *June* 1970.

WALLACE, Robert Johnston; Sheriff Substitute of Caithness, Sutherland, Orkney and Zetland, Lerwick, 1935-61, retired; *b.* Edinburgh, 24 Apr. 1886; *e. s.* of Robert

Walker Wallace, W.S., of Halbeath, Fife, and Mary Parker Willoughby; *m.* 1941, Gladys W. (*d.* 1963) *o. d.* of W. Ferrier, Bournemouth. *Educ.:* Edinburgh Academy; Univ. College, Oxford; Edinburgh Univ. B.A. Oxon, 1909; M.A. 1919; LL.B. Edin. 1912; Admitted to Faculty of Advocates, 1913; served in 1st O.U.V.B. Oxford Light Infantry, 1905-8; 9th Bn. (Highlanders) Royal Scots, 1908-20; Staff Captain and Brigade Major, 1915-16; Attd. R.F.C. and R.A.F. (Gunnery), 1917-19; Captain (retd.). D.L. Zetland, 1953-61. *Recreation:* fishing. *Address:* 2 Darnaway Street, Edinburgh 3. *T.:* Caledonian 3082. *Clubs:* New, Scottish Arts (Edinburgh). [*Died* 11 *Feb.* 1967.

WALLACE, Sir Robert Strachan, Kt., *cr.* 1941; LL.D., M.A. (Aberd.), M.A. (Oxf.); Vice-Chancellor Sydney University, 1927-47; *b.* 1 Aug. 1882; *s.* of late John Wallace, Home Mission Evangelist, U.F. Church of Scotland; *m.* Nan, *d.* of John M'Adam, Aberdeen; three *s.* *Educ.:* Gordon's College, Aberdeen; Aberdeen University; Christ Church, Oxford (Exhibitioner). Assistant Professor and Lecturer in English. Aberdeen University, and Lecturer in Aberdeen Training College, 1907-11; served with A.I.F., 1917-19; Professor of English Language and Literature, University of Melbourne, 1911-27; Dean of the Faculty of Arts, 1914-27; President of the Professorial Board of Melbourne University, 1924-27; Member of the Australian Broadcasting Commission, 1932-35. *Recreation:* golf. *Address:* The University, Sydney, Australia. *Clubs:* Australian, University (Sydney). [*Died* 5 *Sept.* 1961.

WALLACE, Samuel Thomas Dickson, V.C. 1917; B.Sc.; Capt. late R.F.A.; *b.* 7 March 1892; *er. s.* of J. W. Wallace, of Ford, Thornhill, Dumfriesshire; *m.* 1925, Margaret Noël *o. c.* of late Claude Edenborough, of Bramshott, Woking; one *d.* *Educ.:* Dumfries Academy, Edinburgh University. Served European War, 1914-18 (V.C.); Deputy Director of Agriculture for the Central Provinces, India, 1919-32; retired 1932; Flight Lieut. R.A.F.V.R., 1940-43; invalided out of R.A.F. 19 Dec. 1943. *Recreation:* shooting. *Address:* Grey Ghyll, Moffat, Dumfriesshire. *T.:* Moffat 148. [*Died* 2 *Feb.* 1968.

WALLACE, Thomas, C.B.E. 1947; M.C. 1915; V.M.H. 1952; F.R.S. 1953; Emeritus Professor of Horticultural Chemistry, University of Bristol; *b.* 5 Sept. 1891; *s.* of Thomas and Isabella Mary Wallace; *m.* 1st, 1917, Gladys Mary Smith; one *d.* (and one *s.* decd.); 2nd, 1938, Elsie Stella Smyth; one *s.* *Educ.:* Armstrong Coll. (now King's Coll.), Univ. of Durham, B.Sc. 1913; M.Sc. 1919; D.Sc. 1931; F.R.I.C. 1946. Served European War, 1914-18, 3rd Border Regt.; active service, France and Belgium, 1914, Gallipoli, 1915, France and Belgium, 1916; seconded R.E.s (Anti-Gas Dept.), 1918. Research Chemist, Long Ashton Research Station, 1919-23, and Advisory Agricultural Chemist, Bristol Province, Ministry of Agriculture Advisory Service; Deputy Director and Research Chemist, Long Ashton Research Stn., 1924-43; Dir., 1943-57; Dir. Agric. Research Council Unit of Plant Nutrition, at Long Ashton Research Station, 1952-59. Corresp. Institut de France, Acad. des Sciences, 1946; Membre étranger Académie d'Agriculture de France, 1957. *Publications:* Diagnosis of Mineral Deficiencies in Plants—Colour Atlas and Guide, 1st Edn., 1943, 3rd Edn. 1961; (with R. W. Marsh) Science and Fruit, 1953; (with J. T. Martin) Insecticides and Colonial Agricultural Development, 1954; (with R. G. W. Bush) Modern Commercial Fruit Growing, 1956. Author and part author of Bulletins on Fruit Culture published by Min. of Agric.; approx. 100 scientific papers on Fruit Culture, Plant Nutrition, and Soil. Jt. Ed. Jl. Horticultural Science, 1943-58. *Address:* Redwings, Old Church Road, Nailsea, Somerset. *T.:* Nailsea 76. *Club:* Farmers. [*Died* 2 *Feb.* 1965.

WALLACE, Sir William, Kt. 1951; C.B.E. 1944; F.R.S.E.; LL.D.; Consultant, ex-Chairman and Managing Director of Brown Bros. & Company Ltd., engineers, Edinburgh; *b.* 25 August 1881; *s.* of Matthew Wallace, Paisley; *m.* 1916, Christina Gilchrist Stewart, Edinburgh; one *s.* one *d.* *Educ.:* Paisley Grammar School; Anderson College. Marine Engineer; M.I.Mech.E.; M.R.I.N.A.; ex-President now Trustee, Engineering Employers Federation; ex-President Institution of Engineers and Shipbuilders in Scotland; Ex-Pres. Inst. of Marine Engineers; Director of: Henry Robb & Co. Ltd., Shipbuilders; William Beardmore & Co. Ltd., Forgemasters, Parkhead, Glasgow; Alex. Cowan & Sons Ltd.; North British Rubber Co. Ltd.; Income Tax Commissioner, Ancient Royalty of Edinburgh; a Director, Ex-President, Edinburgh Chamber of Commerce; Governor Leith Nautical College; Vice-Pres.: Royal Instn. of Naval Architects; British Welding Research Assoc. Awarded Churchill Gold Medal, 1954. Hon. LL.D. Edinburgh University, 1956. *Recreation:* golf. *Address:* 112 Princes Street, Edinburgh. *T.:* Edinburgh Caledonian 4253. *Clubs:* Royal Automobile; New, Scottish Conservative (Edinburgh); Hon. Co. of Edinburgh Golfers (Muirfield); (formerly Captain) Bruntsfield Links Golfing Society. [*Died* 27 *May* 1963.

WALLACE, William Kelly, C.B.E. 1946; M.I.C.E.; Lieut.-Col. (retired) Engineer and Railway Staff Corps, R.E. (T.A.); *b.* 1883; *s.* of John Orr Wallace; *m.* 1945, Marjorie Glass, *d.* of Humphrey Benjamin Dadd. Formerly Chief Civil Engineer, London, Midland & Scottish Railway Co.; Chm., Building Research Board, Department of Scientific and Industrial Research, 1949-54. President, Institution of Civil Engineers, 1955-56. D.Sc. in Applied Technology (*h.c.*) The Queen's University of Belfast, 1956. *Address:* 51 Ember Lane, Esher, Surrey. *Club:* Athenæum. [*Died* 23 *May* 1969.

WALLACE, William Reeve, C.B.E. 1927; Chief Clerk Judicial Dept. Privy Council Office, 1909-45; *b.* 1 July 1873; *s.* of late William Wallace, Bank of England. *Educ.:* St. Paul's School; abroad. Admitted a Solicitor, 1896; Official Solicitors Dept., 1896-1902; entered Privy Council Office 1902; Acting Superintendent Aliens Officer, 1916-19. *Clubs:* Athenæum, Savile. [*Died* 7 *Dec.* 1966.

WALLACE, William Stewart, M.A. (Oxon), LL.D. (B.C.; McMaster; Toronto), F.R.S.C.; Librarian Emeritus, University of Toronto, since 1954 (Librarian, 1923-54); *b.* Georgetown, Ontario, 23 June 1884; *s.* of Rev. W. G. Wallace; *m.* 1913, Isobel Dora Graeme Robertson, Toronto; one *s.* one *d.* *Educ.:* University of Toronto; Balliol College, Oxford. Professor of English and History, Western University, London, Ont., 1906-7; rofessor of History, McMaster University, Toronto, 1909-20, Special Lecturer in History, University of Toronto, 1910-20; Assistant Librarian, University of Toronto, 1920-22; Associate Librarian, 1922-23; Editor, Canadian Historical Review, 1920-30; Hon Secretary, Champlain Society, Toronto, 1922-43, Pres., 1943-48; Pres. Canadian Library Association, 1950-51. F.R.S.C. 1927. Served overseas, with rank of Major, with the 139th Bn., C.E.F., and the 3rd Reserve Bn., 1916-18; and in Canada with Univ. of Toronto C.O.T.C., 1940-43. *Publications:* The United Empire Loyalists (Chronicles of Canada), 1914; The Family Compact (Chronicles of Canada), 1915; The Maseres Letters, 1920; By Star and Compass, 1922; Sir John Macdonald, 1924; A New History of Great Britain and Canada, 1925; The Dictionary of Canadian Biography, 1926

(3rd ed., 1963); A History of the University of Toronto, 1927; The Growth of Canadian National Feeling 1927; A First Book of Canadian History, 1928; A History of the Canadian People, 1930; Murders and Mysteries, 1931; (ed.) John McLean's Notes of a Twenty-five Years' Service, 1932; Memoirs of Sir George Foster, 1933; (ed.) Documents relating to the North West Company, 1934; (ed.) The Encyclopædia of Canada, 6 vols., 1935-37; (ed.) Royal Canadian Institute Centennial Volume, 1949; A Dictionary of North American Authors, 1951; The Pedlars from Quebec, and other papers, 1954; The Knight of Dundurn, 1960. *Address:* University of Toronto Library, Toronto, Canada. *Clubs:* York, Toronto Golf (Toronto).
[*Died* 11 *March* 1970.

WALLACH, Lewis Charles, C.I.Mech.E.; *b.* 1 July 1871; *m.* Eileen (*d.* 1944), *d.* of C. Nolan; no *c.* *Educ.:* by private tutor. A pioneer of safety appliances for protection of workmen in factories and mines and of introduction of medicinal liquid paraffin for internal use; A.I.Mech.E. 1895; Fell. of Roy. Instit. of Great Britain since 1906; Member Royal Geog. Soc., Royal Institute of Philosophy, Museums Association, American Petroleum Inst. Collector of Old Masters, Old English and French furniture, pewter, miniatures, etc.; library (over 10,000) 16-19th century books, maps and manuscripts; pre-historic, Mexican and Egyptian collections. Has made presentations of works of art, 1939, 1951, 1952, notably Painting of H.M. King George VI to 7th Regt., New York Nat. Guard; a Miniature of George Washington to Mount Vernon Ladies' Association, Washington, D.C.; National Maritime Museum, Greenwich; donation (£1000) to start National Fund for Poliomyelitis Research for study, treatment and cure of poliomyelitis; mem. Council Nat. Fund for Poliomyelitis Research; Vice-Pres. Infantile Paralysis Fellowship. *Publication:* The Prevention of Accidents in Industrial Concerns. *Recreation:* foreign travel. *Address:* The Grange, Northington, Alresford, Hants. *T.:* Alresford 159; Savoy Hotel, W.C.2; Plaza Hotel, New York. *Clubs:* Royal Commonwealth Society; British Schools and Universities (New York).
[*Died* 21 *Aug.* 1964.

WALLER, Brig.-General Richard Lancelot, C.M.G. 1918; *b.* 1875; *s.* of late Major-General W. N. Waller, R.A.; *m.* 1912, Clare Cicely (*d.* 1951), *d.* of E. Crace, of Gininderra, New South Wales; one *s.* (one *d.* decd.). Served South African War, 1899-1902 (Queen's medal and two clasps, King's medal and two clasps); European War, 1914-18 (despatches, C.M.G., Bt. Lieut.-Col.); Lt.-Col. 1921; Col. 1925; late C.R.E., Woolwich; Chief Engineer Scottish Command, 1927-28; Southern Command, 1928-31; retired pay, 1931; Bursar, Sherborne School, 1931-45. *Address:* Lindum House, Lenthay Road, Sherborne, Dorset.
[*Died* 9 *March* 1961.

WALLINGTON, Hon. Sir Hubert Joseph, Kt. 1944; retired as Justice of the High Court, Probate, Divorce and Admiralty Division (1944-60). *m.* 1904, Bertha Mary (*d.* 1945), *d.* of Andrew Smith; one *s.* one *d.*; *m.* 1945, Ella M., *d.* of William James Standen. Admitted a Solicitor, 1899; called to Bar, Gray's Inn, 1911; K.C. 1934; Bencher, 1934; Treasurer, 1946; Vice-Treasurer, 1947; Recorder of Birmingham, 1937-44; H.M. Comr. of Assize on Midland Circuit, 1939; Mem. of National Mark Cttee., 1936-39; sat as Aliens Tribunal for No. 9 Midland Region, 1939; Chairman Local Price Regulation Committee for the same region; Chairman Home Office Advisory Committee on Internees under Regulation 18B, 1940, and Aliens Advisory Committee for the Midland (No. 9) Civil Defence Region, 1940-42. *Recreations:* music and bowls. *Address:* 64 Oakwood Court, Kensington, W.14. *T.:* Western 9296.
[*Died* 19 *Jan.* 1962.

WALMSLEY, His Honour Allan, Q.C., Retired Judge of County Courts; *b.* 22 July 1889; *s.* of George Doxon Walmsley, Darwen, Lancs.; *m.* 1916, Mary Thompson; one *d.* *Educ.:* Blackburn Gram. Sch.; Sedbergh. Solicitor (1st class hons. and Clifford's Inn Prize), 1910; called to Bar (Certif. of honour) 1923; LL.B. London (1st class), 1923; K.C., 1948; Q.C. 1952. Judge of County Courts, 1948-62. *Address:* 21 East Beach, Lytham, Lancs. *T.:* Lytham 7402.
[*Died* 25 *Sept.* 1963.

WALMSLEY, Leo, M.C.; author; *b.* 1892; *y. s.* of J. U. Walmsley, artist; *m.* 1933, *d.* of E. Little, M.A. (marriage dissolved, 1954); three *s.* two *d.*; *m.* 1955, Stephanie, *d.* of Nathaniel Gubbins; one *d.* Served with R.F.C. in East Africa during European War (despatches four times, M.C.). *Publications:* Flying and Sport in East Africa, 1920; The Silver Blimp, 1921; The Lure of Thunder Island, 1923; Three Asses in the Pyrenees, 1924; The Green Rocket; Toro of the Little People, 1926; Three Fevers, 1932 (Film, Turn of the Tide); Phantom Lobster, 1933; Foreigners, 1935; Sally Lunn, 1937; Love in the Sun, 1939; Fishermen at War, 1941; British Ports and Harbours, 1942; So Many Loves, 1944; Sally Lunn (play), 1944; Master Mariner, 1948; Festival Guide Yorkshire and Lancashire, 1951; Invisible Cargo, 1952; The Golden Waterwheel, 1954; The Happy Ending, 1957; Sound of the Sea, 1959; Paradise Creek, 1963; Angler's Moon, 1965. *Recreations:* boats, fishing. *Address:* Bramblewick, Passage St., Fowey, Cornwall. *T.:* Fowey 2297.
[*Died June* 1966.

WALN, Nora; writer; *b.* Grampian Hills, Pennsylvania, U.S.A., 4 June 1895; *d.* of Thomas Lincoln Waln and Lillia Quest; *m.* 1922, George Edward Osland-Hill (*d.* 1958), Dobins, Fulmer, Bucks, England; one *d.* *Educ.:* home and Swarthmore College, Pennsylvania. Member of the Society of Friends; Member of the Kappa Gamma Fraternity (administering K.K.G. Fund for bombed mothers and children since 1940); Member Council, American Outpost in Britain; Member China Convoy Committee of Friends Ambulance Unit; four years in Asia as correspondent of The Saturday Evening Post, in Tokio, Japan (the last six months on the Korean battlefields), 1947-51; late corresp. for The Atlantic Monthly in Germany and Scandinavia, also, May 1951-, for same in Europe. Freelance from 1951, touring Asian countries and America. Hon. M.A. Swarthmore Coll., Pa. Haakon Cross (Norway), 1950. Gold Medal, Distinguished Daughter of Pennsylvania, 1956. *Publications:* The Street of Precious Pearls, 1922; The House of Exile, 1933; Reaching for the Stars, 1939; Surrender the Heart, 1961; Contributor to: Atlantic Monthly, Saturday Evening Post, and other American magazines; broadcast plays for children: If You Were American, 1941. *Recreations:* cooking, riding, flying. *Address:* Dobins, Fulmer, Buckinghamshire, England; Horseshoe Hse., 219 Delancy Street, Philadelphia, Pennsylvania 6, U.S.A. *Clubs:* American Women's, P.E.N., The China Society.
[*Died* 27 *Sept.* 1964.

WALSH, Ernst; *see* Pakenham-Walsh.

WALSH, Rt. Rev. Herbert P.; *see* Pakenham-Walsh.

WALSH, Maurice; Retired Officer of Customs and Excise, Ireland; *b.* Ballydonohue, Co. Kerry, 2 May 1879; *s.* of John Walsh, farmer and land-leaguer, and Elizabeth Buckley; *m.* 1908, Caroline I. J. Begg, Dufftown, Banffshire; three *s.* *Educ.:* Lisselton, Bally-

bunion; St. Michael's College, Listowel. Entered British Civil Service, 1901; transferred to Irish Free State Service, 1922; President, Comaltas Cana, 1929-30; President Irish P.E.N., 1938. 1st Prize Screen Writers' Guild, Hollywood, 1955. *Publications:* Eudmon Blake, 1909; The Key above the Door, 1923; While Rivers Run, 1926; The Small Dark Man, 1929; Blackcock's Feather, 1932; The Road to Nowhere, 1934; Green Rushes, 1935; And no Quarter, 1937; Sons of the Swordmaker, 1938; The Hill is Mine, 1940; Thomasheen James, 1941; Son of Apple, 1942; Spanish Lady, 1943; Man in Brown, 1945; A Man for Castle Gillian, 1948; Trouble in the Glen, 1950; Son of a Tinker, 1952; The Honest Fisherman, 1954; A Strange Woman's Daughter, 1954; Danger under the Moon, 1956; The Smart Fellow, 1964. *Recreations:* fishing, shooting, golf, gardening. *Address:* Green Rushes, Blackrock, Co. Dublin. *T.:* 889480. *Clubs:* P.E.N., Irish.
[*Died* 18 *Feb.* 1964.

WALSH, Maj.-Gen. Ridley P. P.; *see* Pakenham-Walsh.

WALSH, Colonel Robert Henry, D.S.O., 1917; O.B.E. 1931; M.C., late Royal Artillery; *b.* 7 Dec. 1884; *s.* of late Ven. R. Walsh, D.D., Archdeacon of Dublin, *s.* of Rt. Hon. J. E. Walsh, Master of the Rolls, Ireland, and Elizabeth, *d.* of late Rev. J. Carson, D.D., Vice-Provost, Trinity College, Dublin; *m.* 1952, Marjorie, *o. d.* of late John Rutherford-Jones; one *d.* *Educ.:* Marlborough; R.M.A., Woolwich. 2/Lt. R.A., 1904; Lt. 1907; Lt., R.H.A., 1914; Captain, 1914; Major, R.A., 1916; Lt.-Col. 1933; Col. 1937; served at Home, 1904-6; India, 1906-11; visited Tibet and Upper Burma on shooting trips; Home, 1911-14; Staff Officer, Local Forces, Trinidad and Tobago, 1914; served European War, France and Belgium, 1914-18 (twice wounded, D.S.O., M.C., despatches four times); Egyptian Army, 1919-25; Sudan Defence Force, 1925-29; seconded Sudan Political Service, 1919-24; Inspector and D.C. Opari and Latuka Districts Mongalla; 2nd in command, Egyptian Artillery, Khartoum, 1924; commanding Eastern Arab Corps, Eastern Area, Sudan, 1925-29; served at home from 1929; retired pay, 1938; served with R.A.F., 1940-44, Head of R.A.F. Courier Section, Wing Comdr. One of H.M. Body Guard, 1938-54. *Address:* Pont du Val, St. Pierre du Bois, Guernsey, C.I. *Club:* Naval and Military. [*Died* 8 *July* 1968.

WALSINGHAM, 8th Baron (*cr.* 1780); **George de Grey,** D.S.O. 1915; O.B.E. 1957; D.L.; Lt.-Col. Royal Norfolk Regt.; *b.* 1884; *e. s.* of 7th Baron and Elizabeth Henrietta (*d.* 1927), *d.* of Patrick Grant of Glenmoriston; *S.* father, 1929; *m.* 1919, Hyacinth, *o. d.* of late Lt.-Col. L. H. Bouwens, R.A., and late Mrs. Lambart Bouwens, Box House, Putney Heath, S.W.; one *s.* three *d.* *Educ.:* Eton; R.M.C., Sandhurst. Served European War (Mesopotamia), 1914-18, France, 1918 (wounded thrice, despatches five times, Brevet of Major, D.S.O.); retired pay, 1923; re-employed (Commanding a Bn. of Royal Norfolk Regt.), 24 Aug. 1939; retired March 1945. D.L. Norfolk, 1959. O.St.J. *Heir:* *s.* Major Hon. John de Grey, M.C. *Address:* Merton, Thetford, Norfolk. *Clubs:* Army and Navy; Norfolk (Norwich).
[*Died* 29 *Nov.* 1965.

WALTER, Professor Bruno, Orchestra Conductor; *b.* Germany, 1876; became French citizen, 1938; became American citizen, 1946; *m.* 1901; one *d.* *Educ.:* Stern Conservatory of Music, Berlin. Began at Cologne Opera House, 1893; through various Opera-houses until Riga, 1898-1900; Berlin Royal Opera, 1900; Vienna Opera, 1901-12; General Musical Director: Munich Opera, 1913-22; Berlin Municipal Opera, 1925-29; Conductor Leipzig Gewandhaus, 1929-33. Guest Conductor: Covent Garden Opera, London; Met. Opera, N.Y.; Salzburg Music Festival, Edin. Music Festival; N.Y. Philharmonic and other Symphony orchestras throughout U.S. and Europe. Musical Adviser Philharmonic Symphony Soc. of N.Y., 1947-49. Hon. Dr. of Music, Univs. of Calif., Los Angeles, and Edinburgh. Awarded Gold Medal of Royal Philharmonic Society, 1957. Golden Mozart Ring, City of Vienna. Commander French Legion of Honour; Grand Officer Dutch Order of Orange Nassau. *Publications:* Gustav Mahler, 1937: Theme and Variations, 1946; Von der Musik und vom Musizieren, 1957. *Address:* c/o Philharmonic Symphony Society of New York, 113 West 57th St., New York 19, N.Y.
[*Died* 17 *Feb.* 1962.

WALTER, John; *b.* 1873; *s.* of Arthur Fraser Walter of Bear Wood, Wokingham; and *g.g.g.s.* of John Walter, who founded The Times in 1785; *m.* 1st, 1903, Phyllis (*d.* 1937), *y. d.* of Col. and Mrs. C. E. Foster of Long Buckby, Northamptonshire; two *s.* two *d.*; 2nd, 1939, Rosemary, *o. d.* of late James Adair Crawford, I.C.S. *Educ.:* Eton; Christ Church, Oxford (M.A.). Entered The Times Office, 1898; Chairman of Directors of The Times, 1910-23. *Address:* 69 The Drive, Hove, Sussex. *T.:* Hove 735889.
[*Died* 11 *Aug.* 1968.

WALTERS, Air Vice-Marshal Allan Leslie, C.B. 1956; C.B.E. 1946; A.F.C. 1942; Royal Australian Air Force, retd.; *b.* 2 November 1905; *s.* of late Arthur F. Walters, Kalamunda, Western Australia; *m.* 1930, Jean Grace Belford, *d.* of late Rev. G. F. B. Manning, Sydney, N.S.W.; one *d.* *Educ.:* Perth Modern School, W.A.; R.M.C., Duntroon. Joined Australian Staff Corps, 1927; transferred to Royal Australian Air Force, 1930; graduated R.A.F. Staff College, 1936. Served War of 1939-45 (A.F.C., C.B.E.), New Guinea and Australia, Director of Operations Allied Air Forces, S.W. Pacific, 1942; Air Officer Commanding Northern Command, 1945; I.d.c. 1947; A.O.C. Southern Area, R.A.A.F., 1948-50; A.O.C. Overseas H.Q., R.A.A.F., London, 1951-52; Head Australian Joint Services Staff, Washington, 1952-53; Air Officer Commanding Australian Home Command, 1954-57; Air Member for Personnel, R.A.A.F., 1957-59; A.O.C. Support Command, 1959-62, retired 1962. *Address:* Strathbogie, Victoria 3666, Australia. *Club:* Melbourne (Melbourne).
[*Died* 19 *Oct.* 1968.

WALTERS, Hubert Algernon; *b.* 1898; *s.* of late Lt.-Col. Robert Walters and Lilian Laidlaw Walters (*née* Hoole); *m.* 1921, Mary Josephine Robertson; one *s.* *Educ.:* Westminster School. Entered service of Royal Exchange Assurance, 1914. War service, 1915-19. Represented Royal Exchange Assurance in various countries in Europe until 1933; returned to London with exec. appt. for overseas affairs, and has travelled extensively in U.S.A., Canada, Australasia and Africa. Chairman: London Salvage Corps, 1958-60; British Insurance Assoc., 1959-61; Director: Atlas Assurance Co. Ltd.; Car and General Insce. Corp. Ltd.; Local Govt. Guarantee Society Ltd.; Motor Union Insce. Co. Ltd.; United British Insce. Co. Ltd.; General Manager, Royal Exchange Assurance, 1954-61. *Address:* 2 Chalfont Drive, Hove 4, Sussex. *T.:* Brighton 505262. *Club:* Oriental. [*Died* 6 *Dec.* 1969.

WALTHALL, Brig.-Gen. Edward Charles Walthall Delves, C.M.G. 1918; D.S.O. 1900; late R.A.; J.P., D.L.; *b.* 24 April 1874; *e. s.* of late Edward W. D. Walthall of Wistaston Hall, and Caroline Marion, *y. d.* of Charles Augustus Stewart of West Hall, Cheshire; *m.* 1902, Isabel Sybil (*d.* 1956), *yr. d.* of Lt.-Gen. Sir J. B. Edwards, K.C.B., K.C.M.G., *Educ:* Charterhouse; R.M.A. Entered R.A. 1894; Major, 1911; Col. 1919; retired pay, 1921;

served South Africa, 1899-1901 (despatches, Queen's medal 6 clasps, D.S.O.); European War, 1914-18 (despatches, Bt. Lt.-Col., C.M.G. Bt. Col.); Order of Danilo, 3rd class, 1917; Officer of Legion of Honour, Croix de Guerre. Zone Commander Derbyshire Home Guard, 1940-42. *Address:* Alton Manor, Idridgehay, near Derby. *T :* Wirksworth 35. *Club:* Army and Navy. [*Died* 22 *Oct.* 1961.

WALTON, Col. Sir Cusack, Kt., *cr.* 1933; D.S.O. 1916; R.E. (retired); *b.* 1878; *s.* of late F. T. G. Walton, C.I.E.; *m.* 1909, Julia Margaret (Kaisar-i-Hind medal 1933), *d.* of late Rev. D. M. Gardner, D.C.L., late I.C.S. *Educ.:* Clifton College; R.M.A., Woolwich. Commissioned in R.E. 1897; proceeded India, 1899; served on State Railways in India 1901-14 and 1919-32; Agent, North-Western Railway, 1924-32; retired 1933; Hon. Secretary India, Ceylon, and Iran Missions, Church Missionary Society, 1934-38; Order of Crown of Belgium 1925; served European War, 1914-19 (despatches, D.S.O., Legion of Honour, Bt. Lt.-Col.). *Address:* Talacre, 17 Shortheath Road, Farnham, Surrey. *T.:* 5770. [*Died* 27 *Feb.* 1966.

WALTON, Lt.-Col. Edgar Brocas, V.D.; *b.* Port Elizabeth, 10 Sept. 1880; *e. s.* of late Sir Edgar Walton, K.C.M.G.; *m.*; one *d.* *Educ.:* Grey Institute, Port Elizabeth. Served South African War, 1899-1901 (wounded three times, despatches); South African Rebellion and German South-West African Campaign, 1914-15 (despatches); East African Campaign, 1915-17 (despatches); joined the staff of Eastern Province Herald, 1902; acting Editor, 1907; Editor, 1922; Delegate to Imperial Press Conf., 1909 and 1930. Ret., 1948. *Address:* 7 Mill Park Rd., Port Elizabeth, South Africa. *Club:* Port Elizabeth. [*Died* 19 *July* 1964.

WALTON, Henry George, C.S.I. 1932; *b.* 2 Aug. 1876; *m.* 1903, Bertha (*d.* 1959), *d.* of Rev. D. Hutto; two *s.* *Educ.:* Newcastle Grammar School; Jesus College, Cambridge. Entered Indian Civil Service, 1899; Member, Board of Revenue, U.P., 1931; retired, 1934. *Address:* Eskhill, Inveresk, Musselburgh; Midlothian. *T.:* Musselburgh 2193. [*Died* 26 *June* 1962.

WALTON, Sydney, C.B.E.; M.A.; B.Litt.; *b.* Frosterley, County Durham, 25 Oct. 1882; *m.* Emma White (*d.* 1950), Gosforth. *Educ.:* Willington; Univ. Coll., Durham. Began as office boy in Bishop Auckland at age of 13; won an Exhibition in Letters at Durham University; took two degrees with distinction; elected President of Durham University Union and edited The Sphinx; taught in George Dixon Secondary School, Birmingham, for two years, and at Harrow County School for one term; entered journalism and became widely known as publicist; at Ministry of Munitions, then at Ministry of Food; on Lord Rhondda's personal staff, and later principal Private Secretary to Food Controller; Director of Publicity for Victory Loan in 1919; gave voluntary assistance of great value to many Government Departments in the War; for some time on the staff of the Canadian Trade Mission in London. *Publications:* The Sieve of Blindness, a volume of Essays; From the White Cottage (Letters in War Time); Into Italy; Among the Fjords; Lotus Leaves; Sunwards on the Stella; multitudinous newspaper articles. *Recreations:* walks, change of work, talks with friends, a book by the fireside. *Address:* St. James' Court, Buckingham Gate, S.W.1. *T.:* Victoria 2360. [*Died* 12 *Dec.* 1964.

WALWYN, Algernon Edward Vere, C.M.G. 1941; *b.* 17 March 1888; *s.* of Edward Vere Walwyn, Bath; *m.* 1925, Helen Mary Harvey; no *c.* *Educ.:* Bath College; Peterhouse, Cambridge. Assistant District Officer, Nigeria, 1915; Resident, 1932; Secretary, Northern Provinces, 1937; Staff Grade, 1937; retired 1943. *Address:* Grosvenor Square, Rondebosch, Cape Town, South Africa. *T.:* 68268. [*Died* 23 *June* 1970.

WARBURG, Otto Heinrich; Ordre pour le Mérite, also Cross, Star and Shoulder Ribbon (West Germany); Direktor des Max Planck Institute für Zellphysiologie, Berlin-Dahlem; *b.* Freiburg, Baden, 8 Oct. 1883; *s.* of late Emil Warburg, President of Physikalische Reichsanstalt, Wirkl. Geh. Oberregierungsrat and Elizabeth Gaertner; unmarried. *Educ.:* Berlin. Dr. der Chemie. Berlin, 1906; Dr. der Medizin, Heidelberg, 1911. Served European War, 1914-18 (Prussian Horse Guards) (Iron Cross, 1st class). Nobel Prize for Medicine, 1931; Foreign Member Royal Society, 1934; Paul Ehrlich Prize, 1962; Hon. D.Sc. Oxford, 1965. Hon. Freedom of West Berlin, 1963. *Publications:* Stoffwechsel der Tumoren, 1926; Katalytische Wirkungen der lebendigen Substanz, 1928; Schwermetalle als Wirkungsgruppen von Fermenten, 1946; Wasserstoffübertragende Fermente, 1948; Z; Mechanism of Photosynthesis, 1951; Entstehung der Krebszellen, 1955; Weiterentwicklung der zellphysiologischen Methoden, 1962. *Address:* Berlin-Dahlem, Garystrasse 18, Germany. *T.:* Berlin 763592. [*Died* 1 *Aug.* 1970.

WARBURTON, Geoffrey E.; *see* Egerton-Warburton.

WARD, Anthony Edward Walter, C.B. 1968; C.B.E. 1958; Solicitor, Ministry of Social Security (formerly Min. of Pensions and National Insurance), since 1958; *b.* 21 April 1905; *s.* of late Mr. Justice C. G. Ward, Johannesburg; *m.* 1932, Muriel Irene Gertrude, *d.* of late Rev. A. C. Howell; one *d.* (and one *d.* decd.). *Educ.:* Charterhouse; Emmanuel College, Cambridge. Called to the Bar, Inner Temple, 1929; practised at Common Law Bar in London till 1939; Junior Legal Assistant, Law Officers' Dept., 1939-40 and 1945-46. Royal Air Force V.R. Technical Branch, 1940-45; released as Acting Wing Commander. Transferred to Ministry of National Insurance as Legal Assistant, 1946; Senior Legal Assistant, 1947; Assistant Solicitor, 1948. *Publications:* part author of Workmen's Compensation in Halsbury's Laws of England, 2nd Edn., 1938. *Recreation:* reading. *Address:* 12 Woodhall Avenue, Pinner, Middlesex. *T.:* 01-866 4290. *Club:* Oxford and Cambridge. [*Died* 21 *May* 1968.

WARD, Lieut.-Col. Ellacott Leamon, C.B.E. 1919; M.R.C.S. Eng.; L.R.C.P. Lond. 1897; D.P.H., R.C.S. 1908; I.M.S., retired; *b.* 28 April 1873; *s.* of William Philip Ward, Royal Navy; *m.* 1901, Charlotte Lyne, (*d.* 1960), *d.* of W. E. L. Veale, Royal Navy, of Byfield, Mannamead, Plymouth; one *s.* *Educ.:* King's School, Chester; Middlesex Hospital, W. House Physician and House Surgeon, Middlesex Hospital, W.; entered I.M.S. 1899; with 42nd Gurkhas in Chitral, 1900; Punjab Jail Department, 1902; Special Health Officer, Coronation Durbar Camp, Delhi, 1911; Sanitary Adviser, Temporary Works, Delhi, 1912; Kaisar-i-Hind gold medal, 1913; British War Medal; despatches twice. Member, Punjab Legislative Assembly, 1927. Inspector-General of Prisons, Punjab, 1916-28; retired, 1928; organised Punjab Jail Department for War work, and raised two Labour Battalions (Jail) for Mesopotamia; O.St.J. Chairman, Maidstone Medical Board, 1939-47. *Address:* Empacombe, 17 Hatherley Road, Sidcup, Kent. *T.:* Foot's Cray 2415. *Club:* East India and Sports. [*Died* 25 *June* 1968.

WARD, George Edgar Septimus, M.D., F.R.C.P.; Hon. F.F.R.; retired; Emeritus Cons. Physician, Middlesex Hospital, W.1; late temporary Surgeon-Lieutenant Royal Navy; *b.* 7 December 1888; 7th *s.* of late

Dr. William J. C. Ward, Harrogate; *m.* 1918, Una (*d.* 1966), *y. d.* of late Dr. S. Gourley, M.D., West Hartlepool; one *d. Educ.:* Epsom College; Middlesex Hospital Medical School. Formerly Physician in charge of Department of Cardiology, Middlesex Hospital. *Publications:* papers on Diseases of the Heart. *Address:* 7 Fernhill, St. Stephen's Road, Bournemouth. *T.:* Bournemouth 20186. [*Died* 19 *March* 1969.

WARD, Col. Henry C. S.; *see* Swinburne-Ward.

WARD, Joseph, C.M.G. 1919; D.S.O. 1917; L.R.C.P., M.R.C.S.; *s.* of late John Samuel Ward, Sheffield; *m.* 1st, Isabella Frances (*decd.*), *d.* of late Henry Wilton, D.I.R.I.C., Co. Antrim; no *c.*; 2nd, 1921, Eva, *d.* of late H. B. Willis, Tunbridge Wells; one *s. Educ.:* University College, Sheffield; London. Lieutenant R.A.M.C. (vols.), 1906; mobilised 14 Aug. 1914; Capt. R.A.M.C. (T.F.); Major 9 Oct. 1914; a/Lt.-Col. 15 June 1915, to demobilisation 18 April 1919; Lt. Col. late R.A.M.C. (T.F.), retired; served Eur-opean War in France, Dec. 1914-Dec. 1915, Salonica, Dec. 1915-Oct. 1918 (despatches thrice, D.S.O., C.M.G., Commander St Sava, Serbia, Serbian Red Cross); British Medical Representative Sofia, Oct. 1918-Jan. 1919; Administrator and Repatriator, Sick Prisoners of War in Bulgaria, British and Serbian; in command of 81st Fld. Ambulance, Tiflis, Jan.-March 1919. *Address:* 24 Radinden Mano Rd., Hove, Sx. [*Died* 14 *Jan.* 1963.

WARD, Sir Joseph George Davidson, 3rd Bt., *cr.* 1911; *b.* Invercargill, New Zealand, 17 Sept. 1909; *s.* of Sir Cyril R. J. Ward, 2nd Bt., and Elinor Angela (*d.* 1943), *d.* of James Henry Davidson, J.P., Brisbane; *g.s.* of Sir Joseph George Ward, 1st Bt., Prime Minister of New Zealand, 1906-12, 1928-30; *S.* father, 1940; *m.* 1944, Joan Mary Haden, *d.* of Maj. Thomas J. Laffey, N.Z.S.C.; three *s.* three *d. Educ.:* Christ's Coll., and Canterbury Univ. College, Christchurch, N.Z. Law Clerk to Roy Twyneham till 1934; Barrister and Solicitor, 1934; Kinsey & Co. Ltd. 1934-48; N.Z. Shipping Gazette Ltd., 1948-. LL.B. 1934; LL.M. 1935; Notary Public, 1938; Associate Institute of Chartered Shipbrokers, 1938; Canterbury University College Council since 1934, Chm. 1948-51; Consul of Belgium, 1940; Director Royal Humane Society, 1941, Pres. 1946-; Provincial Comr. for Boy Scouts 1942-61; Pres. N.Z. Amateur Fencing Assoc., 1938-54. Chevalier of the Order of the Crown (Belgium), 1950. *Recreations:* gardening, philately, contract bridge. *Heir: s.* Joseph James Laffey Ward, *b.* 11 Nov. 1946. *Address:* Westbrook, 75 Harakeke St., Christchurch, N.Z. *T.A.:* Sureward, Christchurch. *T.:* 43.299. *Clubs:* Canterbury, University, Canterbury Jockey, Officers' (Christchurch). [*Died* 4 *Aug.* 1970.

WARD, Sarah Adelaide, C.B.E. 1961 (O.B.E. 1952); *d.* of John Ainsworth Meaford, Stone; *m.* 1921, William J. Ward; one *d. Educ.:* Orme Girls' School, Newcastle-under-Lyme. Served European War, V.A.D., 1914-18; M.P. (U.) Cannock Div. of Staffs., 1931-35. Served War of 1939-45: Junior Comdr. A.T.S., 1940-43. Prospective Conservative Candidate: Lichfield Div. of Staffs., 1946; Perry Barr Div. of Birmingham, 1951. Member of Staffordshire C.C. since 1950; Chm., Staffs. County Welfare Services Cttee., 1956-64. *Address:* Grange Farm, Walsall Wood, Walsall, Staffs. *T.:* Pelsall 2275. [*Died* 9 *April* 1969.

WARDE, Mrs. Beatrice Lamberton; Typographic Consultant to The Monotype Corporation Ltd.; Founder, Books Across the Sea; a Governor, English-Speaking Union; writer and lecturer on typography; Editor, Monotype Recorder, since 1927; *b.* New York City, 20 Sept. 1900; *d.* of Gustav L. Becker, composer and musical pedagogue, and May Lamberton Becker, editor and author. *Educ.:* Barnard College, Columbia University, B.A. Assistant Librarian and Curator, 1921-25, at the Typographic Library of the American Typefounders' Co.; carried out independent researches in London and Paris on the history of typography. Hon. Fellow, Manchester College of Art. Member: Society of Industrial Artists & Designers; Society of Designer Craftsmen. *Publications:* Type Faces Old and New, Transactions of the Bibliographical Society, 1935; Typography in Art Education, N.S.A.E.; The Crystal Goblet (16 essays on typography); Under pen-name of Paul Beaujon: XVIIIth Century French Typography and Fournier le Jeune, 1926; The "Garamond" Types, 1926; Peace Under Earth, 1938; Contributor to Encyc. Brit., Chambers's Encyc., The Fleuron, and typographical periodicals of Europe and America. *Address:* 2 College Avenue, Epsom, Surrey. *T.:* Epsom 20287. [*Died* 14 *Sept.* 1969.

WARDLAW, Rev. James T. P.; *see* Plowden-Wardlaw.

WARDLAW-MILNE, Sir John (Sydney), K.B.E., *cr.* 1932; 4th *s.* of James Milne, J.P., banker, of Helensburgh, and Elizabeth, *d.* of James Fleming Wardlaw, W.S., Edinburgh; assumed name of Wardlaw-Milne, 1922; *m.* 1st, Aimee Margaret (*d.* 1933), *o. d.* of William Garden, Uttershill, Penicuik; no *c.*; 2nd, 1935, Vyvien Mary Pike (*d.* 1965), *widow* of Lt.-Col. Montague Headland Pike, O.B.E., M.C. For some years Director of Turner Morrison & Co., Bombay and Calcutta; member Bombay Municipal Corporation, 1907-1917; Government Representative, City of Bombay Improvement Trust; Trustee of the Port of Bombay; Chairman and Deputy-Chairman, Bombay Chamber of Commerce. Director Bank of Bombay; Additional Member Governor of Bombay's Legislative Council and Governor-General of India's Council; Lt.-Col. Commanding 4th (Bombay) Artillery, Indian Defence Force, 1915-19; President, Government of India's Advisory War Shipping Committee; Official Lecturer for British Government in U.S.A. upon Mesopotamia and Near East questions; M.P. (U.) Kidderminster Division of Worcestershire, 1922-45; Member of Imperial Economic Committee, 1926-29; Chairman, House of Commons Select Committee on National Expenditure, 1939-45; Chairman, Conservative Foreign Affairs Committee, 1939-1945; also of India and Anglo-Egyptian Committees. Freedom of Kidderminster, 1937. Has travelled extensively in India, Straits, Mesopotamia, China, Canada, and U.S.A. *Publications:* The Key to the War; The A. B. C. of £. s. d.; The G. H. Q. of £. s. d.; several contributions on Eastern War questions. *Address:* Grouville Court, Grouville, Jersey, C.I. *T.:* East 140. *Clubs:* Carlton; Royal Yacht Squadron; Royal Channel Island Yacht; Victoria (Jersey). [*Died* 11 *July* 1967.

WARDLE-SMITH, John Hughes, C.M.G. 1957; H.M. Minister, Rio de Janeiro, since 1963; *b.* 16 Oct. 1909; *s.* of Frederick Wardle-Smith, Carlton, Notts, and Constance L. Hughes, Ashdell Grove, Sheffield. *Educ.:* Marlborough College; St. John's College, Oxford. Joined Foreign Service 1945; 2nd Sec., 1945-46. Head of Chancery, 1946-47, Santiago, Chile; S. American Dept., F.O., 1947-48; 1st Sec., 1948; Far Eastern Dept., F.O., 1948-49; 1st Sec., Cairo, 1949; Counsellor and Head of Chancery, British Embassy Cairo, 1950-52; H.M. Consul-General, Eritrea, 1952-54; Counsellor (Commercial and Economic Affairs), Djakarta, 1955-59; Counsellor (Commercial), Rome, 1959-63. *Address:* British Embassy, Rio de Janeiro, Brazil. *Clubs:* Bath; Island Sailing (Cowes). [*Died* 5 *Aug.* 1968.

WARDROP, General Sir Alexander, G.C.B., *cr.* 1936 (K.C.B., *cr.* 1930; C.B. 1918); C.M.G. 1916; *b.* 15 Sept. 1872; *s.* of late Major-Gen. A. Wardrop and Ann Godden; *m.* 1920, Amy (*d.* 1944), *e. d.* of E. Norton, Uplands, Fareham. *Educ.:* Haileybury; Royal Military Academy. Col. Comdt. Royal Artillery, 1930; G.O.C. Northern Command, 1933-37. Col. Comdt., R.H.A., 1934; A.D.C. General to King George V, 1935. Retired pay, 1937. *Publications:* Modern Pig-sticking, 1914; Indian Big Game, 1923. *Address:* Belmore House, Upham, Hants. *Club:* United Service. [*Died* 22 *June* 1961.

WARE, Sir Frank, Kt., *cr.* 1946, C.I.E. 1937; *b.* Theydon Bois, Essex, 22 Feb. 1886; *s.* of J. W. Ware; *m.* 1921, Martha Turner, M.Sc.; one *s.* two *d.* *Educ.:* Privately; Roy. Veterinary Coll., London. M.R.C.V.S. 1907; F.R.C.V.S. 1921; joined Indian Veterinary Service, 1907; retd., 1947; served as Principal, Madras Veterinary Coll.; Director of Veterinary Services, Madras; Director, Imperial Veterinary Research Institute, Muktesar; Animal Husbandry Commissioner, Imperial Council of Agricultural Research, India; Director of Animal Husbandry, U.P. India. *Publications:* Various in Protozoology, Helminthology and other branches of Veterinary Science. *Address:* Springfield, Highclere, Newbury, Berks. [*Died* 6 *Dec.* 1968.

WARING, Lady Clementine; *see* Waring, Lady S. E. C.

WARING, (Henry) William (Allen). C.M.G. 1945; F.C.A.; Director, Guest Keen & Nettlefolds Ltd.; Deputy Chairman and General Managing Director, G.K.N. Steel Co. Ltd.; Director: Guest Keen & Nettlefolds (South Wales) Ltd.; Tarmac (South Wales) Ltd.; Oxfordshire Ironstone Co. Ltd.; *b.* 7 August 1906; *s.* of late Henry Allen Waring, Indian Police, and Marguerita Lillian Chamier Macleod (who *m.* 1912, H. V. Rabagliati, *q.v.*); *m.* 1st, 1931, Anne Elizabeth Tindal Faithfull (marriage dissolved, 1951); one *s.*; 2nd, 1952, Suzanne Barr Jacob. *Educ.:* Christ's Hospital. Articled to Sir Arthur Roberts, K.B.E., Chartered Accountant, 1924-29; Chartered Accountant with Whinney, Murray & Co. Resident in Berlin and Hamburg, 1929-34; Oslo, 1934-39; attached to British Consulate, Oslo, 1939-40; Assistant to Commercial Counsellor, British Legation, Stockholm, with diplomatic status, 1940-42; Ministry of Supply representative in Stockholm with diplomatic status, 1942-45; Ministry of Economic Warfare representative in Anglo-American ball-bearing negotiations with Sweden, 1944-45; Control Commission for Germany; successively in charge Iron and Steel; Basic Industries; and Dep. Chief Industry Div., 1945-47; Guest Keen Baldwins Iron & Steel Co. Ltd., Cardiff, 1947-51; Director Power and Steel Division, Economic Commn. for Europe, 1951, Industry Division, 1952-56. Director of Belships A/S, Oslo 1936-38; Mannesmannröhren-Werke, Düsseldorf, 1949-51; Managing Director, Brymbo Steel Works Ltd., 1956-60; Chairman: Steel Committee, Economic Commission for Europe, 1959-61. *Publications:* numerous United Nations Economic Publications, since 1952. *Recreations:* sailing, fishing and shooting. *Address:* (office) G.K.N. Steel Co. Ltd., 22 Kingsway, W.C.2; (home) 12 Eaton Row, S.W.1. *T.:* Belgravia 7924. *Clubs:* Turf, Special Forces; Cardiff and County. [*Died* 9 *Jan.* 1962.

WARING, Rev. Canon John, M.A. (T.C.D.); Residentiary Canon of Norwich Cathedral, 1951-66; Residentiary Canon Emeritus, 1966; Canon Treasurer, 1954; *b.* 28 May 1890; *s.* of Samuel Waring, J.P., and Elizabeth Waring; *m.* 1918, Beryl Constance Howard; one *d.* *Educ.:* Royal Belfast Academical Institution; Trinity Coll., Dublin. Deacon, 1913; priest, 1914; Curate: St. James, Dublin, 1913-15; St. Werburgh, Dublin, 1915-16; St. Mark, Dundela, Belfast, 1916-17. Church Missionary Society: Organising Secretary for Ulster, 1917-22, for Salisbury and Winchester, 1922-26; Metropolitan Secretary, 1926-28; Secretary, Missions of Service, 1928-29. Vicar of St. Andrew's, Nottingham, 1929-39; Hon. Canon of Southwell, 1936-39; Vicar and Rural Dean of Rotherham, 1939-45; Canon in Sheffield Cathedral, 1939-45; Proctor in Convocation, Sheffield, 1942-45; Vicar of Dudley, 1945-51; Hon. Canon of Worcester, 1946-51; Rural Dean of Dudley, 1946-51. *Address:* 13 Cecil Road, Norwich, NOR 78D, Norfolk. *T.:* Norwich 22998. [*Died* 27 *Dec.* 1967.

WARING, Mrs. Margaret Alicia, C.B.E. 1933; J.P. Co. Down; *b.* 14 Nov. 1887; *y. d.* of Joseph Charlton Parr of Grappallhen Heyes, Warrington; *m.* 1914, Major Holt Waring, D.L., J.P. of Waringstown, Co. Down (killed in action at Kemmel Hill 18 April 1918); no *c.* M.P. (U.) Iveagh Division, Co. Down, in Ulster Parliament 1929-33. *Address:* Waringstown, Co. Down, Northern Ireland. [*Died* 9 *May* 1968.

WARING, Lady (Susan Elizabeth) Clementine, C.B.E. 1918; *d.* of William Montagu, 10th Marquess of Tweeddale, and Candida Bartolucci; *m.* 1901, Walter Waring, M.P. (*d.* 1930), 1st Life Guards; one *d.* (and one *d.* decd.). *Educ.:* Home; Germany; France. Donor and Administrator of Lennel Auxiliary Hospital for Officers; President Scottish Children's League of Pity, 1893-1950, Assoc. Pres 1950; Organiser W.V.S. Salcombe 1941-42; Co-organised Red Cross Shop, Kingsbridge, 1942-46. Order of Queen Elizabeth of Belgium. *Publication:* Mother and Babe, an anthology for Mothers, 1933. *Recreations:* gardening and travelling. *Address:* The Moult, Salcombe, S. Devon. *T.:* Salcombe 2630; Albany Lodge, Albany Street, N.W.1. *T.:* Euston 2003. *Clubs:* Bath, Royal Over-Seas League. [*Died* 15 *Feb.* 1964.

WARING, William; *see* Waring, H. W. A.

WARLOW-DAVIES, Eric John; Managing Director, Bristol Siddeley Engines Ltd., since 1963; *b.* 4 Jan. 1910; *s.* of Harry Warlow-Davies and Muriel Warlow-Davies (*née* Bate). *Educ.:* Hutchins School, Hobart, Tasmania; University of Tasmania; Oxford University. B.Sc. (Tasmania), 1931; B.A. (Oxon), 1934; D.Phil. (Oxon.), 1937. Mech. Test Dept., R.A.E., 1937; Railway Research Dept., L.M.S., 1938; Rolls-Royce Ltd. 1942; Engine Division, Bristol Aeroplane Co. Ltd., 1953; Director and Chief Engineer (Aero), Bristol Siddeley Engines Ltd., 1961. *Address:* Bristol Siddeley Engines Ltd., Mercury House, 195 Knightsbridge, S.W.7. *T.:* Kensington 7090. [*Died* 28 *June* 1964.

WARNE-BROWNE, Air Marshal Sir Thomas Arthur, K.B.E., *cr.* 1951 (C.B.E. 1944); C.B. 1947; D.S.C.; with R. A. Brand & Co. Ltd., Spray Packaging Division, Letchworth, as Services Liaison, since 1955; *b.* 1898; *s.* of late A. Warne-Browne, Shiplake-on-Thames; *m.* 1926, Ruth, *d.* of late Charles E. Nicholson, O.B.E., Hill Head, Hants.; three *d.* *Educ.:* Malvern. Served European War, 1914-19, with R.N.A.S. and R.A.F. (D.S.C.). Wing Commander, 1937; Group Captain, 1940; Air Commodore, 1943; Air Vice-Marshal, 1946; Acting Air Marshal 1949; Air Marshal 1951; Senior Engineer Staff Officer, H.Q. Coastal Command, 1942-46; A.O.C. No. 43 Group, 1946-47; Senior Technical Staff Officer, R.A.F., Mediterranean and Middle East, 1947-49; Air Officer Commanding-in-Chief, Maintenance Command, 1949-Dec. 1952; retired, Jan. 1953. *Address:* Martins, Chilbolton, Stockbridge, Hants. *Clubs:* Lansdowne, Royal Air Force, Royal Air Force Reserves. [*Died* 13 *Oct.* 1962.

WARNER, Hon. Sir Arthur (George), K.B.E. 1962; Kt. 1956; Member Legislative Council and Minister of Transport, Victorian State Govt., Aust., 1955-64; Chairman: Electronic Industries Ltd.; Australian & International Insurances Ltd.; *b.* 31 July 1899; British; *m.* 1920, Ethel, *d.* of Charles Wakefield, England; two *s.* *Educ.:* Sir George Monarch Gram. School; London Univ. Commenced radio manufacture, 1927; founded Public Co. Electronic Industries Ltd., 1938 and is Dir. of many subsidiary cos., and also of Sutex Ltd. Fellow of Australian Inst. of Accountants; Council Member: Victorian Chamber of Manufactures; Victorian Chamber of Commerce; Inst. of Public Affairs. Entered politics as M.L.C., 1946; Minister of Housing, Materials and State Development, 1947; Dep. Leader of Liberal Party in Upper House, 1947, Leader, 1954. Served European War, 1914-1918, Flight Lt. in Fleet Air Arm; during War of 1939-45, was Controller of Finance, Min. of Munitions, Finance Dir. of Bd. of Area Management, and Chm. of Business Advisory Panel to the Army. *Recreations:* yachting and golf. *Address:* 2 Dudley Street, Brighton, Victoria, Australia. *T.:* XM 3652. *Clubs:* Savage, Royal Brighton and Royal Yacht Club of Victoria, Metropolitan Golf (Melbourne). [*Died* 3 *April* 1966.

WARNER, Edwin Charles, M.D., B.S., B.Sc., F.R.C.P. (Lond.); Consulting Physician, Charing Cross Hosp.; Consultant Physician, New Victoria Hospital, Kingston-on-Thames, and Emer. Cons. Phys., Putney Hosp.; Member of Senate, University of London; Member Council, Royal Society of Medicine; *b.* 10 April 1900, *s.* of late F. Watkin and L. Warner; *m.* 1931, Dora Allsop; one *s.* two *d.* *Educ.:* Guy's Hospital Medical School. Formerly Asst. House Surgeon, House Physician and Senior Medical Registrar, Guy's Hospital; University of London Research Student in Physiology, and Parson's Research Fellow; Demonstrator in Physiology and Pharmacology, Guy's Hospital Medical School; Physician to Children's Dept., Miller General Hospital; Physician to Outpatient Dept., Dreadnought (Seamen's) Hospital; Medical Superintendent, Ashridge (E.M.S.) Hospital, Berkhamsted. Hon. Editor of Proc., Roy. Soc. Med.; Lectr. in Med. and in Therapeutics (formerly Dean) Charing Cross Hosp. Med. School. *Publications:* Editor and contributor, Savill's System of Clinical Medicine, 1944, 1950 and 1964; chapter Recent Advances in Medicine, O'Meara's Med. Guide; contrib. Lancet. *Recreation:* golf. *Address:* 83 Harley House, Regent's Park, N.W.1. *T.:* Welbeck 2581/2. [*Died* 6 *Jan.* 1968.

WARNER, Sir Pelham Francis, Kt. 1937; M.B.E. 1919; Writer on Cricket; *b.* 2 October 1873; *y. s.* of C. W. Warner, C.B.; *m.* 1904, Agnes (*d.* 1955), *d.* of late Henry Arthur Blyth; two *s.* one *d.* *Educ.:* Rugby; Oriel College, Oxford. Barrister-at-law, Inner Temple, 1900. Has played cricket all over the world. Deputy Secretary, M.C.C., 1939-45; President, M.C.C., 1950. *Publications:* Cricket in many Climes; Cricket Across the Seas; How we Recovered the Ashes; M.C.C. in South Africa; The Book of Cricket; England *v.* Australia; Imperial Cricket; Cricket Reminiscences; The Badminton Cricket; My Cricketing Life, 1921; The Fight for the Ashes in 1926; The Fight for the Ashes in 1930; Cricket between Two Wars, 1942; Lord's 1787-1945, 1946; Gentlemen *v.* Players 1787-1949, 1950; Long Innings, 1951. Sometime Editor of The Cricketer. *Clubs:* Buck's, E. India and Sports. [*Died* 30 *Jan.* 1963.

WARR, Very Rev. Charles Laing, G.C.V.O. 1967 (K.C.V.O. 1950; C.V.O. 1937); D.L., Co. of City of Edinburgh, 1953; M.A. Edin. 1914; Hon. D.D. Edin., 1931; Hon. LL.D. St. Andrews, 1937, Edin., 1953; Hon. R.S.A. 1927; Hon. F.R.C.S. Edin., 1955; Hon. F.R.I.B.A. 1957; F.R.S.E.; Dean of the Chapel Royal in Scotland and Dean of the Order of the Thistle since 1926; Chaplain to the Queen since 1952 (to King George V, 1926-36, to King Edward VIII, 1936, to King George VI, 1936-52); Chaplain to H.M. Bodyguard for Scotland (Royal Company of Archers) since 1937; Sub-Prelate of Order of St. John of Jerusalem since 1947 (Chaplain since 1942); Hon. Member of Merchant Company of Edinburgh, 1951; Chaplain: Royal Scottish Academy; Convention of Royal Burghs of Scotland; Royal Highland and Agricultura. Soc.; Royal College of Surgeons of Edinburgh; Merchant Company of Edinburgh; Pres., Eglise Protestante Française d'Edimbourg; Hon. President Scottish Association of Boys' Clubs; Vice-President Scot. Nat. Inst. for War Blinded, Roy. Scot. Soc. for Prevention of Cruelty to Children, Scottish Church Soc., and Trin. Coll. of Music. London; Vice-Patron, A.T.S. and W.R.A.C. Benevolent Funds; Hon. Governor Glasgow Academy; *b.* 20 May 1892: 2nd *s.* of late Rev. Alfred Warr, Minister of Rosneath, Dunbartonshire, and Christian Grey, 5th *d.* of late Adam Laing; *m.* 1918, Christian Lawson Aitken (Ruby) (*d.* 1961), *o. d.* of Robert Rattray Tatlock and Christian Lawson, *o. d.* of Rev. Charles Aitken of Cuparhead, Lanarks., Vicar of Carmenellis, Cornwall; no *c.* *Educ.:* Glasgow Academy; Universities of Edinburgh and Glasgow. Commissioned to 9th Argyll and Sutherland Highlanders, 5 Aug. 1914; dangerously wounded, May 1915; Assistant Minister at Glasgow Cathedral, 1917-18; Minister of St. Paul's, Greenock, 1918-26; Member of Renfrewshire Education Authority, 1923-25; Walker Trust Lecturer, University of St. Andrews, 1936; Pres. Scoto-Russian Fellowship of St. Andrew, 1936-46; Convener Church of Scotland Committee on Huts and Canteens for H.M. Forces, 1939-46; Governor Fettes College, 1926-46; Director Royal Edinburgh Hospital for Sick Children, 1937-47; Governor Princess Margaret Rose Hospital for Crippled Children, 1930-48; Member of Council, National Trust for Scotland, 1932-35, 1940-46, and 1955-60, and of Executive, 1940-46; Hon. President Church Service Society, 1946- (President 1944-46); Convener of Home Mission Cttee. and Vice-Convener of Home Board, 1939-41 and 1947-51; Jt. Convener, National Church Extension Cttee., 1955-58. Minister of St. Giles' Cathedral, Edinburgh, 1926-62. Trustee: of National Library of Scotland, 1926-62; of Iona Cathedral, 1926, 1962. *Publications:* The Unseen Host, 1916; Echoes of Flanders, 1916; Alfred Warr of Rosneath, 1917; Principal Caird, 1926; The Call of the Island, 1929; Scottish Sermons and Addresses, 1930; The Presbyterian Tradition, 1933; Bruce (Walker Trust Lecture), 1936; The Glimmering Landscape, 1960. *Recreations:* music, travel, literature. *Address:* Queen's House, Moray Place, Edinburgh. *T.:* 031-225 2243. *Club:* New (Edinburgh). [*Died* 14 *June* 1969.

WARREN, Arthur George, M.Sc. (Lond.), M.I.E.E. F.Inst.P.; retired; *b.* Bexley, 18 Nov 1887; *m.* 1st, 1915, Mabel Middleton (*d.* 1952), *d.* of James Middleton Smith, Havant and Southsea; 2nd, 1962, Ethel Katherine Inverstein, *widow* of Walter James Powell, Orpington. *Educ.:* University of London; Sherbrooke (Mathematical) Scholar, First class Honours, B.Sc. 1908, M.Sc. 1921, M.I.E.E., Fellow of the Institute of Physics. Lecturer in Mechanical Engineering, East London College, 1908; Head of Engineering Department Aston Technical School, and Lecturer in Design, Birmingham Technical School, 1910; appointed to University of Hong-Kong, 1912; Lecturer in Physics, 1913; Professor of Physics, 1914-18; Professor of Electrical Engineering, 1918-21; Dean of Faculty of Engineering and Consulting Engineer, 1919; Mem. of Senate, elected Mem. of Council and Court. Formerly Assistant Dir., Engineering, Ministry of Supply. *Publications:* Mathematics applied to Electrical Engineering, 1939; (Joint) The New Steam Tables, 1912; Prime Movers, 1921; papers on Physical and Eng. subjects. *Address:* Brasted, Battle Hill, Battle, Sussex. *T.:* 2377.

[*Died* 9 *Jan.* 1967.

WARREN, Clarence Henry; author, broadcaster, reviewer, lecturer; *b.* 12 June 1895; *s.* of Alice and William Warren; unmarried. *Educ.:* Maidstone Grammar School; Goldsmiths' College, University of London. Served European War, 1916-19. English Master, Newport Grammar School, 1922-24; Lecturer, National Portrait Gallery, 1927; B.B.C., 1929-33. *Publications:* A Cotswold Year, 1936; A Boy in Kent, 1937; Happy Countryman, 1939; Corn Country, 1940; England is a Village, 1940; The Land is Yours, 1943; Essex (The County Books), 1950, The Scythe in the Apple Tree, 1953, Tyrolean Journal, 1954, etc. *Recreations:* music and gardens. *Address:* Timbers, Finchingfield, Essex. *T.:* Gt. Bardfield 380.

[*Died* 3 *April* 1966.

WARREN, Rear-Admiral Guy Langton, C.B. 1947; *b.* 13 Feb. 1888; *s.* of Frederic and Margaret Warren, Liverpool; *m.* 1915, Kathleen May, *d.* of late Col. H. H. Peel, C.B.E.; one *s.* one *d.* Britannia, 1903; Commander, 1924; Captain, 1931; Rear-Admiral, 1941; served European War, 1914-18, and War of 1939-45 (despatches, C.B.). *Address:* Keyford, Yeovil, Somerset. *Club:* United Service. [*Died* 11 *Jan.* 1961.

WARREN, Sir (Henry William) Hugh, Kt., *cr.* 1951; D.Sc., M.Sc. (Engineering), M.I.E.E., M.I.Mech.E., F.Inst.P.; Director: Micanite & Insulators Co. Ltd.; British Industrial Plastics Ltd.; *b.* Bristol, 30 June 1891; *s.* of Henry and Eliza Warren; *m.* 1914, May Goude; one *d.* (one *s.* decd.). *Educ.:* Merchant Venturers' Technical Coll., Bristol; Bristol Univ. Demonstrator (Chemistry and Physics), Bristol University, 1907-1911; was with British Thomson-Houston Co. Ltd., successively as Eng. of Insulations, Director of Research (24 years), Director of Engineering, Mng. Director, 1911-47; Managing Director, Associated Electrical Industries Limited, 1948-54, retired 1954. *Publications:* Electrical Insulating Materials, 1931; various technical papers on Electrical Ignition, Synthetic Resins, Engineering Materials, Education, Research, Production of Light, etc.; Miscellaneous essays. *Recreation:* writing. *Address:* Milbury, West Parade, Worthing, Sussex.

[*Died* 18 *June* 1961.

WARREN, Sir Hugh; *see* Warren, Sir Henry W. H.

WARREN, Nigel Sebastian Sommerville, Q.C. 1959; *b.* 14 March 1912; *s.* of Robert Hall Warren and Jean Dorothy Warren, Clifton, Bristol. *Educ.:* Clifton; Hertford College, Oxford (M.A.). 1st class Jurisprudence, 1934. Called to Bar, 1936; Bencher, Lincoln's Inn, 1964. Served War of 1939-45 with Royal Wiltshire Yeomanry; served in Middle East, 1941-June 1945; staff of Judge Advocate-General, 1942-45; Lieutenant-Colonel, 1945. *Address:* 6 Arlington House, S.W.1. *T.:* Hyde Park 4301; Compton House, Compton Bishop, Som. *T.:* Axbridge 257. *Clubs:* Alpine, Beefsteak, Oxford and Cambridge.

[*Died* 18 *July* 1967.

WARREN, Thomas Alfred, C.B.E. 1939; Order of Carlos Miguel de Cespedes, Republic Cuba, 1946; late Director of Education, Wolverhampton; *b.* 10 May 1882; *s.* of Alfred and Selina Warren, Manchester; *m.* 1908, Louisa (*d.* 1955). *d.* of Robert Davidson, Irthington, Carlisle; one *s.* *Educ.:* Manchester Secondary School. Mem. National Youth Cttee., 1940-42; formerly Chief Asst. for Higher Education and Supt. of Evening Schools, Manchester; Asst. Education Sec. Plymouth; President Rotary in Great Britain and Ireland, 1937-38; President Rotary International, 1945-46; Member Departmental Committee on Private Schools, 1930-32. *Publications:* Many educational reports and pamphlets; Youth, written particularly for issue in Rotary *Recreations:* football, cricket, riding. *Address:* Broadwood, 3 Beechey Rd., Bournemouth.

[*Died* 13 *Nov.* 1968.

WARREN, Colonel Sir Thomas Richard Pennefather, 8th Bt. *cr.* 1784; C.B.E. 1919; D.L.; A.M.I.Mech.E.; p.s.c., late R.A.S.C.; Chief Constable of Buckinghamshire, 1928-1953; Barrister-at-Law; *b.* 12 September 1885; *s.* of late Inspector-General T. R. Warren, R.N., and late Harriet Lavina, *d.* of Richard Pennefather, Lakefield, County Tipperary; *S.* kinsman (Sir Augustus George Digby Warren, Bt.) 1958; *m.* Ada Rene Costello, *d.* of late Col. Charles Hely, 12th Regt., of Woodstock, Cappoquin; one *s.* two *d.* *Educ.:* Burney's, Gosport. Joined A.S.C. from R.M.C., Sandhurst; promoted to Capt., Major, Lt.-Col., and Colonel R.A.S.C. 1914-18; served European War on the Staff and also Administrative side of Mechanical Transport (C.B.E., Brevet twice, despatches thrice); seconded from the Army, Oct. 1919, to hold position as Resident Magistrate in Ireland; restored to Regular Army Establishment, Dec. 1920; Passed Staff Coll., Camberley, 1922; Major, 1924; D.A.A. and Q.M.G. Wessex Area; Bt. Lt.-Col. 1928; retired pay, 1928. King's Police Medal, 1952. O.St.J. *Recreations:* shooting, fishing, hunting. *Heir:* *s.* Brian Charles Pennefather Warren [*b.* 4 June 1923. *Educ.:* Bilton Grange; Wellington Coll. Served War of 1939-45, 1941-1945, as Lieut., Irish Guards]. *Address:* Dunmore, Co. Waterford. *Clubs:* Royal Irish Automobile; Gold Staff Officers.

[*Died* 8 *Dec.* 1961.

WARREN, Colonel William Robinson, C.B.E. 1920; D.S.O. 1915; late R.A.; *b* 5 May 1882; *s.* of late Maj.-Gen. L. S. Warren, 65th Regt.; *m.* E. M. Gifford Ottley, *e. d.* of late D. Gifford Ottley. *Educ.:* Cheltenham; R.M.A., Woolwich. Entered R.A. 1900; Lt.-Col. 1925; served European War, 1914-18; North Russia and Baltic, 1919-20 (wounded thrice, despatches eight times, D.S.O., C.B.E., Bt. Lt.-Col.); retired 1929. [*Died* 14 *May* 1969.

WARREN PEARL, Mrs. F.; *see* Pearl, Amy Lea.

WARRINGTON-MORRIS, Air Commodore (retd.) Alfred Drummond, C.B. 1943; C.M.G. 1919; O.B.E. 1918; *b.* 18 Dec. 1883; *m.* 1909, Lilian Ruth Staples (*d.* 1961); no *c.* Served in Royal Navy, 1899-1916. Was Deputy Director of Wireless Telegraphy at Air Ministry; Commandant Royal Observer Corps, 1936-42; Deputy Director Air Training Corps at Air Ministry, 1942-44. *Recreations:* Rugby football, England, 1909; hockey. R.A.F., 1919. *Address:* 17 St. John's Avenue, Putney, S.W.15. *T.:* Putney 4606. [*Died* 24 *March* 1962.

WARWICK, Sir Norman Richard Combe, K.C.V.O. *cr.* 1950 (C.V.O. 1937; M.V.O. 1932); O.B.E. 1918; *b.* 5 Oct. 1892; *s.* of R. H. Warwick, Burgage Manor, Southwell; *m.* 1921, Joyce Huskinson, *d.* of H. C. Ransom, Hale, Winscombe, Somerset; two *s.* *Educ.:* Marlborough; Trinity College, Oxford. Cattle farming in Kenya, 1912; served

European War, 1914-18, with East African Protectorate Force; Trooper East African Mounted Rifles, 1914; Capt. East African Supply Corps, 1917 (O.B.E.); Asst. Political Officer, Tanganyika, 1918; apptd. to Duchy of Lancaster, 1919; Private Secretary to nineteen Chancellors, 1922-45; Chief Clerk, 1927-45; Clerk of the Council, 1945-52. *Address:* Claydene, Cowden, Kent. *Club:* Royal Commonwealth Society.
[*Died* 17 *Sept.* 1962.

WARWICK, Walter Curry; retired, 1962; formerly: Chairman of Houlder Brothers & Co. Ltd. (now President); Furness Houlder Argentine Lines Ltd., Empire Transport Co. Ltd., and British Empire Steam Navigation Co. Ltd.; Chairman and Director various other Shipping Companies; Director Shaw Savill & Albion Co. Ltd.; *b.* 9 Nov. 1877; *s.* of John Joseph Christopher Warwick and Elizabeth Harriet Walton; *m.* 1902, Margaret Hannah Spoor (*d.* 1948); one *s.*; *m.* 1950, Mrs. Mabel Kirtley (*d.* 1961), East Boldon. *Educ.:* Private. Joined Furness Withy & Co. Ltd. in London, 1896; in July 1911, when Furness Withy acquired controlling interest in Houlder Brothers & Co. Ltd. and Associated Companies, became a Managing Director of Houlder Brothers, a Director of Houlder Line Ltd., a Director of Empire Transport Co. Ltd., and other companies. In 1932, when Royal Mail Lines Ltd. was formed and took over the assets of Royal Mail Steam Packet Company, was one of the first Directors of the new Company (Chairman, 1944-60); Chairman, Pacific Steam Navigation Co., 1944-60. *Recreation:* golf. *Address:* 53 Leadenhall Street, E.C.3. *T.A.:* care Houlders Telex London. *T.:* Royal 2020; Walmar, Beech Hill, Hadley Wood, Herts. *T.:* Barnet 0491. *Clubs:* Bath, Argentine, Gresham, Royal Automobile.
[*Died* 20 *May* 1963.

WASON, Lieut.-Gen. Sydney Rigby, C.B. 1941; M.C.; *b.* 27 Sept. 1887; *s.* of James Wason, J.P., Mertonhall, Newton Stewart, Scotland; *m.* 1921, Freda, *d.* of Brig.-General F. Waldron, C.B. *Educ.:* Laleham; Wellington College; R.M.A., Woolwich. Joined Army, 1907; served European War, 1914-18, France, Gallipoli, Egypt, Mesopotamia (despatches, M.C. and 2 bars); G.S.O., Grade 2 at School of Artillery, 55th T.A. Div. and A.H.Q. India; G.S.O. Grade 1, Western Command; Commandant School of Artillery; Major-General, Royal Artillery, B.E.F., 1939-40 (despatches); commanded 1st A.A. Corps, 1940-42; Temp. Lt.-Gen.; retired 1942; Military Correspondent to European Broadcast of B.B.C., 1943-46. *Address:* Wheathill, Sparsholt, Hants. *Club:* Army and Navy.
[*Died* 17 *March* 1969.

WASS, Samuel Hall, M.S., F.R.C.S.: Surgeon, Guy's Hospital, since 1946; *b.* 5 Dec. 1907; *o. s.* of Isaac Wass; *m.* 1st, 1932, Joyce (from whom he obtained a divorce, 1946), *d.* of Rev. Harvey Blackett; two *s.*; 2nd, 1946, June Mary Vaudine, *d.* of Thomas Hugh Connolly Blaikie, O.B.E.; two *s.* *Educ.:* Queen Elizabeth's Grammar School, Mansfield; University College, Nottingham; Guy's Hospital Medical School. M.R.C.S., L.R.C.P., 1934, M.B., B.S. (Lond.), 1934, F.R.C.S. (Eng.), 1935, M.S. (Lond.), 1938. House Appointments, Demonstrator of Anatomy and Physiology, and Surgical Registrar, Guy's Hosp., 1934-46; Clinical Asst., St. Mark's Hosp., 1937-39; late Surgeon, Evelina Hosp. for Sick Children, St. John's Hosp., Lewisham and St. Olave's Hosp. Hunterian Professor, R.C.S., 1946; Hon. Visiting Surgeon, Johns Hopkins Hosp., Baltimore, U.S.A., 1954; Universities of Capetown and Johannesburg, S.A., 1960 and Prince Henry Hospital, Melbourne, Aust., 1961; Examiner in Surgery, Univ. of London, 1947 55, 1958-; Mem. of Court of Examiners, R.C.S., 1955-64; F.R.S. Med. (Member of Council, Sections of Surgery and Proctology); Fellow Assoc. of Surgeons of Great Britain and Ireland; Member, Board of Governors, Guy's Hospital. *Publications:* contrib. to medical literature. *Recreations:* photography, philately. *Address:* 9 Devonshire Place, W.1. *T.:* 01-935 4054; 18 Kensington Mansions, S.W.5. *T.:* 01-370 1880.
[*Died* 10 *Feb.* 1970.

WATERFALL, William Duncan, C.B. 1947; *b.* 28 December 1889; *s.* of Charles and Louisa Maria Waterfall; *m.* 1917, Gertrude Gladys Cornish; one *s.* four *d.* *Educ.:* Manchester Grammar School; Brasenose College, Oxford. Entered Home C.S. (Secretary's Office, G.P.O.), 1913; Principal, 1924; Dep. Regional Director, London Telecommunications Region, P.O., 1936; Dep. Regional Director, N.W. Region, P.O., 1939, and Regional Director, 1942. Director of Savings, General Post Office, 1944-1951. *Recreations:* tennis, chess. *Address:* 8 Sauncey Avenue, Harpenden Herts. *T.:* Harpenden 4141.
[*Died* 23 *Dec.* 1970.

WATERFIELD, Sir (Alexander) Percival, K.B.E. *cr.* 1951; Kt., *cr* 1944; C.B. 1923. First Civil Service Commissioner, 1939-1951; retired, 1951; *b.* 16 May 1888; *y. s* of late William Waterfield, J.P.; Bengal Civil Service; *m.* 1920, Doris Mary, *d.* of Otto Siepmann; two *s.* two *d* *Educ.:* Westminster; Christ Church, Oxford; 1st Cl Mods 1909 and Lit. Hum., 1911; Hertford Scholar, 1909; Prox. acc to Craven Schol., 1909. Hon. LL.D., Ohio Wesleyan Univ., U.S.A., 1948. Entered H.M. Treasury, 1911; Treasury Remembrancer in Ireland, 1920-22; Principal Assistant Secretary, 1934-39; Deputy Secretary, Ministry of Information, 1939-40. Member of Palestine Partition Commission, 1938. Comr. for review of salaries and wages in Malta, 1958 *Recreations:* gardening, chess. *Address:* The Paddock, Sotwell, Wallingford, Berks. *T.:* Wallingford 3225. *Club:* Athenæum.
[*Died* 2 *June* 1965.

WATERFIELD, Lina, O.B.E.; *b.* 1874; *o. c.* of late Sir Maurice Duff Gordon, Bt., of Fyvie, Aberdeenshire, and Frances Waterton; *m.* 1901, Aubrey Waterfield, artist; two *s.* one *d.* *Educ.:* Sacred Heart Convent, Brighton; Sacré Cœur, Paris; with her aunt Mrs. Janet Ross, Florence. Was put in charge of British Mission for I Rapporti Italo-Britannica for Tuscany, 1917; helped to found British Institute in Florence; member of the Academy of Perugia. Italian Corresp., The Observer, Dec. 1921-Feb. 1935; a foreign corresp., Kemsley Press, 1946-50. *Publications:* The Story of Perugia (with Margaret Vaughan); The Story of Assisi; Mediæval Town Series; The Story of Rome; Home Life in Italy; Concise Guide to Florence; Castle in Italy (autobiog.). *Recreations:* travelling, agriculture. *Address:* The Aumbry, Eastry, Kent.
[*Died* 27 *Nov.* 1964.

WATERFIELD, Sir Percival; *see* Waterfield, Sir A. P.

WATERFIELD, Very Rev. Reginald, D.D.; Dean Emeritus; *b.* 20 Dec. 1867; 3rd *s.* of late Edward Waterfield Bengal Civil Service; *m.* 1898, Mary (*d.* 1959), 2nd *d.* of late Thomas James Lawson of Sydney, N.S.W.; one *s.* one *d.* *Educ.:* Winchester Coll. (scholar 1881-86); New Coll., Oxford (scholar 1886-90). 1st Class Classical Moderations, 1888; 1st Class Final School of Literæ Humaniores, 1890. Tutor to Prince Arthur of Connaught, 1892-93; Assistant Master in Rugby School, 1893-99; at Cuddesdon Theological College, parts of 1895 and 1896; Deacon, 1896; Priest, 1897; Principal of Cheltenham College, 1899-1919; Archdeacon of Cirencester (afterwards Cheltenham), 1919;

Hon. Canon Gloucester Cathedral, 1910-19; Dean of Hereford, and Vicar of St. John Baptist, Hereford, 1919-46; Rural Dean of Hereford, 1921-34; Chairman of Cathedrals Commission, 1934-41 (Member, 1930-41). Provincial Grand Master, Freemasons of Herefordshire, 1923-46. *Address:* **Hereford, Swinley Road, Ascot.** *T.*: Ascot 22331
[*Died* 8 *March* 1967.

WATERHOUSE, Rev. Eric Strickland, D Lit., D.D., M A.; Professor of Philosophy of Religion in Univ. of London 1931-51, Emeritus since 1951; *b* 16 Sept 1879; *s.* of J B Waterhouse, M.R.C S, L.R C P, Peatling Magna, Leics.; *m.* Edith, (*d.* 1964) *d.* of Rev. W D. Walters; one *s.* *Educ.:* Rydal School; London University. Wesleyan Minister at Bognor Regis, Wallington, Hither Green, Norbury East Dulwich and Streatham; Lecturer in Philosophy, Richmond Coll., 1920, Principal, 1940-51; Representative of the Faculty of Theology on the Senate of the Univ., 1928-51; Dep. Vice-Chancellor, 1936-37; Chairman of the Board of Studies in Theology, 1932; Examiner at the University; University Extension Lect.; Lecturer, New College, University of London, 1951-54; Treasurer of the Methodist Education Fund, 1934-56. Governor of Queenswood School, Hatfield, and of Penrhos Coll., Colwyn Bay. *Publications:* Modern Theories of Religion; The Psychology of the Christian Life; The Philosophy of Religious Experience; An A B.C of Psychology; Everyman and Christianity; Psychology and Religion—Broadcast Talks; What is Salvation? 1932; The Philosophical Approach to Religion, 1933, The Dawn of Religion, 1936; Psychology and Pastoral Work, 1939; Articles: Pietism and Secularism in Hastings Encyclopædia of Religion and Ethics; regular contributions to the Locomotive Jl. (A. S. L. E. F.), 1935-. *Recreations:* golf. country life. *Address:* 11 Denham Rd., Epsom, Surrey. *T.:* Epsom 1744
[*Died* 10 *April* 1964.

WATERHOUSE, Michael Theodore, C.B.E. 1953; M.C.; Architect; Past President R.I.B.A.; *b.* 1888; *o s.* of late Paul Waterhouse and Lucy Waterhouse, *d.* of Sir Reginald Palgrave, K.C.B.; *m.* 1920, Rissa, *d.* of Lt.-Col. H. F. Barclay; one *s.* three *d.* *Educ.:* Eton; Balliol College, Oxford; Architectural Assoc. Royal Academy Schools. Inns of Court O.T.C. Sqdn., 1912-14; commissioned Aug. 1914, 1/1 Notts Sherwood Rangers Yeomanry; served with Regt. and on Bde. Staff in England, Egypt, Gallipoli, Macedonia, Palestine and Syria, commanding Regt. in Syria; transferred to Inns of Court O.T.C., 1923; Reserve, 1925; H.G. 5th Oxfordshire Bn., 1940-44. Architectural practice general, Domestic, Hospitals, Laboratories, Commercial, Industrial, continuing in the third generation the practice founded 1854 by Alfred Waterhouse, R.A., Past Pres. R.I.B.A.; in partnership with Paul Waterhouse, Past Pres. R.I.B.A., 1920-1925; 1927, joined in partnership by Cedric G. Ripley, F.R.I.B.A. and in 1956 by his son, David Barclay Waterhouse, A.R.I.B.A. A.R.I.B.A. 1920; F.R.I.B.A. 1933; Assoc. Member of Council R.I.B.A. 1921-22, 1923-1929, 1930-33, Hon. Sec., 1941-46, Vice-Pres. 1946-47; Pres. 1948-50. *Recreations:* formerly all outdoor sports. *Address:* The Close, Yattendon, Newbury, Berks. *Clubs:* Bath, Flyfishers'. [*Died* 22 *May* 1968.

WATERHOUSE, Sir Nicholas Edwin, K.B.E., *cr.* 1920; Partner in Price, Waterhouse & Co., 1906-60; President of the Institute of Chartered Accountants, 1928-29; *b.* 24 Aug. 1877; *s.* of Edwin Waterhouse, of Feldemore, Holmbury S. Mary, Surrey. *m.* 1st, 1903, Audrey Lewin (*d.* 1945); no *c.*; 2nd, 1953, Louise How. *Educ.:* Winchester; New Coll., Oxford; M.A. *Address:* Norwood Farm, Effingham, Surrey. [*Died* 28 *Dec.* 1964.

WATERHOUSE, Alderman Thomas, C.B.E. 1945; J.P.; Chairman, 1930-57, Managing Director, 1909-57, Holywell Textile Mills Ltd., retd.; J.P. County of Flint; *b.* 21 Mar. 1878; 2nd *s.* of Thomas Holmes Waterhouse, Bradford and Holywell; *m.* 1915, Doris Helena Gough, Olton, Warwickshire; three *s.* one *d.* *Educ.:* Oswestry High School. Chairman Flintshire Education Committee, 1925-34; Chairman Flintshire County Council, 1938-40; Chairman Flintshire Technical College; Pres. Welsh Textile Manufacturers Assoc. since 1920; President, Flintshire Liberal Assoc.; Vice-Pres. County Councils Assoc., 1954-; Chm. North Wales Development Council; High Sheriff of Flintshire, 1942. *Recreations:* golf, motoring. *Address:* Highfield, Holywell, North Wales. *T.:* Holywell 3021.
[*Died* 3 *July* 1961.

WATERHOUSE, Walter Lawry, C.M.G. 1955; M.C. 1916; Emeritus Professor of Agriculture, University of Sydney, since 1953; *b.* 31 Aug. 1887; *s.* of John Waterhouse, M.A., Head Master, Sydney Boys' High School; *m.* 1924, Dorothy Blair Hazlewood, Epping, N.S.W.; three *d.* *Educ.:* Sydney Boys' High School; University of Sydney. H.D.A. (Diploma of Hawkesbury Agric. Coll., N.S.W.); B.Sc.Agric. (1st Cl. Hons.); Univ. Medal; 1851 Exhibitioner; W. and E. Hall Fellowship; D.I.C. Served European War, 1915-17: Egypt and France (severely wounded, M.C.). Lectr., Sydney University, 1921; D.Sc.Agr. 1929; Reader, 1937; Research Professor 1946, retired 1952, Emeritus Professor 1953. President: Linnean Society of N.S.W., 1935; Roy. Soc. of N.S.W., 1937; Sect. K. of A.N.Z.A.A.S., 1938; Fellow, Aust. Acad. of Science, 1954; Fellow, A.I.A.S., 1960. Farrer Memorial Medal, 1938 and 1949; Clarke Memorial Medal, 1943; Medal of Royal Soc. of N.S.W., 1948; Medal of Aust. Inst. of Agricultural Science, 1949; James Cook Medal, 1952; E. C. Stakman Award, U.S.A., 1956. *Publications:* **numerous in scientific jls.** *Recreations:* horticulture, literature. *Address:* Hazelmere, Chelmsford Avenue, Lindfield, N.S.W. 2070, Australia. *T.:* 46.1162.
[*Died* 9 *Dec.* 1969.

WATERLOW, Colonel Sir (William) James, 2nd Bt., *cr.* 1930; C.B.E. 1964 (M.B.E. 1945); T.D.; M.A.; *b.* 20 March 1905; *s.* of late Sir William Alfred Waterlow, 1st Bt., K.B.E., Lord Mayor of London, 1929-30, and Adelaide Hay (*d.* 1957), *d.* of Thomas Gordon, Grosvenor St., Edinburgh; *S.* father, 1931. *Educ.:* Marlborough; Trinity College Cambridge. Dir., Evans Bros. Ltd.; formerly Dep.-Chm. of Fleetway Publications Ltd. President Caxton Convalescent Home, 1951-61; Chairman, Bd. of Governors, Birkbeck College, 1966-, President Federation of Master Process Engravers, 1951-53, and President London Master Printers Assoc., 1953-54. Pres. Printers Pension Corp., 1958; Pres. Periodical Proprietors Assoc., 1962-64 (Vice-Pres., 1964-); Chm. of Joint Export Cttee. for Newspapers and Periodicals, 1966-. Master of the Guild of St. Bride. Member: Press Council; Upper Warden, Stationers' and Newspapermakers' Co. Jt. Hon. Treas., G.L.A. Conservative Assoc., 1963-69. Served with the City of London Yeo., 1939-45 (despatches); commanded, 1947-50; Hon. Col. 1952-61. *Heir:* *b.* Thomas Gordon Waterlow. *Address:* 1 Welbeck House, Welbeck Street, W.1. *T.:* 01-935 9458. *Clubs:* White's, Bath. [*Died* 20 *Nov.* 1969.

WATERS, Sir George Alexander, Kt., *cr.* 1944; Chevalier de la Légion d'Honneur, 1946; Hon. LL.D., St. Andrews, 1938; M.A.; J.P.; *b.* Thurso, 28 July 1880; *yr s.* of late Matthew Waters, J.P.; *m.* 1912, Mina,

e. d. of late John Waters, bank manager, Thurso; one *d.* *Educ.:* Thurso Academy; George Watson's College, Edinburgh; Edinburgh University. M.A. (First Class Honours in English), 1902; Vans Dunlop Scholar in English Poetry, 1903; studied at Berlin University and the Sorbonne, Paris, 1903-4. Joined editorial staff of the Scotsman, 1905; Editor of the Scotsman, 1924-44. *Address:* 9 Morningside Place, Edinburgh.
[*Died* 15 *Dec.* 1967.

WATERS, John Dallas, C.B. 1936; D.S.O. 1918; D.L., J.P. (Cheshire); K.C.S.G. (with star); late Lt.-Col. Royal Fusiliers; Barrister-at-law, Inner Temple; Deputy Chairman of Quarter Sessions County of Chester, 1932-36, Chairman, 1936-61; *b.* 1889; *s.* of late John Michael Waters; *m.* 1919, Lettice, *e. d.* of 2nd Lord Newton, and *widow* of Capt. J. Egerton-Warburton, Scots Guards. *Educ.:* Beaumont; Merton Coll., Oxford. B.A. European War, 1914-19 (D.S.O., despatches 4 times, 1914-15 Star); Private Secretary to the Lord Chancellor, and Deputy Serjeant-at-Arms in the House of Lords, 1929-1930; Secretary of Commissions to the Lord Chancellor, 1930-40; Registrar, Privy Council, 1940-54. Gold Stick, Coronation of King George VI; Clerk, Committee of Privileges, Coronation of Queen Elizabeth II. *Address:* Ormersfield Farm House, Basingstoke, Hants. *T.:* Fleet 256. *Club:* Travellers'.
[*Died* 31 *Jan.* 1967.

WATKIN, Sir Herbert George, Kt. 1964; B.A., Dip.Ed.; Chairman, Institute of Higher Technical Education, Papua and New Guinea, since 1965; Director-General of Education, Queensland, 1952-64; Deputy-Chancellor of the University of Queensland, 1953-; *m.* 1927, Ettie W. Cairns; one *d.* *Address:* 23 Ontario St., Holland Park, Queensland, Australia. [*Died* 20 *Aug.* 1966.

WATKIN, Morgan, M.A., D.Litt. (Wales), Hon.D. ès L. (Rennes), 1963; Ph.D. (Zürich), 1916; Chevalier de la Légion d'Honneur, Officier de l'Instruction Publique; Commandeur des Palmes Académiques; Cavaliere della Corona d'Italia; Emeritus Professor of French and Romance Philology, University of Wales (Cardiff College); Head of Department of French (1948-50) at University College, Swansea; *b.* 23 June 1878; *s.* of William and Barbara Watkin; *m.* 1911, Lucy (*d.* 1968), *d.* of John and Elizabeth Jenkins, Pontarddulais, Swansea; one *s.* *Educ.:* Univ. Coll., Cardiff; Universities of Paris and Zürich; Italy. Graduated in University of Wales, 1910, in Honours School of French and in Honours School of Celtic; Gilchrist Scholar, 1910; Fellow, 1910-13; Lectr., Univ. of Paris, 1912-15; Prof. of French and Lectr. in Italian, Univ. of S. Africa (Johannesburg), 1917-20; formerly: Chief Examiner in French, and in Italian to Central Welsh Board; Examiner in French, University of London; Member of the Board of Advisors in Romance Philology in the University of London; President of the S. Wales Branch of the M.L.A. (for 30 yrs.); member of Academic Board of the University of Wales; representative of the University of Wales on Board of Electors to Jesus Professorship of Celtic, Univ. of Oxford; sometime Deputy Principal University College, Cardiff. *Publications:* Edition of the Early Welsh translation of the Anglo-Norman Boeve de Haumtone, 1958; The Chronology of the Annales Cambriae and the Liber Landavensis, 1960; La Civilisation française dans les Mabinogion, 1962; The Chronology of the White Book of Rhydderch, on the basis of its Old French graphical phenomena, 1964; The Book of Aneirin, 1965; papers to Hon. Society of Cymmrodorion, etc.; articles on French Influence on Welsh Mediæval Orthography in various publications. *Recreations:* motoring, shooting, and fishing. *Address:* 12 Glyn Rhondda Street, Cardiff; University College, Cardiff.
[*Died* 7 *Sept.* 1970.

WATKINS, Arthur Ernest, M.A.; *b.* 23 April 1898; *s.* of Alfred Charles Watkins, London; *m.* 1923, Amy Marjorie (*d.* 1941), *d.* of Thomas Blanch, O.B.E., Chelsea; one *s.* *Educ.:* Latymer Upper School; St. John's College, Cambridge. Mathematical Tripos, Part 1, 1919; Natural Science Tripos, 1920; Fellow of St. John's College, 1924-27; University Lecturer in Genetics and Cytology, Cambridge, 1931. *Publications:* Heredity and Evolution, 1935; various papers on genetics, cytology, and plant breeding. *Recreations:* gardening, birds, books. *Address:* The Spinney, Clanver End, Royston Rd., Saffron Walden, Essex. *T.:* Newport 443. [*Died* 3 *Jan.* 1967.

WATKINS, Rear-Adm. John Kingdon, C.B. 1967; O.B.E. 1945; Director: Metallurgical Plantmakers Federation; British Metalworking Plant Makers' Association; Ironmaking & Steelmaking Plant Contractors' Association; *b.* 24 February 1913; *s.* of Dr. John Grandisson Watkins, Sidmouth; *m.* 1946, Lettice Marjorie Hellaby; one *s.* two *d.* *Educ.:* Epsom College. Entered Royal Navy, 1930; served in various ships and establishments; H.M.S. Howe, 1941-43; Base Supply Officer, Naples Area, 1943-45 (O.B.E., despatches); Admty., 1945-48; Naval Staff Coll., 1948-51; H.M.S. Forth, 1951-53; H.M.S. Ark Royal, 1954-56; Dep. Dir., Naval War Coll., 1957-1959; Dir. Standing Gp., N.A.T.O., 1959-61; Sec., Chiefs of Staff Cttee., 1961-64, also Dir. Defence Ops. Staff, 1963-64; Rear-Adm. (Personnel), Naval Air Comd., 1964-67. *Recreations:* shooting, fishing, watching Rugby football. *Address:* The Old Rectory, Caston, Nr. Attleborough, Norfolk. *T.:* Caston 353. *Club:* United Service.
[*Died* 13 *May* 1970.

WATKINS, Stanley Heath, M.A., Ph.D.; Emeritus Professor; *b.* Dowlais, Glam.; *s.* of late John Watkins; *m.* Aimée Ophélie Coueslant (*d.* 1944); one *s.* one *d.* *Educ.:* County School, Merthyr; University College, Cardiff; Leipzig University. Lecturer in Education, University College, Cardiff, 1914-1923; Professor of Education, 1923-53, and Acting Principal, 1953, University College, Exeter. *Recreations:* fishing, golf. *Address:* Heathcourt, Pennsylvania Park, Exeter.
[*Died* 24 *Oct.* 1967.

WATKINS, Vernon Phillips; Poet and Lecturer, University College, Swansea (Calouste Gulbenkian Fellow in Poetry); *b.* 27 June 1906; *s.* of William and Sarah Watkins; *m.* 1944, Gwendoline Mary (*née* Davies); four *s.* one *d.* *Educ.:* Repton; Magdalene College, Cambridge. Lloyds Bank, 1925-66. Served R.A.F., 1941-46. F.R.S.L. 1951. Visiting Lecturer on Modern Poetry, University of Washington, U.S.A., 1967-68. D.Litt., University of Wales, 1966. *Publications:* Ballad of the Mari Lwyd and other poems, 1941; The Lamp and the Veil, 1945; The Lady with the Unicorn, 1948; Selected Poems, (America) 1948; Heine's The North Sea (trans. of poems), (America) 1951, (English edn.) 1955; The Death Bell, Poems and Ballads, 1954; Editor, Letters to Vernon Watkins by Dylan Thomas, 1957; Cypress and Acacia, 1959; Affinities, 1962; Selected Poems 1930-1960, 1967. *Recreations:* tennis, walking, swimming, rock-climbing on low rocks, listening to music. *Address:* The Garth, Pennard Cliffs, near Swansea.
[*Died* 8 *Oct.* 1967.

WATKINS, William Henry, F.R.I.B.A.; Chartered Architect; Company Director; *b.* 16 Aug. 1877; *s.* of late Thomas

Watkins and Mary Louise Parsons; *m.* 1st, Violet Georgina Webb; one *s.* one *d.*; 2nd, Nora Frances Thomas. *Educ.:* privately. Pres. Dolphin Soc. and Canynge Soc., Bristol; Gov. Fitzmaurice Gram. Sch.; Ex-Chairman Bristol Hotels, Ltd.; Architect for new St. George's Hospital, Hyde Park Corner; designed many of principal buildings in Bristol and West of England; Architect for Govt. of Trinidad, W. Indies, for Hospitals and Public Buildings; Architect to Stockdale Commission for West Indies to design, Hospitals, etc., in Barbadoes, British Guiana, etc.; Architect to British Guiana, for public buildings; Architect apptd. by Bristol Univ. and Hospital Councils for New Medical Centre, Bristol. Member Company of Wheelwrights; Freeman of City of London. *Recreations:* golf, tennis, gardening. *Address:* Belcombe Court, Bradford-on-Avon, Wilts. *T.A.* and *T.:* Bradford-on-Avon 2357; Northcott Mouth, nr. Bude, N. Cornwall. *Clubs:* Carlton, West Indies, Royal Commonwealth Society; Constitutional (Bristol). [*Died* 30 *Jan.* 1964.

WATKYN-THOMAS, Frederic, William, M.A., M.D., B.Ch. Cantab., F.R.C.S.; Consulting Surgeon University College Hospital, Throat and Ear Department; Consulting Aural Surgeon to the Royal Navy; Member Royal Naval Personnel Research Cttee., and Flying Personnel Research Cttee.; *o. surv. s.* of late W. Watkyn-Thomas, J.P., Papcastle, Cumberland; *m.* 1928, A. M., (Diana), *yr. d.* of late W. N. Clayton, J.P., Clayton West, Yorks. *Educ.:* Tonbridge; Trinity College, Cambridge (Exhibitioner and Prizeman, Benn Levy University Studentship); St. Bartholomew's Hospital (Sen. Entrance Schol., Walsham Prize, Brackenbury and Luther Holden Scholar). A/Major R.A.M.C., B.E.F., 1915-20; M.O. 16/60th Rifles, Surgical Specialist and in charge of Surgical division, E.M.S. London and Capt. of Fire Guard, 1939-45; Formerly Abstract Editor Journal of Laryngology; President Section of Otology, R.S.M.; Member of Council British Assoc. of Laryngology and Otology. *Publications:* Books, articles and papers. *Recreations:* natural history, fishing. *Address:* 4 Gerald Road, Eaton Square, S.W.1. *Club:* United University. [*Died* 31 *Jan.* 1963.

WATNEY, Colonel Sir Frank Dormay, K.C.V.O. *cr.* 1936; C.B.E. 1919; T.D. 1908; Officer of Order of St John of Jerusalem; a Director of the Royal Exchange Assurance, 1920-65; Vice-President Officers' Association; *b.* 25 Jan. 1870; 3rd *s.* of Sir John Watney (*d.* 1923) and Elizabeth (*d.* 1896), *d.* and *co-heir* of Stephen Dendy of Leigh Place, Surrey; *m.* 1896, Margaret Graham, Order of Mercy (*d.* 1951), *o. d.* of Rev. George Richardson of Winchester College; one *s.*; *m.* 1955, Jane, *o. d.* of Edward Arthur Bagot and *widow* of Major-General J. H.-W. Pollard, C.B., C.M.G., D.S.O. *Educ.:* Winchester College. Solicitor, 1893; Clerk to the Mercers' Company, Gresham Committee, and St. Paul's Schools, 1919-40; Lt.-Colonel late commanding 4th Battn. Queen's Royal Regt. 1903-9; Hon. Colonel, 1908; Colone 1918; served European War, Gallipoli, Egypt, France, Salonika, Palestine, 1914-19 (despatches three times, C.B.E., Order of Nile, 3rd Class); D.L. Surrey 1911; one of H.M.'s Lieut. for City of London, 1926; Chairman of Committee, 1947-59. *Address:* 2 The Little Boltons, S.W.10. *Club:* Hurlingham. [*Died* 16 *July* 1965.

WATNEY, Oliver Vernon, J.P.; *b.* 22 Oct. 1902; *o. s.* of late Vernon James Watney and Lady Margaret Watney (*d.* 1943), *d.* of 5th Earl of Portsmouth; *m.* 1934, Christina Margaret, *e. d.* of late Capt. T. A. Nelson, Achnacloich, Argyll. *Educ.:* Eton; Oxford. Master of the Brewers' Company 1934; High Sheriff of Oxfordshire, 1937-38; D.L., 1961. *Recreation:* shooting. *Address:* Cornbury Park, Charlbury, Oxon; Tressady, Rogart, Sutherland; 2 Mansfield Street, W.1. *Clubs:* Brooks's, White's. [*Died* 5 *Aug.* 1966.

WATSON, Sir Alfred Henry, Kt., *cr.* 1932; Ex-Vice-Chm. Union of Britain and India; Ex-Chm., India Section, Empire Press Union; F.J.I.; F.R.S.A.; *b.* Newcastle upon Tyne, 1874; *s.* of late Aaron Watson; *m.* 1st, Isa Morland Beck (*d.* 1927); 2nd, 1940, Rosebud Ada Gros. Journalist, 1890; in Press Gallery, 1893; leader writer and special correspondent, Newcastle Leader, 1894; London correspondent, 1895-1903; joined Westminster Gazette Staff, 1902; news editor, 1903; general manager, 1909; managing editor, 1921; chief leader writer, 1922; editor Weekly Westminster, 1922-24; editor, Statesman, Calcutta, 1925-33; Bengal Correspondent of the Times, 1927-32; Editorial Director, Great Britain and the East, 1940-41, Director, 1941-58; Political Adviser Union of Britain and India, 1933-35; Political Adviser India Burma Assoc., 1942-47. *Publications:* Pamphlets on the Meat Trust, on Tariff Questions and on India. *Address:* 31 Bramerton Road, Beckenham, Kent. *T.:* Beckenham 0016. *Club:* National Liberal (Vice-pres.). [*Died* 1 *March* 1967.

WATSON, A(ndrew) Aiken, Q.C., 1946; *b.* 5 June 1897; *y. s.* of Alexander Watson and Anne Maitland-Johnstone, Renfrewshire; *m.* 1929, Marguerite Jean, *o. d.* of George Anderson, Gordon Hall, Grantown, Morayshire; one *s.* *Educ.:* Johnstone Higher Grade; Glasgow University. Served European War in R.G.A. Signals in France; admitted a Solicitor, 1921, and practised in Edinburgh and Glasgow. Called to Bar, Gray's Inn, 1927; practised on Common Law side. Recorder of Bury St. Edmunds 1947-1949; Recorder of Colchester, 1949-64. Chm. Amalgamated Dental Co. Ltd. and Medical and Industrial Equipment Ltd., 1949-65; Dep. Chm. East Sussex Quarter Sessions, 1947-50; Chairman, Commission of Inquiry to Gold Coast, 1948. *Address:* 51 Castelnau, S.W.13. *T.:* 01-748 5517. *Club:* Devonshire. [*Died* 7 *June* 1969.

WATSON, Sir Angus; *see* Watson, Sir J. A.

WATSON, Arthur E.; *b.* 29 Feb. 1880; *y. s.* of late Aaron Watson, journalist; *m.* 1904, Lily (*d.* 1960), *y. d.* of late Edward Waugh, Whitley Bay, Northumberland, and Gateshead; no *c.* *Educ.:* Rutherford Coll., Newcastle; Alleyn's School, Dulwich; Armstrong College, Newcastle. Began journalistic career on Newcastle Daily Leader, and joined the Daily Telegraph in 1902; Assistant Editor, 1923; Editor, 1924-50; served European War, 1914-18, in France, Royal Field Artillery; acting Major, 1918; Hon. Treasurer of the Institute of Journalists, 1923-28; Chairman of the London District, 1921; Pres., Merton and Morden Conservative Assoc., 1962-68. *Address:* Briar Dene, 15 Langley Rd., Merton Park, S.W.19. *Clubs:* Athenæum, Carlton; Pen and Palette (Newcastle upon Tyne). [*Died* 18 *Sept.* 1969.

WATSON, Sir Arthur Egerton, Kt., *cr.* 1949; C.B. 1938; C.B.E. 1920 (O.B.E. 1918); Civil Servant, retired; *b.* 1882; *m.* Alice, *e. d.* of T. W. Brown, Hornsey; no *c.* Chairman Civil Service Sports Council, 1944-48, Vice-President, 1948. *Address:* 200 Coleherne Court, S.W.5. [*Died* 8 *May* 1967.

WATSON, General Sir Daril G., G.C.B., *cr.* 1947 (K.C.B., *cr.* 1945; C.B. 1942); C.B.E. 1940; M.C.; Legion of Merit (U.S.A.), Degree of Commander; *b.* 17 October 1888; *e. s.* of late J. B. Watson, formerly of Paisley; *m.* 1917, Winifred, *yr. d.* of late Alfred Reynolds, formerly of Hampstead; one *s.* *Educ.:* Mercers' School. Enlisted Army, 1914; commissioned Highland Light Infantry 1915; promotion to D.C.L.I. 1928; Bt. Lt.-Col. 1931; commanded 1st Bn. D.C.L.I. 1934-36; commanded Senior Officers' School, India, 1937-39 B.G.S. Eastern Command, 1939; B.G.S. 3rd Corps, 1939-40; G.O.C. 2nd. Div. 1940-41; D.S.D. War Office, 1941-1942; A.C.I.G.S. 1942; D.A.G. 1942-44; G.O.C.-in-C., Western Command, 1944-46; Quartermaster-General to the Forces, 1946-1947; A.D.C. General to the King, 1946-47; Col., The Duke of Cornwall's Light Infantry, 1947-53; Member of the Railway Executive, 1949-53; Chief of Gen. Services, B.T.C., 1953-54; Secretary-General, B.T.C., Jan.-June 1955. *Address:* Larch Wood, Hadlow Down, Nr. Uckfield, Sussex *Clubs:* United Service, Caledonian. [*Died* 1 *July* 1967.

WATSON, Elliot Lovegood Grant; author; *b* 14 June 1885; *e. s.* of Reginald and Lucy Grant Watson; *m.*1919, Katharine Hanny; two *d.* *Educ.:* Bedales School; Trinity College, Cambridge. Class I. Natural Science Tripos, 1909; Scientific Expedition to N.W. Australia 1910-11 *Publications:* Where Bonds are Loosed; The Mainland; Deliverance; Shadow and Sunlight; The Desert Horizon; English Country Innocent Desires; Daimon; The Lord of the Prophets; Moonlight in Ur; The Common Earth; It's Up to You The Partners, The Nun and the Bandit; Enigmas of Natural History; More Enigmas of Natural History; Man of Valour; Priest Island; Man and His Universe; Country Holiday; Walking with Fancy; The Leaves Return; But to what Purpose, 1946; Departures, 1949; Profitable Wonders 1950; What to Look for in Winter, 1959; What to look for in Summer, 1960; What to look for in Autumn 1960; What to look for in Springtime, 1960; Nature's Changing Course; A Naturalist at Large; The Mystery of Physical Life, 1964; Animals in Splendour and Decline, 1964; Land Journeys and Seafaring, 1968. *Recreation:* gardening. *Address:* 9 Woodbury Avenue, Petersfield, Hants *T.:* Petersfield 3994. [*Died* 21 *May* 1970.

WATSON, Colonel Francis William, C.B. 1955; M.C. 1917 and Bar 1918; T.D. 1943; County Alderman, Bucks., since 1949; *b.* 25 Jan. 1893; 2nd *s.* of Charles Watson, J.P., Leek, Staffs.; *m.* 1st, 1916, Alice Madelein (*d.* 1952), *d.* of late Arthur Collings-Wells, J.P., Caddington Hall, Herts.; one *s.* two *d.*; 2nd, 1958, Joan, *widow* of Capt. I. R. Macbeth; one *d.* *Educ.:* Rugby; King's College, Cambridge. B.A. LL.B. 1914, M.A. 1922. Served European War, 1914-19, Capt. and Adjt. 296th Bde. R.F.A. Major, 99th (Bucks. & Berks. Yeomanry) Fd. Regt. R.A.T.A., 1925-31. Served War of 1939-1945: Lt.-Col. comdg. 99th (Roy. Bucks Yeo.) Fd. Regt. R.A.T.A., 1939-41 (despatches); Colonel, Sen. Mil. Liaison Officer to Regional Comr., N.E. Region, 1941-45. D.L. (Bucks.) 1938, J.P. 1932, C.C. 1935; High Sheriff of Bucks., 1947. Chm. Roy. Bucks. Hosp., Aylesbury, 1935-39; Chm. Bucks. T. & A.F.A., 1936-39 and 1946-54; Chm. Bucks. Educ. Cttee., 1949-58; Vice-Chm. Bucks. C.C., 1957-61. President Old Rugbeian Soc., 1951-1952; Chairman Aylesbury Magistrates Court, 1951-62. *Recreations:* music (piano and organ). *Address:* St. Osyth's, Parson's Fee, Aylesbury, Bucks. *T.:* Aylesbury 4120. [*Died* 10 *June* 1966.

WATSON, Sir Hugh, Kt. 1957; M.A., LL.D.; Deputy Keeper of Her Majesty's Signet, 1954-64; *b.* 4 May 1897; *s.* of William John Watson, LL.D., D.Litt. (Celt.), Professor of Celtic Languages, Univ. of Edinburgh, and Isabella Munro; *m.* 1925, Winifred Margaret, *d.* of Asst. Chief Constable W. D. Paterson, Edinburgh; one *s.* two *d.* *Educ.:* Inverness Royal Acad.; Royal High Sch.; Edinburgh Univ. LL.B. Edinburgh 1924, LL.D. Edinburgh 1964. Chairman, Departmental Cttee. on Marketing of Home Grown Timber, 1954-55; Mem. Cttee. on Crown Lands, 1954-55; Mem. Royal Commn. on Remuneration of Doctors and Dentists, 1957-60; Dep. Governor and Chm. Court of Directors, British Linen Bank, 1963-. Pres., Law Society of Scotland, 1964-66. *Recreation:* golf. *Address:* 1 St. Colme Street, Edinburgh 3. *Clubs:* Caledonian; New (Edinburgh). [*Died* 16 *Oct.* 1966.

WATSON, Sir James Anderson Scott, Kt. 1949; C.B.E. 1946; M.C. 1919; LL.D., D.Sc.; *b.* 16 Nov. 1889; 2nd *s.* of William Watson, farmer, Downieken Dundee; *m.* 1914, Jeanie (*d.* 1962), *e. d.* of Provost Carmichael, Coldstream; (one *s.* killed on active service) three *d.* *Educ.:* Univs. of Edinburgh and Berlin; Iowa State College of Agriculture. Assistant Dept. of Agriculture, University of Edinburgh, 1910; Lecturer, 1911; Commissioned R.F.A. 1915; served in France (M.C.); Professor of Agriculture and Rural Economy, University of Edinburgh, 1922-25; Sibthorpian Professor of Rural Economy and Fellow of St. John's College, Oxford, 1925-44; Agricultural Attaché, British Embassy, Washington, 1942-44; Chief Scientific and Agricultural Adviser to Ministry of Agriculture, and Dir.-Gen. Nat. Agric. Advisory Service, 1948-54. Editor of Journal of Royal Agricultural Society, 1931-45. President, British Agricultural History Society, 1953; Development Commissioner, 1955-56. Gold Medal, Roy. Agric. Soc., 1955. *Publications:* Agriculture — The Science and Practice of British Farming (with J. A. More), 1924 (11th Edn. 1962); Rural Britain Today and Tomorrow, 1934; Great Farmers (with Mrs. Elliot Hobbs), (2nd edn., 1951), 1937; The Farming Year, 1938; History of the Royal Agricultural Society, 1940. *Address:* 4 Sheldon Avenue, N.6. [*Died* 5 *Aug.* 1966.

WATSON, Sir (James) Angus, Kt., *cr.* 1945; D.C.L. (Durham); J.P.; *b.* Ryton-on-Tyne, 15 Jan. 1874; *m. d.* of James Reid two *s* two *d.* *Educ.:* Private School. Founder of Angus Watson & Co. Ltd., with branches throughout the world; Knight of Order of Saint Olaf (Norway); Freeman of City of London; Ex-Chm. Congregational Union England and Wales (1935); Ex-Pres. Tyneside Council of Social Service; late Northern Divisional Food Officer, Ministry of Food, 1939-45 Founder Imperial Canneries, Ltd., Norway. *Recreations:* golf, motoring and walking, farming. *Address:* Whitewell, Jesmond, Newcastle upon Tyne. *T.:* Newcastle 81-0002, Newcastle 24337. [*Died* 31 *Jan.* 1961.

WATSON, Very Rev. Prof. James P.; *see* Pitt-Watson.

WATSON, Lt.-Col. John William; C.I.E. 1919; C.B.E. 1929; Indian Medical Service (ret.); *b.* 8 Nov. 1874; *s.* of Col. John Whaley Watson, Bombay Political Department, and Elizabeth C. Watts; *m.* 1920, Ruth Mary (*d.* 1958), *d.* of late Ernest Charrington and Mrs. W. Hadley of Parkside, Reigate; one *s.* two *d.* *Educ.:* Charterhouse; St. George's Hospital. M.R.C.S. (Eng.), L.R.C.P. (London); M.R.C.P. (London), 1908. Joined Indian Medical Service, 1898; despatches, 1919; retired, 1929. *Address:* 10 New Dover Road, Canterbury, Kent. *T.:* Canterbury 2197. [*Died* 30 *May* 1962.

WATSON, Samuel, C.B.E. 1946; D.C.L., D.L., J.P.; Secretary Durham Miners' Assoc., 1936-63, retd.; *b.* 11 Mar. 1898; *m.*; one *s.* one *d.* *Educ.:* Elementary School, Boldon. Worked in mine, below ground, until 1936. Member: Council, Durham University; Labour Party; Durham County Executive Council, National Health Service

Part-time Member: National Coal Board; Central Electricity Generating Bd. D.C.L. Univ. of Durham, 1955 O.St.J. *Recreations:* reading, walking, unravelling knots. *Address:* Bede Rest, Beech Crest, Durham City. *T.:* Durham 2824 [*Died* 7 *May* 1967.

WATSON, William McLean; *b.* 27 Oct. 1874; *s.* of James Watson, Cowdenbeath; *m.* 1908, Elizabeth Westwood. Student, Ruskin College, 1906-07. M.P. (Lab.) Dunfermline, 1922-31, and 1935-50. *Address:* 136 Halbeath Road, Dunfermline. *T.:* 601. [*Died May* 1962.

WATSON-WILLIAMS, Eric, M.C.; Consultant Surgeon to Ear, Nose and Throat Department, United Bristol Hospitals, since 1955; *b.* 18 Sept. 1890; *m.* 1922, Cresten Margaret Boase; two *s.* two *d.* *Educ.:* Clifton College; Gonville and Caius Coll., Cambridge; King's College Hospital; Middlesex Hospital. Nat. Sci. Tripos (Hons.), B.A., 1912; K.C.H. Jelf and Todd medals, 1914; M.R.C.S. Served 4 Aug. 1914-Jan. 1919; R.A.M.C. (S.R.) France; 14th, 49th, 55th Divs.; Major; M.C. battle of Lys, April 1918. M.B. Cantab. 1919; M.D. 1948. Vice-Pres. Laryngol. B.M.A., 1934; Vice-Pres. Laryngol. R. Soc. Med., 1936; Vice-Pres. Otol. R. Soc. Med., 1936; Long Fox Mem. Lectr., 1944; Pres. S.W. Laryngolog. Assoc., 1947. Member Classical Assoc. *Publications* contribs. to Greece and Rome, Classical Quarterly, Trans. Bristol and Glos. Archæol. Assoc., Classica et Mediævalia Eranos. *Recreations:* fishing, painting. *Address:* Domus, Cranmer Road, Cambridge. *T.:* 52668. [*Died* 26 *Jan.* 1964.

WATT, Very Rev Hugh, D.D.; *b.* 12 Dec. 1879; *s.* of John Watt, J.P., and Agnes Taylor Dickie; *m.* 1908, Mary Smith Taylor; one *s.* two *d.* *Educ.:* Kilmarnock Academy; Universities of Glasgow, Marburg, Berlin, Halle, M.A. (1st Cl. Hon.) Glasgow, 1901; Freeland Scholar, 1904-5; B.D. 1905; Minister at Waterbeck, 1907-12, at Bearsden, North, 1912-19; served with Y.M.C.A. in France, 1915-16; Chaplain in Palestine and France, 1917-18; with Army of Occupation, 1919. Secretary of New College Senate, 1921-45; Secretary of Edinburgh Post-graduate School of Theology, 1937-46; Professor of Church History in New College, 1919-50, and in University of Edinburgh, 1935-50; Principal of New College, Edinburgh, and Dean of the Faculty of Divinity, 1946-50 Moderator of the General Assembly of the Church of Scotland, May 1950-May 1951. Pres. Scottish Church History Soc., 1936-39; Chalmers Lecturer, 1940-44; Stone Lecturer, Princeton, 1948-49. *Publications:* Representative Churchmen of Twenty Centuries, 1926; Thomas Chalmers and the Disruption, 1943; The Published Writings of Thomas Chalmers, 1943; Recalling the Scottish Covenants, 1946; New College—A Centenary History, 1946; John Knox in Controversy, 1950; numerous articles in encyclopædias and journals. *Recreations:* golf and burn-fishing. *Address:* 8 Marchhall Crescent, Edinburgh 9. *T.:* 031-667 1896. [*Died* 5 *Sept.* 1968.

WATT, Dame Katherine Christie, D.B.E., *cr.* 1945 (C.B.E. 1935); R.R.C. 1930; 2nd *d.* of James Christie Watt, Glasgow. *Educ.:* Glasgow; Private Tuition. Trained Nurse; General training, Western Infirmary, Glasgow; Midwifery Training, Middlesex Hospital, London; Founder Member of College of Nursing; served European War, 1916-19; Princess Mary's Royal Air Force Nursing Service, Sister 1919, Matron, 1922-30, Matron-in-Chief, 1930-38; retired list, 1938. Principal Matron, Ministry of Health, 1939; Chief Nursing Officer, 1941; Chief Nursing Adviser, 1948; retired from Ministry of Health, 1950. C.St.J. *Recreation:* golf. *Address:* Barclays Bank, 1 Pall Mall East, S.W.1. *Club:* United Hunts. [*Died* 1 *Nov.* 1963.

WATT, Rev. Lewis, S.J., M.A., B.Sc. (Econ.); Professor of Social Economics at Heythrop College, Oxon; *b.* 1885; *e. s.* of G. A. Watt, L.D.S., W. Hartlepool *Educ.:* Queen Elizabeth's Sch., Darlington. Articled as solicitor, 1902; qualified 1907, received into the Catholic Church, 1906; entered the Society of Jesus in 1908; in addition to the ordinary philosophical and theological course of the Society (7 years), spent 2 years at London School of Economics (B.Sc.Econ., Hons.), and two years in study of moral philosophy at Louvain and Paris; Priest, 1920; professor of moral philosophy to students S.J. 1923-37 and 1946-63; of history of philosophy, 1930-35; and of social economics since 1933. Lecturer in the University of Oxford, 1938-46. M.A. (Oxon) by decree, 1940. *Publications:* Capitalism and Morality; Catholic Social Principles; The Future of Capitalism; Pope Pius XII on World Order; A Handbook to Rerum Novarum; Usury in Catholic Theology; various booklets; many contributions to journals in Europe and U.S.A. *Address:* Heythrop College, Chipping Norton, Oxon. [*Died Feb.* 1965.

WATT, Michael Herbert, C.B.E. 1935; M.D.; F.R.A.C.P.; D.P.H.; *b.* 16 Mar. 1887; *s.* of Rev. Michael Watt, M.A., D.D., and Isabella Shand; *m.* 1913, Mary Roberta McCahon; two *s.* *Educ.:* Otago Boys' High School; Otago Univ. Late Director-General, Dept. of Health, Wellington, N.Z.; Chairman, Council for Medical Research, N.Z., 1938-46. *Address:* 255 The Terrace, Wellington, N.Z. [*Died* 7 *April* 1967.

WATT, Sir Robert (Dickie), Kt. 1960; M.A., B.Sc., N.D.A. (Hons.), N.D.D.; Emeritus Prof. of Agriculture, Univ. of Sydney, Australia, since 1947; *b.* Kilmaurs, Ayrshire, 23 April 1881; *s.* of late John Watt, farmer and land valuator; *m.* 1916, Madge, 4th *d.* of late John Forsyth; one *d.* *Educ.:* Glasgow University; West of Scotland Agricultural College. National Diploma in Dairying, 1902; National Diploma in Agriculture, with Honours and Gold Medal for first place in examination, awarded Carnegie Research Scholarship, 1905; carried out research work on agricultural and dairying problems at Rothamsted, Herts, 1905-7; Assistant Chemist to Transvaal Department of Agriculture, 1907-8; Acting Chief Chemist to same Department, 1908-9; Prof. of Agriculture, Sydney Univ., 1910-46. Farrer Memorial Medallist, 1950. *Publications:* The Romance of the Australian Land Industries; articles in Agric. jours. *Recreations:* formerly general athletics; now golf, bowls, Australian history. *Address:* 48 Towns Road, Vancluse, Sydney, N.S.W. *Club:* Royal Sydney Golf. [*Died* 10 *April* 1965.

WATT, William Warnock, C.B.E. 1958; Member of Board of Governors of Hammersmith Group of Hospitals, 1956-60; Member of Board of Management of Postgraduate Medical School of London, Chairman and Treas. of Finance and Gen. Purposes Cttee. and Chm. of Appeal Fund, 1957-60; *b.* 6 July 1890; *m.* 1st, 1919, Margaret Mitchell Arnott (*d.* 1940); one *s.* one *d.*; 2nd, 1952, Erica Constance Dalgleish. *Educ.:* Whitehill School, Glasgow. Chairman and Managing Director, Ogston and Tennant Ltd., soap manufacturers, Renfrew and Aberdeen, 1929-1934; Vice-Chairman of Board of Management, Lever Brothers Ltd., Port Sunlight, 1935-37; Managing Director, British Oxygen Co. Ltd., 1938-56; Pres. Inst. of Welding, 1941-42; Pres. British Acetylene Assoc., 1942-43; Mem. Admiralty Commn., Admiralty Requirements in Material, 1956-57.

Mem. Treasury Advisory Business (organisation and methods) Panel, 1941-60. Chm. Arc Welding Electrode Section British Electrical and Allied Manufacturers Association, 1939-. Has travelled extensively. *Recreations:* gardening, fishing and philately. *Address:* Sandlands, Sidbury, Nr. Sidmouth, Devon. *T.:* Sidbury 245. *Clubs:* Oriental; Sidmouth. [*Died* 19 *May* 1963.

WATTS, Arthur Frederick; *see* Addenda: II.

WATTS, James, T.D.; M.P. (C.) Moss Side Division of Manchester since Oct. 1959; *b.* 22 Aug. 1903; *s.* of James Watts of Alney Hall, Cheadle, Cheshire and Upper House, Kinder, Hayfield, Derbyshire. *Educ.:* Shrewsbury; New College, Oxford (M.A.). Hon. Major T.A., Cheshire Regt. Served War of 1939-45, in U.K., France, India, Irak, Persia. Politics: Hon. Treas. Manchester City Conservative Assoc., 1933-51, Chm. 1951-53; contested (C.) Gorton Div. of Manchester, 1950. Lord of the Manor of Cheadle Buckley, Cheshire. *Recreation:* conversation. *Address:* 20 Chester St., S.W.1. *T.:* Sloane 3145. *Clubs:* White's, Pratt's, Carlton, Royal Automobile; Union, Clarendon (Manchester). [*Died* 7 *July* 1961.

WAUGH, Sir Arthur Allen, K.C.I.E., *cr.* 1946 (C.I.E. 1937); C.S.I. 1943; late I.C.S.; *b.* 25 July 1891. *Educ.:* George Watson's College, Edinburgh; Edinburgh University, M.A. Entered I.C.S., 1914; Revenue Sec., U.P. Govt., 1934; Settlement Commissioner, United Provinces, 1939; War Production Commissioner and Sec. to Govt., U.P., 1942; Sec. Dept. of Supply, Govt. of India, 1943; Member Governor-General's Exec. Council, India, 1945-46; Controller of Establishments, British Council, 1948-56. Chairman, Salaries Commn., Ghana, 1956-57. Pres., The Folk-lore Soc., 1959-61. *Publication:* (with Gwen Benwell) Sea Enchantress, 1961. *Address:* Ballintua, Mulberry Lane, Ditchling, Sussex. *Club:* Caledonian. [*Died* 12 *Jan.* 1968.

WAUGH, Evelyn Arthur St. John; C.Lit. 1963; Writer; *b.* 1903; 2nd *s.* of late Arthur Waugh; *m.* 1937, Laura, *y. d.* of late Col. Hon. Aubrey Herbert, M.P.; three *s.* three *d.* *Educ.:* Lancing; Hertford College, Oxford. Temp. commn. Roy. Marines, 1939; transferred R.H.G., 1942. *Publications:* Rossetti, 1928; Decline and Fall, 1928; Vile Bodies, 1930; Labels, 1930; Remote People, 1932; Black Mischief, 1932; Ninety-two Days, 1934; Handful of Dust, 1934; Edmund Campion, 1935 (Hawthornden Prize, 1936); Waugh in Abyssinia, 1936; Scoop, 1938; Put Out More Flags, 1942; Work Suspended, 1943; Brideshead Revisited, 1945; Scott-King's Modern Europe; When the Going was Good, 1946; The Loved One, 1948; Helena, 1950; Men at Arms, (James Tait Black Memorial Book Prize), 1952; The Holy Places, 1953; Love Among the Ruins, 1953; Officers and Gentlemen, 1955; The Ordeal of Gilbert Pinfold, 1957; The Life of Ronald Knox, 1959; A Tourist in Africa, 1960; Unconditional Surrender, 1961; Basil Seal Rides Again, 1963; A Little Learning, 1964. *Address:* c/o A. D. Peters, 10 Buckingham Street W.C.2. *Clubs:* White's, St. James'. [*Died* 10 *April* 1966.

WAYLAND, Edward James, C.B.E. 1938; A.R.C.S., M.Inst.M.M., F.G.S., Corresp. Mem. Acad. Roy. Sci. d'outre-mer, Brussels; Hon. Mem. Soc. Géol. de Belg.; Mem. Econ. Geol. America, etc.; *b.* 23 Jan. 1888; *s.* of Edward Wayland and Emily Street; *m.* 1917, Ellen Morrison. *Educ.:* Central Foundational Sch.; City of London Coll.; Royal Coll. of Science; Royal School of Mines. Five years apprenticeship building and architecture; Nat. Sci. Studentship and Lubbock prize, C.L.C.; Nat. Schol. Imp. Coll.; Marshall Research Schol. (palæontology) R.C.S. Egypt 1909, geological research; Portuguese East Africa, 1911, exploring for a Mining Company; Ceylon Government Service (as Assistant Mineral Surveyor), 1912-16; European War, 1916-19; Uganda Government Service, 1919-39 (first as Geological Expert, next as Government Geologist and later as Director of the Geological Survey); returned to England to rejoin military forces; tunnelling in Dover and Gibraltar; then joined Bomb Disposal Co. R.E.; was sent on a one-man secret mission to a neutral country; again joined Bomb Disposal on return; went to Bechuanaland, 1943, on water devel. reconnaissance; formerly Director of the Geological Surveys of Uganda and Bechuanaland from their formation; instigated and ran mid-African Seismological Station at Entebbe. Bigsby Medal, Geol. Soc. Lond.; Victoria Medal, R.G.S. *Publications:* numerous. *Address:* Regency Hotel, Ramsgate, Kent. *Club:* Athenæum. [*Died* 11 *July* 1966.

WAYNE, Naunton; Actor; *b.* 22 June 1901; *s.* of William Thomas Davies, Solicitor, and Annie Elizabeth Davies, Porth (Rhondda Valley), South Wales; changed name by deed-poll from Henry Wayne Davies, 1933; *m.* 1927, Gladys Dove; two *s.* *Educ.:* Clifton College. Started professional career in concert party, 1920; first cabaret engagement, 1927; first Radio performance, 1928; first Music Hall booking, Victoria Palace, 1929; first Revue, Chelsea Follies (as Compère), 1930; first Picture, First Mrs. Fraser, 1931; non-stop Variety, London Pavilion (40 weeks), 1932; Pictures, Going Gay and For Love of You, 1933; Compère for Josephine Baker season, Prince Edward Theatre, 1933; Cochran's Streamline, 1934; Compère, 1066 and All That, 1935; All Wave, Revue, 1936; first straight part, Norman, in Wise Tomorrow, Lyric Theatre, 1937; played same part in New York, 1937; Choose Your Time, Piccadilly Theatre, 1938; Caldicott in film The Lady Vanishes, 1938; Film, A Girl Must Live, 1938; Farce, Giving the Bride Away, St. Martin's Theatre, 1939; Caldicott in films Night Train to Munich and Crooks Tour, 1940; George Black's Black Vanities, Victoria Palace, 1941; Tristan Sprott in J. B. Priestley's Good Night, Children, New Theatre, 1942; Tom Arnold's Sky High Revue, Phœnix Theatre, 1942; Arsenic and Old Lace, Strand Theatre, 1942-46; Clutterbuck, Wyndham's, 1946; Young Wives' Tale, Savoy, 1949; Count Your Blessings, Wyndham's, 1951; Trial and Error, Vaudeville, 1953; Its Different for Men, Duchess Theatre, 1955; One Bright Day, Apollo, 1956; A River Breeze, Phœnix, 1956; The Bride and the Bachelor, Duchess Theatre, 1957; A Day in the Life of . . ., Savoy, 1958; From the French, Strand, 1959; (film), Operation Bullshine, 1959; The Big Killing, Princes, 1962; Vanity Fair, Queen's 1962; Let's Be Frank, Vaudeville, 1963; The Reluctant Peer, Duchess, 1964; Justice is a Woman, Vaudeville, 1966; Oh Clarence!, Lyric, 1968. Music Hall engagements between productions. *Recreations:* golf and photography. *Address:* 6 Vicarage Gardens, S.W.14. *T.:* 01-876 1808. *Clubs:* Green Room, Stage Golfing. [*Died* 17 *Nov.* 1970.

WEATHERBY, Sir Francis, Kt., *cr.* 1953; M.C. 1918; *b.* 15 Sept. 1885; *y. s.* of Edward Weatherby; *m.* 1926, Sheila Neilson; one *s.* *Educ.:* Winchester; Magdalen Coll., Oxford. Formerly Secretary of the Jockey Club. *Address:* Ettington, Nr. Stratford-on-Avon, Warwicks. *Clubs:* Oriental; Jockey. [*Died* 17 *Nov.* 1969.

WEAVER, John Reginald Homer; President of Trinity College, Oxford, 1938-54; formerly Fellow, Tutor, and Librarian of the College; Hon. Fellow 1954; editor, Dictionary of

National Biography, 1928-37; *b.* 1882; *o. s.* of late Rev. John Crowley Weaver, M.A., Vicar of Kempley, Gloucestershire; *m.* 1917, Stella Mary Georgina, *o. d.* of Col. Hampden Acton, R.F.A.; one *s.* *Educ.:* Felsted; Keble Coll., Oxford. Hon. Scholar; B.A. (1st Class Mod. Hist.), 1909; M.A., 1912; Arnold Prize Essay, 1912; F.S.A.; Hon. D.Litt. (Dublin); Hon. Fellow of Keble College and of Trinity College, Dublin; Junior Proctor, 1921; pro-Vice-Chancellor, 1945-52; Member, Hebdomadal Council, 1929-49; F.R.P.S., Professor of Modern History, University of Dublin, 1911-13; War Trade Intelligence Department, Westminster, 1915-19. Chairman of Cttee. Enquiry into Cleaning of Pictures at National Gallery, 1947; Chm. Oxford Diocesan Advisory Committee; Mem. Cathedrals Advisory Cttee. Corresp. Mem., Royal Acad. of History, Madrid. *Publications:* The Chronicle of John of Worcester, 1908; contributor to Vinogradoff and Morgan's Denbigh Survey, 1914; Editor of George's Genealogical Tables, 1915, 1930; Dictionary of National Biography (1912-21), 1928, (1922-1930), 1937; Memoir of H. W. C. Davis, 1933; Ed. (with A. Beardwood) Some Oxfordshire Wills, 1393-1510, 1958. *Recreation:* architectural photography in Spain. *Address:* Romney, Boar's Hill, Oxford. *Club:* Athenæum.
[*Died* 22 *March* 1965.

WEBB, Sir (Ambrose) Henry, Kt., *cr.* 1941; *b.* 13 Aug. 1882; *s.* of Charles Webb, late of Park Place, Tashinny, Co. Longford, and Louisa Marie Bole; *m.* 1910, Agnes, *d.* of Michael Gunn, late of 69 Merrion Square, Dublin; one *s.* *Educ.:* Clifton College; Bath College; Trinity College, Oxford (classical scholar, B.A. 1905); King's Inns, Dublin (Victoria Prize and John Brooke Scholarship, 1908). Called to Irish Bar, 1909; Q.C., 1920; Member General Council of the Bar of Ireland, 1916-21; President of the District Court of Samaria, Palestine, 1921-33; Legal Assessor to Dept. of Development, Palestine, 1931-33; Puisne Judge, Supreme Court of Kenya, 1933-1937; Chief Justice of Sierra Leone, 1938-39; Chief Justice of Tanganyika, 1940-45; retired, 1945. *Recreations:* reading, golf. *Address:* c/o Barclay's Bank, D.C.O., 1 Cockspur St., S.W.1. *Club:* Royal Over-Seas League.
[*Died* 19 *May* 1964.

WEBB, Sir Charles Morgan, Kt., *cr.* 1924; C.I.E. 1921; *b.* Wolverhampton, 30 June 1872; *s.* of late Alfred Webb, merchant, Wolverhampton; *m.* 1899, Lilian Elizabeth Griffiths (*d.* 1959); one *s.* *Educ.:* St. Peter's, Wolverhampton; Mason's College, Birmingham; St. John's Coll., Cambridge. Indian Civil Service, 1895; Deputy Commissioner, Burma, 1901; Settlement Officer, 1903; Superintendent Census Operations, 1910-12; Secretary, Govt. 1914; Chief Secretary, Government of Burma, 1918; First Vice-Chancellor, University of Rangoon, 1920; Chairman, Rangoon Development Trust, 1921. *Publications:* Report on Census Operations for Burma, 1911; The Rise and Fall of the Gold Standard, 1934; Ten Years of Currency Revolution, 1935; Three Million Houses, 1937; The Outlook for Gold, 1938; Monetary Management, 1939. *Recreations:* gardening, walking. *Address:* 68 Wilbury Rd., Hove, Sussex.
[*Died* 20 *June* 1963.

WEBB, Hon. Sir Clifton; *see* Webb, Hon. Sir T. C.

WEBB, Geoffrey Fairbank, C.B.E. 1953; M.A.; F.B.A. 1957; F.S.A.; Hon. A.R.I.B.A., Sec. to Royal Commission on Historical Monuments (England), 1948-62; Member Royal Fine Arts Commission, 1943-62; *b.* 9 May 1898; *s.* of John Racker Webb and Elizabeth Hodgson Fairbank; *m.* 1934, Marjorie Isabel (*d.* 1962), *d.* of late John Holgate Batten. *Educ.:* Birkenhead Sch.; Magdalene Coll., Camb. Able Seaman R.N.V.R. 1917-19; Univ. Demonstrator in the Faculty of Fine Art; Univ. Lecturer, 1938; Slade Prof. of Fine Art in the Univ. of Camb., 1938-49; Lecturer at Courtauld Institute of Fine Art, University of London, 1934-37. Attached to the Naval Staff, 1939-43; Historical Section of War Cabinet Offices, 1943-44; Adviser on Monuments, Fine Arts and Archives, S.H.A.E.F., rank Lt.-Col., 1944; Director, Monuments, Fine Arts and Archives, Control Commission for Germany, British Element, rank Col., 1945 (despatches); Croix de Guerre, 1945; Officer of the Legion of Honour, 1946; Bronze Medal of Freedom (U.S.A.), 1947. *Publications:* Edited Letters of Sir John Vanbrugh, 1928; Life of Sir Christopher Wren, 1937; Architecture in Britain: The Middle Ages 1956; Contributions to Johnson's England, Chapter on Architecture and Garden; Walpole Society, Letters of Nicholas Hawksmoor; Georgian Art, Architecture and Sculpture; Spanish Art, Sculpture; Anne to Victoria, Robert Adam and his Brothers; and to journals. *Recreations:* various. *Address:* Prospect House, Tower Hill, Fishguard, Pembs. *Club:* United University.
[*Died* 17 *July* 1970.

WEBB, Sir Henry; *see* Webb, Sir A. H.

WEBB, Millicent Vere, C.B.E. 1935; L.R.C.P. and S.Ed; F.R.C.O.G.; *b.* Coleshill, Warwickshire, 15 Sept. 1878; *d.* of Vere George Webb, Physician, and Annie Millicent Gilbert. *Educ.:* London School of Medicine for Women. Went to India in 1910 as Missionary; was one of original officers of Women's Medical Service, India, on its formation in 1914 served 1914-21 at Dufferin Hospital, Calcutta; Principal Women's Medical School, Agra, 1921-32; Chief Medical Officer Women's Medical Service, 1932-1936; Superintendent, Victoria Zenana Hospital, Hyderabad, 1936-38; retired, 1938. Gold Kaisar-i-Hind medal, 1916, bar 1934. *Address;* Berners House, London Rd., Maldon, Essex.
[*Died* 3 *Oct.* 1969.

WEBB, Hon. Sir (Thomas) Clifton, K.C.M.G. 1956; Q.C. (New Zealand) 1954; *b.* 8 March 1889; *s.* of Thomas and Penelope Martha Webb; *m.* 1915, Lucy Amelia Nairn; two *d.* *Educ.:* Auckland Grammar School; Auckland University College. Solicitor, 1910; practised Dargaville, 1913-27; shifted to Auckland (Webb, Ross & Griffiths), 1927; served European War, 1917-19, New Zealand Armed Forces; elected M.P. (Kaipara, now Rodney), 1943 Attorney-General and Minister of Justice, 1949-54; Minister of External Affairs and Island Territories, 1951-54; High Commissioner for New Zealand in the United Kingdom, 1954-58. Rep. for N.Z.: Anzus Conf., Honolulu, 1952; U.N. Gen. Assembly, 1952 and 1953; S.E.A.T.O. Conf., Manila, 1954; Foreign Ministers' Conf., Geneva, 1954. *Recreations:* former Auckland provincial Rugby representative; Rugby referee. *Address:* White Haven Flats, Hill St., Wellington, New Zealand. [*Died* 6 *Feb.* 1962.

WEBB, Walter Prescott; Professor of History, University of Texas, U.S.A.; late Harmsworth Professor of American History, Oxford; *b.* 3 April 1888; *s.* of C. P. Webb and Mary Kyle; *m.* 1916, Jane Oliphant (*d.* 1960); one *d.*; *m.* 1961, Terrell D. Maverick. *Educ.:* public schools of Texas; University of Texas (B.A. 1915, Ph.D. 1932); University of Wisconsin; University of Chicago, M.A. Oxford, 1942; Phi Beta Kappa; taught history, public school, 1915-18; Member History Dept. Univ. of Texas, 1918; Consulting Historian, National Park Service, 1937; Harkness Lecturer in American History, University College, London University, 1938. Director Texas State Historical Association, 1938-46. Editor Southwestern Historical Quarterly; Founder Junior Historians. Pres. Mississippi Valley Hist. Assoc., 1954; Pres. American Historical Assoc., 1958. *Publications:* The

Great Plains: A Study in Environment and Institutions, 1931; The Texas Rangers: A Century of Frontier Defense; Divided we Stand: The Crisis of a Frontierless Democracy, 1937; The Great Frontier, 1952; More Water for Texas, 1954; The Story of the Texas Rangers, 1957; An Honest Preface, 1959; articles to Scribner's, Harper's, Southwest Review, etc. *Address:* University Station, Austin, Texas, U.S.A. *T.A.:* Austin, Texas. *T.:* Austin G.R. 8-6889. *Clubs:* University Town and Gown (Austin, Texas), The Headliners. [*Died* 8 *March* 1963.

WEBB, William Harcourt, D.L., J.P.; Major 1/1 Staffordshire Yeomanry; *b.* 27 October 1875; *e. s.* of late Lieutenant-Colonel W. G. Webb, M.P. Kingswinford Div. of Staffords.; *m.* 1911, Winifred Marion (*d.* 1960), *d.* of late R. Cecil Corbett, Stableford, Salop.; three *s.* *Educ.:* Uppingham; Christ Church, Oxford. Served with Staffordshire Yeomanry, Boer War, 1899-1900 (severely wounded); European War, Egypt, 1914-17; M.F.H., Albrighton Woodland, 1920-22; contested Kingswinford Division of Staffordshire, Nov. 1923; High Sheriff of Worcestershire, 1934. *Recreations:* hunting and shooting. *Address:* Spring Grove, Wribbenhall, Bewdley, Worcs. *T.:* 211. *Club:* Bath. [*Died* 2 *March* 1968.

WEBB-JOHNSON, Stanley, C.I.E. 1941; O.B.E. 1930; E.D. 1925; LL.B.; Solicitor; Chief Warden, Wimbledon Civil Defence; on Exec. of Staffordshire Soc. and Ex-Services Assoc.; *b.* 1 Mar. 1888; *m.* 1932, Beryl Buchanan, *d.* of late Steuart and Mabe Binny, Dale House, Hassocks, Sussex; two *s.* *Educ.:* Rossall Sch.; Victoria Univ. LL.B. (1st cl. Hons.); qualified as Solicitor (with Hons. and awarded the Slater Heelis Gold Medal), 1911; Partner in Hasties, 65 Lincoln's Inn Fields, W.C., 1912-14; served throughout European War, 1914-19, Officer with 6th Bn. E. Surrey Regt. and on the Staff, Aden Field Force and G.H.Q., India; then Controller of Enemy Property and legal adviser to Govt. of India, and member of Indian Legislature; President: Delhi and Simla Y.M.C.A., East and West Society, Masonic Fraternity, and Ex-Services Association of India; Hon. A.D.C. to the Viceroy; Colonel A.F.I.; Commanded Delhi Volunteer Force during War of 1939-45. On retirement from India, 1946, was Chairman Pension Appeal Tribunal and Sen. Professional Officer and Legal Adviser, Board of Trade (Enemy Property Dept.); Chairman, English Counties Socs. Conference and Staffordshire Soc. *Publications:* A Digest of Indian Law Cases, a brochure on Conveyancing and Litigation. *Recreations:* hunting, tennis, golf, swimming. *Address:* 14 Raymond Road, S.W.19. *Clubs:* Garrick; Royal Over-Seas League. [*Died* 2 *Dec.* 1965.

WEBB-JONES, James William, M.A.; Headmaster of the Junior School, Wells Cathedral, Wells, since September 1955; *b.* 12 Feb. 1904; *s.* of Ernest William Jones and Aimée Elizabeth Parson; *m.* 1930, Barbara Bindon, *d.* of late Col. R. H. S. Moody, C.B., The Buffs, and The Royal Irish Fusiliers; one *d.* *Educ.:* Cranleigh School; Worcester Coll., Oxford; Grenoble University (Diplôme de Hautes Études). Capt. Worcester College Cricket; Assistant Master St. George's Windsor Castle, 1928; Headmaster, 1934-42; resigned to enter R.A.F.; R.A.F. Education Service, 1942-45; Housemaster, Wellington School, Somerset, 1945-50; Headmaster, Vanbrugh Castle Sch. Blackheath, 1951-55. *Recreations:* cricket, fives, fishing. *Address:* Cathedral Junior School, Wells. [*Died* 29 *Dec.* 1965.

WEBBE, Sir Harold, Kt., *cr.* 1937; C.B.E. 1920; D.L. 1949; Director Mercantile Credit Co. Ltd. etc.; *b.* 30 September 1885; *s.* of late J. H. Webbe, Birmingham; *m.* Constance (*d.* 1956), *d.* of late W. A. Harrison, Edgbaston, Birmingham; two *s.* one *d.* *Educ.:* King Edward's, Birmingham; Queens' Coll., Cambridge; B.A., 27th Wrangler. H.M. Inspector, Bd. of Education, 1910-14; Deputy Director, Surplus Stores Dept. Ministry of Munitions, 1916-18; Member of L.C.C. Education Committee; Member of Consultative Committee, Board of Education, 1925-26; Member of London County Council, 1925-49; Alderman, 1934-39; Chm. Educ. Cttee., L.C.C., 1926-28; Chm. Gen. Purposes Cttee., 1933; Leader of the Municipal Reform Party, L.C.C., 1934-45; M.P. (U.) Cities of London and Westminster, 1950-59 (Abbey Division of Westminster, 1939-50). *Address:* Ash Pollard, Merstham, Surrey. *Clubs:* Athenæum, Carlton. [*Died* 22 *April* 1965.

WEBBER, Sir Robert John, Kt. 1934; J.P.; D.L.; F.Z.S.; F.S.A.; *b.* 14 Nov. 1884; *e. s.* of Charles and Hannah Webber. *Educ.:* Barry School; Cardiff Science and Art School. President of the Newspaper Society of Great Britain and Ireland, 1926-27; Chm., The Press Association, Ltd., 1932-33; Dep. Chairman Reuters, 1932-33; Hon. Mem. of the Institute of Journalists; Chm. of the Federation of Southern Newspaper Owners for many years; founder and first Chairman of the South Wales and Monmouthshire Alliance of Master Printers, and Chairman for several years of the West of England and South Wales Monotype Users Association; Member of Council, Cardiff University College; Member of Government Advisory Council Reconstruction Post War for Wales and Monmouthshire; Chairman, Cardiff Pilotage Board; President, Cardiff Business Club; Hon. Treas., various benevolent funds. K.St.J. *Recreations:* golf, motoring, shooting. *Address:* 109 Cathedral Road, Cardiff. *T.:* Cardiff 32123. *Clubs:* Press, Aldwych; Cardiff and County, Exchange, Radyr, Cardiff (Cardiff); Royal Porthcawl (Porthcawl), Southerndown (Bridgend), Walton Heath (Epsom), and Royal and Ancient. [*Died* 18 *Dec.* 1962.

WEBER, F. Parkes, M.A., M.D. (Cantab.); Fellow of the Royal College of Physicians; Consulting Diagnostician to German Hospital and late Physician to Mount Vernon Hospital for Consumption; *b.* 1863; *e. s.* of late Sir Hermann Weber; *m.* 1921, Hedwig Unger-Laissle, M.D. *Educ.:* Charterhouse; Cambridge; St. Bartholomew's Hospital, London; Paris; Vienna; Hon. F.R.Soc.Med., 1958; Fellow Society of Antiquaries; mem. Brit. Med. Assoc. and Med. Soc. of London; hon. member: Assoc. Phys. Gt. Britain and Ireland; Brit. Assoc. Dermat.; German Soc. Dermat.; Danish Soc. Dermat.; Amer. Clinical and Climatological Assoc.; Hon. Fell. Roy. Numismatic Soc.; Mitchell Lecturer (R.C.P.), 1921; Moxon Medallist (R.C.P.), 1930. *Publications:* On Climate and Mineral Waters, and other medical and scientific and archæological subjects; Aspects of Death and Correlated Aspects of Life in Art, Epigram, and Poetry, 4th edition, 1922; Some Thoughts of a Doctor, 1935; More Thoughts and Comments of a Doctor, 1952; Rare Diseases and Some Debatable Subjects, 2nd ed., 1947; (Ed.), Further Rare Diseases, 1949; Endocrine Tumours, 1936; On Naevi, 1952; Rhymes, Verses and Epigrams, 1955 (priv. printed), Interesting Cases and Pathological Considerations, and a Numismatic Suggestion, 1956; Medical Teleology and Miscellaneous Subjects, 1958; Miscellaneous Notes (seven series), 1960. *Address:* 68 Harley House, N.W.1. *T.:* Welbeck 9441. [*Died* 2 *June* 1962.

WEBER-BROWN, Lt.-Colonel Arthur Miles, M.V.O. 1945; Chairman of United British Securities Trust and Transparent Paper Ltd.; Director of other cos.; *b.* 10 June 1898; *m.* 1927, Joan Mary (marr. diss., 1939), *er. d.* of Major E. G. Gillilan, D.S.O.,

Market Harborough; one *s.* *Educ.:* St. Paul's; R.M.C., Sandhurst. Served European War, 1914-19; Royal Sussex Regt.; invalided on account of wounds, 1923. War of 1939-45, Lieut.-Colonel in offices of the War Cabinet. *Publications:* "Semolina" Series of books for children. *Recreation:* fishing. *Address:* 102 Arlington House, S.W.1. *Clubs:* Boodle's, Pratt's, White's. [*Died* 3 *Sept.* 1965.

WEBSTER, Mrs. Amy Marjorie, F.B.A. 1957; Professor Emeritus of Greek in the University of London, since 1963; *b.* 15 January 1901; *d.* of E. Dale; *m.* 1944, T. B. L. Webster. *Educ.:* Sheffield; Somerville College, Oxford (M.A.). Fellow and Tutor of Lady Margaret Hall, Oxford, 1929-39; seconded to Foreign Office, 1939-1945. Univ. of London, at Birkbeck College: Reader in Classics, 1952-59; Professor of Greek, 1959-63. Hon. Fellow, Somerville College, Oxford, 1962. *Publications:* The Lyric Metres of Greek Drama, 1948; (Ed.) Euripides' Alcestis, 1954; (Ed.) Euripides' Helena, 1967; contributions to various learned journals. *Recreation:* walking. *Address:* 37 Nevern Square, S.W.5. *T.:* Frobisher 3143. [*Died* 4 *Feb.* 1967.

WEBSTER, Sir Charles Kingsley, K.C.M.G., *cr.* 1946; M.A.; Litt.D.; F.B.A. 1930; Stevenson Professor of International History, London School of Economics, 1932 - 53, Professor Emeritus, 1953; *b.* 25 April 1886; *s.* of Daniel Webster of Freshfield, Liverpool; *m.* 1915, Nora Violet, *d.* of late R. P. Harvey of Florence. *Educ.:* Merchant Taylors' School, Crosby; King's College, Cambridge (Scholar 1904; Fell. 1909; Hon. Fell. 1953); Prof. of Modern History, Liverpool Univ., 1914-22; Subaltern R.A.S.C. in England and France, 1915-17; General Staff War Office, 1917-18; Secretary, Military Section British Delegation, Conference of Paris, 1918-19; Wilson Professor of International Politics, Univ. of Wales, Aberystwyth, 1922-32; Ausserordentlich Professor, University of Vienna, 1926; Nobel lecturer, Oslo, 1926; Reader University of Calcutta, 1927; Professor of History, Harvard University, 1928-32; Ford lecturer, Oxford University, 1948; Foreign Research and Press Service, 1939-41; Director of the British Library of Information, New York, 1941-42; Foreign Office, 1943-46; British Delegation Dumbarton Oaks and San Francisco, 1944-45, Preparatory Commission and General Assembly United Nations, London, 1945-46; U.N.E.S.C.O. 1950, 1954; Pres. of the British Acad., 1950-54; Foreign Secretary of British Academy, 1955 - 58; Hon. Associate of Adams House, Harvard Univ., 1932; For. Assoc. Mem., French Acad. of Moral and Political Sciences, 1960. Hon. Doctor of Humane Letters, Williams College, 1942; Hon. Litt.D., Oxford, Wales, 1952, Rome, 1956. *Publications:* The Congress of Vienna, 1814-1815, 1919; British Diplomacy, 1813-15, 1921; The Foreign Policy of Castlereagh, 1815-22, 1925; The Foreign Policy of Castlereagh, 1812-15, 1931; Britain and the Independence of Latin America, 2 vols., 1938; The Foreign Policy of Palmerston, 1830-41, 2 vols., 1951; Contrib. to History of the Second World War, U.K. Military Series, Ed. Sir James Butler: (with Noble Frankland) The Strategic Air Offensive Against Germany, 1939–1945, 4 vols. 1961; The Art and Practice of Diplomacy, 1961; and other works. *Address:* 4 St. John's Lodge, Harley Road, N.W.3. *T.:* Primrose 2030. *Club:* Athenæum. [*Died* 21 *Aug.* 1961.

WEBSTER, David William Ernest; M.P. (C.) for Weston-super-Mare, since June 1958; *b.* 20 Oct. 1923; *s.* of David Waddell Webster, Gowanlea, Arbroath, Scotland; *m.* 1947, Irene Isabella Staig Beasey; two *s.* one *d.* *Educ.:* Fettes College; Downing College, Cambridge. Served R.A.F.V.R. as Flt.-Lt., 1942-47; commissioned Pilot, and Parachute Jumping Instructor, 1944; served India, Pakistan, Canada and U.S.A. Cambridge, 1947-50 (M.A. Hist.). Personal Assistant to Director, The British Oxygen Company, 1950-53; contested (C. and Nat. L.) Bristol North East, 1955; stockbroker, 1956. Parliamentary Private Secretary to Joint Parliamentary Secretaries, Ministry of Pensions and National Insurance, 1958-60; Member, Select Committee of Estimates, 1960-63; Jt. Sec. Conservative Parly. Backbench Transport Cttee, 1961-62; Vice-Chm. Transport Cttee., 1962-63, 1964-; Chm., Conservative Parly. Transport Cttee., 1963-64; Delegate to the Council of Europe and Western European Union, 1963-1967; Opposition front-bench spokesman on Transport, 1965; Member, Select Cttee. on Nationalised Industries, 1966; introduced as Private Member's bill, Merchant Shipping Act, 1964, to ratify Internat. Convention for Safety of Life at Sea. Mem. Speaker's Conf. on Electoral Reform, 1965-1966; Vice-Pres., Economic Cttee. of Council of Europe, 1965-66. *Recreations:* brewing, wine-making, travel. *Address:* House of Commons, S.W.1. *Clubs:* Carlton; Constitutional (Bristol). [*Died* 7 *Jan.* 1969.

WEBSTER, James Alexander, C.B. 1923 D.S.O. 1918; Director of A. Guinness Son & Co., 1937-63; *b.* 1877; *s.* of late John Webster, Barony House, St. Bees, Cumberland; *m.* 1919, Constance, (*d.* 1956), 2nd *d.* of Mr. Richard and Lady Constance Combe of Pierrepont, Farnham, Surrey; one *s.* (and one *s.* killed in action, 1943). *Educ.:* St. Bees; privately; Magdalen Coll., Oxf. 1st; Cl. Classical Mods., and Gaisford Prize, Greek Verse, 1898 2nd Class Lit. Hum. Entered Board of Trade, 1901; Secretary to Royal Commission on Shipping Rings, 1907; Private Secretary to Pres. (Rt. Hon. Winston Churchill and Rt. Hon. Sydney Buxton), 1908-1913, and to Rt. Hon. Winston Churchill as Minister of Munitions (Oct. 1917-May 1918); Principal Asst.-Sec. to Air Ministry, 1921-37; General Secretary of International Conference on Safety of Life at Sea, 1914; served European War, 1914-19, in 8th London Regt. and as Brigade-Major, 53rd Infantry Brigade (Brevet Major, 1917, D.S.O., despatches, Italian Order of St Maurice and St Lazarus). *Address:* The Vale, Windsor Forest, Berks. *Club:* Travellers'. [*Died* 6 *Nov.* 1964.

WEBSTER, Tom; late cartoonist on News Chronicle; late cartoonist on London Daily Mail; *b.* 17 July 1890; *m.* 1935, Ida Michael; one *s.* two *d.* *Educ.:* Wolverhampton. Commenced with the Birmingham Sports Argus, then was political cartoonist on late Daily Citizen; served with Royal Fusiliers during European War; joined Daily Mail, 1919; retired from Daily Mail, 1940. Came out of retirement in 1944 to join Kemsley Newspapers; joined News Chronicle, 1953; retired from News Chronicle, 1956. *Publications:* Tom Webster's Annual; Drawn from Life; All the Best People. *Recreation:* golf. *Address:* 22 Bishopswood Road, Highgate, N.6. *T.:* Mountview 7247. *Clubs:* Savage, Buck's. [*Died* 20 *June* 1962.

WEBSTER, Major William Henry Albert, C.I.E. 1926; Representative of Port of London Authority in S. Africa since 1945; Chief Police Officer, Port of London Authority, 1926, also, on outbreak of War, 1939, commissioned in T.A. Reserve of Officers and appointed Security Control Officer for Port of London; in 1942 attached to British Military Mission S. Africa as Security Liaison Officer (Col.); retd. 1945; of the Inner Temple, Barrister-at-Law; *b.* 18 Oct. 1884; *e. s.* of late J. Webster, J.P., Royal Irish Constabulary, of Ballinacurra, Co. Cork, Ireland; *m.* 1932, Myrta Vivienne Gamble; one *d.* *Educ.:* Christ's Hospital.

Entered the Indian Police Service in 1905 as Assistant Superintendent of Police; was Private Secretary to the Lieutenant-Governor of Burma, 1914-15; served European War, 1917-19, with Burma Rifles; Deputy Inspector-General and Commissioner of Police, Rangoon, 1922-26; King's Police Medal, 1926. *Recreations:* golf, fishing, shooting. *Address:* P.O. Box 3034, Cape Town, South Africa. *Club:* East India and Sports. [*Died* 14 *July* 1968.

WEDD, Brig. William Basil, C.B.E. 1945; D.S.O. 1918; M.C. 1916; E.D.; Retd; *b.* 1 May 1890; *s.* of William Wedd, Toronto, and Amelia Astleford, Pembroke; *m.* 1915, Nora Marsh van Nostrand, Toronto; two *d.* (one *s.* decd.). *Educ.:* Toronto, Canada. Mil. Service: commnd. 2 Queen's Own Rifles of Canada, 1914; Canadian Expeditionary Force, France and Belgium, 1914-19 (despatches, M.C., D.S.O., French Croix de Guerre with Palm); War of 1939-45 (despatches, C.B.E.); Canadian Army, 1940; D.A.A.G., then A.A.G., Canadian Military H.Q., London, till Oct. 1942; Mil. Attaché, Can. Embassy, Washington, 1942-43; Mil. Sec. Can. Mil. H.Q., London, 1943-44; Senior Mil. Gov. Officer H.Q. First Canadian Army, 1944-45 (France, June 1944). Civil: Massey Harris Co. Ltd., Toronto; Toronto, 1919-23; London, Eng., 1924-25; Paris, 1925-27; Bordeaux, 1927-29; Copenhagen, 1929-32; Lille, 1933-40 (Manager for France); Paris, 1945 (European General Manager). Executive Officer, Infrastructure, N.A.T.O., Paris, 1951-1953; Vice-Pres., Massey-Harris-Ferguson (Export) Ltd., London, 1953-57. Comdr. Orange Nassau, Holland, 1945; Comdr. Ouissam Alouite, Morocco, 1950. *Recreations:* sailing, golf, winter sports. *Address:* 14 rue Antoine Roucher, Paris 16me; Upper Canada, Pibonson, Mougins (A.M.), France. *Clubs:* Toronto, Royal Canadian Yacht, Rosedale Golf (Toronto). [*Died* 6 *Nov.* 1966.

WEDDELL, Colonel (Hon. Brig.) John Murray, C.B.E. 1944; F.R.C.S.; late R.A.M.C.; *b.* 20 Jan. 1884; *s.* of Dr. W. H. Weddell, M.R.C.S., L.R.C.P.; *m.* 1926, Hilda Madeline Pearson; one *d.* *Educ.:* Cheltenham College; Christ's College, Cambridge; St. Bartholomew's Hospital. B.A. Cantab. 1906; M.R.C.S., L.R.C.P. London, 1909; F.R.C.S. England, 1927; entered R.A.M.C. 1909; Assistant Professor Military Surgery, R.A.M. College, 1928-32; Professor of Military Surgery R.A.M. College and Consulting Surgeon to the Army, 1935-39; retired pay, 1939; re-employed, 1939; Consulting Surgeon to the Army (B.N.A.F.). *Recreations:* golf, fishing. *Address:* 17 Bentley Road, Cambridge. [*Died* 19 *Feb.* 1966.

WEDDERBURN, Alexander Henry Melvill, C.B.E. 1956; J.P.; Vice-President, General Executive Committee, Queen's Institute of District Nursing, since 1968 (Chairman, 1946-61); Director, Mallet & Wedderburn Ltd. and other companies; *b.* 1 July 1892; *o. s.* of late A. D. O. Wedderburn, C.B.E., K.C.; *m.* 1921, Cynthia Margaret, *e. d.* of late Cecil Lubbock; three *d.* (one *s.* killed in action, Singapore, 1960). *Educ.:* Eton College; Balliol College, Oxford. M.A. (Oxon); Pres. Oxf. Union Soc., 1914. Served European War, 1914-18, Capt. 5th Bn. The Black Watch, France, 1914-19 (wounded, despatches). Barrister, Inner Temple, 1917; practised, 1919-36. J.P. Berkshire, 1943. *Recreation:* formerly rowing (Oxford VIII, 1912 and 1913). *Address:* Parsonage Farm, East Hagbourne, Didcot, Berkshire. *T.:* Didcot 3101. *Clubs:* Brooks's, Leander. [*Died* 23 *Dec.* 1968.

WEDGWOOD, 3rd Baron, *cr.* 1942, of Barlaston, **Hugh Everard Wedgwood**; Farmer, at Hillwood, Molo, Kenya, 1941-1964; *b.* 20 April 1921; *s.* of 2nd Baron Wedgwood and Edith May (Dowager Lady Wedgwood; *née* Telfer); *S.* father 1959; *m.* 1949, Jane Weymouth, *d.* of W. J. Poulton, Kenjockety, Molo, Kenya; one *s.* two *d.* *Educ.:* Bedales School, Petersfield, Hants. The Kenya Regiment, 1939; The Elector's Union 1948-55. Nakuru County Council, 1955-63. *Recreation:* nature study. *Heir:* *s.* Hon. Piers Anthony Weymouth Wedgwood, *b.* 20 Sept. 1954. *Address:* Drywick, Shear Hill, Petersfield, Hants. [*Died* 18 *April* 1970.

WEDGWOOD, Hon. Josiah; President since 1967, Chairman, 1947-67, and Managing Director, 1930-61, Josiah Wedgwood and Sons, Ltd., Potters; *b.* 20 Oct. 1899; 2nd *s.* of 1st Baron Wedgwood, P.C., D.S.O.; *m.* 1919, Dorothy Mary, *d.* of Percy J. Winser, the Moorhouse, Biddulph, Staffs.; two *s.* one *d.* *Educ.:* Bedales School, Hampshire; University College, London and London School of Economics (B.Sc.). R.F.A., 1918-19; Sec. and then Director of Rural Industries Bureau, 1922-26; economic research work, 1926-28; Josiah Wedgwood and Sons, Secretary, 1928; Chairman of Council, Royal College of Art, 1948-49; Director of Bank of England, 1942-46; Director of District Bank, 1948-60; Part-time member of Monopolies and Restrictive Practices Commission, 1949-53. *Publication:* The Economics of Inheritance, 1929 (Penguin Ed., 1939). *Address:* 7 Holland Park Road, W.14. [*Died* 5 *May* 1968.

WEECH, William Nassau, M.A. (Oxon.), F.S.A.; J.P. (Gloucs.); M.R.S.T.; Major T.A. (retd.); Member Councils of Bristol University and Cheltenham Ladies' College; Governor, Blundell's (Tiverton), Cirencester and Lucton Schools; *b.* 6 Sept. 1878; *s.* of late W. J. Weech of Worksop, Notts; *m.* 1908, Gladys Hester, 3rd *d.* of late Deputy-Surg.-Gen. Landale of Dunholme, Cheltenham; two *d.* *Educ.:* Winchester (Scholar); New College, Oxford (Scholar); Lothian Prize Essay, 1903. Assistant Master, Cheltenham College, 1903-11; Headmaster of Sedbergh, 1911-26; Member of Leeds University Court, 1923-27; Occasional Inspector to the Board of Education, 1928-39; C.C. (Gloucs.), 1931-46. Liaison Officer R.O.C., 1940; Headmaster of Lytham School, 1941; Gloucestershire Organiser, University of Bristol Regional Committee on Education for H.M. Forces, 1942; Chairman Cheltenham Youth Committee, 1943-45; Headmaster of Cirencester Grammar School, 1945. *Publications:* Urban VIII; Ancient Times; Editor of History of the World, 2nd edn., 1951; (with Archbishop Clarke) A History of Sedbergh School, 1525-1925. *Recreations:* talking, walking. *Address:* 40 St. Stephen's Road, Cheltenham. *Club:* New (Cheltenham). [*Died* 14 *Jan.* 1961.

WEIGHTMAN, William Henry, C.M.G. 1946; Assistant Secretary, Post Office, 1938-47; *b.* 24 Mar. 1887; *s.* of late H. Herbert Weightman, Architect, Liverpool; *m.* 1912, Grace E. Howes; four *d.* *Educ.:* Liverpool College; St. John's College, Cambridge. Post Office H.Q. 1910. *Address:* 123 North End House, W.14. *T.:* 01-603 2463. *Clubs:* Hamilton, Anglo-Belgian. [*Died* 18 *Dec.* 1970.

WEINBERGER, Jaromir; composer; *b.* 8 Jan 1896; *s.* of Karel and Rúzena Weinberger; *m.* 1931, Jana Lembergrová. *Educ.:* Conservatory of Music, Prague; Leipzig. *Publications:* Opera: Shvanda; Beloved Voice; People of Poker Flat; Wallenstein; For Orchestra: Christmas; Overture to a Puppet Show; Overture to a Cavalier's Play; Passacaglia; Czech Songs and Dances; Under the Spreading Chestnut Tree, Variations and Fugue on an old English tune; Legend of Sleepy Hollow; Song of the High Seas; Two Poems by E. A. Poe; A Bird's Opera; Lincoln Symphony; Czech Rhapsody; Préludes réligieux et profanes; for piano: Spinett Sonate, Gravures; Bible Poems for Organ: The Way to Emmaus and Psalm 150 for high voice and Organ; Sonata for Organ; Saratoga: a Ballet; Religious Preludes for Organ; Ecclesiastes, for soli, chorus and Organ; Meditations; Dedications; Pastorale (for Organ); Songs of the Faith, 14 songs on the text of the New Testament (King James version) for high voice with organ or piano; From Tyrol for full orchestra; Eine Walzerouverture for orchestra; Five Songs from des Knaben Wunderhorn; Ave, a Rhapsody for mixed chorus and orchestra. *Address:* 32 South 45th Street, St. Petersburg, Florida, 33711, U.S.A. [*Died* 9 *Aug.* 1967.

WEIR, Air Vice-Marshal Cecil Thomas, C.B. 1960; C.B.E. 1958; D.F.C. 1944; British Joint Staffs, Washington, since Nov. 1964; *b.* 2 April 1913; *s.* of Cecil H. Weir and Mary Fulton; *m.* 1937, Muriel Lonsdale; one *s.* one *d.* *Educ.:* Brentwood College, Victoria, British Columbia; R.A.F. College, Cranwell. Joined R.A.F., 1931; served War of 1939-45, in Bomber Command, also in U.S.A. and Canada (P.O.W. 1944-45). Group Capt. 1949; Air Cdre. 1957; Senior Air Staff Officer, H.Q., Middle East Air Force, 1958-60; Commandant of School of Land/Air Warfare, 1961; First Commandant of Joint Warfare Establishment (formed in April 1963 by amalgamation of School of Land/Air Warand Amphibious Warfare School), 1963-64. Air Vice-Marshal, 1959. *Address:* c/o Glyn, Mills and Co., Whitehall, S.W.1. *Club:* Royal Air Force. [*Died* 5 *Aug.* 1965.

WEIR, Miss Helen Stuart, R.O.I.; R.B.A.; Artist. Gold Medallist for Sculpture. Former Acting President, Society of Women Artists; Vice-Pres. St. James Society for Deafened Artists; One-Man Exhibitions: Goupil Gall., Cheltenham Art Gallery, Montclair, New Jersey, U.S.A.; Exhibitor, Royal Academy, R. Scottish Academy, R. Hibernian Academy, New English Art Club, Liverpool, Glasgow, Toronto, Auckland, N.Z. *Address:* 79 Campden Hill Court, W.8; Rose Lodge Studio, St. Ives, Cornwall. *Clubs:* Campden Hill; Art, Ridley Art. [*Died* 15 *Oct.* 1969.

WEIR, Neil Archibald Campbell, C.M.G. 1950; O.B.E. 1947; E.D. 1938; F.C.I.S. 1935; *b.* 25 Apr. 1895; *s.* of late Archibald Munday Weir and late Edith Weir, St. Giles, Malvern Link, Worcs.; *m.* 1930, Hermine Anna, *d.* of Rev. C. F. Fyffe, St. Helen's Coll., Southsea, and Fiddington Rectory, Somerset; two *d.* (two *s.* decd.). *Educ.:* The School, Malvern Link; Wellington College, Berks; Keble Coll., Oxford. Served European War, Argyll and Sutherland Highlanders, 1914-20 (wounded twice, despatches); Military Operations Department, War Office. 5th Bn., Gloucestershire Regt., 1920-22; attached to Reserves of Nigeria and Sierra Leone Regts., R. West African Frontier Force, 1930-43. Colonial Administrative Service, 1925-50: Nigeria, 1925-36; Sierra Leone, 1936-43; Senior Comr. and Mem. Exec. and Legislative Councils, The Gambia, 1943-50; Sierra Leone Development Co. Ltd., 1953-54; Chairman: Public Service Commission, Mauritius, 1955-60; Police Service Commission, Mauritius, 1959-60. Chartered Secretary, 1935-. *Address:* Bourne Stream, Holford, Bridgwater, Somerset. *Club:* Royal Commonwealth Society. [*Died* 10 *Jan.* 1967.

WEIR, Major-Gen. (retd.) Sir Norman (William McDonald), K.B.E., *cr.* 1948 (C.B.E. 1942); C.B. 1946; *b.* 6 July 1893; *e. s.* of late Jas. Weir, J.P., Heathcote Valley, N.Z.; *m.* 1917, Alice Dorothy, *y. d.* of John McWhirter, J.P., Hokitika; one *d.* *Educ.:* West Christchurch High School. Cadet, Roy. Mil. Coll., Australia, 1911-14; commissioned into N.Z. Staff Corps: served with Auckland Regt., European War, 1914-1918; subsequently held various Staff appointments, N.Z. Regular Forces; commanded N.Z. Coronation Contingent to England, 1937; commanded Northern Military Dist., 1939-40; Central Mil. Dist., 1941; 4 N.Z. Div. 1942; 6 N.Z. Div. M.E.F. 1943-1944; Q.M.G., N.Z. Army, 1945; Chief of General Staff, N.Z. Army, 1946-49; A.D.C. to King George VI, 1945. Retd. 1949. Colonel N.Z. Scottish Regt., 1949. Officer U.S.A. Legion of Merit, 1944. *Recreations:* fishing, shooting. *Address:* Heathcote, Thornton Rd., Cambridge, N.Z. [*Died* 11 *July* 1961.

WEIR, Ralph Somerville, C.I.E. 1939; M.A.; B.Sc.; Asst. Regional Controller, Ministry of Labour Region, Scotland; *b.* 10 Sept. 1884; *s.* of John Weir, Lesmahagow; *m.* 1913, Ella Plant; one *s.* two *d.* *Educ.:* Glasgow Univ. Joined Indian Educational service, 1917; Director of Public Instruction, U.P., 1936; retired, 1939. *Address:* Dana, Uddingston, Lanarkshire. [*Died* 26 *June* 1962.

WEIR, Maj.-Gen. Sir Stephen (Cyril Ettrick), K.B.E. 1960 (C.B.E. 1944); C.B. 1945; D.S.O. 1941, Bar 1942; Ambassador for New Zealand to Thailand, 1961-67, retired; *b.* 5 October 1905; *s.* of Cochrane and Alison McKay Weir; *m.* 1936, Betty Catherine Winthrop; three *s.* *Educ.:* Otago Boys' High School, Dunedin, N.Z. Trooper, 6 N.Z. Mtd. Rifles, 1923-25; cadet, Royal Military Academy, 1926-27; 2nd Lt. 1927; Lt. 1929, returned to N.Z.; Capt. 1935; B.C. 25 Bty. N.Z.A., Sept.-Dec. 1939. C.O. 7 N.Z. A/TK Regt., Jan.-Feb. 1940; C.O. 6 N.Z. Fd. Regt., Feb. 1940-Dec. 1941; C.R.A. 2 N.Z. Div., Dec. 1941-July 1944; L.O. G.O.C. 8 Army, July-Aug. 1944; C.C.R.A. 10 Corps, Aug.-Sept. 1944; G.O.C. 2 N.Z. Div., Sept.-Oct. 1944; G.O.C. 46 Inf. Div., 1944-46; Comdr. S. Mil. Dist. N.Z., 1948; i.d.c. 1950; Q.M.G. House, War Office, London, 1951; Q.M.G., N.Z. Army, 1952-55; C.G.S., N.Z. Army, 1955-60; Chief Military Adviser to the Govt. of N.Z., 1960-61. Comdr., Legion of Merit (U.S.); Greek Cross of St. Andreas. *Recreations:* show-jumping, horse-racing, ski-ing, farming. *Address:* Snodgrass Road, Te Puna, R.D.2, Tauranga, New Zealand. [*Died* 24 *Sept.* 1969.

WEISS, Prof. Roberto; Prof. of Italian, University of London, since 1946; *b.* Milan, 22 Jan. 1906; *s.* of late Eugenio Weiss and late Rita Fattori; a British subject by naturalisation since 1934; *m.* 1936, Eve Cecil; one *s.* three *d.* *Educ.:* Abroad and at Oxford University (B.A. Passed examinations for D.Phil. but not taken degree formally, Charles Oldham Prize). Special Assistant, Dept. of Western Manuscripts, Bodleian Library, 1932-33; Advanced Research Student, Oxford University, 1934-38; Asst. Editor, Hudson's Bay Record Society, 1937-1938; Assistant Lecturer, 1938-41, Lecturer, 1941-46, Univ. Coll., London. Edmund Gardner Prize for Italian studies, 1943. Served in H.M. Forces, 1942-45. Corresp. Fell., Mediæval Acad. of America, Istituto Veneto di scienze, lettere ed arti, Accademia Patavina di scienze, lettere, ed arti, Arcadia, Accademia Petrarca of Arezzo, Accademia dei Sepolti of Volterra, Accademia degli Incamminati of Modigliana, hon. mem. Deputazione di Storia Patria per le Venezie; Senior editor of Italian Studies. *Publications:* Humanism in England during the Fifteenth Century, 1941, 3rd edn. 1967; The Dawn of Humanism in Italy, 1947; Il primo secolo dell' umanesimo, 1949; Un inedito petrarchesco, 1950; The Greek Culture of South Italy in the Later Middle Ages, Annual Italian Lecture of Brit. Acad. for 1951; Un Umanista Veneziano: Papa Paolo II, 1958; The Medals of Pope Sixtus

IV, 1961; The Spread of Italian Humanism, 1964; Pisanello's Medallion of the Emperor John VIII Palæologus, 1966; The Renaissance Discovery of Classical Antiquity, 1969; articles and reviews in learned periodicals. *Recreations:* painting and wood engraving. *Address:* University College London, Gower Street, W.C.1. *T.:* Euston 7050, Extn. 479; 44 St. Andrew's Rd., Henley-on-Thames. *T.:* Henley-on-Thames 4116.
[*Died* 10 *Aug.* 1969.

WEISZ, Victor, (Vicky), F.S.I.A.; Cartoonist for the Evening Standard since 1958 and for the New Statesman since 1954; *b.* Berlin (then Hungarian citizen), 25 April 1913; *s.* of Desider Weisz. *Educ.:* Berlin Art School. Started career as political cartoonist, 1929; emigrated to England, 1935. Joined staff of News Chronicle, 1941; later joined Daily Mirror. Has exhibited at Lefevre Galleries, London, etc. *Publications:* illustrations for the following, from 1947 onwards: Let Cowards Flinch; Stabs in the Back; Meet the Russians; Real Mackay; Up the Poll!; How to be a Celebrity; also: New Statesman Profiles, 1957; Vicky's World, 1959; Vicky Must Go, 1960; Twists, 1962; Home and Abroad, 1964. *Address:* 22 Upper Wimpole Street, W.1. *T.:* Welbeck 0978. *Club:* Savile.
[*Died* 23 *Feb.* 1966.

WELBOURNE, Edward; *b.* 23 March 1894; *s.* of Edward Welbourne; *m.* 1926, Jeanie Maxwell Myles; one *s.* one *d.* *Educ.:* De Aston School; Emmanuel College. Allen Scholar, 1919; Thirlwall Prizeman, Seeley Medallist and Gladstone Prizeman, 1921; Junior Fellow, 1921, Tutor, 1927, Senior Tutor, 1938, Master, 1951-July 1964 (retired). Emmanuel College, Cambridge. Served European War, 1915-18, Durham L.I. (M.C.). *Address:* Emmanuel College, Cambridge; Granhams, Great Shelford, Cambridge. *T.:* Shelford 3158.
[*Died* 28 *Jan.* 1966.

WELBY, Hugh Robert Everard Earle, C.M.G. 1936; *b.* 1885; *s.* of late Edward M. E. Welby; *m.* 1915, Dorothea Margaret, (*d.* 1965) *d.* of late Charles Martin Green; no *c.* *Educ.:* Eton; Corpus Christi College, Oxford. Kenya Administrative Service, 1911-36; Retired as Provincial Commissioner, 1936; served with East African Forces, Captain unattached list, 1916-1918; J.P Lincolnshire, Parts of Kesteven, 1937. *Recreations:* hunting, shooting. *Address:* The Manor House, Sapperton, nr. Sleaford, Lincs. *T.:* Ingoldsby 273. *Club:* United Service.
[*Died* 18 *April* 1970.

WELCH, James William, M.A., Ph.D. (Cantab.); M.Ed. (Dunelm); Visiting Reader in Philosophy, University of Surrey (formerly Battersea College of Technology), since Oct. 1964; *b.* 15 Feb. 1900; 2nd *s.* of Wm. Lewis and Emily Charlotte Welch. *Educ.:* Sidney Sussex Coll., Cambridge. Curate Gateshead Parish Church, 1926-29; C.M.S. Missionary and Government Supervisor of Mission Schools, Isoko, S. Nigeria, 1929-35; Principal, St. John's Coll., York, 1935-39; Director of Religious Broadcasting, B.B.C., 1939-47; Prebendary of St. Paul's, 1942-47; Chaplain to the King, 1944-47; Hon. Chaplain to Archbishop Wm. Temple (York and Canterbury), 1942-44; Chief Education and Social Science Officer, Overseas Food Corporation, 1948-Aug. 1950; Prof. of Religious Studies and Vice-Principal, Ibadan Univ. Coll., Nigeria, 1950-54. *Address:* 39 Great Cumberland Place, W.1. *T.:* Ambassador 1443; Sarsens, Shipley, Sussex. *T.:* Coolham 354. *Clubs:* Athenæum; Swiss Alpine. [*Died* 22 *Dec.* 1967.

WELCH, Margaret; *see* Kemp-Welch.

WELD, Brigadier Charles Joseph, C.I.E. 1945; M.C. 1918; p.s.c.; retired; *b.* 4 Feb. 1893; *s.* of Henry Joseph Weld, Lymington, Hants; *m.* 1929, Una, *d.* of C. J. Hargreaves; two *d.* *Educ.:* R.M.C., Sandhurst. 2nd Lieut. I.A., 1912; served European War, 1914-19 (despatches); p.s.c. 1928; D.A.Q.M.G., India, 1930-31; Asst. Mil. Sec., India, 1931-33; Lt.-Col., 1936; Operations N.W. Frontier, India, 1936-39 (despatches thrice); G.S.O. 1, Waziristan Dist., 1938-39; Colonel, 1938; Brig., 1940; Comd. a Bde. in M.E.F. (despatches), 1941; Local Maj.-Gen., Cyprus, 1942; Comdr. Rawalpindi Area, 1943-45; A.D.C. to the King 1944; I.A. Liaison Officer, India Office, 1945-47; retired, 1947. Comd. a Bn., Home Guard, 1952-57. *Address:* Highfield Holme, Lymington, Hants. *T.:* Lymington 2651. *Clubs:* United Service; Royal Lymington Yacht.
[*Died* 9 *June* 1962.

WELD, Reverend Walter Joseph, S.J.; *b.* 1881; *s.* of late Walter Weld, Birkdale, and Frances, *d.* of late Herman Walmesley, Gidlow Hall. *Educ.:* Stonyhurst College. Master of Discipline for many years at Beaumont College, where he also taught; Theological Course at Milltown; Superior of Hodder, the Preparatory School of Stonyhurst, 1916; Rector of Stonyhurst College, 1924-29; Rector of Beaumont College, Old Windsor, 1929-37; Guest Master, Stonyhurst College, 1939 Superior of Hodder, 1941; Chaplain, Beaumont College, 1948. Retired, 1959. *Address:* c/o 114 Mount St., W.1.
[*Died* 7 *March* 1969.

WELD-FORESTER, Maj. Hon. Edric A. C.; *see* Forester.

WELD-FORESTER, Lieut.-Comdr. Wolstan Beaumont Charles, C.B.E. 1957; R.N. (retd.); *b.* 27 Aug. 1899; *e. s.* of Hon. Charles Cecil Orlando Weld-Forester and Elspeth Lascelles Mackenzie; *m.* 1932, Anne Grace Christian, *d.* of William Augustus Stirling Home Drummond Moray; one *s.* one *d.* *Educ.:* Royal Naval Colleges, Osborne and Dartmouth. Served European War, 1914-18, retd. 1922. Vice-Consul, Tehran, 1927; Actg. Consul-General, Munich, 1939; Consul: Basra, 1940-42, Suez, 1943-1944, Damascus, 1944-46; First Secretary, British Legation, Addis Ababa, 1947-49; Consul-General: Salonika, 1949-52, Oporto, 1952-55, Nice, 1956-57; retired from Foreign Service, 1957. *Recreations:* riding and shooting. *Address:* el Merahta, The Mountain, Tangier. *T.:* Tangier 16439. *Clubs:* Travellers'; International Sportsmen's; Monte Carlo.
[*Died* 25 *Oct.* 1961.

WELDON, George; Associate Conductor, Hallé Orchestra, since 1952; Conductor and Musical Director, City of Birmingham Symphony Orchestra, 1943-51; Conductor, Sadler's Wells Ballet, 1955-56; *b.* 5 June 1908; *s.* of Major F. H. Weldon, D.S.O., Sherwood Foresters, and Eveleen Weldon. *Educ.:* Sherborne. Before War Dep. Conductor of Hastings Municipal Orchestra; since War has conducted London Symphony Orchestra, London Philharmonic Orchestra, B.B.C. Symphony Orchestra, Philharmonia Orchestra, Hallé Orchestra, Liverpool Philharmonic Orchestra, etc., also International Ballet, etc.; has visited Turkey, North Africa, Yugoslavia, Norway, Germany, Belgium, Holland, France, South Africa, Sweden, on conducting tours. Records for Columbia and H.M.V. *Recreation:* motoring. *Address:* 37 St. John's Wood Road, N.W.8. *T.:* Cunningham 5740. *Club:* Savage.
[*Died* 16 *Aug.* 1963.

WELLBORNE, Lieut.-Colonel Cyril de Montfort, C.I.E. 1936; O.B.E. 1919; Indian Army, retd.; late Inspector-General of Police, Burma; *b.* 2 July 1884; *s.* of Harry de Montfort Wellborne, Wallington, Surrey. *Educ.:* Dulwich College. Served European War, 1915-19, Mesopotamia (despatches four times, O.B.E.); retired, 1939; King's Police Medal, 1930. *Address:* 21 Berkeley Court, Don Rd., St. Helier, Jersey. [*Died* 14 *Nov.* 1965.

WELLER, Rt. Rev. John Reginald, M.A.; Hon. Assistant Bishop of Worcester since 1960; Rector of Holme Pierrepont, 1951-58; *b.* Blackwell Hall, Chesham, Bucks, 6 Oct. 1880; *s.* of Edward Weller and Edith Aylward; *m.* 1st, 1916, Alexina Caley (*d.* 1934), Windsor; no *c.*; 2nd, 1938, Frances M., *d.* of late Capt. Paget Butler, Tupsley, Hereford; one *s.* one *d.* *Educ.:* Selwyn College, Cambridge. Tea planting, Ceylon, 1899; 32nd Battalion I.Y. South Africa, 1901; in United States and Canada, 1903-10; Deacon, 1913; Priest, 1914; Cambridge University Mission, Delhi, 1914; Chaplain, Waziristan, 1917; Divisional Chaplain, 3rd Lahore Division, Mesopotamia, Egypt, and Palestine, 1917-18; Divisional Chaplain, 4th Quetta Division, Afghanistan, 1919; Superintendent, The Missions to Seamen, Melbourne, 1923; Superintendent, The Mersey Mission to Seamen, 1930; Bishop of Falkland Islands, 1934-37; Bishop in Argentina and Eastern South America, 1937-46; Vicar of Edwalton, Notts, 1946-49; Assistant Bishop of Southwell, 1946-52. *Address:* 2 St. Barnabas, Newland, Malvern, Worcs. [*Died* 26 *Oct.* 1969.

WELLES, Sumner; *b.* N.Y. City, 14 Oct. 1892; *s.* of Benjamin Welles and Frances Swan; *m.* 1st, Esther Slater; two *s.*; 2nd, 1925, Mathilde Townsend (*d.* 1949); 3rd, 1952, Baroness von Jeszensky. *Educ.:* Groton School, Groton, Mass.; Harvard Univ., Cambridge, Mass. Sec. of Embassy, Tokyo, 1915-1917, Buenos Aires, 1917-19; asst. chief Latin American Affairs Division, Dept. of State, 1920-21, chief, 1921-22; comr. to Dominican Republic, 1922-25; delegate to Conference on Central American Affairs, Washington, D.C., 1922; personal representative of President to offer mediation in Honduras revolution, 1924; delegate Central American Conference, Amapala, Honduras, 1924; member Dawes Financial Mission to Dominican Republic, 1929; Asst. Sec. of State, 1933; ambassador to Cuba, Apr.-Dec. 1933; again Asst. Sec. of State, Dec. 1933; delegate Inter-American Conference for Maintenance of Peace, Buenos Aires, 1936; Under-Secretary of State of U.S.A., 1937-43; delegate Meeting of the Foreign Ministers of the American Republics for Consultation, Panama, 1939; Chairman, Inter-American Financial and Economic Advisory Committee, 1939-43; special representative of President to report on conditions in Europe, 1940; representative of the U.S. on Provisional Administration of European Colonies and Possessions in the Americas, 1940; member, Central Committee, American Red Cross, rep. State Department, 1941; accompanied President Roosevelt at meeting at sea with Prime Minister Churchill of England, Aug. 1941; representative of U.S. at Third Consultative Meeting of Ministers of Foreign Affairs of American Republics, Rio de Janeiro, 1942. LL.D., Columbia, 1939, Brown, 1939, New York (hon,), 1942; Phi Beta Kappa, Harvard, 1939; Omicron Delta Kappa, Univ. of Maryland, 1939 (hon.); Doctor (hon.) Univ. of Brazil, 1942; Univ. of Toronto, 1943; Lafayette Coll., 1944; Capt. Robert Dollar Memorial Award, 1942; Pres. Freedom House (Award, 1944). Grand Cross, Order of Carlos Manuel de Cespedes (Cuba); Order of Aztec Eagle (Mexico); Grand Cross, Cruzeiro do Sul (Brazil). *Publications:* Naboth's Vineyard, 1928; The World of the Four Freedoms, 1943; The Time for Decision, 1944; Where Are We Heading ?, 1946; We Need Not Fail, 1948; Seven Major Decisions, 1951; Editor: The Intelligent American's Guide to the Peace, 1946; Ciano's Diary, 1946; American Foreign Policy Series. *Recreations:* riding, gardening. *Address:* Bar Harbor, Maine, U.S.A. *Clubs:* Metropolitan (Washington, D.C.); Knickerbocker, Union (New York). [*Died* 24 *Sept.* 1961.

WELLESLEY, Lord George, M.C.; *b.* 29 July 1889; *s.* of 4th Duke of Wellington, K.G.; *m.* 1st, 1917, Lady Richard Wellesley (*d.* 1946); one *s.*; 2nd, 1955, Jean McGillivray. *Educ.:* Wellington College. Capt. Grenadier Guards; Lieut.-Colonel R.F.C.; Wing Commander R.A.F.; retired, 1919 (Mons Star, M.C., despatches). Managing Director of Coxeter & Son Ltd., 1923-40. Rejoined R.A.F.V.R 1940 as Pilot Officer, Acting Sqdn. Ldr.; demobilised, 1945. Royal Humane Society's life-saving medal. *Address:* Flat 5, Woodsford, 14 Melbury Road, W.14. *Club:* Royal Automobile. [*Died* 31 *July* 1967.

WELLINGTON, Arthur Robartes, C.M.G. 1934; late Director of Medical Services, Hong Kong; retired, 1937; *b.* 24 Nov. 1877; *s.* of J. C. Wellington; *m.* Queenie (*d.* 1958), *d.* of Lt.-Col. William Trydell Helden, C.M.G. *Educ.:* Kelly College, Tavistock; St. Mary's Hospital. *Address:* c/o Barclays Bank (France) Ltd., 7 Promenade des Anglais, Nice, France. *Club:* East India and Sports. [*Died* 26 *Oct.* 1961.

WELLINGTON, Gilbert Trevor, C.B.E. 1942; H.M. Coroner, City of Gloucester; *b.* 4 July 1882; *s.* of M. N. Wellington, Churchdown, Gloucestershire; *m.* 1908, Grace Evelyn (*d.* 1960), *d.* of S. R. Alexander, Chiswick; one *s.* *Educ.:* Crypt Sch., Gloucester. Solicitor, 1904; served European War of 1914-18, Lieut. Cavalry, Egypt, Palestine; Lieut. M.G.C., France; H.M. Coroner, City of Gloucester, 1921-37 and 1944-; High Sheriff, City, 1936; Mayor of Gloucester, 1937-43; A.R.P. Controller, 1938-43. *Address:* The Bear Inn, Rodborough Common, Glos. *T.:* (private) Amberley 3105, (office) Gloucester 25164. *Clubs:* Gloucester (Gloucester); Minchinhampton Golf (Minchinhampton). [*Died* 3 *Feb.* 1963.

WELLINGTON, Hubert Lindsay, Hon. A.R.C.A.; *b.* 1879; *s.* of Caleb J. Wellington and Katherine Potter; *m.* Nancy Charlotte Boughtwood (*d.* 1942); two *s.*; 2nd, 1944, Irene Bass, A.R.C.A. *Educ.:* Crypt Grammar School, Glos.; Glos. and Birmingham Schools of Art; Slade School; Paris. Exhibitor New English Art Club, London Group, Venice International Exhibition; Retrospective Exhibition, Agnew's Gallery, 1963. Pictures acquired for: Tate Gallery; Arts Council; Southampton Art Gallery; Ashmolean Museum, Oxford. Taught at Stafford School of Art; War service in Field Survey Bn. Royal Engineers in France; Official Lecturer, National Gallery, 1919-23; Lecturer in Art, Bristol University, Gilchrist Trust, Hermione Lecturer, Dublin, Courtauld Institute; Registrar and Lecturer in Art, Royal College of Art, London, 1923-32; Principal, Edinburgh College of Art, 1932-42; Lecturer, History of Art, Slade School, 1946-1949. *Publications:* William Rothenstein, 1923; Jacob Epstein, 1924; A. Renoir (translation); ed. with introduction, translation of the Journal of Eugène Delacroix, 1951; Art criticism in Saturday Review, Spectator, and Manchester Guardian. *Recreations:* music, travel. *Address:* The White House, North End, nr. Henley-on-Thames. [*Died* 3 *Nov.* 1967.

WELLS, Cyril Mowbray; late Assistant Master at Eton College; *b.* 21 Mar. 1871; *s.* of late William Lewis Wells. *Educ.:* Dulwich College; Trinity College, Cambridge (Scholar); Browne Medallist; 1st class Classical Tripos.

Recreations: cricket, football, fishing, entomology; Cambridge University Cricket Eleven and Football Fifteen, 1891-93; England Football Fifteen, 1892-97; Surrey County Cricket, 1892-93; Middlesex County Cricket, 1895-1909. *Address:* Northwick House, St. John's Wood Road, N.W.8. *Clubs:* East India and Sports, United University.
[*Died* 22 *Aug.* 1963.

WELLS, Sir Frederick Michael, 1st Bt., *cr.* 1948, of Hove; Kt., *cr.* 1947; *b.* 11 Mar. 1884; *s.* of Henry Francis Wells, merchant of City of London and of Essex; *m.* 1907, Catherine Davie (*d.* 1958); two *d.* *Educ.:* St. Bonaventure's Sch.; City of London Coll. Director of The Sanitas Co., Ltd., and all associated companies. Member Courts of Haberdashers' (Master, 1955-56), Carmen's and Painter-Stainers Companies, Livery of Founders' Company and Freeman of Society of Apothecaries of London. Alderman City of London since 1941. Sheriff, 1945-46; Lord Mayor of London, 1947-48. Governor, Nat. Corp. for Care of Old People; Brighton and Hove Charities Fund. *Recreation:* golf. *Address:* The Doone, Byfleet Road, Cobham, Surrey. *Clubs:* Carlton, Royal Automobile, City Livery, Eccentric.
[*Died* 13 *Sept.* 1966 (*ext.*).

WELLS, Rt. Rev. George Anderson, C.M.G. 1918; M.A.; D.D.; *b.* 1877; *s.* of W. J. Wells; *m.* Charlotte M'Donell; one *s.* three *d.* *Educ.:* Manitoba University; St. John's College, Winnipeg. Served South African War, 1901-2; European War, 1914-1918 (C.M.G.); Warden, St. John's College, Winnipeg; Bishop of Cariboo, 1934-40; Prot. Chap.-Gen., Can. Forces, 1940-45. Asst. Bp. to Bp. of Toronto, 1946-52. Formerly Exam. Chap. to Archbp. of Rupertsland, and Clerical Sec., Provincial Synod. *Address:* 4 Astley Av., Rosedale, Toronto 5.
[*Died* 10 *April* 1964.

WELLS, His Honour Henry Bensley; Judge of Marylebone County Court (Circuit 43), 1946-58, retd.; *b.* 12 Jan. 1891; *s.* of late Thomas Edward and Mary Ellen Wells; *m.* 1926, Angela Horatia Emma James, *d.* of late Edward Scott James, Chagford, Devon; two *s.* one *d.* *Educ.:* Winchester; Magdalen College, Oxford. Coxed Oxford University crew in 1911, 1912, 1913 and 1914, and Leander crew at Olympic Games, 1912; Arden Scholar, Gray's Inn, 1913; called to Bar, Gray's Inn, June 1914; 2nd Lieut. 6th London Brigade, R.F.A., in Oct. 1914; served in H.M. Forces until 1919 (M.B.E.); practised at Bar in London and on S.E. Circuit, 1920-34; Judge of County Courts, Circuit 47, 1934-46. *Address:* Hockmoor House, Buckfast, Buckfastleigh, Devon. *T.:* Buckfastleigh 2176. *Clubs:* Junior Carlton, Leander, M.C.C.
[*Died* 4 *July* 1967.

WELLS, Admiral Sir Lionel Victor, K.C.B., *cr.* 1943 (C.B. 1938); D.S.O. 1920; *b.* 28 Nov. 1884; 3rd *s.* of Thomas Wells, Moxley, Staffs; *m.* 1915, Aline Margaret, *y. d.* of Sir Hector Munro, 11th Bart. of Foulis; one *s.* *Educ.:* Stubbington House; Britannia. Entered Navy, 1901; served Persian Gulf, 1911 (medal, one clasp); European War, North Sea and Black Sea (D.S.O.); operations Asia Minor, 1920; Captain, 1924; commanded H.M.S. Diomede, 1929-31; Staff R.N. War College, 1931-33; commanded H.M.S. Eagle, 1933-35; Director Tactical School, 1935-37; A.D.C. to the King, 1935-1936; Rear-Adm. 1936; Rear-Adm. Third Cruiser Squadron, 1937-39; Vice-Adm. 1939; Vice-Adm. Aircraft-Carriers, 1939-40 (despatches twice); Flag Officer Commanding, Orkney and Shetland, 1942-44; Admiral, 1943; retired, 1944. Grand Cross Royal Norwegian Order of St. Olaf, 1945. *Recreation:* fishing. *Address:* Itchen Abbas Cottage, Winchester. *Clubs:* United Service; Hampshire.
[*Died* 22 *April* 1965.

WELLS, Percy Lawrence; M.P. (Lab). Faversham Division of Kent since 1945; J.P. Kent 1938; Govr. Girls County Grammar School, Sittingbourne; Member Central Agricultural Wages Board; *b.* 8 June 1891; *m.* 1919, Florie Lily Peet Fisher; one *d.* *Educ.:* National School, Stone, Greenhithe, Kent. Joined Royal Navy at 16 years of age. Afterwards lived in Canada, U.S.A., Pacific Islands, New Zealand and Australia. District Officer of Transport and General Workers' Union, 1919 until Aug. 1945; Parl. Private Sec. to Foreign Secretary Mr. Ernest Bevin from 1945 until his death, 1951. U.K. Alternate Delegate to Gen. Assembly, U.N.O., 1946; Council of Europe, 1951; member Commonwealth Parliamentary Assoc. Deleg. to Canada, 1952. *Recreations:* gardening, reading, motoring, carpentry. *Address:* Wandella, 4 Park Avenue, Sittingbourne, Kent. *T.A.* and *T.:* Sittingbourne 4246.
[*Died* 3 *April* 1964.

WELLS, Robert Douglas, M.A., F.R.I.B.A.; (ret.); R.B.A. 1928; architect in private practice, retired 1953; landscape painter; *b.* 1875; *s.* of Thomas Wells, 14 Manchester Sq., W.1; *m.* Madeline Rachel (*d.* 1959), *d.* of William Henn Holmes; no *c.* *Educ.:* Uppingham; Trinity Coll., Cambridge. Articled to J. J. Stephenson and Harry Redfern, F.F.R.I.B.A. Architectural Studentship at Athens, 1900-1901; designed number of houses in London and the country including Grandfalls, Newfoundland for the late Lord Northcliffe, and St. Mary's Hall, Putney; exhibitor at R.A., R.I., New English Art Club, International Society of Sculptors, Painters and Gravers, Venice International, Goupil Gallery Salon, various provincial galleries. *Recreations:* travelling and painting. *Address:* 30 Palace Gardens Terrace, Kensington, W.8.
[*Died* 28 *April* 1963.

WELMAN, Captain Arthur Eric Pole, D.S.O. 1918; D.S.C.; R.N. Emergency List; *b.* 1893; *s.* of late Colonel Arthur Pole Welman and late Lady Scott; *m.* 1st, 1920, Eileen, *d.* of late Lieutenant-Comdr. G. R. Maltby, M.V.O., and late Hersey Maltby, *d.* of late Admiral Sir George Elliot; one *s.*; 2nd, 1950, Irene, *d.* of late Vincent King, Southsea, Hants. Served European War, 1914-18; served in Destroyer Flotilla, Harwich, 1914-16; in command of Coastal Motor Boat Flotilla operating upon Belgian Coast and during Blocking Ops. against Zeebrugge and Ostend (despatches thrice, D.S.O. and bar, D.S.C., Croix de Guerre, Legion of Honour, recommended for early promotion); War of 1939-45 (bar to D.S.C.); Acting Capt. Feb. 1945. Naval Attaché Belgrade, 1945-47; reverted to Emergency List, Capt., 1949. Comdt. Metropolitan Special Constabulary, Thames Division, 1936-39. Vice-Pres., Royal Free Hospital, 1932 (Life Governor, 1929). *Address:* Twindown Mead, Middle Chinnock, Nr. Crewkerne, Somerset. *T.:* Chiselborough 221.
[*Died* 7 *March* 1966.

WELSH, James, D.L.; (Hon.) LL.D.; J.P.; *b.* Paisley, 29 Jan. 1881; *m.* 1910, Nell Greig (*d.* 1945); one *s.* *Educ.:* Board School. Lord Provost of Glasgow, 1943-45; M.P. (Lab.) Paisley, 1929-31. Ex-Pres. of Cinematograph Exhibitors' Assoc. *Recreation:* public work. *Address:* 1 Endfield Ave., Glasgow, W.2. *T.:* 041-339 5447.
[*Died* 16 *Dec.* 1969.

WELSH, Air Marshal Sir William Lawrie, K.C.B., *cr.* 1941 (C.B. 1937); D.S.C.; A.F.C.; North American Representative Society of Motor Manufacturers and Traders; *m.* 1922, Ruth Mary (marriage diss., 1947) (Dame Mary Welsh, D.B.E.), *d.* of Dr. W. R. Dalzell, Birkenhead; one *s.*; *m.* 1947, Elysabeth Carrere Barbour, *widow* of

Senator Warren Barbour, U.S.A. Surveyed and pioneered desert Air Route from Jerusalem to Baghdad, 1921. Director of Organisation Air Ministry, 1934-37; Air Member for Supply and Organisation on Air Council, 1937-40; Air Officer Commanding Technical Training Command, 1940-41; Air Officer Commanding-in-Chief, Flying Training Command, 1941-1942; commanded R.A.F. operating with Allied Forces, N.W. Africa, 1942; Head of R.A.F. Delegation, Washington, D.C., 1943-1944; retired, 1944. Officer of the Order of the Couronne, Belgium, 1918; French Croix de Guerre, 1918; Grand Officer Polonia Restituta, Poland, 1943; Commander Legion of Merit, U.S.A. *Address:* 45 High Street, Farmington, Connecticut, U.S.A. *Clubs:* United Service, M.C.C.; Racquet (New York); Metropolitan (Washington, D.C.). [*Died* 2 *Jan.* 1962.

WELSH, Brigadier William Miles Moss O'Donnell, D.S.O. 1919; M.C., R.A.; *o. s.* of late W. O'D. Welsh; *b.* 1888; *m.* 1926, Mary, *o. d.* of late Sir Walter Risley Hearn, K.B.E.; one *s.* one *d.* Served European War, 1914-19 (despatches, D.S.O., M.C.); Iraq rebellion, 1920 (despatches); Major Instructor in Gunnery (Artillery), School of Artillery, 1932-35; Commander of 42nd Anti-Aircraft Brigade, T.A., 1938; Brigade Commander, Paiforce, 1941-44; retired pay, 1945. *Address:* Lismore, Pound Lane, Sonning, Berks. *T.:* Sonning 2570. [*Died* 7 *June* 1965.

WELSTED, Col. Reginald H. P.; *see* Penrose-Welsted.

WENHAM, Sir John (Henry), Kt., *cr.* 1954; J.P., D.L.; Chairman Surrey County Council, 1953-56 (Member, 1929; Alderman 1942; Vice-Chm. 1950-53); *b.* 23 March 1891; *e. s.* of late Henry James Wenham, Witley Manor, Witley, Sy.; *m.* 1930, Maud Jane Elisabeth, M.B.E. 1966, *d.* of late Comdr. Adolf de Bahr, formerly Swedish Naval Attaché in London; one *s.* (one *d.* decd.). *Educ.:* Charterhouse; Trinity College, Cambridge. Served European War, 1914-18, in 2/1st Suffolk Yeo. J.P. 1926, D.L. 1951, for Surrey. Chm. Guildford County Bench, 1943-61; Chm. Surrey Standing Joint Cttee. (now Surrey Police Cttee.), 1947-67; County Council Representative on Thames Conservancy, 1935-; Hon. Treasurer, Guildford Conservative Association, 1925-47. Member Commn. of Inquiry Singapore Riots, 1951. *Recreations:* foreign travel, shooting, fishing and riding. *Address:* Hunts Hill, Normandy, Guildford, Surrey. *T.:* Normandy 2104. [*Died* 25 *Aug.* 1970.

WENTWORTH, Patricia; *see* Turnbull, Mrs. George.

WERTENBAKER, Thomas Jefferson; Ph.D. (Univ. Va.); M.A. (Oxon.); L.H.D. (Lehigh); Litt.D. (William and Mary, and Princeton); Edwards Prof. of Amer. History, Emeritus, Princeton Univ., since 1947; *b.* Charlottesville, Va., 6 Feb. 1879; *s.* of Charles Christian Wertenbaker and Frances Leftwich; *m.* 1916, Sarah Marshall; one *s.* *Educ.:* Univ. of Virginia. Editor Baltimore News, 1906; Associate Professor of History and Economics, Agricultural and Mechanical College of Texas, 1907-9; Instructor Univ. of Virginia, 1909-10; Princeton Univ.: Instructor, 1910-14, Preceptor, 1914-21, Assoc. Prof., 1921-25, Prof., 1925-47; Chairman Dept. of History, 1928-36. Visiting Prof. Univ. of Göttingen, 1931, Ehrenbürger, 1931; Harmsworth Professor of American History, Oxford University, 1939-40, 1944-45; Visiting Prof., Amerika-Institut der Universität München, 1950-51; Visiting Professor, Univ. of Delaware, 1952, Emory Univ., 1953; Thomas Jefferson Research Fell., Univ. of Virginia, 1954-55; John Hay Whitney Prof., Hampden-Sydney Coll., 1957-58. President American Hist. Assoc., 1947; Amer. Phil. Soc.; Amer. Antiquarian Soc.; Nat. Council for Historic Sites and Buildings; Nat. Cttee. on Folk Art in the United States. Editor New York Evening Sun, 1918-23. Member Phi Beta Kappa Phi Kappa Psi. His Majesty's Medal for Service in the Cause of Freedom. *Publications:* Patrician and Plebeian in Virginia; Virginia under the Stuarts; The Planters of Colonial Virginia; The First Americans; The Founding of American Civilization—the Middle Colonies; The Torchbearer of the Revolution; The Old South—the Founding of American Civilization; The Golden Age of Colonial Culture; Princeton, 1746-1806; The Puritan Oligarchy—the Founding of American Civilization; Father Knickerbocker Rebels; New York City during the Revolution, 1948; Give me Liberty, the Struggle for Self-government in Virginia, 1958; The Shaping of Colonial Virginia, 1958; Norfolk, Historic Southern Port. *Address:* 164 Prospect Av., Princeton, N.J., U.S.A. *T.:* WA 4-2218. [*Died April* 1966.

WERTH, Alexander; Author and journalist; *b.* St. Petersburg, 4 Feb. 1901; *m.* 1931, Freda Helen Lendrum; one *d.*; *m.* 1957, Aline B. Dawson; one *s.* *Educ.:* Glasgow Univ. M.A. (1st cl. Hons.), 1922; sub-editor, Glasgow Bulletin, 1924; reviewer, Glasgow Herald, 1923-26; assistant to Columbia University Research Council in Paris, 1927-1928; Paris Correspondent of Glasgow Herald, 1929-31; Paris Correspondent Manchester Guardian, 1931-40, and of Sunday Times, 1937-40; Diplomatic Correspondent Sunday Times, 1940-41; Sunday Times Correspondent and B.B.C. Commentator in Moscow, 1941-46; Moscow Correspondent of the Manchester Guardian, 1946-48; Paris Correspondent, New Statesman and New York Nation, 1949-53, and of New York Nation, 1957-; contributions to many other journals. Senior Simon Research Fellow, Manchester Univ., 1953-55. Visiting Prof. of Modern History, Ohio State Univ., 1957. Soviet Victory Medal. *Publications:* France in Ferment, 1934; The Destiny of France, 1937; France and Munich, 1939; The Last Days of Paris, 1940; Moscow, '41, 1942; The Twilight of France, 1933-40, 1942; Leningrad, 1944; The Year of Stalingrad, 1946; Musical Uproar in Moscow, 1949; France 1940-1955, 1956; The Strange History of Mendès-France, 1957; America in Doubt, 1959; The de Gaulle Revolution, 1960; The Khrushchev Phase, 1961; Russia at War 1941-45, 1964; de Gaulle, 1965. *Recreation:* piano. *Address:* 13 rue Herold, Paris 1. *T.:* Central 16-49; Le Bugue (Dordogne). [*Died* 5 *March* 1969.

WEST, Christopher; Operatic and Theatrical Director; *b.* 27 July 1915; *o. s.* of late Edward and Alice Elizabeth West, Weston-super-Mare; unmarried. *Educ.:* Bristol Gram. Sch.; Roy. Acad. of Dramatic Art. Early career included some time as repertory actor, producer, insurance clerk, drama organiser, tramp; six years in R.A.F.V.R. Joined Sir Barry Jackson's Company, Stratford-on-Avon, 1947, The Old Vic Co. and Shakespeare Memorial Theatre, 1949; Resident Producer, The Royal Opera, Covent Garden, 1950-59. Operatic Productions at Covent Garden include: The Fairy Queen (with Constant Lambert), Rosenkavalier (with Kleiber), The Marriage of Figaro, World Première of The Midsummer Marriage (Tippett), The Bartered Bride, The Magic Flute, Jenufa and Tristan und Isolde (the last four with Kubelik). Directed: World Première of verse play The Hidden King for Edinburgh Festival, 1957; Albert Herring for Wiesbaden Festival, 1953; Jenufa for Chicago Lyric Opera, 1959; Katya Kabanova for Empire State Music

Festival, Orfeo (Monteverdi) and The Prisoner (both with Stokowski) for New York City Opera. Don Carlos, Le Nozze di Figaro, Die Walküre and Madame Butterfly for Chicago Lyric Opera, 1960; Fidelio (with Klemperer), Covent Garden, The Trittico, The Wings of The Dove (World Première) for New York City Opera, Cosi Fan Tutte, Fidelio for Chicago Lyric Opera, 1961; Die Zauberflöte (with Klemperer) and Tristan and Isolde for Covent Garden; Louise for New York City Opera; Orfeo ed Euridice for Chicago Lyric Opera, 1962; American Première of The Long Christmas Dinner (with Hindemith conducting) for Juilliard Opera Theatre; Cincinnati Summer Opera; Ballo in Maschera for Chicago Lyric Opera; La Tosca and The Rape of Lucrece for Washington D.C. Grand opera; The Lady from Colorado, World Première for Central City, Colorado Opera; Katya Kabanova for Juilliard Opera Theater; Il Trovatore for Chicago Lyric Opera; American Premières of Elegy for Young Lovers (Henze conducting), Mines of Sulphur, Ormindo, for Juilliard Opera Theatre; The Marriage of Figaro and American Première of Capriccio for Young Lovers (Henze conducting) for Juilliard Opera Theatre; The Marriage of Figaro and Amer. Première of Capriccio for N.Y.C. Opera, 1965. Director, Juilliard Opera Theatre, Juilliard School of Music, N.Y. City. *Publications:* contrib. to theatrical and musical journals, to broadcasting and television. *Recreations:* piano, cooking, and not listening to opera. *Address:* Apt. 29-G, 185 West End Avenue, New York City 23, N.Y., U.S.A.; c/o Royal Opera House, Covent Garden, W.C.2.
[*Died* 27 *Oct.* 1967.

WEST, Sir Harold (Ernest Georges), Kt. 1948; J.P.; Comp.M.I.Mech.E.; F.B.I.M.; Mem. various University and Industrial cttees.; County Commissioner for South Yorkshire, and Member of Council of Boy Scouts Association; President Economic League (E.M. Region); Mem. Company of Cutlers in Hallamshire; Mem. Council Sheffield Chamber of Commerce; Pres. Soc. of Incorporated Secretaries (Sheffield and District); Life Mem. Court, Univ. of Leeds; *b.* 7 June 1895; *s.* of George Howard West; *m.* 1925, Winifred Mary Eagleton, St. Louis, U.S.A.; one *s.* one *d.* Served European War, 1914-16, Essex Regiment (wounded); Senior Technical Asst. to Surveyor Gen. of Supply, W.O., 1917-19. Chairman, East and West Ridings Cttees. of Business Training Scheme, 1945-48; President The Sheffield Chamber of Commerce, 1948-49; Chairman of Institute of Industrial Administration, 1950-52; Master of Cutlers Company in Hallamshire, 1952-53; Chm. Citizens of Tomorrow Working Party of King George's Jubilee Trust, 1953-55; Chm., Duke of Edinburgh Adv. Cttee., Sheffield, 1955-56, Chm., Sheffield Academic Bd. for Advanced Technology, 1955-57; Chm. Governors, Loughborough College of Technology, 1952-57. *Publications:* The Thorncliffe Experiment in Employee Relationships (Silver Medal, Royal Society of Arts, 1950); various articles on administration and industrial welfare. *Recreations:* scouting, gardening. *Address:* Muswell Lodge, Brincliffe, Sheffield 11. *T.:* Sheffield 50739. *Clubs:* Constitutional, Royal Automobile; Sheffield (Sheffield) [*Died* 8 *Nov.* 1968.

WEST, Ralph Winton, C.B.E. 1958; D.Sc. (Lond.), A.R.C.S. F.R.I.C., F.I.R.I.; Principal, Battersea College of Technology, 1947-1960; *b.* Winchester, 15 Sept. 1895; *y.s.* of late William Freshney West; *m.* 1924, Gwenneth Margaret, *er. d.* of late E. J. Walters; two *s.* one *d.* *Educ.:* Alleyn's School; Imperial College of Science and Technology. Research Asst., Trench Warfare Dept., 1916; served in France, Captain R.E., 1916-19. Senior Demonstrator in Chemistry Dept., Imperial Coll. of Science and Technology, 1919-27; Professor of Organic Chemistry and Head of Chemistry Dept., Egyptian Univ., Cairo, 1927-31; Head of Dept. of Chemistry and Rubber Technology, N. Polytechnic, 1932-47. Member of Council of Instn. of Rubber Industry, 1945-47; Senator of Univ. of London, 1952-56; Mem. Commonwealth Scholarship Commission, 1959-66. *Publications:* contrib. to scientific and technical journals. *Recreations:* gardening and bridge. *Address:* 4 Parkside Rd., Northwood, Middx. *T.:* Northwood 21619.
[*Died* 2 *Jan.* 1968.

WEST, Stewart Ellis Lawrence, C.S.I. 1947; C.I.E. 1943; O.B.E. 1918; M.Inst.T.; V.D.; Chief Transportation Supt., Rhodesia Railways, 1947-53, retd.; *b.* 2 Mar. 1890; *m.* 1918, Vera Muriel, *d.* of Anthony Van Ryneveld, J.P., of Messrs. Dempers Van Ryneveld, Cape Town, and Gertrude Berrange, Graaf Reinet, C.P.; two *s.* Joined Indian State Railways, 1909; Divisional Superintendent, Junior, N.W. Railway, 1934; Divisional Superintendent, Senior, N.W. Railway, 1937; Member Transportation, Railway Dept. (Railway Board), Govt. of India. *Address:* La Rochelle, St. James, Cape Province, S. Africa. *Clubs:* M.C.C., Free Foresters; Western Province, C.C. (Newlands, Cape).
[*Died* 31 *Jan.* 1968.

WEST, Hon. V. S.; *see* Sackville-West.

WESTALL, Bernard Clement, C.B.E. 1945; President, The De La Rue Company, since 1964; *b.* 28 Nov. 1893; *s.* of Rev. Arthur St. Leger Westall and Jessie Margaret (*née* Koe); *m.* 1919, Christine, *d.* of H. W. Rapkin; one *s.* one *d.* *Educ.:* Newbury School; Queens' College, Cambridge. B.A. 1914, M.A. 1919 (Cantab.). European War: commissioned 6th Bn. The Essex Regt., 1914; served in Gallipoli; invalided to Malta, 1915, thence to England; served 10th Bn., The Essex Regt., 1918. With Messrs. Waterlow & Sons, 1919-22; joined Thos. De La Rue & Co. Ltd., 1922; Director, 1928; Joint Managing Director, 1931-34; (sole) Managing Director, 1934-52. Chairman of Thomas De La Rue & Company Limited (subsequently The De La Rue Company Limited), 1944-63. First President of the English Bridge Union. Fellow of the British Institute of Management. *Publications:* (in collaboration with Hubert Phillips) The Book of Indoor Games, 1932; The Complete Book of Card Games, 1933. *Recreations:* bridge, golf, snooker and billiards. *Address:* 2 St. Swithun's Close, East Grinstead, Sussex. *T.:* Sharpthorne 310. *Club:* Garrick. [*Died* 18 *Jan.* 1970.

WESTBROOK, Bernard Anson, C.B.E. 1943 (O.B.E. 1929); Chief Technical Adviser, Fire Service Department, Home Office, 1939, now retired; *b.* 8 March 1884; *s.* of late Edward and Ellen Westbrook; *m.* Winifred (*decd.*), *d.* of late Louis S. and Mary A. Beale; one *d.*; *m.* 1966, Mrs. Rose Thorpe (widow). *Educ.:* Skinners' School, Tunbridge Wells. Chief Officer Calcutta Fire Bde., 1910-36; Fire Adviser, Home Office, 1936-1938; Chief Inspector, Fire Service Dept., Home Office, 1938-39; Seconded, Chief Regional Fire Officer, Midland Regional No. 9 (Birmingham), National Fire Service, 1942-1945; Past President Institution of Fire Engineers; King's Police and Fire Brigades Medal, 1918; various foreign decorations. Served with forces in Mesopotamia during European War to organise fire protection; travelled extensively studying fire protection in foreign countries. [*Died* 3 *Jan.* 1969.

WESTBURY, 4th Baron (*cr.* 1861), **Richard Morland Tollemache Bethell;** Maj. late R.E.; *b.* 9 Oct. 1914; *s.* of late Captain

Hon. Richard Bethell and Evelyn Lucia Millicent, *d.* of late Colonel George Morland Hutton, C.B.; *S.* grandfather, 1930. *Educ.:* Stowe; Trinity College, Cambridge. Served with Royal Engineers, European War. *Publication:* Gusto and Relish, 1955. *Heir: b.* Hon. David Alan Bethell, M.C. 1943, Scots Guards [A.D.C. to the Duke of Gloucester; *b.* 16 July 1922; *m.* 1947, Ursula, *er. d.* of late Hon. Robert James; one *s.* one *d.*]. *Address:* Via Ronciglione 3, Rome, Italy. [*Died* 26 *June* 1961.

WESTMINSTER, 3rd Duke of (*cr.* 1874), **William Grosvenor;** Bt. 1622; Baron Grosvenor, 1761; Earl Grosvenor and Viscount Belgrave, 1764; Marquess of Westminster, 1831; *b.* 23 Dec. 1894; *s.* of Lord Henry George Grosvenor (*d.* 1914), 3rd *s.* of 1st Duke, and Dora Mina Kittina (*d.* 1894), *d.* of James Hay Erskine Wemyss; *S.* cousin 1953. *Heir: cousin,* Gerald Hugh Grosvenor, D.S.O. [*Died* 22 *Feb.* 1963.

WESTMINSTER, 4th Duke of, *cr.* 1874; **Gerald Hugh Grosvenor,** P.C. 1964; D.S.O. 1942; Bt. 1622; Baron Grosvenor, 1761; Earl Grosvenor and Viscount Belgrave, 1764; Marquess of Westminster, 1831; Lt.-Col. (retd.), 9th Lancers; Col. 9th/12th Royal Lancers, since 1961; Hon. Col. Cheshire Yeomanry; Lord Steward of the Queen's Household since 1964; *b.* 13 February 1907; *s.* of Captain Lord Hugh William Grosvenor, 1st Life Guards (killed in action, 1914), and Lady Mabel Florence Mary Crichton, M.B.E. (*d.* 1944); *S.* cousin, 1963; *m.* 1945, Sally, (twin) *d.* of late George Perry. *Educ.:* Eton; Royal Military College, Sandhurst. Joined 9th Lancers, 1926; Lieut.-Col., 1942. Served War of 1939-45 (D.S.O.). Exon, Queen's Bodyguard, Yeomen of the Guard, 1952-64; Hon. Col. Cheshire Yeomanry, 1955. D.L., 1957, High Sheriff, 1959, Cheshire. *Heir: b.*, Lt.-Col. Lord Robert (George) Grosvenor, T.D. *Address:* Saighton Grange, Chester. *T.:* Chester 35070. *Clubs:* Cavalry, Buck's, M.C.C., Jockey. [*Died* 25 *Feb.* 1967.

WESTON, Captain Arthur Fullam, C.M.G. 1919; R.N. retired; *b.* 21 April 1879; *s.* of Major Alfred Weston, late 5th Lancers; *m.* 1910, Elizabeth, *d.* of Captain John Irving, Victoria, British Columbia; one *d.* *Educ.:* St. George's College, Weybridge. Served 10th Cruiser Squadron; sec. to Senior Naval Officer, Liverpool, and Base Officer 10th Cruiser Squadron; retired list, 1934. *Address:* Randalls, 111 Sussex Rd., Petersfield. *T.:* Petersfield 1007. [*Died* 10 *Jan.* 1962.

WESTON, Sir Arthur (Reginald) Astley, Kt. 1956; C.B.E. 1948; retired, 1957, as Legal Adviser and Solicitor to the Ministry of Agriculture, Fisheries and Food, The Commissioners of Crown Lands, The Tithe Redemption Commission and the Forestry Commissioners; *b.* 27 July 1892; *er. s.* of late A. S. Astley Weston, Bristol; *m.* 1921, Margaret Ethelwyn Gibbs (*d.* 1958), Worcester; three *s.* *Educ.:* Dean Close Sch., Cheltenham. Served European War, 1915-19, in France, Italy and Germany (despatches); attached 14th Brigade, Royal Horse Artillery; Captain (R.F.A.), and Adjutant. Entered Ministry of Agriculture and Fisheries, 1921; Legal Adviser, 1949. *Address:* at St. Ebbe's Rectory, Oxford. [*Died* 18 *Oct.* 1969.

WESTON, Hon. Brig. John Leslie, C.B.E. 1940; D.S.O. 1917; late R.A.S.C.; *b.* Leslie Court, Barnwood, 28 January 1882; *s.* of John and Margaret Louisa Weston; *m.* 1st, 1908, Eila Esther (*d.* 1944), *d.* of late D. Lynch, Q.C., Dublin; two *d.*; 2nd, 1944, Lady Betty Butler, *yr. d.* of 7th Earl of Lanesborough. *Educ.:* Clifton College. 5th R. Dublin Fus., 1900-1; 1st R. Inniskilling Fusiliers, 1901-5; Army Service Corps since 1905; served S. African War 1900-2, with 5th R. Dublin Fusiliers and 1st R. Inniskilling Fusiliers (despatches; Queen's medal 3 clasps, King's medal 2 clasps); European War, in France, on Staff 51st (Highland) Division (despatches thrice, D.S.O., Bt. Lt.-Col.); comd. Razani line, Waziristan, 1927; Assistant Director of Supplies and Transport, Southern Command, 1931-33; Brigadier in charge of Administration, Scottish Command, 1933-37; retired pay, 1937; comd., Scottish Border Zone, Home Guard, 1941. *Recreations:* golf and shooting. *Address:* Gifford Bank, Gifford, E. Lothian. *T.:* Gifford 226. *Club:* New (Edinburgh). [*Died* 21 *June* 1963.

WESTWOOD, John David, C.I.E. 1941; V.D.; *b.* 1881; *s.* of late David Westwood, of Valparaiso, Chile; *m.* 1909, Anne McDougall, *d.* of Rev. George Paulin, Muckhart, Perthshire; two *s.* *Educ.:* Dollar Academy; Edinburgh University. After qualification in law, joined Bengal and North-Western Railway in India in 1906; Traffic Manager, 1926-36; Agent and General Manager, 1936-1941; Hon. A.D.C. to Governor of U.P. 1937-40; Transport Adviser to Govt. United Provinces, 1943-44. *Recreation:* golf. *Address:* Lochgreen, Kilmacolm, Renfrewshire. [*Died* 29 *Aug.* 1964.

WETHEY, Capt. Edwin Howard, C.B.E. 1943 (O.B.E. 1918); R.N., retired; *b.* 29 Sept. 1887; *s.* of H. G. Wethey, Clifton; *m.* 1st, 1914, Dorothy Blanche Moore, *d.* of T. F. Cottam, Solicitor, Cheltenham; one *s.* two *d.*; 2nd, 1942, Margaret Isobel Dorothy, *d.* of Lt.-Col. E. W. Skinner, O.B.E., Rye. *Educ.:* Clifton College. Entered Royal Navy, 1905; European War, 1914-19; Naval Mission to Greece, 1919-22; League of Nations, 1927-29; Squadron Supply Officer Med. Fleet in Italo-Abyssinian War, 1935-36; Captain (S) 1937; H.M.S. Caledonia, 1937-38; Fleet Supply Officer, China and Far East, 1938-42; Command Supply Officer, Portsmouth, 1942-43; H.M.S. Excellent, 1943-47. High Sheriff, Sussex, 1953-54. *Recreations:* cricket, tennis, travel. *Address:* Mountsfield, Rye, Sussex. *T.:* Rye 2164. *Club:* Naval and Military. [*Died* 20 *Dec.* 1963.

WEYGAND, Général Maxime; Grand Croix de la Légion d'Honneur, 1924; Médaille Militaire, 1932; Membre de l'Académie française; *b.* 21 January 1867; *m.* 1900, Renée de Forsanz; two *s.* *Educ.:* École spéciale militaire. Officier de Cavalerie; Instructeur à l'École de Cavalerie; Chef d'État-Major du Maréchal Foch, 1914-1923; Haut Commissaire en Syrie, 1923-24; Chef de l'État-Major Général de l'Armée; Commandant en chef de l'Armée française, 1931-35; Commander of French Forces in Near East; Chief of General Staff of National Defence and Commander-in-Chief, French Army, 1940; Minister of National Defence, France, 1940; Governor-General of Algeria and Delegate-General of Vichy Government in French Africa, 1941; Prisoner of the Gestapo in Germany, 1942-45, prisoner in France, 1945-46. Hon. C.B. (U.K.), 1914; Hon. G.C.M.G. (U.K.), 1918; Grand Cross, Virtuti Militari (Poland), 1920. *Publications:* Turenne; Le 11 Novembre; Histoire militaire de Mehemet Ali; Le Général Frère; Histoire de l'armée française; Foch, 1947; Forces de la France, 1948; Trois tomes de Mémoires: I Idéal Vécu, II Mirages et Réalité, III Rappelé au service (Eng. trans.: Recalled to Service); L'Arc de Triomphe, 1960. *Address:* 22 Avenue de Friedland, Paris 8e. [*Died* 28 *Jan.* 1965.

WHARTON, 9th Baron (called out of abeyance, 1916); **Charles John Halswell Kemeys-Tynte;** *b.* 12 Jan. 1908; *s.* of 8th Baron and Dorothy (*d.* 1944), *y. d.* of late Maj.-Gen. Sir Arthur Edward Augustus Ellis,

G.C.V.O., C.S.I.; *S.* father 1934; *m.* 1967, Joanna, *o. d.* of Walter Henry Law-Smith, Adelaide, S. Australia, and *widow* of 6th Baron Tredegar. *Educ.:* Christ Church, Oxford. Served War of 1939-45. Flight Lieutenant, R.A.F.V.R. *Heir: sister,* Hon. Elizabeth Dorothy [*b.* 1906; *m.* 1st, 1933, David George Arbuthnot (marriage dissolved, 1946]; two *d.*; 2nd, 1946, St. John Vintcent (marriage dissolved, 1958). *Club:* Travellers'. [*Died* 11 *July* 1969.

WHATLEY, Norman, M.A.; *b.* 8 September 1884; third *s.* of late A. T. Whatley, B.C.L., M.A., solicitor; *m.* 1914, Norah Radley, *o. d.* of late A. C. M. Croome; one *s.* (and two *s.* killed in action). *Educ.:* Radley; Hertford College, Oxford; British School at Athens; 1st Cl. Mods.; 1st Class Lit. Hum. Editor of The Isis, 1904-1905. Fellow (1907-23), Tutor and Lecturer (1908-23) and Dean (1912-20), of Hertford College; Member of the Hebdomadal Council, 1920-23; Delegate of the Oxford University Press, 1919-23; Councillor, City of Oxford, 1919-22 and 1944-55; Alderman, 1955-61; Headmaster of Clifton Coll., 1923-1939. Mem. Bristol Univ. Council, 1934-39; Mayor of Oxford, 1949-50; Chm. Southern Regional Council for Further Educn., 1953; Chm. Oxfordshire Playing Fields Association, 1945-54; Chairman, City of Oxford Educ. Cttee., 1946-49 and 1952-54. On the Unattached List Territorial Forces; serving with the Oxford University O.T.C. (1909-19); Captain, 1911; served with B.E.F., France. in the Intelligence Corps; Brevet Major, 1919. *Address:* 10 Staverton Road, Oxford. *T.:* Oxford 58708. [*Died* 1 *April* 1965.

WHATMOUGH, Joshua, M.A. (Manc., Cantab.), Hon. A.M. (Harv.) 1942; Hon. Litt.D. (Ire.) 1959; Professor of Comparative Philology, Harvard Univ., 1926-1963; after retirement lectured at Grinnell Coll.; *b.* 30 June 1897; *s.* of late Walter Whatmough, iron-moulder, and Elizabeth Hollows, woollen weaver, Rochdale; *m.* 1930, G. Verona, Barrister-at-Law (author: Annotations on Revised Statutes of Ontario; Canadian Notary), 2nd *d.* of late W. J. Taylor, Toronto; one *s.* one *d.* *Educ.:* public elementary and secondary schools, Rochdale; Manchester University, 1st Cl. Hons. in Classics (Entrance Scholar, Bishop Fraser Scholar, Classical Prose Prizeman, Graduate Scholar, Faulkner Fellow); Emmanuel College, Cambridge (Exhibitioner); Research Student of the University (Craven Award). Lecturer in Classics, Univ. Coll. of N. Wales, 1921-25; Prof. of Latin, Egyptian Univ., Cairo, 1925-1926. Proctor, Harvard, 1927-30; Special Lecturer in Comparative Philology, Univ. of Chicago, 1930 and 1948; Collitz Prof. of Indo-European, Linguistic Inst., 1949; Sather Prof. of Classical Literature, University of Calif., 1955; Lecturer, Lowell Inst., Boston, 1957. Formerly (1929-37) Fellow (and 1935-36, Editor of Publications) American Acad. of Arts and Sciences; Member of Advisory Council, Yenching University, Peiping, 1932-39; Comitato per l'Etruria; sometime member Council Classical Assoc. of England and Wales; Perm. Internat. Com. Linguists, 1950 (delegate to Unesco Phil. and Hist. Council, 1952, 1957 1959); Visiting Cttee. on Mod. Langs., Mass. Inst. Techn., 1947-50; Vice-Pres. and Executive Cttee. member, Linguistic Circle of N.Y., 1947; Pres., Linguistic Society of America, 1951; Cttee. on Dialectology, Brussels, 1953. Originator of Theory of Selective Variation in Language, 1951 and of instruction in Mathematical Linguistics, 1955; Founder, Dept. of Linguistics, Harvard. U.S. representative, Council Indogermanische Gesellschaft, Bern; Comitato Direttive, Instituto per Lingua Messapica. Recipient of Studies Presented on 60th birthday, 1957; World-wide lecture tour, 1958. President 9th International Congress of Linguists, 1961. Hon. Phi Beta Kappa. *Publications:* The Liber Glossarum, 1926 (with W. M. Lindsay and others); Scholia Vallicelliana, 1926; articles on Philology and Linguistics, and editorial adviser, Ency. Brit., 1955-; Venture (Karachi), 1959-; on Italic Religion, Iguvine Tables in Oxford Classical Dictionary, 1949; on Italic Dialects in Dictionary of Languages, 1947; on Etruria in Chambers's Encyclopædia, 1950; on letters of the alphabet, Ency. Americana, 1948; Grolier Enc., 1961; on Iberian, etc. Collier's Enc., 1959; The Prae-Italic Dialects of Italy, 1933; The Foundations of Roman Italy, 1937; Keltika, 1944; Dialects of Ancient Gaul, 1949-51; Language, 1955 (Japanese trans., Tokyo, 1960); Poetic Scientific and Other Forms of Discourse, 1956; Language: the Measure of Man, 1962. Articles and reviews in Classical, etc., jls. of England, Denmark, France, Switzerland, Canada, U.S.A., etc. Editor (1931-34; 1941-1948) Harvard Studies in Class. Philol.; Jt. Editor, Berichte zur Runenforschung, 1939-1941; Associate Editor, Class. Philol. (Chicago), 1945-48; Word (N.Y.), 1947-49; Bibliog. of Statistical Linguistics, 1954; Editor, Trends in European and American Linguistics, 1930-60, 1961. *Recreations:* walking, climbing. *Address:* 17 Central Street, Winchester, Mass., U.S.A. *T.:* Parkview 9-1945. *Club:* Faculty (Cambridge, Mass.). [*Died* 25 *April* 1964.

WHEATLEY, Edith Grace, R.P. 1954; R.W.S. 1952 (A.R.W.S.); R.B.A.; R.G.I.; R.W.E.A.; Painter and Sculptor; *b.* London; 4th *d.* of James Wolfe; *m.* 1912, Prof. John Wheatley (*d.* 1955); one *d.* *Educ.:* privately. Studied Art at the Slade and in Paris; has works in the British Museum and at the Tate Gallery; Exhibitor at Royal Academy; works bought for many important collections and by Canada and S. Africa; for ten years Lecturer in Painting and Sculpture, University of Cape Town. *Recreations:* reading and writing. *Address:* 57 Cadogan Place, S.W.1. *T.:* 01-235 6864; Thakeham, Nr. Pulborough, Sussex. *T.:* West Chiltington 2330. [*Died* 28 *Nov.* 1970.

WHEELER, Sir Arthur F. P., 2nd Bt., *cr.* 1920; *b.* 10 Dec. 1900; *e. s.* of Sir Arthur Wheeler, 1st Bt.; *S.* father 1943; *m.* 1938, Alice Webster Stones. *Educ.:* Charterhouse. *Heir:* *b.* John Hieron, *b.* 22 July 1905. *Address:* Greenhill, Ulverscroft, nr. Markfield, Leics. *T.:* Woodhouse Eaves 209. *Club:* Junior Carlton. [*Died* 16 *Dec.* 1964.

WHEELER, Rear-Admiral (retd.) Aubrey John, C.B. 1949; D.L.; J.P.; *b.* 22 Oct. 1894; *s.* of late H. Wheeler, Grantham, Lincs; *m.* 1919, Edith A., *d.* of late J. Rear, Harlaxton, Grantham; one *s.* one *d.* *Educ.:* King's School, Grantham. Entered R.N. as Asst. Clerk, R.N., 1912; Capt. (S), 1943; Actg. Rear-Adm. (S), 1948; Barrister-at-Law, Gray's Inn, 1925. Served in East Indies, Dardanelles and Grand Fleet during European War, 1914-18; Comdr. (S) H.M.S. Prince of Wales, 1940-41; Fleet Supply Officer, East Indies Fleet, 1945; Deputy Judge-Advocate of the Fleet, 1946-1948; Command Supply Officer, Portsmouth, 1948-50; retired list, 1950. J.P. (Hants.), 1952; D.L., Hampshire, 1958. *Recreations:* golf, sailing. *Address:* Southfields, Beach Rd., Emsworth, Hants. *T.:* Emsworth 2007. *Clubs:* Emsworth Sailing; Royal Naval (Portsmouth). [*Died* 16 *March* 1970.

WHEELER, Brig. Sir (Edward) Oliver, Kt., *cr.* 1943; M.C.; *b.* Ottawa, Canada, 18 April 1890; *s.* of Arthur Oliver Wheeler, Dominion Land Surveyor, and Clara, *d.* of Prof. John Macoun; *m.* 1921, Dorothea Sophie Danielsen, Edgbaston, Birmingham; one *s.* *Educ.:* Trinity College

School, Port Hope, Canada; Royal Military College, Kingston, Canada. 2nd Lt. R.E. 1910; with 1st K.G.O. Sappers and Miners in France, 1914-15, Mesopotamia and India, 1916-18; thereafter on General Staff, Brigade Major (despatches 7 times, M.C., Legion of Honour 5th Class); demobilised and joined Survey of India, 1919; First Mount Everest Expedition, 1921; Director, Survey of India, 1938; Surveyor-General of India, 1941; retired, 1947. *Publications:* technical departmental and articles in Canadian Alpine Journal, etc. *Recreations:* mountaineering, fishing, shooting. *Address:* R.R.2, Vernon, B.C. *Clubs:* Alpine; Alpine of Canada (Pres. 1950-54); American Alpine.
[*Died* 19 *March* 1962.

WHEELER, Dame Olive Annie, D.B.E., *cr.* 1950; Professor Emeritus, University of Wales, 1951; *y. d.* of H. Burford Wheeler, Brecon; unmarried. *Educ.:* Aberystwyth University College; Bedford College, London; University of Paris. M.Sc. and former Fellow of the Univ. of Wales; D.Sc. (Psychology) Univ. of London. Lecturer in Mental and Moral Science, Cheltenham Ladies' College; Lecturer in Education and Dean of the Faculty of Education, Univ. of Manchester; Prof. of Education and Dean of Faculty of Educ., Univ. Coll., Cardiff, 1925-51. Warden, Univ. of Wales Guild of Graduates, 1947-50; contested Univ. of Wales, Parliamentary seat (1922 election). F.B.Ps.S. Member of: Welsh Joint Education Committee; Court and Appointments Board of University of Wales; Council Welsh National School of Medicine; General Advisory Council of the B.B.C. Chairman of South Wales District W.E.A. *Publications:* Anthropomorphism and Science, 1916; The Mind of the Child (Part II. of Nursery School Education, edited by G. Owen), 1920, 1923, and 1928; Bergson and Education, 1922; Youth: The Psychology of Adolescence and its Bearing on the Reorganisation of Adolescent Education, 1929 and 1933; Creative Education and the Future, 1936; Part I of Nursery School Education and the Reorganisation of the Infant School, 1939; The Adventure of Youth, 1945, 1946, and 1950; Part III of Mental Health and Education, 1961. Papers in psychological and educational jls., etc. *Recreation:* golf. *Address:* Woodlands, Bettws-y-coed Road, Cyncoed, Cardiff
[*Died* 26 *Sept.* 1963.

WHEELER, Brig. Sir Oliver; *see* Wheeler, Brig. Sir E. O.

WHEELER, Thomas Sherlock, D.Sc. (N.U.I.); Ph.D. (Lond.); F.R.C.Sc.I.; F.I.C.I; F.R.I.C.; F.Inst.P.; M.I.Chem.E.; M.R.I.A.; Professor (Head of Department) of Chemistry; University College (N.U.I.), Dublin, since 1945; Member Senate, N.U.I.; Member Governing Body and Dean of Faculty of Science, University College, Dublin; Member Governing Boards, Schools of Cosmic and Theoretical Physics, Dublin Inst. for Advanced Studies; Director Irish Peat, Chem. and Industrial Research and Standards Bds.; Mem. Council Roy. Dublin Soc. and Roy. Irish Acad; Mem. Irish Nat. Commission for U.N.E.S.C.O.; Sometime Member for the Republic of Ireland on the O.E.E.C. Technical and Scientific Manpower Cttee.; Chm., Organising Cttee., Dublin (1957) Meeting of the British Assoc. for the Advancement of Science; sometime a Vice-President Royal Inst. of Chemistry; Past-Pres. Irish Chem. Association; sometime Fellow, and Dean of the Faculty of Science, University of Bombay; Foundation Fellow (sometime a Vice-President) National Institute of Sciences of India; *b.* Dublin, 30 April 1899; *e. s.* of late M. R. Wheeler, M.A.; *m.* 1926, Una, 3rd *d.* of late John Sherlock, B.A.; one *s.* two *d.* *Educ.:* Royal College of Science, Dublin; London University. Demonstrator in Chemistry, Royal Technical College, Glasgow, 1920-21; Research Chemist, Royal Naval Cordite Factory, Holton Heath, and Research Department, Royal Arsenal, 1921-28; Research Chemist with Imperial Chemical Industries, Northwich, 1928-31; Principal and Professor of Organic Chemistry, Royal Institute of Science, Bombay, 1931-39; State Chemist, Republic of Ireland, 1939-45. *Publications:* chemical research papers, books and patents. *Recreation:* golf. *Address:* Science Blds., Upper Merrion St., Dublin. *T.:* 61584.
[*Died* 13 *Dec.* 1962.

WHELDON, Sir Wynn Powell, K.B.E., *cr.* 1952; Kt., *cr.* 1939; D.S.O. 1917; LL.D. (Hon.) Wales; Member of Council Honourable Society of Cymmrodorion; Chairman: Festival of Britain 1951 Welsh Cttee.; Court and Council of University of Wales; University College of North Wales; and the Council of Social Service (Wales); *s.* of late Rev. T. J. Wheldon, Bangor, and Mary Elinor Powell; *m.* 1915, Megan Edwards of Canonbury, Prestatyn, *d.* of Hugh Edwards, London; two *s.* two *d.* *Educ.:* Friars School, Bangor; Oswestry High School; U.C.N.W.; St. John's College, Cambridge, M.A., LL.B. Solicitor, 1905; in practice at 63 Queen Victoria Street, E.C.; enlisted Inns of Court O.T.C. Sept. 1914, and gazetted to 14th R.W.F. in Dec. 1914; served in France with that Battalion Dec. 1915-Nov. 1918, and as 2nd in command July 1916 (D.S.O.); Secretary and Registrar of the University College of North Wales, Bangor, 1920-33; Permanent Secretary, Welsh Dept., Bd. of Educn., 1933-45. Chairman Welsh Church Commission, 1945-47. *Address:* Canonbury, Prestatyn, N. Wales. *T.:* 591.
[*Died* 10 *Nov.* 1961.

WHIDDINGTON, Richard, C.B.E. 1946; F.R.S. 1925; M.A. (Camb.); D.Sc. (Lond.); Emeritus Professor since 1951; Cavendish Professor of Physics, University of Leeds, 1919-Sept. 1951; Pro Vice-Chancellor, 1949-51; *b.* London, 25 November 1885; *s.* of late Richard Whiddington and Ada, *d.* of late Richard FitzGerald; *m.* 1919, Katherine Reoch Grant; one *s.* one *d.* *Educ.:* William Ellis School, London; St. John's College, Cambridge (Scholar). Natural Sciences Tripos I and II, 1907 and 1908; Hutchinson Student, 1909; Allen Scholar, 1910; Fellow of St. John's College, 1911-19; Assistant Demonstrator in Cavendish Laboratory, 1909-14; a Supervisor of Natural Sciences, St. John's College, 1912-14. European War, 1914-19, Radio Telegraphy and Telephony Research and Design for Air Services at R.A.E. Farnborough and later as Experimental Officer (Capt. R.F.C.; Major R.A.F.). Hon. Editor Leeds Philosophical and Literary Society Proceedings, 1925-48. In War of 1939-45; Joint Recruiting Board, Univ. of Leeds (Hon. Wing Cdr. R.A.F.V.R.), 1939-40; with Dept. of Scientific Research, Admiralty, London, 1940-42; Deputy Director Scientific Research, Ministry of Supply, London, 1942-1945. Pres. Physical Soc. 1952-54. Scientific Adv. to Central Treaty Organization, 1959-62. *Publications:* numerous papers in scientific journals mainly on electron physics and discharge tubes; (jointly) Science at War. *Recreations:* country and sailing. *Address:* Holme next the Sea, by King's Lynn. *T.:* Holme 225. *Club:* Athenæum.
[*Died* 7 *June* 1970.

WHIPPLE, Dorothy; *m.* A. H. Whipple; no *c.* *Educ.:* English and French Convents. *Publications:* *novels:* Young Anne, 1927; High Wages, 1930; Greenbanks, 1932; They Knew Mr. Knight, 1934 (filmed, 1945); The Priory, 1938; They Were Sisters, 1943 (filmed, 1945); Every Good Deed, 1946; Because of the Lockwoods, 1949; Someone at a Distance, 1953; *autobiography:* The

Other Day, 1936; Random Commentary, 1965; *short stories:* On Approval, 1935; After Tea, 1941; Wednesday, 1961; *for children:* Tale of a Very Little Tortoise, 1962; The Smallest Tortoise of all, 1964; The Little Hedgehog, 1964. *Recreations:* gardening, walking, cooking. *Address:* 3 Whinfield Place, Blackburn, Lancs. *T.:* Blackburn 57201. [*Died* 14 *Sept.* 1966.

WHISTLER, General Sir Lashmer (Gordon), G.C.B. 1957 (K.C.B. 1955; C.B. 1945); K.B.E. 1952; D.S.O. 1940; D.L.; retd.; Col., The Royal Sussex Regt.; Chairman, Army Cadet Force Association, since 1961; Hon. Col. Royal Nigerian Military Forces, 1959; Hon. Col. Royal Sierra Leone Military Forces, 1959; Vice-President, National Small Bore Rifle Assoc. (N.S.R.A.), since 1958; *b.* 3 Sept. 1898; *s.* of Colonel A. E. Whistler, Indian Army and Florence Annie Gordon, *d.* of late Charles Forbes Rivett-Carnac; *m.* 1926, Esmé Keighley; two *d.* *Educ.:* Harrow; R.M.C. Sandhurst. 2nd Lt. Royal Sussex Regt. 1917; Capt. 1932; Major, 1938; Temp. Lt.-Col. 1940; Temp. Brig. 1942; Lt.-Col. 1945; Acting Maj.-Gen., 1944; Temp. Maj.-Gen., 1945; Col. 1946; Maj.-Gen., 1946; Lt.-Gen., 1951; General, 1955. Served European War, 1917-18 (wounded); Palestine, 1937-38; War of 1939-45 (despatches, D.S.O. and two Bars, C.B.); Palestine, 1945-46; Maj.-Gen. British Troops in India, 1947-48; Maj.-Gen. Commanding Troops Sudan, Kaid Sudan Defence Force, 1948-50; Commander, Northumbrian District and a T.A. Division, 1950-51; G.O.C.-in-C., West Africa Command, 1951-53; G.O.C.-in-C., Western Command, Dec. 1953; retired Feb. 1957; Chairman Cttee. on the New Army, Dec. 1957-May 1958. D.L. Sussex, 1957. Comdr. of the Crown of Belgium 2nd class, with palm; Belgian Croix de Guerre, 1940, with palm; Grand Cross, House of Orange. *Address:* Fairlawn, Petersfield, Hants. *T.:* Petersfield 516. *Club:* Naval and Military. [*Died* 4 *July* 1963.

WHITAKER, Sir Arthur; *see* Whitaker, Sir F. A.

WHITAKER, Frank; F.R.S.L.; F.J.I.; Editorial Director of Country Life publications, 1941-59; *b.* Keighley, Yorks; 3rd *s.* of William Henry Whitaker; *m.* 1919, Hilda, *o. d.* of F. W. Thornton, M.R.C.S., L.R.C.P., Huddersfield; one *s.* two *d.* Formerly on editorial staffs of Sheffield Daily Telegraph, Huddersfield Examiner, Daily News, Liverpool Daily Post, Daily Mail, Star, Evening Standard (literary editor); acting editor John O' London's Weekly, 1928-36, editor, 1936-41; editor P.T.O. 1939-40; editor British Trade and Industry, 1942 and 1945 (for export only); editor Country Life, 1940-58. J.P. (Kent), 1950-54. Member Stationers' Company; Conductor, Beckenham Choral Society, 1926-33; Bromley Home Guard Choir, 1945-51. Capt., Addington G.C., 1954-55, Press Golfing Soc., 1938; Langley Park G.C., 1932. *Publications:* Saturday to Monday (with W. T. Williams), 1938; Good and Bad English (with W. Whitten), 1939; edited The Joy of London (essays by W. Whitten), 1943. *Recreations:* music, golf. *Address:* 21 Court Downs Road, Beckenham, Kent. *T.:* Beckenham 2373. *Club:* Reform. [*Died* 17 *Feb.* 1962.

WHITAKER, Sir (Frederick) Arthur, K.C.B., *cr.* 1945 (C.B. 1941); M.Inst.C.E.; *b.* 17 July 1893; *s.* of William Henry Whitaker and Georgina Primrose Foggo; *m.* 1923, Florence, *d.* of John Woods Overend, Liverpool; one *s.* two *d.* *Educ.:* Liverpool Institute High School; Liverpool University. B.Eng. Liverpool with 1st Class Honours, 1914; M.Eng (Liverpool) 1917; joined Civil Engineer-in-Chief's Department in 1915 and served at Rosyth, Port Edgar, Jamaica, Devonport, Malta, Portsmouth and Singapore; Deputy Civil Engineer-in-Chief, Admiralty, 1934; Civil Engineer-in-Chief, Admiralty, 1940-54; Partner, Messrs. Livesey & Henderson, Consulting Engineers, 1954-62. President Inst. C.E. 1957; Mem. Internat. Cons. Cttee. of Suez Canal, 1952. Commander, Legion of Honour, 1947. *Address:* 8 Grosvenor Road, Northwood, Middlesex. [*Died* 13 *June* 1968.

WHITAMORE, Charles Eric, O.B.E. 1941; *b.* Madras, India, 17 Nov. 1890; *s.* of Rev. T. H. Whitamore; *m.* 1921, Virginia, *d.* of J. P. Cook, San Francisco, California; one *s.* *Educ.:* Tonbridge School; France and Germany. Entered H.M. Consular Service in China, 1913; Vice-Consul at Shanghai, Hankow, Canton; Called to Bar, 1931; Consul at Canton, Tsinan; Acting Consul-General at Hankow and Mukden; Consul-General at Kweilin, Chungking; Consul-General, Boston, U.S.A.; retired from H.M. Foreign Service, 1951. *Recreations:* reading, riding, tennis, golf. *Club:* Somerset (Boston, U.S.A.). [*Died* 15 *March* 1965.

WHITBURGH, 1st Baron (*cr.* 1912); **Thomas Banks Borthwick,** Bt., *cr.* 1908; of firm of Thomas Borthwick & Sons Limited, colonial merchants; *b.* 21 Aug. 1874; *s.* of Sir Thomas Borthwick (who was created Baron, but died before patent could be made out) and Letitia Mary (*d.* 1935), *d.* of Thomas Banks, West Derby, Liverpool. *Heir:* (to Baronetcy only) *n.* John Thomas Borthwick (Sir J. T. Borthwick, Bt., M.B.E.) [*b.* 5 Dec. 1917; *m.* 1st, 1939, Irene (marr. diss., 1961), *o. c.* of Joseph Heller; three *s.*; 2nd, 1962, Irene, *d.* of Leo Fink; two *s.*]. *Address:* Whitburgh, Ford, Midlothian. *Club:* Reform. [*Died* 29 *Sept.* 1967 (*barony ext.*).

WHITE, Sir (Alfred Edward) Rowden, Kt. 1961; C.M.G. 1953; M.D., F.R.A.C.P.; Consulting Physician, Australia; Hon. Consultant, St. Vincent's Royal Children and Foundling Hosps.; Chief M.O. to Colonial Mutual Life Assurance Soc.; Mem. War Pensions Assessment Appeal Tribunal; Final Med. Refereee Military Bd.; *b.* 5 Nov. 1876; *s.* of J. and Elizabeth White; unmarried. *Educ.:* Carlton Coll. and Univ. of Melbourne; post-grad. work abroad. Sen. R.M.O., Children's and Alfred Hosps., Melb.: Demr. in Bacteriology, Univ. of Melb. (9 mths.); then priv. practice with Sir Richard Stawell (6 yrs.); Sen. Hon. Phys., Children's Hosp., also St. Vincent's Hosp., Melb. (Med. Tutor, Clin. Instr., Lectr. to students); for periods: Dean of Clin. Sch., St. Vincent's Hosp., also Mem. Faculty of Med., Examr. in Med. for final M.B. (later M.D.), Mem. Standing Cttee. of Convocation, Univ. of Melb. After 34½ years retd., 1942, from active staff of St. Vincent's Hosp. (having been recalled 2 yrs. for Nat. Emergency reasons). Mem. Melb. Permanent Post-Grad. Cttee. from its inception, 1920, until 1940. Council (Emer.) Victorian Br. of B.M.A. (previously Asst. Sec. and Hon. Sec.); a Founder, then Councillor, Assoc. of Physicians of Aust. from its inception until it was absorbed by R.A.C.P., 1937; Councillor, R.A.C.P., until 1951, Vice-Pres., 1943-46. Australian Expedny. Forces (Boulogne, etc.), Med. Specialist, 2½ yrs., latterly Physician-Consultant with rank of Major. Benefactions (sometimes as memorials) totalling over £20,000 have been made to universities, colleges, hospitals, etc., also for the theatre, art, libraries, and for research; over £30,000 (including benefaction of £2000 a year for the A. E. Rowden White and Edward R. White Foundation for Medical Research in the Art and Science of Obstetrics and Gynæcology at Royal Women's Hosp., Melb.) to University of Melbourne; £1100 to

"Como" National Trust. F.A.M.S. 1958; Hon. LL.D. Melb. 1962. *Publications:* contrib. to med. jls. *Recreation:* formerly tennis. *Address:* Altadore, 24 Balmerino Avenue, Toorak, Vic., Australia. *Clubs:* Melbourne (Melb.); Royal Automobile of Victoria; (Life Mem.) Roy. S. Yarra Lawn Tennis, Lawn Tennis Assoc. of Vic.
[*Died* 15 *Jan.* 1963.

WHITE, Ven. Archdeacon Arthur, M.A.; Archdeacon Emeritus, 1959 (Archdeacon of Warrington 1947-58); Vicar of Billinge, Lancs, 1935-50; *b.* 17 Jan. 1880; *s.* of Joseph and Emma White; *m.* 1st, 1909, Elizabeth Herringshaw; one *s.* killed in action, 1942) one *d.*; 2nd, 1955, Dora (*née* Jones). *Educ.:* Deytheur Grammar School, Oswestry; Ystrad Meurig Sch., Cardiganshire; St. David's Coll., Lampeter; Oxford University. Deacon, 1904; priest, 1905; Curate of Holy Trinity, Ashton-in-Makerfield, 1904-1906 and 1909-16; Holy Trinity, Headington Quarry, 1906-9; Vicar of St. James, Wigan, 1916-23; Rector of Golborne, 1923-35; Rural Dean of Winwick, 1930-34; Canon Diocesan of Liverpool Cathedral, 1934; Rural Dean of Wigan, 1946-47. *Address:* 49 Upholland Road, Billinge, Wigan, Lancs. *T.:* Billinge 241. [*Died* 20 *Aug.* 1961.

WHITE, Sir Bernard Kerr, K.B.E., *cr.* 1949; *b.* 15 Dec. 1888; *s.* of late Sir Richard White; *m.* 1914, Madeleine Elisabeth, *er. d.* of late Frederick William Kerr; one *s.* one *d.* *Educ.:* Charterhouse; Pembroke College, Cambridge (B.A.). Called to Bar, Lincoln's Inn, 1913; Asst. Registrar of Friendly Societies, 1926; Dep. Industrial Assurance Commissioner, 1937; Chief Registrar of Friendly Societies and Industrial Assurance Commissioner, 1947-54; Chairman, Leek and Moorlands Building Society, 1962-. *Address:* Norman House, Rye, Sussex. *T.:* Rye 2032. [*Died* 11 *July* 1964.

WHITE, Charles Francis, C.B.E. 1957 (O.B.E. 1942); M.D.; Retired; *b.* 13 Oct. 1890; *s.* of William White, M.D., Hadfield, Derbyshire; *m.* 1916, Edith Celia Reynolds; two *s.* *Educ.:* King Edward VI School, Retford; University of Manchester. M.B., Ch.B., Hons., distinction in Surgery and Obstetrics (Manch.), 1912; M.D. Commend. (Manch.), 1935; D.P.H. (Manch.), 1920; D.T.M. (Liverpool), 1923. Asst. M.O.H., Port of Liverpool, 1920-27; M.O., Min. of Health, 1927-28; M.O.H., Port of London, 1928-37, City of London, 1937-56. European War, 1914-18, Capt. 6th Bn. Cheshire Regt., seconded to Capt. R.A.M.C., 1915 (wounded, despatches); War of 1939-45, in charge of Civil Defence Casualty Services, City of London. Bronze Medal, Royal Humane Society, 1924. Liveryman of: Worshipful Soc. of Apothecaries (Master, 1960-61); Company of Barbers. *Publications:* Aids to Sanitary Science and Law, 1926; contrib. to Lancet, B.M.J., Proc. Roy. Soc. Med., Medical Officer, etc. *Recreation:* living in the country. *Address:* Gosfield Hall, Halstead, Essex. *Club:* City Livery.
[*Died* 20 *June* 1966.

WHITE, Sir Dymoke; *see* White, Sir R. D.

WHITE, Very Rev. Eric M.; *see* Milner-White.

WHITE, Major Frederick Norman, C.I.E. 1916; M.D.; D.P.H.; *b.* 1877; *s.* of late C. F. White; *m.* 1906, Katherine Isabel (*d.* 1961), *d.* of late Captain S. Reid, Devonshire Regt.; one *s.* Entered I.M.S. 1903. Mem. Plague Research Commn., 1908-13; Asst. Dir.-General, Indian Medical Service (Sanitary), 1913; Public Health Commissioner with the Government of India, 1917; retired, 1920; Medical Officer, Ministry of Health, 1919; Member Health Organization, League of Nations, 1920; retired, 1934. Alderman, Oxfordshire County Council, 1946-1961. Pres. Roy. Soc. of Trop. Med. and Hygiene, 1953-55. *Address:* The Park Cottage, Aston Rowant, Oxon. *T.:* Kingston Blount 250. [*Died* 3 *June* 1964.

WHITE, Geoffrey Charles, C.M.G. 1958; O.B.E. 1944; Chief Constable of Kent since Nov. 1958; *b.* 6 Sept. 1912; *yr. s.* of late Capt. F. G. White, R.F.A.; *m.* 1939, Christian Mary Isobel Nicholls, *d.* of late Rev. Ashplant Nicholls, Inverness; one *s.* one *d.* *Educ.:* Brighton College. Royal Tank Corps, S.R.O., 1931-33; Metropolitan Police, 1934-46. Military service in N. Africa, Sicily, Italy, 1941-45 (despatches, 1943); demobilised as Lieut.-Colonel; served on staff of H.Q. 78 Inf. Div. and H.Q. 13 Corps. Deputy Commandant, No. 2 District Police Training Centre, Yorkshire N. Riding, 1946; Assistant Chief Constable of Northumberland, 1947-48; Chief Constable of Warwickshire, 1948-58; Chief Constable of Cyprus (on secondment), 1956-58. O.St.J. 1951. *Recreations:* golf, fishing, painting. *Address:* The Residence, Edinburgh Square, Maidstone, Kent. [*Died* 16 *Oct.* 1961.

WHITE, Geoffrey Henllan, O.B.E. 1960; retired; *b.* 24 March 1873; *s.* of George White, wine merchant, sometime Mayor of Tenby, Co. Pembroke, and Laetitia, *d.* of David Hart, wine merchant, Leytonstone Park, Essex; unmarried. *Educ.:* Whitgift Grammar School, Croydon; Queen Elizabeth's Grammar School, Barnet. Editor of The Complete Peerage, 1941-59. F.S.A.; F.R.Hist.S.; a Vice-President of the Soc. of Genealogists; a member of Council of the Harleian Soc. Hon. M.A. (Oxon.). *Publications:* contributions to Transactions of R.Hist.Soc.; Complete Peerage; Genealogist (New Series); Genealogists' Magazine; Antiquaries Journal; Chambers's Encyclopaedia. *Address:* Charterhouse, E.C.1.
[*Died* 6 *March* 1969.

WHITE, Air Vice-Marshal George Holford, C.B. 1962; C.B.E. 1958 (O.B.E. 1946); F.C.A.; *b.* 16 Oct. 1904; *s.* of George Holford White Dorchester, and Emily Elsie Bord Ryall; unmarried. *Educ.:* Felsted. Chartered Accountant, 1927; R.A.F. Secretarial Br., 1927. Served War of 1939-45: France, West Africa, Western Desert, India. R.A.F. Staff College, 1946; Group Capt., Organisation, R.A.F. Germany 1951; Air Commodore, H.Q. Maintenance Command, 1956; A.O.C., R.A.F. Record Office, 1960; Air Vice-Marshal, Air Officer i/c Administration, Technical Training Comd., R.A.F., 1961; retired, 1963. *Recreations:* cricket (captained R.A.F.), shooting, golf. *Address:* 32 Prince of Wales Road, Dorchester, Dorset. *T.:* 296. *Clubs:* Royal Air Force, M.C.C.; Free Foresters. [*Died* 18 *Jan.* 1965.

WHITE, George Rivers Blanco, Q.C. 1936; Recorder of Croydon, 1940-56; *b.* 8 May 1883; *s.* of Thomas and Margaret Elizabeth Blanco White; *m.* 1908, Amber, *d.* of Hon. William Pember Reeves; one *s.* two *d.* *Educ.:* St. Paul's School (Scholar); Trinity College, Cambridge (Scholar). 2nd Wrangler, 1904; Smith's Prizeman, 1906; called to Bar, Lincoln's Inn, 1907; served European War, R.G.A. in France; Bencher Lincoln's Inn, 1941; Special Divorce Commissioner, 1948-57. *Address:* 44 Downshire Hill, N.W.3. *T.:* Hampstead 1870.
[*Died* 26 *March* 1966.

WHITE, Sir (George) Stanley, 2nd Bart., *cr.* 1904; *b.* 31 July 1882; *s.* of 1st Bt. and Caroline Rosena (*d.* 1915), *d.* of late William Thomas, Bristol; *S.* father, 1916; *m.* 1908, Kate Muriel, *d.* of late Thomas Baker of Durdham Park, Bristol; one *s.* *Educ.:* Clifton. Member of firm of George White & Co., Bristol; Deputy Chairman Bristol Aeroplane Co. Ltd.,

1952. *Heir:* *s.* George Stanley Midelton [*b.* 11 April 1913; *m.* 1939, Diane Eleanor, *d.* of late Bernard Abdy Collins, C.I.E.; one *s.* one *d.*]. *Address:* Hollywood Tower, Cribbs Causeway, Westbury-on-Trym, near Bristol. [*Died* 18 *Jan.* 1964.

WHITE, Rt. Hon. Graham; *see* White, Rt. Hon. H. G.

WHITE, Very Rev. Harold; *see* Costley-White.

WHITE, Henry; M.P. (Lab.) N.E. Div. of Derbyshire, 1942-59; *b.* 5 Aug. 1890; *s.* of late William White, Church Gresley; *m.* 1912, *d.* of Frederick Cook. Vice-Pres. Derbyshire Miners' Assoc., 1938-42. *Address:* Elmfield, Creswell, Worksop, Notts. [*Died* 4 *Feb.* 1964.

WHITE, Rt. Hon. (Henry) Graham, P.C. 1945; *s.* of late John Arnold White and Annie Sinclair, *d.* of late Capt. John Graham of Birkenhead; *m.* 1910, Mary Irene, (*d.* 1962), *d.* of late Rev. Charles Heath of Nether Stowey, Somerset; two *s.* one *d.* *Educ.:* Birkenhead School; Liverpool Univ. Chairman British Association for Labour Legislation; Chairman Advisory Committee on War Risks Insurance; Member Council of Royal Institute of International Affairs; Member Council of Bedford College for Women; Member Council on Aliens; Member of Executive Committee, League of Nations Union, 1923-1924 and 1930; Member of Birkenhead Town Council, 1917-23; Chairman, Higher Education Committee, 1921-22; Chairman Council, Beechcroft Settlement; contested Birkenhead East, 1918, 1924, and 1945; M.P. (L.) Birkenhead East, 1922-24 and 1929-45; Asst. Postmaster-General, 1931-32; Member of Inter-Parliamentary Association; Fellow of Royal Statistical Society; Member Masterman Committee on the political activities of Civil Servants; Mem. of Indian Round Table Conference, 1930; Mem. of Select Committee on Private Schools, 1930; Member of Broadcasting Committee, 1935; Member Rent Restriction Acts Committee, 1937; Member of Distress for Rent Committee, 1938; Member Select Committee on National Expenditure, 1940; Member Executive Committee British Council, 1940; Chairman, Committee on Seamen's Welfare in Ports, 1943; Member: Curtis Committee on the Care of Children; Board of Social Sciences and Administration of Liverpool Univ. Freeman of Birkenhead, 1945. President of Liberal Party, 1954-55; Vice-Pres. 1958-59. LL.D. University of Liverpool, 1955. *Address:* Millfield, Vyner Rd., North Birkenhead. *Clubs:* Reform, Eighty, P.E.P., National Liberal, English-Speaking Union; University (Liverpool). [*Died* 19 *Feb.* 1965.

WHITE, Alderman Henry James; *b.* 20 Dec. 1898; *s.* of J. F. White, Bradford; *m.* 1922, Marie Butterfield; one *s.* one *d.* (and one *s.* decd.). *Educ.:* St. Bede's Grammar School, Bradford. City of Bradford: Councillor, Nov. 1932-; Leader of Conservative Group, 1950-59; Alderman, 1949-; Deputy Lord Mayor, 1938-39; Lord Mayor, May 1954-55. Pres. Bradford Sportsmen's Soc. Pres. Bradford Hosp. Broadcasting Assoc. Served European War 1914-1918, 4 years home and overseas (disability pensioner). K.C.S.G. 1957. *Recreations:* football, cricket, and judging mastiffs (Vice-Pres. and Hon. Judge, Old English Mastiff Club). *Address:* Acre House, Eccleshill, Bradford. *T.:* Bradford 37835. *Clubs:* Albany; Bradford, Columba (Bradford). [*Died* 14 *May* 1961.

WHITE, Herbert Martyn Oliver, M.A.; M.R.I.A.; retired as Professor of English Literature, University of Dublin (1940-1960); *b.* 1885; 3rd *s.* of late Reverend Robert White, Dundonald, County Down; Dublin. Modern Language Scholar, 1911; Senior Mod. B.A. Modern Literature, 1914; M.A., 1919; Pres., University Philosophical Society, 1912; English Lecturer, Ecole Normale Supérieure, Paris, 1919-20; Lecturer, English Language and Literature, University of Sheffield, 1920-31; Lecturer in English Literature, Queen's University of Belfast, 1931-39; Professor of English Literature, Universidad Internacional de Verano, Santander, 1933, 1934. *Publication:* Thomas Purney, 1933. *Address:* 52 Redesdale Road, Mt. Merrion, Dublin. *Club:* Univ. (Dublin). [*Died* 22 *Nov.* 1963.

WHITE, Horace P. W.; *see* Winsbury-White.

WHITE, Kenneth James Macarthur, C.B.E. 1951; Consul-General in H.M. Foreign Service, retired 1954; *b.* Toowoomba, Qld., Australia, 27 Feb. 1894; *s* of late John White, Levernholme, Pollokshields, Glasgow; *m.* 1924, Hilda Morris Fisher (*d.* 1969); two *d.* *Educ.:* Hutchesons', Glasgow; London University. Served European War, 1914-18, France and Flanders, London Scottish, etc. (despatches); various Allied Missions in Central Europe, 1919-20; entered Consular Service, 1920; served successively at Berlin, Punta Arenas, Zürich, Madrid, New Orleans, Savannah, Managua, Pernambuco, Stockholm; Control Commission for Germany at Berlin; Gothenburg, Sweden and San Francisco, U.S.A. *Address:* 18 Woodvale Avenue, Whitecraigs, Renfrewshire. [*Died* 4 *June* 1969.

WHITE, Lt.-Gen. Sir Maurice F. G.; see Grove-White.

WHITE, Oswald, C.M.G. 1931; *b.* 23 Sept. 1884; *m.* 1st, Kathleen Elizabeth (*d.* 1937), *d.* of J. C. Hall, C.M.G., I.S.O.; three *d.*; 2nd, 1937, Margaret Gourley Anderson (*d.* 1968). Student Interpreter in Japan, 1903; Vice-Consul at Osaka, 1914; Consul at Nagasaki, 1920; Dairen, 1925; Consul-General at Seoul, 1927; Osaka, 1931; Mukden, 1938; Tientsin, 1939-41; retired, 1944. *Address:* Leicester Court Hotel, 41 Queen's Gate, S.W.7. [*Died* 29 *Dec.* 1970.

WHITE, Richard Charles B.; *see* Brooman-White.

WHITE, Robert S.; *see* Standish-White.

WHITE, Sir Rowden; *see* White, Sir A. E. R.

WHITE, Sir Rudolph Dymoke, 2nd Bt., *cr.* 1922; late Major Hampshire Carabiniers; D.L., J.P., Alderman, Hants; late Hon. Col. 457 (Wessex) Regt. R.A. (T.A.) (Hampshire Carabiniers Yeomanry); *b.* 11 June 1888; *s.* of Sir Woolmer White, 1st Bt., and Edith Wittcomb, *yr. d.* of George Dawes Monck, of Hilsea, Hants; *S.* father, 1931; *m.* 1912, Isabelle, *yr. d.* of James G. MacGowan; two *s.* two *d.* *Educ.:* Cheltenham; Trinity College, Cambridge, M.A. High Sheriff of Hampshire, 1935. M.P. (U.) Fareham Div. of Hants, 1939-50. President: Royal Counties Agric. Soc., 1959; Royal Norfolk Agricultural Assoc. 1963. British Horse Society, 1966; Coaching Club. *Heir:* *s.* Headley Dymoke White, late Maj. Intelligence Corps [*b.* 15 Apr. 1914; *m.* 1943, Elizabeth Victoria Mary, *er. d.* of Wilfrid Wrightson, Dinsdale Manor, Neasham, Darlington; one *s.* two *d.*]. *Address:* Southleigh Park, near Havant, Hants; Salle Park, Norfolk. *Club:* Cavalry. [*Died* 25 *May* 1968.

WHITE, Sir Stanley, Bt.; *see* White, Sir G. S.

WHITE, Terence Hanbury; Author; *b.* 29 May 1906; *s.* of Garrick Hanbury White and Constance Edith Southcote Aston. *Educ.:*

Cheltenham; Queens' College, Cambridge. Taught at Stowe till 1936. *Publications:* Loved Helen, 1926; Darkness at Pemberley, 1930; Farewell Victoria, 1933; Earth Stopped, 1934; Gone to Ground, 1935; England Have My Bones, 1936; Burke's Steerage, 1938; The Sword in the Stone, 1939 (Book of Month in U.S.A.); The Witch in the Wood, 1940; The Ill-Made Knight, 1941; Mistress Masham's Repose, 1946 (Book of Month in U.S.A.); The Elephant and the Kangaroo, 1947; The Age of Scandal, 1950; The Goshawk, 1951; The Scandalmonger, 1952; The Book of Beasts, 1954; The Master, 1957; The Once and Future King, 1958; The Godstone and the Blackymor, 1959. *Recreation:* animals. *Address:* c/o Jonathan Cape, 30 Bedford Square, W.C.1. *Club:* British Falconers'. [*Died* 17 *Jan.* 1964.

WHITEHEAD, Arnold Sydney, C.B. 1953; C.B.E. 1948; Commissioner of Inland Revenue, Secretary and Director of Establishments, Board of Inland Revenue, 1949-1955; *b.* Leicester, 14 Jan. 1895. *Address:* Pen Gwyn, Coed Celyn Rd., Derwen Fawr, Swansea. [*Died* 23 *May* 1966.

WHITEHOUSE, Wallace Edward, M.B.E. 1943; M.Sc., L.C.P.; Hon. M.I. Fire E.; F.R.Met.S.; F.I.C.D.; *b.* 1882; *s.* of Albert Edward Whitehouse, Wolverhampton; *m.* 1905, Mabel, *d.* of Alfred Hammond of Wordsley; one *s.* (and one *s.* killed in action). *Educ.:* Technical School, Walsall; University College of Wales, Aberystwyth. Secondary School Teacher, 1906-12; Gilchrist Geography Student, 1912; Assistant Lecturer and Lecturer, Geography, Univ. College of Wales, 1913-41; Acting Head of Dept. of Geography, Univ. Coll. of Wales, 1941-46; Divisional Officer (part-time N.F.S.), Region 8 Fire Staff, 1941-48; Assistant Fire Force Commander, 1944-48. Member Nat. Joint Council of Fire Brigades of England and Wales, 1947-53; Mem. of Central Advisory Fire Brigades Council, 1948-57; Div. Officer (part-time) Glam. Fire Service, 1948-61; Mem. of Council of Inst. of Civil Defence, 1950 (Bronze Medallist). Geography and General Knowledge, Examiner, various Bds. *Publications:* Articles on teaching Geography in Geographical Journals and on various European countries, in Ency. Brit. (xiv. edn.), and in Enciclopedia Italiana. Articles on Fire Engineering and Civil Defence. *Recreation:* philately. *Address:* c/o Institution of Fire Engineers, 94 Southwark Bridge Rd., S.E.1. [*Died* 7 *March* 1963.

WHITEHOUSE, Major William Henry, M.B., B.S. 1896; M.D., 1898; D.P.H., R.C.S. (Edin.), F.P.S. (Glasg.) 1899; Barrister-at-Law, Inner Temple, 1908; *b.* 21 April 1873; *s.* of William Henry Whitehouse; *m.* 1913, Constance Mary, (*d.* 1945), *d.* of A. J. Hucklesby, J.P., C.A.; two *s.* *Educ.:* Birmingham University; Durham University. Fellow of Royal Society of Medicine, 1904; Senior Prosector and Asst. in Anatomy, Surgical Officer Skin Hospital and Hon. Surgeon Maternity Hospital, Birmingham, 1907; M.O.H., School M.O., Bacteriologist, Superintendent of the Infectious Diseases Hospitals, Aston Manor, Birmingham, 1908; Member Birmingham Drainage Board, 1909; Member Birmingham City Council, 1909; M.O.H. Metropolitan Borough of Deptford, 1911; H.M. Coroner, County of London, S.E. District, 1920-43; Hon. Treasurer, 1928, and President of the Coroners' Society of England and Wales, 1932; Vice-Pres. Section of Forensic Medicine, B.M.A., 1932; served European War, Major, R.A.M.C.; Deputy Asst. Director of Medical Services and S.S.O. Northern Command (despatches twice). *Publications:* The Prevention of Tuberculosis and Dispensary Treatment; The Problem of Consumption; Facts about Foods; The Problem of the Child; Notes for the guidance of Coroners' Officers; Contributions on various medico-legal subjects. *Recreations:* travel, shooting, farming of pedigree stock. *Address:* Holmwood Place, Four Elms, Edenbridge, Kent. *T.A.:* Four Elms. *T.:* Four Elms 208; 32 Wickham Road, S.E.4. [*Died* 9 *July* 1963.

WHITELAW, Anne Watt; *b.* Edinburgh, 1875; *d.* of late G. E. and Grace Whitelaw, Auckland, New Zealand. *Educ.:* Auckland College and Grammar School; Girton College, Cambridge (Certificated Student). Mathematical Tripos, Class II., 1897; M. A. Dublin, 1905; Assistant Mistress, Wycombe Abbey School, 1897-1906; Headmistress of Girls' Grammar School, Auckland, N.Z., 1906-1910; Headmistress of Wycombe Abbey School, 1910-25; Head of Education Department, Selly Oak Colleges, Birmingham, 1928-30; Head of Talbot Settlement Camberwell, 1932-37. *Address:* 57 Arney Road, Remuera, Auckland, N.Z. [*Died* 11 *Aug.* 1966.

WHITELAW, Major-General John Stewart, C.B. 1951; C.B.E. 1942; retd.; *b.* 26 August 1894; *s.* of Thomas Whitelaw, Hawthorn, Victoria; *m.* 1916, Esther A. Norman; three *s.* *Educ.:* Wesley College, Melbourne; Royal Military College, Duntroon. Entered Army (R.M.C.), 1911; commissioned, 1914. Served A.I.F. 1914-16 (wounded); then with Australian Regular Army in varying Artillery Staff and regimental appointments including Chief Instructor, School of Artillery, and Major-General Royal Artillery at Headquarters, Allied Land Forces, Brigadier and A.D.C. to the Governor-General, 1941; Maj.-Gen. 1942. G.O.C. Western Command, Australia, 1946-1951; retired, 1951. Colonel Commandant, Royal Australian Artillery, 1955-61. *Address:* Woorinyan, Upper Beaconsfield, Vic., Australia. *Club:* Naval and Military (Melbourne). [*Died* 21 *April* 1964.

WHITELEY, General Sir John Francis Martin, G.B.E. 1956 (C.B.E. 1941); K.C.B. 1950 (C.B. 1943); M.C.; late R.E.; *b.* 7 June 1896; *m.* 1929, Margaret Aline Anderson; one *s.* one *d.* 2nd Lt. R.E. 1915; served European War, 1915-18 (despatches, M.C.); D.A.A.G. India, 1932-34; G.S.O. 2 War Office, 1935-38; served War of 1939-45 (despatches five times, C.B.E., C.B.); i.d.c. 1946; Comdt. National Defence Coll. and Canadian Army Staff Coll., Canada, 1947-49; Deputy C.I.G.S., 1949-53; Chairman of British Joint Services Mission, Washington, and U.K. representative on Standing Group of the Military Committee of the North Atlantic Treaty Organisation, 1953-July 1956; retired, 1956. *Club:* Army and Navy. [*Died* 4 *April* 1970.

WHITELEY, Wilfrid, C.B.E. 1950; Political Secretary, retd.; *b.* Huddersfield, 3 Feb. 1882; *s.* of Joe and Martha Whiteley, textile workers, Huddersfield; *m.* 1904; one *s.* two *d.* *Educ.:* Paddock Elementary School, Huddersfield. Started work at a wool warehouse; worked in a newspaper office and provision stores; joined the Socialist movement, 1904; part time Labour agent at Huddersfield, 1909; contested Colne Valley, 1918; sales manager for the National Labour Press, 1919; full time Labour agent at Huddersfield, 1921-26; registration agent to the Ladywood Divisional Labour Party, 1926-29; M.P. (Lab.) Ladywood Division of Birmingham, 1929-31. Agent to West Birmingham Divisional Labour Party, 1932-36; Agent, Elland Divisional Labour Party, 1936-47; Mayor of Brighouse, 1947-50. *Address:* 33 Huddersfield Road, Brighouse, Yorks. [*Died* 4 *April* 1970.

WHITESIDE, Sir Cuthbert William; *see* Addenda: II.

WHITFORD, Air Vice-Marshal Sir John, K.B.E., *cr.* 1949 (C.B.E. 1943; O.B.E. 1935); C.B. 1945; *b.* 1893; *s.* of John

Henry Whitford, Alberta, Canada; *m.* 1918, Vera Treleavan, *d.* of late C. B. Major, Reading; one *s.* Acting Air Vice-Marshal, 1944; Temp. Air Vice-Marshal, 1946; retired, 1949. *Address:* c/o Glyn, Mills & Co. (Holt's Branch), Kirkland House, Whitehall, S.W.1. [*Died* 12 *Aug.* 1966.

WHITHAM, Gilbert Shaw, C.M.G. 1943; C.B.E. 1936; retired; *b.* 1889; *s.* of Joseph Shaw Whitham and Sarah Jane Browett; *m.* 1916, Edith Lena Emma, *d.* of Frederick Stephen Church, King's Commissioner, Gold Coast; one *d.* *Educ.:* privately, Chile, 1910-14; Inns of Court, 1914-15; Commissioned, 1915, York and Lancaster Regt. (wounded); H.M. Factory, Queensferry, 1916-17; Headquarters Dept. of Explosive Supply, 1917-20; Secretary Factories Branch, 1918-20; War Office, 1920, under the Director-General of Factories; Superintendent H.M. Factory, Gretna, 1921; Assistant Director of Ordnance Factories; Director of Industrial Planning (War Office), 1936; Director of Ammunition Production, 1939; Deputy Director-General, Ministry of Supply, 1941; Head of British Mission (Supply) to Turkey, Sept. 1941; Major-Gen. (Hon.) Sept. 1941; Head of Production Office, Palestine, 1942; Director-General of Production Services (Ministry of Supply), 1943; Deputy Chief (General) of the Economic Division, C.C.G. (B.E.), 1945; Chief of the Reparations Deliveries and Restitution Division, Control Commission for Germany (British Element), 1945-50, retd. C.C. Devon, 1956. *Recreation:* gardening. *Address:* 1 Church View, South Zeal, Okehampton, Devon. [*Died* 20 *Aug.* 1970.

WHITING, Frederic, R.S.W., R.P.; R.I. *Educ.:* Deal; St. Mark's College, Chelsea; St. John's Wood Art Schools; Royal Academy Schools; Julien's, Paris. War Correspondent and Artist for the Graphic, China, 1900-1; Russo-Japanese War, 1904-5; paints portraits and figure subjects; Paris Salon, 1914 (mention hon.); Silver Medal, Paris Salon, 1926; joined 18th County of London, Oct. 1914; served European War, 1915-18. *Exhibits:* International, Royal Academy, Royal Institute, etc., and chief provincial galleries. Pictures in Public Galleries in Liverpool, Brighton, Wolverhampton, Glasgow, N.S. Wales; medal for best water colour, Anglo-German Exhibition; holds China medal, British Expeditionary Force, 1901; Japanese War medal and clasp, 1904-5. Imperial War Museum—Gen. Sir William Marshall, Adm. Sir Richard Peirse; equestrian portrait of George V; portrait of the Royal Princesses riding at Windsor, in possession of the King, 1945. *Recreation:* riding. *Address.* 2 Alma Studios, Stratford Road, W.8. *T.:* Western 2167. *Clubs:* Arts, Chelsea Arts. [*Died* 1 *Aug.* 1962.

WHITING, John Robert; playwright; *b.* 15 Nov. 1917; *s.* of Frederick Charles and Dorothy Edith Whiting; *m.* 1940, Asthore Lloyd Mawson; two *s.* two *d.* *Educ.:* Taunton Sch. Roy. Acad. of Dramatic Art, 1935-37. Served War of 1939-45, Royal Artillery. Plays produced: A Penny for a Song, Haymarket, 1951, Aldwych, 1962; Saints' Day, Arts, 1951; Marching Song, St. Martin's 1954; The Gates of Summer, New Theatre, Oxford, 1956; The Devils, Aldwych, 1961, 1962; Conditions of Agreement, posthumous production, Bristol Old Vic. 1965. Plays trans. from the French; film scripts. Member of the Arts Council Drama Panel, 1954-; Theatre Critic, London Magazine, 1961. *Publications:* The Plays of John Whiting, 1957; The Devils, 1961. *Address:* Duddleswell House, Duddleswell, near Uckfield, Sussex. *T.:* Nutley 269. *Club:* Garrick. [*Died* 16 *June* 1963.

WHITLEY, Brig.-Gen. Sir Edward Nathan, K.C.B., *cr.* 1921 (C.B. 1919); C.M.G. 1916; D.S.O. 1918; T.D.; M.A., LL.M.; R.A.; retired; *b.* 1873; *y. s.* of Nathan Whitley, Halifax; *m.* 1902, Julia Kathleen (*d.* 1957), *d.* of late Rev. W. A. Norris of Flore, Northampton; one *s.* one *d.* *Educ.:* Clifton Coll.; Trinity Coll., Cambridge. Served European War, 1914-18 (despatches, C.M.G., D.S.O., C.B.). *Address:* Campfield House, Malton, Yorks. [*Died* 29 *Nov.* 1966.

WHITLEY-JONES, Ernest; Director of: Lloyds Bank Ltd., 1951-61 (Chm. of the Cttee. for South Wales, 1959-61); Bank of British West Africa Ltd., 1947-64 (Dep. Chm. 1954-1964); Premier Investment Co. Ltd. 1951; Argus Press Ltd. 1951; Argus Press Holdings, 1951; *b.* 1 August 1890; *e. s.* of Joseph and Elizabeth Whitley-Jones; *m.* 1st, 1915, Katherine Jones (*d.* 1917); one *d.*; 2nd, 1919, Beatrice E. M. Bright; one *s.* (decd.). *Educ.:* Pwllheli Grammar School. Lloyds Bank Ltd.: Asst. General Manager, 1933; Jt. General Manager, 1941; Dep. Chief General Manager, 1945; Chief General Manager, 1946. Chairman, City of London Savings Committee, 1952-62; Chairman, Chief Exec. Officers, London Clearing Bankers, 1949-50. Fellow Bankers Institute. *Recreations:* golf, ornithology. *Address:* Pyes, Knotty Green, Beaconsfield, Bucks. *T.:* Beaconsfield 342. *Clubs:* Boodle's, Oriental. [*Died* 11 *July* 1965.

WHITMORE, Col. Sir Francis Henry Douglas Charlton, 1st Bt., *cr.* 1954; K.C.B., *cr.* 1941 (C.B. 1935); C.M.G. 1918; D.S.O. 1917; T.D. 1918; T.E.D. 1951; J.P. 1899; D.L. 1907; Lord Lieut. of Essex and Custos Rotulorum, 1936-58, retd.; *b.* 1872; *o. s.* of Thomas Charles Douglas Whitmore, late Capt. R.H.G., of Apley, Salop, Gumley Hall, Leicestershire and Orsett Hall, Essex, D.L., J.P., and Louisa M.E., 5th *d.* of Sir William E. Cradock Hartopp, 3rd Bart.; *m.* 1st, 1900, Violet Frances Elisabeth, O.B.E. (*d.* 1927), *y. d.* of Sir William Hy. Houldsworth, 1st Bt., M.P., D.L., J.P., of Coodham, Ayrshire; 2nd, 1931, Ellis Christense, D.St.J. 1960, *e. d.* of Knud Johnsen, Bergen, Norway; one *s.* one *d.* *Educ.:* Eton. Lord of the Manors of Orsett, Little Thurrock, Stifford, Corringham and North Benfleet; Essex C.C., 1918-26; High Sheriff, Essex, 1922-23; Military Member of Territorial Army Association, County of Essex, since 1908, Chairman, 1929-36; President, 1936; Member of the T.A. Advisory Committee, War Office, 1935-37; Allotments Advisory Cttee., Min. of Agriculture, 1924-48; Hon. Col. Essex Group of Anti-Aircraft Searchlight Companies, R.E. (T.A.), 1926-33; Hon. Colonel 104th (Essex Yeomanry) Regt. R.H.A., 1936, 147 (Essex Yeomanry) Field Regt. R.A., 1940-49, and 17th Light A.-A. Regt. R.A., 1941-47; Hon. Commander Essex Home Guard and J and K Zones, Home Guard, London District, 1940; Hon. Col. 304 Field Regt. R.A., 1947; Hon. Colonel 517 Lt. A.A. Regt R.A., 1947. Lieut. 1 Essex Artillery Volunteers, 1892-95; Major Essex Imperial Yeomanry, 1901; Lieutenant-Colonel commanding Essex Yeo., 1915-18; 10th (P.W.O.) Roy. Hussars, 1918-19; served European War, 1914-19 (wounded twice, despatches four times, C.M.G., D.S.O., T.D.); K.J.St.J. 1937. *Publication:* The 10th P.W.O. Royal Hussars and the Essex Yeomanry in the European War, 1914-19. *Heir:* *s.* John Henry Douglas Whitmore, *b.* 16 Oct. 1937. *Address:* Orsett Hall, Essex. *T.A.:* Orsett. *T.:* Orsett 233. *Clubs:* Cavalry, United Service. [*Died* 12 *June* 1962.

WHITNEY, George; Chairman, Advisory Council, Morgan Guaranty Trust Co.; (President J. P. Morgan & Co. Inc., 1940-50; Chairman, 1950-55); *b.* 9 October 1885; *s.* of George and Elizabeth W. Whitney; *m.* 1914, Martha Beatrix Bacon; one *s.* two *d.* (and one *s.* decd.). *Educ.:* Groton School; Harvard University. Started in banking business with Kidder, Peabody & Co., Boston, 1907; in employ J. P. Morgan & Co., 1915-19. Partner, 1919; Director, General Motors Corporation. *Address:* 23 Wall Street, New York 8, N.Y. *T.A.:* Morgan New York. *T.:* Rector 2-6400. *Clubs:* Racquet & Tennis, Links, Harvard, Piping Rock (N.Y.). [*Died* 22 *July* 1963.

WHITTAKER, Maj.-Gen. Robert Frederick Edward, C.B. 1943; C.B.E. 1945 (O.B.E. 1938); T.D.; General Manager (Administration) Lloyds Bank, 1952-57, ret.; *b.* 18 June 1894; 2nd *s.* of Robert William Whittaker; *m.* 1919, Minnie B. Miles (*d.* 1953); one *d.*; *m.* 1956, Brenda L. Johansen. *Educ.:* Ardingly College. T.A. O.T.C. 1909-1911; R.A. 1914-38; Col. 1938; Brig. 1939; Maj.-Gen. 1945: Divl. Commander. Maj.-Gen., 1940. Banking, 1911; F.I.B. 1940. *Recreation:* Rugby football (Past Pres. and Hon. Treas. Kent County R.F.U.; President, London R.F.U.; Mem. R.F.U. Cttee.). *Address:* 58 Bickenhall Mansions, Gloucester Place, W.1. *T.:* Welbeck 1001.
[*Died* 17 *Feb.* 1967.

WHITTARD, Prof. Walter Frederick, F.R.S. 1957; D.Sc. (Lond.), Ph.D. (Lond. and Camb.), A.R.C.Sc.; Chaning Wills Professor of Geology, University of Bristol, since 1937 (Dean, Faculty of Science, 1945-48); *b.* 26 Oct. 1902; *y. s.* of Thomas W. Whittard and Sarah Cotterell; *m.* 1930, Caroline Margaret, *d.* of Albert W. Sheppard; one *s.* *Educ.:* County Secondary Sch., Battersea; Chelsea Polytechnic; Imperial College of Science and Technology; Sidney Sussex College, Cambridge. D.S.I.R. junior and senior awards, 1924-29; 1851 Senior Studentship, 1929-31; Chief Geologist, Cambridge Expedition to East Greenland, 1929; Assistant Lecturer, 1931-35, Lecturer, 1935-37, in Geology, Imperial College of Science. Pres. Bristol Naturalists' Soc., 1952-54. Vice-President, Palaeontological Association, 1961-62. Fellow Imperial College of Science and Technology, 1964; Murchison Medal, Geological Society of London, 1965. *Publications:* various papers on geology of Shropshire, Bristol district, East Greenland, submarine geology of the English Channel, and on fossil amphibians, trilobites and brachiopods. Joint Editor: Bristol and its Adjoining Counties, 1955; Lexique Stratigraphique International (England, Scotland and Wales) 1958-; Submarine Geology and Geophysics, 1965. *Recreations:* gardening, bookbinding. *Address:* Coombe Farm House, Canford Lane, Westbury-on-Trym, Bristol. *T.:* Bristol 627926.
[*Died* 2 *March* 1966.

WHITTLE, Ven. John Tyler; Archdeacon of Macclesfield, 1950-58, later Archdeacon Emeritus; Rector of Astbury 1951-1962, later Canon Emeritus; *b.* 2 Dec. 1889; *s.* of James and Susan Whittle; *m.* 1920, Florence E. Bowler (*d.* 1960); two *s.* *Educ.:* S. Augustine, Canterbury; Lichfield Coll. Served European War, 1914-18, Combatant Officer (Lieut.) North Stafford Regt. Deacon 1919; Priest, 1920; Curate of St. Thomas, Stockport, 1919-24; Curate of Seaford, Sussex, 1924-28; Vicar of Gatley, 1928-36; Rector of Nantwich, 1936-51. Proctor in Convocation, 1942-; Canon of Chester Cathedral and Rural Dean of Nantwich, 1948-. *Address:* Keverstone Court Hotel, Manor Rd., Bournemouth, Hants. [*Died* 27 *Jan.* 1969.

WHITTY, Maj.-Gen. Henry Martin, C.B. 1945; O.B.E. 1942; *b.* 11 Nov. 1896; 4th *s.* of late Lt.-Col. M. J. Whitty; unmarried. *Educ.:* St. George's College, Woburn Park; R.M.C., Sandhurst. R.A.S.C.; 2nd Lieut., 1914; France and Belgium, 1915-19 (despatches); D.S.T., C.M.F. 1944; D.S.T., M.E.L.F., 1946; Inspector, R.A.S.C., 1948; retd. 1951. Colonel Comandant, R.A.S.C., 1955-59. *Address:* c/o Lloyds Bank Ltd., 6 Pall Mall, S.W.1. *Club:* United Service.
[*Died* 17 *Sept.* 1961.

WHITTY, Brig. Noel Irwine, D.S.O. 1917; *b* Australia, 1885; *s.* of late H. T Whitty, Dewhurst Lodge, Wadhurst; *m* 1918, Lilian Margaret, *e. d.* of J. H E. Garrett, Haywards Heath; one *s.* (and one killed in action 1943) one *d.* *Educ.:* Clifton College; Sandhurst. Joined Queen's Own Royal West Kent Regiment, 1906; European War, Belgium and France, 1915-18 (despatches thrice, D.S.O.); commanded 2nd Battalion The Queen's Own Royal West Kent Regt. 1932-36; Officer i/c Infantry Record and Pay Office, Leith, 1937-38; Commander 133rd (Sussex and Kent) Infantry Brigade, 1938; retired, 1941; Col. Queen's Own Royal West Kent Regt., 1946-48. *Address:* 18 Chelmscote Mansions, Salisbury, Rhodesia. [*Died* 23 *Jan.* 1964.

WHITWILL, Col. Mark, C.B.E. 1949; D.S.O. 1918; M.C. 1917; T.D 1929; Belgian Consul; Shipowner; Chartered Shipbroker; Chairman of Mark Whitwill and Son, Ltd., Bristol; *b.* 17 June 1889; *s.* of Colonel Mark Whitwill, C.B.E., V.D.; *m.* 1st, 1915, Mary Elizabeth Turner; one *s.* three *d.*; 2nd, 1965, Eleanor Elise Neilson. *Educ.:* Clifton College; University College, Oxford. Pres., Bristol Chamber of Commerce, 1939-44; Chairman, South Western Regional Board for Industry, 1944-56. President, Bristol Channel Branch, Institute of Chartered Shipbrokers. T.A. 1912-1933; commanded 48th Div. R.E., 1926-1933. Chevalier de l'Ordre de Léopold (Belgium). *Recreations:* riding, farming. *Address:* The Old Rectory, Stawley, Somerset. *T.:* Greenham 274. *Club:* Constitutional (Bristol). [*Died* 19 *April* 1967.

WHITWORTH, Charles Stanley, C.I.E. 1927; *b.* 14 June 1880; *m.* 1932, Mrs. Mabel Webb, Fishery Cottage, Bray, Berks; one *s.* Attached N.W.R., India, 1909-12; Assistant Coal Superintendent Indian State Railways, 1913-14; services lent to Great Indian Peninsular Railway, 1914-17; Mining Engineer Indian Railway Board and Technical Adviser to Indian Coal Controller, 1918-20; Chief Mining Engineer, Government of India (Rail-Dept.), 1921; retired 1935. Member Indian Coal Committee, 1925; President Indian Coal Grading Board, 1926-7-8-9. *Address:* Islet Park, Maidenhead, Berks. *T.:* Maidenhead 1592. [*Died* 14 *Sept.* 1963.

WHITWORTH, Cyril, C.B.E. 1962 (M.B.E. 1947); *b.* 16 Dec. 1904; *s.* of late James Henry Whitworth and Elizabeth Ann (*née* Walton); *m.* 1928, Dorcas E. Thorne; two *s.* *Educ.:* Grange School, Bradford. Served in Royal Air Force, 1921-30. Appointed to The Residency, later H.M. Embassy, Cairo, 1930; H.M. Legation, Addis Ababa, 1942; H.M. Embassy, Moscow, 1946; Office of the Commissioner General, Singapore, 1948; H.M. Consul, Hanoi, Vietnam, 1951; Foreign Office, 1953; Counsellor, British Embassy, Bonn, 1957; Retired from H.M. Diplomatic Service, June 1963. *Recreations:* golf, photography. *Address:* Cedarhurst, Primrose Ridge, Godalming, Surrey.
[*Died* 16 *Jan.* 1968.

WHYTE, Sir (Alexander) Frederick, K.C.S.I., *cr.* 1925 Kt. *cr.* 1922; M.A., LL.D.; *b.* 30 Sep. 1883; *e. s.* of late Rev. Principal Whyte, D.D.; *m.* 1912, Margaret Emily, *e. d.* of Rev. W. Fairweather, D.D., of Kirkcaldy; one *s.* one *d.* (and one *d.* decd.). M.A. (Edin.), with 1st Class Honours in Modern Languages; one of the founders of The New Europe, and joint-editor; M.P. (L.) Perth City, 1910-18; travelled in United States, 1919-1920; Chairman Indian Red Cross Society, 1923; Hon. LL.D. Edinburgh, 1924; McGill,

1926; University of Michigan, 1926; Dartmouth College, U.S.A., 1926; President of the Legislative Assembly, India, 1920-25; Political Adviser to the National Government of China, 1929-32; Director-General of the English-Speaking Union of the British Empire, 1938; Head of American Division, Ministry of Information, 1939-40. Chm., Reindeer Council of the U.K., 1968-. *Publications:* Asia in the Twentieth Century, 1926; China and Foreign Powers, 1927; The Future of East and West, 1932. *Address:* 33 Sussex Lodge, W.2. *Club:* Athenæum.
[*Died* 30 *July* 1970.

WICKHAM, Brig. John Charles, D.S.O. 1916; late R.E.; p.s.c.; n.s.; *b.* 23 June 1886; *s.* of late Col. Charles Brenton Wickham, R.A.; *m.* 1921, Augusta Phyllis Amyand, *d.* of late Major Arthur Haggard; one *s.* (decd.). *Educ.:* Cheltenham Coll.; R.M.A., Woolwich. Commissioned in R.E. 1904; served Abor Survey Expedition, 1912-13; European War, France, 1914 (wounded, despatches, D.S.O.); North West Frontier, 1930-31; War of 1939-45; A.D.C. to the King, 1940-43; retired, 1943. *Address:* Shoddesden Manor, Nr. Andover, Hants. *T.:* Ludgershall 252. *Club:* United Service. [*Died* 12 *May* 1970.

WICKS, Margaret Campbell Walker, M.A., Ph.D.; retired; *b.* 27 June 1893; *d.* of late George Douglas Wicks and Helen Douglas Wilson. *Educ.:* private school Sale, Cheshire; Edinburgh Ladies' Coll.; Elisabethschule, Hildesheim, Germany; Univs., Edinburgh, London. M.A. Hons. Mod. Lang., 1914; Diploma in Education (Edin.), 1915; Member of V.A.D. Red Cross Station Rest Room and Convalescent Hospital, Edinburgh, 1916; Administrator, Queen Mary's Army Auxiliary Corps, France, 1917-19 (despatches); three months' service on staff of British Empire Leave Club, Cologne, 1920; Certificate in Italian, University of London, 1923; Modern Language Mistress in various schools, 1915-27; Head of German Department, Edinburgh Ladies' College, 1927-34; Ph.D. Edinburgh, 1930; Headmistress, Broughton High School, Salford, 1935-51; retired, 1951; interested in Assoc. of Youth Clubs. *Publication:* Italian Exiles in London, 1816-1848, 1937. *Recreations:* walking, travel, Scottish country dancing, needlework. *Address:* 9 Alnwickhill Road, Edinburgh 9. *Club:* Service Women's.
[*Died* 27 *May* 1970.

WIDGERY, Alban Gregory, M.A. Camb.; Professor, Duke University, U.S.A.; *b.* 9 May 1887; *s.* of J. T. and E. Widgery; *m.* 1915, Marion, *d.* of Alderman W. G. Wilkins, J.P., Derby; two *s.* one *d.* *Educ.:* St. Catharine's College Cambridge (Scholar); Jena; Paris; Burney Prize Essayist and Burney Student, Cambridge. Lecturer, University of Bristol; Assistant to the Professor of Moral Philosophy, University of St. Andrews; Professor of Philosophy and Comparative Religion, Baroda, 1915-22; Lecturer in the Philosophy of Religion, Cambridge Univ., 1922-28; Professor Cornell Univ., 1929-30; Editor of the Indian Philosophical Review, also of the Indian Journal of Sociology; Originator of the Baroda Seminar for Comparative Study of Religions, 1916; President of Baroda University Commission, 1926-28; Tallman Lecturer, Bowdoin College; Upton Lecturer Oxford, 1937; Reynolds' Lecturer, Amherst College; Pres., American Theological Society, 1939-40. *Publications:* Translated, with Introduction, Life's Basis and Life's Ideal by R. Eucken; also Naturalism or Idealism; joint author with H. Weinel of Jesus in the XIXth Century and After; author of Human Needs and the Justification of Religious Beliefs; Immortality and other Essays; The Comparative Study of Religions; Outlines of a Philosophy of Life; Contemporary Thought of Great Britain; Living Religions and Modern Thought, 1936; Christian Ethics in History and Modern Life, 1940; What is Religion?, 1953; Interpretations of History: Confucius to Toynbee, 1961; A Philosopher's Pilgrimage, 1961; Les Grandes Doctrines de l'Histoire, 1965; The Meanings in History, 1967, etc.; General Editor of the Gaekwad Studies in Religion and Philosophy; articles in various journals. *Recreations:* walking, gardening. *Address:* Val Vista, Winchester, Va., U.S.A.
[*Died* 22 *March* 1968.

WIELER, Brig. Leslie Frederic Ethelbert, C.B. 1950; C.B.E. 1947; *b.* 1899; *s.* of late Eric Wieler; *m.* 1929, Elisabeth Anne *d.* of late Eric Parker; two *s.* one *d.* *Educ.:* Malvern; R.M.C., Sandhurst. 2nd Lieut. K.O.Y.L.I., 1919; Adjutant 1st Battn., 1929-32; p.s.c. 1935; Major, 1938; served in Palestine (despatches); War of 1939-45 (despatches); Comd. Infantry Training Centre and 2/4 K.O.Y.L.I., 1941-43; Commandant Army Selection Training Units, 1943-44; Inspector of Physical Training, 1944-48; Provost Marshal, 1948-52; Deputy Comdr., Home Counties District, 1952-54; Major and Resident Governor of H.M. Tower of London, 1955-61. Life Vice-Pres. Amateur Boxing Association; Vice-President International Pentathlon Association. O.St.J. *Address:* Feathercombe, Hambledon, Nr. Godalming, Surrey. *T.:* Hascombe 257. *Clubs:* Army and Navy, British Sportsman's. [*Died* 31 *Jan.* 1965.

WIENER, Professor Norbert; Professor of Mathematics, Massachusetts Institute of Technology, 1932-59, Institute Professor, 1959, Emeritus, 1960; *b.* Columbia, Mo., 26 Nov. 1894; *s.* of Leo Wiener and Bertha Kahn Wiener; *m.* 1926, Margaret Engemann; two *d.* *Educ.:* Ayer, Mass., High School; Tufts Coll.; Harvard Univ.; Cornell Univ. M.A. 1912, Ph.D. 1913, Harvard. John Thornton Kirkland Fell., Harvard, 1913-14, study with Bertrand Russell, Cambridge, and Hilbert, Göttingen; Frederick Sheldon Fell., Harvard, 1914-15, study with Russell and Hardy, Cambridge, and at Columbia Univ. Docent Lectr., Dept. of Philosophy, Harvard, 1915-16; Instructor of Maths., Univ. of Maine, 1916-17; Staff writer for Encycl. Americana, Albany, N.Y., 1918; U.S. Army, Aberdeen Proving Ground, Md., 1918-19; Writer for Boston Herald, 1919; Instructor of Mathematics, M.I.T., 1919-24; Asst. Prof., 1924-29; Assoc. Prof., 1929-32. Guggenheim Fell., study at Göttingen and Copenhagen, 1926-27; Exchange Prof. of Maths., Brown Univ., 1929-30; Lectr. at Cambridge Univ., Eng., 1931-32; Visiting Prof., Tsing Hua Univ., Peiping, 1935-36; Collab. with Dr. Arturo Rosenblueth at Instituto Nacional de Cardiologia, Mexico, 1947; Fulbright Teaching Fell., Univ. of Paris, Collège de France, 1951. Guest Professor: Indian Statistical Inst., Calcutta, 1955-56; Inst. Theoret. Physics, Univ. of Naples, 1960-62. Bowdoin Prize, Harvard, 1914; Boucher Prize, Amer. Math. Soc., 1933; Lord and Taylor Amer. Award, 1949; ASTME Res. Medal, 1960. Member: Royal Society of Arts; American Math. Soc. (Vice-pres., 1935-37); London Math. Soc. Sc.D. (Hon.) Tufts, 1946, University, Mexico, 1951; Sc.D. (Hon.), Grinnell College, 1957. Awards for Design and Research, F.R.S.A. 1960. *Publications:* The Fourier Integral and Certain of Its Applications, 1933; Cybernetics, 1948 (2nd edn., 2 new chapters, 1961); Extrapolation and Interpolation and Smoothing of Stationary Time series with Engineering Applications, 1949; The Human Use of Human Beings, 1950; Ex-Prodigy, 1953; I Am A Mathematician, 1956; Nonlinear Problems in Random Theory, 1958; The Tempter, 1959; numerous contributions to mathematical and scientific journals. *Recreations:* hiking, detective stories. *Address:* 53 Cedar Road, Belmont, Mass. *T.:* Ivanhoe 4-0021. *Club:* Appalachian Mountain. [*Died* 18 *March* 1964.

WIGGINS, Rev. Clare Aveling, C.M.G. 1923; Hon. M.A. (Oxon.); M.R.C.S. Eng., L.R.C.P. Lond.; (retired); *s.* of late William Wiggins, J.P., Watlington, Oxon; *m.* 1904, Ethel Beatrice Elliott; two *s.* two *d.* *Educ.:* Magdalen College School, Oxford; St. Mary's Hospital. Qualified, 1900; Assistant Medical Officer, Fulham Infirmary, 1900; Medical Officer, B.E.A. 1901; transferred to Uganda, 1909; Dep. P.M.O. Uganda, 1911; P.M.O. 1919; Member of the Sleeping Sickness Extended Investigation Commission, 1906-7; D.A.D.M.S. Uganda, with rank of Major, 1914-19; O.C. Base Hospital, Entebbe; O.C. Uganda Native Medical Corps; O.C. Uganda Bearer Corps, and official Censor for Uganda, 1915-19 (despatches twice); Member of the Executive and Legislative Councils of Uganda on their formation in 1920 till 1923; retired from the Uganda Medical Service, 1923; Founder of the Ngora, now Kumi, Leprosy Centre 1927; ordained Deacon, 1942; Priest, 1943, Vicar of Pyrton with Shirburn, 1944-50. *Address:* 111 Cliddesden Road, Basingstoke, Hants. *T.:* 811. [*Died* 7 *July* 1965.

WIGGLESWORTH, Air Commodore (retd.) Cecil George, C.B. 1946; A.F.C. 1918; *b.* 1893; 2nd *s.* of late George Wigglesworth, B.A., B.Sc.; *m.* Margaret Cade, *y. d.* of late Cade Bemrose, Derby; one *s.* one *d.* *Educ.:* Chesterfield; London. Served European War, 1914-18, with R.N.A.S. and R.A.F. Inter-Allied Aeronautical Commission of Control (Germany), 1919-21; Army of Occupation, Constantinople, 1922-23; R.A.F. Far East Flight, 1927-29, Coastal Command, H.Q. (Air Staff), 1931-33; Air Ministry (Operational Requirements), 1935-1939; commanded No. 201 Sqdn., 1933-35, and No. 209 Sqdn., 1939-40; A.O.C. R.A.F. Iceland, 1943-44; Air Attaché, Ankara, 1945-49. *Recreations:* cricket, hockey, golf. *Address:* The Corner House, Woodham Road, Woking, Surrey. *Clubs:* Royal Aero, M.C.C. [*Died* 8 *Aug.* 1961.

WIGHT, Sir Gerald (Robert), Kt., *cr.* 1951; company director (lately president); *b.* 28 May 1898; *s.* of late Arthur Henry Wight and Ivy Maude Wight; *m.* 1936, Rita Betty Robinson; one *s.* three *d.* *Educ.:* Bilton Grange; Charterhouse. Served European War, 1914-18, Royal Flying Corps and R.A.F. (pilot), 1916-19. Joined Alstons Ltd., 1919; Civil Defence Commissioner, Trinidad, 1942; Member Legislative Council for Port of Spain, 1941-1945, and 1950, Deputy Speaker, 1951. Formerly president of Alstons Limited, and chairman of several other companies, until Sept. 1961. *Recreations:* big game, fishing, golf, sailing. *Address:* The Lodge, Wight Road, Maraval, Trinidad, W.I.; Greens Old Farm, Bucklebury Common, Nr. Reading, Berks. *Clubs:* Royal Air Force; Union (Trinidad); Trinidad Yacht. [*Died* 20 *May* 1962.

WIGHTWICK, Humphrey Wolseley, M.C. 1917; Metropolitan Police Magistrate, 1944-61; *b.* 30 Sept. 1889; *s.* of late W. N. Wightwick, Canterbury; *m.* 1924, Diana, *d.* of late Brig.-Gen. R. C. Haig, D.S.O.; three *s.* one *d.* *Educ.:* Radley; Oriel College, Oxford. Barrister, Inner Temple, 1914. Served with 12th Bn. London Regt., 1914-17 (thrice wounded, M.C.); Staff Captain Fifth Army, 1918. *Address:* 40 Wear Bay Road, Folkstone, Kent. *T.:* Folkestone 4228. [*Died* 8 *May* 1962.

WIGLEY, Rev. Henry Townsend; Methodist Minister; *b.* 27 April 1893; *s.* of Rev. Albert J. Wigley and Elizabeth (*née* Townsend); *m.* 1920, Emily Elizabeth Mather (*d.* 1964); two *d.*; *m.* 1966, Hephzibah Richmond. *Educ.:* Liverpool Institute High School; Manchester University. B.A. (Manchester) 1917; B.D. (Manchester) 1920. Entered Methodist Ministry, 1917; Churches in Halifax, Northampton, Orrell (Wigan), and Oldham; Delegate Methodist Ecumenical Conference, Atlanta, U.S.A., 1931; General Christian Endeavour Secretary, Primitive Methodist Church, 1930; Secretary, Young Methodism Department, the Methodist Church, 1933-39; President, Christian Endeavour Union, Great Britain and Ireland, 1938-39; Minister Lodge Lane Methodist Church, Liverpool, 1939-45; General Secretary, Free Church Federal Council, 1945-52; Minister Park Avenue Methodist Church, Northampton, 1952-60. *Publications:* The Distinctive Free Church Witness To-day; Christian Endeavour and Modern Needs. *Recreations:* interested in football, cricket, tennis, and in all forms of transport, particularly railways. *Address:* 116 Coppice Drive, Northampton. *T.:* Northampton 42507. [*Died* 26 *May* 1970.

WIGLEY, Dr. John Edwin Mackonochie; Cons. Physi., St. John's Hospital for Diseases of the Skin; Cons. Physi. for Diseases of the Skin, Charing Cross Hospital; Cons. Physi. for Diseases of the Skin, King Edward Memorial Hospital, Ealing; Consultant Dermatologist, London County Council; lately Dean, Institute of Dermatology; F.R.S.M. (Past Pres. of Dermatological Section); Vice-Pres. St. John's Hospital Dermatological Soc.; Member British Association of Dermatology (Pres. 1952 and 1953); *b.* Holmbury St. Mary, Surrey, 1 Jan. 1892; *s.* of Thomas F. and Lilian S. Wigley; *m.* 1935, Evelyn, *d.* of Stanley Hoare, 17 Cornwall Terrace, Regents Park, N.W.1. *Educ.:* Church of England Grammar School, Melbourne; University of M bourne, Australia. M.B., B.S. (Melb.), 1915; F.R.C.P. Lond. 1938; M.R.C.P. Lond., 1922; Temp. Capt. R A.M.C.; House Surgeon, West London Hospital, 1919, Paddington Green Children's Hospital, 1920, late Physician for Diseases of the Skin; late Consulting Physician King Edward VII Hospital Windsor; House Physician Skin Dept. London Hospital, 1921; Clinical Asst. Skin Dept. London Hospital, 1922-27. *Publications:* articles in Brit. Jl. Dermat. and Syph. *Recreation:* golf. *Address:* 132 Harley Street, W.1. *T.:* Welbeck 3678; 6 Wellington Road, St. John's Wood, N.W.8. *T.:* Primrose 9520. *Clubs:* Public Schools; Hampstead Golf. [*Died* 7 *Aug.* 1962.

WIGRAM, Loftus Edward, M.A., M.B., B.C. (Cantab.); *b.* 31 May 1877; *y. s.* of late Prebendary F. E. Wigram; *m.* 1912, Constance, *d.* of late Rev. Canon W. G. Edwards; two *s.* one *d.* (and one *s.* killed in action, 1944). *Educ.:* Harrow School; Trinity College Cambridge; St. Thomas's Hospital. House Surgeon, St. Thomas's Hospital, 1903-4; Medical Missionary of Church Missionary Society, Peshawar, N.W.F.P., India, 1904-9; Principal, Livingstone College, 1914-21 *Address:* 11 Roselands, Sidmouth, Devon. *T.:* 1737. [*Died* 3 *July* 1963.

WIJEYERATNE, Sir Edwin Aloysius Perera, K.B.E., *cr.* 1953; High Commissioner for Ceylon in India, 1955-57; Barrister-at-Law; *b.* 7 Jan. 1890; *m.* 1921, Leela Petiyagoda; three *s.* (*o. d.* decd.). *Educ.:* St. Joseph's Coll., Colombo. Proctor, Supreme Court, Ceylon and Notary; Advocate, 1929; called to the Bar, Inner Temple, London, 1938; Member State Council, Ceylon, 1931 (Deputy Speaker, 1934); with grant of Independence to Ceylon became Member of Senate, 1947; Minister of Home Affairs and Rural Development, 1948-51; High Comr. for Ceylon in London, 1951-54; Leader, Senate, short period before becoming

High Comr. *Address:* Buddenipola Walauwa, Kegalle, Ceylon. *T.:* 211.
[*Died* 20 *Oct.* 1968.

WIJEYEWARDENE, Hon. Sir (Edwin) Arthur (Lewis), Kt., *cr.* 1949; Chairman; Official Languages Commn., Ceylon, 1951-; Judicial Service Commn., 1949; Land Tenure and Delimitation Commns., 1953; Commission on Higher Education, 1954; Land Commission, 1955; President, Arts Council of Ceylon, 1957; *b.* 21 March 1887; *s.* of D. S. L. Wijeyewardene, Notary Public, and Maria Catherine Perera; *m.* 1921, Lilian Beatrice Perera; one *s.* (and one *s.* one *d.* decd.). *Educ.:* Ananda College, Colombo; St. Thomas' College, Colombo. Advocate of the Supreme Court, Ceylon, 1911; Public Trustee, 1935; Solicitor-General, 1936; Q.C. 1937; Acting Attorney-General, 1938; Puisne Justice, 1938. Officer Administering the Government, Ceylon, 1949; Chief Justice of Ceylon, 1949-50. *Recreations:* chess, walking. *Address:* Vajira Road, Colombo, Ceylon.
[*Died* 4 *Feb.* 1964.

WILCOCK, Group Captain Clifford Arthur Bowman, O.B.E. 1944; A.F.C.; R.A.F.; M.P. (Lab.) North Derby since 1950 (Derby, 1945-50); *m.* Served in London Scottish, Queen's Royal West Surrey Regiment, Royal Flying Corps and R.A.F. (wounded at Ypres). During War of 1939-45 Deputy Director Manning Air Ministry and Senior Personnel Staff Officer Transport Command. Chairman: Cttee. on Licensing, Training and Recruitment of Personnel for Civil Aviation; Director aviation companies. Governor Westminster Hospital; Lloyd's underwriter; Freeman City of London; A.F.R.Ae.S. *Address:* 78 Buckingham Gate, S.W.1. *T.:* Abbey 2345. *Clubs:* Royal Automobile Royal Aero.
[*Died* 14 *Jan.* 1962.

WILDE, Professor Johannes, C.B.E. 1955; Ph.D. (Vienna); F.B.A. 1951; Professor of History of Art, University of London, 1950-1958; Professor Emeritus since 1958; *b.* Budapest, 2 June 1891; *m.* 1930, Julia Gyárfás, Ph.D. *Educ.:* State Gymnasium, Budapest; Universities of Budapest and Vienna. Asst., later Keeper, Museum of Fine Arts, Budapest, 1914-22; Asst., later Keeper, Kunsthistorisches Museum, Vienna, 1923-38; Reader in History of Art, London University, 1947; Dep. Dir. of Courtauld Inst. of Art, 1948-61; Mem., Reviewing Cttee. on Export of Works of Art, 1957-63. Serena Medal of British Academy, 1963. *Publications:* (with A. E. Popham) Italian Drawings of the XV and XVI Centuries at Windsor Castle, 1949; Drawings of Michelangelo and his Studio in the British Museum, 1953; Michelangelo's "Victory", 1954; contrib. to Burlington Magazine, Journal of the Warburg and Courtauld Institutes, and foreign periodicals. *Address:* 131 Burbage Road, Dulwich, S.E.21. *T.:* 01-274 3346.
[*Died* 13 *Sept.* 1970.

WILDING, Longworth Allen, M.A.; author; *b.* 30 January 1902; *er. s.* of late William Owen Wilding, Lyth Hill, Shrewsbury; *m.* 1928, Elizabeth Olga Fenwick, 2nd *d.* of late Rev. William Fenwick Stokes, Master at Rugby School; two *s.* one *d.* *Educ.:* Rossall (scholar); Oriel College, Oxford (Open Classical Scholar). 2nd Class Honours Classical Mods., 1923; 2nd Class Lit. Hum., 1925; B.A., 1925; M.A., 1929; Assistant Master, Bradfield College, 1925-27; Assistant Master, St. Edward's School, Oxford, 1927-36; Headmaster of King's School, Worcester, 1936-39. Assistant Master, Dragon School, Oxford, 1940-61; retired, 1961. *Publications:* Latin Course for Schools, Part 1, 1949; Part 2, 1950; Part 3, 1953; (with *er. s.* R. W. L. Wilding) A Classical Anthology, 1955; Greek for Beginners, 1957. *Address:* 37A St. Margaret's Rd., Oxford.
[*Died* 27 *Aug.* 1963.

WILDMAN-LUSHINGTON, Maj.-Gen. Godfrey Edward, C.B. 1947; C.B.E. 1944; R.M. (retd.); Chairman British Sulphur Corporation Ltd.; *b.* 20 May 1897; *y. s.* of late Capt. Percy Wildman-Lushington, K.O.S.B., Chilham, Kent; *m.* 1920, Kathleen Marianne, *d.* of late S. P. Trounce Truro; one *d.* *Educ.:* Wellington College. First commissioned R.M., 1914; served European War, 1914-19, R.M.A.; R.N.A.S. (pilot) and R.A.F.(despatches); Major-General, 1946; Chief of Staff to Chief of Combined Operations (actg. Maj.-Gen.), 1942-43; Asst. Chief of Staff to Supreme Allied Commander, S.E. Asia, 1944; G.O.C. Commando Group, 1945; A.D.C. to the King, 1946; Chief of Combined Operations, 1947-50; retd. list, 1950. Officier Légion d'Honneur, Croix de Guerre (France); Special Cravat Order of Cloud and Banner (China). *Recreation:* golf. *Address:* Carisbrooke, 8 Middle Avenue, Farnham, Surrey. *T.:* Farnham 6898. *Club:* United Service.
[*Died* 3 *Feb.* 1970.

WILES, Sir Gilbert, K.C.I.E., *cr.* 1938 (C.I.E. 1926); C.S.I. 1931; M.A.; I.C.S. retd.; *b.* 25 March 1880; *m.* 1906, Winifred Mary Pryor one *s.* two *d.* *Educ.:* Perse School; S. Catharine's Coll., Cambridge. I.C.S., 1904, Bombay Presidency; Chairman, Cotton Contracts Board, Bombay, 1918-20; Deputy Secretary to Government, Home Department, 1920; Secretary to Government, General Dept., 1923; Finance Secretary to Govt. of Bombay, 1923-32; Member and Pres., Indian Tariff Board, 1933-35; Chairman, Bombay Port Trust, 1935-37; Chief Secretary Bombay Govt., 1937-39; Adviser to Governor of Bombay, 1939-40; Adviser to Secretary of State for India, 1941-46. *Recreations:* golf, painting and music. *Address:* 9 Grange Road, Cambridge. *T.:* 4056.
[*Died* 11 *Sept.* 1961.

WILES, Sir Harold Herbert, K.B.E., *cr.* 1947 (M.B.E. 1919); C.B. 1944; *b.* 4 July 1892; *s.* of late Reverend J. P. Wiles, M.A., of Cambridge; *m.* 1918, Stella, *d.* of late Rev. J. H. Wilkinson, West Grimstead, Salisbury; three *s.* one *d.* *Educ.:* Perse School; Christ's College, Cambridge (First Class Hons. Classics, 1914). Served in European War (Captain) Wiltshire Regt.; entered Ministry of Labour, 1920; Deputy Secretary, Ministry of Labour and National Service, 1946-55. Member of Interdepartmental Committee on the Rehabilitation of Injured Persons, 1937-39; Member of Interdepartmental Committee on Rehabilitation and Resettlement of Disabled Persons, 1942-43. Chairman, National Advisory Council on Employment of the Disabled, 1955-60. *Address:* Holywell, Buxted, Sussex. *Club:* Oxford and Cambridge.
[*Died* 20 *May* 1965.

WILES, Philip, M.S. (Lond.), F.R.C.S. (Eng.), F.A.C.S.; Emeritus Orthopædic Surgeon, The Middlesex Hospital; Hon. Member Faculty of Medicine, University of the West Indies; Chairman, Scientific Research Council of Jamaica; *b.* 18 August 1899; *s.* of Right Honourable Thomas Wiles, P.C. and Winifred Alice (*née* Crassweller); *m.* 1923, Mary Constance Luff, *d.* of Dr. A. P. and Amy Luff; one *s.* one *d.* *Educ.:* Rugby School; University of London. Lieut. Canadian Field Artillery, Royal Flying Corps, Army Service Corps, 1917-20. Asst. Orthopædic Surgeon, The Middlesex Hosp., 1935. Brigadier R.A.M.C., 1942-45; Consultant Surgeon (Orthopædics) Paiforce and M.E.F.; Consultant Surgeon: Eastern Command, India; 12th Army. President, British Orthopædic Assoc., 1955-57; Pres. Orthopædic Section, Roy. Soc. Med., 1951-52; Emeritus Fellow, British Orthopædic Asso-

ciation; Pres. Orthopædic Section, B.M.A., 1955; Hon. Mem. Amer. Orthopædic Assoc.; Hon. Mem. Amer. Acad. of Orthopædic Surgeons. *Publications:* Essentials of Orthopædics, 4th ed., 1965; Fractures, Dislocations and Sprains, 1960; contrib. to scientific journals. *Address:* Forest Way, Redhills P.O., Jamaica, W.I. *T.:* Redhills 266.
[*Died* 17 *May* 1967.

WILGRESS, L. Dana, C.C. (Canada) 1967; diplomat; *b.* Vancouver, 20 October 1892; *s.* of Henry Trollope Wilgress and Helen Maud Empey; *m.* 1919, Olga Buergin; two *s.* one *d.* *Educ.:* Queens School, Vancouver, British Columbia; Modern Sch., Yokohama, Japan; Univ. School, Victoria, B.C.; McGill University, Montreal. Entered Canadian Trade Commissioner Service, 1914; Trade Commissioner at Omsk, Siberia, 1916; transferred to Vladivostock, 1918; Member of Canadian Economic Mission to Siberia, 1919; Trade Commissioner at Bucharest, Roumania, 1920, at London, 1921, at Hamburg, Germany, 1922-32. Director, Commercial Intelligence Service, Ottawa, 1932; Adviser at Imperial Economic Conference, Ottawa, 1932, at World Economic Conference, London, 1933; Deputy Minister of Trade and Commerce, 1940; Member of Canadian Trade Mission to South America, 1941; Canadian Ambassador, 1944-47 (Minister, 1942-44) to the Union of Soviet Socialist Republics, Moscow; Minister to Switzerland, 1947-49; High Commissioner for Canada in U.K. 1949-52; Under-Secretary of State for External Affairs, Ottawa Canada, 1952-53; Canadian Permanent Representative to N.A.T.O., 1953-58; Canadian Chairman of Canada-U.S. Joint Defence Board, 1959-66. *Address:* 371 Mariposa Avenue, Ottawa, Canada. *Club:* Rideau Country Ottawa).
[*Died* 22 *July* 1969.

WILKES, Richard Leslie Vaughan, C.M.G. 1958; Colonial Civil Service Pensioner; *b.* 8 March 1904; *s.* of late L. C. Vaughan Wilkes and Mrs. L. C. Vaughan Wilkes, St. Cyprian's, Eastbourne; *m.* 1933, Hilary Joan Summerhays; one *s.* *Educ.:* Eton College; Balliol College, Oxford. B.A. (Hons.) Oxon. 1925. Colonial Civil Service, Nigeria, 1928-51. Chairman: Public Service Commission, Sierra Leone, 1954-58; Public Service Commn., Sarawak, 1961-64; Sabah (British North Borneo), 1963-64. *Recreations:* fishing and gardening. *Address:* Wonham Barton Cottage, Bampton, Tiverton, Devon. *T.:* Bampton, 322.
[*Died* 19 *Oct.* 1970.

WILKIE, Alexander Mair, C.M.G. 1962; British Resident Commissioner, New Hebrides, since 1962; *b.* 24 May 1917; *yr. s.* of late Mr. and Mrs. John Wilkie, Glasgow and Helensburgh; *m.* 1955, Margaret Eleanor, *e. d.* of R. J. Fetherston, Tunbridge Wells; two *s.* one *d.* *Educ.:* Hillhead High School; Glasgow University; Christ's College, Cambridge. Apptd. Cadet, Colonial Admin. Service, Kenya Colony, 1940; Military service, 1940-43; D.O., Kenya, 1943-47; Clerk to Exec. and Legislative Councils, Kenya, 1947-50; Asst. Financial Sec., Kenya, 1950-53; seconded to H.M. Treasury, London, 1953-55; Development Sec., Western Pacific High Commn., 1955-57; Financial Secretary, Western Pacific High Commission, 1957-62. *Address:* British Residency, Vila, New Hebrides, Western Pacific; Fotheringhay, Groombridge, Kent. *Club:* The Royal Over-Seas League.
[*Died* 13 *Aug.* 1966.

WILKIE, Hugh Graham, C.M.G. 1946; M.A.; I.C.S., retired; *b.* 13 Mar. 1893; *s.* of Col. David Wilkie, Indian Medical Service; *m.* 1927, Margaret Wilhelmina Owen Stephens; two *d.* *Educ.:* Uppingham School; Brasenose College, Oxford. 1st Class Classical Honour Moderations, 1914; served European War, 1914-18, 5 Aug., 1914-Mar. 1919. First in King Edward's Horse, then commissioned 1915 into R.F.A.; served in France, 1915-16, Mesopotamia, 1917-19 (despatches twice); joined Indian Civil Service, Burma, 1919; Secretary to Govt. first in 1930; Commissioner first in 1939; Chief Secretary to Govt. of Burma, 1941-42, again 1943-44; then after leave 1945 to retirement in 1946 on medical grounds; in 1945 was Representative of Govt. of Burma to arrange for the transfer of Burma from the Military Administration to the Civil Govt. *Address:* 18A, Marlborough Road, Exeter, Devon.
[*Died* 13 *March* 1969.

WILKINSON, Rev. Arthur Rupert B.; *see* Brown-Wilkinson.

WILKINSON, Engineer Rear-Admiral Brian John Hamilton, C.B. 1945; C.B.E. 1942. Served European War, 1914-1919. Engineer Captain, R.N., 1936; Engineer Rear-Admiral, 1943. Served War of 1939-45 (C.B.E., C.B.).
[*Died* 29 *April* 1963.

WILKINSON, Cyril Theodore Anstruther, C.B.E. 1954; Registrar, Probate and Divorce Registry, 1936-59; *b.* 4 Oct. 1884; *o. s.* of Anthony John Anstruther Wilkinson, barrister-at-law; unmarried. *Educ.:* Blundell's. Entered Probate, Divorce and Admiralty Div., 1906; Asst. Registrar, Probate Registry, 1931. Served in Artists' Rifles 1914; 8th London Regt., 1915-19. *Publications:* Consulting Editor: Rayden on Divorce; Tristram and Coote's Probate Practice, 1926-60. *Recreations:* cricket (Surrey County Cricket XI, 1909-20, Captain 1914-1920), hockey (played for England and for Great Britain in Olympic Games, 1920), and golf. *Address:* Belmont Hotel, Sidmouth, Devon. *Clubs:* M.C.C., Royal Commonwealth Society, Free Foresters; Surrey County Cricket, etc.
[*Died* 16 *Dec.* 1970.

WILKINSON, Frank, C.B.E. 1965; Chairman, Training Board for Ceramics, Glass and Mineral Products Industries, since 1965; *b.* 17 April 1900; *s.* of Leonard and Mary Wilkinson; *m.* 1st, 1922, Amelia Barker (*d.* 1958); one *d.*; 2nd, 1965, Vera May Pitt Matthews. Controller Distribution, North German Coal Control, 1945; British Member, Combined Coal Control Group, W. Germany, 1949, British Chairman, 1950. National Coal Board: Shipping Manager, 1952; Regional Sales Manager, 1955; Director-General Marketing, 1958; Member Board, 1960-65. *Address:* The Croft, 16 Langley Way, Watford, Herts. *T.:* Watford 43757. *Club:* Royal Automobile.
[*Died* 21 *Oct.* 1970.

WILKINSON, Sir George (Henry), 1st Bt., *cr.* 1941; K.C.V.O. 1956; one of H.M. Lieutenants for the City of London since 1933; Sheriff City of London, 1931-32; Alderman of Aldersgate Ward City of London, 1933-59; Lord Mayor of London, 1940-41; *b.* 20 July 1885; *e. s.* of George Henry Wilkinson, Dulwich; *m.* 1912, Freda Dorothy (C.St.J.), *d.* of Robert Volland, Dulwich; one *s.* one *d.* Member: Archbp. of Canterbury's Cttee. on the Eccles. Comrs. as Ground Landlords, 1938-39; L.C.C. for City of London, 1937-43; Chm. Ministry of Home Security London Deep Shelter Cttee., 1940-1944; Chm. and Treas. Lord Mayor's National Air Raid Distress Fund, 1941-54; Chm. and Treas. Nat. Greek Relief Fund, 1940-47; Pres. City of London Sqdn. A.T.C., 1941; Y.M.C.A. War Emergency Cttee., 1941-45; Governor of St. Bartholomew's, St. Thomas's and King's Coll. Hosps., 1931-48; Governor Royal Holloway Coll., 1944-48; Trustee Morden Coll., 1943-47; Mem. Bishop of London's Commn. City Churches, 1941-1947; Chm. City of London Employment and Disablement Advisory Cttee., 1937-1947; Chm., London and Home Counties Conciliation Board of Cinematograph Industry, 1941-46; Dep. Chm., Lord Mayor's National Flood Fund, 1946-50; U.N. Appeal for Children, 1947-49; Governor and Almoner Christ's Hospital Schools; Council, St. Bartholomew's Medical College; Vice-Pres. Bridewell Royal Hospital, 1941-60; Chairman of Governors National Corporation for the care of Old People (Nuffield Foundation), 1947-53; Vice-Chm. Lord Mayor's United Nations Appeal for Children, 1948-50; Chm. Co. London Licensing Planning Cttee., 1948-52; Governor, Hon. The Irish Society, 1950-53; Chm. City of London Magistracy Cttee., 1951-59; Dep. Chm. Jamaica Hurricane Relief Fund, 1951-52; Master, 1941, and Hon. Freeman and Treasurer Stationers' and Newspaper Makers' Company; Chairman Executive Committee and Trustee, King George VI Foundation, 1953-60; Vice-Pres. King Edward School, Witley, Surrey, 1941-60; Chm. London Homes for the Elderly, 1945-60; Trustee: Stationers' and Paper Makers' Provident Society; Lord Mayor's National Air Raid Distress Fund; W.V.S. Residential Clubs for Old People; King George VI Foundation; Lambeth Palace Library. Grand Cross, Royal Order of the Phoenix (Greece), 1947; Hon. LL.D., London University, 1957. *Heir: s.* Lieut.-Comdr. L. David Wilkinson, D.S.C., R.N. [*b.* 18 Jan. 1920; *m.* 1946, Sylvia Anne, *o. d.* of Prof. B. A. R. Gater, The Old Mill, Greatham, nr. Liss]. *Address:* Arlington House, St. James's, S.W.1. *Club:* Athenæum. [*Died* 27 *June* 1967.

WILKINSON, Louis Umfreville (Louis Marlow), F.R.S.L.; *b.* 17 Dec. 1881; *s.* of Rev. Walter George and Charlotte Elizabeth Wilkinson; *m.* 1st, Frances Josefa Gregg; 2nd, Ann Reid; 3rd, Diana Bryn; 4th, Joan Lamburn; one *s.* one *d.* (and one *d.* decd.) (all *c.* of first two marriages). *Educ.:* Radley; Pembroke College, Oxford; St. John's College, Cambridge. Lectured on Literature in U.S.A. at intervals, 1905-19; University Extension Lecturer in England, 1909-49; has lectured also in Germany, Holland, Belgium, France, Norway, and Sweden. *Publications:* (novels) The Puppets' Dallying, 1905; The Buffoon, 1916; A Chaste Man, 1917; Brute Gods, 1919; Mr. Amberthwaite, 1928; Two Made their Bed, 1929; Love by Accident, 1929; The Lion Took Fright, 1930; Swan's Milk, 1934; Fool's Quarter Day, 1935; The Devil in Crystal, 1944; Forth, Beast!, 1946; (biographies) Welsh Ambassadors, 1936; Sackville of Drayton, 1948; Seven Friends, 1953; Ed. The Letters of Llewelyn Powys, 1943; Letters of John Cowper Powys to Louis Wilkinson (1935-1956), 1958. *Recreations:* travelling, swimming, walking, wine, reading, the theatre. *Address:* Dove Cottage, Hazelbury Bryan, Dorset. [*Died* 12 *Sept.* 1966.

WILKINSON, Dame Louisa Jane, D.B.E., *cr.* 1948 (C.B.E. 1946; O.B.E. 1943); R.R.C.; *b.* 11 Dec. 1889; *m.* 1917, Capt. R. J. Wilkinson, Royal Irish Fusiliers; no *c.* *Educ.:* Bede Collegiate School Sunderland; Thornbeck Collegiate School, Darlington. Matron-in-Chief, Q.A.I.M.N.S., War Office, 1944-48; formerly Colonel Commandant of Queen Alexandra's Royal Army Nursing Corps. President, Royal College of Nursing, 1948-50. *Address:* Oakhurst, Innhams Wood, Crowborough, Sussex. [*Died* 4 *Dec.* 1968.

WILKINSON, Sir Robert Pelham, Kt., *cr.* 1946; late Deputy Chairman, Stock Exchange; *b.* 1 Oct. 1883; *s.* of Robert Daniel Wilkinson and Kate, *d.* of William Barton Ford; *m.* 1910, Phyllis Marion (*d.* 1944), *d.* of J. C. Barnard, Lincoln's Inn; two *s.* two *d.* *Educ.:* Westminster. Master, Worshipful Company of Needlemakers, 1927; Departmental Committee on Fixed Trusts, 1936; Foreign Transactions Advisory Committee, 1936-39; Departmental Committee on Share-pushing, 1936; Capital Issues Committee, 1939-1946; Departmental Committee on Company Law, 1943-45; Hon. Treas. Chartered Soc. of Physiotherapy; National Savings Committee, 1941-50. *Address:* 41 Hanover House, Regents Park, N.W. *T.:* Primrose 2414. *Clubs:* City of London, Oriental. [*Died* 24 *May* 1962.

WILKINSON, Sir Russell (Facey), K.C.V.O., *cr.* 1930; M.R.C.S. (Eng.); L.R.C.P. (Lond.); Esquire of Order of St. John of Jerusalem; Fellow of Medical Society of London; *b.* 1888; *e. s.* of late C. W. Wilkinson, St. James's House, Monmouth; *m.* 1915, Viva (*d.* 1964), *d.* of late Richard Power; one *s.* (one *d.* decd.). *Educ.:* Eastbourne Coll.; St. Mary's Hosp. Research Scholar in Physiology; served European War, 1914, 1918; Capt. R.A.M.C.; Med Officer, 2nd Middlesex Regt. (1914 Star, wounded, despatches); Medical Officer, Prince of Wales Hospital for Officers, Medical Officer (Personal Staff) and Aide-de-Camp to Prince Arthur of Connaught when Governor-General of Union of South Africa, 1920-23; Physician to late Princess Royal, 1925-31; Physician to Prince and Princess Arthur of Connaught, 1918-38. Served 1940-1945; Colonel, A.M.S.; Military Medical Adviser, Ministry of Supply; Member Penicillin Committee. *Publications:* articles in the Lancet. *Address:* The Glebe House, Assington, Suffolk. *T.:* Boxford 202. *Club:* White's. [*Died* 23 *Dec.* 1968.

WILKINSON, Stephen, F.R.I.B.A.; A.F.C.; Architect; late Chief Architect to Lancashire County Council; *b.* 23rd April 1876; *s.* of George Wilkinson, Manufacturer, Stockport, Cheshire; *m.* Frances Evaline Neave (*d.* 1952); two *d.* *Educ.:* Lincoln; St. George's, Harpenden, Herts. Formerly Chief Architect to North Eastern Railway, and Consulting Architect to L.N.E. Railway; Past Member of Council R.I.B.A. and Past President York and East Yorks Architectural Society. Exhibited Paris International Exposition, 1925, and R.A. 1930-31-32-33-36-37-38-39; Principal works; L.N.E.R. Wagon Works, Darlington and Gosforth; Central Station Hotel, Newcastle; Edge Hill Training College, Ormskirk; County Hall, Preston (extensions); Stretford Technical College; many Grammar schools and Police Stations and hospital works; several public buildings in India. Has given talks from Broadcasting House, London, on aeronautics and war-time experiences in the air, and many lectures on the same subject. Has appeared at West End Theatres; served Boxer Rebellion 1900 (China Medal); Flight Lt. R.F.C., Special Reserve, R.N.A.S., and R.A.F. (A.F.C.) in European War. *Publications:* Lighter than Air; numerous articles in technical press, etc. *Recreations:* theatricals, flying, swimming. *Address:* The White Cottage, Lytham, Lancs. *T.:* 6435. *Clubs:* Royal Aero; Lancs. Aero; Blackpool and Fylde Aero. [*Died* 1 *Jan.* 1962.

WILKINSON, Rev. Canon William Evans; Canon Emeritus of Ripon Cathedral since 1966 (Canon 1948-66); *b.* 11 Dec. 1891; *s.* of William Hardwick and Rosetta Blanche Wilkinson, Handsworth, Birmingham; *m.* 1932, Alice Margaret, *o. d.* of Colonel H. O. Wade, D.S.O., T.D.; two *s.* one *d.* *Educ.:* King Edward's School, Aston, Birmingham; University of Birmingham. Served European War, 1915-19, Royal Fusiliers. Schoolmaster 1919-22; Cuddesdon College, 1923. Ordained Ripon Cathedral for Leeds Parish Church, 1923; Student Christian worker in China, 1927-30; Inspector of Schools and Canon

Missioner, Diocese of Wakefield, 1931-37; Rector of Barnsley, 1937-48. *Address:* Borrage Croft, Ripon, Yorks. *T.:* Ripon 2465. [*Died* 28 *Sept.* 1967.

WILL, Robert Ross, C.I.E. 1928; D.S.O. 1918; V.D.; T.D. 1949; Col. late Comdt. Bengal Artillery, A.F.I.; *b.* Dundee, 22 Oct. 1883; *s.* of late John Will, Dundee; *m.* 1914, Margaret Winifred, *o. c.* of late J. B. Gregory, Tayport, Fife. *Educ.:* Dundee. Major R.F.A. European War (despatches three times, D.S.O. Legion of Honour); Lt.-Col. R.A., 1939-40. *Address:* Tayport, Fife. *Club:* Bengal (Calcutta). [*Died* 10 *Jan.* 1968.

WILLAN, Healey, C.C. (Canada) 1967; Mus.D.; LL.D.; D.Lit.; F.R.C.O.; Organist and Choirmaster, S. Mary Magdalene, Toronto, 1921; University Organist, 1932-1961, retired; *b.* 12 Oct. 1880; *s.* of James Henry Burton and Eleanor Willan; *m.* 1905, Gladys Ellen Hall; three *s.* one *d.* *Educ.:* S. Saviour's Choir School, Eastbourne; privately. Choir-boy, S. Saviour's, Eastbourne, 1888; organist and choirmaster: S. Saviour's, S. Albans, 1896; Christ Church, Wanstead, 1900; S. John Baptist, Kensington, 1903; Toronto Conservatory of Music, 1913-36; S. Paul's Church, Toronto, 1913-21; Prof. in Faculty of Music, Univ. of Toronto, 1936, retired, 1950. A.R.C.O. 1897; F.R.C.O. 1899. Hon. Mus.D. Toronto, 1920; Hon. LL.D. Queen's, 1952. Hon. D.Lit. Manitoba, 1954; Mus.D. Cantuar, 1956; Hon. D.Lit. MacMaster, 1962. Hon Fellow R.S.C.M., 1955. Dir. Gregorian Association of Canada, retd. 1963. *Publications:* 2 operas; 2 symphonies; piano concerto; works for chorus and orchestra; motets a capella; songs; chamber music; organ music; Homage Anthem for Coronation of H.M. Queen Elizabeth II; Anthem for St. Cecilia's Festival, 1953; Magnificat for Northern Cathedral Choirs Festival, 1957; Anthem for Anglican Congress, 1963. Compositions number over 300. *Recreation:* philately. *Address:* 139 Inglewood Drive, Toronto, Canada. *T.:* 489-3179. *Club:* Arts and Letters (Toronto) (affiliated with Savage Club, London). [*Died* 16 *Feb.* 1968.

WILLCOCK, Major Ralph, D.S.O. 1919; B.A.; M.C.; Nursery Business, 1947-68; *b.* 1887; *s.* of George Willcock and Louisa Kate Pink; *m.* 1916, Emily Ruse, Hamilton, Ontario. *Educ.:* Hamilton Public and Collegiate Institutes; McMaster Univ., Toronto. Classics Master, Woodstock College, 1914-16; served European War (Lieutenant, Captain, Major), 1916-19 (D.S.O., M.C. and bar, despatches, two medals, wounded); Classics Master, Woodstock College, 1919-22; Principal, Woodstock College, 1922-26; House Master, Horton Academy, Wolfville, N.S., 1926-28; Supt. Boys' Farm and Training School, Shawbridge, Quebec, Canada, 1928-42; Education Officer, Army, 1943-45; Counsellor, Dept. of Veterans Affairs, Hamilton, Ont., 1945-46. *Address:* 1928 Main W., Apt. 518, Hamilton, Ontario, Canada. *Club:* 1925-26 Rotary (Woodstock). [*Died* 30 *Jan.* 1969.

WILLCOX, Arthur, T.D.; Physician, Middlesex Hospital; Hon. Consultant Physician to the Army; *b.* 27 April 1909; *s.* of Frank Ainsworth Willcox and Clara (*née* Herbert); unmarried. *Educ.:* Gresham's School; Clare College, Cambridge. Exhibitioner, Clare College, 1928; 1st Class Hons., Natural Science Tripos, 1930; Univ. Schol., Middlesex Hosp., 1930; M.R.C.S., L.R.C.P., 1933; M.B., B.Chir., 1934; M.A., M.R.C.P., 1935; M.D. 1939. F.R.C.P. (London), 1946. House appointments, Middlesex and Brompton Hospitals, 1933-35; Medical Registrar, Middlesex Hosp., 1935-38; Elmore Research Student, Cambridge, 1938-39. Served with R.A.M.C. (despatches); T.A., 1939-, now Colonel. Examiner in Medicine: Cambridge Univ., 1947, Sheffield Univ., 1962; Royal College of Physicians, 1962. *Publications:* articles in the Lancet, B.M.J., Proc. Roy. Soc. Med., Trans. Med. Soc. of London, etc. *Recreations:* gardening, music, reading. *Address:* 59 Harley Street, W.1. *T.:* Langham 3978. *Club:* Athenæum. [*Died* 9 *Dec.* 1963.

WILLCOX, Lieut.-General Sir Henry Beresford Dennitts, K.C.I.E., *cr.* 1945; C.B. 1942; D.S.O. 1918; M.C.; *b.* 30 April 1889; *s.* of Edward Dennitts Willcox and Charlotte Beresford; *m.* 1919, Magdalen Philpott; one *s.* *Educ.:* Christchurch, New Zealand; Staff College and Imperial Defence College. Commissioned into the Sherwood Foresters, 1911; served European War, France, Sept. 1914, Palestine, 1917 (D.S.O., M.C., despatches five times, 1914 Star, two medals, thrice wounded): a Commander, 1940-41; a Commander in India, 1942; Chairman of Army Reorganization Committee, to consider India's post-war defence needs, 1944; retired pay, 1946. *Club:* Army and Navy. [*Died* 15 *Aug.* 1968.

WILLES, His Honour Judge Richard Augustus; Barrister-at-law; J.P. Warwickshire, 1917; *b.* 24 Feb. 1881; *yr. s.* of late William Willes, Newbold Comyn, Warwickshire, and Alice, *d.* of late Sir William Cope, Bart., Bramshill, Hampshire; *m.* 1912, Marian, *y. d.* of late Benjamin Harding-Newman, Nelmes, Essex, and Bucklesham Hall, Suffolk; one *s.* Entered R.N., cadet, H.M.S. Britannia, Jan. 1895; served as midshipman in H.M.S. Undaunted, China station, 1897-1901; Boxer medal, 1900; invalided, Acting Sub-Lieutenant R.N., 1901; called to Bar, Lincoln's Inn, 1905; joined the Midland Circuit, 1905; Deputy Chm. Warwickshire Quarter Sessions, 1921-50; Chairman Rating Appeals Committee for the County of Warwick, 1928; Bencher, Lincoln's Inn, 1933; Recorder of Newark-on-Trent, 1932-34 Recorder of Coventry, 1934-41; Judge of County Courts, Circuit No. 19 (Derbyshire), 1941-53; Member of Council, Selden Society, since 1934; Member of Council, Legal Education, 1936-41. *Address:* 37 Goldstone Crescent, Hove, Sussex. *T.:* Brighton 59237. [*Died* 17 *Aug.* 1966.

WILLETT, Captain Basil Rupert, C.B.E. 1943; D.S.C.; M.I.E.E., F.R.S.A.; R.N. (retired); *b.* 23 July 1896; *s.* of William Willett; *m.* 1917, Ivy Christabel Adelaide Tuke Hayter, O.B.E. 1956; two *s.* one *d.* *Educ.:* Osborne and Dartmouth. Lt. R.N. 1917; Comdr. 1931; Staff College, 1932; Experimental Commander H.M. Signal School, 1938; Experimental Captain, 1939; Captain Superintendent Admiralty Signal Establishment, 1941-43; Director of Naval Air Radio, Admiralty and M.A.P., 1944-45. Chevalier, Légion d'Honneur, 1918. *Address:* Spring Lawn House, Bedhampton, Havant, Hants. *T.A.* and *T.:* Havant 3144. *Club:* United Service. [*Died* 29 *June* 1966.

WILLIAMS, 1st Baron, *cr.* 1948, of Ynyshir; **Thomas Edward Williams;** ex-President Co-operative Wholesale Society Ltd.; ex-Part-time Mem. London Transport Executive; Formerly Chairman and Director: New Zealand Produce Assoc. Ltd.; English and Scottish Joint Co-operative Wholesale Society; ex-Member Central Executive Co-operative Union; *b.* 26 July 1892; *s.* of William and Mary Williams; *m.* 1921, Lavinia Northam; one *d.* *Educ.:* Porth County Sch.; Ruskin Coll., Oxford. Mem. Woolwich Borough Council, 1919-22; London County Council, 1932-35 (Chm. Parl. Cttee. and Vice-Chm. Public Assist. Cttee.); Mem. Nat. Exec. Labour Party, 1931-35; contested Finsbury (Lab.), 1931; Ex-Member, National

Council of Labour. President Co-operative Congress, 1952-53. A Commissioner of Crown Estates, 1956-66; ex-part-time Mem., War Works Commn. During War of 1939-45 served on Ministry of Food Tea Distribution Cttee. Commander of the Order of Dannebrog, Denmark. *Heir:* none. *Address:* 35 Foxes' Dale, Blackheath, S.E.3. *T.:* Lee Green 2899. [*Died* 18 *Feb.* 1966 (*ext.*).

WILLIAMS OF BARNBURGH, Baron (Life Peer) *cr.* 1961; **Thomas Williams,** P.C. 1941; LL.D.; *b.* 18 March 1888. Checkweigher at Barnboro' Main, 1916-22. M.P. (Lab.) Don Valley Div. of Yorks., 1922-59. Parliamentary Private Sec. to: Minister of Agriculture, 1924; Minister of Labour, 1929-1931. Parliamentary Secretary, Ministry of Agriculture, 1940-45; Minister of Agriculture and Fisheries, 1945-51. Member, Political Honours Scrutiny Committee, 1961-. Freeman of Doncaster, 1962. *Address:* Town Moor Avenue, Doncaster. [*Died* 29 *March* 1967.

WILLIAMS, Rt. Rev. Aidan; *see* Williams, Rt. Rev. Augustine A.

WILLIAMS, Rt. Rev. Alwyn Terrell Petre, D.D.; *b.* 20 July 1888; *s.* of John Terrell Williams, Barrow-in-Furness, and Adeline Mary Peter; *m.* 1914, Margaret Grace (*d.* 1958), *d.* of Col. Charles Stewart of Tighnduin, Perthshire; no *c. Educ.:* Rossall School; Jesus College, Oxford (Scholar). 1 Cl. Mod. 1908, 1 Lit. Hum. 1910, 1 Hist. 1911; Gladstone Historical Essay, 1909; Fellow of All Souls College, 1911-18; Deacon, 1913; Priest, 1914; Assistant-Master, Winchester College, 1915-16; Second Master, 1916-24; Headmaster, 1924-34; Dean of Christ Church, Oxford, 1934-39; Bishop of Durham, 1939-52; Bishop of Winchester, 1952-61. Prelate to the Most Noble Order of the Garter, 1952-61. Hon. Canon of Winchester, 1928-34; Chaplain to the King, 1931-1934. Examining Chaplain to Bishop of Southwark, then of Oxford; Select Preacher at Oxford, 1924-25; at Cambridge, 1925; Hon. Fellow of Jesus College, 1935; Hon. Student of Christ Church, 1939; Hon. Fellow of All Souls College, 1953. Chairman of the Joint Committee for the New Translation of the Bible, 1950- (The New English Bible: New Testament, 1961). D.D. Oxon. 1925, Durham and St. Andrews, 1939, Glasgow, 1951; D.Litt. Southampton, 1962. *Publication:* The Anglican Tradition in the life of England, 1947. *Recreations:* walking, rowing. *Address:* 3 Hillside, Charmouth, Dorset. *Club:* Athenæum [*Died* 18 *Feb.* 1968.

WILLIAMS, Arthur James, J.P.; Alderman, Cardiff City Council, since 1957; Councillor, since 1935; *b.* 30 Nov. 1880; *s.* of James Edwin Williams, late General Secretary, N.U.R. and Sarah Jane Williams; *m.* 1914, Gwladys Agnes (*d.* 1945); no *c. Educ.:* Pontymoile National School; Ruskin College, Oxford. Entered Railway Service, G.W.R., 1896; became Passenger Guard about 1900. Attended Ruskin College, 1907 and 1908. Organiser, N.U.R., 1909; retired 1940. J.P. for about thirty years. Contested (Lab.) Cardiff East Div., 1918-22. Lord Mayor of Cardiff, 1958-59. *Recreations:* singing and drama. *Address:* 81 Heol Llanishen Fach, Rhiwbina, Cardiff, Glam. *T.:* Cardiff 65363. [*Died* 10 *Oct.* 1962.

WILLIAMS, Rt. Rev. (Augustine) Aidan, O.S.B., D.D.; Titular Abbot of Shrewsbury since 1948; Procurator in Curia for English Benedictine Congregation, 1953; Professor of Moral Theology in the Pontifical Institute Regina Mundi, Rome, 1954; *b.* Dublin, 16 June 1904; *e. s.* of late John Williams and Brigid Anne Rooney. *Educ.:* St. Bede's College, Manchester; Collegio S. Anselmo, Rome. Professed at Belmont, 1922; Rome, 1923-28 (D.D. 1928); Priest, 1927; Professor of Philosophy at Belmont, 1928-39; Senior Classics Master in Abbey School, 1931-40; Abbot of Belmont Abbey, Hereford, 1940-48; resigned 1948; Professor of Theology, St. Gregory's Priory, Portsmouth, Rhode Island, U.S.A., 1948-53. *Publication:* Trans. of The Doctrine of Spiritual Perfection, 1938, from German of Dom Anselm Stolz, O.S.B. *Address:* Pensionato Romano, 18 Via della Traspontina, Rome. [*Died* 7 *Dec.* 1965.

WILLIAMS, Benjamin; *see* Haydn Williams.

WILLIAMS, Sir Benjamin (Allen), Kt. 1965; C.B.E. 1955 (O.B.E. 1946); C.Eng.; *m.* 1911, Kathleen Theresa Roberts; two *s.* Joined Kitchener's Army, 1915; Founded Williams & Williams Ltd. and subsids., 1910; resigned, 1960. Chm., Westool Ltd., 1950-62. Pres., Chester and N. Wales Chamber of Commerce, 1935-; Founder and Chm., City of Chester Nat. Savings Cttee., 1940-55; Founder and Chm., N.W. Region Industrial Adv. Cttee., Nat. Savings, 1940-55; Chm., N.W. Area Trustee Savings Banks Assoc., 1953-59; Chester, Wrexham and N. Wales Savings Bank: Trustee, 1942-; Chm., 1954-; Custodian Trustee, 1956-; Vice-Pres., 1960-. Chm., Chester and Crewe District Cttee., N.W. Regional Bd. for Industry, 1946-61; Mem. N.W. Regional Coun., Fedn. of Brit. Industries, 1951-65 (Vice-Chm., 1960-62); Mem. Grand Coun., Fedn. of Brit. Industries, 1958-62; Mem. N.W. Regional Bd. for Industry, 1956-64. Chm. Exec. Coun. for Co. Borough of Chester, Min. of Health, 1948-; Mem. Chester City Coun. Health Cttee., 1949-65; Chm., Runcorn, Dutton, and Dutton Recovery Hosps., 1948-64; Mem. Gp. XIII Chester and District Hosp. Management Cttee., Liverpool Region, 1948-64. Governor's investigator into industrial conditions in Isle of Man, 1960. Mem. N.W. Industrial Recovery Adv. Coun. and of Home Office Adv. Coun. on Employment of Prisoners since inception. Founder, Past Pres. and Mem., Liverpool Section of Inst. Prod. Engrs., 1947-. M.I.Prod.E.; F.R.H.S.; F.R.A.S.E. Freeman, City of Chester, 1911. Coronation Medal, 1953; Comdr., Order of Crown of Belgium, 1959. *Address:* Greenfield Cottage, Hoole Village, Nr. Chester CH2 2PA. *Club:* Exchange (Liverpool). [*Died* 11 *Oct.* 1968.

WILLIAMS, Bernard Warren, B.A., B.M., B.Ch. (Oxon); F.R.C.S. England; retd.; *b.* Westmoreland, Jamaica, 1895; 3rd *s.* of James Rowland Williams, Kew Park, Jamaica; *m.* 1920, Muriel Burton, 2nd *d.* of 1st Baron Wrenbury; three *s. Educ.:* Oundle School; Exeter College, Oxford; St. Thomas's Hospital. In 2nd King Edward's Horse (Trooper) and R.F.A. (Temp. Capt.) 1914-18; Temp, Lt.-Col. R.A.M.C. i/c Surgical Division 22nd General Hospital, 1940; student St. Thomas's Hospital, 1919-22; 1st Assistant Surgical Unit, St. Thomas's Hospital, 1924; Hunterian Professor, Royal College of Surgeons, England, 1927; Surgeon to out-patients St. Thomas's Hospital, 1928. Formerly: Surg. Mt. Vernon Hosp., Northwood; Cons. Surg. L.C.C. Hosp. Service; Examr. in Path., R.C.S. Eng.; Examr. in Surg., Univ. Oxford; Med. Adv. and Deane Med. Sch., Univ. Coll. of W.I. *Publications:* papers on Medical Research. *Address:* Copse Mountain House, Bethel Town P.O., Westmoreland, Jamaica. *Club:* United University. [*Died* 24 *Sept.* 1970.

WILLIAMS, Sir Charles S.; *see* Stuart-Williams, Sir S. C.

WILLIAMS, Christmas Price, J.P.; *s.* of late Peter Williams, Managing Director of

Brymbo Steel Co.; *m.* 1909, Marion, *d.* of late Thos. Davies, Brymbo. *Educ.:* Wrexham; Mold; Victoria University, Manchester (Honours in Science). M.P. (L.) Wrexham Division, 1924-1929. *Address:* Sanddeth House, Gwersyllt, Wrexham. *Club:* National Liberal. [*Died* 18 *Aug.* 1965.

WILLIAMS, Conrad Veale, C.M.G. 1956; Senior Resident, Northern Region, Nigeria, 1951-56 (retired); *b.* 25 June 1903; *s.* of late J. V. Williams and Deborah Williams; *m.* 1942, Helen Brewer; no *c.* *Educ.:* St. Olave's School; St. John's College, Oxford (B.A.). Administrative Cadet, Nigeria, 1926-1929; Asst. District Officer and District Officer, 1929-45; Senior District Officer, 1945-47; Resident, 1947-51. Executive Council, Northern Region, 1952-54; Actg. Governor, Northern Region, 1955. *Address:* 36 Hyde Park Gate, S.W.7. *T.:* 01-589 2811. *Club:* Junior Carlton. [*Died* 14 *April* 1969.

WILLIAMS, Sir David (Philip), 3rd Bt., *cr.* 1915; D.L.; *b.* 5 Oct. 1909; *s.* of Sir Philip Francis Cunningham Williams, 2nd Bt., and Margaret Williams (*née* Peek); *S.* father 1958; *m.* 1st, 1937, Kathleen Mary Walker (*d.* 1945); one *d.* (one *s.* decd.); 2nd, 1948, Elizabeth Mary Garneys Bond; two *s.* one *d.* *Educ.:* R.N. College, Dartmouth; Trinity College, Oxford (B.A.). Served in R.N.V.R., 1939-45. D.L. Dorset, 1968. *Recreations:* shooting, cricket, sailing. *Heir:* *s.* Robert Philip Nathaniel Williams, *b.* 3 May 1950. *Address:* Bridehead, Dorchester, Dorset. *T.:* Longbredy 232. *Clubs:* M.C.C., Junior Carlton; Royal Dorset Yacht. [*Died* 31 *Oct.* 1970.

WILLIAMS, D(ouglas) Graeme; Editor, Radio Times, since 1954; *b.* 17 Nov. 1909; *s.* of late Graeme Douglas and of Winifred Maude Williams; *m.* 1938, Jean Mary Drusilla White; one *d.* *Educ.:* Downsend, Leatherhead; Wallingbrook, Chulmleigh. Joined B.B.C., 1927; successively Sub-Editor, Art Editor, and Dep. Editor, Radio Times. Served War of 1939-45, in Army, 1942-46; during last two years was member of staff, Army Bureau of Current Affairs. Editor, London Calling, 1950-54. *Publication:* Britain's Neighbours, 1948. *Recreations:* painting in oils, photography, gardening, golf. *Address:* 12 Oakley Street, Chelsea, S.W.3; Birklands, Hayling Is., Hants. *Club:* Hayling Golf. [*Died* 10 *Dec.* 1970.

WILLIAMS, Hon. Sir Dudley, K.B.E., *cr.* 1954; M.C.; B.A., LL.B. (Sydney); retd. as Justice of the High Court of Australia, 1958; *b.* 12 Dec. 1889; *s.* of P. O. Williams, Solicitor, Sydney; *m.* 1919, Catherine Rua Mackenzie Webster (*d.* 1959); one *s.* four *d.* *Educ.:* Sydney Church of England Grammar Sch.; Sydney Univ. Capt. R.F.A. (S.R.) 1915-19 (M.C., despatches twice); admitted to Bar of N.S.W. 1915; commenced practice, 1921; Q.C. 1934; Supreme Court, N.S.W., Nov. 1939-Oct. 1940; resigned on appointment to High Court. *Recreations:* tennis, gardening, motoring. *Address:* 39 Junction Rd., Wahroonga, Sydney, N.S.W., Australia. *Clubs:* Union, Royal Sydney Golf, Royal Sydney Yacht Sqdn. (Sydney). [*Died* 8 *Jan.* 1693.

WILLIAMS, Edward Francis; *see* Francis-Williams, Baron.

WILLIAMS, Rt. Hon. Sir Edward John (commonly known as Ted), P.C. 1945; K.C.M.G., *cr.* 1952; J.P. Glamorgan; J.P. for N.S.W., Australia, 1950; *b.* Victoria, Mon., 1890; *s.* of Emanuel Williams, Duffryn Victoria, Mon.; *m.* 1916, Evelyn James; two *d.* *Educ.:* Elementary Schools; Labour College, London. Secretary to Great Western Collieries, 1909-13; Labour College, 1913-1915; Provincial Lecturer for Labour College; Member Glamorgan County Council, 1928-31; Miners' Agent to Garw District of S. Wales Miners' Federation, 1919-31; M.P. (Lab.) Ogmore Div. of Glamorganshire, 1931-46; Parliamentary Private Secretary to Under-Secretary for Colonies, 1940-41; to Financial Secretary to the Admiralty, 1942-1943; to Parl. Under-Sec. of State for Foreign Affairs, 1943-45; Minister of Information, 1945-46; High Commissioner in Australia, 1946-52. Mem., Nat. Industrial Disputes Tribunal, 1953 until termination, 1959. *Publications:* series of articles to various South Wales and Miners' Journals. *Recreations:* bowling, and all forms of sport and games. *Address:* Canberra, 107 Grove Rd., Bridgend, Glamorgan. [*Died* 16 *May* 1963.

WILLIAMS, Lt.-Col. Eliot; *see* Crawshay-Williams.

WILLIAMS, Eric W.; *see* Watson-Williams.

WILLIAMS, Sir Ernest Hillas, Kt. 1957; J.P.; Chairman, Pensions Appeal Tribunal, 1960; Regional Chairman, Mental Health Review Tribunal for North-West Metropolitan Area, 1960; President, Appeal Tribunal, Wireless Telegraph Act, 1963; *b.* 16 Aug. 1899; *y. s.* of late Hillas Williams; *m.* 1935, Mary Howard, *d.* of late Frank Howard Smith; one *d.* *Educ.:* Mountjoy Sch.; Trinity Coll. Dublin (Sch., Double Sen. Moderator and Gold Medallist, 1922). Colonial Administrative Service, Hong Kong, 1923; various administrative posts; Acting Sec. for Chinese Affairs and Mem. Exec. Council and Legislative Council, 1935 and 1937; Asst. Attorney-General, 1935; Crown Counsel, 1938; Legal Advisory staff, Colonial Office, 1939 and 1946; Hong Kong Volunteer Defence Corps, 1941-45 (P.O.W. Hong Kong and Japan, 1942-45); Puisne Judge, Hong Kong, 1946; Senior Puisne Judge, 1948; Chief Justice of the Borneo Territories Combined Judiciary, 1953-59, retired 1959. Chairman: Compulsory Service Tribunal, Hong Kong, 1940-1941; Evacuation Committee, 1940-41; War Memorial Cttee., Hong Kong, 1947-53; Public Services Commn., Hong Kong, 1952-1953. Retired, 1959. J.P., Surrey, 1961. *Recreations:* golf, walking. *Address:* 42 Dome Hill, Caterham, Surrey. *T.:* Caterham 3347. *Clubs:* Junior Carlton, Royal Commonwealth Society. [*Died* 5 *Feb.* 1965.

WILLIAMS, (Ernest) Rohan, M.D.; F.R.C.P.; F.R.C.S.; F.F.R.; Hon. F.C.R.A.; Hon. Radiologist (1935), Director of Radiological Department (1947), St. Mary's Hospital, London, W.2; Consultant Radiologist, Queen Charlotte's Maternity Hospital; *b.* 21 Dec. 1906; *s.* of Ernest Thomas Williams and Madge Williams (*née* Catleugh); *m.* 1932, Barbara Joyce (*née* Symes); one *s.* one *d.* *Educ.:* Epsom College; St. Mary's Hospital Medical School. Cheadle Gold Medallist, St. Mary's, 1929. M.R.C.S., L.R.C.P. 1929; M.B., B.S. (Lond.) 1930; M.R.C.P. (Lond.) 1931; D.M.R.E. (Camb.) 1932; M.D. (Lond.) 1933; F.R.C.P. 1940; F.F.R. 1937; F.R.C.S. (Eng.) 1961; Hon. Fellow, College of Radiologists of Australasia, 1960; Hon. Fellow, Faculty of Radiology, Royal College of Surgeons, Ireland, 1962. Hon. Radiologist: Willesden General Hospital, 1932-46; Hampstead General Hospital, 1939-48. President: British Institute of Radiology, 1944-45; President Section of Radiology, Royal Society of Medicine, 1955-56. Faculty of Radiologists: Hon. Secretary, 1949-54; Warden of Fellowship, 1956-61, Pres. 1961-; Knox Memorial Lecturer (first), 1957. Co-opted Member of Council, Royal College of Surgeons, 1953-58; Hunterian Professor, R.C.S., 1955-56. Temp. Consultant to World Health Organisation, on

Teaching Mission to Far East, 1952. Visiting Radiologist-in-Chief (*Pro Tem.*) and Merrill Sosman Memorial Lectr., Peter Bent Brigham Hosp.; Visiting Lectr., Harvard Univ. Med. Sch., Boston, U.S.A., 1960; Baker Travelling Prof. of Coll. of Radiologists of Australasia, in Australia and N.Z., 1960 (2 months). *Publications:* contributor to Text Book of X-Ray Diagnosis (by British Authors), 2nd edn. 1950, 3rd edn. 1958. Numerous contributions British Journal of Radiology and Jl. Faculty of Radiologists, especially in field of obstetric radiology. *Recreations:* gardening and photography. *Address:* Sherford, Pine Grove, Totteridge, Herts. *T.:* Hillside 2564. [*Died* 17 *March* 1963.

WILLIAMS, Sir (Evan) Owen, K.B.E., 1924; Civil Engineer and Architect; Private Practice since 1919; in partnership since 1939 with T. S. Vandy, M.I.C.E. (Asst. 1913) and (Son) O. T. Williams, M.I.C.E.; Consulting Engineers for Motorways, Ministry of Transport, since 1945 (First Section London-Birmingham Motorway (M.1) completed Nov. 1959); *b.* 1890; *s.* of Evan Owen Williams; *m.* 1915, Gladys (*d.* 1947), *d.* of Thomas Tustian; one *s.* one *d.*; *m.* 1947, Doreen, *d.* of Percy Harold Baker; one *s.* one *d.* *Educ.:* Tottenham Gram. Sch. B.Sc. London; M.Inst.C.E.; A.F.R.Ae.S.; Consulting Civil Engineer to British Empire Exhibition, 1924. *Works include:* Electric Tramways, London, 1905-11; Concrete ships during Wars; Road Bridges in Great Britain, 1925-30; Parc des Attractions, Paris Exhibition, 1925; Greyhound Racing Stadiums, 1927; first ramped garage, Cumberland Car Park, 1930; Dorchester Hotel (resigned before completion), 1930; Daily Express: London, Manchester, Glasgow, 1930-59; Pioneer Health Centre, 1934; Empire Pool, Wembley, 1934; Synagogue, Dollis Hill, 1936; Daily News Garage, London, 1938; Olympic Games Installation, Wembley Stadium, 1948; B.O.A.C. Headqrs. and Hangers, 1950-54; Daily Mirror, London, 1959 (in collaboration); several factories, notably Boots, Nottingham, 1930-36. *Publication:* (treatise) The Philosophy of Masonry Arches, 1927 (awarded Telford Gold Medal of Inst. Civil Engineers); (with O. T. Williams) (treatise) Design and Construction of M.1, 1961 (awarded Telford Gold Medal of Inst. of Civil Engineers). *Address:* 39 Kings Road, Berkhamsted; 141 Euston Road, N.W.1. *Clubs:* Arts, Garrick. [*Died* 23 *May* 1969.

WILLIAMS, Surgeon Rear-Admiral (D) Frank Reginald Parry, C.B.E. 1950 (O.B.E. 1946); *b.* 19 March 1897; *s.* of Rev. Henry Williams, Vicar of Brownhill, Batley, Yorks; *m.* 1926, Dorothy Ann Bird; one *s.* three *d.* *Educ.:* University College, Cork (B.D.S.). Served European War, 1917-18, with R.F.C.; joined R.N. Dental Service as Surgeon Lieut. (D), 1921; Surgeon Commander (D), 1936; Surgeon Captain (D), 1947; F.D.S.R.C.S.Eng., 1948; F.D.S.R.C.S. Edin., 1951. Deputy Director-General for Dental Services, Admiralty, 1950-54. Surgeon Rear-Admiral (D), 1952. K.H.D.S., 1950, Q.H.D.S., 1953, retired, 1954. *Recreations:* shooting, fishing, golf, sailing. *Address:* Little Chub Tor, Yelverton, Devon. *T.:* Yelverton 885. [*Died* 18 *May* 1965.

WILLIAMS, Brigadier and Chief Paymaster Frederick Christian, C.B. 1953; C.B.E. 1943; M.C.; Royal Army Pay Corps; *b.* 1891. Served European War, 1914-19, in Balkans and Egypt (M.C., 1914-15 star, two medals); served Palestine, 1936-39 (despatches, medal with clasp). Brigadier, 1951. *Address:* c/o Lloyds Bank Ltd., Cox's and King's Branch, 6 Pall Mall, S.W.1. [*Died* 16 *Jan.* 1970.

WILLIAMS, Sir Gwilym Ffrangcon, Kt. 1960; C.B.E. 1953; Vice-Chairman National Savings Committee; *b.* 6 Dec. 1902; *s.* of Illtyd Graham Williams; *m.* 1933, Florence Marion, *d.* of Francis Bardine Harrison. High Sheriff of Breconshire, 1942; High Constable of Miskin Higher, 1939-45. K.St.J. 1968 (C.St.J. 1963). *Address:* 14 Park Lane, Aberdare, Glam. *T.:* 2799. [*Died* 13 *Dec.* 1969.

WILLIAMS, Harold; *see* Heathcote-Williams.

WILLIAMS, Harold Beck, Q.C. 1947; LL.D. (Lond.); J.P.; Solicitor since 1912; *b.* 1889; *s.* of William Alfred Williams; *m.* 1932, Jane, *d.* of William G. Watson, Surbiton, Surrey; one *s.* one *d.* *Educ.:* privately; University College, London. Served European War, 1915-19, Lieut. Hampshire Regiment. Called to the Bar, Middle Temple, 1933, Master of the Bench, 1954. J.P. Surrey, 1950; Middlesex, 1952; Dep.-Chm. of Middlesex Quarter Sessions, 1956-63. Citizen and Bowyer. *Publications:* Improvement of Roads and Bridges, 1935; Public Health Act, 1936; War Damage Act, 1941; an Ed., Ryde on Rating; numerous legal articles and entomological papers. *Recreations:* horticulture, entomology (F.R.Ent.Soc. 1915; Vice-Pres., 1944, 1946, 1955). *Address:* 3 Hunters Close, The Ridings, Aldwick Bay, Bognor Regis, Sussex. *T.:* Pagham 3464. [*Died* 21 *April* 1969.

WILLIAMS, Sir Harold (Herbert), Kt., *cr.* 1951; F.B.A. 1944; F.S.A.; M.A.; Hon. D.Litt., Durham; Barrister-at-law; J.P. Herts; Herts C.C.; *b.* Tokio, 25 July 1880; *e. s.* of late Rev. James Williams and Mary Grindrod; *m.* 1913, Jean (*d.* 1948), *o. d.* of Andrew Chalmers, M.D.; *m.* 1949, Pauline Louise, *e. d.* of Major Campbell-Renton, Mordington and Lamberton, Berwickshire. *Educ.:* abroad; Christ's College, Cambridge. Steel University Student, 1903; Carus Prize, 1903. University Extension Lecturer; also lectured in U.S.A.; in 1915 served with the French forces in the Vosges; later, English forces; President of the Bibliographical Society, 1938-44; Sandars Reader in Bibliography, Cambridge, 1950; Vice-Chairman Herts C.C., 1939-47; Chairman Herts Education Committee, 1939-47; Chairman Herts C.C., 1947-52. *Publications:* Two Centuries of the English Novel, 1911; The Ballad of Two Great Cities, 1912; Discovery, 1913; Modern English Writers, 1918 (3rd and augmented edition, 1924); Outlines of Modern English Literature, 1920; Book Clubs and Printing Societies, 1929; Dean Swift's Library, 1932; The Text of Gulliver's Travels, 1952; edited Collected Works of Herbert Trench and Selected Poems of Herbert Trench, 1924; edited bi-centenary critical edition of Gulliver's Travels, 1926; The Poems of Jonathan Swift, 1937, 2nd edn., 1958; The Journal to Stella, 1948; contributor to English and American Reviews. *Recreations:* travelling, book-collecting, gardening, shooting. *Address:* 43 Albert Court, Kensington Gore, S.W.7. *Club:* Athenæum. [*Died* 24 *Oct.* 1964.

WILLIAMS, Rt. Rev. Henry Herbert, C.H. 1945; D.D.; *b.* Poppleton, York, 19 Dec. 1872; *e. s.* of Rev. J. Williams, Vicar of Poppleton; *m.* 1902, Maud Elizabeth, 3rd *d.* of late J. Y. Sargent, Fellow of Hertford College, Oxford; no *c.* *Educ.:* St. Peter's School, York; Queen's College, Oxford (Hastings Exhibitioner). Second Class Classical Mods., First Lit. Hum.; Aubrey Moore student: Fellow of Hertford College, Oxford, 1898; Deacon, 1900; Priest, 1901; Tutor and Lecturer in Philosophy, Hertford College, Oxford, until 1913; Principal of St. Edmund Hall, Oxford, 1913-1920; Bishop of Carlisle, 1920-46. Hon.

Fellow Queen's, Hertford and St. Edmund Hall; Select Preacher in University of Oxford, 1909-11, 1918-20, and 1938-39; Select Preacher in University of Cambridge, 1922 and 1926; Examining Chaplain to Bishop of Llandaff, 1908-20 *Publications:* articles in Encyclopædia Britannica. *Recreation:* golf. *Address:* 40 King Street, Chester. [*Died* 29 *Sept.* 1961.

WILLIAMS, Hubert Llewelyn, Q.C. 1938; D.L.; J.P.; Stipendiary Magistrate of Swansea, 1950-60; Chairman: Glamorgan County Quarter Sessions, 1949-61; Master of the Bench, Middle Temple, 1947; *b.* 1890; *s.* of Mayberry Williams, Pontypridd; *m.* 1915, Hilda, *d.* of late T. Lumley-Davies and Lady (David Charles) Roberts; no *c.* *Educ.:* Llandovery Coll.; Lincoln Coll., Oxford, M.A. Served four years in Army, European War, 1914-18, two years in France with 250 Siege Battery R.G.A. with rank of Lieut.; called to Bar, 1920; Recorder of Carmarthen, 1941-50; J.P. for Borough of Swansea, 1948; D.L. for County of Glamorgan, 1954. *Address:* Morfryn, Langland Bay, Swansea. *T.:* Swansea 66307. *Clubs:* National Liberal; Cardiff and County (Cardiff). [*Died* 11 *May* 1964.

WILLIAMS, Hugh (Anthony Glanmor); Actor, Playwright; *b.* 6 March 1904; *s.* of Hugh D. A. and Hilda Williams; *m.* 1st, 1925, Gwynne Whitby (marriage dissolved, 1940); two *d.*; 2nd, 1940, Margaret Vyner; two *s.* one *d.* *Educ.:* Haileybury; Switzerland. Served War of 1939-45 with the Devonshire Regt. and G.H.Q. Liaison Regt. First stage appearance 1921; Liverpool Repertory, 1923-26; three consecutive plays at Lyric Theatre; tours of Australia and Canada; The Matriarch, 1929; Grand Hotel, 1931; While Parents Sleep, 1932; The Green Bay Tree, 1933; Hollywood and New York, 1934-35; Pride and Prejudice, 1936; Old Music, 1937; Dear Octopus, 1939; The Seagull, 1956; Plaintiff in a Pretty Hat, 1956; The Happy Men, 1957; The Grass is Greener, 1958; The Irregular Verb to Love, 1961; Past Imperfect, 1964; The Cherry Orchard, 1966; Getting Married, 1967; Let's All Go Down the Strand, 1967. Appeared in films, 1931-54. *Publications:* (with Margaret Vyner) *plays:* Plaintiff in a Pretty Hat; The Happy Man; The Grass is Greener; Double Yolk; The Irregular Verb to Love; Past Imperfect; Charlie Girl; The Flip Side; Let's All Go Down the Strand; His, Hers and Theirs. *Recreations:* lying in the sun, swimming in the sea, reading, drinking, travelling. *Address:* c/o Bryce, Hanmer, 23 Albemarle Street, W.1. *Club:* Bath. [*Died* 7 *Dec.* 1969.

WILLIAMS, Sir Hugh Grenville, 6th Bt., *cr.* 1798; *b.* 26 March 1889; 2nd *s.* of 4th Bt. and Ellinor, *d.* of Willoughby Hurt Sitwell, Ferney Hall, Salop; *S.* brother, 1932; *m.* 1st, 1914, Charlotte Kebbel (divorce, 1921); 2nd, 1922, Maud Beatrice Fraser Marie, *d.* of Comte de Marillac St. Julien; one *s.* decd. Served European War 1914-19 (despatches, M.C. and bar). *Heir: kinsman,* Reginald (Lawrence William) Williams [*b.* 3 May 1900; *m.* 1936, Elinor Meriol Enriqueta Trevor; two *d.*]. [*Died* 9 *Dec.* 1961.

WILLIAMS, Hugh L.; *see* Lloyd-Williams.

WILLIAMS, Sir Ifor, Kt., *cr.* 1947; D.Litt. (Wales); LL.D.(Wales); F.B.A.1938; F.S.A.1939; Chairman: Board of Celtic Studies of Univ. of Wales, 1941-58; Ancient Monuments Board for Wales; Member of Royal Commission on Ancient Monuments in Wales and Monmouthshire, 1943; Pres. Cambrian Archæological Assoc. 1949-51; *b.* 16 April 1881; *s.* of John Williams, Pendinas, Tregarth, Bangor; *m.* 1913, Myfanwy (*d.* 1964), *d.* of Henry Jones, Cae Glas, Pontlyfni; one *s.* one *d.* *Educ.:* Friars Grammar School, Bangor; Clynnog Grammar School; Univ. College, Bangor (Bala Scholarship). U.C.N.W. Open Scholarship, B.A.; Honours (Second Class in Greek), 1905; Honours (First Class in Welsh), 1906; Scholar Assistant in Welsh at U.C.N.W., 1906-7; M.A. (Wales), 1907; thesis on Aneirin Poems; Assistant Lecturer in Welsh at U.C.N.W., 1907-19; Independent Lecturer in Welsh Literature, U.C.N.W., 1919; Professor of Welsh Literature, 1920; Professor of Welsh Language and Literature, University College of North Wales, Bangor, 1929-47. Medallist, Hon. Soc. Cymmrodorion. *Publications:* Breuddwyd Maxen, 1908; Cyfranc Lludd a Llevelys, 1909; Pedair Cainc y Mabinogi, 1911; Cywyddau Dafydd ap Gwilym, 1914; Dafydd ap Gwilym a'r Gler, Transactions of the Cymmrodorion, 1913-1914; Joint Editor of Y Tyddynnwr, 1922-23; Editor of Language and Literature Section, Bulletin of Board of Celtic Studies, 1921-48; General Editor, 1937-48; Poetical Works of Dafydd Nanmor, 1923; Iolo Goch ac Eraill (in collaboration), 1925; Chwedlau Odo, 1926; Ty Dol (Ibsen), 1926; Pedeir Keinc y Mabinogi, 1930; Gwyneddon 3, 1931; The Poems of Llywarch Hên (Sir John Rhys Memorial Lecture, British Academy), 1933; Canu Llywarch Hên, 1935; Epigraphic Notes (Anglesey Inventory), 1937; Canu Aneirin, 1938; Gwaith Guto'r Glyn (in collaboration), 1939; Lectures on Early Welsh Poetry, 1944; Enwau Lleoedd, 1945; Meddwn i, 1946; Armes Prydein, 1955; Chwedl Taliesin, 1957; I Ddifzrru'r Amser 1959; Canu Taliesin, 1960; various articles in Wales, Y Geninen, Y, Traethodydd, Y Beirniad, etc. *Recreation:* motoring. *Address:* Hafod Lwyd, Pontlyfni, Caernarvonshire. [*Died* 4 *Nov.* 1965.

WILLIAMS, Iolo Aneurin; author and journalist; *b.* Middlesbrough, 18 June 1890; *s.* of late Aneurin Williams, M.P.; *m.* 1920, Francion Elinor, *d.* of late A. R. Dixon, Cedaredge, Colorado, U.S.A.; one *s.* two *d.* *Educ.:* Rugby; King's College, Cambridge. Served in or with the Army (chiefly in France), 1914-20; retired as Capt.; Bibliographical Correspondent of London Mercury, 1920-39; part-time on Times since 1936, full-time since 1938; contributor to various journals and newspapers; has broadcast several times; sometime Hon. Secretary of Folk Song Society; a Trustee of the Watts Gallery, Compton; a Vice-President, Bibliographical Society, 1944; Member of Council, National Museum of Wales, 1958-; a Vice-President, Zoological Society of London, 1959-60; member, Welsh Cttee., Arts Council, 1960-; hon. member, Gorsedd of Bards, 1960. Contested (L) Chelsea, 1924 and 1929. *Publications:* Poems, 1915; New Poems, 1919; Byways Round Helicon, 1922; Shorter Poems of the 18th Century, 1923; Seven 18th Century Bibliographies, 1924; Editor: plays of Sheridan, 1926; Elements of Book-Collecting, 1927; Poetry To-day, 1927; Where the Bee Sucks, 1929; The Firm of Cadbury, 1931; Points in 18th Century Verse, 1934; English Folk Song and Dance, 1935; Flowers of Marsh and Stream (King Penguin), 1946; Early English Water-Colours, 1952, etc.; contributions to Dictionary of National Biography, 1937, and Cambridge Bibliography of English Literature, 1940. *Recreations:* natural history and collecting books, drawings, and plants. *Address:* West Hall, Kew Gardens, Surrey. *T.:* Prospect 3504. *Club:* Athenæum. [*Died* 18 *Jan.* 1962.

WILLIAMS, Capt. Jack; *see* Fox-Williams.

WILLIAMS, Capt. James E. L.; *see* Lloyd-Williams.

WILLIAMS, Sir John C. H.; *see* Hanbury-Williams.

WILLIAMS, Sir John L. C. C.; *see* Cecil-Williams.

WILLIAMS, Sir John R. L.; *see* Lort-Williams.

WILLIAMS, Lady Juliet R.; *see* Rhys Williams.

WILLIAMS, Maj.-Gen. Sir Leslie Hamlyn, K.B.E., *cr.* 1946; C.B. 1943; M.C. 1917; Director: Rootes Ltd., 1946; Howard Tenens Ltd. since 1956; Autolifts Engineering Co.; Chairman Grierson Oldham and Adams; Col. Comdt. R.A.O.C. since 1945; *b.* 13 June 1892; *s.* of Alfred Hamlyn and Mildred M. Williams; *m.* 1948, Nancy Mary, *o. d.* of F. G. Perks, Long Eaton; one *s.* one *d.* *Educ.:* Dulwich. London Scottish, 1909; 2nd Lieutenant Suffolk Regiment, 1914; served European War, 1914-1918; attached A.O.D. 1915; D.A.D.O.S. 19th Division, France, 1916-17; A.D.O.S. G.H.Q. Italy, 1918 (despatches, M.C., 1914-15 Star, British War Medal, Victory Medal); Bt. Lieut.-Colonel 1935; Bt. Colonel 1938; D.D.O.S. Served War of 1939-45, War Office, Sept. 1939; Director of Warlike Stores, 1940, and Controller of Ordnance Services, 1942-46, War Office (Africa Star, Burma Star, Italy Star, Defence Medal, General Service Medal); Master of Worshipful Company of Carmen, 1951-52; Knight of Polish Order of Polonia Restituta; Commander Legion of Merit; Commander Order of Crown of Belgium; Commander of Legion of Honour; Croix de Guerre (Belgium). *Recreations:* fishing, motoring. *Address:* Long Grove House, Seer Green, Beaconsfield. *T.:* Jordans 3221.
[*Died* 7 *Aug.* 1965.

WILLIAMS, Llywelyn; M.P. (Lab.) Abertillery Division of Monmouthshire since Nov. 1950; Governor, Westminster Hospital; *b.* 22 July 1911; *s.* of W. Williams, Llanelly; *m.* 1938, Hon. Elsie Macdonald, *d.* of 1st Baron Macdonald of Gwaenysgor, *q.v.*; one *s.* one *d.* *Educ.:* Llanelly Grammar School; Univ. Coll. of Swansea (B.A. Wales); Presbyterian Coll., Carmarthen. Congregational Minister: Bethesda, Bangor, 1936-42; Tabernacle, Abertillery, 1943-46; Welsh Tabernacle, King's Cross, London, 1946-50. *Publication:* History of King's Cross Welsh Tabernacle Church, 1947. *Address:* House of Commons, S.W.1; Hafod y Cwm, Pant Rd., Newbridge, Mon., South Wales. *T.:* Newbridge 229. [*Died* 4 *Feb.* 1965.

WILLIAMS, Orlando (Orlo) Cyprian, C.B. 1941; M.C.; Chevalier, Legion of Honour; D.C.L. 1946; F.R.S.L. 1951; *b.* 4 May 1883; *s.* of late T. Cyprian Williams, Conveyancer to the Supreme Court, Bencher of Lincoln's Inn, and Helen, *d.* of late A. C. Campbell; *m.* 1912, Alice Isabella (*d.* 1953), *d.* of late Rt. Hon. Sir Frederick Pollock, Bart., K.C., 21 Hyde Park Place, W.; one *d.* *Educ.:* Eton (K.S.); Balliol College, Oxford (Domus Exhibitioner), 1st class Hon. Mods. and Lit. Hum.; became Clerk, House of Commons, 1907; lately the Clerk of Committees, House of Commons, retd. 1948. Served in Army, 1915-19, Dardanelles, Egypt, Palestine; G.S.O. 2, Major at G.H.Q., Mediterranean Expdy. Force and at War Office, 1918-19; Lieut. Palace of Westminster Company, Home Guard, 1940-1945; contrib. to Times Literary Supplement and many other periodicals. *Publications:* Life and Letters of John Rickman, 1912; Vie de Bohème, 1913; The Good Englishwoman, 1920; Contemporary Criticism, 1924; The Essay, 1914; Giosuè Carducci, 1914; Three Naughty Children, 1922; Some Great English Novels, 1926; Charles Lamb, 1934; The Historical Development of Private Bill Procedure and Standing Orders in the House of Commons, 1948; The Minute Book of James Courthope (Camden Miscellany vol. XX), 1953; The Topography of the Old House of Commons (Min. of Works), 1953; The Clerical Organisation of the House of Commons, 1661-1850, 1954; trans. several Italian novels and other works. *Recreations:* winner Heavy-Weight Boxing and Foils, Eton, 1901 and 1902, sabres, Oxford *v.* Cambridge, 1903. *Address:* 6 Weller Court, 66 Ladbroke Road, W.11. *T.:* Park 7812. *Clubs:* Athenæum, Garrick.
[*Died* 10 *March* 1967.

WILLIAMS, Sir Owen; *see* Williams, Sir E. O.

WILLIAMS, Owen Herbert, D.Sc. Wales (Hon.); M.B., Ch.B. (Edin.); F.R.C.S. (Eng. and Edin.); D.P.H. (Oxf.); Emeritus Professor of Surgery, University of Liverpool; Hon. Consulting Surgeon, Royal Liverpool United Hospital (Royal Southern Hosp. Branch); Hon. Surgeon, Liverpool Radium Inst.; Vice-President, Univ. College of North Wales, Bangor; Member of the Council of the Welsh National School of Medicine. Member Anglesey Health Committee; *b.* 1884; *s.* of Owen and Jane Williams, Bodrwnsiwn, Anglesey; *m.* 1916, Ethel Kenrick (High Sheriff, Anglesey, 1961), *d.* of William Thomas, Shipowner, Liverpool; one *s.* one *d.* *Educ.:* Beaumaris Grammar School; Univ. of Edinburgh. Major R.A.M.C. (T.F.) (retired); Surgical Specialist 51st (Highland) Casualty Clearing Station, B.E.F. Past Pres. Liverpool Medical Institution. *Publications:* papers in the medical journals. *Recreations:* bird photography, fishing. *Address:* 18 Sefton Park Road, Liverpool 8. *T.:* Lark Lane 1482; Hafod Wen, Rhosneigr, Anglesey. *T.:* Rhosneigr 205. *Clubs:* Royal Automobile; University (Liverpool).
[*Died* 6 *March* 1962.

WILLIAMS, Ralph W. H.; *see* Hodder-Williams.

WILLIAMS, Richard James, R.C.A. 1936 (A.R.C.A. 1919); M.R.S.T.; *b.* Hereford, 16 March 1876; *s.* of Samuel Williams, Hereford; *m.* 1905, Madge Oakey James (*d.* 1958). *Educ.:* Grange Coll., Leominster; Newhaven Gram. Sch.; Hereford County College; Cardiff University College; Art Schools, Hereford, Cardiff, Birmingham and London; Gold Medallist (Cardiff), 1893; Holder of two Art Scholarships, Board of Education and Birmingham School of Art; exhibited at R.I., R.C.A., etc.; represented by engravings, etc. at Victoria and Albert Museum, British Museum, National Museum of Wales, Hereford Art Gallery; work in Studio Specials; teaching posts, Birmingham, Gloucestershire, and Worcester; First Assistant Master, 1908, then Head Master, Worcester School of Art and Crafts; retired, 1939; Art Teachers Diploma, 1919; edited Three Pears Magazine for several years; Illustrator of numerous children's books; Designer of Children's Games and Toys. Four Water Colours in permanent collection, Worcester Art Gallery, Victoria Inst. *Publications;* contributor to many Children's Magazines and Scholastic Publications. *Recreations:* philately, numismatics, anthropology, and cactus culture. *Address:* Ascalon, 37 Hill Avenue, Worcester. [*Died* 5 *Nov* 1964.

WILLIAMS, Lt.-Col. Robert Carlisle, C.M.G. 1919; D.S.O. 1916; late R.A.; *b.* 2 Feb. 1880; 5th *s.* of late G.R.C. Williams, I.C.S.; *m.* 1917, Mary Frances Elizabeth, *d.* of late Carter N. Draper; one *s.* two *d.* *Educ.:* Elizabeth College, Guernsey; R.M.A. Woolwich. First commissioned, June 1899; served S. Africa, 1901-02 (Queen's medal 4 clasps); S. Nigeria, 1906 (medal with clasp); European War, 1914-18 (wounded four times, D.S.O., C.M.G., Croix de Guerre); retired pay, 1926; War of 1939-45, re-employed, 1939-41. *Address:* The Elms, Upton Snodsbury, Worcester.
[*Died* 28 *June* 1964.

WILLIAMS, Rohan; *see* Williams, Ernest R.

WILLIAMS, Theodore Rowland, C.M.G. 1954; farmer since 1926; *b.* 29 Sept. 1889; *s.* of J. R. Williams, M.A., Kew Park, Jamaica, and Margaret, *d.* of General W. T. F. Farewell, Bath; *m.* 1926, Gwendolen Brinley Boatfield, Torrington, Devon; one *s.* two *d.* *Educ.:* Bath College and Trinity College, Oxford. Civil Service of Northern Rhodesia, 1912-25. Since 1926, farming and public service in Jamaica: Custos of Westmoreland, 1944; M.L.C., 1941; M.E.C., 1951. *Recreations:* unaggressive ball games. *Address:* Kew Park, Jamaica. *Club:* Oxford Union. [*Died* 18 *Feb.* 1964.

WILLIAMS, Sir Thomas, Kt. 1964; O.B.E. 1955; *b.* 26 September 1893; *s.* of late James Williams and Mary Ann; *m.* 1920, Nellie, *d.* of James Turner Brown and Lydia Ann Brown; one *s.* two *d.* *Educ.:* Normanton Grammar School; Leeds University. Principal, Johannesburg Teachers Coll., and Hon. Prof. of Educn., Univ. of Witwatersrand, 1935-49; Dir. of European Educn., Northern Rhodesia, 1950-55; Clerk of the House, Northern Rhodesia Legislative Council, 1955-56; Speaker Legislative Assembly, 1956-64. Served European War, 1914-18: Machine Gun Corps, B.E.F., 1916-1919 (Lieut.); served War of 1939-45: S.A. Staff Corps (V), 1940-43 (Major). Chairman, Zambia University Provisional Council, 1964-1965. *Recreations:* bowls, gardening. *Address:* P.O. Box R.W.7 Lusaka, Zambia. *Club:* Lusaka (Zambia). [*Died* 23 *Feb.* 1967.

WILLIAMS, Thomas H.; *see* Hudson-Williams.

WILLIAMS, Walter Naider, M.A., LL.B.; Senior Fellow of Selwyn College, Cambridge, *b* London, 17 Aug. 1880; *s.* of late Walter Williams, formerly of Eastbourne; *m.* 1917, Evelyn Mary, *y. d.* of late Rev. G. M. Russell; one *s.* one *d.* *Educ.:* Eastbourne Coll. (Scholar); Trinity College, Cambridge (Scholar); First Class Classical Tripos, Part I., 1902; First Class Law Tripos, Part I., 1903; Classical Lecturer of Selwyn College, 1905-31; Lecturer at Girton College, 1904-14; Sublector at Trinity College, 1908-10; General Secretary Christian Social Union, 1910-12; Assistant Secretary of Cambridge Local Examinations, 1914-21 and General Secretary, 1921-46; Member Norwood Committee on Secondary Education, 1941; Member Cambridge University Board of Extra-Mural Studies from its inauguration to 1948, President Cambridge Philatelic Society, 1926-1946. *Recreations:* gardening, walking, music; *Address:* Knockbrea, Penn, High Wycombe, Bucks. *T.:* Penn 2303. [*Died* 12 *April* 1966.

WILLIAMS, Maj.-Gen. Weir De Lancey, C.B. 1921; C.M.G. 1917; D.S.O. 1899; *b.* 2 March 1872; *s.* of Sir W. J. Williams, K.C.B.; of Pembroke, Wales; *m.* 1899, Nina Henrietta, *d.* of Col. Field, late 6th Foot; one *d.* *Educ.:* United Services College, Westward Ho! Entered Army, 1891; Captain, 1898; Major, 1909; Lt.-Col. 1915; served Tirah Expedition, 1897 (severely wounded); West Africa, 1898 (severely wounded); South Africa, 1900 (severely wounded, despatches, Queen's medal 2 clasps); European War, 1914-18 (despatches, Bt. Col., C.M.G.); retired pay, 1923. *Recreations:* hunting, fishing, shooting. *Address:* Halcyon Pl., Doyle Rd., Guernsey. [*Died* 28 *Nov.* 1961.

WILLIAMS, Wilfred H.; *see* Howard-Williams.

WILLIAMS, William Daniel, O.B.E. 1944; *b.* 30 March 1888; *s.* of Henry Llewellyn Williams, Parkydrissy, Carmarthen; *m.* 1946, Annie Beatrice, *d.* of D. E. Jones, Eryl Daf, Radyr, Glam.; one *d.* *Educ.:* Queen Elizabeth Grammar School, Carmarthen; University College of Wales, Aberystwyth Solicitor, 1910; Coroner, 1925-65. LL.B. (London) 1911. Served European War, 1914-19; Major, 1918; War of 1939-45, Home Guard, Col. Sector Commander. Carmarthen, 1940-44. Formerly for many years Chm. of Ammanford Gas Co. and Benubor Tea Co. and Director of other companies; Chm. of Carmarthenshire T. and A.F.A., 1951-52 and 1952-53. D.L. Co. of Carmarthen, 1943; Vice-Lieutenant of the County of Carmarthen, 1957-67. *Recreations:* shooting, fishing and golf. *Address:* Parkydrissy, Carmarthen. *T.:* Carmarthen 5193. *Club:* Reform. [*Died* 9 *March* 1970.

WILLIAMS, Sir William Richard, Kt., *cr.* 1930; Railway Traffic Superintendent; *b.* 1879; *s.* of Thomas Williams, Pontypridd; *m.* 1902, Mabel Escott Melluish; no *c.* *Educ.:* Cardiff. Junior Clerk, Rhymney Railway, 1893; in Charge of Traffic Dept., 1905; on grouping of Railways in 1922 appointed by G.W. Railway, Assistant Divisional Superintendent; retired, 1931; Elected Cardiff City Council, 1913; Deputy Lord Mayor, 1921-22; Lord Mayor, 1928-29; Magistrate. Hon. Freedom Cardiff, 1954. *Recreation:* motoring. *Address:* 71 King George Drive, West Heath, Cardiff. [*Died* 28 *June* 1961.

WILLIAMS, William Richard; M.P. (Lab.) Openshaw Division of Manchester since 1955; *b.* 1 March 1895; *s.* of Welsh quarryman; *m.*; three *d.* *Educ.:* Elementary and County Schools. Civil Servant (Post Office), 1912-40; Assistant Secretary, Post Office Workers, 1940-52. M.P. (Lab.) Heston and Isleworth, 1945-50; Droylsden, 1951-55. *Recreation:* bowls. *Address:* 53 Woodbury Drive, Sutton, Surrey. *T.:* Vigilant 7060. [*Died* 11 *Sept.* 1963.

WILLIAMS-DRUMMOND, Sir James H. W.; *see* Drummond.

WILLIAMSON, Sir Horace, Kt., *cr.* 1934; C.I.E. 1922; M.B.E.; *b.* 1880; *s.* of George Williamson, Barrister-at-law; *m.* 1913, Joan Doran Holtz. *Educ.:* Cheltenham Coll. Joined Indian Police, United Provinces, 1900; Superintendent, 1913; Assistant to Inspector-General, 1917; Secretary Indian Disorders Inquiry Committee, 1919-20; Deputy Inspector-General of Police, 1923; Officiating Inspector-General, 1928; Director Intelligence Bureau, Home Department, Government of India, 1931-1936; retired 1936; Member of Council of India, 1936-37; Adviser to Secretary of State for India, 1937-42. King's Police Medal, 1931. *Address:* Beacon Lodge, Crowborough, Sussex. [*Died* 15 *April* 1965.

WILLIAMSON, James Alexander, M.A., D.Lit.; author; *b.* 1886; *s.* of late James Ireland Williamson; *m.* Ruth Chapple. *Educ.:* Watford Grammar School; London University. B.A. 1906, M.A. 1909; Army, 1914-19; D.Lit. 1924; Vice-President Hakluyt Society; Vice-President, Historical Association; Assistant Master, Westminster City School, 1910-37; Ford Lectr., 1939-40; *Publications:* Maritime Enterprise, 1485–1558, 1913; A Short History of British Expansion, 1922, (latest edn., 1963); The English in Guiana, 1923; Europe Overseas, 1925, new edn. 1938; The Caribbee Islands under the Proprietary Patents, 1926; Sir John Hawkins, the Time and the Man, 1927; Voyages of the Cabots, 1929; The Evolution of England, 1931, new edn., 1943; The Observations of Sir Richard Hawkins (edited), 1933; The British Empire and Commonwealth, 1935, (latest edition 1962); The Age of Drake, 1938, latest edition 1964; Dampier's Voyage to New Holland (edited), 1939; The Ocean in English History (Ford Lec-

tures, 1940), 1941; A Notebook of Commonwealth History, 1942, new edn. 1959; Great Britain and the Empire, 1944; Cook and the Opening of the Pacific (Teach Yourself History Library), 1946; Hawkins of Plymouth, 1949; Sir Francis Drake (Collins's Brief Lives), 1951 (Fontana edn., 1961); The Tudor Age, 1953, new edition 1964; George and Robert Stephenson, 1958; The English Channel: a History, 1959; The Cabot Voyages and Bristol Discovery under Henry VII, 1962; school books; contrib. to Blackwood's Magazine, Geogrl. Jl., History, Johnson's England, Cambridge History of the British Empire; joint editor of The Pioneer Histories. *Address:* 2 Laburnum Grove, Chichester, Sussex.
[*Died* 31 *Dec.* 1964.

WILLIAMSON, Thomas Broadwood, C.M.G. 1953; Assistant Secretary, Department of Technical Co-operation, since 1961; *b.* 18 August 1911; 2nd *s.* of William Norman Williamson and Gertrude Louise (*née* Johnson); *m.* 1943, Margaret Frances, *o. d.* of Capt. B. O. M. Davy, R.N. (retd.); one *s.* one *d.* *Educ.:* City of London School; Trinity College, Cambridge. Entered Home Office as Asst. Principal, 1934; Asst. Private Secretary to Home Secretary, 1937-1938; Principal, Home Office, 1938. Served in Berlin with C.C.G., 1945-48. Asst. Secretary, 1946; transferred to Colonial Office, 1948; seconded to Department of Technical Co-operation, 1961. *Recreations:* swimming, church-crawling, watching county cricket. *Address:* 7 Woodside Avenue, Highgate, N.6. *T.:* Tudor 3903. *Club:* Oxford and Cambridge. [*Died* 22 *Feb.* 1963.

WILLIAMSON-NOBLE, Frederick Arnold; Ophthalmic Surgeon; *b.* 26 July 1889; *e. s.* of late G. E. Williamson, F.R.C.S., Newcastle upon Tyne; assumed name Williamson-Noble, 1921; *m.* 1917, Hon. Sheila Black Noble, *er. d.* of 1st Baron Kirkley of Kirkley; one *s.* (elder son killed on active service, Dec. 18, 1945). *Educ:* Oundle School; Cambridge University. B.A., M.B.(Cantab.); F.R.C.S.Eng.; F.R.C.S. Eng. with Ophthalmology; Temporary Surgeon Lt. R.N., 1914-19; Civil Ophthalmic Consultant R.N., 1943; Master Oxon. Ophthalmological Congress, 1947-49; Consulting Ophthalmic Surgeon, St. Mary's Hosp., Paddington and National Hosp. for Diseases of the Nervous System, Queen Square; Consulting Surg. Central London Ophthalmic Hosp.; Fellow Roy. Soc. of Medicine; Member Ophthalmological Society of United Kingdom and of Société Française d'Ophtalmologie; Lettsomian Lecturer Medical Society of London, 1932. *Publications:* Handbook of Ophthalmology (jointly); Chapter on Ophthalmology in Maingot's Surgery; Contributions to various medical journals. *Recreations:* ski-ing, golf, squash rackets. *Address:* 27 Harley Street, W.1. *T.A.* and *T.:* Langham 1631, 01-580 7068. [*Died* 27 *Feb.* 1969.

WILLIS, Maj.-Gen. Edward Henry, C.B. 1918; C.M.G. 1917; *b.* 5 Sept. 1870; *s.* of H. S. Willis of Trowbridge, Wilts; *m.* 1st, 1904, Sarah Augusta (*d.* 1924), 2nd *d.* of Micah Barlow, Bury, Lancs; one *s.*; 2nd, 1925, Ellis Mary (*d.* 1961) *d.* of late Col. A. W. Duke. *Educ.:* Hermitage Sch., Bath; Wolfram's; R.M. Academy, Woolwich. Received commission in R.A. 1890; Capt. 1900; Major, 1907; Lt.-Col., 1914; Maj.-Gen., 1921; served in United Kingdom and Mediterranean till 1897; Queensland, 1897 and 1898; and in the East till August 1914, when he brought the 94th Batt. R.F.A. (Lahore Division) to France; served European War, 1914-18 (despatches five times, Brevet Col., Russian Order of St. Stanislaus, C.M.G., C.B.); Maj.-Gen. R.A. India, 1921-25; Inspector of Royal Artillery, 1927-29; Lieut.-Governor of Jersey and commanding troops in Jersey District, 1929-34; Colonel Commandant R.A., 1933-40; retired pay, 1934. *Address:* Westlands, St. Brelade, Jersey, C.I. *Club:* Naval and Military.
[*Died* 26 *June* 1961.

WILLIS, Captain Frank Reginald, C.B.E. 1935; Royal Navy (retired); *b.* 9 Aug. 1881; 4th *s.* of late James Willis, I.S.O., of H.M. Office of Works; *m.* 1908, Pauline Mann (*d.* 1960); three *d.* *Educ.:* H.M.S. Britannia. Lieut. 1901; Mem of Ordnance Cttee., 1928-1929; Chief Inspector of Naval Ordnance, 1929-36; Naval Ordnance Inspecting Officer, Royal Ordnance Factory, Chorley, 1939 - 45. *Address:* Moor View, Ashwell Lane, Glastonbury, Somerset. [*Died* 8 *April* 1964.

WILLIS, Maj.-Gen. John Christopher Temple, C.B. 1956; C.B.E. 1953; J.P.; R.I.; R.S.M.A.; *b.* 14 May 1900; *s.* of Paymaster Captain G. H. A. Willis and Adela Willis (*née* Frere); *m.* 1927, Ursula Frances Galpin; one *s.* one *d.* *Educ.:* Uppingham; Royal Military Academy, Woolwich. Commissioned R.E. 1919; Malayan Survey Section, R.E., 1923-26; War Office, 1926-30; Ordnance Survey, 1930-34; Survey Instructor, S.M.E., Chatham, 1934-37; Jamaican Survey Section, R.E., 1937-39; Asst. Director of Intelligence (Maps), Air Ministry, 1939-41; Dep. Dir. Mil. Survey, War Office, 1941-45; Dir. of Survey, S.E. Asia Comd., 1945-48; Dep. Dir. Ordnance Survey, 1948-1949; Dir. Mil. Survey, War Office, 1949-53; Dir.-Gen., Ordnance Survey, 1953-57, retired. J.P. 1957. *Publications:* papers and travel articles. *Recreations:* water-colour painting, gardening. *Address:* Wood Hatch, Furze Hill, The Sands, Farnham, Surrey.
[*Died* 12 *Oct.* 1969.

WILLIS, Major Richard Raymond, V.C. 1915; late Lancashire Fusiliers; *b.* 13 Oct. 1876; *s.* of R. A. Willis; *m.* 1907, Maude (*d.* 1960), *d.* of Col. J. A. Temple, I.A., and *niece* of late Sir R. Temple, Bt.; two *s.* one *d.* *Educ.:* Harrow; Sandhurst. Entered army, 1897; Captain, 1900; Major, 1915; served Nile Expedition, 1898 (Egyptian medal with clasp, medal); European War, Dardanelles, 1915 (V.C., chosen by his regiment to receive the decoration for a desperate landing in Gallipoli); France, 1915-18; R.A.F. Education Officer, 1923-29; retired. F.R.G.S. *Address:* Faithfull House, Cheltenham. [*Died* 9 *Feb.* 1966.

WILLISON, Brig. (retd.) Arthur Cecil, D.S.O. 1919; M.C.; J.P.; Royal Tank Regt.; late Sherwood Foresters; *b.* 1896; *m.* 1918, Hyacinth D'Arcy (*d.* 1957), (Kaisar-i-Hind Gold Medal, 1935), *er. d.* of Major Philip Urban Walter Vigors, D.S.O.; one *s.* Served European War, 1914-19 (despatches twice, D.S.O., M.C. and Bar); G.S.O. 3 Intelligence, W. Command, India, 1934; D.A.A.G. Deccan District, India, 1937-39; War of 1939-1945 (Bar to D.S.O., prisoner, but repatriated); G.S.O.1 Intelligence: Far East, 1943; Germany, 1945. J.P. Devon. *Address:* Trentishoe Manor, Parracombe, N. Devon. *T.:* 243. *Club:* Naval and Military.
[*Died* 11 *March* 1966.

WILLMOT, Roger Boulton, C.M.G. 1953; *b.* 16 October 1892; *s.* of late Philip Henry Willmot; *m.* 1936, Thirza, *d.* of late Rev. A. J. Hards; one *d.* *Educ.:* Berkhamsted School. In business in London, 1911-15. European War; commnd. in R.G.A. (S.R.), 1916-19. Board of Trade, London, 1920-24; Calcutta, 1924-35; Trade Commissioner at Singapore, 1935-42. Civil Internee in Singapore with the Japanese, 1942-45. Board of Trade, London, 1946-1947; Trade Comr. in Malaya, Singapore, 1947-49; United Kingdom Senior Trade Commissioner in New Zealand, 1949-55; retired, 1955. *Address:* 6 Kenton Court, Kenton Road, Harrow, Middx. *T.:* Wordsworth 1860. [*Died* 25 *Jan.* 1964.

WILLOUGHBY de ERESBY, Lord; Timothy Gilbert Heathcote-Drummond-Willoughby; *b.* 19 March 1936; *o. s.* of 3rd Earl of Ancaster, T.D. *Educ.:* Eton College. *Recreations:* collecting (very nearly anything), travelling. *Address:* 5 Wilton Row, S.W.1. *T.:* Belgravia 5811. *Club:* Bath.
[*Missing, at sea in August* 1963; *High Court gave leave to presume death in March* 1964.

WILLS, Captain Arnold Stancomb; *b.* 1877; 4th *s.* of Sir Edward Payson Wills, 1st Bt.; *m.* 1905, Hilda C., *d.* of late Edward Lyon; two *s.* Sheriff of Northamptonshire, 1935. *Address:* Middleton, Longparish, Andover, Hampshire. *T.:* Longparish 206. *Clubs:* Cavalry; Royal Yacht Squadron (Cowes).
[*Died* 19 *Jan.* 1961.

WILLS, Edith Agnes, O.B.E. 1966; J.P.; City Councillor, City of Birmingham, 1930, Honorary Councillor, 1968; Director, Birmingham Co-operative Society, since 1932; Chairman Directors, Birmingham Printers Ltd.; *b.* 21 Nov. 1892; *d.* of John Philip and Henrietta Wood; *m.* 1921, Frank Wills; one *s.* *Educ.:* Aston; Birmingham. M.P. (Lab.) Duddeston Division Birmingham, 1945-50. Member, Rating and Valuation Court Panel. *Address:* 164 Pretoria Road, Birmingham 9. *T.:* 021-772 3641.
[*Died* 7 *April* 1970.

WILLS, Sir Gerald, Kt. 1958; M.B.E. 1945; M.A.; J.P.; M.P. (C.) Bridgwater Division of Somerset since 1950; Comptroller of H.M. Household, 1957-58; *b.* 1905. *Educ.:* privately; Trinity College, Cambridge (M.A.). Barrister, Middle Temple, 1932; served War of 1939-45, with R.A. (T.A.) and on Staff; D.A.A.G., H.Q. Southern Command, 1942-45. J.P. (Wiltshire) 1946; contested Bridgwater Division, 1945. Asst. Whip, 1952. Lord Comr. of the Treasury, 1954. *Address:* Milton House, East Knoyle, Salisbury, Wiltshire. *T.:* East Knoyle 397; 42 Eaton Square, S.W.1. *Clubs:* Buck's, Carlton, Pratt's. [*Died* 31 *Oct.* 1969.

WILLS, Richard Lloyd Joseph, C.B.E. 1961; M.C. 1945; Member, British Transport Docks Board, since 1963, Vice-Chairman since 1968, Chairman, 1969; Vice-Chairman, George Wills & Sons (Holdings) Ltd., since 1961; Managing Director: George Wills & Sons Ltd., since 1958; Fowlie Reid and Wills Ltd., since 1967; *b.* 9 Mar. 1914; *s.* of Charles Percy Wills and Clarisse Audrey (*née* Patton-Bethune); *m.* 1948, Joan Eileen (*née* Abercromby); one step *d.* *Educ.:* Harrow School; Corpus Christi College, Cambridge. G. & R. Wills & Co. Ltd., Adelaide, S. Australia, 1931-35; Cambridge, 1935-38; Foreign Service, 1939; served Royal Fusiliers, 1939-40; 2nd Lieut. D.C.L.I., June 1940; No. 3 Commando, 1940-45, Capt., 1941-45. A Vice-Pres., London Chamber of Commerce, 1962-; Pres., Assoc. of British Chambers of Commerce, 1964-66. *Recreations:* fishing, sailing, ski-ing. *Address:* 36 Marlborough Place, N.W.8. *T.:* Maida Vale 3066. *Club:* Devonshire.
[*Died* 25 *Sept.* 1969.

WILLS, Dame Violet Edith, D.B.E., *cr* 1937; *d.* of Sir Edward Payson Wills, 1st Bt., K.C.B. Member of Queen Mary's Institute for District Nursing Committee. Officer Order of St. John of Jerusalem. *Address:* Sungleam, Clevedon, Somerset: Woodside, Stoke Bishop, Bristol. [*Died* 26 *Oct.* 1964.

WILLS, Walter Kenneth, O.B.E.; V.D.; J.P.; M.A., M.B., B.C. (Cantab.), M.R.C.S., L.R.C.P.; *b.* 9 Dec. 1872; *s.* of late Samuel Day Wills, J.P.; *m.* 1st, Kathleen (*d.* 1923), *d.* of late Charles Foulger Tubbs, Plymouth; one *s.* one *d.*; 2nd, 1926, Kathleen Jane (*d.* 1955), *d.* of late Rev. John MacIldowie, Bristol. *Educ.:* Clifton College; St. John's Coll., Cambridge; Guy's Hospital; Vienna. Surgeon-Captain R.N.V.R., retired. *Publications:* medical papers. *Address:* The Old Vicarage, Henbury, Bristol. *T.:* Bristol, Westbury-on-Trym 626551. [*Died* 6 *Jan.* 1968.

WILLYAMS, Bt. Colonel Edward Neynoe, D.S.O. 1917; D.L., J.P. Cornwall; late Duke of Cornwall's L.I.; *b.* 1891; *s.* of late Humphry John Willyams and Margaret, *y. d.* of late Joseph Jowitt, of Bishop Thornton, Ripley; *m.* 1918, Beatrice Jean Blewett, A.R.R.C., late C.A.M.C., *e. d.* of late Coleman and Mary Blewett, Toronto, Canada. *Educ.:* Eton; R.M.C., Sandhurst. Served European War. 1914-18 (D.S.O.); retired pay, 1926; Commanded 4/5th Batt. D.C.L.I. (T.A.) 1929-35; Lt.-Col. Cmdg. No. 3 Stevedore Bn. R.E., France, 1939-40 (despatches); Cmdg. 6th H.D. Bn. The Wiltshire Regt., 1940-41. Sheriff of Cornwall, 1934-35. Hon. Colonel 4/5 D.C.L.I., 1947-58. *Address:* Carnanton, near Newquay, Cornwall. *T.:* St. Mawgan 345. *Club:* United Service. [*Died* 12 *May* 1964.

WILMOT OF SELMESTON, 1st Baron, *cr.* 1950, of Selmeston, Sussex; **John Wilmot,** P.C. 1945; J.P. Co. of London; *b.* 2 April 1895; *s.* of late Charles Wilmot, engraver. Gilbart Prizeman in Banking, King's College, London. Member of Institute of Bankers; Chairman Illingworth Morris & Co. Ltd.; Salts (Saltaire) Ltd.; Edwards High Vacuum Ltd.; West Cumberland Silk Mills Ltd. and other Cos.; contested East Lewisham, 1924, 1929, 1931; M.P. (Lab.) East Fulham, 1933-1935; Kennington Div. of Lambeth, 1939-1945; Deptford, 1945-50. Parliamentary Private Secretary to Minister of Economic Warfare, 1940-42; to President of Board of Trade, 1942-44; Joint Parliamentary Secretary, Ministry of Supply, 1944-45; Minister of Supply, 1945-47. Served in Royal Naval Air Service during European War, 1914-19. Member: Cohen Cttee. on Company Law Reform, 1943-45; Select Cttee. on Rebuilding Houses of Parliament, 1944; Exec. Cttee.: British-American Parl. Assoc. (Chm. 1948-50); Commonwealth Parl. Assoc. (and Vice-Chm. of Council); British Section, Inter-Parliamentary Union; Alderman of L.C.C., 1936-44, Chairman Parliamentary Committee, 1944; Chairman London Fire Brigade, 1938-42; Member of the National Theatre Board; Chairman: Governors of Old Vic; Glyndebourne Festival Society. *Publications:* Banking and Finance, 1935; numerous papers on political, historical and financial subjects. *Recreations:* the theatre, the opera, travel, camping and sailing. *Address:* Cobb Court Farm, Selmeston, Sussex; 8 Buckingham Place, Westminster, S.W.1. *T.:* Victoria 1481. *Clubs:* Garrick, Reform, Savile. [*Died* 22 *July* 1964 (*ext.*).

WILMOT, Harold, C.B.E. 1949; Chairman 1949-65 (Man. Dir., 1938-60) of Beyer, Peacock & Co. Ltd., and its subsidiary cos., retd.; also as Dir., and as Chm., Beyer Peacock (Hymek) Ltd. (1958-65); *b.* 14 Aug. 1895; *o. s.* of late Ernest Luke Wilmot, Matlock, Derbys., and Hannah Elizabeth Wilmot; *m.* 1st, 1925, Margaret Laidlaw (*d.* 1957), *d.* of William Shields, Glasgow; one *s.* one *d.*; 2nd, 1961, Beatrice Emily Farrell (*née* Franklin). *Educ.:* Strutt School, Belper, Derby. Served throughout European War, 1914-18, in 4th Sherwood Foresters and later Royal Engineers. Chas. McNeil & Co. Ltd., Glasgow (special post-war apprenticeship), 1919-24; joined Beyer, Peacock & Co. Ltd., 1925; various exec. positions to General Manager, 1934. Chairman of various subsidiary cos., 1934-65. Pres. Inst. of Cost & Works Accountants, 1943-46, Gold Medallist, 1959; Pres. Locomotive Manufrs. Assoc., 1947-50; Pres. Locomotive & Allied

Manufrs.' Assoc., 1956-58; Vice-Pres., formerly Chm. Council, British Institute of Management, 1956-58. Silver Medal of City of Paris, 1957; Bowie Medal, 1959; Member Advisory Bd. European Productivity Agency (O.E.E.C.), 1958-61; Mem. Working Party of Council of European Industrial Federations, 1958-61; Chairman: Locomotive Manufacturers' Co. Ltd.; Locomotive House Ltd. Elbourne Memorial Lecture, 1959. Member or Fellow of number of learned societies and specialist bodies; was for some years Mem. Grand Council of F.B.I. *Publications:* many papers on industrial finance and management subjects. *Recreations* music, golf. *Address:* Granville House, Limpsfield, Surrey. *T.:* Oxted 2560. *Clubs:* Buck's, Royal Automobile.
[*Died* 12 *May* 1966.

WILMOT, Sir John; *see* Eardley-Wilmot.

WILMOT, May; *see* Eardley-Wilmot.

WILSEY, Maj.-Gen. John Harold Owen, C.B. 1953; C.B.E. 1945; D.S.O. 1945; retired 1956; *b.* 29 Nov. 1904; *y. s.* of late Major Harry Willasey Wilsey; *m.* 1938, Beatrice Sarah Finlay Best, one *s.* one *d.* *Educ.:* Imperial Service College; Royal Military College, Sandhurst Gazetted Dorset Regiment, 1924; Worcestershire Regt., 1936. Served War of 1939-45: N.W. Europe, 1944-45; Comdt. Staff College, Haifa, 1945-46. B.G.S., Rhine Army, 1948; Comd. 5 Inf. Bde., B.A.O.R., 1949-50; Chief of Staff, West Africa Comd., 1950-51; Director of Infantry, War Office, 1952; Director of Staff Duties, W.O., Sept. 1952-Oct. 1954; G.O.C. 2 Infantry Division, Oct. 1954-May 1956. *Address:* Maufant Manor, Jersey, C.I.
[*Died* 20 *July* 1961.

WILSHAW, Sir Edward, K.C.M.G., *cr.* 1939; D.L.; J.P. Essex; LL.D.; President of: Cable & Wireless (Holding) Ltd.; Electra Finance Co. Ltd.; Electra Investments Ltd.; Globe Telegraph & Trust Co. Ltd.; Cables Investment Trust Ltd.; Electra House Ltd.; Direct Spanish Telegraph Co. Ltd.; *b.* 3 June 1879; *s.* of late William George Wilshaw, London; *m.* 1912, Myn, *d.* of late William Moar, Orkney; two *d.* Entered service Eastern Telegraph Company, 1894; and appointed Gen. Man. and Sec. of Imperial and International Communications on amalgamation of Empire cable and wireless services, 1928; Chairman of Empire Rates Conference, 1937; Government approved Chairman and Managing Director of Cable and Wireless Ltd. (the Operating Company), 1936-46; Commander of Order of the Dannebrog; Officer of Order of Leopold; Grand Officer of Order of George I (Greece); Commander Order of Merit (Chile); one of H.M. Lieutenants of City of London; Past Pres. Chartered Institute of Secretaries; Past-Master of Guild of Freemen of the City of London; Vice-President Royal Society of St. George and Past Pres. City Branch; Past Prime Warden of Company of Shipwrights; Liveryman of Company of Coopers; Joint Hon. Treas. Friends of St. Paul's; Mem. St. Paul's Cathedral Trust Council. *Address:* Arundel House, Arundel Street, Victoria Embankment, W.C.2; Barnfield, Denbigh Road, Haslemere, Surrey. *Club:* Royal Automobile.
[*Died* 3 *March* 1968.

WILSON, 1st Baron, *cr.* 1946, of Libya and of Stowlangtoft; **Field-Marshal Henry Maitland Wilson,** G.C.B., *cr.* 1944 (K.C.B., *cr.* 1940; C.B. 1937); G.B.E., *cr.* 1941; D.S.O. 1917; *b.* 1881; *s.* of late Arthur Maitland Wilson, O.B.E., Stowlangtoft Hall, Suffolk; *m.* 1914, Hester Mary, *d.* of Philip James Digby Wykeham, Tythrop House, Oxon; one *s.* one *d.* *Educ.:* Eton. Served S. African War, 1899-1902 (Queen's medal with two clasps, King's medal with two clasps); European War, 1914-17 (despatches, D.S.O.); commanded 1st Batt. Rifle Brigade, 1927-30; G.S.O.I. Staff College, Camberley, 1930-33; Commander 6th Infantry Brigade, 1934-35; Maj.-Gen. 1935; Commander 2nd Division, Aldershot, 1937-1939; Lt.-Gen. 1939; Col. Commandant The Rifle Brigade, 1939-51; General Officer C.-in-C. in Egypt, 1939; Military Governor and G.O.C.-in-C., Cyrenaica, 1941; G.O.C.-in-C., British Troops in Greece, 1941; General, 1941; G.O.C., British Forces in Palestine and Transjordan, 1941; C.-in-C. Allied Forces in Syria, 1941; G.O.C. the Army, 1941; C.-in-C. Persia-Iraq Commnd., 1942-43; C.-in-C., Middle East, 1943; Supreme Allied Commander, Mediterranean Theatre, 1944; Field Marshal, 1944; Head of British Joint Staff Mission in Washington, 1945-47. Constable, H.M. Tower of London, 1955-60. *Heir: s.* Lt.-Col. Hon. Patrick Maitland Wilson, *b.* 14 Sept 1915. *Address:* Wheelwrights, Chilton, Aylesbury, Bucks.
[*Died* 31 *Dec.* 1964.

WILSON, Cecil Claude, C.I.E. 1941; V.D., B.A. (Oxon.); *b.* 11 July 1885; *s.* of late Dr. Ambrose J. Wilson, D.D., formerly Headmaster of Carlisle Grammar School, Melbourne Grammar School, and Lancing College, and Julia Mary Lawrence; *m.* 1919, Elsie Woodthorpe Barry (*d.* 1962); one *d.* *Educ.:* Melbourne Gram. Sch., Victoria, Australia; Lancing College; Cheltenham College; Queen's College, Oxford (Honours Degree in Natural Science, Diploma of Forestry, Blue for boxing). Joined India Forest Service, 1908, as Asst. Conservator; Deputy Conservator, 1912; joined 12th Bengal Lancers in Mesopotamia, 1916-19, as officer of Reserves; Principal Madras Forest College, 1920-23; Conservator of Forests, 1925; in charge of Branch of Forest Economy at Imperial Forest Research Institute at Dehra Dun in N. India, 1925-28; Conservator of Forests, Madras, 1929-38; Major in Indian Army Reserve of Officers, attached Poona Horse, 1927; Chief Conservator of Forests, Madras, 1938; retired 1940. Royal Canadian Artillery (Res.), 1942-44. *Recreations:* polo, fox hunting, fishing, shooting, ski-ing; shooting and photographing big game. *Address:* c/o Messrs. Coutts & Co., 440 Strand, W.C.2. *Club:* East India and Sports.
[*Died* 9 *May* 1968.

WILSON, Charles Erwin; Secretary of Defence, U.S., 1953-57; President, 1941-1953 and Chief Executive Officer, 1946-53, of General Motors Corporation, Detroit; *b.* Minerva, Ohio, 18 July 1890; *s.* of Thomas E. Wilson and Rosalind Unkefer; *m.* 1912, Jessie Ann Curtis; three *s.* three *d.* *Educ.:* Bellevue High School, Pittsburgh; Carnegie Institute of Technology. Employed with Westinghouse Electric and Manufacturing Co., 1909-19; during War, until 1918, was in charge of design and development of Westinghouse radio generators and dynamotors for U.S. Army and Navy; joined General Motors, 1919; general manager, 1925; Vice-President, 1928. M.S.A.E. Holds numerous hon. degrees in Laws, Engineering and Science. Awarded Medal of Merit, by U.S. Govt., 1946. *Address:* Bloomfield Hills, Mich. *Clubs:* Detroit (Detroit); Bloomfield Country, Bloomfield Open Hunt.
[*Died* 26 *Sept.* 1961.

WILSON, Charles Paul, C.V.O. 1939; F.R.C.S.; J.P. 1962; Semon Lecturer (R.S. Med.) 1961; late Senior Ear, Nose and Throat Surgeon, The Middlesex Hospital; *b.* 17 Aug. 1900; *m.* 1924, Margaret Fraser Cameron; one *s.* two *d.* *Educ.:* Walling Brook School, N. Devon. Hunterian Prof., R.C.S., 1955. *Address:* Spindle Bridge, Much Hadham, Herts. *T.:* Much Hadham 2672.
[*Died* 12 *March* 1970.

WILSON, Capt. Sir Frank O'Brien, Kt., *cr.* 1949; C.M.G. 1935; D.S.O. 1916; *b.* 1883; *s.* of late Col. John Gerald Wilson, C.B., of Cliffe Hall, Yorks; *m.* 1919, Elizabeth Frances, *d.* of Sir Arthur Francis Pease, 1st Bt.; two *s.* two *d.* Formerly R.N.; served E. Africa, 1914-18, as Capt. African Mounted Rifles (despatches, D.S.O.). Member, Kenya Land Commission, 1932-33; Chairman, Bd. of Agriculture, 1948-53. *Address:* Kilima Kiu, Ulu, Kenya. [*Died* 7 *April* 1962.

WILSON, Frank Percy, F.B.A.; Hon. LL.D. (Birmingham); Merton Professor of English Literature, in the Univ. of Oxford, 1947-57, now Emeritus Professor; Senior Research Fellow, Merton Coll., 1957-0; Hon. Fellow of Lincoln College; President, Bibliographical Society 1950-52; Oxford Bibliographical Soc., 1956-57; Modern Humanities Research Association, 1961; General Editor Malone Society, 1948-60, President, 1960-; *b.* 11 Oct. 1889; *m.* Joanna, *d.* of Lancelot Perry-Keene; three *s.* one *d.* *Educ.:* King Edward's Grammar School, Camp Hill; King Edward's School, Birmingham; University of Birmingham; Lincoln Coll., Oxf. Lecturer in English, Univ. of Birmingham, 1919-21; Lecturer (1921-25) and Reader (1925-29) in English Literature, Univ. of Oxford; Professor of English Literature, Univ. of Leeds, 1929-36; Hildred Carlile Professor of English Literature in the Univ. of London, at Bedford College, 1936-46; Visiting Fellow, Huntington Library, Cal., 1933, 1952-53, 1958; Leverhulme Research Fellow, 1938-40; Visiting Carnegie Professor, Columbia Univ. and Smith College, 1943; Visiting Professor Stanford Univ., 1952; Fellow, Folger Shakespeare Library, 1957, Alexander Lecturer, Univ. of Toronto, 1943; Clark Lecturer, Trinity College, Cambridge, 1951; Turnbull Lecturer, Johns Hopkins Univ., 1952; Ewing Lecturer, Univ. of Cal. at Los Angeles, 1958. Hon. Mem.: Elizabethan Club, Yale; Tudor and Stuart Club, Johns Hopkins; Modern Language Association of America; Renaissance English Text Soc. *Publications:* Elizabethan and Jacobean, 1945; Shakespeare and the new Bibliography, 1945; Marlowe and the early Shakespeare, 1953; Seventeenth Century Prose: Five Lectures, 1960; etc. *Address:* 30 Cumnor Hill, Oxford. [*Died* 29 *May* 1963.

WILSON, George Frederick, C.B.E. 1944 (O.B.E. 1935); *b.* 18 Dec. 1886; *s.* of late George Wilson; *m.* 1909, Kathleen Ponsford; two *d.* *Educ.:* King Edward's School, Bath. Secretariat, Cyprus, 1904; Comptroller of Customs, 1924; M.L.C. 1925-31; Colonial Treasurer, Cyprus, and Member of Executive Council, 1939-47; retired, 1947. *Recreations:* ornithology, shooting, gardening. *Address:* 2 Aston Road, Ealing, W.5. *Club:* Royal Commonwealth Society. [*Died* 6 *Aug.* 1970.

WILSON, George Hamilton Bracher, C.B.E. 1949; M.C.; A.F.C.; J.P.; Life President, late Chairman, of Raleigh Industries Limited and Subsidiary Companies, and late Director of Tube Investments Limited; *b.* 14 May 1895; *s.* of Charles John Wilson and Jane Wilson (*née* Snook); *m.* 1929, Elizabeth Violet Glen; one *s.* one *d.* *Educ.:* Marlborough College; Pembroke Coll., Cambridge. Served throughout European War, 1914-18, with Army, R.F.C. and R.A.F. Dunlop Rubber Co., 1920; Sturmey Archer Gears Ltd., 1927; succeeded Sir Harold Bowden as Managing Director Raleigh Cycle Co. Ltd., 1938; Chm. of Nottingham Savings Committee, 1939-1948; President: The British Cycle and Motor Cycle Manufacturers and Traders Union Ltd., 1945-48; Motor and Cycle Trades Benevolent Fund, 1950 and 1951; Member Council of F.B.I., North Midland Region, 1947-56; Member Council of Nottingham Univ., 1948; President Nottingham and District Engineering and Allied Employers' Assoc., and Member of Management Board of National Federation, 1949-56; Vice-Chairman of East Midlands Regional Cttee., 1951; Mem. East Midlands Electricity Board; Governor, Loughborough Coll. of Techn., 1952-56. Pres., Nottingham Trustee Savings Bank, 1962. J.P. Notts, 1939; High Sheriff of Notts, 1949. *Address:* The Old Rectory, Plumtree, Notts. *T.:* Plumtree 2126. *Clubs:* Nottingham Borough (Nottingham); Royal Irish Yacht; Royal Norfolk and Suffolk Yacht. [*Died* 19 *Dec.* 1963.

WILSON, Harold Albert, F.R.S. 1906; M.A., D.Sc., M.Sc.; Professor of Physics, Rice Inst. (now University), Houston, 1912-1947, subsq. professor emeritus; *b.* York, 1 Dec. 1874; *s.* of late A. W. Wilson, Neasham House, Darlington; *m.* 1912, Marjorie, *e. d.* of Archdeacon Paterson-Smyth of Montreal, Canada; two *s.* two *d.* *Educ.:* St. Olave's School, York; Yorkshire Coll., Leeds; Berlin University; Trinity Coll., Cambridge. University Scholar, London University, 1896-98; 1851 Exhibition Scholar, 1897-1900; Allen Scholar, Cambridge University, 1900; Fellow of Trinity College, Cambridge, 1901-07; Clerk-Maxwell Student, Cavendish Laboratory, Cambridge, 1901-04; Lecturer on Physics, King's College, London, 1904-05; Professor of Physics, King's College, London, 1905-09; Professor of Physics, McGill University, Montreal, 1909-12; Professor of Natural Philosophy, Glasgow University, 1924-25; Professor of Physics, Chicago University, summers of 1922, 1923, and 1928; Fellow American Phil. Soc.; Technical Expert on Anti-Submarine Devices. Naval Experimental Station, New London, Conn., 1917-19; Physicist, Office of Scientific Research and Development, 1942, 1943. *Publications:* numerous scientific papers in Philosophical Transactions of the Royal Society and other journals; The Electrical Properties of Flames; Experimental Physics; Modern Physics; The Mysteries of the Atom; Electricity. *Address:* Adair Home, 1200 California, Houston 6, Texas, U.S.A. [*Died* 13 *Oct.* 1964.

WILSON, Rt. Rev. Henry Albert, C.B.E. 1953; D.D.; *b* Port Bannatyne, Bute, 6 Sept. 1876; *s.* of Thomas Alexander Wilson, Glasgow, and Mary Proctor, Newtown Butler, Co. Fermanagh; *m.* Dorothy Mary Marston, *d.* of G. Walter Daniels, Hampstead; two *s.* two *d.* *Educ.:* Corpus Christi Coll., Camb. Curate of Christ Church, Hampstead, 1899-1904; Vicar of Norbiton, Kingston-upon-Thames, 1904-16; Rector and Rural Dean of Cheltenham, 1916-28; Bishop of Chelmsford, 1929-50; resigned, 1950. Hon. Canon of Gloucester Cathedral; Hon. Chaplain to Bishop of Gloucester; Proctor in Convocation; President of Cheltenham Conference; Select Preacher at Cambridge-1930, 1939, and 1960, at Oxford, 1932. *Publications:* Episcopacy and Unity, 1912; Faith of a Little Child, 1914; Creed of a Young Churchman, 1916; The Master and His Friends, 1925; At the Lord's Table, 1927; Your Faith or Your Life, 1940; It Can Happen Here!, 1942; Reflections of a Back-Bench Bishop, 1948. *Recreation:* golf. *Address:* Sole Bay House, Southwold, Suffolk. [*Died* 16 *July* 1961.

WILSON, Henry (Leonard), M.D., F.R.C.P.; Hon. Cons. Physician in Psychological Medicine to the London Hospital; ex-Pres., Psychiatric Section, Roy. Soc. Medicine; *b.* 17 May 1897; *s.* of Cecil Henry and Sarah Catherine Wilson, Sheffield; *m.* 1927, Ruth Taylor, Letchworth; two *s.* one *d.* *Educ.:* Stramongate Sch. Kendal; Emmanuel Coll., Camb.; St. Bartholomew's Hosp., London. *Publications:* contributions to scientific journals. *Recreations:* fell walking, water-colour sketching. *Address:* 18 Mount Pleasant, Cambridge. *T.:* 51039. [*Died* 8 *April* 1968.

WILSON, Sir James Robertson, 2nd Bt., of Airdrie, *cr.* 1906; D.L., J.P. for County of Perth; *b.* 5 May 1883; *s.* of Sir John Wilson, 1st Bt. of Airdrie, and Margaret B. M. (*d.* 1885), *d.* of James Robertson, Glasgow; *S.* father, 1918; *m.* 1908, Helen Rae Fife, *e. d.* of late A. Bulloch Graham, Park Gardens, Glasgow; (*s.* killed in action Jan. 1942). *Educ.:* Uppingham; Balliol, Oxford (B.A.); Member of Inner Temple. Contested N.E. Division of Lanarkshire in Unionist interest, 1909; prospective candidate for Falkirk Burghs, 1914; served European War, 1914-17, Gallipoli, Palestine, and Egypt; with A.A. Battery, Sept. 1939-Jan. 1940; Member of Royal Company of Archers (H.M. Bodyguard for Scotland). *Recreations:* hunting, shooting, fishing. *Heir: b.* John Menzies, late Capt. 2nd Life Guards [*b.* 1885; *m.* 1921, Silvia Helena Sophia, *d.* of late W. D. James, C.V.O.; one *d.* Served European War of 1914-18; has been Hon. Attaché at Washington, Petrograd, and Constantinople]. *Address:* Duilater, Callander, Perthshire. *Clubs:* Cavalry; County (Stirling); County and City (Perth).
[*Died* 30 *Sept.* 1964.

WILSON, Sir (James) Steuart, Kt., *cr.* 1948; retd.; *b.* 21 July 1889; *m.* 1st, 1917, Ann Bowles; 2nd, 1937, Mary Daisy Goodchild (*d.* 1960); 3rd, 1962, Margaret (*née* Stewart), *widow* of Leslie Hunter. *Educ.:* Winchester; King's College, Cambridge (M.A.). Professional Musician (Singer), 1912-39; Captain K.R.R.C. 1914-19; Curtis Institute of Music, Philadelphia, 1939-1942; B.B.C. (Overseas Music Director), 1942-45; Music Director, Arts Council of Great Britain, 1945-48; Head of Music, B.B.C., 1948; Deputy General Administrator, Royal Opera House, 1950-55; Principal, Birmingham School of Music, 1957-60. *Address:* Fenn's, Petersfield, Hants. *T.:* 3539. *Club:* Garrick. [*Died* 18 *Dec.* 1966.

WILSON, John Dover, C.H. 1936; M.A.; Litt.D. (Camb.); F.B.A.; Hon. LL.D. (Natal and Edin.); Hon. D.Litt. (Durh. and Leics.); D.-ès-L. hon. (Lille); Hon. D.Lit. (London); Hon. Fell. of Gonville and Caius Coll., Camb.; *b.* London, 13 July 1881; *s.* of Edwin Wilson, scientific artist, Camb.; *m.* 1st, 1906, Dorothy (*d.* 1961), *d.* of late Canon Baldwin, Harston, Cambs.; (one *s.* died on active service, 1944) two *d.*; 2nd, 1963, Elizabeth Wintringham, *d.* of late Sir Joseph Arkwright, F.R.S. *Educ.:* Lancing College; Gonville and Caius College, Cambridge (History Scholar); Members' Prizeman, 1902; Harness Prizeman, 1904; 2nd Class Hist. Tripos, 1903; B.A. 1903; M.A. 1908; Assistant Master Whitgift Grammar School, 1904-05; English Lector in the University of Helsingfors, Finland, 1906-09; Lecturer in English Language and Literature at Goldsmiths' College, University of London, 1909-12; H.M.I. (adult education and Continuation Schools), 1912-24; Professor of Education in the University of London, King's College, 1924-35; Editor of the Journal of Adult Education, 1927-29; Regius Professor of Rhetoric and English Literature, University of Edinburgh, 1935-45; Trustee of Shakespeare's Birthplace since 1931 (Life Trustee, 1951); Trustee Nat. Library of Scotland since 1946 (Vice-Chm., 1951-57); Mem. Gen. Council of Friends of the Nat. Libraries since 1949; Leverhulme Research Fellow: 1933-34, 1945-46; Clark Lecturer, Cambridge, 1942-43; President Scottish Classical Assoc., 1950-51; Chichele Lecturer Oxford, 1949. *Publications:* Life in Shakespeare's England, 1911; The War and Democracy (with four others), 1914; Humanism in the Continuation School (Board of Education Pamphlet), 1921; Shakespeare's hand in the play of Sir Thomas More (with A. W. Pollard and others), 1923; The Essential Shakespeare, 1932; The New Shakespeare (editor), 1921-66; The Schools of England (editor), 1928; M. Arnold's Culture and Anarchy (editor), 1932; The Manuscript of Shakespeare's Hamlet, 1934; What happens in Hamlet, 1935; The Fortunes of Falstaff, 1943; A. W. Pollard: a memoir, 1948; Shakespeare's Happy Comedies, 1962 (new edn. 1969); Shakespeare's Sonnets: an Introduction for Historians and Others, 1963; Milestones on the Dover Road, 1969. *Address:* Three Beeches, Balerno, Midlothian. *T.:* 031-449 3816. [*Died* 15 *Jan.* 1969.

WILSON, John Gideon, C.B.E. 1948; Chairman and Managing Director John and Edward Bumpus, Ltd., 1941-59; *b.* Glasgow, 9 Jan. 1876; *s.* of James and Margaret Wilson, Bookbinders; *m.* 1908, Catherine Smart Provan; one *s.* three *d.* *Educ.:* Board School, Glasgow. Bookseller: John Smith & Son, Glasgow; Constable & Co., London; Jones & Evans; J. & E. Bumpus, Ltd. Liveryman Stationers' Company; Vice-Pres.: Booksellers Association. *Publications:* (Editor) The Odd Volume, 1909-13; The Business of Bookselling, 1930. *Recreation:* books. *Address:* 29 West End Avenue, Pinner, Middx. *T.:* Pinner 0342. *Club:* Savile. [*Died* 6 *Sept.* 1963.

WILSON, John Gray, Q.C. (Scot.) 1956; Sheriff-substitute of the Lothians and Peebles at Edinburgh since 1963 (of Renfrewshire at Paisley, 1958-63); *b.* 10 Oct. 1915; *s.* of Alexander Robertson Wilson and Elizabeth Wyllie Wilson (*née* Murray); *m.* 1943, Nan Macauslan; three *s.* *Educ.:* Irvine Royal Academy; The Edinburgh Academy; Oriel College, Oxford (B.A.); Edinburgh University (LL.B.). Admitted to Faculty of Advocates, 1942. Vis. Lectr., Univ. of the Witwatersrand, (Johannesburg) 1964. *Publications:* Trial of Jeannie Donald, 1953; The Trial of Peter Manuel, 1959; Not Proven, 1960; articles in legal journals in Scotland and elsewhere. *Recreations:* painting, criminology. *Address:* 57 Northumberland St., Edinburgh 3. *T.:* 031-556 2822. *Club:* Scottish Arts (Edinburgh).
[*Died* 28 *Sept.* 1968.

WILSON, Right Rev. John Leonard, K.C.M.G. 1968 (C.M.G. 1946); Prelate of the Most Distinguished Order of Saint Michael and Saint George, since 1963; *b.* 23 Nov. 1897; *s.* of Rev. John and Mary Adelaide Wilson; *m.* 1930, Doris Ruby Phillips, Cairo, Egypt; three *s.* one *d.* *Educ.:* St. John's Leatherhead; Queen's College, Oxford; Wycliffe Hall, Oxford. B.A. 1922; M.A. 1926; Deacon, 1924; Priest, 1926; Curate, St. Michael's Cathedral, Coventry, 1924-27; C.M.S., Egypt, 1928-29; Curate, St. Margaret's, Durham, 1929-30; Vicar of St. Thomas, Eighton Banks, Gateshead on Tyne, 1930-35; of St. Andrew's, Monkwearmouth, 1935-38; Dean of St. John's Cathedral and Archdeacon of Hong Kong, 1938-1941; Interned Changi Camp, Singapore, 1943-45; Bishop of Singapore, 1941-49; Dean of Manchester and Assistant Bishop, 1949-53; Bishop of Birmingham, 1953-69. Select Preacher Oxford, 1948 and 1962, Cambridge, 1949, St. Andrews, 1953, Trinity College, Dublin, 1959. Hon. Fellow, Queen's Coll., Oxford, 1954. Hon. D.D. Lambeth, 1953; Hon. D.Sc. Aston, 1969. *Address:* Brush House, Bainbridge, Leyburn, Yorks. *T.:* Bainbridge 228. [*Died* 18 *Aug.* 1970.

WILSON, Sir John (Menzies), 3rd Bt., *cr.* 1906, of Aidrie; late Captain, 2nd Life Guards; formerly Lieut., Scots Greys; *b.* 12 Feb. 1885; *s.* of Sir John Wilson, 1st Bt. of Airdrie, and Margaret, *d.* of James Robertson, Glasgow; *S.* brother, 1964; *m.* 1921, Silvia Helena Sophia (marriage dissolved, 1948), *d.* of late William Dodge James, C.V.O.; one *d.* *Educ.:* Uppingham. Served European War, 1914-18. Formerly Hon. Attaché, H.M. Embassy: St. Petersburg, 1911-12; Washington, 1912-14; Constantinople, 1914. *Recreations:* hunting, tennis, golf. *Heir: nephew* Thomas Douglas Wilson, M.C., Captain late 15th/19th Hussars [*b.* (posthumous) 10 June 1917; *m.* 1947, Pamela Aileen, 2nd *d.* of Lt.-Col. Sir (G. W.) Edward Hanmer, Bt.; one *s.* three *d.*]. *Address:* Peppers Farm, Burton Lazars, Melton Mowbray, Leics. *Club:* Buck's. [*Died* 22 *Oct.* 1968.

WILSON, Col. John Skinner, C.M.G. 1950; O.B.E. 1943; Hon. Pres. and Life Mem. Council, International Fellowship of Former Scouts and Guides; *b.* 20 May 1888; *s.* of Very Rev. John Skinner Wilson, sometime Dean of Edinburgh, and Liza Mary, *d.* of Norval Clyne, Advocate, Aberdeen; *m.* 1916, Ann Marie (*d.* 1961), *d.* of Robert Huggan, Jedburgh; one *s.* one *d.* *Educ.:* Trinity College, Glenalmond. Indian Police, 1908-23; Senior Deputy Comr. of Police, Calcutta, 1916-23; King's Police Medal, 1920. Camp Chief, Boy Scouts Association, 1923-43; Director, Boy Scouts International Bureau, 1938-53; Hon. Pres. Boy Scouts Internat. Cttee., 1953-57. Served War, 1940-45, Col., G.S., Intelligence Corps and Special Forces Headquarters. Comdr., Order of St. Olav (Norway), 1944; Officer, Legion of Merit (U.S.A.), 1945; King Christian X Liberty Medal (Denmark), 1946. Commander, Order of Sacred Treasure (Japan), 1953. *Publications:* several books on Scouting subjects, including Scouting round the World, 1959. *Recreation:* gardening. *Address:* The Cottage, Pleasant Valley, East Farleigh, Kent. *T.:* Hunton 285. [*Died* 19 *Dec.* 1969.

WILSON, Kenneth Henry, O.B.E. 1949; J.P.; Chairman Albright & Wilson, Ltd., Oldbury, 1932-58, retd., President since 1958; *b.* 7 Sept. 1885; *s.* of G. Edward Wilson and Henrietta R. Pease; *m.* 1911, Mary Isabel, *d.* of George Cadbury; one *s.* four *d.* *Educ.:* Marlborough; Trinity Coll., Cambridge. With Albright & Wilson, 1908; Dir., 1910; Man. Dir. and Chm., 1932-58, Pres., 1958-. Mem. of Oldbury Urban District Council, 1919-58; Charter Mayor of Oldbury, 1935; Alderman of Borough of Oldbury, 1935-58; Worcestershire County Council, 1936, Alderman, 1941-; Chm. Oldbury Local Employment Cttee., 1925-62. Past Pres. and Member of Council Birmingham Chamber of Commerce; Governor, Birmingham Univ. (Mem. Council, 1933-68). High Sheriff of Worcs., 1948-49. Freeman, Borough of Oldbury, 1960. *Recreations:* shooting, farming. *Address:* Park Hall, Kidderminster. *T.:* Blakedown 268. *Club:* Royal Automobile. [*Died* 2 *Sept.* 1969.

WILSON, Major-General Norman Methven, C.I.E. 1939; O.B.E. 1920; *b.* 23 Feb. 1881; *s.* of A. R. Wilson, Public Works Dept., India; *m.* 1908, *d.* of David Dalrymple, Crowborough, Sussex; one *s.* one *d.* *Educ.:* Dollar Academy; St. Bartholomew's Hospital. Entered Indian Medical Service, 1905; Capt. 1908; Major, 1915; Lt. Col., 1924; Col., 1933; Maj.-Gen., 1937; K.H.S., 1937-41; Surgeon-General with Govt. of Madras, 1937; retired, 1941. *Address:* Higher Mead, Chagford, Devon. [*Died* 3 *Dec.* 1961.

WILSON, Rev. Canon Sir Percy M., Bt.; *see* Maryon-Wilson, Rev. Canon Sir G. P.

WILSON, Philip Duncan, A.B., M.D.; Surgeon, U.S.A.; Surgeon-in-Chief, Hospital for Special Surgery, New York City, 1934-55, Surgeon-in-Chief Emeritus, 1955, and Director of Research and Education (Emeritus, 1962); also Emeritus Clinical Professor of Surgery (Orthopædics), Cornell Medical School, N.Y.; *b.* 5 April 1886; *s.* of late Ida Tudor and Dr. Edward J. Wilson, Columbus, Ohio; *m.* 1916, Germaine Porel, Paris; two *s.* one *d.* *Educ.:* Harvard Univ., A.B. 1909; Harvard Medical Sch., M.D. 1912. Surgical interneship, Massachusetts General Hospital, Boston, 1912-14; Member of Harvard Unit to American Ambulance, Neuilly, France, 1915; Voluntary Surgeon French Hospital, Hennqueville, France, 1916; Medical Corps, U.S. Army, Captain and later Major, Orth. Consultant, A.E.F., 1917-19; engaged in practice as specialist in orthopedic surgery, Boston, Mass., attending orthopedic surgeon, Massachusetts General Hospital, Boston, and instructor in surgery Harvard Medical School, 1919-34; Medical Director, American Hospital in Britain, Park Prewett, Basingstoke (later at Churchill Hosp., Oxford), under Emergency Medical Service, Ministry of Health, 1940-42; Orthopædic Consultant to Surgeon General, 1943-46. Fellow and Regent Amer. Coll. of Surgeons, Amer. Med. Assoc., Amer. Acad. Orthopædic Surgeons (Past President). Amer. Orthopædic Assoc., British Orthopædic Assoc., Hon. Fellow: Royal College of Surgeons (Edinburgh); Royal Society Medicine, Society Orthopædica Scandinavica; Member Internat. Soc. Orthopedics and Traumatology, President 9th Congress in Vienna, 1963. Dr. (*h.c.*) University of Paris, 1966. Chevalier of Legion of Honour (France), 1947; Hon. C.B.E. 1948. *Publications:* (with W. A. Cochran) Fractures and Dislocations, 1925, 2nd ed. 1937; Editor and joint author Management of Fractures and Dislocations, 1939; numerous contributions to medical jls. *Recreations:* yachting, golf, fishing. *Address:* 535 East 70 Street, New York 21, N.Y., U.S.A. *Clubs:* Harvard, Century Association (New York). [*Died* 7 *May* 1969.

WILSON, Ralph Darrell, C.B.E. 1952; *b.* 8 Dec. 1892; *s.* of late Rev. Ralph Venables Wilson, R.N., and Emily Darrell; *m.* 1921, Germaine, *d.* of Nicolas Leclercq, Brussels; one *d.* *Educ.:* Epsom Coll. Served in destroyers at Portsmouth and Dover as Sub-Lieut. and Lieut. R.N.V.R.; Naval Interpreter (French and German), 1917; Naval Intelligence Dept., Admiralty, 1918; Vice-Consul New Orleans, 1919, St. Vincent, 1921; Chargé d'Affaires Santo Domingo, 1922; Vice-Consul Rotterdam, 1925, Brussels, 1927; Consul Leipzig, 1931, Lima, 1933, with local rank of Commercial Secretary; acted as Chargé d'Affaires in 1933, 1934 and 1936; Consul Bahia, 1936, Galatz, 1937, Alexandria, 1938; Brussels with local rank of First Secretary, 1944; Consul-General, Algiers, 1945-49; Consul-General, Rotterdam, 1949-1953; retd. 1953. *Address:* 1432 Kelton Ave., Westwood, Los Angeles 24, Calif., U.S.A. [*Died* 26 *June* 1967.

WILSON, Colonel Richard Henry, C.I.E. 1939; M.C.; retired; *b.* 1886; *s.* of late R. A. Wilson, Salisbury; *m.* 1923, Ella Maud, *s.* *d.* of E. J. Gunner, Newport, Isle of Wight; one *s.* two *d.* *Educ.:* Sherborne; R.M.C., Sandhurst. 1st Commission, 1906, York and Lancaster Regt., Indian Army, 1908; Afghanistan, 1919 (M.C.); N.W. Frontier of India, 1930 (despatches); Deputy Mil. Sec. A.H.Q. India, 1936-37; Inspecting Officer and Secretary, Frontier Corps, N.W.F.P., 1937-41. *Address:* 3 Greenbanks Close, Church Hill, Milford-on-Sea, Lymington, Hants. *T.:* Milford-on-Sea 3260. [*Died* 13 *Jan.* 1969.

WILSON, Robert McNair, M.B., Ch.B.; Medical Correspondent of the Times, 1914-42 (now retired); *b.* Glasgow, 22 May 1882; *s.* of Wm. Wilson, West India merchant, Glasgow, and Helen Turner; *m.* 1st, Winifred Paynter; three *s.*; 2nd, Doris May Fischel; two *s.* *Educ.:* Glasgow Academy and University. M.B., Ch.B. (with commendation), 1904. Assistant House Surgeon Norfolk and Norwich Hospital; House Surgeon Glasgow Western Infirmary;

Private Practice in Northumberland and Argyll till 1913; Assistant to late Sir James Mackenzie under Medical Research Committee; Temp. Captain R.A.M.C.; Editor for nine years of Oxford Medical Publications; Consulting Physician to Ministry of Pensions; Contested (L.) Saffron Walden Division, 1922-23. *Publications:* The Beloved Physician (Life of Sir Jas. Mackenzie); Life of Lord Northcliffe; Napoleon, the Man; How our Bodies are Made; The Nervous Heart, the Clinical Study of Heart Disease; Pygmalion; Josephine, the portrait of a woman; Germaine de Stäel, The Woman of Affairs, 1931; The King of Rome, 1932; Monarchy or Money Power, 1933 (U.S. edn. God and the Goldsmiths, 1961); Napoleon's Mother, 1933; Napoleon's Love Story, 1933; Promise to Pay, 1934; Gypsy Queen of Paris, 1934; Young Man's Money; The Mind of Napoleon; The Defeat of Debt; Women of the French Revolution, 1936; Napoleon, 1937; Doctor's Progress: autobiography, 1938; British Medicine, 1941; The Witness of Science, 1942; Housing Finance, 1945; Josephine (reprint under new title of The Empress Josephine), 1952; The New Wealth, 1955. *Recreations:* writing detective stories (under pseudonym of Anthony Wynne), motoring, gardening. *Address:* Ironshill Lodge, Ashurst, Southampton.
[*Died* 29 *Nov.* 1963.

WILSON, Gen. Sir Roger Cochrane, K.C.B., *cr.* 1937 (C.B. 1930); D.S.O. 1918; M.C.; lately serving on Staff of Union Defence Force of South Africa; *b.* 26 Dec. 1882; *s.* of Colonel F. A. Wilson, Indian Staff Corps; *m.* 1905, Marion Blanche Florence Hollway (*d.* 1959); two *s.* two *d.* *Educ.:* Wellington Coll.; R.M.C., Sandhurst. Cheshire Regiment, 1901; 114 Mahrattas, Indian Army, 1904; Staff College, 1914; served Mesopotamia, 1914-18 (D.S.O., M.C., despatches, Croix de Guerre); Major, 1916; Lieut.-Col., 1917; Colonel, 1920; General Staff India, 1922-25; Brigadier Manzai Brigade, Waziristan, 1926-30; Maj.-Gen., 1929; Commandant Indian Staff College, 1931-34; late Colonel 5th R. Bn. 5th Mahratta Light Infantry; G.O.C. Rawalpindi District, 1934-36; Secretary, Military Dept., India Office, 1936-37; Lt.-Gen., 1937; Adjt.-General, India, 1937-41; Gen., 1940; A.D.C. General to the King, 1940-41; retired, 1941. Served in South African Army, 1942-1947. *Recreation:* mountaineering. *Address:* 46 Connaught Road, Fleet, Hants. *Clubs:* Alpine, United Service. [*Died* 5 *Feb.* 1966.

WILSON, Sir Steuart; *see* Wilson, Sir J. S.

WILSON, Ven. Thomas Bowstead, M.A.; Hon. Canon of Worcester Cathedral since 1944; *b.* 15 Aug. 1882; *s.* of Rev. J. Bowstead and Catherine Eliza Wilson, Knightwick, Worcester; *m.* 1912, Winifred Dorothy, *d.* of Dr. James Blamey, Penryn, Cornwall; one *s.* (and one son killed in France 1944) three *d.* *Educ.:* Charterhouse; Pembroke College, Cambridge. President Cambridge University Athletic Club, 1904; Curate Wakefield Cathedral, 1906; Missioner of Pembroke College Mission, 1910; Rector of Suckley, 1912; Vicar of Wolverley, 1924-39; Rector of Hartlebury, 1939-56, resigned; Archdeacon of Worcester, 1944-61, resigned. *Address:* Ryall Hill, Upton-upon-Severn, Worcestershire. *Club:* Worcestershire (Worcester). [*Died* 11 *Oct.* 1961.

WILSON, Maj.-Gen. Thomas Need ham Furnival, C.B. 1946; D.S.O. 1919; M.C.; p.s.c.; of Sandbach and of Coole Lane, Co. Chester; Secretary, King George's Jubilee Trust, 1948; *b.* 20 March 1896; *m.* 1922, Doreen Gordon (marriage dissolved, 1946), *y. d.* of James Wilson, Hockley Lodge, Armagh; one *s.*; *m.* 1946, Margot, *d.* of Capt. R. G. Cruickshank. *Educ.:* West Downs, Winchester; Winchester College; R.M.C., Sandhurst. Served European War, 1914-19 (despatches, D.S.O., M.C.); D.A.A.G. War Office, 1936-38; Military Assistant (G.S.O. 2) to Chief of Imperial General Staff, War Office, 1938; commanded 2nd Battn. Kings' Royal Rifle Corps, 1938-39; Brigadier commanding an Infantry Brigade, 1939-40 (despatches); General Staff, 1940; Acting Maj.-Gen., General Staff, March 1943; Temp. Maj.-Gen., 1944. Retired pay, 1946. *Address:* Buckridges, Sutton Courtenay, nr. Abingdon, Berks. *T.:* Sutton Courtenay 56. *Clubs:* Naval and Military, M.C.C.
[*Died* 15 *May* 1961.

WILSON, Group Captain Walter Carandini, C.B.E. 1944; D.S.O. 1915; M.C. 1914; p.s.c.; *b.* 1885; *s.* of late Robert Walter Wilson, Bannockburn House, Stirling and Donna Marie Emma Carandini, *d.* of Marquis of Sarzano; *m.* 1957, Elizabeth Sale. *Educ.:* Tonbridge School. Entered Leicestershire Regiment 1907. Served European War, 1914-19 (wounded thrice, despatches 5 times, M.C., D.S.O. with bar, O.B.E., Bt. Major, 1914 Star and clasp, British War Medal, Victory Medal, French Silver Gilt Medal of Honour with Swords, Order of St. Vladimir and Order of St. Anne of Russia); France: Staff Capt., 1916; Brevet Major, 1916-17; G.S.O. 2 (temp. Major), 1917-18. G.S.O. 1, British Military Mission to America (temp. Lt.-Col.), 1918-19; G.S.O. 1, Home Forces (temp. Lt.-Col.), 1919; G.S.O. 2, British Military Mission to Finland (temp. Major), 1919; G.S.O. 1, British Military Mission to Finland (temp. Lt.-Col.), 1919-20; G.S.O. 2 (temp.) British Military Mission to Baltic States, 1920; G.S.O. 1 (Intelligence), Dublin District (temp.), 1920-1921; Bde.-Major E.E.F. 1922-24; Commander Co. of Gent. Cadets (G.S.O. 2), Royal Military College, 1924-26; employed with Malay States Vol. Regt. 1926; Commandant (temp.) (local Lt.-Col.), 1926; employed with R.W.A.F.F. 1927-30 (local Col.); commanded 1st Bn. Duke of Wellington's Regt., 1930-32; retired pay, 1932; G.S.O. 1, 42nd Div., Sept. 1939; joined R.A.F. Dec. 1939, Pilot Officer under probation, acting Wing Comdr.; Acting Group Capt. 1942; retired rank Group Capt. 1944. Assistant to Director-General, British Overseas Airways Corporation, Feb. 1944-Sept. 1945. F.R.G.S. *Recreations:* travelling played Rugby football for England. *Address:* Flat 19, 40 Sussex Square, Brighton 7, Sussex. *Club:* Buck's.
[*Died* 12 *April* 1968.

WILSON, Professor William, F.R.S.; Dr.Phil., D.Sc.; Fellow King's College, London: Professor Emeritus of Physics, Univ. of London; native of Holme St. Cuthbert, Cumberland; *b.* 1875; *s.* of W. O. Wilson, Abbey House, Abbey Town, Carlisle; *m.* Rose Blanche (*d.* 1957), *d.* of Henry Heathfield, Stoke Canon, Devon; one *s.* *Educ.:* Royal College of Science and King's College, London; Leipzig. Assistant Lecturer in Physics at King's College, 1906; Senior Lecturer, 1919; Reader in the University of London, 1920; Hildred Carlile Professor, 1921-44. *Publications:* Quantum Theory (Enc. Brit., 14th edit.); Quantum Theory and other articles, Chambers's Encyclopædia; Theoretical Physics; A Hundred Years of Physics; The Microphysical World; Chapters in a Century of Science; Space Time and the Cosmos: Papers in Proc. Roy. Soc., etc. *Address:* 14 Saint Owen Street, Hereford.
[*Died* 14 *Oct.* 1965.

WILSON-FOX, Hon. Mrs. Eleanor Birch, C.B.E. 1918; 5th *d.* of 1st Baron Basing of Hoddington, Winchfield, Hants; *widow* of Henry Wilson-Fox, M.P., Tamworth Division of Warwickshire; one *s.* Chairman Hackney War Pensions Committee, 1914-18; Chairman South African Comforts Committee, 1914-18; Vice-Chairman Society Oversea Settlement of British Women; Vice-Chairman Joint Parliamentary Advisory Council; Vice-Chairman Women's Advisory Committee of Unionist Organization, 1925-28; served on Departmental Committees on Child Adoption, 1924-26, and on Street Offences, 1927-28; Chairman Women's Advisory Committee League of Nations Union, 1931-35. *Address:* 318 Minster House, St. James' Court, S.W.1. [*Died* 7 *Oct.* 1963.

WILTON, George Wilton; retired; Q.C. (Scot.) 1919; *b.* 14 Dec. 1862; *e. s.* of Wilton Wilton, printer, Edinburgh; *m.* 1904, Christina Steel (*d.* 1950), *d.* of Hugh Smith, engineer, Glasgow; two *s.* two *d.* *Educ.:* Royal High Sch., Edin.; B.L. Univ. of Edinburgh, 1887; Lord Rector's Prize Essayist, 1888; University and Law School, Paris. Qualified as Solicitor, 1884; admitted Member of Faculty of Advocates, 1890; English Bar, Middle Temple, 1901; Sheriff-Substitute of Lanarkshire at Lanark, 1927-1939. *Publications:* Company Law and Practice in Scotland, 1912, and other Company Law works; Fingerprints: History, Law and Romance, 1938; Fingerprints: Swan Song of Old "Dr. Fingerprints," 1963. *Address:* c/o Drummonds Bank, 49 Charing Cross, S.W.1. *Club:* Royal Over-Seas League. [*Died* 4 *April* 1964.

WILTSHIRE, Aubrey Roy Liddon, C.M.G. 1919; D.S.O. 1918; M.C.; V.D.; Director: Birmid Auto Castings Pty. Ltd.; Australian Steamships Pty. Ltd.; Caledonian Collieries Ltd.; Cessnock Collieries Ltd.; Coal & Allied Industries Ltd.; Howard Smith Ltd.; Howard Smith Industries Ltd.; Australian Sugar Co. Pty. Ltd.; J. & A. Brown & Abermain Seaham Collieries Ltd.; Melbourne Steamship Co. Ltd.; Lamson Paragon Ltd.; *b.* Longwood, Victoria, 28 May 1891; *s.* of Reverend A. A. Wiltshire; *m.* 1922, Jean, *y. d.* of Dr. William Morrison; two *d.* *Educ.:* Euroa. European War, 1915-19, 22nd Battalion Australian Imperial Force, Egypt, Gallipoli, France and Belgium (M.C., D.S.O., C.M.G., despatches four times). Inspector-General of Administration, Dept. of Defence, 1940-41 (Brigadier); General Manager Bank of Australasia, 1944-1951. Australia and New Zealand Bank, 1951-54; Chairman: Associated Banks, 1950-51; Australian Bankers Association, 1954. Trustee, Royal Soc. of Victoria. *Recreations:* golf, swimming. *Address:* 9/424 Glenferrie Road, Victoria, Australia. *Clubs:* Melbourne, Union. [*Died* 1 *June* 1969.

WILTSHIRE, Samuel Paul, M.A. (Cantab.), D.Sc. (Bristol); Director, Commonwealth Mycological Institute, Ferry Lane, Kew, 1940-56; *b.* 13 Mar. 1891; *s.* of Oliver and Hester Wiltshire, Trowbridge, Wilts; *m.* 1922, Violet Gertrude, *d.* of late Dr. D. H. Scott, F.R.S.; no *c.* *Educ.:* Bristol University; Emmanuel College, Cambridge. Mycologist at Long Ashton Research Station, Bristol, 1919-22; Commonwealth Mycological Institute (then Imperial Bureau of Mycology), 1922. Assistant Director, 1924-1939. *Publications:* papers in scientific journals. *Address:* 24 Lawn Crescent, Kew, Richmond, Surrey. *T.:* Richmond 3151 [*Died* 13 *May* 1967.

WIMBORNE, 2nd Viscount, *cr.* 1918; 3rd Baron, *cr.* 1880; **Ivor Grosvenor Guest**; Baron Ashby St. Ledgers, *cr.* 1910; Bt. 1838; O.B.E. 1953; J.P., D.L. London; *b.* 21 Feb. 1903; *s.* of 1st Viscount and Hon. Alice Katherine Sibell Grosvenor (*d.* 1948), *d.* of 2nd Baron Ebury; *S.* father, 1939; *m.* 1938, Lady Mabel Fox-Strangways, *yr. d.* of 6th Earl of Ilchester, G.B.E.; three *s.* one *d.* *Educ.:* Eton; Trinity Coll., Camb. M.P. (Nat.) Brecon and Radnor, 1935-39. Served in Northamptonshire Yeomanry, 1939-43. Parliamentary Private Secretary to Under-Secretary of State for Air, 1943-45. Governor, Stowe School, 1950 (Chm. 1952-60). *Heir:* *s.* Hon. Ivor Fox-Strangways Guest [*b.* 2 December 1939; *m.* 1966, Victoria Ann, *o. d.* of late Col. Mervyn Vigors, D.S.O., M.C.]. *Address:* 5 Wilton Crescent, S.W.1; Ashby St. Ledgers, Rugby. *Clubs:* White's, Turf, Beefsteak. [*Died* 7 *Jan.* 1967.

WINCHESTER, 16th Marquess of (*cr.* 1551), **Henry William Montagu Paulet,** Baron St. John of Basing, 1539; Earl of Wiltshire, 1550; Premier Marquess of England; H.M.'s Lieutenant and Custos Rotulorum, 1904-17; Chairman Hants County Council, 1904-09; President Territorial Association, 1909-17; *b.* 30 Oct. 1862; *s.* of 14th Marquess and Mary, *d.* of 6th Lord Rokeby; *S.* brother, 1899; *m.* 1st, 1892, Charlotte (G.B.E. 1918, *d.* 1924), *d.* of Col. Howard of Ballina Park, Co. Wicklow, and *widow* of Samuel Garnett of Arch Hall, Co. Meath; 2nd, 1925, Caroline (*d.* 1949), *widow* of Major Claud Marks, D.S.O., Highland Light Infantry; 3rd, 1952, Bapsy Pavry, M.A., *d.* of Most Rev. Khurshedji Pavry, High Priest of the Parsees in India. Late Lt. 3rd Batt. Hampshire Regt.; late Capt. Hampshire Carabineers, I.Y. B.E.F. France, 1915-17; Major 13th Rifle Brigade. *Heir: cousin,* Richard Charles Paulet. [*Died* 28 *June* 1962.

WINCHESTER, 17th Marquess of, *cr.* 1551 - **Richard Charles Paulet**; Baron St. John of Basing, 1539; Earl of Wiltshire, 1550; Premier Marquess of England; *b.* 8 July 1905; *s* of late Major Charles Standish Paulet, M.V.O., and of Lilian J. C., *d.* of Major William Thomas Exham Fosbery; *S. kinsman,* 1962. *Educ.:* Eton. *Heir: kinsman,* Nigel George Paulet, *b.* 23 Dec. 1941. *Address:* c/o Munster & Leinster Bank, Main Street, Wexford, Eire. *Club:* Royal Automobile. [*Died* 5 *March* 1968.

WINCHESTER, Tarleton; retd. as Vice-Pres. (Europe) United States Lines Company (Shipping); *b.* Baltimore, Maryland, 12 Dec. 1895; *s.* of late Marshall Winchester and late Maud Tarleton Winchester; *m.* 1923, Vera Roslington; two *d.*; *m.* 1959, Nancy Hamilton. *Educ.:* Jefferson School, Baltimore, Md.; St. Paul Academy, St. Paul, Minnesota; Trinity College, Port Hope, Ontario. Morning Telegraph, New York, 1914; Paramount Pictures Corp., New York, 1916; Shipping Control Committee, 1918; U.S. Shipping Board, 1920; United States Lines, 1923-62. C.B.E. (Hon.) 1962. *Recreations:* International affairs and commerce, books, theatre. *Address:* Sol de Oro, Pelayo (Algeciras), Spain. *Clubs:* American, Hurlingham. [*Died* 21 *June* 1967.

WINCOTT, Harold Edward, C.B.E. 1963; *b.* 13 September 1906; *s.* of Thomas Edward and Rose Laura Wincott; *m.* 1931, Joyce Mary (*née* White); one *s.* three *d.* (one *s.* decd.). *Educ.:* Hornsey County Sch. Financial News, 1930-38; Editor, Investors Chronicle, 1938-58, Editor-in-Chief, 1958-66. Weekly contrib. to Financial Times, 1950-. Director: Investors Chronicle Ltd.; Throgmorton Publications Ltd.; Banker Ltd.; Provincial Insurance Co. Ltd.; Trades Union Unit Trust Managers Ltd.; Financial Mail (Pty.) Ltd. (S. Africa). *Publications:* The Stock Exchange, 1946; The Business of Capitalism, 1968. *Address:* 15 Conduit House, Hyde Vale, Greenwich, S.E.10. *T.:* Tideway 1376. *Club:* Reform. [*Died* 5 *March* 1969.

WINDHAM, Sir William, Kt., *cr.* 1923; C.B.E. 1917; *b.* 1864; *s.* of late Ashe Windham of Wawne, near Hull, and late Alexa M'Lean; *m.* Blance Marie Titren (*d.* 1933); one *s.* one *d.* *Educ.:* Diocesan College, Cape Town. Public Service: Zululand and Natal, 1883-1900; Transvaal, Sec. for Native Affairs, J.P., M.L.C., M.E.C., 1901-10; England, Bd. of Trade and Min. of Labour, 1912-22; Head of Missions to Canada and

Newfoundland, 1914 and 1915; to France, 1916; to Australia and New Zealand, 1923. *Club:* Royal Commonwealth Society.
[*Died* 21 *March* 1961.

WINDLESHAM, 2nd Baron, *cr.* 1937, of Windlesham; **James Bryan George Hennessy,** Bt., *cr.* 1927; Brigadier, late Grenadier Guards; *b.* 4 Aug. 1903; *s.* of 1st Baron Windlesham, O.B.E., and Ethel Mary (*d.* 1951), *d.* of Charles Reginald Wynter; *S.* father 1953; *m.* 1st, 1929, Angela Mary (*d.* 1956), 2nd *d.* of Julian Duggan, formerly of 2 Lowther Gns., Princes Gate, S.W.; one *s.* three *d.*; 2nd, 1957, Pamela Dinan (*née* Kennedy). *Educ.:* Eton; Royal Military Coll., Sandhurst; Staff College. Served War of 1939-45; retired, 1948. Croix de Guerre (Belgium); Commander Order of George I (Greece); Commander Order of Leopold II (Belgium). *Heir:* *s.* Hon. David James George Hennessy, *b.* 28 Jan. 1932. *Address:* Corke Little, Woodbrook, Nr. Bray, Co. Wicklow. *Club:* Boodle's.
[*Died* 16 *Nov.* 1962.

WINDSOR-CLIVE, Lieut.-Col. George, C.M.G. 1919; *b.* 6 April 1878; *o. s.* of late Lt.-Colonel Hon. G. H. W. Windsor-Clive and Gertrude, *d.* of 19th Baron Clinton; *m.* 1912, Sidney (*d.* 1935), *o. d.* of C. C. Lacaita, Selham House, Petworth, Sussex; three *s.* one *d.* *Educ.:* Eton; R.M.C., Sandhurst. Joined Coldstream Guards, 1897: served South African War; European War, 1914-19 (C.M.G.); retired pay, 1923; Home Guard, 1940-44: M.P. (C.) Ludlow Div. of Shropshire, 1923-45. D.L. Shropshire, 1947-67. *Address:* The Lodge, Ludlow, Salop. *T.:* Ludlow 54. *Clubs:* Guards, Carlton.
[*Died* 25 *June* 1968.

WINDSOR LEWIS, Brigadier James Charles, D.S.O. 1941 (and Bar 1945); M.C.; *b.* 18 March 1907; *s.* of late James Windsor Lewis (killed in action 1916), Llwyndcoed, Glamorgan, and Katherine Henrietta, *d.* of late Major-General Charles Gregorie, C.B.; *m.* 1st, 1941, Audrey (marriage dissolved, 1961), *d.* of Lt.-Col. and the Hon. Mrs. J. F. Harrison, Kings Walden Bury, Hitchin; two *d.*; 2nd, 1961, Mrs. Anne Murray, *d.* of Vice-Admiral the Hon. Rupert and Lady Evelyn Drummond. *Educ.:* Eton; Sandhurst. Joined Welsh Guards, 1927; Adjutant 1st Battalion, 1932-35; Comptroller to Governor-General, South Africa, 1936-37; A.D.C. to Governor-General, Australia, 1938-39; served War of 1939-45 (despatches); Commanded 2nd Bn. Welsh Guards, Dec. 1943-May 1946; Commandant Guards Depot, 1946-48; Military Attaché, Washington, 1948-51; Commanding Welsh Guards, 1951-54; Commander 1st Guards Brigade, 1954-58. *Address:* Beeches Farm, Tunstead, Norwich. *Clubs:* Buck's, Turf, White's.
[*Died* 27 *Oct.* 1964.

WINGE, Ojvind, Dr.phil.; Professor at the Carlsberg Laboratory and Director of the Physiological Department, 1933-56; retired 1956; leader of the Carlsberg Breweries' Experimental Farm, Nordgaarden pr. Herfölge, from 1938; *b.* Aarhus, 19 May 1886; *s.* of Sigfred Winge, Lawyer, and Petra Winge; *m.* 1913, Julie Begtrup Møller; one *s.* *Educ.:* Marselisborg Sch., Aarhus. M.Sc. (Botany) Univ. of Copenhagen, 1910; studies at Univs. of Stockholm, Paris and Chicago; Asst. at Carlsberg Laboratory, 1911-21; Dr.phil. 1917; Prof. of Genetics, Roy. Veterinary and Agricultural College, 1921-33; Lecturer in Genetics, University of Copenhagen, 1929-1935; Lectures at Universities in U.S.A., 1932 and 1957; Hitchcock Professor at California University, 1957; Member of Academies in Copenhagen (Chm. of Science Class, 1946-62), Stockholm, Lund, Oslo, Helsingfors; Foreign Mem. of Roy. Soc., London, 1947 and of National Acad. of Sciences, Washington, 1948, and of Linnean Soc. of London, 1956; Hon. Mem. Danish Mycological Soc., Danish Bot. Soc., Genetic Soc. of Gt. Britain, of Sweden, of Japan, and of Northern Genetic Society. Dr.Sc. *h.c.*: University of Oxford; University of Stockholm. Scheele Medal for Biochemistry (Stockholm) and Prize of Danish Yeast Industry; Emil Chr. Hansen Medal (Copenhagen), 1958; Pres. Danish Royal Horticultural Soc., 1944-52, Co-op. Danish Hort. Societies, 1949-52, and Emil Chr. Hansen Foundation for Microbiology, 1933-1956. *Publications:* A (Danish) Textbook in Genetics, 3rd ed., 1945; A (Danish) Manual in Higher Fungi (with C. Ferdinandsen), 2nd ed., 1943; Genetics in Dogs (Danish), 1945, American edn., 1950; series of papers on botany (Fungi), Cytology and Genetics. *Recreations:* hunting, fishing. *Address:* The Carlsberg Laboratory, Copenhagen (Valby), Denmark. *T.:* Valby 1125.
[*Died* 5 *April* 1964.

WINNINGTON-INGRAM, Ven. Arthur John; Archdeacon of Hereford, 1942-58, Archdeacon Emeritus, 1959; Canon Residentiary of Hereford Cathedral and Treas. 1945-61; *b.* 14 June 1888; *s.* of Edward Henry Winnington-Ingram, formerly Archdeacon of Hereford, and Elizabeth Ruscombe, *d.* of John Anstice; *m.* 1938, Joan Mary, *d.* of Rev. R. A. Lyne; no *c.* *Educ.:* Hereford Cathedral School; St. John's College, Oxford (M.A.); Wells Theological College. Curate, 1912-16, Vicar, 1916-21, Corsham, Wilts; Principal of St. Aidan's College, Ballarat, Australia, and Chaplain to the Bishop of Ballarat, 1921-28; Vicar of Kimbolton with Middleton-on-the-Hill, 1929-36; Rural Dean of Leominster, 1934-36; Prebendary of Hereford Cathedral, 1937-61; Rural Dean of Ledbury, 1937-42; Rector of Ledbury, 1936-1945. *Address:* Little Brendon, Park Road, Winchester, Hants. *T.:* Winchester 3124.
[*Died* 1 *June* 1965.

WINSBURY-WHITE, Horace Powell, M.B., Ch.B., F.R.C.S. Edin., F.R.C.S. Eng.; Commendatore (Italy); Hon. Cons. Surg. St. Peter's, St. Paul's and St. Philip's Hosps., for Genito-Urinary Diseases, London; Hon. cons. Urologist Italian Hospital, and Queen Elizabeth Hospital for Children; *s.* of late John James Winsbury White, J.P., Public Trustee, Blenheim, N.Z.; *m.* 1st, 1924, Concha Marguerite De Courcy Brodie (decd.); 2nd, 1953, Elizabeth, *widow* of Ellwood Holmes; one adopted *s.* *Educ.:* Marlborough College, N.Z.; Univ. of Edinburgh. Co-Founder (with late Frank Kidd) of British Journal of Urology and Editor for 20 years; Cons. Editor, British Journal of Urology. Hunterian Professor Royal College of Surgeons, 1925 and 1933; Guitéras Lecturer, American Urological Association, 1936. Hon. Mem. Amer. Urological Assoc. Corresp. Mem. Assoc. Française d'Urologie; Mem. Internat. Soc. of Urology; Ex-Pres., Sect. of Urology, Roy. Soc. Med. Served European War, Army, 1914-18; War of 1939-45, Emergency Medical Service. *Publications:* Stone in the Urinary Tract (two edns.); contrib. to British Encyclopædia of Medical Practice, Cyclopedia of Medicine (American) and Italian Encyclopedia of Medicine, Brit. Jl. of Urology, etc. Ed. Textbook of Genito-Urinary Surgery (two edns.). *Recreations:* Oriental hardstones; riding, fishing. *Address:* 71 Harley Street, W.1; Walled-garden House, Whitchurch, Reading. *T.:* Pangbourne 220. *Club:* Junior Carlton.
[*Died* 6 *Nov.* 1962.

WINSER, Colonel (Hon. Brig. Gen.) Charles Rupert Peter, C.M.G. 1918; D.S.O. 1916, Bar 1918; *b.* 29 June 1880; *s.* of Rev. C. J. Winser, M.A., late Rector of Adderley, Salop, and *d.* of Sir Rupert Kettle; *m.* 1st, 1914, Adeline Margaret (*d.* 1939), *d.* of William Bouch, Ashorne, Warwick; (two *s.* decd.

and one *s.* killed in action); 2nd, 1945, Gerda Sophie Dorothea, *d.* of Generalintendant G. P. Brammer, Royal Danish Army. *Educ.:* Denstone, Staffs. Joined 3rd South Lancs Militia, 1899; served South Africa, 1900-2; Transport M.I. Coy. Staff; 1st South Lancashire, India, 1903-10; Adjutant 3rd South Lancashire, 1910-12; resigned, 1913, rejoined, Aug. 1914; East Anglia Div. R.F.A. (T.), France, 7th South Lancashire, 1915; to command 19th Batt. Machine Gun Corps, 1917; commanded 41st Infantry Brigade and other brigades (C.M.G., D.S.O., and bar, wounded, despatches). *Address:* Dean Buildings, Chipping Norton, Oxon. *T.:* Chipping Norton 217. *Clubs:* Lansdowne; Mount (Churchill, Oxon.)

[*Died* 16 *May* 1961.

WINSTEDT, Sir Richard (Olaf), K.B.E., *cr.* 1935; C.M.G. 1926; F.B.A. 1945; D.Litt., M.A. (Oxon); Hon. LL.D. (Malaya), 1951; *b.* 2 Aug. 1878; *m.* 1921, Sara O'Flynn, M.B., Ch.B. *Educ.:* Magdalen College School, and New College, Oxford. Cadet Malayan Civil Service, 1902; District Officer, Kuala Pilah, 1913; acting Secretary to the High Commissioner, 1923; Director of Education, Straits Settlements and F.M.S., M.L.C., Straits Settlements 1924-31, and of the Federal Council, F.M.S., 1927-31; President of Raffles College, 1921-1931; General Adviser to the Malay State of Johore, 1931-35; Member of the Colonial Office Advisory Committee on Education, 1936-39; Reader in Malay, London Univ., 1937-47; Pres., Assoc. of British Malaya, 1938; Dir., Royal Asiatic Society, 1940-43, 1946-49, 1952-55, 1958-61, Pres., 1943-46, 1949-52, 1955-58, 1961-64 (Hon. Vice-Pres., 1964), Gold Medallist, 1947; Vice-Pres. of Royal India Soc., 1947-; Mem. of Governing Body of School of Oriental and African Studies, 1939-59; Hon. Fellow, 1947; Vice-Chairman of Executive Committee for Exhibition of Art from India and Pakistan, held at Royal Academy of Arts, London, 1947-48, and headed a delegation to India to arrange for collec-lection of exhibits; Hon. Member of S.E. Asia Inst., U.S.A.; Hon. Mem., Roy. Batavian Soc. and of Kon. Instituut voor Taal-, Land-en Volkenkunde, The Hague. *Publications:* A Malay Grammar; five Malay Dictionaries; The Malay Magician, 1952, revised edn., 1961; Histories of Johore Perak, Selangor and Negri Sembilan, and many other works on Malay subjects; A History of Malaya, 1935, 3rd edn. 1964; A History of Malay Literature, 1940, revised edn. 1961; Britain and Malaya, 1944; The Malays, a Cultural History, 1947, revised edn., 1961; Malaya and its History, 1948, 7th edn., 1965; Malay Proverbs, 1950. *Address:* 10 Ross Court, Putney Hill, S.W.15. *T.:* Putney 2419. *Club:* (Commodore, 1934) Royal Singapore Yacht (Singapore).

[*Died* 2 *June* 1966.

WINSTER, 1st Baron, *cr.* 1942, of Witherslack; **Reginald Thomas Herbert Fletcher,** P.C. 1945; K.C.M.G. 1948; *b.* 27 March 1885; *o. s.* of Nicholas and Dinah Fletcher, Rampholme, Windermere; *m.* 1909, Elspeth, *d.* of Rev. H. J. Lomax, of Abbotswood, Buxted, Sussex, and *g. d.* of Robert Lomax of Great Harwood, Lancashire and of G. C. Dewhurst, Aberuchill Castle, Perthshire. *Address:* Fivewents Way, Crowborough, Sussex. *T.:* Crowborough 607. *Club:* United Service.

[*Died* 7 *June* 1961 (*ext.*).

WINTER, Carl, M.A.; Director and Marlay Curator, Fitzwilliam Museum, since 1946; Fellow of Trinity College, Cambridge; *b.* 10 Jan. 1906; *o. s.* of late Carl Winter and Ethel M. Hardy, Melbourne, Australia; *m.* 1936, Theodora (marriage dissolved, 1953), *er. d.* of Sir Thomas D. Barlow; two *s.* one *d.* *Educ.:* Xavier College, Melbourne; Newman College, University of Melbourne; Exeter College, Oxford. Assistant Keeper, Departments of Engraving, Illustration and Design and of Paintings, Victoria and Albert Museum, 1931; Deputy Keeper, 1945. *Publications:* Elizabethan Miniatures, 1943; The Fitzwilliam Museum, 1958. *Address:* Grove Lodge, Trumpington Street, Cambridge.

[*Died* 21 *May* 1966.

WINTER, Brig.-Gen. Sir Ormonde de l'Epée, K.B.E., *cr.* 1922; C.B. 1919; C.M.G. 1917; D.S.O. 1915; late Royal Field Artillery; *s.* of W. H. and Fanny Cheney Winter, late of Sutton Court Lodge, Chiswick; *m.* 1927, Mrs. Marjorie Effie Pinder, 2nd *d.* of Hon. Ernest Bowes Lyon. *Educ.:* Cheltenham College; R.M.A., Woolwich. Entered Army, 1894; Captain, 1901; Major, 1911; Brig.-Gen., R.A., 1917-19; Col., 1920; served European War, 1914-18 (despatches six times, C.B., C.M.G., D.S.O., and bar, Grand Officer of Aviz); temp. commanded 11th Division during operations which resulted in the fall of Cambrai; appointed head of the boundary commission to Schleswig-Holstein but subsequently transferred as Deputy Chief of Police and Director of Intelligence, Ireland, 1920-22; Director of Resettlement, Irish Office, 1922 (K.B.E.); half pay, 1923; retd. pay, 1924; Director of Communications to International Board for Non-Intervention in Spain, 1938-39; joined British Contingent, International Volunteer Force for Finland, and proceeded to Finland March 1940. Finnish War Medal. *Publications:* Horseshoeing; The History of Racing in India; Winter's Tale, an autobiography, 1955. *Recreations:* racing, G. R. in India for 20 years. *Address:* 32 Sullington Gardens, Worthing, Sussex. *Club:* Naval and Military.

[*Died* 13 *Feb.* 1962.

WINTERBOTHAM, Sir Geoffrey Leonard, Kt., *cr.* 1936; late Partner Wallace and Co., Merchants, Bombay, retired 1939; *s.* of late Sir Henry Winterbotham, K.C.S.I.; *m.* 1917, Hilda, *d.* of late David Norton, C.S.I.; no *c.* *Educ.:* Malvern; Magdalene College, Cambridge. President Associated Chambers of Commerce of India and Ceylon, 1929; President Bombay Chamber of Commerce, 1929 and 1934, M.L.C. Bombay, 1926-35. Chairman, Portsmouth Diocesan Board of Finance. *Address:* Durford Knoll, Petersfield, Hants. *Club:* Oriental.

[*Died* 22 *Jan.* 1966.

WINTERBOTTOM, Richard Emanuel; M.P. (Lab.) Brightside Division of Sheffield since 1950; *b.* 22 July 1899; *s.* of Peter Winterbottom and Annie (*née* Butterworth); *m.* 1925, Lilian Sumner; one *s.* *Educ.:* Clarksfield Council School. Half-timer, cotton mill, 1912-13; Co-operative employee, 1913-1917 and 1919-35; served European War, 1917-19; Area Organiser, Nat. Union of Distributive and Allied Workers, 1935-44; National Organiser, Union of Shop, Distributive and Allied Workers, 1944-50; Parliamentary Private Secretary to the Postmaster-General, 1950-51. *Address:* 64 Firth Park Crescent, Sheffield 5. [*Died* 9 *Feb.* 1968.

WINTERTON, 6th Earl, *cr.* 1766 (Ire.); **Edward Turnour;** Baron Winterton, 1761 (Ire.); Viscount Turnour, 1766 (Ire.); Baron Turnour, of Shillinglee, 1952 (U.K.); P.C. 1924; T.D.; Chm. of the Governors of Raines School, 1944; J.P. and D.L. Sussex; *b.* 4 April 1883; *o. s.* of 5th Earl and Lady Georgiana Susan Hamilton (*d.* 1913), *d.* of 1st Duke of Abercorn, K.G.; *S.* father, 1907; *m.* 1924, Hon. Cecilia Monica Wilson, *o. d.* of 2nd Baron Nunburnholme. *Educ.:* Eton; New College, Oxford. Controlling Editor of The World, 1909-10; served European War in Gallipoli, Palestine, Arabia (despatches twice, Order of the Nile and El Nahada); M.P. (U.) Horsham Division, 1904-18

Horsham and Worthing, 1918-40, Horsham Division, 1940-51; Under-Secretary for India, 1922-24, and November 1924-29; Chancellor of Duchy of Lancaster, 1937-39; Deputy to Secretary of State for Air and Vice-President of Air Council Mar.-May 1938; Member of the Cabinet, Mar. 1938-Jan. 1939; Asst. to Home Sec. June 1938; Paymaster General, Jan.-Nov. 1939; Chairman Select Committee Rebuilding of House of Commons, Jan. 1944 Chairman of and British Government Representative upon Inter-Governmental Cttee. for Refugees, 1938-45. Member Sussex Territorial Force Association, 1909-1945; Chairman, Committee of Management, Soho Hospital for Women, 1911-46. Owns about 2800 acres. *Publications:* Pre-War, 1904-1914; a volume of Reminiscences, 1932; Orders of the Day, 1953; Fifty Tumultuous Years, 1955. *Heir:* (*to Irish titles only*): *kinsman*, Robert Chad Turnour, Flt. Sgt., R.C.A.F. [*b.* 1915; *m.* 1941, Kathleen Whyte, Saskatchewan; no *c.*]. *Address:* Shillinglee Park, Chiddingfold, Surrey. *Clubs:* Turf, Carlton, Beefsteak, Royal Automobile.
[*Died* 26 *Aug.* 1962.

WINTLE, Colonel Charles Edmund Hunter, C.B.E. 1921; D.S.O. 1919; I.A., retired; *e. s.* of Col. A. T Wintle, R.A.; *m.* 1st, 1900, Lucy Eliza, *d.* of Colonel Kilgour, Indian Army; one *s.* two *d.*; 2nd, 1924, Violet (*d.* 1953), *widow* of George Falconer-Taylor, I.F.S.; 3rd, 1954, Constance Leslie Sharpe; 4th, 1964, Esther Lydia Pierce. Served Waziristan Expedition, 1894-95 (medal with clasp); European War, 1914-21 in Iraq, Persia, Persian Gulf, and Mesopotamia (despatches five times D.S.O., French Croix de Guerre with Palm, C.B.E.). *Address:* Ashburnham, Bishop's Down, Tunbridge Wells, Kent. *T.:* Tunbridge Wells 22775. [*Died* 9 *May* 1969.

WISE, 1st Baron, *cr.* 1951, of King's Lynn; **Frederick John Wise**; D.L.; Major; retired chartered surveyor, land agent and farmer; Mayor of King's Lynn, 1958-54; *b.* 10 Apr. 1887; *yr. s.* of Edward and Ellen Clayton Wise, Bury St. Edmunds; *m* 1911, Kate Elizabeth, *e. d.* of late John Michael Sturgeon, Horringer, Bury St. Edmunds; one *s.* three *d.* *Educ.:* King Edward VI School, Bury St. Edmunds. Served European War, 1914-18 with R.F.C., Suffolk Regt. and R.A.F. and War of 1939-45 with R.A.F. M.P. (Lab.) King's Lynn Division of Norfolk, 1945-51. President: Norfolk County Football Assoc.; Norfolk County Schools Athletic Assoc.; Vice-President, The English Schools Athletic Association. F.R.I.C.S. D.L. Norfolk, 1954. *Heir:* *s.* John Clayton Wise [*b.* 11 June 1923; *m.* 1946, Margaret Annie Snead; two *s.*]. *Address:* The Great Wood Cottage, North Elmham, East Dereham, Norfolk. *T.:* Elmham 236.
[*Died* 20 *Nov.* 1968.

WISE, Group Capt. Percival Kinnear, C.M.G. 1919; D.S.O. 1917; *b.* 1885; *s.* of A. G. Wise; *m.* 1st, 1917 (marriage dissolved, 1924); one *d.*; 2nd, 1930, Esmée Lyonelle (who obtained a divorce, 1938), *d.* of Sir Lionel Fletcher, C.B.E.; one *s.* *Educ.:* Wellington Coll. Served European War, 1914-19 (despatches, D.S.O., C.M.G.). *Address:* Fairways, Aldeburgh, Suffolk.
[*Died* 7 *June* 1968.

WISEMAN, Sir William George Eden, 10th Bt., *cr.* 1628; C.B. 1918; Chairman of the Committee in the United States of the Dollar Exports Council; *b.* 1 Feb. 1885; *o. s.* of 9th Bt. and Sarah Elizabeth, 3rd *d.* of Lewis Langworthy of Ellesmere, Putney; *S.* father, 1893; *m.* 1908, Florence Marjorie Hulton, *d.* of Rev. G. F. Sams, Rector of Emberton, Bucks; two *d.* (and one *d.* decd.); *m.* 1944, Joan Mary, *d.* of late A. Phelps; one *s.* *Educ.:* Winchester; Jesus College, Cambridge. Served European War, 1914; Chief Adviser on American Affairs to British Delegation, Paris, 1918-19; Member of the banking firm of Kuhn, Loeb and Co., New York, U.S.A. *Heir:* *s.* John William, *b.* 16 March, 1957. *Address:* 30 Wall Street, New York, U.S.A. *Clubs:* Athenæum, Garrick.
[*Died* 17 *June* 1962.

WISHART, John, C.B.E. 1945; LL.D.1947; M.A.; F.E.I.S.; General Secretary, Educational Institute of Scotland, 1941-46, President, 1946-47; *b.* 1879; *s.* of late Robert Wishart, Glasgow; *m.* 1920, Isabella Mary, *d.* of late James Gulliland, Glasgow; one *d.* *Educ.:* Crookston Street School, Glasgow; Hutchesons' Grammar School, Glasgow; Glasgow University. Teacher in Glasgow Primary and High Schools; Head Teacher Junior Instruction Centres, Glasgow; Organising Secretary of Educational Institute of Scotland and Editor Scottish Educational Journal, 1926. F.Coll.H. (Fellow of the College of Handicraft). *Publications:* Selected English Letters, 1919; articles in various educational journals. *Recreation:* walking. *Address:* 37 Craiglockhart Loan, Edinburgh 11. *T.:* Edinburgh Craiglockhart 1576.
[*Died* 14 *Dec.* 1970.

WISHART, Rear-Admiral John Webster, C.B. 1954; C.B.E. 1950 (O.B.E. 1941); R.A.N. retd.; *b.* 15 September 1892; *s.* of John Wishart, Adelaide and Suva, Fiji; *m.* 1919, Jessie Helena, *d.* of James Couston, Adelaide; one *s.* one *d.* *Educ.:* St. John's Collegiate School, Auckland, New Zealand. Joined R.A.N. as Engineer Sub-Lt., 1915; Engr. Lt. Comdr., 1923; Engr. Commander, 1927; appointed to staff of High Commissioner in London, 1933, to obtain experience at Admiralty at Greenwich and with engineering firms in U.K.; Engr. Capt. and Director of Engineering, 1942; Engr. Rear-Admiral, 1947; 3rd Naval Member of Australian Commonwealth Naval Board, and Chief of Construction, 1948; served on various Defence committees. Retired, 1953. *Recreation:* walking. *Address:* Exeter Road, Croydon, Victoria, Australia. *T.:* Croydon 31085. *Clubs:* Naval and Military, Wallaby (Melbourne).
[*Died* 3 *June* 1968.

WITNEY, John Humphrey, O.B.E. 1946 (M.B.E. 1920); *b.* 23 Feb. 1879; *e. s.* of John Witney, Princes Risborough; *m.* 1911, Dora Ethel Mary, *yr. d.* of John Morrison Stobart, Ryde, Isle of Wight; one *s.* one *d.* (and *er. s.* decd.). *Educ.:* United Westminster School; King's College, London. Entered British Museum, 1896; served European war, 1915-20; Assistant Secretary, British Museum, 1926; Secretary, 1940-46; retired, March 1946. *Recreation:* gardening. *Address:* Longfield, Princes Risborough, Bucks. *T.:* Princes Risborough 254. 254. *Club:* Reform. [*Died* 12 *Nov.* 1964.

WITTS, Major-General Frederick Vavasour Broome, C.B. 1943; C.B.E. 1921; D.S.O. 1917; M.C.; D.L. (Glos.) 1953; C.C. Glos. 1955-61. Lord of the Manor and Patron of the Living of Upper Slaughter, Glos., since 1958; *b.* 30 Jan. 1889; 5th *s.* of late Rev. Canon Broome Witts, Upper Slaughter Manor, Glos.; *m.* 1929, Alice, *e. d.* of late A. E. Wrigley, J.P., Wyck Hill, Glos.; one *s.* three *d.* *Educ.:* Radley; R.M.A., Woolwich (passed in first and out first, King's medal and Pollock medal); Staff Coll., Quetta, 1922. Joined Royal Engineers, 1907; Lt. 1909; Capt. 1914; Bt. Major, 1919; Major, 1924; Bt. Lt.-Col. 1929; Lt.-Col. 1931; Col. 1934; Maj.-Gen. 1939; joined K.G.O. Bengal Sappers and Miners, 1913, and served with them in European War; France, 1915; Mesopotamia, 1916-18, including command of bridging operations over the Tigris at Shumran on 23 Feb. 1917 (despatches three times, wounded once, M.C., D.S.O., French Croix de Guerre, Brevet Major, 1919); served in Kurdistan, 1919, as Brigade-Major (despatches); served in Iraq, 1920, as Brigade-Major to Brig.-Gen. F. E. Coningham (despatches twice, O.B.E., C.B.E.); General Staff War Office, 1923-27; Staff Officer, Royal Engineers, H.Q. Shanghai Defence Force, 1927; O.C. 56th Field Co. R.E., Shanghai Defence Force, 1928; Bulford Camp, 1929; General Staff, Staff College, Camberley, 1930-32; C.R.E. 5th Division, Catterick Camp, 1933-1934; G.S.O.I., 5th Division, Catterick Camp, 1935; Western Desert, Egypt, 1936; Palestine, 1936; Catterick Camp, 1937; Brigadier, General Staff, Western Command, India, 1937-38; Commander 8th (Bareilly) Infantry Brigade, India, 1938-39; Commander 45th (West Country) Division T.A. 1939; D.C.G.S. at G.H.Q. France, Feb.-Apr. 1940; Comdr. 59th (Staffs.) Div. 1940-41; Comdr. Bombay District, 1941-43; Off. G.O.C.-in-C. Southern Army, India, with acting rank of Lt.-Gen., May-June 1942; retired, 1943; Lt.-Govnr. and Sec., Roy. Hosp., Chelsea, 1944-48, Commr., 1948-57. Member Executive Committee Red Cross and St. John Joint War Organization, 1944-47; Member of Joint Cttee., Order of St. John and B.R.C.S. 1945-48, Asst. Dir. of Ambulance, Order of St. John, 1944-48; Memb. of Chap.-Gen. 1945-48; K.St.J. 1956; F.R.G.S. *Publications:* articles in R.U.S.I. and R.E. Journals on Military Bridging in Mesopotamia. *Recreations:* genealogy and crosswords. *Address:* Magpies, Chesterton, Cirencester, Glos. *T.:* Cirencester 3346. *Club:* Army and Navy. [*Died* 10 *March* 1969.

WODEHOUSE, Lt.-Colonel Frederic William, C.I.E. 1912; Indian Army (retired); *b.* 7 April 1867; *s.* of late Lt.-Colonel Charles Wodehouse, C.I.E.; *m.* 1st, 1893, Mary Helen (*d.* 1920), *d.* of late George Nugent Reynolds Lambert, Co. Galway; three *d.*; 2nd, 1940, Hilary Mary, *o. d.* of late William Henry Pell, Holme House, Nottinghamshire. *Educ.:* Westminster School; R.M.C., Sandhurst. Joined South Staffordshire Regt., 1886; transferred Lancashire Fusiliers, 1886; Indian Staff Corps, 1887; held various appointments in the Bombay Political Department; served Chin Lushai, 1889-90 (medal); Resident, Kolhapur, and Political Agent, Southern Mahratta Country States. *Recreations:* shooting, golf, fishing. *Address:* 188 Chatsworth Court, W.8. *T.:* Western 8251. *Club:* United Service. [*Died* 16 *Jan.* 1961.

WODEHOUSE, Helen Marion; *b.* Oct. 1880; *d.* of Philip John Wodehouse, Rector of Bratton Fleming, North Devon, and Marion Bryan Wallas. *Educ.:* Notting Hill High School; Girton College, Cambridge; University of Birmingham. Mathematical Tripos, Class II.; Moral Sciences Tripos, Class I., Div. I.; M.A. and D.Phil. Birmingham; Lecturer in Philosophy, University of Birmingham, 1903-11; Principal, Bingley Training College, Yorkshire, 1911-19; Professor of Education in the University of Bristol, 1919-31; Mistress of Girton Coll., Cambridge, 1931-42. *Publications:* The Logic of Will, 1907; The Presentation of Reality, 1910; Nights and Days, and other Lay Sermons, 1916; God the Prisoner, and other Lay Sermons, 1920; A Survey of the History of Education, 1924; The Scripture Lesson in the Elementary School, 1926; Temples and Treasuries, and other Lay Sermons, 1935; Selves and their Good, 1936; One Kind of Religion, 1944, and articles in periodicals, etc. *Address:* Park Nursing Home, Llandrindod Wells, Radnorshire. [*Died* 20 *Oct.* 1964.

WODEMAN, Guy Stanley, C.M.G. 1939; M.A.; *b.* 16 July 1886; *y. s.* of late Rev. Henry Wodeman, M.A., The Grange, Folkestone; *m.* 1st, 1915, Phyllis Mary (*d.* 1937), *e. d.* of late Ralph Carpenter, Aston Hall, Ches.; 2nd, 1938, Winifred Mary (*d.* 1967), 2nd *d.* of W. B. de Winton, C.I.E; no *c.* *Educ:* Rossall; Jesus Coll., Camb. B.A. (Hons.), 1908; M.A., 1921; passed into Ceylon Civil Service, 1909; Excise Commissioner, 19[illegible]-31; Principal Collector of Customs and Chairman, Colombo Port Commission, 1931-36; Deputy Chief Secretary, 1937-40; Chief Secretary, 1940-42; retired, 1942; Temp. Principal, Colonial Office, 1942-46. *Address:* 33 The Mansions, Old Brompton Rd., S.W.5. *T.:* Frobisher 3810. [*Died* 5 *May* 1970.

WOLFE, Rev. Clarence Albert Edward, M.B.E. 1959; *b.* 24 Feb. 1892; *s.* of late Augustine Wolfe; *m.* 1920, Mary M. Billington; one *s.* one *d.* *Educ.:* Slade Gram. Sch., Bolton; Manchester Univ. (B.A.); St. Aidan's College, Birkenhead. Deacon 1916, priest 1917, Manchester; Curate, St. John's, Cheetham, 1916-20; Curate, St. Anne's-on-Sea, 1920-21; Chaplain, Slade Grammar School, Bolton, 1920-24; Vicar of St. Bartholomew's, Bolton, 1924-26; Sub-Warden, Aberlour Orphanage, 1926-28; Rector of St. Margaret's, Aberlour and Warden of Aberlour Orphanage, 1928-58; Dean of Moray, Ross and Caithness, 1946-60; Rector, Gordon Chapel, Fochabers, 1958-60; Vicar of Glasson, Lancaster, 1960-63. Canon, St. Andrew's Cathedral, Inverness, 1932. *Address:* 5 Beatty Road, Southport, Lancs. [*Died* 2 *Feb.* 1967.

WOLFE, Frederick John; late Chairman, Anglo-American Oil Co. Ltd. (Esso Petroleum Co. Ltd.); *b.* Brantford, Ont., Canada; *s.* of Charles Frederick and Sarah Balfour Wolfe; *m.* Marguerite, *d.* of late Senator John J. Boyce; one *s.* one *d.* Formerly Vice-President, Imperial Oil Ltd., Canada. *Address:* P.O. Box 1128, Nassau, Bahamas. *Clubs:* Carlton; York, National (Toronto); Metropolitan (New York). [*Died* 23 *Jan.* 1962.

WOLFE, Herbert Robert Inglewood, V.R.D. 1955; M.S.; F.R.C.S.; Consultant Surgeon: University College Hospital since 1949; National Temperance Hospital since 1950; Hospital for Tropical Diseases since 1951; Member, Court of Examiners, R.C.S. Eng., 1965; *b.* 16 Oct. 1907; *s.* of John Henry Wolfe and Euphemia Heim (*née* Daniels); *m.* 1946, Lesley Winifred, *d.* of Charles William Norman and Dorothy Winifred Fox; three *s.* one *d.* *Educ.:* Eastbourne College; St. Thomas's Hospital. Casualty Officer, Anaesthetist and House Surgeon, St. Thomas' Hosp., 1933-34; Resident Surgical Officer, Roy. Infirmary, Cardiff, 1935-37. Served in R.N., 1939-46. Asst. in Surgical Unit and Asst. Lecturer in Surgery, Welsh Nat. School of Medicine, 1937-49. *Publications:* papers on surgical subjects in medical journals. *Recreations:* yacht cruising. *Address:* Inglewood, North Square, N.W.11. *T.:* 01-455 7281. *Club:* Junior Carlton. [*Died* 18 *Feb.* 1970.

WOLFFSOHN, Sir Arthur (Norman), Kt. 1961; C.M.G. 1947; O.B.E. 1943; Speaker of the Legislative Assembly of British Honduras, 1954-61; *b.* 30 September 1888; *y. s.* of late Sally Wolffsohn, Belize; *m.* 1924, Stella Erica Laura, *e. d.* of late Henry Denbigh Phillips, Belize; one *s.* one *d.* *Educ.:* Dollar Academy, Clackmannanshire, Scotland. Certified Land Surveyor, 1910; 3rd Scottish Horse Yeomanry, 1914; 6th Bn. The Black Watch, 1916; 3rd (Light) Tank Bn., 1917; Asst. Eng., Sea Defence Dept., British Guiana, 1919; Govt. Surveyor, British Honduras, 1922, Director of Surveys, 1935, Member of Exec. Council, 1936; Colonial Secretary, British Honduras, 1943-49; Acting Director of Public Works, 1941; retired Apr. 1949. Controller of

Imports, British Honduras, 1949-50; President of nominated Belize City Council, 1951; Actg. Conservator of Forests, 1952. *Recreations:* cards and billiards. *Address:* Belize, British Honduras. *Clubs:* Pickwick: Belize (Belize). [*Died* 17 *Nov.* 1967.

WOLFIT, Sir Donald, Kt. 1957; C.B.E. 1950; Actor Manager; President, Royal General Theatrical Fund; *b.* 20 April 1902; *s.* of William Pearce Woolfitt and Emma Tomlinson; *m.* 1st, Chris Frances Castor; one *d.*; 2nd, Susan Katherine Anthony; one *s.* one *d.*; 3rd, Rosalind Iden Payne. *Educ.:* Magnus School, Newark. Began theatrical career 1920. Engagements with Matheson Lang; Fred Terry, Haymarket Theatre; Sir Barry Jackson, Old Vic, and Stratford Memorial Theatre. Appeared in films, 1934, 1935. Commenced Actor management, 1937. Toured all the principal cities Great Britain. London seasons at Kingsway, Strand, St. James', Westminster, Winter Garden, Savoy Theatres with repertoire of Shakespeare and other classics. Presented over 112 perfs. of lunch-time Shakespeare at the Strand Theatre during the Battle of Britain; also 100 performances full Shakespeare repertoire at Scala Theatre, 1944; Shakespeare seasons in Cairo, Paris, Brussels, to H.M. Forces, 1945, Century Theatre, New York, 1947; trans-Canadian Shakespeare Tour, 1948, playing all cities in the Dominion; Season of 126 performances of Shakespeare, Bedford Theatre, Camden Town, 1949; Long John Silver in Treasure Island, Fortune, 1949; presented A New Way to pay old Debts, playing Sir Giles Overreach, Malvern Festival, 1950; presented Twelfth Night on 350th anniversary in Middle Temple Hall before The Queen and Princess Margaret; played Tamburlaine the Great, opening Old Vic Season, 1951, followed by The Clandestine Marriage. Season of classic plays, King's Theatre, Hammersmith, 1953, 280 performances of all his chief parts including Œdipus Rex and Colonus in one evening's programme. Sir Peter Teazle in School for Scandal and Captain Hook in Peter Pan, Scala Theatre, 1953-54; The Strong are Lonely, Piccadilly, Haymarket Theatres and Edinburgh Festival, 1955-56; The Master of Santiago, and Malatesta, Lyric, Hammersmith, 1957; Ghosts, Princes Theatre, 1959; Shakespeare Recital Tour, Kenya, Ethiopia and Italy, 1959; World tour with Shakespeare Recitals, 1960; Cromwell at Drogheda, Leatherhead Theatre, 1961; Fit to Print, Duke of York's, 1962; Tour of So. Af. (Ibsen and Shakespeare), 1962-63; John Gabriel Borkman, Duchess, 1963; All in Good Time, Royale Theatre, New York, 1965; Treasure Island, Mermaid; Robert and Elizabeth, Lyric, 1966. Has presented Ibsen, Shaw, Molière, and Jonson with his own co. Famous rôles: Hamlet, Othello, Shylock, Volpone, Richard III, Lear, Touchstone, Malvolio, Benedick, Macbeth, Solness. *Films include,* 1952: The Ringer; Pickwick Papers; Isn't Life Wonderful?; 1953: Svengali, in film of Trilby; Prize of Gold; 1958: I Accuse; Room at the Top; The Angry Hills; The Rough and the Smooth; House of Seven Hawks; Lawrence of Arabia; Becket; Life at the Top; Decline and Fall. Numerous television appearances and broadcasts. *Publication: autobiography:* First Interval, 1955. *Recreations:* gardening, playwriting. *Address:* Swift Cottage, Ibthorpe, Andover, Hants. *T.:* Hurstbourne Tarrant 245. *Club:* Garrick. [*Died* 17 *Feb.* 1968.

WOLMARK, Alfred Aaran, artist; *b.* Warsaw, 1877, British subject; *s* of Solomon and Gitel Wolmark; *m.* 1911, Bessie Leah Tapper; two *s.* one *d.* *Educ.:* London, studied Art British Museum and Royal Academy of Arts; 1st Silver Medallist for Drawing, R.A.; exhibitor Royal Academy and most Galleries in England and Continent; one man exhibitions in England, France, Germany, Austria, and America; Pioneer of New Movement in Art; Designer Stage work, Stained Glass, Pottery, Furniture, House Decoration; Portraits of famous Shakespearians presented to Shakespeare Memorial Museum, Stratford-on-Avon; works in public Galleries: Tate Gallery, Aberdeen, National Gallery, Stoke on Trent, Derby, Leamington, Southampton, Musée D'Orléans, York, and National Portrait Gallery, London. *Publications:* articles on Art and Decorations in Magazines, and in the Press on beautifying London. *Recreations:* art and reading. *Address:* St. Paul's Studio, 54 Colet Gdns., W.14. *T.:* Riverside 4532. *Club:* Chelsea Arts. [*Died* 6 *Jan.* 1961.

WOLSELEY, Garnet Ruskin, A.R.W.A.; Painter, portrait; *b.* London, 24 May 1884; *s.* of Rev. Robert Warren Wolseley, B.A., and Jean Ruskin, *d.* of late William Richardson, M.D., Tunbridge Wells; *m.* 1937, Joan Alys (*d.* 1943), *d.* of Sir Walter Trevelyan, 8th Bart., and of Lady Trevelyan, Brockenhurst, Hants; one *s.* two *d.* *Educ.:* Slade School of Art, London. Slade Scholarship and Painting Prizes, 1902-1903; has been a frequent exhibitor at R.A. and other leading London and Provincial Exhibitions since 1909; visited America, 1929 and 1930; Principal works: Visions; The Lady Brocket and Children; The Dancing Lesson; served in the Navy, in Eastern waters, 1915-18; has discovered and excavated important prehistoric villages on South Downs, principal relics from which are exhibited in British Museum. *Publications:* Illustrations in Colour and chapter I Sussex in the Past and Sussex Byways (Lady Wolseley); Prehistoric and Roman Sussex, jointly with Reginald A. Smith, F.S.A., Archæologia Vol. LXXVI. *Recreations:* growing rare flowers, fishing. *Address:* Nettlecombe, Williton, Somerset. [*Died* 16 *Nov.* 1967.

WOMERSLEY, Rt. Hon. Sir Walter James, P.C. 1941; 1st Bt., *cr.* 1945; Kt., *cr.* 1934; J.P.; *b.* Bradford, 5 Feb. 1878; *s.* of William and Mary Ann Womersley, Bradford; *m.* 1905, Annie (*d.* 1952), *d.* of John Stamp, Bradford; one *d.* (*er. s.* decd., *yr. s.* killed in action, 1944). *Educ.:* Usher Street Board School, Bradford. Worked as half-timer in a factory at 10 years of age; at 12 worked as shopboy; at 18, appointed manager of a retail shop; at 21 commenced business on own account; late senior partner in Womersley & Stamp, Grimsby; entered Grimsby Town Council, 1911; Mayor of Grimsby, 1922-23; High Steward of Borough, 1950; President Grimsby Chamber of Trade; Vice-Pres. Municipal Corporations Association; Chm. Nat. Chamber of Trade, 1949-54; Chm. Furniture Trades Benevolent Assoc.; M.P. (U.) Grimsby, 1924-45; Parliamentary Private Sec. to Sir Kingsley Wood, Aug.-Oct. 1931; Junior Lord of the Treasury, 1931-35; Assistant Postmaster-General, 1935-39; Minister of Pensions, 1939-45. Knight Commander of the Order of Dannebrog. *Address:* Badminton, 24 Signhills Ave., Cleethorpes, Lincs. *T.:* Cleethorpes 61361. *Clubs:* Constitutional, Carlton; Constitutional (Grimsby). [*Died* 15 *March* 1961.

WOOD, Professor Alfred Cecil; Retd.; Prof. of Modern History, University of Nottingham, 1951-60; *b.* Liverpool, 7 Feb. 1896; *y. s.* of Thomas and Bertha Wood; *m.* 1928, Alice Evelyn Chesters, Nantwich, Cheshire; two *d.* *Educ.:* Liverpool College; Jesus College, Oxford. Served European War, 1915-19, King's Liverpool and Cheshire Regts. (2nd Lieut.; wounded); discharged with permanent disabilities, 1919. Jesus College, Oxford, 1919-21; 1st cl. Hons., History, 1921; B.Litt., 1923; D.Phil. (Oxford), 1933. Lecturer, University College, Nottingham, 1926; Reader, 1946. President

of the Thoroton Society of Nottinghamshire, 1953. *Publications:* History of the Levant Company, 1935; Nottinghamshire in the Civil War, 1937; Memorials of the Holles Family (edited for the Camden Society), 1937; History of Nottinghamshire, 1947; History of University College, Nottingham, 1953; (edited) History of the Willoughby Family by Cassandra, Duchess of Chandos, 1958. Contribs. to English Historical Review, Transactions of Royal Historical Soc., Trans. Thoroton Soc., etc. *Recreations:* reading, walking, gardening. *Address:* 30 Ffforddlas, Prestatyn, Flintshire. *T.:* 2914.
[*Died* 18 *May* 1968.

WOOD, Allan Fergusson; *b.* 1876; 5th *s.* of Wm C Wood, Brinscall, Lancashire; *m* 1907, Rubina, *d.* of Geo. H. Robertson, Llangollen; one *s.* one *d.* *Educ.:* Heversham; Yorkshire Coll. J.P. Beds., 1933; High Sheriff of Bedfordshire, 1943-44. Master Bushmead Beagles, 1932-39. Engineering, 1900-28. *Recreations:* outdoor sports. *Address:* c/o Midland Bank, Nottingham.
[*Died* 6 *Oct.* 1966.

WOOD, Rear-Adm. Arthur Edmund, C.M.G. 1919; R.N., retired; *b.* 1875; 3rd *s.* of late A. H. Wood, Duddleswell Manor, Sussex; *m.* Ruth (*d.* 1957), *o. d.* of Mrs. E. Johnston, Sydney, Australia; one *s.* *Educ.:* H.M.S. Britannia. *Recreations:* cricket, shooting. *Address:* Rytongrove, Ryton, Co. Durham. *Club:* Naval and Military.
[*Died* 30 *Jan.* 1961.

WOOD, Arthur Henry, C.B. 1926; late Assistant Secretary, Board of Education; *b.* 1870; *s.* of Rev. R. Wood, late of Weyleas, Godalming, and Charlotte, *sister* of first Viscount Goschen; *m.* 1st, Adela, *d.* of late Herbert C. Hardy, of Danehurst, Sussex; 2nd, Katharine Mary Altham, *d.* of late Rev. H. A. Cumberlege, Rector of Ockham, Surrey; three *s.* (and one killed in action, 1941); two *d.* *Educ.:* Cranbrook Grammar School; New College, Oxford. *Publications:* The History of West Clandon; The Epic of the Old Testament. *Address:* Dene Court, Shipbourne, Tonbridge, Kent. *T.:* Tonbridge 2545. *Club:* Union (Oxford).
[*Died* 11 *Dec.* 1964.

WOOD, Rt. Rev. Claud Thomas Thellusson, M.C., M.A.; retd.; *b.* 27 Feb. 1885; *s.* of Canon Henry Thellusson and Lucy Elizabeth Wood; *m.* 1928, Sybil Margaret, *d.* of Col. Frederic William Wodehouse, *q.v.*; two *s.* two *d.* *Educ.:* Hawtreys Prep. School; Eton; Trinity College, Cambridge. Deacon, 1908; Priest, 1909; Curate of Hatfield, Herts. 1908-14; Chaplain, Territorial Army, 1914-24; Resident Chaplain to Archbishop of Canterbury, 1919-20; Curate, Croydon Parish Church, 1921-22; Vicar of S. Saviour, Croydon, 1922-30; of Tring, 1930-42; Rural Dean of Berkhamsted, 1934-40; Archdeacon of St. Albans, 1942-51; Bishop Suffragan of Bedford, 1948-Oct. 1953. *Address:* Redcote, Harpenden, Herts. *Club:* United University. [*Died* 17 *Jan.* 1961.

WOOD, Ernest Clement, C.I.E. 1943; I.C.S., retired; *b.* 12 Sept. 1890; *s.* of late James Torrance Wood; *m.* 1925, Lucy Eileen, *d.* of Maj.-Gen. R. W. S. Lyons; three *s.* *Educ.:* Cheltenham Coll.; New Coll., Oxford. Indian Civil Service, 1914. Served European War, 27th Light Cavalry; Asst. to Resident, Travancore and Cochin, 1919; Asst. Settlement Officer, 1920; Sub-Collector, 1922; Private Sec. Govr. of Madras, 1924; Commissioner of Coorg, 1925; Dep. Sec. Finance Dept., Madras, 1926; Collector of various districts in Madras Presidency, 1930-40; Sec. to Madras Govt. Educ. and Public Health Depts., 1940; Member Board of Revenue, Madras, 1943-45; H.M. Treasury, Whitehall, 1946-50. *Recreation:* gardening. *Address:* Floricans, Branksomewood Road, Fleet, Hants. *T.:* Fleet 3813. [*Died* 5 *Oct.* 1970.

WOOD, Mrs. Ethel Mary, C.B.E. 1920; Governor, The Polytechnic, 309 Regent Street, W.1, President of Women's Section; *d.* of late Quintin Hogg; *m.* 1907, Major Herbert Frederic Wood (*d.* 1918), 9th Lancers and R.A.F.; one *d.* Secretary London War Pensions Committee, 1917-21; Chairman Domestic Service Commission, 1923; Hon. Sec. Management Research Groups, 1930-35, 1940-46; Hon. Sec. Committee on Woman Power, 1940-45. *Publications:* Life of Quintin Hogg; Scientific, Management in a Group of Small Factories, 1930; Robert Mitchell, a Life of Service, 1934; Mainly for Men, 1943; The Pilgrimage of Perseverance, 1949; A History of the Polytechnic, 1965. *Address:* 12 Orme Square, W.2. *T.:* 01-229 7630. *Club:* International Sportsmen's.
[*Died* 29 *June* 1970.

WOOD, Herbert George, M.A. (Cantab. and London); Hon. D.D. St. And., 1937, Birmingham, 1957; Hon. Fellow, Jesus Coll., Cambridge, 1956; *b.* London, 2 Sept. 1879; *s.* of Rev. J. R. Wood and Frances Anne Wren; *m.* 1907, Dorothea Wallis (*d.* 1959), Scarborough; two *s.* two *d.* *Educ.:* City of London School; Jesus College, Cambridge (Fellow, 1904). President of the Cambridge Union Society, Lent Term, 1905; Lecturer in History at Jesus College, Cambridge, 1908; Lecturer on New Testament at the Selly Oak Colleges, 1910-40; Director of Studies of Woodbrooke Settlement, Birmingham, 1917-1940; Professor of Theology, Univ. of Birmingham, 1940-46; Dean of the Faculty of Arts, 1943-46; Hulsean Lecturer, Cambridge, 1933-34; Beckly Lecturer, 1935; Dale Lecturer, 1942; Edward Cadbury Lecturer, 1948-49; Arthur Stanley Eddington Memorial Lecturer; Sir William Riddell Memorial Lecturer, 1957. *Publications:* Personal Economy and Social Reform; George Fox; The Kingdom of God in the Teaching of Jesus; Rationalism and Historical Criticism; Venturers for the Kingdom (the Pilgrim Fathers); Quakerism and the Future of the Church; Living Issues in Religious Thought; Why Mr. Bertrand Russell is not a Christian; John William Hoyland of Kingsmead; The Truth and Error of Communism; Christianity and the Nature of History; Communism, Marxist and Christian; Henry T. Hodgkin, a memoir; Did Christ really Live?; Christianity and Civilisation; Religious Liberty Today; F. D. Maurice; T. R. Glover; Why did Christ die?; Belief and Unbelief since 1850; Thought, Life and Time, as reflected in Science and Poetry; Freedom and Necessity in History; Essays in The Englishman's Religion; The Parting of the Roads; Property: its Rights and Duties; The Unity of Civilisation: Christianity and the Crisis; Jesus in the Twentieth Century, 1960. *Recreation:* tennis. *Address:* 26 Linden Road, Bournville, Birmingham 30. *T.A.* and *T.:* Selly Oak 0374
[*Died* 9 *March* 1963.

WOOD, Lieut.-Col. John Nicholas Price; *b.* 9 May 1877; *e. s.* of John Baddeley Wood, Henley Hall, Ludlow, Salop, and Elizabeth Marianne Wood, The Hall, Wirksworth, Derbyshire; *m.* 1932, Eleanor Kaye (*d.* 1948), *o. c.* of Sir Albert Kaye Rollit and *widow* of Major Richard Todd Ellison, 2nd Life Guards, of Boultham Hall, Lincoln; no *c.*; *m.* 1949, Alice Mary (*née* Roddick), *widow* of Lt.-Gen. H. Lumsden, C.B., D.S.O., M.C. *Educ.:* Eton College; Christ Church, Oxford. Joined 12th R. Lancers, 1898; served S. Africa, 1899-1902 (Queen's Medal and 4 clasps, King's Medal and 2 clasps); Capt. 1903; served in India with Regt., 1904-08; Adjutant Lincolnshire Yeomanry, 1908-12; Major, 1912 and retd.; rejoined service, Lt.-Col. 1914; commanded Yeomanries, 1914-19; Home Guard, 1940-42; High Sheriff of Shropshire, 1943-44. *Publication:*

Travel and Sport in Turkestan, 1910. *Address:* Henley Hall, Ludlow. *T.:* Ludlow 99. *Club:* Cavalry. [*Died* 16 *Jan.* 1962.

WOOD, Kenneth Spencer, M.A. (Oxon); Stipendiary Magistrate S. Staffs., 1951-60; Recorder of Smethwick, 1939-51; *b.* 16 Sept. 1897; 2nd *s.* of late Enoch Wood, J.P., West Bromwich, Staffs; *m.* 1924, Winifred Etty, *er. d.* of William Etty Potter, Farnham, Surrey; no *c.* *Educ.:* King Edward's High School, Birmingham; Wadham College, Oxford. Served in European War, 1915-19 with R.N.V.R., R.N.A.S., and R.A.F. (Flight Lieut.) in France and Italy; Barrister, Middle Temple, 1922; Oxford Circuit; re-joined R.A.F. (Pilot Officer), 1940; Flight Lieut., 1941; Squadron Leader, 1942. *Recreations:* reading, theatre-going, travel. *Address:* Casa Rosada, Paguera, Mallorca, Balearics, Spain. *Club:* United University. [*Died* 21 *June* 1963.

WOOD, Paul Hamilton, O.B.E. 1946; M.D., F.R.C.P.; Director, Institute of Cardiology, London; Physician, National Heart Hospital, London; Physician, Cardiac Department, Brompton Hospital, London; *b.* 1907; *s.* of Richard Boardman Wood, B.A., I.C.S.; *m.* 1934, Elizabeth Josephine, *d.* of late John Guthrie, M.S., F.R.C.S., Christchurch, New Zealand; two *s.* one *d.* *Educ.:* Launceston Grammar School, Tasmania; Trinity College, Melbourne University. M.B., B.S. 1931. House Phys. and House Surgeon, Christchurch Hosp., N.Z., 1931-32; Ho. Phys., Brompton Hosp., 1933; Res. M.O., Nat. Heart Hosp., 1934; Brit. Postgraduate Med. Sch.: First Asst., 1935-40; Cons. Phys., 1940-42; Phys. i/c Effort Syndrome Unit, Mill Hill (E.M.S.), 1940-42; Lt.-Col., Officer i/c Med. Div., R.A.M.C., 1942-45 (despatches); served with First Army in N. Africa and Italy; Brig., Cons. Phys. C.M.F., 1945-46; Phys. and Sen. Lectr., Brit. Postgrad. Med. Sch., 1946-48; Dean, Inst. of Cardiology, 1947-50; Cardiologist, Rheumatic Fever Unit, Canadian Red Cross Memorial Hosp., Taplow, 1947-53. Goulstonian Lectr., R.C.P., 1941; Visiting Lectr. Witwatersrand Univ., 1949; St. Cyres Lectr., 1950; Visiting Lectr., Nat. Thoracic Unit, Univ. of N.Z., 1951; Visiting Lectr. (Nuffield) Australia, 1951; Guest Lectr., San Francisco and Los Angeles Heart Assocs., 1953; Strickland Goodall Lectr., Soc. of Apothecaries, 1954; Litchfield Lectr., Univ. of Oxford, 1957; Guest Lectr., Nat. Inst. Cardiovasc. Research, Prague, and Middle East Assembly, Amer. Univ. of Beirut, 1957; Croonian Lectr., R.C.P., 1958; Nathanson Lectr., Univ. S. Cal., 1958; George Fahr Lectr., Univ. of Minn., 1958; Truitt Lectr., Univ. Texas, 1959; Roy Scott Lectr., Western Reserve Univ., Cleveland, 1960; Sims Travelling Prof. (Can.), 1961. Mem. Brit. Cardiac Soc., 1937, and Assoc. of Phys., 1940; Hon. Mem. Australasian Cardiac Soc., 1952, and Indian Cardiac Soc., 1952, Hon. Fell. Amer. College Cardiol., 1959. *Publications:* Diseases of the Heart and Circulation, 1950, 2nd Edn. 1956. Numerous contribs. to Cardiology in Brit. Heart Jl., Amer. Heart Jl., Quarterly Jl. of Med., Brit. Med. Bulletin, B.M.J., Lancet, Brit. Encyclopædia of Medical Practice, The Practitioner, Chambers's Encyclopædia, and Proc. Roy. Soc. Med. *Recreation:* gardening. *Address:* 44 Wimpole St., W.1. *T.:* Welbeck 9363; North Bank, Totteridge Lane, N.20. *T.:* Hillside 5402; Fair Lady Lodge, West Runton, Norfolk. *Club:* Bath. [*Died* 13 *July* 1962.

WOOD, Gen. Robert E., Hon. C.M.G.; Hon. Chairman, Sears, Roebuck and Co.; *b.* Kansas City, Mo., 13 June 1879; *m.* 1908, Mary Hardwick, Augusta, Ga.; one *s.* four *d.* *Educ.:* U.S. Military Academy, graduated 1900; 2nd Lt., 1st Lt., Capt. and Major 3rd Cavalry, U.S. Army; served during Philippine Insurrection 1900-2; Fort Assiniboine, Montana, 1902-3; instructor at West Point, 1903-5; detailed for service in construction of Panama Canal, 1905-15, Assistant Chief Q.M. and Chief Q.M. Panama Canal; Director of Panama Railroad Co.; Retired by special Act of Congress as Major, U.S. Army, 1915; Assistant to President, General Asphalt Company, 1915-17; re-entered service during European War as Colonel of Infantry, later Brigadier-General and Acting Q.M.-General, U.S. Army; (Distinguished Service Medal, U.S.); received Legion of Merit (U.S.) for work in War of 1939-45; re-entered civil life, 1919: Vice-Pres. Montgomery Ward and Co., 1919-1924; Vice-Pres. Sears, Roebuck and Co., 1924-28, Pres. 1928-39, Chm. 1939-54, Chm. Finance Cttee., 1954-56. Knight of Legion of Honour. *Recreations:* riding, hunting, fishing. *Address:* 464 North Mayflower Rd., Lake Forest, Ill., U.S.A. *Clubs:* Chicago, Onwentsia, Old Elm, University and Commercial (Chicago); Army and Navy (Washington). [*Died* 6 *Nov.* 1969.

WOOD, Sir Robert Stanford, K.B.E., *cr.* 1941; C.B. 1939; *b.* 1886; *y. s.* of late Rev. John Roskruge Wood; *m.* 1922, Iris Cecilie, *yr. d.* of late Frederick Arnsby; one *d.* *Educ.:* City of London School; Jesus College, Cambridge (Scholar), Hon. Fellow, 1952. Entered Board of Education, 1911; Principal Private Secretary to President (Lord Eustace Percy), 1926-28; Director of Establishments, 1928-36; Principal Assistant Secretary, Technical Branch 1936-40; Deputy Secretary, 1940-46; Principal, Univ. Coll., Southampton, 1946-52; First Vice-Chancellor, Univ. of Southampton, 1952; retd. Sept. 1952. Hon. LL.D. Southampton. *Address:* 104 Iverna Court, Kensington, W.8. *T.:* Western 6142. *Club:* Oxford and Cambridge. [*Died* 18 *May* 1963.

WOOD, R(onald) McKinnon, O.B.E. 1928 (M.B.E. 1924); M.A.; C.Eng., F.R.Ae.S.; Hon. Fellow, Imperial College of Science and Technology, since 1959; Hon. Fellow, Queen Mary College, since 1967; *b.* 11 May 1892; 4th *s.* of Rt. Hon. Thomas McKinnon Wood, LL.D., D.L. and Isabella Mill (*née* Sandison); *m.* 1918, Gwendolen Elaine Dykes, 5th *d.* of Rt. Hon. Sir Albert Spicer, 1st Bt.; one *s.* one *d.* (and one *s.* decd.). *Educ.:* Highgate Sch.; Merchant Taylors' School, London; Pembroke College, Cambridge. R.A.E., 1914-34 (Head of Aerodynamics Dept., 1919-34). Political work, 1934-40; contested (Lab.) Harborough Div. of Leicestershire, 1935; co-opted Education Cttee. of L.C.C., 1937; M.A.P., 1940-46; Member of L.C.C. for Bethnal Green, 1946-61; Chairman L.C.C. Education Committee, 1950-55; Chairman of L.C.C., 1957-58. *Publications:* contributions to Reports and Memoranda of Aeronautical Research Council, Jl. of Roy. Aeronautical Soc., Encyc. Brit. *Recreation:* gardening. *Address:* The Barn, Upper Vann, Hambledon, Godalming, Surrey. [*Died* 22 *Oct.* 1967.

WOOD, Stuart (Zachary) Taylor, C.M.G. 1943; Commissioner Royal Canadian Mounted Police, 1938-51, retd.; *b.* Napanee, Ont., 17 Oct. 1889; *s.* of Asst. Commissioner Zachary Taylor Wood, C.M.G.; *m.* 1917, Gertrude M., *d.* of John Peterson, Emerson, Manitoba; one *s.* two *d.* (and two *s.* decd.). *Educ.:* Public Schools, Dawson City, Yukon; Upper Canada College; Royal Military College, Kingston, Ont. Inspector in Royal North-West Mounted Police, 1912; Supt. 1931; Asst. Commissioner, 1933; Director of Criminal Investigation at Ottawa, 1936; Registrar-General of Alien Enemies, 1939. Served in Canadian Exped. Force, European War, 1914-18. Religion C. of E. *Address:* 238 Buena Vista, Rockcliffe, Ont., Canada [*Died* 4 *Jan.* 1966.

WOOD, Walter; author; *b.* Bradford, 10 Mar. 1866; *s.* of late William Wood; *m.* 1st, M. A. Baker of Bradford (*d.* 1907); 2nd, 1910, Edith J., 2nd *d.* of Rev. W. G. Berry, M.A., Rector of Shangton, Leicestershire; twin *s.* one *d.* *Educ.:* Borough West School, Bradford. After short spell in wool trade, was on the staff of Yorkshire Observer for ten years; Editor, 1913-46 of Toilers of the Deep, the Magazine of the Royal National Mission to Deep Sea Fishermen. *Publications* include: The Enemy in Our Midst; Men of the North Sea; Survivors' Tales of Great Events (which ran for nearly seven years in The Royal Magazine); A Corner of Spain; North Sea Fishers and Fighters; The Battleship; Fishermen in War Time; Fishing-boats and Barges; The Romance of Regimental Marches (many broadcasts); The Fleeters. *Address:* 99 Steyne Road, Seaford, Sussex. *T.:* Seaford 2946.

[*Died* 26 *Jan.* 1961.

WOOD, William Alfred Rae, C.M.G. 1929; C.I.E. 1919; *b.* Liverpool, 23 Jan. 1878; *s.* of late G. W. T. Wood of Patras, Greece, and London; *m.* 1906, Boon, *d.* of late N. Panyasri of Chieng Rai, Siam; two *d.* *Educ.:* Dulwich College; abroad. Student Interpreter in Siam, 1896; Consul, Chiengmai, 1913-21; Consul-General, Chiengmai, Siam, 1921; retired 1930; has held several Consular and Judicial appointments, all in Siam; C.I.E. for services connected with the War. *Publications:* A History of Siam; Land of Smiles; Consul in Paradise, 1965. *Recreations:* reading, writing, teaching. *Address:* 68 Ban Nong Hoi, Chiengmai, Thailand.

[*Died* 22 *Jan.* 1970.

WOOD, Sir William (Wilkinson), Kt. 1959; *b.* 1879; *s.* of William Wilkinson Wood and Emily Bassett; unmarried. *Educ.:* Leys School, Cambridge. Master of the Company of Cutlers in Hallamshire, 1924 and 1940-44. Town Trustee, 1946-; Town Collector, 1955-59; J.P. City of Sheffield, 1937-; City Councillor, 1917-21. Chairman Hillsborough Conservative Association 35 years. *Recreations:* fishing, golf. *Address:* 67 Stumperlowe Crescent Road, Sheffield 10. *T.:* 31374. *Club:* Sheffield (Sheffield).

[*Died* 12 *Dec.* 1963.

WOODBURN, Lt.-Col. Thomas Stanley; C.B.E. 1918; Australian Imperial Forces; engaged in pastoral and agricultural industry; *b.* Dunkeld, Victoria, 24 June 1881; 3rd *s.* of John Woodburn of Stonehouse, Scotland, and Barbara Young of Motherwell, Scotland; *m.* 1920, Olive Bertha, 3rd *d.* of Henry and Katherine Trompf of Ballarat, Victoria; two *s.* *Educ.:* Hamilton and Western District College, Victoria. Rejected for active service in 1914-15; joined the Overseas Service of the Australian Comforts Fund, an honorary work with A.I.F. troops abroad; served with the 1st and 2nd Australian Divisions in all their front line fighting of 1916 in France; Chief Commissioner of the Fund's activities in the European area of war until end of 1919. *Publication:* European section of the History of the Australian Comforts Fund. *Recreations:* cricket, tennis, golf. *Address:* Wandobah, Dunkeld, Victoria, Australia. *T.:* Dunkeld 10. *Club:* Hamilton (Hamilton).

[*Died* 9 *Jan.* 1965.

WOODCOCK, T. A., M.A.; O.B.E. 1953; retired as Headmaster Ashby-de-la-Zouch Grammar School (1927-58); J.P. Leics.; Chairman Ashby-de-la-Zouch Bench; Commissioner of Income Tax; Chairman Leicestershire County Confirming and Compensation Committee; *b.* Bradford, 1897; *m.* 1922, Miss Steel; one *d.* *Educ.:* Bradford Grammar School. Lieut. Duke of Wellington's West Riding Regt., 1916-19; St. John's College, Oxford, 1919-22; 1st Class Honours Classical Moderations, 1920; 3rd Class Lit. Hum., 1922; Captain, College Rugby XV and Golf Team; Captain School XV and Cricket XI; Assistant Master, Manchester Grammar School, 1922-27. *Recreations:* golf and bowls. *Address:* Baildon, Willesley Close, Ashby-de-la-Zouch. *T.:* Ashby 2531.

[*Died* 16 *Aug.* 1965.

WOODFORD, Thomas Gordon Charles; Headmaster, Leeds Grammar School, since 1954; *b.* 15 Oct. 1911; *s.* of T. W. Woodford, Southampton; *m.* 1939, Joan Audrey Soutar; two *d.* *Educ.:* Regents Park School, Southampton; King Edward VI School, Southampton (Scholar); St. Edmund Hall, Oxford. M.A. (Modern History) and Diploma in Education (Oxon.); Hockey Blue. Asst. Master, Northampton Grammar School, 1934-38; Senior History Master, Trent Coll., Derbyshire, 1938-40. Served in War of 1939-46 (despatches, 1945): Trooper R.T.R., Sandhurst, 1st Derbyshire Yeomanry, Intelligence Staff 1 Corps, College of the Rhine Army (Head of Dept. of Modern Studies). Housemaster, School House, Durham, 1946-50; Headmaster, Richmond School, Yorks., 1950-53. *Publications:* contrib. to Universities Quarterly. *Recreations:* gardening, place-names, reading, motoring, watching school games. *Address:* 22 Weetwood Avenue, Leeds 16.

[*Died* 29 *Oct.* 1962.

WOODFORDE, Very Rev. Dr. Christopher; Dean of Wells since 1959; *b.* 29 Nov. 1907; *s.* of Robert Edmond Heighes Woodforde and Mary Thorne; *m.* 1935, Muriel Carol Isobel Forster (*d.* 1951); one *s.* *Educ.:* King's School, Bruton; Peterhouse, Cambridge. B.A. 1929, M.A. 1933, Litt.D. 1947 (Cantab.), D.Litt. (Oxon.) 1948. Wells Theological College, 1929. Deacon, 1930; Priest, 1932. Curate of: St. Margaret with St. Nicholas, King's Lynn, 1930-32; Louth with Welton-le-Wold, 1932-34; Drayton with Hellesdon, 1934-36; Rector of: Exford, 1936-39; Axbridge, 1939-45; Vicar of Steeple Morden, 1945-48; Fellow and Chaplain of New College, Oxford, 1948-59. Canon and Wiccamical Prebendary in Chichester Cathedral, 1950-53. *Publications:* Stained Glass in Somerset, 1250-1830, 1946; The Norwich School of Glass-Painting in the Fifteenth Century, 1950; The Stained Glass of New College, Oxford, 1951; A Pad in the Straw, 1952; English Stained and Painted Glass, 1954; Record of John: novel, 1962 (posthumous). Many articles on medieval stained glass and glass-painters. *Recreations:* walking, photography. *Address:* 4 Vicars Close, Wells, Somerset. *T.:* Wells 2224.

[*Died* 12 *Aug.* 1962.

WOODGATE, (Hubert) Leslie, O.B.E. 1959; Chorus Master, British Broadcasting Corporation; *b.* 15 April 1902; *s.* of Harry Woodgate, Maresfield, Sussex and Isabella Woodgate, Tarves, Aberdeenshire; *m.* 1926, Lena Mason; one *s.* *Educ.:* Westminster; Roy. Coll. of Music. Stage, with Where the Rainbow Ends and The Luck of the Navy; became B.B.C. official 1929. Hon. A.R.C.M., A.R.C.M. Freeman, City of London; Liveryman, Worshipful Co. of Musicians. *Publications:* Carnegie United Kingdom Award (1923) for A Hymn to the Virgin and The White Island; Several Songs for Solo Voice and Piano, Part Songs, Chamber Music, Orchestral Works, Organ pieces, Oratorio (Simon Peter), etc. *Address:* 6 Clarendon Mews, Hyde Park, W.2. *T.:* Ambassador 2213.

[*Died* 18 *May* 1961.

WOODHAMS, Herbert Martin, C.B.E. 1944; F.R.Ae.S.; M.I.P.E.; retired; Sir W. G. Armstrong Whitworth Aircraft Ltd. (Chairman and Managing Director, 1950-1961); *b.* 11 August 1890; *s.* of Ernest Woodhams; *m.* 1914, Jane Watts; two *s.* two *d.* *Educ.:* Tunbridge Wells. Peter Hooker (Gnôme-Rhône Engs.), 1915; Aircraft Manufacturing Co. Ltd. 1916-19; Chief

Engineer Aircraft Travel and Transport, 1920; Chief Engineer Air Post of Banks, 1921; Asst. Chief Insp. De Havilland Aircraft Ltd., 1922. Chief Insp. Armstrong Whitworth Aircraft Ltd., 1923-26, Asst. Works Manager, 1927-33, Works Manager, 1934-37, General Manager, 1938-41, Director and General Manager, 1942-50. *Address:* Casita, Windy Arbour, Kenilworth, Warwicks. *T.:* Kenilworth 52507. *Clubs:* Royal Automobile, Royal Aero.

[*Died* 12 *Jan.* 1965.

WOODHOUSE, Arthur William Webster, C.B.E. 1920; *b.* at sea, 31 May 1867; *e. s.* of late H.B.M. Consul Arthur Woodhouse and Mary Rachel, *d.* of Richard Webster, Jersey; *m.* 1st, 1892, Selina, *d.* of Henry Rogers, Odessa; 2nd, Marie, *widow* of Vladimir Voznesensky, St. Petersburg; one *d.*, one adopted *d.* (one *s.* decd.). *Educ.:* Oxenford House Academy, Jersey. Entered Consulate-General at Odessa as clerk, 1886; employed on the Afghan Boundary Commission, 1887-88; Vice-Consul, Batoum, 1891; Acting Consul-General at Odessa in each year, 1891-94, and in 1901 and 1903; Vice-Consul at Odessa, 1893; Acting Vice-Consul, Sevastopol, 1894; transferred to Nicolaiev, 1895; to Boston, 1905; Consul at St. Pierre-Miquelon, 1906; transferred to Thorshavn, 1907; to St. Petersburg, 1907; Coronation Medal, 1911; arrested by Bolshevik Forces, 30 Aug. 1918; imprisoned in Troubetskoi Bastion till 6 October, and left Petrograd, 10 Oct. 1918; Consul-General, New Orleans, 1919; Acting Consul-General at Genoa, 1920; H.B.M.'s Consul-General, Gothenburg, Sweden, 1921; retired, 1927. *Recreations:* yachting, reading. *Address:* 30 Cyprus Rd., N.3. *Club:* Royal Over-Seas League.

[*Died* 6 *Jan.* 1961.

WOODROFFE, Brig.-Gen. Charles Richard, C.M.G. 1917; C.V.O. 1922; C.B.E. 1919; late R.A.; *b.* 4 July 1878; *s.* of late G. W. P. Woodroffe, late Royal Horse Guards, nd Alice, *d.* of late Henry Townshend, Caldecote Hall, Nuneaton; *m.* 1st, 1909, Eleanor Mary (*d.* 1918), 2nd *d.* of late Henry Barlow Webb, Holmdale, Holmbury St. Mary; one *s.* two *d.*; 2nd, 1921, Islay, *y. d.* of late Col. A. H. Macdonald Moreton, Coldstream Guards, and Mrs. Macdonald Moreton, Bembridge, Isle of Wight; one *d.* *Educ.:* Radley. Joined R. Sussex Artillery Militia, 1896-98; Royal Artillery, 1898; Captain, 1906; Major, 1914; attached Japanese Army, 1907-8; Japanese Interpreter, 1908; Adjt. R.H.A., 1909-13; Staff Captain, 1913-14; D.A.Q.M.G. 1914-15; A.Q.M.G. 1915-16; D.A. and Q.M.G., 1917-18; retired pay, 1921; served S. Africa, 1899-1902 (despatches, 2 medals 5 clasps); European War, 1914-18 (C.M.G., C.B.E., Bt. Lt.-Col., despatches six times); Military Attaché, Tokio, 1919-21; Military Secretary to Prince of Wales in Japan, 1922; Officer Legion of Honour; Order of Crown of Belgium; Order of the Rising Sun, 2nd Class (Japanese); Order of the Sacred Treasure, 2nd Class (Japanese); Order of the Nile, 2nd Class (Egypt); Croix de Guerre (Belgian and French). *Recreations:* shooting, fishing, yachting. *Address:* North Wells Bungalow, Bembridge, I. of W. *Clubs:* Brooks's, Royal Automobile. [*Died* 18 *Nov.* 1965.

WOODRUFF, Harold Addison, lately Professor of Bacteriology and Director of Bacteriology Department, University of Melbourne; now Professor-Emeritus; *m.* (wife *d.* 1954), *d.* of late Prof. John Glaister; two *s.* *Educ.:* Wesley Coll., Sheffield; Royal Veterinary College, London. Qualified and became M.R.C.V.S. 1898; tutor in Surgery; Professor of Veterinary Science in the Royal Agricultural College, Cirencester, 1899; returned to Royal Veterinary College to occupy chair of Veterinary Hygiene and Materia Medica, 1900; Prof. of Veterinary Medicine, 1908; took up the study of human medicine at University College Hosp.; M.R.C.S., L.R.C.P., 1912; Prof. of Veterinary Pathology and Director of the Veterinary Institute, University of Melbourne, 1913-28; late Major, Australian Army Veterinary Corps, A.I.F.; B.Sc.Melb. 1933. Retired, 1945. *Publications:* The Economics of Feeding Horses. Collaborated in revising Finlay Dun's Veterinary Medicines. *Address:* 48 Fellows St., Kew, Victoria, Australia.

[*Died* 1 *May* 1966.

WOODS, Donald Devereux, F.R.S. 1952; Iveagh Professor of Chemical Microbiology, University of Oxford, since 1955; Fellow of Trinity Coll., Oxford, since 1951; *b.* 16 Feb. 1912; *s.* of Walter James and Violet Mabel Woods; *m.* 1939, Alison L. Woods (*née* Halls); one *d.* *Educ.:* Northgate School, Ipswich; Trinity Hall, Cambridge. M.A. (Cantab.) 1937; Ph.D. (Cantab.) 1937; M.A. (Oxon) 1945. Beit Memorial Research Fellow, 1936; Halley - Stewart Research Fellow, 1939; Member Scientific Staff, Medical Research Council, 1945; Reader in Microbiology, Univ. of Oxford, 1946-55. Member: Biochemical Soc., Soc. for General Microbiology, Soc. of Amer. Bacteriologists. Advisory Editor British Journal of Experimental Pathology; Associate Editor Journal of General Microbiology. *Publications:* contributions to scientific journals. *Address:* 12 St. Margarets Rd., Oxford; Trinity College, Oxford. *T.:* Oxford 55703. *Club:* Athenæum.

[*Died* 6 *Nov.* 1964.

WOODS, Rev. Prof. George Frederick; Professor of Divinity, King's College, University of London, since 1964; *b.* 25 June 1907; *s.* of Rev. Sandford and Mary Edith Woods; unmarried. *Educ.:* The King's School, Macclesfield; Jesus College, Cambridge. Deacon, 1932; Priest, 1933. Curate, Doncaster Parish Church, 1932; Tutor of Ripon Hall, Oxford, 1936; Director of Ordinands, Bristol, 1938; Chaplain of Downing College, Cambridge, 1945; Fellow of Downing College, 1947; Lectr. in Divinity, Univ. of Cambridge, 1947; Dean of Chapel, Downing College, 1959; Hon. Fellow of Downing College, 1964; Hon. Canon of Bristol Cathedral, 1961. Examining Chaplain to: Bishop of Bristol, 1939-; Bishop of Gloucester, 1946-; Bishop of Blackburn, 1960-; Bishop of Winchester, 1965-. Select Preacher: Univ. of Cambridge, 1947, 1949, 1963; Univ. of Oxford, 1965. *Publications:* Theological Explanation, 1958; contrib. to: Soundings, 1962; The Roads Converge, 1963. *Address:* King's College London, Strand, W.C.2. *Club:* National Liberal. [*Died* 31 *May* 1966.

WOODS, Brig.-Gen. Hugh Kennedy, D.S.O. 1919; late Royal Tank Corps; *b.* 1877; *s.* of late Insp.-Gen. Henry Charles Woods, C.B., C.V.O., K.H.P.; *m.* 1914, Therese Elizabeth Eucharis, *d.* of late Rev. F. A. Gace; one *s.* one *d.* (and one *s.* killed in action). Served S. Africa, 1899-1902 (despatches, Queen's medal with five clasps, King's medal with two clasps); European War, 1914-19 (despatches, D.S.O.); retired pay, 1925; Officier Légion d'Honneur; Croix de Guerre. *Address:* Sheko, Palmerston Way, Alverstoke, Hants. *T.:* Gosport 82965.

[*Died* 8 *Dec.* 1964.

WOODS, Sir John (Harold Edmund), G.C.B., *cr.* 1949 (K.C.B., *cr.* 1945; C.B. 1943); M.V.O. 1930; retd. Civil Service; *b.* 20 April 1895; *e. s.* of late Rev. J. H. Woods; *m.* 1930, K. M. Baker; one *s.* one *d.* *Educ.:* Christ's Hosp.; Balliol Coll., Oxford. Served in France during European War as Lieut. in 22nd Bn. R. Fusiliers; invalided as result of wounds. Entered Treasury as Assistant Principal in 1920; Principal Assistant Secretary, 1940-43; Permanent Secretary of Ministry of Production, 1943-1945; Permanent Secretary, Board of Trade, 1945-51; Member of Economic Planning Board, 1947-51; retired, 1951. Director

(1952): The English Electric Co. Ltd.; Marconi's Wireless Telegraph Co. Ltd.; Director: Marconi Internat. Marine Communication Co. Ltd.; Marconi Instruments Ltd.; Indian Steel Works Construction Co. Ltd.; Power and Traction Finance Co. Ltd.; British Newfoundland Corp. etc.; Member, Dollar Exports Council, 1951; Radcliffe Cttee. on the Working of the Monetary System, 1957-59; Mem. Nat. Inst. Econ. and Social Research (Pres. 1952-55); Chm., Advisory Cttee. on Revolving Fund for Industry (Conditional Aid), 1955-58; Chm. of Bd. of Govs., National Hospital for Nervous Diseases, Queen Square; Governor, Administrative Staff College; Member of Waverley Committee on Atomic Energy, 1953. Governor, Christ's Hospital, 1955-; Church Assembly: Mem. Central Bd. of Finance of C. of E.; Mem. Social and Industrial Council. Church Commissioners: Mem. Advisory Panel on Investments, 1959. *Recreation:* golf. *Address:* Burchetts, Haywards Heath, Sussex. *T.:* 230. *Clubs:* Beefsteak, United University. [*Died* 2 *Dec.* 1962.

WOODS, Colonel Philip James, C.M.G. 1919; D.S.O. 1917; *b.* 23 September 1880; *s.* of late Hugh Woods, of St. John's, Hillsborough, Co. Down, and Emily Catherine, *g.d.* of Sir John Puleston, Flintshire; *m.* 1st, 1907, Florence Edith (marriage dissolved 1934), *e. d.* of Stewart Blacker-Quin, Belfast; one *d.*; 2nd, 1934, Veronica, *d.* of George Richard Quested, Kent. *Educ.:* Royal Academical Institution, Belfast; Belfast School of Art. Adopted the profession of Art; served in South Africa in Constabulary eleven months of war and twelve months after peace declared; became interested in the Ulster Volunteer Force, and took a prominent part in the ensuing gun-running, etc.; 1914, Lieutenant in 9th (West Belfast) Royal Irish Rifles; Captain, Nov. 1914; Major, Sept. 1915; second in command, Dec. 1915; Lieut.-Col., Jan. 1917; (D.S.O., Battle of Somme, July 1916); Col. May 1919; commanded 19th Res. Batt. Royal Irish Rifles, Jan. to June, 1918; volunteered for North Russia; landed there, June 1918; transferred to General List; formed, organised and led the Koralian Regt. against Germans and White Finns in Koralia, Aug. 1918 (C.M.G.); promoted Colonel (local), Oct. 1918; Colonel gazetted, 1919; commanding The Koralian Regt. and Allied Forces, Kem and Koralia, North Russia, till evacuated 3 Oct. 1919; appointed to General Staff, Lithuanian Army, as Inspector of Forces, Kovno District, Nov. 1919; posted to Reserve, Royal Ulster Rifles, 1922; M.P. (Northern Ireland) West Belfast, n Ex-Service Interests, May 1923-29. *Recreation:* designing tapestries. *Address:* Long Crendon, Bucks. [*Died* 12 *Sept.* 1961.

WOODTHORPE, John Frederick; Master of Supreme Court, Chancery Division, 1943, retired, 1958; *b.* 9 Jan. 1897; *s.* of late Edmund Woodthorpe, M.A., F.R.I.B.A., formerly of Grayshott House, Grayshott, Hants; *m.*; one *d.* *Educ.:* St. Bees School. Served Royal Norfolk Regiment, European War, 1914-18; Assist. Adjutant 1st Bn. Norfolk Regiment, 1919-22; Staff Officer to O.C. Troops, Belfast, 1921-22; retired owing to ill health caused by wounds, 1922; admitted a solicitor, 1925; partner of Gregory Rowcliffe & Co., 1928-43; formerly a Director of B.A. Collieries Ltd. and Bestwood Coal & Iron Co. Ltd., etc.; Mem. Royal Musical Association, Hellenic Society and Oriental Ceramic Society; Reserve Chm. Nat. Assistance Appeal Tribunal, Bournemouth and Poole. He has written many songs and other music, and contributes articles to art journals on Art and Chinese Pottery and Porcelain. *Recreations:* music, literature, poetry, ceramics. *Address:* c/o Glyn, Mills & Co., Kirkland House, Whitehall, S.W.1. *Club:* Army and Navy. [*Died* 7 *April* 1966.

WOODWARD, Lt.-Gen. Sir Eric (Winslow), K.C.M.G. 1958; K.C.V.O. 1963; C.B. 1956; C.B.E. 1952; D.S.O. 1943; i.d.c. 1948; p.s.c. 1938; *b.* 21 July 1899; *s.* of late Albert William Woodward, Ellangowan, Queensland; *m.* 1927, Amy Freame Weller; one *s.* one *d.* *Educ.:* Toowoomba Grammar School; Royal Mil. College of Australia. Attached 7th (Queen's Own) Hussars, India, 1921; seconded to R.A.A.F., 1925-27; Staff College, Camberley, 1937-38; served War, 1940-45: Libya 1940-41, Greece 1941, Syria 1941, Alamein 1942, Netherlands East Indies 1945; i.d.c. 1948; Aust. Army Rep., U.K., 1949; Adjutant-General, Aust. Mil. Forces, 1951-53; G.O.C. Eastern Command, Australia, 1953-57; Administrator, Commonwealth of Australia, June-August, 1964; Governor of New South Wales, 1957-65. Hon. D.Sc. (N.S.W.); Hon. D.Litt. (Sydney and New England). K.St.J. 1957. Pres. R. Humane Soc. of Aust. (N.S.W.). *Address:* 4 Wongalee Ave., Wahroonga, New South Wales, Australia. [*Died* 29 *Dec.* 1967.

WOODWARD, Oliver Holmes, C.M.G. 1956; M.C., two Bars; *b.* 8 October 1885; *s.* of Sydney Arthur Woodward and Jemima Johnstone Reid; *m.* 1920, Marjorie Moffat Waddell; two *s.* one *d.* *Educ.:* New South Wales State School Primary; Newington College Secondary; Technical Queensland School of Mines. 2nd Lt. 1st Australian Tunnelling Co., Australia Imperial Force, 1915; Captain, 1916 (despatches, M.C. and two bars). Plant Superintendent, Broken Hill Associated Smelters Pty. Ltd., 1920, General Supt. 1934; General Manager, North Broken Hill Ltd., 1935, superannuated 1947. Pres.: Australasian Inst. of Mining and Metallurgy, 1940; Australian Mines and Metals Assoc., 1953 and 1954, Director, 1952-; Director of companies until Dec. 1961. M.I.M.M. *Publications:* contrib. to journals. *Recreation:* gardening. *Address:* No. 6 Senator Street, New Town, Hobart, Tasmania. *T.:* W 2501. *Club:* Athenaeum (Melbourne). [*Died* 24 *Aug.* 1966.

WOOLDRIDGE, Sidney William, C.B.E. 1954; F.R.S. 1959; D.Sc.; F.K.C. 1956; Professor of Geography in University of London, King's College; *b.* 16 November 1900; *s.* of Lewis William Wooldridge and Helen Chadwick; *m.* 1934, Edith Mary Stephens; no *c.* *Educ.:* Glendale County School; King's Coll., London. B.Sc. (Lond.) 1st Class Hons. in Geology, 1921; M.Sc. 1923; D.Sc. 1927; Assistant in Dept. of Geology and Geography, King's College, London, 1922; Lecturer in Geography, 1927; Reader in Geography, 1942; Professor of Geography, Birkbeck College, 1944. Received Daniell-Pidgeon Award and Lyell Fund (Geological Society of London, and Murchison Fund and Victoria Medal of the R.G.S. President, Section E, British Association, 1950. and Institute of British Geographers, 1949-50. Elected New York Acad. of Sciences, 1960. *Publications:* The Physical Basis of Geography (with R. S. Morgan), 1937; Structure, Surface and Drainage of South-East England (with D. L. Linton), 1939; The Spirit and Purpose of Geography (with W. G. East), 1951; The Weald (with F. Goldring), 1953; The Geographer as Scientist, 1956; London's Countryside (with G. E. Hutchings), 1956; papers on the geology, geomorphology, and historical geography of South-East England. *Address:* Dept. of Geography, King's Coll., Strand, W.C.2. [*Died* 25 *April* 1963.

WOOLDRIDGE, Walter Reginald, C.B.E. 1964; Ph.D. (Cantab.), M.Sc. (London), F.R.C.V.S.; F.R.I.C.: scientific director for the Animal Health Trust since 1946; *b.* 11 July 1900; *s.* of Edward and Florence Wooldridge; *m.* 1929, Evelyn, *d.* of late S. S. Champion, Dursley, Glos.; one *s.* one *d.* *Educ.:* Sir Walter St.

John's School, London; Royal Veterinary College (M.R.C.V.S.); Birkbeck Coll. (B.Sc. Hons.); Gonville and Caius College, Cambridge (Ph.D.). Research Institute of Animal Pathology, Cambridge, 1924; Sir William Dunn Institute of Biochemistry, 1925-29; Staff, Food Investigation Board, 1925-26; Frank Smart Research Student, Gonville and Caius College, Cambridge, 1926; Beit Memorial Fellowship for Medical Research, 1927; Lecturer in Biochemistry, 1929-47, London School of Hygiene and Tropical Medicine, University of London; President, 1930, Hon. Sec. 1931-42, Veterinary Research Club; Hon. Secretary, 1938-41, President, 1941-43, British Veterinary Assoc.; Member of Council, R.C.V.S., 1939- (Pres. 1954); Hon. Secretary 1941-43 and 1950-53, Vice-Pres. 1945-50, 1953-56, 1962-64, Vice-Chm., 1958-61, Parliamentary and Scientific Cttee.; Dir. of Veterinary Services, National A.R.P. for Animals, 1941; Executive Officer, England and Wales, Farm Livestock Emergency Service, 1942; Trustee and Chairman of Council, Animal Health Trust, 1942; Member Inter-Departmental Committee on Veterinary Education in Great Britain, 1936-38, recalled 1942-43; Gov., Birkbeck College (Vice-chm. and chm., Finance Cttee., 1946-55, Chm. 1955-), Royal Veterinary Coll., South Eastern Agricultural Coll., Wye, and National College of Food Technology; Gen. Sec. 14th International Veterinary Congress, London, 1949. Member of Senate, University of London, 1952. Fellow, Birkbeck College, London. Hon. Dr. Vet. Sci. (Liverpool), 1961. Master, Worshipful Co. of Farriers, 1964-65; Mem. Court, Worshipful Co. of Farmers; Chm., British Epicure Soc. *Publications:* War Gases and Foodstuffs, 1942; Farm Animals in Health and Disease, 1954; papers on biochemistry, animal health, foodstuffs of animal origin, etc. in Biochemical Journal, Nature, etc. *Recreation:* gardening. *Address:* Bentley Hyde, Priory Drive, Stanmore, Middlesex. *T.:* Grimsdyke 1229. *Clubs:* Athenæum, Farmers', Kennel. [*Died* 31 *Aug.* 1966.

WOOLF, Leonard Sidney; *b.* 25 Nov. 1880; *s.* of Sidney Woolf, Q.C.; *m.* Virginia (*d.* 1941), *y. d.* of late Sir Leslie Stephen, K.C.B. *Educ.:* St. Paul's School; Trinity College, Cambridge. In the Ceylon Civil Service, 1904-11; Editor of The International Review, 1919; Editor of Internat. Section Contemporary Review, 1920 and 1921; Lit. Editor, The Nation, 1923-30; Jt. Editor, Political Quarterly, 1931-59 (Lit. Editor, 1959); founded Hogarth Press, 1917; Member of National Whitley Council for Administrative and Legal Departments of Civil Service, 1938-55. Hon. Litt.D. Sussex. *Publications:* The Village in the Jungle, 1913; The Wise Virgins, 1914; International Government, 1916; Co-operation and the Future of Industry, 1918; The Future of Constantinople, 1917; Empire and Commerce in Africa, 1920; Socialism and Co-operation, 1921; Hunting the Highbrow: Essays, 1927; Imperialism and Civilization, 1928; After the Deluge, Vol. 1. 1931, Vol. 2. 1939; (Editor) The Intelligent Man's Way to Prevent War, 1933; Quack, Quack, 1935; The Hotel, 1939; Barbarians at the Gate, 1939; The War for Peace, 1940; Principia Politica, 1953; (with James Strachey) Letters of Virginia Woolf and Lytton Strachey, 1956; Sowing, 1960; Growing, 1961; Beginning Again, 1964 (W. H. Smith Literary Award, 1965); Downhill all the Way, 1967; A Calendar of Consolation, 1967; The Journey not the Arrival Matters: Autobiography of the years 1939-69, 1969. *Recreation:* gardening. *Address:* 24 Victoria Square, S.W.1. *Club:* Athenæum. [*Died* 14 *Aug.* 1969.

WOOLFE, Brig. Richard Dean Townsend, C.I.E. 1941; M.C.; formerly Controller-General of Inspection, Army Headquarters, India; *b.* 7 Dec. 1888; *m.* 1914, Norah Emily Oldfield; one *s.* one *d.* Served European War, 1914-18 (wounded, despatches, M.C.); Waziristan, 1921-24; retired 1947. *Address:* 36 Pine Walk, Sarisbury, Southampton. *T.:* Locksheath 3713. [*Died* 17 *Jan.* 1966.

WOOLFORD, Sir Eustace Gordon, Kt., *cr.* 1947; O.B.E. 1943; Q.C. 1920; Speaker in the House of Assembly, British Guiana, since 1953; *b.* 15 Dec. 1876; *s.* of J. Barrington Woolford, Solicitor; *m.* 1915; one *s.* three *d.* *Educ.:* Dulwich College, London; Queen's College, British Guiana. Called to Bar, Middle Temple, 1898; Financial Representative for Georgetown, 1910, for New Amsterdam, 1914; Member of Court of Policy for New Amsterdam, 1916; British Guiana Colonisation Delegation to England, 1919; Mayor of Georgetown, 1919-20; British Guiana Constitution Commission, 1927; M.L.C. for New Amsterdam, 1930; Chairman British Guiana Franchise Commission, 1941. Delegate West Indian Conferences Caribbean Commission, 1944, 1946. Speaker, Legislative Council, British Guiana, 1953. *Recreation* reading. *Address:* Demerara Life Buildings, Georgetown, British Guiana. *T.A.:* Woolford, British Guiana. *Club:* West India. [*Died* 20 *May* 1966.

WOOLGAR, Alfred John, B.A. (Lond.), M.A. (Oxon.); *b.* 15 Oct. 1879; *s.* of John Martin Woolgar, Horsham, and Sarah Emma Moxham, High Wycombe; *m.* 1910, Frances Charlotte, *d.* of Henry and Frances Elizabeth Woodall; one *s.* one *d.* *Educ.:* Collyer's School, Horsham; London University; St. John's College, Oxford (Casberd Scholar); First Class Honours in Final School of Modern Languages. Assistant Master: Collyer's School, Oxford High School, Christ's Hospital, St. Olave's School; Principal of George Green's School (co-educational), 1920-1924; Headmaster of Maidstone Grammar School, 1925-41; Assistant Master and Careers Master, St. Paul's School, 1941-45; Member of Headmasters' Conference, 1936-41; Oxford Society, Maidstone and Medway Branch (Chairman, 1938). *Address:* 512 Banbury Road, Oxford. *T:* Oxford 5158. [*Died* 21 *July* 1968.

WOOLL, Edward, O.B.E.; Q.C. 1943; Barrister-at-Law, Leader of Northern Circuit; Recorder of Carlisle, 1929-63; *b.* 31 March 1878; *e. s.* of late Rev. C. W. Wooll, Vicar of Ditton, Lancs; *m.* 1st, 1913, Nora (*d.* 1922), *d.* of late Hugh Goold; two *s.*; 2nd, 1940, Vera, *d.* of late John Moore; one *s.* two *d.* *Educ.:* Liverpool College; New College, Oxford. 1st Class Classical Mods.; called to Bar, Inner Temple, 1903; retired October 1965. Cheshire Yeomanry, 1914-27 (retired Captain); Cavalry Corps H.Q. B.E.F., 1916-19 (despatches twice, O.B.E.); Conservative Candidate St. Helens (Lancs), 1922, and Hull (Central), 1923. *Publications:* Libel (play), 1934; Moral Gestures (play), 1937; The Last Will (play), 1964; There is a Tide, The Lodestar, Libel, The Nettle (novels); Layman's Guide to Libel. *Address:* 2 Pump Court, Temple, E.C.4. *T.:* 01-353 2925; Brunswick House, North Walsham, Norfolk. *T.:* N. Walsham 3270. [*Died* 20 *May* 1970.

WOOLLCOMBE, Captain Charles George Ley, C.B.E. 1943; R.N. (retd.); *b.* 28 April 1884; *s.* of Richard Woollcombe and Caroline Elizabeth Stooks; *m.* 1916, Gladys Mary, M.B.E. 1944, *d.* of Rt. Rev. Frank Gurdon, late Bishop of Hull. *Educ.:* H.M.S. Britannia. China Medal, 1900; qualified in gunnery, 1907; Acting Flag Commander Admiral Sir Berkeley Milne, 1914; 1st Lieut. Whale Island, 1914; served as Gunnery Officer H.M.S. Glorious, 1916-19; Naval Secretary to Ordnance Committee on two occasions; retired, 1929; Captain Supt. National Nautical School, Portishead, 1929-1935; called back, 1940; demobilized Oct. 1945. *Address:* Hackthorn, Beaminster, Dorset. *T.:* Beaminster 231.

[*Died* 18 *Jan.* 1962.

WOOLLCOMBE, Major Malcolm Louis, C.M.G. 1939; O.B.E. 1919; *b.* 8 May 1891; *e. s.* of late Lt.-Gen. Sir Charles Louis Woollcombe, K.C.B., K.C.M.G., and Lady Agnes Meade Woollcombe; *m.* 1919, Eileen Marguerite Conway-Bishop; two *s.* one *d.* *Educ.:* Marlborough College; R.M.A., Woolwich (Infantry Company). Entered Army, 1910; Indian Army, 1911, 28th Light Cavalry; European War, transferred to Lincolnshire Regiment and promoted Captain, 1916; G.S.O.3, France, 1916 (despatches); Brigade Major 35th Infantry Brigade, and served as such in the battle of Arras, 1917; Intelligence, War Office, 1918; Member of Military Section, British Delegation at Peace Conference, 1919; Temp. Major and G.S.O. 2, War Office, 1919-21; retired from Army, 1921; Employed under Foreign Office, 1921-1944. *Address:* 52 Palmeira Avenue, Hove, Sussex. *Club:* Naval and Military.

[*Died* 15 *Feb.* 1968.

WOOLLEY, Rev. Geoffrey Harold, V.C. 1915; O.B.E. 1943; M.C. 1919; M.A.; *b.* 14 May 1892; *s.* of Rev. George H. Woolley; *m.* 1st, 1918, Janet Beatrix (*d.* 1943), *d.* of late Charles Lindsay Orr Ewing, M.P., and *widow* of Captain George Culme-Seymour; (one *s.* killed in Tunisia, 1942) one *d.*; 2nd, 1945, Elcie Elisabeth, *y. d.* of late Alfred Nichols, Worthing; one *s.* *Educ.:* Queen's College, Oxford, M.A. Served European War, 1914-19 (V.C. for conspicuous bravery at Hill 60 on night of 20-21 April 1915; he was the only officer on the hill, but held it under heavy fire until relieved); 9th (County of London) Batt. London Regt. T.F.; General Staff Officer, 3rd grade; Assistant Master of Rugby School; Vicar of Monk Sherborne, near Basingstoke, 1923-27; Asst. Master and Chaplain, Harrow School, 1927-39; C.F., 1940-44; Vicar of Harrow, 1944-52; Rector of West Grinstead, Sussex, 1952-Oct. 1958. *Publications:* The Epic of the Mountain, 1929; Fear and Religion, 1930; A Journey to Palestine, 1935; A Pocket-book of Prayers, 1940; Sometimes a Soldier, 1963. *Address:* Hunters Barn, West Chiltington, Pulborough, Sussex. *Club:* Royal Commonwealth Society.

[*Died* 10 *Dec.* 1968.

WOOLMER, Professor Ronald Francis, V.R.D., B.M., F.F.A.R.C.S.; Professor of Anaesthesia, Royal College of Surgeons of England; Director, Research Dept. of Anaesthetics, since 1957; Surg. Cdr. R.N.V.R.; Consultant in Anaesthetics to Royal Navy; Consultant Anaesthetist, Whittington Hospital; *b.* 17 Feb. 1908; *s* of late H. C. Woolmer; *m.* 1937, Marjorie, *d.* of H. S. Grant; two *d.* *Educ.:* Rugby School; University College, Oxford; St. Thomas's Hospital. B.A. (Hons.) Oxon, 1930; B.M., B.Ch. 1932; F.F.A.R.C.S. 1948. Sen. Res. Anaesthetist, St. Thomas's Hosp., 1934-36; R.M.O. St. Thomas's Home, 1936-38; Anaesthetist Registrar, Westminster Hosp., 1939. Anaesthetist, R.N. Medical Service, 1939-45. Lecturer, Sen. Lecturer and Reader in Anaesth., Univ. of Bristol and Hon. Consultant Anaesthetist, United Bristol Hosp., 1946-56; Mem. Board Faculty of Anaesth., 1948-58. President, Biological Engineering Society; Vice-Pres. International Federation for Medical Electronics. Fellow and Mem. Council, Royal Society Medicine. *Publications:* Conquest of Pain, 1961; various contributions in medical press. *Address:* Royal College of Surgeons of England, Lincoln's Inn Fields, W.C.2. *T.:* Holborn 3474. *Club:* Oriental.

[*Died* 8 *Dec.* 1962.

WOOLTON, 1st Earl of, *cr.* 1956; **Frederick James Marquis,** P.C. 1940; C.H. 1942; Viscount, cr. 1953, Baron, *cr.* 1939, of Liverpool; Kt. 1935; D.L.; J.P.; LL.D. (Hon.), Cambridge, Liverpool, Manchester, McGill (Can.), Hamilton (U.S.A.); Hon. A.R.C.A.; late Chm. and Senr. Managing Dir. Lewis's Investment Trust, Ltd. and its subsidiary companies and other companies; *b.* 24 Aug. 1883; *o. c.* of late Thomas Robert Marquis and Margaret Ormerod, Manchester; *m.* 1st, 1912, Maud (*d.* 1961), *y. d.* of Thomas Smith and Augusta Mathews, Manchester; one *s.* one *d.*; 2nd, 1962, Dr. Margaret Eluned Thomas. *Educ.:* Manchester Grammar School; Manchester Univ. (M.A., B.Sc.). Past Pres. Roy. Statistical Soc.; late Res. Fellow on Economics, Manchester Univ.; Chancellor of Manch. Univ., 1944-; Visitor of Manchester Gram. Sch.; Trustee National Central Library; Chm. of Conservative and Unionist Central Office, 1946-55; lately Hon. Col. 113 Assault Engineer Regt. R.E. (T.A.); sometime Warden Univ. Settlement, Liverpool; Chm. of Exec. Cttee. Brit. Red Cross Society; Director-General of Equipment and Stores in Ministry of Supply, 1939-40; Minister of Food, 1940-43; Member of War Cabinet, 1943-45; Minister of Reconstruction, 1943-1945; Lord President of the Council, 1945 and 1951-52; Chancellor of the Duchy of Lancaster (with a seat in the Cabinet), Dec. 1952-Dec. 1955; President, British Travel and Holidays Association, 1961-63. Hon. Fellow, Downing College, Cambridge, 1963. J.P. Liverpool, 1929; D.L. Lancs, 1941. Hon. Freeman Salters' Company, Master 1951. K.St.J. Chevalier of Legion of Honour; Hon. Freeman, City of Liverpool. *Publication:* Memoirs, 1959. *Heir:* *s.* Viscount Walberton. *Address:* Walberton House, nr. Arundel, Sussex. *Clubs:* Athenæum, Carlton, Brooks's; University (Liverpool).

[*Died* 14 *Dec.* 1964.

WOOLTON, 2nd Earl of, *cr.* 1956; **Roger David Marquis;** Baron Woolton, 1939; Viscount Woolton, 1953; Viscount Walberton, 1956; *b.* 16 July 1922; *o. s.* of 1st Earl of Woolton, P.C., C.H.; *S.* father, 1964; *m.* 1st, 1946, Hon. Lucia Lawson (whom he div., 1953), *d.* of 4th Baron Burnham; 2nd, 1957, Cecily Josephine, *e. d.* of Sir Alexander Gordon Cumming, 5th Bt., and of Countess Cawdor; one *s.* one *d.* *Educ.:* Rugby; Trinity College, Camb. Served War of 1939-45 as Flight-Lt. R.A.F.V.R. Trustee, Chantrey Bequest. *Heir:* *s.* Viscount Walberton. *Address:* 31 Tite St., S.W.3. *T.:* Flaxman 1333. *Clubs:* White's, Pratt's, Brook's.

[*Died* 7 *Jan.* 1969.

WOOTTEN, Major-Gen. Sir George (Frederick), K.B.E. 1958 (C.B.E. 1943); C.B. 1945; D.S.O. 1917; E.D. 1946; Solicitor of the Supreme Court of New South Wales; *b.* 1 May 1893; *s.* of W. F. Wootten; *m.* 1920, Muriel, *e. d.* of J. Kirwan Bisgood, Roehampton; one *s.* (*er. s.* killed on active service in Middle East, 10 May 1943) two *d.* *Educ.:* Royal Military College of Australia, Duntroon. Served European War, 1914-18 (despatches, D.S.O.); p.s.c. (Camberley); served Middle East, 1940-41 (Bar to D.S.O.); Papua, 1942-43 (C.B.E., D.S.C. of U.S.A.); New Guinea, 1943-44 (C.B.); Tarakan, Labuan, Sarawak, Brunei, and Brit. Borneo, 1945. Chm. Repatriation Commn., Commonwealth of Australia, 1945-1958; Chm. A.H.Q. Battle Hons. Cttee. *Address:* 305 Park Regis, Park Street, Sydney, N.S.W. 2000, Australia. *Club:* Imperial Service (Sydney).

[*Died* 30 *March* 1970.

WOOTTON-DAVIES, James Henry, F.R.I.C.; J.P. County Lancaster; Lloyd's Underwriter; *b.* 1884; *m.* 1937, Shirley G. M., 2nd *d.* of late Prof. Charles Bale Wootton; one *s.* *Educ.:* Technical School, Chester.

Chemist; has travelled extensively; M.P. (U.) Heywood and Radcliffe Division of Lancaster, 1940-45. *Recreation:* interested in land reclamation. *Address:* Bronwylfa Hall, near Wrexham. *T.:* Rhos (Wrexham) 321. *Clubs:* Carlton, Constitutional. [*Died* 21 *Dec.* 1964.

WORBOYS, Sir Arthur (Thomas), Kt. 1966; C.B.E. 1953; J.P.; Chairman and a Managing Director of the London Brick Co. Ltd.; Chairman of Transformers (Watford) Ltd. J.P. Bedfordshire 1941; High Sheriff of Bedfordshire, 1952-53. *Address:* Westray, 230 Old Bedford Road, Luton, Bedfordshire. [*Died* 7 *Nov.* 1966.

WORBOYS, Sir Walter (John), Kt. 1958; Chairman since 1960, Managing Director 1963-67, BTR Industries Ltd.; Chairman: British Printing Corporation since 1965; Bristol-BTR (G.R.P.) Ltd.; Director: Imperial Chemical Industries Ltd., 1948-59; Westminster Bank Ltd., since 1956; Westminster Foreign Bank Ltd., 1956-65; Associated Portland Cement Manufrs. Ltd., and British Portland Cement Manufrs. Ltd.; Forestal Land, Timber and Railways Co., Ltd.; *b.* Cottesloe, Western Australia, 22 Feb. 1900; *s.* of late Walter and Amanda Worboys; *m.* 1927, Ethelwynne Bessie Lavers; one *s.* one *d.* *Educ.:* Scotch Coll., W.A.; Univ. of W. Australia (B.Sc. Hons. Chem. and Geol.); Lincoln Coll., Oxford Univ. (Rhodes Schol., D.Phil. Chem). Mem. of the Council of Indust. Design, 1947, Chm., 1953-60; Chm., Assoc. of British Chem. Manufacturers, 1953-56, Pres., 1957-59; F.R.S.A. 1949; Bicentenary Medal, R.S.A., 1956; Mem. of Coun., 1961 (Chm. 1967-); Mem. Coun. of Soc. of Chem. Industry, 1955-58, Gold Medallist 1957; Hon. A.R.I.B.A., 1957; Fell. of Royal Inst. of Chemistry, 1957; Hon. Fell. Soc., Industrial Artists, 1961. Hon. Fell. of Lincoln Coll., Oxford, 1957. F.B.I.M. 1964. Governor, Radley Coll., 1952-62; Chm. Governing Council Roedean School, 1962. Member, Council and Acad. Adv. Cttee., of University of East Anglia, 1964; Chairman Academic Advisory Cttee. for Brunel University, 1964-67; Hon. D.Tech. Brunel University, 1967. Member, Commonwealth Scholarship Commn., 1966-68. *Recreations:* country pursuits, travel. *Address:* Flat 8, 69 Onslow Square, S.W.7. *T.:* 01-589 0941. *Club:* United University. [*Died* 17 *March* 1969.

WORDIE, Sir James Mann, Kt. 1957; C.B.E. 1947; Hon. LL.D. (Glasgow, Hull); Master of St. John's College, Cambridge, 1952-1959 (Fellow 1921. Tutor 1923. Senior Tutor 1933, Pres., 1950); Hon. Fellow, Trinity College, Dublin; *b.* 1889; *y. s.* of late John Wordie, Glasgow; *m.* 1923, Gertrude, 2nd *d.* of late G. T. Henderson; three *s.* two *d.* *Educ.:* Glasgow Academy; Glasgow and Cambridge Universities. Geologist, Chief of Scientific Staff, Shackleton Antarctic Expedition, 1914-17; Lt., R.F.A., served in France; Geologist, Second in Command, Scottish Spitsbergen Expeditions, 1919, 1920; Expeditions to Jan Mayen and East Greenland, 1921, 1923, 1926, 1929; to North West Greenland, Ellesmere Island and Baffin Island, 1934, 1937; S. Orkneys, S. Shetlands, and Graham Land, Antarctica, 1947; President Royal Geographical Society, 1951-54; Chairman Scott Polar Research Institute, 1937-55; Member Discovery Committee, Colonial Office, 1923-49; Chairman, British Mountaineering Council, 1953-1956; Chairman British National Committee for International Geophysical Year, 1954-1958; Back Award, 1920; Founder's Gold Medal, 1933, R.G.S.; Bruce Medallist Roy. Soc. of Edinburgh, 1926; Roy. Scottish Geog. Society's Gold Medal, 1944; Daly Gold Medal, Amer. Geog. Soc., 1952. Commander of Order of St. Olav of Norway. *Recreations:* mountaineering, shooting. *Address:* St. John's College, Cambridge. *T.:* Cambridge 50151. *Clubs:* Athenæum, Travellers', Alpine. [*Died* 16 *Jan.* 1962.

WORLLEDGE, Sir John Leonard, K.B.E., *cr.* 1951; C.M.G. 1945; retired as Director-General of the Overseas Audit Service (1943-1959); *b.* 24 Sept. 1895; 2nd *s.* of late E. C. Worlledge; *m.* 1922, Annie Margaret Glencairn, *o. d.* of late James Paterson, R.S.A.; one *s.* one *d.* Active service in Armed Forces in France and Belgium, 1914-19; Assistant Auditor, Colonial Audit Dept., Kenya, 1920; Senior Asst. Auditor, Kenya, 1925; Auditor British Guiana, 1932-36; Auditor-General, Jamaica, 1936-41; Dep. Dir. of Colonial Audit, 1941-43. *Address:* Field Cottage, Liss, Hants. *T.:* 2212. *Club:* E. India and Sports. [*Died* 19 *April* 1968.

WORMALL, Prof. Arthur, F.R.S. 1956; D.Sc., F.R.I.C.; Hon. Dr. Univ. (São Paulo); Emeritus Professor of Biochemistry and Chemistry, St. Bartholomew's Hospital Medical College, London, since 1963 (Professor, 1936-63); *b.* 17 January 1900; *s.* of James William and Ann Wormall; *m.* 1925, Eva Jackson; two *d.* *Educ.:* The Boys' Modern School, Leeds; University of Leeds. Demonstrator in Biochemistry, University of Leeds, 1922-26; Lecturer in Biochemistry, University of Leeds, 1926-36; Rockefeller Medical Fellow (U.S.A.) 1928-29; research work on sleeping sickness in Uganda, 1930-1931. Director of 1st Latin-American course on radioisotope methodology (São Paulo, Brazil), Jan.-Feb. 1953. *Publications:* scientific papers in the Biochemical Journal, etc. *Recreations:* golf, cricket. *Address:* The Medical College of St. Bartholomew's Hospital, Charterhouse Square. E.C.1. [*Died* 9 *May* 1964.

WORRELL, Sir Frank (Mortimer Maglinne), Kt. 1964; Dean of the Students, University of the West Indies in Trinidad (formerly Warden in Jamaica); *b.* 1924; *s.* of late Athelston Theophilus Worrell; *m.* 1962, Velda Elaine, *d.* of Mervyn Gittens Brewster. *Educ.:* Combermere School, Barbados; Manchester University (B.A. Admin.). Captain of West Indian cricket team for Test Matches against Australia, 1960-61, and Great Britain, 1963. Senator, Jamaica, 1962-64. Consultant on Community Develt., Trinidad Govt., 1964. *Address:* The Univ. of the West Indies, St. Augustine, Trinidad. [*Died* 13 *March* 1967.

WORSLEY, Alexandra Lady, (Alexandra Mary Freesia), C.B.E. 1954 (O.B.E. 1945); Extra Lady in Waiting to Queen Elizabeth the Queen Mother since 1947; 3rd *d.* of 3rd Baron Vivian, P.C., G.C.M.G., C.B.; *m.* 1911, Charles Sackville, Lord Worsley, Lieutenant Royal Horse Guards (killed in action, 1914). Regional Administrator, Women's Voluntary Services, Region 12, 1938-46; Chairman Victoria League, 1948-53. *Address:* 3 Belgrave Place, S.W.1. *T.:* Belgravia 6984. [*Died* 21 *Sept.* 1963.

WORTHAM, Maj.-Gen. Geoffrey Christopher Hale, O.B.E. 1944; Comd., Base Organisation, R.A.O.C., since 1967; *b.* 25 March 1913; *s.* of Brig. P. W. T. Hale-Wortham, C.B.; *m.* 1947, Gillian Constance Doble; one *s.* *Educ.:* Tonbridge School. Commission, Duke of Wellington's Regiment, 1935; served in Malta and India, 1935-38; transferred R.A.O.C., 1939. Served in France, Middle East, Italy, Burma and Malaya, 1940-46. Staff College, Camberley, 1947; R.A.O.C. Officers' School: 1948-50 (Administrative Staff College, Henley, 1949); 1954-56 (Chief Instructor); Egypt and Cyrenaica, 1951-52; War Office: 1952-54;

1957-59; Commandant, Central Ordnance Depot, Didcot, Berkshire, 1959-61; Director, Ordnance Services, F.A.R.E.L.F., 1961-63; Dep. Director, Ordnance Services, War Office, 1963-64; Brig. Q. M.o.D. (Army), 1946-67. *Recreation:* the countryside. *Club;* Army and Navy. [*Died* 10 *Oct.* 1967.

WORTHINGTON, Arthur Furley, M.A.; *b.* 22 June 1874; 2nd *s.* of late Richard Burton Worthington, Indian Civil Service; *m.* 1922, Kathleen Isabel, *y. d.* of late Lt.-Col. F. C. Barker, I.M.S.; no *c.* *Educ.:* Tonbridge; Sidney Sussex College, Cambridge. Entered Malayan Civil Service by competitive examination, 1897; cadet, Perak; held various posts in Federated Malay States; British Adviser, Kelantan, 1922; British Resident, Pahang, Federated Malay States, 1926; Perak, 1929; retired, 1929. *Address:* The Little Close, Pennington, Lymington, Hants. *T.:* 2440. [*Died* 10 *Nov.* 1964.

WORTHINGTON, Charles Edward, C.B.E. 1943; J.P.; *b.* Leicester, 20 Feb. 1897; *s.* of late Charles T. Worthington and Annie Elizabeth Whetstone; *m.* 1921, Winifred Boning Hextall Lovell; one *s.* two *d.* *Educ.:* Wyggeston School, Leicester; Heidelberg, Germany. Lieut. R.F.C., 1916-1919; elected to Leicester City Council, 1936; Lord Mayor of Leicester, 1945-46; President Leicester and County Chamber of Commerce, 1937-39, President East Leicester Conservative Assoc. 1939-45. Civil Defence Controller, Leicester City, 1941-45; Flight Lt. R.A.F.V.R. to command No. 1434 (Leicester Schools) Squadron, A.T.C., 1941-1945. Traffic Commissioner, E. Midlands Area. *Recreation:* yachting. *Address:* 7 Barrington Road, Leicester. *T.A.:* Resolute, Leicester. *T.:* Leicester 707739. *Clubs:* Leicestershire (Leicester); Leicestershire Yacht (Commodore). [*Died* 26 *April* 1970.

WORTHINGTON, Frank, C.B.E. 1920 (O.B.E. 1917); *b.* 1874; *s.* of late J. C. Worthington, of Belcombe Brook, Bradford-on-Avon; *m.* Gladys Elma (*d.* 1940), *o. d.* of late Major K. F. Maclachlan, R.H.A. *Educ.:* Repton. Served in Matabeleland Rebellion (medal 1896); entered Rhodesia C.S., 1896; District Commissioner, 1901; Acting Administrator, 1904; Secretary for Native Affairs, Northern Rhodesia, 1904; Judge of the Administrator's Court, 1907; retired, 1914; Deputy Chief (Postal) Censor, War Office, 1915-19; Deputy Director-General (awards) Ministry of Pensions, 1919, Chief Postal Censor, 1939-40; Member of Standing Inter-departmental Committee on Censorship, Committee of Imperial Defence, 1938-40; Member of Linguists Committee, Ministry of Labour, 1939; Palmes d'Officier de l'Académie Française, 1920. *Publications:* Chiromo the Witch Doctor; The Dancing Poisoners; The Little Wise One; The Zoo on Sunday; Kalula the Hare; III Act Plays, Mavana, I.D.B. *Address:* Westerfield Hall, Ipswich, Suffolk. [*Died* 29 *Jan.* 1964.

WORTHINGTON, Major-General Frederic Frank, C.B. 1943; M.C.; M.M.; C.D.; Major-General, Canadian Army; Civil Defence Co-ordinator, Canada, 1948-57, retired; President of Vicom Ltd.; *b.* 1889; *s.* of Henry Worthington; *m.* 1924, Clara Ellen (Larry), *d.* of Edward Dignum, Toronto, Ontario; one *s* one *d.* Served European War, with Canadian Overseas Forces, 1914-19; served War of 1939-45 (C.B.); Commanded Tank Brigade, 1940; G.O.C. Armd. Div., 1942; Pacific Comd., 1945; Western Comd., 1946. *Address:* (business) P.O. Box 472, Kingston, Ontario, Canada; 9 Ryeburn Dr., P.O. Box 736, R.R.#5, Ottawa, Ontario. *Club:* Rideau (Ottawa). [*Died* 8 *Dec.* 1967

WORTHINGTON, Sir Hubert, Kt 1949; O.B.E. 1929; R.A. 1955 (A.R.A. 1945); M.A.; F.R.I.B.A.; Hon. A.R.C.A.; M.T.P.I.; Senior Partner in the firm of Thomas Worthington & Sons, Manchester, and King's Bench Walk, Temple; *b.* 1886; *y. s.* of late Thomas Worthington, F.R.I.B.A., Alderley Edge, Cheshire; *m.* 1928, Joan, *o. d.* of late Dr. S. M. Banham, The Mill House, Northiam; one *s.* two *d.* *Educ.:* Sedbergh; Manchester University School of Architecture; foreign travel. Articled to his brother, late Sir Percy S. Worthington; Assistant in the office of late Sir E. L. Lutyens, O.M., P.R.A.; Captain in 16th Manchester Regiment, European War (severely wounded); Principal Architect for North Africa and Egypt, Imperial War Graves Commission; Architect to Manchester Cathedral; Planning Consultant: Manchester University and Manchester College of Science and Technology; Member Central Council for the care of Churches. Professor of Architecture, Royal College of Art, South Kensington, 1923-28; Lecturer on Architecture at University of Oxford, 1929; Ferens Lectr. in Fine Art, University Coll., Hull, 1933-34 and 1941; Member of the Royal Fine Art Commission, 1945-50; Member National Consultative Council of the Building and Civil Engineering Industries (Ministry of Works), 1942-45; Past Vice-President R.I.B.A. and Past President Manchester Society of Architects. *Principal Buildings:* Memorial to the Missing, Alamein; Memorial to the Missing, Medjes-el-Bab; Memorial to Missing Airmen, Malta; Radcliffe Library, new wing; St. Catherine's Society Building; Library, New College; Garden Buildings, Merton College; remodelling old Bodleian Library and Radcliffe Camera; Gatehouse Trinity College, New School of Forestry, School of Botany, Besse Building, Pembroke College and Special Faculties Library, Oxford; Harcourt Buildings, etc.; Inner Temple; Repair of King's Bench Walk: Inner Temple Hall (in association with T. W. Sutcliffe); Great Parlour, Merchant Taylors' Hall; new Brewers' Hall, London, E.C.2; Talbot Heath School, Bournemouth; War Memorial Cloister, Sedbergh School; Dining Hall and New Wing, Rossall School; Montague James Schools, new Boarding House, etc., Eton College; Westminster School, Repair of College Building, and Busby Library; Refectory, Mirfield; additions to Chemical Technology Building, etc., Imperial Coll. of Science; repair of Manchester Cathedral after war damage; domestic and ecclesiastical works, and (among hosps. by firm) recent buildings for Manchester Royal Infirmary, Manchester Royal Eye Hosp., new Manchester Dental Hosp. and School, Arts Library, School of Architecture, Woolton Hall, Manchester Univ.; (in association with Messrs. Norman & Dawbarn), Consulting Architect: Hawker Aircraft Head Office, Richmond Rd.; new Town Hall, Maidenhead (in assoc. with Messrs. North and Partners); new Boarding House, Aldenham School in association with Dawe Carter and Partners). During War of 1939-45 work for Ministry of Aircraft Production in factories and airports; Barrowmore Tuberculosis San. *Publications:* papers in R.I.B.A. Jl. on Italian Renaissance architects. *Recreation:* travel. *Address:* The Pantiles, Alderley Edge, Cheshire. *T.:* Alderley 3278; 13 King's Bench Walk, Temple, E.C.4. *T.:* Central 0488; 178 Oxford Road, Manchester. *T.:* Ardwick 4606 (Manchester). *Clubs:* Athenæum; Union (Manchester). [*Died* 26 *July* 1963.

WORTHINGTON, Rear-Adm. Roger Ernest, C.B. 1944; D.S.C. 1917; *b.* 19 November 1889; *s.* of Ernest Andrew Worthington, Queen's Own Royal Yeomanry, J.P., Leek, Staffs; *m.* 1926, Primrose, *d.* of Admiral H. E. Grace, C.B., and *g.d.* of Dr. W. G. Grace; three *d.* *Educ.:* Shrewsbury. Joined R.N 1907. Service includes: European War, 1914-18; N.Z. Expeditionary Force to Samoa, taking summons

to surrender to German Governor at Apia, Aug. 1914; Minelaying Squadron, 1915-1917 (D.S.C.); Secretary to Admiral Commanding Orkneys and Shetlands, 1918-1919; Secretary to Admiral, Submarines, 1927-29; Sec. to C.-in-C., Plymouth, 1935-38; Paymaster-Captain, 1939; Sec. to C.-in-C., the Nore, 1939-41; Deputy Paymaster-Director-General, Admiralty, 1941-44; A.D.C. to the King, 1944; retired list, 1944; Rear-Adm. (S), retired, 1947. *Recreation*: lawn tennis, won Royal Navy and Royal Marine Singles Championship, 1925-6-7. *Address*: Tamar, Beech Grove, Alverstoke, Hants. *Club*: All England Lawn Tennis.
[*Died* 20 *Oct*. 1967.

WRENCH, Sir (John) Evelyn (Leslie), K.C.M.G. 1960 (C.M.G. 1917); Kt. 1932; Hon. LL.D. (St. Andrews); Hon. D.Litt. (Bristol); Major (Royal Air Force), retired; Chairman of The Spectator since 1925; Founder of Overseas League (1910); Founder of the English-Speaking Union of the Commonwealth (1918); Founder of the English-Speaking Union of the United States (1920); Founder of All People's Association (1929-1936); Jt. Founder, Elizabethan Garden, Roanoke Is., N.C., U.S.A. (1952); *b*. Brookeborough, Co. Fermanagh, 29 October 1882; *o. surv. s.* of late Rt. Hon. Frederick Wrench; *m*. 1937, Hylda Henrietta, C.B.E. (*d*. 1955), *widow* of Sir Frederick des Voeux, 7th Bt. *Educ.*: Summer Fields, nr. Oxford; Eton; on the Continent. For four years engaged in postcard publishing business; in 1904 joined Lord Northcliffe's Staff; engaged in journalism till 1912, when he gave up all outside work so as to devote himself to the Overseas Club movement and to other Imperial work; made a tour of self-governing Dominions, 1912-13; Chief Private Sec. first Air Minister, 1917-18; Deputy Controller British Empire and U.S.A. Sections, Ministry of Information, 1918. Undertook lecture tour with Lady Wrench, Canada, U.S., N.Z., and Australia, 1940-41. Arrived India, Nov. 1941. America Relations Officer to Govt. of India, May 1942 to April 1944; Mem., Goodwill Mission to Virginia, 1957; visited Commonwealth Countries and S.E. Asia, 1959-60. Ed. of The Spectator, 1925-32. Senior Trustee Cecil Rhodes Memorial Museum Foundation, Bishops Stortford, Hertfordshire; Pres. Dickens Fellowship, 1961-64. Benjamin Franklin Medal (R.S.A.), 1964. *Publications*: Uphill, 1934; Struggle, 1935; I Loved Germany, 1940; Immortal Years, 1945; Francis Yeats Brown: A Portrait, 1949; Transatlantic London, 1949; Geoffrey Dawson and our Times, 1955; Alfred, Lord Milner, the Man of no illusions, 1958; founded Overseas, journal of Royal Over-Seas League. *Recreations*: promoting Commonwealth unity, British American co-operation, travelling. *Address*: The Mill House, Marlow, Bucks. *Clubs*: Travellers', Beefsteak. [*Died* 11 *Nov*. 1966.

WRENCH, John Mervyn Dallas, C.I.E. 1929; Chief Controller of Standards, Railway Bd., India, 1929-40; *b*. 1883; s. of John Mervyn Wrench, M.I.C.E.; *m*. 1908, Elise, 3rd *d*. of E. W. Mackenzie-Hughes; four *d*. *Educ.*: Bedford. Entered service of Indian State Railways, 1906; District Locomotive Superintendent, 1910; Deputy Locomotive Superintendent, 1919; Locomotive Superintendent, 1921; Chief Mechanical Engineer Great Indian Peninsular Railway, 1923; served in Mesopotamia with rank of Major in Indian Army Reserve of Officers, 1917-19. *Recreations*: golf, tennis. *Address*: c/o Lloyds Bank, 6 Pall Mall, S.W.1. *Club*: East India and Sports.
[*Died* 31 *Aug*. 1961.

WRENCH, Mollie L. S.; *see* Stanley-Wrench.

WRENN, Charles Leslie, M.A. Oxon.; Hon. D.Lit. (Nat. Univ. of Ireland); Hon. Fellow of Pembroke Coll., Oxford; Professor Emeritus, Oxford University; Rawlinson and Bosworth Professor of Anglo-Saxon, Oxford, 1946-63; *b*. Westcliffe-on-Sea, Essex, 30 Dec. 1895; *s*. of late H. W. Wrenn, merchant; *m*. 1919, A. E. Wright, Windsor; one *d*. *Educ.*: privately; Queen's Coll., Oxf. Lecturer in English, Durham University, 1917-20; Principal and Professor of English, Pachaiyappa's College, Madras, 1920-21; Fellow of Madras University, 1920; Head of the Department of English, Univ. of Dacca, 1921-27; Lecturer in English, Leeds Univ. 1928-30; Univ. Lecturer in English Language, Oxford, 1930-39; Professor of English Language and Literature, University of London, 1939-46. Chairman of Council, London University School of Slavonic and East European Studies, 1945-49; Mem., Academic Council, Univ. Coll., N. Staffs, 1950-62; President: Philological Soc., 1944-1948 (Vice-Pres., 1948-); Modern Humanities Research Assoc., 1968. Chm. International Conference of Univ. Professors of English, Oxford, 1950; Pres. Internat. Assoc. of Univ. Professors of English, 1950-1953. Visiting Professor, Universities of Florida, 1956-57, Texas, 1957 and N. Carolina, 1959; Taft Lecturer, University of Cincinatti, 1957; O'Donnell Lectr. in Celtic Studies, Oxford, 1957-58. Alexander White Visiting Prof., Chicago University, 1957; George A. Miller Visiting Prof., Illinois University, 1962; Rose Morgan Visiting Professor, University of Kansas; Visiting Prof., Ibadan Univ., Nigeria, 1964; Berg Professor of English and American Literature, New York Univ., 1964-65. *Publications*: Beowulf, a revision of Clark Hall's translation, with new introduction and notes, 1940, new expanded edition 1949; The Poetry of Caedmon (British Academy Lecture, 1947); The English Language, 1949, 2nd impression, 1952; Beowulf, an edition with commentary, glossary etc. 1953; An Old English Grammar (with R. Quirk), 1955; Supplement to 3rd edn. of R. W. Chambers' Introduction to Beowulf, 1959; A Study of Old English Literature, 1967; Word and Symbol (collected essays), 1967; reviews and articles in Trans. Philological Society, The Year's work in English Studies, Essays and Studies by Members of the English Assoc., Medium Ævum, Review of English Studies, Modern Language Review, The Slavonic Review, History, Chambers's Encyclopædia, Encyclopædia Britannica, New Catholic Encyclopædia, Oxford Slavonic Papers Cymmrodorion, etc. *Recreation*: walking. *Address*: 259A Woodstock Rd., Oxford.
[*Died* 31 *May* 1969.

WRIGHT, Baron (Life Peer), *cr*. 1932, of Durley; **Robert Alderson Wright**; P.C. 1932; G.C.M.G., *cr*. 1948; Kt., *cr*. 1925; F.B.A. 1940; Hon. LL.D. Cambridge, Birmingham, London, and Toronto; a Lord of Appeal in Ordinary, 1932-35, and 1937-47; Hon. Fellow of Trinity College, Cambridge; *b*. 15 Oct. 1869; *s*. of John Wright, South Shields; *m*. 1928, Margery Avis (master of the Tedworth Hounds, 1936, 1937 and jt. master of the Tedworth Woodland 1938, 1939), *d*. of late F. J. Bullows, of Sutton Coldfield. *Educ.*: privately; Trinity College, Cambridge. B.A. 1896; M.A. 1900; Fellow of Trinity College, 1899-1905; called to Bar, Inner Temple, 1900; K.C. 1917; Bencher of the Inner Temple, 1923; Treas., 1946; a Judge of the High Court of Justice, King's Bench Division, 1925-32; Master of the Rolls, 1935-37. Chairman of the Law Revision Committee. Australian Representative 1944, on the United Nations War Crimes Commission, and Chairman from 1945. *Publications*: Legal Essays and Addresses, 1939; many legal articles. *Address*: Durley House, Burbage, Marlborough, Wilts. *T.*:

Burbage, Wilts, 217. *Clubs:* Brooks's, Oxford and Cambridge, Alpine.
[*Died* 27 *June* 1964.

WRIGHT, Arthur Alban, C.M.G. 1937; B.A.; *b.* 24 Oct. 1887; *s.* of late Rev. Alban Henry Wright, M.A., Organising Sec. S.P.G.; *m.* 1914, Margaret Emily, *e. d.* of Robert Malcolm Booth; three *d.* *Educ.:* St. Edmund's School, Canterbury; St. John's College, Oxford. Entered Colonial Civil Service, 1912; Cadet, Fiji, 1912; District Commissioner, 1915; served European War; Provincial Commissioner, Fiji, 1922; Assistant Colonial Secretary, 1928; Secretary for Native Affairs, 1932; Acting Colonial Secretary, 1932-1934; Acting Governor of Fiji, 1935; Administrator of St. Vincent, 1936-38; Administrator of St. Lucia, 1938-43; Acting Governor of the Windward Islands, 1938 and 1939; retired, 1943; Managing Dir., Jamaica Starch and Milling Co. Ltd., 1944-46. *Address:* 4 Martin's Heron, Bracknell, Berks. [*Died* 4 *Jan.* 1967.

WRIGHT, Sir Bernard Swanwick, Kt. *cr.* 1921; D.L. Notts and City and County of City of Nottingham; J.P.; *b.* 9 April 1876; *y. s.* of late Colonel Joseph Wright, J.P.; *m.* 1st, 1901, Florence Mary (*d.* 1944), *y. d.* of late Joseph Burton, Nottingham; one *s.* two *d.*; 2nd, 1949, Jessie Wilkinson, Nottingham. *Educ.:* Clifton Coll. Solicitor; Hon. Freeman of City of Nottingham. *Address:* Haddon House, The Park, Nottingham. [*Died* 14 *Aug.* 1961.

WRIGHT, Frank Arnold, F.R.B.S., retired; *b.* London, 17 May 1874; *s.* of Thomas and Elizabeth Wright of St. Osyth, Essex; *m.* 1900, Ada Emmeline Wells; one *s.* three *d.* *Educ.:* Roan School, Greenwich. Studied Art at Goldsmiths' Institute, New Cross, Royal Academy Schools (Landseer Scholarship); exhibited at Royal Academy, 1903-19; Monument to Seventh Duke of Rutland, Bottesford Church, Lincs; Godman Memorial in Natural History Museum, S. Kensington; War Memorials at Stevenage, Herts, Stock, Essex, Pilsley Church, Derbyshire, St. Osyth, Essex, Lloyd's Register of Shipping, and the Queen's University of Belfast.
[*Died* 26 *Jan.* 1961.

WRIGHT, Frank Joseph Henry, M.B.E. 1966; Music Director, G.L.C. (formerly L.C.C.) Parks Department, since 1955; Member of Corporation, and Examiner, Trinity College of Music, London, since 1963; Professor and Examiner, Guildhall School of Music and Drama since 1945; *b.* Smeaton, Vic., Australia, 2 Aug. 1901; *s.* of late W. Wright and Sarah (*née* Higgins); unmarried. *Educ.:* singing, piano, composition and brass instrs. at Ballarat and Melbourne. Won Australian Cornet Championship, 1919; Open Diploma Award of Associated Board for highest points in Australia (subject singing), 1930. L.R.S.M. (Lond.). Jun. Warden, Worshipful Co. of Musicians; Exec. Mem., Nat. Music Coun. of Gt. Brit., 1959-; Life Mem., Roy. Musical Assoc.; Mem. Internat. Jury, Wereld Muziek-Concours, Holland, 1948-; Music Adviser Sth. Bank Exhibn., Fest. of Brit., 1951. Adjudicated at Nat. Brass Band Fest. 19 times; also at Championships of Aust. and N.Z., and for B.B.C., Challenging Brass, 1967-68. Hon. Editor, The Conductor, since its inception in 1946; edited Brass Today, 1957. Started G.L.C. open-air symphony concerts at: Kenwood Lakeside, 1951; Holland Park, 1955; Crystal Palace Concert Bowl, 1961. Toured W. German Opera Houses as guest of Fed. Republic, 1963. Featured in B.B.C. TV Documentary, The Impresario, 1967. Hon. F.T.C.L., F.G.S.M. *Publications:* Compositions, mainly brass band, include: Diversions on Original Theme, Sirius; Trilogy, Threshold; Suite, Old Westminster; Preludio Marziale; Ceremonial March, Whitehall. Music and script of tutorial (record), Voice of the Cornet. Test pieces scored for Nat. Brass Band Fest., incl. works by R. Vaughan Williams, Bliss, Rubbra, Howells; also scored T. Wood's The Rainbow (A Tale of Dunkirk), commissioned by the Arts Council for Fest. of Britain, 1951. Altogether over 100 works published. *Recreations:* collecting Melba records and Edison phonographs. *Address:* 14 Highbury Grange, N.5. *Club:* City Livery. [*Died* 16 *Nov.* 1970.

WRIGHT, Sir Geoffrey C., Bt.; *see* Cory-Wright.

WRIGHT, George Payling; D.M., F.R.C.P.; Professor Emeritus, University of London, formerly Sir William Dunn Professor of Pathology, Guy's Hospital Medical School; Hon. Consulting Pathologist, Guy's Hosp.; Vice-Chm., Council, Imperial Cancer Research Fund; Mem. Expert Cttee. on Med. Educ., W.H.O.; *b.* 4 April 1898; *s.* of William James Payling Wright and Mary Esther Mandall; *m.* 1937, Helen Margaret, *d.* of late Alexander Goddard, C.B.E.; one *s.* (one *d.* decd.). *Educ.:* Univ. Coll. Sch.; Exeter College, Oxford. Rockefeller travelling Fellow in Medicine; Research Fellow, Harvard University Medical School; Lecturer on Morbid Anatomy, University College Hospital Medical School; Pathologist to U.C.H. Mem. M.R.C., 1956-60. Hon. Member, Berlin Medical Soc. *Publications:* Tuberculosis and Social Conditions in England; An Introduction to Pathology; papers on Epidemiological and Pathological subjects. *Address:* Royal College of Surgeons, Lincoln's Inn Fields, W.C.2; 6 Turner's Wood, N.W.11.
[*Died* 4 *April* 1964.

WRIGHT, Sir Henry (Edward), Kt. 1965; J.P.; *b.* 30 March 1893; *s.* of Henry Edward Wright; *m.* 1921, Florence Minnie Maud Perry; one *s.* two *d.* *Educ.:* Ford Boys' Sch., Devonport, Plymouth. Member of Plymouth City Council, 1927-; Alderman, 1946-; Lord Mayor of Plymouth, 1952-53; J.P., City of Plymouth, 1946-. *Recreations:* reading, walking on Dartmoor. *Address:* 36 Tamar Avenue, Keyham, Plymouth, Devon. [*Died* 2 *Nov.* 1966.

WRIGHT, Sir Leonard (Morton), Kt. 1957; J.P.; Managing Director, L. M. Wright and Co., Tea Importers; *b.* Sydney, Australia, 29 July 1906; 3rd *s.* of George Arthur and Maude C. Wright; *m.* 1936, Cecilia Mary, *o. d.* of Melville Bell, Havelock North, N.Z.; four *s.* (and one *s.* decd.). *Educ.:* Hornsby High School, Sydney. Formed L. M. Wright and Co., 1927 (at age of 20). Director: Union Steam Ship Co.; South British Insurance Co.; Neill Cropper and Co. Ltd.; N.Z. Oil Refinery; N.Z. Steel Co.; Chas. Begg & Co.; D.I.C. Ltd.; McLeod Bros. Ltd.; and other Dunedin, N.Z. commercial firms; City councillor, 1942-1950; Honorary Tea Controller of N.Z., 1941-50. Director N.Z. Govt. Tourist Hotel Corporation, 1954-57. Leader, N.Z. Trade Mission to West Coast America and Canada, 1963. Mayor of Dunedin, New Zealand, 1950-59. J.P. 1950. *Recreations:* tennis, golf, ski-ing, skating; represented Otago Province at athletics; N.Z. Rugby referee, 1936. *Address:* Wychwood, Belmont Lane, Dunedin, New Zealand. *T.:* 83838. *Clubs:* Dunedin, Otago (Dunedin).
[*Died* 22 *Oct.* 1967.

WRIGHT, Sir Norman (Charles), Kt. 1963; C.B. 1955; M.A., D.Sc. (Oxford), Ph.D. (Cambridge); F.R.I.C.; F.R.S.E.; *b.* 19 Feb. 1900; 2nd *s.* of Rev. Francis H. Wright, M.A., late Registrar of University of Reading, and Agnes Mary Dunkley; *m.* 1928, Janet Robison Ledingham, *e. d.* of late Dr.

John Rennie, Aberdeen; one *d*. *Educ.*: University College, Reading; Christ Church, Oxford; Gonville and Caius College, Cambridge. Agricultural Research Scholar, 1922-24; Research Asst., National Institute for Research in Dairying, Univ. of Reading, 1924-26; Commonwealth Fund Fellow, U.S.A., 1926-28, at Cornell Univ., N.Y., and U.S. Dept. of Agriculture, Washington, D.C.; First Director Hannah Dairy Research Institute, Ayr, 1928-47; Hon. Lecturer, Univ. of Glasgow, 1932-47; Chief Scientific Adviser (Food) to the Ministry of Agriculture, Fisheries and Food (formerly Chief Scientific Adviser to the Ministry of Food), 1947-1959; Deputy Director-General Food and Agriculture Organization of the United Nations, 1959-63; Sec., Brit. Assoc. for Advancement of Science, 1963-68. Special Adviser to Imperial Council of Agricultural Res., India, 1936-37; Mem. Scientific Advisory Mission, Middle East Supply Centre, 1944-45; Special Adviser to Govt. of Ceylon, 1945; British Mem. of F.A.O. Mission to Greece, 1946; Chm., Agric. Educ. Assoc., 1948-50; Member: Colonial Agric. Advisory Council 1947-55; Agricultural Research Council, 1950-55; Colonial Research Council, 1950-54; Natural Resources (Technical) Cttee., 1950-55; U.N. Adv. Cttee. on Application of Science and Technology to Development, 1964-; Council of Nestlé Foundation, 1967-; Member Council, Brit. Association for the Advancement of Science, 1950-56; President Sect. M., 1952; Gen. Secretary of the Assoc., 1958-59; Chairman: Food Standards Committee 1947-59; National Food Survey Cttee., 1948-59; F.A.O. Program Cttee. (Rome), 1953-59; successively Chm., Vice-Chm. and member of Committee for Colonial Agricultural Animal Health and Forestry Research, 1946-59. Hon. LL.D. Leeds, 1967. *Publications:* official reports and papers in scientific and tech. jls. *Recreations:* travelling, photography. *Address:* 65 Addison Road, W.14. *T.:* 01-603 8383. *Clubs:* Athenæum, Authors', Farmers'.

[*Died* 16 *July* 1970.

WRIGHT, Philip Arundell, C.M.G. 1962; Chancellor, New England University, Armidale, N.S.W., since 1960 (Deputy Chancellor, 1954-60); *b*. 20 July 1889; *s*. of Albert Andrew Wright and Charlotte May Wright (*née* Mackenzie); *m*. 1st, 1913, Ethel Mabel Bigg; two *s*. one *d*.; 2nd, 1929, Dora Isabella Temperley; one *s*. one *d*. *Educ.*: Bedford Gram. Sch., England; Sydney C. of E. Gram. Sch. Governing Director, P. A. Wright & Sons Pty. Ltd., 1914-; Pres. Graziers Assoc. of N.S.W., 1944; Pres. Graziers Fed. Council of Australia, 1948; Chm. New England Nat. Park Trust, 1931; Pres. New England State Movement, 1948. Hon. D.Sc. Univ. of New England, 1958. *Recreation:* tennis. *Address:* Wallamumbi, Armidale, N.S.W. 2350, Australia. *T.:* 516344 Wollomombi. *Clubs:* Australian (Sydney, N.S.W.); Armidale (Armidale).

[*Died* 30 *Aug*. 1970.

WRIGHT, (Sydney) Fowler; *b*. 6 Jan. 1874; *m*. 1st, 1895, Nellie Ashbarry (*d*. 1918); three *s*. three *d*.; 2nd, 1920, Truda Hancock; one *s*. three *d*. *Educ.*: King Edward's High School, Birmingham. Practised as an accountant in Birmingham since 1895, and retired and taken to literary work during recent years. Editor of Poetry (afterwards Poetry and the Play), 1920-32. *Publications:* Scenes from the Morte d'Arthur, 1920; Some Songs of Bilitis, 1922; a translation of Dante's Inferno, 1928; Poems Chosen (with R. Crompton Rhodes), 1925; The Amphibians, 1925; The Song of Songs, and other Poems, 1925; The Ballad of Elaine, 1926; Deluge, 1927; The Island of Captain Sparrow, 1928; Police and Public, a Political Pamphlet, 1929; The World Below, 1929; Dawn, 1930; The Riding of Lancelot, a Narrative Poem, 1929; Elfwin, 1930; Dream, 1931; Seven Thousand in Israel, 1931; Red Ike (with J. M. Denwood) 1931; The New Gods Lead, short stories, 1932; Beyond the Rim, 1932; The Life of Sir Walter Scott, a biography, 1932; Lord's Right in Languedoc, 1933; Power, 1933; David, 1934; Prelude in Prague, 1935; Four Days War, 1936; The Screaming Lake, 1937; Megiddo's Ridge, 1937; The Hidden Tribe, 1938; The Adventure of Wyndham Smith, 1938; Ordeal of Barata, 1939; Should We Surrender Colonies? 1939; The Siege of Malta, a historical romance, 1942; Residue, poems, 1948; The Witchfinder, short stories, 1946; Vengeance of Gwa, 1946; The Adventure of the Blue Room, 1950; The Throne of Saturn (short stories), 1952; (trans.) Dante's Purgatorio, 1953; Spider's War, 1955; Professor Randall's Experiment, 1955; Outbreak from Earth, 1955; Under Ten, 1955; editor of numerous anthologies. *Novels as Sydney Fowler:* The King against Anne Bickerton, 1930; The Bell Street Murders, 1931; By Saturday, 1931; The Hanging of Constance Hillier, 1931; The Handprint Mystery, 1932; Arresting Delia, 1933; The Secret of the Screen, 1933; Who else but She?, 1934; Three Witnesses, 1935; The Attic Murder, 1936; Was Murder Done?, 1936; Post-mortem Evidence, 1936; Four Callers in Razor Street, 1937; The Jordans Murder, 1938; The Murder in Bethnal Square, 1938; The Wills of Jane Kanwhistle, 1939; The Rissole Mystery, 1942; A Bout with the Mildew Gang, 1942; Second Bout with the Mildew Gang, 1943; The End of the Mildew Gang, 1944; Dinner in New York, 1943; Too Much for Mr. Jellipot, 1945; Who Killed Reynard?, 1947; With Cause Enough?, 1954. *Recreations:* gardening, chess. *Address:* Petersham Cottage, Byfleet, Surrey.

[*Died* 25 *Feb*. 1965.

WROTTESLEY, 4th Baron (*cr*. 1838), **Victor Alexander Wrottesley**; Bt. 1642; *b*. 18 Sept. 1873; *e*. *surv*. *s*. of 3rd Baron and Hon. Augusta Elizabeth Denison, *d*. of 1st Lord Londesborough; *S*. father, 1910. Owns about 5800 acres. *Heir*: *b*. Hon. Walter Bennet Wrottesley [*b*. 28 Sept. 1877; *m*. 1917, Kate May (who obtained a divorce, 1926), *d*. of late Dr. Douglas Harris, Johannesburg; one *s*., *b*. 7 July 1918]. *Address:* Wrottesley, Wolverhampton.

[*Died* 1 *Sept*. 1962.

WYATT, Sir Myles (Dermot Norris), Kt. 1963; C.B.E. 1956; Chm. Air Holdings Ltd; *b*. 2 July 1903; *yr*. *s*. of Arthur Norris Wyatt; *m*. 1929, Dorothy O'Malley; one *s*. one *d*. *Educ.*: Radley; New Coll., Oxford. On leaving Oxford, 1926, joined Comrs. for the Port of Calcutta; retired, 1934. Chairman: British United Airways Ltd.; Airwork Services Ltd.; Aviation Traders (Engineering) Ltd.; Airwork International Ltd.; British Air Ferries Ltd.; Cripplegate Property Holdings Ltd.; Air Holdings Ltd.; Director: Morton Air Services Ltd.; Whitehall Securities Corp. Ltd.; S. Pearson Industries Ltd.; Brit. United Airways (C.I.) Ltd.; Economic Insurance Co. Ltd.; Western Ground Rents Ltd.; Shop Investments Ltd. *Recreations:* sailing, shooting, ski-ing. *Address:* Alresford Hall, Nr. Colchester, Essex. *T.:* Wivenhoe 556. *Clubs:* Brooks's; Royal Yacht Squadron; Royal Ocean Racing; Royal Cruising.

[*Died* 14 *April* 1968.

WYATT, Sir Stanley, Kt., *cr*. 1939; British Member and President, Ottoman Public Debt Council; Vice-President, Caisse Commune des Dettes Publiques Autrichiennes et Hongroises; *b*. 1877; *s*. of Charles Purnell Wyatt; *m*. 1910, Sylvia Neild, *d*. of Edward Neild Shackle, late of Botwell House, Hayes, Middlesex; four *s*. one *d*. *Publication:* Cheneys and Wyatts, 1959. *Address:* 39 Roland Gardens, S.W.7. *T.:* Frobisher 2808.

[*Died* 26 *May* 1968.

WYCHERLEY, Sir (Robert) Bruce, Kt., *cr.* 1953; M.C. and Bar 1918; first President, Abbey National Building Society, since 1964 (Managing Director, 1949-63); Director: Royal Insurance Co. Ltd.; Liverpool & London & Globe Insurance Co. Ltd.; London and Lancashire Insurance Co. Ltd.; South Essex Water Works Co.; *b.* 5 Apr. 1894; *s.* of Rev. Richard Wycherley, Hadnall, Shropshire, and Mary (*née* Bruce); *m.* 1st, 1920, Lena Winifred (*d.* 1942), *d.* of Edward Land Harrison; one *d.*; 2nd, 1943, Margaret Brown, *d.* of William Leitch Morton; one *d.* West Riding Education Dept. (Wakefield), 1911-19 (including four years war service). Served European War, 1914-18, in Army; joined 1/5 Bn. W. Yorkshire Regt., France, 1916, as 2nd Lt. ; demobilised in 1919 from that Regt. with rank of Capt. (M.C. and Bar). Secretary West Riding War Pensions Div. 34, 1919-21; Secretary Halifax District Engineering Employers' Assoc., 1921-29; Asst. Sec., Gen. Manager, and Managing Director, The National Building Soc., 1929-43, and on amalgamation with the Abbey Road Building Soc. in 1944, Joint Managing Director of Abbey National Building Soc., 1944-48. Vice-President, Building Socs. Association (Council Member for over 30 years); Chairman Metropolitan Assoc. of Building Socs., 1934-38; Chairman Building Socs. Assoc., 1943-46; Vice-President Building Socs. Institute. F.C.I.S. (President, 1954). Liveryman (and Member of Court), Worshipful Company of Innholders; Freeman of City of London. War of 1939-45, Major in 54th Kent Bn. Home Guard. *Recreations:* gardening, music. *Address:* High Timber, Chislehurst, Kent. *T.:* Imperial 3961. *Club:* City Livery (Past Pres.). [*Died* 17 *March* 1965.

WYKES, John Arthur; Managing Director, Crown (Lyndhurst) & County Hotels Ltd., Lyndhurst, Hants, since 1937; *b.* 17 Jan. 1891; *s.* of late John Alfred Wykes and late Rose Wykes; *m.* 1920, Doris Mizen; one *s.* one *d.* *Educ.:* St. Thomas's Grammar School; United Kingdom College. Director of Accounts, Mechanical Warfare Dept., Ministry of Munitions, 1916-20; Hoover Ltd.: Chief Accountant, Jan.-Aug. 1921; Secretary, 1921-45; Director and Secretary, 1928; Deputy Managing Director, 1946; Managing Director, 1954-55. Director: County Fire Office Ltd. 1948. *Recreations:* golf, yachting, ski-ing. *Address:* Flaghead, Cliff Drive, Canford Cliffs, Dorset. [*Died* 25 *Jan.* 1970.

WYLIE, David Storer, C.M.G. 1917; C.B.E. 1919; F.R.C.S. (Eng.); F.A.C.S. F.R.A.C.S.; Hon. Consulting Surgeon Palmerston North Hospital; *b.* 21 Sept. 1876, *Educ.:* Manchester Grammar School; Owens College, Manchester; King's College Hospital, London. Civil Surgeon attached R.A.M.C., South African War, 1900-2; Major, N.Z.M.C.. 915; Lieut.-Colonel, 1916; Colonel, 1918, ;erved European War, 1915-18; Director of Hospitals, Health Department, New Zealand, 1920-22; Officer Commanding No. 1 N.Z. General Hospital and Consulting Surgeon n special Military Surgery (C.M.G., C.B.E.). *Recreation:* gardening. *Address:* Otumoetai, Tauranga, New Zealand. [*Died* 23 *Sept.* 1965.

WYLIE, Sir Francis Verner, G.C.I.E., *cr.* 1947 (C.I.E. 1929; K.C.S.I., *cr.* 1938; Commander of the Legion of Honour; *b.* 9 Aug. 1891; *s.* of late David and Margaret (*née* Hyde) Wylie; *m.* Kathleen, Kaisar-i-Hind Gold Medal, *y. d.* of late L. A. Bryne, F.R.C.S.I.; two *s.* *Educ.:* Royal Sch., Dungannon; Trinity Coll., Dublin. Entered I.C.S., 1914; arrived in India, 1915; temporary Commission, Indian Army, 1916-19; Indian Political Service, 1910-38; Gov. of Central Provinces and Berar, 1938-40; Political Adviser to the Crown Representative, 940-41 and 1943-45; Minister to Afghanistan, 1941-43; Gov. of the United Provinces, 1945-47. *Address:* 85 Rivermead Court, S.W.6. *Club:* Athenæum. [*Died* 25 *Nov.* 1970.

WYLIE, Hon. William Evelyn, Q.C. (Ire.); *b.* 1881; *s.* of Rev. R. B. Wylie, M.A., LL.D., Coleraine, Co. Derry, and Marion Drury; *m.* 1913, Ida Moloney (*d.* 1950), Dungarvan, Co. Waterford; one *s.* one *d.* *Educ.:* Coleraine Academical Institution; Trinity College, Dublin (Honour Graduate and Large Gold Medalist); Brook Prizeman in Law, King's Inn, Dublin; called to Bar, 1905; K.C., 1914; Bencher of King's Inn, 1918; Law Adviser to Irish Government, 1919-20; Judge of the Supreme Court of Judicature (Ireland), 1920-24; Judge of High Court Irish Free State, 1924-3 , and late Judicial Commissioner to the Irish Land Commission; Chairman Irish Railway Wages Board, 1924-44; Vice-Chm. Irish Betting Control Board, 1930-45; Pres., Royal Dublin Society, 1939-41, Chairman Executive Cttee. 1937-60; Vice-Chm. Irish Red Cross Soc., 1939-46; mem. Irish Turf Club, steward, 1951-54, and 1957-60; steward Irish Nat. Hunt Steeplechase Cttee., 1947-50; Chm. Irish Racing Board, 1945; held a commn. in H.M. Army (Territorial Force), 1915-18 (despatches); Master Ward Union Hounds, 1925-39. *Recreations:* hunting and riding, golf, motoring. *Clubs:* St. Stephens Green (Dublin), Turf. [*Died* 12 *Oct.* 1964.

WYLLIE, William Gifford, M.D. (Edin.), F.R.C.P. (Lond.); Consulting Physician, Hosp. for Sick Children, Great Ormond St. and Hosp for Nervous Diseases, Maida Vale; 2nd *s.* of Alexander Wyllie of Whitelee, nr. Galashiels; unmarried. *Educ.:* Edinburgh Academy; Univ. of Edinburgh. Temp. Surg. Lieut. R.N., 1915-19. Councillor, R.C.P., 1950; Examr. in Med. R.C.P. *Publications:* papers in the medical journals, etc.; collab. (the nervous system) in Garrod, Batten, Thursfield, and Paterson, Diseases of Children, and in Parsons and Barling, Diseases of Infancy and Childhood. *Recreations:* travel, fishing, gardening. *Address:* 22 Belgrave Crescent, Edinburgh. *T.:* 031-332 6531. *Club:* Junior Carlton. [*Died* 24 *Oct.* 1969.

WYLLY, Col. Guy George Egerton, V.C.; C.B. 1933; D.S.O. 1918; Indian Army, retired; late Corps of Guides, Cavalry; late Tasmanian Imperial Bushmen; *b.* 17 Feb. 1880. Served South Africa, 1900 (V.C., twice wounded, Queen's medal three clasps); European War, 1914-18; Staff Capt. and Brigade-Major, Mhow Cavalry Brig.; G.S.O.2, 4th Divn., B.E.F.; 3rd Aust. Divn. A.I.F.; 1st Anzac Corps (wounded, despatches thrice, D.S.O.); operations N.W. Frontier, India, 1919, against Afghanistan (despatches, medal); N.W. Frontier of India, 1930 (despatches); Chitral Reliefs, 1932 (despatches); operations against Upper Mohmands, 1933 (despatches); Commandant 6th D.C.O. Lancers, 1926-29; A.A. and Q.M.G. Peshawur District, 1929-33; A.D.C. to Lord Kitchener, 1905-09; A.D.C. to the King, 1926-33; retired 1933. *Address:* c/o Lloyds Bank, Ltd., Cox's and King's Branch, 6 Pall Mall, S.W.1. *Club:* United Service. [*Died* 9 *Jan.* 1962.

WYMARK, Patrick Carl, (A. K. A. Cheeseman); actor since 1951; *b.* 11 July 1926; *s.* of Thomas W. Cheeseman and Agnes Maria Cheeseman; *m.* 1950, Olwen Margaret Buck; two *s.* two *d.* *Educ.:* Wintringham Grammar School, Grimsby; University College, London. Old Vic Company, 1951-53; Artist in Residence, Stanford University, California, 1953-54; Shakespeare Memorial Theatre, Stratford-on-Avon, 1955-59, 1960-1962; Fifty-nine Company, Lyric, Hammersmith, 1959; Revue, One to Another, 1959; Open Air Theatre, Regent's Park, 1962, 1963; The Judge, Cambridge, 1967; Edinburgh Festival, 1967; The Cherry Orchard,

Queen's, 1967. Television and film rôles, 1959- ; T.V. series, The Power Game, 1965-1969. *Recreations:* listening to music, golf. *Address:* 77 Parliament Hill, N.W.3. *Clubs:* New Arts, Buckstone, Pickwick. [*Died* 20 *Oct.* 1970.

WYNDHAM, Horace Cowley; author; *b.* Oxfordshire 1873; *s.* of Canon G. J. Cowley-Brown, who assumed by licence name of grandmother (Hannah Cowley, author and playwright). *Educ.:* Glenalmond. Proceeded to France as Railway Transport Officer, 1914; graded as Staff Capt., 1914; to Ordnance Corps, 1917; to Army of the Rhine, 1918 (1914-15 Mons Star; Allies Victory Medal and War Medal); Demobilised 1920; Military interviewing Officer (recruiting panel), 1940-42; A.R.P. duties, 1942-45. *Publications:* The Queen's Service; The King's Scarlet; Audrey, the Actress; Reginald Auberon; The Call of the Drum; Roses and Rue; Chetwynd's Career; Hilary Onslow; Following the Drum; Limelight; Soldiers on Service; The Nineteen Hundreds; Famous Trials Retold; The Mayfair Calendar; Blotted 'Scutcheons; Judicial Dramas; Crime on the Continent; Criminology; Feminine Frailty; Romances of the Peerage; Victorian Sensations; Victorian Parade; The Magnificent Montez, Courtesan and Convert; Dramas of the Law; Mr. Sludge, biography of Daniel Home; Society Sensations; Consider Your Verdict; This was the News; Speranza, Lady Wilde; Chorus to Coronet; and several other books; contributor to Spectator, etc.; also various Encyclopædic articles, two radio plays, and B.B.C. talks. *Recreations:* play-going, travelling. *Address:* Saxlingham Hall, Saxlingham, Norfolk. [*Died* 28 *Dec.* 1970.

WYNN PARRY, Hon. Sir Henry, Kt., 1946; Judge of High Court of Justice, Chancery Division, 1946-60, retd.; *b.* 15 Jan. 1899; *s.* of Robert Henry Parry, F.R.C.S.E. and Margaret Whigham Lorimer; *m.* 1st, 1923, Shelagh Berkeley Moynihan (marr. diss., 1929); one *s.*; 2nd, 1930, Catherine Louise Holliday (*d.* 1963). *Educ.:* Rugby; New College, Oxford. Served European War, 1917-19, Worcestershire Regiment; War of 1939-40, Royal Artillery; B.A. Jurisprudence, 1921; M.A., 1925; B.C.L., 1922: Called to Bar, Lincoln's Inn, 1922; Bencher, 1941, Treas. 1960; Q.C. 1936. Late Dep. Chm., Board of Referees. Chm. Cttee. of Enquiry under British Nationalisation Act, 1948; Chairman Hertford Quarter Sessions, 1950; Chairman Permanent Cttee. on Private International Law appointed by Lord Chancellor, 1952-60; Chm. Council of Legal Education, 1952-63 (Dep. Chm. 1952); Chm. Home Office Departmental Cttee. on Remuneration and Conditions of Service of Prison Officers; Chm. Commonwealth Colonial Office Commn. on Feb. 1962 riots in British Guiana, 1962. *Recreations:* tennis, gardening. *Address:* Hatching Green Lodge, Hatching Green, nr. Harpenden, Hertfordshire. *T.:* Harpenden 262. *Club:* Oxford and Cambridge. [*Died* 10 *Jan.* 1964.

WYNNE, Anthony; *see* Wilson, Robert McNair.

WYNNE, Rev. Arthur Edwin: M.A. Cantab.; *b.* 1864; *s.* of late William Palmer Wynne, Stafford; *m.* 1st, 1895, Georgina, *d.* of John Lovatt; 2nd, 1909, Enid Goymour, *d.* of Goymour Cuthbert; three *s.* two *d.* *Educ.:* King Edward's School, Birmingham; Jesus College, Cambridge. Wrangler, 1885; Mathematical Master and Housemaster, Dover College, 1890-1916; Headmaster of Blundell's School, 1917-30; Priest-in-charge of St. Anne's, Saunton, N. Devon, 1930-45. *Address:* 11x Hungershall Park, Tunbridge Wells, Kent. *T.:* 30695. [*Died* 21 *Aug.* 1964.

WYNNE, Lieut.-Col. Henry Ernest Singleton, C.M.G. 1919; D.S.O. 1915; late R.F.A.; *b.* 4 Jan. 1877; *s.* of late Major Warren R. C. Wynne, R.E., and *g.s.* of Captain John Wynne, R.A.; *m.* 1911, Katherine, *d.* of late Rev. D. W. Kennedy; one *s.* two *d.* *Educ.:* Uppingham; Woolwich. Entered Army, 1896; Captain, 1902; Major, 1913; Lt.-Col. 1916; served South Africa, 1899-1901 (despatches, Queen's medal 5 clasps); Staff Capt. R.A. Highland Div., Scottish Command, 1911-14; Brigade Major, 1914; served European War, 1914-18 (D.S.O., C.M.G., despatches five times); retired pay, 1922; Secretary, City of Edinburgh T.A. Association, 1924-41. *Address:* 41 Ganghill, Guildford, Surrey. [*Died* 25 *March* 1962.

WYNNE FINCH, Colonel Sir William (Heneage), Kt. 1960; M.C. 1916; Lord-Lieutenant of Caernarvonshire, 1941-60; *b.* 18 Jan. 1893; *s.* of late Lt.-Col. C. A. Wynne Finch of Voelas and Cefnamwlch; *m.* 1929, Gladys F., *d.* of late John I. Waterbury, Fairfield, New Jersey, U.S.A.; no *c.* *Educ.:* Eton. 2nd Lieut. Scots Guards, 1912; Capt. 1916; Major, 1923; Lt.-Col. 1931; Col. 1935; served European War, 1914-19 (twice wounded, M.C.); attached Egyptian Army and Sudan Defence Force, 1919-26 (Order of the Nile); commanded 2nd Bn. Scots Guards, 1931-35; retired pay, 1938; Training Officer attached to Territorial Division, 1939-40; A.G.4 Branch War Office, 1940-1941; Commander North-East London Sub-District, 1941-44; Lt.-Col. Commanding Scots Guards, 1944-45. *Recreations:* fishing, shooting. *Address:* Cefnamwlch, Edeyrn, Pwllheli, N. Wales. *T.:* Tudweiliog 209. *Clubs:* Guards, Lansdowne. [*Died* 16 *Dec.* 1961.

WYNTER-MORGAN, Air Cdre. Wilfred; C.B. 1951; C.B.E. 1945; M.C. 1916; R.A.F. retd.; *b.* 19 Nov. 1894; *m.* 1925, Mollie, *d.* of late E. Stafford Herbert and Elizabeth Herbert; one *d.* *Educ.:* Wycliffe College. Gloucestershire Regiment, 1914-1923. Served European War, 1914-18 (despatches, M.C.). R.A.F., 1924-51; No. 4 Flying Training School, Egypt, 1924; No. 60 (B) Sqdn., N.W.F.P., 1925-28; Air H.Q. Iraq, 1932. Specialised in Air Armament, 1929; Air Armament Sch., Eastchurch, 1929-31; H.Q. Central Area, Abingdon 1933-36; Aircraft and Armament Experimental Establishment, Martlesham, 1936-39; Ministry of Aircraft Production and Ministry of Supply, as Dep. Dir. of Armament Development, 1940-45; Vice-Pres. Ordnance Bd., 1947-48; Director of Technical Services (Air) in British Joint Services Mission, Washington, 1948-51. Retired from R.A.F. 1951. Officer American Legion of Merit, 1946. *Address:* Wentworth, Mount Hermon Rd., Woking, Surrey. *T.:* Woking 60995. *Club:* Royal Automobile. [*Died* 27 *March* 1968.

WYNYARD, Diana, C.B.E. 1953; actress; *b.* 16 January 1906; *d.* of Edward T. and Margaret C. Cox; adopted stage name of Wynyard by deed poll, 1936; *m.* 1943, Carol Reed (Kt. 1952), (marr. diss., 1947); *m.* 1951, Tibor Csato (marr. diss., 1958). *Educ.:* Woodford School, Croydon. Went on stage, Globe Theatre, London, Grand Duchess, 1925; toured until 1927; Liverpool Repertory Co., 1927-29; played at St. Martin's Theatre, London, in Sorry You've been Troubled, Honours Easy, Petticoat Influence, Man who Paid the Piper, Lean Harvest, 1929-31; to America, Dec. 1931, N. York, in The Devil; Hollywood, 1932-33, Cavalcade, Reunion in Vienna, etc.; Wild Decembers, London, 1933; Hollywood, Oct. 1933-July 1934, Over the River, etc.; Sweet Aloes, London, 1934; Candida, Pygmalion, 1937; Design for Living, 1938-40; No Time for Comedy, 1941; Watch on the Rhine, 1942-43; with E.N.S.A. England and abroad,

1944; The Wind of Heaven, 1945; Portrait in Black, 1946; The Rossiters, 1947; Stratford Memorial Theatre, Apr.-Nov. 1948 and Apr.-Sept. 1949; to Australia with the Stratford Company, Oct. 1949; played in Captain Carvallo, St. James's, 1950; The Winter's Tale, Phœnix, 1951; Much Ado About Nothing, Phœnix, 1952; The Private Life of Helen, Globe, 1953; Marching Song, St. Martin's, 1954; The Bad Seed, Aldwych, 1955; Hamlet, 1955 (on tour, Russia, London); The Seagull, Saville, 1956; Camino Real, Phœnix, 1957; A Touch of the Sun, Saville, 1958; Cue for Passion (New York) 1958; Heartbreak House (New York) 1959; Toys in the Attic, 1960; The Bird of Time, Savoy, 1961; Photo Finish, Saville, 1962. Hamlet, Old Vic, National Theatre, 1963; Andorra, National Theatre, 1964. *Films:* Gaslight; Kipps; Prime Minister; The Ideal Husband; The Feminine Touch; Island in the Sun. *Address:* c/o Christopher Mann, Ltd., 140 Park Lane, W.1. [*Died* 13 *May* 1964.

WYON, Rev. Allan Gairdner, F.R.B.S.; Sculptor and Medallist; and Clerk in Holy Orders since 1933; Vicar of Newlyn, 1936-55, retired; *b.* 1882; *s.* of Allan Wyon, F.S.A., Chief Engraver of Her Majesty's Seals; *m.* 1910, Eileen May, 3rd *d.* of late Frederick N. le Poer Trench, Q.C., J.P., of Dublin; one *d.* *Educ.:* Highgate School. Studied sculpture at the Royal Academy Schools. Hon. Secretary of Art Workers' Guild, 1924-1930; Exhibits at Royal Academy, Liverpool, Edinburgh, and Salon, etc. *Chief Works:* Pax Dolorosa, in the Glasgow Corporation Art Gallery; A Worshipper, Leicester Corporation Art Gallery; Spirit of Slumber, Auckland, N.Z., Art Gallery; many Memorials to Bishops and other distinguished persons in cathedrals, etc. St. Michael figure on Shrewsbury War Memorial, Richard Corfield Memorial at Marlborough College, and combined Memorial to William Pitt, Earl of Chatham, and William Pitt the Younger, erected at Hayes, Kent; busts of Milton, Chaucer, Darwin, Newton, and others for Nottingham University; portrait reliefs of Lord Rhondda, Lord Manton, and Sir Algernon Methuen; Episcopal Seals of Archbishops of Canterbury and York and many others; medals of King George, Prince of Wales, and numerous others. *Recreation:* wandering in Italy. *Address:* 24 Woollards Lane, Great Shelford, Cambridge. *T.:* Shelford 3373. [*Died* 26 *Feb.* 1962.

Y

YAMIN KHAN, Sir Mohammed, Kt. 1936; C.I.E. 1931; Barrister-at Law; Landholder, United Provinces, India; *m.* cousin; one *d.* *Educ.:* Meerut College; M.A.O. College, Aligarh; Allahabad University; Lincoln's Inn. Started practice at the Bar at Meerut. 1914; Hon. Secretary, U.P. Special War Fund, Meerut, 1915; Hon. Secretary of several other functions connected with war; member of Municipal Board, Meerut, 1916; Vice-Chairman, 1918; Chairman, 1928-31; member of Legislative Assembly from Meerut Division, 1921-23; member of Council of State, 1924-25; member of the 3rd Assembly, 1927-30; went as delegate to the Reserve Bank and Statutory Railway Board Committees, held in London in June and July 1933; became Leader of the United India Party in the Legislative Assembly; nominated to Council of State, Jan. 1935; elected to the Assembly from Agra Division, May 1935. *Recreations:* cricket, hockey, tennis. *Address:* Kothi Junnut Nishan, Meerut, U.P., India. [*Died Feb.* 1966.

YARBOROUGH, 6th Earl of (*cr.* 1837), **Lt.-Col. Hon. Marcus Herbert Pelham;** Baron Yarborough, Baron Worsley, 1794; *b.* 30 June 1893; *s.* of 4th Earl of Yarborough; *S.* brother 1948; *m.* 1919, Hon. Pamela Douglas Pennant; one *s.* one *d.* *Educ.:* Eton; Trinity College, Cambridge (B.A.). Served European War, 1914-18; Lincolnshire Yeomanry and 1st Life Guards, France, 1916-18; Diploma Agriculture, Oxford; served War of 1939-45. *Recreations:* hunting, shooting. *Heir:* *s.* Lord Worsley. *Address:* Brocklesby Park, Habrough, Lincolnshire. *T.:* Roxton 242. *Clubs:* Cavalry, Buck's. [*Died* 2 *Dec.* 1966.

YARROW, Sir Harold (Edgar), 2nd Bt., *cr.* 1916; G.B.E. 1958 (C.B.E. 1918); Chairman of Yarrow & Co. Ltd., Glasgow; Chairman of Clydesdale and North of Scotland Bank; Director of Midland Bank and of Yarrow (Africa) (Pty.) Ltd.; *b.* 11 Aug. 1884; *e. s.* of Sir Alfred Yarrow, 1st Bart. and 1st wife, Minnie Florence Franklin (*d.* 1922); *S.* father 1932; *m.* 1st, 1906, Eleanor Etheldreda (*d.* 1934), *d.* of late Rev. Canon W. H. M. H. Aitken; one *s.* three *d.*; 2nd, 1935, Rosalynde, twin *d.* of late Sir Oliver Lodge, F.R.S.; one *d.* *Educ.:* Bedford Grammar School. Served apprenticeship at Humphrys and Tennant, engineers, Deptford, and at Augustin Normand, Havre; entered works of Yarrow & Co., Ltd., shipbuilders. LL.D., Glasgow University, 1953. *Recreations:* shooting and golf. *Heir:* *s.* Major Eric Grant Yarrow, M.B.E. 1946 [*b.* 23 April 1920; *m.* 1st, 1951, Rosemary Ann (*d.* 1957), *yr. d.* of H. T. Young, Roehampton, S.W.15; 2nd, 1959, Annette Elizabeth Françoise, *d.* of Mr. and Mrs. A. J. E. Steven, Grianach, Ardgay, Ross-shire; twin *s.* Served Burma 1942-45 (M.B.E.)]. *Address:* Overton, Kilmacolm, Renfrewshire. *T.:* Kilmacolm 541. *Club:* Roya Automobile. [*Died* 19 *April* 1962

YATES, John Ernest, C.B. 1950; C.B.E. 1945; D.C.M. 1918; retd.; *b.* 5 Feb. 1887; *er. s.* of late John Yates, Birstall, Leicester; *m.* 1912, *d.* of J. E. Law, Chartered Acct., Northampton. *Educ.:* Alderman Newtons, Leicester. Entered G.P.O. at Leicester, 1902; G.P.O. Headquarters, 1925; Asst. Secretary, 1941; Director of Postal Services, 1947; retired from G.P.O. Hdqtrs. 1950. Served European War in Royal Engineers (Signals), 1915-19. Member Institute of Public Administration. Medal of Freedom with silver Palm (U.S.A.), 1946. *Recreation:* gardening. *Address:* Heathfield Hotel, 236 London Road, Leicester. *T.:* Leicester 75083. *Clubs:* Civil Service, Roadfarers'. [*Died* 23 *Feb.* 1969

YATES, Victor Francis; M.P. (Lab.) Ladywood Division of Birmingham since 1945; *b.* 19 Apr. 1900; unmarried. *Educ.:* Stirchley Elementary School; Industrial Training Course, Birmingham University; Residential Course, Ruskin College, Oxford. Membership Birmingham City Council 6 years; Governor King Edward's Grammar School. *Address:* 7 Umberslade Road, Selly Oak, Birmingham 29. *T.:* Selly Oak 1654. [*Died* 19 *Jan.* 1969.

YEAXLEE, Basil Alfred, C.B.E. 1946; M.A., B.Litt.(Oxon); B.A.; Ph.D.(Lond.); F.B.Ps.S.; University Reader Emeritus, Librarian and Tutor, Mansfield College, Oxford; *b.* 1883; *e. s.* of Alfred George Yeaxlee and Lila, *d.* of Samuel Read; *m.* 1st, 1913, Annie Julie Mary (*d.* 1955), *d.* of Thomas Edward Leadbeater, M.R.C.S., L.R.C.P., and Agnes Crouch Curtis; two *d.*; 2nd, 1958, Margaret Frances Addison, *d.* of late Harold Lewis Tatham. *Educ.:* privately; New College, London; St. Catherine's and Mansfield College, Oxford, 1905-09. Assistant Minister, Emmanuel

Congregational Church, Bootle, Lancs, 1909-1911; Educational Assistant, London Missionary Society, and Editor, United Council for Missionary Education, 1912; Editor, U.C.M.E., 1913-15; Editorial Secretary, National Council of Y.M.C.A.'s, 1915-18, and Secretary, Y.M.C.A. Universities Committee, 1917-20; Secretary, Educational Settlements Association, 1920-28; Member of Ministry of Reconstruction Adult Education Committee, 1917-19; Editor, the New Chronicle of Christian Education, 1928-30; Principal of Westhill Training College, Selly Oak, Birmingham, 1930-35; Editor of Religion in Education, 1933-57; University Reader in Educational Psychology, and Lecturer and Tutor in Dept. of Education, Oxford, 1935-49. Select-Preacher, Univ. of Cambridge, 1944; Secretary, Central Advisory Council for Adult Education in H.M. Forces, 1940-48; Secretary Education Committee, British Council of Churches, 1949-51; Research Secretary, Institute of Christian Education, 1949-53. *Publications:* An Educated Nation; Working Out the Fisher Act; Settlements and their Outlook; Spiritual Values in Adult Education (two vols.); Towards a Full-Grown Man (John Clifford Lectue, 1927); Life-long Education; The Approach to Religious Education; Religion and the Growing Mind; Handbook to the Cambridgeshire Syllabus of Religious Teaching; Handbook to the London Syllabus of Religious Education; The Handbook and Directory of Adult Education (Editor and contributor, 1926-27, 1928-29); Principal Editor and Contributor The Handbook of Christian Teaching, 1939, and Religious Education in Schools, 1954; contrib. to The Outline of Christianity, The Encyclopædia and Dictionary of Education and the Year Book of Education. *Recreation:* gardening. *Address:* Church Cottage, Islip, Oxford. *T.:* Kidlington 2929. [*Died* 23 *Aug.* 1967.

YEO-THOMAS, Wing Comdr. Forest Frederick Edward, G.C. 1946; M.C. and Bar 1944; Representative in France, Federation of British Industries, since 1950; *b.* London, 17 June 1901. Manager for Molyneux in France until War of 1939-45. Joined R.A.F. during the War and became secret agent ("The White Rabbit") about whom a book was written by Bruce Marshall, 1952. Returned to Molyneux after the War but left in 1948 for reasons of health. Légion d'Honneur, Croix de Guerre, Polish Cross of Merit. *Address:* c/o F.B.I., 6 Rue Halévy, Paris IX. *Clubs:* R.A.F.; St. Stephen's Green (Dublin); Union Interallieé (Paris). [*Died* 26 *Feb.* 1964.

YERBURY, Francis Rowland, O.B.E. 1952; Hon. A.R.I.B.A.; Hon. F.I.B.D.; *b.* 1885; *s.* of late Francis William Yerbury; *m.* 1914, Winifred Constance Bendall; one *s.* one *d.* Travelled extensively in Europe and America in the study of modern architecture; Secretary, The Architectural Association, 1911-37. A Founder of the Building Centre and first Director, 1931-61. President D'Honneur, Internat. Conf. of European Building Centres; Vice-Pres. Design and Industries Assoc. Retired. Comdr. of the Swedish Royal Order of Vasa; Knight of Danish Royal Order of the Dannebrog. *Publications:* Modern European Buildings; Modern Swedish Architecture; Old Domestic Architecture of Holland; Modern Danish Architecture; Modern English Homes; Lesser Known Architecture of Spain, etc.; General Editor of Housing, a European Survey of Working-class Housing. *Address:* 2 Clarendon Gardens, London Road, Newbury, Berks. *T.:* Newbury 3906. *Club:* Arts. [*Died* 7 *July* 1970.

YORK, Thomas John Pinches; Head Master of Merchant Taylors' School, Crosby, 1942-64; *b.* 1 Aug. 1898; *s.* of Leonard York; *m.* 1935, Enid Lena, *yr. d.* of late Maj. R. H. Langham, St. Leonards; one *s.* two *d.* *Educ.:* Hereford Cathedral Sch.; Emmanuel College, Cambridge. Rifle Brigade and R.F.C. 1917; Lieut. (Pilot) R.A.F., 1918-19; Asst. Master and a Sixth Form Master at Bedford School, 1923-31; Head Master of Derby School, 1931-42; Pres. Headmasters' Assoc., 1950. General Editor, Nelson's British History. *Publication:* Europe, 1898-1965, 1969. *Address:* 14 High Wickham, Hastings, Sussex. *T.:* Hastings 28198. [*Died* 25 *May* 1970.

YORKE, Francis Reginald Stevens, C.B.E. 1962; F.R.I.B.A.; Architect in private practice in London since 1930, in partnership with E. Rosenberg and C. S. Mardall since 1944; *b.* 3 Dec. 1906; *s.* of Francis Walter Bagnall Yorke and Mary Stevens; *m.* 1930, Thelma Austin Jones; twin *d.* *Educ.:* Chipping Campden; Birmingham Sch. of Architecture and Town Planning, Birmingham Univ. Principal buildings include: Sch. at Stevenage, 1947-49 (Festival of Britain award, 1951); Flats at Stevenage, 1952; residential area Harlow New Town, 1953; factory for Sigmund Pumps at Gateshead, 1948; Merthyr Tydfil College of Further Education, 1954; Bromsgrove Education Centre, 1955-; Hospitals at Londonderry, Crawley and Hull, 1952-61; Gatwick Airport, 1958; Leeds Central Colleges, 1953-. Founder-member of MARS group (Modern Architectural Research group), 1932. Editor of Specification. *Publications:* The Modern House, 1934; The Modern Flat, 1937; (joint) Planning for Re-Construction, 1944; (with F. Gibberd) Modern Flats, 1958. *Recreations:* Guernsey cattle breeding and fishing. *Address:* Greystoke Place, Fetter Lane, E.C.4. *Clubs:* Athenæum, Arts, Savage. [*Died* 10 *June* 1962.

YORKE, Brigadier Philip Gerard, D.S.O. 1919; late R.H.A.; *b.* 1882; *yr. s.* of late Lieut.-Colonel Philip Charles Yorke and late Emily Marion, *d.* of Henry Raikes, Llwynegrin Hall, Flintshire; *m.* 1914, Beryl Emilia, *d.* of late Brigadier-General A. H. C. Phillpotts, late R.H.A.; one *s.* one *d.* *Educ.:* Wellington Coll.; Royal Military Acad., Woolwich. Served European War, 1914-18 (despatches, D.S.O.); Bt. Lt.-Col. 1928; Lt.-Col. 1929; Col. 1932; Brig. 1935; Commander Royal Artillery 49th (West Riding) Division T.A. 1934-35; Brigadier, Royal Artillery, Southern Command, India, 1935-39; retired pay, 1939; recalled Active list Colonel R.A. Aldershot Command, Sept. 1939; retired list, 1941. Mérite Militaire (Spain), 1909. J.P. Somerset. *Address:* Marycourt, Childe Okeford, Blandford, Dorset. *T.:* Childe Okeford 242. *Club:* Army and Navy. [*Died* 27 *Jan.* 1968.

YORKE, Simon; *b.* 24 June 1903; *er. s.* of Philip and Louisa Matilda Yorke. *Educ.:* Cheltenham; Corpus Christi, Cambridge. B.A. Cantab. 1927; High Sheriff of Denbighshire, 1937. *Address:* Erthig, Wrexham. [*Died* 7 *May* 1966.

YOSHIDA, Shigeru; Prime Minister, Japan, 1946-47, and Oct. 1948-Dec. 1954; Foreign Minister, 1945-47, and Oct. 1948-Dec. 1954; Grand Cordon, Supreme Order of the Chrysanthemum, Japan, 1964; *b.* Tokyo, 22 Sept. 1878; *s.* of late Kenzo Yoshida, Tokyo; *m.* Yukiko (author of Whispering Leaves in Grosvenor Square, 1936-37, 1938), *d.* of late Count Makino; two *s.* two *d.* *Educ.:* Law College, Tokyo Imperial University, graduated, 1906. Vice-Consul of Japanese Consulate at Tientsin, 1906; Mukden, 1907; Consulate-General, London, 1908-09; Third Secretary, Rome, 1909-12; Consul, Antung, 1912-16; Consul Tsinan, 1918; on delegation to Paris Peace Conference, 1919; First Secretary, London, 1920-22; Consul-General, Tientsin, 1922-25; Mukden, 1925-28; Vice-Minister for Foreign

Affairs, 1928-30; Ambassador to Italy, 1930-1932; Delegate to Lausanne Reparation Conference, 1932; to Assembly, League of Nations, 1932; on Mission to Europe and America, 1934; Ambassador Extraordinary and Plenipotentiary at the Court of St. James', 1936-38. *Recreation:* riding. *Address:* Kanagawa-ken, Japan. *Club:* Tokio. [*Died* 20 *Oct.* 1967.

YOUARD, Very Rev. Wilfrid Wadham, M.A.; *b.* 1869; *s.* of Rev. H. G. Youard, sometime Vicar of Whitegate, Cheshire; *m.* 1901, Evelyn Constance (*d.* 1962), *d.* of G. F. Malcolmson; one *s.* *Educ.:* Exeter Coll., Oxf.; Lichfield Theological College. Vicar of St. John's, Brighton, 1902-8; Vicar of East Grinstead, 1908-24; Dean and Vicar of Battle, 1924-45. [*Died* 27 *Aug.* 1964.

YOUENS, Rev. Canon Fearnley Algernon Cyril, M.A. (Oxon); Hon. C.F.; Canon Residentiary and Capitular Treasurer of Sheffield Cathedral, 1939, Canon Emeritus, 1965; Vicar of Brodsworth, nr. Doncaster, since 1934; *b.* 29 August 1886; *s.* of James and Annie Youens; *m.* 1913, Dorothy Mary, *o. d.* of William and Annie Ross, Blackpool; four *s.* two *d.* *Educ.:* Oxford; Lincoln. Curate of St. Paul's, Helsby, Ches., 1908-10; South Shore, Blackpool, 1910-13; Chaplain, Anglican Church, Bologna, 1914-15; Curate, Brownswood Park P.C.L., 1915-16; C.F., 1916-21; Org. Sec., Nat. Soc., 1921-30; Sec. of Bishop of Sheffield's 100,000 gns. Appeal, 1930-34; Hon. Clerical Secretary, Sheffield Diocesan Trust and Board of Finance, 1934-38; Member of the Consultative Committee for National Society, 1933; Member of York Convocation and Church Assembly, 1939. Director, Church of England Pensions Board, 1948; Assessor, York Convocation, 1953. *Publications:* An Analysis of Hooker's Ecclesiastical Policy, 1912; The Preacher's Handbook, 1916. *Recreation:* golf. *Address:* Brodsworth Vicarage, near Doncaster. *Club:* Royal Commonwealth Society. [*Died* 29 *Oct.* 1967.

YOUNG, Sir Alastair (Spencer Templeton), 2nd Bt., *cr.* 1945; D.L.; Chairman, James Templeton & Co. Ltd., Glasgow; *b.* 28 June 1918; *s.* of Sir Arthur Stewart Leslie Young, 1st Bt., and Dorothy Spencer; *S.* father 1950; *m.* 1945, Dorothy Constance Marcelle, *widow* of Lt. J. H. Grayburn, V.C., and *d.* of late Lt.-Col. C. E. Chambers; one *s.* one *d.* *Educ.:* Rugby; Trinity College, Oxford. Served War of 1939-45. D.L. Dunbarton, 1962. *Recreation:* yachting. *Heir:* *s.* Stephen Stewart Templeton, *b.* 24 May 1947. *Address:* Ardtarman, Rhu, Dunbartonshire. *Clubs:* Western (Glasgow); Roy. Yacht Sqdn. [*Died* 15 *Oct.* 1963.

YOUNG, Maj.-Gen. Bernard Keith, C.B.E. 1943; M.C. 1917; retired as Director-General of Royal Soc. for the Prevention of Accidents (1951-59); *b.* 11 March 1892; 2nd *s.* of late E. A. Young, Tan y Bryn, Bangor, N. Wales; *m.* 1916, Eileen Mary, *d.* of late W. Dawson, M.Inst.C.E.; two *d.* *Educ.:* Wellington Coll.; R.M.A., Woolwich. 2nd Lt. R.E. 1912; European War, 1914-18, France, Salonica, Palestine; Egyptian Army in the Sudan, 1918-19; Col. 1937; Temp. Brig. 1940; Comdr. Inf. Bde. 1940-1941; Chief Engineer, 1941-45; Mid-East, 1942; Temp. Maj.-Gen. 1943; B.N.A.F. and A.F.H.Q., 1943; retired pay, 1945. *Address:* 2 Mount Pleasant, Guildford, Surrey. *T.:* Guildford 66910. *Club:* United Service. [*Died* 28 *Oct.* 1969.

YOUNG, Douglas: Consul-General (retired 1941); *b.* 11 July 1882; *y. s.* of Charles Woodrow Young; *m.* 2nd, 1929, Nina, *o. d.* of late S. I. Grinevitch, Poltava, Russia. *Educ.:* St. Dunstan's College, S.E.; Trinity College, Cambridge; Paris and Hanover. Passed examination for General Consular Service, 1907; served at Zanzibar, Sevastopol, Bogotá, San Francisco, Rustchuk, Bukarest, Archangel (1915-18), unemployed 1919-24, Sofia, Malaga, Basle and Luanda (local rank Consul-Gen.). *Recreations:* thinking and reading; antiques; numismatics (S.A. Numismatic Soc.). *Address:* 2 Somerfield, Station Rd., Somerset West, C.P. S. Africa. *T.:* 162. [*Died* 30 *April* 1967.

YOUNG, Frederick Hugh, O.B.E. 1918; M.D. (Cantab.), F.R.C.P. (London); Consulting Physician Charing Cross Hospital, Scottish Red Cross Sanatorium, Tor-na-Dee, the Brompton Hospital and St. Bartholomew's Hospital; *b.* 1892; *s.* of F. W. Young, Liverpool; *m.* 1928, Stella Mary, *d.* of E. F. Robinson, Oxted; one *s.* one *d.* *Educ.:* Shrewsbury School; Trinity College, Cambridge; St. Bartholomew's Hospital, London. Member: Association of Physicians of Great Britain and Ireland; Thoracic Society. Weber-Parkes Prize, R.C.P. *Publications:* articles in medical press on tuberculosis and diseases of the respiratory system. *Recreations:* golf, gardening. *Address:* Martins, Icehouse Wood, Oxted, Surrey. *T.:* Oxted 3763. *Club:* Bath. [*Died* 22 *Sept.* 1969.

YOUNG, Gerard Mackworth-, C.I.E. 1929; F.S.A.; Indian Civil Service, retired; Corr. Mem. of the Archæological Institute of Germany; Hon. Fellow of Archæological Soc. of Greece; Commander Order of King George I of Greece; *b.* 7 Apr. 1884; *e. s.* of Sir W. Mackworth Young, K.C.S.I.; *m.* 1916, Natalie, *d.* of Rt. Hon. Sir Walter Hely-Hutchinson, P.C., G.C.M.G.; two *s.* two *d.* *Educ.:* Eton; King's College, Cambridge (B.A. 1906, M.A. 1912). Entered I.C.S. 1908; Under-Secretary to Government, Punjab, 1913-15; Under-Secretary to Government of India, Home Department, 1916-19; Deputy Commissioner of Delhi, 1921-24; Secretary to Government of India, Army Department, 1926-32. Student at British School of Archæology in Athens, 1932-36; Director, 1936-46. Served in British Legation, Athens, 1939-41; re-employed as Joint Secretary, War Dept., Govt. of India, 1941-44; Hon. Officer, Archæological Survey of India, 1944-45. Assumed surname of Mackworth-Young in lieu of Young by deed poll, 1947. *Publications:* articles in various journals; The Epigrams of Callimachus, 1934; Archaic Marble Sculpture from the Acropolis (with Humfry Payne), 1936, and photographs in other archæological publications; What Happens in Singing, 1953. *Address:* Bryn Brith, King's Rd., Windsor, Berks. [*Died* 28 *Nov.* 1965.

YOUNG, Major-General Gordon Drummond, C.I.E. 1947; O.B.E. 1937; M.C. 1918; A.M.I.Mech.E.; *b.* 25 Apr. 1896; *s.* of William Drummond Young, artist, Edinburgh; *m.* 1922, Theodora Mary Elizabeth, *d.* of Gerald Hume Wright, Ash Vale, Surrey; one *s.* two *d.* *Educ.:* George Watson's College, Edinburgh. Mobilized as a Despatch Rider, 4th Aug. 1914, with Lothians & Border Horse, Yeomanry; European War, 1914-18, commissioned to 5th Bn. Royal Scots, 1915; transferred to R.A.S.C., 1916; attached Royal Artillery, 1916-18; served France and Belgium (M.C.). Transferred Indian Army, R.I.A.S.C., 1927; G.S.O. 2, Waziristan District, 1928; Dep. Asst. Dir. Transport Wazir Force and Waziristan District, 1935-39 (despatches twice, O.B.E.). War of 1939-45, D.D.M.E. 10th Army, 1941-1942 (despatches); D.D.M.E., G.H.Q. India, 1943-45; Brigadier, I.E.M.E., H.Q. Southern Command, India, 1945-47; Director of Mechanical Engineering, Supreme Headquarters, India, 1947 (C.I.E.). *Recreations:* riding, shooting, golf, amateur theatricals. *Address:* Orchards, The Avenue, Fleet,

Hants. *T.:* Fleet 397. *Club:* Naval and Military. [*Died* 27 *July* 1964.

YOUNG, Hilda Beatrice (Sister Pauline), C.B.E. 1917; Sister of Charity of St. Vincent de Paul; State Registered Nurse, S.C.M.; M.C.S.P.; Member, Society of Radiographers; *e. d.* of John McKenzie Young, Llandudno, North Wales. *Address:* St. Vincents, Ladbroke Terrace, Notting Hill Gate, W.11. [*Died* 5 *Oct.* 1967.

YOUNG, James, D.S.O. 1919; M.D., F.R.C.S. (Ed.), F.R.C.O.G.; Emeritus Professor of Obstetrics and Gynæcology, University of London; late Director of Obstetrical and Gynæcological Unit, British Postgraduate Medical School, Hammersmith, W.12; Consulting Physician, Royal Maternity Hospital; Consulting Gynæcologist, Royal Infirmary, Edinburgh; Hon. Fellow Edinburgh Obstetrical Society and American Association of Obstetricians and Gynæcologists; Corresponding Fellow of German Gynæcological Society; Fellow Royal Society of Medicine, London; Fellow, Medico-Chirurgical Society, Edinburgh; late Governor, Imperial Cancer Research Fund; Editor, Journal of Obstetrics and Gynæcology of the British Commonwealth; late Examiner for Roy. Coll. of Surgeons, Edinburgh, and Central Midwives Bd. of Scotland; *b.* 1883; *m.* 1919, Eva, *widow* of G. Harvey Webb, Capt. R.A.M.C.; two *s.* two *d. Educ.:* Heriot's School and University, Edinburgh; M.B. with First Class Honours 1905; M.D. with gold medal, 1910. Formerly Resident Surgeon and Gynæcologist, Tutor in Gynæcology, Gynæcologist, Royal Infirmary, Edinburgh; and Physician, Royal Maternity and Simpson Memorial Hospital, Edinburgh; late Lieut.-Colonel R.A.M.C. (T.), served in Gallipoli, Egypt, Palestine, and France, 1915-1919 (D.SO., despatches twice). *Publications:* With the 52nd Division in Three Continents; Text-Book of Gynæcology, 10th edition; Practical Gynæcology for Nurses and Students (with Netta Stewart); Combined Text-book of Obstetrics and Gynæcology (in collaboration), 5th edition; articles in medical journals. *Address:* Little Plaston, Ditchling, Sussex. *T.:* Hassocks 2125. [*Died* 14 *May* 1963.

YOUNG Major-Gen. James Vernon, C.B. 1946; C.B.E. 1944; Vice-Pres. Hamilton Cotton Co. Ltd., Hamilton, Ontario, Canada; *b.* 13 Oct. 1891; *s.* of James M. and G. A. Young; *m.* 1915, Willmot M. Holton; three *s.* (and one killed in action), one *d. Educ.:* Lakefield Preparatory School; Upper Canada College; Royal Military College. Served European War, 1914-18; Master General Ordnance, Canada, 1942-45; Cotton Manufacturer between wars. *Recreations:* golf, tennis. *Address:* Ancaster, Ontario, Canada. *T.:* Ancaster 734. *Clubs:* Hamilton, Hamilton Golf & Country (Hamilton, Ont.). [*Died* 12 *Sept.* 1961.

YOUNG, Brig.-General Sir Julian Mayne, Kt., *cr.* 1941; C.B. 1923; C.M.G. 1915; D.S.O. 1917; *b.* 6 Aug. 1872; *m.* 1902, Gwendoline Mary, *d.* of G. H. B. Young; two *d. Educ.:* Repton School. Entered Army, Lancashire Fusiliers, 1893; Capt., R.A.S.C., 1901; Adjutant, 1908-10; Major, 1911; Lieut.-Colonel, 1915; Colonel, 1919; specially employed War Office, 1912; D.A.Q.M.G. 1914; A.D.T. 1915; D.D.T. 1916; Director of Transport, 1917 (Brig.-Gen.), and Brig.-Gen. Q.M.G.'s Branch, 1918; served S. Africa, 1899-1901 (Queen's medal 5 clasps); European War, 1914-17 (despatches, C.M.G., D.S.O.; Order of St. Maurice and St. Lazarus, Italy; Order of Leopold II of Belgium); retired, 1926; Bursar Repton School, 1926-36. Chief Divisional Food Officer, London and Home Counties, 1940-44 (Divl. Food Officer, London, 1939). *Address:* Edgeworth, Milford-on-Sea, Lymington, Hants. [*Died* 19 *Oct.* 1961.

YOUNG, Brig.-General Julius Ralph, C.B. 1921; late R.E.; *b.* 4 Oct. 1864; 2nd *s.* of late Maj.-Gen. Ralph Young, R.E.; *m.* 1901, Ellinor May Stoward (*d.* 1940); one *d. Educ.:* Clifton College. Commissioned in Royal Engineers, 1884; served South Africa, 1899-1900 (despatches thrice); European War, 1914-19; retired, 1921. *Address:* 53A Carlton Hill, N.W.8. [*Died* 9 *July* 1961.

YOUNG, Brig. Keith de Lorentz, C.I.E. 1942; M.C.; *b.* 5 Aug. 1889; *s.* of Colonel E. A. Young, J.P., Steyning, Sussex; *m.* Ada Lilian, *d.* of H. P. Tollinton, C.I.E., I.C.S.; two *s. Educ.:* Lancing; R.M.C. Sandhurst. 2nd Lt. North Staffordshire Regt., 1909; Lt. Indian Army, 1912; Capt., 1915; Major, 1925; Bt. Lt.-Col., 1931; Lt.-Col. 1934; Col. 1937. Served War of 1914-1918 (France); Staff College, Quetta, 1924; Served on N.W. Frontier, India, 1938; Commandant Indian Military Academy, Dehra Dun; A.D.C. to the King, 1940-43; retired 1943. Re-employed in England, 1943-45. *Address:* Little Court, Rolvenden, Cranbrook, Kent. *T.:* Rolvenden 337. [*Died* 11 *Jan.* 1962.

YOUNG, Norman Egerton, C.B 1953; C.M.G. 1946; M.C. 1919; *b.* 1892; *s.* of late Sir W. Mackworth Young, K.C.S.I. *Educ.:* Eton; Corpus Christi College, Oxford (M.A.). Served European War, 1914-18, with 9th (S) Battalion Royal Sussex Regiment and H.Q. 73rd Inf. Bde. (despatches, M.C.), wounded and P.O.W. in Germany, Mar.-Nov. 1918; entered Treasury 1919; Sec. Cttee. on the Currency and Bank of England Note Issues, 1925; an Asst. Financial Secretary, Sudan Government, 1929-31; Imperial Defence College, 1932; Financial Adviser, British Embassy, Paris, 1939-40; British Government Director, Suez Canal Co., 1939-45. Overseas on other financial duties or missions to: Buenos Aires, 1933; Hong Kong, 1935-36; Rangoon, 1947; Sydney, Tokyo, Singapore, Bangkok and New Delhi, 1948-49; Comptroller General, National Debt Office, 1951-54. *Recreations:* yacht cruising, golf. *Address:* c/o Lloyds Bank Ltd., 16 St. James's St., S.W.1. *Clubs:* Brooks's, United University; Royal Wimbledon Golf; Royal Cornwall Yacht. [*Died* 20 *Dec.* 1964.

YOUNG, Owen D.; Hon. Chairman General Electric Co.; *b.* Van Hornesville, N.Y., 27 Oct. 1874; *s.* of Jacob Smith Young and Ida Brandow, Van Hornesville, Herkimer Co., New York; *m.* 1st, 1898, Josephine Sheldon Edmonds (*d.* 1935); three *s.* one *d.*; 2nd, Mrs. Louise P. Clark. *Educ.:* St. Lawrence University, A.B. 1894, D.H.L. 1923; Boston University Law School, LL.B. 1896; Hon. LL.D. numerous U.S.A. universities; D.C.S., New York University, 1927; Litt.D. Rollins College, 1936. Began practice of law in Boston, 1896; Instructor in Common Law Pleadings, Boston University, 1896-1903; member firm of Tyler and Young, 1907-13; came to New York as Counsel for the General Electric Company, 1913; Vice-President and General Counsel, 1913-22; Chairman of the Board, 1922-39, and 1942-44, now Hon. Chairman; Chairman of the Board, Radio Corporation of America, 1919-29, Chairman of the Executive Committee, 1930-33; Trustee Rockefeller Foundation, 1928-40; Director American and Foreign Power Co.; New York Life Insurance Co.; Chairman, Advisory Board, Transportation Study National Resources Planning Board, 1940-1942; Member, National Patent Planning Commission since 1941; Member, Regional Committee, War Manpower Commission,

1942-45; Class B. Director Federal Reserve Bank of New York, 1923-27; Class C Director, 1927-40; Deputy Chairman, 1927-38; Chairman, 1938-40; alternate member President Wilson's First Industrial Conference; member, Second Industrial Conference, 1919; member, President Harding's Conference on Unemployment, 1921; Chairman, Committee on Unemployment and Business Cycles, 1922; member, First Committee of Experts appointed by Reparation Commission, 1924; Agent-General for Reparation Payments, *ad interim*, 1924; Unofficial Adviser London Conference of Premiers, 1924; Chairman, American Section International Chamber of Commerce, 1925-28, now member Executive Com.; Hon. Economic Adviser Nationalist Govt. of China, 1928; Chairman, Second Committee of Experts appointed by Reparation Commission and German Government, 1929; member, Executive Committee National Business Survey Conference called by President Hoover, 1929; member National Advisory Council National Youth Administration; League of Nations; Member of Board of Regents, Univ. of State of New York, 1934-46; Chm. State of N.Y. temp. commn. on Need for State Univ., 1946-1948; Member: President's Non-Partisan Advisory Cttee. on Foreign Aid; Commn. on Organization of Exec. Branch of Govt. (Hoover Commn.), 1948. Pres.: Holstein-Friesian Assoc. of America, 1948-49; Dairy Cattle Breeding Research Foundation; Dir. American Broadcasting Co. 4th Class Order of the Rising Sun (Japan), 1921; Cross of Commander of the Legion of Honour (France), 1924; Cross of Commander of the Order of Leopold (Belgium), 1925; First Order of the German Red Cross, 1925; Gold Medal, National Institute of Social Sciences, 1923; Roosevelt Medal, 1929; Grand Cross of the Crown, Belgium, 1930; Gold Medal, Society of Arts and Sciences, 1936. *Recreations:* books, fishing. *Address:* Van Hornesville, N.Y., U.S.A.; 570 Lexington Avenue, New York, N.Y., U.S.A. *T.A.:* Genetric. *T.:* Plaza 5-1311. *Clubs:* Harvard, Manhattan, University, Engineers (New York); Tavern (Boston); Mohawk (Schenectady).
[*Died* 11 *July* 1962

YOUNG, William; *see* Addenda: II.

YOUNGMAN, William, D.Sc., Ph.D.; *b.* 6 Aug. 1880; *s.* of William and Catherine Youngman; *m.* 1922, Kathleen Capon; one *s.* one *d.* *Educ.:* East Anglian School; privately; University of London. Professor of Biology, Agra College, 1910; Canning College, Lucknow, 1911; Former Fellow of the Univ. of Allahabad and Member of the Senate; Economic Botanist to the Government of the United Provinces, India, 1918; to the Government of the Central Provinces, 1922; Nominated by Viceroy a Member of the Indian Central Cotton Committee; carried out extensive research and work for the improvement of cotton crop in Central India; Member Legislative Council, Ceylon, 1930-31; Director of Agriculture, Ceylon; Editor of the Tropical Agriculturist, Chairman, Rubber Research Scheme, Ceylon, and of the Coconut Research Scheme, Ceylon, 1930-35. *Publications:* various scientific papers. *Recreations:* tramping, has travelled extensively in the Himalayas; Natural History, shooting. *Address:* 16 Lattice Avenue, Ipswich.
[*Died* 3 *June* 1963.

YUSUF, Sir Mohamad, Kt. 1915; *see* Addenda: II.

YUSUF, Nawab Sir Muhammad, Kt., *cr.* 1933; *b.* June 1895; *s.* of Nawab Muhammad Abdul Majid, C.I.E., and Aziz-un-nisan Begum; *m.* 1910; no *c.* *Educ.:* Muir Central College and Christian College, Allahabad. Called to Bar, Lincoln's Inn, 1914; President, Agra Province, Zamindars' Association; Member Legislative Assembly; Ex-Minister for Local Self-Govt., U.P., India. *Recreations:* cricket, tennis. *Address:* Yusuf Castle, Jaunpur, India; 2 Nawab Yusuf Road, Allahabad, U.P., India. *Club:* United Service (Allahabad).
[*Deceased.*

Z

ZAROUBIN, Georgi Nikolaevitch; A Deputy Foreign Minister, U.S.S.R. since 1958; *b.* 1900; *m.* 1926, Elizaveta Kulkova; one *s.* *Educ.:* Moscow Textile Institute; Stalin Industrial Academy, Occupied various posts in industry, 1924-27; Director of Industrial Academy, 1933-38; Assistant General Commissar of Soviet Sector of International Fair in New York, 1938-40; Ambassador to Canada, 1944-46; Ambassador in Great Britain, 1947-52; Ambassador of the U.S.S.R. to the United States, 1952-58. *Address:* The Ministry of Foreign Affairs, Moscow, U.S.S.R.
[*Died Nov.* 1968.

ZEALLEY, Sir Alec (Thomas Sharland), Kt. 1957; Chairman Remploy Corporation Ltd., 1956-63 (Vice-Chairman, 1964); *b.* 28 January 1893; 2nd *s.* of John and Mary Zealley; *m.* 1920, Nellie Maude, *d.* of Thomas King; three *s.* one *d.* *Educ.:* Wellington School, Somerset; University College, London. Research chemist, Brunner Mond & Co., 1920; General Works Manager, Delegate Director, and Divisional Board Chm., Billingham Div., Imperial Chemical Industries, 1926-51; Director, Imperial Chemical Industries Ltd., 1951-55. Fellow of University College, London, 1960. *Recreations:* walking, archæology (local). *Address:* Coles Mill, Colyton, Devon. *T.:* Colyton 233.
[*Died* 20 *April* 1970.

ZERNIKE, Professor Frits, Sc.D.; retired as Professor of Theoretical and Technical Physics and Theoretical Mechanics, University of Groningen (1910-58); *b.* Amsterdam, 16 July 1888; *s.* of C. F. A. Zernike and Anne (*née* Dieperink); *m.* 1929, Dora van Bommel van Vloten (*d.* 1945); two *c.*; *m.* 1954, Lena Baanders, *widow* of Dr. S. Koperberg. *Educ.:* Univ. of Amsterdam (Sc.D.). Spent entire career at Univ. of Groningen, working on statistical mechanics and optics; Asst. in astronomical laboratory of Prof. J. C. Kapteyn, 1910; Lecturer in Theoretical Physics, University of Groningen, 1915. Visiting Professor, Johns Hopkins Univ., Baltimore, 1948. Developed phase contrast microscope and galvanometer. Mem. Roy. Netherlands Acad. of Sciences, 1946; Hon. Mem. Roy. Microscopical Soc., Lond., 1950; Foreign Mem. Royal Society, 1956. Hon. M.D., University of Amsterdam, 1952; Hon. Sc.D., University of Poitiers, 1955. Gold Medal, Science Faculty, Univ. of Groningen, 1908; Gold Medal Dutch Soc. of Sciences Haarlem), 1912; Rumford Medal, Brit. Roy. Soc., 1952; Nobel Prize for Physics, 1953; Officer, Legion of Honour (France), 1954. *Publications:* Contrib. to learned jls. of Holland, Germany, America, Gt. Brit., etc. *Address:* Physics Laboratory, 34 Westersingel, Groningen, Netherlands ;(home) Verschuurlaan 5, Groningen, Netherlands.
[*Died* 10 *March* 1966.

ZETLAND, 2nd Marquess of (*cr.* 1892). **Lawrence John Lumley Dundas,** K.G., 1942; P.C. 1922; G.C.S.I. *cr.* 1922; G.C.I.E., *cr.* 1917; F.B.A.; Bt. 1762; Baron Dundas, 1794; Earl of Zetland, 1838; Earl of Ronaldshay (U.K.), 1892; *b.* 11 June 1876; *e. surv.* *s.* of 1st Marquess and Lady Lilian Selina Elizabeth Lumley (*d.* 1943), *d.* of 9th Earl of Scarbrough; *S.* father 1929; *m.* 1907, Cicely, 2nd *d.* of Colonel Mervyn Archdale, late 12th Lancers; one *s.* (and one lost his life serving in the R.A.F.) three *d.* *Educ.:*

Harrow; Trinity College, Cambridge. Travelled Ceylon, 1898; India, 1899-1900; Persia, 1900-01; Asiatic Turkey, Persia, Central Asia, Siberia, 1903; Japan, China, Burma, 1906-07; A.D.C. Viceroy's Staff, India, 1900; Capt. 1st N. Riding of Yorkshire Volunteer Artillery; hon. Col. late 62nd (Northumbrian) A.A. Bde., R.A. (T.A.); Major late 4th Bn. Green Howards; M.P. (U.) Hornsey Division Middlesex, 1907-16; Member Royal Commission on the Public Services in India, 1912-14; Governor of Bengal, 1917-22; Secretary of State for India, 1935-40, and Secretary of State for Burma, 1937-40; bore Sword of State at Coronation of King George VI.; President R.G.S., 1922-25, and a Trustee of the Soc. until 1947; Pres., Royal India Soc., 1923-50; Pres. Royal Asiatic Society, 1928-31; Pres. Soc. for the Study of Religions, 1930-51; an Hon. Vice-Pres. Royal Central Asian Society; a Member of the Indian Round Table Conference, 1930-31; and of the Parliamentary Joint Select Committee on India, 1933; Chairman of the National Trust, 1931-45; Lord Lieutenant and Custos Rotulorum, North Riding of Yorkshire, 1945-51; Governor National Bank of Scotland, 1940-52; Provincial Grand Master Freemasons of the North and East Ridings of Yorkshire, 1923-56; a Steward of the Jockey Club, 1928-31; Hon. LL.D., Cambridge; Hon. Litt.D., Leeds; Hon. LL.D., Glasgow; K.St.J. *Publications:* Sport and Politics under an Eastern Sky, 1902; On the Outskirts of Empire in Asia, 1904; A Wandering Student in the Far East, 1908; An Eastern Miscellany, 1911; Lands of the Thunderbolt; Sikhim Chumbi and Bhutan, 1923; India, a Bird's-Eye View, 1924; The Heart of Aryavarta, awarded the gold medal of the Royal Empire Society, 1925; The Life of Lord Curzon, being the authorised biography of Marquis Curzon of Kedleston, K.G., 1928; The Letters of Disraeli to Lady Bradford and Lady Chesterfield, 1929; The Life of Lord Cromer, being the authorised biography of Evelyn Baring, 1st Earl of Cromer, 1932; Steps towards Indian Home Rule, 1935; Essayez, 1957. *Heir:* *s.* Earl of Ronaldshay. *Address:* Aske, Richmond, Yorkshire. *Clubs:* Turf; Jockey (Newmarket).

[*Died* 6 *Feb.* 1961.

ZEUNER, Frederick Everard, Ph.D., D.Sc. (London), F.S.A., F.G.S., F.Z.S.; Professor of Environmental Archæology in University of London since 1946; *b.* Berlin, 8 Mar. 1905; *s.* of Friedrich Hugo Zeuner and Melanie Franziska Tippmann; *m.* 1931, Ilse Henrietta Gustava Levin; two *s.* *Educ.:* Univs. of Berlin, Tübingen, Breslau. Assistant, Institute of Geology and Palæontology, Breslau University, 1925; Ph.D. summa cum laude (Breslau), 1927; venia legendi in Geology and Palæontology (Breslau), 1930; Head Assistant and Lecturer, University of Freiburg i. Br., 1931; Research Associate in palæontology, British Museum (Natural History), London, 1934; Lecturer in Geochronology, London University Institute of Archæology, 1936; war work with Anti-Locust Research Centre, London. Member: Acad. Sci. Halle (Leopoldina); Foreign Member: Acad. Sci., Göttingen, Mayence; Istituto Ital. di Paleont. Umana; Instituto Ital. Preistoria; Archæol. Surv., India; Anthrop. Gesellschaft, Vienna; American Ent. Soc., Phila.; Pres. Geologische Vereinigung, 1954, Vice-Pres. 1951-53, 1955-57; Pres. Internat. Dating Commission INQUA, 1957-; Vice-Pres., Prehist. Soc., 1960; R. Anthrop. Inst., 1963; Pres. Congress Quaternar. Septentrionaux Calais, 1961; Maharaja Shivajirao Lectr., Baroda, 1961; Hon. Prof., Univ. of Baroda, 1962; Guest Professor: Holland, 1938; Madrid, 1953; Berlin, 1954; Vienna, 1956; Laguna, 1958. Archaeological and geological field work in various European countries, Levant, N. Africa, Canaries, India, Australia, E. Africa. *Publications:* Fossil Orthoptera Ensifera (Brit. Mus., 1939); The Pleistocene Period, 1945, 1958; Dating the Past, 1946, 4th edn. 1958 (some foreign edns. of above pubns.); History of Domesticated Animals, 1963; other books and over 200 papers. *Recreation:* nature study. *Address:* London University Institute of Archaeology, Gordon Square, W.C.1.

[*Died* 5 *Nov.* 1963.

ZILLIACUS, Konni; M.P. (Lab.) Gorton Division of Manchester since 1955; author, lecturer, journalist; *b.* Kobe, Japan, 13 Sept. 1894; *s.* of Konni Zilliacus, author and journalist, Finnish-Swedish, and Lilian Maclaurin Grafe, Scottish-American. *Educ.:* primary schooling: Brooklyn, N.Y., Finland and Sweden; secondary schooling; Bedales School, Petersfield, Hants; Yale Univ. Grad. first of his year (Ph.B.) 1915. Served European War, 1914-18. Royal Flying Corps and General List (Intelligence Officer, British Military Mission, Siberia), 1917-19. Member of Information Section, League of Nations Secretariat, 1919-39; Ministry of Information, 1939-45. M.P. for Gateshead, 1945-50 (Lab. 1945-49, Ind May 1949-Feb. 1950). Expelled from Labour Party, May 1949, for persistent opposition to Government's foreign policy; re-admitted Feb. 1952. *Publications:* The League of Nations; The League, the Protocol and the Empire; The Origin, Structure and Working of the League of Nations; Inquest on Peace; The Road to War; Why the League Has Failed; Why We Are Losing The Peace; Between Two Wars?; The Mirror of the Past (Eng. 1944, U.S.A. 1946); Can The Tories Win The Peace, and Why They Lost The Last One; The Mirror of the Present; I Choose Peace (Penguin Special); Tito of Yugoslavia; A New Birth of Freedom?; Mutiny Against Madness; Challenge to Fear; contrib. to periodicals. *Address:* 75 Warrington Crescent, W.9.

[*Died* 6 *July* 1967.

ZOPPI, Count Vittorio; Knight Grand Cross Ordine al Merito della Repubblica Italiana; Hon. G.C.V.O.; *b.* Novara, Italy, 23 February 1898; *s.* of late Gen. Ottavio Zoppi and Ida Poggi. *Educ.:* University of Turin, Italy (Degree in Law). Entered diplomatic service, 1923; served in Consulates at Munich, Algiers, Bona and Nairobi, 1923-28; First Secretary at Addis Ababa, 1928-30; Political dept., Ministry of Foreign Affairs, Rome, 1930-39; during this period acted as Secretary to League of Nations' Permanent Cttee. for Mandated Territories (22nd, 23rd, 24th and 25th sessions); Counsellor to Italian Embassy in Madrid, 1939-42; Consul General in Vichy, 1942-43; recalled to Ministry, May 1943; Director General Political Department, Ministry of Foreign Affairs, Rome, 1945-48; Secretary General to Ministry of Foreign Affairs, 1948-55; Ambassador to the Court of St. James's, 1955-61; Permanent Representative of Italy to U.N., 1961-63; retired. *Address:* Via Petrolini 36, Rome, Italy.

[*Died* 6 *May* 1967

ZOUCHE, 17th Baroness, *cr.* 1308; of Haryngworth; **Mary Cecil Frankland,** *widow* of Sir Frederick Frankland, 10th Bart.; one *s.* one *d.* (*er. s.* killed on active service, 1944); *S. cousin* 1917. *Heir:* *g.s.* Sir James Assheton Frankland. *Address:* Castle Mead, Windsor. *T.:* 64953.

[*Died* 25 *Sept.* 1965.

ZWEIG, Arnold; Author; *b.* Gross-Glogau, Prussia, 10 Nov. 1887; *s.* of Adolf Zweig, saddler and remover, and Bianca van Spandow; *m.* 1916, Margarete Beatrice Zweig; two *s.* *Educ.:* non-classical (technical) school of the 1st grade, Kattowitz, Upper Silesia; studied philosophy, modern languages (English and French) and German literature during seven years at German Universities of Breslau, Munich, Berlin, Göttingen, Rostock, Tübingen. Interest in history,

arts, modern psychology. During European War, private in labour battalion in northern France, Serbia, Verdun; from 1917 till armistice in the press section of Ober-Ost; after the War lived in Upper Bavaria for restoration of his strength; was forced to leave his home in Starnberg by the Hitler Putsch of 1923; lived in Berlin till 1933, whence he was expelled by the same movement; went, after some months of European emigration, to Palestine, where he resided until 1948; has since lived in Berlin. Pres. Deutsche Akad. der Künste, 1950-53, Hon. Pres. 1957-; Pres. E. and W. German P.E.N. Centre, 1958 (P.E.N. Centre of German Democratic Republic, 1967-). Kleist Prize, 1915, for his tragedy Die Sendung Semaels; National Prize, 1951; Lenin Peace Prize, 1958; Dr.phil. *h.c.* Leipzig, 1952; Prof., 1962. *Publications:* before 1914: Claudia (novel) short stories, and two plays; after the War: more plays and short stories, essays on Anti-Semitism (Caliban or Politics and Passions), 1926; The Case of Sergeant Grischa, 1927 (novel); Young Woman of 1914, 1931 (novel); De Vriendt goes home, 1932 (novel); Playthings of Time (short stories), 1934; Education before Verdun, 1935 (novel); Crowning of a King, 1937 (novel); Insulted and Exiled, 1937 (published in German, 1934); (novel) Versunkene Tage, 1938; The Axe of Wandsbek, 1943; Fahrt zum Acheron, 1951; Westlandsaga, 1952; Die Feuerpause, 1954; Soldatenspiele, Früchtekorb, 1956; Die Zeit ist reif, 1957; Fünf Romanzen, 1959; Essays I, 1959; Novellen I and II, 1961; Traum ist teuer, 1962; Jahresringe (poems), 1963; Essays II, 1967. *Recreations:* walking and swimming; collecting of ancient coins; chamber music. *Address:* Homeyerstrasse 13, Berlin-Niederschönhausen, Germany. *Club:* P.E.N. [*Died* 26 *Nov.* 1968.

Printed in Great Britain by R. & R. CLARK, LTD., *Edinburgh*